FOOTBALL CARD PRICE GUIDE

NUMBER 29

THE HOBBY'S MOST RELIABLE AND RELIED UPON SOURCE™

Founder & Advisor: Dr. James Beckett III

Edited by Dan Hitt with the staff of
BECKETT FOOTBALL

Manufactured in the United States of America
Published by Beckett Media LLC

Beckett Media LLC
4635 McEwen Road
Dallas, TX 75244
(972) 991-6657
www.beckett.com

First Printing
ISBN 9781936681938

CONTENTS

PRICE GUIDE

COVER PHOTOS – TOM BRADY – GETTY/JIM ROGASH, ANDREW LUCK – GETTY/JOE ROBBINS

DRAFT PICKS

COLLEGE

CANADIAN

HISTORY OF FOOTBALL CARDS

Until the 1930s, the only set devoted exclusively to football players was the Mayo N302 set. The first bubblegum issue dedicated entirely to football players did not appear until the National Chicle issue of 1935. Before this, athletes from several sports were pictured in the multi-sport Goudey Sport Kings issue of 1933. In that set, football was represented by three legends whose fame has not diminished through the years: Red Grange, Knute Rockne and Jim Thorpe.

But it was not until 1948, and the post-war bubblegum boom, that the next football issues appeared. Bowman and Leaf Gum companies both issued football card sets in that year. From this point on, football cards have been issued annually by one company or another up to the present time, with Topps being the only major card producer until 1989, when Pro Set and Score debuted and sparked a football card boom.

Football cards depicting players from the Canadian Football League (CFL) did not appear until Parkhurst issued a 100-card set in 1952. Four years later, Parkhurst issued another CFL set with 50 small cards this time. Topps began issuing CFL sets in 1958 and continued annually until 1965, although from 1961 to 1965 these cards were printed in Canada by O-Pee-Chee. Post Cereal issued two CFL sets in 1962 and 1963; these cards formed the backs of boxes of Post Cereals distributed in Canada. The O-Pee-Chee company, which has maintained a working relationship with the Topps Gum Company, issued four CFL sets in the years 1968, 1970, 1971, and 1972. Since 1981, the JOGO Novelties Company has been producing a number of CFL sets depicting past and present players.

Returning to American football issues, Bowman resumed its football cards (by then with full-color fronts) from 1950 to 1955. The company twice increased the size of its card during that period. Bowman was unopposed during most of the early 1950s as the sole producer of cards featuring pro football players.

Topps issued its first football card set in 1950 with a group of very small, felt-back cards. In 1951 Topps issued what is referred to as the "Magic Football Card" set. This set of 75 has a scratch-off section on the back which answers a football quiz. Topps did not issue another football set until 1955 when its All-American Football set paid tribute to past college football greats. In January of 1956, Topps Gum Company (of Brooklyn) purchased the Bowman Company (of Philadelphia).

After the purchase, Topps issued sets of National Football League (NFL) players up until 1963. The 1961 Topps football set also included American Football League (AFL) players in the high number series (133-198). Topps sets from 1964 to 1967 contained AFL players only. From 1968 to the present, Topps has issued a major set of football cards each year.

When the AFL was founded in 1960, Fleer produced a 132-card set of AFL players and coaches. In 1961, Fleer issued a 220-card set (even larger than the Topps issue of that year) featuring players from both the NFL and AFL. Apparently, for that one year, Topps and Fleer tested a reciprocal arrangement, trading the card printing rights to each other's contracted players. The 1962 and 1963 Fleer sets feature only AFL players. Both sets are relatively small at 88 cards each.

Post Cereal issued a 200-card set of National League football players in 1962 which contains numerous scarcities, namely those players appearing on unpopular varieties of Post Cereal. From 1964 to 1967, the Philadelphia Gum company issued four 198-card NFL player sets.

In 1984 and 1985, Topps produced a set for the now defunct United States Football League, in addition to its annual NFL set. The 1984 set in particular is scarce, due to both low distribution and the high demand for the extended Rookie Cards of NFL legends Steve Young, Jim Kelly and Reggie White.

The popularity of football cards continued to grow since 1984 and card companies other than Topps noticed the burgeoning interest in football cards, resulting in the two landmark 1989 football sets: a 330-card Score issue, and a 440-card Pro Set release. Score later produced a self-contained 110-card supplemental set, while Pro Set printed 100 Series II cards and a 21-card "Final Update" set. Topps, Pro Set and Score all improved card quality and increased the size of their sets for 1990. That season also marked Fleer's return to football cards and Action Packed's first major set.

In 1991, Pacific, Pro Line, Upper Deck and Wild Card joined a market that was now at least as competitive as the baseball card market. And the premium card trend that began in baseball cards spilled over to the gridiron in the form of Fleer Ultra, Pro Set Platinum, Score Pinnacle, and Topps Stadium Club sets. 1992 brought even more growth with the debuts of All World, Collectors Edge, GameDay, Playoff, Pro Set Power, SkyBox Impact and SkyBox Primetime. The football card market stabilized somewhat in 1993 thanks to an agreement between the long-feuding NFL licensing bodies, NFL Properties and the NFL Players Association. Also helping the stabilization was the emergence of several promising rookies, including Drew Bledsoe, Jerome Bettis and Rick Mirer. Limited production became the industry buzzword in sports cards, and football was no exception. The result was the success of three new product lines: 1993 Playoff Contenders, 1993 Select and 1993 SP. The year 1994 brought further stabilization and limited production. Pro Set and Wild Card dropped out, while no new card companies joined the ranks. However, several new NFL sets were added to the mix by existing manufacturers: Classic NFL Experience, Collector's Choice, Excalibur, Finest and Sportflics. The new trend centered around multi-level parallel sets and interactive game inserts with parallel prizes. Another strong rookie crop and reported production cut backs contributed to strong football card sales throughout 1994. The football card market grew again between 1995 and 1998. Many new sets were released by the major manufacturers and a few new players entered the hobby. Companies continued to push the limits of printing technology with issues printed on plastic, leather, cloth and various metals. Rookie Cards once more came into vogue and the "1-of-1" insert card was born.

In the last years of the decade more changes occurred in the football card market: the Rookie Card phenomenon continued unabated but with a twist. Since 1998, many Rookie Cards have been sequentially numbered and printed to a number of cards less than the veteran cards in the set. Pinnacle Brands ceased to exist in 1998, with the Playoff Company taking over the names of long standing football issues such as Score and Leaf. Many other products began having players sign cards for the set or began featuring game worn cards that include swatches of jerseys, footballs, or helmets.

In addition, professionally graded cards, old and new, have really revitalized the card market. Many collectors and dealers have been able to trade cards over internet services such as Ebay or the many different ways cards are available on Beckett.com. These cards make trading sight unseen much easier than they used to be.

The trend towards short printed Rookie Cards as well as the growing use of memorabilia swatches on cards continued through the first and into the second decades of the 2000s. Many key Rookie Cards are now issued with some combination of either an autograph, uniform swatch, serial numbering, or all three. In addition, the print run of many of these is smaller each and every year. In addition, a significant amount of the autographs are no longer actually signed on the cards but are signed on stickers which are then affixed to the card.

One after-effect of all this emphasis on Rookie and Memorabilia cards is that many supposed "second-tier" players just do not have many cards issued. A notable example was in 2001 when Super Bowl quarterback Tom Brady had less than five cards issued in more than 50 sets. While some collectors are frustrated by the

changing hobby, others are thrilled because there are more choices than ever for the football card fan - and many collectors like it that way.

ACKNOWLEDGMENTS

A great deal of diligence, hard work, and dedicated effort went into this, our 28th Edition. The high standards to which we hold ourselves, however, could not have been met without the expert input and generous amount of time contributed by many people. Our sincere thanks are extended to each and every one of you.

Each year we refine the process of developing the most accurate and up-to-date information for this book. Thanks again to all of the contributors nationwide (listed below) as well as our staff here in Dallas.

A special thank you goes to the following contributors who made an extraordinary contribution to this year's book: Pat Blandford, A.J. Firestone, Mike Hattley, Terrell Irwin, Carl Lamendola, Steve Liskey, Morgan Moore, Jayson Morand, Mike Mosier, and Steve Taft.

At the risk of inadvertently overlooking or omitting the many other key contributors over the years, we would like to individually thank A & J Cards, Jonathan Abraham, Action Sports Cards, Jerry Adamic, Mehdi and Danny Alaei, Aliso Hills Stamp and Coin, Rich Altman, Neil Armstrong, Mike Aronstein, Chris Bak, Tom Barborich, Red Barnes, Bob Bawiel, William E. Baxendale, Dean Bedell, Jerry Bell, Patrick Benes, Bubba Bennett, Chuck Bennett, Carl Berg, Eric Berger, Kevin Bergson, Skip Bertman, Brian L. Bigelow, Lance Billingsley, David Bitar, Mike Blaisdell, Pat Blandford, Jeff Blatt, Mike Bonner, Bill Bossert, Terry Boyd, John Bradley (JOGO), Virgil Burns, Dave Byer, Mike Caffey, David Carenbauer, Dale Carlson, Bud Carter, Sally Carves, Ric Changdie, Dwight Chapin, Don Chubey, Howard Churchill, Ralph Ciarlo, Orr Cihlar, Mike Clark, Craig Coddling, Jon Cohen, Joe Colabella, Collector's Edge, Matt Collett, George Courter, Taylor Crane, Scott Crump, Jim Curie, Alan Custer, Paul Czuchna, Joe Davey, Steve Davidow, Samuel Davis, Tony Wayne Davis, Robert Der, Bill and Diane Dodge, Cliff Dolgins, Rick Donohoo, Patrick Dorsey, Vic Dougan, John Douglas, Joseph Drelich, John Durkos, Al Durso, E&R Galleries, Buck Easley, Ed Emmitt, The End Zone, Joe Ercole, Darrell Ereth, Doak Ewing, Rodney Faciane, Bob Farmer, Terry Faulkner, A.J. Firestone, Fleischman and Walsh, Fleer, Flickball, Gervise Ford, Craig Frank, Mark Franke, Ron Frasier, Steve Freedman, Tom Freeman, Richard Freiburghouse, Craig Friedemann, Larry and Jeff Fritsch, Brian Froehlich, Chris Gala, Mike Gallella, Steven Galletta, Tony Galovich, Gerry Gartland (The Gallagher Archives), Tom Giacchino, Dick Gilkeson, Michael R. Gionet, David Giove, Steve Glass, Steve Gold (AU Sports), Todd Goldenberg, Jeff Goldstein, Mike and Howard Gordon, Gregg Gornes, George Grauer, Joseph Griffin, Bob Grissett, Robert G. Gross, Hall's Nostalgia, Steve Hart, Michael Hattley, Rod Heffern, Kevin Heffner, Dennis Heitland, Jon Helfenstein, Jerry and Etta Hersh, Mike Hersh, Clay Hill, Gary Hlady, Geof Hollenbeck, Russ Hoover, Neil Hoppenworth, Nelson Hu, Don Hurry, John Inouye, Terrell Irwin, Barry Isak, Jeff Issler, Robert R. Jackson, Joe and Mike Jardina, Dan Jaskula, Terry Johnson, Craig Jones, Stewart Jones, Larry Jordon, Jeff Juhnke, Chuck Juliana, Loyd Jungling, Ed Kabala, Wayne Kleman, Andrew Kaiser, Jay and Mary Kasper, Frank and Rose Katen, Jack Kemps, Rick Keplinger, John Kilian, Ron Klassnik, Steve Kluback, Albert Klumpp, Don Knutsen, Raymond Kong, Bob and Bryan Kornfield, Terry Kreider, George Kruk, Thomas Kunnecke, Carl Lamendola, Dan Lavin, Scott Lawson, Walter Ledzki, Marc Lefkowitz, Tom Leon, Irv Lerner, Ed Lim, Lew Lipset, Frank Lopez, Neil Lopez, Joe Lucia, Frank Lucito, Kevin Lynch, Bud Lyle, Jim Macie, Gary Madrack, Paul Marchant, Adam Martin, Chris Martin (Chris Martin Enterprises), Alex McCollum, Bob McDonald, Michael McDonald, Steve McHenry, Mike McKee, Carlos Medina, Fernando Mercado, Joe Merkel, Chris Merrill, Blake Meyer, Lee Milazzo, Wayne Miller, Dick Millerd, Pat Mills, Ron Moermond, Morgan Moore, John Morales, Rev. Michael Moran, Jayson Morand, Michael Moretto, Brian Morris, Rusty Morse, Kyle Morton, Mike and Cindy Mosier, Dick Mueller, Roger Neufeldt, NFL Properties, Don Niemi, Raymond Ng, Steve Novella, Larry Nyeste, Mike O'Brien, Richard Ochoa, John O'Hara, Glenn Olsen, Mike Orth, Pacific Trading Cards, Andrew Pak, Chris Park, Clay Pasternack, Paul and Judy's, John Peavy, Mark Perna, Michael Perrotta, Steve Peters, Ira Petsrillo, Tom Pfirrmann, Playoff Corp, Arto Poladian, Steve Poland, Jack Pollard, Chris Pomerleau, Jeff Porter, Press Pass, Jeff Prillaman, Jonathan Pullano, Loran Pulver, Pat Quinn, Don and Tom Ras, Phil Regli, Owen Ricker, Gavin Riley, Carson Ritchey, Evelyn Roberts, Jim Roberts, Jeff Rogers, Mark Rose, Greg Rosen, Chip Rosenberg, Rotman Productions, Blake and Sheldon Rudman, John Rumierz, George Rusnak, Terry Ryan, Terry Sack, SAGE, Joe Sak, Barry Sanders, John Sandstrom, Kevin Savage, Nathan Schank, Mike Schechter (MSA), R.J. Schulhof, Perry Schwartzberg, Patrick W. Scoggin, Dan Scolman, Rick Scruggs, Burns Searfoss, Eric Shillito, Shinder's Cards, Bob Singer, Sam Sliheet, John Smith, Keith Smith, Rick Smith, Gerry Sobie, Don Spagnolo, John Spalding, John Spano, Carl Specht, Nigel Spill, Sportcards Etc., Vic Stanley, Bill Steinberg, Cary Stephenson, Murvin Sterling Dan Stickney, Jack Stowe, Del Stracke, Richard Strobino, Kevin Struss, Bob Swick, Steve Taft, George Tahinos, Richard Tattoli, Paul S. Taylor, Lee Temanson, Jeff Thomas, Rodney Thomas, Tatoo Thomas, TK Legacy, Bud Tompkins, Steve Tormollen, Topps, Greg Tranter, John Tumazos, Upper Deck, U-Trading Cards (Mike Livingston), Eric Valkys, Wayne Varner, Kevin M. VanderKelen, Rob Veres, Bill Vizas, Tom Wall, Mike Wasserman, Keith Watson, Mark Watson, Brian Wentz, Dale Wesolewski, Bill Wesslund, Mike Wheat, Joe White, Rick Wilson, John Wirtanen, Wizards of the Coast, Jay Wolt, Paul Wright, Darryl Yee, Sheraton Yee, Kit Young, Eugene Zalewski, Robert Zanze, Steve Zeller, Dean Zindler, and Tim Zwick.

Every year we make active solicitations for expert input. We are particularly appreciative of the help (however extensive or cursory) provided for this volume. We receive many inquiries, comments and questions regarding material within this book. In fact, each and every one is read and digested. Time constraints, however, prevent us from personally replying. But keep sharing your knowledge. Even though we cannot respond to each letter, you are making significant contributions to the hobby through your interest and comments.

The effort to continually refine and improve our books also involves a growing number of people and types of expertise on our home team. Our company boasts a substantial Sports Data Publishing team, which strengthens our ability to provide comprehensive analysis of the marketplace.

Our price guide team played a major part in compiling this year's book through dedicated efforts to compile the most complete and accurate checklists and pricing data available. The majority of additions, corrections, and changes to this edition were made by Beckett football senior market analyst Dan Hitt and information analyst Jeff Camay. Their efforts were ably assisted by the rest of the Price Guide team: Lloyd Almonguera, Brian Fleischer, Dave Sliepka, Rob Springs, & AR Tan. Finally, this book could not have been produced without the fine page layout work of Arvind Sidhu & Tom Carroll.

About the Publisher

Based in Dallas, Beckett Media LLC is the leading publisher of sports and specialty market collectible products in the U.S. Beckett operates Beckett.com (www.beckett.com) to deliver the most comprehensive online price guide in the hobby and is the premier publisher of monthly sports and entertainment collectibles magazines.

HOW TO USE AND CONDITION GUIDE

HOW TO USE

Every year this book gets bigger and better with all the new sets coming out and this edition has been enhanced and expanded from the previous volume with new releases, updated prices, and additions to older listings. The Beckett Guide has been successful where other attempts have failed because it is complete, current, and valid. The prices were added to the card lists just prior to printing and reflect not the author's opinions or desires but the going retail prices for each card, based on the marketplace (sports memorabilia conventions and shows, sports card shops, on-line computer trading, auction results, and other firsthand reports of realized prices).

To facilitate proper use of this book, please read the complete introductory section before going to the pricing pages, especially the sections on grading and card conditions.

ADVERTISING

Within this Price Guide you will find advertisements for sports memorabilia material, mail order, and retail sports collectibles establishments. All advertisements were accepted in good faith based on the reputation of the advertiser; however neither the author, the publisher, the distributors, nor the other advertisers in this Price Guide accept any responsibility for any particular advertiser not complying with the terms of his or her ad.

HOW TO COLLECT

PRESERVING YOUR CARDS

Cards are fragile so they must be handled properly in order to retain their value. Careless handling can easily result in damaged cards and lower values. Although there are many collectors who use boxes to store their cards, plastic sheets or single card sleeves and plastic holders are the preferred methods for storing cards. Most card shops and websites (such as Beckett.com), and virtually all card shows, will have these plastic storage materials available for you.

COLLECTING VS. INVESTING

Collecting individual players and complete sets are popular methods for both investment and speculation. There is obviously no guarantee in this book, or anywhere else for that matter, that cards will outperform the stock market or other investment alternatives in the future. After all, football cards do not pay quarterly dividends and cards are not nearly as liquid as stocks or bonds. Nevertheless, investors have sometimes experienced favorable long-term trends in past performance of hot sports collectibles and certain cards have outperformed many traditional investments in some years. Many hobbyists maintain that the best investment is and always will be the building of a collection and the more you learn about your collection and the hobby the better you're likely to make decisions. We're not providing investment tips, but simple information about the current value of football cards. It's up to you to use that information to your best advantage.

UNDERSTANDING CARD VALUES

Why are some cards more valuable than others? Obviously, the economic laws of supply and demand are applicable to card collecting just as they are to any other field where a commodity is bought, sold or traded in a free, unregulated market.

Supply (the number of cards available on the market) is often less than the total number of cards originally produced since attrition tends to diminish that original quantity. Each year a percentage of cards is typically thrown away, destroyed or otherwise lost to collectors. This percentage is much, much smaller today than it was in the past because more and more people have become increasingly aware of the value of cards.

Demand is never equal for all sets so price correlations can be complicated. The demand for a card is influenced by many factors including: (1) the age of the card; (2) the attributes attached to it like autographs or memorabilia; (3) the player(s) portrayed; (4) the attractiveness and popularity of the set; and (5) the physical condition of the card. In general, (1) the older the card, (2) the fewer cards printed, (3) the more famous, popular and talented the player, (4) the more attractive and popular the set, and (5) the better the condition of the card, the higher the value of the card will be. While those guidelines help to establish the value of a card, the countless exceptions and peculiarities make any simple, direct mathematical formula to determine card values impossible.

SET PRICES

A somewhat paradoxical situation exists in the price of a complete set vs. the combined cost of the individual cards in the set. In nearly every case, the sum of the prices for the individual cards is higher than the typical selling price for a complete set. This is prevalent especially in the cards of the past few years. The reasons for this apparent anomaly stem from the habits of collectors and from the carrying costs to dealers. Many collectors pick up only stars, superstars and particular teams. As a result, the dealer is left with a shortage of certain player cards and an abundance of others. He therefore incurs an expense in "carrying" these remainder cards in stock which discourages him from selling them at the same discount a bulk, or "set" sale might afford.

GRADING YOUR CARDS

Each hobby has its own grading terminology and collectors of sports cards are no exception. The one invariable criterion for determining the value of a card is its condition: the better the condition of the card, the more valuable it is. Card grading, however, is subjective. Individual card dealers and collectors often differ in the strictness of their grading, but the stated condition of a card should be determined without regard to whether it is being bought or sold. In the past fifteen years professional third party card grading services (like PSA, SGC, and BGS) have become a staple of the industry and are a valuable resource for collectors and dealers. Their grading scales, standards and terminology are used industry-wide and help to facilitate trade particularly when a transaction occurs by mail.

CENTERING

Current centering terminology typically uses numbers representing the percentage of border on either side of the main design. Obviously, centering is diminished in importance for borderless cards such as Stadium Club. A slightly off-center card (60/40) is one that upon close inspection is found to have one border bigger than the opposite border. This slight degree was once offensive to only purists, but now some hobbyists try to avoid cards that are anything but perfectly centered. Off-Center (70/30) cards have one border that is more than twice as wide as the opposite border. Badly Off-Center (80/20 or worse) and miscut cards have virtually no border on one side of the card which severely lowers the card's value.

CORNER WEAR

Corner wear is the most scrutinized grading criteria in the hobby. These are the major categories of corner wear:

Corner with a slight touch of wear: The corner still is sharp, but there is a slight touch of wear showing. On a dark-bordered card, this shows as a dot of white.

Fuzzy corner: The corner still comes to a point, but the point has just begun to fray. A slightly "dinged" corner is considered the same as a fuzzy corner.

Slightly rounded corner: The fraying of the corner has increased to where there is only a hint of a point. Mild layering may be evident. A "dinged" corner is considered the same as a slightly rounded corner.

Rounded corner: The point is completely gone. Some layering is noticeable.

CREASES

A third common defect is creasing. The degree of creasing in a card is difficult to show in a drawing or picture but will greatly affect the card's value. Any creasing on the average modern era card will render it nearly worthless but three typical categories of severity found on some rare and vintage cards are:

Light Crease: a crease that is barely noticeable upon close inspection. In fact, when cards are in plastic sheets or holders, a light crease may not be seen. A light crease on the front is much more serious than a light crease on the card back only.

Medium Crease: A medium crease is fairly noticeable, but does not overly detract from the appearance of the card. It is an obvious crease, but not one that breaks the picture surface of the card.

Heavy Crease: A heavy crease is one that has torn or broken through the card's picture surface, e.g., puts a tear in the photo surface.

ALTERATIONS

Trimming: This occurs when someone alters the card in order (1) to shave off edge wear, (2) to improve the sharpness of the corners, or (3) to improve centering - obviously their objective is to falsely increase the perceived value of the card to an unsuspecting buyer. The shrinkage usually is evident only if the trimmed card is compared to an adjacent full-sized card or if the trimmed card is measured.

Retouched Borders: This occurs when the borders (especially on those cards with dark borders) are touched up on the edges and corners with magic marker or crayons of appropriate color in order to make the card appear to be Mint.

MISCELLANEOUS FLAWS

There are a number of minor flaws that, depending on severity, may lower a card's condition by one to four grades: bubbles (lumps in surface), gum and wax stains, diamond cutting (slanted borders), notching, off-centered backs, paper wrinkles, scratched-off cartoons or puzzles on back, rubber band marks, scratches, surface impressions and warping. The following are common serious flaws that, depending on severity, lower a card's condition at least four grades and often render it no better than Good: chemical or sun fading, erasure marks, mildew, miscutting (severe off-centering), holes, bleached or retouched borders, tape marks, tears, trimming, water or coffee stains and writing.

CONDITION GUIDE

Gem Mint (Gem Mt) - A card with no flaws or wear even under magnification. This grade is usually reserved for a card certified by a third party grading company.

Mint (Mt): A card with no noticeable flaws or wear. The card has four square corners, 60/40 or better centering from top to bottom and from left to right, original gloss, smooth edges and original color borders. A Mint card does not have distracting print spots, color or focus imperfections.

Near Mint-Mint (NrMt-Mt): A card with one minor flaw. Any one of the following would lower a Mint card to Near Mint-Mint: one corner with a slight touch of wear, barely noticeable print spots, color or focus imperfections. The card must have 60/40 or better centering in both directions, original gloss, smooth edges and original color borders.

Near Mint (NrMt): A card with one minor flaw. Any one of the following would lower a Mint card to Near Mint: one fuzzy corner or two to four corners with slight touches of wear, 70/30 to 60/40 centering, slightly rough edges, minor print spots, color or focus imperfections. The card must have original gloss and original color borders.

Excellent-Mint (ExMt): A card with two or three fuzzy, but not rounded, corners and centering no worse than 80/20. The card may have no more than two of the following: slightly rough edges, very slightly discolored borders, minor print spots, color or focus imperfections. The card must have original gloss.

Excellent (EX): A card with four fuzzy but not rounded corners and centering no worse than 80/20. The card may have a small amount of original gloss lost, rough edges, slightly discolored borders and minor print spots, color or focus imperfections.

Very Good (VG): A card that has been handled but not abused: slightly rounded corners with slight layering, slight notching on edges, a significant amount of gloss lost from the surface but no scuffing and moderate discoloration of borders. The card may have a few light creases.

Good (G), Fair (F), Poor (P): A well-worn, mishandled or abused card: badly rounded and layered corners, scuffing, most or all original gloss missing, seriously discolored borders, moderate or heavy creases, and one or more serious flaws. Good, Fair and Poor cards generally are used only as fillers.

SELLING YOUR CARDS

Just about every collector sells cards or will sell cards eventually. Someday you may be interested in selling your duplicates or maybe even your whole collection. You may sell to other collectors, friends or dealers. You may even sell cards you purchased from a certain dealer back to that same dealer. In any event, it helps to know some of the mechanics of the typical transaction between buyer and seller. Dealers will buy cards in order to resell them to other collectors who are interested in the cards. Dealers will always pay a higher percentage for items that (in their opinion) can be resold quickly, and a much lower percentage for those items that are perceived as having low demand and hence are slow moving. In either case, dealers must buy at a price that allows for the expense of doing business and a margin for profit.

If you have cards for sale, the best advice we can give is that you get several offers for your cards - either from card shops or at a card show - and take the best offer, all things considered. Note, the "best" offer may not be the one for the highest amount. And remember, if a dealer really wants your cards, he won't let you get away without making his best competitive offer. Another alternative is to place your cards in an auction as one or several lots.

Many people think nothing of going into a department store and paying $15 for an item of clothing for which the store paid $5. But if you were selling your $15 card to a dealer and he offered you $5 for it, you might think his mark-up unreasonable. To complete the analogy: most department stores (and card dealers) that consistently pay $10 for $15 items eventually go out of business. An exception is when the dealer has lined up a willing buyer for the item(s) you are attempting to sell, or if the cards are so Hot that it's likely he'll have to hold the cards for only a short period of time. In those cases, an offer of up to 75 percent of book value still will allow the dealer to make a reasonable profit considering the short time he will need to hold the merchandise. In general, however, most cards and collections will bring offers in the range of 25 to 50 percent of retail price. Also consider that most material from the past 20 to 30 years is plentiful. If that's what you're selling, don't be surprised if your best offer is well below that range.

Football

DEALER DIRECTORY

ALASKA

BOSCO'S
2606 Spenard Rd
Anchorage, AK 99503-2309
(907)-274-4112
patmoe@boscos.com

Don's Sportscards
9900 Old Seward Hwy, Ste 8
Anchorage, AK 99515-2249
(907)-349-8804
donssport@aol.com

ARKANSAS

HobbyTown USA
9101 West Markham Street Ste 18
Little Rock, AR 72205
(501)-223-5155
htulittlerock@comcast.net

ARIZONA

Sports Cards Etc.
2506 W Chilton St
Chandler, AZ 85224-1108
(480)-777-2688
weedy@cox.net

Phoenix Card Co-Op
4326 West Bell Rd, Ste 7
Glendale, AZ 85308-3545
(602)-548-1254
phoenixcardcoop@cox.net

CALIFORNIA

The OC Dugout
5655 E. La Palma Ave #123
Anaheim Hills, CA 92807
(714)-997-1111
celebritysluggers@hotmail.com

Taylor Baseball Cards
8682 Beach Blvd, Ste 101
Buena Park, CA 90620-4808
(714)-827-7746
taycard@aol.com

Teammates
4705 Manzanita Ave
Carmichael, CA 95608-0822
(916)-488-2303
teammates1@aol.com

Bases Loaded
3225 West Shaw Ave, Ste 104
Fresno, CA 93711-3227
(559)-225-9321
basloaded@sbcglobal.net

Best Variety Sportscards
358 W Foothill Blvd
Glendora, CA 91741
626-914-CARD
bestvarietycoinerrors.com

Bill's Bullpen
207 4th St
Hollister, CA 95023-3923
(831)-636-1180
billbullpen@aol.com

Baseball Cards Plus
6401 Edinger Ave
Huntington Beach, CA 92647-3341
(714)-898-5648
brian@surfcitycards.com

MVP Sportscards
24881 Alicia Pkwy, Ste J
Laguna, CA 92653-4617
(949)-837-7830

Baseball Fan-Attic
3025 McHenry Ave
Modesto, CA 95350-1466
(209)-342-0420
fanattic@sbcglobal.net

D and P Sports Cards
5968 S Land Park Dr
Sacramento, CA 95822-3313
(916)-391-8750
DNPcards@gmail.com

Sportscard Mania
8301 Folsom Blvd, Ste A
Sacramento, CA 95826-3500
(916)-381-0466
scardmaniac@cs.com

Centre City Sports Collectible
1027 6th Avenue
San Diego, CA 92101
(619)-338-0007
centrecitysport@yahoo.com

Clairemont Sportcards
4941 Clairemont Dr, Ste C
San Diego, CA 92117-2731
(858)-270-4945
clairemontsc@netscape.net

Pro Star Sports and Gaming
414 N Capitol Ave
San Jose, CA 95133
(408)-259-6460
prostargaming@aol.com

The Card Pavilion
2423 N Tustin Ave
Santa Ana, CA 92705-1662
(714)-541-4757
kbuck57@hotmail.com

The Press Boxx
3525 W Walnut Ave
Visalia, CA 93277-4170
(559)-625-2202
thepressboxx@earthlink.net

COLORADO

Mike's Stadium Sports Cards
4022 S Parker Rd
Aurora, CO 80014
303-699-9808
cardmn5150@aol.com

Mike's Stadium Sports Cards
4022 S Parker Rd
Aurora, CO 80014-4131
(303)-699-9808
cardmn5150@aol.com

Dale's Kardz And Koinz
4341 N Academy Blvd
Colorado Springs, CO 80918-6623
(719)-528-5959
dalezkardz@earthlink.net

John's Sports Collectibles
3615 Galley Rd
Colorado Springs, CO 80909-4315
(719)-574-7040

Bill's Sports Collectibles
2335 S Broadway
Denver, CO 80210-5006
(303)-733-4878
billsportscolo@aol.com

FLORIDA

Dan's Sports Cards
6415 Blanding Blvd.
Jacksonville, FL 32244
(904)-777-4548

Dick & Jane's Sportscards
1833 Dean Rd
Jacksonville, FL 32216-4520
(904)-725-2316
dickandjanes@aol.com

Jacksonville Sport Card Center
1370 Cassat Ave
Jacksonville, FL 32205-7063
(904)-387-0260

Orlando Sportscards South
9476 S Orange Blossom Trl
Orlando, FL 32837-8321
(407)-240-0384

Triple Play Sports Card
2219 S Dale Marburry Hwy
Tampa, FL 33629
(813)-831-0652
hcuff7@aol.com

Eric's Baseball Cards
2400 S Hopkins Ave, Ste B
Titusville, FL 32780-5076
(321)-383-0947
mossland@cfl.rr.com

GEORGIA

Sports Legends
310 N Glynn Street
Fayetteville, GA 30214
(678)-817-6769
sportslegendsusa.com

Champion Sportscards & Collectibles
840 Ernest Barrett Pkwy Suite#708
Kennesaw, GA 30144
(770)-427-2220
championsportscards@yahoo.com

J&J's Sports Superstore
2135 East Main Street SW Ste 210
Snellville, GA 30078
770-736-9998
gotbaseballcards.com

IOWA

Midwest Collectibles
3541 N Fairmount St, Ste A
Davenport, IA 52806
(563)-823-1975
midwestcoll@gmail.com

The Silver Card
204 N. Highway 69, Ste D
Huxley, IA 50124-0219
(515)-597-2646
alex@thesilvercard.com

The Rookie
7204 University Ave
Windsor Heights, IA 50324
(515)-255-4675
www.therookiesportscards.com

ILLINOIS

Top Cut Comics
5600 North 2nd St.
Loves Park, IL 611114602
(815)-633-0330
info@topcutcomics.com

Baseball Card Exchange
21686 East Lincoln Hwy Unit C
Lynwood, IL 60411
800-598-8656
bbcexchange.com

Triple Crown Trading Co.
414 B W 5th Ave, Ste B
Naperville, IL 60563-3050
(630)-357-7707
tom@tcrowntom.com

Southside Cards & Collectibles
11325 W 143rd ST
Orland Park, IL 60467
(708)-873-5088
www.southsidecards.com

The Baseball Card King
16030 Lincoln Hwy, Unit 1
Plainfield, IL 60586
(815)-609-7777
thebaseballcardking@comcast.net

INDIANA

Squeeze Play
2109 S Scatterfield Rd
Anderson, IN 46016-5738
(765)-644-5412
squeezeplayonline@sbcglobal.net

MCS Cards Comics and Gaming
107 1/2 W Wabash St;
Bluffton, IN 46714
(260)-824-4576
mcscardscomics@adamswells.com

More Fun Sportscards
706 Joliet St
Dyer, IN 46311-1720
(219)-322-5080
www.morefunsportscards.com

The Book Broker
2717 Covert Ave
Evansville, IN 47714-3950
(812)-479-5647

K&L Cards
265 S State Road 135
Greenwood, IN 46142-1421
(317)-883-2240
lscantcard@aol.com

KANSAS

Oliver Sports Cards and Memorabilia
1303 W 31st S
Wichita, KS 67217
(316)-425-1938
kooluof@cox.net

Rock's Dugout
3232 N Rock Rd
Wichita, KS 67226-1313
(316)-682-7902
jcruocco@hotmail.com

LOUISIANA

Chuck's Field of Dreams
28550 La 43 Hwy
Albany, LA 70711-4301
(225)-567-9200
jaimie@bayoustatesportscards.com

Jason's Sports Cards
5734 S. Sherwood Forest Blvd.
Baton Rouge, LA 70726
(225)-291-4018

Louisianas Double Play
2834 S Sherwood Forest Blvd, Ste C5
Baton Rouge, LA 70816-2246
(225)-296-5812
ladp@cox.net

Wyatt Sports Cards
4636 Hwy. 22
Mandeville, LA 70471
(225)-567-9200

Jaimie' Field of Dreams Sportscards
4715 Pecanland Mall Dr
Monroe, LA 71203-7005
(318)-812-2900
jaimie@bayoustatesportscards.com

MASSACHUSETTS

Slapshot Sportscards
184 Broadway
Saugus, MA 01906-1099
(781)-231-1800
slapshotsport@aol.com

Batter Up Sportscards
1875 Main St
Tewksbury, MA 1876
(978)-640-1586
bjudge3853@aol.com

MARYLAND

Baseball Card Outlet
7502 Eastern Ave
Baltimore, MD 21224-1919
(410)-284-7922
bcoutlet@aol.com

DugoutZone
9210 Baltimore National Pike
Ellicott City, MD 21042-2615
(410)-461-8664
www.dugoutzone.com

Sports Card Heroes
634 Main St
Laurel, MD 20707-4070
(301)-317-4666
rcurre6294@aol.com

Sportscard Depot
2517 Putty Hill Ave
Parkville, MD 21234-4307
(410)-663-4262
edsportcd@aol.com

MICHIGAN

The Stadium
3980 East Wilder Rd
Bay City, MI 48706-2157
(989)-667-0450
dumars1935@charter.net

Lou Brown Cards
3115 28th St SE Space F101
Grand Rapids, MI 49512
CollectAndSave.com

Stadium Cards & Comics
2061 Golfside Dr
Ypsilanti, MI 48197-1303
(734)-434-0283
fennydude@aol.com

MINNESOTA

Pal's Sports Cards
14025 Round Lake Blvd
Andover, MN 55304
(763)-427-4505

Uncommon Sports Cards
6627 Penn Ave S
Richfield, MN 55423-2026
(612)-869-3930
ucards@qwest.net

Three Stars Sportscards
2801 Hamline Ave N
Roseville, MN 55113-1715
(651)-633-6041
wayne@threestarssportscards.com

Billy's Sports Treasures
4809 W 123rd Street
Savage, MN 55378-1364
(952)-808-7754
billyssportstreasures@msn.com

MISSOURI

Coach's Corner Sportscards
110 N Scott Ave, Ste A
Belton, MO 64012-2012
(816)-331-6462

Show-Me Sports Cards Co
706 W. US Highway 40
Blue Springs, MO 64015-4651
(816)-224-3281
nitemayre1@sbcglobal.net

Fastbreak Sports
2825 S Glenstone Ave
Springfield, MO 65804-3732
(888)-543-3411
www.FastbreakSportsFansHQ.com

MISSISSIPPI

Gulf Coast Cards & Sports Memo
2600 Beach Blvd
Biloxi, MS 39531-4606
(228)-388-5178
gulfcoastcards@cableone.net

NORTH CAROLINA

The Dugout Cards & Games
2109 Catawba Valley Blvd. SE
Hickory, NC 28602
(828)-322-4164
www.hickorydugout.com

NORTH DAKOTA

Big Nicks Sports Cards
3902 13th ave S, Ste 100 West Acres Mall
Fargo, ND 58103
(701)-277-1989
bignickscards@cableone.net

NEBRASKA

Sports Center Cards
4725 S 131st St
Omaha, NE 68137-1867
(402)-891-0605

NEW JERSEY

The Hobby Shop
1077-C Hwy 34
Aberdeen, NJ 07747
7325830505 Ext 5
sales@hobbyshopnj.com

Rookies and Stars
1350 Saint Georges Ave
Avenel, NJ 07001-1134
(732)-396-3870
rookies_and_stars@comcast.net

East Coast Connection
288 Ridge Road
Lyndhurst, NJ 07071
201-438-4327
eastcoastconnection.net

New Concept III
676 Stokes Rd
Medford, NJ 08055-2907
(609)-953-0404
newconceptcards@gmail.com

NEW MEXICO

Bubba's Baseball Bullpen
8206 Menaul Blvd NE
Albuquerque, NM 87110-4614
(505)-299-1156
bubbasbaseballbullpen@juno.com

NEVADA

Ultimate Sportscards
3211 N Tenaya Way, Ste 103
Las Vegas, NV 89129-7440
(702)-363-7999

NEW YORK

L. J.'s Sportscards & Collectibles
171 Clinton St
Binghamton, NY 13905-2290
(607)-775-0278
ljssportscards@stny.rr.com

Chameleon Comics
3 Maiden Ln
New York, NY 10038-4008
(212)-587-3411
steve@chameleoncomics.com

Dave & Adam's Card World
1595 Military Road
Niagra Falls, NY 14304
716-299-0777
dacardworld.com

Dave & Adam's Card World
3217F Southwestern Blvd
Orchard Park, NY 14127
716-677-1840
dacardworld.com

Staten Island Sportscards Inc.
27 Seguine Ave, Ste 4
Staten Island, NY 10309-3700
(718)-967-7171
cb7171@aol.com

Dave & Adam's Card World
2217 Sheridan Drive
Tonawanda, NY 14223
716-837-4920
dacardworld.com

First n' Goal Sportscards, Inc.
1060 Niagara Falls Blvd Suite 2
Tonawanda, NY 14150
(716)-835-1553
wheels643@aol.com

DCS Sportscards
3381C Merrick Rd
Wantagh, NY 11793
516-946-6334
dcssportscards.com

A&S Sports LLC
825 Carman Ave
Westbury, NY 11590
(516)-398-7800
www.nysportscards.com

Dave & Adam's Card World
5575 Transit Rd
Williamsville, NY 14221
716-689-2273
dacardworld.com

OHIO

Hooterville Sportscards
5102 Pleasant Ave
Fairfield, OH 45014-2611
(513)-737-9772
hoot369@cinci.rr.com

Sportmark
P O Box 805
Miamisburg, OH 45343
sportmarkcards@gmail.com

OKLAHOMA

Al's Sportscards and Gaming
116 East 15th St
Edmond, OK 73013-4303
(405)-348-7583
Alscards7599@sbcglobal.net

PENNSYLVANIA

Steel City Collectibles
5256 Route 30
Greensburg, PA 15601
724-830-9369
steelcitycollect.com

BJ Sportscards
14 S York Rd
Hatboro, PA 19040-3326
(215)-675-8746
bschn56091@aol.com

Sportscard Playground
297 W County Line Rd
Hatboro, PA 19040-1719
(215)-675-6644
heidig@sportscardplayground.com

The Baseball Card Shop
1891 E State St
Hermitage, PA 16148-1866
(724)-981-4443
info@baseballcardshop.net

Indiana Sportscards
1506 Oakland Ave.
Indiana, PA 15701
(724)-349-1769

Shaffer's Trading Cards
2849 Westbranch Hwy
Lewisburg, PA 17837
(570)-524-4341

Sports Cards Etc
110 West McMurray Road
McMurray, PA 15317
(724)-942-8085

Steel City Collectibles - Ross Park Mall
1000 Ross Park Mall Drive
Pittsburgh, PA 15237
412-366-5858
steelcitycollect.com

Sports Collectors Universe
1348 Mall Run Rd, Uniontown Mall
Uniontown, PA 15401
(724)-437-2030
Btbcompany@aol.com

SOUTH DAKOTA

Triple Play Sports Cards
3816 S Western Ave
Sioux Falls, SD 57105-6511
(605)-332-4815
www.tpsc.net

TENNESSEE

Tennessee Card Company
2829 Bartlett Blvd.
Bartlett, TN 38134-4529
(901)-372-1408
tennesseecardco@bellsouth.net

Sports Treasures LLC
4819 N Broadway St
Knoxville, TN 37918-1708
(865)-688-2273
ebarkley23@comcast.net

Cards-R-Fun
15125 Old Hickory Blvd
Nashville, TN 37211-1318
(615)-832-3216

TEXAS

Superior Sports Investments
P.O. Box 183613
Arlington, TX 76096
(817)-557-9196

Dollars & Cents
500 N Galloway Ave, Ste 128
Mesquite, TX 75149-4339
(972)-289-7970
dollarscents@sbcglobal.net

Triple Cards & Collectibles
2452 Ave K
Plano, TX 75074-5911
(972)-509-5263
triplecard@sbcglobal.net

Sports Cards Plus
2239 Lock Hill Selma Rd
San Antonio, TX 78230
(210)-524-2337
www.sportscardsplussa.com

Whats On Second
4177 Naco Perrin Blvd
San Antonio, TX 78217-2505
(210)-590-8444
whatsonsecond@stic.net

UTAH

House Of Cards & Coins
4700 S 900 E, Ste 28
Salt Lake City, UT 84117-4980
(801)-485-7337
jeff@pntgame.com

VIRGINIA

Blowout Cards - The Fantastic Store
14508 Lee Rd - Unit F
Chantilly, VA 20151
Blowoutcards.com

J & L Sportscards
1867 Seminole Trail
Charlottesville, VA 22901
(434)-973-1704

The Card Cellar
5047 Jefferson Davis Hwy
Fredricksburg, VA 22408-4263

Jerseys Cards And Comics
1818 Todds Ln, Ste G
Hampton, VA 23666-3139
(757)-890-2842

The Tenth Inning
3324 W. Mercury Blvd.
Hampton, VA 23666
(757)-827-1667
thetenthinning79@yahoo.com

Ball Four Sportscards
10924 Hull Street Rd
Midlothian, VA 23112-3316
(804)-745-3687
follow us on facebook

Rick's Cards
689 Stephenson Rd
Stephenson, VA 22656-1736
(540)-662-4401

Collectors Corner
47024 Harry Byrd Hwy, Ste 106
Sterling, VA 20164-1029
(703)-450-7280
cardsharkmurph@aol.com

B&B Cards and Collectibles
4239 Holland Rd, Ste 792
Virginia Beach, VA 23452-1941
(757)-495-5523
rpres73140@aol.com

WASHINGTON

Atomic Cards
2008 S 314th St
Federal Way, WA 98003-5475
(866)-440-9224
westcoastbryan@yahoo.com

D J's Sportcards & Comics
1630 Duvall Ave NE
Renton, WA 98059-3976
(425)-235-4357
dj@djssportscards.com

Card Exchange
14020 Aurora Ave N
Seattle, WA 98133-6915
(206)-440-5467
sportsryter@aol.com

Knutsen's Northwest Sportscards
3816 Bridgeport Way West
University Place, WA 98466
(253)-564-9204
northwestsportscards@yahoo.com

WISCONSIN

Jeff's Sports, Inc.
14165 W Capitol Dr
Brookfield, WI 53005-2316
(262)-781-2546
jeffssports@jeffssports.com

Baseball Card Shoppe
126 Westgate Mall
Madison, WI 53711
(608)-274-8498
waunacard@charter.net

Rich's Sports Cards
3425 Kinzie Ave
Racine, WI 53405
(262)-770-4650
setuprich@yahoo.com

Fred Copp
(847)-967-7824
fcopp@sbcglobal.net

ONLINE

Baseball Card Exchange
bbcexchange.com

Blowout Cards
Blowoutcards.com

CheckOutMyCards
checkoutmycards.com

Collect and Save
CollectAndSave.com

Dave & Adam's Card World
dacardworld.com

DCS Sportscards
dcssportscards.com

DNA Cards
dnacards.net

FootballCardShop
footballcardshop.com

GotBaseballCards.com
770-736-9998
gotbaseballcards.com

Pittsburgh Sports Cards
pittsburghsportscards.com

Wax Box Cards
waxboxcards.com

To be listed in the ***Football Dealer Directory***,
please contact Bill Dumas at (972) 448-9147 or bdumas@beckett.com

1994 A1 Masters of the Grill

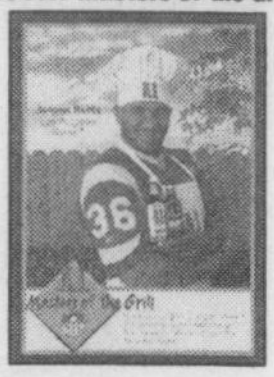

Sponsored by A.1. Steak Sauce, this 28-card standard-size set is actually a recipe card set. Inside gold and black borders, the fronts display a football player wearing his team's jersey, an apron, a hat with A.1. on it, and holding either A.1. steak sauce or barbeque utensils. The player's facsimile autograph appears in one of the upper corners, with player's name and team name immediately below. The backs present a picture of a prepared dish as well as recipe instructions for its preparing the food. The cards are unnumbered and checklisted below in alphabetical order.

COMPLETE SET (28)	10.00	25.00
1 Harris Barton	.40	1.00
2 Jerome Bettis	1.25	3.00
3 Ray Childress	.40	1.00
4 Eugene Chung	.30	.75
5 Jamie Dukes	.30	.75
6 Steve Emtman	.30	.75
7 Burt Grossman	.30	.75
8 Courtney Hall	.30	.75
9 Ken Harvey	.40	1.00
10 Chris Hinton	.30	.75
11 Kent Hull	.30	.75
12 Keith Jackson	.50	1.25
13 Rickey Jackson	.40	1.00
14 Cortez Kennedy	.50	1.25
15 Tim Krumrie	.30	.75
16 Jeff Lageman	.30	.75
17 Greg Lloyd	.50	1.25
18 Howie Long	.60	1.50
19 Hardy Nickerson	.40	1.00
20 Bart Oates	.30	.75
21 Ken Ruettgers	.30	.75
22 Dan Saleaumua	.30	.75
23 Alonzo Spellman	.40	1.00
24 Eric Swann	.50	1.25
25 Pat Swilling	.40	1.00
26 Tommy Vardell	.40	1.00
27 Erik Williams	.40	1.00
28 Gary Zimmerman	.30	.75

1995 Absolute

This 200-card standard-size set was released both through hobby and retail packaging. The hobby product was called Absolute while the retail product was titled Prime. The hobby boxes contained 24 packs per box with eight cards per pack. Cards 179-200 are dedicated to a draft pick subset. These "Absolute" draft pick cards are easy to differentiate from the regular cards as the words "Draft Picks" are emblazoned in large letters at the bottom of the card. In between the words "Draft Picks", the player is identified in white lettering against a black background. The "Prime" cards features full-bleed photos. The player is identified in the upper right corner and the words "Prime Playoff" are in the lower left corner. Against a yellowish background, the backs feature a player photo, some information as well as seasonal and career stats. Two special cards of both Tony Boselli and Kerry Collins were also inserted into both types of packs. Boselli cards were DP1G for the gold version and DP1S for the silver and Collins cards were DP2G for the gold and DP2S for the silver. Rookie Cards include Jeff Blake, Ki-Jana Carter, Kerry Collins, Joey Galloway, Napoleon Kaufman, Steve McNair, Rashaan Salaam, J.J. Stokes, Michael Westbrook and Tyrone Wheatley.

COMPLETE SET (200)	7.50	20.00
1 John Elway	.75	2.00
2 Reggie White	.15	.40
3 Errict Rhett	.07	.20
4 Deion Sanders	.20	.50
5 Rocket Ismail	.07	.20
6 Jerome Bettis	.15	.40
7 Randall Cunningham	.15	.40
8 Mario Bates	.07	.20
9 Dave Brown	.07	.20
10 Stan Humphries	.07	.20
11 Drew Bledsoe	.25	.60
12 Neil O'Donnell	.07	.20
13 Dan Marino	.75	2.00
14 Larry Centers	.07	.20
15 Craig Heyward	.07	.20
16 Bruce Smith	.15	.40
17 Erik Kramer	.02	.10
18 Jeff Blake RC	.40	1.00
19 Vinny Testaverde	.07	.20
20 Barry Sanders	.60	1.50
21 Boomer Esiason	.07	.20
22 Emmitt Smith	.60	1.50
23 Warren Moon	.07	.20
24 Junior Seau	.15	.40
25 Heath Shuler	.07	.20
26 Jackie Harris	.02	.10
27 Terance Mathis	.07	.20
28 Raymont Harris	.02	.10
29 Jim Kelly	.15	.40
30 Dan Wilkinson	.07	.20
31 Herman Moore	.15	.40
32 Shannon Sharpe	.07	.20
33 Antonio Langham	.02	.10
34 Charles Haley	.07	.20
35 Brett Favre	.75	2.00
36 Marshall Faulk	.50	1.25
37 Neil Smith	.07	.20
38 Harvey Williams	.02	.10
39 Johnny Bailey	.02	.10
40 O.J. McDuffie	.15	.40
41 David Palmer	.07	.20
42 Willie McGinest	.07	.20
43 Quinn Early	.07	.20
44 Johnny Johnson	.02	.10
45 Derek Brown TE	.02	.10
46 Charlie Garner	.15	.40
47 Byron Bam Morris	.02	.10
48 Natrone Means	.07	.20
49 Ken Norton Jr.	.07	.20
50 Troy Aikman	.40	1.00
51 Reggie Brooks	.07	.20
52 Trent Dilfer	.15	.40
53 Cortez Kennedy	.07	.20
54 Chuck Levy	.02	.10
55 Jeff George	.07	.20
56 Steve Young	.30	.75
57 Lewis Tillman	.02	.10
58 Carl Pickens	.07	.20
59 Jake Reed	.07	.20
60 Jay Novacek	.07	.20
61 Greg Hill	.07	.20
62 James Jett	.07	.20
63 Terry Kirby	.07	.20
64 Qadry Ismail	.07	.20
65 Ben Coates	.07	.20
66 Kevin Greene	.07	.20
67 Bryant Young	.07	.20
68 Brian Mitchell	.02	.10
69 Steve Walsh	.02	.10
70 Darnay Scott	.07	.20
71 Daryl Johnston	.07	.20
72 Glyn Milburn	.02	.10
73 Tim Brown	.15	.40
74 Isaac Bruce	.30	.75
75 Bernie Parmalee	.07	.20
76 Terry Allen	.07	.20
77 Jim Everett	.02	.10
78 Thomas Lewis	.07	.20
79 Vaughn Hebron	.02	.10
80 Rod Woodson	.07	.20
81 Rick Mirer	.07	.20
82 Dana Stubblefield	.07	.20
83 Bert Emanuel	.15	.40
84 Andre Reed	.07	.20
85 Jeff Graham	.02	.10
86 Johnnie Morton	.07	.20
87 LeShon Johnson	.07	.20
88 Michael Irvin	.15	.40
89 Derrick Alexander WR	.15	.40
90 Lake Dawson	.07	.20
91 Cody Carlson	.02	.10
92 Chris Warren	.07	.20
93 William Floyd	.07	.20
94 Charles Johnson	.07	.20
95 Roosevelt Potts	.02	.10
96 Cris Carter	.15	.40
97 Aaron Glenn	.02	.10
98 Curtis Conway	.15	.40
99 Kevin Williams WR	.07	.20
100 Jerry Rice	.40	1.00
101 Frank Reich	.02	.10
102 Harold Green	.02	.10
103 Russell Copeland	.02	.10
104 Rob Moore	.07	.20
105 Edgar Bennett	.07	.20
106 Darren Carrington	.02	.10
107 Tommy Maddox	.15	.40
108 Dave Meggett	.02	.10
109 Fred Barnett	.07	.20
110 Mark Seay	.07	.20
111 Gus Frerotte	.07	.20
112 Brent Jones	.02	.10
113 Chris Miller	.02	.10
114 Cedric Tillman	.02	.10
115 Mark Ingram	.02	.10
116 Eric Turner	.02	.10
117 Mark Carrier WR	.07	.20
118 Garrison Hearst	.15	.40
119 Craig Erickson	.02	.10
120 Derek Russell	.02	.10
121 Mike Sherrard	.02	.10
122 Horace Copeland	.02	.10
123 Jack Trudeau	.02	.10
124 Leroy Hoard	.02	.10
125 Gary Brown	.02	.10
126 Mel Gray	.02	.10
127 Steve Beuerlein	.07	.20
128 Marcus Allen	.15	.40
129 Irving Fryar	.07	.20
130 Marion Butts	.02	.10
131 Ricky Watters	.07	.20
132 Tony Martin	.07	.20
133 Lawrence Dawsey	.02	.10
134 Ronnie Harmon	.02	.10
135 Herschel Walker	.07	.20
136 Michael Haynes	.07	.20
137 Eric Green	.02	.10
138 Steve Bono	.07	.20
139 Jamir Miller	.02	.10
140 Rod Smith DB	.07	.20
141 Andre Rison	.07	.20
142 Eric Metcalf	.07	.20
143 Michael Timpson	.02	.10
144 Cornelius Bennett	.07	.20
145 Sean Dawkins	.07	.20
146 Scott Mitchell	.07	.20
147 Ray Childress	.02	.10
148 Jim Harbaugh	.07	.20
149 Reggie Cobb	.02	.10
150 Willie Roaf	.02	.10
151 Stevie Anderson	.02	.10
152 Barry Foster	.07	.20
153 Joe Montana	.75	2.00
154 David Klingler	.07	.20
155 Chris Chandler	.07	.20
156 Carnell Lake	.02	.10
157 Calvin Williams	.07	.20
158 Kenneth Davis	.02	.10
159 Tydus Winans	.02	.10
160 Sam Adams	.02	.10
161 Ronald Moore	.02	.10
162 Vincent Brisby	.02	.10
163 Alvin Harper	.02	.10
164 Jake Reed	.07	.20
165 Jeff Hostetler	.07	.20
166 Mark Brunell	.25	.60
167 Leonard Russell	.02	.10
168 Greg Truitt	.02	.10
169 Pete Metzelaars	.02	.10
170 Dave Krieg	.02	.10
171 Lorenzo White	.02	.10
172 Robert Brooks	.15	.40
173 Willie Davis	.07	.20
174 Irving Spikes	.07	.20
175 Rodney Hampton	.07	.20
176 Erric Pegram	.07	.20
177 Brian Blades	.07	.20
178 Shawn Jefferson	.02	.10
179 Tyrone Poole RC	.15	.40
180 Rob Johnson RC	.60	1.50
181 Ki-Jana Carter RC	.15	.40
182 Steve McNair RC	2.00	5.00
183 Michael Westbrook RC	.15	.40
184 Kerry Collins RC	1.25	3.00
185 Kevin Carter RC	.15	.40
186 Tony Boselli RC	.15	.40
187 Joey Galloway RC	1.00	2.50
188 Kyle Brady RC	.15	.40
189 J.J. Stokes RC	.15	.40
190 Warren Sapp RC	1.00	2.50
191 Tyrone Wheatley RC	.60	1.50
192 Napolean Kaufman RC	.75	2.00
193 James O. Stewart RC	.60	1.50
194 Rashaan Salaam RC	.07	.20
195 Ray Zellars RC	.07	.20
196 Todd Collins RC	.07	.20
197 Sherman Williams RC	.02	.10
198 Frank Sanders RC	.15	.40
199 Terrell Fletcher RC	.02	.10
200 Chad May RC	.02	.10
DP1G Tony Boselli Draft Gold	1.50	3.00
DP1S Tony Boselli Draft Silver	.75	2.00
DP2G Kerry Collins Draft Gold	2.00	5.00
DP2S Kerry Collins Draft Silver	2.00	5.00

1995 Absolute Die Cut Helmets

COMPLETE SET (30)	50.00	120.00
RANDOM INSERTS IN ABSOLUTE PAC		
1 Garrison Hearst	1.50	4.00
2 Jim Kelly	1.50	4.00
3 Jeff Blake	4.00	10.00
4 Emmitt Smith	6.00	15.00
5 John Elway	8.00	20.00
6 Brett Favre	8.00	20.00
7 Marshall Faulk	5.00	12.00
8 Marcus Allen	1.50	4.00
9 Jerome Bettis	1.50	4.00
10 Dan Marino	8.00	20.00
11 Cris Carter	1.50	4.00
12 Drew Bledsoe	2.50	6.00
13 Jim Everett	.40	1.00
14 Rodney Hampton	.75	2.00
15 Natrone Means	.75	2.00
16 Steve Young	3.00	8.00
17 Rick Mirer	.75	2.00
18 Errict Rhett	.75	2.00
19 Heath Shuler	.75	2.00
20 Lewis Tillman	.40	1.00
21 Barry Sanders	6.00	15.00
22 Leroy Hoard	.40	1.00
23 Rod Woodson	.75	2.00
24 Gary Brown	.40	1.00
25 Terance Mathis	.75	2.00
26 Frank Reich	.40	1.00
27 Steve Beuerlein	.75	2.00
28 Rocket Ismail	.75	2.00
29 Johnny Johnson	.40	1.00
30 Charlie Garner	1.50	4.00

1995 Absolute/Prime Pigskin Previews

COMPLETE SET (12)	50.00	120.00
COMP.SERIES 1 (6)	25.00	60.00
COMP.SERIES 2 (6)	25.00	60.00
7-12 INSERTS IN PRIME PACKS		
7-12 STATED ODDS 1:145 PRIME		
1 Emmitt Smith	10.00	25.00
2 Steve Young	5.00	12.00
3 Barry Sanders	10.00	25.00
4 Deion Sanders	3.00	8.00
5 Cris Carter	2.50	6.00
6 Errict Rhett	1.25	3.00
7 Dan Marino	12.50	30.00
8 Marshall Faulk	8.00	20.00
9 Natrone Means	1.25	3.00
10 Tim Brown	2.50	6.00
11 Drew Bledsoe	4.00	10.00
12 Marcus Allen	2.50	6.00

1995 Absolute Quad Series

COMPLETE SET (50)	125.00	300.00
RANDOM INSERTS IN ABSOLUTE PAC		
Q1 Joe Montana	25.00	60.00
Dan Marino		
Steve Young		
John Elway		
Q2 Troy Aikman	20.00	50.00
Brett Favre		
Drew Bledsoe		
Rick Mirer		
Q3 Trent Dilfer	5.00	12.00
Heath Shuler		
Mark Brunell		
Jeff Blake		
Q4 Randall Cunningham	2.00	5.00
Warren Moon		
Jim Kelly		
Boomer Esiason		
Q5 Jeff George	3.00	8.00
Dave Brown		
Stan Humphries		
Jim Everett		
Q6 Emmitt Smith	20.00	50.00
Barry Sanders		
Marshall Faulk		
Eric Rhett		
Q7 Marcus Allen	5.00	12.00
Ricky Watters		
William Floyd		
Natrone Means		
Q8 Garrison Hearst	3.00	8.00
Jerome Bettis		
Lewis Tillman		
Gary Brown		
Q9 Michael Irvin	15.00	30.00
Jerry Rice		
Tim Brown		
Cris Carter		
Q10 Pete Metzelaars	3.00	8.00
Byron Bam Morris		
Ben Coates		
Andre Rison		
Q11 Reggie White	6.00	15.00
Bruce Smith		
Deion Sanders		
Junior Seau		
Q12 Rob Moore	3.00	8.00
Larry Centers		
Jamir Miller		
Chuck Levy		
Q13 Craig Heyward UER	3.00	8.00
Terance Mathis		
Bert Emanuel		
Eric Metcalf		
Q14 Kenneth Davis	3.00	8.00
Andre Reed		
Russell Copeland		
Cornelius Bennett		
Q15 Frank Reich	5.00	12.00
Jack Trudeau		
Mark Carrier WR		
Tyrone Poole		
Q16 Jeff Graham	3.00	8.00
Curtis Conway		
Erik Kramer		
Steve Walsh		
Q17 Carl Pickens	3.00	8.00
Darnay Scott		
Harold Green		
David Klingler		
Q18 Vinny Testaverde	2.00	5.00
Derrick Alexander WR		
Leroy Hoard		
Lorenzo White		
Q19 Charles Haley	3.00	8.00
Kevin Williams WR		
Daryl Johnston		
Jay Novacek		
Q20 Glyn Milburn	2.00	5.00
Leonard Russell		
Derek Russell		
Shannon Sharpe		
Q21 Scott Mitchell	3.00	8.00
Brett Perriman		
Herman Moore		
Johnnie Morton		
Q22 Edgar Bennett	3.00	8.00
LeShon Johnson		
Robert Brooks		
Mark Ingram		
Q23 Cody Carlson	2.00	5.00
Mel Gray		
Chris Chandler		
Ray Childress		
Q24 Craig Erickson	3.00	8.00
Jim Harbaugh		
Roosevelt Potts		
Sean Dawkins		
Q25 Steve Beuerlein	5.00	12.00
Rob Johnson		
Cedric Tillman		
Reggie Cobb		
Q26 Greg Hill	3.00	8.00
Willie Davis		
Lake Dawson		
Steve Bono		
Q27 Harvey Williams	2.00	5.00
Jeff Hostetler		
James Jett		
Rocket Ismail		
Q28 Bernie Parmalee	2.00	5.00
Irving Spikes		
Terry Kirby		
Irving Fryar		
Q29 Terry Allen	3.00	8.00
David Palmer		
Qadry Ismail		
Jake Reed		
Q30 Marion Butts	2.00	5.00
Vincent Brisby		
Dave Meggett		
Willie McGinest		
Q31 Willie Roaf	2.00	5.00
Mario Bates		
Quinn Early		
Michael Haynes		
Q32 Herschel Walker	2.00	5.00
Mike Sherrard		
Derek Brown TE		
Thomas Lewis		
Q33 Stevie Anderson	3.00	8.00
Aaron Glenn		
Johnny Johnson		
Ron Moore		
Q34 Calvin Williams	5.00	12.00
Fred Barnett		
Vaughn Hebron		
Charlie Garner		
Q35 Charles Johnson	3.00	8.00
Neil O'Donnell		
Rod Woodson		
Erric Pegram		
Q36 Ronnie Harmon	2.00	5.00
Shawn Jefferson		
Tony Martin		
Mark Seay		
Q37 Brent Jones	3.00	8.00
Dana Stubblefield		
Bryant Young		
Ken Norton		
Q38 Chris Warren	3.00	8.00
Cortez Kennedy		
Sam Adams		
Brian Blades		
Q39 Tommy Maddox	5.00	12.00
Chris Miller		
Johnny Bailey		
Isaac Bruce		
Q40 Lawrence Dawsey	2.00	5.00
Alvin Harper		
Jackie Harris		
Horace Copeland		
Q41 Gus Frerotte	3.00	8.00
Brian Mitchell		
Reggie Brooks		
Tydus Winans		
Q42 Steve McNair	6.00	15.00
Kerry Collins		
Todd Collins		
Chad May		
Q43 Ki-Jana Carter	5.00	12.00
Tyrone Wheatley		
Napoleon Kaufman		
Rashaan Salaam		
Q44 Terrell Fletcher	3.00	8.00
Sherman Williams		
Ray Zellars		
James O.Stewart		
Q45 Michael Westbrook	3.00	8.00
Joey Galloway		
J.J. Stokes		
Frank Sanders		
Q46 Kevin Carter	5.00	12.00
Tony Boselli		
Warren Sapp		
Kyle Brady		
Q47 Greg Truitt	2.00	5.00
Dan Wilkinson		
Eric Turner		
Antonio Langham		
Q48 Carnell Lake	3.00	8.00
Neil Smith		
Rod Smith DB		
Kevin Greene		
Q49 O.J. McDuffie	3.00	8.00
Darren Carrington		
Michael Timpson		
Raymont Harris		
Q50 Rodney Hampton	2.00	5.00
Dave Krieg		
Barry Foster		
Eric Green		

1995 Absolute Unsung Heroes

COMPLETE SET (28)	5.00	12.00
*GOLD/SILVER: SAME VALUE		
GOLD ODDS 1:13 ABSOLUTE		
SILVER ODDS 1:13 PRIME		
1 Garth Jax	.20	.50
2 Craig Heyward	.30	.75
3 Steve Tasker	.30	.75
4 Raymont Harris	.20	.50
5 Jeff Blake	.50	1.25
6 Bob Dahl	.20	.50
7 Jason Garrett	.40	1.00
8 Gary Zimmerman	.20	.50
9 Tom Beer	.20	.50
10 John Jurkovic	.20	.50
11 Spencer Tillman	.20	.50
12 Devon McDonald	.20	.50
13 John Alt	.20	.50
14 Steve Wisniewski	.20	.50
15 Tim Bowens	.20	.50
16 Amp Lee	.20	.50
17 Todd Rucci	.20	.50
18 Tyrone Hughes	.30	.75
19 Michael Strahan	.60	1.50
20 Brad Baxter	.20	.50
21 Mark Bavaro	.20	.50
22 Yancey Thigpen	.60	1.50
23 Courtney Hall	.20	.50
24 Eric Davis	.20	.50
25 Rufus Porter	.20	.50
26 Jackie Slater	.30	.75
27 Courtney Hawkins	.30	.75
28 Gus Frerotte	.30	.75

1996 Absolute Samples

These promo cards were issued to preview the 1996 Playoff Absolute release. Each is very similar to its base brand card in design, except for the word "sample" where the card number otherwise would be.

COMPLETE SET (4)	3.00	8.00
1 Zack Crockett	.50	1.25
2 Terrell Davis	2.00	5.00
3 Rashaan Salaam	.60	1.50
4 Tamarick Vanover	.50	1.25

1996 Absolute

The 1996 Playoff Absolute set was issued in one series totalling 200 cards. The 6-card packs retailed for $3.75 each. Within every pack is five cards and an additional inner pack, featuring one collectible card. This concept from Playoff created three levels of color coded insertion ratios for the base cards: red, white and blue. The red level (1-100) are the most frequently inserted cards. The white level cards (101-150) appear in white inner packs which are found inside the Absolute pack. With one card per pack, the white packs appear approximately 18 per box. The blue level cards (151-200) are the hardest to find and also contain one card per pack. Approximately six packs per box will contain a blue pack, in place of the white pack. Rookie Cards in this set include Tim Biakabutuka, Terry Glenn, Eddie George, Keshawn Johnson, Leeland McElroy, Eric Moulds and Lawrence Phillips.

COMPLETE SET (200)	25.00	60.00
COMP.RED SET (100)	6.00	15.00
1 Jim Kelly	.25	.60
2 Michael Irvin	.25	.60
3 Jim Harbaugh	.10	.30
4 Warren Moon	.10	.30
5 Rick Mirer	.10	.30
6 Drew Bledsoe	.40	1.00
7 Steve Young	.50	1.25
8 Junior Seau	.25	.60
9 Sherman Williams	.05	.15
10 Jay Novacek	.05	.15
11 Bill Brooks	.05	.15
12 Steve Bono	.05	.15
13 Leroy Hoard	.05	.15
14 Willie Jackson	.10	.30
15 Irving Fryar	.10	.30
16 Tony McGee	.05	.15
17 Neil O'Donnell	.10	.30
18 Fred Barnett	.05	.15
19 Erric Pegram	.05	.15
20 Derrick Moore	.05	.15
21 Johnnie Morton	.10	.30
22 James Jett	.10	.30
23 Tim Brown	.25	.60
24 Kevin Miniefield	.05	.15
25 Jim McMahon	.10	.30
26 Brian Blades	.05	.15
27 Henry Ellard	.05	.15
28 Calvin Williams	.05	.15
29 Chris Chandler	.10	.30
30 Rod Woodson	.10	.30
31 Ronnie Harmon	.05	.15
32 Brent Jones	.05	.15
33 Qadry Ismail	.10	.30
34 Steve Tasker	.05	.15
35 Eric Green	.05	.15
36 Brian Mitchell	.05	.15
37 Herschel Walker	.10	.30
38 Sean Dawkins	.05	.15
39 Bryce Paup	.05	.15
40 Dorsey Levens	.25	.60
41 Andre Rison	.10	.30
42 Lamont Warren	.05	.15
43 Earnest Byner	.05	.15
44 Bobby Engram RC	.25	.60
45 Simeon Rice RC	.60	1.50
46 Michael Jackson	.10	.30
47 Marvin Harrison RC	1.50	4.00
48 Thurman Thomas	.25	.60
49 Charles Haley	.10	.30
50 Rob Moore	.10	.30
51 Bryan Cox	.05	.15
52 Horace Copeland	.05	.15
53 Rodney Peete	.05	.15
54 Jeff Graham	.05	.15
55 Charles Johnson	.05	.15
56 Natrone Means	.10	.30
57 Terrell Fletcher	.05	.15
58 Eric Bieniemy	.05	.15
59 Karim Abdul-Jabbar RC	.25	.60
60 Quinn Early	.05	.15
61 Mark Bruener	.05	.15
62 Shawn Jefferson	.05	.15
63 Vinny Testaverde	.10	.30
64 Derrick Mayes RC	.25	.60
65 Mario Bates	.10	.30
66 J.J. Birden	.05	.15
67 Eddie Kennison RC	.25	.60
68 Steve Walsh	.05	.15
69 Mark Chmura	.10	.30
70 Mike Sherrard	.05	.15
71 Boomer Esiason	.10	.30
72 Alex Van Dyke RC	.10	.30
73 Jake Reed	.10	.30
74 Jackie Harris	.05	.15
75 Mark Rypien	.05	.15
76 Chris Calloway	.05	.15
77 Amani Toomer RC	.60	1.50
78 Terrell Davis	1.25	3.00
79 Rocket Ismail	.05	.15
80 Derek Loville	.05	.15
81 Ben Coates	.10	.30
82 Kyle Brady	.05	.15
83 Willie Green	.05	.15
84 Randall Cunningham	.25	.60
85 Amp Lee	.05	.15
86 Bert Emanuel	.10	.30
87 Jason Dunn RC	.10	.30
88 Michael Haynes	.05	.15
89 Robert Green	.05	.15
90 Willie Davis	.05	.15
91 O.J. McDuffie	.10	.30
92 Harold Green	.05	.15
93 Ken Dilger	.10	.30
94 Brett Perriman	.05	.15
95 Eric Zeier	.05	.15
96 Jerome Bettis	.25	.60
97 Rickey Dudley RC	.25	.60
98 Darnay Scott	.10	.30
99 Mark Brunell	.40	1.00
100 Christian Fauria	.05	.15
101 Jeff Blake	.60	1.50
102 Troy Aikman	1.50	4.00
103 John Elway	3.00	8.00
104 Barry Sanders	2.50	6.00
105 Curtis Conway	.60	1.50
106 Wayne Chrebet	.75	2.00
107 Lake Dawson	.30	.75
108 Jerry Rice	1.50	4.00
109 Kevin Williams	.08	.25
110 Zack Crockett	.08	.25
111 Vincent Brisby	.08	.25
112 Rodney Thomas	.08	.25
113 Rodney Hampton	.30	.75
114 Adrian Murrell	.10	.30
115 Bruce Smith	.60	1.50
116 Napoleon Kaufman	.60	1.50
117 Byron Bam Morris	.08	.25
118 Anthony Miller	.30	.75
119 Aaron Hayden RC	.30	.75
120 Joey Galloway	.25	.60
121 Trent Dilfer	.30	.75
122 Stoney Case	.08	.25
123 Tamarick Vanover	.10	.30
124 Eric Metcalf	.30	.75
125 Marcus Allen	.60	1.50
126 James O. Stewart	.30	.75
127 Charlie Garner	.30	.75
128 Yancey Thigpen	.30	.75
129 William Floyd	.30	.75
130 Terry Allen	.30	.75
131 Robert Smith	.30	.75
132 Todd Kinchen	.08	.25
133 Gus Frerotte	.30	.75
134 Frank Sanders	.30	.75
135 Scott Mitchell	.30	.75
136 Greg Hill	.30	.75
137 Edgar Bennett	.30	.75
138 Alvin Harper	.08	.25
139 Reggie White	.60	1.50
140 Craig Heyward	.08	.25
141 Todd Collins	.30	.75
142 Ernie Mills	.08	.25
143 Keyshawn Johnson RC	1.00	2.50
144 Mark Carrier WR	.08	.25
145 Robert Brooks	.60	1.50
146 Bernie Parmalee	.08	.25
147 Carl Pickens	.30	.75
148 Kevin Hardy RC	.60	1.50
149 Jonathan Ogden RC	.60	1.50
150 Lawrence Phillips RC	.60	1.50
151 Emmitt Smith	4.00	10.00
152 Brett Favre	5.00	12.00
153 Dan Marino	5.00	12.00
154 Jim Everett	.25	.60
155 Dave Brown	.50	1.25
156 Jeff Hostetler	.50	1.25
157 Heath Shuler	.50	1.25
158 Daryl Johnston	.50	1.25
159 Terance Mathis	.50	1.25
160 Curtis Martin	2.00	5.00
161 Ray Zellars	.25	.60
162 Ricky Watters	.50	1.25
163 Chris Warren	.50	1.25
164 Larry Centers	.50	1.25
165 Steve McNair	2.00	5.00
166 Terry Kirby	.50	1.25
167 Rob Johnson	1.00	2.50
168 Dave Meggett	.25	.60
169 Antonio Freeman	.25	.60
170 Marshall Faulk	1.50	4.00
171 Andre Hastings	.05	.15
172 Stan Humphries	.50	1.25
173 Errict Rhett	.50	1.25
174 Michael Westbrook	1.00	2.50
175 Deion Sanders	1.50	4.00
176 Jeff George	.50	1.25
177 Cris Carter	1.00	2.50
178 Chris Sanders	.50	1.25
179 Ki-Jana Carter	.50	1.25
180 Kordell Stewart	1.00	2.50
181 Isaac Bruce	1.00	2.50
182 Terry Glenn RC	2.00	5.00
183 Garrison Hearst	.50	1.25
184 Erik Kramer	.25	.60
185 Leeland McElroy RC	.50	1.25
186 Rashaan Salaam	.50	1.25
187 Kimble Anders	.25	.60
188 Chad May	.25	.60
189 Tony Martin	.50	1.25
190 J.J. Stokes	1.00	2.50
191 Darick Holmes	.25	.60
192 Eric Moulds RC	2.50	6.00
193 Shannon Sharpe	.50	1.25
194 Tim Biakabutuka RC	1.00	2.50
195 Eddie George RC	2.50	6.00
196 Mike Alstott RC	2.00	5.00
197 Kerry Collins	1.00	2.50
198 Harvey Williams	.25	.60
199 Herman Moore	.50	1.25
200 Tyrone Wheatley	.50	1.25

1996 Absolute Metal XL

COMPLETE SET (36)	125.00	300.00
COMP.SERIES 1 SET (18)	75.00	200.00
COMP.SERIES 2 SET (18)	40.00	100.00
1-18: STATED ODDS 1:96 ABSOLUTE PACKS		
19-36: STATED ODDS 1:80 PRIME PACKS		
1 Troy Aikman	5.00	12.00
2 Emmitt Smith	12.50	30.00
3 Barry Sanders	8.00	20.00
4 Brett Favre	15.00	40.00
5 Dan Marino	15.00	40.00
6 Jerry Rice	5.00	12.00
7 Marshall Faulk	5.00	12.00
8 Curtis Martin	6.00	15.00
9 Rashaan Salaam	1.50	4.00
10 Harvey Williams	.75	2.00
11 Ricky Watters	1.50	4.00
12 Yancey Thigpen	1.00	2.50
13 Chris Warren	1.50	4.00
14 Errict Rhett	1.50	4.00
15 Terry Allen	1.00	2.50
16 Robert Brooks	2.00	5.00
17 Anthony Miller	1.00	2.50
18 Erik Kramer	.75	2.00
19 Michael Irvin	.75	2.00
20 John Elway	10.00	25.00
21 Jim Harbaugh	.40	1.00
22 Steve Young	1.50	4.00
23 Deion Sanders	5.00	12.00
24 Terrell Davis	4.00	10.00
25 Reggie White	2.00	5.00
26 Herman Moore	1.50	4.00
27 Rodney Hampton	1.00	2.50

28 Cris Carter 3.00 8.00
29 Isaac Bruce 3.00 8.00
30 Kordell Stewart 3.00 8.00
31 Brett Perriman .20 .50
32 Joey Galloway .75 2.00
33 Drew Bledsoe 1.25 3.00
34 J.J. Stokes 3.00 8.00
35 Napoleon Kaufman 2.00 5.00
36 Tim Brown .75 2.00

1996 Absolute Quad Series

COMPLETE SET (35) 200.00 400.00
STATED ODDS 1:24
1 Stoney Case 4.00 10.00
Garrison Hearst
Rob Moore
Frank Sanders
2 J.J.Birden 2.50 6.00
Bert Emanuel
Jeff George
Craig Heyward
3 Todd Collins 6.00 15.00
Bill Brooks
Jim Kelly
Bryce Paup
4 Mark Carrier WR 6.00 15.00
Kerry Collins
Willie Green
Derrick Moore
5 Curtis Conway 4.00 10.00
Robert Green
Erik Kramer
Kevin Miniefield
6 Eric Bieniemy 6.00 15.00
Jeff Blake
Harold Green
Tony McGee
7 Earnest Byner 2.50 6.00
Michael Jackson
Andre Rison
Eric Zeier
8 Michael Irvin 7.50 20.00
Jay Novacek
Deion Sanders
Kevin Williams
9 Terrell Davis 15.00 40.00
John Elway
Anthony Miller
Shannon Sharpe
10 Scott Mitchell 4.00 10.00
Herman Moore
Johnnie Morton
Brett Perriman
11 Edgar Bennett 10.00 25.00
Mark Chmura
Antonio Freeman
Reggie White
12 Chris Chandler 6.00 15.00
Steve McNair
Chris Sanders
Rodney Thomas
13 Zack Crockett 4.00 10.00
Sean Dawkins
Ken Dilger
Jim Harbaugh
14 Mark Brunell 10.00 25.00
Willie Jackson
Rob Johnson
James O.Stewart
15 Marcus Allen 6.00 15.00
Kimble Anders
Lake Dawson
Tamarick Vanover
16 Eric Green 4.00 10.00
Terry Kirby
O.J. McDuffie
Bernie Parmalee
17 Cris Carter 4.00 10.00
Warren Moon
Robert Smith
Chad May
18 Drew Bledsoe 10.00 25.00
Vincent Brisby
Ben Coates
Dave Meggett
19 Mario Bates 2.50 6.00
Jim Everett
Michael Haynes
Ray Zellars
20 Dave Brown 4.00 10.00
Chris Calloway
Rodney Hampton
Tyrone Wheatley
21 Kyle Brady 7.50 20.00
Wayne Chrebet
Adrian Murrell
Neil O'Donnell
22 Tim Brown 6.00 15.00
Jeff Hostetler
Rocket Ismail
Napoleon Kaufman
23 Charlie Garner 4.00 10.00
Rodney Peete
Ricky Watters
Calvin Williams
24 Andre Hastings 6.00 15.00
Ernie Mills
Kordell Stewart
Rod Woodson
25 Terrell Fletcher 6.00 15.00
Ronnie Harmon
Aaron Hayden
Junior Seau
26 William Floyd 12.50 30.00
Derek Loville
J.J.Stokes
Steve Young
27 Brian Blades 6.00 15.00
Christian Fauria
Joey Galloway
Rick Mirer
28 Mark Rypien 6.00 15.00
Isaac Bruce
Todd Kinchen
Steve Walsh
29 Horace Copeland 4.00 10.00
Trent Dilfer
Alvin Harper
James Harris
30 Henry Ellard 6.00 15.00
Gus Frerotte
Heath Shuler
Michael Westbrook
31 Keyshawn Johnson 6.00 15.00
Kevin Hardy
Simeon Rice
Jonathan Ogden
32 Lawrence Phillips 7.50 20.00
Tim Biakabutuka
Terry Glenn
Rickey Dudley
33 Eddie George 12.50 30.00
Marvin Harrison
Eric Moulds
Eddie Kennison
34 Derrick Mayes 6.00 15.00
Karim Abdul-Jabbar
Alex Van Dyke
Bobby Engram
35 Mike Alstott 6.00 15.00
Leeland McElroy
Jason Dunn
Amani Toomer

1996 Absolute Unsung Heroes

COMPLETE SET (30) 10.00 25.00
COMP.SERIES 1 SET (15) 4.00 10.00
COMP.SERIES 2 SET (15) 6.00 15.00
1-15 ODDS 1:24 ABSOLUTE PACKS
16-30 ODDS 1:24 PRIME PACKS
1 Bill Bates 1.00 2.50
2 Jeff Brady .30 .75
3 Ray Brown .30 .75
4 Isaac Bruce 1.00 2.50
5 Larry Centers .50 1.25
6 Mark Chmura .50 1.25
7 Keith Elias .30 .75
8 Robert Green .30 .75
9 Andy Harmon .30 .75
10 Rodney Holman .30 .75
11 Derek Loville .30 .75
12 J.J. McCleskey .30 .75
13 Sam Mills .50 1.25
14 Hardy Nickerson .50 1.25
15 Jessie Tuggle .30 .75
16 Eric Bieniemy .30 .75
17 Blaine Bishop .30 .75
18 Mark Brunell 1.00 2.50
19 Wayne Chrebet 1.00 2.50
20 Vince Evans .30 .75
21 Sam Gash .30 .75
22 Tim Grunhard .30 .75
23 Jim Harbaugh .50 1.25
24 Dwayne Harper .30 .75
25 Bernie Parmalee .30 .75
26 Reggie Rivers .30 .75
27 Eugene Robinson .50 1.25
28 Kordell Stewart 1.00 2.50
29 Steve Tasker 1.00 2.50
30 Bennie Thompson .30 .75

1996 Absolute Xtreme Team

COMPLETE SET (30) 150.00 300.00
STATED ODDS 1:24
1 Troy Aikman 5.00 12.00
2 Emmitt Smith 12.50 30.00
3 Jerry Rice 5.00 12.00
4 Dan Marino 15.00 40.00
5 Brett Favre 15.00 40.00
6 Barry Sanders 8.00 20.00
7 Michael Irvin 2.00 5.00
8 John Elway 10.00 25.00
9 Joey Galloway 1.00 2.50
10 Steve Young 2.00 5.00
11 Deion Sanders 5.00 12.00
12 Terrell Davis 4.00 10.00
13 Herman Moore 1.00 2.50
14 Reggie White 2.00 5.00
15 Cris Carter 2.00 5.00
16 Rodney Hampton 1.00 2.50
17 Isaac Bruce 2.00 5.00
18 Brett Perriman .50 1.25
19 Curtis Conway 2.00 5.00
20 Scott Mitchell 1.00 2.50
21 Rashaan Salaam 1.00 2.50
22 Robert Brooks 2.00 5.00
23 Marshall Faulk 5.00 12.00
24 Curtis Martin 6.00 15.00
25 Harvey Williams .50 1.25
26 Yancey Thigpen 1.00 2.50
27 Chris Warren 1.00 2.50
28 Errict Rhett 1.00 2.50
29 Terry Allen 1.00 2.50
30 Carl Pickens 1.00 2.50

1997 Absolute

The 1997 Playoff Absolute set was issued together as three series totaling 200 cards. The first 100-cards (green bordered) were the easiest to pull with the second 50 (blue bordered) slightly tougher and the final 50 (red bordered) the most difficult to pull. Several insert sets were included with the product which was packaged five-cards and one Chip Shot per pack with 24-packs per box.

COMPLETE SET (200) 30.00 80.00
COMP.GREEN SET (100) 10.00 25.00
1 Marcus Allen .20 .50
2 Eric Bieniemy .07 .20
3 Jason Dunn .07 .20
4 Jim Harbaugh .10 .30
5 Michael Westbrook .10 .30
6 Tiki Barber RC 1.50 4.00
7 Frank Reich .07 .20
8 Irving Fryar .10 .30
9 Courtney Hawkins .07 .20
10 Eric Zeier .10 .30
11 Kent Graham .07 .20
12 Trent Dilfer .20 .50
13 Neil O'Donnell .10 .30
14 Reidel Anthony RC .20 .50
15 Jeff Hostetler .07 .20
16 Lawrence Phillips .07 .20
17 Dave Brown .07 .20
18 Mike Tomczak .07 .20
19 Jake Reed .10 .30
20 Anthony Miller .07 .20
21 Eric Metcalf .10 .30
22 Sedrick Shaw RC .10 .30
23 Anthony Johnson .07 .20
24 Mario Bates .07 .20
25 Dorsey Levens .20 .50
26 Stan Humphries .10 .30
27 Ben Coates .10 .30
28 Tyrone Wheatley .10 .30
29 Adrian Murrell .10 .30
30 William Henderson .10 .30
31 Warrick Dunn RC .75 2.00
32 LeShon Johnson .07 .20
33 James O.Stewart .10 .30
34 Edgar Bennett .10 .30
35 Raymont Harris .07 .20
36 LeRoy Butler .07 .20
37 Darren Woodson .07 .20
38 Darnell Autry RC .10 .30
39 Johnnie Morton .10 .30
40 William Floyd .10 .30
41 Terrell Fletcher .07 .20
42 Leonard Russell .07 .20
43 Henry Ellard .07 .20
44 Terrell Owens .20 .50
45 John Friesz .07 .20
46 Antowain Smith RC .60 1.50
47 Charles Johnson .10 .30
48 Rickey Dudley .10 .30
49 Lake Dawson .07 .20
50 Bert Emanuel .10 .30
51 Zach Thomas .20 .50
52 Earnest Byner .07 .20
53 Yatil Green RC .10 .30
54 Chris Spielman .07 .20
55 Muhsin Muhammad .10 .30
56 Bobby Engram .10 .30
57 Eric Bjornson .07 .20
58 Willie Green .07 .20
59 Derrick Mayes .10 .30
60 Chris Sanders .07 .20
61 Jimmy Smith .10 .30
62 Tony Gonzalez RC 1.00 2.50
63 Rich Gannon .20 .50
64 Stanley Pritchett .07 .20
65 Brad Johnson .20 .50
66 Rodney Peete .07 .20
67 Sam Gash .07 .20
68 Chris Calloway .07 .20
69 Chris T. Jones .07 .20
70 Will Blackwell RC .10 .30
71 Mark Bruener .07 .20
72 Terry Kirby .10 .30
73 Brian Blades .07 .20
74 Craig Heyward .07 .20
75 Jamie Asher .07 .20
76 Terance Mathis .10 .30
77 Troy Davis RC .10 .30
78 Bruce Smith .10 .30
79 Simeon Rice .10 .30
80 Fred Barnett .07 .20
81 Tim Brown .20 .50
82 James Jett .10 .30
83 Mark Carrier WR .07 .20
84 Shawn Jefferson .07 .20
85 Ken Dilger .07 .20
86 Rae Carruth RC .07 .20
87 Keenan McCardell .10 .30
88 Michael Irvin .20 .50
89 Mark Chmura .10 .30
90 Derrick Alexander WR .10 .30
91 Andre Reed .10 .30
92 Ed McCaffrey .10 .30
93 Erik Kramer .07 .20
94 Albert Connell RC .20 .50
95 Frank Wycheck .07 .20
96 Zack Crockett .07 .20
97 Jim Everett .07 .20
98 Michael Haynes .07 .20
99 Jeff Graham .07 .20
100 Brent Jones .10 .30
101 Troy Aikman 1.25 3.00
102 Byron Hanspard RC .10 .30
103 Robert Brooks .50 1.25
104 Karim Abdul-Jabbar .50 1.25
105 Drew Bledsoe .60 1.50
106 Napoleon Kaufman .50 1.25
107 Steve Young .75 2.00
108 Leeland McElroy .07 .20
109 Jamal Anderson .20 .50
110 David LaFleur RC .20 .50
111 Vinny Testaverde .30 .75
112 Eric Moulds .50 1.25
113 Tim Biakabutuka .50 1.25
114 Rick Mirer .20 .50
115 Jeff Blake .50 1.25
116 Jim Schwantz RC .20 .50
117 Herman Moore .30 .75
118 Ike Hilliard RC 1.00 2.50
119 Reggie White .50 1.25
120 Steve McNair .75 2.00
121 Marshall Faulk .75 2.00
122 Natrone Means .30 .75
123 Greg Hill .30 .75
124 O.J. McDuffie .30 .75
125 Robert Smith .30 .75
126 Bryant Westbrook RC .50 1.25
127 Ray Zellars .20 .50
128 Rodney Hampton .30 .75
129 Wayne Chrebet .20 .50
130 Desmond Howard .30 .75
131 Ty Detmer .30 .75
132 Erric Pegram .20 .50
133 Yancey Thigpen .30 .75
134 Danny Wuerffel RC .20 .50
135 Charlie Jones .20 .50
136 Chris Warren .30 .75
137 Isaac Bruce .50 1.25
138 Errict Rhett .30 .75
139 Gus Frerotte .50 1.25
140 Frank Sanders .30 .75
141 Todd Collins .30 .75
142 Jake Plummer RC UER 5.00 12.00
(height listed at 6-24)
143 Darnay Scott .30 .75
144 Rashaan Salaam .50 1.25
145 Terrell Davis .75 2.00
146 Scott Mitchell .30 .75
147 Junior Seau .50 1.25
148 Warren Moon .30 .75
149 Wesley Walls .20 .50
150 Daryl Johnston .30 .75
151 Brett Favre 5.00 12.00
152 Emmitt Smith 4.00 10.00
153 Dan Marino 5.00 12.00
154 Larry Centers .50 1.25
155 Michael Jackson .50 1.25
156 Kerry Collins .20 .50
157 Curtis Conway .50 1.25
158 Peter Boulware RC .75 2.00
159 Carl Pickens .50 1.25
160 Shannon Sharpe .50 1.25
161 Brett Perriman .30 .75
162 Eddie George .75 2.00
163 Mark Brunell 1.50 4.00
164 Tamarick Vanover .50 1.25
165 Cris Carter .75 2.00
166 Corey Dillon RC 6.00 15.00
167 Curtis Martin 1.50 4.00
168 Amani Toomer .50 1.25
169 Jeff George .50 1.25
170 Kordell Stewart .75 2.00
171 Garrison Hearst .50 1.25
172 Tony Banks .50 1.25
173 Mike Alstott .75 2.00
174 Jim Druckenmiller RC .10 .30
175 Chris Chandler .50 1.25
176 Byron Bam Morris .30 .75
177 Billy Joe Hobert .50 1.25
178 Ernie Mills .30 .75
179 Ki-Jana Carter .30 .75
180 Deion Sanders .75 2.00
181 Ricky Watters .50 1.25
182 Shawn Springs RC .75 2.00
183 Barry Sanders 4.00 10.00
184 Antonio Freeman .75 2.00
185 Marvin Harrison .75 2.00
186 Elvis Grbac .50 1.25
187 Terry Glenn .75 2.00
188 Willie Roaf .30 .75
189 Keyshawn Johnson .75 2.00
190 Orlando Pace RC .75 2.00
191 Jerome Bettis .75 2.00
192 Tony Martin .50 1.25
193 Jerry Rice 2.50 6.00
194 Joey Galloway .50 1.25
195 Terry Allen .75 2.00
196 Eddie Kennison .50 1.25
197 Thurman Thomas .75 2.00
198 Darrell Russell RC .30 .75
199 Rob Moore .50 1.25
200 John Elway 5.00 12.00

1997 Absolute Bronze Redemption

COMP.BRONZE SET (200) 100.00 200.00
*BRONZE 1-100: .6X TO 1.5X HI COL.
*BRONZE 101-150: .6X TO 1.5X HI COL.
*BRONZE 151-200: .5X TO 1X HI COL.
BRONZE REDEMPTION SET ODDS 1:1440
COMP.GOLD SET (200) 150.00 400.00
*GOLD 1-100: 1.2X TO 3X HI COL.
*GOLD 101-150: 1.2X TO 3X HI COL.
*GOLD 151-200: .8X TO 2X HI COL.
GOLD REDEMPTION SET ODDS 1:2880
COMP.SILVER SET (200) 150.00 300.00
*SILVER 1-100: 1X TO 2.5X HI COL.
*SILVER 101-150: 1X TO 2.5X HI COL.
*SILVER 151-200: .6X TO 1.5X HI COL.
SILVER REDEMPTION SET ODDS 1:1920
FOIL SET AVAILABLE VIA MAIL REDEMPTION

1997 Absolute Chip Shots Black

COMPLETE SET (200) 60.00 150.00
EACH PRINTED IN BLUE, BLACK, AND RED
*RED CHIP: .4X TO 1X BLACK
ONE PER PACK
1 Marcus Allen .60 1.50
2 Eric Bieniemy .15 .40
3 Jason Dunn .15 .40
4 Jim Harbaugh .30 .75
5 Michael Westbrook .30 .75
6 Tiki Barber 2.00 5.00
7 Frank Reich .15 .40
8 Irving Fryar .30 .75
9 Courtney Hawkins .15 .40
10 Eric Zeier .30 .75
11 Kent Graham .15 .40
12 Trent Dilfer .60 1.50
13 Neil O'Donnell .30 .75
14 Reidel Anthony .30 .75
15 Jeff Hostetler .15 .40
16 Lawrence Phillips .15 .40
17 Dave Brown .15 .40
18 Mike Tomczak .15 .40
19 Jake Reed .30 .75
20 Anthony Miller .15 .40
21 Eric Metcalf .30 .75
22 Sedrick Shaw .30 .75
23 Anthony Johnson .15 .40
24 Mario Bates .15 .40
25 Dorsey Levens .60 1.50
26 Stan Humphries .30 .75
27 Ben Coates .30 .75
28 Tyrone Wheatley .30 .75
29 Adrian Murrell .30 .75
30 William Henderson .30 .75
31 Warrick Dunn 1.00 2.50
32 LeShon Johnson .15 .40
33 James O.Stewart .30 .75
34 Edgar Bennett .30 .75
35 Raymont Harris .15 .40
36 LeRoy Butler .15 .40
37 Darren Woodson .15 .40
38 Darnell Autry .15 .40
39 Johnnie Morton .30 .75
40 William Floyd .15 .40
41 Terrell Fletcher .15 .40
42 Leonard Russell .15 .40
43 Henry Ellard .15 .40
44 Terrell Owens .60 1.50
45 John Friesz .15 .40
46 Antowain Smith .60 1.50
47 Charles Johnson .30 .75
48 Rickey Dudley .30 .75
49 Lake Dawson .15 .40
50 Bert Emanuel .30 .75
51 Zach Thomas .60 1.50
52 Earnest Byner .15 .40
53 Yatil Green .30 .75
54 Chris Spielman .15 .40
55 Muhsin Muhammad .30 .75
56 Bobby Engram .30 .75
57 Eric Bjornson .15 .40
58 Willie Green .15 .40
59 Derrick Mayes .30 .75
60 Chris Sanders .15 .40
61 Jimmy Smith .30 .75
62 Tony Gonzalez 1.25 3.00
63 Rich Gannon .60 1.50
64 Stanley Pritchett .15 .40
65 Brad Johnson .60 1.50
66 Rodney Peete .15 .40
67 Sam Gash .15 .40
68 Chris Calloway .15 .40
69 Chris T. Jones .15 .40
70 Will Blackwell .15 .40
71 Mark Bruener .15 .40
72 Terry Kirby .30 .75
73 Brian Blades .15 .40
74 Craig Heyward .15 .40
75 Jamie Asher .15 .40
76 Terance Mathis .30 .75
77 Troy Davis .30 .75
78 Bruce Smith .30 .75
79 Simeon Rice .30 .75
80 Fred Barnett .15 .40
81 Tim Brown .60 1.50
82 James Jett .30 .75
83 Mark Carrier WR .15 .40
84 Shawn Jefferson .15 .40
85 Ken Dilger .15 .40
86 Rae Carruth .15 .40
87 Keenan McCardell .30 .75
88 Michael Irvin .60 1.50
89 Mark Chmura .30 .75
90 Derrick Alexander WR .30 .75
91 Andre Reed .30 .75
92 Ed McCaffrey .30 .75
93 Erik Kramer .15 .40
94 Albert Connell .15 .40
95 Frank Wycheck .15 .40
96 Zack Crockett .15 .40
97 Jim Everett .15 .40
98 Michael Haynes .15 .40
99 Jeff Graham .15 .40
100 Brent Jones .15 .40
101 Troy Aikman 2.00 5.00
102 Byron Hanspard .30 .75
103 Robert Brooks .30 .75
104 Karim Abdul-Jabbar .60 1.50
105 Drew Bledsoe 1.25 3.00
106 Napoleon Kaufman .60 1.50
107 Steve Young 1.50 4.00
108 Leeland McElroy .15 .40
109 Jamal Anderson .60 1.50
110 David LaFleur .15 .40
111 Vinny Testaverde .30 .75
112 Eric Moulds .60 1.50
113 Tim Biakabutuka .30 .75
114 Rick Mirer .15 .40
115 Jeff Blake .30 .75
116 Jim Schwantz .15 .40
117 Herman Moore .30 .75
118 Ike Hilliard .60 1.50
119 Reggie White .60 1.50
120 Steve McNair 1.00 2.50
121 Marshall Faulk .75 2.00
122 Natrone Means .30 .75
123 Greg Hill .15 .40
124 O.J. McDuffie .30 .75
125 Robert Smith .30 .75
126 Bryant Westbrook .15 .40
127 Ray Zellars .15 .40
128 Rodney Hampton .30 .75
129 Wayne Chrebet .60 1.50
130 Desmond Howard .30 .75
131 Ty Detmer .30 .75
132 Erric Pegram .15 .40
133 Yancey Thigpen .30 .75
134 Danny Wuerffel .60 1.50
135 Charlie Jones .30 .75
136 Chris Warren .30 .75
137 Isaac Bruce .60 1.50
138 Errict Rhett .15 .40
139 Gus Frerotte .15 .40
140 Frank Sanders .15 .40
141 Todd Collins .15 .40
142 Jake Plummer 1.50 4.00
143 Darnay Scott .30 .75
144 Rashaan Salaam .15 .40
145 Terrell Davis 1.00 2.50
146 Scott Mitchell .30 .75
147 Junior Seau .60 1.50
148 Warren Moon .60 1.50
149 Wesley Walls .30 .75
150 Daryl Johnston .30 .75
151 Brett Favre 4.00 10.00
152 Emmitt Smith 3.00 8.00
153 Dan Marino 4.00 10.00
154 Larry Centers .30 .75
155 Michael Jackson .30 .75
156 Kerry Collins .60 1.50
157 Curtis Conway .30 .75
158 Peter Boulware .60 1.50
159 Carl Pickens .30 .75
160 Shannon Sharpe .30 .75
161 Brett Perriman .15 .40
162 Eddie George .60 1.50
163 Mark Brunell 1.25 3.00
164 Tamarick Vanover .30 .75
165 Cris Carter .60 1.50
166 Corey Dillon 2.00 5.00
167 Curtis Martin 1.00 2.50
168 Amani Toomer .30 .75
169 Jeff George .30 .75
170 Kordell Stewart .60 1.50
171 Garrison Hearst .30 .75
172 Tony Banks .60 1.50
173 Mike Alstott .60 1.50
174 Jim Druckenmiller .30 .75
175 Chris Chandler .30 .75
176 Byron Bam Morris .15 .40
177 Billy Joe Hobert .30 .75
178 Ernie Mills .15 .40
179 Ki-Jana Carter .15 .40
180 Deion Sanders .60 1.50
181 Ricky Watters .30 .75
182 Shawn Springs .15 .40
183 Barry Sanders 3.00 8.00
184 Antonio Freeman .60 1.50
185 Marvin Harrison .60 1.50
186 Elvis Grbac .30 .75
187 Terry Glenn .60 1.50
188 Willie Roaf .15 .40
189 Keyshawn Johnson .60 1.50
190 Orlando Pace .60 1.50
191 Jerome Bettis .60 1.50
192 Tony Martin .30 .75
193 Jerry Rice 2.00 5.00
194 Joey Galloway .30 .75
195 Terry Allen .60 1.50
196 Eddie Kennison .30 .75
197 Thurman Thomas .60 1.50
198 Darrell Russell .15 .40
199 Rob Moore .30 .75
200 John Elway 4.00 10.00
S162 Eddie George Sample .40 1.00

1997 Absolute Honors

STATED ODDS 1:7200
PH7 Jerry Rice 40.00 100.00
PH8 Reggie White 20.00 50.00
PH9 John Elway 50.00 120.00

1997 Absolute Leather Quads

COMPLETE SET (18) 200.00 400.00
STATED ODDS 1:144
*GOLD CARDS: 1.2X TO 3X BASIC INSERTS
GOLD REDEMPTION SET ODDS 1:28,800
1 Emmitt Smith 40.00 100.00
Dan Marino
Jerry Rice
Brett Favre
2 Eddie George 12.50 30.00
Curtis Martin
Barry Sanders
Terrell Davis
3 Herman Moore 5.00 12.00
Kordell Stewart
Elvis Grbac
Chris Warren
4 Leeland McElroy 10.00 25.00
Troy Aikman
Zach Thomas
Cris Carter
5 Jim Harbaugh 6.00 15.00
Michael Jackson
Drew Bledsoe
Jamal Anderson
6 John Elway 15.00 40.00
Reggie White
Warren Moon
Terrell Owens
7 Rashaan Salaam 5.00 12.00
Kerry Collins
Shannon Sharpe
Ricky Watters
8 Larry Centers 5.00 12.00
Mario Bates
Eric Moulds
Mark Brunell
9 Jerome Bettis 5.00 12.00
Carl Pickens
Robert Brooks
Karim Abdul-Jabbar
10 Jeff George 7.50 20.00
Tony Martin
Steve Young
Tim Biakabutuka
11 Terry Glenn 5.00 12.00
Jeff Blake
Mike Alstott
Curtis Conway
12 Rick Mirer 5.00 12.00
Anthony Johnson
Antonio Freemn
Joey Galloway
13 Steve McNair 6.00 15.00
Marshall Faulk
Jimmy Smith
Isaac Bruce
14 Vinny Testaverde 5.00 12.00
Rodney Hampton
Deion Sanders
Tony Banks
15 Chris Chandler 5.00 12.00
Thurman Thomas
Marvin Harrison
Lawrence Phillips
16 Greg Hill 5.00 12.00
Gus Frerotte
Napoleon Kaufman
Keyshawn Johnson
17 Terry Allen 3.00 8.00
Eddie Kennison
Errict Rhett
Scott Mitchell
18 Warrick Dunn 7.50 20.00
Jim Druckenmiller
Orlando Pace
Darrell Russell

1997 Absolute Pennants

COMPLETE SET (192) 150.00 300.00
COMMON CARD (1-192) .30 .75
SEMISTARS .60 1.50
UNLISTED STARS 1.25 3.00
ONE PER BOX
*GOLD REDEMPTION : .5X TO 1.2X BASIC INSERT
GOLD REDEMPTION SET ODDS 1:14,400
6 Tiki Barber 4.00 10.00
31 Warrick Dunn 2.00 5.00
62 Tony Gonzalez 2.50 6.00
81 Jerry Rice 4.00 10.00
101 Troy Aikman 4.00 10.00
105 Drew Bledsoe 2.50 6.00
107 Steve Young 3.00 8.00
120 Steve McNair 2.00 5.00
121 Marshall Faulk 1.50 4.00
142 Jake Plummer 3.00 8.00
145 Terrell Davis 2.00 5.00
151 Brett Favre 8.00 20.00
152 Emmitt Smith 6.00 15.00
153 Dan Marino 8.00 20.00
163 Mark Brunell 2.50 6.00
166 Corey Dillon 4.00 10.00
167 Curtis Martin 2.00 5.00
183 Barry Sanders 6.00 15.00
187 John Elway 8.00 20.00

1997 Absolute Pennant Autographs

RANDOMLY INSERTED BOX TOPPER
A1 Kordell Stewart 12.50 30.00
A2 Eddie George 15.00 40.00
A3 Karim Abdul-Jabbar 10.00 25.00
A4 Mike Alstott 15.00 40.00
A5 Terry Glenn 20.00 40.00
A6 Napoleon Kaufman 10.00 25.00
A7 Terry Allen 10.00 25.00
A8 Tim Brown 25.00 50.00

1997 Absolute Reflex

COMMON CARD (1-200) 3.00 8.00
SEMISTARS 5.00 12.00
UNLISTED STARS 8.00 20.00
STATED ODDS 1:288
1 Brett Favre 30.00 80.00
7 Drew Bledsoe 10.00 25.00
8 Curtis Martin 10.00 25.00
16 Mark Brunell 10.00 25.00
19 John Elway 30.00 80.00
20 Terrell Davis 10.00 25.00
23 Steve Young 10.00 25.00
25 Jerry Rice 15.00 40.00
26 Troy Aikman 15.00 40.00
28 Emmitt Smith 25.00 60.00
50 Marshall Faulk 10.00 25.00
57 Dan Marino 30.00 80.00
61 Steve McNair 10.00 25.00
88 Barry Sanders 25.00 60.00
116 Terrell Owens 10.00 25.00
149 Corey Dillon 25.00 60.00
163 Jake Plummer 20.00 50.00

1997 Absolute Unsung Heroes

COMPLETE SET (30) 10.00 25.00
STATED ODDS 1:12
1 Larry Centers .60 1.50
2 Jessie Tuggle .40 1.00
3 Stevon Moore .40 1.00
4 Mark Pike .40 1.00
5 Anthony Johnson .60 1.50
6 Anthony Carter RB .40 1.00
7 Eric Bieniemy .40 1.00
8 Jim Schwantz .40 1.00
9 Tyrone Braxton .40 1.00
10 Bennie Blades .40 1.00
11 Don Beebe .40 1.00
12 Barron Wortham .40 1.00
13 Jason Belser .40 1.00
14 Mickey Washington .40 1.00
15 Dave Szott .40 1.00
16 Zach Thomas .75 2.00
17 Chris Walsh .40 1.00
18 Sam Gash .40 1.00
19 Willie Roaf .40 1.00
20 Charles Way .60 1.50
21 Wayne Chrebet .75 2.00
22 Russell Maryland .40 1.00
23 Michael Zordich .40 1.00
24 Tim Lester .40 1.00
25 Harold Green .40 1.00
26 Rodney Harrison .75 2.00
27 Gary Plummer .40 1.00
28 Winston Moss .40 1.00
29 Robb Thomas .40 1.00
30 Darrick Brownlow .40 1.00

1998 Absolute Hobby

The 1998 Playoff Absolute set consists of 200 standard size cards issued in three card packs printed on 42 pt. brushed silver foil. Each card included a plastic player image laminated between the card's front and back.

COMPLETE SET (200) 40.00 100.00
1 John Elway 4.00 10.00
2 Marcus Nash RC .60 1.50
3 Brian Griese RC 2.50 6.00
4 Terrell Davis 1.00 2.50
5 Rod Smith WR .60 1.50
6 Shannon Sharpe .60 1.50
7 Ed McCaffrey .60 1.50
8 Brett Favre 4.00 10.00
9 Dorsey Levens 1.00 2.50
10 Derrick Mayes .60 1.50
11 Antonio Freeman 1.00 2.50
12 Robert Brooks .60 1.50
13 Mark Chmura .60 1.50
14 Reggie White 1.00 2.50
15 Kordell Stewart 1.00 2.50
16 Hines Ward RC 6.00 12.00
17 Jerome Bettis 1.00 2.50
18 Charles Johnson .40 1.00
19 Courtney Hawkins .40 1.00
20 Will Blackwell .40 1.00
21 Mark Bruener .40 1.00
22 Steve Young 1.50 4.00
23 Jim Druckenmiller .40 1.00
24 Garrison Hearst 1.00 2.50
25 R.W. McQuarters RC 1.00 2.50
26 Marc Edwards .40 1.00
27 Irv Smith .40 1.00
28 Jerry Rice 2.00 5.00
29 Terrell Owens 1.00 2.50
30 J.J. Stokes .60 1.50
31 Elvis Grbac .60 1.50
32 Rashaan Shehee RC 1.00 2.50
33 Donnell Bennett .40 1.00
34 Kimble Anders .60 1.50
35 Ted Popson .40 1.00
36 Derrick Alexander WR .60 1.50
37 Tony Gonzalez 1.00 2.50
38 Andre Rison .60 1.50
39 Brad Johnson 1.00 2.50
40 Randy Moss RC 8.00 20.00
41 Robert Smith 1.00 2.50
42 Leroy Hoard .40 1.00
43 Cris Carter 1.00 2.50
44 Jake Reed .60 1.50
45 Drew Bledsoe 1.50 4.00
46 Tony Simmons RC 1.00 2.50
47 Chris Floyd RC .60 1.50
48 Robert Edwards RC 1.00 2.50
49 Shawn Jefferson .40 1.00
50 Ben Coates .60 1.50
51 Terry Glenn 1.00 2.50
52 Trent Dilfer 1.00 2.50
53 Jacquez Green RC 1.00 2.50
54 Warrick Dunn 1.00 2.50
55 Mike Alstott 1.00 2.50
56 Reidel Anthony .60 1.50
57 Bert Emanuel .60 1.50
58 Warren Sapp .60 1.50
59 Charlie Batch RC 1.25 3.00
60 Germane Crowell RC 1.00 2.50
61 Scott Mitchell .60 1.50
62 Barry Sanders 3.00 8.00
63 Tommy Vardell .40 1.00
64 Herman Moore .60 1.50
65 Johnnie Morton .60 1.50
66 Mark Brunell 1.00 2.50
67 Jonathan Quinn RC 1.25 3.00
68 Fred Taylor RC 2.00 5.00
69 James Stewart .60 1.50
70 Jimmy Smith .60 1.50
71 Damon Jones .40 1.00
72 Keenan McCardell .60 1.50
73 Dan Marino 4.00 10.00
74 Larry Shannon RC .60 1.50
75 John Avery RC 1.00 2.50
76 Troy Drayton .40 1.00
77 Stanley Pritchett .40 1.00
78 Karim Abdul-Jabbar 1.00 2.50
79 O.J. McDuffie .60 1.50
80 Yatil Green .40 1.00
81 Danny Kanell .60 1.50
82 Tiki Barber 1.00 2.50
83 Tyrone Wheatley .60 1.50
84 Charles Way .40 1.00
85 Gary Brown .40 1.00
86 Brian Alford RC .60 1.50
87 Joe Jurevicius RC 1.25 3.00
88 Ike Hilliard .60 1.50
89 Troy Aikman 2.00 5.00
90 Deion Sanders 1.00 2.50
91 Emmitt Smith 3.00 8.00
92 Chris Warren .60 1.50
93 Daryl Johnston .60 1.50
94 Michael Irvin 1.00 2.50
95 David LaFleur .40 1.00
96 Kevin Dyson RC 1.25 3.00
97 Steve McNair 1.00 2.50
98 Eddie George 1.00 2.50
99 Yancey Thigpen .40 1.00
100 Frank Wycheck .40 1.00
101 Glenn Foley .60 1.50
102 Vinny Testaverde .60 1.50
103 Keyshawn Johnson 1.00 2.50

104 Curtis Martin 1.00 2.50
105 Keith Byars .40 1.00
106 Scott Frost RC .60 1.50
107 Wayne Chrebet 1.00 2.50
108 Warren Moon 1.00 2.50
109 Ahman Green RC 3.00 8.00
110 Steve Broussard .40 1.00
111 Ricky Watters .60 1.50
112 Joey Galloway .60 1.50
113 Mike Pritchard .40 1.00
114 Brian Blades .40 1.00
115 Gus Frerotte .40 1.00
116 Skip Hicks RC 1.00 2.50
117 Terry Allen 1.00 2.50
118 Michael Westbrook .60 1.50
119 Jamie Asher .40 1.00
120 Leslie Shepherd .40 1.00
121 Jeff Blake .60 1.50
122 Corey Dillon 1.00 2.50
123 Carl Pickens .60 1.50
124 Tony McGee .40 1.00
125 Darnay Scott .60 1.50
126 Kerry Collins .60 1.50
127 Fred Lane .40 1.00
128 William Floyd .40 1.00
129 Rae Carruth .40 1.00
130 Wesley Walls .60 1.50
131 Muhsin Muhammad .60 1.50
132 Jake Plummer 1.00 2.50
133 Adrian Murrell .60 1.50
134 Michael Pittman RC 2.00 4.00
135 Larry Centers .40 1.00
136 Frank Sanders .60 1.50
137 Rob Moore .60 1.50
138 Andre Wadsworth RC 1.00 2.50
139 Mario Bates .60 1.50
140 Chris Chandler .60 1.50
141 Byron Hanspard .40 1.00
142 Jamal Anderson 1.00 2.50
143 Terance Mathis .60 1.50
144 O.J. Santiago .40 1.00
145 Tony Martin .60 1.50
146 Jammi German RC .60 1.50
147 Jim Harbaugh .60 1.50
148 Errict Rhett .60 1.50
149 Michael Jackson .40 1.00
150 Pat Johnson RC 1.00 2.50
151 Eric Green .40 1.00
152 Doug Flutie 1.00 2.50
153 Rob Johnson .60 1.50
154 Antowain Smith 1.00 2.50
155 Bruce Smith .60 1.50
156 Eric Moulds 1.00 2.50
157 Andre Reed .60 1.50
158 Erik Kramer .40 1.00
159 Darnell Autry .40 1.00
160 Edgar Bennett .40 1.00
161 Curtis Enis RC .60 1.50
162 Curtis Conway .60 1.50
163 E.G. Green RC 1.00 2.50
164 Jerome Pathon RC 1.25 3.00
165 Peyton Manning RC 15.00 30.00
166 Marshall Faulk 1.25 3.00
167 Zack Crockett .40 1.00
168 Ken Dilger .40 1.00
169 Marvin Harrison 1.00 2.50
170 Danny Wuerffel .60 1.50
171 Lamar Smith .60 1.50
172 Ray Zellars .40 1.00
173 Qadry Ismail .60 1.50
174 Sean Dawkins .40 1.00
175 Andre Hastings .40 1.00
176 Jeff George .60 1.50
177 Charles Woodson RC 1.50 4.00
178 Napoleon Kaufman 1.00 2.50
179 Jon Ritchie RC 1.00 2.50
180 Desmond Howard .60 1.50
181 Tim Brown 1.00 2.50
182 James Jett .60 1.50
183 Rickey Dudley .40 1.00
184 Bobby Hoying .60 1.50
185 Rodney Peete .40 1.00
186 Charlie Garner .60 1.50
187 Irving Fryar .60 1.50
188 Chris T. Jones .40 1.00
189 Jason Dunn .40 1.00
190 Tony Banks .60 1.50
191 Robert Holcombe RC 1.00 2.50
192 Craig Heyward .40 1.00
193 Isaac Bruce 1.00 2.50
194 Az-Zahir Hakim RC 1.25 3.00
195 Eddie Kennison .60 1.50
196 Mikhael Ricks RC 1.00 2.50
197 Ryan Leaf RC 1.25 3.00
198 Natrone Means .60 1.50
199 Junior Seau 1.00 2.50
200 Freddie Jones .40 1.00

1998 Absolute Hobby Gold

*GOLD STARS: 10X TO 25X BASIC CARDS
*GOLD RCs: 5X TO 10X
STATED PRINT RUN 25 SERIAL #'d SETS

1998 Absolute Hobby Silver

COMPLETE SET (200) 200.00 400.00
*STARS: 1.25X TO 2.5X BASIC CARDS
*RC'S: .75X TO 1.5X BASIC CARDS
STATED ODDS 1:3 HOBBY

1998 Absolute Retail

COMP.RETAIL SET (200) 40.00 80.00
*RETAIL CARDS: .25X TO .5X HOBBY SSD

1998 Absolute Retail Green

COMPLETE SET (200) 75.00 150.00
*GREEN STARS: 1.2X TO 3X RETAIL
*GREEN RCs: .6X TO 1.5X RETAIL
RANDOM INSERTS IN RETAIL PACKS

1998 Absolute Retail Red

COMPLETE SET (200) 125.00 250.00
*RED RETAIL STARS: 1.2X TO 3X BASIC RETAIL
*RED RETAIL RC'S: .8X TO 2X BASIC RETAIL
RED RETAIL STATED ODDS 1:3 RETAIL

1998 Absolute 7-Eleven

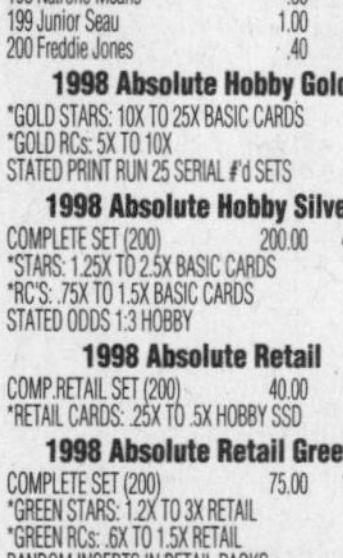

*STARS: 1.2X TO 3X BASIC RETAIL
*ROOKIES: .4X TO 1X BASIC RETAIL

1998 Absolute Checklists

COMPLETE SET (30) 125.00 250.00
STATED ODDS 1:19
*SILVER DIE CUTS: .3X TO .6X BASIC INSERTS
SILVER DIE CUT STATED ODDS 1:25 RETAIL
1 Jake Plummer 3.00 8.00
2 Jamal Anderson 3.00 8.00
3 Jim Harbaugh 2.00 5.00
4 Rob Johnson 2.00 5.00
5 Fred Lane 1.25 3.00
6 Curtis Enis .75 2.00
7 Corey Dillon 3.00 8.00
8 Troy Aikman 6.00 15.00
9 Terrell Davis 3.00 8.00
10 Barry Sanders 10.00 25.00
11 Brett Favre 12.50 30.00
12 Peyton Manning 15.00 40.00
13 Mark Brunell 3.00 8.00
14 Elvis Grbac 2.00 5.00
15 Dan Marino 12.50 30.00
16 Cris Carter 3.00 8.00
17 Drew Bledsoe 5.00 12.00
18 Ray Zellars 1.25 3.00
19 Charles Way 1.25 3.00
20 Curtis Martin 3.00 8.00
21 Napoleon Kaufman 3.00 8.00
22 Irving Fryar 2.00 5.00
23 Kordell Stewart 3.00 8.00
24 Tony Banks 2.00 5.00
25 Ryan Leaf 1.50 4.00
26 Jerry Rice 6.00 15.00
27 Warren Moon 3.00 8.00
28 Warrick Dunn 3.00 8.00
29 Eddie George 3.00 8.00
30 Terry Allen 3.00 8.00

1998 Absolute Draft Picks

COMPLETE SET (36) 75.00 150.00
STATED ODDS 1:10
*BRONZE: .4X TO 1X BASIC GOLD
BRONZE BONUS PACKS 1:4 BOXES
*SILVER DIE CUT: .3X TO .6X GOLD
SILVER DIE CUT STATED ODDS 1:13 RETAIL
*BLUE DIE CUT: .4X TO 1X GOLD
BLUE DIE CUT INSERTED IN SPECIAL RETAIL
1 Peyton Manning 15.00 40.00
2 Ryan Leaf 1.50 4.00
3 Andre Wadsworth 1.25 3.00
4 Charles Woodson 2.00 5.00
5 Curtis Enis .75 2.00
6 Fred Taylor 2.50 6.00
7 Kevin Dyson 1.50 4.00
8 Robert Edwards 1.25 3.00
9 Randy Moss 10.00 25.00
10 R.W. McQuarters 1.25 3.00
11 John Avery 1.25 3.00
12 Marcus Nash .75 2.00
13 Jerome Pathon 1.50 4.00
14 Jacquez Green 1.25 3.00
15 Robert Holcombe 1.25 3.00
16 Pat Johnson 1.25 3.00
17 Germane Crowell 1.25 3.00
18 Tony Simmons 1.25 3.00
19 Joe Jurevicius 1.50 4.00
20 Mikhael Ricks 1.25 3.00
21 Charlie Batch 1.50 4.00
22 Jon Ritchie 1.25 3.00
23 Scott Frost .75 2.00
24 Skip Hicks 1.25 3.00
25 Brian Alford .75 2.00
26 E.G. Green 1.25 3.00
27 Jammi German .75 2.00
28 Ahman Green 4.00 10.00
29 Chris Floyd .75 2.00
30 Larry Shannon .75 2.00
31 Jonathan Quinn 1.50 4.00
32 Rashaan Shehee 1.25 3.00
33 Brian Griese 3.00 8.00
34 Hines Ward 6.00 15.00
35 Michael Pittman 2.00 5.00
36 Az-Zahir Hakim 1.50 4.00

1998 Absolute Honors

COMPLETE SET (3) 60.00 150.00
STATED ODDS 1:3970
PH13 John Elway 30.00 80.00
PH14 Jerome Bettis 12.50 30.00
PH15 Steve Young 20.00 50.00

1998 Absolute Dan Marino Milestones Autographs

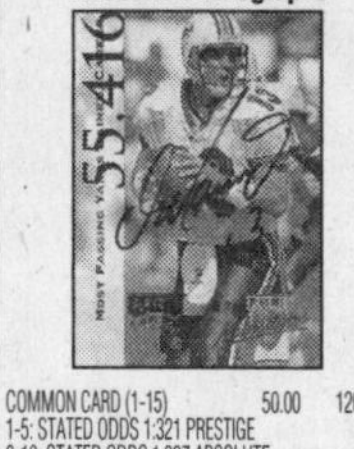

COMMON CARD (1-15) 50.00 120.00
1-5: STATED ODDS 1:321 PRESTIGE
6-10: STATED ODDS 1:397 ABSOLUTE
11-15: STATED ODDS 1:385 MOMENTUM

1998 Absolute Platinum Quads

COMPLETE SET (18) 200.00 500.00
STATED ODDS 1:73
1 Brett Favre 30.00 80.00
John Elway
Barry Sanders
Warrick Dunn
2 Dan Marino 20.00 50.00
Terrell Davis
Napoleon Kaufman
Jerome Bettis
3 Jerry Rice 12.50 30.00
Brad Johnson
Marshall Faulk
Jimmy Smith
4 Troy Aikman 15.00 40.00
Herman Moore
Mark Chmura
Gus Frerotte
5 Steve Young 10.00 25.00
Mike Alstott
Tiki Barber
Keyshawn Johnson
6 Kordell Stewart 10.00 25.00
Robert Brooks
Karim Abdul-Jabbar
Shannon Sharpe
7 Mark Brunell 10.00 25.00
Dorsey Levens
Carl Pickens
Rob Moore
8 Drew Bledsoe 12.50 40.00
Joey Galloway
Tim Brown
Fred Lane
9 Eddie George 10.00 25.00
Rob Johnson
Irving Fryar
Andre Rison
10 Jake Plummer 10.00 25.00
Antonio Freeman
Steve McNair
Warren Moon
11 Emmitt Smith 25.00 60.00
Cris Carter
Junior Seau
Danny Kanell
12 Corey Dillon 10.00 25.00
Jake Reed
Curtis Martin
Bobby Hoying
13 Deion Sanders 10.00 25.00
Jim Druckenmiller
Reidel Anthony
Terry Allen
14 Antowain Smith 10.00 25.00
Wesley Walls
Isaac Bruce
Terry Glenn
15 Charlie Batch 10.00 25.00
Scott Frost
Jonathan Quinn
Brian Griese
16 Kevin Dyson 25.00 50.00
Randy Moss
Marcus Nash
Jerome Pathon
17 Curtis Enis 10.00 25.00
Fred Taylor
Robert Edwards
John Avery
18 Peyton Manning 25.00 60.00
Ryan Leaf
Andre Wadsworth
Charles Woodson

1998 Absolute Red Zone

COMPLETE SET (26) 100.00 200.00
STATED ODDS 1:19
*DIE CUTS: .3X TO .6X BASIC INSERTS
DIE CUT STATED ODDS 1:25 RETAIL
1 Terrell Davis 2.50 6.00
2 Jerome Bettis 2.50 6.00
3 Mike Alstott 2.50 6.00
4 Brett Favre 10.00 25.00
5 Mark Brunell 2.50 6.00
6 Jeff George 1.50 4.00
7 John Elway 10.00 25.00
8 Troy Aikman 5.00 12.00
9 Steve Young 4.00 10.00
10 Kordell Stewart 2.50 6.00
11 Drew Bledsoe 4.00 10.00
12 James Jett 1.50 4.00
13 Dan Marino 10.00 25.00
14 Brad Johnson 2.50 6.00
15 Jake Plummer 2.50 6.00
16 Karim Abdul-Jabbar 2.50 6.00
17 Eddie George 2.50 6.00
18 Warrick Dunn 2.50 6.00
19 Cris Carter 2.50 6.00
20 Barry Sanders 8.00 20.00
21 Corey Dillon 2.50 6.00
22 Steve McNair 2.50 6.00
23 Herman Moore 1.50 4.00
24 Antonio Freeman 2.50 6.00
25 Dorsey Levens 2.50 6.00
26 James Stewart 1.50 4.00

1998 Absolute Shields

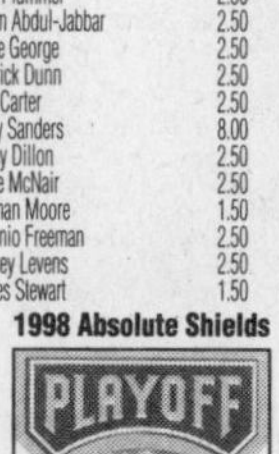

COMP.HOBBY SET (20) 125.00 250.00
STATED ODDS 1:37
*RETAIL DIE CUT CORNER: .25X TO .6X HOBBY
RETAIL DIE CUT CORNER ODDS 1:49 RETAIL
1 Terrell Davis 3.00 8.00
2 Corey Dillon 3.00 8.00
3 Dorsey Levens 2.50 6.00
4 Brett Favre 12.50 30.00
5 Warrick Dunn 3.00 8.00
6 Jerome Bettis 3.00 8.00
7 John Elway 12.50 30.00
8 Troy Aikman 6.00 15.00
9 Mark Brunell 3.00 8.00
10 Kordell Stewart 2.50 6.00
11 Eddie George 3.00 8.00
12 Jerry Rice 6.00 15.00
13 Dan Marino 12.50 30.00
14 Emmitt Smith 10.00 25.00
15 Napoleon Kaufman 2.50 6.00
16 Ryan Leaf 2.50 6.00
17 Curtis Martin 3.00 8.00
18 Peyton Manning 30.00 60.00
19 Cris Carter 3.00 8.00
20 Barry Sanders 10.00 25.00

1998 Absolute Statistically Speaking

COMPLETE SET (18) 100.00 200.00
STATED ODDS 1:55
*DIE CUTS: .3X TO .6X BASIC INSERTS
DIE CUT STATED ODDS 1:73 RETAIL
1 Jerry Rice 6.00 15.00
2 Barry Sanders 10.00 25.00
3 Deion Sanders 3.00 8.00
4 Brett Favre 12.50 30.00
5 Curtis Martin 3.00 8.00
6 Warrick Dunn 3.00 8.00
7 John Elway 12.50 30.00
8 Steve Young 5.00 12.00
9 Cris Carter 3.00 8.00
10 Kordell Stewart 3.00 8.00
11 Terrell Davis 3.00 8.00
12 Irving Fryar 2.00 5.00
13 Dan Marino 12.50 30.00
14 Tim Brown 3.00 8.00
15 Jerome Bettis 3.00 8.00
16 Troy Aikman 6.00 15.00
17 Napoleon Kaufman 3.00 8.00
18 Emmitt Smith 10.00 25.00

1998 Absolute Tandems

COMPLETE SET (6) 60.00 120.00
EACH PLAYER HAS BOTH VERSIONS
STATED ODDS 1:97 RETAIL
1A Terrell Davis ME 6.00 15.00
Curtis Enis
1B Terrell Davis 6.00 15.00
Curtis Enis ME
2A John Elway ME 20.00 50.00
Ryan Leaf
2B John Elway 20.00 50.00
Ryan Leaf ME
3A Brett Favre ME 25.00 60.00
Peyton Manning
3B Brett Favre 25.00 60.00
Peyton Manning ME
4A Randy Moss ME 25.00 50.00
Jerry Rice
4B Randy Moss 25.00 50.00
Jerry Rice ME
5A Barry Sanders ME 10.00 25.00
Fred Taylor
5B Barry Sanders 10.00 25.00
FredTaylor ME
6A Deion Sanders ME 6.00 15.00
Charles Woodson
6B Deion Sanders 6.00 15.00
Charles Woodson ME

1999 Absolute EXP

Released as a 200-card set, 1999 Playoff Absolute EXP is comprised of 160 regular player cards and 40 draft pick cards printed on 20-point stock enhanced with foil stamping. EXP was packaged in eight card packs.

COMPLETE SET (200) 25.00 50.00
1 Tim Couch RC .30 .75
2 Donovan McNabb RC 1.25 3.00
3 Akili Smith RC .25 .60
4 Edgerrin James RC .40 1.00
5 Ricky Williams RC .50 1.25
6 Torry Holt RC .50 1.25
7 Champ Bailey RC .60 1.50
8 David Boston RC .25 .60
9 Chris Claiborne RC .20 .50
10 Chris McAlister RC .25 .60
11 Daunte Culpepper RC .30 .75
12 Cade McNown RC .25 .60
13 Troy Edwards RC .25 .60
14 Kevin Johnson RC .25 .60
15 James Johnson RC .20 .50
16 Rob Konrad RC .20 .50
17 Jim Kleinsasser RC .30 .75
18 Kevin Faulk RC .30 .75
19 Joe Montgomery RC .20 .50
20 Shaun King RC .25 .60
21 Peerless Price RC .25 .60
22 Mike Cloud RC .20 .50
23 Jermaine Fazande RC .20 .50
24 D'Wayne Bates RC .20 .50
25 Brock Huard RC .25 .60
26 Marty Booker RC .25 .60
27 Karsten Bailey RC .20 .50
28 Shawn Bryson RC .20 .50
29 Jeff Paulk RC .20 .50
30 Sedrick Irvin RC .20 .50
31 Craig Yeast RC .20 .50
32 Joe Germaine RC .25 .60
33 Dameane Douglas RC .20 .50
34 Brandon Stokley RC .30 .75
35 Larry Parker RC .25 .60
36 Wane McGarity RC .20 .50
37 Na Brown RC .20 .50
38 Cecil Collins RC .20 .50
39 Darrin Chiaverini RC .20 .50
40 Madre Hill RC .20 .50
41 Adrian Murrell .25 .60
42 Jake Plummer .25 .60
43 Frank Sanders .20 .50
44 Rob Moore .20 .50
45 Andre Wadsworth .20 .50
46 Simeon Rice .20 .50
47 Eric Swann .20 .50
48 Terance Mathis .20 .50
49 Tim Dwight .25 .60
50 Jamal Anderson .25 .60
51 Chris Chandler .25 .60
52 Chris Calloway .20 .50
53 O.J. Santiago .20 .50
54 Jermaine Lewis .20 .50
55 Priest Holmes .30 .75
56 Scott Mitchell .20 .50
57 Tony Banks .25 .60
58 Rod Woodson .30 .75
59 Andre Reed .30 .75
60 Thurman Thomas .30 .75
61 Bruce Smith .30 .75
62 Rob Johnson .25 .60
63 Eric Moulds .25 .60
64 Doug Flutie .30 .75
65 Antowain Smith .20 .50
66 Tim Biakabutuka .25 .60
67 Muhsin Muhammad .25 .60
68 Steve Beuerlein .25 .60
69 Bobby Engram .25 .60
70 Curtis Conway .25 .60
71 Curtis Enis .20 .50
72 Edgar Bennett .25 .60
73 Jeff Blake .25 .60
74 Darnay Scott .20 .50
75 Carl Pickens .25 .60
76 Corey Dillon .25 .60
77 Ty Detmer .25 .60
78 Leslie Shepherd .20 .50
79 Sedrick Shaw .20 .50
80 Rocket Ismail .25 .60
81 Emmitt Smith .75 2.00
82 Michael Irvin .30 .75
83 Troy Aikman .50 1.25
84 Deion Sanders .30 .75
85 Darren Woodson .25 .60
86 Chris Warren .25 .60
87 John Elway 1.00 2.50
88 Brian Griese .25 .60
89 Shannon Sharpe .30 .75
90 Terrell Davis .30 .75
91 Bubby Brister .20 .50
92 Ed McCaffrey .25 .60
93 Rod Smith .25 .60
94 Germane Crowell .20 .50
95 Johnnie Morton .25 .60
96 Barry Sanders .75 2.00
97 Herman Moore .25 .60
98 Charlie Batch .25 .60
99 Mark Chmura .20 .50
100 Derrick Mayes .20 .50
101 Dorsey Levens .25 .60
102 Brett Favre 1.00 2.50
103 Antonio Freeman .25 .60
104 Robert Brooks .25 .60
105 Desmond Howard .25 .60
106 Jerome Pathon .20 .50
107 Marvin Harrison .30 .75
108 Peyton Manning 1.00 2.50
109 E.G. Green .20 .50
110 Tavian Banks .20 .50
111 Keenan McCardell .25 .60
112 Jimmy Smith .25 .60
113 Mark Brunell .25 .60
114 Fred Taylor .25 .60
115 Byron Bam Morris .20 .50
116 Andre Rison .25 .60
117 Elvis Grbac .20 .50
118 Warren Moon .30 .75
119 Tony Gonzalez .30 .75
120 Derrick Alexander WR .20 .50
121 Rashaan Shehee .20 .50
122 Zach Thomas .30 .75
123 Oronde Gadsden .20 .50
124 Dan Marino 1.00 2.50
125 Karim Abdul-Jabbar .25 .60
126 O.J. McDuffie .25 .60
127 Jake Reed .25 .60
128 John Randle .25 .60
129 Randy Moss .30 .75
130 Cris Carter .30 .75
131 Randall Cunningham .30 .75
132 Robert Smith .25 .60
133 Terry Glenn .25 .60
134 Ben Coates .25 .60
135 Drew Bledsoe .30 .75
136 Ty Law .25 .60
137 Tony Simmons .20 .50
138 Eddie Kennison .25 .60
139 Cam Cleeland .20 .50
140 Ike Hilliard .25 .60
141 Joe Jurevicius .20 .50
142 Gary Brown .20 .50
143 Kerry Collins .25 .60
144 Tiki Barber .30 .75
145 Jason Sehorn .25 .60
146 Dedric Ward .20 .50
147 Vinny Testaverde .25 .60
148 Wayne Chrebet .25 .60
149 Curtis Martin .30 .75
150 Keyshawn Johnson .25 .60
151 James Jett .20 .50
152 Napoleon Kaufman .20 .50
153 Tim Brown .30 .75
154 Charles Woodson .30 .75
155 Rickey Dudley .20 .50
156 Charles Johnson .20 .50
157 Duce Staley .25 .60
158 Chris Fuamatu-Ma'afala .20 .50
159 Jerome Bettis .30 .75
160 Kordell Stewart .25 .60
161 Levon Kirkland .20 .50
162 Hines Ward .30 .75
163 Mikhael Ricks .20 .50
164 Natrone Means .25 .60
165 Ryan Leaf .25 .60
166 Jim Harbaugh .25 .60
167 Junior Seau .30 .75
168 Steve Young .40 1.00
169 J.J. Stokes .20 .50
170 Terrell Owens .30 .75
171 Jerry Rice .60 1.50
172 Garrison Hearst .25 .60
173 Ricky Watters .25 .60
174 Jon Kitna .25 .60
175 Joey Galloway .25 .60
176 Ahman Green .25 .60
177 Isaac Bruce .30 .75
178 Marshall Faulk .30 .75
179 Trent Green .25 .60
180 Amp Lee .20 .50
181 Greg Hill .20 .50
182 Warren Sapp .25 .60
183 Hardy Nickerson .20 .50
184 Trent Dilfer .25 .60
185 Reidel Anthony .20 .50
186 Jacquez Green .20 .50
187 Warrick Dunn .25 .60
188 Mike Alstott .30 .75
189 Kevin Dyson .20 .50
190 Eddie George .25 .60
191 Yancey Thigpen .20 .50
192 Steve McNair .30 .75
193 Chris Sanders .20 .50
194 Frank Wycheck .25 .60
195 Darrell Green .30 .75
196 Stephen Alexander .20 .50
197 Albert Connell .20 .50
198 Michael Westbrook .20 .50
199 Brad Johnson .25 .60
200 Skip Hicks .20 .50

1999 Absolute EXP Tools of the Trade

*DEF.PLAYER: 1.5X TO 4X BASIC CARDS
DEFENSIVE STATED PRINT RUN 1000
*RECEIVERS: 2X TO 5X BASIC CARDS
RECEIVER STATED PRINT RUN 750
*RUNNING BACKS: 2.5X TO 6X BASIC CARDS
RUNNING BACK PRINT RUN 500
*QUARTERBACKS: 4X TO 10X BASIC CARDS
QUARTERBACK PRINT RUN 250

1999 Absolute EXP Terrell Davis Salute

COMPLETE SET (5) 15.00 40.00
COMMON CARD (TD6-TD10) 4.00 10.00
STATED ODDS 1:289

1999 Absolute EXP Terrell Davis Salute Autographs

COMMON AUTO/150 20.00 50.00
AUTO STATED PRINT RUN 150

1999 Absolute EXP Extreme Team

COMPLETE SET (36) 60.00 120.00
STATED ODDS 1:25
ET1 Steve Young 2.00 5.00
ET2 Fred Taylor 1.25 3.00
ET3 Kordell Stewart 1.25 3.00
ET4 Emmitt Smith 4.00 10.00
ET5 Barry Sanders 4.00 10.00
ET6 Jerry Rice 3.00 8.00
ET7 Jake Plummer 1.25 3.00
ET8 Eric Moulds 1.25 3.00
ET9 Randy Moss 1.50 4.00
ET10 Steve McNair 1.50 4.00
ET11 Curtis Martin 1.50 4.00
ET12 Dan Marino 5.00 12.00
ET13 Peyton Manning 5.00 12.00
ET14 Jon Kitna 1.25 3.00
ET15 Napoleon Kaufman 1.00 2.50
ET16 Eddie George 1.25 3.00
ET17 Brett Favre 5.00 12.00
ET18 Marshall Faulk 1.50 4.00
ET19 John Elway 5.00 12.00
ET20 Corey Dillon 1.25 3.00
ET21 Terrell Davis 1.50 4.00
ET22 Randall Cunningham 1.50 4.00
ET23 Mark Brunell 1.25 3.00
ET24 Tim Brown 1.50 4.00
ET25 Drew Bledsoe 1.50 4.00
ET26 Jerome Bettis 1.50 4.00
ET27 Charlie Batch 1.25 3.00
ET28 Jamal Anderson 1.25 3.00
ET29 Mike Alstott 1.50 4.00
ET30 Troy Aikman 2.50 6.00
ET31 Dorsey Levens 1.25 3.00
ET32 Joey Galloway 1.25 3.00
ET33 Skip Hicks 1.00 2.50
ET34 Terrell Owens 1.50 4.00
ET35 Keyshawn Johnson 1.25 3.00
ET36 Doug Flutie 1.50 4.00

1999 Absolute EXP Heroes

COMPLETE SET (24) 30.00 60.00
STATED ODDS 1:25
HE1 Terrell Owens 1.00 2.50
HE2 Troy Aikman 1.50 4.00
HE3 Cris Carter 1.00 2.50
HE4 Brett Favre 3.00 8.00
HE5 Jamal Anderson .75 2.00
HE6 Doug Flutie 1.00 2.50
HE7 John Elway 3.00 8.00
HE8 Steve Young 1.25 3.00
HE9 Jerome Bettis 1.00 2.50
HE10 Emmitt Smith 2.50 6.00
HE11 Drew Bledsoe 1.00 2.50
HE12 Fred Taylor .75 2.00
HE13 Dan Marino 3.00 8.00
HE14 Antonio Freeman .75 2.00
HE15 Mark Brunell .75 2.00
HE16 Jake Plummer .75 2.00
HE17 Warrick Dunn .75 2.00
HE18 Peyton Manning 3.00 8.00
HE19 Randy Moss 1.00 2.50
HE20 Barry Sanders 2.50 6.00
HE21 Keyshawn Johnson .75 2.00
HE22 Eddie George .75 2.00
HE23 Terrell Davis 1.00 2.50
HE24 Jerry Rice 2.00 5.00

1999 Absolute EXP Rookie Reflex

COMPLETE SET (18) 25.00 60.00
STATED ODDS 1:49
RR1 Peerless Price 1.00 2.50
RR2 Daunte Culpepper 1.25 3.00
RR3 Joe Montgomery .75 2.00
RR4 David Boston 1.00 2.50
RR5 Shaun King 1.00 2.50
RR6 Champ Bailey 2.50 6.00
RR7 Rob Konrad .50 1.25
RR8 Torry Holt 2.00 5.00
RR9 Kevin Faulk 1.25 3.00
RR10 Ricky Williams 2.00 5.00
RR11 James Johnson .75 2.00
RR12 Edgerrin James 1.50 4.00
RR13 Kevin Johnson 1.00 2.50
RR14 Akili Smith 1.00 2.50
RR15 Troy Edwards 1.00 2.50
RR16 Donovan McNabb 3.00 8.00
RR17 Cade McNown 1.00 2.50
RR18 Tim Couch 1.25 3.00

1999 Absolute EXP Rookies Inserts

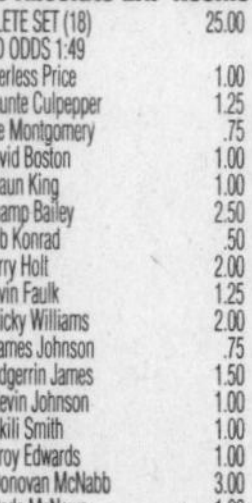

COMPLETE SET (36) 10.00 25.00
STATED ODDS 1:13
AR1 Champ Bailey .75 2.00
AR2 Karsten Bailey .25 .60
AR3 D'Wayne Bates .25 .60
AR4 Marty Booker .30 .75
AR5 David Boston .30 .75
AR6 Shawn Bryson .25 .60
AR7 Chris Claiborne .25 .60
AR8 Mike Cloud .25 .60
AR9 Cecil Collins .25 .60
AR10 Tim Couch .40 1.00
AR11 Daunte Culpepper .40 1.00
AR12 Dameane Douglas .25 .60
AR13 Troy Edwards .30 .75
AR14 Kevin Faulk .40 1.00
AR15 Jermaine Fazande .25 .60
AR16 Joe Germaine .30 .75
AR17 Torry Holt .60 1.50
AR18 Brock Huard .30 .75
AR19 Edgerrin James .50 1.25
AR20 James Johnson .25 .60
AR21 Kevin Johnson .30 .75
AR22 Shaun King .30 .75
AR23 Jim Kleinsasser .40 1.00
AR24 Rob Konrad .25 .60
AR25 Chris McAlister .30 .75
AR26 Travis McGriff .25 .60
AR27 Donovan McNabb 1.00 2.50
AR28 Cade McNown .30 .75
AR29 Joe Montgomery .25 .60
AR30 Larry Parker .30 .75
AR31 Jeff Paulk .25 .60
AR32 Peerless Price .30 .75
AR33 Akili Smith .30 .75
AR34 Brandon Stokley .40 1.00
AR35 Ricky Williams .60 1.50
AR36 Craig Yeast .25 .60

1999 Absolute EXP Barry Sanders Commemorative

COMPLETE SET (5) 30.00 60.00
COMMON CARD (RR2-RR6) 6.00 15.00
STATED ODDS 1:289

1999 Absolute EXP Team Jersey Tandems

STATED ODDS 1:97
TJ1 Jake Plummer 6.00 15.00
David Boston
TJ2 Troy Aikman 20.00 50.00
Emmitt Smith
TJ3 Skip Hicks 6.00 15.00
Brad Johnson
TJ4 Joe Montgomery 6.00 15.00
Ike Hilliard
TJ5 Charles Johnson 15.00 40.00
Donovan McNabb
TJ6 Randy Moss 8.00 20.00
Cris Carter
TJ7 Warrick Dunn 8.00 20.00
Mike Alstott
TJ8 Barry Sanders 20.00 50.00
Charlie Batch
TJ9 Antonio Freeman 25.00 60.00
Brett Favre
TJ10 Curtis Enis 6.00 15.00
Cade McNown
TJ11 Tim Biakabutuka 6.00 15.00
Muhsin Muhammad
TJ12 Eddie Kennison 10.00 25.00
Ricky Williams
TJ13 Steve Young 15.00 40.00
Jerry Rice
TJ14 Marshall Faulk 10.00 25.00
Torry Holt
TJ15 Jamal Anderson 6.00 15.00
Chris Chandler
TJ16 Dan Marino 25.00 60.00
O.J. McDuffie
TJ17 Drew Bledsoe 8.00 20.00
Terry Glenn
TJ18 Eric Moulds 8.00 20.00
Doug Flutie
TJ19 Peyton Manning 25.00 60.00
Edgerrin James
TJ20 Keyshawn Johnson 6.00 15.00
Wayne Chrebet
TJ21 Kordell Stewart 8.00 20.00
Jerome Bettis
TJ22 Mark Brunell 6.00 15.00
Fred Taylor
TJ23 Tim Couch 8.00 20.00
Kevin Johnson
TJ24 Carl Pickens 6.00 15.00
Akili Smith
TJ25 Jermiane Lewis 6.00 15.00
Tony Banks
TJ26 Eddie George 8.00 20.00
Steve McNair
TJ27 Napoleon Kaufman 8.00 20.00
Tim Brown
TJ28 John Elway 25.00 60.00
Terrell Davis
TJ29 Jon Kitna 6.00 15.00
Joey Galloway
TJ30 Andre Rison 6.00 15.00
Elvis Grbac
TJ31 Natrone Means 6.00 15.00
Mikhael Ricks

1999 Absolute SSD

The 1999 Playoff Absolute SSD base set contains 200-cards. The base card design showcases the featured player printed on a animation cell within a card stock frame printed with foil stamping on a solid background color. Cards #1-110 and #161-200 can be found in five different colored borders: Blue, Green, Orange, Purple, and Red. The Purple and Orange borderd cards are the most difficult to find.

COMPLETE SET (200) 125.00 250.00
1 Rob Moore .40 1.00
2 Frank Sanders .40 1.00
3 Jake Plummer .50 1.25
4 Adrian Murrell .50 1.25
5 Chris Chandler .50 1.25
6 Jamal Anderson .50 1.25
7 Tim Dwight .50 1.25
8 Terance Mathis .40 1.00
9 Priest Holmes .60 1.50
10 Jermaine Lewis .40 1.00
11 Antowain Smith .40 1.00
12 Doug Flutie .60 1.50
13 Eric Moulds .50 1.25
14 Muhsin Muhammad .50 1.25
15 Tim Biakabutuka .50 1.25
16 Curtis Enis .40 1.00
17 Curtis Conway .50 1.25
18 Bobby Engram .50 1.25
19 Corey Dillon .50 1.25
20 Carl Pickens .50 1.25
21 Darnay Scott .40 1.00
22 Sedrick Shaw .40 1.00
23 Leslie Shepherd .40 1.00
24 Ty Detmer .50 1.25
25 Deion Sanders .60 1.50
26 Troy Aikman 1.00 2.50
27 Michael Irvin .60 1.50
28 Emmitt Smith 1.50 4.00
29 Rocket Ismail .50 1.25
30 Rod Smith WR .50 1.25
31 Ed McCaffrey .50 1.25
32 Bubby Brister .40 1.00
33 Terrell Davis .60 1.50
34 Shannon Sharpe .60 1.50
35 Brian Griese .50 1.25
36 John Elway 2.00 5.00
37 Charlie Batch .50 1.25
38 Herman Moore .50 1.25
39 Barry Sanders 1.50 4.00
40 Johnnie Morton .50 1.25
41 Antonio Freeman .50 1.25
42 Brett Favre 2.00 5.00
43 Dorsey Levens .50 1.25
44 Derrick Mayes .40 1.00
45 Mark Chmura .40 1.00
46 Peyton Manning 2.00 5.00
47 Marvin Harrison .60 1.50
48 Jerome Pathon .40 1.00
49 Fred Taylor .50 1.25
50 Mark Brunell .50 1.25
51 Jimmy Smith .50 1.25
52 Keenan McCardell .50 1.25
53 Elvis Grbac .40 1.00
54 Andre Rison .50 1.25
55 Byron Bam Morris .40 1.00
56 O.J. McDuffie .50 1.25
57 Karim Abdul-Jabbar .50 1.25
58 Dan Marino 2.00 5.00
59 Oronde Gadsden .40 1.00
60 Robert Smith .50 1.25
61 Randall Cunningham .60 1.50
62 Cris Carter .60 1.50
63 Randy Moss .60 1.50
64 Drew Bledsoe .60 1.50
65 Ben Coates .50 1.25
66 Terry Glenn .50 1.25
67 Cam Cleeland .40 1.00
68 Eddie Kennison .50 1.25
69 Kerry Collins .50 1.25
70 Gary Brown .40 1.00
71 Joe Jurevicius .40 1.00
72 Ike Hilliard .50 1.25
73 Keyshawn Johnson .50 1.25

74 Curtis Martin .60 1.50
75 Wayne Chrebet .50 1.25
76 Tim Brown .60 1.50
77 Napoleon Kaufman .40 1.00
78 James Jett .40 1.00
79 Duce Staley .50 1.25
80 Charles Johnson .40 1.00
81 Kordell Stewart .50 1.25
82 Jerome Bettis .60 1.50
83 Chris Fuamatu-Ma'afala .40 1.00
84 Jim Harbaugh .50 1.25
85 Ryan Leaf .50 1.25
86 Natrone Means .50 1.25
87 Mikhael Ricks .40 1.00
88 Garrison Hearst .50 1.25
89 Jerry Rice 1.25 3.00
90 Terrell Owens .60 1.50
91 J.J. Stokes .40 1.00
92 Steve Young .75 2.00
93 Joey Galloway .50 1.25
94 Jon Kitna .50 1.25
95 Ricky Watters .50 1.25
96 Trent Green .50 1.25
97 Marshall Faulk .60 1.50
98 Isaac Bruce .60 1.50
99 Mike Alstott .60 1.50
100 Warrick Dunn .50 1.25
101 Jacquez Green .40 1.00
102 Reidel Anthony .40 1.00
103 Trent Dilfer .50 1.25
104 Steve McNair .60 1.50
105 Yancey Thigpen .40 1.00
106 Eddie George .50 1.25
107 Kevin Dyson .40 1.00
108 Skip Hicks .40 1.00
109 Brad Johnson .50 1.25
110 Michael Westbrook .40 1.00
111 Thurman Thomas CA 2.00 5.00
112 Andre Reed CA 2.00 5.00
113 Emmitt Smith CA 5.00 12.00
114 Troy Aikman CA 3.00 8.00
115 Deion Sanders CA 2.00 5.00
116 John Elway CA 6.00 15.00
117 Terrell Davis CA 2.00 5.00
118 Barry Sanders CA 5.00 12.00
119 Brett Favre CA 6.00 15.00
120 Warren Moon CA 2.00 5.00
121 Dan Marino CA 6.00 15.00
122 Cris Carter CA 2.00 5.00
124 Tim Brown CA 2.00 5.00
125 Jerome Bettis CA 2.00 5.00
126 Junior Seau CA 2.00 5.00
127 Vinny Testaverde CA 1.50 4.00
127 Jerry Rice CA 4.00 10.00
128 Steve Young CA 2.50 6.00
129 Eddie George CA 1.50 4.00
130 Rob Moore 1.25 3.00
Jake Plummer
Adrian Murrell
Frank Sanders
David Boston
131 Jamal Anderson 1.25 3.00
Chris Chandler
Terance Mathis
Tim Dwight
Jeff Paulk
132 Priest Holmes 1.50 4.00
Chris McAlister
Jermaine Lewis
Brandon Stokely
133 Antowain Smith 2.00 5.00
Thurman Thomas
Shawn Bryson
Doug Flutie
Andre Reed
Eric Moulds
Peerless Price
134 Tim Biakabutuka 1.25 3.00
Muhsin Muhammad
135 Curtis Enis 1.50 4.00
Curtis Conway
Bobby Engram
Cade McNown
Marty Booker
D'Wayne Bates
136 Corey Dillon 1.25 3.00
Carl Pickens
Akili Smith
Darnay Scott
Craig Yeast
137 Sedrick Shaw 1.50 4.00
Tim Couch
Madre Hill
Leslie Shepard
Kevin Johnson
Ty Detmer
Darrin Chiaverini
138 Emmitt Smith 3.00 8.00
Michael Irvin
Deion Sanders
Wane McGarity
Rocket Ismail
Troy Aikman
139 John Elway 3.00 8.00
Terrell Davis
Bubby Brister
Ed McCaffrey
Rod Smith
Brian Griese
Shannon Sharpe
140 Barry Sanders 3.00 8.00
Charlie Batch
Herman Moore
Chris Claiborne
Sedrick Irvin
141 Brett Favre 3.00 8.00
Dorsey Levens
Derrick Mayes
Mark Chmura
Antonio Freeman
142 Peyton Manning 3.00 8.00
Jerome Pathon
Marvin Harrison
Edgerrin James
143 Mark Brunell 1.50 4.00
Fred Taylor
Jimmy Smith
Keenan McCardell
144 Andre Rison 1.25 3.00
Elvis Grbac
Warren Moon
Michael Cloud
Byron Bam Morris
Larry Parker
145 Dan Marino 1.25 3.00
Rob Konrad
Cecil Collins
James Johnson
O.J. McDuffie
Karim Abdul-Jabbar
Oronde Gadsden
146 Randy Moss 1.50 4.00
Robert Smith
Jim Kleinsasser
Randall Cunningham
Cris Carter
Daunte Culpepper
147 Drew Bledsoe 1.25 3.00
Terry Glenn
Ben Coates
Kevin Faulk
148 Ricky Williams 1.50 4.00
Eddie Kennison
Cam Cleeland
149 Kerry Collins 1.25 3.00
Gary Brown
Joe Jurevicius
Ike Hilliard
Joe Montgomery
150 Keyshawn Johnson 1.50 4.00
Wayne Chrebet
Curtis Martin
Vinny Testaverde
151 Tim Brown 2.00 5.00
Napoleon Kaufman
James Jett
Dameane Douglas
152 Duce Staley 2.00 5.00
Donovan McNabb
Na Brown
Charles Johnson
153 Kordell Stewart 2.00 5.00
Jerome Bettis
Chris Fuamatu-Ma'afala
Troy Edwards
154 Jim Harbaugh 2.00 5.00
Mikhael Ricks
Ryan Leaf
Junior Seau
Natrone Means
Jermaine Fazande
155 Steve Young 3.00 8.00
Jerry Rice
Terrell Owens
J.J. Stokes
156 Joey Galloway 1.25 3.00
Jon Kitna
Ricky Watters
Brock Huard
Karsten Bailey
157 Trent Green 1.50 4.00
Torry Holt
Marshall Faulk
Isaac Bruce
Joe Germaine
158 Mike Alstott 1.25 3.00
Warrick Dunn
Reidel Anthony
Jacquez Green
Trent Dilfer
Shaun King
159 Eddie George 1.50 4.00
Yancy Thigpen
Kevin Dyson
Steve McNair
160 Brad Johnson 2.00 5.00
Champ Bailey
Skip Hicks
Michael Westbrook
161 Tim Couch RC .60 1.50
162 Donovan McNabb RC 3.00 8.00
163 Akili Smith RC .50 1.25
164 Edgerrin James RC .75 2.00
165 Ricky Williams RC 1.00 2.50
166 Torry Holt RC 1.00 2.50
167 Champ Bailey RC 1.25 3.00
168 David Boston RC .50 1.25
169 Chris Claiborne RC .40 1.00
170 Chris McAlister RC .50 1.25
171 Daunte Culpepper RC .60 1.50
172 Cade McNown RC .50 1.25
173 Troy Edwards RC .50 1.25
174 Kevin Johnson RC .50 1.25
175 James Johnson RC .40 1.00
176 Rob Konrad RC .40 1.00
177 Jim Kleinsasser RC .60 1.50
178 Kevin Faulk RC .60 1.50
179 Joe Montgomery RC .40 1.00
180 Shaun King RC .50 1.25
181 Peerless Price RC .50 1.25
182 Mike Cloud RC .40 1.00
183 Jermaine Fazande RC .40 1.00
184 D'Wayne Bates RC .40 1.00
185 Brock Huard RC .50 1.25
186 Marty Booker RC .50 1.25
187 Karsten Bailey RC .40 1.00
188 Shawn Bryson RC .40 1.00
189 Jeff Paulk RC .40 1.00
190 Sedrick Irvin RC .40 1.00
191 Craig Yeast RC .40 1.00
192 Joe Germaine RC .50 1.25
193 Dameane Douglas RC .40 1.00
194 Brandon Stokley RC .60 1.50
195 Larry Parker RC .50 1.25
196 Wane McGarity RC .40 1.00
197 Na Brown RC .40 1.00
198 Cecil Collins RC .40 1.00
199 Darrin Chiaverini RC .40 1.00
200 Madre Hill RC .40 1.00

1999 Absolute SSD Coaches Collection Gold

*VETS 1-110: 6X TO 15X BASIC CARDS
*CANTON ABS 111-129: 2.5X TO 6X
*TEAM CLs 130-160: 2X TO 5X
*ROOKIES 161-200: 6X TO 15X
GOLD PRINT RUN 25 SER.#'d SETS

1999 Absolute SSD Coaches Collection Silver

*VETS 1-110: 1.5X TO 4X BASIC CARDS
*CANTON ABS 111-129: .6X TO 1.5X
*TEAM CLs 130-160: .6X TO 1.5X
*SILVER ROOKIES: 1.5X TO 4X
SILVER PRINT RUN 500 SER.#'d SETS

1999 Absolute SSD Green

GREEN BORDER: .4X TO 1X BASIC CARDS

1999 Absolute SSD Honors Gold

*GOLD VETS/25: 8X TO 20X BASIC CARDS
*GOLD ROOK/25: 5X TO 12X BASIC CARDS
GOLD PRINT RUN 25 SER.#'d SETS

1999 Absolute SSD Honors Red

*RED/200: 2X TO 5X BASIC CARDS
RED PRINT RUN 200 SER.#'d SETS

1999 Absolute SSD Honors Silver

*SILVER/100: 3X TO 8X BASIC CARDS
SILVER STATED PRINT RUN 100 SER.#'d SETS

1999 Absolute SSD Orange

*ORANGE: 2.5X TO 6X BASIC CARDS

1999 Absolute SSD Purple

*PURPLE BORDER: .6X TO 1.5X BASIC CARDS

1999 Absolute SSD Red

*RED BORDER: .4X TO 1X BASIC CARDS

1999 Absolute SSD Boss Hogs Autographs

STATED PRINT RUN 400 SER.#'d SETS
BH2 Terrell Davis 12.50 30.00
BH3 Mike Alstott 12.50 30.00
BH4 Jake Plummer 12.50 30.00
BH5 Vinny Testaverde 12.50 30.00
BH6 Cris Carter 15.00 40.00
BH7 Peyton Manning 40.00 100.00
BH8 Natrone Means 12.50 30.00
BH9 Eddie George 12.50 30.00
BH10 Barry Sanders 50.00 120.00

1999 Absolute SSD Force

COMPLETE SET (36) 75.00 150.00
STATED ODDS 1:19
AF1 Steve Young 2.50 6.00
AF2 Fred Taylor 1.50 4.00
AF3 Kordell Stewart 1.50 4.00
AF4 Emmitt Smith 5.00 12.00
AF5 Barry Sanders 5.00 12.00
AF6 Jerry Rice 4.00 10.00
AF7 Jake Plummer 1.50 4.00
AF8 Eric Moulds 1.50 4.00
AF9 Randy Moss 2.00 5.00
AF10 Steve McNair 2.00 5.00
AF11 Curtis Martin 2.00 5.00
AF12 Dan Marino 6.00 15.00
AF13 Peyton Manning 6.00 15.00
AF14 Jon Kitna 1.50 4.00
AF15 Napoleon Kaufman 1.25 3.00
AF16 Keyshawn Johnson 1.50 4.00
AF17 Eddie George 1.50 4.00
AF18 Antonio Freeman 1.50 4.00
AF19 Doug Flutie 2.00 5.00
AF20 Brett Favre 6.00 15.00
AF21 Marshall Faulk 2.00 5.00
AF22 John Elway 6.00 15.00
AF23 Warrick Dunn 1.50 4.00
AF24 Corey Dillon 1.50 4.00
AF25 Terrell Davis 2.00 5.00
AF26 Randall Cunningham 2.00 5.00
AF27 Cris Carter 2.00 5.00
AF28 Mark Brunell 1.50 4.00
AF29 Tim Brown 2.00 5.00
AF30 Drew Bledsoe 2.00 5.00
AF31 Jerome Bettis 2.00 5.00
AF32 Charlie Batch 1.50 4.00
AF33 Jamal Anderson 1.50 4.00
AF34 Mike Alstott 2.00 5.00
AF35 Troy Aikman 3.00 8.00
AF36 Terrell Owens 2.00 5.00

1999 Absolute SSD Heroes

COMPLETE SET (24) 60.00 120.00
STATED ODDS 1:19
*JUMBOS: .3X TO .8X BASIC INSERTS
JUMBOS ONE PER HOBBY BOX
*RED/100: 1.5X TO 4X BASIC INSERTS
HE1 Terrell Owens 1.50 4.00
HE2 Troy Aikman 2.50 6.00
HE3 Cris Carter 1.50 4.00
HE4 Brett Favre 5.00 12.00
HE5 Jamal Anderson 1.25 3.00
HE6 Doug Flutie 1.50 4.00
HE7 John Elway 5.00 12.00
HE8 Steve Young 2.00 5.00
HE9 Jerome Bettis 1.50 4.00
HE10 Emmitt Smith 4.00 10.00
HE11 Drew Bledsoe 1.50 4.00
HE12 Fred Taylor 1.25 3.00
HE13 Dan Marino 5.00 12.00
HE14 Antonio Freeman 1.25 3.00
HE15 Mark Brunell 1.25 3.00
HE16 Jake Plummer 1.25 3.00
HE17 Warrick Dunn 1.25 3.00
HE18 Peyton Manning 5.00 12.00
HE19 Randy Moss 1.50 4.00
HE20 Barry Sanders 4.00 10.00
HE21 Keyshawn Johnson 1.25 3.00
HE22 Eddie George 1.25 3.00
HE23 Terrell Davis 1.50 4.00
HE24 Jerry Rice 3.00 8.00

1999 Absolute SSD Rookie Roundup

COMPLETE SET (18) 25.00 60.00
1ST ROUNDER STATED ODDS 1:46
2ND ROUNDER STATED ODDS 1:69
RR1 Peerless Price 2 1.25 3.00
RR2 Daunte Culpepper 1.50 4.00
RR3 Joe Montgomery 2 1.00 2.50
RR4 David Boston 1.25 3.00
RR5 Shaun King 2 1.25 3.00
RR6 Champ Bailey 3.00 8.00
RR7 Rob Konrad 2 1.00 2.50
RR8 Torry Holt 2.50 6.00
RR9 Kevin Faulk 2 1.50 4.00
RR10 Ricky Williams 2.50 6.00
RR11 James Johnson 2 1.00 2.50
RR12 Edgerrin James 2.00 5.00
RR13 Kevin Johnson 2 1.25 3.00
RR14 Akili Smith 1.25 3.00
RR15 Troy Edwards 1.25 3.00
RR16 Donovan McNabb 4.00 10.00
RR17 Cade McNown 1.25 3.00
RR18 Tim Couch 1.50 4.00

1999 Absolute SSD Rookies Inserts

COMPLETE SET (36) 40.00 80.00
STATED ODDS 1:10
*RED/100: 2X TO 5X BASIC INSERTS
AR1 Champ Bailey 1.50 4.00
AR2 Karsten Bailey .50 1.25
AR3 D'Wayne Bates .50 1.25
AR4 Marty Booker .60 1.50
AR5 David Boston .60 1.50
AR6 Shawn Bryson .50 1.25
AR7 Chris Claiborne .50 1.25
AR8 Mike Cloud .50 1.25
AR9 Cecil Collins .50 1.25
AR10 Tim Couch .75 2.00
AR11 Daunte Culpepper .75 2.00
AR12 Dameane Douglas .50 1.25
AR13 Troy Edwards .60 1.50
AR14 Kevin Faulk .75 2.00
AR15 Jermaine Fazande .50 1.25
AR16 Joe Germaine .60 1.50
AR17 Torry Holt 1.25 3.00
AR18 Brock Huard .60 1.50
AR19 Edgerrin James 1.00 2.50
AR20 James Johnson .50 1.25
AR21 Kevin Johnson .60 1.50
AR22 Shaun King .60 1.50
AR23 Jim Kleinsasser .75 2.00
AR24 Rob Konrad .50 1.25
AR25 Chris McAlister .60 1.50
AR26 Travis McGriff .50 1.25
AR27 Donovan McNabb 3.00 8.00
AR28 Cade McNown .60 1.50
AR29 Joe Montgomery .50 1.25
AR30 Larry Parker .60 1.50
AR31 Jeff Paulk .50 1.25
AR32 Peerless Price .60 1.50
AR33 Akili Smith .60 1.50
AR34 Brandon Stokley .75 2.00
AR35 Ricky Williams 1.25 3.00
AR36 Craig Yeast .50 1.25

1999 Absolute SSD Team Jersey Quad

STATED ODDS 1:73
TQ1 David Boston 6.00 15.00
Adrian Murrell
Jake Plummer
Frank Sanders
TQ2 Troy Aikman 20.00 50.00
Michael Irvin
Deion Sanders
Emmitt Smith
TQ3 Champ Bailey 12.00 30.00
Skip Hicks
Brad Johnson
Michael Westbrook
TQ4 Gary Brown 6.00 15.00
Kerry Collins
Ike Hilliard
Joe Montgomery
TQ5 Na Brown 12.00 30.00
Charles Johnson
Donovan McNabb
Duce Staley
TQ6 Cris Carter 15.00 40.00
Randall Cunningham
Randy Moss
Robert Smith
TQ7 Mike Alstott 8.00 20.00
Anthony Reidel
Trent Dilfer
Warrick Dunn
TQ8 Charlie Batch 20.00 50.00
Herman Moore
Johnnie Morton
Barry Sanders
TQ9 Mark Chmura 25.00 60.00
Brett Favre
Antonio Freeman
Dorsey Levens
TQ10 Curtis Conway 6.00 15.00
Bobby Engram
Curtis Enis
Cade McNown
TQ11 Steve Beuerlein 6.00 15.00
Tim Biakabutuka
Muhsin Muhammad
Wesley Walls
TQ12 Cam Cleeland 10.00 25.00
Eddie Kennison
Willie Roaf
Ricky Williams
TQ13 Garrison Hearst 15.00 40.00
Terrell Owens
Jerry Rice
Steve Young
TQ14 Bruce Isaac 10.00 25.00
Marshall Faulk
Trent Green
Torry Holt
TQ15 Jamal Anderson 6.00 15.00
Chris Chandler
Tim Dwight
Terrance Mathis
TQ16 Karim Abdul-Jabbar 25.00 60.00
Cecil Collins
Dan Marino
O.J. McDuffie
TQ17 Drew Bledsoe 8.00 20.00
Ben Coates
Kevin Faulk
Terry Glenn
TQ18 Doug Flutie 8.00 20.00
Eric Moulds
Peerless Price
Antowain Smith
TQ19 Marvin Harrison 25.00 60.00
Edgerrin James
Peyton Manning
Jerome Pathon
TQ20 Wayne Chrebet 8.00 20.00
Keyshawn Johnson
Curtis Martin
Vinny Testaverde
TQ21 Jerome Bettis 8.00 20.00
Troy Edwards
Kordell Stewart
Hines Ward
TQ22 Mark Brunell 6.00 15.00
Keenan McCardell
Jimmy Smith
Fred Taylor
TQ23 Tim Couch 8.00 20.00
Kevin Johnson
Cedrick Chow
Leslie Shepherd
TQ24 Corey Dillon 6.00 15.00
Carl Pickens
Darnay Scott
Akili Smith
TQ25 Tony Banks 8.00 20.00
Priest Holmes
Jermaine Lewis
Chris McAlister
TQ26 Kevin Dyson 8.00 20.00
Eddie George
Steve McNair
Yancey Thigpen
TQ27 Tim Brown 8.00 20.00
James Jett
Napoleon Kaufman
Charles Woodson
TQ28 Terrell Davis 25.00 60.00
John Elway
Ed McCaffrey
Rod Smith
TQ29 Joey Galloway 6.00 15.00
Ahman Green
Jon Kitna
Ricky Watters
TQ30 Mike Cloud 6.00 15.00
Elvis Grbac
Byron Bam Morris
Andre Rison
TQ31 Ryan Leaf 8.00 20.00
Natrone Means
Mikhael Ricks
Junior Seau

2000 Absolute

Released as a 250-card set, Playoff Absolute features 150 veteran cards and 100 rookie cards sequentially numbered to 3000. Base cards feature player action photos and holographic foil stamping. Absolute was packaged in 20-pack boxes with packs containing six cards and carried a suggested retail price of $3.99.

COMPLETE SET (250) 125.00 250.00
COMP.SET w/o SP's (150) 7.50 20.00
151-250 ROOKIE PRINT RUN 3000
1 Frank Sanders .20 .50
2 Rob Moore .20 .50
3 Jake Plummer .25 .60
4 David Boston .25 .60
5 Chris Chandler .25 .60
6 Tim Dwight .25 .60
7 Terance Mathis .20 .50
8 Jamal Anderson .25 .60
9 Priest Holmes .30 .75
10 Tony Banks .20 .50
11 Jermaine Lewis .20 .50
12 Qadry Ismail .25 .60
13 Brandon Stokley .25 .60
14 Shannon Sharpe .30 .75
15 Trent Dilfer .25 .60
16 Eric Moulds .25 .60
17 Doug Flutie .30 .75
18 Antowain Smith .25 .60
19 Jonathan Linton .20 .50
20 Peerless Price .25 .60
21 Rob Johnson .25 .60
22 Muhsin Muhammad .25 .60
23 Wesley Walls .20 .50
24 Tim Biakabutuka .25 .60
25 Steve Beuerlein .25 .60
26 Patrick Jeffers .25 .60
27 Natrone Means .20 .50
28 Curtis Enis .20 .50
29 Bobby Engram .25 .60
30 Marcus Robinson .25 .60
31 Marty Booker .25 .60
32 Cade McNown .20 .50
33 Darnay Scott .25 .60
34 Carl Pickens .25 .60
35 Corey Dillon .25 .60
36 Akili Smith .20 .50
37 Michael Basnight .20 .50
38 Karim Abdul-Jabbar .25 .60
39 Tim Couch .25 .60
40 Kevin Johnson .20 .50
41 Darrin Chiaverini .20 .50
42 Errict Rhett .25 .60
43 Emmitt Smith .75 2.00
44 Michael Irvin .30 .75
45 Rocket Ismail .25 .60
46 Troy Aikman .50 1.25
47 Jason Tucker .20 .50
48 Randall Cunningham .30 .75
49 Joey Galloway .25 .60
50 Ed McCaffrey .25 .60
51 Rod Smith .25 .60
52 Brian Griese .25 .60
53 John Elway .75 2.00
54 Terrell Davis .30 .75
55 Olandis Gary .25 .60
56 Johnnie Morton .25 .60
57 Charlie Batch .25 .60
58 Barry Sanders .60 1.50
59 Germane Crowell .20 .50
60 Herman Moore .25 .60
61 James Stewart .20 .50
62 Corey Bradford .25 .60
63 Dorsey Levens .25 .60
64 Antonio Freeman .25 .60
65 Brett Favre 1.00 2.50
66 Bill Schroeder .25 .60
67 Marvin Harrison .30 .75
68 Peyton Manning .75 2.00
69 Terrence Wilkins .20 .50
70 Edgerrin James .30 .75
71 Keenan McCardell .25 .60
72 Mark Brunell .25 .60
73 Fred Taylor .30 .75
74 Jimmy Smith .25 .60
75 Elvis Grbac .20 .50
76 Tony Gonzalez .25 .60
77 Donnell Bennett .20 .50
78 Warren Moon .30 .75
79 Kimble Anders .20 .50
80 Dan Marino 1.00 2.50
81 O.J. McDuffie .25 .60
82 Tony Martin .25 .60
83 James Johnson .20 .50
84 Thurman Thomas .30 .75
85 Randy Moss .30 .75
86 Cris Carter .30 .75
87 Robert Smith .25 .60
88 Daunte Culpepper .25 .60
89 Terry Glenn .25 .60
90 Drew Bledsoe .30 .75
91 Kevin Faulk .25 .60
92 Ricky Williams .25 .60
93 Jeff Blake .25 .60
94 Jake Reed .25 .60
95 Amani Toomer .20 .50
96 Kerry Collins .25 .60
97 Tiki Barber .30 .75
98 Ike Hilliard .25 .60
99 Curtis Martin .30 .75
100 Vinny Testaverde .25 .60
101 Wayne Chrebet .25 .60
102 Ray Lucas .20 .50
103 Tyrone Wheatley .20 .50
104 Napoleon Kaufman .25 .60
105 Tim Brown .30 .75
106 Rich Gannon .25 .60
107 Duce Staley .25 .60
108 Donovan McNabb .30 .75
109 Kordell Stewart .25 .60
110 Jerome Bettis .30 .75
111 Troy Edwards .20 .50
112 Junior Seau .30 .75
113 Jim Harbaugh .25 .60
114 Ryan Leaf .25 .60
115 Jermaine Fazande .20 .50
116 Curtis Conway .25 .60
117 Terrell Owens .30 .75
118 Charlie Garner .25 .60
119 Jerry Rice .60 1.50
120 Steve Young .40 1.00
121 Jeff Garcia .20 .50
122 Derrick Mayes .20 .50
123 Ricky Watters .25 .60
124 Jon Kitna .25 .60
125 Sean Dawkins .20 .50
126 Az-Zahir Hakim .20 .50
127 Isaac Bruce .30 .75
128 Marshall Faulk .30 .75
129 Trent Green .25 .60
130 Kurt Warner .50 1.25
131 Torry Holt .30 .75
132 Jacquez Green .20 .50
133 Warren Sapp .25 .60
134 Mike Alstott .30 .75
135 Warrick Dunn .25 .60
136 Shaun King .20 .50
137 Keyshawn Johnson .25 .60
138 Eddie George .25 .60
139 Yancey Thigpen .20 .50
140 Steve McNair .30 .75
141 Kevin Dyson .25 .60
142 Frank Wycheck .25 .60
143 Jevon Kearse .25 .60
144 Stephen Davis .25 .60
145 Brad Johnson .25 .60
146 Michael Westbrook .20 .50
147 Albert Connell .20 .50
148 Bruce Smith .30 .75
149 Jeff George .25 .60
150 Deion Sanders .30 .75
151 Peter Warrick RC 1.25 3.00
152 Courtney Brown RC 1.00 2.50
153 Plaxico Burress RC 1.25 3.00
154 Corey Simon RC 1.00 2.50
155 Thomas Jones RC 1.50 4.00
156 Travis Taylor RC 1.00 2.50
157 Shaun Alexander RC 1.50 4.00
158 Chris Redman RC 1.00 2.50
159 Chad Pennington RC 2.00 5.00
160 Jamal Lewis RC 1.25 3.00
161 Brian Urlacher RC 5.00 12.00
162 Bubba Franks RC 1.25 3.00
163 Dez White RC 1.00 2.50
164 Ahmed Plummer RC .75 2.00
165 Ron Dayne RC 1.25 3.00
166 Shaun Ellis RC 1.25 3.00
167 Sylvester Morris RC .75 2.00
168 Deltha O'Neal RC 1.00 2.50
169 R.Jay Soward RC .75 2.00
170 Sherrod Gideon RC .75 2.00
171 John Abraham RC 1.25 3.00
172 Travis Prentice RC 1.00 2.50
173 Darrell Jackson RC 1.00 2.50
174 Giovanni Carmazzi RC .75 2.00
175 Anthony Lucas RC .75 2.00
176 Danny Farmer RC .75 2.00
177 Dennis Northcutt RC 1.00 2.50
178 Troy Walters RC .75 2.00
179 Laveranues Coles RC 1.25 3.00
180 Kwame Cavil RC .75 2.00
181 Tee Martin RC 1.25 3.00
182 J.R. Redmond RC .75 2.00
183 Tim Rattay RC 1.00 2.50
184 Jerry Porter RC 1.25 3.00
185 Sebastian Janikowski RC 1.25 3.00
186 Michael Wiley RC .75 2.00
187 Reuben Droughns RC 1.25 3.00
188 Trung Canidate RC 1.00 2.50
189 Shyrone Stith RC .75 2.00
190 Ian Gold RC .75 2.00
191 Hank Poteat RC .75 2.00
192 Darren Howard RC .75 2.00
193 Rob Morris RC 1.00 2.50
194 Marc Bulger RC 1.25 3.00
195 Tom Brady RC 50.00 100.00
196 Doug Johnson RC 1.00 2.50
197 Todd Husak RC .75 2.00
198 Gari Scott RC .75 2.00
199 Erron Kinney RC .75 2.00
200 Nate Webster RC .75 2.00
201 Anthony Becht RC 1.00 2.50
202 Sammy Morris RC 1.00 2.50
203 Rondell Mealey RC .75 2.00
204 Doug Chapman RC .75 2.00
205 Rogers Beckett RC .75 2.00
206 Ron Dugans RC .75 2.00
207 Deon Dyer RC .75 2.00
208 Marcus Knight RC .75 2.00
209 Thomas Hamner RC .75 2.00
210 Joe Hamilton RC .75 2.00
211 Todd Pinkston RC .75 2.00
212 Chris Cole RC 1.00 2.50
213 Ron Dixon RC .75 2.00
214 JaJuan Dawson RC .75 2.00
215 Terrelle Smith RC .75 2.00
216 Curtis Keaton RC .75 2.00
217 Keith Bulluck RC 1.00 2.50
218 John Engelberger RC .75 2.00
219 Raynoch Thompson RC .75 2.00
220 Cornelius Griffin RC .75 2.00
221 William Bartee RC .75 2.00
222 Fred Robbins RC .75 2.00
223 Dwayne Goodrich RC .75 2.00
224 Deon Grant RC .75 2.00
225 Jacoby Shepherd RC .75 2.00
226 Ben Kelly RC .75 2.00
227 Corey Moore RC .75 2.00
228 Aaron Shea RC 1.00 2.50
229 Trevor Gaylor RC .75 2.00
230 Frank Moreau RC .75 2.00
231 Avion Black RC .75 2.00
232 Paul Smith RC .75 2.00
233 Dante Hall RC 1.25 3.00
234 Muneer Moore RC .75 2.00
235 James Whalen RC .75 2.00
236 Chad Morton RC 1.25 3.00
237 Frank Murphy RC .75 2.00
238 Mareno Philyaw RC .75 2.00
239 James Williams RC .75 2.00
240 Mike Anderson RC 1.25 3.00
241 Jarious Jackson RC 1.00 2.50
242 Demario Brown RC .75 2.00
243 Chris Coleman RC .75 2.00
244 Rashard Anderson RC .75 2.00
245 John Jones RC .75 2.00
246 Erik Flowers RC .75 2.00
247 JaJuan Seider RC .75 2.00
248 Leon Murray RC .75 2.00
249 Bashir Yamini RC .75 2.00
250 Na'il Diggs RC .75 2.00

2000 Absolute Coaches Honors

*VETS 1-150: 3X TO 8X BASIC CARDS
*ROOKIE 151-250: .8X TO 2X BASIC CARDS
STATED PRINT RUN 300 SER.#'d SETS
195 Tom Brady 125.00 200.00

2000 Absolute Players Honors

UNPRICED PLAYER HONOR PRINT RUN 10

2000 Absolute Boss Hogg Autographs

AUTO/200 ODDS 1:298 HOB, 1:447 RET
STATED PRINT RUN 200 SETS
BH1 Eric Moulds 10.00 25.00
BH2 Cade McNown 8.00 20.00
BH3 Tim Couch 10.00 25.00
BH4 Terrell Davis 12.00 30.00
BH5 Barry Sanders 50.00 100.00
BH6 Peyton Manning 50.00 100.00
BH7 Edgerrin James 12.00 30.00
BH8 Marvin Harrison 12.00 30.00
BH9 Mark Brunell 10.00 25.00
BH11 Dan Marino 60.00 120.00
BH12 Cris Carter 12.00 30.00
BH13 Drew Bledsoe 12.00 30.00
BH14 Ricky Williams 12.00 30.00
BH16 Kurt Warner 20.00 40.00
BH17 Isaac Bruce 12.00 30.00
BH18 Eddie George 10.00 25.00
BH19 Steve McNair 12.00 30.00
BH20 Brad Johnson 10.00 25.00

2000 Absolute Canton Absolutes

COMPLETE SET (30) 60.00 150.00
STATED ODDS 1:39
CA1 Tim Couch 1.50 4.00
CA2 Emmitt Smith 5.00 12.00
CA3 Troy Aikman 3.00 8.00
CA4 John Elway 5.00 12.00
CA5 Terrell Davis 2.00 5.00
CA6 Barry Sanders 4.00 10.00
CA7 Brett Favre 6.00 15.00
CA8 Peyton Manning 5.00 12.00
CA9 Edgerrin James 2.00 5.00
CA10 Mark Brunell 1.50 4.00
CA11 Dan Marino 6.00 15.00
CA12 Randy Moss 2.00 5.00
CA13 Drew Bledsoe 2.00 5.00
CA14 Jerry Rice 4.00 10.00
CA15 Steve Young 2.50 6.00
CA16 Kurt Warner 3.00 8.00
CA17 Eddie George 1.50 4.00
CA18 Deion Sanders 2.00 5.00
CA19 Antonio Freeman 1.50 4.00
CA20 Warren Moon 2.00 5.00
CA21 Cris Carter 2.00 5.00
CA22 Randall Cunningham 2.00 5.00
CA23 Curtis Martin 2.00 5.00
CA24 Tim Brown 2.00 5.00
CA25 Marshall Faulk 2.00 5.00
CA26 Michael Irvin 2.00 5.00
CA27 Thurman Thomas 2.00 5.00
CA28 Vinny Testaverde 1.50 4.00
CA29 Ricky Watters 1.50 4.00
CA30 Jeff George 1.50 4.00

2000 Absolute Extreme Team

COMPLETE SET (40) 60.00 150.00
STATED ODDS 1:18 HOB, 1:27 RET
XT1 Jake Plummer 1.00 2.50
XT2 Tim Couch 1.00 2.50
XT3 Terrell Davis 1.25 3.00
XT4 Brett Favre 4.00 10.00
XT5 Peyton Manning 3.00 8.00
XT6 Edgerrin James 1.25 3.00
XT7 Mark Brunell 1.00 2.50
XT8 Fred Taylor 1.25 3.00
XT9 Randy Moss 1.25 3.00
XT10 Drew Bledsoe 1.25 3.00
XT11 Ricky Williams 1.25 3.00
XT12 Kurt Warner 2.00 5.00
XT13 Eddie George 1.00 2.50
XT14 Cade McNown .75 2.00
XT15 Kevin Johnson 1.00 2.50
XT16 Joey Galloway 1.00 2.50
XT17 Olandis Gary 1.00 2.50
XT18 Dorsey Levens 1.00 2.50
XT19 Marvin Harrison 1.25 3.00
XT20 Daunte Culpepper 1.00 2.50
XT21 Duce Staley 1.00 2.50
XT22 Donovan McNabb 1.25 3.00
XT23 Marshall Faulk 1.25 3.00
XT24 Shaun King .75 2.00
XT25 Keyshawn Johnson 1.00 2.50
XT26 Steve McNair .75 2.00
XT27 Stephen Davis 1.00 2.50
XT28 Brad Johnson 1.00 2.50
XT29 Akili Smith .75 2.00
XT30 Brian Griese 1.00 2.50
XT31 Emmitt Smith 3.00 8.00
XT32 Isaac Bruce 1.25 3.00
XT33 Peter Warrick 1.25 3.00
XT34 Jamal Lewis 1.00 2.50
XT35 Thomas Jones 1.50 4.00
XT36 Plaxico Burress 1.25 3.00
XT37 Travis Taylor 1.00 2.50
XT38 Ron Dayne 1.25 3.00
XT39 Chad Pennington 1.50 4.00
XT40 Shaun Alexander 1.25 3.00

2000 Absolute Ground Hoggs Shoe

STATED ODDS 1:188 HOBBY
FIRST 25 SER.#'D SETS SIGNED
GH1 Jake Plummer/110* 10.00 25.00
GH1AU Jake Plummer AU/25* 40.00 80.00
GH2 Muhsin Muhammad/75 12.00 30.00
GH3 Emmitt Smith/135 30.00 80.00
GH4 Ricky Watters/135 10.00 25.00
GH5 Terrell Davis/135 12.00 30.00
GH6 Brett Favre/135 40.00 100.00
GH7 Dorsey Levens/135 10.00 25.00
GH8 Antonio Freeman/135 10.00 25.00
GH9 Edgerrin James/110* 12.00 30.00
GH9AU Edgerrin James AU/25* 50.00 100.00
GH10 Marvin Harrison/135 12.00 30.00
GH11 Mark Brunell/135 10.00 25.00

GH12 Fred Taylor/135	12.00	30.00
GH13 Jimmy Smith/135	10.00	25.00
GH14 James Johnson/135	8.00	20.00
GH15 Dan Marino/135	40.00	100.00
GH16 Jon Kitna/135	10.00	25.00
GH17 Ricky Williams/100*	12.00	30.00
GH17AU Ricky Williams AU/25*	40.00	80.00
GH18 Curtis Martin/135	12.00	30.00
GH19 Wayne Chrebet/135	10.00	25.00
GH20 Steve Young/135	15.00	40.00
GH21 Junior Seau/135	12.00	30.00
GH22 Kurt Warner/110*	20.00	50.00
GH22AU Kurt Warner AU/25*	50.00	100.00
GH23 Marshall Faulk/135	12.00	30.00
GH24 Eddie George/135	10.00	25.00
GH25 Steve McNair/135	12.00	30.00
GH26 Joey Galloway/135	10.00	25.00
GH27 Jerry Rice/135	25.00	60.00
GH28 Jevon Kearse/135	10.00	25.00
GH29 Stephen Davis/135	10.00	25.00
GH30 Albert Connell/135	8.00	20.00

2000 Absolute Leather and Laces

*COMBO/20: 1X TO 2.5X BASIC INS/350
*COMBO/10: 1.2X TO 3X BASIC INS/175
COMBOS PRINT RUN 10-20

AC83 Albert Connell/175	4.00	10.00
AF86A Antonio Freeman/350	4.00	10.00
AF86B Antonio Freeman/175	5.00	12.00
AS11 Akili Smith/350	3.00	8.00
AS23 Antowain Smith/350	4.00	10.00
BC85 Ben Coates/175	4.00	10.00
BE81 Bobby Engram/175	5.00	12.00
BF4A Brett Favre/350	15.00	40.00
BF4B Brett Favre/175	20.00	50.00
BJ14 Brad Johnson/175	5.00	12.00
BM74 Bruce Matthews/175	5.00	12.00
BS20 Barry Sanders/350	10.00	25.00
BS78 Bruce Smith/350	5.00	12.00
CC80 Curtis Conway/175	5.00	12.00
CC80 Cris Carter/175	6.00	15.00
CD28 Corey Dillon/350	4.00	10.00
CE44 Curtis Enis/350	3.00	8.00
CG25 Charlie Garner/350	4.00	10.00
CM28 Curtis Martin/175	6.00	15.00
CP81 Carl Pickens/175	5.00	12.00
DB89 David Boston/350	3.00	8.00
DC84 Darrin Chiaverini/175	4.00	10.00
DD11 Drew Bledsoe/350	5.00	12.00
DH11 Damon Huard/175	5.00	12.00
DL25A Dorsey Levens/350	4.00	10.00
DL25B Dorsey Levens/175	5.00	12.00
DM5 Donovan McNabb/350	5.00	12.00
DM13 Dan Marino/350	15.00	40.00
DM87 Derrick Mayes/175	4.00	10.00
DS21 Deion Sanders/175	6.00	15.00
DS22 Duce Staley/350	4.00	10.00
DS86 Darnay Scott/175	5.00	12.00
EG27A Eddie George/350	4.00	10.00
EG27B Eddie George/175	5.00	12.00
EJ32 Edgerrin James/175	6.00	15.00
EM80 Eric Moulds/350	4.00	10.00
EM87 Ed McCaffrey/175	5.00	12.00
ER23 Errict Rhett/175	5.00	12.00
ES22 Emmitt Smith/175	15.00	40.00
FS81 Frank Sanders/350	3.00	8.00
FT28A Fred Taylor/350	5.00	12.00
FT28B Fred Taylor/175	6.00	15.00
FW89 Frank Wycheck/175	5.00	12.00
HM84 Herman Moore/175	5.00	12.00
HW86 Hines Ward/175	6.00	15.00
IB80 Isaac Bruce/350	5.00	12.00
JB18 Jeff Blake/175	5.00	12.00
JB36 Jerome Bettis/350	8.00	
JE7 John Elway/175	15.00	40.00
JG5 Jeff Garcia/350	4.00	10.00
JG87 Jammi German/175	4.00	10.00
JH4 Jim Harbaugh/175	5.00	12.00
JJ32 James Johnson/350	3.00	8.00
JK90A Jevon Kearse/350	4.00	10.00
JK90B Jevon Kearse/175	5.00	12.00
JL84 Jermaine Lewis/175	4.00	10.00
JM87 Johnnie Morton/175	5.00	12.00
JR80A Jerry Rice/350	10.00	25.00
JR80B Jerry Rice/175	12.00	30.00
JS33 James Stewart/350	3.00	8.00
JS55 Junior Seau/175	6.00	15.00
JS82 Jimmy Smith/350	4.00	10.00
JS83 J.J. Stokes/175	5.00	12.00
KD87 Kevin Dyson/175	5.00	12.00
KJ19 Keyshawn Johnson/175	5.00	12.00
KJ85 Kevin Johnson/350	3.00	8.00
KM87 Keenan McCardell/350	4.00	10.00
KS10 Kordell Stewart/350	4.00	10.00
KW13A Kurt Warner/350	8.00	20.00
KW13B Kurt Warner/175	10.00	25.00
LK99 Levon Kirkland/175	4.00	10.00
MA40 Mike Alstott/350	5.00	12.00
MB8A Mark Brunell/350	4.00	10.00
MB8B Mark Brunell/175	5.00	12.00
MB35 Michael Basnight/175	4.00	10.00
MF28A Marshall Faulk/175	6.00	15.00
MH88 Marvin Harrison/175	6.00	15.00
MM87 Muhsin Muhammad/350	4.00	10.00
MW82 Michael Westbrook/175	4.00	10.00
NK26 Napoleon Kaufman/175	5.00	12.00
NM20 Natrone Means/175	5.00	12.00
NO14 Neil O'Donnell/175	4.00	10.00
OG86 Oronde Gadsden/175	5.00	12.00
OM81 O.J. McDuffie/175	5.00	12.00
PH33 Priest Holmes/175	6.00	15.00
PM18 Peyton Manning/350	12.00	30.00
PP81 Peerless Price/175	5.00	12.00
PW80 Peter Warrick/350	5.00	12.00
QI87 Qadry Ismail/175	5.00	12.00
RA85 Reidel Anthony/175	4.00	10.00
RC7 Randall Cunningham/175	6.00	15.00
RD83 Rickey Dudley/175	4.00	10.00
RG12 Rich Gannon/175	5.00	12.00
RI81 Rocket Ismail/175	5.00	12.00
RJ11 Rob Johnson/175	5.00	12.00
RM84 Randy Moss/175	6.00	15.00
RS26 Robert Smith/175	5.00	12.00
RS80 Rod Smith/175	5.00	12.00
RW34 Ricky Williams/350	5.00	12.00
RW92 Reggie White/350	5.00	12.00
SD48 Stephen Davis/175	5.00	12.00
SM9A Steve McNair/350	5.00	12.00
SM9B Steve McNair/175	6.00	15.00
SM29 Sam Madison/175	4.00	10.00
SY8 Steve Young/350	6.00	15.00
TA8 Troy Aikman/175	10.00	25.00
TB21 Tim Biakabutuka/350	4.00	10.00
TB81 Tim Brown/350	5.00	12.00
TC2 Tim Couch/350	4.00	10.00
TD7 Trent Dilfer/175	5.00	12.00
TD30 Terrell Davis/175	6.00	15.00
TE81 Troy Edwards/350	3.00	8.00
TG88 Terry Glenn/175	5.00	12.00
TH88 Torry Holt/175	6.00	15.00
TM80 Tony Martin/175	5.00	12.00
TM81 Terance Mathis/175	4.00	10.00
TO81A Terrell Owens/175	6.00	15.00
TO81B Terrell Owens/175	6.00	15.00
TT34 Thurman Thomas/350	5.00	12.00
TW47 Tyrone Wheatley/175	4.00	10.00
VT16 Vinny Testaverde/175	5.00	12.00
WC80 Wayne Chrebet/175	5.00	12.00
WD28 Warrick Dunn/350	4.00	10.00
WS99 Warren Sapp/350	4.00	10.00
YT82 Yancey Thigpen/175	4.00	10.00
ZT54 Zach Thomas/175	6.00	15.00

2000 Absolute Playoff Fever

1 Jake Plummer	1.50	4.00
2 Emmitt Smith	5.00	12.00
3 Troy Aikman	3.00	8.00
4 John Elway	5.00	12.00
5 Terrell Davis	2.00	5.00
6 Charlie Batch	1.50	4.00
7 Barry Sanders	4.00	10.00
8 Brett Favre	6.00	15.00
9 Peyton Manning	5.00	12.00
10 Edgerrin James	2.00	5.00
11 Mark Brunell	1.50	4.00
12 Fred Taylor	2.00	5.00
13 Dan Marino	6.00	15.00
14 Randy Moss	2.00	5.00
15 Drew Bledsoe	2.00	5.00
16 Jerry Rice	4.00	10.00
17 Steve Young	2.50	6.00
18 Kurt Warner	3.00	8.00
19 Eddie George	1.50	4.00
20 Eric Moulds	1.50	4.00
21 Doug Flutie	2.00	5.00
22 Dorsey Levens	1.50	4.00
23 Antonio Freeman	1.50	4.00
24 Marvin Harrison	2.00	5.00
25 Cris Carter	2.00	5.00
26 Curtis Martin	2.00	5.00
27 Marshall Faulk	2.00	5.00
28 Torry Holt	2.00	5.00
29 Keyshawn Johnson	1.50	4.00
30 Mike Alstott	2.00	5.00
31 Shaun King	1.25	3.00
32 Steve McNair	2.00	5.00
33 Stephen Davis	1.50	4.00
34 Brad Johnson	1.50	4.00
35 Ed McCaffrey	1.50	4.00
36 Germane Crowell	1.25	3.00
37 James Stewart	1.25	3.00
38 Jimmy Smith	1.50	4.00
39 Isaac Bruce	2.00	5.00
40 Michael Westbrook	1.25	3.00

2000 Absolute Rookie Reflex

COMPLETE SET (30)	25.00	60.00
STATED ODDS 1:10 HOB, 1:15 RET		
*GOLD/100: 2X TO 5X BASIC INSERTS		
GOLD STATED PRINT RUN 100 SER.#'d SETS		
RR1 Peter Warrick	.75	2.00
RR2 Jamal Lewis	.75	2.00
RR3 Thomas Jones	1.00	2.50
RR4 Plaxico Burress	.75	2.00
RR5 Travis Taylor	.60	1.50
RR6 Ron Dayne	.75	2.00
RR7 Bubba Franks	.75	2.00
RR8 Chad Pennington	1.25	3.00
RR9 Shaun Alexander	1.00	2.50
RR10 Sylvester Morris	.50	1.25
RR11 R.Jay Soward	.50	1.25
RR12 Trung Canidate	.60	1.50
RR13 Dennis Northcutt	.60	1.50
RR14 Todd Pinkston	.50	1.25
RR15 Jerry Porter	.75	2.00
RR16 Travis Prentice	.60	1.50
RR17 Giovanni Carmazzi	.50	1.25
RR18 Ron Dugans	.50	1.25
RR19 Erron Kinney	.50	1.25
RR20 Dez White	.60	1.50
RR21 Chris Cole	.60	1.50
RR22 Doug Chapman	.50	1.25
RR23 Chris Redman	.60	1.50
RR24 J.R. Redmond	.50	1.25
RR25 Laveranues Coles	.75	2.00
RR26 JaJuan Dawson	.50	1.25
RR27 Darrell Jackson	.60	1.50
RR28 Reuben Droughns	.75	2.00
RR29 Curtis Keaton	.50	1.25
RR30 Gari Scott	.50	1.25

2000 Absolute Tag Team Quads

COMPLETE SET (31)	125.00	250.00
STATED ODDS 1:79		
TTQ1 Jake Plummer	5.00	12.00
David Boston		
Thomas Jones		
Frank Sanders		
TTQ2 Jamal Anderson	3.00	8.00
Tim Dwight		
Chris Chandler		
Terance Mathis		
TTQ3 Tony Banks	2.50	6.00
Travis Taylor		
Shannon Sharpe		
Jamal Lewis		
TTQ4 Rob Johnson	3.00	8.00
Eric Moulds		
Antowain Smith		
Peerless Price		
TTQ5 Steve Beuerlein	3.00	8.00
Tim Biakabutuka		
Patrick Jeffers		
Muhsin Muhammad		
TTQ6 Curtis Enis	3.00	8.00
Cade McNown		
Marcus Robinson		
Dez White		
TTQ7 Corey Dillon	4.00	10.00
Akili Smith		
Peter Warrick		
Ron Dugans		
TTQ8 Tim Couch	3.00	8.00
Errict Rhett		
Kevin Johnson		
Courtney Brown		
TTQ9 Rocket Ismail	10.00	25.00
Emmitt Smith		
Troy Aikman		
Joey Galloway		
TTQ10 Terrell Davis	4.00	10.00
Ed McCaffrey		
Olandis Gary		
Brian Griese		
TTQ11 James Stewart	3.00	8.00
Charlie Batch		
Herman Moore		
Germane Crowell		
TTQ12 Brett Favre	12.00	30.00
Bubba Franks		
Dorsey Levens		
Antonio Freeman		
TTQ13 Peyton Manning	10.00	25.00
Marvin Harrison		
Edgerrin James		
Terrence Wilkins		
TTQ14 Keenan McCardell	4.00	10.00
Mark Brunell		
Jimmy Smith		
Fred Taylor		
TTQ15 Elvis Grbac	2.50	6.00
Sylvester Morris		
Tony Gonzalez		
Derrick Alexander WR		
TTQ16 James Johnson	3.00	8.00
O.J. McDuffie		
Tony Martin		
Damon Huard		
TTQ17 Randy Moss	4.00	10.00
Robert Smith		
Cris Carter		
Daunte Culpepper		
TTQ18 Drew Bledsoe	2.50	6.00
Kevin Faulk		
J.R. Redmond		
Terry Glenn		
TTQ19 Sherrod Gideon	4.00	10.00
Jeff Blake		
Ricky Williams		
Jake Reed		
TTQ20 Kerry Collins	4.00	10.00
Amani Toomer		
Ron Dayne		
Ike Hilliard		
TTQ21 Curtis Martin	4.00	10.00
Chad Pennington		
Vinny Testaverde		
Wayne Chrebet		
TTQ22 Tim Brown	4.00	10.00
Napoleon Kaufman		
Rich Gannon		
Tyrone Wheatley		
TTQ23 Donovan McNabb	2.50	6.00
Corey Simon		
Todd Pinkston		
Duce Staley		
TTQ24 Plaxico Burress	4.00	10.00
Troy Edwards		
Kordell Stewart		
Jerome Bettis		
TTQ25 Jim Harbaugh	4.00	10.00
Junior Seau		
Curtis Conway		
Jermaine Fazande		
TTQ26 Charlie Garner	8.00	20.00
Jerry Rice		
Terrell Owens		
Steve Young		
TTQ27 Derrick Mayes	5.00	12.00
Shaun Alexander		
Ricky Watters		
Jon Kitna		
TTQ28 Kurt Warner	6.00	15.00
Torry Holt		
Isaac Bruce		
Marshall Faulk		
TTQ29 Warrick Dunn	4.00	10.00
Keyshawn Johnson		
Shaun King		
Mike Alstott		
TTQ30 Kevin Dyson	4.00	10.00
Eddie George		
Steve McNair		
Jevon Kearse		
TTQ31 Albert Connell	3.00	8.00
Brad Johnson		
Michael Westbrook		
Stephen Davis		

2000 Absolute Tag Team Tandems

COMPLETE SET (62)	75.00	150.00
STATED ODDS 1:71 RETAIL		
1 Jake Plummer	1.50	4.00
David Boston		
2 Thomas Jones	1.50	4.00
Frank Sanders		
3 Jamal Anderson	1.50	4.00
Tim Dwight		
4 Chris Chandler	1.50	4.00
Terance Mathis		
5 Tony Banks	1.50	4.00
Travis Taylor		
6 Shannon Sharpe	1.25	3.00
Jamal Lewis		
7 Eric Moulds	1.50	4.00
Rob Johnson		
8 Antowain Smith	1.50	4.00
Peerless Price		
9 Steve Beuerlein	1.50	4.00
Tim Biakabutuka		
10 Patrick Jeffers	1.50	4.00
Muhsin Muhammad		
11 Cade McNown	1.25	3.00
Curtis Enis		
12 Marcus Robinson	1.50	4.00
Dez White		
13 Corey Dillon	1.50	4.00
Akili Smith		
14 Peter Warrick	2.00	5.00
Ron Dugans		
15 Tim Couch	1.50	4.00
Errict Rhett		
16 Kevin Johnson	1.50	4.00
Courtney Brown		
17 Emmitt Smith	5.00	12.00
Rocket Ismail		
18 Troy Aikman	3.00	8.00
Joey Galloway		
19 Terrell Davis	2.00	5.00
Ed McCaffrey		
20 Brian Griese	1.50	4.00
Olandis Gary		
21 Charlie Batch	1.50	4.00
James Stewart		
22 Germane Crowell	1.50	4.00
Herman Moore		
23 Brett Favre	6.00	15.00
Bubba Franks		
24 Dorsey Levens	1.50	4.00
Antonio Freeman		
25 Peyton Manning	5.00	12.00
Marvin Harrison		
26 Edgerrin James	2.00	5.00
Terrence Wilkins		
27 Mark Brunell	1.50	4.00
Keenan McCardell		
28 Fred Taylor	2.00	5.00
Jimmy Smith		
29 Elvis Grbac	1.25	3.00
Sylvester Morris		
30 Tony Gonzalez	2.00	5.00
Derrick Alexander		
31 James Johnson	1.50	4.00
O.J. McDuffie		
32 Tony Martin	2.00	5.00
Damon Huard		
33 Randy Moss	2.00	5.00
Robert Smith		
34 Cris Carter	2.00	5.00
Daunte Culpepper		
35 Drew Bledsoe	2.00	5.00
Kevin Faulk		
36 Terry Glenn	1.25	3.00
J.R. Redmond		
37 Ricky Williams	2.00	5.00
Sherrod Gideon		
38 Jeff Blake	1.50	4.00
Jake Reed		
39 Amani Toomer	1.50	4.00
Kerry Collins		
40 Ron Dayne	2.00	5.00
Ike Hilliard		
41 Curtis Martin	2.00	5.00
Wayne Chrebet		
42 Chad Pennington	2.00	5.00
Vinny Testaverde		
43 Tim Brown	2.00	5.00
Napoleon Kaufman		
44 Rich Gannon	1.50	4.00
Tyrone Wheatley		
45 Donovan McNabb	1.50	4.00
Corey Simon		
46 Todd Pinkston	1.25	3.00
Duce Staley		
47 Plaxico Burress	2.00	5.00
Troy Edwards		
48 Jerome Bettis	2.00	5.00
Kordell Stewart		
49 Junior Seau	2.00	5.00
Jim Harbaugh		
50 Jermaine Fazande	1.50	4.00
Curtis Conway		
51 Jerry Rice	4.00	10.00
Charlie Garner		
52 Steve Young	2.50	6.00
Terrell Owens		
53 Shaun Alexander	1.50	4.00
Derrick Mayes		
54 Ricky Watters	1.50	4.00
Jon Kitna		
55 Kurt Warner	3.00	8.00
Torry Holt		
56 Marshall Faulk	2.00	5.00
Isaac Bruce		
57 Keyshawn Johnson	1.50	4.00
Warrick Dunn		
58 Shaun King	2.00	5.00
Mike Alstott		
59 Eddie George	1.50	4.00
Kevin Dyson		
60 Steve McNair	2.00	5.00
Jevon Kearse		
61 Brad Johnson	1.50	4.00
Albert Connell		
62 Steve Davis	1.50	4.00
Michael Westbrook		

2000 Absolute Tools of the Trade

TT1-TT20 PRINT RUN 2000
TT21-TT40 PRINT RUN 1500
TT41-TT60 PRINT RUN 1000
*1-20 DIE CUT/25: 4X TO 10X BASIC INSERTS
1-20 DIE CUT PRINT RUN 25
*21-40 DIE CUT/50: 2.5X TO 6X BASIC INSERTS
21-40 DIE CUT PRINT RUN 50
*41-60 DIE CUT/100: 1.2X TO 3X BASIC INSERTS
41-60 DIE CUT PRINT RUN 100

TT1 Jake Plummer	1.00	2.50
TT2 Tim Couch	1.00	2.50
TT3 Troy Aikman	2.00	5.00
TT4 John Elway	3.00	8.00
TT5 Charlie Batch	1.00	2.50
TT6 Brett Favre	4.00	10.00
TT7 Peyton Manning	3.00	8.00
TT8 Mark Brunell	1.00	2.50
TT9 Dan Marino	4.00	10.00
TT10 Drew Bledsoe	1.25	3.00
TT11 Steve Young	1.50	4.00
TT12 Kurt Warner	2.00	5.00
TT13 Cade McNown	.75	2.00
TT14 Daunte Culpepper	1.00	2.50
TT15 Donovan McNabb	1.25	3.00
TT16 Jon Kitna	1.00	2.50
TT17 Steve McNair	1.25	3.00
TT18 Brad Johnson	1.00	2.50
TT19 Akili Smith	.75	2.00
TT20 Chad Pennington	2.00	5.00
TT21 Emmitt Smith	3.00	8.00
TT22 Terrell Davis	1.25	3.00
TT23 Barry Sanders	2.50	6.00
TT24 Edgerrin James	1.25	3.00
TT25 Fred Taylor	1.25	3.00
TT26 Ricky Williams	1.25	3.00
TT27 Eddie George	1.00	2.50
TT28 Jamal Anderson	1.00	2.50
TT29 Corey Dillon	1.00	2.50
TT30 Dorsey Levens	1.00	2.50
TT31 Robert Smith	1.00	2.50
TT32 Curtis Martin	1.25	3.00
TT33 Jerome Bettis	1.25	3.00
TT34 Marshall Faulk	1.25	3.00
TT35 Stephen Davis	1.00	2.50
TT36 Jamal Lewis	1.25	3.00
TT37 Thomas Jones	1.50	4.00
TT38 Ron Dayne	1.25	3.00
TT39 Shaun Alexander	1.50	4.00
TT40 Trung Canidate	1.00	2.50
TT41 Randy Moss	1.50	4.00
TT42 Jerry Rice	3.00	8.00
TT43 Eric Moulds	1.25	3.00
TT44 Kevin Johnson	1.00	2.50
TT45 Joey Galloway	1.25	3.00
TT46 Antonio Freeman	1.25	3.00
TT47 Marvin Harrison	1.50	4.00
TT48 Cris Carter	1.50	4.00
TT49 Tim Brown	1.50	4.00
TT50 Terrell Owens	1.50	4.00
TT51 Keyshawn Johnson	1.25	3.00
TT52 Muhsin Muhammad	1.25	3.00
TT53 Patrick Jeffers	1.25	3.00
TT54 Marcus Robinson	1.25	3.00
TT55 Jimmy Smith	1.25	3.00
TT56 Amani Toomer	1.25	3.00
TT57 Isaac Bruce	1.50	4.00
TT58 Peter Warrick	1.50	4.00
TT59 Plaxico Burress	1.50	4.00
TT60 Travis Taylor	1.25	3.00

2001 Absolute Memorabilia

In July of 2001 Playoff Inc. released its Playoff Absolute Memorabilia product. Its hobby release was packed in boxes of 18 6-card packs along with a signed mini-helmet. The cardfronts featured a foilboard design. The set consisted of 185-cards with 85 of those being short printed rookies. Cards numbered 101-150 were Rookie Premieres that were serial numbered to 1750. Cards that were numbered 151-185 are Rookie Premiere Materials serial numbered to 850, with the first 25 of each card autographed. The Rookie Premiere Materials also had an authentic event-used football swatch.

COMP.SET w/o SP's (100)	12.50	30.00
151-185 RPM PRINT RUN 850		
1 David Boston	.30	.75
2 Jake Plummer	.40	1.00
3 Thomas Jones	.40	1.00
4 Jamal Anderson	.40	1.00
5 Chris Redman	.50	1.25
6 Jamal Lewis	.50	1.25
7 Qadry Ismail	.40	1.00
8 Ray Lewis	.50	1.25
9 Shannon Sharpe	.50	1.25
10 Travis Taylor	.30	.75
11 Trent Dilfer	.40	1.00
12 Elvis Grbac	.40	1.00
13 Eric Moulds	.40	1.00
14 Rob Johnson	.40	1.00
15 Muhsin Muhammad	.40	1.00
16 Brian Urlacher	.60	1.50
17 Cade McNown	.40	1.00
18 Marcus Robinson	.40	1.00
19 Akili Smith	.30	.75
20 Corey Dillon	.40	1.00
21 Peter Warrick	.40	1.00
22 Courtney Brown	.30	.75
23 Tim Couch	.30	.75
24 Emmitt Smith	1.25	3.00
25 Troy Aikman	.75	2.00
26 Brian Griese	.40	1.00
27 Ed McCaffrey	.40	1.00
28 John Elway	1.25	3.00
29 Mike Anderson	.40	1.00
30 Rod Smith	.40	1.00
31 Terrell Davis	.50	1.25
32 Barry Sanders	1.25	3.00
33 James Stewart	.30	.75
34 Ahman Green	.50	1.25
35 Antonio Freeman	.50	1.25
36 Brett Favre	1.50	4.00
37 Edgerrin James	.50	1.25
38 Marvin Harrison	.50	1.25
39 Peyton Manning	1.25	3.00
40 Fred Taylor	.50	1.25
41 Jimmy Smith	.40	1.00
42 Keenan McCardell	.40	1.00
43 Mark Brunell	.40	1.00
44 Sylvester Morris	.30	.75
45 Tony Gonzalez	.50	1.25
46 Dan Marino	1.25	3.00
47 Jay Fiedler	.40	1.00
48 Lamar Smith	.40	1.00
49 Cris Carter	.50	1.25
50 Daunte Culpepper	.40	1.00
51 Randy Moss	.50	1.25
52 Drew Bledsoe	.50	1.25
53 Terry Glenn	.40	1.00
54 Aaron Brooks	.40	1.00
55 Joe Horn	.40	1.00
56 Ricky Williams	.50	1.25
57 Amani Toomer	.40	1.00
58 Ike Hilliard	.40	1.00
59 Kerry Collins	.40	1.00
60 Ron Dayne	.40	1.00
61 Tiki Barber	.50	1.25
62 Chad Pennington	.50	1.25
63 Curtis Martin	.50	1.25
64 Laveranues Coles	.40	1.00
65 Vinny Testaverde	.40	1.00
66 Wayne Chrebet	.40	1.00
67 Charles Woodson	.50	1.25
68 Rich Gannon	.40	1.00
69 Tim Brown	.50	1.25
70 Tyrone Wheatley	.40	1.00
71 Corey Simon	.30	.75
72 Donovan McNabb	.50	1.25
73 Duce Staley	.40	1.00
74 Jerome Bettis	.50	1.25
75 Plaxico Burress	.40	1.00
76 Doug Flutie	.50	1.25
77 Junior Seau	.50	1.25
78 Charlie Garner	.40	1.00
79 Jeff Garcia	.40	1.00
80 Jerry Rice	1.00	2.50
81 Steve Young	.60	1.50
82 Terrell Owens	.50	1.25
83 Darrell Jackson	.40	1.00
84 Ricky Watters	.40	1.00
85 Shaun Alexander	.50	1.25
86 Isaac Bruce	.50	1.25
87 Kurt Warner	.75	2.00
88 Marshall Faulk	.50	1.25
89 Torry Holt	.40	1.00
90 Brad Johnson	.40	1.00
91 Keyshawn Johnson	.40	1.00
92 Mike Alstott	.40	1.00
93 Shaun King	.30	.75
94 Warren Sapp	.40	1.00
95 Warrick Dunn	.50	1.25
96 Eddie George	.50	1.25
97 Jevon Kearse	.40	1.00
98 Steve McNair	.50	1.25
99 Jeff George	.40	1.00
100 Stephen Davis	.40	1.00
101 Jason McKinley RC	1.25	3.00
102 Bobby Newcombe RC	1.50	4.00
103 Cedrick Wilson RC	1.50	4.00
104 Ken-Yon Rambo RC	1.25	3.00
105 Kevin Kasper RC	1.25	3.00
106 Jamal Reynolds RC	1.25	3.00
107 Scotty Anderson RC	1.25	3.00
108 T.J. Houshmandzadeh RC	2.50	6.00
109 Chris Taylor RC	1.25	3.00
110 Vinny Sutherland RC	1.25	3.00
111 Jabari Holloway RC	1.25	3.00
112 Shad Meier RC	1.25	3.00
113 Correll Buckhalter RC	2.00	5.00
114 Dan Alexander RC	1.50	4.00
115 David Allen RC	1.25	3.00
116 LaMont Jordan RC	2.00	5.00
117 Nate Clements RC	1.50	4.00
118 Reggie White RC	1.25	3.00
119 Javon Green RC	1.25	3.00
120 Shaun Rogers RC	2.00	5.00
121 Heath Evans RC	1.50	4.00
122 Moran Norris RC	1.25	3.00
123 Ben Leard RC	1.25	3.00
124 David Rivers RC	1.25	3.00
125 A.J. Feeley RC	1.50	4.00
126 Boo Williams RC	1.25	3.00
127 Ronney Daniels RC	1.25	3.00
128 Alge Crumpler RC	2.00	5.00
129 Todd Heap RC	2.00	5.00
130 Tim Hasselbeck RC	1.50	4.00
131 Josh Booty RC	1.50	4.00
132 Jamie Winborn RC	1.50	4.00
133 Brian Allen RC	1.25	3.00
134 Sedrick Hodge RC	1.25	3.00
135 Tommy Polley RC	1.25	3.00
136 Torrance Marshall RC	1.25	3.00
137 Damione Lewis RC	1.50	4.00
138 Marcus Stroud RC	1.50	4.00
139 Aaron Schobel RC	2.00	5.00
140 DeLawrence Grant RC	1.25	3.00
141 Fred Smoot RC	2.00	5.00
142 Jamar Fletcher RC	1.25	3.00
143 Ken Lucas RC	1.50	4.00
144 Will Allen RC	2.00	5.00
145 Adam Archuleta RC	1.50	4.00
146 Derrick Gibson RC	1.25	3.00
147 Jarrod Cooper RC	1.50	4.00
148 Eddie Berlin RC	1.25	3.00
149 Steve Smith RC	4.00	10.00
150 Willie Middlebrooks RC	1.50	4.00
151 Michael Vick RPM RC	20.00	50.00
152 Drew Brees RPM RC	20.00	50.00
153 Chris Weinke RPM RC	4.00	10.00
154 Marques Tuiasosopo RPM RC	4.00	10.00
155 Mike McMahon RPM RC	4.00	10.00
156 Deuce McAllister RPM RC	5.00	12.00
157 Leonard Davis RPM RC	5.00	12.00
158 LaDainian Tomlinson RPM RC	12.00	30.00
159 Anthony Thomas RPM RC	5.00	12.00
160 Travis Henry RPM RC	4.00	10.00
161 James Jackson RPM RC	3.00	8.00
162 Michael Bennett RPM RC	4.00	10.00
163 Kevan Barlow RPM RC	4.00	10.00
164 Travis Minor RPM RC	4.00	10.00
165 David Terrell RPM RC	4.00	10.00
166 Santana Moss RPM RC	6.00	15.00
167 Rod Gardner RPM RC	4.00	10.00
168 Quincy Morgan RPM RC	4.00	10.00
169 Freddie Mitchell RPM RC	3.00	8.00
170 Reggie Wayne RPM RC	10.00	25.00
171 Koren Robinson RPM RC	4.00	10.00
172 Chad Johnson RPM RC	8.00	20.00
173 Chris Chambers RPM RC	5.00	12.00
174 Josh Heupel RPM RC	5.00	12.00
175 Andre Carter RPM RC	4.00	10.00
176 Justin Smith RPM RC	5.00	12.00
177 Richard Seymour RPM RC	5.00	12.00
178 Dan Morgan RPM RC	4.00	10.00
179 Gerard Warren RPM RC	4.00	10.00
180 Robert Ferguson RPM RC	5.00	12.00
181 Sage Rosenfels RPM RC	5.00	12.00
182 Rudi Johnson RPM RC	5.00	12.00
183 Snoop Minnis RPM RC	3.00	8.00
184 Jesse Palmer RPM RC	4.00	10.00
185 Quincy Carter RPM RC	4.00	10.00

2001 Absolute Memorabilia Rookie Premiere Materials Autographs

FIRST 25 SER.#'d RPM's SIGNED		
151 Michael Vick	100.00	250.00
152 Drew Brees	200.00	400.00
153 Chris Weinke	20.00	50.00
155 Mike McMahon	20.00	50.00
156 Deuce McAllister	25.00	60.00
158 LaDainian Tomlinson	125.00	250.00
159 Anthony Thomas	25.00	60.00
160 Travis Henry	20.00	50.00
162 Michael Bennett	20.00	50.00
163 Kevan Barlow	20.00	50.00
164 Travis Minor	20.00	50.00
165 David Terrell	20.00	50.00
166 Santana Moss	30.00	80.00
168 Quincy Morgan	20.00	50.00
169 Freddie Mitchell	15.00	40.00
170 Reggie Wayne	50.00	125.00
171 Koren Robinson	20.00	50.00
172 Chad Johnson	40.00	100.00
173 Chris Chambers	25.00	60.00
176 Justin Smith	25.00	60.00
180 Robert Ferguson	25.00	60.00
182 Rudi Johnson	25.00	60.00
183 Snoop Minnis	15.00	40.00
184 Jesse Palmer	20.00	50.00

2001 Absolute Memorabilia Spectrum

UNPRICED 1-100 VET PRINT RUN 10
*ROOKIES 101-150: 1.2X TO 3X BASIC CARDS
*RPM ROOKIES 151-185: .8X TO 2X
101-185 ROOKIE PRINT RUN 25

2001 Absolute Memorabilia Ground Hoggs Shoe

GROUND HOGG PRINT RUN 125 SER.#'d SETS		
GH1 Amani Toomer	6.00	15.00
GH2 Antonio Freeman	8.00	20.00
GH3 Brett Favre	25.00	60.00
GH4 Bruce Matthews	6.00	15.00
GH5 Chad Pennington	8.00	20.00
GH6 Champ Bailey	8.00	20.00
GH7 Charles Woodson	8.00	20.00
GH8 Charlie Batch	6.00	15.00
GH9 Chris Samuels	5.00	12.00
GH10 Cris Carter	8.00	20.00
GH11 Curtis Martin	8.00	20.00
GH12 Dan Marino	20.00	50.00
GH13 Darrell Green	8.00	20.00
GH14 Darren Woodson	6.00	15.00
GH15 Daunte Culpepper	6.00	15.00
GH16 Deion Sanders	8.00	20.00
GH17 Derrick Mason	6.00	15.00
GH18 Eddie George	8.00	20.00
GH19 Edgerrin James	8.00	20.00
GH20 Emmitt Smith	20.00	50.00
GH21 Frank Wycheck	5.00	12.00
GH22 Fred Taylor	8.00	20.00
GH23 Ike Hilliard	6.00	15.00
GH24 Isaac Bruce	8.00	20.00
GH25 Jeff George	6.00	15.00
GH26 Jerry Rice	15.00	40.00
GH27 Jessie Armstead	5.00	12.00
GH28 Jevon Kearse	6.00	15.00
GH29 Jimmy Smith	6.00	15.00
GH30 Keyshawn Johnson	6.00	15.00
GH31 Lamar Smith	6.00	15.00
GH32 Laveranues Coles	6.00	15.00
GH33 Mark Brunell	6.00	15.00
GH34 Marshall Faulk	8.00	20.00
GH35 Marvin Harrison	8.00	20.00
GH36 Peerless Price	5.00	12.00
GH37 Peyton Manning	20.00	50.00
GH38 Rocket Ismail	6.00	15.00
GH39 Robert Smith	6.00	15.00
GH40 Ron Dayne	6.00	15.00
GH41 Stephen Davis	6.00	15.00
GH42 Terrell Owens	8.00	20.00
GH43 Terry Glenn	6.00	15.00
GH44 Tyrone Wheatley	6.00	15.00
GH45 Vinny Testaverde	6.00	15.00
GH46 Warren Moon	8.00	20.00
GH47 Warren Sapp	6.00	15.00
GH48 Wayne Chrebet	6.00	15.00
GH49 Willie McGinest	5.00	12.00
GH50 Zach Thomas	8.00	20.00

2001 Absolute Memorabilia Boss Hoggs Shoe

*UNSIGNED BOSS/25: .6X TO 1.5X GROUND		
GH12 Dan Marino AU	150.00	300.00
GH19 Edgerrin James AU	30.00	80.00
GH20 Emmitt Smith AU	150.00	300.00
GH24 Isaac Bruce AU	30.00	80.00
GH26 Jerry Rice AU	125.00	250.00
GH29 Jimmy Smith AU	25.00	60.00
GH34 Marshall Faulk AU	30.00	80.00
GH35 Marvin Harrison AU	30.00	80.00

2001 Absolute Memorabilia Leather and Laces

LL1-LL16 PRINT RUN 825
LL17-LL34 PRINT RUN 550
LL35-LL50 PRINT RUN 275
*COMBOS: .8X TO 2X BASIC INSERTS
LL1-LL16 COMBOS PRINT RUN 75
LL17-LL34 COMBOS PRINT RUN 50
LL35-LL50 COMBOS PRINT RUN 25

LL1 David Boston	3.00	8.00
LL2 Thomas Jones	4.00	10.00
LL3 Akili Smith	3.00	8.00
LL4 Cris Carter	5.00	12.00
LL5 Tiki Barber	5.00	12.00
LL6 Jevon Kearse	4.00	10.00
LL7 Jamal Anderson	4.00	10.00
LL8 Corey Simon	3.00	8.00
LL9 Deion Sanders	5.00	12.00
LL10 Stephen Davis	4.00	10.00
LL11 Peter Warrick	4.00	10.00
LL12 Kerry Collins	4.00	10.00
LL13 Bruce Smith	5.00	12.00
LL14 Jake Plummer	4.00	10.00
LL15 Darren Woodson	4.00	10.00
LL16 Steve McNair	5.00	12.00
LL17 Brian Urlacher	8.00	20.00
LL18 Cade McNown	5.00	12.00
LL19 Marcus Robinson	5.00	12.00
LL20 Corey Dillon	5.00	12.00
LL21 Emmitt Smith	15.00	40.00
LL22 Brett Favre	20.00	50.00
LL23 Peyton Manning	15.00	40.00
LL24 Fred Taylor	6.00	15.00
LL25 Mark Brunell	5.00	12.00
LL26 Dan Marino	15.00	40.00
LL27 Daunte Culpepper	5.00	12.00
LL28 Randy Moss	6.00	15.00
LL29 Drew Bledsoe	6.00	15.00
LL30 Ron Dayne	5.00	12.00
LL31 Donovan McNabb	6.00	15.00
LL32 Jerome Bettis	6.00	15.00
LL33 Jerry Rice	12.00	30.00
LL34 Eddie George	6.00	15.00
LL35 Isaac Bruce	8.00	20.00
LL36 Ray Lewis	8.00	20.00
LL37 Tim Couch	5.00	12.00
LL38 Eric Moulds	6.00	15.00
LL39 Doug Flutie	8.00	20.00
LL40 Edgerrin James	8.00	20.00
LL41 Curtis Martin	8.00	20.00
LL42 Wayne Chrebet	6.00	15.00
LL43 Jamal Lewis	8.00	20.00
LL44 Kurt Warner	12.00	30.00
LL45 Barry Sanders	20.00	50.00
LL46 Marvin Harrison	8.00	20.00
LL47 Ricky Williams	8.00	20.00
LL48 Jimmy Smith	6.00	15.00
LL49 Tim Brown	8.00	20.00
LL50 Troy Aikman	12.00	30.00

2001 Absolute Memorabilia Leather and Laces Autographs

STATED PRINT RUN 25 SER.#'d SETS		
LL10 Stephen Davis	20.00	50.00
LL20 Corey Dillon	20.00	50.00
LL26 Dan Marino	125.00	250.00
LL27 Daunte Culpepper	20.00	50.00
LL40 Edgerrin James	25.00	60.00
LL44 Kurt Warner	40.00	100.00
LL45 Barry Sanders	100.00	200.00
LL46 Marvin Harrison	25.00	60.00
LL47 Ricky Williams	25.00	60.00
LL49 Tim Brown	25.00	60.00

2001 Absolute Memorabilia Mini Helmet Autographs

ONE PER SEALED BOX		
1 Troy Aikman/86	60.00	120.00
2 Troy Aikman CHR/24	90.00	150.00
3 Will Allen/252	10.00	25.00
4 Alex Bannister/250	10.00	25.00
5 Kevan Barlow/226	12.00	30.00
7 Michael Bennett/251	12.00	30.00
8 Cliff Branch/554	12.00	30.00
10 Drew Brees/273	40.00	80.00
11 Drew Brees CHR/24	75.00	150.00
12 Willie Brown/1005	12.00	30.00
13 Quincy Carter/236	15.00	40.00
15 Chris Chambers/242	15.00	40.00
18 Randall Cunningham/70	20.00	40.00
19 Trent Dilfer SB/100	25.00	50.00
20 John Elway/40	125.00	250.00
21 Robert Ferguson/226	12.00	30.00
22 Robert Ferguson CHR/24	30.00	60.00
23 Chuck Foreman/600	12.00	30.00
24 Rich Gannon/1033	12.00	30.00
25 Jeff Garcia/1000	12.00	30.00
26 Rod Gardner/226	12.00	30.00
27 Kevin Greene/474	12.00	30.00
29 John Hannah/500	12.00	30.00
30 Todd Heap/225	15.00	40.00

31 Todd Heap CHR/24 40.00 80.00
32 Travis Henry/225 15.00 40.00
33 Travis Henry CHR/24 30.00 60.00
34 James Jackson/238 10.00 25.00
36 Chad Johnson/249 25.00 60.00
37 Rob Johnson/501 10.00 25.00
38 Rudi Johnson/238 15.00 40.00
40 Charlie Joiner/511 12.00 30.00
40 Gerard Warren/250 12.00 30.00
41 LaMont Jordan/237 15.00 40.00
42 Jevon Kearse/40 30.00 60.00
43 Jim Kelly/20 90.00 150.00
44 Bob Lilly/600 15.00 40.00
45 Peyton Manning/287 90.00 150.00
46 Dan Marino/80 100.00 200.00
47 Harvey Martin/250 50.00 100.00
48 Deuce McAllister/224 15.00 40.00
49 Deuce McAllister CHR/24 40.00 80.00
50 Mike McMahon/289 10.00 25.00
52 Donovan McNabb/58 40.00 80.00
53 Cade McNown/1024 10.00 20.00
54 Snoop Minnis/225 10.00 25.00
55 Snoop Minnis CHR/24 30.00 60.00
56 Travis Minor/250 12.00 30.00
57 Freddie Mitchell/217 12.00 30.00
58 Freddie Mitchell CHR/24 30.00 60.00
59 Quincy Morgan/238 12.00 30.00
61 Santana Moss/238 15.00 40.00
62 Jesse Palmer/250 10.00 25.00
63 Drew Pearson/600 15.00 40.00
64 Jake Plummer/1003 12.00 30.00
66 Ken-Yon Rambo/226 10.00 25.00
67 Ken-Yon Rambo CHR/24 30.00 60.00
68 Koren Robinson/227 10.00 25.00
69 Koren Robinson CHR/23 30.00 60.00
70 Sage Rosenfels/250 10.00 25.00
71 Barry Sanders/20 100.00 175.00
72 Richard Seymour/228 15.00 40.00
73 Richard Seymour CHR/22 40.00 80.00
74 Justin Smith/239 15.00 40.00
76 Charlie Taylor/485 12.00 30.00
77 Anthony Thomas/238 15.00 40.00
79 LaDainian Tomlinson/226 40.00 80.00
80 LaDainian Tomlinson Chrome/24 75.00 150.00
81 Michael Vick/226 50.00 80.00
82 Michael Vick CHR/24 90.00 150.00
83 Kurt Warner/119 50.00 120.00
85 Reggie Wayne/232 15.00 40.00
87 Chris Weinke/226 12.00 30.00
88 Chris Weinke CHR/24 40.00 80.00
89 Ricky Williams/1046 15.00 40.00
90 Steve Young/20 90.00 150.00

2001 Absolute Memorabilia Tools of the Trade

TT1-TT19 JERSEY PRINT RUN 300
TT20-TT30 GLOVE PRINT RUN 50
TT31-TT40 FACEMASK PRINT RUN 125
TT41-TT50 PANTS PRINT RUN 100
TT1 Antonio Freeman JSY 6.00 15.00
TT2 Barry Sanders JSY/275* 15.00 40.00
TT3 Brett Favre JSY 20.00 50.00
TT4 Brian Griese JSY 5.00 12.00
TT5 Donovan McNabb JSY 6.00 15.00
TT6 Daunte Culpepper JSY 5.00 12.00
TT7 Drew Bledsoe JSY/275* 6.00 15.00
TT8 Emmitt Smith JSY 15.00 40.00
TT9 Jamal Lewis JSY 6.00 15.00
TT10 Jimmy Smith JSY 5.00 12.00
TT11 Edgerrin James JSY/275* 6.00 15.00
TT12 Mike Anderson JSY/275* 5.00 12.00
TT13 Peyton Manning JSY 15.00 40.00
TT14 Randy Moss JSY 6.00 15.00
TT15 Rich Gannon JSY 5.00 12.00
TT16 Ricky Williams JSY/275* 6.00 15.00
TT17 Steve McNair JSY 6.00 15.00
TT18 Terrell Owens JSY 6.00 15.00
TT19 Ricky Watters JSY 5.00 12.00
TT20 Warren Sapp JSY 5.00 12.00
TT21 Champ Bailey GLV 12.00 30.00
TT22 Courtney Brown GLV 8.00 20.00
TT23 Deion Sanders GLV 12.00 30.00
TT24 Derrick Mason GLV 10.00 25.00
TT25 Eddie George GLV 12.00 30.00
TT26 Jevon Kearse GLV 10.00 25.00
TT27 Keyshawn Johnson GLV 10.00 25.00
TT28 Ron Dayne GLV 10.00 25.00
TT29 Terry Glenn GLV 10.00 25.00
TT30 Wayne Chrebet GLV 10.00 25.00
TT31 Curtis Martin FM 10.00 25.00
TT32 Corey Dillon FM 8.00 20.00
TT33 Cris Carter FM 10.00 25.00
TT34 Junior Seau FM 10.00 25.00
TT35 Jerome Bettis FM 10.00 25.00
TT36 Warrick Dunn FM 10.00 25.00
TT37 Eric Moulds FM 8.00 20.00
TT38 Stephen Davis FM 8.00 20.00
TT39 Steve Young FM 12.00 30.00
TT40 Troy Aikman FM/100* 15.00 40.00
TT41 Dan Marino Pants/75* 20.00 50.00
TT42 Isaac Bruce Pants 8.00 20.00
TT43 Jerry Rice Pants 15.00 40.00
TT44 John Elway Pants/75* 20.00 50.00
TT45 Kurt Warner Pants/75* 12.00 30.00
TT46 Mark Brunell Pants 6.00 15.00
TT47 Marshall Faulk Pants/75* 8.00 20.00
TT48 Terrell Davis Pants 8.00 20.00
TT49 Tim Couch Pants 5.00 12.00
TT50 Torry Holt Pants 6.00 15.00

2001 Absolute Memorabilia Tools of the Trade Autographs

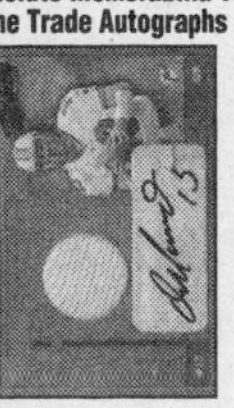

FIRST 25 CARDS OF PRINT RUN SIGNED
TT2 Barry Sanders JSY 100.00 200.00
TT7 Drew Bledsoe JSY 40.00 80.00
TT11 Edgerrin James JSY 40.00 80.00
TT12 Mike Anderson JSY 30.00 60.00
TT16 Ricky Williams JSY 40.00 80.00
TT40 Troy Aikman FM 75.00 150.00
TT41 Dan Marino Pants 125.00 250.00
TT44 John Elway Pants 125.00 250.00
TT45 Kurt Warner Pants 40.00 80.00
TT47 Marshall Faulk Pants 40.00 80.00

2001 Absolute Memorabilia Chicago Collection

NOT PRICED DUE TO SCARCITY

2002 Absolute Memorabilia

Released in October 2002, this 232-card base set includes 150 veterans, 50 rookies, and 32 Rookie Premiere Materials cards that feature one swatch each of event-used footballs and jerseys. The rookie cards are sequentially numbered to 1500 and Rookie Premiere Materials cards are serial #'d 825. Each full box contains two mini-boxes of 9 packs. Each pack contains 6 cards. In addition, each full sealed box contains one Signing Bonus plaque.

COMP.SET w/o SP's (150) 12.50 30.00
151-200 ROOKIE PRINT RUN 1500
201-232 RPM PRINT RUN 825
1 Aaron Brooks .30 .75
2 Ahman Green .30 .75
3 Alge Crumpler .30 .75
4 Amani Toomer .30 .75
5 Andre Carter .25 .60
6 Anthony Thomas .30 .75
7 Antonio Freeman .40 1.00
8 Antowain Smith .30 .75
9 Az-Zahir Hakim .25 .60
10 Bill Schroeder .25 .60
11 Brad Johnson .30 .75
12 Brett Favre 1.00 2.50
13 Brian Griese .30 .75
14 Brian Urlacher .40 1.00
15 Chad Johnson .40 1.00
16 Chad Pennington .40 1.00
17 Champ Bailey .40 1.00
18 Charles Woodson .40 1.00
19 Charlie Batch .25 .60
20 Charlie Garner .30 .75
21 Chris Chambers .30 .75
22 Chris Redman .25 .60
23 Chris Weinke .25 .60
24 Corey Dillon .30 .75
25 Correll Buckhalter .30 .75
26 Cris Carter .40 1.00
27 Curtis Martin .40 1.00
28 Darnay Scott .30 .75
29 Darrell Jackson .30 .75
30 Daunte Culpepper .30 .75
31 David Boston .25 .60
32 David Terrell .25 .60
33 Derrick Alexander .25 .60
34 Derrick Mason .30 .75
35 Deuce McAllister .30 .75
36 Dominic Rhodes .30 .75
37 Donald Hayes .25 .60
38 Donovan McNabb .40 1.00
39 Doug Flutie .40 1.00
40 Drew Bledsoe .40 1.00
41 Drew Brees .60 1.50
42 Duce Staley .30 .75
43 Ed McCaffrey .30 .75
44 Eddie George .30 .75
45 Edgerrin James .30 .75
46 Elvis Joseph .25 .60
47 Emmitt Smith 1.00 2.50
48 Eric Moulds .30 .75
49 Frank Sanders .25 .60
50 Fred Taylor .30 .75
51 Freddie Mitchell .25 .60
52 Garrison Hearst .30 .75
53 Gerard Warren .25 .60
54 Germane Crowell .25 .60
55 Isaac Bruce .40 1.00
56 Jake Plummer .30 .75
57 Jamal Anderson .30 .75
58 Jamal Lewis .30 .75
59 James Allen .25 .60
60 James Jackson .25 .60
61 James Stewart .25 .60
62 Jason Brookins .25 .60
63 Jay Fiedler .30 .75
64 Jeff Garcia .30 .75
65 Jerome Bettis .40 1.00
66 Jerry Rice .75 2.00
67 Jevon Kearse .30 .75
68 Jim Miller .25 .60
69 Jimmy Smith .30 .75
70 Joe Horn .30 .75
71 Joey Galloway .30 .75
72 Jon Kitna .30 .75
73 Junior Seau .40 1.00
74 Keenan McCardell .30 .75
75 Kendrell Bell .25 .60
76 Kerry Collins .30 .75
77 Kevan Barlow .25 .60
78 Kevin Dyson .30 .75
79 Kevin Johnson .25 .60
80 Kevin Kasper .25 .60
81 Keyshawn Johnson .30 .75
82 Kordell Stewart .30 .75
83 Koren Robinson .25 .60
84 Kurt Warner .40 1.00
85 LaDainian Tomlinson .50 1.25
86 Lamar Smith .30 .75
87 Laveranues Coles .30 .75
88 MarTay Jenkins .25 .60
89 Mark Brunell .30 .75
90 Marshall Faulk .40 1.00
91 Marty Booker .30 .75
92 Marvin Harrison .40 1.00
93 Snoop Minnis .25 .60
94 Michael Bennett .30 .75
95 Michael Strahan .40 1.00
96 Michael Vick .60 1.50
97 Mike Alstott .30 .75
98 Mike Anderson .30 .75
99 Mike McMahon .25 .60
100 Muhsin Muhammad .30 .75
101 Nate Clements .25 .60
102 Oronde Gadsden .25 .60
103 Peter Warrick .30 .75
104 Peyton Manning .75 2.00
105 Plaxico Burress .30 .75
106 Priest Holmes .40 1.00
107 Quincy Carter .25 .60
108 Quincy Morgan .25 .60
109 Rocket Ismail .30 .75
110 Randy Moss .40 1.00
111 Ray Lewis .40 1.00
112 Reggie Wayne .40 1.00
113 Rich Gannon .30 .75
114 Rickey Dudley .25 .60
115 Ricky Watters .30 .75
116 Ricky Williams .30 .75
117 Rod Gardner .25 .60
118 Rod Smith .30 .75
119 Robert Ferguson .30 .75
120 Santana Moss .30 .75
121 Shaun Alexander .30 .75
122 Stephen Davis .30 .75
123 Steve McNair .40 1.00
124 Steve Smith .40 1.00
125 Terrell Davis .40 1.00
126 Terrell Owens .40 1.00
127 Terry Glenn .30 .75
128 Thomas Jones .40 1.00
129 Tiki Barber .40 1.00
130 Tim Brown .40 1.00
131 Tim Couch .25 .60
132 Todd Heap .30 .75
133 Todd Pinkston .25 .60
134 Tom Brady 1.00 2.50
135 Tony Boselli .30 .75
136 Tony Gonzalez .40 1.00
137 Torry Holt .40 1.00
138 Travis Henry .25 .60
139 Travis Taylor .25 .60
140 Trent Dilfer .30 .75
141 Trent Green .30 .75
142 Troy Brown .30 .75
143 Troy Hambrick .25 .60
144 Trung Canidate .25 .60
145 Vinny Testaverde .30 .75
146 Warren Sapp .30 .75
147 Warrick Dunn .30 .75
148 Wayne Chrebet .30 .75
149 Wesley Walls .30 .75
150 Zach Thomas .40 1.00
151 Quentin Jammer RC 2.00 5.00
152 Randy Fasani RC 1.50 4.00
153 Kurt Kittner RC 1.25 3.00
154 Chad Hutchinson RC 1.25 3.00
155 Major Applewhite RC 2.00 5.00
156 Wes Pate RC 1.25 3.00
157 J.T. O'Sullivan RC 1.50 4.00
158 Ryan Denney RC 1.25 3.00
159 Ronald Curry RC 1.50 4.00
160 Lamar Gordon RC 1.50 4.00
161 Brian Westbrook RC 3.00 8.00
162 Jonathan Wells RC 2.00 5.00
163 Ricky Williams RC 1.50 4.00
164 Verron Haynes RC 1.25 3.00
165 Josh Scobey RC 1.50 4.00
166 Larry Ned RC 1.25 3.00
167 Adrian Peterson RC 2.00 5.00
168 Chester Taylor RC 2.00 5.00
169 Luke Staley RC 1.25 3.00
170 Damien Anderson RC 1.25 3.00
171 Lee Mays RC 1.25 3.00
172 Deion Branch RC 2.00 5.00
173 Terry Charles RC 1.25 3.00
174 Woody Dantzler RC 1.50 4.00
175 Jason McAddley RC 1.50 4.00
176 Kelly Campbell RC 1.50 4.00
177 Freddie Milons RC 1.25 3.00
178 Kahlil Hill RC 1.25 3.00
179 Brian Poli-Dixon RC 1.25 3.00
180 Mike Echols RC 1.25 3.00
181 Pete Rebstock RC 1.25 3.00
182 Dwight Freeney RC 2.50 6.00
183 Bryan Thomas RC 1.25 3.00
184 Charles Grant RC 2.00 5.00
185 Kalimba Edwards RC 1.50 4.00
186 Ryan Sims RC 2.00 5.00
187 John Henderson RC 1.50 4.00
188 Wendell Bryant RC 1.25 3.00
189 Albert Haynesworth RC 2.00 5.00
190 Larry Tripplett RC 1.25 3.00
191 Phillip Buchanon RC 2.00 5.00
192 Lito Sheppard RC 2.00 5.00
193 Mike Rumph RC 1.25 3.00
194 Levar Fisher RC 1.25 3.00
195 Ed Reed RC 8.00 20.00
196 Rocky Calmus RC 1.50 4.00
197 Michael Lewis RC 2.00 5.00
198 Napoleon Harris RC 1.50 4.00
199 Robert Thomas RC 1.25 3.00
200 Anthony Weaver RC 1.25 3.00
201 Ladell Betts RPM RC 3.00 8.00
202 Antonio Bryant RPM RC 3.00 8.00
203 Reche Caldwell RPM RC 3.00 8.00
204 David Carr RPM RC 3.00 8.00
205 Tim Carter RPM RC 2.50 6.00
206 Eric Crouch RPM RC 3.00 8.00
207 Rohan Davey RPM RC 3.00 8.00
208 Andre Davis RPM RC 2.50 6.00
209 T.J. Duckett RPM RC 3.00 8.00
210 DeShaun Foster RPM RC 3.00 8.00
211 Jabar Gaffney RPM RC 3.00 8.00
212 Daniel Graham RPM RC 2.50 6.00
213 William Green RPM RC 2.50 6.00
214 Joey Harrington RPM RC 3.00 8.00
215 David Garrard RPM RC 4.00 10.00
216 Ron Johnson RPM RC 2.50 6.00
217 Ashley Lelie RPM RC 2.50 6.00
218 Josh McCown RPM RC 3.00 8.00
219 Maurice Morris RPM RC 2.50 6.00
220 Julius Peppers RPM RC 6.00 15.00
221 Clinton Portis RPM RC 8.00 20.00
222 Patrick Ramsey RPM RC 3.00 8.00
223 Antwaan Randle El RPM RC 3.00 8.00
224 Josh Reed RPM RC 2.50 6.00
225 Cliff Russell RPM RC 2.00 5.00
226 Jeremy Shockey RPM RC 5.00 12.00
227 Donte Stallworth RPM RC 3.00 8.00
228 Travis Stephens RPM RC 2.00 5.00
229 Javon Walker RPM RC 3.00 8.00
230 Marquise Walker RPM RC 2.00 5.00
231 Roy Williams RPM RC 3.00 8.00
232 Mike Williams RPM RC 2.00 5.00

2002 Absolute Memorabilia Spectrum

*1-150 VETS/100: 3X TO 8X BASIC CARDS
1-150 VET PRINT RUN 100
*151-200 ROOKIES/50: 1.5X TO 4X
151-200 ROOKIE PRINT RUN 50
*201-232 RPM ROOKIE/25: 1.5X TO 4X
201-232 ROOKIE RPM PRINT RUN 25

2002 Absolute Memorabilia Absolutely Ink

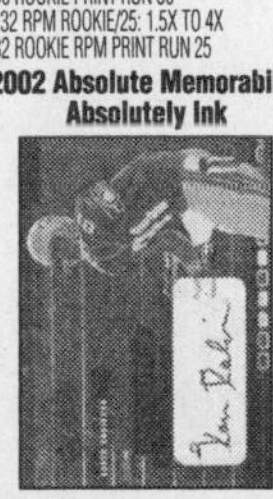

STATED PRINT RUN 30 SER.#'d SETS
AI1 Randy Moss 50.00 120.00
AI2 Brett Favre 125.00 250.00
AI3 Dan Marino 100.00 200.00
AI4 Tim Brown 20.00 50.00
AI5 Todd Heap 15.00 40.00
AI6 Correll Buckhalter 15.00 40.00
AI7 Mike McMahon 12.00 30.00
AI8 John Riggins 25.00 60.00
AI9 Aaron Brooks 15.00 40.00
AI10 David Terrell 12.00 30.00
AI11 Ray Lewis 30.00 60.00
AI12 Torry Holt 20.00 50.00
AI13 Stephen Davis 15.00 40.00
AI14 Mike Anderson 15.00 40.00
AI15 Jimmy Smith 15.00 40.00
AI16 Troy Aikman 50.00 100.00
AI17 Josh Heupel 15.00 40.00
AI18 Marcus Robinson 15.00 40.00
AI19 Kurt Warner 20.00 50.00
AI21 LaMont Jordan 15.00 40.00
AI22 Peter Warrick 15.00 40.00
AI23 Santana Moss 15.00 40.00
AI24 Terrell Owens 20.00 50.00
AI25 Koren Robinson 12.00 30.00
AI26 Quincy Carter 12.00 30.00
AI27 Jamal Lewis 15.00 40.00
AI28 Ronnie Lott 25.00 60.00
AI29 Eric Moulds 15.00 40.00
AI30 Cade McNown 15.00 40.00
AI31 Isaac Bruce 20.00 50.00
AI32 Jesse Palmer 12.00 30.00
AI33 Travis Minor 12.00 30.00
AI36 Damione Lewis 12.00 30.00
AI37 Daunte Culpepper 15.00 40.00
AI39 Phil Simms 20.00 50.00
AI40 Deuce McAllister 15.00 40.00
AI41 Will Allen 12.00 30.00
AI42 Mark Brunell 15.00 40.00
AI43 Edgerrin James 15.00 40.00
AI44 Steve Young 40.00 80.00
AI45 Chris Weinke 12.00 30.00
AI46 Emmitt Smith 125.00 250.00
AI47 Sage Rosenfels 15.00 40.00
AI48 Kevan Barlow 12.00 30.00
AI49 Marshall Faulk 20.00 50.00
AI50 Thurman Thomas 20.00 50.00

2002 Absolute Memorabilia Boss Hoggs Shoe

STATED PRINT RUN 125 SER.#'d SETS
GH1 Edgerrin James 6.00 15.00
GH2 Eddie George 6.00 15.00
GH3 Curtis Martin 8.00 20.00
GH4 Stephen Davis 6.00 15.00
GH5 Lamar Smith 6.00 15.00
GH6 Emmitt Smith 20.00 50.00
GH7 Troy Aikman 12.00 30.00
GH8 Dan Marino 20.00 50.00
GH9 Drew Bledsoe 8.00 20.00
GH10 Zach Thomas 8.00 20.00
GH11 Michael Strahan 8.00 20.00
GH12 Troy Brown 6.00 15.00
GH13 Derrick Mason 6.00 15.00
GH14 Terrell Owens 8.00 20.00
GH15 Isaac Bruce 8.00 20.00

2002 Absolute Memorabilia Ground Hoggs

COMPLETE SET (15) 10.00 25.00
STATED ODDS 1:17
*GOLD: 1X TO 2.5X BASIC INSERTS
GOLD STATED ODDS 1:85
GH1 Edgerrin James 1.00 2.50
GH2 Eddie George 1.00 2.50
GH3 Curtis Martin 1.25 3.00
GH4 Stephen Davis 1.00 2.50
GH5 Lamar Smith 1.00 2.50
GH6 Emmitt Smith 3.00 8.00
GH7 Troy Aikman 2.00 5.00
GH8 Dan Marino 3.00 8.00
GH9 Drew Bledsoe 1.25 3.00
GH10 Zach Thomas 1.25 3.00
GH11 Michael Strahan 1.25 3.00
GH12 Troy Brown 1.00 2.50
GH13 Derrick Mason 1.00 2.50
GH14 Terrell Owens 1.25 3.00
GH15 Isaac Bruce 1.25 3.00

2002 Absolute Memorabilia Leather and Laces

LL1-LL25 PRINT RUN 250
LL26-LL50 PRINT RUN 500
*COMBO/25: 2X TO 5X INSERT/250
*COMBO/50: 1.5X TO 4X INSERT/500
LL1 Kurt Warner 5.00 12.00
LL2 Rod Smith 4.00 10.00
LL3 Curtis Martin 5.00 12.00
LL4 Ahman Green 4.00 10.00
LL5 Daunte Culpepper 4.00 10.00
LL6 David Boston 3.00 8.00
LL7 Brian Urlacher 5.00 12.00
LL8 Dominic Rhodes 4.00 10.00
LL9 Doug Flutie 5.00 12.00
LL10 Kordell Stewart 4.00 10.00
LL11 Antowain Smith 4.00 10.00
LL12 Torry Holt 5.00 12.00
LL13 Eric Moulds 4.00 10.00
LL14 Marvin Harrison 5.00 12.00
LL15 Troy Brown 4.00 10.00
LL16 Garrison Hearst 4.00 10.00
LL17 Mike Anderson 4.00 10.00
LL18 Priest Holmes 5.00 12.00
LL19 David Terrell 3.00 8.00
LL20 Peyton Manning 10.00 25.00
LL21 Isaac Bruce 5.00 12.00
LL22 Randy Moss 5.00 12.00
LL23 Kerry Collins 4.00 10.00
LL24 Shaun Alexander 4.00 10.00
LL25 Terrell Davis 5.00 12.00
LL26 Anthony Thomas 3.00 8.00
LL27 Keyshawn Johnson 3.00 8.00
LL28 Quincy Carter 2.50 6.00
LL29 Rich Gannon 3.00 8.00
LL30 Tom Brady 10.00 25.00
LL31 Aaron Brooks 3.00 8.00
LL32 Tim Brown 4.00 10.00
LL33 Chris Chambers 3.00 8.00
LL34 Stephen Davis 3.00 8.00
LL35 Cris Carter 4.00 10.00
LL36 Brett Favre 10.00 25.00
LL37 Eddie George 3.00 8.00
LL38 Travis Henry 2.50 6.00
LL39 Jerry Rice 8.00 20.00
LL40 Correll Buckhalter 3.00 8.00
LL41 Jeff Garcia 3.00 8.00
LL42 Emmitt Smith 10.00 25.00
LL43 Steve McNair 4.00 10.00
LL44 LaDainian Tomlinson 5.00 12.00
LL45 Ricky Williams 3.00 8.00
LL46 Brian Griese 3.00 8.00
LL47 Terrell Owens 4.00 10.00
LL48 Marshall Faulk 4.00 10.00
LL49 Jake Plummer 3.00 8.00
LL50 Donovan McNabb 4.00 10.00

2002 Absolute Memorabilia Signing Bonus

SER.#'d 5-400; ONE PER BOX
SERIAL #'d UNDER 25 NOT PRICED
4 Jamal Anderson/125 20.00 50.00
5 Mike Anderson/50 25.00 60.00
6 Mike Anderson/150 20.00 50.00
7 Kevan Barlow/100 15.00 40.00
8 Kevan Barlow/300 12.00 30.00
9 Charlie Batch/150 15.00 40.00
10 Charlie Batch/250 12.00 30.00
11 Michael Bennett/50 25.00 60.00
13 Drew Bledsoe/50 50.00 100.00
14 Drew Bledsoe/100 25.00 60.00
15 David Boston/50 20.00 50.00
16 Drew Brees/200 40.00 80.00
17 Drew Brees/400 40.00 80.00
20 Aaron Brooks/100 20.00 50.00
21 Aaron Brooks/200 15.00 40.00
22 Tim Brown/50 50.00 100.00
23 Tim Brown/300 30.00 60.00
25 Isaac Bruce/175 20.00 50.00
26 Isaac Bruce/300 20.00 50.00
28 Mark Brunell/150 20.00 50.00
29 Mark Brunell/350 15.00 40.00
30 Correll Buckhalter/150 20.00 50.00
31 Correll Buckhalter/350 15.00 40.00
32 Cris Carter/50 60.00 120.00
33 Cris Carter/100 25.00 60.00
35 Quincy Carter/250 12.00 30.00
36 Quincy Carter/350 12.00 30.00
38 Chris Chambers/125 20.00 50.00
39 Laveranues Coles/100 20.00 50.00
40 Kerry Collins/200 15.00 40.00
41 Kerry Collins/380 15.00 40.00
43 Daunte Culpepper/100 20.00 50.00
45 Stephen Davis/75 20.00 50.00
46 Stephen Davis/400 15.00 40.00
47 Terrell Davis/50 50.00 120.00
48 Terrell Davis/150 25.00 60.00
50 Corey Dillon/100 20.00 50.00
53 Marshall Faulk/50 30.00 80.00
54 Marshall Faulk/300 20.00 50.00
56 Brett Favre/75 150.00 250.00
57 Robert Ferguson/150 20.00 50.00
58 Robert Ferguson/250 15.00 40.00
60 Jeff Garcia/40 25.00 60.00
61 Rod Gardner/50 20.00 50.00
62 Tony Gonzalez/50 30.00 80.00
63 Tony Gonzalez/150 25.00 60.00
65 Ahman Green/100 20.00 50.00
67 Brian Griese/25 30.00 80.00
68 Brian Griese/175 15.00 40.00
69 Marvin Harrison/50 60.00 100.00
70 Marvin Harrison/150 25.00 60.00
71 Todd Heap/150 20.00 50.00
72 Todd Heap/400 15.00 40.00
73 Torry Holt/100 25.00 60.00
74 Torry Holt/300 20.00 50.00
75 James Jackson/150 15.00 40.00
76 James Jackson/300 12.00 30.00
79 Edgerrin James/150 20.00 50.00
80 Edgerrin James/250 15.00 40.00
81 Chad Johnson/100 25.00 60.00
82 Chad Johnson/250 20.00 50.00
83 Jamal Lewis/100 20.00 50.00
84 Ray Lewis/150 60.00 120.00
85 Ray Lewis/350 50.00 100.00
86 Jamal Lewis/400 15.00 40.00
89 Deuce McAllister/200 15.00 40.00
90 Deuce McAllister/400 15.00 40.00
91 Mike McMahon/150 15.00 40.00
92 Mike McMahon/300 12.00 30.00
93 Quincy Morgan/200 12.00 30.00
94 Quincy Morgan/400 12.00 30.00
95 Santana Moss/200 15.00 40.00
96 Santana Moss/400 15.00 40.00
97 Eric Moulds/125 20.00 50.00
98 Eric Moulds/300 15.00 40.00
100 Terrell Owens/25 50.00 100.00
101 Terrell Owens/75 40.00 80.00
102 Chad Pennington/100 25.00 60.00
103 Chad Pennington/200 20.00 50.00
104 Jake Plummer/100 20.00 50.00
105 Jerry Rice/125 90.00 150.00
107 Junior Seau/25 60.00 120.00
108 Junior Seau/100 30.00 60.00
111 Emmitt Smith/75 150.00 300.00
112 Emmitt Smith/150 125.00 250.00
113 Jimmy Smith/300 15.00 40.00
114 Jimmy Smith/400 15.00 40.00
116 Michael Strahan/90 50.00 80.00
117 David Terrell/200 12.00 30.00
118 David Terrell/400 12.00 30.00
119 Vinny Testaverde/25 30.00 80.00
120 Vinny Testaverde/75 20.00 50.00
122 Anthony Thomas/50 25.00 60.00
123 Anthony Thomas/150 20.00 50.00
124 Brian Urlacher/50 60.00 120.00
125 Brian Urlacher/200 75.00 150.00
126 Michael Vick/75 60.00 100.00
128 Kurt Warner/100 40.00 100.00
129 Kurt Warner/250 30.00 60.00
130 Peter Warrick/150 20.00 50.00
131 Peter Warrick/350 15.00 40.00
132 Ricky Watters/50 25.00 60.00
133 Ricky Watters/200 15.00 40.00
134 Reggie Wayne/75 25.00 60.00
135 Reggie Wayne/200 20.00 50.00
137 Chris Weinke/200 12.00 30.00
138 Chris Weinke/300 12.00 30.00
140 Ricky Williams/75 20.00 50.00

2002 Absolute Memorabilia Tools of the Trade

STATED ODDS 1:17
*GOLD: .8X TO 2X BASIC INSERTS
GOLD STATED ODDS 1:85
TT1 Emmitt Smith 4.00 10.00
TT2 Brett Favre 4.00 10.00
TT3 Donovan McNabb 1.50 4.00
TT4 Brian Griese 1.25 3.00
TT5 Peyton Manning 3.00 8.00
TT6 Kurt Warner 1.50 4.00
TT7 Dan Marino 4.00 10.00
TT8 Shaun Alexander 1.25 3.00
TT9 Anthony Thomas 1.25 3.00
TT10 Troy Aikman 2.50 6.00
TT11 Barry Sanders 2.50 6.00
TT12 Mike Anderson 1.25 3.00
TT13 Jerry Rice 3.00 8.00
TT14 Daunte Culpepper 1.25 3.00
TT15 Chris Chambers 1.25 3.00
TT16 Marshall Faulk 1.50 4.00
TT17 Doug Flutie 1.50 4.00
TT18 Travis Henry 1.00 2.50
TT19 LaDainian Tomlinson 2.00 5.00
TT20 Eddie George 1.25 3.00
TT21 Aaron Brooks 1.25 3.00
TT22 Chris Weinke 1.00 2.50
TT23 Ricky Williams 1.25 3.00
TT24 Jerome Bettis 1.50 4.00
TT25 Ahman Green 1.25 3.00
TT26 Steve Young 2.00 5.00
TT27 Zach Thomas 1.50 4.00
TT28 Randy Moss 1.50 4.00
TT29 Quincy Carter 1.00 2.50
TT30 Jeff Garcia 1.25 3.00
TT31 Tim Brown 1.50 4.00
TT32 Jimmy Smith 1.25 3.00
TT33 Torry Holt 1.50 4.00
TT34 Todd Pinkston 1.00 2.50
TT35 Eric Moulds 1.25 3.00
TT36 Marvin Harrison 1.50 4.00
TT37 Derrick Mason 1.25 3.00
TT38 Troy Brown 1.25 3.00
TT39 Marty Booker 1.25 3.00
TT40 Wayne Chrebet 1.25 3.00
TT41 Darrell Green 1.50 4.00
TT42 Charles Woodson 1.50 4.00
TT43 Bruce Matthews 1.25 3.00
TT44 Tim Couch 1.00 2.50
TT45 Mark Brunell 1.25 3.00
TT46 Hines Ward 1.50 4.00
TT47 Corey Dillon 1.25 3.00
TT48 Edgerrin James 1.25 3.00
TT49 John Elway 3.00 8.00
TT50 Frank Wycheck 1.00 2.50

2002 Absolute Memorabilia Tools of the Trade Materials

TT1-TT30 JSY PRINT RUN 150
TT31-TT42 PRINT RUN 50 SER.#'d SETS
TT43-TT50 FACE MASK PRINT RUN 300
TT1 Emmitt Smith JSY 20.00 50.00
TT2 Brett Favre JSY 20.00 50.00
TT3 Donovan McNabb JSY 8.00 20.00
TT4 Brian Griese JSY 6.00 15.00
TT5 Peyton Manning JSY 15.00 40.00
TT6 Kurt Warner JSY 8.00 20.00
TT7 Dan Marino JSY 20.00 50.00
TT8 Shaun Alexander JSY 6.00 15.00
TT9 Anthony Thomas JSY 6.00 15.00
TT10 Troy Aikman JSY 12.00 30.00
TT11 Barry Sanders JSY 12.00 30.00
TT12 Mike Anderson JSY 6.00 15.00
TT13 Jerry Rice JSY 15.00 40.00
TT14 Daunte Culpepper JSY 6.00 15.00
TT15 Chris Chambers JSY 6.00 15.00
TT16 Marshall Faulk JSY 8.00 20.00
TT17 Doug Flutie JSY 8.00 20.00
TT18 Travis Henry JSY 5.00 12.00
TT19 LaDainian Tomlinson JSY 10.00 25.00
TT20 Eddie George JSY 6.00 15.00
TT21 Aaron Brooks JSY 6.00 15.00
TT22 Chris Weinke JSY 5.00 12.00
TT23 Ricky Williams JSY 6.00 15.00
TT24 Jerome Bettis JSY 8.00 20.00
TT25 Ahman Green JSY 6.00 15.00
TT26 Steve Young JSY 10.00 25.00
TT27 Zach Thomas JSY 8.00 20.00
TT28 Randy Moss JSY 8.00 20.00
TT29 Quincy Carter JSY 5.00 12.00
TT30 Jeff Garcia JSY 6.00 15.00
TT31 Tim Brown GLV 10.00 25.00
TT32 Jimmy Smith GLV 8.00 20.00
TT33 Torry Holt GLV 10.00 25.00
TT34 Todd Pinkston GLV 6.00 15.00
TT35 Eric Moulds GLV 8.00 20.00
TT36 Marvin Harrison GLV 10.00 25.00
TT37 Derrick Mason GLV 8.00 20.00
TT38 Troy Brown GLV 8.00 20.00
TT39 Marty Booker GLV 8.00 20.00
TT40 Wayne Chrebet GLV 8.00 20.00
TT41 Darrell Green GLV 10.00 25.00
TT42 Charles Woodson GLV 10.00 25.00
TT43 Bruce Matthews FM 5.00 12.00
TT44 Tim Couch FM 4.00 10.00
TT45 Mark Brunell FM 5.00 12.00
TT46 Hines Ward FM 6.00 15.00
TT47 Corey Dillon FM 5.00 12.00
TT48 Edgerrin James FM 5.00 12.00
TT49 John Elway FM 12.00 30.00
TT50 Frank Wycheck FM 4.00 10.00

2003 Absolute Memorabilia Samples

*VETS 1-100: .8X TO 2X BASIC CARDS
*ROOKIE 101-150: .2X TO .5X BASIC CARD

2003 Absolute Memorabilia

Released in August of 2003, this set consists of 180 cards, including 100 veterans, 50 rookies serial numbered to 1100, and 30 rookies serial numbered to 750 that contain an event used jersey and football swatch. Each full box contained two min-boxes of nine packs, each with six cards.

COMP.SET w/o SP's (100) 10.00 25.00
1 Jamal Lewis .40 1.00
2 Ray Lewis .50 1.25
3 Todd Heap .40 1.00
4 Drew Bledsoe .50 1.25
5 Travis Henry .30 .75
6 Peerless Price .30 .75
7 Corey Dillon .40 1.00
8 Chad Johnson .50 1.25
9 Tim Couch .30 .75
10 William Green .30 .75
11 Andre Davis .30 .75
12 Brian Griese .40 1.00
13 Ashley Lelie .30 .75
14 Clinton Portis .40 1.00
15 Rod Smith .40 1.00
16 David Carr .40 1.00
17 Corey Bradford .30 .75
18 Jonathan Wells .30 .75
19 Peyton Manning 1.00 2.50
20 Edgerrin James .50 1.25
21 Marvin Harrison .50 1.25
22 Mark Brunell .40 1.00
23 Fred Taylor .40 1.00
24 Jimmy Smith .40 1.00
25 Trent Green .40 1.00
26 Priest Holmes .50 1.25
27 Tony Gonzalez .50 1.25
28 Jay Fiedler .30 .75
29 Ricky Williams .40 1.00
30 Chris Chambers .40 1.00
31 Zach Thomas .50 1.25
32 Tom Brady 1.25 3.00
33 Troy Brown .40 1.00
34 Antowain Smith .40 1.00
35 Chad Pennington .50 1.25
36 Curtis Martin .50 1.25
37 Laveranues Coles .30 .75
38 Rich Gannon .40 1.00
39 Charlie Garner .40 1.00
40 Jerry Rice 1.00 2.50
41 Tim Brown .50 1.25
42 Tommy Maddox .40 1.00
43 Jerome Bettis .50 1.25
44 Plaxico Burress .40 1.00
45 Hines Ward .50 1.25
46 Drew Brees .50 1.25
47 LaDainian Tomlinson .50 1.25
48 Junior Seau .50 1.25
49 Steve McNair .50 1.25
50 Eddie George .40 1.00
51 Jevon Kearse .40 1.00
52 Jake Plummer .40 1.00
53 David Boston .30 .75
54 Marcel Shipp .30 .75
55 Michael Vick .60 1.50
56 T.J. Duckett .40 1.00
57 Warrick Dunn .40 1.00
58 Muhsin Muhammad .40 1.00
59 Julius Peppers .50 1.25
60 Steve Smith .50 1.25
61 Anthony Thomas .40 1.00
62 Brian Urlacher .50 1.25
63 Marty Booker .40 1.00
64 Antonio Bryant .30 .75
65 Chad Hutchinson .30 .75
66 Roy Williams .40 1.00
67 Emmitt Smith 1.25 3.00
68 Joey Harrington .30 .75
69 James Stewart .30 .75
70 Az-Zahir Hakim .30 .75
71 Brett Favre 1.25 3.00
72 Ahman Green .40 1.00
73 Donald Driver .50 1.25
74 Daunte Culpepper .40 1.00
75 Randy Moss .50 1.25
76 Michael Bennett .40 1.00
77 Aaron Brooks .40 1.00
78 Deuce McAllister .40 1.00
79 Donte Stallworth .30 .75
80 Tiki Barber .50 1.25
81 Kerry Collins .40 1.00
82 Jeremy Shockey .50 1.25
83 Donovan McNabb .50 1.25
84 Duce Staley .40 1.00
85 Antonio Freeman .40 1.00
86 Jeff Garcia .40 1.00
87 Terrell Owens .50 1.25
88 Garrison Hearst .40 1.00
89 Matt Hasselbeck .40 1.00
90 Koren Robinson .40 1.00
91 Shaun Alexander .40 1.00
92 Kurt Warner .50 1.25
93 Marshall Faulk .50 1.25
94 Isaac Bruce .50 1.25
95 Brad Johnson .40 1.00
96 Keyshawn Johnson .50 1.25
97 Warren Sapp .40 1.00
98 Patrick Ramsey .40 1.00
99 Rod Gardner .30 .75
100 Stephen Davis .40 1.00
101 Jason Gesser RC 2.00 5.00
102 Brandon Lloyd RC 4.00 10.00
103 Ken Dorsey RC 2.00 5.00
104 Avon Cobourne RC 1.50 4.00
105 Cecil Sapp RC 1.50 4.00
106 Derek Watson RC 1.50 4.00
107 Dwone Hicks RC 1.50 4.00
108 Earnest Graham RC 2.50 6.00
109 LaBrandon Toefield RC 2.00 5.00
110 Quentin Griffin RC 2.00 5.00
111 Sultan McCullough RC 1.50 4.00
112 Lee Suggs RC 2.00 5.00
113 Talman Gardner RC 1.50 4.00
114 Arnaz Battle RC 2.50 6.00
115 Billy McMullen RC 1.50 4.00
116 Doug Gabriel RC 2.00 5.00
117 Justin Gage RC 2.00 5.00
118 Kareem Kelly RC 1.50 4.00
119 Paul Arnold RC 1.50 4.00
120 Sam Aiken RC 2.00 5.00

121 Shaun McDonald RC 2.00 5.00
122 Terrence Edwards 1.50 4.00
123 Walter Young RC 1.50 4.00
124 Ryan Hoag RC 1.50 4.00
125 Jason Witten RC 6.00 15.00
126 Bennie Joppru RC 1.50 4.00
127 George Wrighster RC 1.50 4.00
128 L.J. Smith RC 2.50 6.00
129 Robert Johnson RC 1.50 4.00
130 Chris Kelsay RC 2.00 5.00
131 Cory Redding RC 2.00 5.00
132 DeWayne White RC 1.50 4.00
133 Kenny Peterson RC 2.00 5.00
134 Jerome McDougle RC 1.50 4.00
135 Michael Haynes RC 1.50 4.00
136 Jimmy Kennedy RC 2.00 5.00
137 Kevin Williams RC 2.50 6.00
138 Johnathan Sullivan RC 1.50 4.00
139 Rien Long RC 1.50 4.00
140 Ty Warren RC 2.00 5.00
141 William Joseph RC 1.50 4.00
142 E.J. Henderson RC 2.00 5.00
143 Boss Bailey RC 2.00 5.00
144 Dennis Weathersby RC 1.50 4.00
145 Chris Simms RC 2.50 6.00
146 Rashean Mathis RC 2.00 5.00
147 Charles Rogers RC 2.00 5.00
148 Andre Woolfolk RC 2.00 5.00
149 Troy Polamalu RC 12.50 25.00
150 Mike Doss RC 2.50 6.00
151 Carson Palmer RPM RC 8.00 20.00
152 Byron Leftwich RPM RC 4.00 10.00
153 Kyle Boller RPM RC 4.00 10.00
154 Rex Grossman RPM RC 4.00 10.00
155 Dave Ragone RPM RC 2.50 6.00
156 Kliff Kingsbury RPM RC 3.00 8.00
157 Seneca Wallace RPM RC 4.00 10.00
158 Larry Johnson RPM RC 4.00 10.00
159 Willis McGahee RPM RC 5.00 12.00
160 Justin Fargas RPM RC 4.00 10.00
161 Onterrio Smith RPM RC 2.50 6.00
162 Chris Brown RPM RC 2.50 6.00
163 Musa Smith RPM RC 2.50 6.00
164 Artose Pinner RPM RC 2.50 6.00
165 Andre Johnson RPM RC 10.00 25.00
166 Kelley Washington RPM RC 2.50 6.00
167 Taylor Jacobs RPM RC 2.50 6.00
168 Bryant Johnson RPM RC 4.00 10.00
169 Tyrone Calico RPM RC 3.00 8.00
170 Anquan Boldin RPM RC 6.00 15.00
171 Bethel Johnson RPM RC 2.50 6.00
172 Nate Burleson RPM RC 3.00 8.00
173 Kevin Curtis RPM RC 4.00 10.00
174 Dallas Clark RPM RC 6.00 15.00
175 Teyo Johnson RPM RC 3.00 8.00
176 Terrell Suggs RPM RC 4.00 10.00
177 DeWayne Robertson RPM RC 3.00 8.00
178 Brian St.Pierre RPM RC 3.00 8.00
179 Terence Newman RPM RC 3.00 8.00
180 Marcus Trufant RPM RC 3.00 8.00

2003 Absolute Memorabilia Spectrum

*VETS 1-100: 2.5X TO 6X BASIC CARDS
1-100 PRINT RUN 150 SER.#'d SETS
*ROOKIES 101-150: 1X TO 2.5X
101-150 PRINT RUN 100 SER.#'d SETS
*RPM 151-180: 1X TO 2.5X
151-180 RPM PRINT RUN 25 SER.#'d SETS
149 Troy Polamalu 50.00 100.00

2003 Absolute Memorabilia Absolute Patches

STATED PRINT RUN 25 SER. #'d SETS
AP1 Brett Favre 60.00 150.00
AP2 Brian Urlacher 25.00 60.00
AP3 Clinton Portis 20.00 50.00
AP4 David Carr 20.00 50.00
AP5 Deuce McAllister 20.00 50.00
AP6 Donovan McNabb 25.00 60.00
AP7 Drew Bledsoe 25.00 60.00
AP8 Edgerrin James 25.00 60.00
AP9 Emmitt Smith 60.00 150.00
AP10 Priest Holmes 25.00 60.00
AP11 Jeremy Shockey 25.00 60.00
AP12 Jerry Rice 50.00 125.00
AP13 Joey Harrington 15.00 40.00
AP14 Kurt Warner 25.00 60.00
AP15 LaDainian Tomlinson 25.00 60.00
AP16 Marshall Faulk 25.00 60.00
AP17 Michael Vick 40.00 100.00
AP18 Peyton Manning 50.00 125.00
AP19 Randy Moss 25.00 60.00
AP20 Steve McNair 25.00 60.00

2003 Absolute Memorabilia Absolutely Ink

STATED PRINT RUN 25 SERIAL #'d SETS
AI1 Marty Booker 20.00 50.00
AI2 Ahman Green 20.00 50.00
AI4 Deion Branch 20.00 50.00
AI6 Ed McCaffrey 20.00 50.00
AI7 Eric Moulds 20.00 50.00
AI8 Garrison Hearst 20.00 50.00
AI9 Jeff Garcia 20.00 50.00
AI10 Joe Horn 20.00 50.00
AI11 Jimmy Smith 20.00 50.00
AI12 Kurt Warner 25.00 60.00
AI13 Michael Vick 50.00 100.00
AI14 Patrick Ramsey 20.00 50.00
AI15 Randy Moss 60.00 120.00
AI16 Ricky Williams 20.00 50.00
AI17 Rod Smith 20.00 50.00
AI18 Tim Brown 25.00 60.00
AI19 Tom Brady 175.00 300.00
AI20 Zach Thomas 25.00 60.00

2003 Absolute Memorabilia Boss Hoggs Shoe

STATED PRINT RUN 125 SERIAL #'d SETS
BH1 Amani Toomer 5.00 12.00
BH2 Chad Pennington 6.00 15.00
BH3 Curtis Martin 6.00 15.00
BH4 Daunte Culpepper 5.00 12.00
BH5 Eddie George 5.00 12.00
BH6 Edgerrin James 6.00 15.00
BH7 Emmitt Smith 15.00 40.00
BH8 Fred Taylor 5.00 12.00
BH9 Jerry Rice 12.00 30.00
BH10 Keyshawn Johnson 6.00 15.00
BH11 Marvin Harrison 6.00 15.00
BH12 Peyton Manning 12.00 30.00
BH13 Rich Gannon 5.00 12.00
BH14 Steve McNair 6.00 15.00
BH15 Terrell Owens 6.00 15.00

2003 Absolute Memorabilia Boss Hoggs Shoe Autographs

BH2 Chad Pennington 30.00 80.00
BH5 Eddie George 25.00 60.00
BH9 Jerry Rice
BH11 Marvin Harrison 30.00 80.00
BH13 Rich Gannon 25.00 60.00
BH14 Steve McNair 30.00 80.00
BH15 Terrell Owens 30.00 80.00

2003 Absolute Memorabilia Canton Absolutes Jersey

STATED PRINT RUN 150 SER. #'d SETS
1 Ahman Green 4.00 10.00
2 Anthony Thomas 4.00 10.00
3 Brett Favre 12.00 30.00
4 Chris Chambers 4.00 10.00
5 Clinton Portis 4.00 10.00
6 Curtis Martin 5.00 12.00
7 Daunte Culpepper 4.00 10.00
8 David Carr 4.00 10.00
9 Donovan McNabb 5.00 12.00
10 Donte Stallworth 3.00 8.00
11 Drew Brees 5.00 12.00
12 Eddie George 4.00 10.00
13 Edgerrin James 5.00 12.00
14 Emmitt Smith 12.00 30.00
15 Garrison Hearst 4.00 10.00
16 Isaac Bruce 5.00 12.00
17 Jamal Lewis 4.00 10.00
18 Jeff Garcia 4.00 10.00
19 Jeremy Shockey 5.00 12.00
20 Jerry Rice 10.00 25.00
21 Jevon Kearse 4.00 10.00
22 Jimmy Smith 4.00 10.00
23 Joey Harrington 3.00 8.00
24 Julius Peppers 5.00 12.00
25 Junior Seau 5.00 12.00
26 Keyshawn Johnson 5.00 12.00
27 Kurt Warner 8.00 20.00
28 LaDainian Tomlinson 5.00 12.00
29 Marshall Faulk 5.00 12.00
30 Marvin Harrison 5.00 12.00
31 Michael Bennett 4.00 10.00
32 Michael Vick 6.00 15.00
33 Mike Alstott 5.00 12.00
34 Peyton Manning 10.00 25.00
35 Priest Holmes 5.00 12.00
36 Randy Moss 5.00 12.00
37 Ray Lewis 5.00 12.00
38 Rich Gannon 4.00 10.00
39 Ricky Williams 4.00 10.00
40 Rod Smith 4.00 10.00
41 Roy Williams 4.00 10.00
42 Shaun Alexander 4.00 10.00
43 Stephen Davis 4.00 10.00
44 Steve McNair 5.00 12.00
45 Terrell Owens 5.00 12.00
46 Tim Brown 5.00 12.00
47 T.J. Duckett 4.00 10.00
48 Tom Brady 12.00 30.00
49 Travis Henry 3.00 8.00
50 Zach Thomas 5.00 12.00

2003 Absolute Memorabilia Canton Absolutes Jersey Autographs

16 Isaac Bruce/25* 25.00 60.00
17 Jamal Lewis/25* 20.00 50.00
18 Jeff Garcia/25*
27 Kurt Warner/50* 40.00 80.00
32 Michael Vick/25* 30.00 80.00

2003 Absolute Memorabilia Glass Plaques

ONE PER SEALED BOX
SERIAL #'d UNDER 25 NOT PRICED
1 Shaun Alexander AU/50 25.00 60.00
2 Shaun Alexander JSY/250 12.00 30.00
3 Shaun Alexander JSY-JSY/100 15.00 40.00
4 Mike Alstott AU/25 40.00 100.00
6 Mike Alstott JSY/200 15.00 40.00
7 Michael Bennett AU/50 25.00 60.00
8 Michael Bennett JSY/250 12.00 30.00
10 Jerome Bettis JSY/150 15.00 40.00
11 Jerome Bettis JSY-JSY/50 20.00 50.00
13 Drew Bledsoe JSY/50 20.00 50.00
14 Drew Bledsoe JSY-JSY/25 25.00 60.00
15 David Boston JSY/150 10.00 25.00
16 David Boston JSY-Pants/50 12.00 30.00
18 Terry Bradshaw JSY/250 25.00 60.00
19 Terry Bradshaw JSY-JSY/75 30.00 80.00
21 Tom Brady JSY/150 40.00 100.00
22 Tom Brady JSY-JSY/75 50.00 120.00
23 Drew Brees JSY/150 15.00 40.00
24 Aaron Brooks JSY/150 12.00 30.00
25 Tim Brown AU/25 40.00 100.00
27 Tim Brown JSY/150 15.00 40.00
28 Tim Brown JSY-JSY/75 20.00 50.00
29 Tim Brown Shoes/125 15.00 40.00
30 Isaac Bruce AU/50 30.00 80.00
31 Isaac Bruce JSY/150 15.00 40.00
32 Isaac Bruce JSY-Pants/75 20.00 50.00
33 Mark Brunell JSY/150 12.00 30.00
34 Mark Brunell JSY-Pants/100 15.00 40.00
35 Mark Brunell Shoes/150 12.00 30.00
36 Plaxico Burress JSY/150 12.00 30.00
38 David Carr JSY/150 12.00 30.00
39 Chris Chambers AU/50 25.00 60.00
41 Chris Chambers JSY/200 12.00 30.00
42 Chris Chambers JSY-JSY/50 15.00 40.00
43 Laveranues Coles AU/50 20.00 50.00
44 Laveranues Coles JSY/150 10.00 25.00
45 Laveranues Coles JSY-JSY/50 12.00 30.00
46 Tim Couch JSY/200 10.00 25.00
47 Tim Couch JSY-Pants/75 12.00 30.00
48 Daunte Culpepper JSY/200 12.00 30.00
49 Daunte Culpepper JSY-Shoes/50 15.00 40.00
51 Eric Dickerson JSY/250 12.00 30.00
52 Eric Dickerson JSY-JSY/100 15.00 40.00
53 Corey Dillon JSY/150 12.00 30.00
54 Corey Dillon JSY-GLV/100 15.00 40.00
56 John Elway JSY/250 40.00 100.00
57 John Elway JSY-JSY/75 50.00 125.00
58 John Elway Pants/200 40.00 100.00
59 Marshall Faulk JSY/250 15.00 40.00
60 Marshall Faulk JSY-Pants/150 15.00 40.00
63 Brett Favre JSY/200 40.00 100.00
64 Brett Favre JSY-Shoes/75 50.00 120.00
65 Rich Gannon AU/50 25.00 60.00
66 Rich Gannon JSY/150 12.00 30.00
67 Rich Gannon JSY-Shoes/125 12.00 30.00
68 Jeff Garcia AU/50 25.00 60.00
70 Jeff Garcia JSY/200 12.00 30.00
71 Jeff Garcia JSY-JSY/50 15.00 40.00
72 Jeff Garcia Shoes/125 12.00 30.00
73 Rod Gardner AU/25 25.00 60.00
74 Rod Gardner JSY/200 10.00 25.00
76 Eddie George JSY/150 12.00 30.00
77 Eddie George JSY-GLV/75 15.00 40.00
78 Eddie George Shoes/25 20.00 50.00
79 Ahman Green AU/25 30.00 80.00
81 Ahman Green JSY/150 12.00 30.00
82 Ahman Green JSY-JSY/50 15.00 40.00
83 Brian Griese JSY/150 12.00 30.00
84 Brian Griese JSY-JSY/75 15.00 40.00
85 Joey Harrington AU/25 25.00 60.00
86 Joey Harrington JSY/250 10.00 25.00
87 Marvin Harrison AU/25 40.00 100.00
88 Marvin Harrison JSY/150 15.00 40.00
89 Marvin Harrison JSY-Shoes/50 20.00 50.00
90 Garrison Hearst AU/50 25.00 60.00
91 Garrison Hearst JSY/150 12.00 30.00
92 Travis Henry JSY/200 10.00 25.00
94 Priest Holmes JSY/250 15.00 40.00
95 Priest Holmes JSY-JSY/50 20.00 50.00
96 Torry Holt AU/50 30.00 80.00
97 Torry Holt JSY/150 15.00 40.00
98 Torry Holt JSY-Pants/50 20.00 50.00
99 Edgerrin James JSY/200 15.00 40.00
100 Edgerrin James JSY-JSY/50 20.00 50.00
101 Edgerrin James Shoes/25 25.00 60.00
102 Andre Johnson AU/200 40.00 100.00
103 Keyshawn Johnson GLV/75 20.00 50.00
104 Keyshawn Johnson JSY/150 15.00 40.00
105 Key.Johnson JSY-JSY/100 20.00 50.00
106 Larry Johnson AU/200 15.00 40.00
107 Jevon Kearse JSY/200 12.00 30.00
108 Jevon Kearse JSY-JSY/100 15.00 40.00
109 Jevon Kearse Shoes/100 15.00 40.00
110 Byron Leftwich AU/200 15.00 40.00
111 Jamal Lewis AU/25 30.00 80.00
113 Jamal Lewis JSY/250 12.00 30.00
114 Peyton Manning JSY/250 30.00 80.00
115 Peyton Manning JSY-Shoes/50 40.00 100.00
116 Curtis Martin JSY/150 15.00 40.00
117 Curtis Martin JSY-Pants/100 20.00 50.00
118 Derrick Mason AU/25 30.00 80.00
120 Derrick Mason JSY/100 15.00 40.00
121 Derrick Mason JSY-Shoes/75 15.00 40.00
123 Deuce McAllister JSY/50 15.00 40.00
124 Ed McCaffrey AU/25 30.00 80.00
126 Ed McCaffrey JSY/150 12.00 30.00
127 Donovan McNabb JSY/250 15.00 40.00
128 Donovan McNabb JSY-JSY/100 20.00 50.00
130 Steve McNair JSY/200 15.00 40.00
131 Steve McNair JSY-Shoes/125 15.00 40.00
132 Randy Moss AU/50 30.00 80.00
134 Randy Moss JSY/250 15.00 40.00
135 Randy Moss JSY-JSY/75 20.00 50.00
136 Eric Moulds AU/25 30.00 80.00
138 Eric Moulds JSY/150 12.00 30.00
139 Terrell Owens AU/50 30.00 80.00
140 Terrell Owens JSY/250 15.00 40.00
141 Terrell Owens JSY-JSY/50 20.00 50.00
143 Carson Palmer AU/150 30.00 80.00
144 Chad Pennington AU/25 40.00 100.00
145 Chad Pennington Shoes/50 20.00 50.00
147 Clinton Portis JSY/250 12.00 30.00
148 Clinton Portis JSY-JSY/75 15.00 40.00
150 Jerry Rice JSY/150 30.00 80.00
151 Jerry Rice JSY-JSY/50 40.00 100.00
152 Warren Sapp JSY/150 12.00 30.00
153 Warren Sapp JSY-Shoes/150 12.00 30.00
154 Junior Seau JSY/150 15.00 40.00
155 Junior Seau JSY-JSY/50 20.00 50.00
156 Jeremy Shockey JSY/100 20.00 50.00
157 Jeremy Shockey JSY-JSY/50 20.00 50.00
158 Emmitt Smith JSY/250 40.00 100.00
159 Emmitt Smith JSY-Shoe/50 50.00 125.00
160 Emmitt Smith Shoes/125 40.00 100.00
161 Jimmy Smith AU/50 25.00 60.00
163 Jimmy Smith JSY/150 12.00 30.00
164 Jimmy Smith JSY-Shoes/75 15.00 40.00
165 Rod Smith AU/50 25.00 60.00
166 Rod Smith JSY/200 12.00 30.00
167 Rod Smith JSY-Pants/75 15.00 40.00
168 Fred Taylor JSY/200 12.00 30.00
169 Fred Taylor JSY-Shoes/50 15.00 40.00
170 Anthony Thomas AU/25 30.00 80.00
171 Anthony Thomas JSY/200 12.00 30.00
172 Zach Thomas JSY/100 20.00 50.00
173 Zach Thomas Shoes/200 15.00 40.00
174 LaDainian Tomlinson AU/25 75.00 150.00
176 LaDainian Tomlinson JSY/250 15.00 40.00
177 LaDainian Tomlinson JSY-JSY/50 20.00 50.00
178 Brian Urlacher AU/25 75.00 150.00
180 Brian Urlacher JSY/200 15.00 40.00
181 Brian Urlacher JSY-GLV/100 20.00 50.00
184 Michael Vick JSY/200 20.00 50.00
185 Hines Ward AU/50 30.00 80.00
186 Hines Ward JSY/150 15.00 40.00
187 Kurt Warner AU/200 50.00 100.00
188 Kurt Warner JSY AU/200 50.00 100.00
189 Kurt Warner JSY/250 15.00 40.00
190 Kurt Warner JSY-Shoe/125 15.00 40.00
191 Kurt Warner Pants/150 15.00 40.00
192 Ricky Williams JSY/150 12.00 30.00
193 Roy Williams JSY/250 12.00 30.00
194 Charles Woodson JSY/200 25.00 50.00
195 Charles Woodson JSY-GLV/100 30.00 60.00

2003 Absolute Memorabilia Gridiron Force

RANDOM INSERTS IN RETAIL PACKS
GF1 A.J. Feeley 3.00 8.00
GF2 Amani Toomer 4.00 10.00
GF3 Brian Griese 4.00 10.00
GF4 Charles Woodson 5.00 12.00
GF5 Corey Dillon 4.00 10.00
GF6 Cory Schlesinger 3.00 8.00
GF7 Darren Woodson 4.00 10.00
GF8 David Boston 3.00 8.00
GF9 Derrick Mason 4.00 10.00
GF10 Duce Staley 4.00 10.00
GF11 Eric Moulds 4.00 10.00
GF12 Fred Taylor 4.00 10.00
GF13 Jake Plummer 4.00 10.00
GF14 Jerome Bettis 5.00 12.00
GF15 Donald Driver 5.00 12.00
GF16 Josh Reed 3.00 8.00
GF17 Kerry Collins 4.00 10.00
GF18 Kevin Johnson 3.00 8.00
GF19 Kordell Stewart 4.00 10.00
GF20 Koren Robinson 4.00 10.00
GF21 Muhsin Muhammed 4.00 10.00
GF22 Peerless Price 3.00 8.00
GF23 Peter Warrick 4.00 10.00
GF24 Randy McMichael 3.00 8.00
GF25 Rod Gardner 3.00 8.00
GF26 Ron Dayne 4.00 10.00
GF27 Santana Moss 4.00 10.00
GF28 Terry Glenn 4.00 10.00

2003 Absolute Memorabilia Leather and Laces

LL1-LL20 PRINT RUN 500 SER.#'d SETS
LL21-LL40 PRINT RUN 250 SER.#'d SETS
LL1-LL20 COMBOS PRINT RUN 50 SETS
LL21-LL40 COMBOS PRINT RUN 25 SETS
LL1 Drew Brees 5.00 12.00
LL2 Jeremy Shockey 5.00 12.00
LL3 Antonio Bryant 3.00 8.00
LL4 Marc Bulger 5.00 12.00
LL5 Shaun Alexander 4.00 10.00
LL6 Koren Robinson 4.00 10.00
LL7 Jerry Porter 3.00 8.00
LL8 Joey Harrington 3.00 8.00
LL9 Kevan Barlow 3.00 8.00
LL10 Kurt Warner 5.00 12.00
LL11 Deuce McAllister 4.00 10.00
LL12 Eddie George 4.00 10.00
LL13 Donovan McNabb 5.00 12.00
LL14 Hines Ward 5.00 12.00
LL15 Michael Bennett 4.00 10.00
LL16 Steve McNair 5.00 12.00
LL17 Randy Moss 5.00 12.00
LL18 Mike Alstott 5.00 12.00
LL19 Curtis Martin 5.00 12.00
LL20 Ray Lewis 5.00 12.00
LL21 LaDainian Tomlinson 6.00 15.00
LL22 Marcel Shipp 4.00 10.00
LL23 Emmitt Smith 15.00 40.00
LL24 Marshall Faulk 6.00 15.00
LL25 Rich Gannon 5.00 12.00
LL26 Jerry Rice 12.00 30.00
LL27 Jeff Garcia 5.00 12.00
LL28 Priest Holmes 6.00 15.00
LL29 Michael Vick 8.00 20.00
LL30 Ahman Green 5.00 12.00
LL31 Brett Favre 15.00 40.00
LL32 Peyton Manning 12.00 30.00
LL33 Marvin Harrison 6.00 15.00
LL34 Travis Henry 4.00 10.00
LL35 Peerless Price 4.00 10.00
LL36 Rod Gardner 4.00 10.00
LL37 Terrell Owens 6.00 15.00
LL38 Charlie Garner 5.00 12.00
LL39 Daunte Culpepper 5.00 12.00
LL40 Anthony Thomas 5.00 12.00

2003 Absolute Memorabilia Pro Bowl Souvenirs

*GOLD/25: 1X TO 2.5X PRO BOWL/400-600
*GOLD/25: .8X TO 2X PRO BOWL/250-300
GOLD PRINT RUN 25 SER.#'d SETS
PB1 Eddie George/400 4.00 10.00
PB2 Edgerrin James/300 6.00 15.00
PB3 Tim Brown/600 5.00 12.00
PB4 Tom Brady/600 12.00 30.00
PB5 Jeff Garcia/600 4.00 10.00
PB6 Daunte Culpepper/300 5.00 12.00
PB7 Drew Bledsoe/600 5.00 12.00
PB8 Peyton Manning/250 12.00 30.00
PB9 Mark Brunell/400 4.00 10.00
PB10 Kevin Hardy/600 3.00 8.00
PB11 Jimmy Smith/250 5.00 12.00
PB12 Harvey Martin/500 6.00 15.00
PB13 John Elway/250 15.00 40.00
PB14 Terry Bradshaw/250 10.00 25.00
PB15 Richard Dent/600 6.00 15.00

2003 Absolute Memorabilia Pro Bowl Souvenirs Gold Autographs

RANDOM INSERTS IN PACKS
PB13 John Elway/15 100.00 200.00
PB14 Terry Bradshaw/15 75.00 150.00
PB15 Richard Dent/25 25.00 50.00

2003 Absolute Memorabilia Quad Series

STATED ODDS 1:9
QS1 Drew Bledsoe 2.50 6.00
Travis Henry
Josh Reed
Eric Moulds
QS2 Tim Couch 1.50 4.00
William Green
Andre Davis
Quincy Morgan
QS3 Jake Plummer 2.00 5.00
Clinton Portis
Rod Smith
Ashley Lelie
QS4 David Carr 5.00 12.00
Jonathan Wells
Jabar Gaffney
Corey Bradford
QS5 Peyton Manning 5.00 12.00
Edgerrin James
James Mungro
Marvin Harrison
QS6 Mark Brunell 2.50 6.00
David Garrard
Fred Taylor
Jimmy Smith
QS7 Jay Fiedler 2.50 6.00
Ricky Williams
Chris Chambers
Zach Thomas
QS8 Tom Brady 6.00 15.00
Antowain Smith
Troy Brown
Deion Branch
QS9 Chad Pennington 2.50 6.00
Curtis Martin
LaMont Jordan
Santana Moss
QS10 Rich Gannon 5.00 12.00
Charlie Garner
Jerry Rice
Tim Brown
QS11 Tommy Maddox 2.50 6.00
Antwaan Randle El
Plaxico Burress
Hines Ward
QS12 Drew Brees 2.50 6.00
LaDainian Tomlinson
Quentin Jammer
David Boston
QS13 Steve McNair 2.50 6.00
Eddie George
Derrick Mason
Jevon Kearse
QS14 Michael Vick 3.00 8.00
Warrick Dunn
T.J. Duckett
Peerless Price
QS15 Kordell Stewart 2.50 6.00
Anthony Thomas
David Terrell
Brian Urlacher
QS16 Chad Hutchinson 2.00 5.00
Terry Glenn
Antonio Bryant
Roy Williams
QS17 Joey Harrington 1.50 4.00
James Stewart
Az-Zahir Hakim
Bill Schroeder
QS18 Brett Favre 6.00 15.00
Ahman Green
Donald Driver
Javon Walker
QS19 Daunte Culpepper 2.50 6.00
Michael Bennett
Randy Moss
Byron Chamberlain
QS20 Aaron Brooks 2.00 5.00
Deuce McAllister
Donte Stallworth
Joe Horn
QS21 Kerry Collins 2.50 6.00
Tiki Barber
Amani Toomer
Michael Strahan
QS22 Donovan McNabb 2.50 6.00
A.J. Feeley
Duce Staley
James Thrash
QS23 Jeff Garcia 2.50 6.00
Garrison Hearst
Kevan Barlow
Terrell Owens
QS24 Matt Hasselbeck 2.00 5.00
Shaun Alexander
Koren Robinson
Darrell Jackson
QS25 Kurt Warner 2.50 6.00
Marshall Faulk
Isaac Bruce
Torry Holt
QS26 Brad Johnson 2.50 6.00
Mike Alstott
Keyshawn Johnson
Warren Sapp
QS27 Patrick Ramsey 2.50 6.00
Laveranues Coles
Rod Gardner
Champ Bailey
QS28 Carson Palmer 3.00 8.00
Byron Leftwich
Rex Grossman
Chris Simms
QS29 Larry Johnson 1.50 4.00
Lee Suggs
Chris Brown
Musa Smith
QS30 Andre Johnson 4.00 10.00
Taylor Jacobs
Charles Rogers
Kelley Washington

2004 Absolute Memorabilia

Absolute Memorabilia initially released in mid-August 2004. The base set consists of 150-veterans serial numbered of 1150, 50-rookies numbered of 750 and 33-rookie jersey cards numbered of 750. Hobby boxes contained 6-packs of 4-cards and carried an S.R.P. of $40 per pack. Two parallel sets and a variety of inserts can be found seeded in hobby and retail packs highlighted by the Signature Materials and Signature Spectrum autographs and Tools of the Trade Material inserts.

COMP.SET w/o SP's (150) 40.00 80.00
151-233 PRINT RUN 750 SER.#'d SETS
UNPRICED SPECTRUM PLATINUM #'d TO 1
1 Anquan Boldin 1.25 3.00
2 Emmitt Smith 3.00 8.00
3 Josh McCown 1.00 2.50
4 Marcel Shipp .75 2.00
5 Michael Vick 1.50 4.00
6 Peerless Price .75 2.00
7 T.J. Duckett 1.00 2.50
8 Warrick Dunn 1.00 2.50
9 Jamal Lewis 1.00 2.50
10 Kyle Boller 1.00 2.50
11 Ray Lewis 1.25 3.00
12 Terrell Suggs 1.00 2.50
13 Drew Bledsoe 1.25 3.00
14 Eric Moulds 1.00 2.50
15 Josh Reed .75 2.00
16 Travis Henry .75 2.00
17 DeShaun Foster 1.00 2.50
18 Jake Delhomme 1.00 2.50
19 Julius Peppers 1.00 2.50
20 Muhsin Muhammad 1.00 2.50
21 Stephen Davis 1.00 2.50
22 Steve Smith 1.25 3.00
23 Anthony Thomas 1.00 2.50
24 Brian Urlacher 1.25 3.00
25 Marty Booker 1.00 2.50
26 Rex Grossman 1.00 2.50
27 Carson Palmer 1.25 3.00
28 Chad Johnson 1.25 3.00
29 Corey Dillon 1.00 2.50
30 Peter Warrick 1.00 2.50
31 Rudi Johnson 1.00 2.50
32 Andre Davis .75 2.00
33 Dennis Northcutt .75 2.00
34 Lee Suggs 1.00 2.50
35 Tim Couch 1.00 2.50
36 Jeff Garcia 1.00 2.50
37 William Green .75 2.00
38 Antonio Bryant 1.00 2.50
39 Quincy Carter .75 2.00
40 Roy Williams S 1.00 2.50
41 Terence Newman 1.00 2.50
42 Keyshawn Johnson 1.00 2.50
43 Garrison Hearst 1.00 2.50
44 Champ Bailey 1.00 2.50
45 Ashley Lelie .75 2.00
46 Jake Plummer 1.00 2.50
47 Rod Smith 1.00 2.50
48 Shannon Sharpe 1.25 3.00
49 Charles Rogers .75 2.00
50 Joey Harrington 1.00 2.50
51 Ahman Green 1.00 2.50
52 Brett Favre 3.00 8.00
53 Donald Driver 1.25 3.00
54 Javon Walker .75 2.00
55 Robert Ferguson .75 2.00
56 Andre Johnson 1.25 3.00
57 David Carr .75 2.00
58 Domanick Davis .75 2.00
59 Edgerrin James 1.00 2.50
60 Marvin Harrison 1.25 3.00
61 Peyton Manning 2.50 6.00
62 Reggie Wayne 1.25 3.00
63 Byron Leftwich 1.00 2.50
64 Fred Taylor 1.00 2.50
65 Jimmy Smith 1.00 2.50
66 Dante Hall 1.00 2.50
67 Priest Holmes 1.25 3.00
68 Tony Gonzalez 1.25 3.00
69 Trent Green 1.00 2.50
70 Chris Chambers 1.00 2.50
71 Jay Fiedler .75 2.00
72 David Boston .75 2.00
73 Ricky Williams 1.00 2.50
74 Zach Thomas 1.25 3.00
75 Daunte Culpepper 1.00 2.50
76 Michael Bennett 1.00 2.50
77 Moe Williams .75 2.00
78 Randy Moss 1.25 3.00
79 David Givens .75 2.00
80 Deion Branch 1.00 2.50
81 Kevin Faulk 1.00 2.50
82 Richard Seymour .75 2.00
83 Tom Brady 2.50 6.00
84 Troy Brown 1.00 2.50
85 Ty Law 1.00 2.50
86 Aaron Brooks 1.00 2.50
87 Deuce McAllister 1.00 2.50
88 Donte Stallworth .75 2.00
89 Joe Horn 1.00 2.50
90 Amani Toomer 1.00 2.50
91 Jeremy Shockey 1.00 2.50
92 Kerry Collins 1.00 2.50
93 Michael Strahan 1.25 3.00
94 Tiki Barber 1.25 3.00
95 Chad Pennington 1.25 3.00
96 Curtis Martin 1.25 3.00
97 Santana Moss 1.00 2.50
98 Wayne Chrebet 1.00 2.50
99 Justin McCareins .75 2.00
100 Charles Woodson 1.25 3.00
101 Jerry Porter .75 2.00
102 Jerry Rice 2.50 6.00
103 Rich Gannon 1.00 2.50
104 Tim Brown 1.25 3.00
105 Warren Sapp 1.00 2.50
106 A.J. Feeley .75 2.00
107 Brian Westbrook 1.25 3.00
108 Correll Buckhalter 1.00 2.50
109 Donovan McNabb 1.25 3.00
110 Freddie Mitchell .75 2.00
111 Terrell Owens 1.25 3.00
112 Jevon Kearse 1.00 2.50
113 Todd Pinkston .75 2.00
114 Antwaan Randle El 1.00 2.50
115 Hines Ward 1.25 3.00
116 Jerome Bettis 1.25 3.00
117 Kendrell Bell .75 2.00
118 Plaxico Burress 1.00 2.50
119 Tommy Maddox 1.00 2.50
120 Duce Staley 1:00 2.50
121 Drew Brees 1.25 3.00
122 LaDainian Tomlinson 1.25 3.00
123 Kevan Barlow .75 2.00
124 Tai Streets .75 2.00
125 Tim Rattay .75 2.00
126 Darrell Jackson 1.00 2.50
127 Koren Robinson .75 2.00
128 Matt Hasselbeck 1.00 2.50
129 Shaun Alexander 1.00 2.50
130 Isaac Bruce 1.00 2.50
131 Kurt Warner 1.25 3.00
132 Marc Bulger 1.00 2.50
133 Marshall Faulk 1.25 3.00
134 Torry Holt 1.00 2.50
135 Derrick Brooks 1.00 2.50
136 Keenan McCardell .75 2.00
137 Mike Alstott 1.00 2.50
138 Thomas Jones 1.25 3.00
139 Charlie Garner 1.00 2.50
140 Derrick Mason 1.00 2.50
141 Drew Bennett 1.00 2.50
142 Eddie George 1.00 2.50
143 Keith Bulluck .75 2.00
144 Steve McNair 1.25 3.00
145 LaVar Arrington 1.00 2.50
146 Laveranues Coles .75 2.00
147 Patrick Ramsey 1.00 2.50
148 Rod Gardner .75 2.00
149 Clinton Portis 1.25 3.00
150 Mark Brunell 1.00 2.50
151 Craig Krenzel AU RC 5.00 12.00
152 Andy Hall AU RC 4.00 10.00
153 Josh Harris RC 1.50 4.00
154 Jim Sorgi AU RC 5.00 12.00
155 Jeff Smoker AU RC 5.00 12.00
156 John Navarre AU RC 4.00 10.00
157 Jared Lorenzen AU RC 5.00 12.00
158 Cody Pickett AU RC 5.00 12.00
159 Casey Bramlet RC 1.50 4.00
160 Matt Mauck AU RC 4.00 10.00
161 B.J. Symons AU RC 4.00 10.00
162 Bradlee Van Pelt RC 2.00 5.00
163 Ryan Dinwiddie RC 1.50 4.00
164 Michael Turner RC 3.00 8.00
165 Drew Henson RC 1.50 4.00
166 Troy Fleming RC 1.50 4.00
167 Adimchinobe Echemandu RC 2.00 5.00
168 Quincy Wilson RC 2.00 5.00
169 Derrick Ward RC 2.50 6.00
170 Bruce Perry RC 1.50 4.00
171 Brandon Miree RC 1.50 4.00
172 Jarrett Payton AU RC 5.00 12.00
173 Ran Carthon RC 1.50 4.00
174 Carlos Francis AU RC 4.00 10.00
175 Samie Parker RC 1.50 4.00
176 Jerricho Cotchery RC 2.00 5.00
177 Ernest Wilford RC 2.00 5.00
178 Johnnie Morant RC 1.50 4.00
179 Maurice Mann AU RC 4.00 10.00
180 D.J. Hackett RC 2.00 5.00
181 Drew Carter RC 2.00 5.00
182 P.K. Sam RC 1.50 4.00
183 Jamaar Taylor RC 1.50 4.00
184 Ryan Krause RC 1.50 4.00
185 Triandos Luke RC 1.50 4.00
186 Jeris McIntyre RC 1.50 4.00
187 Clarence Moore AU RC 4.00 10.00
188 Mark Jones RC 1.50 4.00
189 Sloan Thomas AU RC 5.00 12.00
190 Sean Taylor RC 5.00 12.00
191 Derek Abney RC 1.50 4.00
192 Jonathan Vilma RC 2.50 6.00
193 Tommie Harris RC 2.50 6.00
194 D.J. Williams RC 2.50 6.00
195 Will Smith RC 2.00 5.00
196 Kenechi Udeze RC 2.00 5.00
197 Vince Wilfork RC 2.50 6.00
198 Ahmad Carroll RC 1.50 4.00
199 Jason Babin RC 2.50 6.00
200 Chris Gamble RC 2.00 5.00
201 Larry Fitzgerald RPM RC 8.00 20.00
202 DeAngelo Hall RPM RC 3.00 8.00
203 Matt Schaub RPM RC 6.00 15.00
204 Michael Jenkins RPM AU RC 10.00 25.00
205 Devard Darling RPM AU RC 6.00 15.00
206 J.P. Losman RPM RC 2.50 6.00
207 Lee Evans RPM RC 3.00 8.00
208 Keary Colbert RPM AU RC 6.00 15.00
209 Bernard Berrian RPM AU RC 10.00 25.00
210 Chris Perry RPM RC 2.50 6.00
211 Kellen Winslow RPM RC 3.00 8.00
212 Luke McCown RPM RC 2.50 6.00
213 Julius Jones RPM RC 2.50 6.00
214 Darius Watts RPM RC 2.00 5.00
215 Tatum Bell RPM AU RC 8.00 20.00
216 Kevin Jones RPM RC 2.50 6.00
217 Roy Williams RPM RC 3.00 8.00
218 Dunta Robinson RPM RC 2.00 5.00
219 Greg Jones RPM AU RC 6.00 15.00
220 Reggie Williams RPM RC 2.50 6.00
221 Mewelde Moore RPM RC 2.50 6.00
222 Ben Watson RPM RC 3.00 8.00
223 Cedric Cobbs RPM RC 2.00 5.00
224 Devery Henderson RPM AU RC 10.00 25.00
225 Eli Manning RPM RC 20.00 50.00
226 Robert Gallery RPM RC 3.00 8.00
227 Ben Roethlisberger RPM RC 20.00 50.00
228 Philip Rivers RPM RC 10.00 25.00
229 Derrick Hamilton RPM RC 2.00 5.00
230 Rashaun Woods RPM RC 2.00 5.00
231 Steven Jackson RPM RC 5.00 12.00
232 Michael Clayton RPM RC 2.50 6.00
233 Ben Troupe RPM RC 2.50 6.00

2004 Absolute Memorabilia Retail

*RETAIL VETS: .1X TO .3X HOBBY
RETAIL CARDS NOT SERIAL NUMBERED

2004 Absolute Memorabilia Spectrum

*VETS 1-150: 1X TO 2.5X BASIC CARD
*ROOKIES 151-200: .6X TO 1.5X BASIC RCs
*ROOKIES 151-200: .25X TO .6X AUTO RCs
1-200 PRINT RUN 100 SER.#'d SETS
*ROOKIES 201-233: .6X TO 1.5X BASIC RCs
*ROOKIES 201-233: .4X TO 1X AUTO RCs
201-233 RPM PRINT RUN 75 SER.#'d SETS
UNPRICED SPECTRUM PLATINUM #'d TO 1

2004 Absolute Memorabilia Absolute Patches

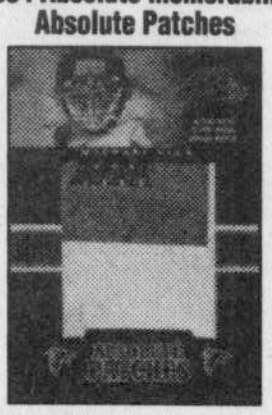

STATED PRINT RUN 25 SER.#'d SETS
UNPRICED SPECTRUM #'d TO 1 SET
AP1 Anquan Boldin 20.00 50.00
AP2 Barry Sanders 40.00 100.00
AP3 Brett Favre 50.00 120.00
AP4 Brian Urlacher 20.00 50.00
AP5 Chad Pennington 20.00 50.00
AP6 Clinton Portis 20.00 50.00
AP7 Dan Marino 50.00 120.00
AP8 Daunte Culpepper 15.00 40.00
AP9 David Carr 12.00 30.00
AP10 Deuce McAllister 15.00 40.00
AP11 Donovan McNabb 20.00 50.00
AP12 Drew Bledsoe 20.00 50.00
AP13 Edgerrin James 15.00 40.00
AP14 Emmitt Smith 50.00 120.00
AP15 Jeremy Shockey 15.00 40.00
AP16 Jerry Rice 40.00 100.00
AP17 John Elway 50.00 120.00
AP18 Joey Harrington 15.00 40.00
AP19 LaDainian Tomlinson 20.00 50.00
AP20 Michael Vick 25.00 60.00
AP21 Peyton Manning 40.00 100.00
AP22 Priest Holmes 20.00 50.00
AP23 Randy Moss 20.00 50.00
AP24 Ricky Williams 15.00 40.00
AP25 Tom Brady 40.00 100.00

2004 Absolute Memorabilia Boss Hoggs

COMPLETE SET (25) 20.00 50.00
STATED PRINT RUN 1000 SER.#'d SETS
BH1 Amani Toomer 1.00 2.50
BH2 Brett Favre 3.00 8.00
BH3 Charles Woodson 1.25 3.00
BH4 Curtis Martin 1.25 3.00
BH5 Eddie George 1.00 2.50
BH6 Edgerrin James 1.00 2.50
BH7 Emmitt Smith 3.00 8.00
BH8 Jeff Garcia 1.00 2.50
BH9 Jerry Rice 2.50 6.00
BH10 Jevon Kearse 1.00 2.50
BH11 Jimmy Smith 1.00 2.50
BH12 Keith Bulluck .75 2.00
BH13 Kurt Warner 1.25 3.00
BH14 Laveranues Coles .75 2.00
BH15 Mark Brunell 1.00 2.50
BH16 Marshall Faulk 1.25 3.00
BH17 Marvin Harrison 1.25 3.00
BH18 Michael Strahan 1.25 3.00
BH19 Michael Vick 1.50 4.00
BH20 Peyton Manning 2.50 6.00
BH21 Rich Gannon 1.00 2.50
BH22 Samari Rolle .75 2.00
BH23 Steve McNair 1.25 3.00
BH24 Tim Brown 1.25 3.00
BH25 Wayne Chrebet 1.00 2.50

2004 Absolute Memorabilia Boss Hoggs Material

STATED PRINT RUN 125 SER.#'d SETS
UNPRICED PRIME SPECTRUM #'d TO 1 SET
BH1 Amani Toomer 4.00 10.00
BH2 Brett Favre 12.00 30.00
BH3 Charles Woodson 5.00 12.00
BH4 Curtis Martin 5.00 12.00
BH5 Eddie George 4.00 10.00
BH6 Edgerrin James 4.00 10.00
BH7 Emmitt Smith 12.00 30.00
BH8 Jeff Garcia 4.00 10.00
BH9 Jerry Rice 10.00 25.00
BH10 Jevon Kearse 4.00 10.00
BH11 Jimmy Smith 4.00 10.00
BH12 Keith Bulluck 3.00 8.00
BH13 Kurt Warner 5.00 12.00
BH14 Laveranues Coles 3.00 8.00
BH15 Mark Brunell 4.00 10.00
BH16 Marshall Faulk 5.00 12.00
BH17 Marvin Harrison 5.00 12.00
BH18 Michael Strahan 5.00 12.00

BH19 Michael Vick 6.00 15.00
BH20 Peyton Manning 10.00 25.00
BH21 Rich Gannon 4.00 10.00
BH22 Samari Rolle 3.00 8.00
BH23 Steve McNair 5.00 12.00
BH24 Tim Brown 5.00 12.00
BH25 Wayne Chrebet 4.00 10.00

2004 Absolute Memorabilia Canton Absolutes Jersey Bronze

BRONZE PRINT RUN 100 SER.#'d SETS
*GOLD/25: .8X TO 2X BRONZE
GOLD PRINT RUN 25 SER.#'d SETS
*SILVER/50: .5X TO 1.2X BRONZE
SILVER PRINT RUN 50 SER.#'d SETS
UNPRICED PLATINUM PRINT RUN 1 SET
CA1 Barry Sanders 10.00 25.00
CA2 Brett Favre 12.00 30.00
CA3 Brian Urlacher 5.00 12.00
CA4 Clinton Portis 5.00 12.00
CA5 Dan Marino 12.00 30.00
CA6 Daunte Culpepper 4.00 10.00
CA7 Deuce McAllister 4.00 10.00
CA8 Donovan McNabb 5.00 12.00
CA9 Earl Campbell 5.00 12.00
CA10 Edgerrin James 4.00 10.00
CA11 Emmitt Smith 12.00 30.00
CA12 Jerry Rice 10.00 25.00
CA13 Jim Kelly 8.00 20.00
CA14 John Elway 12.00 30.00
CA15 LaDainian Tomlinson 5.00 12.00
CA16 Marshall Faulk 5.00 12.00
CA17 Marcus Allen 5.00 12.00
CA18 Michael Vick 6.00 15.00
CA19 Peyton Manning 10.00 25.00
CA20 Priest Holmes 5.00 12.00
CA21 Randy Moss 5.00 12.00
CA22 Ricky Williams 4.00 10.00
CA23 Steve McNair 5.00 12.00
CA24 Tom Brady 10.00 25.00
CA25 Warren Moon 4.00 10.00

2004 Absolute Memorabilia Fans of the Game

COMPLETE SET (4) 3.00 8.00
STATED ODDS 1:12 HOB, 1:24 RET
FG1 Erik Estrada .75 2.00
FG3 Chris Berman 1.00 2.50
FG4 Rich Eisen .75 2.00
FG5 John Clayton .75 2.00

2004 Absolute Memorabilia Fans of the Game Autographs

GOLD/SILVER: SAME PRICE
GOLD/300 INSERTED IN HOBBY PACKS
SILVER INSERTED IN RETAIL PACKS
FG1A Erik Estrada/300 12.50 30.00
FG1B Erik Estrada 12.50 30.00
FG3A Chris Berman/300 20.00 50.00
FG3B Chris Berman 20.00 50.00
FG4A Rich Eisen/300 12.50 30.00
FG4B Rich Eisen 12.50 30.00
FG5A John Clayton/300 7.50 20.00
FG5B John Clayton 7.50 20.00

2004 Absolute Memorabilia Gridiron Force

COMPLETE SET (25) 20.00 50.00
STATED PRINT RUN 1000 SER.#'d SETS
GF1 Aaron Brooks 1.00 2.50
GF2 Anquan Boldin 1.25 3.00
GF3 Brian Urlacher 1.25 3.00
GF4 Byron Leftwich 1.00 2.50
GF5 Chad Johnson 1.25 3.00
GF6 Chad Pennington 1.25 3.00
GF7 Clinton Portis 1.25 3.00
GF8 Daunte Culpepper 1.00 2.50
GF9 David Carr .75 2.00
GF10 Deuce McAllister 1.00 2.50
GF11 Donovan McNabb 1.25 3.00
GF12 Edgerrin James 1.00 2.50
GF13 Emmitt Smith 3.00 8.00
GF14 Jamal Lewis 1.00 2.50
GF15 Jeff Garcia 1.00 2.50
GF16 Jeremy Shockey 1.00 2.50
GF17 Joey Harrington 1.00 2.50
GF18 Koren Robinson .75 2.00
GF19 LaDainian Tomlinson 1.25 3.00
GF20 Plaxico Burress 1.00 2.50
GF21 Priest Holmes 1.25 3.00
GF22 Ricky Williams 1.00 2.50
GF23 Shaun Alexander 1.00 2.50
GF24 Terrell Owens 1.25 3.00
GF25 Tom Brady 2.50 6.00

2004 Absolute Memorabilia Gridiron Force Jersey Bronze

BRONZE PRINT RUN 100 SER.#'d SETS
*GOLD/25: .8X TO 2X BRONZE
GOLD PRINT RUN 25 SER.#'d SETS
*SILVER/50: .5X TO 1.2X BRONZE
SILVER PRINT RUN 50 SER.#'d SETS
UNPRICED PLATINUM PRINT RUN 10 SET
GF1 Aaron Brooks 4.00 10.00
GF2 Anquan Boldin 5.00 12.00
GF3 Brian Urlacher 5.00 12.00
GF4 Byron Leftwich 4.00 10.00
GF5 Chad Johnson 5.00 12.00
GF6 Chad Pennington 5.00 12.00
GF7 Clinton Portis 5.00 12.00
GF8 Daunte Culpepper 4.00 10.00
GF9 David Carr 3.00 8.00
GF10 Deuce McAllister 4.00 10.00
GF11 Donovan McNabb 5.00 12.00
GF12 Edgerrin James 4.00 10.00
GF13 Emmitt Smith 12.00 30.00
GF14 Jamal Lewis 4.00 10.00
GF15 Jeff Garcia 4.00 10.00
GF16 Jeremy Shockey 4.00 10.00
GF17 Joey Harrington 4.00 10.00
GF18 Koren Robinson 3.00 8.00
GF19 LaDainian Tomlinson 5.00 12.00
GF20 Plaxico Burress 4.00 10.00
GF21 Priest Holmes 5.00 12.00
GF22 Ricky Williams 4.00 10.00
GF23 Shaun Alexander 4.00 10.00
GF24 Terrell Owens 5.00 12.00
GF25 Tom Brady 10.00 25.00

2004 Absolute Memorabilia Ground Hoggs Shoe

STATED PRINT RUN 125 SER.#'d SETS
GH1 Amani Toomer 5.00 12.00
GH2 Brett Favre 15.00 40.00
GH3 Curtis Martin 6.00 15.00
GH4 Derrick Brooks 5.00 12.00
GH5 Derrick Mason 5.00 12.00
GH6 Dexter Coakley 4.00 10.00
GH7 Eddie George 5.00 12.00
GH8 Edgerrin James 5.00 12.00
GH9 Emmitt Smith 15.00 40.00
GH10 Jason Taylor 5.00 12.00
GH11 Jerry Rice 12.00 30.00
GH12 Jevon Kearse 5.00 12.00
GH13 Joey Galloway 5.00 12.00
GH14 Junior Seau 6.00 15.00
GH15 Keyshawn Johnson 5.00 12.00
GH16 Kurt Warner 6.00 15.00
GH17 Laveranues Coles 4.00 10.00
GH18 Marvin Harrison 6.00 15.00
GH19 Patrick Surtain 4.00 10.00
GH20 Peyton Manning 12.00 30.00
GH21 Rich Gannon 5.00 12.00
GH22 Samari Rolle 4.00 10.00
GH23 Steve McNair 6.00 15.00
GH24 Terry Glenn 5.00 12.00
GH25 Wayne Chrebet 5.00 12.00

2004 Absolute Memorabilia Leather and Laces

STATED PRINT RUN 250 SER.#'d SETS
*COMBOS/25: 1.2X TO 3X BASIC JSY
LL1 Ahman Green 4.00 10.00
LL2 Anquan Boldin 5.00 12.00
LL3 Brett Favre 12.00 30.00
LL4 Chad Johnson 5.00 12.00
LL5 Chad Pennington 5.00 12.00
LL6 Curtis Martin 5.00 12.00
LL7 Daunte Culpepper 4.00 10.00
LL8 Donovan McNabb 5.00 12.00
LL9 Emmitt Smith 12.00 30.00
LL10 Jake Delhomme 4.00 10.00
LL11 Jamal Lewis 4.00 10.00
LL12 Kevan Barlow 3.00 8.00
LL13 Koren Robinson 3.00 8.00
LL14 Marc Bulger 4.00 10.00
LL15 Marshall Faulk 5.00 12.00
LL16 Matt Hasselbeck 4.00 10.00
LL17 Randy Moss 5.00 12.00
LL18 Ricky Williams 4.00 10.00
LL19 Rudi Johnson 4.00 10.00
LL20 Shaun Alexander 4.00 10.00
LL21 Stephen Davis 4.00 10.00
LL22 Steve McNair 5.00 12.00
LL23 Steve Smith 5.00 12.00
LL24 Terrell Owens 5.00 12.00
LL25 Torry Holt 4.00 10.00

2004 Absolute Memorabilia Marks of Fame

COMPLETE SET (25) 25.00 60.00
STATED PRINT RUN 1000 SER.#'d SETS
MOF1 Aaron Brooks 1.00 2.50
MOF2 Anquan Boldin 1.25 3.00
MOF3 Brett Favre 3.00 8.00
MOF4 Brian Urlacher 1.25 3.00
MOF5 Chad Pennington 1.25 3.00
MOF6 Clinton Portis 1.25 3.00
MOF7 Daunte Culpepper 1.00 2.50
MOF8 David Carr .75 2.00
MOF9 Deuce McAllister 1.00 2.50
MOF10 Donovan McNabb 1.25 3.00
MOF11 Emmitt Smith 3.00 8.00
MOF12 Jamal Lewis 1.00 2.50
MOF13 Jeremy Shockey 1.00 2.50
MOF14 Jerry Rice 2.50 6.00
MOF15 Joey Harrington 1.00 2.50
MOF16 LaDainian Tomlinson 1.25 3.00
MOF17 Marvin Harrison 1.25 3.00
MOF18 Michael Vick 1.50 4.00
MOF19 Peyton Manning 2.50 6.00
MOF20 Priest Holmes 1.25 3.00
MOF21 Ricky Williams 1.00 2.50
MOF22 Steve McNair 1.25 3.00
MOF23 Terrell Owens 1.25 3.00
MOF24 Tom Brady 2.50 6.00
MOF25 Torry Holt 1.00 2.50

2004 Absolute Memorabilia Marks of Fame Material

STATED PRINT RUN 75 SER.#'d SETS
UNPRICED PRIME SPECTRUM 1 SET
MOF1 Aaron Brooks 5.00 12.00
MOF2 Anquan Boldin 6.00 15.00
MOF3 Brett Favre 15.00 40.00
MOF4 Brian Urlacher 6.00 15.00
MOF5 Chad Pennington 6.00 15.00
MOF6 Clinton Portis 6.00 15.00
MOF7 Daunte Culpepper 5.00 12.00
MOF8 David Carr 4.00 10.00
MOF9 Deuce McAllister 5.00 12.00
MOF10 Donovan McNabb 6.00 15.00
MOF11 Emmitt Smith 15.00 40.00
MOF12 Jamal Lewis 5.00 12.00
MOF13 Jeremy Shockey 5.00 12.00
MOF14 Jerry Rice 12.00 30.00
MOF15 Joey Harrington 5.00 12.00
MOF16 LaDainian Tomlinson 6.00 15.00
MOF17 Marvin Harrison 6.00 15.00
MOF18 Michael Vick 8.00 20.00
MOF19 Peyton Manning 12.00 30.00
MOF20 Priest Holmes 6.00 15.00
MOF21 Ricky Williams 5.00 12.00
MOF22 Steve McNair 6.00 15.00
MOF23 Terrell Owens 6.00 15.00
MOF24 Tom Brady 12.00 30.00
MOF25 Torry Holt 5.00 12.00

2004 Absolute Memorabilia Marks of Fame Material Prime

*UNSIGNED PRIME: .6X TO 1.5X BASIC INSERTS
PRIME PRINT RUN 25 SER.#'d SETS
MOF1 Aaron Brooks AU 20.00 50.00
MOF2 Anquan Boldin AU 25.00 60.00
MOF3 Brett Favre AU 150.00 250.00
MOF5 Chad Pennington AU 25.00 60.00
MOF6 Clinton Portis AU 25.00 60.00
MOF8 David Carr AU 15.00 40.00
MOF14 Jerry Rice AU 125.00 200.00
MOF15 Joey Harrington AU 20.00 50.00
MOF16 LaDainian Tomlinson AU 40.00 100.00
MOF19 Peyton Manning AU 60.00 150.00
MOF22 Steve McNair AU 30.00 80.00

2004 Absolute Memorabilia Signature Material

STATED PRINT RUN 19-300
UNPRICED PRIME PRINT RUN 5 SETS
UNPRICED SPECTRUM PRINT RUN 1 SET
SM1 Ahman Green/194 15.00 40.00
SM2 Antwaan Randle El/119 15.00 40.00
SM3 Chris Chambers/94 15.00 40.00
SM4 Deuce McAllister/94 15.00 40.00
SM5 Joe Horn/94 15.00 40.00
SM6 Roy Williams S/194 15.00 40.00
SM7 Shaun Alexander/144 15.00 40.00
SM8 Stephen Davis/144 15.00 40.00
SM9 Tom Brady/194 125.00 250.00
SM10 Joe Namath/94 50.00 100.00
SM11 Terry Bradshaw/19 60.00 120.00
SM12 Jim Kelly/19 40.00 80.00
SM13 Cedric Cobbs/300 8.00 20.00
SM14 Chris Perry/280 10.00 25.00
SM15 Devery Henderson/280 12.00 30.00
SM16 Julius Jones/300 10.00 25.00
SM17 Keary Colbert/300 8.00 20.00
SM18 Kevin Jones/280 10.00 25.00
SM19 Lee Evans/300 12.00 30.00
SM20 Matt Schaub/280 25.00 60.00
SM21 Michael Clayton/300 10.00 25.00
SM22 Philip Rivers/300 30.00 80.00
SM23 Reggie Williams/280 10.00 25.00
SM24 Steven Jackson/280 20.00 50.00
SM25 Tatum Bell/300 10.00 25.00

2004 Absolute Memorabilia Signature Spectrum

RANDOM INSERTS IN PACKS
3 Josh McCown/300 8.00 20.00
10 Kyle Boller/225 8.00 20.00
18 Jake Delhomme/150 8.00 20.00
21 Stephen Davis/50 10.00 25.00
22 Steve Smith/300 12.00 30.00
31 Rudi Johnson/300 8.00 20.00
58 Domanick Davis/300 6.00 15.00
60 Marvin Harrison/25 15.00 40.00
65 Jimmy Smith/125 8.00 20.00
83 Tom Brady/50 150.00 250.00
89 Joe Horn/50 10.00 25.00
93 Michael Strahan/25 15.00 40.00
117 Kendrell Bell/25 10.00 25.00
128 Matt Hasselbeck/125 8.00 20.00
134 Torry Holt/50 10.00 25.00
140 Derrick Mason/125 8.00 20.00
146 Laveranues Coles/25 10.00 25.00
153 Josh Harris/50 8.00 20.00
164 Michael Turner/50 15.00 40.00
165 Drew Henson/300 6.00 15.00
168 Quincy Wilson/50 10.00 25.00
175 Samie Parker/50 8.00 20.00
176 Jerricho Cotchery/50 10.00 25.00
177 Ernest Wilford/50 10.00 25.00
178 Johnnie Morant/75 8.00 20.00
180 D.J. Hackett/50 10.00 25.00
182 P.K. Sam/50 8.00 20.00
192 Jonathan Vilma/50 12.00 30.00
195 Will Smith/25 12.00 30.00
196 Kenechi Udeze/25 12.00 30.00
197 Vince Wilfork/25 15.00 40.00
198 Ahmad Carroll/25 10.00 25.00

2004 Absolute Memorabilia Team Quads

STATED PRINT RUN 250 SER.#'d SETS
UNPRICED SPECTRUM PRINT RUN 5 SETS
TQ1 Anquan Boldin 6.00 15.00
Emmitt Smith
Josh McCown
Marcel Shipp
TQ2 Jamal Lewis 2.50 6.00
Ray Lewis
Terrell Suggs
Kyle Boller
TQ3 Drew Bledsoe 2.50 6.00
Eric Moulds
Travis Henry
Josh Reed
TQ4 Anthony Thomas 2.50 6.00
Brian Urlacher
Rex Grossman
David Terrell
TQ5 Clinton Portis 2.50 6.00
Rod Smith
Jake Plummer
Ashley Lelie
TQ6 Brett Favre 6.00 15.00
Ahman Green
Javon Walker
Donald Driver
TQ7 Edgerrin James 5.00 12.00
Peyton Manning
Marvin Harrison
Reggie Wayne
TQ8 Priest Holmes 2.50 6.00
Trent Green
Tony Gonzalez
Dante Hall
TQ9 Chris Chambers 2.50 6.00
Ricky Williams
Zach Thomas
Jason Taylor
TQ10 Jeremy Shockey 2.50 6.00
Kerry Collins
Michael Strahan
Tiki Barber
TQ11 Chad Pennington 2.50 6.00
Curtis Martin
Santana Moss
John Abraham
TQ12 Jerry Rice 5.00 12.00
Tim Brown
Rich Gannon
Charles Woodson
TQ13 Hines Ward 2.50 6.00
Jerome Bettis
Antwaan Randle El
Plaxico Burress
TQ14 Kurt Warner 2.50 6.00
Marshall Faulk
Marc Bulger
Torry Holt
TQ15 Eddie George 2.50 6.00
Steve McNair
Jevon Kearse
Derrick Mason

2004 Absolute Memorabilia Team Quads Material

STATED PRINT RUN 50 SER.#'d SETS
UNPRICED PRIME PRINT RUN 5 SETS
UNPRICED SPECTRUM PRINT RUN 1 SETS
TQ1 Anquan Boldin 25.00 60.00
Emmitt Smith
Josh McCown
Marcel Shipp
TQ2 Jamal Lewis 12.00 30.00
Ray Lewis
Terrell Suggs
Kyle Boller
TQ3 Drew Bledsoe 12.00 30.00
Eric Moulds
Travis Henry
Josh Reed
TQ4 Anthony Thomas 12.00 30.00
Brian Urlacher
Rex Grossman
David Terrell
TQ5 Clinton Portis 12.00 30.00
Rod Smith
Jake Plummer
Ashley Lelie
TQ6 Brett Favre 30.00 80.00
Ahman Green
Javon Walker
Donald Driver
TQ7 Edgerrin James 25.00 60.00
Peyton Manning
Marvin Harrison
Reggie Wayne
TQ8 Priest Holmes 12.00 30.00
Trent Green
Tony Gonzalez
Dante Hall
TQ9 Chris Chambers 12.00 30.00
Ricky Williams
Zach Thomas
Jason Taylor
TQ10 Jeremy Shockey 12.00 30.00
Kerry Collins
Michael Strahan
Tiki Barber
TQ11 Chad Pennington 12.00 30.00
Curtis Martin
Santana Moss
John Abraham
TQ12 Jerry Rice 25.00 60.00
Tim Brown
Rich Gannon
Charles Woodson
TQ13 Hines Ward 12.00 30.00
Jerome Bettis
Antwaan Randle El
Plaxico Burress
TQ14 Kurt Warner 12.00 30.00
Marshall Faulk
Marc Bulger
Torry Holt
TQ15 Eddie George 12.00 30.00
Steve McNair
Jevon Kearse
Derrick Mason

2004 Absolute Memorabilia Team Tandems

COMPLETE SET (25) 25.00 60.00
STATED PRINT RUN 1000 SER.#'d SETS
*SPECTRUM/25: 2X TO 5X TANDEM/1000
SPECTRUM PRINT RUN 25 SER.#'d SETS
TAN1 Anquan Boldin 3.00 8.00
Emmitt Smith
TAN2 Michael Vick 1.50 4.00
Peerless Price
TAN3 Jamal Lewis 1.25 3.00
Ray Lewis
TAN4 Stephen Davis 1.00 2.50
Julius Peppers
TAN5 Brian Urlacher 1.25 3.00
Anthony Thomas
TAN6 Clinton Portis 1.25 3.00
Rod Smith
TAN7 Charles Rogers 1.00 2.50
Joey Harrington
TAN8 Ahman Green 3.00 8.00
Brett Favre
TAN9 Andre Johnson 1.25 3.00
David Carr
TAN10 Edgerrin James 2.50 6.00
Peyton Manning
TAN11 Byron Leftwich 1.00 2.50
Fred Taylor
TAN12 Priest Holmes 1.25 3.00
Trent Green
TAN13 Chris Chambers 1.00 2.50
Ricky Williams
TAN14 Daunte Culpepper 1.25 3.00
Randy Moss
TAN15 Tom Brady 2.50 6.00
Troy Brown
TAN16 Aaron Brooks 1.00 2.50
Deuce McAllister
TAN17 Jeremy Shockey 1.00 2.50
Kerry Collins
TAN18 Chad Pennington 1.25 3.00
Curtis Martin
TAN19 Jerry Rice 2.50 6.00
Tim Brown
TAN20 Donovan McNabb 1.25 3.00
Correll Buckhalter
TAN21 Drew Brees 1.25 3.00
LaDainian Tomlinson
TAN22 Matt Hasselbeck 1.00 2.50
Shaun Alexander
TAN23 Kurt Warner 1.25 3.00
Marshall Faulk
TAN24 Eddie George 1.25 3.00
Steve McNair
TAN25 Patrick Ramsey 1.00 2.50
Laveranues Coles

2004 Absolute Memorabilia Team Tandems Material

STATED PRINT RUN 125 SER.#'d SETS
*PRIME/25: 1X TO 2.5X TANDEM JSY/125
PRIME PRINT RUN 25 SER.#'d SETS
UNPRICED SPECTRUM PRINT RUN 1 SET
TT1 Anquan Boldin 12.00 30.00
Emmitt Smith
TT2 Michael Vick 6.00 15.00
Peerless Price
TT3 Jamal Lewis 5.00 12.00
Ray Lewis
TT4 Stephen Davis 4.00 10.00
Julius Peppers
TT5 Brian Urlacher 5.00 12.00
Anthony Thomas
TT6 Clinton Portis 5.00 12.00
Rod Smith
TT7 Charles Rogers 4.00 10.00
Joey Harrington
TT8 Ahman Green 12.00 30.00
Brett Favre
TT9 Andre Johnson 5.00 12.00
David Carr
TT10 Edgerrin James 10.00 25.00
Peyton Manning
TT11 Byron Leftwich 4.00 10.00
Fred Taylor
TT12 Priest Holmes 5.00 12.00
Trent Green
TT13 Chris Chambers 4.00 10.00
Ricky Williams
TT14 Daunte Culpepper 5.00 12.00
Randy Moss
TT15 Tom Brady 10.00 25.00
Troy Brown
TT16 Aaron Brooks 4.00 10.00
Deuce McAllister
TT17 Jeremy Shockey 4.00 10.00
Kerry Collins
TT18 Chad Pennington 5.00 12.00
Curtis Martin
TT19 Jerry Rice 10.00 25.00
Tim Brown
TT20 Donovan McNabb 5.00 12.00
Correll Buckhalter
TT21 Drew Brees 5.00 12.00
LaDainian Tomlinson
TT22 Matt Hasselbeck 4.00 10.00
Shaun Alexander
TT23 Kurt Warner 5.00 12.00
Marshall Faulk
TT24 Eddie George 5.00 12.00
Steve McNair
TT25 Patrick Ramsey 4.00 10.00
Laveranues Coles

2004 Absolute Memorabilia Team Trios

STATED PRINT RUN 500 SER.#'d SETS
UNPRICED SPECTRUM PRINT RUN 10 SETS
TTR1 Anquan Boldin 5.00 12.00
Emmitt Smith
Josh McCown
TTR2 Michael Vick 2.50 6.00
Peerless Price
T.J. Duckett
TTR3 Jamal Lewis 2.00 5.00
Ray Lewis
Terrell Suggs
TTR4 Drew Bledsoe 2.00 5.00
Eric Moulds
Travis Henry
TTR5 Anthony Thomas 2.00 5.00
Brian Urlacher
Rex Grossman
TTR6 Chad Johnson 2.00 5.00
Corey Dillon
Peter Warrick
TTR7 Quincy Carter 1.50 4.00
Roy Williams S
Terence Newman
TTR8 Clinton Portis 2.00 5.00
Rod Smith
Jake Plummer
TTR9 Charles Rogers 1.50 4.00
Joey Harrington
James Stewart
TTR10 Ahman Green 5.00 12.00
Brett Favre
Javon Walker
TTR11 Edgerrin James 4.00 10.00
Peyton Manning
Marvin Harrison
TTR12 Byron Leftwich 1.50 4.00
Fred Taylor
Jimmy Smith
TTR13 Priest Holmes 2.00 5.00
Trent Green
Tony Gonzalez
TTR14 Chris Chambers 2.00 5.00
Ricky Williams
Zach Thomas
TTR15 Daunte Culpepper 2.00 5.00
Randy Moss
Michael Bennett
TTR16 Aaron Brooks 1.50 4.00
Deuce McAllister
Joe Horn
TTR17 Jeremy Shockey 2.00 5.00
Kerry Collins
Michael Strahan
TTR18 Chad Pennington 2.00 5.00
Curtis Martin
Santana Moss
TTR19 Jerry Rice 4.00 10.00
Tim Brown
Rich Gannon
TTR20 Hines Ward 2.00 5.00
Jerome Bettis
Antwaan Randle El
TTR21 Drew Brees 2.00 5.00
LaDainian Tomlinson
Doug Flutie
TTR22 Matt Hasselbeck 1.50 4.00
Shaun Alexander
Koren Robinson
TTR23 Kurt Warner 2.00 5.00
Marshall Faulk
Marc Bulger
TTR24 Eddie George 2.00 5.00
Steve McNair
Jevon Kearse
TTR25 Laveranues Coles 1.50 4.00
Patrick Ramsey
LaVar Arrington

2004 Absolute Memorabilia Team Trios Material

STATED PRINT RUN 100 SER.#'d SETS
UNPRICED PRIME PRINT RUN 10 SETS
UNPRICED SPECTRUM PRINT RUN 1 SETS
TTR1 Anquan Boldin 15.00 40.00
Emmitt Smith
Josh McCown
TTR2 Michael Vick 8.00 20.00
Peerless Price
T.J. Duckett
TTR3 Jamal Lewis 6.00 15.00
Ray Lewis
Terrell Suggs
TTR4 Drew Bledsoe 6.00 15.00
Eric Moulds
Travis Henry
TTR5 Anthony Thomas 6.00 15.00
Brian Urlacher
Rex Grossman
TTR6 Chad Johnson 6.00 15.00
Corey Dillon
Peter Warrick
TTR7 Quincy Carter 5.00 12.00
Roy Williams S
Terence Newman
TTR8 Clinton Portis 6.00 15.00
Rod Smith
Jake Plummer
TTR9 Charles Rogers 5.00 12.00
Joey Harrington
James Stewart
TTR10 Ahman Green 15.00 40.00
Brett Favre
Javon Walker
TTR11 Edgerrin James 12.00 30.00
Peyton Manning
Marvin Harrison
TTR12 Byron Leftwich 5.00 12.00
Fred Taylor
Jimmy Smith
TTR13 Priest Holmes 6.00 15.00
Trent Green
Tony Gonzalez
TTR14 Chris Chambers 6.00 15.00
Ricky Williams
Zach Thomas
TTR15 Daunte Culpepper 6.00 15.00
Randy Moss
Michael Bennett
TTR16 Aaron Brooks 5.00 12.00
Deuce McAllister
Joe Horn
TTR17 Jeremy Shockey 6.00 15.00
Kerry Collins
Michael Strahan
TTR18 Chad Pennington 6.00 15.00
Curtis Martin
Santana Moss
TTR19 Jerry Rice 12.00 30.00
Tim Brown
Rich Gannon
TTR20 Hines Ward 6.00 15.00
Jerome Bettis
Antwaan Randle El
TTR21 Drew Brees 6.00 15.00
LaDainian Tomlinson
Doug Flutie
TTR22 Matt Hasselbeck 5.00 12.00
Shaun Alexander
Koren Robinson
TTR23 Kurt Warner 6.00 15.00
Marshall Faulk
Marc Bulger
TTR24 Eddie George 6.00 15.00
Steve McNair
Jevon Kearse
TTR25 Laveranues Coles 5.00 12.00
Patrick Ramsey
LaVar Arrington

2004 Absolute Memorabilia Tools of the Trade

STATED PRINT RUN 250 SER.#'d SETS
UNPRICED SPECTRUM PRINT RUN 10 SETS
TT1 Aaron Brooks 1.50 4.00
TT2 Ahman Green 1.50 4.00
TT3 Andre Johnson 2.00 5.00
TT4 Anquan Boldin 2.00 5.00
TT5 Anthony Thomas 1.50 4.00
TT6 Antwaan Randle El 1.50 4.00
TT7 Ashley Lelie 1.25 3.00
TT8 Brad Johnson 1.50 4.00
TT9 Brett Favre 5.00 12.00
TT10 Brian Urlacher 2.00 5.00
TT11 Byron Leftwich 1.50 4.00
TT12 Chad Johnson 2.00 5.00
TT13 Chad Pennington 2.00 5.00
TT14 Charles Rogers 1.25 3.00
TT15 Charles Woodson 2.00 5.00
TT16 Chris Chambers 1.50 4.00
TT17 Clinton Portis 2.00 5.00
TT18 Corey Dillon 1.50 4.00
TT19 Curtis Martin 2.00 5.00
TT20 Dante Hall 1.50 4.00
TT21 Daunte Culpepper 1.50 4.00
TT22 David Boston 1.25 3.00
TT23 David Carr 1.25 3.00
TT24 Deuce McAllister 1.50 4.00
TT25 Donovan McNabb 2.00 5.00
TT26 Donte Stallworth 1.25 3.00
TT27 Drew Bledsoe 2.00 5.00
TT28 Eddie George 1.50 4.00
TT29 Edgerrin James 1.50 4.00
TT30 Emmitt Smith 5.00 12.00
TT31 Eric Moulds 1.50 4.00
TT32 Fred Taylor 1.50 4.00
TT33 Hines Ward 2.00 5.00
TT34 Isaac Bruce 1.50 4.00
TT35 Jake Plummer 1.50 4.00
TT36 Jamal Lewis 1.50 4.00
TT37 Javon Walker 1.25 3.00
TT38 Jeff Garcia 1.50 4.00
TT39 Jeremy Shockey 1.50 4.00
TT40 Jerome Bettis 2.00 5.00
TT41 Jerry Rice 4.00 10.00
TT42 Jevon Kearse 1.50 4.00
TT43 Joey Harrington 1.50 4.00
TT44 Josh McCown 1.50 4.00
TT45 Julius Peppers 1.50 4.00
TT46 Kendrell Bell 1.25 3.00
TT47 Kerry Collins 1.50 4.00
TT48 Keyshawn Johnson 1.50 4.00
TT49 Koren Robinson 1.25 3.00
TT50 Kurt Warner 2.00 5.00
TT51 Kyle Boller 1.50 4.00
TT52 LaDainian Tomlinson 2.00 5.00
TT53 LaVar Arrington 1.50 4.00
TT54 Laveranues Coles 1.25 3.00
TT55 Marc Bulger 1.50 4.00
TT56 Marcel Shipp 1.25 3.00
TT57 Mark Brunell 1.50 4.00
TT58 Marshall Faulk 2.00 5.00
TT59 Marvin Harrison 2.00 5.00
TT60 Matt Hasselbeck 1.50 4.00
TT61 Michael Bennett 1.50 4.00
TT62 Michael Strahan 2.00 5.00
TT63 Michael Vick 2.50 6.00
TT64 Patrick Ramsey 1.50 4.00
TT65 Peerless Price 1.25 3.00
TT66 Peter Warrick 1.50 4.00
TT67 Peyton Manning 4.00 10.00
TT68 Plaxico Burress 1.50 4.00
TT69 Priest Holmes 2.00 5.00
TT70 Quincy Carter 1.25 3.00
TT71 Randy Moss 2.00 5.00
TT72 Ray Lewis 2.00 5.00
TT73 Reggie Wayne 2.00 5.00
TT74 Rex Grossman 1.50 4.00
TT75 Rich Gannon 1.50 4.00
TT76 Ricky Williams 1.50 4.00
TT77 Rod Smith 1.50 4.00
TT78 Roy Williams S 1.50 4.00
TT79 Santana Moss 1.50 4.00
TT80 Shaun Alexander 1.50 4.00
TT81 Stephen Davis 1.50 4.00
TT82 T.J. Duckett 1.50 4.00
TT83 Terence Newman 1.50 4.00
TT84 Terrell Owens 2.00 5.00
TT85 Terrell Suggs 1.50 4.00
TT86 Tiki Barber 2.00 5.00
TT87 Tim Brown 2.00 5.00
TT88 Tom Brady 4.00 10.00
TT89 Tony Gonzalez 2.00 5.00
TT90 Torry Holt 1.50 4.00
TT91 Travis Henry 1.25 3.00
TT92 Trent Green 1.50 4.00
TT93 Warrick Dunn 1.50 4.00
TT94 Zach Thomas 2.00 5.00
TT95 Barry Sanders 4.00 10.00
TT96 Dan Marino 5.00 12.00
TT97 Deion Sanders 2.00 5.00
TT98 Joe Montana 6.00 15.00
TT99 John Elway 4.00 10.00
TT100 Warren Moon 2.00 5.00

2004 Absolute Memorabilia Tools of the Trade Material Jersey

JERSEY PRINT RUN 100 SER.#'d SETS
UNPRICED PRIME SPEC.PRINT RUN 1 SET
UNPRICED SPECTRUM PRINT RUN 10 SETS
TT1 Aaron Brooks 4.00 10.00
TT2 Ahman Green 4.00 10.00
TT3 Andre Johnson 5.00 12.00
TT4 Anquan Boldin 5.00 12.00
TT5 Anthony Thomas 4.00 10.00
TT6 Antwaan Randle El 4.00 10.00
TT7 Ashley Lelie 3.00 8.00
TT8 Brad Johnson 4.00 10.00
TT9 Brett Favre 12.00 30.00
TT10 Brian Urlacher 5.00 12.00
TT11 Byron Leftwich/50* 4.00 10.00
TT11A Byron Leftwich AU/50* 12.00 30.00
TT12 Chad Johnson AU 15.00 40.00
TT13 Chad Pennington 5.00 12.00
TT14 Charles Rogers 3.00 8.00
TT15 Charles Woodson 5.00 12.00
TT16 Chris Chambers AU 12.00 30.00
TT17 Clinton Portis 5.00 12.00
TT18 Corey Dillon 4.00 10.00
TT19 Curtis Martin 5.00 12.00
TT20 Dante Hall 4.00 10.00
TT21 Daunte Culpepper 4.00 10.00
TT22 David Boston 3.00 8.00
TT23 David Carr/75* 3.00 8.00
TT23A David Carr AU/25* 12.00 30.00
TT24 Deuce McAllister 4.00 10.00
TT25 Donovan McNabb 5.00 12.00
TT26 Donte Stallworth 3.00 8.00
TT27 Drew Bledsoe 5.00 12.00
TT28 Eddie George 4.00 10.00
TT29 Edgerrin James 4.00 10.00
TT30 Emmitt Smith 12.00 30.00
TT31 Eric Moulds 4.00 10.00
TT32 Fred Taylor 4.00 10.00
TT33 Hines Ward AU 30.00 60.00
TT34 Isaac Bruce 4.00 10.00
TT35 Jake Plummer 4.00 10.00
TT36 Jamal Lewis 4.00 10.00
TT37 Javon Walker 3.00 8.00
TT38 Jeff Garcia 4.00 10.00
TT39 Jeremy Shockey 4.00 10.00
TT40 Jerome Bettis 5.00 12.00
TT41 Jerry Rice 10.00 25.00
TT42 Jevon Kearse 4.00 10.00
TT43 Joey Harrington 4.00 10.00
TT44 Josh McCown 4.00 10.00
TT45 Julius Peppers 4.00 10.00
TT46 Kendrell Bell 3.00 8.00
TT47 Kerry Collins 4.00 10.00
TT48 Keyshawn Johnson 4.00 10.00
TT49 Koren Robinson 3.00 8.00
TT50 Kurt Warner 5.00 12.00
TT51 Kyle Boller AU 12.00 30.00
TT52 LaDainian Tomlinson 5.00 12.00
TT53 LaVar Arrington 4.00 10.00
TT54 Laveranues Coles 3.00 8.00
TT55 Marc Bulger 4.00 10.00
TT56 Marcel Shipp 3.00 8.00
TT57 Mark Brunell 4.00 10.00

TT58 Marshall Faulk 5.00 12.00
TT59 Marvin Harrison 5.00 12.00
TT60 Matt Hasselbeck AU 12.00 30.00
TT61 Michael Bennett 4.00 10.00
TT62 Michael Strahan 5.00 12.00
TT63 Michael Vick 6.00 15.00
TT64 Patrick Ramsey 4.00 10.00
TT65 Peerless Price 3.00 8.00
TT66 Peter Warrick 4.00 10.00
TT67 Peyton Manning 10.00 25.00
TT68 Plaxico Burress 4.00 10.00
TT69 Priest Holmes 5.00 12.00
TT70 Quincy Carter 3.00 8.00
TT71 Randy Moss 5.00 12.00
TT72 Ray Lewis 5.00 12.00
TT73 Reggie Wayne 5.00 12.00
TT74 Rex Grossman AU 12.00 30.00
TT75 Rich Gannon 4.00 10.00
TT76 Ricky Williams 4.00 10.00
TT77 Rod Smith 4.00 10.00
TT78 Roy Williams S AU 12.00 30.00
TT79 Santana Moss 4.00 10.00
TT80 Shaun Alexander/50* 4.00 10.00
TT80A Shaun Alexander AU/50* 12.00 30.00
TT81 Stephen Davis 4.00 10.00
TT82 T.J. Duckett 4.00 10.00
TT83 Terence Newman 4.00 10.00
TT84 Terrell Owens 5.00 12.00
TT85 Terrell Suggs 4.00 10.00
TT86 Tiki Barber 5.00 12.00
TT87 Tim Brown 5.00 12.00
TT88 Tom Brady 10.00 25.00
TT89 Tony Gonzalez 5.00 12.00
TT90 Torry Holt/50* 4.00 10.00
TT90A Torry Holt AU/50*
TT91 Travis Henry 3.00 8.00
TT92 Trent Green/25* 6.00 15.00
TT92A Trent Green AU/75* 12.00 30.00
TT93 Warrick Dunn 4.00 10.00
TT94 Zach Thomas 5.00 12.00
TT95 Barry Sanders 12.00 30.00
TT96 Dan Marino 15.00 40.00
TT97 Deion Sanders 10.00 25.00
TT98 Joe Montana/50* 15.00 40.00
TT98A Joe Montana AU/50* 100.00 175.00
TT99 John Elway 15.00 40.00
TT100 Warren Moon/50* 6.00 15.00
TT100A Warren Moon AU/50* 15.00 40.00

2004 Absolute Memorabilia Tools of the Trade Material Jersey Prime

*UNSIGNED PRIME: .8X TO 2X BASIC JSY
COMMON AUTO 20.00 50.00
AUTO SEMISTARS 25.00 60.00
AUTO UNL.STARS 30.00 80.00
PRIME PRINT RUN 25 SER.#'d SETS
TT25 Donovan McNabb AU 40.00 100.00
TT41 Jerry Rice AU 125.00 250.00
TT63 Michael Vick AU 60.00 100.00
TT67 Peyton Manning AU 75.00 150.00
TT88 Tom Brady AU 150.00 300.00
TT95 Barry Sanders AU 100.00 200.00
TT96 Dan Marino AU 125.00 250.00
TT97 Deion Sanders AU 60.00 120.00
TT98 Joe Montana AU 125.00 250.00
TT99 John Elway AU 100.00 200.00

2004 Absolute Memorabilia Tools of the Trade Material Combos

*UNSIGNED COMBO: .5X TO 1.2X BASIC JSY
STATED PRINT RUN 75 SER.#'d SETS
UNPRICED PRIME PRINT RUN 10 SETS
TT13 Chad Pennington Jsy-Pants/50 6.00 15.00
TT13A Chad Pennington Jsy-Pants AU/25 15.00 40.00
TT20 Dante Hall Jsy-Pants AU 12.00 30.00
TT23 David Carr Jsy-Jsy/50* 4.00 10.00
TT23A David Carr Jsy-Jsy AU/25 10.00 25.00
TT27 Drew Bledsoe Jsy-Jsy/25* 8.00 20.00
TT27A Drew Bledsoe Jsy-Jsy AU/50 15.00 40.00
TT28 Eddie George Jsy-Pants/50 5.00 12.00
TT28A Eddie George Jsy-Pants AU/25 12.00 30.00
TT44 Josh McCown Jsy-Pants AU 12.00 30.00
TT48 Keyshawn Johnson Jsy-Shoe AU 12.00 30.00
TT79 Santana Moss Jsy-Pants AU 12.00 30.00
TT86 Tiki Barber Jsy-Pants AU 15.00 40.00
TT90A Torry Holt Jsy-Pants AU/50* 12.00 30.00
TT98 Joe Montana Jsy-Shoe/50 15.00 40.00
TT98A Joe Montana Jsy-Shoe AU/25 125.00 225.00

2004 Absolute Memorabilia Tools of the Trade Material Quads

*UNSIGNED QUADS: 1.5X TO 4X SINGLE JSYs
STATED PRINT RUN 25 SER.#'d SETS
UNPRICED PRIME PRINT RUN 1 SET
TT44 Josh McCown J-J-P-F AU 20.00 50.00
TT79 Santana Moss J-P-F-H AU 25.00 60.00
TT90 Torry Holt J-P-F-H 25.00 60.00
TT96 Dan Marino J-J-P-S AU 175.00 300.00

2004 Absolute Memorabilia Tools of the Trade Material Trios

*TRIOS: .8X TO 2X SINGLE JSY 100
*TRIOS: .6X TO 1.5X SINGLE JSY 50
STATED PRINT RUN 50 SER.#'d SETS
UNPRICED PRIME PRINT RUN 5 SET

2005 Absolute Memorabilia

This 234-card set was released in August, 2005. The set was issued in four-card hobby packs with an $40 SRP which also came four packs to a box. Cards numbered 1-150 feature veteran players in team alphabetical order while cards numbered 151-234 all feature rookies. In that rookie groups cards numbered 151-205 are printed to a stated print run of 999 serial numbered sets and cards numbered 206-234 (which included a player-worn swatch) were issued to a stated print run of 750 serial numbered sets. A way to differentiate the hobby cards from the retail version is that the hobby cards were printed on holofoil stock.

151-205 PRINT RUN 999 SER.#'d SETS
206-234 PRINT RUN 750 SER.#'d SETS
UNPRICED PLATINUM PRINT RUN 1 SET
HOBBY PRINTED ON HOLOFOIL STOCK
1 Anquan Boldin 1.00 2.50
2 Kurt Warner 1.25 3.00
3 Josh McCown 1.00 2.50
4 Larry Fitzgerald 1.25 3.00
5 Alge Crumpler 1.00 2.50
6 Michael Vick 1.25 3.00
7 Peerless Price .75 2.00
8 T.J. Duckett .75 2.00
9 Warrick Dunn 1.00 2.50
10 Deion Sanders 1.50 4.00
11 Derrick Mason 1.00 2.50
12 Ed Reed 1.00 2.50
13 Jamal Lewis 1.00 2.50
14 Kyle Boller 1.00 2.50
15 Ray Lewis 1.25 3.00
16 Todd Heap 1.00 2.50
17 Eric Moulds .75 2.00
18 J.P. Losman .75 2.00
19 Lee Evans 1.00 2.50
20 Travis Henry .75 2.00
21 Willis McGahee 1.25 3.00
22 DeShaun Foster 1.00 2.50
23 Jake Delhomme 1.00 2.50
24 Julius Peppers 1.00 2.50
25 Keary Colbert .75 2.00
26 Stephen Davis 1.00 2.50
27 Steve Smith 1.25 3.00
28 Brian Urlacher 1.25 3.00
29 Muhsin Muhammad 1.00 2.50
30 Thomas Jones 1.25 3.00
31 Rex Grossman 1.00 2.50
32 Carson Palmer 1.25 3.00
33 Chad Johnson 1.00 2.50
34 Peter Warrick .75 2.00
35 Rudi Johnson 1.00 2.50
36 T.J. Houshmandzadeh 1.00 2.50
37 Antonio Bryant .75 2.00
38 Dennis Northcutt .75 2.00
39 Trent Dilfer 1.00 2.50
40 Kellen Winslow 1.00 2.50
41 Lee Suggs .75 2.00
42 Reuben Droughns .75 2.00
43 Drew Bledsoe 1.25 3.00
44 Jason Witten 1.25 3.00
45 Julius Jones .75 2.00
46 Keyshawn Johnson 1.00 2.50
47 Terence Newman .75 2.00
48 Roy Williams S .75 2.00
49 Jake Plummer 1.00 2.50
50 Rod Smith 1.00 2.50
51 Ashley Lelie .75 2.00
52 Tatum Bell .75 2.00
53 Charles Rogers .75 2.00
54 Joey Harrington 1.00 2.50
55 Kevin Jones .75 2.00
56 Roy Williams WR 1.00 2.50
57 Ahman Green 1.00 2.50
58 Brett Favre 3.00 8.00
59 Donald Driver 1.25 3.00
60 Javon Walker .75 2.00
61 Andre Johnson 1.25 3.00
62 David Carr .75 2.00
63 Domanick Davis .75 2.00
64 Brandon Stokley .75 2.00
65 Dallas Clark 1.00 2.50
66 Edgerrin James 1.00 2.50
67 Marvin Harrison 1.25 3.00
68 Peyton Manning 2.50 6.00
69 Reggie Wayne 1.25 3.00
70 Reggie Williams .75 2.00
71 Byron Leftwich 1.00 2.50
72 Fred Taylor 1.00 2.50
73 Jimmy Smith 1.00 2.50
74 Priest Holmes 1.00 2.50
75 Tony Gonzalez 1.00 2.50
76 Dante Hall .75 2.00
77 Trent Green 1.00 2.50
78 Eddie Kennison .75 2.00
79 A.J. Feeley .75 2.00
80 Chris Chambers 1.00 2.50
81 Zach Thomas 1.25 3.00
82 Junior Seau 1.25 3.00
83 Marty Booker .75 2.00
84 Daunte Culpepper 1.00 2.50
85 Nate Burleson .75 2.00
86 Michael Bennett 1.00 2.50
87 Onterrio Smith .75 2.00
88 Corey Dillon 1.00 2.50
89 Deion Branch .75 2.00
90 Tom Brady 2.50 6.00
91 Troy Brown .75 2.00
92 Tedy Bruschi 1.25 3.00
93 Aaron Brooks .75 2.00
94 Donte Stallworth .75 2.00
95 Joe Horn 1.00 2.50
96 Deuce McAllister 1.00 2.50
97 Amani Toomer 1.00 2.50
98 Plaxico Burress 1.00 2.50
99 Jeremy Shockey 1.25 3.00
100 Eli Manning 2.00 5.00
101 Tiki Barber 1.25 3.00
102 Chad Pennington 1.25 3.00
103 Laveranues Coles .75 2.00
104 Curtis Martin 1.25 3.00
105 Justin McCareins .75 2.00
106 Wayne Chrebet 1.00 2.50
107 Jerry Porter .75 2.00
108 LaMont Jordan 1.00 2.50
109 Randy Moss 1.25 3.00
110 Kerry Collins 1.00 2.50
111 Charles Woodson 1.25 3.00
112 Brian Westbrook 1.00 2.50
113 Donovan McNabb 1.25 3.00
114 Jevon Kearse 1.00 2.50
115 Terrell Owens 1.25 3.00
116 Ben Roethlisberger 2.00 5.00
117 Hines Ward 1.25 3.00
118 Duce Staley 1.00 2.50
119 Jerome Bettis 1.25 3.00
120 Antonio Gates 1.25 3.00
121 Eric Parker .75 2.00
122 Keenan McCardell 1.00 2.50
123 Drew Brees 1.25 3.00
124 LaDainian Tomlinson 1.25 3.00
125 Brandon Lloyd .75 2.00
126 Kevan Barlow .75 2.00
127 Tim Rattay .75 2.00
128 Koren Robinson .75 2.00
129 Darrell Jackson .75 2.00
130 Jerry Rice 2.50 6.00
131 Matt Hasselbeck 1.00 2.50
132 Shaun Alexander 1.00 2.50
133 Isaac Bruce 1.00 2.50
134 Marc Bulger 1.00 2.50
135 Marshall Faulk 1.25 3.00
136 Steven Jackson 1.25 3.00
137 Torry Holt 1.00 2.50
138 Brian Griese 1.00 2.50
139 Michael Clayton .75 2.00
140 Michael Pittman .75 2.00
141 Mike Alstott 1.00 2.50
142 Chris Brown .75 2.00
143 Drew Bennett 1.00 2.50
144 Steve McNair 1.25 3.00
145 Clinton Portis 1.00 2.50
146 LaVar Arrington 1.00 2.50
147 Santana Moss 1.00 2.50
148 Patrick Ramsey 1.00 2.50
149 Rod Gardner .75 2.00
150 Sean Taylor 1.25 3.00
151 DeMarcus Ware RC 5.00 12.00
152 Shawne Merriman RC 2.50 6.00
153 Thomas Davis RC 1.50 4.00
154 Derrick Johnson RC 2.00 5.00
155 Travis Johnson RC 1.50 4.00
156 David Pollack RC 2.00 5.00
157 Erasmus James RC 2.00 5.00
158 Marcus Spears RC 2.00 5.00
159 Fabian Washington RC 2.00 5.00
160 Marlin Jackson RC 1.50 4.00
161 Cedric Benson RC 2.50 6.00
162 Matt Roth RC 2.00 5.00
163 Dan Cody RC 2.00 5.00
164 Bryant McFadden RC 2.00 5.00
165 Chris Henry RC 2.50 6.00
166 Brandon Jones RC 2.00 5.00
167 Marion Barber RC 2.50 6.00
168 Brandon Jacobs RC 3.00 8.00
169 Jerome Mathis RC 2.50 6.00
170 Craphonso Thorpe RC 1.50 4.00
171 Alvin Pearman RC 1.50 4.00
172 Darren Sproles RC 2.50 6.00
173 Fred Gibson RC 2.00 5.00
174 Roydell Williams RC 2.00 5.00
175 Airese Currie RC 1.50 4.00
176 Damien Nash RC 2.00 5.00
177 Dan Orlovsky RC 2.50 6.00
178 Adrian McPherson RC 1.50 4.00
179 Larry Brackins RC 1.50 4.00
180 Aaron Rodgers RC 30.00 60.00
181 Cedric Houston RC 2.50 6.00
182 Mike Williams 2.50 6.00
183 Heath Miller RC 3.00 8.00
184 Dante Ridgeway RC 1.50 4.00
185 Craig Bragg RC 1.50 4.00
186 Deandra Cobb RC 1.50 4.00
187 Derek Anderson RC 2.00 5.00
188 Paris Warren RC 2.00 5.00
189 David Greene RC 1.50 4.00
190 Lionel Gates RC 1.50 4.00
191 Anthony Davis RC 1.50 4.00
192 Noah Herron RC 1.50 4.00
193 Ryan Fitzpatrick RC 4.00 10.00
194 J.R. Russell RC 1.50 4.00
195 Jason White RC 2.50 6.00
196 Kay-Jay Harris RC 1.50 4.00
197 Steve Savoy RC 1.50 4.00
198 T.A. McLendon RC 1.50 4.00
199 Taylor Stubblefield RC 1.50 4.00
200 Josh Davis RC 1.50 4.00
201 Shaun Cody RC 2.00 5.00
202 Rasheed Marshall RC 2.00 5.00
203 Chad Owens RC 2.00 5.00
204 Tab Perry RC 1.50 4.00
205 James Kilian RC 1.50 4.00
206 Adam Jones RPM RC 2.50 6.00
207 Alex Smith QB RPM RC 6.00 15.00
208 Antrel Rolle RPM RC 4.00 10.00
209 Andrew Walter RPM RC 3.00 8.00
210 Braylon Edwards RPM RC 5.00 12.00
211 Cadillac Williams RPM RC 4.00 10.00
212 Carlos Rogers RPM RC 4.00 10.00
213 Charlie Frye RPM RC 4.00 10.00
214 Ciatrick Fason RPM RC 2.50 6.00
215 Courtney Roby RPM RC 3.00 8.00
216 Eric Shelton RPM RC 2.50 6.00
217 Frank Gore RPM RC 6.00 15.00
218 J.J. Arrington RPM RC 3.00 8.00
219 Kyle Orton RPM RC 4.00 10.00
220 Jason Campbell RPM RC 5.00 12.00
221 Mark Bradley RPM RC 2.50 6.00
222 Mark Clayton RPM RC 4.00 10.00
223 Matt Jones RPM RC 4.00 10.00
224 Maurice Clarett RPM 3.00 8.00
225 Reggie Brown RPM RC 2.50 6.00
226 Ronnie Brown RPM RC 5.00 12.00
227 Roddy White RPM RC 5.00 12.00
228 Ryan Moats RPM RC 3.00 8.00
229 Roscoe Parrish RPM RC 2.50 6.00
230 Stefan LeFors RPM RC 2.50 6.00
231 Terrence Murphy RPM RC 2.50 6.00
232 Troy Williamson RPM RC 3.00 8.00
233 Vernand Morency RPM RC 3.00 8.00
234 Vincent Jackson RPM RC 5.00 12.00

2005 Absolute Memorabilia Retail

COMPLETE SET (150) 15.00 30.00
*VETERANS: .1X TO .25X BASIC CARDS
*ROOKIES 151-205: .2X TO .5X BASIC CARDS
RETAIL PRINTED ON WHITE STOCK

2005 Absolute Memorabilia Spectrum Black

*VETERANS: 1X TO 2.5X BASIC CARDS
*ROOKIES: .6X TO 1.5X BASIC CARDS
BLACK STATED ODDS 1:12 RETAIL

2005 Absolute Memorabilia Spectrum Blue

*VETERANS: .8X TO 2X BASIC CARDS
*ROOKIES: .5X TO 1.2X BASIC CARDS
BLUE STATED ODDS 1:8 RETAIL
*RPM ROOKIES: .5X TO 1.2X BASIC CARDS
RPM PRINT RUN 75 SER.#'d SETS

2005 Absolute Memorabilia Spectrum Gold

*VETS: 2.5X TO 6X BASIC CARDS
*ROOKIES: 1X TO 2.5X BASIC CARDS
STATED PRINT RUN 25 SER.#'d SETS

2005 Absolute Memorabilia Spectrum Platinum

UNPRICED PLATINUM SER.#'d OF 1

2005 Absolute Memorabilia Spectrum Red

*VETERANS: .8X TO 2X BASIC CARDS
*ROOKIES: .5X TO 1.2X BASIC CARDS
RED STATED ODDS 1:8 RETAIL

2005 Absolute Memorabilia Spectrum Silver

*VETERANS: 1.2X TO 3X BASIC CARDS
*ROOKIES: .8X TO 2X BASIC CARDS
STATED PRINT RUN 100 SER.#'d SETS

2005 Absolute Memorabilia Absolute Heroes Silver

SILVER PRINT RUN 250 SER.#'d SETS
*GOLD/150: .5X TO 1.2X SILVER
*SPECTRUM/25: 1.2X TO 3X SILVER
1 Bo Jackson 4.00 10.00
2 Brian Urlacher 2.50 6.00
3 Brian Westbrook 2.00 5.00
4 Dan Marino 8.00 20.00
5 Domanick Davis 1.50 4.00
6 Donovan McNabb 2.50 6.00
7 Edgerrin James 2.00 5.00
8 Hines Ward 2.50 6.00
9 Jake Delhomme 2.00 5.00
10 Jamal Lewis 2.00 5.00
11 Jeremy Shockey 2.50 6.00
12 Jerry Rice 5.00 12.00
13 Joe Montana 8.00 20.00
14 LaDainian Tomlinson 2.50 6.00
15 Larry Fitzgerald 2.50 6.00
16 Marvin Harrison 2.50 6.00
17 Matt Hasselbeck 2.00 5.00
18 Michael Clayton 1.50 4.00
19 Michael Irvin 3.00 8.00
20 Roy Williams S 1.50 4.00
21 Steve Young 4.00 10.00
22 Steven Jackson 2.50 6.00
23 Terrell Davis 3.00 8.00
24 Troy Aikman 4.00 10.00
25 Walter Payton 8.00 20.00

2005 Absolute Memorabilia Absolute Heroes Material

STATED PRINT RUN 150 SER.#'d SETS
*PRIME/25: 1X TO 2.5X BASIC JSY/150
PRIME PRINT RUN 25 SER.#'d SETS
UNPRICED SPECTRUM PRINT RUN 1 SET
1 Bo Jackson 6.00 15.00
2 Brian Urlacher 4.00 10.00
3 Brian Westbrook 3.00 8.00
4 Dan Marino 12.00 30.00
5 Domanick Davis 2.50 6.00
6 Donovan McNabb 4.00 10.00
7 Edgerrin James 3.00 8.00
8 Hines Ward 4.00 10.00
9 Jake Delhomme 3.00 8.00
10 Jamal Lewis 3.00 8.00
11 Jeremy Shockey 4.00 10.00
12 Jerry Rice 8.00 20.00
13 Joe Montana 12.00 30.00
14 LaDainian Tomlinson 4.00 10.00
15 Larry Fitzgerald 4.00 10.00
16 Marvin Harrison 4.00 10.00
17 Matt Hasselbeck 3.00 8.00
18 Michael Clayton 2.50 6.00
19 Michael Irvin 4.00 10.00
20 Roy Williams S 2.50 6.00
21 Steve Young 6.00 15.00
22 Steven Jackson 4.00 10.00
23 Terrell Davis 4.00 10.00
24 Troy Aikman 6.00 15.00
25 Walter Payton 12.00 30.00

2005 Absolute Memorabilia Absolute Patches

STATED PRINT RUN 25 SER.#'d SETS
UNPRICED SPECTRUM PRINT RUN 1
1 Barry Sanders 40.00 100.00
2 Ben Roethlisberger 40.00 100.00
3 Bo Jackson 40.00 100.00
4 Brett Favre 60.00 150.00
5 Brian Urlacher 30.00 80.00
6 Chad Pennington 25.00 60.00
7 Dan Marino 60.00 150.00
8 Donovan McNabb 25.00 60.00
9 Edgerrin James 20.00 50.00
10 Eli Manning 40.00 100.00
11 Jerry Rice 50.00 125.00
12 Joe Montana 60.00 150.00
13 John Elway 50.00 125.00
14 Julius Jones 15.00 40.00
15 Kevin Jones 15.00 40.00
16 LaDainian Tomlinson 25.00 60.00
17 Michael Irvin 25.00 60.00
18 Peyton Manning 50.00 125.00
19 Priest Holmes 20.00 50.00
20 Randy Moss 25.00 60.00
21 Steve Young 40.00 100.00
22 Terrell Davis 25.00 60.00
23 Tom Brady 50.00 125.00
24 Troy Aikman 40.00 100.00
25 Walter Payton 80.00 200.00

2005 Absolute Memorabilia Canton Absolutes Silver

SILVER PRINT RUN 250 SER.#'d SETS
*GOLD/150: .5X TO 1.2X SILVER
*SPECTRUM/25: 1.2X TO 3X SILVER
1 Chad Pennington 2.50 6.00
2 Curtis Martin 2.50 6.00
3 Dan Marino 8.00 20.00
4 David Carr 1.50 4.00
5 Deion Sanders 3.00 8.00
6 Donovan McNabb 2.50 6.00
7 Drew Bledsoe 2.50 6.00
8 Earl Campbell 3.00 8.00
9 Eli Manning 4.00 10.00
10 Jerry Rice 5.00 12.00
11 Joe Montana 8.00 20.00
12 Joe Namath 5.00 12.00
13 John Elway 6.00 15.00
14 Junior Seau 2.50 6.00
15 Marvin Harrison 2.50 6.00
16 Michael Irvin 3.00 8.00
17 Michael Vick 2.50 6.00
18 Peyton Manning 5.00 12.00
19 Priest Holmes 2.00 5.00
20 Randy Moss 2.50 6.00
21 Ray Lewis 2.50 6.00
22 Steve McNair 2.50 6.00
23 Steve Young 4.00 10.00
24 Troy Aikman 4.00 10.00
25 Walter Payton 8.00 20.00

2005 Absolute Memorabilia Canton Absolutes Jersey Bronze

BRONZE PRINT RUN 150 SER.#'d SETS
*PRIME/25: 1X TO 2.5X BASIC JSY/150
UNPRICED SPECTRUM PRINT RUN 1
1 Chad Pennington 4.00 10.00
2 Curtis Martin 4.00 10.00
3 Dan Marino 12.00 30.00
4 David Carr 2.50 6.00
5 Deion Sanders 5.00 12.00
6 Donovan McNabb 4.00 10.00
7 Drew Bledsoe 4.00 10.00
8 Earl Campbell 5.00 12.00
9 Eli Manning 6.00 15.00
10 Jerry Rice 8.00 20.00
11 Joe Montana 12.00 30.00
12 Joe Namath 8.00 20.00
13 John Elway 10.00 25.00
14 Junior Seau 4.00 10.00
15 Marvin Harrison 4.00 10.00
16 Michael Irvin 4.00 10.00
17 Michael Vick 4.00 10.00
18 Peyton Manning 8.00 20.00
19 Priest Holmes 3.00 8.00
20 Randy Moss 4.00 10.00
21 Ray Lewis 4.00 10.00
22 Steve McNair 4.00 10.00
23 Steve Young 6.00 15.00
24 Troy Aikman 6.00 15.00
25 Walter Payton 12.00 30.00

2005 Absolute Memorabilia Leather

LEATHER PRINT RUN 250 SER.#'d SETS
*LACES/25: .8X TO 2X LEATHER/250
RANDOM INSERTS IN RETAIL PACKS
1 LaDainian Tomlinson 4.00 10.00
2 Rod Smith 3.00 8.00
3 Tim Brown 4.00 10.00
4 Jerry Porter 2.50 6.00
5 Tiki Barber 4.00 10.00
6 Amani Toomer 3.00 8.00
7 Eric Moulds 2.50 6.00
8 Michael Vick 4.00 10.00
9 Josh McCown 3.00 8.00
10 Anquan Boldin 3.00 8.00
11 Shaun Alexander 3.00 8.00
12 Darrell Jackson 2.50 6.00
13 Terrell Owens 4.00 10.00
14 Brian Urlacher 4.00 10.00
15 Zach Thomas 4.00 10.00
16 Chris Chambers 3.00 8.00
17 Keyshawn Johnson 3.00 8.00
18 Chad Johnson 3.00 8.00
19 Corey Dillon 3.00 8.00
20 Peyton Manning 8.00 20.00
21 Marvin Harrison 4.00 10.00
22 LaVar Arrington 3.00 8.00
23 Tom Brady 8.00 20.00
24 Priest Holmes 3.00 8.00
25 Trent Green 3.00 8.00
26 Tony Gonzalez 3.00 8.00
27 Jerry Rice 8.00 20.00
28 Donovan McNabb 4.00 10.00
29 Torry Holt 3.00 8.00
30 Kurt Warner 4.00 10.00
31 Aaron Brooks 2.50 6.00
32 Deuce McAllister 3.00 8.00
33 Joe Horn 3.00 8.00
34 Reggie Wayne 4.00 10.00
35 Charles Woodson 4.00 10.00
36 Curtis Martin 4.00 10.00
37 Duce Staley 3.00 8.00
38 Daunte Culpepper 3.00 8.00
39 Ray Lewis 4.00 10.00
40 Drew Brees 4.00 10.00
41 Larry Fitzgerald 4.00 10.00
42 Hines Ward 4.00 10.00
43 Steve McNair 4.00 10.00
44 Marshall Faulk 4.00 10.00
45 Isaac Bruce 3.00 8.00
46 Freddie Mitchell 2.50 6.00
47 Travis Henry 2.50 6.00
48 Muhsin Muhammad 3.00 8.00
49 Jimmy Smith 3.00 8.00
50 Jerome Bettis 6.00 15.00

2005 Absolute Memorabilia Marks of Fame Silver

SILVER PRINT RUN 250 SER.#'d SETS
*GOLD/150: .5X TO 1.2X SILVER/250
*SPECTRUM/25: 1.2X TO 3X SILVER/250
1 Antonio Gates 2.50 6.00
2 Ben Roethlisberger 4.00 10.00
3 Brian Westbrook 2.00 5.00
4 Chad Johnson 2.00 5.00
5 Domanick Davis 1.50 4.00
6 Hines Ward 2.50 6.00
7 Rudi Johnson 2.00 5.00
8 Chris Brown 1.50 4.00
9 Tatum Bell 1.50 4.00
10 Michael Vick 2.50 6.00
11 Tom Brady 5.00 12.00
12 Willis McGahee 2.50 6.00
13 Ickey Woods 2.00 5.00
14 Earl Campbell 3.00 8.00
15 Joe Namath 5.00 12.00
16 Alex Smith QB 2.00 5.00
17 Troy Williamson 1.00 2.50
18 Ronnie Brown 1.50 4.00
19 Cadillac Williams 1.25 3.00
20 J.J. Arrington 1.00 2.50
21 Jason Campbell 1.50 4.00
22 Mark Clayton 1.25 3.00
23 Reggie Brown .75 2.00
24 Roscoe Parrish .75 2.00
25 Roddy White 1.50 4.00

2005 Absolute Memorabilia Marks of Fame Material Prime

PRIME PRINT RUN 25 SER.#'d SETS
*BASIC JSY/150: .15X TO .4X PRIME/25
UNPRICED SPECTRUM PRINT RUN 1 SET
1 Antonio Gates 10.00 25.00
2 Ben Roethlisberger 15.00 40.00
3 Brian Westbrook 8.00 20.00
4 Chad Johnson 8.00 20.00
5 Domanick Davis 6.00 15.00
6 Hines Ward 10.00 25.00
7 Rudi Johnson 8.00 20.00
8 Chris Brown 6.00 15.00
9 Tatum Bell 6.00 15.00
10 Michael Vick 10.00 25.00
11 Tom Brady 20.00 50.00
12 Willis McGahee 10.00 25.00
13 Ickey Woods 8.00 20.00
14 Earl Campbell 12.00 30.00
15 Joe Namath 20.00 50.00
16 Alex Smith QB 12.00 30.00
17 Troy Williamson 6.00 15.00
18 Ronnie Brown 10.00 25.00
19 Cadillac Williams 8.00 20.00
20 J.J. Arrington 6.00 15.00
21 Jason Campbell 10.00 25.00
22 Mark Clayton 8.00 20.00
23 Reggie Brown 5.00 12.00
24 Roscoe Parrish 5.00 12.00
25 Roddy White 10.00 25.00

2005 Absolute Memorabilia Marks of Fame Material Autographs

STATED PRINT RUN 15-300
*PRIME/25: .6X TO 1.5X BASE AU/150-300
*PRIME/25: .5X TO 1.2X BASE AU/50-100
PRIME PRINT RUN 10-25
UNPRICED PRIME SPECT.PRINT RUN 1
1 Antonio Gates/300 12.00 30.00
2 Ben Roethlisberger/50 75.00 150.00
3 Brian Westbrook/200 10.00 25.00
4 Chad Johnson/150 10.00 25.00
5 Domanick Davis/300 8.00 20.00
6 Hines Ward/150 40.00 80.00
7 Rudi Johnson/250 10.00 25.00
8 Chris Brown/250 8.00 20.00
9 Tatum Bell/300 8.00 20.00
10 Michael Vick/100 40.00 80.00
11 Tom Brady/15 125.00 250.00
12 Willis McGahee/100 12.00 30.00
13 Ickey Woods/300 8.00 20.00
14 Earl Campbell/100 15.00 40.00
15 Joe Namath/150 40.00 100.00
16 Alex Smith QB/150 30.00 60.00
17 Troy Williamson/250 8.00 20.00
18 Ronnie Brown/300 12.00 30.00
19 Cadillac Williams/300 10.00 25.00
20 J.J. Arrington/300 8.00 20.00
21 Jason Campbell/300 12.00 30.00
22 Mark Clayton/300 8.00 20.00
23 Reggie Brown/200 6.00 15.00
24 Roscoe Parrish/200 6.00 15.00
25 Roddy White/200 12.00 30.00

2005 Absolute Memorabilia National Treasures Jerseys

STATED PRINT RUN 50 SER.#'d SETS
*PRIME/25: .6X TO 1.5X BASIC JSY/50
UNPRICED SPECT.PRINT RUN 10
1 Joe Montana 40.00 100.00
Tom Brady
Troy Aikman
2 Steve Young 20.00 50.00
Michael Vick
Donovan McNabb
3 Barry Sanders 25.00 60.00
LaDainian Tomlinson
Kevin Jones
4 Dan Marino 40.00 100.00
Peyton Manning
Eli Manning
5 Daunte Culpepper 15.00 40.00
Steve McNair
Byron Leftwich
6 Marcus Allen 15.00 40.00
Priest Holmes
Edgerrin James
7 Bo Jackson 20.00 50.00
Jamal Lewis
Rudi Johnson
8 Eric Dickerson 15.00 40.00
Marshall Faulk
Steven Jackson
9 Earl Campbell 15.00 40.00
Eddie George
Domanick Davis
10 John Elway 40.00 100.00
Brett Favre
Tom Brady
11 Jerry Rice 30.00 80.00
Marvin Harrison
Torry Holt
12 Michael Irvin 15.00 40.00
Randy Moss
Terrell Owens
13 Joe Namath 25.00 60.00
Chad Pennington
Ben Roethlisberger
14 Trent Green 12.00 30.00
Marc Bulger
Matt Hasselbeck
15 Javon Walker 12.00 30.00
Roy Williams WR
Michael Clayton
16 Hines Ward 15.00 40.00
Chad Johnson
Andre Johnson
17 Ahman Green 12.00 30.00
Shaun Alexander
Deuce McAllister
18 Tony Dorsett 15.00 40.00
Julius Jones
Curtis Martin
19 David Carr 15.00 40.00
Carson Palmer
Kyle Boller
20 Jake Plummer 15.00 40.00
Jake Delhomme
Drew Brees
21 Ray Lewis 15.00 40.00
Brian Urlacher
Lavar Arrington
22 Corey Dillon 12.00 30.00
Willis McGahee
Brian Westbrook
23 John Riggins 15.00 40.00
Terrell Davis
Clinton Portis
24 Jim Brown 40.00 100.00
Walter Payton
Barry Sanders
25 Deion Sanders 20.00 50.00
Roy Williams
Terence Newman
26 Joe Montana 40.00 100.00
Jerry Rice
Steve Young
27 Troy Aikman 20.00 50.00
Tony Dorsett
Michael Irvin
28 Michael Vick 15.00 40.00
Donovan McNabb
Daunte Culpepper
29 John Elway 40.00 100.00
Dan Marino
Ben Roethlisberger
30 Joe Namath 40.00 100.00
Brett Favre
Peyton Manning

2005 Absolute Memorabilia Rookie Jerseys

STATED ODDS 1:8 SPECIAL RETAIL
1 Ronnie Brown 3.00 8.00
2 Troy Williamson 2.00 5.00
3 Carlos Rogers 2.50 6.00
4 Matt Jones 2.50 6.00
5 Jason Campbell 3.00 8.00
6 Roddy White 3.00 8.00
7 Terrence Murphy 1.50 4.00
8 Vincent Jackson 3.00 8.00
9 Charlie Frye 2.50 6.00
10 Ciatrick Fason 1.50 4.00

2005 Absolute Memorabilia Rookie Premiere Materials Oversize

*SINGLES: .6X TO 1.5X BASIC CARDS
STATED PRINT RUN 50 SER.#'d SETS

2005 Absolute Memorabilia Rookie Premiere Materials Triple Spectrum

*SINGLES: 1X TO 2.5X BASIC CARDS
STATED PRINT RUN 75 SER.#'d SETS

2005 Absolute Memorabilia Rookie Reflex Jersey Autographs

STATED PRINT RUN 100 SER.#'d ETS
1 Alex Smith QB 40.00 80.00
2 Braylon Edwards 25.00 60.00
3 Cadillac Williams 20.00 50.00
4 Charlie Frye 20.00 50.00
5 Ciatrick Fason 12.00 30.00
6 Courtney Roby 15.00 40.00
7 Frank Gore 30.00 80.00
8 Jason Campbell 25.00 60.00
9 Kyle Orton 20.00 50.00
10 Mark Bradley 12.00 30.00
11 Mark Clayton 15.00 40.00
12 Matt Jones 15.00 40.00
13 Reggie Brown 12.00 30.00
14 Roddy White 25.00 60.00
15 Ronnie Brown 25.00 60.00
16 Roscoe Parrish 12.00 30.00
17 Stefan LeFors 12.00 30.00
18 Terrence Murphy 12.00 30.00
19 Troy Williamson 15.00 40.00
20 Vincent Jackson 25.00 60.00

2005 Absolute Memorabilia Rookie Reflex Oversized Jersey

STATED PRINT RUN 25 SER.#'d SETS
*PRIME/10: .6X TO 1.5X BASIC INSERTS
1 Alex Smith QB 12.00 30.00
2 Braylon Edwards 10.00 25.00
3 Cadillac Williams 8.00 20.00
4 Charlie Frye 8.00 20.00
5 Ciatrick Fason 5.00 12.00
6 Courtney Roby 6.00 15.00
7 Frank Gore 12.00 30.00
8 Jason Campbell 10.00 25.00
9 Kyle Orton 8.00 20.00
10 Mark Bradley 5.00 12.00
11 Mark Clayton 8.00 20.00
12 Matt Jones 8.00 20.00
13 Reggie Brown 5.00 12.00
14 Roddy White 10.00 25.00
15 Ronnie Brown 10.00 25.00
16 Roscoe Parrish 5.00 12.00
17 Stefan LeFors 5.00 12.00
18 Terrence Murphy 5.00 12.00
19 Troy Williamson 6.00 15.00
20 Vincent Jackson 10.00 25.00

2005 Absolute Memorabilia Spectrum Silver Autographs

STATED PRINT RUN 15-249
UNPRICED PLATINUM PRINT RUN 1 SET
5 Alge Crumpler/99 6.00 15.00
10 Deion Sanders/35 50.00 80.00
11 Derrick Mason/125 6.00 15.00
18 J.P. Losman/99 8.00 20.00
25 Keary Colbert/99 6.00 15.00
43 Drew Bledsoe/35 20.00 40.00
47 Terence Newman/149 8.00 20.00
85 Nate Burleson/75 10.00 25.00
93 Aaron Brooks/75 8.00 20.00
95 Joe Horn/100 8.00 20.00
152 Shawne Merriman/249 12.00 30.00
154 Derrick Johnson/249 10.00 25.00
155 Travis Johnson/249 6.00 15.00
156 David Pollack/249 8.00 20.00
157 Erasmus James/249 10.00 25.00
161 Cedric Benson/99 25.00 60.00
162 Matt Roth/75 10.00 25.00
163 Dan Cody/99 8.00 20.00
164 Bryant McFadden/99 10.00 25.00
165 Chris Henry/99 8.00 20.00
167 Marion Barber/249 8.00 20.00
169 Jerome Mathis/249 6.00 15.00
170 Craphonso Thorpe/249 8.00 20.00
172 Darren Sproles/249 15.00 40.00
173 Fred Gibson/249 8.00 20.00
174 Roydell Williams/249 10.00 25.00
178 Adrian McPherson/199* 6.00 15.00
180 Aaron Rodgers/249 250.00 350.00
181 Cedric Houston/249 10.00 25.00
182 Mike Williams/150 10.00 25.00
183 Heath Miller/249 15.00 40.00
184 Dante Ridgeway/150 6.00 15.00
185 Craig Bragg/150 8.00 20.00
186 Deandra Cobb/99 8.00 20.00
187 Derek Anderson/150 8.00 20.00
188 Paris Warren/249 6.00 15.00
189 David Greene/249 8.00 20.00
190 Lionel Gates/249 8.00 20.00
191 Anthony Davis/249 6.00 15.00
193 Ryan Fitzpatrick/249 20.00 40.00
194 J.R. Russell/249 6.00 15.00
195 Jason White/249 8.00 20.00

2005 Absolute Memorabilia Spectrum Gold Autographs

*GOLD/25-100: .5X TO 1.2X SILVER AU
GOLD STATED PRINT RUN 10-100
CARDS SER.#'d UNDER 25 NOT PRICED
180 Aaron Rodgers/100 300.00 400.00

2005 Absolute Memorabilia Star Gazing Jersey Prime

STATED PRINT RUN 150 SER.#'d SETS
1 Larry Fitzgerald 6.00 15.00
2 Michael Vick AU 30.00 60.00
3 Warrick Dunn 5.00 12.00
4 Willis McGahee AU 20.00 50.00
5 Brian Urlacher AU 25.00 60.00
6 Carson Palmer 6.00 15.00
7 Chad Johnson AU 15.00 40.00
8 Julius Jones AU 12.00 30.00
9 Troy Aikman 10.00 25.00
10 Michael Irvin 8.00 20.00
11 Jake Plummer 5.00 12.00
12 Tatum Bell 4.00 10.00
13 Barry Sanders 12.00 30.00
14 Roy Williams WR AU 15.00 40.00
15 Kevin Jones 4.00 10.00
16 Ahman Green 5.00 12.00
17 Brett Favre 15.00 40.00
18 Andre Johnson AU 20.00 50.00
19 Domanick Davis AU 12.00 30.00
20 Edgerrin James 5.00 12.00
21 Marvin Harrison 6.00 15.00
22 Peyton Manning 12.00 30.00
23 Reggie Wayne AU 20.00 50.00
24 Byron Leftwich 5.00 12.00
25 Priest Holmes 5.00 12.00
26 Dan Marino 20.00 50.00
27 Nate Burleson 4.00 10.00
28 Randy Moss 6.00 15.00
29 Corey Dillon 5.00 12.00
30 Tom Brady 12.00 30.00
31 Eli Manning 10.00 25.00
32 Curtis Martin 6.00 15.00
33 Chad Pennington 6.00 15.00
34 Donovan McNabb 6.00 15.00
35 Terrell Owens 6.00 15.00

36 Ben Roethlisberger 10.00 25.00
37 Hines Ward AU 20.00 50.00
38 Antonio Gates AU 20.00 50.00
39 LaDainian Tomlinson 6.00 15.00
40 Joe Montana 20.00 50.00
41 Jerry Rice 12.00 30.00
42 Matt Hasselbeck 5.00 12.00
43 Shaun Alexander 5.00 12.00
44 Steven Jackson AU 20.00 50.00
45 Torry Holt 5.00 12.00
46 Michael Clayton AU 12.00 30.00
47 Chris Brown AU 12.00 30.00
48 Steve McNair 6.00 15.00
49 Clinton Portis 5.00 12.00
50 LaVar Arrington 5.00 12.00

2005 Absolute Memorabilia Star Gazing Jersey Oversized

OVERSIZED PRINT RUN 25 SER.#'d SETS
UNPRICED OS PRIME PRINT RUN 10
1 Larry Fitzgerald 12.00 30.00
2 Michael Vick 12.00 30.00
3 Warrick Dunn 10.00 25.00
4 Willis McGahee 12.00 30.00
5 Brian Urlacher 12.00 30.00
6 Carson Palmer 12.00 30.00
7 Chad Johnson 10.00 25.00
8 Julius Jones 8.00 20.00
9 Troy Aikman 20.00 50.00
10 Michael Irvin 15.00 40.00
11 Jake Plummer 10.00 25.00
12 Tatum Bell 8.00 20.00
13 Barry Sanders 25.00 60.00
14 Roy Williams WR 10.00 25.00
15 Kevin Jones 8.00 20.00
16 Ahman Green 10.00 25.00
17 Brett Favre 30.00 80.00
18 Andre Johnson 12.00 30.00
19 Domanick Davis 8.00 20.00
20 Edgerrin James 10.00 25.00
21 Marvin Harrison 12.00 30.00
22 Peyton Manning 25.00 60.00
23 Reggie Wayne 12.00 30.00
24 Byron Leftwich 10.00 25.00
25 Priest Holmes 10.00 25.00
26 Dan Marino 40.00 100.00
27 Nate Burleson 8.00 20.00
28 Randy Moss 12.00 30.00
29 Corey Dillon 10.00 25.00
30 Tom Brady 25.00 60.00
31 Eli Manning 20.00 50.00
32 Curtis Martin 12.00 30.00
33 Chad Pennington 12.00 30.00
34 Donovan McNabb 12.00 30.00
35 Terrell Owens 12.00 30.00
36 Ben Roethlisberger 20.00 50.00
37 Hines Ward 12.00 30.00
38 Antonio Gates 12.00 30.00
39 LaDainian Tomlinson 12.00 30.00
40 Joe Montana 40.00 100.00
41 Jerry Rice 25.00 60.00
42 Matt Hasselbeck 10.00 25.00
43 Shaun Alexander 10.00 25.00
44 Steven Jackson 12.00 30.00
45 Torry Holt 10.00 25.00
46 Michael Clayton 8.00 20.00
47 Chris Brown 8.00 20.00
48 Steve McNair 12.00 30.00
49 Clinton Portis 10.00 25.00
50 LaVar Arrington 10.00 25.00

2005 Absolute Memorabilia Team Tandems

STATED PRINT RUN 250 SER.#'d SETS
*SPECTRUM/150: .5X TO 1.2X BASIC INSERTS
1 Anquan Boldin 2.50 6.00
Larry Fitzgerald
2 Michael Vick 2.50 6.00
T.J. Duckett
3 Jamal Lewis 2.50 6.00
Ray Lewis
4 Willis McGahee 2.50 6.00
Drew Bledsoe
5 Jake Delhomme 2.00 5.00
Julius Peppers
6 Brian Urlacher 2.50 6.00
Thomas Jones
7 Carson Palmer 2.50 6.00
Chad Johnson
8 Julius Jones 1.50 4.00
Roy Williams S
9 Joey Harrington 2.00 5.00
Kevin Jones
10 Brett Favre 6.00 15.00
Javon Walker
11 David Carr 1.50 4.00
Domanick Davis
12 Peyton Manning 5.00 12.00
Edgerrin James
13 Byron Leftwich 2.00 5.00
Fred Taylor
14 Priest Holmes 2.00 5.00
Tony Gonzalez
15 Daunte Culpepper 2.50 6.00
Randy Moss
16 Tom Brady 5.00 12.00
Corey Dillon
17 Eli Manning 4.00 10.00
Jeremy Shockey
18 Chad Pennington 2.50 6.00
Curtis Martin
19 Donovan McNabb 2.50 6.00
Terrell Owens
20 Ben Roethlisberger 4.00 10.00
Hines Ward
21 LaDainian Tomlinson 2.50 6.00
Antonio Gates
22 Jerry Rice 5.00 12.00
Kevan Barlow
23 Matt Hasselbeck 2.00 5.00
Shaun Alexander
24 Mike Alstott 2.00 5.00
Michael Clayton
25 Clinton Portis 2.00 5.00
LaVar Arrington

2005 Absolute Memorabilia Team Tandems Material

STATED PRINT RUN 150 SER.#'d SETS
*PRIME/25: .8X TO 2X DUAL JSY/150
UNPRICED SPECTRUM PRINT RUN 1 SET
1 Anquan Boldin 6.00 15.00
Larry Fitzgerald
2 Michael Vick 6.00 15.00
T.J. Duckett
3 Jamal Lewis 6.00 15.00
Ray Lewis
4 Willis McGahee 6.00 15.00
Drew Bledsoe
5 Jake Delhomme 5.00 12.00
Julius Peppers
6 Brian Urlacher 6.00 15.00
Thomas Jones
7 Carson Palmer 6.00 15.00
Chad Johnson
8 Julius Jones 4.00 10.00
Roy Williams S
9 Joey Harrington 5.00 12.00
Kevin Jones
10 Brett Favre 15.00 40.00
Javon Walker
11 David Carr 4.00 10.00
Domanick Davis
12 Peyton Manning 12.00 30.00
Edgerrin James
13 Byron Leftwich 5.00 12.00
Fred Taylor
14 Priest Holmes 5.00 12.00
Tony Gonzalez
15 Daunte Culpepper 6.00 15.00
Randy Moss
16 Tom Brady 12.00 30.00
Corey Dillon
17 Eli Manning 10.00 25.00
Jeremy Shockey
18 Chad Pennington 6.00 15.00
Curtis Martin
19 Donovan McNabb 6.00 15.00
Terrell Owens
20 Ben Roethlisberger 12.00 30.00
Hines Ward
21 LaDainian Tomlinson 6.00 15.00
Antonio Gates
22 Jerry Rice 12.00 30.00
Kevan Barlow
23 Matt Hasselbeck 5.00 12.00
Shaun Alexander
24 Mike Alstott 5.00 12.00
Michael Clayton
25 Clinton Portis 5.00 12.00
LaVar Arrington

2005 Absolute Memorabilia Team Trios

STATED PRINT RUN 150 SER.#'d SETS
*SPECTRUM/100: .5X TO 1.2X BASIC INSERT
1 Anquan Boldin 3.00 8.00
Larry Fitzgerald
Josh McCown
2 Michael Vick 3.00 8.00
T.J. Duckett
Warrick Dunn
3 Brian Urlacher 3.00 8.00
Thomas Jones
Rex Grossman
4 David Carr 3.00 8.00
Domanick Davis
Andre Johnson
5 Peyton Manning 6.00 15.00
Edgerrin James
Marvin Harrison
6 Byron Leftwich 2.50 6.00
Fred Taylor
Jimmy Smith
7 Daunte Culpepper 3.00 8.00
Randy Moss
Michael Bennett
8 Aaron Brooks 2.50 6.00
Deuce McAllister
Donte Stallworth
9 Eli Manning 5.00 12.00
Jeremy Shockey
Michael Strahan
10 Chad Pennington 3.00 8.00
Curtis Martin
Santana Moss
11 Donovan McNabb 2.50 6.00
Terrell Owens
Brian Westbrook
12 Ben Roethlisberger 5.00 12.00
Hines Ward
Duce Staley
13 Antonio Gates 3.00 8.00
LaDainian Tomlinson
Drew Brees
14 Matt Hasselbeck 2.50 6.00
Shaun Alexander
Darrell Jackson
15 Clinton Portis 2.50 6.00
LaVar Arrington
Patrick Ramsey

2005 Absolute Memorabilia Team Trios Material

STATED PRINT RUN 100 SER.#'d SETS
UNPRICED PRIME PRINT RUN 10
UNPRICED SPECTRUM PRINT RUN 1
1 Anquan Boldin 8.00 20.00
Larry Fitzgerald
Josh McCown
2 Michael Vick 8.00 20.00
T.J. Duckett
Warrick Dunn
3 Brian Urlacher 8.00 20.00
Thomas Jones
Rex Grossman
4 David Carr 8.00 20.00
Domanick Davis
Andre Johnson
5 Peyton Manning 15.00 40.00
Edgerrin James
Marvin Harrison
6 Byron Leftwich 6.00 15.00
Fred Taylor
Jimmy Smith
7 Daunte Culpepper 8.00 20.00
Randy Moss
Michael Bennett
8 Aaron Brooks 6.00 15.00
Deuce McAllister
Donte Stallworth
9 Eli Manning 12.00 30.00
Jeremy Shockey
Michael Strahan
10 Chad Pennington 8.00 20.00
Curtis Martin
Santana Moss
11 Donovan McNabb 6.00 15.00
Terrell Owens
Brian Westbrook
12 Ben Roethlisberger 15.00 40.00
Hines Ward
Duce Staley
13 Antonio Gates 8.00 20.00
LaDainian Tomlinson
Drew Brees
14 Matt Hasselbeck 6.00 15.00
Shaun Alexander
Darrell Jackson
15 Clinton Portis 6.00 15.00
LaVar Arrington
Patrick Ramsey

2005 Absolute Memorabilia Team Quads

STATED PRINT RUN 100 SER.#'d SETS
*SPECTRUM/25: .8X TO 2X BASIC INSERT
1 Willis McGahee 4.00 10.00
Drew Bledsoe
Lee Evans
Eric Moulds
2 Jake Delhomme 3.00 8.00
Julius Peppers
DeShaun Foster
Stephen Davis
3 Julius Jones 3.00 8.00
Roy Williams S
Keyshawn Johnson
Terence Newman
4 Brett Favre 10.00 25.00
Ahman Green
Javon Walker
Robert Ferguson
5 Byron Leftwich 3.00 8.00
Fred Taylor
Jimmy Smith
Reggie Williams
6 Tom Brady 8.00 20.00
Corey Dillon
Ty Law
Bethel Johnson
7 Eli Manning 6.00 15.00
Jeremy Shockey
Michael Strahan
Tiki Barber
8 Donovan McNabb 3.00 8.00
Terrell Owens
Brian Westbrook
Jevon Kearse
9 Ben Roethlisberger 8.00 20.00
Hines Ward
Duce Staley
Jerome Bettis
10 Marc Bulger 4.00 10.00
Torry Holt
Steven Jackson
Marshall Faulk

2005 Absolute Memorabilia Team Quads Material

STATED PRINT RUN 50 SER.#'d SETS
UNPRICED PRIME PRINT RUN 5
UNPRICED SPECTRUM PRINT RUN 1
1 Willis McGahee 15.00 40.00
Drew Bledsoe
Lee Evans
Eric Moulds
2 Jake Delhomme 12.00 30.00
Julius Peppers
DeShaun Foster
Stephen Davis
3 Julius Jones 12.00 30.00
Roy Williams S
Keyshawn Johnson
Terence Newman
4 Brett Favre 25.00 60.00
Ahman Green
Javon Walker
Robert Ferguson
5 Byron Leftwich 12.00 30.00
Fred Taylor
Jimmy Smith
Reggie Williams
6 Tom Brady 25.00 60.00
Corey Dillon
Ty Law
Bethel Johnson
7 Eli Manning 25.00 60.00
Jeremy Shockey
Michael Strahan
Tiki Barber
8 Donovan McNabb 12.00 30.00
Terrell Owens
Brian Westbrook
Jevon Kearse
9 Ben Roethlisberger 25.00 60.00
Hines Ward
Duce Staley
Jerome Bettis
10 Marc Bulger 15.00 40.00
Torry Holt
Steven Jackson
Marshall Faulk

2005 Absolute Memorabilia Tools of the Trade Red

RED PRINT RUN 250 SER.#'d SETS
*BLACK/100: .6X TO 1.5X RED/250
UNPRICED BLACK SPECT.PRINT RUN 10
*BLUE/150: .5X TO 1.2X RED/250
*BLUE SPECT/25: 1X TO 2.5X RED/250
*RED SPECT/50: .8X TO 2X RED/250
1 Aaron Brooks 1.50 4.00
2 Ahman Green 2.00 5.00
3 Amani Toomer 2.00 5.00
4 Andre Johnson 2.50 6.00
5 Anquan Boldin 2.00 5.00
6 Antwaan Randle El 2.00 5.00
7 Ashley Lelie 1.50 4.00
8 Ben Roethlisberger 4.00 10.00
9 Brett Favre 6.00 15.00
10 Brian Urlacher 2.50 6.00
11 Brian Westbrook 2.00 5.00
12 Byron Leftwich 2.00 5.00
13 Carson Palmer 2.50 6.00
14 Chad Johnson 2.00 5.00
15 Chad Pennington 2.50 6.00
16 Chris Brown 1.50 4.00
17 Chris Chambers 2.00 5.00
18 Clinton Portis 2.00 5.00
19 Corey Dillon 2.00 5.00
20 Curtis Martin 2.50 6.00
21 Dan Marino 6.00 15.00
22 Darrell Jackson 1.50 4.00
23 Daunte Culpepper 2.00 5.00
24 David Carr 1.50 4.00
25 Deuce McAllister 2.00 5.00
26 Domanick Davis 1.50 4.00
27 Donovan McNabb 2.50 6.00
28 Drew Bledsoe 2.50 6.00
29 Duce Staley 2.00 5.00
30 Earl Campbell 2.50 6.00
31 Edgerrin James 2.00 5.00
32 Eli Manning 4.00 10.00
33 Fred Taylor 2.00 5.00
34 Hines Ward 2.50 6.00
35 Ickey Woods 1.50 4.00
36 Jake Delhomme 2.00 5.00
37 Jake Plummer 2.00 5.00
38 Jamal Lewis 2.00 5.00
39 Javon Walker 1.50 4.00
40 Jeremy Shockey 2.50 6.00
41 Jerry Porter 1.50 4.00
42 Jerry Rice 5.00 12.00
43 Jevon Kearse 2.00 5.00
44 Jimmy Smith 2.00 5.00
45 Joe Montana 6.00 15.00
46 Joey Harrington 2.00 5.00
47 John Elway 5.00 12.00
48 Julius Jones 1.50 4.00
49 Julius Peppers 2.00 5.00
50 Kevin Jones 1.50 4.00
51 Keyshawn Johnson 2.00 5.00
52 Kyle Boller 2.00 5.00
53 LaDainian Tomlinson 2.50 6.00
54 Larry Fitzgerald 2.50 6.00
55 LaVar Arrington 2.00 5.00
56 Laveranues Coles 1.50 4.00
57 Lee Evans 2.00 5.00
58 Lee Suggs 1.50 4.00
59 Marc Bulger 2.00 5.00
60 Marcus Allen 2.50 6.00
61 Marshall Faulk 2.50 6.00
62 Marvin Harrison 2.50 6.00
63 Matt Hasselbeck 2.00 5.00
64 Michael Clayton 1.50 4.00
65 Michael Irvin 2.50 6.00
66 Michael Strahan 2.50 6.00
67 Michael Vick 2.50 6.00
68 Mike Alstott 2.00 5.00
69 Patrick Ramsey 2.00 5.00
70 Peter Warrick 1.50 4.00
71 Peyton Manning 5.00 12.00
72 Priest Holmes 2.00 5.00
73 Randy Moss 2.50 6.00
74 Ray Lewis 2.50 6.00
75 Reggie Wayne 2.50 6.00
76 Rex Grossman 2.00 5.00
77 Roy Williams S 1.50 4.00
78 Roy Williams WR 2.00 5.00
79 Rudi Johnson 2.00 5.00
80 Santana Moss 2.00 5.00
81 Shaun Alexander 2.00 5.00
82 Stephen Davis 2.00 5.00
83 Steve McNair 2.50 6.00
84 Steve Smith 2.50 6.00
85 Steve Young 3.00 8.00
86 Steven Jackson 2.50 6.00
87 T.J. Duckett 1.50 4.00
88 Terrell Davis 2.50 6.00
89 Terrell Owens 2.50 6.00
90 Thomas Jones 2.50 6.00
91 Tiki Barber 2.50 6.00
92 Todd Heap 2.00 5.00
93 Tom Brady 5.00 12.00
94 Tony Gonzalez 2.00 5.00
95 Trent Green 2.00 5.00
96 Troy Aikman 3.00 8.00
97 Walter Payton 6.00 15.00
98 Warrick Dunn 2.00 5.00
99 Willis McGahee 2.50 6.00
100 Zach Thomas 2.50 6.00

2005 Absolute Memorabilia Tools of the Trade Material Black

*BLACK UNSIGNED: .8X TO 2X RED
BLACK PRINT RUN 25 SER.#'d SETS
UNPRICED BLACK SPECT.PRINT RUN 1
1 Aaron Brooks AU 15.00 40.00
9 Brett Favre AU 175.00 300.00
12 Byron Leftwich AU 20.00 50.00
15 Chad Pennington AU 25.00 60.00
17 Chris Chambers AU 20.00 50.00
18 Clinton Portis AU 20.00 50.00
19 Corey Dillon AU 20.00 50.00
21 Dan Marino AU 150.00 300.00
24 David Carr AU 15.00 40.00
25 Deuce McAllister AU 20.00 50.00
30 Earl Campbell AU 25.00 60.00
32 Eli Manning AU 90.00 150.00
42 Jerry Rice AU 150.00 250.00
43 Jevon Kearse AU 20.00 50.00
45 Joe Montana AU 125.00 250.00
47 John Elway AU 100.00 200.00
52 Kyle Boller AU 20.00 50.00
56 Laveranues Coles AU 15.00 40.00
62 Marvin Harrison AU 25.00 60.00
63 Matt Hasselbeck AU 20.00 50.00
64 Michael Clayton AU 15.00 40.00
65 Michael Irvin AU 25.00 60.00
69 Patrick Ramsey AU 20.00 50.00
71 Peyton Manning AU 100.00 200.00
72 Priest Holmes AU 20.00 50.00
84 Steve Smith AU 25.00 60.00
85 Steve Young AU 60.00 120.00
88 Terrell Davis AU 25.00 60.00
95 Trent Green AU 20.00 50.00
96 Troy Aikman AU 50.00 100.00

2005 Absolute Memorabilia Tools of the Trade Material Blue

*BLUE UNSIGNED: .5X TO 1.2X RED JSYs
BLUE PRINT RUN 50 SER.#'d SETS
UNPRICED BLUE SPECTRUM PRINT RUN 5
1 Aaron Brooks AU 10.00 25.00
12 Byron Leftwich AU 12.00 30.00
13 Carson Palmer AU 20.00 50.00
15 Chad Pennington AU 15.00 40.00
17 Chris Chambers AU 12.00 30.00
18 Clinton Portis AU 12.00 30.00
24 David Carr AU 10.00 25.00
25 Deuce McAllister AU 12.00 30.00
30 Earl Campbell AU 15.00 40.00
32 Eli Manning AU 75.00 125.00
36 Jake Delhomme AU 12.00 30.00
43 Jevon Kearse AU 12.00 30.00
44 Jimmy Smith AU 12.00 30.00
45 Joe Montana AU 75.00 150.00
46 Joey Harrington AU 12.00 30.00
47 John Elway AU 75.00 150.00
48 Julius Jones AU 10.00 25.00
52 Kyle Boller AU 12.00 30.00
56 Laveranues Coles AU 10.00 25.00
57 Lee Evans AU 12.00 30.00
63 Matt Hasselbeck AU 12.00 30.00
64 Michael Clayton AU 10.00 25.00
65 Michael Irvin AU 15.00 40.00
72 Priest Holmes AU 12.00 30.00
76 Rex Grossman AU 12.00 30.00
77 Roy Williams S AU 10.00 25.00
84 Steve Smith AU 15.00 40.00
85 Steve Young AU 40.00 80.00
91 Tiki Barber AU 25.00 50.00
92 Todd Heap AU 12.00 30.00

2005 Absolute Memorabilia Tools of the Trade Material Red

RED PRINT RUN 100 SER.#'d SETS
UNPRICED RED SPECT.PRINT RUN 10
1 Aaron Brooks AU 8.00 20.00
2 Ahman Green AU 10.00 25.00
3 Amani Toomer 3.00 8.00
4 Andre Johnson 4.00 10.00
5 Anquan Boldin AU 10.00 25.00
6 Antwaan Randle El 3.00 8.00
7 Ashley Lelie 2.50 6.00
8 Ben Roethlisberger 6.00 15.00
9 Brett Favre 10.00 25.00
10 Brian Urlacher 4.00 10.00
11 Brian Westbrook 3.00 8.00
12 Byron Leftwich 3.00 8.00
13 Carson Palmer 4.00 10.00
14 Chad Johnson 3.00 8.00
15 Chad Pennington 4.00 10.00
16 Chris Brown 2.50 6.00
18 Clinton Portis 3.00 8.00
19 Corey Dillon 3.00 8.00
20 Curtis Martin 4.00 10.00
21 Dan Marino 15.00 40.00
22 Darrell Jackson 2.50 6.00
23 Daunte Culpepper 3.00 8.00
24 David Carr 2.50 6.00
25 Deuce McAllister 3.00 8.00
26 Domanick Davis 2.50 6.00
27 Donovan McNabb 4.00 10.00
28 Drew Bledsoe 4.00 10.00
29 Duce Staley 3.00 8.00
30 Earl Campbell 4.00 10.00
31 Edgerrin James 3.00 8.00
32 Eli Manning AU 60.00 100.00
33 Fred Taylor 3.00 8.00
34 Hines Ward 4.00 10.00
35 Ickey Woods 2.50 6.00
36 Jake Delhomme AU 10.00 25.00
37 Jake Plummer 3.00 8.00
38 Jamal Lewis 3.00 8.00
39 Javon Walker 2.50 6.00
40 Jeremy Shockey 4.00 10.00
41 Jerry Porter 2.50 6.00
42 Jerry Rice 8.00 20.00
43 Jevon Kearse AU 10.00 25.00
44 Jimmy Smith AU 10.00 25.00
45 Joe Montana AU 75.00 150.00
46 Joey Harrington 3.00 8.00
47 John Elway AU 75.00 150.00
48 Julius Jones 2.50 6.00
49 Julius Peppers 3.00 8.00
50 Kevin Jones 2.50 6.00
51 Keyshawn Johnson AU 10.00 25.00
52 Kyle Boller AU 10.00 25.00
53 LaDainian Tomlinson 4.00 10.00
54 Larry Fitzgerald 4.00 10.00
55 LaVar Arrington 3.00 8.00
57 Lee Evans AU 10.00 25.00
58 Lee Suggs 2.50 6.00
59 Marc Bulger 3.00 8.00
60 Marcus Allen 4.00 10.00
61 Marshall Faulk 4.00 10.00
62 Marvin Harrison 4.00 10.00
63 Matt Hasselbeck AU 20.00 40.00
64 Michael Clayton AU 8.00 20.00
65 Michael Irvin AU 20.00 40.00
66 Michael Strahan 4.00 10.00
67 Michael Vick 4.00 10.00
68 Mike Alstott 3.00 8.00
69 Patrick Ramsey AU 10.00 25.00
70 Peter Warrick 2.50 6.00
71 Peyton Manning 8.00 20.00
72 Priest Holmes 3.00 8.00
73 Randy Moss 4.00 10.00
74 Ray Lewis 4.00 10.00
75 Reggie Wayne 4.00 10.00
76 Rex Grossman AU 10.00 25.00
77 Roy Williams S AU 8.00 20.00
78 Roy Williams WR 3.00 8.00
79 Rudi Johnson 3.00 8.00
80 Santana Moss 3.00 8.00
81 Shaun Alexander 3.00 8.00
82 Stephen Davis 3.00 8.00
83 Steve McNair 4.00 10.00
84 Steve Smith AU 12.00 30.00
85 Steve Young 6.00 15.00
86 Steven Jackson AU 12.00 30.00
87 T.J. Duckett 2.50 6.00
88 Terrell Davis 4.00 10.00
89 Terrell Owens 4.00 10.00
90 Thomas Jones 4.00 10.00
91 Tiki Barber AU 20.00 40.00
92 Todd Heap AU 10.00 25.00
93 Tom Brady 8.00 20.00
94 Tony Gonzalez 3.00 8.00
95 Trent Green AU 10.00 25.00
96 Troy Aikman 6.00 15.00
97 Walter Payton 15.00 40.00
98 Warrick Dunn 3.00 8.00
99 Willis McGahee 4.00 10.00
100 Zach Thomas 4.00 10.00

2005 Absolute Memorabilia Tools of the Trade Material Double Red

RED PRINT RUN 100 SER.#'d SETS
*BLACK/25: .6X TO 1.5X RED/100
*BLUE/50: .5X TO 1.2X RED/100
*QUAD RED/25: 1X TO 2.5X DBL RED
UNPRICED QUAD BLACK PRINT RUN 1
UNPRICED QUAD BLUE PRINT RUN 5
*TRIPLE RED/50: .6X TO 1.5X DBL RED
UNPRICED TRIPLE BLACK PRINT RUN 5
UNPRICED BLUE PRINT RUN 10
1 Aaron Brooks 5.00 12.00
2 Ahman Green 6.00 15.00
3 Amani Toomer 6.00 15.00
4 Andre Johnson 8.00 20.00
5 Anquan Boldin 6.00 15.00
7 Ashley Lelie 5.00 12.00
9 Brett Favre 20.00 50.00
10 Brian Urlacher 8.00 20.00
12 Byron Leftwich 6.00 15.00
15 Chad Pennington 8.00 20.00
19 Corey Dillon 6.00 15.00
20 Curtis Martin 8.00 20.00
21 Dan Marino 20.00 50.00
23 Daunte Culpepper 6.00 15.00
24 David Carr 5.00 12.00
26 Domanick Davis 5.00 12.00
27 Donovan McNabb 8.00 20.00
30 Earl Campbell 8.00 20.00
31 Edgerrin James 6.00 15.00
34 Hines Ward 8.00 20.00
36 Jake Delhomme 6.00 15.00
37 Jake Plummer 6.00 15.00
38 Jamal Lewis 6.00 15.00
42 Jerry Rice 15.00 40.00
43 Jevon Kearse 6.00 15.00
45 Joe Montana 20.00 50.00
46 Joey Harrington 6.00 15.00
47 John Elway 15.00 40.00
51 Keyshawn Johnson 6.00 15.00
59 Marc Bulger 6.00 15.00
60 Marcus Allen 8.00 20.00
61 Marshall Faulk 8.00 20.00
63 Matt Hasselbeck 6.00 15.00
66 Michael Strahan 8.00 20.00
67 Michael Vick 8.00 20.00
68 Mike Alstott 6.00 15.00
70 Peter Warrick 5.00 12.00
72 Priest Holmes 6.00 15.00
73 Randy Moss 8.00 20.00
80 Santana Moss 6.00 15.00
81 Shaun Alexander 6.00 15.00
83 Steve McNair 8.00 20.00
84 Steve Smith 8.00 20.00
85 Steve Young 10.00 25.00
88 Terrell Davis 8.00 20.00
91 Tiki Barber 8.00 20.00
94 Tony Gonzalez 6.00 15.00
96 Troy Aikman 10.00 25.00
97 Walter Payton 20.00 50.00
100 Zach Thomas 8.00 20.00

2006 Absolute Memorabilia

This 281-card set was released in August, 2006. The set was issued in the hobby in four-card packs, with an $40 SRP, which came 4 packs to a box. Cards numbered 1-150 feature veterans in alphabetical team order based on where the player played in 2005 while 151-281 feature 2006 rookies. The rookies are broken down into three subsets: Cards numbered 151-220 are issued to a stated print run of 999 serial numbered sets, cards numbered 221-250 are signed by the player and those cards have a stated print run of 349 serial numbered cards (unless specifically noted in our checklist) and cards numbered 251-281 have a player-worn uniform swatch and those cards are issued to a stated print run of 849 serial numbered sets.

151-220 PRINT RUN 999 SER.#'d SETS
221-250 PRINT RUN 349 UNLESS NOTED
251-281 PRINT RUN 849 SER.#'d SETS
HOBBY PRINTED ON HOLOFOIL STOCK
1 Anquan Boldin 1.00 2.50
2 J.J. Arrington .75 2.00
3 Kurt Warner 1.25 3.00
4 Larry Fitzgerald 1.25 3.00
5 Marcel Shipp .75 2.00
6 Alge Crumpler 1.00 2.50
7 Michael Jenkins 1.00 2.50
8 Michael Vick 1.25 3.00
9 T.J. Duckett .75 2.00
10 Warrick Dunn 1.00 2.50
11 Derrick Mason 1.00 2.50
12 Jamal Lewis 1.00 2.50
13 Kyle Boller 1.00 2.50
14 Mark Clayton 1.00 2.50
15 Ray Lewis 1.25 3.00
16 Todd Heap 1.00 2.50
17 Eric Moulds .75 2.00
18 J.P. Losman 1.00 2.50
19 Josh Reed .75 2.00
20 Lee Evans 1.00 2.50
21 Willis McGahee 1.00 2.50
22 DeShaun Foster 1.00 2.50
23 Jake Delhomme 1.00 2.50
24 Julius Peppers 1.00 2.50
25 Keary Colbert .75 2.00
26 Stephen Davis 1.00 2.50
27 Steve Smith 1.25 3.00
28 Brian Urlacher 1.25 3.00
29 Cedric Benson 1.00 2.50
30 Rex Grossman 1.00 2.50
31 Thomas Jones 1.00 2.50
32 Muhsin Muhammad 1.00 2.50
33 Carson Palmer 1.25 3.00
34 Chad Johnson 1.00 2.50
35 Rudi Johnson 1.00 2.50
36 T.J. Houshmandzadeh 1.00 2.50
37 Charlie Frye 1.00 2.50
38 Dennis Northcutt .75 2.00
39 Reuben Droughns 1.00 2.50
40 Braylon Edwards 1.00 2.50
41 Drew Bledsoe 1.25 3.00
42 Jason Witten 1.25 3.00
43 Julius Jones .75 2.00
44 Keyshawn Johnson 1.00 2.50
45 Roy Williams S 1.00 2.50
46 Terry Glenn 1.00 2.50
47 Ashley Lelie .75 2.00
48 Jake Plummer 1.00 2.50
49 Rod Smith 1.00 2.50
50 Tatum Bell .75 2.00
51 Mike Anderson 1.00 2.50
52 Joey Harrington .75 2.00
53 Kevin Jones .75 2.00
54 Mike Williams .75 2.00
55 Roy Williams WR 1.00 2.50
56 Marcus Pollard .75 2.00
57 Aaron Rodgers 2.50 6.00
58 Brett Favre 2.50 6.00
59 Donald Driver 1.25 3.00
60 Javon Walker 1.00 2.50
61 Samkon Gado 1.00 2.50
62 Bubba Franks .75 2.00
63 Andre Johnson 1.25 3.00
64 Corey Bradford .75 2.00
65 David Carr .75 2.00
66 Domanick Davis .75 2.00
67 Jabar Gaffney .75 2.00
68 Edgerrin James 1.00 2.50
69 Dallas Clark 1.00 2.50
70 Marvin Harrison 1.25 3.00
71 Peyton Manning 2.00 5.00
72 Reggie Wayne 1.00 2.50
73 Brandon Stokley 1.00 2.50
74 Byron Leftwich 1.00 2.50
75 Fred Taylor 1.00 2.50
76 Jimmy Smith 1.00 2.50
77 Matt Jones .75 2.00
78 Ernest Wilford .75 2.00
79 Larry Johnson 1.00 2.50
80 Tony Gonzalez 1.00 2.50
81 Trent Green 1.00 2.50
82 Eddie Kennison .75 2.00
83 Dante Hall 1.00 2.50
84 Chris Chambers 1.00 2.50
85 Randy McMichael .75 2.00
86 Terrell Owens 1.25 3.00
87 Ronnie Brown 1.25 3.00
88 Zach Thomas 1.25 3.00
89 Marty Booker .75 2.00
90 Daunte Culpepper 1.00 2.50
91 Mewelde Moore .75 2.00
92 Nate Burleson .75 2.00
93 Troy Williamson .75 2.00
94 Corey Dillon 1.00 2.50
95 David Givens 1.00 2.50
96 Deion Branch 1.00 2.50
97 Tedy Bruschi 1.25 3.00
98 Tom Brady 2.00 5.00
99 Aaron Brooks 1.00 2.50
100 Deuce McAllister 1.00 2.50
101 Donte Stallworth .75 2.00
102 Joe Horn 1.00 2.50
103 Eli Manning 1.50 4.00
104 Jeremy Shockey 1.25 3.00
105 Plaxico Burress 1.00 2.50
106 Tiki Barber 1.25 3.00
107 Chad Pennington 1.00 2.50
108 Curtis Martin 1.25 3.00
109 Laveranues Coles .75 2.00
110 Justin McCareins .75 2.00
111 Kerry Collins 1.00 2.50
112 LaMont Jordan 1.00 2.50
113 Randy Moss 1.25 3.00
114 Jerry Porter .75 2.00
115 Brian Westbrook 1.00 2.50
116 Donovan McNabb 1.25 3.00
117 Reggie Brown .75 2.00
118 Ryan Moats .75 2.00
119 Antwaan Randle El 1.00 2.50
120 Ben Roethlisberger 1.50 4.00
121 Willie Parker 1.00 2.50
122 Hines Ward 1.25 3.00
123 Antonio Gates 1.25 3.00
124 Drew Brees 1.25 3.00
125 Keenan McCardell 1.00 2.50
126 LaDainian Tomlinson 1.25 3.00
127 Alex Smith QB 1.25 3.00
128 Brandon Lloyd .75 2.00
129 Frank Gore 1.25 3.00
130 Kevan Barlow .75 2.00
131 Darrell Jackson 1.00 2.50
132 Joe Jurevicius .75 2.00
133 Matt Hasselbeck 1.00 2.50
134 Shaun Alexander 1.00 2.50
135 Isaac Bruce 1.00 2.50
136 Marc Bulger 1.00 2.50
137 Steven Jackson 1.25 3.00
138 Torry Holt 1.00 2.50
139 Cadillac Williams 1.00 2.50
140 Chris Simms 1.00 2.50
141 Joey Galloway 1.00 2.50
142 Michael Clayton .75 2.00
143 Chris Brown .75 2.00
144 Drew Bennett 1.00 2.50
145 Steve McNair 1.00 2.50
146 Tyrone Calico .75 2.00
147 Clinton Portis 1.25 3.00
148 LaVar Arrington 1.00 2.50
149 Mark Brunell 1.00 2.50
150 Santana Moss 1.00 2.50
151 Greg Jennings RC 5.00 12.00
152 Joseph Addai RC 2.50 6.00
153 Erik Meyer RC 2.00 5.00
154 Drew Olson RC 1.50 4.00
155 Darrell Hackney RC 2.00 5.00
156 Paul Pinegar RC 1.50 4.00
157 Brandon Kirsch RC 2.00 5.00
158 Andre Hall RC 2.00 5.00
159 Taurean Henderson RC 2.50 6.00
160 Derrick Ross RC 2.00 5.00
161 Mike Bell RC 2.50 6.00
162 Wendell Mathis RC 2.00 5.00
163 Gerald Riggs RC 2.00 5.00
164 John David Washington RC 2.00 5.00
165 Devin Aromashodu RC 2.50 6.00
166 Ben Obomanu RC 2.50 6.00
167 David Anderson RC 2.00 5.00
168 Marques Colston RC 5.00 12.00
169 Kevin McMahan RC 2.00 5.00
170 Miles Austin RC 6.00 15.00
171 Martin Nance RC 2.00 5.00
172 Greg Lee RC 1.50 4.00
173 Hank Baskett RC 2.50 6.00
174 Anthony Mix RC 2.00 5.00
175 D'Brickashaw Ferguson RC 2.50 6.00
176 Kamerion Wimbley RC 2.50 6.00
177 Tamba Hali RC 2.50 6.00
178 Mathias Kiwanuka RC 2.50 6.00
179 Brodrick Bunkley RC 2.00 5.00
180 John McCargo RC 1.50 4.00
181 Claude Wroten RC 1.50 4.00
182 Gabe Watson RC 1.50 4.00
183 D'Qwell Jackson RC 2.00 5.00
184 Abdul Hodge RC 1.50 4.00
185 Ernie Sims RC 2.00 5.00
186 Chad Greenway RC 2.50 6.00
187 Bobby Carpenter RC 1.50 4.00
188 Manny Lawson RC 2.00 5.00
189 DeMeco Ryans RC 2.50 6.00
190 Rocky McIntosh RC 2.00 5.00
191 Thomas Howard RC 2.00 5.00
192 Jon Alston RC 1.50 4.00
193 A.J. Nicholson RC 1.50 4.00
194 Tye Hill RC 1.50 4.00
195 Antonio Cromartie RC 2.50 6.00
196 Johnathan Joseph RC 2.00 5.00
197 Kelly Jennings RC 2.00 5.00
198 Jimmy Williams RC 2.50 6.00
199 Ashton Youboty RC 1.50 4.00
200 Alan Zemaitis RC 2.50 6.00
201 Anwar Phillips RC 2.00 5.00
202 Jason Allen RC 2.00 5.00
203 Cedric Griffin RC 2.00 5.00
204 Ko Simpson RC 2.00 5.00
205 Pat Watkins RC 2.00 5.00
206 Donte Whitner RC 2.50 6.00
207 Bernard Pollard RC 2.00 5.00
208 Darnell Bing RC 2.00 5.00
209 De'Arrius Howard RC 2.50 6.00
210 Ethan Kilmer RC 2.00 5.00
211 Bennie Brazell RC 2.00 5.00
212 Haloti Ngata RC 2.50 6.00
213 Jeremy Bloom RC 2.00 5.00
214 Jay Cutler RC 5.00 12.00
215 Marcus Vick RC 1.50 4.00
216 Roman Harper RC 2.00 5.00
217 Anthony Smith RC 2.50 6.00
218 Daniel Bullocks RC 2.50 6.00
219 Eric Smith RC 2.00 5.00
220 Dusty Dvoracek RC 2.50 6.00
221 Brodie Croyle AU RC 6.00 15.00
222 Ingle Martin AU RC 5.00 12.00
223 Reggie McNeal AU RC 5.00 12.00
224 Bruce Gradkowski AU RC 6.00 15.00
225 D.J. Shockley AU RC 5.00 12.00
226 P.J. Daniels AU RC 4.00 10.00
227 Marques Hagans AU RC 4.00 10.00
228 Jerome Harrison RC 5.00 12.00
229 Wali Lundy AU RC 5.00 12.00
230 Cedric Humes AU RC 4.00 10.00
231 Quinton Ganther AU RC 4.00 10.00
232 Garrett Mills AU RC 6.00 15.00
233 Anthony Fasano AU RC 6.00 15.00
234 Tony Scheffler AU RC 8.00 20.00
235 Leonard Pope AU RC 6.00 15.00
236 David Thomas AU RC 5.00 12.00
237 Dominique Byrd AU RC 5.00 12.00
238 Jai Lewis AU/299 RC 5.00 12.00
239 Devin Hester AU RC 30.00 50.00
240 Willie Reid AU RC 5.00 12.00
241 Brad Smith AU RC 6.00 15.00
242 Cory Rodgers AU RC 5.00 12.00
243 Skyler Green AU RC 4.00 10.00
244 Domenik Hixon AU RC 6.00 15.00
245 Mike Hass AU RC 5.00 12.00
246 Jonathan Orr AU/299 RC 5.00 12.00
247 Delanie Walker AU/299 RC 6.00 15.00
248 Adam Jennings AU/299 RC 5.00 12.00
249 Jeff Webb AU/299 RC 5.00 12.00
250 Todd Watkins AU RC 4.00 10.00
251 Chad Jackson RPM RC 2.50 6.00
252 Laurence Maroney RPM RC 3.00 8.00
253 Tarvaris Jackson RPM RC 4.00 10.00

254 Michael Huff RPM RC 3.00 8.00
255 Mario Williams RPM RC 4.00 10.00
256 Marcedes Lewis RPM RC 4.00 10.00
257 Maurice Drew RPM RC 6.00 15.00
258 Vince Young RPM RC 5.00 12.00
259 LenDale White RPM RC 3.00 8.00
260 Reggie Bush RPM RC 8.00 20.00
261 Matt Leinart RPM RC 4.00 10.00
262 Michael Robinson RPM RC 3.00 8.00
263 Vernon Davis RPM RC 5.00 12.00
264 Brandon Williams RPM RC 2.50 6.00
265 Derek Hagan RPM RC 3.00 8.00
266 Jason Avant RPM RC 2.50 6.00
267 Brandon Marshall RPM RC 4.00 10.00
268 Omar Jacobs RPM RC 2.50 6.00
269 Santonio Holmes RPM RC 5.00 12.00
270 Jerious Norwood RPM RC 3.00 8.00
271 Demetrius Williams RPM RC 3.00 8.00
272 Sinorice Moss RPM RC 4.00 10.00
273 Leon Washington RPM RC 3.00 8.00
274 Kellen Clemens RPM RC 3.00 8.00
275 A.J. Hawk RPM RC 4.00 10.00
276 Maurice Stovall RPM RC 2.50 6.00
277 DeAngelo Williams RPM RC 5.00 12.00
278 Charlie Whitehurst RPM RC 4.00 10.00
279 Travis Wilson RPM RC 2.50 6.00
280 Joe Klopfenstein RPM RC 2.50 6.00
281 Brian Calhoun RPM RC 2.50 6.00

2006 Absolute Memorabilia Retail

COMPLETE SET (150) 10.00 25.00
*SINGLES: .1X TO .25X BASIC CARDS
RETAIL PRINTED ON WHITE STOCK

2006 Absolute Memorabilia Spectrum Black

*VETS 1-150: 1X TO 2.5X BASIC CARDS
*ROOKIES 151-220: .6X TO 1.5X
RANDOM INSERTS IN RETAIL PACKS
STATED PRINT RUN 100 SER.#'d SETS

2006 Absolute Memorabilia Spectrum Blue

*VETS 1-150: .8X TO 2X BASIC CARDS
*ROOKIES 151-220: .5X TO 1.2X
RANDOM INSERTS IN RETAIL PACKS
STATED PRINT RUN 250 SER.#'d SETS

2006 Absolute Memorabilia Spectrum Gold

*VETS 1-150: 2X TO 5X BASIC CARDS
*ROOKIES 151-220: 1.2X TO 3X
STATED PRINT RUN 25 SER.#'d SETS

2006 Absolute Memorabilia Spectrum Platinum

UNPRICED PLATINUM PRINT RUN 1

2006 Absolute Memorabilia Spectrum Red

*VETS 1-150: .6X TO 1.5X BASIC CARDS
*ROOKIES 151-220: .4X TO 1X BASIC CARDS
RANDOM INSERTS IN RETAIL PACKS

2006 Absolute Memorabilia Spectrum Silver

*VETS 1-150: 1X TO 2.5X BASIC CARDS
*ROOKIES 151-220: .6X TO 1.5X
STATED PRINT RUN 100 SER.#'d SETS

2006 Absolute Memorabilia Absolute Heroes Silver

SILVER PRINT RUN 250 SER.#'d SETS
*GOLD/100: .5X TO 1.2X SILVER/250
*SPECTRUM/25: 1X TO 2.5X SILVER/250
1 Larry Fitzgerald 2.00 5.00
2 Michael Vick 2.00 5.00
3 Willis McGahee 1.50 4.00
4 Steve Smith 2.00 5.00
5 Carson Palmer 2.00 5.00
6 Julius Jones 1.25 3.00
7 Samkon Gado 1.50 4.00
8 Peyton Manning 3.00 8.00
9 Jimmy Smith 1.50 4.00
10 Larry Johnson 1.50 4.00
11 Ronnie Brown 2.00 5.00
12 Tom Brady 3.00 8.00
13 Eli Manning 2.50 6.00
14 Curtis Martin 2.00 5.00
15 Randy Moss 2.00 5.00
16 Donovan McNabb 2.00 5.00
17 Ben Roethlisberger 2.50 6.00
18 LaDainian Tomlinson 2.00 5.00
19 Alex Smith QB 2.00 5.00
20 Shaun Alexander 1.50 4.00
21 Steven Jackson 2.00 5.00
22 Cadillac Williams 1.50 4.00
23 Chris Brown 1.25 3.00
24 Clinton Portis 2.00 5.00
25 Marvin Harrison 2.00 5.00

2006 Absolute Memorabilia Absolute Heroes Material Autographs

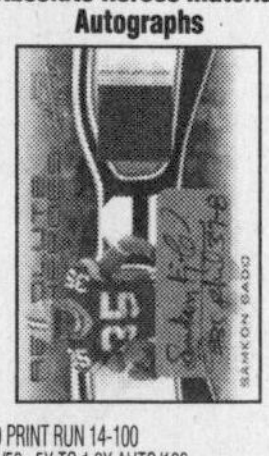

STATED PRINT RUN 14-100
*PRIME/50: .5X TO 1.2X AUTO/100
*PRIME/50: .4X TO 1X AUTO/25
*PRIME/25: .6X TO 1.5X AUTO/100
*PRIME/25: .5X TO 1.2X AUTO/50
UNPRICED PRIME SPECTRUM #'d TO 1
SERIAL #'d UNDER 25 NOT PRICED
1 Larry Fitzgerald/100 25.00 50.00
2 Michael Vick/25 30.00 80.00
3 Willis McGahee/100 10.00 25.00
4 Steve Smith/100 15.00 40.00
6 Julius Jones/25 15.00 40.00
7 Samkon Gado/100 15.00 40.00
8 Peyton Manning/25 90.00 150.00
10 Larry Johnson/100 15.00 40.00
11 Ronnie Brown/100 20.00 50.00
13 Eli Manning/25 60.00 100.00
16 Donovan McNabb/25 35.00 60.00
17 Ben Roethlisberger/25 90.00 150.00
18 LaDainian Tomlinson/25 40.00 80.00
19 Alex Smith QB/50 25.00 50.00
20 Shaun Alexander/25 20.00 50.00
21 Steven Jackson/100 15.00 40.00
22 Cadillac Williams/100 12.00 30.00
23 Chris Brown/25 12.00 30.00
24 Clinton Portis/25
25 Marvin Harrison/25 20.00 50.00

2006 Absolute Memorabilia Absolute Heroes Materials

STATED PRINT RUN 150 SER.#'d SETS
*PRIME/40-50: .6X TO 1.5X BASIC JERSEYS
*PRIME/25-30: .8X TO 2X BASIC JERSEYS
UNPRICED PRIME SPECTRUM #'d TO 1
1 Larry Fitzgerald 4.00 10.00
2 Michael Vick 4.00 10.00
3 Willis McGahee 4.00 10.00
4 Steve Smith 4.00 10.00
5 Carson Palmer 5.00 12.00
6 Julius Jones 4.00 10.00
7 Samkon Gado 3.00 8.00
8 Peyton Manning 6.00 15.00
9 Jimmy Smith 3.00 8.00
10 Larry Johnson 4.00 10.00
11 Ronnie Brown 4.00 12.00
12 Tom Brady 6.00 15.00
13 Eli Manning 6.00 15.00
14 Curtis Martin 4.00 10.00
15 Randy Moss 4.00 10.00
16 Donovan McNabb 4.00 10.00
17 Ben Roethlisberger 8.00 20.00
18 LaDainian Tomlinson 4.00 10.00
19 Alex Smith QB 4.00 10.00
20 Shaun Alexander 5.00 12.00
21 Steven Jackson 4.00 10.00
22 Cadillac Williams 4.00 10.00
23 Chris Brown 2.50 6.00
24 Clinton Portis 4.00 10.00
25 Marvin Harrison 4.00 10.00

2006 Absolute Memorabilia Absolute Patches Prime

STATED PRINT RUN 15-25
UNPRICED SPECTRUM PRINT RUN 1
1 Larry Fitzgerald 20.00 50.00
2 Michael Vick/15 25.00 60.00
3 Willis McGahee 15.00 40.00
4 Steve Smith 20.00 50.00
5 Carson Palmer 20.00 50.00
6 Julius Jones 12.00 30.00
7 Samkon Gado 15.00 40.00
8 Peyton Manning 30.00 80.00
9 Jimmy Smith 15.00 40.00
10 Larry Johnson 15.00 40.00
11 Ronnie Brown 20.00 50.00
12 Tom Brady 30.00 80.00
13 Eli Manning 25.00 60.00
14 Curtis Martin 20.00 50.00
15 Randy Moss 20.00 50.00
16 Donovan McNabb 20.00 50.00
17 Ben Roethlisberger/15 30.00 80.00
18 LaDainian Tomlinson 20.00 50.00
19 Alex Smith QB 20.00 50.00
20 Shaun Alexander 15.00 40.00
21 Steven Jackson 20.00 50.00
22 Cadillac Williams 15.00 40.00
23 Chris Brown 12.00 30.00
24 Clinton Portis 20.00 50.00
25 Marvin Harrison 20.00 50.00
26 Antonio Gates 20.00 50.00
27 Rudi Johnson 15.00 40.00
28 Tiki Barber 20.00 50.00
29 Domanick Davis 12.00 30.00
30 Anquan Boldin 15.00 40.00
31 Torry Holt 15.00 40.00
32 Warrick Dunn 15.00 40.00
33 Zach Thomas 20.00 50.00
34 Chad Johnson 15.00 40.00
35 Brian Urlacher 20.00 50.00
36 Trent Green 15.00 40.00
37 Santana Moss 15.00 40.00
38 Corey Dillon 15.00 40.00

2006 Absolute Memorabilia Canton Absolutes Silver

SILVER PRINT RUN 250 SER.#'d SETS
*GOLD/100: 2.5X TO 1.2X BASIC INSERTS
*SPECTRUM/25: 1X TO 2.5X BASIC INSERTS
1 Derrick Thomas 4.00 10.00
2 Reggie White 3.00 8.00
3 Walter Payton 6.00 15.00
4 Troy Aikman 3.00 8.00
5 Brett Favre 4.00 10.00
6 Shaun Alexander 1.50 4.00
7 Peyton Manning 3.00 8.00
8 Jerome Bettis 2.00 5.00
9 Tom Brady 3.00 8.00
10 Marshall Faulk 1.50 4.00
11 LaDainian Tomlinson 2.00 5.00
12 Jerry Rice 3.00 8.00
13 Ben Roethlisberger 2.50 6.00
14 Corey Dillon 1.50 4.00
15 Curtis Martin 2.00 5.00
16 Dan Marino 5.00 12.00
17 Eric Dickerson 2.00 5.00
18 Marcus Allen 2.00 5.00
19 Marvin Harrison 2.00 5.00
20 Donovan McNabb 2.00 5.00
21 Edgerrin James 1.50 4.00
22 Eli Manning 2.50 6.00
23 Isaac Bruce 1.50 4.00
24 Jeremy Shockey 2.00 5.00
25 John Elway 4.00 10.00

2006 Absolute Memorabilia Canton Absolutes Materials

STATED PRINT RUN 150 SER.#'d SETS
*PRIME/25: .8X TO 2X BASIC JERSEYS
UNPRICED SPECTRUM PRINT RUN 1
1 Derrick Thomas 15.00 30.00
2 Reggie White 8.00 20.00
3 Walter Payton 12.50 30.00
4 Troy Aikman 8.00 20.00
5 Brett Favre 8.00 20.00
6 Shaun Alexander 5.00 12.00
7 Peyton Manning 6.00 15.00
8 Jerome Bettis/57 6.00 15.00
9 Tom Brady 6.00 15.00
10 Marshall Faulk 3.00 8.00
11 LaDainian Tomlinson 4.00 10.00
12 Jerry Rice 6.00 15.00
13 Ben Roethlisberger 8.00 20.00
14 Corey Dillon 3.00 8.00
15 Curtis Martin 4.00 10.00
16 Dan Marino 12.50 30.00
17 Eric Dickerson 4.00 10.00
18 Marcus Allen 4.00 10.00
19 Marvin Harrison 4.00 10.00
20 Donovan McNabb 4.00 10.00
21 Edgerrin James 4.00 10.00
22 Eli Manning 6.00 15.00
23 Isaac Bruce 4.00 10.00
24 Jeremy Shockey 4.00 10.00
25 John Elway 8.00 20.00

2006 Absolute Memorabilia Canton Absolutes Spectrum Autographs

SERIAL #'d UNDER 25 NOT PRICED
7 Peyton Manning/25 60.00 100.00
21 Edgerrin James/50 12.50 30.00

2006 Absolute Memorabilia Marks of Fame Silver

SILVER PRINT RUN 250 SER.#'d SETS
*GOLD/100: .5X TO 1.2X SILVER
*SPECTRUM/25: 1X TO 2.5X SILVER
1 Barry Sanders 4.00 10.00
2 Boomer Esiason 2.00 5.00
3 Dan Marino 5.00 12.00
4 Eric Dickerson 2.00 5.00
5 Joe Montana 5.00 12.00
6 John Elway 4.00 10.00
7 John Riggins 2.00 5.00
8 Marcus Allen 2.00 5.00
9 Steve Largent 2.00 5.00
10 Terrell Davis 1.50 4.00
11 Troy Aikman 3.00 8.00
12 Warren Moon 2.00 5.00
13 Ben Roethlisberger 2.50 6.00
14 Brett Favre 4.00 10.00
15 Carson Palmer 2.00 5.00
16 Eli Manning 2.50 6.00
17 LaDainian Tomlinson 2.00 5.00
18 Michael Vick 2.00 5.00
19 Peyton Manning 3.00 8.00
20 Cadillac Williams 1.50 4.00
21 Larry Johnson 1.50 4.00
22 Shaun Alexander 1.50 4.00
23 Chad Johnson 1.50 4.00
24 Clinton Portis 2.00 5.00
25 Steve Smith 2.00 5.00
26 Vince Young 1.50 4.00
27 Matt Leinart 1.25 3.00
28 Kellen Clemens 1.00 2.50
29 Tarvaris Jackson 1.25 3.00
30 Omar Jacobs .75 2.00
31 Reggie Bush 2.50 6.00
32 Laurence Maroney 1.00 2.50
33 DeAngelo Williams 1.50 4.00
34 LenDale White 1.00 2.50
35 Maurice Drew 2.00 5.00
36 Brian Calhoun .75 2.00
37 Vernon Davis 1.50 4.00
38 Santonio Holmes 1.50 4.00
39 Chad Jackson .75 2.00
40 Sinorice Moss 1.25 3.00
41 Travis Wilson .75 2.00
42 Derek Hagan 1.00 2.50
43 Michael Robinson 1.00 2.50
44 Demetrius Williams 1.00 2.50
45 Mario Williams 1.25 3.00
46 A.J. Hawk 1.25 3.00
47 Michael Huff 1.00 2.50
48 Charlie Whitehurst 1.25 3.00
49 Brandon Marshall 1.25 3.00
50 Leon Washington 1.00 2.50

2006 Absolute Memorabilia Marks of Fame Material Autographs

BASE AUTO PRINT RUN 50-100
UNPRICED SPECTRUM PRINT RUN 1
1 Barry Sanders/50 75.00 135.00
2 Boomer Esiason/50 12.00 30.00
3 Dan Marino/75 75.00 150.00
4 Eric Dickerson/75 20.00 40.00
5 Joe Montana/25 100.00 175.00
6 John Elway/50 75.00 150.00
7 John Riggins/30 20.00 40.00
8 Marcus Allen/75 20.00 40.00
9 Steve Largent/50 20.00 40.00
10 Terrell Davis/75 12.00 30.00
11 Troy Aikman/50 50.00 80.00
12 Warren Moon/50 20.00 40.00
13 Ben Roethlisberger/75 60.00 100.00
14 Brett Favre/75 125.00 200.00
15 Carson Palmer/75 15.00 40.00
16 Eli Manning/75 35.00 60.00
17 LaDainian Tomlinson/75 40.00 80.00
18 Michael Vick/75 30.00 80.00
19 Peyton Manning/75 60.00 120.00
20 Cadillac Williams/100 12.00 30.00
21 Larry Johnson/100 12.00 30.00
22 Shaun Alexander/100 12.00 30.00
23 Chad Johnson/100 20.00 40.00
25 Steve Smith/100 15.00 40.00
26 Vince Young/50 20.00 50.00
27 Matt Leinart/50 12.00 30.00
28 Kellen Clemens/100 12.00 30.00
29 Tarvaris Jackson/100 12.00 30.00
30 Omar Jacobs/100 8.00 20.00
31 Reggie Bush/50 30.00 80.00
32 Laurence Maroney/50 10.00 25.00
33 DeAngelo Williams/50 15.00 40.00
34 LenDale White/50 15.00 40.00
35 Maurice Drew/100 20.00 50.00
36 Brian Calhoun/50 8.00 20.00
37 Vernon Davis/50 15.00 40.00
38 Santonio Holmes/50 20.00 50.00
39 Chad Jackson/100 8.00 20.00
40 Sinorice Moss/50 10.00 25.00
41 Travis Wilson/100 8.00 20.00
42 Derek Hagan/100 8.00 20.00
43 Michael Robinson/100 8.00 20.00
44 Demetrius Williams/100 8.00 20.00
45 Mario Williams/100 12.00 30.00
46 A.J. Hawk/50 25.00 60.00
47 Michael Huff/100 8.00 20.00
48 Charlie Whitehurst/50 10.00 25.00
49 Brandon Marshall/50 10.00 25.00
50 Leon Washington/100 10.00 25.00

2006 Absolute Memorabilia Marks of Fame Material Autographs Prime

*PRIME/25: .6X TO 1.5X JSY AU/75-100
*PRIME/25: .5X TO 1.2X JSY AU/50
*PRIME/25: .4X TO 1X JSY AU/25-30
STATED PRINT RUN 10-25
1 Barry Sanders 100.00 175.00
3 Dan Marino 125.00 225.00
5 Joe Montana 100.00 175.00
6 John Elway 100.00 175.00
13 Ben Roethlisberger 75.00 150.00
14 Brett Favre 150.00 250.00
17 LaDainian Tomlinson 30.00 80.00
19 Peyton Manning 90.00 150.00
26 Vince Young 30.00 80.00
31 Reggie Bush 25.00 60.00

2006 Absolute Memorabilia Marks of Fame Materials

VET PRINT RUN 150 SER.#'d SETS
ROOKIE PRINT RUN 200 SER.#'d SETS
*PRIME/50: .6X TO 1.5X BASIC JERSEYS
*PRIME/25-30: .8X TO 2X BASIC JERSEYS
UNPRICED SPECTRUM PRINT RUN 1
1 Barry Sanders 8.00 20.00
2 Boomer Esiason 4.00 10.00
3 Dan Marino 12.50 30.00
4 Eric Dickerson 4.00 10.00
5 Joe Montana 12.50 30.00
6 John Elway 8.00 20.00
7 John Riggins 4.00 10.00
8 Marcus Allen 4.00 10.00
9 Steve Largent 4.00 10.00
10 Terrell Davis 4.00 10.00
11 Troy Aikman 8.00 20.00
12 Warren Moon 4.00 10.00
13 Ben Roethlisberger 8.00 20.00
14 Brett Favre 8.00 20.00
15 Carson Palmer 5.00 12.00
16 Eli Manning 6.00 15.00
17 LaDainian Tomlinson 4.00 10.00
18 Michael Vick 4.00 10.00
19 Peyton Manning 6.00 15.00
20 Cadillac Williams 3.00 8.00
21 Larry Johnson 4.00 10.00
22 Shaun Alexander 5.00 12.00
23 Chad Johnson 3.00 8.00
24 Clinton Portis 4.00 10.00
25 Steve Smith 4.00 10.00
26 Vince Young 8.00 20.00
27 Matt Leinart 5.00 12.00
28 Kellen Clemens 5.00 12.00
29 Tarvaris Jackson 4.00 10.00
30 Omar Jacobs 4.00 10.00
31 Reggie Bush 10.00 25.00
32 Laurence Maroney 5.00 12.00
33 DeAngelo Williams 6.00 15.00
34 LenDale White 4.00 10.00
35 Maurice Drew 5.00 12.00
36 Brian Calhoun 4.00 10.00
37 Vernon Davis 5.00 12.00
38 Santonio Holmes 5.00 12.00
39 Chad Jackson 3.00 8.00
40 Sinorice Moss 3.00 8.00
41 Travis Wilson 3.00 8.00
42 Derek Hagan 3.00 8.00
43 Michael Robinson 3.00 8.00
44 Demetrius Williams 3.00 8.00
45 Mario Williams 4.00 10.00
46 A.J. Hawk 6.00 15.00
47 Michael Huff 4.00 10.00
48 Charlie Whitehurst 4.00 10.00
49 Brandon Marshall 3.00 8.00
50 Leon Washington 3.00 8.00

2006 Absolute Memorabilia NFL Icons Materials

STATED PRINT RUN 50 SER.#'d SETS
*PRIME/25: .6X TO 1.5X BASIC JERSEYS
UNPRICED SPECTRUM PRINT RUN 5-10
1 John Elway 12.50 30.00
2 Troy Aikman 12.50 30.00
3 Dan Marino 20.00 50.00
4 Walter Payton 20.00 50.00
5 Joe Montana 20.00 50.00
6 Barry Sanders 12.50 30.00
7 Peyton Manning 10.00 25.00
8 Tom Brady 10.00 25.00
9 LaDainian Tomlinson 6.00 15.00
10 Shaun Alexander 8.00 20.00
11 Michael Vick 6.00 15.00
12 Willis McGahee 6.00 15.00
13 Chad Johnson 5.00 12.00
14 Julius Jones 6.00 15.00
15 Kevin Jones 6.00 15.00
16 Brett Favre 12.50 30.00
17 Andre Johnson 5.00 12.00
18 Jimmy Smith 5.00 12.00
19 Larry Johnson 6.00 15.00
20 Chris Chambers 5.00 12.00
21 Daunte Culpepper 6.00 15.00
22 Clinton Portis 6.00 15.00
23 Eli Manning 10.00 25.00
24 Chad Pennington 5.00 12.00
25 Randy Moss 6.00 15.00
26 Donovan McNabb 6.00 15.00
27 Ben Roethlisberger 15.00 40.00
28 Alex Smith QB 6.00 15.00
29 Torry Holt 6.00 15.00
30 Steve McNair 6.00 15.00
31 Jerome Bettis 8.00 20.00
32 Marvin Harrison 6.00 15.00
33 Tiki Barber 6.00 15.00
34 Hines Ward 6.00 15.00
35 Tony Gonzalez 6.00 15.00
36 Carson Palmer 8.00 20.00
37 Jake Delhomme 5.00 12.00
38 Brian Urlacher 6.00 15.00

2006 Absolute Memorabilia Rookie Jerseys

INSERTED IN SPECIAL RETAIL PACKS
1TE A.J. Hawk 4.00 10.00
2TE Brandon Marshall 4.00 10.00
3TE Brandon Williams 2.50 6.00
4TE Brian Calhoun 2.50 6.00
5TE Chad Jackson 2.50 6.00
6TE Charlie Whitehurst 4.00 10.00
7TE DeAngelo Williams 5.00 12.00
8TE Demetrius Williams 3.00 8.00
9TE Derek Hagan 3.00 8.00
10TE Jason Avant 2.50 6.00
11TE Jerious Norwood 3.00 8.00
12TE Joe Klopfenstein 2.50 6.00
13TE Kellen Clemens 3.00 8.00
14TE Laurence Maroney 3.00 8.00
15TE LenDale White 3.00 8.00
16TE Leon Washington 3.00 8.00
17TE Marcedes Lewis 4.00 10.00
18TE Mario Williams 4.00 10.00
19TE Matt Leinart 4.00 10.00
20TE Maurice Drew 6.00 15.00
21TE Maurice Stovall 2.50 6.00
22TE Michael Huff 3.00 8.00
23TE Michael Robinson 3.00 8.00
24TE Omar Jacobs 2.50 6.00
25TE Reggie Bush 8.00 20.00
26TE Santonio Holmes 5.00 12.00
27TE Sinorice Moss 4.00 10.00
28TE Tarvaris Jackson 4.00 10.00
29TE Travis Wilson 2.50 6.00
30TE Vernon Davis 5.00 12.00
31TE Vince Young 5.00 12.00

2006 Absolute Memorabilia Rookie Premiere Materials Autographs

STATED PRINT RUN 100 SER.#'d SETS
*SPECTRUM/50: .6X TO 1.5X BASIC AU/100
251 Chad Jackson 8.00 20.00
252 Laurence Maroney 10.00 25.00
253 Tarvaris Jackson 12.00 30.00
254 Michael Huff 10.00 25.00
255 Mario Williams 12.00 30.00
256 Marcedes Lewis 12.00 30.00
257 Maurice Drew 20.00 50.00
258 Vince Young 15.00 40.00
259 LenDale White 10.00 25.00
260 Reggie Bush 25.00 60.00
261 Matt Leinart 12.00 30.00
262 Michael Robinson 10.00 25.00
263 Vernon Davis 15.00 40.00
264 Brandon Williams 8.00 20.00
265 Derek Hagan 10.00 25.00
266 Jason Avant 8.00 20.00
267 Brandon Marshall 12.00 30.00
268 Omar Jacobs 8.00 20.00
269 Santonio Holmes 15.00 40.00
270 Jerious Norwood 10.00 25.00
271 Demetrius Williams 10.00 25.00
272 Sinorice Moss 12.00 30.00
273 Leon Washington 10.00 25.00
274 Kellen Clemens 10.00 25.00
275 A.J. Hawk 12.00 30.00
276 Maurice Stovall 8.00 20.00
277 DeAngelo Williams 15.00 40.00
278 Charlie Whitehurst 12.00 30.00
279 Travis Wilson 8.00 20.00
280 Joe Klopfenstein 8.00 20.00
281 Brian Calhoun 8.00 20.00

2006 Absolute Memorabilia Rookie Premiere Materials Oversize

*SINGLES: .6X TO 1.5X BASIC CARDS
STATED PRINT RUN 50 SER.#'d SETS
UNPRICED SPECTRUM PRIME PRINT RUN 10

2006 Absolute Memorabilia Rookie Premiere Materials Spectrum Prime

*SINGLES: .5X TO 1.2X BASIC CARDS
STATED PRINT RUN 100 SER.#'d SETS

2006 Absolute Memorabilia Spectrum Gold Autographs

*GOLD/50: .5X TO 1.2X SILVER AUTOS
*GOLD/25: .6X TO 1.5X SILVER AUTOS
SERIAL #'d UNDER 25 NOT PRICED
152 Joseph Addai/50 20.00 50.00
214 Jay Cutler/50 50.00 120.00

2006 Absolute Memorabilia Spectrum Silver Autographs

SERIAL #'d UNDER 25 NOT PRICED
UNPRICED PLATINUM PRINT RUN 1
6 Alge Crumpler/100 5.00 12.00
14 Mark Clayton/100 6.00 15.00
20 Lee Evans/100 5.00 12.00
27 Steve Smith/25 15.00 40.00
35 Rudi Johnson/92 6.00 15.00
36 T.J. Houshmandzadeh/100 6.00 15.00
50 Tatum Bell/100 6.00 15.00
61 Samkon Gado/100 8.00 20.00
66 Domanick Davis/30 6.00 15.00
69 Dallas Clark/100 6.00 15.00
79 Larry Johnson/25 15.00 40.00
96 Deion Branch/100 6.00 15.00
97 Tedy Bruschi/100 35.00 60.00
112 LaMont Jordan/100 6.00 15.00
117 Reggie Brown/100 8.00 20.00
121 Willie Parker/100 20.00 40.00
123 Antonio Gates/100 8.00 20.00
131 Darrell Jackson/100 6.00 15.00
144 Drew Bennett/67 6.00 15.00
151 Greg Jennings/125 15.00 40.00
152 Joseph Addai/125 15.00 40.00
153 Erik Meyer/100 6.00 15.00
154 Drew Olson/76 8.00 20.00
155 Darrell Hackney/70 8.00 20.00
156 Paul Pinegar/100 6.00 15.00
157 Brandon Kirsch/100 8.00 20.00
158 Andre Hall/100 10.00 25.00
159 Taurean Henderson/100 8.00 20.00
160 Derrick Ross/100 6.00 15.00
161 Mike Bell/100 10.00 25.00
162 Wendell Mathis/100 6.00 15.00
163 Gerald Riggs/50 10.00 25.00
165 Devin Aromashodu/100 8.00 20.00
166 Ben Obomanu/100 6.00 15.00
167 David Anderson/100 6.00 15.00
169 Kevin McMahan/100 6.00 15.00
170 Miles Austin/76 50.00 100.00
171 Martin Nance/100 6.00 15.00
172 Greg Lee/100 6.00 15.00
173 Hank Baskett/76 8.00 20.00
174 Anthony Mix/100 6.00 15.00
175 D'Brickashaw Ferguson/150 8.00 20.00
176 Kamerion Wimbley/150 8.00 20.00
177 Tamba Hali/150 8.00 20.00
178 Mathias Kiwanuka/150 10.00 25.00
179 Brodrick Bunkley/150 8.00 20.00
180 John McCargo/150 6.00 15.00
181 Claude Wroten/100 4.00 10.00
182 Gabe Watson/100 6.00 15.00
183 D'Qwell Jackson/100 6.00 15.00
184 Abdul Hodge/100 8.00 20.00
185 Ernie Sims/150
186 Chad Greenway/150 8.00 20.00
187 Bobby Carpenter/150 8.00 20.00
188 Manny Lawson/150 8.00 20.00
189 DeMeco Ryans/100 10.00 25.00
190 Rocky McIntosh/100 8.00 20.00
191 Thomas Howard/100 8.00 20.00
192 Jon Alston/100 8.00 20.00
193 A.J. Nicholson/100 4.00 10.00
194 Tye Hill/150 8.00 20.00
195 Antonio Cromartie/150 8.00 20.00
196 Johnathan Joseph/150 6.00 15.00
197 Kelly Jennings/150 8.00 20.00
198 Jimmy Williams/100 8.00 20.00
199 Ashton Youboty/100 8.00 20.00
200 Alan Zemaitis/100 8.00 20.00
201 Anwar Phillips/50 8.00 20.00
202 Jason Allen/150 8.00 20.00
203 Cedric Griffin/100 6.00 15.00
204 Ko Simpson/100 6.00 15.00
205 Pat Watkins/100 8.00 20.00
206 Donte Whitner/150 8.00 20.00
207 Bernard Pollard/100 6.00 15.00
208 Darnell Bing/100 8.00 20.00
209 De'Arrius Howard/100 8.00 20.00
210 Ethan Kilmer/100 8.00 20.00
211 Bennie Brazell/100 6.00 15.00
212 Haloti Ngata/150 8.00 20.00
213 Jeremy Bloom/100 8.00 20.00
214 Jay Cutler/125 30.00 80.00

2006 Absolute Memorabilia Star Gazing Materials

STATED PRINT RUN 100 SER.#'d SETS
*PRIME/50: .5X TO 1.2X BASIC JERSEYS
*PRIME OVERSIZED/25: .8X TO 2X BASIC JSYs
UNPRICED OVERSIZED SPECTRUM #'d TO 1
1 Chad Jackson 3.00 8.00
2 Laurence Maroney 4.00 10.00
3 Tarvaris Jackson 5.00 12.00
4 Michael Huff 4.00 10.00
5 Mario Williams 5.00 12.00
6 Marcedes Lewis 5.00 12.00
7 Maurice Drew 8.00 20.00
8 Vince Young 6.00 15.00
9 LenDale White 4.00 10.00
10 Reggie Bush 10.00 25.00
11 Matt Leinart 5.00 12.00
12 Michael Robinson 4.00 10.00
13 Vernon Davis 6.00 15.00
14 Brandon Williams 3.00 8.00
15 Derek Hagan 4.00 10.00
16 Jason Avant 3.00 8.00
17 Brandon Marshall 5.00 12.00
18 Omar Jacobs 3.00 8.00
19 Santonio Holmes 6.00 15.00
20 Jerious Norwood 4.00 10.00
21 Demetrius Williams 4.00 10.00
22 Sinorice Moss 5.00 12.00
23 Leon Washington 4.00 10.00
24 Kellen Clemens 4.00 10.00
25 A.J. Hawk 5.00 12.00
26 Maurice Stovall 3.00 8.00
27 DeAngelo Williams 6.00 15.00
28 Charlie Whitehurst 5.00 12.00
29 Travis Wilson 3.00 8.00
30 Joe Klopfenstein 3.00 8.00
31 Brian Calhoun 3.00 8.00

2006 Absolute Memorabilia Team Quads Silver

STATED PRINT RUN 100 SER.#'d SETS
*SPECTRUM: .6X TO 1.5X BASIC INSERTS
SPECTRUM PRINT RUN 25 SER.#'d SETS
1 J.P. Losman 2.50 6.00
Willis McGahee
Eric Moulds
Lee Evans
2 Carson Palmer 3.00 8.00
Chad Johnson
Rudi Johnson
T.J. Houshmandzadeh
3 Drew Bledsoe 3.00 8.00
Julius Jones
Keyshawn Johnson
Roy Williams S
4 Brett Favre 6.00 15.00
Aaron Rodgers
Donald Driver
Ahman Green
5 Peyton Manning 5.00 12.00
Marvin Harrison
Edgerrin James
Reggie Wayne
6 Tom Brady 5.00 12.00
Corey Dillon
David Givens
Deion Branch
7 Eli Manning 4.00 10.00
Tiki Barber
Plaxico Burress
Jeremy Shockey
8 Ben Roethlisberger 4.00 10.00
Hines Ward
Antwaan Randle El
Willie Parker
9 Drew Brees 3.00 8.00
LaDainian Tomlinson
Antonio Gates
Keenan McCardell
10 Marc Bulger 3.00 8.00
Steven Jackson
Torry Holt
Isaac Bruce

2006 Absolute Memorabilia Team Quads Materials

STATED PRINT RUN 50 SER.#'d SETS
UNPRICED PRIME PRINT RUN 5
UNPRICED PRIME SPECTRUM PRINT RUN 1
1 J.P. Losman 12.00 30.00
Willis McGahee
Eric Moulds
Lee Evans
2 Carson Palmer 12.00 30.00
Chad Johnson
Rudi Johnson
T.J. Houshmandzadeh
3 Drew Bledsoe 12.00 30.00
Julius Jones
Keyshawn Johnson
Roy Williams S
4 Brett Favre 40.00 80.00
Aaron Rodgers
Donald Driver
Ahman Green
5 Peyton Manning 20.00 50.00
Marvin Harrison
Edgerrin James
Reggie Wayne
6 Tom Brady 20.00 50.00
Corey Dillon
David Givens
Deion Branch/29
7 Eli Manning 15.00 40.00
Tiki Barber
Plaxico Burress
Jeremy Shockey
8 Ben Roethlisberger 25.00 60.00
Hines Ward
Antwaan Randle El
Willie Parker
9 Drew Brees 15.00 40.00
LaDainian Tomlinson
Antonio Gates
Keenan McCardell
10 Marc Bulger 12.00 30.00
Steven Jackson
Torry Holt
Isaac Bruce

2006 Absolute Memorabilia Team Tandems Silver

STATED PRINT RUN 250 SER.#'d SETS
*SPECTRUM: .5X TO 1.2X BASIC INSERTS
SPECTRUM PRINT RUN 100 SER.#'d SETS
1 Michael Vick 2.00 5.00
Warrick Dunn
2 J.P. Losman 1.50 4.00
Willis McGahee
3 Jake Delhomme 2.00 5.00
Steve Smith
4 Carson Palmer 2.00 5.00
Chad Johnson
5 Drew Bledsoe 2.00 5.00
Julius Jones
6 Jake Plummer 1.50 4.00
Tatum Bell
7 Joey Harrington 1.25 3.00
Kevin Jones
8 Peyton Manning 3.00 8.00
Marvin Harrison
9 Byron Leftwich 1.50 4.00
Jimmy Smith
10 Trent Green 1.50 4.00
Larry Johnson
11 Chris Chambers 2.00 5.00
Ronnie Brown
12 Tom Brady 3.00 8.00
Corey Dillon
13 Eli Manning 2.50 6.00
Tiki Barber
14 Chad Pennington 2.00 5.00
Curtis Martin
15 Kerry Collins 2.00 5.00
Randy Moss
16 Donovan McNabb 2.00 5.00
Brian Westbrook
17 Ben Roethlisberger 2.50 6.00
Hines Ward
18 Drew Brees 2.00 5.00
LaDainian Tomlinson
19 Matt Hasselbeck 1.50 4.00
Shaun Alexander
20 Steven Jackson 2.00 5.00
Torry Holt
21 Cadillac Williams 1.50 4.00
Michael Clayton
22 Steve McNair 1.50 4.00
Drew Bennett
23 Clinton Portis 2.00 5.00
Santana Moss
24 Larry Fitzgerald 2.00 5.00
Anquan Boldin
25 Thomas Jones 1.50 4.00
Cedric Benson

2006 Absolute Memorabilia Team Tandems Materials

STATED PRINT RUN 55-100 SER.#'d SETS
*PRIME: .6X TO 1.5X BASIC JSY/100
*PRIME: .5X TO 1.2X BASIC JSY/50-75
PRIME PRINT RUN 25 SER.#'d SETS
UNPRICED PRIME SPECTRUM PRINT RUN 1
1 Michael Vick 6.00 15.00
Warrick Dunn/100
2 J.P. Losman 5.00 12.00
Willis McGahee/100
3 Jake Delhomme 6.00 15.00
Steve Smith/100
4 Carson Palmer 6.00 15.00
Chad Johnson/100
5 Drew Bledsoe 8.00 20.00
Julius Jones/75
6 Jake Plummer 6.00 15.00
Tatum Bell/70
7 Joey Harrington 5.00 12.00
Kevin Jones/55
8 Peyton Manning 10.00 25.00
Marvin Harrison/100
9 Byron Leftwich 5.00 12.00
Jimmy Smith/100
10 Trent Green 5.00 12.00
Larry Johnson/100
11 Chris Chambers 6.00 15.00
Ronnie Brown/100
12 Tom Brady 10.00 25.00
Corey Dillon/100
13 Eli Manning 8.00 20.00
Tiki Barber/100
14 Chad Pennington 8.00 20.00
Curtis Martin/75
15 Kerry Collins 6.00 15.00
Randy Moss/100
16 Donovan McNabb 6.00 15.00
Brian Westbrook/90
17 Ben Roethlisberger 8.00 20.00
Hines Ward/100
18 Drew Brees 6.00 15.00
LaDainian Tomlinson/100
19 Matt Hasselbeck 5.00 12.00
Shaun Alexander/100
20 Steven Jackson 6.00 15.00
Torry Holt/100
21 Cadillac Williams 6.00 15.00
Michael Clayton/75
22 Steve McNair 6.00 15.00
Drew Bennett/50
23 Clinton Portis 6.00 15.00
Santana Moss/100
24 Larry Fitzgerald 6.00 15.00
Anquan Boldin/100
25 Thomas Jones 6.00 15.00
Cedric Benson/75

2006 Absolute Memorabilia Team Trios Silver

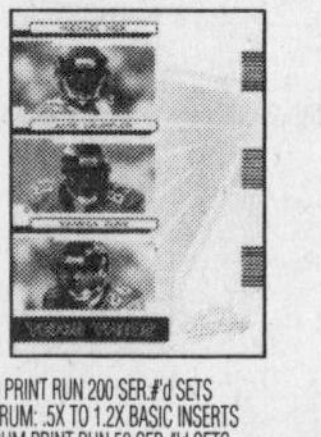

STATED PRINT RUN 200 SER.#'d SETS
*SPECTRUM: .5X TO 1.2X BASIC INSERTS
SPECTRUM PRINT RUN 50 SER.#'d SETS
1 Jake Delhomme 2.50 6.00
Steve Smith
DeShaun Foster
2 Carson Palmer 2.50 6.00
Chad Johnson
Rudi Johnson

3 Drew Bledsoe 2.50 6.00
Keyshawn Johnson
Julius Jones
4 Peyton Manning 4.00 10.00
Marvin Harrison
Edgerrin James
5 Byron Leftwich 2.00 5.00
Jimmy Smith
Fred Taylor
6 Trent Green 2.00 5.00
Tony Gonzalez
Larry Johnson
7 Chris Chambers 2.50 6.00
Ronnie Brown
Zach Thomas
8 Tom Brady 4.00 10.00
Deion Branch
Corey Dillon
9 Eli Manning 3.00 8.00
Plaxico Burress
Tiki Barber
10 Chad Pennington 2.50 6.00
Laveranues Coles
Curtis Martin
11 Ben Roethlisberger 3.00 8.00
Hines Ward
Willie Parker
12 Drew Brees 2.50 6.00
Antonio Gates
LaDainian Tomlinson
13 Matt Hasselbeck 2.00 5.00
Darrell Jackson
Shaun Alexander
14 Marc Bulger 2.50 6.00
Torry Holt
Steven Jackson
15 Michael Vick 2.50 6.00
Alge Crumpler
Warrick Dunn

2006 Absolute Memorabilia Team Trios Materials

STATED PRINT RUN 80-100
*PRIME/15: .6X TO 1.5X TRIO/80-100
UNPRICED PRIME SPECTRUM PRINT RUN 1
1 Jake Delhomme 6.00 15.00
Steve Smith
DeShaun Foster
2 Carson Palmer 6.00 15.00
Chad Johnson
Rudi Johnson
3 Drew Bledsoe 6.00 15.00
Keyshawn Johnson
Julius Jones
4 Peyton Manning 10.00 25.00
Marvin Harrison
Edgerrin James
5 Byron Leftwich 5.00 12.00
Jimmy Smith
Fred Taylor
6 Trent Green 5.00 12.00
Tony Gonzalez
Larry Johnoon
7 Chris Chambers 6.00 15.00
Ronnie Brown
Zach Thomas
8 Tom Brady 10.00 25.00
Deion Branch
Corey Dillon
9 Eli Manning 8.00 20.00
Plaxico Burress
Tiki Barber
10 Chad Pennington 6.00 15.00
Laveranues Coles
Curtis Martin
11 Ben Roethlisberger 8.00 20.00
Hines Ward
Willie Parker
12 Drew Brees 6.00 15.00
Antonio Gates
LaDainian Tomlinson
13 Matt Hasselbeck 5.00 12.00
Darrell Jackson
Shaun Alexander
14 Marc Bulger 6.00 15.00
Torry Holt
Steven Jackson/80
15 Michael Vick 6.00 15.00
Alge Crumpler
Warrick Dunn

2006 Absolute Memorabilia Tools of the Trade Red

RED PRINT RUN 100 SER.#'d SETS
*BLACK: .5X TO 1.2X RED INSERTS
BLACK PRINT RUN 50 SER.#'d SETS
UNPRICED BLACK SPECTRUM PRINT RUN 5
*BLUE: .4X TO 1X RED INSERTS
BLUE PRINT RUN 75 SER.#'d SETS
UNPRICED BLUE SPECTRUM PRINT RUN 10
*RED SPECTRUM: .8X TO 2X RED INSERTS
RED SPECT.PRINT RUN 25 SER.#'d SETS
1 Aaron Brooks 2.00 5.00
2 Aaron Rodgers 5.00 12.00
3 Ahman Green 2.00 5.00
4 Alex Smith QB 2.50 6.00
5 Alge Crumpler 2.00 5.00
6 Amani Toomer 2.00 5.00
7 Andre Johnson 2.50 6.00
8 Anquan Boldin 2.00 5.00
9 Antonio Bryant 1.50 4.00
10 Antonio Gates 2.50 6.00
11 Antwaan Randle El 2.00 5.00
12 Ashley Lelie 1.50 4.00
13 Barry Sanders 5.00 12.00
14 Ben Roethlisberger 3.00 8.00
15 Bernard Berrian 2.00 5.00
16 Bethel Johnson 1.50 4.00
17 Boomer Esiason 2.50 6.00
18 Brandon Stokley 2.00 5.00
19 Brad Johnson 2.00 5.00
20 Brandon Lloyd 1.50 4.00
21 Brett Favre 5.00 12.00
22 Brian Urlacher 2.50 6.00
23 Brian Westbrook 2.00 5.00
24 Byron Leftwich 2.00 5.00
25 Cadillac Williams 2.00 5.00
26 Carson Palmer 2.50 6.00
27 Cedric Benson 2.00 5.00
28 Chad Johnson 2.00 5.00
29 Chad Pennington 2.00 5.00
30 Chris Chambers 2.00 5.00
31 Charles Rogers 2.00 5.00
32 Chris Brown 1.50 4.00
33 Clinton Portis 2.50 6.00
34 Corey Dillon 2.00 5.00
35 Curtis Martin 2.50 6.00
36 Dallas Clark 2.00 5.00
37 Dan Marino 6.00 15.00
38 Dante Hall 2.00 5.00
39 Daunte Culpepper 2.00 5.00
40 Darrell Jackson 2.00 5.00
41 David Carr 1.50 4.00
42 Derrick Brooks 2.00 5.00
43 David Givens 2.00 5.00
44 Deion Sanders 4.00 10.00
45 Derrick Mason 2.00 5.00
46 DeShaun Foster 2.00 5.00
47 Deuce McAllister 2.00 5.00
48 Domanick Davis 1.50 4.00
49 Donovan McNabb 2.50 6.00
50 Donte Stallworth 1.50 4.00
51 Drew Bennett 2.00 5.00
52 Drew Bledsoe 2.50 6.00
53 Drew Brees 2.50 6.00
54 Duce Staley 1.50 4.00
55 Edgerrin James 2.00 5.00
56 Eli Manning 3.00 8.00
57 Eric Dickerson 2.50 6.00
58 Eric Moulds 1.50 4.00
59 Fred Taylor 2.00 5.00
60 Herschel Walker 2.50 6.00
61 Hines Ward 2.50 6.00
62 Isaac Bruce 2.00 5.00
63 Ickey Woods 2.00 5.00
64 Jeff Garcia 2.00 5.00
65 J.P. Losman 2.00 5.00
66 Jabar Gaffney 1.50 4.00
67 Julius Jones 1.50 4.00
68 Jake Delhomme 2.00 5.00
69 Jake Plummer 2.00 5.00
70 Jamal Lewis 2.00 5.00
71 Jason Campbell 2.00 5.00
72 Jason Taylor 2.00 5.00
73 Javon Walker 2.00 5.00
74 Jeremy Shockey 2.50 6.00
75 Jerome Bettis 2.50 6.00
76 Jerry Rice 5.00 12.00
77 Jevon Kearse 2.00 5.00
78 Jimmy Smith 2.00 5.00
79 Joe Montana 6.00 15.00
80 Joey Harrington 1.50 4.00
81 John Elway 5.00 12.00
82 Kevin Jones 1.50 4.00
83 Junior Seau 2.50 6.00
84 Julius Peppers 2.00 5.00
85 Keenan McCardell 2.00 5.00
86 Keyshawn Johnson 2.00 5.00
87 LaDainian Tomlinson 2.50 6.00
88 LaMont Jordan 2.00 5.00
89 Larry Fitzgerald 2.50 6.00
90 LaVar Arrington 2.00 5.00
91 Laveranues Coles 1.50 4.00
92 Lee Evans 2.00 5.00
93 Marcel Shipp 1.50 4.00
94 Marc Bulger 2.00 5.00
95 Marcus Allen 3.00 8.00
96 Mark Brunell 2.00 5.00
97 Marshall Faulk 2.00 5.00
98 Marvin Harrison 2.50 6.00
99 Matt Hasselbeck 2.00 5.00
100 Matt Jones 1.50 4.00
101 Michael Bennett 1.50 4.00
102 Michael Clayton 1.50 4.00
103 Michael Pittman 1.50 4.00
104 Michael Strahan 2.00 5.00
105 Michael Vick 2.50 6.00
106 Muhsin Muhammad 2.00 5.00
107 Peyton Manning 4.00 10.00
108 Priest Holmes 2.00 5.00
109 Randy Moss 2.50 6.00
110 Ray Lewis 2.50 6.00
111 Reggie Brown 1.50 4.00
112 Reggie Wayne 2.00 5.00
113 Reggie White 4.00 10.00
114 Rex Grossman 2.00 5.00
115 Richard Seymour 1.50 4.00
116 Derrick Thomas 5.00 12.00
117 Rod Smith 2.00 5.00
118 Ronnie Brown 2.50 6.00
119 Roy Williams S 2.00 5.00
120 Rudi Johnson 2.00 5.00
121 Samkon Gado 2.00 5.00
122 Santana Moss 2.00 5.00
123 Shaun Alexander 2.00 5.00
124 Stephen Davis 2.00 5.00
125 Steve McNair 2.00 5.00
126 Steve Smith 2.50 6.00
127 Steve Young 4.00 10.00
128 Steven Jackson 2.50 6.00
129 T.J. Houshmandzadeh 2.00 5.00
130 Tatum Bell 1.50 4.00
131 Terrell Davis 3.00 8.00
132 Terrell Owens 2.50 6.00
133 Terry Glenn 2.00 5.00
134 Thomas Jones 2.00 5.00
135 Tiki Barber 2.50 6.00
136 Todd Heap 2.00 5.00
137 Tom Brady 4.00 10.00
138 Tony Gonzalez 2.00 5.00
139 Torry Holt 2.00 5.00
140 Trent Green 2.00 5.00
141 Troy Aikman 4.00 10.00
142 Troy Williamson 1.50 4.00
143 Tyrone Calico 1.50 4.00
144 Walter Payton 6.00 15.00
145 Warren Moon 3.00 8.00
146 Warren Sapp 2.00 5.00
147 Warrick Dunn 2.00 5.00
148 Willie Parker 2.00 5.00
149 Willis McGahee 2.00 5.00
150 Zach Thomas 2.50 6.00

2006 Absolute Memorabilia Tools of the Trade Material Black Spectrum

*BLACK SPECTRUM/35-50: .5X TO 1.2X RED MATERIALS
SERIAL #'d UNDER 25 NOT PRICED
UNPRICED BLACK OVERSIZED PRINT RUN 1
14 Ben Roethlisberger/38 15.00 40.00

2006 Absolute Memorabilia Tools of the Trade Material Blue

*BLUE: .5X TO 1.2X RED MATERIALS
SERIAL #'d UNDER 25 NOT PRICED
UNPRICED BLUE OVERSIZED PRINT RUN 2-5
14 Ben Roethlisberger 12.50 30.00

2006 Absolute Memorabilia Tools of the Trade Material Red

RED STATED PRINT RUN 5-100
1 Aaron Brooks 3.00 8.00
2 Aaron Rodgers 20.00 40.00
3 Ahman Green 3.00 8.00
4 Alex Smith QB 4.00 10.00
5 Alge Crumpler 3.00 8.00
6 Amani Toomer/75 3.00 8.00
7 Andre Johnson 4.00 10.00
8 Anquan Boldin 3.00 8.00
10 Antonio Gates 4.00 10.00
11 Antwaan Randle El 3.00 8.00
12 Ashley Lelie 2.50 6.00
13 Barry Sanders 8.00 20.00
14 Ben Roethlisberger/28 20.00 50.00
15 Bernard Berrian 3.00 8.00
17 Boomer Esiason 4.00 10.00
19 Brad Johnson 3.00 8.00
20 Brandon Lloyd/37 4.00 10.00
21 Brett Favre 8.00 20.00
22 Brian Urlacher 4.00 10.00
23 Brian Westbrook 3.00 8.00
24 Byron Leftwich 3.00 8.00
25 Cadillac Williams 3.00 8.00
26 Carson Palmer 4.00 10.00
27 Cedric Benson 3.00 8.00
28 Chad Johnson 3.00 8.00
29 Chad Pennington 3.00 8.00
30 Chris Chambers 3.00 8.00
31 Charles Rogers 3.00 8.00
32 Chris Brown 2.50 6.00
33 Clinton Portis 4.00 10.00
34 Corey Dillon 3.00 8.00
35 Curtis Martin 4.00 10.00
36 Dallas Clark/75 3.00 8.00
37 Dan Marino 12.50 30.00
38 Dante Hall 3.00 8.00
39 Daunte Culpepper 3.00 8.00
41 David Carr 2.50 6.00
43 David Givens 3.00 8.00
44 Deion Sanders 5.00 12.00
47 Deuce McAllister 3.00 8.00
48 Domanick Davis 2.50 6.00
49 Donovan McNabb 4.00 10.00
50 Donte Stallworth 2.50 6.00
51 Drew Bennett 3.00 8.00
52 Drew Bledsoe 4.00 10.00
53 Drew Brees 4.00 10.00
54 Duce Staley 2.50 6.00
55 Edgerrin James 3.00 8.00
56 Eli Manning 5.00 12.00
57 Eric Dickerson 4.00 10.00
58 Eric Moulds 2.50 6.00
59 Fred Taylor 3.00 8.00
60 Herschel Walker 4.00 10.00
61 Hines Ward 4.00 10.00
62 Isaac Bruce 3.00 8.00
63 Ickey Woods 3.00 8.00
64 Jeff Garcia 3.00 8.00
65 J.P. Losman 3.00 8.00
67 Julius Jones 2.50 6.00
68 Jake Delhomme/82 3.00 8.00
69 Jake Plummer 3.00 8.00
70 Jamal Lewis 3.00 8.00
71 Jason Campbell 3.00 8.00
73 Javon Walker/42 4.00 10.00
74 Jeremy Shockey 4.00 10.00
76 Jerry Rice 8.00 20.00
78 Jimmy Smith 3.00 8.00
79 Joe Montana 10.00 25.00
80 Joey Harrington 2.50 6.00
81 John Elway 8.00 20.00
82 Kevin Jones 2.50 6.00
83 Junior Seau 4.00 10.00
84 Julius Peppers/22
85 Keenan McCardell 3.00 8.00
87 LaDainian Tomlinson 4.00 10.00
88 LaMont Jordan 3.00 8.00
89 Larry Fitzgerald 4.00 10.00
90 LaVar Arrington 3.00 8.00
91 Laveranues Coles 2.50 6.00
92 Lee Evans 3.00 8.00
93 Marcel Shipp/75 2.50 6.00
94 Marc Bulger 3.00 8.00
95 Marcus Allen 5.00 12.00
96 Mark Brunell 3.00 8.00
97 Marshall Faulk 3.00 8.00
98 Marvin Harrison 4.00 10.00
99 Matt Hasselbeck 3.00 8.00
100 Matt Jones 2.50 6.00
102 Michael Clayton 2.50 6.00
103 Michael Pittman 2.50 6.00
104 Michael Strahan 3.00 8.00
105 Michael Vick 4.00 10.00
106 Muhsin Muhammad 3.00 8.00
107 Peyton Manning 6.00 15.00
108 Priest Holmes 3.00 8.00
109 Randy Moss 4.00 10.00
110 Ray Lewis 4.00 10.00
111 Reggie Brown 2.50 6.00
112 Reggie Wayne 3.00 8.00
113 Reggie White 8.00 20.00
114 Rex Grossman 3.00 8.00
115 Richard Seymour 2.50 6.00
116 Derrick Thomas 12.00 30.00
117 Rod Smith 3.00 8.00
118 Ronnie Brown 4.00 10.00
119 Roy Williams S/77 3.00 8.00
120 Rudi Johnson 3.00 8.00
121 Samkon Gado 3.00 8.00
122 Santana Moss 3.00 8.00
123 Shaun Alexander 3.00 8.00
124 Stephen Davis 3.00 8.00
125 Steve McNair 3.00 8.00
127 Steve Young 6.00 15.00
128 Steven Jackson 4.00 10.00
129 T.J. Houshmandzadeh 3.00 8.00
130 Tatum Bell 2.50 6.00
131 Terrell Davis 4.00 10.00
132 Terrell Owens 4.00 10.00
134 Thomas Jones 3.00 8.00
135 Tiki Barber 4.00 10.00
136 Todd Heap 3.00 8.00
137 Tom Brady 6.00 15.00
138 Tony Gonzalez 3.00 8.00
139 Torry Holt 3.00 8.00
140 Trent Green 3.00 8.00
141 Troy Aikman/75 6.00 15.00
142 Troy Williamson 2.50 6.00
144 Walter Payton/75 10.00 25.00
145 Warren Moon/75 5.00 12.00
146 Warren Sapp 3.00 8.00
147 Warrick Dunn/68 4.00 10.00
148 Willie Parker 3.00 8.00
149 Willis McGahee 3.00 8.00
150 Zach Thomas 4.00 10.00

2006 Absolute Memorabilia Tools of the Trade Material Red Oversize

*RED OVER: .8X TO 2X RED MATERIAL
SERIAL #'d UNDER 25 NOT PRICED
14 Ben Roethlisberger/25 30.00 80.00
144 Walter Payton/26 30.00 80.00

2006 Absolute Memorabilia Tools of the Trade Material Double Black Spectrum

*DOUBLE BLK/25: .8X TO 2X RED MATERIAL
SERIAL #'d UNDER 25 NOT PRICED

2006 Absolute Memorabilia Tools of the Trade Material Double Blue

*DOUB.BLUE: .6X TO 1.5X RED MATERIAL
SERIAL #'d UNDER 25 NOT PRICED

2006 Absolute Memorabilia Tools of the Trade Material Double Red

*DOUB.RED/72-100: .5X TO 1.2X RED MAT.
*DOUB.RED/35-67: .6X TO 1.5X RED MAT.
*DOUB.RED/25-26: .8X TO 2X RED MAT.
SERIAL #'d UNDER 25 NOT PRICED

2006 Absolute Memorabilia Tools of the Trade Material Quad Red

*QUAD RED/25: 1X TO 2.5X RED MATERIAL
SERIAL #'d UNDER 25 NOT PRICED
UNPRICED BLACK PRINT RUN 1
UNPRICED BLUE PRINT RUN 3-10

2006 Absolute Memorabilia Tools of the Trade Material Triple Blue

*TRIP.BLUE/25: .8X TO 2X RED MATERIAL
SERIAL #'d UNDER 25 NOT PRICED

2006 Absolute Memorabilia Tools of the Trade Material Triple Red

*TRIP.RED/50: .6X TO 1.5X RED MATERIAL
*TRIP.RED/25-36: .8X TO 2X RED MATERIAL
UNPRICED BLACK PRINT RUN 1-5
SER.#'d UNDER 25 NOT PRICED

2006 Absolute Memorabilia War Room Materials

STATED PRINT RUN 100 SER.#'d SETS
*PRIME/50: .6X TO 1.5X BASIC JERSEYS
*OVERSIZED/25: 1X TO 2.5X BASIC JERSEYS
UNPRICED OVER.SPECTRUM PRINT RUN 10
1 Chad Jackson 3.00 8.00
2 Laurence Maroney 4.00 10.00
3 Tarvaris Jackson 5.00 12.00
4 Michael Huff 4.00 10.00
5 Mario Williams 5.00 12.00
6 Marcedes Lewis 5.00 12.00
7 Maurice Drew 8.00 20.00
8 Vince Young 6.00 15.00
9 LenDale White 4.00 10.00
10 Reggie Bush 10.00 25.00
11 Matt Leinart 5.00 12.00
12 Michael Robinson 4.00 10.00
13 Vernon Davis 6.00 15.00
14 Brandon Williams 3.00 8.00
15 Derek Hagan 4.00 10.00
16 Jason Avant 3.00 8.00
17 Brandon Marshall 5.00 12.00
18 Omar Jacobs 3.00 8.00
19 Santonio Holmes 6.00 15.00
20 Jerious Norwood 4.00 10.00
21 Demetrius Williams 4.00 10.00
22 Sinorice Moss 5.00 12.00
23 Leon Washington 4.00 10.00
24 Kellen Clemens 4.00 10.00
25 A.J. Hawk 5.00 12.00
26 Maurice Stovall 3.00 8.00
27 DeAngelo Williams 6.00 15.00
28 Charlie Whitehurst 5.00 12.00
29 Travis Wilson 3.00 8.00
30 Joe Klopfenstein 3.00 8.00
31 Brian Calhoun 3.00 8.00

2007 Absolute Memorabilia

This 284-card set was released in September, 2007. The set was issued into the hobby in five-card packs, with a $40 SRP, which came six packs to a box. Cards numbered 1-150 feature veterans in team alphabetical order by division while cards numbered 151-284 feature 2007 NFL rookies. The Rookie Cards are broken down thusly: Cards numbered 151-200 were issued to a stated print run of 699 serial numbered sets, cards numbered 201-250 were signed by the player and were issued to a stated print run of 349 serial numbered sets and cards numbered 251-284 had player-worn swatches and were issued to a stated print run of 849 serial numbered sets.

ROOKIE PRINT RUN 699 SER.#'d SETS
AU ROOKIE PRINT RUN 349 SER.#'d SETS
RPM ROOKIE PRINT RUN 849 SER.#'d SETS
UNPRICED SPECTRUM PLATINUM #'d TO 1
1 Tony Romo 1.50 4.00
2 Julius Jones .75 2.00
3 Terry Glenn 1.00 2.50
4 Terrell Owens 1.25 3.00
5 Marion Barber 1.00 2.50
6 Reuben Droughns 1.00 2.50
7 Eli Manning 1.25 3.00
8 Plaxico Burress 1.00 2.50
9 Jeremy Shockey 1.00 2.50
10 Brandon Jacobs 1.00 2.50
11 Donovan McNabb 1.25 3.00
12 Brian Westbrook 1.00 2.50
13 Reggie Brown .75 2.00
14 Hank Baskett 1.00 2.50
15 Jason Campbell 1.00 2.50
16 Clinton Portis 1.00 2.50
17 Santana Moss 1.00 2.50
18 Ladell Betts .75 2.00
19 Brandon Lloyd 1.00 2.50
20 Chris Cooley 1.00 2.50
21 Rex Grossman 1.00 2.50
22 Cedric Benson 1.00 2.50
23 Muhsin Muhammad 1.00 2.50
24 Bernard Berrian .75 2.00
25 Devin Hester 1.25 3.00
26 Brian Urlacher 1.25 3.00
27 Jon Kitna .75 2.00
28 Kevin Jones .75 2.00
29 Roy Williams 1.00 2.50
30 Mike Furrey 1.00 2.50
31 Ernie Sims .75 2.00
32 Tatum Bell .75 2.00
33 Brett Favre 2.50 6.00
34 Vernand Morency 1.00 2.50
35 Donald Driver 1.25 3.00
36 Greg Jennings 1.25 3.00
37 AJ Hawk 1.00 2.50
38 Tarvaris Jackson .75 2.00
39 Chester Taylor .75 2.00
40 Troy Williamson .75 2.00
41 Mewelde Moore .75 2.00
42 Michael Vick 1.25 3.00
43 Warrick Dunn 1.00 2.50
44 Joe Horn 1.00 2.50
45 Alge Crumpler 1.00 2.50
46 Jerious Norwood 1.00 2.50
47 Jake Delhomme 1.00 2.50
48 DeShaun Foster 1.00 2.50
49 Steve Smith 1.00 2.50
50 DeAngelo Williams 1.25 3.00
51 Drew Brees 1.25 3.00
52 Deuce McAllister 1.00 2.50
53 Marques Colston 1.25 3.00
54 Devery Henderson .75 2.00
55 Reggie Bush 1.25 3.00
56 Jeff Garcia 1.00 2.50
57 Cadillac Williams 1.00 2.50
58 Joey Galloway 1.00 2.50
59 Michael Clayton .75 2.00
60 Matt Leinart 1.00 2.50
61 Edgerrin James 1.00 2.50
62 Anquan Boldin 1.00 2.50
63 Larry Fitzgerald 1.25 3.00
64 Marc Bulger 1.00 2.50
65 Steven Jackson 1.25 3.00
66 Torry Holt 1.00 2.50
67 Isaac Bruce 1.00 2.50
68 Randy McMichael .75 2.00
69 Drew Bennett .75 2.00
70 Alex Smith 1.25 3.00
71 Frank Gore 1.25 3.00
72 Darrell Jackson .75 2.00
73 Ashley Lelie 1.00 2.50
74 Vernon Davis 1.00 2.50
75 Matt Hasselbeck 1.00 2.50
76 Shaun Alexander 1.00 2.50
77 Deion Branch 1.00 2.50
78 J.P. Losman .75 2.00
79 Lee Evans 1.00 2.50
80 Josh Reed .75 2.00
81 Daunte Culpepper 1.00 2.50
82 Ronnie Brown 1.00 2.50
83 Chris Chambers 1.00 2.50
84 Marty Booker .75 2.00
85 Zach Thomas 1.00 2.50
86 Tom Brady 2.00 5.00
87 Laurence Maroney 1.00 2.50
88 Randy Moss 1.25 3.00
89 Chad Jackson .75 2.00
90 Ben Watson .75 2.00
91 Donte' Stallworth 1.00 2.50
92 Chad Pennington 1.00 2.50
93 Thomas Jones 1.00 2.50
94 Laveranues Coles .75 2.00
95 Jerricho Cotchery 1.00 2.50
96 Leon Washington 1.00 2.50
97 Steve McNair 1.00 2.50
98 Willis McGahee 1.00 2.50
99 Derrick Mason 1.00 2.50
100 Demetrius Williams .75 2.00
101 Mark Clayton 1.00 2.50
102 Carson Palmer 1.00 2.50
103 Rudi Johnson 1.00 2.50
104 Chad Johnson 1.00 2.50
105 T.J. Houshmandzadeh 1.00 2.50
106 Charlie Frye 1.00 2.50
107 Braylon Edwards 1.00 2.50
108 Travis Wilson .75 2.00
109 Kellen Winslow 1.00 2.50
110 Jamal Lewis 1.00 2.50
111 Ben Roethlisberger 1.25 3.00
112 Willie Parker 1.00 2.50
113 Hines Ward 1.25 3.00
114 Santonio Holmes 1.00 2.50
115 Ahman Green 1.00 2.50
116 Andre Johnson 1.00 2.50
117 Matt Schaub 1.00 2.50
118 DeMeco Ryans 1.00 2.50
119 Owen Daniels .75 2.00
120 Peyton Manning 2.00 5.00
121 Joseph Addai 1.00 2.50
122 Marvin Harrison 1.25 3.00
123 Reggie Wayne 1.00 2.50
124 Dallas Clark .75 2.00
125 Byron Leftwich 1.00 2.50
126 Fred Taylor 1.00 2.50
127 Matt Jones 1.00 2.50
128 Reggie Williams 1.00 2.50
129 Marcedes Lewis .75 2.00
130 Maurice Jones-Drew 1.25 3.00
131 Vince Young 1.00 2.50
132 LenDale White 1.00 2.50
133 Brandon Jones .75 2.00
134 Jay Cutler 1.25 3.00
135 Travis Henry 1.00 2.50
136 Javon Walker 1.00 2.50
137 Rod Smith 1.00 2.50
138 Mike Bell 1.00 2.50
139 Brandon Marshall 1.00 2.50
140 Larry Johnson .75 2.00
141 Eddie Kennison .75 2.00
142 Tony Gonzalez 1.00 2.50
143 Brodie Croyle 1.00 2.50
144 LaMont Jordan 1.00 2.50
145 Ronald Curry 1.00 2.50
146 Philip Rivers 1.25 3.00
147 LaDainian Tomlinson 1.25 3.00
148 Vincent Jackson 1.00 2.50
149 Michael Turner 1.25 3.00
150 Antonio Gates 1.25 3.00
151 A.J. Davis RC 3.00 8.00
152 Aaron Rouse RC 4.00 10.00
153 Ahmad Bradshaw RC 8.00 20.00
154 Alonzo Coleman RC 4.00 10.00
155 Anthony Spencer RC 5.00 12.00
156 Brandon Siler RC 3.00 8.00
157 Buster Davis RC 4.00 10.00
158 Chris Houston RC 4.00 10.00
159 Dallas Baker RC 3.00 8.00
160 Dan Bazuin RC 4.00 10.00
161 Danny Ware RC 5.00 12.00
162 David Ball RC 4.00 10.00
163 David Irons RC 3.00 8.00
164 D'Juan Woods RC 3.00 8.00
165 Earl Everett RC 4.00 10.00
166 Eric Frampton RC 4.00 10.00
167 Eric Weddle RC 5.00 12.00
168 Eric Wright RC 5.00 12.00
169 Fred Bennett RC 3.00 8.00
170 Gary Russell RC 4.00 10.00
171 H.B. Blades RC 3.00 8.00
172 Jarrett Hicks RC 4.00 10.00
173 Jarvis Moss RC 4.00 10.00
174 Jason Snelling RC 5.00 12.00
175 Jerard Rabb RC 4.00 10.00
176 Jemalle Cornelius RC 4.00 10.00
177 Tyler Thigpen RC 5.00 12.00
178 Jon Beason RC 4.00 10.00
179 Jonathan Wade RC 4.00 10.00
180 Jordan Kent RC 4.00 10.00
181 Josh Gattis RC 3.00 8.00
182 Kenneth Darby RC 4.00 10.00
183 DeMarcus Tank Tyler RC 3.00 8.00
184 Levi Brown RC 5.00 12.00
185 Marcus McCauley RC 4.00 10.00
186 Tim Shaw RC 4.00 10.00
187 Michael Okwo RC 4.00 10.00
188 Mike Walker RC 5.00 12.00
189 Nate Ilaoa RC 4.00 10.00
190 Reggie Ball RC 4.00 10.00
191 Rhema McKnight RC 3.00 8.00
192 Zak DeOssie RC 4.00 10.00
193 Rufus Alexander RC 4.00 10.00
194 Ryan McBean RC 5.00 12.00
195 Ryne Robinson RC 4.00 10.00
196 Selvin Young RC 4.00 10.00
197 Steve Breaston RC 5.00 12.00
198 Stewart Bradley RC 4.00 10.00
199 Thomas Clayton RC 4.00 10.00
200 Tim Crowder RC 5.00 12.00
201 Aaron Ross AU RC 6.00 15.00
202 Adam Carriker AU RC 5.00 12.00
204 Amobi Okoye AU RC 6.00 15.00
205 Aundrae Allison AU RC 4.00 10.00
206 Ben Patrick AU RC 5.00 12.00
207 Brandon Meriweather AU RC 6.00 15.00
208 Chansi Stuckey AU RC 6.00 15.00
210 Chris Davis AU RC 4.00 10.00
211 Chris Leak AU RC 5.00 12.00
212 Courtney Taylor AU RC 5.00 12.00
214 Darius Walker AU RC 4.00 10.00
215 Darrelle Revis AU RC 10.00 25.00
216 David Clowney AU RC 5.00 12.00
217 David Harris AU RC 5.00 12.00
218 Daymeion Hughes AU RC 5.00 12.00
219 DeShawn Wynn AU RC 5.00 12.00
220 Dwayne Wright AU RC 5.00 12.00
221 Ikaika Alama-Francis AU RC 6.00 15.00
222 Isaiah Stanback AU RC 4.00 10.00
223 Jacoby Jones AU RC 6.00 15.00
224 Jamaal Anderson AU RC 5.00 12.00
225 James Jones AU RC 6.00 15.00
226 Jared Zabransky AU RC 5.00 12.00
227 Jeff Rowe AU RC 4.00 10.00
228 Joel Filani AU RC 5.00 12.00
229 Jordan Palmer AU RC 5.00 12.00
230 Josh Wilson AU RC 5.00 12.00
231 Kenny Scott AU RC 4.00 10.00
232 Kolby Smith AU RC 5.00 12.00
233 LaMarr Woodley AU RC 15.00 25.00
234 LaRon Landry AU RC 6.00 15.00
235 Laurent Robinson AU RC 6.00 15.00
236 Lawrence Timmons AU RC 6.00 15.00
237 Leon Hall AU RC 5.00 12.00
238 Matt Spaeth AU RC 6.00 15.00
239 Michael Griffin AU RC 6.00 15.00
240 Paul Posluszny AU RC 6.00 15.00
241 Quentin Moses AU RC 5.00 12.00
242 Ray McDonald AU RC 5.00 12.00
243 Reggie Nelson AU RC 5.00 12.00
244 Ronnie McGill AU RC 5.00 12.00
245 Sabby Piscitelli AU RC 6.00 15.00
246 Scott Chandler AU RC 6.00 15.00
247 Toby Korrodi AU RC 5.00 12.00
248 Tyler Palko AU RC 5.00 12.00
249 Victor Abiamiri AU RC 6.00 15.00
250 Zach Miller AU RC 6.00 15.00
251 JaMarcus Russell RPM RC 2.50 6.00
252 Calvin Johnson RPM RC 12.00 30.00
253 Joe Thomas RPM RC 4.00 10.00
254 Gaines Adams RPM RC 4.00 10.00
255 Greg Olsen RPM RC 3.00 8.00
256 Adrian Peterson RPM RC 15.00 40.00
257 Ted Ginn RPM RC 3.00 8.00
258 Patrick Willis RPM RC 8.00 20.00
259 Marshawn Lynch RPM RC 4.00 10.00
260 Brady Quinn RPM RC 4.00 10.00
261 Dwayne Bowe RPM RC 5.00 12.00
262 Robert Meachem RPM RC 4.00 10.00
263 Anthony Gonzalez RPM RC 4.00 10.00
264 Kevin Kolb RPM RC 6.00 15.00
265 John Beck RPM RC 4.00 10.00
266 Drew Stanton RPM RC 2.50 6.00
267 Sidney Rice RPM RC 5.00 12.00
268 Dwayne Jarrett RPM RC 3.00 8.00
269 Kenny Irons RPM RC 2.50 6.00
270 Chris Henry RPM RC 2.50 6.00
271 Steve Smith RPM RC 4.00 10.00
272 Brian Leonard RPM RC 3.00 8.00
273 Brandon Jackson RPM RC 3.00 8.00
274 Lorenzo Booker RPM RC 3.00 8.00
275 Yamon Figurs RPM RC 2.50 6.00
276 Jason Hill RPM RC 4.00 10.00
277 Paul Williams RPM RC 2.50 6.00
278 Tony Hunt RPM RC 2.50 6.00
279 Trent Edwards RPM RC 4.00 10.00
280 Garrett Wolfe RPM RC 2.50 6.00
281 Johnnie Lee Higgins RPM RC 3.00 8.00
282 Michael Bush RPM RC 4.00 10.00
283 Antonio Pittman RPM RC 2.50 6.00
284 Troy Smith RPM RC 4.00 10.00

2007 Absolute Memorabilia Retail

*VET 1-150: .1X TO .25X BASIC CARDS
*ROOKIES 151-200: .4X TO 1X BASIC CARDS
ROOKIES PRINT RUN 699 SER.#'d SETS

2007 Absolute Memorabilia Rookie Premiere Materials AFC/NFC

*SINGLES: .6X TO 1.5X BASE RPM RCs
AFC/NFC PRINT RUN 50 SER.#'d SETS
*PRIME/10: 1.5X TO 4X BASE RPM RCs
SPECTRUM PRIME PRINT RUN 10 SER.#'d SETS

2007 Absolute Memorabilia Rookie Premiere Materials Oversize

*SINGLES: .8X TO 2X BASE RPM RCs
OVERSIZE PRINT RUN 50 SER.#'d SETS
*SPECT/10: 1.5X TO 4X BASE RPM RCs
SPECTRUM PRINT RUN 10 SER.#'d SETS

2007 Absolute Memorabilia Rookie Premiere Materials Spectrum Prime

*SINGLES: .6X TO 1.5X BASE RPM RCs
STATED PRINT RUN 100 SER.#'d SETS

2007 Absolute Memorabilia Spectrum Black

*VETS 1-150: 1X TO 2.5X BASIC CARDS
*ROOKIES 151-200: .6X TO 1.5X BASIC RC/699
*ROOKIES 201-250: .4X TO 1X SPECT.SILVER
STATED PRINT RUN 100 SER.#'d SETS

2007 Absolute Memorabilia Spectrum Blue

*VETS 1-150: .8X TO 2X BASIC CARDS
*ROOKIES 151-200: .5X TO 1.2X BASIC CARDS
*ROOKIES 201-250: .3X TO .8X SPECT.SILVER
BLUE PRINT RUN 250 SER.#'d SETS

2007 Absolute Memorabilia Spectrum Gold

*VETS 1-150: 2X TO 5X BASIC CARDS
*ROOKIES 151-200: 1.2X TO 3X BASIC RC/699
*ROOKIES 201-250: .8X TO 2X SPECT.SILVER
STATED PRINT RUN 25 SER.#'d SETS

2007 Absolute Memorabilia Spectrum Red

*VETS 1-150: .6X TO 1.5X BASIC CARDS
*ROOKIES 151-200: .4X TO 1X BASIC RC/699
*ROOKIES 201-250: .25X TO .6X SPECT.SILVER
RANDOM INSERTS IN RETAIL PACKS

2007 Absolute Memorabilia Spectrum Silver

*VETERANS 1-150: 1X TO 2.5X BASIC CARDS
*ROOKIES 151-200: .5X TO 1.2X RC/699
COMMON ROOKIE 201-250 4.00 10.00
ROOKIE SEMISTARS 201-250 5.00 12.00
ROOKIE UNL.STARS 201-250 6.00 15.00
STATED PRINT RUN 100 SER.#'d SETS
225 James Jones 6.00 15.00
226 Jared Zabransky 5.00 12.00
234 LaRon Landry 6.00 15.00
236 Lawrence Timmons 6.00 15.00
240 Paul Posluszny 6.00 15.00

2007 Absolute Memorabilia Absolute Heroes

STATED PRINT RUN 100 SER.#'d SETS
*GOLD/50: .5X TO 1.2X BASIC INSERTS
GOLD PRINT RUN 50 SER.#'d SETS
*SPECTRUM/25: .8X TO 2X BASIC INSERTS
SPECTRUM PRINT RUN 25 SER.#'d SETS
1 Laurence Maroney 2.00 5.00
2 Leon Washington 2.00 5.00
3 Maurice Jones-Drew 2.50 6.00
4 Mike Bell 2.00 5.00
5 A.J. Hawk 2.00 5.00
6 Andre Johnson 2.00 5.00
7 Anquan Boldin 2.00 5.00
8 Antonio Gates 2.50 6.00
9 Bernard Berrian 1.50 4.00
10 Brandon Jacobs 2.00 5.00
11 Brandon Marshall 2.00 5.00
12 Chester Taylor 1.50 4.00
13 Demetrius Williams 1.50 4.00
14 Joseph Addai 2.00 5.00
15 Matt Leinart 2.00 5.00
16 Philip Rivers 2.50 6.00
17 Tony Romo 3.00 8.00
18 Frank Gore 2.50 6.00
19 Marion Barber 2.50 6.00
20 Fred Taylor 2.00 5.00
21 Larry Fitzgerald 2.50 6.00
22 Michael Vick 2.50 6.00
23 Reggie Wayne 2.00 5.00
24 Reggie Bush 2.50 6.00
25 Vince Young 2.00 5.00

2007 Absolute Memorabilia Absolute Heroes Materials

STATED PRINT RUN 40-200
*PRIME/50: .6X TO 1.5X BASIC JSY/108-200
PRIME PRINT RUN 7-50
UNPRICED PRIME SPECTRUM PRINT RUN 1
1 Laurence Maroney 3.00 8.00
2 Leon Washington 3.00 8.00
3 Maurice Jones-Drew 4.00 10.00
4 Mike Bell 3.00 8.00
5 A.J. Hawk/190 3.00 8.00
6 Andre Johnson 3.00 8.00
7 Anquan Boldin 3.00 8.00
8 Antonio Gates 4.00 10.00
9 Bernard Berrian 2.50 6.00
10 Brandon Jacobs/190 3.00 8.00
11 Brandon Marshall 3.00 8.00
12 Chester Taylor 2.50 6.00
13 Demetrius Williams/40 3.00 8.00
14 Joseph Addai 3.00 8.00
15 Matt Leinart 3.00 8.00
16 Philip Rivers 4.00 10.00
17 Tony Romo 5.00 12.00
18 Frank Gore 4.00 10.00
19 Marion Barber 4.00 10.00
20 Fred Taylor 3.00 8.00
23 Reggie Wayne 3.00 8.00
24 Reggie Bush 4.00 10.00
25 Vince Young/108 3.00 8.00

2007 Absolute Memorabilia Absolute Heroes Materials Autographs

AUTO STATED PRINT RUN 30-50
UNPRICED PRIME SPECTRUM PRINT RUN 1
3 Maurice Jones-Drew 20.00 40.00
4 Mike Bell 10.00 25.00
6 Andre Johnson 10.00 25.00
7 Anquan Boldin 10.00 25.00
8 Antonio Gates 20.00 40.00
9 Bernard Berrian 10.00 25.00
10 Brandon Jacobs 10.00 25.00
11 Brandon Marshall 10.00 25.00
12 Chester Taylor 10.00 25.00
13 Demetrius Williams 10.00 25.00
14 Joseph Addai 20.00 50.00
15 Matt Leinart/30 15.00 40.00
16 Philip Rivers/30 20.00 40.00
17 Tony Romo/30 75.00 150.00
18 Frank Gore 20.00 40.00
19 Marion Barber 20.00 40.00
20 Fred Taylor 10.00 25.00
21 Larry Fitzgerald/30 25.00 50.00
23 Reggie Wayne 20.00 40.00
24 Reggie Bush/30 50.00 120.00
25 Vince Young/30 40.00 80.00

2007 Absolute Memorabilia Absolute Heroes Materials Autographs Prime

*PRIME/25: .6X TO 1.2X BASIC AUTO/30-50
PRIME PRINT RUN 15-25
1 Laurence Maroney
5 A.J. Hawk 25.00 50.00
16 Philip Rivers/15 30.00 60.00
22 Michael Vick 40.00 80.00

2007 Absolute Memorabilia Absolute Patches Prime

STATED PRINT RUN 5-25
UNPRICED SPECTRUM PRINT RUN 1
SERIAL #'d UNDER 15 NOT PRICED
1 Chad Johnson 20.00 50.00
2 Barry Sanders 50.00 125.00
3 Dan Marino 60.00 150.00
4 Joe Montana 60.00 150.00
5 Walter Payton 60.00 150.00
6 Antonio Gates 25.00 60.00
8 Vince Young/15 20.00 50.00
9 Brett Favre 50.00 125.00
10 Brian Urlacher 25.00 60.00
11 Donovan McNabb 25.00 60.00
12 LaDainian Tomlinson 25.00 60.00
13 Larry Johnson 15.00 40.00
14 Peyton Manning 40.00 100.00
15 Steve Smith 20.00 50.00
16 Marvin Harrison 25.00 60.00
17 Torry Holt 20.00 50.00
18 Carson Palmer 20.00 50.00
19 Steven Jackson 25.00 60.00
20 Terrell Owens/24 25.00 60.00

2007 Absolute Memorabilia Canton Absolutes

GOLD PRINT RUN 100 SER.#'d SETS
*GOLD/50: .5X TO 1.2X BASIC INSERTS
GOLD PRINT RUN 50 SER.#'d SETS
*SPECTRUM/25: .8X TO 2X BASIC INSERTS
SPECTRUM PRINT RUN 25 SER.#'d SETS
1 Chad Johnson 2.00 5.00
2 Bo Jackson 3.00 8.00
3 Reggie Bush 2.50 6.00
4 Vince Young 2.00 5.00
5 Ben Roethlisberger 2.50 6.00
6 Brett Favre 5.00 12.00
7 Brian Urlacher 2.50 6.00

8 Corey Dillon 2.00 5.00
9 Curtis Martin 2.50 6.00
10 Donovan McNabb 2.50 6.00
11 Drew Brees 2.50 6.00
12 Eli Manning 2.50 6.00
13 Hines Ward 2.50 6.00
14 LaDainian Tomlinson 2.50 6.00
15 Larry Johnson 1.50 4.00
16 Peyton Manning 4.00 10.00
17 Steve Smith 2.00 5.00
18 Marvin Harrison 2.50 6.00
19 Steve McNair 2.00 5.00
20 Torry Holt 2.00 5.00
21 Deuce McAllister 2.00 5.00
22 Roy Williams WR 2.00 5.00
23 Rudi Johnson 2.00 5.00
24 Steven Jackson 2.50 6.00
25 Shaun Alexander 2.00 5.00

2007 Absolute Memorabilia Canton Absolutes Materials

STATED PRINT RUN 25-200
*PRIME/25: .8X TO 2X BASIC JSY/122-200
*PRIME/25: .5X TO 1.2X BASIC JSY/25
PRIME PRINT RUN 25 SER.#'d SETS
UNPRICED PRIME SPECTRUM PRINT RUN 1
1 Chad Johnson 3.00 8.00
2 Bo Jackson/183 5.00 12.00
3 Reggie Bush 4.00 10.00
4 Vince Young 3.00 8.00
5 Ben Roethlisberger/25 6.00 15.00
6 Brett Favre 8.00 20.00
7 Brian Urlacher 4.00 10.00
8 Corey Dillon 3.00 8.00
9 Curtis Martin 4.00 10.00
10 Donovan McNabb 4.00 10.00
11 Drew Brees 4.00 10.00
12 Eli Manning 4.00 10.00
13 Hines Ward 4.00 10.00
14 LaDainian Tomlinson 4.00 10.00
15 Larry Johnson 2.50 6.00
16 Peyton Manning/122 6.00 15.00
17 Steve Smith 3.00 8.00
18 Marvin Harrison 4.00 10.00
19 Steve McNair 3.00 8.00
20 Torry Holt 3.00 8.00
21 Deuce McAllister 3.00 8.00
22 Roy Williams WR 3.00 8.00
23 Rudi Johnson 3.00 8.00
24 Steven Jackson 4.00 10.00
25 Shaun Alexander 3.00 8.00

2007 Absolute Memorabilia Canton Absolutes Autographs

STATED PRINT RUN 10-27
2 Bo Jackson/25 30.00 60.00
15 Larry Johnson/27 20.00 40.00
24 Steven Jackson/25 20.00 40.00

2007 Absolute Memorabilia College Materials

STATED PRINT RUN 100 SER.#'d SETS
*SPECT.PRIME/10: 2X TO 4X BASIC JSY/100
SPECTRUM PRIME PRINT RUN 5-10
1 Frank Gore 5.00 12.00
2 Robert Meachem 5.00 12.00
3 Dwayne Jarrett 4.00 10.00
4 Steve Smith 5.00 12.00
5 Adrian Peterson 30.00 80.00
6 Brady Quinn 5.00 12.00
7 JaMarcus Russell 3.00 8.00
8 Peyton Manning 15.00 40.00
9 Vince Young 10.00 25.00
10 Reggie Bush 10.00 25.00

2007 Absolute Memorabilia College Materials Autographs

STATED PRINT RUN 25 SER.#'d SETS
UNPRICED SPECTRUM PRIME PRINT RUN 1-5
1 Frank Gore
2 Robert Meachem 25.00 50.00
3 Dwayne Jarrett 25.00 50.00
4 Steve Smith 15.00 40.00
5 Adrian Peterson 175.00 300.00
6 Brady Quinn 100.00 200.00
7 JaMarcus Russell 30.00 80.00
8 Peyton Manning 125.00 200.00
9 Vince Young 40.00 100.00
10 Reggie Bush 50.00 120.00

2007 Absolute Memorabilia Marks of Fame

STATED PRINT RUN 100 SER.#'d SETS
*GOLD/50: .5X TO 1.2X BASIC INSERTS
GOLD PRINT RUN 50 SER.#'d SETS
*SPECTRUM/25: .8X TO 2X BASIC INSERTS
SPECTRUM PRINT RUN 25 SER.#'d SETS
1 Jerious Norwood 2.00 5.00
2 LenDale White 2.00 5.00
3 Brian Westbrook 2.00 5.00
4 Cadillac Williams 2.00 5.00
5 Cedric Benson 2.00 5.00
6 DeAngelo Williams 2.50 6.00
7 DeMeco Ryans 2.00 5.00
8 Devin Hester 2.50 6.00
9 Jay Cutler 2.50 6.00
10 Marques Colston 2.50 6.00
11 Rex Grossman 2.00 5.00
12 Shawne Merriman 2.00 5.00
13 Vernon Davis 2.00 5.00
14 Willie Parker 2.00 5.00
15 Santonio Holmes 2.00 5.00
16 Larry Johnson 1.50 4.00
17 Ted Ginn Jr. 2.00 5.00
18 Joe Thomas 2.50 6.00
19 Brady Quinn 2.50 6.00
20 Brandon Jackson 2.00 5.00
21 Tony Hunt 1.50 4.00
22 Steve Smith 2.50 6.00
23 Dwayne Jarrett 2.00 5.00
24 Drew Stanton 1.50 4.00
25 Antonio Pittman 1.50 4.00
26 Dwayne Bowe 3.00 8.00
27 Anthony Gonzalez 2.50 6.00
28 Lorenzo Booker 2.00 5.00
29 Chris Henry 1.50 4.00
30 Gaines Adams 2.50 6.00
31 Kevin Kolb 4.00 10.00
32 John Beck 2.50 6.00
33 Brian Leonard 2.00 5.00
34 Adrian Peterson 10.00 25.00
35 Greg Olsen 2.00 5.00
36 JaMarcus Russell 1.50 4.00
37 Garrett Wolfe 1.50 4.00
38 Yamon Figurs 1.50 4.00
39 Sidney Rice 3.00 8.00
40 Trent Edwards 2.50 6.00
41 Michael Bush 2.50 6.00
42 Patrick Willis 5.00 12.00
43 Kenny Irons 1.50 4.00
44 Calvin Johnson 8.00 20.00
45 Paul Williams 1.50 4.00
46 Robert Meachem 2.50 6.00
47 Jason Hill 2.50 6.00
48 Marshawn Lynch 2.50 6.00
49 Johnnie Lee Higgins 2.00 5.00
50 Troy Smith 2.50 6.00

2007 Absolute Memorabilia Marks of Fame Materials

STATED PRINT RUN 100-200
*PRIME/50: .6X TO 1.5X BASIC JSY/100-200
PRIME PRINT RUN 50 SER.#'d SETS
UNPRICED SPECTRUM PRINT RUN 1
1 Jerious Norwood 3.00 8.00
2 LenDale White 3.00 8.00
3 Brian Westbrook/100 3.00 8.00
4 Cadillac Williams 3.00 8.00
5 Cedric Benson 3.00 8.00
6 DeAngelo Williams 4.00 10.00
7 DeMeco Ryans 3.00 8.00
8 Devin Hester 4.00 10.00
9 Jay Cutler 4.00 10.00
10 Marques Colston 4.00 10.00
11 Rex Grossman 3.00 8.00
12 Shawne Merriman 3.00 8.00
13 Vernon Davis 3.00 8.00
14 Willie Parker 3.00 8.00
15 Santonio Holmes 3.00 8.00
16 Larry Johnson 2.50 6.00
17 Ted Ginn Jr. 3.00 8.00
18 Joe Thomas 4.00 10.00
19 Brady Quinn 4.00 10.00
20 Brandon Jackson 3.00 8.00
21 Tony Hunt 2.50 6.00
22 Steve Smith 4.00 10.00
23 Dwayne Jarrett 3.00 8.00
24 Drew Stanton 2.50 6.00
25 Antonio Pittman 2.50 6.00
26 Dwayne Bowe 5.00 12.00
27 Anthony Gonzalez 4.00 10.00
28 Lorenzo Booker 3.00 8.00
29 Chris Henry 2.50 6.00
30 Gaines Adams 4.00 10.00
31 Kevin Kolb 6.00 15.00
32 John Beck 4.00 10.00
33 Brian Leonard 3.00 8.00
34 Adrian Peterson 15.00 40.00
35 Greg Olsen 3.00 8.00
36 JaMarcus Russell 2.50 6.00
37 Garrett Wolfe 2.50 6.00
38 Yamon Figurs 2.50 6.00
39 Sidney Rice 5.00 12.00
40 Trent Edwards 4.00 10.00
41 Michael Bush 4.00 10.00
42 Patrick Willis 8.00 20.00
43 Kenny Irons 2.50 6.00
44 Calvin Johnson 12.00 30.00
45 Paul Williams 2.50 6.00
46 Robert Meachem 4.00 10.00
47 Jason Hill 4.00 10.00
48 Marshawn Lynch 4.00 10.00
49 Johnnie Lee Higgins 3.00 8.00
50 Troy Smith 4.00 10.00

2007 Absolute Memorabilia Marks of Fame Materials Autographs

STATED PRINT RUN 30-50
*PRIME/25: .6X TO 1.2X BASIC JSY AU
PRIME PRINT RUN 25 SER.#'d SETS
UNPRICED PRIME SPECT.PRINT RUN 1
1 Jerious Norwood 12.00 30.00
2 LenDale White 12.00 30.00
4 Cadillac Williams 15.00 40.00
5 Cedric Benson 12.00 30.00
6 DeAngelo Williams 10.00 25.00
7 DeMeco Ryans 10.00 25.00
8 Devin Hester/30 25.00 50.00
9 Jay Cutler/30 25.00 50.00
10 Marques Colston 12.00 30.00
11 Rex Grossman 12.00 30.00
13 Vernon Davis 10.00 25.00
14 Willie Parker 15.00 40.00
15 Santonio Holmes 12.00 30.00
16 Larry Johnson 15.00 40.00
17 Ted Ginn Jr. 15.00 40.00
18 Joe Thomas 12.00 30.00
19 Brady Quinn/30 40.00 100.00
20 Brandon Jackson 15.00 40.00
21 Tony Hunt 12.00 30.00
22 Steve Smith 12.00 30.00
23 Dwayne Jarrett 12.00 30.00
24 Drew Stanton 12.00 30.00
25 Antonio Pittman 10.00 25.00
26 Dwayne Bowe 20.00 50.00
27 Anthony Gonzalez 20.00 50.00
28 Lorenzo Booker 10.00 25.00
29 Chris Henry 12.00 30.00
30 Gaines Adams 10.00 25.00
31 Kevin Kolb 15.00 40.00
32 John Beck 12.00 30.00
33 Brian Leonard 12.00 30.00
34 Adrian Peterson/30 125.00 250.00
35 Greg Olsen 15.00 40.00
36 JaMarcus Russell/30 20.00 50.00
37 Garrett Wolfe 12.00 30.00
38 Yamon Figurs 12.00 30.00
39 Sidney Rice 20.00 50.00
40 Trent Edwards 12.00 30.00
41 Michael Bush 12.00 30.00
42 Patrick Willis 20.00 50.00
43 Kenny Irons 12.00 30.00
44 Calvin Johnson/30 50.00 120.00
45 Paul Williams 12.00 30.00
46 Robert Meachem 12.00 30.00
47 Jason Hill 12.00 30.00
48 Marshawn Lynch 15.00 40.00
49 Johnnie Lee Higgins 10.00 25.00
50 Troy Smith 12.00 30.00

2007 Absolute Memorabilia NFL Icons

STATED PRINT RUN 100 SER.#'d SETS
*SPECT/25 .8X TO 2X BASIC INSERTS
SPECTRUM PRINT RUN 25 SER.#'d SETS
1 Barry Sanders 6.00 15.00
2 Bo Jackson 5.00 12.00
3 Bob Griese 4.00 10.00
4 Dan Marino 8.00 20.00
5 Dick Butkus 5.00 12.00
6 Eric Dickerson 3.00 8.00
7 Franco Harris 4.00 10.00
8 Michael Irvin 3.00 8.00
9 Fred Biletnikoff 4.00 10.00
10 Jack Lambert 4.00 10.00
11 James Lofton 2.50 6.00
12 Jerry Rice 6.00 15.00
13 Jim Kelly 5.00 12.00
14 Jim Otto 2.50 6.00
15 Joe Greene 4.00 10.00
16 Joe Montana 8.00 20.00
17 John Hannah 2.50 6.00
18 John Riggins 3.00 8.00
19 Ken Stabler 5.00 12.00
20 Larry Little 2.50 6.00
21 Paul Hornung 4.00 10.00
22 Paul Krause 2.50 6.00
23 Paul Warfield 3.00 8.00
24 Rosey Brown 2.50 6.00
25 Ron Mix 2.50 6.00
26 Steve Young 5.00 12.00
27 Thurman Thomas 3.00 8.00
28 Tony Dorsett 4.00 10.00
29 Walter Payton 8.00 20.00
30 Y.A. Tittle 4.00 10.00

2007 Absolute Memorabilia NFL Icons Materials

STATED PRINT RUN 3-50
*PRIME/20-25: 1X TO 2.5X BASIC JSY/30-50
*PRIME/10: 1.5X TO 4X BASIC JSY/30-50
PRIME PRINT RUN 4-25
*PRIME SPECT/10: 1.5X TO 4X JSY/30-50
PRIME SPECTRUM PRINT RUN 5-10
1 Barry Sanders 10.00 25.00
2 Bo Jackson 8.00 20.00
3 Bob Griese 6.00 15.00
4 Dan Marino 12.00 30.00
5 Dick Butkus 8.00 20.00
6 Eric Dickerson 5.00 12.00
7 Franco Harris 6.00 15.00
8 Michael Irvin 5.00 12.00
9 Fred Biletnikoff 6.00 15.00
10 Jack Lambert 6.00 15.00
11 James Lofton 4.00 10.00
12 Jerry Rice 10.00 25.00
13 Jim Kelly 8.00 20.00
14 Jim Otto 4.00 10.00
15 Joe Greene 6.00 15.00
16 Joe Montana 12.00 30.00
17 John Hannah 4.00 10.00
18 John Riggins 5.00 12.00
20 Larry Little 4.00 10.00
21 Paul Hornung 6.00 15.00
22 Paul Krause/35 4.00 10.00
23 Paul Warfield 5.00 12.00
24 Rosey Brown 4.00 10.00
25 Ron Mix 4.00 10.00
26 Steve Young 8.00 20.00
27 Thurman Thomas 5.00 12.00
28 Tony Dorsett 6.00 15.00
29 Walter Payton 12.00 30.00
30 Y.A. Tittle 6.00 15.00

2007 Absolute Memorabilia Rookie Jersey Collection

RANDOM INSERTS IN RETAIL PACKS
1 Ted Ginn Jr. 3.00 8.00
2 Joe Thomas 4.00 10.00
3 Brady Quinn 4.00 10.00
4 Brandon Jackson 3.00 8.00
5 Tony Hunt 2.50 6.00
6 Steve Smith 4.00 10.00
7 Dwayne Jarrett 3.00 8.00
8 Drew Stanton 2.50 6.00
9 Antonio Pittman 2.50 6.00
10 Dwayne Bowe 5.00 12.00
11 Anthony Gonzalez 4.00 10.00
12 Lorenzo Booker 3.00 8.00
13 Chris Henry 2.50 6.00
14 Gaines Adams 4.00 10.00
15 Kevin Kolb 6.00 15.00
16 John Beck 4.00 10.00
17 Brian Leonard 3.00 8.00
18 Adrian Peterson 15.00 40.00
19 Greg Olsen 3.00 8.00
20 JaMarcus Russell 2.50 6.00
21 Garrett Wolfe 2.50 6.00
22 Yamon Figurs 2.50 6.00
23 Sidney Rice 5.00 12.00
24 Trent Edwards 4.00 10.00
25 Michael Bush 4.00 10.00
26 Patrick Willis 8.00 20.00
27 Kenny Irons 2.50 6.00
28 Calvin Johnson 12.00 30.00
29 Paul Williams 2.50 6.00
30 Robert Meachem 4.00 10.00
31 Jason Hill 4.00 10.00
32 Marshawn Lynch 4.00 10.00
33 Johnnie Lee Higgins 3.00 8.00
34 Troy Smith 4.00 10.00

2007 Absolute Memorabilia Rookie Premiere Materials Autographs

STATED PRINT RUN 100 SER.#'d SETS
*AFC/NFC/25: .6X TO 1.5X BASIC AU/100
AFC/NFC PRINT RUN 25 SER.#'d SETS
UNPRICED AFC/NFC SPECT.#'d TO 5
*EMBOSSED/25: .5X TO 1.2X BASIC AU/100
EMBOSSED HOLOGRAM PRINT RUN 25
UNPRICED EMBOSSED HOLO.PRIME #'d TO 10
*SPEC.PLAT/50: .5X TO 1.2X BASIC AU/100
SPECTRUM PLATINUM PRINT RUN 50 SER.#'d SETS
251 JaMarcus Russell 8.00 20.00
252 Calvin Johnson 60.00 120.00
253 Joe Thomas 12.00 30.00
254 Gaines Adams 12.00 30.00
255 Greg Olsen 10.00 25.00
256 Adrian Peterson 100.00 200.00
257 Ted Ginn 10.00 25.00
258 Patrick Willis 25.00 60.00
259 Marshawn Lynch 15.00 40.00
260 Brady Quinn 12.00 30.00
261 Dwayne Bowe 15.00 40.00
262 Robert Meachem 12.00 30.00
263 Anthony Gonzalez 12.00 30.00
264 Kevin Kolb 20.00 50.00
265 John Beck 12.00 30.00
266 Drew Stanton 8.00 20.00
267 Sidney Rice 15.00 40.00
268 Dwayne Jarrett 10.00 25.00
269 Kenny Irons 8.00 20.00
270 Chris Henry 8.00 20.00
271 Steve Smith 12.00 30.00
272 Brian Leonard 10.00 25.00
273 Brandon Jackson 10.00 25.00
274 Lorenzo Booker 10.00 25.00
275 Yamon Figurs 8.00 20.00
276 Jason Hill 12.00 30.00
277 Paul Williams 8.00 20.00
278 Tony Hunt 8.00 20.00
279 Trent Edwards 12.00 30.00
280 Garrett Wolfe 8.00 20.00
281 Johnnie Lee Higgins 10.00 25.00
282 Michael Bush 12.00 30.00
283 Antonio Pittman 8.00 20.00
284 Troy Smith 12.00 30.00

2007 Absolute Memorabilia Spectrum Silver Autographs

STATED PRINT RUN 25-100 SER.#'d SETS
UNPRICED PLATINUM PRINT RUN 1
53 Marques Colston/100 10.00 25.00
54 Devery Henderson/100 5.00 12.00
140 Larry Johnson/100 12.50 30.00
148 Vincent Jackson/100 5.00 12.00
151 A.J. Davis/50 6.00 15.00
152 Aaron Rouse/50 8.00 20.00
153 Ahmad Bradshaw/50 20.00 50.00
155 Anthony Spencer/50 10.00 25.00
156 Brandon Siler/25 8.00 20.00
158 Chris Houston/50 8.00 20.00
159 Dallas Baker/50 6.00 15.00
160 Dan Bazuin/50 8.00 20.00
161 Danny Ware/56 10.00 25.00
163 David Irons/25 8.00 20.00
165 Earl Everett/25 10.00 25.00
166 Eric Frampton/50 8.00 20.00
169 Fred Bennett/25 8.00 20.00
171 H.B. Blades/25 8.00 20.00
172 Jarrett Hicks/25 10.00 25.00
174 Jason Snelling/50 10.00 25.00
178 Jon Beason/50 8.00 20.00
179 Jonathan Wade/25 10.00 25.00
180 Jordan Kent/50 8.00 20.00
181 Josh Gattis/25 8.00 20.00
182 Kenneth Darby/50 8.00 20.00
184 Levi Brown/25 12.00 30.00
185 Marcus McCauley/25 10.00 25.00
186 Tim Shaw/25 10.00 25.00
187 Michael Okwo/25 10.00 25.00
188 Mike Walker/50 10.00 25.00
189 Nate Ilaoa/50 8.00 20.00
190 Reggie Ball/25 10.00 25.00
191 Rhema McKnight/25 8.00 20.00
193 Rufus Alexander/30 8.00 20.00
194 Ryan McBean/25 12.00 30.00
195 Ryne Robinson/50 8.00 20.00
196 Selvin Young/25 10.00 25.00
197 Steve Breaston/50 10.00 25.00
198 Stewart Bradley/25 10.00 25.00
200 Tim Crowder/50 10.00 25.00

2007 Absolute Memorabilia Spectrum Gold Autographs

SERIAL #'d UNDER 25 NOT PRICED
10 Brandon Jacobs/27 10.00 25.00
53 Marques Colston/50 12.50 30.00
54 Devery Henderson/50 6.00 15.00
55 Reggie Bush/25 60.00 150.00
98 Willis McGahee/50 10.00 25.00
118 DeMeco Ryans/50 6.00 15.00
130 Maurice Jones-Drew/25
140 Larry Johnson/50 15.00 40.00
148 Vincent Jackson/50 6.00 15.00
153 Ahmad Bradshaw/25 30.00 60.00
155 Anthony Spencer/25 12.00 30.00
158 Chris Houston/25 10.00 25.00
159 Dallas Baker/25 8.00 20.00
160 Dan Bazuin/25 10.00 25.00
161 Danny Ware/25 12.00 30.00
174 Jason Snelling/25 12.00 30.00
178 Jon Beason/25 10.00 25.00
180 Jordan Kent/25 10.00 25.00
182 Kenneth Darby/25 10.00 25.00
188 Mike Walker/25 12.00 30.00
189 Nate Ilaoa/25 10.00 25.00
193 Rufus Alexander/25 10.00 25.00
195 Ryne Robinson/25 10.00 25.00
197 Steve Breaston/25 12.00 30.00
200 Tim Crowder/25 12.00 30.00

2007 Absolute Memorabilia Star Gazing

STATED PRINT RUN 100 SER.#'d SETS
*SPECTRUM/25: .8X TO 2X BASIC INSERTS
SPECTRUM PRINT RUN 25 SER.#'d SETS
UNPRICED AUTO PRINT RUN 5
UNPRICED MATERIAL AU PRINT RUN 5
1 Troy Smith 2.00 5.00
2 Dwayne Jarrett 1.50 4.00
3 Ted Ginn Jr. 1.50 4.00
4 John Beck 2.00 5.00
5 Lorenzo Booker 1.50 4.00
6 Antonio Pittman 1.25 3.00
7 Robert Meachem 2.00 5.00
8 Dwayne Bowe 2.50 6.00
9 Anthony Gonzalez 2.00 5.00
10 JaMarcus Russell 1.25 3.00
11 Greg Olsen 1.50 4.00
12 Michael Bush 2.00 5.00
13 Johnnie Lee Higgins 1.50 4.00
14 Kevin Kolb 3.00 8.00
15 Tony Hunt 1.25 3.00
16 Patrick Willis 4.00 10.00
17 Jason Hill 2.00 5.00
18 Gaines Adams 2.00 5.00
19 Trent Edwards 2.00 5.00
20 Marshawn Lynch 2.00 5.00
21 Chris Henry 1.25 3.00
22 Paul Williams 1.25 3.00
23 Sidney Rice 2.50 6.00
24 Adrian Peterson 8.00 20.00
25 Drew Stanton 1.25 3.00
26 Calvin Johnson 6.00 15.00
27 Yamon Figurs 1.25 3.00
28 Brian Leonard 1.50 4.00
29 Garrett Wolfe 1.25 3.00
30 Kenny Irons 1.25 3.00
31 Joe Thomas 2.00 5.00
32 Brady Quinn 2.00 5.00
33 Brandon Jackson 1.50 4.00
34 Steve Smith 2.00 5.00

2007 Absolute Memorabilia Star Gazing Materials

STATED PRINT RUN 100 SER.#'d SETS
*PRIME/50: .5X TO 1.2X BASIC JSY/100
PRIME PRINT RUN 50 SER.#'d SETS
*OVERSIZE/25: .8X TO 2X BASIC JSY/100
OVERSIZE PRINT RUN 25 SER.#'d SETS
*OVER.SPECT/10: 1.2X TO 3X BASIC JSY/100
OVERSIZE SPECTRUM PRINT RUN 10
1 Troy Smith 5.00 12.00
2 Dwayne Jarrett 4.00 10.00
3 Ted Ginn Jr. 4.00 10.00
4 John Beck 5.00 12.00
5 Lorenzo Booker 4.00 10.00
6 Antonio Pittman 3.00 8.00
7 Robert Meachem 5.00 12.00
8 Dwayne Bowe 6.00 15.00
9 Anthony Gonzalez 5.00 12.00
10 JaMarcus Russell 3.00 8.00
11 Greg Olsen 4.00 10.00
12 Michael Bush 5.00 12.00
13 Johnnie Lee Higgins 4.00 10.00
14 Kevin Kolb 8.00 20.00
15 Tony Hunt 3.00 8.00
16 Patrick Willis 10.00 25.00
17 Jason Hill 5.00 12.00
18 Gaines Adams 5.00 12.00
19 Trent Edwards 5.00 12.00
20 Marshawn Lynch 5.00 12.00
21 Chris Henry 3.00 8.00
22 Paul Williams 3.00 8.00
23 Sidney Rice 6.00 15.00
24 Adrian Peterson 25.00 60.00
25 Drew Stanton 3.00 8.00
26 Calvin Johnson 15.00 40.00
27 Yamon Figurs 3.00 8.00
28 Brian Leonard 4.00 10.00
29 Garrett Wolfe 3.00 8.00
30 Kenny Irons 3.00 8.00
31 Joe Thomas 5.00 12.00
32 Brady Quinn 5.00 12.00
33 Brandon Jackson 4.00 10.00
34 Steve Smith 5.00 12.00

2007 Absolute Memorabilia Team Quads

STATED PRINT RUN 100 SER.#'d SETS
*SPECTRUM/25: .6X TO 1.5X BASIC INSERTS
SPECTRUM PRINT RUN 25 SER.#'d SETS
1 Anquan Boldin 3.00 8.00
Matt Leinart
Larry Fitzgerald
Edgerrin James
2 Muhsin Muhammad 2.50 6.00
Rex Grossman
Bernard Berrian
Cedric Benson
3 Carson Palmer 2.50 6.00
Chad Johnson
Rudi Johnson
T.J. Houshmandzadeh
4 Tony Romo 4.00 10.00
Terrell Owens
Julius Jones
Terry Glenn
5 Marvin Harrison 5.00 12.00
Peyton Manning
Reggie Wayne
Joseph Addai
6 Deuce McAllister 3.00 8.00
Drew Brees
Reggie Bush
Marques Colston
7 Plaxico Burress 4.00 10.00
Eli Manning
Jeremy Shockey
Brandon Jacobs
8 Brian Westbrook 3.00 8.00
Donovan McNabb
Correll Buckhalter
Reggie Brown
9 LaDainian Tomlinson 3.00 8.00
Philip Rivers
Antonio Gates
Keenan McCardell
10 Isaac Bruce 3.00 8.00
Steven Jackson
Torry Holt
Marc Bulger

2007 Absolute Memorabilia Team Quads Materials

STATED PRINT RUN 50 SER.#'d SETS
*PRIME/10: 1.2X TO 3X BASIC JSY/50
PRIME PRINT RUN 10 SER.#'d SETS
UNPRICED SPECTRUM PRINT RUN 1
1 Anquan Boldin 10.00 25.00
Matt Leinart
Larry Fitzgerald
Edgerrin James
2 Muhsin Muhammad 8.00 20.00
Rex Grossman
Bernard Berrian
Cedric Benson
3 Carson Palmer 8.00 20.00
Chad Johnson
Rudi Johnson
T.J. Houshmandzadeh
4 Tony Romo 12.00 30.00
Terrell Owens
Julius Jones
Terry Glenn
5 Marvin Harrison 15.00 40.00
Peyton Manning
Reggie Wayne
Joseph Addai
6 Deuce McAllister 10.00 25.00
Drew Brees
Reggie Bush
Marques Colston
7 Plaxico Burress 12.00 30.00
Eli Manning
Jeremy Shockey
Brandon Jacobs
8 Brian Westbrook 10.00 25.00
Donovan McNabb
Correll Buckhalter
Reggie Brown
9 LaDainian Tomlinson 10.00 25.00
Philip Rivers
Antonio Gates
Keenan McCardell
10 Isaac Bruce 10.00 25.00
Steven Jackson
Torry Holt
Marc Bulger

2007 Absolute Memorabilia Team Tandems

STATED PRINT RUN 100 SER.#'d SETS
*SPECTRUM: .5X TO 1.2X BASIC INSERTS
SPECTRUM PRINT RUN 50 SER.#'d SETS
1 Anquan Boldin 3.00 8.00
Larry Fitzgerald
2 Warrick Dunn 2.50 6.00
Alge Crumpler
3 J.P. Losman 2.50 6.00
Lee Evans
4 Jake Delhomme 2.50 6.00
Steve Smith
5 Muhsin Muhammad 2.50 6.00
Bernard Berrian
6 Carson Palmer 2.50 6.00
Chad Johnson
7 Braylon Edwards 2.50 6.00
Kellen Winslow
8 Tony Romo 4.00 10.00
Terrell Owens
9 Brett Favre 6.00 15.00
Donald Driver
10 Marvin Harrison 3.00 8.00
Reggie Wayne
11 Fred Taylor 3.00 8.00
Maurice Jones-Drew
12 Larry Johnson 2.50 6.00
Tony Gonzalez
13 Chris Chambers 2.50 6.00
Ronnie Brown
14 Tom Brady 5.00 12.00
Laurence Maroney
15 Deuce McAllister 3.00 8.00
Reggie Bush
16 Plaxico Burress 2.50 6.00
Jeremy Shockey
17 Laveranues Coles 2.50 6.00
Jerricho Cotchery
18 Brian Westbrook 2.50 6.00
Correll Buckhalter
19 Hines Ward 3.00 8.00
Willie Parker
20 LaDainian Tomlinson 3.00 8.00
Antonio Gates
21 Alex Smith 3.00 8.00
Frank Gore
22 Shaun Alexander 2.50 6.00
Deion Branch
23 Isaac Bruce 2.50 6.00
Torry Holt
24 Clinton Portis 2.50 6.00
Santana Moss
25 Cadillac Williams 2.50 6.00
Mike Alstott

2007 Absolute Memorabilia Team Tandems Materials

STATED PRINT RUN 100 SER.#'d SETS
*PRIME/25: .8X TO 2X BASIC JSY/100
PRIME PRINT RUN 25 SER.#'d SETS
UNPRICED PRIME SPECTRUM PRINT RUN 1
1 Anquan Boldin 5.00 12.00
Larry Fitzgerald
2 Warrick Dunn 4.00 10.00
Alge Crumpler
3 J.P. Losman 4.00 10.00
Lee Evans
4 Jake Delhomme 4.00 10.00
Steve Smith
5 Muhsin Muhammad 4.00 10.00
Bernard Berrian
6 Carson Palmer 4.00 10.00
Chad Johnson
7 Braylon Edwards 4.00 10.00
Kellen Winslow
8 Tony Romo 6.00 15.00
Terrell Owens
9 Brett Favre 10.00 25.00
Donald Driver
10 Marvin Harrison 5.00 12.00
Reggie Wayne
11 Fred Taylor 5.00 12.00
Maurice Jones-Drew
12 Larry Johnson 4.00 10.00
Tony Gonzalez
13 Chris Chambers 4.00 10.00
Ronnie Brown
14 Tom Brady 8.00 20.00
Laurence Maroney
15 Deuce McAllister 5.00 12.00
Reggie Bush
16 Plaxico Burress 4.00 10.00
Jeremy Shockey
17 Laveranues Coles 4.00 10.00
Jerricho Cotchery
18 Brian Westbrook 4.00 10.00
Correll Buckhalter
19 Hines Ward 5.00 12.00
Willie Parker
20 LaDainian Tomlinson 5.00 12.00
Antonio Gates
21 Alex Smith 5.00 12.00
Frank Gore
22 Shaun Alexander 4.00 10.00
Deion Branch
23 Isaac Bruce 4.00 10.00
Torry Holt
24 Clinton Portis 4.00 10.00
Santana Moss
25 Cadillac Williams 4.00 10.00
Mike Alstott

2007 Absolute Memorabilia Team Trios

STATED PRINT RUN 100 SER.#'d SETS
*SPECTRUM/50: .6X TO 1.2X BASIC INSERTS
SPECTRUM PRINT RUN 50 SER.#'d SETS
1 Anquan Boldin 3.00 8.00
Matt Leinart
Larry Fitzgerald
2 Muhsin Muhammad 2.50 6.00
Rex Grossman
Bernard Berrian
3 Carson Palmer 2.50 6.00
Chad Johnson
Rudi Johnson
4 Tony Romo 4.00 10.00
Terrell Owens
Julius Jones
5 Marvin Harrison 5.00 12.00
Peyton Manning
Reggie Wayne
6 Fred Taylor 3.00 8.00
Byron Leftwich
Maurice Jones-Drew
7 Larry Johnson 2.50 6.00
Tony Gonzalez
Eddie Kennison
8 Deuce McAllister 3.00 8.00
Drew Brees
Reggie Bush
9 Plaxico Burress 3.00 8.00
Eli Manning
Jeremy Shockey
10 Brian Westbrook 3.00 8.00
Donovan McNabb
Correll Buckhalter
11 Hines Ward 3.00 8.00
Ben Roethlisberger
Willie Parker
12 LaDainian Tomlinson 3.00 8.00
Philip Rivers
Antonio Gates
13 Alex Smith 3.00 8.00
Frank Gore
Vernon Davis
14 Shaun Alexander 2.50 6.00
Matt Hasselbeck
Deion Branch
15 Isaac Bruce 3.00 8.00
Steven Jackson
Torry Holt

2007 Absolute Memorabilia Team Trios Materials

STATED PRINT RUN 100 SER.#'d SETS
*PRIME/25: .8X TO 2X BASIC JSY/100
PRIME PRINT RUN 25 SER.#'d SETS
UNPRICED PRIME SPECTRUM PRINT RUN 1
1 Anquan Boldin 6.00 15.00
Matt Leinart
Larry Fitzgerald
2 Muhsin Muhammad 5.00 12.00
Rex Grossman
Bernard Berrian
3 Carson Palmer 5.00 12.00
Chad Johnson
Rudi Johnson
4 Tony Romo 8.00 20.00
Terrell Owens
Julius Jones
5 Marvin Harrison 10.00 25.00
Peyton Manning
Reggie Wayne
6 Fred Taylor 6.00 15.00
Byron Leftwich
Maurice Jones-Drew
7 Larry Johnson 5.00 12.00
Tony Gonzalez
Eddie Kennison
8 Deuce McAllister 6.00 15.00
Drew Brees
Reggie Bush
9 Plaxico Burress 6.00 15.00
Eli Manning
Jeremy Shockey
10 Brian Westbrook 6.00 15.00
Donovan McNabb
Correll Buckhalter
11 Hines Ward 6.00 15.00
Ben Roethlisberger
Willie Parker
12 LaDainian Tomlinson 6.00 15.00
Philip Rivers
Antonio Gates
13 Alex Smith 6.00 15.00
Frank Gore
Vernon Davis
14 Shaun Alexander 5.00 12.00
Matt Hasselbeck
Deion Branch
15 Isaac Bruce 6.00 15.00
Steven Jackson
Torry Holt

2007 Absolute Memorabilia Tools of the Trade Red

RED PRINT RUN 100 SER.#'d SETS
*BLUE/75: .4X TO 1X RED/100
BLUE PRINT RUN 75 SER.#'d SETS
*BLACK/50: .5X TO 1.2X RED/100
BLACK PRINT RUN 50 SER.#'d SETS
*RED SPECT/25: .8X TO 2X RED/100
RED SPECTRUM PRINT RUN 25 SER.#'d SETS
*BLUE SPECT/10: 1.2X TO 3X RED/100
BLUE SPECTRUM PRINT RUN 10 SER.#'d SETS
UNPRICED BLACK SPECTRUM PRINT RUN 5
1 Aaron Rodgers 6.00 15.00
2 Ahman Green 2.00 5.00
3 A.J. Hawk 2.00 5.00
4 Alex Smith QB 2.50 6.00
5 Alge Crumpler 2.00 5.00
6 Amani Toomer 2.00 5.00
7 Andre Johnson 2.00 5.00
8 Anquan Boldin 2.00 5.00
9 Anthony Fasano 1.50 4.00
10 Antonio Gates 2.50 6.00
11 John Hannah 2.50 6.00
12 Ben Roethlisberger 2.50 6.00
13 Ben Watson 1.50 4.00
14 Bernard Berrian 1.50 4.00
15 Bobby Carpenter 1.50 4.00
16 Brad Smith 1.50 4.00
17 Brandon Jacobs 2.00 5.00
18 Brandon Jones 1.50 4.00
19 Brandon Marshall 2.00 5.00
20 Brandon Stokley 2.00 5.00
21 Braylon Edwards 2.00 5.00
22 Brett Favre 5.00 12.00
23 Brian Urlacher 2.50 6.00
24 Brian Westbrook 2.00 5.00
25 Brodie Croyle 2.00 5.00
26 Bruce Gradkowski 1.50 4.00
27 Bubba Franks 1.50 4.00
28 Bryant Young 1.50 4.00
29 Byron Leftwich 2.00 5.00
30 Cadillac Williams 2.00 5.00
31 Carson Palmer 2.00 5.00
32 Cedric Benson 2.00 5.00
33 Chad Johnson 2.00 5.00
34 Chad Lewis 1.50 4.00
35 Chad Pennington 2.00 5.00
36 Champ Bailey 2.00 5.00
37 Charlie Frye 2.00 5.00
38 Chester Taylor 1.50 4.00
39 Chris Brown 1.50 4.00
40 Chris Chambers 2.00 5.00
41 Chris Henry 1.50 4.00
42 Chris Simms 1.50 4.00
43 Clinton Portis 2.00 5.00
44 Correll Buckhalter 2.00 5.00
45 Curtis Martin 2.50 6.00
46 D'Brickashaw Ferguson 1.50 4.00
47 Dallas Clark 1.50 4.00
48 Darrell Jackson 1.50 4.00
49 Daunte Culpepper 2.00 5.00
50 DeAngelo Williams 2.50 6.00
51 Deion Branch 2.00 5.00
52 Demetrius Williams 1.50 4.00
53 Derrick Mason 2.00 5.00
54 DeShaun Foster 2.00 5.00
55 Deuce McAllister 2.00 5.00
56 Devin Hester 2.50 6.00
57 Donald Driver 2.50 6.00
58 Donovan McNabb 2.50 6.00
59 Drew Brees 2.50 6.00
60 Eddie Kennison 1.50 4.00
61 Edgerrin James 2.00 5.00
62 Eli Manning 2.50 6.00
63 Frank Gore 2.50 6.00
64 Fred Taylor 2.00 5.00
65 Greg Lewis 1.50 4.00
66 Hank Baskett 2.00 5.00
67 Heath Miller 1.50 4.00
68 Hines Ward 2.50 6.00
69 Isaac Bruce 2.00 5.00
70 J.P. Losman 1.50 4.00
71 Jason Campbell 2.00 5.00
72 Jason Taylor 2.00 5.00
73 Jason Witten 2.50 6.00
74 Jay Cutler 2.50 6.00
75 Jeremy Shockey 2.00 5.00
76 Jerious Norwood 2.00 5.00
77 Jerome Harrison 1.50 4.00
78 Jerricho Cotchery 2.00 5.00
79 Jevon Kearse 2.00 5.00
80 Joe Klopfenstein 1.50 4.00
81 Joey Galloway 2.00 5.00
82 Jon Kitna 1.50 4.00
83 Joseph Addai 2.00 5.00
84 Josh Reed 1.50 4.00
85 Julius Jones 1.50 4.00
86 Julius Peppers 2.00 5.00
87 Keary Colbert 1.50 4.00
88 Keenan McCardell 1.50 4.00
89 Kellen Winslow Jr. 2.00 5.00
90 Kevin Jones 1.50 4.00
91 Keyshawn Johnson 2.00 5.00
92 LaDainian Tomlinson 2.50 6.00
93 Larry Fitzgerald 2.50 6.00
94 Larry Johnson 1.50 4.00
95 Laurence Maroney 2.00 5.00
96 Laveranues Coles 1.50 4.00
97 Lee Evans 2.00 5.00

98 Leon Washington 2.00 5.00
99 Marc Bulger 2.00 5.00
100 Mario Williams 2.00 5.00
101 Marion Barber 2.50 6.00
102 Mark Clayton 2.00 5.00
103 Marvin Harrison 2.50 6.00
104 Mathias Kiwanuka 1.50 4.00
105 Matt Hasselbeck 2.00 5.00
106 Matt Jones 2.00 5.00
107 Matt Leinart 2.00 5.00
108 Maurice Jones-Drew 2.50 6.00
109 Michael Clayton 1.50 4.00
110 Michael Robinson 2.00 5.00
111 Michael Strahan 2.00 5.00
112 Michael Vick 2.50 6.00
113 Muhsin Muhammad 2.00 5.00
114 Nick Barnett 1.50 4.00
115 Peyton Manning 4.00 10.00
116 Philip Rivers 2.50 6.00
117 Plaxico Burress 2.00 5.00
118 Randy Moss 2.50 6.00
119 Reggie Brown 1.50 4.00
120 Reggie Bush 2.50 6.00
121 Reggie Wayne 2.00 5.00
122 Reggie Williams 2.00 5.00
123 Robert Ferguson 1.50 4.00
124 Ronnie Brown 2.00 5.00
125 Roy Williams S 2.00 5.00
126 Roy Williams WR 2.00 5.00
127 Rudi Johnson 2.00 5.00
128 Santana Moss 2.00 5.00
129 Shaun Alexander 2.00 5.00
130 Steve McNair 2.00 5.00
131 Steve Smith 2.00 5.00
132 Steven Jackson 2.50 6.00
133 T.J. Houshmandzadeh 2.00 5.00
134 Terence Newman 1.50 4.00
135 Terrell Owens 2.50 6.00
136 Terry Glenn 2.00 5.00
137 Todd Heap 1.50 4.00
138 Tony Gonzalez 2.00 5.00
139 Torry Holt 2.00 5.00
140 Trent Green 2.00 5.00
141 Troy Polamalu 2.50 6.00
142 Vernon Davis 2.00 5.00
143 Vince Young 2.00 5.00
144 Warrick Dunn 2.00 5.00
145 Willie Parker 2.00 5.00
146 Barry Sanders 6.00 15.00
147 Dan Marino 8.00 20.00
148 Joe Montana 8.00 20.00
149 Steve Largent 4.00 10.00
150 Walter Payton 8.00 20.00

2007 Absolute Memorabilia Tools of the Trade Material Red Oversize

STATED PRINT RUN 7-50
UNPRICED BLUE OVERSIZE PRINT RUN 1-5
22 Brett Favre 12.00 30.00
74 Jay Cutler 6.00 15.00
83 Joseph Addai 5.00 12.00
92 LaDainian Tomlinson 6.00 16.00
107 Matt Leinart 5.00 12.00
115 Peyton Manning 10.00 25.00
120 Reggie Bush/25 8.00 20.00
143 Vince Young 5.00 12.00
146 Barry Sanders 15.00 40.00
147 Dan Marino 20.00 50.00
148 Joe Montana 20.00 50.00
149 Steve Largent 10.00 25.00
150 Walter Payton 12.00 30.00

2007 Absolute Memorabilia Tools of the Trade Material Black Spectrum

COMMON CARD/40-50 3.00 8.00
SEMISTARS/40-50 4.00 10.00
UNL.STARS/40-50 5.00 12.00
COMMON CARD/15-25 4.00 10.00
SEMISTARS/15-25 4.00 12.00
STATED PRINT RUN 4-50
*DBL BLK SPC/25: 1X TO 2.5X BLK SPCT/40-50
*DBLE BLK/25: .8X TO 2X BLK SPEC/15-25
*DBLE BLK/15-20: 1.2X TO 3X BLK SPEC/40-50
UNPRICED BLACK OVER.SPECT.PRINT RUN 1
12 Ben Roethlisberger 5.00 12.00
22 Brett Favre 10.00 25.00
74 Jay Cutler/45 5.00 12.00
83 Joseph Addai 4.00 10.00
92 LaDainian Tomlinson 5.00 12.00
107 Matt Leinart/25 5.00 12.00
115 Peyton Manning 8.00 20.00
120 Reggie Bush 5.00 12.00
143 Vince Young 4.00 10.00
146 Barry Sanders 12.00 30.00
147 Dan Marino 15.00 40.00
148 Joe Montana 15.00 40.00
149 Steve Largent 8.00 20.00
150 Walter Payton 15.00 40.00

2007 Absolute Memorabilia Tools of the Trade Material Autographs Blue

UNPRICED BLUE AU PRINT RUN 4-5
UNPRICED BLACK AU PRINT RUN 1
UNPRICED DOUBLE BLACK AU PRINT RUN 1
UNPRICED DOUBLE BLUE AU PRINT RUN 5
UNPRICED TRIPLE BLUE AU PRINT RUN 4-5
UNPRICED TRIPLE BLACK AU PRINT RUN 4-5

2007 Absolute Memorabilia Tools of the Trade Material Quad Red

STATED PRINT RUN 25 SER.#'d SETS
*BLUE/10: .8X TO 2X RED/25
BLUE PRINT RUN 2-10
UNPRICED BLACK SPECTRUM PRINT RUN 1
6 Amani Toomer 10.00 25.00
8 Anquan Boldin 10.00 25.00
23 Brian Urlacher 12.00 30.00
29 Byron Leftwich 10.00 25.00
30 Cadillac Williams 10.00 25.00
32 Cedric Benson 10.00 25.00
33 Chad Johnson 10.00 25.00
35 Chad Pennington 10.00 25.00
45 Curtis Martin 12.00 30.00
53 Derrick Mason 10.00 25.00
58 Donovan McNabb 12.00 30.00
69 Isaac Bruce 10.00 25.00
72 Jason Taylor 10.00 25.00
93 Larry Fitzgerald 12.00 30.00
96 Laveranues Coles 8.00 20.00
97 Lee Evans 10.00 25.00
103 Marvin Harrison/24 12.00 30.00
111 Michael Strahan 10.00 25.00
112 Michael Vick 12.00 30.00
115 Peyton Manning 20.00 50.00
139 Torry Holt 10.00 25.00
147 Dan Marino 50.00 125.00
149 Steve Largent 25.00 60.00

2007 Absolute Memorabilia Tools of the Trade Material Triple Red

STATED PRINT RUN 13-50
*BLUE/15-25: .8X TO 2X RED/35-50
BLUE PRINT RUN 9-25
UNPRICED BLACK SPECTRUM PRINT RUN 5
6 Amani Toomer 5.00 12.00
7 Andre Johnson 5.00 12.00
8 Anquan Boldin 5.00 12.00
22 Brett Favre 12.00 30.00
23 Brian Urlacher 6.00 15.00
29 Byron Leftwich 5.00 12.00
30 Cadillac Williams/35 5.00 12.00
31 Carson Palmer 5.00 12.00
33 Chad Johnson 5.00 12.00
35 Chad Pennington 5.00 12.00
36 Champ Bailey/40 5.00 12.00
40 Chris Chambers 5.00 12.00
43 Clinton Portis 5.00 12.00
45 Curtis Martin 6.00 15.00
48 Darrell Jackson 4.00 10.00
49 Daunte Culpepper 5.00 12.00
53 Derrick Mason 5.00 12.00
55 Deuce McAllister 5.00 12.00
58 Donovan McNabb 6.00 15.00
60 Eddie Kennison 4.00 10.00
61 Edgerrin James 5.00 12.00
62 Eli Manning 6.00 15.00
68 Hines Ward 6.00 15.00
69 Isaac Bruce 5.00 12.00
75 Jeremy Shockey 5.00 12.00
79 Jevon Kearse 5.00 12.00
81 Joey Galloway 5.00 12.00
92 LaDainian Tomlinson 6.00 15.00
93 Larry Fitzgerald 6.00 15.00
96 Laveranues Coles 4.00 10.00
99 Marc Bulger 5.00 12.00
103 Marvin Harrison/35 6.00 15.00
105 Matt Hasselbeck 5.00 12.00
111 Michael Strahan 5.00 12.00
112 Michael Vick 6.00 15.00
115 Peyton Manning 10.00 25.00
125 Roy Williams 5.00 12.00
129 Shaun Alexander 5.00 12.00
130 Steve McNair 5.00 12.00
131 Steve Smith 5.00 12.00
136 Terry Glenn 5.00 12.00
137 Todd Heap 4.00 10.00
138 Tony Gonzalez 5.00 12.00
139 Torry Holt 5.00 12.00
140 Trent Green 5.00 12.00
144 Warrick Dunn 5.00 12.00
147 Dan Marino 20.00 50.00
148 Joe Montana 20.00 50.00
149 Steve Largent 10.00 25.00

2007 Absolute Memorabilia War Room

STATED PRINT RUN 100 SER.#'d SETS
*SPECTRUM/25: .8X TO 2X BASIC INSERTS
SPECTRUM PRINT RUN 25 SER.#'d SETS
UNPRICED AUTO PRINT RUN 5
UNPRICED MATERIAL AU PRINT RUN 5
1 Ted Ginn Jr. 2.00 5.00
2 Joe Thomas 2.50 6.00
3 Brady Quinn 2.50 6.00
4 Brandon Jackson 2.00 5.00
5 Tony Hunt 1.50 4.00
6 Steve Smith 2.50 6.00
7 Dwayne Jarrett 2.00 5.00
8 Drew Stanton 1.50 4.00
9 Antonio Pittman 1.50 4.00
10 Dwayne Bowe 3.00 8.00
11 Anthony Gonzalez 2.50 6.00
12 Lorenzo Booker 2.00 5.00
13 Chris Henry 1.50 4.00
14 Gaines Adams 2.50 6.00
15 Kevin Kolb 4.00 10.00
16 John Beck 2.50 6.00
17 Brian Leonard 2.00 5.00
18 Adrian Peterson 10.00 25.00
19 Greg Olsen 2.00 5.00
20 JaMarcus Russell 1.50 4.00
21 Garrett Wolfe 1.50 4.00
22 Yamon Figurs 1.50 4.00
23 Sidney Rice 3.00 8.00
24 Trent Edwards 2.50 6.00
25 Michael Bush 2.50 6.00
26 Patrick Willis 5.00 12.00
27 Kenny Irons 1.50 4.00
28 Calvin Johnson 8.00 20.00
29 Paul Williams 1.50 4.00
30 Robert Meachem 2.50 6.00
31 Jason Hill 2.50 6.00
32 Marshawn Lynch 2.50 6.00
33 Johnnie Lee Higgins 2.00 5.00
34 Troy Smith 2.50 6.00

2007 Absolute Memorabilia War Room Materials

STATED PRINT RUN 100 SER.#'d SETS
*PRIME/50: .6X TO 1.5X BASIC JSY/100
PRIME PRINT RUN 50 SER.#'d SETS
*OVERSIZE/25: 1X TO 2.5X BASIC JSY/100
OVERSIZE PRINT RUN 25 SER.#'d SETS
*OVER.SPECT/10: 1.5X TO 4X BASIC JSY/100
OVERSIZE SPECTRUM PRINT RUN 10
1 Ted Ginn Jr. 3.00 8.00
2 Joe Thomas 4.00 10.00
3 Brady Quinn 4.00 10.00
4 Brandon Jackson 3.00 8.00
5 Tony Hunt 2.50 6.00
6 Steve Smith 4.00 10.00
7 Dwayne Jarrett 3.00 8.00
8 Drew Stanton 2.50 6.00
9 Antonio Pittman 2.50 6.00
10 Dwayne Bowe 5.00 12.00
11 Anthony Gonzalez 4.00 10.00
12 Lorenzo Booker 3.00 8.00
13 Chris Henry 2.50 6.00
14 Gaines Adams 4.00 10.00
15 Kevin Kolb 6.00 15.00
16 John Beck 4.00 10.00
17 Brian Leonard 3.00 8.00
18 Adrian Peterson 15.00 40.00
19 Greg Olsen 3.00 8.00
20 JaMarcus Russell 2.50 6.00
21 Garrett Wolfe 2.50 6.00
22 Yamon Figurs 2.50 6.00
23 Sidney Rice 5.00 12.00
24 Trent Edwards 4.00 10.00
25 Michael Bush 4.00 10.00
26 Patrick Willis 8.00 20.00
27 Kenny Irons 2.50 6.00
28 Calvin Johnson 12.00 30.00
29 Paul Williams 2.50 6.00
30 Robert Meachem 4.00 10.00
31 Jason Hill 4.00 10.00
32 Marshawn Lynch 4.00 10.00
33 Johnnie Lee Higgins 3.00 8.00
34 Troy Smith 4.00 10.00

2008 Absolute Memorabilia

This set was released on September 3, 2008. The base set consists of 284 cards. Cards #1-150 feature veterans, while cards #151-250 consist of rookies serial numbered to 799 with some autographed rookie cards serial numbered to 99. Finally, cards #251-284 are autographed rookie jerseys serial numbered of 299.

ROOKIE PRINT RUN 799 SER.#'d SETS
AU ROOKIE PRINT RUN 99 SER.#'d SETS
JSY AU ROOKIE PRINT RUN 299 SER.#'d SETS
1 Anquan Boldin .50 1.25
2 Edgerrin James .50 1.25
3 Kurt Warner .60 1.50
4 Larry Fitzgerald .60 1.50
5 Matt Leinart .60 1.50
6 Jerious Norwood .50 1.25
7 Roddy White .50 1.25
8 Michael Turner .60 1.50
9 Joey Harrington .40 1.00
10 Steve McNair .50 1.25
11 Willis McGahee .50 1.25
12 Derrick Mason .50 1.25
13 Yamon Figurs .40 1.00
14 Ray Lewis .60 1.50
15 Trent Edwards .40 1.00
16 Marshawn Lynch .50 1.25
17 Fred Jackson RC 6.00 15.00
18 Lee Evans .50 1.25
19 Josh Reed .40 1.00
20 Jake Delhomme .50 1.25
21 DeAngelo Williams .50 1.25
22 Steve Smith .50 1.25
23 Jon Beason .40 1.00
24 Rex Grossman .50 1.25
25 Adrian Peterson 1.00 2.50
26 Greg Olsen .50 1.25
27 Devin Hester .60 1.50
28 Brian Urlacher .60 1.50
29 Carson Palmer .60 1.50
30 Chad Johnson .50 1.25
31 Rudi Johnson .50 1.25
32 T.J. Houshmandzadeh .50 1.25
33 Kenny Watson .40 1.00
34 Derek Anderson .40 1.00
35 Jamal Lewis .50 1.25
36 Braylon Edwards .50 1.25
37 Kellen Winslow .50 1.25
38 Josh Cribbs .60 1.50
39 Tony Romo .75 2.00
40 Terrell Owens .60 1.50
41 Jason Witten .60 1.50
42 Marion Barber .50 1.25
43 DeMarcus Ware .50 1.25
44 Jay Cutler .60 1.50
45 Brandon Marshall .50 1.25
46 Selvin Young .40 1.00
47 Brandon Stokley .50 1.25
48 Tony Scheffler .40 1.00
49 Jon Kitna .50 1.25
50 Tatum Bell .40 1.00
51 Roy Williams WR .50 1.25
52 Calvin Johnson .60 1.50
53 Shaun McDonald .40 1.00
54 Aaron Rodgers 1.25 3.00
55 Greg Jennings .60 1.50
56 Donald Driver .50 1.25
57 James Jones .40 1.00
58 Ryan Grant .60 1.50
59 Matt Schaub .50 1.25
60 Ahman Green .50 1.25
61 Andre Johnson .50 1.25
62 Kevin Walter .50 1.25
63 Owen Daniels .40 1.00
64 Peyton Manning 1.00 2.50
65 Reggie Wayne .50 1.25
66 Marvin Harrison .60 1.50
67 Joseph Addai .50 1.25
68 Anthony Gonzalez .40 1.00
69 David Garrard .50 1.25
70 Fred Taylor .50 1.25
71 Maurice Jones-Drew .50 1.25
72 Jerry Porter .40 1.00
73 Reggie Williams .50 1.25
74 Brodie Croyle .50 1.25
75 Tony Gonzalez .50 1.25
76 Larry Johnson .50 1.25
77 Kolby Smith .40 1.00
78 Dwayne Bowe .50 1.25
79 John Beck .40 1.00
80 Ted Ginn .50 1.25
81 Ernest Wilford .40 1.00
82 Ronnie Brown .50 1.25
83 Tarvaris Jackson .50 1.25
84 Adrian Peterson 1.00 2.50
85 Chester Taylor .40 1.00
86 Bernard Berrian .50 1.25
87 Tom Brady 1.00 2.50
88 Laurence Maroney .50 1.25
89 Randy Moss .60 1.50
90 Wes Welker .60 1.50
91 Drew Brees .60 1.50
92 Deuce McAllister .50 1.25
93 Marques Colston .50 1.25
94 Reggie Bush .60 1.50
95 Devery Henderson .40 1.00
96 Eli Manning .60 1.50
97 Brandon Jacobs .50 1.25
98 Derrick Ward .40 1.00
99 Plaxico Burress .50 1.25
100 Steve Smith .50 1.25
101 Kellen Clemens .50 1.25
102 Thomas Jones .50 1.25
103 Laveranues Coles .40 1.00
104 Jerricho Cotchery .50 1.25
105 JaMarcus Russell .50 1.25
106 Justin Fargas .40 1.00
107 Michael Bush .50 1.25
108 Javon Walker .50 1.25
109 Zach Miller .50 1.25
110 Donovan McNabb .60 1.50
111 Brian Westbrook .50 1.25
112 Kevin Curtis .40 1.00
113 Reggie Brown .40 1.00
114 Ben Roethlisberger .60 1.50
115 Willie Parker .50 1.25
116 Santonio Holmes .50 1.25
117 Hines Ward .50 1.25
118 Philip Rivers .60 1.50
119 LaDainian Tomlinson .60 1.50
120 Antonio Gates .60 1.50
121 Vincent Jackson .40 1.00
122 Alex Smith QB .60 1.50
123 Frank Gore .50 1.25
124 Vernon Davis .50 1.25
125 Isaac Bruce .50 1.25
126 Arnaz Battle .40 1.00
127 Matt Hasselbeck .50 1.25
128 Lofa Tatupu .50 1.25
129 Deion Branch .50 1.25
130 Nate Burleson .40 1.00
131 Julius Jones .40 1.00
132 Marc Bulger .50 1.25
133 Steven Jackson .60 1.50
134 Torry Holt .50 1.25
135 Randy McMichael .40 1.00
136 Jeff Garcia .50 1.25
137 Cadillac Williams .50 1.25
138 Warrick Dunn .50 1.25
139 Joey Galloway .50 1.25
140 Michael Clayton .40 1.00
141 Vince Young .50 1.25
142 LenDale White .50 1.25
143 Alge Crumpler .50 1.25
144 Justin Gage .40 1.00
145 Roydell Williams .40 1.00
146 Jason Campbell .50 1.25
147 Clinton Portis .50 1.25
148 Chris Cooley .50 1.25
149 Santana Moss .40 1.00
150 Ladell Betts .40 1.00
151 Adrian Arrington AU RC 5.00 12.00
152 Alex Brink RC 2.50 6.00
153 Ali Highsmith RC 1.50 4.00
154 Allen Patrick AU RC 5.00 12.00
155 Andre Woodson AU RC 6.00 15.00
156 Anthony Alridge RC 2.00 5.00
157 Antoine Cason AU RC 6.00 15.00
158 Aqib Talib AU RC 6.00 15.00
159 Arman Shields RC 2.00 5.00
160 Brad Cottam AU RC 5.00 12.00
161 Brandon Flowers AU RC 6.00 15.00
162 Calais Campbell RC 2.00 5.00
163 Caleb Campbell RC 2.50 6.00
164 Chauncey Washington AU RC 5.00 12.00
165 Chevis Jackson RC 1.50 4.00
166 Chris Long AU RC 6.00 15.00
167 Colt Brennan AU RC 8.00 20.00
168 Cory Boyd AU RC 4.00 10.00
169 Craig Steltz RC 2.00 5.00
170 Curtis Lofton AU RC 5.00 12.00
171 Dan Connor AU RC 6.00 15.00
172 Dantrell Savage RC 2.00 5.00
173 Darius Reynaud RC 1.50 4.00
174 Darrell Strong RC 2.00 5.00
175 Davone Bess RC 2.50 6.00
176 Dennis Dixon AU RC 8.00 20.00
177 Derrick Harvey AU RC 4.00 10.00
178 DJ Hall RC 2.00 5.00
179 Dominique Rodgers-Cromartie AU RC 6.00 15.00
180 Erik Ainge AU RC 6.00 15.00
181 Erin Henderson RC 2.50 6.00
182 Ernie Wheelwright RC 2.00 5.00
183 Fred Davis AU RC 6.00 15.00
184 Joe Jon Finley RC 2.00 5.00
185 Jacob Hester AU RC 6.00 15.00
186 Jacob Tamme AU RC 6.00 15.00
187 Jalen Parmele RC 2.00 5.00
188 Jamar Adams RC 2.00 5.00
189 Jason Rivers RC 2.00 5.00
190 Jaymar Johnson RC 1.50 4.00
191 Jed Collins RC 2.00 5.00
192 Jermichael Finley AU RC 10.00 20.00
193 Jerod Mayo AU RC 6.00 15.00
194 John Carlson AU RC 6.00 15.00
195 Jonathan Hefney RC 2.00 5.00
196 Jordon Dizon AU RC 6.00 15.00
197 Josh Johnson AU RC 6.00 15.00
198 Josh Morgan AU RC 6.00 15.00
199 Justin Forsett AU RC 6.00 15.00
200 Justin Harper RC 2.00 5.00
201 Kalvin McRae RC 1.50 4.00
202 Keenan Burton AU RC 4.00 10.00
203 Keith Rivers AU RC 6.00 15.00
204 Kellen Davis RC 1.50 4.00
205 Kenneth Moore RC 2.00 5.00
206 Kenny Phillips AU RC 8.00 20.00
207 Kentwan Balmer AU RC 5.00 12.00
208 Kevin Robinson AU RC 4.00 10.00
209 Lavelle Hawkins AU RC 4.00 10.00
210 Lawrence Jackson AU RC 5.00 12.00
211 Leodis McKelvin AU RC 5.00 12.00
212 Marcus Henry RC 2.00 5.00
213 Marcus Monk RC 2.00 5.00
214 Marcus Smith AU RC 5.00 12.00
215 Marcus Thomas AU RC 5.00 12.00
216 Mark Bradford RC 1.50 4.00
217 Martellus Bennett AU RC 5.00 12.00
218 Martin Rucker AU RC 5.00 12.00
219 Matt Flynn AU RC 25.00 60.00
220 Mike Jenkins AU RC 6.00 15.00
221 Mike Hart AU RC 6.00 15.00
222 Owen Schmitt RC 2.50 6.00
223 Pat Sims RC 2.00 5.00
224 Paul Hubbard AU/91 RC 5.00 12.00
225 Paul Smith RC 2.50 6.00
226 Peyton Hillis RC 3.00 8.00
227 Phillip Merling RC 2.00 5.00
228 Pierre Garcon RC 3.00 8.00
229 Quentin Groves RC 2.00 5.00
230 Reggie Smith RC 2.00 5.00
231 Robert Killebrew RC 2.00 5.00
232 Ryan Grice-Mullen RC 1.50 4.00
233 Ryan Torain AU RC 6.00 15.00
234 Adarius Bowman RC 2.00 5.00
235 Sam Keller RC 2.00 5.00
236 Sedrick Ellis AU RC 6.00 15.00
237 Shawn Crable RC 1.50 4.00
238 Simeon Castille RC 2.00 5.00
239 Tashard Choice AU RC 5.00 12.00
240 Terrell Thomas RC 2.00 5.00
241 Dorien Bryant RC 2.00 5.00
242 Thomas Brown AU RC 5.00 12.00
243 Tim Hightower AU RC 8.00 20.00
244 Tracy Porter RC 2.50 6.00
245 Vernon Gholston AU RC 5.00 12.00
246 Bernard Morris RC 2.00 5.00
247 Will Franklin 5.00 12.00
248 Xavier Adibi RC 1.50 4.00
249 Xavier Omon RC 2.50 6.00
250 Zackary Bowman RC 2.00 5.00
251 Chad Henne RPM AU RC 15.00 40.00
252 Dustin Keller RPM AU RC 8.00 20.00
253 Jonathan Stewart RPM AU RC 15.00 40.00
254 Steve Slaton RPM AU RC 6.00 15.00
255 Earl Bennett RPM AU RC 6.00 15.00
256 Brian Brohm RPM AU RC 6.00 15.00
257 Jamaal Charles RPM AU RC 15.00 30.00
258 Mario Manningham RPM AU RC 12.50 25.00
259 Felix Jones RPM AU RC 15.00 40.00
260 DeSean Jackson RPM AU RC 15.00 40.00
261 Kevin O'Connell RPM AU RC 5.00 12.00
262 Kevin Smith RPM AU RC 6.00 15.00
263 Jerome Simpson RPM AU RC 6.00 15.00
264 Darren McFadden RPM AU RC 25.00 50.00
265 Harry Douglas RPM AU RC 6.00 15.00
266 John David Booty RPM AU RC 5.00 12.00
267 Rashard Mendenhall RPM AU RC 15.00 40.00
268 Malcolm Kelly RPM AU RC 5.00 12.00
269 Matt Ryan RPM AU RC 30.00 80.00
270 Joe Flacco RPM AU RC 40.00 80.00
271 Early Doucet RPM AU RC 5.00 12.00
272 Andre Caldwell RPM AU RC 5.00 12.00
273 James Hardy RPM AU RC 5.00 12.00
274 Jordy Nelson RPM AU RC 15.00 30.00
275 Glenn Dorsey RPM AU RC EXCH 6.00 15.00
276 Chris Johnson RPM AU RC 40.00 80.00
277 Eddie Royal RPM AU RC 6.00 15.00
278 Matt Forte RPM AU RC 15.00 40.00
279 Ray Rice RPM AU RC 15.00 40.00
280 Devin Thomas RPM AU RC 5.00 12.00
281 Limas Sweed RPM AU RC 6.00 15.00
282 Dexter Jackson RPM AU RC 5.00 12.00
283 Donnie Avery RPM AU RC 5.00 12.00
284 Jake Long RPM AU RC 6.00 15.00

2008 Absolute Memorabilia Retail

*VETS 1-150: .2X TO .5X BASIC CARDS
*ROOKIES 151-250: .4X TO 1X BASIC CARDS
ROOKIES PRINT RUN 799 SER.#'d SETS
PRINTED ON WHITE CARD STOCK
101B Brett Favre 10.00 25.00

2008 Absolute Memorabilia Spectrum Black

*VETERANS 1-150: 1.5X TO 4X BASIC CARDS
*ROOKIES: .5X TO 1.2X SILVER SPECTRUM
RETAIL PACK INSERT PRINT RUN 100

2008 Absolute Memorabilia Spectrum Blue

*VETS 1-150: 1.2X TO 3X BASIC CARDS
*ROOKIES: .4X TO 1X SILVER SPECTRUM
RETAIL PACK INSERT PRINT RUN 250

2008 Absolute Memorabilia Spectrum Gold

*VETS 1-150: 3X TO 8X BASIC CARDS
*ROOKIES: 1X TO 2.5X SILVER SPECTRUM
STATED PRINT RUN 25 SER.#'d SETS

2008 Absolute Memorabilia Spectrum Platinum

UNPRICED PLATINUM PRINT RUN 1

2008 Absolute Memorabilia Spectrum Red

*VETS 1-150: 1X TO 2.5X BASIC CARDS
*ROOKIES: .3X TO .8X SILVER SPECTRUM
RANDOM INSERTS IN RETAIL PACKS

2008 Absolute Memorabilia Spectrum Silver

*VETS 1-150: 1.2X TO 3X BASIC CARDS
COMMON ROOKIE 2.00 5.00
ROOKIE SEMISTARS 2.50 6.00
ROOKIE UNL.STARS 3.00 8.00
STATED PRINT RUN 100 SER.#'d SETS
166 Chris Long 3.00 8.00
167 Colt Brennan 3.00 8.00
175 Davone Bess 3.00 8.00
176 Dennis Dixon 3.00 8.00
180 Erik Ainge 3.00 8.00
185 Jacob Hester 3.00 8.00
193 Jerod Mayo 3.00 8.00
219 Matt Flynn 6.00 15.00
220 Mike Jenkins 3.00 8.00
221 Mike Hart 3.00 8.00
222 Owen Schmitt 3.00 8.00
226 Peyton Hillis 4.00 10.00
243 Tim Hightower 3.00 8.00
245 Vernon Gholston 2.50 6.00

2008 Absolute Memorabilia Absolute Heroes

STATED PRINT RUN 250 SER.#'d SETS
*SPECTRUM/25: 1X TO 2.5X BASIC INSERTS
SPECTRUM PRINT RUN 25 SER.#'d SETS
1 Donovan McNabb 1.50 4.00
2 Vince Young 1.25 3.00
3 Antonio Gates 1.50 4.00
4 Cadillac Williams 1.25 3.00
5 Philip Rivers 1.50 4.00
6 Kevin Curtis 1.00 2.50
7 Andre Johnson 1.25 3.00
8 LaDainian Tomlinson 1.50 4.00
9 Deuce McAllister 1.25 3.00
10 Marc Bulger 1.25 3.00
11 Ben Roethlisberger 1.50 4.00
12 Marvin Harrison 1.50 4.00
13 Eli Manning 1.50 4.00
14 Derrick Mason 1.25 3.00
15 Lee Evans 1.25 3.00
16 Fred Taylor 1.25 3.00
17 Terrell Owens 1.50 4.00
18 Roy Williams WR 1.25 3.00
19 Jon Kitna 1.25 3.00
20 Amani Toomer 1.25 3.00
21 Thomas Jones 1.25 3.00
22 Michael Clayton 1.00 2.50
23 Frank Gore 1.25 3.00
24 Peyton Manning 2.50 6.00
25 Devin Hester 1.50 4.00
26 Ronnie Brown 1.25 3.00
27 Steve Smith 1.25 3.00
28 Deion Branch 1.25 3.00
29 Hines Ward 1.25 3.00
30 Zach Miller 1.25 3.00

2008 Absolute Memorabilia Absolute Heroes Autographs Spectrum

STATED PRINT RUN 10-25
SERIAL #'d UNDER 25 NOT PRICED
30 Zach Miller/25 8.00 20.00

2008 Absolute Memorabilia Absolute Heroes Materials

RETAIL PACK INSERT PRINT RUN 130-200
1 Donovan McNabb 4.00 10.00
2 Vince Young 3.00 8.00
5 Philip Rivers 4.00 10.00
7 Andre Johnson 3.00 8.00
9 Deuce McAllister 3.00 8.00
10 Marc Bulger 3.00 8.00
11 Ben Roethlisberger 4.00 10.00
13 Eli Manning 4.00 10.00
14 Derrick Mason 3.00 8.00
18 Roy Williams WR 3.00 8.00
20 Amani Toomer 3.00 8.00
22 Michael Clayton 2.50 6.00
25 Devin Hester 5.00 12.00
26 Ronnie Brown 3.00 8.00
27 Steve Smith 3.00 8.00
28 Deion Branch/130 3.00 8.00
29 Hines Ward 3.00 8.00

2008 Absolute Memorabilia Absolute Heroes Materials Prime

PRIME PRINT RUN 50 SER.#'d SETS
UNPRICED SPECTRUM PRIME PRINT RUN 1
1 Donovan McNabb 5.00 12.00
3 Antonio Gates 5.00 12.00
4 Cadillac Williams 4.00 10.00
5 Philip Rivers 5.00 12.00
6 Kevin Curtis 3.00 8.00
7 Andre Johnson 4.00 10.00
8 LaDainian Tomlinson 5.00 12.00
9 Deuce McAllister 4.00 10.00
10 Marc Bulger 4.00 10.00
11 Ben Roethlisberger 5.00 12.00
12 Marvin Harrison 5.00 12.00
13 Eli Manning 5.00 12.00
14 Derrick Mason 4.00 10.00
15 Lee Evans 4.00 10.00
16 Fred Taylor 4.00 10.00
17 Terrell Owens 5.00 12.00
18 Roy Williams WR 4.00 10.00
19 Jon Kitna 4.00 10.00
20 Amani Toomer 4.00 10.00
21 Thomas Jones 4.00 10.00
22 Michael Clayton 3.00 8.00
23 Frank Gore 4.00 10.00
26 Ronnie Brown 4.00 10.00
27 Steve Smith 4.00 10.00
28 Deion Branch 4.00 10.00
29 Hines Ward 4.00 10.00

2008 Absolute Memorabilia Absolute Heroes Materials Autographs

STATED PRINT RUN 10-25
UNPRICED PRIME PRINT RUN 5-15
UNPRICED SPECTRUM PRIME PRINT RUN 1
SERIAL #'d UNDER 20 NOT PRICED
9 Deuce McAllister/25 10.00 25.00
18 Roy Williams WR/20 10.00 25.00

2008 Absolute Memorabilia Absolute Patches Prime

STATED PRINT RUN 5-25
UNPRICED SPECTRUM PRIME PRINT RUN 1
1 Tom Brady 40.00 100.00
2 Tony Romo/20 30.00 80.00
5 Eli Manning 25.00 60.00
7 LaDainian Tomlinson 25.00 60.00
8 Adrian Peterson 40.00 100.00
9 Brian Westbrook 20.00 50.00
10 Willie Parker 20.00 50.00
11 Marshawn Lynch 20.00 50.00
12 Joseph Addai 20.00 50.00
13 Ryan Grant 25.00 60.00
15 Randy Moss 25.00 60.00
16 Chad Johnson 20.00 50.00
17 Terrell Owens 25.00 60.00
18 Torry Holt 20.00 50.00
19 Greg Jennings 25.00 60.00
20 Tony Gonzalez 20.00 50.00

2008 Absolute Memorabilia Canton Absolutes

STATED PRINT RUN 250 SER.#'d SETS
*SPECTRUM/25: 1X TO 2.5X BASIC INSERTS
SPECTRUM PRINT RUN 25 SER.#'d SETS
1 Emmitt Smith 4.00 10.00
2 Brett Favre 4.00 10.00
3 Brian Westbrook 1.25 3.00
4 Chad Johnson 1.25 3.00
5 Peyton Manning 2.50 6.00
6 Tom Brady 2.50 6.00
7 Eli Manning 1.50 4.00
8 Terrell Owens 1.50 4.00
9 Randy Moss 1.50 4.00
10 LaDainian Tomlinson 1.50 4.00
11 Edgerrin James 1.25 3.00
12 Tony Gonzalez 1.25 3.00
13 Steve Smith 1.25 3.00
14 Hines Ward 1.25 3.00
15 Steve McNair 1.25 3.00
16 Warrick Dunn 1.25 3.00
17 Isaac Bruce 1.25 3.00
18 Marvin Harrison 1.50 4.00
19 Shaun Alexander 1.25 3.00
20 Torry Holt 1.25 3.00
21 Joey Galloway 1.25 3.00
22 Donovan McNabb 1.50 4.00
23 Tim Brown 1.50 4.00
24 Andre Reed 1.25 3.00
25 Tiki Barber 1.25 3.00
26 Phil Simms 1.50 4.00
27 Michael Strahan 1.50 4.00
28 Jerry Rice 3.00 8.00
29 Michael Irvin 1.50 4.00
30 Darrell Green 1.50 4.00

2008 Absolute Memorabilia Canton Absolutes Autographs Spectrum

UNPRICED AUTO PRINT RUN 10

2008 Absolute Memorabilia Canton Absolutes Materials Autographs

STATED PRINT RUN 5-25
UNPRICED PRIME PRINT RUN 5-20
UNPRICED SPECTRUM PRIME PRINT RUN 1-15
SERIAL #'d UNDER 25 NOT PRICED
30 Darrell Green/25 30.00 60.00

2008 Absolute Memorabilia Canton Absolutes Materials Prime

STATED PRINT RUN 12-25
UNPRICED SPECTRUM PRIME PRINT RUN 1
1 Emmitt Smith 20.00 50.00
3 Brian Westbrook 6.00 15.00
4 Chad Johnson 6.00 15.00
5 Peyton Manning/12 15.00 40.00
6 Tom Brady 12.00 30.00
7 Eli Manning 8.00 20.00
8 Terrell Owens 8.00 20.00
9 Randy Moss 8.00 20.00
10 LaDainian Tomlinson 8.00 20.00
11 Edgerrin James 6.00 15.00
12 Tony Gonzalez 6.00 15.00
13 Steve Smith 6.00 15.00
14 Hines Ward 6.00 15.00
15 Steve McNair 6.00 15.00
16 Warrick Dunn 6.00 15.00
17 Isaac Bruce 6.00 15.00
18 Marvin Harrison 8.00 20.00
19 Shaun Alexander 6.00 15.00
20 Torry Holt 6.00 15.00
21 Joey Galloway 6.00 15.00
22 Donovan McNabb 8.00 20.00
23 Tim Brown 10.00 25.00
24 Andre Reed 8.00 20.00
25 Tiki Barber 6.00 15.00
27 Michael Strahan 8.00 20.00
28 Jerry Rice 15.00 40.00
29 Michael Irvin 8.00 20.00

2008 Absolute Memorabilia College Materials

STATED PRINT RUN 35-100
UNPRICED SPECTRUM PRIME PRINT RUN 1-10
1 Allen Patrick 3.00 8.00
2 Brian Brohm/35 5.00 12.00
3 Chad Henne 4.00 10.00
4 Chris Long 4.00 10.00
5 Dan Connor 4.00 10.00
6 Early Doucet 3.00 8.00
7 Fred Davis 4.00 10.00
8 John David Booty 3.00 8.00
9 Glenn Dorsey 4.00 10.00
10 Keith Rivers 4.00 10.00
11 Kenny Phillips 4.00 10.00
12 Limas Sweed 4.00 10.00
13 Mike Hart 6.00 15.00
14 Brandon Flowers 4.00 10.00
15 Darren McFadden 10.00 25.00
16 Jamaal Charles 6.00 15.00
17 Malcolm Kelly 3.00 8.00
18 Terrell Thomas 3.00 8.00
19 Colt Brennan 4.00 10.00
20 Aqib Talib 4.00 10.00

2008 Absolute Memorabilia College Materials Autographs

STATED PRINT RUN 25 SER.#'d SETS
UNPRICED SPECTRUM PRIME PRINT RUN 5
1 Allen Patrick 10.00 25.00
2 Brian Brohm 10.00 25.00
3 Chad Henne 10.00 25.00
4 Chris Long 10.00 25.00
5 Dan Connor 10.00 25.00
6 Early Doucet 8.00 20.00
7 Fred Davis 10.00 25.00
8 John David Booty 8.00 20.00
9 Glenn Dorsey No AU 6.00 15.00
10 Keith Rivers 10.00 25.00
11 Kenny Phillips 10.00 25.00
12 Limas Sweed 10.00 25.00
13 Mike Hart 15.00 40.00
14 Brandon Flowers 10.00 25.00
15 Darren McFadden 60.00 120.00
16 Jamaal Charles 15.00 40.00
17 Malcolm Kelly 8.00 20.00
18 Terrell Thomas 8.00 20.00
19 Colt Brennan 20.00 50.00
20 Aqib Talib 10.00 25.00

2008 Absolute Memorabilia Gridiron Force

STATED PRINT RUN 250 SER.#'d SETS
*SPECTRUM/25: 1X TO 2.5X BASIC INSERTS
SPECTRUM PRINT RUN 25 SER.#'d SETS
1 Brandon Jacobs 1.25 3.00
2 Brandon Marshall 1.25 3.00
3 Braylon Edwards 1.25 3.00
4 Chris Cooley 1.25 3.00
5 Dallas Clark 1.25 3.00
6 DeAngelo Williams 1.25 3.00
7 DeMeco Ryans 1.25 3.00
8 Devin Hester 1.50 4.00
9 Donald Driver 1.25 3.00
10 Greg Jennings 1.50 4.00
11 Jason Witten 1.50 4.00
12 Marion Barber 1.25 3.00
13 Marshawn Lynch 1.25 3.00
14 Patrick Willis 1.25 3.00
15 Roddy White 1.25 3.00
16 T.J. Houshmandzadeh 1.25 3.00
17 Vincent Jackson 1.00 2.50
18 Wes Welker 1.50 4.00
19 Chester Taylor 1.00 2.50
20 LaMont Jordan 1.25 3.00
21 Marques Colston 1.25 3.00
22 Steven Jackson 1.50 4.00
23 Willis McGahee 1.25 3.00
24 Rudi Johnson 1.25 3.00
25 Jerricho Cotchery 1.25 3.00
26 LaRon Landry 1.25 3.00
27 Drew Brees 1.50 4.00
28 Greg Lewis 1.00 2.50
29 Larry Johnson 1.25 3.00
30 Clinton Portis 1.25 3.00
31 Laurence Maroney 1.25 3.00
32 Joseph Addai 1.25 3.00
33 Shaun Alexander 1.25 3.00
34 Reggie Bush 1.50 4.00
35 Larry Fitzgerald 1.50 4.00
36 Torry Holt 1.25 3.00
37 Matt Hasselbeck 1.25 3.00
38 Plaxico Burress 1.25 3.00
39 Joey Galloway 1.25 3.00
40 Santonio Holmes 1.25 3.00
41 Reggie Wayne 1.25 3.00
42 Willie Parker 1.25 3.00
43 Tony Romo 2.00 5.00
44 Eli Manning 1.50 4.00
45 Carson Palmer 1.50 4.00
46 Cedric Benson 1.25 3.00
47 Shawne Merriman 1.25 3.00
48 Vernon Davis 1.25 3.00
49 Maurice Jones-Drew 1.25 3.00
50 Adrian Peterson 2.50 6.00

2008 Absolute Memorabilia Gridiron Force Autographs Spectrum

STATED PRINT RUN 5-25
SERIAL #'d UNDER 25 NOT PRICED
7 DeMeco Ryans 8.00 20.00
15 Roddy White 8.00 20.00
17 Vincent Jackson 6.00 15.00
19 Chester Taylor 6.00 15.00
20 LaMont Jordan 8.00 20.00
21 Marques Colston 8.00 20.00
24 Rudi Johnson 8.00 20.00
25 Jerricho Cotchery 8.00 20.00
26 LaRon Landry 8.00 20.00
29 Larry Johnson 8.00 20.00
40 Santonio Holmes 8.00 20.00
46 Cedric Benson 8.00 20.00

2008 Absolute Memorabilia Gridiron Force Material Autographs

STATED PRINT RUN 10-25
1 Brandon Jacobs/15 10.00 25.00
5 Dallas Clark/25 10.00 25.00
6 DeAngelo Williams/25 10.00 25.00
7 DeMeco Ryans/25 10.00 25.00
13 Marshawn Lynch/25 10.00 25.00
14 Patrick Willis/25 10.00 25.00
17 Vincent Jackson/25 8.00 20.00
19 Chester Taylor/25 8.00 20.00
20 LaMont Jordan/25 10.00 25.00
21 Marques Colston/25 12.00 30.00
24 Rudi Johnson/20 10.00 25.00
25 Jerricho Cotchery/20 10.00 25.00
26 LaRon Landry/25 10.00 25.00
29 Larry Johnson/25 10.00 25.00
34 Reggie Bush/15 25.00 50.00
40 Santonio Holmes/25 15.00 40.00

46 Cedric Benson/25 10.00 25.00
48 Vernon Davis/20 10.00 25.00
49 Maurice Jones-Drew/25 10.00 25.00

2008 Absolute Memorabilia Gridiron Force Material Autographs Prime

PRIME PRINT RUN 5-25
*JER.NUM/15-25: .4X TO 1X PRIME/15-25
JERSEY NUMBER PRINT RUN 5-25
*POSITION/25: .4X TO 1X PRIME/15-25
POSITION AU PRINT RUN 1-25
10 Greg Jennings/15 15.00 40.00
11 Jason Witten/20 15.00 40.00
12 Marion Barber/20 25.00 50.00
13 Marshawn Lynch/20 10.00 25.00
14 Patrick Willis/25 10.00 25.00
15 Roddy White/20 10.00 25.00
17 Vincent Jackson/20 8.00 20.00
18 Wes Welker/15 30.00 60.00
19 Chester Taylor/15 8.00 20.00
20 LaMont Jordan/25 10.00 25.00
21 Marques Colston/25 12.00 30.00
24 Rudi Johnson/15 10.00 25.00
25 Jerricho Cotchery/15 10.00 25.00
26 LaRon Landry/25 10.00 25.00
29 Larry Johnson/25 10.00 25.00
32 Joseph Addai/15 10.00 25.00
40 Santonio Holmes/20 15.00 40.00
46 Cedric Benson/20 10.00 25.00
48 Vernon Davis/15 10.00 25.00
49 Maurice Jones-Drew/20 10.00 25.00

2008 Absolute Memorabilia Gridiron Force Material Prime Position

STATED PRINT RUN 25 SER.#'d SETS
*JER.NUM/15-25: .4X TO 1X POSITION/25
JERSEY NUMBER PRINT RUN 15-25
*PRIME/50: .3X TO .8X POSITION/25
*PRIME/25-35: .4X TO 1X POSITION/25
PRIME PRINT RUN 3-50
1 Brandon Jacobs 6.00 15.00
2 Brandon Marshall 6.00 15.00
3 Braylon Edwards 6.00 15.00
4 Chris Cooley 6.00 15.00
5 Dallas Clark 6.00 15.00
8 Devin Hester 10.00 25.00
9 Donald Driver 6.00 15.00
10 Greg Jennings 8.00 20.00
11 Jason Witten 8.00 20.00
12 Marion Barber 8.00 20.00
13 Marshawn Lynch 6.00 15.00
14 Patrick Willis 6.00 15.00
15 Roddy White 6.00 15.00
16 T.J. Houshmandzadeh 6.00 15.00
17 Vincent Jackson 5.00 12.00
18 Wes Welker 8.00 20.00
19 Chester Taylor 5.00 12.00
20 LaMont Jordan 6.00 15.00
21 Marques Colston 6.00 15.00
22 Steven Jackson 8.00 20.00
23 Willis McGahee 6.00 15.00
24 Rudi Johnson 6.00 15.00
25 Jerricho Cotchery 6.00 15.00
26 LaRon Landry 6.00 15.00
27 Drew Brees 8.00 20.00
28 Greg Lewis 5.00 12.00
29 Larry Johnson 6.00 15.00
30 Clinton Portis 6.00 15.00
31 Laurence Maroney 6.00 15.00
32 Joseph Addai 6.00 15.00
33 Shaun Alexander 6.00 15.00
34 Reggie Bush 8.00 20.00
36 Torry Holt 6.00 15.00
37 Matt Hasselbeck 6.00 15.00
38 Plaxico Burress 6.00 15.00
39 Joey Galloway 6.00 15.00
40 Santonio Holmes 6.00 15.00
41 Reggie Wayne 6.00 15.00
42 Willie Parker 6.00 15.00
43 Tony Romo 10.00 25.00
44 Eli Manning 8.00 20.00
45 Carson Palmer 8.00 20.00
46 Cedric Benson 6.00 15.00
47 Shawne Merriman 6.00 15.00
48 Vernon Davis 6.00 15.00
49 Maurice Jones-Drew 6.00 15.00
50 Adrian Peterson 15.00 40.00

2008 Absolute Memorabilia Marks of Fame

STATED PRINT RUN 250 SER.#'d SETS
*SPECTRUM/25: 1X TO 2.5X BASIC INSERTS
SPECTRUM PRINT RUN 25 SER.#'d SETS
1 Adrian Peterson 2.50 6.00
2 Anthony Gonzalez 1.00 2.50
3 Brian Westbrook 1.25 3.00
4 Calvin Johnson 1.50 4.00
5 Chris Henry RB 1.25 3.00
6 Earnest Graham 1.00 2.50
7 Frank Gore 1.25 3.00
8 James Jones 1.00 2.50
9 Jerious Norwood 1.25 3.00
10 Justin Fargas 1.00 2.50
11 Kenny Watson 1.00 2.50
12 Kevin Curtis 1.00 2.50
13 Kolby Smith 1.00 2.50
14 Patrick Crayton 1.25 3.00
15 Ryan Grant 1.50 4.00
16 Selvin Young 1.00 2.50
17 Sidney Rice 1.50 4.00
18 Trent Edwards 1.25 3.00
19 Garrett Wolfe 1.25 3.00
20 Anquan Boldin 1.25 3.00
21 Kellen Winslow 1.25 3.00
22 Steve Smith USC 1.25 3.00
23 David Garrard 1.25 3.00
24 Derek Anderson 1.00 2.50
25 Matt Schaub 1.25 3.00
26 Dwayne Bowe 1.25 3.00
27 Kurt Warner 1.50 4.00
28 Brandon Marshall 1.25 3.00
29 Eli Manning 1.50 4.00
30 Jamal Lewis 1.25 3.00
31 LenDale White 1.25 3.00
32 Jay Cutler 1.50 4.00
33 Jason Witten 1.50 4.00
34 Derrick Ward 1.00 2.50
35 Jason Campbell 1.25 3.00
36 Mike Furrey 1.25 3.00
37 Randy Moss 1.50 4.00
38 Santana Moss 1.00 2.50
39 Justin Gage 1.00 2.50
40 Wes Welker 1.50 4.00

2008 Absolute Memorabilia Marks of Fame Autographs Spectrum

STATED PRINT RUN 10-25
9 Jerious Norwood 8.00 20.00
10 Justin Fargas 6.00 15.00
11 Kenny Watson 6.00 15.00
13 Kolby Smith 6.00 15.00
18 Trent Edwards 6.00 15.00
34 Derrick Ward 6.00 15.00
36 Mike Furrey 8.00 20.00

2008 Absolute Memorabilia Marks of Fame Materials

RETAIL PACK INSERT PRINT RUN 15-200
2 Anthony Gonzalez 2.50 6.00
3 Brian Westbrook/135 3.00 8.00
4 Calvin Johnson 4.00 10.00
8 James Jones 2.50 6.00
9 Jerious Norwood 3.00 8.00
10 Justin Fargas 2.50 6.00
14 Patrick Crayton 3.00 8.00
17 Sidney Rice 4.00 10.00
20 Anquan Boldin 3.00 8.00
21 Kellen Winslow 3.00 8.00
22 Steve Smith USC 3.00 8.00
27 Kurt Warner/15 8.00 20.00
29 Eli Manning 4.00 10.00
32 Jay Cutler/75 5.00 12.00
34 Derrick Ward 2.50 6.00
35 Jason Campbell 3.00 8.00
36 Mike Furrey/100 3.00 8.00

2008 Absolute Memorabilia Marks of Fame Materials Prime

PRIME PRINT RUN 1-50
UNPRICED SPECTRUM PRIME PRINT RUN 1
SERIAL #'d UNDER 25 NOT PRICED
1 Adrian Peterson 8.00 20.00
2 Anthony Gonzalez 3.00 8.00
3 Brian Westbrook 4.00 10.00
4 Calvin Johnson 5.00 12.00
7 Frank Gore 4.00 10.00
8 James Jones 3.00 8.00
10 Justin Fargas 3.00 8.00
12 Kevin Curtis 3.00 8.00
14 Patrick Crayton 4.00 10.00
15 Ryan Grant 5.00 12.00
17 Sidney Rice 5.00 12.00
21 Kellen Winslow/45 4.00 10.00
22 Steve Smith USC 4.00 10.00
23 David Garrard 4.00 10.00
24 Derek Anderson 3.00 8.00
26 Dwayne Bowe 4.00 10.00
27 Kurt Warner 5.00 12.00
28 Brandon Marshall 4.00 10.00
29 Eli Manning 5.00 12.00
30 Jamal Lewis 4.00 10.00
31 LenDale White 4.00 10.00
33 Jason Witten 5.00 12.00
34 Derrick Ward 3.00 8.00
35 Jason Campbell/40 4.00 10.00
37 Randy Moss 5.00 12.00
38 Santana Moss 3.00 8.00

2008 Absolute Memorabilia Marks of Fame Materials Autographs

AUTO PRINT RUN 10-100
*PRIME/25: .5X TO 1.2X BASIC AU/100
PRIME PRINT RUN 5-25
UNPRICED SPECTRUM PRIME AU PRINT RUN 1
SERIAL #'d UNDER 15 NOT PRICED
2 Anthony Gonzalez/25 8.00 20.00
3 Brian Westbrook/15 10.00 25.00
4 Calvin Johnson/15 12.00 30.00
7 Frank Gore/15 10.00 25.00
9 Jerious Norwood/25 10.00 25.00
10 Justin Fargas/15 8.00 20.00
14 Patrick Crayton/100 8.00 20.00
17 Sidney Rice/35 12.00 30.00
34 Derrick Ward/25 8.00 20.00
36 Mike Furrey/50 8.00 20.00

2008 Absolute Memorabilia NFL Icons

STATED PRINT RUN 250 SER.#'d SETS
*SPECTRUM/25: 1X TO 2.5X BASIC INSERTS
SPECTRUM PRINT RUN 25 SER.#'d SETS
1 Emmitt Smith 4.00 10.00
2 Brett Favre 4.00 10.00
3 Alan Page 1.50 4.00
4 Billy Sims 1.50 4.00
5 Troy Aikman 2.50 6.00
6 Dan Fouts 2.00 5.00
7 Chuck Foreman 1.25 3.00
8 Earl Campbell 2.00 5.00
9 Jim Brown 2.50 6.00
10 Jim McMahon 2.00 5.00
11 Joe Klecko 1.25 3.00
12 John Elway 3.00 8.00
13 Lawrence Taylor 2.00 5.00
14 Mike Singletary 2.00 5.00
15 Reggie White 2.00 5.00
16 Ronnie Lott 2.00 5.00
17 Roger Staubach 2.50 6.00
18 John Stallworth 1.50 4.00
19 Charlie Joiner 1.25 3.00
20 Jack Youngblood 1.25 3.00
21 Phil Simms 1.50 4.00
22 Andre Reed 1.50 4.00
23 Darrell Green 1.50 4.00
24 Tiki Barber 1.25 3.00
25 Ted Hendricks 1.25 3.00
26 Warren Moon 2.00 5.00
27 Gale Sayers 2.50 6.00
28 LaDainian Tomlinson 1.50 4.00
29 Peyton Manning 2.50 6.00
30 Tom Brady 2.50 6.00

2008 Absolute Memorabilia NFL Icons Materials

STATED PRINT RUN 50 SER.#'d SETS
UNPRICED SPECTRUM PRIME PRINT RUN 1-10
3 Alan Page 6.00 15.00
4 Billy Sims 6.00 15.00
5 Troy Aikman 10.00 25.00
7 Chuck Foreman 5.00 12.00
8 Earl Campbell 8.00 20.00
10 Jim McMahon 8.00 20.00
11 Joe Klecko 5.00 12.00
12 John Elway 12.00 30.00
13 Lawrence Taylor 8.00 20.00
14 Mike Singletary 8.00 20.00
15 Reggie White 10.00 25.00
16 Ronnie Lott 8.00 20.00
17 Roger Staubach 10.00 25.00
18 John Stallworth 6.00 15.00
19 Charlie Joiner 6.00 15.00
20 Jack Youngblood 5.00 12.00
21 Phil Simms 6.00 15.00
23 Darrell Green 6.00 15.00
24 Tiki Barber 6.00 15.00
25 Ted Hendricks 5.00 12.00
26 Warren Moon 8.00 20.00

2008 Absolute Memorabilia NFL Icons Materials Prime

PRIME PRINT RUN 2-25
1 Emmitt Smith 20.00 50.00
3 Alan Page 8.00 20.00
4 Billy Sims 8.00 20.00
7 Chuck Foreman 6.00 15.00
8 Earl Campbell 10.00 25.00
10 Jim McMahon 10.00 25.00
11 Joe Klecko 6.00 15.00
15 Reggie White 12.00 30.00
16 Ronnie Lott 10.00 25.00
17 Roger Staubach 12.00 30.00
18 John Stallworth 8.00 20.00
22 Andre Reed 8.00 20.00
24 Tiki Barber 8.00 20.00
28 LaDainian Tomlinson 10.00 25.00
29 Peyton Manning 15.00 40.00
30 Tom Brady 15.00 40.00

2008 Absolute Memorabilia NFL Icons Materials AFC/NFC

STATED PRINT RUN 25
UNPRICED PRIME PRINT RUN 2-10
UNPRICED SPECTRUM PRIME PRINT RUN 1-5
3 Alan Page 8.00 20.00
4 Billy Sims 8.00 20.00
5 Troy Aikman 12.00 30.00
7 Chuck Foreman 6.00 15.00
8 Earl Campbell 10.00 25.00
9 Jim Brown 12.00 30.00
10 Jim McMahon 10.00 25.00
11 Joe Klecko 6.00 15.00
12 John Elway 15.00 40.00
13 Lawrence Taylor 10.00 25.00
14 Mike Singletary 10.00 25.00
15 Reggie White 10.00 25.00
16 Ronnie Lott 10.00 25.00
17 Roger Staubach 12.00 30.00
18 John Stallworth 8.00 20.00
20 Jack Youngblood 8.00 20.00
21 Phil Simms 8.00 20.00
23 Darrell Green 8.00 20.00
24 Tiki Barber 8.00 20.00
25 Ted Hendricks 6.00 15.00
26 Warren Moon 10.00 25.00
27 Gale Sayers 12.00 30.00

2008 Absolute Memorabilia Rookie Jersey Collection

ONE PER BLASTER RETAIL BOX
1 Brian Brohm 2.50 6.00
2 Chris Johnson 6.00 15.00
3 Darren McFadden 6.00 15.00
4 Devin Thomas 2.00 5.00
5 Donnie Avery 2.00 5.00
6 Earl Bennett 2.50 6.00
7 Eddie Royal 2.50 6.00
8 Harry Douglas 2.00 5.00
9 Jamaal Charles 4.00 10.00
10 Jerome Simpson 2.50 6.00
11 John David Booty 2.50 6.00
12 Jordy Nelson 3.00 8.00
13 Kevin Smith 3.00 8.00
14 Malcolm Kelly 2.00 5.00
15 Matt Forte 4.00 10.00
16 Rashard Mendenhall 5.00 12.00
17 Steve Slaton 2.50 6.00
18 Glenn Dorsey 2.50 6.00
19 Ray Rice 5.00 12.00
20 Matt Ryan 10.00 25.00
21 Mario Manningham 2.50 6.00
22 Limas Sweed 2.50 6.00
23 Kevin O'Connell 2.00 5.00
24 Jonathan Stewart 4.00 10.00
25 Joe Flacco 8.00 20.00
26 James Hardy 2.00 5.00
27 Jake Long 2.50 6.00
28 Felix Jones 4.00 10.00
29 Early Doucet 2.00 5.00
30 Dustin Keller 2.50 6.00
31 Dexter Jackson 2.00 5.00
32 DeSean Jackson 5.00 12.00
33 Chad Henne 2.50 6.00
34 Andre Caldwell 2.00 5.00

2008 Absolute Memorabilia Rookie Premiere Materials AFC/NFC

AFC/NFC PRINT RUN 199
*AFC/NFC SPECT.PRIME/25: .8X TO 2X
AFC/NFC SPECT.PRIME PRINT RUN 25
*NFL/199: .4X TO 1X AFC/NFC/199
NFL PRINT RUN 199
*NFL SPECT.PRIME/100: .5X TO 1.2X
NFL SPECT.PRIME PRINT RUN 100
*OVERSIZE/100: .5X TO 1.2X AFC/NFC/199
OVERSIZE PRINT RUN 100 SER.#'d SETS
UNPRICED OVER.SPECT.PRIME PRINT RUN 10
*JSY NUMBER/100: .5X TO 1.2X AFC/NFC/199
JERSEY NUMBER PRINT RUN 100
UNPRICED JSY NUMB.PRIME PRINT RUN 10
251 Chad Henne 2.50 6.00
252 Dustin Keller 2.50 6.00
253 Jonathan Stewart 4.00 10.00
254 Steve Slaton 2.50 6.00
255 Earl Bennett 2.50 6.00
256 Brian Brohm 2.50 6.00
257 Jamaal Charles 4.00 10.00
258 Mario Manningham 2.50 6.00
259 Felix Jones 4.00 10.00
260 DeSean Jackson 5.00 12.00
261 Kevin O'Connell 2.00 5.00
262 Kevin Smith 2.50 6.00
263 Jerome Simpson 2.50 6.00
264 Darren McFadden 6.00 15.00
265 Harry Douglas 2.00 5.00
266 John David Booty 2.50 6.00
267 Rashard Mendenhall 5.00 12.00
268 Malcolm Kelly 2.00 5.00
269 Matt Ryan 10.00 25.00
270 Joe Flacco 8.00 20.00
271 Early Doucet 2.00 5.00
272 Andre Caldwell 2.00 5.00
273 James Hardy 2.00 5.00
274 Jordy Nelson 3.00 8.00
275 Glenn Dorsey 2.50 6.00
276 Chris Johnson 6.00 15.00
277 Eddie Royal 2.50 6.00
278 Matt Forte 4.00 10.00
279 Ray Rice 5.00 12.00
280 Devin Thomas 2.00 5.00
281 Limas Sweed 2.50 6.00
282 Dexter Jackson 2.00 5.00
283 Donnie Avery 2.00 5.00
284 Jake Long 2.50 6.00

2008 Absolute Memorabilia Rookie Premiere Materials Autographs AFC/NFC

STATED PRINT RUN 25 SER.#'d SETS
*EMB.HOLO/31-35: .3X TO .8X AFC/NFC/25
EMBOSSED HOLO.PRINT RUN 31-35
*EMB.HOLO.PRIM/15: .5X TO 1.2X AFC/NFC/25
UNPRICED PARALLEL PRINT RUNS 5-10
251 Chad Henne 30.00 60.00
252 Dustin Keller 10.00 25.00
253 Jonathan Stewart 15.00 40.00
254 Steve Slaton 10.00 25.00
255 Earl Bennett 10.00 25.00
256 Brian Brohm 10.00 25.00
257 Jamaal Charles 25.00 50.00
258 Mario Manningham 10.00 25.00
259 Felix Jones 25.00 60.00
260 DeSean Jackson 25.00 50.00
261 Kevin O'Connell 8.00 20.00
262 Kevin Smith 10.00 25.00
263 Jerome Simpson 10.00 25.00
264 Darren McFadden 30.00 80.00
265 Harry Douglas 8.00 20.00
266 John David Booty 8.00 20.00
267 Rashard Mendenhall 30.00 60.00
268 Malcolm Kelly 8.00 20.00
269 Matt Ryan 50.00 120.00
270 Joe Flacco 50.00 120.00
271 Early Doucet 8.00 20.00
272 Andre Caldwell 8.00 20.00
273 James Hardy 8.00 20.00
274 Jordy Nelson 25.00 50.00
275 Glenn Dorsey EXCH 10.00 25.00
276 Chris Johnson 60.00 120.00
277 Eddie Royal 10.00 25.00
278 Matt Forte 20.00 50.00
279 Ray Rice 25.00 60.00
280 Devin Thomas 8.00 20.00
281 Limas Sweed 10.00 25.00
282 Dexter Jackson 8.00 20.00
283 Donnie Avery 8.00 20.00
284 Jake Long 10.00 25.00

2008 Absolute Memorabilia Spectrum Gold Autographs

GOLD AUTO PRINT RUN 25 SER.#'d SETS
UNPRICED PLATINUM AU PRINT RUN 1
151 Adrian Arrington 6.00 15.00
154 Allen Patrick 6.00 15.00
155 Andre Woodson 8.00 20.00
157 Antoine Cason 8.00 20.00
158 Aqib Talib 8.00 20.00
160 Brad Cottam 6.00 15.00
161 Brandon Flowers 8.00 20.00
164 Chauncey Washington 6.00 15.00
166 Chris Long 8.00 20.00
167 Colt Brennan 15.00 40.00
168 Cory Boyd 5.00 12.00
170 Curtis Lofton 6.00 15.00
171 Dan Connor 8.00 20.00
176 Dennis Dixon 12.00 30.00
177 Derrick Harvey 5.00 12.00
179 Dominique Rodgers-Cromartie 8.00 20.00
180 Erik Ainge 8.00 20.00
183 Fred Davis 8.00 20.00
185 Jacob Hester 8.00 20.00
186 Jacob Tamme 8.00 20.00
192 Jermichael Finley 15.00 40.00
193 Jerod Mayo 8.00 20.00
194 John Carlson 8.00 20.00
196 Jordon Dizon 8.00 20.00
197 Josh Johnson 8.00 20.00
198 Josh Morgan 8.00 20.00
199 Justin Forsett 8.00 20.00
202 Keenan Burton 5.00 12.00
203 Keith Rivers 8.00 20.00
206 Kenny Phillips 8.00 20.00
207 Kentwan Balmer 6.00 15.00
208 Kevin Robinson 5.00 12.00
209 Lavelle Hawkins 5.00 12.00
210 Lawrence Jackson 6.00 15.00
211 Leodis McKelvin 6.00 15.00
214 Marcus Smith 6.00 15.00
215 Marcus Thomas 6.00 15.00
217 Martellus Bennett 6.00 15.00
218 Martin Rucker 6.00 15.00
219 Matt Flynn 40.00 100.00
220 Mike Jenkins 8.00 20.00
221 Mike Hart 8.00 20.00
223 Ryan Torain 8.00 20.00
236 Sedrick Ellis 8.00 20.00
239 Tashard Choice 6.00 15.00
242 Thomas Brown 6.00 15.00
243 Tim Hightower 20.00 50.00
245 Vernon Gholston 6.00 15.00
247 Will Franklin 6.00 15.00

2008 Absolute Memorabilia Star Gazing Materials

RETAIL PACK INSERT PRINT RUN 250
*PRIME/50: .6X TO 1.5X BASIC JSY/250
PRIME PRINT RUN 50 SER.#'d SETS
*OVER.JER.NUM/25: .8X TO 2X JSY/250
OVERSIZE JER NUM PRINT RUN 25
UNPRICED OVER.JER# PRIME PRINT RUN 10
*OVER.PRIME/25: 1X TO 2.5X JSY/250
OVERSIZED PRIME PRINT RUN 25
UNPRICED OVER.SPECT.PRIME PRINT RUN 10
1 Brian Brohm 2.50 6.00
2 Chris Johnson 6.00 15.00
3 Darren McFadden 6.00 15.00
4 Devin Thomas 2.00 5.00
5 Donnie Avery 2.00 5.00
6 Earl Bennett 2.50 6.00
7 Eddie Royal 2.50 6.00
8 Harry Douglas 2.00 5.00
9 Jamaal Charles 4.00 10.00
10 Jerome Simpson 2.50 6.00
11 John David Booty 2.50 6.00
12 Jordy Nelson 3.00 8.00
13 Kevin Smith 2.50 6.00
14 Malcolm Kelly 2.00 5.00
15 Matt Forte 4.00 10.00
16 Rashard Mendenhall 5.00 12.00
17 Steve Slaton 2.50 6.00
18 Glenn Dorsey 2.50 6.00
19 Ray Rice 5.00 12.00
20 Matt Ryan 10.00 25.00
21 Mario Manningham 2.50 6.00
22 Limas Sweed 2.50 6.00
23 Kevin O'Connell 2.00 5.00
24 Jonathan Stewart 4.00 10.00
25 Joe Flacco 8.00 20.00
26 James Hardy 2.00 5.00
27 Jake Long 2.50 6.00
28 Felix Jones 4.00 10.00
29 Early Doucet 2.00 5.00
30 Dustin Keller 2.50 6.00
31 Dexter Jackson 2.00 5.00
32 DeSean Jackson 5.00 12.00
33 Chad Henne 2.50 6.00
34 Andre Caldwell 2.00 5.00

2008 Absolute Memorabilia Star Gazing Materials Autographs

STATED PRINT RUN 25 SER.#'d SETS
*PRIME/25: .5X TO 1.2X BASIC AU/25
PRIME PRINT RUN 25 SER.#'d SETS
1 Brian Brohm 8.00 20.00
2 Chris Johnson 20.00 50.00
3 Darren McFadden 20.00 50.00
4 Devin Thomas 6.00 15.00
5 Donnie Avery 6.00 15.00
6 Earl Bennett 8.00 20.00
7 Eddie Royal 8.00 20.00
8 Harry Douglas 6.00 15.00
9 Jamaal Charles 12.00 30.00
10 Jerome Simpson 8.00 20.00
11 John David Booty 6.00 15.00
12 Jordy Nelson 25.00 50.00
13 Kevin Smith 8.00 20.00
14 Malcolm Kelly 6.00 15.00
15 Matt Forte 12.00 30.00
16 Rashard Mendenhall 15.00 40.00
17 Steve Slaton 8.00 20.00
18 Glenn Dorsey EXCH 20.00
19 Ray Rice 15.00 40.00
20 Matt Ryan 30.00 80.00
21 Mario Manningham 8.00 20.00
22 Limas Sweed 8.00 20.00
23 Kevin O'Connell 6.00 15.00
24 Jonathan Stewart 12.00 30.00
25 Joe Flacco 25.00 60.00
26 James Hardy 6.00 15.00
27 Jake Long 8.00 20.00
28 Felix Jones 12.00 30.00
29 Early Doucet 6.00 15.00
30 Dustin Keller 8.00 20.00
31 Dexter Jackson 6.00 15.00
32 DeSean Jackson 15.00 40.00
33 Chad Henne 8.00 20.00
34 Andre Caldwell 6.00 15.00

2008 Absolute Memorabilia Team Quads Materials Die Cut

STATED PRINT RUN 100 SER.#'d SETS
*PRIME/25: .5X TO 1.5X BASIC QUAD/100
SPECTRUM PRIME PRINT RUN 25 SER.#'d SETS
1 Tony Romo 15.00 40.00
Terrell Owens
Jason Witten
Marion Barber
2 Trent Edwards 8.00 20.00
Marshawn Lynch
Lee Evans
Josh Reed
3 Donovan McNabb 10.00 25.00
Brian Westbrook
Kevin Curtis
Correll Buckhalter
4 Eli Manning 10.00 25.00
Plaxico Burress
Brandon Jacobs
Jeremy Shockey
5 Drew Brees 12.00 30.00
Marques Colston
Deuce McAllister
Reggie Bush
6 Aaron Rodgers 20.00 50.00
Greg Jennings
Donald Driver
Ryan Grant
7 Ben Roethlisberger 15.00 40.00
Hines Ward
Willie Parker
Santonio Holmes
8 Peyton Manning 12.00 30.00
Reggie Wayne
Marvin Harrison
Joseph Addai
9 Derek Anderson 8.00 20.00
Braylon Edwards
Kellen Winslow
Jamal Lewis
10 Philip Rivers 10.00 25.00
LaDainian Tomlinson
Antonio Gates
Vincent Jackson
11 Alex Smith QB 10.00 25.00
Frank Gore
Vernon Davis
Patrick Willis
12 Matt Leinart 10.00 25.00
Anquan Boldin
Edgerrin James
Larry Fitzgerald
13 Jason Campbell 8.00 20.00
Clinton Portis
Chris Cooley
Santana Moss
14 Matt Schaub 8.00 20.00
Andre Johnson
DeMeco Ryans
Mario Williams
15 Matt Hasselbeck 8.00 20.00
Shaun Alexander
Deion Branch
Nate Burleson
16 Willis McGahee 10.00 25.00
Mark Clayton
Ray Lewis
Terrell Suggs
17 Vince Young 8.00 20.00
LenDale White
Justin Gage
Justin McCareins
18 Jeff Garcia 8.00 20.00
Joey Galloway
Cadillac Williams
Michael Clayton
20 Jon Kitna 10.00 25.00
Roy Williams WR
Calvin Johnson
Mike Furrey

2008 Absolute Memorabilia Team Tandems Materials

STATED PRINT RUN 100 SER.#'d SETS
*SPECT.PRIME/25: .8X TO 2X BASIC TANDEM
SPECTRUM PRIME PRINT RUN 25 SER.#'d SETS
1 Tom Brady 8.00 20.00
Randy Moss
2 Carson Palmer 5.00 12.00
Chad Johnson
3 Philip Rivers 5.00 12.00
LaDainian Tomlinson
4 Eli Manning 5.00 12.00
Plaxico Burress
5 Drew Brees 5.00 12.00
Marques Colston
6 Derek Anderson 4.00 10.00
Braylon Edwards
7 Aaron Rodgers 10.00 25.00
Greg Jennings
8 Tony Romo 6.00 15.00
Terrell Owens
9 Peyton Manning 8.00 20.00
Reggie Wayne
10 Ben Roethlisberger 8.00 20.00
Santonio Holmes

2008 Absolute Memorabilia Team Trios Materials NFL

NFL TRIO PRINT RUN 100
*NFL SPECT.PRIME/25: .8X TO 2X BASIC TRIO
NFL SPECTRUM PRIME PRINT RUN 25
*AFC/NFC/50: .5X TO 1.2X BASIC TRIO
AFC/NFC PRINT RUN 50
*AFC/NFC SPECT.PRIME/25: .8X TO 2X
AFC/NFC SPECT.PRIME PRINT RUN 25
1 Ben Roethlisberger 8.00 20.00
Santonio Holmes
Willie Parker
2 Tom Brady 15.00 40.00
Randy Moss
Wes Welker
3 Peyton Manning 10.00 25.00
Reggie Wayne
Joseph Addai
4 Carson Palmer 6.00 15.00
Chad Johnson
T.J. Houshmandzadeh
5 Tony Romo 12.00 30.00
Terrell Owens
Jason Witten
6 Greg Jennings 8.00 20.00
Donald Driver
Ryan Grant
7 Philip Rivers 8.00 20.00
LaDainian Tomlinson
Antonio Gates
8 Eli Manning 8.00 20.00
Plaxico Burress
Brandon Jacobs
9 Drew Brees 6.00 15.00
Marques Colston
Reggie Bush
10 Derek Anderson 5.00 12.00
Braylon Edwards
Kellen Winslow
11 David Garrard 5.00 12.00
Fred Taylor
Maurice Jones-Drew
12 Trent Edwards 6.00 15.00
Marshawn Lynch
Lee Evans
14 Tony Gonzalez 6.00 15.00
Larry Johnson
Dwayne Bowe
15 Laveranues Coles 5.00 12.00
Thomas Jones
Jerricho Cotchery
16 Marc Bulger 6.00 15.00
Torry Holt
Steven Jackson
17 Jake Delhomme 5.00 12.00
Steve Smith
DeAngelo Williams
18 Tarvaris Jackson 10.00 25.00
Adrian Peterson
Chester Taylor
19 Donovan McNabb 6.00 15.00
Brian Westbrook
Kevin Curtis
20 Matt Leinart 5.00 12.00
Larry Fitzgerald
Anquan Boldin

2008 Absolute Memorabilia Tools of the Trade Red Spectrum

RED PRINT RUN 100 SER.#'d SETS
*BLUE/50: .5X TO 1.2X RED/100
BLUE PRINT RUN 50 SER.#'d SETS
*GREEN/25: 1X TO 2.5X RED/100
GREEN PRINT RUN 25 SER.#'d SETS
*BLACK/10: 1.5X TO 4X RED/100
BLACK PRINT RUN 10 SER.#'d SETS
1 Emmitt Smith 3.00 8.00
2 Brett Favre 3.00 8.00
3 Carson Palmer 1.25 3.00
4 Chad Johnson 1.00 2.50
5 Cedric Benson 1.00 2.50
6 Larry Fitzgerald 1.25 3.00
7 Peyton Manning 2.00 5.00
8 Torry Holt 1.00 2.50
9 Tony Romo 1.50 4.00
10 Marvin Harrison 1.25 3.00
11 Eli Manning 1.25 3.00
12 Marion Barber 1.00 2.50
13 Michael Strahan 1.00 2.50
14 LaDainian Tomlinson 1.25 3.00
15 Tom Brady 2.00 5.00
16 Jerry Rice 2.50 6.00
17 Michael Irvin 1.25 3.00
18 Earl Campbell 1.50 4.00
19 John Elway 2.50 6.00
20 Mike Singletary 1.50 4.00
21 Reggie White 1.50 4.00
22 Roger Staubach 2.00 5.00
23 Phil Simms 1.25 3.00
24 Tiki Barber 1.25 3.00
25 Warren Moon 1.50 4.00
26 Tim Brown 1.50 4.00
27 Reggie Wayne 1.00 2.50
28 Ben Roethlisberger 1.25 3.00
29 Ryan Grant 1.25 3.00
30 Anquan Boldin 1.00 2.50
31 Greg Jennings 1.25 3.00
32 Brian Westbrook 1.25 3.00
33 Antonio Gates 1.25 3.00
34 David Garrard 1.00 2.50
35 Mike Furrey 1.00 2.50
36 Donovan McNabb 1.25 3.00
37 Philip Rivers 1.25 3.00
38 Marques Colston 1.00 2.50
39 Braylon Edwards 1.00 2.50
40 Plaxico Burress 1.00 2.50
41 T.J. Houshmandzadeh 1.00 2.50
42 Terrell Owens 1.25 3.00
43 Brandon Jacobs 1.00 2.50
44 Drew Brees 1.25 3.00
45 Derek Anderson .75 2.00
46 Kellen Winslow 1.00 2.50
47 Fred Taylor 1.00 2.50
48 Marshawn Lynch 1.00 2.50
49 Brandon Marshall 1.00 2.50
50 Dwayne Bowe 1.00 2.50
51 Larry Johnson 1.00 2.50
52 Adrian Peterson 2.00 5.00
53 Calvin Johnson 1.25 3.00
54 Brian Urlacher 1.25 3.00
55 Tony Gonzalez 1.00 2.50
56 Joey Galloway 1.00 2.50
57 Maurice Jones-Drew 1.00 2.50
58 Jake Delhomme 1.00 2.50
59 Steve Smith 1.00 2.50
60 Ray Lewis 1.25 3.00
61 Steven Jackson 1.25 3.00
62 Matt Hasselbeck 1.00 2.50
63 Clinton Portis 1.00 2.50
64 Frank Gore 1.00 2.50
65 Jeremy Shockey 1.00 2.50
66 Aaron Rodgers 2.50 6.00
67 Earnest Graham .75 2.00
68 LaRon Landry 1.00 2.50
69 Jason Witten 1.25 3.00
70 Santana Moss .75 2.00
71 Matt Schaub 1.00 2.50
72 Trent Edwards .75 2.00
73 Jerricho Cotchery 1.00 2.50
74 Kevin Curtis .75 2.00
75 Jamal Lewis 1.00 2.50

2008 Absolute Memorabilia Tools of the Trade Material Black Spectrum

BLACK SPECTRUM PRINT RUN 10-50
1 Emmitt Smith 15.00 40.00
2 Brett Favre 15.00 40.00
3 Carson Palmer 6.00 15.00
4 Chad Johnson 5.00 12.00
5 Cedric Benson 5.00 12.00
8 Torry Holt 5.00 12.00
9 Tony Romo 8.00 20.00
10 Marvin Harrison 6.00 15.00
11 Eli Manning 6.00 15.00
12 Marion Barber 5.00 12.00
13 Michael Strahan 5.00 12.00
14 LaDainian Tomlinson 6.00 15.00
15 Tom Brady 10.00 25.00
16 Jerry Rice 20.00 50.00
17 Michael Irvin/25 8.00 20.00
20 Mike Singletary 8.00 20.00
21 Reggie White 10.00 25.00
23 Phil Simms 6.00 15.00
24 Tiki Barber 5.00 12.00
27 Reggie Wayne 5.00 12.00
28 Ben Roethlisberger 6.00 15.00
29 Ryan Grant 6.00 15.00
32 Brian Westbrook 5.00 12.00
33 Antonio Gates 5.00 12.00
34 David Garrard 5.00 12.00
37 Philip Rivers 6.00 15.00
38 Marques Colston 5.00 12.00
39 Braylon Edwards 5.00 12.00
40 Plaxico Burress 5.00 12.00
41 T.J. Houshmandzadeh 5.00 12.00
42 Terrell Owens 6.00 15.00
43 Brandon Jacobs 5.00 12.00
44 Drew Brees 6.00 15.00
46 Kellen Winslow 5.00 12.00
47 Fred Taylor 5.00 12.00
48 Marshawn Lynch 5.00 12.00
49 Brandon Marshall 5.00 12.00
50 Dwayne Bowe 5.00 12.00
51 Larry Johnson 5.00 12.00
52 Adrian Peterson 10.00 25.00
53 Calvin Johnson 6.00 15.00
54 Brian Urlacher 6.00 15.00
55 Tony Gonzalez 5.00 12.00
56 Joey Galloway 5.00 12.00
57 Maurice Jones-Drew/20 6.00 15.00
58 Jake Delhomme 5.00 12.00
59 Steve Smith 5.00 12.00
60 Ray Lewis 6.00 15.00
61 Steven Jackson 6.00 15.00
62 Matt Hasselbeck 5.00 12.00
63 Clinton Portis 5.00 12.00
64 Frank Gore 5.00 12.00
65 Jeremy Shockey 5.00 12.00
66 Aaron Rodgers 12.00 30.00
69 Jason Witten 6.00 15.00
70 Santana Moss 4.00 10.00
73 Jerricho Cotchery 5.00 12.00
75 Jamal Lewis 5.00 12.00

2008 Absolute Memorabilia Tools of the Trade Material Red

STATED PRINT RUN 100 SER.#'d SETS
2 Brett Favre 12.00 30.00
3 Carson Palmer 5.00 12.00
5 Cedric Benson 4.00 10.00
6 Larry Fitzgerald 5.00 12.00
7 Peyton Manning/45 10.00 25.00
8 Torry Holt 4.00 10.00
9 Tony Romo 6.00 15.00
11 Eli Manning 6.00 15.00
12 Marion Barber 4.00 10.00
13 Michael Strahan 4.00 10.00
16 Jerry Rice 12.00 30.00
18 Earl Campbell/50 8.00 20.00
19 John Elway 10.00 25.00
20 Mike Singletary 6.00 15.00
21 Reggie White 8.00 20.00
22 Roger Staubach 10.00 25.00
23 Phil Simms 5.00 12.00
24 Tiki Barber 4.00 10.00
25 Warren Moon 6.00 15.00
26 Tim Brown 6.00 15.00
28 Ben Roethlisberger 5.00 12.00
29 Ryan Grant/90 5.00 12.00
30 Anquan Boldin 4.00 10.00
32 Brian Westbrook 4.00 10.00
34 David Garrard/99 4.00 10.00
35 Mike Furrey 4.00 10.00
36 Donovan McNabb 5.00 12.00
37 Philip Rivers 5.00 12.00
38 Marques Colston 4.00 10.00
40 Plaxico Burress 4.00 10.00
43 Brandon Jacobs 4.00 10.00
44 Drew Brees 5.00 12.00
46 Kellen Winslow 4.00 10.00
48 Marshawn Lynch 4.00 10.00
50 Dwayne Bowe/55 5.00 12.00
51 Larry Johnson 4.00 10.00
53 Calvin Johnson 5.00 12.00
54 Brian Urlacher 5.00 12.00
55 Tony Gonzalez 5.00 12.00
57 Maurice Jones-Drew 5.00 12.00
59 Steve Smith 4.00 10.00
60 Ray Lewis 5.00 12.00
61 Steven Jackson 5.00 12.00
62 Matt Hasselbeck 4.00 10.00
63 Clinton Portis 4.00 10.00
65 Jeremy Shockey 4.00 10.00
66 Aaron Rodgers 10.00 25.00
68 LaRon Landry 4.00 10.00
70 Santana Moss 3.00 8.00
71 Matt Schaub 4.00 10.00
73 Jerricho Cotchery 4.00 10.00

2008 Absolute Memorabilia Tools of the Trade Material Oversize Red
STATED PRINT RUN 50 SER.#'d SETS
UNPRICED OVERSIZE BLACK PRINT RUN 1-10
UNPRICED OVER.BLACK SPECT.PRINT RUN 1-5
UNPRICED TEAM LOGO GRN PRINT RUN 1-10
UNPRICED TEAM LOGO BLK PRINT RUN 1-10
1 Emmitt Smith 15.00 40.00
2 Brett Favre 15.00 40.00
3 Carson Palmer 6.00 15.00
5 Cedric Benson 5.00 12.00
6 Larry Fitzgerald/40 6.00 15.00
7 Peyton Manning 10.00 25.00
8 Torry Holt 5.00 12.00
9 Tony Romo 8.00 20.00
11 Eli Manning 6.00 15.00
13 Michael Strahan 5.00 12.00
16 Jerry Rice/25 20.00 50.00
18 Earl Campbell 8.00 20.00
19 John Elway 12.00 30.00
21 Reggie White/20 12.00 30.00
22 Roger Staubach 12.00 30.00
23 Phil Simms 6.00 15.00
24 Tiki Barber/40 5.00 12.00
26 Tim Brown/45 8.00 20.00
27 Reggie Wayne 5.00 12.00
30 Anquan Boldin 5.00 12.00
32 Brian Westbrook 5.00 12.00
35 Mike Furrey/15 6.00 15.00
36 Donovan McNabb 6.00 15.00
37 Philip Rivers/15 8.00 20.00
38 Marques Colston/15 6.00 15.00
40 Plaxico Burress/15 6.00 15.00
43 Brandon Jacobs 5.00 12.00
44 Drew Brees 6.00 15.00
46 Kellen Winslow 5.00 12.00
48 Marshawn Lynch 5.00 12.00
51 Larry Johnson 5.00 12.00
53 Calvin Johnson 6.00 15.00
54 Brian Urlacher 6.00 15.00
55 Tony Gonzalez/25 6.00 15.00
57 Maurice Jones-Drew/25 6.00 15.00
59 Steve Smith/20 6.00 15.00
60 Ray Lewis/40 6.00 15.00
61 Steven Jackson/25 8.00 20.00
62 Matt Hasselbeck 5.00 12.00
63 Clinton Portis 5.00 12.00
65 Jeremy Shockey 5.00 12.00
66 Aaron Rodgers 12.00 30.00
73 Jerricho Cotchery 5.00 12.00

2008 Absolute Memorabilia Tools of the Trade Material Oversize Jersey Number Blue
*JER# BLU/15-25: .5X TO 1.2X OVR.RED/40-50
*JER# BLUE/15-25: .4X TO 1X OVER.RED/15-25
JSY NUMBER BLUE PRINT RUN 5-25
UNPRICED JER NUM BLACK PRINT RUN 1-10
39 Braylon Edwards 0.00 15.00

2008 Absolute Memorabilia Tools of the Trade Double Material Black Spectrum
BLACK SPECTRUM PRINT RUN 4-50
1 Emmitt Smith 20.00 50.00
3 Carson Palmer/18 10.00 25.00
4 Chad Johnson 6.00 15.00
5 Cedric Benson 6.00 15.00
8 Torry Holt 6.00 15.00
10 Marvin Harrison 8.00 20.00
12 Marion Barber 6.00 15.00
13 Michael Strahan/25 8.00 20.00
14 LaDainian Tomlinson 8.00 20.00
15 Tom Brady 12.00 30.00
16 Jerry Rice 12.00 30.00
18 Earl Campbell 8.00 20.00
20 Mike Singletary/40 8.00 20.00
21 Reggie White 8.00 20.00
24 Tiki Barber 6.00 15.00
29 Ryan Grant/30 10.00 25.00
30 Anquan Boldin 6.00 15.00
32 Brian Westbrook 6.00 15.00
35 Mike Furrey 6.00 15.00
37 Philip Rivers 8.00 20.00
38 Marques Colston 6.00 15.00
40 Plaxico Burress 6.00 15.00
41 T.J. Houshmandzadeh 6.00 15.00
42 Terrell Owens 8.00 20.00
46 Kellen Winslow 6.00 15.00
48 Marshawn Lynch 6.00 15.00
50 Dwayne Bowe 6.00 15.00
51 Larry Johnson 6.00 15.00
53 Calvin Johnson/25 10.00 25.00
54 Brian Urlacher 8.00 20.00
55 Tony Gonzalez 6.00 15.00
56 Joey Galloway 6.00 15.00
57 Maurice Jones-Drew 6.00 15.00
58 Jake Delhomme 6.00 15.00
61 Steven Jackson 8.00 20.00
62 Matt Hasselbeck 6.00 15.00
63 Clinton Portis 6.00 15.00
65 Jeremy Shockey 6.00 15.00
68 LaRon Landry 6.00 15.00
69 Jason Witten 8.00 20.00
70 Santana Moss 5.00 12.00
72 Trent Edwards 5.00 12.00
73 Jerricho Cotchery 6.00 15.00
74 Kevin Curtis 5.00 12.00

2008 Absolute Memorabilia Tools of the Trade Double Material Blue
*DOUBLE BLUE/100: .5X TO 1.2X RED/100
*DOUBLE BLUE/30-42: .6X TO 1.5X RED/100
*DOUBLE BLUE/18: .8X TO 2X RED/100
RETAIL PACK INSERT PRINT RUN 9-100

2008 Absolute Memorabilia Tools of the Trade Double Material Autographs Black Spectrum
STATED PRINT RUN 1-25
SERIAL #'d UNDER 15 NOT PRICED
4 Chad Johnson/15 12.00 30.00
5 Cedric Benson/25 12.00 30.00
17 Michael Irvin/25 20.00 50.00
20 Mike Singletary/25 25.00 60.00
26 Tim Brown/25 25.00 60.00
31 Greg Jennings/25 20.00 50.00
35 Mike Furrey/25 12.00 30.00
38 Marques Colston/25 12.00 30.00
48 Marshawn Lynch/25 12.00 30.00
51 Larry Johnson/25 12.00 30.00
57 Maurice Jones-Drew/25 12.00 30.00
59 Steve Smith/25 12.00 30.00
61 Steven Jackson/25 15.00 40.00
68 LaRon Landry/25 12.00 30.00
69 Jason Witten/15 30.00 60.00
72 Trent Edwards/25 10.00 25.00
73 Jerricho Cotchery/25 12.00 30.00

2008 Absolute Memorabilia Tools of the Trade Triple Material Autographs Green
GREEN PRINT RUN 5-25
UNPRICED BLACK SPECT.PRINT RUN 1-10
22 Roger Staubach/25 40.00 80.00
68 LaRon Landry/25 12.00 30.00

2008 Absolute Memorabilia Tools of the Trade Triple Material Black Spectrum
STATED PRINT RUN 5-50
1 Emmitt Smith 25.00 60.00
3 Carson Palmer 10.00 25.00
13 Michael Strahan 10.00 25.00
16 Jerry Rice 25.00 60.00
21 Reggie White 15.00 40.00
54 Brian Urlacher 10.00 25.00
57 Maurice Jones-Drew 8.00 20.00
63 Clinton Portis 8.00 20.00
68 LaRon Landry 8.00 20.00

2008 Absolute Memorabilia War Room
STATED PRINT RUN 250 SER.#'d SETS
*SPECTRUM/25: 1X TO 2.5X BASIC INSERTS
SPECTRUM PRINT RUN 25 SER.#'d SETS
1 Andre Caldwell .75 2.00
2 Brian Brohm 1.00 2.50
3 Chad Henne 1.00 2.50
4 Chris Johnson 2.50 6.00
5 Darren McFadden 2.50 6.00
6 DeSean Jackson 2.00 5.00
7 Devin Thomas .75 2.00
8 Dexter Jackson .75 2.00
9 Donnie Avery .75 2.00
10 Dustin Keller 1.00 2.50
11 Earl Bennett 1.00 2.50
12 Early Doucet .75 2.00
13 Eddie Royal 1.00 2.50
14 Felix Jones 1.50 4.00
15 Harry Douglas .75 2.00
16 Jake Long 1.00 2.50
17 Jamaal Charles 1.50 4.00
18 James Hardy .75 2.00
19 Jerome Simpson 1.00 2.50
20 Joe Flacco 3.00 8.00
21 John David Booty .75 2.00
22 Jonathan Stewart 1.50 4.00
23 Jordy Nelson 1.25 3.00
24 Kevin O'Connell .75 2.00
25 Kevin Smith 1.00 2.50
26 Limas Sweed 1.00 2.50
27 Malcolm Kelly .75 2.00
28 Mario Manningham 1.00 2.50
29 Matt Forte 1.50 4.00
30 Matt Ryan 4.00 10.00
31 Rashard Mendenhall 2.00 5.00
32 Ray Rice 2.00 5.00
33 Steve Slaton 1.00 2.50
34 Glenn Dorsey 1.00 2.50

2008 Absolute Memorabilia War Room Materials
RETAIL PACK INSERT PRINT RUN 250
*PRIME/50: .8X TO 2X BASIC JSY/250
PRIME PRINT RUN 50
*OVER.JER NUM/25: 1X TO 2.5X BASIC JSY/250
OVERSIZE JSY NUMBER PRINT RUN 25
UNPRICED OVER.JER# PRIME PRINT RUN 3-10
*OVER.PRIME/25: 1X TO 2.5X BASIC JSY/250
OVERSIZE PRIME PRINT RUN 5-25
UNPRICED OVER.SPECT.PRIME PRINT RUN 3-10
1 Andre Caldwell 2.00 5.00
2 Brian Brohm 2.50 6.00
3 Chad Henne 2.50 6.00
4 Chris Johnson 6.00 15.00
5 Darren McFadden 6.00 15.00
6 DeSean Jackson 5.00 12.00
7 Devin Thomas 2.00 5.00
8 Dexter Jackson 2.00 5.00
9 Donnie Avery 2.00 5.00
10 Dustin Keller 2.50 6.00
11 Earl Bennett 2.50 6.00
12 Early Doucet 2.00 5.00
13 Eddie Royal 2.50 6.00
14 Felix Jones 4.00 10.00
15 Harry Douglas 2.00 5.00
16 Jake Long 2.50 6.00
17 Jamaal Charles 4.00 10.00
18 James Hardy 2.00 5.00
19 Jerome Simpson 2.50 6.00
20 Joe Flacco 8.00 20.00
21 John David Booty 2.00 5.00
22 Jonathan Stewart 4.00 10.00
23 Jordy Nelson 3.00 8.00
24 Kevin O'Connell 2.00 5.00
25 Kevin Smith 2.50 6.00
26 Limas Sweed 2.50 6.00
27 Malcolm Kelly 2.00 5.00
28 Mario Manningham 2.50 6.00
29 Matt Forte 4.00 10.00
30 Matt Ryan 10.00 25.00
31 Rashard Mendenhall 5.00 12.00
32 Ray Rice 5.00 12.00
33 Steve Slaton 2.50 6.00
34 Glenn Dorsey 2.50 6.00

2008 Absolute Memorabilia War Room Materials Autographs
JSY AU PRINT RUN 25 SER.#'d SETS
*PRIME/25: .5X TO 1.2X BASIC JSY AU
PRIME PRINT RUN 25 SER.#'d SETS
1 Andre Caldwell 6.00 15.00
2 Brian Brohm 8.00 20.00
3 Chad Henne 8.00 20.00
4 Chris Johnson 20.00 50.00
5 Darren McFadden 20.00 50.00
6 DeSean Jackson 15.00 40.00
7 Devin Thomas 6.00 15.00
8 Dexter Jackson 6.00 15.00
9 Donnie Avery 6.00 15.00
10 Dustin Keller 8.00 20.00
11 Earl Bennett 8.00 20.00
12 Early Doucet 6.00 15.00
13 Eddie Royal 8.00 20.00
14 Felix Jones 12.00 30.00
15 Harry Douglas 6.00 15.00
16 Jake Long 8.00 20.00
17 Jamaal Charles 12.00 30.00
18 James Hardy 6.00 15.00
19 Jerome Simpson 8.00 20.00
20 Joe Flacco 25.00 60.00
21 John David Booty 6.00 15.00
22 Jonathan Stewart 12.00 30.00
23 Jordy Nelson 25.00 50.00
24 Kevin O'Connell 6.00 15.00
25 Kevin Smith 8.00 20.00
26 Limas Sweed 8.00 20.00
27 Malcolm Kelly 6.00 15.00
28 Mario Manningham 8.00 20.00
29 Matt Forte 12.00 30.00
30 Matt Ryan 30.00 80.00
31 Rashard Mendenhall 15.00 40.00
32 Ray Rice 15.00 40.00
33 Steve Slaton 8.00 20.00
34 Glenn Dorsey EXCH

2009 Absolute Memorabilia
AUTO ROOKIE PRINT RUN 99-149
RPM AUTO PRINT RUN 149-299
1 Kurt Warner .50 1.25
2 Larry Fitzgerald .50 1.25
3 Tim Hightower .30 .75
4 Matt Ryan .50 1.25
5 Michael Turner .40 1.00
6 Roddy White .40 1.00
7 Derrick Mason .40 1.00
8 Joe Flacco .50 1.25
9 Willis McGahee .40 1.00
10 Lee Evans .40 1.00
11 James Hardy .40 1.00
12 Terrell Owens .50 1.25
13 DeAngelo Williams .50 1.25
14 Jake Delhomme .40 1.00
15 Jonathan Stewart .40 1.00
16 Steve Smith .40 1.00
17 Greg Olsen .30 .75
18 Jay Cutler .50 1.25
19 Matt Forte .50 1.25
20 Carson Palmer .50 1.25
21 Cedric Benson .40 1.00
22 Chad Ochocinco .40 1.00
23 Brady Quinn .40 1.00
24 Braylon Edwards .40 1.00
25 Jamal Lewis .40 1.00
26 Marion Barber .40 1.00
27 Tashard Choice .30 .75
28 Tony Romo .75 2.00
29 Brandon Marshall .40 1.00
30 Correll Buckhalter .30 .75
31 Kyle Orton .40 1.00
32 Calvin Johnson .50 1.25
33 Daunte Culpepper .40 1.00
34 Kevin Smith .40 1.00
35 Aaron Rodgers 1.00 2.50
36 Greg Jennings .50 1.25
37 Ryan Grant .40 1.00
38 Andre Johnson .40 1.00
39 Matt Schaub .40 1.00
40 Steve Slaton .40 1.00
41 Anthony Gonzalez .30 .75
42 Joseph Addai .50 1.25
43 Peyton Manning .75 2.00
44 Reggie Wayne .40 1.00
45 David Garrard .40 1.00
46 Maurice Jones-Drew .40 1.00
47 Marcedes Lewis .30 .75
48 Dwayne Bowe .40 1.00
49 Jamaal Charles .50 1.25
50 Matt Cassel .40 1.00
51 Tony Gonzalez .40 1.00
52 Chad Pennington .40 1.00
53 Ted Ginn .40 1.00
54 Ronnie Brown .40 1.00
55 Adrian Peterson .75 2.00
56 Bernard Berrian .40 1.00
57 Visanthe Shiancoe .40 1.00
58 Laurence Maroney .40 1.00
59 Tom Brady .75 2.00
60 Wes Welker .50 1.25
61 Randy Moss .50 1.25
62 Drew Brees .50 1.25
63 Jeremy Shockey .30 .75
64 Reggie Bush .50 1.25
65 Eli Manning .50 1.25
66 Brandon Jacobs .40 1.00
67 Kevin Boss .40 1.00
68 Thomas Jones .40 1.00
69 Jerricho Cotchery .40 1.00
70 Leon Washington .40 1.00
71 Darren McFadden .50 1.25
72 JaMarcus Russell .30 .75
73 Justin Fargas .30 .75
74 Brian Westbrook .40 1.00
75 Kevin Curtis .30 .75
76 Donovan McNabb .50 1.25
77 Ben Roethlisberger .50 1.25
78 Santonio Holmes .40 1.00
79 Rashard Mendenhall .40 1.00
80 Philip Rivers .50 1.25
81 LaDainian Tomlinson .50 1.25
82 Darren Sproles .40 1.00
83 Frank Gore .40 1.00
84 Josh Morgan .30 .75
85 Vernon Davis .40 1.00
86 Matt Hasselbeck .40 1.00
87 T.J. Houshmandzadeh .40 1.00
88 John Carlson .40 1.00
89 Marc Bulger .40 1.00
90 Steven Jackson .40 1.00
91 Donnie Avery .40 1.00
92 Antonio Bryant .30 .75
93 Derrick Ward .30 .75
94 Kellen Winslow Jr. .40 1.00
95 Chris Johnson .50 1.25
96 Brandon Jones .30 .75
97 Justin Gage .30 .75
98 Chris Cooley .40 1.00
99 Clinton Portis .40 1.00
100 Jason Campbell .30 .75
101 Aaron Maybin RC 1.50 4.00
102 Aaron Kelly AU/149 RC 5.00 12.00
103 Aaron Brown RC 2.00 5.00
104 Alphonso Smith RC 1.50 4.00
105 Andre Smith RC 1.50 4.00
106 Anthony Hill RC 1.25 3.00
107 Arian Foster RC 4.00 10.00
108 Asher Allen RC 1.50 4.00
109 Austin Collie AU/149 RC 8.00 20.00
110 B.J. Raji AU/99 RC 6.00 15.00
111 Bernard Scott RC 2.00 5.00
112 Bradley Fletcher RC 1.50 4.00
113 Brandon Tate AU/149 RC 6.00 15.00
114 Brandon Gibson AU/149 RC 6.00 15.00
115 Brian Orakpo AU/99 RC 6.00 15.00
116 Brian Cushing AU/99 RC 6.00 15.00
117 Brian Hartline RC 2.00 5.00
118 Brooks Foster AU/149 RC 4.00 10.00
119 Cameron Morrah AU/149 RC 4.00 10.00
120 Cedric Peerman AU/99 RC 5.00 12.00
121 Chase Coffman AU/149 RC 5.00 12.00
122 Chris Ogbonnaya RC 1.50 4.00
123 Chris Owens RC 1.50 4.00
124 Clay Matthews AU/99 RC 50.00 80.00
125 Clint Sintim AU/99 RC 6.00 15.00
126 Cody Brown RC 1.25 3.00
127 Connor Barwin RC 2.00 5.00
128 Cornelius Ingram AU/149 RC 4.00 10.00
129 Curtis Painter RC 2.00 5.00
130 Darcel McBath RC 1.50 4.00
131 Darius Butler RC 2.00 5.00
132 David Johnson RC 1.50 4.00
133 David Veikune RC 1.50 4.00
134 DeAndre Levy RC 2.00 5.00
135 Demetrius Byrd AU/149 RC 5.00 12.00
136 Devin Moore AU/99 RC 5.00 12.00
137 Davon Drew RC 1.50 4.00
138 Dominique Edison AU/149 RC 4.00 10.00
139 Eddie Williams RC 1.50 4.00
140 Eugene Monroe RC 1.25 3.00
141 Evander Hood RC 2.50 6.00
142 Everette Brown AU/149 RC 5.00 12.00
143 Gartrell Johnson RC 1.25 3.00
144 Hunter Cantwell AU/149 RC 6.00 15.00
145 Jairus Byrd RC 2.00 5.00
146 James Laurinaitis AU/149 RC 6.00 15.00
147 James Casey AU/149 RC 5.00 12.00
148 James Davis RC 2.00 5.00
149 Jared Cook AU/149 RC 6.00 15.00
150 Jarett Dillard AU/149 RC 6.00 15.00
151 Jason Williams RC 2.00 5.00
152 Javarris Williams RC 1.50 4.00
153 Jeremy Childs RC 1.50 4.00
154 Jerraud Powers RC 1.50 4.00
155 Julian Phillips RC 2.00 5.00
156 Johnny Knox AU/149 RC 12.00 30.00
157 Kaluka Maiava RC 2.00 5.00
158 Keith Null RC 1.50 4.00
159 Kenny McKinley AU/149 RC 6.00 15.00
160 Kevin Ogletree AU/149 RC 6.00 15.00
161 Kory Sheets RC 1.50 4.00
162 Lardarius Webb RC 2.00 5.00
163 Larry English AU/99 RC 6.00 15.00
164 Louis Murphy AU/149 RC 6.00 15.00
165 Louis Delmas RC 2.00 5.00
166 Malcolm Jenkins AU/149 RC 6.00 15.00
167 Manuel Johnson RC 1.50 4.00
168 Marko Mitchell RC 1.50 4.00
169 Bear Pascoe RC 1.50 4.00
170 Michael Mitchell RC 1.50 4.00
171 Michael Oher RC 3.00 8.00
172 Mike Teel RC 2.00 5.00
173 Mike Goodson AU/149 RC 6.00 15.00
174 Nathan Brown AU/149 RC 5.00 12.00
175 P.J. Hill AU/149 RC 5.00 12.00
176 Patrick Chung RC 2.00 5.00
177 Peria Jerry RC 1.50 4.00
178 Quan Cosby AU/149 RC 5.00 12.00
179 Quinn Johnson AU/149 RC 5.00 12.00
180 Quinten Lawrence RC 1.25 3.00
181 Rashad Jennings AU/149 RC 6.00 15.00
182 Rashad Johnson RC 1.50 4.00
183 Rey Maualuga AU/99 RC 6.00 15.00
184 Richard Quinn RC 1.50 4.00
185 Robert Ayers RC 2.00 5.00
186 Ron Brace RC 1.50 4.00
187 Ryan Mouton RC 1.50 4.00
188 Sammie Stroughter RC 2.00 5.00
189 Sean Smith RC 2.00 5.00
190 Shawn Nelson AU/149 RC EXCH 5.00 12.00
191 Sherrod Martin RC 1.50 4.00
192 Tiquan Underwood RC 1.50 4.00
193 Tom Brandstater RC 2.00 5.00
194 Tony Fiammetta AU/149 RC 5.00 12.00
195 Travis Beckum AU/149 RC 5.00 12.00
196 Tyrell Sutton RC 1.50 4.00
197 Tyrone McKenzie RC 1.50 4.00
198 Darius Passmore RC 1.50 4.00
199 Vontae Davis AU/149 RC 6.00 15.00
200 William Moore RC 2.00 5.00
201 Matthew Stafford RPM AU/299 RC 60.00 100.00
202 Jason Smith RPM AU/199 RC 5.00 12.00
203 Tyson Jackson RPM AU/149 RC 5.00 12.00
204 Aaron Curry RPM AU/299 RC 6.00 15.00
205 Mark Sanchez RPM AU/299 RC 40.00 80.00
206 Darrius Heyward-Bey RPM AU/199 RC 6.00 15.00
207 Michael Crabtree RPM AU/299 RC 15.00 40.00
208 Knowshon Moreno RPM AU/249 RC 6.00 15.00
209 Josh Freeman RPM AU/199 RC 20.00 40.00
210 Jeremy Maclin RPM AU/199 RC 12.00 30.00
211 Brandon Pettigrew RPM AU/299 RC 6.00 15.00
212 Percy Harvin RPM AU/299 RC 20.00 50.00
213 Donald Brown RPM AU/199 RC 8.00 20.00
214 Hakeem Nicks RPM AU/199 RC 10.00 25.00
215 Kenny Britt RPM AU/299 RC 8.00 20.00
216 Chris Wells RPM AU/249 RC 15.00 40.00
217 Brian Robiskie RPM AU/299 RC 6.00 15.00
218 Pat White RPM AU/149 RC 10.00 25.00
219 Mohamed Massaquoi (RPM AU/149 RC 5.00 12.00
220 LeSean McCoy RPM AU/199 RC 20.00 40.00
221 Shonn Greene RPM AU/299 RC 12.00 30.00
222 Glen Coffee RPM AU/299 RC 5.00 12.00
223 Derrick Williams RPM AU/199 RC 5.00 12.00
224 Javon Ringer RPM AU/299 RC 6.00 15.00
225 Mike Wallace RPM AU/299 RC 20.00 40.00
226 Ramses Barden RPM AU/149 RC 4.00 10.00
227 Patrick Turner RPM AU/299 RC 5.00 12.00
228 Deon Butler RPM AU/299 RC 5.00 12.00
229 Juaquin Iglesias RPM AU/149 RC 5.00 12.00
230 Stephen McGee RPM AU/149 RC 6.00 15.00
231 Mike Thomas RPM AU/149 RC 6.00 15.00
232 Andre Brown RPM AU/249 RC 4.00 10.00
233 Rhett Bomar RPM AU/199 RC 5.00 12.00
234 Nate Davis RPM AU/199 RC 5.00 12.00

2009 Absolute Memorabilia Retail
*VETS 1-100: .25X TO .6X BASIC CARDS
*ROOKIES 101-200: .4X TO 1X BASIC CARDS
ROOKIE STATED PRINT RUN 499

2009 Absolute Memorabilia Spectrum Black
*VETS 1-100: 2X TO 5X BASIC CARDS
RETAIL PACK INSERT PIRNT RUN 50

2009 Absolute Memorabilia Spectrum Blue
*VETS: 1.5X TO 4X BASIC CARDS
RETAIL PACK INSERT PIRNT RUN 75

2009 Absolute Memorabilia Spectrum Red
*VETS 1-100: 1X TO 2.5X BASIC CARDS
RANDOM INSERTS IN RETAIL PACKS

2009 Absolute Memorabilia Spectrum Silver
*VETS 1-100: 3X TO 8X BASIC CARDS
COMMON ROOKIE (101-200) 3.00 8.00
ROOKIE SEMISTARS 4.00 10.00
ROOKIE UNL.STARS 5.00 12.00
STATED PRINT RUN 25 SER.#'d SETS
110 B.J. Raji 5.00 12.00
115 Brian Orakpo 5.00 12.00
116 Brian Cushing 5.00 12.00
124 Clay Matthews 12.00 30.00
141 Evander Hood 6.00 15.00
146 James Laurinaitis 5.00 12.00
156 Johnny Knox 8.00 20.00
183 Rey Maualuga 5.00 12.00
185 Robert Ayers 5.00 12.00

2009 Absolute Memorabilia Absolute Heroes
RANDOM INSERTS IN RETAIL PACKS
*SPECTRUM/25: 1.2X TO 3X BASIC INSERTS
1 Andre Johnson 1.00 2.50
2 Anthony Gonzalez .75 2.00
3 Antonio Bryant .75 2.00
4 Brandon Marshall 1.00 2.50
5 Brandon Jacobs 1.00 2.50
6 Braylon Edwards 1.00 2.50
7 Brian Urlacher 1.25 3.00
8 Brian Westbrook 1.00 2.50
9 Dallas Clark 1.00 2.50
10 David Garrard 1.00 2.50
11 Derrick Mason 1.00 2.50
12 Jerricho Cotchery 1.00 2.50
13 Kerry Collins 1.00 2.50
14 Kurt Warner 1.25 3.00
15 Lee Evans 1.00 2.50
16 Marc Bulger 1.00 2.50
17 Matt Schaub 1.00 2.50
18 Philip Rivers 1.25 3.00
19 Ricky Williams 1.00 2.50
20 Santonio Holmes 1.00 2.50
21 Steve Breaston 1.00 2.50
22 Steve Smith 1.00 2.50
23 Tom Brady 2.00 5.00
24 Tony Romo 2.00 5.00
25 Vince Young 1.00 2.50

2009 Absolute Memorabilia Absolute Heroes Materials Spectrum Prime
STATED PRINT RUN 50 SER.#'d SETS
1 Andre Johnson 4.00 10.00
2 Anthony Gonzalez 3.00 8.00
5 Brandon Jacobs 4.00 10.00
6 Braylon Edwards 4.00 10.00
7 Brian Urlacher 5.00 12.00
8 Brian Westbrook 4.00 10.00
9 Dallas Clark 4.00 10.00
10 David Garrard 4.00 10.00
11 Derrick Mason 4.00 10.00
12 Jerricho Cotchery 4.00 10.00
15 Lee Evans 4.00 10.00
16 Marc Bulger 4.00 10.00
18 Philip Rivers 5.00 12.00
19 Ricky Williams 4.00 10.00
20 Santonio Holmes 4.00 10.00
22 Steve Smith 4.00 10.00
23 Tom Brady 8.00 20.00
24 Tony Romo 8.00 20.00
25 Vince Young 4.00 10.00

2009 Absolute Memorabilia Absolute Heroes Materials Autographs
STATED PRINT RUN 2-25
SERIAL #'d UNDER 15 NOT PRICED
4 Brandon Marshall/25 10.00 25.00
6 Braylon Edwards/15 10.00 25.00
9 Dallas Clark/25 10.00 25.00
20 Santonio Holmes/20 10.00 25.00

2009 Absolute Memorabilia Absolute Patches Spectrum Prime
STATED PRINT RUN 10-25
SERIAL #'d UNDER 15 NOT PRICED
1 Adrian Peterson/21 30.00 80.00
2 Andre Johnson/25 15.00 40.00
3 Brandon Jacobs/25 15.00 40.00
4 Brian Urlacher/15 20.00 50.00
5 Brian Westbrook/25 15.00 40.00
6 Calvin Johnson/25 25.00 60.00
7 Carson Palmer/25 20.00 50.00
8 Chad Ochocinco/25 15.00 40.00
9 Clinton Portis/25 15.00 40.00
10 DeAngelo Williams/25 20.00 50.00
12 Dwayne Bowe/25 15.00 40.00
13 Eli Manning/25 20.00 50.00
14 Frank Gore/25 15.00 40.00
15 Greg Jennings/25 20.00 50.00
16 Joseph Addai/25 20.00 50.00
17 Larry Fitzgerald/25 20.00 50.00
18 Lee Evans/25 15.00 40.00
19 Michael Turner/24 15.00 40.00
21 Philip Rivers/25 20.00 50.00
22 Ray Lewis/25 20.00 50.00
23 Reggie Wayne/25 15.00 40.00
24 Santonio Holmes/25 15.00 40.00
25 Steven Jackson/25 15.00 40.00

2009 Absolute Memorabilia Canton Absolutes
RANDOM INSERTS IN RETAIL PACKS
*SPECTRUM/25: 1.2X TO 3X BASIC INSERTS
1 Kurt Warner 1.25 3.00
2 Peyton Manning 2.00 5.00
3 Eli Manning 1.25 3.00
4 Ben Roethlisberger 1.25 3.00
5 Tom Brady 2.00 5.00
6 Andre Johnson 1.00 2.50
7 Steve Smith 1.00 2.50
8 Randy Moss 1.25 3.00
9 Hines Ward 1.00 2.50
10 Jason Witten 1.25 3.00
11 Chad Ochocinco 1.00 2.50
12 Brian Westbrook 1.00 2.50
13 Donovan McNabb 1.25 3.00
14 LaDainian Tomlinson 1.25 3.00
15 Adrian Peterson 2.00 5.00
16 Clinton Portis 1.00 2.50
17 Tony Romo 2.00 5.00
18 Maurice Jones-Drew 1.00 2.50
19 Greg Jennings 1.25 3.00
20 Tony Gonzalez 1.00 2.50
21 Larry Fitzgerald 1.25 3.00
22 Reggie Wayne 1.00 2.50
23 Brandon Jacobs 1.00 2.50
24 Terrell Owens 1.25 3.00
25 Fred Taylor 1.00 2.50

2009 Absolute Memorabilia Canton Absolutes Materials Spectrum Prime
STATED PRINT RUN 10-50
SERIAL #'d UNDER 15 NOT PRICED
3 Eli Manning/50 5.00 12.00
4 Ben Roethlisberger/50 5.00 12.00
5 Tom Brady/50 8.00 20.00
6 Andre Johnson/50 4.00 10.00
7 Steve Smith/50 4.00 10.00
9 Hines Ward/50 4.00 10.00
10 Jason Witten/50 5.00 12.00
11 Chad Ochocinco/50 4.00 10.00
12 Brian Westbrook/50 4.00 10.00
13 Donovan McNabb/15 8.00 20.00
14 LaDainian Tomlinson/50 5.00 12.00
16 Adrian Peterson/50 8.00 20.00
16 Clinton Portis/50 4.00 10.00
17 Tony Romo/50 8.00 20.00
18 Maurice Jones-Drew/50 4.00 10.00
19 Greg Jennings/50 5.00 12.00
20 Tony Gonzalez/50 4.00 10.00
22 Reggie Wayne/25 5.00 12.00
23 Brandon Jacobs/50 4.00 10.00

2009 Absolute Memorabilia Canton Absolutes Materials Autographs
STATED PRINT RUN 1-25
SERIAL #'d UNDER 15 NOT PRICED
10 Jason Witten/15 20.00 40.00
19 Greg Jennings/20 15.00 30.00
25 Fred Taylor/25 10.00 25.00

2009 Absolute Memorabilia College Materials
STATED PRINT RUN 10-100
1 Brian Orakpo/100 4.00 10.00
2 Brandon Tate/50 4.00 10.00
3 Brian Cushing/75 4.00 10.00
4 Chase Coffman/100 3.00 8.00
5 Chris Wells/75 6.00 15.00
6 Derrick Williams/15 5.00 12.00
8 Graham Harrell/25 5.00 12.00
9 James Laurinaitis/25 5.00 12.00
10 Jeremy Maclin/100 6.00 15.00
11 Josh Freeman/100 8.00 20.00
13 Kenny McKinley/100 4.00 10.00
14 LeSean McCoy/50 8.00 20.00
15 Brandon Gibson/100 4.00 10.00
16 Mark Sanchez/25 20.00 50.00
18 Rey Maualuga/25 5.00 12.00
19 Tyson Jackson/100 3.00 8.00
20 Mohamed Massaquoi/100 3.00 8.00

2009 Absolute Memorabilia College Materials Autographs
STATED PRINT RUN 5-25
SERIAL #'d UNDER 15 NOT PRICED
1 Brian Orakpo/25 8.00 20.00
3 Brian Cushing/25 8.00 20.00
4 Chase Coffman/25 8.00 20.00
5 Chris Wells/25 25.00 50.00
10 Jeremy Maclin/25 12.00 30.00
11 Josh Freeman/25 15.00 40.00
13 Kenny McKinley/25 8.00 20.00
15 Brandon Gibson/25 8.00 20.00
19 Tyson Jackson/25 6.00 15.00
20 Mohamed Massaquoi/25 10.00 25.00

2009 Absolute Memorabilia Gridiron Force
RANDOM INSERTS IN RETAIL PACKS
*SPECTRUM/25: 1.2X TO 3X BASIC INSERTS
1 Aaron Rodgers 2.50 6.00
2 Antonio Gates 1.00 2.50
3 Calvin Johnson 1.25 3.00
4 Cedric Benson 1.00 2.50
5 Clinton Portis 1.00 2.50
6 Donald Driver 1.00 2.50
7 Drew Brees 1.25 3.00
8 Felix Jones 1.25 3.00
9 Jamal Lewis 1.00 2.50
10 Jason Campbell .75 2.00
11 Justin Fargas .75 2.00
12 Justin McCareins .75 2.00
13 Kellen Winslow Jr. 1.00 2.50
14 Kevin Curtis .75 2.00
15 Laveranues Coles .75 2.00
16 Marques Colston 1.00 2.50
17 Matt Leinart 1.00 2.50
18 Peyton Manning 2.00 5.00
19 Ray Lewis 1.25 3.00
20 Reggie Wayne 1.00 2.50
21 Santana Moss 1.00 2.50
22 Todd Heap .75 2.00
23 Trent Edwards .75 2.00
24 Vernon Davis 1.00 2.50
25 Vincent Jackson 1.00 2.50

2009 Absolute Memorabilia Gridiron Force Material Prime Jersey Number
STATED PRINT RUN 25 SER.#'d SETS
1 Aaron Rodgers 12.00 30.00
2 Antonio Gates 5.00 12.00
3 Calvin Johnson 6.00 15.00
5 Clinton Portis 5.00 12.00
6 Donald Driver 5.00 12.00
8 Felix Jones 6.00 15.00
9 Jamal Lewis 5.00 12.00
10 Jason Campbell 4.00 10.00
11 Justin Fargas 4.00 10.00
12 Justin McCareins 4.00 10.00
14 Kevin Curtis 4.00 10.00
16 Marques Colston 5.00 12.00
18 Peyton Manning 10.00 25.00
19 Ray Lewis 6.00 15.00
20 Reggie Wayne 5.00 12.00
21 Santana Moss 5.00 12.00
22 Todd Heap 4.00 10.00
23 Trent Edwards 4.00 10.00
24 Vernon Davis 5.00 12.00
25 Vincent Jackson 5.00 12.00

2009 Absolute Memorabilia Gridiron Force Material Autographs

STATED PRINT RUN 1-50
*JSY #/25-50: .4X TO 1X BASIC JSY AU
*PRIME/25: .6X TO 1.5X BASIC JSY AU/50
*PRIME JSY #/25: .6X TO 1.5X BASIC JSY AU/50
SERIAL #'d UNDER 15 NOT PRICED
14 Kevin Curtis/25 8.00 20.00
16 Marques Colston/50 8.00 20.00
17 Matt Leinart/25 10.00 25.00
25 Vincent Jackson/25 10.00 25.00

2009 Absolute Memorabilia Ground Hoggs
RANDOM INSERTS IN RETAIL PACKS
*SPECTRUM/25: 1.2X TO 3X BASIC INSERTS
1 Adrian Peterson 2.00 5.00
2 Brandon Jacobs 1.00 2.50
3 Brian Westbrook 1.00 2.50
4 Chris Johnson 1.25 3.00
5 Clinton Portis 1.00 2.50
6 DeAngelo Williams 1.25 3.00
7 Derrick Ward .75 2.00
8 Frank Gore 1.00 2.50
9 Joseph Addai 1.25 3.00
10 LaDainian Tomlinson 1.25 3.00
11 Laurence Maroney 1.00 2.50
12 LenDale White 1.00 2.50
13 Marion Barber 1.00 2.50
14 Marshawn Lynch 1.00 2.50
15 Matt Forte 1.25 3.00
16 Maurice Jones-Drew 1.00 2.50
17 Michael Turner 1.00 2.50
18 Reggie Bush 1.25 3.00
19 Ronnie Brown 1.00 2.50
20 Ryan Grant 1.00 2.50
21 Steve Slaton 1.00 2.50
22 Steven Jackson 1.00 2.50
23 Thomas Jones 1.00 2.50
24 Willie Parker .75 2.00
25 Willis McGahee 1.00 2.50

2009 Absolute Memorabilia Ground Hoggs Materials Jersey Number
STATED PRINT RUN 25 SER.#'d SETS
1 Adrian Peterson 10.00 25.00
2 Brandon Jacobs 5.00 12.00
3 Brian Westbrook 5.00 12.00
4 Chris Johnson 6.00 15.00
5 Clinton Portis 5.00 12.00
6 DeAngelo Williams 6.00 15.00
8 Frank Gore 5.00 12.00
9 Joseph Addai 6.00 15.00
10 LaDainian Tomlinson 6.00 15.00
11 Laurence Maroney 5.00 12.00
12 LenDale White 5.00 12.00
13 Marion Barber 5.00 12.00
14 Marshawn Lynch 5.00 12.00
16 Maurice Jones-Drew 5.00 12.00
17 Michael Turner 5.00 12.00
18 Reggie Bush 6.00 15.00
19 Ronnie Brown 5.00 12.00
20 Ryan Grant 5.00 12.00
21 Steve Slaton 5.00 12.00
22 Steven Jackson 5.00 12.00
23 Thomas Jones 5.00 12.00
24 Willie Parker 4.00 10.00
25 Willis McGahee 5.00 12.00

2009 Absolute Memorabilia Ground Hoggs Materials Autographs
STATED PRINT RUN 2-25
*JSY #/25: .4X TO 1X BASIC JSY AU
SERIAL #'d UNDER 15 NOT PRICED
21 Steve Slaton/25 10.00 25.00

2009 Absolute Memorabilia Marks of Fame
RANDOM INSERTS IN RETAIL PACKS
*SPECTRUM/25: 1.2X TO 3X BASIC INSERTS
1 Anquan Boldin 1.00 2.50
2 Bernard Berrian 1.00 2.50
3 Chris Cooley 1.00 2.50
4 DeSean Jackson 1.00 2.50
5 Devin Hester 1.25 3.00
6 Dwayne Bowe 1.00 2.50
7 Earnest Graham .75 2.00
8 Eddie Royal 1.00 2.50
9 Heath Miller 1.00 2.50
10 Jake Delhomme 1.00 2.50
11 Jay Cutler 1.25 3.00
12 Joe Flacco 1.25 3.00
13 John Carlson 1.00 2.50
14 Larry Fitzgerald 1.25 3.00
15 Larry Johnson 1.00 2.50
16 Leon Washington 1.00 2.50
17 Mark Clayton .75 2.00
18 Matt Hasselbeck 1.00 2.50
19 Matt Ryan 1.25 3.00
20 Owen Daniels .75 2.00
21 Roddy White 1.00 2.50
22 Selvin Young .75 2.00
23 T.J. Houshmandzadeh 1.00 2.50
24 Wes Welker 1.25 3.00
25 Zach Miller .75 2.00

2009 Absolute Memorabilia Marks of Fame Materials Spectrum Prime
STATED PRINT RUN 4-50
SERIAL #'d UNDER 15 NOT PRICED
1 Anquan Boldin/50 4.00 10.00
2 Bernard Berrian/50 4.00 10.00
3 Chris Cooley/50 4.00 10.00
5 Devin Hester/49 5.00 12.00
6 Dwayne Bowe/50 4.00 10.00
7 Earnest Graham/50 3.00 8.00
10 Jake Delhomme/30 5.00 12.00
14 Larry Fitzgerald/44 5.00 12.00
15 Larry Johnson/50 4.00 10.00
17 Mark Clayton/50 3.00 8.00
18 Matt Hasselbeck/50 4.00 10.00
19 Matt Ryan/50 5.00 12.00
21 Roddy White/50 4.00 10.00
22 Selvin Young/50 3.00 8.00
24 Wes Welker/50 5.00 12.00
25 Zach Miller/50 3.00 8.00

2009 Absolute Memorabilia Marks of Fame Materials Autographs
STATED PRINT RUN 10-50
*PRIME/25: .6X TO 1.5X BASIC JSY AU/50
2 Bernard Berrian/15 10.00 25.00
15 Larry Johnson/50 8.00 20.00
25 Zach Miller/20 8.00 20.00

2009 Absolute Memorabilia NFL Icons
RANDOM INSERTS IN RETAIL PACKS
*SPECTRUM/25: 1.2X TO 3X BASIC INSERTS
1 Bart Starr 3.00 8.00
2 Andre Johnson 1.00 2.50
3 Ben Roethlisberger 1.25 3.00
4 Brian Westbrook 1.00 2.50
5 Dan Marino 4.00 10.00
6 Deion Sanders 2.00 5.00
7 Donovan McNabb 1.25 3.00
8 Eli Manning 1.25 3.00
9 Emmitt Smith 3.00 8.00
10 Frank Gifford 2.00 5.00
11 Jason Witten 1.25 3.00
12 John Elway 3.00 8.00
13 LaDainian Tomlinson 1.25 3.00
14 Lance Alworth 1.50 4.00
15 Maurice Jones-Drew 1.00 2.50
16 Peyton Manning 2.00 5.00
17 Randy Moss 1.25 3.00
18 Steve Smith 1.00 2.50
19 Tom Brady 2.00 5.00
20 Tony Gonzalez 1.00 2.50

2009 Absolute Memorabilia NFL Icons Materials Spectrum Prime
STATED PRINT RUN 25 SER.#'d SETS
1 Bart Starr 20.00 50.00
2 Andre Johnson 5.00 12.00
3 Ben Roethlisberger 6.00 15.00
4 Brian Westbrook 5.00 12.00
5 Dan Marino 25.00 60.00
6 Deion Sanders 12.00 30.00
7 Donovan McNabb 6.00 15.00
8 Eli Manning 6.00 15.00
9 Emmitt Smith 20.00 50.00
10 Frank Gifford 12.00 30.00
11 Jason Witten 6.00 15.00
12 John Elway 20.00 50.00
13 LaDainian Tomlinson 6.00 15.00
14 Lance Alworth 10.00 25.00
15 Maurice Jones-Drew 5.00 12.00
16 Peyton Manning 10.00 25.00

18 Steve Smith 5.00 12.00
19 Tom Brady 10.00 25.00
20 Tony Gonzalez 5.00 12.00

2009 Absolute Memorabilia NFL Icons Materials Autographs

STATED PRINT RUN 1-25
1 Bart Starr/25 90.00 150.00
5 Dan Marino/15 100.00 200.00
6 Deion Sanders/15 40.00 80.00
9 Emmitt Smith/25 75.00 150.00
10 Frank Gifford/25 25.00 50.00
12 John Elway/25 75.00 150.00
14 Lance Alworth/25 30.00 60.00

2009 Absolute Memorabilia Rookie Jersey Collection

ONE PER BLASTER RETAIL BOX
1 Chris Wells 4.00 10.00
2 Kenny Britt 3.00 8.00
3 Hakeem Nicks 4.00 10.00
4 Donald Brown 2.50 6.00
5 Percy Harvin 4.00 10.00
6 Brandon Pettigrew 2.50 6.00
7 Jeremy Maclin 4.00 10.00
8 Josh Freeman 5.00 12.00
9 Knowshon Moreno 2.50 6.00
10 Michael Crabtree 5.00 12.00
11 Darrius Heyward-Bey 2.50 6.00
12 Mark Sanchez 8.00 20.00
13 Aaron Curry 2.50 6.00
14 Tyson Jackson 2.00 5.00
15 Jason Smith 2.00 5.00
16 Matthew Stafford 12.00 30.00
17 Javon Ringer 2.50 6.00
18 Nate Davis 2.00 5.00
19 Rhett Bomar 2.00 5.00
20 Andre Brown 1.50 4.00
21 Mike Thomas 2.50 6.00
22 Stephen McGee 2.50 6.00
23 Juaquin Iglesias 2.00 5.00
24 Deon Butler 2.00 5.00
25 Patrick Turner 2.00 5.00
26 Ramses Barden 1.50 4.00
27 Mike Wallace 5.00 12.00
28 Brian Robiskie 2.50 6.00
29 Derrick Williams 2.00 5.00
30 Glen Coffee 2.00 5.00
31 Shonn Greene 4.00 10.00
32 LeSean McCoy 5.00 12.00
33 Mohamed Massaquoi 2.00 5.00
34 Pat White 2.50 6.00

2009 Absolute Memorabilia Rookie Premiere Materials AFC/NFC

STATED PRINT RUN 99 SER.#'d SETS
*AFC/NFC SPEC.PRM/25: .8X TO 2X
*NFL SPECT.PRIME/50: .6X TO 1.5X BASIC JSY
*OVER.JSY.#/99: .5X TO 1.2X BASIC JSY
*OVER.JSY.# PRM/10: 1.5X TO 4X BASIC JSY
*OVER.SPEC.PRM/25: 1X TO 2.5X
201 Matthew Stafford 12.00 30.00
202 Jason Smith 2.00 5.00
203 Tyson Jackson 2.00 5.00
204 Aaron Curry 2.50 6.00
205 Mark Sanchez 8.00 20.00
206 Darrius Heyward-Bey 2.50 6.00
207 Michael Crabtree 5.00 12.00
208 Knowshon Moreno 2.50 6.00
209 Josh Freeman 5.00 12.00
210 Jeremy Maclin 4.00 10.00
211 Brandon Pettigrew 2.50 6.00
212 Percy Harvin 4.00 10.00
213 Donald Brown 2.50 6.00
214 Hakeem Nicks 4.00 10.00
215 Kenny Britt 3.00 8.00
216 Chris Wells 4.00 10.00
217 Brian Robiskie 2.50 6.00
218 Pat White 2.50 6.00
219 Mohamed Massaquoi 2.00 5.00
220 LeSean McCoy 5.00 12.00
221 Shonn Greene 4.00 10.00
222 Glen Coffee 2.00 5.00
223 Derrick Williams 2.00 5.00
224 Javon Ringer 2.50 6.00
225 Mike Wallace 5.00 12.00
226 Ramses Barden 1.50 4.00
227 Patrick Turner 2.00 5.00
228 Deon Butler 2.00 5.00
229 Juaquin Iglesias 2.00 5.00
230 Stephen McGee 2.50 6.00
231 Mike Thomas 2.50 6.00
232 Andre Brown 1.50 4.00
233 Rhett Bomar 2.00 5.00
234 Nate Davis 2.00 5.00

2009 Absolute Memorabilia Rookie Premiere Materials Autographs AFC/NFC

*AFC/NFC/25: .5X TO 1.2X BASIC RPM RC
STATED PRINT RUN 25 SER.#'d SETS
201 Matthew Stafford 100.00 175.00
205 Mark Sanchez 60.00 120.00
207 Michael Crabtree 25.00 60.00
212 Percy Harvin 30.00 80.00

2009 Absolute Memorabilia Spectrum Gold Autographs

STATED PRINT RUN 9-100
SERIAL #'d UNDER 23 NOT PRICED
4 Matt Ryan/25 30.00 60.00
11 James Hardy/100 6.00 15.00
27 Tashard Choice/23 6.00 15.00
34 Kevin Smith/30 8.00 20.00
40 Steve Slaton/25 8.00 20.00
49 Jamaal Charles/75 8.00 20.00
79 Rashard Mendenhall/100 6.00 15.00
84 Josh Morgan/100 5.00 12.00
91 Donnie Avery/100 6.00 15.00
93 Derrick Ward/25 6.00 15.00

2009 Absolute Memorabilia Spectrum Platinum Autographs

STATED PRINT RUN 1-25
SERIAL #'d UNDER 15 NOT PRICED
3 Tim Hightower/25 6.00 15.00
11 James Hardy/25 8.00 20.00
21 Cedric Benson/25 8.00 20.00
49 Jamaal Charles/25 10.00 25.00
53 Ted Ginn/15 8.00 20.00
79 Rashard Mendenhall/25 8.00 20.00
84 Josh Morgan/25 6.00 15.00
91 Donnie Avery/25 8.00 20.00

2009 Absolute Memorabilia Star Gazing

RANDOM INSERTS IN RETAIL PACKS
*SPECTRUM/25: 1.2X TO 3X BASIC INSERTS
1 Ramses Barden .50 1.25
2 Mike Wallace 1.50 4.00
3 Darrius Heyward-Bey .75 2.00
4 Derrick Williams .60 1.50
5 Glen Coffee .60 1.50
6 Shonn Greene 1.25 3.00
7 LeSean McCoy 1.50 4.00
8 Mohamed Massaquoi .60 1.50
9 Pat White .75 2.00
10 Brian Robiskie .75 2.00
11 Patrick Turner .60 1.50
12 Deon Butler .60 1.50
13 Juaquin Iglesias .60 1.50
14 Stephen McGee .75 2.00
15 Mike Thomas .75 2.00
16 Andre Brown .50 1.25
17 Rhett Bomar .60 1.50
18 Nate Davis .60 1.50
19 Javon Ringer .75 2.00
20 Matthew Stafford 4.00 10.00
21 Jason Smith .60 1.50
22 Tyson Jackson .60 1.50
23 Aaron Curry .75 2.00
24 Mark Sanchez 2.50 6.00
25 Chris Wells 1.25 3.00
26 Kenny Britt 1.00 2.50
27 Hakeem Nicks 1.25 3.00
28 Donald Brown .75 2.00
29 Percy Harvin 1.25 3.00
30 Brandon Pettigrew .75 2.00
31 Jeremy Maclin 1.25 3.00
32 Josh Freeman 1.50 4.00
33 Knowshon Moreno .75 2.00
34 Michael Crabtree 1.50 4.00

2009 Absolute Memorabilia Star Gazing Materials

RETAIL INSERT PRINT RUN 250
*OVR.JER.# PRM/25: 1X TO 2.5X BASIC JSY
*OVER.PRIME/25: 1X TO 2.5X BASIC JSY
*PRIME/50: .6X TO 1.5X BASIC JSY
1 Ramses Barden 1.50 4.00
2 Mike Wallace 5.00 12.00
3 Darrius Heyward-Bey 2.50 6.00
4 Derrick Williams 2.00 5.00
5 Glen Coffee 2.00 5.00
6 Shonn Greene 4.00 10.00
7 LeSean McCoy 5.00 12.00
8 Mohamed Massaquoi 2.00 5.00
9 Pat White 2.50 6.00
10 Brian Robiskie 2.50 6.00
11 Patrick Turner 2.00 5.00
12 Deon Butler 2.00 5.00
13 Juaquin Iglesias 2.00 5.00
14 Stephen McGee 2.50 6.00
15 Mike Thomas 2.50 6.00
16 Andre Brown 1.50 4.00
17 Rhett Bomar 2.00 5.00
18 Nate Davis 2.00 5.00
19 Javon Ringer 2.50 6.00
20 Matthew Stafford 8.00 20.00
21 Jason Smith 2.00 5.00
22 Tyson Jackson 2.00 5.00
23 Aaron Curry 2.50 6.00
24 Mark Sanchez 8.00 20.00
25 Chris Wells 4.00 10.00
26 Kenny Britt 3.00 8.00
27 Hakeem Nicks 4.00 10.00
28 Donald Brown 2.50 6.00
29 Percy Harvin 4.00 10.00
30 Brandon Pettigrew 2.50 6.00
31 Jeremy Maclin 4.00 10.00
32 Josh Freeman 5.00 12.00
33 Knowshon Moreno 2.50 6.00
34 Michael Crabtree 5.00 12.00

2009 Absolute Memorabilia Star Gazing Materials Autographs

STATED PRINT RUN 25 SER.#'d SETS
1 Ramses Barden 5.00 12.00
2 Mike Wallace 15.00 40.00
3 Darrius Heyward-Bey 8.00 20.00
4 Derrick Williams 6.00 15.00
5 Glen Coffee 6.00 15.00
6 Shonn Greene 12.00 30.00
7 LeSean McCoy 20.00 50.00
8 Mohamed Massaquoi 6.00 15.00
10 Brian Robiskie 8.00 20.00
11 Patrick Turner 6.00 15.00
12 Deon Butler 6.00 15.00
15 Mike Thomas 8.00 20.00
16 Andre Brown 5.00 12.00
17 Rhett Bomar 6.00 15.00
18 Nate Davis 6.00 15.00
19 Javon Ringer 8.00 20.00
20 Matthew Stafford 60.00 120.00
21 Jason Smith 6.00 15.00
22 Tyson Jackson 6.00 15.00
23 Aaron Curry 8.00 20.00
24 Mark Sanchez 50.00 100.00
25 Chris Wells 12.00 30.00
27 Hakeem Nicks 12.00 30.00
28 Donald Brown 8.00 20.00
29 Percy Harvin 40.00 80.00
30 Brandon Pettigrew 8.00 20.00
31 Jeremy Maclin 12.00 30.00
32 Josh Freeman 15.00 40.00
33 Knowshon Moreno 15.00 40.00
34 Michael Crabtree 30.00 60.00

2009 Absolute Memorabilia Team Quads Materials Die Cut

QUAD JERSEY PRINT RUN 10-100
*QUAD PRIM/25: .8X TO 2X BASIC QUAD/100
*QUAD PRIM/25: .6X TO 1.5X QUAD/40-49
*QUAD PRIM/25: .5X TO 1.2X BASIC QUAD/25
2 Marshawn Lynch 6.00 15.00
Lee Evans
Terrell Owens
Trent Edwards
5 Matt Ryan 8.00 20.00
Michael Turner
Roddy White
Jerious Norwood
7 Jason Witten 10.00 25.00
Marion Barber
Terence Newman
Tony Romo
8 Brian Westbrook 6.00 15.00
Donovan McNabb
Kevin Curtis
Reggie Brown
9 Aaron Ross 8.00 20.00
Brandon Jacobs
Eli Manning
Sinorice Moss
10 D'Brickashaw Ferguson 5.00 12.00
Jerricho Cotchery
Jonathan Vilma
Thomas Jones
11 Aaron Rodgers 12.00 30.00
Donald Driver
Greg Jennings
Ryan Grant
12 DeAngelo Williams 6.00 15.00
Jake Delhomme
Steve Smith
Muhsin Muhammad
13 Laurence Maroney 10.00 25.00
(Randy Moss
Tom Brady
Wes Welker
15 Derrick Mason 6.00 15.00
Mark Clayton
Ray Lewis
Willis McGahee
16 Chris Cooley 5.00 12.00
Clinton Portis
Jason Campbell
Santana Moss
17 Devery Henderson 6.00 15.00
Drew Brees
Marques Colston
Reggie Bush
18 Ben Roethlisberger 10.00 25.00
Hines Ward
Santonio Holmes
Willie Parker
20 Brandon Jones 8.00 20.00
Chris Johnson
Justin Gage
LenDale White

2009 Absolute Memorabilia Team Tandems Materials

STATED PRINT RUN 50 SER.#'d SETS
*PRIME/25: .6X TO 1.5X BASIC DUAL/50
1 Lee Evans 6.00 15.00
Terrell Owens
2 Terence Newman 6.00 15.00
Jason Witten
3 Reggie Wayne 6.00 15.00
Joseph Addai
4 Michael Turner 5.00 12.00
Roddy White
5 Brian Urlacher 6.00 15.00
Devin Hester
6 Clinton Portis 5.00 12.00
Chris Cooley
7 Brandon Stokley 5.00 12.00
Brandon Marshall
8 Dwayne Bowe 5.00 12.00
Tony Gonzalez
9 Donald Driver 6.00 15.00
Greg Jennings
10 Carson Palmer 6.00 15.00
Chad Ochocinco

2009 Absolute Memorabilia Team Trios Materials NFL

STATED PRINT RUN 4-50
*PRIME/15-25: .6X TO 1.5X BASIC TRIO/40-50
1 Brian Urlacher 6.00 15.00
Devin Hester
Greg Olsen
2 Carson Palmer/40 6.00 15.00
Chad Ochocinco
Laveranues Coles
3 Lee Evans 6.00 15.00
Marshawn Lynch
Terrell Owens
4 Antonio Gates 6.00 15.00
LaDainian Tomlinson
Philip Rivers
5 Joseph Addai 10.00 25.00
Peyton Manning
Reggie Wayne
6 Jason Witten 10.00 25.00
Marion Barber
Tony Romo
7 Matt Ryan 6.00 15.00
Michael Turner
Roddy White
8 Aaron Ross 6.00 15.00
Brandon Jacobs
Eli Manning
9 Brian Westbrook 6.00 15.00
Donovan McNabb
Greg Lewis
10 Jerricho Cotchery 5.00 12.00
Leon Washington
Thomas Jones
11 Donald Driver 6.00 15.00
Greg Jennings
Ryan Grant
12 DeAngelo Williams 6.00 15.00
Muhsin Muhammad
Steve Smith
13 Laurence Maroney 6.00 15.00
(Randy Moss
Wes Welker
14 Derrick Mason 6.00 15.00
Mark Clayton
Willis McGahee
15 Chris Cooley 5.00 12.00
Clinton Portis
Santana Moss
16 Drew Brees 6.00 15.00
Marques Colston
Reggie Bush
17 Hines Ward 6.00 15.00
Santonio Holmes
Willie Parker
18 Andre Johnson 5.00 12.00
Matt Schaub
Steve Slaton
19 Brandon Jones 5.00 12.00
Justin Gage
LenDale White
20 Adrian Peterson 10.00 25.00
Bernard Berrian
Chester Taylor

2009 Absolute Memorabilia Tools of the Trade Material Red

RETAIL RED PRINT RUN 250
1 Adrian Peterson 5.00 12.00
2 Adrian Wilson 2.00 5.00
3 Alan Faneca 2.00 5.00
4 Albert Haynesworth 2.00 5.00
5 Andre Johnson 2.50 6.00
6 Anquan Boldin 2.50 6.00
7 Chris Cooley 3.00 8.00
8 DeMarcus Ware 3.00 8.00
9 Drew Brees 3.00 8.00
10 Dwight Freeney 2.50 6.00
11 Eli Manning 3.00 8.00
12 James Farrior 2.00 5.00
13 James Harrison 3.00 8.00
14 Jared Allen 3.00 8.00
15 Jay Cutler 3.00 8.00
16 Jon Beason 2.00 5.00
17 Julius Peppers 2.50 6.00
18 Kurt Warner 3.00 8.00
19 Lance Briggs 2.50 6.00
20 Larry Fitzgerald 3.00 8.00
21 Le'Ron McClain 2.50 6.00
22 Mario Williams 2.50 6.00
23 Michael Turner 2.50 6.00
24 Mike Sellers 2.00 5.00
25 Patrick Willis 2.50 6.00
26 Peyton Manning 5.00 12.00
27 Ray Lewis 3.00 8.00
28 Reggie Wayne 2.50 6.00
29 Robert Mathis 2.00 5.00
30 Roddy White 2.50 6.00
31 Ronnie Brown 2.50 6.00
32 Steve Smith 2.50 6.00
33 Terrell Suggs 2.00 5.00
34 Thomas Jones 2.50 6.00
35 Tony Gonzalez 2.50 6.00
36 Troy Polamalu 5.00 12.00
37 Wes Welker 3.00 8.00

2009 Absolute Memorabilia Tools of the Trade Material Black Spectrum

STATED PRINT RUN 4-50
SERIAL #'d UNDER 15 NOT PRICED
1 Adrian Peterson/38 10.00 25.00
2 Adrian Wilson/50 4.00 10.00
3 Alan Faneca/50 4.00 10.00
4 Albert Haynesworth/50 4.00 10.00
5 Andre Johnson/50 5.00 12.00
6 Anquan Boldin/34 5.00 12.00
7 Chris Cooley/30 6.00 15.00
8 DeMarcus Ware/50 6.00 15.00
9 Drew Brees/39 6.00 15.00
10 Dwight Freeney/50 5.00 12.00
11 Eli Manning/25 8.00 20.00
12 James Farrior/28 5.00 12.00
13 James Harrison/36 10.00 25.00
14 Jared Allen/50 6.00 15.00
15 Jay Cutler/30 6.00 15.00
16 Jon Beason/50 4.00 10.00
17 Julius Peppers/50 5.00 12.00
18 Kurt Warner/25 8.00 20.00
19 Lance Briggs/27 6.00 15.00
20 Larry Fitzgerald/25 8.00 20.00
21 Le'Ron McClain/29 6.00 15.00
22 Mario Williams/50 5.00 12.00
23 Michael Turner/24 6.00 15.00
24 Mike Sellers/30 4.00 10.00
25 Patrick Willis/50 5.00 12.00
26 Peyton Manning/50 10.00 25.00
27 Ray Lewis/50 6.00 15.00
28 Reggie Wayne/50 5.00 12.00
29 Robert Mathis/25 5.00 12.00
30 Roddy White/40 5.00 12.00
31 Ronnie Brown/50 5.00 12.00
32 Steve Smith/50 5.00 12.00
33 Terrell Suggs/50 4.00 10.00
34 Thomas Jones/40 5.00 12.00
35 Tony Gonzalez/50 5.00 12.00
36 Troy Polamalu/25 20.00 40.00
37 Wes Welker/49 6.00 15.00
40 Deion Sanders/15 12.00 30.00
43 LaDainian Tomlinson/50 6.00 15.00
44 Willis McGahee/15 6.00 15.00
45 Dwayne Bowe/50 5.00 12.00
46 Braylon Edwards/50 5.00 12.00
47 Brian Urlacher/50 6.00 15.00
49 Cadillac Williams/50 5.00 12.00
50 Carson Palmer/25 8.00 20.00
51 Chad Ochocinco/50 5.00 12.00
52 Tony Romo/25 12.00 30.00
53 Ricky Williams/50 5.00 12.00
55 Maurice Jones-Drew/50 5.00 12.00
56 Marion Barber/25 6.00 15.00
57 Lee Evans/50 5.00 12.00
58 Clinton Portis/25 6.00 15.00
59 Joseph Addai/25 8.00 20.00
60 Jason Campbell/50 4.00 10.00
61 JaMarcus Russell/25 5.00 12.00
63 Hines Ward/50 5.00 12.00
64 Frank Gore/25 6.00 15.00
65 Ed Reed/19 6.00 15.00

2009 Absolute Memorabilia Tools of the Trade Material Oversize Black Spectrum

STATED PRINT RUN 1-50
SERIAL #'d UNDER 15 NOT PRICED

2009 Absolute Memorabilia Tools of the Trade Material Oversize Jersey Number Black

STATED PRINT RUN 1-30
SERIAL #'d UNDER 15 NOT PRICED
1 Adrian Peterson/15 25.00 60.00
13 James Harrison/15 25.00 60.00
36 Troy Polamalu/15 30.00 60.00

2009 Absolute Memorabilia Tools of the Trade Double Material Black Spectrum

STATED PRINT RUN 10-50
SERIAL #'d UNDER 15 NOT PRICED
1 Adrian Peterson/50 12.00 30.00
2 Adrian Wilson/50 5.00 12.00
3 Alan Faneca/50 5.00 12.00
4 Albert Haynesworth/50 5.00 12.00
5 Andre Johnson/50 6.00 15.00
6 Anquan Boldin/50 4.00 10.00
7 Chris Cooley/50 8.00 20.00
8 DeMarcus Ware/50 8.00 20.00
9 Drew Brees/25 10.00 25.00
10 Dwight Freeney/50 6.00 15.00
11 Eli Manning/50 8.00 20.00
12 James Farrior/50 5.00 12.00
13 James Harrison/50 12.00 30.00
14 Jared Allen/50 8.00 20.00
15 Jay Cutler/50 8.00 20.00
16 Jon Beason/50 5.00 12.00
17 Julius Peppers/50 6.00 15.00
18 Kurt Warner/50 8.00 20.00
19 Lance Briggs/50 6.00 15.00
20 Larry Fitzgerald/50 8.00 20.00
21 Le'Ron McClain/50 6.00 15.00
22 Mario Williams/50 6.00 15.00
23 Michael Turner/50 6.00 15.00
24 Mike Sellers/50 5.00 12.00
25 Patrick Willis/50 6.00 15.00
26 Peyton Manning/25 15.00 40.00
27 Ray Lewis/15 12.00 30.00
28 Reggie Wayne/48 6.00 15.00
29 Robert Mathis/50 5.00 12.00
30 Roddy White/50 6.00 15.00
31 Ronnie Brown/50 6.00 15.00
32 Steve Smith/50 6.00 15.00
33 Terrell Suggs/50 5.00 12.00
34 Thomas Jones/50 6.00 15.00
35 Tony Gonzalez/45 6.00 15.00
36 Troy Polamalu/50 12.00 30.00
37 Wes Welker/50 8.00 20.00
39 Dan Marino/40 15.00 40.00
40 Deion Sanders/30 8.00 20.00
41 Emmitt Smith/50 12.00 30.00
43 LaDainian Tomlinson/50 8.00 20.00
44 Willis McGahee/50 6.00 15.00
45 Dwayne Bowe/50 6.00 15.00
47 Brian Urlacher/50 8.00 20.00
49 Cadillac Williams/50 6.00 15.00
50 Carson Palmer/50 8.00 20.00
51 Chad Ochocinco/35 6.00 15.00
53 Ricky Williams/50 6.00 15.00
55 Maurice Jones-Drew/50 6.00 15.00
56 Marion Barber/25 8.00 20.00
57 Lee Evans/50 6.00 15.00
58 Clinton Portis/50 6.00 15.00
59 Joseph Addai/50 8.00 20.00
60 Jason Campbell/50 5.00 12.00
61 JaMarcus Russell/50 5.00 12.00
62 Jake Delhomme/50 6.00 15.00
63 Hines Ward/50 6.00 15.00
64 Frank Gore/25 8.00 20.00
65 Ed Reed/50 6.00 15.00

2009 Absolute Memorabilia Tools of the Trade Triple Material Black Spectrum

STATED PRINT RUN 2-50
SERIAL #'d UNDER 15 NOT PRICED
5 Andre Johnson/20 8.00 20.00
35 Tony Gonzalez/50 6.00 15.00
39 Dan Marino/15 30.00 80.00
47 Brian Urlacher/50 8.00 20.00
50 Carson Palmer/50 8.00 20.00
53 Ricky Williams/50 6.00 15.00
57 Lee Evans/45 6.00 15.00
58 Clinton Portis/25 8.00 20.00
63 Hines Ward/50 6.00 15.00

2009 Absolute Memorabilia War Room

*SPECTRUM/25: 1.2X TO 3X BASIC INSERTS
1 Mike Wallace 1.50 4.00
2 Derrick Williams .60 1.50
3 Shonn Greene 1.25 3.00
4 Mohamed Massaquoi .60 1.50
5 Brian Robiskie .75 2.00
6 Deon Butler .60 1.50
7 Stephen McGee .75 2.00
8 Andre Brown .50 1.25
9 Nate Davis .60 1.50
10 Matthew Stafford 4.00 10.00
11 Tyson Jackson .60 1.50
12 Mark Sanchez 2.50 6.00
13 Kenny Britt 1.00 2.50
14 Donald Brown .75 2.00
15 Brandon Pettigrew .75 2.00
16 Josh Freeman 1.50 4.00
17 Michael Crabtree 1.50 4.00
18 Darrius Heyward-Bey .75 2.00
19 Knowshon Moreno .75 2.00
20 Jeremy Maclin 1.25 3.00
21 Percy Harvin 1.25 3.00
22 Hakeem Nicks 1.25 3.00
23 Chris Wells 1.25 3.00
24 Aaron Curry .75 2.00
25 Jason Smith .60 1.50
26 Javon Ringer .75 2.00
27 Rhett Bomar .60 1.50
28 Mike Thomas .75 2.00
29 Juaquin Iglesias .60 1.50
30 Patrick Turner .60 1.50
31 Pat White .75 2.00
32 LeSean McCoy 1.50 4.00
33 Glen Coffee .60 1.50
34 Ramses Barden .50 1.25

2009 Absolute Memorabilia War Room Materials

RETAIL PACK INSERT PRINT RUN 250
*OVR.JER.# PRM/25: 1X TO 2.5X BASIC JSY
*OVER.PRIME/25: 1X TO 2.5X BASIC JSY
*PRIME/50: .6X TO 1.5X BASIC JSY
1 Mike Wallace 5.00 12.00
2 Derrick Williams 2.00 5.00
3 Shonn Greene 4.00 10.00
4 Mohamed Massaquoi 2.00 5.00
5 Brian Robiskie 2.50 6.00
6 Deon Butler 2.00 5.00
7 Stephen McGee 2.50 6.00
8 Andre Brown 1.50 4.00
9 Nate Davis 2.00 5.00
10 Matthew Stafford 8.00 20.00
11 Tyson Jackson 2.00 5.00
12 Mark Sanchez 8.00 20.00
13 Kenny Britt 3.00 8.00
14 Donald Brown 2.50 6.00
15 Brandon Pettigrew 2.50 6.00
16 Josh Freeman 5.00 12.00
17 Michael Crabtree 5.00 12.00
18 Darrius Heyward-Bey 2.50 6.00
19 Knowshon Moreno 2.50 6.00
20 Jeremy Maclin 4.00 10.00
21 Percy Harvin 4.00 10.00
22 Hakeem Nicks 4.00 10.00
23 Chris Wells 4.00 10.00
24 Aaron Curry 2.50 6.00
25 Jason Smith 2.00 5.00
26 Javon Ringer 2.50 6.00
27 Rhett Bomar 2.00 5.00
28 Mike Thomas 2.50 6.00
29 Juaquin Iglesias 2.00 5.00
30 Patrick Turner 2.00 5.00
31 Pat White 2.50 6.00
32 LeSean McCoy 5.00 12.00
33 Glen Coffee 2.00 5.00
34 Ramses Barden 1.50 4.00

2009 Absolute Memorabilia War Room Materials Autographs

STATED PRINT RUN 25 SER.#'d SETS
1 Mike Wallace 15.00 40.00
2 Derrick Williams 6.00 15.00
3 Shonn Greene 12.00 30.00
4 Mohamed Massaquoi 6.00 15.00
5 Brian Robiskie 8.00 20.00
6 Deon Butler 6.00 15.00
7 Stephen McGee 8.00 20.00
8 Andre Brown 5.00 12.00
9 Nate Davis 6.00 15.00
10 Matthew Stafford 60.00 120.00
11 Tyson Jackson 6.00 15.00
12 Mark Sanchez 50.00 100.00
14 Donald Brown 8.00 20.00
15 Brandon Pettigrew 8.00 20.00
16 Josh Freeman 15.00 40.00
17 Michael Crabtree 25.00 60.00
18 Darrius Heyward-Bey 8.00 20.00
19 Knowshon Moreno 20.00 50.00
20 Jeremy Maclin 12.00 30.00
21 Percy Harvin 30.00 80.00
22 Hakeem Nicks 12.00 30.00
23 Chris Wells 12.00 30.00
24 Aaron Curry 8.00 20.00
25 Jason Smith 6.00 15.00
26 Javon Ringer 8.00 20.00
27 Rhett Bomar 6.00 15.00
28 Mike Thomas 8.00 20.00
30 Patrick Turner 6.00 15.00
32 LeSean McCoy 20.00 50.00
33 Glen Coffee 6.00 15.00
34 Ramses Barden 5.00 12.00

2010 Absolute Memorabilia

101-200 ROOKIE PRINT RUN 299
201-235 RPM AU PRINT RUN 299
EXCH EXPIRATION: 4/13/2012
1 Chris Wells .40 1.00
2 Larry Fitzgerald .50 1.25
3 Matt Leinart .40 1.00
4 Matt Ryan .50 1.25
5 Michael Turner .30 .75
6 Roddy White .40 1.00
7 Anquan Boldin .40 1.00
8 Joe Flacco .50 1.25
9 Ray Rice .40 1.00
10 Lee Evans .40 1.00
11 Marshawn Lynch .40 1.00
12 Ryan Fitzpatrick .50 1.25
13 DeAngelo Williams .40 1.00
14 Matt Moore .40 1.00
15 Steve Smith .40 1.00
16 Devin Hester .50 1.25
17 Jay Cutler .50 1.25
18 Matt Forte .40 1.00
19 Carson Palmer .40 1.00
20 Cedric Benson .40 1.00
21 Chad Ochocinco .40 1.00
22 Jake Delhomme .40 1.00
23 Josh Cribbs .50 1.25
24 Mohamed Massaquoi .40 1.00
25 Felix Jones .40 1.00
26 Jason Witten .50 1.25
27 Miles Austin .50 1.25
28 Tony Romo .60 1.50
29 Eddie Royal .30 .75
30 Knowshon Moreno .40 1.00
31 Kyle Orton .40 1.00
32 Calvin Johnson .50 1.25
33 Matthew Stafford .50 1.25
34 Nate Burleson .30 .75
35 Aaron Rodgers 1.00 2.50
36 Donald Driver .40 1.00
37 Ryan Grant .40 1.00
38 Andre Johnson .40 1.00
39 Matt Schaub .40 1.00
40 Owen Daniels .30 .75
41 Dallas Clark .40 1.00
42 Joseph Addai .40 1.00
43 Peyton Manning .75 2.00
44 Reggie Wayne .40 1.00
45 David Garrard .40 1.00
46 Maurice Jones-Drew .40 1.00
47 Mike Sims-Walker .40 1.00
48 Dwayne Bowe .40 1.00
49 Jamaal Charles .40 1.00
50 Matt Cassel .40 1.00
51 Brandon Marshall .40 1.00
52 Chad Henne .40 1.00
53 Ronnie Brown .40 1.00
54 Adrian Peterson .75 2.00
55 Brett Favre 1.25 3.00
56 Sidney Rice .40 1.00
57 Randy Moss .50 1.25
58 Tom Brady .75 2.00
59 Wes Welker .50 1.25
60 Drew Brees .50 1.25
61 Marques Colston .40 1.00
62 Pierre Thomas .40 1.00
63 Brandon Jacobs .40 1.00
64 Eli Manning .50 1.25
65 Steve Smith USC .40 1.00
66 Braylon Edwards .40 1.00
67 LaDainian Tomlinson .50 1.25
68 Mark Sanchez .50 1.25
69 Shonn Greene .40 1.00
70 Darren McFadden .40 1.00
71 Jason Campbell .40 1.00
72 Louis Murphy .40 1.00
73 DeSean Jackson .40 1.00
74 Kevin Kolb .40 1.00
75 LeSean McCoy .40 1.00
76 Ben Roethlisberger .50 1.25
77 Hines Ward .40 1.00
78 Rashard Mendenhall .40 1.00
79 Antonio Gates .40 1.00
80 Darren Sproles .40 1.00
81 Philip Rivers .50 1.25
82 Vincent Jackson .30 .75
83 Frank Gore .40 1.00
84 Michael Crabtree .50 1.25
85 Vernon Davis .40 1.00
86 Julius Jones .30 .75
87 Matt Hasselbeck .30 .75
88 T.J. Houshmandzadeh .40 1.00
89 Donnie Avery .40 1.00
90 James Laurinaitis .40 1.00
91 Steven Jackson .40 1.00
92 Cadillac Williams .40 1.00
93 Josh Freeman .50 1.25
94 Kellen Winslow Jr. .40 1.00
95 Chris Johnson .50 1.25
96 Kenny Britt .40 1.00
97 Vince Young .30 .75
98 Chris Cooley .40 1.00
99 Clinton Portis .40 1.00
100 Donovan McNabb .50 1.25
101 Aaron Hernandez RC 5.00 12.00
102 Amari Spievey RC 3.00 8.00
103 Victor Cruz RC 10.00 25.00
104 Anthony Davis RC 2.50 6.00
105 Anthony Dixon RC 3.00 8.00
106 Anthony McCoy RC 2.50 6.00
107 Antonio Brown RC 5.00 12.00
108 Blair White RC 3.00 8.00
109 Brandon Ghee RC 2.50 6.00
110 Brandon Graham RC 2.50 6.00
111 Brandon Spikes RC 3.00 8.00
112 Brian Price RC 3.00 8.00
113 Bryan Bulaga RC 3.00 8.00
114 Carlos Dunlap RC 3.00 8.00
115 Carlton Mitchell RC 2.50 6.00
116 Chad Jones RC 3.00 8.00
117 Charles Scott RC 2.50 6.00
118 Chris Cook RC 3.00 8.00
119 Chris McGaha RC 2.00 5.00
120 Corey Wootton RC 2.50 6.00
121 Dan LeFevour RC 3.00 8.00
122 Dan Williams RC 2.50 6.00
123 Daryl Washington RC 2.50 6.00
124 David Gettis RC 3.00 8.00
125 David Reed RC 2.50 6.00
126 Deji Karim RC 3.00 8.00
127 Dennis Pitta RC 3.00 8.00
128 Derrick Morgan RC 2.50 6.00
129 Devin McCourty RC 3.00 8.00
130 Dezmon Briscoe RC 2.50 6.00
131 Dominique Franks RC 2.00 5.00
132 Donald Butler RC 2.00 5.00
133 Earl Thomas RC 3.00 8.00
134 Ed Dickson RC 3.00 8.00
135 Everson Griffen RC 3.00 8.00
136 Freddie Barnes RC 2.50 6.00
137 Garrett Graham RC 2.50 6.00
138 Jacoby Ford RC 3.00 8.00
139 James Starks RC 5.00 12.00
140 Jared Odrick RC 3.00 8.00
141 Jarrett Brown RC 3.00 8.00
142 Jason Pierre-Paul RC 5.00 12.00
143 Jason Worilds RC 3.00 8.00
144 Javier Arenas RC 3.00 8.00
145 Jeremy Williams RC 2.00 5.00
146 Jermaine Cunningham RC 3.00 8.00
147 Jerome Murphy RC 2.50 6.00
148 Jerry Hughes RC 3.00 8.00
149 Jevan Snead RC 3.00 8.00
150 Jimmy Graham RC 6.00 15.00
151 Joe Haden RC 3.00 8.00
152 Joe Webb RC 3.00 8.00
153 John Conner RC 3.00 8.00
154 John Skelton RC 3.00 8.00
155 Joique Bell RC 2.50 6.00
156 Jonathan Crompton RC 2.50 6.00
157 Kareem Jackson RC 3.00 8.00
158 Kerry Meier RC 2.50 6.00
159 Koa Misi RC 3.00 8.00
160 Kyle Williams RC 3.00 8.00
161 Kyle Wilson RC 3.00 8.00
162 Lamarr Houston RC 3.00 8.00
163 LeGarrette Blount RC 5.00 12.00
164 Levi Brown RC 2.50 6.00
165 Linval Joseph RC 2.50 6.00
166 Lonyae Miller RC 2.50 6.00
167 Major Wright RC 3.00 8.00
168 Marc Mariani RC 3.00 8.00
169 Maurkice Pouncey RC 3.00 8.00
170 Mike Iupati RC 3.00 8.00
171 Mike Neal RC 3.00 8.00
172 Morgan Burnett RC 3.00 8.00
173 Myron Lewis RC 2.50 6.00
174 Nate Allen RC 3.00 8.00
175 NaVorro Bowman RC 3.00 8.00
176 Pat Angerer RC 3.00 8.00
177 Patrick Robinson RC 3.00 8.00
178 Perrish Cox RC 2.50 6.00
179 Ricky Sapp RC 2.50 6.00
180 Riley Cooper RC 3.00 8.00
181 Russell Okung RC 3.00 8.00
182 Rusty Smith RC 3.00 8.00
183 Sean Canfield RC 2.50 6.00
184 Sean Lee RC 3.00 8.00
185 Sean Weatherspoon RC 3.00 8.00
186 Sergio Kindle RC 3.00 8.00
187 Seyi Ajirotutu RC 3.00 8.00
188 Shay Hodge RC 2.50 6.00
189 T.J. Ward RC 3.00 8.00
190 Taylor Mays RC 3.00 8.00
191 Terrence Austin RC 2.50 6.00
192 Terrence Cody RC 2.50 6.00
193 Timothy Toone RC 2.50 6.00
194 Tony Moeaki RC 3.00 8.00
195 Tony Pike RC 3.00 8.00
196 Torell Troup RC 2.50 6.00
197 Trent Williams RC 3.00 8.00
198 Trindon Holliday RC 3.00 8.00
199 Tyson Alualu RC 2.50 6.00
200 Zac Robinson RC 2.50 6.00
201 Sam Bradford RPM AU RC 60.00 120.00
202 Jimmy Clausen RPM AU RC 6.00 15.00
203 Colt McCoy RPM AU RC 15.00 40.00
204 Tim Tebow RPM AU RC 75.00 135.00
205 Armanti Edwards RPM AU RC 6.00 15.00
206 C.J. Spiller RPM AU RC 10.00 25.00
207 Jahvid Best RPM AU RC 10.00 25.00
208 Jonathan Dwyer RPM AU RC 6.00 15.00
209 Ryan Mathews RPM AU RC 20.00 50.00
210 Joe McKnight RPM AU RC 6.00 15.00
211 Montario Hardesty RPM AU RC 6.00 15.00
212 Toby Gerhart RPM AU RC 6.00 15.00
213 Ben Tate RPM AU RC 8.00 20.00
214 Dexter McCluster RPM AU RC 6.00 15.00
215 Dez Bryant RPM AU RC 40.00 80.00
216 Golden Tate RPM AU RC 6.00 15.00
217 Arrelious Benn RPM AU RC 6.00 15.00
218 Brandon LaFell RPM AU RC 6.00 15.00
219 Demaryius Thomas RPM AU RC 8.00 20.00
220 Damian Williams RPM AU RC 6.00 15.00
221 Eric Decker RPM AU RC 8.00 20.00
222 Jordan Shipley RPM AU RC 6.00 15.00
223 Mardy Gilyard RPM AU RC 6.00 15.00
224 Mike Williams RPM AU RC 12.00 30.00
225 Andre Roberts RPM AU RC 6.00 15.00
226 Jermaine Gresham RPM AU RC 8.00 20.00
227 Rob Gronkowski RPM AU RC 25.00 40.00
228 Ndamukong Suh RPM AU RC 25.00 50.00
229 Gerald McCoy RPM AU RC 6.00 15.00
230 Rolando McClain RPM AU RC 6.00 15.00
231 Eric Berry RPM AU RC 6.00 15.00
232 Emmanuel Sanders RPM AU RC 10.00 25.00
233 Marcus Easley RPM AU RC 5.00 12.00
234 Taylor Price RPM AU RC 6.00 15.00
235 Mike Kafka RPM AU RC 6.00 15.00

2010 Absolute Memorabilia Retail

COMP.SET w/o RC's (100) 10.00 20.00
*VETS 1-100: .25X TO .6X BASIC CARDS
*ROOKIES 101-200: .4X TO 1X BASIC CARDS
101-200 ROOKIE PRINT RUN 299

2010 Absolute Memorabilia Rookie Premiere Materials Autographs AFC/NFC

*AFC/NFC/25: .5X TO 1.2X BASIC RPM AU RC
AFC/NFC STATED PRINT RUN 25
EXCH EXPIRATION: 4/13/2012
201 Sam Bradford 75.00 150.00
203 Colt McCoy 50.00 120.00
204 Tim Tebow 100.00 175.00
209 Ryan Mathews 40.00 80.00
215 Dez Bryant 60.00 120.00

2010 Absolute Memorabilia Spectrum Black

*VETS 1-100: 2X TO 5X BASIC CARDS
*ROOKIES 101-200: .5X TO 1.2X BASIC CARDS
STATED PRINT RUN 50 SER.#'d SETS

2010 Absolute Memorabilia Spectrum Blue

*VETS 1-100: 2X TO 5X BASIC CARDS
*ROOKIES 101-200: .5X TO 1.2X BASIC CARDS
STATED PRINT RUN 75 SER.#'d SETS

2010 Absolute Memorabilia Spectrum Red
*VETS 1-100: 1.2X TO 3X BASIC CARDS
*ROOKIES 101-200: .3X TO .8X BASIC CARDS
RANDOM INSERT IN RETAIL PACKS

2010 Absolute Memorabilia Spectrum Silver
*VETS 1-100: 2X TO 5X BASIC CARDS
*ROOKIES 101-200: .5X TO 1.2X BASIC CARDS
STATED PRINT RUN 50 SER.#'d SETS
169 Maurkice Pouncey 4.00 10.00

2010 Absolute Memorabilia Absolute Heroes
*SPECTRUM/50: 1X TO 2.5X BASIC INSERTS
1 Andre Johnson 1.00 2.50
2 Braylon Edwards 1.00 2.50
3 Carson Palmer 1.00 2.50
4 Devin Hester 1.25 3.00
5 Eli Manning 1.25 3.00
6 Greg Jennings 1.00 2.50
7 Hines Ward 1.00 2.50
8 Jeremy Maclin 1.00 2.50
9 T.J. Houshmandzadeh 1.00 2.50
10 Jerricho Cotchery 1.00 2.50
11 Joe Flacco 1.25 3.00
12 Johnny Knox 1.00 2.50
13 Kyle Orton 1.00 2.50
14 Larry Fitzgerald 1.25 3.00
15 Marques Colston 1.00 2.50
16 Matt Hasselbeck .75 2.00
17 Matt Ryan 1.25 3.00
18 Matt Schaub 1.00 2.50
19 Pierre Garcon 1.00 2.50
20 Randy Moss 1.25 3.00
21 Roddy White 1.00 2.50
22 Steve Smith 1.00 2.50
23 Steve Smith USC 1.00 2.50
24 Kenny Britt 1.00 2.50
25 Tony Romo 1.50 4.00

2010 Absolute Memorabilia Absolute Heroes Materials Spectrum Prime
STATED PRINT RUN 10-50
1 Andre Johnson/50 4.00 10.00
2 Braylon Edwards/50 4.00 10.00
3 Carson Palmer/50 4.00 10.00
4 Devin Hester/50 5.00 12.00
6 Greg Jennings/50 4.00 10.00
7 Hines Ward/50 4.00 10.00
8 Jeremy Maclin/50 4.00 10.00
10 Jerricho Cotchery/50 4.00 10.00
11 Joe Flacco/50 5.00 12.00
12 Johnny Knox/50 4.00 10.00
13 Kyle Orton/50 4.00 10.00
14 Larry Fitzgerald/25 6.00 15.00
15 Marques Colston/50 4.00 10.00
16 Matt Hasselbeck/50 3.00 8.00
17 Matt Ryan/50 5.00 12.00
20 Randy Moss/50 5.00 12.00
21 Roddy White/50 4.00 10.00
22 Steve Smith/50 4.00 10.00
23 Steve Smith USC/50 4.00 10.00
24 Kenny Britt/50 4.00 10.00
25 Tony Romo/50 6.00 15.00

2010 Absolute Memorabilia Absolute Heroes Materials Autographs
STATED PRINT RUN 5-15
2 Braylon Edwards/15 12.00 30.00
11 Joe Flacco/15 25.00 50.00
13 Kyle Orton/15 15.00 40.00
21 Roddy White/15 12.00 30.00
24 Kenny Britt/15 12.00 30.00
25 Tony Romo/15

2010 Absolute Memorabilia Absolute Patches Spectrum Prime
STATED PRINT RUN 20-25
1 Adrian Peterson/25 40.00 100.00
2 Ahmad Bradshaw/25 20.00 50.00
3 Antonio Gates/25 20.00 50.00
4 Vincent Jackson/25 15.00 40.00
5 Calvin Johnson/25 25.00 60.00
6 Chad Ochocinco/25 20.00 50.00
7 Chris Johnson/20 25.00 60.00
8 Clinton Portis/25 20.00 50.00
9 Darren McFadden/25 20.00 50.00
10 Darren Sproles/25 20.00 50.00
11 DeAngelo Williams/25 20.00 50.00
12 DeMarcus Ware/25 20.00 50.00
13 Devery Henderson/25 15.00 40.00
14 Donald Driver/25 20.00 50.00
15 Dustin Keller/25 20.00 50.00
16 Dwayne Bowe/20 20.00 50.00
17 Felix Jones/25 20.00 50.00
18 Frank Gore/25 20.00 50.00
19 Greg Olsen/25 15.00 40.00
20 Hines Ward/25 20.00 50.00
21 Jeremy Maclin/25 20.00 50.00
22 Jerricho Cotchery/25 20.00 50.00
23 Jonathan Stewart/25 20.00 50.00
24 Johnny Knox/25 20.00 50.00
25 Kenny Britt/25 20.00 50.00
26 Ladell Betts/25 15.00 40.00
27 Marion Barber/25 20.00 50.00
28 Marques Colston/25 20.00 50.00
29 Maurice Jones-Drew/25 20.00 50.00
30 Reggie Bush/25 25.00 60.00
31 Ronnie Brown/25 20.00 50.00
32 Santana Moss/25 20.00 50.00
33 Steve Smith/25 20.00 50.00
34 Steven Jackson/25 20.00 50.00
35 Tom Brady/25 60.00 120.00
36 Troy Polamalu/25 125.00 200.00
37 Vince Young/25 15.00 40.00
38 Visanthe Shiancoe/25 20.00 50.00
39 Wes Welker/25 25.00 60.00
40 Willis McGahee/25 20.00 50.00

2010 Absolute Memorabilia Canton Absolutes
*SPECTRUM/50: 1X TO 2.5X BASIC INSERTS
1 Bart Starr 2.00 5.00
2 Bob Hayes 1.25 3.00
3 Bruce Smith 1.00 2.50
4 Dan Marino 2.50 6.00
5 Deacon Jones 1.00 2.50
6 Derrick Thomas 1.25 3.00
7 Don Maynard 1.00 2.50
8 Earl Campbell 1.25 3.00
9 Emmitt Smith 2.00 5.00
10 Gale Sayers 1.50 4.00
11 Henry Jordan .75 2.00
12 Howie Long 1.25 3.00
13 Jerry Rice 2.00 5.00
14 Joe Greene 1.25 3.00
15 Joe Montana 2.50 6.00
16 Joe Namath 1.50 4.00
17 John Elway 2.00 5.00
18 John Randle .75 2.00
19 Rod Woodson 1.25 3.00
20 Terry Bradshaw 1.50 4.00
21 Thurman Thomas 1.25 3.00
22 Tony Dorsett 1.25 3.00
23 Troy Aikman 1.50 4.00
24 Walter Payton 2.50 6.00
25 Warren Moon 1.25 3.00

2010 Absolute Memorabilia Canton Absolutes Materials Spectrum Prime
STATED PRINT RUN 4-50
2 Bob Hayes/50 8.00 20.00
3 Bruce Smith/50 6.00 15.00
4 Dan Marino/50 15.00 40.00
7 Don Maynard/50 6.00 15.00
9 Emmitt Smith/50 12.00 30.00
10 Gale Sayers/50 10.00 25.00
11 Henry Jordan/50 6.00 15.00
12 Howie Long/50 10.00 25.00
13 Jerry Rice/50 12.00 30.00
15 Joe Montana/25 20.00 50.00
16 Joe Namath/25 12.00 30.00
18 John Randle/50 6.00 15.00
19 Rod Woodson/20 10.00 25.00
20 Terry Bradshaw/50 10.00 25.00
22 Tony Dorsett/50 8.00 20.00
23 Troy Aikman/20 12.00 30.00
24 Walter Payton/25 20.00 50.00

2010 Absolute Memorabilia Canton Absolutes Materials Autographs
STATED PRINT RUN 10-50
*SPECT.PRIM/15: .5X TO 1.2X JSY AU/20-50
1 Bart Starr/25 60.00 120.00
3 Bruce Smith/25 25.00 50.00
5 Deacon Jones/50 15.00 40.00
7 Don Maynard/25 12.00 30.00
8 Earl Campbell/40 20.00 50.00
9 Emmitt Smith/25 100.00 175.00
12 Howie Long/50 25.00 60.00
13 Jerry Rice/15 100.00 200.00
14 Joe Greene/50 20.00 50.00
15 Joe Montana/15 100.00 200.00
16 Joe Namath/25 40.00 80.00
17 John Elway/20 100.00 200.00
18 John Randle/25 15.00 40.00
19 Rod Woodson/35 30.00 60.00
20 Terry Bradshaw/25 50.00 100.00
21 Thurman Thomas/25 15.00 40.00
22 Tony Dorsett/25 20.00 50.00
25 Warren Moon/50 20.00 50.00

2010 Absolute Memorabilia Gridiron Force
*SPECTRUM/50: 1X TO 2.5X BASIC INSERTS
1 Ben Roethlisberger 1.25 3.00
2 Bernard Berrian .75 2.00
3 Brandon Jacobs 1.00 2.50
4 Chad Ochocinco 1.00 2.50
5 Darrelle Revis 1.00 2.50
6 Darren McFadden 1.00 2.50
7 Donald Driver 1.00 2.50
8 Dustin Keller 1.00 2.50
9 Dwayne Bowe 1.00 2.50
10 Greg Olsen .75 2.00
11 Heath Miller 1.00 2.50
12 Jason Witten 1.25 3.00
13 Jay Cutler 1.25 3.00
14 Kevin Boss 1.00 2.50
15 Ladell Betts .75 2.00
16 Lee Evans 1.00 2.50
17 Patrick Willis 1.00 2.50
18 Philip Rivers 1.25 3.00
19 Rashard Mendenhall 1.00 2.50
20 Ray Lewis 1.25 3.00
21 Reggie Wayne 1.00 2.50
22 Santana Moss 1.00 2.50
23 Troy Polamalu 1.25 3.00
24 Vincent Jackson .75 2.00
25 Wes Welker 1.25 3.00

2010 Absolute Memorabilia Gridiron Force Material Prime Jersey Number
STATED PRINT RUN 25-50
1 Ben Roethlisberger/50 8.00 20.00
2 Bernard Berrian/50 4.00 10.00
3 Brandon Jacobs/50 5.00 12.00
4 Chad Ochocinco/50 5.00 12.00
5 Darrelle Revis/50 5.00 12.00
6 Darren McFadden/50 5.00 12.00
7 Donald Driver/50 5.00 12.00
8 Dustin Keller/50 5.00 12.00
9 Dwayne Bowe/50 5.00 12.00
10 Greg Olsen/50 4.00 10.00
11 Heath Miller/25 6.00 15.00
12 Jason Witten/50 6.00 15.00
13 Jay Cutler/25 8.00 20.00
14 Kevin Boss/50 5.00 12.00
15 Ladell Betts/50 4.00 10.00
16 Lee Evans/50 5.00 12.00
17 Patrick Willis/50 5.00 12.00
18 Philip Rivers/50 6.00 15.00
19 Rashard Mendenhall/50 5.00 12.00
20 Ray Lewis/50 8.00 20.00
22 Santana Moss/50 5.00 12.00
23 Troy Polamalu/50 12.00 30.00
24 Vincent Jackson/50 4.00 10.00
25 Wes Welker/50 6.00 15.00

2010 Absolute Memorabilia Ground Hoggs
*SPECTRUM/50: 1X TO 2.5X BASIC INSERTS
1 Adrian Peterson 2.00 5.00
2 Chris Wells 1.00 2.50
3 Cadillac Williams 1.00 2.50
4 Chris Johnson 1.25 3.00
5 Clinton Portis 1.00 2.50
6 Darren Sproles 1.00 2.50
7 DeAngelo Williams 1.00 2.50
8 Felix Jones 1.00 2.50
9 Frank Gore 1.00 2.50
10 Jamaal Charles 1.00 2.50
11 Jonathan Stewart 1.00 2.50
12 Joseph Addai 1.00 2.50
13 Knowshon Moreno 1.00 2.50
14 Laurence Maroney 1.00 2.50
15 Matt Forte 1.00 2.50
16 Maurice Jones-Drew 1.00 2.50
17 Michael Turner .75 2.00
18 Pierre Thomas 1.00 2.50
19 Ray Rice 1.00 2.50
20 Reggie Bush 1.25 3.00
21 Ricky Williams 1.00 2.50
22 Ronnie Brown 1.00 2.50
23 Ryan Grant 1.00 2.50
24 Shonn Greene 1.00 2.50
25 Steven Jackson 1.00 2.50

2010 Absolute Memorabilia Ground Hoggs Materials Jersey Number
STATED PRINT RUN 20-50
1 Adrian Peterson/50 10.00 25.00
2 Chris Wells/50 4.00 10.00
3 Cadillac Williams/50 4.00 10.00
4 Chris Johnson/50 5.00 12.00
5 Clinton Portis/50 4.00 10.00
6 Darren Sproles/50 4.00 10.00
7 DeAngelo Williams/45 4.00 10.00
8 Felix Jones/50 4.00 10.00
9 Frank Gore/50 4.00 10.00
10 Jamaal Charles/50 4.00 10.00
11 Jonathan Stewart/50 4.00 10.00
12 Joseph Addai/50 4.00 10.00
13 Knowshon Moreno/50 4.00 10.00
14 Laurence Maroney/50 4.00 10.00
15 Matt Forte/50 4.00 10.00
16 Maurice Jones-Drew/50 4.00 10.00
19 Ray Rice/50 4.00 10.00
20 Reggie Bush/50 5.00 12.00
21 Ricky Williams/50 4.00 10.00
22 Ronnie Brown/50 4.00 10.00
24 Shonn Greene/20 5.00 12.00
25 Steven Jackson/50 4.00 10.00

2010 Absolute Memorabilia Marks of Fame
*SPECTRUM/50: 1X TO 2.5X BASIC INSERTS
1 Aaron Rodgers 2.50 6.00
2 Antonio Gates 1.00 2.50
3 Brent Celek 1.00 2.50
4 Brett Favre 3.00 8.00
5 Calvin Johnson 1.25 3.00
6 Chris Cooley 1.00 2.50
7 Dallas Clark 1.00 2.50
8 DeSean Jackson 1.00 2.50
9 Devery Henderson .75 2.00
10 Drew Brees 1.25 3.00
11 Josh Cribbs 1.25 3.00
12 LeSean McCoy 1.00 2.50
13 Mark Sanchez 1.25 3.00
14 Matthew Stafford 1.25 3.00
15 Michael Crabtree 1.25 3.00
16 Miles Austin 1.25 3.00
17 Percy Harvin 1.25 3.00
18 Peyton Manning 2.00 5.00
19 Sidney Rice 1.00 2.50
20 Tom Brady 2.00 5.00
21 Tony Gonzalez 1.00 2.50
22 Vernon Davis 1.00 2.50
23 Vince Young .75 2.00
24 Visanthe Shiancoe 1.00 2.50
25 Willis McGahee 1.00 2.50

2010 Absolute Memorabilia Marks of Fame Materials Spectrum Prime
STATED PRINT RUN 15-50
2 Antonio Gates/50 5.00 12.00
3 Brent Celek/50 5.00 12.00
4 Brett Favre/15 40.00 80.00
5 Calvin Johnson/50 6.00 15.00
6 Chris Cooley/50 5.00 12.00
7 Dallas Clark/50 5.00 12.00
9 Devery Henderson/50 4.00 10.00
10 Drew Brees/35 6.00 15.00
12 LeSean McCoy/50 5.00 12.00
13 Mark Sanchez/50 6.00 15.00
14 Matthew Stafford/50 6.00 15.00
17 Percy Harvin/50 6.00 15.00
18 Peyton Manning/50 10.00 25.00
19 Sidney Rice/50 6.00 15.00
20 Tom Brady/50 10.00 25.00
21 Tony Gonzalez/50 5.00 12.00
22 Vernon Davis/50 5.00 12.00
23 Vince Young/50 4.00 10.00
24 Visanthe Shiancoe/50 5.00 12.00
25 Willis McGahee/50 5.00 12.00

2010 Absolute Memorabilia Marks of Fame Materials Autographs
STATED PRINT RUN 1-15
2 Antonio Gates/15 15.00 40.00
3 Brent Celek/15 12.00 30.00
9 Devery Henderson/15 10.00 25.00
10 Drew Brees/15 60.00 120.00
11 Josh Cribbs/15 15.00 40.00
13 Mark Sanchez/15 30.00 60.00
14 Matthew Stafford/15 40.00 80.00
18 Peyton Manning/15 75.00 150.00
19 Sidney Rice/15 12.00 30.00
22 Vernon Davis/15 12.00 30.00

2010 Absolute Memorabilia NFL Icons
*SPECTRUM/50: 1X TO 2.5X BASIC INSERTS
1 Art Monk 1.25 3.00
2 Bernie Kosar 1.00 2.50
3 Bo Jackson 1.50 4.00
4 Boomer Esiason 1.00 2.50
5 Brent Jones .75 2.00
6 Cris Carter 1.25 3.00
7 Curtis Martin 1.00 2.50
8 D.D. Lewis .75 2.00
9 Deion Sanders 1.25 3.00
10 Ed Too Tall Jones 1.00 2.50
11 Eddie George 1.00 2.50
12 Fran Tarkenton 1.25 3.00
13 Harvey Martin .75 2.00
15 Jim Kelly 1.25 3.00
16 Joe Montana 2.50 6.00
17 Junior Seau 1.00 2.50
18 Ken Stabler 1.25 3.00
19 L.C. Greenwood 1.00 2.50
20 Priest Holmes .75 2.00
21 Randall Cunningham 1.00 2.50
22 Raymond Berry 1.00 2.50
23 Rod Smith .75 2.00
24 Roger Craig 1.00 2.50
25 Ronnie Lott 1.25 3.00
26 Steve Largent 1.25 3.00
27 Steve Young 1.50 4.00
28 Terrell Davis 1.25 3.00
29 Todd Christensen .75 2.00
30 Tom Rathman .75 2.00

2010 Absolute Memorabilia NFL Icons Materials Spectrum Prime
STATED PRINT RUN 10-50
1 Art Monk/14 25.00 50.00
2 Bernie Kosar/50 6.00 15.00
3 Bo Jackson/50 10.00 25.00
4 Boomer Esiason/50 6.00 15.00
5 Brent Jones/50 5.00 12.00
6 Cris Carter/50 8.00 20.00
7 Curtis Martin/50 6.00 15.00
8 D.D. Lewis/50 5.00 12.00
9 Deion Sanders/50 8.00 20.00
10 Ed Too Tall Jones/50 6.00 15.00
11 Eddie George/50 6.00 15.00
13 Harvey Martin/25 8.00 20.00
15 Jim Kelly/50 8.00 20.00
16 Joe Montana/25 20.00 50.00
17 Junior Seau/50 6.00 15.00
18 Ken Stabler/50 8.00 20.00
20 Priest Holmes/50 5.00 12.00
22 Raymond Berry/50 6.00 15.00
23 Rod Smith/50 5.00 12.00
24 Roger Craig/50 6.00 15.00
26 Steve Largent/50 8.00 20.00
27 Steve Young/50 10.00 25.00
28 Terrell Davis/50 8.00 20.00
29 Todd Christensen/50 5.00 12.00
30 Tom Rathman/50 5.00 12.00

2010 Absolute Memorabilia NFL Icons Materials Autographs
STATED PRINT RUN 10-50
*SPECT.PRIM/15: .5X TO 1.2X JSY AU/15-50
1 Art Monk/15 75.00 125.00
2 Bernie Kosar/25 15.00 40.00
3 Bo Jackson/25 50.00 100.00
5 Brent Jones/25 15.00 40.00
8 D.D. Lewis/25 12.00 30.00
9 Deion Sanders/25 30.00 60.00
10 Ed Too Tall Jones/25 15.00 40.00
12 Fran Tarkenton/45 20.00 50.00
15 Jim Kelly/25 30.00 60.00
16 Joe Montana/15 100.00 200.00
18 Ken Stabler/50 15.00 40.00
19 L.C. Greenwood/20 15.00 40.00
20 Priest Holmes/25 12.00 30.00
21 Randall Cunningham/50 20.00 50.00
22 Raymond Berry/50 10.00 25.00
23 Rod Smith/25 15.00 40.00
24 Roger Craig/50 10.00 25.00
25 Ronnie Lott/50 15.00 40.00
26 Steve Largent/50 20.00 50.00
27 Steve Young/25 40.00 80.00
28 Terrell Davis/25 20.00 50.00
29 Todd Christensen/25 12.00 30.00
30 Tom Rathman/25 12.00 30.00

2010 Absolute Memorabilia Rookie Jersey Collection
ONE PER BLASTER RETAIL BOX
1 Andre Roberts 2.50 6.00
2 Armanti Edwards 2.50 6.00
3 Arrelious Benn 2.50 6.00
4 Ben Tate 3.00 8.00
5 Brandon LaFell 2.50 6.00
6 C.J. Spiller 4.00 10.00
7 Colt McCoy 5.00 12.00
8 Damian Williams 2.50 6.00
9 Demaryius Thomas 3.00 8.00
10 Dexter McCluster 2.50 6.00
11 Dez Bryant 6.00 15.00
12 Emmanuel Sanders 2.50 6.00
13 Eric Berry 2.50 6.00
14 Eric Decker 3.00 8.00
15 Gerald McCoy 2.50 6.00
16 Golden Tate 2.50 6.00
17 Jahvid Best 4.00 10.00
18 Jermaine Gresham 3.00 8.00
19 Jimmy Clausen 2.50 6.00
20 Joe McKnight 2.50 6.00
21 Jonathan Dwyer 2.50 6.00
22 Jordan Shipley 2.50 6.00
23 Marcus Easley 2.00 5.00
24 Mardy Gilyard 2.50 6.00
25 Mike Kafka 2.50 6.00
26 Mike Williams 4.00 10.00
27 Montario Hardesty 2.50 6.00
28 Ndamukong Suh 5.00 12.00
29 Rob Gronkowski 6.00 15.00
30 Rolando McClain 2.50 6.00
31 Ryan Mathews 5.00 12.00
32 Sam Bradford 8.00 20.00
33 Taylor Price 2.50 6.00
34 Tim Tebow 10.00 25.00
35 Toby Gerhart 2.50 6.00

2010 Absolute Memorabilia Rookie Premiere Materials AFC/NFC
AFC/NFC PRINT RUN 99 SER.#'d SETS
*AFC/NFC SPECTRUM PRIME/25: .8X TO 2X
*NFL SPECTRUM PRIME/50: .6X TO 1.5X
*OVER.JERSEY NUMBER/50: .6X TO 1.5X
*OVER.JSY NUMBER PRIME/10: 1.5X TO 4X
*OVER.SPECTRUM PRIME/25: 1X TO 2.5X
201 Sam Bradford 12.00 30.00
202 Jimmy Clausen 2.50 6.00
203 Colt McCoy 5.00 12.00
204 Tim Tebow 12.00 30.00
205 Armanti Edwards 2.50 6.00
206 C.J. Spiller 4.00 10.00
207 Jahvid Best 4.00 10.00
208 Jonathan Dwyer 2.50 6.00
209 Ryan Mathews 5.00 12.00
210 Joe McKnight 2.50 6.00
211 Montario Hardesty 2.50 6.00
212 Toby Gerhart 2.50 6.00
213 Ben Tate 3.00 8.00
214 Dexter McCluster 2.50 6.00
215 Dez Bryant 8.00 20.00
216 Golden Tate 2.50 6.00
217 Arrelious Benn 2.50 6.00
218 Brandon LaFell 2.50 6.00
219 Demaryius Thomas 3.00 8.00
220 Damian Williams 2.50 6.00
221 Eric Decker 3.00 8.00
222 Jordan Shipley 2.50 6.00
223 Mardy Gilyard 2.50 6.00
224 Mike Williams 4.00 10.00
225 Andre Roberts 2.50 6.00
226 Jermaine Gresham 3.00 8.00
227 Rob Gronkowski 6.00 15.00
228 Ndamukong Suh 5.00 12.00
229 Gerald McCoy 2.50 6.00
230 Rolando McClain 2.50 6.00
231 Eric Berry 2.50 6.00
232 Emmanuel Sanders 2.50 6.00
233 Marcus Easley 2.00 5.00
234 Taylor Price 2.50 6.00
235 Mike Kafka 2.50 6.00

2010 Absolute Memorabilia Spectrum Gold Autographs
1-100 VETERAN PRINT RUN 5-50
101-200 ROOKIE PRINT RUN 99-299
10 Lee Evans/25 8.00 20.00
72 Louis Murphy/50 6.00 15.00
74 Kevin Kolb/25 10.00 25.00
100 Donovan McNabb/15 25.00 50.00
101 Aaron Hernandez/199 8.00 20.00
106 Anthony McCoy/99 5.00 12.00
107 Antonio Brown/99 10.00 25.00
108 Blair White/99 6.00 15.00
110 Brandon Graham/299 4.00 10.00
111 Brandon Spikes/199 5.00 12.00
113 Bryan Bulaga/199 5.00 12.00
114 Carlos Dunlap/199 5.00 12.00
115 Carlton Mitchell/199 4.00 10.00
116 Chad Jones/141 5.00 12.00
117 Charles Scott/299 4.00 10.00
120 Corey Wootton/99 5.00 12.00
121 Dan LeFevour/149 5.00 12.00
124 David Gettis/99 6.00 15.00
128 Derrick Morgan/99 5.00 12.00
129 Devin McCourty/199 5.00 12.00
130 Dezmon Briscoe/99 5.00 12.00
131 Dominique Franks/299 3.00 8.00
133 Earl Thomas/99 6.00 15.00
134 Ed Dickson/199 5.00 12.00
135 Everson Griffen/199 5.00 12.00
136 Freddie Barnes/299 4.00 10.00
137 Garrett Graham/99 5.00 12.00
138 Jacoby Ford/199 12.50 25.00
139 James Starks/99 15.00 40.00
141 Jarrett Brown/99 6.00 15.00
142 Jason Pierre-Paul/199 8.00 20.00
143 Jason Worilds/199 5.00 12.00
145 Jeremy Williams/99 4.00 10.00
148 Jerry Hughes/199 5.00 12.00
149 Jevan Snead/201 5.00 12.00
150 Jimmy Graham/299 15.00 30.00
151 Joe Haden/199 5.00 12.00
154 John Skelton/299 5.00 12.00
155 Joique Bell/199 4.00 10.00
156 Jonathan Crompton/299 4.00 10.00
172 Morgan Burnett/199 5.00 12.00
177 Patrick Robinson/199 5.00 12.00
178 Perrish Cox/199 4.00 10.00
179 Ricky Sapp/299 4.00 10.00
180 Riley Cooper/299 5.00 12.00
183 Sean Canfield/99 5.00 12.00
184 Sean Lee/199 5.00 12.00
185 Sean Weatherspoon/99 6.00 15.00
188 Shay Hodge/299 4.00 10.00
190 Taylor Mays/199 5.00 12.00
195 Tony Pike/99 6.00 15.00
200 Zac Robinson/199 4.00 10.00

2010 Absolute Memorabilia Spectrum Platinum Autographs
1-100 VETERAN PRINT RUN 1-25
101-200 ROOKIE PRINT RUN 19-25
31 Kyle Orton/25 10.00 25.00
48 Dwayne Bowe/25 8.00 20.00
72 Louis Murphy/25 8.00 20.00
96 Kenny Britt/25 8.00 20.00
101 Aaron Hernandez/25 15.00 40.00
105 Anthony Dixon/25 10.00 25.00
106 Anthony McCoy/25 8.00 20.00
107 Antonio Brown/25 15.00 40.00
108 Blair White/25 10.00 25.00
110 Brandon Graham/25 8.00 20.00
111 Brandon Spikes/25 10.00 25.00
113 Bryan Bulaga/25 10.00 25.00
114 Carlos Dunlap/25 10.00 25.00
115 Carlton Mitchell/25 8.00 20.00
116 Chad Jones/25 10.00 25.00
117 Charles Scott/25 8.00 20.00
118 Chris Cook/19 10.00 25.00
120 Corey Wootton/25 8.00 20.00
121 Dan LeFevour/25 10.00 25.00
124 David Gettis/25 10.00 25.00
128 Derrick Morgan/25 8.00 20.00
129 Devin McCourty/25 10.00 25.00
130 Dezmon Briscoe/25 8.00 20.00
133 Earl Thomas/25 10.00 25.00
134 Ed Dickson/25 10.00 25.00
135 Everson Griffen/25 10.00 25.00
136 Freddie Barnes/25 8.00 20.00
137 Garrett Graham/25 8.00 20.00
138 Jacoby Ford/25 25.00 50.00
139 James Starks/25 20.00 50.00
141 Jarrett Brown/25 10.00 25.00
142 Jason Pierre-Paul/25 15.00 40.00
143 Jason Worilds/25 10.00 25.00
145 Jeremy Williams/25 6.00 15.00
148 Jerry Hughes/25 10.00 25.00
149 Jevan Snead/25 10.00 25.00
150 Jimmy Graham/25 30.00 60.00
151 Joe Haden/25 10.00 25.00
154 John Skelton/25 10.00 25.00
155 Joique Bell/25 8.00 20.00
156 Jonathan Crompton/25 8.00 20.00
157 Kareem Jackson/25 10.00 25.00
166 Lonyae Miller/25 8.00 20.00
172 Morgan Burnett/25 10.00 25.00
177 Patrick Robinson/25 10.00 25.00
178 Perrish Cox/25 8.00 20.00
179 Ricky Sapp/25 8.00 20.00
180 Riley Cooper/25 10.00 25.00
183 Sean Canfield/25 8.00 20.00
184 Sean Lee/25 10.00 25.00
185 Sean Weatherspoon/25 10.00 25.00
187 Seyi Ajirotutu/25 10.00 25.00
188 Shay Hodge/25 8.00 20.00
190 Taylor Mays/25 10.00 25.00
195 Tony Pike/25 10.00 25.00
200 Zac Robinson/25 8.00 20.00

2010 Absolute Memorabilia Star Gazing
*SPECTRUM/50: 1X TO 2.5X BASIC INSERTS
1 Tim Tebow 3.00 8.00
2 Sam Bradford 3.00 8.00
3 Brandon LaFell .75 2.00
4 Colt McCoy 1.50 4.00
5 Demaryius Thomas 1.00 2.50
6 Dez Bryant 2.50 6.00
7 Eric Berry .75 2.00
8 Gerald McCoy .75 2.00
9 Jahvid Best 1.25 3.00
10 Jimmy Clausen .75 2.00
11 Jonathan Dwyer .75 2.00
12 Marcus Easley .60 1.50
13 Mike Kafka .75 2.00
14 Montario Hardesty .75 2.00
15 Armanti Edwards .75 2.00
16 C.J. Spiller 1.25 3.00
17 Damian Williams .75 2.00
18 Emmanuel Sanders .75 2.00
19 Toby Gerhart .75 2.00
20 Dexter McCluster .75 2.00
21 Arrelious Benn .75 2.00
22 Jordan Shipley .75 2.00
23 Mardy Gilyard .75 2.00
24 Andre Roberts .75 2.00
25 Jermaine Gresham 1.00 2.50
26 Ndamukong Suh 1.50 4.00
27 Taylor Price .75 2.00
28 Rob Gronkowski 2.00 5.00
29 Rolando McClain .75 2.00
30 Mike Williams 1.25 3.00
31 Ryan Mathews 1.50 4.00
32 Joe McKnight .75 2.00
33 Ben Tate 1.00 2.50
34 Eric Decker 1.00 2.50
35 Golden Tate .75 2.00

2010 Absolute Memorabilia Star Gazing Materials
STATED PRINT RUN 250 SER.#'d SETS
*OVER.JSY NUMBER/10: 1X TO 2.5X
*OVER.JSY NMBR PRIME/25: 1X TO 2.5X
*OVER.SPECTRUM PRIME/15: 1X TO 2.5X
*PRIME/50: .6X TO 1.5X BASIC JSY/250
1 Tim Tebow 10.00 25.00
2 Sam Bradford 10.00 25.00
3 Brandon LaFell 2.50 6.00
4 Colt McCoy 5.00 12.00
5 Demaryius Thomas 3.00 8.00
6 Dez Bryant 8.00 20.00
7 Eric Berry 2.50 6.00
8 Gerald McCoy 2.50 6.00
9 Jahvid Best 4.00 10.00
10 Jimmy Clausen 2.50 6.00
11 Jonathan Dwyer 2.50 6.00
12 Marcus Easley 2.00 5.00
13 Mike Kafka 2.50 6.00
14 Montario Hardesty 2.50 6.00
15 Armanti Edwards 2.50 6.00
16 C.J. Spiller 4.00 10.00
17 Damian Williams 2.50 6.00
18 Emmanuel Sanders 2.50 6.00
19 Toby Gerhart 2.50 6.00
20 Dexter McCluster 2.50 6.00
21 Arrelious Benn 2.50 6.00
22 Jordan Shipley 2.50 6.00
23 Mardy Gilyard 2.50 6.00
24 Andre Roberts 2.50 6.00
25 Jermaine Gresham 3.00 8.00
26 Ndamukong Suh 5.00 12.00
27 Taylor Price 2.50 6.00
28 Rob Gronkowski 6.00 15.00
29 Rolando McClain 2.50 6.00
30 Mike Williams 4.00 10.00
31 Ryan Mathews 5.00 12.00
32 Joe McKnight 2.50 6.00
33 Ben Tate 3.00 8.00
34 Eric Decker 3.00 8.00
35 Golden Tate 2.50 6.00

2010 Absolute Memorabilia Star Gazing Materials Autographs
STATED PRINT RUN 25 SER.#'d SETS
EXCH EXPIRATION: 4/13/2012
1 Tim Tebow 60.00 120.00
2 Sam Bradford 60.00 120.00
3 Brandon LaFell 8.00 20.00
4 Colt McCoy 30.00 60.00
5 Demaryius Thomas 10.00 25.00
6 Dez Bryant 30.00 80.00
7 Eric Berry 8.00 20.00
8 Gerald McCoy 8.00 20.00
9 Jahvid Best 12.00 30.00
10 Jimmy Clausen 8.00 20.00
11 Jonathan Dwyer 8.00 20.00
12 Marcus Easley 6.00 15.00
13 Mike Kafka 8.00 20.00
14 Montario Hardesty 8.00 20.00
15 Armanti Edwards 8.00 20.00
16 C.J. Spiller 12.00 30.00
17 Damian Williams 8.00 20.00
18 Emmanuel Sanders 8.00 20.00
19 Toby Gerhart 8.00 20.00
20 Dexter McCluster 8.00 20.00
21 Arrelious Benn 8.00 20.00
22 Jordan Shipley 8.00 20.00
23 Mardy Gilyard 8.00 20.00
24 Andre Roberts 8.00 20.00
25 Jermaine Gresham 10.00 25.00
26 Ndamukong Suh 30.00 60.00
27 Taylor Price 8.00 20.00
28 Rob Gronkowski 25.00 60.00
29 Rolando McClain 8.00 20.00
30 Mike Williams 12.00 30.00
31 Ryan Mathews 15.00 40.00
32 Joe McKnight 8.00 20.00
33 Ben Tate 10.00 25.00
34 Eric Decker 10.00 25.00
35 Golden Tate 8.00 20.00

2010 Absolute Memorabilia Team Quads Materials Die Cut Spectrum Prime
SPECTRUM PRIME PRINT RUN 15-25
*QUAD MAT/50: .25X TO .6X PRIME/15-25
1 Sidney Rice/25 40.00 100.00
Visanthe Shiancoe
Adrian Peterson
Brett Favre
3 Drew Brees/25 12.00 30.00
Marques Colston
Reggie Bush
Devery Henderson
5 Felix Jones/15 20.00 50.00
Miles Austin
Jason Witten
Tony Romo
6 Eli Manning/25 12.00 30.00
Brandon Jacobs
Ahmad Bradshaw
Steve Smith USC
7 Troy Polamalu/25 15.00 40.00
Ben Roethlisberger
Hines Ward
Heath Miller
8 Jay Cutler/25 15.00 40.00
Matt Forte
Greg Olsen
Johnny Knox
10 Vince Young/25 12.00 30.00
Chris Johnson
Kenny Britt
Justin Gage

2010 Absolute Memorabilia Team Tandems Materials Spectrum Prime
SPECTRUM PRIME PRINT RUN 15-25
*TAND.MAT/85-100: .25X TO .6X PRIME/15-25
*TANDEM MAT/30: .3X TO .8X PRIME/15-25
1 Felix Jones/25 10.00 25.00
Jason Witten
2 Darren Sproles/25 8.00 20.00
Antonio Gates
3 Wes Welker/25 8.00 20.00
Randy Moss
4 Drew Brees/25 8.00 20.00
Marques Colston
5 Greg Jennings/25 8.00 20.00
Ryan Grant
6 Brandon Jacobs/25 8.00 20.00
Ahmad Bradshaw
7 David Garrard/25 6.00 15.00
Maurice Jones-Drew
8 Santana Moss/25 6.00 15.00
Ladell Betts
9 Sidney Rice/25 8.00 20.00
Visanthe Shiancoe
10 Roddy White/15 6.00 15.00
Michael Turner
11 Larry Fitzgerald/25 8.00 20.00
Chris Wells
12 Carson Palmer/25 8.00 20.00
Chad Ochocinco
13 Vince Young/25 6.00 15.00
Kenny Britt
14 Matt Schaub/15 6.00 15.00
Andre Johnson
16 Rashard Mendenhall/25 12.00 30.00
Troy Polamalu
17 Matthew Stafford/25 8.00 20.00
Calvin Johnson
18 DeAngelo Williams/25 6.00 15.00
Steve Smith
19 Frank Gore/25 8.00 20.00
Michael Crabtree
20 Darren McFadden/25 6.00 15.00
Sebastian Janikowski

2010 Absolute Memorabilia Team Trios Materials NFL
STATED PRINT RUN 75 SER.#'d SETS
3 Adrian Peterson 12.00 30.00
Sidney Rice
Percy Harvin
4 Jason Witten 8.00 20.00
DeMarcus Ware
Felix Jones
5 Clinton Portis 5.00 12.00
Santana Moss
Ladell Betts
8 Ray Rice 5.00 12.00
Willis McGahee
Derrick Mason
9 Ahmad Bradshaw 8.00 20.00
Brandon Jacobs
Eli Manning
10 Matt Forte 8.00 20.00
Brian Urlacher
Greg Olsen
11 Dustin Keller 5.00 12.00
Jerricho Cotchery
Shonn Greene
13 Wes Welker 10.00 25.00
Tom Brady
Randy Moss
14 Matt Leinart 6.00 15.00
Larry Fitzgerald
Chris Wells
15 Vince Young 6.00 15.00
Kenny Britt
Chris Johnson
16 Antonio Gates 6.00 15.00
Darren Sproles
Philip Rivers
19 Drew Brees 8.00 20.00
Marques Colston
Reggie Bush
20 Darren McFadden 6.00 15.00
Louis Murphy
Sebastian Janikowski

2010 Absolute Memorabilia Team Trios Materials NFL Spectrum Prime
PRIME STATED PRINT RUN 5-25
1 DeAngelo Williams/25 8.00 20.00
Steve Smith
Jonathan Stewart
2 Hines Ward/25 15.00 40.00
Troy Polamalu
Rashard Mendenhall
3 Adrian Peterson/25 20.00 50.00
Sidney Rice
Percy Harvin
4 Jason Witten/25 12.00 30.00
DeMarcus Ware
Felix Jones
5 Clinton Portis/25 8.00 20.00
Santana Moss
Ladell Betts
7 Frank Gore/25 10.00 25.00
Vernon Davis
Michael Crabtree
8 Ray Rice/25 8.00 20.00
Willis McGahee
Derrick Mason
9 Ahmad Bradshaw/25 12.00 30.00
Brandon Jacobs
Eli Manning
10 Matt Forte/25 12.00 30.00
Brian Urlacher
Greg Olsen
11 Dustin Keller/25 8.00 20.00
Jerricho Cotchery
Shonn Greene
13 Wes Welker/25 15.00 40.00
Tom Brady
Randy Moss
15 Vince Young/25 10.00 25.00
Kenny Britt
Chris Johnson
16 Antonio Gates/25 10.00 25.00
Darren Sproles
Philip Rivers
19 Drew Brees/25 12.00 30.00
Marques Colston
Reggie Bush
20 Darren McFadden/25 10.00 25.00
Louis Murphy
Sebastian Janikowski

2010 Absolute Memorabilia Tools of the Trade Material Red
RETAIL INSERT PRINT RUN 35-250
1 Curtis Martin/168 4.00 10.00
3 Eddie George/250 4.00 10.00
4 Jim Kelly/250 6.00 15.00
5 Marion Barber/225 3.00 8.00
6 Dan Marino/250 10.00 25.00
7 Josh Freeman/250 4.00 10.00
8 Tony Romo/100 5.00 12.00
9 Steve Young/250 6.00 15.00
10 Peyton Manning/75 8.00 20.00
11 Reggie Bush/250 4.00 10.00
12 Brett Favre/100 10.00 25.00
13 Rod Smith/50 5.00 12.00
14 Andre Johnson/70 4.00 10.00
15 Steve Largent/250 5.00 12.00
16 Troy Aikman/250 6.00 15.00
17 Randall Cunningham/250 4.00 10.00
18 Larry Fitzgerald/250 4.00 10.00
19 LeSean McCoy/60 4.00 10.00
20 Brian Urlacher/100 4.00 10.00
21 Terrell Davis/250 4.00 10.00
22 Hines Ward/250 3.00 8.00
23 Reggie Wayne/199 3.00 8.00
24 Chris Wells/60 4.00 10.00
25 Jeremy Maclin/35 5.00 12.00
26 Darren McFadden/250 3.00 8.00
27 Matthew Stafford/250 4.00 10.00
28 Warren Moon/250 5.00 12.00
29 Emmitt Smith/250 8.00 20.00
30 Clinton Portis/250 3.00 8.00
31 Terry Bradshaw/250 6.00 15.00
32 Eli Manning/100 4.00 10.00
33 Carson Palmer/250 3.00 8.00
34 Don Maynard/250 4.00 10.00
35 Cadillac Williams/215 3.00 8.00
36 Derrick Thomas/250 10.00 25.00
37 Tom Brady/100 10.00 25.00
38 John Elway/250 8.00 20.00
39 Junior Seau/250 3.00 8.00
40 Mark Sanchez/100 4.00 10.00
41 Bart Starr/250 8.00 20.00
42 Earl Campbell/250 5.00 12.00
43 Frank Gore/200 3.00 8.00
44 Steven Jackson/95 3.00 8.00

45 L.C. Greenwood/100 4.00 10.00
46 Todd Heap/145 2.50 6.00
47 Vince Young/250 2.50 6.00
48 Tony Dorsett/250 5.00 12.00
49 Jerry Rice/250 8.00 20.00
50 Ricky Williams/250 3.00 8.00

2010 Absolute Memorabilia Tools of the Trade Material Black Spectrum

STATED PRINT RUN 1-50
1 Curtis Martin/50 6.00 15.00
2 Deion Sanders/40 8.00 20.00
3 Eddie George/50 6.00 15.00
4 Jim Kelly/50 12.00 30.00
5 Marion Barber/50 5.00 12.00
6 Dan Marino/50 15.00 40.00
9 Steve Young/50 10.00 25.00
10 Peyton Manning/25 12.00 30.00
11 Reggie Bush/50 6.00 15.00
12 Brett Favre/25 20.00 50.00
13 Rod Smith/50 4.00 10.00
14 Andre Johnson/50 5.00 12.00
15 Steve Largent/50 8.00 20.00
16 Troy Aikman/25 12.00 30.00
18 Larry Fitzgerald/25 8.00 20.00
19 LeSean McCoy/50 5.00 12.00
20 Brian Urlacher/50 6.00 15.00
21 Terrell Davis/50 6.00 15.00
22 Hines Ward/50 5.00 12.00
24 Chris Wells/50 5.00 12.00
25 Jeremy Maclin/50 5.00 12.00
26 Darren McFadden/50 5.00 12.00
27 Matthew Stafford/50 6.00 15.00
29 Emmitt Smith/50 12.00 30.00
30 Clinton Portis/50 5.00 12.00
31 Terry Bradshaw/40 10.00 25.00
32 Eli Manning/25 8.00 20.00
33 Carson Palmer/17 6.00 15.00
34 Don Maynard/25 8.00 20.00
35 Cadillac Williams/50 5.00 12.00
37 Tom Brady/50 15.00 40.00
39 Junior Seau/50 5.00 12.00
40 Mark Sanchez/15 8.00 20.00
41 Bart Starr/25 15.00 40.00
43 Frank Gore/45 5.00 12.00
44 Steven Jackson/35 5.00 12.00
45 L.C. Greenwood/50 6.00 15.00
46 Todd Heap/50 4.00 10.00
47 Vince Young/50 4.00 10.00
48 Tony Dorsett/50 8.00 20.00
49 Jerry Rice/50 12.00 30.00
50 Ricky Williams/50 5.00 12.00

2010 Absolute Memorabilia Tools of the Trade Material Oversize Black Spectrum

STATED PRINT RUN 1-50
4 Jim Kelly/39 15.00 40.00
5 Marion Barber/50 6.00 15.00
11 Reggie Bush/35 8.00 20.00
21 Terrell Davis/30 8.00 20.00
22 Hines Ward/25 15.00 40.00
26 Darren McFadden/20 8.00 20.00
30 Clinton Portis/50 6.00 15.00
35 Cadillac Williams/15 8.00 20.00
37 Tom Brady/50 30.00 80.00
43 Frank Gore/50 6.00 15.00
46 Todd Heap/50 5.00 12.00
47 Vince Young/50 5.00 12.00
50 Ricky Williams/22 8.00 20.00

2010 Absolute Memorabilia Tools of the Trade Material Oversize Jersey Number Black

STATED PRINT RUN 1-25
1 Curtis Martin/19 12.00 30.00
2 Deion Sanders/21 15.00 40.00
3 Eddie George/24 12.00 30.00
5 Marion Barber/25 10.00 25.00
30 Clinton Portis/25 10.00 25.00
31 Terry Bradshaw/18 20.00 50.00
37 Tom Brady/25 25.00 60.00
47 Vince Young/25 8.00 20.00
50 Ricky Williams/25 10.00 25.00

2010 Absolute Memorabilia Tools of the Trade Double Material Black Spectrum

STATED PRINT RUN 1-50
1 Curtis Martin/50 8.00 20.00
2 Deion Sanders/50 10.00 25.00
3 Eddie George/50 8.00 20.00
4 Jim Kelly/50 10.00 25.00
6 Dan Marino/50 20.00 50.00
7 Josh Freeman/18 10.00 25.00
8 Tony Romo/50 10.00 25.00
9 Steve Young/50 12.00 30.00
11 Reggie Bush/50 8.00 20.00
12 Brett Favre/25 25.00 60.00
15 Steve Largent/50 10.00 25.00
16 Troy Aikman/17 15.00 40.00
18 Larry Fitzgerald/30 8.00 20.00
19 LeSean McCoy/50 6.00 15.00
20 Brian Urlacher/50 8.00 20.00
21 Terrell Davis/50 8.00 20.00
22 Hines Ward/50 6.00 15.00
24 Chris Wells/50 6.00 15.00
26 Darren McFadden/50 6.00 15.00
28 Warren Moon/40 10.00 25.00
29 Emmitt Smith/50 15.00 40.00
30 Clinton Portis/50 6.00 15.00
31 Terry Bradshaw/50 12.00 30.00
35 Cadillac Williams/40 6.00 15.00
37 Tom Brady/50 12.00 30.00
39 Junior Seau/50 6.00 15.00
40 Mark Sanchez/30 8.00 20.00
44 Steven Jackson/50 6.00 15.00
45 L.C. Greenwood/30 8.00 20.00
47 Vince Young/50 5.00 12.00
50 Ricky Williams/50 6.00 15.00

2010 Absolute Memorabilia Tools of the Trade Triple Material Black Spectrum

STATED PRINT RUN 1-50
1 Curtis Martin/50 8.00 20.00
3 Eddie George/50 8.00 20.00
6 Dan Marino/50 20.00 50.00
15 Steve Largent/35 10.00 25.00
21 Terrell Davis/25 12.00 30.00
29 Emmitt Smith/30 15.00 40.00
31 Terry Bradshaw/50 12.00 30.00
33 Carson Palmer/50 6.00 15.00
35 Cadillac Williams/45 6.00 15.00
37 Tom Brady/38 12.00 30.00
45 L.C. Greenwood/49 8.00 20.00
50 Ricky Williams/50 6.00 15.00

2010 Absolute Memorabilia War Room

*SPECTRUM/50: 1X TO 2.5X BASIC INSERTS
1 Jordan Shipley .75 2.00
2 Andre Roberts .75 2.00
3 Ndamukong Suh 1.50 4.00
4 Rob Gronkowski 2.00 5.00
5 Mike Williams 1.25 3.00
6 Joe McKnight .75 2.00
7 Eric Decker 1.00 2.50
8 Golden Tate .75 2.00
9 Arrelious Benn .75 2.00
10 Toby Gerhart .75 2.00
11 Damian Williams .75 2.00
12 Armanti Edwards .75 2.00
13 Mike Kafka .75 2.00
14 Jonathan Dwyer .75 2.00
15 Jahvid Best 1.25 3.00
16 Eric Berry .75 2.00
17 Demaryius Thomas 1.00 2.50
18 Tim Tebow 3.00 8.00
19 Dez Bryant 2.50 6.00
20 Montario Hardesty .75 2.00
21 Taylor Price .75 2.00
22 Mardy Gilyard .75 2.00
23 Emmanuel Sanders .75 2.00
24 Brandon LaFell .75 2.00
25 Gerald McCoy .75 2.00
26 Colt McCoy 1.50 4.00
27 Ryan Mathews 1.50 4.00
28 Rolando McClain .75 2.00
29 Dexter McCluster .75 2.00
30 Marcus Easley .60 1.50
31 C.J. Spiller 1.25 3.00
32 Jermaine Gresham 1.00 2.50
33 Ben Tate 1.00 2.50
34 Jimmy Clausen .75 2.00
35 Sam Bradford 3.00 8.00

2010 Absolute Memorabilia War Room Materials

STATED PRINT RUN 250 SER.#'d SETS
*OVER.JSY NUMBER/10: 1X TO 2.5X
*OVER.JSY NMBR PRIME/15: 1X TO 2.5X
*PRIME/50: .6X TO 1.5X BASIC JSY/250
1 Jordan Shipley 2.50 6.00
2 Andre Roberts 2.50 6.00
3 Ndamukong Suh 5.00 12.00
4 Rob Gronkowski 6.00 15.00
5 Mike Williams 4.00 10.00
6 Joe McKnight 2.50 6.00
7 Eric Decker 3.00 8.00
8 Golden Tate 2.50 6.00
9 Arrelious Benn 2.50 6.00
10 Toby Gerhart 2.50 6.00
11 Damian Williams 2.50 6.00
12 Armanti Edwards 2.50 6.00
13 Mike Kafka 2.50 6.00
14 Jonathan Dwyer 2.50 6.00
15 Jahvid Best 4.00 10.00
16 Eric Berry 2.50 6.00
17 Demaryius Thomas 3.00 8.00
18 Tim Tebow 10.00 25.00
19 Dez Bryant 8.00 20.00
20 Montario Hardesty 2.50 6.00
21 Taylor Price 2.50 6.00
22 Mardy Gilyard 2.50 6.00
23 Emmanuel Sanders 2.50 6.00
24 Brandon LaFell 2.50 6.00
25 Gerald McCoy 2.50 6.00
26 Colt McCoy 5.00 12.00
27 Ryan Mathews 5.00 12.00
28 Rolando McClain 2.50 6.00
29 Dexter McCluster 2.50 6.00
30 Marcus Easley 2.00 5.00
31 C.J. Spiller 4.00 10.00
32 Jermaine Gresham 3.00 8.00
33 Ben Tate 3.00 8.00
34 Jimmy Clausen 2.50 6.00
35 Sam Bradford 10.00 25.00

2010 Absolute Memorabilia War Room Materials Autographs

*WAR ROOM: .4X TO 1X STAR GAZING
STATED PRINT RUN 25 SER.#'d SETS
EXCH EXPIRATION: 4/13/2012

2011 Absolute Memorabilia

101-200 ROOKIE PRINT RUN 399
201-236 RPM AU PRINT RUN 199-299
EXCH EXPIRATION: 4/26/2013
1 Larry Fitzgerald .40 1.00
2 Steve Breaston .30 .75
3 Tim Hightower .30 .75
4 Matt Ryan .50 1.25
5 Michael Turner .40 1.00
6 Roddy White .40 1.00
7 Tony Gonzalez .40 1.00
8 Anquan Boldin .40 1.00
9 Joe Flacco .50 1.25
10 Ray Lewis .50 1.25
11 Ray Rice .40 1.00
12 C.J. Spiller .40 1.00
13 Fred Jackson .50 1.25
14 Ryan Fitzpatrick .40 1.00
15 DeAngelo Williams .40 1.00
16 Jonathan Stewart .40 1.00
17 Steve Smith .40 1.00
18 Brian Urlacher .50 1.25
19 Jay Cutler .40 1.00
20 Julius Peppers .40 1.00
21 Matt Forte .40 1.00
22 Carson Palmer .40 1.00
23 Cedric Benson .40 1.00
24 Chad Ochocinco .40 1.00
25 Terrell Owens .50 1.25
26 Colt McCoy .40 1.00
27 Peyton Hillis .40 1.00
28 DeMarcus Ware .40 1.00
29 Dez Bryant .50 1.25
30 Jason Witten .50 1.25
31 Tony Romo .50 1.25
32 Brandon Lloyd .40 1.00
33 Knowshon Moreno .40 1.00
34 Tim Tebow 1.00 2.50
35 Calvin Johnson .50 1.25
36 Matthew Stafford .50 1.25
37 Ndamukong Suh .50 1.25
38 Aaron Rodgers .75 2.00
39 Greg Jennings .40 1.00
40 Jermichael Finley .40 1.00
41 Andre Johnson .40 1.00
42 Arian Foster .40 1.00
43 Matt Schaub .40 1.00
44 Dallas Clark .40 1.00
45 Peyton Manning .75 2.00
46 Reggie Wayne .40 1.00
47 David Garrard .40 1.00
48 Maurice Jones-Drew .40 1.00
49 Dwayne Bowe .40 1.00
50 Jamaal Charles .40 1.00
51 Matt Cassel .40 1.00
52 Brandon Marshall .40 1.00
53 Ronnie Brown .40 1.00
54 Adrian Peterson .60 1.50
55 Percy Harvin .40 1.00
56 Sidney Rice .40 1.00
57 BenJarvus Green-Ellis .40 1.00
58 Tom Brady .75 2.00
59 Wes Welker .50 1.25
60 Drew Brees .50 1.25
61 Marques Colston .40 1.00
62 Reggie Bush .40 1.00
63 Ahmad Bradshaw .40 1.00
64 Brandon Jacobs .40 1.00
65 Eli Manning .50 1.25
66 Hakeem Nicks .40 1.00
67 Braylon Edwards .40 1.00
68 LaDainian Tomlinson .50 1.25
69 Mark Sanchez .50 1.25
70 Darren McFadden .40 1.00
71 Jason Campbell .40 1.00
72 DeSean Jackson .40 1.00
73 Jeremy Maclin .40 1.00
74 LeSean McCoy .40 1.00
75 Michael Vick .50 1.25
76 Ben Roethlisberger .50 1.25
77 Hines Ward .40 1.00
78 Mike Wallace .50 1.25
79 Rashard Mendenhall .40 1.00
80 Troy Polamalu .50 1.25
81 Antonio Gates .40 1.00
82 Philip Rivers .50 1.25
83 Ryan Mathews .40 1.00
84 Frank Gore .40 1.00
85 Michael Crabtree .40 1.00
86 Patrick Willis .40 1.00
87 Vernon Davis .40 1.00
88 Marshawn Lynch .40 1.00
89 Matt Hasselbeck .40 1.00
90 James Laurinaitis .30 .75
91 Sam Bradford .50 1.25
92 Steven Jackson .40 1.00
93 Josh Freeman .50 1.25
94 Kellen Winslow Jr. .40 1.00
95 LeGarrette Blount .40 1.00
96 Chris Johnson .40 1.00
97 Kenny Britt .40 1.00
98 Donovan McNabb .50 1.25
99 Ryan Torain .30 .75
100 Santana Moss .40 1.00
101 Aldrick Robinson RC 1.50 4.00
102 Cecil Shorts RC 2.00 5.00
103 David Ausberry RC 2.00 5.00
104 DeMarco Sampson RC 1.50 4.00
105 Denarius Moore RC 3.00 8.00
106 Dwayne Harris RC 2.50 6.00
107 Greg Salas RC 2.50 6.00
108 Jeremy Kerley RC 2.50 6.00
109 Kealoha Pilares RC 2.50 6.00
110 Kris Durham RC 2.00 5.00
111 Niles Paul RC 2.50 6.00
112 Ronald Johnson RC 2.00 5.00
113 Ryan Whalen RC 2.00 5.00
114 Scotty McKnight RC 2.00 5.00
115 Stephen Burton RC 1.50 4.00
116 Tandon Doss RC 2.00 5.00
117 D.J. Williams RC 2.50 6.00
118 Daniel Hardy RC 2.00 5.00
119 Jordan Cameron RC 2.00 5.00
120 Julius Thomas RC 2.00 5.00
121 Lance Kendricks RC 2.00 5.00
122 Lee Smith RC 2.00 5.00
123 Luke Stocker RC 2.00 5.00
124 Richard Gordon RC 2.00 5.00
125 Robert Housler RC 2.00 5.00
126 Virgil Green RC 2.00 5.00
127 Allen Bradford RC 2.00 5.00
128 Anthony Allen RC 1.50 4.00
129 Baron Batch RC 2.50 6.00
130 Da'Rel Scott RC 2.00 5.00
131 Dion Lewis RC 2.50 6.00
132 Evan Royster RC 2.50 6.00
133 Jacquizz Rodgers RC 2.50 6.00
134 Jay Finley RC 2.00 5.00
135 Johnny White RC 2.00 5.00
136 Roy Helu RC 5.00 12.00
137 Greg McElroy RC 2.50 6.00
138 Nathan Enderle RC 2.50 6.00
139 Ricky Stanzi RC 3.00 8.00
140 T.J. Yates RC 3.00 8.00
141 Terrelle Pryor RC 5.00 12.00
142 Tyrod Taylor RC 2.50 6.00
143 Aaron Williams RC 2.00 5.00
144 Brandon Harris RC 1.50 4.00
145 Jimmy Smith RC 2.50 6.00
146 Marcus Gilchrist RC 1.50 4.00
147 Patrick Peterson RC 4.00 10.00
148 Prince Amukamara RC 2.50 6.00
149 Ras-I Dowling RC 2.50 6.00
150 Adrian Clayborn RC 2.50 6.00
151 Aldon Smith RC 4.00 10.00
152 Brooks Reed RC 2.50 6.00
153 Cameron Heyward RC 2.50 6.00
154 Cameron Jordan RC 2.00 5.00
155 Da'Quan Bowers RC 2.50 6.00
156 J.J. Watt RC 3.00 8.00
157 Jabaal Sheard RC 2.50 6.00
158 Muhammad Wilkerson RC 2.50 6.00
159 Robert Quinn RC 2.50 6.00
160 Akeem Ayers RC 2.00 5.00
161 Bruce Carter RC 2.50 6.00
162 Jonas Mouton RC 2.00 5.00
163 Ryan Kerrigan RC 2.50 6.00
164 Corey Liuget RC 1.50 4.00
165 Jarvis Jenkins RC 1.50 4.00
166 Marvin Austin RC 2.00 5.00
167 Nick Fairley RC 3.00 8.00
168 Phil Taylor RC 2.00 5.00
169 Stephen Paea RC 2.50 6.00
170 Jaiquawn Jarrett RC 2.00 5.00
171 Rahim Moore RC 2.00 5.00
172 Mike Pouncey RC 2.50 6.00
173 Rodney Hudson RC 1.50 4.00
174 Stefen Wisniewski RC 2.50 6.00
175 Danny Watkins RC 2.00 5.00
176 James Carpenter RC 2.50 6.00
177 Orlando Franklin RC 2.00 5.00
178 Anthony Castonzo RC 1.50 4.00
179 Derek Sherrod RC 2.50 6.00
180 Gabe Carimi RC 2.50 6.00
181 Marcus Gilbert RC 2.50 6.00
182 Nate Solder RC 2.50 6.00
183 Tyron Smith RC 3.00 8.00
184 Ahmad Black RC 2.00 5.00
185 Greg Jones RC 2.00 5.00
186 Marcus Cannon RC 1.50 4.00
187 Chris Culliver RC 2.00 5.00
188 Owen Marecic RC 2.50 6.00
189 DeMarcus Van Dyke RC 2.00 5.00
190 Dontay Moch RC 1.50 4.00
191 Quinton Carter RC 1.50 4.00
192 Stanley Havili RC 1.50 4.00
193 Jurrell Casey RC 1.50 4.00
194 Justin Houston RC 2.50 6.00
195 Kelvin Sheppard RC 2.50 6.00
196 Martez Wilson RC 2.50 6.00
197 Mason Foster RC 2.50 6.00
198 Nate Irving RC 2.00 5.00
199 Tyler Sash RC 2.50 6.00
200 Terrell McClain RC 2.00 5.00
201 Andy Dalton RPM AU/299 RC 30.00 60.00
202 Cam Newton RPM AU/199 RC 100.00 175.00
203 A.J. Green RPM AU/199 RC 30.00 60.00
204 Taiwan Jones RPM AU/299 RC 6.00 15.00
205 DeMarco Murray RPM AU/299 RC EXCH 25.00 60.00
206 Torrey Smith RPM AU/299 RC 10.00 25.00
207 Ryan Mallett RPM AU/199 RC 20.00 40.00
208 Stevan Ridley RPM AU/299 RC 6.00 15.00
209 Austin Pettis RPM AU/299 RC 5.00 12.00
210 Shane Vereen RPM AU/299 RC 8.00 20.00
211 Titus Young RPM AU/299 RC 10.00 25.00
212 Mikel Leshoure RPM AU/299 RC 8.00 20.00
213 Christian Ponder RPM AU/199 RC 25.00 60.00
214 Jordan Todman RPM AU/298 RC 4.00 10.00
215 Vincent Brown RPM AU/299 RC 6.00 15.00
216 Von Miller RPM AU/299 RC 12.00 30.00
217 Kyle Rudolph RPM AU/299 RC 6.00 15.00
218 Jonathan Baldwin RPM AU/299 RC 6.00 15.00
219 Jake Locker RPM AU/199 RC 30.00 80.00
220 Jamie Harper RPM AU/299 RC 6.00 15.00
221 Mark Ingram RPM AU/199 RC 25.00 60.00
222 Leonard Hankerson RPM AU/299 RC 6.00 15.00
223 Jerrel Jernigan RPM AU/299 RC 5.00 12.00
224 Delone Carter RPM AU/299 RC 8.00 20.00
225 Blaine Gabbert RPM AU/199 RC 20.00 50.00
226 Julio Jones RPM AU/299 RC 25.00 50.00
227 Marcell Dareus RPM AU/299 RC EXCH 6.00 15.00
228 Ryan Williams RPM AU/299 RC 8.00 20.00
229 Clyde Gates RPM AU/299 RC 5.00 12.00
230 Daniel Thomas RPM AU/299 RC 10.00 25.00
231 Greg Little RPM AU/299 RC 8.00 20.00
232 Colin Kaepernick RPM AU/299 RC 12.00 30.00
233 Alex Green RPM AU/299 RC 6.00 15.00
234 Randall Cobb RPM AU/299 RC 15.00 30.00
235 Bilal Powell RPM AU/299 RC 4.00 10.00
236 Kendall Hunter RPM AU/299 RC 8.00 20.00

2011 Absolute Memorabilia Retail

COMPLETE SET (200) 10.00 25.00
*1-100 VETS: .25X TO .6X BASIC CARDS
*101-200 ROOKIES: .4X TO 1X BASIC CARDS

2011 Absolute Memorabilia Rookie Premiere Materials Autographs AFC/NFC

*AFC/NFC/49: .5X TO 1.2X BASIC RPM AU RC
STATED PRINT RUN 49 SER.#'d SETS
201 Andy Dalton 50.00 100.00
202 Cam Newton 125.00 200.00

2011 Absolute Memorabilia Rookie Premiere Materials Autographs AFC/NFC Spectrum Prime

*AFC/NFC PRIME/25: .6X TO 1.5X RPM AU RC
STATED PRINT RUN 25 SER.#'d SETS
201 Andy Dalton 60.00 120.00
202 Cam Newton 150.00 250.00

2011 Absolute Memorabilia Rookie Premiere Materials Autographs NFL Spectrum Prime

*NFL PRIME/25: .6X TO 1.5X RPM AU RC
STATED PRINT RUN 25 SER.#'d SETS
201 Andy Dalton 60.00 120.00
202 Cam Newton 150.00 250.00

2011 Absolute Memorabilia Rookie Premiere Materials Autographs Oversize

*OVER.AU/18-25: .6X TO 1.5X RPM AU RC
STATED PRINT RUN 18-25
201 Andy Dalton/25 60.00 120.00
202 Cam Newton/25 250.00 400.00

2011 Absolute Memorabilia Spectrum Black

*1-100 VETS/25: 3X TO 8X BASIC CARDS
*101-200 ROOKIES/25: 1X TO 2.5X
STATED PRINT RUN 25 SER.#'d SETS

2011 Absolute Memorabilia Spectrum Blue

*1-100 VETS/100: 1.5X TO 4X BASIC CARDS
*101-200 ROOKIES/100: .5X TO 1.2X
RETAIL BLUE PRINT RUN 100 SER.#'d SETS

2011 Absolute Memorabilia Spectrum Gold

*1-100 VETS/25: 3X TO 8X BASIC CARDS
*101-200 ROOKIES/25: 1X TO 2.5X
STATED PRINT RUN 25 SER.#'d SETS

2011 Absolute Memorabilia Spectrum Red

*1-100 VETS: 1.2X TO 3X BASIC CARDS
*101-200 ROOKIES: .4X TO 1X BASIC CARDS
RANDOM INSERTS IN RETAIL PACKS

2011 Absolute Memorabilia Spectrum Silver

*1-100 VETS/50: 2X TO 5X BASIC CARDS
*101-200 ROOKIES/50: .6X TO 1.5X
STATED PRINT RUN 50 SER.#'d SETS

2011 Absolute Memorabilia Absolute Heroes

RANDOM INSERTS IN PACKS
*SPECTRUM/100: .8X TO 2X BASIC INSERTS
1 Calvin Johnson 1.25 3.00
2 Kellen Winslow Jr. 1.00 2.50
3 Joe Flacco 1.25 3.00
4 Bo Scaife .75 2.00
5 Antonio Gates 1.00 2.50
6 Reggie Wayne 1.00 2.50
7 Mark Sanchez 1.25 3.00
8 Jeremy Maclin 1.00 2.50
9 Danny Amendola 1.00 2.50
10 Aaron Rodgers 2.00 5.00
11 DeSean Jackson 1.00 2.50
12 Mike Wallace 1.25 3.00
13 Dallas Clark 1.00 2.50
14 Wes Welker 1.25 3.00
15 Santonio Holmes 1.00 2.50
16 Brandon Lloyd 1.00 2.50
17 Randy Moss 1.00 2.50
18 Visanthe Shiancoe 1.00 2.50
19 Peyton Manning 2.00 5.00
20 Chris Cooley 1.00 2.50
21 Tom Brady 2.00 5.00
22 Drew Brees 1.25 3.00
23 Percy Harvin 1.00 2.50
24 Matt Cassel 1.00 2.50
25 Hines Ward 1.00 2.50

2011 Absolute Memorabilia Absolute Heroes Materials Autographs

STATED PRINT RUN 5-25
5 Antonio Gates
10 Aaron Rodgers 175.00 300.00
11 DeSean Jackson 12.00 30.00
15 Santonio Holmes 12.00 30.00
20 Chris Cooley 12.00 30.00

2011 Absolute Memorabilia Absolute Heroes Materials Spectrum Prime

STATED PRINT RUN 5-50
1 Calvin Johnson/25 6.00 15.00
2 Kellen Winslow Jr./25 5.00 12.00
3 Joe Flacco/25 6.00 15.00
5 Antonio Gates/50 4.00 10.00
7 Mark Sanchez/25 6.00 15.00
8 Jeremy Maclin/25 5.00 12.00
10 Aaron Rodgers/25 12.00 30.00
11 DeSean Jackson/25 5.00 12.00
12 Mike Wallace/25 6.00 15.00
13 Dallas Clark/25 5.00 12.00
14 Wes Welker/25 6.00 15.00
15 Santonio Holmes/25 5.00 12.00
16 Brandon Lloyd/25 5.00 12.00
18 Visanthe Shiancoe/25 5.00 12.00
20 Chris Cooley/25 5.00 12.00
24 Matt Cassel/25 5.00 12.00
25 Hines Ward/25 5.00 12.00

2011 Absolute Memorabilia Absolute Patches Spectrum Prime

STATED PRINT RUN 5-25
2 Ahmad Bradshaw/25 20.00 50.00
4 Antonio Gates/25 20.00 50.00
17 James Harrison/25 25.00 60.00
22 Michael Turner/25 20.00 50.00
35 Terrell Suggs/25 20.00 50.00

2011 Absolute Memorabilia Canton Absolutes

*SPECTRUM/100: .8X TO 2X BASIC INSERTS
1 Drew Brees 1.25 3.00
2 Ed Reed 1.00 2.50
3 Adam Vinatieri .75 2.00
4 Troy Polamalu 1.25 3.00
5 Charles Woodson 1.25 3.00
6 Brian Urlacher 1.25 3.00
7 Ray Lewis 1.25 3.00
8 LaDainian Tomlinson 1.25 3.00
9 Tom Brady 2.00 5.00
10 Peyton Manning 2.00 5.00
11 Randy Moss 1.00 2.50
12 Terrell Owens 1.25 3.00
13 Tony Gonzalez 1.00 2.50
14 Champ Bailey 1.00 2.50
15 Brett Favre 2.50 6.00
16 Curtis Martin 1.25 3.00
17 Michael Strahan .75 2.00
18 Warren Sapp 1.00 2.50
19 Junior Seau 1.25 3.00
20 Andre Reed 1.00 2.50
21 Cris Carter 1.25 3.00
22 Jerome Bettis 1.25 3.00
23 Shannon Sharpe 1.00 2.50
24 Deion Sanders 1.25 3.00
25 Marshall Faulk 1.00 2.50

2011 Absolute Memorabilia Canton Absolutes Materials Autographs

STATED PRINT RUN 5-25
15 Brett Favre/25 150.00 250.00
18 Warren Sapp/25 20.00 50.00
19 Junior Seau/25 40.00 80.00
20 Andre Reed/25 15.00 40.00
22 Jerome Bettis/25 40.00 80.00
23 Shannon Sharpe/25
25 Marshall Faulk/25 30.00 60.00

2011 Absolute Memorabilia Canton Absolutes Materials Spectrum Prime

STATED PRINT RUN 5-25
2 Ed Reed/25 6.00 15.00
4 Troy Polamalu/25 12.00 30.00
7 Ray Lewis/25 6.00 15.00
13 Tony Gonzalez/25 5.00 12.00
16 Curtis Martin/25 6.00 15.00
18 Warren Sapp/25 5.00 12.00
19 Junior Seau/25 6.00 15.00
21 Cris Carter/25 6.00 15.00
22 Jerome Bettis/25 12.00 30.00
23 Shannon Sharpe/25 6.00 15.00
25 Marshall Faulk/25 6.00 15.00

2011 Absolute Memorabilia Gridiron Force

*SPECTRUM/100: .8X TO 2X BASIC INSERTS
1 Asante Samuel .75 2.00
2 Barrett Ruud .75 2.00
3 Brian Urlacher 1.25 3.00
4 Chad Greenway 1.00 2.50
5 Charles Woodson 1.25 3.00
6 Clay Matthews 1.25 3.00
7 Darrelle Revis 1.00 2.50
8 David Harris .75 2.00
9 DeAngelo Hall .75 2.00
10 DeMarcus Ware 1.00 2.50
11 Dhani Jones .75 2.00
12 Dwight Freeney 1.00 2.50
13 Ed Reed 1.00 2.50
14 James Harrison 1.25 3.00
15 James Laurinaitis .75 2.00
16 Jared Allen 1.00 2.50
17 Jerod Mayo .75 2.00
18 Jon Beason .75 2.00
19 London Fletcher .75 2.00
20 Nnamdi Asomugha 1.00 2.50
21 Patrick Willis 1.00 2.50
22 Stephen Tulloch .75 2.00
23 Tamba Hali .75 2.00
24 Terrell Suggs .75 2.00
25 Troy Polamalu 1.25 3.00

2011 Absolute Memorabilia Gridiron Force Materials Prime Jersey Number

STATED PRINT RUN 25 SER.#'d SETS
1 Asante Samuel 5.00 12.00
2 Barrett Ruud 5.00 12.00
3 Brian Urlacher 8.00 20.00
4 Chad Greenway 6.00 15.00
6 Clay Matthews 8.00 20.00
7 Darrelle Revis 6.00 15.00
8 David Harris 5.00 12.00
9 DeAngelo Hall 5.00 12.00
10 DeMarcus Ware 8.00 20.00
12 Dwight Freeney 6.00 15.00
13 Ed Reed 6.00 15.00
14 James Harrison 8.00 20.00
15 James Laurinaitis 5.00 12.00
16 Jared Allen 8.00 20.00
18 Jon Beason 5.00 12.00
19 London Fletcher 5.00 12.00
20 Nnamdi Asomugha 6.00 15.00
21 Patrick Willis 6.00 15.00
22 Stephen Tulloch 5.00 12.00
23 Tamba Hali 5.00 12.00
24 Terrell Suggs 5.00 12.00
25 Troy Polamalu 10.00 25.00

2011 Absolute Memorabilia Ground Hoggs

*SPECTRUM/100: .8X TO 2X BASIC INSERTS
1 Rashard Mendenhall 1.00 2.50
2 Ryan Grant 1.00 2.50
3 Jonathan Stewart 1.00 2.50
4 LeSean McCoy 1.00 2.50
5 Darren McFadden 1.00 2.50
6 Danny Woodhead 1.25 3.00
7 Knowshon Moreno 1.00 2.50
8 Jahvid Best 1.00 2.50
9 Ryan Mathews 1.00 2.50
10 Ahmad Bradshaw 1.00 2.50
11 Ray Rice 1.00 2.50
12 Tashard Choice .75 2.00
13 C.J. Spiller 1.00 2.50
14 Jamaal Charles 1.00 2.50
15 Michael Turner 1.00 2.50
16 Frank Gore 1.00 2.50
17 Ronnie Brown 1.00 2.50
18 Maurice Jones-Drew 1.00 2.50
19 Matt Forte 1.00 2.50
20 Adrian Peterson 1.50 4.00
21 Cedric Benson 1.00 2.50
22 Chris Johnson 1.00 2.50
23 LaDainian Tomlinson 1.25 3.00
24 Steven Jackson 1.00 2.50
25 Arian Foster 1.00 2.50

2011 Absolute Memorabilia Ground Hoggs Materials Prime Jersey Number

STATED PRINT RUN 1-25
3 Jonathan Stewart/25 6.00 15.00
4 LeSean McCoy/25 6.00 15.00
6 Danny Woodhead/25 12.00 30.00
7 Knowshon Moreno/25 6.00 15.00
8 Jahvid Best/25 6.00 15.00
9 Ryan Mathews/25 6.00 15.00
10 Ahmad Bradshaw/25 6.00 15.00
11 Ray Rice/25 6.00 15.00
12 Tashard Choice/25 5.00 12.00
13 C.J. Spiller/25 6.00 15.00
14 Jamaal Charles/25 6.00 15.00
15 Michael Turner/25 6.00 15.00
18 Maurice Jones-Drew/25 6.00 15.00
19 Matt Forte/25 6.00 15.00
21 Cedric Benson/25 6.00 15.00
22 Chris Johnson/25 6.00 15.00

2011 Absolute Memorabilia Marks of Fame

*SPECTRUM/100: .8X TO 2X BASIC INSERTS
1 Vernon Davis 1.00 2.50
2 Andre Johnson 1.00 2.50
3 Ben Roethlisberger 1.25 3.00
4 Carson Palmer 1.00 2.50
5 Matt Ryan 1.25 3.00
6 Lee Evans 1.00 2.50
7 Donald Driver 1.00 2.50
8 David Garrard 1.00 2.50
9 Miles Austin 1.00 2.50
10 Philip Rivers 1.25 3.00
11 Roddy White 1.00 2.50
12 Matt Schaub 1.00 2.50
13 Josh Freeman 1.25 3.00
14 Eli Manning 1.25 3.00
15 Chad Ochocinco 1.00 2.50
16 Jay Cutler 1.00 2.50
17 Anquan Boldin 1.00 2.50
18 Marques Colston 1.00 2.50
19 Donovan McNabb 1.25 3.00
20 Dwayne Bowe 1.00 2.50
21 Dez Bryant 1.25 3.00
22-Tim Tebow 2.50 6.00
23 Michael Vick 1.25 3.00
24 Greg Jennings 1.00 2.50
25 Sam Bradford 1.25 3.00

2011 Absolute Memorabilia Marks of Fame Materials Autographs

STATED PRINT RUN 10-25
1 Vernon Davis/25 12.00 30.00
2 Andre Johnson/25 EXCH 15.00 40.00
3 Ben Roethlisberger/25 40.00 80.00
8 David Garrard/25
9 Miles Austin/25 40.00 80.00
17 Anquan Boldin/25 12.00 30.00
25 Sam Bradford/25 40.00 80.00

2011 Absolute Memorabilia Marks of Fame Materials Spectrum Prime

1 Vernon Davis/25 5.00 12.00
3 Ben Roethlisberger/25 6.00 15.00
6 Lee Evans/25 5.00 12.00
9 Miles Austin/25 6.00 15.00
10 Philip Rivers/25 6.00 15.00
11 Roddy White/25 5.00 12.00
14 Eli Manning/25 6.00 15.00
16 Jay Cutler/25 5.00 12.00
18 Marques Colston/25 5.00 12.00
19 Donovan McNabb/25 6.00 15.00
20 Dwayne Bowe/25 5.00 12.00
22 Tim Tebow/25 12.00 30.00
23 Michael Vick/25 6.00 15.00
25 Sam Bradford/25 6.00 15.00

2011 Absolute Memorabilia NFL Icons

*SPECTRUM/100: .8X TO 2X BASIC INSERTS
1 Jerry Rice 2.50 6.00
2 Jack Lambert 1.50 4.00
3 Jim Plunkett 1.25 3.00
4 Frank Gifford 1.25 3.00
5 Lee Roy Selmon 1.00 2.50
6 Mark Duper 1.00 2.50
7 Ronnie Lott 1.25 3.00
8 Doug Flutie 1.25 3.00
9 Steve Largent 1.50 4.00
10 Thurman Thomas 1.50 4.00
11 Phil Simms 1.25 3.00
12 Fran Tarkenton 1.50 4.00
13 Daryle Lamonica 1.00 2.50
14 Joe Montana 3.00 8.00
15 Tony Dorsett 1.50 4.00
16 Rod Woodson 1.50 4.00
17 Eric Dickerson 1.25 3.00
18 Reggie White 1.50 4.00
19 Marcus Allen 1.50 4.00
20 Dick Butkus 2.00 5.00
21 Bart Starr 2.50 6.00
22 Franco Harris 1.50 4.00
23 Terry Bradshaw 2.00 5.00
24 Walter Payton 3.00 8.00
25 Derrick Thomas 1.25 3.00
26 Terrell Davis 1.50 4.00
27 Steve Young 2.00 5.00
28 Warren Moon 1.25 3.00
29 Howie Long 1.50 4.00
30 Michael Strahan 1.00 2.50

2011 Absolute Memorabilia NFL Icons Materials Autographs

STATED PRINT RUN 5-25
1 Jerry Rice/25 100.00 175.00
2 Jack Lambert/25 30.00 60.00
3 Jim Plunkett/25 15.00 40.00
5 Lee Roy Selmon/25
6 Mark Duper/25 15.00 40.00
7 Ronnie Lott/25 30.00 60.00
8 Doug Flutie/25 15.00 40.00
9 Steve Largent/25 20.00 50.00
10 Thurman Thomas/25 20.00 40.00
11 Phil Simms/25 20.00 50.00
12 Fran Tarkenton/25 20.00 50.00
13 Daryle Lamonica/25 12.00 30.00
16 Rod Woodson/25 40.00 80.00
19 Marcus Allen/25 20.00 50.00
20 Dick Butkus/25 40.00 80.00
21 Bart Starr/25 40.00 100.00
22 Franco Harris/25 30.00 60.00
23 Terry Bradshaw/25 EXCH 50.00 100.00
27 Steve Young/25 40.00 80.00
28 Warren Moon/25 15.00 40.00
29 Howie Long/25 40.00 80.00

2011 Absolute Memorabilia NFL Icons Materials Spectrum Prime

STATED PRINT RUN 5-25
1 Jerry Rice/25 15.00 40.00
2 Jack Lambert/25 10.00 25.00
3 Jim Plunkett/25 8.00 20.00
5 Lee Roy Selmon/25 6.00 15.00
6 Mark Duper/25 6.00 15.00
8 Doug Flutie/25 8.00 20.00
9 Steve Largent/25 10.00 25.00
10 Thurman Thomas/25 10.00 25.00
11 Phil Simms/25 8.00 20.00
12 Fran Tarkenton/25 10.00 25.00
15 Tony Dorsett/25 10.00 25.00
16 Rod Woodson/25 10.00 25.00
20 Dick Butkus/25 12.00 30.00
21 Bart Starr/25 15.00 40.00
22 Franco Harris/25 10.00 25.00
23 Terry Bradshaw/25 12.00 30.00
24 Walter Payton/25 25.00 60.00
25 Derrick Thomas/25 125.00 200.00
26 Terrell Davis/25 10.00 25.00
27 Steve Young/25 12.00 30.00
28 Warren Moon/25 8.00 20.00

2011 Absolute Memorabilia Rookie Jersey Collection

1 A.J. Green 4.00 10.00
2 Alex Green 2.50 6.00
3 Andy Dalton 5.00 12.00
4 Austin Pettis 2.00 5.00
5 Bilal Powell 2.50 6.00
6 Blaine Gabbert 4.00 10.00
7 Cam Newton 12.00 30.00
8 Christian Ponder 5.00 12.00
9 Clyde Gates 2.00 5.00
10 Colin Kaepernick 3.00 8.00
11 Daniel Thomas 2.50 6.00
12 Delone Carter 2.00 5.00
13 DeMarco Murray 5.00 12.00
14 Greg Little 2.50 6.00
15 Jake Locker 6.00 15.00
16 Jamie Harper 2.50 6.00
17 Jerrel Jernigan 2.00 5.00
18 Jonathan Baldwin 2.50 6.00
19 Jordan Todman 1.50 4.00
20 Julio Jones 4.00 10.00
21 Kendall Hunter 2.50 6.00
22 Kyle Rudolph 2.50 6.00
23 Leonard Hankerson 2.50 6.00
24 Marcell Dareus 2.50 6.00
25 Mark Ingram 5.00 12.00
26 Mikel Leshoure 2.50 6.00
27 Randall Cobb 3.00 8.00
28 Ryan Mallett 5.00 12.00
29 Ryan Williams 3.00 8.00
30 Shane Vereen 2.50 6.00
31 Stevan Ridley 2.50 6.00
32 Taiwan Jones 2.50 6.00
33 Titus Young 3.00 8.00
34 Torrey Smith 3.00 8.00
35 Vincent Brown 2.50 6.00
36 Von Miller 3.00 8.00

2011 Absolute Memorabilia Rookie Premiere Materials AFC/NFC

AFC/NFC PRINT RUN 99 SER.#'d SETS
*AFC/NFC SPECT.PRIME/25: .6X TO 1.5X
*NFL SPECTRUM PRIME/50: .5X TO 1.2X
*OVERSIZE JSY NUMBER/50: .6X TO 1.5X
*OVER.JSY NUMBER PRIME/10: 1.2X TO 3X
*OVER.SPECTRUM PRIME/25: .8X TO 2X
201 Andy Dalton 8.00 20.00
202 Cam Newton 15.00 40.00
203 A.J. Green 6.00 15.00
204 Taiwan Jones 3.00 8.00
205 DeMarco Murray 6.00 15.00
206 Torrey Smith 4.00 10.00
207 Ryan Mallett 6.00 15.00
208 Stevan Ridley 3.00 8.00
209 Austin Pettis 2.50 6.00
210 Shane Vereen 3.00 8.00
211 Titus Young 4.00 10.00
212 Mikel Leshoure 3.00 8.00
213 Christian Ponder 6.00 15.00
214 Jordan Todman 2.00 5.00
215 Vincent Brown 3.00 8.00
216 Von Miller 4.00 10.00
217 Kyle Rudolph 3.00 8.00
218 Jonathan Baldwin 3.00 8.00
219 Jake Locker 8.00 20.00
220 Jamie Harper 3.00 8.00
221 Mark Ingram 6.00 15.00
222 Leonard Hankerson 3.00 8.00
223 Jerrel Jernigan 2.50 6.00
224 Delone Carter 2.50 6.00
225 Blaine Gabbert 5.00 12.00
226 Julio Jones 6.00 15.00
227 Marcell Dareus 3.00 8.00
228 Ryan Williams 4.00 10.00
229 Clyde Gates 2.50 6.00
230 Daniel Thomas 3.00 8.00
231 Greg Little 3.00 8.00
232 Colin Kaepernick 4.00 10.00
233 Alex Green 3.00 8.00
234 Randall Cobb 4.00 10.00
235 Bilal Powell 2.00 5.00
236 Kendall Hunter 3.00 8.00

2011 Absolute Memorabilia Spectrum Gold Autographs

VETERAN STATED PRINT RUN 5-50
ROOKIE STATED PRINT RUN 99-299
*PLAT.ROOK/25: .8X TO 2X GLD AU/99-299
EXCH EXPIRATION: 4/26/2013

6 Roddy White/25	8.00	20.00
9 Joe Flacco/25	20.00	40.00
11 Ray Rice/25 EXCH		
12 C.J. Spiller/50	6.00	15.00
15 DeAngelo Williams/25	8.00	20.00
16 Jonathan Stewart/25	8.00	20.00
21 Matt Forte/25	10.00	25.00
26 Colt McCoy/50	10.00	25.00
27 Peyton Hillis/50	16.00	30.00
29 Dez Bryant/25	20.00	40.00
30 Jason Witten/25	15.00	30.00
32 Brandon Lloyd/25	8.00	20.00
39 Greg Jennings/50	10.00	25.00
42 Arian Foster/50	20.00	40.00
43 Matt Schaub/25		
45 Peyton Manning/18	60.00	120.00
46 Reggie Wayne/25	8.00	20.00
47 David Garrard/25	8.00	20.00
49 Dwayne Bowe/25 EXCH		
50 Jamaal Charles/25	8.00	20.00
51 Matt Cassel/25	8.00	20.00
55 Percy Harvin/25		
56 Sidney Rice/50	6.00	15.00
57 BenJarvus Green-Ellis/50	25.00	50.00
61 Marques Colston/25	10.00	25.00
63 Ahmad Bradshaw/25 EXCH	8.00	20.00
65 Eli Manning/25	30.00	60.00
66 Hakeem Nicks/25		
70 Darren McFadden/25		
73 Jeremy Maclin/25 EXCH	8.00	20.00
74 LeSean McCoy/25	8.00	20.00
75 Michael Vick/15	50.00	100.00
79 Rashard Mendenhall/25 EXCH		
81 Antonio Gates/25	10.00	25.00
83 Ryan Mathews/25 EXCH	10.00	25.00
86 Patrick Willis/25	10.00	25.00
90 James Laurinaitis/50	5.00	12.00
93 Josh Freeman/25	10.00	25.00
97 Kenny Britt/25 EXCH		
99 Ryan Torain/50	6.00	15.00
101 Aldrick Robinson/299	5.00	12.00
102 Cecil Shorts/299	4.00	10.00
105 Denarius Moore/299	10.00	25.00
106 Dwayne Harris/299	5.00	12.00
107 Greg Salas/299	5.00	12.00
108 Jeremy Kerley/299	5.00	12.00
109 Kealoha Pilares/299	8.00	20.00
110 Kris Durham/299	4.00	10.00
111 Niles Paul/299	5.00	12.00
112 Ronald Johnson/299	4.00	10.00
113 Ryan Whalen/299	4.00	10.00
114 Scotty McKnight/299	4.00	10.00
115 Stephen Burton/299	4.00	10.00
116 Tandon Doss/299	4.00	10.00
117 D.J. Williams/299	5.00	12.00
119 Jordan Cameron/299	4.00	10.00
120 Julius Thomas/299	4.00	10.00
121 Lance Kendricks/299	4.00	10.00
123 Luke Stocker/299	4.00	10.00
125 Robert Housler/299	4.00	10.00
127 Allen Bradford/299	4.00	10.00
128 Anthony Allen/299	3.00	8.00
130 Da'Rel Scott/299	4.00	10.00
131 Dion Lewis/299	6.00	12.00
132 Evan Royster/299	5.00	12.00
133 Jacquizz Rodgers/299	5.00	12.00
135 Johnny White/299	4.00	10.00
136 Roy Helu/299	10.00	25.00
137 Greg McElroy/299	5.00	12.00
138 Nathan Enderle/299 EXCH	6.00	15.00
139 Ricky Stanzi/299	6.00	15.00
140 T.J. Yates/299	10.00	25.00
141 Terrelle Pryor/299	20.00	50.00
142 Tyrod Taylor/299	5.00	12.00
143 Aaron Williams/99	5.00	12.00
144 Brandon Harris/299	3.00	8.00
145 Jimmy Smith/299	5.00	12.00
148 Prince Amukamara/299	6.00	15.00
150 Adrian Clayborn/299	6.00	15.00
151 Aldon Smith/299	12.00	30.00
153 Cameron Heyward/299	5.00	12.00
154 Cameron Jordan/299	4.00	10.00
155 Da'Quan Bowers/299	5.00	12.00
156 J.J. Watt/299	6.00	15.00
160 Akeem Ayers/299	4.00	10.00
163 Ryan Kerrigan/299	6.00	15.00
164 Corey Liuget/299	3.00	8.00
168 Phil Taylor/299	4.00	10.00
169 Stephen Paea/299	5.00	12.00
171 Rahim Moore/299	4.00	10.00
178 Anthony Castonzo/299	3.00	8.00
183 Tyron Smith/299	8.00	20.00
184 Ahmad Black/299	4.00	10.00
185 Greg Jones/299	4.00	10.00
186 Marcus Cannon/299	3.00	8.00
188 Owen Marecic/299 EXCH	5.00	12.00
191 Quinton Carter/299	3.00	8.00
192 Stanley Havili/299	3.00	8.00
194 Justin Houston/299	5.00	12.00
196 Martez Wilson/299	5.00	12.00
199 Tyler Sash/299	5.00	12.00

2011 Absolute Memorabilia Star Gazing

*SPECTRUM/50: 1X TO 2.5X BASIC INSERTS

1 Randall Cobb	1.00	2.50
2 Andy Dalton	2.00	5.00
3 Marcell Dareus	.75	2.00
4 Jamie Harper	.75	2.00
5 Delone Carter	.60	1.50
6 Blaine Gabbert	1.25	3.00
7 Vincent Brown	.75	2.00
8 Kyle Rudolph	.75	2.00
9 Shane Vereen	.75	2.00
10 Leonard Hankerson	.75	2.00
11 Austin Pettis	.60	1.50
12 Cam Newton	4.00	10.00
13 Clyde Gates	.60	1.50
14 A.J. Green	1.50	4.00
15 Alex Green	.75	2.00
16 Daniel Thomas	.75	2.00
17 Mikel Leshoure	.75	2.00
18 Stevan Ridley	.75	2.00
19 Von Miller	1.00	2.50
20 Greg Little	.75	2.00
21 Julio Jones	1.50	4.00
22 Taiwan Jones	.75	2.00
23 Jonathan Baldwin	.75	2.00
24 Ryan Williams	1.00	2.50
25 Ryan Mallett	1.50	4.00
26 Mark Ingram	1.50	4.00
27 Jerrel Jernigan	.60	1.50
28 Jake Locker	2.00	5.00
29 Jordan Todman	.50	1.25
30 Christian Ponder	1.50	4.00
31 Bilal Powell	.50	1.25
32 Colin Kaepernick	1.00	2.50
33 Torrey Smith	1.00	2.50
34 Kendall Hunter	.75	2.00
35 DeMarco Murray	1.50	4.00
36 Titus Young	1.00	2.50

2011 Absolute Memorabilia Star Gazing Materials

*OVER.JSY NUM/10: 1X TO 2.5X BSC JSY
*OVER.JSY NUM PRIME/25: .8X TO 2X
*OVER.SPECTRUM PRIME/15: 1.2X TO 3X
*PRIME/50: .6X TO 1.5X BASIC JSY

1 Randall Cobb	3.00	8.00
2 Andy Dalton	5.00	12.00
3 Marcell Dareus	2.50	6.00
4 Jamie Harper	2.50	6.00
5 Delone Carter	2.00	5.00
6 Blaine Gabbert	4.00	10.00
7 Vincent Brown	2.50	6.00
8 Kyle Rudolph	2.50	6.00
9 Shane Vereen	2.50	6.00
10 Leonard Hankerson	2.50	6.00
11 Austin Pettis	2.00	5.00
12 Cam Newton	10.00	25.00
13 Clyde Gates	2.00	5.00
14 A.J. Green	4.00	10.00
15 Alex Green	2.50	6.00
16 Daniel Thomas	2.50	6.00
17 Mikel Leshoure	2.50	6.00
18 Stevan Ridley	2.50	6.00
19 Von Miller	3.00	8.00
20 Greg Little	2.50	6.00
21 Julio Jones	5.00	12.00
22 Taiwan Jones	2.50	6.00
23 Jonathan Baldwin	2.50	6.00
24 Ryan Williams	3.00	8.00
25 Ryan Mallett	5.00	12.00
26 Mark Ingram	5.00	12.00
27 Jerrel Jernigan	2.00	5.00
28 Jake Locker	5.00	12.00
29 Jordan Todman	1.50	4.00
30 Christian Ponder	5.00	12.00
31 Bilal Powell	1.50	4.00
32 Colin Kaepernick	3.00	8.00
33 Torrey Smith	3.00	8.00
34 Kendall Hunter	2.50	6.00
35 DeMarco Murray	5.00	12.00
36 Titus Young	3.00	8.00

2011 Absolute Memorabilia Star Gazing Materials Autographs

STATED PRINT RUN 49 SER.#'d SETS
*PRIME AU/25: .5X TO 1.2X JSY AU/49
EXCH EXPIRATION: 4/26/2013

1 Randall Cobb	10.00	25.00
2 Andy Dalton	30.00	60.00
3 Marcell Dareus	8.00	20.00
4 Jamie Harper	8.00	20.00
5 Delone Carter	6.00	15.00
6 Blaine Gabbert	12.00	30.00
7 Vincent Brown	8.00	20.00
8 Kyle Rudolph	8.00	20.00
9 Shane Vereen	8.00	20.00
10 Leonard Hankerson	8.00	20.00
11 Austin Pettis	6.00	15.00
12 Cam Newton	90.00	150.00
13 Clyde Gates	6.00	15.00
14 A.J. Green	25.00	50.00
15 Alex Green	8.00	20.00
16 Daniel Thomas	8.00	20.00
17 Mikel Leshoure	8.00	20.00
18 Stevan Ridley	8.00	20.00
19 Von Miller	10.00	25.00
20 Greg Little	8.00	20.00
21 Julio Jones	20.00	50.00
22 Taiwan Jones	8.00	20.00
23 Jonathan Baldwin	8.00	20.00
24 Ryan Williams	10.00	25.00
25 Ryan Mallett	15.00	40.00
26 Mark Ingram	15.00	40.00
27 Jerrel Jernigan	6.00	15.00
28 Jake Locker	30.00	60.00
29 Jordan Todman	5.00	12.00
30 Christian Ponder	25.00	60.00
31 Bilal Powell	5.00	12.00
32 Colin Kaepernick	10.00	25.00
33 Torrey Smith	10.00	25.00
34 Kendall Hunter	8.00	20.00
35 DeMarco Murray	30.00	60.00
36 Titus Young	10.00	25.00

2011 Absolute Memorabilia Team Quads Materials Die Cut

STATED PRINT RUN 25-50
*PRIME/20-25: .6X TO 1.5X BASIC QUAD/50

1 Devin Hester/50	10.00	25.00
Jay Cutler		
Johnny Knox		
Matt Forte		
2 Felix Jones/50	10.00	25.00
Jason Witten		
Tashard Choice		
Miles Austin		
3 Dallas Clark/50	15.00	40.00
Peyton Manning		
Pierre Garcon		
Reggie Wayne		
4 Ahmad Bradshaw/25	12.00	30.00
Brandon Jacobs		
Eli Manning		
Steve Smith		
5 Antonio Gates/50	10.00	25.00
Malcom Floyd		
Philip Rivers		
Vincent Jackson		
6 Matt Ryan/50	10.00	25.00
Tony Gonzalez		
Roddy White		
Michael Turner		
7 Anquan Boldin/50	12.00	30.00
Joe Flacco		
Ray Lewis		
Ray Rice		
8 C.J. Spiller/50	12.00	30.00
Fred Jackson		
Lee Evans		
Ryan Fitzpatrick		
9 Andre Johnson/25	10.00	25.00
Arian Foster		
Matt Schaub		
Owen Daniels		
10 Brandon Marshall/50	8.00	20.00
Chad Henne		
Ricky Williams		
Brian Hartline		

2011 Absolute Memorabilia Team Tandems Materials

STATED PRINT RUN 50 SER.#'d SETS
*PRIME/25 .6X TO 1.5X BASIC DUAL/50

1 Ed Reed/50	6.00	15.00
Ray Lewis		
2 C.J. Spiller/50	8.00	20.00
Fred Jackson		
3 Felix Jones/50	6.00	15.00
Miles Austin		
4 Brandon Lloyd/50	5.00	12.00
Eddie Royal		
5 Calvin Johnson/50	6.00	15.00
Ndamukong Suh		
6 Dallas Clark/50	5.00	12.00
Reggie Wayne		
7 Dwayne Bowe/50	5.00	12.00
Jamaal Charles		
8 Tom Brady/50	15.00	40.00
Wes Welker		
9 Devery Henderson/50	5.00	12.00
Marques Colston		
10 Sam Bradford/50	6.00	15.00
Steven Jackson		
11 Jimmy Clausen/50	5.00	12.00
Steve Smith		
12 Brian Urlacher/50	6.00	15.00
Jay Cutler		
13 Carson Palmer/50	5.00	12.00
Jordan Shipley		
14 Dez Bryant/50	6.00	15.00
Tony Romo		
15 Tim Tebow/50	12.00	30.00
Knowshon Moreno		
16 Matthew Stafford/50	6.00	15.00
Jahvid Best		
17 A.J. Hawk/50	10.00	25.00
Clay Matthews		
18 David Garrard/50	5.00	12.00
Maurice Jones-Drew		
19 Bernard Berrian/50	5.00	12.00
Visanthe Shiancoe		
20 Drew Brees/50	6.00	15.00
Pierre Thomas		
21 Shonn Greene/50	5.00	12.00
Dustin Keller		
22 Darren McFadden/50	5.00	12.00
Jason Campbell		
23 LeSean McCoy/50	5.00	12.00
Brent Celek		
24 Hines Ward/50	10.00	25.00
Mike Wallace		
25 Ryan Mathews/50	5.00	12.00
Malcom Floyd		
26 DeAngelo Hall/50	5.00	12.00
LaRon Landry		
27 Ahmad Bradshaw/50	5.00	12.00
Brandon Jacobs		
28 Antonio Gates/50	6.00	15.00
Philip Rivers		
29 Andre Johnson/25	5.00	12.00
Matt Schaub		
30 Josh Cribbs/50	5.00	12.00
Peyton Hillis		

2011 Absolute Memorabilia Team Trios Materials NFL

STATED PRINT RUN 25-75
*PRIME/25: .8X TO 2X BASIC TRIPLE/75

1 Michael Turner	5.00	12.00
Roddy White		
Tony Gonzalez		
2 DeAngelo Williams	5.00	12.00
Steve Smith		
Jonathan Stewart		
3 Cedric Benson	5.00	12.00
Carson Palmer		
Jordan Shipley		
4 Dwayne Bowe	5.00	12.00
Matt Cassel		
Jamaal Charles		
5 Adrian Peterson	10.00	25.00
Percy Harvin		
Visanthe Shiancoe		
7 DeSean Jackson	10.00	25.00
Michael Vick		
Jeremy Maclin		
8 Frank Gore	6.00	15.00
Michael Crabtree		
Vernon Davis		
9 Chris Cooley	6.00	15.00
LaRon Landry		
Santana Moss		
10 Earnest Graham	6.00	15.00
Josh Freeman		
Kellen Winslow Jr.		

2011 Absolute Memorabilia Tools of the Trade Material Red

STATED PRINT RUN 25-250

1 Bernard Berrian/99	3.00	8.00
2 Braylon Edwards/250	3.00	8.00
3 Jabar Gaffney/250	2.50	6.00
4 Fred Jackson/199	6.00	15.00
5 Vincent Jackson/250	3.00	8.00
6 Peyton Manning/25	12.00	30.00
7 Willis McGahee/250	2.50	6.00
8 Jordan Shipley/250	3.00	8.00
9 Darren Sproles/250	3.00	8.00
10 Chad Henne/250	3.00	8.00
11 Sam Hurd/250	2.50	6.00
12 Santana Moss/250	3.00	8.00
13 Cedric Benson/250	3.00	8.00
14 Jason Campbell/250	3.00	8.00
15 Michael Crabtree/250	3.00	8.00
16 Pierre Garcon/250	3.00	8.00
17 Lee Evans/250	3.00	8.00
20 Devery Henderson/250	2.50	6.00
21 Cortland Finnegan/250	3.00	8.00
22 Reggie Bush/250	3.00	8.00
23 Heath Miller/250	3.00	8.00
24 Eddie Royal/250	2.50	6.00
25 Beanie Wells/99	4.00	10.00
26 Felix Jones/250	3.00	8.00
27 Kyle Orton/250	3.00	8.00
28 Malcom Floyd/250	3.00	8.00
30 Marion Barber/250	3.00	8.00
31 Shonn Greene/250	3.00	8.00
32 Devin Hester/250	4.00	10.00
33 Brandon Jacobs/49	4.00	10.00
34 Dustin Keller/199	3.00	8.00
35 Sidney Rice/250	3.00	8.00
36 Johnny Knox/250	3.00	8.00
37 Brent Celek/250	3.00	8.00
38 Todd Heap/250	2.50	6.00
39 Tony Romo/250	4.00	10.00
40 Nate Washington/250	2.50	6.00
41 Matt Hasselbeck/250	3.00	8.00
42 Matthew Stafford/250	4.00	10.00
43 Larry Fitzgerald/250	3.00	8.00
44 Brian Urlacher/250	4.00	10.00
45 Kevin Boss/250	3.00	8.00
46 Kevin Kolb/250	3.00	8.00
47 Cadillac Williams/250	2.50	6.00
48 DeAngelo Williams/99	4.00	10.00
49 Roy Williams WR/250	3.00	8.00
50 Ryan Fitzpatrick/250	3.00	8.00

2011 Absolute Memorabilia Tools of the Trade Material Black Spectrum

STATED PRINT RUN 5-25

5 Vincent Jackson/25	6.00	15.00
7 Willis McGahee/25	5.00	12.00
8 Jordan Shipley/25	6.00	15.00
9 Darren Sproles/25	6.00	15.00
10 Chad Henne/25	6.00	15.00
11 Sam Hurd/25	5.00	12.00
12 Santana Moss/25	6.00	15.00
13 Cedric Benson/25	6.00	15.00
14 Jason Campbell/25	6.00	15.00
16 Pierre Garcon/25	6.00	15.00
17 Lee Evans/25	6.00	15.00
18 Greg Olsen/25	5.00	12.00
19 Hakeem Nicks/25	6.00	15.00
21 Cortland Finnegan/50	6.00	15.00
23 Heath Miller/25	6.00	15.00
24 Eddie Royal/25	5.00	12.00
26 Felix Jones/25	6.00	15.00
27 Kyle Orton/25	6.00	15.00
28 Malcom Floyd/25	6.00	15.00
29 Steve Smith/25	6.00	15.00
30 Marion Barber/25	6.00	15.00
32 Devin Hester/25	8.00	20.00
36 Johnny Knox/25	6.00	15.00
38 Todd Heap/25	5.00	12.00
39 Tony Romo/25	8.00	20.00
40 Nate Washington/25	5.00	12.00
41 Matt Hasselbeck/25	6.00	15.00
42 Matthew Stafford/25	8.00	20.00
43 Larry Fitzgerald/25	6.00	15.00
44 Brian Urlacher/25	8.00	20.00
45 Kevin Boss/25	6.00	15.00
49 Roy Williams WR/25	6.00	15.00
50 Ryan Fitzpatrick/25	6.00	15.00

2011 Absolute Memorabilia Tools of the Trade Double Material Black Spectrum

STATED PRINT RUN 1-25

21 Cortland Finnegan/25	6.00	15.00
30 Marion Barber/25	6.00	15.00
40 Nate Washington/25	5.00	12.00

2011 Absolute Memorabilia Tools of the Trade Triple Material Black Spectrum

STATED PRINT RUN 1-25

2011 Absolute Memorabilia Tools of the Trade Material Autographs Black Spectrum

STATED PRINT RUN 1-25

2 Braylon Edwards/25	12.00	30.00
5 Vincent Jackson/25	12.00	30.00

2011 Absolute Memorabilia War Room

*WAR ROOM: .4X TO 1X STAR GAZING
*WR SPECTRUM/50: 1X TO 2.5X STAR GAZING

2011 Absolute Memorabilia War Room Materials

*WAR ROOM: .4X TO 1X STAR GAZING JSY
*JSY NUMBER/10: 1X TO 2.5X BASIC JSY
*JSY NUMBER PRIME/10: 1.2X TO 3X JSY
*PRIME/50: .6X TO 1.5X STAR GAZING JSY

2011 Absolute Memorabilia War Room Materials Autographs

*WAR ROOM/49: .4X TO 1X STAR GAZING AU/49
WAR ROOM PRINT RUN 49 SER.#'d SETS
*PRIME/25: .5X TO 1.2X JSY AU/49

1989 Action Packed Prototypes

These two prototype cards were issued before the 1989 Test issue was released to show the style of Action Packed cards. The cards were folded by hand when they were made, which is why there is no seam on the back of the card as is typical of other Action Packed cards. The standard-size cards feature on the fronts embossed color photos bordered in gold. The horizontally oriented backs have a mugshot, biography, statistics, and an "Action Note" in the form of a caption to the action shot on the front. The primary stylistic difference between these prototype cards and the test set issued later that year is the location of the card number.

72 Freeman McNeil	8.00	20.00
101 Phil Simms	12.00	30.00

1989 Action Packed Test

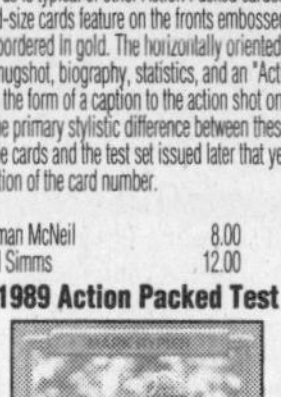

The 1989 Action Packed Football Test set contains 30 standard-size cards. The cards have rounded corners and gold borders. The fronts have "raised" color action shots, and the horizontally-oriented backs feature mug shots and complete stats. The set, which includes ten players each from the Chicago Bears, New York Giants, and Washington Redskins, was packaged in six-card poly packs. These cards were not packaged very well; many cards come creased or bent out of packs, and a typical box will yield quite a few duplicates. Although this is considered to be a limited test issue, the test apparently was successful as there were reports that more than 4300 cases were produced of these cards. Factory sets packaged in small dull-gold colored boxes were also available on a limited basis. The cards are copyrighted by Hi-Pro Marketing of Northbrook, Illinois and the packs are labeled "Action Packed." On the card back of number 6 Dan Hampton it lists his uniform number as 95 which is actually Richard Dent's number; Hampton wears 99 for the Bears. The cards are numbered in alphabetical order within teams, Chicago Bears (1-10), New York Giants (11-20), and Washington Redskins (21-30). Since this set was a test issue, the cards of Dave Meggett and Mark Rypien are not considered true Rookie Cards.

COMPLETE SET (30)	6.00	15.00
1 Neal Anderson	.25	.60
2 Trace Armstrong	.15	.40
3 Kevin Butler	.15	.40
4 Richard Dent	.25	.60
5 Dennis Gentry	.15	.40
6 Dan Hampton UER	.25	.60
7 Jay Hilgenberg	.15	.40
8 Thomas Sanders	.15	.40
9 Mike Singletary	.30	.75
10 Mike Tomczak	.25	.60
11 Raul Allegre	.15	.40
12 Ottis Anderson	.25	.60
13 Mark Bavaro	.25	.60
14 Terry Kinard	.15	.40
15 Lionel Manuel	.15	.40
16 Leonard Marshall	.25	.60
17 Dave Meggett	.30	.75
18 Joe Morris	.25	.60
19 Phil Simms	.60	1.50
20 Lawrence Taylor	.30	.75
21 Kelvin Bryant	.15	.40
22 Darrell Green	.25	.60
23 Dexter Manley	.15	.40
24 Charles Mann	.15	.40
25 Wilber Marshall	.15	.40
26 Art Monk	.30	.75
27 Jamie Morris	.15	.40
28 Tracy Rocker	.15	.40
29 Mark Rypien UER	.25	.60
30 Ricky Sanders	.25	.60

1990 Action Packed

This 280-card standard-size set was issued in two skip-numbered series. The cards are the same style as previous year's "test" issue. The set is organized numerically in alphabetical order within team and teams themselves are in alphabetical order by city. For cards numbered 3, 26, 193 and 222, the action note on the card back does not correspond with the picture on the front. Later in the year Action Packed released these cards in the form of pre-packed ten-card complete team sets. The only Rookie Card of any note is Ken Harvey. A special Braille-backed card of Jim Plunkett was released in both 281-card factory sets and as a random insert in wax packs.

COMPLETE SET (280)	8.00	20.00
COMP.FACT.SET (281)	10.00	25.00
1 Aundray Bruce UER	.02	.10
(Andre on back)		
2 Scott Case	.02	.10
3 Tony Casillas	.02	.10
4 Shawn Collins	.02	.10
5 Marcus Cotton	.02	.10
6 Bill Fralic	.02	.10
7 Tim Green RC	.02	.10
8 Chris Miller	.20	.50
9 Deion Sanders	.50	1.25
10 John Settle	.02	.10
11 Cornelius Bennett	.08	.25
12 Shane Conlan	.02	.10
13 Kent Hull	.02	.10
14 Jim Kelly	.20	.50
15 Mark Kelso	.02	.10
16 Scott Norwood	.02	.10
17 Andre Reed	.20	.50
18 Fred Smerlas	.02	.10
19 Bruce Smith	.20	.50
20 Thurman Thomas	.20	.50
21 Neal Anderson UER	.08	.25
(Action note begins 'Neil ...')		
22 Kevin Butler	.02	.10
23 Richard Dent	.08	.25
24 Dennis Gentry	.02	.10
25 Dan Hampton	.08	.25
26 Jay Hilgenberg	.02	.10
27 Steve McMichael	.08	.25
28 Brad Muster	.02	.10
29 Mike Singletary	.08	.25
30 Mike Tomczak	.08	.25
31 James Brooks	.08	.25
32 Rickey Dixon RC	.02	.10
33 Boomer Esiason	.08	.25
34 David Fulcher	.02	.10
35 Rodney Holman	.02	.10
36 Tim Krumrie	.02	.10
37 Tim McGee	.02	.10
38 Anthony Munoz UER	.08	.25
(Action note says he's blocking Howie Long, but jersey begins with a nine)		
39 Reggie Williams	.02	.10
40 Ickey Woods	.02	.10
41 Thane Gash RC	.02	.10
42 Mike Johnson	.02	.10
43 Bernie Kosar	.08	.25
44 Reggie Langhorne	.02	.10
45 Clay Matthews	.08	.25
46 Eric Metcalf	.20	.50
47 Frank Minnifield	.02	.10
48 Ozzie Newsome	.08	.25
49 Webster Slaughter	.08	.25
50 Felix Wright	.02	.10
51 Troy Aikman	.75	2.00
52 James Dixon	.02	.10
53 Michael Irvin	.20	.50
54 Jim Jeffcoat	.02	.10
55 Ed Too Tall Jones	.08	.25
56 Eugene Lockhart	.02	.10
57 Danny Noonan	.02	.10
58 Paul Palmer	.02	.10
59 Everson Walls	.02	.10
60 Steve Walsh	.08	.25
61 Steve Atwater	.02	.10
62 Tyrone Braxton	.02	.10
63 John Elway	1.25	3.00
64 Bobby Humphrey	.02	.10
65 Mark Jackson	.02	.10
66 Vance Johnson	.02	.10
67 Greg Kragen	.02	.10
68 Karl Mecklenburg	.02	.10
69 Dennis Smith	.08	.25
70 David Treadwell	.02	.10
71 Jim Arnold	.02	.10
72 Jerry Ball	.02	.10
73 Bennie Blades	.02	.10
74 Mel Gray	.08	.25
75 Richard Johnson	.02	.10
76 Eddie Murray	.02	.10
77 Rodney Peete UER	.08	.25
(On back, squeaker misspelled as squeeker)		
78 Barry Sanders	1.25	3.00
79 Chris Spielman	.20	.50
80 Walter Stanley	.02	.10
81 Dave Brown DB	.02	.10
82 Brent Fullwood	.02	.10
83 Tim Harris	.02	.10
84 Johnny Holland	.02	.10
85 Don Majkowski	.02	.10
86 Tony Mandarich	.02	.10
87 Mark Murphy	.02	.10
88 Brian Noble UER	.02	.10
(Fumble recovery stats show 9 instead of 7)		
89 Ken Ruettgers	.02	.10
90 Sterling Sharpe UER	.20	.50
(Born Glenville, Ga. should be Chicago)		
91 Ray Childress	.02	.10
92 Ernest Givins	.08	.25
93 Alonzo Highsmith	.02	.10
94 Drew Hill	.02	.10
95 Bruce Matthews	.08	.25
96 Bubba McDowell	.02	.10
97 Warren Moon	.20	.50
98 Mike Munchak	.08	.25
99 Allen Pinkett	.02	.10
100 Mike Rozier	.02	.10
101 Albert Bentley	.02	.10
102 Duane Bickett	.02	.10
103 Bill Brooks	.02	.10
104 Chris Chandler	.20	.50
105 Ray Donaldson	.02	.10
106 Chris Hinton	.02	.10
107 Andre Rison	.20	.50
108 Keith Taylor	.02	.10
109 Clarence Verdin	.02	.10
110 Fredd Young	.02	.10
111 Deron Cherry	.02	.10
112 Steve DeBerg	.02	.10
113 Dino Hackett	.02	.10
114 Albert Lewis	.02	.10
115 Nick Lowery	.02	.10
116 Christian Okoye	.02	.10
117 Stephone Paige	.02	.10
118 Kevin Ross	.02	.10
119 Derrick Thomas	.20	.50
120 Mike Webster	.08	.25
121 Marcus Allen	.20	.50
122 Eddie Anderson RC	.02	.10
123 Steve Beuerlein	.08	.25
124 Tim Brown	.20	.50
125 Mervyn Fernandez	.02	.10
126 Willie Gault	.08	.25
127 Bob Golic	.02	.10
128 Bo Jackson UER	.25	.60
(Final column in stats has LG, should be TD)		
129 Howie Long	.20	.50
130 Greg Townsend	.02	.10
131 Flipper Anderson	.02	.10
132 Greg Bell	.02	.10
133 Robert Delpino	.02	.10
134 Henry Ellard	.08	.25
135 Jim Everett	.08	.25
136 Jerry Gray	.02	.10
137 Kevin Greene	.08	.25
138 Tom Newberry	.02	.10
139 Jackie Slater	.02	.10
140 Doug Smith	.02	.10
141 Mark Clayton	.08	.25
142 Jeff Cross	.02	.10
143 Mark Duper	.08	.25
144 Ferrell Edmunds	.02	.10
145 Jim C.Jensen	.02	.10
146 Dan Marino	1.25	3.00
147 John Offerdahl	.02	.10
148 Louis Oliver	.02	.10
149 Reggie Roby	.02	.10
150 Sammie Smith	.02	.10
151 Joey Browner	.02	.10
152 Anthony Carter	.08	.25
153 Chris Doleman	.02	.10
154 Steve Jordan	.02	.10
155 Carl Lee	.02	.10
156 Randall McDaniel	.08	.25
157 Keith Millard	.02	.10
158 Herschel Walker	.08	.25
159 Wade Wilson	.08	.25
160 Gary Zimmerman	.07	.20
161 Hart Lee Dykes	.02	.10
162 Irving Fryar	.20	.50
163 Steve Grogan	.08	.25
164 Maurice Hurst RC	.02	.10
165 Fred Marion	.02	.10
166 Stanley Morgan	.02	.10
167 Robert Perryman	.02	.10
168 John Stephens UER	.02	.10
(Taking handoff from Eason& not Grogan)		
169 Andre Tippett	.02	.10
170 Brent Williams	.02	.10
171 John Fourcade	.02	.10
172 Bobby Hebert	.02	.10
173 Dalton Hilliard	.02	.10
174 Rickey Jackson	.08	.25
175 Vaughan Johnson	.02	.10
176 Eric Martin	.02	.10
177 Robert Massey	.02	.10
178 Rueben Mayes UER	.02	.10
(Final column in stats has LG& should be TD)		
179 Sam Mills	.08	.25
180 Pat Swilling	.08	.25
181 Ottis Anderson	.08	.25
182 Carl Banks	.02	.10
183 Mark Bavaro	.02	.10
184 Mark Collins	.02	.10
185 Leonard Marshall	.02	.10
186 Dave Meggett	.08	.25
187 Gary Reasons	.02	.10
188 Phil Simms	.20	.50
189 Lawrence Taylor	.20	.50
190 Odessa Turner RC	.02	.10
191 Kyle Clifton	.02	.10
192 James Hasty	.02	.10
193 Johnny Hector	.02	.10
194 Jeff Lageman	.02	.10
195 Pat Leahy	.02	.10
196 Erik McMillan	.02	.10
197 Ken O'Brien	.02	.10
198 Mickey Shuler	.02	.10
199 Al Toon	.08	.25
200 Jo Jo Townsell	.02	.10
201 Eric Allen UER	.02	.10
(Card has 24 passes defended, Eagles say 25)		
202 Jerome Brown	.02	.10
203 Keith Byars UER	.02	.10
(LG column shows TD's, not longest run)		
204 Cris Carter	.50	1.25
205 Wes Hopkins	.02	.10
(Photo from 1985 season)		
206 Keith Jackson UER	.08	.25
(Born AK, should be AR)		
207 Seth Joyner	.08	.25
(Photo not from an Eagle home game)		
208 Mike Quick	.02	.10
(Photo is from a pre-1985 game)		
209 Andre Waters	.02	.10
210 Reggie White	.20	.50
211 Rich Camarillo	.02	.10
212 Roy Green	.02	.10
213 Ken Harvey RC	.20	.50
214 Gary Hogeboom	.02	.10
215 Tim McDonald	.02	.10
216 Stump Mitchell	.02	.10
217 Luis Sharpe	.02	.10
218 Vai Sikahema	.02	.10
219 J.T. Smith	.02	.10
220 Ron Wolfley	.02	.10
221 Gary Anderson K	.02	.10
222 Bubby Brister UER	.02	.10
(Stats say 0 TD passes in 1989; should be 9)		
223 Merril Hoge	.02	.10
224 Tunch Ilkin	.02	.10
225 Louis Lipps	.08	.25
226 David Little	.02	.10
227 Greg Lloyd	.20	.50
228 Dwayne Woodruff	.02	.10
229 Rod Woodson	.20	.50
(AJR patch is from/1988 season; not 1989)		
230 Tim Worley	.02	.10
231 Marion Butts	.08	.25
232 Gill Byrd	.02	.10
233 Burt Grossman	.02	.10
234 Jim McMahon	.08	.25
235 Anthony Miller UER	.20	.50
(Text says 76 catches, stats say 75)		
236 Leslie O'Neal UER	.08	.25
(Born AK, should be AR)		
237 Gary Plummer	.02	.10
238 Billy Ray Smith	.02	.10
(Action note begins, 'Bily Ray ...')		
239 Tim Spencer	.02	.10
240 Lee Williams	.02	.10
241 Mike Cofer	.02	.10
242 Roger Craig	.08	.25
243 Charles Haley	.08	.25
244 Ronnie Lott	.08	.25
245 Guy McIntyre	.02	.10
246 Joe Montana	1.25	3.00
247 Tom Rathman	.02	.10
248 Jerry Rice	.75	2.00
249 John Taylor	.20	.50
250 Michael Walter	.02	.10
251 Brian Blades	.08	.25
252 Jacob Green	.02	.10
253 Dave Krieg	.08	.25
254 Steve Largent	.20	.50
255 Joe Nash	.02	.10
256 Rufus Porter	.02	.10
257 Eugene Robinson	.02	.10
258 Paul Skansi RC	.02	.10
259 Curt Warner UER	.02	.10
(Yards and attempts are reversed in text)		
260 John L. Williams	.02	.10
261 Mark Carrier WR	.20	.50
262 Reuben Davis	.02	.10
263 Harry Hamilton	.02	.10
264 Bruce Hill	.02	.10
265 Donald Igwebuike	.02	.10
266 Eugene Marve	.02	.10
267 Kevin Murphy	.02	.10
268 Mark Robinson	.02	.10
269 Lars Tate	.02	.10
270 Vinny Testaverde	.08	.25
271 Gary Clark	.20	.50
272 Monte Coleman	.02	.10
273 Darrell Green	.08	.25
274 Charles Mann UER	.02	.10
(CA is not alphabetized on back)		
275 Wilber Marshall	.02	.10
276 Art Monk	.08	.25
277 Gerald Riggs	.02	.10
278 Mark Rypien	.08	.25
279 Ricky Sanders	.02	.10
280 Alvin Walton	.02	.10
NNO Jim Plunkett BR	2.00	4.00
(Braille on card back)		

1990 Action Packed Rookie Update

This 84-card standard-size set was issued to feature most of the rookies who made an impact in the 1990 season that Action Packed did not issue in their regular set. The first 64 cards in the set are 1990 rookies while the last 20 cards are either players who were traded during the off-season or players such as Randall Cunningham who were not included in the regular set. Rookie Cards include Fred Barnett, Reggie Cobb, Barry Foster, Jeff George, Eric Green, Rodney Hampton, Johnny Johnson, Cortez Kennedy, Scott Mitchell, Rob Moore, Junior Seau, Shannon Sharpe, Emmitt Smith, Chris Warren and Calvin Williams. The set was released through both the Action Packed dealer network and via traditional retail outlets and was available both in wax packs and as collated factory sets.

COMPLETE SET (84)	10.00	25.00
COMP.FACT.SET (84)	12.50	30.00
1 Jeff George RC	.75	2.00
2 Richmond Webb RC	.05	.15
3 James Williams DB RC	.05	.15
4 Tony Bennett RC	.08	.25
5 Darrell Thompson RC	.05	.15
6 Steve Broussard RC	.05	.15
7 Rodney Hampton RC	.20	.50
8 Rob Moore RC	.60	1.50
9 Alton Montgomery RC	.05	.15
10 LeRoy Butler RC	.20	.50
11 Anthony Johnson RC	.20	.50
12 Scott Mitchell RC	.20	.50
13 Mike Fox RC	.05	.15
14 Robert Blackmon RC	.05	.15
15 Blair Thomas RC	.05	.15
16 Tony Stargell RC	.05	.15
17 Peter Tom Willis RC	.05	.15
18 Harold Green RC	.08	.25
19 Bernard Clark	.05	.15

20 Aaron Wallace RC	.05	.15
21 Dennis Brown RC	.05	.15
22 Johnny Johnson RC	.08	.25
23 Chris Calloway RC	.05	.15
24 Walter Wilson	.05	.15
25 Dexter Carter RC	.05	.15
26 Percy Snow RC	.05	.15
27 Johnny Bailey RC	.05	.15
28 Mike Bellamy RC	.05	.15
29 Ben Smith RC	.05	.15
30 Mark Carrier DB RC UER	.20	.50
(stats say 54 yards		
in 1989, text has 58)		
31 James Francis RC	.05	.15
32 Lamar Lathon RC	.08	.25
33 Bern Brostek RC	.05	.15
34 Emmitt Smith RC UER	6.00	15.00
(Career yardage on back		
is 4232, should be 3928)		
35 Andre Collins RC UER	.05	.15
(born 1986, should be 1966)		
36 Alexander Wright RC	.05	.15
37 Fred Barnett RC	.20	.50
38 Junior Seau RC	1.50	4.00
39 Cortez Kennedy RC	.20	.50
40 Terry Wooden RC	.05	.15
41 Eric Davis RC	.08	.25
42 Fred Washington RC	.05	.15
43 Reggie Cobb RC	.05	.15
44 Andre Ware RC	.08	.25
45 Anthony Smith RC	.05	.15
46 Shannon Sharpe RC	3.00	8.00
47 Harlon Barnett RC	.05	.15
48 Greg McMurtry RC	.05	.15
49 Stacey Simmons RC	.05	.15
50 Calvin Williams RC	.08	.25
51 Anthony Thompson RC	.05	.15
52 Ricky Proehl RC	.20	.50
53 Tony Jones RC	.05	.15
54 Ray Agnew RC	.05	.15
55 Tommy Hodson RC	.05	.15
56 Ron Cox RC	.05	.15
57 Leroy Hoard RC	.20	.50
58 Eric Green RC UER	.08	.25
(Back photo reversed)		
59 Barry Foster RC	.08	.25
60 Keith McCants RC	.05	.15
61 Oliver Barnett RC	.05	.15
62 Chris Warren RC	.20	.50
63 Pat Terrell RC	.05	.15
64 Renaldo Turnbull RC	.05	.15
65 Chris Chandler	.20	.50
66 Everson Walls	.05	.15
67 Alonzo Highsmith	.05	.15
68 Gary Anderson RB	.05	.15
69 Fred Smerlas	.05	.15
70 Jim McMahon	.08	.25
71 Curt Warner	.05	.15
72 Stanley Morgan	.05	.15
73 Dave Waymer	.05	.15
74 Billy Joe Tolliver	.05	.15
75 Tony Eason	.05	.15
76 Max Montoya	.05	.15
77 Greg Bell	.05	.15
78 Dennis McKinnon	.05	.15
79 Raymond Clayborn	.05	.15
80 Broderick Thomas	.05	.15
81 Timm Rosenbach	.05	.15
82 Tim McKyer	.05	.15
83 Andre Rison	.20	.50
84 Randall Cunningham	.20	.50

1991 Action Packed

This 280-card, standard-size set features action photos on the front that are framed in gold along the left side and on the bottom of the card. The cards are arranged by team. Complete factory sets also included an exclusive subset of 8 Braille cards; card numbers 281-288 which feature the category leaders of the AFC and NFC. They have the same front design as the regular issue, but different borderless embossed color player photos and horizontally oriented backs written in Braille. Two logo cards and an unnumbered checklist card complete the set. There are no key Rookie Cards in this set. Two prototype cards were issued as well and priced below. Each contains the word "prototype" stamped on the card back and neither is considered part of the complete set. We've assigned card numbers to these two for ease in cataloging.

COMPLETE SET (280)	6.00	15.00
COMP.FACT.SET (291)	10.00	25.00
1 Steve Broussard	.02	.10
2 Scott Case	.02	.10
3 Brian Jordan	.07	.20
4 Darion Conner	.02	.10
5 Tim Green	.02	.10
6 Chris Miller	.07	.20
7 Andre Rison	.07	.20
8 Mike Rozier	.02	.10
9 Deion Sanders	.30	.75
10 Jessie Tuggle	.02	.10
11 Leonard Smith	.02	.10
12 Shane Conlan	.02	.10
13 Kent Hull	.02	.10
14 Keith McKeller	.02	.10
15 James Lofton	.07	.20
16 Andre Reed	.07	.20
17 Bruce Smith	.15	.40
18 Darryl Talley	.02	.10
19 Steve Tasker	.07	.20
20 Thurman Thomas	.15	.40
21 Neal Anderson	.07	.20
22 Trace Armstrong	.02	.10
23 Mark Bortz	.02	.10
24 Mark Carrier DB	.07	.20
25 Wendell Davis	.02	.10
26 Richard Dent	.07	.20
27 Jim Harbaugh	.15	.40
28 Jay Hilgenberg	.02	.10
29 Brad Muster	.02	.10
30 Mike Singletary	.07	.20
31 Harold Green	.02	.10
32 James Brooks	.02	.10
33 Eddie Brown	.02	.10
34 Boomer Esiason	.07	.20
35 James Francis	.02	.10
36 David Fulcher	.02	.10
37 Rodney Holman	.02	.10
38 Tim McGee	.02	.10
39 Anthony Munoz	.07	.20
40 Ickey Woods	.02	.10
41 Rob Burnett RC	.07	.20
42 Thane Gash	.02	.10
43 Mike Johnson	.02	.10
44 Brian Brennan	.02	.10
45 Reggie Langhorne	.02	.10
46 Kevin Mack	.02	.10
47 Clay Matthews	.07	.20
48 Eric Metcalf	.07	.20
49 Anthony Pleasant	.02	.10
50 Ozzie Newsome	.07	.20
51 Troy Aikman	.50	1.25
52 Issiac Holt	.02	.10
53 Michael Irvin	.15	.40
54 Jimmie Jones	.02	.10
55 Eugene Lockhart	.02	.10
56 Kelvin Martin	.02	.10
57 Ken Norton Jr.	.07	.20
58 Jay Novacek	.15	.40
59 Emmitt Smith	1.50	4.00
60 Daniel Stubbs	.02	.10
61 Steve Atwater	.02	.10
62 Michael Brooks	.02	.10
63 John Elway	.75	2.00
64 Simon Fletcher	.02	.10
65 Bobby Humphrey	.02	.10
66 Mark Jackson	.02	.10
67 Vance Johnson	.02	.10
68 Karl Mecklenburg	.02	.10
69 Dennis Smith	.02	.10
70 Greg Kragen	.02	.10
71 Jerry Ball	.02	.10
72 Lomas Brown	.02	.10
73 Robert Clark	.02	.10
74 Michael Cofer	.02	.10
75 Mel Gray	.02	.10
76 Richard Johnson	.02	.10
77 Rodney Peete	.07	.20
78 Barry Sanders	.75	2.00
79 Chris Spielman	.07	.20
80 Andre Ware	.07	.20
81 Matt Brock RC	.02	.10
82 LeRoy Butler	.07	.20
83 Tim Harris	.02	.10
84 Perry Kemp	.02	.10
85 Don Majkowski	.02	.10
86 Mark Murphy	.02	.10
87 Brian Noble	.02	.10
88 Sterling Sharpe	.15	.40
89 Darrell Thompson	.02	.10
90 Ed West	.02	.10
91 Ray Childress	.02	.10
92 Ernest Givins	.07	.20
93 Drew Hill	.02	.10
94 Haywood Jeffires	.07	.20
95 Richard Johnson RC	.02	.10
96 Sean Jones	.07	.20
97 Bruce Matthews	.07	.20
98 Warren Moon	.15	.40
99 Mike Munchak	.07	.20
100 Lorenzo White	.02	.10
101 Albert Bentley	.02	.10
102 Duane Bickett	.02	.10
103 Bill Brooks	.02	.10
104 Jeff George	.15	.40
105 Jon Hand	.02	.10
106 Jeff Herrod	.02	.10
107 Jessie Hester	.02	.10
108 Mike Prior UER	.02	.10
(Did not play in '86)		
109 Rohn Stark	.02	.10
110 Clarence Verdin	.02	.10
111 Steve DeBerg	.02	.10
112 Dan Saleaumua	.02	.10
113 Albert Lewis	.02	.10
114 Nick Lowery	.02	.10
115 Christian Okoye	.02	.10
116 Stephone Paige	.02	.10
117 Kevin Ross	.02	.10
118 Dino Hackett	.02	.10
119 Derrick Thomas UER	.15	.40
(Drafted in 1989 not 1990)		
120 Barry Word UER	.02	.10
(Bio says 1105 yards,		
stats say 1015)		
121 Marcus Allen	.15	.40
122 Mervyn Fernandez UER	.02	.10
(Drafted by Raiders)		
123 Willie Gault	.02	.10
124 Bo Jackson	.20	.50
125 Terry McDaniel	.02	.10
126 Don Mosebar	.02	.10
127 Jay Schroeder	.02	.10
128 Greg Townsend UER	.02	.10
(B in DeBerg not in caps)		
129 Aaron Wallace	.02	.10
130 Steve Wisniewski	.02	.10
131 Flipper Anderson	.02	.10
132 Henry Ellard	.07	.20
133 Jim Everett	.07	.20
134 Cleveland Gary	.02	.10
135 Jerry Gray	.02	.10
136 Kevin Greene	.07	.20
137 Buford McGee	.02	.10
138 Vince Newsome	.02	.10
139 Jackie Slater	.02	.10
140 Frank Stams	.02	.10
141 Jeff Cross	.02	.10
142 Mark Duper	.07	.20
143 Ferrell Edmunds	.02	.10
144 Dan Marino	.75	2.00
145 Louis Oliver	.02	.10
146 John Offerdahl	.02	.10
147 Tony Paige	.02	.10
148 Sammie Smith	.02	.10
149 Richmond Webb	.02	.10
150 Jarvis Williams	.02	.10
151 Joey Browner	.02	.10
152 Anthony Carter	.07	.20
153 Chris Doleman	.02	.10
154 Hassan Jones	.02	.10
155 Steve Jordan	.02	.10
156 Carl Lee	.02	.10
157 Randall McDaniel	.05	.15
158 Mike Merriweather	.02	.10
159 Herschel Walker	.07	.20
160 Wade Wilson	.07	.20
161 Ray Agnew	.02	.10
162 Bruce Armstrong	.02	.10
163 Marv Cook	.02	.10
164 Hart Lee Dykes	.02	.10
165 Irving Fryar	.07	.20
166 Tommy Hodson	.02	.10
167 Ronnie Lippett	.02	.10
168 Fred Marion	.02	.10
169 John Stephens	.02	.10
170 Brent Williams	.02	.10
171A Morten Andersen ERR	.02	.10
(Back photo has white		
emblem, should be black)		
171B Morten Andersen COR	.02	.10
172A Gene Atkins ERR	.02	.10
(Back photo has white		
emblem, should be black)		
172B Gene Atkins COR	.02	.10
173A Craig Heyward ERR	.07	.20
(Back photo has white		
emblem, should be black)		
173B Craig Heyward COR	.07	.20
174A Rickey Jackson ERR	.02	.10
(Back photo has white		
emblem, should be black)		
174B Rickey Jackson COR	.02	.10
175A Vaughan Johnson ERR	.02	.10
(Back photo has white		
emblem, should be black)		
175B Vaughan Johnson COR	.02	.10
176A Eric Martin ERR	.02	.10
(Back photo has white		
emblem, should be black)		
176B Eric Martin COR	.02	.10
177A Rueben Mayes ERR	.02	.10
(Back photo has white		
emblem, should be black;		
would have been fifth		
season, not sixth)		
177B Rueben Mayes COR	.02	.10
178A Pat Swilling ERR	.07	.20
(Back photo has white		
emblem, should be black)		
178B Pat Swilling COR	.07	.20
179A Renaldo Turnbull ERR	.07	.20
(Back photo has white		
emblem, should be black)		
179B Renaldo Turnbull COR	.07	.20
180A Steve Walsh ERR	.02	.10
(Back photo has white		
emblem, should be black)		
180B Steve Walsh COR	.02	.10
181 Ottis Anderson	.07	.20
182 Rodney Hampton	.15	.40
183 Jeff Hostetler	.15	.40
184 Pepper Johnson	.02	.10
185 Sean Landeta	.02	.10
186 Dave Meggett	.07	.20
187 Bart Oates	.02	.10
188 Phil Simms	.15	.40
189 Lawrence Taylor	.15	.40
190 Reyna Thompson	.02	.10
191 Brad Baxter	.02	.10
192 Dennis Byrd	.02	.10
193 Kyle Clifton	.02	.10
194 James Hasty	.02	.10
195 Pat Leahy	.02	.10
196 Erik McMillan	.02	.10
197 Rob Moore	.15	.40
198 Ken O'Brien	.02	.10
199 Mark Boyer	.02	.10
200 Al Toon	.07	.20
201 Fred Barnett	.15	.40
202 Jerome Brown	.02	.10
203 Keith Byars	.02	.10
204 Randall Cunningham	.15	.40
205 Wes Hopkins	.02	.10
206 Keith Jackson	.07	.20
207 Seth Joyner	.07	.20
208 Heath Sherman	.02	.10
209 Reggie White	.15	.40
210 Calvin Williams	.07	.20
211 Roy Green	.02	.10
212 Ken Harvey UER	.07	.20
(Tackling Rodney Hampton,		
not Howard Cross)		
213 Luis Sharpe	.02	.10
214 Ernie Jones	.02	.10
215 Tim McDonald	.02	.10
216 Freddie Joe Nunn	.02	.10
217 Ricky Proehl	.02	.10
218 Timm Rosenbach	.02	.10
219 Anthony Thompson	.02	.10
220 Lonnie Young	.02	.10
221 Gary Anderson K	.02	.10
222 Bubby Brister	.02	.10
223 Eric Green	.02	.10
224 Merril Hoge	.02	.10
225 Carnell Lake	.02	.10
226 Louis Lipps	.02	.10
227 David Little	.02	.10
228 Greg Lloyd	.15	.40
229 Gerald Williams	.02	.10
230 Rod Woodson	.15	.40
231 Marion Butts	.02	.10
232 Gill Byrd	.02	.10
233 Burt Grossman	.02	.10
234 Courtney Hall	.02	.10
235 Ronnie Harmon	.02	.10
236 Anthony Miller	.07	.20
237 Leslie O'Neal	.07	.20
238 Junior Seau	.15	.40
239 Billy Joe Tolliver	.02	.10
240 Lee Williams	.02	.10
241 Dexter Carter	.02	.10
242 Kevin Fagan	.02	.10
243 Charles Haley	.07	.20
244 Brent Jones	.15	.40
245 Ronnie Lott	.07	.20
246 Guy McIntyre	.02	.10
247 Joe Montana	.75	2.00
248 Jerry Rice	.50	1.25
249 John Taylor	.07	.20
250 Roger Craig	.07	.20
251 Brian Blades	.07	.20
252 Derrick Fenner	.02	.10
253 Nesby Glasgow UER	.02	.10
(1991 was his 13th		
season, not 12th)		
254 Jacob Green	.02	.10
255 Tommy Kane	.02	.10
256 Dave Krieg	.07	.20
257 Rufus Porter	.02	.10
258 Eugene Robinson	.02	.10
259 Cortez Kennedy	.15	.40
260 John L. Williams	.02	.10
261 Gary Anderson RB	.02	.10
262 Mark Carrier WR	.15	.40
263 Steve Christie	.02	.10
264 Reggie Cobb	.02	.10
265 Paul Gruber	.02	.10
266 Wayne Haddix	.02	.10
267 Bruce Hill	.02	.10
268 Keith McCants	.02	.10
269 Vinny Testaverde	.07	.20
270 Broderick Thomas	.02	.10
271 Earnest Byner	.02	.10
272 Gary Clark	.15	.40
273 Darrell Green	.02	.10
274 Jim Lachey	.02	.10
275 Chip Lohmiller	.02	.10
276 Charles Mann	.02	.10
277 Wilber Marshall	.02	.10
278 Art Monk	.07	.20
279 Mark Rypien	.07	.20
280 Alvin Walton	.02	.10
281 Randall Cunningham BR	.15	.40
NFC Passing Leader		
282 Warren Moon BR	.15	.40
AFC Passing Leader		
283 Barry Sanders BR	1.25	3.00
284 Thurman Thomas BR	.15	.40
AFC Rushing Leader		
285 Jerry Rice BR	.60	1.50
NFC Receiving Leader		
286 Haywood Jeffires BR	.02	.10
AFC Receiving Leader		
287 Charles Haley BR	.02	.10
NFC Sack Leader		
288 Derrick Thomas BR	.15	.40
AFC Sack Leader		
289 NFC Logo Card	.02	.10
290 AFC Logo Card	.02	.10
P1 Randall Cunningham	1.50	4.00
Prototype		
P2 Emmitt Smith Prototype	6.00	15.00
NNO Randall Cunningham	100.00	200.00
(18K Gold Card,		
serial numbered of 26)		
NNO Checklist Card	.07	.20
(Double fold)		

1991 Action Packed 24K Gold

COMPLETE SET (42)	75.00	200.00
1G Andre Rison	2.50	6.00
2G Deion Sanders	4.00	10.00
3G Andre Reed	3.00	8.00
4G Bruce Smith	3.00	8.00
5G Thurman Thomas	3.00	8.00
6G Neal Anderson	2.50	6.00
7G Mark Carrier DB	2.00	5.00
8G Mike Singletary	3.00	8.00
9G Boomer Esiason	2.50	6.00
10G James Francis	2.00	5.00
11G Anthony Munoz	2.50	6.00
12G Troy Aikman	6.00	15.00
13G Emmitt Smith	15.00	40.00
14G John Elway	10.00	25.00
15G Bobby Humphrey	2.00	5.00
16G Barry Sanders	10.00	25.00
17G Don Majkowski	2.00	5.00
18G Sterling Sharpe	2.50	6.00
19G Warren Moon	3.00	8.00
20G Jeff George	2.50	6.00
21G Christian Okoye	2.50	6.00
22G Derrick Thomas	3.00	8.00
23G Barry Word	2.00	5.00
24G Marcus Allen	3.00	8.00
25G Bo Jackson	5.00	12.00
26G Jim Everett	2.50	6.00
27G Cleveland Gary	2.00	5.00
28G Dan Marino	10.00	25.00
29G Herschel Walker	3.00	8.00
30G Ottis Anderson	2.50	6.00
31G Rodney Hampton	2.50	6.00
32G Dave Meggett	2.00	5.00
33G Marion Butts	2.00	5.00
34G Randall Cunningham	3.00	8.00
35G Reggie White	3.00	8.00
36G Jerry Rice	8.00	20.00
37G Eric Green	2.00	5.00
38G Charles Haley	2.50	6.00
39G Ronnie Lott	3.00	8.00
40G Joe Montana	15.00	40.00
41G Vinny Testaverde	2.50	6.00
42G Gary Clark	2.50	6.00

1991 Action Packed Rookie Update

This 84-card standard-size set contains 74 Rookie Cards (including 26 first round draft picks) plus ten traded and update cards. The front design consists of embossed color player photos. Designated rookies have an embossed red helmet with a white "R". The gold indicia and logo are bordered in red instead of black as on the regular set. In red print, the horizontally oriented backs have the player's college regular season and career statistics. An Emmitt Smith rookie prototype card was included as a bonus with each case of 1991 Action Packed Rookie Update foil or sets ordered. Rookie Cards in this set include Bryan Cox, Ricky Ervins, Brett Favre, Alvin Harper, Randal Hill, Herman Moore, Russell Maryland, Erric Pegram, Mike Pritchard, Leonard Russell, Ricky Watters, and Harvey Williams.

COMPLETE SET (84)	7.50	20.00
COMP.FACT.SET (84)	10.00	25.00
1 Herman Moore RC	.08	.25
2 Eric Turner RC	.02	.10
3 Mike Croel RC	.01	.05
4 Alfred Williams RC	.01	.05
5 Stanley Richard RC	.01	.05
6 Russell Maryland RC	.08	.25
7 Pat Harlow RC	.01	.05
8 Alvin Harper RC	.08	.25
9 Mike Pritchard RC	.02	.10
10 Leonard Russell RC	.08	.25
11 Jarrod Bunch RC	.01	.05
12 Dan McGwire RC	.01	.05
13 Bobby Wilson RC	.01	.05
14 Vinnie Clark RC	.01	.05
15 Kelvin Pritchett RC	.02	.10
16 Harvey Williams RC	.08	.25
17 Stan Thomas	.01	.05
18 Todd Marinovich RC	.01	.05
19 Antone Davis RC	.01	.05
20 Greg Lewis RC	.01	.05
21 Brett Favre RC	6.00	15.00
22 Wesley Carroll RC	.01	.05
23 Ed McCaffrey RC	1.25	3.00
24 Reggie Barrett	.01	.05
25 Chris Zorich RC	.08	.25
26 Kenny Walker RC	.01	.05
27 Aaron Craver RC	.01	.05
28 Browning Nagle RC	.01	.05
29 Nick Bell RC	.01	.05
30 Anthony Morgan RC	.01	.05
31 Jesse Campbell RC	.01	.05
32 Eric Bieniemy RC	.01	.05
33 Ricky Ervins RC UER	.02	.10
(Totals don't add up)		
34 Kanavis McGhee RC	.01	.05
35 Shawn Moore RC	.01	.05
36 Todd Lyght RC	.01	.05
37 Eric Swann RC	.08	.25
38 Henry Jones RC	.02	.10
39 Ted Washington RC	.01	.05
40 Charles McRae RC	.01	.05
41 Randal Hill RC	.02	.10
42 Huey Richardson RC	.01	.05
43 Roman Phifer RC	.01	.05
44 Ricky Watters RC	.75	2.00
45 Esera Tuaolo RC	.01	.05
46 Michael Jackson WR RC	.08	.25
47 Shawn Jefferson RC	.02	.10
48 Tim Barnett RC	.01	.05
49 Chuck Webb RC	.01	.05
50 Moe Gardner RC	.01	.05
51 Mo Lewis RC	.02	.10
52 Mike Dumas RC	.01	.05
53 Jon Vaughn RC	.01	.05
54 Jerome Henderson RC	.01	.05
55 Harry Colon RC	.01	.05
56 David Daniels RC	.01	.05
57 Phil Hansen RC	.01	.05
58 Ernie Mills RC	.02	.10
59 John Kasay RC	.02	.10
60 Darren Lewis RC	.01	.05
61 James Joseph RC	.01	.05
62 Robert Wilson RC	.01	.05
63 Lawrence Dawsey RC	.02	.10
64 Mike Jones DE RC	.01	.05
65 Dave McCloughan	.01	.05
66 Erric Pegram RC	.08	.25
67 Aeneas Williams RC	.08	.25
68 Reggie Johnson RC	.01	.05
69 Todd Scott RC	.01	.05
70 James Jones RC	.01	.05
71 Lamar Rogers RC	.01	.05
72 Darryll Lewis RC	.02	.10
73 Bryan Cox RC	.08	.25
74 Leroy Thompson RC	.01	.05
75 Mark Higgs RC	.01	.05
76 John Friesz	.08	.25
77 Tim McKyer	.01	.05
78 Roger Craig	.02	.10
79 Ronnie Lott	.02	.10
80 Steve Young	.40	1.00
81 Percy Snow	.01	.05
82 Cornelius Bennett	.02	.10
83 Johnny Johnson	.01	.05
84 Blair Thomas	.01	.05

1991 Action Packed Rookie Update 24K Gold

COMPLETE SET (26)	150.00	300.00
1G Russell Maryland	7.50	15.00
2G Eric Turner	10.00	20.00
3G Mike Croel	5.00	10.00
4G Todd Lyght	5.00	10.00
5G Eric Swann	10.00	20.00
6G Charles McRae	5.00	10.00
7G Antone Davis	5.00	10.00
8G Stanley Richard	7.50	15.00
9G Herman Moore	10.00	20.00
10G Pat Harlow	5.00	10.00
11G Alvin Harper	10.00	20.00
12G Mike Pritchard	10.00	20.00
13G Leonard Russell	10.00	20.00
14G Huey Richardson	5.00	10.00
15G Dan McGwire	7.50	15.00
16G Bobby Wilson	5.00	10.00
17G Alfred Williams	5.00	10.00
18G Vinnie Clark	5.00	10.00
19G Kelvin Pritchett	7.50	15.00
20G Harvey Williams	10.00	20.00
21G Stan Thomas	5.00	10.00
22G Randal Hill	5.00	10.00
23G Todd Marinovich	7.50	15.00
24G Ted Washington	5.00	10.00
25G Henry Jones	5.00	10.00
26G Jarrod Bunch	5.00	10.00

1991 Action Packed NFLPA Awards

This 16-card standard-size set was produced by Action Packed to honor the athletes who earned various awards in the 1990 NFL season. There were 5,000 sets issued each in their own attractive solid black box; these boxes were individually numbered on the back. The box has the inscription NFLPA/MDA Awards Dinner March 12, 1991 on it. The cards are in the 1991 Action Packed design with a raised, 3-D like photo on the front and a hockey-stick like frame going down the left side of the card and on the bottom identifying the player. The card backs feature a portrait of the player along with biographical information and statistical information where applicable. The cards feature the now-traditional Action Packed rounded corners.

COMPLETE SET (16)	7.50	20.00
1 Jim Lachey	.50	1.25
2 Anthony Munoz	.75	2.00
3 Bruce Smith	.75	2.00
4 Reggie White	1.25	3.00
5 Charles Haley	.50	1.25
6 Derrick Thomas	1.25	3.00
7 Albert Lewis	.50	1.25
8 Mark Carrier DB	.50	1.25
9 Reyna Thompson	.50	1.25
10 Steve Tasker	.75	2.00
11 James Francis	.50	1.25
12 Mark Carrier DB	.75	2.00
13 Johnny Johnson	.50	1.25
14 Eric Green	.50	1.25
15 Warren Moon	1.25	3.00
16 Randall Cunningham	1.25	3.00

1991 Action Packed Whizzer White Award

At the silver anniversary NFLPA/Mackey Awards banquet in Chicago (June 23, 1991), Action Packed presented this 25-card commemorative standard-size set in honor of the 25 winners of the Justice Byron "Whizzer" White Humanitarian Award from 1967-91. Reportedly 3,500 sets were distributed at the dinner and another 5,000 numbered boxed sets were produced for sale into the hobby. The front design features a color embossed action photo, with indicia in silver and the award year inscribed on a silver helmet. The backs have a color head shot, biographical information, career statistics, and a tribute to the player's professional career and community contributions. The card numbering follows chronologically the order in which the award was won, 1967 through 1991, inclusive.

COMPLETE SET (25)	8.00	20.00
1 Bart Starr	2.00	5.00
2 Willie Davis	.30	.75
3 Ed Meador	.20	.50
4 Gale Sayers	1.00	2.50
5 Kermit Alexander	.20	.50
6 Ray May	.20	.50
7 Andy Russell	.20	.50
8 Floyd Little	.20	.50
9 Rocky Bleier	.50	1.25
10 Jim Hart	.20	.50
11 Lyle Alzado	.30	.75
12 Archie Manning	.50	1.25
13 Roger Staubach	2.00	5.00
14 Gene Upshaw	.30	.75
15 Ken Houston	.20	.50
16 Franco Harris	.80	2.00
17 Doug Dieken	.20	.50
18 Rolf Benirschke	.20	.50
19 Reggie Williams	.20	.50
20 Nat Moore	.20	.50
21 George Martin	.20	.50
22 Deron Cherry	.20	.50
23 Mike Singletary	.50	1.25
24 Ozzie Newsome	.30	.75
25 Mike Kenn	.20	.50

1991 Action Packed Withdrawals

These cards apparantly were withdrawn prior to the release of the 1991 Action Packed issue due to the dispute between the NFL Player's Association and NFL Properties. Each card appears to be a standard 1991 Action Packed card, but none were ever included in packs.

14 Jim Kelly	100.00	250.00
44 Bernie Kosar	50.00	125.00
199 Blair Thomas	50.00	125.00
213 Johnny Johnson	50.00	125.00

1992 Action Packed Prototypes

The 1992 Action Packed Prototype set contains three standard-size cards. The card design is very similar to the 1992 Action Packed regular issue cards. The cards were first distributed at the Super Bowl Show in Minneapolis in January, 1992. The cards are overstamped "Prototype" on the back. The Barry Sanders card seems to be a little more difficult to find than the other two cards.

92A Thurman Thomas	.60	1.50
92N Emmitt Smith	4.00	10.00
92P Barry Sanders	4.00	10.00

1992 Action Packed

The 1992 Action Packed football set contains 280 standard-size cards. Cards were issued six per pack. The fronts feature borderless embossed color player photos, accented by either gold and aqua (NFC) or gold and red (AFC) border stripes running down either the left or right side of the card face. The team helmet appears in the lower left or right corner, with the player's name and position printed at the card bottom. The horizontally oriented backs carry biography, player profile, a color head shot, and an "Action Note" in the form of an extended caption to the photo on the front. The cards are numbered on the back and checklisted below alphabetically according to teams. There are no key Rookie Cards in this set. To show support for their injured teammate, a special "thumbs up" logo with Mike Utley's number 60 was placed on the back of all Detroit Lions' cards. The factory set closes with a Braille subset (281-288) and Logo cards (289-290). The inside lid of the factory set box has the set checklist printed on it. The eight Braille cards, available in foil packs as well as factory sets, feature category leaders by division. Action Packed also made 26 18K solid gold Tiffany-designed cards of Action Packed Player of the Year Barry Sanders. Certificates for a chance to win these cards were randomly inserted in the regular series foil packs. Action Packed also produced a 288-card "Mint" parallel version of the regular set. The Mint cards were pacakged seperately in boxes of twenty-four six-card packs.

COMPLETE SET (280)	10.00	25.00
COMP.FACT.SET (292)	12.50	30.00
1 Steve Broussard	.05	.15
2 Michael Haynes	.08	.25
3 Tim McKyer	.05	.15
4 Chris Miller	.08	.25
5 Andre Rison	.08	.25
6 Jessie Tuggle	.05	.15
7 Mike Pritchard	.05	.15
8 Moe Gardner	.05	.15
9 Brian Jordan	.08	.25
10 Mike Kenn and	.05	.15
Chris Hinton		
11 Steve Tasker	.08	.25
12 Cornelius Bennett	.08	.25
13 Shane Conlan	.05	.15
14 Darryl Talley	.05	.15
15 Thurman Thomas	.20	.50
16 James Lofton	.08	.25
17 Don Beebe	.05	.15
18 Jim Ritcher	.05	.15
19 Keith McKeller	.05	.15
20 Nate Odomes	.05	.15
21 Mark Carrier DB	.05	.15
22 Wendell Davis	.05	.15
23 Richard Dent	.08	.25
24 Jim Harbaugh	.20	.50
25 Jay Hilgenberg	.05	.15
26 Steve McMichael	.08	.25
27 Tom Waddle	.05	.15
28 Neal Anderson	.05	.15
29 Brad Muster	.05	.15
30 Shaun Gayle	.05	.15
31 Jim Breech	.05	.15
32 James Brooks	.05	.15
33 James Francis	.05	.15
34 David Fulcher	.05	.15
35 Harold Green	.05	.15
36 Rodney Holman	.05	.15
37 Anthony Munoz	.08	.25
38 Tim Krumrie	.05	.15
39 Tim McGee	.05	.15
40 Eddie Brown	.05	.15
41 Kevin Mack	.05	.15
42 James Jones	.05	.15
43 Vince Newsome	.05	.15
44 Ed King	.05	.15
45 Eric Metcalf	.08	.25
46 Leroy Hoard	.08	.25
47 Stephen Braggs	.05	.15
48 Clay Matthews	.08	.25
49 David Brandon RC	.05	.15
50 Rob Burnett	.05	.15
51 Larry Brown DB	.05	.15
52 Alvin Harper	.08	.25
53 Michael Irvin	.20	.50
54 Ken Norton Jr.	.08	.25
55 Jay Novacek	.08	.25
56 Emmitt Smith	1.50	4.00
57 Tony Tolbert	.05	.15
58 Nate Newton	.08	.25
59 Steve Beuerlein	.08	.25
60 Tony Casillas	.05	.15
61 Steve Atwater	.05	.15
62 Mike Croel	.05	.15
63 Gaston Green	.05	.15
64 Mark Jackson	.05	.15
65 Greg Kragen	.05	.15
66 Karl Mecklenburg	.05	.15
67 Dennis Smith	.05	.15
68 Steve Sewell	.05	.15
69 John Elway	1.25	3.00
70 Simon Fletcher	.05	.15
71 Mel Gray	.05	.15
72 Barry Sanders	1.25	3.00
73 Jerry Ball	.05	.15
74 Bennie Blades	.05	.15
75 Lomas Brown	.05	.15
76 Erik Kramer	.08	.25
77 Chris Spielman	.08	.25
78 Ray Crockett	.05	.15
79 Willie Green	.05	.15
80 Rodney Peete	.08	.25
81 Sterling Sharpe	.20	.50
82 Tony Bennett	.05	.15
83 Chuck Cecil	.05	.15
84 Perry Kemp	.05	.15
85 Brian Noble	.05	.15
86 Darrell Thompson	.05	.15
87 Mike Tomczak	.05	.15
88 Vince Workman	.05	.15
89 Esera Tuaolo	.05	.15
90 Mark Murphy	.05	.15
91 William Fuller	.08	.25
92 Ernest Givins	.08	.25
93 Drew Hill	.05	.15
94 Al Smith	.05	.15
95 Ray Childress	.05	.15
96 Haywood Jeffires	.08	.25
97 Cris Dishman	.05	.15
98 Warren Moon	.20	.50
99 Lamar Lathon	.05	.15
100 Mike Munchak and	.08	.25
Bruce Matthews		
101 Bill Brooks	.05	.15
102 Duane Bickett	.05	.15
103 Eugene Daniel	.05	.15
104 Jeff Herrod	.05	.15
105 Jessie Hester	.05	.15
106 Donnell Thompson	.05	.15
107 Anthony Johnson	.08	.25
108 Jon Hand	.05	.15
109 Rohn Stark	.05	.15
110 Clarence Verdin	.05	.15
111 Derrick Thomas	.20	.50
112 Steve DeBerg	.05	.15
113 Deron Cherry	.05	.15
114 Chris Martin	.05	.15
115 Christian Okoye	.05	.15
116 Dan Saleaumua	.05	.15
117 Neil Smith	.20	.50
118 Barry Word	.05	.15
119 Tim Barnett	.05	.15
120 Albert Lewis	.05	.15
121 Ronnie Lott	.08	.25
122 Marcus Allen	.20	.50
123 Todd Marinovich	.05	.15
124 Nick Bell	.05	.15
125 Tim Brown	.20	.50
126 Ethan Horton	.05	.15
127 Greg Townsend	.05	.15
128 Jeff Gossett and	.05	.15
Jeff Jaeger		
129 Scott Davis	.05	.15
130 Steve Wisniewski and	.05	.15
Don Mosebar		
131 Kevin Greene	.08	.25
132 Roman Phifer	.05	.15
133 Tony Zendejas	.05	.15
134 Pat Terrell	.05	.15
135 Flipper Anderson	.05	.15
136 Robert Delpino	.05	.15
137 Jim Everett	.08	.25
138 Larry Kelm	.05	.15
139 Todd Lyght	.05	.15
140 Henry Ellard	.08	.25
141 Mark Clayton	.08	.25
142 Jeff Cross	.05	.15
143 Mark Duper	.05	.15
144 John Offerdahl	.05	.15
145 Louis Oliver	.05	.15
146 Pete Stoyanovich	.05	.15
147 Richmond Webb	.05	.15
148 Mark Higgs	.05	.15
149 Tony Paige	.05	.15
150 Bryan Cox	.08	.25
151 Anthony Carter	.08	.25
152 Cris Carter	.40	1.00
153 Rich Gannon	.20	.50
154 Steve Jordan	.05	.15
155 Mike Merriweather	.05	.15
156 Henry Thomas	.05	.15
157 Herschel Walker	.08	.25
158 Randall McDaniel	.05	.15
159 Terry Allen	.20	.50
160 Joey Browner	.05	.15
161 Leonard Russell	.08	.25
162 Bruce Armstrong	.05	.15
163 Vincent Brown	.05	.15
164 Hugh Millen	.05	.15
165 Andre Tippett	.05	.15
166 Jon Vaughn	.05	.15
167 Pat Harlow	.05	.15
168 Marv Cook	.05	.15
169 Irving Fryar	.08	.25
170 Maurice Hurst	.05	.15
171 Pat Swilling	.08	.25
172 Vince Buck	.05	.15
173 Rickey Jackson	.05	.15
174 Sam Mills	.05	.15
175 Bobby Hebert	.05	.15
176 Vaughan Johnson	.05	.15
177 Floyd Turner	.05	.15
178 Fred McAfee RC	.05	.15
179 Morten Andersen	.05	.15
180 Eric Martin	.05	.15
181 Rodney Hampton	.20	.50
182 Pepper Johnson	.05	.15
183 Leonard Marshall	.05	.15
184 Stephen Baker	.05	.15
185 Mark Ingram	.05	.15
186 Dave Meggett	.08	.25
187 Bart Oates	.05	.15
188 Mark Collins	.05	.15
189 Myron Guyton	.05	.15

190 Jeff Hostetler	.08	.25
191 Jeff Lageman	.05	.15
192 Brad Baxter	.05	.15
193 Mo Lewis	.05	.15
194 Chris Burkett	.05	.15
195 James Hasty	.05	.15
196 Rob Moore	.08	.25
197 Kyle Clifton	.05	.15
198 Terance Mathis	.08	.25
199 Marvin Washington	.05	.15
200 Lonnie Young	.05	.15
201 Reggie White	.20	.50
202 Eric Allen	.05	.15
203 Fred Barnett	.08	.25
204 Keith Byars	.05	.15
205 Seth Joyner	.08	.25
206 Clyde Simmons	.05	.15
207 Jerome Brown	.05	.15
208 Wes Hopkins	.05	.15
209 Keith Jackson	.08	.25
210 Calvin Williams	.08	.25
211 Aeneas Williams	.08	.25
212 Ken Harvey	.05	.15
213 Ernie Jones	.05	.15
214 Freddie Joe Nunn	.05	.15
215 Rich Camarillo	.05	.15
216 Johnny Johnson	.05	.15
217 Tim McDonald	.05	.15
218 Eric Swann	.08	.25
219 Eric Hill	.05	.15
220 Anthony Thompson	.05	.15
221 Hardy Nickerson	.20	.50
222 Barry Foster	.08	.25
223 Louis Lipps	.05	.15
224 Greg Lloyd	.08	.25
225 Neil O'Donnell	.20	.50
226 Jerrol Williams	.05	.15
227 Eric Green	.05	.15
228 Rod Woodson	.20	.50
229 Carnell Lake	.05	.15
230 Dwight Stone	.05	.15
231 Marion Butts	.05	.15
232 John Friesz	.08	.25
233 Burt Grossman	.05	.15
234 Ronnie Harmon	.05	.15
235 Gill Byrd	.05	.15
236 Rod Bernstine	.05	.15
237 Courtney Hall	.05	.15
238 Nate Lewis	.05	.15
239 Joe Phillips	.05	.15
240 Henry Rolling	.05	.15
241 Keith Henderson	.05	.15
242 Guy McIntyre	.05	.15
243 Bill Romanowski	.05	.15
244 Don Griffin	.05	.15
245 Dexter Carter	.05	.15
246 Charles Haley	.08	.25
247 Brent Jones	.08	.25
248 John Taylor	.08	.25
249 Steve Young	.60	1.50
250 Larry Roberts	.05	.15
251 Brian Blades	.08	.25
252 Jacob Green	.05	.15
253 John Kasay	.05	.15
254 Cortez Kennedy	.08	.25
255 Rufus Porter	.05	.15
256 John L. Williams	.05	.15
257 Tommy Kane	.05	.15
258 Eugene Robinson	.05	.15
259 Terry Wooden	.05	.15
260 Chris Warren	.20	.50
261 Lawrence Dawsey	.05	.15
262 Mark Carrier WR	.08	.25
263 Keith McCants	.05	.15
264 Jesse Solomon	.05	.15
265 Vinny Testaverde	.08	.25
266 Ricky Reynolds	.05	.15
267 Broderick Thomas	.05	.15
268 Gary Anderson RB	.05	.15
269 Reggie Cobb	.05	.15
270 Tony Covington	.05	.15
271 Darrell Green	.05	.15
272 Charles Mann	.05	.15
273 Wilber Marshall	.05	.15
274 Gary Clark	.20	.50
275 Chip Lohmiller	.05	.15
276 Earnest Byner	.05	.15
277 Jim Lachey	.05	.15
278 Art Monk	.08	.25
279 Mark Rypien	.05	.15
280 Mark Schlereth RC	.05	.15
281 Mark Rypien BR NFC Passing Yardage Leader	.08	.25
282 Warren Moon BR AFC Passing Yardage Leader	.20	.50
283 Emmitt Smith BR	.75	2.00
284 Thurman Thomas BR AFC Rushing Leader	.20	.50
285 Michael Irvin BR NFC Receiving Leader	.20	.50
286 Haywood Jeffires BR AFC Receiving Leader	.08	.25
287 Pat Swilling BR NFC Sack Leader	.08	.25
288 Ronnie Lott BR AFC Interception Leader	.20	.50
289 NFC Logo (Only available in factory sets)	.05	.15
290 AFC Logo (Only available in factory sets)	.05	.15
43G Barry Sanders 24K Gold	6.00	15.00
44G Barry Sanders 24K Gold	6.00	15.00
NNO Barry Sanders 18K	250.00	400.00

1992 Action Packed Mint Parallel

COMPLETE SET (288)	1,000.00	2,500.00
*MINT CARDS: 30X TO 80X BASIC CARDS		
P1 Barry Sanders Promo	25.00	50.00

1992 Action Packed 24K Gold

COMPLETE SET (42)	150.00	400.00
RANDOM INSERTS IN FOIL PACKS		
1G Michael Haynes	4.00	10.00
2G Chris Miller	4.00	10.00
3G Andre Rison	5.00	12.00
4G Cornelius Bennett	4.00	10.00
5G James Lofton	4.00	10.00
6G Thurman Thomas	5.00	12.00
7G Neal Anderson	3.00	8.00
8G Michael Irvin	5.00	12.00
9G Emmitt Smith	25.00	50.00
10G Mike Croel	3.00	8.00
11G John Elway	20.00	50.00
12G Gaston Green	3.00	8.00
13G Barry Sanders	20.00	50.00
14G Sterling Sharpe	5.00	12.00
15G Ernest Givins	3.00	8.00
16G Drew Hill	4.00	10.00
17G Haywood Jeffires	4.00	10.00
18G Warren Moon	5.00	12.00
19G Christian Okoye	4.00	10.00
20G Derrick Thomas	5.00	12.00
21G Ronnie Lott	4.00	10.00
22G Todd Marinovich	3.00	8.00
23G Henry Ellard	4.00	10.00
24G Mark Clayton	4.00	10.00
25G Herschel Walker	4.00	10.00
26G Irving Fryar	4.00	10.00
27G Leonard Russell	4.00	10.00
28G Pat Swilling	4.00	10.00
29G Rodney Hampton	4.00	10.00
30G Rob Moore	4.00	10.00
31G Seth Joyner	3.00	8.00
32G Reggie White	5.00	12.00
33G Eric Green	4.00	10.00
34G Rod Woodson	5.00	12.00
35G Marion Butts	3.00	8.00
36G Charles Haley	4.00	10.00
37G John Taylor	4.00	10.00
38G Steve Young	10.00	25.00
39G Earnest Byner	4.00	10.00
40G Gary Clark	5.00	12.00
41G Art Monk	4.00	10.00
42G Mark Rypien	4.00	10.00
13GAU Barry Sanders AUTO Signed 24K Gold Card	50.00	120.00

1992 Action Packed Rookie Update

This 84-card standard-size set features 25 first round draft choices pictured in their NFL uniforms and some of the league's outstanding veteran players. Cards were issued in six-card packs. Action Packed guaranteed one 1st round draft pick in each seven-card foil pack. The foil packs also included randomly inserted 24K gold cards of the quarterbacks and 1st round draft choices as well as a special "Neon Deion Sanders" card featuring neon fluorescent orange and numbered "84N". No factory sets were made. The fronts feature full-bleed embossed color player photos that are edged on one side by black and gold foil stripes. The player's name and position are gold-foil stamped at the bottom alongside a representation of the team helmet. The horizontal backs display a color head shot, biography, statistics, and career summary. A black stripe at the bottom carries the card number and an autograph slot. Players aligned with both NFL Properties and the NFL Players Association appear together in this set. Rookie Cards in this set include Edgar Bennett, Terrell Buckley, Marco Coleman,Quentin Coryatt, Steve Emtman, Sean Gilbert, Johnny Mitchell and Carl Pickens. Action Packed also produced a 24K Gold "Mint" rookie/update set. The 24K gold "Mint" cards were sold in separately issued six-card packs, with seven packs to a box. Each of the 250 "Mint" cards of each player were individually numbered (1/250, 2/250, etc.).

COMPLETE SET (84)	5.00	12.00
1 Steve Emtman RC	.05	.15
2 Quentin Coryatt RC	.05	.15
3 Sean Gilbert RC	.08	.25
4 John Fina RC	.05	.15
5 Alonzo Spellman RC	.08	.25
6 Amp Lee RC	.05	.15
7 Robert Porcher RC	.20	.50
8 Jason Hanson RC	.08	.25
9 Ty Detmer	.20	.50
10 Ray Roberts RC	.05	.15
11 Bob Whitfield RC	.05	.15
12 Greg Skrepenak RC	.05	.15
13 Vaughn Dunbar RC	.05	.15
14 Siran Stacy RC	.05	.15
15 Mark D'Onofrio RC	.05	.15
16 Tony Sacca RC	.05	.15
17 Dana Hall RC	.05	.15
18 Courtney Hawkins RC	.08	.25
19 Shane Collins RC	.05	.15
20 Tony Smith RC	.05	.15
21 Rod Smith RC	.05	.15
22 Troy Auzenne RC	.05	.15
23 David Klingler RC	.05	.15
24 Darryl Williams RC	.05	.15
25 Carl Pickens RC	.20	.50
26 Ricardo McDonald RC	.05	.15
27 Tommy Vardell RC	.05	.15
28 Kevin Smith RC	.05	.15
29 Rodney Culver RC	.05	.15
30 Jimmy Smith RC	2.00	5.00
31 Robert Jones RC	.05	.15
32 Tommy Maddox RC	1.25	3.00
33 Shane Dronett RC	.05	.15
34 Terrell Buckley RC	.05	.15
35 Santana Dotson RC	.08	.25
36 Edgar Bennett RC	.20	.50
37 Ashley Ambrose RC	.20	.50
38 Dale Carter RC	.08	.25
39 Chester McGlockton RC	.08	.25
40 Steve Israel RC	.05	.15
41 Marc Boutte RC	.05	.15
42 Marco Coleman RC	.05	.15
43 Troy Vincent RC	.05	.15
44 Mark Wheeler RC	.05	.15
45 Darren Perry RC	.05	.15
46 Eugene Chung RC	.05	.15
47 Derek Brown TE RC	.05	.15
48 Phillippi Sparks RC	.05	.15
49 Johnny Mitchell RC	.05	.15
50 Kurt Barber RC	.05	.15
51 Leon Searcy RC	.05	.15
52 Chris Mims RC	.05	.15
53 Keith Jackson	.08	.25
54 Charles Haley	.08	.25
55 Dave Krieg	.08	.25
56 Dan McGwire	.05	.15
57 Phil Simms	.08	.25
58 Bobby Humphrey	.05	.15
59 Jerry Rice	1.00	2.50
60 Joe Montana	1.50	4.00
61 Junior Seau	.20	.50
62 Leslie O'Neal	.08	.25
63 Anthony Miller	.08	.25
64 Timm Rosenbach	.05	.15
65 Herschel Walker	.08	.25
66 Randal Hill	.05	.15
67 Randall Cunningham	.20	.50
68 Al Toon	.08	.25
69 Browning Nagle	.05	.15
70 Lawrence Taylor	.20	.50
71 Dan Marino	1.50	4.00
72 Eric Dickerson	.08	.25
73 Harvey Williams	.20	.50
74 Jeff George	.20	.50
75 Russell Maryland	.05	.15
76 Troy Aikman	.75	2.00
77 Michael Dean Perry	.08	.25
78 Bernie Kosar	.08	.25
79 Boomer Esiason	.08	.25
80 Mike Singletary	.08	.25
81 Bruce Smith	.20	.50
82 Andre Reed	.08	.25
83 Jim Kelly	.20	.50
84 Deion Sanders	.40	1.00
84N Deion Sanders Neon orange card	4.00	10.00

1992 Action Packed Rookie Update Mint Parallel

COMPLETE SET (84)	600.00	1,500.00
*MINT CARDS: 30X TO 80X BASIC CARDS		

1992 Action Packed Rookie Update 24K Gold

COMPLETE SET (35)	200.00	400.00
RANDOM INSERTS IN FOIL PACKS		
1G Steve Emtman	5.00	12.00
2G Quentin Coryatt	5.00	12.00
3G Sean Gilbert	5.00	12.00
4G Terrell Buckley	5.00	12.00
5G David Klingler	6.00	15.00
6G Troy Vincent	6.00	15.00
7G Tommy Vardell	5.00	12.00
8G Leon Searcy	2.50	6.00
9G Marco Coleman	5.00	12.00
10G Eugene Chung	2.50	6.00
11G Derek Brown TE	5.00	12.00
12G Johnny Mitchell	6.00	15.00
13G Chester McGlockton	6.00	15.00
14G Kevin Smith	5.00	12.00
15G Dana Hall	5.00	12.00
16G Tony Smith	2.50	6.00
17G Dale Carter	5.00	12.00
18G Vaughn Dunbar	5.00	12.00
19G Alonzo Spellman	6.00	15.00
20G Chris Mims	6.00	15.00
21G Robert Jones	5.00	12.00
22G Tommy Maddox	10.00	25.00
23G Robert Porcher	5.00	12.00
24G John Fina	2.50	6.00
25G Darryl Williams	2.50	6.00
26G Jim Kelly	6.00	15.00
27G Randall Cunningham	6.00	15.00
28G Dan Marino	25.00	60.00
29G Troy Aikman	20.00	40.00
30G Boomer Esiason	5.00	12.00
31G Bernie Kosar	5.00	12.00
32G Jeff George	6.00	15.00
33G Phil Simms	5.00	12.00
34G Ray Roberts	2.50	6.00
35G Bob Whitfield	2.50	6.00

1992 Action Packed Mackey Award

Only 2,000 numbered sets of these three 24K gold standard-size cards were produced for the attendees al the 1992 NFLPA Mackey Awards Banquet.

COMPLETE SET (3)	30.00	75.00
92W Reggie White	10.00	25.00
HOF John Mackey	6.00	15.00
HUD Jack Kemp	16.00	40.00

1992 Action Packed NFLPA/MDA Award 24K

This 16-card, 24K gold standard-size set was produced by Action Packed to honor NFL Players of the Year for the 1991 season. Cards come packed in an attractive black box imprinted on front with NFLPA/MDA Awards Dinner, March 5, 1992. Only 1,000 sets were produced, and banquet attendees each received a set stamped "Banquet Edition." Card fronts feature a raised-print player photo and team helmet. The Action Packed logo appears in the upper left corner of red cards (AFC) and in the upper right on blue cards (NFC). Players' names appear at the lower right or left of each card offsetting the logo. Handsomely designed with 24K gold borders and lettering, horizontally designed backs feature biographical and statistical information and a head shot of each player within a 24K gold box. Featuring the traditional rounded corners, cards are numbered in the lower left corner.

COMPLETE SET (16)	60.00	120.00
1 Steve Wisniewski	2.00	5.00
2 Jim Lachey	2.00	5.00
3 Reggie White	6.00	12.00
4 William Fuller	2.00	5.00
5 Derrick Thomas	4.00	8.00
6 Pat Swilling	2.00	5.00
7 Darrell Green	4.00	8.00
8 Ronnie Lott	6.00	12.00
9 Steve Tasker	4.00	8.00
10 Mel Gray	2.00	5.00
11 Aeneas Williams	2.00	5.00
12 Mike Croel	2.00	5.00
13 Leonard Russell	2.00	5.00
14 Lawrence Dawsey	2.00	5.00
15 Barry Sanders	16.00	40.00
16 Thurman Thomas	6.00	12.00

1993 Action Packed Troy Aikman Promos

COMMON CARD (TA2-TA3)	4.00	10.00

1993 Action Packed Emmitt Smith Promos

COMPLETE SET (5)	14.00	35.00
COMMON CARD (ES1-ES5)	2.00	5.00
ES2 Emmitt Smith	4.00	10.00
ES3 Emmitt Smith	4.00	10.00
ES5 Emmitt Smith (Running to right; ball in left arm)	3.20	8.00

1993 Action Packed Prototypes

COMPLETE SET (6)	12.00	30.00
FB1 Emmitt Smith	4.00	10.00
FB2 Thurman Thomas	1.20	3.00
FB3 Steve Young	1.60	4.00
FB4 Barry Sanders	4.00	10.00
FB5 Barry Foster	.60	1.50
FB6 Warren Moon	1.20	3.00

1993 Action Packed

The 1993 Action Packed football set consists of 222 standard-size cards. A 60-card Rookie Update series begins at card number 163, where the first series leaves off. It features players selected in the early rounds of the NFL draft wearing their NFL uniforms. The fronts feature an embossed color player cut-out against a full-bleed background that consists of a tilted colored panel bordered on two sides by foil. Depending on the round the player was drafted, the foil varies from gold (first round, 163-192); to silver (second round, 193-210); to bronze (third round, 211-215). Players drafted after the third round have their panels bordered in a non-foil sky blue color (cards 217-222). The horizontal backs carry a color close-up photo, '92 college season and NCAA career statistics, biography and college career highlights.

COMPLETE SET (222)	20.00	50.00
COMP.SERIES 1 (162)	10.00	25.00
COMP.SERIES 2 (60)	10.00	25.00
1 Michael Haynes	.10	.30
2 Chris Miller	.10	.30
3 Andre Rison	.10	.30
4 Jim Kelly	.25	.60
5 Andre Reed	.10	.30
6 Thurman Thomas	.25	.60
7 Jim Harbaugh	.25	.60
8 Harold Green	.05	.15
9 David Klingler	.05	.15
10 Bernie Kosar	.10	.30
11 Troy Aikman	.75	2.00
12 Michael Irvin	.25	.60
13 Emmitt Smith	1.25	3.00
14 John Elway	1.25	3.00
15 Barry Sanders	1.25	3.00
16 Brett Favre	1.50	4.00
17 Sterling Sharpe	.25	.60
18 Ernest Givins	.10	.30
19 Haywood Jeffires	.10	.30
20 Warren Moon	.25	.60
21 Lorenzo White	.05	.15
22 Jeff George	.25	.60
23 Joe Montana	1.25	3.00
24 Jim Everett	.10	.30
25 Cleveland Gary	.05	.15
26 Dan Marino	1.25	3.00
27 Terry Allen	.25	.60
28 Rodney Hampton	.10	.30
29 Phil Simms	.10	.30
30 Fred Barnett	.10	.30
31 Randall Cunningham	.25	.60
32 Gary Clark	.10	.30
33 Barry Foster	.10	.30
34 Neil O'Donnell	.25	.60
35 Stan Humphries	.10	.30
36 Anthony Miller	.10	.30
37 Jerry Rice	1.00	2.50
38 Ricky Watters	.25	.60
39 Steve Young	.60	1.50
40 Chris Warren	.10	.30
41 Reggie Cobb	.05	.15
42 Mark Rypien	.05	.15
43 Deion Sanders	.50	1.25
44 Henry Jones	.05	.15
45 Bruce Smith	.25	.60
46 Richard Dent	.10	.30
47 Tommy Vardell	.05	.15
48 Charles Haley	.10	.30
49 Ken Norton Jr.	.10	.30
50 Jay Novacek	.10	.30
51 Simon Fletcher	.05	.15
52 Pat Swilling	.05	.15
53 Tony Bennett	.05	.15
54 Reggie White	.25	.60
55 Ray Childress	.05	.15
56 Quentin Coryatt	.10	.30
57 Steve Emtman	.05	.15
58 Derrick Thomas	.25	.60
59 James Lofton	.10	.30
60 Marco Coleman	.05	.15
61 Bryan Cox	.05	.15
62 Troy Vincent	.05	.15
63 Chris Doleman	.05	.15
64 Audray McMillian	.05	.15
65 Vaughn Dunbar	.05	.15
66 Rickey Jackson	.05	.15
67 Lawrence Taylor	.25	.60
68 Ronnie Lott	.10	.30
69 Rob Moore	.10	.30
70 Browning Nagle	.05	.15
71 Eric Allen	.05	.15
72 Tim Harris	.05	.15
73 Clyde Simmons	.05	.15
74 Steve Beuerlein	.10	.30
75 Randal Hill	.05	.15
76 Darren Perry	.05	.15
77 Rod Woodson	.25	.60
78 Marion Butts	.05	.15
79 Chris Mims	.05	.15
80 Junior Seau	.25	.60
81 Cortez Kennedy	.10	.30
82 Santana Dotson	.10	.30
83 Earnest Byner	.05	.15
84 Charles Mann	.05	.15
85 Pierce Holt	.05	.15
86 Mike Pritchard	.10	.30
87 Cornelius Bennett	.10	.30
88 Neal Anderson	.05	.15
89 Carl Pickens	.10	.30
90 Eric Metcalf	.10	.30
91 Michael Dean Perry	.10	.30
92 Alvin Harper	.10	.30
93 Robert Jones	.05	.15
94 Steve Atwater	.05	.15
95 Rod Bernstine	.05	.15
96 Herman Moore	.25	.60
97 Chris Spielman	.10	.30
98 Terrell Buckley	.05	.15
99 Dale Carter	.05	.15
100 Terry McDaniel	.05	.15
101 Tim Brown	.25	.60
102 Gaston Green	.05	.15
103 Howie Long	.25	.60
104 Todd Marinovich	.05	.15
105 Anthony Smith	.05	.15
106 Flipper Anderson	.05	.15
107 Henry Ellard	.10	.30
108 Mark Higgs	.05	.15
109 Keith Jackson	.10	.30
110 Irving Fryar	.10	.30
111 Cris Carter	.25	.60
112 Leonard Russell	.10	.30
113 Wayne Martin	.05	.15
114 Mark Jackson	.05	.15
115 Dave Meggett	.05	.15
116 Brad Baxter	.05	.15
117 Boomer Esiason	.10	.30
118 Johnny Johnson	.05	.15
119 Seth Joyner	.05	.15
120 Kevin Greene	.10	.30
121 Greg Lloyd	.10	.30
122 Brent Jones	.10	.30
123 Amp Lee	.05	.15
124 Tim McDonald	.05	.15
125 Darrell Green	.05	.15
126 Art Monk	.10	.30
127 Tony Smith	.05	.15
128 Bill Brooks	.05	.15
129 Kenneth Davis	.05	.15
130 Donnell Woolford	.05	.15
131 Derrick Fenner	.05	.15
132 Michael Jackson	.10	.30
133 Mark Clayton	.05	.15
134 Al Smith	.05	.15
135 Curtis Duncan	.05	.15
136 Rodney Culver	.05	.15
137 Harvey Williams	.10	.30
138 Neil Smith	.25	.60
139 Marcus Allen	.25	.60
140 Eric Dickerson	.10	.30
141 Sean Gilbert	.10	.30
142 Shane Conlan	.05	.15
143 Todd Scott	.05	.15
144 Vincent Brown	.05	.15
145 Andre Tippett	.05	.15
146 Jon Vaughn	.05	.15
147 Marv Cook	.05	.15
148 Morten Andersen	.05	.15
149 Sam Mills	.05	.15
150 Mark Collins	.05	.15
151 Heath Sherman	.05	.15
152 Johnny Bailey	.05	.15
153 Eric Green	.05	.15
154 Ronnie Harmon	.05	.15
155 Gill Byrd	.05	.15
156 Leslie O'Neal	.10	.30
157 Rufus Porter	.05	.15
158 Eugene Robinson	.05	.15
159 Broderick Thomas	.05	.15
160 Lawrence Dawsey	.05	.15
161 Anthony Munoz	.10	.30
162 Wilber Marshall	.05	.15
163 Drew Bledsoe RC	2.50	6.00
164 Rick Mirer RC	.25	.60
165 Garrison Hearst RC	.75	2.00
166 Marvin Jones RC	.05	.15
167 John Copeland RC	.10	.30
168 Eric Curry RC	.05	.15
169 Curtis Conway RC	.50	1.25
170 Willie Roaf RC	.10	.30
171 Lincoln Kennedy RC	.05	.15
172 Jerome Bettis RC	4.00	8.00
173 Dan Williams RC	.05	.15
174 Patrick Bates RC	.05	.15
175 Brad Hopkins RC	.05	.15
176 Steve Everitt RC	.05	.15
177 W.Simmons RC UER College touchdowns and yards are in wrong columns	.05	.15
178 Tom Carter RC	.10	.30
179 Ernest Dye RC	.05	.15
180 Lester Holmes	.05	.15
181 Irv Smith RC	.05	.15
182 Robert Smith RC	1.25	3.00
183 Darrien Gordon RC	.05	.15
184 Deon Figures RC	.05	.15
185 Leonard Renfro RC	.05	.15
186 O.J. McDuffie RC	.25	.60
187 Dana Stubblefield RC	.25	.60
188 Todd Kelly RC	.05	.15
189 Thomas Smith RC	.10	.30
190 George Teague RC	.10	.30
191 Wilber Marshall	.05	.15
192 Reggie White	.25	.60
193 Carlton Gray RC	.05	.15
194 Chris Slade RC	.10	.30
195 Ben Coleman RC	.05	.15
196 Ryan McNeil RC	.25	.60
197 Demetrius DuBose RC	.05	.15
198 Coleman Rudolph RC	.05	.15
199 Tony McGee RC	.10	.30
200 Troy Drayton RC	.10	.30
201 Natrone Means RC	.25	.60
202 Glyn Milburn RC	.25	.60
203 Chad Brown RC	.10	.30
204 Reggie Brooks RC	.10	.30
205 Kevin Williams RC	.25	.60
206 Micheal Barrow RC	.25	.60
207 Roosevelt Potts RC	.05	.15
208 Victor Bailey RC	.05	.15
209 Qadry Ismail RC	.25	.60
210 Vincent Brisby RC	.25	.60
211 Billy Joe Hobert RC	.25	.60
212 Lamar Thomas RC	.05	.15
213 Jason Elam RC	.25	.60
214 Andre Hastings RC	.10	.30
215 Terry Kirby RC	.25	.60
216 Joe Montana	1.25	3.00
217 Derrick Lassic RC	.05	.15
218 Mark Brunell RC	1.50	4.00
219 Vaughn Hebron RC	.05	.15
220 Troy Brown RC	6.00	15.00
221 Derek Brown RBK RC	.05	.15
222 Rocket Ismail	.10	.30

1993 Action Packed 24K Gold

RANDOM INS.IN BOTH SERIES PACK		
1G Troy Aikman	10.00	25.00
2G Randall Cunningham	6.00	15.00
3G John Elway	20.00	50.00
4G Jim Everett	5.00	12.00
5G Brett Favre	20.00	50.00
6G Jim Harbaugh	6.00	15.00
7G Jeff Hostetler	5.00	12.00
8G Jim Kelly	6.00	15.00
9G David Klingler	5.00	12.00
10G Bernie Kosar	5.00	12.00
11G Dan Marino	20.00	50.00
12G Chris Miller	5.00	12.00
13G Boomer Esiason	5.00	12.00
14G Warren Moon	6.00	15.00
15G Neil O'Donnell	0.00	15.00
16G Mark Rypien	5.00	12.00
17G Phil Simms	5.00	12.00
18G Steve Young	8.00	20.00
19G Fred Barnett	5.00	12.00
20G Gary Clark	5.00	12.00
21G Mark Clayton	5.00	12.00
22G Ernest Givins	5.00	12.00
23G Michael Haynes	3.00	8.00
24G Michael Irvin	6.00	15.00
25G Haywood Jeffires	3.00	8.00
26G Anthony Miller	5.00	12.00
27G Andre Reed	6.00	15.00
28G Jerry Rice	10.00	25.00
29G Andre Rison	6.00	15.00
30G Sterling Sharpe	6.00	15.00
31G Terry Allen	6.00	15.00
32G Reggie Cobb	3.00	8.00
33G Barry Foster	5.00	12.00
34G Cleveland Gary	3.00	8.00
35G Harold Green	3.00	8.00
36G Rodney Hampton	5.00	12.00
37G Barry Sanders	15.00	40.00
38G Emmitt Smith	20.00	50.00
39G Thurman Thomas	6.00	15.00
40G Chris Warren	6.00	15.00
41G Ricky Watters	6.00	15.00
42G Lorenzo White	3.00	8.00
43G Drew Bledsoe	12.50	30.00
44G Rick Mirer	6.00	15.00
45G Garrison Hearst	6.00	15.00
46G Marvin Jones	3.00	8.00
47G John Copeland	5.00	12.00
48G Eric Curry	5.00	12.00
49G Curtis Conway	6.00	15.00
50G Willie Roaf	5.00	12.00
51G Lincoln Kennedy	3.00	8.00
52G Jerome Bettis	15.00	30.00
53G Dan Williams	3.00	8.00
54G Patrick Bates	3.00	8.00
55G Brad Hopkins	3.00	8.00
56G Steve Everitt	5.00	12.00
57G Wayne Simmons	5.00	12.00
58G Tom Carter	5.00	12.00
59G Ernest Dye	3.00	8.00
60G Lester Holmes	0.00	0.00
61G Irv Smith	5.00	12.00
62G Robert Smith	6.00	15.00
63G Darrien Gordon	3.00	8.00
64G Deon Figures	3.00	8.00
65G Leonard Renfro	3.00	8.00
66G O.J. McDuffie	6.00	15.00
67G Dana Stubblefield	5.00	12.00
68G Todd Kelly	3.00	8.00
69G Thomas Smith	5.00	12.00
70G George Teague	5.00	12.00
71G Wilber Marshall	3.00	8.00
72G Reggie White	6.00	15.00

1993 Action Packed Mint Parallel

*MINT CARDS: 30X TO 80X BASIC CARDS
STATED PRINT RUN 500 SER.#'d SETS

1993 Action Packed Moving Targets

COMPLETE SET (12)	5.00	10.00
MT1 Fred Barnett	.20	.50
MT2 Gary Clark	.20	.50
MT3 Mark Clayton	.08	.25
MT4 Ernest Givins	.20	.50
MT5 Michael Haynes	.20	.50
MT6 Michael Irvin	.40	1.00
MT7 Haywood Jeffires	.20	.50
MT8 Anthony Miller	.20	.50
MT9 Andre Reed	.20	.50
MT10 Jerry Rice	2.00	4.00
MT11 Andre Rison	.20	.50
MT12 Sterling Sharpe	.40	1.00

1993 Action Packed Quarterback Club

COMPLETE SET (18)	8.00	20.00
*BRAILLE: 1.2X TO 3X BASIC INSERTS		
*MINT CARDS: 25X to 60X BASIC INSERTS		
QB1 Troy Aikman	1.25	2.50
QB2 Randall Cunningham	.30	.75
QB3 John Elway	2.00	4.00
QB4 Jim Everett	.15	.40
QB5 Brett Favre	2.50	5.00
QB6 Jim Harbaugh	.30	.75
QB7 Jeff Hostetler	.15	.40
QB8 Jim Kelly	.30	.75
QB9 David Klingler	.07	.20
QB10 Bernie Kosar	.15	.40
QB11 Dan Marino	2.00	4.00
QB12 Chris Miller	.15	.40
QB13 Boomer Esiason	.15	.40
QB14 Warren Moon	.30	.75
QB15 Neil O'Donnell	.30	.75
QB16 Mark Rypien	.07	.20
QB17 Phil Simms	.15	.40
QB18 Steve Young	1.00	2.00

1993 Action Packed Rookie Update Previews

COMPLETE SET (3)	2.40	6.00
RU1 Troy Aikman	1.50	2.00
RU2 Brett Favre	1.50	4.00
RU3 Neil O'Donnell	.40	1.00

1993 Action Packed Rushers

COMPLETE SET (12)	6.00	12.00
RB1 Terry Allen	.30	.75
RB2 Reggie Cobb	.07	.20
RB3 Barry Foster	.15	.40
RB4 Cleveland Gary	.07	.20
RB5 Harold Green	.07	.20
RB6 Rodney Hampton	.15	.40
RB7 Barry Sanders	1.50	4.00
RB8 Emmitt Smith	1.50	4.00
RB9 Thurman Thomas	.30	.75
RB10 Chris Warren	.15	.40
RB11 Ricky Watters	.30	.75
RB12 Lorenzo White	.07	.20

1993 Action Packed Emmitt Smith Mint Collection

This 2-card set was issued in honor of Emmitt Smith's 1993 season MVP performance. Each card is essentially a 24K Gold serial numbered parallel to his base card and Rusher insert card. The set was issued in a black factory box with each set serial numbered of 1486.

COMPLETE SET (2)	60.00	150.00
13 Emmitt Smith	30.00	75.00
RB8 Emmitt Smith	30.00	75.00

1993 Action Packed NFLPA Awards

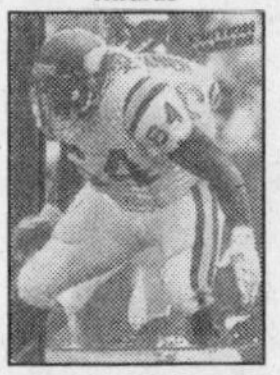

Held on March 4, 1993 in Washington, D.C., and sponsored by Action Packed, the 20th annual NFLPA banquet honored outstanding professional football players from the 1992 season. The set was produced to benefit the District of Columbia's Special Olympics. Reportedly less than 2,000 sets were produced. This 17-card standard-size set features the players selected as the best at their position by their peers and was issued in a special black box. The fronts feature an embossed action player photo overlapping a black-bordered gold stripe. The backs have a player photo and the award recipient's statistics.

COMPLETE SET (17)	20.00	50.00
1 Randall McDaniel	1.20	3.00
2 Bruce Matthews	1.20	3.00
3 Richmond Webb	1.20	3.00
4 Cortez Kennedy	1.60	4.00
5 Clyde Simmons	1.20	3.00
6 Wilber Marshall	1.20	3.00
7 Junior Seau	2.00	5.00
8 Henry Jones	1.20	3.00
9 Audray McMillian	1.20	3.00
10 Mel Gray	1.20	3.00
11 Steve Tasker	1.60	4.00
12 Marco Coleman	1.20	3.00
13 Santana Dotson	1.20	3.00
14 Vaughn Dunbar	1.20	3.00
15 Carl Pickens	2.00	5.00
16 Barry Foster	1.20	3.00
17 Steve Young	6.00	15.00

1994 Action Packed Prototypes

FB941 Troy Aikman/1994 Action Packed	1.25	3.00
FB942 Jeff Hostetler Quarterback Challenge	.40	1.00
FB943 Emmitt Smith Warp Speed	2.00	5.00
FB944 Jerry Rice Catching Fire	1.50	4.00
FB945 Barry Foster Fantasy Forecast	40	1.00
RL1 Troy Aikman Rocket Launcher	1.50	4.00
RM1 Emmitt Smith Rocket Man	2.50	6.00
RU941 Drew Bledsoe Rookie Update	.75	2.00
RU942 Derrick Lassic Rookie Update	.40	1.00
RU943 Rick Mirer (Golden Domers)	.40	1.00
RU944 Jerome Bettis (Golden Domers)	.75	2.00
MNF941 Steve Young Sept. 12, 1994 S.F. at Cleveland Monday Night Football	1.00	2.50
MNF942 Steve Young Monday Night Moment	1.00	2.50
MNF943 Barry Foster Monday Night Moment	.40	1.00
SL2 Jerry Rice Stat Leader	2.00	5.00

1994 Action Packed

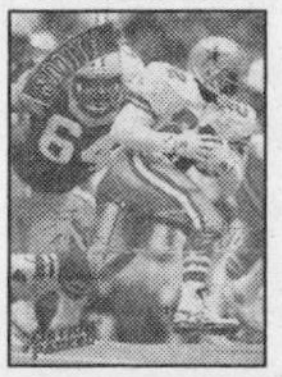

The 1994 Action Packed football set contains 198 standard-size cards. The cards were issued in two series of 120 and 78. The 120th card has a special twist. It is a Troy Aikman Back-To-Back Super Bowl card with Troy on the front holding up a number 1 of his first Super Bowl and on the back holding two fingers up to signify his second win. There are 12 Braille cards in this set. The cards are numbered on the back and checklisted below according to teams. Second series cards include rookies and traded players, Quarterback Club (172-184) and Golden Domers (193-198). Rookie Cards include Derrick Alexander, Mario Bates, Isaac Bruce, Lake Dawson, Trent Dilfer, Bert Emanuel, Marshall Faulk, William Floyd, Gus Frerotte, Greg Hill, Charles Johnson, Byron Bam Morris, Errict Rhett, Darnay Scott and Heath Shuler.

COMPLETE SET (198)	20.00	50.00
COMP.SERIES 1 (120)	10.00	25.00
COMP.SERIES 2 (78)	10.00	25.00
1 Michael Haynes	.10	.30
2 Andre Rison	.10	.30
3 Mike Pritchard	.05	.15
4 Erric Pegram	.05	.15
5 Deion Sanders	.30	.75
6 Jim Kelly	.25	.60
7 Andre Reed	.10	.30
8 Thurman Thomas	.25	.60

9 Bruce Smith .25 .60
10 Cornelius Bennett .10 .30
11 Nate Odomes .05 .15
12 Richard Dent .10 .30
13 Donnell Woolford .05 .15
14 Harold Green .05 .15
15 David Klingler .05 .15
16 Eric Metcalf .10 .30
17 Michael Dean Perry .10 .30
18 Michael Jackson .10 .30
19 Vinny Testaverde .10 .30
20 Troy Aikman .60 1.50
21 Michael Irvin .25 .60
22 Emmitt Smith 1.00 2.50
23 Jay Novacek .10 .30
24 Alvin Harper .10 .30
25 Charles Haley .10 .30
26 John Elway 1.25 3.00
27 Shannon Sharpe .10 .30
28 Rod Bernstine .05 .15
29 Simon Fletcher .05 .15
30 Barry Sanders 1.00 2.50
31 Herman Moore .25 .60
32 Pat Swilling .05 .15
33 Chris Spielman .10 .30
34 Brett Favre 1.25 3.00
35 Sterling Sharpe UER .25 .60
(Photo on back is Shannon Sharpe)
36 Reggie White .25 .60
37 Jackie Harris .05 .15
38 Tony Bennett .05 .15
39 LeRoy Butler .05 .15
40 Warren Moon .25 .60
41 Ernest Givins .10 .30
42 Haywood Jeffires .10 .30
43 Webster Slaughter .05 .15
44 Ray Childress .05 .15
45 Gary Brown .05 .15
46 Jeff George .25 .60
47 Roosevelt Potts .05 .15
48 Quentin Coryatt .05 .15
49 Joe Montana 1.25 3.00
50 Derrick Thomas .25 .60
51 Neil Smith .10 .30
52 Marcus Allen .25 .60
53 Willie Davis .10 .30
54 Jerome Bettis .40 1.00
55 Sean Gilbert .05 .15
56 Chris Miller .05 .15
57 Jeff Hostetler .10 .30
58 Tim Brown .25 .60
59 Anthony Smith .05 .15
60 Greg Townsend .05 .15
61 Terry McDaniel .05 .15
62 Dan Marino 1.25 3.00
63 Irving Fryar .10 .30
64 Keith Jackson .05 .15
65 Terry Kirby .25 .60
66 Bryan Cox .05 .15
67 Chris Doleman .05 .15
68 Cris Carter .30 .75
69 John Randle .10 .30
70 Drew Bledsoe .60 1.50
71 Ben Coates .10 .30
72 Vincent Brisby .10 .30
73 Rickey Jackson .05 .15
74 Eric Martin .05 .15
75 Renaldo Turnbull .05 .15
76 Rodney Hampton .10 .30
77 Mike Sherrard .05 .15
78 Phil Simms .10 .30
79 Keith Hamilton .05 .15
80 Rob Moore .10 .30
81 Brad Baxter .05 .15
82 Boomer Esiason .10 .30
83 Johnny Johnson .05 .15
84 Ronnie Lott .10 .30
85 Randall Cunningham .25 .60
86 Herschel Walker .10 .30
87 Eric Allen .05 .15
88 Clyde Simmons .05 .15
89 Seth Joyner .05 .15
90 Calvin Williams .10 .30
91 Garrison Hearst .25 .60
92 Steve Beuerlein .10 .30
93 Ricky Proehl .05 .15
94 Ronald Moore .05 .15
95 Barry Foster .05 .15
96 Neil O'Donnell .25 .60
97 Eric Green .05 .15
98 Rod Woodson .10 .30
99 Greg Lloyd .10 .30
100 Kevin Greene .10 .30
101 Stan Humphries .10 .30
102 Anthony Miller .10 .30
103 Junior Seau .25 .60
104 Leslie O'Neal .05 .15
105 Ronnie Harmon .05 .15
106 Jerry Rice .60 1.50
107 Ricky Watters .10 .30
108 Steve Young .50 1.25
109 Brent Jones .10 .30
110 John Taylor .10 .30
111 Rick Mirer .25 .60
112 Chris Warren .10 .30
113 Cortez Kennedy .10 .30
114 Brian Blades .10 .30
115 Eugene Robinson .05 .15
116 Reggie Cobb .05 .15
117 Hardy Nickerson .10 .30
118 Reggie Brooks .10 .30
119 Darrell Green .05 .15
120 Troy Aikman .75 2.00
Back to Back
121 Dan Wilkinson RC .10 .30
122 Marshall Faulk RC 3.00 8.00
123 Heath Shuler RC .25 .60
124 Willie McGinest RC .25 .60
125 Trev Alberts RC .10 .30
126 Trent Dilfer RC .75 2.00
127 Bryant Young RC .40 1.00
128 Sam Adams RC .10 .30
129 Antonio Langham RC .10 .30
130 Jamir Miller RC .10 .30
131 John Thierry RC .05 .15
132 Aaron Glenn RC .25 .60
133 Joe Johnson RC .05 .15
134 Bernard Williams .05 .15
135 Wayne Gandy .05 .15
136 Charles Johnson RC .25 .60
137 Dewayne Washington RC .10 .30
138 Todd Steussie RC .10 .30
139 Tim Bowens RC .10 .30
140 Johnnie Morton RC 1.00 2.50
141 Rob Fredrickson RC .10 .30
142 Shante Carver RC .05 .15
143 Thomas Lewis RC .10 .30
144 Greg Hill RC .25 .60
145 Henry Ford .05 .15
146 Jeff Burris RC .10 .30
147 William Floyd RC .25 .60
148 Der. Alexander WR RC .25 .60
149 Darnay Scott RC .50 1.25
150 Isaac Bruce RC 3.00 6.00
151 Errict Rhett RC .25 .60
152 Kevin Lee RC .05 .15
153 Chuck Levy RC .05 .15
154 David Palmer RC .25 .60
155 Ryan Yarborough RC .05 .15
156 Charlie Garner RC .75 2.00
157 Mario Bates RC .25 .60
158 Bert Emanuel RC .25 .60
159 Bucky Brooks RC .05 .15
160 Donnell Bennett RC .25 .60
161 Tydus Winans RC .05 .15
162 Andre Coleman RC .05 .15
163 Calvin Jones RC .05 .15
164 LeShon Johnson RC .10 .30
165 Doug Brien RC .05 .15
166 Byron Bam Morris RC .10 .30
167 Lake Dawson RC .10 .30
168 Perry Klein RC .05 .15
169 Doug Nussmeier RC .05 .15
170 Lamont Warren RC .05 .15
171 Gus Frerotte RC 1.00 2.50
172 Troy Aikman QC .60 1.50
173 Randall Cunningham QC .25 .60
174 John Elway QC 1.00 2.50
175 Jim Everett QC .05 .15
176 Drew Bledsoe QC .40 1.00
177 Jim Kelly QC .10 .30
178 Dan Marino QC 1.00 2.50
179 Chris Miller QC .05 .15
180 Warren Moon QC .10 .30
181 Rick Mirer QC .25 .60
182 Jeff Hostetler QC .05 .15
183 Brett Favre QC 1.25 2.50
184 Steve Young QC .40 1.00
185 Anthony Miller .10 .30
186 Michael Haynes .10 .30
187 Mike Pritchard .05 .15
188 Jeff George .25 .60
189 Lewis Tillman .05 .15
190 Ken Norton .10 .30
191 Erik Kramer .10 .30
192 Richard Dent .10 .30
193 Rick Mirer GD .25 .60
194 Jerome Bettis GD .25 .60
195 Reggie Brooks GD .05 .15
196 Tom Carter GD .05 .15
197 Irv Smith GD .05 .15
198 Rocket Ismail GD .10 .30

1994 Action Packed Braille

30 Barry Sanders 2.50 5.00
36 Reggie White .60 1.25
38 Tony Bennett .10 .30
40 Warren Moon .60 1.25
59 Anthony Smith .10 .30
70 Drew Bledsoe 1.50 3.00
78 Phil Simms .25 .60
82 Boomer Esiason .25 .60
98 Rod Woodson .25 .60
108 Steve Young 1.25 2.50
113 Cortez Kennedy .25 .60
118 Reggie Brooks .25 .60

1994 Action Packed Gold Signatures

6 Jim Kelly 1.00 2.00
15 David Klingler .20 .50
20 Troy Aikman 2.50 5.00
21 Michael Irvin 1.00 2.00
22 Emmitt Smith 4.00 8.00
26 John Elway 5.00 10.00
30 Barry Sanders 4.00 8.00
34 Brett Favre 5.00 10.00
40 Warren Moon 1.00 2.00
56 Chris Miller .20 .50
57 Jeff Hostetler .40 1.00
62 Dan Marino 5.00 10.00
70 Drew Bledsoe 2.50 5.00
78 Phil Simms .40 1.00
82 Boomer Esiason .40 1.00
85 Randall Cunningham 1.00 2.00
96 Neil O'Donnell 1.00 2.00
106 Jerry Rice 2.50 5.00
108 Steve Young 2.00 4.00
111 Rick Mirer 1.00 2.00

1994 Action Packed 24K Gold

COMPLETE SET (55) 200.00 400.00
STATED ODDS 1:96
G1 Troy Aikman 6.00 15.00
G2 Randall Cunningham 3.00 8.00
G3 John Elway 12.50 30.00
G4 Boomer Esiason 2.50 6.00
G5 Jim Everett 2.50 6.00
G6 Brett Favre 12.50 30.00
G7 Jerry Rice 8.00 20.00
G8 Jeff Hostetler 2.00 5.00
G9 Jim Kelly 4.00 10.00
G10 David Klingler 2.00 5.00
G11 Bernie Kosar 2.50 6.00
G12 Dan Marino 12.50 30.00
G13 Chris Miller 2.00 5.00
G14 Warren Moon 3.00 8.00
G15 Neil O'Donnell 2.50 6.00
G16 Michael Irvin 4.00 10.00
G17 Phil Simms 3.00 8.00
G18 Steve Young 5.00 12.00
G19 Rick Mirer 2.50 6.00
G20 Drew Bledsoe 4.00 10.00
G21 Jerry Rice 8.00 20.00
G22 Sterling Sharpe 3.00 8.00
G23 Michael Irvin 4.00 10.00
G24 Andre Rison 2.50 6.00
G25 Anthony Miller 2.50 6.00
G26 Tim Brown 3.00 8.00
G27 Andre Reed 3.00 8.00
G28 Herman Moore 2.50 6.00
G29 Irving Fryar 2.50 6.00
G30 Shannon Sharpe 3.00 8.00
G31 Emmitt Smith 12.50 30.00
G32 Barry Sanders 10.00 25.00
G33 Thurman Thomas 3.00 8.00
G34 Jerome Bettis 5.00 12.00
G35 Barry Foster 2.00 5.00
G36 Ricky Watters 2.50 6.00
G37 Rodney Hampton 2.00 5.00
G38 Chris Warren 2.00 5.00
G39 Erric Pegram 2.00 5.00
G40 Reggie Brooks 2.00 5.00
G41 Marcus Allen 3.00 8.00
G42 Ronald Moore 2.00 5.00
G43 Troy Aikman QC 8.00 20.00
G44 Randall Cunningham QC 4.00 10.00
G45 John Elway QC 15.00 40.00
G46 Jim Everett QC 2.50 6.00
G47 Drew Bledsoe QC 5.00 12.00
G48 Jim Kelly QC 5.00 12.00
G49 Dan Marino QC 15.00 40.00
G50 Chris Miller QC 2.50 6.00
G51 Warren Moon QC 4.00 10.00
G52 Rick Mirer QC 4.00 10.00
G53 Jeff Hostetler QC 2.50 6.00
G54 Brett Favre QC 15.00 40.00
G55 Steve Young QC 6.00 15.00

1994 Action Packed Catching Fire

COMPLETE SET (10) 4.00 10.00
R1 Jerry Rice 1.50 3.00
R2 Sterling Sharpe .60 1.25
R3 Michael Irvin .60 1.25
R4 Andre Rison .25 .60
R5 Anthony Miller .25 .60
R6 Tim Brown .60 1.25
R7 Andre Reed .25 .60
R8 Herman Moore .60 1.25
R9 Irving Fryar .25 .60
R10 Shannon Sharpe .25 .60

1994 Action Packed Fantasy Forecast

COMPLETE SET (42) 6.00 15.00
FF1 Rodney Hampton .07 .20
FF2 Steve Young .40 1.00
FF3 Michael Irvin .15 .40
FF4 Emmitt Smith 1.00 2.00
FF5 Troy Aikman .40 1.00
FF6 Jerry Rice .40 1.00
FF7 Brett Favre 1.00 2.00
FF8 Jerome Bettis .30 .75
FF9 Reggie Brooks .07 .20
FF10 John Elway 1.00 2.00
FF11 Jim Kelly .15 .40
FF12 Dan Marino 1.00 2.00
FF13 Randall Cunningham .15 .40
FF14 Sterling Sharpe .15 .40
FF15 Chris Warren .07 .20
FF16 Andre Rison .07 .20
FF17 Mike Pritchard .02 .10
FF18 Barry Sanders 1.00 2.00
FF19 Marcus Allen .15 .40
FF20 Thurman Thomas .15 .40
FF21 Erric Pegram .02 .10
FF22 Barry Foster .02 .10
FF23 Anthony Miller .07 .20
FF24 Shannon Sharpe .07 .20
FF25 Tim Brown .15 .40
FF26 Ricky Watters .07 .20
FF27 Ernest Givins .07 .20
FF28 Cris Carter .20 .50
FF29 Willie Davis .07 .20
FF30 Warren Moon .15 .40
FF31 Joe Montana 1.00 2.00
FF32 Herman Moore .15 .40
FF33 Terry Kirby .15 .40
FF34 Eric Green .02 .10
FF35 Michael Jackson .07 .20
FF36 Johnny Johnson .02 .10
FF37 Calvin Williams .07 .20
FF38 Michael Haynes .07 .20
FF39 Irving Fryar .07 .20
FF40 Gary Brown .02 .10
FF41 Jeff Hostetler .07 .20
FF42 Keith Jackson .02 .10

1994 Action Packed Quarterback Challenge

COMPLETE SET (12) 8.00 20.00
ONE PER SPECIAL RETAIL PACK
FA1 Steve Young .60 1.25
FA2 John Elway 1.50 3.00
FA3 Troy Aikman .75 1.50
FA4 Randall Cunningham .25 .60
FA5 Warren Moon .25 .60
FA6 Brett Favre 1.50 3.00
FA7 Rick Mirer .25 .60
FA8 Drew Bledsoe .75 1.50
FA9 Boomer Esiason .10 .30
FA10 Jeff Hostetler .10 .30
FA11 Jim Kelly .25 .60
FA12 Dan Marino 1.50 3.00

1994 Action Packed Quarterback Club

COMPLETE SET (20) 8.00 20.00
QB1 Troy Aikman .75 1.50
QB2 Randall Cunningham .25 .60
QB3 John Elway 1.50 3.00
QB4 Boomer Esiason .10 .30
QB5 Jim Everett .05 .15
QB6 Brett Favre 1.50 3.00
QB7 Jerry Rice .75 1.50
QB8 Jeff Hostetler .10 .30
QB9 Jim Kelly .25 .60
QB10 David Klingler .05 .15
QB11 Bernie Kosar .05 .15
QB12 Dan Marino 1.50 3.00
QB13 Chris Miller .05 .15
QB14 Warren Moon .25 .60
QB15 Neil O'Donnell .25 .60
QB16 Michael Irvin .25 .60
QB17 Phil Simms .10 .30
QB18 Steve Young .60 1.25
QB19 Rick Mirer .25 .60
QB20 Drew Bledsoe .75 1.50

1994 Action Packed Warp Speed

COMPLETE SET (12) 4.00 10.00
WS1 Emmitt Smith 1.50 3.00
WS2 Barry Sanders 1.50 3.00
WS3 Thurman Thomas .30 .75
WS4 Jerome Bettis .60 1.25
WS5 Barry Foster .07 .20
WS6 Ricky Watters .15 .40
WS7 Rodney Hampton .15 .40
WS8 Chris Warren .15 .40
WS9 Erric Pegram .07 .20
WS10 Reggie Brooks .15 .40
WS11 Marcus Allen .30 .75
WS12 Ronald Moore .07 .20

1994 Action Packed Badge of Honor Pins

This set of 25 pins measures approximately 1 1/2" by 1". The pins came in packs of four inside a cardboard holder. The back of the holder contained a checklist for the set. Each box contained three packs of 4-pins along with one of five different black pin "albums" to house five of the pins. On a bronze background, the fronts feature color player portraits with a gold border. The player's last name appears in gold lettering at the bottom. The Action Packed logo is above the picture, while the year 1994 inside a football icon is below. The backs carry the copyrights "1994 Action Packed" and "1994 NFL/NFL QB Club." The pins are unnumbered and checklisted below in alphabetical order. A 24K Gold parallel version of each pin was also produced and randomly inserted in packs.

COMPLETE SET (25) 12.00 30.00
*24K GOLD PINS: 7.5X TO 20X
1 Troy Aikman .80 2.00
2 Drew Bledsoe .80 2.00
3 Bubby Brister .10 .30
4 Randall Cunningham .30 .75
5 John Elway 1.60 4.00
6 Boomer Esiason .20 .50
7 Jim Everett .10 .30
8 Brett Favre 1.60 4.00
9 Jim Harbaugh .20 .50
10 Jeff Hostetler .10 .30
11 Michael Irvin .30 .75
12 Jim Kelly .30 .75
13 David Klingler .10 .30
14 Bernie Kosar .10 .30
15 Dan Marino 1.60 4.00
16 Chris Miller .10 .30
17 Rick Mirer .10 .30
18 Warren Moon .30 .75
19 Neil O'Donnell .10 .30
20 Jerry Rice .80 2.00
21 Mark Rypien .10 .30
22 Barry Sanders 1.60 4.00
23 Phil Simms .20 .50
24 Emmitt Smith 1.20 3.00
25 Steve Young .60 1.50

1994 Action Packed Mammoth

COMPLETE SET (25) 45.00 100.00
MM1 Troy Aikman 3.00 8.00
MM2 Drew Bledsoe 2.50 6.00
MM3 Barry Sanders 5.00 12.00
MM4 Chris Miller .75 2.00
MM5 Randall Cunningham 1.60 4.00
MM6 John Elway 5.00 12.00
MM7 Boomer Esiason 1.50 3.00
MM8 Jim Everett .75 2.00
MM9 Brett Favre 5.00 12.00
MM10 Jim Harbaugh 1.50 3.00
MM11 Jeff Hostetler .75 2.00
MM12 Michael Irvin 1.60 4.00
MM13 Jim Kelly 1.60 4.00
MM14 David Klingler .75 2.00
MM15 Bernie Kosar .75 2.00
MM16 Dan Marino 5.00 12.00
MM17 Rick Mirer .75 2.00
MM18 Warren Moon 1.60 4.00
MM19 Neil O'Donnell .75 2.00
MM20 Jerry Rice 3.00 8.00
MM21 Mark Rypien .75 2.00
MM22 Phil Simms 1.50 3.00
MM23 Emmitt Smith 4.00 10.00
MM24 Steve Young 2.00 5.00
MM26 Bubby Brister .75 2.00
2MM1 Troy Aikman 3.00 8.00
Series 2 card
numbered MM1-2
2MM2 Michael Irvin 1.60 4.00
Series 2 card
numbered MM2-2
2MM6 Emmitt Smith 4.00 10.00
Series 2 card
numbered MM6-2
P1 Troy Aikman 3.00 8.00
Prototype
Numbered MMP
P2 Emmitt Smith 12.00 30.00
Prototype 24K Gold
Numbered MMP1G
reportedly 2500 made
P3 Troy Aikman 8.00 20.00
Prototype 24K Gold
Numbered MMP2G
reportedly 1000 made

1994 Action Packed CoaStars

Issued in six-card shrink wrapped retail sheets, these "coaster cards" have rounded corners and measure roughly 3 1/4" by 3 1/4". The front of each features a borderless player action shot that is full color within the 2 3/4" diameter central circle. The player's name and position appear in an arc at the upper right. The back features a borderless color player action shot, with the player's name and '93 away statistics appearing near the bottom. The coasters are numbered on the front but have been listed below in 6-card panels since that is the most common form in which they are traded.

COMPLETE SET (5) 10.00 20.00
1 Troy Aikman 2.00 4.00
Bubby Brister
Randall Cunningham
John Elway
Warren Moon
Jerry Rice
2 Troy Aikman 2.00 4.00
Rick Mirer
Chris Miller
Phil Simms
Bernie Kosar
Barry Sanders
3 Drew Bledsoe 3.00 6.00
Dan Marino
Neil O'Donnell
Jim Kelly
Jim Everett
David Klingler
4 Drew Bledsoe 1.50 3.00
Emmitt Smith
Mark Rypien
Boomer Esiason
Steve Young
Jim Harbaugh
5 John Elway 3.00 6.00
Jim Kelly
Troy Aikman
Jerry Rice
Dan Marino
Emmitt Smith

1995 Action Packed Promos

1 Jerry Rice 1.00 2.50
2 Emmitt Smith 1.60 4.00
AF4 Steve Young .80 2.00
(Armed Forces)
RM1 Emmitt Smith 2.00 5.00
NNO Action Packed Ad Card .20 .50

1995 Action Packed

This 126-card standard size set is the first Action Packed set issued by Pinnacle Brands. The fronts display full-bleed, embossed color action photos, with the team's helmet, player's name and the words "Action Packed 1995" on the right side for veterans and on the left side for rookies. The backs feature statistics, a player photo, and brief biographical information. Rookie Cards include Ki-Jana Carter, Kerry Collins, Joey Galloway, Steve McNair, Rashaan Salaam, J.J. Stokes, Michael Westbrook and Tyrone Wheatley.

COMPLETE SET (126) 7.50 20.00
1 Jerry Rice .60 1.50
2 Emmitt Smith 1.00 2.50
3 Drew Bledsoe .40 1.00
4 Ben Coates .08 .25
5 Jim Everett .02 .10
6 Warren Moon .08 .25
7 Herman Moore .20 .50
8 Deion Sanders .40 1.00
9 Rick Mirer .08 .25
10 Natrone Means .08 .25
11 Jeff Blake RC .50 1.25
12 William Floyd .08 .25
13 Steve Young .50 1.25
14 John Elway 1.25 3.00
15 Brett Favre 1.25 3.00
16 Marshall Faulk .75 2.00
17 Heath Shuler .08 .25
18 Ricky Watters .08 .25
19 Michael Haynes .08 .25
20 Troy Aikman .60 1.50
21 Dan Marino 1.25 3.00
22 Byron Bam Morris .02 .10
23 Marcus Allen .20 .50
24 Carl Pickens .08 .25
25 Rodney Hampton .08 .25
26 Dave Brown .08 .25
27 Jerome Bettis .20 .50
28 Jim Kelly .20 .50
29 Andre Reed .08 .25
30 Michael Irvin .20 .50
31 Barry Sanders 1.00 2.50
32 Chris Warren .08 .25
33 Jeff Hostetler .08 .25
34 Alvin Harper .02 .10
35 Rob Moore .08 .25
36 Steve McNair RC 2.00 5.00
37 Rashaan Salaam RC .08 .25
38 Joey Galloway RC 1.00 2.50
39 J.J. Stokes RC .20 .50
40 Michael Westbrook RC .20 .50
41 Kerry Collins RC 1.25 3.00
42 Ki-Jana Carter RC .20 .50
43 Boomer Esiason .08 .25
44 Chris Spielman .08 .25
45 Vinny Testaverde .08 .25
46 Kevin Williams WR .08 .25
47 Ronnie Harmon .02 .10
48 Fred Barnett .08 .25
49 Harvey Williams .02 .10
50 Reggie White .20 .50
51 Brent Jones .02 .10
52 Henry Ellard .08 .25
53 Cris Carter .20 .50
54 Leroy Hoard .02 .10
55 Trent Dilfer .20 .50
56 Raymont Harris .02 .10
57 Garrison Hearst .20 .50
58 Lewis Tillman .02 .10
59 Mark Brunell .40 1.00
60 Bruce Smith .20 .50
61 Lake Dawson .08 .25
62 Bert Emanuel .20 .50
63 Eric Green .02 .10
64 Barry Foster .08 .25
65 Jeff Graham .02 .10
66 Curtis Conway .20 .50
67 Herschel Walker .08 .25
68 Edgar Bennett .08 .25
69 Mario Bates .08 .25
70 Irving Fryar .08 .25
71 Gary Brown .02 .10
72 Cortez Kennedy .08 .25
73 John Taylor .02 .10
74 Jeff George .08 .25
75 Shannon Sharpe .08 .25
76 Andre Rison .08 .25
77 Mike Sherrard .02 .10
78 Errict Rhett .08 .25
79 Junior Seau .20 .50
80 Willie Davis .08 .25
81 Craig Erickson .02 .10
82 Torrance Small .02 .10
83 Randall Cunningham .20 .50
84 Robert Brooks .20 .50
85 Terance Mathis .08 .25
86 Rod Woodson .08 .25
87 Anthony Miller .08 .25
88 Stan Humphries .08 .25
89 Chris Miller .02 .10
90 Steve Beuerlein .08 .25
91 Steve Bono .08 .25
92 Frank Reich .02 .10
93 Cory Fleming .02 .10
94 Isaac Bruce .30 .75
95 Dave Meggett .02 .10
96 Jackie Harris .02 .10
97 J.J. Birden .02 .10
98 Flipper Anderson .02 .10
99 Johnnie Morton .08 .25
100 Michael Timpson .02 .10
101 Derek Brown RBK .02 .10
102 Ricky Ervins .02 .10
103 Der.Alexander DE RC .02 .10
104 Dave Barr RC .02 .10
105 Tony Boselli RC .20 .50
106 Kyle Brady RC .20 .50
107 Mark Bruener RC .08 .25
108 Kevin Carter RC .20 .50
109 Neil O'Donnell .08 .25
110 Derrick Alexander WR .20 .50
111 Charlie Garner .20 .50
112 Darnay Scott .08 .25
113 Scott Mitchell .08 .25
114 Charles Johnson .08 .25
115 Greg Hill .08 .25
116 Ty Law RC 1.00 2.50
117 Frank Sanders RC .20 .50
118 James O. Stewart RC .75 2.00
119 James A.Stewart RC .02 .10
120 Kordell Stewart RC 1.00 2.50
121 Rob Johnson RC .60 1.50
122 John Walsh RC .02 .10
123 Stoney Case RC .02 .10
124 Tyrone Wheatley RC .75 2.00
125 Sherman Williams RC .02 .10
126 Ray Zellars RC .08 .25

1995 Action Packed Quick Silver

COMPLETE SET (126) 40.00 100.00
*STARS: 2.5X TO 6X BASIC CARDS
*RCs: 1.5X TO 4X BASIC CARDS
STATED ODDS 1:6

1995 Action Packed 24K Gold

COMPLETE SET (21) 75.00 200.00
STATED ODDS 1:72
1G Jerry Rice 8.00 20.00
2G Emmitt Smith 12.50 30.00
3G Drew Bledsoe 3.00 8.00
4G Warren Moon 2.50 6.00
5G Deion Sanders 4.00 10.00
6G Natrone Means 2.00 5.00
7G Steve Young 5.00 12.00
8G John Elway UER 12.50 30.00
Last year is shown as 994
9G Brett Favre 12.50 30.00
10G Marshall Faulk 8.00 20.00
11G Heath Shuler 2.00 5.00
12G Troy Aikman 6.00 15.00
13G Dan Marino 12.50 30.00
14G Jerome Bettis 3.00 8.00
15G Jim Kelly 4.00 10.00
16G Michael Irvin 4.00 10.00
17G Barry Sanders 10.00 25.00
18G Steve McNair 8.00 20.00
19G Rashaan Salaam 2.00 5.00
20G Kerry Collins 4.00 15.00
21G Ki-Jana Carter 2.00 5.00

1995 Action Packed Armed Forces

COMPLETE SET (12) 25.00 60.00
STATED ODDS 1:24
*BRAILLES: .5X TO 1.2X BASIC INSERTS
BRAILLE STATED ODDS 1:96
AF1 Drew Bledsoe 2.00 5.00
AF2 Dan Marino 6.00 15.00
AF3 Troy Aikman 3.00 8.00
AF4 Steve Young 2.50 6.00
AF5 Brett Favre 6.00 15.00
AF6 Heath Shuler .50 1.25
AF7 Dave Brown .50 1.25
AF8 Jeff Blake 1.00 2.50
AF9 John Elway 6.00 15.00
AF10 Rick Mirer .50 1.25
AF11 Kerry Collins 2.50 6.00
AF12 Steve McNair 4.00 10.00

1995 Action Packed G-Force

COMPLETE SET (12) 10.00 20.00
RANDOM INSERTS IN PACKS
GF1 Emmitt Smith 5.00 10.00
GF2 Barry Sanders 5.00 10.00
GF3 Marshall Faulk 4.00 8.00
GF4 Natrone Means .40 1.00
GF5 Chris Warren .40 1.00
GF6 Jerome Bettis 1.00 2.00
GF7 Errict Rhett .40 1.00
GF8 Byron Bam Morris .15 .40
GF9 Ki-Jana Carter .30 .75
GF10 Mario Bates .40 1.00
GF11 Ricky Watters .40 1.00
GF12 Tyrone Wheatley 1.50 3.00

1995 Action Packed Rocket Men

COMPLETE SET (18) 50.00 100.00
STATED ODDS 1:12 JUM
RM1 Marshall Faulk 5.00 10.00
RM2 Emmitt Smith 6.00 12.00
RM3 Barry Sanders 6.00 12.00
RM4 Natrone Means .60 1.25
RM5 Errict Rhett .60 1.25
RM6 Ki-Jana Carter .40 1.00
RM7 Tyrone Wheatley 2.00 4.00
RM8 Drew Bledsoe 2.50 5.00
RM9 Dan Marino 8.00 15.00
RM10 Steve Young 3.00 6.00
RM11 Troy Aikman 4.00 8.00
RM12 Brett Favre 8.00 15.00
RM13 Kerry Collins 2.50 6.00
RM14 Steve McNair 5.00 10.00
RM15 Heath Shuler .60 1.25
RM16 Jerry Rice 4.00 8.00
RM17 Michael Irvin 1.25 2.50
RM18 Herman Moore 1.25 2.50
RM1P Emmitt Smith Promo .75 2.00

1995 Action Packed Brian Piccolo

This single card was issued by Action Packed to honor the 25th anniversary of the passing of Brian Piccolo. Ech card was serial numbered to 2500.

1 Brian Piccolo 5.00

1996 Action Packed Promos

This three-card set was issued to preview the 1996 Action Packed series. The cards are identical to their regular issue counterparts, except for the word "Promo" printed in black on the card back.

COMPLETE SET (4) 8.00 20.00
1 Emmitt Smith 1.60 4.00
3 Jerry Rice Studs 6.00 15.00
16 Steve Young .80 2.00
105 Neil O'Donnell .40 1.00

1996 Action Packed

The 1996 Action Packed set was issued by Pinnacle in one series totalling 126 standard-size cards. The set was issued in three different pack forms. Retail and Hobby packs each contained five cards per pack while the magazine packs contained four cards per pack. For the first time, these cards had square corners instead of the traditional round corners. Cards numbered 115-126 are a subset titled "Eyeing the Storm". There are no Rookie Cards in this set.

COMPLETE SET (126) 12.50 25.00
1 Emmitt Smith 1.50 3.00
2 Dan Marino 1.50 4.00
3 Isaac Bruce .25 .60
4 Eric Zeier .05 .15
5 Ben Coates .10 .30
6 Jim Kelly .25 .60
7 Rodney Hampton .10 .30
8 Greg Lloyd .10 .30
9 Reggie White .25 .60
10 Derrick Thomas .25 .60
11 Jerry Rice .75 2.00
12 Drew Bledsoe .40 1.00
13 Cris Carter .25 .60
14 Troy Aikman .75 2.00
15 Steve McNair .60 1.50
16 Steve Young .60 1.50
17 Ricky Watters .10 .30
18 Brett Favre 2.00 4.00
19 Michael Westbrook .25 .60
20 Charles Haley .10 .30
21 Heath Shuler .10 .30
22 Tim Brown .25 .60
23 Kerry Collins .25 .60
24 Hugh Douglas .10 .30
25 Marcus Allen .25 .60
26 Steve Bono .05 .15
27 Curtis Martin .60 1.50
28 Wayne Chrebet .40 1.00
29 Dave Brown .05 .15
30 James O. Stewart .10 .30
31 Chris Sanders .10 .30
32 Deion Sanders .40 1.00
33 Rodney Thomas .05 .15
34 Rashaan Salaam .10 .30
35 Curtis Conway .25 .60
36 Harvey Williams .05 .15
37 William Floyd .10 .30
38 Carl Pickens .10 .30
39 Herman Moore .10 .30
40 Stan Humphries .10 .30
41 Orlando Thomas .05 .15
42 Bert Emanuel .10 .30
43 Yancey Thigpen .10 .30
44 Darick Holmes .05 .15
45 Mario Bates .10 .30
46 Greg Hill .10 .30
47 Errict Rhett .10 .30
48 Erik Kramer .05 .15
49 Garrison Hearst .10 .30
50 Jim Everett .05 .15
51 Barry Sanders 1.25 3.00
52 Eric Metcalf .05 .15
53 Marshall Faulk .30 .75
54 Junior Seau .25 .60
55 Bruce Smith .10 .30
56 Kordell Stewart .25 .60
57 Edgar Bennett .10 .30
58 Joey Galloway .25 .60
59 Jeff Hostetler .05 .15
60 Frank Sanders .10 .30
61 John Elway 1.50 4.00
62 Tyrone Wheatley .10 .30
63 Jeff George .10 .30
64 Ken Norton, Jr. .05 .15
65 Bryan Cox .05 .15
66 Bryce Paup .05 .15
67 Larry Centers .10 .30
68 Bernie Parmalee .05 .15
69 Jeff Graham .05 .15
70 Rick Mirer .10 .30
71 Chris Warren .10 .30
72 Charlie Garner .10 .30
73 Robert Brooks .25 .60
74 Jim Harbaugh .10 .30
75 Tamarick Vanover .10 .30
76 Napoleon Kaufman .25 .60
77 Warren Moon .10 .30
78 Vincent Brisby .05 .15
79 Ki-Jana Carter .10 .30
80 Michael Irvin .25 .60
81 Trent Dilfer .25 .60
82 Byron Bam Morris .05 .15
83 Mark Brunell .40 1.00
84 Jeff Blake .25 .60
85 Kevin Williams .05 .15
86 Rod Woodson .10 .30
87 Andre Reed .10 .30
88 Erric Pegram .05 .15
89 Anthony Miller .10 .30
90 Gus Frerotte .10 .30
91 Quinn Early .05 .15
92 Daryl Johnston .10 .30
93 Tony Martin .10 .30
94 Terrell Davis .60 1.50
95 Brent Jones .05 .15
96 Mark Chmura .10 .30
97 Kyle Brady .05 .15
98 J.J. Stokes .25 .60
99 Rodney Peete .05 .15
100 Natrone Means .10 .30
101 Sherman Williams .05 .15
102 Brian Blades .05 .15
103 Brett Perriman .05 .15
104 Antonio Freeman .25 .60
105 Neil O'Donnell .10 .30
106 Craig Heyward .05 .15
107 Derek Loville .05 .15
108 Jay Novacek .05 .15
109 Scott Mitchell .10 .30
110 Bill Brooks .05 .15
111 Shannon Sharpe .10 .30
112 Jake Reed .10 .30
113 Derrick Moore .05 .15
114 Steve Atwater .05 .15

115 Darren Woodson ETS	.10	.30
116 Junior Seau ETS	.25	.60
117 Quentin Coryatt ETS	.05	.15
118 Bruce Smith ETS	.10	.30
119 Rod Woodson ETS	.10	.30
120 Charles Haley ETS	.10	.30
121 Derrick Thomas ETS	.10	.30
122 Ken Norton, Jr. ETS	.05	.15
123 Steve Atwater ETS	.05	.15
124 Greg Lloyd ETS	.10	.30
125 Reggie White ETS	.25	.60
126 Bryan Cox ETS	.05	.15

1996 Action Packed Artist's Proofs

COMPLETE SET (126)	200.00	400.00

*AP STARS: 4X TO 10X BASIC CARDS
STATED ODDS 1:24 HOB, 1:30 RET

1996 Action Packed 24K Gold

COMPLETE SET (14)	100.00	200.00
STATED ODDS 1:72 HOB/RET		
1 Brett Favre	12.50	30.00
2 Michael Irvin	4.00	10.00
3 Drew Bledsoe	3.00	8.00
4 Jerry Rice	8.00	20.00
5 Troy Aikman	6.00	15.00
6 Dan Marino	12.50	30.00
7 Errict Rhett	2.00	5.00
8 Curtis Martin	3.00	8.00
9 Steve Young	5.00	12.00
10 Barry Sanders	10.00	25.00
11 Marshall Faulk	2.50	6.00
12 Isaac Bruce	2.50	6.00
13 John Elway	12.50	30.00
14 Emmitt Smith	12.50	30.00

1996 Action Packed Ball Hog

COMPLETE SET (12)	20.00	50.00
STATED ODDS 1:23HOB/RET, 1:29MAG		
1 Carl Pickens	.60	1.50
2 Terrell Davis	3.00	8.00
3 Jerry Rice	4.00	10.00
4 Barry Sanders	6.00	15.00
5 Marshall Faulk	1.50	4.00
6 Isaac Bruce	1.25	3.00
7 Michael Irvin	1.25	3.00
8 Cris Carter	1.25	3.00
9 Rashaan Salaam	.60	1.50
10 Herman Moore	.60	1.50
11 Chris Warren	.60	1.50
12 Emmitt Smith	6.00	15.00

1996 Action Packed Jumbos

COMPLETE SET (4)	6.00	15.00
ONE PER RETAIL BOX		
1 Emmitt Smith	2.50	6.00
2 Drew Bledsoe	.75	2.00
3 Troy Aikman	1.50	4.00
4 Brett Favre	3.00	8.00

1996 Action Packed Longest Yard

COMPLETE SET (12)	50.00	120.00
STATED ODDS 1:24 MAG		
1 Brett Favre Robert Brooks	12.50	30.00
2 Tamarick Vanover	1.00	2.50
3 Joey Galloway	2.00	5.00
4 Kerry Collins	2.00	5.00
5 Jeff Blake	2.00	5.00
6 Jerry Rice	6.00	15.00
7 Barry Sanders	10.00	25.00
8 Rodney Thomas	.50	1.25
9 Herman Moore	1.00	2.50
10 Emmitt Smith	10.00	25.00
11 Terrell Davis	5.00	12.00
12 Cris Carter	2.00	5.00

1996 Action Packed Sculptor's Proof

COMPLETE SET (14)	100.00	250.00
REDEMPT.ODDS 1:192H/R, 1:288MAG		
1 Dan Marino	12.50	30.00
2 Deion Sanders	3.00	8.00
3 Joey Galloway	2.00	5.00
4 Brett Favre	12.50	30.00
5 Barry Sanders	10.00	25.00
6 Michael Irvin	2.00	5.00
7 Drew Bledsoe	3.00	8.00
8 Emmitt Smith	10.00	25.00
9 Curtis Martin	5.00	12.00
10 Steve Young	5.00	12.00
11 John Elway	12.50	30.00
12 Jerry Rice	6.00	15.00
13 Errict Rhett	1.00	2.50
14 Troy Aikman	6.00	15.00

1996 Action Packed Studs

COMPLETE SET (6)	50.00	120.00
STATED ODDS 1:161 HOB/RET		
STATED PRINT RUN 1500 #'d SETS		
*24K STUDS: .6X TO 1.5X BASIC INSERTS		
24K PRINT RUN 200 SERIAL #'d SETS		
1 Emmitt Smith	20.00	50.00
2 Deion Sanders	12.50	30.00
3 Jerry Rice	15.00	40.00
4 Michael Irvin	7.50	20.00
5 Kordell Stewart	7.50	20.00
6 Ricky Watters	6.00	15.00

1997 Action Packed

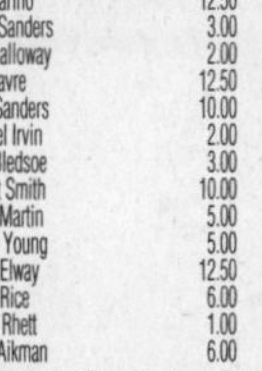

The 1997 Action Packed set was issued in one series totaling 125 cards and was distributed in five card packs with a suggested retail price of $2.99. The fronts feature embossed color action player photos on a pebble-grained pigskin background. The backs carry another player photo with a faded background version of it and career statistics. Three promo cards were produced to promote the set.

COMPLETE SET (125)	12.00	30.00
1 Jerry Rice	1.25	2.50
2 Troy Aikman	1.25	2.50
3 Ricky Watters	.25	.60
4 Dan Marino	2.00	5.00
5 Emmitt Smith	2.00	4.00
6 Warren Moon	.40	1.00
7 Rashaan Salaam	.15	.40
8 Drew Bledsoe	.60	1.50
9 Eddie George	.40	1.00
10 John Elway	2.00	5.00
11 Robert Brooks	.25	.60
12 Scott Mitchell	.25	.60
13 Isaac Bruce	.40	1.00
14 Marshall Faulk	.50	1.25
15 Steve Bono	.25	.60
16 Barry Sanders	1.50	4.00
17 Brett Favre	2.50	5.00
18 Curtis Martin	.50	1.25
19 Keyshawn Johnson	.40	1.00
20 Dave Brown	.15	.40
21 Frank Sanders	.25	.60
22 Gus Frerotte	.15	.40
23 Eric Metcalf	.25	.60
24 Thurman Thomas	.40	1.00
25 Steve Young	.60	1.50
26 Alvin Harper	.15	.40
27 Mark Brunell	.60	1.50
28 Kordell Stewart	.40	1.00
29 Terry Glenn	.40	1.00
30 Junior Seau	.40	1.00
31 Karim Abdul-Jabbar	.25	.60
32 Jeff Hostetler	.15	.40
33 Rodney Hampton	.25	.60
34 Irving Fryar	.25	.60
35 Cris Carter	.40	1.00
36 James O.Stewart	.25	.60
37 Marcus Allen	.40	1.00
38 Napoleon Kaufman	.40	1.00
39 Shannon Sharpe	.25	.60
40 LeShon Johnson	.15	.40
41 Tony Banks	.25	.60
42 Lawrence Phillips	.15	.40
43 Kerry Collins	.40	1.00
44 Curtis Conway	.25	.60
45 Jim Harbaugh	.25	.60
46 Garrison Hearst	.25	.60
47 Trent Dilfer	.40	1.00
48 Terance Mathis	.25	.60
49 Jerome Bettis	.40	1.00
50 Chris Sanders	.15	.40
51 Deion Sanders	.40	1.00
52 Herman Moore	.25	.60
53 Elvis Grbac	.25	.60
54 O.J. McDuffie	.25	.60
55 Ben Coates	.25	.60
56 Jim Kelly	.40	1.00
57 J.J. Stokes	.25	.60
58 Terrell Davis	.50	1.25
59 Stan Humphries	.25	.60
60 Carl Pickens	.25	.60
61 Neil O'Donnell	.25	.60
62 Edgar Bennett	.25	.60
63 Yancey Thigpen	.25	.60
64 Bert Emanuel	.25	.60
65 Amani Toomer	.25	.60
66 Jeff Blake	.25	.60
67 Eddie Kennison	.25	.60
68 Jason Dunn	.15	.40
69 Rob Moore	.25	.60
70 Andre Rison	.25	.60
71 Vinny Testaverde	.25	.60
72 Henry Ellard	.15	.40
73 Dale Carter	.15	.40
74 Tony Martin	.25	.60
75 Jim Everett	.15	.40
76 Joey Galloway	.25	.60
77 Mike Alstott	.40	1.00
78 Kevin Hardy	.15	.40
79 Jake Reed	.25	.60
80 Tim Brown	.40	1.00
81 Sean Dawkins	.15	.40
82 Bobby Engram	.25	.60
83 Michael Irvin	.40	1.00
84 Rickey Dudley	.25	.60
85 Chris Chandler	.25	.60
86 Keith Jackson	.15	.40
87 Muhsin Muhammad	.25	.60
88 Tamarick Vanover	.25	.60
89 Chris Warren	.25	.60
90 Johnnie Morton	.25	.60
91 Terry Allen	.40	1.00
92 Stanley Pritchett	.15	.40
93 Charles Johnson	.25	.60
94 Chris T. Jones	.15	.40
95 Winslow Oliver	.15	.40
96 Anthony Miller	.15	.40
97 Tyrone Wheatley	.25	.60
98 Robert Smith	.25	.60
99 Eric Moulds	.40	1.00
100 Hardy Nickerson	.15	.40
101 Derrick Alexander WR	.25	.60
102 Michael Haynes	.15	.40
103 Jamal Anderson	.40	1.00
104 Marvin Harrison	.40	1.00
105 Antonio Freeman	.40	1.00
106 Dorsey Levens	.40	1.00
107 Natrone Means	.25	.60
108 Keenan McCardell	.25	.60
109 Mark Chmura	.25	.60
110 Darren Woodson	.15	.40
111 Brett Favre DD	1.25	2.50
112 Emmitt Smith DD	.75	2.00
113 Junior Seau DD	.40	1.00
114 Jerry Rice DD	.50	1.25
115 Barry Sanders DD	.75	2.00
116 Bruce Smith DD	.15	.40
117 Troy Aikman DD	.50	1.25
118 Bryan Cox DD	.15	.40
119 Zach Thomas DD	.40	1.00
120 Reggie White DD	.40	1.00
121 Ben Coates DD	.25	.60
122 Jerome Bettis DD	.40	1.00
123 Michael Irvin DD	.25	.60
124 Quentin Coryatt DD	.15	.40
125 Checklist Card	.15	.40
P28 Kordell Stewart Promo	.75	2.00
P45 Jim Harbaugh Promo	.20	.50

1997 Action Packed First Impressions

COMPLETE SET (125)	200.00	400.00

*SINGLES: 2X TO 5X BASIC CARDS
STATED ODDS 1:12 HOB, 1:15 MAG

1997 Action Packed Gold Impressions

COMPLETE SET (125)	400.00	800.00

*SINGLES: 4X TO 10X BASIC CARDS
STATED ODDS 1:35 HOB, 1:44 MAG

1997 Action Packed 24K Gold

COMPLETE SET (15)	100.00	200.00
STATED ODDS 1:71 HOB, 1:89 MAG		
1 Brett Favre	12.50	30.00
2 Steve Young	4.00	10.00
3 Terrell Davis	3.00	8.00
4 Barry Sanders	10.00	25.00
5 Isaac Bruce	3.00	8.00
6 Deion Sanders	4.00	10.00
7 Dan Marino	12.50	30.00
8 Jim Harbaugh	2.50	6.00
9 Jerry Rice	8.00	20.00
10 John Elway	12.50	30.00
11 Herman Moore	2.00	5.00
12 Troy Aikman	6.00	15.00
13 Emmitt Smith	10.00	25.00
14 Drew Bledsoe	3.00	8.00
15 Eddie George	2.50	6.00

1997 Action Packed Crash Course

COMPLETE SET (18)	30.00	80.00
STATED ODDS 1:23 HOB, 1:29 MAG		
1 Dan Marino	8.00	20.00
2 Troy Aikman	4.00	10.00
3 Barry Sanders	6.00	15.00
4 Emmitt Smith	6.00	15.00
5 Brett Favre	8.00	20.00
6 John Elway	8.00	20.00
7 Keyshawn Johnson	1.50	4.00
8 Jim Harbaugh	1.00	2.50
9 Kerry Collins	1.50	4.00
10 Karim Abdul-Jabbar	1.00	2.50
11 Eddie Kennison	1.00	2.50
12 Curtis Martin	2.00	5.00
13 Tony Banks	1.00	2.50
14 Dorsey Levens	1.50	4.00
15 Jerome Bettis	1.50	4.00
16 Drew Bledsoe	2.50	6.00
17 Marvin Harrison	1.50	4.00
18 Jerry Rice	4.00	10.00

1997 Action Packed Pinnacle Scoring Core Preview

COMPLETE SET (12)	40.00	100.00
RANDOM INSERTS IN AP EXTRA POINTS		
1 Karim Abdul-Jabbar	2.00	5.00
2 Troy Aikman	8.00	20.00
3 Tim Biakabutuka	2.00	5.00
4 Drew Bledsoe	5.00	12.00
5 Robert Brooks	2.00	5.00
6 Mark Brunell	5.00	12.00
7 John Elway	15.00	40.00
8 Terry Glenn	3.00	8.00
9 Garrison Hearst	2.00	5.00
10 Michael Irvin	3.00	8.00
11 Shannon Sharpe	2.00	5.00
12 Steve Young	5.00	12.00

1997 Action Packed Studs

COMPLETE SET (9)	75.00	150.00
STATED ODDS 1:167 HOB, 1:209 MAG		
STATED PRINT RUN 1500 #'d SETS		
1 Deion Sanders	10.00	25.00
2 Barry Sanders	20.00	50.00
3 Eddie George	7.50	20.00
4 Jerry Rice	15.00	40.00
5 Kordell Stewart	6.00	15.00
6 Emmitt Smith	15.00	40.00
7 Terrell Davis	10.00	25.00
8 Keyshawn Johnson	7.50	20.00
9 Robert Smith	6.00	15.00
P4 Jerry Rice Promo Studs Card	2.00	5.00

1990 Action Packed All-Madden

This 58-card standard-size set honors the members of the annual team selected by CBS analyst John Madden. The set was released both in six-card packs as well as in a factory set. This set features a borderless design on the front and an action shot of the player and a brief description on the back about what qualifies the player to be on the All-Madden Team. The back also features a portrait shot of the player and a portrait shot of John Madden as well. The set also has some of the features standard in Action Packed sets, rounded corners, and the All-Madden Team logo in embossed, raised letters as well as the players' photos being raised. The Neal Anderson prototype (P12) is not included in the complete set as it was passed out to dealers prior to the mass distribution of the set. The Anderson prototype was also available as a special magazine insert in SCD.

COMPLETE SET (58)	4.00	10.00
COMP.FACT SET (58)	5.00	10.00
1 Joe Montana	.75	2.00
2 Jerry Rice	.50	1.25
3 Charles Haley	.08	.25
4 Steve Wisniewski	.08	.25
5 Dave Meggett	.08	.25
6 Ottis Anderson	.08	.25
7 Nate Newton	.08	.25
8 Warren Moon	.15	.40
9 Emmitt Smith	1.25	3.00
10 Jackie Slater	.05	.15
11 Pepper Johnson	.05	.15
12 Lawrence Taylor	.15	.40
13 Sterling Sharpe	.15	.40
14 Sean Landeta	.05	.15
15 Richard Dent (tackling Jim Kelly)	.08	.25
16 Neal Anderson	.08	.25
17 Bruce Matthews	.08	.25
18 Matt Millen	.08	.25
19 Reggie White	.15	.40
20 Greg Townsend	.08	.25
21 Troy Aikman	.50	1.25
22 Don Mosebar	.05	.15
23 Jeff Zimmerman	.05	.15
24 Rod Woodson	.15	.40
25 Keith Byars	.08	.25
26 Randall Cunningham	.15	.40
27 Reyna Thompson	.05	.15
28 Marcus Allen	.15	.40
29 Gary Clark	.15	.40
30 Anthony Carter	.08	.25
31 Bubba Paris	.05	.15
32 Ronnie Lott	.08	.25
33 Erik Howard	.05	.15
34 Ernest Givins	.08	.25
35 Mike Munchak	.08	.25
36 Jim Lachey	.05	.15
37 Merril Hoge UER (Back photo reversed)	.05	.15
38 Darrell Green	.08	.25
39 Pierce Holt	.05	.15
40 Jerome Brown	.08	.25
41 William Perry UER (Back photo reversed)	.08	.25
42 Michael Carter	.05	.15
43 Keith Jackson	.08	.25
44 Kevin Fagan	.05	.15
45 Mark Carrier DB	.08	.25
46 Fred Barnett	.08	.25
47 Barry Sanders	.75	2.00
48 Pat Swilling and Rickey Jackson	.08	.25
49 Sam Mills and Vaughan Johnson	.05	.15
50 Jacob Green	.05	.15
51 Stan Brock	.05	.15
52 Dan Hampton	.08	.25
53 Brian Noble	.05	.15
54 John Elliott	.05	.15
55 Matt Bahr	.05	.15
56 Bill Parcells CO	.08	.25
57 Art Shell CO	.08	.25
58 All-Madden Team Trophy	.05	.15
P12 Neal Anderson (Prototype)	.40	1.00

1991 Action Packed All-Madden

In its second year, this 52-card standard-size set honors the selections to the All-Madden Team. The cards were issued in foil packs as well as in factory sets. Each of the cards in the set was also available in a randomly inserted 24K Gold parallel version.

COMPLETE SET (52)	4.00	10.00
COMP.FACT SET (52)	5.00	10.00
1 Mark Rypien	.08	.25
2 Erik Kramer	.08	.25
3 Jim McMahon	.08	.25
4 Jesse Sapolu	.05	.15
5 Jay Hilgenberg	.05	.15
6 Howard Ballard	.05	.15
7 Lomas Brown	.05	.15
8 John Elliott	.05	.15
9 Joe Jacoby	.05	.15
10 Jim Lachey	.05	.15
11 Anthony Munoz	.08	.25
12 Nate Newton	.05	.15
13 Will Wolford	.05	.15
14 Jerry Ball	.05	.15
15 Jerome Brown	.08	.25
16 William Perry	.08	.25
17 Charles Mann	.05	.15
18 Clyde Simmons	.05	.15
19 Reggie White	.15	.40
20 Eric Allen	.05	.15
21 Darrell Green	.05	.15
22 Bennie Blades	.05	.15
23 Chuck Cecil	.05	.15
24 Rickey Dixon	.05	.15
25 David Fulcher	.05	.15
26 Ronnie Lott	.15	.40
27 Emmitt Smith	1.25	3.00
28 Neal Anderson	.08	.25
29 Robert Delpino	.05	.15
30 Barry Sanders	.75	2.00
31 Thurman Thomas	.15	.40
32 Cornelius Bennett	.08	.25
33 Rickey Jackson	.08	.25
34 Seth Joyner	.08	.25
35 Wilber Marshall	.05	.15
36 Clay Matthews	.08	.25
37 Chris Spielman	.08	.25
38 Pat Swilling	.08	.25
39 Fred Barnett	.08	.25
40 Gary Clark	.08	.25
41 Michael Irvin	.15	.40
42 Art Monk	.08	.25
43 Jerry Rice	.50	1.25
44 John Taylor	.08	.25
45 Tom Waddle	.05	.15
46 Kevin Butler	.05	.15
47 Bill Bates	.08	.25
48 Greg Manusky	.05	.15
49 Elvis Patterson	.05	.15
50 Steve Tasker	.08	.25
51 John Daly (Golfer)	.15	.40
52 All-Madden Team Trophy	.05	.15

1991 Action Packed All-Madden 24K Gold

COMPLETE SET (52)	150.00	300.00

*24K GOLD CARDS: 10X TO 25X

1992 Action Packed All-Madden

For the third consecutive year, Action Packed has issued a 55-card standard-size set to honor the toughest players in the game as picked by sportscaster John Madden. For hobby dealers only, Action Packed inserted two prototype cards of upcoming products in each display box of All-Madden Team foil packs. Moreover, 24K Gold leaf versions of each card were randomly inserted in foil packs.

COMPLETE SET (55)	4.00	10.00
1 Emmitt Smith	.75	2.00
2 Reggie White	.15	.40
3 Deion Sanders	.40	1.00
4 Wilber Marshall	.05	.15
5 Barry Sanders	.75	2.00
6 Derrick Thomas	.08	.25
7 Troy Aikman	.50	1.25
8 Eric Allen	.05	.15
9 Cris Carter	.15	.40
10 Jerry Rice	.50	1.25
11 Rickey Jackson	.05	.15
12 Dubba McDowell	.06	.16
13 Jack Del Rio	.05	.15
14 Nate Newton	.05	.15
15 John Elliott	.05	.15
16 Fred Barnett	.05	.15
17 Mike Singletary	.08	.25
18 Lawrence Taylor	.08	.25
19 Bruce Matthews	.05	.15
20 Pat Swilling	.08	.25
21 Charles Haley	.08	.25
22 Andre Rison	.15	.40
23 Seth Joyner	.08	.25
24 Steve Young	.40	1.00
25 Gary Clark	.08	.25
26 Jerry Ball	.05	.15
27 Michael Irvin	.15	.40
28 Haywood Jeffires	.08	.25
29 Kevin Ross	.05	.15
30 Chris Doleman	.05	.15
31 Vai Sikahema	.05	.15
32 Ricky Watters	.08	.25
33 Henry Thomas	.05	.15
34 Mike Kenn	.05	.15
35 Erik Williams	.08	.25
36 Neil Smith	.15	.40
37 Mark Schlereth	.05	.15
38 Steve Wallace	.05	.15
39 Randall McDaniel	.05	.15
40 Kurt Gouveia	.05	.15
41 Al Noga	.05	.15
42 Tom Rathman	.05	.15
43 Harris Barton	.05	.15
44 Mel Gray	.05	.15
45 Keith Byars	.05	.15
46 Todd Scott	.05	.15
47 Brent Jones	.05	.15
48 Audray McMillian	.05	.15
49 Ray Childress	.05	.15
50 Dennis Smith	.05	.15
51 Mark McMillian	.05	.15
52 Sean Gilbert	.05	.15
53 Pierce Holt	.05	.15
54 Daryl Johnston	.08	.25
55 Madden Cruiser (Bus)	.05	.15

1992 Action Packed All-Madden 24K Gold

COMPLETE SET (55)	200.00	400.00

*24K GOLDS: 10X TO 25X BASIC CARDS

1993 Action Packed All-Madden

COMPLETE SET (42)	4.00	10.00
1 Troy Aikman	.50	1.25
2 Bill Bates	.08	.25
3 Mark Bavaro	.07	.20
4 Jim Burt	.07	.20
5 Gary Clark	.07	.20
6 Richard Dent	.08	.25
7 Gary Fencik	.07	.20
8 Darrell Green	.07	.20
9 Roy Green	.07	.20
10 Russ Grimm	.07	.20
11 Charles Haley	.07	.20
12 Dan Hampton	.07	.20
13 Lester Hayes	.07	.20
14 Mike Haynes	.07	.20
15 Jay Hilgenberg	.07	.20
16 Michael Irvin	.15	.40
17 Joe Jacoby	.07	.20
18 Steve Largent	.15	.40
19 Howie Long	.15	.40
20 Ronnie Lott	.08	.25
21 Dan Marino	.75	2.00
22 Jim McMahon	.08	.25
23 Matt Millen	.07	.20
24 Art Monk	.08	.25
25 Joe Montana	.75	2.00
26 Anthony Munoz	.08	.25
27 Nate Newton	.07	.20
28 Walter Payton	.15	.40
29 William Perry	.08	.25
30 Jack Reynolds	.07	.20
31 Jerry Rice	.50	1.25
32 Barry Sanders	.75	2.00
33 Sterling Sharpe	.08	.25
34 Mike Singletary	.08	.25
35 Jackie Slater	.07	.20
36 Emmitt Smith	.75	2.00
37 Pat Summerall	.08	.25
38 Lawrence Taylor	.15	.40
39 Jeff Van Note	.07	.20
40 Reggie White	.15	.40
41 Otis Wilson	.07	.20
42 Jack Youngblood	.07	.20
P1 Troy Aikman Prototype	1.00	2.50
NNO Uncut Sheet AUTO/1000 (signed by John Madden)	40.00	80.00

1993 Action Packed All-Madden 24K Gold

COMPLETE SET (12)	150.00	300.00
1G Troy Aikman	12.50	30.00
2G Michael Irvin	5.00	12.00
3G Ronnie Lott	3.00	8.00
4G Dan Marino	20.00	50.00
5G Joe Montana	20.00	50.00
6G Walter Payton	7.50	20.00
7G Jerry Rice	12.50	30.00
8G Barry Sanders	20.00	50.00
9G Sterling Sharpe	3.00	8.00
10G Emmitt Smith	20.00	50.00
11G Lawrence Taylor	5.00	12.00
12G Reggie White	7.50	20.00

1994 Action Packed All-Madden

COMPLETE SET (41)	4.00	10.00
1 Emmitt Smith	.75	2.00
2 Jerome Bettis	.30	.75
3 Steve Young	.30	.75
4 Jerry Rice	.50	1.25
5 Richard Dent	.08	.25
6 Junior Seau	.15	.40
7 Harris Barton	.05	.15
8 Steve Wallace	.05	.15
9 Keith Byars	.05	.15
10 Michael Irvin	.15	.40
11 Joe Montana	.75	2.00
12 Jesse Sapolu	.05	.15
13 Rickey Jackson	.05	.15
14 Ronnie Lott	.08	.25
15 Donnell Woolford	.05	.15
16 Reggie White	.15	.40
17 John Taylor	.05	.15
18 Bruce Matthews	.05	.15
19 Ronald Moore	.05	.15
20 Bill Bates	.08	.25
21 Steve Hendrickson	.05	.15
22 Eric Allen	.05	.15
23 Monte Coleman	.05	.15
24 Mark Collins	.05	.15
25 Barry Sanders	.75	2.00
26 Erik Williams	.05	.15
27 Phil Simms	.08	.25
28 Chris Zorich	.05	.15
29 Troy Aikman	.50	1.25
30 Charles Haley	.05	.15
31 Darrell Green	.05	.15
32 Sean Gilbert	.05	.15
33 Kevin Gogan	.05	.15
34 Rodney Hampton	.08	.25
35 Chris Doleman	.05	.15
36 Nate Newton	.05	.15
37 Jackie Slater	.05	.15
38 Ricky Watters	.08	.25
39 LeRoy Butler	.05	.15
40 Gary Clark	.05	.15
41 Sterling Sharpe	.08	.25
P1 Emmitt Smith Prototype	1.00	2.50
NNO Uncut Sheet AUTO/1000 (signed by John Madden)	40.00	80.00

1994 Action Packed All-Madden 24K Gold

COMPLETE SET (41)	250.00	500.00
*24K GOLDS: 10X TO 25X BASIC CARDS		
1G Emmitt Smith	20.00	50.00
2G Jerome Bettis	8.00	20.00
3G Steve Young	8.00	20.00
4G Jerry Rice	12.50	30.00
5G Richard Dent	2.50	6.00
6G Junior Seau	4.00	10.00
7G Harris Barton	1.50	4.00
8G Steve Wallace	1.50	4.00
9G Keith Byars	1.50	4.00
10G Michael Irvin	4.00	10.00
11G Joe Montana	20.00	50.00
12G Jesse Sapolu	1.50	4.00
13G Rickey Jackson	1.50	4.00
14G Ronnie Lott	2.50	6.00
15G Donnell Woolford	1.50	4.00
16G Reggie White	4.00	10.00
17G John Taylor	1.50	4.00
18G Bruce Matthews	1.50	4.00
19G Ronald Moore	1.50	4.00
20G Bill Bates	2.50	6.00
21G Steve Hendrickson	1.50	4.00
22G Eric Allen	1.50	4.00
23G Monte Coleman	1.50	4.00
24G Mark Collins	1.50	4.00
25G Barry Sanders	20.00	50.00
26G Erik Williams	1.50	4.00
27G Phil Simms	2.50	6.00
28G Chris Zorich	1.50	4.00
29G Troy Aikman	12.50	30.00
30G Charles Haley	1.50	4.00
31G Darrell Green	1.50	4.00
32G Sean Gilbert	1.50	4.00
33G Kevin Gogan	1.50	4.00
34G Rodney Hampton	2.50	6.00
35G Chris Doleman	1.50	4.00
36G Nate Newton	1.50	4.00
37G Jackie Slater	1.50	4.00
38G Ricky Watters	2.50	6.00
39G LeRoy Butler	1.50	4.00
40G Gary Clark	1.50	4.00
41G Sterling Sharpe	2.50	6.00

1993 Action Packed Monday Night Football Prototypes

COMPLETE SET (6)	10.00	25.00
MN1 Barry Sanders	4.00	10.00
MN2 Steve Young	1.60	4.00
MN3 Emmitt Smith	4.00	10.00
MN4 Thurman Thomas	1.00	2.50
MN5 Barry Foster	.60	1.50
MN6 Warren Moon	1.00	2.50

1993 Action Packed Monday Night Football

COMPLETE SET (81)	4.00	10.00
1 Michael Irvin	.10	.30
2 Charles Haley	.02	.10
3 Art Monk	.07	.20
4 Earnest Byner	.02	.10
5 Tom Rathman	.02	.10
6 John Taylor	.02	.10
7 Bernie Kosar	.02	.10
8 Clay Matthews	.02	.10
9 Simon Fletcher	.02	.10
10 John Elway	.80	2.00
11 Joe Montana	.80	2.00
12 Derrick Thomas	.07	.20
13 Rod Woodson	.10	.30
14 Gary Anderson K	.02	.10
15 Chris Miller	.07	.20
16 Andre Rison	.07	.20
17 Mark Rypien	.02	.10
18 Charles Mann	.02	.10
19 John Offerdahl	.02	.10
20 Pete Stoyanovich	.02	.10
21 Warren Moon	.10	.30
22 Lorenzo White	.02	.10
23 Haywood Jeffires	.02	.10
24 Andre Reed	.07	.20
25 Darryl Talley	.02	.10
26 Tim Brown	.10	.30
27 Howie Long	.10	.30
28 Steve Atwater	.02	.10
29 Karl Mecklenburg	.02	.10
30 Chris Doleman	.02	.10
31 Terry Allen	.10	.30
32 Richard Dent	.02	.10
33 Neal Anderson	.02	.10
34 Darrell Green	.02	.10
35 Chip Lohmiller	.02	.10
36 Jim Kelly	.10	.30
37 Cornelius Bennett	.02	.10
38 Brett Favre	.80	2.00
39 Sterling Sharpe	.07	.20
40 Reggie White	.10	.30
41 Neil Smith	.02	.10
42 Nick Lowery	.02	.10
43 Thurman Thomas	.10	.30
44 Bruce Smith	.10	.30
45 Barry Foster	.02	.10
46 Neil O'Donnell	.07	.20
47 Rickey Jackson	.02	.10
48 Morten Andersen	.02	.10
49 Brent Jones	.02	.10
50 Ricky Watters	.07	.20
51 Leslie O'Neal	.02	.10
52 Marion Butts	.02	.10
53 Anthony Miller	.07	.20
54 Jeff George	.07	.20
55 Steve Emtman	.02	.10
56 Herschel Walker	.07	.20
57 Randall Cunningham	.10	.30
58 Clyde Simmons	.02	.10
59 Emmitt Smith	.80	2.00
60 Ken Norton Jr.	.07	.20
61 Troy Aikman	.40	1.00
62 Eric Green	.02	.10
63 Greg Lloyd	.07	.20
64 Bryan Cox	.02	.10
65 Mark Higgs	.02	.10
66 Phil Simms	.07	.20
67 Lawrence Taylor	.07	.20
68 Rodney Hampton	.07	.20
69 Wayne Martin	.02	.10
70 Vaughn Dunbar	.02	.10
71 Keith Jackson	.07	.20
72 Dan Marino	.80	2.00
73 Junior Seau	.07	.20
74 Stan Humphries	.07	.20
75 Fred Barnett	.07	.20
76 Seth Joyner	.02	.10
77 Steve Young	.30	.75
78 Jerry Rice	.40	1.00
79 Dan Dierdorf ANN	.07	.20
80 Frank Gifford ANN	.10	.30
81 Al Michaels ANN	.07	.20
HW1 Hank Williams Jr.	.30	.75

1993 Action Packed Monday Night Football Mint Parallel

COMPLETE SET (81)	500.00	800.00

*MINT CARDS: 30X TO 80X BASIC CARDS

1993 Action Packed Monday Night Football 24K Gold

COMPLETE SET (81)	160.00	400.00

*24K GOLDS: 12X TO 30X BASIC CARDS

1994 Action Packed Monday Night Football

COMPLETE SET (71)	4.00	10.00
1 Jeff Hostetler	.07	.20
2 Terry McDaniel	.02	.10
3 Steve Young	.30	.75
4 Jerry Rice	.40	1.00
5 Donnell Woolford	.02	.10
6 Eric Allen	.02	.10
7 Herschel Walker	.07	.20
8 Barry Sanders	.80	2.00
9 Herman Moore	.10	.30
10 Emmitt Smith	.60	1.50
11 Michael Irvin	.10	.30
12 John Elway	.80	2.00
13 Jim Kelly	.10	.30
14 Andre Reed	.07	.20
15 Gary Brown	.02	.10
16 Ernest Givins	.02	.10
17 Barry Foster	.07	.20
18 Rod Woodson	.07	.20
19 Warren Moon	.10	.30
20 Cris Carter	.10	.30
21 Rodney Hampton	.07	.20
22 Derrick Thomas	.07	.20
23 Marcus Allen	.10	.30
24 Shannon Sharpe	.07	.20
25 Cody Carlson	.02	.10
26 Haywood Jeffires	.02	.10
27 Randall Cunningham	.10	.30
28 Calvin Williams	.02	.10
29 Brett Favre	.80	2.00
30 Sterling Sharpe	.07	.20
31 Chris Zorich	.02	.10
32 Dante Jones	.02	.10
33 Mike Sherrard	.02	.10
34 Keith Hamilton	.02	.10
35 Charles Haley	.02	.10
36 Thurman Thomas	.10	.30
37 Bruce Smith	.07	.20
38 Greg Lloyd	.02	.10
39 Michael Brooks	.02	.10
40 Jumbo Elliott	.02	.10
41 Ray Childress	.02	.10
42 Bruce Matthews	.02	.10
43 Ricky Watters	.07	.20

44 Brent Jones	.07	.20
45 Morten Andersen	.02	.10
46 Tim Brown	.10	.30
47 Anthony Smith	.02	.10
48 Natrone Means	.10	.30
49 Rickey Jackson	.02	.10
50 Joe Montana	.80	2.00
51 Neil Smith	.07	.20
52 Dan Marino	.80	2.00
53 Keith Jackson	.02	.10
54 Troy Aikman	.40	1.00
55 Jay Novacek	.07	.20
56 Junior Seau	.07	.20
57 John Taylor	.07	.20
58 Tim McDonald	.02	.10
59 John Randle	.07	.20
60 Henry Thomas	.02	.10
61 Don Meredith	.10	.30
Howard Cosell		
Frank Gifford		
62 Howard Cosell	.10	.30
Don Meredith		
63 The Entertainers ANN	.10	.30
Don Meredith		
Howard Cosell		
Frank Gifford		
64 Howard Cosell ANN	.10	.30
65 Don Meredith ANN	.10	.30
Howard Cosell ANN		
Frank Gifford ANN		
66 Keith Jackson ANN	.02	.10
67 Don Meredith ANN	.10	.30
68 Howard Cosell ANN	.10	.30
69 Chris Hinton	.02	.10
Donning a Dierdorf (mask)		
70 Brent Musburger ANN	.02	.10
71 Lynn Swann ANN	.07	.20

1994 Action Packed Monday Night Football Silver

COMPLETE SET (12)	120.00	300.00
1S Steve Young	10.00	25.00
2S Jerry Rice	12.00	30.00
3S Barry Sanders	20.00	50.00
4S Emmitt Smith	16.00	40.00
5S John Elway	20.00	50.00
6S Jim Kelly	6.00	15.00
7S Warren Moon	6.00	15.00
8S Randall Cunningham	6.00	15.00
9S Brett Favre	20.00	50.00
10S Dan Marino	20.00	50.00
11S Troy Aikman	12.00	30.00
12S Howard Cosell ANN	6.00	15.00
Speaking of Sports		

1995 Action Packed Monday Night Football Promos

1 Steve Young	.80	2.00
3A Troy Aikman	1.20	3.00
3B Drew Bledsoe	1.20	3.00
Night Flights card		
NNO NMFB Ad Card	.20	.50

1995 Action Packed Monday Night Football

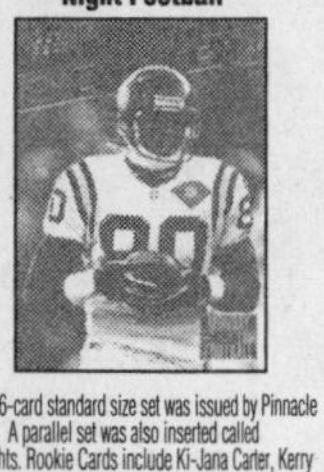

This 126-card standard size set was issued by Pinnacle Brands. A parallel set was also inserted called Highlights. Rookie Cards include Ki-Jana Carter, Kerry Collins, Joey Galloway, Steve McNair, Rashaan Salaam, Kordell Stewert, J.J. Stokes and Michael Westbrook in the subset "The Night is Young".

COMPLETE SET (126)	10.00	15.00
1 Jerry Rice	.40	1.00
2 Barry Sanders	.75	2.00
3 Troy Aikman	.40	1.00
4 Jerome Bettis	.08	.25
5 Tim Brown	.08	.25
6 Marcus Allen	.08	.25
7 Jeff Blake RC	.30	.75
8 Rodney Hampton	.05	.15
9 Reggie White	.08	.25
10 Warren Moon	.08	.25
11 William Floyd	.02	.10
12 Cris Carter	.08	.25
13 Stan Humphries	.05	.15
14 Herschel Walker	.05	.15
15 Dave Brown	.02	.10
16 Jim Everett	.02	.10
17 Mario Bates	.05	.15
18 Terance Mathis	.02	.10
19 Chris Spielman	.02	.10
20 Neil O'Donnell	.05	.15
21 Anthony Miller	.02	.10
22 Steve Bono	.05	.15
23 Henry Ellard	.02	.10
24 Dave Meggett	.02	.10
25 Flipper Anderson	.02	.10
26 Rocket Ismail	.05	.15
27 Leroy Hoard	.02	.10
28 Steve Young	.30	.75
29 Marshall Faulk	.20	.50
30 Dan Marino	.75	2.00
31 Errict Rhett	.05	.15
32 Michael Irvin	.08	.25
33 Byron Bam Morris	.02	.10
34 Heath Shuler	.05	.15
35 Jim Kelly	.08	.25
36 Deion Sanders	.25	.60
37 Jeff Hostetler	.05	.15
38 Jeff George	.08	.25
39 Alvin Harper	.02	.10
40 Barry Foster	.02	.10
41 Craig Erickson	.02	.10
42 Vinny Testaverde	.05	.15
43 Andre Reed	.05	.15
44 Eric Green	.02	.10
45 Bruce Smith	.05	.15
46 Frank Reich	.02	.10
47 Shannon Sharpe	.05	.15
48 Chris Miller	.02	.10
49 Darnay Scott	.05	.15
50 Eric Metcalf	.05	.15
51 Mike Sherrard	.02	.10
52 Lorenzo White	.02	.10
53 Scott Mitchell	.05	.15
54 Jay Novacek	.02	.10
55 Emmitt Smith	.60	1.50
56 Drew Bledsoe	.40	1.00
57 Natrone Means	.05	.15
58 John Elway	.75	2.00
59 Herman Moore	.20	.50
60 Brett Favre	.75	2.00
61 Ricky Watters	.05	.15
62 Andre Rison	.05	.15
63 Junior Seau	.05	.15
64 Randall Cunningham	.08	.25
65 Chris Warren	.05	.15
66 Garrison Hearst	.08	.25
67 Ben Coates	.05	.15
68 Rick Mirer	.05	.15
69 Johnny Mitchell	.02	.10
70 Trent Dilfer	.08	.25
71 Carl Pickens	.05	.15
72 Craig Heyward	.02	.10
73 Greg Lloyd	.02	.10
74 Boomer Esiason	.05	.15
75 Greg Hill	.02	.10
76 Lewis Tillman	.02	.10
77 Willie Davis	.02	.10
78 Brent Jones	.02	.10
79 Michael Haynes	.02	.10
80 Daryl Johnston	.05	.15
81 Steve Beuerlein	.05	.15
82 Ki-Jana Carter NY RC	.08	.25
83 Steve McNair NY RC	.75	2.00
84 Michael Westbrook NY RC	.40	1.00
85 Kerry Collins NY RC	1.00	2.50
86 Joey Galloway NY RC	.50	1.25
87 Kyle Brady NY RC	.08	.25
88 J.J. Stokes NY RC	.30	.75
89 Tyrone Wheatley NY RC	.40	1.00
90 Rashaan Salaam NY RC	.08	.25
91 Napoleon Kaufman NY RC	.40	1.00
92 Frank Sanders NY RC	.30	.75
93 Stoney Case NY RC	.02	.10
94 Todd Collins NY RC	.50	1.25
95 James O. Stewart NY RC	.50	1.25
96 Kordell Stewart NY RC	.60	1.50
97 Joe Aska NY	.05	.15
98 Terrell Fletcher NY RC	.02	.10
99 Rob Johnson NY RC	.40	1.00
100 Steve Young C	.15	.40
101 Jerry Rice C	.20	.50
102 Emmitt Smith C	.40	1.00
103 Barry Sanders C	.40	1.00
104 Marshall Faulk C	.15	.40
105 Drew Bledsoe C	.20	.50
106 Dan Marino C	.40	1.00
107 Troy Aikman C	.20	.50
108 John Elway C	.40	1.00
109 Brett Favre C	.40	1.00
110 Michael Irvin C	.08	.25
111 Heath Shuler C	.05	.15
112 Warren Moon C	.08	.25
113 Chris Warren C	.05	.15
114 Natrone Means C	.05	.15
115 Errict Rhett C	.05	.15
116 Byron Bam Morris C	.02	.10
117 Randall Cunningham C	.08	.25
118 Jim Kelly C	.08	.25
119 Jeff Hostetler C	.02	.10
120 Barry Foster C	.02	.10
121 Jim Everett C	.05	.15
122 Neil O'Donnell C	.05	.15
123 Jerome Bettis C	.08	.25
124 Ricky Watters C	.05	.15
125 Joe Montana C	.75	2.00
126 Rodney Hampton C	.05	.15

1995 Action Packed Monday Night Football Highlights

COMP.HIGHLIGHTS SET (126)	60.00	150.00
*HIGHLIGHTS STARS: 3X TO 8X		
*HIGHLIGHTS RCs: 1.2X TO 3X		

1995 Action Packed Monday Night Football 24K Gold

COMPLETE SET (12)	125.00	300.00
1 Emmitt Smith	15.00	40.00
2 Barry Sanders	20.00	50.00
3 Marshall Faulk	7.50	20.00
4 Dan Marino	20.00	50.00
5 Steve Young	10.00	25.00
6 Drew Bledsoe	10.00	25.00
7 Troy Aikman	12.50	30.00
8 John Elway	20.00	50.00
9 Brett Favre	25.00	50.00
10 Ki-Jana Carter	4.00	10.00
11 Steve McNair	12.50	30.00
12 Kerry Collins	8.00	20.00

1995 Action Packed Monday Night Football Night Flight

COMPLETE SET (12)	45.00	60.00
1 Steve Young	2.00	5.00
2 Dan Marino	5.00	12.00
3 Drew Bledsoe	2.00	5.00
4 Troy Aikman	2.50	6.00
5 John Elway	5.00	12.00
6 Brett Favre	5.00	12.00
7 Heath Shuler	.75	2.00
8 Dave Brown	.75	2.00
9 Steve McNair	2.50	6.00
10 Kerry Collins	2.00	5.00
11 Warren Moon	1.25	3.00
12 Jeff Hostetler	.75	2.00

1995 Action Packed Monday Night Football Reverse Angle

COMPLETE SET (18)	30.00	60.00
1 Emmitt Smith	3.00	8.00
2 Barry Sanders	4.00	10.00
3 Steve Young	1.50	4.00
4 Marshall Faulk	1.25	3.00
5 Randall Cunningham	1.00	2.50
6 Deion Sanders	1.25	3.00
7 John Elway	4.00	10.00
8 Brett Favre	4.00	10.00
9 William Floyd	.60	1.50
10 Ricky Watters	1.00	2.50
11 Ben Coates	.60	1.50
12 Rod Woodson	.60	1.50
13 Marcus Allen	1.00	2.50
14 Eric Metcalf	.60	1.50
15 Keith Byars	.60	1.50
16 Jerry Rice	2.00	5.00
17 Alvin Harper	.60	1.50
18 Eric Green	.60	1.50

1995 Action Packed Rookies/Stars Prototypes

This four-card set was produced to promote the release of the 1995 Action Packed Rookies/Stars release. Each of the three player cards is essentially a parallel of the base issue with the word "prototype" stamped on the back.

12 Barry Sanders	1.00	2.50
18 Dan Marino	1.00	2.50
38 Troy Aikman	.60	1.50
NNO Ad Card	.20	.50

1995 Action Packed Rookies/Stars

This 105-card standard size set was issued by Pinnacle Brands. The fronts display full-bleed, embossed color action photos, with the player's name and team logo running along the bottom of the card. The Action Packed Rookies and Stars logo is located in the top left hand corner. The horizontal backs feature season and career statistics, a player photo as well as biographical information. A parallel set called Stargazers was also inserted into packs. Rookie Cards include Ki-Jana Carter, Kerry Collins, Joey Galloway, Curtis Martin, Steve McNair, Rashaan Salaam, Kordell Stewert, J.J. Stokes and Michael Westbrook.

COMPLETE SET (105)	7.50	20.00
1 Steve Young	.50	1.25
2 Steve Bono	.08	.25
3 Natrone Means	.08	.25
4 Steve Beuerlein	.08	.25
5 Neil O'Donnell	.08	.25
6 Marshall Faulk	.75	2.00
7 Ricky Watters	.08	.25
8 Gary Brown	.02	.10
9 Jeff Hostetler	.08	.25
10 Robert Brooks	.20	.50
11 Johnny Mitchell	.02	.10
12 Barry Sanders	1.00	2.50
13 Dave Brown	.08	.25
14 John Elway	1.25	3.00
15 Garrison Hearst	.20	.50
16 Jim Everett	.02	.10
17 Michael Irvin	.20	.50
18 Dan Marino	1.25	3.00
19 Jeff George	.08	.25
20 Ben Coates	.08	.25
21 Charles Johnson	.08	.25
22 Carl Pickens	.08	.25
23 Deion Sanders	.40	1.00
24 Errict Rhett	.08	.25
25 Steve Walsh	.02	.10
26 Bruce Smith	.20	.50
27 Andre Rison	.08	.25
28 Warren Moon	.08	.25
29 Terry Allen	.08	.25
30 Desmond Howard	.08	.25
31 Shannon Sharpe	.08	.25
32 Dave Krieg	.02	.10
33 Byron Bam Morris	.02	.10
34 Rodney Hampton	.08	.25
35 Scott Mitchell	.08	.25
36 Alvin Harper	.02	.10
37 Robert Smith	.20	.50
38 Troy Aikman	.60	1.50
39 William Floyd	.08	.25
40 Randall Cunningham	.20	.50
41 Mario Bates	.08	.25
42 Reggie White	.20	.50
43 Chris Chandler	.08	.25
44 Erik Kramer	.02	.10
45 Emmitt Smith	1.00	2.50
46 Irving Fryar	.08	.25
47 Jeff Blake RC	.30	.75
48 Drew Bledsoe	.40	1.00
49 Anthony Miller	.08	.25
50 Marcus Allen	.20	.50
51 Leroy Hoard	.02	.10
52 Stan Humphries	.08	.25
53 Eric Green	.02	.10
54 Herschel Walker	.08	.25
55 Junior Seau	.20	.50
56 Terance Mathis	.08	.25
57 Boomer Esiason	.08	.25
58 Lorenzo White	.02	.10
59 Tim Brown	.20	.50
60 Brett Favre	1.25	3.00
61 Craig Erickson	.02	.10
62 Rod Woodson	.08	.25
63 Frank Reich	.02	.10
64 Cris Carter	.20	.50
65 Jerry Rice	.60	1.50
66 Greg Hill	.08	.25
67 Andre Reed	.08	.25
68 Trent Dilfer	.20	.50
69 Eric Metcalf	.08	.25
70 Jim Kelly	.20	.50
71 Herman Moore	.20	.50
72 Vinny Testaverde	.08	.25
73 Jeff Graham	.02	.10
74 Edgar Bennett	.08	.25
75 Jerome Bettis	.20	.50
76 Heath Shuler	.08	.25
77 Chris Warren	.08	.25
78 Reggie Brooks	.08	.25
79 Rick Mirer	.08	.25
80 Chris Miller	.02	.10
81 Napoleon Kaufman RC	.50	1.25
82 Christian Fauria RC	.08	.25
83 Todd Collins RC	.60	1.50
84 J.J. Stokes RC	.20	.50
85 Mark Bruener RC	.08	.25
86 Frank Sanders RC	.20	.50
87 Chad May RC	.02	.10
88 Kordell Stewart RC	.60	1.50
89 Ki-Jana Carter RC	.20	.50
90 Curtis Martin RC	1.25	3.00
91 Sherman Williams RC	.02	.10
92 Terrell Davis RC	1.00	2.50
93 Chris Sanders RC	.08	.25
94 Kyle Brady RC	.20	.50
95 Tyrone Wheatley RC	.50	1.25
96 Rodney Thomas RC	.08	.25
97 James O. Stewart RC	.50	1.25
98 Kerry Collins RC	1.00	2.50
99 Rashaan Salaam RC	.08	.25
100 Stoney Case RC	.02	.10
101 Steve McNair RC	1.25	3.00
102 Joey Galloway RC	.60	1.50
103 Michael Westbrook RC	.20	.50
104 Eric Zeier RC	.20	.50
105 Ray Zellars RC	.08	.25

1995 Action Packed Rookies/Stars Stargazers

COMPLETE SET (105)	80.00	200.00
*STARS: 5X TO 12X BASIC CARDS		
*RCs: 3X TO 8X BASIC CARDS		
STATED ODDS 1:6		

1995 Action Packed Rookies/Stars 24K Gold

COMPLETE SET (14)	150.00	300.00
STATED ODDS 1:72		
1 Steve Young	8.00	20.00
2 Brett Favre	20.00	50.00
3 Rashaan Salaam	1.25	3.00
4 Tyrone Wheatley	6.00	15.00
5 Marshall Faulk	12.50	30.00
6 Rick Mirer	1.50	4.00
7 Troy Aikman	10.00	25.00
8 John Elway	20.00	50.00
9 Dan Marino	20.00	50.00
10 Barry Sanders	15.00	40.00
11 Jerry Rice	10.00	25.00
12 Emmitt Smith	15.00	40.00
13 Michael Irvin	3.00	8.00
14 Drew Bledsoe	6.00	15.00

1995 Action Packed Rookies/Stars Bustout

COMPLETE SET (12)	25.00	50.00
STATED ODDS 1:12		
1 Marshall Faulk	6.00	12.00
2 Barry Sanders	8.00	15.00
3 Emmitt Smith	8.00	15.00
4 Natrone Means	.75	1.50
5 Errict Rhett	.75	1.50
6 Byron Bam Morris	.25	.60
7 Terry Allen	.75	1.50
8 Rodney Hampton	.75	1.50
9 Ricky Watters	.75	1.50
10 Chris Warren	.75	1.50
11 Jerome Bettis	1.50	3.00
12 Gary Brown	.25	.60

1995 Action Packed Rookies/Stars Closing Seconds

COMPLETE SET (12)	60.00	120.00
STATED ODDS 1:36 HOB		
1 Dan Marino	12.50	25.00
2 Steve Young	5.00	10.00
3 Jerry Rice	6.00	12.00
4 Emmitt Smith	10.00	20.00
5 Barry Sanders	10.00	20.00
6 Brett Favre	12.50	25.00
7 Drew Bledsoe	4.00	8.00
8 Troy Aikman	6.00	12.00
9 John Elway	12.50	25.00
10 Dave Brown	1.00	2.00
11 Warren Moon	1.00	2.00
12 Jim Kelly	2.00	4.00

1995 Action Packed Rookies/Stars Instant Impressions

COMPLETE SET (12)	30.00	60.00
STATED ODDS 1:24		
1 Ki-Jana Carter	1.00	2.00
2 Steve McNair	6.00	12.00
3 Kerry Collins	3.00	8.00
4 Michael Westbrook	1.00	2.00
5 Joey Galloway	3.00	6.00
6 J.J. Stokes	1.00	2.00
7 Rashaan Salaam	.40	1.00
8 Tyrone Wheatley	2.50	5.00
9 Eric Zeier	1.00	2.00
10 Curtis Martin	6.00	12.00
11 Napoleon Kaufman	2.50	5.00
12 Kyle Brady	1.00	2.00

2010 Adrenalyn XL

1 Adrian Wilson	.15	.40
2 Andre Roberts RC	.60	1.50
3 Anthony Becht	.15	.40
4 Chris Wells	.20	.50
5 Clark Haggans	.15	.40
6 Darnell Dockett	.15	.40
7 Dominique Rodgers-Cromartie	.15	.40
8 Joey Porter	.15	.40
9 Larry Fitzgerald	.25	.60
10 Matt Leinart	.20	.50
11 Steve Breaston	.15	.40
12 Tim Hightower	.15	.40
13 Curtis Lofton	.15	.40
14 Erik Coleman	.15	.40
15 Jason Snelling	.20	.50
16 Jerious Norwood	.15	.40
17 John Abraham	.15	.40
18 Jonathan Babineaux	.15	.40
19 Matt Ryan	.25	.60
20 Michael Jenkins	.15	.40
21 Michael Turner	.15	.40
22 Mike Peterson	.15	.40
23 Roddy White	.20	.50
24 Tony Gonzalez	.20	.50
25 Anquan Boldin	.20	.50
26 Dawan Landry	.15	.40
27 Derrick Mason	.20	.50
28 Ed Reed	.20	.50
29 Joe Flacco	.25	.60
30 Mark Clayton	.15	.40
31 Ray Lewis	.25	.60
32 Ray Rice	.20	.50
33 Terrell Suggs	.15	.40
34 Todd Heap	.15	.40
35 Trevor Pryce	.15	.40
36 Willis McGahee	.20	.50
37 Aaron Schobel	.15	.40
38 Bryan Scott	.15	.40
39 C.J. Spiller RC	1.00	2.50
40 Derek Schouman	.15	.40
41 Fred Jackson	.25	.60
42 George Wilson	.15	.40
43 Jairus Byrd	.20	.50
44 James Hardy	.15	.40
45 Kyle Williams	.15	.40
46 Lee Evans	.20	.50
47 Marcus Stroud	.15	.40
48 Marshawn Lynch	.20	.50
49 Paul Posluszny	.20	.50
50 Trent Edwards	.15	.40
51 Brandon LaFell RC	.60	1.50
52 Charles Godfrey	.15	.40
53 Chris Gamble	.15	.40
54 Dante Rosario	.15	.40
55 DeAngelo Williams	.20	.50
56 James Anderson	.15	.40
57 Jimmy Clausen RC	.60	1.50
58 Jon Beason	.15	.40
59 Jonathan Stewart	.20	.50
60 Matt Moore	.20	.50
61 Richard Marshall	.15	.40
62 Steve Smith	.20	.50
63 Tyler Brayton	.15	.40
64 Brian Urlacher	.25	.60
65 Charles Tillman	.15	.40
66 Chester Taylor	.15	.40
67 Danieal Manning	.15	.40
68 Devin Hester	.25	.60
69 Earl Bennett	.20	.50
70 Greg Olsen	.15	.40
71 Hunter Hillenmeyer	.15	.40
72 Jay Cutler	.25	.60
73 Johnny Knox	.20	.50
74 Julius Peppers	.20	.50
75 Lance Briggs	.20	.50
76 Matt Forte	.20	.50
77 Zack Bowman	.15	.40
78 Antonio Bryant	.15	.40
79 Antwan Odom	.15	.40
80 Bernard Scott	.15	.40
81 Carson Palmer	.20	.50
82 Cedric Benson	.20	.50
83 Dhani Jones	.15	.40
84 Jermaine Gresham RC	.75	2.00
85 Chad Ochocinco	.20	.50
86 Johnathan Joseph	.15	.40
87 Jordan Shipley RC	.60	1.50
88 Keith Rivers	.15	.40
89 Leon Hall	.15	.40
90 Rey Maualuga	.15	.40
91 Roy Williams S	.20	.50
92 Abram Elam RC	.25	.60
93 Ben Watson	.15	.40
94 Colt McCoy RC	1.25	3.00
95 D'Qwell Jackson	.15	.40
96 Eric Barton	.15	.40
97 Eric Wright	.15	.40
98 Jake Delhomme	.20	.50
99 Jerome Harrison	.15	.40
100 Josh Cribbs	.25	.60
101 Mohamed Massaquoi	.20	.50
102 Montario Hardesty RC	.60	1.50
103 Sheldon Brown	.15	.40
104 Anthony Spencer	.15	.40
105 Bradie James	.15	.40
106 DeMarcus Ware	.20	.50
107 Dez Bryant RC	2.00	5.00
108 Felix Jones	.20	.50
109 Jason Witten	.25	.60
110 Keith Brooking	.15	.40
111 Marion Barber	.20	.50
112 Mike Jenkins	.15	.40
113 Miles Austin	.25	.60
114 Roy Williams WR	.20	.50
115 Tony Romo	.30	.75
116 Andre Goodman	.15	.40
117 Brandon Stokley	.15	.40
118 Brian Dawkins	.20	.50
119 Champ Bailey	.20	.50
120 D.J. Williams	.15	.40
121 Daniel Graham	.15	.40
122 Demaryius Thomas RC	.75	2.00
123 Eddie Royal	.15	.40
124 Elvis Dumervil	.15	.40
125 Knowshon Moreno	.20	.50
126 Kyle Orton	.20	.50
127 Mario Haggan	.15	.40
128 Renaldo Hill	.15	.40
129 Tim Tebow RC	5.00	12.00
130 Brandon Pettigrew	.15	.40
131 Bryant Johnson	.15	.40
132 Calvin Johnson	.25	.60
133 Cliff Avril	.15	.40
134 DeAndre Levy	.15	.40
135 Jahvid Best RC	1.00	2.50
136 Kevin Smith	.20	.50
137 Kyle Vanden Bosch	.15	.40
138 Louis Delmas	.15	.40
139 Marvin White	.15	.40
140 Matthew Stafford	.25	.60
141 Nate Burleson	.15	.40
142 Ndamukong Suh RC	1.25	3.00
143 A.J. Hawk	.20	.50
144 Aaron Rodgers	.50	1.25
145 Brandon Jackson	.15	.40
146 Charles Woodson	.25	.60
147 Clay Matthews	.25	.60
148 Donald Driver	.20	.50
149 Greg Jennings	.20	.50
150 Jermichael Finley	.20	.50
151 Jordy Nelson	.25	.60
152 Nick Barnett	.15	.40
153 Nick Collins	.15	.40
154 Ryan Grant	.20	.50
155 Andre Davis	.15	.40
156 Andre Johnson	.20	.50
157 Ben Tate RC	.75	2.00
158 Brian Cushing	.15	.40
159 DeMeco Ryans	.15	.40
160 Glover Quin	.15	.40
161 Kareem Jackson RC	.60	1.50
162 Kevin Walter	.20	.50
163 Mario Williams	.20	.50
164 Matt Schaub	.20	.50
165 Owen Daniels	.15	.40
166 Steve Slaton	.15	.40
167 Anthony Gonzalez	.15	.40
168 Antoine Bethea	.15	.40
169 Austin Collie	.20	.50
170 Bob Sanders	.20	.50
171 Clint Session	.15	.40
172 Dallas Clark	.20	.50
173 Donald Brown	.20	.50
174 Dwight Freeney	.20	.50
175 Joseph Addai	.20	.50
176 Peyton Manning	.40	1.00
177 Reggie Wayne	.20	.50
178 Robert Mathis	.15	.40
179 Aaron Kampman	.20	.50
180 Daryl Smith	.15	.40
181 David Garrard	.20	.50
182 Derek Cox	.15	.40
183 Derrick Harvey	.15	.40
184 Gerald Alexander	.15	.40
185 Justin Durant	.15	.40
186 Marcedes Lewis	.15	.40
187 Maurice Jones-Drew	.20	.50
188 Mike Sims-Walker	.20	.50
189 Mike Thomas	.20	.50
190 Rashad Jennings	.15	.40
191 Rashean Mathis	.15	.40
192 Troy Williamson	.15	.40
193 Brandon Flowers	.15	.40
194 Chris Chambers	.20	.50
195 Demorrio Williams	.15	.40
196 Dexter McCluster RC	.60	1.50
197 Dwayne Bowe	.20	.50
198 Eric Berry RC	.60	1.50
199 Glenn Dorsey	.15	.40
200 Jamaal Charles	.20	.50
201 Leonard Pope	.15	.40
202 Matt Cassel	.20	.50
203 Mike Vrabel	.15	.40
204 Tamba Hali	.15	.40
205 Thomas Jones	.20	.50
206 Anthony Fasano	.15	.40
207 Brandon Marshall	.20	.50
208 Chad Henne	.20	.50
209 Channing Crowder	.15	.40
210 Davone Bess	.15	.40
211 Greg Camarillo	.15	.40
212 Karlos Dansby	.15	.40
213 Ricky Williams	.20	.50
214 Ronnie Brown	.20	.50
215 Vontae Davis	.15	.40
216 Yeremiah Bell	.15	.40
217 Adrian Peterson	.40	1.00
218 Antoine Winfield	.15	.40
219 Bernard Berrian	.15	.40
220 Brett Favre	1.50	4.00
221 Cedric Griffin	.15	.40
222 E.J. Henderson	.15	.40
223 Jared Allen	.25	.60
224 Percy Harvin	.25	.60
225 Sidney Rice	.20	.50
226 Toby Gerhart RC	.60	1.50
227 Visanthe Shiancoe	.20	.50
228 Devin McCourty RC	.60	1.50
229 Jerod Mayo	.20	.50
230 Julian Edelman	.15	.40
231 Laurence Maroney	.20	.50
232 Randy Moss	.25	.60
233 Rob Gronkowski RC	1.50	4.00
234 Sammy Morris	.15	.40
235 Tom Brady	.40	1.00
236 Ty Warren	.15	.40
237 Vince Wilfork	.15	.40
238 Wes Welker	.25	.60
239 Alex Brown	.15	.40
240 Devery Henderson	.15	.40
241 Drew Brees	.25	.60
242 Jeremy Shockey	.20	.50
243 Jonathan Vilma	.15	.40
244 Lance Moore	.20	.50
245 Marques Colston	.20	.50
246 Pierre Thomas	.20	.50
247 Reggie Bush	.25	.60
248 Roman Harper	.15	.40
249 Scott Shanle	.15	.40
250 Tracy Porter	.15	.40
251 Ahmad Bradshaw	.20	.50
252 Antrel Rolle	.15	.40
253 Brandon Jacobs	.20	.50
254 Eli Manning	.25	.60
255 Hakeem Nicks	.20	.50
256 Justin Tuck	.20	.50
257 Kevin Boss	.20	.50
258 Mario Manningham	.20	.50
259 Mathias Kiwanuka	.15	.40
260 Michael Boley	.15	.40
261 Osi Umenyiora	.15	.40
262 Steve Smith USC	.20	.50
263 Terrell Thomas	.15	.40
264 Antonio Cromartie	.15	.40
265 Bart Scott	.15	.40
266 Braylon Edwards	.20	.50
267 Darrelle Revis	.20	.50
268 Dustin Keller	.20	.50
269 Jerricho Cotchery	.20	.50
270 Jim Leonhard	.15	.40
271 Kris Jenkins	.15	.40
272 LaDainian Tomlinson	.25	.60
273 Mark Sanchez	.25	.60
274 Santonio Holmes	.20	.50
275 Shaun Ellis	.15	.40
276 Shonn Greene	.20	.50
277 Bruce Gradkowski	.15	.40
278 Chaz Schilens	.15	.40
279 Darren McFadden	.20	.50
280 Darrius Heyward-Bey	.20	.50
281 Kamerion Wimbley	.15	.40
282 Kirk Morrison	.15	.40
283 Louis Murphy	.20	.50
284 Michael Bush	.15	.40
285 Nnamdi Asomugha	.20	.50
286 Richard Seymour	.15	.40
287 Rolando McClain RC	.60	1.50
288 Tyvon Branch	.15	.40
289 Zach Miller	.20	.50
290 Brent Celek	.20	.50
291 DeSean Jackson	.20	.50
292 Ellis Hobbs	.15	.40
293 Hank Baskett	.15	.40
294 Jeremy Maclin	.20	.50
295 Kevin Kolb	.20	.50
296 LeSean McCoy	.20	.50
297 Michael Vick	.30	.75
298 Mike Patterson	.15	.40
299 Quintin Mikell	.15	.40
300 Stewart Bradley	.15	.40
301 Antwaan Randle El	.15	.40
302 Ben Roethlisberger	.25	.60
303 Brett Keisel	.20	.50
304 Bryant McFadden	.15	.40
305 Heath Miller	.20	.50
306 Hines Ward	.20	.50
307 James Farrior	.15	.40
308 James Harrison	.25	.60
309 Mewelde Moore	.15	.40
310 Mike Wallace	.20	.50
311 Rashard Mendenhall	.20	.50
312 Troy Polamalu	.25	.60
313 William Gay	.15	.40
314 Antonio Gates	.20	.50
315 Darren Sproles	.20	.50
316 Eric Weddle	.15	.40
317 Kevin Ellison	.15	.40
318 Legedu Naanee	.15	.40
319 Malcom Floyd	.20	.50
320 Philip Rivers	.25	.60
321 Quentin Jammer	.15	.40
322 Ryan Mathews RC	1.25	3.00
323 Shaun Phillips	.15	.40
324 Shawne Merriman	.20	.50
325 Stephen Cooper	.15	.40
326 Vincent Jackson	.15	.40
327 Alex Smith QB	.20	.50
328 Dashon Goldson	.15	.40
329 Frank Gore	.20	.50
330 Glen Coffee	.20	.50
331 Josh Morgan	.20	.50
332 Manny Lawson	.15	.40
333 Michael Crabtree	.25	.60
334 Michael Lewis	.15	.40
335 Patrick Willis	.20	.50
336 Takeo Spikes	.15	.40
337 Vernon Davis	.20	.50
338 Aaron Curry	.20	.50
339 Colin Cole RC	.15	.40
340 Deion Branch	.15	.40
341 Golden Tate RC	.60	1.50
342 John Carlson	.15	.40
343 Josh Wilson	.15	.40
344 Julius Jones	.15	.40
345 Justin Forsett	.20	.50
346 Lofa Tatupu	.15	.40
347 Marcus Trufant	.15	.40
348 Matt Hasselbeck	.15	.40
349 T.J. Houshmandzadeh	.20	.50
350 Chris Long	.15	.40
351 Daniel Fells RC	.60	1.50
352 Danny Amendola	.25	.60
353 Donnie Avery	.20	.50
354 James Butler	.15	.40
355 James Laurinaitis	.20	.50
356 Kenneth Darby	.15	.40
357 Leonard Little	.15	.40
358 Mardy Gilyard RC	.60	1.50
359 Oshiomogho Atogwe	.15	.40
360 Ron Bartell	.15	.40
361 Sam Bradford RC	2.50	6.00
362 Steven Jackson	.20	.50
363 Aqib Talib	.15	.40
364 Arrelious Benn RC	.60	1.50
365 Barrett Ruud	.15	.40
366 Cadillac Williams	.20	.50
367 Derrick Ward	.15	.40
368 Earnest Graham	.15	.40
369 Geno Hayes	.15	.40
370 Gerald McCoy RC	.60	1.50
371 Josh Freeman	.25	.60
372 Kellen Winslow Jr.	.20	.50
373 Michael Clayton	.15	.40
374 Ronde Barber	.15	.40
375 Tanard Jackson	.15	.40
376 Bo Scaife	.15	.40
377 Chris Hope	.15	.40
378 Chris Johnson	.25	.60
379 Cortland Finnegan	.15	.40
380 Javon Ringer	.15	.40
381 Justin Gage	.15	.40
382 Kenny Britt	.20	.50
383 Michael Griffin	.15	.40
384 Nate Washington	.15	.40
385 Stephen Tulloch	.15	.40
386 Vince Young	.15	.40
387 William Hayes	.15	.40
388 Albert Haynesworth	.15	.40
389 Brian Orakpo	.15	.40
390 Chris Cooley	.20	.50
391 Clinton Portis	.20	.50
392 DeAngelo Hall	.15	.40
393 Devin Thomas	.15	.40
394 Donovan McNabb	.25	.60
395 LaRon Landry	.15	.40
396 Larry Johnson	.20	.50
397 London Fletcher	.15	.40
398 Willie Parker	.15	.40
399 Reed Doughty	.15	.40
400 Santana Moss	.20	.50

2010 Adrenalyn XL Extra

STATED ODDS 1:8 BOOSTER		
E1 Adrian Wilson	1.00	2.50
E2 Tony Gonzalez	1.25	3.00
E3 Joe Flacco	1.50	4.00
E4 Paul Posluszny	1.25	3.00
E5 Jon Beason	1.00	2.50
E6 Matt Forte	1.25	3.00
E7 Cedric Benson	1.25	3.00
E8 Jerome Harrison	1.00	2.50
E9 Jason Witten	1.50	4.00
E10 Brian Dawkins	1.25	3.00
E11 Kevin Smith	1.25	3.00
E12 Greg Jennings	1.25	3.00
E13 Mario Williams	1.25	3.00
E14 Dallas Clark	1.25	3.00
E15 Mike Sims-Walker	1.25	3.00
E16 Thomas Jones	1.25	3.00
E17 Ricky Williams	1.25	3.00
E18 Jared Allen	1.50	4.00
E19 Wes Welker	1.50	4.00
E20 Marques Colston	1.25	3.00
E21 Justin Tuck	1.25	3.00
E22 Santonio Holmes	1.25	3.00
E23 Richard Seymour	1.00	2.50
E24 Kevin Kolb	1.25	3.00
E25 Ben Roethlisberger	1.50	4.00
E26 Shawne Merriman	1.25	3.00
E27 Vernon Davis	1.25	3.00
E28 Julius Jones	1.00	2.50
E29 Donnie Avery	1.25	3.00
E30 Kellen Winslow Jr.	1.25	3.00
E31 Kenny Britt	1.25	3.00
E32 Clinton Portis	1.25	3.00

2010 Adrenalyn XL Extra Signature

STATED ODDS 1:8 BOOSTER		
ES1 Tim Hightower	2.00	5.00
ES2 Michael Turner	2.00	5.00
ES3 Anquan Boldin	2.50	6.00
ES4 Fred Jackson	3.00	8.00
ES5 DeAngelo Williams	2.50	6.00
ES6 Brian Urlacher	3.00	8.00
ES7 Chad Ochocinco	2.50	6.00
ES8 Mohamed Massaquoi	2.50	6.00
ES9 DeMarcus Ware	2.50	6.00
ES10 Knowshon Moreno	2.50	6.00
ES11 Matthew Stafford	3.00	8.00
ES12 Charles Woodson	3.00	8.00
ES13 Matt Schaub	2.50	6.00
ES14 Reggie Wayne	2.50	6.00
ES15 David Garrard	2.50	6.00
ES16 Dwayne Bowe	2.50	6.00
ES17 Ronnie Brown	2.50	6.00
ES18 Brett Favre	8.00	20.00
ES19 Randy Moss	3.00	8.00
ES20 Reggie Bush	3.00	8.00
ES21 Brandon Jacobs	2.50	6.00
ES22 Darrelle Revis	2.50	6.00
ES23 Nnamdi Asomugha	2.50	6.00
ES24 LeSean McCoy	2.50	6.00
ES25 Troy Polamalu	3.00	8.00
ES26 Antonio Gates	2.50	6.00
ES27 Frank Gore	2.50	6.00
ES28 Matt Hasselbeck	2.00	5.00
ES29 James Laurinaitis	2.50	6.00
ES30 Cadillac Williams	2.50	6.00
ES31 Vince Young	2.00	5.00
ES32 Albert Haynesworth	2.00	5.00

2010 Adrenalyn XL Special

STATED ODDS 1:2 BOOSTER		
S1 Joey Porter	.50	1.25
S2 Matt Leinart	.60	1.50
S3 John Abraham	.50	1.25
S4 Roddy White	.60	1.50
S5 Ed Reed	.60	1.50
S6 Ray Rice	.60	1.50
S7 Aaron Schobel	.50	1.25
S8 Lee Evans	.60	1.50
S9 Jonathan Stewart	.60	1.50
S10 Matt Moore	.60	1.50
S11 Devin Hester	.75	2.00
S12 Julius Peppers	.60	1.50
S13 Dhani Jones	.50	1.25
S14 Rey Maualuga	.50	1.25
S15 Jake Delhomme	.60	1.50
S16 Sheldon Brown	.50	1.25
S17 Marion Barber	.60	1.50

S18 Miles Austin	.75	2.00
S19 Elvis Dumervil	.50	1.25
S20 Kyle Orton	.60	1.50
S21 Julian Peterson	.50	1.25
S22 Nate Burleson	.50	1.25
S23 A.J. Hawk	.60	1.50
S24 Ryan Grant	.60	1.50
S25 DeMeco Ryans	.50	1.25
S26 Steve Slaton	.50	1.25
S27 Dwight Freeney	.60	1.50
S28 Joseph Addai	.60	1.50
S29 Aaron Kampman	.60	1.50
S30 Rashean Mathis	.50	1.25
S31 Demorrio Williams	.50	1.25
S32 Jamaal Charles	.60	1.50
S33 Karlos Dansby	.50	1.25
S34 Vontae Davis	.50	1.25
S35 Percy Harvin	.75	2.00
S36 Sidney Rice	.60	1.50
S37 Jerod Mayo	.60	1.50
S38 Vince Wilfork	.50	1.25
S39 Jeremy Shockey	.60	1.50
S40 Jonathan Vilma	.50	1.25
S41 Kevin Boss	.60	1.50
S42 Mathias Kiwanuka	.50	1.25
S43 LaDainian Tomlinson	.75	2.00
S44 Shonn Greene	.60	1.50
S45 Darrius Heyward-Bey	.60	1.50
S46 Zach Miller	.60	1.50
S47 Brent Celek	.60	1.50
S48 Jeremy Maclin	.60	1.50
S49 James Harrison	.75	2.00
S50 Rashard Mendenhall	.60	1.50
S51 Darren Sproles	.60	1.50
S52 Vincent Jackson	.50	1.25
S53 Alex Smith QB	.60	1.50
S54 Michael Crabtree	.75	2.00
S55 Jordan Babineaux	.50	1.25
S56 Lofa Tatupu	.50	1.25
S57 Chris Long	.50	1.25
S58 Sam Bradford	2.50	6.00
S59 Michael Clayton	.50	1.25
S60 Ronde Barber	.50	1.25
S61 Cortland Finnegan	.50	1.25
S62 Justin Gage	.50	1.25
S63 London Fletcher	.50	1.25
S64 Santana Moss	.60	1.50

2010 Adrenalyn XL Ultimate Signature

STATED ODDS 1:23 BOOSTER

U1 Larry Fitzgerald	3.00	8.00
U2 Matt Ryan	3.00	8.00
U3 Ray Lewis	3.00	8.00
U4 Trent Edwards	2.00	5.00
U5 Steve Smith	2.50	6.00
U6 Jay Cutler	3.00	8.00
U7 Carson Palmer	2.50	6.00
U8 Josh Cribbs	3.00	8.00
U9 Tony Romo	4.00	10.00
U10 Champ Bailey	2.50	6.00
U11 Calvin Johnson	3.00	8.00
U12 Aaron Rodgers	6.00	15.00
U13 Andre Johnson	2.50	6.00
U14 Peyton Manning	5.00	12.00
U15 Maurice Jones-Drew	2.50	6.00
U16 Matt Cassel	2.50	6.00
U17 Brandon Marshall	2.50	6.00
U18 Adrian Peterson	5.00	12.00
U19 Tom Brady	5.00	12.00
U20 Drew Brees	3.00	8.00
U21 Eli Manning	3.00	8.00
U22 Mark Sanchez	3.00	8.00
U23 Darren McFadden	2.50	6.00
U24 DeSean Jackson	2.50	6.00
U25 Hines Ward	2.50	6.00
U26 Philip Rivers	3.00	8.00
U27 Patrick Willis	2.50	6.00
U28 T.J. Houshmandzadeh	2.50	6.00
U29 Steven Jackson	2.50	6.00
U30 Josh Freeman	3.00	8.00
U31 Chris Johnson	3.00	8.00
U32 Donovan McNabb	3.00	8.00

2011 Adrenalyn XL Super Bowl XLV Promos

These two cards were released at the 2011 Super Bowl Card Show in Dallas as part of a wrapper redemption program at the Panini booth.

1 Dez Bryant	5.00	12.00
2 Tim Tebow	10.00	25.00

2011 Adrenalyn XL

1 Adrian Wilson	.15	.40
2 Beanie Wells	.20	.50
3 Darnell Dockett	.15	.40
4 Jay Feely	.15	.40
5 Kevin Kolb	.20	.50
6 Larry Fitzgerald	.20	.50
7 Paris Lenon	.15	.40
8 Patrick Peterson RC	1.00	2.50
9 Ryan Williams RC	.75	2.00
10 Todd Heap	.15	.40
11 Brent Grimes RC	.60	1.50
12 Curtis Lofton	.15	.40
13 John Abraham	.15	.40
14 Julio Jones RC	1.25	3.00
15 Matt Bryant RC	.40	1.00
16 Matt Ryan	.25	.60
17 Michael Turner	.20	.50
18 Ray Edwards	.15	.40
19 Roddy White	.20	.50
20 Tony Gonzalez	.20	.50
21 Anquan Boldin	.20	.50
22 Billy Cundiff	.15	.40
23 Ed Reed	.20	.50
24 Haloti Ngata	.15	.40
25 Joe Flacco	.25	.60
26 Ray Lewis	.25	.60
27 Ray Rice	.20	.50
28 Ricky Williams	.20	.50
29 Terrell Suggs	.15	.40
30 Torrey Smith RC	.75	2.00
31 C.J. Spiller	.20	.50
32 Donald Jones	.15	.40
33 Fred Jackson	.25	.60
34 Jairus Byrd	.15	.40
35 Marcell Dareus RC	.60	1.50
36 Rian Lindell	.15	.40
37 Ryan Fitzpatrick	.20	.50
38 Shawne Merriman	.15	.40
39 Steve Johnson	.20	.50
40 Terrence McGee	.15	.40
41 Cam Newton RC	3.00	8.00
42 Charles Johnson	.15	.40
43 Chris Gamble	.15	.40
44 DeAngelo Williams	.20	.50
45 Greg Olsen	.15	.40
46 James Anderson	.15	.40
47 Jon Beason	.15	.40
48 Jonathan Stewart	.20	.50
49 Olindo Mare	.15	.40
50 Steve Smith	.20	.50
51 Brian Urlacher	.25	.60
52 Charles Tillman	.15	.40
53 Devin Hester	.25	.60
54 Jay Cutler	.20	.50
55 Johnny Knox	.20	.50
56 Julius Peppers	.20	.50
57 Lance Briggs	.20	.50
58 Marion Barber	.20	.50
59 Matt Forte	.20	.50
60 Robbie Gould	.15	.40
61 A.J. Green RC	1.25	3.00
62 Andy Dalton RC	1.50	4.00
63 Cedric Benson	.20	.50
64 Jermaine Gresham	.20	.50
65 Jordan Shipley	.20	.50
66 Keith Rivers	.15	.40
67 Leon Hall	.15	.40
68 Mike Nugent	.15	.40
69 Reggie Nelson	.15	.40
70 Rey Maualuga	.15	.40
71 Ben Watson	.15	.40
72 Colt McCoy	.20	.50
73 D'Qwell Jackson	.15	.40
74 Jabaal Sheard RC	.60	1.50
75 Joe Haden	.15	.40
76 Josh Cribbs	.20	.50
77 Mohamed Massaquoi	.20	.50
78 Peyton Hillis	.20	.50
79 Phil Dawson	.15	.40
80 T.J. Ward	.15	.40
81 Anthony Spencer	.15	.40
82 David Buehler RC	.40	1.00
83 DeMarcus Ware	.20	.50
84 Dez Bryant	.25	.60
85 Felix Jones	.20	.50
86 Jason Witten	.25	.60
87 Jay Ratliff	.20	.50
88 Mike Jenkins	.15	.40
89 Miles Austin	.20	.50
90 Tony Romo	.25	.60
91 Brandon Lloyd	.20	.50
92 Brian Dawkins	.20	.50
93 Champ Bailey	.20	.50
94 Elvis Dumervil	.15	.40
95 Knowshon Moreno	.20	.50
96 Kyle Orton	.20	.50
97 Matt Prater RC	.40	1.00
98 Tim Tebow	.50	1.25
99 Von Miller RC	.75	2.00
100 Willis McGahee	.15	.40
101 Brandon Pettigrew	.15	.40
102 Calvin Johnson	.25	.60
103 Jahvid Best	.20	.50
104 Jason Hanson	.15	.40
105 Louis Delmas	.15	.40
106 Matthew Stafford	.25	.60
107 Ndamukong Suh	.25	.60
108 Nick Fairley RC	.75	2.00
109 Stephen Tulloch	.15	.40
110 Titus Young RC	.75	2.00
111 Aaron Rodgers	.40	1.00
112 A.J. Hawk	.20	.50
113 Charles Woodson	.25	.60
114 Clay Matthews	.25	.60
115 Donald Driver	.20	.50
116 Greg Jennings	.20	.50
117 Jermichael Finley	.20	.50
118 Mason Crosby	.15	.40
119 Nick Collins	.15	.40
120 Ryan Grant	.20	.50
121 Andre Johnson	.20	.50
122 Arian Foster	.20	.50
123 Brian Cushing	.15	.40
124 DeMeco Ryans	.15	.40
125 Johnathan Joseph	.15	.40
126 Kevin Walter	.20	.50
127 Mario Williams	.15	.40
128 Matt Schaub	.20	.50
129 Neil Rackers	.15	.40
130 Owen Daniels	.15	.40
131 Adam Vinatieri	.15	.40
132 Antoine Bethea	.15	.40
133 Dallas Clark	.20	.50
134 Dwight Freeney	.20	.50
135 Ernie Sims	.15	.40
136 Joseph Addai	.20	.50
137 Peyton Manning	.40	1.00
138 Pierre Garcon	.20	.50
139 Reggie Wayne	.20	.50
140 Robert Mathis	.15	.40
141 Aaron Kampman	.20	.50
142 Blaine Gabbert RC	1.00	2.50
143 Luke McCown	.15	.40
144 Dawan Landry	.15	.40
145 Josh Scobee	.15	.40
146 Marcedes Lewis	.15	.40
147 Maurice Jones-Drew	.20	.50
148 Mike Thomas	.20	.50
149 Paul Posluszny	.15	.40
150 Rashean Mathis	.15	.40
151 Brandon Flowers	.15	.40
152 Dwayne Bowe	.20	.50
153 Eric Berry	.20	.50
154 Glenn Dorsey	.15	.40
155 Jamaal Charles	.20	.50
156 Jonathan Baldwin RC	.60	1.50
157 Matt Cassel	.20	.50
158 Ryan Succop	.15	.40
159 Tamba Hali	.15	.40
160 Thomas Jones	.20	.50
161 Anthony Fasano	.15	.40
162 Brandon Marshall	.20	.50
163 Cameron Wake	.15	.40
164 Chad Henne	.20	.50
165 Dan Carpenter RC	.40	1.00
166 Daniel Thomas RC	.60	1.50
167 Karlos Dansby	.15	.40
168 Reggie Bush	.20	.50
169 Vontae Davis	.15	.40
170 Yeremiah Bell	.15	.40
171 Adrian Peterson	.30	.75
172 Antoine Winfield	.15	.40
173 Christian Ponder RC	1.25	3.00
174 Donovan McNabb	.25	.60
175 E.J. Henderson	.15	.40
176 Jared Allen	.20	.50
177 Kevin Williams	.15	.40
178 Percy Harvin	.20	.50
179 Ryan Longwell	.15	.40
180 Visanthe Shiancoe	.20	.50
181 Aaron Hernandez	.20	.50
182 Albert Haynesworth	.15	.40
183 BenJarvus Green-Ellis	.20	.50
184 Chad Ochocinco	.20	.50
185 Devin McCourty	.15	.40
186 Jerod Mayo	.15	.40
187 Stephen Gostkowski	.15	.40
188 Tom Brady	.40	1.00
189 Vince Wilfork	.15	.40
190 Wes Welker	.25	.60
191 Cameron Jordan RC	.50	1.25
192 Darren Sproles	.20	.50
193 Drew Brees	.25	.60
194 Garrett Hartley	.15	.40
195 Jonathan Vilma	.15	.40
196 Lance Moore	.20	.50
197 Mark Ingram RC	1.25	3.00
198 Marques Colston	.20	.50
199 Roman Harper	.15	.40
200 Will Smith	.15	.40
201 Ahmad Bradshaw	.20	.50
202 Antrel Rolle	.15	.40
203 Brandon Jacobs	.20	.50
204 Eli Manning	.25	.60
205 Hakeem Nicks	.20	.50
206 Justin Tuck	.20	.50
207 Lawrence Tynes	.15	.40
208 Mario Manningham	.20	.50
209 Michael Boley	.15	.40
210 Terrell Thomas	.15	.40
211 Antonio Cromartie	.15	.40
212 Darrelle Revis	.20	.50
213 David Harris	.15	.40
214 Jim Leonhard	.15	.40
215 LaDainian Tomlinson	.25	.60
216 Mark Sanchez	.25	.60
217 Nick Folk	.15	.40
218 Plaxico Burress	.20	.50
219 Santonio Holmes	.20	.50
220 Shonn Greene	.20	.50
221 Darren McFadden	.20	.50
222 Jacoby Ford	.20	.50
223 Jason Campbell	.20	.50
224 Kevin Boss	.20	.50
225 Louis Murphy	.20	.50
226 Michael Huff	.15	.40
227 Richard Seymour	.15	.40
228 Rolando McClain	.15	.40
229 Sebastian Janikowski	.20	.50
230 Tyvon Branch	.15	.40
231 Alex Henery RC	.50	1.25
232 Brent Celek	.20	.50
233 DeSean Jackson	.20	.50
234 Dominique Rodgers-Cromartie	.15	.40
235 Jason Babin	.15	.40
236 Jeremy Maclin	.20	.50
237 LeSean McCoy	.20	.50
238 Michael Vick	.25	.60
239 Nnamdi Asomugha	.20	.50
240 Trent Cole	.15	.40
241 Aaron Smith	.15	.40
242 Ben Roethlisberger	.25	.60
243 Heath Miller	.20	.50
244 Hines Ward	.20	.50
245 James Harrison	.25	.60
246 LaMarr Woodley	.15	.40
247 Mike Wallace	.25	.60
248 Rashard Mendenhall	.20	.50
249 Shaun Suisham	.15	.40
250 Troy Polamalu	.25	.60
251 Antonio Gates	.20	.50
252 Bob Sanders	.15	.40
253 Eric Weddle	.15	.40
254 Mike Tolbert	.20	.50
255 Nate Kaeding	.15	.40
256 Philip Rivers	.25	.60
257 Ryan Mathews	.20	.50
258 Shaun Phillips	.15	.40
259 Takeo Spikes	.15	.40
260 Vincent Jackson	.20	.50
261 Aldon Smith RC	1.00	2.50
262 Alex Smith QB	.20	.50
263 Braylon Edwards	.20	.50
264 Carlos Rogers	.15	.40
265 David Akers	.15	.40
266 Frank Gore	.20	.50
267 Justin Smith	.15	.40
268 Michael Crabtree	.20	.50
269 Patrick Willis	.20	.50
270 Vernon Davis	.20	.50
271 Aaron Curry	.15	.40
272 Chris Clemons	.15	.40
273 David Hawthorne	.15	.40
274 Jeff Reed	.15	.40
275 Marcus Trufant	.15	.40
276 Marshawn Lynch	.20	.50
277 Mike Williams USC	.20	.50
278 Sidney Rice	.20	.50
279 Tarvaris Jackson	.15	.40
280 Zach Miller	.20	.50
281 Al Harris	.15	.40
282 Chris Long	.15	.40
283 Danny Amendola	.20	.50
284 Donnie Avery	.15	.40
285 James Laurinaitis	.15	.40
286 Josh Brown	.15	.40
287 Mike Sims-Walker	.20	.50
288 Quintin Mikell	.15	.40
289 Sam Bradford	.25	.60
290 Steven Jackson	.20	.50
291 Adrian Clayborn RC	.60	1.50
292 Aqib Talib	.15	.40
293 Arrelious Benn	.20	.50
294 Connor Barth RC	.40	1.00
295 Gerald McCoy	.15	.40
296 Josh Freeman	.25	.60
297 Kellen Winslow Jr.	.20	.50
298 LeGarrette Blount	.20	.50
299 Mike Williams	.20	.50
300 Ronde Barber	.15	.40
301 Barrett Ruud	.15	.40
302 Chris Johnson	.20	.50
303 Cortland Finnegan	.15	.40
304 Jake Locker RC	1.50	4.00
305 Javon Ringer	.15	.40
306 Kenny Britt	.20	.50
307 Matt Hasselbeck	.20	.50
308 Michael Griffin	.15	.40
309 Rob Bironas	.15	.40
310 Will Witherspoon	.15	.40
311 Anthony Armstrong	.20	.50
312 Brian Orakpo	.20	.50
313 Chris Cooley	.20	.50
314 DeAngelo Hall	.15	.40
315 Graham Gano RC	.40	1.00
316 LaRon Landry	.15	.40
317 London Fletcher	.15	.40
318 Rex Grossman	.20	.50
319 Santana Moss	.20	.50
320 Tim Hightower	.15	.40

2011 Adrenalyn XL Extra

1 Kevin Kolb	1.25	3.00
2 Michael Turner	1.25	3.00
3 Ed Reed	1.25	3.00
4 Marcell Dareus	1.00	2.50
5 Cam Newton	5.00	12.00
6 Devin Hester	1.50	4.00
7 Keith Rivers	1.00	2.50
8 Josh Cribbs	1.25	3.00
9 Jason Witten	1.50	4.00
10 Knowshon Moreno	1.25	3.00
11 Matthew Stafford	1.50	4.00
12 Charles Woodson	1.50	4.00
13 Matt Schaub	1.25	3.00
14 Reggie Wayne	1.25	3.00
15 Luke McCown	1.00	2.50
16 Tamba Hali	1.00	2.50
17 Cameron Wake	1.00	2.50
18 Percy Harvin	1.25	3.00
19 Jerod Mayo	1.00	2.50
20 Jonathan Vilma	1.00	2.50
21 Justin Tuck	1.25	3.00
22 Santonio Holmes	1.25	3.00
23 Jacoby Ford	1.25	3.00
24 DeSean Jackson	1.25	3.00
25 James Harrison	1.50	4.00
26 Eric Weddle	1.00	2.50
27 Vernon Davis	1.25	3.00
28 Marshawn Lynch	1.25	3.00
29 Chris Long	1.00	2.50
30 Kellen Winslow Jr.	1.25	3.00
31 Barrett Ruud	1.00	2.50
32 Chris Cooley	1.25	3.00

2011 Adrenalyn XL Extra Signature

1 Adrian Wilson	2.00	5.00
2 Roddy White	2.50	6.00
3 Joe Flacco	3.00	8.00
4 Steve Johnson	2.50	6.00
5 Steve Smith	2.50	6.00
6 Julius Peppers	2.50	6.00
7 Cedric Benson	2.50	6.00
8 Colt McCoy	2.50	6.00
9 DeMarcus Ware	2.50	6.00
10 Champ Bailey	2.50	6.00
11 Ndamukong Suh	3.00	8.00
12 Clay Matthews	3.00	8.00
13 Arian Foster	2.50	6.00
14 Dwight Freeney	2.50	6.00
15 Paul Posluszny	2.00	5.00
16 Dwayne Bowe	2.50	6.00
17 Reggie Bush	2.50	6.00
18 Jared Allen	2.50	6.00
19 Wes Welker	3.00	8.00
20 Marques Colston	2.50	6.00
21 Hakeem Nicks	2.50	6.00
22 Mark Sanchez	3.00	8.00
23 Richard Seymour	2.00	5.00
24 Nnamdi Asomugha	2.50	6.00
26 Ben Roethlisberger	3.00	8.00
26 Antonio Gates	2.50	6.00
27 Frank Gore	2.50	6.00
28 Sidney Rice	2.50	6.00
29 Sam Bradford	3.00	8.00
30 Ronde Barber	2.00	5.00
31 Cortland Finnegan	2.00	5.00
32 London Fletcher	2.00	5.00

2011 Adrenalyn XL Special

1 Todd Heap	.50	1.25
2 Curtis Lofton	.50	1.25
3 Ray Rice	.60	1.50
4 Fred Jackson	.75	2.00
5 DeAngelo Williams	.60	1.50
6 Jay Cutler	.60	1.50
7 A.J. Green	1.00	2.50
8 Joe Haden	.50	1.25
9 Dez Bryant	.75	2.00
10 Elvis Dumervil	.50	1.25
11 Jahvid Best	.60	1.50
12 Greg Jennings	.60	1.50
13 Mario Williams	.50	1.25
14 Adam Vinatieri	.50	1.25
15 Marcedes Lewis	.50	1.25
16 Matt Cassel	.60	1.50
17 Karlos Dansby	.50	1.25
18 Visanthe Shiancoe	.60	1.50
19 Aaron Hernandez	.60	1.50
20 Mark Ingram	1.50	4.00
21 Ahmad Bradshaw	.60	1.50
22 LaDainian Tomlinson	.75	2.00
23 Sebastian Janikowski	.60	1.50
24 LeSean McCoy	.60	1.50
25 Hines Ward	.60	1.50
26 Vincent Jackson	.60	1.50
27 Michael Crabtree	.60	1.50
28 Zach Miller	.60	1.50
29 James Laurinaitis	.50	1.25
30 LeGarrette Blount	.60	1.50
31 Rob Bironas	.50	1.25
32 Brian Orakpo	.60	1.50

2011 Adrenalyn XL Ultimate Signature

1 Larry Fitzgerald	2.50	6.00
2 Matt Ryan	3.00	8.00
3 Ray Lewis	3.00	8.00
4 Ryan Fitzpatrick	2.50	6.00
5 Jon Beason	2.00	5.00
6 Brian Urlacher	3.00	8.00
7 Rey Maualuga	2.00	5.00
8 Peyton Hillis	2.50	6.00
9 Tony Romo	3.00	8.00
10 Brandon Lloyd	2.50	6.00
11 Calvin Johnson	3.00	8.00
12 Aaron Rodgers	5.00	12.00
13 Andre Johnson	2.50	6.00
14 Peyton Manning	5.00	12.00
15 Maurice Jones-Drew	2.50	6.00
16 Jamaal Charles	2.50	6.00
17 Brandon Marshall	2.50	6.00
18 Adrian Peterson	4.00	10.00
19 Tom Brady	5.00	12.00
20 Drew Brees	3.00	8.00
21 Eli Manning	3.00	8.00
22 Darrelle Revis	2.50	6.00
23 Darren McFadden	2.50	6.00
24 Michael Vick	3.00	8.00
25 Troy Polamalu	3.00	8.00
26 Philip Rivers	3.00	8.00
27 Patrick Willis	2.50	6.00
28 Aaron Curry	2.00	5.00
29 Steven Jackson	2.50	6.00
30 Josh Freeman	3.00	8.00
31 Chris Johnson	2.50	6.00
32 Santana Moss	2.50	6.00

1972 All Pro Graphics

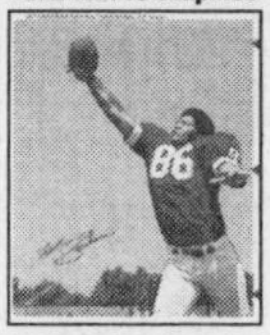

These 8 1/2" by 10 1/2" color photos were produced by All Pro Graphics Inc. of Miami Florida. Each card carries an attractive color photo of the player with a facsimile signature on the front and the player's name above the photo. The cardbacks include biographical player information and carry the company name "Dimensional Sales Corporation, All Pro Graphics" all in lower case letters. Any additions to the checklist below are appreciated.

1 Buck Buchanan	7.50	15.00
2 Nick Buoniconti	7.50	15.00
3 Mike Curtis	6.00	12.00
4 Len Dawson	12.50	25.00
5 Mel Farr	5.00	10.00
6 Ted Hendricks	6.00	12.00
7 Leroy Kelly	7.50	15.00
8 Jim Kiick	6.00	12.00
9 Willie Lanier	6.00	12.00
10 Archie Manning	10.00	20.00
11 Earl Morrall	6.00	12.00
12 Steve Owens	6.00	12.00
13 Altie Taylor	5.00	10.00
14 Otis Taylor	6.00	12.00
15 Garo Yepremian	6.00	12.00

1973 All Pro Graphics

These 8" by 10" color photos were produced by All Pro Graphics Inc. of Miami Florida around 1973. Each blankbacked photo carries an attractive color photo of the player with a facsimile signature. Below the photo are the manufacturer's name on the left and the player's name on the right side. This list is thought to be incomplete as All Pro Graphics issued many photos in varying styles over a number of years. Any additions are appreciated.

1 John Brockington	6.00	12.00
2 Wally Chambers	5.00	10.00
3 Mike Curtis	6.00	12.00
4 Roman Gabriel	7.50	15.00
5 Joe Greene	12.00	20.00
6 John Hadl	7.50	15.00
7 Ron Johnson	5.00	10.00
8 Steve Owens	7.50	15.00
9 Alan Page	7.50	15.00
10 Jim Plunkett	7.50	15.00
11 Jan Stenerud	6.00	12.00

1991 All World Troy Aikman Promos

This set consists of six standard-size cards. The cards feature the same color action photo of Aikman, with ball cocked behind his head ready to pass. On the first three cards, the top of the photo is oval-shaped and framed by yellow stripes. The space above the oval as well as the stripe at the bottom carrying player information are purple. The outer border is green. Inside green borders, the horizontal back has a color close-up photo, biography (there were French, Spanish, and English versions), and statistics. On the second three cards listed below, the player photo is tilted slightly to the right and framed by a thin green border. Yellow stripes above and below the picture carry information, and the outer border is black-and-white speckled. The backs have a similar design and display a close-up color head shot and biographical and statistical information on a pastel green panel. All versions use the same color action photo, but differ in that the photo is cropped differently on the green-border cards compared to the speckled-border cards. All cards are numbered on the back as number 1.

COMPLETE SET (6)	6.00	15.00
COMMON CARD (1A-1F)	1.20	3.00

1992 All World

The 1992 All World NFL football set contains 300 standard-size cards. The production run was reported to be 8000 foil cases, but many collectors feel the actual print run number fell slightly short of 8000. There are 12 cards per foil pack and 26 per rack pack. Ten rookies and ten "Legends in the Making" cards, embossed with gold-foil stars, were randomly inserted in the foil packs. Likewise, autographed cards by Joe Namath (1,000), Jim Brown (1,000), and Desmond Howard (2,500) were inserted in both foil and rack packs. Although the player's name is not printed on the front, his autograph and number do appear. A special double-fold card (TR1) of the three autographed cards was inserted only in the rack packs. It is distinguished from the regular issue triple cards by foil-stamping. The regular card backs have a second color player photo, with player information (biography and player profile) in a horizontally oriented box alongside the picture. Topical subsets featured include Legends in the Making (1-10) and Greats of the Game (266-300). Rookie Cards include Edgar Bennett, Steve Bono, Terrell Buckley, Dale Carter, Marco Coleman, Quentin Coryatt, Vaughn Dunbar, Steve Emtman, Desmond Howard (AW had exclusive rights), Carl Pickens, and Tommy Vardell. A Desmond Howard promo card was released and is priced at the end of our checklist.

COMPLETE SET (300)	6.00	15.00
1 Emmitt Smith LM	.25	.60
2 Thurman Thomas LM	.02	.10
3 Deion Sanders LM	.08	.25
4 Randall Cunningham LM	.02	.10
5 Michael Irvin LM	.02	.10
6 Bruce Smith LM	.02	.10
7 Jeff George LM	.02	.10
8 Derrick Thomas LM	.02	.10
9 Andre Rison LM	.08	.25
10 Troy Aikman LM	.15	.40
11 Quentin Coryatt RC	.01	.05
12 Carl Pickens RC	.08	.25
13 Steve Emtman RC	.01	.05
14 Derek Brown TE RC	.01	.05
15 Desmond Howard RC	.20	.50
16 Troy Vincent RC	.01	.05
17 David Klingler RC	.01	.05
18 Vaughn Dunbar RC	.01	.05
19 Terrell Buckley RC	.01	.05
20 Jimmy Smith RC	1.25	3.00
21 Marquez Pope RC	.01	.05
22 Kurt Barber RC	.01	.05
23 Robert Harris RC	.01	.05
24 Tony Sacca RC	.01	.05
25 Alonzo Spellman RC	.02	.10
26 Shane Collins RC	.01	.05
27 Chris Mims RC	.01	.05
28 Siran Stacy RC	.01	.05
29 Edgar Bennett RC	.08	.25
30 Sean Gilbert RC	.02	.10
31 Eugene Chung RC	.01	.05
32 Levon Kirkland RC	.01	.05
33 Chuck Smith RC	.01	.05
34 Chester McGlockton RC	.02	.10
35 Ashley Ambrose RC	.08	.25
36 Phillippi Sparks RC	.01	.05
37 Darryl Williams RC	.01	.05
38 Tracy Scroggins RC	.01	.05
39 Mike Gaddis RC	.01	.05
40 Tony Brooks RC	.01	.05
41 Steve Israel RC	.01	.05
42 Patrick Rowe RC	.01	.05
43 Shane Dronett RC	.01	.05
44 Mike Pawlawski RC	.01	.05
45 Dale Carter RC	.02	.10
46 Tyji Armstrong RC	.01	.05
47 Kevin Smith RC	.01	.05
48 Courtney Hawkins RC	.02	.10
49 Marco Coleman RC	.01	.05
50 Tommy Vardell RC	.01	.05
51 Ray Ethridge RC	.01	.05
52 Robert Porcher RC	.08	.25
53 Todd Collins RC	.01	.05
54 Robert Jones RC	.01	.05
55 Tommy Maddox RC	.75	2.00
56 Dana Hall RC	.01	.05
57 Leon Searcy RC	.01	.05
58 Robert Brooks RC	.30	.75
59 Darren Woodson RC	.08	.25
60 Jeremy Lincoln RC	.01	.05
61 Sean Jones	.01	.05
62 Howie Long	.08	.25
63 Rich Gannon	.08	.25
64 Keith Byars	.01	.05
65 John Taylor	.02	.10
66 Burt Grossman	.01	.05
67 Chris Hinton	.01	.05
68 Brad Muster	.01	.05
69 Cris Dishman	.01	.05
70 Russell Maryland	.01	.05
71 Harvey Williams	.02	.10
72 Broderick Thomas	.01	.05
73 Louis Lipps	.01	.05
74 Erik Kramer	.01	.05
75 David Fulcher	.01	.05
76 Andre Tippett	.01	.05
77 Timm Rosenbach	.01	.05
78 Mark Rypien	.01	.05
79 James Lofton	.02	.10
80 Dan Saleaumua	.01	.05
81 John L. Williams	.01	.05
82 Kevin Fagan	.01	.05
83 Flipper Anderson	.01	.05
84 Michael Dean Perry	.02	.10
85 Mark Higgs	.01	.05
86 Pat Swilling	.01	.05
87 Pierce Holt	.01	.05
88 John Elway	.50	1.25
89 Bill Brooks	.02	.10
90 Rob Moore	.02	.10
91 Junior Seau	.08	.25
92 Wendell Davis	.01	.05
93 Brian Noble	.01	.05
94 Ernest Givins	.02	.10
95 Phil Simms	.02	.10
96 Eric Dickerson	.02	.10
97 Bennie Blades	.01	.05
98 Gary Anderson RB	.01	.05
99 Erric Pegram	.01	.05
100 Hart Lee Dykes	.01	.05
101 Charles Haley	.02	.10
102 Bruce Smith	.08	.25
103 Nick Lowery	.01	.05
104 Webster Slaughter	.01	.05
105 Ray Childress	.01	.05
106 Gene Atkins	.01	.05
107 Bruce Armstrong	.01	.05
108 Anthony Miller	.08	.25
109 Eric Thomas	.01	.05
110 Greg Townsend	.01	.05
111 Anthony Carter	.02	.10
112 James Hasty	.01	.05
113 Chris Miller	.01	.05
114 Sammie Smith	.01	.05
115 Bubby Brister	.02	.10
116 Mark Clayton	.02	.10
117 Richard Johnson	.01	.05
118 Bernie Kosar	.02	.10
119 Lionel Washington	.01	.05
120 Gary Clark	.02	.10
121 Anthony Munoz	.08	.25
122 Brent Jones	.02	.10
123 Thurman Thomas	.08	.25
124 Lee Williams	.01	.05
125 Jessie Hester	.01	.05
126 Andre Ware	.02	.10
127 Patrick Hunter	.01	.05
128 Erik Howard	.01	.05
129 Keith Jackson	.02	.10
130 Troy Aikman	.30	.75
131 Mike Singletary	.02	.10
132 Carnell Lake	.01	.05
133 Jeff Hostetler	.02	.10
134 Alonzo Highsmith	.01	.05
135 Vaughan Johnson	.01	.05
136 Louis Oliver	.01	.05
137 Mel Gray	.02	.10
138 Al Toon	.02	.10
139 Bubba McDowell	.01	.05
140 Ronnie Lott	.02	.10
141 Deion Sanders	.20	.50
142 Jim Harbaugh	.08	.25
143 Gary Zimmerman	.02	.10
144 Ernie Jones	.01	.05
145 Cortez Kennedy	.02	.10
146 Jeff Cross	.01	.05
147 Floyd Turner UER (Bio says he was drafted in 4th round)	.01	.05
148 Mike Tomczak	.01	.05
149 Lorenzo White	.01	.05
150 Mark Carrier DB	.01	.05
151 John Stephens	.01	.05
152 Jerry Rice	.30	.75
153 Jim Kelly	.08	.25
154 Al Smith	.01	.05
155 Duane Bickett	.01	.05
156 Brett Perriman	.08	.25
157 Boomer Esiason	.02	.10
158 Neil Smith	.08	.25
159 Eddie Anderson	.01	.05
160 Browning Nagle	.01	.05
161 John Friesz	.02	.10
162 Robert Delpino	.01	.05
163 Darren Lewis	.01	.05
164 Roger Craig	.02	.10
165 Keith McCants	.01	.05
166 Stephone Paige	.01	.05
167 Steve Broussard	.01	.05
168 Gaston Green	.01	.05
169 Ethan Horton	.01	.05
170 Lewis Billups	.01	.05
171 Mike Merriweather	.01	.05
172 Randall Cunningham	.08	.25
173 Leonard Marshall	.01	.05
174 Jay Novacek	.02	.10
175 Irving Fryar	.02	.10
176 Randal Hill	.01	.05
177 Keith Henderson	.01	.05
178 Brad Baxter	.01	.05
179 William Fuller	.01	.05
180 Leslie O'Neal	.02	.10
181 Steve Smith	.01	.05
182 Joe Montana UER (Born 1956, not 1965)	.50	1.25
183 Eric Green	.02	.10
184 Rodney Peete	.02	.10
185 Lawrence Dawsey	.02	.10
186 Brian Mitchell	.02	.10
187 Rickey Jackson	.01	.05
188 Christian Okoye	.02	.10
189 David Wyman	.01	.05
190 Jessie Tuggle	.01	.05
191 Ronnie Harmon	.01	.05
192 Andre Reed	.08	.25
193 Chris Doleman	.02	.10
194 Leroy Hoard	.01	.05
195 Mark Ingram	.01	.05
196 Willie Gault	.02	.10
197 Eugene Lockhart	.01	.05
198 Jim Everett	.02	.10
199 Doug Smith	.01	.05
200 Clarence Verdin	.01	.05
201 Steve Bono RC	.08	.25
202 Mark Vlasic	.01	.05
203 Fred Barnett	.02	.10
204 Henry Thomas	.01	.05
205 Shaun Gayle	.01	.05
206 Rod Bernstine	.01	.05
207 Harold Green	.02	.10
208 Dan McGwire	.01	.05
209 Marv Cook	.01	.05
210 Emmitt Smith	.60	1.50
211 Merril Hoge	.01	.05
212 Darion Conner	.01	.05
213 Mike Sherrard	.01	.05
214 Jeff George	.08	.25
215 Craig Heyward	.02	.10
216 Henry Ellard	.02	.10
217 Lawrence Taylor	.08	.25
218 Jerry Ball	.01	.05
219 Tom Rathman	.01	.05
220 Warren Moon	.08	.25
221 Ricky Proehl	.01	.05
222 Sterling Sharpe	.08	.25
223 Earnest Byner	.01	.05
224 Jay Schroeder	.01	.05
225 Vance Johnson	.01	.05
226 Cornelius Bennett	.02	.10
227 Ken O'Brien	.01	.05
228 Ferrell Edmunds	.01	.05
229 Eric Allen	.01	.05
230 Derrick Thomas	.08	.25
231 Cris Carter	.20	.50
232 Jon Vaughn	.01	.05
233 Eric Metcalf	.02	.10
234 William Perry	.02	.10
235 Vinny Testaverde	.02	.10
236 Chip Banks	.01	.05
237 Brian Blades	.02	.10
238 Calvin Williams	.01	.05
239 Andre Rison	.08	.25
240 Neil O'Donnell	.02	.10
241 Michael Irvin	.08	.25
242 Gary Plummer	.01	.05
243 Nick Bell	.01	.05
244 Ray Crockett	.01	.05
245 Sam Mills	.01	.05
246 Haywood Jeffires	.01	.05
247 Steve Young	.25	.60
248 Martin Bayless	.01	.05
249 Dan Marino	.50	1.25
250 Carl Banks	.01	.05
251 Keith McKeller	.01	.05
252 Aaron Wallace	.01	.05
253 Lamar Lathon	.01	.05
254 Derrick Fenner	.01	.05
255 Vai Sikahema	.01	.05
256 Keith Sims	.01	.05
257 Rohn Stark	.01	.05
258 Reggie Roby	.01	.05
259 Tony Zendejas	.01	.05
260 Harris Barton	.01	.05
261 Checklist 1-100	.01	.05
262 Checklist 101-200	.01	.05
263 Checklist 201-300	.01	.05
264 Rookies Checklist	.01	.05
265 Greats Checklist	.01	.05
266 Joe Namath GG	.08	.25
267 Joe Namath GG	.08	.25
268 Joe Namath GG	.08	.25
269 Joe Namath GG	.08	.25

270 Joe Namath GG	.08	.25
271 Jim Brown GG	.08	.25
272 Jim Brown GG	.08	.25
273 Jim Brown GG	.08	.25
274 Jim Brown GG	.08	.25
275 Jim Brown GG	.08	.25
276 Vince Lombardi GG	.08	.25
277 Jim Thorpe GG	.01	.05
278 Tom Fears GG	.01	.05
279 John Henry Johnson GG	.01	.05
280 Gale Sayers GG	.02	.10
281 Willie Brown GG	.01	.05
282 Doak Walker GG	.01	.05
283 Dick Lane GG	.01	.05
284 Otto Graham GG	.02	.10
285 Hugh McElhenny GG	.01	.05
286 Roger Staubach GG	.08	.25
287 Steve Largent GG	.08	.25
288 Otis Taylor GG	.01	.05
289 Sam Huff GG	.01	.05
290 Harold Carmichael GG	.01	.05
291 Steve Van Buren GG	.01	.05
292 Gino Marchetti GG	.01	.05
293 Tony Dorsett GG	.02	.10
294 Leo Nomellini GG	.01	.05
295 Jack Lambert GG	.01	.05
296 Joe Theismann GG	.02	.10
297 Bobby Layne GG	.01	.05
298 John Stallworth GG	.01	.05
299 Paul Hornung GG	.02	.10
300 Don Maynard GG	.01	.05
A1 Desmond Howard AU/1000	10.00	25.00
A2 Jim Brown AU/1000	25.00	50.00
A3 Joe Namath AU/1000	25.00	60.00
P1 Desmond Howard	.40	1.00
(Promo; Numbered P)		
TRI Desmond Howard	1.25	3.00
Jim Brown		
Joe Namath		
(Triplefolder)		

1992 All World Greats/Rookies

COMPLETE SET (20)	4.00	10.00
ONE PER RACK PACK		
SG1 Troy Aikman	.75	2.00
SG2 Thurman Thomas	.30	.75
SG3 Andre Rison	.20	.50
SG4 Emmitt Smith	1.50	4.00
SG5 Derrick Thomas	.30	.75
SG6 Joe Namath	.30	.75
SG7 Jim Brown	.30	.75
SG8 Roger Staubach	.30	.75
SG9 Gale Sayers	.20	.50
SG10 Jim Thorpe	.20	.50
SG11 Quentin Coryatt	.20	.50
SG12 Carl Pickens	.30	.75
SG13 Steve Emtman	.08	.25
SG14 Derek Brown TE	.08	.25
SG15 Desmond Howard	.30	.75
SG16 Troy Vincent	.08	.25
SG17 David Klinger	.20	.50
SG18 Vaughn Dunbar	.08	.25
SG19 Terrell Buckley	.08	.25
SG20 Jimmy Smith	1.25	3.00

1992 All World Legends/Rookies

COMPLETE SET (20)	15.00	35.00
RANDOM INSERTS IN FOIL PACKS		
L1 Emmitt Smith	4.00	10.00
L2 Thurman Thomas	.75	2.00
L3 Deion Sanders	1.25	3.00
L4 Randall Cunningham	.75	2.00
L5 Michael Irvin	.75	2.00
L6 Bruce Smith	.40	1.00
L7 Jeff George	.40	1.00
L8 Derrick Thomas	.40	1.00
L9 Andre Rison	.40	1.00
L10 Troy Aikman	2.00	5.00
L11 Quentin Coryatt	.40	1.00
L12 Carl Pickens	.75	2.00
L13 Steve Emtman	.40	1.00
L14 Derek Brown TE	.40	1.00
L15 Desmond Howard	.40	1.00
L16 Troy Vincent	.40	1.00
L17 David Klinger	.40	1.00
L18 Vaughn Dunbar	.40	1.00
L19 Terrell Buckley	.40	1.00
L20 Jimmy Smith	2.50	6.00

1966 American Oil All-Pro

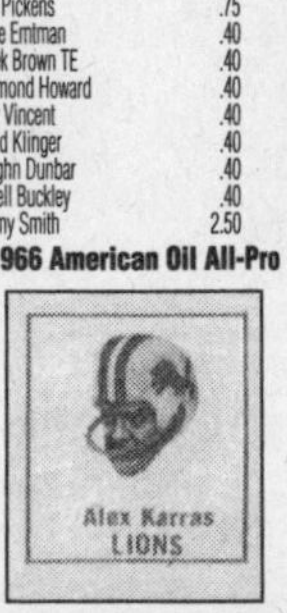

The 1966 American Oil All-Pro set featured 20 stamps, each measuring approximately 15/16" by 1 1/8". To participate in the contest, the consumer needed to acquire an 8 1/2" by 11" collection sheet from a participating American Oil dealer. This sheet is horizontally oriented and presents rules governing the contest as well as 20 slots in which to paste the stamps. The 20 slots are arranged in five rows in the shape of an inverted triangle (6, 5, 4, 3, and 2 stamps per row as one moves from top to bottom) with the prizes listed to the left of each row. The consumer also received envelopes from participating dealers that contained small sheets of three perforated player stamps each. Each 3-stamp sheet was numbered with a letter as noted below making some of the stamps known double prints. Each stamp features a color head shot with the player wearing his helmet. After separating the stamps, the consumer was instructed to paste them on the matching squares of the collection sheet. If all the stamps in a particular prize group row were collected, the consumer won that particular prize. Top prize for all six stamps in the top group was a 1967 Ford Mustang. The other prizes were $250, $25, $5, and $1 for five-, four-, three-, and two-stamp prize groups respectively. Prizes were to be redeemed within 15 days after the closing of the promotion, but no later than March 1, 1967 in any event. Complete three stamp panels carry a 50 percent premium. The stamps are blank backed and unnumbered, and have been checklisted below alphabetically. Wayne Walker and Tommy Nobis were required to win $1; Herb Adderley and Dave Parks and Lenny Moore were required to win $5; John Unitas and Dave Jones, Mick Tingelhoff, and Alex Karras were required to win $25; Dick Butkus and Charley Johnson, Gary Ballman, Frank Ryan, and Willie Davis were required to win $250; and Gary Collins and Tucker Frederickson, Pete Retzlaff, Sam Huff, Gale Sayers, and Bob Lilly were required to win the 1967 Mustang. The winner cards indicated below are not priced (and not considered necessary for a complete set) since each is thought to have been largely redeemed and very few sales have been reported on existing copies. A 3-stamp advertising strip (roughly 3 1/4" by 6 3/4") was also produced and listed below.

COMPLETE SET (15)	250.00	500.00
WRAPPER	5.00	12.00
1 Herb Adderley		
(Winner $5)		
2 Gary Ballman C	15.00	30.00
3 Dick Butkus		
(Winner $250)		
4 Gary Collins		
(Winner Car)		
5 Willie Davis H	20.00	35.00
6 Tucker Frederickson B/D	15.00	30.00
7 Sam Huff B	20.00	35.00
8 Charley Johnson C/L	15.00	30.00
9 Deacon Jones D	20.00	35.00
10 Alex Karras C	20.00	35.00
11 Bob Lilly F	30.00	50.00
12 Lenny Moore F	30.00	50.00
13 Tommy Nobis H/K	15.00	30.00
14 Dave Parks F	15.00	30.00
15 Pete Retzlaff H	15.00	30.00
16 Frank Ryan K	15.00	30.00
17 Gale Sayers B/L	50.00	80.00
18 Mick Tingelhoff D/K	15.00	30.00
19 Johnny Unitas		
(Winner $25)		
20 Wayne Walker L	100.00	200.00
(Winner $1)		
NNO Saver Sheet	50.00	100.00
NNO Ad Strip	75.00	150.00
Dave Parks		
Bob Lilly		
Lenny Moore		

1967 American Oil All-Pro

The 1967 American Oil All-Pro set featured 21-stamps with each measuring approximately 7/8" by 1 1/8". The contestant needed to acquire an 8 1/2" by 11" collection sheet from a participating American Oil dealer on which he would place the stamps. The sheet was arranged in five rows with the prize level listed above each row. Each 3-stamp sheet was numbered with a letter as noted below. The consumer received envelopes from participating dealers that contained sheets of two perforated player stamps and one Mustang car stamp. Note that the Jim Taylor sheet contained a "Service Award" stamp instead of a second player. If all stamps in a particular prize group were collected, the consumer won that particular prize: the grand prize of a 1968 Ford Mustang, $100, $25, $5, or $1 cash. The $1 prize could be won by acquiring the stamps of Johnny Morris, Tommy Nobis, and Jim Taylor. The $5 prize required the stamps of Timmy Brown, Jimmy Orr, Fran Tarkenton, and Brady Keys. The $25 prize required stamps of John Unitas, Bob Hayes, Bill Brown, and Junior Coffey. The $100 prize required Gary Collins, Sonny Jurgensen, Charley Johnson, Gale Sayers, and Merlin Olsen. To win the 1968 Mustang required stamps of Bart Starr, Wayne Walker, Charley Taylor, Larry Wilson, and Ken Willard. The "winning" player for each prize group is fairly scarce, (and not neccessary for a complete set) since each is thought to have been largely redeemed. Each stamp front features a color action player photo. The stamps are blank-backed and unnumbered and have been checklisted below alphabetically.

COMPLETE SET (19)	350.00	600.00
1 Bill Brown F	15.00	30.00
2 Timmy Brown J	15.00	30.00
3 Junior Coffey H	15.00	30.00
4 Gary Collins E	15.00	30.00
5 Bob Hayes D	25.00	40.00
6 Charley Johnson J	15.00	30.00
7 Sonny Jurgensen B	30.00	50.00
8 Brady Keys B	15.00	30.00
9 Johnny Morris A/M/P	15.00	30.00
10 Tommy Nobis	60.00	100.00
($1 winner)		
11 Merlin Olsen M/P	25.00	35.00
12 Jimmy Orr H	15.00	30.00
13 Gale Sayers	60.00	100.00
($100 winner)		
14 Bart Starr A	60.00	100.00
15 Fran Tarkenton	30.00	50.00
($5 winner)		
16 Charley Taylor E	20.00	35.00
17 Jim Taylor N	40.00	75.00
18 John Unitas		
($25 winner)		
19 Wayne Walker		
(Winner 1968 Mustang)		
20 Ken Willard F	15.00	30.00
21 Larry Wilson A/D	18.00	30.00
NNO Saver Sheet	50.00	100.00

1968 American Oil Mr. and Mrs.

This 32-card set was produced by Glendinning Companies and distributed by the American Oil Company. The cards measure approximately 2 1/8" by 3 7/16". The set is made up of 16 player cards and 16 wife/family cards that were originally connected by perforation in pairs. The cards were distributed as pieces of the "Mr. and Mrs. NFL" game. If a matched pair (i.e. a player card and his wife/family card) were obtained, the holder was an instant winner of either a 1969 Ford (choice of Mustang Mach I or Country Squire), $500, $100, $10, $5, $1, or 50-cents. The cards are most frequently found as detached halves. The horizontally oriented fronts feature action color player photos or color family photos featuring the wife. On the player card, the player's name is printed above the picture. On the wife card, the woman's married name (i.e. Mrs. Bobby Mitchell) and a caption defining the activity shown are above the picture. Each card is bordered in a different color and the prize corresponding to that card is printed in the border. The backs of the cards vary. In each pair that were originally connected, the wife card back features contest rules in a blue box on a red background with darker red car silhouettes. The player card back carries the game title (Mr. and Mrs. NFL), the American Oil Company logo, and the words "Win 1969 Fords and Cash" on the same background. In addition, attached to each pair at either end and forming a 12" strip, two more cardlike pieces contained further information and a game piece for predicting the 1969 Super Bowl scores. The smaller of the two (approximately 1 7/8" by 2 1/8") is printed with the NFL players and the corresponding prizes. The larger of the two (2 1/8" by 3 1/4") is the game piece for the second part of the contest with blanks for recording a score prediction for one NFL and one AFL team. This piece was mailed in to Super Bowl Scoreboard in New York. Each correct entry would share equally in the $100,000 Super Bowl Scoreboard cash prize. The cards are checklisted below alphabetically. The prize corresponding to each married couple is listed under the tougher of the pair. Prices listed are for single cards. Complete two-card panels are valued at approximately double the value of the individual cards. There are 16 tougher pieces that were the cards needed to win prizes. These 16 are not considered necessary for a complete set.

COMPLETE SET (16)	100.00	200.00
1 Kermit Alexander	250.00	400.00
(Winner $100)		
2 Mrs. Kermit Alexander	6.00	12.00
Jogging with Family		
3 Jim Bakken	6.00	12.00
4 Mrs. Jim Bakken	50.00	80.00
(Winner $1)		
5 Gary Collins		
(Winner $500)		
6 Mrs. Gary Collins	6.00	12.00
Enjoying the Outdoors		
7 Jim Grabowski		
(Winner 1969 Ford)		
8 Mrs. Jim Grabowski	6.00	12.00
At the Fireside		
9 Earl Gros	50.00	80.00
(Winner $1)		
10 Mrs. Earl Gros	6.00	12.00
At the Park		
11 Deacon Jones	12.00	20.00
12 Mrs. Deacon Jones		
(Winner $500)		
13 Billy Lothridge		
(Winner $10)		
14 Mrs. Billy Lothridge	6.00	12.00
And Baby Daughter		
15 Tom Matte	10.00	15.00
16 Mrs. Tom Matte		
(Winner 50-cents)		
17 Bobby Mitchell		
(Winner $5)		
18 Mrs. Bobby Mitchell	6.00	12.00
At a Backyard Barbecue		
19 Joe Morrison	6.00	12.00
20 Mrs. Joe Morrison		
(Winner 1969 Ford)		
21 Dave Osborn	6.00	12.00
22 Mrs. Dave Osborn		
(Winner $5)		
23 Dan Reeves	40.00	80.00
(Winner 50 cents)		
24 Mrs. Dan Reeves	6.00	12.00
Enjoying the Children		
25 Gale Sayers	25.00	40.00
26 Mrs. Gale Sayers		
(Winner $100)		
27 Norm Snead	60.00	100.00
(Winner $1)		
28 Mrs. Norm Snead	6.00	12.00
On the Family Boat		
29 Steve Stonebreaker	6.00	12.00
30 Mrs. Steve	6.00	
Stonebreaker		
(Winner $10)		
31 Wayne Walker	50.00	80.00
(Winner 50-cents)		
32 Mrs. Wayne Walker	6.00	12.00
At a Family Picnic		

1968 American Oil Winners Circle

This set of 12 perforated game cards measures approximately 2 5/8" by 2 1/8". There are "left side" and "right side" game cards which had to be matched to win a car or a cash prize. The "right side" game cards have a color drawing of a sports personality in a circle on the left, surrounded by laurel leaf twigs, and a short career summary on the right. There is a color bar on the bottom of the game piece carrying a dollar amount and the words "right side". The "left side" game cards carry a rectangular drawing of a sports personality or a photo of a Camaro or a Corvette. A different color bar with a dollar amount and the words "left side" are under the picture. On a dark blue background, the "right side" backs carry the rules of the game, and the "left side" cards show a "Winners Circle". The cards are unnumbered and checklisted below in alphabetical order.

COMPLETE SET (12)	75.00	150.00
11 Gale Sayers	7.50	15.00
Left side		
12 Bart Starr	10.00	20.00
Right side		

1961 American Tract Society

These cards are quite attractive and feature the "pure card" concept that is always popular with collectors (no card borders simply pure photo on front). The cards are numbered on the back and are skip-numbered below due to the fact that these singles are part of a much larger (sport and non-sport) set. The issue features Christian ballplayers giving first-person testimonies on the cardbacks describing how Jesus has changed their lives. These cards are often referred to as "Tracards." Each measures approximately 2 3/4" X 3 1/2". Many of the baseball subjects contain variations. No known variations exist for the football cards.

21 Donn Moomaw	10.00	20.00
50 Joe Romig	10.00	20.00

1994 AmeriVox Quarterback Legends Phone Cards

This set of 5-phone cards was issued by AmeriVox mounted on a large cardboard backer. The backer contained brief information about each player and was serial numbered of 2000-sets produced. The cards themselves feature artist's renderings of the player along with the QB Legends logo. Each carried an initial phone time value of $10.

COMPLETE SET (5)	15.00	25.00
1 George Blanda	3.00	6.00
2 Len Dawson	3.00	5.00
3 Otto Graham	4.00	8.00
4 Bob Griese	3.00	5.00
5 Sonny Jurgensen	3.00	5.00

1993 Anti-Gambling Postcards

COMPLETE SET (13)	6.00	15.00
9 Jim Kelly FB	1.00	2.50
10 Bernie Kosar FB	.60	1.50

1987 A Question of Sport UK

These cards are part of a British board game "A Question of Sport" in which participants attempt to name an athlete by seeing a picture of them. These white bordered, full color cards measure 2 1/4" by 3 1/2" and have a back that contains only the player's name on a green background. The copyright on the box is 1986, but the game was released in early 1987. We've arranged the unnumbered cards alphabetically below.

COMPLETE SET (240)	20.00	40.00
69 Eric Dickerson	.40	1.00
84 John Elway	1.50	4.00
155 Dan Marino	1.50	4.00
163 Joe Montana	2.00	5.00
166 Joe Morris	.40	1.00

1992 A Question of Sport UK

These cards are part of a British board game "A Question of Sport" in which participants attempt to name an athlete by seeing a picture of them. These white bordered, full color cards measure 2 1/4" by 3 1/2" and have a back that contains only the player's name. We've arranged the unnumbered cards alphabetically below.

COMPLETE SET (80)	20.00	50.00
54 Joe Montana	2.00	5.00

1994 A Question of Sport UK

These cards are part of a British board game "A Question of Sport" in which participants attempt to name an athlete by seeing a picture of them. These white bordered, full color cards measure 2 1/4" by 3 1/2" and have a back that contains only the player's name surrounded by a blue border on white card stock. We've arranged the unnumbered cards alphabetically below.

COMPLETE SET (79)	20.00	50.00
46 Dan Marino	2.00	5.00
48 Joe Montana	2.00	5.00
58 Jerry Rice	1.50	4.00

1991 Arena Holograms

The 1991 Arena Hologram cards were distributed through hobby dealers and feature famous athletes. According to Arena, production quantities were limited to 250,000 of each card. The standard-size hologram cards have on the horozontially oriented backs a color photo of the player in a tuxedo. Ken Griffey Jr. Frank Thomas, David Robinson, Joe Montana and Barry Sanders all signed cards with each being serial numbered by hand. A card-sized certificate of authenticity was also issued with each signed card.

COMPLETE SET (5)	3.20	8.00
1 Joe Montana	.80	2.00
4 Barry Sanders	.60	1.50
AU4 Barry Sanders AU/1000	40.00	75.00
AU6 Joe Montana AU/2500	40.00	75.00

1991 Arena Holograms 12th National

These standard-size cards have on their fronts a 3-D silver-colored emblem on a white background with orange borders. Though the back of each card salutes a different superstar, the players themselves are not pictured; instead, one finds pictures of a football; hockey stick and puck; basketball; and baseball in glove respectively. The cards are numbered on the front.

COMPLETE SET (4)	4.00	10.00
1 Joe Montana	1.25	3.00

1992 Arena Holograms

The 1992 Arena Hologram Joe Montana card is very much like the 1991 release. The cardbacks are essentially the same except for the card number (1 versus 1A) and the print run; 99,000 for the 1992 card. The photo on the '92 card shows Montana against a background image of the Golden Gate Bridge.

1A Joe Montana	1.25	3.00

1998 Arizona Rattlers AFL

This set was sponsored by Elete Cards, Inc. and features members of the Arizona Rattlers of the Arena Football League. Each card includes the team name and player name running vertically on the left hand side of the front along with a color player photo. The cardbacks are also printed in color and feature another player photo and a player bio.

COMPLETE SET (27)	15.00	30.00
1 Darrin Kenney	.50	1.25
2 Tom Gibson	.50	1.25
3 Bryan Hooks	.50	1.25
4 Barry Voorhees	.50	1.25
5 Junior Green	.50	1.25
6 Tony Henderson	.50	1.25
7 Marvin Bagley	.50	1.25
8 Flint Fleming	.50	1.25
9 Sherdrick Bonner	.60	1.50
10 Hunkie Cooper	.50	1.25
11 Randy Gatewood	.50	1.25
12 Bob McMillen	.50	1.25
13 Shawn Parnell	.50	1.25
14 Calvin Schexnayder	.50	1.25
15 Bo Kelly	.50	1.25
16 Donnie Davis	.50	1.25
17 Cedric Walker	.50	1.25
18 Cecil Doggette	.50	1.25
19 Mark Tucker	.50	1.25
20 Herb Duncan	.50	1.25
21 Joe Burch	.50	1.25
22 Craig Ritter	.50	1.25
23 Tim Watson	.50	1.25
24 Brian Easter	.50	1.25
25 Danny White CO	1.25	3.00
GM		
26 Jayme Washel	.50	1.25
27 Cedric Tillman	.50	1.25

1984 Arizona Wranglers Carl's Jr.

This ten-card USFL set was sponsored by Carl's Jr. Restaurants and distributed by the local police department in Tempe, Arizona. The cards measure approximately 2 1/2" by 3 5/8". On the front, the company logo and name appears in the lower right hand corner, and the USFL logo in the lower left hand corner. These emblems and the team name "Arizona Wranglers" on the top are in red print. The black and white posed photo in the middle has the player's name and position below in black ink. The back includes biographical information and an advertisement for Carl's Jr. Restaurants. The cards are listed below alphabetically, with the jersey number after the player's name.

COMPLETE SET (10)	50.00	80.00
1 George Allen CO	20.00	40.00
2 Luther Bradley 27	2.00	5.00
3 Trumaine Johnson 2	2.00	5.00
4 Greg Landry 11	7.50	15.00
5 Kit Lathrop 70	2.00	5.00
6 John Lee 64	2.00	5.00
7 Keith Long 33	2.00	5.00
8 Alan Risher 7	2.00	5.00
9 Tim Spencer 46	4.00	8.00
10 Lenny Willis 89	2.00	5.00

1984 Arizona Wranglers Team Sheets

These eight (approximately) 8" by 10" glossy, horizontally oriented sheets feature the 1984 Arizona Wranglers of the USFL. Each sheet features two rows of four black-and-white photos each, with player identification printed immediately beneath the picture. The team and USFL logos fill out the bottom corners. The backs are blank. Each sheet is numbered at the bottom in the middle "X of 8."

COMPLETE SET (8)	30.00	60.00
1 Edward Diethrich PRES	6.00	12.00
Bill Harris VP		
George Allen CO		
G. Bruce Allen GM		
Robert Barnes		
Dennis Bishop		
Mack Boatner		
Luther Bradley		
2 Clay Brown	4.00	8.00
Eddie Brown		
Wamon Buggs		
Bob Clasby		
Frank Corral		
Doug Cozen		
Doug Dennison		
Robert Dillon		
3 Larry Douglas	4.00	8.00
Joe Ehrmann		
Nick Eyre		
Jim Fahnhorst		
Doak Field		
Bruce Gheesling		
Frank Giddens		
Alfondia Hill		
4 Dave Huffman	5.00	10.00
Hubert Hurst		
Donnie Johnson		
Randy Johnson RB		
Trumaine Johnson		
Jeff Kiewel		
Bruce Laird		
Greg Landry		
5 Kit Lathrop	4.00	8.00
John Lee		
Alva Liles		
Dan Lloyd		
Kevin Long		
Karl Lorch		
Andy Melontree		
Frank Minnifield		
6 Tom Piette	4.00	5.00
Tom Porras		
Paul Ricker		
Alan Risher		
Don Schwartz		
Bobby Scott		
Lance Shields		
Ed Smith		
7 Robert Smith	6.00	12.00
Tim Spencer		
John Stadnik		
Mark Stevenson		
Dave Steif		
Gerry Sullivan		
Ted Sutton		
Motrandy Taylor		
8 Rob Taylor T	6.00	12.00
Tom Thayer		
Todd Thomas		
Ted Walton		
Stan White		
Lenny Willis		
Tim Wrightman		
Wilbur Young		

2007 Artifacts

This 200-card set was released in June, 2007. The set was issued into the hobby in four-card packs, with a $9.99 SRP which came 10 packs to a box. Cards numbered 1-100 feature veterans in their 2006 team alphabetical order while cards numbered 101-200 feature 2007 NFL rookies. Cards numbered 101-150 and 151-200 are both sequenced in first name alphabetical order.

COMP.SET w/o RC's (100)	15.00	40.00
1 Matt Leinart	.40	1.00
2 Edgerrin James	.40	1.00
3 Larry Fitzgerald	.50	1.25
4 Anquan Boldin	.40	1.00
5 Michael Vick	.50	1.25
6 Warrick Dunn	.40	1.00
7 Alge Crumpler	.40	1.00
8 Steve McNair	.40	1.00
9 Willis McGahee	.40	1.00
10 Mark Clayton	.40	1.00
11 J.P. Losman	.30	.75
12 Anthony Thomas	.30	.75
13 Lee Evans	.40	1.00
14 Jake Delhomme	.40	1.00
15 DeShaun Foster	.40	1.00
16 Steve Smith	.40	1.00
17 Rex Grossman	.40	1.00
18 Cedric Benson	.40	1.00
19 Brian Urlacher	.50	1.25
20 Carson Palmer	.40	1.00
21 Rudi Johnson	.40	1.00
22 Chad Johnson	.40	1.00
23 T.J. Houshmandzadeh	.40	1.00
24 Charlie Frye	.40	1.00
25 Braylon Edwards	.40	1.00
26 Kellen Winslow	.40	1.00
27 Tony Romo	.60	1.50
28 Julius Jones	.30	.75
29 Terrell Owens	.50	1.25
30 Terry Glenn	.40	1.00
31 Jay Cutler	.50	1.25
32 Travis Henry	.40	1.00
33 Javon Walker	.40	1.00
34 Jon Kitna	.30	.75
35 Kevin Jones	.30	.75
36 Roy Williams WR	.40	1.00
37 Mike Furrey	.40	1.00
38 Brett Favre	1.00	2.50
39 Greg Jennings	.50	1.25
40 Donald Driver	.50	1.25
41 David Carr	.40	1.00
42 Ron Dayne	.40	1.00
43 Andre Johnson	.40	1.00
44 Peyton Manning	.75	2.00
45 Joseph Addai	.40	1.00
46 Marvin Harrison	.50	1.25
47 Reggie Wayne	.40	1.00
48 David Garrard	.40	1.00
49 Fred Taylor	.40	1.00
50 Maurice Jones-Drew	.50	1.25
51 Trent Green	.40	1.00
52 Larry Johnson	.30	.75
53 Tony Gonzalez	.40	1.00
54 Daunte Culpepper	.40	1.00
55 Ronnie Brown	.40	1.00
56 Chris Chambers	.40	1.00
57 Tarvaris Jackson	.30	.75
58 Chester Taylor	.30	.75
59 Travis Taylor	.30	.75
60 Tom Brady	.75	2.00
61 Laurence Maroney	.40	1.00
62 Reche Caldwell	.30	.75
63 Drew Brees	.50	1.25
64 Deuce McAllister	.40	1.00
65 Reggie Bush	.50	1.25
66 Marques Colston	.50	1.25
67 Eli Manning	.50	1.25
68 Brandon Jacobs	.40	1.00
69 Plaxico Burress	.40	1.00
70 Chad Pennington	.40	1.00
71 Leon Washington	.40	1.00
72 Laveranues Coles	.30	.75
73 Ronald Curry	.40	1.00
74 LaMont Jordan	.40	1.00
75 Randy Moss	.50	1.25
76 Donovan McNabb	.50	1.25
77 Brian Westbrook	.40	1.00
78 Reggie Brown	.30	.75
79 Ben Roethlisberger	.50	1.25
80 Willie Parker	.40	1.00
81 Hines Ward	.50	1.25
82 Santonio Holmes	.40	1.00
83 Philip Rivers	.50	1.25
84 LaDainian Tomlinson	.50	1.25
85 Antonio Gates	.50	1.25
86 Matt Hasselbeck	.40	1.00
87 Shaun Alexander	.40	1.00
88 Deion Branch	.40	1.00
89 Marc Bulger	.40	1.00
90 Steven Jackson	.50	1.25
91 Torry Holt	.40	1.00
92 Chris Simms	.30	.75
93 Cadillac Williams	.40	1.00
94 Joey Galloway	.40	1.00
95 Vince Young	.40	1.00
96 LenDale White	.40	1.00
97 Drew Bennett	.30	.75
98 Jason Campbell	.40	1.00
99 Clinton Portis	.40	1.00
100 Santana Moss	.40	1.00
101 Aaron Ross RC	2.50	6.00
102 Aaron Rouse RC	2.00	5.00
103 Alvin Banks RC	2.00	5.00
104 Anthony Spencer RC	2.50	6.00
105 Ben Patrick RC	2.00	5.00
106 Brandon Siler RC	1.50	4.00
107 Buster Davis RC	2.00	5.00
108 Clark Harris RC	2.00	5.00
109 Chris Henry RC	1.50	4.00
110 Chris Houston RC	2.00	5.00
111 Courtney Taylor RC	2.00	5.00
112 Dallas Baker RC	1.50	4.00
113 Danny Ware RC	2.50	6.00
114 Darius Walker RC	1.50	4.00
115 Darrelle Revis RC	4.00	10.00
116 David Ball RC	2.00	5.00
117 D'Juan Woods RC	1.50	4.00
118 Drew Tate RC	2.00	5.00
119 Dwayne Wright RC	2.00	5.00
120 Isaiah Stanback RC	1.50	4.00
121 Garrett Wolfe RC	1.50	4.00
122 Gary Russell RC	2.00	5.00
123 Jared Zabransky RC	2.00	5.00
124 Jarvis Moss RC	2.00	5.00
125 Jason Hill RC	2.50	6.00
126 Justin Harrell RC	2.00	5.00
127 John Beck RC	2.50	6.00
128 Johnnie Lee Higgins RC	2.00	5.00
129 Kolby Smith RC	2.00	5.00
130 LaMarr Woodley RC	2.50	6.00
131 Le'Ron McClain RC	2.50	6.00
132 Levi Brown RC	2.50	6.00
133 Mason Crosby RC	2.00	5.00
134 Matt Moore RC	2.50	6.00
135 Matt Trannon RC	1.50	4.00
136 Ahmad Bradshaw RC	4.00	10.00
137 Michael Griffin RC	2.50	6.00
138 Paul Williams RC	1.50	4.00
139 Rhema McKnight RC	1.50	4.00
140 Martrez Milner RC	1.50	4.00
141 Scott Chandler RC	2.50	6.00
142 Selvin Young RC	2.00	5.00
143 Steve Breaston RC	2.50	6.00
144 Matt Spaeth RC	2.50	6.00
145 DeMarcus Tank Tyler RC	1.50	4.00
146 Thomas Clayton RC	2.00	5.00
147 Tim Crowder RC	2.50	6.00
148 Tony Ugoh RC	2.00	5.00
149 Trent Edwards RC	2.50	6.00
150 Tyler Palko RC	2.00	5.00
151 Adam Carriker RC	2.00	5.00
152 Adrian Peterson RC	10.00	25.00
153 Alan Branch RC	2.00	5.00
154 Amobi Okoye RC	2.50	6.00
155 Anthony Gonzalez RC	2.50	6.00
156 Antonio Pittman RC	1.50	4.00
157 Aundrae Allison RC	1.50	4.00
158 Brady Quinn RC	2.50	6.00
159 Brandon Jackson RC	2.00	5.00
160 Brian Leonard RC	2.00	5.00
161 Calvin Johnson RC	8.00	20.00
162 Chansi Stuckey RC	2.50	6.00
163 Charles Johnson RC	1.50	4.00
164 Chris Leak RC	2.00	5.00
165 Craig Buster Davis RC	2.00	5.00
166 David Clowney RC	2.00	5.00
167 Daymeion Hughes RC	2.00	5.00
168 DeShawn Wynn RC	2.00	5.00
169 Drew Stanton RC	1.50	4.00
170 Dwayne Bowe RC	3.00	8.00
171 Dwayne Jarrett RC	2.00	5.00
172 Gaines Adams RC	2.50	6.00
173 Greg Olsen RC	2.00	5.00
174 Jamaal Anderson RC	2.00	5.00
175 JaMarcus Russell RC	1.50	4.00
176 Joe Thomas RC	2.50	6.00
177 Joel Filani RC	2.00	5.00
178 Jordan Palmer RC	2.00	5.00
179 Kenneth Darby RC	2.00	5.00
180 Kenny Irons RC	1.50	4.00
181 Kevin Kolb RC	4.00	10.00
182 LaRon Landry RC	2.50	6.00
183 Lawrence Timmons RC	2.50	6.00
184 Leon Hall RC	2.00	5.00
185 Lorenzo Booker RC	2.00	5.00
186 Marcus McCauley RC	2.00	5.00
187 Marshawn Lynch RC	2.50	6.00
188 Michael Bush RC	2.50	6.00
189 Patrick Willis RC	5.00	12.00
190 Paul Posluszny RC	2.50	6.00
191 Quentin Moses RC	2.00	5.00
192 Reggie Nelson RC	2.00	5.00
193 Robert Meachem RC	2.50	6.00
194 Sidney Rice RC	3.00	8.00
195 Steve Smith USC RC	2.50	6.00
196 Ted Ginn Jr. RC	2.00	5.00
197 Tony Hunt RC	1.50	4.00
198 Troy Smith RC	2.50	6.00
199 Tyrone Moss RC	1.50	4.00
200 Zach Miller RC	2.50	6.00

2007 Artifacts Bronze

*ROOKIES 101-200: 2X TO 5X BASIC CARDS
STATED PRINT RUN 25 SER.#'d SETS

2007 Artifacts Gold

*VETS/70-99: 3X TO 8X BASIC CARDS
*VETS/45-69: 4X TO 10X BASIC CARDS
*VETS/30-44: 5X TO 12X BASIC CARDS
*VETS/20-29: 6X TO 15X BASIC CARDS
*VETS/10-19: 8X TO 20X BASIC CARDS
*ROOKIES 101-200: 1X TO 2.5X BASIC CARDS
ROOKIES PRINT RUN 99 SER.#'d SETS

2007 Artifacts Green

*VETS 1-100: 3X TO 8X BASIC CARDS
*ROOKIES 101-200: 1X TO 2.5X BASIC CARDS
STATED PRINT RUN 99 SER.#'d SETS

2007 Artifacts Red

*VETS: 3X TO 8X BASIC CARDS
STATED PRINT RUN 99 SER.#'d SETS

2007 Artifacts AFC/NFC Apparel

STATED PRINT RUN 325 SER.#'d SETS
*RED/250: .4X TO 1X BASIC JSYs
RED PRINT RUN 250 SER.#'d SETS
*GOLD/99: .5X TO 1.2X BASIC JSYs
GOLD PRINT RUN 99 SER.#'d SETS
*BRONZE/75: .5X TO 1.2X BASIC JSYs
BRONZE PRINT RUN 75 SER.#'d SETS
*GREEN: X TO X BASIC INSERTS
*PATCH/50: .8X TO 2X BASIC JSYs
PATCH PRINT RUN 50 SER.#'d SETS
*PATCH RED/25: 1X TO 2.5X BASIC JSYs
PATCH RED PRINT RUN 25 SER.#'d SETS

AB Anquan Boldin	3.00	8.00
AG Ahman Green	3.00	8.00
AJ Andre Johnson	3.00	8.00
BD Brian Dawkins	3.00	8.00
BE Braylon Edwards	3.00	8.00
BF Brett Favre	8.00	20.00
BR Ben Roethlisberger	4.00	10.00
BU Brian Urlacher	4.00	10.00
BW Brian Westbrook	3.00	8.00
CJ Chad Johnson	3.00	8.00
CP1 Carson Palmer	3.00	8.00
CP2 Clinton Portis	3.00	8.00
DB Drew Brees	4.00	10.00
DC David Carr	3.00	8.00
EM Eli Manning	4.00	10.00
HW Hines Ward	4.00	10.00
JO LaMont Jordan	3.00	8.00
KJ Kevin Jones	2.50	6.00
LF Larry Fitzgerald	4.00	10.00
LJ Larry Johnson	2.50	6.00
LM Laurence Maroney	3.00	8.00
LT LaDainian Tomlinson	4.00	10.00
MB Marc Bulger	3.00	8.00
MF Marshall Faulk	3.00	8.00
MH Marvin Harrison	4.00	10.00
ML Matt Leinart	3.00	8.00
MV Michael Vick	4.00	10.00
PM Peyton Manning	8.00	20.00
RB1 Ronnie Brown	3.00	8.00
RB2 Reggie Bush	4.00	10.00
RL Ray Lewis	4.00	10.00
RM Randy Moss	4.00	10.00
SA Shaun Alexander	3.00	8.00
SJ Steven Jackson	4.00	10.00
SM Santana Moss	3.00	8.00
TB1 Tatum Bell	2.50	6.00
TB2 Tom Brady	6.00	15.00
TG Tony Gonzalez	3.00	8.00
TO Terrell Owens	4.00	10.00
WM Willis McGahee	3.00	8.00

2007 Artifacts AFC/NFC Apparel Autographs

STATED PRINT RUN 15 SER.#'d SETS
UNPRICED PATCH AUTOS #'d TO 5
UNPRICED RARE AUTOS #'d TO 1

2007 Artifacts Awesome Artifacts

STATED PRINT RUN 50 SER.#'d SETS
*PATCH/10: 1X TO 2.5X BASIC JSYs
PATCH PRINT RUN 10 SER.#'d SETS

AAAB Anquan Boldin	8.00	20.00
AABE Tatum Bell	6.00	15.00
AABF Brett Favre	20.00	50.00
AABR Ben Roethlisberger	10.00	25.00
AABU Reggie Bush	10.00	25.00
AACB Champ Bailey	8.00	20.00
AACP Carson Palmer	8.00	20.00
AADB Drew Brees	10.00	25.00
AADM Donovan McNabb	10.00	25.00
AAEM Eli Manning	10.00	25.00
AAHA Matt Hasselbeck	8.00	20.00
AAHW Hines Ward	10.00	25.00
AAJD Jake Delhomme	8.00	20.00
AAKJ Kevin Jones	6.00	15.00
AALF Larry Fitzgerald	10.00	25.00
AALJ Larry Johnson	6.00	15.00
AALM Laurence Maroney	8.00	20.00
AALT LaDainian Tomlinson	10.00	25.00
AAMB Marc Bulger	8.00	20.00
AAMF Marshall Faulk	8.00	20.00
AAMH Marvin Harrison	10.00	25.00
AAML Matt Leinart	8.00	20.00
AAMV Michael Vick	10.00	25.00
AAPE Chad Pennington	8.00	20.00
AAPM Peyton Manning	20.00	50.00
AAPR Philip Rivers	10.00	25.00
AARB Ronnie Brown	8.00	20.00
AARL Ray Lewis	10.00	25.00
AARW Reggie Wayne	8.00	20.00
AASA Shaun Alexander	8.00	20.00
AASJ Steven Jackson	10.00	25.00
AATB Tom Brady	15.00	40.00
AATG Trent Green	8.00	20.00
AATP Troy Polamalu	15.00	40.00
AAUR Brian Urlacher	10.00	25.00
AAWI Roy Williams WR	8.00	20.00
AAWP Willie Parker	8.00	20.00

2007 Artifacts NFL Artifacts

STATED PRINT RUN 325 SER.#'d SETS
*RED/250: .4X TO 1X BASIC JSYs
RED PRINT RUN 250 SER.#'d SETS
*GOLD/99: .5X TO 1.2X BASIC JSYs
GOLD PRINT RUN 99 SER.#'d SETS
*BRONZE/75: .5X TO 1.2X BASIC JSYs
BRONZE PRINT RUN 75 SER.#'d SETS
*GREEN: X TO X BASIC JSYs
*PATCH/50: .8X TO 2X BASIC JSYs
PATCH PRINT RUN 50 SER.#'d SETS
*PATCH RED/25: 1X TO 2.5X BASIC JSYs
PATCH RED PRINT RUN 25 SER.#'d SETS

NFLAB Anquan Boldin	3.00	8.00
NFLAG Ahman Green	3.00	8.00
NFLAJ Andre Johnson	3.00	8.00
NFLBD Brian Dawkins	3.00	8.00
NFLBE Ben Roethlisberger	4.00	10.00
NFLBF Brett Favre	8.00	20.00
NFLBL Byron Leftwich	3.00	8.00
NFLBR Tom Brady	6.00	15.00
NFLBU Brian Urlacher	4.00	10.00
NFLBW Brian Westbrook	3.00	8.00
NFLCA David Carr	3.00	8.00
NFLCM Curtis Martin	4.00	10.00
NFLCP Carson Palmer	3.00	8.00
NFLCW Cadillac Williams	3.00	8.00
NFLDB Drew Bledsoe	4.00	10.00
NFLDC Daunte Culpepper	3.00	8.00
NFLDM Donovan McNabb	4.00	10.00
NFLDR Drew Brees	4.00	10.00
NFLED Braylon Edwards	3.00	8.00
NFLEM Eli Manning	4.00	10.00
NFLFG Frank Gore	4.00	10.00
NFLGR Trent Green	3.00	8.00
NFLHA Marvin Harrison	4.00	10.00
NFLHW Hines Ward	4.00	10.00
NFLJD Jake Delhomme	3.00	8.00
NFLJO LaMont Jordan	3.00	8.00
NFLJP Jake Plummer	3.00	8.00
NFLJS Jeremy Shockey	3.00	8.00
NFLJU Julius Peppers	3.00	8.00
NFLKC Kevin Curtis	2.50	6.00
NFLKJ Kevin Jones	2.50	6.00
NFLLF Larry Fitzgerald	4.00	10.00
NFLLJ Larry Johnson	2.50	6.00
NFLLM Laurence Maroney	3.00	8.00
NFLLT LaDainian Tomlinson	4.00	10.00
NFLMA Dan Marino	12.00	30.00
NFLMB Marc Bulger	3.00	8.00
NFLMC Deuce McAllister	3.00	8.00
NFLMF Marshall Faulk	3.00	8.00
NFLMH Matt Hasselbeck	3.00	8.00
NFLML Matt Leinart	3.00	8.00
NFLMV Michael Vick	4.00	10.00
NFLMW Mike Williams	2.50	6.00
NFLPH Priest Holmes	3.00	8.00
NFLPM Peyton Manning	8.00	20.00
NFLPR Philip Rivers	4.00	10.00
NFLRB Reggie Bush	4.00	10.00
NFLRJ Rudi Johnson	3.00	8.00
NFLRL Ray Lewis	4.00	10.00
NFLRM Randy Moss	4.00	10.00
NFLRO Ronnie Brown	3.00	8.00
NFLSA Shaun Alexander	3.00	8.00
NFLSJ Steven Jackson	4.00	10.00
NFLSM Santana Moss	3.00	8.00
NFLTA Lofa Tatupu	3.00	8.00
NFLTB Tatum Bell	2.50	6.00
NFLTE Tedy Bruschi	4.00	10.00
NFLTG Tony Gonzalez	3.00	8.00
NFLTO Terrell Owens	4.00	10.00
NFLWM Willis McGahee	3.00	8.00

2007 Artifacts NFL Artifacts Autographs

AUTO PRINT RUN 15 SER.#'d SETS
UNPRICED PATCH AU PRINT RUN 5
UNPRICED RARE AUTO PRINT RUN 1

2007 Artifacts NFL Artifacts Dual

STATED PRINT RUN 99 SER.#'d SETS
*PATCH/25: .8X TO 2X BASIC JSYs
PATCH PRINT RUN 25 SER.#'d SETS

DJ Marc Bulger Steven Jackson	6.00	15.00
BL Reggie Bush Matt Leinart	15.00	40.00
BM Tom Brady Laurence Maroney	8.00	20.00
BU Brian Urlacher Champ Bailey	8.00	20.00
CJ David Carr Andre Johnson	5.00	12.00
DD Drew Brees Deuce McAllister	6.00	15.00
EF Braylon Edwards Charlie Frye	5.00	12.00
FG Brett Favre Ahman Green	15.00	40.00
FR Brett Favre Ben Roethlisberger	15.00	40.00
HA Matt Hasselbeck Shaun Alexander	6.00	15.00
HW Marvin Harrison Reggie Wayne	6.00	15.00
JB Larry Johnson Tatum Bell	6.00	15.00
JO Chad Johnson Terrell Owens	6.00	15.00
JU Thomas Jones Brian Urlacher	8.00	20.00
KT Kevin Jones Tatum Bell	5.00	12.00
LC Matt Leinart Jay Cutler	10.00	25.00
LF Matt Leinart Larry Fitzgerald	10.00	25.00
MB Peyton Manning Tom Brady	15.00	40.00
MD Curtis Martin Corey Dillon	6.00	15.00
MH Peyton Manning Marvin Harrison	12.00	30.00
MM Dan Marino Peyton Manning	25.00	60.00
MR Eli Manning Philip Rivers	6.00	15.00
MS Eli Manning Jeremy Shockey	6.00	15.00
MW Donovan McNabb Brian Westbrook	8.00	20.00
OJ Terrell Owens Julius Jones	6.00	15.00
PE Peyton Manning Eli Manning	12.00	30.00
PL Julius Peppers Ray Lewis	6.00	15.00
PP Carson Palmer Chad Pennington	6.00	15.00
PR Peyton Manning Reggie Wayne	12.00	30.00
PW Chad Pennington Curtis Martin	6.00	15.00
RL Reggie Bush Laurence Maroney	12.00	30.00
RT Philip Rivers LaDainian Tomlinson	6.00	15.00
RW Ben Roethlisberger Hines Ward	8.00	20.00
SB Steve Smith Anquan Boldin	5.00	12.00
TJ LaDainian Tomlinson Larry Johnson	6.00	15.00
UB Brian Urlacher Tedy Bruschi	6.00	15.00
VC Michael Vick Alge Crumpler	6.00	15.00
VM Michael Vick Donovan McNabb	8.00	20.00
WF Roy Williams WR Larry Fitzgerald	6.00	15.00
WP Hines Ward Willie Parker	8.00	20.00

2007 Artifacts NFL Artifacts Triple

STATED PRINT RUN 75 SER.#'d SETS
*PATCH/15: .8X TO 2X BASIC JSYs
PATCH PRINT RUN 15 SER.#'d SETS

BHL Marc Bulger Matt Hasselbeck Matt Leinart	10.00	25.00
BMD Reggie Bush Laurence Maroney Maurice Jones-Drew	20.00	40.00
BPG Drew Brees Chad Pennington Trent Green	6.00	15.00
BRD Champ Bailey Ed Reed Brian Dawkins	10.00	25.00
FBM Brett Favre Tom Brady Peyton Manning	30.00	60.00
FBR Brett Favre Tom Brady Ben Roethlisberger	30.00	60.00
GCS Antonio Gates Alge Crumpler Jeremy Shockey	6.00	15.00
JJB Steven Jackson Kevin Jones Ronnie Brown	8.00	20.00
JSF Chad Johnson Steve Smith Larry Fitzgerald	10.00	25.00
LBW Matt Leinart Reggie Bush Mike Williams	20.00	40.00
LFB Matt Leinart Larry Fitzgerald Anquan Boldin	12.00	30.00
MHW Peyton Manning Marvin Harrison Reggie Wayne	20.00	50.00
MRR Eli Manning Philip Rivers Ben Roethlisberger	10.00	25.00
MVP Donovan McNabb Michael Vick Carson Palmer	10.00	25.00
PLU Julius Peppers Ray Lewis Brian Urlacher	10.00	25.00
RPW Ben Roethlisberger Willie Parker Hines Ward	15.00	40.00
RTO Philip Rivers LaDainian Tomlinson Antonio Gates	12.00	30.00
TAJ LaDainian Tomlinson Shaun Alexander Larry Johnson	10.00	25.00
WMW Hines Ward Eric Moulds Roy Williams WR	6.00	15.00
YLC Vince Young Matt Leinart Jay Cutler	10.00	25.00

2007 Artifacts NFL Equipment

UNPRICED EQUIPMENT PRINT RUN 15

2007 Artifacts NFL Facts

NFAB Anquan Boldin	1.50	4.00
NFAC Antonio Cromartie	1.25	3.00
NFAG Antonio Gates	2.00	5.00
NFAH Anttaj Hawthorne	1.25	3.00
NFAJ Adam Jones	1.25	3.00
NFAL Shaun Alexander	1.50	4.00
NFAR Aaron Rodgers	5.00	12.00
NFAS Alex Smith QB	2.00	5.00
NFAV Jason Avant	1.25	3.00
NFAW Andrew Walter	1.25	3.00
NFAY Ashton Youboty	1.25	3.00
NFBB Bernard Berrian	1.25	3.00
NFBC Brian Calhoun	1.25	3.00
NFBD Brian Dawkins	1.50	4.00
NFBE Braylon Edwards	1.50	4.00
NFBET Josh Betts	1.25	3.00
NFBG Bruce Gradkowski	1.25	3.00
NFBH Ben Hartsock	1.25	3.00
NFBI Darnell Bing	1.25	3.00
NFBJ Brad Johnson	1.50	4.00
NFBL Byron Leftwich	1.50	4.00
NFBM Brandon Marshall	1.50	4.00
NFBN Brandon Jacobs	1.50	4.00
NFBP Brodney Pool	1.25	3.00
NFBR Mark Brunell	1.50	4.00
NFBS Brad Smith	1.25	3.00
NFBT Ben Troupe	1.25	3.00
NFBU Marc Bulger	1.50	4.00
NFBW Ben Watson	1.25	3.00
NFBY Dominique Byrd	1.25	3.00
NFCB Chris Brown	1.25	3.00
NFCE Cedric Benson	1.50	4.00
NFCF Ciatrick Fason	1.25	3.00
NFCG Chris Gamble	1.25	3.00
NFCH Chris Henry	1.25	3.00
NFCJ Chad Jackson	1.25	3.00
NFCL Brandon Chillar	1.25	3.00
NFCO Keary Colbert	1.25	3.00
NFCP Carson Palmer	1.50	4.00
NFCR Carlos Rogers	1.25	3.00
NFCRU Alge Crumpler	1.50	4.00
NFCU Jay Cutler	2.00	5.00
NFCW Corey Webster	1.25	3.00
NFDA Derek Anderson	1.25	3.00
NFDB Drew Bledsoe	2.00	5.00
NFDC Deuce McAllister	1.50	4.00
NFDE DeAngelo Hall	1.50	4.00
NFDF D'Brickashaw Ferguson	1.25	3.00
NFDG David Givens	1.25	3.00
NFDH Derek Hagan	1.25	3.00
NFDJ D.J. Shockley	1.25	3.00
NFDM Derrick Mason	1.50	4.00
NFDO Dan Orlovsky	1.25	3.00
NFDR Drew Bennett	1.25	3.00
NFDS Darren Sproles	1.50	4.00
NFEJ Edgerrin James	1.50	4.00
NFEL John Elway	3.00	8.00
NFEM Eli Manning	2.00	5.00
NFER Erasmus James	1.25	3.00
NFES Eric Shelton	1.25	3.00
NFEW Ernest Wilford	1.25	3.00
NFFG Frank Gore	2.00	5.00
NFFO DeShaun Foster	1.50	4.00
NFFR Charlie Frye	1.50	4.00
NFGA Robert Gallery	1.25	3.00
NFGJ Greg Jones	1.25	3.00
NFGL Greg Lee	1.25	3.00
NFGN Chad Greenway	1.25	3.00
NFGO Tony Gonzalez	1.50	4.00
NFGR Ahman Green	1.50	4.00
NFHA Dante Hall	1.50	4.00
NFHAC Darrell Hackney	1.25	3.00
NFHAR Jerome Harrison	1.25	3.00
NFHAS Mike Hass	1.25	3.00
NFHE Devery Henderson	1.25	3.00
NFHI Tye Hill	1.25	3.00
NFHK A.J. Hawk	1.50	4.00
NFHM Heath Miller	1.25	3.00
NFHO T.J. Houshmandzadeh	1.50	4.00
NFHOW Thomas Howard	1.25	3.00
NFIB Isaac Bruce	1.50	4.00
NFJA Joseph Addai	1.50	4.00
NFJB James Butler	1.25	3.00
NFJC Jason Campbell	1.50	4.00
NFJE Jerricho Cotchery	1.50	4.00
NFJEN Greg Jennings	2.00	5.00
NFJF Justin Fargas	1.25	3.00
NFJG Joey Galloway	1.50	4.00
NFJH Joe Horn	1.50	4.00
NFJJ Julius Jones	1.25	3.00
NFJL J.P. Losman	1.25	3.00
NFJM Johnnie Morant	1.25	3.00
NFJN Jerious Norwood	1.50	4.00
NFJO Chad Johnson	1.50	4.00
NFJP Jim Plunkett	1.50	4.00
NFJT Joe Theismann	2.00	5.00
NFJV Jonathan Vilma	1.50	4.00
NFJW Jimmy Williams	1.25	3.00
NFKA Kay-Jay Harris	1.25	3.00
NFKB Kyle Boller	1.25	3.00
NFKC Kellen Clemens	1.50	4.00
NFKE Keyshawn Johnson	1.50	4.00
NFKH Kelly Holcomb	1.25	3.00
NFKJ Kelly Jennings	1.25	3.00
NFKL Joe Klopfenstein	1.25	3.00
NFKM Kirk Morrison	1.25	3.00
NFKN Kevin Burnett	1.25	3.00
NFKU Kenechi Udeze	1.25	3.00
NFKV Kevin Jones	1.25	3.00
NFKW Kellen Winslow	1.50	4.00
NFLA Larry Johnson	1.25	3.00
NFLC Luis Castillo	1.25	3.00
NFLE Marcedes Lewis	1.25	3.00
NFLF Larry Fitzgerald	2.00	5.00
NFLJ LaMont Jordan	1.50	4.00
NFLL Brandon Lloyd	1.50	4.00
NFLM Laurence Maroney	1.50	4.00
NFLO Lofa Tatupu	1.50	4.00
NFLP Leonard Pope	1.25	3.00
NFLT LaDainian Tomlinson	2.00	5.00
NFLU Luke McCown	1.25	3.00
NFLW LenDale White	1.50	4.00
NFMA Mark Bradley	1.25	3.00
NFMAR Mario Williams	1.50	4.00
NFMB Marion Barber	2.00	5.00
NFMC Michael Clayton	1.25	3.00
NFMD Maurice Jones-Drew	2.00	5.00
NFME Mewelde Moore	1.25	3.00
NFMH Michael Huff	1.50	4.00
NFMI Mike Bell	1.50	4.00
NFMJ Marlin Jackson	1.25	3.00
NFML Matt Leinart	1.50	4.00
NFMM Marcus McNeill	1.25	3.00
NFMN Martin Nance	1.25	3.00
NFMO Ryan Moats	1.25	3.00
NFMOS Sinorice Moss	1.50	4.00
NFMQ Mike Quick	1.25	3.00
NFMR Michael Robinson	1.50	4.00
NFMS Maurice Stovall	1.25	3.00
NFMV Michael Vick	2.00	5.00
NFMW Mike Williams	1.25	3.00
NFNB Nate Burleson	1.25	3.00
NFOD Owen Daniels	1.25	3.00
NFOJ Omar Jacobs	1.25	3.00
NFOL Drew Olson	1.25	3.00
NFPE Chris Perry	1.25	3.00
NFPM Peyton Manning	3.00	8.00
NFPN Chad Pennington	1.50	4.00
NFPR Philip Rivers	2.00	5.00
NFRB Ronnie Brown	1.50	4.00
NFRC Reche Caldwell	1.25	3.00
NFRE Reggie Bush	2.00	5.00
NFRG Rex Grossman	1.50	4.00
NFRI Rocket Ismail	1.50	4.00
NFRJ Rudi Johnson	1.50	4.00
NFRM Reggie McNeal	1.25	3.00
NFRO Ben Roethlisberger	2.00	5.00
NFROD Cory Rodgers	1.25	3.00
NFRU Barrett Ruud	1.25	3.00
NFRW Roy Williams WR	1.50	4.00
NFRY Courtney Roby	1.25	3.00
NFSA Santana Moss	1.50	4.00
NFSAM B.J. Sams	1.25	3.00
NFSC Matt Schaub	1.50	4.00
NFSH Santonio Holmes	1.50	4.00
NFSI Ernie Sims	1.25	3.00
NFSJ Steven Jackson	2.00	5.00
NFSM Shawne Merriman	1.50	4.00
NFSP Samie Parker	1.25	3.00
NFSS Steve Smith	1.50	4.00
NFTA Tarvaris Jackson	1.25	3.00
NFTB Tatum Bell	1.25	3.00
NFTD Thomas Davis	1.25	3.00
NFTE Terrence Whitehead	1.25	3.00
NFTG Trent Green	1.50	4.00
NFTH Tommie Harris	1.25	3.00
NFTJ Taylor Jacobs	1.25	3.00
NFTO Todd Heap	1.25	3.00
NFTR Travis Henry	1.50	4.00
NFTS Terrell Suggs	1.50	4.00
NFTT Tyson Thompson	1.25	3.00
NFTW Travis Wilson	1.25	3.00
NFTY Troy Williamson	1.25	3.00
NFVD Vernon Davis	1.50	4.00
NFVM Vernand Morency	1.50	4.00
NFVW Vince Wilfork	1.25	3.00
NFVY Vince Young	1.50	4.00
NFWA Kelley Washington	1.25	3.00
NFWAS Leon Washington	1.50	4.00
NFWAY Reggie Wayne	1.50	4.00
NFWB Will Blackmon	1.25	3.00
NFWE Brian Westbrook	1.50	4.00
NFWH Roddy White	1.50	4.00
NFWHI Charlie Whitehurst	1.25	3.00
NFWI Roy Williams S	1.50	4.00
NFWIL Demetrius Williams	1.25	3.00
NFWL Reggie Williams	1.50	4.00
NFWM Willis McGahee	1.50	4.00
NFWP Willie Parker	1.50	4.00
NFWS Will Smith	1.25	3.00

2007 Artifacts NFL Facts Autographs

AC Antonio Cromartie	5.00	12.00
AH Anttaj Hawthorne	5.00	12.00
AJ Adam Jones	5.00	12.00
AR Aaron Rodgers	125.00	200.00
AS Alex Smith QB	8.00	20.00
AV Jason Avant	5.00	12.00
AW Andrew Walter	5.00	12.00
AY Ashton Youboty	5.00	12.00
BB Bernard Berrian	5.00	12.00
BC Brian Calhoun	5.00	12.00
BD Brian Dawkins	20.00	40.00
BE Braylon Edwards	6.00	15.00
BET Josh Betts	5.00	12.00
BG Bruce Gradkowski	5.00	12.00
BH Ben Hartsock	5.00	12.00
BI Darnell Bing	5.00	12.00
BJ Brad Johnson	6.00	15.00
BL Byron Leftwich	6.00	15.00
BN Brandon Jacobs	6.00	15.00
BP Brodney Pool	5.00	12.00
BR Mark Brunell	6.00	15.00
BS Brad Smith	5.00	12.00
BT Ben Troupe	5.00	12.00
BU Marc Bulger	6.00	15.00
BW Ben Watson	5.00	12.00
BY Dominique Byrd	5.00	12.00
CB Chris Brown	5.00	12.00
CF Ciatrick Fason	5.00	12.00
CG Chris Gamble	5.00	12.00
CH Chris Henry	5.00	12.00
CJ Chad Jackson	5.00	12.00
CL Brandon Chillar	5.00	12.00
CO Keary Colbert	5.00	12.00
CP Carson Palmer	15.00	40.00
CR Carlos Rogers	5.00	12.00
CRU Alge Crumpler	6.00	15.00
CU Jay Cutler	30.00	60.00
CW Corey Webster	5.00	12.00
DA Derek Anderson	5.00	12.00
DB Drew Bledsoe	10.00	25.00
DC Deuce McAllister	6.00	15.00
DE DeAngelo Hall	6.00	15.00
DG David Givens	5.00	12.00
DH Derek Hagan	5.00	12.00
DJ D.J. Shockley	6.00	12.00
DM Derrick Mason	6.00	15.00
DO Dan Orlovsky	5.00	12.00
DR Drew Bennett	5.00	12.00
DS Darren Sproles	6.00	15.00
EJ Edgerrin James	6.00	15.00
EM Eli Manning	50.00	100.00
ER Erasmus James	5.00	12.00
ES Eric Shelton	5.00	12.00
EW Ernest Wilford	5.00	12.00
FG Frank Gore	8.00	20.00
FO DeShaun Foster	6.00	15.00
FR Charlie Frye	6.00	15.00
GA Robert Gallery	5.00	12.00
GJ Greg Jones	5.00	12.00
GL Greg Lee	5.00	12.00
GR Ahman Green	6.00	15.00
HA Dante Hall	6.00	15.00
HAC Darrell Hackney	5.00	12.00
HAR Jerome Harrison	5.00	12.00
HAS Mike Hass	5.00	12.00
HE Devery Henderson	5.00	12.00
HI Tye Hill	5.00	12.00
HK A.J. Hawk	15.00	30.00
HM Heath Miller	5.00	12.00
HO T.J. Houshmandzadeh	6.00	15.00
HOW Thomas Howard	5.00	12.00
IB Isaac Bruce	6.00	15.00
JA Joseph Addai	6.00	15.00
JB James Butler	5.00	12.00
JC Jason Campbell	6.00	15.00
JE Jerricho Cotchery	6.00	15.00
JEN Greg Jennings	8.00	20.00
JF Justin Fargas	5.00	12.00
JG Joey Galloway	6.00	15.00
JH Joe Horn	6.00	15.00
JJ Julius Jones	5.00	12.00
JL J.P. Losman	5.00	12.00
JM Johnnie Morant	5.00	12.00
JN Jerious Norwood	6.00	15.00
JO Chad Johnson	6.00	15.00
JP Jim Plunkett	10.00	25.00
JT Joe Theismann	12.00	30.00
JV Jonathan Vilma	6.00	15.00
JW Jimmy Williams	5.00	12.00
KA Kay-Jay Harris	5.00	12.00
KB Kyle Boller	5.00	12.00
KC Kellen Clemens	6.00	15.00
KE Keyshawn Johnson	6.00	15.00
KH Kelly Holcomb	5.00	12.00
KJ Kelly Jennings	5.00	12.00
KL Joe Klopfenstein	5.00	12.00
KM Kirk Morrison	5.00	12.00
KN Kevin Burnett	5.00	12.00
KU Kenechi Udeze	5.00	12.00
KV Kevin Jones	5.00	12.00
KW Kellen Winslow	6.00	15.00
LA Larry Johnson	5.00	12.00
LC Luis Castillo	5.00	12.00
LE Marcedes Lewis	5.00	12.00
LJ LaMont Jordan	6.00	15.00
LL Brandon Lloyd	6.00	15.00
LM Laurence Maroney	6.00	15.00
LP Leonard Pope	5.00	12.00
LT LaDainian Tomlinson	40.00	80.00
LU Luke McCown	5.00	12.00
LW LenDale White	6.00	15.00
MA Mark Bradley	5.00	12.00
MAR Mario Williams	6.00	15.00
MB Marion Barber	8.00	20.00
MC Michael Clayton	5.00	12.00
MD Maurice Jones-Drew	8.00	20.00
ME Mewelde Moore	5.00	12.00
MH Michael Huff	6.00	15.00
MI Mike Bell	6.00	15.00
MJ Marlin Jackson	5.00	12.00
ML Matt Leinart	20.00	40.00
MM Marcus McNeill	5.00	12.00
MN Martin Nance	5.00	12.00
MO Ryan Moats	5.00	12.00
MOS Sinorice Moss	6.00	15.00
MQ Mike Quick	5.00	12.00
MR Michael Robinson	6.00	15.00
MS Maurice Stovall	5.00	12.00
MV Michael Vick	30.00	60.00
NB Nate Burleson	5.00	12.00
OD Owen Daniels	5.00	12.00
OJ Omar Jacobs	5.00	12.00
OL Drew Olson	5.00	12.00
PE Chris Perry	5.00	12.00
PN Chad Pennington	6.00	15.00
RB Ronnie Brown	6.00	15.00
RC Reche Caldwell	5.00	12.00
RE Reggie Bush	30.00	60.00
RG Rex Grossman	6.00	15.00
RI Rocket Ismail	6.00	15.00
RJ Rudi Johnson	6.00	15.00
RM Reggie McNeal	5.00	12.00
ROD Cory Rodgers	5.00	12.00
RU Barrett Ruud	5.00	12.00
RW Roy Williams WR	6.00	15.00
RY Courtney Roby	5.00	12.00
SA Santana Moss	6.00	15.00
SAM B.J. Sams	5.00	12.00
SC Matt Schaub	6.00	15.00
SH Santonio Holmes	6.00	15.00
SI Ernie Sims	5.00	12.00
SM Shawne Merriman	6.00	15.00
SP Samie Parker	5.00	12.00
TA Tarvaris Jackson	5.00	12.00
TB Tatum Bell	5.00	12.00
TD Thomas Davis	5.00	12.00
TE Terrence Whitehead	5.00	12.00
TG Trent Green	6.00	15.00
TH Tommie Harris	5.00	12.00
TJ Taylor Jacobs	5.00	12.00
TO Todd Heap	5.00	12.00
TR Travis Henry	6.00	15.00
TS Terrell Suggs	8.00	20.00
TT Tyson Thompson	5.00	12.00
TW Travis Wilson	5.00	12.00
TY Troy Williamson	5.00	12.00
VD Vernon Davis	6.00	15.00
VM Vernand Morency	6.00	15.00
VW Vince Wilfork	5.00	12.00
VY Vince Young	25.00	50.00
WA Kelley Washington	5.00	12.00
WAS Leon Washington	6.00	15.00
WAY Reggie Wayne	6.00	15.00
WB Will Blackmon	5.00	12.00
WE Brian Westbrook	6.00	15.00
WH Roddy White	6.00	15.00
WHI Charlie Whitehurst	5.00	12.00
WI Roy Williams S	6.00	15.00
WIL Demetrius Williams	5.00	12.00
WL Reggie Williams	6.00	15.00
WM Willis McGahee	6.00	15.00
WP Willie Parker	6.00	15.00
WS Will Smith	5.00	12.00

2007 Artifacts Photo Shoot Flashback Fabrics

STATED PRINT RUN 350 SER.#'d SETS
*GREEN: .3X TO .8X BASIC INSERTS

AH A.J. Hawk	4.00	10.00
AJ Adam Jones	3.00	8.00
AS Alex Smith QB	5.00	12.00
AW Andrew Walter	3.00	8.00
BB Bernard Berrian	3.00	8.00
BE Braylon Edwards	4.00	10.00
BL Byron Leftwich	4.00	10.00
BR Ben Roethlisberger	5.00	12.00
BW Ben Watson	3.00	8.00
CF Charlie Frye	4.00	10.00
CJ Chad Jackson	3.00	8.00
CL Michael Clayton	3.00	8.00
CP Carson Palmer	4.00	10.00
CR Carlos Rogers	3.00	8.00
CW Cadillac Williams	4.00	10.00
DC Dallas Clark	3.00	8.00
DH DeAngelo Hall	4.00	10.00
DW DeAngelo Williams	5.00	12.00
EM Eli Manning	5.00	12.00
JC Jason Campbell	4.00	10.00
JJ Julius Jones	3.00	8.00
JL J.P. Losman	3.00	8.00
JN Jerious Norwood	4.00	10.00
JO Andre Johnson	4.00	10.00
KC Kellen Clemens	4.00	10.00
KJ Kevin Jones	3.00	8.00
KW Kellen Winslow	4.00	10.00
LE Lee Evans	4.00	10.00
LF Larry Fitzgerald	5.00	12.00
LM Laurence Maroney	4.00	10.00
LW LenDale White	4.00	10.00
MC Mark Clayton	4.00	10.00
MD Maurice Jones-Drew	5.00	12.00
MJ Michael Jenkins	4.00	10.00
ML Matt Leinart	4.00	10.00
MS Matt Schaub	4.00	10.00
PE Chris Perry	3.00	8.00
PR Philip Rivers	5.00	12.00
RB Reggie Bush	5.00	12.00
RO Ronnie Brown	4.00	10.00
RW Reggie Williams	4.00	10.00
SH Santonio Holmes	4.00	10.00
SJ Steven Jackson	5.00	12.00
TB Tatum Bell	3.00	8.00
TW Troy Williamson	3.00	8.00
VD Vernon Davis	4.00	10.00
VY Vince Young	4.00	10.00
WA Leon Washington	4.00	10.00
WH Roddy White	4.00	10.00
WI Roy Williams WR	4.00	10.00

2007 Artifacts Photo Shoot Flashback Fabrics Autographs

UNPRICED AUTO PRINT RUN 10

2007 Artifacts Rookie Autographs

STATED PRINT RUN 10-30
SERIAL #'d TO 10 NOT PRICED

109 Chris Henry/25	10.00	25.00
111 Courtney Taylor/30	12.00	30.00
112 Dallas Baker/25	10.00	25.00
114 Darius Walker/25	10.00	25.00
115 Darrelle Revis/30	25.00	60.00
118 Drew Tate/30	12.00	30.00
119 Dwayne Wright/25	12.00	30.00
121 Garrett Wolfe/25	10.00	25.00
122 Gary Russell/25	12.00	30.00
125 Jason Hill/25	15.00	40.00
127 John Beck/25	15.00	40.00
128 Johnnie Lee Higgins/25	12.00	30.00
134 Matt Moore/30	15.00	40.00
137 Michael Griffin/30	15.00	40.00
139 Rhema McKnight/25	10.00	25.00
141 Scott Chandler/30	15.00	40.00
142 Selvin Young/25	12.00	30.00
149 Trent Edwards/25	15.00	40.00
150 Tyler Palko/30	12.00	30.00
151 Adam Carriker/30	12.00	30.00
153 Alan Branch/30	12.00	30.00
154 Amobi Okoye/25	15.00	40.00
155 Anthony Gonzalez/25	40.00	80.00
156 Antonio Pittman/25	10.00	25.00
157 Aundrae Allison/30	10.00	25.00
159 Brandon Jackson/25	12.00	30.00
160 Brian Leonard/25	12.00	30.00
164 Chris Leak/30	12.00	30.00
165 Craig Buster Davis/25	12.00	30.00
166 David Clowney/25	12.00	30.00
167 Daymeion Hughes/30	12.00	30.00
169 Drew Stanton/25	10.00	25.00
170 Dwayne Bowe/25	40.00	80.00
171 Dwayne Jarrett/25	12.00	30.00
172 Gaines Adams/25	15.00	40.00
173 Greg Olsen/25	12.00	30.00
174 Jamaal Anderson/30	12.00	30.00
176 Joe Thomas/25	15.00	40.00
177 Joel Filani/30	12.00	30.00
180 Kenny Irons/25	10.00	25.00
182 LaRon Landry/25	15.00	40.00
183 Lawrence Timmons/30	15.00	40.00
184 Leon Hall/25	12.00	30.00
186 Marcus McCauley/30	12.00	30.00
188 Michael Bush/25	30.00	60.00
189 Patrick Willis/25	40.00	80.00
190 Paul Posluszny/25	15.00	40.00
191 Quentin Moses/25	12.00	30.00
193 Robert Meachem/25	15.00	40.00
194 Sidney Rice/25	20.00	50.00
195 Steve Smith USC/25	15.00	40.00
199 Tyrone Moss/30	10.00	25.00

1978 Atlanta Convention

This 24-card standard-size set features circular black-and-white player photos framed in light green and bordered in white. The player's name is printed in black across the top with his position, team name, and logo at the bottom. The white backs carry the player's name and career information. The cards are unnumbered and checklisted below in alphabetical order. Almost all of the players in this set played for the Braves at one time.

COMPLETE SET (24)	7.50	15.00
19 Tommy Nobis	.75	1.50

1988 Athletes in Action

The set features six Texas Rangers (1-6) and six Dallas Cowboys (7-12). The cards are standard size, 2 1/2" by 3 1/2". The fronts display color action player photos bordered in white. The words "Athletes in Action" are printed in black across the lower edge of the picture. The backs carry a player quote, a salvation message, and the player's favorite Scripture.

COMPLETE SET (12)	5.00	12.00
7 Tom Landry CO	1.25	3.00
8 Steve Pelluer	.50	1.25
9 Gordon Banks	.50	1.25
10 Bill Bates	.60	1.50
11 Doug Cosbie	.50	1.25
12 Herschel Walker	.75	2.00

1996 Athletes In Action

This set was sponsored and distributed by Athletes in Action. Each card includes a color photo on the front with an inspirational message from the player on the back.

COMPLETE SET (10)	5.00	10.00
1 Cris Carter	1.50	4.00
2 Howard Cross	.40	1.00
3 Trent Dilfer	.50	1.25
4 Irving Fryar	.60	1.50
5 Brent Jones	.40	1.00
6 Jolin Kidd	.40	1.00
7 Doug Pelfrey	.40	1.00
8 Frank Reich	.40	1.00
9 Ken Ruettgers	.40	1.00
10 Steve Wallace	.40	1.00

2002 Atomic

Released in June 2002, this 150-card base set includes 100 vetarans and 50 rookies prodcued in a die cut design. The rookies are shortprinted (serial numbered of 465) and inserted in hobby packs at a rate of 4:21 and retail packs at a rate of 1:25. Hobby product contains 5 cards per pack/20 packs per box/16 boxes per case. The S.R.P. is $5.99. Retail product contains 3 cards per pack/24 packs ber box/16 boxes per case. The S.R.P. is $2.99. Cards numbered from 1-100 feature veterans while cards numbered 101 through 150 feature rookies. Please note that cards 151-170, that feature rookies which made their name during the 2002 season, were only available in packs of 2002 Pacific Heads Update.

COMP.SET w/o SP's (100)	20.00	50.00
1 David Boston	.40	1.00
2 Thomas Jones	.60	1.50
3 Jake Plummer	.50	1.25
4 Jamal Anderson	.50	1.25
5 Warrick Dunn	.50	1.25
6 Michael Vick	1.00	2.50
7 Jamal Lewis	.50	1.25
8 Chris Redman	.40	1.00
9 Travis Taylor	.40	1.00
10 Travis Henry	.40	1.00
11 Eric Moulds	.50	1.25
12 Peerless Price	.40	1.00
13 Muhsin Muhammad	.50	1.25
14 Lamar Smith	.50	1.25
15 Chris Weinke	.40	1.00
16 Marty Booker	.50	1.25
17 Jim Miller	.40	1.00
18 Anthony Thomas	.50	1.25
19 Corey Dillon	.50	1.25
20 Jon Kitna	.50	1.25
21 Peter Warrick	.50	1.25
22 Tim Couch	.40	1.00
23 Kevin Johnson	.40	1.00
24 Quincy Morgan	.40	1.00
25 Quincy Carter	.40	1.00
26 Joey Galloway	.50	1.25
27 Emmitt Smith	1.50	4.00
28 Terrell Davis	.60	1.50

29 Brian Griese	.50	1.25
30 Ed McCaffrey	.50	1.25
31 Rod Smith	.50	1.25
32 Scotty Anderson	.40	1.00
33 Az-Zahir Hakim	.40	1.00
34 Mike McMahon	.40	1.00
35 Brett Favre	1.50	4.00
36 Terry Glenn	.50	1.25
37 Ahman Green	.50	1.25
38 James Allen	.40	1.00
39 Corey Bradford	.40	1.00
40 Jermaine Lewis	.40	1.00
41 Marvin Harrison	.60	1.50
42 Edgerrin James	.50	1.25
43 Peyton Manning	1.25	3.00
44 Mark Brunell	.50	1.25
45 Jimmy Smith	.50	1.25
46 Fred Taylor	.50	1.25
47 Tony Gonzalez	.60	1.50
48 Trent Green	.50	1.25
49 Priest Holmes	.60	1.50
50 Chris Chambers	.50	1.25
51 Jay Fiedler	.50	1.25
52 Ricky Williams	.50	1.25
53 Michael Bennett	.50	1.25
54 Daunte Culpepper	.50	1.25
55 Randy Moss	.60	1.50
56 Tom Brady	1.50	4.00
57 Troy Brown	.50	1.25
58 Antowain Smith	.50	1.25
59 Aaron Brooks	.50	1.25
60 Joe Horn	.50	1.25
61 Deuce McAllister	.50	1.25
62 Tiki Barber	.60	1.50
63 Kerry Collins	.50	1.25
64 Ron Dayne	.50	1.25
65 Wayne Chrebet	.50	1.25
66 Curtis Martin	.60	1.50
67 Vinny Testaverde	.50	1.25
68 Tim Brown	.60	1.50
69 Rich Gannon	.50	1.25
70 Charlie Garner	.50	1.25
71 Jerry Rice	1.25	3.00
72 Correll Buckhalter	.50	1.25
73 Donovan McNabb	.60	1.50
74 Duce Staley	.50	1.25
75 Jerome Bettis	.60	1.50
76 Kordell Stewart	.50	1.25
77 Hines Ward	.60	1.50
78 Isaac Bruce	.60	1.50
79 Marshall Faulk	.60	1.50
80 Torry Holt	.60	1.50
81 Kurt Warner	.60	1.50
82 Drew Brees	1.00	2.50
83 Tim Dwight	.40	1.00
84 Doug Flutie	.60	1.50
85 LaDainian Tomlinson	.75	2.00
86 Jeff Garcia	.50	1.25
87 Garrison Hearst	.50	1.25
88 Terrell Owens	.60	1.50
89 Shaun Alexander	.50	1.25
90 Trent Dilfer	.50	1.25
91 Darrell Jackson	.50	1.25
92 Mike Alstott	.50	1.25
93 Brad Johnson	.50	1.25
94 Keyshawn Johnson	.50	1.25
95 Eddie George	.50	1.25
96 Derrick Mason	.50	1.25
97 Steve McNair	.60	1.50
98 Stephen Davis	.50	1.25
99 Rod Gardner	.40	1.00
100 Jacquez Green	.40	1.00
101 Damien Anderson RC	1.50	4.00
102 Ladell Betts RC	2.50	6.00
103 Antonio Bryant RC	2.50	6.00
104 Reche Caldwell RC	2.50	6.00
105 Kelly Campbell RC	2.00	5.00
106 David Carr RC	2.50	6.00
107 Rohan Davey RC	2.50	6.00
108 Andre Davis RC	2.00	5.00
109 T.J. Duckett RC	2.50	6.00
110 DeShaun Foster RC	2.50	6.00
111 David Garrard RC	3.00	8.00
112 Lamar Gordon RC	2.00	5.00
113 William Green RC	2.00	5.00
114 Joey Harrington RC	2.50	6.00
115 Kurt Kittner RC	1.50	4.00
116 Ashley Lelie RC	2.00	5.00
117 Josh McCown RC	2.50	6.00
118 Clinton Portis RC	3.00	8.00
119 Patrick Ramsey RC	2.50	6.00
120 Antwaan Randle El RC	2.50	6.00
121 Josh Reed RC	2.00	5.00
122 Luke Staley RC	1.50	4.00
123 Donte Stallworth RC	2.50	6.00
124 Marquise Walker RC	1.50	4.00
125 Brian Westbrook RC	4.00	10.00
126 Jason McAddley RC	2.00	5.00
127 Josh Scobey RC	2.00	5.00
128 Kahlil Hill RC	1.50	4.00
129 Ron Johnson RC	2.00	5.00
130 Julius Peppers RC	5.00	12.00
131 Adrian Peterson RC	2.50	6.00
132 Woody Dantzler RC	2.00	5.00
133 Roy Williams RC	2.50	6.00
134 Najeh Davenport RC	2.50	6.00
135 Javon Walker RC	2.50	6.00
136 Jabar Gaffney RC	2.50	6.00
137 John Henderson RC	2.00	5.00
138 Leonard Henry RC	1.50	4.00
139 Daniel Graham RC	2.00	5.00
140 Jeremy Shockey RC	4.00	10.00
141 Ronald Curry RC	2.00	5.00
142 Napoleon Harris RC	2.00	5.00
143 Freddie Milons RC	1.50	4.00
144 Lito Sheppard RC	2.50	6.00
145 Eric Crouch RC	2.50	6.00
146 Robert Thomas RC	1.50	4.00
147 Quentin Jammer RC	2.50	6.00
148 Maurice Morris RC	2.00	5.00
149 Travis Stephens RC	1.50	4.00
150 Cliff Russell RC	1.50	4.00
151 Dameon Hunter RC	1.50	4.00
152 Javin Hunter RC	1.50	4.00
153 Tellis Redmon RC	1.50	4.00
154 Chester Taylor RC	2.50	6.00
155 Randy Fasani RC	2.00	5.00
156 Jamin Elliott RC	1.50	4.00
157 Chad Hutchinson RC	1.50	4.00
158 Eddie Drummond RC	1.50	4.00
159 Craig Nall RC	2.00	5.00
160 Jarrod Baxter RC	1.50	4.00
161 Jonathan Wells RC	2.50	6.00
162 Shaun Hill RC	3.00	8.00
163 Deion Branch RC	2.50	6.00
164 J.T. O'Sullivan RC	2.00	5.00
165 Tim Carter RC	2.00	5.00
166 Daryl Jones RC	1.50	4.00
167 Lee Mays RC	1.50	4.00
168 Seth Burford RC	1.50	4.00
169 Brandon Doman RC	1.50	4.00
170 Jerramy Stevens RC	2.50	6.00

2002 Atomic Gold

*VETS/80-98: 2.5X TO 6X BASIC CARDS
*ROOKIES/80-98: .8X TO 2X
*VETS/30-49: 4X TO 10X BASIC CARDS
*ROOKIES/30-49: 1.2X TO 3X
*VETS/20-29: 5X TO 12X BASIC CARDS
*ROOKIES/20-29: 1.5X TO 4X
GOLD PRINT RUN 1-98
SERIAL #'d UNDER 20 NOT PRICED

2002 Atomic Non Die Cut

*VETS 1-100: 1X TO 2.5X BASIC CARDS
*ROOKIES 101-150: .25X TO .6X
NON DIE-CUT/600 ODDS 13:21
STATED PRINT RUN 600 SER.#'d SETS

2002 Atomic Red

*VETS 1-100: 1.5X TO 4X BASIC CARDS
*ROOKIES 101-150: .4X TO 1X
STATED ODDS 4:21

2002 Atomic Retail Rookies

*ROOKIES: .08X TO .2X BASE CARD HI
RETAIL VERSION NOT SERIAL #'d

2002 Atomic Arms Race

COMPLETE SET (18)	20.00	50.00
STATED ODDS 1:21		
1 Michael Vick	2.00	5.00
2 Tim Couch	.75	2.00
3 Brian Griese	1.00	2.50
4 Joey Harrington	1.25	3.00
5 Brett Favre	3.00	8.00
6 David Carr	1.25	3.00
7 Peyton Manning	2.50	6.00
8 Mark Brunell	1.00	2.50
9 Daunte Culpepper	1.00	2.50
10 Tom Brady	3.00	8.00
11 Aaron Brooks	1.00	2.50
12 Donovan McNabb	1.25	3.00
13 Kurt Warner	1.25	3.00
14 Drew Brees	2.00	5.00
15 Doug Flutie	1.25	3.00
16 Jeff Garcia	1.00	2.50
17 Steve McNair	1.25	3.00
18 Patrick Ramsey	1.25	3.00

2002 Atomic Countdown To Stardom

COMPLETE SET (18)	12.00	30.00
STATED ODDS 2:21		
1 Josh McCown	.75	2.00
2 T.J. Duckett	.75	2.00
3 Josh Reed	.60	1.50
4 DeShaun Foster	.75	2.00
5 William Green	.60	1.50
6 Antonio Bryant	.75	2.00
7 Ashley Lelie	.60	1.50
8 Clinton Portis	1.00	2.50
9 Joey Harrington	.75	2.00
10 Javon Walker	.75	2.00
11 David Carr	.75	2.00
12 Jabar Gaffney	.75	2.00
13 Donte Stallworth	.75	2.00
14 Brian Westbrook	1.25	3.00
15 Lamar Gordon	.60	1.50
16 Reche Caldwell	.75	2.00
17 Maurice Morris	.60	1.50
18 Patrick Ramsey	.75	2.00

2002 Atomic Fusion Force

COMPLETE SET (18)	30.00	80.00
STATED ODDS 1:41		
1 T.J. Duckett	1.50	4.00
2 Michael Vick	2.50	6.00
3 DeShaun Foster	1.50	4.00
4 Anthony Thomas	1.25	3.00
5 William Green	1.25	3.00
6 Emmitt Smith	4.00	10.00
7 Terrell Davis	1.50	4.00
8 Ashley Lelie	1.25	3.00
9 Joey Harrington	1.50	4.00
10 Brett Favre	4.00	10.00
11 David Carr	1.50	4.00
12 Randy Moss	1.50	4.00
13 Donte Stallworth	1.50	4.00
14 Jerry Rice	3.00	8.00
15 Marshall Faulk	1.50	4.00
16 Kurt Warner	1.50	4.00
17 LaDainian Tomlinson	2.00	5.00
18 Patrick Ramsey	1.50	4.00

2002 Atomic Game Worn Jerseys

STATED ODDS 3:21 HOBBY		
*GOLD/25: 1X TO 2.5X BASIC JERSEYS		
GOLD PRINT RUN 25 SER.#'d SETS		
1 David Boston/350	3.00	8.00
2 Freddie Jones/277	3.00	8.00
3 Joel Makovicka/238	3.00	8.00
4 Jake Plummer/132	4.00	10.00
5 Jamal Anderson/333	4.00	10.00
6 Warrick Dunn/106	4.00	10.00
7 Shawn Jefferson/261	3.00	8.00
8 Maurice Smith/259	3.00	8.00
9 Dave Moore/277	3.00	8.00
10 Peerless Price/249	3.00	8.00
11 Jay Riemersma/251	3.00	8.00
12 Lamar Smith/259	4.00	10.00
13 Rabih Abdullah/270	3.00	8.00
14 Chris Chandler/352	4.00	10.00
15 Brian Urlacher/141	5.00	12.00
16 Dez White/246	3.00	8.00
17 Corey Dillon/210	4.00	10.00
18 Scott Mitchell/268	4.00	10.00
19 Akili Smith/264	4.00	10.00
20 Takeo Spikes/283	3.00	8.00
21 Tim Couch/261	3.00	8.00
22 Jammi German/276	3.00	8.00
23 Jamel White/270	3.00	8.00
24 La'Roi Glover/279	3.00	8.00
25 Emmitt Smith/257	12.00	30.00
26 Darren Woodson/281	4.00	10.00
27 Mike Anderson/333	4.00	10.00
28 Terrell Davis/270	5.00	12.00
29 Gus Frerotte/272	4.00	10.00
30 Brian Griese/125	4.00	10.00
31 Howard Griffith/264	3.00	8.00
32 Deltha O'Neal/231	3.00	8.00
33 Shannon Sharpe/278	5.00	12.00
34 Charlie Batch/257	3.00	8.00
35 Az-Zahir Hakim/59	3.00	8.00
36 Brett Favre/247	12.00	30.00
37 Antonio Freeman/358	5.00	12.00
39 Ahman Green/242	4.00	10.00
40 Dorsey Levens/219	4.00	10.00
41 James Allen/241	3.00	8.00
42 Avion Black/262	3.00	8.00
43 Jermaine Lewis/283	3.00	8.00
44 Charlie Rogers/296	3.00	8.00
45 Qadry Ismail/275	4.00	10.00
46 Trent Green/346	4.00	10.00
47 Tony Richardson/282	3.00	8.00
48 Ricky Williams/348	4.00	10.00
49 Cris Carter/199	5.00	12.00
50 Corey Chavous/262	3.00	8.00
51 Daunte Culpepper/346	4.00	10.00
52 Jim Kleinsasser/273	5.00	12.00
53 Randy Moss/179	5.00	12.00
54 Tom Brady/95	12.00	30.00
55 Donald Hayes/264	3.00	8.00
56 Curtis Jackson/206	3.00	8.00
57 Patrick Pass/254	3.00	8.00
58 Aaron Brooks/267	4.00	10.00
59 Bryan Cox/276	4.00	10.00
60 Jerome Pathon/80	3.00	8.00
61 Robert Wilson/287	3.00	8.00
62 Tiki Barber/153	5.00	12.00
63 Kerry Collins/111	4.00	10.00
64 Ron Dayne/354	4.00	10.00
65 Laveranues Coles/243	4.00	10.00
66 James Jett/287	4.00	10.00
67 Randy Jordan/238	3.00	8.00
68 Jerry Rice/323	10.00	25.00
69 Cecil Martin/267	3.00	8.00
70 Donovan McNabb/357	5.00	12.00
71 Brian Mitchell/266	4.00	10.00
72 Jerome Bettis/337	5.00	12.00
73 Mark Bruener/289	4.00	10.00
74 Troy Edwards/262	3.00	8.00
75 Kordell Stewart/340	4.00	10.00
76 Isaac Bruce/351	5.00	12.00
77 Trung Canidate/300	3.00	8.00
78 Ernie Conwell/266	3.00	8.00
79 Marshall Faulk/355	5.00	12.00
80 Torry Holt/77	5.00	12.00
81 Kurt Warner/191	8.00	20.00
82 Aeneas Williams /268	4.00	10.00
83 Stephen Alexander/261	3.00	8.00
84 Drew Brees/248	8.00	20.00
85 Tim Dwight/112	3.00	8.00
86 Terrell Fletcher/262	3.00	8.00
87 Doug Flutie/328	5.00	12.00
88 Ronney Jenkins/292	3.00	8.00
89 Fred Beasley/244	3.00	8.00
90 Shaun Alexander/356	4.00	10.00
91 Itula Mili/262	3.00	8.00
92 Ken Dilger/253	4.00	10.00
93 Michael Pittman/229	4.00	10.00
94 Eddie George/183	4.00	10.00
95 Jevon Kearse/253	4.00	10.00
96 Erron Kinney/247	3.00	8.00
97 Steve McNair/371	5.00	12.00
98 Dameyune Craig/265	3.00	8.00
99 Stephen Davis/304	4.00	10.00

2002 Atomic Game Worn Jersey Patches

PATCH/2-150 ODDS 1:21 HOBBY		
1 David Boston/100	5.00	12.00
3 Joel Makovicka/100	5.00	12.00
5 Jamal Anderson/100	6.00	15.00
6 Warrick Dunn/32	8.00	20.00
7 Shawn Jefferson/100	5.00	12.00
8 Maurice Smith/100	5.00	12.00
9 Dave Moore/100	5.00	12.00
11 Jay Riemersma/29	6.00	15.00
12 Lamar Smith/100	6.00	15.00
13 Rabih Abdullah/100	5.00	12.00
14 Chris Chandler/30	8.00	20.00
16 Dez White/76	5.00	12.00
17 Corey Dillon/80	6.00	15.00
18 Scott Mitchell/100	6.00	15.00
19 Akili Smith/100	6.00	15.00
20 Takeo Spikes/100	5.00	12.00
21 Tim Couch/75	5.00	12.00
22 Jammi German/150	5.00	12.00
23 Jamel White/100	5.00	12.00
24 La'Roi Glover/100	5.00	12.00
25 Emmitt Smith/38	30.00	80.00
26 Darren Woodson/100	6.00	15.00
27 Mike Anderson/75	6.00	15.00
28 Terrell Davis/75	8.00	20.00
29 Gus Frerotte/100	6.00	15.00
31 Howard Griffith/100	5.00	12.00
33 Shannon Sharpe/100	8.00	20.00
35 Az-Zahir Hakim/60	5.00	12.00
36 Brett Favre/100	20.00	50.00
37 Antonio Freeman/100	8.00	20.00
39 Ahman Green/100	6.00	15.00
40 Dorsey Levens/100	6.00	15.00
43 Jermaine Lewis/150	5.00	12.00
44 Charlie Rogers/100	5.00	12.00
45 Qadry Ismail/100	6.00	15.00
46 Trent Green/100	6.00	15.00
47 Tony Richardson/100	5.00	12.00
48 Ricky Williams/95	6.00	15.00
49 Cris Carter/80	8.00	20.00
50 Corey Chavous/100	5.00	12.00
51 Daunte Culpepper/75	6.00	15.00
52 Jim Kleinsasser/100	8.00	20.00
53 Randy Moss/28	20.00	50.00
54 Tom Brady/50	25.00	60.00
55 Donald Hayes/150	5.00	12.00
56 Curtis Jackson/150	5.00	12.00
57 Patrick Pass/100	5.00	12.00
58 Aaron Brooks/100	6.00	15.00
59 Bryan Cox/100	6.00	15.00
61 Robert Wilson/100	5.00	12.00
62 Tiki Barber/25	12.00	30.00
64 Ron Dayne/75	6.00	15.00
65 Laveranues Coles/90	6.00	15.00
66 James Jett/100	6.00	15.00
67 Randy Jordan/100	5.00	12.00
68 Jerry Rice/75	15.00	40.00
69 Cecil Martin/100	5.00	12.00
70 Donovan McNabb/95	8.00	20.00
71 Brian Mitchell/100	6.00	15.00
72 Jerome Bettis/75	8.00	20.00
73 Mark Bruener/100	6.00	15.00
74 Troy Edwards/100	5.00	12.00
75 Kordell Stewart/75	6.00	15.00
76 Isaac Bruce/99	8.00	20.00
77 Trung Canidate/100	5.00	12.00
78 Ernie Conwell/100	5.00	12.00
79 Marshall Faulk/95	8.00	20.00
80 Torry Holt/100	8.00	20.00
81 Kurt Warner/20	20.00	40.00
82 Aeneas Williams/38	8.00	20.00
85 Tim Dwight/25	8.00	20.00
86 Terrell Fletcher/22	8.00	20.00
87 Doug Flutie/20	12.00	30.00
88 Ronney Jenkins/21	8.00	20.00
89 Fred Beasley/100	5.00	12.00
90 Shaun Alexander/95	6.00	15.00
91 Itula Mili/100	5.00	12.00
92 Ken Dilger/100	6.00	15.00
93 Michael Pittman/110	6.00	15.00
94 Eddie George/75	6.00	15.00
96 Erron Kinney/100	5.00	12.00
97 Steve McNair/80	8.00	20.00

2002 Atomic Super Colliders

COMPLETE SET (9)	7.50	15.00
STATED ODDS 1:21		
1 Anthony Thomas	.75	2.00
2 Corey Dillon	.75	2.00
3 Emmitt Smith	2.50	6.00
4 Edgerrin James	.75	2.00
5 Ricky Williams	.75	2.00
6 Jerome Bettis	1.00	2.50
7 Marshall Faulk	1.00	2.50
8 LaDainian Tomlinson	1.25	3.00
9 Shaun Alexander	.75	2.00

1998 Aurora

The 1998 Pacific Aurora set was issued in one series totalling 200 cards. The 6-card packs retail for $2.99 each. Each card is printed on super-thick 24-point card. Each gold-foiled card features color action photography with a head shot of the featured player in the upper right corner. The backs offer the latest player information and statistics along with a challenging trivia question.

COMPLETE SET (200)	30.00	60.00
1 Rob Moore	.25	.60
2 Jake Plummer	.40	1.00
3 Frank Sanders	.25	.60
4 Eric Swann	.15	.40
5 Jamal Anderson	.40	1.00
6 Chris Chandler	.25	.60
7 Byron Hanspard	.15	.40
8 Terance Mathis	.25	.60
9 O.J. Santiago	.15	.40
10 Chuck Smith	.15	.40
11 Jessie Tuggle	.15	.40
12 Jay Graham	.15	.40
13 Jim Harbaugh	.25	.60
14 Michael Jackson	.15	.40
15 Pat Johnson RC	.60	1.50
16 Jermaine Lewis	.25	.60
17 Errict Rhett	.25	.60
18 Rod Woodson	.25	.60
19 Quinn Early	.15	.40
20 Andre Reed	.25	.60
21 Antowain Smith	.40	1.00
22 Bruce Smith	.25	.60
23 Thurman Thomas	.40	1.00
24 Ted Washington	.15	.40
25 Michael Bates	.15	.40
26 Rae Carruth	.15	.40
27 Kerry Collins	.25	.60
28 Fred Lane	.15	.40
29 Wesley Walls	.25	.60
30 Edgar Bennett	.15	.40
31 Curtis Conway	.25	.60
32 Curtis Enis RC	.40	1.00
33 Walt Harris	.15	.40
34 Erik Kramer	.15	.40
35 Barry Minter	.15	.40
36 Jeff Blake	.25	.60
37 Corey Dillon	.40	1.00
38 Carl Pickens	.25	.60
39 Darnay Scott	.25	.60
40 Troy Aikman	.75	2.00
41 Michael Irvin	.40	1.00
42 Deion Sanders	.40	1.00
43 Emmitt Smith	1.50	3.00
44 Chris Warren	.25	.60
45 Terrell Davis	.40	1.00
46 John Elway	1.50	4.00
47 Brian Griese RC	1.50	4.00
48 Ed McCaffrey	.25	.60
49 John Mobley	.15	.40
50 Shannon Sharpe	.25	.60
51 Neil Smith	.25	.60
52 Rod Smith WR	.25	.60
53 Stephen Boyd	.15	.40
54 Scott Mitchell	.25	.60
55 Herman Moore	.25	.60
56 Johnnie Morton	.25	.60
57 Robert Porcher	.15	.40
58 Barry Sanders	1.25	3.00
59 Robert Brooks	.25	.60
60 Mark Chmura	.25	.60
61 Brett Favre	2.00	4.00
62 Antonio Freeman	.40	1.00
63 Vonnie Holliday RC	.60	1.50
64 Dorsey Levens	.40	1.00
65 Ross Verba	.15	.40
66 Reggie White	.40	1.00
67 Elijah Alexander	.15	.40
68 Ken Dilger	.15	.40
69 Marshall Faulk	.50	1.25
70 Marvin Harrison	.40	1.00
71 Peyton Manning RC	10.00	20.00
72 Bryan Barker	.15	.40
73 Mark Brunell	.40	1.00
74 Keenan McCardell	.25	.60
75 Jimmy Smith	.25	.60
76 James Stewart	.25	.60
77 Derrick Alexander WR	.25	.60
78 Kimble Anders	.25	.60
79 Donnell Bennett	.15	.40
80 Elvis Grbac	.25	.60
81 Andre Rison	.25	.60
82 Rashaan Shehee RC	.60	1.50
83 Derrick Thomas	.40	1.00
84 Karim Abdul-Jabbar	.40	1.00
85 Trace Armstrong	.15	.40
86 Charles Jordan	.15	.40
87 Dan Marino	1.50	4.00
88 O.J. McDuffie	.25	.60
89 Zach Thomas	.40	1.00
90 Cris Carter	.40	1.00
91 Charles Evans	.15	.40
92 Andrew Glover	.15	.40
93 Brad Johnson	.40	1.00
94 Randy Moss RC	5.00	12.00
95 John Randle	.25	.60
96 Jake Reed	.25	.60
97 Robert Smith	.40	1.00
98 Bruce Armstrong	.15	.40
99 Drew Bledsoe	.60	1.50
100 Ben Coates	.25	.60
101 Robert Edwards RC	.60	1.50
102 Terry Glenn	.40	1.00
103 Willie McGinest	.15	.40
104 Sedrick Shaw	.15	.40
105 Tony Simmons RC	.60	1.50
106 Chris Slade	.15	.40
107 Billy Joe Hobert	.15	.40
108 Qadry Ismail	.25	.60
109 Heath Shuler	.15	.40
110 Lamar Smith	.25	.60
111 Ray Zellars	.15	.40
112 Tiki Barber	.40	1.00
113 Chris Calloway	.15	.40
114 Ike Hilliard	.25	.60
115 Joe Jurevicius RC	.75	2.00
116 Danny Kanell	.25	.60
117 Amani Toomer	.25	.60
118 Charles Way	.15	.40
119 Tyrone Wheatley	.25	.60
120 Wayne Chrebet	.40	1.00
121 John Elliott	.15	.40
122 Glenn Foley	.25	.60
123 Scott Frost RC	.15	.40
124 Aaron Glenn	.15	.40
125 Keyshawn Johnson	.40	1.00
126 Curtis Martin	.40	1.00
127 Vinny Testaverde	.25	.60
128 Tim Brown	.40	1.00
129 Rickey Dudley	.15	.40
130 Jeff George	.25	.60
131 James Jett	.25	.60
132 Napoleon Kaufman	.40	1.00
133 Darrell Russell	.15	.40
134 Charles Woodson RC	1.00	2.50
135 James Darling RC	.15	.40
136 Koy Detmer	.40	1.00
137 Irving Fryar	.25	.60
138 Charlie Garner	.25	.60
139 Bobby Hoying	.25	.60
140 Chad Lewis	.25	.60
141 Duce Staley	.50	1.25
142 Kevin Turner	.15	.40
143 Jerome Bettis	.40	1.00
144 Will Blackwell	.15	.40
145 Mark Bruener	.15	.40
146 Dermontti Dawson	.15	.40
147 Charles Johnson	.15	.40
148 Levon Kirkland	.15	.40
149 Tim Lester	.15	.40
150 Kordell Stewart	.40	1.00
151 Tony Banks	.25	.60
152 Isaac Bruce	.40	1.00
153 Robert Holcombe RC	.60	1.50
154 Eddie Kennison	.25	.60
155 Amp Lee	.15	.40
156 Jerald Moore	.15	.40
157 Charlie Jones	.15	.40
158 Freddie Jones	.15	.40
159 Ryan Leaf RC	.75	2.00
160 Natrone Means	.25	.60
161 Junior Seau	.40	1.00
162 Bryan Still	.15	.40
163 Marc Edwards	.15	.40
164 Merton Hanks	.15	.40
165 Garrison Hearst	.40	1.00
166 Terrell Owens	.40	1.00
167 Jerry Rice	.75	2.00
168 J.J. Stokes	.25	.60
169 Bryant Young	.15	.40
170 Steve Young	.50	1.25
171 Chad Brown	.15	.40
172 Joey Galloway	.25	.60
173 Walter Jones	.15	.40
174 Cortez Kennedy	.15	.40
175 Jon Kitna	.40	1.00
176 James McKnight	.40	1.00
177 Warren Moon	.40	1.00
178 Michael Sinclair	.15	.40
179 Mike Alstott	.40	1.00
180 Reidel Anthony	.25	.60
181 Derrick Brooks	.40	1.00
182 Trent Dilfer	.40	1.00
183 Warrick Dunn	.40	1.00
184 Hardy Nickerson	.15	.40
185 Warren Sapp	.25	.60
186 Willie Davis	.15	.40
187 Eddie George	.40	1.00
188 Steve McNair	.40	1.00
189 Jon Runyan	.15	.40
190 Chris Sanders	.15	.40
191 Frank Wycheck	.15	.40
192 Stephen Alexander RC	.60	1.50
193 Terry Allen	.40	1.00
194 Stephen Davis	.15	.40
195 Cris Dishman	.15	.40
196 Gus Frerotte	.15	.40
197 Darrell Green	.25	.60
198 Skip Hicks RC	.60	1.50
199 Dana Stubblefield	.15	.40
200 Michael Westbrook	.25	.60
S1 Warrick Dunn Sample	.40	1.00

1998 Aurora Championship Fever

COMP.GOLD SET (50)	20.00	50.00
OVERALL ODDS ONE PER PACK		
*COPPER/20: 15X TO 40X BASIC INSERTS		
COPPER/20 INSERTED IN HOBBY PACKS		
*PLAT.BLUE/100: 4X TO 10X BASIC INSERTS		
PLAT.BLUE/100 INSERTED IN HOB/RET		
*RED: 1.2X TO 3X BASIC INSERTS		
RED ODDS 4:25 SPECIAL RETAIL		
*SILVER/250: 2X TO 5X BASIC INSERTS		
SILVER/250 INSERTED IN RETAIL PACKS		
1 Jake Plummer	.40	1.00
2 Antowain Smith	.40	1.00
3 Bruce Smith	.50	1.25
4 Kerry Collins	.40	1.00
5 Kevin Greene	.40	1.00
6 Jeff Blake	.40	1.00
7 Corey Dillon	.40	1.00
8 Carl Pickens	.30	.75
9 Troy Aikman	1.00	2.50
10 Michael Irvin	.50	1.25
11 Deion Sanders	.50	1.25
12 Emmitt Smith	1.50	4.00
13 Terrell Davis	.50	1.25
14 John Elway	2.00	5.00
15 Shannon Sharpe	.50	1.25
16 Herman Moore	.30	.75
17 Barry Sanders	1.50	4.00
18 Brett Favre	2.00	5.00
19 Antonio Freeman	.40	1.00
20 Dorsey Levens	.40	1.00
21 Marshall Faulk	.50	1.25
22 Peyton Manning	4.00	10.00
23 Mark Brunell	.40	1.00
24 Elvis Grbac	.30	.75
25 Andre Rison	.40	1.00
26 Rashaan Shehee	.30	.75
27 Derrick Thomas	.50	1.25
28 Dan Marino	2.00	5.00
29 Cris Carter	.50	1.25
30 Robert Smith	.40	1.00
31 Drew Bledsoe	.50	1.25
32 Robert Edwards	.30	.75
33 Terry Glenn	.40	1.00
34 Danny Kanell	.30	.75
35 Keyshawn Johnson	.40	1.00
36 Tim Brown	.50	1.25
37 Napoleon Kaufman	.30	.75
38 Bobby Hoying	.30	.75
39 Jerome Bettis	.50	1.25
40 Kordell Stewart	.40	1.00
41 Ryan Leaf	.30	.75
42 Jerry Rice	1.00	2.50
43 Steve Young	.60	1.50
44 Joey Galloway	.40	1.00
45 Mike Alstott	.50	1.25
46 Trent Dilfer	.40	1.00
47 Warrick Dunn	.40	1.00
47AU Warrick Dunn AUTO/100	20.00	50.00
48 Eddie George	.50	1.25
49 Steve McNair	.50	1.25
50 Gus Frerotte	.30	.75

1998 Aurora Cubes

COMPLETE SET (20)	75.00	150.00
ONE PER HOBBY BOX		
1 Corey Dillon	2.00	5.00
2 Troy Aikman	4.00	10.00
3 Emmitt Smith	6.00	15.00
4 Terrell Davis	2.00	5.00
5 John Elway	8.00	20.00
6 Barry Sanders	6.00	15.00
7 Brett Favre	8.00	20.00
8 Dorsey Levens	2.00	5.00
9 Peyton Manning	12.50	30.00
10 Mark Brunell	2.00	5.00
11 Dan Marino	8.00	20.00
12 Drew Bledsoe	3.00	8.00
13 Napoleon Kaufman	2.00	5.00
14 Jerome Bettis	2.00	5.00
15 Kordell Stewart	2.00	5.00
16 Ryan Leaf	1.25	3.00
17 Jerry Rice	4.00	10.00
18 Steve Young	2.50	6.00
19 Warrick Dunn	2.00	5.00
20 Eddie George	2.00	5.00

1998 Aurora Face Mask Cel Fusions

COMPLETE SET (20)	150.00	250.00
STATED ODDS 1:73		
1 Corey Dillon	3.00	8.00
2 Troy Aikman	6.00	15.00
3 Emmitt Smith	10.00	25.00
4 Terrell Davis	3.00	8.00
5 John Elway	12.50	30.00
6 Barry Sanders	10.00	25.00
7 Brett Favre	12.50	30.00
8 Antonio Freeman	3.00	8.00
9 Peyton Manning	15.00	40.00
10 Mark Brunell	3.00	8.00
11 Dan Marino	12.50	30.00
12 Drew Bledsoe	5.00	12.00
13 Napoleon Kaufman	3.00	8.00
14 Jerome Bettis	3.00	8.00
15 Kordell Stewart	3.00	8.00
16 Ryan Leaf	1.50	4.00
17 Jerry Rice	6.00	15.00
18 Steve Young	4.00	10.00
19 Warrick Dunn	3.00	8.00
20 Eddie George	3.00	8.00

1998 Aurora Gridiron Laser Cuts

COMPLETE SET (20)	30.00	80.00
STATED ODDS 4:37 HOBBY		
1 Jake Plummer	1.50	4.00
2 Corey Dillon	1.50	4.00
3 Troy Aikman	3.00	8.00
4 Emmitt Smith	5.00	12.00
5 Terrell Davis	1.50	4.00
6 John Elway	6.00	15.00
7 Barry Sanders	5.00	12.00
8 Brett Favre	6.00	15.00
9 Peyton Manning	12.50	30.00
10 Mark Brunell	1.50	4.00
11 Dan Marino	6.00	15.00
12 Drew Bledsoe	2.50	6.00
13 Jerome Bettis	1.50	4.00
14 Kordell Stewart	1.50	4.00
15 Ryan Leaf	1.25	3.00
16 Jerry Rice	3.00	8.00
17 Steve Young	2.00	5.00
18 Warrick Dunn	1.50	4.00
19 Eddie George	1.50	4.00
20 Steve McNair	1.50	4.00

1998 Aurora NFL Command

STATED ODDS 1:361		
1 Terrell Davis	4.00	10.00
2 John Elway	15.00	40.00
3 Barry Sanders	12.50	30.00
4 Brett Favre	15.00	40.00
5 Peyton Manning	30.00	80.00
6 Mark Brunell	4.00	10.00
7 Dan Marino	15.00	40.00
8 Drew Bledsoe	6.00	15.00
9 Ryan Leaf	4.00	10.00
10 Warrick Dunn	4.00	10.00

1999 Aurora

This 200 card set, issued in August 1999, was released in six card packs. These cards are sequenced in alphabetical order by teams which are also in alphabetical order. Rookie Cards in this set include Tim Couch, Edgerrin James and Ricky Williams. Terrell Owens signed 197 cards which were radomly inserted into packs.

COMPLETE SET (150)	15.00	40.00
1 David Boston RC	.30	.75
2 Larry Centers	.20	.50
3 Rob Moore	.15	.40
4 Adrian Murrell	.20	.50
5 Jake Plummer	.20	.50
6 Jamal Anderson	.20	.50
7 Chris Chandler	.20	.50
8 Tim Dwight	.20	.50
9 Terance Mathis	.15	.40
10 O.J. Santiago	.15	.40
11 Priest Holmes	.25	.60
12 Michael Jackson	.15	.40
13 Jermaine Lewis	.15	.40
14 Ray Lewis	.25	.60
15 Michael McCrary	.15	.40
16 Doug Flutie	.25	.60
17 Eric Moulds	.20	.50
18 Peerless Price RC	.30	.75
19 Antowain Smith	.15	.40
20 Bruce Smith	.25	.60
21 Steve Beuerlein	.20	.50
22 Tim Biakabutuka	.20	.50
23 Kevin Greene	.20	.50
24 Muhsin Muhammad	.20	.50
25 Wesley Walls	.20	.50
26 Curtis Conway	.20	.50
27 Bobby Engram	.20	.50
28 Curtis Enis	.15	.40
29 Erik Kramer	.20	.50
30 Cade McNown RC	.30	.75
31 Jeff Blake	.20	.50
32 Corey Dillon	.20	.50
33 Carl Pickens	.20	.50
34 Darnay Scott	.15	.40
35 Akili Smith RC	.30	.75
36 Tim Couch RC	.40	1.00
37 Ty Detmer	.20	.50
38 Kevin Johnson RC	.30	.75
39 Terry Kirby	.15	.40
40 Troy Aikman	.40	1.00
41 Michael Irvin	.25	.60
42 Rocket Ismail	.20	.50
43 Deion Sanders	.25	.60
44 Emmitt Smith	.60	1.50
45 Bubby Brister	.15	.40
46 Terrell Davis	.25	.60
47 Brian Griese	.20	.50
48 Ed McCaffrey	.20	.50
49 Shannon Sharpe	.25	.60
50 Rod Smith	.20	.50
51 Charlie Batch	.20	.50
52 Sedrick Irvin RC	.25	.60
53 Herman Moore	.20	.50
54 Johnnie Morton	.20	.50
55 Barry Sanders	.60	1.50
56 Robert Brooks	.20	.50
57 Brett Favre	.75	2.00
58 Antonio Freeman UER (photo on back is Dorsey Levens)	.20	.50
59 Dorsey Levens	.20	.50
60 Derrick Mayes	.15	.40
61 Marvin Harrison	.25	.60
62 Edgerrin James RC	.50	1.25
63 Peyton Manning	.75	2.00
64 Jerome Pathon	.15	.40
65 Tavian Banks	.15	.40
66 Mark Brunell	.20	.50
67 Keenan McCardell	.20	.50
68 Jimmy Smith	.20	.50
69 Fred Taylor	.20	.50
70 Derrick Alexander	.15	.40
71 Kimble Anders	.15	.40
72 Mike Cloud RC	.25	.60
73 Elvis Grbac	.15	.40
74 Andre Rison	.20	.50
75 Karim Abdul-Jabbar	.20	.50
76 James Johnson RC	.25	.60
77 Dan Marino	.75	2.00
78 O.J. McDuffie	.20	.50
79 Lamar Thomas	.15	.40
80 Cris Carter	.25	.60
81 Daunte Culpepper RC	.40	1.00
82 Randall Cunningham	.25	.60
83 Randy Moss	.25	.60
84 John Randle	.20	.50
85 Robert Smith	.20	.50
86 Drew Bledsoe	.25	.60
87 Ben Coates	.20	.50
88 Kevin Faulk RC	.40	1.00
89 Terry Glenn	.20	.50
90 Ty Law	.20	.50
91 Cam Cleeland	.15	.40
92 Andre Hastings	.15	.40
93 Billy Joe Hobert	.15	.40
94 Ricky Williams RC	.60	1.50
95 Tiki Barber	.25	.60
96 Kent Graham	.15	.40
97 Ike Hilliard	.20	.50
98 Charles Way	.15	.40
99 Wayne Chrebet	.20	.50
100 Keyshawn Johnson	.20	.50
101 Curtis Martin	.25	.60
102 Vinny Testaverde	.20	.50
103 Dedric Ward	.15	.40
104 Tim Brown	.25	.60
105 Rickey Dudley	.15	.40
106 James Jett	.15	.40
107 Napoleon Kaufman	.15	.40
108 Charles Woodson	.25	.60
109 Jeff Graham	.15	.40
110 Charles Johnson	.15	.40
111 Donovan McNabb RC	2.00	5.00
112 Duce Staley	.20	.50
113 Jerome Bettis	.25	.60
114 Troy Edwards RC	.30	.75
115 Courtney Hawkins	.15	.40
116 Kordell Stewart	.20	.50
117 Amos Zereoue RC	.30	.75
118 Isaac Bruce	.25	.60

119 Marshall Faulk	.25	.60
120 Joe Germaine RC	.30	.75
121 Torry Holt RC	.60	1.50
122 Amp Lee	.15	.40
123 Charlie Jones	.15	.40
124 Ryan Leaf	.20	.50
125 Natrone Means	.20	.50
126 Junior Seau	.25	.60
127 Garrison Hearst	.20	.50
128 Terrell Owens	.25	.60
129 Jerry Rice	.50	1.25
130 J.J. Stokes	.15	.40
131 Steve Young	.30	.75
132 Chad Brown	.15	.40
133 Joey Galloway	.20	.50
134 Brock Huard RC	.30	.75
135 Jon Kitna	.20	.50
136 Ricky Watters	.20	.50
137 Mike Alstott	.25	.60
138 Reidel Anthony	.15	.40
139 Trent Dilfer	.20	.50
140 Warrick Dunn	.20	.50
141 Jacquez Green	.15	.40
142 Shaun King RC	.30	.75
143 Eddie George	.20	.50
144 Steve McNair	.25	.60
145 Yancey Thigpen	.15	.40
146 Frank Wycheck	.20	.50
147 Champ Bailey RC	.75	2.00
148 Skip Hicks	.15	.40
149 Brad Johnson	.20	.50
150 Michael Westbrook	.15	.40
AU1 T.Owens AUTO/197	20.00	40.00

1999 Aurora Pinstripes

*PINSTRIPES: .4X TO 1X BASIC CARDS

1999 Aurora Premiere Date

*VETS: 10X TO 25X BASIC CARDS
*ROOKIES: 6X TO 15X BASIC CARDS
*PINSTRIPE PD: .4X TO 1X PREM.DATE
PREMIERE DATE/77 ODDS 1:25 HOB
PREMIERE DATE PRINT RUN 77

1999 Aurora Canvas Creations

COMPLETE SET (10)	40.00	100.00
STATED ODDS 1:193		
1 Troy Aikman	5.00	12.00
2 Terrell Davis	3.00	8.00
3 Barry Sanders	8.00	20.00
4 Brett Favre	10.00	25.00
5 Peyton Manning	10.00	25.00
6 Dan Marino	10.00	25.00
7 Randy Moss	3.00	8.00
8 Drew Bledsoe	3.00	8.00
9 Steve Young	4.00	10.00
10 Jon Kitna	2.50	6.00

1999 Aurora Championship Fever

COMPLETE SET (20)	20.00	40.00
STATED ODDS 4:25		
*COPPER/20: 10X TO 25X BASIC INSERTS		
*PLAT.BLUE/100: 5X TO 12X BASIC INSERTS		
*SILVER/250: 3X TO 8X BASIC INSERTS		
1 Jake Plummer	.40	1.00
2 Jamal Anderson	.40	1.00
3 Tim Couch	.50	1.25
4 Troy Aikman	.75	2.00
5 Emmitt Smith	1.25	3.00
6 Terrell Davis	.50	1.25
7 Barry Sanders	1.25	3.00
8 Brett Favre	1.50	4.00
9 Peyton Manning	1.50	4.00
10 Fred Taylor	.40	1.00
11 Dan Marino	1.50	4.00
12 Randy Moss	.50	1.25
13 Drew Bledsoe	.50	1.25
14 Ricky Williams	.75	2.00
15 Keyshawn Johnson	.40	1.00
16 Terrell Owens	.50	1.25
17 Jerry Rice	1.00	2.50
18 Steve Young	.60	1.50
19 Jon Kitna	.40	1.00
20 Eddie George	.40	1.00

1999 Aurora Complete Players

STATED PRINT RUN 299 SER.#'d SETS		
*HOLOGOLD/25: 1.5X TO 4X BASIC INSERT		
HOLOGOLD/25 INSERTS IN HOB/RET		
1 Troy Aikman	5.00	12.00
2 Terrell Davis	3.00	8.00
3 Barry Sanders	8.00	20.00
4 Brett Favre	10.00	25.00
5 Peyton Manning	10.00	25.00
6 Dan Marino	10.00	25.00
7 Randy Moss	3.00	8.00
8 Drew Bledsoe	3.00	8.00
9 Jerry Rice	6.00	15.00
10 Steve Young	4.00	10.00

1999 Aurora Leather Bound

COMPLETE SET (20)	50.00	100.00
STATED ODDS 2:25 HOBBY		
1 Jake Plummer	1.00	2.50
2 Jamal Anderson	1.00	2.50
3 Tim Couch	1.00	2.50
4 Troy Aikman	2.00	5.00
5 Emmitt Smith	3.00	8.00
6 Terrell Davis	1.25	3.00
7 Barry Sanders	3.00	8.00
8 Brett Favre	4.00	10.00
9 Peyton Manning	4.00	10.00
10 Fred Taylor	1.00	2.50
11 Dan Marino	4.00	10.00
12 Randy Moss	1.25	3.00
13 Drew Bledsoe	1.25	3.00
14 Ricky Williams	1.50	4.00
15 Curtis Martin	1.25	3.00
16 Jerome Bettis	1.25	3.00
17 Jerry Rice	2.50	6.00
18 Steve Young	1.50	4.00
19 Jon Kitna	1.00	2.50
20 Eddie George	1.00	2.50

1999 Aurora Styrotechs

COMPLETE SET (20)	60.00	120.00
STATED ODDS 1:25		
1 Jake Plummer	1.25	3.00
2 Jamal Anderson	1.25	3.00
3 Tim Couch	1.25	3.00
4 Troy Aikman	2.50	6.00
5 Emmitt Smith	4.00	10.00
6 Terrell Davis	1.50	4.00
7 Barry Sanders	4.00	10.00
8 Brett Favre	5.00	12.00
9 Peyton Manning	5.00	12.00
10 Fred Taylor	1.25	3.00
11 Dan Marino	5.00	12.00
12 Randy Moss	1.50	4.00
13 Drew Bledsoe	1.50	4.00
14 Ricky Williams	2.00	5.00
15 Curtis Martin	1.50	4.00
16 Jerry Rice	3.00	8.00
17 Steve Young	2.00	5.00
18 Joey Galloway	1.25	3.00
19 Jon Kitna	1.25	3.00
20 Eddie George	1.25	3.00

2000 Aurora

Released as a 150-card set, Aurora features a card design that utilizes both portrait photography and acton photography. A color player portrait photo is placed on the left side of the card, while a black and white player action photo is set against a circle in the upper right hand corner of the card. Background colors are set to match the featured player's team colors, and cards are accented with gold foil highlights. Aurora was packaged in 36-pack boxes with packs containing six cards each.

COMPLETE SET (150)	12.50	30.00
1 David Boston	.15	.40
2 Thomas Jones RC	.50	1.25
3 Rob Moore	.15	.40
4 Jake Plummer	.20	.50
5 Frank Sanders	.15	.40
6 Jamal Anderson	.20	.50
7 Chris Chandler	.20	.50
8 Tim Dwight	.20	.50
9 Doug Johnson RC	.30	.75
10 Tony Banks	.15	.40
11 Qadry Ismail	.20	.50
12 Jamal Lewis RC	.40	1.00
13 Chris Redman RC	.30	.75
14 Travis Taylor RC	.30	.75
15 Doug Flutie	.25	.60
16 Rob Johnson	.20	.50
17 Eric Moulds	.20	.50
18 Peerless Price	.20	.50
19 Antowain Smith	.20	.50
20 Steve Beuerlein	.20	.50
21 Tim Biakabutuka	.20	.50
22 Patrick Jeffers	.20	.50
23 Muhsin Muhammad	.20	.50
24 Curtis Enis	.15	.40
25 Cade McNown	.15	.40
26 Marcus Robinson	.20	.50
27 Dez White RC	.30	.75
28 Corey Dillon	.20	.50
29 Ron Dugans RC	.25	.60
30 Darnay Scott	.20	.50
31 Akili Smith	.15	.40
32 Peter Warrick RC	.40	1.00
33 Tim Couch	.20	.50
34 JaJuan Dawson RC	.25	.60
35 Kevin Johnson	.15	.40
36 Dennis Northcutt RC	.30	.75
37 Travis Prentice RC	.30	.75
38 Troy Aikman	.40	1.00
39 Rocket Ismail	.20	.50
40 Emmitt Smith	.60	1.50
41 Jason Tucker	.15	.40
42 Terrell Davis	.25	.60
43 Olandis Gary	.20	.50
44 Brian Griese	.20	.50
45 Ed McCaffrey	.20	.50
46 Rod Smith	.20	.50
47 Charlie Batch	.20	.50
48 Germane Crowell	.15	.40
49 Reuben Droughns RC	.40	1.00
50 Herman Moore	.20	.50
51 Barry Sanders	.50	1.25
52 Brett Favre	.75	2.00
53 Bubba Franks RC	.40	1.00
54 Antonio Freeman	.20	.50
55 Dorsey Levens	.20	.50
56 Bill Schroeder	.20	.50
57 Marvin Harrison	.25	.60
58 Edgerrin James	.25	.60
59 Peyton Manning	.60	1.50
60 Terrence Wilkins	.15	.40
61 Mark Brunell	.20	.50
62 Keenan McCardell	.20	.50
63 Jimmy Smith	.20	.50
64 R.Jay Soward RC	.25	.60
65 Shyrone Stith RC	.25	.60
66 Fred Taylor	.25	.60
67 Derrick Alexander	.15	.40
68 Donnell Bennett	.15	.40
69 Tony Gonzalez	.25	.60
70 Elvis Grbac	.15	.40
71 Sylvester Morris RC	.25	.60
72 Damon Huard	.20	.50
73 James Johnson	.15	.40
74 Dan Marino	.75	2.00
75 Tony Martin	.20	.50
76 O.J. McDuffie	.20	.50
77 Quinton Spotwood RC	.25	.60
78 Cris Carter	.25	.60
79 Daunte Culpepper	.20	.50
80 Randy Moss	.25	.60
81 Robert Smith	.20	.50
82 Troy Walters RC	.25	.60
83 Drew Bledsoe	.25	.60
84 Tom Brady RC	10.00	25.00
85 Kevin Faulk	.20	.50
86 Terry Glenn	.20	.50
87 J.R. Redmond RC	.25	.60
88 Marc Bulger RC	.40	1.00
89 Sherrod Gideon RC	.25	.60
90 Keith Poole	.15	.40
91 Ricky Williams	.25	.60
92 Kerry Collins	.20	.50
93 Ron Dayne RC	.40	1.00
94 Ike Hilliard	.20	.50
95 Amani Toomer	.20	.50
96 Wayne Chrebet	.20	.50
97 Laveranues Coles RC	.40	1.00
98 Curtis Martin	.25	.60
99 Chad Pennington RC	.60	1.50
100 Vinny Testaverde	.20	.50
101 Tim Brown	.25	.60
102 Rich Gannon	.20	.50
103 Napoleon Kaufman	.20	.50
104 Jerry Porter RC	.40	1.00
105 Tyrone Wheatley	.15	.40
106 Charles Johnson	.15	.40
107 Donovan McNabb	.25	.60
108 Todd Pinkston RC	.25	.60
109 Duce Staley	.20	.50
110 Jerome Bettis	.25	.60
111 Plaxico Burress RC	.40	1.00
112 Troy Edwards	.15	.40
113 Richard Huntley	.15	.40
114 Tee Martin RC	.40	1.00
115 Kordell Stewart	.20	.50
116 Isaac Bruce	.25	.60
117 Trung Canidate RC	.30	.75
118 Marshall Faulk	.25	.60
119 Torry Holt	.25	.60
120 Kurt Warner	.40	1.00
121 Jermaine Fazande	.15	.40
122 Trevor Gaylor RC	.25	.60
123 Jim Harbaugh	.20	.50
124 Junior Seau	.25	.60
125 Giovanni Carmazzi RC	.25	.60
126 Charlie Garner	.20	.50
127 Terrell Owens	.25	.60
128 Jerry Rice	.50	1.25
129 J.J. Stokes	.20	.50
130 Steve Young	.30	.75
131 Shaun Alexander RC	.50	1.25
132 Christian Fauria	.15	.40
133 Jon Kitna	.20	.50
134 Derrick Mayes	.15	.40
135 Ricky Watters	.20	.50
136 Mike Alstott	.25	.60
137 Warrick Dunn	.20	.50
138 Jacquez Green	.15	.40
139 Joe Hamilton RC	.25	.60
140 Shaun King	.15	.40
141 Eddie George	.20	.50
142 Jevon Kearse	.20	.50
143 Steve McNair	.25	.60
144 Yancey Thigpen	.15	.40
145 Frank Wycheck	.20	.50
146 Albert Connell	.15	.40
147 Stephen Davis	.20	.50
148 Todd Husak RC	.25	.60
149 Brad Johnson	.20	.50
150 Michael Westbrook	.15	.40
S1 Jon Kitna Sample	.40	1.00

2000 Aurora Pinstripes

COMPLETE SET (50)	30.00	50.00
*VETERANS: 1.2X TO 3X BASIC CARDS		
*ROOKIES: .8X TO 2X BASIC CARDS		

2000 Aurora Premiere Date

*VETERANS: 8X TO 20X BASIC CARDS		
*ROOKIES: 5X TO 12X BASIC CARDS		
*PD PINSTRIPE: .4X TO 1X PREM.DATE		
STATED PRINT RUN 85 SER.#'d SETS		
84 Tom Brady	150.00	300.00

2000 Aurora Autographs

ANNOUNCED PRINT RUNS BELOW		
2 Thomas Jones/350*	10.00	25.00
12 Jamal Lewis/325*	8.00	20.00
14 Travis Taylor/150*	8.00	20.00
26 Marcus Robinson/350*	8.00	20.00
27 Dez White/350*	8.00	20.00
29 Ron Dugans/250*	6.00	15.00
32 Peter Warrick	10.00	25.00
34 JaJuan Dawson/350*	6.00	15.00
43 Olandis Gary/350*	8.00	20.00
49 Reuben Droughns/350*	10.00	25.00
61 Mark Brunell/100*	10.00	25.00
63 Jimmy Smith/350*	8.00	20.00
66 Fred Taylor	10.00	25.00
71 Sylvester Morris/350*	6.00	15.00
77 Quinton Spotwood/350*	6.00	15.00
88 Marc Bulger/350*	10.00	25.00
93 Ron Dayne/150*	10.00	25.00
97 Laveranues Coles/250*	10.00	25.00
99 Chad Pennington/150*	12.00	30.00
131 Shaun Alexander/350*	10.00	25.00
139 Joe Hamilton/350*	6.00	15.00
147 Stephen Davis/335*	8.00	20.00

2000 Aurora Championship Fever

COMPLETE SET (20)	12.50	30.00
STATED ODDS 4:37		
*COPPER/160: 2X TO 5X BASIC INSERTS		
*PLAT.BLUE/145: 2X TO 5X BASIC INSERTS		
PLAT.BLUE PRINT RUN 145 SER.#'d SETS		
*SILVER/310: .8X TO 2X BASIC INSERTS		
SILVER PRINT RUN 310 SER.#'d SETS		
1 Thomas Jones	.60	1.50
2 Jamal Lewis	.50	1.25
3 Peter Warrick	.50	1.25
4 Tim Couch	.40	1.00
5 Emmitt Smith	1.25	3.00
6 Olandis Gary	.40	1.00
7 Marvin Harrison	.50	1.25
8 Edgerrin James	.50	1.25
9 Mark Brunell	.40	1.00
10 Fred Taylor	.50	1.25
11 Randy Moss	.50	1.25
12 Chad Pennington	.75	2.00
13 Plaxico Burress	.50	1.25
14 Marshall Faulk	.50	1.25
15 Kurt Warner	.75	2.00
16 Shaun Alexander	.60	1.50
17 Jon Kitna	.40	1.00
17AU Jon Kitna AUTO	6.00	15.00
18 Eddie George	.40	1.00
19 Shaun King	.30	.75
20 Stephen Davis	.40	1.00

2000 Aurora Game Worn Jerseys

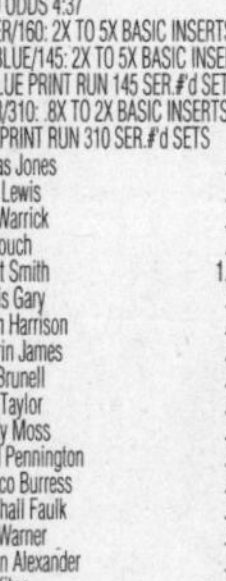

UNPRICED PATCH PRINT RUN 10		
1 Olandis Gary	6.00	15.00
2 Brett Favre	25.00	60.00
3 Mark Brunell	6.00	15.00
4 Cris Carter	8.00	20.00
5 Randy Moss	8.00	20.00
6 Ricky Williams	8.00	20.00
7 Donovan McNabb	8.00	20.00
8 Duce Staley	6.00	15.00
9 Junior Seau	8.00	20.00
10 Steve McNair	8.00	20.00

2000 Aurora Helmet Styrotechs

COMPLETE SET (20)	40.00	80.00
STATED ODDS 1:37		
1 Jake Plummer	1.25	3.00
2 Cade McNown	1.00	2.50
3 Tim Couch	1.25	3.00
4 Troy Aikman	2.50	6.00
5 Emmitt Smith	4.00	10.00
6 Barry Sanders	3.00	8.00
7 Terrell Davis	1.50	4.00
8 Brett Favre	5.00	12.00
9 Edgerrin James	1.50	4.00
10 Peyton Manning	4.00	10.00
11 Mark Brunell	1.25	3.00
12 Fred Taylor	1.50	4.00
13 Drew Bledsoe	1.50	4.00
14 Ricky Williams	1.50	4.00
15 Randy Moss	1.50	4.00
16 Kurt Warner	2.50	6.00
17 Jerry Rice	3.00	8.00
18 Jon Kitna	1.25	3.00
19 Shaun King	1.00	2.50
20 Eddie George	1.25	3.00

2000 Aurora Rookie Draft Board

COMPLETE SET (20)	20.00	50.00
STATED ODDS 2:37 HOB		
1 Thomas Jones	.75	2.00
2 Jamal Lewis	.60	1.50
3 Chris Redman	.50	1.25
4 Travis Taylor	.50	1.25
5 Peter Warrick	.60	1.50
6 Dez White	.50	1.25
7 Dennis Northcutt	.50	1.25
8 Travis Prentice	.50	1.25
9 Reuben Droughns	.60	1.50
10 R.Jay Soward	.40	1.00
11 Sylvester Morris	.40	1.00
12 J.R. Redmond	.40	1.00
13 Ron Dayne	.60	1.50
14 Laveranues Coles	.60	1.50
15 Chad Pennington	1.00	2.50
16 Plaxico Burress	.60	1.50
17 Tee Martin	.60	1.50
18 Trung Canidate	.50	1.25
19 Giovanni Carmazzi	.40	1.00
20 Shaun Alexander	.75	2.00

2000 Aurora Team Players

COMP.HOBBY SET (10)	7.50	20.00
COMP.RETAIL SET (10)	7.50	20.00
1A-10A STATED ODDS 1:37 HOBBY		
1B-10B STATED ODDS 1:37 RETAIL		
1A Troy Aikman	1.25	3.00
1B Emmitt Smith	2.00	5.00
2A Terrell Davis	.75	2.00
2B Brian Griese	.60	1.50
3A Antonio Freeman	.60	1.50
3B Brett Favre	2.50	6.00
4A Peyton Manning	2.00	5.00
4B Edgerrin James	.75	2.00
5A Fred Taylor	.75	2.00
5B Mark Brunell	.60	1.50
6A Randy Moss	.75	2.00
6B Cris Carter	.75	2.00
7A Marshall Faulk	.75	2.00
7B Kurt Warner	1.25	3.00
8A Jerry Rice	1.50	4.00
8B Terrell Owens	.75	2.00
9A Steve McNair	.75	2.00
9B Eddie George	.60	1.50
10A Stephen Davis	.60	1.50
10B Brad Johnson	.60	1.50

1945 Autographs Playing Cards

Cards from this set are part of a playing card game released in 1945 by Leister Game Co. of Toledo Ohio. The cards feature a photo of a famous person, such as an actor or writer, or athlete on the top half of the card with his signature across the middle. A photo appears in the upper left hand corner along with some biographical information about him printed in orange in the center. The bottom half of the cardfront features a drawing along with information about a second personality in the same field or vocation. Those two characters are featured on another card with the positions reversed top and bottom. Note that a card number was also used in the upper left corner with each pair being featured on two of the same card number. We've listed the player who's photo appears on the card first, followed by the personality featured at the bottom of the card.

COMPLETE SET (55)	200.00	400.00
7A Bernie Bierman CO Knute Rockne CO	10.00	20.00
7A Knute Rockne CO Bernie Bierman	10.00	20.00
10 Tom Harmon Red Grange	12.50	25.00
10 Red Grange Tom Harmon	12.50	25.00

1959 Bazooka

The 1959 Bazooka football cards made up the back of the Bazooka Bubble Gum boxes of that year. The cards are blank backed and measure approximately 2 13/16" by 4 15/16". Comparable to the Bazooka baseball cards of that year, they are relatively difficult to obtain and fairly attractive considering they form part of the box. The full boxes contained 20 pieces of chewing gum. The cards are unnumbered but have been numbered alphabetically in the checklist below for your convenience. The cards marked with SP in the checklist below were apparently printed in shorter supply and are more difficult to find. The catalog number for this set is R414-15A. The value of complete intact boxes would be 50 percent greater than the prices listed below.

COMPLETE SET (18)	6,000.00	9,500.00
1 Alan Ameche	175.00	300.00
2 Jon Arnett	150.00	250.00
3 Jim Brown	500.00	800.00
4 Rick Casares	200.00	350.00
5A Charley Conerly SP ERR (Baltimore Colts)	350.00	600.00
5B Charley Conerly SP COR (New York Giants)	350.00	600.00
6 Howard Ferguson	175.00	300.00
7 Frank Gifford	200.00	350.00
8 Lou Groza SP	1,250.00	2,000.00
9 Bobby Layne	200.00	350.00
10 Eddie LeBaron	175.00	300.00
11 Woodley Lewis	150.00	250.00
12 Ollie Matson	175.00	300.00
13 Joe Perry	175.00	300.00
14 Pete Retzlaff	150.00	250.00
15 Tobin Rote	150.00	250.00
16 Y.A. Tittle	250.00	400.00
17 Tom Tracy SP	1,200.00	2,000.00
18 Johnny Unitas	400.00	750.00

1971 Bazooka

The 1971 Bazooka football cards were issued as twelve panels of three on the backs of Bazooka Bubble Gum boxes. Consequently, cards are seen in panels of three or as individual cards which have been cut from panels of three. The individual cards measure approxiamtely 1 15/16" by 2 5/8" and the panels of three measure 2 5/8" by 5 7/8". The 36 individual blank-backed cards are numbered on the card front. The checklist below presents prices for the individual cards. Complete panels are worth 25 percent more than the sum of the individual players making up the panel; complete boxes are worth approximately 50 percent more (i.e., an additional 25 percent premium) than the sum of the three players on the box. With regard to cut single cards, the mid-panel cards (2, 5, 8, ...) seem to be somewhat easier to find in nice shape.

COMPLETE SET (36)	300.00	450.00
1 Joe Namath	25.00	50.00
2 Larry Brown	6.00	12.00
3 Bobby Bell	6.00	12.00
4 Dick Butkus	18.00	30.00
5 Charlie Sanders	6.00	12.00
6 Chuck Howley	6.00	12.00
7 Gale Gillingham	5.00	10.00
8 Leroy Kelly	6.00	12.00
9 Floyd Little	6.00	12.00
10 Dan Abramowicz	5.00	10.00
11 Sonny Jurgensen	10.00	20.00
12 Andy Russell	5.00	10.00
13 Tommy Nobis	6.00	12.00
14 O.J. Simpson	10.00	20.00
15 Tom Woodeshick	5.00	10.00
16 Roman Gabriel	6.00	12.00
17 Claude Humphrey	5.00	10.00
18 Merlin Olsen	7.50	15.00
19 Daryle Lamonica	6.00	12.00
20 Fred Cox	5.00	10.00
21 Bart Starr	30.00	50.00
22 John Brodie	7.50	15.00
23 Jim Nance	5.00	10.00
24 Gary Garrison	5.00	10.00
25 Fran Tarkenton	12.50	25.00
26 Johnny Robinson	5.00	10.00
27 Gale Sayers	18.00	30.00
28 Johnny Unitas	30.00	50.00
29 Jerry LeVias	5.00	10.00
30 Virgil Carter	5.00	10.00
31 Bill Nelsen	5.00	10.00
32 Dave Osborn	5.00	10.00
33 Matt Snell	5.00	10.00
34 Larry Wilson	6.00	12.00
35 Bob Griese	15.00	25.00
36 Lance Alworth	10.00	20.00

1972 Bazooka Official Signals

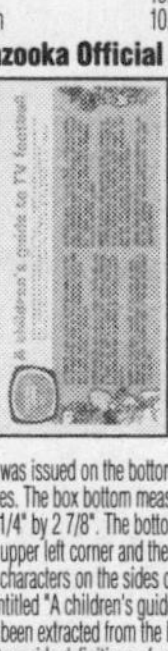

This 12-card set was issued on the bottom of Bazooka Bubble Gum boxes. The box bottom measures approximately 6 1/4" by 2 7/8". The bottoms are numbered in the upper left corner and the text appears between cartoon characters on the sides of the bottom. The material is entitled "A children's guide to TV football," having been extracted from the book Football Lingo. Cards 1-8 provide definitions of numerous terms associated with football. Card number 9 lists the six different officials and describes their responsibilities. Cards 10-12 picture the officials' signals and explain their meanings. The value of complete intact boxes would be 50 percent greater than the prices listed below.

COMPLETE SET (12)	62.50	125.00
1 Football Lingo Automatic through Bread and Butter Play	6.00	12.00
2 Football Lingo Broken-Field Runner through Dive	6.00	12.00
3 Football Lingo Double-Coverage through Interference	6.00	12.00
4 Football Lingo Game Plan through Lateral Pass	6.00	12.00
5 Football Lingo Interception through Man-to-Man Coverage	6.00	12.00
6 Football Lingo Killing the Clock through Punt	6.00	12.00
7 Football Lingo Belly Series through Quick Whistle	6.00	12.00
8 Football Lingo Prevent Defense through Primary Receiver	6.00	12.00
9 Officials' Duties Referee through Line Judge	6.00	12.00
10 Officials' Duties	6.00	12.00
11 Officials' Signals	6.00	12.00
12 Officials' Signals	6.00	12.00

2004 Bazooka

Bazooka initially released in early September 2004. The base set consists of 220-cards including 55 rookies at the end of the set. Hobby boxes contained 24-packs of 8-cards and carried an S.R.P. of $2 per pack. Two parallel sets and a variety of inserts can be found seeded in hobby and retail packs highlighted by an assortment of jersey memorabilia inserts.

COMPLETE SET (220)	20.00	50.00
1 Peyton Manning	.60	1.50
2 Rod Gardner	.20	.50
3 Marc Bulger	.25	.60
4 Champ Bailey	.25	.60
5 Moe Williams	.20	.50
6 Andre' Davis	.20	.50
7 Corey Dillon	.25	.60
8 Trent Green	.25	.60
9 Daunte Culpepper	.25	.60
10 Chad Pennington	.30	.75
11 Hines Ward	.30	.75
12 Tim Brown	.30	.75
13 Jerome Pathon	.20	.50
14 Drew Brees	.30	.75
15 Eddie George	.25	.60
16 Duce Staley	.25	.60
17 Marques Tuiasosopo	.20	.50
18 Willis McGahee	.30	.75
19 T.J. Duckett	.25	.60
20 Brian Urlacher	.30	.75
21 Ashley Lelie	.25	.60
22 Robert Ferguson	.20	.50
23 Tai Streets	.20	.50
24 Junior Seau	.30	.75
25 Priest Holmes	.30	.75
26 Ty Law	.25	.60
27 Correll Buckhalter	.25	.60
28 Plaxico Burress	.25	.60
29 Brad Johnson	.25	.60
30 Shaun Alexander	.25	.60
31 Mark Brunell	.25	.60
32 Julian Peterson	.25	.60
33 Marcel Shipp	.25	.60
34 Kyle Boller	.25	.60
35 Rudi Johnson	.25	.60
36 Quincy Carter	.20	.50
37 Jabar Gaffney	.20	.50
38 Reggie Wayne	.25	.60
39 Deion Branch	.25	.60
40 Terrell Owens	.30	.75
41 Chris Brown	.25	.60
42 Bobby Engram	.25	.60
43 Josh Reed	.25	.60
44 Thomas Jones	.30	.75
45 Stephen Davis	.25	.60
46 Mike Anderson	.25	.60
47 Javon Walker	.25	.60
48 Edgerrin James	.30	.75
49 Randy McMichael	.20	.50
50 Deuce McAllister	.25	.60
51 Nate Burleson	.25	.60
52 Jevon Kearse	.25	.60
53 Jay Fiedler	.20	.50
54 Patrick Ramsey	.25	.60
55 Brian Westbrook	.30	.75
56 Tyrone Calico	.25	.60
57 Alge Crumpler	.25	.60
58 Josh McCown	.25	.60
59 Quincy Morgan	.20	.50
60 Jeff Garcia	.30	.75
61 Garrison Hearst	.25	.60
62 Chad Johnson	.30	.75
63 Byron Leftwich	.30	.75
64 Donald Driver	.25	.60
65 Ricky Williams	.25	.60
66 Todd Pinkston	.20	.50
67 Amani Toomer	.25	.60
68 David Givens	.25	.60
69 Jerome Bettis	.30	.75
70 Derrick Mason	.25	.60
71 Darrell Jackson	.25	.60
72 Kassim Osgood	.20	.50
73 Todd Heap	.25	.60
74 Warrick Dunn	.25	.60
75 Brett Favre	.75	2.00
76 Chris Chambers	.25	.60
77 Fred Taylor	.25	.60
78 Charles Rogers	.25	.60
79 Onterrio Smith	.20	.50
80 Joe Horn	.25	.60
81 Justin McCareins	.20	.50
82 Ike Hilliard	.20	.50
83 Kevan Barlow	.20	.50
84 Charlie Garner	.25	.60
85 Anquan Boldin	.30	.75
86 Anthony Thomas	.25	.60
87 Julius Peppers	.25	.60
88 Dat Nguyen	.20	.50
89 Peerless Price	.20	.50
90 Randy Moss	.30	.75
91 Jamie Sharper	.20	.50
92 Travis Henry	.20	.50
93 Terrell Suggs	.25	.60
94 Joey Galloway	.25	.60
95 Torry Holt	.30	.75
96 Freddie Mitchell	.20	.50
97 Jerry Porter	.25	.60
98 Dwight Freeney	.25	.60
99 Joey Harrington	.25	.60
100 Michael Vick	.40	1.00
101 Kelley Washington	.20	.50
102 Marty Booker	.20	.50
103 Tim Rattay	.20	.50
104 Derrick Brooks	.25	.60
105 Laveranues Coles	.25	.60
106 Ray Lewis	.30	.75
107 Jon Kitna	.25	.60
108 Terry Glenn	.25	.60
109 Steve Smith	.30	.75
110 Ahman Green	.25	.60
111 Andre Johnson	.30	.75
112 Dallas Clark	.25	.60
113 Kevin Faulk	.25	.60
114 Michael Bennett	.25	.60
115 Tony Gonzalez	.30	.75
116 Michael Strahan	.30	.75
117 Tommy Maddox	.25	.60
118 Isaac Bruce	.25	.60
119 Brandon Lloyd	.25	.60
120 Steve McNair	.30	.75
121 Keith Brooking	.20	.50
122 Drew Bledsoe	.30	.75
123 Peter Warrick	.25	.60
124 Antonio Bryant	.25	.60
125 Clinton Portis	.30	.75
126 Kelly Holcomb	.20	.50
127 Jake Delhomme	.25	.60
128 Rod Smith	.25	.60
129 Lee Suggs	.25	.60
130 Domanick Davis	.20	.50
131 Carson Palmer	.30	.75
132 Kerry Collins	.25	.60
133 Teyo Johnson	.20	.50
134 Curtis Martin	.30	.75
135 Matt Hasselbeck	.25	.60
136 Cedrick Wilson	.20	.50
137 Eric Moulds	.25	.60
138 Keyshawn Johnson	.25	.60
139 Dante Hall	.25	.60
140 Jamal Lewis	.25	.60
141 Kelly Campbell	.20	.50
142 Jeremy Shockey	.25	.60
143 Jerry Rice	.60	1.50
144 Kurt Warner	.30	.75
145 Jake Plummer	.25	.60
146 Keenan McCardell	.20	.50
147 Jimmy Smith	.25	.60
148 Zach Thomas	.30	.75
149 Eddie Kennison	.25	.60
150 Tom Brady	.60	1.50
151 Donte' Stallworth	.20	.50
152 John Abraham	.20	.50
153 Koren Robinson	.20	.50
154 Rex Grossman	.25	.60
155 Donovan McNabb	.30	.75
156 David Carr	.20	.50
157 David Boston	.20	.50
158 Tiki Barber	.30	.75
159 Santana Moss	.25	.60
160 LaDainian Tomlinson	.30	.75
161 Justin Fargas	.25	.60
162 Troy Brown	.25	.60
163 Marshall Faulk	.30	.75
164 Aaron Brooks	.25	.60
165 Marvin Harrison	.30	.75
166 Kevin Jones RC	.50	1.25
167 Michael Clayton RC	.50	1.25
168 Bernard Berrian RC	.60	1.50
169 Ben Watson RC	.60	1.50
170 Philip Rivers RC	2.50	6.00
171 Vince Wilfork RC	.60	1.50
172 Jason Babin RC	.60	1.50
173 Marcus Tubbs RC	.40	1.00
174 Sean Taylor RC	1.25	3.00
175 Larry Fitzgerald RC	1.50	4.00
176 Craig Krenzel RC	.50	1.25
177 Cedric Cobbs RC	.40	1.00
178 Lee Evans RC	.60	1.50
179 Johnnie Morant RC	.40	1.00
180 Kellen Winslow RC	.60	1.50
181 Mewelde Moore RC	.50	1.25
182 Carlos Francis RC	.40	1.00
183 Josh Harris RC	.40	1.00
184 Julius Jones RC	.50	1.25
185 Reggie Williams RC	.50	1.25
186 DeAngelo Hall RC	.60	1.50
187 D.J. Williams RC	.60	1.50
188 Cody Pickett RC	.50	1.25
189 Dunta Robinson RC	.40	1.00
190 J.P. Losman RC	.50	1.25
191 Jonathan Vilma RC	.60	1.50
192 Jericho Cotchery RC	.50	1.25
193 Keary Colbert RC	.40	1.00
194 Ben Troupe RC	.50	1.25
195 Drew Henson RC	.40	1.00
196 Chris Gamble RC	.50	1.25
197 Samie Parker RC	.40	1.00
198 Tatum Bell RC	.50	1.25
199 Robert Gallery RC	.60	1.50
200 Eli Manning RC	4.00	10.00
201 Ahmad Carroll RC	.40	1.00
202 Devery Henderson RC	.60	1.50
203 Matt Schaub RC	1.25	3.00
204 Greg Jones RC	.40	1.00
205 Roy Williams RC	.60	1.50
206 Tommie Harris RC	.60	1.50
207 Jeff Smoker RC	.50	1.25
208 Kenechi Udeze RC	.50	1.25
209 Derrick Hamilton RC	.40	1.00
210 Ben Roethlisberger RC	4.00	10.00
211 Darius Watts RC	.40	1.00
212 John Navarre RC	.40	1.00
213 Ernest Wilford RC	.50	1.25
214 Rashaun Woods RC	.40	1.00
215 Steven Jackson RC	1.00	2.50
216 Michael Jenkins RC	.60	1.50
217 Will Smith RC	.50	1.25
218 Devard Darling RC	.40	1.00
219 Chris Perry RC	.50	1.25
220 Luke McCown RC	.50	1.25

2004 Bazooka Gold

COMPLETE SET (220)	40.00	80.00
*GOLD STARS: 1.2X TO 3X BASE CARD HI		
*GOLD ROOKIES: .8X TO 2X BASE CARD HI		
ONE GOLD PER PACK		

2004 Bazooka Minis

COMPLETE SET (220)	40.00	80.00
*MINI STARS: 1.2X TO 3X BASE CARD HI		
*MINI ROOKIES: .8X TO 2X BASE CARD HI		
MINI STATED ODDS 1:1		

2004 Bazooka All-Stars Jerseys

STATED ODDS 1:17		
BASAB Alex Bannister	3.00	8.00
BASAC Alge Crumpler	3.00	8.00
BASAW Aeneas Williams	3.00	8.00
BASBM Brock Marion	3.00	8.00
BASCC Corey Chavous	3.00	8.00
BASCH Casey Hampton	3.00	8.00
BASCM Chris McAlister	3.00	8.00
BASDB Dre Bly	3.00	8.00
BASDM Derrick Mason	3.00	8.00
BASER Ed Reed	4.00	10.00
BASFA Flozell Adams	3.00	8.00
BASFB Fred Beasley	3.00	8.00

BASJA Jerry Azumah 3.00 8.00
BASJO Jonathan Ogden 3.00 8.00
BASJP Julian Peterson 3.00 8.00
BASJW Jeff Wilkins 3.00 8.00
BASJWO Jerome Woods 3.00 8.00
BASKJ Kris Jenkins 3.00 8.00
BASKM Kevin Mawae 3.00 8.00
BASKBU Keith Bulluck 3.00 8.00
BASLG La'Roi Glover 3.00 8.00
BASLL Leonard Little 3.00 8.00
BASMR Marco Rivera 3.00 8.00
BASMV Mike Vanderjagt 3.00 8.00
BASOP Orlando Pace 3.00 8.00
BASPS Patrick Surtain 3.00 8.00
BASRB Ruben Brown 3.00 8.00
BASRS Richard Seymour 4.00 10.00
BASRW Roy Williams S 4.00 10.00
BASSE Shaun Ellis 3.00 8.00
BASTR Tony Richardson 3.00 8.00
BASTS Takeo Spikes 3.00 8.00
BASTV Troy Vincent 3.00 8.00
BASWJ Walter Jones 3.00 8.00
BASWS Will Shields 3.00 8.00

2004 Bazooka College Collection Jerseys

STATED ODDS 1:115
BCCAB Anquan Boldin 4.00 10.00
BCCCP Carson Palmer 5.00 12.00
BCCCPI Cody Pickett 4.00 10.00
BCCDA Derek Abney 3.00 8.00
BCCDD Devard Darling 3.00 8.00
BCCJRT J.R. Tolver 3.00 8.00
BCCLD Lane Danielsen 3.00 8.00
BCCMS Matt Schaub 8.00 20.00
BCCWW Wes Welker 12.50 25.00

2004 Bazooka Comics

COMPLETE SET (24) 10.00 25.00
STATED ODDS 1:4
1 Anquan Boldin .75 2.00
2 Brett Favre 2.00 5.00
3 Bruce Smith .75 2.00
4 Clinton Portis .75 2.00
5 Dante Hall .60 1.50
6 Domanick Davis .50 1.25
7 Jamal Lewis .60 1.50
8 Jerry Rice 1.50 4.00
9 LaDainian Tomlinson .75 2.00
10 Marvin Harrison .75 2.00
11 Mike Vanderjagt .50 1.25
12 New England Patriots .50 1.25
13 Peyton Manning 1.50 4.00
14 Priest Holmes .75 2.00
15 Randy Moss .75 2.00
16 Shannon Sharpe .75 2.00
17 Steve McNair .75 2.00
18 Terrell Suggs .60 1.50
19 Tom Brady 1.50 4.00
20 Tony Gonzalez .75 2.00
21 Torry Holt .60 1.50
22 Michael Vick 1.00 2.50
23 Ricky Williams .60 1.50
24 Jake Delhomme .60 1.50

2004 Bazooka Originals Jerseys

STATED ODDS 1:21
BOBB Bernard Berrian 2.50 6.00
BOBR Ben Roethlisberger 8.00 20.00
BOBT Ben Troupe 2.00 5.00
BOBW Ben Watson 2.00 5.00
BOCC Cedric Cobbs 2.00 5.00
BOCP Chris Perry 2.50 6.00
BODD Devard Darling 2.00 5.00
BODH DeAngelo Hall 2.50 6.00
BODHA Derrick Hamilton 2.00 5.00
BODHE Devery Henderson 2.00 5.00
BODR Dunta Robinson 2.00 5.00
BODW Darius Watts 2.00 5.00
BOEM Eli Manning 8.00 20.00
BOGJ Greg Jones 2.50 6.00
BOJJ Julius Jones 3.00 8.00
BOJPL J.P. Losman 2.50 6.00
BOKC Keary Colbert 2.00 5.00
BOKJ Kevin Jones 3.00 8.00
BOKW Kellen Winslow Jr. 2.50 6.00
BOLE Lee Evans 2.50 6.00
BOLF Larry Fitzgerald 5.00 12.00
BOLM Luke McCown 2.50 6.00
BOMC Michael Clayton 2.50 6.00
BOMJ Michael Jenkins 2.00 5.00
BOMM Mewelde Moore 2.00 5.00
BOMS Matt Schaub 5.00 12.00
BOPR Philip Rivers 5.00 12.00
BORG Robert Gallery 2.00 5.00
BORW Roy Williams WR 2.50 6.00
BORWI Reggie Williams 2.00 5.00
BORWO Rashaun Woods 2.50 6.00
BOSJ Steven Jackson 5.00 12.00
BOTB Tatum Bell 2.50 6.00

2004 Bazooka Rookie Roundup Jerseys

STATED ODDS 1:115
RRBT Ben Troupe 3.00 8.00
RRDR Dunta Robinson 2.50 6.00
RRJT Joey Thomas 2.50 6.00
RRKR Keiwan Ratliff 2.50 6.00
RRKS Keith Smith 2.50 6.00
RRPR Philip Rivers 10.00 20.00
RRRC Ricardo Colclough 3.00 8.00
RRRG Robert Gallery 3.00 8.00
RRTA Tim Anderson 4.00 10.00

2004 Bazooka Stickers

STATED ODDS 1:4
1 Champ Bailey .60 1.50
Ty Law
DeAngelo Hall
Dunta Robinson
2 Jevon Kearse 1.00 2.50
Julius Peppers
Dwight Freeney
Michael Strahan
3 John Abraham 1.25 3.00
Brian Urlacher
Junior Seau
Jonathan Vilma
4 Julian Peterson .60 1.50
Dat Nguyen
Jamie Sharper
Terrell Suggs
5 Derrick Brooks 1.00 2.50
Ray Lewis
Keith Brooking
Zach Thomas
6 Peyton Manning 2.50 6.00
Brett Favre
Donovan McNabb
Michael Vick
7 Chad Pennington 2.50 6.00
Daunte Culpepper
Tom Brady
Steve McNair
8 Mark Brunell 1.00 2.50
Jeff Garcia
Kurt Warner
Kerry Collins
9 Kyle Boller 1.25 3.00
Carson Palmer
Rex Grossman
Byron Leftwich
10 Trent Green 1.00 2.50
Marc Bulger
Matt Hasselbeck
Jake Delhomme
11 Jon Kitna 1.00 2.50
Drew Brees
Jay Fiedler
Kelly Holcomb
12 Tim Rattay .50 1.25
Josh McCown
Marques Tuiasosopo
Quincy Carter
13 Brad Johnson 1.00 2.50
Tommy Maddox
Drew Bledsoe
Jake Plummer
14 David Carr 1.00 2.50
Aaron Brooks
Joey Harrington
Patrick Ramsey
15 Corey Dillon .60 1.50
Duce Staley
Charlie Garner
Garrison Hearst
16 Eddie George 1.00 2.50
Stephen Davis
Jerome Bettis
Curtis Martin
17 Deuce McAllister 1.00 2.50
Clinton Portis
LaDainian Tomlinson
Ahman Green
18 Priest Holmes 1.25 3.00
Jamal Lewis
Ricky Williams
Marshall Faulk
19 Rudi Johnson 1.00 2.50
Lee Suggs
Domanick Davis
Brian Westbrook
20 Justin Fargas 1.00 2.50
Chris Brown
Willis McGahee
Onterrio Smith
21 Fred Taylor 1.00 2.50
Shaun Alexander
Edgerrin James
Travis Henry
22 Mike Anderson .60 1.50
Correll Buckhalter
Kevin Faulk
Moe Williams
23 Warrick Dunn .60 1.50
Tiki Barber
Michael Bennett
Thomas Jones
24 Marcel Shipp .60 1.50
Kevan Barlow
T.J. Duckett
Anthony Thomas
25 Randy McMichael .60 1.50
Alge Crumpler
Dallas Clark
Teyo Johnson
26 Tony Gonzalez 1.00 2.50
Jeremy Shockey
Todd Heap
Dante Hall
27 Amani Toomer .60 1.50
Joe Horn
Jimmy Smith
Eric Moulds
28 Isaac Bruce .60 1.50
Keenan McCardell
Donald Driver
Tim Brown
29 Isaac Bruce 1.00 2.50
Keenan McCardell
Donald Driver
Tim Brown
30 Jerry Rice 2.00 5.00
Rod Smith
Troy Brown
Terry Glenn
31 Derrick Mason 1.00 2.50
Hines Ward
Laveranues Coles
Darrell Jackson
32 Santana Moss 1.00 2.50
Steve Smith
Jerry Porter
Chris Chambers
33 Kelly Campbell .50 1.25
Kassim Osgood
Brandon Lloyd
Robert Ferguson
34 David Boston 1.00 2.50
Terrell Owens
Joey Galloway
Keyshawn Johnson
35 Randy Moss 1.25 3.00
Chad Johnson
Marvin Harrison
Torry Holt
36 Rod Gardner .60 1.50
Reggie Wayne
Justin McCareins
Quincy Morgan
37 Plaxico Burress .60 1.50
Ashley Lelie
Koren Robinson
Donte' Stallworth
38 Peerless Price .60 1.50
Marty Booker
Eddie Kennison
Todd Pinkston
39 Ike Hilliard .50 1.25
Jerome Pathon
Tai Streets
Bobby Engram
40 Andre' Davis .50 1.25
Josh Reed
Jabar Gaffney
Antonio Bryant
41 Nate Burleson .60 1.50
Deion Branch
Kelley Washington
Javon Walker
42 Cedrick Wilson .60 1.50
David Givens
Peter Warrick
Freddie Mitchell
43 Vince Wilfork 1.00 2.50
Tommie Harris
Teddy Lehman
D.J. Williams
44 Will Smith 1.00 2.50
Kenechi Udeze
Jason Babin
Robert Gallery
45 Eli Manning 4.00 10.00
Philip Rivers
Ben Roethlisberger
J.P. Losman
46 Steven Jackson 2.00 5.00
Chris Perry
Kevin Jones
Tatum Bell
47 Darius Watts 1.25 3.00
Keary Colbert
Derrick Hamilton
Bernard Berrian
48 Kellen Winslow 1.00 2.50
Ben Watson
Ben Troupe
Devard Darling
49 Josh Harris .75 2.00
Jeff Smoker
John Navarre
Cody Pickett
50 Larry Fitzgerald 2.50 6.00
Roy Williams
Reggie Williams
Lee Evans
51 Matt Schaub 2.00 5.00
Luke McCown
Craig Krenzel
Drew Henson
52 Carlos Francis .75 2.00
Samie Parker
Jerricho Cotchery
Ernest Wilford
53 Sean Taylor 1.00 2.50
Ahmad Carroll
Chris Gamble
Johnnie Morant
54 Julius Jones 1.25 3.00
Greg Jones
Mewelde Moore
Cedric Cobbs
55 Michael Clayton 1.50 4.00
Michael Jenkins
Rashaun Woods
Devery Henderson

2004 Bazooka Tattoos

COMPLETE SET (33) 6.00 15.00
STATED ODDS 1:6
1 Arizona Cardinals .30 .75
2 Atlanta Falcons .30 .75
3 Baltimore Ravens .30 .75
4 Buffalo Bills .40 1.00
5 Carolina Panthers .30 .75
6 Chicago Bears .40 1.00
7 Cincinnati Bengals .30 .75
8 Cleveland Browns .30 .75
9 Dallas Cowboys .50 1.25
10 Denver Broncos .40 1.00
11 Detroit Lions .30 .75
12 Green Bay Packers .50 1.25
13 Houston Texans .30 .75
14 Indianapolis Colts .30 .75
15 Jacksonville Jaguars .30 .75
16 Kansas City Chiefs .40 1.00
17 Miami Dolphins .40 1.00
18 Minnesota Vikings .30 .75
19 New England Patriots .40 1.00
20 New Orleans Saints .30 .75
21 New York Giants .40 1.00
22 New York Jets .40 1.00
23 Oakland Raiders .50 1.25
24 Philadelphia Eagles .30 .75
25 Pittsburgh Steelers .40 1.00
26 St. Louis Rams .30 .75
27 San Diego Chargers .30 .75
28 San Francisco 49ers .50 1.25
29 Seattle Seahawks .30 .75
30 Tampa Bay Buccaneers .30 .75
31 Tennessee Titans .30 .75
32 Washington Redskins .50 1.25
33 Bazooka Logo .30 .75

2005 Bazooka

This 220-card set was released in August, 2005. The set was issued into the hobby in six-card packs with an $1.99 SRP which came 24 packs to a box. Cards numbered 1-165 feature veterans while cards 166-220 feature 2005 rookies.

COMPLETE SET (220) 20.00 50.00
COMP.SET w/o RC's (165) 10.00 25.00
1 Willis McGahee .30 .75
2 Aaron Brooks .20 .50
3 Allen Rossum .20 .50
4 Brett Favre .75 2.00
5 Donovan McNabb .30 .75
6 Torry Holt .25 .60
7 Michael Vick .30 .75
8 David Carr .20 .50
9 Eric Moulds .20 .50
10 Chad Pennington .30 .75
11 Larry Fitzgerald .30 .75
12 Tom Brady .60 1.50
13 Derrick Brooks .25 .60
14 Brandon Stokley .20 .50
15 Justin McCareins .20 .50
16 Champ Bailey .25 .60
17 Jake Delhomme .25 .60
18 Peyton Manning .60 1.50
19 Keyshawn Johnson .25 .60
20 Daunte Culpepper .25 .60
21 Chester Taylor .25 .60
22 Kurt Warner .30 .75
23 Cedrick Wilson .20 .50
24 Brian Westbrook .25 .60
25 Rodney Harrison .25 .60
26 Clinton Portis .25 .60
27 A.J. Feeley .20 .50
28 Curtis Martin .30 .75
29 Chris Perry .20 .50
30 Randy Moss .30 .75
31 Darrell Jackson .20 .50
32 Edgerrin James .25 .60
33 Ben Roethlisberger .50 1.25
34 Kevin Jones .20 .50
35 LaMont Jordan .25 .60
36 Jerome Bettis .30 .75
37 Ahman Green .25 .60
38 Tyrone Calico .20 .50
39 Anquan Boldin .25 .60
40 Dante Hall .20 .50
41 Todd Heap .25 .60
42 Corey Dillon .25 .60
43 Julius Peppers .25 .60
44 Antonio Bryant .20 .50
45 Dunta Robinson .20 .50
46 Michael Pittman .20 .50
47 Billy Volek .20 .50
48 Jimmy Smith .25 .60
49 Carson Palmer .30 .75
50 Derrick Blaylock .20 .50
51 Deuce McAllister .25 .60
52 Ray Lewis .30 .75
53 Chad Johnson .25 .60
54 Zach Thomas .30 .75
55 Julius Jones .20 .50
56 D.J. Williams .20 .50
57 Stephen Davis .25 .60
58 Greg Jones .20 .50
59 J.P. Losman .20 .50
60 Trent Green .25 .60
61 Drew Bennett .25 .60
62 Joe Horn .25 .60
63 Mewelde Moore .20 .50
64 Alge Crumpler .25 .60
65 Javon Walker .20 .50
66 Jake Plummer .25 .60
67 Aaron Stecker .20 .50
68 Keary Colbert .20 .50
69 Joey Harrington .25 .60
70 Brian Urlacher .30 .75
71 Jeremy Shockey .30 .75
72 Duce Staley .25 .60
73 Tim Rattay .20 .50
74 Jerry Porter .20 .50
75 Steven Jackson .30 .75
76 David Givens .20 .50
77 Byron Leftwich .25 .60
78 T.J. Duckett .20 .50
79 Jason Witten .30 .75
80 Andre Johnson .30 .75
81 Amani Toomer .25 .60
82 Kellen Winslow .25 .60
83 Kyle Boller .25 .60
84 Santana Moss .25 .60
85 Antonio Gates .30 .75
86 Lee Evans .25 .60
87 Larry Johnson .25 .60
88 Plaxico Burress .25 .60
89 Reuben Droughns .20 .50
90 Eli Manning .50 1.25
91 Lito Sheppard .25 .60
92 DeAngelo Hall .25 .60
93 Josh McCown .25 .60
94 Eric Parker .20 .50
95 Drew Brees .30 .75
96 Fred Taylor .25 .60
97 Jonathan Vilma .25 .60
98 Michael Strahan .30 .75
99 Dwight Freeney .25 .60
100 Kerry Collins .25 .60
101 Hines Ward .30 .75
102 Lee Suggs .20 .50
103 Luke McCown .20 .50
104 Laveranues Coles .20 .50
105 LaDainian Tomlinson .30 .75
106 Jeff Garcia .25 .60
107 Michael Clayton .20 .50
108 DeShaun Foster .25 .60
109 Rex Grossman .25 .60
110 Priest Holmes .25 .60
111 Roy Williams WR .25 .60
112 Drew Henson .20 .50
113 Derrick Mason .25 .60
114 Michael Bennett .25 .60
115 Chris Simms .25 .60
116 Isaac Bruce .25 .60
117 Deion Branch .20 .50
118 Rudi Johnson .25 .60
119 Nate Burleson .20 .50
120 Warrick Dunn .25 .60
121 Brian Griese .25 .60
122 T.J. Houshmandzadeh .25 .60
123 Jamaar Taylor .20 .50
124 Drew Bledsoe .30 .75
125 Najeh Davenport .25 .60
126 Charles Rogers .20 .50
127 Ronald Curry .20 .50
128 Chris Brown .20 .50
129 Doug Gabriel .20 .50
130 Todd Pinkston .20 .50
131 Marc Bulger .25 .60
132 Marshall Faulk .30 .75
133 Marvin Harrison .30 .75
134 Matt Hasselbeck .25 .60
135 Tiki Barber .30 .75
136 Muhsin Muhammad .25 .60
137 Kevan Barlow .20 .50
138 Chris Chambers .25 .60
139 Donald Driver .30 .75
140 Jamal Lewis .25 .60
141 Rashaun Woods .20 .50
142 Steve McNair .30 .75
143 Reggie Wayne .30 .75
144 Jevon Kearse .25 .60
145 Domanick Davis .20 .50
146 Donte Stallworth .20 .50
147 Chris Gamble .20 .50
148 Philip Rivers .30 .75
149 Sean Taylor .30 .75
150 Antwaan Randle El .25 .60
151 Koren Robinson .20 .50
152 Tatum Bell .20 .50
153 Tony Gonzalez .25 .60
154 Reggie Williams .20 .50
155 Onterrio Smith .20 .50
156 Patrick Ramsey .25 .60
157 Thomas Jones .30 .75
158 Michael Jenkins .25 .60
159 Rod Smith .25 .60
160 Trent Dilfer .25 .60
161 Randy McMichael .20 .50
162 Terrell Owens .30 .75
163 Travis Henry .20 .50
164 Travis Taylor .20 .50
165 Shaun Alexander .25 .60
166 J.J. Arrington RC .50 1.25
167 Cedric Benson RC .60 1.50
168 Carlos Rogers RC .60 1.50
169 Troy Williamson RC .50 1.25
170 Ronnie Brown RC .75 2.00
171 Jason Campbell RC .75 2.00
172 Alvin Pearman RC .40 1.00
173 Reggie Brown RC .40 1.00
174 Lionel Gates RC .40 1.00
175 Derek Anderson RC .50 1.25
176 Craphonso Thorpe RC .40 1.00
177 Frank Gore RC 1.00 2.50
178 David Greene RC .40 1.00
179 Vincent Jackson RC .75 2.00
180 Adam Jones RC .50 1.25
181 Derrick Johnson RC .50 1.25
182 Stefan LeFors RC .40 1.00
183 Heath Miller RC .75 2.00
184 Ryan Moats RC .50 1.25
185 Vernand Morency RC .50 1.25
186 Brandon Jacobs RC .75 2.00
187 Kyle Orton RC .60 1.50
188 Roscoe Parrish RC .40 1.00
189 Courtney Roby RC .50 1.25
190 Aaron Rodgers RC 6.00 12.00
191 Marion Barber RC .60 1.50
192 Antrel Rolle RC .60 1.50
193 Airese Currie RC .40 1.00
194 Alex Smith QB RC 1.00 2.50
195 Andrew Walter RC .50 1.25
196 Roddy White RC .75 2.00
197 Cadillac Williams RC .60 1.50
198 Mike Williams .60 1.50
199 Rasheed Marshall RC .50 1.25
200 Charlie Frye RC .60 1.50
201 Justin Miller RC .50 1.25
202 Fabian Washington RC .50 1.25
203 Mark Bradley RC .40 1.00
204 Adrian McPherson RC .40 1.00
205 Marcus Spears RC .50 1.25
206 Matt Jones RC .60 1.50
207 Darren Sproles RC .60 1.50
208 Eric Shelton RC .40 1.00
209 Fred Gibson RC .50 1.25
210 Anthony Davis RC .40 1.00
211 Mark Clayton RC .60 1.50
212 Braylon Edwards RC .75 2.00
213 Ciatrick Fason RC .40 1.00
214 DeMarcus Ware RC 1.25 3.00
215 Dan Orlovsky RC .60 1.50
216 Maurice Clarett .50 1.25
217 Erasmus James RC .50 1.25
218 Chris Henry RC .60 1.50
219 Jerome Mathis RC .60 1.50
220 Terrence Murphy RC .40 1.00

2005 Bazooka Blue

COMPLETE SET (220) 40.00 80.00
*VETS: 1X TO 2.5X BASIC CARDS
*ROOKIES: .6X TO 1.5X BASIC CARDS
ONE BLUE CARD PER PACK

2005 Bazooka Gold

*VETS: 1X TO 2.5X BASIC CARDS
*ROOKIES: .6X TO 1.5X BASIC CARDS
ONE GOLD CARD PER PACK

2005 Bazooka All-Stars Jerseys

GROUP A ODDS 1:259
GROUP B ODDS 1:75
GROUP C ODDS 1:69
GROUP D ODDS 1:84
BAAF Alan Faneca B 8.00 20.00
BAAJ Andre Johnson C 4.00 10.00
BABD Brian Dawkins A 3.00 8.00
BABW Brian Waters D 2.50 6.00
BADB Dre Bly A 2.50 6.00
BAIR Ike Reese B 2.50 6.00
BAJH Jeff Hartings B 5.00 12.00
BAJHO Joe Horn B 3.00 8.00
BAJL John Lynch B 3.00 8.00
BAJT Jeremiah Trotter A 2.50 6.00
BAKW Kevin Williams C 2.50 6.00
BALG La'Roi Glover D 2.50 6.00
BALI Larry Izzo C 2.50 6.00
BALS Lito Sheppard A 3.00 8.00
BAMB Matt Birk D 2.50 6.00
BAMR Marco Rivera C 2.50 6.00
BAMS Marcus Stroud C 2.50 6.00
BAMW Marcus Washington B 2.50 6.00
BAOK Olin Kreutz C 3.00 8.00
BAOP Orlando Pace C 2.50 6.00
BARJ Rudi Johnson B 3.00 8.00
BASA Sam Adams C 2.50 6.00
BASH Steve Hutchinson D 3.00 8.00
BASL Shane Lechler B 2.50 6.00
BATJ Tory James C 2.50 6.00
BATM Terrence McGee B 3.00 8.00
BATP Troy Polamalu D 12.50 25.00
BATS Terrell Suggs D 3.00 8.00
BATS Takeo Spikes B 2.50 6.00
BAWH William Henderson B 4.00 10.00
BAWJ Walter Jones D 2.50 6.00
BAWS Will Shields C 2.50 6.00

2005 Bazooka Comics

STATED ODDS 1:4
1 Peyton Manning 1.25 3.00
2 Ben Roethlisberger 1.00 2.50
3 Jonathan Vilma .50 1.25
4 Torry Holt .50 1.25
5 Peyton Manning 1.25 3.00
6 Curtis Martin .60 1.50
7 Ed Reed .50 1.25
8 Jerome Bettis .60 1.50
9 Reggie Wayne .60 1.50
10 Drew Brees .60 1.50
11 Randy Moss .60 1.50
12 Michael Vick .60 1.50
13 Brett Favre 1.50 4.00
14 Daunte Culpepper .50 1.25
15 Terrell Owens .60 1.50
16 Tom Brady 1.25 3.00
17 LaDainian Tomlinson .60 1.50
18 Donovan McNabb .60 1.50
19 Alex Smith QB 1.00 2.50
20 Aaron Rodgers 5.00 12.00
21 Cadillac Williams .60 1.50
22 Cedric Benson .60 1.50
23 Mike Williams .60 1.50
24 Braylon Edwards .75 2.00

2005 Bazooka Originals Jerseys

STATED ODDS 1:15
BOAJ Adam Jones 1.50 4.00
BOARO Antrel Rolle 2.50 6.00
BOAS Alex Smith QB 4.00 10.00
BOAW Andrew Walter 2.00 5.00
BOBE Braylon Edwards 3.00 8.00
BOCF Ciatrick Fason 1.50 4.00
BOCFR Charlie Frye 2.50 6.00
BOCR Courtney Roby 2.00 5.00
BOCRO Carlos Rogers 2.50 6.00
BOCW Cadillac Williams 2.50 6.00
BOES Eric Shelton 1.50 4.00
BOFG Frank Gore 4.00 10.00
BOJC Jason Campbell 3.00 8.00
BOJJA J.J. Arrington 2.00 5.00
BOKO Kyle Orton 2.50 6.00
BOMB Mark Bradley 1.50 4.00
BOMC Maurice Clarett 1.50 4.00
BOMCL Mark Clayton 2.00 5.00
BOMJ Matt Jones 2.00 5.00
BORB Ronnie Brown 3.00 8.00
BORBR Reggie Brown 1.50 4.00
BORM Ryan Moats 1.50 4.00
BORP Roscoe Parrish 1.50 4.00
BORW Roddy White 3.00 8.00
BOSL Stefan LeFors 1.50 4.00
BOTM Terrence Murphy 1.50 4.00
BOTW Troy Williamson 2.00 5.00
BOVJ Vincent Jackson 3.00 8.00
BOVM Vernand Morency 2.00 5.00

2005 Bazooka Rookie Threads

STATED ODDS 1:69
BZRAJ Adam Jones 2.00 5.00
BZRAR Antrel Rolle 3.00 8.00
BZRAW Andrew Walter 2.50 6.00
BZRCF Ciatrick Fason 2.00 5.00
BZRCF Charlie Frye 3.00 8.00
BZRCR Courtney Roby 2.50 6.00
BZRFG Frank Gore 5.00 12.00
BZRJC Jason Campbell 4.00 10.00
BZRKO Kyle Orton 3.00 8.00
BZRMB Mark Bradley 2.00 5.00
BZRMC Mark Clayton 2.50 6.00
BZRRW Roddy White 4.00 10.00
BZRTM Terrence Murphy Grn 2.00 5.00
BZRTM2 Terrence Murphy Wht 2.00 5.00
BZRVJ Vincent Jackson 4.00 10.00
BZRVM Vernand Morency 2.00 5.00

2005 Bazooka Stickers

STATED ODDS 1:4
1 Champ Bailey .60 1.50
Chris Gamble
DeAngelo Hall
Dunta Robinson
2 D.J. Williams .75 2.00
Jonathan Vilma
Lito Sheppard
Sean Taylor
3 Brian Urlacher .75 2.00
Derrick Brooks
Ray Lewis
Zach Thomas
4 Dwight Freeney .75 2.00
Jevon Kearse
Julius Peppers
Michael Strahan
5 Alge Crumpler .75 2.00
Antonio Gates
Jeremy Shockey
Kellen Winslow
6 Jason Witten .75 2.00
Randy McMichael
Todd Heap
Tony Gonzalez
7 Brian Westbrook .60 1.50
Donovan McNabb
Terrell Owens
Todd Pinkston
8 Chad Pennington .75 2.00
Kyle Boller
Marc Bulger
Tim Rattay
9 Chris Simms .75 2.00
Daunte Culpepper
Michael Vick
Philip Rivers
10 Billy Volek .60 1.50
Jake Delhomme
Kerry Collins
Trent Dilfer
11 A.J. Feeley .75 2.00
David Carr
Drew Brees
Josh McCown
12 Ben Roethlisberger 1.25 3.00
Drew Henson
Joey Harrington
Patrick Ramsey
13 Brian Griese .60 1.50
Byron Leftwich
J.P. Losman
Rex Grossman
14 Brett Favre 2.00 5.00
Jake Plummer
Kurt Warner
Luke McCown
15 Aaron Brooks 1.50 4.00
Jeff Garcia
Matt Hasselbeck
Peyton Manning
16 Carson Palmer .75 2.00
Drew Bledsoe
Steve McNair
Trent Green
17 Aaron Stecker .60 1.50
Clinton Portis
Fred Taylor
Julius Jones
18 Jamal Lewis .75 2.00
Michael Pittman
Onterrio Smith
Thomas Jones
19 Jerome Bettis .75 2.00
Shaun Alexander
T.J. Duckett
Tatum Bell
20 Curtis Martin .75 2.00
Deuce McAllister
Najeh Davenport
Willis McGahee
21 Chris Brown .75 2.00
Dante Hall
Larry Johnson
Steven Jackson
22 Ahman Green .75 2.00
Chester Taylor
Michael Bennett
Tiki Barber
23 Edgerrin James .60 1.50
Kevan Barlow
Priest Holmes
Stephen Davis
24 Derrick Blaylock .75 2.00
LaDainian Tomlinson
Reuben Droughns
Rudi Johnson
25 Chris Perry .50 1.25
Domanick Davis
Lee Suggs
Mewelde Moore
26 DeShaun Foster .60 1.50
Greg Jones
LaMont Jordan
Warrick Dunn
27 Duce Staley .75 2.00
Kevin Jones
Marshall Faulk
Travis Henry
28 Corey Dillon 1.50 4.00
Deion Branch
Rodney Harrison
Tom Brady
29 Antonio Bryant .60 1.50
Darrell Jackson
David Givens
Roy Williams WR
30 Anquan Boldin .60 1.50
Antwaan Randle El
Brandon Stokley
T.J. Houshmanzadeh
31 Isaac Bruce .60 1.50
Jamaar Taylor
Jimmy Smith
Nate Burleson
32 Chad Johnson .75 2.00
Jerry Porter
Keary Colbert
Reggie Wayne
33 Doug Gabriel .75 2.00
Hines Ward
Michael Clayton
Rod Smith
34 Javon Walker .75 2.00
Larry Fitzgerald
Laveranues Coles
Lee Evans
35 Amani Toomer .60 1.50
Keyshawn Johnson
Muhsin Muhammad
Ronald Curry
36 Charles Rogers .60 1.50
Michael Jenkins
Santana Moss
Travis Taylor
37 Derrick Mason .60 1.50
Eric Parker
Joe Horn
Rashaun Woods
38 Donte Stallworth .75 2.00
Drew Bennett
Eric Moulds
Randy Moss
39 Cedrick Wilson .60 1.50
Chris Chambers
Plaxico Burress
Torry Holt
40 Donald Driver .75 2.00
Justin McCareins
Koren Robinson
Marvin Harrison
41 Allen Rossum .75 2.00
Andre Johnson
Reggie Williams
Tyrone Calico
42 Aaron Rodgers 5.00 12.00
Alex Smith QB
Andrew Walter
Eli Manning
43 Adrian McPherson .60 1.50
Charlie Frye
Dan Orlovsky
Kyle Orton
44 David Greene .75 2.00
Derek Anderson
Jason Campbell
Stefan LeFors
45 Alvin Pearman .75 2.00
Cedric Benson
J.J. Arrington
Ronnie Brown
46 Frank Gore 1.00 2.50
Lionel Gates
Ryan Moats
Vernand Morency
47 Brandon Jacobs .75 2.00
Cadillac Williams
Darren Sproles
Marion Barber
48 Anthony Davis .50 1.25
Ciatrick Fason
Eric Shelton
Maurice Clarett
49 DeMarcus Ware 1.25 3.00
Derrick Johnson
Erasmus James
Marcus Spears
50 Antrel Rolle .75 2.00
Carlos Rogers
Fabian Washington
Justin Miller
51 Adam Jones .75 2.00
Courtney Roby
Heath Miller
Jerome Mathis
52 Craphonso Thorpe .75 2.00
Reggie Brown
Troy Williamson
Vincent Jackson
53 Airese Currie .75 2.00
Mike Williams
Roddy White
Roscoe Parrish
54 Fred Gibson .60 1.50
Mark Bradley
Matt Jones
Rasheed Marshall
55 Braylon Edwards .75 2.00
Chris Henry
Mark Clayton
Terrence Murphy

2005 Bazooka Window Clings

COMPLETE SET (34)	6.00	15.00
STATED ODDS 1:6		
1 Arizona Cardinals	.30	.75
2 Atlanta Falcons	.30	.75
3 Baltimore Ravens	.30	.75
4 Buffalo Bills	.40	1.00
5 Carolina Panthers	.30	.75
6 Chicago Bears	.40	1.00
7 Cincinnati Bengals	.30	.75
8 Cleveland Browns	.30	.75
9 Dallas Cowboys	.50	1.25
10 Denver Broncos	.40	1.00
11 Detroit Lions	.30	.75
12 Green Bay Packers	.50	1.25
13 Houston Texans	.30	.75
14 Indianapolis Colts	.30	.75
15 Jacksonville Jaguars	.30	.75
16 Kansas City Chiefs	.40	1.00
17 Miami Dolphins	.40	1.00
18 Minnesota Vikings	.30	.75
19 New England Patriots	.40	1.00
20 New Orleans Saints	.30	.75
21 New York Giants	.40	1.00
22 New York Jets	.40	1.00
23 Oakland Raiders	.50	1.25
24 Philadelphia Eagles	.30	.75
25 Pittsburgh Steelers	.40	1.00
26 St. Louis Rams	.30	.75
27 San Diego Chargers	.30	.75
28 San Francisco 49ers	.50	1.25
29 Seattle Seahawks	.30	.75
30 Tampa Bay Buccaneers	.30	.75
31 Tennessee Titans	.30	.75
32 Washington Redskins	.50	1.25
33 NFL Shield	.30	.75
34 Bazooka Joe	.30	.75

1964 Bears McCarthy Postcards

This 11-card set of the Chicago Bears features posed and action player photos taken by J.D. McCarthy and printed on postcard-size cards. Each is unnumbered and checklisted below in alphabetical order.

COMPLETE SET (11)	45.00	90.00
1 Charlie Bivins	2.50	5.00
2 Ronnie Bull	4.00	8.00
3 Mike Ditka	15.00	25.00
4 John Farrington	2.50	5.00
5 Sid Luckman CO	7.50	15.00
6 Joe Marconi	4.00	8.00
7 Billy Martin HB (Running pose)	2.50	5.00
8 Billy Martin E (Portrait)	2.50	5.00
9 Johnny Morris	4.00	8.00
10 Mike Rabold	2.50	5.00
11 Gene Schroeder CO	2.50	5.00

1967 Bears Pro's Pizza

These cards are actually discs that measure roughly 4 3/4" in diameter. They were printed on Pro's Pizza packages sold in the Chicago area and at stadiums. The player's image, with the athlete dressed in street clothes, appears on the front and the backs are blank.

COMPLETE SET (12)	3,000.00	4,500.00
1 Doug Atkins	175.00	300.00
2 Ronnie Bull	150.00	250.00
3 Dick Butkus	500.00	800.00
4 Mike Ditka	500.00	800.00
5 Dick Evey	150.00	250.00
6 Johnny Morris	150.00	250.00
7 Richie Petitbon	150.00	250.00
8 Jim Purnell	150.00	250.00
9 Mike Pyle	150.00	250.00
10 Gale Sayers	500.00	800.00
11 Roosevelt Taylor	150.00	250.00
12 Bob Wetoska	150.00	250.00

1967 Bears Team Issue

These black and white player photos were released by the Chicago Bears around 1967. Each measures approximately 5" by 7" and includes the player's name, his position (spelled out in full) and team name below the photo. They are blankbacked and unnumbered. Any additions to this list are appreciated.

COMPLETE SET (10)	75.00	125.00
1 Ronnie Bull	6.00	12.00
2 Rudy Bukich	5.00	10.00
3 Jack Concannon	5.00	10.00
4 Joe Fortunato	5.00	10.00
5 Richie Petitbon	6.00	12.00
6 Jim Purnell	5.00	10.00
7 Mike Pyle	5.00	10.00
8 Mike Rabold	5.00	10.00
9 Gale Sayers	15.00	30.00
10 Roosevelt Taylor	6.00	12.00

1968-69 Bears Team Issue

The Chicago Bears issued these black and white glossy photos for fans primarily for autograph purposes and mail requests. Each measures roughly 8" by 10" and includes the player's name and team name below the photo. Many also include the player's position or abbreviated position initials below the photo. As is common with many team issued photos, they were issued during more than one season and many contain different printed type styles and sizes. Any additions to this checklist are appreciated.

COMPLETE SET (43)	200.00	400.00
1 Doug Buffone	5.00	10.00
2 Ronnie Bull	6.00	12.00
3 Dick Butkus	15.00	30.00
4 Jim Cadile	5.00	10.00
5 Virgil Carter	5.00	10.00
6 Jack Concannon	5.00	10.00
7 Frank Cornish (name only on front)	5.00	10.00
8 Frank Cornish (position and team on front)	5.00	10.00
9 Austin Denney	5.00	10.00
10 Dick Evey (no position on front)	5.00	10.00
11 Dick Evey (position intials on front)	5.00	10.00
12 Bobby Joe Green	5.00	10.00
13 Willie Holman	5.00	10.00
14 Mike Hull	5.00	10.00
15 Randy Jackson	5.00	10.00
16 John Johnson DT	5.00	10.00
17 Jimmy Jones TE	5.00	10.00
18 Doug Kriewald	5.00	10.00
19 Rudy Kuechenberg	5.00	10.00
20 Ralph Kurek	5.00	10.00
21 Andy Livingston	5.00	10.00
22 Garry Lyle	5.00	10.00
23 Wayne Mass	5.00	10.00
24 Bennie McRae	5.00	10.00
25 Ed O'Bradovich	5.00	10.00
26 Richie Petitbon	6.00	12.00
27 Loyd Phillips (cutting to his left)	5.00	10.00
28 Loyd Phillips (cutting to his right)	5.00	10.00
29 Brian Piccolo (cutting to his right)	15.00	30.00
30 Brian Piccolo (moving to his right)	15.00	30.00
31 Bob Pickens	5.00	10.00
32 Jim Purnell	5.00	10.00
33 Mike Pyle	5.00	10.00
34 Larry Rakestraw	5.00	10.00
35 Mike Reilly	5.00	10.00
36 Gale Sayers (portrait)	18.00	30.00
37 Gale Sayers (posed action, ball in right arm, no position mentioned)	18.00	30.00
38 Gale Sayers (posed action, ball in left arm, position initials)	18.00	30.00
39 Joe Taylor	5.00	10.00
40 Roosevelt Taylor	6.00	12.00
41 Cecil Turner	5.00	10.00
42 Bob Wallace	5.00	10.00
43 Bob Wetoska	5.00	10.00

1968 Bears Tasco Prints

1 Dick Butkus	20.00	40.00
2 Gale Sayers	20.00	40.00

1969 Bears Kroger

Similar to the Chiefs set issued the same year, this eight-card release was sponsored by Kroger Stores and measures approximately 8" by 9 3/4." The fronts feature a color painting of the player by artist John Wheeldon with the player's name inscribed across the bottom of the picture. The back has player biographical and statistical information and a brief note about the artist.

COMPLETE SET (8)	150.00	300.00
1 Dick Butkus	40.00	80.00
2 Virgil Carter	8.00	12.00
3 Jack Concannon	10.00	15.00
4 Dick Gordon	8.00	12.00
5 Bennie McRae	8.00	12.00
6 Brian Piccolo	60.00	100.00
7 Gale Sayers	35.00	60.00
8 Roosevelt Taylor	10.00	15.00

1971 Bears Team Issue

These twelve black and white photos were released as a set by the Chicago Bears in 1971. Each measures approximately 4 1/2" by 7" and includes the player's name and team name below the photo. They are blankbacked and unnumbered.

COMPLETE SET (12)	75.00	125.00
1 Doug Buffone	5.00	10.00
2 Dick Butkus	12.50	25.00
3 Rich Coady	5.00	10.00
4 Jack Concannon	5.00	10.00
5 Bobby Douglass	6.00	12.00
6 Dick Gordon	5.00	10.00
7 Jim Grabowski	5.00	10.00
8 Willie Holman	5.00	10.00
9 Randy Jackson	5.00	10.00
10 Gale Sayers	12.50	25.00
11 George Seals	5.00	10.00
12 Aaron Thomas	5.00	10.00

1973 Bears Team Issue Color

The NFLPA worked with many teams in 1973 to issued photo packs to be sold at stadium concession stands. Each measures approximately 7" by 8-5/8" and features a color player photo with a blank back. A small sheet with a player checklist was included in each 12-photo pack. These twelve color photos are thought to have also been released by Jewel Foods in Chicago.

COMPLETE SET (12)	40.00	80.00
1 Doug Buffone	5.00	8.00
2 Dick Butkus	10.00	20.00
3 Bobby Douglass UER name misspelled Douglas	5.00	10.00
4 George Farmer	5.00	8.00
5 Carl Garrett	5.00	8.00
6 Jimmy Gunn	5.00	8.00
7 Jim Harrison	5.00	8.00
8 Willie Holman	5.00	8.00
9 Mac Percival	5.00	8.00
10 Jim Seymour	5.00	8.00
11 Don Shy	5.00	8.00
12 Cecil Turner	5.00	8.00

1973 Bears Team Sheets

This set of photos of the Chicago Bears was distributed on glossy paper stock each measuring approximately 8" by 10". The fronts feature black-and-white player and/or coach portraits with eight pictures to a sheet along with the Bears helmet and team name. The backs are blank and the sheets are not numbered.

COMPLETE SET (7)	35.00	60.00
1 Lionel Antoine	5.00	8.00
Bob Asher		
Rich Coady		
Craig Cotton		
Glen Holloway		
Randy Jackson		
Bob Newton		
Bob Parsons		
2 Doug Buffone	6.00	12.00
Dick Butkus		
Wally Chambers		
Jimmy Gunn		
Willie Holman		
Tony McGee DT		
Jim Osborne		
Andy Rice		
3 Gail Clark	5.00	8.00
Allan Ellis		
Conrad Graham		
Roger Lawson		
Don Rives		
Reggie Sanderson		
Moo Porcival		
Mirro Rodor		
4 Craig Clemons	5.00	8.00
Dave Hale		
Larry Horton		
Gary Hrivnak		
Ernie Janet		
Bob Jeter		
Garry Lyle		
Bob Pifferini		
5 Bobby Douglass	6.00	10.00
George Farmer		
Gary Huff		
Carl Garrett		
Jim Harrison		
Gary Kozins		
Joe Moore		
Earl Thomas		
6 Abe Gibron	5.00	8.00
Zeke Bratkowski		
Chuck Cherundolo		
Whitey Dovell		
Jim Carr CO		
Perry Moss CO		
Jerry Stoltz		
Abe Gibron		
7 George Halas Sr.	10.00	20.00
Charlie Ford		
Bobby Joe Green		
George Halas Jr.		
Ike Hill		
Tom Reynolds		
Joe Taylor		
Cecil Turner		

1974 Bears Team Sheets

This set of photos of the Chicago Bears was distributed on six glossy sheets with each measuring approximately 8" by 10". The fronts feature black-and-white player or coach portraits with eight pictures to a sheet along with the year of issue. The backs are blank and the sheets are numbered on the fronts 1-5.

COMPLETE SET (5)	25.00	40.00
1 Sheet 1:	6.00	10.00
Abe Gibron		
Zeke Bratkowski		
Chuck Cherundolo		
Whitey Dovall		
Jim Carr		
Ralph Goldston		
Bob Lloyd		
Jerry Stoltz		
2 Sheet 2:	10.00	15.00
George Halas, Chairman		
Doug Buffone		
Randy Jackson		
George Halas Jr., President		
Ike Hill		
Perry Williams		
Joe Taylor		
Bo Rather		
3 Sheet 3:	5.00	8.00
Joe Barnes		
Wayne Wheeler		
Wally Chambers		
Jimmy Gunn		
Norm Hodgins		
Clifton Taylor		
Jim Osborne		
Jim Kelly		
4 Sheet 4:	5.00	8.00
Lionel Antoine		
Bob Asher		
Rich Coady		
Fred Pagac		
Don Hultz		
Bob Newton		
Bob Parsons		
5 Sheet 5:	5.00	8.00
Craig Clemons		
Rich Harris		
Dave Gallagher		
Gary Hrivnak		
Ernie Janet		
Mel Tom		
GaRry Lyle		
Bob Pifferini		

1976 Bears Coke Discs

The cards in this 22-player disc set are unnumbered so they are listed below alphabetically. All players in the set are members of the Chicago Bears suggesting that these cards were issued as part of a local Chicago Coca-Cola promotion. The discs measure approximately 3 3/8" in diameter but with the hang tab intact the whole card is 5 1/4" long. There are two versions of the Doug Plank disc (green and yellow) and two versions of Clemons (yellow and orange); both of these variations were printed in the same quantities as all the other cards in the set and hence are not that difficult to find. The discs were produced by Mike Schechter Associates (MSA). These cards are frequently found with their hang tabs intact and hence they are priced that way in the list below. The back of each disc contains the phrase, "Coke adds life to ... halftime fun." The set price below includes all the variation cards. The set is also noteworthy in that it contains another card (albeit round) of Walter Payton in 1976, the same year as his Topps Rookie Card.

COMPLETE SET (24)	50.00	100.00
1 Lionel Antoine	1.00	2.50
2 Bob Avellini	1.25	3.00
3 Waymond Bryant	1.00	2.50
4 Doug Buffone	1.25	3.00
5 Wally Chambers	1.25	3.00
6A Craig Clemons (Yellow border)	1.00	2.50
6B Craig Clemons (Orange border)	1.00	2.50
7 Allan Ellis	1.00	2.50
8 Roland Harper	1.00	2.50
9 Mike Hartenstine	1.00	2.50
10 Noah Jackson	1.00	2.50
11 Virgil Livers	1.00	2.50
12 Jim Osborne	1.00	2.50
13 Bob Parsons	1.25	3.00
14 Walter Payton	40.00	75.00
15 Dan Peiffer	1.00	2.50
16A Doug Plank (Yellow border)	1.25	3.00
16B Doug Plank (Green border)	1.25	3.00
17 Bo Rather	1.00	2.50
18 Don Rives	1.00	2.50
19 Jeff Sevy	1.00	2.50
20 Ron Shanklin	1.00	2.50
21 Revie Sorey	1.00	2.50
22 Roger Stillwell	1.00	2.50

1980 Bears Team Sheets

This set of photos was released by the Bears. Each measures roughly 8" by 10" and features 8-players or coaches on each sheet. The sheets are blankbacked and numbered on the fronts of 7.

COMPLETE SET (7)	20.00	40.00
1 Neill Armstrong	2.50	5.00
Jerry Frei		
Dale Haupt		
Hank Kuhlmann		
Jim LaRue		
Ken Meyer		
Ted Plumb		
Buddy Ryan		
2 Ted Albrecht	4.00	8.00
Bob Avellini		
Brian Baschnagel		
Gary Campbell		
Mike Cobb		
Robin Earl		
Allan Ellis		
Vince Evans		
3 Gary Fencik	4.00	8.00
Robert Fisher		
Wentford Gaines		
Kris Haines		
Dan Hampton		
Roland Harper		
Al Harris		
Mike Hartenstine		
4 Bruce Herron	2.50	5.00
Tom Hicks		
Noah Jackson		
Dan Jiggetts		
Lee Kunz		
Greg Latta		
Dennis Lick		
Virgil Livers		
5 Willie McClendon	7.50	15.00
Rocco Moore		
Jerry Muckensturm		
Dan Neal		
Jim Osborne		
Alan Page		
Bob Parsons		
Walter Payton		
6 Mike Phipps	4.00	8.00
Doug Plank		
Ron Rydalch		
Terry Schmidt		
James Scott		
Brad Shearer		
John Skibinski		
Revie Sorey		
7 Matt Suhey	2.50	5.00
Paul Tabor		
Bob Thomas		
Mike Ulmer		
Lenny Walterscheid		
Rickey Watts		
Dave Williams RB		
Otis Wilson		

1981 Bears Police

The 1981 Chicago Bears police set contains 24 unnumbered cards. The cards measure approximately 2 5/8" by 4 1/8". Although uniform numbers appear on the fronts of the cards, they have been listed alphabetically in the checklist below. The set is sponsored by the Kiwanis Club, the local law enforcement agency and the Chicago Bears. Appearing on the backs along with a Chicago Bears helmet are "Chicago Bears Tips". The card backs have blue print with orange accent. The Kiwanis logo and Chicago Bears helmet appear on the fronts of the cards.

COMPLETE SET (24)	12.50	25.00
1 Ted Albrecht	.30	.75
2 Neill Armstrong CO	.40	1.00
3 Brian Baschnagel	.40	1.00
4 Gary Campbell	.30	.75
5 Robin Earl	.30	.75
6 Allan Ellis	.30	.75
7 Vince Evans	.60	1.50
8 Gary Fencik	.50	1.25
9 Dan Hampton	1.00	2.50
10 Roland Harper	.40	1.00
11 Mike Hartenstine	.30	.75
12 Tom Hicks	.30	.75
13 Noah Jackson	.40	1.00
14 Dennis Lick	.30	.75
15 Jerry Muckensturm	.30	.75
16 Dan Neal	.30	.75
17 Jim Osborne	.30	.75
18 Alan Page	1.00	2.50
19 Walter Payton	6.00	12.00
20 Doug Plank	.40	1.00
21 Terry Schmidt	.30	.75
22 James Scott	.30	.75
23 Revie Sorey	.40	1.00
24 Rickey Watts	.30	.75

1987 Bears Ace Fact Pack

This 33-card set was made in West Germany (by Ace Fact Pack) for distribution in England. The cards measure approximately 2 1/4" by 3 5/8" and feature rounded corners and a playing card type design on the back. The 22 player cards in the set have been checklisted below in alphabetical order.

COMPLETE SET (33)	125.00	250.00
1 Todd Bell	1.50	4.00
2 Mark Bortz	1.50	4.00
3 Kevin Butler	2.00	5.00
4 Jim Covert	2.00	5.00
5 Richard Dent	4.00	10.00
6 Dave Duerson	1.50	4.00
7 Gary Fencik	2.00	5.00
8 Willie Gault	2.00	5.00
9 Dan Hampton	4.00	10.00
10 Jay Hilgenberg	2.00	5.00
11 Wilber Marshall	2.00	5.00
12 Jim McMahon	12.50	25.00
13 Steve McMichael	2.50	6.00
14 Emery Moorehead	1.50	4.00
15 Keith Ortega	1.50	4.00
16 Walter Payton	50.00	100.00
17 William Perry	3.00	8.00
18 Mike Richardson	1.50	4.00
19 Mike Singletary	12.50	25.00
20 Matt Suhey	2.00	5.00
21 Keith Van Horne	1.50	4.00
22 Otis Wilson	1.50	4.00
23 Bears Helmet	1.50	4.00
24 Bears Information	1.50	4.00
25 Bears Uniform	1.50	4.00
26 Game Record Holders	1.50	4.00
27 Season Record Holders	1.50	4.00
28 Career Record Holders	1.50	4.00
29 Record 1967-86	1.50	4.00
30 1986 Team Statistics	1.50	4.00
31 All-Time Greats	1.50	4.00
32 Roll of Honour	1.50	4.00
33 Soldier Field	1.50	4.00

1994 Bears 75th Anniversary Sheets

COMPLETE SET (10)	20.00	50.00
1 George Halas OWN CO (Vs. Eagles; 8/5/94)	2.00	5.00
2 Doug Atkins	1.20	3.00
George Connor		
George Blanda (Vs. Giants; 8/27/94)		
3 Walter Payton (Vs. Bucs; 9/4/94)	10.00	15.00
4 Dan Fortmann	2.00	5.00
Mike Ditka		
Paddy Driscoll (Vs. Vikings; 9/18/94)		
5 Dick Butkus (Vs. Bills; 10/2/94)	3.20	8.00
6 Bill George	2.00	5.00
Red Grange		
Ed Healey (Vs. Saints; 10/9/94)		
7 Gale Sayers (Vs. Packers; 10/31/94)	3.20	8.00
8 Bill Hewitt	1.60	4.00
Stan Jones		
Sid Luckman (Vs. Lions; 11/20/94)		
9 Roy(Link) Lyman	1.20	3.00
George Musso		
George McAfee (Vs. Rams; 12/18/94)		
10 Bronko Nagurski	1.60	4.00
Bulldog Turner		
Joe Stydahar		
George Trafton (Vs. Patriots; 12/24/94)		

1994 Bears Toyota

1 Dick Butkus	15.00	30.00
2 Gale Sayers	15.00	30.00

1995 Bears Program Sheets

These eight sheets measure approximately 8" by 10" and appeared in regular-season issues of the Bears' GameDay program. The set features large action photos of various individuals involved in the Chicago Bears Super Bowl XX championship. The sheets are listed below in chronological order.

COMPLETE SET (8)	20.00	50.00
1 Mike Ditka/9/3/95 vs Vikings	2.40	6.00
2 Walter Payton/9/11/95 vs Packers	4.80	12.00
3 Jim McMahon/10/8/95 vs Panthers	2.40	6.00
4 Mike Singletary	3.20	8.00
Gary Fencik		
5 Richard Dent/11/5/95 vs Steelers	2.40	6.00
6 William Perry/11/19/95 vs Lions	2.40	6.00
7 Otis Wilson/12/17/95 vs Buccaneers	2.00	5.00
8 Wilber Marshall/12/24/95 vs Eagles	2.00	5.00

1995 Bears Super Bowl XX 10th Anniversary Kemper

The Chicago Bears, in conjunction with Kemper Mutual Funds, produced this 20-card set commemorating the 10th anniversary of the Chicago Bears winning Super Bowl XX. The fronts feature color action player photos from that championship team with the player's name, position, and jersey number in a vertical blue strip on the left. The backs display a small player portrait with the player's name, biographical information, and 1985 season and postseason highlights. The cards are unnumbered and checklisted below in alphabetical order.

COMPLETE SET (20)	10.00	25.00
1 Mark Bortz	.40	1.00
2 Kevin Butler	.40	1.00
3 Jim Covert	.40	1.00
4 Richard Dent	.60	1.50
5 Dave Duerson	.40	1.00
6 Gary Fencik	.40	1.00
7 Willie Gault	.60	1.50
8 Dan Hampton	.60	1.50
9 Jay Hilgenberg	.40	1.00
10 Wilber Marshall	.60	1.50
11 Dennis McKinnon	.40	1.00
12 Jim McMahon	1.20	3.00
13 Steve McMichael	.40	1.00
14 Walter Payton	3.20	8.00
15 William Perry	.60	1.50
16 Mike Singletary	1.00	2.50
17 Matt Suhey	.40	1.00
18 Tom Thayer	.40	1.00
19 Keith Van Horne	.40	1.00
20 Otis Wilson	.40	1.00

1995 Bears Super Bowl XX Montgomery Ward Cards/Coins

The Chicago Bears, in conjunction with Montgomery Ward Stores, produced this 8-card and 8-coin set commemorating the 10th anniversary of the Chicago Bears winning Super Bowl XX. The card fronts feature color action player photos from that championship team with the player's name and position in a diagonal blue and orange strip. The backs display the complete 8-card checklist and individual card numbers. We've listed the cards below using a "CA" prefix. The coin fronts feature a player from the championship team with the player's name and jersey number. The backs display the Bears Super Bowl XX logo. The coins are unnumbered but have been listed below alphabetically using a "CO" prefix. A cardboard holder was produced to house the set that featured all the players included in the set.

COMP.CARD/COIN SET (16)	9.60	24.00
COMPLETE CARD SET (8)	4.80	12.00
COMPLETE COIN SET (8)	4.80	12.00
CA1 Mike Ditka CO/'85 Super Bowl	.80	2.00
CA2 Kevin Butler	.50	1.25
CA3 Dan Hampton	.50	1.25
CA4 Richard Dent	.60	1.50
CA5 Gary Fencik	.50	1.25
CA6 Walter Payton	.50	1.25
CA7 Jim McMahon	.75	2.00
CA8 Mike Ditka	.80	2.00
CO1 Kevin Butler	.50	1.25
CO2 Richard Dent	.60	1.50
CO3 Mike Ditka CO	.80	2.00
CO4 Gary Fencik	.50	1.25
CO5 Dan Hampton	.50	1.25
CO6 Jim McMahon	.75	2.00
CO7 Walter Payton	2.40	6.00
CO8 Super Bowl Trophy	.50	1.25
NNO Set Display Holder	.40	1.00
Mike Ditka		
Jim McMahon		
Richard Dent		
Walter Payton		
Gary Fencik		
William Perry		
Dan Hampton		

1996 Bears Illinois State Lottery

These "cards" were actually issued as Illinois State Lottery tickets. It is common to find them stratched since the potential lottery prize far outweighed the value of the ticket unscratched. Each includes a small color photo of the player along with the rules for the contest.

COMPLETE SET (5)	1.20	3.00
1 Richard Dent	.20	.50
2 Mike Ditka	.40	1.00
3 Dan Hampton	.20	.50
4 William Perry	.08	.25
5 Gale Sayers	.40	1.00

1997 Bears Collector's Choice

Upper Deck released several team sets in 1997 in a blister pack wrapper. Each of the 14-cards in this set are very similar to the base Collector's Choice cards except for the card numbering on the back. A cover/checklist card was added featuring the team helmet.

COMPLETE SET (14)	1.25	3.00
CH1 Raymont Harris	.08	.25
CH2 Jeff Jaeger	.07	.20
CH3 Curtis Conway	.08	.25
CH4 Walt Harris	.07	.20
CH5 Bobby Engram	.08	.25
CH6 Rick Mirer	.08	.25
CH7 Rashaan Salaam	.08	.25
CH8 Darnell Autry	.08	.25
CH9 Alonzo Spellman	.07	.20
CH10 Bryan Cox	.07	.20
CH11 Tom Carter	.07	.20
CH12 Tyrone Hughes	.07	.20
CH13 Anthony Marshall	.07	.20
CH14 Chicago Bears CL	.07	.20

1997 Bears Score

This 15-card set of the Chicago Bears was distributed in five-card packs with a suggested retail price of $1.99. The fronts feature color action player photos with white borders and the player's name and team logo printed in team color foil at the bottom. The backs carry player information and career statistics. Platinum Team parallel cards were randomly seeded in packs featuring all foil cardfronts.

COMPLETE SET (15)	2.40	6.00
*PLATINUM TEAMS: 1X TO 2X		
1 Rashaan Salaam	.15	.40
2 Curtis Conway	.15	.40
3 Erik Kramer	.15	.40
4 Bobby Engram	.30	.75
5 Bryan Cox	.08	.25
6 Walt Harris	.08	.25
7 Raymont Harris	.30	.75
8 Michael Timpson	.08	.25
9 Tony Carter	.08	.25
10 Alonzo Spellman	.08	.25
11 Donnell Woolford	.08	.25
12 Barry Minter	.08	.25
13 Mark Carrier DB	.08	.25
14 Marty Carter	.08	.25
15 Rick Mirer	.30	.75

1998 Bears Fan Convention

COMPLETE SET (56)	10.00	25.00
1 Doug Atkins	.30	.75
2 Bob Avellini	.08	.25
3 Brian Baschnagel	.08	.25
4 Mark Bortz	.08	.25
5 Doug Buffone	.08	.25
6 Ronnie Bull	.08	.25
7 Dick Butkus	2.00	4.00
8 Marty Carter	.08	.25
9 George Connor	.15	.40
10 Curtis Conway	.30	.75
11 Jim Covert	.08	.25
12 Wendell Davis WR	.08	.25
13 Richard Dent	.30	.75
14 Bobby Douglass	.08	.25
15 Dave Duerson	.08	.25
16 Bobby Engram	.15	.40
17 Willie Gault	.15	.40
18 George Halas	1.00	2.50
19 Dan Hampton	.15	.40
20 Roland Harper	.08	.25
21 Mike Hartenstine	.08	.25
22 Andy Heck	.08	.25
23 Jay Hilgenberg	.08	.25
24 Jeff Jaeger	.08	.25
25 Dan Jiggetts	.15	.40
26 Glen Kozlowski	.08	.25
27 Sid Luckman	.60	1.50
28 Dennis McKinnon	.08	.25
29 Jim McMahon	.40	1.00
30 Barry Minter	.08	.25
31 Emery Moorehead	.08	.25
32 Jim Morrissey	.08	.25
33 Brad Muster	.08	.25
34 Jim Osborne	.08	.25
35 Walter Payton	4.00	8.00

36 Todd Perry	.08	.25
37 Doug Plank	.08	.25
38 Mike Pyle	.08	.25
39 Ron Rivera	.08	.25
40 Thomas Sanders	.08	.25
41 Gale Sayers	2.00	4.00
42 Terry Schmidt	.08	.25
43 Carl Simpson	.08	.25
44 Mike Singletary	.30	.75
45 Ed Sprinkle	.08	.25
46 Matt Suhey	.08	.25
47 John Thierry	.08	.25
48 Bob Thomas	.08	.25
49 James Thornton	.08	.25
50 Chris Villarrial	.08	.25
51 Tom Waddle	.08	.25
52 Bill Wade	.15	.40
53 Ryan Wetnight	.08	.25
54 James Williams T	.08	.25
55 Otis Wilson	.08	.25
56 Announcers	.08	.25
Wayne Larrivee		
Hub Arkush		
Tom Thayer		

1999 Bears Fan Convention

This set was distributed at the 1999 Chicago Bears Fan Convention in complete set form. Each card features a white border with the Fan Convention logo and a player photo on the front and player information on the back. The cards were not numbered.

COMPLETE SET (45)	10.00	25.00
1 Brian Baschnagel	.08	.25
2 Mark Bortz	.08	.25
3 Doug Buffone	.08	.25
4 Ronnie Bull	.08	.25
5 Rick Casares	.15	.40
6 George Connor	.15	.40
7 Jim Covert	.08	.25
8 Richard Dent	.30	.75
9 Allan Ellis	.08	.25
10 Curtis Enis	.75	2.00
11 Gary Fencik	.08	.25
12 Jim Flanigan	.08	.25
13 George Halas	.80	2.00
14 Dan Hampton	.15	.40
15 Roland Harper	.08	.25
16 Walt Harris	.08	.25
17 Mike Hartenstine	.08	.25
18 Jay Hilgenberg	.08	.25
19 Dick Jauron CO	.15	.40
20 Stan Jones	.30	.75
21 Glen Kozlowski	.08	.25
22 Ricardo McDonald	.08	.25
23 Dennis McKinnon	.08	.25
24 Glyn Milburn	.08	.25
25 Barry Minter	.08	.25
26 Emery Moorehead	.08	.25
27 Jim Morrissey	.08	.25
28 Jim Osborne	.08	.25
29 Tony Parrish	.08	.25
30 Walter Payton	3.00	6.00
31 Doug Plank	.08	.25
32 Mike Pyle	.08	.25
33 Marcus Robinson	2.40	6.00
34 Todd Sauerbrun	.08	.25
35 Gale Sayers	1.20	3.00
36 Mike Singletary	.30	.75
37 Tom Thayer	.08	.25
38 Jim Thornton	.08	.25
39 Tom Waddle	.08	.25
40 Bill Wade	.15	.40
41 Mike Wells	.08	.25
42 Ryan Wetnight	.08	.25
43 Otis Wilson	.08	.25
44 Bears Fan Club Logo	.08	.25
45 Checklist Card	.08	.25

2003 Bears Upper Deck Van Kampen

This set was sponsored by Van Kampen Investments, produced by Upper Deck, and features 5-young members of the Chicago Bears. The cards are printed in a horizontal format and are numbered on the backs.

COMPLETE SET (5)	10.00	20.00
1 Michael Haynes	1.25	3.00
2 Rex Grossman	5.00	12.00
3 Charles Tillman	1.25	3.00
4 Lance Briggs	1.25	3.00
5 Justin Gage	1.50	4.00

2004 Bears Legends Activa Medallions

COMPLETE SET (21)	40.00	80.00
1 Doug Atkins	1.50	4.00
2 Brian Baschnagel	1.25	3.00
3 George Blanda	1.50	4.00
4 Doug Buffone	1.25	3.00
5 Ronnie Bull	1.25	3.00
6 Dick Butkus	2.00	5.00
7 Mike Ditka	1.50	4.00
8 Bobby Douglass	1.25	3.00
9 Gary Fencik	1.25	3.00
10 Bill George	1.25	3.00
11 Red Grange	2.00	5.00
12 George Halas	2.00	5.00
13 Dan Hampton	1.25	3.00
14 Sid Luckman	1.50	4.00
15 Jim McMahon	1.50	4.00
16 Bronko Nagurski	2.00	5.00
17 Walter Payton	2.50	6.00
18 Richie Petitbon	1.25	3.00
19 Brian Piccolo	2.50	6.00
20 Gale Sayers	2.00	5.00
21 Mike Singletary	1.50	4.00

2005 Bears Playoff Prestige National Convention

This set was issued for the 2005 National Sport Collectors Convention held in Chicago. Collectors who purchased the early bird VIP card show package received this 6-card set featuring members of the Chicago Bears. The cards were produced in the design of a Playoff Prestige product but included a special "2005 Chicago National" logo printed on the cardfronts

COMPLETE SET (6)	6.00	15.00
1 Brian Urlacher	1.25	3.00
2 Rex Grossman	.75	2.00
3 Thomas Jones	.75	2.00
4 Kyle Orton	1.00	2.50
5 Cedric Benson	1.25	3.00
6 Mark Bradley	.75	2.00

2005 Bears Super Bowl XX Activa Medallions

COMPLETE SET (25)	30.00	60.00
1 Mark Bortz	1.25	3.00
2 Maury Buford	1.25	3.00
3 Kevin Butler	1.25	3.00
4 Jim Covert	1.25	3.00
5 Richard Dent	1.50	4.00
6 Mike Ditka	1.50	4.00
7 Dave Duerson	1.25	3.00
8 Gary Fencik	1.25	3.00
9 Leslie Frazier	1.25	3.00
10 Willie Gault	1.25	3.00
11 Dan Hampton	1.50	4.00
12 Wilber Marshall	1.25	3.00
13 Dennis McKinnon	1.25	3.00
14 Jim McMahon	1.50	4.00
15 Steve McMichael	1.25	3.00
16 Emery Moorehead	1.25	3.00
17 Walter Payton	2.50	6.00
18 William Perry	1.25	3.00
19 Ron Rivera	1.25	3.00
20 Mike Singletary	1.50	4.00
21 Matt Suhey	1.25	3.00
22 Tom Thayer	1.25	3.00
23 Keith Van Horne	1.25	3.00
24 Otis Wilson	1.25	3.00
25 Bears Logo	1.00	2.50

2005 Bears Topps National Convention

This set was issued at the Topps booth at the 2005 National Sports Collectors Convention in Chicago. Collectors who presented 5-Topps football wrappers from packs opened at the show received a complete set. While no mention of the card show is given on the cards, they were produced with the Topps 50th Anniversary logo printed in yellow on the cardfronts and a special card numbering scheme XX of 6.

COMPLETE SET (6)	4.00	8.00
1 Rex Grossman	.40	1.00
2 Brian Urlacher	.60	1.50
3 Cedric Benson	.60	1.50
4 Mark Bradley	.40	1.00
5 Kyle Orton	.50	1.25
6 Gale Sayers	.60	1.50

2006 Bears Topps

COMPLETE SET (12)	3.00	6.00
CHI1 Nathan Vasher	.20	.50
CHI2 Thomas Jones	.25	.60
CHI3 Kyle Orton	.30	.75
CHI4 Alex Brown	.20	.50
CHI5 Lance Briggs	.25	.60
CHI6 Mark Bradley	.20	.50
CHI7 Rex Grossman	.25	.60
CHI8 Cedric Benson	.25	.60
CHI9 Brian Urlacher	.30	.75
CHI10 Brian Griese	.25	.60
CHI11 Muhsin Muhammad	.25	.60
CHI12 Devin Hester	.60	1.50

2007 Bears Topps

COMPLETE SET (12)	2.50	5.00
1 Brian Urlacher	.30	.75
2 Rex Grossman	.25	.60
3 Cedric Benson	.25	.60
4 Bernard Berrian	.20	.50
5 Desmond Clark	.20	.50
6 Devin Hester	.30	.75
7 Tommie Harris	.20	.50
8 Alex Brown	.20	.50
9 Robbie Gould	.20	.50
10 Mike Brown	.25	.60
11 Muhsin Muhammad	.25	.60
12 Greg Olsen	.25	.60

2007 Bears Upper Deck

This set was issued in two perforated 9-card panels; one panel featuring offensive players and the other defensive players. A Jewel-Osco ad card was also included on each panel.

COMPLETE SET (18)	6.00	12.00
1 Devin Hester	.50	1.25
2 Robbie Gould	.30	.75
3 Desmond Clark	.30	.75
4 Bernard Berrian	.30	.75
5 NFC Champs Sheet 1	.20	.50
6 Muhsin Muhammad	.40	1.00
7 Greg Olsen	.40	1.00
8 Olin Kreutz	.30	.75
9 Cedric Benson	.40	1.00
10 Tommie Harris	.30	.75
11 Ricky Manning	.30	.75
12 Hunter Hillenmeyer	.30	.75
13 Brian Urlacher	.50	1.25
14 NFC Champs Sheet 2	.20	.50
15 Lance Briggs	.30	.75
16 Nathan Vasher	.30	.75
17 Charles Tillman	.30	.75
18 Brendon Ayanbadejo	.30	.75

2008 Bears Topps

COMPLETE SET (12)	2.50	5.00
1 Brian Urlacher	.30	.75
2 Devin Hester	.30	.75
3 Desmond Clark	.20	.50
4 Tommie Harris	.20	.50
5 Cedric Benson	.25	.60
6 Lance Briggs	.20	.50
7 Rex Grossman	.25	.60
8 Adrian Peterson	.50	1.25
9 Greg Olsen	.25	.60
10 Adewale Ogunleye	.20	.50
11 Matt Forte	.60	1.50
12 Earl Bennett	.40	1.00

2010 Bears Chicago Tribune Fathead Tradeables

These six Bears Fathead Tradeables were issued inside copies of the Chicago Tribune sold through Jewel-Osco stores in the Chicago area. Each unnumbered Fathead features a sticker back that includes an advertisement for the paper which differeniates it from base set.

COMPLETE SET (6)	5.00	12.00
1 Lance Briggs	.75	2.00
2 Jay Cutler	1.00	2.50
3 Matt Forte	.75	2.00
4 Devin Hester	1.00	2.50
5 Julius Peppers	.75	2.00
6 Brian Urlacher	1.00	2.50

1968 Bengals Royal Crown Photos

These black and white blankbacked photos measure roughly 4" by 5 5/8" and feature members of the Bengals. Printed below the player photo are "Compliments of Royal Crown Cola" along with the player's name. A facsimile autograph is also included across each photo.

1 Frank Buncom	10.00	20.00
2 Sherrill Headrick	10.00	20.00
3 Dewey Warren	10.00	20.00
4 Ernie Wright	10.00	20.00

1968 Bengals Team Issue

The Cincinnati Bengals issued and distributed these player photos. Each measures approximately 8 1/2" by 11" and features a black and white photo. The player's name and position appear in the bottom border below the photo.

COMPLETE SET (15)	100.00	200.00
1 Al Beauchamp	7.50	15.00
2 Paul Brown CO	15.00	25.00
3 Frank Buncom	7.50	15.00
4 Greg Cook	7.50	15.00
5 Sherrill Headrick	7.50	15.00
6 Bob Johnson	7.50	15.00
7 Warren McVea	7.50	15.00
8 Jess Phillips	7.50	15.00
10 Fletcher Smith	7.50	15.00
11 Bill Staley	7.50	15.00
12 John Stofa	7.50	15.00
13 Bob Trumpy	7.50	15.00
14 Dewey Warren	7.50	15.00
15 Ernie Wright	7.50	15.00
16 Sam Wyche	10.00	20.00

1969 Bengals Tresler Comet

The 1969 Tresler Comet set contains 20 cards featuring Cincinnati Bengals only. The cards measure 2 1/2" by 3 1/2". The set is quite attractive in its sepia and orange color front with a facsimile autograph of the player portrayed. The cards are unnumbered but have been listed below in alphabetical order for convenience. The card of Bob Johnson is much scarcer than the other cards, although some collectors and dealers consider Howard Fest, Harry Gunner, and Warren McVea to be somewhat more difficult to find as well. The backs contain biographical and statistical data of the player and the Tresler Comet logo. An offer to obtain a free set of these cards at a Tresler Comet (gasoline) dealer is stated at the bottom on the back.

COMPLETE SET (20)	300.00	450.00
1 Al Beauchamp	5.00	10.00
2 Bill Bergey	6.00	12.00
3 Royce Berry	5.00	10.00
4 Paul Brown CO	25.00	40.00
5 Frank Buncom	5.00	10.00
6 Greg Cook	5.00	10.00
7 Howard Fest SP	30.00	50.00
8 Harry Gunner SP	30.00	50.00
9 Bobby Hunt	5.00	10.00
10 Bob Johnson SP	75.00	125.00
11 Charley King	5.00	10.00
12 Dale Livingston	5.00	10.00
13 Warren McVea SP	30.00	50.00
14 Bill Peterson	5.00	10.00
15 Jess Phillips	5.00	10.00
16 Andy Rice	5.00	10.00
17 Bill Staley	5.00	10.00
18 Bob Trumpy	6.00	12.00
19 Ernie Wright	5.00	10.00
20 Sam Wyche	7.50	15.00

1971 Bengals Team Issue

The Bengals issued this photo pack set in 1971. Each borderless photo measures roughly 4 3/4" by 6 3/4" and features a facsimile autograph of the player over the photo. The cardbacks are blank and unnumbered. The set was typically released in an envelope labeled "Travel With the Champs" with the checklist on the outside of the envelope.

COMPLETE SET (6)	30.00	60.00
1 Virgil Carter	6.00	12.00
2 Greg Cook	6.00	12.00
3 Bob Johnson	6.00	12.00
4 Horst Muhlman	6.00	12.00
5 Lamar Parrish	6.00	12.00
6 Mike Reid	7.50	15.00

1972-74 Bengals Team Issue

The Bengals issued this set of player photos in the mid-1970s. Each measures roughly 8" by 10" and was printed on glossy black and white stock. The photos are blankbacked and unnumbered and checklisted below in alphabetical order. Each photo typically includes the player's name, position (spelled out) and team name below the photo seperated by dashes. The type sizes and styles vary with many of the photos in this list suggesting that they were issued in different years. Any additions to the list below are appreciated.

1 Doug Adams	5.00	10.00
2 Ken Anderson	7.50	15.00
3 Ken Avery	5.00	10.00
4 Al Beauchamp	5.00	10.00
5A Royce Berry wht jsy	5.00	10.00
5B Royce Berry brwn jsy	5.00	10.00
6 Lyle Blackwood	5.00	10.00
7 Paul Brown CO	7.50	15.00
8 Ron Carpenter	5.00	10.00
9 Virgil Carter wht jsy	5.00	10.00
10 Tommy Casanova	5.00	10.00
11 Al Chandler	5.00	10.00
12 Steve Chomyszak	5.00	10.00
13 Boobie Clark	6.00	12.00
14 Charles Clark	5.00	10.00
15 Wayne Clark	5.00	10.00
16 Bruce Coslet	5.00	10.00
17 Neal Craig	5.00	10.00
18 Isaac Curtis	5.00	10.00
19 Charles Davis	5.00	10.00
20 Doug Dressler	5.00	10.00
21 Lenvil Elliott	5.00	10.00
22 Mike Ernst	5.00	10.00
23 Howard Fest	5.00	10.00
24 Dave Green	5.00	10.00
25 Vern Holland	5.00	10.00
26 Bernard Jackson	5.00	10.00
27 Bob Johnson wht jsy	6.00	12.00
28 Ken Johnson DT	5.00	10.00
29 Charlie Joiner	7.50	15.00
30 Evan Jolitz wht jsy	5.00	10.00
31 Bob Jones S	5.00	10.00
32 Tim Kearney	5.00	10.00
33 Bill Kollar	5.00	10.00
34 Dave Lapham	5.00	10.00
35 Steve Lawson	5.00	10.00
36 Jim LeClair	5.00	10.00
37 Dave Lewis wht jsy	5.00	10.00
38 Pat Matson	5.00	10.00
39 Rufus Mayes	5.00	10.00
40 John McDaniel	5.00	10.00
41 Horst Muhlmann	5.00	10.00
42 Chip Myers	5.00	10.00
43 Lemar Parrish	6.00	12.00
44 Ron Pritchard	5.00	10.00
45 Mike Reid	6.00	12.00
46 Ken Riley	6.00	12.00
47 Paul Robinson wht jsy	5.00	10.00
48 Ken Sawyer wht jsy	5.00	10.00
49 John Shinners	5.00	10.00
50 Fletcher Smith	5.00	10.00
51 Bob Trumpy	6.00	12.00
52 Stan Walters	5.00	10.00
53 Sherman White	5.00	10.00
54 Fred Willis wht jsy	5.00	10.00

1976 Bengals MSA Cups

This set of plastic cups was issued for the Cincinnati Bengals in 1976 and licensed through MSA. Each features an artist's rendering of a Bengals' player. Some players also appeared in the nationally issued 1976 MSA Cups set with only slight differences in each. The unnumbered cups are listed below alphabetically. Confirmed additions to this checklist are appreciated.

1 Ken Anderson	5.00	10.00
2 Archie Griffin	4.00	8.00
3 Essex Johnson	3.00	6.00

1975-77 Bengals Team Issue

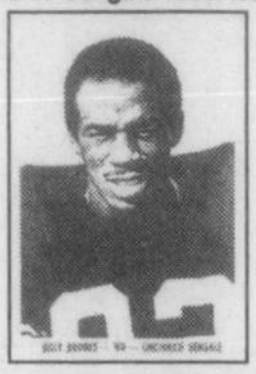

The Bengals issued this set of player photos between 1975 and 1977. Each measures roughly 5" by 8" with a black and white photo. The photos are blankbacked and unnumbered and checklisted below in alphabetical order. Each card includes the player's name, position initials and team name below the photo in large all capital letters. They look very similar to the 1978-79 photos but feature a larger type size. The white border below the player image is generally smaller as well but some players were also issued with a larger border and larger type size which would indicate a multiple year issue.

1 Al Beauchamp	4.00	8.00
2 Lyle Blackwood	4.00	8.00
3 Billy Brooks	4.00	8.00
4A Bob Brown	4.00	8.00
(jersey numbers not showing)		
4B Bob Brown	4.00	8.00
(jersey numbers showing)		
5 Glenn Bujnoch	4.00	8.00
6 Gary Burley	4.00	8.00
7 Glenn Cameron	4.00	8.00
8 Ron Carpenter	4.00	8.00
9 Tommy Casanova	4.00	8.00
10 Boobie Clark	4.00	8.00
11 Marvin Cobb	4.00	8.00
12 Bruce Coslet	4.00	8.00
13 Brad Cousino	4.00	8.00
14 Isaac Curtis	5.00	10.00
15 Tony Davis	4.00	8.00
16 Lenvil Elliott	4.00	8.00
17 Greg Fairchild	4.00	8.00
18 Howard Fest	4.00	8.00
19 Stan Fritts	4.00	8.00
20A Vern Holland	4.00	8.00
(smiling pose)		
20B Vern Holland	4.00	8.00
(not smiling)		
21 Ron Hunt	4.00	8.00
22 Bob Johnson	4.00	8.00
23 Essex Johnson	4.00	8.00
24 Ken Johnson	4.00	8.00
25 Charlie Joiner	6.00	12.00
26 Bill Kollar	4.00	8.00
27 Al Krevis	4.00	8.00
28A Dave Lapham	4.00	8.00
(jersey numbers cut off)		
28B Dave Lapham	4.00	8.00
(jersey numbers fully visible)		
29 Jim LeClair	4.00	8.00
30 Rufus Mayes	4.00	8.00
31A John McDaniel	4.00	8.00
(jersey numbers fully visible)		
31B John McDaniel	4.00	8.00
(jersey numbers cut in half)		
32 Pat McInally	4.00	8.00
33 Maulty Moore	4.00	8.00
34 Melvin Morgan	4.00	8.00
35 Jack Novak	4.00	8.00
36 Lemar Parrish	5.00	10.00
37 Scott Perry	4.00	8.00
38A Ron Pritchard	4.00	8.00
(wearing a crew cut)		
38B Ron Pritchard	4.00	8.00
(wearing longer hair style)		
39 John Reaves	4.00	8.00
40 Ken Riley	5.00	10.00
41 Willie Shelby	4.00	8.00
42A John Shinners	4.00	8.00
(jersey numbers fully visible)		
42B John Shinners	4.00	8.00
(jersey numbers cut in half)		
43 Rick Walker	4.00	8.00
44 Sherman White	4.00	8.00
45 Ed Williams	4.00	8.00
46A Reggie Williams	5.00	10.00
(jersey numbers fully visible)		
46B Reggie Williams	5.00	10.00
(jersey numbers cut in half)		

1978-79 Bengals Team Issue

The Bengals issued this set of player photos in 1978. The 5 x 8 black and white photos are blankbacked and unnumbered and checklisted below in alphabetical order. Each card includes the player's name, position (spelled out) and team name below the photo. They look very similar to the 1975-77 photos but feature a smaller type size and a larger white border below the player image.

COMPLETE SET (30)	100.00	200.00
1 Ken Anderson	6.00	12.00
2 Chris Bahr	4.00	8.00
3 Don Bass	4.00	8.00
4 Louis Breeden	4.00	8.00
5 Ross Browner	4.00	8.00
6 Glenn Bujnoch	4.00	8.00
7 Gary Burley	4.00	8.00
8 Blair Bush	4.00	8.00
9 Glenn Cameron	4.00	8.00
10 Marvin Cobb	4.00	8.00
11 Jim Corbett	4.00	8.00
12 Tom DePaso	4.00	8.00
13 Tom Dinkel	4.00	8.00
14 Mark Donahue	4.00	8.00
15 Eddie Edwards	4.00	8.00
16 Lenvil Elliott	4.00	8.00
17 Archie Griffin	6.00	12.00
18 Ray Griffin	4.00	8.00
19 Bo Harris	4.00	8.00
20 Ron Hunt	4.00	8.00
21 Pete Johnson	5.00	10.00
22 Dave Lapham	4.00	8.00
23 Dennis Law	4.00	8.00
24 Jim LeClair	4.00	8.00
25 Pat McInally	4.00	8.00
26 Ken Riley	5.00	10.00
27 Ron Shumon	4.00	8.00
28 Dave Turner	4.00	8.00
29 Ted Vincent	4.00	8.00
30 Wilson Whitley	4.00	8.00

1982 Bengals Nu-Maid Butter Tubs

This set of butter cups or tubs was released by Nu-Maid and Miami Margarine in 1982 in the Cincinnati area. Each includes color illustrations of the featured player and measures roughly 3 3/4" tall and 3" in diameter.

COMPLETE SET (7)	25.00	40.00
1 Ken Anderson	5.00	10.00
2 Cris Collinsworth	4.00	8.00
3 Archie Griffin	4.00	8.00
4 Pete Johnson	3.00	6.00
5 Jim LeClair	3.00	6.00
6 Anthony Munoz	5.00	10.00
7 Reggie Williams	3.00	6.00

1997 Bengals Team Sheets

COMPLETE SET (9)	15.00	30.00
1 Mike Brown PRES	1.50	4.00
Bruce Coslet CO		
Dick LeBeau CO		
Ken Anderson CO		
Paul Alexander CO		
Jim Anderson CO		
Louie Cioffi CO		
Mark Duffner CO		
2 John Garrett CO	1.50	4.00
Ray Horton CO		
Tim Krumrie CO		
Al Roberts CO		
Kim Wood CO		
Bob Wylie CO		
Ashley Ambrose		
Willie Anderson		
3 Marco Battaglia	2.00	5.00
Eric Bieniemy		
Ken Blackman		
Jeff Blake		
Rich Braham		
Darrick Brilz		
Anthony Brown		
Scott Brumfield		
4 Brentson Buckner	2.00	5.00
Steve Bush		
Ki-Jana Carter		
Andre Collins		
John Copeland		
Canute Curtis		
Corey Dillon		
Gerald Dixon		
5 Ty Douthard	3.00	8.00
David Dunn		
Boomer Esiason		
James Francis		
Scottie Graham		
Billy Granville		
Brock Gutierrez		
James Hundon		
6 Mike Jenkins	1.50	4.00
Lee Johnson		
Rod Jones		
Roger Jones		
Jevon Langford		
Anthone Lott		
Tremain Mack		
Ricardo McDonald		
7 Tony McGee	2.00	5.00
Brian Milne		
Greg Myers		
Bo Orlando		
Rod Payne		
Doug Pelfrey		
Carl Pickens		
Andre Purvis		
8 Kevin Sargent	2.00	5.00
Corey Sawyer		
Darnay Scott		
Sam Shade		
Jimmy Spencer		
Ramondo Stallings		
Steve Tovar		
Greg Truitt		
9 Tom Tumulty	1.50	4.00
Gunnard Twyner		
Kimo Von Oelhoffen		
Joe Walter		
Erik Wilhelm		
Dan Wilkinson		
Reinard Wilson		
Lawrence Wright		

1998 Bengals Team Sheets

COMPLETE SET (6)	10.00	25.00
1 Bruce Coslet CO	1.50	4.00
Dick LeBeau Asst. CO		
Ken Anderson CO		
Paul Alexander CO		
Jim Anderson CO		
Louie Cioffi CO		
Mark Duffner CO		
John Garrett CO		
Ray Horton CO		
Tim Krumrie CO		
Al Roberts CO		
Kim Wood CO		
2 Bob Wylie	2.00	5.00
Ashley Ambrose		
Willie Anderson		
Michael Bankston		
Marco Battaglia		
Myron Bell		
Brandon Bennett		
Eric Bieniemy		
Ken Blackman		
Jeff Blake		
Rich Braham		
Darrick Brilz		
3 Anthony Brown	2.00	5.00
Steve Bush		
Ki-Jana Carter		
John Copeland		
Harry Deligianis		
Corey Dillon		
Mike Doughty		
Steve Foley		
James Francis		
Damon Gibson		
Mike Goff		
Billy Granville		
4 Artrell Hawkins	1.50	4.00
James Hundon		
Willie Jackson		
Lee Johnson		
Rod Jones		
Paul Justin		
Eric Kresser		
Jevon Langford		
Tremain Mack		
Ric Mathias		
Tony McGee		
Brian Milne		
5 Greg Myers	2.00	5.00
Neil O?ÇODonnell		
Rod Payne		
Doug Pelfrey		
Carl Pickens		
Andre Purvis		
Thomas Randolph		
Adrian Ross		
Kevin Sargent		
Corey Sawyer		
Darnay Scott		
Sam Shade		
6 Scott Shaw	1.50	4.00
Brian Simmons		
Clyde Simmons		
Takeo Spikes		
Glen Steele		
Mike Thompson		
Greg Truitt		
Tom Tumulty		
Damiam Vaughn		
Kimo von Oelhoffen		
Stepfret Williams		
Reinard Wilson		

2003 Bengals Upper Deck Gold Star Chili

This set was sponsored by Gold Star Chili, produced by Upper Deck, and features members of the Cincinnati Bengals. The cards are printed in a horizontal format and are numbered on the backs.

COMPLETE SET (17)	10.00	20.00
1 Jon Kitna	.75	2.00
2 Carson Palmer	2.50	6.00
3 Tory James	.30	.75
4 Corey Dillon	.75	2.00
5 Kevin Hardy	.30	.75
6 Brian Simmons	.30	.75
7 Willie Anderson	.30	.75
8 Matt O'Dwyer	.30	.75
9 Levi Jones	.30	.75
10 Peter Warrick	.75	2.00
11 Reggie Kelly	.30	.75
12 Chad Johnson	.40	1.00
13 Justin Smith	.40	1.00
14 Tony Williams	.30	.75
15 John Thornton	.30	.75
16 Marvin Lewis CO	.75	2.00
NNO Coupon Card	.40	1.00

2006 Bengals Topps

COMPLETE SET (12)	3.00	5.00
CIN1 Deltha O'Neal	.20	.50
CIN2 Chad Johnson	.25	.60
CIN3 Carson Palmer	.30	.75
CIN4 Shayne Graham	.20	.50
CIN5 Chris Perry	.25	.60
CIN6 Rudi Johnson	.25	.60
CIN7 Odell Thurman	.20	.50
CIN8 T.J. Houshmandzadeh	.25	.60
CIN9 David Pollack	.20	.50
CIN10 Tory James	.20	.50
CIN11 Reggie McNeal	.25	.60
CIN12 Johnathan Joseph	.25	.60

2007 Bengals Activa Medallions

COMPLETE SET (22)	30.00	60.00
1 Paul Brown	1.50	4.00
2 Ken Anderson	1.50	4.00
3 James Brooks	1.25	3.00
4 Cris Collinsworth	1.50	4.00
5 Isaac Curtis	1.25	3.00
6 Boomer Esiason	1.50	4.00
7 David Fulcher	1.25	3.00
8 Anthony Munoz	1.50	4.00
9 Ken Riley	1.25	3.00
10 Ickey Woods	1.25	3.00
11 Willie Anderson	1.25	3.00
12 Robert Geathers	1.25	3.00
13 Shayne Graham	1.25	3.00
14 T.J. Houshmandzadeh	1.50	4.00
15 Chad Johnson	1.50	4.00
16 Rudi Johnson	1.25	3.00
17 Levi Jones	1.25	3.00
18 Johnathan Joseph	1.25	3.00
19 Marvin Lewis	1.25	3.00
20 Carson Palmer	2.00	5.00
21 Justin Smith	1.25	3.00
22 40th Anniversary Logo	1.25	3.00

2007 Bengals Topps

COMPLETE SET (12)	2.50	5.00
1 Carson Palmer	.25	.60
2 Rudi Johnson	.25	.60
3 Chad Johnson	.25	.60
4 Madieu Williams	.20	.50
5 T.J. Houshmandzadeh	.25	.60
6 Robert Geathers	.20	.50

7 Landon Johnson	.20	.50
8 Kenny Irons	.20	.50
9 Justin Smith	.20	.50
10 Shayne Graham	.20	.50
11 Leon Hall	.25	.60
12 Johnathan Joseph	.20	.50

2008 Bengals Topps

COMPLETE SET (12)	2.50	5.00
1 Carson Palmer	.30	.75
2 Chad Johnson	.25	.60
3 Kenny Watson	.20	.50
4 T.J. Houshmandzadeh	.25	.60
5 Rudi Johnson	.25	.60
6 Leon Hall	.20	.50
7 Keith Rivers	.30	.75
8 Reggie Kelly	.20	.50
9 Johnathan Joseph	.20	.50
10 Dexter Jackson	.25	.60
11 Jerome Simpson	.30	.75
12 Andre Caldwell	.25	.60

1951 Berk Ross

The 1951 Berk Ross set consists of 72 cards (each measuring approximately 2 1/16" by 2 1/2") with tinted photographs, divided evenly into four series (designated in the checklist as A, B, C and D). The cards were marketed in boxes containing two card panels, without gum, and the set includes stars of other sports as well as baseball players. The set is sometimes still found in the original packaging. Intact panels command a premium over the listed prices. The catalog designation for this set is W532-1. In every series the first ten cards are baseball players; the set has a heavy emphasis on Yankees and Phillies players as they were in the World Series the year before. The set includes the first card of Bob Cousy as well as a card of Whitey Ford in his Rookie Card year.

COMPLETE SET (72)	900.00	1,500.00
14-Jan Leon Hart Football	7.50	15.00
15-Jan James Martin Football	6.00	12.00
14-Feb Doak Walker Football	10.00	20.00
15-Feb Emil Sitko Football	6.00	12.00
14-Mar Wade Walker Football	7.50	15.00
15-Mar Rodney Franz Football	6.00	12.00
14-Apr Arnold Galiffa Football	6.00	12.00
15-Apr Charlie Justice Football	7.50	15.00

1960 Bills Team Issue

Issued by the team, this set of 40 black-and-white photos each measures roughly 4 7/8" by 6 3/4" and was given to 1960 Bills season ticketholders in complete set form. The photos are unnumbered and checklisted below in alphabetical order. The photos are frequently found personally autographed.

COMPLETE SET (40)	250.00	400.00
1 Bill Atkins	7.50	15.00
2 Bob Barrett	7.50	15.00
3 Phil Blazer	7.50	15.00
4 Bob Brodhead	7.50	15.00
5 Dick Brubaker	7.50	15.00
6 Bernie Buzyniski UER (name spelled Burzinski)	7.50	15.00
7 Wray Carlton	7.50	15.00
8 Don Chelf	7.50	15.00
9 Monte Crockett	7.50	15.00
10 Bob Dove CO	7.50	15.00
11 Elbert Dubenion	10.00	20.00
12 Fred Ford	7.50	15.00
13 Dick Gallagher GM	7.50	15.00
14 Darrell Harper	7.50	15.00
15 Harvey Johnson CO	7.50	15.00
16 John Johnson	7.50	15.00
17 Billy Kinard	7.50	15.00
18 Joe Kulbacki	7.50	15.00
19 John Laraway	7.50	15.00
20 Richie Lucas	7.50	15.00
21 Archie Matsos	7.50	15.00
22 Rich McCabe	7.50	15.00
23 Dan McGrew	7.50	15.00
24 Chuck McMurtry	7.50	15.00
25 Ed Meyer	7.50	15.00
26 Ed Muelhaupt	7.50	15.00
27 Tom O'Connell	7.50	15.00
28 Harold Olson	7.50	15.00
29 Buster Ramsey CO	7.50	15.00
30 Floyd Reid CO	7.50	15.00
31 Tom Rychlec	7.50	15.00
32 Joe Schaffer	7.50	15.00
33 John Scott	7.50	15.00
34 Bob Sedlock	7.50	15.00
35 Carl Smith	7.50	15.00
36 Jim Sorey	7.50	15.00
37 Laverne Torczon	7.50	15.00
38 Jim Wagstaff	7.50	15.00
39 Ralph Wilson OWN	10.00	20.00
40 Mack Yoho	7.50	15.00

1963 Bills Jones-Rich Dairy

This set of 40-crude drawings features members of the Buffalo Bills and were produced in a variety of versions and variations, but not all players have been verified for all versions. These "cards" are actually either blankbacked cardboard cut-outs from the sides of milk cartons or actual cap liners originally inserted into milk bottles. The bottle cap liners were produced with or without a small pull-out tab on the fronts and include the Jones-Rich logo on the backs. The flat (non-tab) version of the bottle caps liners were also produced in two versions with one being printed with a slightly larger player name printed on the front and larger company logo printed on the back. It is not yet known which players appeared in the large versus small print or the flat versus tab cap version. The milk carton version was produced in both a red and black ink variety with a further slight difference being found in the red ink variety (some can be found with a red ink circle around the player image along with the yellow ink dotted line). Most, if not all, of the players appear to be available in both varieties as well as both milk cap versions. The black ink carton variety seems to be very difficult to find. These circular cards measure approximately 1" in diameter and are frequently found miscut, i.e., off-centered. A display sheet that featured Bill's owner, Ralph Wilson, and Head Coach, Lou Saban, was also produced to house some of the caps and liners. Collectors at the time were challenged to complete a line-up of the 1963 Bills team, attach the caps and liners to the sheet and mail it in for a chance to win tickets to a Bill's game. The ACC catalog designation for this set is F118-1.

*CAP LINERS: .5X TO 1.2X CARTON CUT-OUTS		
1 Ray Abruzzese	150.00	300.00
2 Art Baker	150.00	300.00
3 Stew Barber	200.00	350.00
4 Glenn Bass	150.00	300.00
5 Dave Behrman	150.00	300.00
6 Al Bemiller	150.00	300.00
7 Wray Carlton	150.00	300.00
8 Carl Charon	150.00	300.00
9 Monte Crockett	150.00	300.00
10 Wayne Crow	150.00	300.00
11 Tom Day	150.00	300.00
12 Elbert Dubenion	200.00	350.00
13 Jim Dunaway	200.00	350.00
14 Booker Edgerson	150.00	300.00
15 Cookie Gilchrist	250.00	400.00
16 Dick Hudson	150.00	300.00
17 Frank Jackunas	150.00	300.00
18 Harry Jacobs	150.00	300.00
19 Jack Kemp	500.00	800.00
20 Roger Kochman	150.00	300.00
21 Daryle Lamonica	250.00	400.00
22 Charley Leo	150.00	300.00
23 Marv Matuszak	150.00	300.00
24 Bill Miller	150.00	300.00
25 Leroy Moore	150.00	300.00
26 Harold Olson	150.00	300.00
27 Herb Paterra	150.00	300.00
28 Ken Rice	150.00	300.00
29 Henry Rivera	150.00	300.00
30 Ed Rutkowski	150.00	300.00
31 George Saimes	150.00	300.00
32 Tom Sestak	150.00	300.00
33 Billy Shaw	250.00	400.00
34 Mike Stratton	150.00	300.00
35 Gene Sykes	150.00	300.00
36 John Tracey	150.00	300.00
37 Ernie Warlick	150.00	300.00
38 Willie West	150.00	300.00
39 Mack Yoho	150.00	300.00
40 Cid Youngelman	150.00	300.00
NNO Display Sheet	500.00	750.00

1965 Bills Matchbooks

This 1965 Buffalo Bills release contains at least 3-different matchbooks. Each features a Bills player printed in blue on white paper stock along with the team's 1965 season schedule. Any additions to the checklist below would be greatly appreciated.

COMPLETE SET (3)	40.00	75.00
1 Elbert Dubenion	18.00	30.00
2 Billy Shaw	20.00	35.00
3 Tom Sestak	15.00	25.00

1965 Bills Super Duper Markets

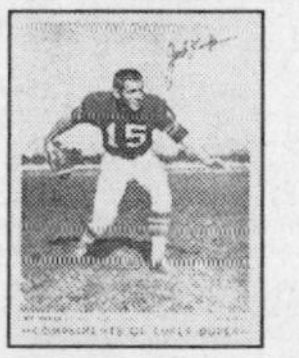

Super Duper Food Markets offered these black-and-white (approximately 8 1/2" by 11") Buffalo Bills photos to shoppers during the fall of 1965. The photos were a weekly giveaway during the football season by Super Duper markets in western New York. The photos are unnumbered and checklisted below in alphabetical order.

COMPLETE SET (10)	150.00	250.00
1 Glenn Bass	7.50	15.00
2 Elbert Dubenion	10.00	20.00
3 Billy Joe	7.50	15.00
4 Jack Kemp	50.00	100.00
5 Daryle Lamonica	25.00	40.00
6 Tom Sestak	7.50	15.00
7 Billy Shaw	10.00	20.00
8 Mike Stratton	7.50	15.00
9 Ernie Warlick	7.50	15.00
10 Team Photo	15.00	30.00

1965 Bills Team Issue

Issued by the team, this set of black-and-white photos each measures roughly 8" by 10" and was issued to fulfill fan requests and for player appearances in the mid 1960s. Unless noted below, the text within the bottom border includes the player's name in all caps, his position in lower case letters, and the team name in all caps. The photos are unnumbered, blankbacked, and checklisted below in alphabetical order.

1 Cookie Gilchrist	7.50	15.00
2 Daryle Lamonica	10.00	20.00
3 Tom Janik Horizontal pose SAFETY, TOM JANIK, BUFFALO BILLS	6.00	12.00

1965 Bills Volpe Tumblers

These Bills artist's renderings were part of a plastic cup tumbler produced in 1965 and distributed through Sunoco gasoline stations. The noted sports artist Volpe created the artwork which includes an action scene and a player portrait. These paper inserts are unnumbered, each measures approximately 5" by 8 1/2" and is curved in the shape required to fit inside a plastic cup.

COMPLETE SET (12)	300.00	500.00
1 Glenn Bass	25.00	40.00
2 Butch Byrd	30.00	50.00
3 Wray Carlton	25.00	40.00
4 Tom Day	25.00	40.00
5 Billy Joe	30.00	50.00
6 Jack Kemp	60.00	100.00
7 Daryle Lamonica	40.00	75.00
8 Lou Saban CO	30.00	50.00
9 George Saimes	25.00	40.00
10 Tom Sestak	25.00	40.00
11 Billy Shaw	35.00	60.00
12 Mike Stratton	30.00	50.00

1966 Bills Matchbooks

The 1966 Bills Matchbook set features the team's 1966 season schedule along with a blue player photo and sponsor logos. Any additions to the checklist below would be greatly appreciated.

COMPLETE SET (4)	100.00	175.00
1 Butch Byrd	7.50	15.00
2 Elbert Dubenion	18.00	30.00
3 Jack Kemp	75.00	125.00
4 Mike Stratton	15.00	25.00

1967 Bills Jones-Rich Dairy

Through a special mail-in offer, Jones-Rich Milk Co. offered this set of six Buffalo Bills' highlight action photos from the 1965 and 1966 seasons. These black-and-white photos measure approximately 8 1/2" by 11".

COMPLETE SET (6)	75.00	125.00
1 George Butch Byrd	12.50	25.00
2 Wray Carlton	12.50	25.00
3 Hagood Clarke	10.00	20.00
4 Paul Costa	10.00	20.00
5 Jim Dunaway	10.00	20.00
6 Jack Spikes	12.50	25.00

1967 Bills Matchbooks

The 1967 Buffalo Bills matchbook set contains 4-different matchbooks. Each includes the team's 1967 season schedule along with a player photo printed in blue ink. Any additions to the checklist below would be greatly appreciated.

COMPLETE SET (4)	50.00	00.00
1 Bobby Burnett	15.00	25.00
2 Butch Byrd	18.00	30.00
3 Roland McDole	15.00	25.00
4 Ed Rutkowski	15.00	25.00

1967 Bills Team Issue

Issued by the team, this set of black-and-white photos each measures roughly 8" by 10" and was issued to fulfill fan requests and for player appearances in the mid 1960s. Unless noted below, the text within the bottom border includes on the far left the photographer's ID, then (in all caps) the player's position, his name, and the team name, followed by the team logo on the far right. The photos are unnumbered, blankbacked, and checklisted below in alphabetical order.

1 Joe Collier CO	6.00	12.00
2 Jack Kemp	20.00	35.00

1968 Bills Matchbooks

This Buffalo Bills matchbook set contains only one known matchbook. It includes the team's 1968 season schedule along with a player photo printed in black ink. Any additions to the checklist below would be appreciated.

1 Keith Lincoln	25.00	40.00

1972 Bills Buffalo News Posters

These posters were created by the Buffalo News and issued as "pages" in the daily newspapers during the 1972 season. Each large poster includes a color artist's rendition of a Bills player on the front with a typical newspaper page back. We've included the date when the photo appeared when known.

COMPLETE SET (10)	50.00	100.00
1 Paul Costa (10/14/1972)	4.00	10.00
2 Al Cowlings (10/28/1972)	4.00	10.00
3 Paul Guidry (10/21/1972)	4.00	10.00
4 J.D. Hill (9/23/1972)	4.00	10.00
5 Spike Jones (11/11/1972)	4.00	10.00
6 Reggie McKenzie (11/18/1972)	6.00	15.00
7 Wayne Patrick (10/7/1972)	4.00	10.00
8 Walt Patulski (11/4/1972)	4.00	10.00
9 Dennis Shaw (9/16/1972)	5.00	12.00
10 O.J. Simpson (9/30/1972)	12.50	25.00

1973 Bills Buffalo News Posters

These posters were created by the Buffalo News and issued as "pages" in the daily newspapers during the 1973 season. Each large poster includes a color artist's rendition of a Bills player on the front with a typical newspaper page back. We've included the date when the photo appeared when known. Any additions to this list are appreciated.

COMPLETE SET (16)	75.00	150.00
1 Jim Braxton	4.00	10.00
2 Bob Chandler (11/10/1973)	5.00	12.00
3 Jim Cheyunski (10/6/1973)	4.00	10.00
4 Earl Edwards (11/3/1973)	4.00	10.00
5 Joe Ferguson (10/20/1973)	6.00	15.00
6 Tony Greene (12/1/1973)	4.00	10.00
7 Bob James (9/22/1973)	4.00	10.00
8 Bruce Jarvis (9/29/1973)	4.00	10.00
9 Reggie McKenzie	6.00	15.00
10 Ahmad Rashad	6.00	15.00
11 Lou Saban CO (9/15/1973)	4.00	10.00
12 Paul Seymour (11/17/1973)	4.00	10.00
13 Dennis Shaw (10/13/1973)	5.00	12.00
14 O.J. Simpson (11/24/1973)	15.00	30.00
15 John Skorupan (12/8/1973)	4.00	10.00
16 Larry Watkins (10/21/1973)	4.00	10.00

1973 Bills Team Issue Color

The NFLPA worked with many teams in 1973 to issued photo packs to be sold at stadium concession stands. Each measures approximately 7" by 8-5/8" and features a color player photo with a blank back. A small sheet with a player checklist was included in each 6-photo pack.

COMPLETE SET (12)	40.00	80.00
1 Jim Braxton	4.00	8.00
2 Bob Chandler	4.00	8.00
3 Jim Cheyunski	4.00	8.00
4 Earl Edwards	4.00	8.00
5 Joe Ferguson	5.00	10.00
6 Dave Foley	4.00	8.00
7 Robert James	4.00	8.00
8 Reggie McKenzie	4.00	8.00
9 Jerry Patton	4.00	8.00
10 Walt Patulski	4.00	8.00
11 John Skorupan	4.00	8.00
12 O.J. Simpson	10.00	20.00

1974 Bills Buffalo News Posters

These posters were created by the Buffalo News and issued as "pages" in the daily newspapers during the 1974 season. Each large poster includes a color artist's rendition of a Bills player on the front with a typical newspaper page back. We've included the date when the photo appeared when known. Any additions to this list are appreciated.

COMPLETE SET (12)	60.00	120.00
1 Doug Allen (9/28/1974)	4.00	10.00
2 Jim Braxton (11/16/1974)	4.00	10.00
3 Joe DeLamielleure (11/9/1974)	6.00	15.00
4 Reuben Gant (10/12/1974)	4.00	10.00
5 Dwight Harrison (12/7/1974)	4.00	10.00
6 Mike Kadish (11/30/1974)	4.00	10.00
7 John Leypoldt (10/23/1974)	4.00	10.00
8 Reggie McKenzie (11/3/1974)	6.00	15.00
9 Mike Montler (12/14/1974)	4.00	10.00
10 Walt Patulski (9/21/1974)	4.00	10.00
11 Ahmad Rashad (11/23/1974)	6.00	15.00
12 O.J. Simpson (9/14/1974)	12.50	25.00

1975 Bills Buffalo News Posters

These posters were created by the Buffalo News and issued as "pages" in the daily newspapers during the 1975 season. Each large poster includes a color artist's rendition of a Bills player on the front with a typical newspaper page back. We've included the date when the photo appeared when known. Any additions to this list are appreciated.

COMPLETE SET (13)	50.00	100.00
1 Marv Bateman (12/1/1975)	3.00	8.00
2 Bo Cornell (10/25/1975)	3.00	8.00
3 Don Croft (10/4/1975)	3.00	8.00
4 Dave Foley (10/16/1975)	3.00	8.00
5 Gary Hayman (10/18/1975)	3.00	8.00
6 John Holland (12/13/1975)	3.00	8.00
7 Merv Krakau (11/22/1975)	3.00	8.00
8 Gary Marangi (10/11/1975)	3.00	8.00
9 Willie Parker (12/6/1975)	3.00	8.00
10 Tom Ruud (11/8/1975)	3.00	8.00
11 Pat Toomay (9/27/1975)	3.00	8.00
12 Vic Washington (11/20/1975)	3.00	8.00
13 Jeff Winans (11/29/1975)	3.00	8.00

1976 Bills Buffalo News Posters

These posters were created by the Buffalo News and issued as "pages" in the daily newspapers during the 1976 season. Each large poster includes a color artist's rendition of a Bills player on the front with a typical newspaper page back. We've included the date when the photo appeared when known. Any additions to this list are appreciated.

COMPLETE SET (11)	40.00	80.00
1 Bill Adams (10/9/1976)	3.00	8.00
2 Mario Clark (12/4/1976)	3.00	8.00
3 Joe Ferguson (10/23/1976)	5.00	12.00
4 Steve Freeman (11/13/1976)	3.00	8.00
5 Dan Jilek (10/2/1976)	3.00	8.00
6 Doug Jones (11/27/1976)	3.00	8.00
7 Ken Jones (11/20/1976)	3.00	8.00
8 Merv Krakau (10/16/1976)	3.00	8.00
9 Gary Marangi (10/30/1976)	3.00	8.00
10 Eddie Ray (12/11/1976)	3.00	8.00
11 Sherman White (12/6/1976)	3.00	8.00

1976 Bills McDonald's

This set of three photos was sponsored by McDonald's in conjunction with WBEN-TV. These "Player of the Week" photos were given away free with the purchase of a Quarter Pounder at participating McDonald's restaurants of Western New York. The offer was valid while supplies lasted but ended Nov. 28, 1976. Each photo measures approximately 8" by 10" and features a posed color close-up photo bordered in white. The player's name and team name are printed in black in the bottom white border, and his facsimile autograph is inscribed across the photo toward the lower right corner. The top portion of the back has biographical information, career summary, and career statistics (except the McKenzie back omits statistics). Inside a rectangle, the bottom portion describes the promotion and presents the 1976-77 football schedule on WBEN-TV. The photos are unnumbered and are checklisted below alphabetically.

COMPLETE SET (3)	12.50	25.00
1 Bob Chandler	4.00	8.00
2 Joe Ferguson	6.00	12.00
3 Reggie McKenzie	4.00	8.00

1977 Bills Buffalo News Posters

These posters were created by the Buffalo News and issued as "pages" in the daily newspapers during the 1977 season. Each large poster includes a color artist's rendition of a Bills player on the front with a typical newspaper page back. We've included the date when the photo appeared when known. Any additions to this list are appreciated.

COMPLETE SET (8)	30.00	60.00
1 Joe Devlin (10/8/1977)	3.00	8.00
2 Phil Dokes (11/13/1977)	3.00	8.00
3 Bill Dunstan (10/22/1977)	3.00	8.00
4 Roland Hooks (10/29/1977)	3.00	8.00
5 Ken Johnson (12/3/1977)	3.00	8.00
6 Keith Moody (10/15/1977)	3.00	8.00
7 Shane Nelson (11/20/1977)	3.00	8.00
8 Ben Williams (11/27/1977)	3.00	8.00

1978 Bills Buffalo News Posters

These posters were created by the Buffalo News and issued as "pages" in the daily newspapers during the 1978 season. Each large poster includes a color artist's rendition of a Bills player on the front with a typical newspaper page back. We've included the date when the photo appeared when known. Any additions to this list are appreciated.

1 Dee Hardison (10/29/1978)	6.00	8.00
2 Scott Hutchinson (11/12/1978)	6.00	8.00
3 Frank Lewis (11/5/1978)	4.00	10.00
4 Terry Miller (10/15/1978)	6.00	8.00
5 Charles Romes (10/22/1978)	6.00	8.00
6 Lucius Sanford (11/19/1978)	6.00	8.00

1978 Bills Postcards

These Bills Team Issue photos were sent out to fans requesting autographs. The cardbacks include a message from the player to fans along with an area for the fan's name and address similar to a postcard. We've included prices below for unsigned copies of the cards. Two different Simpson photos were released that contain the same cardback.

COMPLETE SET (5)	20.00	40.00
1 Jim Braxton	2.00	4.00
2 Bob Chandler	3.00	6.00
3 Joe Ferguson	3.00	6.00
4 O.J. Simpson (cutting to the left)	7.50	15.00
5 O.J. Simpson (hurdling a defender)	7.50	15.00

1978 Bills Team Issue

This set of 8" by 10" black and white photos was issued by the Bills around 1978. Each photo was produced in one of two styles: with player name, position, and team name below the photo, or with jersey number, player name, position, and team name below. All photos also include the photographer's notation (Photo by Robert L. Smith) below the photo. Each is blankbacked and listed alphabetically below.

COMPLETE SET (22)	35.00	60.00
1 Mario Celotto	2.00	4.00
2 Mike Collier	2.00	4.00
3 Elbert Drungo	2.00	4.00
4 Mike Franckowiak	2.00	4.00
5 Tom Graham	2.00	4.00
6 Will Grant	2.00	4.00
7 Tony Greene	2.00	4.00
8 Dee Hardison	2.00	4.00
9 Scott Hutchinson	2.00	4.00
10 Dennis Johnson	2.00	4.00
11 Ken Johnson	2.00	4.00
12 Mike Kadish	2.00	4.00
13 Frank Lewis	2.50	5.00
14 John Little	2.00	4.00
15 Carson Long	2.00	4.00
16 David Mays	2.00	4.00
17 Terry Miller	2.00	4.00
18 Keith Moody	2.00	4.00
19 Bill Munson	2.50	5.00
20 Shane Nelson	2.00	4.00
21 Lucius Sanford	2.00	4.00
22 Connie Zelencik	2.00	4.00

1979 Bills Bell's Market

The 1979 Bell's Market Buffalo Bills set contains 11 photos which were issued one per week, with purchase, at Bell's Markets during the football season. The cards measure approximately 7 5/8" by 10" and were printed on thin stock. The Bills' logo as well as the Bell's Markets logo appears on the back along with information and statistics about the players. The cards show the player portrayed in action in full color. The photos are unnumbered and are listed below in alphabetical order by name.

COMPLETE SET (11)	20.00	40.00
1 Curtis Brown	1.50	3.00
2 Bob Chandler	3.00	6.00
3 Joe DeLamielleure	2.00	4.00
4 Joe Ferguson	4.00	8.00
5 Reuben Gant	2.00	4.00
6 Dee Hardison	1.50	3.00
7 Frank Lewis	2.00	4.00
8 Reggie McKenzie	2.00	4.00
9 Terry Miller	2.00	4.00
10 Shane Nelson	1.50	3.00
11 Lucius Sanford	1.50	3.00

1979 Bills Buffalo News Posters

These posters were created by the Buffalo News and issued as "pages" in the daily newspapers during the 1979 season. Each large poster includes a color artist's rendition of a Bills player on the front with a typical newspaper page back. We've included the date when the photo appeared when known. Any additions to this list are appreciated.

1 Curtis Brown (11/25/1979)	3.00	8.00
2 Jerry Butler (10/14/1979)	4.00	10.00
3 Jim Haslett (10/28/1979)	3.00	8.00
4 Isiah Robertson (12/9/1979)	4.00	10.00
5 Fred Smerlas (9/1/1979)	3.00	8.00

1980 Bills Bell's Market

The 1980 Bell's Market Buffalo Bills cards were available in ten strips of two (connected together by a perforation) or singly as 20 individual cards. The individual cards measure approximately 2 1/2" by 3 1/2". The cards are in full color and contain a red frame line on the front. The back features blue printing listing player biographies, statistics and the Bell's Markets logo. The prices below are for the individual cards. The value of a connected pair is approximately the sum of the two individual cards listed below. The pairings were as follows: 1-2, 3-4, 5-6, 7-8, 9-10, 11-12, 13-14, 15-16, 17-18, and 19-20.

COMPLETE SET (20)	5.00	10.00
1 Curtis Brown	.20	.50
2 Shane Nelson	.20	.50
3 Jerry Butler	.30	.75
4 Joe Ferguson	.60	1.50
5 Joe Cribbs	.40	1.00
6 Reggie McKenzie	.30	.75
7 Joe Devlin	.30	.75
8 Ken Jones	.20	.50
9 Steve Freeman	.20	.50
10 Mike Kadish	.20	.50
11 Jim Haslett	.75	2.00
12 Isiah Robertson	.30	.75
13 Frank Lewis	.30	.75
14 Jeff Nixon	.20	.50
15 Nick Mike-Mayer	.20	.50
16 Jim Ritcher	.30	.75
17 Charles Romes	.20	.50
18 Fred Smerlas	.40	1.00
19 Ben Williams	.20	.50
20 Roland Hooks	.20	.50

1980 Bills Buffalo News Posters

These posters were created by the Buffalo News and issued as "pages" in the daily newspapers during the 1979 season. Each large poster includes a color artist's rendition of a Bills player on the front with a typical newspaper page back. We've included the date when the photo appeared when known. Any additions to this list are appreciated.

COMPLETE SET (9)	30.00	60.00
1 Joe Cribbs (10/19/1980)	4.00	10.00
2 Conrad Dobler (10/26/1980)	4.00	10.00
3 Joe Ferguson (9/28/1980)	4.00	10.00
4 Roosevelt Leaks (11/9/1980)	3.00	8.00
5 Reggie McKenzie (10/5/1980)	5.00	12.00
6 Nick Mike-Mayer (11/2/1980)	3.00	8.00
7 Jeff Nixon (10/12/1980)	3.00	8.00
8 Lou Piccone (11/16/1980)	3.00	8.00
9 Team Picture (12/21/1980)	4.00	10.00

1981 Bills Buffalo News Posters

These posters were created by the Buffalo News and issued as "pages" in the daily newspapers during the 1981 season. Each poster is smaller than what was issued in prior years and an actual player photo is included instead of a color artist's rendition. The backs are a typical newspaper page. We've included the date when the photo appeared when known.

COMPLETE SET (16)	40.00	80.00
1 Mark Brammer 11/1/1981	3.00	6.00
2 Curtis Brown 9/20/1981	3.00	6.00
3 Jerry Butler 11/15/1981	4.00	8.00
4 Greg Cater 11/29/1981	3.00	6.00
5 Joe Cribbs 12/13/1981	4.00	8.00
6 Conrad Dobler 10/11/1981	4.00	8.00
7 Joe Ferguson 9/6/1981	4.00	8.00
8 Will Grant 9/13/1981	3.00	6.00
9 Shane Nelson 12/6/1981	3.00	6.00
10 Lou Piccone 11/22/1981	3.00	6.00
11 Charles Romes 10/18/1981	3.00	6.00
12 Lucius Sanford 10/4/1981	3.00	6.00
13 Fred Smerlas 10/25/1981	3.00	6.00
14 Sherman White 11/8/1981	3.00	6.00
15 Ben Williams 9/27/1981	3.00	6.00
16 Team Picture 12/20/1981	4.00	8.00

1982 Bills Buffalo News Posters

These posters were created by the Buffalo News and issued as "pages" in the daily newspapers during the 1981 season. Each poster is smaller than what was issued in prior years and an actual player photo is included instead of a color artist's rendition. The backs are a typical newspaper page. We've included the date when the photo appeared when known.

COMPLETE SET (8)	25.00	50.00
1 Mario Clark 10/31/1982	3.00	6.00
2 Joe Devlin 10/17/1982	3.00	6.00
3 Ken Jones 10/3/1982	3.00	6.00
4 Frank Lewis 9/26/1982	4.00	8.00
5 Reggie McKenzie 10/24/1982	5.00	10.00
6 Booker Moore 9/12/1982	3.00	6.00
7 Jeff Nixon 9/19/1982	3.00	6.00
8 Perry Tuttle 10/10/1982	3.00	6.00

1983 Bills Buffalo News Posters

These posters were created by the Buffalo News and issued as "pages" in the daily newspapers during the 1981 season. Each poster is smaller than what was issued in prior years and an actual player photo is included instead of a color artist's rendition. The backs are a typical newspaper page. We've included the date when the photo appeared when known.

COMPLETE SET (16)	40.00	80.00
1 Buster Barnett 10/30/1983	3.00	6.00
2 Jon Borchardt 10/9/1983	3.00	6.00
3 Greg Cater 11/6/1983	3.00	6.00
4 Byron Franklin 11/27/1983	3.00	6.00
5 Steve Freeman 10/16/1983	3.00	6.00
6 Tony Hunter 9/4/1983	3.00	6.00
7 Trey Junkin 11/20/1983	3.00	6.00
8 Chris Keating 12/4/1983	3.00	6.00
9 Matt Kofler 9/18/1983	3.00	6.00
10 Rod Kush 9/25/1983	3.00	6.00
11 Roosevelt Leaks 12/11/1983	4.00	8.00
12 Eugene Marve 10/2/1983	3.00	6.00
13 Jim Ritcher 11/13/1983	3.00	6.00
14 Fred Smerlas 10/23/1983	3.00	6.00
15 Darryl Talley 9/11/1983	4.00	8.00
16 Team Picture 12/18/1983	4.00	8.00

1986 Bills Sealtest

These panels were issued on the sides of half-gallon Sealtest milk cartons. The Freeman and Marve panels were issued on the sides of vitamin D cartons, and the Kelly and Romes panels appeared on two percent lowfat cartons. The panels measure approximately 3 5/8" by 7 5/8" and feature a black and white head shot of the player, biographical information, statistics, and career highlights, all in black lettering. The panels are unnumbered and listed below in alphabetical order.

COMPLETE SET (6)	20.00	40.00
1 Greg Bell SP	4.00	10.00
2 Jerry Butler SP	4.00	10.00
3 Steve Freeman	2.00	5.00
4 Jim Kelly	8.00	20.00
5 Eugene Marve	2.00	5.00
6 Charles Romes	2.00	5.00

1987 Bills Police

This eight-card set of Buffalo Bills is numbered on the back. The card backs are printed in gray and black ink on white card stock. Cards measure approximately 2 5/8" by 4 1/8". The set was sponsored by the Buffalo Bills, Erie and Niagara County Sheriff's Departments, Louis Rich Turkey Products, Claussen Pickles, and WBEN Radio.

Uniform numbers are printed on the card front along with the player's name and position. The photos in the set were taken by Robert L. Smith, the Bills' official team photographer.

COMPLETE SET (8)	7.50	15.00
1 Marv Levy CO	.75	2.00
2 Bruce Smith	2.00	5.00
3 Joe Devlin	.60	1.50
4 Jim Kelly	2.50	6.00
5 Eugene Marve	.60	1.50
6 Andre Reed	1.50	4.00
7 Pete Metzelaars	.75	2.00
8 John Kidd	.60	1.50

1988 Bills Police

This eight-card set of Buffalo Bills is numbered in the upper right corner of each reverse. Cards measure approximately 2 5/8" by 4 1/8". The set was sponsored by the Buffalo Bills, Erie and Niagara County Sheriff's Departments, Louis Rich Turkey Products, and WBEN Radio. Uniform numbers are printed on the card front along with the player's name and position. The photos in the set were taken by several photographers, each of whom is credited on the lower right front beside the respective photo.

COMPLETE SET (8)	5.00	10.00
1 Steve Tasker	.75	2.00
2 Cornelius Bennett	1.00	2.50
3 Shane Conlan	.60	1.50
4 Mark Kelso	.60	1.50
5 Will Wolford	.60	1.50
6 Chris Burkett	.60	1.50
7 Kent Hull	.60	1.50
8 Art Still	.60	1.50

1989 Bills Police

This eight-card set of Buffalo Bills is numbered in the upper right corner of each reverse. Cards measure approximately 2 1/2" by 3 1/2". The set was sponsored by the Buffalo Bills, Erie County Sheriff's Department, Louis Rich Turkey Products, and WBEN Radio. Uniform numbers are printed on the card front along with the player's name and position. The photos in the set were taken by several photographers, each of whom is credited on the lower right front beside the respective photo.

COMPLETE SET (8)	6.00	12.00
1 Leon Seals	.30	1.50
2 Thurman Thomas	2.00	5.00
3 Jim Ritcher	.60	1.50
4 Scott Norwood	.60	1.50
5 Darryl Talley	.75	2.00
6 Nate Odomes	.60	1.50
7 Leonard Smith	.60	1.50
8 Ray Bentley	.60	1.50

1990 Bills Police

This eight-card set was sponsored by Blue Shield of Western New York, and its company logo graces both sides of the card. The oversized cards measure approximately 4" by 6". The color action player photos on the fronts have red borders on a white card face. The Bills' helmet and player identification appear above the picture, while biography is given below the picture. In black print, the back has career summary, statistics, and "Tips from the Sheriff" in the form of anti-drug and alcohol messages. The cards are unnumbered and checklisted below in alphabetical order.

COMPLETE SET (8)	6.00	15.00
1 Carlton Bailey	.40	1.00
2 Kirby Jackson	.40	1.00
3 Jim Kelly	2.50	6.00
4 James Lofton	.75	2.00
5 Keith McKeller	.40	1.00
6 Mark Pike	.40	1.00
7 Andre Reed	1.25	3.00
8 Jeff Wright	.40	1.00

1991 Bills Buffalo News Posters

These posters were created by the Buffalo News and issued as "pages" in the daily newspapers during the 1991 season. Each large poster includes a color image of a Bills player on the front with a typical newspaper page back. We've included the date when the photo appeared when known.

COMPLETE SET (16)	25.00	50.00
1 Howard Ballard 10/17/1991	1.25	3.00
2 Don Beebe 10/9/1991	1.50	4.00
3 Cornelius Bennett 10/2/1991	1.50	4.00
4 Shane Conlan 9/25/1991	1.25	3.00
5 Kent Hull 10/30/1991	1.25	3.00
6 Jim Kelly 9/5/1991	4.00	10.00
7 James Lofton 10/23/1991	2.00	5.00
8 Keith McKeller 12/18/1991	1.25	3.00
9 Scott Norwood 12/11/1991	1.25	3.00
10 Nate Odomes 11/21/1991	1.25	3.00
11 Andre Reed 9/19/1991	2.00	5.00
12 Leon Seals 11/27/1991	1.25	3.00
13 Bruce Smith 9/11/1991	2.00	5.00
14 Darryl Talley 11/6/1991	1.25	3.00
15 Thurman Thomas 11/13/1991	2.50	6.00
16 Jeff Wright 12/4/1991	1.25	3.00

1991 Bills Police

This eight-card Police standard-size set was sponsored by Blue Shield of Western New York. The cards are printed on white card stock. The top portion of the front features the player's name centered above the team name, with the team helmet and Blue Shield logo on either side. The center features an action player photo while biographical information is printed below. The three-sectioned front is separated by red borders. The backs have player profile, career statistics, and safety tips sponsored by the Erie County Sheriff's Department. The cards are unnumbered and checklisted below alphabetically.

COMPLETE SET (8)	2.40	6.00
1 Howard Ballard	.30	.75
2 Don Beebe	.50	1.25
3 John Davis	.30	.75
4 Kenneth Davis	.50	1.25
5 Mark Kelso	.30	.75
6 Frank Reich	.60	1.50
7 Butch Rolle	.30	.75
8 J.D. Williams	.30	.75

1992 Bills Buffalo News Posters

These posters were created by the Buffalo News and issued as "pages" in the daily newspapers during the 1992 season. Each large poster includes a color image of a Bills player on the front with a typical newspaper page back. We've included the date when the photo appeared when known.

COMPLETE SET (15)	20.00	40.00
1 Carlton Bailey 9/9/1992	1.25	3.00
2 Steve Christie 9/24/1992	1.50	4.00
3 Kenneth Davis 11/18/1992	1.50	4.00
4 Phil Hansen 11/11/1992	1.25	3.00
5 Henry Jones 12/9/1992	1.50	4.00
6 Mark Kelso 9/30/1992	1.25	3.00
7 Brad Lamb 11/4/1992	1.25	3.00
7 Pete Metzelaars 10/22/1992	1.25	3.00
9 Chris Mohr 10/30/1992	1.25	3.00
10 Chris Mohr 11/29/1992	1.25	3.00
11 Nate Odomes 9/16/1992	1.25	3.00
12 Frank Reich 10/7/1992	1.50	4.00
13 Jim Ritcher 12/16/1992	1.25	3.00
14 Steve Tasker 11/25/1992	1.50	4.00
15 Will Wolford 10/15/1992	1.25	3.00

1992 Bills Police

This seven-card set was sponsored by Blue Shield of Western New York. The oversized cards measure approximately 4" by 6" and are printed on white card stock. The top portion of the front features the player's name centered above the team name, with the team helmet and Blue Shield logo on either side. The center features an action color player photo while biographical information is printed below. The three-section front is separated by red borders. The backs have player profile, career statistics, and safety tips sponsored by the Erie County Sheriff's Department. The cards are unnumbered and checklisted below alphabetically.

COMPLETE SET (7)	6.00	12.00
1 Carlton Bailey	.75	2.00
2 Steve Christie	.75	2.00
3 Shane Conlan	.75	2.00
4 Phil Hansen	.75	2.00
5 Henry Jones	1.00	2.50
6 Chris Mohr	.75	2.00
7 Thurman Thomas	2.00	5.00

1993 Bills Buffalo News Posters

These posters were created by the Buffalo News and issued as "pages" in the daily newspapers during the 1993 season. Each large poster includes a color image of a Bills player on the front with a typical newspaper page back. We've included the date when the photo appeared when known.

COMPLETE SET (14)	25.00	50.00
1 Howard Ballard 12/23/1993	1.25	3.00
2 Cornelius Bennett 10/14/1993	1.50	4.00
3 Bill Brooks 11/10/1993	1.50	4.00
4 Russell Copeland 10/6/1993	1.25	3.00
5 Kenneth Davis 12/8/1993	1.50	4.00
6 John Fina 11/18/1993	1.25	3.00
7 Keith Goganious 12/30/1993	1.25	3.00
8 Kent Hull 12/15/1993	1.25	3.00
9 Jim Kelly 9/22/1993	4.00	10.00
10 Andre Reed 9/29/1993	2.00	5.00
11 Darryl Talley 11/23/1993	1.25	3.00
12 Steve Tasker 11/3/1993	1.50	4.00
13 Nate Turner 10/28/1993	1.25	3.00
14 James Williams 10/21/1993	1.25	3.00

1994 Bills Buffalo News Posters

These posters were created by the Buffalo News and issued as "pages" in the daily newspapers during the 1994 season. Each large poster includes a color image of a Bills player on the front with a typical newspaper page back. We've included the date when the photo appeared when known.

COMPLETE SET (16)	25.00	50.00
1 Don Beebe 11/2/1994	1.50	4.00
2 Cornelius Bennett 9/14/1994	1.50	4.00
3 Jeff Burris 10/19/1994	1.25	3.00
4 Jerry Crafts 11/23/1994	1.25	3.00
5 Kenneth Davis 10/12/1994	1.50	4.00
6 Carwell Gardner 9/28/1994	1.25	3.00
7 Henry Jones 11/9/1994	1.50	4.00
8 Yonel Jordan 12/21/1994	1.25	3.00
9 Jim Kelly 10/27/1994	4.00	10.00
10 Mark Maddox 12/7/1994	1.25	3.00
11 Pete Metzelaars 12/15/1994	1.25	3.00
12 Andre Reed 10/6/1994	2.00	5.00
13 Frank Reich 11/30/1994	1.50	4.00
14 Bruce Smith 9/8/1994	2.00	5.00
15 Darryl Talley 11/16/1994	1.25	3.00
16 Thurman Thomas 9/21/1994	3.00	8.00

1994 Bills Police

COMPLETE SET (6)	5.00	10.00
1 Bill Brooks	1.00	2.50
2 Kenneth Davis	1.00	2.50
3 John Fina	.75	2.00
4 Phil Hansen	.75	2.00
5 Pete Metzelaars	1.00	2.50
6 Marvcus Patton	.75	2.00

1995 Bills Buffalo News Posters

These posters were created by the Buffalo News and issued as "pages" in the daily newspapers during the 1995 season. Each large poster includes a color image of a Bills player on the front with a typical newspaper page back. We've included the date when the photo appeared when known.

COMPLETE SET (16)	20.00	40.00
1 Justin Armour 10/12/1995	1.00	2.50
2 Bill Brooks 10/25/1995	1.25	3.00
3 Ruben Brown 10/18/2005	1.00	2.50
4 Jeff Burris 9/20/1995	1.00	2.50
5 Russell Copeland 9/27/1995	1.00	2.50
6 John Fina 11/2/1995	1.00	2.50
7 Darick Holmes 11/9/1995	1.00	2.50
8 Kent Hull 11/29/1995	1.00	2.50
9 Jerry Ostroski 12/6/1995	1.00	2.50
10 Bryce Paup 11/15/1995	1.25	3.00
11 Andre Reed 9/13/1995	1.50	4.00
12 Kurt Schulz 10/5/1995	1.25	3.00
13 Bruce Smith 9/6/1995	1.50	4.00
14 Thomas Smith 12/13/1995	1.00	2.50
15 Steve Tasker 12/20/1995	1.25	3.00
16 Ted Washington 11/21/1995	1.00	2.50

1995 Bills Police

This six-card set of the Buffalo Bills was sponsored by Coca-Cola and the Erie County Office of Sheriff. The cards measure approximately 4" by 6" and feature a color action player photo set on a colorful stone-look background. The backs carry player information and a safety tip. The cards are unnumbered and checklisted below in alphabetical order.

COMPLETE SET (6)	5.00	10.00
1 Jeff Burris	.75	2.00
2 Joe Ferguson All-Time Great	1.00	2.50
3 Kent Hull	.75	2.00
4 Adam Lingner	.75	2.00
5 Glenn Parker	.75	2.00
6 Andre Reed	1.50	4.00

1996 Bills Buffalo News Posters

These posters were created by the Buffalo News and issued as "pages" in the daily newspapers during the 1996 season. Each large poster includes a color image of a Bills player on the front with a typical newspaper page back. We've included the date when the photo appeared when known.

COMPLETE SET (15)	20.00	40.00
1 Jeff Burris 11/21/1996	1.00	2.50
2 Todd Collins 10/3/1996	1.00	2.50
3 Quinn Early 9/25/1996	1.25	3.00
4 Jim Jeffcoat 9/11/1996	1.00	2.50
5 Lonnie Johnson 10/9/1996	1.00	2.50
6 Tony Kline 9/19/1996	1.00	2.50
7 Mark Maddox 10/31/1996	1.00	2.50
8 Gabe Northern 10/23/1996	1.00	2.50
9 Bryce Paup 11/6/1996	1.25	3.00
10 Andre Reed 11/26/1996	1.50	4.00
11 Sam Rogers 11/13/1996	1.00	2.50
12 Chris Spielman 9/5/1996	1.25	3.00
13 Steve Tasker 12/11/1996	1.25	3.00
14 Thurman Thomas 12/18/1996	1.50	4.00
15 David White 12/6/1996	1.00	2.50

1996 Bills Police

This five-card set of the Buffalo Bills was sponsored by Coca-Cola and the Erie County Sheriff's Office. The cards measure approximately 4" by 6" and feature a color action player photo with the sponsor logos on the cardfront. The cards are unnumbered but have been checklisted below in alphabetical order.

COMPLETE SET (5)	3.00	8.00
1 Ruben Brown	.75	2.00
2 Mark Maddox	.75	2.00
3 Bryce Paup	1.00	2.50
4 Mark Pike	.75	2.00
5 Kurt Schulz	.75	2.00

1997 Bills Buffalo News Posters

These posters were created by the Buffalo News and issued as "pages" in the daily newspapers during the 1997 season. Each large poster includes a color image of a Bills player on the front with a typical newspaper page back. We've included the date when the photo appeared when known.

COMPLETE SET (16)	20.00	40.00
1 Ruben Brown 10/15/1997	1.00	2.50
2 Todd Collins 9/3/1997	1.00	2.50
3 John Fina 9/24/1997	1.00	2.50
4 Phil Hansen 11/26/1997	1.00	2.50
5 Ken Irvin 10/30/1997	1.00	2.50
6 Lonnie Johnson 10/8/1997	1.00	2.50
7 Henry Jones 11/5/1997	1.25	3.00
8 Eric Moulds 10/22/1997	1.50	4.00
9 Gabe Northern 11/12/1997	1.00	2.50
10 Andre Reed 12/10/1997	1.50	4.00
11 Antowain Smith 12/3/1997	2.00	5.00
12 Thomas Smith 9/10/1997	1.00	2.50
13 Chris Spielman 9/17/1997	1.25	3.00
14 Thurman Thomas 10/1/1997	1.50	4.00
15 Ted Washington 12/17/1997	1.25	3.00
16 Dusty Zeigler 11/19/1997	1.00	2.50

1998 Bills Buffalo News Posters

These posters were created by the Buffalo News and issued as "pages" in the daily newspapers during the 1998 season. Each large poster includes a color image of a Bills player on the front with a typical newspaper page back. We've included the date when the photo appeared when known.

COMPLETE SET (16)	15.00	30.00
1 Ruben Brown 12/1/1998	.75	2.00
2 Sam Cowart 10/21/1998	.75	2.00
3 Quinn Early 10/7/1998	1.00	2.50
4 Doug Flutie 10/14/1998	2.00	5.00
5 Sam Gash 9/23/1998	.75	2.00
6 John Holecek 12/15/1998	.75	2.00
7 Ken Irvin 12/8/1998	.75	2.00
8 Chris Mohr 11/4/1998	.75	2.00
9 Gabe Northern 11/10/1998	.75	2.00
10 Jerry Ostroski 12/23/1998	.75	2.00
11 Jay Riemersma 11/25/1998	.75	2.00
12 Sam Rogers 9/16/1998	.75	2.00
13 Antowain Smith 11/18/1998	1.25	3.00
14 Ted Washington 10/27/1998	1.00	2.50
15 Marcellus Wiley 9/30/1998	.75	2.00
16 Kevin Williams 9/9/1998	.75	2.00

1998 Bills Police

This set was sponsored by Pepsi and the Erie County Sheriff's Office. The cards measure approximately 4" by 6" and feature a color action player photo with the sponsor logos on the cardfront. The cards are unnumbered but have been checklisted below in alphabetical order.

COMPLETE SET (5)	5.00	10.00
1 Steve Christie	1.00	2.50
2 Phil Hansen	1.00	2.50
3 Henry Jones	1.00	2.50
4 Andre Reed	1.50	4.00
5 Ted Washington	1.00	2.50

1999 Bills Bookmarks

This set of bookmarks was distributed by Buffalo area libraries. Each features one Bills player along with the title "Rush for Reading" on the front. The backs include a smaller photo of the player along with his vital statistics. Sponsors included Blue Cross and Blue Shield, Buffalo Bills Youth Foundation and Just Buffalo Literary Center. Each bookmark measures roughly 2 1/2" by 7 1/2" and was printed on thin glossy stock.

COMPLETE SET (5)	6.00	12.00
1 John Fina	1.25	3.00
2 Sam Gash	1.25	3.00
3 John Holecek	1.25	3.00
4 Gabe Northern	1.25	3.00
5 Marcellus Wiley	1.25	3.00

1999 Bills Buffalo News Posters

These posters were created by the Buffalo News and issued as "pages" in the daily newspapers during the 1999 season. Each large poster includes a color image of a Bills player on the front with a typical newspaper page back. We've included the date when the photo appeared when known.

COMPLETE SET (16)	15.00	30.00
1 Ruben Brown 11/17/1999	.75	2.00
2 Sam Cowart 11/10/1999	.75	2.00
3 Doug Flutie 9/15/1999	2.00	5.00
4 Phil Hansen 10/20/1999	.75	2.00
5 John Holecek 10/6/1999	.75	2.00
6 Henry Jones 12/22/1999	1.00	2.50
7 Eric Moulds 10/13/1999	1.25	3.00
8 Peerless Price/12/1/1999	1.50	4.00
9 Andre Reed 10/27/1999	1.25	3.00
10 Kurt Schulz 11/24/1999	1.00	2.50
11 Antowain Smith 9/29/1999	1.25	3.00
12 Thurman Thomas 12/15/1999	1.25	3.00
13 Ted Washington 9/22/1999	1.00	2.50
14 Marcellus Wiley 12/8/1999	.75	2.00
15 Kevin Williams 11/3/1999	.75	2.00
16 Antoine Winfield 12/29/1999	.75	2.00

2000 Bills Bookmarks

This set of bookmarks was sponsored by Blue Cross and Blue Shield and distributed in the Buffalo area. Each features one Bills player along with the title "Rush for Reading" on the front. The backs include a smaller photo of the player along with his vital statistics. Each measures roughly 2 1/2" by 7 1/2" and was printed on thin glossy stock. An additional bookmark was released for the Summer reading program, but is not considered part of the complete set.

COMPLETE SET (4)	5.00	10.00
1 Sam Cowart	.75	2.00
2 Doug Flutie	2.00	5.00
3 Peerless Price	1.25	3.00
4 Jay Riemersma	.75	2.00
5 Marcellus Wiley	1.25	3.00

2000 Bills Buffalo News Posters

These posters were created by the Buffalo News and issued as "pages" in the daily newspapers during the 2000 season. Each large poster includes a color image of a Bills player on the front with a typical newspaper page back. We've included the date when the photo appeared when known.

COMPLETE SET (8)	7.50	15.00
1 Sam Cowart 10/25/2000	.75	2.00
2 John Fina 10/4/2000	.75	2.00
3 John Holecek 10/18/2000	.75	2.00
4 Rob Johnson 11/22/2000	1.00	2.50
5 Henry Jones 12/6/2000	1.00	2.50
6 Sammy Morris 12/13/2000	1.25	3.00
7 Peerless Price 11/15/2000	1.25	3.00
8 Sam Rogers 11/8/2000	.75	2.00

2000 Bills Xerox

These oversized cards (measuring roughly 4 1/4" by 6 1/2") were sponsored by Xerox and feature members of the Buffalo Bills. Each was printed on thin white coated paper stock with a color photo of the featured player on the front and vital stats on the back. The cards were issued to promote Xerox's DocuColor 2060 Digital Press which was used to print the cards. The unnumbered cards are listed below aphabetically.

COMPLETE SET (32)	30.00	50.00
1 Avion Black	.50	1.25
2 Ruben Brown	.50	1.25
3 Bobby Collins	.50	1.25
4 Sam Cowart	.50	1.25
5 John Fina	.50	1.25
6 Erik Flowers	.50	1.25
7 Doug Flutie	2.00	5.00
8 Drew Haddad	.50	1.25
9 Phil Hansen	.50	1.25
10 Robert Hicks	.50	1.25
11 John Holecek	.50	1.25
12 Ken Irvin	.50	1.25
13 Sheldon Jackson	.50	1.25
14 Rob Johnson	1.25	3.00
15 Henry Jones	.75	2.00
16 Jonathan Linton	.75	2.00
17 Corey Moore	.50	1.25
18 Sammy Morris	1.00	2.50
19 Eric Moulds	1.25	3.00
20 Keith Newman	.50	1.25
21 Jerry Ostroski	.50	1.25
22 Joe Panos	.50	1.25
23 DaShon Polk	.50	1.25
24 Peerless Price	2.50	6.00
25 Jay Riemersma	.50	1.25
26 Sam Rogers	.50	1.25
27 Antowain Smith	1.25	3.00
28 Travares Tillman	.50	1.25
29 Ted Washington	.75	2.00
30 Marcellus Wiley	.75	2.00
31 Pat Williams	.75	2.00
32 Antoine Winfield	.50	1.25

2001 Bills Bookmarks

Blue Cross Blue Shield of Western New York sponsored this set of player bookmarks that was distributed in the Buffalo area. Each features one Bills player along with the title "Rush for Reading" on the front at the top. The backs include a smaller photo of the player along with his vital statistics. Each measures roughly 2 1/2" by 7 1/2" and was printed on thin glossy stock. An additional bookmark was released for the Summer reading program, but is not considered part of the complete set.

COMPLETE SET (4)	3.00	8.00
1 Rob Johnson	1.25	3.00
2 Keion Carpenter	.75	2.00
3 Kenyatta Wright	.75	2.00
4 Jonas Jennings	.75	2.00
5 Sammy Morris (Summer Reading Program)	1.25	3.00

2002 Bills Bookmarks

For the fourth year, Blue Cross and Blue Shield sponsored a set of player bookmarks that was distributed in the Buffalo area. Each features one Bills player along with the title "Rush for Reading" on the front. The backs include a smaller photo of the player along with his vital statistics. Each measures roughly 2 1/2" by 7 1/2" and was printed on thin glossy stock. An additional bookmark was released for the Summer reading program, but is not considered part of the complete set.

COMPLETE SET (5)	5.00	10.00
1 Drew Bledsoe	2.00	5.00
2 Larry Centers	1.25	3.00
3 Tony Driver	.75	2.00
4 Brian Moorman	.75	2.00
5 Gregg Williams CO	.75	2.00
6 Sammy Morris (Summer Program; Jersey #33)	1.25	3.00

2002 Bills Buffalo News Posters

These posters were created by the Buffalo News and issued as "pages" in the daily newspapers during the 2002 season. Each large poster includes a color image of a Bills player on the front with a typical newspaper page back. We've included the date when the photo appeared when known.

COMPLETE SET (6)	6.00	12.00
1 Travis Henry 10/12/2002	1.25	3.00
2 Eric Moulds 11/23/2002	1.25	3.00
3 Keith Newman 11/16/2002	.75	2.00
4 Eddie Robinson 9/26/2002	.75	2.00
5 Trey Teague 9/20/2002	.75	2.00
6 Pat Williams 10/17/2002	.75	2.00

2003 Bills Bookmarks

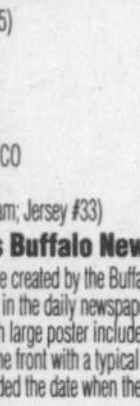

For the third straight year, Blue Cross Blue Shield of Western New York sponsored a set of bookmarks that was distributed in the Buffalo area. Each features one Bills player along with the title "Rush for Reading" on the front at the top. The backs include an additional photo of the player along with his vital statistics. Each measures roughly 2 1/2" by 7 1/2" and was printed on very thin high gloss stock. An additional bookmark was released for the Summer reading program and sponsored by UPS. It is priced below, but is not considered part of the complete set.

COMPLETE SET (6)	4.00	10.00
1 Drew Bledsoe	2.00	5.00
2 Sam Gash	.75	2.00
3 Brian Moorman	.75	2.00
4 Gregg Williams CO	.75	2.00
5 Mike Williams	.75	2.00
6 Coy Wire	.75	2.00
7 Sammy Morris (Summer Program; Jersey #31)	1.25	3.00

2004 Bills Tops Grocery

These large cards (measuring roughly 3 7/8" by 5 1/8") were issued by Tops Grocery Stores in the Buffalo area and could be exchanged at Bills home games for a chance to win a variety of prizes.

COMPLETE SET (5)	4.00	10.00
1 Drew Bledsoe	1.25	3.00
2 London Fletcher	.75	2.00
3 Travis Henry	.75	2.00
4 Pat Williams	1.00	2.50
5 Coy Wire	.75	2.00

2004 Bills Xerox

These slightly oversized cards (measuring roughly 2 1/2" by 3 3/4") were sponsored by Xerox and feature members of the Buffalo Bills. Each was printed on thin white coated paper stock with a color photo of the featured player on the front with a thin blue border. A slightly smaller "mini" version of card was also issued measuring roughly 2 1/4" by 3 1/4". The unnumbered cards are listed below aphabetically.

COMPLETE SET (11)	6.00	15.00
*MINI: .4X TO 1X BASIC CARDS		
1 Sam Adams	.60	1.50
2 Drew Bledsoe	1.00	2.50
3 Lee Evans	1.00	2.50
4 London Fletcher	.60	1.50
5 Travis Henry	.60	1.50
6 J.P. Losman	.75	2.00
7 Willis McGahee	1.00	2.50
8 Lawyer Milloy	.60	1.50
9 Eric Moulds	.75	2.00
10 Takeo Spikes	.60	1.50
11 Pat Williams	.75	2.00

2005 Bills Merrick Mint Quarters

COMPLETE SET (11)	60.00	100.00
1 Nate Clements	5.00	10.00
2 Lee Evans	5.00	10.00
3 London Fletcher	5.00	10.00
4 J.P. Losman	5.00	10.00
5 Willis McGahee	5.00	10.00
6 Lawyer Milloy	5.00	10.00
7 Eric Moulds	5.00	10.00
8 Aaron Schobel	5.00	10.00
9 Takeo Spikes	5.00	10.00
10 Bills red helmet	5.00	10.00
11 Bills white helmet	5.00	10.00

2005 Bills Xerox

These slightly oversized cards (measuring roughly 2 1/2" by 3 3/4") were sponsored by Xerox and feature members of the Buffalo Bills. Each was printed on white paper stock with a color photo of the featured player on the front with a thick light blue border. The unnumbered cards are listed below aphabetically.

COMPLETE SET (6)	4.00	10.00
1 London Fletcher	.60	1.50
2 J.P. Losman	.60	1.50
3 Willis McGahee	1.00	2.50
4 Eric Moulds	.60	1.50
5 Mike Mularkey	.60	1.50
6 Takeo Spikes	.60	1.50

2006 Bills Topps

COMPLETE SET (12)	3.00	6.00
BUF1 Willis McGahee	.25	.60
BUF2 Roscoe Parrish	.20	.50
BUF3 London Fletcher	.20	.50
BUF4 Lee Evans	.25	.60
BUF5 J.P. Losman	.25	.60
BUF6 Aaron Schobel	.20	.50
BUF7 Takeo Spikes	.20	.50
BUF8 Troy Vincent	.20	.50
BUF9 Kelly Holcomb	.20	.50
BUF10 Josh Reed	.20	.50
BUF11 Ashton Youboty	.20	.50
BUF12 Nate Clements	.20	.50

2006 Bills Xerox

These slightly oversized cards (measuring roughly 2 1/2" by 3 3/4") were sponsored by Xerox and feature members of the Buffalo Bills. Each was printed on white paper stock with a color photo of the featured player on the front with a white border at the top but full-bleed sides. The unnumbered cards are listed below aphabetically.

COMPLETE SET (6)	4.00	10.00
1 Nate Clements	.60	1.50
2 Lee Evans	.75	2.00
3 London Fletcher	.60	1.50
4 Willis McGahee	.75	2.00
5 Terrence McGee	.60	1.50
6 Takeo Spikes	.60	1.50

2007 Bills Blue Cross Blue Shield

These oversized cards (measuring roughly 3" by 4-1/2") were sponsored by Blue Cross Blue Shield and feature members of the Buffalo Bills. Each was printed on white paper stock with a color photo of the featured player on the front and the back as well as a "What Moves U" message. The unnumbered cards are listed below aphabetically.

COMPLETE SET (4)	5.00	12.00
1 Lee Evans	1.25	3.00
2 Chris Kelsay	1.00	2.50
3 Rian Lindell	1.00	2.50
4 Marshawn Lynch	1.50	4.00

2007 Bills Topps

COMPLETE SET (12)	3.00	6.00
1 J.P. Losman	.20	.50
2 Lee Evans	.25	.60
3 Peerless Price	.20	.50
4 Aaron Schobel	.20	.50
5 Anthony Thomas	.20	.50
6 Rian Lindell	.20	.50
7 Josh Reed	.20	.50
8 Terrence McGee	.20	.50
9 Donte Whitner	.20	.50
10 Marshawn Lynch	.30	.75
11 Paul Posluszny	.30	.75
12 Trent Edwards	.30	.75

2008 Bills Topps

COMPLETE SET (12)	2.50	5.00
1 Trent Edwards	.20	.50
2 Marshawn Lynch	.25	.60
3 J.P. Losman	.20	.50
4 Aaron Schobel	.20	.50
5 Angelo Crowell	.20	.50
6 Lee Evans	.25	.60
7 Josh Reed	.20	.50
8 Donte Whitner	.20	.50
9 Terrence McGee	.20	.50
10 Roscoe Parrish	.20	.50
11 James Hardy	.25	.60
12 Leodis McKelvin	.30	.75

2009 Bills Breast Cancer Awareness

This three card set was issued at a Bills game in 2009. Each unnumbered card was created by one of the three NFL licensed manufacturers and features the pink ribbon breast cancer awareness logo on the fronts.

COMPLETE SET (3)	2.50	5.00
1 Trent Edwards Panini	.75	2.00
2 Lee Evans Upper Deck	.75	2.00
3 Paul Posluszny Topps	3.00	8.00

2009 Bills Buffalo News Posters

These posters were created by the Buffalo News and issued as "pages" in the daily newspapers during the 2009 season. Each large poster includes a color image of a Bills player(s) on the front with a typical newspaper page back. We've included the date released for each poster.

COMPLETE SET (15)	10.00	25.00
1 Trent Edwards Lee Evans Josh Reed Terrell Owens (9/23/2009)	1.00	2.50
2 Fred Jackson (9/30/2009)	.75	2.00
3 Aaron Schobel (10/7/2009)	.75	2.00
4 Terrell Owens (10/14/2009)	1.00	2.50
5 Terrence McGee (10/21/2009)	.75	2.00
6 Jairus Byrd (10/28/2009)	.75	2.00
7 Bills All-Time Team (11/14/2009)	.75	2.00
8 Jim Kelly 50 yrs. (11/11/2009)	1.25	3.00
9 Thurman Thomas 50 yrs. (11/18/2009)	1.00	2.50
10 James Lofton 50 yrs. Pete Metzelaars Eric Moulds Andre Reed (11/25/2009	.75	2.00
11 Reuben Brown 50 yrs. Joe DeLamielleure Kent Hull	.75	2.00

Jim Ritcher		
Billy Shaw		
12 Tom Sestak 50 yrs.	1.00	2.50
Fred Smerlas		
Bruce Smith		
(12/9/2009)		
13 Cornelius Bennett 50 yrs.	.75	2.00
Shane Conlan		
Mike Stratton		
Darryl Talley		
(12		
14 Butch Byrd 50 yrs.	.75	2.00
Henry Jones		
Nate Odomes		
George Saimes		
(12/23/2009)		
15 Steve Christie 50 yrs.	.75	2.00
Brian Moorman		
Steve Tasker		
Marv Levy CO		
(12/30/2		

2009 Bills NOCO Medallions

This set of coins or medallions was issued by NOCO Express stores in the Buffalo area over a series of weeks during the 2009 NFL season. Each features a past Bufallo Bill great and an album was issued as well to house the collection. NOCO offered each coin at an SRP of $2.99 and the complete set at $49.99.

COMPLETE SET (14)	30.00	50.00
1 Ruben Brown	1.25	3.00
2 Joe DeLamielleure	1.25	3.00
3 Kent Hull	1.25	3.00
4 Jim Kelly	2.00	5.00
5 Marv Levy CO	1.25	3.00
6 James Lofton	1.50	4.00
7 Pete Metzelaars	1.25	3.00
8 Eric Moulds	1.25	3.00
9 Andre Reed	1.50	4.00
10 Jim Ritcher	1.25	3.00
11 Billy Shaw	1.25	3.00
12 Steve Tasker	1.25	3.00
13 Thurman Thomas	1.50	4.00
NNO Album	1.25	3.00

2010 Bills Dick's Sporting Goods

This set was released by Dick's Sporting Goods Stores in the Buffalo area in 2010. Each features a large color image of a Bills player along with a $10 store coupon attached below the image. With the coupon attached, the cards measure roughly 5" by 9".

COMPLETE SET (3)	3.00	7.50
1 David Nelson	1.00	2.50
2 Garrison Sanborn	1.00	2.50
3 Jonathan Stupar	1.00	2.50

1974 Birmingham Americans WFL Cups

These plastic drinking cups were sponsored by Jack's Hamburgers and WBRC-TV Channel 6 in Birmingham and feature members of the WFL Birmingham Americans. Each week of the WFL season a different player was featured on a cup. Any additions to the list below are appreciated.

1 John Andrews	7.50	15.00
2 George Mira	7.50	15.00
3 Paul Robinson	7.50	15.00

1975 Birmingham Vulcans WFL Team Issue 8X10

These photos measure roughly 8" x 10" and include a large black and white player image on the front with only the player's name below photo. The backs are blank.

1 Matthew Reed	7.50	15.00

1975 Birmingham Vulcans WFL Team Issue Dual Photo 8X10

These photos measure roughly 8" x 10" and Include black and white images with a smaller head-and-shoulders photo to the left with the player's name and team logo beneath it and a larger action shot to the right. The backs are blank.

1 William Bryant	7.50	15.00
2 Denny Duron	7.50	15.00
3 Larry Estes	7.50	15.00
4 Mike Hayes	7.50	15.00
5 Dennis Homan	7.50	15.00
6 Pat Kelley	7.50	15.00
7 Steve Manstedt	7.50	15.00
8 Johnny Musso	7.50	15.00
9 Ted Powell	7.50	15.00
10 Joe Profit	7.50	15.00
11 Matthew Reed	7.50	15.00
12 Ron Slovensky	7.50	15.00
13 Bob Tatarek	7.50	15.00
14 Larry Willingham	7.50	15.00
15 Wimpy Winther	7.50	15.00
16 Jesse Wolf	7.50	15.00

2000 Birmingham Steeldogs AFL2

This set was given out as a promotional item at a Steeldogs Arena 2 League football game. Each card features a color photo of the player along with his jersey number. The unnumbered cardbacks feature a short player bio. The cards measure slightly larger than standard size at 2 9/16" by 3 9/16".

COMPLETE SET (20)	5.00	10.00
1 Fred Bishop	.25	.60
2 Donald Blackmon	.25	.60
3 Cedrick Buchannon	.25	.60
4 Chris Edwards	.25	.60
5 Tommy Harrison	.25	.60
6 Bobby Humphrey CO	.40	1.00
7 James Lewis	.25	.60
8 Anthony Jordan	.25	.60
9 Wes Mitchem	.25	.60
10 Sterrick Morgan	.25	.60
11 Alphonso Pugue	.25	.60
12 Robert Poole	.25	.60
13 Jackie Rowan	.25	.60
14 Steve Stanley	.25	.60
15 Brandon Stewart	.25	.60
16 Wayne Thomas	.25	.60
17 Mo Thompson	.25	.60
18 Adlai Trone	.25	.60
19 Troy Williams	.25	.60
20 Chris Windsor	.25	.60

2002 Birmingham Steeldogs AFL2

This set was issued to promote the Steeldogs Arena League football team. Each standard-sized card features a color photo of the player printed on thin card stock. The unnumbered cardbacks feature a short player bio and a small photo.

COMPLETE SET (21)	5.00	10.00
1 Johnny Anderson	.25	.60
2 Cedrick Buchannon	.25	.60
3 Michael Feagin	.25	.60
4 Jeff Hannah	.25	.60
5 Terrance Harris	.25	.60
6 Jimmi Henson	.25	.60
7 Bobby Humphrey CO	.40	1.00
8 Larry Huntington	.25	.60
9 Terrance Ingram	.25	.60
10 Anthony Jordan	.25	.60
11 Montressa Kirby	.25	.60
12 James Lewis	.25	.60
13 William Mayes	.25	.60
14 Jimmy Moore	.25	.60
15 Paul Morgan	.25	.60
16 Ozell Powell	.25	.60
17 Ernest Ross	.25	.60
18 Jackie Rowan	.25	.60
19 Wayne Thomas	.25	.60
20 Jerry Turner	.25	.60
21 DeJuan Washington	.25	.60

1997 Black Diamond

The 1997 Upper Deck Black Diamond set totals 180-cards and was distributed in six card packs with a suggested retail of $3.49. The set was produced essentially in three series together: Black Diamond (1-90), Double Black Diamond (91-150) inserted one in every four packs, and Triple Black Diamond (151-180) inserted one in every 30 packs. The fronts feature color action player photos reproduced on Light F/X card stock with one, two, or three Black Diamonds on the front designating its rarity. The backs carry player information and statistics.

COMPLETE SET (180)	150.00	300.00
COMP.SERIES 1 (90)	12.50	25.00
1 Alfred Williams	.15	.40
2 Alvin Harper	.15	.40
3 Andre Hastings	.15	.40
4 Andre Reed	.25	.60
5 Anthony Johnson	.15	.40
6 Anthony Miller	.15	.40
7 Byron Bam Morris	.15	.40
8 Bobby Hebert	.15	.40
9 Bobby Taylor	.15	.40
10 Boomer Esiason	.25	.60
11 Brett Perriman	.15	.40
12 Brian Blades	.15	.40
13 Bryan Cox	.15	.40
14 Bryant Young	.15	.40
15 Bryce Paup	.15	.40
16 Carnell Lake	.15	.40
17 Cedric Jones	.15	.40
18 Chad Brown	.15	.40
19 Charlie Garner	.25	.60
20 Chris Chandler	.25	.60
21 Cornelius Bennett	.15	.40
22 Cortez Kennedy	.15	.40
23 Cris Carter	.40	1.00
24 Dale Carter	.15	.40
25 Daryl Gardener	.15	.40
26 Derrick Alexander WR	.25	.60
27 Derrick Mayes	.25	.60
28 Don Beebe	.15	.40
29 Eric Allen	.15	.40
30 Eric Moulds	.40	1.00
31 Errict Rhett	.15	.40
32 Frank Sanders	.25	.60
33 Glyn Milburn	.15	.40
34 Henry Ellard	.15	.40
35 Jamal Anderson	.40	1.00
36 James O. Stewart	.25	.60
37 Jason Dunn	.15	.40
38 Jerry Rice	1.25	3.00
39 Jim Everett	.15	.40
40 Jim Kelly	.40	1.00
41 Joey Galloway	.25	.60
42 John Carney	.15	.40
43 John Elway	2.00	5.00
44 John Randle	.25	.60
45 Karim Abdul-Jabbar	.25	.60
46 Keenan McCardell	.25	.60
47 Ken Dilger	.15	.40
48 Ken Norton	.15	.40
49 Ki-Jana Carter	.15	.40
50 Kordell Stewart	.40	1.00
51 Lawrence Phillips	.15	.40
52 Leslie O'Neal	.15	.40
53 Mark Chmura	.25	.60
54 Marshall Faulk	.50	1.25
55 Michael Haynes	.15	.40
56 Michael Irvin	.40	1.00
57 Michael Jackson	.25	.60
58 Michael Westbrook	.25	.60
59 Mike Tomczak	.15	.40
60 Napoleon Kaufman	.40	1.00
61 Neil O'Donnell	.25	.60
62 Neil Smith	.25	.60
63 O.J. McDuffie	.25	.60
64 Orlando Thomas	.15	.40
65 Rashaan Salaam	.15	.40
66 Regan Upshaw	.15	.40
67 Rick Mirer	.15	.40
68 Rob Moore	.25	.60
69 Ronnie Harmon	.15	.40
70 Sam Mills	.15	.40
71 Sean Dawkins	.15	.40
72 Shawn Jefferson	.15	.40
73 Stan Humphries	.25	.60
74 Stepfret Williams	.15	.40
75 Stephen Davis	.40	1.00
76 Steve Atwater	.15	.40
77 Terance Mathis	.25	.60
78 Terrell Fletcher	.15	.40
79 Terry Glenn	.40	1.00
80 Terry McDaniel	.15	.40
81 Tony McGee	.15	.40
82 Trent Dilfer	.40	1.00
83 Troy Drayton	.15	.40
84 Ty Detmer	.25	.60
85 Tyrone Hughes	.15	.40
86 Walt Harris	.15	.40
87 Wayne Chrebet	.40	1.00
88 Wesley Walls	.25	.60
89 Willie Davis	.15	.40
90 Willie McGinest	.15	.40
91 Adrian Murrell	.75	2.00
92 Alex Molden	.50	1.25
93 Alex Van Dyke	.75	2.00
94 Andre Coleman	.50	1.25
95 Ben Coates	1.25	3.00
96 Bobby Engram	.75	2.00
97 Bruce Smith	1.25	3.00
98 Charles Johnson	1.25	3.00
99 Chris Sanders	1.25	3.00
100 Chris T. Jones	1.25	3.00
101 Chris Warren	.75	2.00
102 Darnay Scott	1.25	3.00
103 Dave Brown	.75	2.00
104 Derrick Thomas	1.25	3.00
105 Drew Bledsoe	2.50	6.00
106 Edgar Bennett	1.25	3.00
107 Emmitt Smith	7.50	15.00
108 Eric Bjornson	.50	1.25
109 Eric Metcalf	1.25	3.00
110 Garrison Hearst	.75	2.00
111 Gus Frerotte	.75	2.00
112 Hardy Nickerson	.50	1.25
113 Herman Moore	.75	2.00
114 Hugh Douglas	.50	1.25
115 Irving Fryar	.75	2.00
116 J.J. Stokes	.75	2.00
117 Jake Reed	.75	2.00
118 Jeff Hostetler	.75	2.00
119 Jeff Lewis	.75	2.00
120 Jim Harbaugh	.75	2.00
121 Johnnie Morton	.75	2.00
122 Jonathan Ogden	.50	1.25
123 Kevin Carter	.75	2.00
124 Kevin Greene	.75	2.00
125 Kevin Hardy	.75	2.00
126 Leeland McElroy	.50	1.25
127 Mike Alstott	1.25	3.00
128 Muhsin Muhammad	1.25	3.00
129 Natrone Means	.75	2.00
130 Quentin Coryatt	.50	1.25
131 Ray Lewis	1.50	4.00
132 Ray Zellars	.50	1.25
133 Rickey Dudley	.75	2.00
134 Ricky Watters	.75	2.00
135 Robert Smith	1.25	3.00
136 Scott Mitchell	.75	2.00
137 Sean Gilbert	.50	1.25
138 Shannon Sharpe	.75	2.00
139 Simeon Rice	.75	2.00
140 Stanley Pritchett	.50	1.25
141 Steve McNair	2.00	5.00
142 Steve Young	4.00	8.00
143 Tamarick Vanover	.75	2.00
144 Terry Allen	.75	2.00
145 Thurman Thomas	1.25	3.00
146 Tony Banks	1.25	3.00
147 Tony Martin	.75	2.00
148 Tyrone Wheatley	1.25	3.00
149 Vinny Testaverde	.75	2.00
150 Zach Thomas	1.25	3.00
151 Amani Toomer	3.00	8.00
152 Barry Sanders	10.00	25.00
153 Bobby Hoying	3.00	8.00
154 Brett Favre	12.50	30.00
155 Carl Pickens	3.00	8.00
156 Curtis Conway	3.00	8.00
157 Curtis Martin	5.00	12.00
158 Dan Marino	12.50	30.00
159 Deion Sanders	3.00	8.00
160 Eddie George	.40	1.00
161 Eddie Kennison	2.00	5.00
162 Elvis Grbac	3.00	8.00
163 Isaac Bruce	3.00	8.00
164 Jeff Blake	2.00	5.00
165 Jerome Bettis	3.00	8.00
166 Junior Seau	3.00	8.00
167 Kerry Collins	2.00	5.00
168 Keyshawn Johnson	3.00	8.00
169 Larry Centers	2.00	5.00
170 Marcus Allen	3.00	8.00
171 Mark Brunell	4.00	10.00
172 Marvin Harrison	3.00	8.00
173 Reggie White	3.00	8.00
174 Rodney Hampton	2.00	5.00
175 Terrell Davis	5.00	12.00
176 Tim Brown	3.00	8.00
177 Todd Collins	2.00	5.00
178 Troy Aikman	6.00	15.00
179 Tim Biakabutuka	2.00	5.00
180 Warren Moon	3.00	8.00
BD1 Troy Aikman Promo	.75	2.00

1997 Black Diamond Gold

*SINGLES: 2.5X TO 6X BASE CARD HI
SINGLE GOLD STATED ODDS 1:15
*DOUBLES: 1.5X TO 4X BASE CARD HI
DOUBLE GOLD ODDS 1:46
*TRIPLES: 2X TO 5X BASE CARD HI
TRIPLE GOLD STATED PRINT RUN 50 SETS

1997 Black Diamond Title Quest

COMPLETE SET (20)	400.00	800.00
STATED PRINT RUN 100 SERIAL #'d SETS		
1 Dan Marino	50.00	120.00
2 Jerry Rice	25.00	60.00
3 Drew Bledsoe	20.00	40.00
4 Emmitt Smith	40.00	100.00
5 Troy Aikman	25.00	60.00
6 Steve Young	20.00	50.00
7 Brett Favre	50.00	120.00
8 John Elway	50.00	120.00
9 Barry Sanders	40.00	100.00
10 Jerome Bettis	12.50	30.00
11 Deion Sanders	12.50	30.00
12 Karim Abdul-Jabbar	5.00	12.00
13 Terrell Davis	15.00	40.00
14 Marshall Faulk	15.00	40.00
15 Curtis Martin	15.00	40.00
16 Eddie George	12.50	30.00
17 Steve McNair	15.00	40.00
18 Terry Glenn	7.50	20.00
19 Joey Galloway	7.50	20.00
20 Keyshawn Johnson	12.50	30.00

1998 Black Diamond

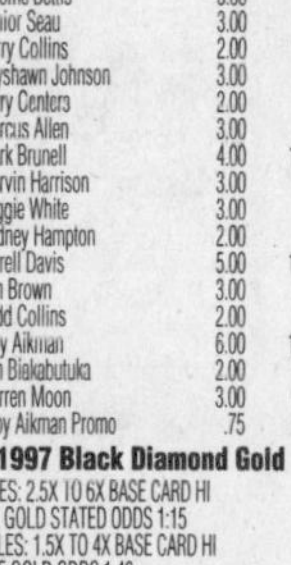

The 1998 Black Diamond set was issued in one series totalling 150 cards. The fronts feature color action player photos reproduced on Light F/X card stock with one, two, three, or four Black Diamonds on the front designating its rarity. The backs carry player information and statistics.

COMPLETE SET (150)	20.00	40.00
1 Kent Graham	.15	.40
2 Darrell Russell	.15	.40
3 Jim Harbaugh	.25	.60
4 Cornelius Bennett	.15	.40
5 Troy Vincent	.15	.40
6 Natrone Means	.25	.60
7 Michael Jackson	.15	.40
8 Will Blackwell	.15	.40
9 Greg Hill	.15	.40
10 Andre Reed	.25	.60
11 Darren Bennett	.15	.40
12 Dan Marino	1.50	4.00
13 Tim Biakabutuka	.25	.60
14 Terrell Owens	.40	1.00
15 Cris Carter	.40	1.00
16 Darnell Autry	.15	.40
17 Joey Galloway	.25	.60
18 Terry Glenn	.40	1.00
19 Ki-Jana Carter	.15	.40
20 Isaac Bruce	.40	1.00
21 Shawn Jefferson	.15	.40
22 Michael Irvin	.40	1.00
23 Warren Sapp	.25	.60
24 Dave Brown	.15	.40
25 Terrell Davis	.40	1.00
26 Frank Wycheck	.15	.40
27 Neil O'Donnell	.25	.60
28 Scott Mitchell	.25	.60
29 Michael Westbrook	.25	.60
30 Tim Brown	.40	1.00
31 Antonio Freeman	.40	1.00
32 Jake Plummer	.40	1.00
33 Irving Fryar	.25	.60
34 Quentin Coryatt	.15	.40
35 Jamal Anderson	.40	1.00
36 Jerome Bettis	.40	1.00
37 Keenan McCardell	.25	.60
38 Derrick Alexander WR	.25	.60
39 Stan Humphries	.15	.40
40 Andre Rison	.25	.60
41 Bruce Smith	.25	.60
42 Garrison Hearst	.40	1.00
43 Zach Thomas	.40	1.00
44 Rae Carruth	.15	.40
45 Kevin Greene	.25	.60
46 Robert Smith	.40	1.00
47 Curtis Conway	.25	.60
48 Christian Fauria	.15	.40
49 Curtis Martin	.40	1.00
50 Dan Wilkinson	.15	.40
51 Eddie Kennison	.25	.60
52 Mark Fields	.15	.40
53 Anthony Miller	.15	.40
54 Mike Alstott	.40	1.00
55 Tiki Barber	.40	1.00
56 Neil Smith	.25	.60
57 Gus Frerotte	.15	.40
58 Adrian Murrell	.25	.60
59 Johnnie Morton	.25	.60
60 O.J. McDuffie	.25	.60
61 Napoleon Kaufman	.40	1.00
62 Robert Brooks	.25	.60
63 Byron Hanspard	.15	.40
64 Ty Detmer	.25	.60
65 Mark Brunell	.40	1.00
66 Byron Bam Morris	.15	.40
67 Kordell Stewart	.40	1.00
68 Elvis Grbac	.25	.60
69 Antowain Smith	.40	1.00
70 Junior Seau	.40	1.00
71 Tony Gonzalez	.40	1.00
72 Anthony Johnson	.15	.40
73 Steve Young	.50	1.25
74 Brian Manning	.15	.40
75 Erik Kramer	.15	.40
76 Warren Moon	.40	1.00
77 Torrian Gray	.15	.40
78 Carl Pickens	.25	.60
79 Tony Banks	.25	.60
80 Willie McGinest	.15	.40
81 Deion Sanders	.40	1.00
82 Warrick Dunn	.40	1.00
83 Danny Wuerffel	.25	.60
84 Rod Smith WR	.25	.60
85 Steve McNair	.40	1.00
86 Danny Kanell	.25	.60
87 Herman Moore	.25	.60
88 Brian Mitchell	.15	.40
89 James Farrior	.15	.40
90 Reggie White	.40	1.00
91 Simeon Rice	.25	.60
92 James Jett	.25	.60
93 Marshall Faulk	.50	1.25
94 Chris Chandler	.25	.60
95 Mike Mamula	.15	.40
96 Jimmy Smith	.25	.60
97 Jamie Sharper	.15	.40
98 Carnell Lake	.15	.40
99 Marcus Allen	.40	1.00
100 Thurman Thomas	.40	1.00
101 Freddie Jones	.15	.40
102 Karim Abdul-Jabbar	.40	1.00
103 Kerry Collins	.25	.60
104 Jerry Rice	.75	2.00
105 Brad Johnson	.40	1.00
106 Raymont Harris	.15	.40
107 Lamar Smith	.25	.60
108 Drew Bledsoe	.60	1.50
109 Corey Dillon	.40	1.00
110 Lawrence Phillips	.15	.40
111 Heath Shuler	.15	.40
112 Emmitt Smith	1.25	3.00
113 Reidel Anthony	.25	.60
114 Ike Hilliard	.25	.60
115 Shannon Sharpe	.25	.60
116 Chris Sanders	.15	.40
117 Keyshawn Johnson	.40	1.00
118 Barry Sanders	1.25	3.00
119 Cris Dishman	.15	.40
120 Jeff George	.25	.60
121 Dorsey Levens	.40	1.00
122 Rob Moore	.25	.60
123 Ricky Watters	.25	.60
124 Marvin Harrison	.40	1.00
125 Vinny Testaverde	.25	.60
126 Charles Johnson	.15	.40
127 Renaldo Wynn	.15	.40
128 Todd Collins QB	.15	.40
129 Tony Martin	.25	.60
130 Derrick Thomas	.40	1.00
131 Wesley Walls	.25	.60
132 Rod Woodson	.25	.60
133 Troy Drayton	.15	.40
134 Bryan Cox	.15	.40
135 Shawn Springs	.15	.40
136 Jake Reed	.25	.60
137 Jeff Blake	.25	.60
138 Craig Heyward	.15	.40
139 Ben Coates	.25	.60
140 Troy Aikman	.75	2.00
141 Trent Dilfer	.40	1.00
142 Troy Davis	.15	.40
143 John Elway	1.50	4.00
144 Eddie George	.40	1.00
145 Rodney Hampton	.25	.60
146 Ed McCaffrey	.25	.60
147 Terry Allen	.40	1.00
148 Wayne Chrebet	.40	1.00
149 Brett Favre	1.50	4.00
150 Daryl Johnston	.25	.60

1998 Black Diamond Double

COMPLETE SET (150)	50.00	100.00
*DOUBLE STARS: 1X TO 2X BASIC CARDS		
STATED ODDS ONE PER PACK		

1998 Black Diamond Quadruple

*QUAD.STARS: 10X TO 25X BASIC CARDS
QUADRUPLE STATED PRINT RUN 50 SETS

1998 Black Diamond Triple

COMPLETE SET (150)	150.00	300.00
*TRIPLE STARS: 2.5X TO 6X BASIC CARDS		
STATED ODDS 1:5		

1998 Black Diamond Premium Cut

COMPLETE SET (30)	100.00	200.00
SINGLE DIAMOND STATED ODDS 1:7		
*DOUBLE DIAMONDS: .6X TO 1.5X BASIC CARDS		
DOUBLE DIAMOND STATED ODDS 1:15		
*TRIPLE DIAMONDS: .8X TO 2X BASIC CARDS		
TRIPLE DIAMOND STATED ODDS 1:30		
*QUAD VERTICALS: 1.5X TO 4X		
QUAD VERTICAL STATED ODDS 1:180		
PC1 Karim Abdul-Jabbar	2.50	6.00
PC2 Troy Aikman	5.00	12.00
PC3 Kerry Collins	1.50	4.00
PC4 Drew Bledsoe	4.00	10.00
PC5 Barry Sanders	8.00	20.00
PC6 Marcus Allen	2.50	6.00
PC7 John Elway	10.00	25.00
PC8 Adrian Murrell	1.50	4.00
PC9 Junior Seau	2.50	6.00
PC10 Eddie George	2.50	6.00
PC11 Antowain Smith	2.50	6.00
PC12 Reggie White	2.50	6.00
PC13 Dan Marino	10.00	25.00
PC14 Joey Galloway	1.50	4.00
PC15 Kordell Stewart	2.50	6.00
PC16 Terry Allen	2.50	6.00
PC17 Napoleon Kaufman	2.50	6.00
PC18 Curtis Martin	2.50	6.00
PC19 Steve Young	3.00	8.00
PC20 Rod Smith WR	1.50	4.00
PC21 Mark Brunell	2.50	6.00
PC22 Emmitt Smith	8.00	20.00
PC23 Rae Carruth	1.00	2.50
PC24 Brett Favre	10.00	25.00
PC25 Jeff George	1.50	4.00
PC26 Terry Glenn	2.50	6.00
PC27 Warrick Dunn	2.50	6.00
PC28 Herman Moore	1.50	4.00
PC29 Cris Carter	2.50	6.00
PC30 Terrell Davis	2.50	6.00

1998 Black Diamond Premium Cut Quadruple Horizontal

PC1 Karim Abdul-Jabbar	7.50	20.00
PC2 Troy Aikman	100.00	200.00
PC3 Kerry Collins	7.50	20.00
PC4 Drew Bledsoe	40.00	100.00
PC5 Barry Sanders	125.00	250.00
PC6 Marcus Allen	12.50	30.00
PC7 John Elway	200.00	400.00
PC8 Adrian Murrell	6.00	15.00
PC9 Junior Seau	7.50	20.00
PC10 Eddie George	12.50	30.00
PC11 Antowain Smith	7.50	20.00
PC12 Reggie White	7.50	20.00
PC13 Dan Marino	175.00	300.00
PC14 Joey Galloway	6.00	15.00
PC15 Kordell Stewart	15.00	40.00
PC16 Terry Allen	7.50	20.00
PC17 Napoleon Kaufman	7.50	20.00
PC18 Curtis Martin	12.50	30.00
PC19 Steve Young	40.00	100.00
PC20 Rod Smith WR	6.00	15.00
PC21 Mark Brunell	12.50	30.00
PC22 Emmitt Smith	125.00	250.00
PC23 Rae Carruth	6.00	15.00
PC24 Brett Favre	150.00	300.00
PC25 Jeff George	6.00	15.00
PC26 Terry Glenn	7.50	20.00
PC27 Warrick Dunn	100.00	250.00
PC28 Herman Moore	7.50	20.00
PC29 Cris Carter	12.50	30.00
PC30 Terrell Davis	15.00	40.00

1998 Black Diamond Rookies

The 1998 Black Diamond Rookies set was issued in one series totalling 120 cards and distributed in six-card packs with a suggested retail price of $3.99. The fronts feature color action photos of 90 top veterans and 30 rookie players reproduced on Light F/X foil cards with one, two, three, or four Black Diamonds on the front designating its rarity. The backs carry player information and statistics. The 30 Rookie cards were seeded in packs at the rate of 1:4.

COMPLETE SET (120)	50.00	100.00
1 Jake Plummer	.30	.75
2 Adrian Murrell	.20	.50
3 Frank Sanders	.20	.50
4 Jamal Anderson	.30	.75
5 Chris Chandler	.20	.50
6 Tony Martin	.20	.50
7 Jim Harbaugh	.20	.50
8 Errict Rhett	.20	.50
9 Michael Jackson	.10	.30
10 Rob Johnson	.20	.50
11 Antowain Smith	.30	.75
12 Thurman Thomas	.30	.75
13 Fred Lane	.10	.30
14 Kerry Collins	.10	.30
15 Rae Carruth	.10	.30
16 Erik Kramer	.10	.30
17 Edgar Bennett	.10	.30
18 Curtis Conway	.20	.50
19 Corey Dillon	.30	.75
20 Neil O'Donnell	.20	.50
21 Carl Pickens	.20	.50
22 Troy Aikman	.60	1.50
23 Emmitt Smith	1.00	2.50
24 Deion Sanders	.30	.75
25 John Elway	1.25	3.00
26 Terrell Davis	.30	.75
27 Rod Smith	.20	.50
28 Barry Sanders	1.00	2.50
29 Johnnie Morton	.20	.50
30 Herman Moore	.20	.50
31 Brett Favre	1.25	3.00
32 Antonio Freeman	.30	.75
33 Dorsey Levens	.30	.75
34 Marshall Faulk	.40	1.00
35 Marvin Harrison	.30	.75
36 Zack Crockett	.10	.30
37 Mark Brunell	.30	.75
38 Jimmy Smith	.20	.50
39 Keenan McCardell	.20	.50
40 Elvis Grbac	.20	.50
41 Andre Rison	.20	.50
42 Derrick Alexander	.20	.50
43 Dan Marino	1.25	3.00
44 Karim Abdul-Jabbar	.30	.75
45 Zach Thomas	.30	.75
46 Brad Johnson	.30	.75
47 Cris Carter	.30	.75
48 Robert Smith	.30	.75
49 Drew Bledsoe	.50	1.25
50 Terry Glenn	.30	.75
51 Ben Coates	.20	.50
52 Danny Wuerffel	.20	.50
53 Lamar Smith	.20	.50
54 Sean Dawkins	.10	.30
55 Danny Kanell	.20	.50
56 Tiki Barber	.30	.75
57 Ike Hilliard	.20	.50
58 Curtis Martin	.30	.75
59 Vinny Testaverde	.20	.50
60 Keyshawn Johnson	.30	.75
61 Napoleon Kaufman	.30	.75
62 Jeff George	.20	.50
63 Tim Brown	.30	.75
64 Bobby Hoying	.20	.50
65 Charlie Garner	.20	.50
66 Duce Staley	.40	1.00
67 Kordell Stewart	.30	.75
68 Jerome Bettis	.30	.75
69 Charles Johnson	.10	.30
70 Tony Banks	.20	.50
71 Isaac Bruce	.30	.75
72 Eddie Kennison	.20	.50
73 Natrone Means	.20	.50
74 Bryan Still	.10	.30
75 Junior Seau	.30	.75
76 Steve Young	.40	1.00
77 Jerry Rice	.60	1.50
78 Garrison Hearst	.30	.75
79 Ricky Watters	.20	.50
80 Joey Galloway	.20	.50
81 Warren Moon	.10	.30
82 Warrick Dunn	.30	.75
83 Trent Dilfer	.30	.75
84 Bert Emanuel	.20	.50
85 Steve McNair	.30	.75
86 Eddie George	.30	.75
87 Yancey Thigpen	.10	.30
88 Leslie Shepherd	.10	.30
89 Terry Allen	.30	.75
90 Michael Westbrook	.20	.50
91 Peyton Manning RC	15.00	30.00
92 Jacquez Green RC	.75	2.00
93 Fred Taylor RC	1.50	4.00
94 Terry Fair RC	.75	2.00
95 Pat Johnson RC	.75	2.00
96 Corey Chavous RC	1.00	2.50
97 Randy Moss RC	8.00	20.00
98 Curtis Enis RC	.50	1.25
99 Rashaan Shehee RC	.75	2.00
100 Kevin Dyson RC	1.00	2.50
101 Shaun Williams RC	.75	2.00
102 Grant Wistrom RC	.75	2.00
103 John Avery RC	.75	2.00
104 Brian Griese RC	2.00	5.00
105 Ryan Leaf RC	1.00	2.50
106 Jerome Pathon RC	1.00	2.50
107 Sam Cowart RC	.75	2.00
108 Germane Crowell RC	.75	2.00
109 Ahman Green RC	5.00	12.00
110 Greg Ellis RC	.50	1.25
111 Robert Holcombe RC	.75	2.00
112 Marcus Nash RC	.50	1.25
113 Duane Starks RC	.50	1.25
114 Andre Wadsworth RC	.75	2.00
115 Takeo Spikes RC	1.00	2.50
116 Eric Brown RC	.50	1.25
117 Robert Edwards RC	.75	2.00
118 Charlie Batch RC	1.00	2.50
119 Mikhael Ricks RC	.75	2.00
120 Charles Woodson RC	1.25	3.00
S13 Dan Marino SAMPLE	.75	2.00

1998 Black Diamond Rookies Double

COMP.DOUBLE SET (120)	125.00	250.00
*DOUBLE STARS: 1.25X TO 3X BASIC CARDS		
*DOUBLE RCs: .6X TO 1.5X BASIC CARDS		
DOUBLE VETERAN PRINT RUN 3000 SETS		
DOUBLE ROOKIE PRINT RUN 2500 SETS		

1998 Black Diamond Rookies Quadruple

*QUAD VETS: 8X TO 20X BASIC CARDS		
*QUAD ROOKIES: 2X TO 5X		
91 Peyton Manning	100.00	200.00

1998 Black Diamond Rookies Triple

COMPLETE SET (120)	250.00	500.00
*TRIPLE STARS: 2.5X TO 6X BASIC CARDS		
*TRIPLE RCs: 1X TO 2.5X		

1998 Black Diamond Rookies Jumbos

COMPLETE SET (8)	16.00	40.00
91 Peyton Manning	5.00	12.00
97 Randy Moss	3.00	8.00
98 Curtis Enis	.80	2.00
100 Kevin Dyson	.80	2.00
104 Brian Griese	3.00	6.00
105 Ryan Leaf	2.00	4.00
118 Charlie Batch	2.00	5.00
120 Charles Woodson	1.20	3.00

1998 Black Diamond Rookies Sheer Brilliance

COMPLETE SET (30)	100.00	200.00
EXTREMES SER.#'d TO PLAYER'S JERSEY NO.		
B1 Dan Marino/1300	6.00	15.00
B2 Troy Aikman/800	5.00	12.00
B3 Brett Favre/400	12.50	30.00
B4 Ryan Leaf/1600	1.25	3.00
B5 Peyton Manning/1800	12.00	30.00
B6 Barry Sanders/2000	5.00	12.00
B7 Emmitt Smith/2200	4.00	10.00
B8 John Elway/700	10.00	25.00
B9 Steve Young/800	3.00	8.00
B10 Steve McNair/900	2.50	6.00
B11 Antowain Smith/2300	1.25	3.00
B12 Corey Dillon/2800	1.00	2.50
B13 Terrell Davis/3000	1.25	3.00
B14 Mark Brunell/800	4.00	10.00
B15 Charles Woodson/2400	2.00	5.00
B16 Brian Griese/1400	4.00	10.00
B17 Curtis Martin/2800	1.25	3.00
B18 Keyshawn Johnson/1900	1.25	3.00
B19 Kordell Stewart/1000	1.25	3.00
B20 Eddie George/2700	1.25	3.00
B21 Drew Bledsoe/1100	4.00	10.00
B22 Jake Plummer/1600	1.25	3.00
B23 Warren Moon/100	7.50	20.00
B24 Curtis Enis/3900	1.00	2.50
B25 John Avery/2000	1.00	2.50
B26 Randy Moss/1800	8.00	20.00
B27 Rob Johnson/1100	1.50	4.00
B28 Warrick Dunn/2800	1.25	3.00
B29 Terry Allen/2100	1.25	3.00
B30 Robert Smith/2600	1.25	3.00

1998 Black Diamond Rookies Extreme Brilliance

STATED PRINT RUN 1-39		
B6 Barry Sanders/20	125.00	250.00
B7 Emmitt Smith/22	100.00	200.00
B11 Antowain Smith/23	20.00	50.00
B12 Corey Dillon/28	20.00	50.00
B13 Terrell Davis/30	30.00	80.00
B15 Charles Woodson/24	25.00	60.00
B17 Curtis Martin/28	20.00	50.00
B20 Eddie George/27	20.00	50.00
B24 Curtis Enis/39	15.00	40.00
B25 John Avery/20	12.00	30.00
B28 Warrick Dunn/28	20.00	50.00
B29 Terry Allen/21	20.00	50.00
B30 Robert Smith/26	15.00	40.00

1998 Black Diamond Rookies White Onyx

COMPLETE SET (30)	100.00	200.00
STATED PRINT RUN 2250 SERIAL #'d SETS		
UNPRICED BLACK ONYZ #'d TO 1		
ON1 Peyton Manning	25.00	50.00
ON2 Corey Dillon	2.00	5.00
ON3 Jerome Bettis	2.00	5.00
ON4 Brett Favre	8.00	20.00
ON5 Napoleon Kaufman	2.00	5.00
ON6 Joey Galloway	1.25	3.00
ON7 John Elway	8.00	20.00
ON8 Troy Aikman	4.00	10.00
ON9 Robert Smith	2.00	5.00
ON10 Kordell Stewart	2.00	5.00
ON11 Garrison Hearst	2.00	5.00
ON12 Curtis Enis	1.00	2.50
ON13 Dan Marino	8.00	20.00
ON14 Jimmy Smith	1.25	3.00
ON15 Steve Young	2.50	6.00
ON16 Ryan Leaf	2.00	5.00
ON17 Steve McNair	2.00	5.00
ON18 Randy Moss	12.00	30.00
ON19 Curtis Martin	2.00	5.00
ON20 Barry Sanders	6.00	15.00
ON21 Rob Johnson	1.25	3.00
ON22 Emmitt Smith	6.00	15.00
ON23 Jake Plummer	2.00	5.00
ON24 Antonio Freeman	2.00	5.00
ON25 Mark Brunell	2.00	5.00
ON26 Warrick Dunn	2.00	5.00
ON27 Eddie George	2.00	5.00
ON28 Jerry Rice	4.00	10.00
ON29 Drew Bledsoe	3.00	8.00
ON30 Terrell Davis	2.00	5.00

1999 Black Diamond

Released as a 150-card base set, the 1999 Upper Deck Black diamond features 110 regular issue veteran cards and 40 rookie subset cards inserted at one in four packs. Cards fronts are all foil and are enhanced with laser etching. Black Diamond was released both as Hobby and Retail, and was packaged in 30-pack boxes containg 6-cards per pack and carried a suggested retail of $3.99.

COMPLETE SET (150)	60.00	120.00
COMP.SET w/o SPs (110)	10.00	20.00
1 Adrian Murrell	.30	.75
2 Jake Plummer	.30	.75
3 Rob Moore	.25	.60
4 Frank Sanders	.25	.60
5 Jamal Anderson	.30	.75
6 Terance Mathis	.25	.60
7 Chris Chandler	.30	.75
8 Tim Dwight	.30	.75
9 Jermaine Lewis	.25	.60
10 Priest Holmes	.40	1.00
11 Peter Boulware	.25	.60
12 Doug Flutie	.40	1.00
13 Antowain Smith	.25	.60
14 Eric Moulds	.30	.75
15 Bruce Smith	.40	1.00
16 Rae Carruth	.25	.60
17 Muhsin Muhammad	.30	.75
18 Wesley Walls	.30	.75
19 Tim Biakabutuka	.30	.75
20 Curtis Enis	.25	.60
21 Curtis Conway	.30	.75
22 Bobby Engram	.30	.75
23 Darnay Scott	.25	.60
24 Corey Dillon	.30	.75
25 Jeff Blake	.30	.75
26 Ty Detmer	.30	.75
27 Terry Kirby	.25	.60
28 Leslie Shepherd	.25	.60
29 Emmitt Smith	1.00	2.50
30 Troy Aikman	.60	1.50
31 Michael Irvin	.40	1.00
32 Rocket Ismail	.30	.75
33 Brian Griese	.30	.75
34 Terrell Davis	.40	1.00
35 Shannon Sharpe	.40	1.00
36 Rod Smith	.30	.75
37 Barry Sanders	1.00	2.50
38 Herman Moore	.30	.75
39 Charlie Batch	.30	.75
40 Johnnie Morton	.30	.75
41 Brett Favre	1.25	3.00
42 Dorsey Levens	.30	.75
43 Antonio Freeman	.30	.75
44 Mark Chmura	.25	.60
45 Peyton Manning	1.25	3.00
46 Jerome Pathon	.25	.60
47 Marvin Harrison	.40	1.00
48 Fred Taylor	.30	.75
49 Mark Brunell	.30	.75
50 Jimmy Smith	.30	.75
51 Keenan McCardell	.30	.75
52 Andre Rison	.30	.75

53 Elvis Grbac .25 .60
54 Derrick Alexander WR .25 .60
55 Tony Gonzalez .40 1.00
56 Dan Marino 1.25 3.00
57 Oronde Gadsden .25 .60
58 O.J. McDuffie .30 .75
59 Randy Moss .40 1.00
60 Randall Cunningham .40 1.00
61 Cris Carter .40 1.00
62 Robert Smith .30 .75
63 Drew Bledsoe .40 1.00
64 Terry Glenn .30 .75
65 Ben Coates .30 .75
66 Billy Joe Hobert .25 .60
67 Eddie Kennison .30 .75
68 Cam Cleeland .25 .60
69 Gary Brown .25 .60
70 Ike Hilliard .30 .75
71 Amani Toomer .30 .75
72 Vinny Testaverde .30 .75
73 Keyshawn Johnson .30 .75
74 Curtis Martin .40 1.00
75 Wayne Chrebet .30 .75
76 Tim Brown .40 1.00
77 Rickey Dudley .25 .60
78 Napoleon Kaufman .25 .60
79 Charles Woodson .40 1.00
80 Duce Staley .30 .75
81 Doug Pederson .25 .60
82 Charles Johnson .25 .60
83 Kordell Stewart .30 .75
84 Jerome Bettis .40 1.00
85 Courtney Hawkins .25 .60
86 Isaac Bruce .40 1.00
87 Marshall Faulk .40 1.00
88 Trent Green .30 .75
89 Jim Harbaugh .30 .75
90 Junior Seau .40 1.00
91 Natrone Means .30 .75
92 Lawrence Phillips .30 .75
93 Steve Young .50 1.25
94 Terrell Owens .40 1.00
95 Jerry Rice .75 2.00
96 Jon Kitna .30 .75
97 Ricky Watters .30 .75
98 Joey Galloway .30 .75
99 Shawn Springs .25 .60
100 Warrick Dunn .30 .75
101 Trent Dilfer .30 .75
102 Reidel Anthony .25 .60
103 Mike Alstott .40 1.00
104 Steve McNair .40 1.00
105 Eddie George .30 .75
106 Kevin Dyson .25 .60
107 Yancey Thigpen .25 .60
108 Michael Westbrook .25 .60
109 Brad Johnson .30 .75
110 Skip Hicks .25 .60
111 Tim Couch RC 1.25 3.00
112 Akili Smith RC 1.00 2.50
113 Ricky Williams RC 2.00 5.00
114 Donovan McNabb RC 6.00 15.00
115 Edgerrin James RC 1.50 4.00
116 Cade McNown RC 1.00 2.50
117 Daunte Culpepper RC 1.25 3.00
118 Shaun King RC 1.00 2.50
119 Brock Huard RC 1.00 2.50
120 Joe Germaine RC 1.00 2.50
121 Troy Edwards RC 1.00 2.50
122 Champ Bailey RC 2.50 6.00
123 Kevin Faulk RC 1.25 3.00
124 David Boston RC 1.00 2.50
125 Kevin Johnson RC 1.00 2.50
126 Torry Holt RC 2.00 5.00
127 James Johnson RC .75 2.00
128 Peerless Price RC 1.00 2.50
129 D'Wayne Bates RC .75 2.00
130 Cecil Collins RC .75 2.00
131 Na Brown RC .75 2.00
132 Rob Konrad RC .75 2.00
133 Joel Makovicka RC .75 2.00
134 Dameane Douglas RC .75 2.00
135 Scott Covington RC .75 2.00
136 Daylon McCutcheon RC .75 2.00
137 Chris Claiborne RC .75 2.00
138 Karsten Bailey RC .75 2.00
139 Mike Cloud RC .75 2.00
140 Sean Bennett RC .75 2.00
141 Jermaine Fazande RC .75 2.00
142 Chris McAlister RC 1.00 2.50
143 Ebenezer Ekuban RC .75 2.00
144 Jeff Paulk RC .75 2.00
145 Jim Kleinsasser RC 1.25 3.00
146 Bobby Collins RC .75 2.00
147 Andy Katzenmoyer RC 1.00 2.50
148 Jevon Kearse RC 1.25 3.00
149 Amos Zereoue RC 1.00 2.50
150 Sedrick Irvin RC .75 2.00
WPBD Walter Payton 1,000.00 1,500.00
Jersey AUTO/34

1999 Black Diamond Diamond Cut

COMPLETE SET (150) 100.00 200.00
*DIAMOND CUT STARS: 1.5X TO 4X
1-110 STATED ODDS 1:7
*DIAMOND CUT RCs: .5X TO 1.2X
111-150 STATED ODDS 1:12

1999 Black Diamond Final Cut

*FINAL CUT STARS: 10X TO 25X
1-110 FINAL CUT PRINT RUN 100 SER.#'d SETS
*FINAL CUT RCs: 2.5X TO 6X
111-150 FINAL CUT PRINT RUN 50 SER.#'d SETS

1999 Black Diamond A Piece of History

COMPLETE SET (26) 300.00 600.00
H STATED ODDS 1:179 HOBBY
HR STATED ODDS 1:359 HOB/RET
*DOUBLE DIAMONDS: .8X TO 2X
DOUBLE H STATED ODDS 1:1079 HOBBY
DOUBLE HR ODDS 1:1079 HOB/RET
AS Akili Smith H 6.00 15.00
BF Brett Favre H/R 20.00 50.00
BG Brian Griese H 7.50 20.00
BH Brock Huard H 6.00 15.00
CB Charlie Batch H/R 7.50 20.00
CM Cade McNown H/R 5.00 12.00
DC Daunte Culpepper H/R 15.00 40.00
DF Doug Flutie H/R 7.50 20.00
DM Dan Marino H/R 25.00 60.00
EJ Edgerrin James H 15.00 40.00
ES Emmitt Smith H 15.00 40.00
HM Herman Moore H 5.00 12.00
JP Jake Plummer H 6.00 15.00
JR Jerry Rice H/R 15.00 40.00
RM Randy Moss H 15.00 40.00
RW Ricky Williams H/R 10.00 25.00
SY Steve Young H/R 12.50 30.00
TA Troy Aikman H/R 15.00 40.00
TB Tim Brown H/R 7.50 20.00
TC Tim Couch H 7.50 20.00
TD Terrell Davis H 7.50 20.00
TH Torry Holt H/R 7.50 20.00
WD Warrick Dunn H 7.50 20.00
DBL Drew Bledsoe H 10.00 25.00
DBO David Boston H 6.00 15.00
DMC Donovan McNabb H/R 20.00 50.00

1999 Black Diamond Diamonation

COMPLETE SET (20) 20.00 50.00
STATED ODDS 1:6
D1 Brett Favre 3.00 8.00
D2 Eddie George 1.00 2.50
D3 Terrell Davis 1.00 2.50
D4 Jerome Bettis 1.00 2.50
D5 Randall Cunningham 1.00 2.50
D6 Jon Kitna 1.00 2.50
D7 Troy Aikman 2.00 5.00
D8 Marshall Faulk 1.25 3.00
D9 Steve Young 1.25 3.00
D10 Warrick Dunn 1.00 2.50
D11 Jake Plummer .60 1.50
D12 Fred Taylor 1.00 2.50
D13 Antonio Freeman 1.00 2.50
D14 Peyton Manning 3.00 8.00
D15 Randy Moss 2.50 6.00
D16 Steve McNair 1.00 2.50
D17 Emmitt Smith 2.00 5.00
D18 Terrell Owens 1.00 2.50
D19 Kordell Stewart .60 1.50
D20 Ricky Williams 1.50 4.00

1999 Black Diamond Gallery

COMPLETE SET (10) 20.00 50.00
STATED ODDS 1:14
G1 Akili Smith 1.25 3.00
G2 Barry Sanders 5.00 12.00
G3 Curtis Martin 1.50 4.00
G4 Drew Bledsoe 2.00 5.00
G5 Emmitt Smith 3.00 8.00
G6 Keyshawn Johnson 1.50 4.00
G7 Jerry Rice 3.00 8.00
G8 Tim Couch 1.50 4.00
G9 Terrell Owens 1.50 4.00
G10 Troy Aikman 3.00 8.00

1999 Black Diamond Might

COMPLETE SET (10) 10.00 25.00
STATED ODDS 1:12
DM1 Antowain Smith 1.00 2.50
DM2 Steve McNair 1.00 2.50
DM3 Corey Dillon 1.00 2.50
DM4 Dan Marino 3.00 8.00
DM5 Eddie George 1.00 2.50
DM6 Jerome Bettis 1.00 2.50
DM7 Jerry Rice 2.00 5.00
DM8 Randall Cunningham 1.00 2.50
DM9 Brian Griese 1.00 2.50
DM10 Joey Galloway .60 1.50

1999 Black Diamond Myriad

COMPLETE SET (10) 25.00 60.00
STATED ODDS 1:29
M1 Barry Sanders 5.00 12.00
M2 Randy Moss 4.00 10.00
M3 Terrell Davis 1.50 4.00
M4 Brett Favre 5.00 12.00
M5 Jamal Anderson 1.50 4.00
M6 Mark Brunell 1.50 4.00
M7 Donovan McNabb 12.50 30.00
M8 Steve Young 2.00 5.00
M9 Ricky Williams 5.00 12.00
M10 Warrick Dunn 1.50 4.00

1999 Black Diamond Skills

COMPLETE SET (10) 40.00 80.00
STATED ODDS 1:29
S1 Drew Bledsoe 2.00 5.00
S2 Fred Taylor 1.50 4.00
S3 Dan Marino 5.00 12.00
S4 Jake Plummer 1.00 2.50
S5 Kurt Warner 7.50 20.00
S6 Marshall Faulk 2.00 5.00
S7 Randy Moss 4.00 10.00
S8 Peyton Manning 5.00 12.00
S9 Keyshawn Johnson 1.50 4.00
S10 Tim Couch 1.50 4.00

2000 Black Diamond

Released in October of 2000, Black Diamond Features a 180 card base set comprised of 120 veteran cards, 30 Rookie Gems sequentially numbered to 2400, and 30 Rookie Jersey Gems showcasing a swatch of a jersey in the shape of an "R" and inserted at one in 23 Hobby and one in 72 Retail packs. Black Diamond was packaged in 24-pack boxes with packs containing six cards and carried a suggested retial price of $3.99

COMP.SET w/o SP's (120) 6.00 15.00
151-180 ROOKIE JSY ODDS 1:23H, 1:72R
1 Jake Plummer .25 .60
2 David Boston .20 .50
3 Frank Sanders .20 .50
4 Tim Dwight .25 .60
5 Chris Chandler .25 .60
6 Jamal Anderson .25 .60
7 Shawn Jefferson .20 .50
8 Terance Mathis .20 .50
9 Qadry Ismail .25 .60
10 Tony Banks .20 .50
11 Shannon Sharpe .30 .75
12 Peerless Price .25 .60
13 Rob Johnson .25 .60
14 Eric Moulds .25 .60
15 Antowain Smith .25 .60
16 Muhsin Muhammad .25 .60
17 Patrick Jeffers .25 .60
18 Steve Beuerlein .25 .60
19 Tim Biakabutuka .25 .60
20 Cade McNown .20 .50
21 Marcus Robinson .25 .60
22 Eddie Kennison .20 .50
23 Bobby Engram .25 .60
24 Akili Smith .20 .50
25 Corey Dillon .25 .60
26 Darnay Scott .25 .60
27 Tim Couch .25 .60
28 Kevin Johnson .20 .50
29 Errict Rhett .25 .60
30 Troy Aikman .50 1.25
31 Emmitt Smith .75 2.00
32 Rocket Ismail .25 .60
33 Joey Galloway .25 .60
34 Terrell Davis .30 .75
35 Olandis Gary .25 .60
36 Brian Griese .25 .60
37 Ed McCaffrey .25 .60
38 Rod Smith .25 .60
39 Charlie Batch .25 .60
40 Germane Crowell .20 .50
41 Johnnie Morton .25 .60
42 James Stewart .20 .50
43 Brett Favre 1.00 2.50
44 Antonio Freeman .25 .60
45 Dorsey Levens .25 .60
46 Peyton Manning .75 2.00
47 Edgerrin James .30 .75
48 Marvin Harrison .30 .75
49 Terrence Wilkins .20 .50
50 Mark Brunell .25 .60
51 Fred Taylor .30 .75
52 Jimmy Smith .25 .60
53 Keenan McCardell .25 .60
54 Elvis Grbac .20 .50
55 Tony Gonzalez .30 .75
56 Derrick Alexander .20 .50
57 James Johnson .20 .50
58 Tony Martin .25 .60
59 Damon Huard .25 .60
60 Oronde Gadsden .25 .60
61 Randy Moss .30 .75
62 Robert Smith .25 .60
63 Cris Carter .30 .75
64 Daunte Culpepper .25 .60
65 Drew Bledsoe .30 .75
66 Terry Glenn .25 .60
67 Sean Morey RC .20 .50
68 Ricky Williams .30 .75
69 Keith Poole .20 .50
70 Jake Reed .25 .60
71 Jeff Blake .25 .60
72 Kerry Collins .25 .60
73 Amani Toomer .25 .60
74 Joe Montgomery .20 .50
75 Ike Hilliard .25 .60
76 Ray Lucas .20 .50
77 Curtis Martin .30 .75
78 Vinny Testaverde .25 .60
79 Wayne Chrebet .25 .60
80 Tim Brown .30 .75
81 Rich Gannon .25 .60
82 Tyrone Wheatley .20 .50
83 Rickey Dudley .20 .50
84 Napoleon Kaufman .25 .60
85 Duce Staley .25 .60
86 Donovan McNabb .30 .75
87 Torrance Small .20 .50
88 Charles Johnson .20 .50
89 Kent Graham .20 .50
90 Troy Edwards .20 .50
91 Jerome Bettis .30 .75
92 Kordell Stewart .25 .60
93 Marshall Faulk .30 .75
94 Kurt Warner .50 1.25
95 Torry Holt .30 .75
96 Isaac Bruce .30 .75
97 Jermaine Fazande .20 .50
98 Ryan Leaf .25 .60
99 Jeff Graham .20 .50
100 Moses Moreno .20 .50
101 Jerry Rice .60 1.50
102 Terrell Owens .30 .75
103 Jeff Garcia .25 .60
104 Ricky Watters .25 .60
105 Jon Kitna .25 .60
106 Derrick Mayes .20 .50
107 Charlie Rogers .20 .50
108 Warrick Dunn .25 .60
109 Shaun King .20 .50
110 Mike Alstott .30 .75
111 Keyshawn Johnson .25 .60
112 Eddie George .25 .60
113 Steve McNair .30 .75
114 Kevin Dyson .25 .60
115 Kevin Daft .20 .50
116 Jevon Kearse .25 .60
117 Brad Johnson .25 .60
118 Stephen Davis .25 .60
119 Michael Westbrook .20 .50
120 Jeff George .25 .60
121 Kwame Cavil RC .50 1.25
122 Corey Moore RC .50 1.25
123 Sebastian Janikowski RC .75 2.00
124 Troy Walters RC .50 1.25
125 Mike Anderson RC .75 2.00
126 Tom Brady RC 40.00 80.00
127 Spergon Wynn RC .60 1.50
128 Tim Rattay RC .60 1.50
129 Giovanni Carmazzi RC .50 1.25
130 Chris Cole RC .60 1.50
131 Demario Brown RC .50 1.25
132 Chris Coleman RC .50 1.25
133 Michael Wiley RC .50 1.25
134 JaJuan Dawson RC .50 1.25
135 Deon Dyer RC .50 1.25
136 Trevor Gaylor RC .50 1.25
137 Todd Husak RC .50 1.25
138 Darrell Jackson RC .60 1.50
139 Erron Kinney RC .50 1.25
140 Anthony Lucas RC .50 1.25
141 Rondell Mealey RC .50 1.25
142 Chad Morton RC .75 2.00
143 Leon Murray RC .50 1.25
144 Mareno Philyaw RC .50 1.25
145 Gari Scott RC .50 1.25
146 Paul Smith RC .50 1.25
147 Terrelle Smith RC .50 1.25
148 Shyrone Stith RC .50 1.25
149 Bashir Yamini RC .50 1.25
150 Windrell Hayes RC .50 1.25
151 Courtney Brown 3.00 8.00
JSY RC
152 Corey Simon JSY RC 3.00 8.00
153 R.Jay Soward JSY RC 2.50 6.00
154 Chris Redman JSY RC 3.00 8.00
155 Joe Hamilton JSY RC 2.50 6.00
156 Chad Pennington 6.00 15.00
JSY RC
157 Tee Martin JSY RC 4.00 10.00
158 Ron Dayne JSY RC 4.00 10.00
159 Shaun Alexander JSY RC 5.00 12.00
160 Thomas Jones JSY RC 5.00 12.00
161 Reuben Droughns 4.00 10.00
JSY RC
162 Jamal Lewis JSY RC 4.00 10.00
163 J.R. Redmond JSY RC 2.50 6.00
164 Travis Prentice JSY RC 3.00 8.00
165 Trung Canidate JSY RC 3.00 8.00
166 Brian Urlacher JSY RC 15.00 40.00
167 Anthony Becht JSY RC 3.00 8.00
168 Bubba Franks JSY RC 4.00 10.00
169 Peter Warrick JSY RC 4.00 10.00
170 Plaxico Burress JSY RC 4.00 10.00
171 Sylvester Morris JSY RC 2.50 6.00
172 Dez White JSY RC 3.00 8.00
173 Travis Taylor JSY RC 3.00 8.00
174 Todd Pinkston JSY RC 2.50 6.00
175 Dennis Northcutt 3.00 8.00
JSY RC
176 Jerry Porter JSY RC 4.00 10.00
177 Laveranues Coles 4.00 10.00
JSY RC
178 Danny Farmer JSY RC 2.50 6.00
179 Curtis Keaton JSY RC 2.50 6.00
180 Ron Dugans JSY RC 2.50 6.00

2000 Black Diamond Gold

*VETS 1-120: 1.2X TO 3X BASIC CARDS
1-120 VETERAN PRINT RUN 1000
*ROOKIES 121-150: .5X TO 1.2X
121-150 ROOKIE PRINT RUN 500
*ROOKIE JSY 151-180.: .6X TO 1.5X
151-180 ROOKIE JSY PRINT RUN 100
126 Tom Brady 100.00 200.00

2000 Black Diamond Diamonation

COMPLETE SET (10) 3.00 8.00
STATED ODDS 1:8
D1 Marshall Faulk .50 1.25
D2 Marcus Robinson .40 1.00
D3 Eddie George .40 1.00
D4 Kurt Warner .75 2.00
D5 Amani Toomer .40 1.00
D6 Muhsin Muhammad .40 1.00
D7 Jevon Kearse .40 1.00
D8 Jon Kitna .40 1.00
D9 Terrell Davis .50 1.25
D10 Tony Gonzalez .50 1.25

2000 Black Diamond Might

COMPLETE SET (15) 7.50 20.00
STATED ODDS 1:11
DM1 Fred Taylor .60 1.50
DM2 Edgerrin James .60 1.50
DM3 Cade McNown .40 1.00
DM4 Randy Moss .60 1.50
DM5 Shaun King .40 1.00
DM6 Keyshawn Johnson .50 1.25
DM7 Jamal Anderson .50 1.25
DM8 Ricky Williams .60 1.50
DM9 Jerry Rice 1.25 3.00
DM10 Isaac Bruce .60 1.50
DM11 Peyton Manning 1.50 4.00
DM12 Mark Brunell .50 1.25
DM13 Tim Couch .50 1.25
DM14 Akili Smith .40 1.00
DM15 Emmitt Smith 1.50 4.00

2000 Black Diamond Skills

COMPLETE SET (15) 7.50 20.00
STATED ODDS 1:11
DS1 Eddie George .50 1.25
DS2 Brett Favre 2.00 5.00
DS3 Marshall Faulk .60 1.50
DS4 Rob Johnson .50 1.25
DS5 Kevin Johnson .40 1.00
DS6 Randy Moss .60 1.50
DS7 Peyton Manning 1.50 4.00
DS8 Kurt Warner 1.00 2.50
DS9 Jake Plummer .50 1.25
DS10 Troy Aikman 1.00 2.50
DS11 Daunte Culpepper .50 1.25
DS12 Drew Bledsoe .60 1.50
DS13 Vinny Testaverde .50 1.25
DS14 Marvin Harrison .60 1.50
DS15 Charlie Batch .50 1.25

1993 Bleachers Troy Aikman Promos

COMPLETE SET (4) 1.20 3.00
COMMON CARD (1-4) .40 1.00

1993 Bleachers 23K Troy Aikman

COMPLETE SET (3) 6.00 15.00
COMMON CARD (1-3) 2.00 5.00
P1 Troy Aikman Promo 2.00 5.00
(Cowboys)

1994 Bleachers 23K Troy Aikman

Bleachers again produced a 23K Gold card of Troy Aikman in 1994. The gold card was issued in a blue box along with a more traditional appearing card. The 2-card set was limited to 10,000 produced.

COMMON CARD (1-2) 2.00 5.00

1995 Bleachers 23K Emmitt Smith

Issued in a cello-wrapped cardboard sleeve, these four standard-size cards capture Emmitt Smith during his high school, collegiate, and pro career. The fronts of the regular-issue cards feature color player photos inside a 23K gold outer border and a black-and-white inner border. The back carries at the top the set's production number (of 10,000). Below are biography, statistics, a color head shot, and gold-foil on black autographs and images at the bottom. The promo card has a full-bleed color player photo on its front, and an advertisement and career summary on its back. Each set included a certificate of authenticity.

COMPLETE SET (3) 6.00 15.00
COMMON CARD (1-3) 2.50 6.00
NNO Emmitt Smith Promo 1.20 3.00
Escambia High School

1994-97 Bleachers

This card group features embossed player images on 23 Karat all-gold sculptured cards. Each card was sold individually and packaged in a clear acrylic holder along with a Certificate of Authenticity inside a collectible foil-stamped box. The cards are unnumbered and checklisted below in alphabetical order. Each card is serially numbered. The continuation line includes: year, brand, and number of cards issued when known.

1 Troy Aikman 4.80 12.00
(3-Time Champs)/1996 Classic 10,000
2 Troy Aikman 4.80 12.00
(Diamond Star)/1995 Classic 10,000
3 Troy Aikman 6.00 15.00
Emmitt Smith
(Texas Terminators #1)/1995 10,000
4 Troy Aikman 6.00 15.00
Emmitt Smith
(Texas Terminators #2)/1995 10,000
5 Troy Aikman 8.00 20.00
Emmitt Smith
(Jumbo, 1995 4,995)
6 Drew Bledsoe/1995 Classic 10,000 4.80 12.00
7 Marshall Faulk/1994 Classic 10,000 4.00 10.00
8 John Elway 2.40 6.00
(1997 Gems of the NFL)
9 Brett Favre/1996 Score Board 10,000 8.00 20.00
10 Brett Favre (Diamond Star) 8.00 20.00
1996 ScoreBoard 10,000
11 Brett Favre/1997 Score Board 10,000 8.00 20.00
12 Eddie George/1997 Classic 1,996 8.00 20.00
13 Keyshawn Johnson/1996 10,000 4.00 10.00
14 Dan Marino/1995 Upper Deck 10,000 8.00 20.00
15 Joe Montana/1995 Upper Deck 10,000 4.80 12.00
16 Joe Montana 4.80 12.00
(Diamond Star)/1995 Upper Deck 10,000
17 Joe Namath/1997 10,000 4.80 12.00
18 Emmitt Smith 6.00 15.00
(1995 MVP; 10,000)
19 Emmitt Smith 6.00 15.00
((Season TD Record)
(1996 Classic 20,000)
20 Emmitt Smith 6.00 15.00
(Diamond Star)/1996 Classic 10,000
21 Emmitt Smith 6.00 15.00
3 time rushing champion/1995/20,000
22 Super Bowl XXX 3.20 8.00
(Color Logo)/1996 Score Board 1,996
23 Super Bowl XXX 2.40 6.00
(Gold)/1996 Score Board 7,850
24 Super Bowl XXXI 3.20 8.00
(Color Logo)/1997 Score Board 1,997
25 Super Bowl XXXI 2.40 6.00
(Gold)/1997 Score Board 4,850
26 Super Bowl Champions 2.40 6.00
1997 Score Board 50,000

2007 Bloomington Extreme

COMPLETE SET (30) 6.00 12.00
1 Team Card .20 .50
2 Ted Schmitz CO .20 .50
3 Reggie Gray .20 .50
4 Steve LaFalce .20 .50
5 Peter Christofilakos .20 .50
6 Dusty Burk .20 .50
7 Glenn Johnson .20 .50
8 Tom Kudyba .20 .50
9 Mike Crumpier .20 .50
10 Dion Brown .20 .50
11 Shatone Powers .20 .50
12 Lamar Baker .20 .50
13 Rocky Harvey .20 .50
14 Terrill Mayberry .20 .50
15 Jason Hutton .20 .50
16 Dorian Pitts .20 .50
17 Ramon Barber .20 .50
18 Eric Johnson DL .20 .50
19 Martin Wilson .20 .50
20 Calvin Jones .20 .50
21 Rachman Crable .20 .50
22 Chad Walker .20 .50
23 Quince Holman .20 .50
24 Luke Wickman .20 .50
25 Evan Triggs .20 .50
26 Jamarkus Gorman .20 .50
27 Chris Burgess .20 .50
28 Nick Ruud .20 .50
29 James Walton .20 .50
30 Dance Team .20 .50

1948 Bowman

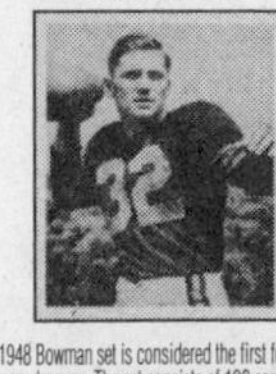

The 1948 Bowman set is considered the first football set of the modern era. The set consists of 108 cards measuring 2 1/16" by 2 1/2". Cards were issued in one-card penny packs. The entire front is comprised of a black and white photo. The backs contain a write-up and an offer for a football. The cards were printed in three sheets; the third sheet (containing all the card numbers divisible by three, i.e., 3, 6, 9, 12, 15, etc.) being printed in much lesser quantities. Hence, cards with numbers divisible by three are substantially more valuable than the other cards in the set. The second sheet (numbers 2, 5, 8, 11, 14, etc.) is also regarded as slightly tougher to obtain than the first sheet (numbers 1, 4, 7, 10, 13, etc.) which contains the most plentiful cards. An album with which to house the set was produced. Key Rookie Cards in this set are Sammy Baugh, Charley Conerly, Sid Luckman, Johnny Lujack, Pete Pihos, Bulldog Turner, Steve Van Buren, and Bob Waterfield.

COMPLETE SET (108) 4,500.00 7,000.00
WRAPPER (1-CENT) 150.00 250.00
1 Joe Tereshinski RC 80.00 150.00
2 Larry Olsonoski RC 15.00 25.00
3 Johnny Lujack SP RC 250.00 350.00
4 Ray Poole RC 12.00 20.00
5 Bill DeCorrevont RC 15.00 25.00
6 Paul Briggs SP RC 65.00 100.00
7 Steve Van Buren RC 125.00 200.00
8 Kenny Washington RC 40.00 60.00
9 Nolan Luhn SP RC 65.00 100.00
10 Chris Iversen RC 12.00 20.00
11 Jack Wiley RC 15.00 25.00
12 Charley Conerly SP RC 250.00 350.00
13 Hugh Taylor RC 15.00 25.00
14 Frank Seno RC 15.00 25.00
15 Gil Bouley SP RC 65.00 100.00
16 Tommy Thompson RC 20.00 35.00
17 Charley Trippi RC 60.00 100.00
18 Vince Banonis SP RC 65.00 100.00
19 Art Faircloth RC 12.00 20.00
20 Clyde Goodnight RC 15.00 25.00
21 Bill Chipley SP RC 65.00 100.00
22 Sammy Baugh RC 350.00 500.00
23 Don Kindt RC 15.00 25.00
24 John Koniszewski SP RC 65.00 100.00
25 Pat McHugh RC 12.00 20.00
26 Bob Waterfield RC 125.00 200.00
27 Tony Compagno SP RC 65.00 100.00
28 Paul Governali RC 15.00 25.00
29 Pat Harder RC 40.00 60.00
30 Vic Lindskog SP RC 65.00 100.00
31 Salvatore Rosato RC 12.00 20.00
32 John Mastrangelo RC 15.00 25.00
33 Fred Gehrke SP RC 65.00 100.00
34 Bosh Pritchard RC 12.00 20.00
35 Mike Micka RC 15.00 25.00
36 Bulldog Turner SP RC 150.00 250.00
37 Len Younce RC 12.00 20.00
38 Pat West RC 15.00 25.00
39 Russ Thomas SP RC 65.00 100.00
40 James Peebles RC 12.00 20.00
41 Bob Skoglund RC 15.00 25.00
42 Walt Stickle SP RC 65.00 100.00
43 Whitey Wistert RC 15.00 25.00
44 Paul Christman RC 40.00 60.00
45 Jay Rhodemyre SP RC 65.00 100.00
46 Tony Minisi RC 12.00 20.00
47 Bob Mann RC 15.00 25.00
48 Mal Kutner SP RC 75.00 125.00
49 Dick Poillon RC 12.00 20.00
50 Charles Cherundolo RC 15.00 25.00
51 Gerald Cowhig SP RC 65.00 100.00
52 Neill Armstrong RC 15.00 25.00
53 Frank Maznicki RC 15.00 25.00
54 John Sanchez SP RC 65.00 100.00
55 Frank Reagan RC 12.00 20.00
56 Jim Hardy RC 15.00 25.00
57 John Badaczewski SP 65.00 100.00
58 Robert Nussbaumer RC 12.00 20.00
59 Mervin Pregulman RC 15.00 25.00
60 Elbie Nickel SP RC 75.00 125.00
61 Alex Wojciechowicz RC 90.00 150.00
62 Walt Schlinkman RC 15.00 25.00
63 Pete Pihos SP RC 150.00 225.00
64 Joseph Sulaitis RC 12.00 20.00
65 Mike Holovak RC 30.00 50.00
66 Cy Souders SP RC 65.00 100.00
67 Paul McKee RC 12.00 20.00
68 Bill Moore RC 15.00 25.00
69 Frank Minini SP RC 65.00 100.00
70 Jack Ferrante RC 12.00 20.00
71 Les Horvath RC 35.00 50.00
72 Ted Fritsch Sr. SP RC 75.00 125.00
73 Tex Coulter RC 15.00 25.00
74 Boley Dancewicz RC 15.00 25.00
75 Dante Mangani SP RC 65.00 100.00
76 James Hefti RC 12.00 20.00
77 Paul Sarringhaus RC 15.00 25.00
78 Joe Scott SP RC 65.00 100.00
79 Bucko Kilroy RC 15.00 25.00
80 Bill Dudley RC 75.00 125.00
81 Mar.Goldberg SP RC 75.00 125.00
82 John Cannady RC 12.00 20.00
83 Perry Moss RC 15.00 25.00
84 Harold Crisler SP RC 75.00 125.00
85 Bill Gray RC 12.00 20.00
86 John Clement RC 15.00 25.00
87 Dan Sandifer SP RC 65.00 100.00
88 Ben Kish RC 12.00 20.00
89 Herbert Banta RC 15.00 25.00
90 Bill Garnaas SP RC 65.00 100.00
91 Jim White RC 15.00 25.00
92 Frank Barzilauskas RC 15.00 25.00
93 Vic Sears SP RC 65.00 100.00
94 John Adams RC 12.00 20.00
95 George McAfee RC 90.00 150.00
96 Ralph Heywood SP RC 65.00 100.00
97 Joe Muha RC 12.00 20.00
98 Fred Enke RC 15.00 25.00
99 Harry Gilmer SP RC 100.00 175.00
100 Bill Miklich RC 12.00 20.00
101 Joe Gottlieb RC 15.00 25.00
102 Bud Angsman SP RC 75.00 125.00
103 Tom Farmer RC 12.00 20.00
104 Bruce Smith RC 40.00 75.00
105 Bob Cifers SP RC 65.00 100.00
106 Ernie Steele RC 12.00 20.00
107 Sid Luckman RC 175.00 300.00
108 Buford Ray SP RC 250.00 400.00
NNO Album 200.00 350.00

1950 Bowman

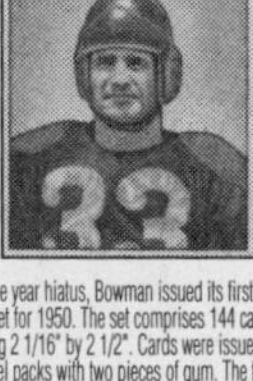

After a one year hiatus, Bowman issued its first color football set for 1950. The set comprises 144 cards measuring 2 1/16" by 2 1/2". Cards were issued in six-card nickel packs with two pieces of gum. The fronts contain a black and white photo that was colored in. The card backs, which contain a write-up, feature black printing except for the player's name and the logo for the "5-Star Bowman Picture Card Collectors Club" which are both in red. The set features the Rookie Cards of Tony Canadeo, Glenn Davis, Tom Fears, Otto Graham, Lou Groza, Elroy Hirsch, Dante Lavelli, Marion Motley, Joe Perry, and Y.A. Tittle. With a few exceptions the set numbering is arranged so that trios of players from the same team are numbered together in sequence.

COMPLETE SET (144) 3,000.00 4,500.00
WRAPPER (5-CENT) 100.00 175.00
1 Doak Walker 150.00 250.00
2 John Greene RC 18.00 25.00
3 Bob Nowasky RC 18.00 25.00
4 Jonathan Jenkins RC 18.00 25.00
5 Y.A. Tittle RC 175.00 250.00
6 Lou Groza RC 100.00 175.00
7 Alex Agase RC 20.00 30.00
8 Mac Speedie RC 30.00 50.00
9 Tony Canadeo RC 50.00 90.00
10 Larry Craig RC 20.00 30.00
11 Ted Fritsch Sr. 20.00 30.00
12 Joe Golding RC 18.00 25.00
13 Martin Ruby RC 18.00 25.00
14 George Taliaferro 20.00 30.00
15 Tank Younger RC 30.00 50.00
16 Glenn Davis RC 75.00 125.00
17 Bob Waterfield 75.00 125.00
18 Val Jansante RC 18.00 25.00
19 Joe Geri RC 18.00 25.00
20 Jerry Nuzum RC 18.00 25.00
21 Elmer Bud Angsman 18.00 25.00
22 Billy Dewell 18.00 25.00
23 Steve Van Buren 50.00 90.00
24 Cliff Patton RC 18.00 25.00
25 Bosh Pritchard 18.00 25.00
26 John Lujack 50.00 80.00
27 Sid Luckman 75.00 125.00
28 Bulldog Turner 35.00 60.00
29 Bill Dudley 35.00 60.00
30 Hugh Taylor 20.00 30.00
31 George Thomas RC 18.00 25.00
32 Ray Poole 18.00 25.00
33 Travis Tidwell RC 18.00 25.00
34 Gail Bruce RC 18.00 25.00
35 Joe Perry RC 125.00 200.00
36 Frankie Albert RC 30.00 50.00
37 Bobby Layne 125.00 200.00
38 Leon Hart 25.00 40.00
39 Bob Hoernschemeyer RC 20.00 30.00
40 Dick Barwegan RC 18.00 25.00
41 Adrian Burk RC 20.00 30.00
42 Barry French RC 18.00 25.00
43 Marion Motley RC 150.00 250.00
44 Jim Martin 20.00 30.00
45 Otto Graham RC 300.00 450.00
46 Al Baldwin RC 18.00 25.00
47 Larry Coutre RC 20.00 30.00
48 John Rauch 18.00 25.00
49 Sam Tamburo RC 18.00 25.00
50 Mike Swistowicz RC 18.00 25.00
51 Tom Fears RC 90.00 150.00
52 Elroy Hirsch RC 125.00 225.00
53 Dick Huffman RC 18.00 25.00
54 Bob Gage RC 18.00 25.00
55 Buddy Tinsley RC 18.00 25.00
56 Bill Blackburn RC 18.00 25.00
57 John Cochran RC 18.00 25.00
58 Bill Fischer 18.00 25.00
59 Whitey Wistert 20.00 30.00
60 Clyde Scott RC 18.00 25.00
61 Walter Barnes RC 18.00 25.00
62 Bob Perina RC 18.00 25.00
63 Bill Wightkin RC 18.00 25.00
64 Bob Goode RC 18.00 25.00
65 Al Demao RC 18.00 25.00
66 Harry Gilmer 20.00 30.00
67 Bill Austin RC 18.00 25.00
68 Joe Scott 18.00 25.00
69 Tex Coulter 20.00 30.00
70 Paul Salata RC 18.00 25.00
71 Emil Sitko RC 20.00 30.00
72 Bill Johnson C RC 18.00 25.00
73 Don Doll RC 18.00 25.00
74 Dan Sandifer RC 18.00 25.00
75 John Panelli RC 18.00 25.00
76 Bill Leonard RC 18.00 25.00
77 Bob Kelly RC 18.00 25.00
78 Dante Lavelli RC 100.00 175.00
79 Tony Adamle RC 20.00 30.00
80 Dick Wildung RC 18.00 25.00
81 Tobin Rote RC 30.00 50.00
82 Paul Burris RC 18.00 25.00
83 Lowell Tew RC 18.00 25.00
84 Barney Poole RC 18.00 25.00
85 Fred Naumetz RC 18.00 25.00
86 Dick Hoerner RC 18.00 25.00
87 Bob Reinhard RC 18.00 25.00
88 Howard Hartley RC 18.00 25.00
89 Darrell Hogan RC 18.00 25.00
90 Jerry Shipkey RC 18.00 25.00
91 Frank Tripucka 20.00 30.00
92 Garrard Ramsey RC 18.00 25.00
93 Pat Harder 20.00 30.00
94 Vic Sears RC 18.00 25.00
95 Tommy Thompson 20.00 30.00
96 Bucko Kilroy 20.00 30.00
97 George Connor 30.00 50.00
98 Fred Morrison RC 18.00 25.00
99 Jim Keane RC 18.00 25.00
100 Sammy Baugh 150.00 250.00
101 Harry Ulinski RC 18.00 25.00
102 Frank Spaniel RC 18.00 25.00
103 Charley Conerly 50.00 90.00
104 Dick Hensley RC 18.00 25.00
105 Eddie Price RC 18.00 25.00
106 Ed Carr RC 18.00 25.00
107 Leo Nomellini 45.00 75.00
108 Verl Lillywhite RC 18.00 25.00
109 Wallace Triplett RC 18.00 25.00
110 Joe Watson RC 18.00 25.00
111 Cloyce Box RC 20.00 30.00
112 Billy Stone RC 18.00 25.00
113 Earl Murray RC 18.00 25.00
114 Chet Mutryn RC 20.00 30.00
115 Ken Carpenter RC 20.00 30.00
116 Lou Rymkus RC 20.00 30.00
117 Dub Jones RC 20.00 30.00
118 Clayton Tonnemaker 18.00 25.00
119 Walt Schlinkman RC 18.00 25.00
120 Billy Grimes RC 18.00 25.00
121 George Ratterman RC 20.00 30.00
122 Bob Mann 18.00 25.00
123 Buddy Young RC 30.00 50.00
124 Jack Zilly RC 18.00 25.00
125 Tom Kalmanir RC 18.00 25.00
126 Frank Sinkovitz RC 18.00 25.00
127 Elbert Nickel 20.00 30.00
128 Jim Finks RC 40.00 75.00
129 Charley Trippi 35.00 60.00
130 Tom Wham RC 18.00 25.00
131 Ventan Yablonski RC 18.00 25.00
132 Chuck Bednarik 75.00 125.00
133 Joe Muha 18.00 25.00
134 Pete Pihos 45.00 80.00
135 Washington Serini RC 18.00 25.00
136 George Gulyanics RC 18.00 25.00
137 Ken Kavanaugh 20.00 30.00

138 Howie Livingston RC	18.00	25.00
139 Joe Tereshinski	18.00	25.00
140 Jim White	18.00	25.00
141 Gene Roberts RC	18.00	25.00
142 Bill Swiacki	20.00	30.00
143 Norm Standlee RC	18.00	25.00
144 Knox Ramsey RC	50.00	100.00

1951 Bowman

The 1951 Bowman set of 144 numbered cards witnessed an increase in card size from previous Bowman football sets. Cards were issued in six-card nickel packs and one-card penny packs. The cards were enlarged from the previous year to 2 1/16" by 3 1/8". The set is very similar in format to the baseball card set of that year. The fronts feature black and white photos that were colored in. The player's name is in a bar toward the bottom that runs from the right border toward the middle of the photo. A team logo or mascot is on top of the bar. The card backs are printed in maroon and blue on gray card stock and contain a write-up. The set features the Rookie Cards of Tom Landry, Emlen Tunnell, and Norm Van Brocklin. The Bill Walsh in this set went to Notre Dame and is not the Bill Walsh who coached the San Francisco 49ers in the 1980s. The set numbering is arranged so that two, three, or four players from the same team are together. Three blank backed proof cards have recently been uncovered and added to the listings below. The proofs are very similar to the corresponding base card. However, the artwork varies somewhat versus the base card.

COMPLETE SET (144)	2,500.00	3,500.00
WRAPPER (1-CENT)	150.00	250.00
WRAPPER (5-CENT)	175.00	300.00
1 Weldon Humble RC	50.00	80.00
2 Otto Graham	150.00	250.00
3 Mac Speedie	20.00	35.00
4 Norm Van Brocklin RC	200.00	300.00
5 Woodley Lewis RC	15.00	25.00
6 Tom Fears	30.00	50.00
7 George Musacco RC	12.00	20.00
8 George Taliaferro	15.00	25.00
9 Barney Poole	12.00	20.00
10 Steve Van Buren	35.00	60.00
11 Whitey Wistert	15.00	25.00
12 Chuck Bednarik	50.00	80.00
13 Bulldog Turner	30.00	50.00
14 Bob Williams RC	12.00	20.00
15 John Lujack	35.00	60.00
16 Roy Rebel Steiner	12.00	20.00
17 Jug Girard	15.00	25.00
18 Bill Neal RC	12.00	20.00
19 Travis Tidwell	12.00	20.00
20 Tom Landry RC	350.00	500.00
21 Arnie Weinmeister RC	35.00	60.00
22 Joe Gori	12.00	20.00
23 Bill Walsh RC	15.00	30.00
24 Fran Rogel	12.00	20.00
25 Doak Walker	35.00	60.00
26 Leon Hart	20.00	35.00
27 Thurman McGraw RC	12.00	20.00
28 Buster Ramsey	12.00	20.00
29 Frank Tripucka	20.00	35.00
30 Don Paul DB RC	12.00	20.00
31 Alex Loyd RC	12.00	20.00
32 Y.A. Tittle	75.00	135.00
33 Verl Lillywhite	12.00	20.00
34 Sammy Baugh	110.00	175.00
35 Chuck Drazenovich RC	12.00	20.00
36 Bob Goode	12.00	20.00
37 Horace Gillom RC	15.00	25.00
38 Lou Rymkus	15.00	25.00
39 Ken Carpenter	12.00	20.00
40 Bob Waterfield	45.00	75.00
41 Vitamin Smith RC	15.00	25.00
42 Glenn Davis	35.00	60.00
43 Dan Edwards RC	12.00	20.00
44 John Rauch	12.00	20.00
45 Zollie Toth RC	12.00	20.00
46 Pete Pihos	35.00	60.00
47 Russ Craft RC	12.00	20.00
48 Walter Barnes	12.00	20.00
49 Fred Morrison	12.00	20.00
50 Ray Bray RC	12.00	20.00
51 Ed Sprinkle RC	15.00	25.00
52 Floyd Reid RC	12.00	20.00
53 Billy Grimes	12.00	20.00
54 Ted Fritsch Sr.	15.00	25.00
55 Al DeRogatis RC	15.00	25.00
56 Charley Conerly	45.00	75.00
57 Jon Baker RC	12.00	20.00
58 Tom McWilliams	12.00	20.00
59 Jerry Shipkey	12.00	20.00
60 Lynn Chandnois RC	15.00	25.00
61 Don Doll	12.00	20.00
62 Lou Creekmur	30.00	50.00
63 Bob Hoernschemeyer	15.00	25.00
64 Tom Wham	12.00	20.00
65 Bill Fischer	12.00	20.00
66 Robert Nussbaumer	12.00	20.00
67 Gordy Soltau RC	12.00	20.00
68 Visco Grgich RC	12.00	20.00
69 John Strzykalski RC	12.00	20.00
70 Pete Stout RC	12.00	20.00
71 Paul Lipscomb RC	12.00	20.00
72 Harry Gilmer	20.00	35.00
73 Dante Lavelli	30.00	50.00
74 Dub Jones	15.00	25.00
75 Lou Groza	45.00	75.00
76 Elroy Hirsch	45.00	75.00
77 Tom Kalmanir	12.00	20.00
78 Jack Zilly	12.00	20.00
79 Bruce Alford RC	12.00	20.00
80 Art Weiner	12.00	20.00
81 Brad Ecklund RC	12.00	20.00
82 Bosh Pritchard	12.00	20.00
83 John Green RC	12.00	20.00
84 Ebert Van Buren RC	12.00	20.00
85 Julie Rykovich RC	12.00	20.00
86 Fred Davis	12.00	20.00
87 John Hoffman RC	12.00	20.00
88 Tobin Rote	15.00	25.00
89 Paul Burris	12.00	20.00
90 Tony Canadeo	30.00	50.00
91 Emlen Tunnell RC	60.00	100.00
92 Otto Schnellbacher RC	12.00	20.00
93 Ray Poole	12.00	20.00
94 Darrell Hogan	12.00	20.00
95 Frank Sinkovitz	12.00	20.00
96 Ernie Stautner	60.00	100.00
97 Elmer Bud Angsman	12.00	20.00
98 Jack Jennings RC	12.00	20.00
99 Jerry Groom RC	12.00	20.00
100 John Prchlik RC	12.00	20.00
101 J. Robert Smith RC	12.00	20.00
102 Bobby Layne	75.00	135.00
103 Frankie Albert	20.00	35.00
104 Gail Bruce	12.00	20.00
105 Joe Perry	45.00	75.00
106 Leon Heath RC	12.00	20.00
107 Ed Quirk RC	12.00	20.00
108 Hugh Taylor	15.00	25.00
109 Marion Motley	60.00	100.00
110 Tony Adamle	12.00	20.00
111 Alex Agase	15.00	25.00
112 Tank Younger	20.00	35.00
113 Bob Boyd RC	12.00	20.00
114 Jerry Williams RC	12.00	20.00
115 Joe Golding	12.00	20.00
116 Sherman Howard RC	12.00	20.00
117 John Wozniak RC	12.00	20.00
118 Frank Reagan	12.00	20.00
119 Vic Sears	12.00	20.00
120 Clyde Scott	12.00	20.00
121 George Gulyanics	12.00	20.00
122 Bill Wightkin	12.00	20.00
123 Chuck Hunsinger RC	12.00	20.00
124 Jack Cloud	12.00	20.00
125 Abner Wimberly RC	12.00	20.00
126 Dick Wildung	12.00	20.00
127 Eddie Price	12.00	20.00
128 Joe Scott	12.00	20.00
129 Jerry Nuzum	12.00	20.00
130 Jim Finks	20.00	35.00
131 Bob Gage	12.00	20.00
132 Bill Swiacki	15.00	25.00
133 Joe Watson	12.00	20.00
134 Ollie Cline RC	12.00	20.00
135 Jack Lininger RC	12.00	20.00
136 Fran Polsfoot RC	12.00	20.00
137 Charley Trippi	30.00	50.00
138 Ventan Yablonski	12.00	20.00
139 Emil Sitko	12.00	20.00
140 Leo Nomellini	30.00	60.00
141 Norm Standlee	12.00	20.00
142 Eddie Saenz RC	12.00	20.00
143 Al Demao	12.00	20.00
144 Bill Dudley	75.00	150.00
NNO Darrell Hogan Proof	75.00	125.00
NNO Bob Gage Proof	75.00	125.00
NNO Johnny Lujack Proof	175.00	300.00

1952 Bowman Large

One of two different sized sets produced by Bowman in 1952, the large version measures 2 1/2" by 3 3/4". Cards were issued in five-card, five-cent packs. The 144-card issue is identical to the smaller version in every respect except size. Either horizontal or vertical fronts contain a player portrait, a white banner with the player's name and a bar containing the team name and logo. Horizontal backs have a small write-up, previous year's stats and biographical information. Certain numbers were systematically printed in lesser quantities due to the fact that Bowman apparently could not fit each 72-card series on their respective sheets. The affected cards are those which are divisible by nine (i.e. 9, 18, 27 etc.) and those which are numbered one more than those divisible by nine (i.e. 10, 19, 28 etc.). These short-print cards are marked in the checklist below by SP. The set features NFL veterans and college players that entered the pro ranks in '52. The set features the Rookie Cards of Paul Brown, Jack Christiansen, Art Donovan, Frank Gifford, George Halas, Yale Lary, Gino Marchetti, Ollie Matson, Hugh McElhenny, and Andy Robustelli. The last card in the set, No. 144 Jim Lansford, is among the toughest football cards to acquire. It is generally accepted among hobbyists that the card was located at the bottom right corner of the production sheet and was subject to much abuse including numerous poor cuts. The problem was such that many copies never made it out of the factory as they were discarded. This card is also indicated below by SP.

COMPLETE SET (144)	9,500.00	12,500.00
WRAPPER (5-CENT)	30.00	60.00
1 Norm Van Brocklin SP	350.00	500.00
2 Otto Graham	200.00	300.00
3 Doak Walker	60.00	100.00
4 Steve Owen CO RC	50.00	80.00
5 Frankie Albert	30.00	50.00
6 Laurie Niemi RC	20.00	35.00
7 Chuck Hunsinger	20.00	35.00
8 Ed Modzelewski	30.00	50.00
9 Joe Spencer SP RC	40.00	75.00
10 Chuck Bednarik SP	200.00	350.00
11 Barney Poole	20.00	35.00
12 Charley Trippi	40.00	75.00
13 Tom Fears	40.00	75.00
14 Paul Brown CO RC	150.00	250.00
15 Leon Hart	30.00	50.00
16 Frank Gifford RC	350.00	500.00
17 Y.A.Tittle	200.00	300.00
18 Charlie Justice SP	100.00	175.00
19 George Connor SP	100.00	175.00
20 Lynn Chandnois	20.00	35.00
21 Billy Howton RC	30.00	50.00
22 Kenneth Snyder RC	20.00	35.00
23 Gino Marchetti RC	150.00	250.00
24 John Karras	20.00	35.00
25 Tank Younger	30.00	50.00
26 Tommy Thompson LB RC	20.00	35.00
27 Bob Miller SP RC	200.00	300.00
28 Kyle Rote SP RC	100.00	175.00
29 Hugh McElhenny RC	150.00	250.00
30 Sammy Baugh	225.00	350.00
31 Jim Dooley RC	25.00	45.00
32 Ray Mathews	20.00	35.00
33 Fred Cone RC	20.00	35.00
34 Al Pollard RC	20.00	35.00
35 Brad Ecklund	20.00	35.00
36 John Hancock SP RC	250.00	350.00
37 Elroy Hirsch SP	125.00	200.00
38 Keever Jankovich RC	20.00	35.00
39 Emlen Tunnell	75.00	125.00
40 Steve Dowden RC	20.00	35.00
41 Claude Hipps RC	20.00	35.00
42 Norm Standlee	20.00	35.00
43 Dick Todd CO RC	20.00	35.00
44 Babe Parilli	30.00	50.00
45 Steve Van Buren SP	200.00	300.00
46 Art Donovan SP RC	250.00	350.00
47 Bill Fischer	20.00	35.00
48 George Halas CO RC	160.00	275.00
49 Jerrell Price	20.00	35.00
50 John Sandusky RC	25.00	40.00
51 Ray Beck	20.00	35.00
52 Jim Martin	25.00	45.00
53 Joe Bach CO RC	20.00	35.00
54 Glen Christian SP RC	40.00	75.00
55 Andy Davis SP RC	40.00	75.00
56 Tobin Rote	25.00	50.00
57 Wayne Millner CO RC	50.00	90.00
58 Zollie Toth	20.00	35.00
59 Jack Jennings	20.00	35.00
60 Bill McColl RC	20.00	35.00
61 Les Richter RC	35.00	60.00
62 Walt Michaels RC	25.00	45.00
63 Charley Conerly SP	500.00	750.00
64 Howard Hartley SP	40.00	75.00
65 Jerome Smith RC	20.00	35.00
66 James Clark RC	20.00	35.00
67 Dick Logan RC	20.00	35.00
68 Wayne Robinson RC	20.00	35.00
69 James Hammond RC	20.00	35.00
70 Gene Schroeder RC	20.00	35.00
71 Tex Coulter	25.00	45.00
72 John Schweder SP RC	400.00	600.00
73 Vitamin Smith SP	75.00	125.00
74 Joe Campanella RC	25.00	40.00
75 Joe Kuharich CO RC	30.00	50.00
76 Herman Clark RC	25.00	40.00
77 Dan Edwards	25.00	40.00
78 Bobby Layne	175.00	300.00
79 Bob Hoernschemeyer	30.00	50.00
80 John Carr Blount RC	25.00	40.00
81 John Kastan SP RC	90.00	150.00
82 Harry Minarik SP RC	90.00	150.00
83 Joe Perry	75.00	125.00
84 Buddy Parker CO RC	30.00	50.00
85 Andy Robustelli RC	125.00	200.00
86 Dub Jones	30.00	50.00
87 Mal Cook RC	25.00	40.00
88 Billy Stone	25.00	40.00
89 George Taliaferro	30.00	50.00
90 Thomas Johnson SP RC	90.00	150.00
91 Leon Heath SP	60.00	100.00
92 Pete Pihos	60.00	100.00
93 Fred Benners RC	25.00	40.00
94 George Tarasovic RC	25.00	40.00
95 Buck Shaw CO RC	25.00	40.00
96 Bill Wightkin	25.00	40.00
97 John Wozniak	25.00	40.00
98 Bobby Dillon RC	30.00	50.00
99 Joe Stydahar SP RC	450.00	650.00
100 Dick Alban SP RC	90.00	150.00
101 Arnie Weinmeister	35.00	60.00
102 Bobby Cross RC	25.00	40.00
103 Don Paul DB	25.00	40.00
104 Buddy Young	35.00	60.00
105 Lou Groza	75.00	125.00
106 Ray Pelfrey RC	25.00	40.00
107 Maurice Nipp RC	25.00	40.00
108 Hubert Johnston SP RC	450.00	650.00
109 Vol.Quinlan SP RC	60.00	100.00
110 Jack Simmons RC	25.00	40.00
111 George Ratterman	30.00	50.00
112 John Badaczewski RC	25.00	40.00
113 Bill Reichardt	25.00	40.00
114 Art Weiner	25.00	40.00
115 Keith Flowers RC	25.00	40.00
116 Russ Craft	25.00	40.00
117 Jim O'Donahue SP RC	90.00	150.00
118 Darrell Hogan SP	60.00	100.00
119 Frank Ziegler RC	25.00	40.00
120 Dan Towler	35.00	60.00
121 Fred Williams RC	25.00	40.00
122 Jimmy Phelan CO RC	25.00	40.00
123 Eddie Price	25.00	40.00
124 Chet Ostrowski RC	25.00	40.00
125 Leo Nomellini	60.00	100.00
126 Steve Romanik SP RC	200.00	300.00
127 Ollie Matson SP RC	200.00	300.00
128 Dante Lavelli	50.00	90.00
129 Jack Christiansen RC	100.00	175.00
130 Dom Moselle RC	25.00	40.00
131 John Rapacz RC	25.00	40.00
132 Chuck Ortmann UER RC	25.00	40.00
133 Bob Williams	25.00	40.00
134 Chuck Ulrich RC	25.00	40.00
135 Gene Ronzani CO SP RC	450.00	650.00
136 Bert Rechichar SP	60.00	100.00
137 Bob Waterfield	75.00	125.00
138 Bobby Walston RC	30.00	50.00
139 Jerry Shipkey	25.00	40.00
140 Yale Lary RC	125.00	200.00
141 Gordy Soltau	25.00	40.00
142 Tom Landry	450.00	600.00
143 John Papit RC	25.00	40.00
144 Jim Lansford SP RC	1,800.00	3,000.00

1952 Bowman Small

One of two different sized sets issued by Bowman in 1952, this 144-card set is identical in every respect to the large version except for the smaller size of 2 1/16" by 3 1/8". Cards were issued in one-card penny packs. The fronts are either horizontal or vertical and feature a player protrait, a white banner with the player's name and a bar containing the team name and logo. All backs are horizontal and contain a brief write-up, previous year's stats and a bio. The set features NFL veterans and college players that entered the pro ranks in '52. The set features the Rookie Cards of Paul Brown, Jack Christiansen, Art Donovan, Frank Gifford, George Halas, Yale Lary, Gino Marchetti, Ollie Matson, Hugh McElhenny, and Andy Robustelli.

COMPLETE SET (144)	3,500.00	5,000.00
WRAPPER (1-CENT)	40.00	60.00
1 Norm Van Brocklin	200.00	350.00
2 Otto Graham	125.00	200.00
3 Doak Walker	35.00	60.00
4 Steve Owen CO RC	35.00	60.00
5 Frankie Albert	20.00	35.00
6 Laurie Niemi RC	15.00	25.00
7 Chuck Hunsinger	15.00	25.00
8 Ed Modzelewski	20.00	35.00
9 Joe Spencer RC	15.00	25.00
10 Chuck Bednarik	45.00	75.00
11 Barney Poole	15.00	25.00
12 Charley Trippi	35.00	60.00
13 Tom Fears	35.00	60.00
14 Paul Brown CO RC	90.00	150.00
15 Leon Hart	20.00	35.00
16 Frank Gifford RC	200.00	400.00
17 Y.A. Tittle	75.00	125.00
18 Charlie Justice	30.00	50.00
19 George Connor	20.00	35.00
20 Lynn Chandnois	15.00	25.00
21 Billy Howton RC	25.00	40.00
22 Kenneth Snyder RC	15.00	25.00
23 Gino Marchetti RC	75.00	125.00
24 John Karras	15.00	25.00
25 Tank Younger	20.00	35.00
26 Tommy Thompson LB RC	15.00	25.00
27 Bob Miller RC	15.00	25.00
28 Kyle Rote RC	30.00	50.00
29 Hugh McElhenny RC	100.00	175.00
30 Sammy Baugh	150.00	250.00
31 Jim Dooley RC	18.00	30.00
32 Ray Mathews	15.00	25.00
33 Fred Cone RC	15.00	25.00
34 Al Pollard RC	15.00	25.00
35 Brad Ecklund	15.00	25.00
36 John Lee Hancock RC	15.00	25.00
37 Elroy Hirsch	35.00	60.00
38 Keever Jankovich	15.00	25.00
39 Emlen Tunnell	30.00	50.00
40 Steve Dowden RC	15.00	25.00
41 Claude Hipps	15.00	25.00
42 Norm Standlee	15.00	25.00
43 Dick Todd CO RC	15.00	25.00
44 Babe Parilli	20.00	35.00
45 Steve Van Buren	40.00	75.00
46 Art Donovan RC	125.00	200.00
47 Bill Fischer	15.00	25.00
48 George Halas CO RC	150.00	250.00
49 Jerrell Price	15.00	25.00
50 John Sandusky RC	15.00	25.00
51 Ray Beck	15.00	25.00
52 Jim Martin	18.00	30.00
53 Joe Bach CO RC	15.00	25.00
54 Glen Christian RC	15.00	25.00
55 Andy Davis RC	15.00	25.00
56 Tobin Rote	18.00	30.00
57 Wayne Millner CO RC	30.00	50.00
58 Zollie Toth	15.00	25.00
59 Jack Jennings	15.00	25.00
60 Bill McColl RC	15.00	25.00
61 Les Richter RC	30.00	50.00
62 Walt Michaels RC	18.00	30.00
63 Charley Conerly	40.00	75.00
64 Howard Hartley	15.00	25.00
65 Jerome Smith RC	15.00	25.00
66 James Clark	15.00	25.00
67 Dick Logan	15.00	25.00
68 Wayne Robinson RC	15.00	25.00
69 James Hammond	15.00	25.00
70 Gene Schroeder RC	15.00	25.00
71 Tex Coulter	18.00	30.00
72 John Schweder	15.00	25.00
73 Vitamin Smith	20.00	35.00
74 Joe Campanella RC	18.00	30.00
75 Joe Kuharich CO RC	20.00	35.00
76 Herman Clark	18.00	30.00
77 Dan Edwards	18.00	30.00
78 Bobby Layne	90.00	150.00
79 Bob Hoernschemeyer	20.00	35.00
80 John Carr Blount RC	18.00	30.00
81 John Kastan RC	18.00	30.00
82 Harry Minarik	18.00	30.00
83 Joe Perry	40.00	75.00
84 Buddy Parker CO RC	20.00	35.00
85 Andy Robustelli RC	75.00	125.00
86 Dub Jones	20.00	35.00
87 Mal Cook	18.00	30.00
88 Billy Stone	18.00	30.00
89 George Taliaferro	20.00	35.00
90 Thomas Johnson RC	18.00	30.00
91 Leon Heath	18.00	30.00
92 Pete Pihos	35.00	50.00
93 Fred Benners	18.00	30.00
94 George Tarasovic RC	18.00	30.00
95 Buck Shaw CO RC	18.00	30.00
96 Bill Wightkin	18.00	30.00
97 John Wozniak	18.00	30.00
98 Bobby Dillon RC	20.00	35.00
99 Joe Stydahar CO RC	35.00	60.00
100 Dick Alban RC	18.00	30.00
101 Arnie Weinmeister	25.00	40.00
102 Bobby Cross RC	18.00	30.00
103 Don Paul	18.00	30.00
104 Buddy Young	25.00	40.00
105 Lou Groza	45.00	75.00
106 Ray Pelfrey	18.00	30.00
107 Maurice Nipp RC	18.00	30.00
108 Hubert Johnston RC	18.00	30.00
109 Volney Quinlan RC	18.00	30.00
110 Jack Simmons RC	18.00	30.00
111 George Ratterman	20.00	35.00
112 John Badaczewski	18.00	30.00
113 Bill Reichardt	18.00	30.00
114 Art Weiner	18.00	30.00
115 Keith Flowers RC	18.00	30.00
116 Russ Craft	18.00	30.00
117 Jim O'Donahue RC	18.00	30.00
118 Darrell Hogan	18.00	30.00
119 Frank Ziegler RC	18.00	30.00
120 Deacon Dan Towler	25.00	40.00
121 Fred Williams RC	18.00	30.00
122 Jimmy Phelan CO RC	18.00	30.00
123 Eddie Price	18.00	30.00
124 Chet Ostrowski RC	18.00	30.00
125 Leo Nomellini	40.00	75.00
126 Steve Romanik RC	18.00	30.00
127 Ollie Matson RC	75.00	125.00
128 Dante Lavelli	35.00	60.00
129 Jack Christiansen RC	50.00	80.00
130 Dom Moselle RC	18.00	30.00
131 John Rapacz RC	18.00	30.00
132 Chuck Ortmann UER RC	18.00	30.00
133 Bob Williams	18.00	30.00
134 Chuck Ulrich RC	18.00	30.00
135 Gene Ronzani CO RC	18.00	30.00
136 Bert Rechichar	20.00	35.00
137 Bob Waterfield	45.00	75.00
138 Bobby Walston RC	20.00	35.00
139 Jerry Shipkey	18.00	30.00
140 Yale Lary RC	50.00	80.00
141 Gordy Soltau	18.00	30.00
142 Tom Landry	250.00	400.00
143 John Papit RC	18.00	30.00
144 Jim Lansford RC	100.00	175.00

1953 Bowman

The 1953 Bowman set of 96 cards measures approximately 2 1/2" by 3 3/4". Cards were issued in five-card, five-cent packs. The set is somewhat smaller in number than would be thought since Bowman was the only major producer of football cards during this year. The fronts feature a player portrait with a football that contains player and team names. Horizontal backs contain a brief write-up, previous year's stats, a bio and a quiz. There are 24 cards marked SP in the checklist below which are considered in shorter supply than the other cards in the set. The Bill Walsh in this set went to Notre Dame and is not the Bill Walsh who coached the San Francisco 49ers in the 1980s. The most notable Rookie Card in this set is Eddie LeBaron.

COMPLETE SET (96)	2,500.00	3,500.00
WRAPPER (5-CENT)	90.00	150.00
1 Eddie LeBaron RC	75.00	125.00
2 John Dottley	18.00	30.00
3 Babe Parilli	20.00	35.00
4 Bucko Kilroy	20.00	35.00
5 Joe Tereshinski	18.00	30.00
6 Doak Walker	45.00	75.00
7 Fran Polsfoot	18.00	30.00
8 Sisto Averno RC	18.00	30.00
9 Marion Motley	45.00	75.00
10 Pat Brady RC	18.00	30.00
11 Norm Van Brocklin	75.00	125.00
12 Bill McColl	18.00	30.00
13 Jerry Groom	18.00	30.00
14 Al Pollard	18.00	30.00
15 Dante Lavelli	30.00	50.00
16 Eddie Price	18.00	30.00
17 Charley Trippi	30.00	50.00
18 Elbert Nickel	20.00	35.00
19 George Taliaferro	20.00	35.00
20 Charley Conerly	50.00	80.00
21 Bobby Layne	75.00	125.00
22 Elroy Hirsch	60.00	100.00
23 Jim Finks	25.00	40.00
24 Chuck Bednarik	45.00	75.00
25 Kyle Rote	25.00	40.00
26 Otto Graham	100.00	175.00
27 Harry Gilmer	20.00	35.00
28 Tobin Rote	20.00	35.00
29 Billy Stone	18.00	30.00
30 Buddy Young	25.00	40.00
31 Leon Hart	25.00	40.00
32 Hugh McElhenny	45.00	75.00
33 Dale Samuels	18.00	30.00
34 Lou Creekmur	30.00	50.00
35 Tom Catlin RC	18.00	30.00
36 Tom Fears	35.00	60.00
37 George Connor	25.00	40.00
38 Bill Walsh C	18.00	30.00
39 Leo Sanford SP RC	30.00	50.00
40 Horace Gillom	20.00	35.00
41 John Schweder SP	30.00	50.00
42 Tom O'Connell RC	18.00	30.00
43 Frank Gifford SP	175.00	300.00
44 Frank Continetti SP RC	30.00	50.00
45 John Olszewski SP RC	30.00	50.00
46 Dub Jones	20.00	35.00
47 Don Paul LB SP RC	30.00	50.00
48 Gerald Weatherly RC	18.00	30.00
49 Fred Bruney SP RC	30.00	50.00
50 Jack Scarbath RC	18.00	30.00
51 John Karras	18.00	30.00
52 Al Conway RC	18.00	30.00
53 Emlen Tunnell SP	75.00	125.00
54 Gern Nagler SP RC	30.00	50.00
55 Kenneth Snyder SP	30.00	50.00
56 Y.A. Tittle	90.00	150.00
57 John Rapacz SP	30.00	50.00
58 Harley Sewell SP RC	30.00	50.00
59 Don Bingham RC	18.00	30.00
60 Darrell Hogan	18.00	30.00
61 Tony Curcillo RC	18.00	30.00
62 Ray Renfro SP RC	35.00	60.00
63 Leon Heath	18.00	30.00
64 Tex Coulter SP	30.00	50.00
65 Dewayne Douglas RC	18.00	30.00
66 J. Robert Smith SP	30.00	50.00
67 Bob McChesney SP RC	30.00	50.00
68 Dick Alban SP	30.00	50.00
69 Andy Kozar RC	18.00	30.00
70 Merwin Hodel SP RC	30.00	50.00
71 Thurman McGraw	18.00	30.00
72 Cliff Anderson RC	18.00	30.00
73 Pete Pihos	35.00	60.00
74 Julie Rykovich	18.00	30.00
75 John Kreamcheck SP RC	30.00	50.00
76 Lynn Chandnois	18.00	30.00
77 Cloyce Box SP	30.00	50.00
78 Ray Mathews	18.00	30.00
79 Bobby Walston	20.00	35.00
80 Jim Dooley	18.00	30.00
81 Pat Harder SP	30.00	50.00
82 Jerry Shipkey	18.00	30.00
83 Bobby Thomason RC	18.00	30.00
84 Hugh Taylor	20.00	35.00
85 George Ratterman	20.00	35.00
86 Don Stonesifer RC	18.00	30.00
87 John Williams SP RC	30.00	50.00
88 Leo Nomellini	30.00	50.00
89 Frank Ziegler	18.00	30.00
90 Don Paul UER (19th in punt returns& should be 9th) Chicago Cardinals	18.00	30.00
91 Tom Dublinski	18.00	30.00
92 Ken Carpenter	18.00	30.00
93 Ted Marchibroda RC	25.00	40.00
94 Chuck Drazenovich	18.00	30.00
95 Lou Groza SP	75.00	125.00
96 William Cross SP RC	50.00	100.00

1954 Bowman

Measuring 2 1/2" by 3 3/4", the 1954 set consists of 128 cards. Cards were issued in seven-card five-cent packs and one-card penny packs. Toward the bottom of the photo is a white banner that contains the player's name, team name and mascot. The card backs feature the player's name in black print inside a red outline of a football. The player's statistical information from the previous season and a quiz are also on back. The "Whizzer" White in the set (125) is not Byron White, the Supreme Court Justice, but Wilford White. Wilford is the father of former Dallas Cowboys quarterback Danny White. The Bill Walsh in this set went to Notre Dame and is not the Bill Walsh who coached the San Francisco 49ers in the 1980s. The mid-series, cards 65-96, is very tough to find in relationship to other series. Rookie Cards in this set include Doug Atkins and George Blanda.

COMPLETE SET (128)	1,200.00	1,800.00
WRAPPER (1-CENT)	10.00	15.00
WRAPPER (5-CENT)	25.00	30.00
1 Ray Mathews	15.00	30.00
2 John Huzvar RC	3.00	5.00
3 Jack Scarbath	3.00	5.00
4 Doug Atkins RC	30.00	50.00
5 Bill Stits RC	3.00	5.00
6 Joe Perry	18.00	30.00
7 Kyle Rote	7.50	15.00
8 Norm Van Brocklin	25.00	50.00
9 Pete Pihos	12.00	20.00
10 Babe Parilli	4.00	8.00
11 Zeke Bratkowski RC	15.00	25.00
12 Ollie Matson	15.00	25.00
13 Pat Brady	3.00	5.00
14 Fred Enke	3.00	5.00
15 Harry Ulinski	3.00	5.00
16 Bob Garrett RC	3.00	5.00
17 Bill Bowman RC	3.00	5.00
18 Leo Rucka RC	3.00	5.00
19 John Cannady	3.00	5.00
20 Tom Fears	15.00	25.00
21 Norm Willey RC	3.00	5.00
22 Floyd Reid	3.00	5.00
23 George Blanda RC	100.00	175.00
24 Don Doheney RC	3.00	5.00
25 John Schweder	3.00	5.00
26 Bert Rechichar	3.00	5.00
27 Harry Dowda RC	3.00	5.00
28 John Sandusky	3.00	5.00
29 Les Bingaman RC	7.50	15.00
30 Joe Arenas RC	3.00	5.00
31 Ray Wietecha RC	3.00	5.00
32 Elroy Hirsch	18.00	30.00
33 Harold Giancanelli RC	3.00	5.00
34 Billy Howton	4.00	8.00
35 Fred Morrison	3.00	5.00
36 Bobby Cavazos RC	3.00	5.00
37 Darrell Hogan	3.00	5.00
38 Buddy Young	4.00	8.00
39 Charlie Justice	12.00	20.00
40 Otto Graham	50.00	80.00
41 Doak Walker	20.00	35.00
42 Y.A.Tittle	35.00	60.00
43 Buford Long RC	3.00	5.00
44 Volney Quinlan	3.00	5.00
45 Bobby Thomason	3.00	5.00
46 Fred Cone	3.00	5.00
47 Gerald Weatherly	3.00	5.00
48 Don Stonesifer	3.00	5.00
49A Lynn Chandnois ERR (Name spelled Chadnois on back)	3.00	5.00
49B Lynn Chandnois COR (correct name Chandnois on back)	3.00	5.00
50 George Taliaferro	3.00	5.00
51 Dick Alban	3.00	5.00
52 Lou Groza	20.00	35.00
53 Bobby Layne	35.00	60.00
54 Hugh McElhenny	20.00	40.00
55 Frank Gifford UER (Avg. gain 7.83, should be 3.1)	60.00	100.00
56 Leon McLaughlin RC	3.00	5.00
57 Chuck Bednarik	20.00	40.00
58 Art Hunter RC	3.00	5.00
59 Bill McColl	3.00	5.00
60 Charley Trippi	15.00	25.00
61 Jim Finks	7.50	15.00
62 Bill Lange G RC	3.00	5.00
63 Laurie Niemi	3.00	5.00
64 Ray Renfro	4.00	8.00
65 Dick Chapman SP RC	15.00	25.00
66 Bob Hantla SP RC	15.00	25.00
67 Ralph Starkey SP RC	15.00	25.00
68 Don Paul LB SP	15.00	25.00
69 Kenneth Snyder SP	15.00	25.00
70 Tobin Rote SP	18.00	30.00
71 Art DeCarlo SP RC	15.00	25.00
72 Tom Keane SP RC	15.00	25.00
73 Hugh Taylor SP	18.00	30.00
74 Warren Lahr SP RC	15.00	25.00
75 Jim Neal SP RC	15.00	25.00
76 Leo Nomellini SP	35.00	60.00
77 Dick Yelvington SP RC	15.00	25.00
78 Les Richter SP	18.00	30.00
79 Bucko Kilroy SP	18.00	30.00
80 John Martinkovic SP RC	15.00	25.00
81 Dale Dodrill SP RC	15.00	25.00
82 Ken Jackson SP RC	15.00	25.00
83 Paul Lipscomb SP	15.00	25.00
84 John Bauer SP RC	15.00	25.00
85 Lou Creekmur SP	20.00	50.00
86 Eddie Price SP	15.00	25.00
87 Kenneth Farragut SP RC	15.00	25.00
88 Dave Hanner SP RC	18.00	30.00
89 Don Boll SP RC	15.00	25.00
90 Chet Hanulak SP RC	15.00	25.00
91 Thurman McGraw SP	15.00	25.00
92 Don Heinrich SP RC	18.00	30.00
93 Dan McKown SP RC	15.00	25.00
94 Bob Fleck SP RC	15.00	25.00
95 Jerry Hilgenberg SP RC	15.00	25.00
96 Bill Walsh C SP	15.00	25.00
97A Tom Finnin ERR	35.00	60.00
97B Tom Finnan COR RC	4.00	8.00
98 Paul Barry RC	3.00	5.00
99 Chick Jagade	3.00	5.00
100 Jack Christiansen	12.00	20.00
101 Gordy Soltau	3.00	5.00
102A Emlen Tunnel ERR	15.00	25.00
102B Emlen Tunnell COR two L's almost touching	12.00	20.00
102C Emlen Tunnell COR Two L's normally spaced	12.00	20.00
103 Stan West RC	3.00	5.00
104 Jerry Williams	3.00	5.00
105 Veryl Switzer RC	3.00	5.00
106 Billy Stone	3.00	5.00
107 Jerry Watford RC	3.00	5.00
108 Elbert Nickel	4.00	8.00
109 Ed Sharkey RC	3.00	5.00
110 Steve Meilinger RC	3.00	5.00
111 Dante Lavelli	12.00	20.00
112 Leon Hart	7.50	15.00
113 Charley Conerly	18.00	30.00
114 Richard Lemmon RC	3.00	5.00
115 Al Carmichael RC	3.00	5.00
116 George Connor	12.00	20.00
117 John Olszewski	3.00	5.00
118 Ernie Stautner	15.00	25.00
119 Ray Smith RC	3.00	5.00
120 Neil Worden RC	3.00	5.00
121 Jim Dooley	3.00	5.00
122 Arnold Galiffa	3.00	5.00
123 Kline Gilbert RC	3.00	5.00
124 Bob Hoernschemeyer	4.00	8.00
125 Wilford White RC	7.50	15.00
126 Art Spinney RC	3.00	5.00
127 Joe Koch RC	3.00	5.00
128 John Lattner RC	40.00	80.00

1955 Bowman

The 1955 Bowman set of 160 cards was Bowman's last sports issue before the company was purchased by Topps in January of 1956. The cards were issued in seven-card, five-cent packs and one-card penny packs and measure approximately 2 1/2" by 3 3/4". The fronts contain player photos with the player name and team logo at the bottom and the team name at the top. The card backs are printed in red and blue on gray card stock and a short player bio is included. On the bottom of most of the card backs is a play diagram. Cards 65-160 are slightly more difficult to obtain. The notable Rookie Cards in this set are Alan Ameche, Len Ford, Frank Gatski, John Henry Johnson, Mike McCormack, Jim Ringo, Bob St. Clair, and Pat Summerall.

COMPLETE SET (160)	1,000.00	1,600.00
WRAPPER (1-CENT)	150.00	225.00
WRAPPER (5-CENT)	60.00	120.00
1 Doak Walker	40.00	75.00
2 Mike McCormack RC	18.00	30.00
3 John Olszewski	3.00	5.00
4 Dorne Dibble RC	3.00	5.00
5 Lindon Crow RC	3.00	5.00
6 Hugh Taylor UER (First word in bio should be Bones)	4.00	8.00
7 Frank Gifford	35.00	60.00
8 Alan Ameche RC	25.00	40.00
9 Don Stonesifer	3.00	5.00
10 Pete Pihos	7.50	15.00
11 Bill Austin	3.00	5.00
12 Dick Alban	3.00	5.00
13 Bobby Walston	4.00	8.00
14 Len Ford RC	25.00	40.00
15 Jug Girard	3.00	5.00
16 Charley Conerly	15.00	25.00
17 Volney Peters RC	3.00	5.00
18 Max Boydston RC	3.00	5.00
19 Leon Hart	6.00	12.00
20 Bert Rechichar	3.00	5.00
21 Lee Riley RC	3.00	5.00
22 Johnny Carson RC	3.00	5.00
23 Harry Thompson	3.00	5.00
24 Ray Wietecha	3.00	5.00
25 Ollie Matson	15.00	25.00
26 Eddie LeBaron	7.50	15.00
27 Jack Simmons	3.00	5.00
28 Jack Christiansen	7.50	15.00
29 Bucko Kilroy	4.00	8.00
30 Tom Keane	3.00	5.00
31 Dave Leggett RC	3.00	5.00
32 Norm Van Brocklin	25.00	40.00
33 Harlon Hill RC	6.00	12.00
34 Robert Haner RC	3.00	5.00
35 Veryl Switzer	3.00	5.00
36 Dick Stanfel RC	6.00	12.00
37 Lou Groza	15.00	25.00
38 Tank Younger	6.00	12.00
39 Dick Flanagan RC	3.00	5.00
40 Jim Dooley	3.00	5.00
41 Ray Collins RC	3.00	5.00
42 John Henry Johnson RC	25.00	40.00
43 Tom Fears	7.50	15.00
44 Joe Perry	18.00	30.00
45 Gene Brito RC	3.00	5.00
46 Bill Johnson	3.00	5.00
47 Deacon Dan Towler	6.00	12.00
48 Dick Moegle RC	4.00	8.00
49 Kline Gilbert	3.00	5.00
50 Les Gobel RC	3.00	5.00
51 Ray Krouse RC	3.00	5.00
52 Pat Summerall RC	35.00	70.00
53 Ed Brown RC	7.50	15.00
54 Lynn Chandnois	3.00	5.00
55 Joe Heap RC	3.00	5.00
56 John Hoffman	3.00	5.00
57 Howard Ferguson RC	3.00	5.00
58 Bobby Watkins RC	3.00	5.00
59 Charlie Ane RC	3.00	5.00
60 Ken MacAfee E RC	4.00	8.00
61 Ralph Guglielmi RC	4.00	8.00
62 George Blanda	35.00	60.00
63 Kenneth Snyder	3.00	5.00
64 Chet Ostrowski	3.00	5.00
65 Buddy Young	7.50	15.00
66 Gordy Soltau	5.00	8.00
67 Eddie Bell RC	5.00	8.00
68 Ben Agajanian RC	6.00	12.00
69 Tom Dahms RC	5.00	8.00
70 Jim Ringo RC	30.00	50.00
71 Bobby Layne	45.00	75.00
72 Y.A. Tittle	45.00	75.00
73 Bob Gaona RC	5.00	8.00
74 Tobin Rote	6.00	12.00
75 Hugh McElhenny	18.00	30.00
76 John Kreamcheck	5.00	8.00
77 Al Dorow RC	6.00	12.00
78 Bill Wade	7.50	15.00

79 Dale Dodrill 5.00 8.00
80 Chuck Drazenovich 5.00 8.00
81 Billy Wilson RC 6.00 12.00
82 Les Richter 6.00 12.00
83 Pat Brady 5.00 8.00
84 Bob Hoernschemeyer 6.00 12.00
85 Joe Arenas 5.00 8.00
86 Len Szafaryn UER RC 5.00 8.00
(Listed as Ben on front)
87 Rick Casares RC 12.00 20.00
88 Leon McLaughlin 5.00 8.00
89 Charley Toogood RC 5.00 8.00
90 Tom Bettis RC 5.00 8.00
91 John Sandusky 5.00 8.00
92 Bill Wightkin 5.00 8.00
93 Darrel Brewster RC 5.00 8.00
94 Marion Campbell 7.50 15.00
95 Floyd Reid 5.00 8.00
96 Chick Jagade 5.00 8.00
97 George Taliaferro 5.00 8.00
98 Carlton Massey RC 5.00 8.00
99 Fran Rogel 5.00 8.00
100 Alex Sandusky RC 5.00 8.00
101 Bob St. Clair RC 30.00 50.00
102 Al Carmichael 5.00 8.00
103 Carl Taseff RC 5.00 8.00
104 Leo Nomellini 15.00 25.00
105 Tom Scott 5.00 8.00
106 Ted Marchibroda 7.50 15.00
107 Art Spinney 5.00 8.00
108 Wayne Robinson 5.00 8.00
109 Jim Ricca RC 5.00 8.00
110 Lou Ferry RC 5.00 8.00
111 Roger Zatkoff RC 5.00 8.00
112 Lou Creekmur 7.50 15.00
113 Kenny Konz RC 5.00 8.00
114 Doug Eggers RC 5.00 8.00
115 Bobby Thomason 5.00 8.00
116 Bill McPeak RC 5.00 8.00
117 William Brown RC 5.00 8.00
118 Royce Womble RC 5.00 8.00
119 Frank Gatski RC 20.00 35.00
120 Jim Finks 7.50 15.00
121 Andy Robustelli 15.00 25.00
122 Bobby Dillon 5.00 8.00
123 Leo Sanford 5.00 8.00
124 Elbert Nickel 6.00 12.00
125 Wayne Hansen RC 5.00 8.00
126 Buck Lansford RC 5.00 8.00
127 Gern Nagler 5.00 8.00
128 Jim Salsbury RC 5.00 8.00
129 Dale Atkeson RC 5.00 8.00
130 John Schweder 5.00 8.00
131 Dave Hanner 6.00 12.00
132 Eddie Price 5.00 8.00
133 Vic Janowicz 15.00 30.00
134 Ernie Stautner 15.00 25.00
135 James Parmer RC 5.00 8.00
136 Emlen Tunnell UER 12.00 20.00
(Misspelled Tunnel
on card front)
137 Kyle Rote UER 7.50 15.00
(Longest gain 1.8 yards,
should be 18 yards)
138 Norm Willey 5.00 8.00
139 Charley Trippi 12.00 20.00
140 Billy Howton 6.00 12.00
141 Bobby Clatterbuck RC 5.00 8.00
142 Bob Boyd 5.00 8.00
143 Bob Toneff UER RC 6.00 12.00
(name misspelled Toneoff)
144 Jerry Helluin RC 5.00 8.00
145 Adrian Burk 5.00 8.00
146 Walt Michaels 6.00 12.00
147 Zollie Toth 5.00 8.00
148 Frank Varrichione RC 5.00 8.00
149 Dick Bielski RC 5.00 8.00
150 George Ratterman 6.00 12.00
151 Mike Jarmoluk RC 5.00 8.00
152 Tom Landry 125.00 200.00
153 Ray Renfro 6.00 12.00
154 Zeke Bratkowski 6.00 12.00
155 Jerry Norton RC 5.00 8.00
156 Maurice Bassett RC 5.00 8.00
157 Volney Quinlan 5.00 8.00
158 Chuck Bednarik 18.00 30.00
159 Don Colo RC 5.00 8.00
160 L.G. Dupre RC 20.00 40.00

1991 Bowman

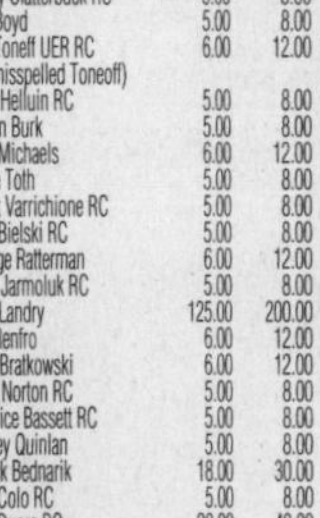

Resurrected by Topps after a 36 year hiatus, Bowman returned to the football card playing field with a 561-card standard-size set. The cards retain some of the qualities from early Bowman products. As far as layout, the backs resemble those of the 1950s. They are printed in black and green on gray and have a write-up, bio and stats from the previous season. The cards are checklisted below alphabetically according to teams. Subsets include Rookie Superstars (1-11), League Leaders (273-283) and Road to Super Bowl XXV (547-557). Rookie Cards include Alvin Harper, Randal Hill, Derek Loville, Herman Moore, Mike Pritchard, Ricky Watters, and Harvey Williams.

COMPLETE SET (561) 5.00 12.00
COMP.FACT.SET (561) 6.00 15.00
1 Jeff George RS .08 .25
2 Richmond Webb RS .01 .05
3 Emmitt Smith RS .50 1.25
4 Mark Carrier DB RS UER .01 .05
5 Steve Christie RS .01 .05
6 Keith Sims RS .01 .05
7 Rob Moore RS UER .08 .25
(Yards misspelled as
yarders on back)
8 Johnny Johnson RS .01 .05
9 Eric Green RS .01 .05
10 Ben Smith RS .01 .05
11 Tory Epps RS .01 .05
12 Andre Rison .02 .10
13 Shawn Collins .01 .05
14 Chris Hinton .01 .05
15 Deion Sanders UER .15 .40
(Bio says he played for
Georgia, College listed
should be Florida State)
16 Darion Conner .01 .05
17 Michael Haynes .08 .25
18 Chris Miller .02 .10
19 Jessie Tuggle .01 .05
20 Scott Fulhage .01 .05
21 Bill Fralic .01 .05
22 Floyd Dixon .01 .05
23 Oliver Barnett .01 .05
24 Mike Rozier .01 .05
25 Tory Epps .01 .05
26 Tim Green .01 .05
27 Steve Broussard .01 .05
28 Bruce Pickens RC .01 .05
29 Mike Pritchard RC .08 .25
30 Andre Reed .02 .10
31 Darryl Talley .01 .05
32 Nate Odomes .01 .05
33 Jamie Mueller .01 .05
34 Leon Seals .01 .05
35 Keith McKeller .01 .05
36 Al Edwards .01 .05
37 Butch Rolle .01 .05
38 Jeff Wright RC .01 .05
39 Will Wolford .01 .05
40 James Williams .01 .05
41 Kent Hull .01 .05
42 James Lofton .02 .10
43 Frank Reich .02 .10
44 Bruce Smith .08 .25
45 Thurman Thomas .08 .25
46 Leonard Smith .01 .05
47 Shane Conlan .01 .05
48 Steve Tasker .02 .10
49 Ray Bentley .01 .05
50 Cornelius Bennett .02 .10
51 Stan Thomas .01 .05
52 Shaun Gayle .01 .05
53 Wendell Davis .01 .05
54 James Thornton .01 .05
55 Mark Carrier DB .02 .10
56 Richard Dent .02 .10
57 Ron Morris .01 .05
58 Mike Singletary .02 .10
59 Jay Hilgenberg .01 .05
60 Donnell Woolford .01 .05
61 Jim Covert .01 .05
62 Jim Harbaugh .08 .25
63 Neal Anderson .02 .10
64 Brad Muster .01 .05
65 Kevin Butler .01 .05
66 Trace Armstrong UER .01 .05
67 Ron Cox .01 .05
68 Peter Tom Willis .01 .05
69 Johnny Bailey .01 .05
70 Mark Bortz UER .01 .05
71 Chris Zorich RC .08 .25
72 Lamar Rogers RC .01 .05
73 David Grant UER .01 .05
74 Lewis Billups .01 .05
75 Harold Green .02 .10
76 Ickey Woods .01 .05
77 Eddie Brown .01 .05
78 David Fulcher .01 .05
79 Anthony Munoz .02 .10
80 Carl Zander .01 .05
81 Rodney Holman .01 .05
82 James Brooks .02 .10
83 Tim McGee .01 .05
84 Boomer Esiason .02 .10
85 Leon White .01 .05
86 James Francis UER .01 .05
87 Mitchell Price RC .01 .05
88 Ed King RC .01 .05
89 Eric Turner RC .02 .10
90 Rob Burnett RC .02 .10
91 Leroy Hoard .02 .10
92 Kevin Mack UER .01 .05
93 Thane Gash UER .01 .05
94 Gregg Rakoczy .01 .05
95 Clay Matthews .02 .10
96 Eric Metcalf .02 .10
97 Stephen Braggs .01 .05
98 Frank Minnifield .01 .05
99 Reggie Langhorne .01 .05
100 Mike Johnson .01 .05
101 Brian Brennan .01 .05
102 Anthony Pleasant .01 .05
103 Godfrey Myles UER RC .01 .05
104 Russell Maryland RC .08 .25
105 James Washington RC .01 .05
106 Nate Newton .02 .10
107 Jimmie Jones .01 .05
108 Jay Novacek .08 .25
109 Alexander Wright .01 .05
110 Jack Del Rio .02 .10
111 Jim Jeffcoat .01 .05
112 Mike Saxon .01 .05
113 Troy Aikman .30 .75
114 Issiac Holt .01 .05
115 Ken Norton .02 .10
116 Kelvin Martin .01 .05
117 Emmitt Smith 1.00 2.50
118 Ken Willis .01 .05
119 Daniel Stubbs .01 .05
120 Michael Irvin .08 .25
121 Danny Noonan .01 .05
122 Alvin Harper RC UER .08 .25
(Drafted in first round,
not second)
123 Reggie Johnson RC .01 .05
124 Vance Johnson .01 .05
125 Steve Atwater .01 .05
126 Greg Kragen .01 .05
127 John Elway .50 1.25
128 Simon Fletcher .01 .05
129 Wymon Henderson .01 .05
130 Ricky Nattiel .01 .05
131 Shannon Sharpe .20 .50
132 Ron Holmes .01 .05
133 Karl Mecklenburg .01 .05
134 Bobby Humphrey .01 .05
135 Clarence Kay .01 .05
136 Dennis Smith .01 .05
137 Jim Juriga .01 .05
138 Melvin Bratton .01 .05
139 Mark Jackson UER .01 .05
140 Michael Brooks .01 .05
141 Alton Montgomery .01 .05
142 Mike Croel RC .01 .05
143 Mel Gray .02 .10
144 Michael Cofer .01 .05
145 Jeff Campbell .01 .05
146 Dan Owens .01 .05
147 Robert Clark UER .01 .05
148 Jim Arnold .01 .05
149 William White .01 .05
150 Rodney Peete .02 .10
151 Jerry Ball .01 .05
152 Bennie Blades .01 .05
153 Barry Sanders UER .50 1.25
154 Andre Ware .02 .10
155 Lomas Brown .01 .05
156 Chris Spielman .02 .10
157 Kelvin Pritchett RC .02 .10
158 Herman Moore RC .08 .25
159 Chris Jacke .01 .05
160 Tony Mandarich .01 .05
161 Perry Kemp .01 .05
162 Johnny Holland .01 .05
163 Mark Lee .01 .05
164 Anthony Dilweg .01 .05
165 Scott Stephen RC .01 .05
166 Ed West .01 .05
167 Mark Murphy .01 .05
168 Darrell Thompson .01 .05
169 James Campen RC .01 .05
170 Jeff Query .01 .05
171 Brian Noble .01 .05
172 Sterling Sharpe UER .08 .25
(Card says he gained/3314 yards in 1990)
173 Robert Brown .01 .05
174 Tim Harris .01 .05
175 LeRoy Butler .02 .10
176 Don Majkowski .01 .05
177 Vinnie Clark RC .01 .05
178 Esera Tuaolo RC .01 .05
179 Lorenzo White UER .01 .05
180 Warren Moon .08 .25
181 Sean Jones .02 .10
182 Curtis Duncan .01 .05
183 Al Smith .01 .05
184 Richard Johnson CB RC .01 .05
185 Tony Jones WR .01 .05
186 Bubba McDowell .01 .05
187 Bruce Matthews .02 .10
188 Ray Childress .01 .05
189 Haywood Jeffires .02 .10
190 Ernest Givins .02 .10
191 Mike Munchak .02 .10
192 Greg Montgomery .01 .05
193 Cody Carlson RC .01 .05
194 Johnny Meads .01 .05
195 Drew Hill UER .01 .05
196 Mike Dumas RC .01 .05
197 Darryll Lewis RC .02 .10
198 Rohn Stark .01 .05
199 Clarence Verdin UER .01 .05
200 Mike Prior .01 .05
201 Eugene Daniel .01 .05
202 Dean Biasucci .01 .05
203 Jeff Herrod .01 .05
204 Keith Taylor .01 .05
205 Jon Hand .01 .05
206 Pat Beach .01 .05
207 Duane Bickett .01 .05
208 Jessie Hester UER .01 .05
209 Chip Banks .01 .05
210 Ray Donaldson .01 .05
211 Bill Brooks .01 .05
212 Jeff George .08 .25
213 Tony Siragusa RC .20 .50
214 Albert Bentley .01 .05
215 Joe Valerio RC .01 .05
216 Chris Martin .01 .05
217 Christian Okoye .01 .05
218 Stephone Paige .01 .05
219 Percy Snow .01 .05
220 David Szott RC .01 .05
221 Derrick Thomas .08 .25
222 Todd McNair .01 .05
223 Albert Lewis .01 .05
224 Neil Smith .08 .25
225 Barry Word .01 .05
226 Robb Thomas .01 .05
227 John Alt .01 .05
228 Jonathan Hayes .01 .05
229 Kevin Ross .01 .05
230 Nick Lowery .01 .05
231 Tim Grunhard .01 .05
232 Dan Saleaumua .01 .05
233 Steve DeBerg .01 .05
234 Harvey Williams RC .08 .25
235 Nick Bell RC UER .01 .05
(Lives in Nevada,
not California)
236 Mervyn Fernandez UER .01 .05
237 Howie Long .08 .25
238 Marcus Allen .08 .25
239 Eddie Anderson .01 .05
240 Ethan Horton .01 .05
241 Lionel Washington .01 .05
242 Steve Wisniewski UER .01 .05
243 Bo Jackson UER .10 .30
(Drafted by Raiders,
should say drafted by
Tampa Bay in '86)
244 Greg Townsend .01 .05
245 Jeff Jaeger .01 .05
246 Aaron Wallace .01 .05
247 Garry Lewis .01 .05
248 Steve Smith .01 .05
249 Willie Gault UER .01 .05
250 Scott Davis .01 .05
251 Jay Schroeder .01 .05
252 Don Mosebar .01 .05
253 Todd Marinovich RC .01 .05
254 Irv Pankey .01 .05
255 Flipper Anderson .01 .05
256 Tom Newberry .01 .05
257 Kevin Greene .02 .10
258 Mike Wilcher .01 .05
259 Bern Brostek .01 .05
260 Buford McGee .01 .05
261 Cleveland Gary .01 .05
262 Jackie Slater .01 .05
263 Henry Ellard .02 .10
264 Alvin Wright .01 .05
265 Darryl Henley RC .01 .05
266 Damone Johnson RC .01 .05
267 Frank Stams .01 .05
268 Jerry Gray .01 .05
269 Jim Everett .02 .10
270 Pat Terrell .01 .05
271 Todd Lyght RC .01 .05
272 Aaron Cox .01 .05
273 Barry Sanders LL .20 .50
274 Jerry Rice LL .15 .40
Receiving Leader
275 Derrick Thomas LL .08 .25
Sack Leader
276 Mark Carrier DB LL .02 .10
Interception Leader
277 Warren Moon LL .08 .25
Passing Yardage Leader
278 Randall Cunningham LL .02 .10
Rushing Average Leader
279 Nick Lowery LL .01 .05
280 Clarence Verdin LL .01 .05
281 Thurman Thomas LL .08 .25
Yards From Scrimmage
Leader
282 Mike Horan LL .01 .05
283 Flipper Anderson LL .01 .05
284 John Offerdahl .01 .05
285 Dan Marino UER .50 1.25
(2637 yards gained,
should be 3563)
286 Mark Clayton .02 .10
287 Tony Paige .01 .05
288 Keith Sims .01 .05
289 Jeff Cross .01 .05
290 Pete Stoyanovich .01 .05
291 Ferrell Edmunds .01 .05
292 Reggie Roby .01 .05
293 Louis Oliver .01 .05
294 Jarvis Williams .01 .05
295 Sammie Smith .01 .05
296 Richmond Webb .01 .05
297 J.B. Brown .01 .05
298 Jim C.Jensen .01 .05
299 Mark Duper .02 .10
300 David Griggs .01 .05
301 Randal Hill RC .02 .10
302 Aaron Craver RC .01 .05
303 Keith Millard .01 .05
304 Steve Jordan .01 .05
305 Anthony Carter .02 .10
306 Mike Merriweather .01 .05
307 Audray McMillian RC UER .01 .05
308 Randall McDaniel .02 .10
309 Gary Zimmerman .02 .10
310 Carl Lee .01 .05
311 Reggie Rutland .01 .05
312 Hassan Jones .01 .05
313 Kirk Lowdermilk UER .01 .05
314 Herschel Walker .02 .10
315 Chris Doleman .01 .05
316 Joey Browner .01 .05
317 Wade Wilson .02 .10
318 Henry Thomas .01 .05
319 Rich Gannon .08 .25
320 Al Noga UER .01 .05
321 Pat Harlow RC .01 .05
322 Bruce Armstrong .01 .05
323 Maurice Hurst .01 .05
324 Brent Williams .01 .05
325 Chris Singleton .01 .05
326 Jason Staurovsky .01 .05
327 Marvin Allen .01 .05
328 Hart Lee Dykes .01 .05
329 Johnny Rembert .01 .05
330 Andre Tippett .01 .05
331 Greg McMurtry .01 .05
332 John Stephens .01 .05
333 Ray Agnew .01 .05
334 Tommy Hodson .01 .05
335 Ronnie Lippett .01 .05
336 Marv Cook .01 .05
337 Tommy Barnhardt RC .01 .05
338 Dalton Hilliard .01 .05
339 Sam Mills .01 .05
340 Morten Andersen .01 .05
341 Stan Brock .01 .05
342 Brett Maxie .01 .05
343 Steve Walsh .01 .05
344 Vaughan Johnson .01 .05
345 Rickey Jackson .01 .05
346 Renaldo Turnbull .01 .05
347 Joel Hilgenberg .01 .05
348 Toi Cook RC .01 .05
349 Robert Massey .01 .05
350 Pat Swilling .02 .10
351 Eric Martin .01 .05
352 Rueben Mayes UER .01 .05
353 Vince Buck .01 .05
354 Brett Perriman .08 .25
355 Wesley Carroll RC .01 .05
356 Jarrod Bunch RC .01 .05
357 Pepper Johnson .01 .05
358 Dave Meggett .02 .10
359 Mark Collins .01 .05
360 Sean Landeta .01 .05
361 Maurice Carthon .01 .05
362 Mike Fox UER .01 .05
363 Jeff Hostetler .02 .10
364 Phil Simms .02 .10
365 Leonard Marshall .01 .05
366 Gary Reasons .01 .05
367 Rodney Hampton .08 .25
368 Greg Jackson RC .01 .05
369 Jumbo Elliott .01 .05
370 Bob Kratch RC .01 .05
371 Lawrence Taylor .08 .25
372 Erik Howard .01 .05
373 Carl Banks .01 .05
374 Stephen Baker .01 .05
375 Mark Ingram .02 .10
376 Browning Nagle RC .01 .05
377 Jeff Lageman .01 .05
378 Ken O'Brien .01 .05
379 Al Toon .02 .10
380 Joe Prokop .01 .05
381 Tony Stargell .01 .05
382 Blair Thomas .01 .05
383 Erik McMillan .01 .05
384 Dennis Byrd .01 .05
385 Freeman McNeil .01 .05
386 Brad Baxter .01 .05
387 Mark Boyer .01 .05
388 Terance Mathis .02 .10
389 Jim Sweeney .01 .05
390 Kyle Clifton .01 .05
391 Pat Leahy .01 .05
392 Rob Moore .08 .25
393 James Hasty .01 .05
394 Blaise Bryant .01 .05
395A J.Campbell RC ERR .40 1.00
(Photo actually
Dan McGwire; see 509)
395B Jesse Campbell RC COR .01 .05
396 Keith Jackson .02 .10
397 Jerome Brown .01 .05
398 Keith Byars .01 .05
399 Seth Joyner .02 .10
400 Mike Bellamy .01 .05
401 Fred Barnett .08 .25
402 Reggie Singletary RC .01 .05
403 Reggie White .08 .25
404 Randall Cunningham .08 .25
405 Byron Evans .01 .05
406 Wes Hopkins .01 .05
407 Ben Smith .01 .05
408 Roger Ruzek .01 .05
409 Eric Allen UER .01 .05
410 Anthony Toney UER .01 .05
411 Clyde Simmons .01 .05
412 Andre Waters .01 .05
413 Calvin Williams .02 .10
414 Eric Swann RC .08 .25
415 Eric Hill .01 .05
416 Tim McDonald .01 .05
417 Luis Sharpe .01 .05
418 Ernie Jones UER .01 .05
419 Ken Harvey .02 .10
420 Ricky Proehl .01 .05
421 Johnny Johnson .01 .05
422 Anthony Bell .01 .05
423 Timm Rosenbach .01 .05
424 Rich Camarillo .01 .05
425 Walter Reeves .01 .05
426 Freddie Joe Nunn .01 .05
427 Anthony Thompson UER .01 .05
428 Bill Lewis .01 .05
429 Jim Wahler RC .01 .05
430 Cedric Mack .01 .05
431 Mike Jones DE RC .01 .05
432 Ernie Mills RC .02 .10
433 Tim Worley .01 .05
434 Greg Lloyd .08 .25
435 Dermontti Dawson .01 .05
436 Louis Lipps .01 .05
437 Eric Green .01 .05
438 Donald Evans .01 .05
439 D.J. Johnson .01 .05
440 Tunch Ilkin .01 .05
441 Bubby Brister .01 .05
442 Chris Calloway .01 .05
443 David Little .01 .05
444 Thomas Everett .01 .05
445 Carnell Lake .01 .05
446 Rod Woodson .08 .25
447 Gary Anderson K .01 .05
448 Merril Hoge .01 .05
449 Gerald Williams .01 .05
450 Eric Moten RC .01 .05
451 Marion Butts .02 .10
452 Leslie O'Neal .02 .10
453 Ronnie Harmon .01 .05
454 Gill Byrd .01 .05
455 Junior Seau .08 .25
456 Nate Lewis RC .01 .05
457 Leo Goeas .01 .05
458 Burt Grossman .01 .05
459 Courtney Hall .01 .05
460 Anthony Miller .02 .10
461 Gary Plummer .01 .05
462 Billy Joe Tolliver .01 .05
463 Lee Williams .01 .05
464 Arthur Cox .01 .05
465 John Kidd UER .01 .05
466 Frank Cornish .01 .05
467 John Carney .01 .05
468 Eric Bieniemy RC .01 .05
469 Don Griffin .01 .05
470 Jerry Rice .30 .75
471 Keith DeLong .01 .05
472 John Taylor .02 .10
473 Brent Jones .08 .25
474 Pierce Holt .01 .05
475 Kevin Fagan .01 .05
476 Bill Romanowski .01 .05
477 Dexter Carter .01 .05
478 Guy McIntyre .01 .05
479 Joe Montana .50 1.25
480 Charles Haley .02 .10
481 Mike Cofer .01 .05
482 Jesse Sapolu .01 .05
483 Eric Davis .01 .05
484 Mike Sherrard .01 .05
485 Steve Young .30 .75
486 Darryl Pollard .01 .05
487 Tom Rathman .01 .05
488 Michael Carter .01 .05
489 Ricky Watters RC .60 1.50
490 John Johnson RC .01 .05
491 Eugene Robinson .01 .05
492 Andy Heck .01 .05
493 John L. Williams .01 .05
494 Norm Johnson .01 .05
495 David Wyman .01 .05
496 Derrick Fenner UER .01 .05
497 Rick Donnelly .01 .05
498 Tony Woods .01 .05
499 Derrick Loville RC .01 .05
500 Dave Krieg .02 .10
501 Joe Nash .01 .05
502 Brian Blades .02 .10
503 Cortez Kennedy .08 .25
504 Jeff Bryant .01 .05
505 Tommy Kane .01 .05
506 Travis McNeal .01 .05
507 Terry Wooden .01 .05
508 Chris Warren .08 .25
509A Dan McGwire RC ERR .01 .05
509B Dan McGwire COR RC .01 .05
510 Mark Robinson .01 .05
511 Ron Hall .01 .05
512 Paul Gruber .01 .05
513 Harry Hamilton .01 .05
514 Keith McCants .01 .05
515 Reggie Cobb .01 .05
516 Steve Christie UER .01 .05
517 Broderick Thomas .01 .05
518 Mark Carrier WR .08 .25
519 Vinny Testaverde .02 .10
520 Ricky Reynolds .01 .05
521 Jesse Anderson .01 .05
522 Reuben Davis .01 .05
523 Wayne Haddix .01 .05
524 Gary Anderson RB UER .01 .05
525 Bruce Hill .01 .05
526 Kevin Murphy .01 .05
527 Lawrence Dawsey RC .02 .10
528 Ricky Ervins RC .02 .10
529 Charles Mann .01 .05
530 Jim Lachey .01 .05
531 Mark Rypien UER .02 .10
(No stat for percentage;/2,0703 yards, sic)
532 Darrell Green .01 .05
533 Stan Humphries .08 .25
534 Jeff Bostic UER .01 .05
535 Earnest Byner .01 .05
536 Art Monk UER .02 .10
(Bio says 718 receptions,
should be 730)
537 Don Warren .01 .05
538 Darryl Grant .01 .05
539 Wilber Marshall .01 .05
540 Kurt Gouveia RC .01 .05
541 Markus Koch .01 .05
542 Andre Collins .01 .05
543 Chip Lohmiller .01 .05
544 Alvin Walton .01 .05
545 Gary Clark .08 .25
546 Ricky Sanders .01 .05
547 Redskins vs. Eagles .01 .05
548 Bengals vs. Oilers .01 .05
549 Dolphins vs. Chiefs .01 .05
550 Bears vs. Saints UER .01 .05
551 Bills vs. Dolphins .02 .10
(Thurman Thomas)
552 49ers vs. Redskins .01 .05
553 Giants vs. Bears .01 .05
554 Raiders vs. Bengals .02 .10
(Bo Jackson)
555 AFC Championship .01 .05
556 NFC Championship .01 .05
557 Super Bowl XXV .01 .05
558 Checklist 1-140 .01 .05
559 Checklist 141-280 .01 .05
560 Checklist 281-420 UER .01 .05
561 Checklist 421-561 UER .01 .05

1992 Bowman

The 1992 Bowman football set consists of 573 standard-size glossy cards that were issued 14 per foil pack. The set includes 45 foil cards that are broken into three subsets: 28 Team Leader (TL) cards, 12 Playoff Star (PS) cards and five cards highlighting the longest plays (LP) of the 1991 season (field goal, run, reception, kick return, and punt). The foil cards were issued one per pack and include a number of short-prints which are designated by SP in the checklist below. Rookie Cards include Steve Bono and Jackie Harris.

COMPLETE SET (573) 25.00 50.00
1 Reggie White .40 1.00
2 Johnny Meads .08 .25
3 Chip Lohmiller .08 .25
4 James Lofton .20 .50
5 Ray Horton .08 .25
6 Rich Moran .08 .25
7 Howard Cross .08 .25
8 Mike Horan .08 .25
9 Erik Kramer .20 .50
10 Steve Wisniewski .08 .25
11 Michael Haynes .20 .50
12 Donald Evans .08 .25
13 Michael Irvin FOIL .40 1.00
14 Gary Zimmerman .08 .25
15 John Friesz .20 .50
16 Mark Carrier WR .40 1.00
17 Mark Duper .08 .25
18 James Thornton .08 .25
19 Jon Hand .08 .25
20 Sterling Sharpe .40 1.00
21 Jacob Green .08 .25
22 Wesley Carroll .08 .25
23 Clay Matthews .20 .50
24 Kevin Greene .20 .50
25 Brad Baxter .08 .25
26 Don Griffin .08 .25
27 Robert Delpino FOIL SP .60 1.50
28 Lee Johnson .08 .25
29 Jim Wahler .08 .25
30 Leonard Russell .20 .50
31 Eric Moore .08 .25
32 Dino Hackett .08 .25
33 Simon Fletcher .08 .25
34 Al Edwards .08 .25
35 Brad Edwards .08 .25
36 James Joseph .08 .25
37 Rodney Peete .20 .50
38 Ricky Reynolds .08 .25
39 Eddie Anderson .08 .25
40 Ken Clarke .08 .25
41 Tony Bennett FOIL .20 .50
42 Larry Brown DB .08 .25
43 Ray Childress .08 .25
44 Mike Kenn .08 .25
45 Vestee Jackson .08 .25
46 Neil O'Donnell .20 .50
47 Bill Brooks .08 .25
48 Kevin Butler .08 .25
49 Joe Phillips .08 .25
50 Cortez Kennedy .20 .50
51 Rickey Jackson .08 .25
52 Vinnie Clark .08 .25
53 Michael Jackson .20 .50
54 Ernie Jones .08 .25
55 Tom Newberry .08 .25
56 Pat Harlow .08 .25
57 Craig Taylor .08 .25
58 Joe Prokop .08 .25
59 Warren Moon FOIL SP .75 2.00
60 Jeff Lageman .08 .25
61 Neil Smith .40 1.00
62 Jim Jeffcoat .08 .25
63 Bill Fralic .08 .25
64 Mark Schlereth RC .08 .25
65 Keith Byars .08 .25
66 Jeff Hostetler .20 .50
67 Joey Browner .08 .25
68 Bobby Hebert FOIL SP .60 1.50
69 Keith Sims .08 .25
70 Warren Moon .40 1.00
71 Pio Sagapolutele RC .08 .25
72 Cornelius Bennett .20 .50
73 Greg Davis .08 .25
74 Ronnie Harmon .08 .25
75 Ron Hall .08 .25
76 Howie Long .40 1.00
77 Greg Lewis .08 .25
78 Carnell Lake .08 .25
79 Ray Crockett .08 .25
80 Tom Waddle .08 .25
81 Vincent Brown .08 .25
82 Bill Brooks FOIL .20 .50
83 John L. Williams .08 .25
84 Floyd Turner .08 .25
85 Scott Radecic .08 .25
86 Anthony Munoz .20 .50
87 Lonnie Young .08 .25
88 Dexter Carter .08 .25
89 Tony Zendejas .08 .25
90 Tim Jorden .08 .25
91 LeRoy Butler .08 .25
92 Richard Brown RC .08 .25
93 Erric Pegram .20 .50
94 Sean Landeta .08 .25
95 Clyde Simmons .08 .25
96 Martin Mayhew .08 .25
97 Jarvis Williams .08 .25
98 Barry Word .08 .25
99 John Taylor FOIL .20 .50
100 Emmitt Smith 3.00 8.00
101 Leon Seals .08 .25
102 Marion Butts .08 .25
103 Mike Merriweather .08 .25
104 Ernest Givins .20 .50
105 Wymon Henderson .08 .25
106 Robert Wilson .08 .25
107 Bobby Hebert .08 .25
108 Terry McDaniel .08 .25
109 Jerry Ball .08 .25
110 John Taylor .20 .50
111 Rob Moore .20 .50
112 Thurman Thomas FOIL .40 1.00
113 Checklist 1-115 .08 .25
114 Brian Blades .20 .50
115 Larry Kelm .08 .25
116 James Francis .08 .25
117 Rod Woodson .40 1.00
118 Trace Armstrong .08 .25
119 Eugene Daniel .08 .25
120 Andre Tippett .08 .25
121 Chris Jacke .08 .25
122 Jessie Tuggle .08 .25
123 Chris Chandler .40 1.00
124 Tim Johnson .08 .25
125 Mark Collins .08 .25
126 Aeneas Williams FOIL SP .60 1.50
127 James Jones .08 .25
128 George Jamison .08 .25
129 Deron Cherry .08 .25
130 Mark Clayton .20 .50
131 Keith DeLong .08 .25
132 Marcus Allen .40 1.00
133 Joe Walter RC .08 .25
134 Reggie Rutland .08 .25
135 Kent Hull .08 .25
136 Jeff Feagles .08 .25
137 Ronnie Lott FOIL SP .75 2.00
138 Henry Rolling .08 .25
139 Gary Anderson RB .08 .25
140 Morten Andersen .08 .25
141 Cris Dishman .08 .25
142 David Treadwell .08 .25
143 Kevin Gogan .08 .25
144 James Hasty .08 .25
145 Robert Delpino .08 .25
146 Patrick Hunter .08 .25
147 Gary Anderson K .08 .25
148 Chip Banks .08 .25
149 Dan Fike .08 .25
150 Chris Miller .20 .50
151 Hugh Millen .08 .25
152 Courtney Hall .08 .25
153 Gary Clark .20 .50
154 Michael Brooks .08 .25
155 Jay Hilgenberg .08 .25
156 Tim McDonald .08 .25
157 Andre Tippett FOIL .20 .50
158 Doug Riesenberg .08 .25
159 Bill Maas .08 .25
160 Fred Barnett .20 .50
161 Pierce Holt .08 .25
162 Brian Noble .08 .25
163 Harold Green .08 .25
164 Joel Hilgenberg .08 .25
165 Mervyn Fernandez .08 .25
166 John Offerdahl .08 .25
167 Shane Conlan .08 .25
168 Mark Higgs FOIL SP .60 1.50
169 Bubba McDowell .08 .25
170 Barry Sanders 2.50 6.00
171 Larry Roberts .08 .25
172 Herschel Walker .20 .50
173 Steve McMichael .20 .50
174 Kelly Stouffer .08 .25
175 Louis Lipps .08 .25
176 Jim Everett .20 .50
177 Tony Tolbert .08 .25
178 Mike Baab .08 .25
179 Eric Swann .20 .50
180 Emmitt Smith FOIL SP 5.00 12.00
181 Tim Brown .40 1.00
182 Dennis Smith .08 .25
183 Moe Gardner .08 .25
184 Derrick Walker .08 .25
185 Reyna Thompson .08 .25
186 Esera Tuaolo .08 .25
187 Jeff Wright .08 .25
188 Mark Rypien .08 .25
189 Quinn Early .20 .50
190 Christian Okoye .08 .25
191 Keith Jackson .20 .50
192 Doug Smith .08 .25
193 John Elway FOIL 4.00 10.00
194 Reggie Cobb .08 .25
195 Reggie Roby .08 .25
196 Clarence Verdin .08 .25
197 Jim Breech .08 .25
198 Jim Sweeney .08 .25
199 Marv Cook .08 .25
200 Ronnie Lott .20 .50
201 Mel Gray .20 .50
202 Maury Buford .08 .25
203 Lorenzo Lynch .08 .25
204 Jesse Sapolu .08 .25
205 Steve Jordan .08 .25
206 Don Majkowski .08 .25
207 Flipper Anderson .08 .25
208 Ed King .08 .25
209 Tony Woods .08 .25
210 Ron Heller .08 .25
211 Greg Kragen .08 .25
212 Scott Case .08 .25
213 Tommy Barnhardt .08 .25
214 Charles Mann .08 .25
215 David Griggs .08 .25
216 Kenneth Davis FOIL SP .60 1.50
217 Lamar Lathon .08 .25
218 Nate Odomes .08 .25
219 Vinny Testaverde .20 .50
220 Rod Bernstine .08 .25
221 Barry Sanders FOIL 4.00 10.00
222 Carlton Haselrig RC .08 .25
223 Steve Beuerlein .20 .50
224 John Alt .08 .25
225 Pepper Johnson .08 .25
226 Checklist 116-230 .08 .25
227 Irv Eatman .08 .25
228 Greg Townsend .08 .25
229 Mark Jackson .08 .25
230 Robert Blackmon .08 .25
231 Terry Allen .40 1.00
232 Bennie Blades .08 .25
233 Sam Mills FOIL .40 1.00
234 Richmond Webb .08 .25
235 Richard Dent .20 .50
236 Alonzo Mitz RC .08 .25
237 Steve Young 2.00 5.00
238 Pat Swilling .08 .25
239 James Campen .08 .25
240 Earnest Byner .08 .25
241 Pat Terrell .08 .25
242 Carwell Gardner .08 .25
243 Charles McRae .08 .25
244 Vince Newsome .08 .25
245 Eric Hill .08 .25
246 Steve Young FOIL 2.00 5.00
247 Nate Lewis .08 .25
248 William Fuller .08 .25
249 Andre Waters .08 .25
250 Dean Biasucci .08 .25
251 Andre Rison .20 .50
252 Brent Williams .08 .25
253 Todd McNair .08 .25
254 Jeff Davidson RC .08 .25
255 Art Monk .20 .50
256 Kirk Lowdermilk .08 .25
257 Bob Golic .08 .25
258 Michael Irvin .40 1.00
259 Eric Green .08 .25
260 David Fulcher FOIL .20 .50

261 Damone Johnson	.08	.25
262 Marc Spindler	.08	.25
263 Alfred Williams	.08	.25
264 Donnie Elder	.08	.25
265 Keith McKeller	.08	.25
266 Steve Bono RC	.40	1.00
267 Jumbo Elliott	.08	.25
268 Randy Hilliard RC	.08	.25
269 Rufus Porter	.08	.25
270 Neal Anderson	.08	.25
271 Dalton Hilliard	.08	.25
272 Michael Zordich RC	.08	.25
273 Cornelius Bennett FOIL	.20	.50
274 Louie Aguiar RC	.08	.25
275 Aaron Craver	.08	.25
276 Tony Bennett	.08	.25
277 Terry Wooden	.08	.25
278 Mike Munchak	.20	.50
279 Chris Hinton	.08	.25
280 John Elway	2.50	6.00
281 Randall McDaniel	.08	.25
282 Brad Baxter FOIL	.20	.50
283 Wes Hopkins	.08	.25
284 Scott Davis	.08	.25
285 Mark Tuinei	.08	.25
286 Broderick Thompson	.08	.25
287 Henry Ellard	.20	.50
288 Adrian Cooper	.08	.25
289 Don Warren	.08	.25
290 Rodney Hampton	.20	.50
291 Kevin Ross	.08	.25
292 Mark Carrier DB	.08	.25
293 Ian Beckles	.08	.25
294 Gene Atkins	.08	.25
295 Mark Rypien FOIL	.20	.50
296 Eric Metcalf	.20	.50
297 Howard Ballard	.08	.25
298 Nate Newton	.08	.25
299 Dan Owens	.08	.25
300 Tim McGee	.08	.25
301 Greg McMurtry	.08	.25
302 Walter Reeves	.08	.25
303 Jeff Herrod	.08	.25
304 Darren Comeaux	.08	.25
305 Pete Stoyanovich	.08	.25
306 Johnny Holland	.08	.25
307 Jay Novacek	.20	.50
308 Steve Broussard	.08	.25
309 Darrell Green	.08	.25
310 Sam Mills	.08	.25
311 Tim Barnett	.08	.25
312 Steve Atwater	.08	.25
313 Tom Waddle FOIL	.20	.50
314 Felix Wright	.08	.25
315 Sean Jones	.08	.25
316 Jim Harbaugh	.40	1.00
317 Eric Allen	.08	.25
318 Don Mosebar	.08	.25
319 Rob Taylor	.08	.25
320 Terance Mathis	.20	.50
321 Leroy Hoard	.20	.50
322 Kenneth Davis	.08	.25
323 Guy McIntyre	.08	.25
324 Deron Cherry FOIL	.20	.50
325 Tunch Ilkin	.08	.25
326 Willie Green	.08	.25
327 Darryl Henley	.08	.25
328 Shawn Jefferson	.08	.25
329 Greg Jackson	.08	.25
330 John Roper	.08	.25
331 Bill Lewis	.08	.25
332 Rodney Holman	.08	.25
333 Bruce Armstrong	.08	.25
334 Robb Thomas	.08	.25
335 Alvin Harper	.20	.50
336 Brian Jordan	.20	.50
337 Morten Andersen FOIL	.20	.50
338 Dermontti Dawson	.08	.25
339 Checklist 231-345	.08	.25
340 Louis Oliver	.08	.25
341 Paul McJulien RC	.08	.25
342 Karl Mecklenburg	.08	.25
343 Lawrence Dawsey	.20	.50
344 Kyle Clifton	.08	.25
345 Jeff Bostic	.08	.25
346 Cris Carter	.60	1.50
347 Al Smith	.08	.25
348 Mark Kelso	.08	.25
349 Art Monk FOIL	.40	1.00
350 Michael Carter	.08	.25
351 Ethan Horton	.08	.25
352 Andy Heck	.08	.25
353 Gill Fenerty	.08	.25
354 David Brandon RC	.08	.25
355 Anthony Johnson	.40	1.00
356 Mike Golic	.08	.25
357 Ferrell Edmunds	.08	.25
358 Dennis Gibson	.08	.25
359 Gill Byrd	.08	.25
360 Todd Lyght	.08	.25
361 Jayice Pearson RC	.08	.25
362 John Rade	.08	.25
363 Keith Van Horne	.08	.25
364 John Kasay	.08	.25
365 Brod. Thomas FOIL SP	.60	1.50
366 Ken Harvey	.08	.25
367 Rich Gannon	.40	1.00
368 Darrell Thompson	.08	.25
369 Jon Vaughn	.08	.25
370 Jesse Solomon	.08	.25
371 Erik McMillan	.08	.25
372 Bruce Matthews	.08	.25
373 Wilber Marshall	.08	.25
374 Brian Blades FOIL SP	.60	1.50
375 Vance Johnson	.08	.25
376 Eddie Brown	.08	.25
377 Don Beebe	.08	.25
378 Brent Jones	.20	.50
379 Matt Bahr	.08	.25
380 Dwight Stone	.08	.25
381 Tony Casillas	.08	.25
382 Jay Schroeder	.08	.25
383 Byron Evans	.08	.25
384 Dan Saleaumua	.08	.25
385 Wendell Davis	.08	.25
386 Ron Holmes	.08	.25
387 George Thomas RC	.08	.25
388 Ray Berry	.08	.25
389 Eric Martin	.08	.25
390 Kevin Mack	.08	.25
391 Natu Tuatagaloa RC	.08	.25
392 Bill Romanowski	.08	.25
393 Nick Bell FOIL SP	.60	1.50
394 Grant Feasel	.08	.25
395 Eugene Lockhart	.08	.25
396 Lorenzo White	.08	.25
397 Mike Farr	.08	.25
398 Eric Bieniemy	.08	.25
399 Kevin Murphy	.08	.25
400 Luis Sharpe	.08	.25
401 Jessie Tuggle FOIL SP	.60	1.50
402 Cleveland Gary	.08	.25
403 Tony Mandarich	.08	.25
404 Bryan Cox	.20	.50
405 Marvin Washington	.08	.25
406 Fred Stokes	.08	.25
407 Duane Bickett	.08	.25
408 Leonard Marshall	.08	.25
409 Barry Foster	.20	.50
410 Thurman Thomas	.40	1.00
411 Willie Gault	.20	.50
412 Vinson Smith RC	.08	.25
413 Mark Bortz	.08	.25
414 Johnny Johnson	.08	.25
415 Rodney Hampton FOIL	.40	1.00
416 Steve Wallace	.08	.25
417 Fuad Reveiz	.08	.25
418 Derrick Thomas	.20	.50
419 Jackie Harris RC	.40	1.00
420 Derek Russell	.08	.25
421 David Grant	.08	.25
422 Tommy Kane	.08	.25
423 Stan Brock	.08	.25
424 Haywood Jeffires	.20	.50
425 Broderick Thomas	.08	.25
426 John Kidd	.08	.25
427 Shawn McCarthy RC	.20	.50
428 Jim Arnold	.08	.25
429 Scott Fulhage	.08	.25
430 Jackie Slater	.08	.25
431 Scott Galbraith RC	.08	.25
432 Roger Ruzek	.08	.25
433 Irving Fryar	.20	.50
434A Der. Thomas FOIL ERR	.40	1.00
Misnumbered 494		
434B Der. Thomas FOIL COR	.40	1.00
Numbered 434		
435 D.J. Johnson	.08	.25
436 Jim C.Jensen	.08	.25
437 James Washington	.08	.25
438 Phil Hansen	.08	.25
439 Rohn Stark	.08	.25
440 Jarrod Bunch	.08	.25
441 Todd Marinovich	.08	.25
442 Brett Perriman	.40	1.00
443 Eugene Robinson	.08	.25
444 Robert Massey	.08	.25
445 Nick Lowery	.08	.25
446 Rickey Dixon	.08	.25
447 Jim Lachey	.08	.25
448 Johnny Hector FOIL	.20	.50
449 Gary Plummer	.08	.25
450 Robert Brown	.08	.25
451 Gaston Green	.08	.25
452 Checklist 346-459	.08	.25
453 Darion Conner	.08	.25
454 Mike Cofer	.08	.25
455 Craig Heyward	.20	.50
456 Anthony Carter	.20	.50
457 Pat Coleman RC	.08	.25
458 Jeff Bryant	.08	.25
459 Mark Gunn RC	.08	.25
460 Stan Thomas	.08	.25
461 Simon Fletcher FOIL SP	.60	1.50
462 Roy Agnew	.08	.25
463 Jessie Hester	.08	.25
464 Rob Burnett	.08	.25
465 Mike Croel	.08	.25
466 Mike Pitts	.08	.25
467 Darryl Talley	.08	.25
468 Rich Camarillo	.08	.25
469 Reggie White FOIL	.40	1.00
470 Nick Bell	.08	.25
471 Tracy Hayworth RC	.08	.25
472 Eric Thomas	.08	.25
473 Paul Gruber	.08	.25
474 David Richards	.08	.25
475 T.J. Turner	.08	.25
476 Mark Ingram	.08	.25
477 Tim Grunhard	.08	.25
478 Marion Butts FOIL	.20	.50
479 Tom Rathman	.08	.25
480 Brian Mitchell	.20	.50
481 Bryce Paup	.40	1.00
482 Mike Pritchard	.20	.50
483 Ken Norton Jr.	.20	.50
484 Roman Phifer	.08	.25
485 Greg Lloyd	.20	.50
486 Brett Maxie	.08	.25
487 Richard Dent FOIL SP	.60	1.50
488 Curtis Duncan	.08	.25
489 Chris Burkett	.08	.25
490 Travis McNeal	.08	.25
491 Carl Lee	.08	.25
492 Clarence Kay	.08	.25
493 Tom Thayer	.08	.25
494 Erik Kramer FOIL SP	.75	2.00
(See also 434A)		
495 Perry Kemp	.08	.25
496 Jeff Jaeger	.08	.25
497 Eric Sanders	.08	.25
498 Burt Grossman	.08	.25
499 Ben Smith	.08	.25
500 Keith McCants	.08	.25
501 John Stephens	.08	.25
502 John Rienstra	.08	.25
503 Jim Ritcher	.08	.25
504 Harris Barton	.08	.25
505 Andre Rison FOIL SP	.75	2.00
506 Chris Martin	.08	.25
507 Freddie Joe Nunn	.08	.25
508 Mark Higgs	.08	.25
509 Norm Johnson	.08	.25
510 Stephen Baker	.08	.25
511 Ricky Sanders	.08	.25
512 Ray Donaldson	.08	.25
513 David Fulcher	.08	.25
514 Gerald Williams	.08	.25
515 Toi Cook	.08	.25
516 Chris Warren	.40	1.00
517 Jeff Gossett	.08	.25
518 Ken Lanier	.08	.25
519 H.Jeffires FOIL SP	.75	2.00
520 Kevin Glover	.08	.25
521 Mo Lewis	.08	.25
522 Bern Brostek	.08	.25
523 Bo Orlando RC	.08	.25
524 Mike Saxon	.08	.25
525 Seth Joyner	.08	.25
526 John Carney	.08	.25
527 Jeff Cross	.08	.25
528 G.Anderson K FOIL SP	.60	1.50
529 Chuck Cecil	.08	.25
530 Tim Green	.08	.25
531 Kevin Porter	.08	.25
532 Chris Spielman	.20	.50
533 Willie Drewrey	.08	.25
534 Chris Singleton UER	.08	.25
(Card has wrong score for Super Bowl XX)		
535 Matt Stover	.08	.25
536 Andre Collins	.08	.25
537 Erik Howard	.08	.25
538 Steve Tasker	.20	.50
539 Anthony Thompson	.08	.25
540 Charles Haley	.20	.50
541 Mike Merriweather FOIL	.20	.50
542 Henry Thomas	.08	.25
543 Scott Stephen	.08	.25
544 Bruce Kozerski	.08	.25
545 Tim McKyer	.08	.25
546 Chris Doleman	.08	.25
547 Riki Ellison	.08	.25
548 Mike Prior	.08	.25
549 Dwayne Harper	.08	.25
550 Bubby Brister	.08	.25
551 Dave Meggett	.20	.50
552 Greg Montgomery	.08	.25
553 Kevin Mack FOIL	.20	.50
554 Mark Stepnoski	.20	.50
555 Kenny Walker	.08	.25
556 Eric Moten	.08	.25
557 Michael Stewart	.08	.25
558 Calvin Williams	.20	.50
559 Johnny Hector	.08	.25
560 Tony Paige	.08	.25
561 Tim Newton	.08	.25
562 Brad Muster	.08	.25
563 Aeneas Williams	.20	.50
564 Herman Moore	.40	1.00
565 Checklist 460-573	.08	.25
566 Jerome Henderson	.08	.25
567 Danny Copeland	.08	.25
568 Alexander Wright FOIL	.20	.50
569 Tim Harris	.08	.25
570 Jonathan Hayes	.08	.25
571 Tony Jones	.08	.25
572 Carlton Bailey RC	.08	.25
573 Vaughan Johnson	.08	.25

1993 Bowman

The 423 standard-size cards comprising the 1993 Bowman set feature full-bleed photos. Each foil pack contained one foil card and each jumbo pack contained two foil cards. A solid Rookie Card crop includes Jerome Bettis, Drew Bledsoe, Vincent Brisby, Reggie Brooks, Mark Brunell, Curtis Conway, Troy Drayton, Garrison Hearst, Qadry Ismail, O.J. McDuffie, Natrone Means, Rick Mirer, Robert Smith, Dana Stubblefield and Kevin Williams.

COMPLETE SET (423)	12.00	30.00
1 Troy Aikman FOIL	1.50	3.00
2 John Parrella RC	.07	.20
3 Dana Stubblefield RC	.30	.75
4 Mark Higgs	.07	.20
5 Tom Carter RC	.15	.40
6 Nate Lewis	.07	.20
7 Vaughn Hebron RC	.07	.20
8 Ernest Givins	.15	.40
9 Vince Buck	.07	.20
10 Levon Kirkland	.07	.20
11 J.J. Birden	.07	.20
12 Steve Jordan	.07	.20
13 Simon Fletcher	.07	.20
14 Willie Green	.07	.20
15 Pepper Johnson	.07	.20
16 Roger Harper RC	.07	.20
17 Rob Moore	.15	.40
18 David Lang	.07	.20
19 David Klingler	.07	.20
20 Garrison Hearst RC	.75	2.00
21 Anthony Johnson	.15	.40
22 Eric Curry RC	.15	.40
23 Nolan Harrison	.07	.20
24 Earl Dotson RC	.07	.20
25 Leonard Russell	.15	.40
26 Doug Riesenberg	.07	.20
27 Dwayne Harper	.07	.20
28 Richard Dent	.15	.40
29 Victor Bailey RC	.07	.20
30 Junior Seau	.30	.75
31 Steve Tasker	.15	.40
32 Kurt Gouveia	.07	.20
33 Renaldo Turnbull UER	.07	.20
(Listed as wide receiver)		
34 Dale Carter	.07	.20
35 Russell Maryland	.07	.20
36 Dana Hall	.07	.20
37 Marco Coleman	.07	.20
38 Greg Montgomery	.07	.20
39 Deon Figures RC	.07	.20
40 Troy Drayton RC	.15	.40
41 Eric Metcalf	.15	.40
42 Michael Husted RC	.07	.20
43 Harry Newsome	.07	.20
44 Kelvin Pritchett	.07	.20
45 Andre Rison FOIL	.30	.75
46 John Copeland RC	.15	.40
47 Greg Biekert RC	.07	.20
48 Johnny Johnson	.07	.20
49 Chuck Cecil	.07	.20
50 Rick Mirer RC	.60	1.50
51 Rod Bernstine	.07	.20
52 Steve McMichael	.15	.40
53 Roosevelt Potts RC	.07	.20
54 Mike Sherrard	.07	.20
55 Terrell Buckley	.07	.20
56 Eugene Chung	.07	.20
57 Kimble Anders RC	.30	.75
58 Daryl Johnston	.30	.75
59 Harris Barton	.07	.20
60 Thurman Thomas FOIL	.60	1.50
61 Eric Martin	.07	.20
62 Reggie Brooks RC	.15	.40
63 Eric Bieniemy	.07	.20
64 John Offerdahl	.07	.20
65 Wilber Marshall	.07	.20
66 Mark Carrier WR	.15	.40
67 Merril Hoge	.07	.20
68 Cris Carter	.30	.75
69 Marty Thompson RC	.07	.20
70 Randall Cunningham FOIL	.60	1.50
71 Winston Moss	.07	.20
72 Doug Pelfrey RC	.07	.20
73 Jackie Slater	.07	.20
74 Pierce Holt	.07	.20
75 Hardy Nickerson	.15	.40
76 Chris Burkett	.07	.20
77 Michael Brandon	.07	.20
78 Tom Waddle	.07	.20
79 Walter Reeves	.07	.20
80 Lawrence Taylor FOIL	.30	.75
81 Wayne Simmons RC	.07	.20
82 Brent Williams	.07	.20
83 Shannon Sharpe	.30	.75
84 Robert Blackmon	.07	.20
85 Keith Jackson	.15	.40
86 A.J. Johnson	.07	.20
87 Ryan McNeil RC	.30	.75
88 Michael Dean Perry	.15	.40
89 Russell Copeland RC	.15	.40
90 Sam Mills	.07	.20
91 Courtney Hall	.07	.20
92 Gino Torretta RC	.15	.40
93 Artie Smith RC	.07	.20
94 David Whitmore	.07	.20
95 Charles Haley	.15	.40
96 Rod Woodson	.30	.75
97 Lorenzo White	.07	.20
98 Tom Scott RC	.07	.20
99 Tyji Armstrong	.07	.20
100 Boomer Esiason	.15	.40
101 Rocket Ismail FOIL	.30	.75
102 Mark Carrier DB	.07	.20
103 Broderick Thompson	.07	.20
104 Bob Whitfield	.07	.20
105 Ben Coleman RC	.07	.20
106 Jon Vaughn	.07	.20
107 Marcus Buckley RC	.07	.20
108 Cleveland Gary	.07	.20
109 Ashley Ambrose	.07	.20
110 Reggie White FOIL	.60	1.50
111 Arthur Marshall RC	.07	.20
112 Greg McMurtry	.07	.20
113 Mike Johnson	.07	.20
114 Tim McGee	.07	.20
115 John Carney	.07	.20
116 Neil Smith	.30	.75
117 Mark Stepnoski	.07	.20
118 Don Beebe	.07	.20
119 Scott Mitchell	.30	.75
120 Randall McDaniel	.07	.20
121 Chidi Ahanotu RC	.07	.20
122 Ray Childress	.07	.20
123 Tony McGee RC	.15	.40
124 Marc Boutte	.07	.20
125 Ronnie Lott	.15	.40
126 Jason Elam RC	.30	.75
127 Martin Harrison RC	.07	.20
128 Leonard Renfro RC	.07	.20
129 Jessie Armstead RC	.15	.40
130 Quentin Coryatt	.15	.40
131 Luis Sharpe	.07	.20
132 Bill Maas	.07	.20
133 Jesse Solomon	.07	.20
134 Kevin Greene	.15	.40
135 Derek Brown RBK RC	.15	.40
136 Greg Townsend	.07	.20
137 Neal Anderson	.07	.20
138 John L. Williams	.07	.20
139 Vincent Brisby RC	.30	.75
140 Barry Sanders FOIL	2.00	5.00
141 Charles Mann	.07	.20
142 Ken Norton	.15	.40
143 Eric Moten	.07	.20
144 John Alt	.07	.20
145 Dan Footman RC	.07	.20
146 Bill Brooks	.07	.20
147 James Thornton	.07	.20
148 Martin Mayhew	.07	.20
149 Andy Harmon	.15	.40
150 Dan Marino FOIL	2.50	6.00
151 Micheal Darrow RC	.30	.75
152 Flipper Anderson	.07	.20
153 Jackie Harris	.07	.20
154 Todd Kelly RC	.07	.20
155 Dan Williams RC	.07	.20
156 Harold Green	.07	.20
157 David Treadwell	.07	.20
158 Chris Doleman	.07	.20
159 Eric Hill	.07	.20
160 Lincoln Kennedy RC	.07	.20
161 Devon McDonald RC	.07	.20
162 Natrone Means RC	.30	.75
163 Rick Hamilton RC	.07	.20
164 Kelvin Martin	.07	.20
165 Jeff Hostetler	.15	.40
166 Mark Brunell RC	1.50	4.00
167 Tim Barnett	.07	.20
168 Ray Crockett	.07	.20
169 William Perry	.15	.40
170 Michael Irvin	.30	.75
171 Marvin Washington	.07	.20
172 Irving Fryar	.15	.40
173 Scott Sisson RC	.07	.20
174 Gary Anderson K	.07	.20
175 Bruce Smith	.30	.75
176 Clyde Simmons	.07	.20
177 Russell White RC	.15	.40
178 Irv Smith RC	.07	.20
179 Mark Wheeler	.07	.20
180 Warren Moon	.30	.75
181 Del Speer RC	.07	.20
182 Henry Thomas	.07	.20
183 Keith Kartz	.07	.20
184 Ricky Ervins	.07	.20
185 Phil Simms	.15	.40
186 Tim Brown	.30	.75
187 Willis Peguese	.07	.20
188 Rich Moran	.07	.20
189 Robert Jones	.07	.20
190 Craig Heyward	.15	.40
191 Ricky Watters	.30	.75
192 Stan Humphries	.15	.40
193 Larry Webster	.07	.20
194 Brad Baxter	.07	.20
195 Randal Hill	.07	.20
196 Robert Porcher	.07	.20
197 Patrick Robinson RC	.07	.20
198 Ferrell Edmunds	.07	.20
199 Melvin Jenkins	.07	.20
200 Joe Montana FOIL	2.50	6.00
201 Marv Cook	.07	.20
202 Henry Ellard	.15	.40
203 Calvin Williams	.15	.40
204 Craig Erickson	.15	.40
205 Steve Atwater	.07	.20
206 Najee Mustafaa	.07	.20
207 Darryl Talley	.07	.20
208 Jarrod Bunch	.07	.20
209 Tim McDonald	.07	.20
210 Patrick Bates RC	.07	.20
211 Sean Jones	.07	.20
212 Leslie O'Neal	.15	.40
213 Mike Golic	.07	.20
214 Mark Clayton	.07	.20
215 Leonard Marshall	.07	.20
216 Curtis Conway RC	.60	1.50
217 Andre Hastings RC	.15	.40
218 Barry Word	.07	.20
219 Will Wolford	.07	.20
220 Desmond Howard	.15	.40
221 Rickey Jackson	.07	.20
222 Alvin Harper	.15	.40
223 William White	.07	.20
224 Steve Broussard	.07	.20
225 Aeneas Williams	.07	.20
226 Michael Brooks	.07	.20
227 Reggie Cobb	.07	.20
228 Derrick Walker	.07	.20
229 Marcus Allen	.30	.75
230 Jerry Ball	.07	.20
231 J.B. Brown	.07	.20
232 Terry McDaniel	.07	.20
233 LeRoy Butler	.07	.20
234 Kyle Clifton	.07	.20
235 Henry Jones	.07	.20
236 Shane Conlan	.07	.20
237 Michael Bates RC	.07	.20
238 Vincent Brown	.07	.20
239 William Fuller	.07	.20
240 Ricardo McDonald	.07	.20
241 Gary Zimmerman	.07	.20
242 Fred Barnett	.15	.40
243 Elvis Grbac RC	1.50	4.00
244 Myron Baker RC	.07	.20
245 Steve Emtman	.07	.20
246 Mike Compton RC	.30	.75
247 Mark Jackson	.07	.20
248 Santo Stephens RC	.07	.20
249 Tommie Agee	.07	.20
250 Broderick Thomas	.07	.20
251 Fred Baxter RC	.07	.20
252 Andre Collins	.07	.20
253 Ernest Dye RC	.07	.20
254 Raylee Johnson RC	.15	.40
255 Rickey Dixon	.07	.20
256 Ron Heller	.07	.20
257 Joel Steed	.07	.20
258 Everett Lindsay RC	.07	.20
259 Tony Smith	.07	.20
260 Sterling Sharpe UER	.30	.75
(Edgar Bennett is pictured on front)		
261 Tommy Vardell	.07	.20
262 Morten Andersen	.07	.20
263 Eddie Robinson	.07	.20
264 Jerome Bettis RC	4.00	8.00
265 Alonzo Spellman	.07	.20
266 Harvey Williams	.15	.40
267 Jason Belser RC	.07	.20
268 Derek Russell	.07	.20
269 Derrick Lassic RC	.07	.20
270 Steve Young FOIL	1.50	3.00
271 Adrian Murrell RC	.30	.75
272 Lewis Tillman	.07	.20
273 O.J. McDuffie RC	.30	.75
274 Marty Carter	.07	.20
275 Ray Seals	.07	.20
276 Earnest Byner	.07	.20
277 Marion Butts	.07	.20
278 Chris Spielman	.15	.40
279 Carl Pickens	.15	.40
280 Drew Bledsoe RC	2.50	6.00
281 Mark Kelso	.07	.20
282 Eugene Robinson	.07	.20
283 Eric Allen	.07	.20
284 Ethan Horton	.07	.20
285 Greg Lloyd	.15	.40
286 Anthony Carter	.15	.40
287 Edgar Bennett	.30	.75
288 Bobby Hebert	.07	.20
289 Haywood Jeffires	.15	.40
290 Glyn Milburn RC	.30	.75
291 Bernie Kosar	.15	.40
292 Jumbo Elliott	.07	.20
293 Jessie Hester	.07	.20
294 Brent Jones	.15	.40
295 Carl Banks	.07	.20
296 Brian Washington	.07	.20
297 Steve Beuerlein	.15	.40
298 John Lynch RC	.75	2.00
299 Troy Vincent	.07	.20
300 Emmitt Smith FOIL	2.50	5.00
301 Chris Zorich	.07	.20
302 Wade Wilson	.07	.20
303 Darrien Gordon RC	.07	.20
304 Fred Stokes	.07	.20
305 Nick Lowery	.07	.20
306 Rodney Peete	.07	.20
307 Chris Warren	.15	.40
308 Herschel Walker	.15	.40
309 Aundray Bruce	.07	.20
310 Barry Foster FOIL	.15	.40
311 George Teague RC	.15	.40
312 Darryl Williams	.07	.20
313 Thomas Smith RC	.15	.40
314 Dennis Brown	.07	.20
315 Marvin Jones RC	.15	.40
316 Andre Tippett	.07	.20
317 Demetrius DuBose RC	.07	.20
318 Kirk Lowdermilk	.07	.20
319 Shane Dronett	.07	.20
320 Terry Kirby RC	.30	.75
321 Qadry Ismail RC	.30	.75
322 Lorenzo Lynch	.07	.20
323 Willie Drewrey	.07	.20
324 Jessie Tuggle	.07	.20
325 Leroy Hoard	.15	.40
326 Mark Collins	.07	.20
327 Darrell Green	.07	.20
328 Anthony Miller	.15	.40
329 Brad Muster	.07	.20
330 Jim Kelly FOIL	.60	1.50
331 Sean Gilbert	.15	.40
332 Tim McKyer	.07	.20
333 Scott Mersereau	.07	.20
334 Willie Davis	.30	.75
335 Brett Favre FOIL	3.00	6.00
336 Kevin Gogan	.07	.20
337 Jim Harbaugh	.30	.75
338 James Trapp RC	.07	.20
339 Pete Stoyanovich	.07	.20
340 Jerry Rice FOIL	1.50	3.00
341 Gary Anderson RB	.07	.20
342 Carlton Gray RC	.07	.20
343 Dermontti Dawson	.07	.20
344 Ray Buchanan RC	.30	.75
345 Derrick Fenner	.07	.20
346 Dennis Smith	.07	.20
347 Todd Rucci RC	.07	.20
348 Seth Joyner	.07	.20
349 Jim McMahon	.15	.40
350 Rodney Hampton	.15	.40
351 Al Smith	.07	.20
352 Steve Everitt RC	.07	.20
353 Vinnie Clark	.07	.20
354 Eric Swann	.15	.40
355 Brian Mitchell	.15	.40
356 Will Shields RC	.30	.75
357 Cornelius Bennett	.15	.40
358 Darrin Smith RC	.15	.40
359 Chris Mims	.07	.20
360 Blair Thomas	.07	.20
361 Dennis Gibson	.07	.20
362 Santana Dotson	.15	.40
363 Mark Ingram	.07	.20
364 Don Mosebar	.07	.20
365 Ty Detmer	.30	.75
366 Bob Christian RC	.07	.20
367 Adrian Hardy	.07	.20
368 Vaughan Johnson	.07	.20
369 Jim Everett	.15	.40
370 Ricky Sanders	.07	.20
371 Jonathan Hayes	.07	.20
372 Bruce Matthews	.07	.20
373 Darren Drozdov RC	.30	.75
374 Scott Brumfield RC	.07	.20
375 Cortez Kennedy	.15	.40
376 Tim Harris	.07	.20
377 Neil O'Donnell	.30	.75
378 Robert Smith RC	1.25	3.00
379 Mike Caldwell RC	.07	.20
380 Burt Grossman	.07	.20
381 Corey Miller	.07	.20
382 Kevin Williams RC	.15	.40
383 Ken Harvey	.07	.20
384 Greg Robinson RC	.07	.20
385 Harold Alexander RC	.07	.20
386 Andre Reed	.15	.40
387 Reggie Langhorne	.07	.20
388 Courtney Hawkins	.07	.20
389 James Hasty	.07	.20
390 Pat Swilling	.07	.20
391 Chris Slade RC	.15	.40
392 Keith Byars	.07	.20
393 Dalton Hilliard	.07	.20
394 David Williams	.07	.20
395 Terry Obee RC	.07	.20
396 Heath Sherman	.07	.20
397 John Taylor	.15	.40
398 Irv Eatman	.07	.20
399 Johnny Holland	.07	.20
400 John Elway FOIL	2.50	6.00
401 Clay Matthews	.15	.40
402 Dave Meggett	.07	.20
403 Eric Green	.07	.20
404 Bryan Cox	.07	.20
405 Jay Novacek	.15	.40
406 Kenneth Davis	.07	.20
407 Lamar Thomas RC	.07	.20
408 Lance Gunn RC	.07	.20
409 Audray McMillian	.07	.20
410 Derrick Thomas FOIL	.60	1.50
411 Rufus Porter	.07	.20
412 Coleman Rudolph RC	.07	.20
413 Mark Rypien	.07	.20
414 Duane Bickett	.07	.20
415 Chris Singleton	.07	.20
416 Mitch Lyons RC	.07	.20
417 Bill Fralic	.07	.20
418 Gary Plummer	.07	.20
419 Ricky Proehl	.07	.20
420 Howie Long	.30	.75
421 Willie Roaf RC	.30	.75
422 Checklist 1-212	.07	.20
423 Checklist 213-423	.07	.20

1994 Bowman

The 1994 Bowman set consists of 390 standard-size cards. The set includes a 30-card foil subset (215-244, one per pack) of rookies. Rookie Cards include Mario Bates, Isaac Bruce, Lake Dawson, Trent Dilfer, Bert Emanuel, William Floyd, Marshall Faulk, Gus Frerotte, Charles Johnson, Errict Rhett, Darnay Scott and Heath Shuler.

COMPLETE SET (390)	20.00	50.00
1 Dan Wilkinson RC	.15	.40
2 Marshall Faulk RC	6.00	15.00
3 Heath Shuler RC	.30	.75
4 Willie McGinest RC	.30	.75
5 Trent Dilfer RC	1.25	3.00
6 Brent Jones	.15	.40
7 Sam Adams RC	.15	.40
8 Randy Baldwin	.07	.20
9 Jamir Miller RC	.15	.40
10 John Thierry RC	.07	.20
11 Aaron Glenn RC	.30	.75
12 Joe Johnson RC	.07	.20
13 Bernard Williams RC	.07	.20
14 Wayne Gandy RC	.07	.20
15 Aaron Taylor RC	.07	.20
16 Charles Johnson RC	.30	.75
17 Dewayne Washington RC	.15	.40
18 Bernie Kosar	.15	.40
19 Johnnie Morton RC	1.00	2.50
20 Rob Fredrickson RC	.15	.40
21 Shante Carver RC	.07	.20
22 Thomas Lewis RC	.15	.40
23 Greg Hill RC	.30	.75
24 Cris Dishman	.07	.20
25 Jeff Burris RC	.15	.40
26 Isaac Davis RC	.07	.20
27 Bert Emanuel RC	.30	.75
28 Allen Aldridge RC	.07	.20
29 Kevin Lee RC	.07	.20
30 Chris Brantley RC	.07	.20
31 Rich Braham RC	.07	.20
32 Ricky Watters	.15	.40
33 Quentin Coryatt	.07	.20
34 Hardy Nickerson	.15	.40
35 Johnny Johnson	.07	.20
36 Ken Harvey	.07	.20
37 Chris Zorich	.07	.20
38 Chris Warren	.15	.40
39 David Palmer RC	.30	.75
40 Chris Miller	.07	.20
41 Ken Ruettgers	.07	.20
42 Joe Panos RC	.07	.20
43 Mario Bates RC	.30	.75
44 Harry Colon	.07	.20
45 Barry Foster	.07	.20
46 Steve Tasker	.15	.40
47 Richmond Webb	.07	.20
48 James Folston RC	.07	.20
49 Erik Williams	.07	.20
50 Rodney Hampton	.15	.40
51 Derek Russell	.07	.20
52 Greg Montgomery	.07	.20
53 Anthony Phillips	.07	.20
54 Andre Coleman RC	.07	.20
55 Gary Brown	.07	.20
56 Neil Smith	.15	.40
57 Myron Baker	.07	.20
58 Sean Dawkins RC	.30	.75
59 Marvin Washington	.07	.20
60 Steve Beuerlein	.15	.40
61 Brenston Buckner RC	.07	.20
62 William Gaines RC	.07	.20
63 LeShon Johnson RC	.15	.40
64 Errict Rhett RC	.30	.75
65 Jim Everett	.15	.40
66 Desmond Howard	.15	.40
67 Jack Del Rio	.07	.20
68 Isaac Bruce RC	6.00	12.00
69 Van Malone RC	.07	.20
70 Jim Kelly	.30	.75
71 Leon Lett	.07	.20
72 Greg Robinson	.07	.20
73 Ryan Yarborough RC	.07	.20
74 Terry Wooden	.07	.20
75 Eric Allen	.07	.20
76 Ernest Givins	.15	.40
77 Marcus Spears RC	.07	.20
78 Thomas Randolph RC	.07	.20
79 Willie Clark RC	.07	.20
80 John Elway	1.50	4.00
81 Aubrey Beavers RC	.07	.20
82 Jeff Cothran RC	.07	.20
83 Norm Johnson	.07	.20
84 Donnell Bennett RC	.30	.75
85 Phillippi Sparks	.07	.20
86 Scott Mitchell	.15	.40
87 Bucky Brooks RC	.07	.20
88 Courtney Hawkins	.07	.20
89 Kevin Greene	.15	.40
90 Doug Nussmeier RC	.07	.20
91 Floyd Turner	.07	.20
92 Anthony Newman	.07	.20
93 Vinny Testaverde	.15	.40
94 Ronnie Lott	.15	.40
95 Troy Aikman	.75	2.00
96 John Taylor	.15	.40
97 Henry Ellard	.15	.40
98 Carl Lee	.07	.20
99 Terry McDaniel	.07	.20
100 Joe Montana	1.50	4.00
101 David Klingler	.07	.20
102 Bruce Walker RC	.07	.20
103 Rick Cunningham RC	.07	.20
104 Robert Delpino	.07	.20
105 Mark Ingram	.07	.20
106 Leslie O'Neal	.07	.20
107 Darrell Thompson	.07	.20
108 Dave Meggett	.07	.20
109 Chris Gardocki	.07	.20
110 Andre Rison	.15	.40
111 Kelvin Martin	.07	.20
112 Marcus Robertson	.07	.20
113 Jason Gildon RC	1.25	3.00
114 Mel Gray	.07	.20
115 Tommy Vardell	.07	.20
116 Dexter Carter	.07	.20
117 Scottie Graham RC	.15	.40
118 Horace Copeland	.07	.20
119 Cornelius Bennett	.15	.40
120 Chris Maumalanga RC	.07	.20
121 Mo Lewis	.07	.20
122 Toby Wright RC	.07	.20
123 George Hegamin RC	.07	.20
124 Chip Lohmiller	.07	.20
125 Calvin Jones RC	.07	.20
126 Steve Shine	.07	.20
127 Chuck Levy RC	.07	.20
128 Sam Mills	.07	.20
129 Terance Mathis	.15	.40
130 Randall Cunningham	.30	.75
131 John Fina	.07	.20
132 Reggie White	.30	.75
133 Tom Waddle	.07	.20
134 Chris Calloway	.07	.20
135 Kevin Mawae RC	.30	.75
136 Lake Dawson RC	.15	.40
137 Alai Kalaniuhalu	.07	.20
138 Tom Nalen RC	.30	.75
139 Cody Carlson	.07	.20
140 Dan Marino	1.50	4.00
141 Harris Barton	.07	.20
142 Don Mosebar	.07	.20
143 Romeo Bandison	.07	.20
144 Bruce Smith	.30	.75
145 Warren Moon	.30	.75
146 David Lutz	.07	.20
147 Dermontti Dawson	.07	.20
148 Ricky Proehl	.07	.20
149 Lou Benfatti RC	.07	.20
150 Craig Erickson	.07	.20
151 Sean Gilbert	.07	.20
152 Zefross Moss	.07	.20
153 Darnay Scott RC	.50	1.25
154 Courtney Hall	.07	.20
155 Brian Mitchell	.07	.20
156 Joe Burch UER RC	.07	.20
157 Terry Mickens	.07	.20
158 Jay Novacek	.15	.40
159 Chris Gedney	.07	.20
160 Bruce Matthews	.07	.20
161 Mario Perry RC	.07	.20
162 Vince Buck	.07	.20
163 Michael Bates	.07	.20
164 Willie Davis	.15	.40
165 Mike Pritchard	.07	.20
166 Doug Riesenberg	.07	.20
167 Herschel Walker	.15	.40
168 Tim Ruddy RC	.07	.20
169 William Floyd RC	.30	.75
170 John Randle	.15	.40
171 Winston Moss	.07	.20
172 Thurman Thomas	.30	.75
173 Eric England RC	.07	.20
174 Vincent Brisby	.15	.40
175 Greg Lloyd	.15	.40
176 Paul Gruber	.07	.20
177 Brad Ottis RC	.07	.20
178 George Teague	.07	.20
179 Willie Jackson RC	.30	.75
180 Barry Sanders	1.25	3.00
181 Brian Washington	.07	.20
182 Michael Jackson	.15	.40
183 Jason Mathews RC	.07	.20
184 Chester McGlockton	.07	.20
185 Tydus Winans RC	.07	.20
186 Michael Haynes	.15	.40
187 Erik Kramer	.15	.40
188 Chris Doleman	.07	.20
189 Haywood Jeffires	.15	.40
190 Larry Whigham RC	.07	.20
191 Shawn Jefferson	.07	.20
192 Pete Stoyanovich	.07	.20
193 Rod Bernstine	.07	.20
194 William Thomas	.07	.20
195 Marcus Allen	.30	.75
196 Dave Brown	.15	.40
197 Harold Bishop RC	.07	.20
198 Lorenzo Lynch	.07	.20
199 Dwight Stone	.07	.20
200 Jerry Rice	.75	2.00
201 Rocket Ismail	.15	.40
202 LeRoy Butler	.07	.20
203 Glenn Parker	.07	.20
204 Bruce Armstrong	.07	.20
205 Shane Conlan	.07	.20
206 Russell Maryland	.07	.20
207 Herman Moore	.30	.75
208 Eric Martin	.07	.20
209 John Friesz	.15	.40
210 Boomer Esiason	.15	.40
211 Jim Harbaugh	.30	.75
212 Harold Green	.07	.20

213 Perry Klein RC	.07	.20
214 Eric Metcalf	.15	.40
215 Steve Everitt	.07	.20
216 Victor Bailey	.07	.20
217 Lincoln Kennedy	.07	.20
218 Glyn Milburn	.15	.40
219 John Copeland	.07	.20
220 Drew Bledsoe	.75	2.00
221 Kevin Williams	.15	.40
222 Roosevelt Potts	.07	.20
223 Troy Drayton	.07	.20
224 Terry Kirby	.30	.75
225 Ronald Moore	.07	.20
226 Tyrone Hughes	.15	.40
227 Wayne Simmons	.07	.20
228 Tony McGee	.07	.20
229 Derek Brown RBK	.07	.20
230 Jason Elam	.15	.40
231 Qadry Ismail	.30	.75
232 O.J. McDuffie	.30	.75
233 Mike Caldwell	.07	.20
234 Reggie Brooks	.15	.40
235 Rick Mirer	.30	.75
236 Steve Tovar	.07	.20
237 Patrick Robinson	.07	.20
238 Tom Carter	.07	.20
239 Ben Coates	.15	.40
240 Jerome Bettis	.50	1.25
241 Garrison Hearst	.30	.75
242 Natrone Means	.30	.75
243 Dana Stubblefield	.15	.40
244 Willie Roaf	.07	.20
245 Cortez Kennedy	.15	.40
246 Todd Steussie RC	.15	.40
247 Pat Coleman	.07	.20
248 David Wyman	.07	.20
249 Jeremy Lincoln	.07	.20
250 Carlester Crumpler	.07	.20
251 Dale Carter	.07	.20
252 Corey Raymond RC	.07	.20
253 Bryan Cox	.07	.20
254 Charlie Garner RC	1.25	3.00
255 Jeff Hostetler	.15	.40
256 Shane Bonham RC	.07	.20
257 Thomas Everett	.07	.20
258 John Jackson	.07	.20
259 Terry Irving RC	.07	.20
260 Corey Sawyer	.15	.40
261 Rob Waldrop RC	.07	.20
262 Curtis Conway	.30	.75
263 Winfred Tubbs RC	.15	.40
264 Sean Jones	.07	.20
265 James Washington	.07	.20
266 Lonnie Johnson RC	.07	.20
267 Rob Moore	.15	.40
268 Flipper Anderson	.07	.20
269 Jon Hand	.07	.20
270 Joe Patton RC	.07	.20
271 Howard Ballard	.07	.20
272 Fernando Smith RC	.07	.20
273 Jessie Tuggle	.07	.20
274 John Alt	.07	.20
275 Corey Miller	.07	.20
276 Gus Frerotte RC	1.25	3.00
277 Jeff Cross	.07	.20
278 Kevin Smith	.07	.20
279 Corey Louchiey RC	.07	.20
280 Micheal Barrow	.07	.20
281 Jim Flanigan RC	.15	.40
282 Calvin Williams	.15	.40
283 Jeff Jaeger	.07	.20
284 John Reece RC	.07	.20
285 Jason Hanson	.07	.20
286 Kurt Haws RC	.07	.20
287 Eric Davis	.07	.20
288 Maurice Hurst	.07	.20
289 Kirk Lowdermilk	.07	.20
290 Rod Woodson	.15	.40
291 Andre Reed	.15	.40
292 Vince Workman	.07	.20
293 Wayne Martin	.07	.20
294 Keith Lyle RC	.07	.20
295 Brett Favre	1.50	4.00
296 Doug Brien RC	.07	.20
297 Junior Seau	.30	.75
298 Randall McDaniel	.07	.20
299 Johnny Mitchell	.07	.20
300 Emmitt Smith	1.25	3.00
301 Michael Brooks	.07	.20
302 Steve Jackson	.07	.20
303 Jeff George	.30	.75
304 Irving Fryar	.15	.40
305 Derrick Thomas	.30	.75
306 Dante Jones	.07	.20
307 Darrell Green	.07	.20
308 Mark Bavaro	.07	.20
309 Eugene Robinson	.07	.20
310 Shannon Sharpe	.15	.40
311 Michael Timpson	.07	.20
312 Kevin Mitchell RC	.07	.20
313 Stevon Moore	.07	.20
314 Eric Swann	.15	.40
315 James Bostic RC	.30	.75
316 Robert Brooks	.30	.75
317 Pete Pierson RC	.07	.20
318 Jim Sweeney	.07	.20
319 Anthony Smith	.07	.20
320 Rohn Stark	.07	.20
321 Gary Anderson K	.07	.20
322 Robert Porcher	.07	.20
323 Darryl Talley	.07	.20
324 Stan Humphries	.15	.40
325 Shelly Hammonds RC	.07	.20
326 Jim McMahon	.15	.40
327 Lamont Warren RC	.07	.20
328 Chris Penn RC	.07	.20
329 Tony Woods	.07	.20
330 Raymont Harris RC	.30	.75
331 Mitch Davis RC	.07	.20
332 Michael Irvin	.30	.75
333 Kent Graham	.15	.40
334 Brian Blades	.15	.40
335 Lomas Brown	.07	.20
336 Willie Drewrey	.07	.20
337 Russell Freeman	.07	.20
338 Eric Zomalt RC	.07	.20
339 Santana Dotson	.15	.40
340 Sterling Sharpe	.15	.40
341 Ray Crittenden RC	.07	.20
342 Perry Carter RC	.07	.20
343 Austin Robbins	.07	.20
344 Mike Wells RC	.07	.20
345 Toddrick McIntosh RC	.07	.20
346 Mark Carrier WR	.15	.40
347 Eugene Daniel	.07	.20
348 Tre Johnson RC	.07	.20
349 D.J. Johnson	.07	.20
350 Steve Young	.60	1.50
351 Jim Pyne RC	.07	.20
352 Jocelyn Borgella RC	.07	.20
353 Pat Carter	.07	.20
354 Sam Rogers RC	.07	.20
355 Jason Sehorn RC	.50	1.25
356 Darren Carrington	.07	.20
357 Lamar Smith RC	1.50	4.00
358 James Burton RC	.07	.20
359 Darrin Smith	.07	.20
360 Marco Coleman	.07	.20
361 Webster Slaughter	.07	.20
362 Lewis Tillman	.07	.20
363 David Alexander	.07	.20
364 Bradford Banta RC	.07	.20
365 Erric Pegram	.07	.20
366 Mike Fox	.07	.20
367 Jeff Lageman	.07	.20
368 Kurt Gouveia	.07	.20
369 Tim Brown	.30	.75
370 Seth Joyner	.07	.20
371 Irv Eatman	.07	.20
372 Dorsey Levens RC	1.50	4.00
373 Anthony Pleasant	.07	.20
374 Henry Jones	.07	.20
375 Cris Carter	.40	1.00
376 Morten Andersen	.07	.20
377 Neil O'Donnell	.30	.75
378 Tyronne Drakeford RC	.07	.20
379 John Carney	.07	.20
380 Vincent Brown	.07	.20
381 J.J. Birden	.07	.20
382 Chris Spielman	.15	.40
383 Mark Bortz	.07	.20
384 Ray Childress	.07	.20
385 Carlton Bailey	.07	.20
386 Charles Haley	.15	.40
387 Shane Dronett	.07	.20
388 Jon Vaughn	.07	.20
389 Checklist 1-195	.07	.20
390 Checklist 196-390	.07	.20

1995 Bowman

This 357-card standard size set was issued by Topps. Parallel sets of the expansion team cards and rookie draft picks were included. The expansion team parallel had extra gold foil while the draft pick parallel had a "First Round" stamp on the front. Rookie Cards in this set include Jeff Blake, Ki-Jana Carter, Kerry Collins, Joey Galloway, Napoleon Kaufman, Steve McNair, Curtis Martin, Rashan Salaam, Chris Sanders, Kordell Stewart, J.J. Stokes, Rodney Thomas, Tamarick Vanover and Michael Westbrook.

COMPLETE SET (357)	25.00	60.00
1 Ki-Jana Carter RC	.30	.75
2 Tony Boselli RC	.30	.75
3 Steve McNair RC	3.00	8.00
4 Michael Westbrook RC	.25	.60
5 Kerry Collins RC	2.00	5.00
6 Kevin Carter RC	.30	.75
7 Mike Mamula RC	.07	.20
8 Joey Galloway RC	1.50	4.00
9 Kyle Brady RC	.30	.75
10 J.J. Stokes RC	.30	.75
11 Derrick Alexander DE RC	.07	.20
12 Warren Sapp RC	1.50	4.00
13 Mark Fields RC	.30	.75
14 Ruben Brown RC	.30	.75
15 Ellis Johnson RC	.07	.20
16 Hugh Douglas RC	.30	.75
17 Mike Pelton RC	.07	.20
18 Napoleon Kaufman RC	1.25	3.00
19 James O. Stewart RC	1.00	2.50
20 Luther Elliss RC	.07	.20
21 Rashaan Salaam RC	.15	.40
22 Tyrone Poole RC	.30	.75
23 Ty Law RC	1.25	3.00
24 Korey Stringer RC	.25	.60
25 Billy Milner RC	.07	.20
26 Devin Bush RC	.07	.20
27 Mark Bruener RC	.15	.40
28 Derrick Brooks RC	1.50	4.00
29 Blake Brockermeyer RC	.07	.20
30 Alundis Brice RC	.07	.20
31 Trezelle Jenkins RC	.07	.20
32 Craig Newsome RC	.07	.20
33 Fred Barnett	.10	.30
34 Ray Childress	.05	.15
35 Chris Miller	.05	.15
36 Charles Haley	.10	.30
37 Ray Crittenden	.05	.15
38 Gus Frerotte	.10	.30
39 Jeff George	.10	.30
40 Dan Marino	1.25	3.00
41 Shawn Lee	.05	.15
42 Herman Moore	.25	.60
43 Chris Calloway	.05	.15
44 Jeff Graham	.05	.15
45 Ray Buchanan	.05	.15
46 Doug Pelfrey	.05	.15
47 Lake Dawson	.10	.30
48 Glenn Parker	.05	.15
49 Terry McDaniel	.05	.15
50 Rod Woodson	.10	.30
51 Santana Dotson	.05	.15
52 Anthony Miller	.10	.30
53 Bo Orlando	.05	.15
54 David Palmer	.10	.30
55 William Floyd	.10	.30
56 Edgar Bennett	.10	.30
57 Jeff Blake RC	1.00	2.50
58 Anthony Pleasant	.05	.15
59 Quinn Early	.10	.30
60 Bobby Houston	.05	.15
61 Terrell Fletcher RC	.07	.20
62 Gary Brown	.05	.15
63 Dwayne Sabb	.05	.15
64 Roman Phifer	.05	.15
65 Sherman Williams RC	.07	.20
66 Roosevelt Potts	.05	.15
67 Darnay Scott	.10	.30
68 Charlie Garner	.25	.60
69 Bert Emanuel	.25	.60
70 Herschel Walker	.10	.30
71 Lorenzo Styles RC	.07	.20
72 Andre Coleman	.05	.15
73 Tyronne Drakeford	.05	.15
74 Jay Novacek	.10	.30
75 Raymont Harris	.05	.15
76 Tamarick Vanover RC	.30	.75
77 Tom Carter	.05	.15
78 Eric Green	.05	.15
79 Patrick Hunter	.05	.15
80 Jeff Hostetler	.10	.30
81 Robert Blackmon	.05	.15
82 Anthony Cook RC	.07	.20
83 Craig Erickson	.05	.15
84 Glyn Milburn	.05	.15
85 Greg Lloyd	.10	.30
86 Brent Jones	.05	.15
87 Barrett Brooks RC	.07	.20
88 Alvin Harper	.05	.15
89 Sean Jones	.05	.15
90 Cris Carter	.25	.60
91 Russell Copeland	.05	.15
92 Frank Sanders RC	.30	.75
93 Mo Lewis	.05	.15
94 Michael Haynes	.10	.30
95 Andre Rison	.10	.30
96 Jesse James RC	.07	.20
97 Stan Humphries	.10	.30
98 James Hasty	.05	.15
99 Ricardo McDonald	.05	.15
100 Jerry Rice	.60	1.50
101 Chris Hudson RC	.07	.20
102 Dave Meggett	.05	.15
103 Brian Mitchell	.05	.15
104 Mike Johnson	.05	.15
105 Kordell Stewart RC	1.50	4.00
106 Michael Brooks	.05	.15
107 Steve Walsh	.05	.15
108 Eric Metcalf	.10	.30
109 Ricky Watters	.10	.30
110 Brett Favre	1.25	3.00
111 Aubrey Beavers	.05	.15
112 Brian Williams LB RC	.07	.20
113 Eugene Robinson	.05	.15
114 Matt O'Dwyer RC	.07	.20
115 Micheal Barrow	.05	.15
116 Rocket Ismail	.10	.30
117 Scott Gragg RC	.07	.20
118 Leon Lett	.05	.15
119 Reggie Roby	.05	.15
120 Marshall Faulk	.75	2.00
121 Jack Jackson RC	.07	.20
122 Keith Byars	.05	.15
123 Eric Hill	.05	.15
124 Todd Sauerbrun RC	.07	.20
125 Dexter Carter	.05	.15
126 Vinny Testaverde	.10	.30
127 Shane Conlan	.05	.15
128 Terrance Shaw RC	.07	.20
129 Willie Roaf	.05	.15
130 Jim Kelly	.25	.60
131 Neil O'Donnell	.10	.30
132 Ray McElroy RC	.07	.20
133 Ed McDaniel	.05	.15
134 Brian Gelzheiser RC	.07	.20
135 Marcus Allen	.25	.60
136 Carl Pickens	.10	.30
137 Mike Verstegen RC	.07	.20
138 Chris Mims	.05	.15
139 Darryl Pounds RC	.07	.20
140 Emmitt Smith	1.25	2.50
141 Mike Frederick RC	.07	.20
142 Henry Ellard	.10	.30
143 Willie McGinest	.10	.30
144 Michael Roan RC	.07	.20
145 Chris Spielman	.10	.30
146 Darryl Talley	.05	.15
147 Randall Cunningham	.25	.60
148 Andrew Greene RC	.07	.20
149 George Teague	.05	.15
150 Tyrone Hughes	.10	.30
151 Ron Davis RC	.07	.20
152 Stevon Moore	.05	.15
153 Merton Hanks	.05	.15
154 Darren Perry	.05	.15
155 Dave Brown	.10	.30
156 Mike Morton RC	.07	.20
157 Seth Joyner	.05	.15
158 Bryan Cox	.05	.15
159 Corey Fuller RC	.07	.20
160 John Elway	1.25	3.00
161 Dewayne Washington	.10	.30
162 Chris Warren	.10	.30
163 Jeff Kopp RC	.07	.20
164 Sean Dawkins	.10	.30
165 Mark Carrier DB	.05	.15
166 Andre Hastings	.10	.30
167 Derek West RC	.07	.20
168 Glenn Montgomery	.05	.15
169 Trent Dilfer	.25	.60
170 Rob Johnson RC	1.00	2.50
171 Todd Scott	.05	.15
172 Charles Johnson	.10	.30
173 Kez McCorvey RC	.07	.20
174 Rob Fredrickson	.05	.15
175 Corey Sawyer	.05	.15
176 Brett Perriman	.10	.30
177 Ken Dilger RC	.30	.75
178 Dana Stubblefield	.10	.30
179 Eric Allen	.05	.15
180 Drew Bledsoe	.40	1.00
181 Tyrone Davis RC	.07	.20
182 Reggie Brooks	.10	.30
183 Dale Carter	.10	.30
184 William Henderson RC	1.25	3.00
185 Reggie White	.25	.60
186 Lorenzo White	.05	.15
187 Leslie O'Neal	.10	.30
188 Stoney Case RC	.07	.20
189 Jeff Burris	.05	.15
190 Leroy Hoard	.05	.15
191 Thomas Randolph	.05	.15
192 Rodney Thomas RC	.15	.40
193 Quentin Coryatt	.10	.30
194 Terry Wooden	.05	.15
195 David Sloan RC	.07	.20
196 Bernie Parmalee	.10	.30
197 Zack Crockett RC	.15	.40
198 Troy Aikman	.60	1.50
199 Bruce Smith	.25	.60
200 Eric Zeier RC	.30	.75
201 Anthony Smith	.05	.15
202 Jake Reed	.10	.30
203 Hardy Nickerson	.05	.15
204 Patrick Riley RC	.07	.20
205 Bruce Matthews	.05	.15
206 Larry Centers	.10	.30
207 Troy Drayton	.05	.15
208 John Burrough RC	.07	.20
209 Jason Elam	.10	.30
210 Donnell Woolford	.05	.15
211 Sam Shade RC	.07	.20
212 Kevin Greene	.10	.30
213 Ronald Moore	.05	.15
214 Shane Hannah RC	.07	.20
215 Jim Everett	.05	.15
216 Scott Mitchell	.10	.30
217 Antonio Freeman RC	1.25	3.00
218 Tony McGee	.05	.15
219 Clay Matthews	.10	.30
220 Neil Smith	.10	.30
221 Mark Williams FOIL	.15	.40
222 Derrick Graham FOIL RC	.15	.40
223 Mike Hollis FOIL	.15	.40
224 Darion Conner FOIL	.15	.40
225 Steve Beuerlein FOIL	.15	.40
226 Rod Smith DB FOIL	.15	.40
227 James Williams FOIL	.15	.40
228 Bob Christian FOIL	.15	.40
229 Jeff Lageman FOIL	.15	.40
230 Frank Reich FOIL	.15	.40
231 Harry Colon FOIL	.15	.40
232 Carlton Bailey FOIL	.15	.40
233 Mickey Washington FOIL	.15	.40
234 Shawn Bouwens FOIL	.15	.40
235 Don Beebe FOIL	.15	.40
236 Kelvin Pritchett FOIL	.15	.40
237 Tommy Barnhardt FOIL	.15	.40
238 Mike Dumas FOIL	.15	.40
239 Brett Maxie FOIL	.15	.40
240 Desmond Howard FOIL	.15	.40
241 Sam Mills FOIL	.15	.40
242 Keith Goganious FOIL	.15	.40
243 Bubba McDowell FOIL	.15	.40
244 Vinnie Clark FOIL	.15	.40
245 Lamar Lathon FOIL	.15	.40
246 Bryan Barker FOIL	.15	.40
247 Darren Carrington FOIL	.15	.40
248 Jay Barker RC	.07	.20
249 Eric Davis	.05	.15
250 Heath Shuler	.10	.30
251 Donta Jones RC	.07	.20
252 LeRoy Butler	.05	.15
253 Michael Zordich	.05	.15
254 Cortez Kennedy	.10	.30
255 Brian DeMarco RC	.07	.20
256 Randal Hill	.05	.15
257 Michael Irvin	.25	.60
258 Natrone Means	.10	.30
259 Linc Harden RC	.07	.20
260 Jerome Bettis	.25	.60
261 Tony Bennett	.05	.15
262 Dameian Jeffries RC	.07	.20
263 Cornelius Bennett	.10	.30
264 Chris Zorich	.05	.15
265 Bobby Taylor RC	.30	.75
266 Terrell Buckley	.05	.15
267 Troy Dumas RC	.07	.20
268 Rodney Hampton	.10	.30
269 Steve Everitt	.05	.15
270 Mel Gray	.05	.15
271 Antonio Armstrong RC	.07	.20
272 Jim Harbaugh	.10	.30
273 Gary Clark	.05	.15
274 Tau Pupua RC	.07	.20
275 Warren Moon	.10	.30
276 Corey Croom	.05	.15
277 Tony Berti RC	.07	.20
278 Shannon Sharpe	.10	.30
279 Boomer Esiason	.10	.30
280 Aeneas Williams	.05	.15
281 Lethon Flowers RC	.07	.20
282 Derek Brown TE	.05	.15
283 Charlie Williams RC	.07	.20
284 Dan Wilkinson	.10	.30
285 Mike Sherrard	.05	.15
286 Evan Pilgrim RC	.07	.20
287 Kimble Anders	.10	.30
288 Greg Jefferson RC	.07	.20
289 Ken Norton	.10	.30
290 Terance Mathis	.10	.30
291 Torey Hunter RC	.07	.20
292 Ken Harvey	.05	.15
293 Irving Fryar	.10	.30
294 Michael Reed RC	.07	.20
295 Andre Reed	.10	.30
296 Vencie Glenn	.05	.15
297 Corey Swinson	.05	.15
298 Harvey Williams	.05	.15
299 Willie Davis	.10	.30
300 Barry Sanders	1.00	2.50
301 Curtis Martin RC	3.00	8.00
302 Johnny Mitchell	.05	.15
303 Daryl Johnston	.10	.30
304 Lorenzo Lynch	.05	.15
305 Christian Fauria RC	.15	.40
306 Sean Gilbert	.10	.30
307 Ray Zellars RC	.15	.40
308 William Strong RC	.07	.20
309 Jack Del Rio	.05	.15
310 Junior Seau	.25	.60
311 Justin Armour RC	.07	.20
312 Eric Bjornson RC	.07	.20
313 Vincent Brown	.05	.15
314 Darius Holland RC	.07	.20
315 Chad May RC	.07	.20
316 Simon Fletcher	.05	.15
317 Roell Preston RC	.10	.30
318 John Thierry	.05	.15
319 Orlando Thomas RC	.07	.20
320 Zach Wiegert RC	.07	.20
321 Derrick Alexander WR	.25	.60
322 Chris Cowart RC	.07	.20
323 Chris Sanders RC	.15	.40
324 Robert Brooks	.25	.60
325 Todd Collins RC	1.00	2.50
326 Ken Irvin RC	.07	.20
327 Erric Pegram	.10	.30
328 Damien Covington RC	.07	.20
329 Brendan Stai RC	.07	.20
330 James A.Stewart RC	.07	.20
331 Jessie Tuggle	.05	.15
332 Marco Coleman	.05	.15
333 Steve Young	.50	1.25
334 Greg Hill	.10	.30
335 Darryl Williams	.05	.15
336 Calvin Williams	.10	.30
337 Cris Dishman	.05	.15
338 Anthony Morgan	.05	.15
339 Renaldo Turnbull	.05	.15
340 Rick Mirer	.10	.30
341 Tim Brown	.25	.60
342 Dennis Gibson	.05	.15
343 Brad Baxter	.05	.15
344 Henry Jones	.05	.15
345 Johnny Bailey	.05	.15
346 Rocket Ismail	.10	.30
347 Richmond Webb	.05	.15
348 Robert Jones	.05	.15
349 Garrison Hearst	.25	.60
350 Errict Rhett	.10	.30
351 Steve Atwater	.05	.15
352 Joe Cain	.05	.15
353 Ben Coates	.10	.30
354 Aaron Glenn	.05	.15
355 Antonio Langham	.05	.15
356 Eugene Daniel	.05	.15
357 Tim Bowens	.05	.15

1995 Bowman Expansion Team Gold

EXPANSION GOLDS: 1.5X TO 3X BASIC CARDS
STATED ODDS 1:12

1995 Bowman First Round Picks

COMPLETE SET (27)	30.00	60.00
STATED ODDS 1:12		
1 Ki-Jana Carter	.60	1.50
2 Tony Boselli	.60	1.50
3 Steve McNair	6.00	15.00
4 Michael Westbrook	.50	1.25
5 Kerry Collins	4.00	10.00
6 Kevin Carter	.60	1.50
7 Mike Mamula	.15	.40
8 Joey Galloway	3.00	8.00
9 Kyle Brady	.60	1.50
10 J.J.Stokes	.60	1.50
11 Derrick Alexander DE	.15	.40
12 Warren Sapp	3.00	8.00
13 Mark Fields	.60	1.50
14 Ruben Brown	.60	1.50
15 Ellis Johnson	.15	.40
16 Hugh Douglas	.60	1.50
18 Napoleon Kaufman	2.50	6.00
19 James O. Stewart	2.00	5.00
20 Luther Elliss	.15	.40
21 Rashaan Salaam	.30	.75
22 Tyrone Poole	.60	1.50
23 Ty Law	2.50	6.00
28 Derrick Brooks	3.00	8.00
32 Craig Newsome	.15	.40
76 Tamarick Vanover	.60	1.50
92 Frank Sanders	.60	1.50
200 Eric Zeier	.60	1.50

1998 Bowman

The 1998 Bowman set was issued in one series totalling 220 standard size cards. The 10-card packs retail for $2.50 each. The cards feature 150 veteran players and 70 prospects. The gold-foil fronts feature a silver and blue logo design for the prospect cards, while the veteran cards show a silver and red design. A 220-card Bowman Inter-State parallel set was also produced which indicated what state the pictured player was from. The card backs display a custom-tailored vanity plate. One card from this parallel set was inserted in every pack.

COMPLETE SET (220)	20.00	50.00
1 Peyton Manning RC	10.00	25.00
2 Keith Brooking RC	.60	1.50
3 Duane Starks RC	.30	.75
4 Takeo Spikes RC	.60	1.50
5 Andre Wadsworth RC	.50	1.25
6 Greg Ellis RC	.30	.75
7 Brian Griese RC	1.25	3.00
8 Germane Crowell RC	.50	1.25
9 Jerome Pathon RC	.60	1.50
10 Ryan Leaf RC	.60	1.50
11 Fred Taylor RC	1.00	2.50
12 Robert Edwards RC	.50	1.25
13 Grant Wistrom RC	.50	1.25
14 Robert Holcombe RC	.50	1.25
15 Tim Dwight RC	.60	1.50
16 Jacquez Green RC	.50	1.25
17 Marcus Nash RC	.30	.75
18 Jason Peter RC	.30	.75
19 Anthony Simmons RC	.50	1.25
20 Curtis Enis RC	.30	.75
21 John Avery RC	.50	1.25
22 Pat Johnson RC	.50	1.25
23 Joe Jurevicius RC	.60	1.50
24 Brian Simmons RC	.50	1.25
25 Kevin Dyson RC	.60	1.50
26 Skip Hicks RC	.50	1.25
27 Hines Ward RC	3.00	8.00
28 Tavian Banks RC	.50	1.25
29 Ahman Green RC	2.00	5.00
30 Tony Simmons RC	.50	1.25
31 Charles Johnson	.10	.30
32 Freddie Jones	.10	.30
33 Joey Galloway	.20	.50
34 Tony Banks	.20	.50
35 Jake Plummer	.30	.75
36 Reidel Anthony	.20	.50
37 Steve McNair	.30	.75
38 Michael Westbrook	.20	.50
39 Chris Sanders	.10	.30
40 Isaac Bruce	.30	.75
41 Charlie Garner	.20	.50
42 Wayne Chrebet	.30	.75
43 Michael Strahan	.20	.50
44 Brad Johnson	.30	.75
45 Mike Alstott	.30	.75
46 Tony Gonzalez	.30	.75
47 Johnnie Morton	.20	.50
48 Darnay Scott	.20	.50
49 Rae Carruth	.10	.30
50 Terrell Davis	.30	.75
51 Jermaine Lewis	.20	.50
52 Frank Sanders	.20	.50
53 Byron Hanspard	.10	.30
54 Gus Frerotte	.10	.30
55 Terry Glenn	.30	.75
56 J.J. Stokes	.20	.50
57 Will Blackwell	.10	.30
58 Keyshawn Johnson	.30	.75
59 Tiki Barber	.30	.75
60 Dorsey Levens	.30	.75
61 Zach Thomas	.30	.75
62 Corey Dillon	.30	.75
63 Antowain Smith	.30	.75
64 Michael Sinclair	.10	.30
65 Rod Smith	.20	.50
66 Trent Dilfer	.30	.75
67 Warren Sapp	.20	.50
68 Charles Way	.10	.30
69 Tamarick Vanover	.10	.30
70 Drew Bledsoe	.50	1.25
71 John Mobley	.10	.30
72 Kerry Collins	.20	.50
73 Peter Boulware	.10	.30
74 Simeon Rice	.20	.50
75 Eddie George	.30	.75
76 Fred Lane	.10	.30
77 Jamal Anderson	.30	.75
78 Antonio Freeman	.30	.75
79 Jason Sehorn	.20	.50
80 Curtis Martin	.30	.75
81 Bobby Hoying	.20	.50
82 Garrison Hearst	.30	.75
83 Glenn Foley	.20	.50
84 Danny Kanell	.20	.50
85 Kordell Stewart	.30	.75
86 O.J. McDuffie	.20	.50
87 Marvin Harrison	.30	.75
88 Bobby Engram	.20	.50
89 Chris Slade	.10	.30
90 Warrick Dunn	.30	.75
91 Ricky Watters	.20	.50
92 Rickey Dudley	.10	.30
93 Terrell Owens	.30	.75
94 Karim Abdul-Jabbar	.30	.75
95 Napoleon Kaufman	.30	.75
96 Darrell Green	.20	.50
97 Levon Kirkland	.10	.30
98 Jeff George	.20	.50
99 Andre Hastings	.10	.30
100 John Elway	1.25	3.00
101 John Randle	.20	.50
102 Andre Rison	.20	.50
103 Keenan McCardell	.20	.50
104 Marshall Faulk	.40	1.00
105 Emmitt Smith	1.00	2.50
106 Robert Brooks	.20	.50
107 Scott Mitchell	.20	.50
108 Shannon Sharpe	.20	.50
109 Deion Sanders	.30	.75
110 Jerry Rice	.60	1.50
111 Erik Kramer	.10	.30
112 Michael Jackson	.10	.30
113 Aeneas Williams	.10	.30
114 Terry Allen	.30	.75
115 Steve Young	.40	1.00
116 Warren Moon	.30	.75
117 Junior Seau	.30	.75
118 Jerome Bettis	.30	.75
119 Irving Fryar	.20	.50
120 Barry Sanders	1.00	2.50
121 Tim Brown	.30	.75
122 Chad Brown	.10	.30
123 Ben Coates	.20	.50
124 Robert Smith	.30	.75
125 Brett Favre	1.25	3.00
126 Derrick Thomas	.30	.75
127 Reggie White	.30	.75
128 Troy Aikman	.60	1.50
129 Jeff Blake	.20	.50
130 Mark Brunell	.30	.75
131 Curtis Conway	.20	.50
132 Wesley Walls	.20	.50
133 Thurman Thomas	.30	.75
134 Chris Chandler	.20	.50
135 Dan Marino	1.25	3.00
136 Larry Centers	.10	.30
137 Shawn Jefferson	.10	.30
138 Andre Reed	.20	.50
139 Jake Reed	.20	.50
140 Cris Carter	.30	.75
141 Elvis Grbac	.20	.50
142 Mark Chmura	.20	.50
143 Michael Irvin	.30	.75
144 Carl Pickens	.20	.50
145 Herman Moore	.20	.50
146 Marvin Jones	.10	.30
147 Terance Mathis	.20	.50
148 Rob Moore	.20	.50
149 Bruce Smith	.20	.50
150 Rob Johnson CL	.10	.30
151 Leslie Shepherd	.10	.30
152 Chris Spielman	.10	.30
153 Tony McGee	.10	.30
154 Kevin Smith	.10	.30
155 Bill Romanowski	.10	.30
156 Stephen Boyd	.10	.30
157 James Stewart	.20	.50
158 Jason Taylor	.20	.50
159 Troy Drayton	.10	.30
160 Mark Fields	.10	.30
161 Jessie Armstead	.10	.30
162 James Jett	.20	.50
163 Bobby Taylor	.10	.30
164 Kimble Anders	.20	.50
165 Jimmy Smith	.20	.50
166 Quentin Coryatt	.10	.30
167 Bryant Westbrook	.10	.30
168 Neil Smith	.20	.50
169 Darren Woodson	.10	.30
170 Ray Buchanan	.10	.30
171 Earl Holmes	.10	.30
172 Ray Lewis	.30	.75
173 Steve Broussard	.10	.30
174 Derrick Brooks	.30	.75
175 Ken Harvey	.10	.30
176 Darryll Lewis	.10	.30
177 Derrick Rodgers	.10	.30
178 James McKnight	.30	.75
179 Cris Dishman	.10	.30
180 Hardy Nickerson	.10	.30
181 Charles Woodson RC	.75	2.00
182 Randy Moss RC	5.00	12.00
183 Stephen Alexander RC	.50	1.25
184 Samari Rolle RC	.30	.75
185 Jamie Duncan RC	.30	.75
186 Lance Schulters RC	.30	.75
187 Tony Parrish RC	.60	1.50
188 Corey Chavous RC	.60	1.50
189 Jammi German RC	.30	.75
190 Sam Cowart RC	.50	1.25
191 Donald Hayes RC	.50	1.25
192 R.W. McQuarters RC	.50	1.25
193 Az-Zahir Hakim RC	.60	1.50
194 C.Fuamatu-Ma'afala RC	.50	1.25
195 Allen Rossum RC	.50	1.25
196 Jon Ritchie RC	.50	1.25
197 Blake Spence RC	.30	.75
198 Brian Alford RC	.30	.75
199 Fred Weary RC	.30	.75
200 Rod Rutledge RC	.30	.75
201 Michael Myers RC	.30	.75
202 Rashaan Shehee RC	.50	1.25
203 Donovin Darius RC	.50	1.25
204 E.G. Green RC	.50	1.25
205 Vonnie Holliday RC	.50	1.25
206 Charlie Batch RC	.60	1.50
207 Michael Pittman RC	.75	2.00
208 Artrell Hawkins RC	.30	.75
209 Jonathan Quinn RC	.60	1.50
210 Kailee Wong RC	.30	.75
211 DeShea Townsend RC	.30	.75
212 Patrick Surtain RC	.60	1.50
213 Brian Kelly RC	.50	1.25
214 Tebucky Jones RC	.30	.75
215 Pete Gonzalez RC	.30	.75
216 Shaun Williams RC	.50	1.25
217 Scott Frost RC	.30	.75
218 Leonard Little RC	.60	1.50
219 Alonzo Mayes RC	.30	.75
220 Cordell Taylor RC	.30	.75

1998 Bowman Golden Anniversary

*STARS: 25X TO 60X BASIC CARDS
*RCs: 6X TO 15X BASIC CARDS
STATED ODDS 1:180
STATED PRINT RUN 50 SERIAL #'d SETS

1 Peyton Manning	175.00	300.00

1998 Bowman Interstate

COMPLETE SET (220)	75.00	200.00

*STARS: 1.5X TO 3X BASIC CARDS
*RC'S: .6X TO 1.5X BASIC CARDS
STATED ODDS 1:1

1998 Bowman Rookie Autographs

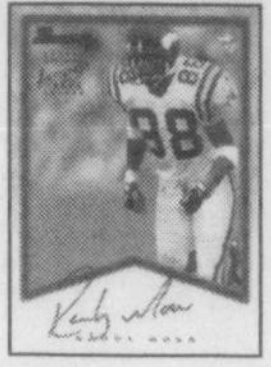

BLUE STATED ODDS 1:360

A1 Peyton Manning	350.00	500.00
A2 Andre Wadsworth	10.00	25.00
A3 Brian Griese	15.00	40.00
A4 Ryan Leaf	10.00	25.00
A5 Fred Taylor	12.50	30.00
A6 Robert Edwards	10.00	25.00
A7 Randy Moss	75.00	150.00
A8 Curtis Enis	10.00	25.00
A9 Kevin Dyson	10.00	25.00
A10 Charles Woodson	200.00	350.00
A11 Tim Dwight	12.50	30.00

1998 Bowman Rookie Autographs Gold

*GOLD FOILS: 1.2X TO 3X BLUE

1 Peyton Manning	800.00	1,200.00

1998 Bowman Rookie Autographs Silver

*SILVER FOIL: .6X TO 1.5X BLUE

1 Peyton Manning	500.00	800.00

1998 Bowman Chrome Preview

COMPLETE SET (10)	20.00	50.00
STATED ODDS 1:12		
*REFRACTORS: .75X TO 2X BASIC INSERTS		
REFRACTOR STATED ODDS 1:48		
BCP1 Peyton Manning	12.00	30.00
BCP2 Curtis Enis	.60	1.50
BCP3 Kevin Dyson	1.25	3.00
BCP4 Robert Edwards	.60	1.50
BCP5 Ryan Leaf	1.25	3.00
BCP6 Brett Favre	6.00	15.00
BCP7 John Elway	6.00	15.00
BCP8 Barry Sanders	5.00	12.00
BCP9 Kordell Stewart	1.50	4.00
BCP10 Terrell Davis	1.50	4.00

1998 Bowman Scout's Choice

COMPLETE SET (14)	20.00	50.00
STATED ODDS 1:12		
SC1 Peyton Manning	15.00	30.00
SC2 John Avery	1.00	2.50
SC3 Grant Wistrom	1.00	2.50
SC4 Kevin Dyson	1.25	3.00
SC5 Andre Wadsworth	1.00	2.50
SC6 Joe Jurevicius	1.25	3.00
SC7 Charles Woodson	1.50	4.00
SC8 Takeo Spikes	1.25	3.00
SC9 Fred Taylor	2.00	5.00
SC10 Ryan Leaf	1.25	3.00
SC11 Robert Edwards	1.00	2.50
SC12 Randy Moss	8.00	20.00
SC13 Pat Johnson	1.00	2.50
SC14 Curtis Enis	.60	1.50

1999 Bowman

The 1999 Bowman set was released in mid October of 1999 as a 220-card single series set featuring 150 veteran players along with 70 rookie cards. The veteran cards are done in a silver and red design action shot and the rookies are done in a silver and blue logo design. Key rookies found within this set include Ricky Williams, Edgerrin James, and Tim Couch. A 220-card Bowman Interstate Parallel was also produced at a rate of 1 per pack which shows which state each player originated from. Also exists is a 220 card Bowman Gold Parallel which is identical to the regular base set card exept for the Team name being done in a gold foil. Authentic Signed Rookie autographed cards are also randomly inserted in packs. Also included is the 10 card Late Bloomers/Early Risers insert set featuring top second year players as well as veteran stars such as Dan Marino and Mark Brunell.

COMPLETE SET (220)	15.00	40.00
1 Dan Marino	.75	2.00
2 Michael Westbrook	.15	.40
3 Yancey Thigpen	.15	.40
4 Tony Martin	.20	.50
5 Michael Strahan	.20	.50
6 Dedric Ward	.15	.40
7 Joey Galloway	.20	.50
8 Bobby Engram	.20	.50
9 Frank Sanders	.15	.40
10 Jake Plummer	.20	.50
11 Eddie Kennison	.20	.50
12 Curtis Martin	.25	.60
13 Chris Spielman	.20	.50
14 Trent Dilfer	.20	.50
15 Tim Biakabutuka	.20	.50
16 Elvis Grbac	.15	.40
17 Charlie Batch	.20	.50
18 Takeo Spikes	.15	.40
19 Tony Banks	.20	.50
20 Doug Flutie	.25	.60
21 Ty Law	.20	.50
22 Isaac Bruce	.25	.60
23 James Jett	.15	.40
24 Kent Graham	.15	.40
25 Derrick Mayes	.15	.40
26 Amani Toomer	.20	.50
27 Ray Lewis	.25	.60
28 Shawn Springs	.15	.40
29 Warren Sapp	.20	.50
30 Jamal Anderson	.20	.50
31 Byron Bam Morris	.15	.40
32 Johnnie Morton	.20	.50
33 Terance Mathis	.15	.40
34 Terrell Davis	.25	.60
35 John Randle	.20	.50
36 Vinny Testaverde	.20	.50
37 Junior Seau	.25	.60
38 Reidel Anthony	.15	.40
39 Brad Johnson	.20	.50

40 Emmitt Smith .60 1.50
41 Mo Lewis .15 .40
42 Terry Glenn .20 .50
43 Dorsey Levens .20 .50
44 Thurman Thomas .25 .60
45 Rob Moore .15 .40
46 Corey Dillon .20 .50
47 Jessie Armstead .20 .50
48 Marshall Faulk .25 .60
49 Charles Woodson .25 .60
50 John Elway .75 2.00
51 Kevin Dyson .15 .40
52 Tony Simmons .15 .40
53 Keenan McCardell .20 .50
54 O.J. Santiago .15 .40
55 Jermaine Lewis .15 .40
56 Herman Moore .20 .50
57 Gary Brown .15 .40
58 Jim Harbaugh .20 .50
59 Mike Alstott .25 .60
60 Brett Favre .75 2.00
61 Tim Brown .25 .60
62 Steve McNair .25 .60
63 Ben Coates .20 .50
64 Jerome Pathon .15 .40
65 Ray Buchanan .15 .40
66 Troy Aikman .40 1.00
67 Andre Reed .25 .60
68 Bubby Brister .15 .40
69 Karim Abdul-Jabbar .20 .50
70 Peyton Manning .75 2.00
71 Charles Johnson .15 .40
72 Natrone Means .20 .50
73 Michael Sinclair .15 .40
74 Skip Hicks .15 .40
75 Derrick Alexander .15 .40
76 Wayne Chrebet .20 .50
77 Rod Smith .20 .50
78 Carl Pickens .20 .50
79 Adrian Murrell .20 .50
80 Fred Taylor .20 .50
81 Eric Moulds .20 .50
82 Lawrence Phillips .20 .50
83 Marvin Harrison .25 .60
84 Cris Carter .25 .60
85 Ike Hilliard .20 .50
86 Hines Ward .25 .60
87 Terrell Owens .25 .60
88 Ricky Proehl .15 .40
89 Bert Emanuel .20 .50
90 Randy Moss .25 .60
91 Aaron Glenn .15 .40
92 Robert Smith .20 .50
93 Andre Hastings .15 .40
94 Jake Reed .20 .50
95 Curtis Enis .15 .40
96 Andre Wadsworth .15 .40
97 Ed McCaffrey .20 .50
98 Zach Thomas .25 .60
99 Kerry Collins .20 .50
100 Drew Bledsoe .25 .60
101 Germane Crowell .15 .40
102 Bryan Still .15 .40
103 Chad Brown .15 .40
104 Jacquez Green .15 .40
105 Garrison Hearst .20 .50
106 Napoleon Kaufman .15 .40
107 Ricky Watters .20 .50
108 O.J. McDuffie .20 .50
109 Keyshawn Johnson .20 .50
110 Jerome Bettis .25 .60
111 Duce Staley .20 .50
112 Curtis Conway .20 .50
113 Chris Chandler .20 .50
114 Marcus Nash .15 .40
115 Stephen Alexander .15 .40
116 Darnay Scott .15 .40
117 Bruce Smith .25 .60
118 Priest Holmes .25 .60
119 Mark Brunell .20 .50
120 Jerry Rice .50 1.25
121 Randall Cunningham .25 .60
122 Scott Mitchell .15 .40
123 Antonio Freeman .20 .50
124 Kordell Stewart .20 .50
125 Jon Kitna .20 .50
126 Ahman Green .20 .50
127 Warrick Dunn .20 .50
128 Robert Brooks .20 .50
129 Derrick Thomas .25 .60
130 Steve Young .30 .75
131 Peter Boulware .15 .40
132 Michael Irvin .25 .60
133 Shannon Sharpe .25 .60
134 Jimmy Smith .20 .50
135 John Avery .15 .40
136 Fred Lane .15 .40
137 Trent Green .20 .50
138 Andre Rison .20 .50
139 Antowain Smith .15 .40
140 Eddie George .20 .50
141 Jeff Blake .20 .50
142 Rocket Ismail .20 .50
143 Rickey Dudley .15 .40
144 Courtney Hawkins .15 .40
145 Mikhael Ricks .15 .40
146 J.J. Stokes .15 .40
147 Levon Kirkland .15 .40
148 Deion Sanders .25 .60
149 Barry Sanders .60 1.50
150 Tiki Barber .25 .60
151 David Boston RC .30 .75
152 Chris McAlister RC .30 .75
153 Peerless Price RC .30 .75
154 D'Wayne Bates RC .25 .60
155 Cade McNown RC .30 .75
156 Akili Smith RC .30 .75
157 Kevin Johnson RC .30 .75
158 Tim Couch RC .40 1.00
159 Sedrick Irvin RC .25 .60
160 Chris Claiborne RC .25 .60
161 Edgerrin James RC .50 1.25
162 Mike Cloud RC .25 .60
163 Cecil Collins RC .25 .60
164 James Johnson RC .25 .60
165 Rob Konrad RC .25 .60
166 Daunte Culpepper RC .40 1.00
167 Kevin Faulk RC .40 1.00
168 Donovan McNabb RC 3.00 8.00
169 Troy Edwards RC .30 .75
170 Amos Zereoue RC .30 .75
171 Karsten Bailey RC .25 .60
172 Brock Huard RC .30 .75
173 Joe Germaine RC .30 .75
174 Torry Holt RC .60 1.50
175 Shaun King RC .30 .75
176 Jevon Kearse RC .40 1.00
177 Champ Bailey RC .75 2.00
178 Ebenezer Ekuban RC .25 .60
179 Andy Katzenmoyer .30 .75
180 Antoine Winfield RC .25 .60
181 Jermaine Fazande RC .25 .60
182 Ricky Williams RC .60 1.50
183 Joel Makovicka RC .25 .60
184 Reginald Kelly RC .25 .60
185 Brandon Stokley RC .40 1.00
186 L.C. Stevens RC .25 .60
187 Marty Booker RC .30 .75
188 Jerry Azumah .25 .60
189 Ted White RC .25 .60
190 Scott Covington RC .25 .60
191 Tim Alexander RC .25 .60
192 Darrin Chiaverini RC .25 .60
193 Dat Nguyen RC .40 1.00
194 Wane McGarity RC .25 .60
195 Al Wilson RC .40 1.00
196 Travis McGriff RC .25 .60
197 Stacey Mack RC .25 .60
198 Antuan Edwards RC .25 .60
199 Aaron Brooks RC .40 1.00
200 De'Mond Parker RC .25 .60
201 Jed Weaver RC .25 .60
202 Madre Hill RC .25 .60
203 Jim Kleinsasser RC .40 1.00
204 Michael Bishop RC .30 .75
205 Michael Basnight RC .25 .60
206 Sean Bennett RC .25 .60
207 Dameane Douglas RC .25 .60
208 Na Brown RC .25 .60
209 Patrick Kerney RC .30 .75
210 Malcolm Johnson RC .25 .60
211 Dre Bly RC .40 1.00
212 Terry Jackson RC .25 .60
213 Eugene Baker RC .25 .60
214 Autry Denson RC .25 .60
215 Darnell McDonald RC .25 .60
216 Charlie Rogers RC .25 .60
217 Joe Montgomery RC .25 .60
218 Cecil Martin RC .25 .60
219 Larry Parker RC .30 .75
220 Mike Peterson RC .30 .75

1999 Bowman Gold

*1-150 VETS: 6X TO 15X BASIC CARDS
*151-220 ROOKIES: 4X TO 10X
STATED PRINT RUN 99 SER.#'d SETS

1999 Bowman Interstate

COMPLETE SET (220) 60.00 150.00
*1-150 VETS: 1.2X TO 3X BASIC CARDS
*151-220 ROOKIES: .8X TO 2X
ONE INTERSTATE PER PACK

1999 Bowman Autographs

GOLD STATED ODDS 1:850
SILVER STATED ODDS 1:212
BLUE STATED ODDS 1:180
A1 Randy Moss G 40.00 100.00
A2 Akili Smith G 10.00 25.00
A3 Edgerrin James G 20.00 50.00
A4 Ricky Williams G 15.00 40.00
A5 Torry Holt G 12.00 30.00
A6 Daunte Culpepper G 15.00 40.00
A8 Tim Couch S 10.00 25.00
A9 Champ Bailey S 12.00 30.00
A10 David Boston S 7.50 20.00
A11 Chris Claiborne S 7.50 20.00
A12 Chris McAlister S 7.50 20.00
A13 Rob Konrad S 6.00 15.00
A14 Mike Cloud S 6.00 15.00
A15 Jermaine Fazande S 6.00 15.00
A16 Brock Huard S 10.00 25.00
A17 Joe Germaine S 6.00 15.00
A18 Sedrick Irvin S 6.00 15.00
A19 Cecil Collins S 6.00 15.00
A20 Karsten Bailey S 6.00 15.00
A21 Antoine Winfield S 7.50 20.00
A22 Cade McNown B 5.00 12.00
A23 Troy Edwards B 6.00 15.00
A24 Jevon Kearse B 10.00 25.00
A26 Kevin Johnson B 5.00 12.00
A27 James Johnson B 6.00 15.00
A28 Kevin Faulk B 7.50 20.00
A29 Shaun King B 6.00 15.00
A30 Peerless Price B 7.50 20.00
A31 D'Wayne Bates B 5.00 12.00
A32 Amos Zereoue B 6.00 15.00

1999 Bowman Late Bloomers/Early Risers

COMPLETE SET (10) 10.00 25.00
STATED ODDS 1:12
U1 Fred Taylor .75 2.00
U2 Peyton Manning 2.50 6.00
U3 Dan Marino 2.50 6.00
U4 Barry Sanders 2.50 6.00
U5 Randy Moss 2.00 5.00
U6 Mark Brunell .75 2.00
U7 Jamal Anderson .75 2.00
U8 Curtis Martin .75 2.00
U9 Wayne Chrebet .50 1.25
U10 Terrell Davis .75 2.00

1999 Bowman Scout's Choice

COMPLETE SET (21) 25.00 50.00
STATED ODDS 1:12
SC1 David Boston .60 1.50
SC2 Champ Bailey .75 2.00
SC3 Edgerrin James 2.50 6.00
SC4 Mike Cloud .50 1.25
SC5 Kevin Faulk .60 1.50
SC6 Troy Edwards .50 1.25
SC7 Cecil Collins .25 .60
SC8 Peerless Price .60 1.50
SC9 Torry Holt 1.50 4.00
SC10 Rob Konrad .60 1.50
SC11 Akili Smith .50 1.25
SC12 Daunte Culpepper 2.50 6.00
SC13 D'Wayne Bates .50 1.25
SC14 Donovan McNabb 3.00 8.00
SC15 James Johnson .50 1.25
SC16 Cade McNown .50 1.25
SC17 Kevin Johnson .60 1.50
SC18 Ricky Williams 1.25 3.00
SC19 Karsten Bailey .50 1.25
SC20 Tim Couch .60 1.50
SC21 Shaun King .50 1.25

2000 Bowman Promos

This 6-card set was released at various Topps sponsored events and through its dealer network to promote the 2000 Bowman football release. The cards look very similar to the base set except for the card numbering on the backs.

COMPLETE SET (6) 2.00 5.00
PP1 Stephen Davis .50 1.25
PP2 Charlie Batch .30 .75
PP3 Patrick Jeffers .20 .50
PP4 Torry Holt .50 1.25
PP5 Akili Smith .20 .50
PP6 Fred Taylor .50 1.25

2000 Bowman

Released in early October, Bowman features a 240-card base set. Card numbers 1-140 picture veterans, card numbers 141-165 focus on NFL Europe Prospects, and card numbers 166-240 picture 2000 NFL Draft Picks. Base cards are full color action shots with a brown and black border and gold foil highlights. Bowman was packaged in 24-pack boxes with each pack containing 10 cards and carried a suggested retail price of $3.00. Hobby Collector Packs were released as well, and were packaged in 12-pack boxes with packs containing 21 cards and carried a suggested retail price of $6.00.

COMPLETE SET (240) 30.00 80.00
1 Eddie George .20 .50
2 Ike Hilliard .20 .50
3 Terrell Owens .25 .60
4 James Stewart .15 .40
5 Joey Galloway .20 .50
6 Jake Reed .20 .50
7 Derrick Alexander .15 .40
8 Jeff George .20 .50
9 Kerry Collins .20 .50
10 Tony Gonzalez .25 .60
11 Marcus Robinson .20 .50
12 Charles Woodson .25 .60
13 Germane Crowell .15 .40
14 Yancey Thigpen .15 .40
15 Tony Martin .20 .50
16 Frank Sanders .15 .40
17 Napoleon Kaufman .20 .50
18 Jay Fiedler .20 .50
19 Patrick Jeffers .20 .50
20 Steve McNair .25 .60
21 Herman Moore .20 .50
22 Tim Brown .25 .60
23 Olandis Gary .20 .50
24 Corey Dillon .20 .50
25 Warren Sapp .20 .50
26 Curtis Enis .15 .40
27 Vinny Testaverde .20 .50
28 Tim Biakabutuka .20 .50
29 Kevin Johnson .15 .40
30 Charlie Batch .20 .50
31 Jermaine Fazande .15 .40
32 Shaun King .15 .40
33 Errict Rhett .20 .50
34 O.J. McDuffie .20 .50
35 Bruce Smith .25 .60
36 Antonio Freeman .20 .50
37 Tim Couch .20 .50
38 Duce Staley .20 .50
39 Jeff Blake .20 .50
40 Jim Harbaugh .20 .50
41 Jeff Graham .15 .40
42 Drew Bledsoe .25 .60
43 Mike Alstott .25 .60
44 Terance Mathis .15 .40
45 Antowain Smith .20 .50
46 Johnnie Morton .20 .50
47 Chris Chandler .20 .50
48 Keith Poole .15 .40
49 Ricky Watters .20 .50
50 Darnay Scott .20 .50
51 Damon Huard .20 .50
52 Peerless Price .20 .50
53 Brian Griese .20 .50
54 Frank Wycheck .20 .50
55 Kevin Dyson .20 .50
56 Junior Seau .25 .60
57 Curtis Conway .20 .50
58 Jamal Anderson .20 .50
59 Jim Miller .15 .40
60 Rob Johnson .20 .50
61 Mark Brunell .20 .50
62 Wayne Chrebet .20 .50
63 James Johnson .15 .40
64 Sean Dawkins .15 .40
65 Stephen Davis .20 .50
66 Daunte Culpepper .20 .50
67 Doug Flutie .25 .60
68 Pete Mitchell .15 .40
69 Bill Schroeder .20 .50
70 Terrence Wilkins .15 .40
71 Cade McNown .15 .40
72 Muhsin Muhammad .20 .50
73 E.G. Green .15 .40
74 Edgerrin James .25 .60
75 Troy Edwards .15 .40
76 Terry Glenn .20 .50
77 Tony Banks .15 .40
78 Derrick Mayes .15 .40
79 Curtis Martin .25 .60
80 Kordell Stewart .20 .50
81 Amani Toomer .20 .50
82 Dorsey Levens .20 .50
83 Brad Johnson .20 .50
84 Ed McCaffrey .20 .50
85 Charlie Garner .20 .50
86 Brett Favre .75 2.00
87 J.J. Stokes .20 .50
88 Steve Young .30 .75
89 Jonathan Linton .15 .40
90 Isaac Bruce .25 .60
91 Shawn Jefferson .15 .40
92 Rod Smith .20 .50
93 Champ Bailey .20 .50
94 Ricky Williams .25 .60
95 Priest Holmes .25 .60
96 Corey Bradford .15 .40
97 Eric Moulds .20 .50
98 Warrick Dunn .20 .50
99 Jevon Kearse .20 .50
100 Albert Connell .15 .40
101 Az-Zahir Hakim .15 .40
102 Marvin Harrison .25 .60
103 Qadry Ismail .20 .50
104 Oronde Gadsden .20 .50
105 Rob Moore .15 .40
106 Marshall Faulk .25 .60
107 Steve Beuerlein .20 .50
108 Torry Holt .25 .60
109 Donovan McNabb .25 .60
110 Rich Gannon .20 .50
111 Jerome Bettis .25 .60
112 Peyton Manning .60 1.50
113 Cris Carter .25 .60
114 Jake Plummer .20 .50
115 Kent Graham .15 .40
116 Keenan McCardell .20 .50
117 Tim Dwight .20 .50
118 Fred Taylor .25 .60
119 Jerry Rice .50 1.25
120 Michael Westbrook .15 .40
121 Kurt Warner .40 1.00
122 Jimmy Smith .20 .50
123 Emmitt Smith .60 1.50
124 Terrell Davis .25 .60
125 Randy Moss .25 .60
126 Akili Smith .15 .40
127 Rocket Ismail .20 .50
128 Jon Kitna .20 .50
129 Elvis Grbac .15 .40
130 Wesley Walls .15 .40
131 Torrance Small .15 .40
132 Tyrone Wheatley .15 .40
133 Carl Pickens .20 .50
134 Zach Thomas .25 .60
135 Jacquez Green .15 .40
136 Robert Smith .20 .50
137 Keyshawn Johnson .20 .50
138 Matthew Hatchette .15 .40
139 Troy Aikman .40 1.00
140 Charles Johnson .15 .40
141 Terry Battle EP .15 .40
142 Pepe Pearson EP RC .15 .40
143 Cory Sauter EP .15 .40
144 Brian Shay EP .15 .40
145 Marcus Crandell EP RC .15 .40
146 Danny Wuerffel EP .25 .60
147 L.C. Stevens EP .15 .40
148 Ted White EP .15 .40
149 Matt Lytle EP RC .15 .40
150 Vershan Jackson EP RC .15 .40
151 Mario Bailey EP .15 .40
152 Darryl Daniel EP RC .15 .40
153 Sean Morey EP RC .15 .40
154 Jim Kubiak EP RC .15 .40
155 Aaron Stecker EP RC .20 .50
156 Damon Dunn EP RC .15 .40
157 Kevin Daft EP .15 .40
158 Corey Thomas EP .15 .40
159 Deon Mitchell EP RC .20 .50
160 Todd Floyd EP RC .15 .40
161 Norman Miller EP RC .15 .40
162 Jeremaine Copeland EP .15 .40
163 Michael Blair EP .15 .40
164 Ron Powlus EP RC .25 .60
165 Pat Barnes EP .20 .50
166 Dez White RC .30 .75
167 Trung Canidate RC .30 .75
168 Thomas Jones RC .50 1.25
169 Courtney Brown RC .30 .75
170 Jamal Lewis RC .40 1.00
171 Chris Redman RC .30 .75
172 Ron Dayne RC .40 1.00
173 Chad Pennington RC .60 1.50
174 Plaxico Burress RC .40 1.00
175 R.Jay Soward RC .25 .60
176 Travis Taylor RC .30 .75
177 Shaun Alexander RC .50 1.25
178 Brian Urlacher RC 2.50 6.00
179 Danny Farmer RC .25 .60
180 Tee Martin RC .40 1.00
181 Sylvester Morris RC .25 .60
182 Curtis Keaton RC .25 .60
183 Peter Warrick RC .40 1.00
184 Anthony Becht RC .30 .75
185 Travis Prentice RC .30 .75
186 J.R. Redmond RC .25 .60
187 Bubba Franks RC .40 1.00
188 Ron Dugans RC .25 .60
189 Reuben Droughns RC .40 1.00
190 Corey Simon RC .30 .75
191 Joe Hamilton RC .25 .60
192 Laveranues Coles RC .40 1.00
193 Todd Pinkston RC .25 .60
194 Jerry Porter RC .40 1.00
195 Dennis Northcutt RC .30 .75
196 Tim Rattay RC .30 .75
197 Giovanni Carmazzi RC .25 .60
198 Mareno Philyaw RC .25 .60
199 Avion Black RC .25 .60
200 Chafie Fields RC .25 .60
201 Rondell Mealey RC .25 .60
202 Troy Walters RC .25 .60
203 Frank Moreau RC .25 .60
204 Vaughn Sanders RC .25 .60
205 Sherrod Gideon RC .25 .60
206 Doug Chapman RC .25 .60
207 Marcus Knight RC .25 .60
208 Jamel White RC .25 .60
209 Windrell Hayes RC .25 .60
210 Reggie Jones RC .25 .60
211 Jarious Jackson RC .30 .75
212 Ronney Jenkins RC .25 .60
213 Quinton Spotwood RC .25 .60
214 Rob Morris RC .30 .75
215 Gari Scott RC .25 .60
216 Kevin Thompson RC .25 .60
217 Trevor Insley RC .25 .60
218 Frank Murphy RC .25 .60
219 Patrick Pass RC .30 .75
220 Mike Anderson RC .40 1.00
221 Derrius Thompson RC .25 .60
222 John Abraham RC .40 1.00
223 Dante Hall RC .40 1.00
224 Chad Morton RC .40 1.00
225 Ahmed Plummer RC .25 .60
226 Julian Peterson RC .40 1.00
227 Mike Green RC .40 1.00
228 Michael Wiley RC .25 .60
229 Spergon Wynn RC .30 .75
230 Trevor Gaylor RC .25 .60
231 Doug Johnson RC .30 .75
232 Marc Bulger RC .40 1.00
233 Ron Dixon RC .25 .60
234 Aaron Shea RC .30 .75
235 Thomas Hamner RC .25 .60
236 Tom Brady RC 30.00 60.00
237 Deltha O'Neal RC .30 .75
238 Todd Husak RC .25 .60
239 Erron Kinney RC .25 .60
240 JaJuan Dawson RC .25 .60

2000 Bowman Gold

*VETS 1-165: 6X TO 15X BASIC CARDS
*ROOKIE 166-240: 5X TO 12X BASIC CARDS
GOLD/99 STATED ODDS 1:60
GOLD PRINT RUN 99 SER.#'d SETS
236 Tom Brady 250.00 400.00

2000 Bowman ROY Promotion

*ROOKIES: 2.5X TO 6X BASIC CARDS
STATED ODDS 1:76
178 Brian Urlacher WIN 40.00 80.00
220 Mike Anderson WIN 20.00 50.00
236 Tom Brady 300.00 500.00

2000 Bowman Autographs

GROUP A STATED ODDS 1:7680
GROUP B STATED ODDS 1:480
GROUP C STATED ODDS 1:320
GROUP D STATED ODDS 1:111
GROUP E STATED ODDS 1:138
GROUP F STATED ODDS 1:14346
OVERALL ODDS 1:46 HOBBY
AB Anthony Becht S 5.00 12.00
BU Brian Urlacher B 25.00 50.00
CB Courtney Brown G 6.00 15.00
CK Curtis Keaton B 4.00 10.00
CP Chad Pennington G 12.00 30.00
CR Chris Redman G 6.00 15.00
CS Corey Simon B 5.00 12.00
DF Danny Farmer S 4.00 10.00
DN Dennis Northcutt B 5.00 12.00
DW Dez White B 5.00 12.00
GC Giovanni Carmazzi S 4.00 10.00
JH Joe Hamilton B 4.00 10.00
JL Jamal Lewis S 6.00 15.00
JP Jerry Porter G 8.00 20.00
LC Laveranues Coles B 6.00 15.00
MB Marc Bulger S 6.00 15.00
PB Plaxico Burress G 8.00 20.00
PW Peter Warrick G 8.00 20.00
RD Ron Dayne G 8.00 20.00
SA Shaun Alexander G 10.00 25.00
SM Sylvester Morris B 4.00 10.00
TC Trung Canidate S 5.00 12.00
TG Trevor Gaylor S 4.00 10.00
TJ Thomas Jones G 10.00 25.00
TM Tee Martin B 6.00 15.00
TP Travis Prentice B 5.00 12.00
TR Tim Rattay B 5.00 12.00
TT Travis Taylor S 5.00 12.00
DFR Bubba Franks S 6.00 15.00
RDR Reuben Droughns S 6.00 15.00
RDU Ron Dugans B 4.00 10.00
TPI Todd Pinkston G 5.00 12.00

2000 Bowman Bowman's Best Previews

COMPLETE SET (10) 8.00 20.00
STATED ODDS 1:24, 1:11 HCP
BBP1 Peyton Manning 2.00 5.00
BBP2 Stephen Davis .60 1.50
BBP3 Marshall Faulk .75 2.00
BBP4 Marvin Harrison .75 2.00
BBP5 Brett Favre 2.50 6.00
BBP6 Terrell Davis .75 2.00
BBP7 Eddie George .60 1.50
BBP8 Kurt Warner 1.25 3.00
BBP9 Edgerrin James .75 2.00
BBP10 Randy Moss .75 2.00

2000 Bowman Breakthrough Discoveries

COMPLETE SET (10) 3.00 8.00
STATED ODDS 1:12, 1:5 HCP
BD1 Jerry Rice 1.00 2.50
BD2 Kurt Warner .75 2.00
BD3 Wayne Chrebet .40 1.00
BD4 Isaac Bruce .50 1.25
BD5 Steve McNair .50 1.25
BD6 Shannon Sharpe .50 1.25
BD7 Andre Reed .50 1.25
BD8 Jimmy Smith .40 1.00
BD9 Darrell Green .40 1.00
BD10 Randy Moss .50 1.25

2000 Bowman Draft Day Relics

STATED ODDS 1:386, 1:196 HCP
CB Courtney Brown 6.00 15.00
CS Chris Samuels 6.00 15.00
PW Peter Warrick 8.00 20.00
TJ Thomas Jones 10.00 25.00

2000 Bowman Road to Success

COMPLETE SET (10) 8.00 20.00
STATED ODDS 1:18, 1:8 HCP
R1 Chad Pennington 1.00 2.50
Randy Moss
R2 Jamal Lewis .60 1.50
Peyton Manning
R3 R.Jay Soward .40 1.00
Keyshawn Johnson
R4 Thomas Jones .75 2.00
Germane Crowell
R5 Giovanni Carmazzi .50 1.25
Wayne Chrebet
R6 Travis Taylor .50 1.25
Ike Hilliard
R7 Plaxico Burress .60 1.50
Muhsin Muhammad
R8 Todd Pinkston .40 1.00
Brett Favre
R9 Sylvester Morris .40 1.00
Jimmy Smith
R10 Peter Warrick .60 1.50
Deion Sanders

2000 Bowman Rookie Rising

COMPLETE SET (10) 2.50 6.00
STATED ODDS 1:12, 1:5 HCP
RR1 Jevon Kearse .50 1.25
RR2 Edgerrin James .60 1.50
RR3 Champ Bailey .50 1.25
RR4 Zach Thomas .60 1.50
RR5 Marvin Harrison .60 1.50
RR6 Kevin Johnson .40 1.00
RR7 Curtis Martin .60 1.50
RR8 Jerome Bettis .60 1.50
RR9 Fred Taylor .60 1.50
RR10 Terry Glenn .50 1.25

2000 Bowman Scout's Choice

COMPLETE SET (20) 7.50 20.00
STATED ODDS 1:18, 1:8 HCP
SC1 Shaun Alexander .50 1.25
SC2 Bubba Franks .40 1.00
SC3 Travis Prentice .30 .75
SC4 Peter Warrick .40 1.00
SC5 Plaxico Burress .40 1.00
SC6 Corey Simon .30 .75
SC7 Courtney Brown .30 .75
SC8 Tee Martin .40 1.00
SC9 Brian Urlacher 1.50 4.00
SC10 J.R. Redmond .25 .60
SC11 Anthony Becht .30 .75
SC12 Thomas Jones .50 1.25
SC13 Giovanni Carmazzi .25 .60
SC14 Jamal Lewis .40 1.00
SC15 Ron Dayne .40 1.00
SC16 R.Jay Soward .25 .60
SC17 Travis Taylor .30 .75
SC18 Chad Pennington .60 1.50
SC19 Sylvester Morris .25 .60
SC20 Chris Redman .30 .75

2001 Bowman

Issued in October 2001, this 275 card set continued the Topps tradition of using this brand to feature many young players. The cards were issued in ten-card packs with a SRP of $3 or 21-card HTA packs with a SRP of $6. The regular packs came 24 packs to a box while the HTA packs came 12 packs to a box. Cards from 1-130 are veterans while cards 131 through 275 are rookies.

COMPLETE SET (275) 25.00 60.00
1 Emmitt Smith .60 1.50
2 James Stewart .15 .40
3 Jeff Graham .15 .40
4 Keyshawn Johnson .20 .50
5 Stephen Davis .20 .50
6 Chad Lewis .15 .40
7 Drew Bledsoe .25 .60
8 Fred Taylor .25 .60
9 Mike Anderson .20 .50
10 Tony Gonzalez .25 .60
11 Aaron Brooks .20 .50
12 Vinny Testaverde .20 .50
13 Jerome Bettis .25 .60
14 Marshall Faulk .25 .60
15 Jeff Garcia .20 .50
16 Terry Glenn .20 .50
17 Jay Fiedler .20 .50
18 Ahman Green .25 .60
19 Cade McNown .20 .50
20 Rob Johnson .20 .50
21 Jamal Anderson .20 .50
22 Corey Dillon .20 .50
23 Jake Plummer .20 .50
24 Rod Smith .20 .50
25 Trent Green .25 .60
26 Ricky Williams .25 .60
27 Charlie Garner .20 .50
28 Shaun Alexander .25 .60
29 Jeff George .20 .50
30 Torry Holt .20 .50
31 James Thrash .20 .50
32 Rich Gannon .20 .50
33 Ron Dayne .20 .50
34 Dedric Ward .15 .40
35 Edgerrin James .25 .60
36 Cris Carter .25 .60
37 Derrick Mason .20 .50
38 Brad Johnson .20 .50
39 Charlie Batch .20 .50
40 Joey Galloway .20 .50
41 James Allen .15 .40
42 Tim Biakabutuka .15 .40
43 Ray Lewis .25 .60
44 David Boston .15 .40
45 Kevin Johnson .15 .40
46 Jimmy Smith .20 .50
47 Joe Horn .20 .50
48 Terrell Owens .25 .60
49 Eddie George .25 .60
50 Brett Favre .75 2.00
51 Wayne Chrebet .20 .50
52 Hines Ward .25 .60
53 Warrick Dunn .25 .60
54 Matt Hasselbeck .25 .60
55 Tiki Barber .25 .60
56 Lamar Smith .20 .50
57 Tim Couch .15 .40
58 Eric Moulds .20 .50
59 Shawn Jefferson .15 .40
60 Donald Hayes .15 .40
61 Brian Urlacher .30 .75
62 Steve McNair .25 .60
63 Kurt Warner .40 1.00
64 Tim Brown .25 .60
65 Troy Brown .20 .50
66 Albert Connell .15 .40
67 Peyton Manning .60 1.50
68 Peter Warrick .20 .50
69 Elvis Grbac .20 .50
70 Chris Chandler .20 .50
71 Akili Smith .15 .40
72 Keenan McCardell .20 .50
73 Kerry Collins .20 .50
74 Junior Seau .25 .60
75 Donovan McNabb .25 .60
76 Tony Banks .15 .40
77 Steve Beuerlein .20 .50
78 Daunte Culpepper .20 .50
79 Darrell Jackson .20 .50
80 Isaac Bruce .25 .60
81 Tyrone Wheatley .20 .50
82 Derrick Alexander .15 .40
83 Germane Crowell .15 .40
84 Jon Kitna .20 .50
85 Jamal Lewis .25 .60
86 Ed McCaffrey .20 .50
87 Mark Brunell .20 .50
88 Jeff Blake .20 .50
89 Duce Staley .20 .50
90 Doug Flutie .25 .60
91 Kordell Stewart .20 .50
92 Randy Moss .25 .60
93 Marvin Harrison .25 .60
94 Muhsin Muhammad .20 .50
95 Brian Griese .20 .50
96 Antonio Freeman .25 .60
97 Amani Toomer .20 .50
98 Oronde Gadsden .15 .40
99 Curtis Martin .25 .60
100 Jerry Rice .50 1.25
101 Michael Pittman .20 .50
102 Shannon Sharpe .25 .60
103 Peerless Price .15 .40
104 Bill Schroeder .20 .50
105 Ike Hilliard .20 .50
106 Freddie Jones .15 .40
107 Tai Streets .15 .40
108 Ricky Watters .20 .50
109 Az-Zahir Hakim .15 .40
110 Jacquez Green .15 .40
111 Bobby Shaw .15 .40
112 Johnnie Morton .20 .50
113 Laveranues Coles .20 .50
114 Chad Pennington .25 .60
115 Champ Bailey .25 .60
116 Charles Woodson .25 .60
117 Curtis Conway .20 .50
118 Marcus Robinson .20 .50
119 Michael Westbrook .15 .40
120 Mike Alstott .20 .50
121 Priest Holmes .25 .60
122 Qadry Ismail .20 .50
123 Rocket Ismail .20 .50
124 Shawn Bryson .15 .40
125 Jeff Lewis .15 .40
126 Jeremy Mcdaniel .15 .40
127 Terance Mathis .15 .40
128 Travis Prentice .15 .40
129 Warren Sapp .20 .50
130 Jevon Kearse .20 .50
131 George Layne RC .30 .75
132 Correll Buckhalter RC .50 1.25
133 Tony Stewart RC .40 1.00
134 Chris Barnes RC .30 .75
135 A.J. Feeley RC .40 1.00
136 Margin Hooks RC .30 .75
137 Anthony Henry RC .50 1.25
138 Dwight Smith RC .30 .75
139 Torrance Marshall RC .30 .75
140 Gary Baxter RC .30 .75
141 Derek Combs RC .30 .75
142 Marcus Bell DT RC .30 .75
143 Delawrence Grant RC .30 .75
144 Jameel Cook RC .40 1.00
145 Eric Downing RC .30 .75
146 Marlon McCree RC .30 .75
147 Tay Cody RC .30 .75
148 Mario Monds RC .30 .75
149 Kenny Smith RC .30 .75
150 Sedrick Hodge RC .30 .75
151 Marcus Stroud RC .40 1.00
152 Steve Smith RC 1.00 2.50
153 Tyrone Robertson RC .30 .75
154 James Reed RC .30 .75
155 Kris Kocurek RC .30 .75
156 Dan O'Leary RC .30 .75
157 Harold Blackmon RC .30 .75
158 Fred Smoot RC .50 1.25
159 Billy Baber RC .30 .75
160 Jarrod Cooper RC .40 1.00
161 Travis Henry RC .40 1.00
162 David Terrell RC .40 1.00
163 Josh Heupel RC .50 1.25
164 Drew Brees RC 6.00 15.00
165 T.J. Houshmandzadeh RC .60 1.50
166 Rod Gardner RC .40 1.00
167 Richard Seymour RC .50 1.25
168 Koren Robinson RC .40 1.00
169 Scotty Anderson RC .30 .75
170 Marques Tuiasosopo RC .40 1.00
171 John Capel RC .30 .75
172 LaMont Jordan RC .50 1.25
173 James Jackson RC .30 .75
174 Bobby Newcombe RC .40 1.00
175 Anthony Thomas RC .50 1.25
176 Dan Alexander RC .40 1.00
177 Quincy Carter RC .40 1.00
178 Morlon Greenwood RC .30 .75
179 Robert Ferguson RC .50 1.25
180 Sage Rosenfels RC .50 1.25
181 Michael Stone RC .30 .75
182 Chris Weinke RC .40 1.00
183 Travis Minor RC .40 1.00
184 Gerard Warren RC .40 1.00
185 Jamar Fletcher RC .30 .75
186 Andre Carter RC .40 1.00
187 Deuce McAllister RC .50 1.25
188 Dan Morgan RC .40 1.00
189 Todd Heap RC .50 1.25
190 Snoop Minnis RC .30 .75
191 Will Allen RC .50 1.25
192 Freddie Mitchell RC .30 .75
193 Rudi Johnson RC .50 1.25
194 Kevan Barlow RC .40 1.00
195 Jamie Winborn RC .40 1.00
196 Onomo Ojo RC .30 .75
197 Leonard Davis RC .50 1.25
198 Santana Moss RC .60 1.50
199 Chris Chambers RC .50 1.25
200 Michael Vick RC 5.00 12.00
201 Michael Bennett RC .40 1.00
202 Mike McMahon RC .40 1.00
203 Jonathan Carter RC .30 .75
204 Jamal Reynolds RC .30 .75
205 Justin Smith RC .50 1.25
206 Quincy Morgan RC .40 1.00
207 Chad Johnson RC .75 2.00
208 Jesse Palmer RC .40 1.00
209 Reggie Wayne RC 1.00 2.50
210 LaDainian Tomlinson RC 5.00 12.00
211 Andre King RC .30 .75
212 Richmond Flowers RC .30 .75
213 Derrick Blaylock RC .40 1.00
214 Cedrick Wilson RC .40 1.00
215 Zeke Moreno RC .40 1.00
216 Tommy Polley RC .30 .75
217 Damione Lewis RC .40 1.00
218 Aaron Schobel RC .50 1.25
219 Alge Crumpler RC .50 1.25
220 Nate Clements RC .40 1.00
221 Quentin McCord RC .40 1.00
222 Ken-Yon Rambo RC .30 .75
223 Milton Wynn RC .30 .75
224 Derrick Gibson RC .30 .75
225 Chris Taylor RC .30 .75
226 Corey Hall RC .30 .75
227 Vinny Sutherland RC .30 .75
228 Kendrell Bell RC .50 1.25
229 Casey Hampton RC .50 1.25
230 Demetric Evans RC .30 .75
231 Brian Allen RC .30 .75
232 Rodney Bailey RC .30 .75
233 Otis Leverette RC .30 .75
234 Ron Edwards RC .30 .75
235 Michael Jameson RC .30 .75
236 Markus Steele RC .30 .75
237 Jimmy Williams RC .30 .75
238 Roger Knight RC .30 .75
239 Randy Garner RC .30 .75
240 Raymond Perryman RC .30 .75
241 Karon Riley RC .30 .75
242 Adam Archuleta RC .40 1.00
243 Arnold Jackson RC .30 .75

244 Ryan Pickett RC	.30	.75
245 Shad Meier RC	.30	.75
246 Reggie Germany RC	.30	.75
247 Justin McCareins RC	.40	1.00
248 Idrees Bashir RC	.30	.75
249 Josh Booty RC	.40	1.00
250 Eddie Berlin RC	.30	.75
251 Heath Evans RC	.40	1.00
252 Alex Bannister RC	.30	.75
253 Corey Alston RC	.30	.75
254 Reggie White RC	.30	.75
255 Orlando Huff RC	.30	.75
256 Ken Lucas RC	.40	1.00
257 Matt Stewart RC	.30	.75
258 Cedric Scott RC	.30	.75
259 Ronney Daniels RC	.30	.75
260 Kevin Kasper RC	.30	.75
261 Tony Driver RC	.40	1.00
262 Kyle Vanden Bosch RC	.50	1.25
263 T.J. Turner RC	.30	.75
264 Eric Westmoreland RC	.30	.75
265 Ronald Flemons RC	.30	.75
266 Eric Kelly RC	.30	.75
267 Moran Norris RC	.30	.75
268 Darnerien McCants RC	.40	1.00
269 James Boyd RC	.30	.75
270 Keith Adams RC	.30	.75
271 Brandon Manumaleuna RC	.40	1.00
272 Dee Brown RC	.30	.75
273 Ross Kolodziej RC	.30	.75
274 Boo Williams RC	.30	.75
275 Patrick Chukwurah RC	.30	.75

2001 Bowman Gold

*VETS 1-100: 1.2X TO 3X BASIC CARDS
*ROOKIES 101-275: .6X TO 1.5X
STATED ODDS ONE PER PACK

2001 Bowman 1996 Rookies

COMPLETE SET (15)	10.00	25.00
STATED ODDS 1:4		
BRC1 Eric Moulds	1.25	3.00
BRC2 Ray Lewis	1.50	4.00
BRC3 Tim Biakabutuka	1.00	2.50
BRC4 Eddie George	1.50	4.00
BRC5 Marvin Harrison	1.50	4.00
BRC6 Joe Horn	1.25	3.00
BRC7 Muhsin Muhammad	1.25	3.00
BRC8 Mike Alstott	1.25	3.00
BRC9 Amani Toomer	1.25	3.00
BRC10 Terrell Owens	1.50	4.00
BRC11 Keyshawn Johnson	1.25	3.00
BRC12 Terry Glenn	1.25	3.00
BRC13 Zach Thomas	1.50	4.00
BRC14 Stephen Davis	1.25	3.00
BRC15 La'Roi Glover	1.00	2.50

2001 Bowman Rookie Autographs

GROUP A STATED ODDS 1:5339
GROUP B STATED ODDS 1:2373
GROUP C STATED ODDS 1:2669
GROUP D STATED ODDS 1:1068
GROUP E STATED ODDS 1:3051
GROUP F STATED ODDS 1:1335
GROUP G STATED ODDS 1:428
GROUP H STATED ODDS 1:1186
GROUP I STATED ODDS 1:119
GROUP J STATED ODDS 1:548
OVERALL STATED ODDS 1:61

BABN Bobby Newcombe H	5.00	12.00
BACC Chris Chambers D	6.00	15.00
BACJ Chad Johnson G	8.00	20.00
BACW Chris Weinke D	5.00	12.00
BADA Dan Alexander I	5.00	12.00
BADB Drew Brees B	100.00	175.00
BADM Dan Morgan I	5.00	12.00
BADR David Rivers J	4.00	10.00
BADT David Terrell D	5.00	12.00
BAJB Josh Booty I	5.00	12.00
BAJH Josh Heupel I	6.00	15.00
BAJJ James Jackson I	4.00	10.00
BAJP Jesse Palmer F	5.00	12.00
BAKB Kevan Barlow G	5.00	12.00
BAKR Koren Robinson C	5.00	12.00
BAKW Kenyatta Walker I	4.00	10.00
BAKYR Ken-Yon Rambo D	4.00	10.00
BAMB Michael Bennett A	5.00	12.00
BAMV Michael Vick B	90.00	150.00
BAQM Quincy Morgan E	5.00	12.00
BARG Rod Gardner G	5.00	12.00
BASM Santana Moss C	8.00	20.00
BATH Travis Henry G	5.00	12.00
BATM Travis Minor I	5.00	12.00

2001 Bowman Rookie Relics

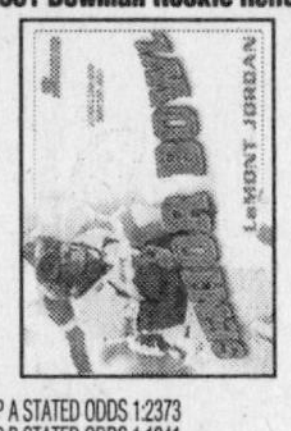

GROUP A STATED ODDS 1:2373
GROUP B STATED ODDS 1:1941
GROUP C STATED ODDS 1:1780
GROUP D STATED ODDS 1:419
GROUP E STATED ODDS 1:1127
GROUP F STATED ODDS 1:356
GROUP G STATED ODDS 1:856
GROUP H STATED ODDS 1:382
GROUP I STATED ODDS 1:36
OVERALL STATED ODDS 1:25

BJAA Adam Archuleta E	4.00	10.00
BJAC Alge Crumpler A	6.00	15.00
BJBA Brian Allen I	3.00	8.00
BJBJ Bhawoh Jue I	4.00	10.00
BJBN Bobby Newcombe C	4.00	10.00
BJCT Chris Taylor I	3.00	8.00
BJDB Drew Brees H	15.00	40.00
BJDBU Derrick Burgess I	5.00	12.00
BJDG Derrick Gibson F	3.00	8.00
BJEW Eric Westmoreland I	3.00	8.00
BJFS Fred Smoot F	5.00	12.00
BJJB Jeff Backus I	3.00	8.00
BJJC Jarrod Cooper I	4.00	10.00
BJJH Jabari Holloway I	3.00	8.00
BJJHE Jamie Henderson I	4.00	10.00
BJJJ Jonas Jennings I	3.00	8.00
BJJP Jesse Palmer D	4.00	10.00
BJKK Kevin Kasper I	3.00	8.00
BJLJ LaMont Jordan H	5.00	12.00
BJLM Leonard Myers I	3.00	8.00
BJLT LaDainian Tomlinson G	15.00	40.00
BJMF Mario Fatefehi I	3.00	8.00
BJMMC Mike McMahon F	4.00	10.00
BJMS Michael Stone I	3.00	8.00
BJRG Reggie Germany I	3.00	8.00
BJRW Reggie Wayne D	10.00	25.00
BJSH Steve Hutchinson I	5.00	12.00
BJSR Sage Rosenfels B	6.00	15.00
BJSS Steve Smith I	10.00	25.00
BJTD Tony Dixon I	3.00	8.00
BJTM Travis Minor D	4.00	10.00
BJTS Tony Stewart I	4.00	10.00
BJZM Zeke Moreno I	4.00	10.00

2001 Bowman Rookie Relics Autographs

STATED ODDS 1:1780		
BJABN Bobby Newcombe	10.00	25.00
BJADB Drew Brees	125.00	200.00
BJALJ LaMont Jordan	12.00	30.00
BJALT LaDainian Tomlinson	75.00	150.00
BJARW Reggie Wayne	25.00	60.00

2001 Bowman Rookie Reprints

COMPLETE SET (15)	10.00	25.00
STATED ODDS 1:6		
RAA Alan Ameche	.75	2.00
RAD Art Donovan	1.00	2.50
RBH Bill Howton	.75	2.00
RBT Bulldog Turner	1.00	2.50
RCC Charlie Conerly	1.00	2.50
REH Elroy Hirsch	1.25	3.00
RET Emlen Tunnell	.75	2.00
RFG Frank Gifford	1.50	4.00
RGM Gino Marchetti	.75	2.00
RLG Lou Groza	1.00	2.50
RNV Norm Van Brocklin	1.25	3.00
ROG Otto Graham	1.25	3.00
RSB Sammy Baugh	1.50	4.00
RSL Sid Luckman	1.00	2.50
RTF Tom Fears	.75	2.00
RYT Y.A Tittle	1.50	4.00

2001 Bowman Rookie Reprints Seat Relics

STATED ODDS 1:713		
RREGB George Blanda	6.00	15.00
RREGM Gino Marchetti	4.00	10.00
RRESB Sammy Baugh	7.50	20.00

2002 Bowman

Released in October, 2002. This set contains 145 rookies and 130 veterans. The Hobby S.R.P. is $3.00/pack. Each hobby pack contains 10 cards. HTA Jumbo S.R.P. is $10.00/pack. Each HTA pack contains 35 cards. Cards numbered 1 through 110 feature veterans while cards numbered 111 through 275 feature rookies.

COMPLETE SET (275)	20.00	50.00
1 Emmitt Smith	.60	1.50
2 Drew Brees	.40	1.00
3 Duce Staley	.20	.50
4 Curtis Martin	.25	.60
5 Isaac Bruce	.25	.60
6 Stephen Davis	.20	.50
7 Darrell Jackson	.20	.50
8 James Stewart	.15	.40
9 Tim Couch	.15	.40
10 Travis Henry	.15	.40
11 Thomas Jones	.25	.60
12 Jamal Lewis	.20	.50
13 Chris Chambers	.20	.50
14 Jeff Blake	.20	.50
15 Plaxico Burress	.20	.50
16 Michael Pittman	.20	.50
17 Jeff Garcia	.20	.50
18 Tim Brown	.25	.60
19 Kent Graham	.15	.40
20 Shannon Sharpe	.25	.60
21 Corey Dillon	.20	.50
22 Muhsin Muhammad	.20	.50
23 Tony Gonzalez	.25	.60
24 Qadry Ismail	.20	.50
25 Mike McMahon	.15	.40
26 Edgerrin James	.20	.50
27 Daunte Culpepper	.20	.50
28 Deuce McAllister	.20	.50
29 Kerry Collins	.20	.50
30 Eddie George	.20	.50
31 Torry Holt	.25	.60
32 Todd Pinkston	.15	.40
33 Quincy Carter	.15	.40
34 Rod Smith	.20	.50
35 Michael Vick	.40	1.00
36 Jim Miller	.15	.40
37 Troy Brown	.20	.50
38 Wayne Chrebet	.20	.50
39 Curtis Conway	.20	.50
40 Reidel Anthony	.15	.40
41 Mark Brunell	.20	.50
42 Chris Weinke	.15	.40
43 Eric Moulds	.20	.50
44 Ike Hilliard	.20	.50
45 Jay Fiedler	.20	.50
46 Keyshawn Johnson	.20	.50
47 Rod Gardner	.15	.40
48 Chris Redman	.15	.40
49 James Allen	.15	.40
50 Kordell Stewart	.20	.50
51 Priest Holmes	.25	.60
52 Anthony Thomas	.20	.50
53 Peter Warrick	.20	.50
54 Jake Plummer	.20	.50
55 Jerry Rice	.50	1.25
56 Joe Horn	.20	.50
57 Derrick Mason	.20	.50
58 Kurt Warner	.25	.60
59 Antowain Smith	.20	.50
60 Randy Moss	.25	.60
61 Warrick Dunn	.20	.50
62 Laveranues Coles	.20	.50
63 LaDainian Tomlinson	.30	.75
64 Michael Westbrook	.15	.40
65 Travis Taylor	.15	.40
66 Brian Griese	.20	.50
67 Bill Schroeder	.15	.40
68 Ahman Green	.20	.50
69 Jimmy Smith	.20	.50
70 Charlie Garner	.20	.50
71 Terrell Owens	.25	.60
72 Brad Johnson	.20	.50
73 James Thrash	.20	.50
74 Marvin Harrison	.25	.60
75 Brett Favre	.60	1.50
76 Rocket Ismail	.20	.50
77 David Boston	.15	.40
78 Jermaine Lewis	.15	.40
79 Aaron Brooks	.20	.50
80 Shaun Alexander	.20	.50
81 Steve McNair	.25	.60
82 Marshall Faulk	.25	.60
83 Terrell Davis	.25	.60
84 Corey Bradford	.15	.40
85 David Terrell	.15	.40
86 Kevin Johnson	.15	.40
87 Jon Kitna	.20	.50
88 Az-Zahir Hakim	.15	.40
89 Drew Bledsoe	.25	.60
90 Garrison Hearst	.20	.50
91 Doug Flutie	.25	.60
92 Jerome Bettis	.25	.60
93 Vinny Testaverde	.20	.50
94 Tiki Barber	.25	.60
95 Johnnie Morton	.20	.50
96 Lamar Smith	.20	.50
97 Marcus Robinson	.20	.50
98 Fred Taylor	.20	.50
99 Tom Brady	.60	1.50
100 Peyton Manning	.50	1.25
101 Donovan McNabb	.25	.60
102 Rich Gannon	.20	.50
103 Hines Ward	.25	.60
104 Michael Bennett	.20	.50
105 Ricky Williams	.20	.50
106 Germane Crowell	.15	.40
107 Joey Galloway	.20	.50
108 Amani Toomer	.20	.50
109 Trent Green	.20	.50
110 Terry Glenn	.20	.50
111 Donte Stallworth RC	.50	1.25
112 Mike Williams RC	.30	.75
113 Kurt Kittner RC	.30	.75
114 Josh Reed RC	.40	1.00
115 Raonall Smith RC	.30	.75
116 David Garrard RC	.60	1.50
117 Eric Crouch RC	.50	1.25
118 Bryan Thomas RC	.30	.75
119 Levi Jones RC	.30	.75
120 Andre Davis RC	.40	1.00
121 Herb Haygood RC	.30	.75
122 Josh McCown RC	.50	1.25
123 Quentin Jammer RC	.50	1.25
124 Cliff Russell RC	.30	.75
125 Jeremy Shockey RC	.75	2.00
126 Jamin Elliott RC	.30	.75
127 Roy Williams RC	.50	1.25
128 Marquise Walker RC	.30	.75
129 Kalimba Edwards RC	.40	1.00
130 Daniel Graham RC	.40	1.00
131 Freddie Milons RC	.30	.75
132 Anthony Weaver RC	.30	.75
133 Jake Schifino RC	.30	.75
134 Antonio Bryant RC	.50	1.25
135 DeShaun Foster RC	.50	1.25
136 Antwaan Randle El RC	.50	1.25
137 William Green RC	.40	1.00
138 Ed Reed RC	2.00	5.00
139 Maurice Morris RC	.40	1.00
140 Joey Harrington RC	.50	1.25
141 T.J. Duckett RC	.50	1.25
142 Javon Walker RC	.50	1.25
143 Albert Haynesworth RC	.50	1.25
144 Julius Peppers RC	1.00	2.50
145 Clinton Portis RC	.60	1.50
146 Craig Nall RC	.40	1.00
147 Ashley Lelie RC	.40	1.00
148 Reche Caldwell RC	.50	1.25
149 Rohan Davey RC	.50	1.25
150 Patrick Ramsey RC	.50	1.25
151 Jabar Gaffney RC	.50	1.25
152 Tank Williams RC	.40	1.00
153 Ron Johnson RC	.40	1.00
154 Ladell Betts RC	.50	1.25
155 Brian Westbrook RC	.75	2.00
156 Jamar Martin RC	.40	1.00
157 Travis Stephens RC	.30	.75
158 Tim Carter RC	.40	1.00
159 Darrell Hill RC	.30	.75
160 Luke Staley RC	.30	.75
161 Randy Fasani RC	.40	1.00
162 Matt Schobel RC	.50	1.25
163 Jon McGraw RC	.30	.75
164 Dwight Freeney RC	.60	1.50
165 Chad Hutchinson RC	.30	.75
166 Adrian Peterson RC	.50	1.25
167 Josh Scobey RC	.40	1.00
168 Jonathan Wells RC	.50	1.25
169 Sam Simmons RC	.30	.75
170 Jerramy Stevens RC	.50	1.25
171 Jason McAddley RC	.40	1.00
172 Ken Simonton RC	.30	.75
173 Chester Taylor RC	.50	1.25
174 Brandon Doman RC	.30	.75
175 Javin Hunter RC	.30	.75
176 Eddie Drummond RC	.30	.75
177 Andre Lott RC	.30	.75
178 Travis Fisher RC	.40	1.00
179 Jarvis Green RC	.30	.75
180 Ross Tucker RC	.30	.75
181 Lamont Brightful RC	.30	.75
182 Rocky Calmus RC	.40	1.00
183 Wes Pate RC	.30	.75
184 Lamar Gordon RC	.40	1.00
185 Terry Jones RC	.30	.75
186 Kyle Johnson RC	.30	.75
187 Daryl Jones RC	.30	.75
188 Tellis Redmon RC	.30	.75
189 Howard Green RC	.30	.75
190 Jarrod Baxter RC	.30	.75
191 Delvon Flowers RC	.30	.75
192 Kevin Curtis RC	.30	.75
193 Kelly Campbell RC	.40	1.00
194 Eddie Freeman RC	.30	.75
195 Atrews Bell RC	.30	.75
196 Omar Easy RC	.40	1.00
197 Jeremy Allen RC	.30	.75
198 Andra Davis RC	.30	.75
199 Jack Brewer RC	.30	.75
200 Mike Rumph RC	.30	.75
201 Seth Burford RC	.30	.75
202 Marquand Manuel RC	.30	.75
203 Marques Anderson RC	.40	1.00
204 Ben Leber RC	.30	.75
205 Ryan Denney RC	.30	.75
206 Justin Peelle RC	.30	.75
207 Lito Sheppard RC	.50	1.25
208 Damien Anderson RC	.30	.75
209 Lamont Thompson RC	.40	1.00
210 David Priestley RC	.30	.75
211 Michael Lewis RC	.50	1.25
212 Lee Mays RC	.30	.75
213 Alan Harper RC	.30	.75
214 Verron Haynes RC	.30	.75
215 Chris Hope RC	.50	1.25
216 David Thornton RC	.30	.75
217 Derek Ross RC	.40	1.00
218 Brett Keisel RC	2.50	6.00
219 Joseph Jefferson RC	.30	.75
220 Andre Goodman RC	.30	.75
221 Robert Royal RC	.50	1.25
222 Sheldon Brown RC	.50	1.25
223 DeVeren Johnson RC	.30	.75
224 Rock Cartwright RC	.50	1.25
225 Quincy Monk RC	.30	.75
226 Nick Rogers RC	.30	.75
227 Kendall Simmons RC	.30	.75
228 Joe Burns RC	.30	.75
229 Wesly Mallard RC	.30	.75
230 Chris Cash RC	.30	.75
231 David Givens RC	.50	1.25
232 John Owens RC	.30	.75
233 Jarrett Ferguson RC	.30	.75
234 Randy McMichael RC	.50	1.25
235 Chris Baker RC	.30	.75
236 Rashad Bauman RC	.30	.75
237 Matt Murphy RC	.30	.75
238 LaVar Glover RC	.40	1.00
239 Steve Bellisari RC	.30	.75
240 Chad Williams RC	.30	.75
241 Kevin Thomas RC	.30	.75
242 Carlos Hall RC	.30	.75
243 Nick Greisen RC	.30	.75
244 Justin Bannan RC	.30	.75
245 Charles Hill RC	.30	.75
246 Mark Anelli RC	.30	.75
247 Coy Wire RC	.40	1.00
248 Darnell Sanders RC	.30	.75
249 Larry Foote RC	.75	2.00
250 David Carr RC	.50	1.25
251 Ricky Williams RC	.40	1.00
252 Napoleon Harris RC	.40	1.00
253 Ennis Haywood RC	.30	.75
254 Keyuo Craver RC	.30	.75
255 Kahlil Hill RC	.30	.75
256 J.T. O'Sullivan RC	.40	1.00
257 Woody Dantzler RC	.40	1.00
258 Phillip Buchanon RC	.50	1.25
259 Charles Grant RC	.50	1.25
260 Dusty Bonner RC	.30	.75
261 James Allen RC	.30	.75
262 Ronald Curry RC	.40	1.00
263 Deion Branch RC	.50	1.25
264 Larry Ned RC	.30	.75
265 Mel Mitchell RC	.30	.75
266 Kendall Newson RC	.30	.75
267 Shaun Hill RC	.60	1.50
268 David Pugh RC	.30	.75
269 Dante Wesley RC	.30	.75
270 Josh Mallard RC	.30	.75
271 Akin Ayodele RC	.40	1.00
272 Pete Hunter RC	.30	.75
273 Kevin McCadam RC	.30	.75
274 Jeff Kelly RC	.30	.75
275 John Henderson RC	.40	1.00

2002 Bowman Gold

*VETS 1-100: 10X TO 25X BASIC CARDS
*ROOKIES 111-275: 6X TO 15X
GOLD/50 ODDS 1:67 HOB, 1:19 HTA
STATED PRINT RUN 50 SER.#'d SETS

2002 Bowman Silver

*VETS 1-110: 3X TO 8X BASIC CARDS
*ROOKIES 111-275: 2.5X TO 6X
SILVER/250 ODDS 1:13 HOB, 1:4 HTA
STATED PRINT RUN 250 SER.#'d SETS

2002 Bowman Uncirculated

*SEALED ROOKIES: 1.2X TO 3X
ANNC'd UNCIRCULATED PRINT RUN 290

2002 Bowman Draft Day Relics

JSY STATED ODDS 1:109H, 1:31HTA
HAT STATED ODDS 1:1850H, 530HTA
OVERALL ODDS 1:103 HOB, 1:30 HTA

DDHBM Bryant McKinnie Hat	8.00	20.00
DDHDC David Carr Hat	12.00	30.00
DDHJP Julius Peppers Hat	15.00	40.00
DDHMW Mike Williams Hat	8.00	20.00
DDHQJ Quentin Jammer Hat	12.00	30.00
DDJBM Bryant McKinnie JSY	4.00	10.00
DDJDC David Carr JSY	6.00	15.00
DDJJP Julius Peppers JSY	8.00	20.00
DDJMW Mike Williams JSY	4.00	10.00
DDJQJ Quentin Jammer JSY	6.00	15.00

2002 Bowman Fabric of the Future

GROUP A ODDS 1:2308H, 1:662HTA
GROUP B ODDS 1:168H, 1:48HTA
GROUP C ODDS 1:185H, 1:53HTA
OVERALL ODDS 1:85H, 1:25HTA

FFAB Alex Brown B	5.00	12.00
FFDB Deion Branch C	5.00	12.00
FFDC David Carr B	5.00	12.00
FFDF DeShaun Foster A	5.00	12.00
FFEF Eddie Freeman B	3.00	8.00
FFHG Herb Haygood B	3.00	8.00
FFJM Josh McCown C	5.00	12.00
FFJW Javon Walker B	5.00	12.00
FFJWE Jonathan Wells C	5.00	12.00
FFKC Kelly Campbell B	4.00	10.00
FFKK Kurt Kittner B	3.00	8.00
FFLG Lamar Gordon B	4.00	10.00
FFTC Tim Carter C	4.00	10.00
FFTJ Terry Jones Jr. B	3.00	8.00
FFTS Travis Stephens C	3.00	8.00
FFTW Tank Williams B	4.00	10.00
FFWD Woody Dantzler B	4.00	10.00

2002 Bowman Flashback Autographs

GROUP A ODDS 1:3070H, 1:883HTA
GROUP B ODDS 1:2308H, 1:662HTA
GROUP C ODDS 1:1711H, 1:488HTA
OVERALL ODDS 1:412H, 1:118HTA
GROUP D ODDS 1:922H, 1:263HTA

RFABF Brett Favre A	100.00	200.00
RFABS Bill Schroeder C	6.00	15.00
RFACC Chris Chambers A	12.00	30.00
RFAJG Jeff Garcia C	8.00	20.00
RFALJ LaMont Jordan D	8.00	20.00
RFALS Lamar Smith B	8.00	20.00
RFALT LaDainian Tomlinson D	30.00	60.00
RFAMR Marcus Robinson B	8.00	20.00

2002 Bowman Flashback Jerseys

GROUP A ODDS 1:308H, 1:88HTA
GROUP B ODDS 1:185, 1:53HTA
OVERALL ODDS 1:116, 1:34HTA

RFRCJ Chad Johnson A	5.00	12.00
RFRCW Chris Weinke A	3.00	8.00
RFRDM Deuce McAllister B	4.00	10.00
RFRDT David Terrell B	3.00	8.00
RFRKB Kevan Barlow B	3.00	8.00
RFRMM Snoop Minnis A	3.00	8.00
RFRMV Michael Vick B	8.00	20.00
RFRMMC Mike McMahon A	3.00	8.00
RFRQM Quincy Morgan A	3.00	8.00
RFRRG Rod Gardner B	3.00	8.00
RFRSM Santana Moss A	4.00	10.00

2002 Bowman Signs of the Future

GROUP A ODDS 1:18612H, 1:5297HTA
GROUP B ODDS 1:9306H, 1:2649HTA
GROUP C ODDS 1:659H, 1:188HTA
GROUP D ODDS 1:171H, 1:49HTA
OVERALL ODDS 1:133H, 1:39HTA

SFAB Antonio Bryant C	8.00	20.00
SFDC David Carr B	8.00	20.00
SFDG David Garrard D	10.00	25.00
SFDRC Reche Caldwell D	8.00	20.00
SFJG Jabar Gaffney C	8.00	20.00
SFJH Joey Harrington A	15.00	40.00
SFJM Josh McCown D	8.00	20.00
SFJS Jeremy Shockey D	12.00	30.00
SFJW Javon Walker C	8.00	20.00
SFLB Ladell Betts D	8.00	20.00
SFMM Maurice Morris D	6.00	15.00
SFNH Napoleon Harris C	6.00	15.00
SFPR Patrick Ramsey D	8.00	20.00
SFQJ Quentin Jammer D	8.00	20.00
SFRD Rohan Davey D	8.00	20.00
SFTC Tim Carter D	6.00	15.00
SFTJD T.J. Duckett C	8.00	20.00
SFTS Travis Stephens D	5.00	12.00
SFWG William Green C	6.00	15.00

2002 Bowman Signs of the Future Red Ink

STATED ODDS 1:251 HTA
STATED PRINT RUN 50 SER.#'d SETS

SFAB Antonio Bryant	12.00	30.00
SFDC David Carr	12.00	30.00
SFDG David Garrard	15.00	40.00
SFDG Daniel Graham	10.00	25.00
SFDRC Reche Caldwell	12.00	30.00
SFJG Jabar Gaffney	12.00	30.00
SFJH Joey Harrington	12.00	30.00
SFJM Josh McCown	12.00	30.00
SFJS Jeremy Shockey	20.00	50.00
SFJW Javon Walker	12.00	30.00
SFLB Ladell Betts	12.00	30.00
SFMM Maurice Morris	10.00	25.00
SFNH Napoleon Harris	10.00	25.00
SFPR Patrick Ramsey	12.00	30.00
SFQJ Quentin Jammer	12.00	30.00
SFRD Rohan Davey	12.00	30.00
SFTC Tim Carter	10.00	25.00
SFTJD T.J. Duckett	12.00	30.00
SFTS Travis Stephens	8.00	20.00
SFWG William Green	10.00	25.00

2003 Bowman

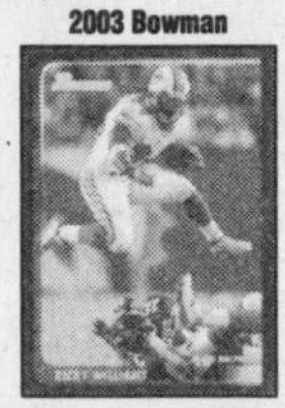

Released in October of 2003, this set consists of 275 cards including 110 veterans and 165 rookies. Hobby boxes contained 24 packs of 10 cards. SRP was $3.00. HTA jumbo boxes contained 10 packs of 35 cards and had an SRP of $10.00.

COMPLETE SET (273)	40.00	80.00
1 Brett Favre	.75	2.00
2 Jeremy Shockey	.30	.75
3 Fred Taylor	.25	.60
4 Rich Gannon	.25	.60
5 Joey Galloway	.25	.60
6 Ray Lewis	.30	.75
7 Jeff Blake	.25	.60
8 Stacey Mack	.20	.50
9 Matt Hasselbeck	.25	.60
10 Laveranues Coles	.20	.50
11 Brad Johnson	.25	.60
12 Tommy Maddox	.25	.60
13 Curtis Martin	.30	.75
14 Tom Brady	.75	2.00
15 Ricky Williams	.25	.60
16 Stephen Davis	.25	.60
17 Chad Johnson	.30	.75
18 Joey Harrington	.20	.50
19 Tony Gonzalez	.30	.75
20 Peerless Price	.20	.50
21 LaDainian Tomlinson	.30	.75
22 James Thrash	.20	.50
23 Charlie Garner	.25	.60
24 Eddie George	.25	.60
25 Terrell Owens	.30	.75
26 Brian Urlacher	.30	.75
27 Eric Moulds	.25	.60
28 Emmitt Smith	.75	2.00
29 Tim Couch	.20	.50
30 Jake Plummer	.25	.60
31 Marvin Harrison	.30	.75
32 Chris Chambers	.25	.60
33 Tiki Barber	.30	.75
34 Kurt Warner	.30	.75
35 Michael Pittman	.20	.50
36 Kevin Dyson	.20	.50
37 Clinton Portis	.25	.60
38 Peyton Manning	.60	1.50
39 Travis Taylor	.20	.50
40 Jeff Garcia	.25	.60
41 Patrick Ramsey	.25	.60
42 Shaun Alexander	.25	.60
43 Joe Horn	.25	.60
44 Daunte Culpepper	.25	.60
45 Travis Henry	.20	.50
46 Brian Finneran	.20	.50
47 William Green	.20	.50
48 Kordell Stewart	.25	.60
49 Reggie Wayne	.30	.75
50 Priest Holmes	.30	.75
51 Jay Fiedler	.20	.50
52 Corey Dillon	.25	.60
53 Jamal Lewis	.25	.60
54 Mark Brunell	.25	.60
55 Santana Moss	.25	.60
56 Duce Staley	.25	.60
57 Torry Holt	.30	.75
58 Rod Gardner	.20	.50
59 Kerry Collins	.25	.60
60 Randy Moss	.30	.75
61 Jerry Porter	.20	.50
62 Plaxico Burress	.25	.60
63 Steve McNair	.30	.75
64 Muhsin Muhammad	.25	.60
65 Drew Bledsoe	.30	.75
66 T.J. Duckett	.25	.60
67 Ahman Green	.25	.60
68 Rod Smith	.25	.60
69 Jimmy Smith	.25	.60
70 Trent Green	.25	.60
71 Tim Brown	.30	.75
72 Jerome Bettis	.30	.75
73 Isaac Bruce	.30	.75
74 Derrick Mason	.25	.60
75 Donovan McNabb	.30	.75
76 Deuce McAllister	.25	.60
77 Zach Thomas	.30	.75
78 Garrison Hearst	.25	.60
79 Koren Robinson	.25	.60
80 Marshall Faulk	.30	.75
81 Keyshawn Johnson	.30	.75
82 Jake Delhomme	.30	.75
83 Marty Booker	.25	.60
84 James Stewart	.20	.50
85 Corey Bradford	.20	.50
86 Derrius Thompson	.20	.50
87 Edgerrin James	.30	.75
88 Darrell Jackson	.25	.60
89 Hines Ward	.30	.75
90 David Boston	.20	.50
91 Curtis Conway	.20	.50
92 David Patten	.20	.50
93 Michael Bennett	.25	.60
94 Todd Pinkston	.20	.50
95 Jerry Rice	.60	1.50
96 Jon Kitna	.25	.60
97 Ed McCaffrey	.25	.60
98 Donald Driver	.30	.75
99 Anthony Thomas	.25	.60
100 Michael Vick	.40	1.00
101 Terry Glenn	.25	.60
102 Quincy Morgan	.20	.50
103 David Carr	.25	.60
104 Troy Brown	.25	.60
105 Aaron Brooks	.25	.60
106 Amani Toomer	.25	.60
107 Drew Brees	.30	.75
108 Chad Hutchinson	.20	.50
109 Warrick Dunn	.25	.60
110 Chad Pennington	.30	.75
111 Carson Palmer RC	1.25	3.00
112 Brian St.Pierre RC	.50	1.25
113 Keenan Howry RC	.40	1.00
114 Sultan McCullough RC	.40	1.00
115 Terence Newman RC	.50	1.25
116 Kelley Washington RC	.40	1.00
117 Musa Smith RC	.40	1.00
118 Kevin Williams RC	.60	1.50
119 Jordan Gross RC	.40	1.00
120 Lance Briggs RC	1.50	4.00
121 Victor Hobson RC	.40	1.00
122 Bryant Johnson RC	.60	1.50
123 Travis Anglin RC	.40	1.00
124 Artose Pinner RC	.40	1.00
125 Willis McGahee RC	.75	2.00
126 Rashean Mathis RC	.50	1.25
127 B.J. Askew RC	.50	1.25
128 DeWayne White RC	.40	1.00
129 Kevin Curtis RC	.60	1.50
130 Tyrone Calico RC	.50	1.25
131 Julian Battle RC	.50	1.25
132 Ricky Manning RC	.50	1.25
133 Cory Redding RC	.50	1.25
134 Michael Haynes RC	.40	1.00
135 Dallas Clark RC	1.00	2.50
136 Shaun McDonald RC	.50	1.25
137 Marcus Trufant RC	.50	1.25
138 Kareem Kelly RC	.40	1.00
139 Sam Aiken RC	.50	1.25
140 Terrell Suggs RC	.60	1.50
141 Gibran Hamdan RC	.40	1.00
142 Bobby Wade RC	.50	1.25
143 Aaron Walker RC	.50	1.25
144 Calvin Pace RC	.50	1.25
145 Quentin Griffin RC	.50	1.25
146 Ken Dorsey RC	.50	1.25
147 Jerome McDougle RC	.40	1.00
148 Earnest Graham RC	.60	1.50
149 Rashad Moore RC	.40	1.00
150 Charles Rogers RC	.50	1.25
151 Cecil Sapp RC	.40	1.00
152 Cato June RC	.75	2.00
153 Ahmaad Galloway RC	.50	1.25
154 William Joseph RC	.40	1.00
155 Anquan Boldin RC	1.00	2.50
156 L.J. Smith RC	.60	1.50
157 Antwoine Sanders RC	.40	1.00
158 Justin Griffith RC	.50	1.25
159 Kevin Garrett RC	.40	1.00
160 Teyo Johnson RC	.50	1.25
161 Chris Crocker RC	.50	1.25
162 Brad Banks RC	.50	1.25
163 Justin Gage RC	.50	1.25
164 Doug Gabriel RC	.50	1.25
165 Terry Pierce RC	.40	1.00
166 Bradie James RC	.60	1.50
167 Bennie Joppru RC	.40	1.00
168 Malaefou Mackenzie RC	.40	1.00
169 Terrence Edwards RC	.40	1.00
170 E.J. Henderson RC	.50	1.25
171 Tony Romo RC	10.00	25.00
172 DeWayne Robertson RC	.50	1.25
173 Dwone Hicks RC	.40	1.00
174 Carl Ford RC	.40	1.00
175 Byron Leftwich RC	.60	1.50
176 Ken Hamlin RC	.60	1.50
177 Domanick Davis RC	.50	1.25
178 Adrian Madise RC	.40	1.00
179 Siddeeq Shabazz RC	.40	1.00
180 Dave Ragone RC	.40	1.00
181 Mike Seidman RC	.40	1.00
182 Brooks Bollinger RC	.50	1.25
183 DeAndrew Rubin RC	.40	1.00
184 Mike Pinkard RC	.40	1.00
185 Nate Burleson RC	.50	1.25
186 LaBrandon Toefield RC	.50	1.25
187 Angelo Crowell RC	.50	1.25
188 J.R. Tolver RC	.50	1.25
189 Osi Umenyiora RC	.75	2.00
190 Larry Johnson RC	.60	1.50
191 Nick Barnett RC	.60	1.50
192 Brandon Drumm RC	.40	1.00
193 Rien Long RC	.40	1.00
194 Zuriel Smith RC	.40	1.00
195 Onterrio Smith RC	.40	1.00
196 Ronald Bellamy RC	.50	1.25
197 Kenny Peterson RC	.50	1.25
198 Charles Tillman RC	.75	2.00
199 Chaun Thompson RC	.40	1.00
200 Andre Johnson RC	1.50	4.00
201 Gerald Hayes RC	.50	1.25
202 Terrence Holt RC	.50	1.25
203 Ovie Mughelli RC	.50	1.25
204 Talman Gardner RC	.40	1.00
205 Bethel Johnson RC	.40	1.00
206 Avon Cobourne RC	.40	1.00
207 Brandon Lloyd RC	1.00	2.50
208 Andre Woolfolk RC	.50	1.25
209 George Wrighster RC	.40	1.00
210 Justin Fargas RC	.60	1.50
211 Jimmy Kennedy RC	.50	1.25
212 Arnaz Battle RC	.60	1.50
213 Marquel Blackwell RC	.40	1.00
214 Walter Young RC	.40	1.00
215 Kliff Kingsbury RC	.50	1.25
216 Kawika Mitchell RC	.60	1.50
217 Drayton Florence RC	.60	1.50
218 Jeremi Johnson RC	.40	1.00
219 Billy McMullen RC	.40	1.00
220 Lee Suggs RC	.50	1.25
221 David Kircus RC	.60	1.50
222 Rod Babers RC	.40	1.00
223 Jon Olinger RC	.40	1.00
224 Ty Warren RC	.50	1.25
225 Kyle Boller RC	.60	1.50
226 Danny Curley RC	.40	1.00
227 Andrew Pinnock RC	.50	1.25
228 Kirk Farmer RC	.50	1.25
229 Tully Banta-Cain RC	.60	1.50
230 Alonzo Jackson RC	.40	1.00
231 Anthony Adams RC	.50	1.25
232 Trent Smith RC	.50	1.25
233 Seneca Wallace RC	.60	1.50
234 Shane Walton RC	.40	1.00
235 Chris Brown RC	.40	1.00
236 Dahrran Diedrick RC	.40	1.00
237 Juston Wood RC	.40	1.00
238 Mike Doss RC	.60	1.50
239 Visanthe Shiancoe RC	.60	1.50
240 Rex Grossman RC	.60	1.50
241 David Young RC	.40	1.00
242 Jimmy Wilkerson RC	.50	1.25
243 Jason Witten RC	1.50	4.00
244 Dennis Weathersby RC	.40	1.00
245 Taylor Jacobs RC	.40	1.00
246 Chris Davis RC	.50	1.25
247 LaTarence Dunbar RC	.40	1.00
248 Eugene Wilson RC	.60	1.50
249 Ryan Hoag RC	.40	1.00
250 Chris Simms RC	.60	1.50
251 Ike Taylor RC	1.25	3.00
252 Brock Forsey RC	.50	1.25
253 Curt Anes RC	.40	1.00
254 Taco Wallace RC	.40	1.00
255 Johnathan Sullivan RC	.40	1.00
256 David Tyree RC	.60	1.50
257 Troy Polamalu RC	10.00	20.00
258 Nate Hybl RC	.50	1.25
259 Spencer Nead RC	.40	1.00
260 Boss Bailey RC	.50	1.25
261 LaMarcus McDonald RC	.40	1.00
262 Casey Moore RC	.40	1.00
263 Pisa Tinoisamoa RC	.60	1.50
264 Willie Ponder RC	.40	1.00
265 Donald Lee RC	.50	1.25
266 Nnamdi Asomugha RC	2.00	5.00
267 Sammy Davis RC	.50	1.25
268 Joffrey Reynolds RC	.40	1.00
269 Eddie Moore RC	.40	1.00
270 Tony Hollings RC	.50	1.25
271 Nick Maddox RC	.40	1.00
272 Kevin Walter RC	1.00	2.50
273 Dan Klecko RC	.50	1.25
274 Antwan Peek RC	.40	1.00
275 Tyler Brayton RC	.50	1.25

2003 Bowman Uncirculated Gold

*GOLD: 3X TO 8X BASIC CARDS
STATED ODDS ONE PER HTA BOX

171 Tony Romo	30.00	80.00
257 Troy Polamalu	60.00	120.00

2003 Bowman Uncirculated Silver

*ROOKIES: 3X TO 8X BASIC CARDS
ONE EXCH CARD PER HTA BOX
STATED PRINT RUN 111 SETS

171 Tony Romo	40.00	100.00
257 Troy Polamalu	50.00	100.00

2003 Bowman Draft Day Selection Relics

JSY STATED ODDS 1:79H, 1:37HTA
HAT STATED ODDS 1:1352H, 1:415HTA
DHBL Byron Leftwich Cap 4.00 10.00
DHCP Carson Palmer Cap 10.00 25.00
DHCR Charles Rogers Cap 3.00 8.00
DHDR DeWayne Robertson Cap 3.00 8.00
DHJK Jimmy Kennedy Cap 3.00 8.00
DHTN Terence Newman Cap 3.00 8.00
DJBL Byron Leftwich JSY 3.00 8.00
DJCP Carson Palmer JSY 8.00 20.00
DJCR Charles Rogers JSY 2.50 6.00
DJDRO DeWayne Robertson JSY 2.50 6.00
DJJK Jimmy Kennedy JSY 2.50 6.00
DJTN Terence Newman JSY 2.50 6.00
DJTS Terrell Suggs JSY 3.00 8.00

2003 Bowman Fabric of the Future

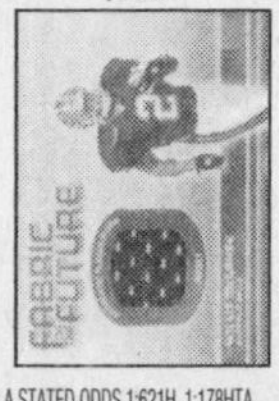

GROUP A STATED ODDS 1:621H, 1:178HTA
GROUP B STATED ODDS 1:724H, 1:218HTA
GROUP C STATED ODDS 1:55H, 1:26HTA
FAAB Anquan Boldin A 5.00 12.00
FAAJ Andre Johnson A 8.00 20.00
FAAP Artose Pinner A 2.50 6.00
FABJ Bryant Johnson C 3.00 8.00
FABL Byron Leftwich A 3.00 8.00
FABSP Brian St.Pierre A 2.50 6.00
FACB Chris Brown C 2.00 5.00
FACP Carson Palmer A 10.00 25.00
FACR Charles Rogers C 2.50 6.00
FADR Dave Ragone C 2.50 6.00
FAJF Justin Fargas B 3.00 8.00
FAKB Kyle Boller A 3.00 8.00
FAKK Kliff Kingsbury C 2.50 6.00
FALJ Larry Johnson C 3.00 8.00
FAOS Onterrio Smith C 2.00 5.00
FARG Rex Grossman B 3.00 8.00
FATJ Taylor Jacobs A 2.00 5.00
FATJO Teyo Johnson C 2.50 6.00
FAWM Willis McGahee C 4.00 10.00

2003 Bowman Fabric of the Future Doubles

DUAL JSY/50 ODDS 1:3475H, 1:999HTA
STATED PRINT RUN 50 SER.#'d SETS
FADBG Kyle Boller 6.00 15.00
Rex Grossman
FADMJ Willis McGahee 5.00 12.00
Larry Johnson
FADPL Carson Palmer 8.00 20.00
Byron Leftwich
FADRJ Charles Rogers 10.00 25.00
Andre Johnson
FADSR Chris Simms 6.00 15.00
Dave Ragone

2003 Bowman Franchise Future Jerseys

DUAL JSY/50 ODDS 1:1738H, 1:495HTA
STATED PRINT RUN 50 SER.#'d SETS
FFBM Drew Bledsoe 5.00 12.00
Willis McGahee
FFCJ David Carr 15.00 40.00
Andre Johnson
FFDP Corey Dillon 8.00 20.00
Carson Palmer
FFDW Corey Dillon 5.00 12.00
Kelley Washington
FFLB Ray Lewis 6.00 15.00
Kyle Boller
FFLS Ray Lewis 6.00 15.00
Terrell Suggs
FFMC Steve McNair 6.00 15.00
Tyrone Calico
FFPR Chad Pennington 6.00 15.00
DeWayne Robertson
FFSL Jimmy Smith 6.00 15.00
Byron Leftwich
FFUG Brian Urlacher 6.00 15.00
Rex Grossman

2003 Bowman Franchise Jerseys

GROUP A/99 ODDS 1:8838H, 1:2448HTA
GROUP B/199 ODDS 1:473H, 1:139HTA
STATED PRINT RUN 99-199
FRBU Brian Urlacher/199 4.00 10.00
FRCD Corey Dillon/199 3.00 8.00
FRCP Chad Pennington/199 4.00 10.00
FRDB Drew Bledsoe/199 4.00 10.00
FRDC David Carr/199 3.00 8.00
FRDM Deuce McAllister/199 3.00 8.00
FRJS Jimmy Smith/199 3.00 8.00
FRRL Ray Lewis/199 4.00 10.00
FRSM Steve McNair/99 4.00 10.00
FRTB Tim Brown/199 4.00 10.00

2003 Bowman Future Jerseys

JSY/199 ODDS 1:425H, 1:128HTA
STATED PRINT RUN 199 SER.#'d SETS
FUAJ Andre Johnson 10.00 25.00
FUBL Byron Leftwich 4.00 10.00
FUCP Carson Palmer 8.00 20.00
FUDR DeWayne Robertson 3.00 8.00
FUKB Kyle Boller 4.00 10.00
FUKW Kelley Washington 2.50 6.00
FURG Rex Grossman 4.00 10.00
FUTC Tyrone Calico 3.00 8.00
FUTS Terrell Suggs 4.00 10.00
FUWM Willis McGahee 5.00 12.00

2003 Bowman Paydirt Previews

STATED ODDS 1:869H, 1:251HTA
*GOLD/25: .8X TO 2X BASIC PYLON
GOLD/25 ODDS 1:3475H, 1:999HTA
PYPBJ Bryant Johnson 4.00 10.00
PYPCP Carson Palmer 10.00 25.00
PYPCS Chris Simms 4.00 10.00
PYPDR Dave Ragone 2.50 6.00
PYPJF Justin Fargas 4.00 10.00
PYPKB Kyle Boller 4.00 10.00
PYPLJ Larry Johnson 4.00 10.00
PYPTC Tyrone Calico 3.00 8.00
PYPTG Talman Gardner 2.50 6.00
PYPTJ Taylor Jacobs 2.50 6.00

2003 Bowman Pigskin Previews

STATED ODDS 1:869H, 1:251HTA
*GOLD/25: .8X TO 2X BASIC FB
GOLD/25 ODDS 1:3475H, 1:999HTA
PGPCP Carson Palmer 12.00 30.00
PGPCS Chris Simms 4.00 10.00
PGPDR Dave Ragone 2.50 6.00
PGPJF Justin Fargas 4.00 10.00
PGPKB Kyle Boller 4.00 10.00
PGPLJ Larry Johnson 4.00 10.00
PGPTG Talman Gardner 2.50 6.00
PGPTJ Taylor Jacobs 2.50 6.00
PGPTC Tyrone Calico 3.00 8.00

2003 Bowman Signs of the Future Autographs

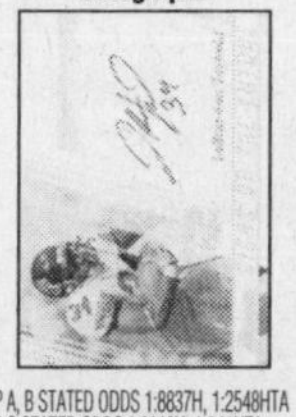

GROUP A, B STATED ODDS 1:8837H, 1:2548HTA
GROUP C STATED ODDS 1:2918H, 1:941HTA
GROUP D STATED ODDS 1:1242H, 1:455HTA
GROUP E, F STATED ODDS 1:1748H, 1:785HTA
GROUP G STATED ODDS 1:2494H, 1:941HTA
GROUP H STATED ODDS 1:1830H, 698HTA
GROUP I STATED ODDS 1:869H, 309HTA
GROUP J STATED ODDS 1:351H, 1:111HTA
GROUP K STATED ODDS 1:519H, 158HTA
GROUP L STATED ODDS 1:157H, 1:64HTA
GROUP M STATED ODDS 1:39H, 1:18HTA
SFAC Avon Cobourne I 3.00 8.00
SFAJ Andre Johnson C 25.00 50.00
SFBB Brad Banks F 4.00 10.00
SFBJ Bryant Johnson D 5.00 12.00
SFBM Billy McMullen M 3.00 8.00
SFCB Chris Brown D 3.00 8.00
SFCS Chris Simms A 8.00 20.00
SFEG Earnest Graham M 5.00 12.00
SFJF Justin Fargas K 5.00 12.00
SFJT Jason Thomas F 3.00 8.00
SFKB Kyle Boller D 5.00 12.00
SFKD Ken Dorsey A 6.00 15.00
SFKK Kareem Kelly M 3.00 8.00
SFKW Kelley Washington G 3.00 8.00
SFLJ Larry Johnson B 12.00 30.00
SFLT LaBrandon Toefield M 4.00 10.00
SFMB Marquel Blackwell M 3.00 8.00
SFMS Musa Smith L 3.00 8.00
SFNB Nate Burleson M 4.00 10.00
SFOS Onterrio Smith H 3.00 8.00
SFQG Quentin Griffin M 4.00 10.00
SFRG Rex Grossman E 15.00 40.00
SFRL ReShard Lee J 5.00 12.00
SFSA Sam Aiken M 4.00 10.00
SFTC Tyrone Calico L 4.00 10.00
SFTG Talman Gardner M 3.00 8.00
SFTJ Teyo Johnson L 4.00 10.00
SFTJA Taylor Jacobs E 3.00 8.00
SFTS Terrell Suggs J 10.00 25.00

2003 Bowman Signs of the Future Autographs Doubles

STATED ODDS 1:3475H, 1:999 HTA
STATED PRINT RUN 50 SER.#'d SETS
SFDBG Kyle Boller 20.00 50.00
Rex Grossman
SFDJF Larry Johnson 20.00 50.00
Justin Fargas
SFDJW Taylor Jacobs 15.00 40.00
Kelley Washington
SFDPL Carson Palmer 30.00 80.00
Byron Leftwich

2003 Bowman Signs of the Future Autographs Triples

STATED ODDS 1:11456H, 1:3264HTA
STATED PRINT RUN 25 SER.#'d SETS
JSF Larry Johnson 30.00 80.00
Onterrio Smith
Justin Fargas

2004 Bowman

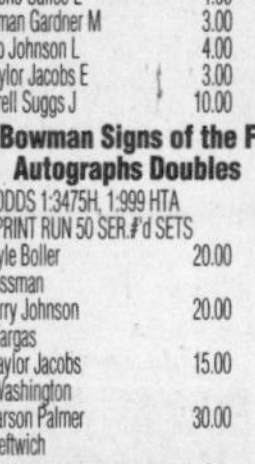

Bowman initially released in late October 2004. The base set consists of 275-cards including 165-rookies. Hobby boxes contained 24-packs of 10-cards and carried an S.R.P. of $3 per pack. Three parallel sets were issued including the hobby only First Edition release and the one-per box Uncirculated Gold sealed card. A variety of inserts can be found seeded in hobby and retail packs highlighted by the Coaches Autographs and Rookie Autographs signed Inserts.

COMPLETE SET (275) 30.00 60.00
1 Brett Favre .75 2.00
2 Jay Fiedler .10 .30
3 Andre Davis .10 .30
4 Travis Henry .20 .50
5 Jimmy Smith .20 .50
6 Santana Moss .25 .60
7 Correll Buckhalter .25 .60
8 Randy Moss .30 .75
9 Edgerrin James .25 .60
10 Marc Bulger .25 .60
11 Derrick Mason .20 .50
12 Mark Brunell .25 .60
13 Donte' Stallworth .20 .50
14 Deion Branch .30 .75
15 Jake Plummer .20 .50
16 Steve Smith .30 .75
17 Jon Kitna .20 .50
18 Andre Johnson .30 .75
19 A.J. Feeley .20 .50
20 Drew Bledsoe .30 .75
21 Antonio Bryant .25 .60
22 Reggie Wayne .30 .75
23 Thomas Jones .30 .75
24 Alge Crumpler .25 .60
25 Anquan Boldin .30 .75
26 Tim Rattay .10 .30
27 Charlie Garner .20 .50
28 James Thrash .10 .30
29 Koren Robinson .20 .50
30 Terrell Owens .30 .75
31 Amani Toomer .20 .50
32 Kelly Campbell .10 .30
33 Patrick Ramsey .25 .60
34 Plaxico Burress .20 .50
35 Chad Pennington .30 .75
36 Fred Taylor .20 .50
37 Domanick Davis .20 .50
38 DeShaun Foster .20 .50
39 T.J. Duckett .20 .50
40 Ahman Green .25 .60
41 Lee Suggs .25 .60
42 Tony Gonzalez .30 .75
43 Rich Gannon .20 .50
44 Kevan Barlow .20 .50
45 Torry Holt .25 .60
46 Aaron Brooks .25 .60
47 Tyrone Calico .20 .50
48 Keenan McCardell .10 .30
49 Hines Ward .30 .75
50 LaDainian Tomlinson .30 .75
51 Dante Hall .25 .60
52 Marcus Pollard .10 .30
53 Corey Dillon .20 .50
54 Justin McCareins .20 .50
55 Stephen Davis .25 .60
56 Jeff Garcia .25 .60
57 Ashley Lelie .20 .50
58 Javon Walker .20 .50
59 Kyle Boller .30 .75
60 Chad Johnson .30 .75
61 Anthony Thomas .20 .50
62 Byron Leftwich .25 .60
63 David Boston .20 .50
64 Onterrio Smith .20 .50
65 Deuce McAllister .25 .60
66 Antwaan Randle El .25 .60
67 Justin Fargas .20 .50
68 Laveranues Coles .20 .50
69 Quincy Morgan .20 .50
70 Priest Holmes .30 .75
71 Robert Ferguson .20 .50
72 Charles Rogers .20 .50
73 Drew Brees .30 .75
74 Matt Hasselbeck .25 .60
75 Peyton Manning .60 1.50
76 Rudi Johnson .25 .60
77 Jake Delhomme .25 .60
78 Tiki Barber .30 .75
79 Brad Johnson .20 .50
80 Steve McNair .30 .75
81 Willis McGahee .30 .75
82 Josh McCown .25 .60
83 Garrison Hearst .20 .50
84 Quincy Carter .20 .50
85 Ricky Williams .25 .60
86 Trent Green .25 .60
87 Curtis Martin .30 .75
88 Jerry Porter .20 .50
89 Brian Westbrook .30 .75
90 Clinton Portis .30 .75
91 Eric Moulds .20 .50
92 Marcel Shipp .20 .50
93 Joey Harrington .25 .60
94 David Carr .20 .50
95 Marvin Harrison .30 .75
96 Joe Horn .25 .60
97 Chris Chambers .25 .60
98 Darrell Jackson .25 .60
99 Eddie George .20 .50
100 Donovan McNabb .30 .75
101 Marshall Faulk .30 .75
102 Rex Grossman .25 .60
103 Tai Streets .10 .30
104 Jeremy Shockey .30 .75
105 Jamal Lewis .25 .60
106 Tom Brady .60 1.50
107 Shaun Alexander .25 .60
108 Carson Palmer .30 .75
109 Daunte Culpepper .25 .60
110 Michael Vick .40 1.00
111 Eli Manning RC 7.50 15.00
112 Kevin Jones RC .50 1.25
113 Philip Rivers RC 2.50 6.00
114 Ben Roethlisberger RC 6.00 15.00
115 Roy Williams RC .60 1.50
116 Tommie Harris RC .60 1.50
117 Vontez Duff RC .40 1.00
118 Karlos Dansby RC .60 1.50
119 Thomas Tapeh RC .50 1.25
120 Matt Schaub RC 1.25 3.00
121 Dexter Reid RC .40 1.00
122 Jonathan Smith RC .40 1.00
123 Ricardo Colclough RC .50 1.25
124 Jeff Dugan RC .40 1.00
125 Larry Fitzgerald RC 2.50 6.00
126 Gibril Wilson RC .60 1.50
127 Sean Taylor RC 1.25 3.00
128 Marquise Hill RC .40 1.00
129 Ernest Wilford RC .50 1.25
130 Cedric Cobbs RC .40 1.00
131 Rich Gardner RC .50 1.25
132 Chris Cooley RC .60 1.50
133 Kenechi Udeze RC .50 1.25
134 John Navarre RC .40 1.00
135 Ben Troupe RC .60 1.50
136 Dave Ball RC .50 1.25
137 Antwan Odom RC .50 1.25
138 Stuart Schweigert RC .50 1.25
139 Derek Abney RC .40 1.00
140 Keary Colbert RC .40 1.00
141 Jeris McIntyre RC .40 1.00
142 Matt Kranchick RC .50 1.25
143 Rodney Leisle RC .40 1.00
144 Vince Wilfork RC .60 1.50
145 Lee Evans RC .60 1.50
146 Darnell Dockett RC .40 1.00
147 Jeremy LeSueur RC .40 1.00
148 Gilbert Gardner RC .40 1.00
149 Amon Gordon RC .40 1.00
150 Darius Watts RC .40 1.00
151 Junior Siavii RC .60 1.50
152 Igor Olshansky RC .50 1.25
153 Courtney Watson RC .40 1.00
154 D.J. Williams RC .60 1.50
155 Mewelde Moore RC .50 1.25
156 Teddy Lehman RC .40 1.00
157 Nathan Vasher RC .60 1.50
158 Randy Starks RC .40 1.00
159 Isaac Sopoaga RC .40 1.00
160 Drew Henson RC .40 1.00
161 Erik Coleman RC .50 1.25
162 Robert Kent RC .40 1.00
163 Jammal Lord RC .40 1.00
164 Richard Seigler RC .40 1.00
165 Jeff Smoker RC .50 1.25
166 Niko Koutouvides RC .40 1.00
167 Adimchinobe Echemandu RC .50 1.25
168 Matt Mauck RC .40 1.00
169 Brandon Miree RC .40 1.00
170 Dunta Robinson RC .40 1.00
171 B.J. Symons RC .60 1.50
172 Courtney Anderson RC .40 1.00
173 Bruce Perry RC .40 1.00
174 Shaun Phillips RC .60 1.50
175 Greg Jones RC .40 1.00
176 Ryan Krause RC .40 1.00
177 Charlie Anderson RC .40 1.00
178 Tank Johnson RC .40 1.00
179 Dwan Edwards RC .40 1.00
180 Julius Jones RC .50 1.25
181 Chad Lavalais RC .40 1.00
182 Tim Anderson RC .60 1.50
183 Jarrett Payton RC .60 1.50
184 Matt Ware RC .60 1.50
185 DeAngelo Hall RC .60 1.50
186 Ben Hartsock RC .40 1.00
187 Bradlee Van Pelt RC .60 1.50
188 Michael Boulware RC .60 1.50
189 Keith Smith RC .40 1.00
190 Michael Jenkins RC .60 1.50
191 Quincy Wilson RC .50 1.25
192 Dontarrious Thomas RC .50 1.25
193 Sloan Thomas RC .50 1.25
194 Tony Hargrove RC .40 1.00
195 Ben Watson RC .60 1.50
196 Craig Krenzel RC .50 1.25
197 Jason Babin RC .60 1.50
198 Jim Sorgi RC .50 1.25
199 Triandos Luke RC .40 1.00
200 Kellen Winslow RC .60 1.50
201 Patrick Crayton RC .60 1.50
202 Michael Waddell RC .40 1.00
203 Chris Gamble RC .50 1.25
204 Josh Harris RC .40 1.00
205 Devard Darling RC .40 1.00
206 Shawntae Spencer RC .40 1.00
207 Will Smith RC .50 1.25
208 Samie Parker RC .40 1.00
209 Darrion Scott RC .60 1.50
210 Chris Perry RC .50 1.25
211 P.K. Sam RC .40 1.00
212 Woo Woller RC 2.50 6.00
213 Ryan Dinwiddie RC .40 1.00
214 Rod Davis RC .40 1.00
215 Casey Clausen RC .50 1.25
216 Clarence Moore RC .40 1.00
217 D.J. Hackett RC .50 1.25
218 Casey Bramlet RC .40 1.00
219 Jared Lorenzen RC .50 1.25
220 Devery Henderson RC .60 1.50
221 Sean Jones RC .50 1.25
222 Maurice Mann RC .40 1.00
223 Jared Allen RC 1.50 4.00
224 Bruce Thornton RC .40 1.00
225 Talum Bell RC .50 1.25
226 Leon Joe RC .40 1.00
227 Tim Euhus RC .40 1.00
228 John Standeford RC .40 1.00
229 Reggie Torbor RC .40 1.00
230 Rashaun Woods RC .40 1.00
231 Jason Shivers RC .40 1.00
232 Jason Peters RC .50 1.25
233 Ahmad Carroll RC .40 1.00
234 Jason David RC .60 1.50
235 Keyaron Fox RC .50 1.25
236 Corey Williams RC .50 1.25
237 Raheem Orr RC .40 1.00
238 Carlos Francis RC .40 1.00
239 Von Hutchins RC .40 1.00
240 Marcus Tubbs RC .60 1.50
241 Daryl Smith RC .40 1.00
242 Robert Gallery RC .60 1.50
243 Sean Tufts RC .40 1.00
244 Marquis Cooper RC .40 1.00
245 Bernard Berrian RC .60 1.50
246 Derrick Strait RC .40 1.00
247 Travis LaBoy RC .60 1.50
248 Johnnie Morant RC .40 1.00
249 Caleb Miller RC .40 1.00
250 Michael Clayton RC .50 1.25
251 Will Poole RC .60 1.50
252 Andy Hall RC .40 1.00
253 Demorrio Williams RC .60 1.50
254 Chris Thompson RC .40 1.00
255 Derrick Hamilton RC .40 1.00
256 Glenn Earl RC .40 1.00
257 Jonathan Vilma RC .60 1.50
258 Donnell Washington RC .50 1.25
259 Drew Carter RC .50 1.25
260 Steven Jackson RC 1.00 2.50
261 Jamaar Taylor RC .40 1.00
262 Nate Lawrie RC .40 1.00
263 Cody Pickett RC .50 1.25
264 Keiwan Ratliff RC .40 1.00
265 Luke McCown RC .50 1.25
266 Jerricho Cotchery RC .50 1.25
267 Joey Thomas RC .40 1.00
268 Shawn Andrews RC .60 1.50
269 Derrick Ward RC .60 1.50
270 Reggie Williams RC .50 1.25
271 Rod Rutherford RC .40 1.00
272 Michael Turner RC .75 2.00
273 Michael Gaines RC .40 1.00
274 Will Allen RC .50 1.25
275 J.P. Losman RC .50 1.25

2004 Bowman First Edition

COMPLETE SET (275) 60.00 120.00
*FIRST EDIT.VETS: .8X TO 2X BASE CARD
*FIRST ED.ROOKIES: .6X TO 1.5X BASE CARD HI

2004 Bowman Gold

COMPLETE SET (110) 12.50 30.00
*GOLD STARS: 1X TO 2.5X BASE CARD HI
ONE GOLD PER PACK

2004 Bowman Uncirculated Gold

*GOLD BORDER: 2.5X TO 6X BASIC CARDS
ANNOUNCED PRINT RUN 110 SETS

2004 Bowman Uncirculated White

*UNCIR.WHITE VETS: 3X TO 8X BASIC CARD
*UNCIR.WHITE ROOKIES: 2X TO 5X
ONE WHITE BORDER PER HOB/HTA BOX
STATED PRINT RUN 165 SER.#'d SETS

2004 Bowman Coaches Autographs

BRC STATED ODDS 1:2160 HOB
BRP STATED ODDS 1:1440 HOB
BRCJM Jim Mora Jr. 10.00 25.00
BRCMM Mike Mularkey 7.50 20.00
BRPGK Gary Kubiak 7.50 20.00
BRPSP Sean Payton 75.00 125.00

2004 Bowman Draft Day Selections Relics

CAP & JSY-CAP/25 ODDS 1:8640 HOB
JSY GROUP A ODDS 1:1728 H
JSY GROUP B ODDS 1:1481 H
JSY GROUP C ODDS 1:788 H
JSY GROUP D ODDS 1:540 H
JSY GROUP E ODDS 1:465 H
DHBR Ben Roethlisberger Cap 60.00 120.00
DHDH DeAngelo Hall Cap
DHKW Kellen Winslow Cap
DHRG Robert Gallery Cap
DHRW Roy Williams WR Cap
DJBR Ben Roethlisberger Jsy B 20.00 50.00
DJDEM Eli Manning Jsy-Jsy/500 20.00 50.00
DJDH DeAngelo Hall Jsy B 5.00 12.00
DJEM Eli Manning Jsy A 20.00 50.00
DJHBR Ben Roethlisberger Jsy-Cap 100.00 200.00
DJHDH DeAngelo Hall Jsy-Cap 12.50 30.00
DJHRG Robert Gallery Jsy-Cap 12.50 30.00
DJHRW Roy Williams WR Jsy-Cap 20.00 50.00
DJKW Kellen Winslow Jsy D 5.00 12.00
DJRG Robert Gallery Jsy C 5.00 12.00
DJRW Roy Williams WR Jsy E 5.00 12.00

2004 Bowman Fabric of the Future

GROUP A ODDS 1:2908 H
GROUP B ODDS 1:1728 H
GROUP C ODDS 1:717 H
GROUP D ODDS 1:575 H
GROUP E ODDS 1:949 H
GROUP F ODDS 1:182 H
GROUP G ODDS 1:480 H
GROUP H ODDS 1:92 H
GROUP I ODDS 1:126 H
FFBR Ben Roethlisberger D 15.00 40.00
FFBT Ben Troupe C 3.00 8.00
FFDH DeAngelo Hall D 4.00 10.00
FFDR Dunta Robinson A 3.00 8.00
FFEM Eli Manning B 15.00 40.00
FFKJ Kevin Jones F 3.00 8.00
FFKW Kellen Winslow Jr. G 4.00 10.00
FFLE Lee Evans H 4.00 10.00
FFLM Luke McCown F 3.00 8.00
FFMJ Michael Jenkins E 4.00 10.00
FFPR Philip Rivers C 10.00 25.00
FFRW Roy Williams WR I 4.00 10.00
FFRWI Reggie Williams H 3.00 8.00
FFSJ Steven Jackson I 6.00 15.00
FFTB Tatum Bell H 3.00 8.00

2004 Bowman Fabric of the Future Doubles

STATED ODDS 1:2936 HOB
STATED PRINT RUN 50 SER.#'d SETS
FFDEJ Lee Evans 6.00 15.00
Michael Jenkins
FFDHR DeAngelo Hall 6.00 15.00
Dunta Robinson
FFDJB Kevin Jones 5.00 12.00
Tatum Bell
FFDMW Eli Manning 20.00 50.00
Reggie Williams
FFDWT Kellen Winslow Jr. 6.00 15.00
Ben Troupe

2004 Bowman Fast Forward Dual Jersey

STATED PRINT RUN 199 SER.#'d SETS
FFWBR Tom Brady 15.00 40.00
Philip Rivers
FFWCR Daunte Culpepper 20.00 50.00
Ben Roethlisberger
FFWFJ Marshall Faulk 6.00 15.00
Steven Jackson
FFWHW Torry Holt 4.00 10.00
Roy Williams WR
FFWMM Josh McCown 3.00 8.00
Luke McCown

2004 Bowman Rookie Autographs Blue

BLUE STATED ODDS 1:766 HOB
111 Eli Manning 100.00 175.00
112 Kevin Jones 15.00 40.00
113 Philip Rivers 50.00 100.00
114 Ben Roethlisberger 90.00 150.00
115 Roy Williams WR 20.00 50.00

2004 Bowman Rookie Autographs Red

*RED AUTO/25: .8X TO 2X BLUE AUTO
RED/25 STATED ODDS 1:7033 HOB
111 Eli Manning 250.00 400.00
114 Ben Roethlisberger 200.00 400.00

2004 Bowman Signs of the Future Autographs

GROUP A ODDS 1:2160 H
GROUP B ODDS 1:3398 H
GROUP C ODDS 1:1938 H
GROUP D ODDS 1:1239 H
GROUP E ODDS 1:866 H
GROUP F ODDS 1:192 H
GROUP G ODDS 1:443 H
GROUP H ODDS 1:91 H
GROUP I ODDS 1:345 H
GROUP J ODDS 1:69 H
SFCC Cedric Cobbs 3.00 8.00
SFCCL Casey Clausen H 4.00 10.00
SFCP Cody Pickett H 4.00 10.00
SFCPE Chris Perry H 4.00 10.00
SFEW Ernest Wilford J 4.00 10.00
SFGJ Greg Jones F 3.00 8.00
SFJC Jerricho Cotchery J 4.00 10.00
SFJH Josh Harris H 3.00 8.00
SFJN John Navarre J 3.00 8.00
SFJPL J.P. Losman C 4.00 10.00
SFJS Jeff Smoker I 4.00 10.00
SFKC Keary Colbert E 3.00 8.00
SFKJ Kevin Jones A 6.00 15.00
SFLE Lee Evans G 5.00 12.00
SFMC Michael Clayton D 4.00 10.00
SFMJ Michael Jenkins J 5.00 12.00
SFMM Mewelde Moore H 4.00 10.00
SFMS Matt Schaub F 10.00 25.00
SFPR Philip Rivers A 30.00 50.00
SFRWO Rashaun Woods B 4.00 10.00
SFTB Tatum Bell F 4.00 10.00

2004 Bowman Signs of the Future Autographs Dual

STATED ODDS 1:4383 HOB
STATED PRINT RUN 50 SER.#'d SETS
SFDFE Larry Fitzgerald 20.00 50.00
Lee Evans
SFDJJ Steven Jackson 12.00 30.00
Kevin Jones
SFDLC J.P. Losman 6.00 15.00
Michael Clayton
SFDMR Eli Manning 75.00 150.00
Philip Rivers

2005 Bowman

This 275-card set was released in October, 2005. The set was issued in the hobby in 10-card packs with an $3 SRP which came 24 packs to a box. Cards numbered 1-109 feature veterans while cards numbered 110-275 feature NFL rookies.

COMP.SET w/o AU's (270) 25.00 60.00
UNPRICED GOLD PRINT RUN 1
UNPRICED PRINT PLATES SER.#'d TO 1
1 Peyton Manning .60 1.50
2 Antonio Gates .30 .75
3 Priest Holmes .25 .60
4 Anquan Boldin .25 .60
5 Donovan McNabb .30 .75
6 Drew Bennett .25 .60
7 Michael Vick .30 .75
8 David Carr .20 .50
9 Drew Brees .30 .75
10 Trent Green .25 .60
11 Drew Bledsoe .30 .75
12 Randy Moss .30 .75
13 Terrell Owens .30 .75
14 Donte Stallworth .20 .50
15 Alge Crumpler .25 .60
16 Jake Plummer .25 .60
17 Curtis Martin .30 .75
18 Jason Witten .30 .75
19 Tom Brady .60 1.50
20 Thomas Jones .30 .75
21 Tiki Barber .30 .75
22 Maurice Carthon CO .20 .50
23 Rex Grossman .25 .60
24 Brett Favre .75 2.00
25 Marshall Faulk .30 .75
26 LaMont Jordan .25 .60
27 Kurt Warner .30 .75
28 Corey Dillon .25 .60
29 Julius Jones .20 .50
30 Ahman Green .25 .60
31 Jamal Lewis .25 .60
32 Ben Roethlisberger .50 1.25
33 Keary Colbert .20 .50
34 Mike Nolan CO RC .25 .60
35 Joey Harrington .25 .60
36 Brian Westbrook .25 .60
37 Domanick Davis .20 .50
38 Carson Palmer .30 .75
39 Stephen Davis .25 .60
40 Eli Manning .50 1.25
41 Edgerrin James .25 .60
42 Jonathan Vilma .25 .60
43 Brad Childress CO RC .25 .60
44 Willis McGahee .30 .75
45 Steve McNair .30 .75
46 Plaxico Burress .25 .60
47 Rudi Johnson .25 .60
48 Jerry Porter .20 .50
49 Chad Pennington .30 .75
50 Charles Rogers .20 .50
51 Patrick Ramsey .25 .60
52 Dwight Freeney .25 .60
53 Brian Griese .25 .60
54 Jerome Bettis .30 .75
55 Tim Lewis CO .20 .50
56 Aaron Brooks .20 .50
57 Matt Hasselbeck .25 .60
58 Chris Chambers .25 .60
59 Kyle Boller .25 .60
60 Brandon Lloyd .20 .50
61 Marc Bulger .25 .60
62 Isaac Bruce .25 .60
63 Jake Delhomme .25 .60
64 Chad Johnson .25 .60
65 Shaun Alexander .25 .60
66 Kevin Jones .20 .50
67 Eric Moulds .20 .50
68 Laveranues Coles .20 .50
69 A.J. Feeley .20 .50
70 Sean Taylor .30 .75
71 Romeo Crennel CO RC .30 .75
72 Ashley Lelie .20 .50
73 Nick Saban CO RC .25 .60
74 Deuce McAllister .25 .60
75 Kerry Collins .25 .60
76 Chris Brown .20 .50
77 Steven Jackson .30 .75
78 Nate Burleson .20 .50
79 LaDainian Tomlinson .30 .75
80 Darrell Jackson .20 .50
81 Torry Holt .25 .60
82 Lee Suggs .20 .50
83 Lee Evans .25 .60
84 Santana Moss .25 .60
85 Jeremy Shockey .30 .75
86 Hines Ward .30 .75
87 Muhsin Muhammad .25 .60
88 Daunte Culpepper .25 .60
89 Deion Branch .20 .50
90 DeShaun Foster .25 .60
91 Travis Henry .20 .50
92 Jerry Rice .60 1.50
93 Reggie Wayne .30 .75
94 Roy Williams WR .25 .60
95 Michael Jenkins .25 .60
96 Tatum Bell .20 .50
97 Andre Johnson .30 .75
98 Dante Hall .20 .50
99 Javon Walker .20 .50
100 Larry Fitzgerald .30 .75
101 Joe Horn .25 .60
102 Marvin Harrison .30 .75
103 Fred Taylor .25 .60
104 Byron Leftwich .25 .60
105 Tony Gonzalez .25 .60
106 T.J. Houshmandzadeh .25 .60
107 J.P. Losman .20 .50
108 Michael Clayton .20 .50
109 Clinton Portis .25 .60
110 Ted Cottrell CO RC .20 .50
111 Braylon Edwards RC .75 2.00
112 Aaron Rodgers RC 8.00 20.00
113 Ronnie Brown RC .75 2.00
114 Alex Smith QB RC 1.00 2.50
115 Cadillac Williams RC .60 1.50
116 Ciatrick Fason RC .40 1.00
117 Derrick Johnson RC .50 1.25
118 Carlos Rogers RC .60 1.50
119 Ryan Moats RC .40 1.00
120 Alvin Pearman RC .40 1.00
121 Stefan LeFors RC .40 1.00
122 Brandon Jacobs RC .75 2.00
123 Kyle Orton RC .60 1.60
124 Marion Barber RC .60 1.50
125 Mark Bradley RC .40 1.00
126 Travis Johnson RC .40 1.00
127 Antrel Rolle RC .60 1.50
128 Jason Campbell RC .75 2.00
129 DeMarcus Ware RC 1.25 3.00
130 Frank Gore RC 1.00 2.50
131 Justin Miller RC .50 1.25
132 J.J. Arrington RC .50 1.25
133 Marcus Spears RC .50 1.25
134 Roddy White RC .75 2.00
135 Fabian Washington RC .50 1.25
136 Vincent Jackson RC .75 2.00
137 Erasmus James RC .50 1.25
138 Roscoe Parrish RC .40 1.00
139 Airese Currie RC .40 1.00
140 Heath Miller RC .75 2.00
141 Mike Patterson RC .40 1.00
142 Troy Williamson RC .50 1.25
143 Terrence Murphy RC .40 1.00
144 Dan Orlovsky RC .60 1.50
145 Eric Shelton RC .40 1.00
146 Thomas Davis RC .40 1.00
147 Cedric Benson RC .60 1.50
148 Noah Herron RC .40 1.00
149 Vernand Morency RC .40 1.00
150 Darren Sproles RC .60 1.50
151 Alex Smith TE RC .40 1.00
152 Mark Clayton RC .50 1.25
153 Craphonso Thorpe RC .40 1.00
154 Mike Williams .60 1.50
155 Anthony Davis RC .40 1.00
156 Charlie Frye RC .60 1.50
157 Fred Gibson RC .50 1.25
158 Reggie Brown RC .40 1.00
159 Andrew Walter RC .50 1.25
160 Adam Jones RC .40 1.00
161 David Greene RC .40 1.00
162 Maurice Clarett .40 1.00
163 Courtney Roby RC .50 1.25
164 Derek Anderson RC .50 1.25
165 Matt Jones RC .50 1.25
166 Chris Henry RC .60 1.50
167 Shaun Cody RC .50 1.25
168 Khalif Barnes RC .40 1.00
169 Matt Roth RC .50 1.25
170 Lionel Gates RC .40 1.00
171 Kevin Burnett RC .50 1.25
172 Taylor Stubblefield RC .40 1.00
173 Zach Tuiasosopo RC .40 1.00
174 Alex Barron RC .40 1.00
175 Mike Nugent RC .50 1.25
176 Barrett Ruud RC .60 1.50
177 Brock Berlin RC .50 1.25
178 Kirk Morrison RC .60 1.50
179 David Pollack RC .50 1.25
180 Ryan Fitzpatrick RC 1.00 2.50
181 Kay-Jay Harris RC .40 1.00
182 Dan Cody RC .50 1.25
183 Chad Owens RC .50 1.25
184 Stanley Wilson RC .50 1.25
185 Rasheed Marshall RC .50 1.25
186 Bryant McFadden RC .50 1.25
187 Joel Dreessen RC .50 1.25
188 Donte Nicholson RC .40 1.00
189 Scott Starks RC .50 1.25
190 Walter Reyes RC .40 1.00
191 Stanford Routt RC .50 1.25
192 Lance Mitchell RC .50 1.25
193 Rian Wallace RC .50 1.25
194 Timmy Chang RC .50 1.25
195 Oshiomogho Atogwe RC .60 1.50
196 Larry Brackins RC .40 1.00
197 Jovan Witherspoon RC .40 1.00
198 Boomer Grigsby RC .60 1.50
199 Darryl Blackstock RC .40 1.00
200 Jerome Mathis RC .60 1.50
201 Ellis Hobbs RC .60 1.50
202 Dante Ridgeway RC .40 1.00
203 James Kilian RC .40 1.00

204 Patrick Estes RC .40 1.00
205 Justin Tuck RC .75 2.00
206 Channing Crowder RC .50 1.25
207 Dustin Fox RC .50 1.25
208 Marlin Jackson RC .40 1.00
209 Luis Castillo RC .50 1.25
210 Paris Warren RC .50 1.25
211 J.R. Russell RC .40 1.00
212 Cedric Houston RC .60 1.50
213 Corey Webster RC .50 1.25
214 Craig Bragg RC .40 1.00
215 Tab Perry RC .40 1.00
216 Ryan Riddle RC .40 1.00
217 Gino Guidugli RC .40 1.00
218 Deandra Cobb RC .40 1.00
219 Travis Daniels RC .50 1.25
220 Marcus Maxwell RC .40 1.00
221 Eric King RC .40 1.00
222 Matt Cassel RC 1.25 3.00
223 Justin Green RC .60 1.50
224 Steve Savoy RC .40 1.00
225 Shawne Merriman RC .60 1.50
226 Damien Nash RC .50 1.25
227 T.A. McLendon RC .40 1.00
228 Vincent Fuller RC .50 1.25
229 Jordan Beck RC .50 1.25
230 Lofa Tatupu RC .60 1.50
231 Will Peoples RC .50 1.25
232 Chad Friehauf RC .50 1.25
233 Brady Poppinga RC .60 1.50
234 Anttaj Hawthorne RC .40 1.00
235 Adrian McPherson RC .40 1.00
236 Nick Collins RC .60 1.50
237 Roydell Williams RC .50 1.25
238 Craig Ochs RC .50 1.25
239 Billy Bajema RC .40 1.00
240 Jon Goldsberry RC .60 1.50
241 Jared Newberry RC .50 1.25
242 Odell Thurman RC .60 1.50
243 Kelvin Hayden RC .50 1.25
244 Jamaal Brimmer RC .40 1.00
245 Jonathan Babineaux RC .50 1.25
246 Bo Scaife RC .50 1.25
247 Chris Spencer RC .60 1.50
248 Manuel White RC .50 1.25
249 Josh Davis RC .40 1.00
250 Bryan Randall RC .50 1.25
251 James Butler RC .50 1.25
252 Harry Williams RC .50 1.25
253 Leroy Hill RC .60 1.50
254 Josh Bullocks RC .50 1.25
255 Alfred Fincher RC .50 1.25
256 Antonio Perkins RC .50 1.25
257 Bobby Purify RC .50 1.25
258 Rick Razzano RC .40 1.00
259 Darrent Williams RC .60 1.50
260 Darian Durant RC .40 1.00
261 Fred Amey RC .40 1.00
262 Ronald Bartell RC .50 1.25
263 Kerry Rhodes RC .50 1.25
264 Jerome Carter RC .40 1.00
265 Marcus Randall RC .50 1.25
266 Nehemiah Broughton RC .50 1.25
267 Keron Henry RC .40 1.00
268 Jerome Collins RC .50 1.25
269 Trent Cole RC .60 1.50
270 Alphonso Hodge RC .40 1.00
271 Brandon Jones RC .50 1.25
272 Chase Lyman RC .40 1.00
273 Marviel Underwood RC .50 1.25
274 Maurice Washington RC .40 1.00
275 Madison Hedgecock RC .60 1.50

2005 Bowman Bronze

COMPLETE SET (275) 75.00 150.00
*VETS: 1X TO 2.5X BASIC CARDS
*ROOKIES: .8X TO 2X BASIC CARDS
ONE BRONZE PER PACK

2005 Bowman First Edition

COMPLETE SET (275) 60.00 120.00
*VETS: .8X TO 2X BASIC CARDS
*ROOKIES: .6X TO 1.5X BASIC CARDS

2005 Bowman Silver

*VETS:/200 2X TO 5X BASIC CARDS
*ROOKIES/200: 1.2X TO 3X BASIC CARDS
SILVER/200 ODDS 1:12 H/R, 1:6 JUM

2005 Bowman Coaches Autographs

PROSPECT ODDS 1:2058H, 1:398J, 1:2139R
COACH ROOK.ODDS 1:4171H, 1:792J, 1:4598R
BCPBC Brad Childress 12.00 30.00
BCPMC Maurice Carthon 10.00 25.00
BCPTC Ted Cottrell 10.00 25.00
BCPTL Tim Lewis 10.00 25.00
BRCMN Mike Nolan 12.00 30.00
BRCRC Romeo Crennel 12.00 30.00

2005 Bowman Draft Day Selections Relics

GROUP A JERSEY 1:1208H, 1:365J, 1:1282R
GROUP B JERSEY 1:305H, 1:92J, 1:321R
CAP & JSY-CAP/25 ODDS 1:15,244H, 1:4557J
UNPRICED 1/1 STATED ODDS 1:147,360
DHAR Antrel Rolle Cap 15.00 30.00
DHARO Aaron Rodgers Cap 50.00 100.00
DHCB Cedric Benson Cap 15.00 40.00
DHRB Ronnie Brown Cap 25.00 50.00
DJAR Antrel Rolle Jsy A 6.00 15.00
DJARO Aaron Rodgers Jsy B 30.00 60.00
DJCB Cedric Benson Jsy B 6.00 15.00
DJHAR Antrel Rolle Jsy-Cap 12.50 30.00
DJHARO Aaron Rodgers Jsy-Cap 50.00 100.00
DJHCB Cedric Benson Jsy-Cap 15.00 40.00
DJHRB Ronnie Brown Jsy-Cap 25.00 50.00
DJRB Ronnie Brown Jsy B 10.00 20.00

2005 Bowman Fabric of the Future

GROUP A ODDS 1:1364H, 1:400J, 1:1472R
GROUP B ODDS 1:43 H, 1:18 J, 1:132 R
*GOLD/100: .6X TO 1.5X BASIC JSY
GOLD/100 ODDS 1:1002H, 1:330J, 1:1074R
UNPRICED LETTER PRINT RUN 1
FFARO Antrel Rolle B 4.00 10.00
FFAS Alex Smith QB B 6.00 15.00
FFAW Andrew Walter B 3.00 8.00
FFCR Carlos Rogers A 4.00 10.00
FFES Eric Shelton B 2.50 6.00
FFFG Frank Gore B 6.00 15.00
FFJJA J.J. Arrington B 3.00 8.00
FFMC Maurice Clarett B 2.50 6.00
FFRB Reggie Brown B 2.50 6.00
FFRM Ryan Moats B 2.50 6.00
FFRP Roscoe Parrish B 2.50 6.00
FFRW Roddy White B 5.00 12.00
FFSL Stefan LeFors B 2.50 6.00
FFVJ Vincent Jackson B 5.00 12.00
FFVM Vernand Morency B 2.50 6.00

2005 Bowman Fabric of the Future Doubles

DOUBLE/50 ODDS 1:6056H, 1:2170J, 1:6624R
FFDCJ Mark Clayton 8.00 20.00
Matt Jones
FFDEW Braylon Edwards
Troy Williamson
FFDRJ Antrelle Rolle
Adam Jones
FFDSC Alex Smith QB 15.00 40.00
Jason Campbell
FFDWB Cadillac Williams 15.00 40.00
Ronnie Brown

2005 Bowman Rookie Autographs

STATED ODDS 1:1249 H, 1:249 J, 1:1485 R
111 Braylon Edwards 15.00 40.00
112 Aaron Rodgers 250.00 400.00
113 Ronnie Brown 15.00 40.00
114 Alex Smith QB 30.00 60.00
115 Cadillac Williams 12.00 30.00

2005 Bowman Signs of the Future Autographs

GROUP A ODDS 1:7247H, 1:2940J, 1:7997R
GROUP B ODDS 1:1373H, 1:1072J, 1:1764R
GROUP C ODDS 1:408H, 1:229J, 1:476R
GROUP D ODDS 1:1107H, 1:779J, 1:1230R
GROUP E ODDS 1:385H, 1:171J, 1:634R
GROUP F ODDS 1:557H, 1:432J, 1:758R
GROUP G ODDS 1:200H, 1:80J, 1:756R
GROUP H ODDS 1:292H, 1:126J, 1:1171R
GROUP I ODDS 1:193H, 1:84J, 1:1688R
GROUP J ODDS 1:156H, 1:58J, 1:649R
GROUP K ODDS 1:86H, 1:36J, 1:130R
SFAM Adrian McPherson J
SFAP Alvin Pearman G 3.00 8.00
SFAR Antrel Rolle C 5.00 12.00
SFAS Alex Smith QB E 25.00 50.00
SFBE Braylon Edwards A 6.00 15.00
SFBJ Brandon Jacobs H 8.00 20.00
SFCBR Craig Bragg K 3.00 8.00
SFCF Ciatrick Fason C 3.00 8.00
SFCFR Charlie Frye B 5.00 12.00
SFCFRE Charles Frederick F 3.00 8.00
SFCH Cedric Houston E 5.00 12.00
SFCO Chad Owens K 4.00 10.00
SFCR Courtney Roby K 4.00 10.00
SFCT Craphonso Thorpe C 3.00 8.00
SFDJ Derrick Johnson I 4.00 10.00
SFDO Dan Orlovsky D 5.00 12.00
SFDP David Pollack B 4.00 10.00
SFES Eric Shelton C 3.00 8.00
SFFG Frank Gore J 8.00 20.00
SFHM Heath Miller C 6.00 15.00
SFJC Jason Campbell C 6.00 15.00
SFLM Lance Mitchell G 4.00 10.00
SFMB Mark Bradley K 3.00 8.00
SFMBA Marion Barber C 5.00 12.00
SFMC Mark Clayton C 4.00 10.00
SFMCL Maurice Clarett E 3.00 8.00
SFMW Mike Williams D 5.00 12.00
SFRB Reggie Brown B 3.00 8.00
SFRM Ryan Moats H 3.00 8.00
SFRP Roscoe Parrish J 3.00 8.00
SFRW Roddy White I 6.00 15.00
SFSL Stefan LeFors K 3.00 8.00
SFTM Terrence Murphy I 3.00 8.00
SFTS Taylor Stubblefield F 3.00 8.00
SFTW Troy Williamson G 4.00 10.00
SFVJ Vincent Jackson E 6.00 15.00
SFVM Vernand Morency G 3.00 8.00

2005 Bowman Signs of the Future Autographs Dual

DUAL AU/50 ODDS 1:7247H, 1:1248J, 1:7997R
SFDBB Ronnie Brown 40.00 100.00
Cedric Benson
SFDBW Ronnie Brown 75.00 150.00
Cadillac Williams
SFDSR Alex Smith QB 200.00 350.00
Aaron Rodgers
SFDWC Troy Williamson 20.00 50.00
Mark Clayton
SFDWE Mike Williams 50.00 120.00
Braylon Edwards

2005 Bowman Throwback Threads Jerseys

STATED ODDS 1:76 H, 1:32 J, 1:137 R
*GOLD/50: .6X TO 1.5X BASIC JSY
GOLD/50 ODDS 1:2695 H, 1:701J, 1:2484R
BRTAW Andrew Walter 3.00 8.00
BRTCF Ciatrick Fason 2.50 6.00
BRTCR Courtney Roby 3.00 8.00
BRTCFR Charlie Frye 4.00 10.00
BRTES Eric Shelton 2.50 6.00
BRTFG Frank Gore 6.00 15.00
BRTKO Kyle Orton 4.00 10.00
BRTMB Mark Bradley 2.50 6.00
BRTRM Ryan Moats 3.00 8.00
BRTRP Roscoe Parrish 2.50 6.00
BRTSL Stefan LeFors 2.50 6.00
BRTVJ Vincent Jackson 5.00 12.00
BRTVM Vernand Morency 3.00 8.00

2006 Bowman

This 275-card set was released in October, 2006. The set was issued into the hobby in 10-card packs, with a $3 SRP, which came 24 packs to a box. Cards numbered 1-100 feature veterans (and a couple of newly-hired head coaches) while cards numbered 101-275 feature 2006 rookies.

COMPLETE SET (275) 25.00 60.00
UNPRICED PRINT PLATES SER.#'d TO 1
UNPRICED RED SER.#'d TO 1
1 Plaxico Burress .25 .60
2 Lee Evans .25 .60
3 Shaun Alexander .25 .60
4 Muhsin Muhammad .25 .60
5 Jamal Lewis .25 .60
6 Brett Favre .60 1.50
7 Jake Plummer .25 .60
8 Clinton Portis .30 .75
9 Deuce McAllister .25 .60
10 Rod Marinelli CO RC .20 .50
11 Tom Brady .50 1.25
12 Torry Holt .25 .60
13 T.J. Houshmandzadeh .25 .60
14 Rudi Johnson .25 .60
15 Priest Holmes .25 .60
16 Tatum Bell .20 .50
17 Carson Palmer .30 .75
18 Jeremy Shockey .30 .75
19 Willis McGahee .25 .60
20 Shawne Merriman .25 .60
21 Alge Crumpler .25 .60
22 Terrell Owens .30 .75
23 Marion Barber .30 .75
24 Fred Taylor .25 .60
25 Dante Hall .25 .60
26 Steve Smith .30 .75
27 Mike McCarthy CO RC .20 .50
28 Brad Johnson .25 .60
29 Reggie Wayne .25 .60
30 David Carr .20 .50
31 DeShaun Foster .25 .60
32 Julius Jones .20 .50
33 Tony Gonzalez .25 .60
34 Chad Johnson .25 .60
35 Javon Walker .25 .60
36 Curtis Martin .30 .75
37 Marc Bulger .25 .60
38 Peyton Manning .50 1.25
39 LaMont Jordan .25 .60
40 LaDainian Tomlinson .30 .75
41 Tiki Barber .30 .75
42 Darrell Jackson .25 .60
43 Byron Leftwich .25 .60
44 J.P. Losman .25 .60
45 Dwight Freeney .25 .60
46 Kevin Jones .20 .50
47 Drew Brees .30 .75
48 Isaac Bruce .25 .60
49 Hines Ward .30 .75
50 Drew Bledsoe .30 .75
51 Randy Moss .30 .75
52 Roy Williams WR .25 .60
53 Edgerrin James .25 .60
54 Donte Stallworth .20 .50
55 Odell Thurman .20 .50
56 Chester Taylor .25 .60
57 Ahman Green .25 .60
58 Steven Jackson .30 .75
59 Randy McMichael .20 .50
60 Larry Fitzgerald .30 .75
61 Ben Roethlisberger .40 1.00
62 Charlie Frye .25 .60
63 Daunte Culpepper .25 .60
64 Keary Colbert .20 .50
65 Santana Moss .25 .60
66 Patrick Ramsey .25 .60
67 Mark Clayton .25 .60
68 Jonathan Vilma .25 .60
69 Gary Kubiak CO .20 .50
70 Michael Jenkins .25 .60
71 Jake Delhomme .25 .60
72 Marvin Harrison .30 .75
73 Aaron Rodgers .60 1.50
74 Trent Green .25 .60
75 Andre Johnson .30 .75
76 Chris Chambers .25 .60
77 Matt Hasselbeck .25 .60
78 Chris Brown .20 .50
79 Reggie Brown .20 .50
80 Eli Manning .40 1.00
81 Warrick Dunn .25 .60
82 Kurt Warner .30 .75
83 Corey Dillon .25 .60
84 Antonio Gates .30 .75
85 Anquan Boldin .25 .60
86 Terry Glenn .25 .60
87 Donovan McNabb .30 .75
88 Steve McNair .25 .60
89 Drew Bennett .25 .60
90 Jason Witten .30 .75
91 Alex Smith QB .30 .75
92 Joe Horn .25 .60
93 Eric Moulds .20 .50
94 Domanick Davis .20 .50
95 Billy Volek .20 .50
96 Deion Branch .25 .60
97 Chris Cooley .25 .60
98 Todd Heap UER .25 .60
(front photo is Jason Witten)
99 Larry Johnson .25 .60
100 Chad Pennington .25 .60
101 Willie Parker .25 .60
102 Brandon Lloyd .20 .50
103 Cadillac Williams .25 .60
104 Rod Smith .25 .60
105 Philip Rivers .30 .75
106 Ronnie Brown .30 .75
107 Reuben Droughns .25 .60
108 Braylon Edwards .25 .60
109 Joey Galloway .25 .60
110 Michael Vick .30 .75
111 Reggie Bush RC 1.25 3.00
112 Matt Leinart RC .60 1.50
113 Vince Young RC .75 2.00
114 Jay Cutler RC 1.25 3.00
115 Santonio Holmes RC .75 2.00
116 LenDale White RC .50 1.25
117 DeAngelo Williams RC .75 2.00
118 Mario Williams RC .60 1.50
119 A.J. Hawk RC .60 1.50
120 Joseph Addai RC .60 1.50
121 Leonard Pope RC .60 1.50
122 Tamba Hali RC .60 1.50
123 Bruce Gradkowski RC .60 1.50
124 Jerome Harrison RC .60 1.50
125 Jason Allen RC .50 1.25
126 Laurence Maroney RC .50 1.25
127 Mathias Kiwanuka RC .60 1.50
128 Brodrick Bunkley RC .50 1.25
129 Brian Calhoun RC .40 1.00
130 Bobby Carpenter RC .40 1.00
131 Johnathan Joseph RC .50 1.25
132 Maurice Stovall RC .40 1.00
133 Anthony Fasano RC .60 1.50
134 Travis Wilson RC .40 1.00
135 Chad Jackson RC .40 1.00
136 D'Brickashaw Ferguson RC .60 1.50
137 Tarvaris Jackson RC .60 1.50
138 Omar Jacobs RC .40 1.00
139 Reggie McNeal RC .50 1.25
140 Jerious Norwood RC .50 1.25
141 Haloti Ngata RC .60 1.50
142 Jason Avant RC .40 1.00
143 Brandon Marshall RC .60 1.50
144 Tye Hill RC .40 1.00
145 Manny Lawson RC .50 1.25
146 Brandon Williams RC .40 1.00
147 Demetrius Williams RC .50 1.25
148 Michael Huff RC .50 1.25
149 Mike Hass RC .50 1.25
150 Vernon Davis RC .75 2.00
151 Donte Whitner RC .60 1.50
152 Marcedes Lewis RC .60 1.50
153 Michael Robinson RC .50 1.25
154 Maurice Drew RC 1.00 2.50
155 Sinorice Moss RC .60 1.50
156 Brodie Croyle RC .60 1.50
157 Derek Hagan RC .50 1.25
158 Chad Greenway RC .60 1.50
159 Kellen Clemens RC .50 1.25
160 Skyler Green RC .40 1.00
161 Devin Hester RC 1.25 3.00
162 Jeremy Bloom RC .50 1.25
163 Ashton Youboty RC .40 1.00
164 Kamerion Wimbley RC .60 1.50
165 Charlie Whitehurst RC .60 1.50
166 Devin Aromashodu RC .60 1.50
167 Darnell Bing RC .50 1.25
168 Adam Jennings RC .50 1.25
169 Joe Klopfenstein RC .40 1.00
170 Jeff Webb RC .50 1.25
171 D.J. Shockley RC .50 1.25
172 Daniel Bullocks RC .60 1.50
173 Marcus Vick RC .40 1.00
174 Greg Jennings RC 1.25 3.00
175 David Thomas RC .50 1.25
176 Thomas Howard RC .50 1.25
177 Todd Watkins RC .40 1.00
178 Leon Washington RC .50 1.25
179 Winston Justice RC .50 1.25
180 Lawrence Vickers RC .50 1.25
181 Bernard Pollard RC .50 1.25
182 Davin Joseph RC .50 1.25
183 Abdul Hodge RC .40 1.00
184 Pat Watkins RC .50 1.25
185 Jon Alston RC .50 1.25
186 Ernie Sims RC .50 1.25
187 Jovon Bouknight RC .50 1.25
188 D'Qwell Jackson RC .50 1.25
189 Wali Lundy RC .50 1.25
190 Corey Bramlet RC .50 1.25
191 Jonathan Orr RC .50 1.25
192 Gerald Riggs RC .50 1.25
193 Antonio Cromartie RC .60 1.50
194 Will Blackmon RC .50 1.25
195 Chris Gocong RC .50 1.25
196 David Pittman RC .60 1.50
197 Quinn Sypniewski RC .50 1.25
198 A.J. Nicholson RC .40 1.00
199 Richard Marshall RC .50 1.25
200 Kevin McMahan RC .50 1.25
201 Cedric Humes RC .40 1.00
202 J.D. Runnels RC .50 1.25
203 Darryl Tapp RC .50 1.25
204 Charles Davis RC .50 1.25
205 Brad Smith RC .60 1.50
206 Tim Massaquoi RC .50 1.25
207 Nate Salley RC .50 1.25
208 Matt Shelton RC .60 1.50
209 Brett Basanez RC .60 1.50
210 Demario Minter RC .50 1.25
211 Marques Hagans RC .40 1.00
212 Rocky Mcintosh RC .50 1.25
213 Anthony Mix RC .50 1.25
214 Hank Baskett RC .60 1.50
215 Jimmy Williams RC .60 1.50
216 Andre Hall RC .50 1.25
217 Cody Hodges RC .50 1.25
218 Greg Lee RC .40 1.00
219 Danieal Manning RC .60 1.50
220 Jason Hatcher RC .60 1.50
221 Ben Obomanu RC .60 1.50
222 Dusty Dvoracek RC .60 1.50
223 Ingle Martin RC .50 1.25
224 Marcus McNeill RC .50 1.25
225 DeMeco Ryans RC .60 1.50
226 Dwayne Slay RC .50 1.25
227 Domenik Hixon RC .60 1.50
228 John David Washington RC .50 1.25
229 P.J. Daniels RC .40 1.00
230 Kelly Jennings RC .50 1.25
231 Josh Betts RC .50 1.25
232 Marques Colston RC 1.25 3.00
233 John McCargo RC .40 1.00
234 P.J. Pope RC .60 1.50
235 Gabe Watson RC .40 1.00
236 Paul Pinegar RC .40 1.00
237 Ray Edwards RC .60 1.50
238 Elvis Dumervil RC .60 1.50
239 Travis Lulay RC .50 1.25
240 Alan Zemaitis RC .60 1.50
241 Bennie Brazell RC .50 1.25
242 Jeff King RC .50 1.25
243 Damien Rhodes RC .50 1.25
244 Orien Harris RC .50 1.25
245 David Anderson RC .50 1.25
246 Roman Harper RC .50 1.25
247 Garrett Mills RC .60 1.50
248 Anthony Schlegel RC .50 1.25
249 David Kirtman RC .50 1.25
250 Omar Gaither RC .60 1.50
251 Freddie Keiaho RC .50 1.25
252 J.J. Outlaw RC .50 1.25
253 Willie Reid RC .50 1.25
254 Tony Scheffler RC .60 1.50
255 Dee Webb RC .50 1.25
256 Drew Olson RC .40 1.00
257 Tim Day RC .50 1.25
258 Martin Nance RC .50 1.25
259 Spencer Havner RC .50 1.25
260 Ko Simpson RC .50 1.25
261 Jesse Mahelona RC .50 1.25
262 Owen Daniels RC .60 1.50
263 Mike Bell RC .60 1.50
264 Anwar Phillips RC .50 1.25
265 Erik Meyer RC .50 1.25
266 Delanie Walker RC .60 1.50
267 Dominique Byrd RC .50 1.25
268 Eric Smith RC .50 1.25
269 Darrell Hackney RC .50 1.25
270 Freddie Roach RC .50 1.25
271 James Anderson RC .40 1.00
272 Anthony Smith RC .60 1.50
273 Quinton Ganther RC .40 1.00
274 Nick Mangold RC .50 1.25
275 Gerris Wilkinson RC .40 1.00

2006 Bowman Blue

*VETERANS: 1.5X TO 4X BASIC CARDS
*ROOKIES: .8X TO 2X BASIC CARDS
STATED PRINT RUN 500 SER.#'d SETS

2006 Bowman Gold

*VETERANS: .8X TO 2X BASIC CARDS
*ROOKIES: .6X TO 1.5X BASIC CARDS
ONE GOLD PER PACK

2006 Bowman White

*VETERANS: 2.5X TO 6X BASIC CARDS
*ROOKIES: 1.5X TO 4X BASIC CARDS
STATED PRINT RUN 125 SER.#'d SETS

2006 Bowman Rookie Autographs

AUTO/199 ODDS 1:2500 RETAIL
UNPRICED PRINT PLATES #'d TO 1
111 Reggie Bush 30.00 80.00
112 Matt Leinart 10.00 25.00
113 Vince Young 12.00 30.00
114 Jay Cutler 60.00 120.00
115 Santonio Holmes 12.00 30.00
116 LenDale White 8.00 20.00
117 DeAngelo Williams 12.00 30.00
118 Mario Williams 10.00 25.00
119 A.J. Hawk 10.00 25.00
120 Joseph Addai 10.00 25.00

2006 Bowman Draft Day Selections Relics

CAP ODDS 1:14,500 RET
JERSEY ODDS 1:275 RET
JERSEY/CAP/25 ODDS 1:28,000 RET
NFL LOGO 1/1 CARDS NOT PRICED
DHDF D'Brickashaw Ferguson Cap
DHML Matt Leinart Cap
DHMW Mario Williams Cap
DHRB Reggie Bush Cap
DHVD Vernon Davis Cap
DHVY Vince Young Cap
DJDF D'Brickashaw Ferguson Jsy 3.00 8.00
DJML Matt Leinart Jsy 5.00 12.00
DJMW Mario Williams Jsy 4.00 10.00
DJRB Reggie Bush Jsy 10.00 25.00
DJHDF D'Brickashaw Ferguson Jsy-Cap/25 10.00 25.00
DJHML Matt Leinart Jsy-Cap/25 20.00 50.00
DJHMW Mario Williams Jsy-Cap/25 20.00 40.00
DJHRB Reggie Bush Jsy-Cap/25 50.00 120.00

2006 Bowman Fabric of the Future

GROUP A ODDS 1:5275 H, 1:5300 R
GROUP B ODDS 1:112 H, 1:160 R
GROUP C ODDS 1:200 H, 1:210 R
*GOLD/100: .6X TO 1.5X BASIC INSERTS
GOLD/100 ODDS 1:1000 RET
UNPRICED LOGO PATCHES #'d TO 1
FFAH A.J. Hawk B 1.50 4.00
FFBC Brian Calhoun C 2.50 6.00
FFCJ Chad Jackson B 2.50 6.00
FFCW Charlie Whitehurst C 3.00 8.00
FFDH Derek Hagan B 2.50 6.00
FFDW DeAngelo Williams A 5.00 12.00
FFKC Kellen Clemens C 3.00 8.00
FFLM Laurence Maroney B 4.00 10.00
FFLW LenDale White C 4.00 10.00
FFMD Maurice Drew B 4.00 10.00
FFMH Michael Huff B 3.00 8.00
FFML Matt Leinart B 5.00 12.00
FFMR Michael Robinson C 2.50 6.00
FFMW Mario Williams B 3.00 8.00
FFRB Reggie Bush B 8.00 20.00
FFSH Santonio Holmes B 4.00 10.00
FFSM Sinorice Moss B 2.50 6.00
FFTJ Tarvaris Jackson C 3.00 8.00
FFVD Vernon Davis B 4.00 10.00
FFVY Vince Young B 6.00 15.00

2006 Bowman Fabric of the Future Dual

DUAL/50 ODDS 1:900 RET
HD Santonio Holmes 8.00 20.00
Vernon Davis
LB Matt Leinart 15.00 40.00
Reggie Bush
WB Lendale White 20.00 50.00
Reggie Bush
WW DeAngelo Williams 10.00 25.00
Mario Williams
YL Vince Young 12.00 30.00
Matt Leinart

2006 Bowman Rookie Coaches Autographs

STATED ODDS 1:5250 RET
BRCMM Mike McCarthy 15.00 40.00
BRCRM Rod Marinelli 4.00 10.00

2006 Bowman Rookie Rewind Jerseys

GROUP A ODDS 1:1450 HOB/RET
GROUP B ODDS 1:45 HOB, 1:260 RET
*GOLD/50: 1X TO 2.5X BASIC INSERTS
GOLD/50 ODDS 1:3200 RET
BRRAH A.J. Hawk B 4.00 10.00
BRRCJ Chad Jackson B 2.50 6.00
BRRDW DeAngelo Williams B 4.00 10.00
BRRKC Kellen Clemens B 2.50 6.00
BRRLM Laurence Maroney B 3.00 8.00
BRRLW LenDale White B 3.00 8.00
BRRMH Michael Huff B 2.50 6.00
BRRML Matt Leinart B 4.00 10.00
BRRMW Mario Williams B 2.50 6.00
BRRRB Reggie Bush B 6.00 15.00
BRRSH Santonio Holmes A 3.00 8.00
BRRSM Sinorice Moss B 2.50 6.00
BRRTJ Tarvaris Jackson B 2.50 6.00
BRRVD Vernon Davis B 3.00 8.00
BRRVY Vince Young B 5.00 12.00

2006 Bowman Signs of the Future

GROUP A ODDS 1:850 H, 1:1500 R
GROUP B ODDS 1:745 H, 1:750 R
GROUP C ODDS 1:1700 H/R
GROUP D ODDS 1:420 H, 1:440 R
GROUP E ODDS 1:300 H, 1:310 R
GROUP F ODDS 1:33 H, 1:89 R
*GOLD/50: .6X TO 1.5X BASIC INSERTS
GOLD/50 ODDS 1:1200 R
SFAF Anthony Fasano F 5.00 12.00
SFBC Brodie Croyle A 20.00 40.00
SFBM Brandon Marshall A 10.00 20.00
SFBS Brad Smith E 4.00 10.00
SFBW Brandon Williams F 5.00 12.00
SFCG Chad Greenway F 4.00 10.00
SFCJ Chad Jackson A 6.00 15.00
SFDA Devin Aromashodu A 5.00 12.00
SFDF D'Brickashaw Ferguson F 4.00 10.00
SFDH Derek Hagan B 4.00 10.00
SFDM DonTrell Moore F 4.00 10.00
SFDO Drew Olson D 5.00 12.00
SFDT David Thomas F 5.00 12.00
SFGJ Greg Jennings F 10.00 25.00
SFIM Ingle Martin E 5.00 12.00
SFJA Joseph Addai B 15.00 40.00
SFJK Joe Klopfenstein F 3.00 8.00
SFJN Jerious Norwood F 7.50 15.00
SFJW Jeff Webb F 4.00 10.00
SFKC Kellen Clemens F 7.50 15.00
SFLP Leonard Pope F 3.00 8.00
SFLW Leon Washington F 12.00 30.00
SFMD Maurice Drew F 15.00 30.00
SFMH Mike Hass F 4.00 10.00
SFML Marcedes Lewis D 4.00 10.00
SFMN Martin Nance F 4.00 10.00
SFMR Michael Robinson F 5.00 12.00
SFMS Maurice Stovall F 5.00 12.00
SFOJ Omar Jacobs D 4.00 10.00
SFSG Skyler Green E 4.00 10.00
SFTJ Tarvaris Jackson F 6.00 15.00
SFTW Todd Watkins C 5.00 12.00
SFTWI Travis Wilson F 3.00 8.00
SFBCA Brian Calhoun E 4.00 10.00
SFMHU Michael Huff B 6.00 15.00

2006 Bowman Signs of the Future Dual

DUAL/50 ODDS 1:9200 RET
UNPRICED GOLD PRINT RUN 10 SETS
BY Reggie Bush 60.00 150.00
Vince Young
JH Chad Jackson 20.00 50.00
Santonio Holmes
LC Matt Leinart 60.00 150.00
Jay Cutler
MA Laurence Maroney 25.00 60.00
Joseph Addai
WW Lendale White 40.00 80.00
DeAngelo Williams

2007 Bowman

This 275-card set was released in October, 2007. The set was issued into the hobby in 10-card packs, with a $3 SRP, which came 24 packs to a box. Cards numbered 1-110 feature veterans while cards 111-275 feature 2007 NFL rookies.

COMPLETE SET (275) 20.00 50.00
UNPRICED PRINT.PLATE PRINT RUN 1
UNPRICED RED PRINT RUN 1
1 Matt Leinart .25 .60
2 Matt Schaub .25 .60
3 Jason Campbell .25 .60
4 Steve McNair .25 .60
5 J.P. Losman .20 .50
6 Jake Delhomme .25 .60
7 Rex Grossman .25 .60
8 Carson Palmer .25 .60
9 Tony Romo .40 1.00
10 Jay Cutler .30 .75
11 Brett Favre .60 1.50
12 Peyton Manning .50 1.25
13 Trent Green .25 .60
14 Tom Brady .50 1.25
15 Drew Brees .30 .75
16 Eli Manning .30 .75
17 Chad Pennington .25 .60
18 Donovan McNabb .30 .75
19 Ben Roethlisberger .30 .75
20 Philip Rivers .30 .75
21 Alex Smith QB .30 .75
22 Matt Hasselbeck .25 .60
23 Marc Bulger .25 .60
24 Vince Young .25 .60
25 Edgerrin James .25 .60
26 Warrick Dunn .25 .60
27 Jamal Lewis .25 .60
28 Willis McGahee .25 .60
29 DeShaun Foster .25 .60
30 DeAngelo Williams .30 .75
31 Cedric Benson .25 .60
32 Thomas Jones .25 .60
33 Rudi Johnson .25 .60
34 Julius Jones .20 .50
35 Dominic Rhodes .25 .60
36 Joseph Addai .25 .60
37 Fred Taylor .25 .60
38 Maurice Jones-Drew .30 .75
39 Larry Johnson .20 .50
40 Ronnie Brown .25 .60
41 Chester Taylor .20 .50
42 Laurence Maroney .25 .60
43 Deuce McAllister .25 .60
44 Reggie Bush .30 .75
45 Brandon Jacobs .25 .60
46 Brian Westbrook .25 .60
47 Willie Parker .25 .60
48 LaDainian Tomlinson .30 .75
49 Frank Gore .30 .75
50 Shaun Alexander .25 .60
51 Steven Jackson .30 .75
52 Cadillac Williams .25 .60
53 Clinton Portis .25 .60
54 Michael Turner .30 .75
55 Anquan Boldin .25 .60
56 Larry Fitzgerald .30 .75
57 Derrick Mason .25 .60
58 Lee Evans .25 .60
59 Steve Smith .25 .60
60 Muhsin Muhammad .25 .60
61 Chad Johnson .25 .60
62 T.J. Houshmandzadeh .25 .60
63 Braylon Edwards .25 .60
64 Terrell Owens .30 .75
65 Terry Glenn .25 .60
66 Javon Walker .25 .60
67 Mike Furrey .25 .60
68 Roy Williams WR .25 .60
69 Donald Driver .30 .75
70 Greg Jennings .30 .75
71 Andre Johnson .25 .60
72 Reggie Wayne .25 .60
73 Marvin Harrison .30 .75
74 Matt Jones .25 .60
75 Chris Chambers .25 .60
76 Troy Williamson .20 .50
77 Devery Henderson .20 .50
78 Joe Horn .25 .60
79 Marques Colston .30 .75
80 Plaxico Burress .25 .60
81 Amani Toomer .25 .60
82 Jerricho Cotchery .25 .60
83 Laveranues Coles .20 .50
84 Randy Moss .30 .75
85 Donte Stallworth .25 .60
86 Reggie Brown .20 .50
87 Hines Ward .30 .75
88 Santonio Holmes .25 .60
89 Keenan McCardell .20 .50
90 Eric Parker .20 .50
91 Arnaz Battle .20 .50
92 Antonio Bryant .20 .50
93 Deion Branch .25 .60
94 Darrell Jackson .20 .50
95 Kevin Curtis .20 .50
96 Torry Holt .25 .60
97 Isaac Bruce .25 .60
98 Antwaan Randle El .20 .50
99 Santana Moss .25 .60
100 Alge Crumpler .25 .60
101 Kellen Winslow .25 .60
102 Tony Gonzalez .25 .60
103 Jeremy Shockey .25 .60
104 Antonio Gates .30 .75
105 Vernon Davis .25 .60
106 Tarvaris Jackson .20 .50
107 Travis Henry .25 .60
108 Drew Bennett .20 .50
109 Todd Heap .20 .50
110 Byron Leftwich .25 .60
111 JaMarcus Russell RC .40 1.00
112 Brady Quinn RC .60 1.50
113 Drew Stanton RC .40 1.00
114 Troy Smith RC .60 1.50
115 Kevin Kolb RC 1.00 2.50
116 Trent Edwards RC .60 1.50
117 John Beck RC .60 1.50
118 Jordan Palmer RC .50 1.25
119 Chris Leak RC .50 1.25
120 Isaiah Stanback RC .40 1.00
121 Tyler Palko RC .50 1.25
122 Jared Zabransky RC .50 1.25
123 Jeff Rowe RC .40 1.00
124 Zac Taylor RC .50 1.25
125 Lester Ricard RC .50 1.25
126 Adrian Peterson RC 6.00 15.00
127 Marshawn Lynch RC .60 1.50
128 Brandon Jackson RC .50 1.25
129 Michael Bush RC .60 1.50
130 Kenny Irons RC .40 1.00
131 Antonio Pittman RC .40 1.00
132 Tony Hunt RC .40 1.00
133 Darius Walker RC .40 1.00
134 Dwayne Wright RC .50 1.25
135 Lorenzo Booker RC .50 1.25
136 Kenneth Darby RC .50 1.25
137 Chris Henry RB RC .40 1.00
138 Selvin Young RC .50 1.25
139 Brian Leonard RC .50 1.25
140 Ahmad Bradshaw RC 1.00 2.50
141 Gary Russell RC .50 1.25
142 Kolby Smith RC .50 1.25
143 Thomas Clayton RC .50 1.25
144 Garrett Wolfe RC .40 1.00
145 Calvin Johnson RC 2.00 5.00
146 Ted Ginn Jr. RC .50 1.25
147 Dwayne Jarrett RC .50 1.25
148 Dwayne Bowe RC .75 2.00
149 Sidney Rice RC .75 2.00
150 Robert Meachem RC .60 1.50
151 Anthony Gonzalez RC .60 1.50
152 Craig Buster Davis RC .50 1.25
153 Aundrae Allison RC .40 1.00
154 Chansi Stuckey RC .60 1.50
155 David Clowney RC .50 1.25
156 Steve Smith USC RC .60 1.50
157 Courtney Taylor RC .50 1.25
158 Paul Williams RC .40 1.00
159 Johnnie Lee Higgins RC .50 1.25
160 Rhema McKnight RC .40 1.00
161 Jason Hill RC .60 1.50
162 Dallas Baker RC .40 1.00

163 Greg Olsen RC .50 1.25
164 Yamon Figurs RC .40 1.00
165 Scott Chandler RC .60 1.50
166 Matt Spaeth RC .60 1.50
167 Ben Patrick RC .50 1.25
168 Clark Harris RC .50 1.25
169 Martrez Milner RC .40 1.00
170 Joe Newton RC .40 1.00
171 Alan Branch RC .50 1.25
172 Amobi Okoye RC .60 1.50
173 DeMarcus Tank Tyler RC .40 1.00
174 Justin Harrell RC .50 1.25
175 Brandon Mebane RC .50 1.25
176 Gaines Adams RC .60 1.50
177 Jamaal Anderson RC .50 1.25
178 Adam Carriker RC .50 1.25
179 Jarvis Moss RC .50 1.25
180 Charles Johnson RC .40 1.00
181 Anthony Spencer RC .60 1.50
182 Quentin Moses RC .50 1.25
183 LaMarr Woodley RC .60 1.50
184 Victor Abiamiri RC .60 1.50
185 Ray McDonald RC .50 1.25
186 Tim Crowder RC .60 1.50
187 Patrick Willis RC 1.25 3.00
188 Brandon Siler RC .40 1.00
189 David Harris RC .50 1.25
190 Buster Davis RC .50 1.25
191 Lawrence Timmons RC .60 1.50
192 Paul Posluszny RC .60 1.50
193 Jon Beason RC .50 1.25
194 Rufus Alexander RC .50 1.25
195 Earl Everett RC .50 1.25
196 Stewart Bradley RC .50 1.25
197 Prescott Burgess RC .50 1.25
198 Leon Hall RC .50 1.25
199 Darrelle Revis RC 1.00 2.50
200 Aaron Ross RC .60 1.50
201 Daymeion Hughes RC .50 1.25
202 Marcus McCauley RC .50 1.25
203 Chris Houston RC .50 1.25
204 Tanard Jackson RC .40 1.00
205 Jonathan Wade RC .50 1.25
206 Josh Wilson RC .50 1.25
207 Eric Wright RC .60 1.50
208 A.J. Davis RC .40 1.00
209 David Irons RC .40 1.00
210 LaRon Landry RC .60 1.50
211 Reggie Nelson RC .50 1.25
212 Michael Griffin RC .60 1.50
213 Brandon Meriweather RC .60 1.50
214 Eric Weddle RC .60 1.50
215 Aaron Rouse RC .50 1.25
216 Josh Gattis RC .40 1.00
217 Joe Thomas RC .60 1.50
218 Levi Brown RC .60 1.50
219 Tony Ugoh RC .50 1.25
220 Ryan Kalil RC .50 1.25
221 Joe Staley RC .50 1.25
222 Steve Breaston RC .60 1.50
223 Jacoby Jones RC .60 1.50
224 Ryne Robinson RC .50 1.25
225 Chris Davis RC .40 1.00
226 Le'Ron McClain RC .60 1.50
227 Joel Filani RC .50 1.25
228 Gerald Alexander RC .40 1.00
229 Justise Hairston RC .50 1.25
230 Nate Ilaoa RC .50 1.25
231 Brett Ratliff RC .60 1.50
232 Kyle Steffes RC .40 1.00
233 Jesse Pellot-Rosa RC .40 1.00
234 Roy Hall RC .60 1.50
235 Brannon Condren RC .40 1.00
236 Clint Session RC .50 1.25
237 Dan Bazuin RC .50 1.25
238 Michael Okwo RC .50 1.25
239 Kevin Payne RC .40 1.00
240 Legedu Naanee RC .60 1.50
241 Jarrett Hicks RC .50 1.25
242 Sonny Shackelford RC .40 1.00
243 Arron Sears RC .50 1.25
244 Justin Durant RC .50 1.25
245 Ikaika Alama-Francis RC .60 1.50
246 Sabby Piscitelli RC .60 1.50
247 Quincy Black RC .60 1.50
248 Jay Alford RC 1.00 2.50
249 Anthony Waters RC .50 1.25
250 Laurent Robinson RC .60 1.50
251 Brian Robison RC .60 1.50
252 Jay Moore RC .50 1.25
253 Stephen Nicholas RC .50 1.25
254 John Bowie RC .40 1.00
255 Brian Smith RC .40 1.00
256 Marvin White RC .40 1.00
257 Fred Bennett RC .40 1.00
258 Kevin Boss RC 1.00 2.50
259 Dante Rosario RC .60 1.50
260 Brent Celek RC .60 1.50
261 Orenthal O'Neal RC .40 1.00
262 Reagan Mauia RC .40 1.00
263 Deon Anderson RC .50 1.25
264 Tyler Ecker RC .50 1.25
265 Michael Allan RC .40 1.00
266 Jordan Kent RC .50 1.25
267 John Broussard RC .50 1.25
268 Chandler Williams RC .50 1.25
269 Jason Snelling RC .60 1.50
270 Derek Stanley RC .50 1.25
271 Zach Miller RC .60 1.50
272 Ramzee Robinson RC .40 1.00
273 Michael Johnson RC .50 1.25
274 Syndric Steptoe RC .50 1.25
275 Tarell Brown RC .60 1.50

2007 Bowman Blue

*VETS 1-110: 2X TO 5X BASIC CARDS
*ROOKIES 111-275: 1X TO 2.5X BASIC CARDS
BLUE/500 ODDS 1:13 HOB

2007 Bowman Gold

*VETS 1-110: 1.2X TO 3X BASIC CARDS
*ROOKIES 111-275: .6X TO 1.5X BASIC CARDS
ONE GOLD PER PACK

2007 Bowman Orange

*VETS 1-110: 2.5X TO 6X BASIC CARDS
*ROOKIES 111-275: 1.2X TO 3X BASIC CARDS
ORANGE/250 ODDS 1:26 HOB

2007 Bowman Draft Day Selections Relics

CAP ODDS 1:3650 HOB
JERSEY GROUP A ODDS 1:345 HOB
JERSEY GROUP B ODDS 1:291 HOB
JERSEY-CAP ODDS 1:16,416 HOB
DCAP Adrian Peterson Cap 25.00 60.00
DCBQ Brady Quinn Cap 12.00 30.00
DCGA Gaines Adams Cap 6.00 15.00
DCJR JaMarcus Russell Cap 10.00 25.00
DJAP Adrian Peterson Jsy A 15.00 40.00
DJBQ Brady Quinn Jsy B 8.00 20.00
DJCJ Calvin Johnson Jsy B 8.00 20.00
DJGA Gaines Adams Jsy B 4.00 10.00
DJJR JaMarcus Russell Jsy A 6.00 15.00
DJCAP Adrian Peterson Jsy-Cap
DJCBQ Brady Quinn Jsy-Cap
DJCGA Gaines Adams Jsy-Cap
DJCJR JaMarcus Russell Jsy-Cap

2007 Bowman Fabric of the Future

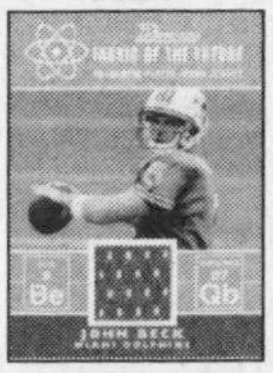

STATED ODDS 1:30 HOB
*GOLD/100: .5X TO 1.2X BASIC INSERTS
GOLD/100 ODDS 1:458 HOB
FFAG Anthony Gonzalez 2.50 6.00
FFAP Adrian Peterson 15.00 40.00
FFAPI Antonio Pittman 3.00 8.00
FFBJ Brandon Jackson 3.00 8.00
FFBL Brian Leonard 3.00 8.00
FFBQ Brady Quinn 6.00 15.00
FFCH Chris Henry RB 3.00 8.00
FFCJ Calvin Johnson 8.00 20.00
FFDB Dwayne Bowe 5.00 12.00
FFDJ Dwayne Jarrett 3.00 8.00
FFDS Drew Stanton 3.00 8.00
FFGA Gaines Adams 3.00 8.00
FFGO Greg Olsen 2.00 5.00
FFGW Garrett Wolfe 3.00 8.00
FFJB John Beck 3.00 8.00
FFJH Jason Hill 3.00 8.00
FFJLH Johnnie Lee Higgins 3.00 8.00
FFJR JaMarcus Russell 1.50 4.00
FFJT Joe Thomas 3.00 8.00
FFKI Kenny Irons 3.00 8.00
FFKK Kevin Kolb 4.00 10.00
FFLB Lorenzo Booker 3.00 8.00
FFMB Michael Bush 3.00 8.00
FFML Marshawn Lynch 2.50 6.00
FFPW Patrick Willis 5.00 12.00
FFPWI Paul Williams 3.00 8.00
FFRM Robert Meachem 3.00 8.00
FFSR Sidney Rice 5.00 12.00
FFSS Steve Smith USC 2.50 6.00
FFTE Trent Edwards 2.50 6.00
FFTG Ted Ginn Jr. 2.00 5.00
FFTH Tony Hunt 3.00 8.00
FFTS Troy Smith 2.50 6.00
FFYF Yamon Figurs 3.00 8.00

2007 Bowman Fabric of the Future Dual

DUAL/50 ODDS 1:7359
*GOLD/25: .6X TO 1.5X BASIC DUALS
DUAL GOLD/25 ODDS 1:14,850 HOB
GB Ted Ginn Jr. 6.00 15.00
Dwayne Bowe
PJ Adrian Peterson 20.00 50.00
Calvin Johnson
PQ Adrian Peterson 15.00 40.00
Brady Quinn
RJ JaMarcus Russell 12.00 30.00
Calvin Johnson
RQ JaMarcus Russell 8.00 20.00
Brady Quinn

2007 Bowman Rookie Autographs

GROUP A/25 ODDS 1:14,000 HOB
GROUP B/199 ODDS 1:303 HOB
BAVAG Anthony Gonzalez/199 10.00 25.00
BAVAP Adrian Peterson/25 150.00 300.00
BAVBJ Brandon Jackson/199 8.00 20.00
BAVBL Brian Leonard/199 8.00 20.00
BAVBQ Brady Quinn/199 25.00 60.00
BAVCD Craig Buster Davis/199 8.00 20.00
BAVCH Chris Henry RB/199 6.00 15.00
BAVCJ Calvin Johnson/25 75.00 150.00
BAVDB Dwayne Bowe/199 30.00 60.00
BAVDS Drew Stanton/199 6.00 15.00
BAVGA Gaines Adams/199 10.00 25.00
BAVJB John Beck/199 12.00 30.00
BAVJH Jason Hill/199 10.00 25.00
BAVJR JaMarcus Russell/25 12.00 30.00
BAVKK Kevin Kolb/199 15.00 40.00
BAVMB Michael Bush/199 10.00 25.00
BAVML Marshawn Lynch/199 12.00 30.00
BAVRM Robert Meachem/199 10.00 25.00
BAVSS Steve Smith USC/199 10.00 25.00
BAVTG Ted Ginn Jr/199 8.00 20.00

2007 Bowman Rookie Coaches Autographs

STATED ODDS 1:1030 HOB
BP Bobby Petrino 6.00 15.00
CC Cam Cameron 8.00 20.00
KW Ken Whisenhunt 6.00 15.00
LK Lane Kiffin 6.00 15.00

2007 Bowman Signs of the Future

GROUP A ODDS 1:2753 HOB
GROUP B ODDS 1:3300 HOB
GROUP C ODDS 1:327 HOB
GROUP D ODDS 1:97 HOB
GROUP E ODDS 1:916 HOB
GROUP F ODDS 1:273 HOB
GROUP G ODDS 1:60 HOB
*GOLD/50: .5X TO 1.2X BASIC GRP A
*GOLD/50: .6X TO 1.5X BASIC GRP B-G
GOLD/50 ODDS 1:650 HOB
SFAA Aundrae Allison D 3.00 8.00
SFAG Anthony Gonzalez B 5.00 12.00
SFBQ Brady Quinn A 50.00 120.00
SFCD Chris Davis C 3.00 8.00
SFCL Chris Leak G 4.00 10.00
SFCT Courtney Taylor C 4.00 10.00
SFDT Drew Tate G 4.00 10.00
SFDW Dwayne Wright D 4.00 10.00
SFDWA Darius Walker D 3.00 8.00
SFGW Garrett Wolfe D 3.00 8.00
SFJF Joel Filani G 4.00 10.00
SFJHA Justise Hairston D 4.00 10.00
SFJH Jason Hill G 5.00 12.00
SFJP Jordan Palmer D 4.00 10.00
SFJR Jeff Rowe D 3.00 8.00
SFKD Kenneth Darby G 4.00 10.00
SFKS Kolby Smith G 4.00 10.00
SFLB Lorenzo Booker C 4.00 10.00
SFLG Luke Getsy D 5.00 12.00
SFLR Laurent Robinson C 5.00 12.00
SFLT Lawrence Timmons F 5.00 12.00
SFML Marshawn Lynch A 12.00 30.00
SFMM Matt Moore G 5.00 12.00
SFPW Paul Williams D 3.00 8.00
SFRH Roy Hall F 5.00 12.00
SFRM Rhema McKnight E 3.00 8.00
SFRR Ryne Robinson G 4.00 10.00
SFSB Steve Breaston G 5.00 12.00
SFTE Trent Edwards C 5.00 12.00
SFTP Tyler Palko D 4.00 10.00
SFZM Zach Miller F 5.00 12.00
SFZT Zac Taylor G 4.00 10.00

2007 Bowman Signs of the Future Dual

DUAL/50 ODDS 1:4200 HOB
UNPRICED DUAL GOLD/10 ODDS 1:22,464
EL Trent Edwards 15.00 40.00
Marshawn Lynch
JM Dwayne Jarrett 10.00 25.00
Robert Meachem
QG Brady Quinn 15.00 40.00
Ted Ginn Jr.
SB Drew Stanton 12.00 30.00
John Beck
WD Paul Williams 10.00 25.00
Chris Davis

2008 Bowman

This set was released on October 29, 2008. The base set consists of 275 cards. Cards 1-110 feature veterans, and cards 111-275 are rookies.

COMPLETE SET (275) 30.00 60.00
1 Drew Brees .25 .60
2 Tom Brady .40 1.00
3 Peyton Manning .40 1.00
4 Carson Palmer .25 .60
5 Ben Roethlisberger .25 .60
6 Eli Manning .25 .60
7 Tony Romo .30 .75
8 Vince Young .20 .50
9 Matt Hasselbeck .20 .50
10 David Garrard .20 .50
11 Jay Cutler .25 .60
12 Derek Anderson .15 .40
13 Philip Rivers .25 .60
14 Donovan McNabb .25 .60
15 Matt Leinart .25 .60
16 Jason Campbell .20 .50
17 JaMarcus Russell .20 .50
18 Jeff Garcia .20 .50
19 Brodie Croyle .20 .50
20 Marc Bulger .20 .50
21 Trent Edwards .15 .40
22 Kyle Boller .15 .40
23 Tarvaris Jackson .20 .50
24 Matt Schaub .20 .50
25 Aaron Rodgers .50 1.25
26 Steven Jackson .25 .60
27 Willie Parker .20 .50
28 Clinton Portis .20 .50
29 Adrian Peterson .40 1.00
30 LaDainian Tomlinson .25 .60
31 Marion Barber .20 .50
32 Brian Westbrook .20 .50
33 Fred Taylor .20 .50
34 Marshawn Lynch .20 .50
35 Joseph Addai .20 .50
36 Willis McGahee .20 .50
37 Frank Gore .20 .50
38 Julius Jones .15 .40
39 Thomas Jones .20 .50
40 Cedric Benson .20 .50
41 LenDale White .20 .50
42 Ryan Grant .25 .60
43 Laurence Maroney .20 .50
44 Brandon Jacobs .20 .50
45 Jamal Lewis .20 .50
46 Larry Johnson .20 .50
47 Rudi Johnson .20 .50
48 Ahmad Bradshaw .20 .50
49 Justin Fargas .15 .40
50 Reggie Bush .25 .60
51 Maurice Jones-Drew .20 .50
52 Michael Turner .25 .60
53 Ronnie Brown .20 .50
54 DeAngelo Williams .20 .50
55 Edgerrin James .20 .50
56 Chad Johnson .20 .50
57 Reggie Wayne .20 .50
58 Anquan Boldin .20 .50
59 Randy Moss .25 .60
60 Plaxico Burress .20 .50
61 Terrell Owens .25 .60
62 Andre Johnson .20 .50
63 Larry Fitzgerald .25 .60
64 Braylon Edwards .20 .50
65 Steve Smith .20 .50
66 Greg Jennings .25 .60
67 Torry Holt .20 .50
68 T.J. Houshmandzadeh .20 .50
69 Jerricho Cotchery .20 .50
70 Joey Galloway .20 .50
71 Santonio Holmes .20 .50
72 Lee Evans .20 .50
73 Dwayne Bowe .20 .50
74 Laurent Robinson .15 .40
75 Wes Welker .25 .60
76 Roy Williams WR .20 .50
77 Brandon Marshall .20 .50
78 Hines Ward .20 .50
79 Donald Driver .20 .50
80 Calvin Johnson .25 .60
81 Marques Colston .20 .50
82 Chris Chambers .20 .50
83 Amani Toomer .20 .50
84 Bernard Berrian .20 .50
85 Sidney Rice .25 .60
86 Anthony Gonzalez .15 .40
87 Steve Smith USC .20 .50
88 Ted Ginn Jr. .20 .50
89 Isaac Bruce .20 .50
90 Derrick Mason .20 .50
91 Roddy White .20 .50
92 Bobby Engram .15 .40
93 Reggie Williams .20 .50
94 Donte Stallworth .15 .40
95 Santana Moss .15 .40
96 Laveranues Coles .15 .40
97 Jerry Porter .15 .40
98 Shaun McDonald .15 .40
99 Dallas Clark .20 .50
100 Tony Gonzalez .20 .50
101 Kellen Winslow .20 .50
102 Antonio Gates .25 .60
103 Jason Witten .25 .60
104 Chris Cooley .20 .50
105 Brett Favre .60 1.50
106 Bob Sanders .20 .50
107 John Harbaugh CO .15 .40
108 Jon Kitna .20 .50
109 Tony Sparano CO .15 .40
110 Mike Smith CO .15 .40
111 Ryan Clady RC .60 1.50
112 Branden Albert RC .60 1.50
113 Gosder Cherilus RC .50 1.25
114 Duane Brown RC .50 1.25
115 Brandon Flowers RC .60 1.50
116 Quentin Groves RC .50 1.25
117 Jason Jones RC .60 1.50
118 Kendall Langford RC .60 1.50
119 Brad Cottam RC .50 1.25
120 Antwaun Molden RC .50 1.25
121 Bryan Smith RC .50 1.25
122 DaJuan Morgan RC .50 1.25
123 Craig Stevens RC .40 1.00
124 Tom Zbikowski RC .60 1.50
125 Andre Fluellen RC .50 1.25
126 Cliff Avril RC .50 1.25
127 Tyvon Branch RC .50 1.25
128 Justin King RC .50 1.25
129 Jeremy Thompson RC .40 1.00
130 William Hayes RC .40 1.00
131 Will Franklin RC .50 1.25
132 Marcus Smith RC .50 1.25
133 Dwight Lowery RC .60 1.50
134 Reggie Corner RC .40 1.00
135 Kenny Iwebema RC .40 1.00
136 Quintin Demps RC .60 1.50
137 Jack Williams RC .40 1.00
138 Craig Steltz RC .50 1.25
139 Bryan Kehl RC .50 1.25
140 Justin Tryon RC .40 1.00
141 Arman Shields RC .50 1.25
142 Paul Hubbard RC .50 1.25
143 Jonathan Wilhite RC .50 1.25
144 Thomas DeCoud RC .40 1.00
145 Derek Fine RC .50 1.25
146 Stanford Keglar RC .40 1.00
147 Kenneth Moore RC .50 1.25
148 Robert James RC .40 1.00
149 Jalen Parmele RC .60 1.50
150 Brandon Carr RC .50 1.25
151 Gary Barnidge RC .40 1.00
152 Zack Bowman RC .50 1.25
153 Lex Hilliard RC .60 1.50
154 Mario Urrutia RC .40 1.00
155 Adrian Arrington RC .50 1.25
156 Jerome Felton RC .40 1.00
157 Chaz Schilens RC .60 1.50
158 Steve Johnson RC 1.00 2.50
159 Tim Hightower RC .60 1.50
160 Alex Brink RC .60 1.50
161 Brett Swain RC .50 1.25
162 Matt Slater RC .60 1.50
163 Justin Harper RC .50 1.25
164 Kevin Robinson RC .50 1.25
165 Pierre Garcon RC .75 2.00
166 Matt Ryan RC 2.50 6.00
167 Brian Brohm RC .60 1.50
168 Andre Woodson RC .60 1.50
169 Chad Henne RC .60 1.50
170 Joe Flacco RC 2.00 5.00
171 John David Booty RC .50 1.25
172 Colt Brennan RC .60 1.50
173 Dennis Dixon RC .60 1.50
174 Erik Ainge RC .60 1.50
175 Josh Johnson RC .60 1.50
176 Kevin O'Connell RC .50 1.25
177 Matt Flynn RC 1.25 3.00
178 Jaymar Johnson RC .40 1.00
179 Marcus Thomas RC .50 1.25
180 Darren McFadden RC 1.50 4.00
181 Rashard Mendenhall RC 1.25 3.00
182 Jonathan Stewart RC 1.00 2.50
183 Felix Jones RC 1.00 2.50
184 Jamaal Charles RC 1.00 2.50
185 Chris Johnson RC 1.50 4.00
186 Ray Rice RC 1.25 3.00
187 Mike Hart RC .60 1.50
188 Kevin Smith RC .60 1.50
189 Steve Slaton RC .60 1.50
190 Matt Forte RC 1.00 2.50
191 Tashard Choice RC .50 1.25
192 Cory Boyd RC .40 1.00
193 Allen Patrick RC .50 1.25
194 Thomas Brown RC .50 1.25
195 Justin Forsett RC .60 1.50
196 Harry Douglas RC .50 1.25
197 DeSean Jackson RC 1.25 3.00
198 Malcolm Kelly RC .50 1.25
199 Limas Sweed RC .60 1.50
200 Mario Manningham RC .60 1.50
201 James Hardy RC .50 1.25
202 Early Doucet RC .50 1.25
203 Donnie Avery RC .50 1.25
204 Dexter Jackson RC .50 1.25
205 Devin Thomas RC .50 1.25
206 Jordy Nelson RC .75 2.00
207 Keenan Burton RC .40 1.00
208 Earl Bennett RC .60 1.50
209 Jerome Simpson RC .60 1.50
210 Andre Caldwell RC .50 1.25
211 Josh Morgan RC .60 1.50
212 Eddie Royal RC .60 1.50
213 Fred Davis RC .60 1.50
214 John Carlson RC .60 1.50
215 Martellus Bennett RC .50 1.25
216 Martin Rucker RC .50 1.25
217 Jermichael Finley RC .60 1.50
218 Dustin Keller RC .60 1.50
219 Jacob Tamme RC .60 1.50
220 Kellen Davis RC .40 1.00
221 Owen Schmitt RC .60 1.50
222 Jacob Hester RC .60 1.50
223 Chris Williams RC .50 1.25
224 Jake Long RC .60 1.50
225 Sam Baker RC .40 1.00
226 Jeff Otah RC .50 1.25
227 Glenn Dorsey RC .60 1.50
228 Sedrick Ellis RC .60 1.50
229 Kentwan Balmer RC .50 1.25
230 Pat Sims RC .50 1.25
231 Marcus Harrison RC .50 1.25
232 Dre Moore RC .50 1.25
233 Paul Smith RC .60 1.50
234 Trevor Laws RC .60 1.50
235 Chris Long RC .60 1.50
236 Vernon Gholston RC .50 1.25
237 Derrick Harvey RC .40 1.00
238 Calais Campbell RC .50 1.25
239 Phillip Merling RC .50 1.25
240 Chris Ellis RC .40 1.00
241 Lawrence Jackson RC .50 1.25
242 Dan Connor RC .60 1.50
243 Curtis Lofton RC .50 1.25
244 Jerod Mayo RC .60 1.50
245 Tavares Gooden RC .50 1.25
246 Kyle Wright RC .50 1.25
247 Philip Wheeler RC .50 1.25
248 Marcus Monk RC .60 1.50
249 Jonathan Goff RC .40 1.00
250 Keith Rivers RC .60 1.50
251 Lavelle Hawkins RC .50 1.25
252 Xavier Adibi RC .40 1.00
253 Chauncey Washington RC .50 1.25
254 Bruce Davis RC .50 1.25
255 Jordon Dizon RC .60 1.50
256 Shawn Crable RC .40 1.00
257 Geno Hayes RC .40 1.00
258 Dominique Rodgers-Cromartie RC .60 1.50
259 Chevis Jackson RC .40 1.00
260 Terrence Wheatley RC .40 1.00
261 Mike Jenkins RC .60 1.50
262 Aqib Talib RC .60 1.50
263 Leodis McKelvin RC .50 1.25
264 Terrell Thomas RC .50 1.25
265 Reggie Smith RC .50 1.25
266 Antoine Cason RC .60 1.50
267 Patrick Lee RC .50 1.25
268 Tracy Porter RC .60 1.50
269 Charles Godfrey RC .60 1.50
270 Kenny Phillips RC .60 1.50
271 Marcus Henry RC .50 1.25
272 DJ Hall RC .50 1.25
273 Xavier Omon RC .60 1.50
274 Tyrell Johnson RC .60 1.50
275 Ryan Torain RC .60 1.50

2008 Bowman Blue

*VETS 1-110: 2.5X TO 6X BASIC CARDS
*ROOKIES 111-275: 1X TO 2.5X BASIC CARDS
BLUE/500 ODDS 1:11 HOB

2008 Bowman Gold

*VETS 1-110: 1.2X TO 3X BASIC CARDS
*ROOKIES 111-275: .6X TO 1.5X BASIC CARDS
ONE GOLD PER PACK

2008 Bowman Orange

*VETS 1-110: 3X TO 8X BASIC CARDS
*ROOKIES 111-275: 1.2X TO 3X BASIC CARDS
ORANGE/250 ODDS 1:21 HOB

2008 Bowman Red

UNPRICED RED 1/1 ODDS 1:2540

2008 Bowman Draft Day Selections Relics

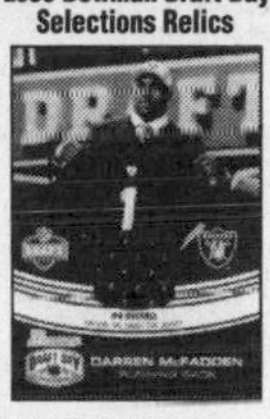

GROUP A JSY ODDS 1:578 HOB
GROUP B JSY ODDS 1:685 HOB
CAP STATED ODDS 1:5300 HOB
JSY-CAP/25 ODDS 1:18,124 HOB
DCCL Chris Long Cap 10.00 25.00
DCDM Darren McFadden Cap 12.00 30.00
DCJL Jake Long Cap 10.00 25.00
DCMR Matt Ryan Cap 20.00 50.00
DCVG Vernon Gholston Cap 10.00 25.00
DJCL Chris Long Jsy B 5.00 12.00
DJDM Darren McFadden Jsy A 8.00 20.00
DJJL Jake Long Jsy A 5.00 12.00
DJMR Matt Ryan Jsy A 8.00 20.00
DJVG Vernon Gholston Jsy B 5.00 12.00
DJCCL Chris Long Jsy-Cap/25
DJCDM Darren McFadden Jsy-Cap/25 25.00 60.00
DJCJL Jake Long Jsy-Cap/25
DJCMR Matt Ryan Jsy-Cap/25
DJCVG Vernon Gholston Jsy-Cap/25

2008 Bowman Fabric of the Future

GROUP A ODDS 1:115 HOB
GROUP B ODDS 1:59 HOB
*GOLD/100: .6X TO 1.5X BASIC JSY
GOLD/100 ODDS 1:1312 HOB
FFAC Andre Caldwell B 2.50 6.00
FFDJ Dexter Jackson B 2.50 6.00
FFDJ DeSean Jackson A 6.00 15.00
FFDK Dustin Keller B 3.00 8.00
FFDT Devin Thomas B 2.50 6.00
FFEB Earl Bennett B 3.00 8.00
FFED Early Doucet A 2.50 6.00
FFER Eddie Royal B 3.00 8.00
FFGD Glenn Dorsey B 3.00 8.00
FFJB John David Booty A 2.50 6.00
FFJC Jamaal Charles B 5.00 12.00
FFJD Harry Douglas B 2.50 6.00
FFJL Jake Long A 3.00 8.00
FFJN Jordy Nelson A 4.00 10.00
FFJS Jerome Simpson B 3.00 8.00
FFKO Kevin O'Connell B 2.50 6.00
FFKS Kevin Smith A 3.00 8.00
FFMF Matt Forte A 5.00 12.00
FFMM Mario Manningham A 3.00 8.00
FFSS Steve Slaton A 3.00 8.00

2008 Bowman Fabric of the Future Dual

DUAL/50 ODDS 1:10,611 HOB
DUAL GOLD/25 ODDS 1:21,781 HOB
FFDAT Donnie Avery
Devin Thomas
FFDMJ Darren McFadden
Felix Jones
FFDRF Matt Ryan
Joe Flacco
FFDRM Matt Ryan 10.00 25.00
Darren McFadden
FFDSM Jonathan Stewart
Rashard Mendenhall

2008 Bowman Signs of the Future

GROUP A ODDS 1:4414 HOB
GROUP B ODDS 1:795 HOB
GROUP C ODDS 1:154 HOB
GROUP D ODDS 1:49 HOB
*GOLD/50: .6X TO 1.5X BASIC AUTO
GOLD/50 ODDS 1:706 HOB
SFAA Adrian Arrington C 4.00 10.00
SFAA Anthony Alridge D 4.00 10.00
SFAC Andre Caldwell C 4.00 10.00
SFAP Allen Patrick C 4.00 10.00
SFBB Brian Brohm A 6.00 15.00
SFCW Chauncey Washington C 4.00 10.00
SFDH DJ Hall C 4.00 10.00
SFDM Darren McFadden A 25.00 60.00
SFDR Darius Reynaud C 3.00 8.00
SFDS Dantrell Savage D 4.00 10.00
SFEB Earl Bennett B 5.00 12.00
SFHD Harry Douglas B 4.00 10.00
SFJF Justin Forsett D 5.00 12.00
SFJF Joe Flacco A 40.00 80.00
SFJJ Josh Johnson B 5.00 12.00
SFJJ Jaymar Johnson D 3.00 8.00
SFJS Jonathan Stewart A 15.00 40.00
SFKB Keenan Burton D 3.00 8.00
SFMF Matt Flynn C 20.00 50.00
SFMF Matt Forte D 15.00 40.00
SFMH Marcus Henry C 4.00 10.00
SFMR Matt Ryan A 50.00 120.00
SFMS Marcus Smith D 4.00 10.00
SFPS Paul Smith C 5.00 12.00
SFRT Ryan Torain C 5.00 12.00
SFSK Sam Keller D 4.00 10.00
SFTC Tashard Choice B 4.00 10.00
SFXO Xavier Omon D 5.00 12.00

2008 Bowman Signs of the Future Dual

DUAL AUTO/50 ODDS 1:3923
UNPRICED GOLD/10 ODDS 1:32,100
SFDDL Glenn Dorsey EXCH 12.00 30.00
Jake Long
SFDHM Chad Henne 20.00 50.00
Mario Manningham
SFDJS Chris Johnson 40.00 80.00
Kevin Smith
SFDNH Jordy Nelson 20.00 40.00
James Hardy
SFDRM Matt Ryan 60.00 120.00
Darren McFadden

2010 Bowman Target Exclusive

ONE PER SPECIAL TARGET BOX OVERALL
*GOLD: .6X TO 1.5X BASIC INSERTS
TC1 Tim Tebow 3.00 8.00
TC2 C.J. Spiller 1.25 3.00
TC3 Dez Bryant 2.50 6.00
TC4 Golden Tate .75 2.00
TC5 Sam Bradford 3.00 8.00
TC6 Ryan Mathews 1.50 4.00
TC7 Jahvid Best 1.25 3.00
TC8 Colt McCoy 1.50 4.00
TC9 Demaryius Thomas 1.00 2.50
TC10 Jimmy Clausen .75 2.00
TC11 Ndamukong Suh 1.50 4.00
TC12 Arrelious Benn .75 2.00
TC13 Ben Tate 1.00 2.50
TC14 Jonathan Dwyer .75 2.00
TC15 Eric Berry .75 2.00

2010 Bowman Wal-Mart Exclusive

ONE PER SPECIAL WAL-MART BOX OVERALL
*GOLD: .6X TO 1.5X BASIC INSERTS
WC1 Tim Tebow 3.00 8.00
WC2 C.J. Spiller 1.25 3.00
WC3 Dez Bryant 2.50 6.00
WC4 Golden Tate .75 2.00
WC5 Sam Bradford 3.00 8.00
WC6 Ryan Mathews 1.50 4.00
WC7 Jahvid Best 1.25 3.00
WC8 Colt McCoy 1.50 4.00
WC9 Demaryius Thomas 1.00 2.50
WC10 Jimmy Clausen .75 2.00
WC11 Ndamukong Suh 1.50 4.00
WC12 Arrelious Benn .75 2.00
WC13 Ben Tate 1.00 2.50
WC14 Jonathan Dwyer .75 2.00
WC15 Eric Berry .75 2.00

2011 Bowman Target Exclusive

ODDS 1:6 TARGET, 1:1 TRGT BLASTER
*GRAY: .5X TO 1.2X BASIC INSERTS
TC1 Blaine Gabbert 1.50 4.00
TC2 Jake Locker 2.50 6.00
TC3 Cam Newton 6.00 15.00
TC4 Ryan Mallett 2.00 5.00
TC5 Mark Ingram 2.00 5.00
TC6 Ryan Williams 1.25 3.00
TC7 Mikel Leshoure 1.00 2.50
TC8 A.J. Green 2.00 5.00
TC9 Julio Jones 2.00 5.00
TC10 Jonathan Baldwin 1.00 2.50
TC11 Marcell Dareus 1.00 2.50
TC12 Von Miller 1.25 3.00
TC13 Andy Dalton 2.50 6.00
TC14 Kyle Rudolph 1.00 2.50
TC15 Christian Ponder 2.00 5.00

2011 Bowman Wal-Mart Exclusive

ODDS 1:6 WAL-MART, 1:1 WLMRT BLASTER
*GRAY: .5X TO 1.2X BASIC INSERTS
WC1 Blaine Gabbert 1.50 4.00
WC2 Jake Locker 2.50 6.00
WC3 Cam Newton 6.00 15.00
WC4 Ryan Mallett 2.00 5.00
WC5 Mark Ingram 2.00 5.00
WC6 Ryan Williams 1.25 3.00
WC7 Mikel Leshoure 1.00 2.50
WC8 A.J. Green 2.00 5.00
WC9 Julio Jones 2.00 5.00
WC10 Jonathan Baldwin 1.00 2.50
WC11 Marcell Dareus 1.00 2.50
WC12 Von Miller 1.25 3.00
WC13 Andy Dalton 2.50 6.00
WC14 Kyle Rudolph 1.00 2.50
WC15 Christian Ponder 2.00 5.00

2012 Bowman

COMP.SET w/o SP's (200) 30.00 80.00
THREE ROOKIES PER PACK OVERALL
ROOKIE SP ODDS 1:39 HOB/RET
MANN/TEBOW SP ODDS 1:488 HOB/RET
1 Cam Newton .50 1.25
2 Miles Austin .25 .60
3 Hakeem Nicks .25 .60
4 Michael Vick .30 .75
5 Brandon Marshall .20 .50
6 Brandon Lloyd .25 .60
7 Eric Decker .25 .60
8 Eli Manning .30 .75
9 Carson Palmer .25 .60
10 LeSean McCoy .25 .60
11 Andy Dalton .30 .75
12 Steve Breaston .20 .50
13 Fred Jackson .25 .60
14 Beanie Wells .25 .60
15 Greg Jennings .25 .60
16 DeSean Jackson .25 .60
17 Frank Gore .25 .60
18 Anquan Boldin .25 .60
19 Vincent Jackson .25 .60
20 Calvin Johnson .30 .75
21 Ryan Mathews .25 .60
22 Josh Freeman .25 .60
23 Rashard Mendenhall .25 .60
24 Aaron Hernandez .25 .60
25 Chris Johnson .25 .60
26 Jason Witten .30 .75
27 Mike Williams .25 .60
28 Tony Romo .30 .75
29 Mark Sanchez .25 .60
30 Arian Foster .25 .60
31 Dwayne Bowe .25 .60
32 Cedric Benson .25 .60
33 Von Miller .25 .60
34 Denarius Moore .20 .50
35 Matt Ryan .25 .60
36 Mike Wallace .25 .60
37 Steve Johnson .25 .60
38 Matt Flynn .25 .60
39 Patrick Willis .25 .60
40 Adrian Peterson .30 .75
41 Santonio Holmes .25 .60
42 Victor Cruz .30 .75
43 Roddy White .25 .60
44 Jason Pierre-Paul .25 .60
45 Matthew Stafford .30 .75
46 Ahmad Bradshaw .25 .60
47 Fred Davis .20 .50
48 Matt Hasselbeck .25 .60
49 Jermichael Finley .25 .60
50 Tom Brady .50 1.25
51 Steven Jackson .25 .60
52 Jay Cutler .25 .60
53 Sam Bradford .30 .75
54 Ryan Fitzpatrick .25 .60
55 Michael Bush .20 .50
56 Mario Williams .20 .50
57 Jeremy Maclin .25 .60
58 Michael Turner .25 .60
59 Wes Welker .30 .75
60 Ray Rice .25 .60
61 Marshawn Lynch .25 .60
62 Torrey Smith .20 .50
63 A.J. Green .25 .60
64 Darren Sproles .25 .60
65 Julio Jones .25 .60
66 Philip Rivers .25 .60
67 Alex Smith QB .25 .60
68 DeMarco Murray .25 .60
69 Rob Gronkowski .25 .60
70 Drew Brees .30 .75
71 DeMarcus Ware .25 .60
72 Larry Fitzgerald .25 .60
73 Matt Schaub .25 .60
74 Vernon Davis .25 .60
75 Maurice Jones-Drew .25 .60
76 Joe Flacco .25 .60
77 Dez Bryant .30 .75
78 Colt McCoy .25 .60
79 Reggie Bush .25 .60
80 Andre Johnson .25 .60
81 Willis McGahee .20 .50
82 Percy Harvin .25 .60
83 Tony Gonzalez .25 .60
84 Steve Smith .25 .60
85 LeGarrette Blount .20 .50
86 Jordy Nelson .25 .60
87 Shonn Greene .25 .60
88 Jared Allen .25 .60
89 Plaxico Burress .25 .60
90 Matt Forte .25 .60
91 Antonio Brown .25 .60
92 Jimmy Graham .25 .60
93 Marques Colston .25 .60
94 Doug Baldwin .25 .60
95 David Nelson .20 .50
96 Darren McFadden .25 .60
97 Ben Tate .20 .50
98 Ben Roethlisberger .30 .75
99 James Starks .25 .60
100 Aaron Rodgers .50 1.25
101 Fletcher Cox RC .50 1.25
102 Dont'a Hightower RC .75 2.00
103A Chris Polk RC .60 1.50
cutting to his right
103B Chris Polk SP 5.00 12.00
cutting to his left
104A Ryan Lindley RC .50 1.25
throwing pose
104B Ryan Lindley SP 4.00 10.00
both hands on football
105 Jerel Worthy RC .60 1.50
106 Alfonzo Dennard RC .50 1.25
107A Kellen Moore RC .75 2.00
white jersey
107B Kellen Moore SP 6.00 15.00
blue jersey
108 Tank Carder RC .50 1.25
109A Jarius Wright RC .50 1.25
running to his right
109B Jarius Wright SP 5.00 12.00
running to his left
110A Ryan Tannehill RC 1.25 3.00
dropping back
110B Ryan Tannehill SP 10.00 25.00
passing pose
111A Isaiah Pead RC .50 1.25
right hand at chin
111B Isaiah Pead SP 4.00 10.00
right hand at waist
112 Ronnie Hillman RC .60 1.50
113A Coby Fleener RC .60 1.50
football at chest
113B Coby Fleener SP 5.00 12.00
football at waist
114A Tommy Streeter RC .50 1.25
mouth closed
114B Tommy Streeter SP 4.00 10.00
mouth open
115 Cam Johnson RC .50 1.25
116A Russell Wilson RC .75 2.00
set to pass
116B Russell Wilson SP 6.00 15.00
dropping back
117A Nick Toon RC .60 1.50
117B Nick Toon SP 5.00 12.00
118 Tauren Poole RC .40 1.00
119A Robert Turbin RC .50 1.25
119B Robert Turbin SP 4.00 10.00
120A Trent Richardson RC 1.50 4.00
left hand at waist
120B Trent Richardson SP 12.00 30.00
left hand at chin
121 Brock Osweiler RC .60 1.50
122 Zach Brown RC .40 1.00
123A Jeff Fuller RC .60 1.50
white Jersey
123B Jeff Fuller SP 5.00 12.00
green jersey
124A Jordan White RC .40 1.00
running pose
124B Jordan White SP 3.00 8.00
catching pose
125 Gerell Robinson RC .50 1.25
126 Chandler Jones RC .50 1.25
127 Vick Ballard RC .40 1.00
128 Matt Kalil RC .60 1.50

129A Kendall Wright RC .60 1.50
football in right hand
129B Kendall Wright SP 5.00 12.00
football in both hands
130A Justin Blackmon RC 1.00 2.50
green jersey
130B Justin Blackmon SP 8.00 20.00
white jersey
131 Davin Meggett RC .40 1.00
132A LaMichael James RC 1.00 2.50
white jersey
132B LaMichael James SP 8.00 20.00
red jersey
133 Cordy Glenn RC .40 1.00
134 Courtney Upshaw RC .60 1.50
135 Patrick Witt RC .40 1.00
136 Greg Childs RC .50 1.25
137A Alshon Jeffery RC .75 2.00
running pose
137B Alshon Jeffery SP 6.00 15.00
catching pose
138 Rishard Matthews RC .50 1.25
139A Jacory Harris RC .40 1.00
set to pass
139B Jacory Harris SP 3.00 8.00
scrambling pose
140A Michael Floyd RC 1.00 2.50
football at waist
140B Michael Floyd SP 8.00 20.00
football near chin
141 Eric Page RC .40 1.00
142A Chandler Harnish RC .50 1.25
blue jersey
142B Chandler Harnish SP 4.00 10.00
white jersey
143 Mark Barron RC .75 2.00
144 Jared Crick RC .50 1.25
145A Kirk Cousins RC .75 2.00
facing forward
145B Kirk Cousins SP 6.00 15.00
back to camera
146 Chase Minnifield RC .40 1.00
147 Lavonte David RC .60 1.50
148 Whitney Mercilus RC .50 1.25
149A Bernard Pierce RC .50 1.25
running pose
149B Bernard Pierce SP 4.00 10.00
catching pose
150A Andrew Luck RC 3.00 8.00
holding football
150B Andrew Luck SP 25.00 50.00
without football
151A A.J. Jenkins RC .60 1.50
white pants
151B A.J. Jenkins SP 5.00 12.00
orange pants
152A Mohamed Sanu RC .50 1.25
with football
152B Mohamed Sanu SP 4.00 10.00
without football
153A David Wilson RC 1.00 2.50
blue helmet
153B David Wilson SP 8.00 20.00
white helmet
154 Riley Reiff RC .50 1.25
155A Doug Martin RC .75 2.00
155B Doug Martin SP 6.00 15.00
156 Nick Perry RC .50 1.25
157 Michael Brockers RC .50 1.25
158 Vinny Curry RC .50 1.25
159 Orson Charles RC .50 1.25
160A Morris Claiborne RC 1.00 2.50
blue helmet
160B Morris Claiborne SP 10.00 25.00
silver helmet
161A Brandon Weeden RC 1.00 2.50
brown jersey
161B Brandon Weeden SP 8.00 20.00
white jersey
162 Marc Tyler RC .50 1.25
163A Bobby Rainey RC .50 1.25
white pants
163B Bobby Rainey SP 4.00 10.00
purple pants
164 Dan Herron RC .50 1.25
165A Cyrus Gray RC .50 1.25
white jersey
165B Cyrus Gray SP 4.00 10.00
red jersey
166 Chris Rainey RC .50 1.25
167 Markelle Martin RC .40 1.00
168A Brian Quick RC .60 1.50
with football
168B Brian Quick SP 5.00 12.00
without football
169 Devon Still RC .50 1.25
170A Quinton Coples RC .50 1.25
white pants
170B Quinton Coples SP 4.00 10.00
green pants
171A Nick Foles RC .75 2.00
171B Nick Foles SP 6.00 15.00
172A T.Y. Hilton RC .50 1.25
running forward
172B T.Y. Hilton SP 4.00 10.00
running to his left
173 David DeCastro RC .60 1.50
174A Lamar Miller RC .60 1.50
football in left arm
174B Lamar Miller SP 5.00 12.00
football in right arm
175 Billy Winn RC .50 1.25
176A Dwayne Allen RC .50 1.25
without football
176B Dwayne Allen SP 4.00 10.00
with football
177 Peter Konz RC .30 .75
178 Janoris Jenkins RC .50 1.25
179 Chris Givens RC .40 1.00
180A Melvin Ingram RC .60 1.50
running to his left
180B Melvin Ingram SP 5.00 12.00
running to his right
181A DeVier Posey RC .50 1.25
without football
181B DeVier Posey SP 4.00 10.00
with football
182A Rueben Randle RC .50 1.25
football at waist
182B Rueben Randle SP 4.00 10.00
football at shoulder
183 Juron Criner RC .40 1.00
184 Brandon Bolden RC .50 1.25
185A Dre Kirkpatrick RC .75 2.00
white jersey
185B Dre Kirkpatrick SP 6.00 15.00
orange jersey
186A Austin Davis RC .50 1.25
186B Austin Davis SP 4.00 10.00
187A Jermaine Kearse RC .50 1.25
187B Jermaine Kearse SP 4.00 10.00
188 Brandon Thompson RC .40 1.00
189A Marvin McNutt RC .50 1.25
football in right hand
189B Marvin McNutt SP 4.00 10.00
football in both hands
190 Luke Kuechly RC .60 1.50
191A Dwight Jones RC .40 1.00
191B Dwight Jones SP 3.00 8.00
192 Dontari Poe RC .50 1.25
193 B.J. Cunningham RC .40 1.00
194 Marvin Jones RC .40 1.00
195 Andre Branch RC .40 1.00
196A Case Keenum RC .60 1.50
white jersey
196B Case Keenum SP 5.00 12.00
blue jersey
197A Ryan Broyles RC .50 1.25
blue jersey
197B Ryan Broyles SP 4.00 10.00
white jersey
198A Joe Adams RC .50 1.25
left hand at waist
198B Joe Adams SP 4.00 10.00
left hand at chest
199 Stephen Hill RC .50 1.25
200A Robert Griffin III RC 3.00 8.00
passing pose
200B Robert Griffin III SP 25.00 50.00
running pose
PMSP Peyton Manning SP 25.00 60.00
TTSP Tim Tebow SP 15.00 40.00

2012 Bowman Gold

*GOLD: .8X TO 2X BASIC CARDS
RANDOM INSERTS IN RETAIL PACKS

2012 Bowman Green

*GREEN/25: 6X TO 15X BASIC CARDS
GREEN/25 ODDS 1:390 HOB/RET

2012 Bowman Purple

*PURPLE: .6X TO 1.5X BASIC CARDS
THREE PER SPECIAL RETAIL PACK

2012 Bowman Silver

*SILVER/99: 3X TO 8X BASIC CARDS
SILVER/99 ODDS 1:98 HOB/RET

2012 Bowman Accolades

STATED ODDS 1:12 RETAIL
BACAL Andrew Luck 4.00 10.00
BACDA Dwayne Allen .60 1.50
BACJB Justin Blackmon 1.25 3.00
BACLK Luke Kuechly .75 2.00
BACMC Morris Claiborne 1.25 3.00
BACRG Robert Griffin III 3.00 8.00
BACTR Trent Richardson 2.00 5.00
BACAL2 Andrew Luck 4.00 10.00
BACAL3 Andrew Luck 4.00 10.00
BACRG2 Robert Griffin III 3.00 8.00

2012 Bowman Accolades Autographs

STATED ODDS 1:699 RETAIL
BACAAL Andrew Luck 125.00 250.00
BACADA Dwayne Allen 10.00 25.00
BACAJB Justin Blackmon 25.00 50.00
BACALK Luke Kuechly 12.00 30.00
BACARG Robert Griffin III 200.00 400.00
BACATR Trent Richardson
BACAAL2 Andrew Luck 125.00 250.00
BACAAL3 Andrew Luck 125.00 250.00
BACARG2 Robert Griffin III 200.00 400.00

2012 Bowman All-American Autographs

STATED ODDS 1:3100 RET
BAAAAL Andrew Luck 150.00 250.00
BAAACF Coby Fleener 12.00 30.00
BAAADA Dwayne Allen 10.00 25.00
BAAADS Devon Still 10.00 25.00
BAAAJB Justin Blackmon 25.00 50.00
BAAAJW Jerel Worthy 12.00 30.00
BAAAKW Kendall Wright 12.00 30.00
BAAALK Luke Kuechly 12.00 30.00
BAAAMK Matt Kalil 12.00 30.00
BAAARB Ryan Broyles 40.00 80.00
BAAARG Robert Griffin III 100.00 200.00
BAAATR Trent Richardson 40.00 80.00

2012 Bowman All-Americans

STATED ODDS 1:6 RETAIL
BAAAL Andrew Luck 3.00 8.00
BAACF Coby Fleener .60 1.50
BAADA Dwayne Allen .50 1.25
BAADK Dre Kirkpatrick .75 2.00
BAADS Devon Still .50 1.25
BAAJB Justin Blackmon 1.00 2.50
BAAJW Jerel Worthy .60 1.50
BAAKW Kendall Wright .60 1.50
BAALJ LaMichael James 1.00 2.50
BAALK Luke Kuechly .60 1.50
BAAMC Morris Claiborne 1.00 2.50
BAAMI Melvin Ingram .60 1.50
BAAMK Matt Kalil .60 1.50
BAARB Ryan Broyles .50 1.25
BAARG Robert Griffin III 2.50 6.00
BAATR Trent Richardson 1.50 4.00

2012 Bowman Autographs Dual

DUAL AU/25 ODDS 1:386 HOB,1:11,515 RET
BDAHM Jacory Harris
Lamar Miller
BDALG Andrew Luck 600.00 800.00
Robert Griffin III
BDAMM Kellen Moore
Doug Martin
BDAPK Chris Polk 15.00 40.00
Jermaine Kearse
BDARK Trent Richardson 100.00 175.00
Dre Kirkpatrick
BDATM Von Miller 60.00 120.00
Ryan Tannehill
BDAVW Michael Vick
David Wilson
BDAWA Jarius Wright 25.00 50.00
Joe Adams

2012 Bowman Autographs Triple

TRIPLE AU/25 ODDS 1:740 HOB,1:24,700 RET
BTAFWJ Michael Floyd
Kendall Wright
Alshon Jeffery
BTAHMS Jacory Harris
Lamar Miller
Tommy Streeter
BTAMTG Von Miller 60.00 120.00
Ryan Tannehill
Cyrus Gray
BTATGF Ryan Tannehill 50.00 100.00
Cyrus Gray
Jeff Fuller

2012 Bowman Combine Competition

STATED ODDS 1:4 HOB/RET
CCCI Quinton Coples .60 1.50
Melvin Ingram
CCCK Morris Claiborne 1.00 2.50
Dre Kirkpatrick
CCCP Morris Claiborne 1.00 2.50
Patrick Peterson
CCFC Nick Foles .75 2.00
Kirk Cousins
CCFW Michael Floyd 1.00 2.50
Kendall Wright
CCGN Robert Griffin III 2.50 6.00
Cam Newton
CCHJ Stephen Hill .50 1.25
Calvin Johnson
CCJP LaMichael James 1.00 2.50
Chris Polk
CCLG Andrew Luck 3.00 8.00
Robert Griffin III
CCLH Ryan Lindley .50 1.25
Chandler Harnish
CCLN Andrew Luck 3.00 8.00
Cam Newton
CCMR Lamar Miller .60 1.50
Chris Rainey
CCMW Doug Martin 1.00 2.50
David Wilson
CCPS Dontari Poe .50 1.25
Ndamukong Suh
CCSR Mohamed Sanu .50 1.25
Rueben Randle

2012 Bowman Inside the Numbers

STATED ODDS 1:8 HOB/RET
ITNAB Ahmad Bradshaw .60 1.50
ITNAF Arian Foster .60 1.50
ITNAJ Andre Johnson .60 1.50
ITNAS Alex Smith QB .60 1.50
ITNBG Blaine Gabbert .60 1.50
ITNBT Ben Tate .50 1.25
ITNBW Beanie Wells .60 1.50
ITNCN Cam Newton 1.25 3.00
ITNDB Drew Brees .75 2.00
ITNDK Dustin Keller .50 1.25
ITNGO Greg Olsen .50 1.25
ITNJF Jacoby Ford .50 1.25
ITNJM Jeremy Maclin .60 1.50
ITNLB LeGarrette Blount .50 1.25
ITNMC Marques Colston .60 1.50
ITNMF Matt Forte .60 1.50
ITNML Marshawn Lynch .60 1.50
ITNMR Matt Ryan .60 1.50
ITNMS Mark Sanchez .60 1.50
ITNMV Michael Vick .75 2.00
ITNMW Mike Wallace .60 1.50
ITNPH Percy Harvin .60 1.50
ITNPT Pierre Thomas .60 1.50
ITNPW Patrick Willis .60 1.50
ITNRG Rob Gronkowski .60 1.50
ITNRH Roy Helu .60 1.50
ITNRL Ray Lewis .75 2.00
ITNRM Rashard Mendenhall .60 1.50
ITNRW Roddy White .60 1.50
ITNSB Sam Bradford .75 2.00
ITNSG Shonn Greene .60 1.50
ITNSH Santonio Holmes .60 1.50
ITNSJ Steve Johnson .60 1.50
ITNVM Von Miller .60 1.50
ITNABR Antonio Brown .60 1.50
ITNMFL Malcom Floyd .50 1.25
ITNMSC Matt Schaub .60 1.50
ITNMWI Mike Williams .60 1.50
ITNPHI Peyton Hillis .50 1.25
ITNRMA Ryan Mathews .60 1.50

2012 Bowman Inside the Numbers Autographs

STATED ODDS 1:117 HOB, 1:1606 RET
ITNAAB Ahmad Bradshaw 8.00 20.00
ITNABG Blaine Gabbert 8.00 20.00
ITNACN Cam Newton 40.00 80.00
ITNAJM Jeremy Maclin 8.00 20.00
ITNAMS Mark Sanchez
ITNAMV Michael Vick
ITNAPH Percy Harvin 8.00 20.00
ITNAPW Patrick Willis 15.00 40.00
ITNARH Roy Helu 8.00 20.00
ITNASB Sam Bradford 20.00 40.00
ITNAVM Von Miller 8.00 20.00
ITNAABR Antonio Brown 12.00 30.00
ITNAMSC Matt Schaub

2012 Bowman Inside the Numbers Relics

STATED ODDS 1:35 RETAIL
ITNRAB Ahmad Bradshaw 3.00 8.00
ITNRAD Andy Dalton 4.00 10.00
ITNRAF Arian Foster 3.00 8.00
ITNRAG A.J. Green 3.00 8.00
ITNRBG Blaine Gabbert 3.00 8.00
ITNRBT Ben Tate 2.50 6.00
ITNRCN Cam Newton 6.00 15.00
ITNRCP Christian Ponder 3.00 8.00
ITNRDB Drew Brees 4.00 10.00
ITNRDK Dustin Keller 2.50 6.00
ITNRDM DeMarco Murray 3.00 8.00
ITNRDT Daniel Thomas 3.00 8.00
ITNRGL Greg Little 2.50 6.00
ITNRGO Greg Olsen 2.50 6.00
ITNRJF Jacoby Ford 2.50 6.00
ITNRJJ Julio Jones 3.00 8.00
ITNRJL Jake Locker 3.00 8.00
ITNRJM Jeremy Maclin 3.00 8.00
ITNRMA Miles Austin 3.00 8.00
ITNRMF Matt Forte 3.00 8.00
ITNRMI Mark Ingram 3.00 8.00
ITNRMR Matt Ryan 3.00 8.00
ITNRMS Mark Sanchez 3.00 8.00
ITNRMSC Matt Schaub 3.00 8.00
ITNRMV Michael Vick 4.00 10.00
ITNRMWI Mike Williams 3.00 8.00
ITNRPH Percy Harvin 3.00 8.00
ITNRPT Pierre Thomas 3.00 8.00
ITNRRG Rob Gronkowski 4.00 10.00
ITNRRH Roy Helu 3.00 8.00
ITNRRL Ray Lewis 4.00 10.00
ITNRRMA Ryan Mathews 3.00 8.00
ITNRRW Roddy White 3.00 8.00
ITNRSB Sam Bradford 4.00 10.00
ITNRSG Shonn Greene 3.00 8.00
ITNRSJ Steve Johnson 3.00 8.00
ITNRTS Torrey Smith 2.50 6.00
ITNRVM Von Miller 3.00 8.00

2012 Bowman Inside the Numbers Relic Autographs

STATED ODDS 1:207 HOB, 1:8680 RET
ITNARAB Ahmad Bradshaw 12.00 30.00
ITNARBG Blaine Gabbert 12.00 30.00
ITNARJM Jeremy Maclin 12.00 30.00
ITNARMS Mark Sanchez
ITNARMSC Matt Schaub
ITNARMV Michael Vick
ITNARPH Percy Harvin 12.00 30.00
ITNARRH Roy Helu 12.00 30.00
ITNARSB Sam Bradford
ITNARVM Von Miller 12.00 30.00

2012 Bowman Rookie Autographs

ONE AU PER HOBBY PACK OVERALL
EXCH EXPIRATION: 5/31/2015
103 Chris Polk SP 6.00 15.00
104 Ryan Lindley 4.00 10.00
105 Jerel Worthy 5.00 12.00
107 Kellen Moore 6.00 15.00
109 Jarius Wright SP 4.00 10.00
110 Ryan Tannehill 10.00 25.00
111 Isaiah Pead SP 4.00 10.00
112 Ronnie Hillman 5.00 12.00
113 Coby Fleener 6.00 15.00
114 Tommy Streeter SP 4.00 10.00
117 Nick Toon SP 6.00 15.00
119 Robert Turbin SP 5.00 12.00
120 Trent Richardson SP 30.00 60.00
121 Brock Osweiler SP 8.00 20.00
123 Jeff Fuller 5.00 12.00
129 Kendall Wright SP 8.00 12.00
130 Justin Blackmon
132 LaMichael James 15.00 30.00
135 Patrick Witt 3.00 8.00
136 Greg Childs 4.00 10.00
137 Alshon Jeffery SP 15.00 30.00
139 Jacory Harris 4.00 10.00
140 Michael Floyd 8.00 20.00
142 Chandler Harnish 4.00 10.00
143 Mark Barron 6.00 15.00
145 Kirk Cousins SP 8.00 20.00
149 Bernard Pierce SP 4.00 10.00
150 Andrew Luck SP 150.00 300.00
152 Mohamed Sanu SP 6.00 15.00
153 David Wilson SP 15.00 30.00
155 Doug Martin SP 8.00 20.00
161 Brandon Weeden SP 15.00 30.00
165 Cyrus Gray SP 4.00 10.00
166 Chris Rainey 8.00 20.00
168 Brian Quick SP 8.00 20.00
169 Devon Still SP 4.00 10.00
171 Nick Foles 6.00 15.00
172 T.Y. Hilton SP 5.00 12.00
173 David DeCastro 8.00 20.00
174 Lamar Miller 5.00 12.00
176 Dwayne Allen 6.00 15.00
178 Janoris Jenkins 4.00 10.00
179 Chris Givens 4.00 10.00
180 Melvin Ingram 5.00 12.00
181 DeVier Posey SP 4.00 10.00
182 Rueben Randle SP 8.00 20.00
183 Juron Criner 4.00 10.00
185 Dre Kirkpatrick EXCH 6.00 15.00
187 Jermaine Kearse 4.00 10.00
189 Marvin McNutt 4.00 10.00
191 Dwight Jones 3.00 8.00
192 Dontari Poe 4.00 10.00
196 Case Keenum 5.00 12.00
197 Ryan Broyles 4.00 10.00
198 Joe Adams 4.00 10.00
200 Robert Griffin III SP 150.00 300.00

2012 Bowman Rookie Autographs Red Ink

RED INK/15: X TO X BASIC AU
RED INK/15* ODDS 1:55 HOBBY
150 Andrew Luck 400.00 600.00
200 Robert Griffin III 400.00 600.00

2012 Bowman Rookie Team Helmet Autographs

STATED ODDS 1:1 HOB OVERALL, 1:88 RET
BCRAAJ Alshon Jeffery 15.00 30.00
BCRAAL Andrew Luck 175.00 300.00
BCRABO Brock Osweiler 15.00 40.00
BCRABP Bernard Pierce 5.00 12.00
BCRABQ Brian Quick 6.00 15.00
BCRABW Brandon Weeden 20.00 40.00
BCRACF Coby Fleener 8.00 20.00
BCRACG Cyrus Gray 5.00 12.00
BCRACP Chris Polk 6.00 15.00
BCRADA Dwayne Allen 5.00 12.00
BCRADJ Dwight Jones 5.00 12.00
BCRADK Dre Kirkpatrick 8.00 20.00
BCRADM Doug Martin 10.00 25.00
BCRADP DeVier Posey 5.00 12.00
BCRADS Devon Still 5.00 12.00
BCRADW David Wilson 20.00 50.00
BCRAIP Isaiah Pead 5.00 12.00
BCRAJA Joe Adams 5.00 12.00
BCRAJB Justin Blackmon 30.00 60.00
BCRAJF Jeff Fuller 6.00 15.00
BCRAJK Jermaine Kearse 5.00 12.00
BCRAKC Kirk Cousins 15.00 40.00
BCRAKM Kellen Moore 8.00 20.00
BCRAKW Kendall Wright 8.00 20.00
BCRALJ LaMichael James 12.00 30.00
BCRALK Luke Kuechly 6.00 15.00
BCRALM Lamar Miller 8.00 20.00
BCRAMF Michael Floyd EXCH 25.00 50.00
BCRAMK Matt Kalil 6.00 15.00
BCRAMM Marvin McNutt 5.00 12.00
BCRAMS Mohamed Sanu 8.00 20.00
BCRANF Nick Foles 8.00 20.00
BCRANT Nick Toon 8.00 20.00
BCRARG Robert Griffin III 150.00 300.00
BCRARR Rueben Randle 8.00 20.00
BCRART Ryan Tannehill 40.00 80.00
BCRATH T.Y. Hilton 6.00 15.00
BCRATR Trent Richardson 40.00 80.00
BCRATS Tommy Streeter 5.00 12.00
BCRACGR Chris Givens 4.00 10.00
BCRAJWR Jarius Wright 6.00 15.00
BCRARTU Robert Turbin 5.00 12.00

2012 Bowman Rookie Team Helmet Autographs Red Ink

RED INK/15: 1X TO 2.5X BASIC INSERTS
RED INK/15* ODDS 1:75 HOBBY
BCRAAL Andrew Luck 400.00 600.00
BCRARG Robert Griffin III 400.00 600.00

2012 Bowman Industry Summit Autographs

LAS VEGAS INDUSTRY SUMMIT EXCLUSIVE
UNPRICED DUE TO SCARCITY
1 Andy Dalton/6
3 Blaine Gabbert/3
4 Christian Ponder/6
7 Hakeem Nicks/11
8 Jason Pierre-Paul/11
11 Mark Ingram/3
15 Rob Gronkowski/11
17 Torrey Smith/11

1998 Bowman Chrome

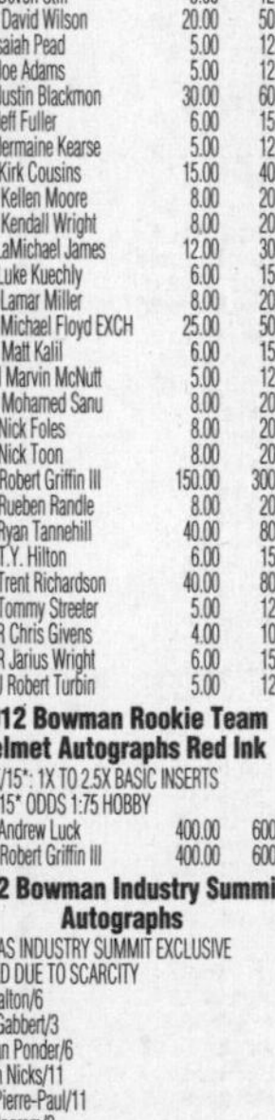

The 1998 Bowman Chrome set was issued in one series totalling 220 cards and was distributed in four-card packs with a suggested retail price of $3. The set features color action photos of 150 veteran players and 70 top prospects printed on chromium metalized cards. The veteran cards display a silver and red design, while the prospect cards carry a silver and blue logo design.

COMPLETE SET (220) 50.00 100.00
1 Peyton Manning RC 15.00 40.00
2 Keith Brooking RC 1.50 4.00
3 Duane Starks RC .75 2.00
4 Takeo Spikes RC 1.50 4.00
5 Andre Wadsworth RC 1.25 3.00
6 Greg Ellis RC .75 2.00
7 Brian Griese RC 3.00 8.00
8 Germane Crowell RC 1.25 3.00
9 Jerome Pathon RC 1.50 4.00
10 Ryan Leaf RC 1.50 4.00
11 Fred Taylor RC 2.50 6.00
12 Robert Edwards RC 1.25 3.00
13 Grant Wistrom RC 1.25 3.00
14 Robert Holcombe RC 1.25 3.00
15 Tim Dwight RC 1.50 4.00
16 Jacquez Green RC 1.25 3.00
17 Marcus Nash RC .75 2.00
18 Jason Peter RC .75 2.00
19 Anthony Simmons RC 1.25 3.00
20 Curtis Enis RC .75 2.00
21 John Avery RC 1.25 3.00
22 Pat Johnson RC 1.25 3.00
23 Joe Jurevicius RC 1.50 4.00
24 Brian Simmons RC 1.25 3.00
25 Kevin Dyson RC 1.50 4.00
26 Skip Hicks RC 1.25 3.00
27 Hines Ward RC 7.50 15.00
28 Tavian Banks RC 1.25 3.00
29 Ahman Green RC 4.00 10.00
30 Tony Simmons RC 1.25 3.00
31 Charles Johnson .20 .50
32 Freddie Jones .20 .50
33 Joey Galloway .30 .75
34 Tony Banks .30 .75
35 Jake Plummer .50 1.25
36 Reidel Anthony .30 .75
37 Steve McNair .50 1.25
38 Michael Westbrook .30 .75
39 Chris Sanders .20 .50
40 Isaac Bruce .20 .50
41 Charlie Garner .30 .75
42 Wayne Chrebet .50 1.25
43 Michael Strahan .30 .75
44 Brad Johnson .50 1.25
45 Mike Alstott .20 .50
46 Tony Gonzalez .50 1.25
47 Johnnie Morton .30 .75
48 Darnay Scott .30 .75
49 Rae Carruth .20 .50
50 Terrell Davis .50 1.25
51 Jermaine Lewis .30 .75
52 Frank Sanders .30 .75
53 Byron Hanspard .20 .50
54 Gus Frerotte .20 .50
55 Terry Glenn .50 1.25
56 J.J. Stokes .30 .75
57 Will Blackwell .20 .50
58 Keyshawn Johnson .50 1.25
59 Tiki Barber .50 1.25
60 Dorsey Levens .50 1.25
61 Zach Thomas .50 1.25
62 Corey Dillon .50 1.25
63 Antowain Smith .50 1.25
64 Michael Sinclair .20 .50
65 Rod Smith .30 .75
66 Trent Dilfer .50 1.25
67 Warren Sapp .30 .75
68 Charles Way .20 .50
69 Tamarick Vanover .20 .50
70 Drew Bledsoe .75 2.00
71 John Mobley .20 .50
72 Kerry Collins .30 .75
73 Peter Boulware .20 .50
74 Simeon Rice .30 .75
75 Eddie George .50 1.25
76 Fred Lane .20 .50
77 Jamal Anderson .50 1.25
78 Antonio Freeman .50 1.25
79 Jason Sehorn .30 .75
80 Curtis Martin .50 1.25
81 Bobby Hoying .30 .75
82 Garrison Hearst .50 1.25
83 Glenn Foley .30 .75
84 Danny Kanell .30 .75
85 Kordell Stewart .50 1.25
86 O.J. McDuffie .30 .75
87 Marvin Harrison .50 1.25
88 Bobby Engram .30 .75
89 Chris Slade .20 .50
90 Warrick Dunn .50 1.25
91 Ricky Watters .30 .75
92 Rickey Dudley .20 .50
93 Terrell Owens .50 1.25
94 Karim Abdul-Jabbar .50 1.25
95 Napoleon Kaufman .50 1.25
96 Darrell Green .30 .75
97 Levon Kirkland .20 .50
98 Jeff George .30 .75
99 Andre Hastings .20 .50
100 John Elway 2.00 5.00
101 John Randle .30 .75
102 Andre Rison .30 .75
103 Keenan McCardell .30 .75
104 Marshall Faulk .60 1.50
105 Emmitt Smith 1.50 4.00
106 Robert Brooks .30 .75
107 Scott Mitchell .30 .75
108 Shannon Sharpe .30 .75
109 Deion Sanders .50 1.25
110 Jerry Rice 1.00 2.50
111 Erik Kramer .20 .50
112 Michael Jackson .20 .50
113 Aeneas Williams .20 .50
114 Terry Allen .50 1.25
115 Steve Young .60 1.50
116 Warren Moon .50 1.25
117 Junior Seau .50 1.25
118 Jerome Bettis .50 1.25
119 Irving Fryar .30 .75
120 Barry Sanders 1.50 4.00
121 Tim Brown .20 .50
122 Chad Brown .20 .50
123 Ben Coates .30 .75
124 Robert Smith .50 1.25
125 Brett Favre 2.00 5.00
126 Derrick Thomas .50 1.25
127 Reggie White .50 1.25
128 Troy Aikman 1.00 2.50
129 Jeff Blake .30 .75
130 Mark Brunell .50 1.25
131 Curtis Conway .30 .75
132 Wesley Walls .30 .75
133 Thurman Thomas .50 1.25
134 Chris Chandler .30 .75
135 Dan Marino 2.00 5.00
136 Larry Centers .20 .50
137 Shawn Jefferson .20 .50
138 Andre Reed .30 .75
139 Jake Reed .30 .75
140 Cris Carter .50 1.25
141 Elvis Grbac .30 .75
142 Mark Chmura .30 .75
143 Michael Irvin .50 1.25
144 Carl Pickens .30 .75
145 Herman Moore .30 .75
146 Marvin Jones .20 .50
147 Terance Mathis .30 .75
148 Rob Moore .30 .75
149 Bruce Smith .30 .75
150 Rob Johnson CL .20 .50
151 Leslie Shepherd .20 .50
152 Chris Spielman .20 .50
153 Tony McGee .20 .50
154 Kevin Smith .20 .50
155 Bill Romanowski .20 .50
156 Stephen Boyd .20 .50
157 James Stewart .30 .75
158 Jason Taylor .30 .75
159 Troy Drayton .20 .50
160 Mark Fields .20 .50
161 Jessie Armstead .20 .50
162 James Jett .30 .75
163 Bobby Taylor .20 .50
164 Kimble Anders .30 .75
165 Jimmy Smith .30 .75
166 Quentin Coryatt .20 .50
167 Bryant Westbrook .20 .50
168 Neil Smith .30 .75
169 Darren Woodson .20 .50
170 Ray Buchanan .20 .50
171 Earl Holmes .20 .50
172 Ray Lewis .50 1.25
173 Steve Broussard .20 .50
174 Derrick Brooks .50 1.25
175 Ken Harvey .20 .50
176 Darryll Lewis .20 .50
177 Derrick Rodgers .20 .50
178 James McKnight .50 1.25
179 Cris Dishman .20 .50
180 Hardy Nickerson .20 .50
181 Charles Woodson RC 2.00 5.00
182 Randy Moss RC 8.00 20.00
183 Stephen Alexander RC 1.25 3.00
184 Samari Rolle RC .75 2.00
185 Jamie Duncan RC .75 2.00
186 Lance Schulters RC .75 2.00
187 Tony Parrish RC 1.50 4.00
188 Corey Chavous RC 1.50 4.00
189 Jammi German RC .75 2.00
190 Sam Cowart RC 1.25 3.00
191 Donald Hayes RC 1.25 3.00
192 R.W. McQuarters RC 1.25 3.00
193 Az-Zahir Hakim RC 1.50 4.00
194 C.Fuamatu-Ma'afala RC 1.25 3.00
195 Allen Rossum RC .75 2.00
196 Jon Ritchie RC 1.25 3.00
197 Blake Spence RC .75 2.00
198 Brian Alford RC .75 2.00
199 Fred Weary RC .75 2.00
200 Rod Rutledge RC .75 2.00
201 Michael Myers RC .75 2.00
202 Rashaan Shehee RC 1.25 3.00
203 Donovin Darius RC 1.25 3.00
204 E.G. Green RC 1.25 3.00
205 Vonnie Holliday RC 1.25 3.00
206 Charlie Batch RC 1.50 4.00
207 Michael Pittman RC 1.50 4.00
208 Artrell Hawkins RC .75 2.00
209 Jonathan Quinn RC 1.50 4.00
210 Kailee Wong RC .75 2.00
211 Deshea Townsend RC .75 2.00
212 Patrick Surtain RC 1.50 4.00
213 Brian Kelly RC 1.25 3.00
214 Tebucky Jones RC .75 2.00
215 Pete Gonzalez RC .75 2.00
216 Shaun Williams RC 1.25 3.00
217 Scott Frost RC .75 2.00
218 Leonard Little RC 1.50 4.00
219 Alonzo Mayes RC .75 2.00
220 Cordell Taylor RC .75 2.00

1998 Bowman Chrome Golden Anniversary

*GOLD.ANN.STARS: 15X TO 40X
*GOLD.ANN.RCs: 2X TO 5X
STATED ODDS 1:138
STATED PRINT RUN 50 SERIAL #'d SETS
REF.STATED PRINT RUN 5 SERIAL #'d SETS
1 Peyton Manning 200.00 350.00
27 Hines Ward 60.00 120.00
182 Randy Moss 75.00 150.00

1998 Bowman Chrome Golden Anniversary Refractors

GOLD.ANNIV REF/5 ODDS 1:1072 HOB
NOT PRICED DUE TO SCARCITY

1998 Bowman Chrome Interstate

COMPLETE SET (220) 400.00 800.00
*INTERSTATE STARS: 1X TO 2.5X BASIC CARDS
*INTERSTATE ROOKIES: .6X TO 1.2X
STATED ODDS 1:4

1998 Bowman Chrome Interstate Refractors

*INTERSTATE REF.STARS: 3X TO 8X BASIC CARDS
*INTERSTATE REF.RCs: 1.5X TO 4X BASIC CARDS
STATED ODDS 1:24
1 Peyton Manning 125.00 200.00

1998 Bowman Chrome Refractors

*REFRACTOR STARS: 2X TO 5X BASIC CARDS
*REFRACT.ROOKIES: 1.2X TO 3X
STATED ODDS 1:12
1 Peyton Manning 60.00 120.00

1999 Bowman Chrome

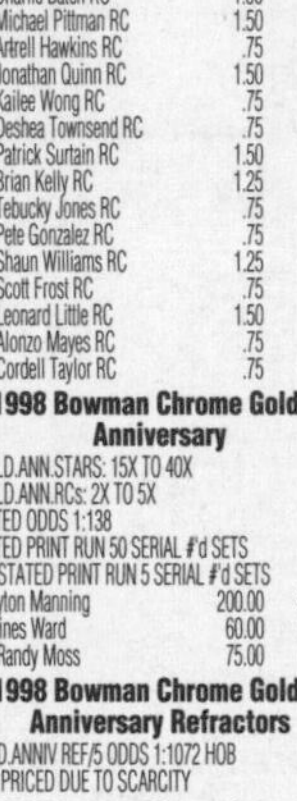

The 1999 Bowman Chrome set was releases as a 220-card set parallels the base 1999 Bowman release. The set contains 150 veteran cards and 70 top rookies on an enhanced all-foil card stock. Each rookie card features the "Bowman Chrome Rookie" logo, and highlights and trim appear in blue, while on veteran cards they appear in red. 1999 Bowman chrome was packaged in 24-pack boxes containing four cards per pack. Packs carried a suggested retail price of $3.00.

COMPLETE SET (220) 40.00 80.00
1 Dan Marino 1.25 3.00
2 Michael Westbrook .25 .60
3 Yancey Thigpen .25 .60
4 Tony Martin .30 .75
5 Michael Strahan .30 .75
6 Dedric Ward .25 .60
7 Joey Galloway .30 .75
8 Bobby Engram .30 .75
9 Frank Sanders .25 .60
10 Jake Plummer .30 .75
11 Eddie Kennison .30 .75
12 Curtis Martin .40 1.00
13 Chris Spielman .30 .75
14 Trent Dilfer .30 .75
15 Tim Biakabutuka .30 .75
16 Elvis Grbac .25 .60
17 Charlie Batch .30 .75
18 Takeo Spikes .25 .60
19 Tony Banks .30 .75
20 Doug Flutie .40 1.00
21 Ty Law .30 .75
22 Isaac Bruce .40 1.00
23 James Jett .25 .60
24 Kent Graham .25 .60
25 Derrick Mayes .25 .60
26 Amani Toomer .30 .75
27 Ray Lewis .40 1.00
28 Shawn Springs .25 .60
29 Warren Sapp .30 .75
30 Jamal Anderson .30 .75
31 Byron Bam Morris .25 .60
32 Johnnie Morton .30 .75
33 Terance Mathis .25 .60
34 Terrell Davis .40 1.00
35 John Randle .30 .75
36 Vinny Testaverde .30 .75
37 Junior Seau .40 1.00
38 Reidel Anthony .25 .60
39 Brad Johnson .30 .75
40 Emmitt Smith 1.00 2.50
41 Mo Lewis .25 .60
42 Terry Glenn .30 .75
43 Dorsey Levens .30 .75
44 Thurman Thomas .40 1.00
45 Rob Moore .25 .60
46 Corey Dillon .30 .75
47 Jessie Armstead .30 .75
48 Marshall Faulk .40 1.00
49 Charles Woodson .40 1.00
50 John Elway 1.25 3.00
51 Kevin Dyson .25 .60
52 Tony Simmons .25 .60
53 Keenan McCardell .30 .75
54 O.J. Santiago .25 .60
55 Jermaine Lewis .25 .60
56 Herman Moore .30 .75
57 Gary Brown .25 .60
58 Jim Harbaugh .30 .75
59 Mike Alstott .40 1.00
60 Brett Favre 1.25 3.00
61 Tim Brown .40 1.00
62 Steve McNair .40 1.00
63 Ben Coates .30 .75
64 Jerome Pathon .25 .60
65 Ray Buchanan .25 .60
66 Troy Aikman .60 1.50
67 Andre Reed .40 1.00
68 Bubby Brister .25 .60
69 Karim Abdul-Jabbar .30 .75
70 Peyton Manning 1.25 3.00
71 Charles Johnson .25 .60
72 Natrone Means .30 .75
73 Michael Sinclair .25 .60
74 Skip Hicks .25 .60
75 Derrick Alexander .25 .60
76 Wayne Chrebet .30 .75
77 Rod Smith .30 .75
78 Carl Pickens .30 .75
79 Adrian Murrell .30 .75
80 Fred Taylor .30 .75
81 Eric Moulds .30 .75
82 Lawrence Phillips .30 .75
83 Marvin Harrison .40 1.00
84 Cris Carter .40 1.00
85 Ike Hilliard .30 .75
86 Hines Ward .40 1.00
87 Terrell Owens .40 1.00
88 Ricky Proehl .25 .60
89 Bert Emanuel .30 .75
90 Randy Moss .40 1.00
91 Aaron Glenn .25 .60
92 Robert Smith .30 .75
93 Andre Hastings .25 .60
94 Jake Reed .30 .75
95 Curtis Enis .25 .60
96 Andre Wadsworth .25 .60
97 Ed McCaffrey .30 .75
98 Zach Thomas .40 1.00
99 Kerry Collins .30 .75
100 Drew Bledsoe .40 1.00
101 Germane Crowell .25 .60
102 Bryan Still .25 .60
103 Chad Brown .25 .60
104 Jacquez Green .25 .60
105 Garrison Hearst .30 .75
106 Napoleon Kaufman .25 .60
107 Ricky Watters .30 .75
108 O.J. McDuffie .30 .75
109 Keyshawn Johnson .30 .75
110 Jerome Bettis .40 1.00
111 Duce Staley .30 .75
112 Curtis Conway .30 .75
113 Chris Chandler .30 .75
114 Marcus Nash .25 .60
115 Stephen Alexander .25 .60
116 Darnay Scott .25 .60
117 Bruce Smith .40 1.00
118 Priest Holmes .40 1.00
119 Mark Brunell .30 .75
120 Jerry Rice .75 2.00
121 Randall Cunningham .40 1.00
122 Scott Mitchell .25 .60
123 Antonio Freeman .30 .75
124 Kordell Stewart .30 .75
125 Jon Kitna .30 .75
126 Ahman Green .30 .75
127 Warrick Dunn .30 .75
128 Robert Brooks .30 .75
129 Derrick Thomas .40 1.00
130 Steve Young .50 1.25
131 Peter Boulware .25 .60
132 Michael Irvin .40 1.00
133 Shannon Sharpe .40 1.00
134 Jimmy Smith .30 .75
135 John Avery .25 .60
136 Fred Lane .25 .60
137 Trent Green .30 .75
138 Andre Rison .30 .75
139 Antowain Smith .25 .60
140 Eddie George .30 .75
141 Jeff Blake .30 .75
142 Rocket Ismail .30 .75
143 Rickey Dudley .25 .60
144 Courtney Hawkins .25 .60
145 Mikhael Ricks .25 .60

146 J.J. Stokes	.25	.60
147 Levon Kirkland	.25	.60
148 Deion Sanders	.40	1.00
149 Barry Sanders	1.00	2.50
150 Tiki Barber	.40	1.00
151 David Boston RC	.50	1.25
152 Chris McAlister RC	.50	1.25
153 Peerless Price RC	.50	1.25
154 D'Wayne Bates RC	.40	1.00
155 Cade McNown RC	.50	1.25
156 Akili Smith RC	.50	1.25
157 Kevin Johnson RC	.50	1.25
158 Tim Couch RC	.60	1.50
159 Sedrick Irvin RC	.40	1.00
160 Chris Claiborne RC	.40	1.00
161 Edgerrin James RC	.75	2.00
162 Mike Cloud RC	.40	1.00
163 Cecil Collins RC	.40	1.00
164 James Johnson RC	.40	1.00
165 Rob Konrad RC	.40	1.00
166 Daunte Culpepper RC	.60	1.50
167 Kevin Faulk RC	.60	1.50
168 Donovan McNabb RC	4.00	10.00
169 Troy Edwards RC	.50	1.25
170 Amos Zereoue RC	.50	1.25
171 Karsten Bailey RC	.40	1.00
172 Brock Huard RC	.50	1.25
173 Joe Germaine RC	.50	1.25
174 Torry Holt RC	1.00	2.50
175 Shaun King RC	.50	1.25
176 Jevon Kearse RC	.60	1.50
177 Champ Bailey RC	1.25	3.00
178 Ebenezer Ekuban RC	.40	1.00
179 Andy Katzenmoyer RC	.50	1.25
180 Antoine Winfield RC	.40	1.00
181 Jermaine Fazande RC	.40	1.00
182 Ricky Williams RC	1.00	2.50
183 Joel Makovicka RC	.40	1.00
184 Reginald Kelly RC	.40	1.00
185 Brandon Stokley RC	.60	1.50
186 L.C. Stevens RC	.40	1.00
187 Marty Booker RC	.50	1.25
188 Jerry Azumah RC	.40	1.00
189 Ted White RC	.40	1.00
190 Scott Covington RC	.40	1.00
191 Tim Alexander RC	.40	1.00
192 Darrin Chiaverini RC	.40	1.00
193 Dat Nguyen RC	.60	1.50
194 Wane McGarity RC	.40	1.00
195 Al Wilson RC	.60	1.50
196 Travis McGriff RC	.40	1.00
197 Stacey Mack RC	.40	1.00
198 Antuan Edwards RC	.40	1.00
199 Aaron Brooks RC	.60	1.50
200 De'Mond Parker RC	.40	1.00
201 Jed Weaver RC	.40	1.00
202 Madre Hill RC	.40	1.00
203 Jim Kleinsasser RC	.60	1.50
204 Michael Bishop RC	.50	1.25
205 Michael Basnight RC	.40	1.00
206 Sean Bennett RC	.40	1.00
207 Dameane Douglas RC	.40	1.00
208 Na Brown RC	.40	1.00
209 Patrick Kerney RC	.50	1.25
210 Malcolm Johnson RC	.40	1.00
211 Dre Bly RC	.60	1.50
212 Terry Jackson RC	.40	1.00
213 Eugene Baker RC	.40	1.00
214 Autry Denson RC	.40	1.00
215 Darnell McDonald RC	.40	1.00
216 Charlie Rogers RC	.40	1.00
217 Joe Montgomery RC	.40	1.00
218 Cecil Martin RC	.40	1.00
219 Larry Parker RC	.50	1.25
220 Mike Peterson RC	.50	1.25

1999 Bowman Chrome Gold

*VETS 1-150: 2.5X TO 6X BASIC CARDS
*ROOKIES 151-220: 1.5X TO 4X
STATED ODDS 1:24

1999 Bowman Chrome Gold Refractors

*VETS 1-150: 10X TO 25X BASIC CARDS
*ROOKIES 151-220: 6X TO 15X
GOLD REF/25 STATED ODDS 1:253
STATED PRINT RUN 25 SER.#'d SETS

1999 Bowman Chrome Interstate

COMPLETE SET (220)	200.00	400.00

*VETS 1-150: 1X TO 2.5X BASIC CARDS
*ROOKIES 151-220: .6X TO 1.5X
STATED ODDS 1:4

1999 Bowman Chrome Interstate Refractors

*VETS 1-150: 5X TO 12X BASIC CARDS
*ROOKIES 151-220: 3X TO 8X
STATED PRINT RUN 100 SER.#'d SETS

1999 Bowman Chrome Refractors

COMPLETE SET (220)	400.00	800.00

*VETS 1-150: 2X TO 5X BASIC CARDS
*ROOKIES 151-220: 1.2X TO 3X
STATED ODDS 1:12

1999 Bowman Chrome Scout's Choice

COMPLETE SET (21)	25.00	50.00
STATED ODDS 1:12		
*REFRACTORS: 1X TO 2.5X BASIC INSERTSL.		
REFRACTOR STATED ODDS 1:60		
SC1 David Boston	.40	1.00
SC2 Champ Bailey	.60	1.50
SC3 Edgerrin James	2.00	5.00
SC4 Mike Cloud	.25	.60
SC5 Kevin Faulk	.40	1.00
SC6 Troy Edwards	.25	.60
SC7 Cecil Collins	.20	.50
SC8 Peerless Price	.40	1.00
SC9 Torry Holt	1.25	3.00
SC10 Rob Konrad	.40	1.00
SC11 Akili Smith	.25	.60
SC12 Daunte Culpepper	2.00	5.00
SC13 D'Wayne Bates	.25	.60
SC14 Donovan McNabb	2.50	6.00
SC15 James Johnson	.25	.60
SC16 Cade McNown	.25	.60
SC17 Kevin Johnson	.40	1.00
SC18 Ricky Williams	1.00	2.50
SC19 Karsten Bailey	.25	.60
SC20 Tim Couch	.40	1.00
SC21 Shaun King	.25	.60

1999 Bowman Chrome Stock in the Game

COMPLETE SET (18)	20.00	40.00
STATED ODDS 1:21		
*REFRACTORS: 1X TO 2.5X BASIC INSERTS		
REFRACTOR STATED ODDS 1:105		
S1 Joe Germaine	.30	.75
S2 Jevon Kearse	.60	1.50
S3 Sedrick Irvin	.30	.75
S4 Brock Huard	.30	.75
S5 Amos Zereoue	.30	.75
S6 Andy Katzenmoyer	.30	.75
S7 Randy Moss	2.50	6.00
S8 Jake Plummer	1.00	2.50
S9 Keyshawn Johnson	.60	1.50
S10 Fred Taylor	1.00	2.50
S11 Eddie George	1.00	2.50
S12 Peyton Manning	3.00	8.00
S13 Dan Marino	3.00	8.00
S14 Terrell Davis	1.00	2.50
S15 Brett Favre	3.00	8.00
S16 Jamal Anderson	.60	1.50
S17 Steve Young	1.25	3.00
S18 Jerry Rice	2.00	5.00

2000 Bowman Chrome

Released in Late December 2000, Bowman Chrome features a 270-card base set divided up into 140 Veteran Cards, 105 Rookie Cards, and 25 NFL Europe Prospects. Cards utilize the same base design as 2000 Bowman consisting of a full color player action shot and black and brown borders, but are enhanced with an all foil card stock. Several rookie cards were limited to just 499 copies which were inserted in packs at the rate of one in 134. Bowman Chrome was packaged in 24-pack boxes with packs containing four cards and carried a suggested retial price of $3.00.

SP ROOKIE/499 ODDS 1:134		
1 Eddie George	.30	.75
2 Ike Hilliard	.30	.75
3 Terrell Owens	.40	1.00
4 James Stewart	.25	.60
5 Joey Galloway	.30	.75
6 Jake Reed	.30	.75
7 Derrick Alexander	.25	.60
8 Jeff George	.30	.75
9 Kerry Collins	.30	.75
10 Tony Gonzalez	.40	1.00
11 Marcus Robinson	.30	.75
12 Charles Woodson	.40	1.00
13 Germane Crowell	.25	.60
14 Yancey Thigpen	.25	.60
15 Tony Martin	.30	.75
16 Frank Sanders	.25	.60
17 Napoleon Kaufman	.30	.75
18 Jay Fiedler	.30	.75
19 Patrick Jeffers	.30	.75
20 Steve McNair	.40	1.00
21 Herman Moore	.30	.75
22 Tim Brown	.40	1.00
23 Olandis Gary	.30	.75
24 Corey Dillon	.30	.75
25 Warren Sapp	.30	.75
26 Curtis Enis	.25	.60
27 Vinny Testaverde	.30	.75
28 Tim Biakabutuka	.30	.75
29 Kevin Johnson	.25	.60
30 Charlie Batch	.30	.75
31 Jermaine Fazande	.25	.60
32 Shaun King	.25	.60
33 Errict Rhett	.30	.75
34 O.J. McDuffie	.30	.75
35 Bruce Smith	.40	1.00
36 Antonio Freeman	.30	.75
37 Tim Couch	.30	.75
38 Duce Staley	.30	.75
39 Jeff Blake	.30	.75
40 Jim Harbaugh	.30	.75
41 Jeff Graham	.25	.60
42 Drew Bledsoe	.40	1.00
43 Mike Alstott	.40	1.00
44 Terance Mathis	.25	.60
45 Antowain Smith	.30	.75
46 Johnnie Morton	.30	.75
47 Chris Chandler	.30	.75
48 Keith Poole	.25	.60
49 Ricky Watters	.30	.75
50 Darnay Scott	.30	.75
51 Damon Huard	.30	.75
52 Peerless Price	.30	.75
53 Brian Griese	.30	.75
54 Frank Wycheck	.30	.75
55 Kevin Dyson	.30	.75
56 Junior Seau	.40	1.00
57 Curtis Conway	.30	.75
58 Jamal Anderson	.30	.75
59 Jim Miller	.25	.60
60 Rob Johnson	.30	.75
61 Mark Brunell	.30	.75
62 Wayne Chrebet	.30	.75
63 James Johnson	.25	.60
64 Sean Dawkins	.25	.60
65 Stephen Davis	.30	.75
66 Daunte Culpepper	.30	.75
67 Doug Flutie	.40	1.00
68 Pete Mitchell	.25	.60
69 Bill Schroeder	.30	.75
70 Terrence Wilkins	.25	.60
71 Cade McNown	.25	.60
72 Muhsin Muhammad	.30	.75
73 E.G. Green	.25	.60
74 Edgerrin James	.40	1.00
75 Troy Edwards	.25	.60
76 Terry Glenn	.30	.75
77 Tony Banks	.25	.60
78 Derrick Mayes	.25	.60
79 Curtis Martin	.40	1.00
80 Kordell Stewart	.30	.75
81 Amani Toomer	.30	.75
82 Dorsey Levens	.30	.75
83 Brad Johnson	.30	.75
84 Ed McCaffrey	.30	.75
85 Charlie Garner	.30	.75
86 Brett Favre	1.25	3.00
87 J.J. Stokes	.30	.75
88 Steve Young	.50	1.25
89 Jonathan Linton	.25	.60
90 Isaac Bruce	.40	1.00
91 Shawn Jefferson	.25	.60
92 Rod Smith	.30	.75
93 Champ Bailey	.30	.75
94 Ricky Williams	.40	1.00
95 Priest Holmes	.40	1.00
96 Corey Bradford	.25	.60
97 Eric Moulds	.30	.75
98 Warrick Dunn	.30	.75
99 Jevon Kearse	.30	.75
100 Albert Connell	.25	.60
101 Az-Zahir Hakim	.25	.60
102 Marvin Harrison	.40	1.00
103 Qadry Ismail	.30	.75
104 Oronde Gadsden	.30	.75
105 Rob Moore	.25	.60
106 Marshall Faulk	.40	1.00
107 Steve Beuerlein	.30	.75
108 Torry Holt	.40	1.00
109 Donovan McNabb	.40	1.00
110 Rich Gannon	.30	.75
111 Jerome Bettis	.40	1.00
112 Peyton Manning	1.00	2.50
113 Cris Carter	.40	1.00
114 Jake Plummer	.30	.75
115 Kent Graham	.25	.60
116 Keenan McCardell	.30	.75
117 Tim Dwight	.30	.75
118 Fred Taylor	.40	1.00
119 Jerry Rice	.75	2.00
120 Michael Westbrook	.25	.60
121 Kurt Warner	.60	1.50
122 Jimmy Smith	.30	.75
123 Emmitt Smith	1.00	2.50
124 Terrell Davis	.40	1.00
125 Randy Moss	.40	1.00
126 Akili Smith	.25	.60
127 Rocket Ismail	.30	.75
128 Jon Kitna	.30	.75
129 Elvis Grbac	.25	.60
130 Wesley Walls	.25	.60
131 Torrance Small	.25	.60
132 Tyrone Wheatley	.25	.60
133 Carl Pickens	.30	.75
134 Zach Thomas	.40	1.00
135 Jacquez Green	.25	.60
136 Robert Smith	.30	.75
137 Keyshawn Johnson	.30	.75
138 Matthew Hatchette	.25	.60
139 Troy Aikman	.60	1.50
140 Charles Johnson	.25	.60
141 Terry Battle EP	.25	.60
142 Pepe Pearson EP RC	.25	.60
143 Cory Sauter EP	.25	.60
144 Brian Shay EP	.25	.60
145 Marcus Crandell EP RC	.25	.60
146 Danny Wuerffel EP	.40	1.00
147 L.C. Stevens EP	.25	.60
148 Ted White EP	.25	.60
149 Matt Lytle EP RC	.25	.60
150 Vershan Jackson EP RC	.25	.60
151 Mario Bailey EP	.25	.60
152 Darryl Daniel EP RC	.25	.60
153 Sean Morey EP RC	.25	.60
154 Jim Kubiak EP RC	.25	.60
155 Aaron Stecker EP RC	.30	.75
156 Damon Dunn EP RC	.25	.60
157 Kevin Daft EP	.25	.60
158 Corey Thomas EP	.25	.60
159 Deon Mitchell EP RC	.30	.75
160 Todd Floyd EP RC	.25	.60
161 Norman Miller EP RC	.25	.60
162 Jeremaine Copeland EP	.25	.60
163 Michael Blair EP	.25	.60
164 Ron Powlus EP RC	.40	1.00
165 Pat Barnes EP	.30	.75
166 Dez White RC	1.25	3.00
167 Trung Canidate SP RC	8.00	20.00
168 Thomas Jones SP RC	12.00	30.00
169 Courtney Brown SP RC	8.00	20.00
170 Jamal Lewis SP RC	10.00	25.00
171 Chris Redman SP RC	8.00	20.00
172 Ron Dayne SP RC	10.00	25.00
173 Chad Pennington SP RC	15.00	40.00
174 Plaxico Burress SP RC	10.00	25.00
175 R.Jay Soward SP RC	6.00	15.00
176 Travis Taylor SP RC	8.00	20.00
177 Shaun Alexander SP RC	12.00	30.00
178 Brian Urlacher RC	6.00	15.00
179 Danny Farmer RC	1.00	2.50
180 Tee Martin SP RC	10.00	25.00
181 Sylvester Morris SP RC	6.00	15.00
182 Curtis Keaton RC	1.00	2.50
183 Peter Warrick SP RC	10.00	25.00
184 Anthony Becht RC	1.25	3.00
185 Travis Prentice SP RC	8.00	20.00
186 J.R. Redmond SP RC	6.00	15.00
187 Bubba Franks SP RC	10.00	25.00
188 Ron Dugans SP RC	6.00	15.00
189 Reuben Droughns RC	1.50	4.00
190 Corey Simon RC	1.25	3.00
191 Joe Hamilton RC	1.00	2.50
192 Laveranues Coles RC	1.50	4.00
193 Todd Pinkston SP RC	6.00	15.00
194 Jerry Porter SP RC	10.00	25.00
195 Dennis Northcutt RC	1.25	3.00
196 Tim Rattay RC	1.25	3.00
197 Giovanni Carmazzi RC	1.00	2.50
198 Mareno Philyaw RC	1.00	2.50
199 Avion Black RC	1.00	2.50
200 Chafie Fields RC	1.00	2.50
201 Rondell Mealey RC	1.00	2.50
202 Troy Walters RC	1.00	2.50
203 Frank Moreau RC	1.00	2.50
204 Vaughn Sanders RC	1.00	2.50
205 Sherrod Gideon RC	1.00	2.50
206 Doug Chapman RC	1.00	2.50
207 Marcus Knight RC	1.00	2.50
208 Jamel White RC	1.00	2.50
209 Windrell Hayes RC	1.00	2.50
210 Reggie Jones RC	1.00	2.50
211 Jarious Jackson RC	1.25	3.00
212 Ronney Jenkins RC	1.00	2.50
213 Quinton Spotwood RC	1.00	2.50
214 Rob Morris RC	1.25	3.00
215 Gari Scott RC	1.00	2.50
216 Kevin Thompson RC	1.00	2.50
217 Trevor Insley RC	1.00	2.50
218 Frank Murphy RC	1.00	2.50
219 Patrick Pass RC	1.25	3.00
220 Mike Anderson RC	1.50	4.00
221 Derrius Thompson RC	1.00	2.50
222 John Abraham RC	1.50	4.00
223 Dante Hall RC	1.50	4.00
224 Chad Morton RC	1.50	4.00
225 Ahmed Plummer RC	1.00	2.50
226 Julian Peterson RC	1.50	4.00
227 Mike Green RC	1.50	4.00
228 Michael Wiley RC	1.00	2.50
229 Spergon Wynn RC	1.25	3.00
230 Trevor Gaylor RC	1.00	2.50
231 Doug Johnson RC	1.25	3.00
232 Marc Bulger RC	1.50	4.00
233 Ron Dixon RC	1.00	2.50
234 Aaron Shea RC	1.25	3.00
235 Thomas Hamner RC	1.00	2.50
236 Tom Brady RC	50.00	100.00
237 Deltha O'Neal RC	1.25	3.00
238 Todd Husak RC	1.00	2.50
239 Erron Kinney RC	1.00	2.50
240 JaJuan Dawson RC	1.00	2.50
241 Nick Williams	.25	.60
242 Deon Grant RC	1.00	2.50
243 Brad Hoover RC	1.25	3.00
244 Kamil Loud	.25	.60
245 Rashard Anderson RC	1.00	2.50
246 Clint Stoerner RC	1.50	4.00
247 Antwan Harris RC	1.00	2.50
248 Jason Webster RC	1.00	2.50
249 Kevin McDougal RC	1.00	2.50
250 Tony Scott RC	1.00	2.50
251 Thabiti Davis RC	1.00	2.50
252 Ian Gold RC	1.00	2.50
253 Sammy Morris RC	1.25	3.00
254 Raynoch Thompson RC	1.00	2.50
255 Jeremy McDaniel	.25	.60
256 Terrelle Smith RC	1.00	2.50
257 Deon Dyer RC	1.00	2.50
258 Na'il Diggs RC	1.00	2.50
259 Brandon Short RC	1.00	2.50
260 Mike Brown RC	1.50	4.00
261 John Engelberger RC	1.00	2.50
262 Rogers Beckett RC	1.00	2.50
263 JaJuan Seider RC	1.00	2.50
264 Desmond Kitchings RC	1.00	2.50
265 Reggie Davis RC	1.00	2.50
266 Corey Moore RC	1.00	2.50
267 Cornelius Griffin RC	1.00	2.50
268 Stockar McDougle RC	1.00	2.50
269 James Williams RC	1.00	2.50
270 Darrell Jackson RC	1.25	3.00

2000 Bowman Chrome Refractors

*VETS 1-165: 1.5X TO 4X BASIC CARDS		
1-165 VETERAN STATED ODDS 1:12		
*ROOKIE 166-270: 1.5X TO 4X BASIC CARD		
166-270 ROOKIE ODDS 1:281		
*ROOKIE/99: .6X TO 1.5X BASIC RC/499		
ROOKIE SP/99 ODDS 1:659		
ROOKIE SP PRINT RUN 99		
236 Tom Brady	350.00	600.00

2000 Bowman Chrome By Selection

COMPLETE SET (10)	10.00	25.00
STATED ODDS 1:24 H/R		
*REFRACTOR: 1.2X TO 3X BASIC INSERTS		
REFRACTOR STATED ODDS 1:240 H/R		
B1 Troy Aikman / Drew Bledsoe	1.25	3.00
B2 Marshall Faulk / Donovan McNabb	.75	2.00
B3 Ricky Williams / Jamal Lewis	.75	2.00
B4 Randy Moss / Sylvester Morris	.50	1.25
B5 Shaun Alexander / Marvin Harrison	1.00	2.50
B6 Tim Couch / Peyton Manning	.60	1.50
B7 Edgerrin James / Peter Warrick	.75	2.00
B8 Jimmy Smith / Todd Pinkston	.50	1.25
B9 Steve McNair / Akili Smith	.75	2.00
B10 Plaxico Burress / Joey Galloway	.75	2.00

2000 Bowman Chrome Ground Breakers

COMPLETE SET (10)	4.00	10.00
STATED ODDS 1:12 H/R		
*REFRACTOR: 1.2X TO 3X BASIC INSERTS		
REFRACTOR STATED ODDS 1:120 H/R		
GB1 Edgerrin James	.60	1.50
GB2 Eddie George	.50	1.25
GB3 Jerome Bettis	.60	1.50
GB4 Fred Taylor	.60	1.50
GB5 Curtis Martin	.60	1.50
GB6 Errict Rhett	.50	1.25
GB7 Marshall Faulk	.60	1.50
GB8 Karim Abdul-Jabbar	.40	1.00
GB9 Olandis Gary	.50	1.25
GB10 Terrell Davis	.60	1.50

2000 Bowman Chrome Rookie Autographs

FIRST 25 ROOKIE CARDS WERE SIGNED		
AUTO/25* ODDS 1:5247 HOB, 1:5292 RET		
168 Thomas Jones	90.00	150.00
170 Jamal Lewis	50.00	120.00
172 Ron Dayne	30.00	80.00
173 Chad Pennington	100.00	200.00
174 Plaxico Burress	50.00	120.00
175 R.Jay Soward	20.00	50.00
177 Shaun Alexander	100.00	200.00
101 Sylvester Morris	20.00	50.00
183 Peter Warrick	30.00	80.00
185 Travis Prentice	25.00	60.00

2000 Bowman Chrome Rookie of the Year Jumbos

COMPLETE SET (10)	4.00	10.00
STATED ODDS ONE PER BOX		
R1 Santana Dotson	.50	1.25
R2 Jerome Bettis	.75	2.00
R3 Marshall Faulk	.75	2.00
R4 Curtis Martin	.75	2.00
R5 Eddie George	.60	1.50
R6 Warrick Dunn	.60	1.50
R7 Charles Woodson	.75	2.00
R8 Randy Moss	.75	2.00
R9 Jevon Kearse	.60	1.50
R10 Edgerrin James	.75	2.00

2000 Bowman Chrome Scout's Choice Update

COMPLETE SET (10)	7.50	20.00
STATED ODDS 1:24 H/R		
*REFRACTOR: 1.2X TO 3X BASIC INSERTS		
REFRACTOR STATED ODDS 1:240 H/R		
SCU1 Shaun Alexander	.75	2.00
SCU2 Brian Urlacher	2.50	6.00
SCU3 Courtney Brown	.50	1.25
SCU4 Jamal Lewis	.60	1.50
SCU5 Sylvester Morris	.40	1.00
SCU6 Plaxico Burress	.60	1.50
SCU7 Ron Dayne	.60	1.50
SCU8 Thomas Jones	.75	2.00
SCU9 Corey Simon	.50	1.25
SCU10 Travis Taylor	.50	1.25

2000 Bowman Chrome Shattering Performers

COMPLETE SET (20)	15.00	40.00
STATED ODDS 1:16 H/R		
*REFRACTOR: 1.2X TO 3X BASIC INSERTS		
REFRACTOR STATED ODDS 1:160 H/R		
SP1 Kurt Warner	1.25	3.00
SP2 Peyton Manning	2.00	5.00
SP3 Brian Griese	.60	1.50
SP4 Daunte Culpepper	.60	1.50
SP5 Elvis Grbac	.50	1.25
SP6 Stephen Davis	.60	1.50
SP7 Charlie Garner	.60	1.50
SP8 Mike Anderson	.75	2.00
SP9 Marshall Faulk	.75	2.00
SP10 Robert Smith	.60	1.50
SP11 Tiki Barber	.75	2.00
SP12 Edgerrin James	.75	2.00
SP13 Isaac Bruce	.75	2.00
SP14 Rod Smith	.60	1.50
SP15 Jimmy Smith	.60	1.50
SP16 Torry Holt	.75	2.00
SP17 Keenan McCardell	.60	1.50
SP18 Marcus Robinson	.60	1.50
SP19 Marvin Harrison	.75	2.00
SP20 Randy Moss	.75	2.00

2001 Bowman Chrome

This 255 card set was released in four card packs which came packaged 24 to a box. Cards numbered 1-110 featured vets while cards numbered 111-255 featured rookies and were inserted at a rate of one every three packs. These rookie cards are serial numbered to 1999 and were printed with Refractor printing technology.

COMPLETE SET (255)	150.00	300.00
COMP.SET w/o SP's (110)	10.00	25.00
ROOKIE/1999 ODDS 1:3 HOBBY		
1 Emmitt Smith	1.00	2.50
2 James Stewart	.25	.60
3 Jeff Graham	.25	.60
4 Keyshawn Johnson	.30	.75
5 Stephen Davis	.30	.75
6 Chad Lewis	.25	.60
7 Drew Bledsoe	.40	1.00
8 Fred Taylor	.40	1.00
9 Mike Anderson	.30	.75
10 Tony Gonzalez	.40	1.00
11 Aaron Brooks	.30	.75
12 Vinny Testaverde	.30	.75
13 Jerome Bettis	.40	1.00
14 Marshall Faulk	.40	1.00
15 Jeff Garcia	.30	.75
16 Terry Glenn	.30	.75
17 Jay Fiedler	.30	.75
18 Ahman Green	.40	1.00
19 Cade McNown	.30	.75
20 Rob Johnson	.30	.75
21 Jamal Anderson	.30	.75
22 Corey Dillon	.30	.75
23 Jake Plummer	.30	.75
24 Rod Smith	.30	.75
25 Trent Green	.40	1.00
26 Ricky Williams	.40	1.00
27 Charlie Garner	.30	.75
28 Shaun Alexander	.40	1.00
29 Jeff George	.30	.75
30 Torry Holt	.30	.75
31 James Thrash	.30	.75
32 Rich Gannon	.30	.75
33 Ron Dayne	.30	.75
34 Dedric Ward	.25	.60
35 Edgerrin James	.40	1.00
36 Cris Carter	.40	1.00
37 Derrick Mason	.30	.75
38 Brad Johnson	.30	.75
39 Charlie Batch	.30	.75
40 Joey Galloway	.30	.75
41 James Allen	.25	.60
42 Tim Biakabutuka	.25	.60
43 Ray Lewis	.40	1.00
44 David Boston	.25	.60
45 Kevin Johnson	.25	.60
46 Jimmy Smith	.30	.75
47 Joe Horn	.30	.75
48 Terrell Owens	.40	1.00
49 Eddie George	.40	1.00
50 Brett Favre	1.25	3.00
51 Wayne Chrebet	.30	.75
52 Hines Ward	.40	1.00
53 Warrick Dunn	.40	1.00
54 Matt Hasselbeck	.40	1.00
55 Tiki Barber	.40	1.00
56 Lamar Smith	.30	.75
57 Tim Couch	.25	.60
58 Eric Moulds	.30	.75
59 Shawn Jefferson	.25	.60
60 Donald Hayes	.25	.60
61 Brian Urlacher	.50	1.25
62 Steve McNair	.40	1.00
63 Kurt Warner	.60	1.50
64 Tim Brown	.40	1.00
65 Troy Brown	.30	.75
66 Albert Connell	.25	.60
67 Peyton Manning	1.00	2.50
68 Peter Warrick	.30	.75
69 Elvis Grbac	.30	.75
70 Chris Chandler	.30	.75
71 Akili Smith	.25	.60
72 Keenan McCardell	.30	.75
73 Kerry Collins	.30	.75
74 Junior Seau	.40	1.00
75 Donovan McNabb	.40	1.00
76 Tony Banks	.25	.60
77 Steve Beuerlein	.30	.75
78 Daunte Culpepper	.30	.75
79 Darrell Jackson	.30	.75
80 Isaac Bruce	.40	1.00
81 Tyrone Wheatley	.30	.75
82 Derrick Alexander	.25	.60
83 Germane Crowell	.25	.60
84 Jon Kitna	.30	.75
85 Jamal Lewis	.40	1.00
86 Ed McCaffrey	.30	.75
87 Mark Brunell	.30	.75
88 Jeff Blake	.30	.75
89 Duce Staley	.30	.75
90 Doug Flutie	.40	1.00
91 Kordell Stewart	.30	.75
92 Randy Moss	.40	1.00
93 Marvin Harrison	.40	1.00
94 Muhsin Muhammad	.30	.75
95 Brian Griese	.30	.75
96 Antonio Freeman	.40	1.00
97 Amani Toomer	.30	.75
98 Orondo Gadsden	.25	.60
99 Curtis Martin	.40	1.00
100 Jerry Rice	.75	2.00
101 Michael Pittman	.30	.75
102 Shannon Sharpe	.40	1.00
103 Peerless Price	.25	.60
104 Bill Schroeder	.30	.75
105 Ike Hilliard	.30	.75
106 Freddie Jones	.25	.60
107 Tai Streets	.25	.60
108 Ricky Watters	.30	.75
109 Az-Zahir Hakim	.25	.60
110 Jacquez Green	.25	.60
111 George Layne RC	2.00	5.00
112 Correll Buckhalter RC	3.00	8.00
113 Tony Stewart RC	2.50	6.00
114 Chris Barnes RC	2.00	5.00
115 A.J. Feeley RC	2.50	6.00
116 Margin Hooks RC	2.00	5.00
117 Anthony Henry RC	3.00	8.00
118 Dwight Smith RC	2.00	5.00
119 Torrance Marshall RC	2.00	5.00
120 Gary Baxter RC	2.00	5.00
121 Derek Combs RC	2.00	5.00
122 Marcus Bell RC	2.00	5.00
123 DeLawrence Grant RC	2.00	5.00
124 Jameel Cook RC	2.50	6.00
125 Eric Downing RC	2.00	5.00
126 Marlon McCree RC	2.00	5.00
127 Tay Cody RC	2.00	5.00
128 Mario Monds RC	2.00	5.00
129 Kenny Smith RC	2.00	5.00
130 Sedrick Hodge RC	2.00	5.00
131 Marcus Stroud RC	2.50	6.00
132 Steve Smith RC	10.00	25.00
133 Tyrone Robertson RC	2.00	5.00
134 James Reed RC	2.00	5.00
135 Kris Kocurek RC	2.00	5.00
136 Dan O'Leary RC	2.00	5.00
137 Harold Blackmon RC	2.00	5.00
138 Fred Smoot RC	3.00	8.00
139 Billy Baber RC	2.00	5.00
140 Jarrod Cooper RC	2.50	6.00
141 Travis Henry RC	2.50	6.00
142 David Terrell RC	2.50	6.00
143 Josh Heupel RC	3.00	8.00
144 Drew Brees RC	60.00	100.00
145 T.J. Houshmandzadeh RC	4.00	10.00
146 Rod Gardner RC	2.50	6.00
147 Richard Seymour RC	3.00	8.00
148 Koren Robinson RC	2.50	6.00
149 Scotty Anderson RC	2.00	5.00
150 Marques Tuiasosopo RC	2.50	6.00
151 John Capel RC	2.00	5.00
152 LaMont Jordan RC	3.00	8.00
153 James Jackson RC	2.00	5.00
154 Bobby Newcombe RC	2.50	6.00
155 Anthony Thomas RC	3.00	8.00
156 Dan Alexander RC	2.50	6.00
157 Quincy Carter RC	2.50	6.00
158 Morlon Greenwood RC	2.00	5.00
159 Robert Ferguson RC	3.00	8.00
160 Sage Rosenfels RC	3.00	8.00
161 Michael Stone RC	2.00	5.00
162 Chris Weinke RC	2.50	6.00
163 Travis Minor RC	2.50	6.00
164 Gerard Warren RC	2.50	6.00
165 Jamar Fletcher RC	2.00	5.00
166 Andre Carter RC	2.50	6.00
167 Deuce McAllister RC	3.00	8.00
168 Dan Morgan RC	2.50	6.00
169 Todd Heap RC	3.00	8.00
170 Snoop Minnis RC	2.00	5.00
171 Will Allen RC	3.00	8.00
172 Freddie Mitchell RC	2.00	5.00
173 Rudi Johnson RC	3.00	8.00
174 Kevan Barlow RC	2.50	6.00
175 Jamie Winborn RC	2.50	6.00
176 Onome Ojo RC	2.00	5.00
177 Leonard Davis RC	3.00	8.00
178 Santana Moss RC	4.00	10.00
179 Chris Chambers RC	3.00	8.00
180 Michael Vick RC	30.00	60.00
181 Michael Bennett RC	2.50	6.00
182 Mike McMahon RC	2.50	6.00
183 Jonathan Carter RC	2.00	5.00
184 Jamal Reynolds RC	2.00	5.00
185 Justin Smith RC	3.00	8.00
186 Quincy Morgan RC	2.50	6.00
187 Chad Johnson RC	10.00	25.00
188 Jesse Palmer RC	2.50	6.00
189 Reggie Wayne RC	10.00	25.00
190 LaDainian Tomlinson RC	30.00	60.00
191 Andre King RC	2.00	5.00
192 Richmond Flowers RC	2.00	5.00
193 Derrick Blaylock RC	2.50	6.00
194 Cedrick Wilson RC	2.50	6.00
195 Zeke Moreno RC	2.50	6.00
196 Tommy Polley RC	2.00	5.00
197 Damione Lewis RC	2.50	6.00
198 Aaron Schobel RC	3.00	8.00
199 Alge Crumpler RC	3.00	8.00
200 Nate Clements RC	2.50	6.00
201 Quentin McCord RC	2.50	6.00
202 Ken-Yon Rambo RC	2.00	5.00
203 Milton Wynn RC	2.00	5.00
204 Derrick Gibson RC	2.00	5.00
205 Chris Taylor RC	2.00	5.00
206 Corey Hall RC	2.00	5.00
207 Vinny Sutherland RC	2.00	5.00
208 Kendrell Bell RC	3.00	8.00
209 Casey Hampton RC	3.00	8.00
210 Demetric Evans RC	2.00	5.00
211 Brian Allen RC	2.00	5.00
212 Rodney Bailey RC	2.00	5.00
213 Otis Leverette RC	2.00	5.00
214 Ron Edwards RC	2.00	5.00
215 Michael Jameson RC	2.00	5.00
216 Markus Steele RC	2.00	5.00
217 Jimmy Williams RC	2.00	5.00
218 Roger Knight RC	2.00	5.00
219 Randy Garner RC	2.00	5.00
220 Raymond Perryman RC	2.00	5.00
221 Karon Riley RC	2.00	5.00
222 Adam Archuleta RC	2.50	6.00
223 Arnold Jackson RC	2.00	5.00
224 Ryan Pickett RC	2.00	5.00
225 Shad Meier RC	2.00	5.00
226 Reggie Germany RC	2.00	5.00
227 Justin McCareins RC	2.50	6.00
228 Idrees Bashir RC	2.00	5.00
229 Josh Booty RC	2.50	6.00
230 Eddie Berlin RC	2.00	5.00
231 Heath Evans RC	2.50	6.00
232 Alex Bannister RC	2.00	5.00
233 Corey Alston RC	2.00	5.00
234 Reggie White RC	2.00	5.00
235 Orlando Huff RC	2.00	5.00
236 Ken Lucas RC	2.50	6.00
237 Matt Stewart RC	2.00	5.00
238 Cedric Scott RC	2.00	5.00
239 Ronney Daniels RC	2.00	5.00
240 Kevin Kasper RC	2.00	5.00
241 Tony Driver RC	2.50	6.00
242 Kyle Vanden Bosch RC	3.00	8.00
243 T.J. Turner RC	2.00	5.00
244 Eric Westmoreland RC	2.00	5.00
245 Ronald Flemons RC	2.00	5.00
246 Eric Kelly RC	2.00	5.00
247 Moran Norris RC	2.00	5.00
248 Darnerien McCants RC	2.50	6.00
249 James Boyd RC	2.00	5.00
250 Keith Adams RC	2.00	5.00
251 Brandon Manumaleuna RC	2.50	6.00
252 Dee Brown RC	2.00	5.00
253 Ross Kolodziej RC	2.00	5.00
254 Boo Williams RC	2.00	5.00
255 Patrick Chukwurah RC	2.00	5.00

2001 Bowman Chrome Gold Refractors

*STARS: 5X TO 12X BASIC CARDS		
*ROOKIES: 1.2X TO 3X BASIC CARDS		
STATED PRINT RUN 99 SER.#'d SETS		
STATED ODDS 1:38 HOBBY		
144 Drew Brees	175.00	300.00
180 Michael Vick	125.00	250.00
190 LaDainian Tomlinson	125.00	250.00

2001 Bowman Chrome Xfractors

*VETS 1-110: 2.5X TO 6X BASIC CARDS		
*ROOKIES 111-255: .8X TO 2X		
STATED ODDS 1:23 HOBBY		
144 Drew Brees	100.00	175.00
180 Michael Vick	60.00	150.00
190 LaDainian Tomlinson	60.00	150.00

2001 Bowman Chrome 1996 Rookies

COMPLETE SET (15)	15.00	40.00
STATED ODDS 1:16 HOBBY		
BRC1 Eric Moulds	1.50	4.00
BRC2 Ray Lewis	2.50	6.00
BRC3 Tim Biakabutuka	1.50	4.00
BRC4 Eddie George	2.50	6.00
BRC5 Marvin Harrison	2.50	6.00
BRC6 Joe Horn	1.50	4.00
BRC7 Muhsin Muhammad	1.50	4.00
BRC8 Mike Alstott	2.50	6.00
BRC9 Amani Toomer	1.50	4.00
BRC10 Terrell Owens	2.50	6.00
BRC11 Keyshawn Johnson	2.50	6.00
BRC12 Terry Glenn	1.50	4.00
BRC13 Zach Thomas	2.50	6.00
BRC14 Stephen Davis	2.50	6.00
BRC15 La'Roi Glover	1.00	2.50

2001 Bowman Chrome Autographs

GROUP A STATED ODDS 1:947		
GROUP B STATED ODDS 1:473		
OVERALL STATED ODDS 1:315 HOBBY		
ROOKIE STATED ODDS 1:772 HOBBY		
BCAT Anthony Thomas	12.00	30.00
BCBN Bobby Newcombe	10.00	25.00
BCCC Chris Chambers	12.00	30.00
BCCJ Chad Johnson	60.00	150.00
BCCW Chris Weinke	10.00	25.00
BCDA Dan Alexander	10.00	25.00
BCDB Drew Brees	400.00	700.00
BCDBO David Boston	8.00	20.00
BCDM1 Derrick Mason	10.00	25.00
BCDM3 Dan Morgan	10.00	25.00
BCDT David Terrell	10.00	25.00
BCJH Josh Heupel	12.00	30.00
BCJHO Joe Horn	10.00	25.00
BCJJ James Jackson	8.00	20.00
BCJP Jesse Palmer	10.00	25.00
BCKB Kevan Barlow	10.00	25.00
BCLJ LaMont Jordan	12.00	30.00
BCLT LaDainian Tomlinson	250.00	500.00
BCMB Michael Bennett	10.00	25.00
BCMV Michael Vick	300.00	600.00
BCQC Quincy Carter	10.00	25.00
BCQM Quincy Morgan	10.00	25.00
BCRG Rod Gardner	10.00	25.00
BCRGE Reggie Germany	8.00	20.00
BCRW Reggie Wayne	125.00	250.00
BCSM Santana Moss	15.00	40.00
BCTH Travis Henry	10.00	25.00
BCTM Travis Minor	10.00	25.00

2001 Bowman Chrome Draft Day Relics

JSY STATED ODDS 1:131 HOBBY		
CAP STATED ODDS 1:2129 HOBBY		
DHDT David Terrell Cap	7.50	20.00
DHJS Justin Smith Cap	7.50	20.00
DHLD Leonard Davis Cap	7.50	20.00
DHLT LaDainian Tomlinson Cap	15.00	40.00
DHMV Michael Vick Cap	15.00	40.00
DJDT David Terrell JSY	4.00	10.00
DJJS Justin Smith JSY	4.00	10.00
DJKW Kenyatta Walker JSY	4.00	10.00
DJLD Leonard Davis JSY	4.00	10.00
DJLT LaDainian Tomlinson JSY	15.00	40.00
DJMV Michael Vick JSY	15.00	40.00

2001 Bowman Chrome Rookie Relics

GROUP A STATED ODDS 1:9648		
GROUP B STATED ODDS 1:1730		
GROUP C STATED ODDS 1:902		
GROUP D STATED ODDS 1:2376		
GROUP E STATED ODDS 1:664		
GROUP F STATED ODDS 1:379		
GROUP G STATED ODDS 1:505		
GROUP H STATED ODDS 1:676		
GROUP I STATED ODDS 1:574		
GROUP J STATED ODDS 1:789		
OVERALL STATED ODDS 1:78		
BCRBA Brian Allen	3.00	8.00
BCRBJ Bhawoh Jue	4.00	10.00

BCRDB Drew Brees	15.00	40.00
BCRDBU Derrick Burgess	5.00	12.00
BCREW Eric Westmoreland	3.00	8.00
BCRJB Jeff Backus	3.00	8.00
BCRJC Jarrod Cooper	4.00	10.00
BCRJH Jabari Holloway	3.00	8.00
BCRJJ Jonas Jennings	3.00	8.00
BCRJP Jesse Palmer	4.00	10.00
BCRJHE Jamie Henderson	4.00	10.00
BCRKK Kevin Kasper	3.00	8.00
BCRLJ LaMont Jordan	5.00	12.00
BCRLM Leonard Myers	3.00	8.00
BCRMF Mario Fatafehi	3.00	8.00
BCRMS Michael Stone	3.00	8.00
BCRRG Reggie Germany	3.00	8.00
BCRRW Reggie Wayne	10.00	25.00
BCRSH Steve Hutchinson	5.00	12.00
BCRSS Steve Smith	10.00	25.00
BCRTD Tony Dixon	3.00	8.00
BCRTS Tony Stewart	4.00	10.00
BCRZM Zeke Moreno	4.00	10.00

2001 Bowman Chrome Rookie Reprints

COMPLETE SET (16)	20.00	40.00
STATED ODDS 1:24 HOBBY		
RAA Alan Ameche	1.25	3.00
RAD Art Donovan	1.50	4.00
RBH Bill Howton	1.25	3.00
RBT Bulldog Turner	1.50	4.00
RCC Charlie Conerly	1.50	4.00
REH Elroy Hirsch	2.00	5.00
RET Emlen Tunnell	1.25	3.00
RFG Frank Gifford	2.50	6.00
RGM Gino Marchetti	1.25	3.00
RLG Lou Groza	1.50	4.00
RNV Norm Van Brocklin	2.00	5.00
ROG Otto Graham	2.00	5.00
RSB Sammy Baugh	2.50	6.00
RSL Sid Luckman	1.50	4.00
RTF Tom Fears	1.25	3.00
RYT Y.A Tittle	2.50	6.00

2002 Bowman Chrome

Released in December 2002, this set features 110 veterans and 140 rookies. Cards 111-220 were inserted at a rate of 1:2. Cards 221-250 were signed and inserted at the following rates: Group A 1:134, Group B 1:162, Group C 1:140, Group D 1:91, Group E 1:68, and Group F 1:150. Boxes contained 18 packs of 4 cards.

COMP.SET w/o SP's (110)	10.00	25.00
1 Emmitt Smith	1.00	2.50
2 Drew Brees	.60	1.50
3 Duce Staley	.30	.75
4 Curtis Martin	.40	1.00
5 Isaac Bruce	.40	1.00
6 Stephen Davis	.30	.75
7 Darrell Jackson	.30	.75
8 James Stewart	.25	.60
9 Tim Couch	.25	.60
10 Travis Henry	.25	.60
11 Thomas Jones	.40	1.00
12 Jamal Lewis	.30	.75
13 Chris Chambers	.30	.75
14 Jeff Blake	.30	.75
15 Plaxico Burress	.30	.75
16 Michael Pittman	.30	.75
17 Jeff Garcia	.30	.75
18 Tim Brown	.40	1.00
19 Kent Graham	.25	.60
20 Shannon Sharpe	.40	1.00
21 Corey Dillon	.30	.75
22 Muhsin Muhammad	.30	.75
23 Tony Gonzalez	.40	1.00
24 Qadry Ismail	.30	.75
25 Mike McMahon	.25	.60
26 Edgerrin James	.30	.75
27 Daunte Culpepper	.30	.75
28 Deuce McAllister	.30	.75
29 Kerry Collins	.30	.75
30 Eddie George	.30	.75
31 Torry Holt	.40	1.00
32 Todd Pinkston	.25	.60
33 Quincy Carter	.25	.60
34 Rod Smith	.30	.75
35 Michael Vick	.60	1.50
36 Jim Miller	.25	.60
37 Troy Brown	.30	.75
38 Wayne Chrebet	.30	.75
39 Curtis Conway	.30	.75
40 Reidel Anthony	.25	.60
41 Mark Brunell	.30	.75
42 Chris Weinke	.25	.60
43 Eric Moulds	.30	.75
44 Ike Hilliard	.30	.75
45 Jay Fiedler	.30	.75
46 Keyshawn Johnson	.30	.75
47 Rod Gardner	.25	.60
48 Chris Redman	.25	.60
49 James Allen	.25	.60
50 Kordell Stewart	.30	.75
51 Priest Holmes	.40	1.00
52 Anthony Thomas	.30	.75
53 Peter Warrick	.30	.75
54 Jake Plummer	.30	.75
55 Jerry Rice	.75	2.00
56 Joe Horn	.30	.75
57 Derrick Mason	.30	.75
58 Kurt Warner	.40	1.00
59 Antowain Smith	.30	.75
60 Randy Moss	.40	1.00
61 Warrick Dunn	.30	.75
62 Laveranues Coles	.30	.75
63 LaDainian Tomlinson	.50	1.25
64 Michael Westbrook	.25	.60
65 Travis Taylor	.25	.60
66 Brian Griese	.30	.75
67 Bill Schroeder	.25	.60
68 Ahman Green	.30	.75
69 Jimmy Smith	.30	.75
70 Charlie Garner	.30	.75
71 Terrell Owens	.40	1.00
72 Brad Johnson	.30	.75
73 James Thrash	.30	.75
74 Marvin Harrison	.40	1.00
75 Brett Favre	1.00	2.50
76 Rocket Ismail	.30	.75
77 David Boston	.25	.60
78 Jermaine Lewis	.25	.60
79 Aaron Brooks	.30	.75
80 Shaun Alexander	.30	.75
81 Steve McNair	.40	1.00
82 Marshall Faulk	.40	1.00
83 Terrell Davis	.40	1.00
84 Corey Bradford	.25	.60
85 David Terrell	.25	.60
86 Kevin Johnson	.25	.60
87 Jon Kitna	.30	.75
88 Az-Zahir Hakim	.25	.60
89 Drew Bledsoe	.40	1.00
90 Garrison Hearst	.30	.75
91 Doug Flutie	.40	1.00
92 Jerome Bettis	.40	1.00
93 Vinny Testaverde	.30	.75
94 Tiki Barber	.40	1.00
95 Johnnie Morton	.30	.75
96 Lamar Smith	.30	.75
97 Marcus Robinson	.30	.75
98 Fred Taylor	.30	.75
99 Tom Brady	1.00	2.50
100 Peyton Manning	.75	2.00
101 Donovan McNabb	.40	1.00
102 Rich Gannon	.30	.75
103 Hines Ward	.40	1.00
104 Michael Bennett	.30	.75
105 Ricky Williams	.30	.75
106 Germane Crowell	.25	.60
107 Joey Galloway	.30	.75
108 Amani Toomer	.30	.75
109 Trent Green	.30	.75
110 Terry Glenn	.30	.75
111 Donte Stallworth RC	1.50	4.00
112 Mike Williams RC	1.00	2.50
113 Kurt Kittner RC	1.00	2.50
114 Josh Reed RC	1.25	3.00
115 Raonall Smith RC	1.00	2.50
116 David Garrard RC	2.00	5.00
117 Eric Crouch RC	1.50	4.00
118 Levi Jones RC	1.00	2.50
119 Quentin Jammer RC	1.50	4.00
120 Cliff Russell RC	1.00	2.50
121 Jamin Elliott RC	1.00	2.50
122 Roy Williams RC	1.50	4.00
123 Marquise Walker RC	1.00	2.50
124 Kalimba Edwards RC	1.25	3.00
125 Daniel Graham RC	1.25	3.00
126 Anthony Weaver RC	1.00	2.50
127 Antonio Bryant RC	1.50	4.00
128 DeShaun Foster RC	1.50	4.00
129 Antwaan Randle El RC	1.50	4.00
130 William Green RC	1.25	3.00
131 Joey Harrington RC	1.50	4.00
132 T.J. Duckett RC	1.50	4.00
133 Javon Walker RC	1.50	4.00
134 Albert Haynesworth RC	1.50	4.00
135 Julius Peppers RC	3.00	8.00
136 Clinton Portis RC	2.00	5.00
137 Ashley Lelie RC	1.25	3.00
138 Reche Caldwell RC	1.50	4.00
139 Rohan Davey RC	1.50	4.00
140 Patrick Ramsey RC	1.50	4.00
141 Ron Johnson RC	1.25	3.00
142 Jamar Martin RC	1.25	3.00
143 Travis Stephens RC	1.00	2.50
143AU Travis Stephens AU	4.00	10.00
144 Darrell Hill RC	1.00	2.50
145 Jon McGraw RC	1.00	2.50
146 Javin Hunter RC	1.00	2.50
146AU Javin Hunter AU	4.00	10.00
147 Eddie Drummond RC	1.00	2.50
148 Andre Lott RC	1.00	2.50
149 Travis Fisher RC	1.25	3.00
150 Lamont Brightful RC	1.00	2.50
151 Rocky Calmus RC	1.25	3.00
152 Wes Pate RC	1.00	2.50
152AU Wes Pate AU	4.00	10.00
153 Lamar Gordon RC	1.25	3.00
154 Terry Jones RC	1.00	2.50
155 Kyle Johnson RC	1.00	2.50
155AU Kyle Johnson AU	4.00	10.00
156 Daryl Jones RC	1.00	2.50
157 Tellis Redmon RC	1.00	2.50
158 Jarrod Baxter RC	1.00	2.50
159 Delvon Flowers RC	1.00	2.50
160 Kelly Campbell RC	1.25	3.00
161 Eddie Freeman RC	1.00	2.50
162 Atrews Bell RC	1.00	2.50
163 Omar Easy RC	1.25	3.00
164 Jeremy Allen RC	1.00	2.50
165 Andra Davis RC	1.00	2.50
166 Mike Rumph RC	1.00	2.50
167 Seth Burford RC	1.00	2.50
168 Marquand Manuel RC	1.00	2.50
169 Marques Anderson RC	1.25	3.00
170 Ben Leber RC	1.00	2.50
171 Ryan Denney RC	1.00	2.50
172 Justin Peelle RC	1.00	2.50
173 Lito Sheppard RC	1.50	4.00
174 Damien Anderson RC	1.00	2.50
175 Lamont Thompson RC	1.25	3.00
176 David Priestley RC	1.00	2.50
177 Michael Lewis RC	1.50	4.00
178 Lee Mays RC	1.00	2.50
179 Alan Harper RC	1.00	2.50
180 Verron Haynes RC	1.00	2.50
181 Chris Hope RC	1.50	4.00
182 Derek Ross RC	1.25	3.00
183 Joseph Jefferson RC	1.00	2.50
184 Carlos Hall RC	1.00	2.50
185 Robert Royal RC	1.50	4.00
186 Sheldon Brown RC	1.50	4.00
187 DeVeren Johnson RC	1.00	2.50
188 Rock Cartwright RC	1.50	4.00
189 Kendall Simmons RC	1.00	2.50
190 Joe Burns RC	1.00	2.50
191 David Givens RC	1.50	4.00
192 John Owens RC	1.00	2.50
193 Jarrett Ferguson RC	1.00	2.50
194 Randy McMichael RC	1.50	4.00
195 Chris Baker RC	1.00	2.50
196 Rashad Bauman RC	1.00	2.50
197 Matt Murphy RC	1.00	2.50
198 Steve Bellisari RC	1.00	2.50
199 Jeff Kelly RC	1.00	2.50
200 Mark Anelli RC	1.00	2.50
201 Darnell Sanders RC	1.00	2.50
202 Coy Wire RC	1.25	3.00
203 Ricky Williams RC	1.25	3.00
204 Napoleon Harris RC	1.25	3.00
205 Ennis Haywood RC	1.00	2.50
206 Keyuo Craver RC	1.00	2.50
207 Kahlil Hill RC	1.00	2.50
208 J.T. O'Sullivan RC	1.25	3.00
209 Woody Dantzler RC	1.25	3.00
210 Phillip Buchanon RC	1.50	4.00
211 Charles Grant RC	1.50	4.00
212 Dusty Bonner RC	1.00	2.50
213 James Allen RC	1.00	2.50
214 Ronald Curry RC	1.25	3.00
215 Deion Branch RC	1.50	4.00
216 Larry Ned RC	1.00	2.50
217 Kendall Newson RC	1.00	2.50
218 Shaun Hill RC	2.00	5.00
219 Akin Ayodele RC	1.25	3.00
220 John Henderson RC	1.25	3.00
221 Andre Davis AU A RC	5.00	12.00
222 Bryan Thomas AU A RC	4.00	10.00
223 Brian Westbrook AU C RC	20.00	50.00
224 Chad Hutchinson AU C RC	4.00	10.00
225 Craig Nall AU D RC	5.00	12.00
226 David Carr AU A RC	10.00	25.00
227 Dwight Freeney AU D RC	25.00	40.00
228 Adrian Peterson AU A RC	8.00	20.00
229 Randy Fasani AU E RC	5.00	12.00
230 Ed Reed AU A RC	35.00	60.00
231 Freddie Milons AU B RC	4.00	10.00
232 Herb Haygood AU E RC	4.00	10.00
233 Jabar Gaffney AU A RC	6.00	15.00
234 Josh McCown AU A RC	12.00	30.00
235 Jeremy Shockey AU A RC	15.00	40.00
236 Jake Schifino AU F RC	4.00	10.00
237 Josh Scobey AU E RC	5.00	12.00
238 Jonathan Wells AU D RC	6.00	15.00
239 Ladell Betts AU A RC	8.00	20.00
240 Luke Staley AU E RC	4.00	10.00
241 Maurice Morris AU B RC	5.00	12.00
242 Matt Schobel AU D RC	6.00	15.00
243 Sam Simmons AU C RC	4.00	10.00
244 Tim Carter AU A RC	5.00	12.00
245 Tank Williams AU E RC	5.00	12.00
246 Jerramy Stevens AU A RC	6.00	15.00
247 Jason McAddley AU C RC	5.00	12.00
248 Ken Simonton AU D RC	4.00	10.00
249 Chester Taylor AU F RC	8.00	20.00
250 Brandon Doman AU C RC	4.00	10.00

2002 Bowman Chrome Refractors

*VETS 1-110: 1.5X TO 4X BASIC CARDS
*ROOKIES 111-220: 1X TO 2.5X
REFRACTOR/500 ODDS 1:6
STATED PRINT RUN 500 SER.#'d SETS

2002 Bowman Chrome Refractors Gold

*VETS 1-110: 5X TO 12X BASIC CARDS
*ROOKIES 111-220: 2.5X TO 6X
REFRACTOR GOLD/50 ODDS 1:60
STATED PRINT RUN 50 SER.#'d SETS

2002 Bowman Chrome Xfractors

*VETS 1-110: 2.5X TO 6X BASIC CARDS
*ROOKIES 111-220: 1.5X TO 4X
1-220 XFRACTOR/250 ODDS 1:12
1-220 PRINT RUN 250 SER.#'d SETS
*ROOKIE AU 221-250: .8X TO 2X
221-250 ROOKIE AU/250 ODDS 1:391

230 Ed Reed AU	75.00	150.00

2002 Bowman Chrome Uncirculated

*ROOKIES: .8X TO 2X BASIC CARDS
ANNC'd UNSIGNED PRINT RUN 172
UNPRICED ANNC'd AUTO PRINT RUN 10

2003 Bowman Chrome

Released in November of 2003, this set consists of 246 cards, including 110 veterans and 136 rookies. Rookies 221-246 feature authentic player autographs and are seeded as follows: Group A: 1:3897, Group B: 1:333, Group C: 1:195, Group D: 1:28, and Group E: 1:99. In addition, Gold Refractor Rookie Autographs are seeded 1:542. Please note that card #180 (Rex Grossman) can be found signed and unsigned. Taylor Jacobs, Bryant Johnson, Talman Gardner, and LaBrandon Toefield were issued as exchange cards in packs with an expiration date of 11/30/2005. Boxes contained 18 packs of 4 cards. SRP was $4.00.

COMP.SET w/o SP's (110)	10.00	25.00
COMP.SET w/o AU's (220)	50.00	100.00
ROOKIE AU GROUP A ODDS 1:3897		
ROOKIE AU GROUP B ODDS 1:333		
ROOKIE AU GROUP C ODDS 1:195		
ROOKIE AU GROUP D ODDS 1:28		
ROOKIE AU GROUP E ODDS 1:99		
1 Brett Favre	1.00	2.50
2 Jeremy Shockey	.40	1.00
3 Fred Taylor	.30	.75
4 Rich Gannon	.30	.75
5 Joey Galloway	.30	.75
6 Ray Lewis	.40	1.00
7 Jeff Blake	.30	.75
8 Stacey Mack	.25	.60
9 Matt Hasselbeck	.30	.75
10 Laveranues Coles	.25	.60
11 Brad Johnson	.30	.75
12 Tommy Maddox	.30	.75
13 Curtis Martin	.40	1.00
14 Tom Brady	1.00	2.50
15 Ricky Williams	.30	.75
16 Stephen Davis	.30	.75
17 Chad Johnson	.40	1.00
18 Joey Harrington	.25	.60
19 Tony Gonzalez	.40	1.00
20 Peerless Price	.25	.60
21 LaDainian Tomlinson	.40	1.00
22 James Thrash	.25	.60
23 Charlie Garner	.30	.75
24 Eddie George	.30	.75
25 Terrell Owens	.40	1.00
26 Brian Urlacher	.40	1.00
27 Eric Moulds	.30	.75
28 Emmitt Smith	1.00	2.50
29 Tim Couch	.25	.60
30 Jake Plummer	.30	.75
31 Marvin Harrison	.40	1.00
32 Chris Chambers	.30	.75
33 Tiki Barber	.40	1.00
34 Kurt Warner	.40	1.00
35 Michael Pittman	.25	.60
36 Kevin Dyson	.25	.60
37 Clinton Portis	.30	.75
38 Peyton Manning	.75	2.00
39 Travis Taylor	.25	.60
40 Jeff Garcia	.30	.75
41 Patrick Ramsey	.30	.75
42 Shaun Alexander	.30	.75
43 Joe Horn	.30	.75
44 Daunte Culpepper	.30	.75
45 Travis Henry	.25	.60
46 Brian Finneran	.25	.60
47 William Green	.25	.60
48 Kordell Stewart	.30	.75
49 Reggie Wayne	.40	1.00
50 Priest Holmes	.40	1.00
51 Jay Fiedler	.25	.60
52 Corey Dillon	.30	.75
53 Jamal Lewis	.30	.75
54 Mark Brunell	.30	.75
55 Santana Moss	.30	.75
56 Duce Staley	.30	.75
57 Torry Holt	.40	1.00
58 Rod Gardner	.25	.60
59 Kerry Collins	.30	.75
60 Randy Moss	.40	1.00
61 Jerry Porter	.25	.60
62 Plaxico Burress	.30	.75
63 Steve McNair	.40	1.00
64 Muhsin Muhammad	.30	.75
65 Drew Bledsoe	.40	1.00
66 T.J. Duckett	.30	.75
67 Ahman Green	.30	.75
68 Rod Smith	.30	.75
69 Jimmy Smith	.30	.75
70 Trent Green	.30	.75
71 Tim Brown	.40	1.00
72 Jerome Bettis	.40	1.00
73 Isaac Bruce	.40	1.00
74 Derrick Mason	.30	.75
75 Donovan McNabb	.40	1.00
76 Deuce McAllister	.30	.75
77 Zach Thomas	.40	1.00
78 Garrison Hearst	.30	.75
79 Koren Robinson	.30	.75
80 Marshall Faulk	.40	1.00
81 Keyshawn Johnson	.40	1.00
82 Jake Delhomme	.40	1.00
83 Marty Booker	.30	.75
84 James Stewart	.25	.60
85 Corey Bradford	.25	.60
86 Derrius Thompson	.25	.60
87 Edgerrin James	.40	1.00
88 Darrell Jackson	.30	.75
89 Hines Ward	.40	1.00
90 David Boston	.25	.60
91 Curtis Conway	.25	.60
92 David Patten	.25	.60
93 Michael Bennett	.30	.75
94 Todd Pinkston	.25	.60
95 Jerry Rice	.75	2.00
96 Jon Kitna	.30	.75
97 Ed McCaffrey	.30	.75
98 Donald Driver	.40	1.00
99 Anthony Thomas	.30	.75
100 Michael Vick	.50	1.25
101 Terry Glenn	.30	.75
102 Quincy Morgan	.25	.60
103 David Carr	.30	.75
104 Troy Brown	.30	.75
105 Aaron Brooks	.30	.75
106 Amani Toomer	.30	.75
107 Drew Brees	.40	1.00
108 Chad Hutchinson	.25	.60
109 Warrick Dunn	.30	.75
110 Chad Pennington	.40	1.00
111 Brian St.Pierre RC	1.50	4.00
112 Keenan Howry RC	1.25	3.00
113 Sultan McCullough RC	1.25	3.00
114 Terence Newman RC	1.50	4.00
115 Kelley Washington RC	1.25	3.00
116 Musa Smith RC	1.25	3.00
117 Victor Hobson RC	1.25	3.00
118 Travis Anglin RC	1.25	3.00
119 Artose Pinner RC	1.25	3.00
120 Rashean Mathis RC	1.50	4.00
121 DeWayne White RC	1.25	3.00
122 Kevin Curtis RC	2.00	5.00
123 Tyrone Calico RC	1.50	4.00
124 Ricky Manning RC	1.50	4.00
125 Cory Redding RC	1.50	4.00
126 Dallas Clark RC	3.00	8.00
127 Marcus Trufant RC	1.50	4.00
128 Terrell Suggs RC	2.00	5.00
129 Aaron Walker RC	1.50	4.00
130 Calvin Pace RC	1.50	4.00
131 Ken Dorsey RC	1.50	4.00
132 Earnest Graham RC	2.00	5.00
133 Cecil Sapp RC	1.25	3.00
134 William Joseph RC	1.25	3.00
135 Anquan Boldin RC	3.00	8.00
136 Justin Griffith RC	1.50	4.00
137 Teyo Johnson RC	1.50	4.00
138 Chris Crocker RC	1.50	4.00
139 Doug Gabriel RC	1.50	4.00
140 Terry Pierce RC	1.25	3.00
141 Bradie James RC	2.00	5.00
142 Terrence Edwards RC	1.25	3.00
143 E.J. Henderson RC	1.50	4.00
144 Tony Romo RC	15.00	40.00
145 DeWayne Robertson RC	1.50	4.00
146 Dwone Hicks RC	1.25	3.00
147 Carl Ford RC	1.25	3.00
148 Ken Hamlin RC	2.00	5.00
149 Adrian Madise RC	1.25	3.00
150 Siddeeq Shabazz RC	1.25	3.00
151 Dave Ragone RC	1.25	3.00
152 Mike Seidman RC	1.25	3.00
153 DeAndrew Rubin RC	1.25	3.00
154 Mike Pinkard RC	1.25	3.00
155 Nate Burleson RC	1.50	4.00
156 Angelo Crowell RC	1.50	4.00
157 J.R. Tolver RC	1.50	4.00
158 Osi Umenyiora RC	2.50	6.00
159 Nick Barnett RC	2.00	5.00
160 Brandon Drumm RC	1.25	3.00
161 Rien Long RC	1.25	3.00
162 Zuriel Smith RC	1.25	3.00
163 Onterrio Smith RC	1.25	3.00
164 Kenny Peterson RC	1.50	4.00
165 Chaun Thompson RC	1.25	3.00
166 Terrence Holt RC	1.50	4.00
167 Ovie Mughelli RC	1.50	4.00
168 Bethel Johnson RC	1.25	3.00
169 Avon Cobourne RC	1.25	3.00
170 Andre Woolfolk RC	1.50	4.00
171 George Wrighster RC	1.25	3.00
172 Justin Fargas RC	2.00	5.00
173 Marquel Blackwell RC	1.25	3.00
174 Walter Young RC	1.25	3.00
175 Kawika Mitchell RC	2.00	5.00
176 Drayton Florence RC	2.00	5.00
177 Jeremi Johnson RC	1.25	3.00
178 Lee Suggs RC	1.50	4.00
179 David Kircus RC	2.00	5.00
180 Rex Grossman RC	2.00	5.00
180AU Rex Grossman AU B	15.00	40.00
181 Jon Olinger RC	1.25	3.00
182 Dan Curley RC	1.25	3.00
183 Andrew Pinnock RC	1.50	4.00
184 Kirk Farmer RC	1.50	4.00
185 Charles Rogers RC	1.50	4.00
186 Alonzo Jackson RC	1.25	3.00
187 Trent Smith RC	1.50	4.00
188 Seneca Wallace RC	2.00	5.00
189 Shane Walton RC	1.25	3.00
190 Chris Brown RC	1.25	3.00
191 Dahrran Diedrick RC	1.25	3.00
192 Juston Wood RC	1.25	3.00
193 Mike Doss RC	2.00	5.00
194 Visanthe Shiancoe RC	2.00	5.00
195 Andre Johnson RC	5.00	12.00
196 Dennis Weathersby RC	1.25	3.00
197 Chris Davis RC	1.50	4.00
198 LaTarence Dunbar RC	1.25	3.00
199 Eugene Wilson RC	2.00	5.00
200 Ryan Hoag RC	1.25	3.00
201 Chris Simms RC	2.00	5.00
202 Curt Anes RC	1.25	3.00
203 Taco Wallace RC	1.25	3.00
204 David Tyree RC	2.00	5.00
205 Nate Hybl RC	1.50	4.00
206 Willis McGahee RC	2.50	6.00
207 Casey Moore RC	1.25	3.00
208 Pisa Tinoisamoa RC	2.00	5.00
209 Willie Ponder RC	1.25	3.00
210 Donald Lee RC	1.50	4.00
211 Nnamdi Asomugha RC	4.00	10.00
212 Sammy Davis RC	1.50	4.00
213 Joffrey Reynolds RC	1.25	3.00
214 Eddie Moore RC	1.25	3.00
215 Tony Hollings RC	1.50	4.00
216 Nick Maddox RC	1.25	3.00
217 Kevin Walter RC	3.00	8.00
218 Dan Klecko RC	1.50	4.00
219 Antwan Peek RC	1.25	3.00
220 Tyler Brayton RC	1.50	4.00
221 Byron Leftwich AU B RC	8.00	20.00
222 Bobby Wade AU D RC	5.00	12.00
223 Jerome McDougle AU C RC	5.00	12.00
224 Michael Haynes AU D RC	4.00	10.00
225 Taylor Jacobs AU C RC	5.00	12.00
226 Shaun McDonald AU D RC	5.00	12.00
228 Talman Gardner AU D RC	4.00	10.00
229 Domanick Davis AU D RC	5.00	12.00
230 Jason Witten AU D RC	30.00	60.00
231 Kyle Boller AU B RC	8.00	20.00
232 L.J. Smith AU C RC	8.00	20.00
233 Boss Bailey AU C RC	6.00	15.00
234 Billy McMullen AU D RC	4.00	10.00
235 Larry Johnson AU B RC	15.00	40.00
236 Kareem Kelly AU E RC	4.00	10.00
237 Carson Palmer AU A RC	50.00	120.00
238 Quentin Griffin AU D RC	5.00	12.00
239 Kevin Garrett AU E RC	4.00	10.00
240 Charles Tillman AU E RC	8.00	20.00
241 Arnaz Battle AU D RC	8.00	20.00
242 Brooks Bollinger AU E RC	5.00	12.00
243 LaBrandon Toefield AU D RC	5.00	12.00
244 Sam Aiken AU D RC	5.00	12.00
245 Justin Gage AU D RC	5.00	12.00
246 Gibran Hamdan AU D RC	4.00	10.00

2003 Bowman Chrome Refractors

*VETS 1-110: 2X TO 5X BASIC CARDS
*ROOKIES 111-220: .8X TO 2X
REFRACTOR/500 ODDS 1:7
STATED PRINT RUN 500 SER.#'d SETS

144 Tony Romo	30.00	80.00

2003 Bowman Chrome Uncirculated Blue Refractors

ONE EXCH CARD PER BOX
STATED PRINT RUN 235 SETS

144 Tony Romo	40.00	100.00

2003 Bowman Chrome Gold Refractors

*VETS 1-110: 6X TO 15X BASIC CARDS
*ROOKIES 111-220: 2.5X TO 6X
1-220 STATED ODDS 1:67
*ROOKIE AUs 221-246: 1.5X TO 4X
221-246 STATED ODDS 1:542
STATED PRINT RUN 50 SER.#'d SETS

144 Tony Romo	100.00	200.00
230 Jason Witten AU	100.00	200.00
235 Larry Johnson AU	25.00	60.00
237 Carson Palmer AU	100.00	200.00

2003 Bowman Chrome Red Refractors

*ROOKIES 111-220: 1.2X TO 3X
OVERALL ODDS ONE PER BOX
111-220 PRINT RUN 235 SER.#'d SETS
221-246 UNPRICED AU PRINT RUN 10
#'d/10 NOT PRICED DUE TO SCARCITY

144 Tony Romo	40.00	100.00

2003 Bowman Chrome Xfractors

*VETS 1-110: 2.5X TO 6X BASIC CARDS
*ROOKIES 111-220: 1X TO 2.5X
XFRACTOR/250 STATED ODDS 1:13
STATED PRINT RUN 250 SER.#'d SETS

144 Tony Romo	40.00	100.00

2004 Bowman Chrome

Bowman Chrome initially released in early December 2004. The base set consists of 245-cards including 110-rookies (issued one per pack) and 25-autographed rookie cards. Six of the signed rookies were serial numbered to just 199-copies. Hobby boxes contained 18-packs of 4-cards and carried an S.R.P. of $4 per pack. Six parallel sets can be found seeded in hobby and retail packs.

COMP.SET w/o SP's (220)	75.00	150.00
COMP.SET w/o RC's (110)	12.50	30.00
ROOKIE AU/199 GROUP A ODDS 1:603		
ROOKIE AU GROUP B ODDS 1:1293		
ROOKIE AU GROUP C ODDS 1:359		
ROOKIE AU GROUP D ODDS 1:21		
1 Brett Favre	1.00	2.50
2 Jay Fiedler	.25	.60
3 Andre Davis	.25	.60
4 Travis Henry	.25	.60
5 Jimmy Smith	.30	.75
6 Santana Moss	.30	.75
7 Correll Buckhalter	.30	.75
8 Randy Moss	.40	1.00
9 Edgerrin James	.30	.75
10 Marc Bulger	.30	.75
11 Derrick Mason	.30	.75
12 Mark Brunell	.30	.75
13 Donte Stallworth	.25	.60
14 Deion Branch	.30	.75
15 Jake Plummer	.30	.75
16 Steve Smith	.40	1.00
17 Jon Kitna	.30	.75
18 Andre Johnson	.40	1.00
19 A.J. Feeley	.25	.60
20 Drew Bledsoe	.40	1.00
21 Antonio Bryant	.30	.75
22 Reggie Wayne	.40	1.00
23 Thomas Jones	.40	1.00
24 Alge Crumpler	.30	.75
25 Anquan Boldin	.40	1.00
26 Tim Rattay	.25	.60
27 Charlie Garner	.30	.75
28 James Thrash	.25	.60
29 Koren Robinson	.25	.60
30 Terrell Owens	.40	1.00
31 Amani Toomer	.30	.75
32 Kelly Campbell	.25	.60
33 Patrick Ramsey	.30	.75
34 Plaxico Burress	.30	.75
35 Chad Pennington	.40	1.00
36 Fred Taylor	.30	.75
37 Domanick Davis	.25	.60
38 DeShaun Foster	.30	.75
39 T.J. Duckett	.30	.75
40 Ahman Green	.30	.75
41 Lee Suggs	.30	.75
42 Tony Gonzalez	.40	1.00
43 Rich Gannon	.30	.75
44 Kevan Barlow	.25	.60
45 Torry Holt	.30	.75
46 Aaron Brooks	.30	.75
47 Tyrone Calico	.30	.75
48 Keenan McCardell	.25	.60
49 Hines Ward	.40	1.00
50 LaDainian Tomlinson	.40	1.00
51 Dante Hall	.30	.75
52 Marcus Pollard	.25	.60
53 Corey Dillon	.30	.75
54 Justin McCareins	.25	.60
55 Stephen Davis	.30	.75
56 Jeff Garcia	.30	.75
57 Ashley Lelie	.25	.60
58 Javon Walker	.25	.60
59 Kyle Boller	.30	.75
60 Chad Johnson	.40	1.00
61 Anthony Thomas	.30	.75
62 Byron Leftwich	.30	.75
63 David Boston	.25	.60
64 Onterrio Smith	.25	.60
65 Deuce McAllister	.30	.75
66 Antwaan Randle El	.30	.75
67 Justin Fargas	.30	.75
68 Laveranues Coles	.25	.60
69 Quincy Morgan	.25	.60
70 Priest Holmes	.40	1.00
71 Robert Ferguson	.25	.60
72 Charles Rogers	.25	.60
73 Drew Brees	.40	1.00
74 Matt Hasselbeck	.30	.75
75 Peyton Manning	.75	2.00
76 Rudi Johnson	.30	.75
77 Jake Delhomme	.30	.75
78 Tiki Barber	.40	1.00
79 Brad Johnson	.30	.75
80 Steve McNair	.40	1.00
81 Willis McGahee	.40	1.00
82 Josh McCown	.30	.75
83 Garrison Hearst	.30	.75
84 Quincy Carter	.25	.60
85 Ricky Williams	.30	.75
86 Trent Green	.30	.75
87 Curtis Martin	.40	1.00
88 Jerry Porter	.25	.60
89 Brian Westbrook	.40	1.00
90 Clinton Portis	.40	1.00
91 Eric Moulds	.30	.75
92 Marcel Shipp	.25	.60
93 Joey Harrington	.30	.75
94 David Carr	.25	.60
95 Marvin Harrison	.40	1.00
96 Joe Horn	.30	.75
97 Chris Chambers	.30	.75
98 Darrell Jackson	.30	.75
99 Eddie George	.30	.75
100 Donovan McNabb	.40	1.00
101 Marshall Faulk	.40	1.00
102 Rex Grossman	.30	.75
103 Tai Streets	.25	.60
104 Jeremy Shockey	.30	.75
105 Jamal Lewis	.30	.75
106 Tom Brady	.75	2.00
107 Shaun Alexander	.30	.75
108 Carson Palmer	.40	1.00
109 Daunte Culpepper	.30	.75
110 Michael Vick	.50	1.25
111 Roethlis AU/199 RC	150.00	250.00
112 Tommie Harris RC	1.50	4.00
113 Thomas Tapeh RC	1.25	3.00
114 Matt Schaub RC	3.00	8.00
115 Jonathan Smith RC	1.00	2.50
116 Ricardo Colclough RC	1.25	3.00
117 Jeff Dugan RC	1.00	2.50
118 Larry Fitzgerald RC	4.00	10.00
119 Gibril Wilson RC	1.50	4.00
120 Sean Taylor RC	3.00	8.00
121 Marquise Hill RC	1.00	2.50
122 Cedric Cobbs RC	1.00	2.50
123 Rich Gardner RC	1.25	3.00
124 Chris Cooley RC	1.50	4.00
125 Ben Troupe RC	1.25	3.00
126 Antwan Odom RC	1.25	3.00
127 Stuart Schweigert RC	1.25	3.00
128 Derek Abney RC	1.00	2.50
129 Keary Colbert RC	1.00	2.50
130 Jeris McIntyre RC	1.00	2.50
131 Matt Kranchick RC	1.25	3.00
132 Rodney Leisle RC	1.00	2.50
133 Vince Wilfork RC	1.50	4.00
134 Darnell Dockett RC	1.00	2.50
135 Jeremy LeSueur RC	1.00	2.50
136 Gilbert Gardner RC	1.00	2.50
137 Amon Gordon RC	1.00	2.50
138 Darius Watts RC	1.00	2.50
139 Junior Siavii RC	1.00	2.50
140 Igor Olshansky RC	1.25	3.00
141 Mewelde Moore RC	1.25	3.00
142 Nathan Vasher RC	1.50	4.00
143 Randy Starks RC	1.00	2.50
144 Isaac Sopoaga RC	1.00	2.50
145 Drew Henson RC	1.00	2.50
146 Erik Coleman RC	1.25	3.00
147 Robert Kent RC	1.00	2.50
148 Jammal Lord RC	1.00	2.50
149 Richard Seigler RC	1.00	2.50
150 Niko Koutouvides RC	1.00	2.50
151 Brandon Miree RC	1.00	2.50
152 Dunta Robinson RC	1.00	2.50
153 Courtney Anderson RC	1.00	2.50
154 Bruce Perry RC	1.00	2.50
155 Shaun Phillips RC	1.50	4.00
156 Greg Jones RC	1.00	2.50
157 Tank Johnson RC	1.00	2.50
158 Dwan Edwards RC	1.00	2.50
159 Julius Jones RC	1.25	3.00
160 Chad Lavalais RC	1.00	2.50
161 Tim Anderson RC	1.25	3.00
162 Jarrett Payton RC	1.25	3.00
163 Matt Ware RC	1.50	4.00
164 DeAngelo Hall RC	1.50	4.00
165 Ben Hartsock RC	1.00	2.50
166 Keith Smith RC	1.00	2.50
167 Michael Jenkins RC	1.50	4.00
168 Quincy Wilson RC	1.25	3.00
169 Dontarrious Thomas RC	1.25	3.00
170 Tony Hargrove RC	1.00	2.50
171 Ben Watson RC	1.50	4.00
172 Triandos Luke RC	1.00	2.50
173 Kellen Winslow RC	1.50	4.00
174 Patrick Crayton RC	1.50	4.00
175 Devard Darling RC	1.00	2.50
176 Shawntae Spencer RC	1.00	2.50
177 Will Smith RC	1.25	3.00
178 Darrion Scott RC	1.25	3.00
179 Wes Welker RC	6.00	15.00
180 Ryan Dinwiddie RC	1.00	2.50
181 Rod Davis RC	1.00	2.50
182 Casey Clausen RC	1.25	3.00
183 Clarence Moore RC	1.00	2.50
184 D.J. Hackett RC	1.25	3.00
185 Devery Henderson RC	1.50	4.00
186 Sean Jones RC	1.25	3.00
187 Bruce Thornton RC	1.00	2.50
188 Tatum Bell RC	1.25	3.00
189 Tim Euhus RC	1.00	2.50
190 John Standeford RC	1.00	2.50
191 Reggie Torbor RC	1.00	2.50
192 Rashaun Woods RC	1.00	2.50
193 Jason Shivers RC	1.00	2.50
194 Ahmad Carroll RC	1.00	2.50
195 Keyaron Fox RC	1.25	3.00
196 Von Hutchins RC	1.00	2.50
197 Marcus Tubbs RC	1.00	2.50
198 Daryl Smith RC	1.00	2.50
199 Robert Gallery RC	1.50	4.00
200 Marquis Cooper RC	1.00	2.50
201 Bernard Berrian RC	1.50	4.00
202 Derrick Strait RC	1.00	2.50
203 Travis LaBoy RC	1.25	3.00
204 Caleb Miller RC	1.00	2.50
205 Michael Clayton RC	1.25	3.00
206 Will Poole RC	1.50	4.00
207 Derrick Hamilton RC	1.00	2.50
208 Glenn Earl RC	1.00	2.50
209 Donnell Washington RC	1.25	3.00
210 Nate Lawrie RC	1.00	2.50
211 Keiwan Ratliff RC	1.00	2.50
212 Luke McCown RC	1.25	3.00
213 Joey Thomas RC	1.00	2.50
214 Shawn Andrews RC	1.25	3.00
215 Derrick Ward RC	1.50	4.00
216 Reggie Williams RC	1.25	3.00
217 Rod Rutherford RC	1.00	2.50
218 Michael Gaines RC	1.00	2.50
219 Will Allen RC	1.25	3.00
220 J.P. Losman RC	1.25	3.00
221 Roy Williams AU/199 RC	15.00	40.00
222 Kevin Jones AU/199 RC	10.00	25.00
223 Philip Rivers AU/199 RC	60.00	120.00
224 Steven Jackson AU/199 RC	40.00	100.00
225 Eli Manning AU/199 RC	175.00	300.00
226 Cody Pickett AU D RC	5.00	12.00
227 P.K. Sam AU D RC	4.00	10.00
228 Maurice Mann AU D RC	4.00	10.00
229 Andy Hall AU D RC	4.00	10.00
230 Chris Perry AU D RC	5.00	12.00
231 Ernest Wilford AU C RC	5.00	12.00
232 Kenechi Udeze AU D RC	5.00	12.00
233 Michael Boulware AU D RC	6.00	15.00
234 B.J. Symons AU D RC	4.00	10.00
235 Jared Lorenzen AU D RC	5.00	12.00
236 Matt Mauck AU D RC	4.00	10.00
237 Carlos Francis AU D RC	4.00	10.00
238 Michael Turner AU D RC	15.00	40.00
239 Lee Evans AU B RC	10.00	25.00
240 Jerricho Cotchery AU D RC	5.00	12.00
241 John Navarre AU D RC	4.00	10.00
242 Jonathan Vilma AU D RC	6.00	15.00
243 Josh Harris AU D RC	4.00	10.00
244 Jeff Smoker AU C RC	5.00	12.00
245 Jamaar Taylor AU D RC	4.00	10.00

2004 Bowman Chrome Blue Refractors

UNPRICED BLUE REF.PRINT RUN 1 SET

2004 Bowman Chrome Gold Refractors

*STARS: 8X TO 20X BASE CARD HI
*ROOKIES: 3X TO 8X BASE CARD HI
1-220 STATED ODDS 1:59
*ROOKIE AUTOS: 1.2X TO 3X BASE CARD HI
ROOKIE AUTO STATED ODDS 1:646
STATED PRINT RUN 50 SER.#'d SETS

111 Ben Roethlisberger AU	300.00	500.00
223 Philip Rivers AU	200.00	350.00
224 Steven Jackson AU	100.00	250.00
225 Eli Manning AU	350.00	500.00

2004 Bowman Chrome Red Refractors

*ROOKIES 112-220: 2X TO 5X
112-220 PRINT RUN 210 SER.#'d SETS
UNPRICED 111/221-245 AU PRINT RUN 10
ONE RED REFRACTOR PER HOBBY BOX

2004 Bowman Chrome Refractors

*STARS: 2X TO 5X BASE CARD HI
*ROOKIES: .8X TO 2X BASE CARD HI
STATED ODDS 1:6
STATED PRINT RUN 500 SER.#'d SETS

2004 Bowman Chrome Uncirculated White Refractors

*ROOKIES 112-220: 1.5X TO 4X
STATED PRINT RUN 210 SETS

2004 Bowman Chrome Xfractors

*STARS: 2.5X TO 6X BASE CARD HI
*ROOKIES: 1.2X TO 3X BASE CARD HI
STATED ODDS 1:12
STATED PRINT RUN 250 SER.#'d SETS

2004 Bowman Chrome Super Bowl XXXIX Unsigned Draft Picks

This set was released in factory set form by Topps in a clear plastic box at the Super Bowl XXXIX Card Show in Jacksonville. The cards are nearly identical to the basic issue Bowman Chrome signed Rookie Cards except for the obvious lack of autographs and lack of the Topps Authenticity hologram on the backs. Note also that the in-pack signed cards also have a ghosted out box on the fronts in which the players affixed their signatures.

COMPLETE SET (26) 75.00 150.00
111 Ben Roethlisberger 25.00 50.00
221 Roy Williams WR 3.00 8.00
222 Kevin Jones 2.50 6.00
223 Philip Rivers 12.00 30.00
224 Steven Jackson 5.00 12.00
225 Eli Manning 25.00 50.00
226 Cody Pickett 2.50 6.00
227 P.K. Sam 2.00 5.00
228 Maurice Mann 2.00 5.00
229 Andy Hall 2.00 5.00
230 Chris Perry 2.50 6.00
231 Ernest Wilford 2.50 6.00
232 Kenechi Udeze 2.50 6.00
233 Michael Boulware 3.00 8.00
234 B.J. Symons 2.00 5.00
235 Jared Lorenzen 2.50 6.00
236 Matt Mauck 2.00 5.00
237 Carlos Francis 2.00 5.00
238 Michael Turner 4.00 10.00
239 Lee Evans 3.00 8.00
240 Jerricho Cotchery 2.50 6.00
241 John Navarre 2.00 5.00
242 Jonathan Vilma 3.00 8.00
243 Josh Harris 2.00 5.00
244 Jeff Smoker 2.50 6.00
245 Jamaar Taylor 2.00 5.00

2005 Bowman Chrome

This 259-card set was released in January, 2006. The set was issued in the hobby in four-card packs wirth an $4 SRP which came 18 packs to a box. Cards numbered 1-109 feature veterans while cards 110-259 feature rookies. Cards numbered 221-259 were signed by the player and a few players (221-227) signed fewer cards (199 serial numbered sets). Those rookies with 199 serial numbered signatures were inserted at a stated rate of one in 685 hobby and one in 1348 retail packs. The other signed rookies were inserted at different rates depending on what autograph group they belonged to.

COMP.SET w/o AU's (220) 40.00 100.00
COMP.SET w/o RC's (110) 12.50 30.00
ROOK.AU GROUP A ODDS 1:381 H, 1:1011 R
ROOK.AU GROUP B ODDS 1:156 H, 1:449 R
ROOK.AU GROUP C ODDS 1:318 H, 1:899 R
ROOK.AU GROUP D ODDS 1:296 H, 1:899 R
ROOK.AU GROUP E ODDS 1:281 H, 1:809 R
ROOK.AU GROUP F ODDS 1:132 H, 404 R
ROOK.AU GROUP G ODDS 1:30 H, 1:108 R
ROOKIE AU/199 ODDS 1:685 H, 1:1348 R
UNPRICED PRINT.PLATE 1/1 ODDS 1:975 H
1 Peyton Manning .75 2.00
2 Priest Holmes .30 .75
3 Anquan Boldin .30 .75
4 Michael Vick .40 1.00
5 Drew Brees .40 1.00
6 Terrell Owens .40 1.00
7 Curtis Martin .40 1.00
8 Tom Brady .75 2.00
9 Maurice Carthon CO .25 .60
10 Brett Favre 1.00 2.50
11 Marshall Faulk .40 1.00
12 Corey Dillon .30 .75
13 Julius Jones .25 .60
14 Jamal Lewis .30 .75
15 Keary Colbert .25 .60
16 Joey Harrington .30 .75
17 Domanick Davis .25 .60
18 Eli Manning .60 1.50
19 Brad Childress CO .30 .75
20 Steve McNair .40 1.00
21 Plaxico Burress .30 .75
22 Chad Pennington .40 1.00
23 Patrick Ramsey .30 .75
24 Brian Griese .30 .75
25 Matt Hasselbeck .30 .75
26 Chris Chambers .30 .75
27 Marc Bulger .30 .75
28 Jake Delhomme .30 .75
29 Shaun Alexander .30 .75
30 Laveranues Coles .25 .60
31 A.J. Feeley .25 .60
32 Ashley Lelie .25 .60
33 Deuce McAllister .30 .75
34 Chris Brown .25 .60
35 Nate Burleson .25 .60
36 Darrell Jackson .25 .60
37 Lee Evans .30 .75
38 Jeremy Shockey .40 1.00
39 Muhsin Muhammad .30 .75
40 Deion Branch .25 .60
41 DeShaun Foster .30 .75
42 Reggie Wayne .40 1.00
43 Michael Jenkins .30 .75
44 Andre Johnson .40 1.00
45 Javon Walker .25 .60
46 Joe Horn .30 .75
47 Fred Taylor .30 .75
48 Tony Gonzalez .30 .75
49 J.P. Losman .25 .60
50 Clinton Portis .30 .75
51 Randy Moss .40 1.00
52 Jake Plummer .30 .75
53 Tiki Barber .40 1.00
54 Edgerrin James .30 .75
55 Jerome Bettis .40 1.00
56 Brandon Lloyd .25 .60
57 Romeo Crennel CO .40 1.00
58 Antonio Gates .40 1.00
59 Donovan McNabb .40 1.00
60 Drew Bennett .30 .75
61 David Carr .25 .60
62 Trent Green .30 .75
63 Drew Bledsoe .40 1.00
64 Donte Stallworth .25 .60
65 Alge Crumpler .30 .75
66 Jason Witten .40 1.00
67 Thomas Jones .40 1.00
68 Rex Grossman .30 .75
69 LaMont Jordan .30 .75
70 Kurt Warner .40 1.00
71 Ahman Green .30 .75
72 Ben Roethlisberger .60 1.50
73 Mike Nolan CO .30 .75
74 Brian Westbrook .30 .75
75 Carson Palmer .40 1.00
76 Stephen Davis .30 .75
77 Jonathan Vilma .30 .75
78 Willis McGahee .40 1.00
79 Rudi Johnson .30 .75
80 Jerry Porter .25 .60
81 Charles Rogers .25 .60
82 Dwight Freeney .30 .75
83 Tim Lewis CO .25 .60
84 Aaron Brooks .25 .60
85 Kyle Boller .30 .75
86 Isaac Bruce .30 .75
87 Chad Johnson .30 .75
88 Kevin Jones .25 .60
89 Eric Moulds .25 .60
90 Sean Taylor .40 1.00
91 Chris Perry .25 .60
92 Kerry Collins .30 .75
93 Steven Jackson .40 1.00
94 LaDainian Tomlinson .40 1.00
95 Torry Holt .30 .75
96 Lee Suggs .25 .60
97 Santana Moss .30 .75
98 Hines Ward .40 1.00
99 Daunte Culpepper .30 .75
100 Travis Henry .25 .60
101 Ricky Williams .30 .75
102 Roy Williams WR .30 .75
103 Tatum Bell .25 .60
104 Dante Hall .25 .60
105 Larry Fitzgerald .40 1.00
106 Marvin Harrison .40 1.00
107 Byron Leftwich .30 .75
108 T.J. Houshmandzadeh .30 .75
109 Michael Clayton .25 .60
110 Ted Cottrell CO .25 .60
111 Carlos Rogers RC 1.25 3.00
112 Kyle Orton RC 1.25 3.00
113 Marion Barber RC 1.25 3.00
114 Mark Bradley RC .75 2.00
115 Travis Johnson RC .75 2.00
116 Antrel Rolle RC 1.25 3.00
117 Jason Campbell RC 1.50 4.00
118 Justin Miller RC 1.00 2.50
119 J.J. Arrington RC 1.00 2.50
120 Marcus Spears RC 1.00 2.50
121 Vincent Jackson RC 1.50 4.00
122 Erasmus James RC 1.00 2.50
123 Heath Miller RC 1.50 4.00
124 Eric Shelton RC .75 2.00
125 Cedric Benson RC 1.25 3.00
126 Mark Clayton RC 1.00 2.50
127 Anthony Davis RC .75 2.00
128 Charlie Frye RC 1.25 3.00
129 Fred Gibson RC 1.00 2.50
130 Reggie Brown RC .75 2.00
131 Andrew Walter RC 1.00 2.50
132 Adam Jones RC .75 2.00
133 David Greene RC .75 2.00
134 Maurice Clarett .75 2.00
135 Roscoe Parrish RC .75 2.00
136 Chris Henry RC 1.25 3.00
137 Mike Nugent RC 1.00 2.50
138 Kevin Burnett RC 1.00 2.50
139 Matt Roth RC 1.00 2.50
140 Barrett Ruud RC 1.25 3.00
141 Kirk Morrison RC 1.25 3.00
142 Brock Berlin RC 1.00 2.50
143 Bryant McFadden RC 1.00 2.50
144 Scott Starks RC 1.00 2.50
145 Stanford Routt RC 1.00 2.50
146 Oshiomogho Atogwe RC 1.25 3.00
147 Jovan Witherspoon RC .75 2.00
148 Boomer Grigsby RC 1.25 3.00
149 Lance Mitchell RC 1.00 2.50
150 Darryl Blackstock RC .75 2.00
151 Ellis Hobbs RC 1.25 3.00
152 James Kilian RC .75 2.00
153 Willie Parker .30 .75
154 Justin Tuck RC 1.50 4.00
155 Luis Castillo RC 1.00 2.50
156 Paris Warren RC 1.00 2.50
157 Corey Webster RC 1.00 2.50
158 Tab Perry RC .75 2.00
159 Rian Wallace RC 1.00 2.50
160 Joel Dreessen RC 1.00 2.50
161 Khalif Barnes RC .75 2.00
162 David Pollack RC 1.00 2.50
163 Zach Tuiasosopo RC .75 2.00
164 Ryan Riddle RC .75 2.00
165 Travis Daniels RC 1.00 2.50
166 Eric King RC .75 2.00
167 Justin Green RC 1.25 3.00
168 Manuel White RC 1.00 2.50
169 Jordan Beck RC 1.00 2.50
170 Lofa Tatupu RC 1.25 3.00
171 Will Peoples RC 1.00 2.50
172 Chad Friehauf RC 1.00 2.50
173 Brady Poppinga RC 1.25 3.00
174 Anttaj Hawthorne RC .75 2.00
175 Nick Collins RC 1.25 3.00
176 Craig Ochs RC 1.00 2.50
177 Billy Bajema RC .75 2.00
178 Jon Goldsberry RC 1.25 3.00
179 Jared Newberry RC 1.00 2.50
180 Odell Thurman RC 1.25 3.00
181 Kelvin Hayden RC 1.00 2.50
182 Jamaal Brimmer RC .75 2.00
183 Jonathan Babineaux RC 1.00 2.50
184 Bo Scaife RC 1.00 2.50
185 Bryan Randall RC 1.00 2.50
186 James Butler RC 1.00 2.50
187 Harry Williams RC 1.00 2.50
188 Leroy Hill RC 1.25 3.00
189 Josh Bullocks RC 1.00 2.50
190 Alfred Fincher RC 1.00 2.50
191 Antonio Perkins RC 1.00 2.50
192 Bobby Purify RC 1.00 2.50
193 Darrent Williams RC 1.25 3.00
194 Darian Durant RC .75 2.00
195 Fred Amey RC .75 2.00
196 Ronald Bartell RC 1.00 2.50
197 Kerry Rhodes RC 1.00 2.50
198 Jerome Carter RC .75 2.00
199 Roddy White RC 1.50 4.00
200 Nehemiah Broughton RC 1.00 2.50
201 Keron Henry RC .75 2.00
202 Jerome Collins RC 1.00 2.50
203 Trent Cole RC 1.25 3.00
204 Alphonso Hodge RC .75 2.00
205 Marviel Underwood RC 1.00 2.50
206 Marlin Jackson RC .75 2.00
207 Madison Hedgecock RC 1.25 3.00
208 Chris Spencer RC 1.25 3.00
209 Vincent Fuller RC 1.00 2.50
210 Marcus Maxwell RC .75 2.00
211 Dustin Fox RC 1.00 2.50
212 Timmy Chang RC 1.00 2.50
213 Walter Reyes RC .75 2.00
214 Donte Nicholson RC .75 2.00
215 Stanley Wilson RC 1.00 2.50
216 Dan Cody RC 1.00 2.50
217 Alex Barron RC .75 2.00
218 Taylor Stubblefield RC .75 2.00
219 Shaun Cody RC 1.00 2.50
220 Steve Savoy RC .75 2.00
221 Aaron Rodgers AU/199 RC 500.00 750.00
222 Alex Smith QB AU/199 RC 60.00 100.00
223 Braylon Edwards AU/199 RC 25.00 60.00
224 Cadillac Williams AU/199 RC 15.00 40.00
225 Mike Williams AU/199 12.00 30.00
226 Ronnie Brown AU/199 RC 30.00 60.00
227 Troy Williamson AU/199 RC 10.00 25.00
228 Dante Ridgeway AU B RC 4.00 10.00
229 Channing Crowder AU G RC 5.00 12.00
230 Chase Lyman AU E RC 4.00 10.00
231 Courtney Roby AU F RC 5.00 12.00
232 Damien Nash AU G RC 5.00 12.00
233 Dan Orlovsky AU C RC 6.00 15.00
234 Fabian Washington AU B RC 5.00 12.00
235 Shawne Merriman AU B RC 10.00 25.00
236 Cedric Houston AU G RC 6.00 15.00
237 Alex Smith TE AU D RC 4.00 10.00
238 Brandon Jones AU B RC 5.00 12.00
239 Alvin Pearman AU G RC 4.00 10.00
240 Derek Anderson AU C RC 5.00 12.00
241 J.R. Russell AU G RC 4.00 10.00
242 Jerome Mathis AU F RC 6.00 15.00
243 Josh Davis AU A RC 4.00 10.00
244 Kay-Jay Harris AU G RC 4.00 10.00
245 Rasheed Marshall AU F RC 5.00 12.00
246 Matt Jones AU/199 RC 10.00 25.00
247 Chad Owens AU G RC 5.00 12.00
248 Larry Brackins AU A RC 4.00 10.00
249 Matt Cassel AU G RC 12.00 30.00
250 Noah Herron AU G RC 4.00 10.00
251 Roydell Williams AU G RC 5.00 12.00
252 Ryan Fitzpatrick AU F RC 12.00 30.00
253 Derrick Johnson AU E RC 5.00 12.00
254 DeMarcus Ware AU D RC 20.00 40.00
255 Brandon Jacobs AU A RC 20.00 40.00
256 Craig Bragg AU G RC 4.00 10.00
257 Ryan Moats AU G RC 4.00 10.00
258 Stefan LeFors AU G RC 4.00 10.00
259 Frank Gore AU B RC 25.00 50.00

2005 Bowman Chrome Blue Refractors

*VETS: 2.5X TO 6X BASIC CARDS
*ROOKIES: .8X TO 2X BASIC CARDS
BLUE REF/250 ODDS 1:24 H, 1:23 R

2005 Bowman Chrome Bronze Refractors

*VETS: 3X TO 8X BASIC CARDS
*ROOKIES 111-220: 1X TO 2.5X BASIC CARDS
1-220 BRONZE REF/150 ODDS 1:39H, 1:40R
*BRONZE AU/50: .8X TO 2X BASE AU
*BRONZE AU/50: .4X TO 1X BASE AU/199
AU BRONZE REF/50 ODDS 1:630 H, 1:815 R
221 Aaron Rodgers AU 700.00 1,000.00
222 Alex Smith QB AU 100.00 175.00

2005 Bowman Chrome Gold Refractors

UNPRICED GOLD REF.1/1 ODDS 1:5904 H/R

2005 Bowman Chrome Red Refractors

*VETS: 2X TO 5X BASIC CARDS
*ROOKIES: .6X TO 1.5X BASIC CARDS
STATED ODDS 1:5

2005 Bowman Chrome Silver Refractors

*VETS: 5X TO 12X BASIC CARDS
*ROOKIE 111-220: 1.5X TO 4X BASIC CARD
1-220 SILVER REF/50 ODDS 1:118H, 1:119R
UNPRICED AU SILVER REF. PRINT RUN 10

2005 Bowman Chrome Uncirculated Green Refractors

*ROOKIES/399: .8X TO 2X BASIC CARDS

2005 Bowman Chrome Uncirculated Green Xfractors

*ROOKIES: 2X TO 5X BASIC CARDS
STATED PRINT RUN 50 SER.#'d SETS

2005 Bowman Chrome Felt Back Flashback

FELT BACK/199 ODDS 1:399 H, 1:533 R
1 Randy Moss 8.00 20.00
2 Michael Vick 8.00 20.00
3 Brett Favre 20.00 50.00
4 LaDainian Tomlinson 8.00 20.00
5 Marvin Harrison 8.00 20.00
6 Curtis Martin 8.00 20.00
7 Peyton Manning 15.00 40.00
8 Tom Brady 15.00 40.00
9 Daunte Culpepper 6.00 15.00
10 Shaun Alexander 6.00 15.00
11 Ronnie Brown 10.00 25.00
12 Alex Smith QB 12.00 30.00
13 Cadillac Williams 8.00 20.00
14 Troy Williamson 6.00 15.00
15 Braylon Edwards 10.00 25.00

2006 Bowman Chrome

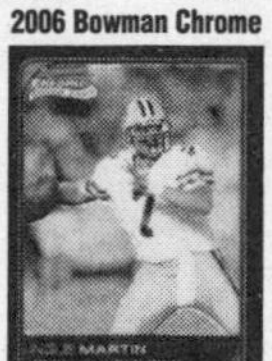

This 275-card set was released in January, 2007. The set was issued in four-card packs, with a $4 SRP, which came 18 packs to a box. Cards numbered 1-110 and 221-275 are 2006 rookies. Interestingly, cards numbered 1-55 were inserted in 2006 Bowman packs.

COMPLETE SET (275) 100.00 200.00
COMP.SHORT SET (55) 15.00 40.00
COMP.VET SET (110) 8.00 20.00
1-55 INSERTED IN BOWMAN PACKS
UNPRICED RED REF. SER.#'d TO 5
UNPRICED SUPERFRACT.1/1 ODDS 1:4687
UNPRICED PRINT PLATE/1 ODDS 1:1177
1 Devin Aromashodu RC .75 2.00
2 Daniel Bullocks RC .75 2.00
3 Winston Justice RC .60 1.50
4 Lawrence Vickers RC .60 1.50
5 Bernard Pollard RC .60 1.50
6 Abdul Hodge RC .50 1.25
7 Jovon Bouknight RC .60 1.50
8 Wali Lundy RC .60 1.50
9 Jonathan Orr RC .60 1.50
10 Gerald Riggs RC .60 1.50
11 Chris Gocong RC .60 1.50
12 David Kirtman RC .60 1.50
13 Quinn Sypniewski RC .60 1.50
14 Richard Marshall RC .60 1.50
15 Darryl Tapp RC .60 1.50
16 Charles Davis RC .60 1.50
17 Tim Massaquoi RC .60 1.50
18 DeMario Minter RC .60 1.50
19 Hank Baskett RC .75 2.00
20 Andre Hall RC .60 1.50
21 Cody Hodges RC .60 1.50
22 Greg Lee RC .50 1.25
23 Danieal Manning RC .75 2.00
24 Jason Hatcher RC .60 1.50
25 Ben Obomanu RC .75 2.00
26 Dusty Dvoracek RC .75 2.00
27 Domenik Hixon RC .75 2.00
28 Josh Betts RC .60 1.50
29 Marques Colston RC 1.50 4.00
30 P.J. Pope RC .75 2.00
31 Gabe Watson RC .50 1.25
32 Alan Zemaitis RC .75 2.00
33 Jeff King RC .60 1.50
34 Damien Rhodes RC .60 1.50
35 Orien Harris RC .60 1.50
36 David Anderson RC .60 1.50
37 Garrett Mills RC .75 2.00
38 Anthony Schlegel RC .60 1.50
39 Omar Gaither RC .60 1.50
40 Freddie Keiaho RC .60 1.50
41 J.J. Outlaw RC .60 1.50
42 Tony Scheffler RC .75 2.00
43 Dee Webb RC .60 1.50
44 Drew Olson RC .50 1.25
45 Martin Nance RC .60 1.50
46 Ko Simpson RC .60 1.50
47 Jesse Mahelona RC .60 1.50
48 Owen Daniels RC .75 2.00
49 Delanie Walker RC .75 2.00
50 Eric Smith RC .60 1.50
51 Darrell Hackney RC .60 1.50
52 Freddie Roach RC .60 1.50
53 James Anderson RC .50 1.25
54 Anthony Smith RC .75 2.00
55 Gerris Wilkinson RC .50 1.25
56 Tamba Hali RC 1.50 4.00
57 Jerome Harrison RC 1.50 4.00
58 Jason Allen RC 1.25 3.00
59 Brodrick Bunkley RC 1.25 3.00
60 Bobby Carpenter RC 1.00 2.50
61 Johnathan Joseph RC 1.25 3.00
62 Travis Wilson RC 1.00 2.50
63 Reggie McNeal RC 1.25 3.00
64 Haloti Ngata RC 1.50 4.00
65 Manny Lawson RC 1.25 3.00
66 Donte Whitner RC 1.50 4.00
67 Derek Hagan RC 1.25 3.00
68 Devin Hester RC 3.00 8.00
69 Jeremy Bloom RC 1.25 3.00
70 Ashton Youboty RC 1.00 2.50
71 Kamerion Wimbley RC 1.50 4.00
72 Charlie Whitehurst RC 1.50 4.00
73 Darnell Bing RC 1.25 3.00
74 Adam Jennings RC 1.25 3.00
75 Tim Day RC 1.25 3.00
76 Jeff Webb RC 1.25 3.00
77 D.J. Shockley RC 1.25 3.00
78 Marcus Vick RC 1.00 2.50
79 Thomas Howard RC 1.25 3.00
80 Todd Watkins RC 1.00 2.50
81 Davin Joseph RC 1.25 3.00
82 Pat Watkins RC 1.25 3.00
83 Jon Alston RC 1.00 2.50
84 Ernie Sims RC 1.25 3.00
85 D'Qwell Jackson RC 1.25 3.00
86 Corey Bramlet RC 1.25 3.00
87 Antonio Cromartie RC 1.50 4.00
88 A.J. Nicholson RC 1.00 2.50
89 Kevin McMahan RC 1.25 3.00
90 J.D. Runnels RC 1.25 3.00
91 Nate Salley RC 1.25 3.00
92 Matt Shelton RC 1.50 4.00
93 Brett Basanez RC 1.50 4.00
94 Rocky McIntosh RC 1.25 3.00
95 Anthony Mix RC 1.25 3.00
96 Jimmy Williams RC 1.50 4.00
97 Marcus McNeill RC 1.25 3.00
98 DeMeco Ryans RC 1.50 4.00
99 Dwayne Slay RC 1.25 3.00
100 John David Washington RC 1.25 3.00
101 P.J. Daniels RC 1.00 2.50
102 Kelly Jennings RC 1.25 3.00
103 John McCargo RC 1.00 2.50
104 Paul Pinegar RC 1.00 2.50
105 Ray Edwards RC 1.50 4.00
106 Elvis Dumervil RC 1.50 4.00
107 Travis Lulay RC 1.25 3.00
108 Bennie Brazell RC 1.25 3.00
109 Dominique Byrd RC 1.25 3.00
110 Nick Mangold RC 1.25 3.00
111 Plaxico Burress .30 .75
112 Shaun Alexander .30 .75
113 Muhsin Muhammad .30 .75
114 Jake Plummer .30 .75
115 Deuce McAllister .30 .75
116 T.J. Houshmandzadeh .30 .75
117 Carson Palmer .40 1.00
118 Willis McGahee .30 .75
119 Terrell Owens .40 1.00
120 Fred Taylor .30 .75
121 Dante Hall .30 .75
122 Brad Johnson .30 .75
123 Reggie Wayne .30 .75
124 DeShaun Foster .30 .75
125 Tony Gonzalez .30 .75
126 Javon Walker .30 .75
127 Marc Bulger .30 .75
128 LaDainian Tomlinson .40 1.00
129 Byron Leftwich .30 .75
130 Dwight Freeney .30 .75
131 Kevin Jones .25 .60
132 Hines Ward .40 1.00
133 Randy Moss .40 1.00
134 Edgerrin James .30 .75
135 Ahman Green .30 .75
136 Steven Jackson .40 1.00
137 Ben Roethlisberger .50 1.25
138 Daunte Culpepper .30 .75
139 Santana Moss .30 .75
140 Jonathan Vilma .30 .75
141 Gary Kubiak CO .25 .60
142 Marvin Harrison .40 1.00
143 Trent Green .30 .75
144 Chris Chambers .30 .75
145 Chris Brown .25 .60
146 Eli Manning .50 1.25
147 Corey Dillon .30 .75
148 Anquan Boldin .30 .75
149 Donovan McNabb .40 1.00
150 Drew Bennett .30 .75
151 Jason Witten .40 1.00
152 Eric Moulds .25 .60
153 Billy Volek .25 .60
154 Chris Cooley .30 .75
155 Larry Johnson .30 .75
156 Willie Parker .30 .75
157 Cadillac Williams .30 .75
158 Philip Rivers .40 1.00
159 Reuben Droughns .30 .75
160 Joey Galloway .30 .75
161 Lee Evans .30 .75
162 Jamal Lewis .30 .75
163 Brett Favre .75 2.00
164 Clinton Portis .40 1.00
165 Rod Marinelli CO .25 .60
166 Tom Brady .00 1.50
167 Torry Holt .30 .75
168 Rudi Johnson .30 .75
169 Priest Holmes .30 .75
170 Tatum Bell .25 .60
171 Jeremy Shockey .40 1.00
172 Shawne Merriman .30 .75
173 Alge Crumpler .30 .75
174 Marion Barber .40 1.00
175 Steve Smith .40 1.00
176 Mike McCarthy CO .25 .60
177 David Carr .25 .60
178 Julius Jones .25 .60
179 Chad Johnson .30 .75
180 Curtis Martin .40 1.00
181 Peyton Manning .60 1.50
182 LaMont Jordan .30 .75
183 Tiki Barber .40 1.00
184 Darrell Jackson .30 .75
185 J.P. Losman .30 .75
186 Drew Brees .40 1.00
187 Isaac Bruce .30 .75
188 Drew Bledsoe .40 1.00
189 Roy Williams WR .30 .75
190 Donte Stallworth .25 .60
191 Odell Thurman .25 .60
192 Chester Taylor .30 .75
193 Randy McMichael .25 .60
194 Larry Fitzgerald .40 1.00
195 Charlie Frye .30 .75
196 Keary Colbert .25 .60
197 Patrick Ramsey .30 .75
198 Mark Clayton .30 .75
199 Michael Jenkins .30 .75
200 Jake Delhomme .30 .75
201 Aaron Rodgers .75 2.00
202 Andre Johnson .40 1.00
203 Matt Hasselbeck .30 .75
204 Reggie Brown .25 .60
205 Warrick Dunn .30 .75
206 Kurt Warner .40 1.00
207 Antonio Gates .40 1.00
208 Terry Glenn .30 .75
209 Steve McNair .30 .75
210 Alex Smith QB .40 1.00
211 Joe Horn .30 .75
212 Domanick Davis .25 .60
213 Deion Branch .30 .75
214 Todd Heap .30 .75
215 Chad Pennington .30 .75
216 Brandon Lloyd .25 .60
217 Rod Smith .30 .75
218 Ronnie Brown .40 1.00
219 Braylon Edwards .30 .75
220 Michael Vick .40 1.00
221 Vince Young RC 2.00 5.00
222 Jay Cutler RC 3.00 8.00
223 Reggie Bush RC 3.00 8.00
224 Matt Leinart RC 1.50 4.00
225 Vernon Davis RC 2.00 5.00
226 A.J. Hawk RC 1.50 4.00
227 Santonio Holmes RC 2.00 5.00
228 DeAngelo Williams RC 2.00 5.00
229 LenDale White RC 1.25 3.00
230 Sinorice Moss RC 1.50 4.00
231 Joseph Addai RC 1.50 4.00
232 Mike Bell RC 1.50 4.00
233 Will Blackmon RC 1.25 3.00
234 Brian Calhoun RC 1.00 2.50
235 Kellen Clemens RC 1.25 3.00
236 Brodie Croyle RC 1.50 4.00
237 Maurice Drew RC 2.50 6.00
238 Anthony Fasano RC 1.50 4.00
239 D'Brickashaw Ferguson RC 1.50 4.00
240 Quinton Ganther RC 1.00 2.50
241 Bruce Gradkowski RC 1.50 4.00
242 Skyler Green RC 1.00 2.50
243 Chad Greenway RC 1.50 4.00
244 Marques Hagans RC 1.00 2.50
245 Michael Huff RC 1.25 3.00
246 Cedric Humes RC 1.00 2.50
247 Tarvaris Jackson RC 1.50 4.00
248 Omar Jacobs RC 1.00 2.50
249 Greg Jennings RC 3.00 8.00
250 Mathias Kiwanuka RC 1.50 4.00
251 Joe Klopfenstein RC 1.00 2.50
252 Marcedes Lewis RC 1.50 4.00
253 Brandon Marshall RC 1.50 4.00
254 Ingle Martin RC 1.25 3.00
255 Dontrell Moore RC 1.25 3.00
256 Jerious Norwood RC 1.25 3.00
257 Leonard Pope RC 1.50 4.00
258 Willie Reid RC 1.25 3.00
259 Michael Robinson RC 1.25 3.00
260 Brad Smith RC 1.50 4.00
261 Maurice Stovall RC 1.00 2.50
262 David Thomas RC 1.25 3.00
263 Leon Washington RC 1.25 3.00
264 Brandon Williams RC 1.00 2.50
265 Demetrius Williams RC 1.25 3.00
266 Tye Hill RC 1.00 2.50
267 Mike Hass RC 1.25 3.00
268 Jason Avant RC 1.00 2.50
269 Chad Jackson RC 1.00 2.50
270 Laurence Maroney RC 1.25 3.00
271 Anwar Phillips RC 1.25 3.00
272 David Kirtman RC 1.25 3.00
273 Roman Harper RC 1.25 3.00
274 Spencer Havner RC 1.25 3.00
275 Erik Meyer RC 1.25 3.00

2006 Bowman Chrome Blue Refractors

*BLUE REF 1-55: 3X TO 8X BASIC CARDS
1-55 BLUE REF/150 ODDS 1:262 BOWMAN
*BLUE REF 111-220: 4X TO 10X BASIC CARDS
*BLUE REF 56-110/221-275: 1.5X TO 4X
56-275 BLUE REF/150 ODDS 1:44

2006 Bowman Chrome Gold Refractors

*GOLD REF 1-55: 4X TO 10X BASIC CARDS
1-55 GOLD REF/50 ODDS 1:770 BOWMAN
*GOLD REF 111-220: 5X TO 12X BASIC CARDS
*GOLD REF 56-110/221-275: 2X TO 5X
56-275 GOLD REF/50 ODDS 1:133

2006 Bowman Chrome Orange Refractors

*ORANGE 1-55: 5X TO 12X BASIC CARDS
1-55 ORANGE/25 ODDS 1:1525 BOWMAN
*ORANGE 111-220: 8X TO 20X BASIC CARDS
*ORANGE 56-110/221-275: 2.5X TO 6X
56-275 ORANGE/25 ODDS 1:267
221 Vince Young 40.00 100.00
222 Jay Cutler 50.00 120.00
223 Reggie Bush 60.00 150.00

2006 Bowman Chrome Red Refractors

1-55 RED REF. ODDS 1:7600 BOWMAN
56-275 RED REF ODDS 1:1335 CHROME
UNPRICED RED REF PRINT RUN 5

2006 Bowman Chrome Refractors

*REF 1-55: 2X TO 5X BASIC CARDS
1-55 REF/500 ODDS 1:80 BOWMAN
*REF 111-220: 2X TO 5X BASIC CARDS
*REF 56-110-221-275: 1X TO 2.5X
56-275 REFRACTOR ODDS 1:4

2006 Bowman Chrome Superfractors

UNPRICED SUPERFRACTOR 1/1 ODDS 1:4687

2006 Bowman Chrome Uncirculated Rookies

*UNCIRC/519: 1X TO 2.5X BASIC CARDS
UNCIRCULATED/519 ODDS 1:BOX

2006 Bowman Chrome Xfractors

*XFRACTOR 1-55: 2.5X TO 6X BASIC CARDS
XFRACTOR/250 ODDS 1:155 BOWMAN
*XFRACTOR 111-220: 2.5X TO 6X
*XFRACTOR 56-110/221-275: 1.2X TO 3X
56-220 XFRACTOR/250 ODDS 1:27

2006 Bowman Chrome Felt Back Flashback

STATED PRINT RUN 199 SER.#'d SETS
*REF/25: 1X TO 2.5X BASIC INSERTS
1 Santonio Holmes 8.00 20.00
2 Vince Young 8.00 20.00
3 Matt Leinart 6.00 15.00
4 Reggie Bush 12.00 30.00
5 Vernon Davis 8.00 20.00
6 Joseph Addai 6.00 16.00
7 Omar Jacobs 4.00 10.00
8 Jay Cutler 12.00 30.00
9 D'Brickashaw Ferguson 6.00 15.00
10 Laurence Maroney 5.00 12.00
11 DeAngelo Williams 8.00 20.00
12 Tarvaris Jackson 6.00 15.00
13 LenDale White 5.00 12.00
14 Sinorice Moss 6.00 15.00
15 Chad Jackson 4.00 10.00

2006 Bowman Chrome Rookie Autographs

AUTO/199 STATED ODDS 1:615
AUTO GROUP A ODDS 1:320
AUTO GROUP B ODDS 1:220
AUTO GROUP C ODDS 1:208
AUTO GROUP D ODDS 1:29
UNPRICED PRINT PLATE/1 ODDS 1:5503
UNPRICED RED REF/5 ODDS 1:6550
UNPRICED SUPERFRACT/1 ODDS 1:21,768
UNPRICED UNCIRCULATED PRINT RUN 10
221 Vince Young/199 25.00 60.00
222 Jay Cutler/199 40.00 100.00
223 Reggie Bush/199 40.00 80.00
224 Matt Leinart/199 10.00 25.00
225 Vernon Davis/199 25.00 50.00
226 A.J. Hawk/199 10.00 25.00
227 Santonio Holmes/199 12.00 30.00
228 DeAngelo Williams/199 12.00 30.00
229 LenDale White/199 8.00 20.00
230 Sinorice Moss/199 10.00 25.00
231 Joseph Addai A 6.00 15.00
232 Mike Bell D 5.00 12.00
233 Will Blackmon C 4.00 10.00
234 Brian Calhoun A 4.00 10.00
236 Brodie Croyle A 6.00 15.00
237 Maurice Drew A 10.00 25.00
238 Anthony Fasano D 5.00 12.00
239 D'Brickashaw Ferguson B 5.00 12.00
240 Quinton Ganther D 3.00 8.00
241 Bruce Gradkowski A 6.00 15.00
242 Skyler Green A 4.00 10.00
243 Chad Greenway D 5.00 12.00
244 Marques Hagans D 3.00 8.00
245 Michael Huff A 5.00 12.00
246 Cedric Humes D 3.00 8.00
247 Tarvaris Jackson D 5.00 12.00
248 Omar Jacobs A 4.00 10.00
249 Greg Jennings A 15.00 40.00
250 Mathias Kiwanuka D 5.00 12.00
251 Joe Klopfenstein C 3.00 8.00
252 Marcedes Lewis A 6.00 15.00
253 Brandon Marshall D 10.00 25.00
254 Ingle Martin D 4.00 10.00
256 Jerious Norwood C 4.00 10.00
257 Leonard Pope D 5.00 12.00
258 Willie Reid D 4.00 10.00
259 Michael Robinson B 4.00 10.00
260 Brad Smith A 6.00 15.00
261 Maurice Stovall B 3.00 8.00
262 David Thomas D 4.00 10.00
263 Leon Washington A 5.00 12.00
264 Brandon Williams D 3.00 8.00
265 Demetrius Williams A 5.00 12.00
266 Tye Hill D 3.00 8.00
268 Jason Avant B 3.00 8.00
269 Chad Jackson A 4.00 10.00
270 Laurence Maroney A 5.00 12.00

2006 Bowman Chrome Rookie Autographs Blue Refractors

*BLUE REF/75: .8X TO 2X BASIC AUTO
*BLUE REF/75: .6X TO 1.5X GROUP A AU
*BLUE REF/75: .4X TO 1X BASIC AU/199
BLUE REFRACTOR/75 ODDS 1:349
221 Vince Young 30.00 80.00
222 Jay Cutler 40.00 100.00
223 Reggie Bush 40.00 100.00

2006 Bowman Chrome Rookie Autographs Gold Refractors

*GOLD REF/50: 1.2X TO 3X BASIC AUTO
*GOLD REF/50: 1X TO 2.5X GROUP A AU
*GOLD REF/50: .6X TO 1.5X AUTO/199
GOLD REFRACT/50 ODDS 1:527
221 Vince Young 50.00 120.00
222 Jay Cutler 60.00 150.00
223 Reggie Bush 60.00 150.00

2006 Bowman Chrome Rookie Autographs Orange Refractors

*ORANGE REF/25: 2X TO 5X BASIC AUTO
*ORANGE REF/25: 1.5X TO 4X GROUP A AU
*ORANGE REF/25: 1X TO 2.5X AUTO/199
ORANGE REF/25 ODDS 1:1075

2007 Bowman Chrome

This 220-card set was released in November, 2007. Cards numbered 1-110 all are 2007 NFL rookies while cards 111-220 feature veterans. Cards numbered 1-55 were inserted earlier in the year in the 2007 Bowman product.

COMPLETE SET (220) 40.00 100.00
COMP.SHORT SET (55) 8.00 20.00
COMP.VET SET (110) 6.00 15.00
1-55 INSERTED IN BOWMAN PACKS
UNPRICED 1-55 RED REF/5 ODDS 1:6884 BOW
UNPR.56-220 RED REF/5 ODDS 1:1628 CHR
UNPR.1-55 SUPERFR/1 ODDS 1:14,227 BOW
UNPR.56-220 SUPERFR/1 ODDS 1:6528 CHR
UNPRICED PRINT.PLATE/1 ODDS 1:1632 CHR
BC1 Kenny Irons RC .40 1.00
BC2 David Clowney RC .50 1.25
BC3 Courtney Taylor RC .50 1.25
BC4 Amobi Okoye RC .60 1.50
BC5 Jamaal Anderson RC .50 1.25
BC6 Adam Carriker RC .50 1.25
BC7 Jarvis Moss RC .50 1.25
BC8 Anthony Spencer RC .60 1.50
BC9 Jon Beason RC .50 1.25
BC10 Darrelle Revis RC 1.00 2.50
BC11 Aaron Ross RC .60 1.50
BC12 Reggie Nelson RC .50 1.25
BC13 Michael Griffin RC .60 1.50
BC14 Brandon Meriweather RC .60 1.50
BC15 Tyler Palko RC .50 1.25
BC16 Jared Zabransky RC .50 1.25
BC17 Lester Ricard RC .50 1.25
BC18 Darius Walker RC .40 1.00
BC19 Ahmad Bradshaw RC 1.00 2.50
BC20 Thomas Clayton RC .50 1.25
BC21 Rhema McKnight RC .40 1.00
BC22 Scott Chandler RC .60 1.50
BC23 Matt Spaeth RC .60 1.50
BC24 Ben Patrick RC .50 1.25
BC25 Clark Harris RC .50 1.25
BC26 Martrez Milner RC .40 1.00
BC27 Joe Newton RC .40 1.00
BC28 DeMarcus Tank Tyler RC .40 1.00
BC29 Justin Harrell RC .50 1.25
BC30 LaMarr Woodley RC .60 1.50
BC31 David Harris RC .50 1.25
BC32 Buster Davis RC .50 1.25
BC33 Rufus Alexander RC .50 1.25
BC34 Earl Everett RC .50 1.25
BC35 Stewart Bradley RC .50 1.25
BC36 Prescott Burgess RC .50 1.25
BC37 Daymeion Hughes RC .50 1.25
BC38 Marcus McCauley RC .50 1.25
BC39 Chris Houston RC .50 1.25
BC40 David Irons RC .40 1.00
BC41 Levi Brown RC .60 1.50
BC42 Joe Staley RC .50 1.25
BC43 Steve Breaston RC .60 1.50
BC44 Le'Ron McClain RC .60 1.50
BC45 Joel Filani RC .50 1.25
BC46 Justise Hairston RC .50 1.25
BC47 Nate Ilaoa RC .50 1.25
BC48 Brett Ratliff RC .60 1.50
BC49 Roy Hall RC .60 1.50
BC50 Legedu Naanee RC .60 1.50
BC51 Jarrett Hicks RC .50 1.25
BC52 Sonny Shackelford RC .40 1.00
BC53 Jordan Kent RC .50 1.25
BC54 John Broussard RC .50 1.25
BC55 Chandler Williams RC .50 1.25
BC56 JaMarcus Russell RC 1.00 2.50
BC57 Brady Quinn RC 1.50 4.00
BC58 Drew Stanton RC 1.00 2.50
BC59 Troy Smith RC 1.50 4.00
BC60 Kevin Kolb RC 2.50 6.00
BC61 Trent Edwards RC 1.50 4.00
BC62 John Beck RC 1.50 4.00
BC63 Jordan Palmer RC 1.25 3.00
BC64 Chris Leak RC 1.25 3.00
BC65 Adrian Peterson RC 6.00 15.00
BC66 Marshawn Lynch RC 1.50 4.00
BC67 Brandon Jackson RC 1.25 3.00
BC68 Michael Bush RC 1.50 4.00
BC69 Antonio Pittman RC 1.00 2.50
BC70 Tony Hunt RC 1.00 2.50
BC71 Lorenzo Booker RC 1.25 3.00
BC72 Chris Henry RC 1.00 2.50
BC73 Brian Leonard RC 1.25 3.00
BC74 Garrett Wolfe RC 1.00 2.50
BC75 Calvin Johnson RC 6.00 15.00
BC76 Ted Ginn RC 1.25 3.00
BC77 Dwayne Jarrett RC 1.25 3.00
BC78 Dwayne Bowe RC 2.00 5.00
BC79 Sidney Rice RC 2.00 5.00
BC80 Robert Meachem RC 1.50 4.00
BC81 Anthony Gonzalez RC 1.50 4.00
BC82 Craig Buster Davis RC 1.25 3.00
BC83 Aundrae Allison RC 1.00 2.50
BC84 Chansi Stuckey RC 1.50 4.00
BC85 Alan Branch RC 1.25 3.00

BC86 Steve Smith USC RC 1.50 4.00
BC87 Paul Williams RC 1.00 2.50
BC88 Johnnie Lee Higgins RC 1.25 3.00
BC89 Jason Hill RC 1.50 4.00
BC90 Greg Olsen RC 1.25 3.00
BC91 Yamon Figurs RC 1.00 2.50
BC92 Gaines Adams RC 1.50 4.00
BC93 Patrick Willis RC 3.00 8.00
BC94 Joe Thomas RC 1.50 4.00
BC95 Isaiah Stanback RC 1.00 2.50
BC96 Paul Posluszny RC 1.50 4.00
BC97 Jeff Rowe RC 1.00 2.50
BC98 Zac Taylor RC 1.25 3.00
BC99 Dwayne Wright RC 1.25 3.00
BC100 Kenneth Darby RC 1.25 3.00
BC101 Selvin Young RC 1.25 3.00
BC102 Gary Russell RC 1.25 3.00
BC103 Kolby Smith RC 1.25 3.00
BC104 Dallas Baker RC 1.00 2.50
BC105 Jacoby Jones RC 1.50 4.00
BC106 Ryne Robinson RC 1.25 3.00
BC107 Chris Davis RC 1.00 2.50
BC108 Laron Landry RC 1.50 4.00
BC109 Leon Hall RC 1.25 3.00
BC110 Lawrence Timmons RC 1.50 4.00
BC111 Matt Leinart .30 .75
BC112 Jason Campbell .30 .75
BC113 J.P. Losman .25 .60
BC114 Rex Grossman .30 .75
BC115 Tony Romo .50 1.25
BC116 Brett Favre .75 2.00
BC117 Trent Green .30 .75
BC118 Drew Brees .40 1.00
BC119 Chad Pennington .30 .75
BC120 Ben Roethlisberger .40 1.00
BC121 Alex Smith QB .40 1.00
BC122 Marc Bulger .30 .75
BC123 Edgerrin James .30 .75
BC124 Jamal Lewis .30 .75
BC125 DeShaun Foster .30 .75
BC126 Cedric Benson .30 .75
BC127 Rudi Johnson .30 .75
BC128 Dominic Rhodes .30 .75
BC129 Fred Taylor .30 .75
BC130 Larry Johnson .25 .60
BC131 Chester Taylor .25 .60
BC132 Deuce McAllister .30 .75
BC133 Brandon Jacobs .30 .75
BC134 Willie Parker .30 .75
BC135 Frank Gore .40 1.00
BC136 Steven Jackson .40 1.00
BC137 Clinton Portis .30 .75
BC138 Anquan Boldin .30 .75
BC139 Derrick Mason .30 .75
BC140 Steve Smith .30 .75
BC141 Chad Johnson .30 .75
BC142 Braylon Edwards .30 .75
BC143 Terry Glenn .30 .75
BC144 Mike Furrey .30 .75
BC145 Donald Driver .40 1.00
BC146 Andre Johnson .30 .75
BC147 Marvin Harrison .40 1.00
BC148 Chris Chambers .30 .75
BC149 Devery Henderson .25 .60
BC150 Marques Colston .40 1.00
BC151 Amani Toomer .30 .75
BC152 Laveranues Coles .25 .60
BC153 Donte Stallworth .30 .75
BC154 Hines Ward .40 1.00
BC155 Keenan McCardell .25 .60
BC156 Arnaz Battle .25 .60
BC157 Deion Branch .30 .75
BC158 Kevin Curtis .25 .60
BC159 Isaac Bruce .30 .75
BC160 Santana Moss .30 .75
BC161 Kellen Winslow .30 .75
BC162 Jeremy Shockey .30 .75
BC163 Vernon Davis .30 .75
BC164 Travis Henry .30 .75
BC165 Todd Heap .25 .60
BC166 Matt Schaub .30 .75
BC167 Steve McNair .30 .75
BC168 Jake Delhomme .30 .75
BC169 Carson Palmer .30 .75
BC170 Jay Cutler .40 1.00
BC171 Peyton Manning .60 1.50
BC172 Tom Brady .60 1.50
BC173 Eli Manning .40 1.00
BC174 Donovan McNabb .40 1.00
BC175 Philip Rivers .40 1.00
BC176 Matt Hasselbeck .30 .75
BC177 Vince Young .30 .75
BC178 Warrick Dunn .30 .75
BC179 Willis McGahee .30 .75
BC180 DeAngelo Williams .40 1.00
BC181 Thomas Jones .30 .75
BC182 Julius Jones .25 .60
BC183 Joseph Addai .30 .75
BC184 Maurice Jones-Drew .40 1.00
BC185 Ronnie Brown .30 .75
BC186 Laurence Maroney .30 .75
BC187 Reggie Bush .40 1.00
BC188 Brian Westbrook .30 .75
BC189 LaDainian Tomlinson .40 1.00
BC190 Shaun Alexander .30 .75
BC191 Cadillac Williams .30 .75
BC192 Michael Turner .40 1.00
BC193 Larry Fitzgerald .40 1.00
BC194 Lee Evans .30 .75
BC195 Muhsin Muhammad .30 .75
BC196 T.J. Houshmandzadeh .30 .75
BC197 Terrell Owens .40 1.00
BC198 Javon Walker .30 .75
BC199 Roy Williams WR .30 .75
BC200 Greg Jennings .40 1.00
BC201 Reggie Wayne .30 .75
BC202 Matt Jones .30 .75
BC203 Troy Williamson .25 .60
BC204 Joe Horn .30 .75
BC205 Plaxico Burress .30 .75
BC206 Jerricho Cotchery .30 .75
BC207 Randy Moss .40 1.00
BC208 Reggie Brown .25 .60
BC209 Santonio Holmes .30 .75
BC210 Eric Parker .25 .60
BC211 Antonio Bryant .25 .60
BC212 Darrell Jackson .25 .60
BC213 Torry Holt .30 .75
BC214 Antwaan Randle El .25 .60
BC215 Alge Crumpler .30 .75
BC216 Tony Gonzalez .30 .75
BC217 Antonio Gates .40 1.00
BC218 Tarvaris Jackson .25 .60
BC219 Drew Bennett .25 .60
BC220 Byron Leftwich .30 .75

2007 Bowman Chrome Blue Refractors

*1-55 BLUE REF/150: 2.5X TO 6X
*56-110 BLUE REF/150: 1X TO 2.5X
*111-220 BLUE REF/150: 3X TO 8X
1-55 BLUE REF/150 ODDS 1:228 BOW
56-220 BLUE REF/150 ODDS 1:55 CHR
65 Adrian Peterson 40.00 100.00

2007 Bowman Chrome Gold Refractors

*1-55 GOLD REF/50: 4X TO 10X BASIC CARDS
*56-110 GOLD REF/50: 1.5X TO 4X
*111-220 GOLD REF/50: 5X TO 12X
1-55 GOLD REF/50 ODDS 1:685 BOW
56-220 GOLD REF/50 ODDS 1:164 CHR
65 Adrian Peterson 75.00 150.00

2007 Bowman Chrome Orange Refractors

*1-55 ORNGE REF/25: 5X TO 12X BASIC CARDS
*56-110 ORNGE REF/25: 2X TO 5X
*111-220 ORNGE REF/25: 6X TO 15X
1-55 ORANGE REF/25 ODDS 1:1377 BOW HOB
56-220 ORNGE REF/25 ODDS 1:327 CHR
65 Adrian Peterson 125.00 250.00
75 Calvin Johnson 50.00 100.00

2007 Bowman Chrome Refractors

*1-55 REFRACT/500: 1.5X TO 4X BASIC CARDS
*56-110 REF: .6X TO 1.5X BASIC CARDS
*111-220 REF: 2X TO 5X BASIC CARDS
1-55 REF/500 ODDS 1:68 BOW
56-220 REFRACTOR ODDS 1:4 CHR
65 Adrian Peterson 10.00 25.00

2007 Bowman Chrome Uncirculated Rookies

*ROOKIES/1079: .8X TO 2X BASIC CARDS
UNCIRCULATED/1079 ONE PER CHROME BOX
BC65 Adrian Peterson 12.00 30.00

2007 Bowman Chrome Xfractors

*1-55 XFRACT/275: 2X TO 5X BASIC CARDS
*56-110 XFRACT/250: .8X TO 2X BASIC CARDS
*111-220 XFRACT/250: 2.5X TO 6X
1-55 XFRACTOR/275 ODDS 1:124 BOW
56-220 XFRACTOR/250 ODDS 1:33 CHR
65 Adrian Peterson 12.00 30.00

2007 Bowman Chrome Rookie Autographs

UNPRICED PRINT.PLATE ODDS 1:6700
UNPRICED RED REF/5 ODDS 1:5655
UNPRICED SUPERFR/1 ODDS 1:20,368
UNPRICED UNCIRC AUTO PRINT RUN 10
BC56 JaMarcus Russell B 5.00 12.00
BC57 Brady Quinn B 12.00 30.00
BC58 Drew Stanton C 5.00 12.00
BC59 Troy Smith C 8.00 20.00
BC60 Kevin Kolb D 10.00 25.00
BC61 Trent Edwards E 5.00 12.00
BC62 John Beck D 6.00 15.00
BC63 Jordan Palmer E 4.00 10.00
BC64 Chris Leak K 4.00 10.00
BC65 Adrian Peterson B 100.00 200.00
BC66 Marshawn Lynch C 10.00 25.00
BC67 Brandon Jackson I 4.00 10.00
BC68 Michael Bush I 5.00 12.00
BC69 Antonio Pittman D 3.00 8.00
BC70 Tony Hunt J 3.00 8.00
BC71 Lorenzo Booker G 4.00 10.00
BC72 Chris Henry K 3.00 8.00
BC73 Brian Leonard C 6.00 15.00
BC74 Garrett Wolfe J 3.00 8.00
BC75 Calvin Johnson A 75.00 150.00
BC76 Ted Ginn C 6.00 15.00
BC77 Dwayne Jarrett C 6.00 15.00
BC78 Dwayne Bowe C 10.00 25.00
BC79 Sidney Rice C 20.00 50.00
BC80 Robert Meachem C 8.00 20.00
BC81 Anthony Gonzalez E 5.00 12.00
BC82 Craig Buster Davis L 4.00 10.00
BC83 Aundrae Allison G 3.00 8.00
BC84 Chansi Stuckey J 5.00 12.00
BC85 Alan Branch H 4.00 10.00
BC86 Steve Smith USC E 5.00 12.00
BC87 Paul Williams I 3.00 8.00
BC88 Johnnie Lee Higgins L 4.00 10.00
BC89 Jason Hill K 5.00 12.00
BC90 Greg Olsen E 4.00 10.00
BC91 Yamon Figurs L 3.00 8.00
BC92 Gaines Adams C 8.00 20.00
BC93 Patrick Willis D 10.00 25.00
BC94 Joe Thomas E 5.00 12.00
BC95 Isaiah Stanback K 3.00 8.00
BC96 Paul Posluszny E 5.00 12.00
BC97 Jeff Rowe I 3.00 8.00
BC99 Dwayne Wright I 4.00 10.00
BC100 Kenneth Darby L 4.00 10.00
BC101 Selvin Young L 4.00 10.00
BC102 Gary Russell I 4.00 10.00
BC103 Kolby Smith K 4.00 10.00
BC104 Dallas Baker J 3.00 8.00
BC105 Jacoby Jones L 5.00 12.00
BC106 Ryne Robinson J 4.00 10.00
BC107 Chris Davis L 3.00 8.00
BC108 LaRon Landry I 5.00 12.00
BC109 Leon Hall F 4.00 10.00
BC110 Lawrence Timmons F 5.00 12.00

2007 Bowman Chrome Rookie Autographs Blue Refractors

*BLUE REF/75: .5X TO 1.2X GROUP B/C AU
*BLUE REF/75: .6X TO 1.5X GROUP D AU
*BLUE REF/75: .8X TO 2X BASIC AUTO
BLUE REF/25 GROUP A ODDS 1:50,900
BLUE REF/75 GROUP B ODDS 1:309
BC57 Brady Quinn 20.00 50.00
BC65 Adrian Peterson 150.00 300.00
BC75 Calvin Johnson/25 100.00 200.00

2007 Bowman Chrome Rookie Autographs Gold Refractors

*GOLD REF/50: .6X TO 1.5X GROUP B/C AU
*GOLD REF/50: 1X TO 2.5X GROUP D AU
*GOLD REF/50: 1.2X TO 3X BASIC AUTO
GOLD REF/15 GROUP A ODDS 1:92,545
GOLD REF/50 GROUP B ODDS 1:467
BC57 Brady Quinn 25.00 60.00
BC65 Adrian Peterson 200.00 400.00
BC75 Calvin Johnson/15 125.00 250.00

2007 Bowman Chrome Rookie Autographs Orange Refractors

*ORANGE REF/25: 1X TO 2.5X GROUP C AU
*ORANGE REF/25: 1.2X TO 3X GROUP D AU
*ORANGE REF/25: 1.5X TO 4X BASIC AUTO
UNPRICED ORG/10 GRP A ODDS 1:169,666
ORANGE REF/25 GROUP B ODDS 1:955
BC57 Brady Quinn 30.00 80.00
BC65 Adrian Peterson 300.00 600.00
BC75 Calvin Johnson/10 200.00 400.00

2008 Bowman Chrome

This set was released on November 19, 2008. The base set consists of 220 cards. Cards 1-110 feature rookies, and cards 111-220 are veterans. Cards 1-55 can be found in regular Bowman packs.

COMPLETE SET (220) 40.00 80.00
COMP.SER.1 SET (55) 10.00 25.00
COMP.SER.2 SET (165) 30.00 60.00
1-55 INSERTED TWO PER BOWMAN PACK
UNPRICED 56-220 PRINT PLATE/1 ODDS 1:797 BOW CHR
BC1 Ryan Clady RC .50 1.25
BC2 Branden Albert RC .50 1.25
BC3 Gosder Cherilus RC .40 1.00
BC4 Duane Brown RC .40 1.00
BC5 Brandon Flowers RC .50 1.25
BC6 Quentin Groves RC .40 1.00
BC7 Jason Jones RC .50 1.25
BC8 Kendall Langford RC .50 1.25
BC9 Brad Cottam RC .40 1.00
BC10 Antwaun Molden RC .40 1.00
BC11 Bryan Smith RC .40 1.00
BC12 DaJuan Morgan RC .40 1.00
BC13 Craig Stevens RC .30 .75
BC14 Tom Zbikowski RC .50 1.25
BC15 Andre Fluellen RC .40 1.00
BC16 Cliff Avril RC .40 1.00
BC17 Tyvon Branch RC .40 1.00
BC18 Justin King RC .40 1.00
BC19 Jeremy Thompson RC .30 .75
BC20 William Hayes RC .30 .75
BC21 Will Franklin RC .40 1.00
BC22 Marcus Smith RC .40 1.00
BC23 Dwight Lowery RC .50 1.25
BC24 Reggie Corner RC .30 .75
BC25 Kenny Iwebema RC .30 .75
BC26 Quintin Demps RC .50 1.25
BC27 Jack Williams RC .30 .75
BC28 Craig Steltz RC .40 1.00
BC29 Bryan Kehl RC .40 1.00
BC30 Justin Tryon RC .30 .75
BC31 Arman Shields RC .40 1.00
BC32 Paul Hubbard RC .40 1.00
BC33 Jonathan Wilhite RC .40 1.00
BC34 Thomas DeCoud RC .30 .75
BC35 Derek Fine RC .40 1.00
BC36 Stanford Keglar RC .30 .75
BC37 Kenneth Moore RC .40 1.00
BC38 Robert James RC .30 .75
BC39 Jalen Parmele RC .40 1.00
BC40 Brandon Carr RC .40 1.00
BC41 Gary Barnidge RC .30 .75
BC42 Zack Bowman RC .40 1.00
BC43 Lex Hilliard RC .50 1.25
BC44 Mario Urrutia RC .30 .75
BC45 Adrian Arrington RC .40 1.00
BC46 Jerome Felton RC .30 .75
BC47 Chaz Schilens RC .50 1.25
BC48 Steve Johnson RC .75 2.00
BC49 Tim Hightower RC .50 1.25
BC50 Alex Brink RC .50 1.25
BC51 Brett Swain RC .40 1.00
BC52 Matt Slater RC .50 1.25
BC53 Justin Harper RC .40 1.00
BC54 Kevin Robinson RC .30 .75
BC55 Pierre Garcon RC .60 1.50
BC56 John David Booty RC .75 2.00
BC57 Brian Brohm RC 1.00 2.50
BC58 Kevin O'Connell RC .75 2.00
BC59 Matt Ryan RC 4.00 10.00
BC60 Chad Henne RC 1.00 2.50
BC61 Joe Flacco RC 3.00 8.00
BC62 Colt Brennan RC 1.00 2.50
BC63 Paul Smith RC 1.00 2.50
BC64 Eric Ainge RC 1.00 2.50
BC65 Kyle Wright RC .75 2.00
BC66 Josh Johnson RC 1.00 2.50
BC67 Dennis Dixon RC 1.00 2.50
BC68 Andre Woodson RC 1.00 2.50
BC69 Matt Forte RC 1.50 4.00
BC70 Felix Jones RC 1.50 4.00
BC71 Darren McFadden RC 2.50 6.00
BC72 Rashard Mendenhall RC 2.00 5.00
BC73 Ray Rice RC 2.00 5.00
BC74 Steve Slaton RC 1.00 2.50
BC75 Jonathan Stewart RC 1.50 4.00
BC76 Chris Johnson RC 2.50 6.00
BC77 Kevin Smith RC 1.00 2.50
BC78 Jamaal Charles RC 1.50 4.00
BC79 Ryan Torain RC 1.00 2.50
BC80 Mike Hart RC 1.00 2.50
BC81 Chauncey Washington RC .75 2.00
BC82 Dustin Keller RC 1.00 2.50
BC83 John Carlson RC 1.00 2.50
BC84 Andre Caldwell RC .75 2.00
BC85 Dexter Jackson RC .75 2.00
BC86 Malcolm Kelly RC .75 2.00
BC87 Donnie Avery RC .75 2.00
BC88 Devin Thomas RC .75 2.00
BC89 Jordy Nelson RC 1.25 3.00
BC90 James Hardy RC .75 2.00
BC91 Eddie Royal RC 1.00 2.50
BC92 Jerome Simpson RC 1.00 2.50
BC93 DeSean Jackson RC 2.00 5.00
BC94 Limas Sweed RC 1.00 2.50
BC95 Earl Bennett RC 1.00 2.50
BC96 Early Doucet RC .75 2.00
BC97 Harry Douglas RC .75 2.00
BC98 Mario Manningham RC 1.00 2.50
BC99 Lavelle Hawkins RC .60 1.50
BC100 Marcus Monk RC .75 2.00
BC101 Marcus Henry RC .75 2.00
BC102 Tashard Choice RC .75 2.00
BC103 DJ Hall RC .75 2.00
BC104 Jake Long RC 1.00 2.50
BC105 Jacob Hester RC 1.00 2.50
BC106 Owen Schmitt RC 1.00 2.50
BC107 Jerod Mayo RC 1.00 2.50
BC108 Chris Long RC 1.00 2.50
BC109 Vernon Gholston RC .75 2.00
BC110 Glenn Dorsey RC 1.00 2.50
BC111 Drew Brees .40 1.00
BC112 Tom Brady .60 1.50
BC113 Peyton Manning .60 1.50
BC114 Carson Palmer .40 1.00
BC115 Ben Roethlisberger .40 1.00
BC116 Eli Manning .40 1.00
BC117 Tony Romo .50 1.25
BC118 Vince Young .30 .75
BC119 Matt Hasselbeck .30 .75
BC120 David Garrard .30 .75
BC121 Jay Cutler .40 1.00
BC122 Derek Anderson .25 .60
BC123 Philip Rivers .40 1.00
BC124 Donovan McNabb .40 1.00
BC125 Matt Leinart .40 1.00
BC126 Jason Campbell .30 .75
BC127 JaMarcus Russell .30 .75
BC128 Jeff Garcia .30 .75
BC129 Brodie Croyle .30 .75
BC130 Marc Bulger .30 .75
BC131 Trent Edwards .25 .60
BC132 Kyle Boller .25 .60
BC133 Tarvaris Jackson .30 .75
BC134 Matt Schaub .30 .75
BC135 Aaron Rodgers .75 2.00
BC136 Steven Jackson .40 1.00
BC137 Willie Parker .30 .75
BC138 Clinton Portis .30 .75
BC139 Adrian Peterson .60 1.50
BC140 LaDainian Tomlinson .40 1.00
BC141 Marion Barber .30 .75
BC142 Brian Westbrook .30 .75
BC143 Fred Taylor .30 .75
BC144 Marshawn Lynch .30 .75
BC145 Joseph Addai .30 .75
BC146 Willis McGahee .30 .75
BC147 Frank Gore .30 .75
BC148 Julius Jones .25 .60
BC149 Thomas Jones .30 .75
BC150 Cedric Benson .30 .75
BC151 LenDale White .30 .75
BC152 Ryan Grant .40 1.00
BC153 Laurence Maroney .30 .75
BC154 Brandon Jacobs .30 .75
BC155 Jamal Lewis .30 .75
BC156 Larry Johnson .30 .75
BC157 Rudi Johnson .30 .75
BC158 Ahmad Bradshaw .30 .75
BC159 Justin Fargas .25 .60
BC160 Reggie Bush .40 1.00
BC161 Maurice Jones-Drew .30 .75
BC162 Michael Turner .40 1.00
BC163 Ronnie Brown .30 .75
BC164 DeAngelo Williams .30 .75
BC165 Edgerrin James .30 .75
BC166 Chad Johnson .30 .75
BC167 Reggie Wayne .30 .75
BC168 Anquan Boldin .30 .75
BC169 Randy Moss .40 1.00
BC170 Plaxico Burress .30 .75
BC171 Terrell Owens .40 1.00
BC172 Andre Johnson .30 .75
BC173 Larry Fitzgerald .40 1.00
BC174 Braylon Edwards .30 .75
BC175 Steve Smith .30 .75
BC176 Greg Jennings .40 1.00
BC177 Torry Holt .30 .75
BC178 T.J. Houshmandzadeh .30 .75
BC179 Jerricho Cotchery .30 .75
BC180 Joey Galloway .30 .75
BC181 Santonio Holmes .30 .75
BC182 Lee Evans .30 .75
BC183 Dwayne Bowe .30 .75
BC184 Laurent Robinson .25 .60
BC185 Wes Welker .40 1.00
BC186 Roy Williams WR .30 .75
BC187 Brandon Marshall .30 .75
BC188 Hines Ward .30 .75
BC189 Donald Driver .30 .75
BC190 Calvin Johnson .40 1.00
BC191 Marques Colston .30 .75
BC192 Chris Chambers .30 .75
BC193 Amani Toomer .30 .75
BC194 Bernard Berrian .30 .75
BC195 Sidney Rice .40 1.00
BC196 Anthony Gonzalez .25 .60
BC197 Steve Smith USC .30 .75
BC198 Ted Ginn Jr. .30 .75
BC199 Isaac Bruce .30 .75
BC200 Derrick Mason .30 .75
BC201 Roddy White .30 .75
BC202 Bobby Engram .25 .60
BC203 Reggie Williams .30 .75
BC204 Donte Stallworth .25 .60
BC205 Santana Moss .25 .60
BC206 Laveranues Coles .25 .60
BC207 Jerry Porter .25 .60
BC208 Shaun McDonald .25 .60
BC209 Dallas Clark .30 .75
BC210 Tony Gonzalez .30 .75
BC211 Kellen Winslow .30 .75
BC212 Antonio Gates .40 1.00
BC213 Jason Witten .40 1.00
BC214 Chris Cooley .30 .75
BC215 Brett Favre 1.00 2.50
BC216 Bob Sanders .30 .75
BC217 John Harbaugh CO RC .25 .60
BC218 Jon Kitna .30 .75
BC219 Tony Sparano CO RC .25 .60
BC220 Mike Smith CO RC .25 .60

2008 Bowman Chrome Blue Refractors

*1-55 ROOKIES: 2.5X TO 6X BASIC CARDS
1-55 BLUE REF/150 ODDS 1:192 BOW
*56-110 ROOKIES: 1.2X TO 3X BASIC CARDS
*111-220 VETS: 2.5X TO 6X BASIC CARDS
56-110 BLUE REF/150 ODDS 1:31 BOW CHR
BC59 Matt Ryan 25.00 50.00

2008 Bowman Chrome Gold Refractors

*1-55 ROOKIES: 4X TO 10X BASIC CARDS
1-55 GOLD REF/50 ODDS 1:575 BOW
*56-110 ROOKIES: 2.5X TO 6X BASIC CARDS
*111-220 VETS: 5X TO 12X BASIC CARDS
56-220 GOLD REF/50 ODDS 1:93 BOW CHR
BC59 Matt Ryan 60.00 100.00

2008 Bowman Chrome Orange Refractors

*1-55 ROOKIES: 6X TO 15X BASIC CARDS
1-55 ORANGE REF/25 ODDS 1:1139 BOW
*56-110 ROOKIES: 4X TO 10X BASIC CARDS
*111-220 VETS: 8X TO 20X BASIC CARDS
56-220 ORANGE REF/25 ODDS 1:185 BOW CHR
BC59 Matt Ryan 75.00 150.00

2008 Bowman Chrome Red Refractors

UNPRICED 1-55 RED REF/5 ODDS 1:4800 BOW
UNPRICED 56-220 RED REF/5 ODDS 1:940 BOW CHR

2008 Bowman Chrome Refractors

*1-55 ROOKIES: 1.5X TO 4X BASIC CARDS
1-55 REFRACTOR/500 ODDS 1:57 BOW
*56-110 ROOKIES: .6X TO 1.5X BASIC CARDS
*111-220 VETS: 1.2X TO 3X BASIC CARDS
56-220 REF INSERTED IN BOW CHR

2008 Bowman Chrome Rookies Bronze

*BRONZE/329: .8X TO 2X BASIC CARDS
BRONZE/329 ODDS 1:36 BOW CHR

2008 Bowman Chrome Rookies Silver

*SILVER: 1X TO 2.5X BASIC INSERTS
SILVER/199 ODDS 1:54 BOW CHR

2008 Bowman Chrome Superfractors

UNPRICED 1-55 SUPER/1 ODDS 1:11,770 BOW
UNPRICED 56-220 SUPER/1 ODDS 1:3200 BOW CHR

2008 Bowman Chrome Xfractors

*1-55 ROOKIES: 2X TO 5X BASIC CARDS
1-55 XFRACTOR/275 ODDS 1:103 BOW
*56-110 ROOKIES: 1X TO 2.5X BASIC CARDS
*111-220 VETS: 2X TO 5X BASIC CARDS
56-220 XFRCT/250 ODDS 1:19 BOW CHR

2008 Bowman Chrome Rookie Autographs

GROUP A ODDS 1:1380 HOB
GROUP B ODDS 1:865 HOB
GROUP C ODDS 1:878 HOB
GROUP D ODDS 1:172 HOB
GROUP E ODDS 1:662 HOB
GROUP F ODDS 1:134 HOB
GROUP G ODDS 1:33 HOB
UNPRICED RED REF/5 ODDS 1:2225 BOW CHR
UNPRICED SUPER/1 ODDS 1:10,481 BOW CHR
UNPRICED PRNT PLTE/1 ODDS 1:3518 BW CHR
UNPRICED SILVER/10 ODDS 1:1170 BOW CHR
BC59 Matt Ryan A 75.00 150.00
BC60 Chad Henne B 25.00 60.00
BC61 Joe Flacco A 60.00 120.00
BC70 Felix Jones A 30.00 60.00
BC71 Darren McFadden A 40.00 80.00
BC73 Ray Rice B 30.00 60.00
BC76 Chris Johnson C 50.00 100.00

2008 Bowman Chrome Rookie Autographs Blue Refractors

*BLUE REFRACT/35: .6X TO 1.5X GREEN AU
BLUE REFRACT/35 ODDS 1:371 BOW CHR
BC59 Matt Ryan 125.00 250.00
BC61 Joe Flacco 90.00 150.00
BC71 Darren McFadden 50.00 120.00
BC76 Chris Johnson 100.00 200.00

2008 Bowman Chrome Rookie Autographs Gold Refractors

*GOLD REFRACT/25: .8X TO 2X GREEN AU
GOLD REFRACT/25 ODDS 1:532 BOW CHR
UNPRICED GOLD REF JSY AU PRINT RUN 10
BC59 Matt Ryan 125.00 250.00
BC61 Joe Flacco 125.00 200.00
BC71 Darren McFadden 100.00 175.00
BC73 Ray Rice 75.00 150.00
BC76 Chris Johnson 100.00 200.00

2008 Bowman Chrome Rookie Autographs Green

GREEN AU/150 ODDS 1:93 BOWMAN
BC56 John David Booty 6.00 15.00
BC57 Brian Brohm 8.00 20.00
BC58 Kevin O'Connell 6.00 15.00
BC59 Matt Ryan 75.00 150.00
BC60 Chad Henne 20.00 50.00
BC61 Joe Flacco 60.00 120.00
BC62 Colt Brennan 8.00 20.00
BC63 Paul Smith 8.00 20.00
BC64 Erik Ainge 8.00 20.00
BC66 Josh Johnson 8.00 20.00
BC67 Dennis Dixon 10.00 25.00
BC68 Andre Woodson 8.00 20.00
BC69 Matt Forte 15.00 40.00
BC70 Felix Jones 20.00 50.00
BC71 Darren McFadden 40.00 80.00
BC72 Rashard Mendenhall 20.00 50.00
BC73 Ray Rice 25.00 60.00
BC74 Steve Slaton 8.00 20.00
BC75 Jonathan Stewart 12.00 30.00
BC76 Chris Johnson 75.00 150.00
BC77 Kevin Smith 8.00 20.00
BC78 Jamaal Charles 12.00 30.00
BC79 Ryan Torain 8.00 20.00
BC80 Mike Hart 8.00 20.00
BC81 Chauncey Washington 6.00 15.00
BC82 Dustin Keller 8.00 20.00
BC83 John Carlson 8.00 20.00
BC84 Andre Caldwell 6.00 15.00
BC85 Dexter Jackson 6.00 15.00
BC86 Malcolm Kelly 6.00 15.00
BC87 Donnie Avery 6.00 15.00
BC88 Devin Thomas 6.00 15.00
BC89 Jordy Nelson 20.00 40.00
BC90 James Hardy 6.00 15.00
BC91 Eddie Royal 8.00 20.00
BC92 Jerome Simpson 8.00 20.00
BC93 DeSean Jackson 25.00 50.00
BC94 Limas Sweed 8.00 20.00
BC95 Earl Bennett 8.00 20.00
BC96 Early Doucet 6.00 15.00
BC97 Harry Douglas 6.00 15.00
BC98 Mario Manningham 12.50 25.00
BC99 Lavelle Hawkins 5.00 12.00
BC100 Marcus Monk 6.00 15.00
BC101 Marcus Henry 6.00 15.00
BC102 Tashard Choice 6.00 15.00
BC103 DJ Hall 6.00 15.00
BC104 Jake Long 8.00 20.00
BC105 Jacob Hester 8.00 20.00
BC106 Owen Schmitt 8.00 20.00
BC107 Jerod Mayo 8.00 20.00
BC108 Chris Long 8.00 20.00
BC109 Vernon Gholston 6.00 15.00
BC110 Glenn Dorsey EXCH 8.00 20.00

2008 Bowman Chrome Rookie Autographs Orange Refractors

*ORANGE REFRACT/15: 1X TO 2.5X GREEN AU
ORANGE REFRACT/15 ODDS 1:760 BOW CHR
BC59 Matt Ryan 200.00 400.00
BC61 Joe Flacco 150.00 300.00
BC71 Darren McFadden 125.00 200.00
BC76 Chris Johnson 150.00 300.00

2008 Bowman Chrome Rookie Coaches Autographs

STATED ODDS 1:1550 BOW HOB
BRCJH John Harbaugh 8.00 20.00
BRCJZ Jim Zorn
BRCMS Mike Smith 8.00 20.00
BRCTS Tony Sparano 10.00 25.00

2009 Bowman Chrome

COMPLETE SET (165) 40.00 100.00
1 Drew Brees .30 .75
2 Ben Roethlisberger .30 .75
3 Eli Manning .30 .75
4 Tony Romo .50 1.25
5 Philip Rivers .30 .75
6 Aaron Rodgers .60 1.50
7 Marc Bulger .25 .60
8 Jay Cutler .30 .75
9 Matt Ryan .30 .75
10 Tom Brady .50 1.25
11 Carson Palmer .30 .75
12 Peyton Manning .50 1.25
13 Kerry Collins .25 .60
14 Kurt Warner .30 .75
15 Jason Campbell .20 .50
16 Chad Pennington .25 .60
17 Trent Edwards .20 .50
18 Matt Schaub .25 .60
19 Donovan McNabb .30 .75
20 Jared Allen .30 .75
21 Kyle Orton .25 .60
22 JaMarcus Russell .20 .50
23 Joe Flacco .30 .75
24 Jake Delhomme .25 .60
25 David Garrard .25 .60
26 Matt Cassel .25 .60
27 Derek Anderson .20 .50
28 Steven Jackson .25 .60
29 Clinton Portis .25 .60
30 Adrian Peterson .50 1.25
31 LaDainian Tomlinson .30 .75
32 Marion Barber .25 .60
33 Brian Westbrook .25 .60
34 Frank Gore .25 .60
35 Chris Johnson .30 .75
36 Michael Turner .25 .60
37 Brandon Jacobs .25 .60
38 Steve Slaton .25 .60
39 Matt Forte .30 .75
40 Leon Washington .25 .60
41 Fred Taylor .25 .60
42 Joseph Addai .30 .75
43 Willis McGahee .25 .60
44 Marshawn Lynch .25 .60
45 Thomas Jones .25 .60
46 DeAngelo Williams .30 .75
47 Earnest Graham .20 .50
48 Jamal Lewis .25 .60
49 John Carlson .25 .60
50 Ryan Grant .25 .60
51 Ronnie Brown .25 .60
52 Jonathan Stewart .25 .60
53 Kevin Boss .25 .60
54 Darren McFadden .30 .75
55 Maurice Jones-Drew .25 .60
56 LenDale White .25 .60
57 Pierre Thomas .25 .60
58 LaMarr Woodley .20 .50
59 Warrick Dunn .25 .60
60 Sammy Morris .20 .50
61 Reggie Bush .30 .75
62 Kevin Smith .25 .60
63 Ricky Williams .25 .60
64 Felix Jones .30 .75
65 Anquan Boldin .25 .60
66 Andre Johnson .25 .60
67 Larry Fitzgerald .30 .75
68 Steve Smith .25 .60
69 Greg Jennings .30 .75
70 Santana Moss .25 .60
71 Brandon Marshall .25 .60
72 T.J. Houshmandzadeh .25 .60
73 Eddie Royal .25 .60
74 Chad Ochocinco .25 .60
75 Troy Polamalu .30 .75
76 Terrell Owens .30 .75
77 Braylon Edwards .25 .60
78 Randy Moss .30 .75
79 Reggie Wayne .25 .60
80 Wes Welker .30 .75
81 Roddy White .25 .60
82 Dwayne Bowe .25 .60
83 Lance Moore .25 .60
84 Tim Hightower .20 .50
85 Antonio Bryant .20 .50
86 Jerricho Cotchery .25 .60
87 Laveranues Coles .20 .50
88 Derrick Mason .25 .60
89 Peyton Hillis .30 .75
90 Greg Camarillo .25 .60
91 DeSean Jackson .25 .60
92 Ed Reed .25 .60
93 Lee Evans .25 .60
94 Hines Ward .25 .60
95 Calvin Johnson .30 .75
96 Steve Smith USC .25 .60
97 Bernard Berrian .25 .60
98 Chris Cooley .25 .60
99 Tony Gonzalez .25 .60
100 Kevin Walter .25 .60
101 Antonio Gates .25 .60
102 Jason Witten .30 .75
103 Dallas Clark .25 .60
104 Joey Porter .25 .60
105 Patrick Willis .25 .60
106 DeMarcus Ware .25 .60
107 James Harrison .30 .75
108 Charles Woodson .30 .75
109 Oshiomogho Atogwe .20 .50
110 Justin Tuck .25 .60
111 Matthew Stafford RC 6.00 15.00
112 Josh Freeman RC 2.00 5.00
113 Nate Davis RC .75 2.00
114 Rhett Bomar RC .75 2.00
115 Mark Sanchez RC 3.00 8.00
116 Chris Wells RC 1.50 4.00
117 Javon Ringer RC 1.00 2.50
118 Deon Butler RC .75 2.00
119 Brandon Pettigrew RC 1.00 2.50
120 LeSean McCoy RC 2.00 5.00
121 Darrius Heyward-Bey RC 1.00 2.50
122 Ramses Barden RC .60 1.50
123 Derrick Williams RC .75 2.00
124 Hakeem Nicks RC 1.50 4.00
125 Aaron Curry RC 1.00 2.50
126 Patrick Turner RC .75 2.00
127 Knowshon Moreno RC 1.00 2.50
128 Brian Robiskie RC 1.00 2.50
129 Stephen McGee RC 1.00 2.50
130 Kenny Britt RC 1.25 3.00
131 Mohamed Massaquoi RC .75 2.00
132 Donald Brown RC 1.00 2.50
133 Juaquin Iglesias RC .75 2.00
134 Andre Brown RC .60 1.50
135 Michael Crabtree RC 2.00 5.00
136 Glen Coffee RC .75 2.00
137 Shonn Greene RC 1.50 4.00
138 Percy Harvin RC 1.50 4.00
139 Pat White RC 1.00 2.50
140 Jeremy Maclin RC 1.50 4.00
141 Jason Smith RC .75 2.00
142 Tyson Jackson RC .75 2.00
143 Mike Wallace RC 2.00 5.00
144 Mike Thomas RC 1.00 2.50
145 B.J. Raji RC 1.00 2.50
146 Aaron Maybin RC .75 2.00
147 Brian Orakpo RC 1.00 2.50
148 Malcolm Jenkins RC 1.00 2.50
149 Brian Cushing RC 1.00 2.50
150 Brian Hartline RC 1.00 2.50
151 Mike Goodson RC 1.00 2.50
152 Louis Murphy RC 1.00 2.50
153 Austin Collie RC 1.00 2.50
154 Gartrell Johnson RC .60 1.50
155 Johnny Knox RC 1.50 4.00
156 Kenny McKinley RC 1.00 2.50
157 Jarett Dillard RC 1.00 2.50
158 Brooks Foster RC .60 1.50
159 Tom Brandstater RC 1.00 2.50
160 Mike Teel RC 1.00 2.50
161 Cedric Peerman RC .75 2.00
162 Brandon Gibson RC 1.00 2.50
163 James Davis RC 1.00 2.50
164 Curtis Painter RC 1.00 2.50
165 Brandon Tate RC 1.00 2.50

2009 Bowman Chrome Blue Refractors

*VETS 1-110: 4X TO 10X BASIC CARDS
*ROOKIES 111-165: 1X TO 2.5X BASIC CARDS
BLUE REF/150 ODDS 1:20 HOB
111 Matthew Stafford 30.00 80.00

2009 Bowman Chrome Gold Refractors

*VETS 1-110: 6X TO 15X BASIC CARDS
*ROOKIES 111-165: 2X TO 5X BASIC CARDS
GOLD REF/50 ODDS 1:59 HOB
111 Matthew Stafford 60.00 150.00

2009 Bowman Chrome Green Refractors

*VETS 1-110: 5X TO 12X BASIC CARDS
*ROOKIES 111-165: 1.2X TO 3X BASIC CARDS
GREEN REF/99 ODDS 1:30
111 Matthew Stafford 40.00 100.00

2009 Bowman Chrome Orange Refractors

*VETS 1-110: 8X TO 20X BASIC CARDS
*ROOKIES 111-165: 2.5X TO 6X BASIC CARDS
ORANGE REF/25 ODDS 1:118 HOB
111 Matthew Stafford 100.00 200.00
115 Mark Sanchez 40.00 100.00

2009 Bowman Chrome Refractors

*VETS 1-110: 2X TO 5X BASIC CARDS
*ROOKIES 111-165: .5X TO 1.2X BASIC CARDS
REFRACTOR STATED ODDS 1:4

2009 Bowman Chrome Rookies Bronze

*ROOKIES 111-165: .6X TO 1.5X BASIC CARDS
BRONZE ROOKIE PRINT RUN 225 SER.#'d SETS

2009 Bowman Chrome Rookies Silver

*ROOKIES 111-165: 1X TO 2.5X BASIC CARDS
SILVER ROOKIE PRINT RUN 99 SER.#'d SETS

2009 Bowman Chrome Xfractors

*VETS 1-110: 2.5X TO 6X BASIC CARDS
*ROOKIES 111-165: .6X TO 1.5X BASIC CARDS
XFRACTOR/250 ODDS 1:12 HOB

2009 Bowman Chrome NFL Letter Autographs

JL James Laurinaitis/22*
TB Tom Brandstater/22*

2009 Bowman Chrome Rookie Autographs

GROUP A ODDS 1:655 HOB
GROUP B ODDS 1:165 HOB
GROUP C ODDS 1:174 HOB
GROUP D ODDS 1:186 HOB
GROUP E ODDS 1:39 HOB
111 Matthew Stafford A 90.00 150.00
112 Josh Freeman A 30.00 60.00
113 Nate Davis E 4.00 10.00
114 Rhett Bomar E 4.00 10.00
115 Mark Sanchez A 40.00 100.00
116 Chris Wells B 10.00 25.00
117 Javon Ringer D 5.00 12.00
118 Deon Butler E 4.00 10.00
119 Brandon Pettigrew B 5.00 12.00
120 LeSean McCoy B 20.00 50.00
121 Darrius Heyward-Bey A 5.00 12.00
122 Ramses Barden E 3.00 8.00
123 Derrick Williams D 4.00 10.00
124 Hakeem Nicks B 10.00 25.00
125 Aaron Curry B 5.00 12.00
126 Patrick Turner E 4.00 10.00
127 Knowshon Moreno A 12.00 30.00
128 Brian Robiskie B 6.00 15.00
129 Stephen McGee C 6.00 15.00
130 Kenny Britt B 10.00 25.00
131 Mohamed Massaquoi C 4.00 10.00
132 Donald Brown B 8.00 20.00
133 Juaquin Iglesias C 4.00 10.00
134 Andre Brown E 3.00 8.00
135 Michael Crabtree A 25.00 50.00

136 Glen Coffee C	4.00	10.00
137 Shonn Greene C	12.00	30.00
138 Percy Harvin C	25.00	50.00
139 Pat White B	5.00	12.00
140 Jeremy Maclin B	15.00	40.00
141 Jason Smith B	4.00	10.00
142 Tyson Jackson C	4.00	10.00
143 Mike Wallace D	15.00	40.00
144 Mike Thomas E	5.00	12.00
147 Brian Orakpo D	5.00	12.00
149 Brian Cushing D	5.00	12.00
150 Brian Hartline E	5.00	12.00
151 Mike Goodson E	5.00	12.00
153 Austin Collie E	6.00	15.00
154 Gartrell Johnson E	3.00	8.00
155 Johnny Knox E	10.00	25.00
157 Jarett Dillard E	5.00	12.00
158 Brooks Foster E	3.00	8.00
159 Tom Brandstater E	5.00	12.00
160 Mike Teel E	5.00	12.00
161 Cedric Peerman E	4.00	10.00
162 Brandon Gibson E	5.00	12.00
163 James Davis E	5.00	12.00
164 Curtis Painter E	5.00	12.00
165 Brandon Tate E	5.00	12.00

2009 Bowman Chrome Rookie Autographs Blue Refractors

*BLUE REF/35: .6X TO 1.5X BASIC AUTO
BLUE REF/35 ODDS 1:222 HOB

111 Matthew Stafford	150.00	250.00
112 Josh Freeman	60.00	120.00
115 Mark Sanchez	75.00	150.00

2009 Bowman Chrome Rookie Autographs Gold Refractors

*GOLD REF/25: 1X TO 2.5X BASIC AUTO
GOLD REF/25 ODDS 1:308 HOB

111 Matthew Stafford	200.00	350.00
112 Josh Freeman	75.00	150.00
115 Mark Sanchez	100.00	200.00

2009 Bowman Chrome Rookie Autographs Orange Refractors

*ORANGE REF/15: 1.2X TO 3X BASIC AUTO
ORANGE REF/15 ODDS 1:498 HOB

111 Matthew Stafford	250.00	400.00
112 Josh Freeman	100.00	200.00
115 Mark Sanchez	150.00	300.00

2010 Bowman Chrome Rookie Preview Inserts

STATED ODDS 1:12 TOPPS CHROME HOB
*REFRACT/99: 2.5X TO 6X BASIC INSERTS

BCR1 Tim Tebow	4.00	10.00
BCR2 C.J. Spiller	1.50	4.00
BCR3 Dez Bryant	3.00	8.00
BCR4 Golden Tate	1.00	2.50
BCR5 Sam Bradford	4.00	10.00
BCR6 Ryan Mathews	2.00	5.00
BCR7 Jahvid Best	1.50	4.00
BCR8 Colt McCoy	2.00	5.00
BCR9 Demaryius Thomas	1.25	3.00
BCR10 Jimmy Clausen	1.00	2.50
BCR11 Ndamukong Suh	2.00	5.00
BCR12 Arrelious Benn	1.00	2.50
BCR13 Ben Tate	1.25	3.00
BCR14 Jonathan Dwyer	1.00	2.50
BCR15 Eric Berry	1.00	2.50
BCR16 Damian Williams	1.00	2.50
BCR17 Armanti Edwards	1.00	2.50
BCR18 Emmanuel Sanders	1.00	2.50
BCR19 Rolando McClain	1.00	2.50
BCR20 Andre Roberts	1.00	2.50
BCR21 Eric Decker	1.25	3.00
BCR22 Joe McKnight	1.00	2.50
BCR23 Brandon LaFell	1.00	2.50
BCR24 Jordan Shipley	1.00	2.50
BCR25 Rob Gronkowski	2.50	6.00
BCR26 Dexter McCluster	1.00	2.50
BCR27 Jermaine Gresham	1.25	3.00
BCR28 Montario Hardesty	1.00	2.50
BCR29 Toby Gerhart	1.00	2.50
BCR30 Gerald McCoy	1.00	2.50

2010 Bowman Chrome Rookie Preview Inserts Autographs

AU/25 ODDS 1:2058 TOPPS CHROME

BCRA1 Tim Tebow	200.00	350.00
BCRA2 C.J. Spiller	30.00	80.00
BCRA3 Dez Bryant	100.00	200.00
BCRA4 Golden Tate	20.00	50.00
BCRA5 Sam Bradford	150.00	300.00
BCRA6 Ryan Mathews	60.00	120.00
BCRA7 Jahvid Best	40.00	80.00
BCRA8 Colt McCoy	75.00	150.00
BCRA9 Demaryius Thomas	40.00	80.00
BCRA10 Jimmy Clausen	20.00	50.00
BCRA11 Ndamukong Suh	75.00	150.00
BCRA12 Arrelious Benn	20.00	50.00
BCRA13 Ben Tate	40.00	80.00
BCRA14 Jonathan Dwyer	20.00	50.00
BCRA15 Eric Berry	20.00	50.00
BCRA16 Damian Williams	20.00	50.00
BCRA17 Armanti Edwards	20.00	50.00
BCRA18 Emmanuel Sanders	20.00	50.00
BCRA19 Rolando McClain	20.00	50.00
BCRA20 Andre Roberts	20.00	50.00
BCRA21 Eric Decker	25.00	60.00
BCRA22 Joe McKnight	20.00	50.00
BCRA23 Brandon LaFell	20.00	50.00
BCRA24 Jordan Shipley	20.00	50.00
BCRA25 Rob Gronkowski	100.00	175.00
BCRA26 Dexter McCluster	20.00	50.00
BCRA27 Jermaine Gresham	25.00	60.00
BCRA28 Montario Hardesty	20.00	50.00
BCRA29 Toby Gerhart	20.00	50.00
BCRA30 Gerald McCoy	20.00	50.00

2011 Bowman Chrome Rookie Preview Inserts

COMPLETE SET (30)	25.00	50.00

STATED ODDS 1:12 TOPPS CHROME HOB
*REFRACTOR/99: 3X TO 8X BASIC INSERTS

BCR1 Blaine Gabbert	1.50	4.00
BCR2 Jake Locker	2.50	6.00
BCR3 Cam Newton	5.00	12.00
BCR4 Ryan Mallett	2.00	5.00
BCR5 Mark Ingram	2.00	5.00
BCR6 Ryan Williams	1.25	3.00
BCR7 Mikel Leshoure	1.00	2.50
BCR8 A.J. Green	2.00	5.00
BCR9 Julio Jones	2.00	5.00
BCR10 Jon Baldwin	1.00	2.50
BCR11 Marcell Dareus	1.00	2.50
BCR12 Von Miller	1.25	3.00
BCR13 Andy Dalton	2.50	6.00
BCR14 Kyle Rudolph	1.00	2.50
BCR15 Christian Ponder	2.00	5.00
BCR16 Blaine Gabbert	1.50	4.00
BCR17 Jake Locker	2.50	6.00
BCR18 Cam Newton	5.00	12.00
BCR19 Ryan Mallett	2.00	5.00
BCR20 Mark Ingram	2.00	5.00
BCR21 Ryan Williams	1.25	3.00
BCR22 Mikel Leshoure	1.00	2.50
BCR23 A.J. Green	2.00	5.00
BCR24 Julio Jones	2.00	5.00
BCR25 Jon Baldwin	1.00	2.50
BCR26 Marcell Dareus	1.00	2.50
BCR27 Von Miller	1.25	3.00
BCR28 Andy Dalton	2.50	6.00
BCR29 Kyle Rudolph	1.00	2.50
BCR30 Christian Ponder	2.00	5.00

2011 Bowman Chrome Rookie Preview Inserts Autographs

STATED ODDS 1:477 TOP.CHROME HOB

BCAR1 Blaine Gabbert	30.00	80.00
BCAR2 Jake Locker	50.00	120.00
BCAR3 Cam Newton	250.00	450.00
BCAR4 Ryan Mallett	40.00	100.00
BCAR5 Mark Ingram	40.00	100.00
BCAR6 Ryan Williams	20.00	50.00
BCAR8 A.J. Green	40.00	100.00
BCAR9 Julio Jones		
BCAR10 Jon Baldwin	20.00	50.00
BCAR12 Von Miller	25.00	60.00
BCAR13 Andy Dalton EXCH	75.00	135.00
BCAR15 Christian Ponder	75.00	125.00
BCAR16 Blaine Gabbert	30.00	80.00
BCAR17 Jake Locker	50.00	120.00
BCAR18 Cam Newton	250.00	450.00
BCAR19 Ryan Mallett	40.00	100.00
BCAR20 Mark Ingram	40.00	100.00
BCAR21 Ryan Williams	20.00	50.00
BCAR23 A.J. Green	40.00	100.00
BCAR24 Julio Jones		
BCAR25 Jon Baldwin	20.00	50.00
BCAR27 Von Miller	25.00	60.00
BCAR28 Andy Dalton EXCH	75.00	135.00
BCAR30 Christian Ponder	75.00	125.00

2009 Bowman Draft

COMPLETE SET (220)	20.00	40.00
1 Drew Brees	.25	.60
2 Ben Roethlisberger	.25	.60
3 Eli Manning	.25	.60
4 Tony Romo	.40	1.00
5 Philip Rivers	.25	.60
6 Aaron Rodgers	.50	1.25
7 Brett Favre	.60	1.50
8 Jay Cutler	.25	.60
9 Matt Ryan	.25	.60
10 Tom Brady	.40	1.00
11 Carson Palmer	.25	.60
12 Peyton Manning	.40	1.00
13 Kerry Collins	.20	.50
14 Kurt Warner	.25	.60
15 Jason Campbell	.15	.40
16 Chad Pennington	.20	.50
17 Trent Edwards	.15	.40
18 Matt Schaub	.20	.50
19 Donovan McNabb	.25	.60
20 Jared Allen	.25	.60
21 Kyle Orton	.20	.50
22 JaMarcus Russell	.15	.40
23 Joe Flacco	.25	.60
24 Jake Delhomme	.20	.50
25 David Garrard	.20	.50
26 Matt Cassel	.20	.50
27 Derek Anderson	.15	.40
28 Steven Jackson	.20	.50
29 Clinton Portis	.20	.50
30 Adrian Peterson	.40	1.00
31 LaDainian Tomlinson	.25	.60
32 Marion Barber	.20	.50
33 Brian Westbrook	.20	.50
34 Frank Gore	.20	.50
35 Chris Johnson	.25	.60
36 Michael Turner	.20	.50
37 Brandon Jacobs	.20	.50
38 Steve Slaton	.20	.50
39 Matt Forte	.25	.60
40 Leon Washington	.20	.50
41 Fred Taylor	.20	.50
42 Joseph Addai	.25	.60
43 Willis McGahee	.20	.50
44 Marshawn Lynch	.20	.50
45 Thomas Jones	.20	.50
46 DeAngelo Williams	.25	.60
47 Earnest Graham	.15	.40
48 Jamal Lewis	.20	.50
49 John Carlson	.20	.50
50 Ryan Grant	.20	.50
51 Ronnie Brown	.20	.50
52 Jonathan Stewart	.20	.50
53 Kevin Boss	.20	.50
54 Darren McFadden	.25	.60
55 Maurice Jones-Drew	.20	.50
56 LenDale White	.20	.50
57 Pierre Thomas	.20	.50
58 LaMarr Woodley	.15	.40
59 Warrick Dunn	.20	.50
60 Sammy Morris	.15	.40
61 Reggie Bush	.25	.60
62 Kevin Smith	.20	.50
63 Ricky Williams	.20	.50
64 Felix Jones	.25	.60
65 Anquan Boldin	.20	.50
66 Andre Johnson	.20	.50
67 Larry Fitzgerald	.25	.60
68 Steve Smith	.20	.50
69 Greg Jennings	.25	.60
70 Santana Moss	.20	.50
71 Brandon Marshall	.20	.50
72 T.J. Houshmandzadeh	.20	.50
73 Eddie Royal	.20	.50
74 Chad Johnson	.20	.50
75 Troy Polamalu	.25	.60
76 Terrell Owens	.25	.60
77 Braylon Edwards	.20	.50
78 Randy Moss	.25	.60
79 Reggie Wayne	.20	.50
80 Wes Welker	.25	.60
81 Roddy White	.20	.50
82 Dwayne Bowe	.20	.50
83 Lance Moore	.20	.50
84 Tim Hightower	.15	.40
85 Antonio Bryant	.15	.40
86 Jerricho Cotchery	.20	.50
87 Laveranues Coles	.15	.40
88 Derrick Mason	.20	.50
89 Peyton Hillis	.25	.60
90 Greg Camarillo	.20	.50
91 DeSean Jackson	.20	.50
92 Ed Reed	.20	.50
93 Lee Evans	.20	.50
94 Hines Ward	.20	.50
95 Calvin Johnson	.25	.60
96 Steve Smith USC	.20	.50
97 Bernard Berrian	.20	.50
98 Chris Cooley	.20	.50
99 Tony Gonzalez	.20	.50
100 Kevin Walter	.20	.50
101 Antonio Gates	.20	.50
102 Jason Witten	.25	.60
103 Dallas Clark	.20	.50
104 Joey Porter	.20	.50
105 Patrick Willis	.20	.50
106 DeMarcus Ware	.20	.50
107 James Harrison	.25	.60
108 Charles Woodson	.25	.60
109 Oshiomogho Atogwe	.15	.40
110 Justin Tuck	.20	.50
111 Matthew Stafford RC	3.00	8.00
112 Brian Orakpo RC	.60	1.50
113 Michael Oher RC	1.00	2.50
114 Michael Crabtree RC	1.25	3.00
115 Andre Smith RC	.50	1.25
116 Knowshon Moreno RC	.60	1.50
117 Aaron Curry RC	.60	1.50
118 Gartrell Johnson RC	.40	1.00
119 Jason Smith RC	.50	1.25
120 James Laurinaitis RC	.60	1.50
121 Chris Wells RC	1.00	2.50
122 Glen Coffee RC	.50	1.25
123 Eugene Monroe RC	.40	1.00
124 Rey Maualuga RC	.60	1.50
125 Malcolm Jenkins RC	.60	1.50
126 Michael Johnson RC	.40	1.00
127 Javon Ringer RC	.60	1.50
128 B.J. Raji RC	.60	1.50
129 Donald Brown RC	.60	1.50
130 Clint Sintim RC	.60	1.50
131 Brian Cushing RC	.60	1.50
132 Brandon Pettigrew RC	.60	1.50
133 Alphonso Smith RC	.50	1.25
134 Vontae Davis RC	.60	1.50
135 Jeremy Maclin RC	1.00	2.50
136 John Parker Wilson RC	.60	1.50
137 Peria Jerry RC	.50	1.25
138 Chase Coffman RC	.50	1.25
139 Darius Butler RC	.60	1.50
140 Jamon Meredith RC	.50	1.25
141 Alex Mack RC	.50	1.25
142 Jarett Dillard RC	.60	1.50
143 Mike Mickens RC	.50	1.25
144 William Moore RC	.60	1.50
145 Austin Collie RC	.60	1.50
146 Fili Moala RC	.50	1.25
147 Percy Harvin RC	1.00	2.50
148 Jared Cook Jr. RC	.60	1.50
149 Rashad Jennings RC	.60	1.50
150 Rhett Bomar RC	.50	1.25
151 Sen'Derrick Marks RC	.40	1.00
152 Duke Robinson RC	.40	1.00
153 Everette Brown RC	.50	1.25
154 Darrius Heyward-Bey RC	.60	1.50
155 Jeremy Childs RC	.50	1.25
156 Darius Passmore RC	.50	1.25
157 Brooks Foster RC	.40	1.00
158 Tyson Jackson RC	.50	1.25
159 James Casey RC	.50	1.25
160 Marcus Freeman RC	.60	1.50
161 Max Unger RC	.50	1.25
162 Josh Freeman RC	1.25	3.00
163 Victor Harris RC	.60	1.50
164 Derrick Williams RC	.50	1.25
165 Jonathan Luigs RC	.40	1.00
166 Graham Harrell RC	.60	1.50
167 Pat White RC	.60	1.50
168 Chase Daniel RC	.60	1.50
169 Mike Goodson RC	.60	1.50
170 LeSean McCoy RC	1.25	3.00
171 James Davis RC	.60	1.50
172 Ramses Barden RC	.40	1.00
173 Juaquin Iglesias RC	.50	1.25
174 Cedric Peerman RC	.50	1.25
175 Kenny Britt RC	.75	2.00
176 Marlon Lucky RC	.50	1.25
177 Mohamed Massaquoi RC	.50	1.25
178 Louis Murphy RC	.60	1.50
179 Tyrell Sutton RC	.50	1.25
180 Andre Brown RC	.40	1.00
181 Brandon Tate RC	.60	1.50
182 Kory Sheets RC	.50	1.25
183 Arian Foster RC	1.25	3.00
184 Demetrius Byrd RC	.50	1.25
185 Hunter Cantwell RC	.60	1.50
186 Brandon Gibson RC	.60	1.50
187 Brian Robiskie RC	.60	1.50
188 Dannell Ellerbe RC	.50	1.25
189 Cornelius Ingram RC	.40	1.00
190 Mark Sanchez RC	2.00	5.00
191 Kenny McKinley RC	.60	1.50
192 Travis Beckum RC	.50	1.25
193 Jeremiah Johnson RC	.60	1.50
194 P.J. Hill RC	.50	1.25
195 Deon Butler RC	.50	1.25
196 Clay Matthews RC	1.50	4.00
197 Patrick Chung RC	.60	1.50
198 Patrick Turner RC	.50	1.25
199 Darry Beckwith RC	.50	1.25
200 Nate Davis RC	.50	1.25
201 Stephen McGee RC	.60	1.50
202 Aaron Kelly RC	.50	1.25
203 Ian Johnson RC	.60	1.50
204 Brian Hoyer RC	.60	1.50
205 Shonn Greene RC	1.00	2.50
206 Sammie Stroughter RC	.60	1.50
207 Cullen Harper RC	.60	1.50
208 Devin Moore RC	.50	1.25
209 Quan Cosby RC	.50	1.25
210 Hakeem Nicks RC	1.00	2.50
211 Kevin Ellison RC	.50	1.25
212 Phil Loadholt RC	.50	1.25
213 Scott McKillop RC	.50	1.25
214 Brad Lester RC	.40	1.00
215 Michael Hamlin RC	.50	1.25
216 Fenuki Tupou RC	.40	1.00
217 Terrance Taylor RC	.50	1.25
218 Zack Follett RC	.40	1.00
219 Aaron Maybin RC	.50	1.25
220 Worrell Williams RC	.50	1.25

2009 Bowman Draft Blue

*VETS: 3X TO 8X BASIC CARDS
*ROOKIES: 1X TO 2.5X BASIC CARDS
BLUE/199 ODDS 1:32 HOB

2009 Bowman Draft Bronze

*VETS: 4X TO 10X BASIC CARDS
*ROOKIES: 1.2X TO 3X BASIC CARDS
BRONZE/99 ODDS 1:67 HOB

2009 Bowman Draft Gold

*VETS: 12X TO 30X BASIC CARDS
*ROOKIES: 3X TO 8X BASIC CARDS
GOLD/10 ODDS 1:668 HOB

2009 Bowman Draft Orange

COMPLETE SET (220)	75.00	150.00

*VETS: 1.2X TO 3X BASIC CARDS
*ROOKIES: .5X TO 1.2X BASIC CARDS
ONE BASE PARALLEL PER PACK

2009 Bowman Draft Silver

*VETS: 5X TO 12X BASIC CARDS
*ROOKIES: 1.5X TO 4X BASIC CARDS
SILVER/50 ODDS 1:131 HOB

2009 Bowman Draft White

COMPLETE SET (220)	100.00	200.00

*VETS: 1.5X TO 4X BASIC CARDS
*ROOKIES: .6X TO 1.5X BASIC CARDS
WHITE/299 ODDS 1:22 HOB

2009 Bowman Draft All-Star Alumni

COMPLETE SET (10)	6.00	15.00

STATED ODDS 1:6
*BRONZE/99: 1X TO 2.5X BASIC INSERTS
BRONZE PRINT RUN 99 SER.#'d SETS
*GOLD/10: 4X TO 10X BASIC INSERTS
GOLD PRINT RUN 10 SER.#'d SETS
*SILVER/50: 1.2X TO 3X BASIC INSERTS
SILVER PRINT RUN 50 SER.#'d SETS

AA1 Matt Ryan	.75	2.00
AA2 Eli Manning	.75	2.00
AA3 Peyton Manning	1.25	3.00
AA4 Adrian Peterson	1.25	3.00
AA5 Andre Johnson	.60	1.50
AA6 Steve Slaton	.60	1.50
AA7 Matt Forte	.75	2.00
AA8 Larry Fitzgerald	.75	2.00
AA9 Eddie Royal	.60	1.50
AA10 DeAngelo Williams	.75	2.00

2009 Bowman Draft All-Star Alumni Combos

COMPLETE SET (10)	8.00	20.00

STATED ODDS 1:12
*BRONZE/99: .8X TO 2X BASIC INSERTS
BRONZE PRINT RUN 99 SER.#'d SETS
*GOLD/10: 3X TO 8X BASIC INSERTS
GOLD PRINT RUN 10 SER.#'d SETS
*SILVER/50: 1X TO 2.5X BASIC INSERTS
SILVER PRINT RUN 50 SER.#'d SETS

AAC1 Matt Ryan Mathias Kiwanuka	1.00	2.50
AAC2 Eli Manning Patrick Willis	1.00	2.50
AAC3 Peyton Manning Jerod Mayo	1.50	4.00
AAC4 Andre Johnson Kellen Winslow	.75	2.00
AAC5 Joseph Addai Dwayne Bowe	1.00	2.50
AAC6 Marshawn Lynch DeSean Jackson	.75	2.00
AAC7 Brandon Marshall Kevin Smith	.75	2.00
AAC8 Reggie Bush Troy Polamalu	1.00	2.50
AAC9 Tom Brady Braylon Edwards	1.50	4.00
AAC10 Larry Fitzgerald Darrelle Revis	1.00	2.50

2009 Bowman Draft College Letter Patch Autographs

GROUP A ODDS 1:915
GROUP B ODDS 1:1250
GROUP C ODDS 1:375
GROUP D ODDS 1:336
GROUP E ODDS 1:160
GROUP F ODDS 1:125
GROUP G ODDS 1:104
TOTAL PRINT RUNS GIVEN BELOW
EXCH EXPIRATION: 5/31/2012

AB Andre Brown F/920* (serial numbered to 184)	5.00	12.00
AC Austin Collie E/690* (serial numbered to 115)	10.00	25.00
ACU Aaron Curry A/100* (serial numbered to 20)	20.00	50.00
AF Arian Foster D/468* (serial numbered to 78)	30.00	60.00
AK Aaron Kelly F/920* (serial numbered to 184)	6.00	15.00
BC Brian Cushing A/63* (serial numbered to 9)	12.00	30.00
BF Brooks Foster G/1038* (serial numbered to 173)	5.00	12.00
BG Brandon Gibson G/1038 (serial numbered to 173)	8.00	20.00
BO Brian Orakpo C/270* (serial numbered to 45)	15.00	40.00
BP Brandon Pettigrew D/360* (serial numbered to 40)	8.00	20.00
CC Chase Coffman B/105* (serial numbered to 15)	8.00	20.00
CD Chase Daniel A/72* (serial numbered to 12)	12.00	30.00
CH Cullen Harper D/480* (serial numbered to 80)	8.00	20.00
CP Cedric Peerman E/700* (serial numbered to 100)	6.00	15.00
CW Chris Wells A/60* (serial numbered to 12)	25.00	60.00
DB Donald Brown C/275* (serial numbered to 55)	10.00	25.00
DBY Demetrius Byrd F/920* (serial numbered to 230)	6.00	15.00
DHB Darrius Heyward-Bey B/130* (serial numbered to 13)	10.00	25.00
DM Devin Moore D/460* (serial numbered to 92)	6.00	15.00
DP Darius Passmore G/1040* (serial numbered to 130)	6.00	15.00
DW Derrick Williams C/232* (serial numbered to 29)	8.00	20.00
GC Glen Coffee E/690* (serial numbered to 115)	12.00	30.00
GH Graham Harrell A/84* (serial numbered to 12)	20.00	50.00
GJ Gartrell Johnson F/945* (serial numbered to 135)	5.00	12.00
HN Hakeem Nicks A/85* (serial numbered to 17)	20.00	50.00
IJ Ian Johnson G/1050* (serial numbered to 150)	8.00	20.00
JC Jeremy Childs F/930* (serial numbered to 155)	6.00	15.00
JCO Jared Cook D/360* (serial numbered to 90)	8.00	20.00
JD Jarett Dillard G/1050* (serial numbered to 150)	8.00	20.00
JDA James Davis C	10.00	25.00
JF Josh Freeman B/112* (serial numbered to 112)	20.00	50.00
JI Juaquin Iglesias B	8.00	20.00
JJ Jeremiah Johnson E/700 (serial numbered to 100)	8.00	20.00
JL James Laurinaitis B/132* (serial numbered to 12)	15.00	40.00
JM Jeremy Maclin A/54* (serial numbered to 9)	20.00	50.00
JMS Matthew Stafford A/64* (serial numbered to 8)	75.00	150.00
JPW John Parker Wilson B/120* (serial numbered to 10)	10.00	25.00
JR Javon Ringer C/240* (serial numbered to 40)	10.00	25.00
JW Jaison Williams G/1040* (serial numbered to 130)	6.00	15.00
KB Kenny Britt C/230* (serial numbered to 46)	12.00	30.00
KM Knowshon Moreno A/78* (serial numbered to 13)	25.00	60.00
KS Kory Sheets G/1050* (serial numbered to 175)	6.00	15.00
LM Louis Murphy F/930* (serial numbered to 155)	8.00	20.00
LMC LeSean McCoy C/260* (serial numbered to 52)	25.00	60.00
MC Michael Crabtree A/56* (serial numbered to 7)	30.00	80.00
MJ Malcolm Jenkins A/56* (serial numbered to 8)	12.00	30.00
MJO Michael Johnson D/455* (serial numbered to 65)	5.00	12.00
ML Marlon Lucky G/1035* (serial numbered to 207)	6.00	15.00
MM Mohamed Massaquoi E/702* (serial numbered to 78)	6.00	15.00
MS Mark Sanchez A/56* (serial numbered to 8)	75.00	150.00
ND Nate Davis A/100* (serial numbered to 20)	10.00	25.00
PH Percy Harvin A/90* (serial numbered to 15)	50.00	120.00
PJH P.J. Hill E/692* (serial numbered to 173)	6.00	15.00
PW Pat White A/85* (serial numbered to 17)	20.00	50.00
QC Quan Cosby F/920* (serial numbered to) 184	6.00	15.00
RB Ramses Barden C/240* (serial numbered to 40)	6.00	15.00
RBO Rhett Bomar B115* (serial numbered to 23)	8.00	20.00
RJ Rashad Jennings C232* (serial numbered to 29)	10.00	25.00
RM Rey Maualuga A/64* (serial numbered to 8)	12.00	30.00
SG Shonn Greene C/216* (serial numbered to 36)	20.00	50.00
SS Sammie Stroughter F/920* (serial numbered to 92)	8.00	20.00
TS Tyrell Sutton E/690* (serial numbered to 115)	6.00	15.00

2009 Bowman Draft College Logo Patch Autographs

VARIATIONS: .4X TO 1X BASIC INSERTS
GROUP A/25 ODDS 1:5800
GROUP B/40 ODDS 1:1700
GROUP C/75 ODDS 1:399
GROUP D/250 ODDS 1:224
GROUP E/300 ODDS 1:301
EXCH EXPIRATION: 5/31/2012

AB Andre Brown/300 NCS	5.00	12.00
AC Austin Collie/250 BYU	10.00	25.00
AF Arian Foster/75 T	40.00	80.00
BG Brandon Gibson/300 Cougars	8.00	20.00
CD Chase Daniel/40 Missouri	12.00	30.00
CP Cedric Peerman/250 V	6.00	15.00
CW Chris Wells/40 Ohio State	30.00	80.00
DB Donald Brown/40 UConn	12.00	30.00
DM Devin Moore/75 UW	8.00	20.00
DW Derrick Williams/75 paw print	15.00	40.00
GC Glen Coffee/250 A	12.00	30.00
GH Graham Harrell/40 TT	20.00	50.00
HN Hakeem Nicks/75 NC	15.00	40.00
IJ Ian Johnson	8.00	20.00
JC Jared Cook/75 C	10.00	25.00
JD Jarett Dillard/300 R	8.00	20.00
JF Josh Freeman/75 wildcat head	20.00	50.00
JI Juaquin Iglesias/75 OU	8.00	20.00
JJ Jeremiah Johnson/250 O	8.00	20.00
JL James Laurinaitis/75 Ohio State	15.00	40.00
JM Jeremy Maclin/40 Missouri	20.00	50.00
KB Kenny Britt/75 R	12.00	30.00
KM Knowshon Moreno/25 G	40.00	100.00
KS Kory Sheets P	6.00	15.00
LM Louis Murphy/300 Gators	8.00	20.00
MC Michael Crabtree/25 TT	40.00	100.00
MM Mohamed Massaquoi/250 G	6.00	15.00
MS Matthew Stafford/25 G	75.00	150.00
ND Nate Davis/40 Hemet	10.00	25.00
PH Percy Harvin/40 Gators	50.00	120.00
QC Quan Cosby/300 UT	6.00	15.00
RB Ramses Barden/75 CP	15.00	30.00
RJ Rashad Jennings/75 LU	10.00	25.00
TS Tyrell Sutton/250 NU	6.00	15.00
WM William Moore/75 Missouri	10.00	25.00
JDA James Davis/75 EXCH	10.00	25.00
JPW John Parker Wilson/75 A	15.00	30.00
LMC LeSean McCoy/40	25.00	60.00
MSA Mark Sanchez/25 USC	75.00	150.00
PJH P.J. Hill/250 W	6.00	15.00
RBO Rhett Bomar/75 SH Paw	8.00	20.00

2009 Bowman Draft Rivals

COMPLETE SET (10)	10.00	25.00

STATED ODDS 1:12
*BRONZE/99: .8X TO 2X BASIC INSERTS
BRONZE PRINT RUN 99 SER.#'d SETS
*GOLD/10: 3X TO 8X BASIC INSERTS
GOLD PRINT RUN 10 SER.#'d SETS
*SILVER/50: 1X TO 2.5X BASIC INSERTS
SILVER PRINT RUN 50 SER.#'d SETS

R1 Jeremy Maclin Vontae Davis	1.00	2.50
R2 Pat White LeSean McCoy	1.25	3.00
R3 Javon Ringer Derrick Williams	.60	1.50
R4 Terrance Taylor Chris Wells	1.00	2.50
R5 Knowshon Moreno Percy Harvin	1.00	2.50
R6 Jeremiah Johnson Sammie Stroughter	.60	1.50
R7 James Laurinaitis Deon Butler	.60	1.50
R8 Andre Smith Sen'Derrick Marks	.50	1.25
R9 Marlon Lucky Juaquin Iglesias	.50	1.25
R10 Worrell Williams Rey Maualuga	.60	1.50

2009 Bowman Draft Rookie All-Stars

COMPLETE SET (20)	20.00	40.00

STATED ODDS 1:6
*BRONZE/99: .8X TO 2X BASIC INSERTS
BRONZE PRINT RUN 99 SER.#'d SETS
*GOLD/10: 3X TO 8X BASIC INSERTS
GOLD PRINT RUN 10 SER.#'d SETS
*SILVER/50: 1X TO 2.5X BASIC INSERTS
SILVER PRINT RUN 50 SER.#'d SETS

AS1 Knowshon Moreno	.60	1.50
AS2 Brian Orakpo	.60	1.50
AS3 Rey Maualuga	.60	1.50
AS4 Chris Wells	1.00	2.50
AS5 Michael Crabtree	1.25	3.00
AS6 Aaron Curry	.60	1.50
AS7 Jeremy Maclin	1.00	2.50
AS8 Chase Coffman	.50	1.25
AS9 Darrius Heyward-Bey	.60	1.50
AS10 Matthew Stafford	3.00	8.00
AS11 Vontae Davis	.60	1.50
AS12 James Davis	.60	1.50
AS13 Percy Harvin	1.00	2.50
AS14 Brandon Pettigrew	.60	1.50
AS15 Malcolm Jenkins	.60	1.50
AS16 Shonn Greene	1.00	2.50
AS17 Javon Ringer	.60	1.50
AS18 LeSean McCoy	1.25	3.00
AS19 Hakeem Nicks	1.00	2.50
AS20 Mark Sanchez	2.00	5.00

2009 Bowman Draft Rookie All-Stars Combos

COMPLETE SET (10)	8.00	20.00

STATED ODDS 1:12
*BRONZE/99: .8X TO 2X BASIC INSERTS
BRONZE PRINT RUN 99 SER.#'d SETS
*GOLD/10: 3X TO 8X BASIC INSERTS
GOLD PRINT RUN 10 SER.#'d SETS
*SILVER/50: 1X TO 2.5X BASIC INSERTS
SILVER PRINT RUN 50 SER.#'d SETS

ASC1 Louis Murphy Percy Harvin	1.00	2.50
ASC2 Matthew Stafford Knowshon Moreno	3.00	8.00
ASC3 Chase Daniel Chase Coffman	.60	1.50
ASC4 Malcolm Jenkins James Laurinaitis	.60	1.50
ASC5 Mark Sanchez Clay Matthews	2.00	5.00
ASC6 Graham Harrell Michael Crabtree	1.25	3.00
ASC7 Brian Cushing Rey Maualuga	.60	1.50
ASC8 Aaron Curry Alphonso Smith	.60	1.50
ASC9 Cullen Harper James Davis	.60	1.50
ASC10 Juaquin Iglesias Duke Robinson	.50	1.25

2009 Bowman Draft Rookie Autographs

GROUP A ODDS 1:229
GROUP B ODDS 1:66
GROUP C ODDS 1:1050
GROUP D ODDS 1:200
GROUP E ODDS 1:725
GROUP F ODDS 1:575
EXCH EXPIRATION: 5/31/2012

111 Matthew Stafford A	60.00	120.00
112 Brian Orakpo A	6.00	15.00
114 Michael Crabtree A	25.00	60.00
116 Knowshon Moreno A	20.00	50.00
117 Aaron Curry A	6.00	15.00
118 Gartrell Johnson B	4.00	10.00
120 James Laurinaitis A	6.00	15.00
121 Chris Wells A	20.00	50.00
122 Glen Coffee B	5.00	12.00
124 Rey Maualuga A	6.00	15.00
125 Malcolm Jenkins A	6.00	15.00
126 Michael Johnson A	4.00	10.00
127 Javon Ringer A	6.00	15.00
129 Donald Brown A	6.00	15.00
131 Brian Cushing A	6.00	15.00
132 Brandon Pettigrew A	6.00	15.00
135 Jeremy Maclin A	15.00	40.00
136 John Parker Wilson B	6.00	15.00
138 Chase Coffman A	5.00	12.00
142 Jarett Dillard B	6.00	15.00
145 Austin Collie E	8.00	20.00
147 Percy Harvin A	25.00	60.00
148 Jared Cook A	6.00	15.00
149 Rashad Jennings A	6.00	15.00
150 Rhett Bomar A	5.00	12.00
154 Darrius Heyward-Bey A	6.00	15.00
155 Jeremy Childs B	5.00	12.00
156 Darius Passmore B	5.00	12.00
157 Brooks Foster B	4.00	10.00
159 James Casey	5.00	12.00
162 Josh Freeman A	12.00	30.00
164 Derrick Williams A	5.00	12.00
166 Graham Harrell A	10.00	25.00
167 Pat White A	6.00	15.00
168 Chase Daniel A	6.00	15.00
170 LeSean McCoy A	15.00	40.00
171 James Davis A	6.00	15.00
172 Ramses Barden A	4.00	10.00
173 Juaquin Iglesias A	5.00	12.00
174 Cedric Peerman D	5.00	12.00
175 Kenny Britt A	8.00	20.00
176 Marlon Lucky B	5.00	12.00
177 Mohamed Massaquoi B	5.00	12.00
179 Tyrell Sutton B	5.00	12.00
180 Andre Brown B	4.00	10.00
182 Kory Sheets D	5.00	12.00
183 Arian Foster B	40.00	80.00
184 Demetrius Byrd B	5.00	12.00
186 Brandon Gibson B	6.00	15.00
190 Mark Sanchez A	50.00	120.00
193 Jeremiah Johnson B	6.00	15.00
194 P.J. Hill B	5.00	12.00
200 Nate Davis A	5.00	12.00
201 Stephen McGee	6.00	15.00
202 Aaron Kelly B	5.00	12.00
203 Ian Johnson D	6.00	15.00
205 Shonn Greene A	10.00	25.00
206 Sammie Stroughter F	6.00	15.00
207 Cullen Harper A	6.00	15.00
208 Devin Moore B	5.00	12.00
209 Quan Cosby C	5.00	12.00
210 Hakeem Nicks A	12.00	30.00

2009 Bowman Draft Rookie Autographs Bronze

BRONZE/99 STATED ODDS 1:115
*SILVER/50: .5X TO 1.2X BRONZE/99 AU
SILVER/50 ODDS 1:220
EXCH EXPIRATION: 5/31/2012

111 Matthew Stafford	75.00	150.00
112 Brian Orakpo	8.00	20.00
114 Michael Crabtree	30.00	80.00
116 Knowshon Moreno	20.00	50.00
117 Aaron Curry	8.00	20.00
118 Gartrell Johnson	5.00	12.00
120 James Laurinaitis	8.00	20.00
121 Chris Wells	12.00	30.00
122 Glen Coffee	6.00	15.00
124 Rey Maualuga	8.00	20.00
125 Malcolm Jenkins	8.00	20.00
126 Michael Johnson	5.00	12.00
127 Javon Ringer	8.00	20.00
129 Donald Brown	8.00	20.00
131 Brian Cushing	8.00	20.00
132 Brandon Pettigrew	8.00	20.00
135 Jeremy Maclin	12.00	30.00
136 John Parker Wilson	8.00	20.00
138 Chase Coffman	6.00	15.00
142 Jarett Dillard	8.00	20.00
145 Austin Collie	10.00	25.00
147 Percy Harvin	30.00	80.00
148 Jared Cook	8.00	20.00
149 Rashad Jennings	8.00	20.00
150 Rhett Bomar	6.00	15.00
154 Darrius Heyward-Bey	8.00	20.00
155 Jeremy Childs	6.00	15.00
156 Darius Passmore	6.00	15.00
157 Brooks Foster	5.00	12.00
159 James Casey	6.00	15.00
162 Josh Freeman	15.00	40.00
164 Derrick Williams	6.00	15.00
166 Graham Harrell	12.00	30.00
167 Pat White	8.00	20.00
168 Chase Daniel	8.00	20.00
170 LeSean McCoy	15.00	40.00
171 James Davis	8.00	20.00
172 Ramses Barden	5.00	12.00
173 Juaquin Iglesias	6.00	15.00
174 Cedric Peerman	6.00	15.00
175 Kenny Britt	10.00	25.00
176 Marlon Lucky	6.00	15.00
177 Mohamed Massaquoi	6.00	15.00
179 Tyrell Sutton	6.00	15.00
180 Andre Brown	5.00	12.00
182 Kory Sheets	6.00	15.00
183 Arian Foster	40.00	100.00
184 Demetrius Byrd	6.00	15.00
186 Brandon Gibson	8.00	20.00
190 Mark Sanchez	75.00	150.00
193 Jeremiah Johnson	8.00	20.00
194 P.J. Hill	6.00	15.00
200 Nate Davis	6.00	15.00
201 Stephen McGee	8.00	20.00
202 Aaron Kelly	6.00	15.00
203 Ian Johnson	8.00	20.00
205 Shonn Greene	12.00	30.00
206 Sammie Stroughter	8.00	20.00
207 Cullen Harper	8.00	20.00
208 Devin Moore	6.00	15.00
209 Quan Cosby	6.00	15.00
210 Hakeem Nicks	15.00	40.00

2009 Bowman Draft Superlatives

COMPLETE SET (10)	6.00	15.00

STATED ODDS 1:6
*BRONZE/99: 1X TO 2.5X BASIC INSERTS
BRONZE PRINT RUN 99 SER.#'d SETS
*GOLD/10: 4X TO 10X BASIC INSERTS
GOLD PRINT RUN 10 SER.#'d SETS
*SILVER/50: 1.2X TO 3X BASIC INSERTS
SILVER PRINT RUN 50 SER.#'d SETS

S1 Chase Coffman	.40	1.00
S2 Brian Orakpo	.50	1.25
S3 Aaron Curry	.50	1.25
S4 Andre Smith	.40	1.00
S5 Rey Maualuga	.50	1.25
S6 Graham Harrell	.50	1.25
S7 Shonn Greene	.75	2.00
S8 Brian Orakpo	.50	1.25
S9 Michael Crabtree	1.00	2.50
S10 Malcolm Jenkins	.50	1.25

2000 Bowman Reserve

Released in late November 2000, Bowman Reserve features a 125-card base set consisting of 100 Veterans and 25 Rookies sequentially numbered to 999. Base cards are printed on an all foil chromium refractor stock and carry an embossed Bowman Reserve logo behind action photography. Bowman Reserve was released in boxes containing 10 packs and one Rookie Autographed Mini Helmet. Boxes carried a suggested retail price of $129.99.

COMP.SET w/o RCs (100)	15.00	40.00
1 Chad Pennington RC	6.00	15.00
2 Shaun Alexander RC	5.00	12.00
3 Thomas Jones RC	5.00	12.00
4 Courtney Brown RC	3.00	8.00
5 Curtis Keaton RC	2.50	6.00
6 Jerry Porter RC	4.00	10.00
7 Jamal Lewis RC	4.00	10.00
8 Ron Dayne RC	4.00	10.00
9 R.Jay Soward RC	2.50	6.00
10 Tee Martin RC	4.00	10.00
11 Travis Taylor RC	3.00	8.00
12 Plaxico Burress RC	4.00	10.00
13 Giovanni Carmazzi RC	2.50	6.00
14 Sylvester Morris RC	2.50	6.00
15 Chris Redman RC	3.00	8.00
16 Trung Canidate RC	3.00	8.00
17 J.R. Redmond RC	2.50	6.00
18 Bubba Franks RC	4.00	10.00
19 Travis Prentice RC	3.00	8.00
20 Peter Warrick RC	4.00	10.00
21 Frank Sanders	.25	.60
22 Edgerrin James	.40	1.00
23 Marcus Robinson	.30	.75
24 Mike Alstott	.40	1.00
25 Jerry Rice	.75	2.00
26 Marshall Faulk	.40	1.00
27 Brad Johnson	.30	.75
28 Elvis Grbac	.25	.60
29 Wayne Chrebet	.30	.75
30 Akili Smith	.25	.60
31 Rob Johnson	.30	.75
32 Brett Favre	1.25	3.00
33 Ricky Williams	.40	1.00
34 Donovan McNabb	.40	1.00
35 Cris Carter	.40	1.00
36 Ricky Watters	.30	.75
37 Steve McNair	.40	1.00
38 Stephen Davis	.30	.75
39 Fred Taylor	.40	1.00
40 Rocket Ismail	.30	.75
41 Terry Glenn	.30	.75
42 Ed McCaffrey	.30	.75
43 Patrick Jeffers	.30	.75
44 Jake Plummer	.30	.75
45 Doug Flutie	.40	1.00
46 Terrell Davis	.40	1.00

47 Marvin Harrison	.40	1.00
48 Amani Toomer	.30	.75
49 Tyrone Wheatley	.25	.60
50 Charlie Garner	.30	.75
51 Jevon Kearse	.30	.75
52 Michael Westbrook	.25	.60
53 Eddie George	.30	.75
54 Robert Smith	.30	.75
55 Keyshawn Johnson	.30	.75
56 Torry Holt	.40	1.00
57 Jon Kitna	.30	.75
58 Curtis Conway	.30	.75
59 Jeff Garcia	.30	.75
60 Randy Moss	.40	1.00
61 Jimmy Smith	.30	.75
62 James Stewart	.25	.60
63 Troy Aikman	.60	1.50
64 Cade McNown	.25	.60
65 Natrone Means	.30	.75
66 Jamal Anderson	.30	.75
67 Warrick Dunn	.30	.75
68 Kordell Stewart	.30	.75
69 Duce Staley	.30	.75
70 Rich Gannon	.30	.75
71 Curtis Martin	.40	1.00
72 Kerry Collins	.30	.75
73 Jeff Blake	.30	.75
74 Drew Bledsoe	.40	1.00
75 Kevin Dyson	.30	.75
76 Tony Gonzalez	.40	1.00
77 Mark Brunell	.30	.75
78 Peyton Manning	1.00	2.50
79 Dorsey Levens	.30	.75
80 Germane Crowell	.25	.60
81 Brian Griese	.30	.75
82 Steve Beuerlein	.30	.75
83 Eric Moulds	.30	.75
84 Tony Banks	.25	.60
85 Chris Chandler	.30	.75
86 Isaac Bruce	.40	1.00
87 Terrell Owens	.40	1.00
88 Jerome Bettis	.40	1.00
89 Daunte Culpepper	.30	.75
90 Emmitt Smith	1.00	2.50
91 Curtis Enis	.25	.60
92 Shaun King	.25	.60
93 Tim Brown	.40	1.00
94 Antonio Freeman	.30	.75
95 Charlie Batch	.30	.75
96 Tim Couch	.30	.75
97 Corey Dillon	.30	.75
98 Muhsin Muhammad	.30	.75
99 Joey Galloway	.30	.75
100 Kurt Warner	.60	1.50
101 David Boston	.25	.60
102 Rod Smith	.30	.75
103 Derrick Mayes	.25	.60
104 Tony Martin	.30	.75
105 Darnay Scott	.30	.75
106 Joe Horn	.30	.75
107 Troy Edwards	.25	.60
108 James Johnson	.25	.60
109 Vinny Testaverde	.30	.75
110 Qadry Ismail	.30	.75
111 Andre Reed	.40	1.00
112 Zach Thomas	.40	1.00
113 Ike Hilliard	.30	.75
114 Herman Moore	.30	.75
115 Kevin Johnson	.25	.60
116 Shawn Jefferson	.25	.60
117 Terance Mathis	.25	.60
118 Peerless Price	.30	.75
119 Bert Emanuel	.25	.60
120 Terrence Wilkins	.25	.60
121 Mike Anderson RC	4.00	10.00
122 Dez White RC	3.00	8.00
123 Todd Pinkston RC	2.50	6.00
124 Reuben Droughns RC	4.00	10.00
125 Danny Farmer RC	2.50	6.00

2000 Bowman Reserve Autographs

STATED ODDS 1:10 HOBBY		
DC Daunte Culpepper	6.00	15.00
EJ Edgerrin James	8.00	20.00
GC Germane Crowell	5.00	12.00
KJ Kevin Johnson	5.00	12.00
MF Marshall Faulk	20.00	50.00
MR Marcus Robinson	6.00	15.00
TG Tony Gonzalez	15.00	30.00
TH Torry Holt	8.00	20.00

2000 Bowman Reserve Mini Helmet Autographs

ONE PER HOBBY GIFT BOX		
1 Shaun Alexander	20.00	50.00
2 Courtney Brown	12.50	25.00
3 Plaxico Burress	20.00	50.00
4 Trung Canidate	12.50	25.00
5 Giovanni Carmazzi	12.50	25.00
6 Laveranues Coles	12.50	25.00
7 Ron Dayne	15.00	40.00
8 Danny Farmer	12.50	25.00
9 Darrell Jackson	15.00	40.00
10 Thomas Jones	15.00	40.00
11 Jamal Lewis	15.00	40.00
12 Sylvester Morris	12.50	25.00
13 Chad Pennington	30.00	60.00
14 Todd Pinkston	12.50	25.00
15 Travis Prentice	12.50	25.00
16 Chris Redman	12.50	25.00
17 J.R. Redmond	12.50	25.00
18 R.Jay Soward	12.50	25.00
19 Brian Urlacher	50.00	100.00
20 Peter Warrick	15.00	40.00
21 Dez White	12.50	25.00
22 Mike Anderson	15.00	40.00

2000 Bowman Reserve Pro Bowl Jerseys

STATED ODDS 1:10 HOBBY		
PBBJ Brad Johnson	8.00	20.00
PBBM Bruce Matthews	8.00	20.00
PBCB Chad Brown	6.00	15.00
PBCC Cris Carter	10.00	25.00
PBCD Corey Dillon	8.00	20.00
PBCK Cortez Kennedy	6.00	15.00
PBCL Carnell Lake	6.00	15.00
PBCW Charles Woodson	10.00	25.00
PBDB Derrick Brooks	10.00	25.00
PBDR Darrell Russell	6.00	15.00
PBEG Eddie George	8.00	20.00
PBEJ Edgerrin James	10.00	25.00
PBEM Emmitt Smith	25.00	60.00
PBFW Frank Wycheck	8.00	20.00
PBGM Glyn Milburn	6.00	15.00
PBHN Hardy Nickerson	6.00	15.00
PBIB Isaac Bruce	10.00	25.00
PBJA Jessie Armstead	6.00	15.00
PBJK Jevon Kearse	8.00	20.00
PBJS Jimmy Smith	8.00	20.00
PBKH Kevin Hardy	6.00	15.00
PBKJ Keyshawn Johnson	8.00	20.00
PBKM Kevin Mawae	6.00	15.00
PBKW Kurt Warner	15.00	40.00
PBLM Lawyer Milloy	6.00	15.00
PBMA Mike Alstott	10.00	25.00
PBMB Mark Brunell	8.00	20.00
PBMF Marshall Faulk	10.00	25.00
PBMH Marvin Harrison	10.00	25.00
PBMM Michael McCrary	6.00	15.00
PBMS Michael Strahan	8.00	20.00
PBPB Peter Boulware	6.00	15.00
PBRG Rich Gannon	8.00	20.00
PBRM Randall McDaniel	8.00	20.00
PBRM Randy Moss	10.00	25.00
PBRP Robert Porcher	6.00	15.00
PBRW Rod Woodson	10.00	25.00
PBSB Steve Beuerlein	8.00	20.00
PBSD Stephen Davis	8.00	20.00
PBSG Sam Gash	6.00	15.00
PBSM Sam Madison	6.00	15.00
PBTG Tony Gonzalez	10.00	25.00
PBTL Todd Lyght	6.00	15.00
PBTT Tom Tupa	6.00	15.00
PBWR Willie Roaf	6.00	15.00
PBWS Warren Sapp	8.00	20.00
PBWW Wesley Walls	6.00	15.00

2000 Bowman Reserve Rookie Autographs

OVERALL STAT.ODDS 1:41 RETAIL		
CB Courtney Brown	6.00	15.00
CP Chad Pennington	15.00	40.00
CR Chris Redman	6.00	15.00
DW Dez White	6.00	15.00
JL Jamal Lewis	12.00	30.00
JR J.R. Redmond	5.00	12.00
PB Plaxico Burress	12.50	25.00
PW Peter Warrick	8.00	20.00
RD Ron Dayne	8.00	20.00
RS R.Jay Soward	5.00	12.00
SA Shaun Alexander	10.00	25.00
SM Sylvester Morris	5.00	12.00
TC Trung Canidate	6.00	15.00
TJ Thomas Jones	10.00	25.00
TP Travis Prentice	6.00	15.00

2000 Bowman Reserve Rookie Premier Jerseys

RPW Peter Warrick	8.00	20.00
RRDU Ron Dugans	5.00	12.00

2006 Bowman Sterling

This 195-card set was released in November, 2006. The set was issued in five-card packs, with a $50 SRP, which came six packs to a box. The set is a mix of rookies, some of whom signed their cards, and veterans with game-worn jersey swatches. A few of the veterans also signed their cards.

COMP.RC SET (50)	20.00	50.00
1 Jon Alston RC	.75	2.00
2 Daniel Bullocks RC	1.25	3.00
3 Damien Rhodes RC	1.00	2.50
4 Josh Betts RC	1.00	2.50
5 Garrett Mills RC	1.25	3.00
6 Anthony Schlegel RC	1.00	2.50
7 Lawrence Vickers RC	1.00	2.50
8 Abdul Hodge RC	.75	2.00
9 Kevin McMahan RC	1.00	2.50
10 Orien Harris RC	1.00	2.50
11 Charles Davis RC	1.00	2.50
12 Haloti Ngata RC	1.25	3.00
13 Kelly Jennings RC	1.00	2.50
14 Corey Bramlet RC	1.00	2.50
15 Manny Lawson RC	1.00	2.50
16 David Kirtman RC	1.00	2.50
17 Jeremy Bloom RC	1.00	2.50
18 Jason Allen RC	1.00	2.50
19 Owen Daniels RC	1.25	3.00
20 Ray Edwards RC	1.25	3.00
21 DeMario Minter RC	1.00	2.50
22 Ernie Sims RC	1.00	2.50
23 Jovon Bouknight RC	1.00	2.50
24 Sinorice Moss RC	1.25	3.00
25 Travis Lulay RC	1.00	2.50
26 Quinn Sypniewski RC	1.00	2.50
27 T.J. Rushing RC	.75	2.00
28 J.J. Outlaw RC	1.00	2.50
29 Donte Whitner RC	1.25	3.00
30 Freddie Keiaho RC	1.00	2.50
31 Rocky McIntosh RC	1.00	2.50
32 Tamba Hali RC	1.25	3.00
33 Johnathan Joseph RC	1.00	2.50
34 Omar Gaither RC	1.00	2.50
35 Elvis Dumervil RC	1.25	3.00
36 Thomas Howard RC	1.00	2.50
37 Gabe Watson RC	.75	2.00
38 Tony Scheffler RC	1.25	3.00
39 Tim Massaquoi RC	1.00	2.50
40 Chris Gocong RC	1.00	2.50
41 Ko Simpson RC	1.00	2.50
42 D'Qwell Jackson RC	1.00	2.50
43 James Anderson RC	.75	2.00
44 P.J. Pope RC	1.25	3.00
45 Bennie Brazell RC	1.00	2.50
46 Jeff King RC	1.00	2.50
47 Dusty Dvoracek RC	1.25	3.00
48 Dee Webb RC	1.00	2.50
49 Jimmy Williams RC	1.25	3.00
50 Danieal Manning RC	1.25	3.00
AC1 Antonio Cromartie AU RC	5.00	12.00
AC2 Alge Crumpler JSY	4.00	10.00
AF Anthony Fasano AU RC	5.00	12.00
AH1 A.J. Hawk JSY RC	3.00	8.00
AH2 A.J. Hawk JSY AU	20.00	50.00
AHA Andre Hall AU RC	4.00	10.00
AJ Adam Jennings AU RC	4.00	10.00
AW Al Wilson JSY	3.00	8.00
AY Ashton Youboty AU RC	3.00	8.00
AZ Alan Zemaitis AU RC	5.00	12.00
BB Brett Basanez AU RC	5.00	12.00
BC1 Brian Calhoun JSY RC	2.00	5.00
BC2 Brian Calhoun JSY AU	5.00	12.00
BCR Brodie Croyle AU RC SP	12.00	30.00
BF Brett Favre JSY	10.00	25.00
BG Bruce Gradkowski AU RC	5.00	12.00
BM Brandon Marshall JSY RC	3.00	8.00
BO Ben Obomanu AU RC	5.00	12.00
BS1 Bob Sanders JSY	4.00	10.00
BS2 Brad Smith AU RC SP	5.00	12.00
BW1 Brandon Williams JSY RC	2.00	5.00
BW2 Brandon Williams JSY AU	5.00	12.00
CB1 Chris Brown JSY	3.00	8.00
CB2 Chris Brown JSY AU	5.00	12.00
CG Chad Greenway AU RC	5.00	12.00
CH Cedric Humes AU RC	3.00	8.00
CHO Cody Hodges AU RC	4.00	10.00
CJ Chad Jackson JSY RC	2.00	5.00
CM Curtis Martin JSY	5.00	12.00
CP Carson Palmer JSY	5.00	12.00
CW Charlie Whitehurst JSY RC	3.00	8.00
DAN David Anderson AU RC	4.00	10.00
DB1 Derrick Burgess JSY	3.00	8.00
DB2 Dominique Byrd AU RC	4.00	10.00
DEH Derek Hagan JSY RC	2.50	6.00
DEW Demetrius Williams JSY RC	2.50	6.00
DF Dwight Freeney JSY	4.00	10.00
DFE D'Brickashaw Ferguson AU RC SP	5.00	12.00
DHA Darrell Hackney AU RC SP	4.00	10.00
DHE Devin Hester AU RC	30.00	60.00
DHI Domenik Hixon AU RC	5.00	12.00
DM Donovan McNabb JSY	5.00	12.00
DOL Drew Olson AU RC	3.00	8.00
DON Deltha O'Neal JSY SP		
DRY DeMeco Ryans AU RC	5.00	12.00
DS1 Darren Sharper JSY	4.00	10.00
DS2 D.J. Shockley AU RC	4.00	10.00
DT David Thomas AU RC	4.00	10.00
DW DeAngelo Williams JSY RC	4.00	10.00
DWA Delanie Walker AU RC	5.00	12.00
GJ Greg Jennings AU RC	20.00	35.00
HB Hank Baskett AU RC	5.00	12.00
IM Ingle Martin AU RC	4.00	10.00
JA1 Joseph Addai AU RC	15.00	40.00
JA2 Jason Avant JSY RC	2.00	5.00
JD Jake Delhomme JSY	4.00	10.00
JH Jerome Harrison AU RC	5.00	12.00
JJ Julius Jones JSY	3.00	8.00
JK1 Joe Klopfenstein JSY RC	2.00	5.00
JK2 Joe Klopfenstein JSY AU	5.00	12.00
JL Jamal Lewis JSY	4.00	10.00
JM Jerome Mathis JSY	3.00	8.00
JN1 Jerious Norwood JSY RC	2.50	6.00
JN2 Jerious Norwood AU	4.00	10.00
JN3 Jerious Norwood JSY AU	6.00	15.00
JO Jonathan Orr AU RC	4.00	10.00
JP Julius Peppers JSY	4.00	10.00
JS Jeremy Shockey JSY	5.00	12.00
JSM Jimmy Smith JSY	4.00	10.00
JT Jeremiah Trotter JSY	3.00	8.00
JW Javon Walker JSY	4.00	10.00
JWE Jeff Webb AU RC	4.00	10.00
KC1 Kellen Clemens JSY RC	2.50	6.00
KC2 Kellen Clemens JSY AU	6.00	15.00
KR Koren Robinson JSY	3.00	8.00
KW Kamerion Wimbley AU RC	5.00	12.00
LB Lance Briggs JSY	4.00	10.00
LE Lee Evans JSY	4.00	10.00
LF Larry Fitzgerald JSY	5.00	12.00
LJ Larry Johnson JSY	4.00	10.00
LM Laurence Maroney JSY RC	2.50	6.00
LN Lorenzo Neal JSY	3.00	8.00
LP Leonard Pope AU RC SP	5.00	12.00
LW LenDale White JSY RC	2.50	6.00
LWA1 Leon Washington JSY RC	2.50	6.00
LWA2 Leon Washington JSY AU	6.00	15.00
MB Marion Barber JSY	4.00	10.00
MBE Mike Bell AU RC	5.00	12.00
MD Maurice Drew JSY RC	5.00	12.00
MH Marvin Harrison JSY	5.00	12.00
MHA Marques Hagans AU RC	3.00	8.00
MHU Michael Huff JSY RC	2.50	6.00
MIH Mike Hass AU RC SP	4.00	10.00
MK Mathias Kiwanuka AU RC	5.00	12.00
ML Matt Leinart JSY RC	3.00	8.00
MLE Marcedes Lewis JSY RC	3.00	8.00
MN Martin Nance AU RC	4.00	10.00
MR1 Michael Robinson JSY RC	2.50	6.00
MR2 Michael Robinson JSY AU	6.00	15.00
MS Michael Strahan JSY	4.00	10.00
MST Marcus Stroud JSY	3.00	8.00
MST1 Maurice Stovall JSY RC	2.00	5.00
MST2 Maurice Stovall AU	3.00	8.00
MV Michael Vick JSY	5.00	12.00
MW1 Mario Williams JSY RC	3.00	8.00
MW2 Mario Williams JSY AU	8.00	20.00
OJ Omar Jacobs JSY RC	2.00	5.00
OU Osi Umenyiora JSY	4.00	10.00
PB Plaxico Burress JSY	4.00	10.00
PM Peyton Manning JSY	8.00	20.00
PP Paul Pinegar AU RC SP	3.00	8.00
QG Quinton Ganther AU RC	3.00	8.00
RB1 Reggie Bush JSY RC	10.00	25.00
RB2 Reggie Bush JSY AU SP	50.00	100.00
RB3 Ronnie Brown JSY	5.00	12.00
RBA Ronde Barber JSY	4.00	10.00
RJ Rudi Johnson JSY AU	6.00	15.00
RM Reggie McNeal AU RC	4.00	10.00
RS Rod Smith JSY	4.00	10.00
RW Reggie Wayne JSY	4.00	10.00
RWI Roy Williams S JSY	4.00	10.00
SG Skyler Green AU RC SP	3.00	8.00
SH1 Santonio Holmes JSY RC	4.00	10.00
SH2 Santonio Holmes JSY AU SP	20.00	50.00
SMO Santana Moss JSY	4.00	10.00
SR Shaun Rogers JSY	3.00	8.00
SS Steve Smith JSY AU SP	20.00	40.00
TB Tatum Bell JSY AU	5.00	12.00
TBA Tiki Barber JSY	5.00	12.00
TG Tony Gonzalez JSY	4.00	10.00
TH Tommie Harris JSY	3.00	8.00
THO Torry Holt JSY	4.00	10.00
TJ1 Tarvaris Jackson JSY RC	3.00	8.00
TJ2 Tarvaris Jackson JSY AU	10.00	25.00
TW Travis Wilson JSY RC	2.00	5.00
TYH Tye Hill AU RC	3.00	8.00
VD1 Vernon Davis JSY RC	4.00	10.00
VD2 Vernon Davis JSY AU SP	25.00	50.00
VY1 Vince Young JSY RC	10.00	25.00
VY2 Vince Young JSY AU SP	30.00	80.00
WB Will Blackmon AU RC	4.00	10.00
WD Warrick Dunn JSY	4.00	10.00
WJ Winston Justice AU RC	4.00	10.00
WR Willie Reid AU RC	4.00	10.00
ZT Zach Thomas JSY	5.00	12.00

2006 Bowman Sterling Black Refractors

*ROOKIES 1-50: 3X TO 8X BASIC CARDS
*VET JSYs: .8X TO 2X BASIC CARDS
*ROOKIE JSYs: .8X TO 2X BASIC CARDS
*ROOKIE AUs: .8X TO 2X BASIC CARDS
*VET JSY AU: .8X TO 2X BASIC CARDS
*ROOKIE JSY AU: .8X TO 2X BASIC CARDS
STATED PRINT RUN 25 SER.#'d SETS

DHE Devin Hester AU	90.00	150.00
RB2 Reggie Bush AU JSY	150.00	300.00
VY2 Vince Young AU JSY	125.00	250.00

2006 Bowman Sterling Red Refractors

UNPRICED RED REF PRINT RUN 1

2006 Bowman Sterling Refractors

*ROOKIES 1-50: 1.5X TO 4X BASIC CARDS
*VET JSYs: .5X TO 1.2X BASIC CARDS
*ROOK JSYs: .5X TO 1.2X BASIC CARDS
*ROOK AUs: .5X TO 1.2X BASIC CARDS
*VET JSY AU: .4X TO 1X BASIC CARDS
*ROOK JSY AU: .4X TO 1X BASIC CARDS
STATED PRINT RUN 199 SER.#'d SETS

DHE Devin Hester AU	50.00	100.00
JA1 Joseph Addai AU	12.00	30.00
VY2 Vince Young JSY AU	40.00	100.00

2006 Bowman Sterling Gold Relic Autographs

BF Brett Favre/50	100.00	200.00
CB Chris Brown/250	5.00	12.00
EM Eli Manning/100	50.00	80.00
JJ Julius Jones/75	20.00	50.00
LJ Larry Johnson/250	10.00	25.00
MH Marvin Harrison/50	25.00	60.00
MV Michael Vick/50	40.00	80.00
PM Peyton Manning/100	100.00	175.00
SMO Santana Moss/50	20.00	50.00

2006 Bowman Sterling Gold Rookie Autographs

PRINT RUN 450-900 SER.#'d SETS		
AF Anthony Fasano/900	6.00	15.00
BCR Brodie Croyle/900	6.00	15.00
BG Bruce Gradkowski/900	6.00	15.00
BO Ben Obomanu/900	6.00	15.00
BS Brad Smith/500	6.00	15.00
CG Chad Greenway/900	6.00	15.00
CHO Cody Hodges/900	5.00	12.00
DAN David Anderson/900	5.00	12.00
DHA Darrell Hackney/500	5.00	12.00
DHI Domenik Hixon/450	6.00	15.00
DS D.J. Shockley/900	5.00	12.00
DT David Thomas/900	5.00	12.00
GJ Greg Jennings/900	15.00	40.00
HB Hank Baskett/500	6.00	15.00
IM Ingle Martin/900	5.00	12.00
JA Joseph Addai/900	8.00	20.00
JH Jerome Harrison/900	6.00	15.00
JN Jerious Norwood/900	5.00	12.00
LP Leonard Pope/900	6.00	15.00
MBE Mike Bell/900	6.00	15.00
MHA Marques Hagans/450	4.00	10.00
MIH Mike Hass/900	5.00	12.00
MST Maurice Stovall/900	4.00	10.00
RM Reggie McNeal/900	5.00	12.00
SG Skyler Green/700	4.00	10.00
WB Will Blackmon/900	5.00	12.00
WR Willie Reid/900	5.00	12.00

2006 Bowman Sterling Dual Autographs

STATED PRINT RUN 20-600		
CAB Joseph Addai/600	12.00	30.00
Mike Bell		
CBS Reggie Bush/20	125.00	250.00
Emmitt Smith		
CCC Jay Cutler/50	60.00	120.00
Kellen Clemens		
CCF Kellen Clemens/20	250.00	400.00
Brett Favre		
CDL Vernon Davis/600	15.00	40.00
Marcedes Lewis		
CHJ Santonio Holmes/200	15.00	40.00
Chad Jackson		
CJS Chad Johnson/20	40.00	100.00
Steve Smith		
CJT Bo Jackson/20	75.00	150.00
LaDainian Tomlinson		
CLM Matt Leinart/20	125.00	250.00
Joe Montana		
CMB Laurence Maroney/600	10.00	25.00
Mike Bell		
CMH Sinorice Moss/400	12.00	30.00
Santonio Holmes		
CMM Peyton Manning/20	175.00	350.00
Eli Manning		
CNE Joe Namath/20	150.00	300.00
John Elway		
CVF Michael Vick/20	250.00	400.00
Brett Favre		
CWH Mario Williams/300	20.00	50.00
A.J. Hawk		
CWW LenDale White/50	30.00	80.00
DeAngelo Williams		
CYC Vince Young/20	60.00	120.00
Earl Campbell		

2007 Bowman Sterling

This 208-card set was released in September, 2007. The set was issued into the hobby in five-card packs, with a $50 SRP, which came six packs to a box. The set contains a mix of Rookie Cards (1-50); veteran cards with game-worn jersey swatches and Rookie Cards with either player-worn jersey swatches or Rookie Cards with both player-worn swatches and a signature.

UNPRICED PRINT.PLATES #'d TO 1		
1 Levi Brown RC	2.50	6.00
2 Darrelle Revis RC	4.00	10.00
3 Lawrence Timmons RC	2.50	6.00
4 Justin Harrell RC	2.00	5.00
5 Jarvis Moss RC	2.00	5.00
6 Michael Griffin RC	2.50	6.00
7 Aaron Ross RC	2.50	6.00
8 Reggie Nelson RC	2.00	5.00
9 Brandon Meriweather RC	2.50	6.00
10 Jon Beason RC	2.00	5.00
11 Anthony Spencer RC	2.50	6.00
12 David Irons RC	1.50	4.00
13 Matt Spaeth RC	2.50	6.00
14 Zak DeOssie RC	2.00	5.00
15 Matt Moore RC	2.50	6.00
16 Brett Ratliff RC	2.50	6.00
17 John Broussard RC	2.00	5.00
18 Chandler Williams RC	2.00	5.00
19 Chansi Stuckey RC	2.50	6.00
20 Derek Stanley RC	2.00	5.00
21 Ahmad Bradshaw RC	4.00	10.00
22 Jason Snelling RC	2.50	6.00
23 Tyler Palko RC	2.00	5.00
24 Tyrone Moss RC	1.50	4.00
25 Drew Tate RC	2.00	5.00
26 Joe Staley RC	2.00	5.00
27 Ben Grubbs RC	2.00	5.00
28 Eric Weddle RC	2.50	6.00
29 Chris Houston RC	2.00	5.00
30 Justin Durant RC	2.00	5.00
31 Eric Wright RC	2.50	6.00
32 Josh Wilson RC	2.00	5.00
33 Tim Crowder RC	2.50	6.00
34 Victor Abiamiri RC	2.50	6.00
35 Ramzee Robinson RC	1.50	4.00
36 Jonathan Wade RC	2.00	5.00
37 Aaron Rouse RC	2.00	5.00
38 Daymeion Hughes RC	2.00	5.00
39 Ray McDonald RC	2.00	5.00
40 Tanard Jackson RC	1.50	4.00
41 Martrez Milner RC	1.50	4.00
42 Le'Ron McClain RC	2.50	6.00
43 Kevin Boss RC	4.00	10.00
44 C.J. Gaddis RC	1.50	4.00
45 Rufus Alexander RC	2.00	5.00
46 Courtney Taylor RC	2.00	5.00
47 Prescott Burgess RC	2.00	5.00
48 Jordan Kent RC	2.00	5.00
49 Ben Patrick RC	2.00	5.00
50 Tyler Thigpen RC	2.50	6.00
AA Aundrae Allison AU RC	2.50	6.00
AB Anquan Boldin JSY	4.00	10.00
ABR Alan Branch AU RC	3.00	8.00
AC Adam Carriker AU RC	3.00	8.00
ACR Alge Crumpler JSY	4.00	10.00
AG1 Anthony Gonzalez JSY RC	3.00	8.00
AG2 Anthony Gonzalez JSY AU	6.00	15.00
AGA Antonio Gates JSY	5.00	12.00
AJ Andre Johnson JSY	4.00	10.00
AO Amobi Okoye AU RC	4.00	10.00
AP1 Antonio Pittman JSY RC	2.00	5.00
AP2 Antonio Pittman JSY AU	4.00	10.00
APE1 Adrian Peterson JSY RC	12.00	30.00
APE2 Adrian Peterson JSY AU	125.00	250.00
AS Aaron Schobel JSY	3.00	8.00
AT Adalius Thomas JSY	3.00	8.00
AW Adrian Wilson JSY	3.00	8.00
BE Braylon Edwards JSY	4.00	10.00
BF Brett Favre JSY	10.00	25.00
BJ1 Brandon Jackson JSY RC	2.50	6.00
BJ2 Brandon Jackson JSY AU	5.00	12.00
BL1 Brian Leonard JSY RC	2.50	6.00
BL2 Brian Leonard JSY AU	5.00	12.00
BQ1 Brady Quinn JSY RC	3.00	8.00
BQ2 Brady Quinn JSY AU	20.00	50.00
BW Brian Westbrook JSY	4.00	10.00
CD Craig Buster Davis AU RC	3.00	8.00
CDA Chris Davis AU RC	2.50	6.00
CH1 Chris Henry JSY RC	2.00	5.00
CH2 Chris Henry JSY AU	4.00	10.00
CJ Chad Johnson JSY	4.00	10.00
CJO1 Calvin Johnson JSY RC	10.00	25.00
CJO2 Calvin Johnson JSY AU	75.00	150.00
CL Chris Leak AU RC	3.00	8.00
CM Chris McAlister JSY	3.00	8.00
CP Chad Pennington JSY	4.00	10.00
CPO Clinton Portis JSY	4.00	10.00
DB1 Dwayne Bowe JSY RC	4.00	10.00
DB2 Dwayne Bowe JSY AU	10.00	25.00
DBA Dallas Baker AU RC	2.50	6.00
DC David Clowney AU RC	3.00	8.00
DD Donald Driver JSY	5.00	12.00
DH DeAngelo Hall JSY	4.00	10.00
DHA David Harris AU RC	3.00	8.00
DJ1 Dwayne Jarrett JSY RC	2.50	6.00
DJ2 Dwayne Jarrett JSY AU	5.00	12.00
DM Deuce McAllister JSY	4.00	10.00
DS1 Drew Stanton JSY RC	2.00	5.00
DS2 Drew Stanton JSY AU	4.00	10.00
DW Darius Walker AU RC	2.50	6.00
DWA DeMarcus Ware JSY	4.00	10.00
DWR Dwayne Wright AU RC	3.00	8.00
EJ Edgerrin James JSY	4.00	10.00
ER Ed Reed JSY	4.00	10.00
FG Frank Gore JSY	5.00	12.00
GA1 Gaines Adams JSY RC	3.00	8.00
GA2 Gaines Adams JSY AU	6.00	15.00
GO1 Greg Olsen JSY RC	2.50	6.00
GO2 Greg Olsen JSY AU	5.00	12.00
GR Gary Russell AU RC	3.00	8.00
GW1 Garrett Wolfe JSY RC	2.00	5.00
GW2 Garrett Wolfe JSY AU	4.00	10.00
IS Isaiah Stanback AU RC	2.50	6.00
JA Jamaal Anderson AU RC	3.00	8.00
JAD Joseph Addai JSY	4.00	10.00
JB1 John Beck JSY RC	3.00	8.00
JB2 John Beck JSY AU	6.00	15.00
JC Jerricho Cotchery JSY	4.00	10.00
JF Joel Filani AU RC	3.00	8.00
JH1 Jason Hill JSY RC	3.00	8.00
JH2 Jason Hill JSY AU	6.00	15.00
JHA Justise Hairston AU RC	3.00	8.00
JJ Jacoby Jones AU RC	4.00	10.00
JJO James Jones AU RC	4.00	10.00
JL J.P. Losman JSY	3.00	8.00
JLH1 Johnnie Lee Higgins JSY RC	2.50	6.00
JLH2 Johnnie Lee Higgins JSY AU	5.00	12.00
JLY John Lynch JSY	4.00	10.00
JM Justin Miller JSY	3.00	8.00
JP Jordan Palmer AU RC	3.00	8.00
JPE Julian Peterson JSY	3.00	8.00
JR1 JaMarcus Russell JSY RC	2.00	5.00
JR2 JaMarcus Russell JSY AU	12.00	30.00
JRO Jeff Rowe AU RC	2.50	6.00
JT Jason Taylor JSY	4.00	10.00
JTH1 Joe Thomas JSY RC	3.00	8.00
JTH2 Joe Thomas JSY AU	6.00	15.00
JW Javon Walker JSY	4.00	10.00
JZ Jared Zabransky AU RC	3.00	8.00
KD Ken Darby AU RC	3.00	8.00
KI1 Kenny Irons JSY RC	2.00	5.00
KI2 Kenny Irons JSY AU	4.00	10.00
KK1 Kevin Kolb JSY RC	5.00	12.00
KK2 Kevin Kolb JSY AU	10.00	25.00
KS Kolby Smith AU RC	3.00	8.00
LB1 Lorenzo Booker JSY RC	2.50	6.00
LB2 Lorenzo Booker JSY AU	5.00	12.00
LC Laveranues Coles JSY	3.00	8.00
LG Luke Getsy AU RC	4.00	10.00
LH Leon Hall AU RC	3.00	8.00
LN Legedu Naanee AU RC	4.00	10.00
LR Laurent Robinson AU RC	6.00	15.00
LW LaMarr Woodley AU RC	6.00	15.00
MB Marc Bulger JSY	4.00	10.00
MBU1 Michael Bush JSY RC	3.00	8.00
MBU2 Michael Bush JSY AU	6.00	15.00
MH Matt Hasselbeck JSY	4.00	10.00
ML1 Marshawn Lynch JSY RC	3.00	8.00
ML2 Marshawn Lynch JSY AU	20.00	40.00
MS Michael Strahan JSY	4.00	10.00
MST Mack Strong JSY	3.00	8.00
MW Mike Walker AU RC	4.00	10.00
PB Plaxico Burress JSY	4.00	10.00
PP Paul Posluszny AU RC	4.00	10.00
PW1 Patrick Willis JSY RC	6.00	15.00
PW2 Patrick Willis JSY AU	15.00	40.00
PWI1 Paul Williams JSY RC	2.00	5.00
PWI2 Paul Williams JSY AU	4.00	10.00
RB Reggie Brown JSY	3.00	8.00
RBR Ronnie Brown JSY	4.00	10.00
RH Roy Hall AU RC	4.00	10.00
RM Rhema McKnight AU RC	2.50	6.00
RMA Rashean Mathis JSY	3.00	8.00
RME1 Robert Meachem JSY RC	3.00	8.00
RME2 Robert Meachem JSY AU	6.00	15.00
RR Ryne Robinson AU RC	3.00	8.00
RW Reggie Wayne JSY	4.00	10.00
RWI Roy Williams S JSY	4.00	10.00
RWL Roy Williams WR JSY	4.00	10.00
SB Steve Breaston AU RC	4.00	10.00
SC Scott Chandler AU RC	4.00	10.00
SH Steve Hutchinson JSY	4.00	10.00
SJ Steven Jackson JSY	5.00	12.00
SR1 Sidney Rice JSY RC	4.00	10.00
SR2 Sidney Rice JSY AU	8.00	20.00
SS1 Steve Smith USC JSY RC	3.00	8.00
SS2 Steve Smith USC JSY AU	10.00	25.00
SSM Steve Smith JSY	4.00	10.00
SY Selvin Young AU RC	3.00	8.00
TC Thomas Clayton AU RC	3.00	8.00
TE1 Trent Edwards JSY RC	3.00	8.00
TE2 Trent Edwards JSY AU	6.00	15.00
TG1 Ted Ginn JSY RC	2.50	6.00
TG2 Ted Ginn JSY AU	5.00	12.00
TH1 Tony Hunt JSY RC	2.00	5.00
TH2 Tony Hunt JSY AU	4.00	10.00
THO T.J. Houshmandzadeh JSY	4.00	10.00
TS1 Troy Smith JSY RC	3.00	8.00
TS2 Troy Smith JSY AU	10.00	25.00
WD Warrick Dunn JSY	4.00	10.00
WP Willie Parker JSY	4.00	10.00
WPI Willie Parker PB JSY	4.00	10.00
WS Will Smith JSY	3.00	8.00
YF1 Yamon Figurs JSY RC	2.00	5.00
YF2 Yamon Figurs JSY AU	4.00	10.00
ZM Zach Miller AU RC	4.00	10.00
ZT Zac Taylor AU RC	3.00	8.00
ZTH Zach Thomas JSY	4.00	10.00

2007 Bowman Sterling Black Refractors

*ROOKIES 1-50: 1.5X TO 4X BASIC CARDS
*VET JSYs: .8X TO 2X BASIC CARDS
*ROOKIE AUs: .8X TO 2X BASIC CARDS
*ROOKIE JSY: 1X TO 2.5X BASIC CARDS
*ROOK JSY AU/25: 1X TO 2.5X
JSY AU/10 CARDS NOT PRICED
STATED PRINT RUN 10-25

2007 Bowman Sterling Refractors

*ROOKIES 1-50: .6X TO 2X BASIC CARDS
*VET JSYs: .5X TO 1.2X BASIC CARDS
*ROOK AUs: .5X TO 1.2X BASIC CARDS
*ROOKIE JSY: .6X TO 1.5X BASIC CARDS
*ROOK JSY AU/199: .5X TO 1.2X
STATED PRINT RUN 25-199

APE2 Adrian Peterson JSY AU/25	250.00	500.00
BQ2 Brady Quinn JSY AU/25	30.00	80.00
CJO2 Calvin Johnson JSY AU/25	150.00	250.00
JR2 JaMarcus Russell JSY AU/25	20.00	50.00

2007 Bowman Sterling Red Refractors

UNPRICED RED REF. PRINT RUN 1

2007 Bowman Sterling Dual Autograph Gold Refractors

STATED PRINT RUN 20-400		
AA Jamaal Anderson/250	8.00	20.00
Gaines Adams		
BL Reggie Bush/20	75.00	150.00
Matt Leinart		
BO Alan Branch/400	8.00	20.00
Amobi Okoye		
BS Reggie Bush/20	125.00	250.00
Barry Sanders		
BST John Beck/150	12.00	30.00
Drew Stanton		
EK Trent Edwards/150	20.00	50.00
Kevin Kolb		
EM John Elway/20	250.00	400.00
Dan Marino		
FJ Marshall Faulk/20	50.00	120.00
Steven Jackson		
II Kenny Irons/250	8.00	20.00
David Irons		
JB Dwayne Jarrett/150	25.00	50.00
Dwayne Bowe		
JT Larry Johnson/20	40.00	100.00
LaDainian Tomlinson		
LB Brian Leonard/250	8.00	20.00
Michael Bush		
LP Marshawn Lynch/25	200.00	400.00
Adrian Peterson		
MB Joe Montana/20	300.00	400.00
Tom Brady		
MW Shawne Merriman/250	15.00	40.00
Patrick Willis		
NS Joe Namath/20	175.00	300.00
Bart Starr		
OM Greg Olsen/250	10.00	25.00
Zach Miller		
PG Antonio Pittman/250	12.00	30.00
Anthony Gonzalez		
QM Brady Quinn/20	150.00	300.00
Joe Montana		
RJ JaMarcus Russell/20	40.00	100.00
Calvin Johnson		
RJO Jerry Rice/20	200.00	350.00
Calvin Johnson		
RQ JaMarcus Russell/20	30.00	80.00
Brady Quinn		
SA Roger Staubach/20	125.00	200.00
Troy Aikman		
SG Troy Smith/250	12.00	30.00
Ted Ginn Jr.		
SJ Steve Smith USC/150	12.00	30.00
Dwayne Jarrett		
SM Phil Simms/20	100.00	175.00
Eli Manning		
WJ Roy Williams WR/20	50.00	120.00
Calvin Johnson		
YC Vince Young/20	60.00	120.00
Earl Campbell		

2007 Bowman Sterling Gold Relic Autographs

STATED PRINT RUN 25-250		
AG Anthony Gonzalez/250	12.00	30.00
AP Adrian Peterson/25	250.00	500.00
BJ Brandon Jackson/250	10.00	25.00
BL Brian Leonard/150	10.00	25.00
BQ Brady Quinn/25	40.00	100.00
CH Chris Henry/150	8.00	20.00
CJ Calvin Johnson/25	125.00	250.00
DB Dwayne Bowe/150	15.00	40.00
DJ Dwayne Jarrett/150	10.00	25.00
DS Drew Stanton/150	8.00	20.00
FG Frank Gore/25	20.00	40.00
GA Gaines Adams/250	12.00	30.00
GO Greg Olsen/250	10.00	25.00
JB John Beck/250	12.00	30.00
JH Johnnie Lee Higgins/250	10.00	25.00
JR JaMarcus Russell/25	20.00	50.00
KI Kenny Irons/150	8.00	20.00
KK Kevin Kolb/150	20.00	50.00
LJ Larry Johnson/25	20.00	50.00
MB Michael Bush/150	12.00	30.00
ML Matt Leinart/25	25.00	60.00
MLY Marshawn Lynch/100	15.00	40.00
RB Reggie Bush/25	30.00	80.00
RM Robert Meachem/150	12.00	30.00
SR Sidney Rice/150	15.00	40.00
SS Steve Smith USC/150	12.00	30.00
TG Ted Ginn/100	12.00	30.00
TS Troy Smith/150	12.00	30.00
VY Vince Young/25	25.00	60.00
YF Yamon Figurs/25	8.00	20.00

2007 Bowman Sterling Gold Rookie Autographs

STATED PRINT RUN 25-1800		
AG Anthony Gonzalez/250	6.00	15.00
AP Adrian Peterson/25	200.00	400.00
AR Aaron Ross/1800	5.00	12.00
BL Brian Leonard/400	5.00	12.00
BQ Brady Quinn/25	30.00	80.00
CD Craig Buster Davis/250	5.00	12.00
CH Chris Henry/400	4.00	10.00
CJ Calvin Johnson/25	125.00	200.00
CS Chansi Stuckey/1800	5.00	12.00
CT Courtney Taylor/1800	4.00	10.00
DB Dwayne Bowe/100	10.00	25.00
DJ Dwayne Jarrett/100	6.00	15.00
DS Drew Stanton/100	5.00	12.00
DT Drew Tate/1800	4.00	10.00
GO Greg Olsen/250	5.00	12.00
JB John Beck/250	6.00	15.00
JF Joel Filani/1000	4.00	10.00
JR JaMarcus Russell/25	15.00	40.00
KI Kenny Irons/50	6.00	15.00
KK Kevin Kolb/100	12.00	30.00
LT Lawrence Timmons/1800	5.00	12.00
ML Marshawn Lynch/50	15.00	30.00
MM Matt Moore/1800	5.00	12.00
RM Robert Meachem/100	10.00	25.00
SR Sidney Rice/100	10.00	25.00
SS Steve Smith USC/100	10.00	25.00
TG Ted Ginn Jr/50	8.00	20.00
TM Tyrone Moss/1800	3.00	8.00
TP Tyler Palko/1800	4.00	10.00
ZD Zak DeOssie/1800	4.00	10.00

2008 Bowman Sterling

This set was released on August 27, 2008. The base set consists of 195 cards. Cards 1-50 feature rookies, cards 51-100 are jersey cards of vererans serial numbered of 389, and cards 101-195 are different types of rookie cards. Some are autographed, some contain jerseys and are serial numbered of 569, and others are autographed jerseys.

JSY VET/389 ODDS 1:4		
JSY ROOKIE/569 ODDS 1:4		
UNPRICED PRINT.PLATES #'d TO 1		
UNPRICED RED REFRACTOR #'d TO 1		
1 Leodis McKelvin RC	1.50	4.00
2 Antoine Cason RC	2.00	5.00
3 Brandon Flowers RC	2.00	5.00
4 Tracy Porter RC	2.00	5.00

5 Patrick Lee RC 1.50 4.00
6 Terrence Wheatley RC 1.25 3.00
7 Terrell Thomas RC 1.50 4.00
8 Charles Godfrey RC 2.00 5.00
9 Chevis Jackson RC 1.25 3.00
10 Reggie Smith RC 1.50 4.00
11 Antwaun Molden RC 1.50 4.00
12 Lawrence Jackson RC 1.50 4.00
13 Josh Morgan RC 2.00 5.00
14 Calais Campbell RC 1.50 4.00
15 Quentin Groves RC 1.50 4.00
16 Tim Hightower RC 2.00 5.00
17 Kendall Langford RC 2.00 5.00
18 Chris Ellis RC 1.25 3.00
19 Bryan Smith RC 1.50 4.00
20 Cliff Avril RC 1.50 4.00
21 Sedrick Ellis RC 2.00 5.00
22 Kentwan Balmer RC 1.50 4.00
23 Trevor Laws RC 2.00 5.00
24 Pat Sims RC 1.50 4.00
25 Andre Fluellen RC 1.50 4.00
26 Marcus Harrison RC 1.50 4.00
27 Branden Albert RC 2.00 5.00
28 Matt Slater RC 2.00 5.00
29 Curtis Lofton RC 1.50 4.00
30 Jordon Dizon RC 2.00 5.00
31 Tavares Gooden RC 1.50 4.00
32 Shawn Crable RC 1.25 3.00
33 Bruce Davis RC 1.50 4.00
34 Philip Wheeler RC 1.50 4.00
35 Ryan Clady RC 2.00 5.00
36 Xavier Omon RC 2.00 5.00
37 Gosder Cherilus RC 1.50 4.00
38 Jalen Parmele RC 1.50 4.00
39 Duane Brown RC 1.50 4.00
40 Tyrell Johnson RC 2.00 5.00
41 Tom Zbikowski RC 2.00 5.00
42 Thomas DeCoud RC 1.25 3.00
43 Martellus Bennett RC 1.50 4.00
44 Brad Cottam RC 1.50 4.00
45 Marcus Thomas RC 1.50 4.00
46 Jermichael Finley RC 2.00 5.00
47 Kenneth Moore RC 1.50 4.00
48 Arman Shields RC 1.50 4.00
49 Thomas Brown RC 1.50 4.00
50 Will Franklin RC 1.50 4.00
51 Drew Brees JSY 4.00 10.00
52 Tom Brady JSY 6.00 15.00
53 Peyton Manning JSY 6.00 15.00
54 Carson Palmer JSY 4.00 10.00
55 Ben Roethlisberger JSY 4.00 10.00
56 Eli Manning JSY 4.00 10.00
57 Tony Romo JSY 5.00 12.00
58 Vince Young JSY 3.00 8.00
59 Steven Jackson JSY 4.00 10.00
60 Willie Parker JSY 3.00 8.00
61 Clinton Portis JSY 3.00 8.00
62 Adrian Peterson JSY 8.00 20.00
63 LaDainian Tomlinson JSY 4.00 10.00
64 Marion Barber JSY 3.00 8.00
65 Brian Westbrook JSY 3.00 8.00
66 Fred Taylor JSY 3.00 8.00
67 Marshawn Lynch JSY 3.00 8.00
68 Joseph Addai JSY 3.00 8.00
69 Willis McGahee JSY 3.00 8.00
70 Frank Gore JSY 3.00 8.00
71 Chad Johnson JSY 3.00 8.00
72 Reggie Wayne JSY 3.00 8.00
73 Anquan Boldin JSY 3.00 8.00
74 Randy Moss JSY 4.00 10.00
75 Plaxico Burress JSY 3.00 8.00
76 Terrell Owens JSY 4.00 10.00
77 Andre Johnson JSY 3.00 8.00
78 Larry Fitzgerald JSY 4.00 10.00
79 Braylon Edwards JSY 3.00 8.00
80 Steve Smith JSY 3.00 8.00
81 Derek Anderson JSY 2.50 6.00
82 Edgerrin James JSY 3.00 8.00
83 Brendon Ayanbadejo JSY 2.50 6.00
84 Rob Bironas JSY 2.50 6.00
85 Shane Lechler JSY 2.50 6.00
86 Darren Sharper JSY 3.00 8.00
87 Brian Westbrook JSY 3.00 8.00
88 Nick Folk JSY 3.00 8.00
89 Tony Richardson JSY 2.50 6.00
90 Torry Holt JSY 3.00 8.00
91 Aaron Kampman JSY 4.00 10.00
92 Dan Koppen JSY 2.50 6.00
93 Mike Vrabel JSY 3.00 8.00
94 Terence Newman JSY 3.00 8.00
95 T.J. Houshmandzadeh JSY 3.00 8.00
96 Jared Allen JSY 4.00 10.00
97 James Harrison JSY RC 20.00 35.00
98 Chris Cooley JSY 3.00 8.00
99 Vince Wilfork JSY 2.50 6.00
100 Ken Hamlin JSY 3.00 8.00
101 Dominique Rodgers-Cromartie AU RC 5.00 12.00
102 Mike Jenkins AU RC 5.00 12.00
103 Aqib Talib AU RC 5.00 12.00
104 Vernon Gholston AU RC 4.00 10.00
105 Derrick Harvey AU RC 3.00 8.00
106 Owen Schmitt AU RC 5.00 12.00
107 Keith Rivers AU RC 5.00 12.00
108 Dan Connor AU RC 5.00 12.00
109 Sam Baker AU RC 3.00 8.00
110 Dennis Dixon AU RC 8.00 20.00
111 Josh Johnson AU RC 5.00 12.00
112 Erik Ainge AU RC 5.00 12.00
113 Colt Brennan AU RC 8.00 20.00
114 Andre Woodson AU RC 5.00 12.00
115 Matt Flynn AU RC 25.00 50.00
116 Anthony Morelli AU RC 4.00 10.00
117 Kyle Wright AU RC 4.00 10.00
118 Tashard Choice AU RC 4.00 10.00
119 Jacob Hester AU RC 5.00 12.00
120 Mike Hart AU RC 5.00 12.00
121 Anthony Alridge AU RC 4.00 10.00
122 Justin Forsett AU RC 5.00 12.00
123 Jerod Mayo AU RC 8.00 20.00
124 Allen Patrick AU RC 4.00 10.00
125 Ryan Torain AU RC 5.00 12.00
126 Chauncey Washington AU RC 4.00 10.00
127 DaJuan Morgan AU RC 4.00 10.00
128 Chris Long AU RC 5.00 12.00
129 Kenny Phillips AU RC 5.00 12.00
130 John Carlson AU RC 5.00 12.00
131 Fred Davis AU RC 5.00 12.00
132 Martin Rucker AU RC 4.00 10.00
133 Paul Smith AU RC 5.00 12.00
134 Keenan Burton AU RC 3.00 8.00
135 Adrian Arrington AU RC 4.00 10.00
136 Marcus Smith AU RC 5.00 12.00
137 DJ Hall AU RC 4.00 10.00
138 Marcus Monk AU RC 4.00 10.00
139 Darius Reynaud AU RC 3.00 8.00
140 Marcus Henry AU RC 4.00 10.00
141 Glenn Dorsey JSY RC 2.50 6.00
142A Jake Long JSY RC 2.50 6.00
142B Jake Long JSY AU 8.00 20.00
143A John David Booty JSY RC 2.00 5.00
143B John David Booty JSY AU 6.00 15.00
144A Brian Brohm JSY RC 2.50 6.00
144B Brian Brohm JSY AU 8.00 20.00
145 Kevin O'Connell JSY RC 2.00 5.00
146A Matt Ryan JSY RC 6.00 15.00
146B Matt Ryan JSY AU 60.00 120.00
147A Chad Henne JSY RC 6.00 15.00
147B Chad Henne JSY AU 25.00 60.00
148A Joe Flacco JSY RC 8.00 20.00
148B Joe Flacco JSY AU 50.00 100.00
149 Matt Forte JSY RC 4.00 10.00
150A Felix Jones JSY RC 4.00 10.00
150B Felix Jones JSY AU 25.00 60.00
151A Darren McFadden JSY RC 6.00 15.00
151B Darren McFadden JSY AU 30.00 60.00
152A Rashard Mendenhall JSY RC 5.00 12.00
152B Rashard Mendenhall JSY AU 25.00 60.00
153A Ray Rice JSY RC 5.00 12.00
153B Ray Rice JSY AU 30.00 60.00
154A Steve Slaton JSY RC 2.50 6.00
154B Steve Slaton JSY AU 8.00 20.00
155A Jonathan Stewart JSY RC 5.00 12.00
155B Jonathan Stewart JSY AU 12.00 30.00
156A Chris Johnson JSY RC 6.00 15.00
156B Chris Johnson JSY AU 30.00 80.00
157A Kevin Smith JSY RC 2.50 6.00
157B Kevin Smith JSY AU 8.00 20.00
158A Jamaal Charles JSY RC 4.00 10.00
158B Jamaal Charles JSY AU 12.00 30.00
159 Dustin Keller JSY RC 2.50 6.00
160 Andre Caldwell JSY RC 2.00 5.00
161 Dexter Jackson JSY RC 2.00 5.00
162A Malcolm Kelly JSY RC 2.00 5.00
162B Malcolm Kelly JSY AU 6.00 15.00
163A Donnie Avery JSY RC 2.00 5.00
163B Donnie Avery JSY AU 6.00 15.00
164 Devin Thomas JSY RC 2.00 5.00
165 Jordy Nelson JSY RC 3.00 8.00
166A James Hardy JSY RC 2.00 5.00
166B James Hardy JSY AU 6.00 15.00
167 Eddie Royal JSY RC 2.50 6.00
168 Jerome Simpson JSY RC 2.50 6.00
169A DeSean Jackson JSY RC 5.00 12.00
169B DeSean Jackson JSY AU 25.00 50.00
170A Limas Sweed JSY RC 2.50 6.00
170B Limas Sweed JSY AU 8.00 20.00
171 Earl Bennett JSY RC 2.50 6.00
172 Early Doucet JSY RC 2.00 5.00
173 Harry Douglas JSY RC 2.00 5.00
174 Mario Manningham JSY RC 2.50 6.00

2008 Bowman Sterling Black Refractors

*ROOKIES 1-50: 1X TO 2.5X BASIC CARDS
1-50 ROOKIE/50 ODDS 1:25
*VET JSYs 51-100: .6X TO 1.5X BASIC JSY
51-100 VET JSY/50 ODDS 1:26
*ROOKIE AU 101-140: .6X TO 1.5X BASIC AU
101-140 ROOKIE AU/50 ODDS 1:33
*ROOK.JSY/50: .8X TO 2X BASIC JSY
141-174 ROOKIE JSY/50 ODDS 1:38
*ROOK.JSY AU/50: .6X TO 1.5X BASIC JSY AU
141-174 ROOK.JSY AU/50 ODDS 1:65
113 Colt Brennan AU 12.00 30.00
146B Matt Ryan JSY AU 100.00 200.00
148B Joe Flacco JSY AU 75.00 150.00
150B Felix Jones JSY AU 50.00 120.00
151B Darren McFadden JSY AU 40.00 100.00
153B Ray Rice JSY AU 50.00 100.00
155B Jonathan Stewart JSY AU 50.00 100.00
156B Chris Johnson JSY AU 90.00 150.00

2008 Bowman Sterling Gold Refractors

*ROOKIES 1-50: 1.2X TO 3X BASIC CARDS
1-50 ROOKIE/25 ODDS 1:50
*VET JSYs 51-100: .8X TO 2X BASIC JSY
51-100 VET JSY/25 ODDS 1:53
*ROOKIE AU 101-140: .8X TO 2X BASIC AU
101-140 ROOKIE AU/25 ODDS 1:66
*ROOK.JSY/50: 1X TO 2.5X BASIC JSY
141-174 ROOKIE JSY/50 ODDS 1:77
*ROOK.JSY AU/25: .8X TO 2X BASIC JSY AU
141-174 ROOK.JSY AU/25 ODDS 1:131
115 Matt Flynn AU 40.00 100.00
146B Matt Ryan JSY AU 100.00 200.00
147B Chad Henne JSY AU 75.00 150.00
148B Joe Flacco JSY AU 100.00 200.00
150B Felix Jones JSY AU 75.00 150.00
151B Darren McFadden JSY AU 50.00 120.00
152B Rashard Mendenhall JSY AU 75.00 150.00
153B Ray Rice JSY AU 75.00 150.00
155B Jonathan Stewart JSY AU 50.00 120.00
156B Chris Johnson JSY AU 125.00 250.00

2008 Bowman Sterling Refractors

*ROOKIES 1-50: .8X TO 2X BASIC CARDS
1-50 ROOKIE/199 ODDS 1:7
*VET JSYs 51-100: .5X TO 1.2X BASIC JSY
51-100 VET JSY/199 ODDS 1:7
*ROOKIE AU 101-140: .5X TO 1.2X BASIC AU
101-140 ROOKIE AU/199 ODDS 1:8
*ROOK.JSY/199: .6X TO 1.5X BASIC JSY
141-174 ROOKIE JSY/199 ODDS 1:10
*ROOK.JSY AU/199: .5X TO 1.2X BASIC JSY AU
141-174 ROOK.JSY AU/199 ODDS 1:27
141-174 ROOK.JSY AU/99 ODDS 1:80
115 Matt Flynn AU 40.00 80.00
146B Matt Ryan JSY AU/99 60.00 150.00
147B Chad Henne JSY AU/99 40.00 80.00
148B Joe Flacco JSY AU/99 50.00 120.00
150B Felix Jones JSY AU/99 40.00 80.00
151B Darren McFadden JSY AU/99 30.00 60.00
152B Rashard Mendenhall JSY AU/99 30.00 60.00
153B Ray Rice JSY AU 30.00 60.00
155B Jonathan Stewart JSY AU/99 20.00 50.00
156B Chris Johnson JSY AU 30.00 80.00

2008 Bowman Sterling Blue Refractor Rookie Autographs

ISSUED VIA MAIL AS BONUS CARDS
BA1 Matt Ryan 40.00 100.00
BA2 Ryan Torain 5.00 12.00
BA3 Darren McFadden 25.00 60.00
BA4 Tashard Choice 4.00 10.00
BA5 Keenan Burton 3.00 8.00
BA6 Andre Caldwell 4.00 10.00
BA7 Kenny Phillips 5.00 12.00
BA8 Dan Connor 5.00 12.00
BA9 Mike Jenkins 5.00 12.00
BA10 Derrick Harvey 3.00 8.00

2008 Bowman Sterling Dual Autograph Gold Refractors

GROUP A ODDS 1:327
GROUP B ODDS 1:26
A1 Matt Ryan A 125.00 250.00
Darren McFadden
A2 Matt Ryan A 200.00 400.00
Tom Brady
A3 Adrian Peterson A 100.00 200.00
Darren McFadden
A4 Eli Manning A 60.00 120.00
Mario Manningham
A5 Marion Barber B 40.00 100.00
Felix Jones
A6 Brian Westbrook B 50.00 100.00
DeSean Jackson
A7 Joe Flacco A 100.00 200.00
Peyton Manning
A8 Braylon Edwards A 20.00 40.00
Derek Anderson
A9 Randy Moss A 200.00 400.00
Tom Brady
A10 Erik Ainge B 10.00 25.00
Dustin Keller
A11 Marcus Monk B 8.00 20.00
Keenan Burton
A12 Dominique Rodgers-Cromartie B 10.00 25.00
Mike Jenkins
A13 Mike Hart B 20.00 50.00
Chad Henne
A14 Vernon Gholston B 10.00 25.00
Chris Long
A15 Jacob Hester A 30.00 60.00
LaDainian Tomlinson
A16 John David Booty B 8.00 20.00
Chauncey Washington
A17 Matt Flynn B 15.00 40.00
Kyle Wright
A18 Allen Patrick B 10.00 25.00
Ryan Torain
A19 Adrian Arrington B 10.00 25.00
Mario Manningham
A20 Josh Johnson B 10.00 25.00
Anthony Morelli

2008 Bowman Sterling Dual Autograph Relic Gold

GROUP A/25 ODDS 1:374
GROUP B/75 ODDS 1:37
AR1 Darren McFadden/25 40.00 100.00
Felix Jones
AR2 Matt Ryan/25 125.00 250.00
Darren McFadden
AR3 Matt Ryan/25 75.00 150.00
Brian Brohm
AR4 Jonathan Stewart/25 60.00 120.00
Rashard Mendenhall
AR5 Joe Flacco/75 50.00 120.00
Ray Rice
AR6 Chad Henne/75 12.00 30.00
Mario Manningham
AR7 Early Doucet/75 EXCH 12.00 30.00
Glenn Dorsey
AR8 Jake Long/75 25.00 60.00
Chad Henne
AR9 Brian Brohm/75 12.00 30.00
Chad Henne
AR10 Dustin Keller/75 12.00 30.00
Jake Long
AR11 Kevin O'Connell/75 10.00 25.00
John David Booty
AR12 Chris Johnson/75 40.00 100.00
Matt Forte
AR13 Matt Ryan/25 75.00 150.00
Harry Douglas
AR14 Steve Slaton/75 20.00 50.00
Jamaal Charles
AR15 Glenn Dorsey/75 EXCH 12.00 30.00
Jake Long
AR16 Kevin Smith/75 30.00 80.00
Ray Rice
AR17 Donnie Avery/75 10.00 25.00
Devin Thomas
AR18 Devin Thomas/75 10.00 25.00
Malcolm Kelly
AR19 Jordy Nelson/75 15.00 40.00
James Hardy
AR20 DeSean Jackson/75 25.00 60.00
Jerome Simpson
AR21 Jerome Simpson/75 12.00 30.00
Andre Caldwell
AR22 Mario Manningham/75 12.00 30.00
Dexter Jackson
AR23 Darren McFadden/25 50.00 120.00
Jonathan Stewart
AR24 Felix Jones/75 40.00 100.00
Chris Johnson
AR25 Eddie Royal/75 12.00 30.00
Earl Bennett
AR26 Joe Flacco/75 40.00 100.00
Donnie Avery
AR27 Joe Flacco/25 125.00 250.00
Matt Ryan
AR28 Andre Caldwell/75 10.00 25.00
Harry Douglas
AR29 Earl Bennett/75 20.00 50.00
Matt Forte
AR30 Chris Johnson/75 30.00 80.00
Kevin Smith

2008 Bowman Sterling Gold Relic Autographs

GROUP C/235 ODDS 1:34
GROUP B/100 ODDS 1:70
GROUP A/20 ODDS 1:254
52 Tom Brady/20 200.00 350.00
53 Peyton Manning/20 100.00 175.00
56 Eli Manning/20 75.00 150.00
62 Adrian Peterson/20 100.00 175.00
68 Joseph Addai/20 20.00 40.00
81 Derek Anderson/20 20.00 40.00
143 John David Booty/235 5.00 12.00
144 Brian Brohm/20 15.00 40.00
145 Kevin O'Connell/100 8.00 20.00
146 Matt Ryan/20 150.00 300.00
147 Chad Henne/100 10.00 25.00
148 Joe Flacco/20 125.00 225.00
149 Matt Forte/235 20.00 50.00
150 Felix Jones/20 50.00 120.00
151 Darren McFadden/20 60.00 120.00
152 Rashard Mendenhall/20 40.00 80.00
153 Ray Rice/100 20.00 50.00
154 Steve Slaton/100 10.00 25.00
155 Jonathan Stewart/20 40.00 100.00
156 Chris Johnson/235 30.00 80.00
157 Kevin Smith/235 6.00 15.00
158 Jamaal Charles/100 15.00 40.00
159 Dustin Keller/235 6.00 15.00
162 Malcolm Kelly/235 5.00 12.00
163 Donnie Avery/235 EXCH
164 Devin Thomas/100 8.00 20.00
165 Jordy Nelson/100 25.00 50.00
166 James Hardy/100 8.00 20.00
169 DeSean Jackson/235 25.00 60.00
170 Limas Sweed/100 10.00 25.00

2008 Bowman Sterling Gold Rookie Autographs

GROUP D/1050 ODDS 1:6
GROUP C/400 ODDS 1:18
GROUP B/250 ODDS 1:42
GROUP A/25 ODDS 1:523
115 Matt Flynn/400 30.00 60.00
116 Anthony Morelli/1050 3.00 8.00
117 Kyle Wright/400 4.00 10.00
118 Tashard Choice/400 4.00 10.00
121 Anthony Alridge/1050 3.00 8.00
122 Justin Forsett/400 5.00 12.00
124 Allen Patrick/1050 3.00 8.00
125 Ryan Torain/1050 4.00 10.00
127 DaJuan Morgan/1050 3.00 8.00
134 Keenan Burton/1050 2.50 6.00
135 Adrian Arrington/1050 3.00 8.00
137 DJ Hall/400 4.00 10.00
138 Marcus Monk/1050 3.00 8.00
142 Jake Long/250 8.00 20.00
146 Matt Ryan/25 75.00 150.00
148 Joe Flacco/25 75.00 150.00
149 Matt Forte/1050 20.00 50.00
151 Darren McFadden/25 60.00 120.00
152 Rashard Mendenhall/25 40.00 80.00
155 Jonathan Stewart/25 40.00 80.00
156 Chris Johnson/400 25.00 60.00
160 Andre Caldwell/1050 3.00 8.00
167 Eddie Royal/250 5.00 12.00
168 Jerome Simpson/250 6.00 15.00
171 Earl Bennett/400 5.00 12.00
172 Early Doucet/250 5.00 12.00
173 Harry Douglas/400 4.00 10.00
174 Mario Manningham/250 6.00 15.00

2008 Bowman Sterling Jerseys Blue

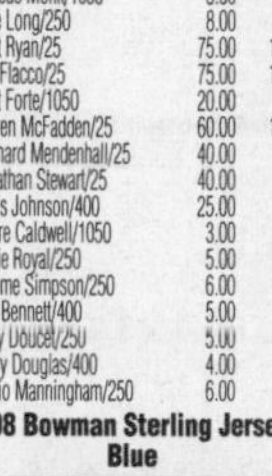

*BLUE VETS: .4X TO 1X BASIC JSY
BLUE VETS/349 ODDS 1:4
*BLUE ROOKIES: .4X TO 1X BASIC JSY
BLUE ROOKIE/399 ODDS 1:5

2008 Bowman Sterling Jerseys Green

*GREEN VETS: .4X TO 1X BASIC JSY
GREEN VET/249 ODDS 1:6
*GREEN ROOKIE: .5X TO 1.2X BASIC JSY
GREEN ROOKIE/299 ODDS 1:7

2008 Bowman Sterling Jerseys Large Swatch

*LARGE SWATCH: .5X TO 1.2X BASIC JSY
LARGE SWATCH/309 ODDS 1:6

2008 Bowman Sterling Rookie Blue Refractors

COMPLETE SET (10) 20.00 50.00
BS1 Matt Ryan 6.00 15.00
BS2 Joe Flacco 5.00 12.00
BS3 Darren McFadden 4.00 10.00
BS4 Jonathan Stewart 2.50 6.00
BS5 Matt Forte 2.50 6.00
BS6 Ray Rice 3.00 8.00
BS7 Chris Johnson 4.00 10.00
BS8 DeSean Jackson 3.00 8.00
BS9 Eddie Royal 1.50 4.00
BS10 Jerod Mayo 1.50 4.00

2009 Bowman Sterling

1-50 ROOKIE PRINT RUN 799
VET JERSEY PRINT RUN 719-999
1 Eugene Monroe RC 1.25 3.00
2 Sean Smith RC 2.00 5.00
3 Andre Smith RC 1.50 4.00
4 B.J. Raji RC 2.00 5.00
5 Peria Jerry RC 1.50 4.00
6 Tony Fiammetta RC 1.50 4.00
7 Jairus Byrd RC 2.00 5.00
8 Louis Murphy RC 2.00 5.00
9 David Veikune RC 1.50 4.00
10 Alphonso Smith RC 1.50 4.00
11 Alex Mack RC 1.50 4.00
12 Jeremiah Johnson RC 2.00 5.00
13 Vontae Davis RC 2.00 5.00
14 Javarris Williams RC 1.50 4.00
15 Darius Butler RC 2.00 5.00
16 Everette Brown RC 1.50 4.00
17 Quinn Johnson RC 1.50 4.00
18 Robert Ayers RC 2.00 5.00
19 Patrick Chung RC 2.00 5.00
20 Richard Quinn RC 1.50 4.00
21 Fili Moala RC 1.50 4.00
22 Louis Delmas RC 2.00 5.00
23 Paul Kruger RC 1.50 4.00
24 Connor Barwin RC 2.00 5.00
25 Victor Harris RC 2.00 5.00
26 Dear Pascoe RC 1.50 4.00
27 Michael Mitchell RC 1.50 4.00
28 Larry English RC 2.00 5.00
29 Bernard Scott RC 2.00 5.00
30 Rashad Johnson RC 1.50 4.00
31 Ron Brace RC 1.50 4.00
32 Jake O'Connell RC 1.25 3.00
33 Gerald McRath RC 1.50 4.00
34 Eric Wood RC 1.50 4.00
35 Asher Allen RC 1.50 4.00
36 Darcel McBath RC 1.50 4.00
37 Mike Mickens RC 1.50 4.00
38 Eben Britton RC 1.50 4.00
39 Frank Summers RC 2.00 5.00
40 Kevin Barnes RC 1.50 4.00
41 Max Unger RC 1.50 4.00
42 Tyrone McKenzie RC 1.50 4.00
43 Michael Oher RC 3.00 8.00
44 Andy Levitre RC 1.50 4.00
45 Marcus Freeman RC 2.00 5.00
46 Scott McKillop RC 1.50 4.00
47 Evander Hood RC 2.50 6.00
48 Quinten Lawrence RC 1.25 3.00
49 Phil Loadholt RC 1.50 4.00
50 Clint Sintim RC 2.00 5.00
51 Ben Roethlisberger JSY/249 4.00 10.00
52 Clinton Portis JSY/39 5.00 12.00
53A Steven Jackson JSY/719 2.50 6.00
54 Jamaal Charles JSY/999 3.00 8.00
55 Wes Welker JSY/189 4.00 10.00
56A Jonathan Stewart JSY/189 3.00 8.00
57 Aaron Rodgers JSY/249 15.00 40.00
58 Thomas Jones JSY/249 3.00 8.00
59 Calvin Johnson JSY/719 3.00 8.00
60 Andre Johnson JSY/189 3.00 8.00
61 Matt Forte JSY/999 3.00 8.00
62 Hines Ward JSY/39 5.00 12.00
63 JaMarcus Russell JSY/189 2.50 6.00
64 Jerricho Cotchery JSY/249 3.00 8.00
65A Ray Rice JSY/999 3.00 8.00
66 Eddie Royal JSY/999 2.50 6.00
67 Brian Westbrook JSY/249 3.00 8.00
68A Dwayne Bowe JSY/249 3.00 8.00
69A Marshawn Lynch JSY/249 3.00 8.00
70 Larry Fitzgerald JSY/249 4.00 10.00
71A Philip Rivers JSY/249 4.00 10.00
72 Jake Long JSY/999 2.00 5.00
73 Steve Smith USC JSY/999 2.50 6.00
74 Brady Quinn JSY/189 3.00 8.00
75 Steve Smith JSY/249 3.00 8.00
76 Donovan McNabb JSY/249 4.00 10.00
77 Jordy Nelson JSY/999 3.00 8.00
78 Dustin Keller JSY/999 2.00 5.00
79 Chester Taylor JSY/249 2.50 6.00
80A DeAngelo Williams JSY/999 3.00 8.00
81 Ronnie Brown JSY/719 2.50 6.00
82 Santana Moss JSY/249 3.00 8.00
83 Lee Evans JSY/719 2.50 6.00
84 Donnie Avery JSY/999 2.50 6.00
85 Maurice Jones-Drew JSY/249 3.00 8.00
86 Anthony Gonzalez JSY/39 4.00 10.00
87 Joseph Addai JSY/189 4.00 10.00
88 Marques Colston JSY/249 3.00 8.00
89 Willie Parker JSY/189 2.50 6.00
90 Ted Ginn JSY/249 3.00 8.00
91 Greg Olsen JSY/719 2.00 5.00
92 Brian Urlacher JSY/719 3.00 8.00
93 Donald Driver JSY/249 3.00 8.00
94 Trent Edwards JSY/189 2.50 6.00
95 Antonio Gates JSY/999 2.50 6.00
96 Ryan Grant JSY/249 3.00 8.00
97 Santonio Holmes JSY/189 3.00 8.00
98A Chad Ochocinco JSY/249 3.00 8.00
99A Brandon Marshall JSY/999 2.50 6.00
100 Anquan Boldin JSY/719 2.50 6.00
101 Brandon Gibson AU/399 RC 4.00 10.00
102 Malcolm Jenkins AU/499 RC 4.00 10.00
103 Ian Johnson AU/999 RC 3.00 8.00
104 William Moore AU/999 RC 3.00 8.00
105 Brian Cushing AU/499 RC 4.00 10.00
106 Gartrell Johnson AU/499 RC 2.50 6.00
107 Rashad Jennings AU/999 RC 3.00 8.00
108 Devin Moore AU/699 RC 2.50 6.00
109 Rey Maualuga AU/299 RC 5.00 12.00
110 Cedric Peerman AU/999 RC 2.50 6.00
111 Kory Sheets AU/999 RC 2.50 6.00
112 Jaison Williams AU/999 RC 2.50 6.00
113 Jeremy Childs AU/999 RC 2.50 6.00
114 Demetrius Byrd AU/999 RC 2.50 6.00
115 Arian Foster AU/599 RC 60.00 120.00
116 Manuel Johnson AU/299 RC 4.00 10.00
117 Jarett Dillard AU/399 RC 4.00 10.00
118 James Laurinaitis AU/299 RC 6.00 15.00
119 James Davis AU/999 RC 3.00 8.00
120 Marlon Lucky AU/999 RC 2.50 6.00
121 P.J. Hill AU/699 RC 2.50 6.00
122 Sammie Stroughter AU/299 RC 5.00 12.00
123 Quan Cosby AU/299 RC 4.00 10.00
124 Tyrell Sutton AU/399 RC 3.00 8.00
125 Mike Goodson AU RC 3.00 8.00
126 Chase Coffman AU/399 RC 3.00 8.00
127 Kenny McKinley AU/299 RC 5.00 12.00
128 Cornelius Ingram AU/499 RC 2.50 6.00
129 Marko Mitchell AU/499 RC 3.00 8.00
130 Chase Daniel AU/299 RC 5.00 12.00
131 Brooks Foster AU/999 RC 2.00 5.00
132 Mike Teel AU/299 RC 5.00 12.00
133 Aaron Kelly AU/999 RC 2.50 6.00
134 Brian Hoyer AU/299 RC 10.00 25.00
135 Johnny Knox AU/499 RC 15.00 30.00
136 Brandon Tate AU/499 RC 4.00 10.00
137 Tiquan Underwood AU/499 RC 3.00 8.00
138 Travis Beckum AU/499 RC 3.00 8.00
139 Brian Hartline AU/499 RC 6.00 15.00
140 Shawn Nelson AU/699 RC 2.50 6.00
141 Chris Ogbonnaya AU/899 RC 2.50 6.00
142 Tom Brandstater AU/299 RC 5.00 12.00
143 Curtis Painter AU/499 RC 4.00 10.00
144 Jarod Cook AU/499 RC 4.00 10.00
145 James Casey AU/999 RC 2.50 6.00
146A Matthew Stafford JSY/749 RC 12.00 30.00
146B Matthew Stafford JSY AU/40 125.00 200.00
147A Josh Freeman JSY/749 RC 5.00 12.00
147B Josh Freeman JSY AU/40 30.00 80.00
148A Nate Davis JSY/749 RC 2.00 5.00
148B Nate Davis JSY AU/250 6.00 15.00
149A Rhett Bomar JSY/749 RC 2.00 5.00
150A Mark Sanchez JSY/749 RC 8.00 20.00
150B Mark Sanchez JSY AU/40 50.00 120.00
151A Chris Wells JSY/749 RC 4.00 10.00
151B Chris Wells JSY AU/100 20.00 50.00
152A Javon Ringer JSY/749 RC 2.50 6.00
152B Javon Ringer JSY AU/599 6.00 15.00
153A Deon Butler JSY/749 RC 2.00 5.00
154A Brandon Pettigrew JSY/749 RC 2.50 6.00
154B Brandon Pettigrew JSY AU/600 6.00 15.00
155A LeSean McCoy JSY/749 RC 5.00 12.00
155B LeSean McCoy JSY AU/150 25.00 50.00
156A Darrius Heyward-Bey JSY/749 RC 2.50 6.00
156B Darrius Heyward-Bey JSY AU/40 15.00 40.00
157A Ramses Barden JSY/749 RC 1.50 4.00
157B Ramses Barden JSY AU/600 4.00 10.00
158A Derrick Williams JSY/749 RC 2.00 5.00
158B Derrick Williams JSY AU/600 5.00 12.00
159 Tyson Jackson JSY/749 RC 2.00 5.00
160A Hakeem Nicks JSY/749 RC 4.00 10.00
161 Mike Wallace JSY/749 RC 5.00 12.00
162 Jason Smith JSY/749 RC 2.00 5.00
163A Aaron Curry JSY/749 RC 3.00 8.00
163B Aaron Curry JSY AU/400 6.00 15.00
164A Patrick Turner JSY/749 RC 2.00 5.00
165A Knowshon Moreno JSY/749 RC 2.50 6.00
165B Knowshon Moreno JSY AU/40 15.00 40.00
166A Brian Robiskie JSY/749 RC 2.50 6.00
166B Brian Robiskie JSY AU/400 6.00 15.00
167A Stephen McGee JSY/749 RC 2.50 6.00
167B Stephen McGee JSY AU/500 6.00 15.00
168A Kenny Britt JSY/749 RC 3.00 8.00
168B Kenny Britt JSY AU/500 8.00 20.00
169A Mohamed Massaquoi JSY/749 RC 2.00 5.00
169B Mohamed Massaquoi JSY AU/200 6.00 15.00
170A Donald Brown JSY/749 RC 2.50 6.00
170B Donald Brown JSY AU/40 15.00 40.00
171 Mike Thomas JSY/749 RC 2.50 6.00
172A Juaquin Iglesias JSY/749 RC 2.00 5.00
173A Andre Brown JSY/749 RC 1.50 4.00
173B Andre Brown JSY AU/500 4.00 10.00
174A Glen Coffee JSY/749 RC 2.00 5.00
174B Glen Coffee JSY AU/500 5.00 12.00
175A Michael Crabtree JSY/749 RC 5.00 12.00
175B Michael Crabtree JSY AU/40 30.00 80.00
176A Shonn Greene JSY/749 RC 4.00 10.00
176B Shonn Greene JSY AU/500 10.00 25.00
177A Percy Harvin JSY/749 RC 4.00 10.00
177B Percy Harvin JSY AU/200 30.00 80.00
178A Pat White JSY/749 RC 2.50 6.00
178B Pat White JSY AU/50 15.00 40.00
179A Jeremy Maclin JSY/749 RC 4.00 10.00
179B Jeremy Maclin JSY AU/50 15.00 40.00
180A Peyton Manning JSY AU/30 60.00 120.00
181A Greg Jennings JSY AU/300 8.00 20.00
182 Jamaal Charles JSY AU/425 8.00 20.00
183A Adrian Peterson JSY AU/30 75.00 150.00
184 Donnie Avery JSY AU/425 5.00 12.00
185 Harry Douglas JSY AU/500 4.00 10.00
186 Devin Thomas JSY AU/300 4.00 10.00
187A Darren McFadden JSY AU/30 25.00 60.00
188A Tony Romo JSY AU/30 40.00 80.00
189A Frank Gore JSY AU/30 15.00 40.00
190A Tom Brady JSY AU/30 125.00 250.00
191A Joe Flacco JSY AU/50 30.00 60.00
192 Drew Brees JSY AU/30 40.00 80.00
193A LaDainian Tomlinson JSY AU/30 25.00 50.00
194A Reggie Bush JSY AU/30 20.00 50.00
195 Rashard Mendenhall JSY AU/30 15.00 40.00

2009 Bowman Sterling Black Refractors

*1-50 ROOKIES: 1.2X TO 3X BASIC RCs
1-50 ROOKIES PRINT RUN 50
*VET JSY/50: .5X TO 1.2X REFRCT.JSY/199
*VET JSY/15: .5X TO 1.2X REFRCT.JSY/25
51-100 VET JERSEY PRINT RUN 15-50
*ROOK AU/25: .5X TO 1.2X REFRACT.AU/75
101-145 ROOKIE AUTO PRINT RUN 25
*ROOK JSY/50: .5X TO 1.2X REFRACT.JSY/199
146-179 ROOKIE JERSEY PRINT RUN 50
*VET JSY AU/15: .5X TO 1.2X REF.JSY AU/25
*RK JSY AU/15: .5X TO 1.2X REF.JSY AU/25
146B Matthew Stafford JSY AU 175.00 300.00
147B Josh Freeman JSY AU 75.00 150.00
150B Mark Sanchez JSY AU 125.00 250.00
177B Percy Harvin JSY AU 60.00 120.00

2009 Bowman Sterling Gold Refractors

*1-50 ROOKIES: 1.5X TO 4X BASIC RCs
1-50 ROOKIES PRINT RUN 25
*VET JSY/25: .6X TO 1.5X REFRCT.JSY/199
*VET JSY/10: .6X TO 1.5X REFRCT.JSY/25
51-100 VET JERSEY PRINT RUN 10-25
*ROOK JSY/25: .6X TO 1.5X REFRACT.JSY/199
146-179 ROOKIE JERSEY PRINT RUN 25

2009 Bowman Sterling Refractors

*1-50 ROOKIES: .6X TO 1.5X BASIC RCs
1-50 ROOKIE PRINT RUN 299
COMMON VET JSY/199 2.50 6.00
VET JSY/199 SEMIS 3.00 8.00
VET JSY/199 UNL.STARS 4.00 10.00
COMMON VET JSY/25 6.00 15.00
VET JSY/25 UNL.STARS 8.00 20.00
51-100 VET JERSEY PRINT RUN 25-199
COMMON ROOKIE AU/75 5.00 12.00
ROOKIE AU/75 UNL.STR 6.00 15.00
101-145 ROOKIE AUTO PRINT RUN 75
COMMON ROOKIE JSY/199 2.50 6.00
ROOKIE JSY/199 UNL.STR 3.00 8.00
ROOKIE JERSEY PRINT RUN 199
COMMON ROOKIE JSY AU/25 10.00 25.00
*VET JSY AU: .6X TO 1.5X JSY AU/300-500
*VET JSY AU: .4X TO 1X BSE JSY AU/30-50
146-195 JERSEY AUTO PRINT RUN 25
51 Ben Roethlisberger JSY 4.00 10.00
105 Brian Cushing AU 6.00 15.00
109 Rey Maualuga AU 6.00 15.00
117 Jarett Dillard AU 8.00 20.00
118 James Laurinaitis AU 8.00 20.00
119 James Davis AU 8.00 20.00
130 Chase Daniel AU 6.00 15.00
134 Brian Hoyer AU 10.00 25.00
135 Johnny Knox AU 25.00 50.00
139 Brian Hartline AU 8.00 20.00
146A Matthew Stafford JSY 20.00 50.00
146B Matthew Stafford JSY AU 125.00 200.00
147A Josh Freeman JSY 6.00 15.00
147B Josh Freeman JSY AU 30.00 60.00
148A Nate Davis JSY 2.50 6.00
148B Nate Davis JSY AU 8.00 20.00
150A Mark Sanchez JSY 10.00 25.00
150B Mark Sanchez JSY AU 100.00 200.00
151A Chris Wells JSY 5.00 12.00
151B Chris Wells JSY AU 15.00 40.00
154A Brandon Pettigrew JSY 3.00 8.00
154B Brandon Pettigrew JSY AU 10.00 25.00
155A LeSean McCoy JSY 6.00 15.00
155B LeSean McCoy JSY AU 20.00 50.00
156A Darrius Heyward-Bey JSY 3.00 8.00
156B Darrius Heyward-Bey JSY AU 10.00 25.00
160A Hakeem Nicks JSY 5.00 12.00
161 Mike Wallace JSY 6.00 15.00
163A Aaron Curry JSY 3.00 8.00
163B Aaron Curry JSY AU 10.00 25.00
165A Knowshon Moreno JSY 3.00 8.00
165B Knowshon Moreno JSY AU 25.00 60.00
168A Kenny Britt JSY 4.00 10.00
168B Kenny Britt JSY AU 12.00 30.00
170A Donald Brown JSY 3.00 8.00
170B Donald Brown JSY AU 20.00 50.00
174A Glen Coffee JSY 2.50 6.00
174B Glen Coffee JSY AU 8.00 20.00
175A Michael Crabtree JSY 6.00 15.00
175B Michael Crabtree JSY AU 30.00 80.00
176A Shonn Greene JSY 5.00 12.00
176B Shonn Greene JSY AU 15.00 40.00
177A Percy Harvin JSY 5.00 12.00
177B Percy Harvin JSY AU 40.00 100.00
178A Pat White JSY 3.00 8.00
178B Pat White JSY AU 25.00 60.00
179A Jeremy Maclin JSY 5.00 12.00
179B Jeremy Maclin JSY AU 15.00 40.00

2009 Bowman Sterling Xfractors

*1-50 ROOKIES: .8X TO 2X BASIC RCs
1-50 ROOKIE PRINT RUN 100
51-195 UNPRICED PRINT RUN 5

2009 Bowman Sterling Dual Autograph Gold Refractors

STATED PRINT RUN 10-125
SERIAL #'d UNDER 15 NOT PRICED
EXCH EXPIRATION: 8/31/2012
BM Donald Brown/15 30.00 80.00
Knowshon Moreno
BR Kenny Britt/125 12.00 30.00
Javon Ringer
BW Deon Butler/125 10.00 25.00
Derrick Williams
CI Jay Cutler/25 30.00 60.00
Juaquin Iglesias
FM Josh Freeman/25 30.00 60.00
Stephen McGee
HM Percy Harvin/125 30.00 60.00
Jeremy Maclin
HW Santonio Holmes/125 25.00 50.00
Mike Wallace
JB Brandon Jacobs/75 10.00 25.00
Andre Brown
JG Thomas Jones/75 20.00 50.00
Shonn Greene
JM DeSean Jackson/15 30.00 60.00
Jeremy Maclin
MH Darren McFadden/15 30.00 60.00
Darrius Heyward-Bey
MM LeSean McCoy/75 25.00 50.00
Jeremy Maclin
MW LeSean McCoy/15 50.00 100.00
Chris Wells
PH Adrian Peterson/15 150.00 300.00
Percy Harvin
PW Brandon Pettigrew/125 10.00 25.00
Derrick Williams
TW Mike Thomas/125 12.00 30.00
Mike Wallace
WF Kellen Winslow Jr./15 30.00 60.00
Josh Freeman
WR LenDale White/125 15.00 40.00
Javon Ringer
WT Pat White/125 25.00 60.00
Patrick Turner

2010 Bowman Sterling

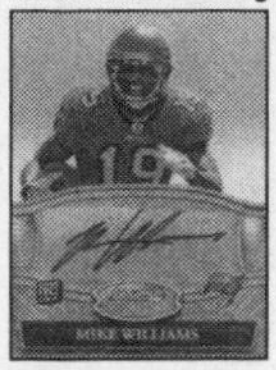

EXCH EXPIRATION: 12/31/2013
1 Javier Arenas RC 1.50 4.00
2 Deji Karim RC 1.50 4.00
3 Chris Cook RC 1.50 4.00
4 Derrick Morgan RC 1.25 3.00
5 Carlos Dunlap RC 1.50 4.00
6 Bryan Bulaga RC 1.50 4.00
7 Akwasi Owusu-Ansah RC 1.50 4.00
8 Nate Allen RC 1.50 4.00
9 Brian Price RC 1.50 4.00
10 Dan Williams RC 1.25 3.00
11 Terrence Cody RC 1.25 3.00
12 Mike Iupati RC 1.50 4.00
13 Joe Haden RC 1.50 4.00
14 Russell Okung RC 1.50 4.00
15 Devin McCourty RC 1.50 4.00
16 Dezmon Briscoe RC 1.25 3.00
17 Daryl Washington RC 1.25 3.00
18 Trent Williams RC 1.50 4.00
19 Brandon Spikes RC 1.50 4.00
20 Jared Odrick RC 1.50 4.00
21 Victor Cruz RC 6.00 15.00
22 Charles Brown RC 1.25 3.00
23 Everson Griffen RC 1.50 4.00
24 Dorin Dickerson RC 1.00 2.50
25 Jerry Hughes RC 1.50 4.00
26 Linval Joseph RC 1.25 3.00
27 Tony Moeaki RC 1.50 4.00
28 Ed Dickson RC 1.50 4.00
29 Patrick Robinson RC 1.50 4.00
30 Corey Wootton RC 1.25 3.00
31 Morgan Burnett RC 1.50 4.00
32 Taylor Mays RC 1.50 4.00
33 Maurkice Pouncey RC 1.50 4.00
34 Brandon Graham RC 1.25 3.00
35 Rodger Saffold RC 1.00 2.50
36 Koa Misi RC 1.50 4.00
37 Jerome Murphy RC 1.25 3.00
38 Kyle Wilson RC 1.50 4.00
39 Lamarr Houston RC 1.50 4.00
40 LeGarrette Blount RC 3.00 8.00
41 Vladimir Ducasse RC 1.50 4.00
42 Cam Thomas RC 1.25 3.00
43 Jermaine Cunningham RC 1.50 4.00
44 Antonio Brown RC 2.50 6.00
45 David Gettis RC 1.50 4.00
46 Dominique Franks RC 1.00 2.50
47 Garrett Graham RC 1.25 3.00
48 Jason Worilds RC 1.50 4.00
49 Keiland Williams RC 1.50 4.00
50 Sam Shields RC 3.00 8.00
BSAAB Arrelious Benn AU B 5.00 12.00
BSAAD Anthony Dixon AU D 4.00 10.00
BSAAH Aaron Hernandez AU D 8.00 20.00
BSAAM Anthony McCoy AU D 3.00 8.00
BSAAR Andre Roberts AU B 5.00 12.00
BSABL Brandon LaFell AU C 4.00 10.00
BSACJS C.J. Spiller AU A 8.00 20.00
BSACMI Carlton Mitchell AU D 3.00 8.00
BSACS Charles Scott AU D 3.00 8.00
BSADD Dennis Dixon AU D 5.00 12.00
BSADM Dexter McCluster AU B 5.00 12.00
BSADR David Reed AU D 3.00 8.00
BSADS Darryl Sharpton AU D RC 2.50 6.00
BSADT Demaryius Thomas AU A 6.00 15.00
BSADW Damian Williams AU C 4.00 10.00
BSAEB Eric Berry AU C 10.00 25.00
BSAED Eric Decker AU C 5.00 12.00
BSAES Emmanuel Sanders AU D 4.00 10.00
BSAGJ Greg Jennings AU A 8.00 20.00
BSAGM Gerald McCoy AU A 5.00 12.00
BSAGT Golden Tate AU B 5.00 12.00
BSAHN Hakeem Nicks AU B 8.00 20.00
BSAJB Jahvid Best AU A 8.00 20.00
BSAJC Jonathan Crompton AU D RC 3.00 8.00
BSAJD Jonathan Dwyer AU C 6.00 15.00
BSAJF Jacoby Ford AU D 6.00 15.00
BSAJG Jimmy Graham AU C 15.00 30.00
BSAJJ James Jones AU D 3.00 8.00
BSAJP Jason Pierre-Paul AU D RC 8.00 20.00
BSAJS Jordan Shipley AU D 4.00 10.00
BSAJSK John Skelton AU D 4.00 10.00
BSAKJ Kareem Jackson AU D RC 4.00 10.00
BSAME Marcus Easley AU C 3.00 8.00
BSAMG Mardy Gilyard AU D 4.00 10.00
BSAMH Montario Hardesty AU B 5.00 12.00
BSAMW Mike Williams AU D 10.00 25.00
BSANS Ndamukong Suh AU A 25.00 50.00
BSAPH Percy Harvin AU A 20.00 40.00
BSARAB Arrelious Benn JSY AU B 8.00 20.00
BSARAD Anthony Dixon JSY AU D 6.00 15.00
BSARAE Armanti Edwards JSY AU C 6.00 15.00
BSARAP Adrian Peterson JSY AU A 60.00 120.00
BSARAR Andre Roberts JSY AU C 6.00 15.00
BSARBE Braylon Edwards JSY AU D 6.00 15.00
BSARBL Brandon LaFell JSY AU C 6.00 15.00
BSARBT Ben Tate JSY AU A 8.00 20.00
BSARC Riley Cooper AU D 4.00 10.00
BSARCJS C.J. Spiller JSY AU A 20.00 40.00
BSARCM Colt McCoy JSY AU A 15.00 40.00
BSARDBR Drew Brees JSY AU A 40.00 80.00
BSARDM Dexter McCluster JSY AU B 6.00 15.00
BSARDT Demaryius Thomas JSY AU A 8.00 20.00
BSARDW Damian Williams JSY AU C 6.00 15.00
BSAREB Eric Berry JSY AU B 12.00 30.00
BSARED Eric Decker JSY AU C 8.00 20.00
BSARES Emmanuel Sanders JSY AU D 6.00 15.00
BSARFJ Felix Jones JSY AU A 10.00 25.00
BSARG Rob Gronkowski AU C 15.00 40.00
BSARGM Gerald McCoy JSY AU A 6.00 15.00
BSARGT Golden Tate JSY AU B 6.00 15.00
BSARJB Jahvid Best JSY AU A 15.00 40.00
BSARJC Jimmy Clausen JSY AU A 6.00 15.00
BSARJD Jonathan Dwyer JSY AU C 6.00 15.00
BSARJG Jimmy Graham JSY AU D 25.00 50.00
BSARJS Jordan Shipley JSY AU D 6.00 15.00
BSARLT LaDainian Tomlinson JSY AU A 20.00 40.00
BSARM Ryan Mathews AU A 20.00 50.00
BSARMC Matt Cassel JSY AU B 8.00 20.00
BSARME Marcus Easley JSY AU B 5.00 12.00
BSARMG Mardy Gilyard JSY AU C 6.00 15.00
BSARMH Montario Hardesty JSY AU A 6.00 15.00
BSARMJD Maurice Jones-Drew JSY AU A 10.00 25.00
BSARMK Mike Kafka JSY AU A 6.00 15.00
BSARMW Mike Williams JSY AU D 10.00 25.00
BSARNS Ndamukong Suh JSY AU A 30.00 60.00
BSARR Ray Rice AU A EXCH 8.00 20.00
BSARRC Riley Cooper JSY AU B 6.00 15.00

BSARRG Rob Gronkowski JSY AU C 25.00 50.00
BSARRM Ryan Mathews JSY AU A 20.00 50.00
BSARRME Robert Meachem JSY AU A 6.00 15.00
BSARSB Sam Bradford JSY AU A 75.00 150.00
BSARSC Sean Canfield JSY AU C 5.00 12.00
BSARTG Toby Gerhart JSY AU B 6.00 15.00
BSARTP Taylor Price JSY AU C 6.00 15.00
BSARTT Tim Tebow JSY AU A 100.00 175.00
BSASB Sam Bradford AU A 60.00 120.00
BSASC Sean Canfield AU D 3.00 8.00
BSASG Shonn Greene AU A 6.00 15.00
BSASL Sean Lee AU C RC 6.00 15.00
BSASR Sidney Rice AU A 10.00 25.00
BSASW Sean Weatherspoon AU D RC 4.00 10.00
BSATA Tyson Alualu AU D RC 3.00 8.00
BSATG Toby Gerhart AU B 5.00 12.00
BSATPR Taylor Price AU D 4.00 10.00
BSATT Tim Tebow AU A 75.00 150.00
BSATW T.J. Ward AU D RC 4.00 10.00
BSAVJ Vincent Jackson AU A 6.00 15.00
BSAZR Zac Robinson AU D 3.00 8.00
BSRAB Arrelious Benn JSY B RC 3.00 8.00
BSRAD Anthony Dixon JSY A RC 4.00 10.00
BSRAE Armanti Edwards JSY B RC 3.00 8.00
BSRAH Aaron Hernandez JSY A RC 6.00 15.00
BSRAM Anthony McCoy JSY B RC 2.50 6.00
BSRAP Adrian Peterson JSY B 6.00 15.00
BSRAR Andre Roberts JSY B RC 3.00 8.00
BSRAS Alex Smith QB JSY A 4.00 10.00
BSRBL Brandon LaFell JSY B RC 3.00 8.00
BSRBS Bob Sanders JSY A 4.00 10.00
BSRBT Ben Tate JSY B RC 4.00 10.00
BSRBU Brian Urlacher JSY A 5.00 12.00
BSRCB Cedric Benson JSY A 4.00 10.00
BSRCBA Champ Bailey JSY A 5.00 12.00
BSRCC Chris Cooley JSY A 5.00 12.00
BSRCJS C.J. Spiller JSY B RC 4.00 10.00
BSRCM Colt McCoy JSY B RC 6.00 15.00
BSRCMI Carlton Mitchell JSY A RC 3.00 8.00
BSRCS Charles Scott JSY A RC 3.00 8.00
BSRDB Dez Bryant JSY B RC 8.00 20.00
BSRDJW D.J. Williams JSY A 3.00 8.00
BSRDL Dan LeFevour JSY A RC 4.00 10.00
BSRDM Dexter McCluster JSY B RC 3.00 8.00
BSRDMC Donovan McNabb JSY A 5.00 12.00
BSRDR David Reed JSY A RC 3.00 8.00
BSRDT Demaryius Thomas JSY B RC 4.00 10.00
BSRDW Damian Williams JSY B RC 3.00 8.00
BSREB Eric Berry JSY B RC 4.00 10.00
BSRED Eric Decker JSY B RC 4.00 10.00
BSRES Emmanuel Sanders JSY B RC 3.00 8.00
BSRET Earl Thomas JSY A RC 4.00 10.00
BSRGM Gerald McCoy JSY A RC 4.00 10.00
BSRGT Golden Tate JSY B RC 3.00 8.00
BSRJB Jahvid Best JSY B RC 4.00 10.00
BSRJC Jimmy Clausen JSY B RC 3.00 8.00
BSRJD Jonathan Dwyer JSY B RC 3.00 8.00
BSRJF Jacoby Ford JSY A RC 8.00 20.00
BSRJG Jimmy Graham JSY A RC 8.00 20.00
BSRJGR Jermaine Gresham JSY B RC 4.00 10.00
BSRJM Joe McKnight JSY B RC 3.00 8.00
BSRJN Jordy Nelson JSY A 4.00 10.00
BSRJS Jordan Shipley JSY B RC 3.00 8.00
BSRJSK John Skelton JSY A RC 4.00 10.00
BSRJST James Starks JSY B RC 5.00 12.00
BSRJWI Jason Witten JSY A 5.00 12.00
BSRKO Kyle Orton JSY A 4.00 10.00
BSRKS Kevin Smith JSY A 4.00 10.00
BSRMB Marion Barber JSY A 4.00 10.00
BSRMBU Michael Bush JSY A 3.00 8.00
BSRME Marcus Easley JSY B RC 2.50 6.00
BSRMG Mardy Gilyard JSY B RC 3.00 8.00
BSRMH Montario Hardesty JSY B RC 3.00 8.00
BSRMK Mike Kafka JSY B RC 3.00 8.00
BSRML Matt Leinart JSY A 4.00 10.00
BSRMW Mike Williams JSY B RC 4.00 10.00
BSRMWI Mario Williams JSY A 4.00 10.00
BSRNS Ndamukong Suh JSY B RC 6.00 15.00
BSRRC Riley Cooper JSY A RC 4.00 10.00
BSRRG Rob Gronkowski JSY B RC 8.00 20.00
BSRRM Ryan Mathews JSY B RC 5.00 12.00
BSRRMC Rolando McClain JSY B RC 3.00 8.00
BSRRS Richard Seymour JSY A 3.00 8.00
BSRSB Sam Bradford JSY B RC 10.00 25.00
BSRSC Sean Canfield JSY A RC 3.00 8.00
BSRSM Santana Moss JSY A 4.00 10.00
BSRSS Steve Slaton JSY A 3.00 8.00
BSRTG Toby Gerhart JSY B RC 3.00 8.00
BSRTH Tommie Harris JSY A 3.00 8.00
BSRTHE Todd Heap JSY A 3.00 8.00
BSRTP Tony Pike JSY A RC 4.00 10.00
BSRTPR Taylor Price JSY B RC 3.00 8.00
BSRTT Tim Tebow JSY B RC 12.50 30.00
BSRVJ Vincent Jackson JSY A 3.00 8.00
BSRZR Zac Robinson JSY A RC 3.00 8.00

2010 Bowman Sterling Black Refractors

*1-50 ROOKIES: 1X TO 2.5X BASIC CARDS
*ROOKIE AU: .6X TO 1.5X BASIC AU A-B
*ROOKIE AU: .8X TO 2X BASIC AU C-D
*ROOKIE JSY: .5X TO 1.2X BASIC JSY A-B
*ROOKIE JSY: .6X TO 1.5X BASIC JSY C-D
*VET AU: .6X TO 1.5X BASIC CARDS
*VET JSY: .5X TO 1.2X BASIC CARDS
STATED PRINT RUN 50 SER.#'d SETS
EXCH EXPIRATION: 12/31/2013
BSABW Chris Wells AU EXCH 8.00 20.00
BSACM Colt McCoy AU 20.00 50.00
BSADBR Drew Brees AU 40.00 80.00
BSAJCL Jimmy Clausen AU 8.00 20.00
BSASB Sam Bradford AU 75.00 150.00
BSATT Tim Tebow AU 100.00 175.00

2010 Bowman Sterling Blue Refractors

*1-50 ROOKIES: .8X TO 2X BASIC CARDS
*ROOKIE AU: .5X TO 1.2X BASIC AU A-B
*ROOKIE AU: .6X TO 1.5X BASIC AU C-D
*ROOKIE JSY: .4X TO 1X BASIC JSY A-B
*ROOKIE JSY: .5X TO 1.2X BASIC JSY C-D
*ROOKIE JSY AU: .5X TO 1.2X BASIC CARDS
*VET AU: .6X TO 1.5X BASIC CARDS
*VET JSY: .4X TO 1X BASIC CARDS
*VET JSY AU: .5X TO 1.2X BASIC CARDS
STATED PRINT RUN 99 SER.#'d SETS
EXCH EXPIRATION: 12/31/2013

2010 Bowman Sterling Gold Refractors

*1-50 ROOKIES: 2X TO 5X BASIC CARDS
*ROOKIE AU: 1X TO 2.5X BASIC AU A-B
*ROOKIE AU: 1.2X TO 3X BASIC AU C-D
*ROOKIE JSY: .6X TO 1.5X BASIC JSY A-B
*ROOKIE JSY: .8X TO 2X BASIC JSY C-D
*ROOKIE JSY AU: 1.2X TO 3X BASIC CARDS
*VET AU: .8X TO 2X BASIC CARDS
*VET JSY: .6X TO 1.5X BASIC CARDS
*VET JSY AU: .8X TO 2X BASIC CARDS
STATED PRINT RUN 25 SER.#'d SETS
EXCH EXPIRATION: 12/31/2013
BSACM Colt McCoy AU 75.00 150.00
BSADB Dez Bryant AU 75.00 150.00
BSADBR Drew Brees AU 50.00 100.00
BSAJCL Jimmy Clausen AU 12.00 30.00
BSARAP Adrian Peterson JSY AU 75.00 150.00
BSARCM Colt McCoy JSY AU 40.00 100.00
BSARNS Ndamukong Suh JSY AU 75.00 150.00
BSARSB Sam Bradford JSY AU 200.00 350.00
BSARTT Tim Tebow JSY AU 250.00 400.00
BSASB Sam Bradford AU 125.00 250.00
BSATT Tim Tebow AU 175.00 300.00
BSRSB Sam Bradford JSY 25.00 60.00
BSRTT Tim Tebow JSY 30.00 80.00

2010 Bowman Sterling Refractors

*1-50 ROOKIES: .6X TO 1.5X BASIC CARDS
*ROOKIE JSY: .4X TO 1X BASIC JSY A
*ROOKIE JSY: .5X TO 1.2X BASIC JSY B
*VETERAN JSY: .4X TO 1X BASIC CARDS
STATED PRINT RUN 299 SER.#'d SETS

2010 Bowman Sterling Dual Autographs

STATED PRINT RUN 25 SER.#'d SETS
BC Sam Bradford 100.00 200.00
Jimmy Clausen
BM Sam Bradford 100.00 200.00
Colt McCoy
BT Eric Berry 30.00 60.00
Earl Thomas
MB Ryan Mathews 40.00 80.00
Jahvid Best
MBE Dexter McCluster 30.00 60.00
Jahvid Best
MH Colt McCoy 40.00 80.00
Montario Hardesty
MM Ryan Mathews 40.00 80.00
Dexter McCluster
MS Gerald McCoy 30.00 60.00
Ndamukong Suh
SB C.J. Spiller 30.00 60.00
Jahvid Best
SM C.J. Spiller 40.00 80.00
Ryan Mathews
ST C.J. Spiller 25.00 50.00
Demaryius Thomas

2010 Bowman Sterling Dual Autographed Relic Black Refractors

STATED PRINT RUN 25 SER.#'d SETS
*BASIC DUAL: .4X TO 1X BLACK REF/25
EXCH EXPIRATION: 12/31/2013
BC Sam Bradford 100.00 200.00
Jimmy Clausen
BD Arrelious Benn 20.00 50.00
Eric Decker
BG Sam Bradford EXCH 100.00 200.00
Mardy Gilyard
BM Sam Bradford 100.00 200.00
Colt McCoy
BTH Eric Berry 30.00 60.00
Earl Thomas
BW Dez Bryant 60.00 120.00
Mike Williams
CL Jimmy Clausen 20.00 50.00
Brandon LaFell
CT Jimmy Clausen 15.00 40.00
Golden Tate
DR Eric Decker 20.00 50.00
Andre Roberts
DT Jonathan Dwyer 20.00 50.00
Demaryius Thomas
GD Toby Gerhart 20.00 50.00
Eric Decker
GDW Toby Gerhart 15.00 40.00
Jonathan Dwyer
GH Rob Gronkowski 60.00 100.00
Aaron Hernandez
HD Montario Hardesty
Jonathan Dwyer
LE Brandon LaFell 12.00 30.00
Armanti Edwards
LW Brandon LaFell 15.00 40.00
Mike Williams
MB Ryan Mathews 40.00 80.00
Jahvid Best
MBE Dexter McCluster 30.00 60.00
Jahvid Best
MH Colt McCoy 40.00 80.00
Montario Hardesty
MM Ryan Mathews 40.00 80.00
Dexter McCluster
MS Gerald McCoy 30.00 60.00
Ndamukong Suh
MSH Colt McCoy 30.00 80.00
Jordan Shipley
MT Dexter McCluster 20.00 50.00
Demaryius Thomas
PG Taylor Price 25.00 50.00
Rob Gronkowski
RG Andre Roberts EXCH 12.00 30.00
Mardy Gilyard
SB C.J. Spiller 30.00 60.00
Jahvid Best
SD Emmanuel Sanders 15.00 40.00
Jonathan Dwyer
SE C.J. Spiller 20.00 50.00
Marcus Easley
SS Jordan Shipley 15.00 40.00
Emmanuel Sanders
ST C.J. Spiller 20.00 50.00
Demaryius Thomas
TD Demaryius Thomas 20.00 50.00
Eric Decker
TDI Ben Tate 15.00 40.00
Anthony Dixon
TT Golden Tate 15.00 40.00
Ben Tate
TTH Golden Tate 20.00 50.00
Demaryius Thomas
WB Mike Williams 20.00 40.00
Arrelious Benn

2010 Bowman Sterling Dual Jersey Box Topper

ONE PER HOBBY BOX
*BLACK REF/25: .6X TO 1.5X BASIC INSERTS
*BLUE REF/50: .5X TO 1.2X BASIC INSERTS
*REF/69: .5X TO 1.2X BASIC INSERTS
BB Dez Bryant 6.00 15.00
Jahvid Best
BC Sam Bradford 8.00 20.00
Jimmy Clausen
BG Sam Bradford 8.00 20.00
Mardy Gilyard
BM Eric Berry 2.50 6.00
Dexter McCluster
BMC Sam Bradford 8.00 20.00
Colt McCoy
BS Jahivd Best 5.00 12.00
C.J. Spiller
BT Eric Berry 5.00 12.00
Earl Thomas
BTE Dez Bryant 6.00 15.00
Demaryius Thomas
BW Dez Bryant 6.00 15.00
Mike Williams
CL Jimmy Clausen 2.50 6.00
Brandon LaFell
CT Jimmy Clausen 2.50 6.00
Golden Tate
DS Jonathan Dwyer 4.00 10.00
Emmanuel Sanders
DT Jonathan Dwyer 4.00 10.00
Demaryius Thomas
GM Antonio Gates 6.00 15.00
Ryan Mathews
MH Colt McCoy 5.00 12.00
Montario Hardesty
MS Colt McCoy 5.00 12.00
Jordan Shipley
PG Adrian Peterson 6.00 15.00
Toby Gerhart
RB Tony Romo 6.00 15.00
Dez Bryant
SE C.J. Spiller 4.00 10.00
Marcus Easley
ST Steve Slaton 4.00 10.00
Ben Tate
TD Tim Tebow 8.00 20.00
Eric Decker
TDE Demaryius Thomas 5.00 12.00
Eric Decker
TT Tim Tebow 8.00 20.00
Demaryius Thomas
WB Mike Williams 4.00 10.00
Arrelious Benn
WM Patrick Willis 3.00 8.00
Rolando McClain

2011 Bowman Sterling

EXCH EXPIRATION: 12/31/2014
1 Patrick Peterson RC 2.00 5.00
2 Aldon Smith RC 2.00 5.00
3 J.J. Watt RC 1.50 4.00
4 Nick Fairley RC 1.50 4.00
5 Robert Quinn RC 1.25 3.00
6 Ryan Kerrigan RC 1.25 3.00
7 James Carpenter RC 1.25 3.00
8 Jacquizz Rodgers RC 1.25 3.00
9 Niles Paul RC 1.25 3.00
10 Derek Sherrod RC 1.25 3.00
11 Aaron Williams RC 1.00 2.50
12 Akeem Ayers RC 1.00 2.50
13 Tandon Doss RC 1.00 2.50
14 Cecil Shorts RC 1.00 2.50
15 Lance Kendricks RC 1.00 2.50
16 Marvin Austin RC 1.00 2.50
17 Rob Housler RC 1.00 2.50
18 Roy Helu RC 2.50 6.00
19 Tyrod Taylor RC 1.25 3.00
20 Casey Matthews RC 1.25 3.00
21 Julius Thomas RC 1.00 2.50
22 Johnny White RC 1.00 2.50
23 Jeremy Kerley RC 1.25 3.00
24 Denarius Moore RC 1.50 4.00
25 T.J. Yates RC 1.50 4.00
26 Da'Rel Scott RC 1.00 2.50
27 Nathan Enderle RC 1.25 3.00
28 Ryan Whalen RC 1.00 2.50
29 Muhammad Wilkerson RC 1.25 3.00
30 Greg Jones RC 1.00 2.50
31 Virgil Green RC 1.00 2.50
32 Ryan Taylor RC 1.00 2.50
33 Justin Houston RC 1.25 3.00
34 Brooks Reed RC 1.25 3.00
35 Mike Pouncey RC 1.25 3.00
36 Prince Amukamara RC 1.25 3.00
37 Jimmy Smith RC 1.25 3.00
38 Da'Quan Bowers RC 1.25 3.00
39 Greg Salas RC 1.25 3.00
40 Dion Lewis RC 1.25 3.00
41 Mark Herzlich RC 1.00 2.50
42 Jabaal Sheard RC 1.25 3.00
43 Adrian Clayborn RC 1.25 3.00
44 Cameron Heyward RC 1.25 3.00
45 Tyron Smith RC 1.50 4.00
46 Rahim Moore RC 1.00 2.50
48 Ricky Stanzi RC 1.50 4.00
49 Anthony Allen RC .75 2.00
50 Kris Durham RC 1.00 2.50
BSAAA Akeem Ayers AU 3.00 8.00
BSAAB Ahmad Bradshaw AU 6.00 15.00
BSAABR Antonio Brown AU 12.50 25.00
BSAAC Adrian Clayborn AU 5.00 12.00
BSAAG Alex Green AU 4.00 10.00
BSAAP Austin Pettis AU 3.00 8.00
BSAAS Aldon Smith AU 15.00 30.00
BSAAW Adrian Wilson AU 5.00 12.00
BSABL Brandon Lloyd AU 5.00 12.00
BSABP Bilal Powell AU 2.50 6.00
BSADA Darvin Adams AU 3.00 8.00
BSADB Davone Bess AU 5.00 12.00
BSADBO Da'Quan Bowers AU 4.00 10.00
BSADC Delone Carter AU 3.00 8.00
BSADH Dwayne Harris AU 4.00 10.00
BSADL Dion Lewis AU 4.00 10.00
BSADM DeMarco Murray AU 20.00 40.00
BSADT Daniel Thomas AU 4.00 10.00
BSAEG Edmond Gates AU 3.00 8.00
BSAGL Greg Little AU 4.00 10.00
BSAGM Greg McElroy AU 4.00 10.00
BSAGS Greg Salas AU 4.00 10.00
BSAJB Jon Baldwin AU 5.00 12.00
BSAJG Jabar Gaffney AU 5.00 12.00
BSAJH Jamie Harper AU 4.00 10.00
BSAJHO Justin Houston AU 4.00 10.00
BSAJJE Jerrel Jernigan AU 3.00 8.00
BSAJR Jacquizz Rodgers AU 4.00 10.00
BSAJT Jordan Todman AU 2.50 6.00
BSAKH Kendall Hunter AU 5.00 12.00
BSALH Leonard Hankerson AU 4.00 10.00
BSALS Luke Stocker AU RC 3.00 8.00
BSAMF Malcom Floyd AU 6.00 15.00
BSAML Mikel Leshoure AU 4.00 10.00
BSAMLE Marcedes Lewis AU 5.00 12.00
BSAMM Mike McNeill AU 4.00 10.00
BSAMP Mike Pouncey AU RC 4.00 10.00
BSAMT Mike Thomas AU 5.00 12.00
BSAMW Mike Wallace AU 10.00 25.00
BSARC Randall Cobb AU 8.00 20.00
BSARMA Robert Mathis AU 6.00 15.00
BSART Ryan Torain AU 5.00 12.00
BSARW Ryan Williams AU 5.00 12.00
BSASR Stevan Ridley AU 4.00 10.00
BSASV Shane Vereen AU 4.00 10.00
BSATJ Taiwan Jones AU 4.00 10.00
BSATS Torrey Smith AU 8.00 20.00
BSATT Tyrod Taylor AU 4.00 10.00
BSATTO Terrence Toliver AU 3.00 8.00
BSATY Titus Young AU 5.00 12.00
BSAVB Vincent Brown AU 4.00 10.00
BSRAD Andy Dalton JSY RC 6.00 15.00
BSRAG Alex Green JSY RC 2.50 6.00
BSRAH Albert Haynesworth JSY 2.50 6.00
BSRAJG A.J. Green JSY RC 5.00 12.00
BSRAJH A.J. Hawk JSY 3.00 8.00
BSRAP Austin Pettis JSY RC 2.00 5.00
BSRAS Alex Smith QB JSY 3.00 8.00
BSRBG Blaine Gabbert JSY RC 4.00 10.00
BSRBP Bilal Powell JSY RC 1.50 4.00
BSRBU Brian Urlacher JSY 4.00 10.00
BSRCC Chris Cooley JSY 4.00 10.00
BSRCK Colin Kaepernick JSY RC 3.00 8.00
BSRCN Cam Newton JSY RC 12.00 30.00
BSRCP Christian Ponder JSY RC 5.00 12.00
BSRCS Cecil Shorts JSY 2.00 5.00
BSRDC Delone Carter JSY RC 2.00 5.00
BSRDHE Devin Hester JSY 4.00 10.00
BSRDL Dion Lewis JSY 2.50 6.00
BSRDM DeMarco Murray JSY RC 5.00 12.00
BSRDT Daniel Thomas JSY RC 2.50 6.00
BSRDW DeAngelo Williams JSY 3.00 8.00
BSREG Edmond Gates JSY RC 2.00 5.00
BSREM Eli Manning JSY 4.00 10.00
BSRER Eddie Royal JSY 2.50 6.00
BSRGL Greg Little JSY RC 2.50 6.00
BSRGS Greg Salas JSY 2.50 6.00
BSRJB Jon Baldwin JSY RC 2.50 6.00
BSRJH Jamie Harper JSY RC 2.50 6.00
BSRJJ Julio Jones JSY RC 5.00 12.00
BSRJJE Jerrel Jernigan JSY RC 2.00 5.00
BSRJL Jake Locker JSY RC 5.00 12.00
BSRJP Julius Peppers JSY 3.00 8.00
BSRJT Jordan Todman JSY RC 1.50 4.00
BSRKH Kendall Hunter JSY RC 2.50 6.00
BSRKO Kyle Orton JSY 3.00 8.00
BSRKR Kyle Rudolph JSY RC 2.50 6.00
BSRLH Leonard Hankerson JSY RC 2.50 6.00
BSRMD Marcell Dareus JSY RC 2.50 6.00
BSRMF Matt Forte JSY 3.00 8.00
BSRMI Mark Ingram JSY RC 5.00 12.00
BSRML Mikel Leshoure JSY RC 2.50 6.00
BSRPA Prince Amukamara JSY 2.50 6.00
BSRRC Randall Cobb JSY RC 3.00 8.00
BSRRM Ryan Mallett JSY RC 5.00 12.00
BSRRR Ray Rice JSY 3.00 8.00
BSRRW Ryan Williams JSY RC 3.00 8.00
BSRSB Sam Bradford JSY 4.00 10.00
BSRSR Stevan Ridley JSY RC 2.50 6.00
BSRSV Shane Vereen JSY RC 2.50 6.00
BSRTJ Taiwan Jones JSY RC 2.50 6.00
BSRTR Tony Romo JSY 4.00 10.00
BSRTS Torrey Smith JSY RC 3.00 8.00
BSRTY Titus Young JSY RC 3.00 8.00
BSRVB Vincent Brown JSY RC 2.50 6.00
BSRVM Von Miller JSY RC 3.00 8.00
BSARAG Alex Green JSY AU 6.00 15.00
BSARAJG A.J. Green JSY AU 25.00 50.00
BSARAP Austin Pettis JSY AU 5.00 12.00
BSARBP Bilal Powell JSY AU 4.00 10.00
BSARCB Champ Bailey JSY AU 15.00 30.00
BSARCK Colin Kaepernick JSY AU 8.00 20.00
BSARCP Christian Ponder JSY AU 20.00 40.00
BSARDC Delone Carter JSY AU 5.00 12.00
BSARDH DeAngelo Hall JSY AU 6.00 15.00
BSARDK Dustin Keller JSY AU 6.00 15.00
BSARDM DeMarco Murray JSY AU EXCH 25.00 50.00
BSARDMA Derrick Mason JSY AU 6.00 15.00
BSARDT Daniel Thomas JSY AU 6.00 15.00
BSARGL Greg Little JSY AU 6.00 15.00
BSARGO Greg Olsen JSY AU 6.00 15.00
BSARJB Jon Baldwin JSY AU 6.00 15.00
BSARJH Jamie Harper JSY AU 5.00 12.00
BSARJJE Jerrel Jernigan JSY AU 5.00 12.00
BSARJR Jacquizz Rodgers JSY AU 6.00 15.00
BSARJT Jordan Todman JSY AU 4.00 10.00
BSARKH Kendall Hunter JSY AU 6.00 15.00
BSARKR Kyle Rudolph JSY AU 6.00 15.00
BSARLH Leonard Hankerson JSY AU 6.00 15.00
BSARMD Marcell Dareus JSY AU 6.00 15.00
BSARML Mikel Leshoure JSY AU 6.00 15.00
BSARNF Nick Fairley JSY AU 8.00 20.00
BSARRC Randall Cobb JSY AU 12.00 30.00
BSARRM Ryan Mallett JSY AU 20.00 40.00
BSARRW Ryan Williams JSY AU 8.00 20.00
BSARSJ Steve Johnson JSY AU 12.00 30.00
BSARSR Stevan Ridley JSY AU 6.00 15.00
BSARSRI Sidney Rice JSY AU 8.00 20.00
BSARSV Shane Vereen JSY AU 6.00 15.00
BSARTJ Taiwan Jones JSY AU 6.00 15.00
BSARTS Torrey Smith JSY AU 8.00 20.00
BSARTY Titus Young JSY AU 8.00 20.00
BSARVB Vincent Brown JSY AU 6.00 15.00
BSARVM Von Miller JSY AU 10.00 25.00
BSARZM Zach Miller JSY AU 6.00 15.00

2011 Bowman Sterling Black Refractors

*1-50 ROOKIES/50: 1.2X TO 3X BASIC CARDS
*VETERAN AU/50: .6X TO 1.5X BASIC AU
*ROOKIE AU/50: .8X TO 2X BASIC AU
STATED PRINT RUN 50 SER.#'d SETS
BSARH Roy Helu AU 30.00 60.00
BSATP Terrelle Pryor AU 20.00 50.00

2011 Bowman Sterling Blue Refractors

*1-50 ROOKIES/99: 1X TO 2.5X BASIC CARDS
*VETERAN AU/99: .5X TO 1.2X BASIC AU
*ROOKIE AU/99: .6X TO 1.5X BASIC AU
*VETERAN JSY/99: .5X TO 1.2X BASIC JSY
*ROOKIE JSY/99: .6X TO 1.5X BASIC JSY
*VET JSY AU/50: .5X TO 1.2X BASIC JSY AU
*ROOK.JSY AU/99: .5X TO 1.2X BASE JSY AU
STATED PRINT RUN 99 SER.#'d SETS
EXCH EXPIRATION: 12/31/2014
BSAAF Arian Foster AU 30.00 60.00
BSARM Ryan Mallett AU 20.00 50.00
BSARAD Andy Dalton JSY AU 40.00 80.00
BSARJJ Julio Jones JSY AU 30.00 60.00

2011 Bowman Sterling Gold Refractors

*1-50 ROOKIES/25: 1.5X TO 4X BASIC CARDS
*VETERAN JSY/25: .8X TO 2X BASIC JSY
*ROOKIE JSY/25: 1X TO 2.5X BASIC JSY
*VETERAN AU/25: .8X TO 2X BASIC AU
*ROOKIE AU/25: 1X TO 2.5X BASIC AU
*VET JSY AU/25: .6X TO 1.5X BASIC JSY AU
*ROOK.JSY AU/25: 1X TO 2.5X BASE JSY AU
STATED PRINT RUN 25 SER.#'d SETS
BSAAD Andy Dalton AU 75.00 125.00
BSAAF Arian Foster AU 40.00 80.00
BSAAJG A.J. Green AU 50.00 100.00
BSAAS Aldon Smith AU 75.00 150.00
BSACK Colin Kaepernick AU 25.00 50.00
BSACN Cam Newton AU 200.00 350.00
BSACP Christian Ponder AU 40.00 80.00
BSAJL Jake Locker AU 75.00 150.00
BSAMI Mark Ingram AU 50.00 100.00
BSAPM Peyton Manning AU 75.00 150.00
BSARH Roy Helu AU 40.00 80.00
BSARM Ryan Mallett AU
BSATP Terrelle Pryor AU 25.00 60.00
BSARAD Andy Dalton JSY AU 100.00 175.00
BSARBG Blaine Gabbert JSY AU 40.00 100.00
BSARCN Cam Newton JSY AU 300.00 450.00
BSARJJ Julio Jones JSY AU
BSARJL Jake Locker JSY AU 100.00 175.00
BSARMI Mark Ingram JSY AU 50.00 120.00

2011 Bowman Sterling Pulsar Refractors

*1-50 ROOK/15: 2.5X TO 6X BASIC CARDS
*VETERAN JSY/15: 1.2X TO 3X BASIC JSY
*ROOKIE JSY/15: 1.5X TO 4X BASIC JSY
*VET AU/15: .5X TO 1.2X GOLD REF/25
*ROOK.AU/15: .5X TO 1.2X GOLD REF/25
*VET JSY AU/15: .5X TO 1.2X GOLD REF/25
*ROOK.JSY AU/15: .5X TO 1.2X GLD REF/25
STATED PRINT RUN 15 SER.#'d SETS
BSAAD Andy Dalton AU 100.00 175.00
BSAAJG A.J. Green AU 90.00 150.00
BSAAS Aldon Smith AU 125.00 200.00
BSACN Cam Newton AU 250.00 400.00
BSAJL Jake Locker AU 100.00 200.00
BSAMI Mark Ingram AU 60.00 150.00
BSARM Ryan Mallett AU
BSARAD Andy Dalton JSY AU 125.00 200.00
BSARAJG A.J. Green JSY AU 100.00 175.00
BSARCN Cam Newton JSY AU 350.00 600.00
BSARDM DeMarco Murray JSY AU EXCH 100.00175.00
BSARJJ Julio Jones JSY AU
BSARJL Jake Locker JSY AU 125.00 200.00

2011 Bowman Sterling Refractors

*1-50 ROOKIES/299: .6X TO 1.5X BASIC CARDS
*VETERAN JSY/299: .4X TO 1X BASIC JSY
*ROOKIE JSY/299: .4X TO 1X BASIC JSY
STATED PRINT RUN 299 SER.#'d SETS

2011 Bowman Sterling Dual Autographs

STATED PRINT RUN 25 SER.#'d SETS
BSDABS Jon Baldwin 20.00 50.00
Torrey Smith
BSDACG Randall Cobb 40.00 80.00
Alex Green
BSDADG Andy Dalton 90.00 150.00
A.J. Green
BSDAKH Colin Kaepernick 30.00 60.00
Kendall Hunter
BSDALG Jake Locker 50.00 100.00
Blaine Gabbert
BSDALY Mikel Leshoure 12.00 30.00
Titus Young
BSDAMD Von Miller 20.00 50.00
Marcell Dareus
BSDANI Cam Newton 125.00 200.00
Mark Ingram
BSDAPR Christian Ponder 40.00 80.00
Kyle Rudolph
BSDAVR Shane Vereen 12.00 30.00
Stevan Ridley

2011 Bowman Sterling Dual Autographed Relics Pulsar Refractors

STATED PRINT RUN 5-60
BSPDARAG A.J. Green
Greg Little
BSPDARBR Bilal Powell/60 8.00 20.00
Stevan Ridley
BSPDARBS Jon Baldwin/10
Torrey Smith
BSPDARCA Cam Newton/5
A.J. Green
BSPDARCG Randall Cobb/35 30.00 60.00
Alex Green
BSPDARCY Randall Cobb/35 15.00 40.00
Titus Young
BSPDARDG Andy Dalton
A.J. Green
BSPDARDM Marcell Dareus/10
Von Miller
BSPDARDP Andy Dalton
Christian Ponder
BSPDARGL Blaine Gabbert/5
Jake Locker
BSPDARGS A.J. Green
Torrey Smith
BSPDARHC Jamie Harper/60 10.00 25.00
Delone Carter
BSPDARHJ Leonard Hankerson/35 12.00 30.00
Jerrel Jernigan
BSPDARHP Leonard Hankerson/60 12.00 30.00
Niles Paul
BSPDARID Mark Ingram/10
Marcell Dareus
BSPDARIL Mark Ingram
Mikel Leshoure
BSPDARKH Colin Kaepernick
Kendall Hunter
BSPDARLH Greg Little/35 12.00 30.00
Leonard Hankerson
BSPDARLHA Jake Locker
Jamie Harper
BSPDARLY Mikel Leshoure
Titus Young
BSPDARMH DeMarco Murray EXCH 40.00 80.00
Kendall Hunter
BSPDARMR Ryan Mallett/5
Stevan Ridley
BSPDARMV Ryan Mallett
Shane Vereen
BSPDARNG Cam Newton/5
Blaine Gabbert
BSPDARNI Cam Newton
Mark Ingram
BSPDARPR Christian Ponder
Kyle Rudolph
BSPDARSD Torrey Smith/60 15.00 40.00
Tandon Doss
BSPDARTB Jordan Todman/60 10.00 25.00
Vincent Brown
BSPDARTG Daniel Thomas/60 12.00 30.00
Edmond Gates
BSPDARTJ Jordan Todman/60 10.00 25.00
Taiwan Jones
BSPDARTP Daniel Thomas/60 12.00 30.00
Bilal Powell
BSPDARVP Shane Vereen/60 8.00 20.00
Bilal Powell
BSPDARVR Shane Vereen/60 10.00 25.00
Stevan Ridley
BSPDARWH Ryan Williams/35 12.00 30.00
Kendall Hunter
BSPDARYP Titus Young/35 10.00 25.00
Austin Pettis

2011 Bowman Sterling Dual Jersey Box Topper

ONE DUAL JSY PER HOBBY BOX
*BLACK REF/25: .8X TO 2X BASIC DUAL
*BLUE REF/50: .6X TO 1.5X BASIC DUAL
*PULSAR REF/15: 1X TO 2.5X BASIC DUAL
*REFRACT/75: .5X TO 1.2X BASIC DUAL
BSDRBM Tom Brady 8.00 20.00
Ryan Mallett
BSDRBS Jon Baldwin 4.00 10.00
Torrey Smith
BSDRCB Randall Cobb 4.00 10.00
Alex Green
BSDRDM Andy Dalton 8.00 20.00
Ryan Mallett
BSDRFB Larry Fitzgerald 3.00 8.00
Jon Baldwin
BSDRGD A.J. Green 10.00 25.00
Andy Dalton
BSDRGJ A.J. Green 8.00 20.00
Julio Jones
BSDRGP Blaine Gabbert 6.00 15.00
Christian Ponder
BSDRIJ Mark Ingram 8.00 20.00
Julio Jones
BSDRIW Mark Ingram 5.00 12.00
Ryan Williams
BSDRJD Julio Jones 6.00 15.00
Marcell Dareus
BSDRKH Colin Kaepernick 4.00 10.00
Kendall Hunter
BSDRLH Jake Locker 6.00 15.00
Jamie Harper
BSDRLY Mikel Leshoure 5.00 12.00
Titus Young
BSDRMH Santana Moss 3.00 8.00
Leonard Hankerson
BSDRMJ Darren McFadden 4.00 10.00
Taiwan Jones
BSDRMR Ryan Mallett 5.00 12.00
Stevan Ridley
BSDRNC Jordy Nelson 6.00 15.00
Randall Cobb
BSDRNL Cam Newton 12.00 30.00
Jake Locker
BSDRPM Adrian Peterson 6.00 15.00
DeMarco Murray
BSDRRP Kyle Rudolph 6.00 15.00
Christian Ponder
BSDRTB Jordan Todman 3.00 8.00
Vincent Brown
BSDRTR Michael Turner 3.00 8.00
Jacquizz Rodgers
BSDRVR Shane Vereen 3.00 8.00
Stevan Ridley
BSDRYP Titus Young 4.00 10.00
Austin Pettis

2011 Bowman Sterling Relics Jumbo Black Refractors

STATED PRINT RUN 50 SER.#'d SETS
BSRJRAD Andy Dalton 10.00 25.00
BSRJRAG Alex Green 5.00 12.00
BSRJRAP Austin Pettis 4.00 10.00
BSRJRBG Blaine Gabbert 8.00 20.00
BSRJRBP Bilal Powell 3.00 8.00
BSRJRCK Colin Kaepernick 6.00 15.00
BSRJRCN Cam Newton 25.00 60.00
BSRJRCP Christian Ponder 8.00 20.00
BSRJRCS Cecil Shorts 4.00 10.00
BSRJRDC Delone Carter 4.00 10.00
BSRJRDL Dion Lewis 5.00 12.00
BSRJRDM DeMarco Murray 8.00 20.00
BSRJRDT Daniel Thomas 5.00 12.00
BSRJREG Edmond Gates 4.00 10.00
BSRJRGL Greg Little 5.00 12.00
BSRJRGS Greg Salas 5.00 12.00
BSRJRJB Jon Baldwin 5.00 12.00
BSRJRJH Jamie Harper 5.00 12.00
BSRJRJJ Julio Jones 10.00 25.00
BSRJRJL Jake Locker 10.00 25.00
BSRJRJT Jordan Todman 3.00 8.00
BSRJRKH Kendall Hunter 5.00 12.00
BSRJRKR Kyle Rudolph 5.00 12.00
BSRJRLH Leonard Hankerson 5.00 12.00
BSRJRMD Marcell Dareus 5.00 12.00
BSRJRMI Mark Ingram 8.00 20.00
BSRJRML Mikel Leshoure 5.00 12.00
BSRJRPA Prince Amukamara 5.00 12.00
BSRJRRC Randall Cobb 6.00 15.00
BSRJRRM Ryan Mallett 8.00 20.00
BSRJRRW Ryan Williams 6.00 15.00
BSRJRSR Stevan Ridley 5.00 12.00
BSRJRSV Shane Vereen 5.00 12.00
BSRJRTJ Taiwan Jones 5.00 12.00
BSRJRTS Torrey Smith 6.00 15.00
BSRJRTY Titus Young 6.00 15.00
BSRJRVB Vincent Brown 5.00 12.00
BSRJRVM Von Miller 6.00 15.00
BSRJRAJG A.J. Green 8.00 20.00
BSRJRJJE Jerrel Jernigan 4.00 10.00

1995 Bowman's Best

This 180 card set was issued by Topps and broken down into two subsets: Bowman's Best Black for veterans (V1-V90) and Bowman's Best Blue for rookies (R1-R90). Rookie Cards in this set include Mark Bruener, Ki-Jana Carter, Kerry Collins, Joey Galloway, Darrick Holmes, Napoleon Kaufman, Steve McNair, Curtis Martin, Chris Sanders, Frank Sanders, Rashaan Salaam, Kordell Stewart, Tamarick Vanover and Michael Westbrook

COMPLETE SET (180) 40.00 100.00
R1 Ki-Jana Carter RC .60 1.50
R2 Tony Boselli RC .60 1.50
R3 Steve McNair RC 6.00 15.00
R4 Michael Westbrook RC .60 1.50
R5 Kerry Collins RC 2.50 6.00
R6 Kevin Carter RC .60 1.50
R7 Mike Mamula RC .15 .40
R8 Joey Galloway RC 2.50 6.00
R9 Kyle Brady RC .60 1.50
R10 Ray McElroy RC .15 .40
R11 Derrick Alexander DE RC .15 .40
R12 Warren Sapp RC 2.50 6.00
R13 Mark Fields RC .60 1.50
R14 Ruben Brown RC .60 1.50
R15 Ellis Johnson RC .15 .40
R16 Hugh Douglas RC .60 1.50
R17 Alundis Brice RC .15 .40
R18 Napoleon Kaufman RC 2.00 5.00
R19 James O. Stewart RC 1.25 3.00
R20 Luther Elliss RC .15 .40
R21 Rashaan Salaam RC .30 .75
R22 Tyrone Poole RC .60 1.50
R23 Ty Law RC 1.50 4.00
R24 Korey Stringer RC .50 1.25
R25 Billy Milner RC .15 .40
R26 Roell Preston RC .30 .75
R27 Mark Bruener RC .30 .75
R28 Derrick Brooks RC 2.50 6.00
R29 Blake Brockermeyer RC .15 .40
R30 Mike Frederick RC .15 .40
R31 Trezelle Jenkins RC .15 .40
R32 Craig Newsome RC .15 .40
R33 Matt O'Dwyer RC .15 .40
R34 Terrance Shaw RC .15 .40
R35 Anthony Cook RC .15 .40
R36 Darick Holmes RC .30 .75
R37 Cory Raymer RC .15 .40
R38 Zach Wiegert RC .15 .40
R39 Sam Shade RC .15 .40
R40 Brian DeMarco RC .15 .40
R41 Ron Davis RC .15 .40
R42 Orlando Thomas RC .15 .40
R43 Derek West RC .15 .40
R44 Ray Zellars RC .30 .75
R45 Todd Collins RC 2.00 5.00
R46 Linc Harden RC .15 .40
R47 Frank Sanders RC .60 1.50
R48 Ken Dilger RC .60 1.50
R49 Barrett Robbins RC .15 .40
R50 Bobby Taylor RC 1.00 2.50
R51 Terrell Fletcher RC .15 .40
R52 Jack Jackson RC .15 .40
R53 Jeff Kopp RC .15 .40
R54 Brendan Stai RC .15 .40
R55 Corey Fuller RC .15 .40
R56 Todd Sauerbrun RC .15 .40
R57 Dameian Jeffries RC .15 .40
R58 Troy Dumas RC .15 .40
R59 Charlie Williams RC .15 .40
R60 Kordell Stewart RC 2.50 6.00
R61 Jay Barker RC .15 .40
R62 Jesse James RC .15 .40
R63 Shane Hannah RC .15 .40
R64 Rob Johnson RC 1.50 4.00
R65 Darius Holland RC .15 .40
R66 William Henderson RC 2.00 5.00
R67 Chris Sanders RC .30 .75
R68 Darryl Pounds RC .15 .40
R69 Melvin Tuten RC .15 .40
R70 David Sloan RC .15 .40
R71 Chris Hudson RC .15 .40
R72 William Strong RC .15 .40
R73 Brian Williams LB RC .15 .40
R74 Curtis Martin RC 6.00 15.00
R75 Mike Verstegen RC .15 .40
R76 Justin Armour RC .15 .40
R77 Lorenzo Styles RC .15 .40
R78 Oliver Gibson RC .15 .40
R79 Zack Crockett RC .30 .75
R80 Tau Pupua RC .15 .40
R81 Tamarick Vanover RC .60 1.50
R82 Steve McLaughlin RC .15 .40
R83 Sean Harris RC .15 .40
R84 Eric Zeier RC .60 1.50
R85 Rodney Young RC .15 .40
R86 Chad May RC .15 .40
R87 Evan Pilgrim RC .15 .40
R88 James A.Stewart RC .15 .40
R89 Torey Hunter RC .15 .40
R90 Antonio Freeman RC 1.50 4.00
V1 Rob Moore .25 .60
V2 Craig Heyward .25 .60
V3 Jim Kelly .50 1.25
V4 John Kasay .10 .30
V5 Jeff Graham .10 .30
V6 Jeff Blake RC 1.00 2.50
V7 Antonio Langham .10 .30
V8 Troy Aikman 1.25 3.00
V9 Simon Fletcher .10 .30
V10 Barry Sanders 2.00 5.00
V11 Edgar Bennett .25 .60
V12 Ray Childress .10 .30
V13 Ray Buchanan .10 .30
V14 Desmond Howard .25 .60
V15 Dale Carter .25 .60
V16 Troy Vincent .10 .30
V17 David Palmer .25 .60
V18 Ben Coates .25 .60
V19 Derek Brown .10 .30
V20 Dave Brown .25 .60
V21 Mo Lewis .10 .30
V22 Harvey Williams .10 .30
V23 Randall Cunningham .50 1.25
V24 Kevin Greene .25 .60
V25 Junior Seau .50 1.25
V26 Merton Hanks .10 .30
V27 Cortez Kennedy .25 .60
V28 Troy Drayton .10 .30
V29 Hardy Nickerson .10 .30
V30 Brian Mitchell .10 .30
V31 Raymont Harris .10 .30
V32 Keith Goganious .10 .30
V33 Andre Reed .25 .60
V34 Terance Mathis .25 .60
V35 Garrison Hearst .50 1.25
V36 Glyn Milburn .10 .30
V37 Emmitt Smith 2.00 5.00
V38 Vinny Testaverde .25 .60
V39 Darnay Scott .25 .60
V40 Mickey Washington .10 .30
V41 Craig Erickson .10 .30
V42 Chris Chandler .50 1.25
V43 Brett Favre 2.50 6.00
V44 Scott Mitchell .25 .60
V45 Chris Slade .10 .30
V46 Warren Moon .25 .60
V47 Dan Marino 2.50 6.00
V48 Greg Hill .25 .60
V49 Rocket Ismail .25 .60
V50 Bobby Houston .10 .30
V51 Rodney Hampton .25 .60
V52 Jim Everett .10 .30
V53 Rick Mirer .25 .60
V54 Steve Young 1.00 2.50
V55 Dennis Gibson .10 .30
V56 Rod Woodson .25 .60
V57 Calvin Williams .25 .60
V58 Tom Carter .10 .30
V59 Trent Dilfer .50 1.25
V60 Shane Conlan .10 .30
V61 Cornelius Bennett .25 .60
V62 Eric Metcalf .25 .60
V63 Frank Reich .10 .30
V64 Eric Hill .10 .30
V65 Erik Kramer .10 .30
V66 Michael Irvin .50 1.25
V67 Tony McGee .10 .30
V68 Andre Rison .25 .60
V69 Shannon Sharpe .25 .60
V70 Quentin Coryatt .25 .60
V71 Robert Brooks .50 1.25
V72 Steve Beuerlein .25 .60
V73 Herman Moore .50 1.25
V74 Jack Del Rio .10 .30
V75 Dave Meggett .10 .30
V76 Pete Stoyanovich .10 .30
V77 Neil Smith .25 .60
V78 Corey Miller .10 .30
V79 Tim Brown .50 1.25
V80 Tyrone Hughes .25 .60
V81 Boomer Esiason .25 .60
V82 Natrone Means .25 .60
V83 Chris Warren .25 .60
V84 Byron Bam Morris .10 .30
V85 Jerry Rice 1.25 3.00
V86 Michael Zordich .10 .30
V87 Errict Rhett .25 .60
V88 Henry Ellard .25 .60
V89 Chris Miller .10 .30
V90 John Elway 2.50 6.00

1995 Bowman's Best Refractors

COMPLETE SET (180)	200.00	500.00
*STARS: 1.2X TO 3X BASIC CARDS		
*ROOKIES: 1.2X TO 2.3X BASIC CARDS		
STATED ODDS 1:6		

1995 Bowman's Best Mirror Images Draft Picks

COMPLETE SET (15)	10.00	25.00
STATED ODDS 1:4		
*REFRACTORS: 2.5X TO 5X BASIC INSERTS		
REFRACTOR STATED ODDS 1:36		
1 Ki-Jana Carter	.75	2.00
Dan Wilkinson		
2 Marshall Faulk	2.00	5.00
Tony Boselli		
3 Steve McNair	3.00	8.00
Heath Shuler		
4 Michael Westbrook	.75	2.00
Willie McGinest		
5 Kerry Collins	1.50	4.00
Trev Alberts		
6 Trent Dilfer	.75	2.00
Kevin Carter		
7 Bryant Young	.75	2.00
Mike Mamula		
8 Joey Galloway	1.50	4.00
Sam Adams		
9 Antonio Langham	.50	1.25
Kyle Brady		
10 J.J.Stokes	.75	2.00
Jamir Miller		
11 John Thierry	.75	2.00
Derrick Alexander DE		
12 Aaron Glenn	.50	1.25
Warren Sapp		
13 Joe Johnson	.75	2.00
Mark Fields		
14 Bernard Williams	.75	2.00
Ruben Brown		
15 Wayne Gandy	.50	1.25
Ellis Johnson		

1996 Bowman's Best

The 1996 Bowman's Best set was issued in one series totalling 180 cards. The six-card packs retail for $5.00 each. The fronts of the 135 veterans' cards feature color action player photos in a gold design. The cards for the 45 draft picks display color action player photos in a silver design. The backs carry player information and statistics.

COMPLETE SET (180)	40.00	80.00
1 Emmitt Smith	1.25	3.00
2 Kordell Stewart	.30	.75
3 Mark Chmura	.20	.50
4 Sean Dawkins	.10	.30
5 Steve Young	.60	1.50
6 Tamarick Vanover	.20	.50
7 Scott Mitchell	.20	.50
8 Aaron Hayden	.10	.30
9 William Thomas	.10	.30
10 Dan Marino	1.50	4.00
11 Curtis Conway	.30	.75
12 Steve Atwater	.10	.30
13 Derrick Brooks	.30	.75
14 Rick Mirer	.20	.50
15 Mark Brunell	.40	1.00
16 Garrison Hearst	.20	.50
17 Eric Turner	.10	.30
18 Mark Carrier WR	.10	.30
19 Darnay Scott	.20	.50
20 Steve McNair	.60	1.50
21 Jim Everett	.10	.30
22 Wayne Chrebet	.40	1.00
23 Ben Coates	.20	.50
24 Harvey Williams	.10	.30
25 Michael Westbrook	.30	.75
26 Kevin Carter	.10	.30
27 Dave Brown	.10	.30
28 Jake Reed	.20	.50
29 Thurman Thomas	.30	.75
30 Jeff George	.20	.50
31 Carnell Lake	.10	.30
32 J.J. Stokes	.30	.75
33 Jay Novacek	.10	.30
34 Brett Perriman	.10	.30
35 Robert Brooks	.30	.75
36 Neil Smith	.20	.50
37 Chris Zorich	.10	.30
38 Micheal Barrow	.10	.30
39 Quentin Coryatt	.10	.30
40 Kerry Collins	.30	.75
41 Aeneas Williams	.10	.30
42 James O.Stewart	.20	.50
43 Warren Moon	.20	.50
44 Willie McGinest	.10	.30
45 Rodney Hampton	.20	.50
46 Jeff Hostetler	.10	.30
47 Darrell Green	.10	.30
48 Warren Sapp	.10	.30
49 Troy Drayton	.10	.30
50 Junior Seau	.30	.75
51 Mike Mamula	.10	.30
52 Antonio Langham	.10	.30
53 Eric Metcalf	.10	.30
54 Adrian Murrell	.20	.50
55 Joey Galloway	.30	.75
56 Anthony Miller	.20	.50
57 Carl Pickens	.20	.50
58 Bruce Smith	.20	.50
59 Merton Hanks	.10	.30
60 Troy Aikman	.75	2.00
61 Erik Kramer	.10	.30
62 Tyrone Poole	.10	.30
63 Michael Jackson	.20	.50
64 Rob Moore	.20	.50
65 Marcus Allen	.30	.75
66 Orlando Thomas	.10	.30
67 Dave Meggett	.10	.30
68 Trent Dilfer	.30	.75
69 Herman Moore	.20	.50
70 Brett Favre	1.50	4.00
71 Blaine Bishop	.10	.30
72 Eric Allen	.10	.30
73 Bernie Parmalee	.10	.30
74 Kyle Brady	.10	.30
75 Terry McDaniel	.10	.30
76 Rodney Peete	.10	.30
77 Yancey Thigpen	.20	.50
78 Stan Humphries	.20	.50
79 Craig Heyward	.10	.30
80 Rashaan Salaam	.20	.50
81 Shannon Sharpe	.20	.50
82 Jim Harbaugh	.20	.50
83 Vinnie Clark	.10	.30
84 Steve Bono	.10	.30
85 Drew Bledsoe	.40	1.00
86 Ken Norton	.10	.30
87 Brian Mitchell	.10	.30
88 Hardy Nickerson	.10	.30
89 Todd Lyght	.10	.30
90 Barry Sanders	1.25	3.00
91 Robert Blackmon	.10	.30
92 Larry Centers	.20	.50
93 Jim Kelly	.30	.75
94 Lamar Lathon	.10	.30
95 Cris Carter	.30	.75
96 Hugh Douglas	.20	.50
97 Michael Strahan	.20	.50
98 Lee Woodall	.10	.30
99 Michael Irvin	.30	.75
100 Marshall Faulk	.40	1.00
101 Terance Mathis	.10	.30
102 Eric Zeler	.10	.30
103 Marty Carter	.10	.30
104 Steve Tovar	.10	.30
105 Isaac Bruce	.30	.75
106 Tony Martin	.20	.50
107 Dale Carter	.10	.30
108 Terry Kirby	.20	.50
109 Tyrone Hughes	.10	.30
110 Bryce Paup	.10	.30
111 Errict Rhett	.20	.50
112 Ricky Watters	.20	.50
113 Chris Chandler	.20	.50
114 Edgar Bennett	.20	.50
115 John Elway	1.50	4.00
116 Sam Mills	.10	.30
117 Seth Joyner	.10	.30
118 Jeff Lageman	.10	.30
119 Chris Calloway	.10	.30
120 Curtis Martin	.60	1.50
121 Ken Harvey	.10	.30
122 Eugene Daniel	.10	.30
123 Tim Brown	.30	.75
124 Mo Lewis	.10	.30
125 Jeff Blake	.30	.75
126 Jessie Tuggle	.10	.30
127 Vinny Testaverde	.20	.50
128 Chris Warren	.20	.50
129 Terrell Davis	.60	1.50
130 Greg Lloyd	.20	.50
131 Deion Sanders	.40	1.00
132 Derrick Thomas	.30	.75
133 Darryll Lewis	.10	.30
UER back Daryl Lewis		
134 Reggie White	.30	.75
135 Jerry Rice	.75	2.00
136 Tony Banks RC	.30	.75
137 Derrick Mayes RC	.30	.75
138 Leeland McElroy RC	.20	.50
139 Bryan Still RC	.20	.50
140 Tim Biakabutuka RC	.30	.75
141 Rickey Dudley RC	.30	.75
142 Tory James RC	.20	.50
143 Lawyer Milloy RC	.50	1.25
144 Mike Ulufale RC	.10	.30
145 Bobby Engram RC	.30	.75
146 Willie Anderson RC	.10	.30
147 Terrell Owens RC	6.00	15.00
148 Jonathan Ogden RC	.30	.75
149 Darrius Johnson RC	.10	.30
150 Kevin Hardy RC	.30	.75
151 Simeon Rice RC	.60	1.50
152 Alex Molden RC	.10	.30
153 Cedric Jones RC	.10	.30
154 Duane Clemons RC	.10	.30
155 Karim Abdul-Jabbar RC	.30	.75
156 Dedric Mathis RC	.10	.30
157 John Michels RC	.10	.30
158 Winslow Oliver RC	.10	.30
159 Stepfret Williams RC	.10	.30
160 Eddie Kennison RC	.30	.75
161 Marcus Coleman RC	.10	.30
162 Tedy Bruschi RC	6.00	15.00
163 Detron Smith RC	.10	.30
164 Ray Lewis RC	15.00	40.00
165 Marvin Harrison RC	6.00	15.00
166 Je'rod Cherry RC	.10	.30
167 Jerris McPhail RC	.10	.30
168 Eric Moulds RC	2.00	5.00
169 Walt Harris RC	.10	.30
170 Eddie George RC	3.00	8.00
171 Jermaine Lewis RC	.30	.75
172 Jeff Lewis RC	.20	.50
173 Ray Mickens RC	.10	.30
174 Amani Toomer RC	2.00	5.00
175 Zach Thomas RC	1.25	3.00
176 Lawrence Phillips RC	.20	.50
177 John Mobley RC	.10	.30
178 Anthony Dorsett RC	.10	.30
179 DeRon Jenkins RC	.10	.30
180 Keyshawn Johnson RC	2.50	6.00

1996 Bowman's Best Atomic Refractors

*ATOMIC REF.VETS: 4X TO 10X		
*ATOMIC REF.ROOKIES: 2X TO 5X		
STATED ODDS 1:48 HOBBY, 1:80 RETAIL		
162 Tedy Bruschi	50.00	100.00
164 Ray Lewis	125.00	250.00

1996 Bowman's Best Refractors

COMP.REF.SET (180)	125.00	250.00
*REFRACT.VETS: 1.2X TO 3X BASE CARD		
*REFRACTOR ROOKIES: .8X TO 2X		
STATED ODDS 1:12 HOBBY, 1:20 RETAIL		
162 Tedy Bruschi	25.00	60.00
164 Ray Lewis	50.00	120.00

1996 Bowman's Best Bets

COMPLETE SET (9)	15.00	30.00
STATED ODDS 1:12 HOBBY, 1:20 RETAIL		
*ATOMIC REF: 1.2X TO 3X BASIC INSERTS		
ATOMIC ODDS 1:96 HOB, 1:160 RET		
*REFRACTORS: .8X TO 2X BASIC INSERTS		
REFRACTOR ODDS 1:48 HOB, 1:80 RET		
1 Keyshawn Johnson	1.50	4.00
2 Lawrence Phillips	.10	.30
3 Tim Biakabutuka	.25	.60
4 Eddie George	2.00	5.00
5 John Mobley	.05	.15
6 Eddie Kennison	.25	.60
7 Marvin Harrison	4.00	10.00
8 Amani Toomer	1.25	3.00
9 Bobby Engram	.25	.60

1996 Bowman's Best Cuts

COMPLETE SET (15)	30.00	80.00
STATED ODDS 1:24 HOBBY, 1:40 RETAIL		
*ATOMIC REF: 1X TO 2.5X BASIC INSERTS		
ATOMIC ODDS 1:96 HOB, 1:160 RET		
*REFRACTORS: .6X TO 1.5X BASIC INSERTS		
REFRACTOR ODDS 1:48 HOB. 1:96 RET		
1 Dan Marino	5.00	12.00
2 Emmitt Smith	4.00	10.00
3 Rashaan Salaam	.50	1.25
4 Herman Moore	.50	1.25
5 Brett Favre	5.00	12.00
6 Marshall Faulk	1.25	3.00
7 John Elway	5.00	12.00
8 Curtis Martin	2.00	5.00
9 Deion Sanders	1.25	3.00
10 Jerry Rice	2.50	6.00
11 Terrell Davis	2.00	5.00
12 Kerry Collins	1.00	2.50
13 Steve Young	2.00	5.00
14 Troy Aikman	2.50	6.00
15 Barry Sanders	4.00	10.00

1996 Bowman's Best Mirror Images

COMPLETE SET (9)	40.00	100.00
STATED ODDS 1:48 HOBBY, 1:80 RETAIL		
*ATOMIC REF: 1X TO 2.5X BASIC INSERTS		
ATOMIC ODDS 1:192 HOB, 1:320 RET		
*REFRACTORS: .6X TO 1.5X BASIC INSERTS		
REFRACTOR ODDS 1:96 HOB, 1:160 RET		
1 Steve Young	10.00	25.00
Kerry Collins		
Dan Marino		
Mark Brunell		
2 Brett Favre	10.00	25.00
Elvis Grbac		
John Elway		
Drew Bledsoe		
3 Troy Aikman	5.00	12.00
Gus Frerotte		
Jim Harbaugh		
Jeff Blake		
4 Emmitt Smith	7.50	20.00
Errict Rhett		
Chris Warren		
Curtis Martin		
5 Barry Sanders	7.50	20.00
Rashaan Salaam		
Thurman Thomas		
Terrell Davis		
6 Rodney Hampton	4.00	10.00
Lawrence Phillips		
Marcus Allen		
Marshall Faulk		
7 Jerry Rice	5.00	12.00
Isaac Bruce		
Tim Brown		
Joey Galloway		
8 Cris Carter	3.00	8.00
Curtis Conway		
Carl Pickens		
Keyshawn Johnson		
9 Robert Brooks	2.00	5.00
Michael Westbrook		
Anthony Miller		
O.J. McDuffie		

1996 Bowman's Best Super Bowl XXXI

*SUPER BOWL XXXI: 1.5X TO 4X BASIC CARDS

1997 Bowman's Best

The 1997 Bowman's Best set was issued in one series totalling 125 cards and was distributed in six-card packs with a suggested retail price of $5. The fronts feature color action photos of 95 veteran players with a gold design and 30 top rookies on silver-designed cards. The backs carry player information and statistics.

COMPLETE SET (125)	12.50	30.00
1 Brett Favre	1.50	4.00
2 Larry Centers	.25	.60
3 Trent Dilfer	.40	1.00
4 Rodney Hampton	.25	.60
5 Wesley Walls	.25	.60
6 Jerome Bettis	.40	1.00
7 Keyshawn Johnson	.40	1.00
8 Keenan McCardell	.25	.60
9 Terry Allen	.40	1.00
10 Troy Aikman	.75	2.00
11 Tony Banks	.25	.60
12 Ty Detmer	.25	.60
13 Chris Chandler	.25	.60
14 Marshall Faulk	.50	1.25
15 Heath Shuler	.15	.40
16 Stan Humphries	.25	.60
17 Bryan Cox	.15	.40
18 Chris Spielman	.15	.40
19 Derrick Thomas	.40	1.00
20 Steve Young	.50	1.25
21 Desmond Howard	.25	.60
22 Jeff Blake	.25	.60
23 Michael Jackson	.25	.60
24 Cris Carter	.40	1.00
25 Joey Galloway	.25	.60
26 Simeon Rice	.25	.60
27 Reggie White	.40	1.00
28 Dave Brown	.15	.40
29 Mike Alstott	.40	1.00
30 Emmitt Smith	1.25	3.00
31 Anthony Johnson	.15	.40
32 Mark Brunell	.50	1.25
33 Ricky Watters	.25	.60
34 Terrell Davis	.50	1.25
35 Ben Coates	.25	.60
36 Gus Frerotte	.15	.40
37 Andre Reed	.25	.60
38 Isaac Bruce	.40	1.00
39 Junior Seau	.40	1.00
40 Eddie George	.40	1.00
41 Adrian Murrell	.25	.60
42 Jake Reed	.25	.60
43 Karim Abdul-Jabbar	.25	.60
44 Scott Mitchell	.25	.60
45 Ki-Jana Carter	.15	.40
46 Curtis Conway	.25	.60
47 Jim Harbaugh	.25	.60
48 Tim Brown	.40	1.00
49 Mario Bates	.15	.40
50 Jerry Rice	.75	2.00
51 Byron Bam Morris	.15	.40
52 Marcus Allen	.40	1.00
53 Errict Rhett	.15	.40
54 Steve McNair	.50	1.25
55 Kerry Collins	.40	1.00
56 Bert Emanuel	.25	.60
57 Curtis Martin	.50	1.25
58 Bryce Paup	.15	.40
59 Brad Johnson	.40	1.00
60 John Elway	1.50	4.00
61 Natrone Means	.25	.60
62 Deion Sanders	.40	1.00
63 Tony Martin	.25	.60
64 Michael Westbrook	.25	.60
65 Chris Calloway	.15	.40
66 Antonio Freeman	.40	1.00
67 Rob Johnson	.40	1.00
68 Kent Graham	.15	.40
69 O.J. McDuffie	.25	.60
70 Barry Sanders	1.25	3.00
71 Chris Warren	.25	.60
72 Kordell Stewart	.40	1.00
73 Thurman Thomas	.40	1.00
74 Marvin Harrison	.40	1.00
75 Carl Pickens	.25	.60
76 Brent Jones	.15	.40
77 Irving Fryar	.25	.60
78 Neil O'Donnell	.25	.60
79 Elvis Grbac	.25	.60
80 Drew Bledsoe	.50	1.25
81 Shannon Sharpe	.25	.60
82 Vinny Testaverde	.25	.60
83 Chris Sanders	.15	.40
84 Herman Moore	.25	.60
85 Jeff George	.25	.60
86 Bruce Smith	.25	.60
87 Robert Smith	.25	.60
88 Kevin Hardy	.15	.40
89 Kevin Greene	.25	.60
90 Dan Marino	1.50	4.00
91 Michael Irvin	.40	1.00
92 Garrison Hearst	.25	.60
93 Lake Dawson	.15	.40
94 Lawrence Phillips	.15	.40
95 Terry Glenn	.40	1.00
96 Jake Plummer RC	2.00	5.00
97 Byron Hanspard RC	.25	.60
98 Bryant Westbrook RC	.15	.40
99 Troy Davis RC	.25	.60
100 Danny Wuerffel RC	.40	1.00
101 Tony Gonzalez RC	2.50	6.00
102 Jim Druckenmiller RC	.25	.60
103 Kevin Lockett RC	.25	.60
104 Renaldo Wynn RC	.15	.40
105 James Farrior RC	.40	1.00
106 Rae Carruth RC	.15	.40
107 Tom Knight RC	.15	.40
108 Corey Dillon RC	2.00	5.00
109 Kenny Holmes RC	.40	1.00
110 Orlando Pace RC	.40	1.00
111 Reidel Anthony RC	.40	1.00
112 Chad Scott RC	.25	.60
113 Antowain Smith RC	1.25	3.00
114 David LaFleur RC	.15	.40
115 Yatil Green RC	.25	.60
116 Darrell Russell RC	.15	.40
117 Joey Kent RC	.40	1.00
118 Darnell Autry RC	.25	.60
119 Peter Boulware RC	.40	1.00
120 Shawn Springs RC	.25	.60
121 Ike Hilliard RC	.60	1.50
122 Dwayne Rudd RC	.40	1.00
123 Reinard Wilson RC	.25	.60
124 Michael Booker RC	.15	.40
125 Warrick Dunn RC	1.50	4.00

1997 Bowman's Best Atomic Refractors

COMPLETE SET (125)	300.00	600.00
*ATOMIC REF.STARS: 3X TO 8X BASIC CARDS		
*ATOMIC REF.RCs: 1.5X TO 4X BASIC CARDS		
ATOMIC REF.STATED ODDS 1:24		

1997 Bowman's Best Refractors

COMPLETE SET (125)	200.00	400.00
*REFRACTOR STARS: 2X TO 5X BASIC CARDS		
*REFRACTOR RCs: 1.25X TO 3X		
REFRACTOR STATED ODDS 1:12		

1997 Bowman's Best Autographs

COMPLETE SET (10)	75.00	150.00
BASE AUTOGRAPH STATED ODDS 1:131		
*ATOMIC REFRACTORS: 1.5X TO 4X		
ATOMIC REFRACTOR ODDS 1:4733		
*REFRACTORS: .8X TO 2X		
REFRACTOR STATED ODDS 1:1578		
22 Jeff Blake	6.00	15.00
44 Scott Mitchell	6.00	15.00
47 Jim Harbaugh	15.00	30.00
99 Troy Davis	6.00	15.00
102 Jim Druckenmiller	6.00	15.00
113 Antowain Smith	12.50	30.00
114 David LaFleur	6.00	15.00
120 Shawn Springs	6.00	15.00
121 Ike Hilliard	7.50	20.00
125 Warrick Dunn	20.00	40.00

1997 Bowman's Best Cuts

COMPLETE SET (20)	40.00	100.00
STATED ODDS 1:24		
*ATOMIC REF: 1X TO 2.5X BASIC INSERTS		
ATOMIC REF.STATED ODDS 1:96		
*REFRACTORS: .6X TO 1.5X BASIC INSERTS		
REFRACTOR STATED ODDS 1:48		
BC1 Orlando Pace	.60	1.50
BC2 Eddie George	1.25	3.00
BC3 John Elway	5.00	12.00
BC4 Tony Gonzalez	3.00	8.00
BC5 Brett Favre	5.00	12.00
BC6 Shawn Springs	.40	1.00
BC7 Warrick Dunn	2.50	6.00
BC8 Troy Aikman	2.50	6.00
BC9 Terry Glenn	1.25	3.00
BC10 Dan Marino	5.00	12.00
BC11 Jake Plummer	2.50	6.00
BC12 Ike Hilliard	1.00	2.50
BC13 Emmitt Smith	4.00	10.00
BC14 Steve Young	1.50	4.00
BC15 Barry Sanders	4.00	10.00
BC16 Jim Druckenmiller	.40	1.00
BC17 Drew Bledsoe	1.50	4.00
BC18 Antowain Smith	2.00	5.00
BC19 Mark Brunell	1.50	4.00
BC20 Jerry Rice	2.50	6.00

1997 Bowman's Best Mirror Images

COMPLETE SET (10)	50.00	120.00
STATED ODDS 1:48		
*ATOMIC REFRACT: 1X TO 2.5X BASIC INSERTS		
ATOMIC REF.STATED ODDS 1:192		
*REFRACTORS: .6X TO 1.5X BASIC INSERTS		
REFRACTOR STATED ODDS 1:96		
MI1 Brett Favre	10.00	25.00
Gus Frerotte		
John Elway		
Mark Brunell		
MI2 Steve Young	10.00	25.00
Tony Banks		
Dan Marino		
Drew Bledsoe		
MI3 Troy Aikman	6.00	15.00
Kerry Collins		
Vinny Testaverde		
Kordell Stewart		
MI4 Emmitt Smith	7.50	20.00
Dorsey Levens		
Marcus Allen		
Eddie George		
MI5 Barry Sanders	7.50	20.00
Errict Rhett		
Thurman Thomas		
Curtis Martin		
MI6 Ricky Watters	5.00	12.00
Jamal Anderson		
Chris Warren		
Terrell Davis		
MI7 Jerry Rice	6.00	15.00
Isaac Bruce		
Tony Martin		
Marvin Harrison		
MI8 Herman Moore	2.00	5.00
Curtis Conway		
Tim Brown		
Terry Glenn		
MI9 Michael Irvin	1.50	4.00
Eddie Kennison		
Carl Pickens		
Keyshawn Johnson		
MI10 Wesley Walls	1.50	4.00
Jason Dunn		
Shannon Sharpe		
Rickey Dudley		

1997-98 Bowman's Best Jumbos

This set of 16-cards was sold in complete set form (for $59.95) directly to collectors through Topps' TSC Zone magazine/catalog. Each set included 16-cards, of which three were Refractors and one an Atomic Refractor. A certificate of authenticity accompanied each set with each numbered of 500-sets produced. Thus these "factory sets" would essentially need to be broken to put together a complete 16-card set of any one version. Each card is a parallel to its base 1997 Bowman's Best card except for the card numbering. Super Bowl and Pro Bowl logo versions were produced as well and distributed at those corresponding events.

COMPLETE SET (16)	24.00	60.00
*ATOMIC REFRACT: 2X TO 5X BASE CARD		
*REFRACTORS: 1.2X TO 3X BASE CARD		
1 Brett Favre	4.00	10.00
2 Barry Sanders	4.00	10.00
3 Emmitt Smith	3.20	8.00
4 John Elway	4.00	10.00
5 Tim Brown	1.25	3.00
6 Eddie George	.75	2.00
7 Troy Aikman	2.00	5.00
8 Drew Bledsoe	1.50	4.00
9 Dan Marino	4.00	10.00
10 Jerry Rice	2.00	5.00
11 Junior Seau	.75	2.00
12 Antowain Smith	.75	2.00
13 Warrick Dunn	1.25	3.00
14 Jim Druckenmiller	.50	1.25
15 Terrell Davis	3.20	8.00
16 Curtis Martin	1.20	3.00

1997-98 Bowman's Best Pro Bowl Jumbos

This oversized card (4" by 6") set was distributed by Topps to card dealers at the 1998 Pro Bowl show in Hawaii. Each card is essentially an enlarged parallel of a base 1997 Bowman's Best football card. A Pro Bowl logo has been added to each card as well as an additional card number (of 16-cards in the set). Both Refractor and Atomic Refractor parallels were produced for all 16-cards in the set. Reportedly, just 100-Refractor sets and 25-Atomic Refractor sets were produced.

COMPLETE SET (16)	24.00	60.00
*ATOMIC REFRACT: 15X TO 30X BASE CARD		
*REFRACTORS: 6X TO 15X BASE CARD		
1 Brett Favre	4.00	10.00
2 Barry Sanders	4.00	10.00
3 Emmitt Smith	3.20	8.00
4 John Elway	4.00	10.00
5 Tim Brown	.80	2.00
6 Eddie George	1.60	4.00
7 Troy Aikman	2.00	5.00
8 Drew Bledsoe	2.00	5.00
9 Dan Marino	4.00	10.00
10 Jerry Rice	2.00	5.00
11 Junior Seau	.50	1.25
12 Antowain Smith	1.20	3.00
13 Warrick Dunn	1.50	4.00
14 Jim Druckenmiller	.50	1.25
15 Terrell Davis	3.20	8.00
16 Curtis Martin	1.20	3.00

1997-98 Bowman's Best Pro Bowl Promos 5X7

This six card set was issued to promote the Bowman brand and feature players in the 1998 Pro Bowl. These cards were issued at the Pro Bowl show in Hawaii and at their measurement of 5"x7" are slightly bigger than the 4' by 6' versions usually seen.

COMPLETE SET (6)	16.00	40.00
*ATOMIC REFRACT: 15X TO 30X BASE CARD		
*REFRACTORS: 7.5X TO 15X BASE CARD		
1 Brett Favre	4.00	10.00
2 Barry Sanders	4.00	10.00
3 Emmitt Smith	3.20	8.00
4 John Elway	4.00	10.00
5 Tim Brown	1.20	3.00
6 Eddie George	1.60	4.00

1997-98 Bowman's Best Super Bowl Jumbos

This oversized card (4" by 6") set was distributed by Topps to card dealers at the 1998 Super Bowl Show. Each card is essentially an enlarged parallel of a base 1997 Bowman's Best football card. The Super Bowl logo was added to each card.

COMPLETE SET (16)	24.00	60.00
*REFRACTORS: 6X TO 15X BASE CARD		
1 Brett Favre	4.00	10.00
2 Barry Sanders	4.00	10.00
3 Emmitt Smith	3.20	8.00
4 John Elway	4.00	10.00
5 Tim Brown	.80	2.00
6 Eddie George	1.60	4.00
7 Troy Aikman	2.00	5.00
8 Drew Bledsoe	2.00	5.00
9 Dan Marino	4.00	10.00
10 Jerry Rice	2.00	5.00
11 Junior Seau	.50	1.25
12 Antowain Smith	1.20	3.00
13 Warrick Dunn	1.50	4.00
14 Jim Druckenmiller	.50	1.25
15 Terrell Davis	3.20	8.00
16 Curtis Martin	1.20	3.00

1998 Bowman's Best

The 1998 Bowman's Best set was issued in one series totalling 125 cards and was distributed in six-card packs with a suggested retail price of $5. The fronts feature color action photos of 100 key veterans with a radiant gold design and 25 top rookies printed on silver-designed cards all printed on 26 pt. stock. The backs carry player information.

COMPLETE SET (125)	30.00	80.00
1 Emmitt Smith	1.25	3.00
2 Reggie White	.40	1.00
3 Jake Plummer	.40	1.00
4 Ike Hilliard	.15	.40
5 Isaac Bruce	.15	.40
6 Trent Dilfer	.40	1.00
7 Ricky Watters	.25	.60
8 Jeff George	.25	.60
9 Wayne Chrebet	.40	1.00
10 Brett Favre	1.50	4.00
11 Terry Allen	.40	1.00
12 Bert Emanuel	.15	.40
13 Andre Reed	.25	.60
14 Andre Rison	.25	.60
15 Jeff Blake	.25	.60
16 Steve McNair	.40	1.00
17 Joey Galloway	.25	.60
18 Irving Fryar	.25	.60
19 Dorsey Levens	.40	1.00
20 Jerry Rice	.75	2.00
21 Kerry Collins	.25	.60
22 Michael Jackson	.15	.40
23 Kordell Stewart	.40	1.00
24 Junior Seau	.40	1.00
25 Jimmy Smith	.25	.60
26 Michael Westbrook	.25	.60
27 Eddie George	.40	1.00
28 Cris Carter	.40	1.00
29 Jason Sehorn	.25	.60
30 Warrick Dunn	.40	1.00
31 Garrison Hearst	.40	1.00
32 Erik Kramer	.15	.40
33 Chris Chandler	.25	.60
34 Michael Irvin	.40	1.00
35 Marshall Faulk	.50	1.25
36 Warren Moon	.40	1.00
37 Rickey Dudley	.15	.40
38 Drew Bledsoe	.60	1.50
39 Antowain Smith	.40	1.00
40 Terrell Davis	.40	1.00
41 Gus Frerotte	.15	.40
42 Robert Brooks	.25	.60
43 Tony Banks	.25	.60
44 Terrell Owens	.40	1.00
45 Edgar Bennett	.15	.40
46 Rob Moore	.25	.60
47 J.J. Stokes	.25	.60
48 Yancey Thigpen	.15	.40
49 Elvis Grbac	.25	.60
50 John Elway	1.50	4.00
51 Charles Johnson	.15	.40
52 Karim Abdul-Jabbar	.40	1.00
53 Carl Pickens	.25	.60
54 Peter Boulware	.15	.40
55 Chris Warren	.15	.40
56 Terance Mathis	.25	.60
57 Andre Hastings	.15	.40
58 Jake Reed	.25	.60
59 Mike Alstott	.15	.40
60 Mark Brunell	.40	1.00
61 Herman Moore	.25	.60
62 Troy Aikman	.75	2.00
63 Fred Lane	.15	.40
64 Rod Smith	.25	.60
65 Terry Glenn	.40	1.00
66 Jerome Bettis	.40	1.00
67 Derrick Thomas	.40	1.00
68 Marvin Harrison	.40	1.00
69 Adrian Murrell	.15	.40
70 Curtis Martin	.40	1.00
71 Bobby Hoying	.25	.60
72 Darrell Green	.25	.60
73 Sean Dawkins	.15	.40
74 Robert Smith	.40	1.00
75 Antonio Freeman	.40	1.00
76 Scott Mitchell	.25	.60
77 Curtis Conway	.25	.60
78 Rae Carruth	.15	.40
79 Jamal Anderson	.40	1.00
80 Dan Marino	1.50	4.00
81 Brad Johnson	.40	1.00
82 Danny Kanell	.25	.60
83 Charlie Garner	.25	.60
84 Rob Johnson	.25	.60
85 Natrone Means	.25	.60
86 Tim Brown	.40	1.00
87 Keyshawn Johnson	.40	1.00
88 Ben Coates	.25	.60
89 Derrick Alexander	.25	.60
90 Steve Young	.50	1.25
91 Shannon Sharpe	.25	.60
92 Corey Dillon	.40	1.00
93 Bruce Smith	.25	.60
94 Errict Rhett	.25	.60
95 Jim Harbaugh	.15	.40
96 Napoleon Kaufman	.40	1.00
97 Glenn Foley	.25	.60
98 Tony Gonzalez	.40	1.00
99 Keenan McCardell	.25	.60
100 Barry Sanders	1.25	3.00
101 Charles Woodson RC	1.25	3.00
102 Tim Dwight RC	1.00	2.50
103 Marcus Nash RC	.50	1.25
104 Joe Jurevicius RC	1.00	2.50
105 Jacquez Green RC	.75	2.00
106 Kevin Dyson RC	1.00	2.50
107 Keith Brooking RC	1.00	2.50
108 Andre Wadsworth RC	.75	2.00
109 Randy Moss RC	5.00	12.00
110 Robert Edwards RC	.75	2.00
111 Pat Johnson RC	.75	2.00
112 Peyton Manning RC	12.50	25.00
113 Duane Starks RC	.50	1.25
114 Grant Wistrom RC	.75	2.00
115 Anthony Simmons RC	.75	2.00
116 Takeo Spikes RC	1.00	2.50
117 Tony Simmons RC	.75	2.00
118 Jerome Pathon RC	1.00	2.50
119 Ryan Leaf RC	1.00	2.50
120 Skip Hicks RC	.75	2.00
121 Curtis Enis RC	.50	1.25
122 Germane Crowell RC	.75	2.00
123 John Avery RC	.75	2.00
124 Hines Ward RC	5.00	10.00
125 Fred Taylor RC	1.50	4.00

1998 Bowman's Best Atomic Refractors

*VETS/100: 10X TO 25X BASIC CARDS		
*ROOKIES: 4X TO 10X BASIC CARDS		
STATED ODDS 1:103		
112 Peyton Manning	125.00	250.00

1998 Bowman's Best Refractors

COMPLETE SET (125)	250.00	500.00
*STARS: 3X TO 8X BASIC CARDS		
*ROOKIES: 1.2X TO 3X BASIC CARDS		
STATED ODDS 1:25		

1998 Bowman's Best Autographs

STATED ODDS 1:158		
1A Jake Plummer	10.00	25.00
1B Jake Plummer	10.00	25.00
2A Jason Sehorn	7.50	20.00
2B Jason Sehorn	7.50	20.00
3A Corey Dillon	10.00	25.00
3B Corey Dillon	10.00	25.00
4A Tim Brown	15.00	40.00
4B Tim Brown	15.00	40.00
5A Keenan McCardell	7.50	20.00
5B Keenan McCardell	7.50	20.00
6A Kordell Stewart	7.50	20.00
6B Kordell Stewart	10.00	20.00
7A Peyton Manning	250.00	400.00
7B Peyton Manning	250.00	400.00
8A Danny Kanell	7.50	20.00
8B Danny Kanell	7.50	20.00
9A Fred Taylor	20.00	40.00
(The Ryan Leaf trade card was redeemed for a Fred Taylor autograph)		
9B Fred Taylor	20.00	40.00
(Ryan Leaf trade card was redeemed for a Fred Taylor autograph)		
10A Curtis Enis	6.00	15.00
10B Curtis Enis	6.00	15.00

1998 Bowman's Best Autographs Atomic Refractors

*ATOMIC REF: 1.2X TO 3X BASIC AU		
7A Peyton Manning	1,000.00	1,800.00
7B Peyton Manning	1,000.00	1,800.00

1998 Bowman's Best Autographs Refractors

*REFRACTOR: .8X TO 2X BASIC AU		
7A Peyton Manning	350.00	600.00
7B Peyton Manning	350.00	600.00

1998 Bowman's Best Mirror Image Fusion

COMPLETE SET (20)	75.00	150.00
STATED ODDS 1:48		
*ATOMIC REF/25: 4X TO 10X BASIC INSERTS		
*REFRACTOR/100: 1.5X TO 4X BASIC INSERTS		
MI1 Terrell Davis	2.50	6.00
John Avery		
MI2 Emmitt Smith	6.00	15.00
Curtis Enis		
MI3 Barry Sanders	6.00	15.00
Skip Hicks		
MI4 Eddie George	2.50	6.00
Robert Edwards		
MI5 Jerome Bettis	2.50	6.00
Fred Taylor		
MI6 Mark Brunell	2.50	6.00
Ryan Leaf		
MI7 John Elway	7.50	20.00
Brian Griese		
MI8 Dan Marino	15.00	30.00
Peyton Manning		
MI9 Brett Favre	6.00	15.00
Charlie Batch		
MI10 Drew Bledsoe	3.00	8.00
Jonathan Quinn		
MI11 Tim Brown	2.50	6.00
Kevin Dyson		
MI12 Herman Moore	1.50	4.00
Germane Crowell		
MI13 Joey Galloway	1.50	4.00
Jerome Pathon		
MI14 Cris Carter	2.50	6.00
Jacquez Green		
MI15 Jerry Rice	12.50	25.00
Randy Moss		
MI16 Junior Seau	2.50	6.00
Takeo Spikes		
MI17 John Randle	1.50	4.00
Jason Peter		
MI18 Reggie White	1.50	4.00
Andre Wadsworth		
MI19 Peter Boulware	1.50	4.00
Anthony Simmons		
MI20 Derrick Thomas	1.50	4.00
Brian Simmons		

1998 Bowman's Best Performers

COMPLETE SET (10)	20.00	40.00
STATED ODDS 1:12		

*ATOMIC REFRACTOR/50: 4X TO 10X
ATOMIC REFRACTOR/50 ODDS 1:2521
*REFRACTORS: 1.5X TO 4X
REFRACTOR/200 ODDS 1:630
BP1 Peyton Manning 12.50 25.00
BP2 Charles Woodson 1.25 3.00
BP3 Skip Hicks .75 2.00
BP4 Andre Wadsworth .75 2.00
BP5 Randy Moss 6.00 15.00
BP6 Marcus Nash .50 1.25
BP7 Ahman Green 3.00 8.00
BP8 Anthony Simmons .75 2.00
BP9 Tavian Banks 1.25 3.00
BP10 Ryan Leaf 1.00 2.50

1998-99 Bowman's Best Super Bowl Promos

These cards were distributed as a wrapper redemption at the 1999 Super Bowl Card Show. Each is essentially a parallel version to the base 1998 Bowman's Best card including the Super Bowl XXXIII logo on the cardfronts.

COMPLETE SET (6) 16.00 40.00
101 Charles Woodson 1.50 4.00
110 Robert Edwards 1.00 2.50
112 Peyton Manning 15.00 25.00
119 Ryan Leaf 2.00 5.00
121 Curtis Enis 1.00 2.50
125 Fred Taylor 4.00 8.00

1999 Bowman's Best Previews

COMPLETE SET (6) 6.00 15.00
PP1 Brett Favre 2.00 5.00
PP2 Warrick Dunn .75 2.00
PP3 Herman Moore .60 1.50
PP4 Tim Couch .75 2.00
PP5 Curtis Martin 1.00 2.50
PP6 Mark Brunell .75 2.00

1999 Bowman's Best

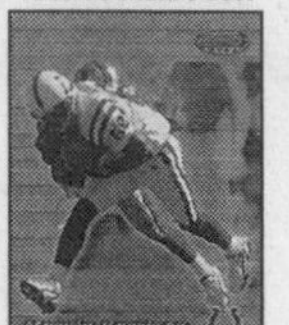

Released as a 133-card set, the 1999 Bowman's Best is comprised of 90 Star Veteran cards, 10 Best Performers cards and 33 Rookie cards inserted at one per pack. Base cards are all foil and feature laser etched highlights in the background. Bowman's Best was packaged in 24-pack boxes with six cards per pack.

COMPLETE SET (133) 30.00 80.00
1 Randy Moss .30 .75
2 Skip Hicks .20 .50
3 Robert Smith .25 .60
4 Drew Bledsoe .30 .75
5 Tim Brown .30 .75
6 Marshall Faulk .30 .75
7 Terance Mathis .20 .50
8 Sean Dawkins .20 .50
9 Ed McCaffrey .25 .60
10 Jamal Anderson .25 .60
11 Antonio Freeman .25 .60
12 Terry Kirby .20 .50
13 Vinny Testaverde .25 .60
14 Eddie George .25 .60
15 Ricky Watters .25 .60
16 Johnnie Morton .25 .60
17 Natrone Means .25 .60
18 Terry Glenn .25 .60
19 Michael Westbrook .20 .50
20 Doug Flutie .30 .75
21 Jake Plummer .25 .60
22 Darnay Scott .20 .50
23 Andre Rison .25 .60
24 Jon Kitna .25 .60
25 Dan Marino 1.00 2.50
26 Ike Hilliard .25 .60
27 Warrick Dunn .25 .60
28 Jerome Bettis .30 .75
29 Curtis Conway .25 .60
30 Emmitt Smith .75 2.00
31 Jimmy Smith .25 .60
32 Isaac Bruce .30 .75
33 Jerry Rice .60 1.50
34 Curtis Martin .30 .75
35 Steve McNair .30 .75
36 Jeff Blake .25 .60
37 Rob Moore .20 .50
38 Dorsey Levens .25 .60
39 Terrell Davis .30 .75
40 John Elway 1.00 2.50
41 Trent Dilfer .25 .60
42 Joey Galloway .25 .60
43 Keyshawn Johnson .25 .60
44 O.J. McDuffie .25 .60
45 Fred Taylor .25 .60
46 Andre Reed .30 .75
47 Frank Sanders .20 .50
48 Keenan McCardell .25 .60
49 Elvis Grbac .20 .50
50 Barry Sanders .75 2.00
51 Terrell Owens .30 .75
52 Trent Green .25 .60
53 Brad Johnson .25 .60
54 Rich Gannon .25 .60
55 Randall Cunningham .30 .75
56 Tony Martin .25 .60
57 Rod Smith .25 .60
58 Eric Moulds .25 .60
59 Yancey Thigpen .20 .50
60 Brett Favre 1.00 2.50
61 Cris Carter .30 .75
62 Marvin Harrison .30 .75
63 Chris Chandler .25 .60
64 Antowain Smith .20 .50
65 Carl Pickens .25 .60
66 Shannon Sharpe .30 .75
67 Mike Alstott .30 .75
68 J.J. Stokes .20 .50
69 Ben Coates .25 .60
70 Peyton Manning 1.00 2.50
71 Duce Staley .25 .60
72 Michael Irvin .30 .75
73 Tim Biakabutuka .25 .60
74 Priest Holmes .30 .75
75 Steve Young .40 1.00
76 Jerome Pathon .20 .50
77 Wayne Chrebet .25 .60
78 Bert Emanuel .25 .60
79 Curtis Enis .20 .50
80 Mark Brunell .25 .60
81 Herman Moore .25 .60
82 Corey Dillon .25 .60
83 Jim Harbaugh .25 .60
84 Gary Brown .20 .50
85 Kordell Stewart .25 .60
86 Garrison Hearst .25 .60
87 Rocket Ismail .25 .60
88 Charlie Batch .25 .60
89 Napoleon Kaufman .20 .50
90 Troy Aikman .50 1.25
91 Brett Favre BP .75 2.00
92 Randy Moss BP .25 .60
93 Terrell Davis BP .25 .60
94 Barry Sanders BP .60 1.50
95 Peyton Manning BP .75 2.00
96 Troy Edwards BP .20 .50
97 Cade McNown BP .20 .50
98 Edgerrin James BP .30 .75
99 Torry Holt BP .40 1.00
100 Tim Couch BP .25 .60
101 Chris Claiborne RC .40 1.00
102 Brock Huard RC .50 1.25
103 Amos Zereoue RC .50 1.25
104 Sedrick Irvin RC .40 1.00
105 Kevin Faulk RC .60 1.50
106 Ebenezer Ekuban RC .40 1.00
107 Daunte Culpepper RC .60 1.50
108 Rob Konrad RC .40 1.00
109 James Johnson RC .40 1.00
110 Kurt Warner RC 4.00 10.00
111 Mike Cloud RC .40 1.00
112 Andy Katzenmoyer RC .50 1.25
113 Jevon Kearse RC .60 1.50
114 Akili Smith RC .50 1.25
115 Edgerrin James RC .75 2.00
116 Cecil Collins RC .40 1.00
117 Chris McAlister RC .50 1.25
118 Donovan McNabb RC 2.50 6.00
119 Kevin Johnson RC .50 1.25
120 Torry Holt RC 1.00 2.50
121 Antoine Winfield RC .40 1.00
122 Michael Bishop RC .50 1.25
123 Joe Germaine RC .50 1.25
124 David Boston RC .50 1.25
125 D'Wayne Bates RC .40 1.00
126 Champ Bailey RC 1.25 3.00
127 Cade McNown RC .50 1.25
128 Shaun King RC .50 1.25
129 Peerless Price RC .50 1.25
130 Troy Edwards RC .50 1.25
131 Karsten Bailey RC .40 1.00
132 Tim Couch RC .60 1.50
133 Ricky Williams RC 1.00 2.50
C1 Rookie Class Photo 2.00 5.00

1999 Bowman's Best Atomic Refractors

*VETS 1-100: 6X TO 15X BASIC CARDS
*ROOKIES 101-133: 4X TO 10X
1-133 ATOMIC REF/100 ODDS 1:69
C1 ROOKIE CLASS/35 ODDS 1:26,880

1999 Bowman's Best Refractors

*VETS 1-100: 3X TO 8X BASIC CARDS
*ROOKIES 101-133: 2X TO 5X
1-133 REFRACTOR/400 ODDS 1:17
C1 ROOKIE CLASS REF/125 ODDS 1:7429

1999 Bowman's Best Autographs

A1-A2 STATED ODDS 1:915
ROY1 STATED ODDS 1:9129
A1 Fred Taylor 12.50 30.00
A2 Jake Plummer 12.50 30.00
ROY1 Randy Moss ROY 50.00 100.00

1999 Bowman's Best Franchise Best

COMPLETE SET (9) 25.00 50.00
STATED ODDS 1:20
FB1 Dan Marino 5.00 12.00
FB2 Fred Taylor 1.50 4.00
FB3 Emmitt Smith 3.00 8.00
FB4 Terrell Davis 1.50 4.00
FB5 Brett Favre 5.00 12.00
FB6 Tim Couch 1.50 4.00
FB7 Peyton Manning 5.00 12.00
FB8 Eddie George 1.50 4.00
FB9 Randy Moss 4.00 10.00

1999 Bowman's Best Franchise Favorites

STATED ODDS 1:153
F1 T.Dorsett 4.00 10.00
R.Staubach
F2 Randy Moss 6.00 15.00
Fran Tarkenton

1999 Bowman's Best Franchise Favorites Autographs

FA1 STATED ODDS 1:4599
FA2/FA5 COMBINED STATED ODDS 1:1017
FA3/FA6 COMBINED STATED ODDS 1:9129
FA4 STATED ODDS 1:9129
OVERALL STATED ODDS 1:703
FA1 Tony Dorsett 35.00 60.00
FA2 Roger Staubach 50.00 80.00
FA3 Tony Dorsett 90.00 150.00
Roger Staubach
FA4 Randy Moss 50.00 100.00
FA5 Fran Tarkenton 30.00 50.00
FA6 Randy Moss 100.00 200.00
Fran Tarkenton

1999 Bowman's Best Future Foundations

COMPLETE SET (18) 25.00 50.00
STATED ODDS 1:20
FF1 Tim Couch .60 1.50
FF2 David Boston .60 1.50
FF3 Donovan McNabb 3.00 8.00
FF4 Troy Edwards .50 1.25
FF5 Ricky Williams 1.25 3.00
FF6 Daunte Culpepper 2.50 6.00
FF7 Torry Holt 1.50 4.00
FF8 Cade McNown .50 1.25
FF9 Akili Smith .50 1.25
FF10 Edgerrin James 2.50 6.00
FF11 Cecil Collins .30 .75
FF12 Peerless Price .60 1.50
FF13 Kevin Johnson .60 1.50
FF14 Champ Bailey .75 2.00
FF15 Mike Cloud .50 1.25
FF16 D'Wayne Bates .50 1.25
FF17 Shaun King .50 1.25
FF18 James Johnson .50 1.25

1999 Bowman's Best Honor Roll

COMPLETE SET (8) 20.00 40.00
STATED ODDS 1:40
H1 Peyton Manning 6.00 15.00
H2 Drew Bledsoe 2.50 6.00
H3 Doug Flutie 2.00 5.00
H4 Tim Couch 2.00 5.00
H5 Charles Woodson 1.25 3.00
H6 Ricky Williams 2.50 6.00
H7 Tim Brown 2.00 5.00
H8 Eddie George 2.00 5.00

1999 Bowman's Best Legacy

COMPLETE SET (3) 10.00 25.00
STATED ODDS 1:102
L1 Ricky Williams 3.00 8.00
L2 Earl Campbell 3.00 8.00
L3 Ricky Williams 6.00 15.00
Earl Campbell

1999 Bowman's Best Legacy Autographs

LA1 STATED ODDS 1:4599
LA2 STATED ODDS 1:2040
LA3 STATED ODDS 1:18,108
OVERALL STATED ODDS 1:1311
LA1 Ricky Williams 20.00 50.00
LA2 Earl Campbell 20.00 50.00
LA3 Ricky Williams 100.00 200.00
Earl Campbell

1999 Bowman's Best Rookie Locker Room Autographs

RA1/RA4/RA5 STATED ODDS 1:305
RA2/RA3 STATED ODDS 1:915
RA1 Tim Couch 7.50 20.00
RA3 Edgerrin James 20.00 50.00
RA4 David Boston 7.50 20.00
RA5 Torry Holt 10.00 25.00

1999 Bowman's Best Rookie Locker Room Jerseys

STATED ODDS 1:229
RU2 Donovan McNabb 25.00 60.00
RU3 Kevin Faulk 7.50 20.00
RU5 Torry Holt 12.50 30.00
RU6 Ricky Williams 12.50 30.00

2000 Bowman's Best

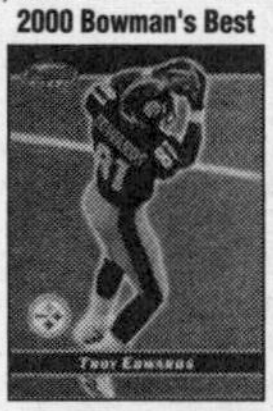

Released in mid-November 2000, Bowman's Best features a 150-card base set consisting of 90 veteran cards, 10 dual player Best Performer cards, and 50 rookies inserted at the rate of one in 11 and sequentially numbered to 1499. Base cards are all refractive foil with a border along the top and full beed photography along the sides and bottom. Bowman's Best was packaged in 24-pack boxes with packs containing five cards and carried a suggested retail price of $5.00.

COMP.SET w/o SP's (100) 7.50 20.00
1 Troy Edwards .20 .50
2 Kurt Warner .50 1.25
3 Steve McNair .30 .75
4 Terry Glenn .25 .60
5 Charlie Batch .25 .60
6 Patrick Jeffers .25 .60
7 Jake Plummer .25 .60
8 Derrick Alexander .20 .50
9 Joey Galloway .25 .60
10 Tony Banks .20 .50
11 Robert Smith .25 .60
12 Jerry Rice .60 1.50
13 Jeff Garcia .25 .60
14 Michael Westbrook .20 .50
15 Curtis Conway .25 .60
16 Brian Griese .25 .60
17 Peyton Manning .75 2.00
18 Daunte Culpepper .25 .60
19 Frank Sanders .20 .50
20 Muhsin Muhammad .25 .60
21 Corey Dillon .25 .60
22 Brett Favre 1.00 2.50
23 Warrick Dunn .25 .60
24 Tim Brown .30 .75
25 Kerry Collins .25 .60
26 Brad Johnson .25 .60
27 Rocket Ismail .25 .60
28 Jamal Anderson .25 .60
29 Jimmy Smith .25 .60
30 Torry Holt .30 .75
31 Duce Staley .25 .60
32 Drew Bledsoe .30 .75
33 Jerome Bettis .30 .75
34 Keyshawn Johnson .25 .60
35 Fred Taylor .30 .75
36 Akili Smith .20 .50
37 Rob Johnson .25 .60
38 Elvis Grbac .20 .50
39 Antonio Freeman .25 .60
40 Curtis Enis .20 .50
41 Terance Mathis .20 .50
42 Terrell Davis .30 .75
43 Randy Moss .30 .75
44 Jon Kitna .25 .60
45 Curtis Martin .30 .75
46 Terrell Owens .30 .75
47 Robert Smith .25 .60
48 Albert Connell .20 .50
49 Edgerrin James .30 .75
50 Tony Gonzalez .30 .75
51 Eric Moulds .25 .60
52 Natrone Means .25 .60
53 Carl Pickens .25 .60
54 Mark Brunell .25 .60
55 Rob Moore .20 .50
56 Marshall Faulk .30 .75
57 Stephen Davis .25 .60
58 Rich Gannon .25 .60
59 Ricky Williams .30 .75
60 Emmitt Smith .75 2.00
61 Germane Crowell .20 .50
62 Doug Flutie .30 .75
63 O.J. McDuffie .25 .60
64 Chris Chandler .25 .60
65 Qadry Ismail .25 .60
66 Tim Couch .25 .60
67 James Stewart .20 .50
68 Marvin Harrison .30 .75
69 Cris Carter .30 .75
70 Cade McNown .20 .50
71 Marcus Robinson .25 .60
72 Steve Beuerlein .25 .60
73 Jevon Kearse .25 .60
74 Eddie George .25 .60
75 Donovan McNabb .30 .75
76 Jeff Blake .25 .60
77 Wayne Chrebet .25 .60
78 Kordell Stewart .25 .60
79 Steve Young .40 1.00
80 Mike Alstott .30 .75
81 Ricky Watters .25 .60
82 Charlie Garner .25 .60
83 Troy Aikman .50 1.25
84 Dorsey Levens .25 .60
85 Ike Hilliard .25 .60
86 Shaun King .20 .50
87 Isaac Bruce .30 .75
88 Tyrone Wheatley .20 .50
89 Amani Toomer .25 .60
90 Ed McCaffrey .25 .60
91 Edgerrin James .20 .50
Marshall Faulk
92 Drew Bledsoe .20 .50
Brad Johnson
93 Jimmy Smith .20 .50
Randy Moss
94 Eddie George .20 .50
Stephen Davis
95 Mark Brunell .30 .75
Troy Aikman
96 Marvin Harrison .20 .50
Cris Carter
97 Curtis Martin .50 1.25
Emmitt Smith
98 Tim Brown .20 .50
Isaac Bruce
99 Fred Taylor .20 .50
Ricky Williams
100 Kurt Warner .50 1.25
Peyton Manning
101 Shaun Alexander RC 3.00 8.00
102 Thomas Jones RC 3.00 8.00
103 Courtney Brown RC 2.00 5.00
104 Curtis Keaton RC 1.50 4.00
105 Jerry Porter RC 2.50 6.00
106 Corey Simon RC 2.00 5.00
107 Dez White RC 2.00 5.00
108 Jamal Lewis RC 2.50 6.00
109 Ron Dayne RC 2.50 6.00
110 R.Jay Soward RC 1.50 4.00
111 Tee Martin RC 2.50 6.00
112 Brian Urlacher RC 10.00 25.00
113 Reuben Droughns RC 2.50 6.00
114 Travis Taylor RC 2.00 5.00
115 Plaxico Burress RC 2.50 6.00
116 Chad Pennington RC 4.00 10.00
117 Sylvester Morris RC 1.50 4.00
118 Ron Dugans RC 1.50 4.00
119 Joe Hamilton RC 1.50 4.00
120 Chris Redman RC 2.00 5.00
121 Trung Canidate RC 2.00 5.00
122 J.R. Redmond RC 1.50 4.00
123 Danny Farmer RC 1.50 4.00
124 Todd Pinkston RC 1.50 4.00
125 Dennis Northcutt RC 2.00 5.00
126 Laveranues Coles RC 2.50 6.00
127 Bubba Franks RC 2.50 6.00
128 Travis Prentice RC 2.00 5.00
129 Peter Warrick RC 2.50 6.00
130 Anthony Becht RC 2.00 5.00
131 Ike Charlton RC 1.50 4.00
132 Shaun Ellis RC 2.50 6.00
133 Sean Morey RC 1.50 4.00
134 Sebastian Janikowski RC 2.50 6.00
135 Aaron Stecker RC 2.00 5.00
136 Ronney Jenkins RC 1.50 4.00
137 Jamel White RC 1.50 4.00
138 Nick Williams 1.50 4.00
139 Andy McCullough 1.50 4.00
140 Kevin Daft 1.50 4.00
141 Thomas Hamner RC 1.50 4.00
142 Tim Rattay RC 2.00 5.00
143 Spergon Wynn RC 2.00 5.00
144 Brandon Short RC 1.50 4.00
145 Chad Morton RC 2.50 6.00
146 Gari Scott RC 1.50 4.00
147 Frank Murphy RC 1.50 4.00
148 James Williams RC 1.50 4.00
149 Windrell Hayes RC 1.50 4.00
150 Doug Johnson RC 2.00 5.00

2000 Bowman's Best Acetate Parallel

*VETS 1-100: 3X TO 8X BASIC CARDS
*ROOKIES 101-150: .5X TO 1.2X
ACETATE/250 STATED ODDS 1:22
ACETATE PRINT RUN 250 SER.#'d SETS

2000 Bowman's Best Autographs

GROUP 1 VETS STATED ODDS 1:8369
GROUP 2 VETS STATED ODDS 1:3348
OVERALL STATED ODDS 1:2395
GROUP A ROOKIES STATED ODDS 1:98
GROUP B ROOKIES STATED ODDS 1:1860
GROUP C ROOKIES STATED ODDS 1:8369
GROUP D ROOKIES STATED ODDS 1:837
OVERALL ROOKIE STATED ODDS 1:83
BBBU Brian Urlacher 25.00 60.00
BBCB Courtney Brown SP 6.00 15.00
BBCP Chad Pennington 12.00 30.00
BBDF Danny Farmer 5.00 12.00
BBJH Joe Hamilton 5.00 12.00
BBJL Jamal Lewis 8.00 20.00
BBJM Joe Montana 60.00 120.00
BBJR J.R. Redmond 5.00 12.00
BBLC Laveranues Coles 8.00 20.00
BBPB Plaxico Burress 15.00 30.00
BBPW Peter Warrick 8.00 20.00
BBRD Ron Dayne 8.00 20.00
BBRDR Reuben Droughns 8.00 20.00
BBRDU Ron Dugans 5.00 12.00
BBRM Randy Moss 40.00 80.00
BBRS R.Jay Soward 5.00 12.00
BBSA Shaun Alexander 10.00 25.00
BBSM Sylvester Morris 5.00 12.00
BBTJ Thomas Jones 10.00 25.00
BBTM Tee Martin 8.00 20.00
BBTPR Travis Prentice 6.00 15.00

2000 Bowman's Best Best of the Game Autographs

STATED ODDS 1:837
BG1 Edgerrin James 15.00 40.00
BG2 Kurt Warner 25.00 50.00

2000 Bowman's Best Bets

COMPLETE SET (13) 6.00 15.00
STATED ODDS 1:19
B1 Jamal Lewis .40 1.00
B2 Plaxico Burress .40 1.00
B3 Chad Pennington .60 1.50
B4 Sylvester Morris .25 .60
B5 Shaun Alexander .50 1.25
B6 Peter Warrick .40 1.00
B7 Travis Taylor .30 .75
B8 Courtney Brown .30 .75
B9 R.Jay Soward .25 .60
B10 Ron Dayne .40 1.00
B11 Jerry Porter .40 1.00
B12 Curtis Keaton .25 .60
B13 Thomas Jones .50 1.25

2000 Bowman's Best Franchise 2000

COMPLETE SET (20) 12.50 30.00
STATED ODDS 1:12
F1 Curtis Martin .60 1.50
F2 Eddie George .50 1.25
F3 Emmitt Smith 1.50 4.00
F4 Stephen Davis .50 1.25
F5 Cade McNown .40 1.00
F6 Drew Bledsoe .60 1.50
F7 Zach Thomas .60 1.50
F8 Mark Brunell .50 1.25
F9 Tim Brown .60 1.50
F10 Akili Smith .40 1.00
F11 Peyton Manning 1.50 4.00
F12 Terrell Davis .60 1.50
F13 Brett Favre 2.00 5.00
F14 Randy Moss .60 1.50
F15 Kurt Warner 1.00 2.50
F16 Ricky Williams .60 1.50
F17 Jerry Rice 1.25 3.00
F18 Jake Plummer .50 1.25
F19 Tim Couch .50 1.25
F20 Warren Sapp .50 1.25

2000 Bowman's Best Pro Bowl Jerseys

STATED ODDS 1:112
BJQB Brad Johnson 6.00 15.00
CWCB Charles Woodson 8.00 20.00
DBOLB Derrick Brooks 8.00 20.00
EJRB Edgerrin James 8.00 20.00
IBWR Isaac Bruce 8.00 20.00
JKDE Jevon Kearse 6.00 15.00
JSWR Jimmy Smith 6.00 15.00
KJWR Keyshawn Johnson 6.00 15.00
KWQB Kurt Warner 12.00 30.00
MBQB Mark Brunell 6.00 15.00
MFRB Marshall Faulk 8.00 20.00
MHWR Marvin Harrison 8.00 20.00
RMWR Randy Moss 8.00 20.00
SDRB Stephen Davis 6.00 15.00

2000 Bowman's Best Year by Year

COMPLETE SET (12) 6.00 15.00
STATED ODDS 1:20
Y1 Peyton Manning 1.50 4.00
Randy Moss
Y2 Keyshawn Johnson .50 1.25
Eddie George
Y3 Tim Brown .60 1.50
Thurman Thomas
Y4 Drew Bledsoe .60 1.50
Jerome Bettis
Y5 Edgerrin James .60 1.50
Ricky Williams
Y6 Troy Aikman 1.00 2.50
Deion Sanders
Y7 Isaac Bruce .60 1.50
Marshall Faulk
Y8 Junior Seau 1.50 4.00
Emmitt Smith
Y9 Curtis Martin .60 1.50
Terrell Davis
Y10 Brad Johnson .50 1.25
Jimmy Smith
Y11 Brett Favre 2.00 5.00
Ricky Watters
Y12 Peter Warrick .60 1.50
Plaxico Burress

2000 Bowman's Best Promos

COMPLETE SET (6) 1.50 4.00
PP1 Kurt Warner .30 .75
PP2 Marvin Harrison .30 .75
PP3 Terrell Davis .30 .75
PP4 Marshall Faulk .30 .75
PP5 Stephen Davis .20 .50
PP6 Eddie George .20 .50

2001 Bowman's Best

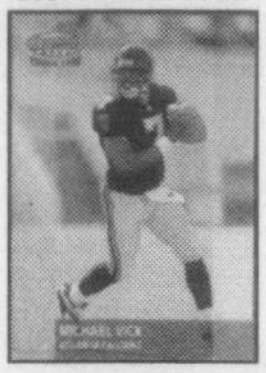

This 170 card set was issued in November, 2001. The set was issued in five card packs with a SRP of $5. The packs come 24 to a box and either six or 12 boxes to a case. The first 90 cards were all veteran cards, cards 91-100 are two player best performer cards, cards 101-120 are rookie relics and cards 121-170 are all rookies. The rookie relic cards are serial numbered to 999 while the other rookies are serial numbered to 1499.

COMP.SET w/o SP's (100) 7.50 20.00
1 Jerry Rice .60 1.50
2 Doug Flutie .30 .75
3 Drew Bledsoe .30 .75
4 Edgerrin James .30 .75
5 Muhsin Muhammad .25 .60
6 Charlie Batch .25 .60
7 Marshall Faulk .30 .75
8 Trent Green .30 .75
9 Rich Gannon .25 .60
10 Emmitt Smith .75 2.00
11 Steve McNair .30 .75
12 Darrell Jackson .25 .60
13 Amani Toomer .25 .60
14 Jimmy Smith .25 .60
15 Kevin Johnson .20 .50
16 Ray Lewis .30 .75
17 Peter Warrick .25 .60
18 Cris Carter .30 .75
19 Jerome Bettis .30 .75
20 Keyshawn Johnson .25 .60
21 Joey Galloway .25 .60
22 Chris Chandler .25 .60
23 Brett Favre 1.00 2.50
24 Aaron Brooks .25 .60
25 Kurt Warner .50 1.25
26 Jeff Graham .20 .50
27 Curtis Martin .30 .75
28 Mike Anderson .25 .60
29 Eric Moulds .25 .60
30 David Boston .20 .50
31 Elvis Grbac .25 .60
32 James Stewart .20 .50
33 Randy Moss .30 .75
34 Donovan McNabb .30 .75
35 Matt Hasselbeck .30 .75
36 Stephen Davis .25 .60
37 Brad Johnson .25 .60
38 Jamal Anderson .25 .60
39 Tim Biakabutuka .20 .50
40 Antonio Freeman .30 .75
41 Mark Brunell .25 .60
42 Tiki Barber .30 .75
43 Charlie Garner .25 .60
44 Eddie George .30 .75
45 Ricky Williams .30 .75
46 Rob Johnson .25 .60
47 Jake Plummer .25 .60
48 Peyton Manning .75 2.00
49 Lamar Smith .25 .60
50 Corey Dillon .25 .60
51 Derrick Alexander .20 .50
52 Troy Brown .25 .60
53 Wayne Chrebet .25 .60
54 Shaun Alexander .30 .75
55 Jeff George .25 .60
56 Tim Brown .30 .75
57 Brian Griese .25 .60
58 Cade McNown .25 .60
59 Jamal Lewis .30 .75
60 Germane Crowell .20 .50
61 Junior Seau .30 .75
62 Warrick Dunn .30 .75
63 Isaac Bruce .30 .75
64 Terry Glenn .25 .60
65 Fred Taylor .30 .75
66 Tim Couch .20 .50
67 Akili Smith .20 .50
68 Tony Gonzalez .30 .75
69 Kerry Collins .25 .60
70 James Thrash .25 .60
71 Terrell Owens .30 .75
72 Derrick Mason .25 .60
73 Tyrone Wheatley .25 .60
74 Oronde Gadsden .20 .50
75 Ahman Green .30 .75
76 Jon Kitna .25 .60
77 Tony Banks .20 .50
78 Marvin Harrison .30 .75
79 Daunte Culpepper .25 .60
80 Vinny Testaverde .25 .60
81 Chad Lewis .20 .50
82 Torry Holt .25 .60
83 Jeff Garcia .25 .60
84 Rod Smith .25 .60
85 Marcus Robinson .25 .60
86 Keenan McCardell .25 .60
87 Joe Horn .25 .60
88 Kordell Stewart .25 .60
89 Jay Fiedler .25 .60
90 Ed McCaffrey .25 .60
91 Eddie George .30 .75
Stephen Davis
92 Peyton Manning .75 2.00
Jeff Garcia
93 Rod Smith .25 .60
Torry Holt
94 Edgerrin James .30 .75
Marshall Faulk
95 Elvis Grbac .25 .60
Daunte Culpepper
96 Marvin Harrison .30 .75
Randy Moss
97 Mike Anderson .75 2.00
Emmitt Smith
98 Brian Griese .50 1.25
Kurt Warner
99 Muhsin Muhammad .25 .60
Ed McCaffrey
100 Eric Moulds .30 .75
Terrell Owens
101 David Terrell JSY RC 2.50 6.00
102 Kevan Barlow JSY RC 2.50 6.00
103 Quincy Morgan JSY RC 2.50 6.00
104 Chris Weinke JSY RC 2.50 6.00
105 Josh Heupel JSY RC 3.00 8.00
106 Chris Chambers JSY RC 3.00 8.00
107 Reggie Wayne JSY RC 6.00 15.00
108 Gerard Warren JSY RC 2.50 6.00
109 Freddie Mitchell JSY RC 2.00 5.00
110 Anthony Thomas JSY RC 3.00 8.00
111 Robert Ferguson JSY RC 3.00 8.00
112 Deuce McAllister JSY RC 3.00 8.00
113 Travis Henry JSY RC 2.50 6.00
114 Rod Gardner JSY RC 2.50 6.00
115 Michael Bennett JSY RC 2.50 6.00
116 Santana Moss JSY RC 4.00 10.00
117 Chad Johnson JSY RC 5.00 12.00
118 Jesse Palmer JSY RC 2.50 6.00
119 James Jackson JSY RC 2.00 5.00
120 Dan Morgan JSY RC 2.50 6.00
121 Drew Brees RC 20.00 40.00
122 Travis Minor RC 1.50 4.00
123 Quincy Carter RC 1.50 4.00
124 LaDainian Tomlinson RC 15.00 30.00
125 Michael Vick RC 15.00 30.00
126 Ryan Pickett RC 1.25 3.00
127 Mike McMahon RC 1.50 4.00
128 Alex Bannister RC 1.25 3.00
129 A.J. Feeley RC 1.50 4.00
130 Shad Meier RC 1.25 3.00
131 Jamie Winborn RC 1.50 4.00
132 Fred Smoot RC 2.00 5.00
133 Milton Wynn RC 1.25 3.00
134 Onome Ojo RC 1.25 3.00
135 Jonathan Carter RC 1.25 3.00
136 Todd Heap RC 2.00 5.00
137 Bobby Newcombe RC 1.50 4.00
138 Tony Stewart RC 1.50 4.00
139 Torrance Marshall RC 1.25 3.00
140 Jamal Reynolds RC 1.25 3.00
141 Jamar Fletcher RC 1.25 3.00
142 Richard Seymour RC 2.00 5.00
143 Tay Cody RC 1.25 3.00
144 Koren Robinson RC 1.50 4.00
145 Eddie Berlin RC 1.25 3.00
146 Damione Lewis RC 1.50 4.00
147 Marques Tuiasosopo RC 1.50 4.00
148 Snoop Minnis RC 1.25 3.00
149 Chris Barnes RC 1.25 3.00
150 Leonard Davis RC 2.00 5.00
151 Vinny Sutherland RC 1.25 3.00
152 Rudi Johnson RC 2.00 5.00
153 Derrick Gibson RC 1.25 3.00
154 Dan Alexander RC 1.50 4.00
155 Darnerien McCants RC 1.50 4.00
156 Adam Archuleta RC 1.50 4.00
157 Correll Buckhalter RC 2.00 5.00
158 LaMont Jordan RC 2.00 5.00
159 Quentin McCord RC 1.50 4.00
160 Justin Smith RC 2.00 5.00
161 Nate Clements RC 1.50 4.00
162 Alge Crumpler RC 2.00 5.00
163 Dan O'Leary RC 1.25 3.00
164 Sage Rosenfels RC 2.00 5.00
165 Andre Carter RC 1.50 4.00
166 Marcus Stroud RC 1.50 4.00
167 Will Allen RC 2.00 5.00
168 Tommy Polley RC 1.25 3.00
169 Justin McCareins RC 1.50 4.00
170 Josh Booty RC 1.50 4.00

2001 Bowman's Best Autographs

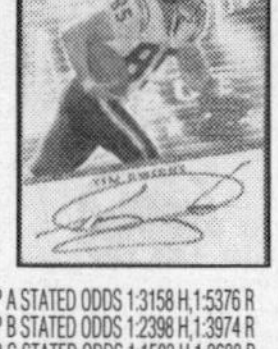

GROUP A STATED ODDS 1:3158 H,1:5376 R
GROUP B STATED ODDS 1:2398 H,1:3974 R
GROUP C STATED ODDS 1:1593 H,1:2688 R
GROUP D STATED ODDS 1:530 H,1:880 R
GROUP E STATED ODDS 1:53 H,1:88 R
GROUP F STATED ODDS 1:868 H,1:1451 R
GROUP G STATED ODDS 1:340 H,1:568 R
GROUP H STATED ODDS 1:502 H,1:838 R
GROUP I STATED ODDS 1:68 H,1:113 R
OVERALL STATED ODDS 1:23 H,1:39 R
BBAT Anthony Thomas I 6.00 15.00
BBBU Brian Urlacher 40.00 80.00
BBCC Chris Chambers E 6.00 15.00
BBCJ Chad Johnson H 15.00 40.00
BBCW Chris Weinke E 5.00 12.00
BBDA Dan Alexander E 5.00 12.00
BBDBR Drew Brees E 90.00 150.00
BBDMO Dan Morgan I 5.00 12.00
BBDR David Rivers I 4.00 10.00
BBDT David Terrell G 5.00 12.00
BBEM Eric Moulds E 5.00 12.00
BBJH Joe Horn E 5.00 12.00
BBJHE Josh Heupel I 6.00 15.00
BBJJ James Jackson E 4.00 10.00
BBJL Jamal Lewis C 6.00 15.00
BBJP Jesse Palmer D 5.00 12.00
BBKB Kevan Barlow E 5.00 12.00
BBLS Lamar Smith E 5.00 12.00
BBLT LaDainian Tomlinson I 75.00 125.00
BBMB Michael Bennett E 5.00 12.00
BBMV Michael Vick A 75.00 135.00
BBQM Quincy Morgan E 5.00 12.00
BBRF Robert Ferguson E 6.00 15.00
BBRG Rod Gardner D 5.00 12.00
BBRM Randy Moss C 30.00 60.00
BBRW Reggie Wayne E 25.00 50.00
BBSD Stephen Davis F 5.00 12.00
BBSM Santana Moss E 8.00 20.00
BBSMO Sammy Morris E 5.00 12.00
BBTD Tim Dwight I 5.00 12.00
BBTH Travis Henry E 5.00 12.00
BBTO Terrell Owens E 15.00 40.00
BBTW Terrence Wilkins G 4.00 10.00

2001 Bowman's Best Bets

COMPLETE SET (10) 10.00 25.00
STATED ODDS 1:12 HOB/RET
BB1 Drew Brees 3.00 8.00
BB2 Michael Vick 2.00 5.00
BB3 David Terrell .40 1.00
BB4 Michael Bennett .40 1.00
BB5 LaDainian Tomlinson 1.50 4.00
BB6 Koren Robinson .40 1.00
BB7 Chris Weinke .40 1.00
BB8 Rod Gardner .40 1.00

BB9 Reggie Wayne	1.00	2.50
BB10 Deuce McAllister	.50	1.25
BB11 Freddie Mitchell	.30	.75
BB12 Chad Johnson	.75	2.00
BB13 Santana Moss	.60	1.50

2001 Bowman's Best Franchise Favorites Relics

GROUP A STATED ODDS 1:9648H,1:16,619R
GROUP B STATED ODDS 1:1593 H,1:2688 R
GROUP C STATED ODDS 1:1360 H,1:2285 R
GROUP D STATED ODDS 1:1059 H,1:1760 R
OVERALL STATED ODDS 1:414 H, 1:692 R

FFCC Daunte Culpepper A	20.00	50.00
Cris Carter		
FFGJ Eddie George D	12.00	30.00
Edgerrin James		
FFSG Jimmy Smith B	7.50	20.00
Tony Gonzalez		
FFWW Charles Woodson C	10.00	25.00
Rod Woodson		

2001 Bowman's Best Impact Players

COMPLETE SET (2θ)	6.00	15.00
STATED ODDS 1:4 HOB/RET		
IP1 Randy Moss	.50	1.25
IP2 Peyton Manning	1.25	3.00
IP3 Eddie George	.50	1.25
IP4 Elvis Grbac	.40	1.00
IP5 Marshall Faulk	.50	1.25
IP6 Marvin Harrison	.50	1.25
IP7 Tony Gonzalez	.50	1.25
IP8 Corey Dillon	.40	1.00
IP9 Rod Smith	.40	1.00
IP10 Daunte Culpepper	.40	1.00
IP11 Edgerrin James	.50	1.25
IP12 Terrell Owens	.50	1.25
IP13 Eric Moulds	.40	1.00
IP14 Kurt Warner	.75	2.00
IP15 Donovan Mcnabb	.50	1.25
IP16 Isaac Bruce	.50	1.25
IP17 Jeff Garcia	.40	1.00
IP18 Cris Carter	.50	1.25
IP19 Stephen Davis	.40	1.00
IP20 Torry Holt	.40	1.00

2001 Bowman's Best Vintage Best

COMPLETE SET (10)	5.00	12.00
STATED ODDS 1:4 HOB/RET		
VBDB Dick Butkus	.60	1.50
VBDJ Deacon Jones	.40	1.00
VBED Eric Dickerson	.40	1.00
VBFG Frank Gifford	.50	1.25
VBGS Gale Sayers	.60	1.50
VBJB Jim Brown	.75	2.00
VBJM Joe Montana	2.00	5.00
VBJN Joe Namath	.75	2.00
VBLT Lawrence Taylor	.50	1.25
VBPH Paul Hornung	.50	1.25

2002 Bowman's Best

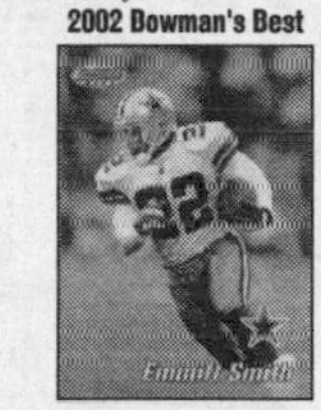

Released in mid-November 2002, this set consists of 90 veterans, 27 rookie jerseys, and 50 rookie autographs. The rookie autographs were inserted at an overall rate of 1:3 packs. Boxes contained 10-packs of 5-cards each. The pack SRP was $15.

COMP.SET w/o SP's (90)	15.00	40.00
ROOKIE AU STATED ODDS 1:3		
1 Peyton Manning	1.00	2.50
2 Chris Weinke	.30	.75
3 Daunte Culpepper	.40	1.00
4 Deuce McAllister	.40	1.00
5 Duce Staley	.40	1.00
6 Koren Robinson	.30	.75
7 Emmitt Smith	1.25	3.00
8 Jamal Lewis	.40	1.00
9 Jake Plummer	.40	1.00
10 Tim Brown	.50	1.25
11 LaDainian Tomlinson	.60	1.50
12 Derrick Mason	.40	1.00
13 Keyshawn Johnson	.40	1.00
14 Priest Holmes	.50	1.25
15 Marcus Robinson	.40	1.00
16 Drew Bledsoe	.50	1.25
17 Troy Brown	.40	1.00
18 Ahman Green	.40	1.00
19 Edgerrin James	.40	1.00
20 Hines Ward	.50	1.25
21 Marshall Faulk	.50	1.25
22 Rod Gardner	.30	.75
23 Amani Toomer	.40	1.00
24 Ricky Williams	.40	1.00
25 Peter Warrick	.40	1.00
26 Ray Lewis	.50	1.25
27 Warrick Dunn	.40	1.00
28 Jermaine Lewis	.30	.75
29 Mark Brunell	.40	1.00
30 Randy Moss	.50	1.25
31 Laveranues Coles	.40	1.00
32 Kordell Stewart	.40	1.00
33 Darrell Jackson	.40	1.00
34 Jeff Garcia	.40	1.00
35 Eddie George	.40	1.00
36 Tim Dwight	.30	.75
37 Trent Green	.40	1.00
38 Quincy Carter	.30	.75
39 Mike McMahon	.30	.75
40 Corey Dillon	.40	1.00
41 Corey Bradford	.30	.75
42 Aaron Brooks	.40	1.00
43 Todd Pinkston	.30	.75
44 Isaac Bruce	.50	1.25
45 Shane Matthews	.30	.75
46 Eric Moulds	.40	1.00
47 Anthony Thomas	.40	1.00
48 David Boston	.30	.75
49 Kevin Johnson	.30	.75
50 Brett Favre	1.25	3.00
51 Ron Dayne	.40	1.00
52 Donovan McNabb	.50	1.25
53 Brad Johnson	.40	1.00
54 Garrison Hearst	.40	1.00
55 Jimmy Smith	.40	1.00
56 Muhsin Muhammad	.40	1.00
57 Michael Vick	.75	2.00
58 Kerry Collins	.40	1.00
59 Jerome Bettis	.50	1.25
60 Trent Dilfer	.40	1.00
61 Torry Holt	.50	1.25
62 Stephen Davis	.40	1.00
63 Steve McNair	.50	1.25
64 Marvin Harrison	.50	1.25
65 Zach Thomas	.50	1.25
66 Antowain Smith	.40	1.00
67 Joe Horn	.40	1.00
68 Jim Miller	.30	.75
69 Travis Taylor	.30	.75
70 James Allen	.30	.75
71 Tom Brady	1.25	3.00
72 Tiki Barber	.50	1.25
73 Doug Flutie	.50	1.25
74 Rich Gannon	.40	1.00
75 Kurt Warner	.50	1.25
76 Michael Pittman	.40	1.00
77 Curtis Martin	.50	1.25
78 Plaxico Burress	.40	1.00
79 Terrell Owens	.50	1.25
80 Tony Gonzalez	.50	1.25
81 Michael Bennett	.40	1.00
82 Brian Griese	.40	1.00
83 Tim Couch	.30	.75
84 Shaun Alexander	.40	1.00
85 Drew Brees	.75	2.00
86 Vinny Testaverde	.40	1.00
87 Chris Chambers	.40	1.00
88 David Terrell	.30	.75
89 Rod Smith	.40	1.00
90 Jerry Rice	1.00	2.50
91 David Carr JSY RC	3.00	8.00
92 Joey Harrington JSY RC	3.00	8.00
93 Marquise Walker JSY RC	2.00	5.00
94 Ladell Betts JSY RC	3.00	8.00
95 David Garrard JSY RC	4.00	10.00
96 Antwaan Randle El JSY RC	3.00	8.00
97 Antonio Bryant JSY RC	3.00	8.00
98 Eric Crouch JSY RC	3.00	8.00
99 Tim Carter JSY RC	2.50	6.00
100 William Green JSY RC	2.50	6.00
101 Rohan Davey JSY RC	3.00	8.00
102 Julius Peppers JSY RC	6.00	15.00
103 Donte Stallworth JSY RC	3.00	8.00
104 Ashley Lelie JSY RC	2.50	6.00
105 Jeremy Shockey JSY RC	5.00	12.00
106 Javon Walker JSY RC	3.00	8.00
107 Patrick Ramsey JSY RC	3.00	8.00
108 Roy Williams JSY RC	3.00	8.00
109 T.J. Duckett JSY RC	3.00	8.00
110 Jabar Gaffney JSY RC	3.00	8.00
111 Andre Davis JSY RC	2.50	6.00
112 Reche Caldwell JSY RC	3.00	8.00
113 Josh McCown JSY RC	3.00	8.00
114 Maurice Morris JSY RC	2.50	6.00
115 Ron Johnson JSY RC	2.50	6.00
116 DeShaun Foster JSY RC	3.00	8.00
117 Clinton Portis JSY RC	4.00	10.00
*118 Aaron Lockett AU RC	3.00	8.00
119 Robert Thomas AU RC	3.00	8.00
121 Atrews Bell AU RC	3.00	8.00
122 Brandon Doman AU RC	3.00	8.00
124 Bryan Thomas AU RC	3.00	8.00
125 Bryant McKinnie AU RC	3.00	8.00
126 Chad Hutchinson AU RC	3.00	8.00
127 Charles Grant AU RC	5.00	12.00
128 Chester Taylor AU RC	5.00	12.00
129 Craig Nall AU RC	4.00	10.00
130 Deion Branch AU RC	6.00	15.00
131 Doug Jolley AU RC	3.00	8.00
132 Dwight Freeney AU RC	10.00	25.00
133 Ed Reed AU RC	30.00	60.00
134 Freddie Milons AU RC	3.00	8.00
135 Herb Haygood AU RC	3.00	8.00
136 J.T. O'Sullivan AU RC	4.00	10.00
137 Jake Schifino AU RC	3.00	8.00
138 Jason McAddley AU RC	4.00	10.00
139 Jeff Kelly AU RC	3.00	8.00
140 Jerramy Stevens AU RC	5.00	12.00
141 John Henderson AU RC	4.00	10.00
142 Jonathan Wells AU RC	5.00	12.00
143 Josh Scobey AU RC	4.00	10.00
144 Kelly Campbell AU RC	4.00	10.00
145 Kahlil Hill AU RC	3.00	8.00
146 Kalimba Edwards AU RC	4.00	10.00
147 Ken Simonton AU RC	3.00	8.00
148 Kurt Kittner AU RC	3.00	8.00
149 Lamar Gordon AU RC	4.00	10.00
150 Leonard Henry AU RC	3.00	8.00
151 Lito Sheppard AU RC	5.00	12.00
152 Luke Staley AU RC	3.00	8.00
153 Matt Schobel AU RC	5.00	12.00
154 Mike Rumph AU RC	3.00	8.00
155 Najeh Davenport AU RC	5.00	12.00
156 Napoleon Harris AU RC	4.00	10.00
158 Quentin Jammer AU RC	5.00	12.00
159 Randy Fasani AU RC	4.00	10.00
160 Ronald Curry AU RC	4.00	10.00
161 Ryan Sims AU RC	5.00	12.00
162 Sam Simmons AU RC	3.00	8.00
163 Seth Burford AU RC	3.00	8.00
164 Tellis Redmon AU RC	3.00	8.00
165 Terry Charles AU RC	3.00	8.00
166 Tracey Wistrom AU RC	4.00	10.00
167 Verron Haynes AU RC	3.00	8.00
168 Wes Pate AU RC	3.00	8.00
169 Wendell Bryant AU RC	3.00	8.00
170 Damien Anderson AU RC	3.00	8.00

2002 Bowman's Best Blue

*VETS 1-90: 2X TO 5X BASIC CARDS
1-90 VET/300 ODDS 1:5
1-90 VET PRINT RUN 300
*ROOKIE JSY 91-117: .5X TO 1.2X
ROOKIE JSY/399 ODDS 1:13
ROOKIE JSY PRINT RUN 399 SER.#'d SETS
*ROOKIE AU 118-170: .5X TO 1.2X
ROOKIE AU/399 ODDS 1:6
ROOKIE AU PRINT RUN 399 SER.#'d SETS

2002 Bowman's Best Gold

*VETS 1-90: 10X TO 25X BASIC CARDS
1-90 VETERAN/25 ODDS 1:62
1-90 VETERAN PRINT RUN 25
*ROOKIE JSY 91-117: 1.5X TO 3X
91-117 ROOKIE JSY/99 ODDS 1:51
91-117 ROOKIE JSY PRINT RUN 99
*ROOKIE AU 118-170: 1X TO 2.5X
118-170 ROOKIE AU/99 ODDS 1:26
118-170 ROOKIE AU PRINT RUN 99

2002 Bowman's Best Red

*VETS: 3X TO 8X BASIC CARDS
1-90 VETERAN/200 ODDS 1:9
1-90 VETERAN PRINT RUN 200
*ROOKIE JSY 91-117: 1X TO 2X
91-117 ROOKIE JSY/199 ODDS 1:25
ROOKIE JSY PRINT RUN 199 SER.#'d SETS
*ROOKIE AU 118-170: .8X TO 1.5X
118-170 ROOKIE AU/199 ODDS 1:13
ROOKIE AU PRINT RUN 199 SER.#'d SETS

2002 Bowman's Best Uncirculated

*SEALED JSY: 1.5X TO 4X BASIC JSY
*SEALED AU: 1X TO 3X BASIC AU
EXCH CARD STATED ODDS 1:89
ANNOUNCED PRINT RUN 20

2003 Bowman's Best

Released in October of 2003, this set consists of 173 cards including 80 veterans and 95 rookies. Rookies 81-90 are not short printed. Rookies 91-115 feature jersey swatches, and were inserted at a rate of 1:5. Rookies 116-175 feature authentic player autographs and were inserted at a rate of 1:136. Boxes contained 10 packs of 5 cards. Please note that cards 270 and 275 were never released.

COMP.SET w/o SP's (80)	12.50	30.00
ROOKIE JSY STATED ODDS 1:5		
ROOKIE AU STATED ODDS 1:136		
1 Terrell Owens	.60	1.50
2 Peerless Price	.40	1.00
3 Joey Harrington	.40	1.00
4 Ricky Williams	.50	1.25
5 David Boston	.40	1.00
6 Troy Brown	.50	1.25
7 Deuce McAllister	.50	1.25
8 Marvin Harrison	.60	1.50
9 Ahman Green	.50	1.25
10 Emmitt Smith	1.50	4.00
11 Brian Urlacher	.60	1.50
12 Jamal Lewis	.50	1.25
13 Keyshawn Johnson	.60	1.50
14 Kurt Warner	.60	1.50
15 Rod Gardner	.40	1.00
16 Plaxico Burress	.50	1.25
17 Chad Pennington	.60	1.50
18 Jeremy Shockey	.60	1.50
19 Donovan McNabb	.60	1.50
20 T.J. Duckett	.50	1.25
21 Fred Taylor	.50	1.25
22 Daunte Culpepper	.50	1.25
23 Tiki Barber	.60	1.50
24 Brian Griese	.50	1.25
25 Chad Johnson	.60	1.50
26 Julius Peppers	.60	1.50
27 Chad Hutchinson	.40	1.00
28 Eddie George	.50	1.25
29 Torry Holt	.60	1.50
30 Drew Brees	.60	1.50
31 Rich Gannon	.50	1.25
32 Trent Green	.50	1.25
33 Clinton Portis	.50	1.25
34 Tom Brady	1.50	4.00
35 Aaron Brooks	.50	1.25
36 Ray Lewis	.60	1.50
37 David Carr	.50	1.25
38 Chris Chambers	.50	1.25
39 Brad Johnson	.50	1.25
40 Tommy Maddox	.50	1.25
41 Curtis Martin	.60	1.50
42 Travis Henry	.40	1.00
43 Brett Favre	1.50	4.00
44 Randy Moss	.60	1.50
45 Jimmy Smith	.50	1.25
46 Joey Galloway	.50	1.25
47 Derrick Mason	.50	1.25
48 Darrell Jackson	.50	1.25
49 Curtis Conway	.40	1.00
50 Michael Vick	.75	2.00
51 Rod Smith	.50	1.25
52 Muhsin Muhammad	.50	1.25
53 Drew Bledsoe	.60	1.50
54 Michael Bennett	.50	1.25
55 Joe Horn	.50	1.25
56 Stephen Davis	.50	1.25
57 Isaac Bruce	.60	1.50
58 Shaun Alexander	.50	1.25
59 Jerry Rice	1.25	3.00
60 Peyton Manning	1.25	3.00
61 Tony Gonzalez	.60	1.50
62 Jake Plummer	.50	1.25
63 Tim Couch	.40	1.00
64 Marty Booker	.50	1.25
65 Corey Dillon	.50	1.25
66 Steve McNair	.60	1.50
67 Jeff Garcia	.50	1.25
68 Hines Ward	.60	1.50
69 Laveranues Coles	.40	1.00
70 Amani Toomer	.50	1.25
71 Eric Moulds	.50	1.25
72 Donald Driver	.60	1.50
73 Jay Fiedler	.40	1.00
74 Charlie Garner	.50	1.25
75 Priest Holmes	.60	1.50
76 Edgerrin James	.60	1.50
77 Kerry Collins	.50	1.25
78 LaDainian Tomlinson	.60	1.50
79 Mark Brunell	.50	1.25
80 Marshall Faulk	.60	1.50
81 Lee Suggs RC	1.25	3.00
82 William Joseph RC	1.00	2.50
83 Brandon Lloyd RC	2.50	6.00
84 Nick Barnett RC	1.50	4.00
85 Andre Woolfolk RC	1.25	3.00
86 Jimmy Kennedy RC	1.25	3.00
87 Kliff Kingsbury RC	1.25	3.00
88 Andrew Williams RC	1.00	2.50
89 Mike Doss RC	1.50	4.00
90 Troy Polamalu RC	15.00	30.00
91 Bryant Johnson JSY RC	3.00	8.00
92 Justin Fargas JSY RC	3.00	8.00
93 Terence Newman JSY RC	2.50	6.00
94 Brian St.Pierre JSY RC	2.50	6.00
95 DeWayne Robertson JSY RC	2.50	6.00
96 Dave Ragone JSY RC	2.00	5.00
97 Teyo Johnson JSY RC	2.50	6.00
98 Bethel Johnson JSY RC	2.00	5.00
00 Tyrone Calico JSY RC	2.50	6.00
100 Carson Palmer JSY RC	10.00	25.00
101 Marcus Trufant JSY RC	2.50	6.00
102 Nate Burleson JSY RC	2.50	6.00
103 Musa Smith JSY RC	2.00	5.00
104 Anquan Boldin JSY RC	6.00	15.00
105 Chris Simms JSY RC	3.00	8.00
106 Taylor Jacobs JSY RC	2.00	5.00
107 Dallas Clark JSY RC	5.00	12.00
108 Seneca Wallace JSY RC	3.00	8.00
109 Ken Dorsey JSY RC	2.50	6.00
110 Willis McGahee JSY RC	6.00	15.00
111 Chris Brown JSY RC	2.00	5.00
112 Terrell Suggs JSY RC	3.00	8.00
113 Kelley Washington JSY RC	2.00	5.00
114 Onterrio Smith JSY RC	2.00	5.00
115 Rex Grossman JSY RC	3.00	8.00
116 LaBrandon Toefield AU RC	4.00	10.00
117 Sam Aiken AU RC	4.00	10.00
118 Malaefou Mackenzie AU RC	3.00	8.00
119 David Tyree AU RC	5.00	12.00
120 Jerome McDougle AU RC	3.00	8.00
121 DeWayne White AU RC	3.00	8.00
122 Zuriel Smith AU RC	3.00	8.00
123 Shaun McDonald AU RC	4.00	10.00
124 Andre Johnson AU/199 RC	40.00	80.00
125 Ahmaad Galloway AU RC	4.00	10.00
126 Keenan Howry AU RC	3.00	8.00
127 Kareem Kelly AU RC	3.00	8.00
128 Brooks Bollinger AU RC	4.00	10.00
129 Arnaz Battle AU RC	5.00	12.00
130 Adrian Madise AU RC	3.00	8.00
131 LaTarence Dunbar AU RC	3.00	8.00
132 L.J. Smith AU RC	5.00	12.00
133 D.J. Askew AU RC	4.00	10.00
134 Michael Haynes AU RC	3.00	8.00
135 David Kircus AU RC	5.00	12.00
136 Kyle Boller AU/199 RC	8.00	20.00
137 Domanick Davis AU RC	4.00	10.00
138 Osi Umenyiora AU RC	20.00	40.00
139 Robby Wade AU RC	4.00	10.00
140 Boss Bailey AU RC	4.00	10.00
141 Billy McMullen AU RC	3.00	8.00
142 Doug Gabriel AU RC	4.00	10.00
143 J.R. Tolver AU RC	4.00	10.00
144 Gibran Hamdan AU RC	3.00	8.00
145 Walter Young AU RC	3.00	8.00
146 Carl Ford AU RC	3.00	8.00
147 Andrew Pinnock AU RC	4.00	10.00
148 Byron Leftwich AU/199 RC	15.00	40.00
149 Ty Warren AU RC	4.00	10.00
150 Visanthe Shiancoe AU RC	5.00	12.00
151 Justin Gage AU RC	4.00	10.00
152 Brock Forsey AU RC	4.00	10.00
153 Casey Moore AU RC	3.00	8.00
154 Juston Wood AU RC	3.00	8.00
155 Aaron Walker AU RC	4.00	10.00
156 Trent Smith AU RC	4.00	10.00
157 Travis Anglin AU RC	3.00	8.00
158 Jeremi Johnson AU RC	3.00	8.00
159 Justin Griffith AU RC	4.00	10.00
160 Chris Davis AU RC	4.00	10.00
161 J.T. Wall AU RC	3.00	8.00
162 Larry Johnson AU/199 RC	8.00	20.00
163 Jon Olinger AU RC	3.00	8.00
164 Donald Lee AU RC	4.00	10.00
165 Taco Wallace AU RC	3.00	8.00
166 DeAndrew Rubin AU RC	3.00	8.00
167 Ryan Hoag AU RC	3.00	8.00
168 Kevin Williams AU RC	6.00	15.00
169 Ovie Mughelli AU RC	4.00	10.00
171 Brandon Drumm AU RC	3.00	8.00
172 Brad Banks AU RC	4.00	10.00
173 Talman Gardner AU RC	3.00	8.00
174 Jason Witten AU RC	20.00	40.00

2003 Bowman's Best Blue

*VETS 1-80: 1X TO 2.5X BASE CARD		
*ROOKIES 81-90: .8X TO 2X BASE CARD		
OVERALL BLUE STATED ODDS 1:3		
*ROOKIE JSYs: .5X TO 1.2X BASE CARD HI		
ROOKIE JSY BLUE STATED ODDS 1:12		
*ROOKIE AUs: .5X TO 1.2X BASE CARD HI		
*ROOK.AU/50: .6X TO 1.5X BASE AU/199		
ROOKIE AU BLUE STATED ODDS 1:5		
BLUE PRINT RUN 499 SER.#'d SETS		
90 Troy Polamalu	40.00	80.00

2003 Bowman's Best Red

*VETS 1-80: 3X TO 8X BASE CARDS		
*ROOKIES 81-90: 2.5X TO 6X BASE CARD		
*ROOK.JSY: 1X TO 2.5X BASE CARD		
ROOKIE JSY RED STATED ODDS 1:110		
*ROOK.AU/50: 1X TO 2.5X BASE AU RC		
*ROOK.AU/25: 1X TO 2.5X BASE AU/199		
ROOKIE AU RED STATED ODDS 1:50		
OVERALL RED/25-50 ODDS 1:30		
RED PRINT RUN 50 SER.#'d SETS		
90 Troy Polamalu	100.00	175.00

2003 Bowman's Best Best Coverage Jersey Duals

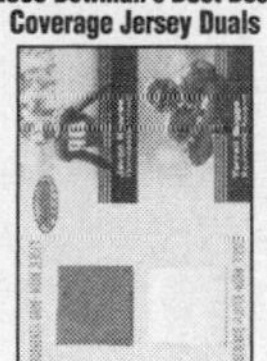

DUAL JSY/25 ODDS 1:464		
STATED PRINT RUN 25 SER.#'d SETS		
BCFB Brett Favre	30.00	80.00
Kyle Boller		
BCGJ Eddie George	12.00	30.00
Larry Johnson		
BCJJ Keyshawn Johnson	12.00	30.00
Bryant Johnson		
BCKS Jevon Kearse	12.00	30.00
Terrell Suggs		
BCOR Terrell Owens	12.00	30.00
Charles Rogers		
BCRJ Jerry Rice	25.00	60.00
Andre Johnson		
BCSJ Jimmy Smith	8.00	20.00
Taylor Jacobs		
BCTF Fred Taylor	12.00	30.00
Justin Fargas		
BCTM LaDainian Tomlinson	15.00	40.00
Willis McGahee		
BCWP Kurt Warner	25.00	60.00
Carson Palmer		

2003 Bowman's Best Double Coverage Autographs

DUAL AUTO/50 ODDS 1:454		
STATED PRINT RUN 50 SER.#'d SETS		
DCABG Kyle Boller	20.00	50.00
Rex Grossman		
DCAMJ Willis McGahee	25.00	60.00
Larry Johnson		
DCAPL Carson Palmer	50.00	120.00
Byron Leftwich		

2003 Bowman's Best Double Coverage Jerseys

DUAL JSY/50 ODDS 1:151		
STATED PRINT RUN 50 SER.#'d SETS		
DCRBC Nate Burleson	5.00	12.00
Kevin Curtis		
DCRBG Kyle Boller	5.00	12.00
Rex Grossman		
DCRBJ Anquan Boldin	8.00	20.00
Bethel Johnson		
DCRCJ Dallas Clark	8.00	20.00
Teyo Johnson		
DCRCW Tyrone Calico	4.00	10.00
Kelley Washington		
DCRFB Justin Fargas	5.00	12.00
Chris Brown		
DCRJJ Bryant Johnson	3.00	8.00
Taylor Jacobs		
DCRMJ Willis McGahee	6.00	15.00
Larry Johnson		
DCRNT Terence Newman	4.00	10.00
Marcus Trufant		
DCRPL Carson Palmer	15.00	40.00
Byron Leftwich		
DCRRJ Charles Rogers	12.00	30.00
Andre Johnson		
DCRRW Dave Ragone	5.00	12.00
Seneca Wallace		
DCRSR Terrell Suggs	5.00	12.00
DeWayne Robertson		
DCRSS Musa Smith	3.00	8.00
Onterrio Smith		
DCRSPK Brian St.Pierre	4.00	10.00
Kliff Kingsbury		

2003 Bowman's Best Single Coverage Autographs

AUTO/100 STATED ODDS 1:151		
STATED PRINT RUN 100 SER.#'d SETS		
SCADD Donald Driver	15.00	40.00
SCAHW Hines Ward	20.00	50.00
SCAJT Jason Taylor	12.00	30.00
SCALC Laveranues Coles	8.00	20.00
SCAMH Marvin Harrison	12.00	30.00
SCAMS Michael Strahan	12.00	30.00
SCATH Travis Henry	8.00	20.00
SCATM Tommy Maddox	10.00	25.00

2003 Bowman's Best Single Coverage Jerseys

JSY/100 STATED ODDS 1:151		
STATED PRINT RUN 100 SER.#'d SETS		
SCREG Eddie George	4.00	10.00
SCRFT Fred Taylor	4.00	10.00
SCRJK Jevon Kearse	4.00	10.00
SCRJR Jerry Rice	10.00	25.00
SCRJS Jimmy Smith	4.00	10.00
SCRKJ Keyshawn Johnson	5.00	12.00
SCRKW Kurt Warner	5.00	12.00
SCRLT LaDainian Tomlinson	5.00	12.00
SCRTO Terrell Owens	5.00	12.00

2003 Bowman's Best Ultimate Coverage Jersey Autographs

DUAL JSY AUTO/25 ODDS 1:921		
UCBG Kyle Boller	40.00	100.00
Rex Grossman		
UCMJ Willis McGahee	40.00	100.00
Larry Johnson		
UCPL Carson Palmer	100.00	200.00
Byron Leftwich		

2004 Bowman's Best

Bowman?CÔs Best initially released in late November 2004. The base set consists of 188-cards including 10-rookie cards, 25-rookie jersey cards, and 58-rookie autographed cards. Five of the signed rookies were serial numbered to just 199-copies. Hobby boxes contained 10-packs of 5-cards and carried an S.R.P. of $15 per pack. Two parallel sets and a variety of inserts can be found seeded in hobby and retail packs highlighted by the Double Coverage Autographs and Ultimate Coverage Jersey Autograph inserts.

COMP.SET w/o SP's (100)	25.00	50.00
RC JSY GROUP A ODDS 1:130		
RC JSY GROUP B ODDS 1:236		
RC JSY GROUP C ODDS 1:86		
RC JSY GROUP D ODDS 1:38		
RC JSY GROUP E ODDS 1:31		
RC JSY GROUP F ODDS 1:27		
RC JSY GROUP G ODDS 1:50		
RC.JSY GROUP H ODDS 1:89		
RC JSY GROUP I ODDS 1:29		
RC AU/199 STATED ODDS 1:311		
RC AU STATED ODDS 1:3		
1 Brett Favre	1.25	3.00
2 Chris Chambers	.40	1.00
3 Kyle Boller	.40	1.00
4 Brian Urlacher	.50	1.25
5 Marvin Harrison	.50	1.25
6 Matt Hasselbeck	.40	1.00
7 Aaron Brooks	.40	1.00
8 Curtis Martin	.50	1.25
9 Keenan McCardell	.30	.75
10 Terrell Owens	.50	1.25
11 Jimmy Smith	.40	1.00
12 Garrison Hearst	.40	1.00
13 Joe Horn	.40	1.00
14 David Carr	.30	.75
15 Tom Brady	1.00	2.50
16 Shaun Alexander	.40	1.00
17 Tommy Maddox	.40	1.00
18 Tiki Barber	.50	1.25
19 Trent Green	.40	1.00
20 Anquan Boldin	.50	1.25
21 Peerless Price	.30	.75
22 Jake Delhomme	.40	1.00
23 Eric Moulds	.40	1.00
24 Quincy Carter	.30	.75
25 Steve McNair	.50	1.25
26 Tim Rattay	.30	.75
27 Laveranues Coles	.30	.75
28 Corey Dillon	.40	1.00
29 Byron Leftwich	.40	1.00
30 Chad Pennington	.50	1.25
31 Koren Robinson	.30	.75
32 Plaxico Burress	.40	1.00
33 Steve Smith	.50	1.25
34 Warrick Dunn	.40	1.00
35 Jamal Lewis	.40	1.00
36 Charles Rogers	.30	.75
37 Tony Gonzalez	.50	1.25
38 Jake Plummer	.40	1.00
39 Chad Johnson	.50	1.25
40 Peyton Manning	1.00	2.50
41 Daunte Culpepper	.40	1.00
42 Fred Taylor	.40	1.00
43 Amani Toomer	.40	1.00
44 Santana Moss	.40	1.00
45 Deuce McAllister	.40	1.00
46 Rex Grossman	.40	1.00
47 Ray Lewis	.50	1.25
48 Hines Ward	.50	1.25
49 Darrell Jackson	.40	1.00
50 Randy Moss	.50	1.25
51 Carson Palmer	.50	1.25
52 Rod Smith	.40	1.00
53 Drew Bledsoe	.50	1.25
54 Brad Johnson	.40	1.00
55 Travis Henry	.30	.75
56 Joey Harrington	.40	1.00
57 Edgerrin James	.40	1.00
58 Kurt Warner	.50	1.25
59 Josh McCown	.40	1.00
60 Clinton Portis	.50	1.25
61 Brian Westbrook	.50	1.25
62 Marc Bulger	.40	1.00
63 Charlie Garner	.40	1.00
64 Torry Holt	.40	1.00
65 LaDainian Tomlinson	.50	1.25
66 Mark Brunell	.40	1.00
67 Derrick Mason	.40	1.00
68 Andre Johnson	.50	1.25
69 Keyshawn Johnson	.40	1.00
70 Ahman Green	.40	1.00
71 Rudi Johnson	.40	1.00
72 Stephen Davis	.40	1.00
73 Jeff Garcia	.40	1.00
74 Michael Strahan	.50	1.25
75 Michael Vick	.60	1.50
76 Ricky Williams	.40	1.00
77 Domanick Davis	.30	.75
78 Priest Holmes	.50	1.25
79 Marshall Faulk	.50	1.25
80 Donovan McNabb	.50	1.25
81 Dunta Robinson RC	1.00	2.50
82 Robert Gallery RC	1.50	4.00
83 Ben Troupe RC	1.25	3.00
84 Antwan Udom RC	1.25	3.00
85 Brandon Mirco RC	1.00	2.50
86 Darnell Dockett RC	1.00	2.50
87 Vince Wilfork RC	1.50	4.00
88 Randy Starks RC	1.00	2.50
89 Chris Cooley RC	1.50	4.00
90 Dwan Edwards RC	1.00	2.50
91 Patrick Crayton RC	1.50	4.00
92 Sean Jones RC	1.25	3.00
93 Sean Ryan RC	1.00	2.50
94 Chris Gamble RC	1.25	3.00
95 Will Smith RC	1.25	3.00
96 Sloan Thomas RC	1.25	3.00
97 Tim Euhus RC	1.00	2.50
98 Tommie Harris RC	1.50	4.00
99 Will Poole RC	1.50	4.00
100 Karlos Dansby RC	1.50	4.00
101 Bernard Berrian JSY RC D	2.50	6.00
102 DeAngelo Hall JSY RC A	2.50	6.00
103 Mewelde Moore JSY RC G	2.00	5.00
104 Rashaun Woods JSY RC G	1.50	4.00
105 Reggie Williams JSY RC	2.00	5.00
106 Derrick Hamilton JSY RC F	1.50	4.00
107 Kellen Winslow JSY RC C	2.50	6.00
108 Devard Darling JSY RC D	1.50	4.00
109 Michael Clayton JSY RC B	2.00	5.00
110 Larry Fitzgerald JSY RC E	6.00	15.00
111 Greg Jones JSY RC E	1.50	4.00
112 Chris Perry JSY RC H	2.00	5.00
113 Lee Evans JSY RC F	2.50	6.00
114 Tatum Bell JSY RC E	2.00	5.00
115 Steven Jackson JSY RC I	6.00	15.00
116 Matt Schaub JSY RC A	6.00	15.00
117 Ben Troupe JSY	2.00	5.00
118 Devery Henderson JSY RC F	2.50	6.00
119 Ben Watson JSY RC E	2.50	6.00
120 J.P. Losman JSY RC I	2.00	5.00
121 Keary Colbert JSY RC F	1.50	4.00
122 Darius Watts JSY RC C	1.50	4.00
123 Cedric Cobbs JSY RC D	1.50	4.00
124 Luke McCown JSY RC A	2.00	5.00
125 Michael Jenkins JSY RC A	2.50	6.00
126 Eli Manning AU/199 RC	25.00	200.00
127 Roy Williams AU/199 RC	15.00	40.00
128 Kevin Jones AU/199 RC	10.00	25.00
129 Philip Rivers AU/199 RC	40.00	100.00
130 Ben Roethlisberger AU/199 RC	100.00	175.00
131 Carlos Francis AU RC	3.00	8.00
132 Bradlee Van Pelt AU RC	4.00	10.00
133 Michael Turner AU RC	10.00	25.00
134 Kenechi Udeze AU RC	4.00	10.00
135 Jeff Smoker AU RC	4.00	10.00
136 Josh Harris AU RC	3.00	8.00
137 Derrick Strait AU RC	3.00	8.00
138 Jonathan Vilma AU RC	5.00	12.00
139 Triandos Luke AU RC	3.00	8.00
140 Jim Sorgi AU RC	4.00	10.00
141 Ryan Krause AU RC	3.00	8.00
142 Julius Jones AU RC	4.00	10.00
143 Mark Jones AU RC	0.00	0.00
144 P.K. Sam AU RC	3.00	8.00
145 B.J. Symons AU RC	3.00	8.00
146 Adimchinobe Echemandu AU RC	4.00	10.00
147 Casey Bramlet AU RC	3.00	8.00
148 Clarence Moore AU RC	3.00	8.00
149 D.J. Williams AU RC	5.00	12.00
150 Jeris McIntyre AU RC	3.00	8.00
151 Jerricho Cotchery AU RC	4.00	10.00
152 Andy Hall AU RC	3.00	8.00
153 Samie Parker AU RC	3.00	8.00
154 Maurice Mann AU RC	3.00	8.00
155 Jonathan Smith AU RC	3.00	8.00
156 Derrick Ward AU RC	5.00	12.00
157 D.J. Hackett AU RC	4.00	10.00
158 Craig Krenzel AU RC	4.00	10.00
159 Jared Lorenzen AU RC	4.00	10.00
160 Cody Pickett AU RC	4.00	10.00
161 Jamaar Taylor AU RC	3.00	8.00
162 Michael Boulware AU RC	5.00	12.00
163 Matt Mauck AU RC	3.00	8.00
164 John Navarre AU RC	3.00	8.00
165 Ahmad Carroll AU RC	3.00	8.00
166 Bruce Perry AU RC	3.00	8.00
167 Erik Jensen AU RC	3.00	8.00
168 Matt Kranchick AU RC	4.00	10.00
169 Courtney Anderson AU RC	3.00	8.00
170 Nate Lawrie AU RC	3.00	8.00
171 Thomas Tapeh AU RC	4.00	10.00
172 Courtney Watson AU RC	3.00	8.00
173 Drew Carter AU RC	4.00	10.00
174 Ricardo Colclough AU RC	4.00	10.00
175 Dontarrious Thomas AU RC	4.00	10.00
176 Ernest Wilford AU RC	4.00	10.00
177 Quincy Wilson AU RC	4.00	10.00
178 Derek Abney AU RC	3.00	8.00
179 Jeff Dugan AU RC	3.00	8.00
180 Ben Hartsock AU RC	3.00	8.00
181 Matt Kegel AU RC	5.00	12.00
182 Derrick Knight AU RC	3.00	8.00
183 Teddy Lehman AU RC	3.00	8.00
184 Johnnie Morant AU RC	3.00	8.00
185A Bob Sanders AU RC Long AU	75.00	150.00
185B Bob Sanders AU RC Short AU	25.00	60.00
186 Michael Gaines AU RC	3.00	8.00
187 Daryl Smith AU RC	3.00	8.00
188 Jason Babin AU RC	5.00	12.00

2004 Bowman's Best Green

*STARS: .8X TO 2X BASIC CARDS		
*ROOKIES 81-100: .6X TO 1.5X BASIC CARDS		
1-100 GREEN STATED ODDS 1:3		
*ROOKIE JSYs 101-125: .5X TO 1.2X		
*ROOKIE AUs 126-188: .5X TO 1.2X		
GREEN AU STATED ODDS 1:5		
GREEN PRINT RUN 499 SER.#'d SETS		
185 Bob Sanders AU	50.00	100.00

2004 Bowman's Best Red

*STARS: 2.5X TO 6X BASIC CARDS		
*ROOKIES 81-100: 2X TO 5X BASIC CARDS		
*ROOKIE JSYs 101-125: 1X TO 2.5X		
*ROOKIE AUs 126-188: 1X TO 2.5X		
RED STATED ODDS 1:26		
RED AU STATED ODDS 1:46		
RED PRINT RUN 50 SER.#'d SETS		
185 Bob Sanders AU	100.00	175.00

2004 Bowman's Best Best Coverage Jersey Duals

STATED ODDS 1:1088		
STATED PRINT RUN 25 SER.#'d SETS		
BCBF Anquan Boldin	20.00	50.00
Larry Fitzgerald		
BCBR Tom Brady	30.00	60.00
Philip Rivers		
BCMM Peyton Manning	50.00	100.00
Eli Manning		
BCMR Eli Manning	60.00	120.00
Ben Roethlisberger		
BCWJ Ricky Williams	15.00	40.00
Kevin Jones		

2004 Bowman's Best Double Coverage Autographs

STATED ODDS 1:532		
STATED PRINT RUN 50 SER.#'d SETS		
DCAJE Steven Jackson	40.00	80.00
Lee Evans		
DCAMF Eli Manning	75.00	150.00
Larry Fitzgerald		
DCAPJ Chris Perry	20.00	50.00
Kevin Jones		
DCARW Philip Rivers	50.00	100.00
Roy Williams WR		

2004 Bowman's Best Double Coverage Jerseys

GROUP A STATED ODDS 1:5747		
GROUP B STATED ODDS 1:295		
STATED PRINT RUN 50 SER.#'d SETS		
DCEJ Lee Evans	6.00	15.00
Michael Jenkins		
DCFW Larry Fitzgerald	12.00	30.00
Reggie Williams		
DCJB Julius Jones	5.00	12.00
Tatum Bell		
DCJJ Steven Jackson	10.00	25.00
Kevin K.Jones B		
DCMR Eli Manning/25	75.00	150.00
Ben Roethlisberger A		
DCPJ Chris Perry	5.00	12.00
Greg Jones		
DCRL Philip Rivers	15.00	30.00
J.P. Losman B		
DCSM Matt Schaub	10.00	25.00
Luke McCown		
DCWC Roy Williams WR	6.00	15.00
Michael Clayton		
DCWW Kellen Winslow	6.00	15.00
Ben Watson		

2004 Bowman's Best Single Coverage Autographs

STATED ODDS 1:532		
STATED PRINT RUN 50 SER.#'d SETS		
SCACP Chad Pennington	15.00	40.00
SCADD Domanick Davis	10.00	25.00
SCADH Dante Hall	12.00	30.00
SCAPM Peyton Manning	40.00	80.00

2004 Bowman's Best Single Coverage Jerseys

STATED ODDS 1:265		
STATED PRINT RUN 50 SER.#'d SETS		
SCAB Anquan Boldin	6.00	15.00
SCCB Champ Bailey	5.00	12.00
SCCC Chris Chambers	5.00	12.00
SCDB Drew Bledsoe	6.00	15.00
SCES Emmitt Smith	15.00	40.00
SCPM Peyton Manning	12.00	30.00
SCRW Ricky Williams	5.00	12.00
SCTB Tom Brady	12.00	30.00

2004 Bowman's Best Ultimate Coverage Jersey Autographs

STATED ODDS 1:1087		
STATED PRINT RUN 25 SER.#'d SETS		
UCFW Larry Fitzgerald	50.00	100.00
Roy Williams WR		
UCJP Steven Jackson	50.00	100.00
Chris Perry		
UCJR Kevin Jones	100.00	200.00
Ben Roethlisberger		
UCMR Eli Manning	125.00	250.00
Philip Rivers		

2005 Bowman's Best

This 172-card set was released in November, 2005. The set was issued in the hobby through five-card packs with a $10 SRP which came 10 packs to a box. Cards numbered 1-50 feature veterans while cards numbered 51-167 feature rookies. Five different players were issued in both signed an unsigned versions. Cards numbered 51-100 (with the exception of the few variations specifically notated) had neither signatures nor player-worn jersey swatches. Cards numbered 101-127 had player-worn jersey swatches and cards numbered 128-167 were all signed by the player. The rookie jersey cards were issued to a stated print run of 799 serial numbered sets and were inserted at a stated rate of one in 14. The signed rookie cards were issued either to a stated print run of 199 or 999 serial numbered sets. The cards numbered to 199 were inserted at a stated rate of one in 296 and the cards numbered to 999 were inserted at a stated rate of one in eight. A few players did not return their signatures in time for pack out and those cards could be redeemed until October 31, 2007.

COMP.SET w/o SPs (100)	15.00	40.00
ROOKIE JSY STATED ODDS 1:14		
ROOKIE JSY PRINT RUN 799 SER.#'d SETS		
ROOKIE AU/999 STATED ODDS 1:8		
ROOKIE AU/199 STATED ODDS 1:296		
ROOKIE AU PRINT RUN 999 SER.#'d SETS		
UNPRICED GOLD PRINT RUN 1 SET		
UNPRICED PRINT.PLATE PRINT RUN 1 SET		
1 Tiki Barber	.40	1.00
2 Peyton Manning	.75	2.00
3 Tony Gonzalez	.30	.75
4 Terrell Owens	.40	1.00
5 Brett Favre	1.00	2.50
6 Rudi Johnson	.30	.75
7 Hines Ward	.40	1.00
8 Andre Johnson	.40	1.00
9 Tom Brady	.75	2.00
10 LaDainian Tomlinson	.40	1.00
11 Daunte Culpepper	.30	.75
12 Muhsin Muhammad	.30	.75
13 Dwight Freeney	.30	.75
14 Curtis Martin	.40	1.00
15 Eli Manning	.60	1.50
16 Willis McGahee	.40	1.00
17 Steve McNair	.40	1.00
18 Jamal Lewis	.30	.75
19 Reggie Wayne	.40	1.00
20 Trent Green	.30	.75
21 Isaac Bruce	.30	.75
22 Edgerrin James	.30	.75
23 Marc Bulger	.30	.75
24 Torry Holt	.30	.75
25 Deuce McAllister	.30	.75
26 Jake Plummer	.30	.75
27 Randy Moss	.40	1.00
28 Drew Brees	.40	1.00
29 Ahman Green	.30	.75
30 Marvin Harrison	.40	1.00
31 Michael Vick	.40	1.00
32 Julius Jones	.25	.60
33 Matt Hasselbeck	.30	.75
34 Priest Holmes	.30	.75
35 Drew Bennett	.30	.75
36 Donovan McNabb	.40	1.00
37 Chad Johnson	.30	.75
38 Fred Taylor	.30	.75
39 Chris Brown	.25	.60
40 Jake Delhomme	.30	.75
41 Joe Horn	.30	.75
42 Chad Pennington	.40	1.00
43 Corey Dillon	.30	.75
44 Byron Leftwich	.30	.75
45 Javon Walker	.25	.60
46 Ben Roethlisberger	.60	1.50
47 Eric Moulds	.25	.60
48 Domanick Davis	.25	.60
49 Steven Jackson	.40	1.00
50 Shaun Alexander	.30	.75
51 Stanford Routt RC	1.25	3.00
52 Marion Barber RC	1.50	4.00
53 Matt Roth RC	1.25	3.00
54 James Kilian RC	1.00	2.50
55 Alex Barron RC	1.00	2.50
56 Madison Hedgecock RC	1.50	4.00
57 Patrick Estes RC	1.00	2.50
58 Bryant McFadden RC	1.25	3.00
59 Dan Cody RC	1.25	3.00
60 Justin Miller RC	1.25	3.00
61 Paris Warren RC	1.25	3.00
62 Marcus Spears RC	1.25	3.00
63 Odell Thurman RC	1.50	4.00
64 Craphonso Thorpe RC	1.00	2.50
65 Dustin Fox RC	1.25	3.00
66 David Pollack RC	1.25	3.00
67 Anthony Davis RC	1.00	2.50
68 Mike Nugent RC	1.25	3.00
69 David Greene RC	1.00	2.50
70 Rick Razzano RC	1.00	2.50
70AU Rick Razzano AU	3.00	8.00
71 Mike Patterson RC	1.00	2.50
72 Derek Anderson RC	1.25	3.00
72AU Derek Anderson AU	4.00	10.00
73 Marlin Jackson RC	1.00	2.50
73AU Marlin Jackson AU	3.00	8.00
74 Boomer Grigsby RC	1.50	4.00
75 Kevin Burnett RC	1.25	3.00
76 Ryan Riddle RC	1.00	2.50
77 Brock Berlin RC	1.25	3.00
78 Khalif Barnes RC	1.00	2.50
79 Marcus Maxwell RC	1.00	2.50
80 Fred Gibson RC	1.25	3.00
81 T.A. McLendon RC	1.00	2.50
82 Kirk Morrison RC	1.50	4.00
83 Sean Considine RC	1.00	2.50
84 Luis Castillo RC	1.25	3.00
85 Darryl Blackstock RC	1.00	2.50
86 Airese Currie RC	1.00	2.50
87 Corey Webster RC	1.25	3.00
88 Kurt Campbell RC	1.00	2.50
89 Ellis Hobbs RC	1.50	4.00
90 Timmy Chang RC	1.25	3.00
91 Travis Johnson RC	1.00	2.50
92 Eric Moore RC	1.00	2.50
93 Barrett Ruud RC	1.50	4.00
94 Erasmus James RC	1.25	3.00
95 Anttaj Hawthorne RC	1.00	2.50
96 Manuel White RC	1.25	3.00
97 Rian Wallace RC	1.25	3.00
98 Justin Tuck RC	2.00	5.00
99 Travis Daniels RC	1.25	3.00
100 Donte Nicholson RC	1.00	2.50
101 Matt Jones JSY RC	2.00	5.00
102 J.J. Arrington JSY RC	2.00	5.00
103 Mark Bradley JSY RC	1.50	4.00
104 Reggie Brown JSY RC	1.50	4.00
105 Jason Campbell JSY RC	3.00	8.00
106 Maurice Clarett JSY	1.50	4.00
107 Mark Clayton JSY RC	2.00	5.00
108 Braylon Edwards JSY RC	3.00	8.00
109 Ciatrick Fason JSY RC	1.50	4.00
110 Charlie Frye JSY RC	2.50	6.00
111 Frank Gore JSY RC	4.00	10.00
112 Vincent Jackson JSY RC	3.00	8.00
113 Adam Jones JSY RC	1.50	4.00
114 Stefan LeFors JSY	1.50	4.00
114AU Stefan LeFors AU RC	3.00	8.00
115 Ryan Moats JSY	1.50	4.00
115AU Ryan Moats AU RC	3.00	8.00
116 Vernand Morency JSY RC	1.50	4.00
117 Terrence Murphy JSY RC	1.50	4.00
118 Kyle Orton JSY RC	2.50	6.00
119 Roscoe Parrish JSY RC	1.50	4.00
120 Courtney Roby JSY RC	2.00	5.00
121 Carlos Rogers JSY RC	2.50	6.00
122 Antrel Rolle JSY RC	2.50	6.00
123 Eric Shelton JSY RC	1.50	4.00
124 Andrew Walter JSY RC	2.00	5.00
125 Roddy White JSY RC	3.00	8.00
126 Cadillac Williams JSY RC	2.50	6.00
127 Troy Williamson JSY RC	2.00	5.00
128 Cedric Benson AU/199 RC	15.00	40.00
129 Aaron Rodgers AU/199 RC	350.00	500.00
130 Alex Smith QB AU/199 RC	40.00	80.00
131 Mike Williams AU/199	8.00	20.00
132 Ronnie Brown AU/199 RC	20.00	50.00
133 Adrian McPherson AU RC	3.00	8.00
134 Brandon Jacobs AU RC	12.50	30.00
135 Chad Owens AU RC	4.00	10.00
136 Chase Lyman AU RC	3.00	8.00
137 Chris Henry AU RC	5.00	12.00
138 Craig Bragg AU RC	3.00	8.00
139 Damien Nash AU RC	4.00	10.00
140 Dante Ridgeway AU RC	3.00	8.00
141 Darren Sproles AU RC	8.00	20.00
142 Deandra Cobb AU RC	3.00	8.00
143 Gino Guidugli AU RC	3.00	8.00
144 J.R. Russell AU RC	3.00	8.00
145 Jerome Mathis AU RC	5.00	12.00
146 Josh Davis AU RC	3.00	8.00
147 Kay-Jay Harris AU RC	3.00	8.00
148 Larry Brackins AU RC	3.00	8.00
149 Matt Cassel AU RC	10.00	25.00
150 Noah Herron AU RC	3.00	8.00
151 Rasheed Marshall AU RC	4.00	10.00
152 Roydell Williams AU RC	4.00	10.00
153 Ryan Fitzpatrick AU RC	10.00	25.00
154 Steve Savoy AU RC	3.00	8.00
155 Tab Perry AU RC	3.00	8.00
156 Shawne Merriman AU RC	5.00	12.00
157 Charles Frederick AU RC	3.00	8.00
158 Alvin Pearman AU RC	3.00	8.00
159 Channing Crowder AU RC	4.00	10.00
160 Fabian Washington AU RC	4.00	10.00
161 Dan Orlovsky AU RC	5.00	12.00
162 Derrick Johnson AU RC	4.00	10.00
163 Alex Smith TE AU RC	3.00	8.00
164 Cedric Houston AU RC	5.00	12.00
165 Brandon Jones AU RC	4.00	10.00
166 DeMarcus Ware AU RC	12.50	30.00
167 Lionel Gates AU RC	3.00	8.00

2005 Bowman's Best Blue

*VETS 1-50: 1.2X TO 3X BASIC CARDS
*ROOK.51-100: .5X TO 1.2X BASIC CARDS
BLUE 1-100 STATED ODDS 1:3
1-100 PRINT RUN 1399 SER.#'d SETS
*ROOKIE JSYs 101-127: .5X TO 1.2X
BLUE JSY STATED ODDS 1:37
*ROOKIE AUs: .5X TO 1.2X BASE CARDS
BLUE AU STATED ODDS 1:25
101-167 PRINT RUN 299 SER.#'d SETS

2005 Bowman's Best Bronze

*VETS 1-50: 2.5X TO 6X BASIC CARDS
*ROOK.51-100: 1X TO 2.5X BASIC CARDS
BRONZE 1-100 STATED ODDS 1:15
1-100 PRINT RUN 199 SER.#'d SETS
*ROOKIE JSYs 101-127: .6X TO 1.5X
BRONZE JSY STATED ODDS 1:111
*ROOKIE AUs: .6X TO 1.5X BASE CARDS
BRONZE AU STATED ODDS 1:75
101-167 PRINT RUN 99 SER.#'d SETS

2005 Bowman's Best Gold

GOLD 1-100 STATED ODDS 1:2340
GOLD JSY STATED ODDS 1:8796
GOLD AU STATED ODDS 1:5943
UNPRICED GOLD PRINT RUN 1 SET

2005 Bowman's Best Green

*VETS 1-50: 1.5X TO 4X BASIC CARDS
*ROOK.51-100: .6X TO 1.5X BASIC CARDS
GREEN 1-100 STATED ODDS 1:4
1-100 PRINT RUN 799 SER.#'d SETS
*ROOKIE JSYs 101-127: .4X TO 1X
GREEN JSY STATED ODDS 1:19
*ROOKIE AUs: .4X TO 1X BASE CARDS
GREEN AU STATED ODDS 1:13
101-167 PRINT RUN 599 SER.#'d SETS

2005 Bowman's Best Red

*VETS 1-50: 2X TO 5X BASIC CARDS
*ROOK.51-100: .8X TO 2X BASIC CARDS
RED 1-100 STATED ODDS 1:6
1-100 PRINT RUN 499 SER.#'d SETS
*ROOKIE JSYs 101-127: .5X TO 1.2X
RED JSY STATED ODDS 1:55
*ROOKIE AUs: .5X TO 1.2X BASE CARDS
RED AU STATED ODDS 1:37
101-167 PRINT RUN 199 SER.#'d SETS

2005 Bowman's Best Silver

*VETS 1-50: 5X TO 12X BASIC CARDS
*ROOK.51-100: 1.5X TO 4X BASIC CARDS
SILVER 1-100 STATED ODDS 1:117
*ROOKIE JSYs 101-127: .8X TO 2X
SILVER JSY STATED ODDS 1:471
*ROOKIE AUs: .8X TO 2X BASE CARDS
SILVER AU STATED ODDS 1:318
1-167 PRINT RUN 25 SER.#'d SETS

153 Ryan Fitzpatrick AU	75.00	150.00

2005 Bowman's Best Best Coverage Jersey Duals

DUAL/25 STATED ODDS 1:1278		
BCRAT J.J. Arrington	12.50	30.00
LaDainian Tomlinson		
BCRBV Michael Vick		
Ronnie Brown		
BCRCF Brett Favre		
Jason Campbell		
BCRCH Mark Clayton	10.00	25.00
Torry Holt		
BCREH Braylon Edwards	20.00	50.00
Marvin Harrison		
BCRJM Matt Jones	20.00	50.00
Randy Moss		
BCRJR Adam Jones	10.00	25.00
Ed Reed		
BCRSB Alex Smith QB	30.00	80.00
Tom Brady		
BCRWC Daunte Culpepper	10.00	25.00
Troy Williamson		
BCRWG Ahman Green	30.00	60.00
Cadillac Williams		

2005 Bowman's Best Double Coverage Autographs

DUAL AU/50 STATED ODDS 1:1525		
DCABW Mike Williams	40.00	100.00
Ronnie Brown		
DCACW Cadillac Williams	40.00	100.00
Earl Campbell		
DCAEW Braylon Edwards	30.00	80.00
Troy Williamson		
DCARS Aaron Rodgers	250.00	400.00
Alex Smith QB		

2005 Bowman's Best Double Coverage Jerseys

DUAL/50 STATED ODDS 1:609		
DCRBM Reggie Brown	5.00	12.00
Ryan Moats		
DCRCE Braylon Edwards	10.00	25.00
Mark Clayton		
DCRCG Frank Gore	6.00	15.00
Maurice Clarett		
DCRFA Ciatrick Fason	5.00	12.00
J.J. Arrington		
DCRFC Charlie Frye	6.00	15.00
Jason Campbell		
DCRJR Adam Jones	5.00	12.00
Antrel Rolle		
DCRSW Alex Smith QB	10.00	25.00
Andrew Walter		
DCRWB Cadillac Williams	15.00	40.00
Ronnie Brown		
DCRWJ Matt Jones	5.00	12.00
Troy Williamson		
DCRWJA Roddy White		
Vincent Jackson		

2005 Bowman's Best Single Coverage Autographs

AUTO/50 STATED ODDS 1:1221		
SCABR Ben Roethlisberger	75.00	135.00
SCADB Deion Branch	15.00	30.00
SCAJB Jim Brown	60.00	120.00
SCAJN Joe Namath	50.00	100.00
SCAPM Peyton Manning	60.00	120.00

2005 Bowman's Best Single Coverage Jerseys

JERSEY/50 STATED ODDS 1:604		
SCRAJ Adam Jones	5.00	12.00
SCRAS Alex Smith QB	10.00	25.00
SCRBE Braylon Edwards	8.00	20.00
SCRCW Cadillac Williams	6.00	15.00
SCRJA J.J. Arrington	5.00	12.00
SCRJC Jason Campbell	8.00	20.00
SCRMC Mark Clayton	6.00	15.00
SCRMJ Matt Jones	6.00	15.00
SCRRB Ronnie Brown	8.00	20.00
SCRTW Troy Williamson	5.00	12.00

2005 Bowman's Best Ultimate Coverage Jersey Autographs

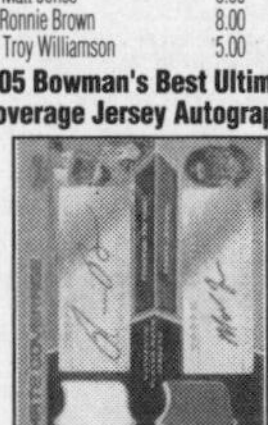

DUAL AU/25 STATED ODDS 1:2533		
UCBJ Matt Jones	60.00	120.00
Ronnie Brown		
UCEC Braylon Edwards	50.00	120.00
Mark Clayton		
UCSC Alex Smith QB	50.00	120.00
Jason Campbell		
UCSM Alex Smith QB	100.00	200.00
Peyton Manning		
UCWW Cadillac Williams	40.00	100.00
Troy Williamson		

1977 Bowmar Reading Kit

The 50-card series consisting of the Bowmar NFL Reading Kit was originally issued to promote reading within school classrooms. The cards would be used to reward school children who correctly answered the questions relating to the biography on the cards. It was distributed in complete set form along with study materials, card dividers, and a colorful storage box. Each card measures roughly 8 3/8" by 13" and includes a color photo on front with a text intensive cardback.

COMPLETE SET (50)	100.00	200.00
1 Terry Metcalf	2.00	4.00
2 O.J. Simpson	2.00	4.00
3 Paul Brown	4.00	8.00
4 George Izo	2.00	4.00
5 Ernie Davis	4.00	8.00
6 Fred Gehrke	2.00	4.00
Bob Waterfield		
7 Bronko Nagurski	2.00	4.00
8 Don Hutson	2.00	4.00
9 Growth of Pro	.75	2.00
Football Helmets		
10 The Men in the Striped	.75	2.00
Shirts (Referees)		
11 Bert Jones	2.00	4.00
12 Jack Lambert	4.00	8.00
13 Charley Taylor	2.00	4.00
14 Frank Gifford	4.00	8.00
15 Roger Staubach	7.50	15.00
16 Joe Namath	10.00	20.00
17 Teddy Roosevelt	2.00	4.00
18 Sammy Baugh	4.00	8.00
19 George Halas	4.00	8.00
20 Y. A. Tittle	4.00	8.00
21 Dan Abramowicz	2.00	4.00
22 Fran Tarkenton	4.00	8.00
23 Johnny Unitas	10.00	20.00
24 Vince Lombardi	6.00	12.00
25 Raiders	2.00	4.00
Dolphins		
Larry Csonka		
Clarence Davis		
26 Ken Houston	2.00	4.00
27 Don Shula	5.00	10.00
28 The Small Man	2.00	4.00
in Pro Football		
Eddie LeBaron		
Tommy McDonald		
Greg Pruitt		
Clarence Davis		
29 Jim Brown	7.50	15.00
30 Franco Harris	2.00	4.00
31 Lydell Mitchell	2.00	4.00
Franco Harris		
32 Players No One Watches	2.00	4.00
Reggie McKenzie		
Dave Foley		
Tom Mack		
33 Gale Sayers	4.00	8.00
34 Tom Dempsey	2.00	4.00
35 Sonny Jurgensen	2.00	4.00
36 George Blanda	2.00	4.00
37 Bart Starr	10.00	20.00
38 Chuck Noll	6.00	12.00
Terry Bradshaw		
39 Longest Football	2.00	4.00
Game Ever Played		
Garo Yepremian		
Jim Kiick		
40 Rocky Bleier	2.00	4.00
41 Walter Payton	15.00	25.00
42 Ken Anderson	2.00	4.00
43 Stadiums: From the	.75	2.00
Coliseum to the Superdome		
44 Coldest Championship	5.00	10.00
Game (Bart Starr)		
45 Jim Bakken	2.00	4.00
46 PP and K: A Super Bowl	.75	2.00
for Young Players		
47 Game that Made	2.00	4.00
Pro Football		
Johnny Unitas		
Frank Gifford		
Gene Lipscomb		
48 Purple People Eaters	2.00	4.00
Carl Eller		
Jim Marshall		
Alan Page		
49 Super Game	4.00	8.00
Roger Staubach		
Jack Lambert		
Preston Pearson		
50 Pro Bowl: A Dream	2.00	4.00
that Came True		
George Preston Marshall		

1987 Bowmar Reading Kit

This set is essentially a re-issue of the 50-card 1977 release, but has been paired down to only 40-cards. The Bowmar NFL Reading Kit was originally issued to promote reading within school classrooms. The large cards would be used to reward school children who correctly answered the questions relating to the biography on the cards. It was distributed in complete set form along with study materials, card dividers, and a colorful storage box. Each card measures roughly 8 3/8" by 13" and includes a color photo on front with a text intensive cardback.

COMPLETE SET (40)	125.00	200.00
1 Dan Marino	15.00	25.00
2 O.J. Simpson	2.00	4.00
3 Walter Payton	15.00	25.00
4 George Izo	2.00	4.00
5 Ernie Davis	4.00	8.00
6 Fred Gehrke	2.00	4.00
Bob Waterfield		
7 Bronko Nagurski	2.00	4.00
8 Joe Morris	2.00	4.00
Lionel James		
9 Growth of Pro	2.00	4.00
Football Helmets		
10 The Men in the Striped	2.00	4.00
Shirts (Referees)		
11 Frank Gifford	4.00	8.00
12 Roger Staubach	6.00	12.00
13 Joe Namath	12.00	20.00
14 Teddy Roosevelt	.75	2.00
15 William Perry	2.00	4.00
16 George Halas	4.00	8.00
17 Eat to Win	.75	2.00
18 Fran Tarkenton	4.00	8.00
19 Johnny Unitas	7.50	15.00
20 Vince Lombardi	5.00	10.00
21 Marcus Allen	5.00	10.00
22 Don Shula	4.00	8.00
23 Monday Night Football	4.00	8.00
O.J. Simpson		
Frank Gifford		
Don Meredith		
Howard Cosell		
24 Jim Brown	5.00	10.00
25 Franco Harris	2.00	4.00
26 Players No One Watches	2.00	4.00
Reggie McKenzie		
Dave Foley		
Tom Mack		
27 Gale Sayers	4.00	8.00
28 Tom Dempsey	2.00	4.00
29 Stadiums: From the	.75	2.00
Coliseum to the Superdome		
30 Eric Dickerson	2.00	4.00
Craig James		
31 Dan Fouts	4.00	8.00
32 Chuck Noll	6.00	12.00
Terry Bradshaw		
33 Longest Football	2.00	4.00
Game Ever Played		
Garo Yepremian		
Jim Kiick		
34 Ken Anderson	2.00	4.00
35 Coldest Championship	4.00	8.00
Game (Bart Starr)		
36 Jim Bakken	2.00	4.00
37 Game that Made	2.00	4.00
Pro Football		
Johnny Unitas		
Frank Gifford		
Gene Lipscomb		
38 Purple People Eaters	2.00	4.00
39 Super Game	4.00	8.00
Roger Staubach		
Jack Lambert		
Preston Pearson		
40 Pro Bowl: A Dream	2.00	4.00
that Came True		
George Preston Marshall		

1950 Bread for Health

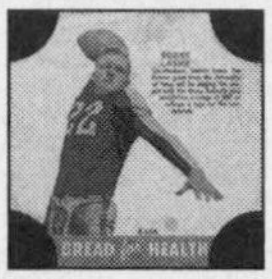

The 1950 Bread for Health football card (actually bread end labels) set contains 32 bread-end labels of players in the National Football League. The cards (actually paper thin labels) measure approximately 2 3/4" by 2 3/4". These labels are not usually found in top condition due to the difficulty in removing them from the bread package. While all the bakeries who issued this set are not presently known, Fisher's Bread in the New Jersey, New York and Pennsylvania area and NBC Bread in the Michigan area are two of the bakeries that have been confirmed to date. As with many of the bread label sets of the early 1950's, an album to house the set was probably issued. Each label contains the B.E.B. copyright found on so many of the labels of this period. Labels which contain "Bread for Energy" at the bottom are not a part of the set but part of a series of movie, western and sport stars issued during the same approximate time period. The catalog designation for this set is D290-15. The cards are unnumbered but are arranged alphabetically below for convenience.

COMPLETE SET (32)	12,000.00	18,000.00
1 Frankie Albert	300.00	500.00
2 Elmer Bud Angsman	250.00	450.00
3 Dick Barwegan	250.00	450.00
4 Sammy Baugh	800.00	1,200.00
5 Charley Conerly	350.00	600.00
6 Glenn Davis	300.00	500.00
7 Don Doll	250.00	450.00
8 Tom Fears	300.00	500.00
9 Harry Gilmer	300.00	500.00
10 Otto Graham	800.00	1,200.00
11 Pat Harder	300.00	500.00
12 Bobby Layne	600.00	1,000.00
13 Sid Luckman	600.00	1,000.00
14 Johnny Lujack	400.00	750.00
15 John Panelli	250.00	450.00
16 Barney Poole	300.00	500.00
17 George Ratterman	300.00	500.00
18 Tobin Rote	300.00	500.00
19 Jack Russell	350.00	600.00
20 Lou Rymkus	300.00	500.00
21 Joe Signiago	250.00	450.00
22 Mac Speedie	350.00	600.00
23 Bill Swiacki	250.00	450.00
24 Tommy Thompson	250.00	450.00
25 Y.A. Tittle	600.00	1,000.00
26 Clayton Tonnemaker	250.00	450.00
27 Charley Trippi	300.00	500.00
28 Bulldog Turner	350.00	600.00
29 Steve Van Buren	350.00	600.00
30 Bill Walsh	300.00	500.00
31 Bob Waterfield	400.00	750.00
32 Jim White	250.00	450.00

1951 Bread For Energy

The 1951 Bread for Energy bread end labels set contains 11 known labels of players in the National Football League, professional basketball, pro boxing, and famous actors. Each measures approximately 2 3/4" by 2 3/4" with the corners cut out in typical bread label style. These labels are not usually found in top condition due to the difficulty in removing them from the bread package. While all the bakeries who issued this set are not presently known, Junge's Brand Bread in the New England area is one bakery that has been confirmed. As with many of the bread label sets of the early 1950's, an album to house the set was probably issued. Each label was printed with a red, yellow, and blue background. The cards are unnumbered but are arranged alphabetically within subject below.

33 Otto Graham FB	1,000.00	1,500.00
34 Johnny Lujack FB	400.00	700.00
35 Johnny Rauch FB	300.00	500.00
36 Buddy Young FB	300.00	500.00

1985 Breakers Team Issue

These 5" by 7" black and white photos were issued by the 1985 Portland Breakers of the USFL. Unless noted below, each includes a studio portrait of the featured player with a dress shirt on - not a jersey. The player's name, jersey number and position are typed on the back of each. The Tim Mazzetti includes his name printed below the photo with the team name "New Orleans Breakers" as well.

COMPLETE SET (10)	25.00	50.00
1 Jearld Baylis	2.50	5.00
2 Allen Hughes	2.50	5.00
3 Dan Hurley	2.50	5.00
4 Louis Jackson	2.50	5.00
5 Tim Mazzetti	2.50	5.00
6 Ben Needham	2.50	5.00
7 Joe Restic	2.50	5.00
8 Matt Robinson	3.00	6.00
9 Dan Ross	3.00	6.00
10 Vince Williams	2.50	5.00

2011 Breast Cancer Awareness

Cards from this set were issued four at a time at home games for each team in 2011. Each card was created by one of the two NFL licensed manufacturers for one of their brands (Topps or Panini Gridiron Gear) and features the pink ribbon breast cancer awareness logo on the front. Gridiron Gear cards were also inserted into 2011 Gridiron Gear packs.

1 Beanie Wells PGG/250	.75	2.00
2 Kevin Kolb PGG/250	.75	2.00
3 Larry Fitzgerald T	.75	2.00
4 Adrian Wilson T	.60	1.50
5 Tony Gonzalez T	.75	2.00
6 TBD		
7 TBD		
8 John Abraham T	.60	1.50
9 Joe Flacco T	1.00	2.50
10 TBD		
11 Ray Rice PGG/250	.75	2.00
12 Ed Reed T	.75	2.00
13 Steve Johnson PGG/250	.75	2.00
14 Ryan Fitzpatrick T	.75	2.00
15 Marcell Dareus PGG/250	.75	2.00
16 C.J. Spiller T	.75	2.00
17 Cam Newton T	4.00	10.00
18 Steve Smith T	.75	2.00
19 Jonathan Stewart PGG/250	.75	2.00
20 DeAngelo Williams PGG/250	.75	2.00
21 Lance Briggs T	.75	2.00
22 Jay Cutler PGG/250	.75	2.00
23 Matt Forte T	.75	2.00
24 Brian Urlacher PGG/250	1.00	2.50
25 A.J. Green PGG/250	1.50	4.00
26 Andy Dalton PGG/250	2.00	5.00
27 Jermaine Gresham T	.75	2.00
28 Jordan Shipley T	.75	2.00
29 Josh Cribbs T	.75	2.00
30 Greg Little PGG/250	.75	2.00
31 Peyton Hillis PGG/250	.75	2.00
32 Colt McCoy T	.75	2.00
33 TBD		
34 Felix Jones T	.75	2.00
35 Tony Romo T	1.00	2.50
36 TBD		
37 Von Miller PGG/250	1.00	2.50
38 Champ Bailey T	.75	2.00
39 Kyle Orton T	.75	2.00
40 Tim Tebow PGG/250	2.00	5.00
41 Jahvid Best T	.75	2.00
42 Calvin Johnson PGG/250	1.00	2.50
43 Matthew Stafford T	1.00	2.60
44 Ndamukong Suh PGG/250	1.00	2.50
45 A.J. Hawk T	.75	2.00
46 Aaron Rodgers T	1.50	4.00
47 Charles Woodson PGG/250	1.00	2.50
48 Clay Matthews PGG/250	1.00	2.50
49 Andre Johnson PGG/250	.75	2.00
50 Matt Schaub T	.75	2.00
51 Mario Williams T	.60	1.50
52 Arian Foster PGG/250	.75	2.00
53 TBD		
54 Dwight Freeney T	.75	2.00
55 Peyton Manning T	1.50	4.00
56 TBD		
57 David Garrard T	.75	2.00
58 Maurice Jones-Drew T	.75	2.00
59 TBD		
60 Blaine Gabbert PGG/250	1.25	3.00
61 Dwayne Bowe PGG/250	.75	2.00
62 Matt Cassel T	.75	2.00
63 Derrick Johnson T	.60	1.50
64 Jamaal Charles PGG/250	.75	2.00
65 Davone Bess T	.60	1.50
66 Daniel Thomas PGG/250	.75	2.00
67 Chad Henne T	.75	2.00
68 TBD		
69 TBD		
70 Christian Ponder PGG/250	1.50	4.00
71 Percy Harvin T	.75	2.00
72 Adrian Peterson T	1.25	3.00
73 Chad Ochocinco PGG/250	.75	2.00
74 Wes Welker T	1.00	2.50
75 Jerod Mayo T	.60	1.50
76 TBD		
77 Drew Brees T	1.00	2.50
78 TBD		
79 Jonathan Vilma T	.60	1.50
80 Mark Ingram PGG/250	1.50	4.00
81 Ahmad Bradshaw PGG/250	.75	2.00
82 Eli Manning T	1.00	2.50
83 Hakeem Nicks PGG/250	.75	2.00
84 Justin Tuck T	.75	2.00
85 TBD		
86 Mark Sanchez T	1.00	2.50
87 Nick Mangold T	.60	1.50
88 Darrelle Revis PGG/250	.75	2.00
89 Michael Bush T	.60	1.50
90 TBD		
91 TBD		
92 Richard Seymour T	.60	1.50
93 DeSean Jackson PGG/250	.75	2.00
94 LeSean McCoy PGG/250	.75	2.00
95 Asante Samuel T	.60	1.50
96 Michael Vick T	1.00	2.50
97 Mike Wallace PGG/250	1.00	2.50
98 Ben Roethlisberger T	1.00	2.50
99 Hines Ward PGG/250	.75	2.00
100 Troy Polamalu T	1.00	2.50
101 TBD		
102 Vincent Jackson PGG/250	.75	2.00
103 Philip Rivers T	1.00	2.50
104 Ryan Mathews T	.75	2.00
105 Michael Crabtree T	.75	2.00
106 Josh Morgan PGG/250	.75	2.00
107 Frank Gore T	.75	2.00
108 TBD		
109 Earl Thomas T	.60	1.50
110 TBD		
111 Sidney Rice PGG/250	.75	2.00
112 Mike Williams USC T	.75	2.00
113 TBD		
114 Steven Jackson T	.75	2.00
115 TBD		
116 Chris Long T	.60	1.50
117 LeGarrette Blount T	.75	2.00
118 Josh Freeman T	1.00	2.50
119 Mike Williams PGG/250	.75	2.00
120 Kellen Winslow PGG/250	.75	2.00
121 Matt Hasselbeck T	.75	2.00
122 Akeem Ayers PGG/250	.60	1.50
123 TBD		
124 Nate Washington T	.60	1.50
125 Chris Cooley T	.75	2.00
126 LaRon Landry T	.60	1.50
127 TBD		
128 TBD		

1992 Breyers Bookmarks

This 66-card set (of bookmarks) was produced by Breyers to promote reading in the home cities of eleven NFL teams. The bookmarks measure approximately 2" by 8". The fronts feature a cut-out player photo superimposed on a yellow background decorated with open books. A lighter yellow panel above the player contains a player profile and a biography. The player's name appears in a black stripe that borders the panel. The Breyers logo and the words "Reading Team" appear on an electronic billboard design. The backs list book selections found at the library, the American Library Association logo, and the sponsor logo. The cards are numbered on the front and are arranged in team order.

COMPLETE SET (66)	100.00	250.00
1 Greg Townsend	1.00	2.50
2 Steve Wisniewski	1.00	2.50
3 Art Shell CO	1.60	4.00
4 Jeff Jaeger	1.00	2.50
5 Lisa O'Day	1.00	2.50
(Cheerleader)		
6 Los Angeles Raiders	1.00	2.50
Helmet and SB trophies		
7 Jerry Rice	6.00	15.00
8 Don Griffin	1.00	2.50
9 John Taylor	1.00	2.50
10 Joe Montana	25.00	40.00
11 Michael Walter	1.00	2.50
12 San Francisco 49ers	1.00	2.50
Helmet		
13 Junior Seau	1.60	4.00
14 John Friesz	1.00	2.50
15 Ronnie Harmon	1.00	2.50
16 Marion Butts	1.00	2.50
17 Gill Byrd	1.00	2.50
18 San Diego Chargers	1.00	2.50
Helmet		
19 Kelly Stouffer	1.00	2.50
20 John Kasay	1.00	2.50
21 Andy Heck	1.00	2.50
22 Jacob Green	1.00	2.50
23 Eugene Robinson	1.00	2.50
24 Seattle Seahawks	1.00	2.50
Helmet		
25 Pat Swilling	1.60	4.00
26 Vaughan Johnson	1.00	2.50
27 Bobby Hebert	1.00	2.50
28 Floyd Turner	1.00	2.50
29 Rickey Jackson	1.00	2.50
30 New Orleans Saints	1.00	2.50
Helmet		
31 Harvey Williams	1.60	4.00
32 Derrick Thomas	2.00	5.00
33 Bill Maas	1.00	2.50
34 Tim Grunhard	1.00	2.50
35 Jonathan Hayes	1.00	2.50
36 Kansas City Chiefs	1.00	2.50
Mascot		
37 Rich Gannon		
38 Tim Irwin	1.00	2.50
39 Audray McMillian	1.00	2.50
40 Gary Zimmerman	1.00	2.50
41 Hassan Jones	1.00	2.50
42 Minnesota Vikings	1.00	2.50
Helmet		
43 Eric Green	1.00	2.50
44 Louis Lipps	1.00	2.50
45 Rod Woodson	1.60	4.00
46 Merril Hoge	1.00	2.50
47 Gary Anderson RB	1.00	2.50
48 Pittsburgh Steelers/60-Season Emblem	1.00	2.50
49 Anthony Johnson	1.00	2.50
50 Bill Brooks	1.00	2.50
51 Jeff Herrod	1.00	2.50
52 Mike Prior	1.00	2.50
53 Jeff George	1.60	4.00
54 Indianapolis Colts	1.00	2.50
Ted Marchibroda CO		
55 Troy Aikman	6.00	15.00
56 Jay Novacek	1.60	4.00
57 Emmitt Smith	18.00	30.00
58 Michael Irvin	2.40	6.00
59 Dorie Braddy	1.00	2.50
(Cheerleader)		
60 Dallas Cowboys	1.00	2.50
Super Bowl trophy		
61 Clay Matthews	1.60	4.00
62 Tommy Vardell	1.00	2.50
63 Eric Turner	1.00	2.50
64 Mike Johnson	1.00	2.50
65 James Jones	1.00	2.50
66 Cleveland Browns	1.00	2.50
Helmet		

1990 British Petroleum

This 36-card standard-size set was issued two cards at a time by British Petroleum gas stations throughout

California in association with Talent Network Inc. of Skokie, Illinois. There were five winning player cards issued in the following quantities. Andre Tippett: $5 - 990 cards, Freeman McNeil: $10 - 325 cards, Clay Matthews: $100 - 18 cards, Tim Harris: $1,000 - three cards, and Deion Sanders $10,000 - one card. Most of these winning cards are not valued as collectibles in the checklist below as they were more valuable as prize winners. The set has multiple players numbered 1, 3, 6, 8, and 10, and we have arranged each group of same-numbered cards into alphabetical order. Each game piece was two NFL football cards inside a cardboard frame, with full-color head shots in uniform of the player. Cards are frequently found in less than Mint condition due to the fact that glue was applied to the obverses of the cards in the manufacturing process. There were 36 cards in the set, and the object of the game was to collect two adjacent numbers, 1-2, 3-4, 5-6, 7-8, or 9-10. One number was easy to get, but the other was difficult. The game redemptions expired in October 1991. Each card was produced in two different card back variations: black with contest rules and advertising design featuring full color football scene.

COMPLETE SET (36)	40.00	80.00
*CONTEST BACK: .4X TO 1X		
1A John Elway	5.00	12.00
1B Boomer Esiason	.40	1.00
1C Jim Everett	.40	1.00
1D Bernie Kosar	.40	1.00
1E Karl Mecklenburg	.30	.75
1F Bruce Smith	.75	2.00
2 Deion Sanders/1* (Winning card)		
3A Roger Craig	.40	1.00
3B Randall Cunningham	.75	2.00
3C Keith Jackson	.40	1.00
3D Dan Marino	6.00	15.00
3E Freddie Joe Nunn	.30	.75
3F Jerry Rice	3.00	8.00
3G Vinny Testaverde	.40	1.00
3H John L. Williams	.30	.75
4 Tim Harris/3* (Winning card)		
5 Clay Matthews/18* (Winning card)		
6A Neal Anderson	.30	.75
6B Duane Bickett	.30	.75
6C Ronnie Lott	.75	2.00
6D Anthony Munoz	.40	1.00
6E Christian Okoye	.30	.75
6F Barry Sanders	5.00	12.00
7 Freeman McNeil/325* (Winning card)		
8A Cornelius Bennett	.40	1.00
8B Anthony Carter	.40	1.00
8C Jim Kelly	1.50	4.00
8D Louis Lipps	.30	.75
8E Phil Simms	.75	2.00
8F Billy Ray Smith	.30	.75
8G Lawrence Taylor	.75	2.00
9 Andre Tippett/990* (Winning card)		
10A Bo Jackson	.75	2.00
10B Howie Long	.75	2.00
10C Don Majkowski	.30	.75
10D Art Monk	.40	1.00
10E Warren Moon	.40	1.00
10F Mike Singletary	.75	2.00
10G Al Toon	.40	1.00
10H Herschel Walker	.75	2.00
10I Reggie White	1.25	3.00

1962 Broncos Team Issue

The Broncos issued several series of player photos in the early 1960s with some invariably being released in multiple years. Each of the photos in this group are black-and-white and measure approximately 8" by 10" and are blankbacked. The line of text below the image contains the following from left to right: player name and team name in all caps.

1 George Herring (dropping back to pass)	7.50	15.00
2 George Herring (running pose)	7.50	15.00
3 George Herring (punting pose)	7.50	15.00
4 Tom Higginbotham	7.50	15.00

1963 Broncos Team Issue

The Broncos issued several series of player photos in the early 1960s with some invariably being released in multiple years. Each of the photos in this group are black-and-white and measure approximately 8" by 10" and are blankbacked. The line of text below the image contains the following from left to right: player name, position spelled out, height, weight and team name in all caps.

1 George Herring (portrait)	7.50	15.00
2 George Herring (handing off the ball)	7.50	15.00
3 Jack Hill	7.50	15.00
4 Jerry Hopkins	7.50	15.00

1967-68 Broncos Team Issue

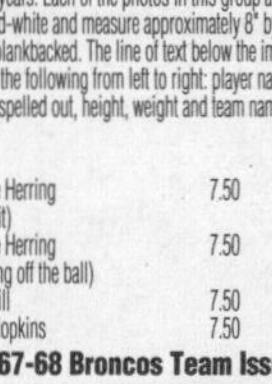

The Broncos issued several series of player photos in the late 1960s through early 1970s with many invariably being released in multiple years. The format is the same for most of the sets with only subtle differences in the type (size and style) and information contained below the photo. Each of the photos in this group are black-and-white measuring approximately 5" by 7" and are blankbacked and unnumbered. The line of text contains the following from left to right: player name, position (completely spelled out), height, weight, and team name. We've included what is thought to be the year of issue. The 1967 photos were printed with both upper and lower case lettering, while the 1968 issue was done in all caps. We've listed the only known photos in the set.

COMPLETE SET (4)	25.00	50.00
1 Carl Cunningham 67	7.50	15.00
2 Al Denson 67	7.50	15.00
3 Wallace Dickey 68	7.50	15.00
4 Charlie Greer 68	7.50	15.00

1969 Broncos Team Issue

The Broncos issued several series of player photos in the 1960s and 1970s with many invariably being released in multiple years. The format is the same for most of the sets with only subtle differences in the type (size and style) and information contained below the photo. Each of these black-and-white photos measures approximately 5" by 7" and is blankbacked and unnumbered. The line of text for the 1969 issue contains the following from left to right: player name (in all caps), position (spelled out in all caps), height, weight, and team name (in all caps). We've listed the only known photos in the set.

COMPLETE SET (16)	100.00	200.00
1 Tom Beer	7.50	15.00
2 Phil Brady	7.50	15.00
3 Sam Brunelli	7.50	15.00
4 George Burrell	7.50	15.00
5 Grady Cavness	7.50	15.00
6 Ken Criter	7.50	15.00
7 Al Denson	7.50	15.00
8 John Embree	7.50	15.00
9 Walter Highsmith	7.50	15.00
10 Gus Hollomon	7.50	15.00
11 Pete Liske	7.50	15.00
12 Rex Mirich	7.50	15.00
13 Tom Oberg	7.50	15.00
14 Frank Richter	7.50	15.00
15 Paul Smith	7.50	15.00
16 Bob Young	7.50	15.00

1970 Broncos Carlson-Frink Dairy Coaches

These large (roughly 6" by 11 7/8") cards were issued by Carlson-Frink Dairy in the Denver area about 1970. Each is blankbacked and features a black and white photo of a then current Denver Broncos coach. A written "Football Tip" is also included below the coach's photo. The set includes just one unique photo for each coach but it is included on five different card numbers that begin with the first initial of the coach's last name. The "Football Tip" is unique to each of the five cards per coach. Lou Saban has also been found only in an unnumbered card version. Any confirmed additions to this list are appreciated.

COMPLETE SET (36)	2,500.00	4,000.00
COMP.SHORT SET (0)	500.00	800.00
C1 Joe Collier	60.00	100.00
C2 Joe Collier	60.00	100.00
C3 Joe Collier	60.00	100.00
C4 Joe Collier	60.00	100.00
C5 Joe Collier	60.00	100.00
D1 Whitey Dovell	60.00	100.00
D2 Whitey Dovell	60.00	100.00
D3 Whitey Dovell	60.00	100.00
D4 Whitey Dovell	60.00	100.00
D5 Whitey Dovell	60.00	100.00
E1 Hunter Enis	60.00	100.00
E2 Hunter Enis	60.00	100.00
E3 Hunter Enis	60.00	100.00
E4 Hunter Enis	60.00	100.00
E5 Hunter Enis	60.00	100.00
G1 Fred Gehrke	60.00	100.00
G2 Fred Gehrke	60.00	100.00
G3 Fred Gehrke	60.00	100.00
G4 Fred Gehrke	60.00	100.00
G5 Fred Gehrke	60.00	100.00
J1 Stan Jones	75.00	125.00
J2 Stan Jones	75.00	125.00
J3 Stan Jones	75.00	125.00
J4 Stan Jones	75.00	125.00
J5 Stan Jones	75.00	125.00
M1 Dick MacPherson	60.00	100.00
M2 Dick MacPherson	60.00	100.00
M3 Dick MacPherson	60.00	100.00
M4 Dick MacPherson	60.00	100.00
M5 Dick MacPherson	60.00	100.00
R1 Sam Rutigliano	75.00	125.00
R2 Sam Rutigliano	75.00	125.00
R3 Sam Rutigliano	75.00	125.00
R4 Sam Rutigliano	75.00	125.00
R5 Sam Rutigliano	75.00	125.00
S1 Lou Saban	75.00	125.00
S2 Lou Saban	75.00	125.00
S3 Lou Saban	75.00	125.00
S4 Lou Saban	75.00	125.00
S5 Lou Saban	75.00	125.00
NNO Lou Saban	75.00	125.00

1970 Broncos Team Issue

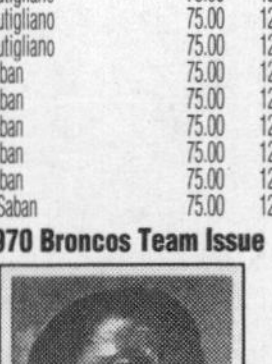

The Broncos issued several series of player photos in the 1960s and 1970s with many invariably being released in multiple years. The format is the same for most of the sets with only subtle differences in the type (size and style) and information contained below the photo. Each of these black-and-white photos measures approximately 5" by 7" and is blankbacked and unnumbered. The line of text for the 1970 issue contains the following from left to right: player name (in upper and lower case), position (initials), and team name (in upper and lower case). We've listed the only known photos in the set.

COMPLETE SET (11)	50.00	100.00
1 Bob Anderson	6.00	12.00
2 Dave Costa	6.00	12.00
3 Ken Criter	6.00	12.00
4 Mike Current	6.00	12.00
5 Fred Forsberg	6.00	12.00
6 Charles Greer	6.00	12.00
7 Larry Kaminski	6.00	12.00
8 Fran Lynch	6.00	12.00
9 Mike Schnitker	6.00	12.00
10 Paul Smith	6.00	12.00
11 Dave Washington	6.00	12.00

1970 Broncos Texaco

The Broncos and Texaco released this set in 1970. Each card is actually an artist's rendering in an 8" by 10" format. The backs are unnumbered and contain extensive player information as well information about the artist, Von Schroeder.

COMPLETE SET (10)	100.00	175.00
1 Bob Anderson RB	7.50	15.00
2 Dave Costa	7.50	15.00
3 Pete Duranko	7.50	15.00
4 George Goeddeke SP	15.00	30.00
5 Mike Haffner	7.50	15.00
6 Rich Jackson	7.50	15.00
7 Larry Kaminski	7.50	15.00
8 Floyd Little	10.00	20.00
9 Pete Liske SP	15.00	30.00
10 Bill Van Heusen	7.50	15.00

1971 Broncos Team Issue 5x7

The Broncos issued several series of player photos in the 1960s and 1970s with many invariably being released in multiple years. The format is the same for most of the sets with only subtle differences in the type (size and style) and information contained below the photo. Each of these black-and-white photos measures approximately 5" by 7" and is blankbacked and unnumbered. The line of text for the 1971 issue contains the following from left to right: player name (in upper and lower case), height, weight, position (initials), and team name (in upper and lower case). We've listed the only known photos in the set.

COMPLETE SET (6)	25.00	40.00
1 Jack Gehrke	4.00	8.00
2 Dwight Harrison	4.00	8.00
3 Randy Montgomery	4.00	8.00
4 Steve Ramsey	4.00	8.00
5 Roger Shoals	4.00	8.00
6 Olen Underwood	4.00	8.00

1971-72 Broncos Team Issue 8x10

The Broncos issued several series of player photos in the 1960s and 1970s with many invariably being released in multiple years. The format is roughly the same for most of the sets with only subtle differences in the type (size and style) and information contained below the photo. Each of these black-and-white photos measures approximately 8" by 10" and is blankbacked and unnumbered.

COMPLETE SET (10)	50.00	100.00
1 Lyle Alzado	7.50	15.00
2 Mike Current	5.00	10.00
3 Fred Forsberg	5.00	10.00
4 Charles Greer	5.00	10.00
5 Don Horn	5.00	10.00
6 Bill McKoy	5.00	10.00
7 George Saimes	5.00	10.00
8 Paul Smith	5.00	10.00
9 Bill Thompson	5.00	10.00
10 Jim Turner Don Horn	5.00	10.00

1972 Broncos Team Issue

The Broncos issued several series of player photos in the 1960s and 1970s with many invariably being released in multiple years. The format is the same for most of the sets with only subtle differences in the type (size and style) and information contained below the photo. Each of these black-and-white photos measures approximately 5" by 7" and is blankbacked and unnumbered. The line of text for the 1972 issue contains the following from left to right: player name (in all caps), position (initials in all caps), and team city and team name (in all caps). We've listed only the known photos in the set, additions to this list are welcomed.

COMPLETE SET (6)	25.00	50.00
1 Carter Campbell	5.00	10.00
2 Cornell Gordon	5.00	10.00
3 Larron Jackson position GUARD spelled out	5.00	10.00
4 Tommy Lyons	5.00	10.00
5 Bobby Maples	5.00	10.00
6 Jerry Simmons	5.00	10.00

1973 Broncos Team Issue

The Broncos issued several series of player photos in the 1960s and 1970s with many invariably being released in multiple years. The format is the same for most of the sets with only subtle differences in the type (size and style) and information contained below the photo. Each of these black-and-white photos measures approximately 5" by 7" and is blankbacked and unnumbered. The line of text for the 1973 issue contains the following from left to right: player name (in all caps), position (initials in all caps) followed by a comma, and team city and team name (in all caps). We've listed only the known photos in the set, additions to this list are welcomed.

COMPLETE SET (16)	75.00	150.00
1 Lyle Alzado	6.00	12.00
2 Otis Armstrong	6.00	12.00
3 Barney Chavous	5.00	10.00
4 Mike Current	5.00	10.00
5 Joe Dawkins	5.00	10.00
6 John Grant	5.00	10.00
7 Larron Jackson position initial G only	5.00	10.00
8 Calvin Jones	5.00	10.00
9 Larry Kaminski	5.00	10.00
10 Bill Laskey	5.00	10.00
11 Tom Lyons	5.00	10.00
12 Randy Montgomery	5.00	10.00
13 Riley Odoms	5.00	10.00
14 Oliver Ross	5.00	10.00
15 Ed Smith	5.00	10.00
16 Bill Van Heusen	5.00	10.00

1975 Broncos Team Issue

The Broncos issued several series of player photos in the 1960s and 1970s with many invariably being released in multiple years. The format is very similar for most of the sets with only subtle differences in the type (size and style) and information contained below the photo. Each of these black-and-white photos measures approximately 5" by 7" and is blankbacked and unnumbered. The line of text for the 1975 issue contains the following from left to right: player name (in all caps), position (initials in all caps), and team city (in all caps). We've listed only the known photos in the set, additions to this list are welcomed.

COMPLETE SET (15)	60.00	120.00
1 Stan Rogers	5.00	10.00
2 John Rowser	5.00	10.00
3 Bob Swenson	5.00	10.00
4 Paul Smith	5.00	10.00
5 Jeff Severson	5.00	10.00
6 Boyd Brown	5.00	10.00
7 Rubin Carter	5.00	10.00
8 Jack Dolbin	5.00	10.00
9 Mike Franckowiak	5.00	10.00
10 Randy Gradishar	6.00	12.00
11 Paul Howard	5.00	10.00
12 Claudie Minor	5.00	10.00
13 Phil Olsen	5.00	10.00
14 Steve Ramsey	5.00	10.00
15 Joe Rizzo	5.00	10.00

1976 Broncos Team Issue

The Broncos issued several series of player photos in the 1960s and 1970s with many invariably being released in multiple years. The format is very similar for most of the sets with only subtle differences in the type (size and style) and information contained below the photo. Each of these black-and-white photos measures approximately 5" by 7" and is blankbacked and unnumbered. The line of text for the 1975 issue contains the following from left to right: player name (in upper and lower case letters), position (initials or spelled out fully in upper and lower case), and team city (in upper and lower case). We've listed only the known photos in the set, additions to this list are welcomed.

1 Randy Poltl	5.00	10.00
2 Earlie Thomas	5.00	10.00

1977 Broncos Burger King Glasses

Burger King restaurants released this set of 6-drinking glasses during the 1977 NFL season in Denver area stores. Each features a black and white photo of a Broncos player with his name and team name below the picture.

COMPLETE SET (6)	45.00	90.00
1 Lyle Alzado	12.50	25.00
2 Randy Gradishar	10.00	20.00
3 Tom Jackson	10.00	20.00
4 Craig Morton	12.50	25.00
5 Haven Moses	7.50	15.00
6 Riley Odoms	7.50	15.00

1977 Broncos Orange Crush Cans

This can set features player images of the Denver Broncos printed on Orange Crush Soda cans. The set is unnumbered and checklisted below in alphabetical order. Reportedly, there were 64-different cans made. Any additions to the below list are appreciated.

COMPLETE SET (64)	200.00	350.00
1 Henry Allison	2.50	5.00
2 Lyle Alzado	5.00	10.00
3 Steve Antonopulos TR	2.50	5.00
4 Otis Armstrong	4.00	8.00
5 Rick Baska	2.50	5.00
6 Ronnie Bill EQ MGR	2.50	5.00
7 Marv Braden CO	2.50	5.00
8 Rubin Carter	2.50	5.00
9 Barney Chavous	3.00	6.00
10 Joe Collier CO	2.50	5.00
11 Bucky Dilts	2.50	5.00
12 Jack Dolbin	3.00	6.00
13 Larry Elliot EQ MGR	2.50	5.00
14 Larry Evans	2.50	5.00
15 Dave Frei DIR	2.50	5.00
16 Steve Foley	3.00	6.00
17 Ron Egloff	2.50	5.00
18 Bob Gambold CO	2.50	5.00
19 Fred Gehrke GM	2.50	5.00
20 Tom Glassic	2.50	5.00
21 Randy Gradishar	5.00	10.00
22 John Grant	2.50	5.00
23 Ken Gray CO	2.50	5.00
24 Paul Howard	2.50	5.00
25 Allen Hurst TR	2.50	5.00
26 Glenn Hyde	2.50	5.00
27 Bernard Jackson	2.50	5.00
28 Tom Jackson	5.00	10.00
29 Jim Jensen	2.50	5.00
30 Stan Jones CO	4.00	8.00
31 Rob Lytle	3.00	6.00
32 Jon Keyworth	3.00	6.00
33 Brison Manor	2.50	5.00
34 Bobby Maples	2.50	5.00
35 Andy Maurer	2.50	5.00
36 Red Miller CO	4.00	8.00
37 Claudie Minor	2.50	5.00
38 Mike Montler	2.50	5.00
39 Myrel Moore CO	2.50	5.00
40 Craig Morton	5.00	10.00
41 Haven Moses	4.00	8.00
42 Rob Nairne	2.50	5.00
43 Riley Odoms	3.00	6.00
44 Babe Parilli CO	3.00	6.00
45 Bob Peck	2.50	5.00
46 Craig Penrose	2.50	5.00
47 Lonnie Perrin	2.50	5.00
48 Fran Polsfoot CO	2.50	5.00
49 Randy Poltl	2.50	5.00
50 Randy Rich	2.50	5.00
51 Larry Riley	2.50	5.00
52 Joe Rizzo	2.50	5.00
53 Paul Roach CO	2.50	5.00
54 Steve Schindler	2.50	5.00
55 John Schultz	2.50	5.00
56 Paul Smith	3.00	6.00
57 Gail Stuckey	2.50	5.00
58 Bob Swenson	2.50	5.00
59 Bill Thompson	3.00	6.00
60 Godwin Turk	2.50	5.00
61 Jim Turner	3.00	6.00
62 Rick Upchurch	4.00	8.00
63 Norris Weese	2.50	5.00
64 Louis Wright	3.00	6.00

1980 Broncos Stamps Police

The 1980 Denver Broncos set are not cards but stamps each measuring approximately 3" by 3". Each stamp actually contains three smaller stamps, two player stamps and the Denver Broncos logo stamp. The set is co-sponsored by Albertson's, the Kiwanis Club, and the local law enforcement agency. A different stamp pair was given away each week for nine weeks by Albertson's food stores in the Denver Metro area. The set is unnumbered, although player uniform numbers appear on each small stamp. The set has been listed below in alphabetical order based on the player stamp on the left side. The back of each pair states "Support your local Law Enforcement Agency" and gives instructions on how to reach the police by phone. The backs of the stamps contain 1980 NFL and NFL Player's Association copyright dates. There was also a poster (to hold the stamps) issued which originally was priced at 99 cents. It was a color action picture of four Broncos tackling a Chargers running back measuring approximately 21" by 29"; the poster is much more difficult to find now than the set of stamps.

COMPLETE SET (9)	7.50	15.00
1 Barney Chavous and Rubin Carter	.60	1.50
2 Bernard Jackson and Haven Moses	.60	1.50
3 Tom Jackson and Riley Odoms	1.25	3.00
4 Brison Manor and Steve Foley	.60	1.50
5 Claudie Minor and Randy Gradishar	.60	1.50
6 Craig Morton and Tom Glassic	1.25	3.00
7 Jim Turner and Bob Swenson	.75	2.00
8 Rick Upchurch and Bill Thompson	1.00	2.50
9 Louis Wright and Joe Rizzo	.75	2.00

1982 Broncos Police

The 1982 Denver Broncos set contains 15 unnumbered cards. The cards measure approximately 2 5/8" by 4 1/8". The uniform numbers, which appear on the fronts of the cards, are used in the checklist below. The set was sponsored by the Colorado Springs Police Department and features "Broncos Tips" and the Broncos helmet logo on the back. Card backs feature black print on white card stock. The fronts contain both the Denver helmet logo and the logo of the Colorado Springs Police Department. The cards of Barney Chavous and Randy Gradishar are supposedly harder to find than the other cards in the set, with Chavous considered the more difficult of the two. In addition Riley Odoms and Dave Preston seem to be harder to find.

COMPLETE SET (15)	75.00	150.00
7 Craig Morton	4.00	10.00
11 Luke Prestridge	1.50	4.00
20 Louis Wright	1.50	4.00
24 Rick Parros	1.50	4.00
36 Bill Thompson	1.50	4.00
41 Rob Lytle	1.50	4.00
46 Dave Preston SP	4.00	10.00
51 Bob Swenson	1.50	4.00
53 Randy Gradishar SP	20.00	50.00
57 Tom Jackson	4.00	10.00
60 Paul Howard	1.50	4.00
68 Rubin Carter	1.50	4.00
79 Barney Chavous SP	20.00	50.00
80 Rick Upchurch	2.50	6.00
88 Riley Odoms SP	4.00	10.00

1984 Broncos KOA

These cards were issued as part of a KOA "Match 'N Win" and KOA/Denver Broncos Silver Anniversary Sweepstakes. They were distributed at any participating Dairy Queen or Safeway in the Metro Denver area between September 17 and November 11, 1984. The cards measure approximately 2" by 4", with a tab at the bottom (measuring 1 1/8" in length). The front has a black and white photo of the player from the waist up. Above the photo the card reads "KOA Official Denver Broncos Memory Series" in blue print with white outlining. The lower portion of the photo is covered over by three items: 1) player number, name, and position; 2) a logo of the original American Football League and the sponsor's name or logo (Rocky Mountain News, Kodak, Dairy Queen, Wood Bros. Homes, KMGH-TV-7 Denver, Safeway, and Armour). The picture and these items are enframed by a color border on a color background. There were three each of eight different color schemes used. The tab portion of the card has three silver footballs that were to be scratched off with a coin. The back lists the rules governing the sweepstakes. There are four players marked as SP in the checklist below who are supposedly tougher to find than the others; they are Bobby Anderson, Randy Gradishar, Floyd Little, and Claudie Minor. The cards are unnumbered but are listed below in uniform number order. The prices listed refer to unscratched cards.

COMPLETE SET (24)	100.00	200.00
7 Craig Morton	6.00	12.00
11 Bob Anderson SP	6.00	12.00
12 Charley Johnson	5.00	10.00
15 Jim Turner	4.00	8.00
21 Gene Mingo	4.00	8.00
22 Fran Lynch	4.00	8.00
23 Goose Gonsoulin	4.00	8.00
24 Otis Armstrong	5.00	10.00
24 Willie Brown	6.00	12.00
25 Haven Moses	5.00	10.00
36 Bill Thompson	4.00	8.00
42 Bill Van Heusen	4.00	8.00
44 Floyd Little SP	10.00	20.00
53 Randy Gradishar SP	10.00	20.00
71 Claudie Minor SP	6.00	12.00
72 Sam Brunelli	4.00	8.00
74 Mike Current	4.00	8.00
75 Eldon Danenhauer	4.00	8.00
78 Marv Montgomery	4.00	8.00
81 Billy Masters	4.00	8.00
82 Bob Scarpitto	4.00	8.00
87 Lionel Taylor	5.00	10.00
87 Rich Jackson	4.00	8.00
88 Riley Odoms	4.00	8.00

1984 Broncos Pizza Hut Glasses

This set of small glasses was distributed and sponsored by Pizza Hut to commemorate the Denver Broncos 25th anniversary. Each glass includes color artist's renderings of 6-different Broncos all-time greats.

COMPLETE SET (4)	15.00	25.00
1 Lyle Alzado Tom Glassic Goose Gonsoulin Tom Jackson Frank Tripucka Steve Watson	5.00	12.00
2 Bill Bryan Craig Morton Haven Moses Bill Thompson Rick Upchurch Billy Van Heusen	3.00	8.00
3 Barney Chavous Randy Gradishar Riley Odoms Paul Smith Jim Turner Louis Wright	3.00	8.00
4 Rich Jackson Charley Johnson Floyd Little Claudie Minor Bob Swenson Lionel Taylor	2.00	5.00

1987 Broncos Ace Fact Pack

This 33-card set measures approximately 2 1/4" by 3 5/8". This set consists of 22 player cards and 11 organizational cards. These cards, which were issued in Great Britain and made in West Germany (by Ace Fact Pack), have a playing card design on the back. The cards are checklisted below in alphabetical order.

COMPLETE SET (33)	150.00	300.00
1 Keith Bishop	1.25	3.00
2 Bill Bryan	1.25	3.00
3 Mark Cooper (John Elway in photo)	1.25	3.00
4 John Elway	125.00	250.00
5 Steve Foley	1.25	3.00
6 Mike Harden	1.25	3.00
7 Ricky Hunley	1.25	3.00
8 Vance Johnson	2.00	5.00
9 Rulon Jones	1.25	3.00
10 Rich Karlis	1.25	3.00
11 Clarence Kay	1.25	3.00
12 Ken Lanier	1.25	3.00
13 Karl Mecklenburg	3.00	8.00
14 Chris Norman	1.25	3.00
15 Jim Ryan	1.25	3.00
16 Dennis Smith	2.00	5.00
17 Dave Studdard	1.25	3.00
18 Andre Townsend	1.25	3.00
19 Steve Watson	2.00	5.00
20 Gerald Willhite	1.25	3.00
21 Sammy Winder	2.00	5.00
22 Louis Wright	2.00	5.00
23 Broncos Helmet	1.25	3.00
24 Broncos Information	1.25	3.00
25 Broncos Uniform	1.25	3.00
26 Game Record Holders	1.25	3.00
27 Season Record Holders	1.25	3.00
28 Career Record Holders	1.25	3.00
29 Record 1967-86	1.25	3.00
30 1986 Team Statistics	1.25	3.00
31 All-Time Greats	1.25	3.00
32 Roll of Honour	1.25	3.00
33 Denver Mile High Stadium	1.25	3.00

1987 Broncos Orange Crush

This nine-card set of Denver Broncos' ex-players was sponsored by Orange Crush and KOA Radio. The cards are standard size, 2 1/2" by 3 1/2", and feature black and white photos inside a blue and orange frame. The set is a salute to the "Ring of Famers," Denver's best players in its history as a franchise. Card backs (written in black, orange, and blue on white card stock) feature a capsule biography and indicate the year of induction into the Ring of Fame. Reportedly 1.35 million cards were distributed over a three-week period at participating 7-Eleven and Albertsons stores in Denver and surrounding areas.

COMPLETE SET (9)	4.00	8.00
1 Bill Thompson	.40	1.00
2 Lionel Taylor	.50	1.25
3 Goose Gonsoulin	.30	.75
4 Paul Smith	.30	.75
5 Rich Jackson	.30	.75
6 Charley Johnson	.40	1.00
7 Floyd Little	.75	2.00
8 Frank Tripucka	.40	1.00
9 Gerald Phipps (Owner 1960-1981)	.30	.75

1997 Broncos Collector's Choice

Upper Deck released several team sets in 1997 in a blister pack wrapper. Each of the 14-cards in this set are very similar to the base Collector's Choice cards except for the card numbering on the cardback. A cover/checklist card was added featuring the team helmet.

COMPLETE SET (14)	1.60	4.00
DN1 Tory James	.02	.10
DN2 Terrell Davis	.50	1.25
DN3 Tyrone Braxton	.02	.10
DN4 John Mobley	.05	.15
DN5 Bill Romanowski	.02	.10
DN6 Vaughn Hebron	.02	.10
DN7 Trevor Pryce	.05	.15
DN8 Alfred Williams	.02	.10
DN9 John Elway	.60	1.50
DN10 Shannon Sharpe	.08	.25
DN11 Steve Atwater	.05	.15
DN12 Neil Smith	.08	.25
DN13 Darrien Gordon	.05	.15
DN14 Broncos Logo Checklist (John Elway on back)	.20	.50

1997 Broncos Score

This 15-card set of the Denver Broncos was distributed in five-card packs with a suggested retail price of $1.99. The fronts feature color action player photos with white borders and the player's name and team logo printed in team color foil at the bottom. The backs carry player information and career statistics. Platinum Team parallel cards were randomly seeded in packs featuring all foil cardfronts.

COMPLETE SET (15)	4.00	10.00
*PLATINUM TEAMS: 1X TO 2X		
1 John Elway	1.20	3.00
2 Shannon Sharpe	.30	.75
3 Anthony Miller	.15	.40
4 Terrell Davis	1.00	2.50
5 Bill Romanowski	.08	.25
6 Ed McCaffrey	.15	.40
7 John Mobley	.15	.40
8 Alfred Williams	.08	.25
9 Steve Atwater	.15	.40
10 Jeff Lewis	.15	.40
11 Aaron Craver	.08	.25
12 Rod Smith WR	.50	1.25
13 Tyrone Braxton	.08	.25
14 Ray Crockett	.08	.25
15 Allen Aldridge	.08	.25

2006 Broncos Topps

COMPLETE SET (12)	3.00	6.00
DEN1 Domonique Foxworth	.20	.50
DEN2 Rod Smith	.25	.60
DEN3 John Lynch	.20	.50
DEN4 Tatum Bell	.20	.50
DEN5 Brandon Marshall	.30	.75
DEN6 D.J. Williams	.20	.50
DEN7 Jake Plummer	.25	.60
DEN8 Ashley Lelie	.20	.50
DEN9 Ron Dayne	.25	.60
DEN10 Champ Bailey	.25	.60
DEN11 Javon Walker	.25	.60
DEN12 Jay Cutler	1.50	4.00

2007 Broncos Topps

COMPLETE SET (12)	2.50	5.00
1 Jay Cutler	.30	.75
2 Rod Smith	.25	.60
3 Champ Bailey	.25	.60
4 Mike Bell	.25	.60
5 Travis Henry	.25	.60
6 Brandon Marshall	.25	.60

7 Elvis Dumervil	.20	.50
8 Javon Walker	.25	.60
9 Dre Bly	.20	.50
10 Jason Elam	.20	.50
11 John Lynch	.25	.60
12 D J Williams	.20	.50

2008 Broncos Topps

COMPLETE SET (12)	2.50	5.00
1 Jay Cutler	.30	.75
2 Selvin Young	.20	.50
3 Brandon Marshall	.25	.60
4 Champ Bailey	.25	.60
5 Tony Scheffler	.20	.50
6 Travis Henry	.20	.50
7 Brandon Stokley	.25	.60
8 Dre Bly	.20	.50
9 Elvis Dumervil	.20	.50
10 D.J. Williams	.20	.50
11 John Lynch	.25	.60
12 Eddie Royal	.40	1.00

1986 Brownell Heisman

This large-sized black and white set features drawings of past Heisman Trophy winners by Art Brownell. The set (first 50-cards) was originally available as part of a promotion. They are unnumbered and blank backed so they have been assigned numbers below in chronological order according to when each player won the Heisman Trophy. Since Archie Griffin of Ohio State won the Heisman in both 1974 and 1975 there is only one card for him. The Vinny Testaverde and Tim Brown cards were produced at a later date. The cards measure approximately 7 15/16" by 10".

COMPLETE SET (52)	350.00	600.00
1 Jay Berwanger	5.00	10.00
2 Larry Kelley	5.00	10.00
3 Clint Frank	5.00	10.00
4 Davey O'Brien	5.00	10.00
5 Nile Kinnick	10.00	20.00
6 Tom Harmon	5.00	10.00
7 Bruce Smith	5.00	10.00
8 Frank Sinkwich	5.00	10.00
9 Angelo Bertelli	5.00	10.00
10 Les Horvath	5.00	10.00
11 Doc Blanchard	6.00	12.00
12 Glenn Davis	6.00	12.00
13 Johnny Lujack	10.00	20.00
14 Doak Walker	7.50	15.00
15 Leon Hart	5.00	10.00
16 Vic Janowicz	6.00	12.00
17 Dick Kazmaier	5.00	10.00
18 Bill Vessels	5.00	10.00
19 John Lattner	6.00	12.00
20 Alan Ameche	6.00	12.00
21 Howard Cassady	5.00	10.00
22 Paul Hornung	10.00	20.00
23 John David Crow	5.00	10.00
24 Pete Dawkins	5.00	10.00
25 Billy Cannon	6.00	12.00
26 Joe Bellino	5.00	10.00
27 Ernie Davis	18.00	30.00
28 Terry Baker	5.00	10.00
29 Roger Staubach	25.00	40.00
30 John Huarte	5.00	10.00
31 Mike Garrett	5.00	10.00
32 Steve Spurrier	7.50	15.00
33 Gary Beban	5.00	10.00
34 O.J. Simpson	10.00	20.00
35 Steve Owens	5.00	10.00
36 Jim Plunkett	6.00	12.00
37 Pat Sullivan	5.00	10.00
38 Johnny Rodgers	5.00	10.00
39 John Cappelletti	5.00	10.00
40 Archie Griffin	6.00	12.00
41 Tony Dorsett	12.50	25.00
42 Earl Campbell	10.00	20.00
43 Billy Sims	5.00	10.00
44 Charles White	5.00	10.00
45 George Rogers	5.00	10.00
46 Marcus Allen	12.50	25.00
47 Herschel Walker	6.00	12.00
48 Mike Rozier	5.00	10.00
49 Doug Flutie	10.00	20.00
50 Bo Jackson	6.00	12.00
51 Vinny Testaverde	7.50	15.00
52 Tim Brown	12.50	25.00

1946 Browns Sears

These eight cards measure approximately 2 1/2" by 4". They were issued by Sears and Roebuck and feature players from the debut season of the Cleveland Browns. The cards were printed on heavy white paper stock and include a black and white photo of the featured player on the front with a team schedule on back. Cardfronts also included a message to follow the Browns and shop at Sears Stores. Several very early cards of Hall of Famers are included in this set. We have checklisted this set in alphabetical order.

COMPLETE SET (8)	1,000.00	1,800.00
1 Ernie Blandin	90.00	150.00
2 Jim Daniell	90.00	150.00
3 Fred Evans	90.00	150.00
4 Frank Gatski	150.00	250.00
5 Otto Graham	350.00	600.00
6 Dante Lavelli	175.00	300.00
7 Mel Maceau	90.00	150.00
8 George Young	125.00	200.00

1948 Browns Sohio

These large (measure either 8" by 9 7/8" or 7 3/4" by 9 7/8") black and white photos are issued by Cleveland area Sohio stores in 1948. They are very simiar to the 1949 release and were printed on heavy card stock and each includes a black and white photo along with brief biographical information on the cardfronts and "Compliments of Sohio" printed within the bottom border. Since the photos are unnumbered, we have sequenced them in alphabetical order.

COMPLETE SET (3)	150.00	300.00
1 Horace Gillom	25.00	50.00
2 Marion Motley	100.00	175.00
3 Bill Willis	40.00	80.00
(measures 7 3/4" by 9 7/8")		

1949 Browns Sohio

These large black and white photos were issued by Cleveland area Sohio stores in 1949 as a complete set in an envelope. The exact size of each photo varies slightly by as much as 1/16" but roughly each measures 8" by 9 3/4". They were printed on heavy card stock and each includes a black and white photo along with brief biographical information on the cardfronts. Since the photos are unnumbered, we have sequenced them in alphabetical order. Note that most of the photos in this release have been reproduced with slight differences in paper stock and size.

COMPLETE SET (11)	500.00	800.00
1 Bob Gaudio	25.00	40.00
2 Otto Graham	175.00	300.00
3 Lou Groza	90.00	150.00
4 Lin Houston	25.00	40.00
5 Weldon Humble	25.00	40.00
6 Tommy James	25.00	40.00
7 Edgar Jones	30.00	50.00
8 Dante Lavelli	60.00	100.00
9 Marion Motley	100.00	175.00
10 Lou Saban	30.00	50.00
11 Mac Speedie	50.00	80.00

1950 Browns Team Issue 6x9

This set of team-issued photos measures approximately 6 1/4" by 9" and was printed on thin paper stock and issued as a set. The fronts feature black-and-white posed action shots framed by white borders with a facsimile autogrpah near the bottoom of the photo. The cardbacks are blank and unnumbered and the photos are checklisted below in alphabetical order.

COMPLETE SET (25)	600.00	1,000.00
1 Tony Adamle	18.00	30.00
2 Paul Brown	50.00	80.00
3 Rex Bumgardner	18.00	30.00
4 Frank Gatski	30.00	50.00
5 Abe Gibron	18.00	30.00
6 Otto Graham	125.00	200.00
7 Forrest Grigg	18.00	30.00
8 Lou Groza	60.00	100.00
9 Hal Herring	18.00	30.00
10 Lin Houston	18.00	30.00
11 Tommy James	18.00	30.00
12 Dub Jones	20.00	35.00
13 Warren Lahr	18.00	30.00
14 Dante Lavelli	40.00	75.00
15 Cliff Lewis	18.00	30.00
16 Dom Moselle	18.00	30.00
17 Marion Motley	60.00	100.00
18 Derrell F. Palmer	18.00	30.00
19 Don Phelps	18.00	30.00
20 John Russell	18.00	30.00
21 Lou Rymkus	20.00	35.00
22 Mac Speedie	30.00	50.00
23 Thomas Thompson	18.00	30.00
24 Bill Willis	35.00	60.00
25 George Young	25.00	40.00

1950 Browns Team Issue 8x10

This set of Cleveland Browns photos measures approximately 8" by 10" and features black and white posed action shots framed by white borders. The year is an estimate based upon when the players appeared on the same Browns' team. The player's name appears in a small white box close to the bottom of the photo and the cardbacks are blank. Each is unnumbered and checklisted below in alphabetical order. It is thought that the set could have been released by Sohio. These photos are identical to the 1954 set and some players may have been issued both years. Any additions to either checklist is appreciated.

COMPLETE SET (11)	400.00	750.00
1 Tony Adamle	25.00	40.00
2 Otto Graham	125.00	200.00
3 Horace Gillom	25.00	40.00
4 Chubby Grigg	25.00	40.00
5 Lou Groza	75.00	125.00
6 Lin Houston	25.00	40.00
7 Dub Jones	30.00	50.00
8 Dante Lavelli	40.00	75.00
9 Marion Motley	75.00	125.00
10 Mac Speedie	35.00	60.00
11 Bill Willis	35.00	60.00

1951 Browns Team Issue 6x9

This set of team-issued photos measures approximately 6 1/2" by 9" and features black and white posed action shots framed by white borders. The set was distributed in an attractive off-white envelope with orange and brown trim titled "Cleveland Browns Photographs". The set is similar to the 1950 issue, but the player's name appears in script close to the photo. The backs are blank. The cards are unnumbered and checklisted below in alphabetical order.

COMPLETE SET (25)	600.00	1,000.00
1 Tony Adamle	18.00	30.00
2 Alex Agase	18.00	30.00
3 Rex Bumgardner	18.00	30.00
4 Emerson Cole	18.00	30.00
5 Len Ford	35.00	60.00
6 Frank Gatski	30.00	50.00
7 Horace Gillom	18.00	30.00
8 Ken Gorgal	18.00	30.00
9 Otto Graham	125.00	200.00
10 Forrest Grigg	18.00	30.00
11 Lou Groza	60.00	100.00
12 Hal Herring	18.00	30.00
13 Lin Houston	18.00	30.00
14 Weldon Humble	18.00	30.00
15 Tommy James	18.00	30.00
16 Dub Jones	20.00	35.00
17 Warren Lahr	18.00	30.00
18 Dante Lavelli	40.00	75.00
19 Cliff Lewis	18.00	30.00
20 Marion Motley	60.00	100.00
21 Lou Rymkus	20.00	35.00
22 Mac Speedie	30.00	50.00
23 Tommy Thompson	18.00	30.00
24 Bill Willis	35.00	60.00
25 George Young	25.00	40.00

1952 Browns Team Issue

This set of team-issued photos measures approximately 8" by 10" and features black and white posed action shots framed by white borders. Each photo was issued with the player's name, position, and team name stamped on the back making it quite different than other Browns photos of the era. The photos are unnumbered and checklisted below in alphabetical order.

1 Doug Atkins	25.00	40.00
2 Darrel Brewster	15.00	30.00
3 Ken Carpenter	15.00	30.00
4 Tom Catlin	15.00	30.00
5 Don Colo	15.00	30.00
6 Gene Donaldson	15.00	30.00
7 Abe Gibron	15.00	30.00
8 Horace Gillom	15.00	30.00
9 Jerry Helluin	15.00	30.00
10 Sherm Howard	15.00	30.00
11 Dub Jones	20.00	35.00
12 Warren Lahr	15.00	30.00
13 Chuck Noll	30.00	50.00
14 Derrell Palmer	15.00	30.00
15 George Ratterman	15.00	30.00
16 Ray Renfro	20.00	35.00
17 John Sandusky	15.00	30.00
18 Tommy Thompson	15.00	30.00

1953 Browns Carling Beer

This set of ten black and white posed action shots was sponsored by Carling Black Label Beer and features members of the Cleveland Browns. The pictures measure approximately 8" by 12 1/4" and have white borders. The sponsor's name and the team name appear below the picture in black lettering. The photos are very similar to the 1954 issue but with several different players and four players with different images. Each is unnumbered and the backs are blank. The serial number in the lower right corner on the fronts reads "DBL 54" plus a unique letter for each player. The photos were shot against a background of an open field with trees.

COMPLETE SET (10)	250.00	400.00
54F Dante Lavelli	25.00	40.00
(holding the football)		
54G Otto Graham	75.00	125.00
(jump pass photo)		
54H Lou Groza	40.00	75.00
(wearing helmet in photo)		
54J Dub Jones	20.00	35.00
54K Ken Gorgal	18.00	30.00
54L Len Ford	25.00	40.00
(is smiling in photo)		
54M Bill Willis	25.00	40.00
54N Tommy Thompson	18.00	30.00
54O Frank Gatski	20.00	35.00
54P Chick Jagade	18.00	30.00

1953 Browns Team Issue

The Cleveland Browns issued and distributed this 12-photo set. Each measures approximately 8 1/2" by 10 1/4" and features a black and white photo. The player's name and position appear in a small white box near the photo.

COMPLETE SET (12)	300.00	450.00
1 Len Ford	20.00	35.00
2 Frank Gatski	20.00	35.00
3 Abe Gibron	15.00	25.00
4 Ken Gorgal	12.00	20.00
5 Otto Graham	75.00	135.00
6 Lou Groza	35.00	60.00
7 Harry Jagade	12.00	20.00
8 Dub Jones	15.00	25.00
9 Dante Lavelli	30.00	50.00
10 Ray Renfro	15.00	25.00
11 Tommy Thompson	15.00	25.00
12 Bill Willis	20.00	35.00

1954 Browns Fisher Foods

This 10-card set features 8 1/2" by 10 1/2" black-and-white photos of the 1954 Cleveland Browns sponsored by Fisher Foods. The photos are very similar to many of the Browns Team Issue sets of the era but can be differentiated by the "Fisher Foods" type within the bottom border. Some or all of the photos an also be found missing the Fisher Foods name. The backs are blank. The cards are unnumbered and checklisted below in alphabetical order.

COMPLETE SET (10)	250.00	400.00
1 Darrel Brewster	12.00	20.00
2 Tom Catlin	12.00	20.00
3 Len Ford	20.00	35.00
4 Otto Graham	60.00	100.00
5 Lou Groza	30.00	50.00
6 Kenny Konz	15.00	25.00
7 Dante Lavelli	25.00	40.00
8 Mike McCormack	20.00	35.00
9 Fred Morrison	12.00	20.00
10 Chuck Noll	60.00	100.00

1954 Browns Team Issue

This photo set features 8 1/2" by 10 1/2" black-and-white photos of the 1954 Cleveland Browns. The photos are very similar to many of the Browns Team Issue sets of the era and are identical to the Fisher Foods set except for the omission of the company name in the bottom border. The player's name and position appear inside a box found near the player's image. The backs are blank. The cards are unnumbered and checklisted below in alphabetical order.

COMPLETE SET (10)	250.00	400.00
1 Tom Catlin	12.00	20.00
2 Len Ford	20.00	35.00
3 Abe Gibron	12.00	20.00
4 Otto Graham	60.00	100.00
5 Lou Groza	30.00	50.00
6 Dante Lavelli	25.00	40.00
7 Mike McCormack	20.00	35.00
8 Fred Morrison	12.00	20.00
9 Chuck Noll	60.00	100.00
10 Tommy Thompson	12.00	20.00

1954 Browns Team Issue 8x10

The Cleveland Browns released this set of photos with each measuring approximately 8" by 10" - slightly smaller than the Fisher Foods photos. The photos feature black and white posed action shots framed by white borders with just the player's name on the front. The year is an estimate based upon when the players appeared on the same Browns' team. Each is blankbacked and unnumbered and checklisted below in alphabetical order. It is thought that the set could have been released by Sohio. These photos are identical in style to the 1947 set and some players may have been issued both years. Any additions to either checklist is appreciated.

COMPLETE SET (8)	90.00	150.00
1 Darrell Brewster	12.00	20.00
2 Len Ford	15.00	25.00
3 Kenny Konz	12.00	20.00
4 Warren Lahr	12.00	20.00
5 Mike McCormack	15.00	25.00
6 Fred Morrison	12.00	20.00
7 Don Phelps	12.00	20.00
8 Tommy Thompson	12.00	20.00

1955-56 Browns Team Issue

This set consists of 8 1/2" by 10" posed player photos, with white borders and blank backs. Most of the photos are poses shot from the waist up; a few (Colo, Ford, and Lahr) picture the player in an action pose. The player's name and position are printed in the bottom white border in large letters. The photos are unnumbered and checklisted below in alphabetical order.

COMPLETE SET (23)	250.00	400.00
1 Maurice Bassett	7.50	15.00
2 Harold Bradley	7.50	15.00
3 Darrell(Pete) Brewster	7.50	15.00
4 Don Colo	7.50	15.00
5 Len Ford	15.00	25.00
6 Bobby Freeman	7.50	15.00
7 Bob Gain	7.50	15.00
8 Frank Gatski	15.00	25.00
9 Abe Gibron	7.50	15.00
10 Lou Groza	25.00	40.00
11 Tommy James	7.50	15.00
12 Dub Jones	10.00	20.00
13 Kenny Konz	7.50	15.00
14 Warren Lahr	7.50	15.00
15 Dante Lavelli	18.00	30.00
16 Carlton Massey	7.50	15.00
17 Mike McCormack	15.00	25.00
18 Walt Michaels	10.00	20.00
19 Chuck Noll	40.00	75.00
20 Babe Parilli	10.00	20.00
21 Don Paul	7.50	15.00
22 Ray Renfro	10.00	20.00
23 George Ratterman	10.00	20.00

1954 Browns Carling Beer

This set of black and white posed action shots was sponsored by Carling Black Label Beer and features members of the Cleveland Browns. The pictures measure approximately 8" by 12 1/4" and have white borders. The sponsor's name and the team name appear below the picture in black lettering. The photos are very similar to the 1953 issue with several new players and updated pictures on four players. Each of the backs are blank and the photo numbering in the lower right corner reads "DBL 54" followed by a unique letter for each player. We've included those numbers/letters below when known. The photos were shot against a background of an open field with trees.

COMPLETE SET (10)	300.00	500.00
1 Darrel Brewster	18.00	30.00
2 Tom Catlin	18.00	30.00
3 Len Ford	25.00	40.00
(not smiling in photo)		
4 Otto Graham	75.00	125.00
(passing pose, feet on the ground)		
5 Lou Groza	40.00	75.00
(no helmet in photo)		
6 Kenny Konz	18.00	30.00
7 Dante Lavelli	25.00	40.00
(ball is in the air)		
8 Mike McCormack	20.00	35.00
9 Fred Morrison	18.00	30.00
10 Chuck Noll	50.00	100.00

1955 Browns Color Postcards

Measuring approximately 6" by 9", these color postcards feature Cleveland Browns players. The cards have rounded corners are are thought to have been distributed directly by the Browns.

COMPLETE SET (6)	125.00	225.00
1 Maurice Bassett	12.50	25.00
2 Don Colo	12.50	25.00
3 Frank Gatski	25.00	40.00
4 Lou Groza	40.00	75.00
5 Dante Lavelli	35.00	60.00
6 George Ratterman	12.50	25.00

1956 Browns Team Issue

This set was issued by the Cleveland Browns. Each photo is very similar to the 1954-55 set except for the size which is 6 3/4" by 8 1/2." All are black and white player photos with white borders and blankbacks. The player's name and position are printed in the bottom white border. The photos are unnumbered and checklisted below in alphabetical order.

COMPLETE SET (7)	125.00	200.00
1 Otto Graham	35.00	60.00
2 Dante Lavelli	15.00	25.00
3 Carlton Massey	7.50	15.00
4 Chuck Noll	25.00	50.00
5 Babe Parilli	10.00	20.00
6 George Ratterman	10.00	20.00
7 Ray Renfro	10.00	20.00

1958 Browns Carling Beer

This set of black-and-white posed action shots was sponsored by Carling Black Label Beer and features members of the Cleveland Browns. The pictures measure approximately 8 1/2" by 11 1/2" and have white borders. The sponsor's name and the team name appear below the picture in black lettering. The backs are blank and the pictures are numbered on the fronts with a "DBL" prefix on the card numbers.

COMPLETE SET (10)	350.00	600.00
227A Ray Renfro	20.00	40.00
227B Jim Brown	150.00	250.00
227C Art Hunter	20.00	40.00
227D Lowe Wren	20.00	40.00
227E Vince Costello	20.00	40.00
227F Chuck Noll	60.00	120.00
227G Paul Wiggin	20.00	40.00
227H Lou Groza	30.00	60.00
227I Bob Gain	20.00	40.00
227J Milt Plum	25.00	50.00

1958-59 Browns Team Issue

These cards are an unnumbered, blank-backed, team issue set of black and white photographs of the Cleveland Browns measuring approximately 8 1/2" by 10 1/2". The set features posed action shots of players whose name and position appear in a white reverse-out block burned into the bottom of each picture. The photos are very similar to the 1961 Browns Team Issue therefore differences are included below for player in both sets. The unnumbered cards are listed below alphabetically.

COMPLETE SET (28)	175.00	300.00
1 Leroy Bolden	6.00	12.00
2 Lew Carpenter	6.00	12.00
3 Tom Catlin	6.00	12.00
4 Don Colo	6.00	12.00
5 Vince Costello	6.00	12.00
6 Galen Fiss	6.00	12.00
(kneeling pose)		
7 Bob Gain	6.00	12.00
(four point stance)		
8 Gene Hickerson	10.00	20.00
9 Art Hunter	6.00	12.00
10 Hank Jordan	10.00	20.00
11 Ken Konz	6.00	12.00
12 Warren Lahr	6.00	12.00
13 Willie McClung	6.00	12.00
14 Mike McCormack	7.50	15.00
(three point stance)		
15 Walt Michaels	7.50	15.00
16 Bobby Mitchell	10.00	20.00
(running cutting pose)		
17 Ed Modzelewski	6.00	12.00
18 Jim Ninowski	6.00	12.00
19 Chuck Noll	12.50	25.00
20 Fran O'Brien	6.00	12.00
21 Bernie Parrish	6.00	12.00
22 Don Paul	6.00	12.00
23 Milt Plum	7.50	15.00
(wearing a black belt)		
24 Bill Quinlan	6.00	12.00
25 Ray Renfro	7.50	15.00
(three point stance)		
26 Jim Shofner	7.50	15.00
(back-pedaling pose)		
27 Paul Wiggin	6.00	12.00
(kneeling pose with helmet)		
28 Lowe Wren	6.00	12.00

1959 Browns Carling Beer

This set of black and white posed action shots was sponsored by Carling Black Label Beer and features members of the Cleveland Browns. The pictures measure approximately 8 1/2" by 11 1/2" and have white borders. The sponsor's name and the team name appear below the picture in black lettering. The backs are typically blank and were printed on glossy paper stock. The pictures are numbered in the lower right corner on the fronts. The photos were shot against a background of an open field with trees. The set is dated by the fact that Billy Howton's last year with Cleveland was 1959. This set was reprinted in the late 1980's; the reprints are on slightly thicker cardboard stock and typically show the Henry M. Barr stamp on the back.

COMPLETE SET (10)	350.00	600.00
302A Leroy Bolden	25.00	40.00
302B Vince Costello	25.00	40.00
302C Galen Fiss	25.00	40.00
302D Jim Brown	100.00	200.00
302E Lou Groza	40.00	75.00
302F Walt Michaels	30.00	50.00
302G Bobby Mitchell	35.00	60.00
302J Bob Gain	25.00	40.00
302K Bill Howton	30.00	50.00
302H Milt Plum	30.00	50.00

1959 Browns Shell Posters

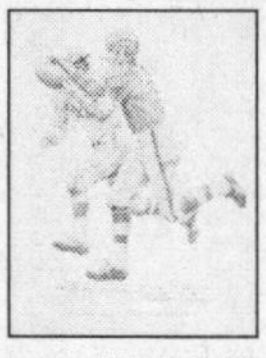

This set of posters was distributed by Shell Oil in 1959. The pictures are black and white drawings with a light sepia color and measure approximately 11 3/4" by 13 3/4". The unnumbered posters are arranged alphabetically by the player's last name and feature members of the Cleveland Browns. Any additions to this list are appreciated.

COMPLETE SET (4)	75.00	125.00
1 Preston Carpenter	15.00	25.00
2 Lou Groza	30.00	50.00
3 Milt Plum	18.00	30.00
4 Jim Ray Smith	15.00	25.00

1960 Browns Team Issue

These large photos are an unnumbered, blank-backed, team issue set of black and white photographs of the Cleveland Browns. Each measures approximately 6" by 9 1/8" and was printed on thin glossy paper stock. The set features posed action shots of players with a facsimile autograph across the image. The cardbacks are blank and they are listed below alphabetically.

COMPLETE SET (32)	300.00	500.00
1 Sam Baker	6.00	12.00
2 Jim Brown	50.00	80.00
3 Paul Brown CO	15.00	30.00
4 Vince Costello	6.00	12.00
5 Len Dawson	30.00	50.00
6 Bob Denton	6.00	12.00
7 Ross Fichtner	6.00	12.00
8 Galen Fiss	6.00	12.00
9 Don Fleming	6.00	12.00
10 Bobby Franklin	6.00	12.00
11 Bob Gain	6.00	12.00
12 Prentice Gautt	6.00	12.00
13 Gene Hickerson	10.00	20.00
14 Jim Houston	6.00	12.00
15 Rich Kreitling	6.00	12.00
16 Dave Lloyd	6.00	12.00
17 Mike McCormack	10.00	20.00
18 Walt Michaels	7.50	15.00
19 Bobby Mitchell	12.50	25.00
20 John Morrow	6.00	12.00
21 Rich Mostardo	6.00	12.00
22 Fred Murphy	6.00	12.00
23 Gern Nagler	6.00	12.00
24 Bernie Parrish	6.00	12.00
25 Floyd Peters	6.00	12.00
26 Milt Plum	7.50	15.00
27 Jim Prestel	6.00	12.00
28 Dick Schafrath	7.50	15.00
29 Jim Shofner	7.50	15.00
30 Jim Ray Smith	6.00	12.00
31 Paul Wiggin	6.00	12.00
32 John Wooten	6.00	12.00

1961 Browns Carling Beer

This set of ten black and white posed action shots was sponsored by Carling Black Label Beer and features members of the Cleveland Browns. The pictures measure approximately 8 1/2" by 11 1/2" and have white borders. The sponsor's name and the team name appear below the picture in black lettering. The banks are blank. The pictures are numbered in the lower right corner on the fronts. The set is dated by the fact that Jim Houston's first year was 1960 and Bobby Mitchell and Milt Plum's last year with the Browns was 1961.

COMPLETE SET (10)	350.00	600.00
439A Milt Plum	30.00	50.00
439B Mike McCormack	30.00	50.00
439C Bob Gain	25.00	40.00
439D John Morrow	25.00	40.00
439E Jim Brown	100.00	200.00
439F Bobby Mitchell	35.00	60.00
439G Bobby Franklin	25.00	40.00
439H Jim Ray Smith	25.00	40.00
439K Jim Houston	25.00	40.00
439L Ray Renfro	30.00	50.00

1961 Browns National City Bank

The 1961 National City Bank Cleveland Browns football card set contains 36 brown and white cards each measuring approximately 2 1/2" by 3 9/16". The cards were issued in sheets of six cards, with each sheet of six given a set number and each individual card within the sheet given a player number. In the checklist below the cards have been numbered consecutively from one to 36. On the actual card, set/sheet number one will appear on cards 1 through 6, set number two on cards 7 through 12, etc. The front of the card states that the card is a "Quarterback Club Brownie Card". The backs of the cards contain the card number, a short biography and an ad for the National City Bank. Cards still in uncut (sheet of six) form are valued at one to two times the sum of the single card prices listed below. Len Dawson's card predates his 1963 Fleer Rookie Card by two years. It has been reported that cards #25-30 are in shorter supply than the rest.

COMPLETE SET (36)	1,200.00	2,000.00
1 Mike McCormack	30.00	60.00
2 Jim Brown	300.00	500.00
3 Leon Clarke	20.00	35.00
4 Walt Michaels	25.00	40.00
5 Jim Ray Smith	20.00	35.00
6 Quarterback Club Membership Card	40.00	80.00
7 Len Dawson	250.00	400.00
8 John Morrow	20.00	35.00
9 Bernie Parrish	25.00	40.00
10 Floyd Peters	25.00	40.00
11 Paul Wiggin	25.00	40.00
12 John Wooten	25.00	40.00
13 Ray Renfro	25.00	40.00
14 Galen Fiss	20.00	35.00
15 Dave Lloyd	20.00	35.00
16 Dick Schafrath	30.00	50.00
17 Ross Fichtner	20.00	35.00
18 Gern Nagler	20.00	35.00
19 Rich Kreitling	20.00	35.00
20 Duane Putnam	20.00	35.00
21 Vince Costello	20.00	35.00
22 Jim Shofner	25.00	40.00
23 Sam Baker	25.00	40.00
24 Bob Gain	25.00	40.00
25 Lou Groza	100.00	175.00
26 Don Fleming	35.00	60.00
27 Tom Watkins	30.00	50.00
28 Jim Houston	35.00	60.00
29 Larry Stephens	30.00	50.00
30 Bobby Mitchell	90.00	150.00
31 Bobby Franklin	20.00	35.00
32 Charley Ferguson	20.00	35.00
33 Johnny Brewer	20.00	35.00
34 Bob Crespino	20.00	35.00
35 Milt Plum	35.00	60.00
36 Preston Powell	20.00	35.00

1961 Browns Team Issue Large

These large photo cards are an unnumbered, blank-backed, team issue set of black and white photographs of the Cleveland Browns measuring approximately 8 1/2" by 10 1/2". The set features posed action shots of players whose name and position appear in a white reverse-out block burned into the bottom of each picture. The cards are listed below alphabetically.

COMPLETE SET (20) 175.00 300.00
1 Jim Brown 50.00 75.00
2 Galen Fiss 6.00 12.00
(back-pedaling pose)
3 Don Fleming 6.00 12.00
4 Bobby Franklin 6.00 12.00
5 Bob Gain 6.00 12.00
(charging pose)
6 Jim Houston 6.00 12.00
7 Rich Kreitling 6.00 12.00
8 Dave Lloyd 6.00 12.00
9 Mike McCormack 12.00 20.00
(kneeling pose)
10 Bobby Mitchell 15.00 25.00
(kneeling pose)
11 John Morrow 6.00 12.00
12 Bernie Parrish 6.00 12.00
13 Milt Plum 7.50 15.00
(wearing a white belt)
14 Ray Renfro 7.50 15.00
(catching a pass)
15 Dick Schafrath 7.50 15.00
16 Jim Shofner 7.50 15.00
(kneeling pose)
17 Jim Ray Smith 6.00 12.00
18 Tom Watkins 6.00 12.00
19 Paul Wiggin 6.00 12.00
(three point stance)
20 John Wooten 6.00 12.00

1961 Browns Team Issue Small

These photos are an unnumbered, blank-backed, team issue set of black and white images of the Cleveland Browns. The photos are virtually identical to the 1960 Team Issue set except for the slightly different size. Each measures approximately 6 1/8" by 9" and was printed on thin glossy paper stock. The set features posed action shots of players with a facsimile autograph across the image. Many of the same photos were used for the 1961 Browns National City card set. The cardbacks are blank and the photos are listed below alphabetically.

COMPLETE SET (30) 200.00 350.00
1 Sam Baker 5.00 10.00
2 Jim Brown 50.00 75.00
3 Paul Brown CO 15.00 25.00
4 Vince Costello 5.00 10.00
5 Len Dawson 25.00 40.00
6 Charley Ferguson 5.00 10.00
7 Ross Fichtner 5.00 10.00
8 Galen Fiss 5.00 10.00
9 Don Fleming 5.00 10.00
10 Bobby Franklin 5.00 10.00
11 Bob Gain 5.00 10.00
12 Prentice Gautt 5.00 10.00
13 Lou Groza 15.00 25.00
14 Jim Houston 5.00 10.00
15 Dave Lloyd 5.00 10.00
16 Mike McCormack 7.50 15.00
17 Walt Michaels 6.00 12.00
18 Bobby Mitchell 10.00 20.00
19 John Morrow 5.00 10.00
20 Bernie Parrish 5.00 10.00
21 Floyd Peters 5.00 10.00
22 Milt Plum 6.00 12.00
23 Preston Powell 5.00 10.00
24 Duane Putnam 5.00 10.00
25 Ray Renfro 6.00 12.00
26 Jim Shofner 6.00 12.00
27 Jim Ray Smith 5.00 10.00
28 Tom Watkins 5.00 10.00
29 Paul Wiggin 5.00 10.00
30 John Wooten 5.00 10.00

1963 Browns Team Issue

These large photos measure approximately 7 1/2" by 9 1/2" and feature a black-and-white player photo on blankbacked glossy paper stock. Each includes the player's name, position (initials) and team name in the bottom border. They are very similar in design to the 1964-66 set, but can be differentiated by the 1/4" space between the player's name, position, and team name. The photos are unnumbered and checklisted below in alphabetical order.

COMPLETE SET (28) 150.00 250.00
1 Johnny Brewer 5.00 10.00
2 Monte Clark 5.00 10.00
3 Blanton Collier CO 5.00 10.00
4 Gary Collins 6.00 12.00
5 Vince Costello 5.00 10.00
6 Bob Crespino 5.00 10.00
7 Ross Fichtner 5.00 10.00
8 Galen Fiss 5.00 10.00
9 Bob Gain 5.00 10.00
10 Bill Glass 5.00 10.00
11 Ernie Green 6.00 12.00
12 Lou Groza 10.00 20.00
13 Gene Hickerson 7.50 15.00
14 Jim Houston 5.00 10.00
15A Tom Hutchinson 5.00 10.00
(catching a pass)
15B Tom Hutchinson 5.00 10.00
(kneeling pose)
16 Rich Kreitling 5.00 10.00
17 Mike Lucci 6.00 12.00
18 John Morrow 5.00 10.00
19 Jim Ninowski 6.00 12.00
20 Frank Parker 5.00 10.00
(charging pose)
21 Bernie Parrish 5.00 10.00
22 Ray Renfro 6.00 12.00
23 Dick Schafrath 5.00 10.00
24 Jim Shofner 6.00 12.00
25 Ken Webb 5.00 10.00
26 Paul Wiggin 5.00 10.00
27 John Wooten 5.00 10.00
(running to his left)

1964-66 Browns Team Issue

These large photos measure approximately 7 3/8" by 9 3/8" and feature a black-and-white player photo on blankbacked glossy paper stock. Each includes the player's name, position (initials) and team name in the bottom border. They are very similar in design to the 1963 set, but can be differentiated by the 1" space between the player's name, position, and team name. The Blanton Collier and John Wooten photos are the only exception to this design. Some players were issued over several years with no differences in the photos or only very slight differences in the photo cropping or text as noted below. Each photo is unnumbered and checklisted below in alphabetical order.

COMPLETE SET (42) 250.00 400.00
1 Walter Beach 5.00 10.00
2 Larry Benz 5.00 10.00
3 John Brewer 5.00 10.00
4 John Brown T 5.00 10.00
5 Jim Brown 35.00 60.00
6 Monte Clark 5.00 10.00
7 Blanton Collier CO 5.00 10.00
8 Gary Collins 6.00 12.00
(white stripe on football)
9 Gary Collins 6.00 12.00
(different pose,
no stripe on football)
10 Vince Costello 5.00 10.00
(left foot 1-inch
above bottom border)
11 Vince Costello 5.00 10.00
(different pose
left foot on bottom border)
12 Galen Fiss 5.00 10.00
(pose in set position)
13 Galen Fiss 5.00 10.00
(pose in kneeling position)
14 Bill Glass DE 5.00 10.00
(left foot touching right border)
15 Bill Glass DE 5.00 10.00
(same pose; left foot/1/4-inch off right border)
16 Ernie Green 5.00 10.00
17 Lou Groza 12.00 20.00
18 Gene Hickerson 7.50 15.00
(position listed as OG)
19 Gene Hickerson 7.50 15.00
(position (spelled out) listed as G)
20 Jim Houston LB 5.00 10.00
(right foot 1-1/2-in
from left border)
21 Jim Houston LB 5.00 10.00
(right foot 1-in
from left border)
22 Jim Kanicki 5.00 10.00
(left foot 1/4-in off right border)
23 Jim Kanicki 5.00 10.00
(different pose; left foot/1-1/2-in off right border)
24 Leroy Kelly 12.00 20.00
25 Dick Modzelewski 5.00 10.00
26 Milt Morin 5.00 10.00
27 John Morrow 5.00 10.00
(head is 7/8-in from top border)
28 John Morrow 5.00 10.00
(same pose; head
is 5/8-in from top border)
29 Jim Ninowski 6.00 12.00
30 Frank Parker 5.00 10.00
(kneeling pose)
31 Bernie Parrish 5.00 10.00
32 Walter Roberts 5.00 10.00
33 Frank Ryan 6.00 12.00
(right foot touching ground)
34 Frank Ryan 6.00 12.00
(left foot touching ground)
35 Dick Schafrath 5.00 10.00
(position listed as OT)
36 Dick Schafrath 5.00 10.00
(position listed as T)
37 Paul Warfield 15.00 25.00
(looking to his right)
38 Paul Warfield 15.00 25.00
(looking to his left)
39 Paul Wiggin 5.00 10.00
(in 3-point stance;/names have 1-inch between them)
40 Paul Wiggin 5.00 10.00
(in 3-point stance;
names have 1/4-inch between them)
41 John Wooten 5.00 10.00
(kneeling pose;/(position listed as OG)
42 John Wooten 5.00 10.00
(running pose;/(position listed as G)

1965 Browns Volpe Tumblers

These Browns artist's renderings were part of a plastic cup tumbler product produced in 1965, which celebrated the 1964 Browns World Championship. These cups were promoted by Fisher's, Fazio's and Costa's Supermarkets in Cleveland. The noted sports artist Volpe created the artwork which includes an action scene and a player portrait. The "cards" are unnumbered, each measures approximately 5" by 8 1/2" and is curved in the shape required to fit inside a plastic cup.

COMPLETE SET (12) 350.00 600.00
1 Jim Brown 75.00 125.00
2 Blanton Collier CO 20.00 35.00
3 Gary Collins 25.00 40.00
4 Vince Costello 20.00 35.00
5 Bill Glass 20.00 35.00
6 Lou Groza 40.00 75.00
7 Jim Houston 25.00 40.00
8 Jim Kanicki 20.00 35.00
9 Dick Modzelewski 25.00 40.00
10 Frank Ryan 25.00 40.00
11 Dick Schafrath 25.00 40.00
12 Paul Warfield 40.00 75.00

1966 Browns Team Sheets

Each of these team issued sheets features four black and white player photos and measures roughly 8" x10". The player's name, position and team name appear below each photo and the cardbacks are blank. Any additions to list below are appreciated.

COMPLETE SET (8) 25.00 50.00
1 Erich Barnes 2.50 5.00
Bob Matheson
Jack Gregory
Larry Conjar
2 Johnny Brewer 2.50 5.00
Jim Houston
Jim Kanicki
Paul Wiggin
3 Gary Collins 3.00 6.00
Frank Ryan
Fred Hoaglin
John Wooten
4 Ben Davis 2.50 5.00
Ralph Smith
Dick Schafrath
Milt Morin
5 Ross Fichtner 6.00 12.00
Mike Howell
Monte Clark
Paul Warfield
6 Gene Hickerson 5.00 10.00
Blanton Collier CO
Ernie Green
Leroy Kelly
7 Walter Johnson 6.00 12.00
Bill Glass
Ernie Kellerman
Lou Groza
8 Gary Lane 2.50 5.00
Dale Lindsey
Vince Costello
Frank Parker

1968 Browns Team Issue 7x8

The Cleveland Browns issued and distributed this set of player photos around 1968. Each measures approximately 6 7/8" by 8 1/2" and features a black and white photo on the front and a blank back. The player's name, position (spelled out), and team name appear in the bottom border below the photo. There is also a facsimile autograph of the featured player printed on each photo. Any additions to this list are appreciated.

COMPLETE SET (7) 50.00 100.00
1 Gary Collins 6.00 12.00
2 Ernie Green 5.00 10.00
3 Leroy Kelly 10.00 20.00
4 Bill Nelsen 6.00 12.00
5 Frank Ryan 6.00 12.00
6 Dick Schafrath 6.00 12.00
7 Paul Warfield 12.50 25.00

1968 Browns Team Issue 8x10

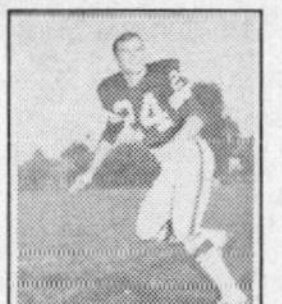

The Cleveland Browns issued and distributed this set of player photos. Each measures approximately 8" by 10" and features a black and white photo. The player's name and position appear in the bottom border below the photo. Any additions to this list are appreciated.

COMPLETE SET (12) 75.00 135.00
1 Don Cockroft 5.00 10.00
2 Gary Collins 6.00 12.00
3 Ernie Green 5.00 10.00
4 Jack Gregory 5.00 10.00
5 Gene Hickerson 7.50 15.00
6 Ernie Kellerman 5.00 10.00
7 Leroy Kelly 10.00 20.00
8 Milt Morin 5.00 10.00
9 Frank Ryan 6.00 12.00
10 Marvin Upshaw 5.00 10.00
11 Paul Warfield 12.50 25.00
12 Coaching Staff 6.00 12.00

1968 Browns Team Sheets

These 8" by 10" sheets were issued primarily to the media for use as player images for print. Each features 7 or 8-players and coaches with the player's name beneath his picture. The sheets are blankbacked and unnumbered. Any additions to this list are appreciated.

1 Blanton Collier CO 6.00 15.00
Jim Houston
Ernie Kellerman
Gene Hickerson
Leroy Kelly
Paul Warfield
Dick Schafrath
2 Mike Howell 5.00 12.00
Jim Kanicki
Jack Gregory
Gary Collins
Dale Lindsey
Bob Matheson
Alvin Mitchell
Bill Nelsen

1969 Browns Team Issue

The Cleveland Browns issued and distributed this set of player photos in the late 1960s. They closely resemble other photos issued by the team throughout the decade. Each measures approximately 7 1/2" by 9 1/2" and features a black and white photo. The player's name, position (spelled out completely), and team name appear in the bottom border below the photo with roughly a 1/2" to 1" white space between the words.

COMPLETE SET (27) 150.00 225.00
1 Bill Andrews 5.00 10.00
2 Erich Barnes 5.00 10.00
3 Monte Clark 5.00 10.00
4 Don Cockroft 5.00 10.00
5 Gary Collins 6.00 12.00
6 Ben Davis 5.00 10.00
7 John DeMarie 5.00 10.00
8 Jack Gregory 5.00 10.00
9 Gene Hickerson 7.50 15.00
10 Fred Hoaglin 5.00 10.00
11 Jim Houston 5.00 10.00
12 Mike Howell 5.00 10.00
13 Ron Johnson 6.00 12.00
14 Jim Kanicki 5.00 10.00
15 Walter Johnson 5.00 10.00
16 Ernie Kellerman 5.00 10.00
17 Leroy Kelly 12.00 20.00
18 Dale Lindsey 5.00 10.00
19 Bob Matheson 5.00 10.00
20 Reece Morrison 5.00 10.00
21 Milt Morin 5.00 10.00
22 Bill Nelsen 6.00 12.00
23 Dick Schafrath 5.00 10.00
24 Ron Snidow 5.00 10.00
25 Walt Sumner 5.00 10.00
26 Marvin Upshaw 5.00 10.00
27 Paul Warfield 12.50 25.00

1971 Browns Boy Scouts

These standard sized cards were issued for the Boy Scouts as rewards for the 1971 "Roundup" membership drive in the Cleveland area. Each was printed on thin stock and features a black and white photo of a Browns player on the front and Boy Scouts membership information on the backs. The cards are often found with the player's autograph on the back as well as the member's hand written name.

1 Jim Houston 20.00 50.00
2 Leroy Kelly 40.00 75.00
3 Bill Nelsen 35.00 60.00
4 Bo Scott 20.00 50.00

1978 Browns Wendy's

This set of oversized (roughly 5" by 7") black and white photos was sponsored by Wendy's. Each includes a Browns player photo with the player's name below the photo and to the left and the Wendy's logo to the right. The backs are blank and unnumbered. Any additions to the list below are appreciated.

COMPLETE SET (19) 100.00 200.00
1 Dick Ambrose 6.00 12.00
2 Ron Bolton 6.00 12.00
3 Larry Collins 6.00 12.00
4 Oliver Davis 6.00 12.00
5 Johnny Evans 6.00 12.00
6 Ricky Feacher 6.00 12.00
7 Dave Graf 6.00 12.00
8 Charlie Hall 6.00 12.00
9 Calvin Hill 7.50 15.00
10 Gerald Irons 6.00 12.00
11 Robert L. Jackson 6.00 12.00
12 Ricky Jones 6.00 12.00
13 Clay Mathews 10.00 20.00
14 Cleo Miller 6.00 12.00
15 Mark Miller 6.00 12.00
16 Sam Rutigliano CO 6.00 12.00
17 Henry Sheppard 6.00 12.00
18 Mickey Sims 6.00 12.00
19 Gerry Sullivan 6.00 12.00

1979 Browns Team Sheets

The 1979 Browns Team Issue Sheets were issued to fans and total six known sheets. Each measures roughly 8" by 10" and includes seven or eight small black and white player photos.

COMPLETE SET (6) 12.50 25.00
1 Clinton Burrell 1.50 3.00
Clarence Scott
Willis Adams
Lawrence Johnson
Cody Risien
Keith Wright
John Smith
2 Oliver Davis 2.50 5.00
Ricky Feacher
Charlie Hall
Don Cockroft
Doug Dieken
Lyle Alzado
George Buehler
Rich Dimler
3 Jack Gregory 1.50 3.00
Dave Graf
Cleo Miller
Ricky Jones
Gerald Irons
Robert L. Jackson
Matt Miller
Johnny Evans
4 Art Modell 2.50 5.00
Sam Rutigliano
Jerry Sherk
Greg Pruitt
Dave Logan
Calvin Hill
Tom DeLeone
Thom Darden
5 Henry Sheppard 3.00 6.00
Mike Pruitt
Gerry Sullivan
Curtis Weathers
Ozzie Newsome
Ron Bolton
Randy Rich
Pat Moriarty
6 Mickey Sims 2.50 5.00
Mark Miller
Clay Matthews
Robert E. Jackson
Brian Sipe
Mike St. Clair
Dick Ambrose
Reggie Rucker

1981 Browns Team Issue

This set of 8" by 10" glossy photos was released by the team for fan mail requests and player appearances. Each is blankbacked with many being found with the photographer, Henry Barr Studios, notation on the backs along with a stamped player name. Otherwise, there is no player name or team name for identification on the fronts. Any additions to this list are appreciated.

COMPLETE SET (13) 30.00 60.00
1 Lyle Alzado 5.00 10.00
(jersey #77)
2 Dick Ambrose 3.00 6.00
(jersey #52)
3 Ron Bolton 3.00 6.00
(jersey #28)
4 Steve Cox 3.00 6.00
(jersey #15)
5 Thom Darden 3.00 6.00
(jersey #27)
6 Joe DeLamielleure 4.00 8.00
(jersey #64)
7 Ricky Feacher 3.00 6.00
(jersey #83)
8 Dino Hall 3.00 6.00
(jersey #26)
9 Bob Jackson 3.00 6.00
(jersey #68)
10 R.L. Jackson 3.00 6.00
(jersey #56)
11 Dave Logan 4.00 8.00
(jersey #85)
12 Paul McDonald 3.00 6.00
(jersey #16)
13 Mike Pruitt 4.00 8.00
(jersey #43)

1981 Browns Wendy's Glasses

Each of these drinking glasses include a front and back picture of a Cleveland Browns player. The front picture is a brown and white drawing of a player within a star, with the players name below the drawing. The back contained an action drawing of that particular player. Wendy's stores sponsored the promotion and distributed the glasses in 1981. The set is catalogued in alphabetical order below.

COMPLETE SET (4) 15.00 30.00
1 Lyle Alzado 5.00 10.00
2 Doug Dieken 3.00 6.00
3 Mike Pruitt 4.00 8.00
4 Brian Sipe 4.00 8.00

1982 Browns Nu-Maid Butter Tubs

This set of butter cups or tubs was released by Nu-Maid and Miami Margarine in 1982. Each includes color illustrations of the featured player and measures roughly 3 3/4" tall and 3" in diameter.

COMPLETE SET (7) 15.00 30.00
1 Tom Cousineau 2.50 5.00
2 Doug Dieken 2.50 5.00
3 Dave Logan 2.50 5.00
4 Ozzie Newsome 4.00 8.00
5 Mike Pruitt 3.00 6.00
6 Dan Ross 2.50 5.00
7 Clarence Scott 2.50 5.00

1984 Browns Team Sheets

These 8" by 10" sheets were issued primarily to the media for use as player images for print. Each features 8-players or coaches with the player's jersey number, name, and position beneath his picture. The sheets are blankbacked and unnumbered.

COMPLETE SET (8) 16.00 40.00
1 Willis Adams 2.00 5.00
Dick Ambrose
Mike Baab
Matt Bahr
Keith Baldwin
Chip Banks
Rickey Bolden
Brian Brennan
2 Clinton Burrell 2.50 6.00
Earnest Byner
Reggie Camp
Bill Contz
Tom Cousineau
Steve Cox
Bruce Davis
Johnny Davis
3 Joe DeLamielleure 2.50 6.00
Tom Deleone
Doud Dieken
Hanford Dixon
Jim Dumont
Paul Farren
Ricky Feacher
Tom Flick
4 Elvis Franks 2.00 5.00
Bob Golic
Boyce Green
Al Gross
Carl Hairston
Duriel Harris
Harry Holt
Robert Jackson
5 Eddie Johnson 4.00 10.00
Lawrence Johnson
David Marshall
Clay Matthews
Paul McDonald
Frank Minnifield
Ozzie Newsome
Scott Nicolas
6 Art Modell 6.00 15.00
Bill Davis
Paul Warfield
Calvin Hill
Marty Schottenheimer
Joe Scannella
Curtis Weathers
Charles White
7 Terry Nugent 4.00 10.00
Rod Perry
Mike Pruitt
Dave Puzzuoli
Chris Rockins
Don Rogers
Tim Stracka
Dwight Walker
8 Sam Rutigliano CO 2.00 5.00
(Five photos on the single sheet)

1985 Browns Coke/Mr. Hero

This 48-card set was issued as six sheets of eight cards each featuring players on the Cleveland Browns. Each card measures approximately 2 3/4" by 3 1/4". Each sheet was numbered; the sheet number is given after each player in the checklist below. The cards are otherwise unnumbered except for uniform number as they are listed below. The bottom of each sheet had coupons for discounts on food and drink from the sponsors.

COMPLETE SET (48) 10.00 25.00
7 Jeff Gossett 4 .30 .75
9 Matt Bahr 1 .30 .75
16 Paul McDonald 4 .30 .75
18 Gary Danielson 5 .30 .75
19 Bernie Kosar 6 1.00 2.50
20 Don Rogers 4 .30 .75
22 Felix Wright 2 .30 .75
26 Greg Allen 3 .20 .50
27 Al Gross 2 .20 .50
29 Hanford Dixon 5 .30 .75
30 Boyce Green 1 .20 .50
31 Frank Minnifield 1 .30 .75
34 Kevin Mack 3 .50 1.25
37 Chris Rockins 1 .20 .50
38 Johnny Davis 5 .20 .50
44 Earnest Byner 2 .60 1.50
47 Larry Braziel 4 .20 .50
50 Tom Cousineau 6 .30 .75
51 Eddie Johnson 2 .20 .50
55 Curtis Weathers 1 .20 .50
56 Chip Banks 6 .30 .75
57 Clay Matthews 5 .60 1.50
58 Scott Nicolas 1 .20 .50
61 Mike Baab 4 .30 .75
62 George Lilja 5 .20 .50
63 Cody Risien 6 .20 .50
65 Mark Krerowicz 3 .20 .50
68 Robert Jackson G 4 .20 .50
69 Dan Fike 2 .20 .50
72 Dave Puzzuoli 1 .20 .50
74 Paul Farren 2 .20 .50
77 Rickey Bolden 3 .30 .75
78 Carl Hairston 2 .30 .75
79 Bob Golic 6 .30 .75
80 Willis Adams 2 .20 .50
81 Harry Holt 3 .20 .50
82 Ozzie Newsome 3 1.00 2.50
83 Fred Banks 3 .20 .50
84 Glen Young 1 .20 .50
85 Clarence Weathers 6 .20 .50
86 Brian Brennan 5 .30 .75
87 Travis Tucker 6 .20 .50
88 Reggie Langhorne 5 .30 .75
89 John Jefferson 4 .40 1.00
91 Sam Clancy 4 .30 .75
96 Reggie Camp 5 .20 .50
99 Keith Baldwin 6 .20 .50
NNO Action Photo 3 .60 1.50
(Clay Matthews tackling
Eric Dickerson)

1987 Browns Louis Rich

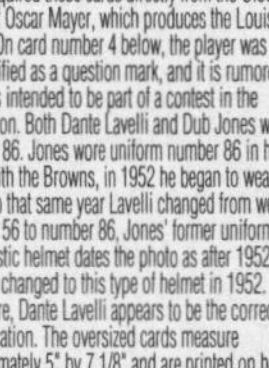

This five-card set was originally produced as a food product insert for Louis Rich products. Apparently, the promotion was canceled, and collectors were known to have acquired these cards directly from the Cleveland office of Oscar Mayer, which produces the Louis Rich brand. On card number 4 below, the player was unidentified as a question mark, and it is rumored that this was intended to be part of a contest in the promotion. Both Dante Lavelli and Dub Jones were number 86. Jones wore uniform number 86 in his earlier years with the Browns, in 1952 he began to wear number 40. Also that same year Lavelli changed from wearing number 56 to number 86, Jones' former uniform number. The plastic helmet dates the photo as after 1952 since the Browns changed to this type of helmet in 1952. Therefore, Dante Lavelli appears to be the correct identification. The oversized cards measure approximately 5" by 7 1/8" and are printed on heavy white card stock. The fronts feature full-bleed sepia-toned player photos. An orange diagonal cuts across the lower left corner and carries the set title ("Memorable Moments by Louis Rich"), uniform number, and player's name. The backs are blank. The cards are unnumbered and checklisted below in alphabetical order.

COMPLETE SET (5) 35.00 60.00
1 Jim Brown 12.50 25.00
Bobby Mitchell
2 Otto Graham 7.50 15.00
3 Lou Groza 5.00 10.00
4 Dante Lavelli 5.00 10.00
(Question Mark)
5 Marion Motley 5.00 10.00

1987 Browns Oh Henry Cups

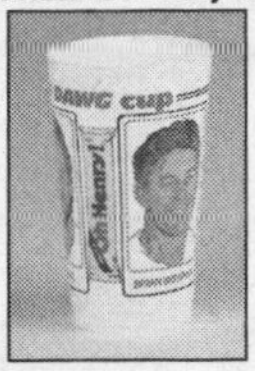

This set of 20-ounce cups was sponsored by Oh Henry! and distributed in the Cleveland area. Each includes a picture of three-Browns players and sponsor logos. Any additions to the list below are appreciated.

1 Brian Brennan 3.00 8.00
Earnest Byner
Bob Golic
2 Curtis Dickey 4.00 10.00
Kevin Mack
Ozzie Newsome

1987 Browns Team Issue

The Cleveland Browns issued this set of black and white player photos. Each card measures roughly 5" by 7" and includes the player's jersey number, name, position initials, and team name below the photo. The cards are blankbacked and unnumbered.

COMPLETE SET (9) 16.00 40.00
1 Mike Baab 2.00 5.00
2 Earnest Byner 3.00 8.00
3 Reggie Camp 2.00 5.00
4 Bob Golic 2.00 5.00
5 Al Gross 2.00 5.00
6 Mike Junkin 2.00 5.00
7 Reggie Langhorne 2.50 6.00
8 Gerald McNeil 2.00 5.00
9 Frank Minnifield 2.50 6.00

1989 Browns Wendy's Cups

This set of 32-ounce cups was sponsored and distributed by Wendy's Restaurant in the Cleveland area. Each includes a picture of two-Browns players and sponsor logos. Any additions to the list below are appreciated.

COMPLETE SET (3) 8.00 20.00
1 Ozzie Newsome 3.00 8.00
Cody Risien
2 Hanford Dixon 2.50 6.00
Frank Minnifield
3 Brian Brennan 2.50 6.00
Webster Slaughter

1992 Browns Sunoco

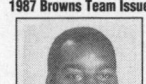

Featuring Cleveland Browns' Hall of Famers, this 24-card set was produced by NFL Properties for an Ohio-area promotion sponsored by Sunoco. Two AM radio stations, WMMS 100.7 and WHK 14.20, cosponsored the set. The cards were available in cello packs that contained a cover card, a player card, and an official sweepstakes entry blank. Some packs contained autograph cards of featured players who were still living. The grand prize offered to the winner was a trip for two to the Super Bowl in Pasadena, California. One player card shown at the Pro Football Hall of Fame would entitle the holder to receive up to three complimentary admissions when up to three admissions were purchased. The offer expired August 31, 1993. The fronts of the cover cards have the words "The Cleveland Browns' Collection" printed in black near the top. A Browns helmet is near the center with the player's name printed below it. The words "Hall of Famer Limited Edition" are printed at the bottom with the Sunoco logo. The backs are simple showing only the Pro Football Hall of Fame logo and sponsors' logos. The player cards exhibit a mix of color and black-and-white full-bleed photos with the player's last name printed in oversized orange letters at the bottom. The Sunoco logo is superimposed on the player's name. The backs are sandstone-textured in varying pastel shades and display a ghosted picture of the player. A career summary and the year the player was inducted into the Hall of Fame are overprinted in black. The player cards are numbered on the back. The cover cards are unnumbered but are checklisted below as they appear in the set and assigned corresponding card numbers with a "C" suffix. There was also an album produced for this set.

COMPLETE SET (24)	6.00	15.00
COMMON CARD (1-12)	.30	.75
COMMON COVER CARD (1-12C)	.10	.25
1 Otto Graham (Player card)	.80	2.00
1C Otto Graham (Cover card)	.08	.25
2 Paul Brown CO (Player card)	.60	1.50
2C Paul Brown CO (Cover card)	.08	.25
3 Marion Motley (Player card)	.60	1.50
3C Marion Motley (Cover card)	.08	.25
4 Jim Brown (Player card)	1.60	4.00
4C Jim Brown (Cover card)	.20	.50
5 Lou Groza (Player card)	.60	1.50
5C Lou Groza (Cover card)	.08	.25
6 Dante Lavelli (Player card)	.50	1.25
6C Dante Lavelli (Cover card)	.08	.25
7 Len Ford (Player card)	.30	.75
7C Len Ford (Cover card)	.08	.25
8 Bill Willis (Player card)	.30	.75
8C Bill Willis (Cover card)	.08	.25
9 Bobby Mitchell (Player card)	.50	1.25
9C Bobby Mitchell (Cover card)	.08	.25
10 Paul Warfield (Player card)	.60	1.50
10C Paul Warfield (Cover card)	.08	.25
11 Mike McCormack (Player card)	.30	.75
11C Mike McCormack (Cover card)	.08	.25
12 Frank Gatski (Player card)	.30	.75
12C Frank Gatski (Cover card)	.08	.25

1999 Browns Giant Eagle Cards

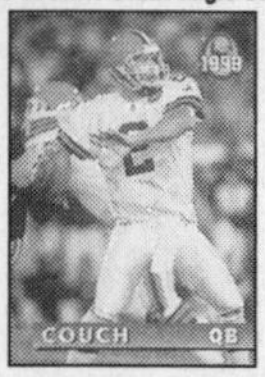

This set was distributed in 4-card packs over the course of 6-weeks during the 1999 NFL season by participating Giant Eagle stores in the Northeast Ohio area. Each card includes a full color player photo on the front along with the player's last name and year.

COMPLETE SET (24)	8.00	20.00
1 Ty Detmer	.30	.75
2 Marc Edwards	.20	.50
3 Jim Pyne	.20	.50
4 Kevin Johnson	1.60	4.00
5 Jerry Ball	.20	.50
6 John Jurkovic	.20	.50
7 Marlon Forbes	.20	.50
8 Marquez Pope	.20	.50
9 Orlando Brown	.20	.50
10 Daylon McCutcheon	.20	.50
11 Irv Smith	.20	.50
12 Dave Wohlabaugh	.20	.50
13 Terry Kirby	.20	.50
14 Lomas Brown	.20	.50
15 Jamir Miller	.20	.50
16 John Thierry	.20	.50
17 Corey Fuller	.20	.50
18 Chris Spielman	.30	.75
19 Roy Barker	.20	.50
20 Antonio Langham	.20	.50
21 Tim Couch	4.00	10.00
22 Derrick Alexander DE	.20	.50
23 Chris Gardocki	.20	.50
24 Leslie Shepherd	.20	.50
NNO Card Album	1.60	4.00

1999 Browns Giant Eagle Coins

This set was distributed over the course of 6-weeks during the 1999 NFL season by participating Giant Eagle stores in the Northeast Ohio area along with the card set. Each coin includes a player image on the front along with the player's name. A backer board was also included with each coin that featured a player photo and brief bio very similar to a card. We've priced the coin/backer board combos below.

COMPLETE SET (8)	8.00	20.00
1 Jerry Ball	.40	1.00
2 Orlando Brown	.40	1.00
3 Tim Couch	6.00	15.00
4 Ty Detmer	.60	1.50
5 Corey Fuller	.40	1.00
6 John Jurkovic	.40	1.00
7 Terry Kirby	.40	1.00
8 Chris Spielman	.60	1.50

2004 Browns Donruss Playoff National

This 6-card set was issued vto persons who purchased the VIP package at the 2004 National convention in Cleveland. Each card features bronze foil highlights on the front and is number "x/6" on the back. A silver foil version of the Kellen Winslow Jr. card was also produced and given away. It features Pepsi and Pizza Hut sponsorship logos on the front and no card number on the back.

COMPLETE SET (6)	6.00	15.00
1 Kellen Winslow Jr.	3.00	8.00
2 Quincy Morgan	.75	2.00
3 Andre Davis	.50	1.25
4 William Green	.75	2.00
5 Lee Suggs	1.00	2.50
6 Jeff Garcia	1.00	2.50
NNO Kellen Winslow Jr. Silver	2.00	5.00

2004 Browns Fleer Tradition National

This set was issued as a 9-card perforated sheet inserted into 525,000 issues of the July 18, 2004 Cleveland Plain Dealer newspaper. A 10th card of Kellen Winslow Jr. was distributed only at the Fleer booth at The Natonal. Each card was produced in the design of the 2004 Fleer Tradition set with an orange border instead of white. The cards are also re-numbered 1-10. Finally a cut version of the 10-card set, along with a Kellen Winslow Jr. Throwback Threads card, was also issued to persons purchasing the VIP package for the show.

COMPLETE SET (10)	5.00	12.00
1 Jeff Garcia	.60	1.50
2 Lee Suggs	.60	1.50
3 Quincy Morgan	.50	1.25
4 William Green	.50	1.25
5 Andre Davis	.30	.75
6 Courtney Brown	.50	1.25
7 Dennis Northcutt	.30	.75
8 Luke McCown	.60	1.50
9 Andra Davis	.30	.75
10 Kellen Winslow Jr.	2.00	5.00
NNO Kellen Winslow Jr. Throwback Threads (no swatch on card)	5.00	12.00

2006 Browns Topps

COMPLETE SET (12)	3.00	6.00
CLE1 Lee Suggs	.20	.50
CLE2 Charlie Frye	.25	.60
CLE3 Braylon Edwards	.25	.60
CLE4 Kamerion Wimbley	.30	.75
CLE5 Dennis Northcutt	.20	.50
CLE6 Reuben Droughns	.25	.60
CLE7 Ken Dorsey	.15	.40
CLE8 Kellen Winslow	.25	.60
CLE9 Willie McGinest	.20	.50
CLE10 Joe Jurevicius	.20	.50
CLE11 D'Qwell Jackson	.25	.60
CLE12 Travis Wilson	.20	.50

2007 Browns Topps

COMPLETE SET (12)	4.00	8.00
1 Braylon Edwards	.25	.60
2 Kellen Winslow	.25	.60
3 Charlie Frye	.25	.60
4 Joe Jurevicius	.20	.50
5 Kamerion Wimbley	.20	.50
6 Jerome Harrison	.20	.50
7 Jamal Lewis	.25	.60
8 Sean Jones	.20	.50
9 Phil Dawson	.20	.50
10 Andra Davis	.20	.50
11 Brady Quinn	.50	1.25
12 Joe Thomas	.30	.75

2008 Browns Topps

COMPLETE SET (12)	2.00	4.00
1 Kellen Winslow	.25	.60
2 Derek Anderson	.20	.50
3 Jamal Lewis	.25	.60
4 Braylon Edwards	.25	.60
5 Donte Stallworth	.20	.50
6 Joe Jurevicius	.20	.50
7 Sean Jones	.20	.50
8 Joe Thomas	.25	.60
9 Brady Quinn	.25	.60
10 Joshua Cribbs	.30	.75
11 Martin Rucker	.25	.60
12 Beau Bell	.25	.60

1978 Buccaneers Team Issue

These 8" by 10" black and white Photos were issued by the Buccaneers for player signing sessions and to fill fan requests. Each includes the player's name, his position initials and the team name below the player photo in all capital letters. It is believed that there were more photos issued in the series, thus any additional submissions would be welcomed.

1 Ricky Bell	3.00	6.00
2 Dave Pear	2.50	5.00
3 Lee Roy Selmon	6.00	12.00

1978 Buccaneers Team Sheets

This set consists of 8" by 10" glossy photo sheets that display eight black-and-white player/coach photos. Each individual photo on the sheet measures approximately 2 1/8" by 3 1/4". Two Buccaneers logos appear in the upper left and right corners of the sheet. The backs are blank. The sheets are unnumbered and checklisted below alphabetically according to the player featured in the upper left corner.

COMPLETE SET (4)	20.00	40.00
1 Ricky Bell	7.50	15.00
Morris Owens		
Jimmie Giles		
Dave Pear		
Lee Roy Selmon		
Dewey Selmon		
Gary Huff		
John McKay CO		
2 Mike Boryla	4.00	8.00
Louis Carter		
Wally Chambers		
Dave Green		
David Lewis		
Dan Medlin		
Mike Washington		
Steve Wilson		
3 Cedric Brown	4.00	8.00
Mark Cotney		
Darryl Carlton		
Rockne Freitas		
Cecil Johnson		
John McKay		
Isaav Hagins		
Don Hardeman		
4 Doug Williams	6.00	12.00
Jeris White		
Jeff Winans		
Johnny Davis		
Ernie Holmes		
Dave Reavis		
Brett Moritz		
Richard Wood		

1979 Buccaneers Team Issue

These 8 1/2" by 11" black and white blank backed photos were given out for publicity purposes by the Buccaneers. Each includes the player's name, his position (spelled out) and the team name below the player photo. It is believed that there were more photos issued in the series, thus any additional submissions would be welcomed.

1 Jimmy DuBose	2.50	5.00
2 Doug Williams	4.00	8.00

1980 Buccaneers Police

This set is complete at 56 cards measuring approximately 2 5/8" by 4 1/8". Since there are no numbers on the cards, the set has been listed in alphabetical order by player. In addition to player cards, an assortment of coaches, mascots, and Swash-Buc-Lers (cheerleaders) are included. The set was sponsored by the Greater Tampa Chamber of Commerce Law Enforcement Council, the local law enforcement agencies, and Coca-Cola. Tips from the Buccaneers are written on the backs. The fronts contain the Tampa Bay helmet logo. Cards are also available with a tougher Paradyne (Corporation) cardback sponsorship.

COMPLETE SET (56)	75.00	150.00
*PARADYNE BACKS: 1.5X TO 2.5X		
1 Ricky Bell	3.00	8.00
2 Rick Berns	2.00	4.00
3 Tom Blanchard	1.50	3.00
4 Scot Brantley	1.50	3.00
5 Aaron Brown	1.50	3.00
6 Cedric Brown	1.50	3.00
7 Mark Cotney	1.50	3.00
8 Randy Crowder	1.50	3.00
9 Gary Davis	1.50	3.00
10 Johnny Davis	2.00	4.00
11 Tony Davis	1.50	3.00
12 Jerry Eckwood	2.50	5.00
13 Chuck Fusina	2.00	4.00
14 Jimmie Giles	2.50	5.00
15 Isaac Hagins	1.50	3.00
16 Charley Hannah	1.50	3.00
17 Andy Hawkins	1.50	3.00
18 Kevin House	2.50	5.00
19 Cecil Johnson	1.50	3.00
20 Gordon Jones	2.00	4.00
21 Curtis Jordan	1.50	3.00
22 Bill Kollar	1.50	3.00
23 Jim Leonard	1.50	3.00
24 David Lewis	2.00	4.00
25 Reggie Lewis	1.50	3.00
26 David Logan	2.00	4.00
27 Larry Mucker	1.50	3.00
28 Jim O'Bradovich	2.00	4.00
29 Mike Rae	1.50	3.00
30 Dave Reavis	1.50	3.00
31 Danny Reece	1.50	3.00
32 Greg Roberts	1.50	3.00
33 Gene Sanders	1.50	3.00
34 Dewey Selmon	2.50	5.00
35 Lee Roy Selmon	10.00	20.00
36 Ray Snell	1.50	3.00
37 Dave Stalls	1.50	3.00
38 Norris Thomas	1.50	3.00
39 Mike Washington	1.50	3.00
40 Doug Williams	5.00	10.00
41 Steve Wilson	1.50	3.00
42 Richard Wood	2.00	4.00
43 George Yarno	1.50	3.00
44 Garo Yepremian	2.50	5.00
45 Logo Card	1.50	3.00
46 Team Photo	2.50	5.00
47 Hugh Culverhouse OWN	2.00	4.00
48 John McKay CO	2.00	4.00
49 Mascot Capt. Crush	1.50	3.00
50 Cheerleaders: Swash-Buc-Lers	2.00	4.00
51 Swash-Buc-Lers (Buzz)	2.00	4.00
52 Swash-Buc-Lers (Check with me)	2.00	4.00
53 Swash-Buc-Lers (Gap Two)	2.00	4.00
54 Swash-Buc-Lers (Gas)	2.00	4.00
55 Swash-Buc-Lers (Pass Protection)	2.00	4.00
56 Swash-Buc-Lers (Post Pattern)	2.00	4.00

1980 Buccaneers Team Issue

These paper thin 5" by 7" black and white blank backed photos were given out for publicity purposes. Each includes the player's name (all caps), a facsimile signature, and the team name (all caps) below the player photo. It is believed that there were more photos issued in the series, thus any additional submissions would be welcomed.

COMPLETE SET (5)	12.50	25.00
1 Jerry Eckwood	2.50	5.00
2 Lee Roy Selmon	4.00	8.00
3 1980 Team Photo	2.50	5.00
4 Doug Williams	4.00	8.00
5 Garo Yepremian	2.50	5.00

1982 Buccaneers Shell

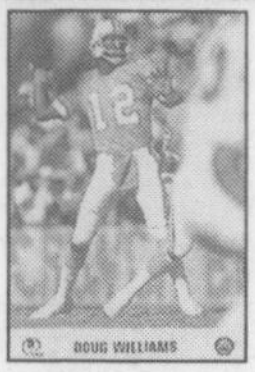

Sponsored by Shell Oil Co., these 32 paper-thin blank-backed cards measure approximately 1 1/2" by 2 1/2" and feature color action player photos. The photos are borderless, except at the bottom, where the player's name, his team's helmet, and the Shell logo appear in a white margin. The cards are unnumbered and checklisted below in alphabetical order.

COMPLETE SET (32)	25.00	50.00
1 Theo Bell	.50	1.25
2 Scot Brantley	.50	1.25
3 Cedric Brown	.50	1.25
4 Bill Capece	.50	1.25
5 Neal Colzie	.50	1.25
6 Mark Cotney	.50	1.25
7 Hugh Culverhouse OWN	.50	1.25
8 Jeff Davis	.50	1.25
9 Jerry Eckwood	.50	1.25
10 Sean Farrell	.50	1.25
11 Jimmie Giles	.60	1.50
12 Hugh Green	.60	1.50
13 Charley Hannah	.50	1.25
14 Andy Hawkins	.50	1.25
15 John Holt	.50	1.25
16 Kevin House	.60	1.50
17 Cecil Johnson	.50	1.25
18 Gordon Jones	.50	1.25
19 David Logan	.50	1.25
20 John McKay CO	.60	1.50
21 James Owens	.50	1.25
22 Greg Roberts	.50	1.25
23 Gene Sanders	.50	1.25
24 Lee Roy Selmon	5.00	10.00
25 Ray Snell	.50	1.25
26 Larry Swider	.50	1.25
27 Norris Thomas	.50	1.25
28 Mike Washington	.50	1.25
29 James Wilder	.60	1.50
30 Doug Williams	3.00	6.00
31 Steve Wilson	.50	1.25
32 Richard Wood	.50	1.25

1984 Buccaneers Police

This unnumbered 56-card set features the Tampa Bay Buccaneers players, cheerleaders, and other personnel. Cards measure approximately 2 5/8" by 4 1/8". Backs are printed in red ink on thin white card stock and feature "Kids and Kops Tips from the Buccaneers". Cards were sponsored by the Greater Tampa Chamber of Commerce Community Security Council and the local law enforcement agencies. In action (IA) cards were issued as an additional card for three players. The cards are essentially ordered below alphabetically according to the player's name with the exception of the non-player cards who are listed first.

COMPLETE SET (56)	30.00	75.00
1 Swash-Buc-Lers	.75	2.00
2 Hugh Culverhouse OWN	.40	1.00
3 John McKay (25 Years as Head Coach)	.60	1.50
4 John McKay CO	.60	1.50
5 Defensive Action	.60	1.50
6 Fred Acorn	.40	1.00
7 Obed Ariri	.40	1.00
8 Adger Armstrong	.40	1.00
9 Jerry Bell	.40	1.00
10 Theo Bell	.60	1.50
11 Byron Braggs	.40	1.00
12 Scot Brantley	.40	1.00
13 Cedric Brown	.40	1.00
14 Keith Browner	.40	1.00
15 John Cannon	.40	1.00
16 Jay Carroll	.40	1.00
17 Gerald Carter	.40	1.00
18 Melvin Carver	.40	1.00
19 Jeremiah Castille	.40	1.00
20 Mark Cotney	.40	1.00
21 Steve Courson	.40	1.00
22 Jeff Davis	.40	1.00
23 Steve DeBerg	2.00	5.00
24 Sean Farrell	.40	1.00
25 Frank Garcia	.40	1.00
26 Jimmie Giles	.75	2.00
27 Hugh Green	1.25	3.00
28 Hugh Green IA	.60	1.50
29 Randy Grimes	.40	1.00
30 Ron Heller	.60	1.50
31 John Holt	.40	1.00
32 Kevin House	.75	2.00
33 Noah Jackson	.40	1.00
34 Cecil Johnson	.40	1.00
35 Ken Kaplan	.40	1.00
36 Blair Kiel	.60	1.50
37 David Logan	.60	1.50
38 Brison Manor	.40	1.00
39 Michael Morton	.40	1.00
40 James Owens	.40	1.00
41 Beasley Reece	.60	1.50
42 Gene Sanders	.40	1.00
43 Lee Roy Selmon	6.00	12.00
44 Lee Roy Selmon IA	3.00	8.00
45 Danny Spradlin	.40	1.00
46 Kelly Thomas	.40	1.00
47 Norris Thomas	.40	1.00
48 Jack Thompson	.75	2.00
49 Perry Tuttle	.40	1.00
50 Chris Washington	.40	1.00
51 Mike Washington	.40	1.00
52 James Wilder	.75	2.00
53 James Wilder IA	.60	1.50
54 Steve Wilson	.40	1.00
55 Mark White	.40	1.00
56 Richard Wood	.60	1.50

1989 Buccaneers Police

This ten-card set measures 2 5/8" by 4 1/8" and features members of the Tampa Bay Buccaneers. The fronts of the cards feature an action color shot along with the identification of the player and his position and uniform number. The back of the card features biographical information, some text, one line of career statistics, and the card number. This set was sponsored by IMC Fertilizer, Inc. and the Polk County Law Enforcement Office.

COMPLETE SET (10)	20.00	50.00
1 Vinny Testaverde	15.00	25.00
2 Mark Carrier WR	3.00	8.00
3 Randy Grimes	1.25	3.00
4 Paul Gruber	2.00	5.00
5 Ron Hall	2.00	5.00
6 William Howard	1.25	3.00
7 Curt Jarvis	1.25	3.00
8 Ervin Randle	1.25	3.00
9 Ricky Reynolds	2.00	5.00
10 Rob Taylor	1.25	3.00

2006 Buccaneers Topps

COMPLETE SET (12)	3.00	6.00
TB1 Chris Simms	.25	.60
TB2 Simeon Rice	.20	.50
TB3 Michael Clayton	.20	.50
TB4 Derrick Brooks	.25	.60
TB5 Cadillac Williams	.25	.60
TB6 Joey Galloway	.25	.60
TB7 Edell Shepherd	.20	.50
TB8 Mike Alstott	.20	.50
TB9 Ronde Barber	.25	.60
TB10 Alex Smith TE	.20	.50
TB11 Maurice Stovall	.20	.50
TB12 Bruce Gradkowski	.30	.75

2007 Buccaneers Topps

COMPLETE SET (12)	2.00	5.00
1 Alex Smith TE	.20	.50
2 Cadillac Williams	.25	.60
3 Michael Clayton	.20	.50
4 Bruce Gradkowski	.20	.50
5 Cato June	.20	.50
6 Chris Simms	.20	.50
7 Joey Galloway	.25	.60
8 Derrick Brooks	.25	.60
9 Ronde Barber	.25	.60
10 Jeff Garcia	.25	.60
11 Mike Alstott	.25	.60
12 Gaines Adams	.30	.75

2008 Buccaneers Topps

COMPLETE SET (12)	2.00	4.00
1 Joey Galloway	.25	.60
2 Jeff Garcia	.25	.60
3 Brian Griese	.20	.50
4 Warrick Dunn	.25	.60
5 Earnest Graham	.20	.50
6 Gaines Adams	.20	.50
7 Cadillac Williams	.25	.60
8 Ike Hilliard	.20	.50
9 Ronde Barber	.20	.50
10 Derrick Brooks	.25	.60
11 Aqib Talib	.40	1.00
12 Dexter Jackson	.30	.75

2009 Buccaneers Donruss Super Bowl XLIII Promos

This set was issued at the Donruss/Playoff booth during the 2009 Super Bowl Card Show in Tampa, Florida. A complete set was given to any collector that opened a specified number of football card packs at the booth during the show.

COMPLETE SET (4)	3.00	6.00
1 Derrick Brooks	.75	2.00
2 Earnest Graham	.60	1.50
3 Ronde Barber	.60	1.50
4 Jeff Garcia	.75	2.00

2009 Buccaneers Upper Deck Super Bowl XLIII Promos

This set was issued at the Upper Deck booth during the 2009 Super Bowl Card Show in Tampa, Florida. A complete set was given to any collector that opened a specified number of football card packs at the booth during the show.

COMPLETE SET (4)	3.00	6.00
5 Derrick Brooks	.75	2.00
6 Antonio Bryant	.60	1.50
7 Jeff Garcia	.75	2.00
8 Aqib Talib	.60	1.50

1976 Buckmans Discs

The 1976 Buckmans football disc set of 20 is unnumbered and features star players from the National Football League. The circular cards measure approximately 3 3/8" in diameter. The players' pictures are in black and white with a colored arc serving as the disc border. Four stars complete the border at the top. The backs of the most common version contain the address of the Buckmans Ice Cream outlet in Rochester, New York. A much scarcer blankbacked version of the set was also prodcued and though to have been issued in packages of Safelon lunch bags. Another version that reads "Customized Sports Discs" on the back exists and is thought to have been issued as promotional pieces or samples. The MSA marking, signifying Michael Schechter Associates, is featured on the backs as well. Since the set is unnumbered, the cards are listed below alphabetically by player's name.

COMPLETE SET (20)	40.00	80.00
*BLANKBACK: 4X TO 10X		
*CUSTOMIZED: 8X TO 20X		
1 Otis Armstrong	1.00	2.50
2 Steve Bartkowski	1.00	2.50
3 Terry Bradshaw	15.00	25.00
4 Doug Buffone	.75	2.00
5 Wally Chambers	.75	2.00
6 Chuck Foreman	1.00	2.50
7 Roman Gabriel	1.25	3.00
8 Mel Gray	1.00	2.50
9 Franco Harris	5.00	10.00
10 James Harris	1.00	2.50
11 Jim Hart	1.00	2.50
12 Gary Huff	.75	2.00
13 Billy Kilmer	1.00	2.50
14 Terry Metcalf	1.00	2.50
15 Jim Otis	.75	2.00
16 Jim Plunkett	1.25	3.00
17 Greg Pruitt	1.00	2.50
18 Roger Staubach	15.00	25.00
19 Jan Stenerud	1.00	2.50
20 Roger Wehrli	1.00	2.50

2002 Buffalo Destroyers AFL

This set was sponsored by Dave and Adams Card World and features members of the 2002 Buffalo Destroyers Arena Football League team. Each includes a color player photo on the front and a brief player bio on back.

COMPLETE SET (17)	6.00	15.00
1 Thomas Bailey	.40	1.00
2 Ray Bentley CO	.30	.75
3 Eddie Brown	.40	1.00
4 David Caldwell	.30	.75
5 Derrick Chachere	.30	.75
6 Bret Cooper	.30	.75
7 Lamart Cooper UER (name misspelled Lamont)	.40	1.00
8 Jerry Crafts	.30	.75
9 Kerwin Hairston	.30	.75
10 Carlos James	.30	.75
11 Corey Johnson	.30	.75
12 Juan Long	.30	.75
13 Kevin Mason	.30	.75
14 Steve McLaughlin	.30	.75
15 Fred McNair	.50	1.25
16 Hardy Mitchell	.30	.75
17 Cover Card	.30	.75

1972 Burger King Ice Milk Cups

These white cups with brown detail were issued in 1972 by Burger King to promote their Ice Milk dessert. These cups are approximately 4" high and feature a detailed portrait on the front of the cup with a biography on the back and a Burger King logo at the bottom. The cups are listed below in alphabetical order. These thin cups are condition sensitive since they are highly susceptible to cracking.

1 Dan Abramowicz	6.00	12.00
2 Julius Adams	6.00	12.00
3 Bob Anderson	6.00	12.00
4 Dick Anderson	6.00	12.00
5 George Andrie	6.00	12.00
6 Jim Bakken	6.00	12.00
7 Pete Banaszak	6.00	12.00
8 Pete Beathard	6.00	12.00
9 Bill Bergey	7.50	15.00
10 Forrest Blue	6.00	12.00
11 Terry Bradshaw	20.00	40.00
12 John Brockington	6.00	12.00
13 Buck Buchanan	7.50	15.00
14 Norm Bulaich	6.00	12.00
15 Nick Buoniconti	7.50	15.00
16 Virgil Carter	6.00	12.00
17 Richard Caster	6.00	12.00
18 Jack Concannon	6.00	12.00
19 Dave Costa	6.00	12.00
20 Larry Csonka	10.00	20.00
21 Mike Curtis	6.00	12.00
22 Len Dawson	12.50	25.00
23 Bobby Douglass	6.00	12.00
24 Bobby Duhon	6.00	12.00
25 Carl Eller	7.50	15.00
26 Mel Farr	6.00	12.00
27 Manny Fernandez	6.00	12.00
28 John Fuqua	7.50	15.00
29 Walt Garrison	6.00	12.00
30 John Gilliam	6.00	12.00
31 Dick Gordon	6.00	12.00
32 Joe Greene	10.00	20.00
33 Bob Griese	12.50	25.00
34 John Hadl	7.50	15.00
35 Don Hansen	6.00	12.00
36 Cliff Harris	7.50	15.00
37 Dave Herman	6.00	12.00
38 J.D. Hill	6.00	12.00
39 Jim Houston	6.00	12.00
40 Delles Howell	6.00	12.00
41 Rich Jackson	6.00	12.00
42 Ron Johnson	6.00	12.00
43 Walter Johnson	6.00	12.00
44 Clint Jones	6.00	12.00
45 Deacon Jones	10.00	20.00
46 Lee Roy Jordan	10.00	20.00
47 Leroy Kelly	10.00	20.00
48 Leroy Keyes	6.00	12.00
49 Jim Kiick	7.50	15.00
50 George Kunz	6.00	12.00
51 Jake Kupp	6.00	12.00
52 Greg Landry	7.50	15.00
53 Willie Lanier	7.50	15.00
54 Pete Liske	6.00	12.00
55 Floyd Little	7.50	15.00
56 Mike Lucci	6.00	12.00
57 Jim Lynch	6.00	12.00
58 Milt Morin	6.00	12.00
59 Earl Morrall	7.50	15.00
60 Mercury Morris	7.50	15.00
61 Haven Moses	6.00	12.00
62 John Niland	6.00	12.00
63 Frank Nunley	6.00	12.00
64 Merlin Olsen	10.00	20.00
65 Steve Owens	7.50	15.00
66 Lemar Parrish	6.00	12.00
67 Dan Pastorini	6.00	12.00
68 Jim Plunkett	10.00	20.00
69 Ed Podolak	6.00	12.00
70 Ron Pritchard	6.00	12.00
71 Isiah Robertson	6.00	12.00
72 Dave Robinson	6.00	12.00
73 Tim Rossovich	6.00	12.00
74 Andy Russell	7.50	15.00
75 Charlie Sanders	7.50	15.00
76 Jake Scott	7.50	15.00
77 George Seals	6.00	12.00
78 Dennis Shaw	6.00	12.00
79 Jackie Smith	7.50	15.00
80 Jerry Smith	6.00	12.00
81 Royce Smith	6.00	12.00
82 Jack Snow	6.00	12.00
83 Walt Sweeney	6.00	12.00
84 Steve Tannen	6.00	12.00
85 Fran Tarkenton	12.50	25.00
86 Altie Taylor	6.00	12.00
87 Otis Taylor	7.50	15.00
88 Billy Truax	6.00	12.00
89 Bob Tucker	6.00	12.00
90 Randy Vataha	6.00	12.00
91 Paul Warfield	10.00	20.00
92 Gene Washington	7.50	15.00
93 George Webster	6.00	12.00
94 Dave Wilcox	7.50	15.00
95 Ken Willard	6.00	12.00
96 Larry Wilson	10.00	20.00
97 Garo Yepremian	6.00	12.00

1995 Burger King/Sports Illustrated College Legends Cups

In 1995, Burger King in conjunction with Sports Illustrated produced a series of 32 oz. Stadium style drinking cups which featured an array of notable college players by position on each cup. These colorful cups were produced by both Alpha Products and Packer Plastics.

COMPLETE SET	16.00	40.00
1 Bobby Bowden	4.80	12.00
Woody Hayes		
Lou Holtz		
Tom Osborne		
Joe Paterno		
Eddie Robinson		
John Robinson		
Bo Schembechler		
Barry Switzer		
2 Defense	2.40	6.00
Cornelius Bennett		
Hugh Green		
Joe Greene		
3 Kerry Collins	4.80	12.00
Ty Detmer		
Doug Flutie		
Jim McMahon		
Warren Moon		
Vinny Testaverde		
Charlie Ward		
Andre Ware		
4 Tim Brown	3.20	8.00
Anthony Carter		
Irving Fryar		
Desmond Howard		
Rocket Ismail		
J.J. Stokes		
Michael Westbrook		
5 Marcus Allen	4.80	12.00
Ki-Jana Carter		
Tony Dorsett		
Archie Griffin		
Bo Jackson		
Rashaan Salaam		
Billy Sims		
Herschel Walker		

1932 Briggs Chocolate

This set was issued by C.A. Briggs Chocolate company in 1932. The cards feature 31-different sports with each card including an artist's rendering of a sporting event. Although players are not named, it is thought that most were modeled after famous athletes of the time. The cardbacks include a written portion about the sport and an offer from Briggs for free baseball equipment for building a compete set of cards.

11 Football (thought to be Red Grange)	800.00	1,200.00

1976 Canada Dry Cans

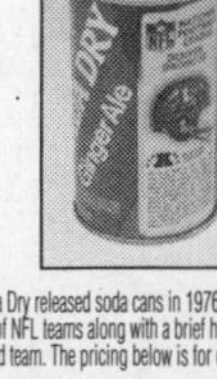

Canada Dry released soda cans in 1976 featuring the logos of NFL teams along with a brief history of the featured team. The pricing below is for opened cans.

COMPLETE SET (28)	100.00	200.00
1 Atlanta Falcons	4.00	8.00
2 Baltimore Colts	4.00	8.00
3 Buffalo Bills	5.00	10.00
4 Chicago Bears	4.00	8.00
5 Cincinnati Bengals	4.00	8.00
6 Cleveland Browns	5.00	10.00
7 Dallas Cowboys	7.50	15.00
8 Denver Broncos	4.00	8.00
9 Detroit Lions	4.00	8.00
10 Green Bay Packers	7.50	15.00
11 Houston Oilers	4.00	8.00
12 Kansas City Chiefs	4.00	8.00
13 Los Angeles Rams	4.00	8.00
14 Miami Dolphins	7.50	15.00

15 Minnesota Vikings 5.00 10.00
16 New England Patriots 4.00 8.00
17 New Orleans Saints 4.00 8.00
18 New York Giants 5.00 10.00
19 New York Jets 5.00 10.00
20 Oakland Raiders 7.50 15.00
21 Philadelphia Eagles 4.00 8.00
22 Pittsburgh Steelers 5.00 10.00
23 St. Louis Cardinals 4.00 8.00
24 San Diego Chargers 4.00 8.00
25 San Francisco 49ers 5.00 10.00
26 Seattle Seahawks 4.00 8.00
27 Tampa Bay Buccaneers 4.00 8.00
28 Washington Redskins 7.50 15.00

1964 Caprolan Nylon All-Star Buttons

These buttons were issued in the mid-1960s and feature a black and white image of an AFL or NFL player. The fronts also feature the words " A Caprolan Nylon All-Star Performer" along with the player's name printed in blue ink above the photo. Any additions to this list are appreciated.

COMPLETE SET (5) 75.00 150.00
1 Maxie Baughan 15.00 30.00
2 Gino Cappelletti 15.00 30.00
3 Matt Hazeltine UER 15.00 30.00
(name misspelled Mat)
4 Merlin Olsen 20.00 40.00
5 Andy Robustelli 20.00 40.00

1967 Caprolan Nylon Photos

These 8" x 10" glossy black-and-white photos were issued to promote the Caprolan company. Each includes the player's name, team name, and "A Caprolan All-Star" below the image.

1 Gary Ballman 12.50 25.00
2 Gino Cappelletti 12.50 25.00
3 Mike Ditka 20.00 40.00
4 Matt Hazeltine 12.50 25.00
5 Pete Retzlaff 12.50 25.00
6 Andy Robustelli 15.00 30.00
7 Frank Ryan 12.50 25.00

1953 Cardinals Team Issue

Photos in this set of the Chicago Cardinals measure approximately 8" by 10" and feature a black-and-white player image on the front printed on high gloss stock. The player's name and position can sometimes be found written on the backs but no player identification is otherwise given. The photos are unnumbered and checklisted below in alphabetical order.

COMPLETE SET (31) 350.00 600.00
1 Cliff Anderson 10.00 20.00
2 Roy Barni 10.00 20.00
3 Tom Bienemann 10.00 20.00
4 Al Campana 10.00 20.00
5 Nick Chickillo 10.00 20.00
6 Dilly Cross 10.00 20.00
7 Tony Curcillo 10.00 20.00
8 Jerry Groom 10.00 20.00
9 Ed Husmann 10.00 20.00
10 Don Joyce 10.00 20.00
11 Ed Listopad 10.00 20.00
12 Ollie Matson 15.00 30.00
13 Gern Nagler 10.00 20.00
14 Johnny Olszewski 10.00 20.00
15 John Panelli 10.00 20.00
16 Volney Peters 10.00 20.00
17 Gordon Polofsky 10.00 20.00
18 Jim Psaltis 10.00 20.00
19 Ray Ramsey 10.00 20.00
20 Jack Simmons 10.00 20.00
21 Emil Sitko 10.00 20.00
22 Don Stonesifer 10.00 20.00
23 Joe Stydahar CO 12.50 25.00
24 Leo Sugar 10.00 20.00
25 Dave Suminski 10.00 20.00
26 Pat Summerall 15.00 30.00
27 Bill Svoboda 10.00 20.00
28 Charley Trippi 12.50 25.00
29 Fred Wallner 10.00 20.00
30 Jerry Watford 10.00 20.00
31 Team Photo 12.50 25.00

1960 Cardinals Mayrose Franks

The Mayrose Franks set of 11 cards features players on the St. Louis (Football) Cardinals and first hit store shelves in Septmber 1960. The cards are plastic coated (they were intended as inserts in hot dog and bacon packages) with slightly rounded corners and are numbered. The cards measure approximately 2 1/2" by 3 1/2". The fronts, with a black and white photograph of the player and a red background, contain the card number, player statistics and the Cardinal's logo. The backs contain a description of the Big Mayrose Football Contest.

COMPLETE SET (11) 80.00 125.00
1 Don Gillis 6.00 12.00
2 Frank Fuller 6.00 12.00
3 George Izo 6.00 12.00
4 Woodley Lewis 6.00 12.00
5 King Hill 6.00 12.00
6 John David Crow 7.50 15.00
7 Bill Stacy 6.00 12.00
8 Ted Bates 6.00 12.00
9 Mike McGee 6.00 12.00
10 Bobby Joe Conrad 6.00 12.00
11 Ken Panfil 6.00 12.00

1961 Cardinals Jay Publishing

This 12-card set features (approximately) 5" by 7" black-and-white player photos. The pictures show players in traditional poses with the quarterback preparing to throw, the runner heading downfield, and the defensive player ready for the tackle. These cards were packaged 12 to a packet and originally sold for 25 cents. The backs are blank. The cards are unnumbered and checklisted below in alphabetical order.

COMPLETE SET (12) 40.00 80.00
1 Joe Childress 4.00 8.00
2 Sam Etcheverry 4.00 8.00
3 Ed Henke 4.00 8.00
4 Jimmy Hill 4.00 8.00
5 Bill Koman 4.00 8.00
6 Roland McDole 4.00 8.00
7 Mike McGee 4.00 8.00
8 Dale Meinert 4.00 8.00
9 Jerry Norton 4.00 8.00
10 Sonny Randle 4.00 8.00
11 Joe Robb 4.00 8.00
12 Billy Stacy 4.00 8.00

1963-64 Cardinals Team Issue

The Cardinals likely issued these photos over a period of years during the mid-1960s. Each measures approximately 5" by 7" and features a black and white player photo along with player information below the photo. Some photos contain only the player's name, positon and team name in all caps, while others also include the player's height and weight with the team name in upper and lower case letters. They are unnumbered and blankbacked and listed below alphabetically.

COMPLETE SET (15) 100.00 175.00
1 Taz Anderson 6.00 12.00
2 Garland Boyette 6.00 12.00
3 Don Brumm 6.00 12.00
4A Jim Burson 6.00 12.00
(Jimmy on front)
4B Jim Burson 6.00 12.00
(Jim on front)
5 Irv Goode 6.00 12.00
6 John Houser 6.00 12.00
7 Bill Koman 6.00 12.00
8 Ernie McMillan 6.00 12.00
9A Luke Owens 6.00 12.00
(white jersey)
9B Luke Owens 6.00 12.00
(red jersey)
10 Bob Paremore 6.00 12.00
11A Bob Reynolds 6.00 12.00
(white jersey)
11B Bob Reynolds 6.00 12.00
(red jersey)
12 Joe Robb 6.00 12.00
13 Sam Silas 6.00 12.00
14 Jerry Stovall 6.00 12.00
15A Bill Triplett 6.00 12.00
(white jersey)
15B Bill Triplett 6.00 12.00
(red jersey)

1965 Cardinals Big Red Biographies

This set was featured during the 1965 football season as the side panels of half-gallon milk cartons from Adams Dairy in St. Louis. When cut, the cards measure approximately 3 1/16" by 5 9/16". The printing on the cards is in purple and orange. All cards feature members of the St. Louis Cardinals. The catalog designation for this set is F112. The Cardinals logo in the upper right hand corner varies slightly on some cards, but no variations of the same card are known. The list below contains those cards known at this time; any additions to the list would be welcomed. The cards have blank backs as is the case with most milk carton issues. Complete milk cartons would be valued at double the prices listed below.

COMPLETE SET (27) 3,000.00 5,000.00
1 Monk Bailey 150.00 250.00
2 Jim Bakken 175.00 300.00
3 Don Brumm 150.00 250.00
4 Jim Burson 150.00 250.00
5 Joe Childress 150.00 250.00
6 Willis Crenshaw 150.00 250.00
7 Bob DeMarco 150.00 250.00
8 Pat Fischer 150.00 250.00
9 Billy Gambrell 150.00 250.00
10 Irv Goode 150.00 250.00
11 Ken Gray 150.00 250.00
12 Charley Johnson 175.00 300.00
13 Bill Koman 150.00 250.00
14 Dave Meggysey 150.00 250.00
15 Dale Meinert 150.00 250.00
16 Mike Melinkovich 150.00 250.00
17 Sonny Randle 150.00 250.00
18 Bob Reynolds 150.00 250.00
19 Joe Robb 150.00 250.00
20 Marion Rushing 150.00 250.00
21 Sam Silas 150.00 250.00
22 Carl Silvestri 150.00 250.00
23 Dave Simmons 150.00 250.00
24 Jackie Smith 200.00 350.00
25 Bill(Thunder) Thornton 150.00 250.00
26 Bill Triplett 150.00 250.00
27 Herschel Turner 150.00 250.00

1965 Cardinals McCarthy Postcards

This two-card set features posed player photos of the Cardinals team printed on postcard-size cards. The cards are unnumbered and checklisted below in alphabetical order.

1 Dick Lane 2.50 5.00
2 Ollie Matson 2.50 5.00

1965 Cardinals Team Issue

This 10-card set of the St. Louis Cardinals measures approximately 7 3/8" by 9 3/8" and features black-and-white player photos in a white border. The player's name, position and team are printed in the wide bottom margin. The backs are blank. The cards are unnumbered and checklisted below in alphabetical order.

COMPLETE SET (10) 60.00 120.00
1 Don Brumm 6.00 12.00
2 Bobby Joe Conrad 6.00 12.00
3 Bob DeMarco 6.00 12.00
4 Charley Johnson 7.50 15.00
5 Ernie McMillan 6.00 12.00
6 Dale Meinert 6.00 12.00
7 Luke Owens 6.00 12.00
8 Sonny Randle 6.00 12.00
9 Joe Robb 6.00 12.00
10 Jerry Stovall 6.00 12.00

1967 Cardinals Team Issue

These photos are very similar in design to several other Cardinals Team Issue releases. Like the other sets, this set was likely released over a period of years. Each photo measures approximately 5" by 7" and features a black and white player photo along with player information below the photo. The player's name and positon are in all caps with the team name in upper and lower case letters. They are unnumbered and blankbacked and listed below alphabetically.

COMPLETE SET (16) 90.00 150.00
1 Don Brumm 6.00 12.00
2 Charlie Bryant 6.00 12.00
3 Jim Burson 6.00 12.00
4 Irv Goode 6.00 12.00
5 Mal Hammack 6.00 12.00
6 Bill Koman 6.00 12.00
7 Chuck Logan 6.00 12.00
8 Dave Long 6.00 12.00
9 John McDowell 6.00 12.00
10 Ernie McMillan 6.00 12.00
(weight 260)
11 Dave O'Brien OL 6.00 12.00
12 Bob Reynolds 6.00 12.00
(weight 260)
13 Joe Robb 6.00 12.00
14 Roy Shivers 6.00 12.00
15 Chuck Walker 6.00 12.00
16 Bobby Williams DB 6.00 12.00

1969 Cardinals Team Issue

These photos are very similar in design to several other Cardinals Team Issue releases. Like the other sets, this set was likely released over a period of years. Each photo measures approximately 5" by 7" and features a black and white player photo along with player information below the photo. The player's name and positon are in all caps with the team name in upper and lower case letters. The type size and style differs slightly from one photo to the next, but all include a slightly wider or round letter "C" in the word Cardinals than the 1971 set. They are unnumbered and blankbacked and listed below alphabetically.

COMPLETE SET (31) 150.00 250.00
1 Robert Atkins 5.00 10.00
2 Jim Bakken 6.00 12.00
3 Bob Brown 5.00 10.00
4 Terry Brown 5.00 10.00
5 Willis Crenshaw 5.00 10.00
6 Jerry Daanen 5.00 10.00
7 Irv Goode 5.00 10.00
8 Chip Healy 5.00 10.00
9 Fred Heron 5.00 10.00
10 King Hill 5.00 10.00
11 Fred Hyatt 5.00 10.00
12 Rolf Krueger 5.00 10.00
13 MacArthur Lane 6.00 12.00
14 Ernie McMillan 5.00 10.00
15 Wayne Mulligan 5.00 10.00
16 Dave Olerich 5.00 10.00
17 Bob Reynolds 5.00 10.00
18 Jamie Rivers 5.00 10.00
19 Johnny Roland 5.00 10.00
20 Rocky Rosema 5.00 10.00
21 Bob Rowe 5.00 10.00
22 Lonnie Sanders 5.00 10.00
23 Joe Schmiesing 5.00 10.00
24 Roy Shivers 5.00 10.00
25 Cal Snowdon 5.00 10.00
26 Rick Sortun 5.00 10.00
27 Chuck Walker 5.00 10.00
28 Clyde Williams 5.00 10.00
29 Dave Williams 5.00 10.00
30 Charley Winner CO 5.00 10.00
31 Nate Wright 5.00 10.00

1971 Cardinals Team Issue

These photos are very similar in design to many other Cardinals Team Issue set listings. Like the others, these photos were likely released over a period of years. Each photo measures approximately 5" by 7" and features a black and white player photo along with player information below the photo. The player's name and positon are in all caps with the team name in upper and lower case letters. The type size and style differs slightly from one photo to the next, but all include a slightly more narrow letter "C" in the word Cardinals than the 1969 set. They are unnumbered and blankbacked and listed below alphabetically.

COMPLETE SET (22) 100.00 175.00
1 Tom Banks 5.00 10.00
2 Dale Hackbart 5.00 10.00
3 Jim Hargrove 5.00 10.00
4 Fred Heron 5.00 10.00
(weight 255)
5 Bob Hollway CO 5.00 10.00
(large print)
6 Mike McGill 5.00 10.00
7 Dave Meggysey 5.00 10.00
8 Terry Miller LB 5.00 10.00
9 Don Parish 5.00 10.00
10 Charlie Pittman 5.00 10.00
11 Rocky Rosema 5.00 10.00
12 Lonnie Sanders 5.00 10.00
13 Joe Schmiesing 5.00 10.00
14 Mike Siwek 5.00 10.00
15 Larry Stegent 5.00 10.00
16 Norm Thompson 5.00 10.00
17 Tim Van Galder 5.00 10.00
18 Chuck Walker 5.00 10.00
19 Dave Williams 5.00 10.00
20 Larry Willingham 5.00 10.00
21 Nate Wright 5.00 10.00
22 Ron Yankowski 5.00 10.00

1972 Cardinals Team Issue

The Cardinals issued these photos likely over a period of years. Each measures approximately 5" by 7" and features a black and white player photo along with the player's name, positon, height, weight, and team name below the photo. The type size and style used is virtually the same for all of the photos and the team name reads "St. Louis Cardinals." The player's name is printed in upper and lower case letters. They are unnumbered and blankbacked and listed below alphabetically.

COMPLETE SET (37) 125.00 225.00
1 Jeff Allen 4.00 8.00
2 Tom Banks 4.00 8.00
3 Craig Baynham 4.00 8.00
4 Pete Beathard 4.00 8.00
5 Tom Beckman 4.00 8.00
6 Terry Brown 4.00 8.00
7 Gary Cuozzo 5.00 10.00
8 Paul Dickson 4.00 8.00
9 Miller Farr 4.00 8.00
10 Walker Gillette 4.00 8.00
11 John Gilliam 5.00 10.00
12 Dale Hackbart 4.00 8.00
13 Jim Hargrove 4.00 8.00
14 Jim Hart 6.00 12.00
15 Fred Heron 4.00 8.00
16 George Hoey 4.00 8.00
17 Bob Hollway CO 4.00 8.00
18 Chuck Hutchison 4.00 8.00
19 Fred Hyatt 4.00 8.00
20 Martin Imhof 4.00 8.00
21 Jeff Lyman 4.00 8.00
22 Mike McGill 4.00 8.00
23 Ernie McMillan 4.00 8.00
24 Terry Miller 4.00 8.00
25 Bobby Moore 10.00 20.00
(Ahmad Rashad)
26 Wayne Mulligan 4.00 8.00
27 Bob Reynolds 4.00 8.00
28 Jamie Rivers 4.00 8.00
29 Johnny Roland 5.00 10.00
30 Bob Rowe 4.00 8.00
31 Roy Shivers 4.00 8.00
32 Tim Van Galder 4.00 8.00
33 Chuck Walker 4.00 8.00
34 Eric Washington 4.00 8.00
35 Clyde Williams 4.00 8.00
36 Larry Willingham 4.00 8.00
37 Ron Yankowski 4.00 8.00

1973 Cardinals Team Issue

The Cardinals issued these photos likely over a period of years as this set looks very similar to the 1972 issue. Each measures approximately 5" by 7" and features a black and white player photo along with the player's name, positon, height, weight, and team name below the photo. The type size and style used is different than the 1972 set and varies slightly from photo to photo. The team name reads "St. Louis Football Cardinals" on all these photos unless noted below. They are unnumbered and blankbacked and listed below alphabetically.

COMPLETE SET (43) 150.00 250.00
1 Donny Anderson 5.00 10.00
2 Tom Banks 4.00 8.00
3 Chuck Beatty 4.00 8.00
4 Tom Beckman 4.00 8.00
5 Willie Belton 4.00 8.00
6 Leon Burns 4.00 8.00
7 Dave Butz 4.00 8.00
8 Steve Conley 4.00 8.00
9 Dwayne Crump 4.00 8.00
10 Ron Davis 4.00 8.00
11 Rod Dowhower CO 4.00 8.00
12 Miller Farr 4.00 8.00
13 Ken Garrett 4.00 8.00
14 Joe Gibbs CO 15.00 30.00
15 Walker Gillette 4.00 8.00
16 Jim Hanifan CO 4.00 8.00
17 Sid Hall CO 4.00 8.00
18 Chuck Hutchison 4.00 8.00
19 Fred Hyatt 4.00 8.00
20 Martin Imhoff 4.00 8.00
21 Gary Keithley 4.00 8.00
(St.Louis Cardinals team name)
22 Don Maynard 6.00 12.00
23 Ernie McMillan 4.00 8.00
25 Terry Miller 4.00 8.00
26 Wayne Mulligan 4.00 8.00
27 Jim Otis 5.00 10.00
28 Marv Owens 4.00 8.00
29 Ara Person 4.00 8.00
30 Ahmad Rashad 7.50 15.00
31 John Richardson 4.00 8.00
32 Jamie Rivers 4.00 8.00
33 Johnny Roland 4.00 8.00
34 Don Shy 4.00 8.00
35 Jackie Simpson CO 4.00 8.00
36 Maurice Spencer 4.00 8.00
37 Jeff Staggs 4.00 8.00
38 Norm Thompson 4.00 8.00
39 Jim Tolbert 4.00 8.00
40 Eric Washington 4.00 8.00
41 Bob Wicks 4.00 8.00
42 Ray Willsey CO 4.00 8.00
43 Bob Young 4.00 8.00
24A Terry Metcalf 5.00 10.00
(St.Louis Cardinals team name)
24B Terry Metcalf 5.00 10.00
(St.Louis Football Cardinals is the team name)

1974 Cardinals Team Issue

The Cardinals issued these photos likely over a period of years as this set looks very similar to the 1972 and 1973 issues. Each measures approximately 5" by 7" and features a black and white player photo along with the player's name, positon, height, weight, and team name below the photo. The type size and style used is different than the 1972 and 1973 sets with the 1974 printing being slightly larger. The team name reads "St. Louis Football Cardinals" on all these photos with most, but not all, being in all capitals letters. They are unnumbered and blankbacked and listed below alphabetically.

COMPLETE SET (17) 50.00 100.00
1 Tom Banks 4.00 8.00
2 Jim Champion CO 4.00 8.00
3 Gene Hamlin 4.00 8.00
4 Reggie Harrison 4.00 8.00
5 Eddie Moss 4.00 8.00
6 Steve Neils 4.00 8.00
7 Jim Otis 5.00 10.00
8 Ken Reaves 4.00 8.00
9 Hal Roberts 4.00 8.00
10 Hurles Scales 4.00 8.00
11 Wayne Sevier CO 4.00 8.00
12 Dennis Shaw 4.00 8.00
13 Maurice Spencer 4.00 8.00
14 Larry Stallings 4.00 8.00
15 Scott Stringer 4.00 8.00
16 Earl Thomas 4.00 8.00
17 Cal Withrow 4.00 8.00

1976 Cardinals Team Issue

The St. Louis Cardinals issued this series of player photos quite possibly over a number of years. Each photo is very similar in design and is only differentiated by the size and type style of the print. The unnumbered black and white photos measure approximately 5 1/8" by 7" and all, except John Zook, include the player's name, position, height and weight below the photo along with "St. Louis Football Cardinals." The team name printed on the cards varies in size and print type from photo to photo. Although they likely were issued over a period of years, we've included them all as a 1976 release since all players performed for that year's team.

COMPLETE SET (51) 150.00 300.00
1 Mark Arneson 4.00 8.00
2 Jim Bakken 5.00 10.00
3 Rodrigo Barnes 4.00 8.00
4 Al Beauchamp 4.00 8.00
5 Bob Bell 4.00 8.00
6 Tom Brahaney 4.00 8.00
7 Leo Brooks 4.00 8.00
8 J.V. Cain 4.00 8.00
9 Don Coryell CO 5.00 10.00
10 Dwayne Crump 4.00 8.00
11 Charlie Davis 4.00 8.00
12 Mike Dawson 4.00 8.00
13 Dan Dierdorf 6.00 12.00
(jersey #72)
14 Conrad Dobler 5.00 10.00
15 Bill Donckers 4.00 8.00
16 Clarence Duren 4.00 8.00
17 Roger Finnie 4.00 8.00
18 Carl Gersbach 4.00 8.00
19 Harry Gilmer CO 5.00 10.00
20 Mel Gray 5.00 10.00
21 Tim Gray 4.00 8.00
22 Gary Hammond 4.00 8.00
23 Ike Harris 4.00 8.00
24 Jim Hart 5.00 10.00
(1/5 of jersey number showing)
25 Steve Jones 4.00 8.00
26 Terry Joyce 4.00 8.00
27 Tim Kearney 4.00 8.00
28 Jerry Latin 4.00 8.00
29 Mike McGraw 4.00 8.00
30 Terry Metcalf 5.00 10.00
31 Wayne Morris 4.00 8.00
32 Steve Neils 4.00 8.00
33 Brad Oates 4.00 8.00
34 Steve Okoniewski 4.00 8.00
35 Walt Patulski 4.00 8.00
36 Ken Reaves 4.00 8.00
37 Mike Sensibaugh 4.00 8.00
38 Jeff Severson 4.00 8.00
39 Jackie Smith 6.00 12.00
40 Larry Stallings 4.00 8.00
41 Norm Thompson 4.00 8.00
42 Pat Tilley 5.00 10.00
43 Jim Tolbert 4.00 8.00
44 Marvin Upshaw 4.00 8.00
45 Roger Wehrli 5.00 10.00
46 Jeff West 4.00 8.00
47 Ray White 4.00 8.00
48 Sam Wyche 5.00 10.00
49 Ron Yankowski 4.00 8.00
50 Bob Young 4.00 8.00
51 John Zook 4.00 8.00

1977-78 Cardinals Team Issue

The St. Louis Cardinals issued this series of player photos quite possibly over a number of years. Each photo is nearly identical in design. The unnumbered black and white photos measure approximately 5 1/8" by 7" and all include the player's name, position, height and weight below the photo along with "ST. LOUIS FOOTBALL CARDINALS" in all capital letters. We've cataloged them all as a 1977-78 release since all of the players performed during those years and the type style matches on each photo.

COMPLETE SET (28) 100.00 200.00
1 Kurt Allerman 4.00 8.00
2 Dan Audick 4.00 8.00
3 John Barefield 4.00 8.00
4 Tim Black 4.00 8.00
5 Dan Brooks CO 4.00 8.00
6 Duane Carrell 4.00 8.00
7 Al Chandler 4.00 8.00
8 Jim Childs 4.00 8.00
9 George Collins 4.00 8.00
10 Dan Dierdorf 5.00 10.00
11 Bob Giblin 4.00 8.00
12 Randy Gill 4.00 8.00
13 Doug Greene 4.00 8.00
14 Ken Greene 4.00 8.00
15 Willard Harrell 4.00 8.00
16 Jim Hart 5.00 10.00
17 Steve Little 4.00 8.00
18 Steve Pisarkiewicz 4.00 8.00
19 Bob Pollard 4.00 8.00
20 Eason Ramson 4.00 8.00
21 Keith Simons 4.00 8.00
22 Perry Smith 4.00 8.00
23 Dave Stief 4.00 8.00
24 Terry Stieve 4.00 8.00
25 Ken Stone 4.00 8.00
26 Pat Tilley 5.00 10.00
27 Eric Williams 4.00 8.00
28 Keith Wortman 4.00 8.00

1980 Cardinals Police

The 15-card 1980 St. Louis Cardinals set was sponsored by the local law enforcement agency, the St. Louis Cardinals, KMOX Radio (which broadcasts the Cardinals' games), and Community Federal Savings and Loan: the last three of which have their logos on the backs of the cards. The cards measure approximately 2 5/8" by 4 1/8". The set is unnumbered but has been listed by player uniform number in the checklist below. The backs present "Cardinal Tips" and information on how to contact a police officer by telephone. Card backs feature black print with red trim on white card stock. Ottis Anderson appears in his Rookie Card year.

COMPLETE SET (15) 7.50 15.00
17 Jim Hart .75 2.00
22 Roger Wehrli .60 1.50
24 Wayne Morris .30 .75
32 Ottis Anderson 1.25 2.50
33 Theotis Brown .30 .75
37 Ken Greene .30 .75
55 Eric Williams .30 .75
56 Tim Kearney .30 .75
59 Calvin Favron .30 .75
68 Terry Stieve .30 .75
72 Dan Dierdorf 1.50 3.00
73 Mike Dawson .30 .75
82 Bob Pollard .30 .75
83 Pat Tilley .50 1.25
85 Mel Gray .60 1.50

1980 Cardinals Team Issue

The St. Louis Cardinals issued this series of player photos around 1980. Each photo is very similar in design to the 1976 issue and is only differentiated by slight differences in type size and style. The unnumbered black and white photos measure approximately 5 1/8" by 7" and all include the player's name, position, height and weight below the photo along with "St. Louis Football Cardinals."

COMPLETE SET (12) 30.00 60.00
1 Mark Arneson 3.00 6.00
2 Tom Banks 3.00 6.00
3 Joe Bostic 4.00 8.00
4 Barney Cotton 3.00 6.00
4 Dan Dierdorf 5.00 10.00
(jersey #64)
5 Calvin Favron 3.00 6.00
6 Harry Gilmer CO 4.00 8.00
7 Tim Kearney 3.00 6.00
7 Jim Hart 4.00 8.00
(1/3 of jersey number showing)
8 Dave Stief 3.00 6.00
9 Ken Stone 3.00 6.00
10 Ron Yankowski 3.00 6.00

1982 Cardinals Nu-Maid Butter Tubs

This set of butter cups or tubs was released by Nu-Maid and Miami Margarine in 1982. Each includes color illustrations of the featured player and measures roughly 3 3/4" tall and 3" in diameter.

COMPLETE SET (6) 12.50 25.00
1 Ottis Anderson 3.00 6.00
2 Dan Dierdorf 4.00 8.00
3 Roy Green 2.50 5.00
4 Curtis Greer 2.50 5.00
5 Neil Lomax 2.50 5.00
6 Pat Tilley 2.50 5.00

1988 Cardinals Holsum

This 12-card standard-size full-color set features players of the Phoenix Cardinals; cards were available only in Holsum Bread packages. The set was co-produced by Mike Schechter Associates on behalf of the NFL Players Association. Card fronts have a color photo within a green border and the backs are printed in black ink on white card stock.

COMPLETE SET (12) 20.00 50.00
1 Roy Green 2.50 6.00
2 Stump Mitchell 2.00 5.00
3 J.T. Smith 2.00 5.00
4 E.J. Junior 2.00 5.00
5 Cedric Mack 1.50 4.00
6 Curtis Greer 1.50 4.00
7 Lonnie Young 1.50 4.00
8 David Galloway 1.50 4.00
9 Luis Sharpe 1.50 4.00
10 Leonard Smith 1.50 4.00
11 Ron Wolfley 1.50 4.00
12 Earl Ferrell 1.50 4.00

1988 Cardinals Smokey

This set of Phoenix Cardinals was issued through local Fire Prevention agencies and sponsored by Blue Cross/Blue Shield. Each unnumbered card is oversized (roughly 5" by 7") and includes a message from Smokey the Bear on the cardback.

COMPLETE SET (16) 25.00 60.00
1 Carl Carter 1.50 4.00
2 David Galloway 1.50 4.00
3 Roy Green 2.00 5.00
4 Don Holmes 1.50 4.00
5 Shawn Knight 1.50 4.00
6 Cedric Mack 1.50 4.00
7 Jay Novacek 2.50 6.00
8 Walter Reeves 1.50 4.00
9 J.T. Smith 2.00 5.00
10 Lance Smith 1.50 4.00
11 Tom Tupa 1.50 4.00
12 Jim Wahler 1.50 4.00
13 Karl Wilson 1.50 4.00

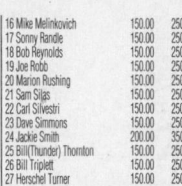

14 Ron Wolfley	1.50	4.00
15 Lonnie Young	1.50	4.00
16 Michael Zordich	1.50	4.00

1989 Cardinals Holsum

The 1989 Holsum Phoenix Cardinals set features 16 standard-size cards. The set was co-produced by Mike Schechter Associates on behalf of the NFL Players Association. The fronts have helmetless color mug shots; the vertically oriented backs have bios, stats, and card numbers.

COMPLETE SET (16)	12.50	25.00
1 Roy Green	1.00	2.50
2 J.T. Smith	.75	2.00
3 Neil Lomax	.75	2.00
4 Stump Mitchell	.75	2.00
5 Vai Sikahema	.75	2.00
6 Lonnie Young	.60	1.50
7 Robert Awalt	.60	1.50
8 Cedric Mack	.60	1.50
9 Earl Ferrell	.60	1.50
10 Ron Wolfley	.60	1.50
11 Bob Clasby	.60	1.50
12 Luis Sharpe	.60	1.50
13 Steve Alvord	.60	1.50
14 David Galloway	.60	1.50
15 Freddie Joe Nunn	.60	1.50
16 Niko Noga	.60	1.50

1989 Cardinals Police

The 1989 Police Phoenix Cardinals set contains 15 cards measuring approximately 2 5/8" by 4 3/16". The fronts have white borders and color action photos; the vertically oriented backs have brief bios, career highlights, and safety messages. The set features members of the Phoenix Cardinals. The set was also sponsored by Louis Rich Meats and KTSP-TV. The cards are unnumbered except for uniform number which is prominently displayed on both sides of the card. Two cards were given out every two weeks during the season. It has been reported that 1.6 million cards were produced; 100,000 of each player. Derek Kennard's card was supposedly withdrawn at some time during the promotion after he was arrested. Reportedly, Freddie Joe Nunn was also planned for inclusion in this set but was withdrawn as well.

COMPLETE SET (15)	10.00	25.00
5 Gary Hogeboom	.50	1.25
24 Ron Wolfley	.40	1.00
30 Stump Mitchell	.50	1.25
31 Earl Ferrell	.40	1.00
36 Vai Sikahema	.50	1.25
43 Lonnie Young	.40	1.00
46 Tim McDonald	.75	2.00
65 David Galloway	.40	1.00
67 Luis Sharpe	.50	1.25
70 Derek Kennard SP	3.00	8.00
79 Bob Clasby	.40	1.00
80 Robert Awalt	.40	1.00
81 Roy Green	.60	1.50
84 J.T. Smith	.50	1.25
85 Jay Novacek	1.50	4.00

1990 Cardinals Police

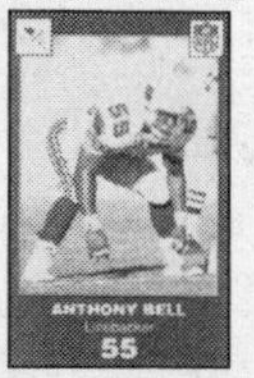

This 16-card police set was sponsored by Louis Rich Meats and KTSP-TV. The cards measure approximately 2 5/8" by 4 1/4". The color action player photos on the fronts have maroon borders, with player information below the pictures in the bottom border. The team and NFL logos overlay the upper corners of the pictures. The backs have biography, a "Cardinal Rule" in the form of a safety tip, and sponsor logos. The cards are unnumbered (except for the prominent display of the player's uniform number) and checklisted below in alphabetical order.

COMPLETE SET (16)	3.20	8.00
1 Anthony Bell	.20	.50
2 Joe Bugel CO	.20	.50
3 Rich Camarillo	.10	.30
4 Roy Green	.40	1.00
5 Ken Harvey	.40	1.00
6 Eric Hill	.50	1.25
7 Tim McDonald	.30	.75
8 Tootie Robbins	.10	.30
9 Timm Rosenbach	.30	.75
10 Luis Sharpe	.20	.50
11 Vai Sikahema	.20	.50
12 J.T. Smith	.30	.75
13 Lance Smith	.10	.30
14 Jim Wahler	.10	.30
15 Ron Wolfley	.10	.30
16 Lonnie Young	.10	.30

1992 Cardinals Police

Sponsored by KTVK-TV (Channel 3) and the Arizona Public Service Co., this 16-card set measures the standard-size. The fronts display color player photos bordered above and partially on the left by stripes that fade from red to yellow. In the lower left corner, an electronic scoreboard gives the player's jersey number and position. Beneath the team name and logo, the player's name and jersey number are printed between two red stripes toward the bottom of the card. The horizontal backs present biographical information and, on a red panel, recycling and conservation tips. The cards are unnumbered and checklisted below in alphabetical order.

COMPLETE SET (16)	4.80	12.00
1 Joe Bugel CO	.20	.50
2 Rich Camarillo	.20	.50
3 Ed Cunningham	.20	.50
4 Greg Davis	.20	.50
5 Ken Harvey	.40	1.00
6 Randal Hill	.30	.75
7 Ernie Jones	.30	.75
8 Mike Jones	.20	.50
9 Tim McDonald	.40	1.00
10 Freddie Joe Nunn	.20	.50
11 Ricky Proehl	.30	.75
12 Timm Rosenbach	.20	.50
13 Tony Sacca	.30	.75
14 Lance Smith	.20	.50
15 Eric Swann	.60	1.50
16 Aeneas Williams	.50	1.25

1994 Cardinals Police

The cards are unnumbered, but listed below alphabetically. They feature a color player photo surrounded by a maroon and orange border. The set is thought to be complete at four cards.

COMPLETE SET (4)	4.00	10.00
1 Greg Davis	1.00	2.50
2 Anthony Edwards	1.00	2.50
3 Terry Hoage	1.00	2.50
4 Aeneas Williams	1.40	3.50

2006 Cardinals Topps

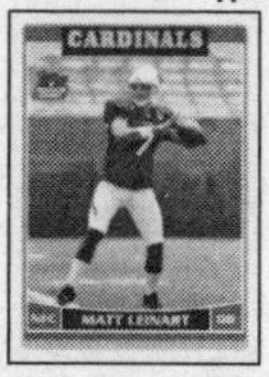

COMPLETE SET (12)	5.00	8.00
ARI1 J.J. Arrington	.20	.50
ARI2 Antrel Rolle	.20	.50
ARI3 Karlos Dansby	.20	.50
ARI4 Kurt Warner	.30	.75
ARI5 Neil Rackers	.20	.50
ARI6 Anquan Boldin	.25	.60
ARI7 Larry Fitzgerald	.30	.75
ARI8 Edgerrin James	.25	.60
ARI9 Adrian Wilson	.20	.50
ARI10 Bryant Johnson	.20	.50
ARI11 Matt Leinart	.75	2.00
ARI12 Leonard Pope	.30	.75

2007 Cardinals Topps

COMPLETE SET (12)	2.50	5.00
1 Matt Leinart	.25	.60
2 Edgerrin James	.25	.60
3 Larry Fitzgerald	.30	.75
4 Anquan Boldin	.25	.60
5 Kurt Warner	.25	.60
6 Bryant Johnson	.20	.50
7 Leonard Pope	.20	.50
8 Marcel Shipp	.20	.50
9 Adrian Wilson	.20	.50
10 Karlos Dansby	.20	.50
11 Neil Rackers	.20	.50
12 Levi Brown	.30	.75

2008 Cardinals Donruss Playoff Super Bowl XLII Card Show

These cards were issued at the 2008 Super Bowl Card Show. Collectors could obtain one card in exchange for wrappers from 2007 Donruss Playoff football card packs opened at the show.

COMPLETE SET (4)	1.50	4.00
9 Karlos Dansby	.30	.75
10 Matt Leinart	.60	1.50
11 Anquan Boldin	.40	1.00
12 Larry Fitzgerald	.40	1.00

2008 Cardinals Topps

COMPLETE SET (12)	2.50	5.00
1 Matt Leinart	.30	.75
2 Kurt Warner	.30	.75
3 Edgerrin James	.25	.60
4 Larry Fitzgerald	.30	.75
5 Anquan Boldin	.25	.60
6 Antrel Rolle	.20	.50
7 Darnell Dockett	.20	.50
8 Roderick Hood	.20	.50
9 Karlos Dansby	.20	.50
10 Leonard Pope	.20	.50
11 Early Doucet	.30	.75
12 Calais Campbell	.30	.75

2008 Cardinals Topps Super Bowl XLII Card Show

These cards were issued at the 2008 Super Bowl Card Show. Collectors could obtain one card in exchange for wrappers from 2007 Topps football card packs opened at the show.

COMPLETE SET (4)	1.50	4.00
1 Larry Fitzgerald	.40	1.00
2 Matt Leinart	.60	1.50
3 Anquan Boldin	.40	1.00
4 Kurt Warner	.50	1.25

2008 Cardinals Upper Deck Super Bowl XLII Card Show

These cards were issued at the 2008 Super Bowl Card Show. Collectors could obtain one card in exchange for wrappers from 2007 Upper Deck football card packs opened at the show.

5 Matt Leinart	.60	1.50
7 Edgerrin James	.50	1.25
8 Adrian Wilson	.30	.75

2009 Cardinals Donruss Super Bowl XLIII

This set was issued at the Donruss/Playoff booth during the 2009 Super Bowl Card Show in Tampa, Florida. A complete set of Steelers and Cardinals was given to any collector that purchased a Score Super Bowl XLIII factory set at the booth during the show.

COMPLETE SET (9)	4.00	8.00
1 Kurt Warner	.60	1.50
2 Larry Fitzgerald	.60	1.50
3 Anquan Boldin	.50	1.25
4 Edgerrin James	.50	1.25
5 Tim Hightower	.40	1.00
6 Steve Breaston	.50	1.25
7 Dominique Rodgers-Cromartie	.40	1.00
8 Karlos Dansby	.40	1.00
9 Adrian Wilson	.40	1.00

1993 Cardz Flintstones NFL Promos

COMPLETE SET (6)	1.60	4.00
1 Fred Flintstone	.30	.75
2 Fred Flintstone	.30	.75
3 Fred and Barney	.30	.75
4 Fred and Barney	.30	.75
5 Fred Flintstone	.30	.75
6 Fred, Barney and Dino	.30	.75

1993 Cardz Flintstones NFL

COMPLETE SET (114)	3.20	8.00
COMMON CARD (1-110)	.04	.10

1998 Cris Carter Energizer/Target

These oversized cards (roughly 5" x 7") were released at Target stores and feature different photos and stats on the career of Cris Carter. Each cardback contains player information, a serial number of 5400-sets produced, and and a card number.

COMPLETE SET (4)	6.00	15.00
COMMON CARD (1-4)	1.60	4.00

1989 CBS Television Announcers

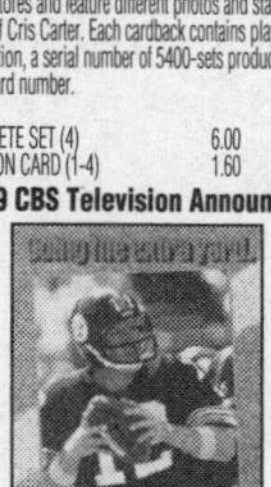

This ten-card set (with cards measuring approximately 2 3/4" by 3 7/8") features those members of the 1989 CBS Football Announcing team who had been involved in professional football. The front of the card features a color action shot from the person's professional career bordered in orange and superimposed over a green football field with a white yard stripe. The words "Going the extra yard" appear in red block lettering at the card top, while the words "NFL on CBS" appear in the lower right corner. The backs are horizontally oriented and have a black and white studio portrait head shot of the announcer. Biography and career highlights are bordered in red. It has been reported that 500 sets were distributed to various CBS outlets and publication sources. The set was split into two series of five announcers each and are unnumbered.

COMPLETE SET (10)	200.00	350.00
WRAPPER	7.50	15.00
1 Terry Bradshaw	40.00	80.00
2 Dick Butkus	25.00	50.00
3 Irv Cross	5.00	10.00
4 Dan Fouts	12.50	25.00
5 Pat Summerall	10.00	20.00
6 Gary Fencik	5.00	10.00
7 Dan Jiggetts	5.00	10.00
8 John Madden	30.00	60.00
9 Ken Stabler	40.00	80.00
10 Hank Stram	7.50	15.00

2008 Celebrity Cuts

COMPLETE SET (100)	125.00	200.00
STATED PRINT RUN 499 SERIAL #'d SETS		
46 Knute Rockne	2.00	5.00

2008 Celebrity Cuts Century Gold

*GOLD: .75X TO 2X BASIC
RANDOM INSERTS IN PACKS
STATED PRINT RUN 25 SERIAL #'d SETS

2008 Celebrity Cuts Century Silver

*SILVER: .6X TO 1.5X BASIC
RANDOM INSERTS IN PACKS
STATED PRINT RUN 50 SERIAL #'d SETS

2008 Celebrity Cuts Century Material

RANDOM INSERTS IN PACKS		
PRINT RUNS B/WN 5-100 COPIES		
NO PRICING ON QTY OF 5		
46 Knute Rockne Jkt/100	30.00	60.00

2008 Celebrity Cuts Century Material Prime

RANDOM INSERTS IN PACKS		
PRINT RUNS B/WN 1-50 COPIES PER		
NO PRICING ON QTY OF 12 OR LESS		
46 Knute Rockne Jkt/50	40.00	80.00

2008 Celebrity Cuts Century Material Combo

RANDOM INSERTS IN PACKS		
PRINT RUNS B/WN 5-50 COPIES PER		
NO PRICING ON QTY OF 10 OR LESS		
46 Knute Rockne Jkt/50	40.00	80.00

2008 CenTex Barracudas IFL

COMPLETE SET (8)	4.00	8.00
1 James Brown	.75	2.00
2 Olan Coleman	.40	1.00
3 Tim Cook	.40	1.00
4 Lance Garner	.40	1.00
5 Rolandus Johnson	.40	1.00
6 Roderick Knight	.40	1.00
7 Taurean Robinson	.40	1.00
8 J.R. Turner	.40	1.00

2009 Certified

COMP.SET w/o RC's (125)	20.00	40.00
ROOKIE AUTO PRINT RUN 99-499		
ROOKIE JSY AU PRINT RUN 229-399		
1 Anquan Boldin	.30	.75
2 Edgerrin James	.30	.75
3 Kurt Warner	.40	1.00
4 Larry Fitzgerald	.40	1.00
5 Tim Hightower	.25	.60
6 Jerious Norwood	.30	.75
7 Matt Ryan	.40	1.00
8 Michael Turner	.30	.75
9 Roddy White	.30	.75
10 Derrick Mason	.30	.75
11 Joe Flacco	.40	1.00
12 Ray Rice	.40	1.00
13 Willis McGahee	.30	.75
14 James Hardy	.30	.75
15 Lee Evans	.30	.75
16 Terrell Owens	.40	1.00
17 Marshawn Lynch	.30	.75
18 DeAngelo Williams	.40	1.00
19 Jake Delhomme	.30	.75
20 Jonathan Stewart	.30	.75
21 Steve Smith	.30	.75
22 Brian Urlacher	.40	1.00
23 Greg Olsen	.25	.60
24 Jay Cutler	.40	1.00
25 Matt Forte	.40	1.00
26 Carson Palmer	.40	1.00
27 Cedric Benson	.30	.75
28 Chad Ochocinco	.30	.75
29 Laveranues Coles	.25	.60
30 Brady Quinn	.30	.75
31 Braylon Edwards	.30	.75
32 Jamal Lewis	.30	.75
33 Jason Witten	.40	1.00
34 Marion Barber	.30	.75
35 Roy Williams WR	.30	.75
36 Tony Romo	.60	1.50
37 Brandon Marshall	.30	.75
38 Correll Buckhalter	.25	.60
39 Eddie Royal	.30	.75
40 Kyle Orton	.30	.75
41 Calvin Johnson	.40	1.00
42 Daunte Culpepper	.30	.75
43 Kevin Smith	.30	.75
44 Aaron Rodgers	.75	2.00
45 A.J. Hawk	.30	.75
46 Donald Driver	.30	.75
47 Greg Jennings	.40	1.00
48 Ryan Grant	.30	.75
49 Andre Johnson	.30	.75
50 Matt Schaub	.30	.75
51 Owen Daniels	.25	.60
52 Steve Slaton	.30	.75
53 Anthony Gonzalez	.25	.60
54 Dallas Clark	.30	.75
55 Joseph Addai	.40	1.00
56 Peyton Manning	.60	1.50
57 Reggie Wayne	.30	.75
58 David Garrard	.30	.75
59 Torry Holt	.30	.75
60 Maurice Jones-Drew	.30	.75
61 Dwayne Bowe	.30	.75
62 Larry Johnson	.30	.75
63 Matt Cassel	.30	.75
64 Tony Gonzalez	.30	.75
65 Chad Pennington	.30	.75
66 Ricky Williams	.30	.75
67 Ronnie Brown	.30	.75
68 Ted Ginn	.30	.75
69 Adrian Peterson	.60	1.50
70 Bernard Berrian	.30	.75
71 Brett Favre	5.00	12.00
72 Laurence Maroney	.30	.75
73 Randy Moss	.40	1.00
74 Tom Brady	.60	1.50
75 Wes Welker	.40	1.00
76 Drew Brees	.40	1.00
77 Jeremy Shockey	.25	.60
78 Lance Moore	.30	.75
79 Marques Colston	.30	.75
80 Reggie Bush	.40	1.00
81 Brandon Jacobs	.30	.75
82 Eli Manning	.40	1.00
83 Kevin Boss	.30	.75
84 Jerricho Cotchery	.30	.75
85 Leon Washington	.30	.75
86 Thomas Jones	.30	.75
87 Darren McFadden	.40	1.00
88 JaMarcus Russell	.25	.60
89 Justin Fargas	.25	.60
90 Zach Miller	.25	.60
91 Brian Westbrook	.30	.75
92 DeSean Jackson	.30	.75
93 Donovan McNabb	.40	1.00
94 Kevin Curtis	.25	.60
95 Ben Roethlisberger	.40	1.00
96 Willie Parker	.25	.60
97 Santonio Holmes	.30	.75
98 Hines Ward	.30	.75
99 Antonio Gates	.30	.75
100 LaDainian Tomlinson	.40	1.00
101 Philip Rivers	.40	1.00
102 Vincent Jackson	.30	.75
103 Frank Gore	.30	.75
104 Patrick Willis	.30	.75
105 Isaac Bruce	.30	.75
106 Vernon Davis	.30	.75
107 Julius Jones	.25	.60
108 Matt Hasselbeck	.30	.75
109 Deion Branch	.30	.75
110 T.J. Houshmandzadeh	.30	.75
111 Donnie Avery	.30	.75
112 Marc Bulger	.30	.75
113 Steven Jackson	.30	.75
114 Antonio Bryant	.25	.60
115 Cadillac Williams	.30	.75
116 Derrick Ward	.25	.60
117 Kellen Winslow Jr.	.30	.75
118 Chris Johnson	.40	1.00
119 Justin Gage	.25	.60
120 Kerry Collins	.30	.75
121 LenDale White	.30	.75
122 Chris Cooley	.30	.75
123 Clinton Portis	.30	.75
124 Jason Campbell	.25	.60
125 Santana Moss	.30	.75
126 Aaron Brown RC	1.50	4.00
127 Aaron Kelly AU/499 RC	3.00	8.00
128 Aaron Maybin RC	1.25	3.00
129 Anthony Hill RC	1.00	2.50
130 Austin Collie AU/399 RC	5.00	12.00
131 B.J. Raji AU/199 RC	4.00	10.00
132 Bear Pascoe RC	1.25	3.00
133 Bernard Scott RC	1.50	4.00
134 Brandon Gibson AU/399 RC	4.00	10.00
135 Brandon Tate AU/299 RC	4.00	10.00
136 Brian Cushing AU/199 RC	4.00	10.00
137 Brian Hartline RC	1.50	4.00
138 Brian Orakpo AU/199 RC	4.00	10.00
139 Brooks Foster AU/399 RC	2.50	6.00
140 Cameron Morrah AU/399 RC	2.50	6.00
141 Cedric Peerman AU/149 RC	3.00	8.00
142 Chase Coffman AU/399 RC	3.00	8.00
143 Chris Ogbonnaya RC	1.25	3.00
144 Clay Matthews AU/199 RC	30.00	60.00
145 Clint Sintim AU/199 RC	4.00	10.00
146 Cornelius Ingram AU/399 RC	2.50	6.00
147 Curtis Painter RC	1.50	4.00
148 Dan Gronkowski RC	1.00	2.50
149 Darius Passmore RC	1.25	3.00
150 David Johnson RC	1.25	3.00
151 Davon Drew RC	1.25	3.00
152 Demetrius Byrd AU/249 RC	3.00	8.00
153 Devin Moore AU/199 RC	3.00	8.00
154 Dominique Edison AU/399 RC	2.50	6.00
155 Eddie Williams RC	1.25	3.00
156 Everette Brown AU/299 RC	3.00	8.00
157 Frank Summers RC	1.50	4.00
158 Fui Vakapuna RC	1.25	3.00
159 Gartrell Johnson RC	1.00	2.50
160 Hunter Cantwell AU/399 RC	4.00	10.00
161 James Casey AU/199 RC	3.00	8.00
162 James Laurinaitis AU/299 RC	6.00	15.00
163 James Davis RC	1.50	4.00
164 Jared Cook AU/299 RC	4.00	10.00
165 Jarett Dillard AU/399 RC	4.00	10.00
166 Javarris Williams RC	1.25	3.00
167 John Phillips RC	1.50	4.00
168 Johnny Knox AU/499 RC	8.00	20.00
169 Keith Null RC	1.25	3.00
170 Kenny McKinley AU/399 RC	4.00	10.00
171 Kevin Ogletree AU/499 RC	6.00	15.00
172 Kory Sheets AU/249 RC	3.00	8.00
173 Larry English AU/99 RC	4.00	10.00
174 Louis Murphy AU/299 RC	8.00	20.00
175 Louis Delmas RC	1.50	4.00
176 Malcolm Jenkins AU/299 RC	4.00	10.00
177 Manuel Johnson RC	1.25	3.00
178 Marko Mitchell RC	1.25	3.00
179 Michael Mitchell RC	1.25	3.00
180 Mike Goodson No AU/399 RC	2.00	5.00
181 Mike Teel RC	1.50	4.00
182 Nathan Brown RC	1.25	3.00
183 P.J. Hill AU/499 RC	3.00	8.00
184 Patrick Chung RC	1.50	4.00
185 Quan Cosby AU/349 RC	3.00	8.00
186 Quinn Johnson AU/399 RC	3.00	8.00
187 Quinten Lawrence RC	1.00	2.50
188 Rashad Jennings AU/499 RC	4.00	10.00
189 Rey Maualuga AU/199 RC	4.00	10.00
190 Richard Quinn RC	1.25	3.00
191 Robert Ayers RC	1.50	4.00
192 Sammie Stroughter RC	1.50	4.00
193 Shawn Nelson No AU/299 RC	1.25	3.00
194 Sherrod Martin RC	1.25	3.00
195 Tiquan Underwood RC	1.25	3.00
196 Tom Brandstater AU/99 RC	4.00	10.00
197 Tony Fiammetta AU/399 RC	3.00	8.00
198 Travis Beckum AU/399 RC	3.00	8.00
199 Tyrell Sutton AU/499 RC	3.00	8.00
200 Vontae Davis AU/299 RC	4.00	10.00
201 Barry Sanders JSY/250	8.00	20.00
202 Brett Favre JSY/250	12.00	30.00
203 Charlie Joiner JSY/250	3.00	8.00
204 Dan Marino JSY/250	10.00	25.00
205 Emmitt Smith JSY/250	8.00	20.00
206 Eric Dickerson JSY/250	4.00	10.00
207 Franco Harris JSY/250	5.00	12.00
208 Gene Upshaw JSY/250	3.00	8.00
209 Jerry Rice JSY/250	8.00	20.00
210 Jim Brown JSY/150	6.00	15.00
211 Joe Montana JSY/250	10.00	25.00
212 Joe Namath JSY/100	6.00	15.00
213 John Elway JSY/250	8.00	20.00
214 Lawrence Taylor JSY/250	5.00	12.00
215 Merlin Olsen JSY/250	4.00	10.00
216 Roger Staubach JSY/250	6.00	15.00
217 Ronnie Lott JSY/250	5.00	12.00
218 Steve Largent JSY/250	5.00	12.00
219 Thurman Thomas JSY/250	5.00	12.00
220 Troy Aikman JSY/250	6.00	15.00
221 Matthew Stafford JSY AU/249 RC	60.00	100.00
222 Jason Smith JSY AU/249 RC	5.00	12.00
223 Tyson Jackson JSY AU/229 RC	5.00	12.00
224 Aaron Curry JSY AU/249 RC	6.00	15.00
225 Mark Sanchez JSY AU/249 RC	40.00	100.00
226 Darrius Heyward-Bey JSY AU/249 RC	6.00	15.00
227 Michael Crabtree JSY AU/249 RC	15.00	40.00
228 Knowshon Moreno JSY AU/249 RC	12.00	30.00
229 Josh Freeman JSY AU/249 RC	20.00	50.00
230 Jeremy Maclin JSY AU/249 RC	10.00	25.00
231 Brandon Pettigrew JSY AU/399 RC	6.00	15.00
232 Percy Harvin JSY AU/249 RC	20.00	50.00
233 Donald Brown JSY AU/249 RC	8.00	20.00
234 Hakeem Nicks JSY AU RC/249	10.00	25.00
235 Kenny Britt JSY AU/399 RC	8.00	20.00
236 Chris Wells JSY AU/249 RC	10.00	25.00
237 Brian Robiskie JSY AU/399 RC	6.00	15.00
238 Pat White JSY AU/249 RC	6.00	15.00
239 Mohamed Massaquoi JSY AU/249 RC	8.00	20.00
240 LeSean McCoy JSY AU/249 RC	12.00	30.00
241 Shonn Greene JSY AU/399 RC	12.00	30.00
242 Glen Coffee JSY AU/399 RC	5.00	12.00
243 Derrick Williams JSY AU/249 RC	5.00	12.00
244 Javon Ringer JSY AU/399 RC	6.00	15.00
245 Mike Wallace JSY AU/399 RC	12.00	30.00
246 Ramses Barden JSY AU/249 RC	4.00	10.00
247 Patrick Turner JSY AU/349 RC	5.00	12.00
248 Deon Butler JSY AU/399 RC	5.00	12.00
249 Juaquin Iglesias JSY AU/249 RC	5.00	12.00
250 Stephen McGee JSY AU/249 RC	6.00	15.00
251 Mike Thomas JSY AU/249 RC	6.00	15.00
252 Andre Brown JSY AU/249 RC	4.00	10.00
253 Rhett Bomar JSY AU/249 RC	5.00	12.00
254 Nate Davis JSY AU/249 RC	5.00	12.00

2009 Certified Mirror Blue

*1-125 VETS: 4X TO 10X BASIC CARDS		
*126-200 ROOKIES: .5X TO 1.2X MIRROR RED		
1-200 MIRROR BLUE PRINT RUN 100		
*ROOK.JSY AU/50: .6X TO 1.5X BASIC CARD		
*ROOK.JSY AU/25: .8X TO 2X BASIC CARDS		
201-234 JSY AU MIRR.BLUE PRINT RUN 25-50		
71 Brett Favre	15.00	40.00
221 Matthew Stafford JSY AU/25	100.00	200.00
225 Mark Sanchez JSY AU/25	100.00	200.00
227 Michael Crabtree JSY AU/25	40.00	100.00
228 Knowshon Moreno JSY AU/25	25.00	60.00
232 Percy Harvin JSY AU/25	50.00	120.00

2009 Certified Mirror Gold

*1-125 VETS: 6X TO 15X BASIC CARDS		
*126-200 ROOKIES: .8X TO 2X MIRROR RED		
1-200 MIRROR GOLD PRINT RUN 25		
*201-234 JSY AU/25: .8X TO 2X BASIC CARDS		
201-234 JSY AU MIR.GOLD PRINT RUN 10-25		
71 Brett Favre	40.00	80.00

2009 Certified Mirror Red

*MIRROR RED: 3X TO 8X BASIC CARDS		
COMMON ROOKIE	2.00	5.00
ROOKIE SEMISTARS	2.50	6.00
ROOKIE UNL.STARS	3.00	8.00
MIRROR RED PRINT RUN 250		
71 Brett Favre	12.00	30.00
130 Austin Collie	3.00	8.00
131 B.J. Raji	3.00	8.00
136 Brian Cushing	3.00	8.00
138 Brian Orakpo	3.00	8.00
144 Clay Matthews	8.00	20.00
162 James Laurinaitis	3.00	8.00
168 Johnny Knox	5.00	12.00
189 Rey Maualuga	3.00	8.00
191 Robert Ayers	3.00	8.00

2009 Certified Certified Potential

STATED PRINT RUN 1000 SER.#'d SETS		
*BLUE/50: .6X TO 1.5X BASIC INSERTS		
*GOLD/25: .8X TO 2X BASIC INSERTS		
*RED/100: .5X TO 1.2X BASIC INSERTS		
1 Glen Coffee	.60	1.50
2 LeSean McCoy	1.50	4.00
3 Rhett Bomar	.60	1.50
4 Ramses Barden	.50	1.25
5 Deon Butler	.60	1.50
6 Stephen McGee	.75	2.00
7 Andre Brown	.50	1.25
8 Nate Davis	.60	1.50
9 Javon Ringer	.75	2.00
10 Matthew Stafford	4.00	10.00
11 Tyson Jackson	.60	1.50
12 Mark Sanchez	2.50	6.00
13 Michael Crabtree	1.50	4.00
14 Josh Freeman	1.50	4.00
15 Brandon Pettigrew	.75	2.00
16 Donald Brown	.75	2.00
17 Kenny Britt	1.00	2.50
18 Brian Robiskie	.75	2.00
19 Pat White	.75	2.00
20 Mohamed Massaquoi	.60	1.50
21 Shonn Greene	1.25	3.00
22 Chris Wells	1.25	3.00
23 Hakeem Nicks	1.25	3.00
24 Percy Harvin	1.25	3.00
25 Jeremy Maclin	1.25	3.00
26 Knowshon Moreno	.75	2.00
27 Darrius Heyward-Bey	.75	2.00
28 Aaron Curry	.75	2.00
29 Jason Smith	.60	1.50
30 Derrick Williams	.60	1.50
31 Mike Wallace	1.50	4.00
32 Patrick Turner	.60	1.50
33 Juaquin Iglesias	.60	1.50
34 Mike Thomas	.75	2.00

2009 Certified Certified Potential Autographs

STATED PRINT RUN 10-25		
1 Glen Coffee/25	6.00	15.00
5 Deon Butler/25	6.00	15.00
9 Javon Ringer/25	8.00	20.00
15 Brandon Pettigrew/25	8.00	20.00
17 Kenny Britt/25	10.00	25.00
21 Shonn Greene/25	12.00	30.00
31 Mike Wallace/25	15.00	40.00

2009 Certified Certified Potential Materials

STATED PRINT RUN 100 SER.#'d SETS		
*PRIME/25: .8X TO 2X BASIC JSY		
PRIME PRINT RUN 25 SER.#'d SETS		
1 Glen Coffee	2.00	5.00
2 LeSean McCoy	5.00	12.00
3 Rhett Bomar	2.00	5.00
4 Ramses Barden	1.50	4.00
5 Deon Butler	2.00	5.00
6 Stephen McGee	2.50	6.00
7 Andre Brown	1.50	4.00
8 Nate Davis	2.00	5.00
9 Javon Ringer	2.50	6.00
10 Matthew Stafford	6.00	15.00
11 Tyson Jackson	2.00	5.00
12 Mark Sanchez	8.00	20.00
13 Michael Crabtree	5.00	12.00
14 Josh Freeman	5.00	12.00
15 Brandon Pettigrew	2.50	6.00
16 Donald Brown	2.50	6.00
17 Kenny Britt	3.00	8.00
18 Brian Robiskie	2.50	6.00
19 Pat White	2.50	6.00
20 Mohamed Massaquoi	2.00	5.00
21 Shonn Greene	4.00	10.00
22 Chris Wells	5.00	12.00
23 Hakeem Nicks	4.00	10.00
24 Percy Harvin	4.00	10.00
25 Jeremy Maclin	5.00	12.00
26 Knowshon Moreno	2.50	6.00
27 Darrius Heyward-Bey	2.50	6.00
28 Aaron Curry	2.50	6.00
29 Jason Smith	2.00	5.00
30 Derrick Williams	2.00	5.00
31 Mike Wallace	5.00	12.00
32 Patrick Turner	2.00	5.00
33 Juaquin Iglesias	2.00	5.00
34 Mike Thomas	2.50	6.00

2009 Certified Fabric of the Game

STATED PRINT RUN 10-99		
SERIAL #'d UNDER 19 NOT PRICED		
2 Aaron Ross/99	2.50	6.00
4 A.J. Hawk/99	3.00	8.00
5 Alan Page/99	4.00	10.00
6 Alex Karras/99	4.00	10.00
7 Andre Johnson/60	3.00	8.00
11 Antonio Gates/99	3.00	8.00
12 Bart Starr/99	8.00	20.00
14 Ben Watson/99	2.50	6.00
16 Bertrand Berry/99	2.50	6.00
17 Bob Griese/99	5.00	12.00
18 Bob Sanders/99	3.00	8.00
20 Terence Newman/99	2.50	6.00
22 Brandon Stokley/99	3.00	8.00
27 Cadillac Williams/50	4.00	10.00
28 Carson Palmer/99	4.00	10.00
30 Chris Cooley/99	3.00	8.00
34 Dan Fouts/99	5.00	12.00
35 Darrelle Revis/99	3.00	8.00
37 Dave Casper/99	3.00	8.00
38 D'Brickashaw Ferguson/99	2.50	6.00
41 DeMeco Ryans/90	3.00	8.00
42 Derek Anderson/99	2.50	6.00
43 Derrick Mason/35	4.00	10.00
45 Devery Henderson/99	2.50	6.00
46 Devin Hester/99	4.00	10.00
48 Donovan McNabb/99	4.00	10.00
49 Drew Brees/99	4.00	10.00
51 Dwight Freeney/99	3.00	8.00
52 Earl Campbell/99	5.00	12.00
54 Edgerrin James/19	5.00	12.00
55 Eli Manning/99	4.00	10.00
59 Hank Baskett/99	2.50	6.00
61 Jamal Lewis/99	3.00	8.00
62 JaMarcus Russell/99	2.50	6.00
68 Jevon Kearse/88	3.00	8.00
69 Jim Kelly/99	5.00	12.00
71 John Mackey/99	4.00	10.00
73 Joseph Addai/99	4.00	10.00
74 Josh Reed/99	2.50	6.00
78 Justin McCareins/99	2.50	6.00
79 Keith Bulluck/99	2.50	6.00
84 Lance Alworth/99	4.00	10.00
85 LaRon Landry/99	2.50	6.00
89 Len Dawson/99	5.00	12.00
91 Lenny Moore/99	4.00	10.00
93 Mario Williams/99	3.00	8.00
95 Mark Clayton/99	2.50	6.00
97 Mathias Kiwanuka/99	2.50	6.00
99 Matt Hasselbeck/99	3.00	8.00
100 Matt Ryan/99	4.00	10.00
102 Maurice Jones-Drew/99	3.00	8.00
104 Mike Brown/99	2.50	6.00
105 Nate Burleson/99	2.50	6.00
106 Nick Barnett/99	2.50	6.00
108 Ozzie Newsome/99	4.00	10.00
109 Patrick Crayton/99	2.50	6.00
111 Paul Hornung/99	5.00	12.00
112 Peyton Manning/99	6.00	15.00
113 Philip Rivers/99	4.00	10.00
115 Ray Lewis/99	5.00	12.00
116 Reggie Brown/99	2.50	6.00
119 Richard Seymour/99	2.50	6.00
120 Ricky Williams/99	3.00	8.00
122 Roger Craig/99	4.00	10.00
124 Ryan Grant/60	3.00	8.00
127 Sebastian Janikowski/99	2.50	6.00
128 Shaun Ellis/99	2.50	6.00
129 Sidney Rice/99	3.00	8.00
130 Sinorice Moss/99	3.00	8.00
131 Sonny Jurgensen/99	4.00	10.00
132 Steve Slaton/99	3.00	8.00
133 Steve Smith/99	3.00	8.00
134 Steve Smith USC/99	3.00	8.00
135 Steve Young/99	6.00	15.00
136 Steven Jackson/99	3.00	8.00
138 Terrell Suggs/99	2.50	6.00
139 Thomas Jones/99	3.00	8.00
140 Todd Heap/55	3.00	8.00
141 Tom Brady/99	6.00	15.00
143 Tony Romo/99	6.00	15.00
144 Trent Edwards/99	2.50	6.00
146 Vincent Jackson/99	3.00	8.00
147 Warren Moon/99	5.00	12.00
149 Willis McGahee/99	3.00	8.00
150 Zach Miller/99	2.50	6.00

2009 Certified Fabric of the Game NFL Die Cut Prime

COMMON CARD/15-25	6.00	15.00
SEMISTARS/15-25	8.00	20.00
UNL.STARS/15-25	10.00	25.00
NFL DC PRIME PRINT RUN 1-25		
34 Dan Fouts/25	12.00	30.00
52 Earl Campbell/25	12.00	30.00
69 Jim Kelly/25	12.00	30.00
100 Matt Ryan/25	10.00	25.00
135 Steve Young/25	15.00	40.00
141 Tom Brady/25	15.00	40.00
143 Tony Romo/25	15.00	40.00

2009 Certified Fabric of the Game Prime

PRIME STATED PRINT RUN 1-50		
13 Ben Roethlisberger/50	5.00	12.00
34 Dan Fouts/25	8.00	20.00
100 Matt Ryan/50	5.00	12.00
135 Steve Young/50	8.00	20.00
141 Tom Brady/50	8.00	20.00
143 Tony Romo/35	8.00	20.00

2009 Certified Fabric of the Game Team Die Cut

STATED PRINT RUN 2-25		
12 Bart Starr/25	20.00	50.00
34 Dan Fouts/25	12.00	30.00
69 Jim Kelly/25	12.00	30.00
89 Len Dawson/20	12.00	30.00
100 Matt Ryan/25	10.00	25.00
111 Paul Hornung/25	12.00	30.00
112 Peyton Manning/25	15.00	40.00
135 Steve Young/25	15.00	40.00
141 Tom Brady/24	15.00	40.00
143 Tony Romo/25	15.00	40.00

2009 Certified Fabric of the Game Jersey Number Autographs

STATED PRINT RUN 2-25		
4 A.J. Hawk/25	15.00	40.00
5 Alan Page/25	20.00	50.00
6 Alex Karras/25	20.00	50.00
7 Andre Johnson/15	15.00	40.00
12 Bart Starr/25	75.00	125.00
17 Bob Griese/25	25.00	60.00
34 Dan Fouts/25	25.00	60.00

37 Dave Casper/25 15.00 40.00
41 DeMeco Ryans/25 15.00 40.00
45 Devery Henderson/25 12.00 30.00
49 Drew Brees/15 40.00 80.00
52 Earl Campbell/25 25.00 60.00
59 Hank Baskett/25 12.00 30.00
63 James Jones/25 12.00 30.00
69 Jim Kelly/25 25.00 60.00
71 John Mackey/25 20.00 50.00
84 Lance Alworth/25 25.00 60.00
85 LaRon Landry/25 12.00 30.00
89 Len Dawson/25 25.00 60.00
91 Lenny Moore/25 20.00 50.00
96 Marques Colston/25 15.00 40.00
108 Ozzie Newsome/25 20.00 50.00
109 Patrick Crayton/25 12.00 30.00
111 Paul Hornung/25 25.00 60.00
122 Roger Craig/25 20.00 50.00
129 Sidney Rice/25 15.00 40.00
131 Sonny Jurgensen/25 20.00 50.00
135 Steve Young/25 30.00 80.00
146 Vincent Jackson/25 15.00 40.00
147 Warren Moon/25 25.00 60.00

2009 Certified Fabric of the Game College

STATED PRINT RUN 20-100
*PRIME/20-25: .8X TO 2X BASIC JSY/100
*PRIME/25: .5X TO 1.2X BASIC JSY/20
1 Matthew Stafford/100 8.00 20.00
2 Tyson Jackson/100 2.50 6.00
3 Mark Sanchez/20 15.00 40.00
4 Brian Orakpo/100 3.00 8.00
6 Brian Cushing/100 3.00 8.00
7 Josh Freeman/100 6.00 15.00
8 Jeremy Maclin/100 6.00 15.00
9 Donald Brown/100 3.00 8.00
10 Chris Wells/100 5.00 12.00
11 James Laurinaitis/100 3.00 8.00
12 Rey Maualuga/100 3.00 8.00
13 Mohamed Massaquoi/100 2.50 6.00
14 LeSean McCoy/100 6.00 15.00
15 Derrick Williams/100 2.50 6.00
16 Brandon Tate/100 3.00 8.00
17 Ramses Barden/100 2.00 5.00
18 Chase Coffman/100 2.50 6.00
19 Juaquin Iglesias/100 2.50 6.00
20 Kenny McKinley/100 3.00 8.00
21 Rhett Bomar/100 2.50 6.00
23 Brandon Gibson/100 3.00 8.00
24 Graham Harrell/100 3.00 8.00
25 Quan Cosby/100 2.50 6.00

2009 Certified Fabric of the Game College Combos

STATED PRINT RUN 50 SER.#'d SETS
1 Malcolm Kelly 4.00 10.00
Juaquin Iglesias
2 Limas Sweed 5.00 12.00
Brian Orakpo
3 Glenn Dorsey 4.00 10.00
Tyson Jackson
4 Jamaal Charles 5.00 12.00
Quan Cosby
5 Dan Connor 4.00 10.00
Derrick Williams
6 Keith Rivers 5.00 12.00
Brian Cushing
7 Chase Coffman 8.00 20.00
Jeremy Maclin
9 Larry Fitzgerald 8.00 20.00
LeSean McCoy
10 Matthew Stafford 12.00 30.00
Mark Sanchez

2009 Certified Freshman Fabric Jumbo

STATED PRINT RUN 100 SER.#'d SETS
*MIRROR BLUE/50: .5X TO 1.2X BASIC JSY/99
*MIRROR GOLD/25: .8X TO 2X BASIC JSY/99
221 Matthew Stafford 10.00 25.00
222 Jason Smith 2.50 6.00
223 Tyson Jackson 2.50 6.00
224 Aaron Curry 3.00 8.00
225 Mark Sanchez 12.00 30.00
226 Darrius Heyward-Bey 3.00 8.00
227 Michael Crabtree 6.00 15.00
228 Knowshon Moreno 3.00 8.00
229 Josh Freeman 6.00 15.00
230 Jeremy Maclin 5.00 12.00
231 Brandon Pettigrew 3.00 8.00
232 Percy Harvin 5.00 12.00
233 Donald Brown 3.00 8.00
234 Hakeem Nicks 5.00 12.00
235 Kenny Britt 4.00 10.00
236 Chris Wells 5.00 12.00
237 Brian Robiskie 3.00 8.00
238 Pat White 3.00 8.00
239 Mohamed Massaquoi 2.50 6.00
240 LeSean McCoy 6.00 15.00
241 Shonn Greene 5.00 12.00
242 Glen Coffee 2.50 6.00
243 Derrick Williams 2.50 6.00
244 Javon Ringer 3.00 8.00
245 Mike Wallace 6.00 15.00
246 Ramses Barden 2.00 5.00
247 Patrick Turner 2.50 6.00
248 Deon Butler 2.50 6.00
249 Juaquin Iglesias 2.50 6.00
250 Stephen McGee 3.00 8.00
251 Mike Thomas 3.00 8.00
252 Andre Brown 2.00 5.00
253 Rhett Bomar 2.50 6.00
254 Nate Davis 2.50 6.00

2009 Certified Gold Team

STATED PRINT RUN 1000 SER.#'d SETS
*MIRROR/100: .8X TO 2X BASIC INSERTS
1 Tom Brady 2.00 5.00
2 Adrian Peterson 2.00 5.00
3 Tony Romo 2.00 5.00
4 Ben Roethlisberger 1.25 3.00
5 Brian Westbrook 1.00 2.50
6 Clinton Portis 1.00 2.50
7 Andre Johnson 1.00 2.50
8 Larry Fitzgerald 1.25 3.00
9 Calvin Johnson 1.25 3.00
10 Reggie Bush 1.25 3.00

2009 Certified Gold Team Materials Prime

STATED PRINT RUN 25 SER.#'d SETS
*BASE MATER/250: .25X TO .6X PRIME/25
1 Tom Brady 10.00 25.00
3 Tony Romo 8.00 20.00
5 Brian Westbrook 5.00 12.00
7 Andre Johnson 5.00 12.00
10 Reggie Bush 6.00 15.00

2009 Certified Mirror Blue Materials

1-122 MIRROR BLUE VET PRINT RUN 15-100
*LEGEND JSY/35-50: .6X TO 1.5X BASE JSY
201-220 MIRR.BLUE LEGEND PRINT RUN 35-50
*MIRR.RED LEGEND/50-100: .3X TO .8X
1 Anquan Boldin/100 3.00 8.00
2 Edgerrin James/100 3.00 8.00
4 Larry Fitzgerald/65 4.00 10.00
7 Matt Ryan/100 4.00 10.00
8 Michael Turner/100 3.00 8.00
10 Derrick Mason/100 3.00 8.00
13 Willis McGahee/100 3.00 8.00
16 Terrell Owens/100 4.00 10.00
17 Marshawn Lynch/100 3.00 8.00
19 Jake Delhomme/100 3.00 8.00
21 Steve Smith/100 3.00 8.00
24 Jay Cutler/15 6.00 15.00
26 Carson Palmer/100 4.00 10.00
27 Cedric Benson/35 4.00 10.00
29 Laveranues Coles/70 2.50 6.00
30 Brady Quinn/100 3.00 8.00
32 Jamal Lewis/100 3.00 8.00
34 Marion Barber/35 4.00 10.00
36 Tony Romo/100 5.00 12.00
38 Correll Buckhalter/100 2.50 6.00
45 A.J. Hawk/100 3.00 8.00
52 Steve Slaton/100 3.00 8.00
54 Dallas Clark/100 3.00 8.00
55 Joseph Addai/100 4.00 10.00
56 Peyton Manning/100 6.00 15.00
57 Reggie Wayne/100 3.00 8.00
59 Torry Holt/100 3.00 8.00
60 Maurice Jones-Drew/100 3.00 8.00
66 Ricky Williams/100 3.00 8.00
74 Tom Brady/100 6.00 15.00
76 Drew Brees/100 4.00 10.00
77 Jeremy Shockey/100 2.50 6.00
79 Marques Colston/60 3.00 8.00
80 Reggie Bush/70 4.00 10.00
82 Eli Manning/100 4.00 10.00
84 Jerricho Cotchery/100 3.00 8.00
86 Thomas Jones/100 3.00 8.00
87 Darren McFadden/100 4.00 10.00
88 JaMarcus Russell/100 2.50 6.00
89 Justin Fargas/100 2.50 6.00
90 Zach Miller/100 2.50 6.00
93 Donovan McNabb/100 4.00 10.00
96 Willie Parker/100 2.50 6.00
97 Santonio Holmes/100 3.00 8.00
99 Antonio Gates/100 3.00 8.00
101 Philip Rivers/100 4.00 10.00
102 Vincent Jackson/100 3.00 8.00
108 Matt Hasselbeck/100 3.00 8.00
109 Deion Branch/100 3.00 8.00
112 Marc Bulger/100 3.00 8.00
113 Steven Jackson/100 3.00 8.00
115 Cadillac Williams/100 3.00 8.00
122 Chris Cooley/95 3.00 8.00
201 Barry Sanders/50 12.00 30.00
202 Brett Favre/50 20.00 50.00
203 Charlie Joiner/50 5.00 12.00
204 Dan Marino/50 15.00 40.00
205 Emmitt Smith/50 12.00 30.00
206 Eric Dickerson/50 6.00 15.00
207 Franco Harris/50 8.00 20.00
208 Gene Upshaw/50 5.00 12.00
209 Jerry Rice/50 12.00 30.00
210 Jim Brown/50 10.00 25.00
211 Joe Montana/50 15.00 40.00
212 Joe Namath/35 10.00 25.00
213 John Elway/50 12.00 30.00
214 Lawrence Taylor/50 8.00 20.00
215 Merlin Olsen/50 6.00 15.00
216 Roger Staubach/50 10.00 25.00
217 Ronnie Lott/50 8.00 20.00
218 Steve Largent/50 8.00 20.00
219 Thurman Thomas/50 8.00 20.00
220 Troy Aikman/50 10.00 25.00

2009 Certified Mirror Gold Materials

I-125 VETERAN PRINT RUN 5-50
*201-220 LEGEND/16-25: .8X TO 2X BASE JSY
201-220 LEGEND PRINT RUN 8-25
7 Matt Ryan/50 5.00 12.00
36 Tony Romo/50 6.00 15.00
74 Tom Brady/50 8.00 20.00

2009 Certified Mirror Red Materials

*MIRR.RED LEGEND/50-100: .3X TO .8X
201-220 LEGEND PRINT RUN 50-100

2009 Certified Mirror Gold Signatures

5-116 VET MIRROR GOLD PRINT RUN 10-25
*127-200 ROOK.AU/25: .8X TO 2X BASE AU RC
127-200 ROOKIE MIRR.GOLD PRINT RUN 25
201-220 LEGEND JSY AU MIRR.GOLD PRINT RUN 13-25
SERIAL #'d UNDER 20 NOT PRICED
5 Tim Hightower/25 5.00 12.00
6 Jerious Norwood/25 6.00 15.00
12 Ray Rice/25 8.00 20.00
14 James Hardy/25 6.00 15.00
25 Matt Forte/25 10.00 25.00
43 Kevin Smith/25 6.00 15.00
45 A.J. Hawk/25 6.00 15.00
52 Steve Slaton/25 6.00 15.00
76 Drew Brees/25 50.00 100.00
79 Marques Colston/25 6.00 15.00
94 Kevin Curtis/25 5.00 12.00
102 Vincent Jackson/25 6.00 15.00
104 Patrick Willis/25 6.00 15.00
111 Donnie Avery/24 6.00 15.00
116 Derrick Ward/25 5.00 12.00
201 Barry Sanders JSY/25 75.00 150.00
202 Brett Favre JSY/25 125.00 200.00
204 Dan Marino JSY/25 125.00 200.00
205 Emmitt Smith JSY/20 90.00 150.00
206 Eric Dickerson JSY/25 25.00 60.00
207 Franco Harris JSY/25 25.00 60.00
208 Gene Upshaw JSY/25 15.00 40.00
209 Jerry Rice JSY/25 75.00 150.00
210 Jim Brown JSY/25 40.00 80.00
211 Joe Montana JSY/25 75.00 150.00
212 Joe Namath JSY/25 50.00 100.00
213 John Elway JSY/25 75.00 150.00
214 Lawrence Taylor JSY/25 25.00 60.00
215 Merlin Olsen JSY/25 20.00 50.00
216 Roger Staubach JSY/25 40.00 80.00
217 Ronnie Lott JSY/25 25.00 60.00
218 Steve Largent JSY/25 25.00 60.00
219 Thurman Thomas JSY/25 25.00 60.00
220 Troy Aikman JSY/25 30.00 80.00

2009 Certified Rookie Fabric of the Game

STATED PRINT RUN 100 SER.#'d SETS
*TEAM DC/25: .8X TO 2X BASIC JSY/100
1 Tyson Jackson 2.00 5.00
2 Mark Sanchez 8.00 20.00
3 Michael Crabtree 5.00 12.00
4 Josh Freeman 5.00 12.00
5 Brandon Pettigrew 2.50 6.00
6 Donald Brown 2.50 6.00
7 Kenny Britt 3.00 8.00
8 Brian Robiskie 2.50 6.00
9 Mohamed Massaquoi 2.00 5.00
10 Shonn Greene 4.00 10.00
11 Derrick Williams 2.00 5.00
12 Mike Wallace 5.00 12.00
13 Patrick Turner 2.00 5.00
14 Juaquin Iglesias 2.00 5.00
15 Mike Thomas 2.50 6.00
16 Rhett Bomar 2.00 5.00
17 Andre Brown 1.50 4.00
18 Nate Davis 2.00 5.00
19 Javon Ringer 2.50 6.00
20 Stephen McGee 2.50 6.00
21 Deon Butler 2.00 5.00
22 Ramses Barden 1.50 4.00
23 Chris Wells 5.00 12.00
24 Glen Coffee 2.00 5.00
25 LeSean McCoy 5.00 12.00
26 Pat White 2.50 6.00
27 Matthew Stafford 6.00 15.00
28 Jason Smith 2.00 5.00
29 Aaron Curry 2.50 6.00
30 Darrius Heyward-Bey 2.50 6.00
31 Knowshon Moreno 2.50 6.00
32 Jeremy Maclin 5.00 12.00
33 Percy Harvin 4.00 10.00
34 Hakeem Nicks 4.00 10.00

2009 Certified Rookie Fabric of the Game Jersey Number Autographs

STATED PRINT RUN 10-25
5 Brandon Pettigrew/25 10.00 25.00
7 Kenny Britt/25 12.00 30.00
8 Brian Robiskie/25 10.00 25.00
10 Shonn Greene/25 15.00 40.00
12 Mike Wallace/25 20.00 50.00
19 Javon Ringer/25 10.00 25.00
21 Deon Butler/25 8.00 20.00
24 Glen Coffee/25 8.00 20.00

2009 Certified Rookie Fabric of the Game Combos

STATED PRINT RUN 100 SER.#'d SETS
*PRIME/25: .6X TO 1.5X BASIC COMBO/100
1 Matthew Stafford 8.00 20.00
Brandon Pettigrew
2 Pat White 3.00 8.00
Patrick Turner
3 Jason Smith 2.50 6.00
Tyson Jackson
4 Mark Sanchez 12.00 30.00
Shonn Greene
5 Javon Ringer 4.00 10.00
Kenny Britt
6 Jeremy Maclin 5.00 12.00
LeSean McCoy
7 Darrius Heyward-Bey 6.00 15.00
Michael Crabtree
8 Knowshon Moreno 5.00 12.00
Chris Wells
9 Brian Robiskie 3.00 8.00
Mohamed Massaquoi
10 Glen Coffee 2.50 6.00
Nate Davis
11 Stephen McGee 6.00 15.00
Josh Freeman
12 Hakeem Nicks 5.00 12.00
Ramses Barden
13 Rhett Bomar 5.00 12.00
Percy Harvin
14 Matthew Stafford 12.00 30.00
Mark Sanchez
15 Derrick Williams 2.50 6.00
Deon Butler

2009 Certified Souvenir Stamps College Materials

STATED PRINT RUN 99 SER.#'d SETS
*PRIME/25: .6X TO 1.5X BASIC JSY/99
1 Chris Wells 5.00 12.00
2 Donald Brown 3.00 8.00
3 Jeremy Maclin 5.00 12.00
4 Josh Freeman 6.00 15.00
5 Brandon Tate 3.00 8.00
6 Derrick Williams 2.50 6.00
7 LeSean McCoy 6.00 15.00
8 Mohamed Massaquoi 2.50 6.00
9 Mark Sanchez 12.00 30.00
10 Tyson Jackson 2.50 6.00
11 Matthew Stafford 10.00 25.00
12 Juaquin Iglesias 2.50 6.00
13 Brian Orakpo 3.00 8.00
14 Brian Cushing 3.00 8.00
15 James Laurinaitis 5.00 12.00
16 Rey Maualuga 3.00 8.00
17 Chase Coffman 2.50 6.00
18 Brandon Gibson 3.00 8.00
19 Graham Harrell 3.00 8.00
20 Quan Cosby 2.50 6.00
21 Jeremiah Johnson 3.00 8.00
22 Kenny McKinley 3.00 8.00

2009 Certified Souvenir Stamps Material Pro Team Logos

STATED PRINT RUN 99 SER.#'d SETS
*PRIME/25: .6X TO 1.5X BASIC JSY/99
*1969 STAMP/50: .5X TO 1.2X BASIC JSY/99
1 Shonn Greene 5.00 12.00
2 Hakeem Nicks 5.00 12.00
3 Jeremy Maclin 5.00 12.00
4 Darrius Heyward-Bey 3.00 8.00
5 Jason Smith 2.50 6.00
6 Mike Wallace 6.00 15.00
7 Juaquin Iglesias 2.50 6.00
8 Rhett Bomar 2.50 6.00
9 Glen Coffee 2.50 6.00
10 LeSean McCoy 6.00 15.00
11 Deon Butler 2.50 6.00
12 Andre Brown 2.00 5.00
13 Javon Ringer 3.00 8.00
14 Tyson Jackson 2.50 6.00
15 Michael Crabtree 6.00 15.00
16 Brandon Pettigrew 3.00 8.00
17 Kenny Britt 4.00 10.00
18 Pat White 3.00 8.00
19 Mike Thomas 3.00 8.00
20 Patrick Turner 2.50 6.00
21 Derrick Williams 2.50 6.00
22 Aaron Curry 3.00 8.00
23 Knowshon Moreno 3.00 8.00
24 Percy Harvin 5.00 12.00
25 Chris Wells 5.00 12.00
26 Mohamed Massaquoi 2.50 6.00
27 Brian Robiskie 3.00 8.00
28 Donald Brown 3.00 8.00
29 Josh Freeman 6.00 15.00
30 Mark Sanchez 12.00 30.00
31 Matthew Stafford 8.00 20.00
32 Nate Davis 2.50 6.00
33 Stephen McGee 3.00 8.00
34 Ramses Barden 2.00 5.00

2009 Certified Souvenir Stamps Material Autographs Pro Team Logos

PRO TEAM LOGO AU PRINT RUN 15-20
*1969 STAMP MAT.AU/20: .4X TO 1X
*PRO TEAM LOGO PRIME AU/15: .4X TO 1X
1 Shonn Greene/20 15.00 40.00
2 Hakeem Nicks/20 15.00 40.00
3 Jeremy Maclin/15 15.00 40.00
4 Darrius Heyward-Bey/20 10.00 25.00
5 Jason Smith/20 8.00 20.00
6 Mike Wallace/20 20.00 50.00
7 Juaquin Iglesias/15 8.00 20.00
8 Rhett Bomar/20 8.00 20.00
9 Glen Coffee/20 8.00 20.00
10 LeSean McCoy/15 20.00 50.00
11 Deon Butler/20 8.00 20.00
12 Andre Brown/20 6.00 15.00
13 Javon Ringer/20 10.00 25.00
14 Tyson Jackson/15 8.00 20.00
15 Michael Crabtree/20 50.00 100.00
16 Brandon Pettigrew/20 10.00 25.00
17 Kenny Britt/20 12.00 30.00
18 Pat White/20 10.00 25.00
19 Mike Thomas/20 10.00 25.00
20 Patrick Turner/20 8.00 20.00
21 Derrick Williams/15 8.00 20.00
22 Aaron Curry/20 10.00 25.00
23 Knowshon Moreno/20 40.00 80.00
24 Percy Harvin/20 40.00 80.00
25 Chris Wells/15 15.00 40.00
26 Mohamed Massaquoi/15 8.00 20.00
27 Brian Robiskie/20 10.00 25.00
28 Donald Brown/15 10.00 25.00
29 Josh Freeman/15 20.00 50.00
30 Mark Sanchez/15 75.00 150.00
31 Matthew Stafford/15 75.00 150.00
32 Nate Davis/20 8.00 20.00
33 Stephen McGee/20 10.00 25.00
34 Ramses Barden/20 6.00 15.00

2010 Certified

COMP.SET w/o SP's (150) 15.00 40.00
151-170 LEGEND JSY PRINT RUN 150-250
171-270 ROOKIE PRINT RUN 999
271-304 ROOK.JSY AU PRINT RUN 199-699
EXCH EXPIRATION: 5/3/2012
1 Chris Wells .30 .75
2 Larry Fitzgerald .40 1.00
3 Tim Hightower .25 .60
4 Steve Breaston .25 .60
5 Matt Ryan .40 1.00
6 Michael Turner .25 .60
7 Roddy White .30 .75
8 Tony Gonzalez .30 .75
9 Michael Jenkins .25 .60
10 Anquan Boldin .30 .75
11 Derrick Mason .30 .75
12 Joe Flacco .40 1.00
13 Ray Lewis .40 1.00
14 Ray Rice .30 .75
15 Fred Jackson .40 1.00
16 Lee Evans .30 .75
17 Marshawn Lynch .30 .75
18 Ryan Fitzpatrick .40 1.00
19 DeAngelo Williams .30 .75
20 Jonathan Stewart .30 .75
21 Matt Moore .30 .75
22 Steve Smith .30 .75
23 Brian Urlacher .40 1.00
24 Devin Hester .40 1.00
25 Greg Olsen .25 .60
26 Jay Cutler .40 1.00
27 Matt Forte .30 .75
28 Leon Hall .25 .60
29 Carson Palmer .30 .75
30 Cedric Benson .30 .75
31 Chad Ochocinco .30 .75
32 Terrell Owens .40 1.00
33 Ben Watson .25 .60
34 Jake Delhomme .30 .75
35 Jerome Harrison .25 .60
36 Josh Cribbs .40 1.00
37 Mohamed Massaquoi .30 .75
38 Felix Jones .30 .75
39 Jason Witten .40 1.00
40 Marion Barber .30 .75
41 Miles Austin .40 1.00
42 Tony Romo .50 1.25
43 Eddie Royal .25 .60
44 Brandon Lloyd .30 .75
45 Knowshon Moreno .30 .75
46 Kyle Orton .30 .75
47 Brandon Pettigrew .25 .60
48 Calvin Johnson .40 1.00
49 Matthew Stafford .40 1.00
50 Nate Burleson .25 .60
51 Aaron Rodgers .75 2.00
52 Donald Driver .30 .75
53 Greg Jennings .30 .75
54 Jermichael Finley .30 .75
55 Ryan Grant .30 .75
56 Andre Johnson .30 .75
57 Kevin Walter .30 .75
58 Matt Schaub .30 .75
59 Owen Daniels .25 .60
60 Arian Foster .30 .75
61 Austin Collie .30 .75
62 Dallas Clark .30 .75
63 Joseph Addai .30 .75
64 Peyton Manning .60 1.50
65 Pierre Garcon .30 .75
66 Reggie Wayne .30 .75
67 David Garrard .30 .75
68 Maurice Jones-Drew .30 .75
69 Mike Sims-Walker .30 .75
70 Mike Thomas .30 .75
71 Chris Chambers .30 .75
72 Dwayne Bowe .30 .75
73 Jamaal Charles .30 .75
74 Matt Cassel .30 .75
75 Thomas Jones .30 .75
76 Brandon Marshall .30 .75
77 Brian Hartline .30 .75
78 Chad Henne .30 .75
79 Davone Bess .25 .60
80 Anthony Fasano .25 .60
81 Ronnie Brown .30 .75
82 Adrian Peterson .60 1.50
83 Bernard Berrian .25 .60
84 Brett Favre 1.00 2.50
85 Percy Harvin .40 1.00
86 Sidney Rice .30 .75
87 Visanthe Shiancoe .30 .75
88 Laurence Maroney .30 .75
89 Randy Moss .40 1.00
90 Tom Brady .60 1.50
91 Wes Welker .40 1.00
92 Devery Henderson .25 .60
93 Drew Brees .40 1.00
94 Jeremy Shockey .30 .75
95 Marques Colston .30 .75
96 Pierre Thomas .30 .75
97 Brandon Jacobs .30 .75
98 Ahmad Bradshaw .30 .75
99 Eli Manning .40 1.00
100 Hakeem Nicks .30 .75
101 Steve Smith USC .30 .75
102 Braylon Edwards .30 .75
103 Jerricho Cotchery .30 .75
104 LaDainian Tomlinson .40 1.00
105 Mark Sanchez .40 1.00
106 Santonio Holmes .30 .75
107 Shonn Greene .30 .75
108 Darren McFadden .30 .75
109 Jason Campbell .30 .75
110 Darrius Heyward-Bey .30 .75
111 Zach Miller .30 .75
112 Brent Celek .30 .75
113 DeSean Jackson .30 .75
114 Jeremy Maclin .30 .75
115 Michael Vick .50 1.25
116 LeSean McCoy .30 .75
117 Antwaan Randle El .25 .60
118 Ben Roethlisberger .40 1.00
119 Heath Miller .30 .75
120 Hines Ward .30 .75
121 Rashard Mendenhall .30 .75
122 Troy Polamalu .40 1.00
123 Antonio Gates .30 .75
124 Darren Sproles .30 .75
125 Philip Rivers .40 1.00
126 Vincent Jackson .25 .60
127 Brian Westbrook .30 .75
128 Frank Gore .30 .75
129 Josh Morgan .30 .75
130 Michael Crabtree .40 1.00
131 Vernon Davis .30 .75
132 Deion Branch .25 .60
133 John Carlson .25 .60
134 Julius Jones .25 .60
135 Matt Hasselbeck .25 .60
136 T.J. Houshmandzadeh .30 .75
137 Donnie Avery .30 .75
138 James Laurinaitis .30 .75
139 Steven Jackson .30 .75
140 Cadillac Williams .30 .75
141 Josh Freeman .40 1.00
142 Kellen Winslow Jr. .30 .75
143 Bo Scaife .25 .60
144 Chris Johnson .40 1.00
145 Kenny Britt .30 .75
146 Vince Young .25 .60
147 Chris Cooley .30 .75
148 Clinton Portis .30 .75
149 Donovan McNabb .40 1.00
150 Santana Moss .30 .75
151 Jerry Rice JSY/250 6.00 15.00
153 Irving Fryar JSY/250 4.00 10.00
154 John Taylor JSY/150 4.00 10.00
155 Paul Warfield JSY/250 4.00 10.00
156 Emmitt Smith JSY/250 8.00 20.00
157 Bruce Smith JSY/150 4.00 10.00
158 Cris Carter JSY/250 5.00 12.00
159 Rickey Jackson JSY/250 4.00 10.00
160 Len Dawson JSY/150 6.00 15.00
161 Lenny Moore JSY/250 4.00 10.00
162 Jack Youngblood JSY/250 4.00 10.00
163 Terry Bradshaw JSY/250 6.00 15.00
164 Todd Christensen JSY/250 4.00 10.00
165 Earl Campbell JSY/195 5.00 12.00
166 Raymond Berry JSY/250 4.00 10.00
167 Bo Jackson JSY/250 6.00 15.00
168 Curtis Martin JSY/150 4.00 10.00
169 Ernie Davis JSY/150 30.00 50.00
170 Ronnie Lott JSY/250 5.00 12.00
171 Aaron Hernandez RC 3.00 8.00
172 Andrew Quarless RC 2.00 5.00
173 Lamarr Houston RC 2.00 5.00
174 Anthony Armstrong RC 3.00 8.00
175 Anthony Dixon RC 2.00 5.00
176 Anthony McCoy RC 1.50 4.00
177 Antonio Brown RC 3.00 8.00
178 Cody Grimm RC 2.50 6.00
179 Blair White RC 2.00 5.00
180 Brandon Banks RC 2.50 6.00
181 Brandon Graham RC 1.50 4.00
182 Brandon Spikes RC 2.00 5.00
183 Brody Eldridge RC 2.00 5.00
184 Bryan Bulaga RC 2.00 5.00
185 Carlos Dunlap RC 2.00 5.00
186 Carlton Mitchell RC 1.50 4.00
187 Chad Jones RC 2.00 5.00
188 Chris Cook RC 2.00 5.00
189 Chris Gronkowski RC 2.00 5.00
190 Chris Ivory RC 2.50 6.00
191 Clay Harbor RC 2.00 5.00
192 Corey Wootton RC 1.50 4.00
193 Dan LeFevour RC 2.00 5.00
194 Danario Alexander RC 2.00 5.00
195 Daryl Washington RC 1.50 4.00
196 David Gettis RC 2.00 5.00
197 David Nelson RC 2.00 5.00
198 David Reed RC 1.50 4.00
199 Deji Karim RC 2.00 5.00
200 Dennis Pitta RC 2.00 5.00
201 Derrick Morgan RC 1.50 4.00
202 Devin McCourty RC 2.00 5.00
203 Dezmon Briscoe RC 1.50 4.00
204 Dominique Curry RC 1.50 4.00
205 Dominique Franks RC 1.25 3.00
206 Donald Jones RC 2.00 5.00
207 Isaac Redman RC 15.00 30.00
208 Duke Calhoun RC 1.50 4.00
209 Earl Thomas RC 2.00 5.00
210 Ed Dickson RC 2.00 5.00
211 Everson Griffen RC 2.00 5.00
212 Fendi Onobun RC 1.50 4.00
213 Garrett Graham RC 1.50 4.00
214 Jacoby Ford RC 2.00 5.00
215 James Starks RC 3.00 8.00
216 Jarrett Brown RC 2.00 5.00
217 Javier Arenas RC 2.00 5.00
218 Jason Pierre-Paul RC 3.00 8.00
219 Jason Worilds RC 2.00 5.00
220 Jeremy Horne RC 1.50 4.00
221 Jerry Hughes RC 2.00 5.00
222 Jimmy Graham RC 4.00 10.00
223 Joe Haden RC 2.00 5.00
224 Joe Webb RC 2.00 5.00
225 John Conner RC 2.00 5.00
226 John Skelton RC 2.00 5.00
227 T.J. Ward RC 2.00 5.00
228 Joique Bell RC 1.50 4.00
229 Tyson Alualu RC 1.50 4.00
230 Jonathan Stupar RC 2.00 5.00
231 Mickey Shuler RC 2.00 5.00
232 Kareem Jackson RC 2.00 5.00
233 Keiland Williams RC 2.00 5.00
234 Keith Toston RC 2.00 5.00
235 Kerry Meier RC 1.50 4.00
236 Kyle Williams RC 2.00 5.00
237 Kyle Wilson RC 2.00 5.00
238 Lonyae Miller RC 1.50 4.00
239 Marc Mariani RC 2.00 5.00
240 Marlon Moore RC 2.00 5.00
241 Matt Willis RC 2.00 5.00
242 Max Hall RC 2.00 5.00
243 Max Komar RC 2.00 5.00
244 Michael Hoomanawanui RC 2.00 5.00
245 Morgan Burnett RC 2.00 5.00
246 Nate Allen RC 2.00 5.00
247 Nate Byham RC 1.50 4.00
248 NaVorro Bowman RC 2.00 5.00
249 Koa Misi RC 2.00 5.00
250 Patrick Robinson RC 2.00 5.00
251 Perrish Cox RC 1.50 4.00
252 Preston Parker RC 1.50 4.00
253 Ricky Sapp RC 1.50 4.00
254 Riley Cooper RC 2.00 5.00
255 Roberto Wallace RC 1.50 4.00
256 Russell Okung RC 2.00 5.00
257 Rusty Smith RC 2.00 5.00
258 Sean Canfield RC 1.50 4.00
259 Sean Lee RC 2.00 5.00
260 Sean Weatherspoon RC 2.00 5.00
261 Sergio Kindle RC 2.00 5.00
262 Seyi Ajirotutu RC 2.00 5.00
263 Stephen Williams RC 2.00 5.00
264 Taylor Mays RC 2.00 5.00
265 Jared Odrick RC 2.00 5.00
266 Thaddeus Lewis RC 1.50 4.00
267 Tony Moeaki RC 2.00 5.00
268 Tony Pike RC 2.00 5.00
269 Trent Williams RC 2.00 5.00
270 Victor Cruz RC 6.00 15.00
271 Andre Roberts JSY AU/699 RC 5.00 12.00
272 Armanti Edwards JSY AU/699 RC 5.00 12.00
273 Arrelious Benn JSY AU/499 RC 5.00 12.00
274 Ben Tate JSY AU/699 RC 6.00 15.00
275 Brandon LaFell JSY AU/599 RC 5.00 12.00
276 C.J. Spiller JSY AU/349 RC 10.00 25.00
277 Colt McCoy JSY AU/349 RC 25.00 50.00
278 Damian Williams JSY AU/599 RC 5.00 12.00
279 Demaryius Thomas JSY AU/599 RC 8.00 20.00
281 Dez Bryant JSY AU/349 RC 30.00 60.00
282 Emmanuel Sanders JSY AU/699 RC 5.00 12.00
283 Eric Berry JSY AU/699 RC 5.00 12.00
284 Eric Decker JSY AU/699 RC 6.00 15.00
285 Gerald McCoy JSY AU/199 RC 6.00 15.00
286 Golden Tate JSY AU/349 RC 6.00 15.00
287 Jahvid Best JSY AU/499 RC 15.00 30.00
288 Jermaine Gresham JSY AU/699 RC 6.00 15.00
289 Jimmy Clausen JSY AU/299 RC 6.00 15.00
290 Joe McKnight JSY AU/699 RC 6.00 15.00
292 Jordan Shipley JSY AU/599 RC 5.00 12.00
293 Marcus Easley JSY AU/699 RC 4.00 10.00
294 Mardy Gilyard JSY AU/699 RC 5.00 12.00
295 Mike Kafka JSY AU/699 RC 5.00 12.00
296 Mike Williams JSY AU/699 RC 12.00 30.00
297 Montario Hardesty JSY AU/699 RC 5.00 12.00
298 Ndamukong Suh JSY AU/599 RC 25.00 50.00
299 Rob Gronkowski JSY AU/699 RC 15.00 40.00
300 Rolando McClain JSY AU/699 RC 5.00 12.00
301 Ryan Mathews JSY AU/349 RC 20.00 40.00
302 Sam Bradford JSY AU/299 RC 60.00 120.00
303 Taylor Price JSY AU/699 RC 5.00 12.00
304 Tim Tebow JSY AU/299 RC 75.00 135.00
305 Toby Gerhart JSY AU/599 RC 5.00 12.00

2010 Certified Mirror Blue

*VETS: 3X TO 8X BASIC CARDS
*RK.JSY AU: .6X TO 1.5X JSY AU RC/499-699
*RK.JSY AU: .5X TO 1.2X JSY AU RC/199-349
STATED PRINT RUN 50 SER.#'d SETS
EXCH EXPIRATION: 5/3/2012
277 Colt McCoy JSY AU 40.00 80.00
281 Dez Bryant JSY AU 50.00 100.00
302 Sam Bradford JSY AU 60.00 120.00
304 Tim Tebow JSY AU 60.00 120.00

2010 Certified Mirror Gold

*VETS: 5X TO 12X BASIC CARDS
*RK.JSY AU: 1.5X TO 4X JSY AU RC/499-699
*RK.JSY AU: 1.2X TO 3X JSY AU RC/199-349
STATED PRINT RUN 25 SER.#'d SETS
EXCH EXPIRATION: 5/3/2012
276 C.J. Spiller JSY AU 50.00 120.00
277 Colt McCoy JSY AU 100.00 175.00
281 Dez Bryant JSY AU 125.00 200.00
287 Jahvid Best JSY AU 60.00 120.00
302 Sam Bradford JSY AU 150.00 300.00
304 Tim Tebow JSY AU 175.00 300.00

2010 Certified Mirror Red

*VETS 1-150: 2.5X TO 6X BASIC CARDS
1-150 VETERAN PRINT RUN 250
*LEGEND JSY: .5X TO 1.2X BASIC CARDS
151-170 LEGEND JSY PRINT RUN 60-100
152 Jack Lambert JSY/60 8.00 20.00

2010 Certified Platinum Blue

*VETS: 3X TO 8X BASIC CARDS
STATED PRINT RUN 100 SER.#'d SETS

2010 Certified Platinum Red

*VETS/999: 1.5X TO 4X BASIC CARDS
STATED PRINT RUN 999 SER.#'d SETS

2010 Certified Certified Potential

STATED PRINT RUN 999 SER.#'d SETS
*BLUE/50: .6X TO 1.5X BASIC INSERT/999
*GOLD/25: .8X TO 2X BASIC INSERT/999
*RED/100: .5X TO 1.2X BASIC INSERT/999
1 Dez Bryant 2.50 6.00
2 Eric Decker 1.00 2.50
3 Jahvid Best 1.25 3.00
4 Joe McKnight .75 2.00
5 Marcus Easley .60 1.50
6 Mike Williams 1.25 3.00
7 Sam Bradford 3.00 8.00
8 Toby Gerhart .75 2.00
9 Brandon LaFell .75 2.00
10 Colt McCoy 1.50 4.00
11 Jordan Shipley .75 2.00
12 Dexter McCluster .75 2.00
13 Eric Berry .75 2.00
14 Andre Roberts .75 2.00
15 Gerald McCoy .75 2.00
16 Ryan Mathews 1.50 4.00
17 Taylor Price .75 2.00
18 Ndamukong Suh 1.50 4.00
19 Damian Williams .75 2.00
20 Golden Tate .75 2.00
21 Rob Gronkowski 2.00 5.00
22 C.J. Spiller 1.25 3.00
23 Armanti Edwards .75 2.00
24 Tim Tebow 3.00 8.00
25 Jermaine Gresham 1.00 2.50
26 Emmanuel Sanders .75 2.00
27 Mardy Gilyard .75 2.00
28 Rolando McClain .75 2.00
29 Demaryius Thomas 1.00 2.50
30 Arrelious Benn .75 2.00
31 Jonathan Dwyer .75 2.00
32 Mike Kafka .75 2.00
33 Jimmy Clausen .75 2.00
34 Montario Hardesty .75 2.00
35 Ben Tate 1.00 2.50

2010 Certified Certified Potential Autographs

STATED PRINT RUN 25-50
EXCH EXPIRATION: 5/3/2012
1 Dez Bryant/50 30.00 60.00
2 Eric Decker/50 8.00 20.00
3 Jahvid Best/50 12.00 30.00
4 Joe McKnight/50 6.00 15.00
5 Marcus Easley/50 5.00 12.00
6 Mike Williams/50 12.00 30.00
7 Sam Bradford/25 50.00 100.00
8 Toby Gerhart/50 6.00 15.00
9 Brandon LaFell/50 6.00 15.00
10 Colt McCoy/25 30.00 60.00
11 Jordan Shipley/50 6.00 15.00
13 Eric Berry/50 12.00 30.00
14 Andre Roberts/50 6.00 15.00
16 Ryan Mathews/50 12.00 30.00
17 Taylor Price/50 6.00 15.00
18 Ndamukong Suh/50 20.00 40.00
19 Damian Williams/50 6.00 15.00
20 Golden Tate/50 6.00 15.00
21 Rob Gronkowski/50 15.00 40.00
22 C.J. Spiller/25 12.00 30.00
23 Armanti Edwards/50 6.00 15.00
24 Tim Tebow/25 50.00 100.00
25 Jermaine Gresham/50 8.00 20.00
26 Emmanuel Sanders/50 6.00 15.00
27 Mardy Gilyard/50 6.00 15.00
28 Rolando McClain/50 6.00 15.00
29 Demaryius Thomas/50 8.00 20.00
30 Arrelious Benn/50 6.00 15.00
31 Jonathan Dwyer/50 6.00 15.00
32 Mike Kafka/50 6.00 15.00
33 Jimmy Clausen/25 8.00 20.00
34 Montario Hardesty/50 6.00 15.00
35 Ben Tate/50 8.00 20.00

2010 Certified Certified Potential Materials

STATED PRINT RUN 75-250
*PRIME/50: .6X TO 1.5X BASIC JSY/250
*PRIME/50: .5X TO 1.2X BASIC JSY/75
1 Dez Bryant/250 6.00 15.00
2 Eric Decker/250 3.00 8.00
3 Jahvid Best/250 5.00 12.00
4 Joe McKnight/250 2.50 6.00
5 Marcus Easley/250 2.00 5.00
6 Mike Williams/250 4.00 10.00
7 Sam Bradford/250 8.00 20.00
8 Toby Gerhart/250 2.50 6.00
9 Brandon LaFell/250 2.50 6.00
10 Colt McCoy/250 5.00 12.00
11 Jordan Shipley/250 2.50 6.00
12 Dexter McCluster/250 2.50 6.00
13 Eric Berry/250 2.50 6.00
14 Andre Roberts/250 2.50 6.00
15 Gerald McCoy/250 2.50 6.00
16 Ryan Mathews/75 5.00 12.00
17 Taylor Price/250 2.50 6.00
18 Ndamukong Suh/250 5.00 12.00
19 Damian Williams/250 2.50 6.00
20 Golden Tate/250 2.50 6.00
21 Rob Gronkowski/250 6.00 15.00
22 C.J. Spiller/250 4.00 10.00
23 Armanti Edwards/250 2.50 6.00
24 Tim Tebow/250 8.00 20.00
25 Jermaine Gresham/250 3.00 8.00
26 Emmanuel Sanders/250 2.50 6.00
27 Mardy Gilyard/250 2.50 6.00
28 Rolando McClain/250 2.50 6.00
29 Demaryius Thomas/250 3.00 8.00
30 Arrelious Benn/250 2.50 6.00
31 Jonathan Dwyer/250 2.50 6.00
32 Mike Kafka/250 2.50 6.00
33 Jimmy Clausen/250 2.50 6.00
34 Montario Hardesty/250 2.50 6.00
35 Ben Tate/250 3.00 8.00

2010 Certified Fabric of the Game

STATED PRINT RUN 35-250
1 Adrian Peterson/250 6.00 15.00
3 Alan Page/250 4.00 10.00
4 Alex Karras/250 4.00 10.00
11 Bart Starr/250 8.00 20.00
13 Bernie Kosar/250 4.00 10.00
14 Bill Bates/250 4.00 10.00
15 Bo Jackson/250 6.00 15.00
16 Bob Griese/250 5.00 12.00
17 Bob Hayes/100 5.00 12.00
18 Bob Lilly/250 4.00 10.00
19 Boomer Esiason/250 4.00 10.00
20 Brent Jones/50 4.00 10.00
21 Brett Favre/125 10.00 25.00
23 Buck Buchanan/250 5.00 12.00
25 Carson Palmer/250 3.00 8.00
26 Cedric Benson/125 3.00 8.00
27 Charles Woodson/250 5.00 12.00
28 Charley Taylor/250 3.00 8.00
29 Charlie Joiner/250 3.00 8.00
30 Chuck Howley/250 4.00 10.00
31 Cliff Harris/120 4.00 10.00
32 Clinton Portis/125 3.00 8.00
33 Craig James/250 3.00 8.00
34 Dan Fouts/250 5.00 12.00
35 Dan Marino/250 8.00 20.00
36 Darren Woodson/35 8.00 20.00
37 D.D. Lewis/250 4.00 10.00
38 Deacon Jones/250 4.00 10.00
40 Deion Sanders/250 5.00 12.00
42 Derrick Thomas/250 10.00 25.00
44 Dick Butkus/250 6.00 15.00
45 Don Maynard/250 4.00 10.00
46 Don Meredith/100 10.00 25.00
48 Doug Flutie/250 4.00 10.00
51 Ed Too Tall Jones/250 4.00 10.00
52 Ed McCaffrey/250 3.00 8.00
53 Eddie George/250 4.00 10.00
54 Eddie Royal/200 2.50 6.00
55 Emmitt Smith/250 8.00 20.00
56 Forrest Gregg/250 5.00 12.00
57 Fran Tarkenton/250 5.00 12.00
58 Franco Harris/250 5.00 12.00
60 Fred Biletnikoff/250 5.00 12.00
61 Gale Sayers/250 6.00 15.00
62 Greg Olsen/250 2.50 6.00
63 Harvey Martin/100 4.00 10.00
64 Henry Ellard/250 3.00 8.00
65 Hank Jordan/250 5.00 12.00
67 Howie Long/250 5.00 12.00
68 Jackie Slater/250 3.00 8.00
69 Jared Allen/250 4.00 10.00
70 Jason Witten/250 4.00 10.00
71 Jay Cutler/250 4.00 10.00
72 Jerricho Cotchery/250 3.00 8.00
73 Jerry Rice/250 6.00 15.00
74 Jim Brown/250 8.00 20.00
75 Jim Kelly/250 5.00 12.00
76 Jim McMahon/250 4.00 10.00
77 Jim Otto/250 3.00 8.00
78 Jim Plunkett/200 4.00 10.00
79 Joe Flacco/250 4.00 10.00

80 Joe Greene/160 6.00 15.00
81 Joe Klecko/140 3.00 8.00
82 Joe Montana/250 8.00 20.00
83 Joe Namath/250 8.00 20.00
85 John Elway/250 8.00 20.00
86 John Taylor/35 6.00 15.00
87 Joseph Addai/250 3.00 8.00
89 Josh Freeman/115 4.00 10.00
90 Junior Seau/250 4.00 10.00
91 Justin Gage/140 2.50 6.00
92 Ken Stabler/250 6.00 15.00
94 Keyshawn Johnson/170 3.00 8.00
95 Joe Perry/100 6.00 15.00
96 Laurence Maroney/250 3.00 8.00
97 L.C. Greenwood/250 4.00 10.00
98 Len Dawson/100 5.00 12.00
100 Mark Sanchez/250 4.00 10.00
102 Knowshon Moreno/250 3.00 8.00
104 Merlin Olsen/250 4.00 10.00
106 Michael Irvin/250 6.00 15.00
107 Mohamed Massaquoi/165 3.00 8.00
109 Ozzie Newsome/250 4.00 10.00
110 Paul Warfield/100 4.00 10.00
111 Peyton Manning/250 6.00 15.00
112 Phil Simms/250 4.00 10.00
113 Philip Rivers/250 4.00 10.00
115 Randy Moss/100 4.00 10.00
116 Randy White/140 5.00 12.00
117 Ray Lewis/250 5.00 12.00
119 Raymond Berry/250 4.00 10.00
122 Rickey Jackson/250 3.00 8.00
123 Robert Meachem/250 3.00 8.00
124 Rod Smith/250 3.00 8.00
125 Rod Woodson/250 6.00 15.00
126 Roger Craig/250 4.00 10.00
127 Roger Staubach/250 6.00 15.00
128 Santana Moss/100 3.00 8.00
129 Sidney Rice/250 3.00 8.00
130 Sonny Jurgensen/250 5.00 12.00
131 Steve Largent/250 5.00 12.00
133 Steve Smith USC/125 3.00 8.00
134 Steven Jackson/125 3.00 8.00
135 Terrell Davis/150 5.00 12.00
136 Terry Bradshaw/250 6.00 15.00
137 Thurman Thomas/145 5.00 12.00
138 Brian Orakpo/250 3.00 8.00
139 Tom Rathman/250 3.00 8.00
140 Tony Dorsett/250 5.00 12.00
141 Tony Romo/125 5.00 12.00
142 Troy Aikman/250 6.00 15.00
143 Troy Polamalu/215 6.00 15.00
144 Vince Young/250 2.50 6.00
145 Walter Payton/250 15.00 30.00
146 Warren Moon/130 6.00 15.00
147 Wayne Chrebet/100 3.00 8.00
148 William Perry/250 3.00 8.00
149 Willie Brown/250 3.00 8.00
150 Bo Scaife/250 2.50 6.00

2010 Certified Fabric of the Game NFL Die Cut Prime

STATED PRINT RUN 1-25
1 Adrian Peterson/25 20.00 50.00
5 Andre Johnson/25 10.00 25.00
7 Antwaan Randle El/25 8.00 20.00
10 Barry Sanders/25 25.00 60.00
15 Bo Jackson/15 20.00 50.00
16 Bob Griese/25 15.00 40.00
24 Calvin Johnson/25 12.00 30.00
25 Carson Palmer/25 10.00 25.00
26 Cedric Benson/25 10.00 25.00
27 Charles Woodson/25 12.00 30.00
30 Chuck Howley/15 12.00 30.00
32 Clinton Portis/25 10.00 25.00
34 Dan Fouts/25 15.00 40.00
36 Darren Woodson/25 20.00 50.00
37 D.D. Lewis/25 12.00 30.00
39 DeAngelo Williams/25 10.00 25.00
41 DeMarcus Ware/25 10.00 25.00
42 Derrick Thomas/25 40.00 100.00
47 Donald Driver/25 10.00 25.00
48 Doug Flutie/25 12.00 30.00
50 Dustin Keller/25 10.00 25.00
51 Ed Too Tall Jones/25 12.00 30.00
52 Ed McCaffrey/25 10.00 25.00
54 Eddie Royal/25 8.00 20.00
55 Emmitt Smith/25 25.00 60.00
57 Fran Tarkenton/25 15.00 40.00
62 Greg Olsen/25 8.00 20.00
64 Henry Ellard/25 10.00 25.00
66 Hines Ward/20 10.00 25.00
67 Howie Long/25 15.00 40.00
69 Jared Allen/25 12.00 30.00
70 Jason Witten/25 12.00 30.00
72 Jerricho Cotchery/25 10.00 25.00
73 Jerry Rice/25 20.00 50.00
78 Jim Plunkett/25 12.00 30.00
82 Joe Montana/25 25.00 60.00
84 Tom Brady/25 20.00 50.00
87 Joseph Addai/25 10.00 25.00
90 Junior Seau/25 12.00 30.00
94 Keyshawn Johnson/25 10.00 25.00
96 Laurence Maroney/25 10.00 25.00
101 Marshawn Lynch/25 10.00 25.00
102 Knowshon Moreno/25 10.00 25.00
106 Michael Irvin/25 12.00 30.00
107 Mohamed Massaquoi/25 10.00 25.00
111 Peyton Manning/25 20.00 50.00
113 Philip Rivers/25 12.00 30.00
115 Randy Moss/25 12.00 30.00
117 Ray Lewis/25 15.00 40.00
120 Reggie Bush/25 12.00 30.00
123 Robert Meachem/25 10.00 25.00
124 Rod Smith/25 10.00 25.00
126 Roger Craig/25 12.00 30.00
128 Santana Moss/25 10.00 25.00
129 Sidney Rice/25 10.00 25.00
131 Steve Largent/25 15.00 40.00
132 Steve Smith/25 10.00 25.00
134 Steven Jackson/25 10.00 25.00
135 Terrell Davis/25 15.00 40.00
138 Brian Orakpo/25 10.00 25.00
143 Troy Polamalu/25 20.00 50.00
144 Vince Young/25 8.00 20.00
147 Wayne Chrebet/25 10.00 25.00
150 Bo Scaife/25 8.00 20.00

2010 Certified Fabric of the Game Prime

PRIME STATED PRINT RUN 2-50
1 Adrian Peterson/50 10.00 25.00
3 Alan Page/25 8.00 20.00
4 Alex Karras/21 8.00 20.00
5 Andre Johnson/50 5.00 12.00
7 Antwaan Randle El/50 4.00 10.00
10 Barry Sanders/50 12.00 30.00
13 Bernie Kosar/50 6.00 15.00
14 Bill Bates/45 6.00 15.00
16 Bob Griese/50 8.00 20.00
17 Bob Hayes/20 10.00 25.00
23 Buck Buchanan/25 8.00 20.00
24 Calvin Johnson/50 6.00 15.00
25 Carson Palmer/15 6.00 15.00
26 Cedric Benson/50 5.00 12.00
27 Charles Woodson/50 10.00 25.00
30 Chuck Howley/25 8.00 20.00
32 Clinton Portis/50 5.00 12.00
33 Craig James/50 5.00 12.00
34 Dan Fouts/25 10.00 25.00
36 Darren Woodson/50 10.00 25.00
37 D.D. Lewis/25 8.00 20.00
39 DeAngelo Williams/50 5.00 12.00
41 DeMarcus Ware/30 5.00 12.00
42 Derrick Thomas/50 25.00 60.00
44 Dick Butkus/25 12.00 30.00
45 Don Maynard/15 8.00 20.00
46 Don Meredith/25 20.00 50.00
47 Donald Driver/50 5.00 12.00
48 Doug Flutie/50 6.00 15.00
50 Dustin Keller/30 5.00 12.00
51 Ed Too Tall Jones/50 6.00 15.00
52 Ed McCaffrey/50 5.00 12.00
53 Eddie George/50 6.00 15.00
54 Eddie Royal/50 4.00 10.00
55 Emmitt Smith/50 12.00 30.00
57 Fran Tarkenton/50 8.00 20.00
58 Franco Harris/25 10.00 25.00
60 Fred Biletnikoff/25 10.00 25.00
61 Gale Sayers/50 10.00 25.00
62 Greg Olsen/50 4.00 10.00
63 Harvey Martin/25 6.00 15.00
64 Henry Ellard/50 5.00 12.00
65 Hank Jordan/15 10.00 25.00
66 Hines Ward/50 5.00 12.00
68 Jackie Slater/25 6.00 15.00
69 Jared Allen/50 6.00 15.00
70 Jason Witten/50 6.00 15.00
72 Jerricho Cotchery/50 5.00 12.00
73 Jerry Rice/25 12.00 30.00
74 Jim Brown/15 15.00 40.00
75 Jim Kelly/20 10.00 25.00
76 Jim McMahon/25 8.00 20.00
77 Jim Otto/25 6.00 15.00
78 Jim Plunkett/50 6.00 15.00
79 Joe Flacco/30 6.00 15.00
82 Joe Montana/50 12.00 30.00
83 Joe Namath/15 15.00 40.00
84 Tom Brady/50 10.00 25.00
90 Junior Seau/50 6.00 15.00
91 Justin Gage/20 5.00 12.00
92 Ken Stabler/25 12.00 30.00
93 Kevin Boss/40 6.00 20.00
94 Keyshawn Johnson/50 5.00 12.00
95 Joe Perry/15 12.00 30.00
96 Laurence Maroney/50 5.00 12.00
98 Len Dawson/15 10.00 25.00
101 Marshawn Lynch/50 5.00 12.00
102 Knowshon Moreno/50 5.00 12.00
106 Michael Irvin/50 6.00 15.00
107 Mohamed Massaquoi/50 5.00 12.00
108 Owen Daniels/35 4.00 10.00
110 Paul Warfield/15 8.00 20.00
111 Peyton Manning/50 10.00 25.00
112 Phil Simms/25 8.00 20.00
113 Philip Rivers/48 6.00 15.00
114 Priest Holmes/35 5.00 12.00
115 Randy Moss/50 6.00 15.00
117 Ray Lewis/50 8.00 20.00
118 Ray Rice/35 5.00 12.00
120 Reggie Bush/50 6.00 15.00
122 Rickey Jackson/15 6.00 15.00
123 Robert Meachem/50 5.00 12.00
124 Rod Smith/50 5.00 12.00
126 Roger Craig/50 6.00 15.00
128 Santana Moss/50 5.00 12.00
129 Sidney Rice/50 5.00 12.00
131 Steve Largent/50 8.00 20.00
132 Steve Smith/50 5.00 12.00
133 Steve Smith USC/50 5.00 12.00
134 Steven Jackson/50 5.00 12.00
135 Terrell Davis/50 8.00 20.00
137 Thurman Thomas/50 8.00 20.00
138 Brian Orakpo/50 5.00 12.00
139 Tom Rathman/50 5.00 12.00
143 Troy Polamalu/50 12.00 30.00
144 Vince Young/50 4.00 10.00
145 Walter Payton/25 25.00 60.00
147 Wayne Chrebet/50 5.00 12.00
148 William Perry/25 6.00 15.00
149 Willie Brown/25 6.00 15.00
150 Bo Scaife/50 4.00 10.00

2010 Certified Fabric of the Game Team Die Cut

STATED PRINT RUN 5-25
1 Adrian Peterson/15 15.00 40.00
3 Alan Page/25 10.00 25.00
11 Bart Starr/25 20.00 50.00
14 Bill Bates/15 10.00 25.00
15 Bo Jackson/25 15.00 40.00
16 Bob Griese/20 12.00 30.00
18 Bob Lilly/25 10.00 25.00
19 Boomer Esiason/25 10.00 25.00
23 Buck Buchanan/25 12.00 30.00
25 Carson Palmer/25 8.00 20.00
27 Charles Woodson/25 10.00 25.00
28 Charley Taylor/25 8.00 20.00
29 Charlie Joiner/25 8.00 20.00
30 Chuck Howley/25 10.00 25.00
32 Clinton Portis/15 8.00 20.00
34 Dan Fouts/25 12.00 30.00
35 Dan Marino/25 20.00 50.00
37 D.D. Lewis/25 10.00 25.00
38 Deacon Jones/25 10.00 25.00
40 Deion Sanders/25 12.00 30.00
42 Derrick Thomas/15 40.00 100.00
44 Dick Butkus/25 15.00 40.00
45 Don Maynard/25 10.00 25.00
48 Doug Flutie/25 10.00 25.00
51 Ed Too Tall Jones/25 10.00 25.00
52 Ed McCaffrey/25 8.00 20.00
53 Eddie George/25 10.00 25.00
54 Eddie Royal/25 6.00 15.00
55 Emmitt Smith/25 20.00 50.00
56 Forrest Gregg/25 12.00 30.00
57 Fran Tarkenton/25 12.00 30.00
58 Franco Harris/25 12.00 30.00
60 Fred Biletnikoff/25 12.00 30.00
61 Gale Sayers/25 15.00 40.00
62 Greg Olsen/25 6.00 15.00
64 Henry Ellard/25 8.00 20.00
65 Hank Jordan/25 12.00 30.00
68 Jackie Slater/25 8.00 20.00
69 Jared Allen/25 10.00 25.00
71 Jay Cutler/25 10.00 25.00
72 Jerricho Cotchery/15 8.00 20.00
74 Jim Brown/25 20.00 50.00
75 Jim Kelly/25 12.00 30.00
76 Jim McMahon/25 10.00 25.00
77 Jim Otto/25 8.00 20.00
78 Jim Plunkett/25 10.00 25.00
79 Joe Flacco/25 10.00 25.00
80 Joe Greene/25 15.00 40.00
82 Joe Montana/25 20.00 50.00
83 Joe Namath/25 20.00 50.00
85 John Elway/25 20.00 50.00
87 Joseph Addai/25 8.00 20.00
89 Josh Freeman/25 10.00 25.00
90 Junior Seau/25 10.00 25.00
92 Ken Stabler/25 15.00 40.00
94 Keyshawn Johnson/25 8.00 20.00
100 Mark Sanchez/25 10.00 25.00
102 Knowshon Moreno/25 8.00 20.00
104 Merlin Olsen/25 10.00 25.00
106 Michael Irvin/25 10.00 25.00
107 Mohamed Massaquoi/25 8.00 20.00
109 Ozzie Newsome/25 10.00 25.00
111 Peyton Manning/25 15.00 40.00
112 Phil Simms/25 10.00 25.00
116 Randy White/25 12.00 30.00
117 Ray Lewis/25 12.00 30.00
118 Ray Rice/15 8.00 20.00
119 Raymond Berry/25 10.00 25.00
122 Rickey Jackson/25 8.00 20.00
123 Robert Meachem/25 8.00 20.00
124 Rod Smith/25 8.00 20.00
126 Roger Craig/25 10.00 25.00
127 Roger Staubach/25 12.00 30.00
129 Sidney Rice/25 8.00 20.00
130 Sonny Jurgensen/25 12.00 30.00
131 Steve Largent/25 12.00 30.00
136 Terry Bradshaw/25 15.00 40.00
138 Brian Orakpo/25 8.00 20.00
139 Tom Rathman/25 8.00 20.00
140 Tony Dorsett/25 12.00 30.00
142 Troy Aikman/25 15.00 40.00
144 Vince Young/25 6.00 15.00
145 Walter Payton/25 30.00 80.00
146 Warren Moon/25 15.00 40.00
147 Wayne Chrebet/15 8.00 20.00
149 Willie Brown/25 8.00 20.00
150 Bo Scaife/25 6.00 15.00

2010 Certified Fabric of the Game Combos Prime

PRIME PRINT RUN 25 SER.#'d SETS
*BASE CMBO/70-100: .25X TO .6X PRIME/25
1 Tom Brady 20.00 50.00
Peyton Manning
2 Larry Fitzgerald 8.00 20.00
Chris Wells
3 Sidney Rice 12.00 30.00
Charles Woodson
4 Frank Gore 6.00 15.00
Patrick Willis
5 Brian Urlacher 8.00 20.00
Devin Hester
6 Adrian Peterson 10.00 25.00
Chris Johnson
7 Randy Moss 8.00 20.00
Darrelle Revis
8 Reggie Bush 8.00 20.00
Devery Henderson
9 Ricky Williams 6.00 15.00
Jamaal Charles
10 DeSean Jackson 6.00 15.00
Terence Newman
11 Andre Johnson 8.00 20.00
Calvin Johnson
12 Tony Romo 10.00 25.00
Eli Manning
14 Marion Barber 6.00 15.00
Felix Jones
15 DeMarcus Ware 6.00 15.00
Will Smith

2010 Certified Fabric of the Game Jersey Number Autographs

STATED PRINT RUN 5-25
EXCH EXPIRATION: 5/3/2012
1 Adrian Peterson/15
3 Alan Page/25 15.00 40.00
4 Alex Karras/25 15.00 40.00
11 Bart Starr/25 75.00 135.00
13 Bernie Kosar/25 15.00 40.00
14 Bill Bates/25 20.00 50.00
15 Bo Jackson/25 40.00 80.00
16 Bob Griese/25 EXCH 20.00 50.00
18 Bob Lilly/25 20.00 50.00
19 Boomer Esiason/25 15.00 40.00
20 Brent Jones/25 12.00 30.00
21 Brett Favre/10
24 Calvin Johnson/15 20.00 50.00
25 Carson Palmer/9
26 Cedric Benson/15 12.00 30.00
28 Charley Taylor/25 12.00 30.00
29 Charlie Joiner/25 12.00 30.00
30 Chuck Howley/25 15.00 40.00
33 Craig James/25 12.00 30.00
34 Dan Fouts/25 25.00 60.00
35 Dan Marino/25 100.00 175.00
36 Darren Woodson/25 25.00 50.00
37 D.D. Lewis/25 15.00 40.00
38 Deacon Jones/25 15.00 40.00
40 Deion Sanders/25 40.00 80.00
44 Dick Butkus/25 40.00 80.00
45 Don Maynard/25 15.00 40.00
48 Doug Flutie/25 15.00 40.00
51 Ed Too Tall Jones/25 20.00 50.00
52 Ed McCaffrey/25 12.00 30.00
53 Eddie George/25 20.00 50.00
55 Emmitt Smith/10
56 Forrest Gregg/25 12.00 30.00
57 Fran Tarkenton/25 25.00 60.00
58 Franco Harris/25 25.00 50.00
60 Fred Biletnikoff/25 20.00 50.00
61 Gale Sayers/25 30.00 60.00
64 Henry Ellard/25 15.00 40.00
67 Howie Long/25 30.00 60.00
68 Jackie Slater/25 EXCH
70 Jason Witten/10
71 Jay Cutler/15 20.00 50.00
73 Jerry Rice/5
74 Jim Brown/25 50.00 100.00
75 Jim Kelly/25 25.00 60.00
76 Jim McMahon/25 15.00 40.00
77 Jim Otto/25 15.00 40.00
78 Jim Plunkett/25 15.00 40.00
79 Joe Flacco/10
80 Joe Greene/25 30.00 60.00
81 Joe Klecko/25 12.00 30.00
82 Joe Montana/13
83 Joe Namath/21 50.00 100.00
84 Tom Brady/12
85 John Elway/25 75.00 150.00
86 John Taylor/25 15.00 40.00
90 Junior Seau/25 40.00 80.00
92 Ken Stabler/25 40.00 80.00
94 Keyshawn Johnson/25 12.00 30.00
95 Joe Perry/25 EXCH 30.00 60.00
97 L.C. Greenwood/25 15.00 40.00
98 Len Dawson/25 20.00 50.00
100 Mark Sanchez/25 40.00 80.00
102 Knowshon Moreno/5
104 Merlin Olsen/12
106 Michael Irvin/25 40.00 80.00
109 Ozzie Newsome/25 15.00 40.00
110 Paul Warfield/25 15.00 40.00
111 Peyton Manning/25 75.00 150.00
112 Phil Simms/25 25.00 50.00
113 Philip Rivers/10
114 Priest Holmes/19 12.00 30.00
116 Randy White/25 25.00 50.00
118 Ray Rice/25 15.00 40.00
119 Raymond Berry/25 15.00 40.00
122 Rickey Jackson/10
124 Rod Smith/25 15.00 40.00
125 Rod Woodson/25 40.00 80.00
126 Roger Craig/25 15.00 40.00
127 Roger Staubach/25 60.00 120.00
129 Sidney Rice/25 15.00 40.00
130 Sonny Jurgensen/25 20.00 50.00
131 Steve Largent/25 20.00 50.00
135 Terrell Davis/25 20.00 50.00
137 Thurman Thomas/25 30.00 60.00
139 Tom Rathman/25 12.00 30.00
140 Tony Dorsett/25 40.00 80.00
141 Tony Romo/10
142 Troy Aikman/25 40.00 80.00
143 Troy Polamalu/25 125.00 250.00
144 Vince Young/10
146 Warren Moon/25 40.00 80.00
147 Wayne Chrebet/25 12.00 30.00
148 William Perry/25 15.00 40.00
149 Willie Brown/25 15.00 40.00

2010 Certified Gold Team

STATED PRINT RUN 999 SER.#'d SETS
*MIRROR/100: .8X TO 2X BASIC INSERTS
1 Chris Johnson 1.25 3.00
2 Steven Jackson 1.00 2.50
3 Peyton Manning 2.00 5.00
4 Wes Welker 1.25 3.00
5 Brett Favre 3.00 8.00
6 Adrian Peterson 2.00 5.00
7 Larry Fitzgerald 1.25 3.00
8 Andre Johnson 1.00 2.50
9 Drew Brees 1.25 3.00
10 Aaron Rodgers 2.50 6.00

2010 Certified Gold Team Materials

STATED PRINT RUN 100-250
2 Steven Jackson/100 3.00 8.00
3 Peyton Manning/125 6.00 15.00
5 Brett Favre/125 10.00 25.00
6 Adrian Peterson/250 6.00 15.00

2010 Certified Gold Team Materials Prime

STATED PRINT RUN 10-50
1 Chris Johnson/50 6.00 15.00
2 Steven Jackson/50 5.00 12.00
*3 Peyton Manning/50 10.00 25.00
4 Wes Welker/50 6.00 15.00
5 Brett Favre/10
6 Adrian Peterson/50 10.00 25.00
8 Andre Johnson/50 5.00 12.00

2010 Certified Mirror Blue Materials

*LEGEND JSY: .6X TO 1.5X BASIC JSY
BLUE STATED PRINT RUN 15-100
12 Joe Flacco/100 4.00 10.00
13 Ray Lewis/100 5.00 12.00
19 DeAngelo Williams/40 4.00 10.00
20 Jonathan Stewart/20 5.00 12.00
24 Devin Hester/100 4.00 10.00
25 Greg Olsen/100 2.50 6.00
26 Jay Cutler/100 4.00 10.00
27 Matt Forte/100 3.00 8.00
29 Carson Palmer/100 3.00 8.00
30 Cedric Benson/100 3.00 8.00
31 Chad Ochocinco/40 4.00 10.00
32 Terrell Owens/100 4.00 10.00
37 Mohamed Massaquoi/100 3.00 8.00
38 Felix Jones/100 3.00 8.00
39 Jason Witten/100 4.00 10.00
40 Marion Barber/100 3.00 8.00
42 Tony Romo/100 5.00 12.00
43 Eddie Royal/100 2.50 6.00
45 Knowshon Moreno/100 3.00 8.00
46 Kyle Orton/100 3.00 8.00
48 Calvin Johnson/60 5.00 12.00
53 Greg Jennings/15 5.00 12.00
55 Ryan Grant/100 3.00 8.00
58 Matt Schaub/100 3.00 8.00
62 Dallas Clark/100 3.00 8.00
63 Joseph Addai/100 3.00 8.00
64 Peyton Manning/100 6.00 15.00
67 David Garrard/100 3.00 8.00
68 Maurice Jones-Drew/100 3.00 8.00
69 Mike Sims-Walker/100 3.00 8.00
72 Dwayne Bowe/100 3.00 8.00
73 Jamaal Charles/100 3.00 8.00
74 Matt Cassel/100 3.00 8.00
76 Brandon Marshall/40 4.00 10.00
82 Adrian Peterson/100 6.00 15.00
84 Brett Favre/100 10.00 25.00
85 Percy Harvin/100 4.00 10.00
86 Sidney Rice/100 3.00 8.00
88 Laurence Maroney/100 3.00 8.00
89 Randy Moss/100 4.00 10.00
90 Tom Brady/100 6.00 15.00
92 Devery Henderson/100 2.50 6.00
94 Jeremy Shockey/100 3.00 8.00
102 Braylon Edwards/100 3.00 8.00
103 Jerricho Cotchery/100 3.00 8.00
105 Mark Sanchez/100 4.00 10.00
108 Darren McFadden/100 3.00 8.00
109 Jason Campbell/100 3.00 8.00
112 Brent Celek/100 3.00 8.00
119 Heath Miller/25 5.00 12.00
121 Rashard Mendenhall/100 3.00 8.00
122 Troy Polamalu/100 4.00 10.00
123 Antonio Gates/100 3.00 8.00
125 Philip Rivers/100 4.00 10.00
126 Vincent Jackson/100 2.50 6.00
128 Frank Gore/100 3.00 8.00
131 Vernon Davis/100 3.00 8.00
139 Steven Jackson/100 3.00 8.00
141 Josh Freeman/100 4.00 10.00
143 Bo Scaife/100 2.50 6.00
144 Chris Johnson/100 4.00 10.00
145 Kenny Britt/100 3.00 8.00
146 Vince Young/100 2.50 6.00
148 Clinton Portis/100 3.00 8.00
150 Santana Moss/100 3.00 8.00
151 Jerry Rice/50 12.00 30.00
152 Jack Lambert/50 10.00 25.00
153 Irving Fryar/50 5.00 12.00
154 John Taylor/50 5.00 12.00
155 Paul Warfield/50 6.00 15.00
156 Emmitt Smith/50 12.00 30.00
157 Bruce Smith/50 6.00 15.00
158 Cris Carter/50 8.00 20.00
159 Rickey Jackson/50 5.00 12.00
160 Len Dawson/50 8.00 20.00
161 Lenny Moore/50 6.00 15.00
162 Jack Youngblood/50 5.00 12.00
163 Terry Bradshaw/50 10.00 25.00
164 Todd Christensen/50 5.00 12.00
165 Earl Campbell/50 8.00 20.00
166 Raymond Berry/50 6.00 15.00
167 Bo Jackson/50 10.00 25.00
168 Curtis Martin/50 6.00 15.00
169 Ernie Davis/50 30.00 80.00
170 Ronnie Lott/50 8.00 20.00
271 Andre Roberts/50 4.00 10.00
272 Armanti Edwards/50 4.00 10.00
273 Arrelious Benn/50 4.00 10.00
274 Ben Tate/50 5.00 12.00
275 Brandon LaFell/50 4.00 10.00
276 C.J. Spiller/50 6.00 15.00
277 Colt McCoy/50 8.00 20.00
278 Damian Williams/50 4.00 10.00
279 Demaryius Thomas/50 5.00 12.00
280 Dexter McCluster/50 4.00 10.00
281 Dez Bryant/50 10.00 25.00
282 Emmanuel Sanders/50 4.00 10.00
283 Eric Berry/50 4.00 10.00
284 Eric Decker/50 5.00 12.00
285 Gerald McCoy/50 4.00 10.00
286 Golden Tate/50 4.00 10.00
287 Jahvid Best/50 8.00 25.00
288 Jermaine Gresham/50 5.00 12.00
289 Jimmy Clausen/50 4.00 10.00
290 Joe McKnight/50 4.00 10.00
291 Jonathan Dwyer/50 4.00 10.00
292 Jordan Shipley/50 4.00 10.00
293 Marcus Easley/50 3.00 8.00
294 Mardy Gilyard/50 4.00 10.00
295 Mike Kafka/50 4.00 10.00
296 Mike Williams/50 6.00 15.00
297 Montario Hardesty/50 4.00 10.00
298 Ndamukong Suh/50 8.00 20.00
299 Rob Gronkowski/50 10.00 25.00
300 Rolando McClain/50 4.00 10.00
301 Ryan Mathews/50 8.00 20.00
302 Sam Bradford/50 12.00 30.00
303 Taylor Price/50 4.00 10.00
304 Tim Tebow/50 12.00 30.00
305 Toby Gerhart/50 4.00 10.00

2010 Certified Mirror Gold Materials

*GLD LEG/25: .8X TO 2X BASE JSY
*GLD ROOKIE/25: .6X TO 1.5X BLUE/50
GOLD STATED PRINT RUN 15-50
1 Chris Wells/5
5 Matt Ryan/15 6.00 15.00
7 Roddy White/50 4.00 10.00
12 Joe Flacco/50 5.00 12.00
13 Ray Lewis/50 6.00 15.00
14 Ray Rice/50 4.00 10.00
16 Lee Evans/50 4.00 10.00
17 Marshawn Lynch/50 4.00 10.00
19 DeAngelo Williams/50 4.00 10.00
20 Jonathan Stewart/50 4.00 10.00
22 Steve Smith/50 4.00 10.00
24 Devin Hester/50 5.00 12.00
25 Greg Olsen/50 3.00 8.00
26 Jay Cutler/50 5.00 12.00
27 Matt Forte/50 4.00 10.00
29 Carson Palmer/50 4.00 10.00
30 Cedric Benson/50 4.00 10.00
31 Chad Ochocinco/50 4.00 10.00
37 Mohamed Massaquoi/50 4.00 10.00
38 Felix Jones/50 4.00 10.00
39 Jason Witten/50 5.00 12.00
40 Marion Barber/50 4.00 10.00
42 Tony Romo/50 6.00 15.00
43 Eddie Royal/50 3.00 8.00
45 Knowshon Moreno/50 4.00 10.00
46 Kyle Orton/50 4.00 10.00
48 Calvin Johnson/50 5.00 12.00
49 Matthew Stafford/20 6.00 15.00
52 Donald Driver/50 4.00 10.00
55 Ryan Grant/50 4.00 10.00
56 Andre Johnson/50 4.00 10.00
62 Dallas Clark/50 4.00 10.00
63 Joseph Addai/50 4.00 10.00
64 Peyton Manning/50 8.00 20.00
67 David Garrard/50 4.00 10.00
68 Maurice Jones-Drew/50 4.00 10.00
69 Mike Sims-Walker/50 4.00 10.00
72 Dwayne Bowe/50 4.00 10.00
73 Jamaal Charles/50 4.00 10.00
74 Matt Cassel/50 4.00 10.00
81 Ronnie Brown/50 4.00 10.00
82 Adrian Peterson/50 8.00 20.00
83 Bernard Berrian/50 3.00 8.00
84 Brett Favre/25 15.00 40.00
85 Percy Harvin/50 5.00 12.00
86 Sidney Rice/50 4.00 10.00
87 Visanthe Shiancoe/50 4.00 10.00
88 Laurence Maroney/50 4.00 10.00
89 Randy Moss/50 5.00 12.00
90 Tom Brady/50 8.00 20.00
91 Wes Welker/50 5.00 12.00
92 Devery Henderson/50 3.00 8.00
94 Jeremy Shockey/50 4.00 10.00
97 Brandon Jacobs/50 4.00 10.00
98 Ahmad Bradshaw/50 4.00 10.00
102 Braylon Edwards/50 4.00 10.00
103 Jerricho Cotchery/50 4.00 10.00
108 Darren McFadden/50 4.00 10.00
112 Brent Celek/50 4.00 10.00
117 Antwaan Randle El/50 3.00 8.00
120 Hines Ward/50 4.00 10.00
121 Rashard Mendenhall/50 4.00 10.00
122 Troy Polamalu/50 5.00 12.00
123 Antonio Gates/50 4.00 10.00
124 Darren Sproles/50 4.00 10.00
125 Philip Rivers/50 5.00 12.00
126 Vincent Jackson/50 3.00 8.00
128 Frank Gore/50 4.00 10.00
131 Vernon Davis/50 4.00 10.00
132 Deion Branch/50 3.00 8.00
139 Steven Jackson/50 4.00 10.00
140 Cadillac Williams/50 4.00 10.00
143 Bo Scaife/50 3.00 8.00
144 Chris Johnson/50 5.00 12.00
145 Kenny Britt/50 4.00 10.00
146 Vince Young/50 3.00 8.00
147 Chris Cooley/50 4.00 10.00
148 Clinton Portis/50 4.00 10.00
150 Santana Moss/50 4.00 10.00
151 Jerry Rice/25 15.00 40.00
153 Irving Fryar/25 6.00 15.00
154 John Taylor/25 6.00 15.00
155 Paul Warfield/25 8.00 20.00
156 Emmitt Smith/25 15.00 40.00
157 Bruce Smith/25 8.00 20.00
158 Cris Carter/25 10.00 25.00
159 Rickey Jackson/25 6.00 15.00
160 Len Dawson/25 10.00 25.00
161 Lenny Moore/25 8.00 20.00
163 Terry Bradshaw/25 12.00 30.00
164 Todd Christensen/25 6.00 15.00
167 Bo Jackson/25 12.00 30.00
168 Curtis Martin/25 8.00 20.00
169 Ernie Davis/25 40.00 100.00

2010 Certified Mirror Blue Signatures

BLUE PRINT RUN 50 SER.#'d SETS
*RED/200-250: .3X TO .8X BLUE AU/50
EXCH EXPIRATION: 5/3/2012
171 Aaron Hernandez 10.00 25.00
175 Anthony Dixon 6.00 15.00
176 Anthony McCoy 5.00 12.00
177 Antonio Brown 10.00 25.00
179 Blair White 6.00 15.00
181 Brandon Graham 5.00 12.00
182 Brandon Spikes 6.00 15.00
184 Bryan Bulaga 6.00 15.00
185 Carlos Dunlap 6.00 15.00
186 Carlton Mitchell 5.00 12.00
187 Chad Jones 6.00 15.00
189 Chris Gronkowski 6.00 15.00
192 Corey Wootton 5.00 12.00
193 Dan LeFevour 6.00 15.00
194 Danario Alexander 6.00 15.00
196 David Gettis 6.00 15.00
199 Deji Karim 6.00 15.00
201 Derrick Morgan 5.00 12.00
202 Devin McCourty 6.00 15.00
203 Dezmon Briscoe 5.00 12.00
204 Dominique Curry 5.00 12.00
205 Dominique Franks 4.00 10.00
206 Donald Jones 6.00 15.00
209 Earl Thomas 6.00 15.00
210 Ed Dickson 6.00 15.00
211 Everson Griffen 6.00 15.00
212 Fendi Onobun 5.00 12.00
213 Garrett Graham 5.00 12.00
214 Jacoby Ford 12.00 30.00
215 James Starks 25.00 60.00
216 Jarrett Brown 6.00 15.00
217 Javier Arenas 8.00 20.00
218 Jason Pierre-Paul 15.00 30.00
219 Jason Worilds 6.00 15.00
221 Jerry Hughes 6.00 15.00
222 Jimmy Graham 12.00 30.00
223 Joe Haden 6.00 15.00
225 John Conner 6.00 15.00
226 John Skelton 6.00 15.00
228 Joique Bell 5.00 12.00
229 Tyson Alualu 5.00 12.00
231 Mickey Shuler 6.00 15.00
235 Kerry Meier 5.00 12.00
238 Lonyae Miller 5.00 12.00
244 Michael Hoomanawanui 6.00 15.00
245 Morgan Burnett 6.00 15.00
249 Koa Misi 6.00 15.00
250 Patrick Robinson 6.00 15.00
251 Perrish Cox 5.00 12.00
252 Preston Parker 5.00 12.00
253 Ricky Sapp 5.00 12.00
254 Riley Cooper 6.00 15.00
257 Rusty Smith 15.00 30.00
258 Sean Canfield 5.00 12.00
259 Sean Lee 6.00 15.00
260 Sean Weatherspoon 6.00 15.00
261 Sergio Kindle 6.00 15.00
262 Seyi Ajirotutu 6.00 15.00
264 Taylor Mays 6.00 15.00
266 Thaddeus Lewis 5.00 12.00
268 Tony Pike 6.00 15.00

2010 Certified Mirror Gold Signatures

*GOLD ROOK.171-268: .5X TO 1.2X BLUE AU
GOLD STATED PRINT RUN 5-25
EXCH EXPIRATION: 5/3/2012
1 Chris Wells/25 10.00 25.00
7 Roddy White/25 10.00 25.00
8 Tony Gonzalez/15 10.00 25.00
14 Ray Rice/25 12.00 30.00
20 Jonathan Stewart/15 10.00 25.00
36 Josh Cribbs/25 12.00 30.00
38 Felix Jones/25 12.00 30.00
45 Knowshon Moreno/25 10.00 25.00
46 Kyle Orton/25 10.00 25.00
55 Ryan Grant/25 12.00 30.00
58 Matt Schaub/25 10.00 25.00
61 Austin Collie/25 12.00 30.00
62 Dallas Clark/15 15.00 40.00
64 Peyton Manning/18 60.00 120.00
72 Dwayne Bowe/15 10.00 25.00
73 Jamaal Charles/25 10.00 25.00
83 Bernard Berrian/25 8.00 20.00
86 Sidney Rice/25 10.00 25.00
87 Visanthe Shiancoe/15 EXCH
97 Brandon Jacobs/15 10.00 25.00
102 Braylon Edwards/25 10.00 25.00
106 Santonio Holmes/25 10.00 25.00
107 Shonn Greene/25 10.00 25.00
112 Brent Celek/25 12.00 30.00
114 Jeremy Maclin/25 10.00 25.00
119 Heath Miller/25 10.00 25.00
121 Rashard Mendenhall/25 10.00 25.00
122 Troy Polamalu/25 100.00 175.00
126 Vincent Jackson/25 8.00 20.00
140 Cadillac Williams/15 10.00 25.00
145 Kenny Britt/25 10.00 25.00
147 Chris Cooley/15
149 Donovan McNabb/25 25.00 50.00
151 Jerry Rice JSY/25 75.00 150.00
153 Irving Fryar JSY/25 15.00 40.00
154 John Taylor JSY/25 15.00 40.00
155 Paul Warfield JSY/24
157 Bruce Smith JSY/25 30.00 60.00
159 Rickey Jackson JSY/25 30.00 60.00
160 Len Dawson JSY/25 25.00 60.00
161 Lenny Moore JSY/25 20.00 50.00
164 Todd Christensen JSY/25 20.00 50.00
168 Curtis Martin JSY/25 30.00 60.00

2010 Certified Rookie Fabric of the Game

STATED PRINT RUN 35-250
*TEAM DC/25: .8X TO 2X BASIC JSY/250
*TEAM DC/25: .5X TO 1.2X BASIC JSY/35
1 Colt McCoy/250 5.00 12.00
2 Sam Bradford/250 10.00 25.00
3 Jordan Shipley/250 2.50 6.00
4 Gerald McCoy/250 2.50 6.00
5 Rob Gronkowski/250 6.00 15.00
6 Emmanuel Sanders/250 2.50 6.00
7 Arrelious Benn/250 2.50 6.00
8 Ben Tate/250 3.00 8.00
9 Dez Bryant/250 8.00 20.00
10 Dexter McCluster/250 2.50 6.00
11 Mike Kafka/250 2.50 6.00
12 Tim Tebow/250 10.00 25.00
13 Mike Williams/250 4.00 10.00
14 Eric Berry/250 2.50 6.00
15 Eric Decker/250 3.00 8.00
16 C.J. Spiller/250 4.00 10.00
17 Ndamukong Suh/250 5.00 12.00
18 Marcus Easley/250 2.00 5.00
19 Taylor Price/250 2.50 6.00
20 Montario Hardesty/250 2.50 6.00
21 Rolando McClain/250 2.50 6.00
22 Jahvid Best/250 5.00 12.00
23 Brandon LaFell/250 2.50 6.00
24 Mardy Gilyard/250 2.50 6.00
25 Jonathan Dwyer/250 2.50 6.00
26 Andre Roberts/250 2.50 6.00
27 Jermaine Gresham/250 3.00 8.00
28 Toby Gerhart/250 2.50 6.00
29 Ryan Mathews/35 8.00 20.00
30 Joe McKnight/250 2.50 6.00
31 Jimmy Clausen/250 2.50 6.00
32 Damian Williams/250 2.50 6.00
33 Armanti Edwards/250 2.50 6.00
34 Demaryius Thomas/250 3.00 8.00
35 Golden Tate/250 2.50 6.00

2010 Certified Rookie Fabric of the Game Jersey Number Autographs

STATED PRINT RUN 25 SER.#'d SETS
EXCH EXPIRATION: 5/3/2012
1 Colt McCoy 40.00 80.00
2 Sam Bradford 75.00 150.00
3 Jordan Shipley 10.00 25.00
4 Gerald McCoy 10.00 25.00
5 Rob Gronkowski 30.00 60.00
6 Emmanuel Sanders 10.00 25.00
7 Arrelious Benn 10.00 25.00
8 Ben Tate 12.00 30.00
9 Dez Bryant 50.00 100.00
11 Mike Kafka 10.00 25.00
12 Tim Tebow 75.00 150.00
13 Mike Williams 20.00 50.00
14 Eric Berry 10.00 25.00
15 Eric Decker 12.00 30.00
16 C.J. Spiller 15.00 40.00
17 Ndamukong Suh 30.00 60.00
18 Marcus Easley 8.00 20.00
19 Taylor Price 10.00 25.00
20 Montario Hardesty 10.00 25.00
21 Rolando McClain 10.00 25.00
22 Jahvid Best 20.00 50.00
23 Brandon LaFell 10.00 25.00
24 Mardy Gilyard 10.00 25.00
25 Jonathan Dwyer 10.00 25.00
26 Andre Roberts 10.00 25.00
27 Jermaine Gresham 12.00 30.00
28 Toby Gerhart 10.00 25.00
29 Ryan Mathews 20.00 50.00
30 Joe McKnight 10.00 25.00
31 Jimmy Clausen 10.00 25.00
32 Damian Williams 10.00 25.00
33 Armanti Edwards 10.00 25.00
34 Demaryius Thomas 12.00 30.00
35 Golden Tate 10.00 25.00

2010 Certified Shirt Off My Back Combos Prime

PRIME PRINT RUN 25 SER.#'d SETS
*BASE COMBO/100: .25X TO .6X PRIME/25
1 Bernard Berrian 6.00 15.00
Visanthe Shiancoe
2 Cadillac Williams 6.00 15.00
Ronnie Brown
3 Carson Palmer 8.00 20.00
Mark Sanchez
4 Donald Driver 6.00 15.00
Greg Jennings
6 Brandon Jacobs 8.00 20.00
Ahmad Bradshaw
7 Louis Murphy 6.00 15.00
Darren McFadden
9 Joe Flacco 8.00 20.00
Ray Rice
10 DeAngelo Williams 6.00 15.00
Jonathan Stewart
12 Philip Rivers 8.00 20.00
Eli Manning
13 Santana Moss 6.00 15.00
Chris Cooley
14 Vince Young 5.00 12.00
Bo Scaife
15 Joseph Addai 6.00 15.00
Marshawn Lynch

2010 Certified Shirt Off My Back Materials

STATED PRINT RUN 55-250
1 Antonio Gates/250 3.00 8.00
4 Steven Jackson/125 3.00 8.00
6 Maurice Jones-Drew/250 3.00 8.00
7 Tony Romo/125 5.00 12.00
8 Frank Gore/250 3.00 8.00
9 Vernon Davis/250 3.00 8.00
10 Kenny Britt/55 4.00 10.00
13 Steve Slaton/250 2.50 6.00
14 Vincent Jackson/250 2.50 6.00
15 Darren McFadden/250 3.00 8.00
17 Reggie Bush/110 4.00 10.00
18 Laurence Maroney/70 4.00 10.00
20 Mark Sanchez/250 4.00 10.00
21 Kevin Kolb/250 3.00 8.00
22 Brett Favre/100 10.00 25.00
24 Philip Rivers/150 4.00 10.00
25 Percy Harvin/250 4.00 10.00
27 Carson Palmer/125 3.00 8.00
28 Jason Witten/250 4.00 10.00
30 Vince Young/250 2.50 6.00
31 Matt Forte/250 3.00 8.00
32 Jeremy Shockey/250 3.00 8.00
33 Charles Woodson/125 4.00 10.00

2010 Certified Shirt Off My Back Materials Prime

COMMON CARD/35-50 4.00 10.00
SEMISTARS/35-50 5.00 12.00
UNL.STARS/35-50 6.00 15.00
COMMON CARD/15-20 6.00 15.00
UNL.STARS/15-20 8.00 20.00
STATED PRINT RUN 10-50
1 Antonio Gates/50 5.00 12.00
2 Lee Evans/50 5.00 12.00
3 Chad Ochocinco/50 5.00 12.00
4 Steven Jackson/50 5.00 12.00
6 Maurice Jones-Drew/50 5.00 12.00
7 Tony Romo/50 8.00 20.00
8 Frank Gore/50 5.00 12.00
9 Vernon Davis/50 5.00 12.00
10 Kenny Britt/35 5.00 12.00
11 Matt Ryan/20 8.00 20.00
12 Chris Cooley/50 6.00 15.00
13 Steve Slaton/50 4.00 10.00
14 Vincent Jackson/50 4.00 10.00
15 Darren McFadden/50 5.00 12.00
16 DeMarcus Ware/20 6.00 15.00
17 Reggie Bush/50 6.00 15.00
18 Laurence Maroney/50 5.00 12.00
20 Mark Sanchez/15 8.00 20.00
21 Kevin Kolb/50 5.00 12.00
22 Brett Favre/10
23 Ronnie Brown/50 5.00 12.00
24 Philip Rivers/50 6.00 15.00
25 Percy Harvin/45 6.00 15.00
26 Darren Sproles/50 5.00 12.00
27 Carson Palmer/50 5.00 12.00
28 Jason Witten/50 6.00 15.00
30 Vince Young/50 4.00 10.00
31 Matt Forte/50 5.00 12.00
32 Jeremy Shockey/50 5.00 12.00
33 Charles Woodson/50 6.00 15.00
35 Clinton Portis/50 5.00 12.00

2010 Certified National Convention

COMPLETE SET (6)	12.00	30.00
*BLUE/25: 1.2X TO 3X BASIC CARDS		
*GREEN/50: 1X TO 2.5X BASIC CARDS		
CM Colt McCoy	2.00	5.00
DM Donovan McNabb	1.25	3.00
PM Peyton Manning	2.00	5.00
RL Ray Lewis	1.25	3.00
SB Sam Bradford	4.00	10.00
TT Tim Tebow	4.00	10.00

2011 Certified

COMP.SET w/o SP's (150)	15.00	40.00
151-250 ROOKIE PRINT RUN 999		
251-286 JSY AU RC PRINT RUN 299-499		
287-306 LEGEND JSY PRINT RUN 49-99		
EXCH EXPIRATION: 5/23/2013		
1 Beanie Wells	.30	.75
2 Larry Fitzgerald	.30	.75
3 Steve Breaston	.25	.60
4 Tim Hightower	.25	.60
5 Jason Snelling	.30	.75
6 Matt Ryan	.40	1.00
7 Michael Turner	.30	.75
8 Roddy White	.30	.75
9 Tony Gonzalez	.30	.75
10 Anquan Boldin	.30	.75
11 Joe Flacco	.40	1.00
12 Ray Lewis	.40	1.00
13 Ray Rice	.30	.75
14 Todd Heap	.25	.60
15 C.J. Spiller	.30	.75
16 Fred Jackson	.40	1.00
17 Lee Evans	.30	.75
18 Ryan Fitzpatrick	.30	.75
19 Steve Johnson	.30	.75
20 DeAngelo Williams	.30	.75
21 Mike Goodson	.25	.60
22 Brandon LaFell	.25	.60
23 Steve Smith	.30	.75
24 Brian Urlacher	.40	1.00
25 Devin Hester	.40	1.00
26 Jay Cutler	.30	.75
27 Julius Peppers	.30	.75
28 Matt Forte	.30	.75
29 Carson Palmer	.30	.75
30 Dhani Jones	.25	.60
31 Chad Ochocinco	.30	.75
32 Jordan Shipley	.30	.75
33 Jermaine Gresham	.30	.75
34 Ben Watson	.25	.60
35 Colt McCoy	.30	.75
36 Josh Cribbs	.30	.75
37 Peyton Hillis	.30	.75
38 Dez Bryant	.40	1.00
39 Felix Jones	.30	.75
40 Jason Witten	.40	1.00
41 Miles Austin	.30	.75
42 Tony Romo	.40	1.00
43 Brandon Lloyd	.30	.75
44 Eddie Royal	.25	.60
45 Jabar Gaffney	.25	.60
46 Knowshon Moreno	.30	.75
47 Tim Tebow	.75	2.00
48 Brandon Pettigrew	.25	.60
49 Calvin Johnson	.40	1.00
50 Jahvid Best	.30	.75
51 Matthew Stafford	.40	1.00
52 Ndamukong Suh	.40	1.00
53 Aaron Rodgers	.60	1.50
54 Clay Matthews	.40	1.00
55 Donald Driver	.30	.75
56 Greg Jennings	.30	.75
57 Charles Woodson	.40	1.00
58 Andre Johnson	.30	.75
59 Arian Foster	.30	.75
60 Brian Cushing	.25	.60
61 Kevin Walter	.30	.75
62 Matt Schaub	.30	.75
63 Austin Collie	.30	.75
64 Dallas Clark	.30	.75
65 Dwight Freeney	.30	.75
66 Peyton Manning	.60	1.50
67 Reggie Wayne	.30	.75
68 Paul Posluszny	.25	.60
69 Marcedes Lewis	.25	.60
70 Maurice Jones-Drew	.30	.75
71 Mike Sims-Walker	.30	.75
72 Mike Thomas	.30	.75
73 Dwayne Bowe	.30	.75
74 Jamaal Charles	.30	.75
75 Matt Cassel	.30	.75
76 Tony Moeaki	.25	.60
77 Brandon Marshall	.30	.75
78 Brian Hartline	.25	.60
79 Chad Henne	.30	.75
80 Davone Bess	.25	.60
81 Ronnie Brown	.30	.75
82 Adrian Peterson	.50	1.25
83 Percy Harvin	.30	.75
84 Sidney Rice	.30	.75
85 Jared Allen	.30	.75
86 Visanthe Shiancoe	.30	.75
87 Jerod Mayo	.25	.60
88 Danny Woodhead	.40	1.00
89 Deion Branch	.25	.60
90 Tom Brady	.60	1.50
91 Wes Welker	.40	1.00
92 Drew Brees	.40	1.00
93 Lance Moore	.30	.75
94 Marques Colston	.30	.75
95 Pierre Thomas	.30	.75
96 Reggie Bush	.30	.75
97 Brandon Jacobs	.30	.75
98 Eli Manning	.40	1.00
99 Hakeem Nicks	.30	.75
100 Mario Manningham	.30	.75
101 Steve Smith USC	.30	.75
102 Braylon Edwards	.30	.75
103 LaDainian Tomlinson	.40	1.00
104 Mark Sanchez	.40	1.00
105 Santonio Holmes	.30	.75
106 Shonn Greene	.30	.75
107 Darren McFadden	.30	.75
108 Nnamdi Asomugha	.30	.75
109 Louis Murphy	.30	.75
110 Jacoby Ford	.30	.75
111 DeSean Jackson	.30	.75
112 Jeremy Maclin	.30	.75
113 LeSean McCoy	.30	.75
114 Michael Vick	.40	1.00
115 Ben Roethlisberger	.40	1.00
116 Hines Ward	.30	.75
117 Mike Wallace	.40	1.00
118 Rashard Mendenhall	.30	.75
119 Troy Polamalu	.40	1.00
120 Antonio Gates	.30	.75
121 Malcom Floyd	.30	.75
122 Mike Tolbert	.30	.75
123 Philip Rivers	.40	1.00
124 Ryan Mathews	.30	.75
125 Frank Gore	.30	.75
126 Michael Crabtree	.30	.75
127 Patrick Willis	.30	.75
128 Vernon Davis	.30	.75
129 John Carlson	.25	.60
130 Marshawn Lynch	.30	.75
131 Matt Hasselbeck	.30	.75
132 Mike Williams USC	.30	.75
133 Danny Amendola	.30	.75
134 James Laurinaitis	.25	.60
135 Sam Bradford	.40	1.00
136 Steven Jackson	.30	.75
137 Cadillac Williams	.25	.60
138 Josh Freeman	.40	1.00
139 Kellen Winslow Jr.	.30	.75
140 LeGarrette Blount	.30	.75
141 Mike Williams	.30	.75
142 Bo Scaife	.25	.60
143 Chris Johnson	.30	.75
144 Kenny Britt	.30	.75
145 Nate Washington	.25	.60
146 Stephen Tulloch	.25	.60
147 Chris Cooley	.30	.75
148 Donovan McNabb	.40	1.00
149 London Fletcher	.25	.60
150 Santana Moss	.30	.75
151 Aaron Williams RC	1.50	4.00
152 Adrian Clayborn RC	2.00	5.00
153 Ahmad Black RC	1.50	4.00
154 Akeem Ayers RC	1.50	4.00
155 Aldon Smith RC	3.00	8.00
156 Aldrick Robinson RC	1.25	3.00
157 Allen Bradford RC	1.50	4.00
158 Anthony Allen RC	1.25	3.00
159 Anthony Castonzo RC	1.25	3.00
160 Baron Batch RC	2.00	5.00
161 Brandon Harris RC	1.25	3.00
162 Brooks Reed RC	2.00	5.00
163 Bruce Carter RC	2.00	5.00
164 Cameron Heyward RC	2.00	5.00
165 Cameron Jordan RC	1.50	4.00
166 Cecil Shorts RC	1.50	4.00
167 Chris Culliver RC	1.50	4.00
168 Corey Liuget RC	1.25	3.00
169 D.J. Williams RC	2.00	5.00
170 Danny Watkins RC	1.50	4.00
171 Da'Quan Bowers RC	2.00	5.00
172 Da'Rel Scott RC	1.50	4.00
173 David Ausberry RC	1.50	4.00
174 DeMarco Sampson RC	1.25	3.00
175 DeMarcus Van Dyke RC	1.50	4.00
176 Denarius Moore RC	2.50	6.00
177 Derek Sherrod RC	2.00	5.00
178 Dion Lewis RC	2.00	5.00
179 Dontay Moch RC	1.25	3.00
180 Dwayne Harris RC	2.00	5.00
181 Evan Royster RC	2.00	5.00
182 Gabe Carimi RC	2.00	5.00
183 Greg Jones RC	1.50	4.00
184 Greg McElroy RC	2.00	5.00
185 Greg Salas RC	2.00	5.00
186 J.J. Watt RC	2.50	6.00
187 Jabaal Sheard RC	2.00	5.00
188 Jacquizz Rodgers RC	2.00	5.00
189 Jaiquawn Jarrett RC	1.50	4.00
190 James Carpenter RC	2.00	5.00
191 Jarvis Jenkins RC	1.25	3.00
192 Jay Finley RC	1.50	4.00
193 Jeremy Kerley RC	2.00	5.00
194 Jimmy Smith RC	2.00	5.00
195 Johnny White RC	1.50	4.00
196 Jonas Mouton RC	1.50	4.00
197 Jordan Cameron RC	1.50	4.00
198 Julius Thomas RC	1.50	4.00
199 Jurrell Casey RC	1.25	3.00
200 Justin Houston RC	2.00	5.00
201 Kealoha Pilares RC	2.00	5.00
202 Kelvin Sheppard RC	2.00	5.00
203 Kris Durham RC	1.50	4.00
204 Lance Kendricks RC	1.50	4.00
205 Lee Smith RC	1.50	4.00
206 Luke Stocker RC	1.50	4.00
207 Marcus Cannon RC	1.25	3.00
208 Marcus Gilbert RC	2.00	5.00
209 Marcus Gilchrist RC	1.25	3.00
210 Martez Wilson RC	2.00	5.00
211 Marvin Austin RC	1.50	4.00
212 Mason Foster RC	2.00	5.00
213 Mike Pouncey RC	2.00	5.00
214 Muhammad Wilkerson RC	2.00	5.00
215 Nate Irving RC	1.50	4.00
216 Nate Solder RC	2.00	5.00
217 Nathan Enderle RC	2.00	5.00
218 Nick Fairley RC	2.50	6.00
219 Niles Paul RC	2.00	5.00
220 Orlando Franklin RC	1.50	4.00
221 Owen Marecic RC	2.00	5.00
222 Patrick Peterson RC	3.00	8.00
223 Phil Taylor RC	1.50	4.00
224 Prince Amukamara RC	2.00	5.00
225 Quinton Carter RC	1.25	3.00
226 Rahim Moore RC	1.50	4.00
227 Ras-I Dowling RC	2.00	5.00
228 Richard Gordon RC	1.50	4.00
229 Ricky Stanzi RC	2.50	6.00
230 Robert Housler RC	1.50	4.00
231 Robert Quinn RC	2.00	5.00
232 Rodney Hudson RC	1.25	3.00
233 Ronald Johnson RC	1.50	4.00
234 Roy Helu RC	4.00	10.00
235 Ryan Kerrigan RC	2.00	5.00
236 Ryan Whalen RC	1.50	4.00
237 Scotty McKnight RC	1.50	4.00
238 Shane Bannon RC	1.25	3.00
239 Stanley Havili RC	1.25	3.00
240 Stefen Wisniewski RC	2.00	5.00
241 Stephen Burton RC	1.25	3.00
242 Stephen Paea RC	2.00	5.00
243 T.J. Yates RC	2.50	6.00
244 Tandon Doss RC	1.50	4.00
245 Terrell McClain RC	1.50	4.00
246 Terrelle Pryor RC	2.50	6.00
247 Tyler Sash RC	2.00	5.00
248 Tyrod Taylor RC	2.00	5.00
249 Tyron Smith RC	2.50	6.00
250 Virgil Green RC	1.50	4.00
251 Andy Dalton JSY AU/499 RC	30.00	60.00
252 Cam Newton JSY AU/299 RC	100.00	175.00
253 A.J. Green JSY AU/299 RC EXCH	15.00	40.00
254 Taiwan Jones JSY AU/499 RC EXCH	6.00	15.00
255 DeMarco Murray JSY AU/499 RC	25.00	60.00
256 Torrey Smith JSY AU/499 RC	10.00	25.00
257 Ryan Mallett JSY AU/299 RC	15.00	40.00
258 Stevan Ridley JSY AU/499 RC EXCH	6.00	15.00
259 Austin Pettis JSY AU/499 RC	5.00	12.00
260 Shane Vereen JSY AU/499 RC EXCH	6.00	15.00
261 Titus Young JSY AU/499 RC EXCH	8.00	20.00
262 Mikel Leshoure JSY AU/499 RC	6.00	15.00
263 Christian Ponder JSY AU/299 RC	25.00	50.00
264 Jordan Todman JSY AU/499 RC EXCH	4.00	10.00
265 Vincent Brown JSY AU/499 RC EXCH	6.00	15.00
266 Von Miller JSY AU/499 RC EXCH	10.00	25.00
267 Kyle Rudolph JSY AU/499 RC EXCH	6.00	15.00
268 Jonathan Baldwin JSY AU/499 RC EXCH	6.00	15.00
269 Jake Locker JSY AU/299 RC	25.00	60.00
270 Jamie Harper JSY AU/499 RC EXCH	6.00	15.00
271 Mark Ingram JSY AU/299 RC	15.00	40.00
272 Leonard Hankerson JSY AU/499 RC	6.00	15.00
273 Jerrel Jernigan JSY AU/499 RC	5.00	12.00
274 Delone Carter JSY AU/499 RC	5.00	12.00
275 Blaine Gabbert JSY AU/299 RC	12.00	30.00
276 Julio Jones JSY AU/499 RC	15.00	40.00
277 Marcell Dareus JSY AU/499 RC EXCH	6.00	15.00
278 Ryan Williams JSY AU/499 RC EXCH	8.00	20.00
279 Clyde Gates JSY AU/499 RC	5.00	12.00
280 Daniel Thomas JSY AU/499 RC EXCH	6.00	15.00
281 Greg Little JSY AU/499 RC EXCH	6.00	15.00
282 Colin Kaepernick JSY AU/499 RC	8.00	20.00
283 Alex Green JSY AU/499 RC	6.00	15.00
284 Randall Cobb JSY AU/499 RC EXCH	8.00	20.00
285 Bilal Powell JSY AU/499 RC EXCH	4.00	10.00
286 Kendall Hunter JSY AU/499 RC	8.00	20.00
287 Dan Marino JSY/99	12.00	30.00
288 Barry Sanders JSY/99	10.00	25.00
289 Brett Favre JSY/99	12.00	30.00
290 Bart Starr JSY/49	12.00	30.00
291 Deion Sanders JSY/99	8.00	20.00
292 Emmitt Smith JSY/99	10.00	25.00
293 Gale Sayers JSY/49	8.00	20.00
294 Jerry Rice JSY/99	10.00	25.00
295 Jim Brown JSY/49	10.00	25.00
296 Joe Montana JSY/99	12.00	30.00
297 Joe Namath JSY/99	10.00	25.00
298 John Elway JSY/99	10.00	25.00
299 Marshall Faulk JSY/99	5.00	12.00
300 Jim Kelly JSY/99	6.00	15.00
301 Terry Bradshaw JSY/49	10.00	25.00
302 Derrick Thomas JSY/49	25.00	50.00
303 Bob Griese JSY/99	6.00	15.00
304 Phil Simms JSY/99	5.00	12.00
305 Troy Aikman JSY/99	8.00	20.00
306 Dick Lane JSY/99	5.00	12.00

2011 Certified Mirror Blue

*VETS/100: 3X TO 8X BASIC CARDS		
1-150 VETERAN PRINT RUN 100		
*RK.JSY AU/50: .6X TO 1.5X JSY AU/499		
*RK.JSY AU/50: .5X TO 1.2X JSY AU/299		
251-286 ROOKIE JSY AU PRINT RUN 50		
*LEGEND JSY/50: .5X TO 1.2X JSY/99		
*LEGEND JSY/25: .5X TO 1.2X JSY/49		
287-306 LEGEND JSY PRINT RUN 25-50		
252 Cam Newton JSY AU/50	150.00	250.00

2011 Certified Mirror Gold

*1-150 VETS/25: 5X TO 12X BASIC CARDS		
*ROOK.JSY AU/25: 1.2X TO 3X AU RC/499		
*ROOK.JSY AU/25: 1X TO 2.5X AU RC/200		
*LEG.JSY/25: .6X TO 1.5X JSY/49-99		
STATED PRINT RUN 25 SER.#'d SETS		
251 Andy Dalton JSY AU	100.00	200.00
252 Cam Newton JSY AU	200.00	350.00
255 DeMarco Murray JSY AU	75.00	150.00
263 Christian Ponder JSY AU	90.00	150.00
269 Jake Locker JSY AU	75.00	150.00
271 Mark Ingram JSY AU	50.00	120.00
276 Julio Jones JSY AU	60.00	120.00

2011 Certified Mirror Red

*1-150 VETS/250: 2.5X TO 6X BASIC CARDS
1-150 VETERAN PRINT RUN 250
*LEG JSY/75-100: .4X TO 1X JSY/99
*LEG JSY/75-100: .3X TO .8X JSY/49
*LEG JSY/50: .4X TO 1X JSY/49
287-306 LEGEND JSY PRINT RUN 75-100

2011 Certified Platinum Blue

*VETS/100: 3X TO 8X BASIC CARDS
STATED PRINT RUN 100 SER.#'d SETS

2011 Certified Platinum Gold

*VETS/25: 5X TO 12X BASIC CARDS
STATED PRINT RUN 25 SER.#'d SETS

2011 Certified Platinum Red

*VETS 1-150: 1.5X TO 4X BASIC CARDS
RANDOM INSERTS IN PACKS

2011 Certified Certified Potential

STATED PRINT RUN 999 SER.#'d SETS		
1 A.J. Green	2.00	5.00
2 Alex Green	1.00	2.50
3 Andy Dalton	2.50	6.00
4 Austin Pettis	.75	2.00
5 Bilal Powell	.60	1.50
6 Blaine Gabbert	1.50	4.00
7 Cam Newton	5.00	12.00
8 Christian Ponder	2.00	5.00
9 Clyde Gates	.75	2.00
10 Colin Kaepernick	1.25	3.00
11 Daniel Thomas	1.00	2.50
12 Delone Carter	.75	2.00
13 DeMarco Murray	2.00	5.00
14 Greg Little	1.00	2.50
15 Jake Locker	2.50	6.00
16 Jamie Harper	1.00	2.50
17 Jerrel Jernigan	.75	2.00
18 Jonathan Baldwin	1.00	2.50
19 Jordan Todman	.60	1.50
20 Julio Jones	2.00	5.00
21 Kendall Hunter	1.00	2.50
22 Kyle Rudolph	1.00	2.50
23 Leonard Hankerson	1.00	2.50
24 Marcell Dareus	1.00	2.50
25 Mark Ingram	2.00	5.00
26 Mikel Leshoure	1.00	2.50
27 Randall Cobb	1.25	3.00
28 Ryan Mallett	2.00	5.00
29 Ryan Williams	1.25	3.00
30 Shane Vereen	1.00	2.50
31 Stevan Ridley	1.00	2.50
32 Taiwan Jones	1.00	2.50
33 Titus Young	1.25	3.00
34 Torrey Smith	1.25	3.00
35 Vincent Brown	1.00	2.50
36 Von Miller	1.25	3.00

2011 Certified Certified Potential Autographs

STATED PRINT RUN 25-50		
1 A.J. Green/35	25.00	50.00
2 Alex Green/50	6.00	15.00
3 Andy Dalton/50	30.00	60.00
4 Austin Pettis/50	5.00	12.00
5 Bilal Powell/50	4.00	10.00
6 Blaine Gabbert/35	10.00	25.00
7 Cam Newton/35	75.00	150.00
8 Christian Ponder/35	25.00	50.00
9 Clyde Gates/50	5.00	12.00
10 Colin Kaepernick/50	8.00	20.00
11 Daniel Thomas/50	6.00	15.00
12 Delone Carter/50	5.00	12.00
13 DeMarco Murray/50	30.00	60.00
14 Greg Little/50	6.00	15.00
15 Jake Locker/35	40.00	80.00
16 Jamie Harper/50	6.00	15.00
17 Jerrel Jernigan/50	5.00	12.00
18 Jonathan Baldwin/50	8.00	20.00
19 Jordan Todman/50	4.00	10.00
20 Julio Jones/50	20.00	40.00
21 Kendall Hunter/50	8.00	20.00
22 Kyle Rudolph/50	6.00	15.00
23 Leonard Hankerson/50	6.00	15.00
24 Marcell Dareus/50 EXCH	6.00	15.00
25 Mark Ingram/35	25.00	50.00
26 Mikel Leshoure/50	6.00	15.00
27 Randall Cobb/50	8.00	20.00
28 Ryan Mallett/35	12.00	30.00
29 Ryan Williams/50	8.00	20.00
30 Shane Vereen/50	6.00	15.00
31 Stevan Ridley/50	6.00	15.00
32 Taiwan Jones/50	6.00	15.00
33 Titus Young/50	8.00	20.00
34 Torrey Smith/50	10.00	25.00
35 Vincent Brown/50	6.00	15.00
36 Von Miller/25	10.00	25.00

2011 Certified Certified Potential Materials

STATED PRINT RUN 250 SER.#'d SETS		
*PRIME/50: .6X TO 1.5X BASIC JSY/250		
1 A.J. Green	5.00	12.00
2 Alex Green	2.50	6.00
3 Andy Dalton	6.00	15.00
4 Austin Pettis	2.00	5.00
5 Bilal Powell	1.50	4.00
6 Blaine Gabbert	4.00	10.00
7 Cam Newton	12.00	30.00
8 Christian Ponder	5.00	12.00
9 Clyde Gates	2.00	5.00
10 Colin Kaepernick	3.00	8.00
11 Daniel Thomas	2.50	6.00
12 Delone Carter	2.00	5.00
13 DeMarco Murray	5.00	12.00
14 Greg Little	2.50	6.00
15 Jake Locker	6.00	15.00
16 Jamie Harper	2.50	6.00
17 Jerrel Jernigan	2.00	5.00
18 Jonathan Baldwin	2.50	6.00
19 Jordan Todman	1.50	4.00
20 Julio Jones	5.00	12.00
21 Kendall Hunter	2.50	6.00
22 Kyle Rudolph	2.50	6.00
23 Leonard Hankerson	2.50	6.00
24 Marcell Dareus	2.50	6.00
25 Mark Ingram	5.00	12.00
26 Mikel Leshoure	2.50	6.00
27 Randall Cobb	3.00	8.00
28 Ryan Mallett	5.00	12.00
29 Ryan Williams	3.00	8.00
30 Shane Vereen	2.50	6.00
31 Stevan Ridley	2.50	6.00
32 Taiwan Jones	2.50	6.00
33 Titus Young	3.00	8.00
34 Torrey Smith	3.00	8.00
35 Vincent Brown	2.50	6.00
36 Von Miller	3.00	8.00

2011 Certified Fabric of the Game

STATED PRINT RUN 20-250		
1 Adrian Peterson/150	5.00	12.00
2 Anquan Boldin/25	5.00	12.00
3 Arian Foster/25	8.00	20.00
4 Santana Moss/150	3.00	8.00
5 Dallas Clark/25	5.00	12.00
6 Carson Palmer/25	5.00	12.00
7 Beanie Wells/25	5.00	12.00
8 Ben Roethlisberger/25	6.00	15.00
9 Bo Scaife/49	3.00	8.00
10 Ray Rice/25	5.00	12.00
11 Devin Hester/25	6.00	15.00
12 Darrelle Revis/25	5.00	12.00
13 Clay Matthews/25	8.00	20.00
14 Tim Tebow/25	12.00	30.00
16 LeSean McCoy/25	5.00	12.00
17 Jonathan Stewart/25	5.00	12.00
18 Knowshon Moreno/25	5.00	12.00
19 Tony Romo/25	6.00	15.00
21 Louis Murphy/25	5.00	12.00
22 Peyton Hillis/25	5.00	12.00
23 Ryan Fitzpatrick/25	5.00	12.00
25 Dwight Freeney/25	5.00	12.00
27 James Harrison/25	8.00	20.00
28 Ray Lewis/25	6.00	15.00
29 Peyton Manning/99	6.00	15.00
30 Ryan Mathews/25	5.00	12.00
32 Patrick Willis/250	3.00	8.00
33 Matt Schaub/25	5.00	12.00
35 Lee Evans/49	4.00	10.00
36 Marques Colston/250	3.00	8.00
37 Jason Witten/250	4.00	10.00
38 Eddie George/49	5.00	12.00
39 Ed Too Tall Jones/49	4.00	10.00
40 Eric Dickerson/49	5.00	12.00
41 Forrest Gregg/25	5.00	12.00
42 Fran Tarkenton/25	8.00	20.00
43 Franco Harris/25	8.00	20.00
44 Fred Biletnikoff/25	6.00	15.00
45 Fred Dryer/250	3.00	8.00
46 Garo Yepremian/49	4.00	10.00
47 Gene Upshaw/150	3.00	8.00
48 George Blanda/25	6.00	15.00
49 Henry Jordan/250	4.00	10.00
50 Howie Long/25	8.00	20.00
51 Priest Holmes/25	5.00	12.00
52 Randall Cunningham/250	4.00	10.00
53 Randy White/49	6.00	15.00
54 Raymond Berry/25	6.00	15.00
55 Richard Dent/25	5.00	12.00
56 Rod Woodson/25	10.00	25.00
57 Jan Stenerud/25	5.00	12.00
58 Dan Hampton/250	3.00	8.00
59 Steve Bartkowski/49	5.00	12.00
60 Steve Young/250	6.00	15.00
62 Thurman Thomas/25	8.00	20.00
63 Jay Novacek/25	6.00	15.00
64 Warren Sapp/250	4.00	10.00
66 Willie Brown/25	5.00	12.00
67 Bernie Kosar/25	6.00	15.00
68 Bert Jones/20	5.00	12.00
69 Billy Sims/55	5.00	12.00
70 Daryle Lamonica/25	5.00	12.00
71 Bob Hayes/25	8.00	20.00
72 Bob Lilly/25	6.00	15.00
73 Don Maynard/25	6.00	15.00
74 Doug Flutie/250	4.00	10.00
75 Carl Eller/25	5.00	12.00
76 Alan Page/25	6.00	15.00
77 Alex Karras/25	6.00	15.00
78 Dick Butkus/25	10.00	25.00
79 Bo Jackson/49	8.00	20.00
80 Chuck Foreman/49	4.00	10.00
81 John Fuqua/49	5.00	12.00
82 John Hadl/49	4.00	10.00
84 John Matuszak/250	5.00	12.00
85 Junior Seau/49	6.00	15.00
86 Keith Jackson/100	5.00	12.00
87 Ken Anderson/100	4.00	10.00
88 Keyshawn Johnson/20	6.00	15.00
89 Larry Little/49	4.00	10.00
90 Lee Roy Selmon/49	6.00	15.00
91 Len Dawson/49	6.00	15.00
92 Marcus Allen/250	5.00	12.00
94 Mark Carrier DB/250	3.00	8.00
95 Mark Duper/49	4.00	10.00
97 Michael Irvin/250	5.00	12.00
98 Mike Alstott/49	4.00	10.00
99 Irving Fryar/49	4.00	10.00
100 Dan Fouts/49	6.00	15.00

2011 Certified Fabric of the Game NFL Die Cut Prime

STATED PRINT RUN 5-25		
1 Adrian Peterson/25	10.00	25.00
2 Anquan Boldin/25	6.00	15.00
4 Santana Moss/25	6.00	15.00
5 Dallas Clark/15	6.00	15.00
10 Ray Rice/25	6.00	15.00
13 Clay Matthews/25	10.00	25.00
14 Tim Tebow/25	15.00	40.00
17 Jonathan Stewart/25	6.00	15.00
18 Knowshon Moreno/25	6.00	15.00
19 Tony Romo/25	8.00	20.00
20 DeAngelo Hall/25	5.00	12.00
21 Louis Murphy/15	6.00	15.00
24 Danny Woodhead/20	12.00	30.00
25 Dwight Freeney/25	6.00	15.00
26 David Harris/25	5.00	12.00
27 James Harrison/25	10.00	25.00
28 Ray Lewis/24	8.00	20.00
30 Ryan Mathews/25	6.00	15.00
31 Roddy White/25	6.00	15.00
32 Patrick Willis/15	6.00	15.00
36 Marques Colston/25	6.00	15.00
37 Jason Witten/25	8.00	20.00
38 Eddie George/25	8.00	20.00
40 Eric Dickerson/25	8.00	20.00
41 Forrest Gregg/25	6.00	15.00
42 Fran Tarkenton/15	10.00	25.00
43 Franco Harris/25	10.00	25.00
44 Fred Biletnikoff/25	8.00	20.00
51 Priest Holmes/25	6.00	15.00
52 Randall Cunningham/25	8.00	20.00
53 Randy White/25	10.00	25.00
54 Raymond Berry/25	8.00	20.00
55 Richard Dent/25	6.00	15.00
56 Rod Woodson/25	12.00	30.00
59 Steve Bartkowski/25	8.00	20.00
60 Steve Young/15	12.00	30.00
62 Thurman Thomas/15	10.00	25.00
63 Jay Novacek/25	8.00	20.00
64 Warren Sapp/25	8.00	20.00
65 Wayne Chrebet/25	6.00	15.00
66 Willie Brown/15	6.00	15.00
67 Bernie Kosar/25	8.00	20.00
69 Billy Sims/15	8.00	20.00
71 Bob Hayes/25	10.00	25.00
72 Bob Lilly/25	8.00	20.00
74 Doug Flutie/25	8.00	20.00
76 Alan Page/25	8.00	20.00
78 Dick Butkus/25	12.00	30.00
79 Bo Jackson/15	12.00	30.00
80 Chuck Foreman/15	6.00	15.00
82 John Hadl/25	6.00	15.00
86 Keith Jackson/25	10.00	25.00
87 Ken Anderson/25	8.00	20.00
88 Keyshawn Johnson/15	8.00	20.00
89 Larry Little/20	6.00	15.00
90 Lee Roy Selmon/25	10.00	25.00
92 Marcus Allen/25	10.00	25.00
93 Curtis Martin/25	10.00	25.00
94 Mark Carrier DB/25	6.00	15.00
95 Mark Duper/25	6.00	15.00
98 Mike Alstott/15	6.00	15.00
100 Dan Fouts/25	10.00	25.00

2011 Certified Fabric of the Game Prime

STATED PRINT RUN 5-50		
1 Adrian Peterson/50	8.00	20.00
2 Anquan Boldin/50	5.00	12.00
4 Santana Moss/50	5.00	12.00
8 Ben Roethlisberger/15	8.00	20.00
10 Ray Rice/50	5.00	12.00
12 Darrelle Revis/25	6.00	15.00
13 Clay Matthews/50	8.00	20.00
14 Tim Tebow/50	12.00	30.00
17 Jonathan Stewart/50	5.00	12.00
18 Knowshon Moreno/50	5.00	12.00
19 Tony Romo/50	6.00	15.00
20 DeAngelo Hall/50	4.00	10.00
21 Louis Murphy/25	6.00	15.00
24 Danny Woodhead/25	12.00	30.00
25 Dwight Freeney/50	5.00	12.00
26 David Harris/25	5.00	12.00
27 James Harrison/50	8.00	20.00
30 Ryan Mathews/50	5.00	12.00
31 Roddy White/50	5.00	12.00
32 Patrick Willis/50	5.00	12.00
35 Lee Evans/50	5.00	12.00
36 Marques Colston/50	5.00	12.00
37 Jason Witten/50	6.00	15.00
38 Eddie George/50	6.00	15.00
40 Eric Dickerson/50	6.00	15.00
41 Forrest Gregg/50	5.00	12.00
42 Fran Tarkenton/25	10.00	25.00
43 Franco Harris/50	8.00	20.00
44 Fred Biletnikoff/25	8.00	20.00
48 George Blanda/50	6.00	15.00
51 Priest Holmes/50	5.00	12.00
52 Randall Cunningham/50	6.00	15.00
53 Randy White/50	8.00	20.00
54 Raymond Berry/50	6.00	15.00
55 Richard Dent/50	5.00	12.00
56 Rod Woodson/50	10.00	25.00
59 Steve Bartkowski/50	6.00	15.00
60 Steve Young/25	12.00	30.00
62 Thurman Thomas/25	10.00	25.00
63 Jay Novacek/50	6.00	15.00
64 Warren Sapp/50	6.00	15.00
65 Wayne Chrebet/50	5.00	12.00
66 Willie Brown/50	5.00	12.00
67 Bernie Kosar/50	6.00	15.00
71 Bob Hayes/50	8.00	20.00
72 Bob Lilly/50	6.00	15.00
74 Doug Flutie/50	6.00	15.00
76 Alan Page/45	6.00	15.00
78 Dick Butkus/50	10.00	25.00
80 Chuck Foreman/25	6.00	15.00
81 John Fuqua/25	8.00	20.00
82 John Hadl/50	5.00	12.00
84 John Matuszak/25	10.00	25.00
85 Junior Seau/15	10.00	25.00
86 Keith Jackson/50	8.00	20.00
87 Ken Anderson/50	6.00	15.00
88 Keyshawn Johnson/30	6.00	15.00
89 Larry Little/50	5.00	12.00
90 Lee Roy Selmon/50	8.00	20.00
92 Marcus Allen/50	8.00	20.00
93 Curtis Martin/50	8.00	20.00
94 Mark Carrier DB/50	5.00	12.00
95 Mark Duper/50	5.00	12.00
98 Mike Alstott/50	5.00	12.00
100 Dan Fouts/25	10.00	25.00

2011 Certified Fabric of the Game Team Die Cut

STATED PRINT RUN 5-25		
1 Adrian Peterson/25	8.00	20.00
2 Anquan Boldin/25	5.00	12.00
4 Santana Moss/25	5.00	12.00
5 Dallas Clark/25	5.00	12.00
7 Beanie Wells/25	5.00	12.00
8 Ben Roethlisberger/25	6.00	15.00
9 Bo Scaife/25	4.00	10.00
12 Darrelle Revis/25	5.00	12.00
13 Clay Matthews/25	8.00	20.00
16 LeSean McCoy/25	5.00	12.00
18 Knowshon Moreno/25	5.00	12.00
19 Tony Romo/25	6.00	15.00
21 Louis Murphy/25	5.00	12.00
24 Danny Woodhead/15	10.00	25.00
25 Dwight Freeney/25	5.00	12.00
27 James Harrison/25	6.00	15.00
29 Peyton Manning/15	10.00	25.00
32 Patrick Willis/25	5.00	12.00
33 Matt Schaub/25	5.00	12.00
35 Lee Evans/25	5.00	12.00
36 Marques Colston/25	5.00	12.00
37 Jason Witten/25	6.00	15.00
38 Eddie George/25	6.00	15.00
39 Ed Too Tall Jones/25	5.00	12.00
40 Eric Dickerson/25	6.00	15.00
45 Fred Dryer/25	5.00	12.00
46 Garo Yepremian/25	5.00	12.00
47 Gene Upshaw/25	5.00	12.00
49 Henry Jordan/25	6.00	15.00
52 Randall Cunningham/25	6.00	15.00
55 Richard Dent/25	5.00	12.00
57 Jan Stenerud/25	5.00	12.00
58 Dan Hampton/25	5.00	12.00
59 Steve Bartkowski/25	6.00	15.00
60 Steve Young/25	10.00	25.00
61 Ted Hendricks/25	5.00	12.00
63 Jay Novacek/25	6.00	15.00
64 Warren Sapp/25	6.00	15.00
67 Bernie Kosar/25	6.00	15.00
69 Billy Sims/25	6.00	15.00
74 Doug Flutie/25	6.00	15.00
77 Alex Karras/25	6.00	15.00
80 Chuck Foreman/25	5.00	12.00
82 John Hadl/25	5.00	12.00
84 John Matuszak/25	8.00	20.00
85 Junior Seau/25	8.00	20.00
86 Keith Jackson/25	8.00	20.00
87 Ken Anderson/25	6.00	15.00
90 Lee Roy Selmon/25	8.00	20.00
92 Marcus Allen/25	8.00	20.00
94 Mark Carrier DB/25	5.00	12.00
95 Mark Duper/25	5.00	12.00
97 Michael Irvin/25	8.00	20.00
98 Mike Alstott/25	5.00	12.00

2011 Certified Fabric of the Game Combos

STATED PRINT RUN 50-150		
*PRIME/14-25: .6X TO 1.5X BASIC COMBO		
2 Troy Aikman/150 Sam Bradford	8.00	20.00
3 Bernie Kosar/150 Colt McCoy	5.00	12.00
4 Troy Polamalu/100 Ed Reed	6.00	15.00
5 Rod Woodson/75 Darrelle Revis	6.00	15.00
6 Joe Namath/100 Sam Bradford	8.00	20.00
7 Randall Cunningham/150 Michael Vick	6.00	15.00
8 Ed Too Tall Jones/100 DeMarcus Ware	5.00	12.00
9 Eric Dickerson/150 Darren McFadden	5.00	12.00
10 Eddie George/150 Chris Johnson	5.00	12.00
11 Carl Eller/150 Jared Allen	8.00	20.00
12 Gale Sayers/150 Matt Forte	8.00	20.00
13 Franco Harris/50 John Fuqua	8.00	20.00

2011 Certified Fabric of the Game. Jersey Number Autographs

STATED PRINT RUN 4-25		
12 Darrelle Revis/25	15.00	40.00
16 LeSean McCoy/15	15.00	40.00
18 Knowshon Moreno/15	15.00	40.00
29 Peyton Manning/15	60.00	120.00
32 Patrick Willis/25	20.00	50.00
33 Matt Schaub/15	15.00	40.00
35 Lee Evans/15	15.00	40.00
37 Jason Witten/15		
39 Ed Too Tall Jones/25	15.00	40.00
40 Eric Dickerson/25	20.00	50.00
41 Forrest Gregg/25	15.00	40.00
43 Franco Harris/25	40.00	80.00
44 Fred Biletnikoff/25	20.00	50.00
47 Gene Upshaw/15	15.00	40.00
50 Howie Long/25	25.00	60.00
51 Priest Holmes/25	15.00	40.00
52 Randall Cunningham/25	25.00	60.00
53 Randy White/25	20.00	50.00
54 Raymond Berry/25	20.00	50.00
57 Jan Stenerud/25	15.00	40.00
59 Steve Bartkowski/25	15.00	40.00
66 Willie Brown/25	15.00	40.00
70 Daryle Lamonica/25	15.00	40.00
72 Bob Lilly/25	20.00	50.00
73 Don Maynard/25	20.00	50.00
76 Alan Page/25	20.00	50.00
77 Alex Karras/25	20.00	50.00
79 Bo Jackson/25	40.00	80.00
85 Junior Seau/25	40.00	80.00
88 Keyshawn Johnson/15	15.00	40.00
89 Larry Little/20	15.00	40.00
90 Lee Roy Selmon/25	20.00	50.00
91 Len Dawson/25	25.00	60.00
92 Marcus Allen/25	25.00	60.00
95 Mark Duper/25	15.00	40.00
97 Michael Irvin/25	25.00	60.00
98 Mike Alstott/25	15.00	40.00

2011 Certified Gold Team

STATED PRINT RUN 999 SER.#'d SETS		
1 Andre Johnson	1.00	2.50
2 Michael Vick	1.25	3.00
3 Aaron Rodgers	2.00	5.00
4 Peyton Manning	2.00	5.00
5 Larry Fitzgerald	1.00	2.50
6 Ray Lewis	1.25	3.00
7 Darrelle Revis	1.00	2.50
8 Tom Brady	2.00	5.00
9 Adrian Peterson	1.50	4.00
10 Troy Polamalu	1.25	3.00

2011 Certified Gold Team Materials

STATED PRINT RUN 10-250		
*PRIME/50: .6X TO 1.5X BASIC JSY/100-125		
1 Andre Johnson/28	6.00	15.00
2 Michael Vick/250	4.00	10.00
3 Aaron Rodgers/125	12.00	30.00
4 Peyton Manning/10		
5 Larry Fitzgerald/100	4.00	10.00
6 Ray Lewis/250	4.00	10.00
7 Darrelle Revis/100	4.00	10.00
8 Tom Brady/200	6.00	15.00
9 Adrian Peterson/100	6.00	15.00

2011 Certified Hometown Heroes Autographs

STATED PRINT RUN 1-30		
4 Asante Samuel/30 EXCH		
5 Brandon Meriweather/25	6.00	15.00
18 Jared Allen/20	25.00	50.00

2011 Certified Hometown Heroes Materials

STATED PRINT RUN 25-250		
1 Aaron Rodgers/125	12.00	30.00
2 Adrian Peterson/150	5.00	12.00
3 Antonio Gates/250	3.00	8.00
6 Brian Urlacher/250	4.00	10.00
7 Calvin Johnson/150	4.00	10.00
8 Ben Roethlisberger/200	4.00	10.00
10 Chris Johnson/200	3.00	8.00
11 DeMarcus Ware/250	4.00	10.00
12 DeSean Jackson/250	3.00	8.00
14 Dwayne Bowe/25	6.00	15.00
15 Eli Manning/250	4.00	10.00
16 Frank Gore/250	3.00	8.00
17 Hines Ward/250	4.00	10.00
18 Jared Allen/250	4.00	10.00
19 Joe Flacco/250	4.00	10.00
20 Larry Fitzgerald/100	4.00	10.00
21 Mark Sanchez/250	4.00	10.00
22 Matt Ryan/250	4.00	10.00
23 Maurice Jones-Drew/100	4.00	10.00
24 Michael Turner/250	3.00	8.00
25 Miles Austin/250	4.00	10.00
26 Percy Harvin/250	3.00	8.00
27 Reggie Wayne/250	3.00	8.00
28 Santana Moss/50	5.00	12.00
29 Steve Smith/100	4.00	10.00
30 Steven Jackson/250	3.00	8.00
31 Tom Brady/100	8.00	20.00
33 Vernon Davis/150	3.00	8.00
34 Wes Welker/50	6.00	15.00

2011 Certified Hometown Heroes Materials Prime

STATED PRINT RUN 1-50		
2 Adrian Peterson/50	12.00	30.00
3 Antonio Gates/50	8.00	20.00
6 Brian Urlacher/25	12.00	30.00
7 Calvin Johnson/50	10.00	25.00
10 Chris Johnson/50	8.00	20.00
11 DeMarcus Ware/50	10.00	25.00
12 DeSean Jackson/50	8.00	20.00
14 Dwayne Bowe/50	8.00	20.00
15 Eli Manning/15	12.00	30.00
18 Jared Allen/50	10.00	25.00
23 Maurice Jones-Drew/50	8.00	20.00
24 Michael Turner/50	8.00	20.00
25 Miles Austin/50	10.00	25.00
27 Reggie Wayne/25	10.00	25.00
28 Santana Moss/50	8.00	20.00
29 Steve Smith/25	10.00	25.00
30 Steven Jackson/50	8.00	20.00
33 Vernon Davis/50	8.00	20.00
34 Wes Welker/50	10.00	25.00

2011 Certified Hometown Heroes Materials Autographs Prime

STATED PRINT RUN 1-25		
4 Asante Samuel/25 EXCH		
18 Jared Allen/20	40.00	80.00
28 Santana Moss/20		

2011 Certified Mirror Gold Materials

MIRROR GOLD PRINT RUN 5-25		
*BLUE/50: .3X TO .8X GOLD JSY/25		
7 Michael Turner/25	5.00	12.00
8 Roddy White/25	5.00	12.00
9 Tony Gonzalez/25	5.00	12.00
10 Anquan Boldin/25	5.00	12.00
12 Ray Lewis/25	6.00	15.00
13 Ray Rice/25	5.00	12.00
15 C.J. Spiller/25	5.00	12.00
16 Fred Jackson/25	8.00	20.00
17 Lee Evans/25	5.00	12.00
20 DeAngelo Williams/25	5.00	12.00
23 Steve Smith/25	5.00	12.00
24 Brian Urlacher/25	6.00	15.00
26 Jay Cutler/25	5.00	12.00
27 Julius Peppers/25	5.00	12.00
28 Matt Forte/25	5.00	12.00
32 Jordan Shipley/25	5.00	12.00
35 Colt McCoy/25	5.00	12.00
37 Peyton Hillis/25	5.00	12.00
39 Felix Jones/25	5.00	12.00
40 Jason Witten/25	6.00	15.00
41 Miles Austin/25	6.00	15.00
42 Tony Romo/25	6.00	15.00
43 Brandon Lloyd/25	5.00	12.00
46 Knowshon Moreno/25	5.00	12.00
47 Tim Tebow/25	12.00	30.00
49 Calvin Johnson/25	6.00	15.00
50 Jahvid Best/25	5.00	12.00
52 Ndamukong Suh/25	6.00	15.00
53 Aaron Rodgers/25	15.00	40.00
54 Clay Matthews/25	6.00	15.00
65 Dwight Freeney/25	5.00	12.00
67 Reggie Wayne/25	5.00	12.00
70 Maurice Jones-Drew/25	5.00	12.00
72 Mike Thomas/25	5.00	12.00
73 Dwayne Bowe/25	5.00	12.00
74 Jamaal Charles/25	5.00	12.00
75 Matt Cassel/25	5.00	12.00
77 Brandon Marshall/25	5.00	12.00
78 Brian Hartline/25	4.00	10.00
79 Chad Henne/25	5.00	12.00
82 Adrian Peterson/25	8.00	20.00
85 Jared Allen/25	6.00	15.00
86 Visanthe Shiancoe/25	5.00	12.00
91 Wes Welker/25	6.00	15.00
94 Marques Colston/25	5.00	12.00
98 Eli Manning/25	6.00	15.00
99 Hakeem Nicks/25	5.00	12.00
103 LaDainian Tomlinson/25	6.00	15.00
105 Santonio Holmes/25	5.00	12.00
107 Darren McFadden/25	5.00	12.00

109 Louis Murphy/25	5.00	12.00
110 Jacoby Ford/25	5.00	12.00
111 DeSean Jackson/25	5.00	12.00
112 Jeremy Maclin/25	5.00	12.00
117 Mike Wallace/25	6.00	15.00
118 Rashard Mendenhall/25	5.00	12.00
119 Troy Polamalu/25	8.00	20.00
120 Antonio Gates/25	5.00	12.00
121 Malcom Floyd/25	5.00	12.00
123 Philip Rivers/25	6.00	15.00
124 Ryan Mathews/25	5.00	12.00
127 Patrick Willis/25	5.00	12.00
128 Vernon Davis/25	5.00	12.00
134 James Laurinaitis/25	4.00	10.00
135 Sam Bradford/25	6.00	15.00
136 Steven Jackson/25	5.00	12.00
139 Kellen Winslow Jr./25	5.00	12.00
143 Chris Johnson/25	5.00	12.00
144 Kenny Britt/25	5.00	12.00
145 Nate Washington/25	4.00	10.00
147 Chris Cooley/25	5.00	12.00
149 London Fletcher/15	6.00	15.00
150 Santana Moss/25	5.00	12.00
251 Andy Dalton/25	15.00	40.00
252 Cam Newton/25	30.00	80.00
253 A.J. Green/25	12.00	30.00
254 Taiwan Jones/25	6.00	15.00
255 DeMarco Murray/25	12.00	30.00
256 Torrey Smith/25	8.00	20.00
257 Ryan Mallett/25	12.00	30.00
258 Stevan Ridley/25	6.00	15.00
259 Austin Pettis/25	5.00	12.00
260 Shane Vereen/25	6.00	15.00
261 Titus Young/25	8.00	20.00
262 Mikel Leshoure/25	6.00	15.00
263 Christian Ponder/25	12.00	30.00
264 Jordan Todman/25	4.00	10.00
265 Vincent Brown/25	6.00	15.00
266 Von Miller/25	8.00	20.00
267 Kyle Rudolph/25	6.00	15.00
268 Jonathan Baldwin/25	6.00	15.00
269 Jake Locker/25	15.00	40.00
270 Jamie Harper/25	6.00	15.00
271 Mark Ingram/25	12.00	30.00
272 Leonard Hankerson/25	6.00	15.00
273 Jerrel Jernigan/25	5.00	12.00
274 Delone Carter/25	5.00	12.00
275 Blaine Gabbert/25	10.00	25.00
276 Julio Jones/25	12.00	30.00
277 Marcell Dareus/25	6.00	15.00
278 Ryan Williams/25	8.00	20.00
279 Clyde Gates/25	5.00	12.00
280 Daniel Thomas/25	6.00	15.00
281 Greg Little/25	6.00	15.00
282 Colin Kaepernick/25	8.00	20.00
283 Alex Green/25	6.00	15.00
284 Randall Cobb/25	8.00	20.00
285 Bilal Powell/25	4.00	10.00
286 Kendall Hunter/25	6.00	15.00

2011 Certified Mirror Gold Signatures

*GOLD ROOKIE/25: .8X TO 2X RED/100-250
STATED PRINT RUN 25 SER.#'d SETS

246 Terrelle Pryor	30.00	60.00
287 Dan Marino JSY/25	100.00	200.00
288 Barry Sanders JSY/25	60.00	120.00
289 Brett Favre JSY/25	100.00	200.00
291 Deion Sanders JSY/25	40.00	80.00
292 Emmitt Smith JSY/25	100.00	175.00
294 Jerry Rice JSY/25 EXCH	100.00	175.00
295 Jim Brown JSY/25 EXCH	40.00	80.00
296 Joe Montana JSY/25	100.00	200.00
297 Joe Namath JSY/25	100.00	200.00
298 John Elway JSY/25	90.00	150.00
299 Marshall Faulk JSY/25	30.00	60.00
300 Jim Kelly JSY/25	30.00	60.00
303 Bob Griese JSY/25	30.00	60.00
304 Phil Simms JSY/25	30.00	60.00
305 Troy Aikman JSY/25 EXCH	40.00	80.00

2011 Certified Mirror Red Signatures

MIRROR RED AU PRINT RUN 100-250
*MIRR.BLUE/50-100: .5X TO 1.2X RED/100-250

152 Adrian Clayborn/250	5.00	12.00
153 Ahmad Black/250	4.00	10.00
154 Akeem Ayers/250	4.00	10.00
155 Aldon Smith/250	8.00	20.00
156 Aldrick Robinson/250	3.00	8.00
157 Allen Bradford/250	4.00	10.00
158 Anthony Allen/250	3.00	8.00
159 Anthony Castonzo/250	3.00	8.00
161 Brandon Harris/250	3.00	8.00
164 Cameron Heyward/250	5.00	12.00
165 Cameron Jordan/250	4.00	10.00
166 Cecil Shorts/250	4.00	10.00
168 Corey Liuget/250	3.00	8.00
169 D.J. Williams/250	5.00	12.00
171 Da'Quan Bowers/250	5.00	12.00
172 Da'Rel Scott/250	4.00	10.00
176 Denarius Moore/250	10.00	25.00
178 Dion Lewis/250	5.00	12.00
180 Dwayne Harris/250	5.00	12.00
181 Evan Royster/250	5.00	12.00
183 Greg Jones/250	4.00	10.00
184 Greg McElroy/250	6.00	15.00
185 Greg Salas/250	5.00	12.00
186 J.J. Watt/250	6.00	15.00
188 Jacquizz Rodgers/250	5.00	12.00
193 Jeremy Kerley/250	5.00	12.00
194 Jimmy Smith/250	5.00	12.00
195 Johnny White/250	4.00	10.00
197 Jordan Cameron/250	4.00	10.00
198 Julius Thomas/250	4.00	10.00
200 Justin Houston/250	5.00	12.00
201 Kealoha Pilares/250	5.00	12.00
203 Kris Durham/250	4.00	10.00
204 Lance Kendricks/250	4.00	10.00
206 Luke Stocker/250	4.00	10.00
207 Marcus Cannon/100	3.00	8.00
210 Martez Wilson/250	5.00	12.00
217 Nathan Enderle/250	5.00	12.00
219 Niles Paul/250	5.00	12.00
221 Owen Marecic/250	5.00	12.00
223 Phil Taylor/250	4.00	10.00
224 Prince Amukamara/250	6.00	15.00
225 Quinton Carter/250	3.00	8.00
226 Rahim Moore/250	4.00	10.00
229 Ricky Stanzi/250	6.00	15.00
230 Robert Housler/250	4.00	10.00
233 Ronald Johnson/250	4.00	10.00
234 Roy Helu/250	10.00	25.00
235 Ryan Kerrigan/250	6.00	15.00
236 Ryan Whalen/250	4.00	10.00
237 Scotty McKnight/250	4.00	10.00
238 Shane Bannon/250	3.00	8.00
239 Stanley Havili/250	3.00	8.00
241 Stephen Burton/250	3.00	8.00
242 Stephen Paea/150	5.00	12.00
243 T.J. Yates/250	6.00	15.00
244 Tandon Doss/250	4.00	10.00
247 Tyler Sash/250	5.00	12.00
248 Tyrod Taylor/250	5.00	12.00
249 Tyron Smith/250	6.00	15.00

2011 Certified Rookie Fabric of the Game

STATED PRINT RUN 150-250
*TEAM DC/25: .8X TO 2X JSY/150-250
*TEAM DC/10: 1.2X TO 3X JSY/150-250

1 Clyde Gates/250	2.00	5.00
2 Jonathan Baldwin/250	2.50	6.00
3 A.J. Green/250	5.00	12.00
4 Mark Ingram/250	5.00	12.00
5 Von Miller/250	3.00	8.00
6 Torrey Smith/250	3.00	8.00
7 Blaine Gabbert/250	4.00	10.00
8 Greg Little/250	2.50	6.00
9 Ryan Mallett/250	5.00	12.00
10 Kendall Hunter/250	2.50	6.00
11 Andy Dalton/250	6.00	15.00
12 Colin Kaepernick/250	3.00	8.00
13 Stevan Ridley/250	2.50	6.00
14 Mikel Leshoure/250	2.50	6.00
15 Jamie Harper/250	2.50	6.00
16 Austin Pettis/250	2.00	5.00
17 Alex Green/250	2.50	6.00
18 Jake Locker/250	6.00	15.00
19 Kyle Rudolph/250	2.50	6.00
20 Ryan Williams/250	3.00	8.00
21 Titus Young/250	3.00	8.00
22 Randall Cobb/250	3.00	8.00
23 Delone Carter/250	2.00	5.00
24 Cam Newton/250	12.00	30.00
25 Bilal Powell/250	1.50	4.00
26 Jerrel Jernigan/250	2.00	5.00
27 Vincent Brown/150	2.50	6.00
28 DeMarco Murray/250	5.00	12.00
29 Christian Ponder/250	5.00	12.00
30 Julio Jones/250	5.00	12.00
31 Shane Vereen/250	2.50	6.00
32 Taiwan Jones/250	2.50	6.00
33 Daniel Thomas/250	2.50	6.00
34 Jordan Todman/250	1.50	4.00
35 Leonard Hankerson/250	2.50	6.00
36 Marcell Dareus/250	2.50	6.00

2011 Certified Rookie Fabric of the Game Jersey Number Autographs

STATED PRINT RUN 25-50
*PRIME/15-25: .5X TO 1.2X AU/25-50

1 Clyde Gates/50	8.00	20.00
2 Jonathan Baldwin/50	12.00	30.00
3 A.J. Green/30	40.00	80.00
4 Mark Ingram/30	40.00	80.00
5 Von Miller/25	15.00	40.00
6 Torrey Smith/50	15.00	40.00
7 Blaine Gabbert/30	15.00	40.00
8 Greg Little/50	10.00	25.00
9 Ryan Mallett/30	20.00	50.00
10 Kendall Hunter/50	12.00	30.00
11 Andy Dalton/50	50.00	100.00
12 Colin Kaepernick/50	12.00	30.00
13 Stevan Ridley/50	10.00	25.00
14 Mikel Leshoure/50	10.00	25.00
15 Jamie Harper/50	10.00	25.00
16 Austin Pettis/50	8.00	20.00
17 Alex Green/50	10.00	25.00
18 Jake Locker/30	50.00	120.00
19 Kyle Rudolph/50	10.00	25.00
20 Ryan Williams/50	12.00	30.00
21 Titus Young/50	12.00	30.00
22 Randall Cobb/50	12.00	30.00
23 Delone Carter/50	8.00	20.00
24 Cam Newton/30	125.00	200.00
25 Bilal Powell/50	6.00	15.00
26 Jerrel Jernigan/50	8.00	20.00
27 Vincent Brown/50	10.00	25.00
28 DeMarco Murray/50	50.00	100.00
29 Christian Ponder/30	40.00	80.00
30 Julio Jones/50	30.00	60.00
31 Shane Vereen/50	10.00	25.00
32 Taiwan Jones/50	10.00	25.00
33 Daniel Thomas/50	10.00	25.00
34 Jordan Todman/50	6.00	15.00
35 Leonard Hankerson/50	10.00	25.00
36 Marcell Dareus/50 EXCH	10.00	25.00

2011 Certified Shirt Off My Back Materials

*JSY/150-250: .4X TO 1X FOTG/150-250
*PRIME/50: .6X TO 1.5X JSY/150-250
STATED PRINT RUN 150-250

2011 Certified Shirt Off My Back Materials Combos

STATED PRINT RUN 25-100
*PRM/18-25: .8X TO 2X CMBO/50-100
*PRIME/25: .5X TO 1.2X COMBO/25

1 A.J. Green/100	8.00	20.00
Andy Dalton		
2 Steve Smith/100	15.00	40.00
Cam Newton		
3 Matt Ryan/100	6.00	15.00
Julio Jones		
4 Marques Colston/100	6.00	15.00
Mark Ingram		
5 Adrian Peterson/100	8.00	20.00
Christian Ponder		
6 Calvin Johnson/75	6.00	15.00
Mikel Leshoure		
7 Maurice Jones-Drew/50	5.00	12.00
Blaine Gabbert		
8 Dwayne Bowe/25	8.00	20.00
Jonathan Baldwin		
9 Tony Romo/100	6.00	15.00
DeMarco Murray		
10 Dallas Clark/100	4.00	10.00
Delone Carter		
11 Antonio Gates/100	5.00	12.00
Vincent Brown		
12 Kenny Britt/100	8.00	20.00
Jake Locker		
13 Chris Cooley/100	5.00	12.00
Leonard Hankerson		
14 Vernon Davis/100	6.00	15.00
Colin Kaepernick		
15 Joe Flacco/100	6.00	15.00
Torrey Smith		

1968 Champion Corn Flakes

These cards were thought to have been issued on Champion Corn Flakes boxes around 1968, but the year has yet to have been confirmed. Each card measures approximately 2 1/16" by 3 3/16, is blankbacked, and features perforations on the edges. The cardfronts feature a color action player photo surrounded by a thin black border on three sides with the player's name and number at the bottom within a thick black border. The cards are apparently reprints of Sports Illustrated posters that were made available in the late 1960s. The card number consists of a numerical team code and AFL or NFL league letter assigned to each team (Examples: 7N for Packers and NFL, 6A for Chiefs and AFL) followed by the player's jersey number. Any additional confirmed information or additions to this list are appreciated. The recently discovered Floyd Little and Lance Rentzel cards were apparently issued without a player image on the cardfronts and have not yet been priced due to perceived scarcity.

1A35 Jim Nance	35.00	60.00
1N34 Junior Coffey	35.00	60.00
1N60 Tommy Nobis	50.00	80.00
2A15 Jack Kemp	125.00	200.00
2N41 Tom Matte	50.00	80.00
2N88 John Mackey	50.00	80.00
3A42 Warren McVea UER	35.00	60.00
(name misspelled McVey)		
3N40 Gale Sayers	175.00	300.00
3N51 Dick Butkus	175.00	300.00
4A44 Floyd Little ERR No Photo		
4N13 Frank Ryan	50.00	80.00
4N44 Leroy Kelly	60.00	100.00
5A90 George Webster	50.00	80.00
5N19 Lance Rentzel ERR No Photo		
5N30 Dan Reeves	60.00	100.00
5N74 Bob Lilly	125.00	200.00
6A16 Len Dawson	125.00	200.00
6A21 Mike Garrett	35.00	60.00
6N20 Lem Barney	50.00	80.00
6N24 Mel Farr	35.00	60.00
7A12 Bob Griese	150.00	250.00
7A39 Larry Csonka	150.00	250.00
Bob Griese in background		
7N15 Bart Starr	300.00	500.00
7N33 Jim Grabowski	50.00	80.00
7N66 Ray Nitschke	125.00	200.00
8A12 Joe Namath	300.00	500.00
8A13 Don Maynard	90.00	150.00
8A83 George Sauer	50.00	80.00
8N18 Roman Gabriel	60.00	100.00
8N75 Deacon Jones	60.00	100.00
9A13 Daryle Lamonica	60.00	100.00
9A40 Pete Banaszak	35.00	60.00
9N30 Bill Brown RB	35.00	60.00
9N84 Gene Washington Vik	35.00	60.00
10A19 Lance Alworth	125.00	200.00
10A21 John Hadl	60.00	100.00
10N17 Billy Kilmer	50.00	80.00
10N31 Jim Taylor	125.00	200.00
11N45 Homer Jones	35.00	60.00
12N16 Norm Snead	50.00	80.00
12N18 Ben Hawkins	35.00	60.00
13N10 Kent Nix	35.00	60.00
13N24 Andy Russell	50.00	80.00
13N47 Marv Woodson	35.00	60.00
14N12 Charley Johnson	50.00	80.00
14N25 Jim Bakken	35.00	60.00
15N12 John Brodie	75.00	125.00
16N9 Sonny Jurgensen	90.00	150.00
16N42 Charley Taylor	50.00	80.00

1960 Chargers Team Issue 5x7

The Chargers released these photos in 1960 - their only year in Los Angeles. Each measures approximately 5" by 7" and includes a black and white photo on the cardfront with a blankback. The player's name appears below the photo to the left with the team name oriented to the right.

1 Charlie Flowers	7.50	15.00
2 Jim Sears	7.50	15.00

1960 Chargers Team Issue 8x10

The Chargers released these photos in 1960 - their only year in Los Angeles. Each measures approximately 5" by 7" and includes a black and white photo on the cardfront with a blankback. The player's name appears below the photo to the left with the team name oriented to the right.

1 Howie Ferguson	10.00	20.00
2 Jack Kemp	20.00	40.00

1961 Chargers Golden Tulip

The 1961 Golden Tulip Chips football card set contains 22 black and white cards featuring San Diego (Los Angeles in 1960) Chargers AFL players. The cards measure approximately 2" by 3" and are commonly found with roughly cut or irregularly shaped edges. The fronts contain the player's name, a short biography, and vital statistics. The backs, which are the same for all cards, contain an ad for XETV television, a premium offer for (approximately) 8" by 10" photos and an ad for a free ticket contest. The cards are unnumbered but have been numbered in alphabetical order in the checklist below for your convenience. The catalog designation for this set is F395.

COMPLETE SET (22)	1,200.00	1,800.00
1 Ron Botchan	40.00	75.00
2 Howard Clark	40.00	75.00
3 Fred Cole	40.00	75.00
4 Sam DeLuca	40.00	75.00
5 Orlando Ferrante	40.00	75.00
6 Charlie Flowers	40.00	75.00
7 Dick Harris	40.00	75.00
8 Emil Karas	40.00	75.00
9 Jack Kemp	300.00	500.00
10 Dave Kocourek	40.00	75.00
11 Bob Laraba	40.00	75.00
12 Paul Lowe	50.00	100.00
13 Paul Maguire	50.00	100.00
14 Charlie McNeil	40.00	75.00
15 Ron Mix	75.00	150.00
16 Ron Nery	40.00	75.00
17 Don Norton	40.00	75.00
18 Volney Peters	40.00	75.00
19 Don Rogers	40.00	75.00
20 Maury Schleicher	50.00	100.00
21 Ernie Wright	50.00	100.00
22 Bob Zeman	40.00	75.00

1961 Chargers Golden Tulip Premiums

These oversized (roughly 8" by 10") photos were issued as premiums for collectors in 1961. Each was mailed in exchange for 5-Golden Tulip cards of the featured player. The photos are black and white and include a facsimile player autograph on the front along with a small Golden Tulip Potato Chips logo.

1 Charlie Flowers	125.00	200.00
2 Dick Harris	125.00	200.00
3 Jack Kemp	350.00	600.00
4 Dave Kocourek	125.00	200.00
5 Paul Maguire	150.00	250.00
6 Charlie McNeil	125.00	200.00
7 Ron Mix	175.00	300.00
8 Don Norton	125.00	200.00
9 Volney Peters	125.00	200.00
10 Don Rogers	125.00	200.00
11 Ernie Wright	150.00	250.00
12 Bob Zeman	125.00	200.00

1961-64 Chargers Team Issue 8x10

The Chargers released these photos over a number of seasons. Each measures approximately 8" by 10" and includes a black and white photo on the cardfront with a blankback. The player's name appears below the photo and to the left with the team name oriented to the right. As is common with many team issued photos, the text style and size varies slightly from photo to photo. We've noted known photo variations below and added a number in parenthesis for other players with reported variations.

1 Chuck Allen	7.50	15.00
2 Lance Alworth (2)	15.00	30.00
3 Lance Alworth	12.50	25.00
Dave Kocourek		
Reg Carolan		
4 Lance Alworth	12.50	25.00
Don Norton		
Dave Kocourek		
Reg Carolan		
5 Ernie Barnes	7.50	15.00
6 George Blair	7.50	15.00
7 Frank Buncom	7.50	15.00
8 Reg Carolan	7.50	15.00
9 Ron Carpenter	7.50	15.00
10 Bert Coan	7.50	15.00
11 Sam DeLuca (2)	7.50	15.00
12 Hunter Enis	7.50	15.00
13 Earl Faison	7.50	15.00
14 Claude Gibson	7.50	15.00
15 Sid Gillman	10.00	20.00
16 Ken Graham	7.50	15.00
17 George Gross	7.50	15.00
18 Sam Gruneisen	7.50	15.00
19 John Hadl	12.50	25.00
20 John Hadl	12.50	25.00
Willie Frazier		
21 Dick Harris	7.50	15.00
22 Bill Hudson	7.50	15.00
Richard Hudson		
23 Richard Hudson	7.50	15.00
24 Bob Jackson	7.50	15.00
25 Emil Karas	7.50	15.00
26A Jack Kemp	15.00	30.00
(passing, crowd background)		
26B Jack Kemp	15.00	30.00
(standing, empty stadium)		
26C Jack Kemp	15.00	30.00
(close-up, ball in hands)		
27 Keith Kinderman	7.50	15.00
28 Gary Kirner	7.50	15.00
29 Dave Kocourek (2)	7.50	15.00
30 Ernie Ladd (3)	10.00	20.00
31 Bob Lane (2)	7.50	15.00
32 Keith Lincoln (3)	10.00	20.00
33 Paul Lowe (2)	10.00	20.00
34A Jacque MacKinnon	7.50	15.00
(diving catch, empty stadium)		
34B Jacque MacKinn	7.50	15.00
(rushing forward, empty onstadium)		
34C Jacque MacKinnon	7.50	15.00
(diving catch, rural background)		
34D Jacque MacKinnon	7.50	15.00
(rushing right, fence background)		
35 Joe Madro	7.50	15.00
36A Paul Maguire	10.00	20.00
([punting, ball near foot)		
36B Paul Maguire	10.00	20.00
([punting, no ball in photo)		
37 Charlie McNeil (2)	7.50	15.00
38 Tommy Minter	7.50	15.00
39 Bob Mitinger	7.50	15.00
40 Ron Mix	12.50	25.00
41 Ron Nery	7.50	15.00
42 Don Norton	7.50	15.00
43 Ernie Park	7.50	15.00
44 Bob Petrich (2)	7.50	15.00
45 Bo Roberson	7.50	15.00
46 Jerry Robinson	7.50	15.00
47 Don Rogers	7.50	15.00
48 Tobin Rote (2)	10.00	20.00
49 Tobin Rote	10.00	20.00
Keith Linclon		
50 Alvin Roy	10.00	20.00
Keith Linclon		
51 Henry Schmidt	7.50	15.00
52 Pat Shea	7.50	15.00
53 Walt Sweeney (2)	7.50	15.00
54 Jim Warren	7.50	15.00
55 Dick Westmoreland (2)	7.50	15.00
56 Bud Whitehead	7.50	15.00
57 Ernie Wright (2)	7.50	15.00
58 1964 Coaching Staff	7.50	15.00
59 1961 Team Photo	10.00	20.00
60 1962 Team Photo	10.00	20.00
61 1963 Team Photo	10.00	20.00
62 1964 Team Photo	10.00	20.00

1962 Chargers Golden Arrow Dairy Bottle Caps

This set of milk caps was issued in 1962, and possibly 1963, by the Golden Arrow Dairy in the San Diego area. Each blankbacked paper milk bottle cap features a black and white drawing of a player or other AFL or team subject along with the team name printed above and his position printed bleow the image. These milk caps are exceedingly scarce and were cataloged for the first time in 2008. The saver sheet is a white paper poster with a football field printed on it along with spaces to align the milk caps into a football play formation. The saver sheet reports that 35 different player caps were produced, therefore it is thought that our list below is not fully complete.

1 Chuck Allen	75.00	150.00
2 Lance Alworth	175.00	300.00
3 Ernie Barnes	75.00	150.00
4 Jim Bates	75.00	150.00
5 Frank Buncom	75.00	150.00
6 Bert Coan	75.00	150.00
7 Earl Faison	75.00	150.00
8 Joe Foss Comm.	75.00	150.00
9 Claude Gibson	75.00	150.00
10 Sid Gillman CO	100.00	200.00
11 George Gross	75.00	150.00
12 John Hadl	150.00	250.00
13 Dick Harris	75.00	150.00
14 Barron Hilton Pres.	75.00	150.00
15 Bill Hudson	75.00	150.00
16 Dick Hudson	75.00	150.00
17 Bob Jackson	75.00	150.00
18 Emil Karas	75.00	150.00
19 Jack Kemp	200.00	400.00
20 Ernie Ladd	100.00	200.00
21 Keith Lincoln	100.00	200.00
22 Paul Lowe	100.00	200.00
23 Jacque MacKinnon	75.00	150.00
24 Paul Maguire	100.00	200.00
25 Bob Mitinger	75.00	150.00
26 Ron Mix	150.00	250.00
27 Ron Nery	75.00	150.00
28 Don Norton	75.00	150.00
29 Sherman Plunkett	75.00	150.00
30 Don Rogers	75.00	150.00
31 Tobin Rote	100.00	200.00
32 Maury Schleicher	75.00	150.00
33 Mark Schmidt	75.00	150.00
34 Bud Whitehead	75.00	150.00
35 Ernie Wright	75.00	150.00
36 Saver Sheet	75.00	150.00

1962 Chargers Union Oil

The set was sponsored by Union 76. All players featured in the set are members of the San Diego Chargers. They are derived from sketches by the artist, Patrick. The cards are black and white, approximately 6" by 8" with player biography and Union Oil logo on backs. The catalog designation for the set is U035-2. The cards were reportedly issued with an album with 24 spaces for the photos. The key cards in this set are quarterback Jack Kemp, who would later gain fame as a politician, as well as cards issued during the rookie season of future Hall of Famer Lance Alworth and star quarterback John Hadl.

COMPLETE SET (16)	350.00	600.00
1 Chuck Allen	10.00	20.00
2 Lance Alworth	75.00	125.00
3 Earl Faison	10.00	20.00
4 John Hadl	25.00	40.00
5 Dick Harris	10.00	20.00
6 Bill Hudson	10.00	20.00
7 Jack Kemp	125.00	250.00
8 Dave Kocourek	10.00	20.00
9 Ernie Ladd	20.00	35.00
10 Keith Lincoln	12.50	25.00
11 Paul Lowe	12.50	25.00
12 Charlie McNeil	10.00	20.00
13 Ron Mix	20.00	35.00
14 Ron Nery	10.00	20.00
15 Don Norton	10.00	20.00
16 Team Photo	15.00	30.00

1964 Chargers Team Issue

Photos from this set, measuring approximately 5 1/2" by 8 1/2", were issued over a number of years. Each features black and white close-up player photos on off-white linen weave paper (same as 1965-67 Chargers Team Issue). The player's facsimile autograph is centered beneath each picture above the team name. The 1964 issue has biographical and statistical information on the backs that helps to identify the year of issue. Because the set is unnumbered, players and coaches are listed alphabetically.

COMPLETE SET (36)	150.00	300.00
1 Chuck Allen	6.00	12.00
2 Lance Alworth	12.50	25.00
3 George Blair	6.00	12.00
4 Frank Buncom	6.00	12.00
5 Earl Faison	6.00	12.00
6 Sid Gillman CO	7.50	15.00
7 George Gross	6.00	12.00
8 Sam Gruneisen	6.00	12.00
9 Walt Hackett CO	6.00	12.00
10 John Hadl	10.00	20.00
11 Dick Harris	6.00	12.00
12 Bob Jackson	6.00	12.00
13 Emil Karas	6.00	12.00
14 Dave Kocourek	6.00	12.00
15 Ernie Ladd	7.50	15.00
16 Keith Lincoln	7.50	15.00
17 Paul Lowe	7.50	15.00
18 Jacque MacKinnon	6.00	12.00
19 Joe Madro CO	6.00	12.00
20 Gerry McDougall	6.00	12.00
21 Charlie McNeil	6.00	12.00
22 Bob Mitinger	6.00	12.00
23 Ron Mix	10.00	20.00
24 Chuck Noll CO	10.00	20.00
25 Don Norton	6.00	12.00
26 Bob Petrich	6.00	12.00
27 Jerry Robinson	6.00	12.00
28 Don Rogers	6.00	12.00
29 Tobin Rote	7.50	15.00
30 Hank Schmidt	6.00	12.00
31 Pat Shea	6.00	12.00
32 Walt Sweeney	7.50	15.00
33 Dick Westmoreland	6.00	12.00
34 Bud Whitehead	6.00	12.00
35 Ernie Wright	6.00	12.00
36 1963 Team Photo	7.50	15.00

1965-67 Chargers Team Issue

This team issue set, with photos measuring approximately 5 1/2" by 8 1/2", was issued over at least a couple of years, with a few personnel changes reflected each year. This series features black and white close-up player photos on off-white linen weave paper. The player's facsimile autograph is centered beneath each picture above the team name. Some photos were issued with biographical information on the back (primarily in 1964 and 1966), while others have blank backs (issued primarily in 1967). We've included known variations below, but the checklist is thought to be incomplete. Because the set is unnumbered, players and coaches are listed alphabetically. This set is interesting in that it features an early issue of Bum Phillips.

1A Chuck Allen	6.00	12.00
blank backed		
1B Chuck Allen/1966 bio on back	6.00	12.00
2A Jim Allison	6.00	12.00
blank backed		
2B Jim Allison/1966 bio on back	6.00	12.00
3A Lance Alworth	25.00	40.00
blank backed		
3B Lance Alworth/1966 bio on back	25.00	40.00
4A Tom Bass CO	6.00	12.00
blank backed		
4B Tom Bass CO/1966 bio on back	6.00	12.00
5A Joe Beauchamp	6.00	12.00
blank backed		
6A Frank Buncom	6.00	12.00
blank backed		
6B Frank Buncom/1966 bio on back	6.00	12.00
7A Ron Carpenter	6.00	12.00
blank backed		
7B Ron Carpenter/1966 bio on back	6.00	12.00
8A Richard Degen	6.00	12.00
blank backed		
9A Steve DeLong	6.00	12.00
blank backed		
9B Steve DeLong/1966 bio on back	6.00	12.00
10A Speedy Duncan	6.00	12.00
blank backed		
10B Speedy Duncan/1966 bio on back	6.00	12.00
11A Earl Faison	6.00	12.00
(1966 bio on back		
12A John Farris	6.00	12.00
(blank backed		
12B John Farris	6.00	12.00
(1966 bio on back		
13A Gene Foster	6.00	12.00
blank backed		
13B Gene Foster/1966 bio on back	6.00	12.00
14A Willie Frazier	6.00	12.00
blank backed		
15A Gary Garrison	6.00	12.00
blank backed		
15B Gary Garrison/1966 bio on back	6.00	12.00
16A Sid Gillman CO	7.50	15.00
blank backed		
16B Sid Gillman CO	7.50	15.00
coaching record on back		
through 1965)		
17A Kenny Graham	6.00	12.00
blank backed)		
17B Kenny Graham/1966 bio on back)	6.00	12.00
18A Jim Griffin	6.00	12.00
(blank backed)		
18B Jim Griffin	6.00	12.00
(1966 bio on back)		
19A George Gross	6.00	12.00
blank backed)		
19B George Gross/1967 bio on back)	6.00	12.00
20A Sam Gruneisen	6.00	12.00
blank backed)		
20B Sam Gruneisen/1966 bio on back)	6.00	12.00
21A Walt Hackett CO	6.00	12.00
(blank backed)		
22A John Hadl	15.00	25.00
(blank backed)		
22B John Hadl	15.00	25.00
(1966 bio on back)		
23A Dick Harris	6.00	12.00
blank backed)		
23B Dick Harris/1966 bio on back)	6.00	12.00
24A Dan Henning	6.00	12.00
blank backed)		
25A Bob Horton	6.00	12.00
26A Harry Johnston CO	6.00	12.00
blank backed)		
27A Howard Kindig	6.00	12.00
blank backed)		
28A Gary Kirner	6.00	12.00
(blank backed)		
28B Gary Kirner	6.00	12.00
(1966 bio on back)		
29A Dave Kocourek	6.00	12.00
(1966 bio on back)		
30A Ernie Ladd	7.50	15.00
(1966 bio on back)		
31A Mike London	6.00	12.00
(1966 bio on back)		
32A Jacque MacKinnon	6.00	12.00
blank backed)		
32B Jacque MacKinnon/1966 bio on back)	6.00	12.00
33A Joe Madro CO	6.00	12.00
blank backed)		
33B Joe Madro CO/1966 bio on back)	6.00	12.00
34A Lloyd McCoy	6.00	12.00
(blank backed)		
35A Ed Mitchell	6.00	12.00
blank backed)		
35B Ron Mix	10.00	20.00
blank backed)		
36A Fred Moore	6.00	12.00
blank backed)		
36B Fred Moore/1966 bio on back)	6.00	12.00
37A Chuck Noll CO	10.00	20.00
(blank backed)		
38A Don Norton	6.00	12.00
blank backed)		
38B Don Norton/1966 bio on back)	6.00	12.00
39A Terry Owens	6.00	12.00
blank backed)		
39B Terry Owens	6.00	12.00
(1966 bio on back)		
40A Bob Petrich	6.00	12.00
(blank backed)		
40B Bob Petrich	6.00	12.00
(1966 bio on back)		
41A Bum Phillips CO	7.50	15.00
blank backed)		
42A Dave Plump	6.00	12.00
blank backed)		
43A Rick Redman	6.00	12.00
blank backed)		
43B Rick Redman/1966 bio on back)	6.00	12.00
44A Houston Ridge	6.00	12.00
blank backed)		
45A Hank Schmidt	6.00	12.00
(blank backed)		
46A Pat Shea	6.00	12.00
blank backed)		
46B Pat Shea	6.00	12.00
(1966 bio on back)		
47A Jackie Simpson CO	6.00	12.00
blank backed)		
48A Walt Sweeney	7.50	15.00
blank backed)		
48B Walt Sweeney/1966 bio on back)	7.50	15.00
49A Sammy Taylor	6.00	12.00
49B Steve Tensi	6.00	12.00
blank backed)		
50A Herb Travenio	6.00	12.00
51A John Travis	6.00	12.00
blank backed)		
52A Dick Van Raaphorst	6.00	12.00
blank backed)		
53A Charlie Waller CO	6.00	12.00
blank backed)		
53B Charlie Waller CO/1966 bio on back)	6.00	12.00
54A Bud Whitehead	6.00	12.00
blank backed)		
54B Bud Whitehead/1966 bio on back)	6.00	12.00
55A Nat Whitmyer	6.00	12.00
blank backed)		
55B Nat Whitmyer/1966 bio on back)	6.00	12.00
56A Ernie Wright	7.50	15.00
blank backed)		
56B Ernie Wright/1966 bio on back)	7.50	15.00
57A Bob Zeman	6.00	12.00
(1966 bio on back)		
58A 1965 Team Photo	10.00	20.00
58B 1966 Team Photo	10.00	20.00

1966-68 Chargers Team Issue 5X7

The Chargers released these photos over a number of seasons. Each measures approximately 5" by 7" and includes a black and white photo on the cardfront with a blankback. The player's name appears below the photo to the left with his position centered. The Chargers' team name appears on the right and is in the style with the goalpost shaped H. The type styles and sizes can vary slightly from photo to photo.

COMPLETE SET (15)	60.00	120.00
1 Harold Akin	5.00	10.00
2 Scott Appleton	5.00	10.00
3 Tom Denman CO	5.00	10.00
4 Ken Dyer	5.00	10.00
5 Willie Frazier	5.00	10.00
6 Barron Hilton OWN	5.00	10.00
7 Brad Hubbert	5.00	10.00
8 Harry Johnston CO	5.00	10.00
9 Irv Kaze OFF	5.00	10.00
10 Paul Lowe	6.00	12.00
11 Don Norton	5.00	10.00
12 Dick Van Raaphorst	5.00	10.00
13 Charlie Waller CO	5.00	10.00
14 Bob Wells	5.00	10.00
15 Bob Zeman	5.00	10.00

1968 Chargers Team Issue 7x9

The Chargers released these photos over a number of seasons. Each measures approximately 7" by 9" and includes a black and white photo on the cardfront with a blankback. The player's name appears below the photo to the left with his position centered. The Chargers' team name appears on the right and is in the style with the goalpost shaped H. The type styles and sizes can vary slightly from photo to photo.

COMPLETE SET (23)	100.00	200.00
1 Chuck Allen	5.00	10.00
2A Lance Alworth	12.50	25.00
(catching a pass)		
2B Lance Alworth	12.50	25.00
(portrait holding football)		
3 Scott Appleton	5.00	10.00
4 Jon Brittenum	5.00	10.00
5 Steve DeLong	5.00	10.00
6 Les Duncan	6.00	12.00
7 Dick Farley	5.00	10.00
8 Gene Foster	5.00	10.00
9 Willie Frazier	5.00	10.00
10 Gary Garrison	5.00	10.00
11 Ken Graham	5.00	10.00
12 Sam Gruneisen	5.00	10.00
13 John Hadl	7.50	15.00
14 Bob Howard	5.00	10.00
15 Gary Kirner	5.00	10.00
16 Larry Little	10.00	20.00
17 Ron Mix	10.00	20.00
18 Terry Owens	5.00	10.00
19 Dick Post	5.00	10.00
20 Rick Redman	5.00	10.00
21 Houston Ridge	5.00	10.00
22 Jeff Staggs	5.00	10.00
23 Walt Sweeney	5.00	10.00

1968 Chargers Team Issue 8x11

This set featuring members of the 1968 San Diego Chargers features sepia toned player photos measuring approximately 8 1/2" by 11". The backs are blank. The cards are unnumbered and checklisted below in alphabetical order. The 1968 photos are nearly identical to the 1969 issue but can be differentiated by the slightly larger type size. Also, most of the photos were produced with the facsimile autograph appearing over the image of the player.

COMPLETE SET (8)	50.00	100.00
1 Lance Alworth	12.50	25.00
(catching pass over head)		
2 Harold Akin	7.50	15.00
3 Bob Howard	6.00	12.00
4 Chuck Allen	6.00	12.00
5 Ron Mix	7.50	15.00
6 Dick Post	6.00	12.00
7 Jeff Staggs	6.00	12.00
8 Walt Sweeney	6.00	12.00

1968 Chargers Volpe Tumblers

These Chargers artist's renderings were part of a plastic cup tumbler product produced in 1968 and distributed by White Front Stores. The noted sports artist Volpe created the artwork which includes an action scene and a player portrait. Each is unnumbered, measures approximately 5" by 8 1/2" when flat, and is curved in the shape required to fit inside a plastic cup. The manufacturer notation PGC (Programs General Corp) is printed on each piece as well. There are thought to be 6-cups included in this set. Any additions to this list are appreciated.

1 Chuck Allen	20.00	40.00
2 Kenny Graham	20.00	40.00
3 John Hadl	25.00	50.00
4 Dick Post	20.00	40.00

1969 Chargers Team Issue 8x11

This set of the 1969 San Diego Chargers was issued by the team. Each features a black-and-white player photo measuring approximately 8 1/2" by 11". The backs are blank. The cards are unnumbered and checklisted below in alphabetical order. The 1969 photos are nearly identical to the 1968 issue but can be differentiated by the smaller type size. Also all of the photos were produced with the facsimile autograph appearing away from the player image.

COMPLETE SET (11)	60.00	120.00
1 Lance Alworth	10.00	20.00
(kneeling, hand on football)		
2 Les Duncan	5.00	10.00
3 Gary Garrison	5.00	10.00
4 Kenny Graham	5.00	10.00
5 John Hadl	7.50	15.00
6 Ron Mix	7.50	15.00
7 Dick Post	5.00	10.00
8 Jeff Staggs	5.00	10.00
9 Walt Sweeney	6.00	12.00
10 Russ Washington	5.00	10.00
11 Team Photo	6.00	12.00

1970 Chargers Team Issue 8X10

This set of photos featuring the 1970 San Diego Chargers was issued by the team. Each features a black-and-white player photo measuring approximately 8" by 10" with blank backs. The player's name is included below the image oriented to the left with his position in the center and the Chargers' team name to the right. Each player is pictured in a posed kneeling photo with his hand on his helmet which includes the player's jersey number. The photos are unnumbered and checklisted below in alphabetical order.

COMPLETE SET (20)	75.00	150.00
1 Lance Alworth	10.00	20.00
2 Bob Babich	5.00	10.00
3 Pete Barnes	5.00	10.00
4 Joe Beauchamp	5.00	10.00
5 Ron Billingsley	5.00	10.00
6 Gene Ferguson	5.00	10.00
7 Gene Foster	5.00	10.00
8 Mike Garrett	6.00	12.00
9 Gary Garrison	5.00	10.00
10 Ira Gordon	5.00	10.00
11 Sam Gruneisen	5.00	10.00
12 Jim Hill	5.00	10.00
13 Bob Howard	5.00	10.00
14 Joe Owens	5.00	10.00
15 Dennis Partee	5.00	10.00
16 Dick Post	5.00	10.00
17 Jeff Staggs	5.00	10.00
18 Walt Sweeney	6.00	12.00
19 Jim Tolbert	5.00	10.00
20 Russ Washington	5.00	10.00

1974 Chargers Team Issue

Photos in this set were issued by the team to fulfill fan requests. Each features a black-and-white player photo measuring approximately 8 1/2" by 11" with blank backs. The team name "Chargers" is printed to the far left below the image and the player's name and position (spelled out) are oriented to the far right side. The photos are unnumbered and checklisted below in alphabetical order.

1 Harrison Davis	5.00	10.00
2 Jesse Freitas	5.00	10.00
3 John Teerlink	5.00	10.00

1976 Chargers Dean's Photo

This 10-card set was sponsored by Dean's Photo Service and features nine San Diego Chargers' players. The cards were released on an uncut perforated sheet with each card measuring approximately 5" by 8." The player photos are black and white, but the team helmet is printed in color. The cards are blank backed and unnumbered.

COMPLETE SET (10)	30.00	60.00
1 Pat Currin	2.50	5.00
2 Chris Fletcher	2.50	5.00
3 Dan Fouts	10.00	20.00
4 Gary Garrison	3.00	6.00
5 Louie Kelcher	3.00	6.00
6 Joe Washington	3.00	6.00
7 Russ Washington	2.50	5.00
8 Doug Wilkerson	2.50	5.00
9 Don Woods	2.50	5.00
10 Schedule Card	2.50	5.00
Dean's coupons attached		

1976 Chargers Team Sheets

The San Diego Chargers issued these sheets of black-and-white player photos around 1976. Each measures roughly 8" by 10 1/4" and was printed on glossy stock with white borders. Each sheet includes photos of 3-players and/or coaches. Below each player's image is his jersey number, his name, position and the team name. The photos are blankbacked.

COMPLETE SET (16)	75.00	125.00
1 Charles Anthony	5.00	10.00
Doug Wilkerson		
Louie Kelcher		
2 Ken Bernich	4.00	8.00
Mark Markovich		
Floyd Rice		
3 Bob Brown	4.00	8.00
Coy Bacon		
Dwight McDonald		
4 Booker Brown	4.00	8.00
Billy Shields		
Ira Gordon		
5 Earnel Durden CO	4.00	8.00
Bobb McKittrick CO		
Howard Mudd CO		
6 Rudy Feldman CO	4.00	8.00
Dick Coury CO		
George Dickson CO		
7 Jesse Freitas	4.00	8.00
Mike Williams		
Glen Bonner		
8 Mike Fuller	4.00	8.00
Chris Fletcher		
Sam Williams		
9 Gary Garrison	5.00	10.00
Dennis Partee		
Don Woods		
10 Don Goode	4.00	8.00
Ed Flanagan		
Carl Gersbach		
11 Neal Jeffrey	10.00	20.00
Dan Fouts		
Ray Wersching		
12 Dave Lowe	4.00	8.00
Terry Owens		
John Teerlinck		
13 Tommy Prothro CO	5.00	10.00
John David Crow CO		
Jackie Simpson CO		
14 Bob Thomas	4.00	8.00
Joe Beauchamp		
Bo Matthews		
15 Charles Wadnelk	4.00	8.00
Harrison Davis		
Wayne Stewart		
16 Russ Washington	5.00	10.00
Fred Dean		
Gary Johnson		

1981 Chargers Jack in the Box Prints

These large prints were issued by Jack in the Box stores in 1981. Each features an artist's rendering of a group of Chargers players on the front and a write-up of the featured players on the back.

COMPLETE SET (4)	30.00	75.00
1 Charger Power	8.00	20.00
Chuck Muncie		
Ed White		
Doug Wilkerson		
2 Air Coryell	12.00	30.00
Dan Fouts		
Charlie Joiner		
Kellen Winslow		
3 Powerline	10.00	15.00
Fred Dean		
Gary Johnson		
Leroy Jones		
Louie Kelcher		
4 Very Special Teams	10.00	15.00
Rolf Benirschke		
three other players		

1981 Chargers Police

The 1981 San Diego Chargers set contains 24 unnumbered cards of 22 subjects. The cards measure approximately 2 5/8" by 4 1/8". The cards are listed in the checklist below by the uniform number which appears on the fronts of the cards. The set is sponsored by the Kiwanis Club, the local law enforcement agency, and Pepsi-Cola. A Chargers helmet logo and "Chargers Tips" appear on the card backs. The card backs have black print with blue trim on white card stock. The Kiwanis and Chargers helmet logos appear on the fronts. Fouts and Winslow each exist with two different safety tips on the backs; the variations are distinguished below by the first few words of the safety tip. The complete set price below includes the variation cards.

COMPLETE SET (24)	40.00	75.00
6 Rolf Benirschke	1.00	2.50
14A Dan Fouts	6.00	15.00
(After a team ...)		
14B Dan Fouts	3.00	8.00
(Once you've ...)		
18 Charlie Joiner	2.00	5.00
25 John Cappelletti	1.00	2.50
28 Willie Buchanon	.75	2.00
29 Mike Williams	.75	2.00
43 Bob Gregor	.75	2.00
44 Pete Shaw	.75	2.00
46 Chuck Muncie	1.00	2.50
51 Woodrow Lowe	.75	2.00
57 Linden King	.75	2.00
59 Cliff Thrift	.75	2.00
62 Don Macek	.75	2.00
63 Doug Wilkerson	.75	2.00
66 Billy Shields	.75	2.00
67 Ed White	.75	2.00
68 Leroy Jones	.75	2.00
70 Russ Washington	.75	2.00
74 Louie Kelcher	1.00	2.50
79 Gary Johnson	.75	2.00
80A Kellen Winslow	5.00	12.00
(Go all out ...)		
80B Kellen Winslow	3.00	8.00
(The length of ...)		
NNO Don Coryell CO	1.00	2.50

1982 Chargers Police

The 1982 San Diego Chargers Police set contains 16 unnumbered cards. The cards measure approximately 2 5/8" by 4 1/8". Although uniform numbers appear on the fronts of the cards, the set has been listed below in alphabetical order. The set is sponsored by the Kiwanis Club, the local law enforcement agency, and Pepsi-Cola. Chargers Tips, in addition to the helmet logo of the Chargers, the Pepsi-Cola logo and a police logo appear on the backs. Card backs have black printing with blue accent on white backs. The Kiwanis logo and Chargers helmet appear on the fronts of the cards.

COMPLETE SET (16)	20.00	40.00
1 Rolf Benirschke	1.00	2.50
2 James Brooks	1.50	4.00
3 Wes Chandler	1.50	4.00
4 Dan Fouts	3.00	8.00
5 Tim Fox	1.00	2.50
6 Gary Johnson	1.00	2.50
7 Charlie Joiner	2.50	6.00
8 Louie Kelcher	1.00	2.50
9 Linden King	.75	2.00
10 Bruce Laird	.75	2.00
11 David Lewis	.75	2.00
12 Don Macek	.75	2.00
13 Billy Shields	.75	2.00
14 Eric Sievers	.75	2.00
15 Russ Washington	.75	2.00
16 Kellen Winslow	3.00	8.00

1985 Chargers Kodak

This set was sponsored by Kodak and measures approximately 5 1/2" by 8 1/2". The fronts have white borders and action color photos. The player's name, position, and a Chargers helmet icon appear below the picture. The backs have biographical information. The set is listed below in alphabetical order by player's name. It is thought that the checklist could be incomplete. Any additions to this list are appreciated.

COMPLETE SET (43)	50.00	100.00
1 Jesse Bendross	.75	2.00
2 Rolf Benirschke	1.25	3.00
3 Carlos Bradley	.75	2.00
4 Maury Buford	.75	2.00
5 Gill Byrd	1.25	3.00
6 Wes Chandler	2.00	5.00
7 Sam Claphan	.75	2.00
8 Don Coryell CO	1.25	3.00
9 Bobby Duckworth	.75	2.00
10 Chuck Ehin	.75	2.00
11 Bill Elko	.75	2.00
12 Keith Ferguson	.75	2.00
13 Dan Fouts	6.00	15.00
14 Andrew Gissinger	.75	2.00
15 Derrel Gofourth	.75	2.00
16 Mike Green	.75	2.00
17 Keith Guthrie	.75	2.00
18 Pete Holohan	.75	2.00
19 Earnest Jackson	1.25	3.00
20 Lionel James	1.25	3.00
21 Charlie Joiner	4.00	10.00
22 Bill Kay	.75	2.00
23 Linden King	.75	2.00
24 Chuck Loewen	.75	2.00
25 Woodrow Lowe	.75	2.00
26 Don Macek	.75	2.00
27 Bruce Mathison	.75	2.00
28 Buford McGee	.75	2.00
29 Dennis McKnight	.75	2.00
30 Miles McPherson	.75	2.00
31 Derrie Nelson	.75	2.00
32 Vince Osby	.75	2.00
33 Fred Robinson	.75	2.00
34 Eric Sievers	.75	2.00
35 Billy Ray Smith	1.25	3.00
36 Lucious Smith	.75	2.00
37 Cliff Thrift	.75	2.00
38 John Turner	.75	2.00
39 Danny Walters	.75	2.00
40 Ed White	.75	2.00
41 Doug Wilkerson	.75	2.00
42 Lee Williams	1.25	3.00
43 Kellen Winslow	4.00	10.00

1986 Chargers Kodak

This set of 48-photos featuring the San Diego Chargers was sponsored by Kodak and measures approximately 5 1/2" by 8 1/2". The fronts feature color action photos with white borders. Biographical information is given below the photo between the Chargers' helmet on the left and the Kodak logo on the right. The backs are blank. The photos are unnumbered and checklisted below in alphabetical order.

COMPLETE SET (48)	50.00	100.00
1 Curtis Adams	.75	2.00
2 Gary Anderson RB	1.50	4.00
3 Jesse Bendross	.75	2.00
4 Rolf Benirschke	1.25	3.00
5 Carlos Bradley	.75	2.00
6 Gill Byrd	1.25	3.00
7 Wes Chandler	1.25	3.00
8 Sam Claphan	.75	2.00
9 Don Coryell CO	1.25	3.00
10 Jeffery Dale	.75	2.00
11 Wayne Davis	.75	2.00
12 Jerry Doerger	.75	2.00
13 Chuck Ehin	.75	2.00
14 Chris Faulkner	.75	2.00
15 Mark Fellows	.75	2.00
16 Dan Fouts	5.00	12.00
17 Mike Green	.75	2.00
18 Mike Guendling	.75	2.00
19 John Hendy	.75	2.00
20 Mark Herrmann	.75	2.00
21 Pete Holohan	1.25	3.00
22 Lionel James	1.25	3.00
23 Trumaine Johnson	.75	2.00
24 Charlie Joiner	3.00	8.00
25 David King	.75	2.00
26 Linden King	.75	2.00
27 Gary Kowalski	.75	2.00
28 Jim Lachey	1.25	3.00
29 Woodrow Lowe	.75	2.00
30 Don Macek	.75	2.00
31 Buford McGee	.75	2.00
32 Dennis McKnight	.75	2.00
33 Ralf Mojsiejenko	.75	2.00
34 Derrie Nelson	.75	2.00
35 Ron O'Bard	.75	2.00
36 Fred Robinson	.75	2.00
37 Eric Sievers	.75	2.00
38 Tony Simmons DE	.75	2.00
39 Billy Ray Smith	1.25	3.00
40 Lucious Smith	.75	2.00
41 Alex G. Spanos PRES	.75	2.00
42 Tim Spencer	1.25	3.00
43 Bob Thomas	.75	2.00
44 Rich Umphrey	.75	2.00
45 Danny Walters	.75	2.00
46 Ed White	.75	2.00
47 Lee Williams	1.25	3.00
48 Earl Wilson	.75	2.00

1987 Chargers Junior Chargers Tickets

This 11" by 8 1/2" perforated sheet features two rows of six coupons each. The coupons resemble tickets, with each coupon measuring approximately 1 7/8" by 4 1/4". They were given to members of the Coca-Cola Junior Chargers club. Edged below by a mustard stripe, a powder blue strip at the top carries the coupon's subtitle. The large middle panel of the ticket carries a color action player photo with white borders and the player's name immediately below. Another powder blue stripe at the bottom of the coupon reads "Sec. Row Seat" in imitation of an actual ticket. The horizontal backs vary in their content, consisting of either a membership card, season schedule, Coca-Cola Junior Chargers club, preseason pass, or various coupons to attractions in the San Diego area. The coupons are unnumbered and are listed below in alphabetical order by subject.

COMPLETE SET (12)	20.00	35.00
1 Gary Anderson RB	1.50	4.00
2 Rolf Benirschke	1.25	3.00
3 Wes Chandler	1.50	4.00
4 Jeffery Dale	1.25	3.00
5 Dan Fouts	2.50	6.00
6 Pete Holohan	1.25	3.00
7 Lionel James	1.25	3.00
8 Don Macek	1.25	3.00
9 Dennis McKnight	1.25	3.00
10 Al Saunders CO	1.25	3.00
11 Billy Ray Smith	1.25	3.00
12 Kellen Winslow	2.00	5.00

1987 Chargers Police

The 1987 San Diego Chargers Police set contains 21 numbered cards. The cards measure approximately 2 5/8" by 4 1/8". Uniform numbers appear on the fronts of the cards. The set is sponsored by the San Diego Chargers, Oscar Mayer, and local law enforcement agencies. The Chargers helmet logo, "Chargers Tips," and the Oscar Mayer logo appear on the backs. Card backs have black printing on white backs. The Chargers helmet along with height, weight, age, and experience statistics appear on the fronts of the cards. Card 13 was never issued apparently for superstitious reasons. Cards 3 (Benirschke released) and 17 (Walters arrested) were distributed in lesser quantities and hence are a little tougher to find, especially Benirschke. Chip Banks (22) was the player substituted in the set for Rolf Benirschke.

COMPLETE SET (21)	10.00	25.00
1 Alex Spanos OWN	.30	.75
2 Gary Anderson RB	.60	1.50
3 Rolf Benirschke SP	2.50	6.00
4 Gill Byrd	.30	.75
5 Wes Chandler	.60	1.50
6 Sam Claphan	.30	.75
7 Jeffery Dale	.30	.75
8 Pete Holohan	.30	.75
9 Lionel James	.30	.75
10 Jim Lachey	.30	.75
11 Woodrow Lowe	.30	.75
12 Don Macek	.30	.75
14 Dan Fouts	1.50	4.00
15 Eric Sievers	.30	.75
16 Billy Ray Smith	.30	.75
17 Danny Walters SP	2.00	5.00
18 Lee Williams	.30	.75
19 Kellen Winslow	1.25	3.00
20 Al Saunders CO	.30	.75
21 Dennis McKnight	.30	.75
22 Chip Banks	.30	.75

1987 Chargers Smokey

This 48-card set features players of the San Diego Chargers in a set sponsored by the California Forestry Department. The cards measure approximately 5 1/2" by 8 1/2"; card fronts show a full-color action photo of the player. Card backs have a forestry safety tip cartoon with Smokey the Bear. Cards are unnumbered but are ordered below in alphabetical order according to the subject's last name. Cards of Donald Brown, Mike Douglas, and Fred Robinson were withdrawn after they were cut from the team and the card of Don Coryell was withdrawn after he was replaced as head coach.

COMPLETE SET (48)	50.00	100.00
1 Curtis Adams	.75	2.00
2 Ty Allert	.75	2.00
3 Gary Anderson RB	1.25	3.00
4 Rolf Benirschke	1.00	2.50
5 Thomas Benson	1.00	2.50
6 Donald Brown SP	3.00	8.00
7 Gill Byrd	1.00	2.50
8 Wes Chandler	1.40	3.50
9 Sam Claphan	.75	2.00
10 Don Coryell CO SP	3.00	8.00
11 Jeffery Dale	.75	2.00
12 Wayne Davis	.75	2.00
13 Mike Douglass SP	3.00	8.00
14 Chuck Ehin	.75	2.00
15 James Fitzpatrick	.75	2.00
16 Tom Flick	.75	2.00
17 Dan Fouts	4.00	10.00
18 Dee Hardison	.75	2.00
19 Andy Hawkins	.75	2.00
20 John Hendy	.75	2.00
21 Mark Herrmann	1.00	2.50
22 Pete Holohan	1.00	2.50
23 Lionel James	1.00	2.50
24 Trumaine Johnson	.75	2.00
25 Charlie Joiner	2.50	6.00
26 Gary Kowalski	.75	2.00
27 Jim Lachey	1.00	2.50
28 Jim Leonard	.75	2.00
29 Woodrow Lowe	.75	2.00
30 Don Macek	.75	2.00
31 Buford McGee	.75	2.00
32 Dennis McKnight	.75	2.00
33 Ralf Mojsiejenko	.75	2.00
34 Derrie Nelson	.75	2.00
35 Leslie O'Neal	1.50	4.00
36 Gary Plummer	1.00	2.50
37 Fred Robinson SP	3.00	8.00
38 Eric Sievers	.75	2.00
39 Billy Ray Smith	1.00	2.50
40 Tim Spencer	1.00	2.50
41 Kenny Taylor	.75	2.00
42 Terry Unrein	.75	2.00
43 Jeff Walker	.75	2.00
44 Danny Walters	.75	2.00
45 Lee Williams	1.00	2.50
46 Earl Wilson	.75	2.00
47 Kellen Winslow	3.00	8.00
48 Kevin Wyatt	.75	2.00

1988 Chargers Police

The 1988 Police San Diego Chargers set contains 12 cards each measuring approximately 2 5/8" by 4". The fronts are white and navy blue with color photos, and the backs feature career highlights and safety tips.

COMPLETE SET (12)	3.00	8.00
1 Gary Anderson RB	.40	1.00
2 Rod Bernstine	.40	1.00
3 Gill Byrd	.30	.75
4 Vencie Glenn	.30	.75
5 Lionel James	.30	.75
6 Babe Laufenberg	.30	.75
7 Don Macek	.20	.50
8 Mark Malone	.30	.75
9 Dennis McKnight	.20	.50
10 Anthony Miller	.75	2.00
11 Billy Ray Smith	.30	.75
12 Lee Williams	.30	.75

1988 Chargers Smokey

This 52-card set features players of the San Diego Chargers in a set sponsored by the California Forestry Department. The cards measure approximately 5" by 8"; card fronts show a full-color action photo of the player. Card backs have a forestry safety tip cartoon with Smokey Bear. Cards are unnumbered but are ordered below in numerical order according to the subject's uniform number as listed on the card's front and back. There is a variation on the Spanos card, which was originally issued indicating he bought the Chargers in 1987 and was quickly corrected to 1984. There are 35 cards which are easier to obtain as they were available all year and 18 cards (marked below by SP) who are more difficult to find as their cards were withdrawn after they were cut from the team, retired, traded, or put on injured reserve. The set is considered complete with only one Spanos card

COMPLETE SET (52)	30.00	60.00
2 Ralf Mojsiejenko	.60	1.50
9 Mark Herrmann SP	.75	2.00
10 Vince Abbott	.60	1.50
13 Mark Vlasic	.60	1.50
14 Dan Fouts	1.50	4.00
20 Barry Redden	.60	1.50
22 Gill Byrd	.75	2.00
23 Danny Walters SP	.75	2.00
25 Vencie Glenn	.60	1.50
26 Lionel James	.75	2.00
27 Daniel Hunter SP	.75	2.00
34 Elvis Patterson	.60	1.50
36 Mike Davis SP	.75	2.00
40 Gary Anderson RB	1.00	2.50
42 Curtis Adams	.60	1.50
43 Tim Spencer	.75	2.00
44 Martin Bayless	.60	1.50
50 Gary Plummer	.75	2.00
52 Jeff Jackson	.60	1.50
54 Billy Ray Smith	.75	2.00
55 Steve Busick SP	.75	2.00
56 Chip Banks SP	.75	2.00
57 Thomas Benson SP	.75	2.00
58 David Brandon	.60	1.50
60 Dennis McKnight	.60	1.50
61 Ken Dallafior	.60	1.50
62 Don Macek	.60	1.50
68 Gary Kowalski	.60	1.50
69 Les Miller	.60	1.50
70 James Fitzpatrick	.60	1.50
71 Mike Charles	.60	1.50
72 Karl Wilson	.60	1.50
74 Jim Lachey SP	1.25	3.00
75 Joe Phillips	.60	1.50
76 Broderick Thompson	.60	1.50
77 Sam Claphan SP	.75	2.00
78 Chuck Ehin SP	.75	2.00
79 Curtis Rouse SP	.75	2.00
80 Kellen Winslow	1.50	4.00
81 Timmie Ware SP	.75	2.00
82 Rod Bernstine	.75	2.00
85 Eric Sievers	.60	1.50
86 Jamie Holland	.60	1.50
88 Pete Holohan SP	.75	2.00
89 Wes Chandler SP	1.50	4.00
92 Dee Hardison SP	.75	2.00
94 Randy Kirk	.60	1.50
96 Keith Baldwin SP	.75	2.00
98 Terry Unrein SP	.75	2.00
99 Lee Williams	.60	1.50
NNO Al Saunders CO	.60	1.50
NNO Alex G. Spanos ERR SP	2.00	5.00
Chairman of the Board		
(Purchased team 1987)		
NNO Alex G. Spanos COR	.60	1.50
Chairman of the Board		
(Purchased team 1984)		

1989 Chargers Junior Chargers Tickets

This perforated sheet features two rows of six cards each. If the cards were separated, they would measure 1 7/8" by 3 5/8". The color action player photos are bordered in white and the cards are designed like game tickets. A bonus gift is listed at the top of each card and the player's name printed below the photo. The set was sponsored by Ralph's and XTRA. The backs contain information about the bonus gift or discount available to the ticket holder. The coupons are unnumbered and are listed below in alphabetical order by subject.

COMPLETE SET (12)	12.50	25.00
1 Gary Anderson RB	1.50	3.00
2 Gill Byrd	1.25	2.50
3 Quinn Early	1.50	3.00
4 Vencie Glenn	1.25	2.50
5 Jamie Holland	.75	2.00
6 Don Macek	.75	2.00
7 Dennis McKnight	.75	2.00
8 Anthony Miller	1.50	3.00
9 Ralf Mojsiejenko	.75	2.00
10 Leslie O'Neal	1.25	2.50
11 Billy Ray Smith	1.25	2.50
12 Lee Williams	1.25	2.50

1989 Chargers Knudsen Dairy Milk Cartons

This set of six half-gallon milk cartons features an image of a Chargers player and a safety tip to youngsters on one of its panels. Each was printed in blue on white stock and issued by Knudsen's Dairy.

COMPLETE SET (5)	20.00	40.00
1 Gill Byrd	4.00	8.00
2 Don Macek	4.00	8.00
3 Anthony Miller	5.00	10.00
4 Leslie O'Neal	5.00	10.00
5 Gary Plummer	4.00	8.00

1989 Chargers Police

The 1989 Police San Diego Chargers set contains 12 cards measuring approximately 2 5/8" by 4 3/16". The fronts have white borders and color action photos; the vertically oriented backs have brief bios, career highlights, and safety messages. The set was sponsored by Louis Rich Co. The set was given away in two six-card panels; the first group at the Chargers' October 22nd home game and the other at the November 5th game.

COMPLETE SET (12)	4.00	10.00
1 Tim Spencer	.30	.75
2 Vencie Glenn	.30	.75
3 Gill Byrd	.30	.75
4 Jim McMahon	.60	1.50
5 David Richards	.20	.50
6 Don Macek	.20	.50
7 Billy Ray Smith	.30	.75
8 Gary Plummer	.30	.75
9 Lee Williams	.30	.75
10 Leslie O'Neal	.40	1.00
11 Anthony Miller	.60	1.50
12 Broderick Thompson	.20	.50

1989 Chargers Smokey

This 48-card set is very similar in style to the Smokey Chargers set of the previous year. This set gives the 1989 date on the bottom of every reverse. Cards are unnumbered except for uniform number which appears on the card front and back. The cards are ordered below by uniform number. The cards measure approximately 5" by 8". Each card back shows a different fire safety cartoon.

COMPLETE SET (48)	25.00	60.00
2 Ralf Mojsiejenko	.60	1.50
6 Steve DeLine	.60	1.50
10 Vince Abbott	.60	1.50
13 Mark Vlasic	.60	1.50
16 Mark Malone	.75	2.00
20 Barry Redden	.60	1.50
22 Gill Byrd	.75	2.00
23 Roy Bennett	.60	1.50
25 Vencie Glenn	.75	2.00
26 Lionel James	.75	2.00
30 Sam Seale	.60	1.50
31 Leonard Coleman	.60	1.50
34 Elvis Patterson	.60	1.50
40 Gary Anderson RB	.75	2.00
42 Curtis Adams	.60	1.50
43 Tim Spencer	.75	2.00
44 Martin Bayless	.60	1.50
48 Pat Miller	.60	1.50
50 Gary Plummer	.75	2.00
51 Cedric Figaro	.60	1.50
52 Jeff Jackson	.60	1.50
53 Chuck Faucette	.60	1.50
54 Billy Ray Smith	.75	2.00
57 Keith Browner	.60	1.50
58 David Brandon	.60	1.50
59 Ken Woodard	.60	1.50
60 Dennis McKnight	.60	1.50
61 Ken Dallafior	.60	1.50
65 David Richards	.60	1.50
66 Dan Rosado	.60	1.50
69 Les Miller	.60	1.50
70 James Fitzpatrick	.60	1.50
71 Mike Charles	.60	1.50
72 Karl Wilson	.60	1.50
73 Darrick Brilz	.60	1.50
75 Joe Phillips	.75	2.00
76 Broderick Thompson	.60	1.50
82 Rod Bernstine	.75	2.00
83 Anthony Miller	1.25	3.00
86 Jamie Holland	.60	1.50
87 Quinn Early	.75	2.00
88 Arthur Cox	.60	1.50

89 Darren Flutie 1.25 3.00
91 Leslie O'Neal .75 2.00
93 Tyrone Keys .60 1.50
95 Joe Campbell .60 1.50
97 George Hinkle .60 1.50
99 Lee Williams .75 2.00

1990 Chargers Junior Chargers Tickets

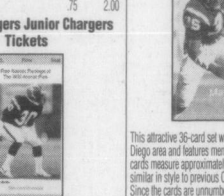

Cards from this set resemble game tickets with each being a coupon good for discounts from local businesses. Each measures approximately 1 7/8" by 4 1/4" with the small lower portion of the coupon intact. They were given to members of the Junior Chargers club. Each coupon carries its own subtitle near the top. The large middle panel of the ticket carries a color action player photo with white borders and the player's name immediately below. A yellow stripe at the bottom of the coupon reads "Sec. Row Seat" similar to an actual ticket. The horizontal backs vary in their content, consisting of either a membership card, season schedule, Coca-Cola Junior Chargers club, preseason pass, or various coupons to attractions in the San Diego area. The coupons are unnumbered and are listed below in alphabetical order by subject.

COMPLETE SET (12) 12.50 25.00
1 Joe Phillips .75 2.00
2 Quinn Early 1.50 3.00
3 Arthur Cox .75 2.00
4 Joe Caravello .75 2.00
5 Courtney Hall .75 2.00
6 Tim Spencer 1.25 2.50
7 Darrin Nelson .75 2.00
8 Billy Joe Tolliver 1.25 2.50
9 Anthony Miller 1.50 3.00
10 Sam Seale .75 2.00
11 Burt Grossman .75 2.00
12 Gary Plummer 1.25 2.50

1990 Chargers Knudsen

This six-card set (of bookmarks) which measures approximately 2" by 8" was produced by Knudsen's to help promote readership by people under 15 years old in the San Diego area. They were given out in San Diego libraries on a weekly basis. The set was sponsored by Knudsen, American Library Association, and the San Diego Public Library. Between the Knudsen company name, the front features a color action photo of the player superimposed on a football stadium. The field is green, the bleachers are yellow with gray print, and the scoreboard above the player reads "The Reading Team". The box below the player gives brief biographical information and player highlights. The back has logos of the sponsors and describes two books that are available at the public library. We have checklisted this set in alphabetical order because they are otherwise unnumbered except for the player's uniform number displayed on the card front.

COMPLETE SET (6) 6.00 15.00
1 Marion Butts 1.20 3.00
2 Anthony Miller 1.60 4.00
3 Leslie O'Neal 1.20 3.00
4 Gary Plummer 1.20 3.00
5 Billy Ray Smith 1.00 2.50
6 Billy Joe Tolliver 1.00 2.50

1990 Chargers Police

This 12-card set measures approximately 2 5/8" by 4 1/8" and features members of the 1990 San Diego Chargers. The set was sponsored by Louis Rich Meats. The card fronts have full-color photos framed by solid blue borders while the backs have brief biographies of the players and limited personal information. There is also a safety tip on the back of the card. The set was issued in two six-card panels or sheets (but is also found as individual cards). The cards are numbered on the back.

COMPLETE SET (12) 3.20 8.00
1 Martin Bayless .20 .50
2 Marion Butts .30 .75
3 Gill Byrd .20 .50
4 Burt Grossman .20 .50
5 Ronnie Harmon .30 .75
6 Anthony Miller .50 1.25
7 Leslie O'Neal .40 1.00
8 Joe Phillips .20 .50
9 Gary Plummer .20 .50
10 Billy Ray Smith .20 .50
11 Billy Joe Tolliver .30 .75
12 Lee Williams .30 .75

1990 Chargers Smokey

This attractive 36-card set was distributed in the San Diego area and features members of the Chargers. The cards measure approximately 5" by 8" and are very similar in style to previous Chargers Smokey issues. Since the cards are unnumbered except for uniform number, they are ordered below in that manner. The cardbacks contain a fire safety cartoon and very brief biographical information.

COMPLETE SET (36) 16.00 40.00
11 Billy Joe Tolliver .50 1.25
13 Mark Vlasic .50 1.25
15 David Archer 1.00 2.50
20 Darrin Nelson .40 1.00
22 Gill Byrd .50 1.25
24 Lester Lyles .40 1.00
25 Vencie Glenn .50 1.25
30 Sam Seale .40 1.00
31 Craig McEwen .40 1.00
35 Marion Butts .50 1.25
43 Tim Spencer .50 1.25
44 Martin Bayless .40 1.00
46 Joe Caravello .40 1.00
50 Gary Plummer .50 1.25
51 Cedric Figaro .40 1.00
53 Courtney Hall .40 1.00
54 Billy Ray Smith .50 1.25
58 David Brandon .40 1.00
59 Ken Woodard .40 1.00
60 Dennis McKnight .40 1.00
65 David Richards .40 1.00
69 Les Miller .40 1.00
75 Joe Phillips .50 1.25
76 Broderick Thompson .40 1.00
78 Joel Patten .40 1.00
79 Joey Howard .40 1.00
80 Wayne Walker .40 1.00
82 Rod Bernstine .50 1.25
83 Anthony Miller 1.00 2.50
85 Andy Parker .40 1.00
87 Quinn Early .60 1.50
88 Arthur Cox .40 1.00
91 Leslie O'Neal .60 1.50
92 Burt Grossman .50 1.25
97 George Hinkle .40 1.00
99 Lee Williams .50 1.25

1991 Chargers Vons

The 12-card Vons Chargers set was issued on panels measuring approximately 6 5/8" by 3 1/2". Two perforated lines divide the panels into three sections: a standard size (2 1/2" by 3 1/2") player card, a 1991 Junior Charger Official Membership Card, and a Sea World of California discount coupon. The player cards have color action player photos on the fronts, with yellow borders on a white card face. A Charger helmet and the words "Junior Chargers" appear at the top of the card. In a horizontal format with dark blue print, the back has biography, career highlights, and sponsors' logos. The cards are unnumbered and checklisted below in alphabetical order.

COMPLETE SET (12) 4.00 10.00
1 Rod Bernstine .30 .75
2 Gill Byrd .30 .75
3 Burt Grossman .30 .75
4 Ronnie Harmon .30 .75
5 Anthony Miller .60 1.50
6 Leslie O'Neal .40 1.00
7 Gary Plummer .30 .75
8 Junior Seau .80 2.00
9 Billy Ray Smith .30 .75
10 Broderick Thompson .20 .50
11 Billy Joe Tolliver .30 .75
12 Lee Williams .30 .75

1992 Chargers Louis Rich

Sponsored by Louis Rich, this 52-card oversized set measures approximately 5" by 8". The fronts feature full-bleed glossy color action photos that are framed by a thin white line. The player's jersey number, name, and position appear at the lower left corner, while the sponsor logo and a replica of the team helmet are printed in the lower right corner. In addition to biographical information, the backs are dominated by a large advertisement for Louis Rich products. The cards are unnumbered and checklisted below in alphabetical order.

COMPLETE SET (52) 20.00 40.00
1 Sam Anno .40 1.00
2 Johnnie Barnes .40 1.00
3 Rod Bernstine .50 1.25
4 Eric Bieniemy .50 1.25
5 Anthony Blaylock .40 1.00
6 Brian Brennan .40 1.00
7 Marion Butts .60 1.50
8 Gill Byrd .50 1.25
9 John Carney .50 1.25
10 Darren Carrington .40 1.00
11 Robert Claborne .40 1.00
12 Floyd Fields .40 1.00
13 Donald Frank .40 1.00
14 Bob Gagliano .40 1.00
15 Leo Goeas .40 1.00
16 Burt Grossman .40 1.00
17 Courtney Hall .40 1.00
18 Delton Hall .40 1.00
19 Ronnie Harmon .50 1.25
20 Steve Hendrickson .40 1.00
21 Stan Humphries .60 1.50
22 Shawn Jefferson .50 1.25
23 John Kidd .40 1.00
24 Shawn Lee .40 1.00
25 Nate Lewis .50 1.25
26 Eugene Marve .40 1.00
27 Deems May .40 1.00
28 Anthony Miller .60 1.50
29 Chris Mims .50 1.25
30 Eric Moten .40 1.00
31 Kevin Murphy .40 1.00
32 Pat O'Hara .40 1.00
33 Leslie O'Neal .50 1.25
34 Gary Plummer .50 1.25
35 Marquez Pope .40 1.00
36 Alfred Pupunu .40 1.00
37 Stanley Richard .40 1.00
38 David Richards .40 1.00
39 Henry Rolling .40 1.00
40 Bobby Ross CO .50 1.25
41 Junior Seau 1.00 2.50
42 Harry Swayne .40 1.00
43 Broderick Thompson .40 1.00
44 George Thornton .40 1.00
45 Peter Tuipulotu .40 1.00
46 Sean Vanhorse .40 1.00
47 Derrick Walker .40 1.00
48 Reggie E. White .40 1.00
49 Curtis Whitley .40 1.00
50 Blaise Winter .40 1.00
51 Duane Young .40 1.00
52 Mike Zandofsky .40 1.00

1993 Chargers D.A.R.E.

The San Diego Chargers issued this 30-card set sponsored by the local Police and the D.A.R.E. program. Each cardfront includes a color photo surrounded by a yellow border. Cardbacks include a short player bio and a public service message. The unnumbered cards are arranged below alphabetically.

COMPLETE SET (30) 3.20 8.00
1 Sam Anno .07 .20
2 Stan Brock .07 .20
3 Marion Butts .10 .30
4 Gill Byrd .07 .20
5 John Carney .10 .30
6 Darren Carrington .07 .20
7 Brian Davis .07 .20
8 Donald Frank .07 .20
9 John Friesz .10 .30
10 Burt Grossman .07 .20
11 Courtney Hall .07 .20
12 Ronnie Harmon .10 .30
13 Steve Hendrickson .07 .20
14 Stan Humphries .20 .50
15 John Kidd .07 .20
16 Shawn Lee .07 .20
17 Nate Lewis .07 .20
18 Joe Milinichik .07 .20
19 Anthony Miller .20 .50
20 Chris Mims .07 .20
21 Gary Plummer .10 .30
22 Bobby Ross CO .10 .30
23 Junior Seau .40 1.00
24 Alex Spanos OWN .07 .20
25 Harry Swayne .07 .20
26 Sean Vanhorse .07 .20
27 Derrick Walker .07 .20
28 Jerrol Williams .07 .20
29 Blaise Winter .07 .20
30 Mike Zandofsky .07 .20

1993 Chargers Police

COMPLETE SET (32) 6.00 15.00
1 Darrien Gordon .15 .40
2 Natrone Means 1.00 2.50
3 John Friesz .15 .40
4 Stan Humphries .40 1.00
5 Anthony Miller .40 1.00
6 Marion Butts .30 .75
7 Ronnie Harmon .30 .75
8 Stanley Richard .15 .40
9 Leslie O'Neal .30 .75
10 Harry Swayne .08 .25
11 Junior Seau .60 1.50
12 Courtney Hall .15 .40
13 Gary Plummer .15 .40
14 Eric Moten .08 .25
15 Chris Mims .30 .75
16 Burt Grossman .15 .40
17 Blaise Winter .08 .25
18 Donald Frank .08 .25
19 Sean Vanhorse .08 .25
20 John Carney .08 .25
21 Floyd Fields .08 .25
22 Gill Byrd .15 .40
23 Shawn Jefferson .15 .40
24 Shawn Lee .08 .25
25 Alfred Pupunu .15 .40
26 Marquez Pope .08 .25
27 Darren Carrington .08 .25
28 Duane Young .08 .25
29 Derrick Walker .08 .25
30 Deems May .08 .25
31 Nate Lewis .15 .40
32 Bobby Ross CO .30 .75
Clarence Tuck
(CHP Chief)

1994 Chargers Castrol

COMPLETE SET (52) 20.00 40.00
1 Johnnie Barnes .40 1.00
2 Eric Bieniemy .50 1.25
3 David Binn .40 1.00
4 Stan Brock .40 1.00
5 Jeff Brohm .40 1.00
6 Lewis Bush .40 1.00
7 John Carney .50 1.25
8 Darren Carrington .40 1.00
9 Eric Castle .40 1.00
10 Willie Clark .40 1.00
11 Joe Cocozzo .40 1.00
12 Andre Coleman .40 1.00
13 Rodney Culver .40 1.00
14 Isaac Davis .40 1.00
15 Reuben Davis .40 1.00
16 Greg Engel .40 1.00
17 Dennis Gilbert .40 1.00
18 Gale Gilbert .40 1.00
19 Darrien Gordon .50 1.25
20 David Griggs .40 1.00
21 Courtney Hall .40 1.00
22 Ronnie Harmon .50 1.25
23 Dwayne Harper .40 1.00
24 Rodney Harrison 1.50 4.00
25 Steve Hendrickson .40 1.00
26 Stan Humphries .60 1.50
27 Shawn Jefferson .50 1.25
28 Raylee Johnson .40 1.00
29 Eric Jonassen .40 1.00
30 Aaron Laing .40 1.00
31 Shawn Lee .40 1.00
32 Deems May .40 1.00
33 Natrone Means 1.00 2.50
34 Joe Milinichik .40 1.00
35 Doug Miller .40 1.00
36 Chris Mims .40 1.00
37 Shannon Mitchell .40 1.00
38 Leslie O'Neal .60 1.50
39 Vaughn Parker .40 1.00
40 John Parrella .40 1.00
41 Alfred Pupunu .40 1.00
42 Stanley Richard .40 1.00
43 Junior Seau 1.20 3.00
44 Mark Seay .40 1.00
45 Harry Swayne .40 1.00
46 Cornell Thomas .40 1.00
47 Sean Van Horse .40 1.00
48 Bryan Wagner .40 1.00
49 Reggie E. White .40 1.00
50 Curtis Whitley .40 1.00
51 Duane Young .40 1.00
52 Lonnie Young .40 1.00

1994 Chargers Pro Mags/Pro Tags

COMPLETE SET (12) 10.00 25.00
1 Stan Humphries .80 2.00
2 Tony Martin .80 2.00
3 Natrone Means 1.00 2.50
4 Leslie O'Neal .60 1.50
5 Junior Seau 1.20 3.00
6 Mark Seay .60 1.50
7 Stan Humphries .80 2.00
8 Tony Martin .80 2.00
9 Natrone Means 1.00 2.50
10 Leslie O'Neal .60 1.50
11 Junior Seau 1.20 3.00
12 Mark Seay .60 1.50

1995 Chargers Police

This 16-card set of the San Diego Chargers sponsored by the California Highway patrol features color player photos with a white inner and blue outer border. The backs carry player information and a safety message.

COMPLETE SET (16) 3.20 8.00
1 John Carney .25 .60
2 Stan Humphries .30 .75
3 Natrone Means .40 1.00
4 Darrien Gordon .20 .50
5 Courtney Hall .20 .50
6 Junior Seau .50 1.25
7 Harry Swayne .20 .50
8 Tony Martin .30 .75
9 Mark Seay .20 .50
10 Chris Mims .25 .60
11 Shawn Lee .20 .50
12 Leslie O'Neal .25 .60
13 Reuben Davis .20 .50
14 Darren Bennett .25 .60
15 Gale Gilbert .20 .50
16 Bobby Ross CO .25 .60
Chief Don Watkins

2006 Chargers Topps

COMPLETE SET (12) 3.00 6.00
SD1 Vincent Jackson .25 .60
SD2 LaDainian Tomlinson .30 .75
SD3 Eric Parker .20 .50
SD4 Antonio Gates .30 .75
SD5 Shawne Merriman .25 .60
SD6 Darren Sproles .30 .75
SD7 Donnie Edwards .20 .50
SD8 Philip Rivers .30 .75
SD9 Keenan McCardell .25 .60
SD10 Quentin Jammer .20 .50
SD11 Antonio Cromartie .30 .75
SD12 Charlie Whitehurst .30 .75

2007 Chargers Topps

COMPLETE SET (12) 2.50
1 Philip Rivers .30 .75
2 LaDainian Tomlinson .30 .75
3 Antonio Gates .30 .75
4 Eric Parker .20 .50
5 Shaun Phillips .20 .50
6 Vincent Jackson .25 .60
7 Shawne Merriman .25 .60
8 Michael Turner .30 .75
9 Luis Castillo .20 .50
10 Nate Kaeding .20 .50
11 Craig Davis .25 .60
12 Eric Weddle .30 .75

2008 Chargers Topps

COMPLETE SET (12) 2.50 5.00
1 Antonio Gates .30 .75
2 LaDainian Tomlinson .30 .75
3 Philip Rivers .30 .75
4 Shawne Merriman .25 .60
5 Antonio Cromartie .25 .60
6 Chris Chambers .25 .60
7 Jamal Williams .20 .50
8 Shaun Phillips .20 .50
9 Vincent Jackson .20 .50
10 Luis Castillo .20 .50
11 Clinton Hart .20 .50
12 Jacob Hester .40 1.00

1993 Charlotte Rage AFL

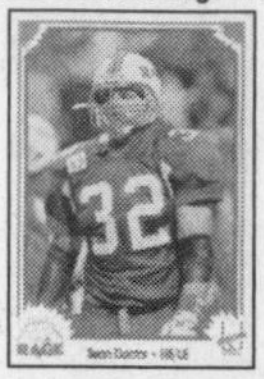

This set was issued by the Charlotte Rage and sponsored by Matthews Equipment. Each card includes a color photo of the featured player or personality on the front with a blue and red striped framed on a white border. The cardbacks include a sponsorship logo with a player bio and stats.

1 Davis Smith .75 2.00
2 Mike Black .75 2.00
3 Andre Johnson .75 2.00
4 Peda Samuel .75 2.00
5 Tony Kimbrough .75 2.00
6 Andy Kelly 1.50 4.00
7 Chris Poston .75 2.00
8 John Burch .75 2.00
9 Tiger Greene 1.00 2.50
10 Steve Wilks .75 2.00
11 Sean Doctor .75 2.00
12 Terry Langston .75 2.00
13 Junior Jackson .75 2.00
14 Tony Bowick .75 2.00
15 Scott Miller .75 2.00
16 Pete Antoniou .75 2.00
17 Danny Smith .75 2.00
18 Mike Renna .75 2.00
19 Ryan Bethea .75 2.00
20 Kubanai Kalombo .75 2.00
21 Marlin Brown .75 2.00
22 Billy Marsh .75 2.00
23 Matthews Equip. Employees .75 2.00
24 Mascot .75 2.00
25 Cheerleaders .75 2.00
26 Assistant Coaches .75 2.00
Charlie Harbison
Steve Patton
Jim Washburn
27 Cliff Stoudt CO 1.00 2.50
28 Cover Card .75 2.00

1970 Chase and Sanborn Stickers

This 26-card set features colored stickers of team logos on silver backgrounds. The backs carry a Chase and Sanborn Coffee send-in ad for a complete set of the 26 NFL team emblems. The cards are unnumbered and checklisted below in alphabetical order according to team nickname.

COMPLETE SET (26) 150.00 300.00
1 Chicago Bears 7.50 15.00
2 Cincinnati Bengals 7.50 15.00
3 Buffalo Bills 7.50 15.00
4 Denver Broncos 7.50 15.00
5 Cleveland Browns 7.50 15.00
6 St.Louis Cardinals 7.50 15.00
7 San Diego Chargers 7.50 15.00
8 Kansas City Chiefs 7.50 15.00
9 Baltimore Colts 7.50 15.00
10 Dallas Cowboys 10.00 20.00
11 Miami Dolphins 7.50 15.00
12 Philadelphia Eagles 7.50 15.00
13 Atlanta Falcons 7.50 15.00
14 San Francisco 49ers 7.50 15.00
15 New York Giants 7.50 15.00
16 New York Jets 7.50 15.00
17 Detroit Lions 7.50 15.00
18 Houston Oilers 7.50 15.00
19 Green Bay Packers 10.00 20.00
20 New England Patriots 7.50 15.00
21 Oakland Raiders 10.00 20.00
22 Los Angeles Rams 7.50 15.00
23 Washington Redskins 10.00 20.00
(yellow Helmet)
24 New Orleans Saints 7.50 15.00
25 Pittsburgh Steelers 7.50 15.00
26 Minnesota Vikings 7.50 15.00

1969 Chemtoy AFL Superballs

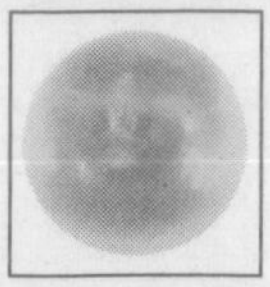

These little high bouncing 1" balls were produced by Chemtoy and featured AFL players. The player's picture is on the front with their name and team affiliation on the back of the paper piece inside the ball. Since these are not numbered, we have sequenced them in alphabetical order.

COMPLETE SET (26) 600.00 1,000.00
1 Lance Alworth 60.00 100.00
2 Pete Beathard 18.00 30.00
3 Bobby Bell 30.00 50.00
4 Emerson Boozer 18.00 30.00
5 Nick Buoniconti 35.00 60.00
6 Billy Cannon 25.00 40.00
7 Gino Cappelletti 25.00 40.00
8 Jack Clancy 18.00 30.00
9 Larry Csonka 60.00 100.00
10 Ben Davidson 25.00 40.00
11 Len Dawson 60.00 100.00
12 Mike Garrett 18.00 30.00
13 Bob Griese 80.00 120.00
14 John Hadl 30.00 50.00
15 Jack Kemp 90.00 150.00
16 Don Maynard 50.00 80.00
17 Ron McDole 18.00 30.00
18 Ron Mix 30.00 50.00
20 Dick Post 18.00 30.00
20 Jim Otto 30.00 50.00
21 George Saimes 18.00 30.00
22 George Sauer 18.00 30.00
23 Jan Stenerud 30.00 50.00
24 Matt Snell 25.00 40.00
25 Jim Turner 18.00 30.00
26 George Webster 18.00 30.00

1983 Chicago Blitz Team Sheets

Each of these sheets measures approximately 10" by 8" and features two rows with four players per row. The first sheet presents the coaching staff, while the other seven sheets feature players. The individual photos measure 2 1/4" by 2 1/2" and have white borders. The photos are head-and-shoulders shots, with player information immediately below. A title between two team logos running across the bottom of the sheets completes them. The sheets are unnumbered.

COMPLETE SET (7) 16.00 40.00
1 George Allen HCO 6.00 15.00
Joe Haering
Paul Lanham
John Payne
John Teerlink
Dick Walker
Charlie Waller
Ray Wietecha
2 Luther Bradley 4.00 10.00
Eddie Brown
Virgil Livers
Frank Minnifield
Lance Shields
Don Schwartz
Maurice Tyler
Ted Walton
3 Mack Boatner 2.00 5.00
Frank Collins
Frank Corral
Doug Cozen
Doug Dennison
John Roveto
Jim Stone
Tim Wrightman
4 Robert Barnes 2.00 5.00
Bruce Branch
Nick Eyre
Tim Norman
Wally Pesuit
Mark Stevenson
Rob Taylor T
Steve Tobin
5 Junior Ah You 2.00 5.00
Mark Buben
Bob Cobb
Joe Ehrmann
Kit Lathrop
Karl Lorch
Troy Thomas
6 Jim Fahnhorst 2.00 5.00
Joe Federspiel
Doak Field
Bruce Gheesling
Andy Melontree
Ed Smith
Stan White
Kari Yli-Renko
7 Marcus Anderson 2.00 5.00
Larry Douglas
Marc May
Pat Schmidt
Lenny Willis
Warren Anderson CO
Chris Pagnucco CO
Bruce Allen GM

2003 Chicago Rush AFL

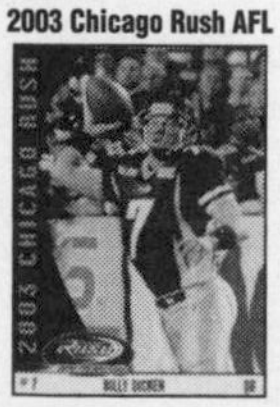

This set was produced by Multi-Ad, sponsored by Cort Furniture, and distributed by the Rush. Each card was produced with a dark blue border on one side with the year of issue and the team name. The cardbacks are numbered in small print at the bottom and feature brief player bios.

COMPLETE SET (30) 6.00 12.00
1 Team Photo .20 .50
2 Dameon Porter .30 .75
3 Anthony Ladd .20 .50
4 Chad Salisbury .30 .75
5 Cedric Walker .20 .50
6 Billy Dicken .40 1.00
7 Cornelius Bonner .30 .75
8 Lindsay Fleshman .30 .75
9 Brian Ah Yat .20 .50
10 Marvin Taylor .20 .50
11 Keith Gispert .20 .50
12 Antonio Chatman .20 .50
13 Levelle Brown .20 .50
14 DeJuan Alfonzo .20 .50
15 Jamie McGourty .20 .50
16 Bob McMillen .20 .50
17 Frank Moore .20 .50
18 Tony Bowick .20 .50
19 Marcus McKenzie .20 .50
20 Furnell Hankton .20 .50
21 James Baron .20 .50
22 Riley Kleinhesselink .20 .50
23 Jerry Montgomery .20 .50
24 John Moyer .20 .50
25 Mike Hohensee CO .20 .50
26 Assistant Coaches .20 .50
Walt Housman
Stan Davis
Dave Witthun
27 Rush Dancers .20 .50
28 Rush Logo .20 .50
29 AFL NBC Logo .20 .50
30 Cort Furniture Logo .20 .50

2004 Chicago Rush AFL

This set was produced by Multi-Ad and distributed by the Rush. Each card is horizontal in format and produced with a dark blue border on the right side with the year of issue in the center and the player image to the left. The cardbacks are numbered and feature brief player bios.

COMPLETE SET (30) 6.00 12.00
1 Cover Card .20 .50
2 Raymond Philyaw .30 .75
3 Sam Clemons .30 .75
4 Chad Salisbury .30 .75
5 Greg Williams S .30 .75
6 Corey Sawyer .30 .75
7 Lindsay Fleshman .30 .75
8 Kareem Larrimore .30 .75
9 Jeremy McDaniel .20 .50
10 Keith Gispert .20 .50
11 Etu Molden .20 .50
12 Levelle Brown .20 .50
13 Donnie Caldwell .20 .50
14 DeJuan Alfonzo .20 .50
15 Jamie McGourty .20 .50
16 Bob McMillen .20 .50
17 Colin Greczek .20 .50
18 Frank Moore .20 .50
19 Salem Simon .20 .50
20 James Baron .20 .50
21 Riley Kleinhesselink .20 .50
22 John Thomas .20 .50
23 John Sikora .20 .50
24 John Moyer .20 .50
25 Mike Hohensee CO .20 .50
26 Assistant Coaches .20 .50
Dave Witthun
Walt Housman
Brian Schwartze
27 Rush Dancers .20 .50
28 Lindsay Fleshman .20 .50
Season Ticket Ad
29 AFL on NBC Ad .20 .50
30 Cort Furniture Coupon .20 .50

2006 Chicago Rush AFL

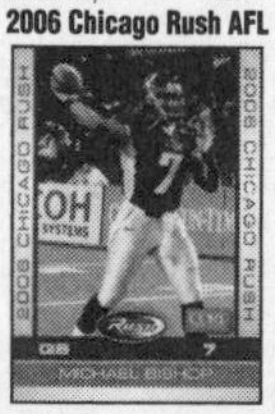

COMPLETE SET (36) 10.00 20.00
1 CORT Sponsor Card .30 .75
2 Carlos Wright .30 .75
3 C.J. Johnson .30 .75
4 Russell Shaw .30 .75
5 Dan Frantz .30 .75
6 Nick Myers .30 .75
7 Marvin Taylor .30 .75
8 Michael Bishop .50 1.25
9 Asad Abdul-Khaliq .30 .75
10 Bobby Sippio .40 1.00
11 Matt D'Orazio .30 .75
12 Woody Dantzler .40 1.00
13 Todd Howard .30 .75
14 Buchie Ibeh .30 .75
15 Etu Molden .30 .75
16 Levelle Brown .30 .75
17 Dennison Robinson .30 .75
18 Marcus Moore .30 .75
19 DeJuan Alfonzo .30 .75
20 Jeremy Unertl .30 .75
21 Bob McMillen .30 .75
22 Curtis Eason .30 .75
23 Khreem Smith .30 .75
24 Tango McCauley .30 .75
25 Frank Moore .30 .75
26 Brian Sump .30 .75
27 D.J. Bleisath .30 .75
28 Charlie Cook .30 .75
29 Joe Peters .30 .75

30 Darain Tate .30 .75
31 John Sikora .30 .75
32 John Moyer .30 .75
33 Mike Hohensee CO .30 .75
34 Asst Coaches .30 .75
35 Rush Dancers .30 .75
36 Grabowski (Mascot) .30 .75

2007 Chicago Rush AFL

COMPLETE SET (36) 6.00 12.00
1 Sponsor Card .20 .50
2 Woody Dantzler .40 1.00
3 Russell Shaw .20 .50
4 Bobby Sippio .30 .75
5 Dan Frantz .20 .50
6 Nick Myers .20 .50
7 James Sadler .20 .50
8 Russ Michna .20 .50
9 Matt D'Orazio .30 .75
10 Rob Mager .20 .50
11 Kevin Beard .20 .50
12 Etu Molden .30 .75
13 Rui Nakanishi .20 .50
14 Jonathan Ordway .20 .50
15 Dennison Robinson .20 .50
16 DeJuan Alfonzo .20 .50
17 Jeremy Unertl .20 .50
18 Bob McMillen .20 .50
19 Curtis Eason .20 .50
20 Frank Moore .20 .50
21 D.J. Bleisath .20 .50
22 Jason Thomas .20 .50
23 Joe Peters .20 .50
24 Robert Boss .20 .50
25 E.J. Burt .20 .50
26 Demetrios Walker .20 .50
27 John Sikora .20 .50
28 John Moyer .20 .50
29 Mike Hohensee (HC) .20 .50
30 Asst Coaches .20 .50
31 Rush Dancers .20 .50
32 Grabowski (Mascot) .20 .50
33 Team Records .20 .50
34 Team Records .20 .50
35 Arena Bowl XX .20 .50
36 Team Schedule .20 .50

2008 Chicago Rush AFL

COMPLETE SET (36) 6.00 12.00
1 Cort Ad Card .20 .50
2 Damian Harrell .40 1.00
3 Donovan Morgan .20 .50
4 Talib Wise .20 .50
5 Dan Frantz .20 .50
6 Carlos Hendricks .20 .50
7 Reggie Gray .20 .50
8 James Sadler .20 .50
9 Russ Michna .20 .50
10 Ryan Dennard .20 .50
11 Clinton Solomon .20 .50
12 Rob Mager .20 .50
13 Sherdrick Bonner .30 .75
14 Liam Ezekiel .20 .50
15 Jonathan Ordway .20 .50
16 Dennison Robinson .20 .50
17 DeJuan Alfonzo .20 .50
18 Matt Kinsinger .20 .50
19 Jeremy Unertl .20 .50
20 Dan Alexander .30 .75
21 Beau Elliott .20 .50
22 Khreem Smith .20 .50
23 Nick Zeck .20 .50
24 Travis Latendresse .20 .50
25 Joe Peters .20 .50
26 Robert Boss .20 .50
27 James Baron .20 .50
28 Demetrios Walker .20 .50
29 John Sikora .20 .50
30 John Moyer .20 .50
31 Mike Hohensee CO .20 .50
32 Assistant Coaches .20 .50
Scott Bailey
Walt Hoisman
Ryan Leonard
Bob McMillen
33 Adrenaline Dancers .20 .50
34 Grabowski - Mascot .20 .50
35 Rush Team Records .20 .50
36 Rush Team Records .20 .50

1963-65 Chiefs Fairmont Dairy

These cards were featured as the side panels of half-gallon milk cartons in the Kansas City area by Fairmont Dairy. Similar cards were apparently issued during more than one season as there are several styles with different sizes and colors. Any one individual card can be identified using either the age of the player or "years pro" that is printed on the card. The cards below were likely issued between 1963 and 1965 based upon this information or have not been confirmed as to year of issue. When cut, each card measures approximately 2 1/4" by 3 1/4" to the outside dotted line. The printing on the cards is in red and may also have been printed in black as well. The fronts feature close-up player photos with the player's biographical information appearing to the right. The cards have blank backs as is the case with most milk carton issues. Complete milk cartons would be valued at double the prices listed below. Additions to the list below are welcomed.

1 Bobby Bell 150.00 250.00
(Age: 23; 1963 issue
2 Len Dawson 300.00 500.00
(Age: 28; 1963 issue)
3 Dave Grayson 60.00 100.00
4 Abner Haynes 90.00 150.00
5 Sherrill Headrick 75.00 125.00
6 Dave Hill 60.00 100.00
(Age: 24; 1965 issue)
7 Bobby Hunt 60.00 100.00
(Age: 23; 1963 issue)
8 Frank Jackson 60.00 100.00
9 Curtis McClinton 75.00 125.00
(Age: 25; 1964 issue)
10 Bobby Ply 60.00 100.00
11 Al Reynolds 60.00 100.00
(Age: 26; 1964 issue)
12 Smokey Stover 60.00 100.00

1965 Chiefs Team Issue 8 x 10

This set of photos was released around 1965. Each features a Chiefs player on glossy photographic stock measuring roughly 8" by 10." The player's position (initials), name and team name is spelled out below the player's photo. The photo backs are blank and can often be found with a photographer's imprint and year of issue. These photos look very similar to the 1967 set, but the team name is roughly 1 3/4" to 1 7/8" long. Any additions to this list are appreciated.

COMPLETE SET (17) 100.00 200.00
1 Pete Beathard 7.50 15.00
2 Buck Buchanan 12.50 25.00
3 Ed Budde 7.50 15.00
4 Chris Burford 7.50 15.00
5 Len Dawson 20.00 35.00
6 Sherrill Headrick 7.50 15.00
7 Mack Lee Hill 7.50 15.00
8 E.J. Holub 7.50 15.00
9 Bobby Hunt 7.50 15.00
10 Frank Jackson 7.50 15.00
11 Ed Lothamer 7.50 15.00
12 Jerry Mays 7.50 15.00
13 Curtis McClinton 10.00 20.00
14 Johnny Robinson 10.00 20.00
15 Jim Tyrer 10.00 20.00
16 Fred Williamson 10.00 20.00
17 Jerrel Wilson 7.50 15.00

1966 Chiefs Team Issue

The Kansas City Chiefs issued these player photos around 1966. Some likely were released over a period years. The type style and size varies slightly from photo to photo. Each measures roughly 7 1/4" by 9 1/2" and features a black and white photo. They are unnumbered and checklisted below in alphabetical order. Any additions to the list are appreciated.

COMPLETE SET (15) 125.00 250.00
1 Pete Beathard 7.50 15.00
2 Bobby Bell 10.00 20.00
3 Tommy Brooker 7.50 15.00
4 Ed Budde 7.50 15.00
5 Bert Coan 7.50 15.00
6 Len Dawson 15.00 30.00
7 Mike Garrett 7.50 15.00
8 Sherrill Headrick 7.50 15.00
9 Jerry Mays 7.50 15.00
10 Curtis McClinton 7.50 15.00
11 Bobby Ply 7.50 15.00
12 Johnny Robinson 7.50 15.00
13 Hank Stram CO 12.50 25.00
14 Otis Taylor 10.00 20.00
15 Fred Williamson 10.00 20.00

1967 Chiefs Fairmont Dairy

These cards were featured as the side panels of half-gallon milk cartons in the Kansas City area by Fairmont Dairy. Similar cards were apparently issued during more than one season as there are several styles with different sizes and colors. Any one individual card can be identified using the age of the player that is printed on the card. The cards below were issued in 1967 based upon this information and we've noted that below when known. When cut, each card measures approximately 2 3/8" by 3 3/8" to the outside dotted line. The printing on all confirmed cards is in red but may also have been printed in black as well. The fronts feature a close-up player photo with the player's team, his name, position, height, weight, age, and college information appearing to the right. The cards have blank backs as is the case with most milk carton issues. Complete milk cartons would be valued at double the prices listed below. Additions to the list below are welcomed.

COMPLETE SET (23) 1,500.00 2,500.00
1 Fred Arbanas 75.00 125.00
(Age: 28)
2 Pete Beathard 75.00 125.00
(Age: 25)
3 Bobby Bell 100.00 200.00
(Age: 27)
4 Aaron Brown 60.00 100.00
(Age: 23)
5 Buck Buchanan 100.00 200.00
(Age: 26)
6 Ed Budde 60.00 100.00
(Age: 26)
7 Chris Burford 75.00 125.00
(Age: 29)
8 Bert Coan 60.00 100.00
(Age: 27)
9 Len Dawson 250.00 400.00
(Age: 32)
10 Mike Garrett 75.00 125.00
(Age: 23)
11 Jon Gilliam 60.00 100.00
(Age: 28)
12 E.J. Holub 75.00 125.00
(Age: 28)
13 Bobby Hunt 60.00 100.00
(Age: 27)
14 Chuck Hurston 60.00 100.00
(Age: 24)
15 Ed Lothamer 60.00 100.00
(Age: 25)
16 Curtis McClinton 75.00 125.00
(Age: 28)
17 Curt Merz 60.00 100.00
(Age: 29)
18 Willie Mitchell 60.00 100.00
(Age: 27)
19 Johnny Robinson 75.00 125.00
(Age: 28)
20 Otis Taylor 90.00 150.00
(Age: 25)
21 Jim Tyrer 75.00 125.00
(Age: 28)
22 Fred Williamson UER 90.00 150.00
(Age: 29 on card; should have read Age: 30)
23 Jerrel Wilson 60.00 100.00
(Age: 25)

1967 Chiefs Team Issue

This set of photos was released around 1967. Each features a Chiefs player on glossy stock measuring roughly 8" by 10." The player's name and team name is spelled out below the player's photo with some photos also including the player's position listed before his name. These photos look very similar to the 1965 set, but the team name is roughly 1 1/2" long. Any additions to this list are appreciated.

COMPLETE SET (11) 100.00 175.00
1 Bobby Bell 10.00 20.00
2 Aaron Brown 7.50 15.00
3 Ed Budde 7.50 15.00
4 Chris Burford 7.50 15.00
5 Bert Coan 7.50 15.00
6 Len Dawson 15.00 30.00
7 Willie Lanier 10.00 20.00
8 Curt Merz 7.50 15.00
9 Jan Stenerud 10.00 20.00
10 Otis Taylor 10.00 20.00
11 Jim Tyrer 10.00 20.00

1968 Chiefs Fairmont Dairy

These cards were featured as the side panels of half-gallon milk cartons in the Kansas City area by Fairmont Dairy. Similar cards were apparently issued during more than one season as there are several styles with different sizes and colors. Any one individual card can be identified using the "years pro" of the player that is printed on the card. The cards below were issued in 1968 based upon this information and we've noted that below when known. When cut, each card measures approximately 2 3/8" by 3 3/8" to the outside dotted lines. The printing on the confirmed cards is in red but may also have been printed in black as well. The fronts feature close-up player photos with the player's team, his jersey number, his name, position, biographical information, and years pro appearing to the right. Most were printed with a very thin (roughly 1/16") white border, while a few featured a thicker (roughly 1/4") white border. The cards have blank backs as is the case with most milk carton issues. Complete milk cartons would be valued at double the prices listed below. Additions to the list below are welcomed.

COMPLETE SET (23) 1,500.00 2,500.00
1 Bud Abell 60.00 100.00
(Years Pro 3)
2 Fred Arbanas 75.00 125.00
(Years Pro 8)
3 Aaron Brown 60.00 100.00
(Years Pro 2)
4 Buck Buchanan 100.00 200.00
(Years Pro 6)
5 Ed Budde 60.00 100.00
(Years Pro 6)
6 Wendell Hayes 75.00 125.00
(Years Pro 4)
7 Dave Hill 60.00 100.00
(Years Pro 6)
8 E.J. Holub 75.00 125.00
(Years Pro 8)
9 Jim Kearney 60.00 100.00
(Years Pro 4)
10 Ernie Ladd 90.00 150.00
(Years Pro 8)
11 Willie Lanier 100.00 200.00
(Years Pro 2)
12 Jacky Lee 75.00 125.00
(Years Pro 9)
13 Ed Lothamer 60.00 100.00
(Years Pro 5)
14 Jim Lynch 60.00 100.00
(Years Pro 2)
15 Jerry Mays 60.00 100.00
(Years Pro 8)
16 Curtis McClinton 75.00 125.00
(Years Pro 7)
17 Willie Mitchell 60.00 100.00
(Years Pro 5)
18 Johnny Robinson 75.00 125.00
(Years Pre 9)
19 Noland Smith 60.00 100.00
(Years Pro 2)
20 Jan Stenerud 90.00 150.00
(Years Pro 2)
21 Otis Taylor 90.00 150.00
(Years Pro 4)
22 Jim Tyrer 75.00 125.00
(Years Pro 8)
23 Jerrell Wilson 60.00 100.00
(Years Pro 6)

1968 Chiefs Team Issue

The Chiefs issued these player photos in the late 1960s. Each photo measures roughly 8 1/2" by 10 5/16" and features a black and white photo along with a white facsimile autograph. The Len Dawson can be found with either a white or black signature. The player's position initials, name, and team name appear below the photo. They are unnumbered and checklisted below in alphabetical order.

COMPLETE SET (22) 150.00 300.00
1 Bobby Bell 10.00 20.00
2 Buck Buchanan 10.00 20.00
3 Reg Carolan 7.50 15.00
4 Len Dawson 15.00 30.00
(white signature)
5 Len Dawson 15.00 30.00
(black signature)
6 Mike Garrett 7.50 15.00
7 E.J. Holub 7.50 15.00
8 Jim Kearney 7.50 15.00
9 Ernie Ladd 7.50 15.00
10 Willie Lanier 10.00 20.00
11 Jacky Lee 7.50 15.00
12 Ed Lothamer 7.50 15.00
13 Curtis McClinton 7.50 15.00
14 Willie Mitchell 7.50 15.00
15 Frank Pitts 7.50 15.00
16 Johnny Robinson 7.50 15.00
17 Goldie Sellers 7.50 15.00
18 Noland Smith 7.50 15.00
19 Hank Stram CO 12.50 25.00
20 Otis Taylor 10.00 20.00
21 Fred Williamson 10.00 20.00
22 Jerrel Wilson 7.50 15.00

1969 Chiefs Fairmont Dairy

These cards were featured as the side panels of half-gallon milk cartons in the Kansas City area by Fairmont Dairy. Similar cards were apparently issued during more than one season as there are several styles with different sizes and colors. Any one individual card can be identified using either the age of the player or "years pro" that is printed on the card. The cards below were issued in 1969 based upon this information and we've noted that below when known. When cut, each card measures approximately 1 5/8" by 3 1/2" to the outside dotted line. The printing on the confirmed cards is in red but some may also have been printed in black ink as well. The fronts feature close-up player photos with the player's team, his jersey number, his name, position, biographical information, and years pro appearing to the right. The cards have blank backs as is the case with most milk carton issues. Complete milk cartons would be valued at double the prices listed below. Additions to the list below are welcomed.

COMPLETE SET (23) 1,500.00 2,500.00
1 Fred Arbanas 60.00 100.00
2 Aaron Brown 60.00 100.00
3 Buck Buchanan 100.00 200.00
4 Ed Budde 60.00 100.00
5 George Daney 60.00 100.00
6 Len Dawson 200.00 350.00
7 Wendell Hayes 75.00 125.00
8 E.J. Holub 75.00 125.00
9 Ernie Ladd 90.00 150.00
10 Mike Livingston 75.00 125.00
11 Ed Lothamer 60.00 100.00
12 Jim Marsalis 60.00 100.00
(First Year Pro)
13 Jerry Mays 60.00 100.00
14 Curtis McClinton 75.00 125.00
15 Willie Mitchell 60.00 100.00
16 Mo Moorman 60.00 100.00
17 Frank Pitts 60.00 100.00
18 Gloster Richardson 60.00 100.00
19 Johnny Robinson 75.00 125.00
20 Otis Taylor 90.00 150.00
21 Emmitt Thomas 75.00 125.00
22 Jim Tyrer 60.00 100.00
23 Jerrel Wilson 60.00 100.00

1969 Chiefs Kroger

This eight-card, unnumbered set was sponsored by Kroger and measures approximately 8" by 9 3/4". The front features a color painting of the player by artist John Wheeldon, with the player's name inscribed across the bottom of the picture. The back has biographical and statistical information about the player and a brief note about the artist.

COMPLETE SET (8) 75.00 150.00
1 Buck Buchanan 10.00 20.00
2 Len Dawson 25.00 40.00
3 Mike Garrett 7.50 15.00
4 Willie Lanier 10.00 20.00
5 Jerry Mays 7.50 15.00
6 Johnny Robinson 7.50 15.00
7 Jan Stenerud 10.00 20.00
8 Jim Tyrer 7.50 15.00

1969 Chiefs Team Issue

These photos of the Kansas City Chiefs measures approximately 8 1/2" by 10 3/8" and feature black-and-white player images with a white border. The player's name and team name are included below each photo. The backs are blank and unnumbered so the photos are checklisted below in alpabetical order.

COMPLETE SET (5) 25.00 50.00
1 Caesar Belser 6.00 12.00
2 Curley Culp 6.00 12.00
3 George Daney 6.00 12.00
4 Mo Moorman 6.00 12.00
5 Frank Pitts 6.00 12.00

1970 Chiefs Team Issue

This 17-card set of the Kansas City Chiefs measures approximately 8" by 10 3/8" and features black-and-white player photos with a white border. The player's facsimile autograph appears across the photo with his name and team name below each photo. The backs are blank and unnumbered so the photos are checklisted below in alpabetical order.

COMPLETE SET (17) 75.00 150.00
1 Fred Arbanas 5.00 10.00
2 Bobby Bell 7.50 15.00
3 Aaron Brown 5.00 10.00
4 Billy Cannon 6.00 12.00
5 Robert Holmes 5.00 10.00
6 Mike Livingston 5.00 10.00
7 Jim Lynch 5.00 10.00
8 Jim Marsalis 5.00 10.00
9 Warren McVea 5.00 10.00
10 Willie Mitchell 5.00 10.00
11 Mo Moorman 5.00 10.00
12 Ed Podolak 5.00 10.00
13 Bob Stein 5.00 10.00
14 Jan Stenerud 7.50 15.00
15 Morris Stroud 5.00 10.00
16 Otis Taylor 6.00 12.00
17 Jerrel Wilson 5.00 10.00

1971 Chiefs Team Issue

This set of photos is a team-issued set. Each photo measures approximately 7 1/4" by 10" and features a black-and-white head shot bordered in white. The player's name and team name are printed in the lower white border, while the player's facsimile autograph is inscribed across the picture. The backs carry biography and career summary; some of the backs also have statistics. The photos are unnumbered and checklisted below in alphabetical order.

COMPLETE SET (13) 60.00 120.00
1 Bobby Bell 7.50 15.00
(Years Pro-9)
2 Wendell Hayes 5.00 10.00
(Years Pro-7)
3 Ed Lothamer 5.00 10.00
(Years Pro-7)
4 Jim Lynch 5.00 10.00
(Years Pro-5)
5 Mike Oriard 5.00 10.00
6 Jack Rudnay 5.00 10.00
(Years Pro-2)
7 Sid Smith 5.00 10.00
(Years Pro-2)
8 Bob Stein 5.00 10.00
(Years Pro-3)
9 Jan Stenerud 7.50 15.00
(Years Pro-5)
10 Hank Stram CO 7.50 15.00
11 Otis Taylor 6.00 12.00
(Years Pro-7)
12 Jim Tyrer 6.00 12.00
(Years Pro-11)
13 Marvin Upshaw 5.00 10.00

1972 Chiefs Team Issue

This set of photos was released by the Chiefs. Each photo measures approximately 7 1/4" by 10" and features a black-and-white head shot bordered in white. The player's name and team name are printed in the lower white border, while the player's facsimile autograph is inscribed across the picture. The backs on most carry biography and career summaries and other statistics while some were issued blankbacked as well. The photos are unnumbered and checklisted below in alphabetical order. Any additions to this list are appreciated.

COMPLETE SET (34) 150.00 300.00
1 Mike Adamle 5.00 10.00
2 Nate Allen 5.00 10.00
(blankbacked)
3 Buck Buchanan 7.50 15.00
(Years Pro 10)
4 Ed Budde 5.00 10.00
5 Curley Culp 5.00 10.00
6 George Daney 5.00 10.00
(blankbacked)
7 Willie Frazier 5.00 10.00
8 Wendell Hayes 5.00 10.00
9 Dave Hill 5.00 10.00
10 Dennis Homan 5.00 10.00
11 Bruce Jankowski 5.00 10.00
12 Jim Kearney 5.00 10.00
13 Jeff Kinney 5.00 10.00
14A Willie Lanier 7.50 15.00
(blankbacked)
14B Willie Lanier 7.50 15.00
(stats on back)
15 Mike Livingston 5.00 10.00
16 Ed Lothamer 5.00 10.00
17 Jim Lynch 5.00 10.00
(blankbacked)
18 Jim Marsalis 5.00 10.00
(Years Pro-4)
19 Larry Marshall 5.00 10.00
(1972 Draftee)
20 Mo Moorman 5.00 10.00
21 Mike Oriard 5.00 10.00
22 Jim Otis 5.00 10.00
23 Ed Podolak 5.00 10.00
24 Kerry Reardon 5.00 10.00
(Years Pro-2)
25 Jack Rudnay 5.00 10.00
26A Mike Sensibaugh 5.00 10.00
(blankbacked)
26B Mike Sensibaugh 5.00 10.00
(stats on back)
27 Sid Smith 5.00 10.00
28 Jan Stenerud 7.50 15.00
(Years Pro-6)
29 Otis Taylor 6.00 12.00
30 Jim Tyrer 5.00 10.00
(Years Pro-12)
31 Clyde Werner 5.00 10.00
(Years Pro-3)
32 Jerrel Wilson 5.00 10.00
(Years Pro-10)
33 Elmo Wright 5.00 10.00
(Years Pro-2)
34 Wilbur Young 5.00 10.00
(Years Pro-2)

1973 Chiefs Team Issue Color

The NFLPA worked with many teams in 1973 to issued photo packs to be sold at stadium concession stands. Each measures approximately 7" by 8-5/8" and features a color player photo with a blank back. A small sheet with a player checklist was included in each 6-photo pack.

COMPLETE SET (6) 30.00 60.00
1 Len Dawson 7.50 15.00
2 Bobby Bell 5.00 10.00
3 Willie Lanier 5.00 10.00
4 Jan Stenerud 5.00 10.00
5 Otis Taylor 4.00 8.00
6 Aaron Brown 4.00 8.00

1973-74 Chiefs Team Issue 5x7

This 18-card set of the Kansas City Chiefs measures approximately 5" by 7" and features black-and-white player photos with a white border. The backs are blank. The cards are unnumbered and checklisted below in alpabetical order.

COMPLETE SET (18) 60.00 120.00
1 Bob Briggs 4.00 8.00
2 Larry Brunson 4.00 8.00
3 Gary Butler 4.00 8.00
4 Dean Carlson 4.00 8.00
5 Tom Condon 4.00 8.00
6 George Daney 4.00 8.00
7 Andy Hamilton 4.00 8.00
8 Dave Hill 4.00 8.00
9 Jim Kearney 4.00 8.00
10 Mike Livingston 4.00 8.00
11 Jim Marsalis 4.00 8.00
12 Darry Pearson 4.00 8.00
13 Francis Peay 4.00 8.00
14 Kerry Reardon 4.00 8.00
15 Mike Sensibaugh 4.00 8.00
16 Bill Thomas 4.00 8.00
17 Marvin Upshaw 4.00 8.00
18 Clyde Werner 4.00 8.00

1973 Chiefs Team Issue 7x10

This set of the Kansas City Chiefs measures approximately 7 1/4" by 10 1/2" and features black-and-white player photos with a white border. The player's facsimile autograph appears across the photo with his name, position (initials), and team name below each photo. The backs are blank. The cards are unnumbered and checklisted below in alpabetical order.

COMPLETE SET (12) 50.00 100.00
1 Pete Beathard 5.00 10.00
2 Gary Butler 5.00 10.00
3 Dean Carlson 5.00 10.00
4 Willie Ellison 5.00 10.00
5 Andy Hamilton 5.00 10.00
6 Pat Holmes 5.00 10.00
7 Leroy Keyes 5.00 10.00
8 John Lohmeyer 5.00 10.00
9 Al Palewicz 5.00 10.00
10 Francis Peay 5.00 10.00
11 George Seals 5.00 10.00
12 Wayne Walton 5.00 10.00

1974 Chiefs Team Issue 7x10

Photos in this set of the Kansas City Chiefs measure approximately 7 1/4" by 10 1/4" and feature a black-and-white player image with a white border. The player's facsimile autograph appears across the photo with his name, position initials (unless noted below) and team name below each photo in small (1/8") letters. The backs are blank. The cards are unnumbered and checklisted below in alphabetical order.

COMPLETE SET (14) 50.00 100.00
1 Bobby Bell 5.00 10.00
(no position listed)
2 Larry Brunson 4.00 8.00
3 Tom Condon 4.00 8.00
4 Len Dawson 7.50 15.00
(no position listed)
5 Charlie Getty 4.00 8.00
6 Woody Green 4.00 8.00
7 Dave Jaynes 4.00 8.00
8 Doug Jones 4.00 8.00
9 Tom Keating 4.00 8.00
10 Cleo Miller 4.00 8.00
11 Jim Nicholson 4.00 8.00
12 Bill Thomas 4.00 8.00
13 Bob Thornbladh 4.00 8.00
14 Marvin Upshaw 4.00 8.00
(no position listed)

1975 Chiefs Team Issue

Each of these photos measures approximately 7 1/4" by 10" and features a black-and-white head shot bordered in white. The player's name, his position (initials), and team name are printed in the lower white border, while the player's facsimile autograph is inscribed across the picture. The player name and position is printed in a different font (resembles typewriter print) than the 1976 Issue. The backs carry a player biography and career summary; some of the backs also have statistics. The photos are unnumbered and checklisted below in alphabetical order. Any additions to this list are appreciated.

COMPLETE SET (19) 75.00 150.00
1 Tony Adams 4.00 8.00
2 Charlie Ane III 4.00 8.00
3 Ken Avery 4.00 8.00
4 Charlie Getty 4.00 8.00
(NFL Experience: 2)
5 Woody Green 4.00 8.00
6 Tim Kearney 4.00 8.00
7 Morris LaGrand 4.00 8.00
8 MacArthur Lane 4.00 10.00
9 Willie Lanier 5.00 10.00
10 Jim Lynch 4.00 8.00
(NFL Experience: 9)
11 Bob Maddox 4.00 8.00
12 Don Martin 4.00 8.00
13 Billy Masters 4.00 8.00
14 John Matuszak 5.00 10.00
15 Bill Peterson 4.00 8.00
16 Jan Stenerud 6.00 12.00
17 Charlie Thomas 4.00 8.00
18 Walter White 4.00 8.00
19 Paul Wiggin CO 4.00 8.00

1976 Chiefs Team Issue

This set of photos was released by the Chiefs with each measuring approximately 7 1/4" by 10." The photos include a black-and-white head shot bordered in white. The player's name appears at the left with his position (initials) in the middle and team name printed in script to the right all within the lower white border. The player's facsimile autograph is inscribed across the picture. The backs carry biography and career summary; some of the backs also have statistics. The photos are unnumbered and checklisted below in alphabetical order. Any additions to this list are appreciated.

COMPLETE SET (31) 100.00 200.00
1 Tony Adams 4.00 8.00
(NFL Experience: Free Agent)
2 Billy Andrews 4.00 8.00
(NFL Experience: 10)
3 Charlie Ane III 4.00 8.00
(NFL Experience: 2)
4 Gary Barbaro 4.00 8.00
(NFL stats go thru 1975)
5 Larry Brunson 4.00 8.00
6 Tim Collier 4.00 8.00
(NFL stats go thru 1975)
7 Tom Condon 4.00 8.00
(NFL Experience: 3)
8 Jimbo Elrod 4.00 8.00
9 Lawrence Estes 4.00 8.00
10 Tim Gray 4.00 8.00
11 Matt Herkenhoff 4.00 8.00
(NFL Experience: 1)
12 MacArthur Lane 5.00 10.00
13 Willie Lee 4.00 8.00
14 John Lohmeyer 4.00 8.00
(NFL Experience: 3)
15 Henry Marshall 5.00 10.00
16 Billy Masters 4.00 8.00
17 Pat McNeil 4.00 8.00
18 Mike Nott 4.00 8.00
19 Orrin Olsen 4.00 8.00
20 Whitney Paul 4.00 8.00
21 Jack Rudnay 4.00 8.00
(NFL Experience: 7)
22 Keith Simons 4.00 8.00
23 Jan Stenerud 5.00 10.00
(NFL Experience: 10)
24 Steve Taylor 4.00 8.00
25 Emmitt Thomas 5.00 10.00

26 Rod Walters	4.00	8.00
27 Walter White	4.00	8.00
28 Larry Williams	4.00	8.00
29 Jerrel Wilson	4.00	8.00
30 Jim Wolf	4.00	8.00
31 Wilbur Young	4.00	8.00
(NFL Experience: 6)		

1977 Chiefs Team Issue

This set of photos was released by the Chiefs with each measuring approximately 7 1/4" by 10." The photos include a black-and-white head shot bordered in white. The player's name appears at the left with his position in the middle and team name printed in script to the right all below the photo. The player's facsimile autograph is inscribed across the picture. The backs carry biographical information and/or a career summary and statistics. The photos are unnumbered and checklisted below in alphabetical order. Any additions to this list are appreciated.

COMPLETE SET (10)	40.00	80.00
1 Mark Bailey	4.00	8.00
(NFL stats go thru 1976)0		
2 Tom Bettis CO	4.00	8.00
(bio goes through early 1977)		
3 John Brockington	5.00	10.00
(NFL stats go thru 1976)		
4 Ricky Davis	4.00	8.00
(NFL Experience: 3)		
5 Cliff Frazier	4.00	8.00
(NFL Experience: 1)		
6 Darius Helton	4.00	8.00
(was 1977 draft pick)		
7 Thomas Howard	4.00	8.00
(NFL stats go thru 1976)		
8 Dave Rozumek	4.00	8.00
(NFL Experience: 2)		
9 Bob Simmons	4.00	8.00
(NFL Experience: 1)		
10 Ricky Wesson	4.00	8.00
(blankbacked)		

1979 Chiefs Frito Lay

These black and white photos include the player's name, position (initials) and team name below the picture on the front. The cardbacks contain an extensive player bio and career statistics.

COMPLETE SET (8)	30.00	60.00
1 Brad Budde	4.00	8.00
(blankbacked)		
2 Steve Gaunty	4.00	8.00
(NFL Experience: R)		
3 Dave Lindstrom	4.00	8.00
(NFL Experience: 2)		
4 Arnold Morgado	4.00	8.00
(NFL Experience: 3)		
5 Tony Samuels	4.00	8.00
(NFL Experience: 3)		
6 Bob Simmons	4.00	8.00
(NFL Experience: 3)		
7 Jan Stenerud	5.00	10.00
(NFL Experience: 13)		
8 Art Still	4.00	8.00
(NFL Experience: 2)		

1979 Chiefs Police

The 1979 Kansas City Chiefs Police set consists of ten cards co-sponsored by Hardee's Restaurants and the Kansas City (Missouri) Police Department, in addition to the Chiefs' football club. The cards measure approximately 2 5/8" by 4 1/8". The card backs discuss a football term and related legal/safety issue in a section entitled "Chief's Tips". The set is unnumbered but the player's uniform number appears on the front of the cards; the cards are numbered and ordered below by uniform number. The Chiefs' helmet logo is found on both the fronts and backs of the cards.

COMPLETE SET (10)	7.50	15.00
1 Bob Grupp	.75	1.50
4 Steve Fuller	1.00	2.00
22 Ted McKnight	.75	1.50
24 Gary Green	.75	1.50
26 Gary Barbaro	.75	1.50
32 Tony Reed	1.00	2.00
58 Jack Rudnay	.75	1.50
67 Art Still	1.00	2.00
73 Bob Simmons	.75	1.50
NNO Marv Levy CO	2.00	4.00

1979 Chiefs Team Issue

This set of Kansas City Chiefs players measures approximately 5" by 7" and features black-and-white player photos with a white border. The fronts include the player's name, position initials, and team name below the photo. The backs contain a player profile and stats but no sponsor logos. The cards are unnumbered and checklisted below in alpabetical order.

COMPLETE SET (20)	75.00	150.00
1 Mike Bell	4.00	8.00
2 Jerry Blanton	4.00	8.00
3 M.L. Carter	4.00	8.00
4 Earl Gant	4.00	8.00
5 Steve Gaunty	4.00	8.00
6 Bob Grupp	4.00	8.00
7 Charles Jackson	4.00	8.00
8 Gerald Jackson	4.00	8.00
9 Ken Kremer	4.00	8.00
10 Dave Lindstrom	4.00	8.00
11 Frank Manumaleuga	4.00	8.00
12 Arnold Morgado	4.00	8.00
13 Horace Perkins	4.00	8.00
14 Cal Peterson	4.00	8.00
15 Jerry Reese	4.00	8.00
16 Tony Samuels	4.00	8.00
17 Bob Simmons	4.00	8.00
18 J.T. Smith	5.00	10.00
19 Art Still	4.00	8.00
20 Mike Williams	4.00	8.00

1980 Chiefs Frito Lay

These black and white photos include the player's name, position initials and team name below the picture on the front. The cardbacks contain an extensive player bio and career statistics along with the Frito Lay logo.

COMPLETE SET (35)	125.00	250.00
1 Gary Barbaro	4.00	8.00
(NFL stats go thru 1979)		
2 Ed Beckman	4.00	8.00
(NFL stats go thru 1979)		
3 Mike Bell	4.00	8.00
(NFL Experience: 2)		
4 Horace Belton	4.00	8.00
5 Jerry Blanton	4.00	8.00
(NFL Experience: 2)		
6 Brad Budde	4.00	8.00
(1980 Draftee)		
7 Carlos Carson	4.00	8.00
(NFL stats go thru 1979)		
8 M.L. Carter	4.00	8.00
9 Herb Christopher	4.00	8.00
10 Tom Clements	5.00	10.00
11 Paul Dombrowski	4.00	8.00
(NFL Experience: R)		
12 Steve Fuller	4.00	8.00
(NFL Experience: 2)		
13 Charlie Getty	4.00	8.00
14 Gary Green	4.00	8.00
(NFL stats go thru 1979)		
15 Bob Grupp	4.00	8.00
(NFL stats go thru 1979)		
16 James Hadnot	4.00	8.00
(NFL stats go thru 1979)		
17 Eric Harris	4.00	8.00
18 Matt Herkenhoff	4.00	8.00
(NFL Experience: 5)		
19 Thomas Howard	4.00	8.00
20 Charles Jackson	4.00	8.00
21 Dave Lindstrom	4.00	8.00
(NFL Experience: 3)		
22 Mike Livingston	4.00	8.00
(NFL Experience: 12)		
23 Nick Lowery	4.00	8.00
(NFL Experience: 1)		
24 Dino Mangiero	4.00	8.00
25 Frank Manumaleuga	4.00	8.00
26 Henry Marshall	4.00	8.00
(NFL stats go thru 1979)		
27 Ted McKnight	4.00	8.00
(NFL stats go thru 1979)		
28 Don Parrish	4.00	8.00
29 Whitney Paul	4.00	8.00
(NFL stats go thru 1979)		
30 Cal Peterson	4.00	8.00
(NFL Experience: 5)		
31 Jim Rourke	4.00	8.00
(NFL Experience: 1)		
32 J.T. Smith	5.00	10.00
(NFL stats go thru 1979)		
33 Gary Spani	4.00	8.00
(NFL Experience: 3)		
34 Art Still	4.00	8.00
(NFL Experience: 3)		
35 Mike Williams	4.00	8.00
(NFL stats go thru 1979)		

1980 Chiefs Police

The unnumbered, ten-card, 1980 Kansas City Chiefs Police set has been listed by the player's uniform number in the checklist below. The cards measure approximately 2 5/8" by 4 1/8". The Stenerud card was supposedly distributed on a limited basis and is thus more difficult to obtain. In addition to the Chiefs and the local law enforcement agencies, the set is sponsored by the Kiwanis Club and Frito-Lay, whose logos appear on the backs of the cards. The 1980 date can be found on the back of the cards as can "Chiefs Tips".

COMPLETE SET (10)	5.00	10.00
1 Bob Grupp	.40	1.00
3 Jan Stenerud SP	2.00	4.00
32 Tony Reed	.50	1.25
53 Whitney Paul	.40	1.00
59 Gary Spani	.40	1.00
67 Art Still	.60	1.50
86 J.T. Smith	.60	1.50
99 Mike Bell	.40	1.00
NNO Defensive Team	.50	1.25
NNO Offensive Team	.50	1.25

1980 Chiefs Team Issue

The Kansas City Chiefs issued this set of unnumbered photos that measure approximately 5" by 7" and contain black and white player photos. Each is similar to the Frito Lay photos except that there are no sponsor logos and the backs are blank. Any additions to this checklist would be appreciated.

COMPLETE SET (34)	125.00	250.00
1 Earl Gant	4.00	8.00
2 Bob Grupp	4.00	8.00
3 James Hadnot	4.00	8.00
4 Larry Heater	4.00	8.00
5 Matt Herkenhoff	4.00	8.00
6 Sylvester Hicks	4.00	8.00
7 Thomas Howard	4.00	8.00
8 Charles Jackson	4.00	8.00
9 Gerald Jackson	4.00	8.00
10 Bill Kellar	4.00	8.00
11 Bill Kenney	4.00	8.00
12 Bruce Kirchner	4.00	8.00
13 Ken Kremer	4.00	8.00
14 Frank Manumaleuga	4.00	8.00
15 Dale Markham	4.00	8.00
16 Henry Marshall	4.00	8.00
17 Ted McKnight	4.00	8.00
18 Arnold Morgado	4.00	8.00
19 Don Parrish	4.00	8.00
20 Cal Peterson	4.00	8.00
21 Tony Reed	4.00	8.00
22 Jerry Reese	4.00	8.00
23 Stan Rome	4.00	8.00
24 Donovan Rose	4.00	8.00
25 Jim Rourke	4.00	8.00
26 Jack Rudnay	4.00	8.00
27 Tony Samuels	4.00	8.00
28 Bob Simmons	4.00	8.00
29 Franky Smith	4.00	8.00
30 Kelvin Smith	4.00	8.00
31 Sam Stepney	4.00	8.00
32 Rod Walters	4.00	8.00
33 Mike Williams	4.00	8.00
34 Cecil Youngblood	4.00	8.00

1981 Chiefs Frito Lay

These black and white photos include the player's name, position (initials) and team name below the picture on the front. The cardbacks contain an extensive player bio and career statistics.

1 Mike Bell	4.00	8.00
2 Jerry Blanton	4.00	8.00
3 Curtis Bledsoe	4.00	8.00
4 Lloyd Burruss	4.00	8.00
(NFL stats go thru 1980)		
5 Phil Cancik	4.00	8.00
6 Frank Case	4.00	8.00
7 Deron Cherry	4.00	8.00
8 Tom Condon	4.00	8.00
(NFL Experience: 8)		
9 Joe Delaney	5.00	10.00
(NFL stats go thru 1980)		
10 Bob Gagliano	4.00	8.00
11 Eric Harris	4.00	8.00
(NFL stats go thru 1980)		
12 Marvin Harvey	4.00	8.00
13 Billy Jackson	4.00	8.00
14 Dave Klug	4.00	8.00
15 Dave Lindstrom	4.00	8.00
16 Henry Marshall	4.00	8.00
17 Stan Rome	4.00	8.00
18 Jack Rudnay	4.00	8.00
(NFL Experience: 12)		
19 Willie Scott	4.00	8.00
(NFL stats go thru 1980)		
20 Bob Simmons	4.00	8.00
21 J.T. Smith	5.00	10.00
22 Art Still	4.00	8.00
23 Roger Taylor	4.00	8.00
24 Todd Thomas	4.00	8.00

1981 Chiefs Police

The 1981 Kansas City Chiefs Police set consists of ten cards, some of which have more than one player pictured. The cards are numbered on the back as well as prominently displaying the player's uniform number on the fronts of the cards. The cards measure approximately 2 5/8" by 4 1/8". The set is sponsored by the area law enforcement agency, the Kiwanis Club, Frito-Lay, and the Kansas City Chiefs. The Kiwanis Club and Frito-Lay logos, in addition to the Chiefs helmet logo, appear on the backs of the cards. Also "Chiefs Tips" are featured on the card backs. The card backs have black print with red accent on white card stock.

COMPLETE SET (10)	1.50	4.00
1 Warpaint and Carla	.15	.40
(Mascots)		
2 Art Still	.30	.75
3 Steve Fuller and	.20	.50
Jack Rudnay		
4 Gary Green	.20	.50
5 Tom Condon	.30	.75
Marv Levy CO		
6 J.T. Smith	.30	.75
7 Gary Spani and	.15	.40
Whitney Paul		
8 Nick Lowery and	.30	.75
Steve Fuller		
9 Gary Barbaro	.20	.50
10 Henry Marshall	.15	.40

1982 Chiefs Nu-Maid Butter Tubs

This set of butter cups or tubs was released by Nu-Maid and Miami Margarine in 1982. Each includes color illustrations of the featured player and measures roughly 3 3/4" tall and 3" in diameter.

1 Gary Barbaro	2.50	5.00
2 Joe Delaney	2.50	5.00
3 Jack Rudnay	2.50	5.00
4 Gary Spani	2.50	5.00
5 Art Still	2.50	5.00

1982 Chiefs Police

The 1982 Kansas City Chiefs Police set features ten numbered (on back) cards, some of which portray more than one player. The cards measure approximately 2 5/8" by 4 1/8". The backs deviate somewhat from a standard police set in that a cartoon is utilized to drive home the sage "Chiefs Tips". This set is sponsored by the local law enforcement agency, Frito-Lay, and the Kiwanis Club. The backs contain a 1982 date and logos of the Kiwanis, Frito-Lay, and the Chiefs. Card backs have black print with red accent on white card stock. Each player's uniform number is given on the front of the card.

COMPLETE SET (10)	2.00	5.00
1 Bill Kenney and	.25	.60
Jack Rudnay		
2 Steve Fuller and	.40	1.00
Nick Lowery		
3 Matt Herkenhoff	.20	.50
4 Art Still	.30	.75
5 Gary Spani	.20	.50
6 James Hadnot	.25	.60
7 Mike Bell	.25	.60
8 Carol Canfield	.20	.50
(Chiefette)		
9 Gary Green	.25	.60
10 Joe Delaney	.40	1.00

1982 Chiefs Team Issue

This set of Kansas City Chiefs players measures approximately 5" by 7" and features black-and-white player photos with a white border. The fronts include the player's name, position initials, and team name below the photo. The backs contain a player profile and stats but no sponsor logos. The cards are unnumbered and checklisted below in alpabetical order.

1 Mike Bell	4.00	8.00
(NFL Experience: 4)		
2 Dean Prater	4.00	8.00
(NFL Experience: 1)		

1983 Chiefs Frito Lay

The Kansas City Chiefs issued this set sponsored by Frito Lay. The cards are unnumbered, measure approximately 5" by 7", and contain black and white player photos. The cards can be distinguished from other Chiefs Frito Lay issues by the biographical information contained on the cardback. We've noted the NFL experince years that are included on the cardbacks for easier identification. Seven lines of large text type are presented. Any additions to this checklist would be appreciated.

COMPLETE SET (14)	50.00	100.00
1 Tom Condon	4.00	8.00
(NFL Experience: 10)		
2 Ellis Gardner	4.00	8.00
(NFL Experience: R)		
3 Anthony Hancock	4.00	8.00
(NFL Experience: 2)		
4 Louis Haynes	4.00	8.00
(NFL Experience: 2)		
5 Matt Herkenhoff	4.00	8.00
(NFL Experience: 8)		
6 Thomas Howard	4.00	8.00
(NFL stats go thru 1982)		
7 Billy Jackson	4.00	8.00
(NFL stats go thru 1982)		
8 Charles Jackson	4.00	8.00
(NFL Experience: 6)		
9 Van Jakes	4.00	8.00
(NFL Experience: R)		
10 Dave Klug	4.00	8.00
(NFL Experience: 3)		
11 Dave Lindstrom	4.00	8.00
(blankbacked)		
12 Adam Lingner	4.00	8.00
(NFL Experience: R)		
13 Nick Lowery	4.00	8.00
(NFL stats go thru 1982)		
14 John Zamberlin	4.00	8.00
(NFL Experience: 5)		

1983 Chiefs Police

The 1983 Kansas City Chiefs set contains ten numbered cards. The cards measure approximately 2 5/8" by 4 1/8". Sponsored by Frito-Lay, the local law enforcement agency, the Kiwanis Club, and KCTV-5, the set features cartoon "Chiefs Tips" and Crime Tips on the backs. A 1983 date plus logos of the Chiefs, Frito-Lay, the Kiwanis, and KCTV-5 also appear on the backs. Uniform numbers are given on the front of the player's card.

COMPLETE SET (10)	2.00	5.00
1 John Mackovic CO	.40	1.00
2 Tom Condon	.20	.50
3 Gary Spani	.20	.50
4 Carlos Carson	.30	.75
5 Brad Budde	.25	.60
6 Lloyd Burruss	.20	.50
7 Gary Green	.25	.60
8 Mike Bell	.25	.60
9 Nick Lowery	.40	1.00
10 Sandi Byrd	.20	.50
(Chiefette)		

1983 Chiefs Team Issue

This set of Kansas City Chiefs players measures approximately 5" by 7" and features black-and-white player photos with a white border. The fronts include the player's name, position initials, and team name below the photo. The backs contain a player profile and stats but no sponsor logos. The cards are unnumbered and checklisted below in alphabetical order.

COMPLETE SET (20)	60.00	120.00
1 Jim Arnold	4.00	8.00
(NFL Experience: R)		
2 Ed Beckman	4.00	8.00
(NFL Experience: 7)		
3 Todd Blackledge	4.00	8.00
(NFL Experience: R)		
4 Jerry Blanton	4.00	8.00
(NFL Experience: 5)		
5 Carlos Carson	4.00	8.00
(NFL Experience: 4)		
6 Calvin Daniels	4.00	8.00
(NFL Experience: 2)		
7 Albert Lewis	5.00	10.00
(NFL Experience: R)		
8 Dave Lindstrom	4.00	8.00
(NFL Experience: 6)		
9 David Lutz	4.00	8.00
(NFL Experience: R)		
10 Kyle McNorton	4.00	8.00
(NFL Experience: 1)		
11 Stephone Paige	4.00	8.00
(NFL Experience: R)		
12 Steve Potter	4.00	8.00
(NFL Experience: 3)		
13 Lawrence Ricks	4.00	8.00
(NFL Experience: R)		
14 Durwood Roquemore	4.00	8.00
(NFL Experience: 2)		
15 Bob Rush	4.00	8.00
(NFL Experience: 6)		
16 Willie Scott	4.00	8.00
(NFL Experience: 3)		
17 Lucious Smith	4.00	8.00
(NFL Experience: 4)		
18 Ken Thomas	4.00	8.00
(NFL Experience: R)		
19 James Walker	4.00	8.00
(NFL Experience: 1)		
20 Ron Wetzel	4.00	8.00
(NFL Experience: R)		

1984 Chiefs Police

This numbered (on back) ten-card set features the Kansas City Chiefs. Backs contain a "Chiefs Tip" and a "Crime Tip," each with an accompanying cartoon. Cards measure approximately 2 5/8" by 4 1/8". Cards were also sponsored by Frito-Lay and KCTV.

COMPLETE SET (10)	2.00	5.00
1 John Mackovic CO	.30	.75
2 Deron Cherry	.40	1.00
3 Bill Kenney	.25	.60
4 Henry Marshall	.20	.50
5 Nick Lowery	.30	.75
6 Theotis Brown	.25	.60
7 Stephone Paige	.50	1.25
8 Gary Spani and	.30	.75
Art Still		
9 Albert Lewis	.40	1.00
10 Carlos Carson	.30	.75

1984 Chiefs QuikTrip

This 16-card set was sponsored by QuikTrip and measures approximately 5" by 7". The front features a black and white posed photo of the player and the back is blank.

COMPLETE SET (16)	60.00	120.00
1 Mike Bell	4.00	8.00
2 Todd Blackledge	4.00	8.00
3 Brad Budde	4.00	8.00
4 Lloyd Burruss	4.00	8.00
5 Carlos Carson	4.00	8.00
6 Gary Green	4.00	8.00
7 Anthony Hancock	4.00	8.00
8 Eric Harris	4.00	8.00
9 Lamar Hunt OWN	5.00	10.00
10 Bill Kenney	4.00	8.00
11 Ken Kremer	4.00	8.00
12 Nick Lowery	4.00	8.00
13 John Mackovic CO	4.00	8.00
14 J.T. Smith	4.00	8.00
15 Gary Spani	4.00	8.00
16 Art Still	4.00	8.00

1984 Chiefs Team Issue

This set of Kansas City Chiefs players measures approximately 5" by 7" and features black-and-white player photos with a white border. The fronts include the player's name, position initials, and team name below the photo. The backs contain a player profile and stats but no sponsor logos. The cards are unnumbered and checklisted below in alphabetical order. Any additions to this list are appreciated.

1 Brad Budde	4.00	8.00
(NFL Experience: 5)		
2 Bill Kenney	4.00	8.00
(NFL Experience: 6)		
3 Scott Radecic	4.00	8.00
(no NFL Experience line)		

1985 Chiefs Frito Lay

The Kansas City Chiefs issued this set sponsored by Frito Lay. The cards are unnumbered, measure approximately 5" by 7", and contain black and white player photos. The cards can be distinguished from other Chiefs Frito Lay issues by the biographical information contained on the cardback. Many lines of text are presented with almost a full cardback of information. Any additions to this checklist would be appreciated.

COMPLETE SET (4)	15.00	30.00
1 Pete Koch	4.00	8.00
(NFL Experience: 2)		
2 Adam Lingner	4.00	8.00
(NFL Experience: 2)		
3 Jeff Paine	4.00	8.00
(NFL Experience: 2)		
4 Mark Robinson	4.00	8.00
(NFL Experience: 2)		

1985 Chiefs Police

This ten-card set features the Kansas City Chiefs. Cards in the set measure approximately 2 5/8" by 4 1/8". The card back gives the card number and the year of issue; printing is in black and red on white card stock. The set was sponsored by Frito-Lay, KCTV-5, and area law enforcement agencies. Two cartoons are featured on the back of each card picturing a Chiefs Tip and a Crime Tip.

COMPLETE SET (10)	2.00	5.00
1 John Mackovic CO	.30	.75
2 Herman Heard	.20	.50
3 Bill Kenney	.30	.75
4 Deron Cherry	.30	.75
Lloyd Burruss		
5 Jim Arnold	.20	.50
6 Kevin Ross	.25	.60
7 David Lutz	.20	.50
8 Chiefettes Cheerleaders	.20	.50
9 Bill Maas	.30	.75
10 Art Still	.30	.75

1985 Chiefs Team Issue

This set of Kansas City Chiefs players measures approximately 5" by 7" and features black-and-white player photos with a white border. The fronts include the player's name, position initials, and team name below the photo. The backs contain a player profile and stats but no sponsor logos. The cards are unnumbered and checklisted below in alphabetical order.

COMPLETE SET (7)	25.00	50.00
1 Deron Cherry	4.00	8.00
(NFL stats go thru 1984)		
2 Jeff Paine	4.00	8.00
(NFL Experience: 2)		
3 Jerry Blanton	4.00	8.00
(NFL Experience: 7)		
4 Anthony Hancock	4.00	8.00
(NFL Experience: 4)		
5 Carlos Carson	4.00	8.00
(NFL Experience: 6)		
6 Mark Robinson	4.00	8.00
(NFL Experience: 2)		
7 Todd Blackledge	4.00	8.00
(NFL Experience: 3)		

1986 Chiefs Frito Lay

The Kansas City Chiefs issued this set sponsored by Frito Lay. The cards are unnumbered, measure approximately 5" by 7", and contain black and white player photos. The cards can be distinguished from other Chiefs Frito Lay issues by the biographical information contained on the cardback. We've noted the NFL experince years that are included on the cardbacks for easier identification. Seven lines of large text type are presented. Any additions to this checklist would be appreciated.

COMPLETE SET (7)	25.00	50.00
1 Mark Adickes	4.00	8.00
(NFL Experience: 1)		
2 Tom Baugh	4.00	8.00
(NFL Experience: R)		
3 Lewis Colbert	4.00	8.00
(NFL Experience: left blank)		
4 Rick Donnalley	4.00	8.00
(NFL Experience: 5)		
5 Dino Hackett	4.00	8.00
(no NFL Experience mentioned)		
6 Bill Kenney	4.00	8.00
(NFL Experience: 8)		
7 Pete Koch	4.00	8.00
(NFL Experience: 3)		

1986 Chiefs Louis Rich

The Kansas City Chiefs issued this set sponsored by Louis Rich and The Kansas City Star. The cards are blankbacked, unnumbered, measure approximately 5" by 7", and contain black and white player photos. The cards can be distinguished from other Chiefs Louis Rich issues by the team name appearing in all upper case letters below the player photo. Any additions to this list are appreciated.

COMPLETE SET (5)	20.00	40.00
1 Carlos Carson	4.00	8.00
2 Calvin Daniels	4.00	8.00
3 Herman Heard	4.00	8.00
4 Albert Lewis	5.00	10.00
5 John Mackovic CO	4.00	8.00

1986 Chiefs Police

This ten-card set features the Kansas City Chiefs. Cards in the set measure approximately 2 5/8" by 4 1/8" and the card back gives the card number and the year of issue. Printing is in black and red on white card stock. The set was sponsored by Frito-Lay, KCTV-5, and area law enforcement agencies. Two cartoons are featured on the back of each card picturing a "Chiefs Tip" and a "Crime Tip".

COMPLETE SET (10)	2.50	6.00
1 John Mackovic CO	.30	.75
2 Willie Lanier	.60	1.50
(Hall of Fame)		
3 Stephone Paige	.30	.75
4 Brad Budde	.20	.50
5 Nick Lowery	.25	.60
6 Scott Radecic	.20	.50
7 Mike Pruitt	.25	.60
8 Albert Lewis	.30	.75
9 Todd Blackledge	.25	.60
10 Deron Cherry	.25	.60

1986 Chiefs Team Issue

The Kansas City Chiefs issued this set of unnumbered photos that measure approximately 5" by 7" and contain black and white player photos. Each is similar to the 1986 Frito Lay photos except that there are no sponsor logos and the backs are blank. Note also that the design is nearly identical to the 1980 Cheifs Team Issue photos except that the player's name is slightly (1/32") larger on the 1986 issue. Any additions to this checklist would be appreciated.

COMPLETE SET (16)	50.00	100.00
1 Boyce Green	4.00	8.00
2 Anthony Hancock	4.00	8.00
3 Emile Harry	4.00	8.00
4 Greg Hill	4.00	8.00
5 Eric Holle	4.00	8.00
6 Brian Jozwiak	4.00	8.00
7 Bill Kenney	4.00	8.00
8 Pete Koch	4.00	8.00
9 Kit Lathrop	4.00	8.00
10 Adam Lingner	4.00	8.00
11 Aaron Pearson	4.00	8.00
12 Mike Pruitt	5.00	10.00
13 Frank Seurer	4.00	8.00
14 Jeff Smith	4.00	8.00
15 Gary Spani	4.00	8.00
16 Art Still	4.00	8.00

1987 Chiefs Louis Rich

The Kansas City Chiefs issued this set sponsored by Louis Rich and The Kansas City Star. The cards are blankbacked, unnumbered, measure approximately 5" by 7", and contain black and white player photos. The cards can be distinguished from other Chiefs Louis Rich issues by the team name appearing in all lower case letters below the player photo. There are 16-known cards in the set. Any additions to this checklist would be appreciated.

COMPLETE SET (16)	40.00	80.00
1 John Alt	3.00	6.00
2 Carlos Carson	3.00	6.00
3 Deron Cherry	3.00	6.00
4 Sherman Cocroft	3.00	6.00
5 Irv Eatman	3.00	6.00
6 Frank Gansz	3.00	6.00
7 Dino Hackett	3.00	6.00
8 Jonathan Hayes	3.00	6.00
9 Bill Kenney	3.00	6.00
10 Albert Lewis	4.00	8.00
11 Nick Lowery	3.00	6.00
12 Bill Maas	3.00	6.00
13 Christian Okoye	4.00	8.00
14 Stephone Paige	3.00	6.00
15 Paul Palmer	3.00	6.00
16 Kevin Ross	3.00	6.00

1987 Chiefs Police

This ten-card set features the Kansas City Chiefs. Cards in the set measure approximately 2 5/8" by 4 1/8". The card back gives the card number and the year of issue; printing is in black and red on white card stock. The set was sponsored by Frito-Lay, US Sprint, KCTV-5, and area law enforcement agencies. Two cartoons are featured on the back of each card picturing a "Chiefs Tip" and a "Crime Tip". Reportedly more than 4.5 million cards were given out by over 275 different police departments.

COMPLETE SET (10)	1.50	4.00
1 Frank Gansz CO	.15	.40
2 Tim Cofield	.15	.40
3 Deron Cherry	.25	.60
and Albert Lewis		
4 Chiefs Cheerleaders	.15	.40
5 Jeff Smith	.15	.40
6 Rick Donnalley	.15	.40
7 Lloyd Burruss	.20	.50
and Kevin Ross		

8 Dino Hackett	.15	.40
9 Bill Maas	.15	.40
10 Carlos Carson	.25	.60

1987 Chiefs Price Chopper

The Kansas City Chiefs issued this set sponsored by Price Chopper. Each card measures approximately 5" by 7" with a black and white player photo on the front. The cardbacks feature a brief player bio and vital statistics along with a "Compliments of Price Chopper" notation at the bottom. The team name appears on the cardfront in all upper case letters below the player photo and to the left. The player's name and position (initial) appear below the photo and to the right of the team name. Any additions to this checklist would be appreciated.

1 Tom Baugh (NFL Experience: 2)	3.00	6.00
2 Lloyd Burruss (NFL Experience: 7)	3.00	6.00

1988 Chiefs Gatorade

The Kansas City Chiefs issued this set sponsored by Gatorade. The cardbacks contain the player's name, biographical information and a Gatorade sponsorship logo. Each measures approximately 5" by 7", and features a typical black and white player photo. The team name appears on the cardfront in all lower case letters below the player photo. Any additions to this checklist would be appreciated.

COMPLETE SET (10)	25.00	50.00
1 Kelly Goodburn (NFL Experience: 2)	3.00	6.00
2 Emile Harry (NFL Experience: 2)	3.00	6.00
3 Bill Kenney (NFL Experience: 10)	3.00	6.00
4 Albert Lewis (NFL Experience: 6)	3.00	6.00
5 Nick Lowery (NFL Experience: 9)	3.00	6.00
6 Bill Maas (blankbacked)	3.00	6.00
7 Stephone Paige (NFL Experience: 6)	3.00	6.00
8 Kevin Ross (NFL Experience: 5)	3.00	6.00
9 Angelo Snipes (NFL Experience: 3)	3.00	6.00
10 Kitrick Taylor (NFL Experience: 1)	3.00	6.00

1988 Chiefs Police

The 1988 Police Kansas City Chiefs set contains ten numbered cards each measuring approximately 2 5/8" by 4 1/8". There are nine player cards and one coach card. The backs have one "Chiefs Tip" and one "Crime Tip."

COMPLETE SET (10)	2.00	5.00
1 Frank Gansz CO	.20	.50
2 Bill Kenney	.25	.60
3 Carlos Carson	.25	.60
4 Paul Palmer	.25	.60
5 Christian Okoye	.30	.75
6 Mark Adickes	.20	.50
7 Bill Maas	.20	.50
8 Albert Lewis	.30	.75
9 Deron Cherry	.25	.60
10 Stephone Paige	.30	.75

1989 Chiefs Price Chopper/Farmland

The Kansas City Chiefs issued this set with each photo sponsored by either Price Chopper or Farmland, but not both. Each card measures approximately 5" by 7" with a black and white player photo on the front. The cardbacks feature a brief player bio and vital statistics along with a "Compliments of Price Chopper" or "Compliments of Farmland" notation at the bottom. The team name appears on the cardfront in all lower case letters below the player photo and to the left. The player's name and position (initial) appear below the team name with the sponsorship logo printed on the far right. Any additions to this checklist would be appreciated.

COMPLETE SET (4)	12.50	25.00
1 Deron Cherry (Price Chopper)	2.00	5.00
2 Stephone Paige (Price Chopper)	2.00	5.00
3 Neil Smith (Price Chopper)	3.00	8.00
4 Derrick Thomas (Farmland)	6.00	12.00

1989 Chiefs Police

The 1989 Police Kansas City Chiefs set contains ten cards measuring approximately 2 5/8" by 4 1/8". The fronts have white borders and color action photos; the horizontally-oriented backs have safety tips. The set was sponsored by Western Auto and KCTV Channel 5. These cards were printed on very thin stock.

COMPLETE SET (10)	2.00	5.00
1 Marty Schottenheimer CO	.30	.75
2 Irv Eatman	.20	.50
3 Kevin Ross	.25	.60
4 Bill Maas	.20	.50
5 Chiefs Cheerleaders	.20	.50
6 Carlos Carson	.25	.60
7 Steve DeBerg	.30	.75
8 Jonathan Hayes	.25	.60
9 Deron Cherry	.25	.60
10 Dino Hackett	.20	.50

1991 Chiefs Star Price Chopper

The Kansas City Chiefs issued this set sponsored by The Kansas City Star and Price Chopper stores. The cardbacks are blank and each measures approximately 5" by 7" with a black and white player photo on the front. The team name appears on the cardfront in all lower case letters below the player photo. The player's name and position (initials) appear below the photo in all caps as well. The two sponsor logos appear on either side of the player name. Note that the basic Price Chopper logo is the one used. Any additions to this checklist would be appreciated.

COMPLETE SET (4)	8.00	20.00
1 Derrick Thomas	3.00	6.00
2 Steve DeBerg	1.50	4.00
3 Neil Smith	2.00	5.00
4 Nick Lowery	2.00	5.00

1991 Chiefs Team Issue

The Chiefs issued these 5" by 7" black and white photos in 1991. Each includes a portrait shot of the featured player with his name, position initials, and team name below the photo in all capital letters. They are nearly identical to the 1993 photos, but the team name in 1991 is slightly larger in size (roughly 1 3/4" long). The photo backs are blank.

COMPLETE SET (4)	6.00	15.00
1 Tim Barnett	1.50	4.00
2 Todd McNair	1.50	4.00
3 Tom Sims	1.50	4.00
4 Neil Smith	2.00	5.00

1992 Chiefs Intimidator Bio Sheets

Produced by Intimidator, each of these bio sheets measures approximately 8 1/2" by 10 1/2" and was printed on thick card stock. The fronts display a large glossy color player photo framed by gold foil. The backs carry two black-and-white player photos, pro career summary, college career summary, and personal as well as biographical information. The bio sheets are unnumbered and checklisted below in alphabetical order.

COMPLETE SET (12)	15.00	30.00
1 Dave Krieg	1.50	4.00
2 Albert Lewis	1.25	3.00
3 Nick Lowery	1.25	3.00
4 Bill Maas	1.00	2.50
5 Christian Okoye	1.50	4.00
6 Kevin Ross	1.25	3.00
7 Dan Saleaumua	1.00	2.50
8 Neil Smith	1.50	4.00
9 Percy Snow	1.00	2.50
10 Derrick Thomas	3.00	8.00
11 Harvey Williams	1.25	3.00
12 Barry Word	1.25	3.00

1993 Chiefs Team Issue

The Chiefs issued these 5" by 7" black and white photos in 1993. Each includes a portrait shot of the featured player with his name, position initials, and team name below the photo in all capital letters. They are nearly identical to the 1991 photos, but the team name in 1993 is slightly smaller in size (roughly 1 3/8" to 1 1/2" long). The photo backs are blank.

COMPLETE SET (24)	40.00	80.00
1 Kimble Anders	1.50	4.00
2 Erick Anderson	1.50	4.00
3 Bryan Barker	1.50	4.00
4 J.J. Birden	1.50	4.00
5 Matt Blundin	1.50	4.00
6 Dale Carter	2.00	5.00
7 Keith Cash	1.50	4.00
8 Derrick Graham	1.50	4.00
9 Tim Grunhard	1.50	4.00
10 Tony Hargain	1.50	4.00
11 Jonathan Hayes	1.50	4.00
12 Fred Jones	1.50	4.00
13 Darren Mickell	1.50	4.00
14 Charles Mincy	1.50	4.00
15 Tracy Rogers	1.50	4.00
16 Will Shields	1.50	4.00
17 Ricky Siglar	1.50	4.00
18 Tracy Simien	1.50	4.00
19 Tony Smith	1.50	4.00
20 Jay Taylor	1.50	4.00
21 Doug Terry	1.50	4.00
22 Bennie Thompson	1.50	4.00
23 Joe Valerio	1.50	4.00
24 Todd Young	1.50	4.00

1996 Chiefs Star Price Chopper

The Kansas City Chiefs issued this set sponsored by The Kansas City Star and Price Chopper. The cardbacks are blank and each measures approximately 5" by 7" with a black and white player photo on the front. The team name appears on the cardfront in all upper case letters below the player photo and to the left. The player's name and position (initial) appear below the photo in all caps as well. The two sponsor logos appear on either side of the player name. Note that the Price Chopper "Best Price" logo is the one used. Any additions to this checklist would be appreciated.

COMPLETE SET (15)	25.00	50.00
1 Marcus Allen	3.00	6.00
2 Kimble Anders	1.50	4.00
3 Donnell Bennett	1.50	4.00
4 Steve Bono	1.50	4.00
5 Vaughn Booker	1.50	4.00
6 Mark Collins	1.50	4.00
7 Jeff Criswell	1.50	4.00
8 Anthony Davis	1.50	4.00
9 Len Dawson	3.00	6.00
10 Pellom McDaniels	1.50	4.00
11 Dan Saleaumua	1.50	4.00
12 Derrick Thomas	3.00	6.00
13 Reggie Tongue	1.50	4.00
14 Tamarick Vanover	1.50	4.00
15 Jerome Woods	1.50	4.00

1997 Chiefs Score

This 15-card set of the Kansas City Chiefs was distributed in five-card packs with a suggested retail price of $1.99. The fronts feature color action player photos with white borders and the player's name and team logo printed in team color foil at the bottom. The backs carry player information and career statistics. Platinum Team parallel cards were randomly seeded in packs featuring all foil cardfronts.

COMPLETE SET (15)	2.00	5.00
*PLATINUM TEAMS: 1X TO 2X		
1 Lake Dawson	.15	.40
2 Tamarick Vanover	.15	.40
3 Marcus Allen	.30	.75
4 Neil Smith	.15	.40
5 Derrick Thomas	.30	.75
6 Kimble Anders	.15	.40
7 Chris Penn	.08	.25
8 Elvis Grbac	.15	.40
9 Mark Collins	.08	.25
10 Greg Hill	.15	.40
11 Reggie Tongue	.08	.25
12 James Hasty	.08	.25
13 Dale Carter	.08	.25
14 Jerome Woods	.08	.25
15 Sean LaChapelle	.08	.25

2006 Chiefs Donruss Thanksgiving Classic

COMPLETE SET (7)	4.00	8.00
KC1 Trent Green	.60	1.50
KC2 Larry Johnson	.60	1.50
KC3 Eddie Kennison	.50	1.25
KC4 Tony Gonzalez	.60	1.50
KC5 Tamba Hali	.75	2.00
KC6 Marcus Allen	1.00	2.50
NNO Cover Card CL	.20	.50

2006 Chiefs Topps

COMPLETE SET (12)	3.00	6.00
KC1 Derrick Johnson	.20	.50
KC2 Larry Johnson	.25	.60
KC3 Trent Green	.25	.60
KC4 Samie Parker	.20	.50
KC5 Tony Gonzalez	.25	.60
KC6 Dante Hall	.25	.60
KC7 Eddie Kennison	.20	.50
KC8 Priest Holmes	.25	.60
KC9 Patrick Surtain	.20	.50
KC10 Sammy Knight	.15	.40
KC11 Tamba Hali	.30	.75
KC12 Brodie Croyle	.30	.75

2007 Chiefs Topps

COMPLETE SET (12)	2.50	5.00
1 Tony Gonzalez	.25	.60
2 Trent Green	.25	.60
3 Larry Johnson	.20	.50
4 Derrick Johnson	.20	.50
5 Eddie Kennison	.20	.50
6 Samie Parker	.20	.50
7 Tamba Hali	.20	.50
8 Damon Huard	.25	.60
9 Dwayne Bowe	.40	1.00
10 Jared Allen	.30	.75
11 Ty Law	.25	.60
12 Donnie Edwards	.20	.50

2008 Chiefs Topps

COMPLETE SET (12)	2.50	5.00
1 Napoleon Harris	.20	.50
2 Dwayne Bowe	.25	.60
3 Tony Gonzalez	.25	.60
4 Damon Huard	.20	.50
5 Larry Johnson	.25	.60
6 Tamba Hali	.20	.50
7 Brodie Croyle	.25	.60
8 Kolby Smith	.20	.50
9 Donnie Edwards	.20	.50
10 Derrick Johnson	.20	.50
11 Glenn Dorsey	.40	1.00
12 Jamaal Charles	.60	1.50

1970 Chiquita Team Logo Stickers

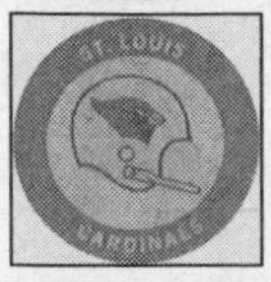

In 1970, Chiquita produced team logo stickers for the 26 pro football teams. We have sequenced these unnumbered stickers alphabetically below. Both Boston and New England Patriots versions of that team's sticker were issued allowing that these stickers may have first appeared in the late 1960s.

COMPLETE SET (26)	175.00	350.00
1 Atlanta Falcons	6.00	12.00
2 Baltimore Colts	7.50	15.00
3 Boston Patriots	20.00	40.00
4 Buffalo Bills	7.50	15.00
5 Chicago Bears	7.50	15.00
6 Cincinnati Bengals	6.00	12.00
7 Cleveland Browns	7.50	15.00
8 Dallas Cowboys	10.00	20.00
9 Denver Broncos	7.50	15.00
10 Detroit Lions	6.00	12.00
11 Green Bay Packers	10.00	20.00
12 Houston Oilers	6.00	12.00
13 Kansas City Chiefs	6.00	12.00
14 Los Angeles Rams	6.00	12.00
15 Miami Dolphins	7.50	15.00
16 Minnesota Vikings	7.50	15.00
17 New England Patriots	6.00	12.00
18 New Orleans Saints	6.00	12.00
19 New York Giants	7.50	15.00
20 New York Jets	7.50	15.00
21 Oakland Raiders	10.00	20.00
22 Philadelphia Eagles	6.00	12.00
23 Pittsburgh Steelers	10.00	20.00
24 San Diego Chargers	6.00	12.00
25 San Francisco 49ers	7.50	15.00
26 St. Louis Cardinals	6.00	12.00
27 Washington Redskins	7.50	15.00

1972 Chiquita NFL Slides

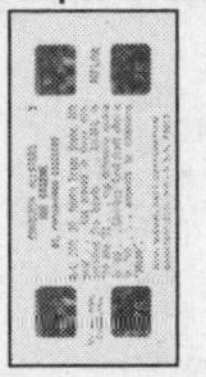

This set consists of 13-slides and a plastic viewer for viewing the slides. Each slide measures approximately 3 9/16" by 1 3/4" and features two players (one on each side); each of the 26 NFL teams is represented by one player. Each side has a player summary on its middle portion, with two small color action slides at each end stacked one above the other. When the slide is placed in the viewer, the two bottom slides, which are identical, reveal the first player. Flipping the slide over reveals the other player biography and enables one to view the other two slides, which show the second player. The text on each slide can be found printed in either black or blue ink. Each side of the slides is numbered as listed below. The set is considered complete without the viewer. In 1972, collectors could receive a viewer and a complete set of 13-slides by sending in 35-cents, 5-NFL Logo Stickers from Chiquita bananas, and a cash register receipt showing $15 worth of produce purchases made at the store.

COMPLETE SET (13)	40.00	100.00
*BLUE: .5X TO 1.2X BLACK		
1 Joe Greene/2 Bob Lilly	12.50	30.00
3 Bill Bergey/4 Gary Collins	5.00	12.00
5 Walt Sweeney/6 Bubba Smith	4.00	10.00
7 Larry Wilson/8 Fred Carr	5.00	12.00
9 Mac Percival/10 John Brodie	5.00	12.00
11 Lem Barney/12 Ron Yary	5.00	12.00
13 Curt Knight/14 Alvin Haymond	4.00	10.00
15 Floyd Little/16 Gerry Philbin	5.00	12.00
17 Jim Mitchell/18 Paul Costa	4.00	10.00
19 Jake Kupp/20 Ben Hawkins	4.00	10.00
21 Johnny Robinson/22 George Webster	4.00	10.00
23 Mercury Morris/24 Willie Brown	6.00	15.00
25 Ron Johnson/26 Jon Morris	4.00	10.00
NNO Yellow Viewer	6.00	15.00
NNO Red Viewer	6.00	15.00
NNO Blue Viewer	6.00	15.00

1970 Clark Volpe

This 66-card set is actually a collection of team sets. Each team subset contains between six and nine cards. These unnumbered cards are listed below alphabetically by player within team as follows: Chicago Bears (1-8), Cincinnati Bengals (9-14), Cleveland Browns (15-21), Detroit Lions (22-30), Green Bay Packers (31-39), Kansas City Chiefs (40-48), Minnesota Vikings (49-57), St. Louis Cardinals (58-66). The cards measure approximately 7 1/2" by 9 15/16" (or 7 1/2" by 14" with mail-in tab intact). The back of the (top) drawing portion describes the mail-in offers for tumblers, posters, etc. The bottom tab is a business-reply mail-in card addressed to Clark Oil and Refining Corporation to the attention of Alex Karras. The artist for these drawings was Nicholas Volpe. The cards are typically found with tabs intact and hence they are priced that way below.

COMPLETE SET (66)	200.00	400.00
1 Ronnie Bull	4.00	8.00
2 Dick Butkus	15.00	30.00
3 Lee Roy Caffey	4.00	8.00
4 Bobby Douglass	4.00	8.00
5 Dick Gordon	4.00	8.00
6 Bennie McRae	4.00	8.00
7 Ed O'Bradovich	4.00	8.00
8 George Seals	4.00	8.00
9 Bill Bergey	5.00	10.00
10 Jess Phillips	4.00	8.00
11 Mike Reid	5.00	10.00
12 Paul Robinson	4.00	8.00
13 Bob Trumpy	5.00	10.00
14 Sam Wyche	5.00	10.00
15 Erich Barnes	4.00	8.00
16 Gary Collins	4.00	8.00
17 Gene Hickerson	5.00	10.00
18 Jim Houston	4.00	8.00
19 Leroy Kelly	6.00	12.00
20 Ernie Kellerman	4.00	8.00
21 Bill Nelsen	4.00	8.00
22 Lem Barney	6.00	12.00
23 Mel Farr	4.00	8.00
24 Larry Hand	4.00	8.00
25 Alex Karras	7.50	15.00
26 Mike Lucci	4.00	8.00
27 Bill Munson	4.00	8.00
28 Charlie Sanders	5.00	10.00
29 Tom Vaughn	4.00	8.00
30 Wayne Walker	4.00	8.00
31 Lionel Aldridge	4.00	8.00
32 Donny Anderson	5.00	10.00
33 Ken Bowman	4.00	8.00
34 Carroll Dale	4.00	8.00
35 Jim Grabowski	4.00	8.00
36 Ray Nitschke	7.50	15.00
37 Dave Robinson	5.00	10.00
38 Travis Williams	4.00	8.00
39 Willie Wood	6.00	12.00
40 Fred Arbanas	4.00	8.00
41 Bobby Bell	6.00	12.00
42 Aaron Brown	4.00	8.00
43 Buck Buchanan	6.00	12.00
44 Len Dawson	12.50	25.00
45 Jim Marsalis	4.00	8.00
46 Jerry Mays	4.00	8.00
47 Johnny Robinson	4.00	8.00
48 Jim Tyrer	4.00	8.00
49 Bill Brown	5.00	10.00
50 Fred Cox	4.00	8.00
51 Gary Cuozzo	4.00	8.00
52 Carl Eller	6.00	12.00
53 Jim Marshall	6.00	12.00
54 Dave Osborn	4.00	8.00
55 Alan Page	7.50	15.00
56 Mick Tingelhoff	5.00	10.00
57 Gene Washington Vik	4.00	8.00
58 Pete Beathard	4.00	8.00
59 John Gilliam	4.00	8.00
60 Jim Hart	5.00	10.00
61 Johnny Roland	4.00	8.00
62 Jackie Smith	6.00	12.00
63 Larry Stallings	4.00	8.00
64 Roger Wehrli	5.00	10.00
65 Dave Williams	4.00	8.00
66 Larry Wilson	6.00	12.00

1992 Classic NFL Game

The 1992 Classic NFL Game football set consists of 60 standard-size cards, a travel game board, player piece and die, rules, and scoreboard. Apparently cards number 13 and 51 were never issued. The game board included with each 60-card blister pack featured a football field and a list of plays at each end with the outcome of each play determining by a roll of the die. The board is folded in half and measures approximately 15 1/2" by 6" after unfolding. The rules for the game are printed on the backs of the Andre Ware and Cris Dishman cards. The cards measure the standard size. The fronts feature color player photos with a dusty rose inner border and a dark blue outer border. The player's name and position appear in a black bar at the lower right corner. The horizontal backs are white and carry a second color player photo, a "personal bio" feature, and five trivia questions with answers.

COMPLETE SET (60)	2.40	6.00
1 Steve Atwater	.01	.05
2 Louis Oliver	.01	.05
3 Ronnie Lott	.02	.10
4 Reggie White	.07	.20
5 Cortez Kennedy	.02	.10
6 Derrick Thomas	.07	.20
7 Pat Swilling	.02	.10
8 Cornelius Bennett	.02	.10
9 Mark Rypien	.02	.10
10 Todd Marinovich	.01	.05
11 Steve Young	.30	.75
12 Warren Moon	.07	.20
14 Hugh Millen	.01	.05
15 John Friesz	.02	.10
16 John Elway	.60	1.50
17 Chris Miller	.02	.10
18 Jim Everett	.02	.10
19 Emmitt Smith	.60	1.50
20 Johnny Johnson	.01	.05
21 Thurman Thomas	.07	.20
22 Leonard Russell	.02	.10
23 Rodney Hampton	.02	.10
24 Marion Butts	.02	.10
25 Neal Anderson	.02	.10
26 Barry Sanders	.60	1.50
27 Dexter Carter	.01	.05
28 Gaston Green	.01	.05
29 Barry Word	.01	.05
30 Eric Bieniemy	.01	.05
31 Nick Bell	.01	.05
32 Reggie Cobb	.01	.05
33 Jay Novacek	.07	.20
34 Keith Jackson	.02	.10
35 Eric Green	.02	.10
36 Lawrence Dawsey	.02	.10
37 Mike Pritchard	.01	.05
38 Michael Haynes	.02	.10
39 James Lofton	.02	.10
40 Art Monk	.02	.10
41 Herman Moore	.10	.30
42 Andre Rison	.07	.20
43 Wendell Davis	.01	.05
44 Sterling Sharpe	.02	.10
45 Fred Barnett	.02	.10
46 Rob Moore	.02	.10
47 Gary Clark	.02	.10
48 Wesley Carroll	.01	.05
49 Michael Irvin	.07	.20
50 John Taylor	.02	.10
52 Ray Bentley	.01	.05
53 Eric Swann	.02	.10
54 Amp Lee	.01	.05
55 Darryl Williams	.01	.05
56 Wilber Marshall	.01	.05
57 Siran Stacy	.01	.05
58 Chip Lohmiller	.01	.05
59 Rodney Culver	.02	.10
60 Tommy Vardell	.02	.10
NNO Cris Dishman (Rules on back)	.01	.05
NNO Andre Ware (Rules on back)	.02	.10

1992 Classic Show Promos 20

COMPLETE SET (20)	15.00	30.00
4 David Klingler (1992 Sports Spectacular) Houston	.20	.50
6 Quentin Coryatt (July 1992 Arlington Marcus show)	.20	.50
18 David Klingler (1992 Tri-Star Houston) Houston	.20	.50

1992 Classic World Class Athletes

Packaged in a high impact clam shell, this 60-card standard-size set features current and past world class athletes. The production run was 295,000 sets, and an enclosed certificate of limited edition carries the set serial number. A few athletes had autographs randomly inserted into the factory sets. We have noted those cards at the end of our checklist.

COMP.FACT SET (60)	1.60	4.00
55 Carl Lewis Track and Field	.05	.15
56 Carl Lewis Track and Field	.05	.15
57 Carl Lewis Track and Field	.08	.25

1993 Classic TONX

These 150 TONX (or player caps) were sold in a clear plastic bag; the attached paper display tag advertises that 123 players and 27 quarterbacks from all NFL teams are featured in the set. Each tonx measures approximately 1 5/8" in diameter and features a full-bleed color action player photo.

COMPLETE SET (150)	125.00	200.00
1 Troy Aikman	2.50	6.00
2 Eric Allen	.30	.75
3 Terry Allen	.60	1.50
4 Morten Andersen	.30	.75
5 Neal Anderson	.30	.75
6 Flipper Anderson	.30	.75
7 Steve Atwater	.30	.75
8 Carl Banks	.30	.75
9 Patrick Bates	.30	.75
10 Cornelius Bennett	.40	1.00
11 Rod Bernstine	.30	.75
12 Jerome Bettis	3.00	8.00
13 Steve Beuerlein	.40	1.00
14 Bennie Blades	.30	.75
15 Brian Blades	.40	1.00
16 Drew Bledsoe	2.00	5.00
17 Tim Brown	.75	2.00
18 Terrell Buckley	.30	.75
19 Marion Butts	.40	1.00
20 Mark Carrier DB	.30	.75
21 Anthony Carter	.40	1.00
22 Cris Carter	.75	2.00
23 Dale Carter	.40	1.00
24 Ray Childress	.40	1.00
25 Gary Clark	.40	1.00
26 Reggie Cobb	.30	.75
27 Marco Coleman	.30	.75
28 Curtis Conway	.50	1.25
29 John Copeland	.40	1.00
30 Quentin Coryatt	.30	.75
31 Randall Cunningham	.60	1.50
32 Eric Curry	.40	1.00
33 Lawrence Dawsey	.30	.75
34 Chris Doleman	.40	1.00
35 Vaughn Dunbar	.30	.75
36 Henry Ellard	.40	1.00
37 John Elway	6.00	12.00
38 Steve Emtman	.30	.75
39 Ricky Ervins	.30	.75
40 Jim Everett	.30	.75
41 Brett Favre	6.00	12.00
42 Barry Foster	.40	1.00
43 Cleveland Gary	.30	.75
44 Jeff George	.50	1.25
45 Sean Gilbert	.40	1.00
46 Ernest Givins	.30	.75
47 Harold Green	.30	.75
48 Kevin Greene	.40	1.00
49 Paul Gruber	.30	.75
50 Charles Haley	.40	1.00
51 Rodney Hampton	.40	1.00
52 Jim Harbaugh	.60	1.50
53 Ronnie Harmon	.30	.75
54 Michael Haynes	.40	1.00
55 Garrison Hearst	.75	2.00
56 Randal Hill	.30	.75
57 Merril Hoge	.30	.75
58 Pierce Holt	.30	.75
59 Jeff Hostetler	.40	1.00
60 Stan Humphries	.40	1.00
61 Michael Irvin	.75	2.00
62 Keith Jackson	.40	1.00
63 Rickey Jackson	.30	.75
64 Haywood Jeffires	.30	.75
65 Pepper Johnson	.30	.75
66 Brent Jones	.40	1.00
67 Marvin Jones	.30	.75
68 Seth Joyner	.40	1.00
69 Jim Kelly	1.25	3.00
70 Cortez Kennedy	.40	1.00
71 David Klingler	.30	.75
72 Bernie Kosar	.40	1.00
73 Reggie Langhorne	.30	.75
74 Mo Lewis	.30	.75
75 Howie Long	.75	2.00
76 Ronnie Lott	.40	1.00
77 Charles Mann	.30	.75
78 Dan Marino	6.00	12.00
79 Todd Marinovich	.30	.75
80 Eric Martin	.30	.75
81 Clay Matthews	.40	1.00
82 Ed McCaffrey	.60	1.50
83 O.J. McDuffie	.60	1.50
84 Steve McMichael	.30	.75
85 Audray McMillian	.30	.75
86 Greg McMurtry	.30	.75
87 Karl Mecklenburg	.30	.75
88 Dave Meggett	.30	.75
89 Eric Metcalf	.40	1.00
90 Anthony Miller	.40	1.00
91 Chris Miller	.30	.75
92 Sam Mills	.30	.75
93 Rick Mirer	.60	1.50
94 Johnny Mitchell	.30	.75
95 Art Monk	.40	1.00
96 Joe Montana	7.50	15.00
97 Warren Moon	.60	1.50
98 Rob Moore	.40	1.00
99 Brad Muster	.30	.75
100 Browning Nagle	.30	.75
101 Ken Norton Jr.	.40	1.00
102 Jay Novacek	.60	1.50
103 Neil O'Donnell	.60	1.50
104 Leslie O'Neal	.40	1.00
105 Louis Oliver	.30	.75
106 Rodney Peete	.40	1.00
107 Michael Dean Perry	.40	1.00
108 Carl Pickens	.40	1.00
109 Ricky Proehl	.30	.75
110 Andre Reed	.60	1.50
111 Jerry Rice	3.00	8.00
112 Andre Rison	.60	1.50
113 Leonard Russell	.40	1.00
114 Mark Rypien	.30	.75
115 Barry Sanders	4.00	10.00
116 Deion Sanders	1.50	4.00
117 Junior Seau	.60	1.50
118 Shannon Sharpe	.60	1.50
119 Sterling Sharpe	.40	1.00
120 Clyde Simmons	.30	.75
121 Wayne Simmons	.30	.75
122 Phil Simms	.40	1.00
123 Bruce Smith	.60	1.50
124 Emmitt Smith	5.00	12.00
126 Alonzo Spellman	.30	.75
127 Pat Swilling	.40	1.00
128 John Taylor	.40	1.00
129 Lawrence Taylor	.60	1.50
130 Broderick Thomas	.30	.75
131 Derrick Thomas	.60	1.50
132 Thurman Thomas	.60	1.50
133 Andre Tippett	.30	.75
134 Jessie Tuggle	.30	.75
135 Tommy Vardell	.30	.75
136 Jon Vaughn	.30	.75
137 Clarence Verdin	.30	.75
138 Herschel Walker	.40	1.00
139 Andre Ware	.30	.75
140 Chris Warren	.40	1.00
141 Ricky Watters	.60	1.50
142 Lorenzo White	.30	.75
143 Reggie White	.60	1.50
144 Alfred Williams	.30	.75
145 Calvin Williams	.40	1.00
146 Harvey Williams	.40	1.00
147 John L. Williams	.30	.75
148 Rod Woodson	.60	1.50
149 Barry Word	.30	.75
150 Steve Young	2.00	5.00

1993 Classic TONX Previews

NNO Troy Aikman	2.00	5.00
NNO Michael Irvin	1.25	3.00

1993 Classic TONX QB Club

These cards are actually round discs (sometimes called POGs) produced by Classic and named TONX. Each features an image of a quarterback club member and measures roughly 1-1/2" round.

1 Troy Aikman	8.00	20.00
2 Bubby Brister	3.00	8.00
3 Randall Cunningham	4.00	10.00
4 John Elway	12.00	30.00
5 Jim Everett	3.00	8.00
6 Boomer Esiason	4.00	10.00
7 Jim Kelly	5.00	12.00
8 Dan Marino	12.00	30.00
9 Jim Harbaugh	4.00	10.00
10 Jeff Hostetler	3.00	8.00
11 Warren Moon	4.00	10.00
12 Bernie Kosar	4.00	10.00
13 Mark Rypien	3.00	8.00
14 Chris Miller	3.00	8.00
15 David Klingler	3.00	8.00
17 Steve Young	6.00	15.00
18 Brett Favre	12.00	30.00
19 Neil O'Donnell	3.00	8.00

1993-94 Classic C3 Gold Crown Cut Lasercut

COMPLETE SET (21)	10.00	25.00
7 Drew Bledsoe	1.00	2.50
8 Rick Mirer	.40	1.00
9 Garrison Hearst	.40	1.00
10 Terry Kirby	.40	1.00
11 Glyn Milburn	.40	1.00
12 Reggie Brooks	.40	1.00
13 Jerome Bettis	.75	2.00
NNO Drew Bledsoe/5000 Rick Mirer Presidential Membership	1.25	3.00

1994 Classic C3 Gold Crown Club

COMPLETE SET (4)	6.00	15.00
CC3 Emmitt Smith	4.00	10.00

1994 Classic International Promos

COMPLETE SET (4)	3.00	8.00
1 Troy Aikman FB	1.25	3.00
3 Marshall Faulk FB	1.25	3.00

1994 Classic National Promos

COMPLETE SET (5)	6.00	15.00
4 Heath Shuler FB	.75	2.00
5 Emmitt Smith FB	2.00	5.00

1995 Classic $3 Phone Cards

COMPLETE SET (6)	6.00	15.00
1 Troy Aikman	1.50	4.00
2 Ki-Jana Carter	.75	2.00
3 Kerry Collins	1.00	2.50

4 Marshall Faulk 1.00 2.50
5 Steve McNair 1.00 2.50
6 Steve Young 1.25 3.00

1995 Classic Draft Day Jaguars

COMPLETE SET (5) 8.00 20.00
JJ1 Kerry Collins 1.50 4.00
(no card number on back)
JJ2 Steve McNair 4.80 12.00
JJ3 Tony Boselli .80 2.00
JJ4 Kevin Carter
JJ5 Ki-Jana Carter 1.20 3.00

1996 Classic NFL Draft Day

This 15-card set was distributed at the 1996 NFL Draft in New York. It was designed to match the top picks with the team that selected them; therefore three players appear with three different team options. NFL veterans and the previous Heisman Award winner are also included. Each set came with a certificate of authenticity numbered of 9,996.

COMPLETE SET (15) 12.00 30.00
1A Keyshawn Johnson 1.20 3.00
Jets
1B Keyshawn Johnson 1.50 3.00
Jaguars
1C Keyshawn Johnson .60 1.50
Redskins
2A Kevin Hardy .80 2.00
Jaguars
2B Kevin Hardy .40 1.00
Redskins
2C Kevin Hardy .40 1.00
Cardinals
3A Terry Glenn .80 2.00
Patriots
3B Terry Glenn .80 2.00
Giants
3C Terry Glenn .80 2.00
Jets
4 Eddie George 2.00 5.00
5 Emmitt Smith 1.60 4.00
6 Troy Aikman 1.00 2.50
7 Drew Bledsoe 1.00 2.50
8 Kerry Collins 1.00 2.50
9 Title Card .40 1.00
Checklist Back

1996 Classic SP Autographs

This eight-card set was offered as a mail-in order from Score Board Inc. (Classic) and Scott Paper Company. Each card was personally autographed by the player featured on the front and is accompanied by a Score Board certificate of authenticity. The cards were initially offered for $7.95 each with two UPCs or $10.95 without UPC labels. Complete could be had for $54.95 with eight UPCs or $64.95 without. Although the cards contain the 1995 date on the copyright line, they were first offered in early 1996.

COMPLETE SET (8) 40.00 100.00
SP1 Kyle Brady 4.80 12.00
SP2 Kerry Collins 10.00 20.00
SP3 Ron Jaworski 4.80 12.00
SP4 Napoleon Kaufman 6.00 15.00
SP5 Jim Kiick 4.80 12.00
SP6 Steve McNair 14.00 35.00
SP7 Jim Plunkett 6.00 15.00
SP8 Randy White 6.00 15.00

1994 Classic NFL Experience Promos

COMPLETE SET (6) 6.00 15.00
1 Troy Aikman 1.60 4.00
2 Jerry Rice 1.60 4.00
3 Emmitt Smith 2.40 6.00
4 Derrick Thomas .50 1.25
5 Thurman Thomas .80 2.00
6 Rod Woodson .50 1.25

1994 Classic NFL Experience

These 100 standard-size cards were released by Classic Games in celebration of Super Bowl XXVIII. Classic produced 1,500 sequentially numbered cases that were offered to hobby dealers only. Cards from the 10-card 1994 Classic NFL Experience LPs and 1,994 Troy Aikman Super Bowl XXVII MVP cards were randomly inserted in the eight-card foil packs.

COMPLETE SET (100) 4.00 10.00
1 Checklist 1 .01 .05
2 Checklist 2 .01 .05
3 Bobby Hebert .01 .05
4 Erric Pegram .01 .05
5 Andre Rison .02 .10
6 Deion Sanders .15 .40
7 Cornelius Bennett .02 .10
8 Jim Kelly .07 .20
9 Andre Reed .02 .10
10 Bruce Smith .07 .20
11 Thurman Thomas .07 .20
12 Curtis Conway .07 .20
13 Jim Harbaugh .07 .20
14 John Copeland .01 .05
15 David Klingler .01 .05
16 Carl Pickens .02 .10
17 Eric Metcalf .02 .10
18 Vinny Testaverde .02 .10
19 Eric Turner .01 .05
20 Tommy Vardell .01 .05
21 Troy Aikman .30 .75
22 Michael Irvin .07 .20
23 Emmitt Smith .50 1.25
24 Kevin Williams WR .02 .10
25 John Elway .60 1.50
26 Glyn Milburn .02 .10
27 Shannon Sharpe .02 .10
28 Herman Moore .07 .20
29 Rodney Peete .01 .05
30 Barry Sanders .50 1.25
31 Pat Swilling .01 .05
32 Brett Favre .60 1.50
33 Sterling Sharpe .02 .10
34 Reggie White .07 .20
35 Haywood Jeffires .02 .10
36 Warren Moon .07 .20
37 Webster Slaughter .01 .05
38 Lorenzo White .01 .05
39 Quentin Coryatt .01 .05
40 Jeff George .07 .20
41 Roosevelt Potts .01 .05
42 Marcus Allen .07 .20
43 Joe Montana .60 1.50
44 Neil Smith .02 .10
45 Derrick Thomas .07 .20
46 Tim Brown .07 .20
47 Jeff Hostetler .02 .10
48 Rocket Ismail .02 .10
49 Anthony Smith .01 .05
50 Jerome Bettis .15 .40
51 Jim Everett .02 .10
52 T.J. Rubley RC .01 .05
53 Keith Jackson .01 .05
54 Terry Kirby .07 .20
55 Dan Marino .60 1.50
56 O.J. McDuffie .07 .20
57 Scott Mitchell .02 .10
58 Cris Carter .15 .40
59 Chris Doleman .01 .05
60 Robert Smith .07 .20
61 Drew Bledsoe .25 .60
62 Vincent Brisby .02 .10
63 Derek Brown RBK .01 .05
64 Willie Roaf .01 .05
65 Irv Smith .01 .05
66 Renaldo Turnbull .01 .05
67 Rodney Hampton .02 .10
68 Phil Simms .02 .10
69 Lawrence Taylor .07 .20
70 Boomer Esiason .02 .10
71 Marvin Jones .01 .05
72 Ronnie Lott .02 .10
73 Johnny Mitchell .01 .05
74 Rob Moore .02 .10
75 Victor Bailey .01 .05
76 Randall Cunningham .07 .20
77 Ken O'Brien .01 .05
78 Steve Beuerlein .02 .10
79 Garrison Hearst .07 .20
80 Ronald Moore .01 .05
81 Ricky Proehl .01 .05
82 Deon Figures .01 .05
83 Barry Foster .01 .05
84 Neil O'Donnell .07 .20
85 Rod Woodson .02 .10
86 Natrone Means .07 .20
87 Anthony Miller .02 .10
88 Junior Seau .07 .20
89 Jerry Rice .30 .75
90 Ricky Watters .02 .10
91 Steve Young .30 .75
92 Brian Blades .02 .10
93 Cortez Kennedy .02 .10
94 Rick Mirer .07 .20
95 Reggie Cobb .02 .10
96 Eric Curry .01 .05
97 Craig Erickson .01 .05
98 Reggie Brooks .02 .10
99 Desmond Howard .02 .10
100 Mark Rypien .01 .05
QB1 Troy Aikman AU/2500 40.00 80.00
(issued via QVC)
SP1 Troy Aikman SB MVP/1994 15.00 40.00

1994 Classic NFL Experience LPs

COMPLETE SET (10) 20.00 50.00
LP1 Jerome Bettis 4.00 10.00
LP2 Drew Bledsoe 6.00 15.00
LP3 Reggie Brooks 1.00 2.50
LP4 Garrison Hearst 2.00 5.00
LP5 Derek Brown RBK .50 1.25
LP6 Terry Kirby 2.00 5.00
LP7 Natrone Means 2.00 5.00
LP8 Glyn Milburn 1.00 2.50
LP9 Rick Mirer 2.00 5.00
LP10 Robert Smith 2.00 5.00

1994 Classic NFL Experience Super Bowl Heroes

COMPLETE SET (5) 5.00 12.00
SBH1 Jerry Rice 1.25 3.00
SBH2 Joe Montana 2.00 5.00
SBH3 Emmitt Smith 1.50 4.00
SBH4 Troy Aikman 1.00 2.50
SBH5 Lawrence Taylor .60 1.50

1995 Classic Draft Day Autographs

Cards from this set were issued in Summer 1995 to honor the NFL Draft. The fronts display a color player photo and a 1995 NFL Draft emblem. On a background consisting of an enlarged version of the 1995 NFL Draft emblem, the back carries the announced print run (of 500) and a brief congratulatory message.

1 Kerry Collins 15.00 30.00
2 Steve McNair 30.00 60.00

1995 Classic National

This 20-card multi-sport set was issued by Classic to commemorate the 16th National Sports Collectors Convention in St. Louis. The set included a certificate of limited edition, with the serial number out of 9,995 sets produced. One thousand Sprint 20-minute phone cards featuring Ki-Jana Carter were also distributed.

COMPLETE SET (20) 8.00 20.00
NC2 Emmitt Smith 1.50 4.00
NC3 Troy Aikman 1.00 2.50
NC6 Steve Young .75 2.00
NC8 Marshall Faulk .75 2.00
NC10 Drew Bledsoe .75 2.00
NC11 Ki-Jana Carter .20 .50
NC12 Kerry Collins .40 1.00
NNO Ki-Jana Carter .75 2.00
(Phone Card)

1995 Classic NFL Experience

This 110-card standard-size set features color player action shots with team color-coded borders. This set also includes a Miami Dolphins commemorative card featuring legendary head coach Don Shula and quarterback Dan Marino (on average of one per box), and 1,995 sequentially numbered "Emmitt Zone" insert cards. Gold cards were inserted one per hobby pack. The cards are grouped alphabetically within teams and checklisted below according to teams. There was an Emmitt Smith Preview card issued for the set one per box in 1994 Classic Images. It is priced with the Images set. For the 1995 Super Bowl NFL Experience Card Show in Miami, Classic issued a commemorative sheet (roughly 8-3/4" by 11-1/2") honoring the 49ers and Chargers. The blankbacked sheet includes the cardfronts of three players from each of the two teams.

COMPLETE SET (110) 4.00 10.00
1 Seth Joyner .01 .05
2 Clyde Simmons .01 .05
3 Ronald Moore .01 .05
4 Andre Rison .02 .10
5 Bert Emanuel .07 .20
6 Jeff George .02 .10
7 Terance Mathis .02 .10
8 Jim Kelly .07 .20
9 Thurman Thomas .07 .20
10 Andre Reed .02 .10
11 Bruce Smith .07 .20
12 Cornelius Bennett .02 .10
13 Steve Walsh .01 .05
14 Lewis Tillman .01 .05
15 Chris Zorich .01 .05
16 Jeff Blake RC .25 .60
17 Darnay Scott .02 .10
18 Dan Wilkinson .02 .10
19 Eric Metcalf .02 .10
20 Antonio Langham .01 .05
21 Pepper Johnson .01 .05
22 Eric Turner .01 .05
23 Leroy Hoard .01 .05
24 Vinny Testaverde .02 .10
25 Troy Aikman .30 .75
26 Emmitt Smith .50 1.25
27 Michael Irvin .07 .20
28 Alvin Harper .01 .05
29 Charles Haley .02 .10
30 John Elway .60 1.50
31 Leonard Russell .01 .05
32 Shannon Sharpe .02 .10
33 Herman Moore .07 .20
34 Barry Sanders .50 1.25
35 Brett Favre .60 1.50
36 Sterling Sharpe .02 .10
37 Reggie White .07 .20
38 Gary Brown .01 .05
39 Haywood Jeffires .01 .05
40 Quentin Coryatt .02 .10
41 Marshall Faulk .40 1.00
42 Tony Bennett .01 .05
43 Joe Montana .60 1.50
44 Marcus Allen .07 .20
45 Derrick Thomas .07 .20
46 Neil Smith .02 .10
47 Tim Brown .07 .20
48 Jeff Hostetler .02 .10
49 Terry McDaniel .01 .05
50 Jerome Bettis .07 .20
51 Sean Gilbert .02 .10
52 Dan Marino .60 1.50
53 Irving Fryar .02 .10
54 Keith Jackson .01 .05
55 Bernie Parmalee .02 .10
56 Tim Bowens .01 .05
57 Cris Carter .07 .20
58 Terry Allen .02 .10
59 Warren Moon .02 .10
60 John Randle .02 .10
61 Jake Reed .02 .10
62 Drew Bledsoe .20 .50
63 Marion Butts .01 .05
64 Ben Coates .02 .10
65 Derek Brown RBK .01 .05
66 Jim Everett .01 .05
67 Michael Haynes .02 .10
68 Darion Conner .01 .05
69 Rodney Hampton .02 .10
70 Dave Meggett .01 .05
71 Boomer Esiason .02 .10
72 Johnny Johnson .01 .05
73 Ronnie Lott .02 .10
74 Rob Moore .02 .10
75 Mo Lewis .01 .05
76 Randall Cunningham .07 .20
77 Herschel Walker .02 .10
78 Charlie Garner .07 .20
79 Calvin Williams .02 .10
80 Fred Barnett .02 .10
81 William Fuller .01 .05
82 Eric Allen .01 .05
83 Barry Foster .02 .10
84 Neil O'Donnell .02 .10
85 Rod Woodson .02 .10
86 Kevin Greene .02 .10
87 Byron Bam Morris .01 .05
88 Darren Perry .01 .05
89 Greg Lloyd .02 .10
90 Steve Young .25 .60
91 Ricky Watters .02 .10
92 Jerry Rice .30 .75
93 Ken Norton Jr. .02 .10
94 Deion Sanders .15 .40
95 Stan Humphries .02 .10
96 Natrone Means .02 .10
97 Junior Seau .07 .20
98 Leslie O'Neal .02 .10
99 Chris Mims .01 .05
100 Rick Mirer .02 .10
101 Chris Warren .02 .10
102 Brian Blades .02 .10
103 Trent Dilfer .07 .20
104 Errict Rhett .02 .10
105 Heath Shuler .02 .10
106 Henry Ellard .02 .10
107 Ken Harvey .01 .05
108 Gus Frerotte .02 .10
109 Checklist 1 .02 .10
110 Checklist 2 .02 .10
SP1 Marshall Faulk Promo .40 1.00
(Throwbacks card with
Super Bowl XXIX Logo)
SP1S Marshall Faulk Promo 4.00 10.00
(Throwbacks card with
Super Bowl XXIX Logo
Spanish print on back)
EZ1 Emmitt Smith Zone/1995 10.00 25.00
GC1 Dan Marino .75 2.00
Don Shula
Play Card
Super Bowl pack insert
GC2 Dan Marino 1.25 3.00
Don Shula
VIP Card
Super Bowl pack insert
MD1 Dan Marino 1.25 3.00
Don Shula
Dolphins Commemorative
regular pack insert
PC1 Marshall Faulk Promo .40 1.00
(Throwbacks card)
NNO Super Bowl XXIX Sheet .75 2.00
(numbered of 10,000)
Deion Sanders
Steve Young
Jerry Rice
Junior Seau
Natrone Means
Stan Humphries

1995 Classic NFL Experience Gold

COMPLETE SET (110) 20.00 40.00
*GOLD CARDS: 1.2X to 3X BASIC CARDS
ONE PER PACK

1995 Classic NFL Experience Rookies

COMPLETE SET (10) 4.00 8.00
STATED ODDS 1:6 HOB, 1:5 JUM
*SPANISH: .8X TO 2X BASIC INSERTS
R1 Marshall Faulk 4.00 10.00
R2 Bert Emanuel .75 2.00
R3 Charlie Garner .75 2.00
R4 Errict Rhett .40 1.00
R5 Byron Bam Morris .20 .50
R6 Heath Shuler .40 1.00
R7 Trent Dilfer .75 2.00
R8 Darnay Scott .40 1.00
R9 Tim Bowens .20 .50
R10 Antonio Langham .20 .50

1995 Classic NFL Experience Super Bowl Game

COMPLETE SET (20) 10.00 20.00
ONE PER SPECIAL JUMBO PACK
A0 Marshall Faulk .75 2.00
A1 Natrone Means .07 .20
A2 Thurman Thomas .15 .40
A3 Joe Montana 1.25 3.00
A4 John Elway 1.25 3.00
A5 Rick Mirer .07 .20
A6 Drew Bledsoe WIN .40 1.00
A7 Dan Marino 1.25 3.00
A8 Jim Kelly .15 .40
A9 Marcus Allen .15 .40
N0 Troy Aikman .60 1.50
N1 Steve Young .50 1.25
N2 Jerome Bettis .15 .40
N3 Barry Sanders 1.00 2.50
N4 Randall Cunningham .15 .40
N5 Andre Rison .07 .20
N6 Jerry Rice .60 1.50
N7 Emmitt Smith 1.00 2.50
N8 Michael Irvin .15 .40
N9 Sterling Sharpe WIN Exp .07 .20

1995 Classic NFL Experience Super Bowl Inserts

This five-card set was sold on Home Shopping Network with the regular 1994 NFL Experience set. It was made exclusively for them. The fronts feature color player action shots with the player's name and a Super Bowl XXX highlight at the bottom in a red stripe. The backs carry another color player action shot with the player's name, position, and team name below it along with a brief biography of the player.

COMPLETE SET (5) 4.80 12.00
SBF1 Jerry Rice 1.60 4.00
SBF2 Ricky Watters .80 2.00
SBF3 Natrone Means .80 2.00
SBF4 Steve Young 1.20 3.00
SBF5 Steve Young 1.20 3.00

1995 Classic NFL Experience Throwbacks

COMPLETE SET (28) 50.00 100.00
STATED ODDS 1:12 HOB, 1:10 JUM
T1 Seth Joyner .15 .40
T2 Andre Rison .30 .75
T3 Thurman Thomas .60 1.50
T4 Lewis Tillman .15 .40
T5 Dan Wilkinson .30 .75
T6 Eric Metcalf .30 .75
T7 Emmitt Smith 4.00 10.00
T8 John Elway 5.00 12.00
T9 Barry Sanders 4.00 10.00
T10 Reggie White .60 1.50
T11 Haywood Jeffires .15 .40
T12 Marshall Faulk 3.00 8.00
T13 Joe Montana 5.00 12.00
T14 Jeff Hostetler .30 .75
T15 Jerome Bettis .60 1.50
T16 Dan Marino 5.00 12.00
T17 Warren Moon .30 .75
T18 Drew Bledsoe 1.50 4.00
T19 Jim Everett .15 .40
T20 Dave Meggett .15 .40
T21 Ronnie Lott .30 .75
T22 Randall Cunningham .60 1.50
T23 Rod Woodson .30 .75
T24 Natrone Means .30 .75
T25 Rick Mirer .30 .75
T26 Steve Young 2.00 5.00
T27 Trent Dilfer .60 1.50
T28 Henry Ellard .30 .75
T7AU Emmitt Smith AUTO 75.00 125.00
(1995 cards signed)

1996 Classic NFL Experience

This 125 card standard-size set was issued in 10 card packs, with 24 cards in a box and 16 boxes in a case. There were also factory sets issued with Emmitt Smith featured on the front, and was released as part of a retail package that included 12-packs of 1996 NFL Experience as well. There are no key Rookie Cards in this set. Special Super Bowl packs were issued with special parallel versions of these cards. An Emmitt Smith Sculpted Promo card (#XXX) was produced to preview the set. We've included it below in the price listings.

COMPLETE SET (125) 4.00 10.00
COMP.FACT SET (130) 6.00 15.00
1 Emmitt Smith .50 1.25
2 Jerry Rice .30 .75
3 Carl Pickens .02 .10
4 Curtis Conway .07 .20
5 Isaac Bruce .07 .20
6 Marshall Faulk .15 .40
7 Errict Rhett .02 .10
8 Troy Aikman .30 .75
9 Jeff Hostetler .01 .05
10 Dan Marino .60 1.50
11 Barry Sanders .50 1.25
12 Drew Bledsoe .15 .40
13 Ricky Watters .02 .10
14 Natrone Means .02 .10
15 Chris Warren .02 .10
16 Jim Kelly .07 .20
17 Jeff George .02 .10
18 Garrison Hearst .02 .10
19 Brett Favre .60 1.50
20 John Elway .60 1.50
21 Robert Smith .02 .10
22 Steve Bono .01 .05
23 Byron Bam Morris .01 .05
24 Jim Everett .01 .05
25 Steve Young .25 .60
26 Rodney Hampton .02 .10
27 Terry Allen .02 .10
28 Chris Chandler .02 .10
29 Mark Carrier WR .01 .05
30 Desmond Howard .02 .10
31 Erik Kramer .01 .05
32 Irving Fryar .02 .10
33 Jeff Blake .07 .20
34 Vinny Testaverde .02 .10
35 Stan Humphries .02 .10
36 Tim Brown .07 .20
37 Trent Dilfer .07 .20
38 Jim Harbaugh .02 .10
39 Warren Moon .02 .10
40 Ben Coates .02 .10
41 Boomer Esiason .02 .10
42 Rodney Peete .01 .05
43 Gus Frerotte .02 .10
44 Jerome Bettis .07 .20
45 Dave Brown .01 .05
46 William Floyd .02 .10
47 Andre Rison .02 .10
48 Robert Brooks .07 .20
49 Marcus Allen .07 .20
50 Rick Mirer .02 .10
51 Alvin Harper .01 .05
52 Chris Miller .01 .05
53 Eric Metcalf .01 .05
54 Dave Krieg .01 .05
55 Darnay Scott .02 .10
56 Cris Carter .07 .20
57 Lake Dawson .01 .05
58 Haywood Jeffires .01 .05
59 Herman Moore .02 .10
60 Michael Irvin .07 .20
61 Anthony Miller .02 .10
62 Troy Vincent .01 .05
63 Jake Reed .02 .10
64 Michael Haynes .01 .05
65 Scott Mitchell .02 .10
66 Roman Phifer .01 .05
67 Harvey Williams .01 .05
68 Darren Perry .01 .05
69 Brian Mitchell .01 .05
70 Derek Loville .01 .05
71 Junior Seau .07 .20
72 Bruce Smith .02 .10
73 Willie Davis .01 .05
74 Charles Haley .02 .10
75 Mike Sherrard .01 .05
76 Pat Swilling .01 .05
77 Yancey Thigpen .02 .10
78 Bryce Paup .01 .05
79 Eric Green .01 .05
80 Deion Sanders .15 .40
81 Mario Bates .02 .10
82 John Randle .02 .10
83 Charlie Garner .02 .10
84 Chris Doleman .01 .05
85 Robert Porcher .01 .05
86 Rob Moore .02 .10
87 Anthony Pleasant .01 .05
88 Bryan Cox .01 .05
89 Greg Hill .02 .10
90 Reggie White .07 .20
91 Shannon Sharpe .02 .10
92 Leroy Hoard .01 .05
93 John Copeland .01 .05
94 Tony Martin .02 .10
95 Greg Lloyd .02 .10
96 Tony Bennett .01 .05
97 Alonzo Spellman .01 .05
98 Wayne Martin .01 .05
99 Craig Heyward .01 .05
100 Leslie O'Neal .01 .05
101 Andy Harmon .01 .05
102 Edgar Bennett .02 .10
103 Derrick Moore .01 .05
104 Terrell Davis .20 .50
105 Kerry Collins .07 .20
106 Rodney Thomas .01 .05
107 Mark Brunell .15 .40
108 Curtis Martin .20 .50
109 Tyrone Wheatley .02 .10
110 Rashaan Salaam .02 .10
111 Kevin Carter .01 .05
112 Joey Galloway .07 .20
113 Mike Mamula .01 .05
114 Kyle Brady .01 .05
115 James O.Stewart .02 .10
116 Michael Westbrook .07 .20
117 J.J. Stokes .07 .20
118 Wayne Chrebet .15 .40
119 Warren Sapp .01 .05
120 Hugh Douglas .02 .10
121 Jim Flanigan .01 .05
122 Chester McGlockton .01 .05
123 Shawn Lee .01 .05
124 Emmitt Smith CL .10 .30
125 Kerry Collins CL .02 .10
P1 Emmitt Smith Promo .75 2.00
Sculpted card, #XXX

1996 Classic NFL Experience Printer's Proofs

COMPLETE SET (125) 80.00 200.00
*STARS: 5X TO 12X BASIC CARDS
STATED ODDS 1:20
STATED PRINT RUN 499 #'d SETS

1996 Classic NFL Experience Super Bowl Gold

COMPLETE GOLD SET (125) 20.00 50.00
*GOLD CARDS: 1.5X TO 4X BASIC CARDS
STATED PRINT RUN 799 #'d SETS

1996 Classic NFL Experience Super Bowl Red

COMPLETE RED SET (125) 150.00 300.00
*RED CARDS: 15X TO 40X BASIC CARDS
STATED ODDS 1:8 SUPER BOWL PACKS
STATED PRINT RUN 150 #'d SETS

1996 Classic NFL Experience Class of 1995

COMPLETE SET (5) 2.50 6.00
ONE SET PER NFL EXP.FACTORY SET
FI1 Steve Young .75 2.00
FI2 Emmitt Smith 1.50 4.00
FI3 Deion Sanders .50 1.25
FI4 Rashaan Salaam .10 .30
FI5 Kerry Collins .25 .60

1996 Classic NFL Experience Emmitt Zone

COMMON CARD (1-5) 20.00 50.00
NNO Emmitt Smith 1.25 3.00
Emmitt Zone Phone Card

1996 Classic NFL Experience Super Bowl Die Cut Promos

COMPLETE SET (10) 10.00 20.00
1C Jim Kelly .60 1.50
2C Dan Marino 2.50 6.00
3C Greg Lloyd .30 .75
4C Marcus Allen .60 1.50
5C Tim Brown .60 1.50
6C Emmitt Smith 2.00 5.00
7C Steve Young 1.00 2.50
8C Rashaan Salaam .30 .75
9C Brett Favre 2.50 6.00
10C Isaac Bruce .60 1.50

1996 Classic NFL Experience Super Bowl Die Cut Contest

COMPLETE SET (20) 30.00 80.00
STATED ODDS 1:12 SUPER BOWL PACKS
1A Jim Kelly .60 1.50
1B Jim Kelly .60 1.50
2A Dan Marino 5.00 12.00
2B Dan Marino 5.00 12.00
3A Greg Lloyd .30 .75
3B Greg Lloyd .30 .75
4A Marcus Allen .60 1.50
4B Marcus Allen .60 1.50
5A Tim Brown .60 1.50
5B Tim Brown .60 1.50
6A Emmitt Smith 4.00 10.00
6B Emmitt Smith 4.00 10.00
7A Steve Young 2.00 5.00
7B Steve Young 2.00 5.00
8A Rashaan Salaam .30 .75
8B Rashaan Salaam .30 .75
9A Brett Favre 5.00 12.00
9B Brett Favre 5.00 12.00
10A Isaac Bruce .60 1.50
10B Isaac Bruce .60 1.50

1996 Classic NFL Experience Super Bowl Game

COMPLETE SET (20) 10.00 25.00
STATED ODDS 1:4 HOB, 1:1 SUPER BOWL
A0 Drew Bledsoe .60 1.50
A1 John Elway 2.50 6.00
A2 Harvey Williams .07 .20
A3 Marshall Faulk .60 1.50
A4 Jim Kelly .30 .75
A5 Carl Pickens .15 .40
A6 Stan Humphries .15 .40
A7 Dan Marino 2.50 6.00
A8 Steve Bono .07 .20
A9 Napoleon Kaufman .30 .75
N0 Isaac Bruce .30 .75
N1 Steve Young 1.00 2.50
N2 Michael Westbrook .30 .75
N3 Troy Aikman 1.25 3.00
N4 Barry Sanders 2.00 5.00
N5 Rashaan Salaam .15 .40
N6 Emmitt Smith 2.00 5.00
N7 Jerry Rice 1.25 3.00
N8 Deion Sanders .60 1.50
N9 Kerry Collins .30 .75

1996 Classic NFL Experience Super Bowl Game Redemption

COMPLETE SET (5) 3.00 6.00
SBR1 Jay Novacek .20 .50
SBR2 Yancey Thigpen .20 .50
SBR3 Emmitt Smith 1.25 2.50
SBR4 Byron Bam Morris .20 .50
SBR5 Troy Aikman .75 2.00

1996 Classic NFL Experience Sculpted

COMPLETE SET (20) 40.00 100.00
STATED ODDS 1:15 HOBBY
S1 Kerry Collins .75 2.00
S2 Jeff Blake .75 2.00
S3 Vinny Testaverde .40 1.00
S4 Emmitt Smith 5.00 12.00
S5 Troy Aikman 3.00 8.00
S6 Deion Sanders 1.50 4.00
S7 John Elway 6.00 15.00
S8 Barry Sanders 5.00 12.00
S9 Brett Favre 6.00 15.00
S10 Marshall Faulk 1.50 4.00
S11 Steve Bono .20 .50
S12 Dan Marino 6.00 15.00
S13 Robert Smith .40 1.00
S14 Drew Bledsoe 1.50 4.00
S15 Natrone Means .40 1.00
S16 Steve Young 2.50 6.00
S17 Jerry Rice 3.00 8.00
S18 Isaac Bruce .75 2.00
S19 Errict Rhett .40 1.00
S20 Michael Westbrook .75 2.00

1996 Classic NFL Experience X

COMPLETE SET (10) 30.00 80.00
STATED ODDS 1:70 HOBBY
X1 Kerry Collins 1.50 4.00
X2 Rashaan Salaam .75 2.00
X3 Michael Westbrook 1.50 4.00
X4 Terrell Davis 4.00 10.00
X5 Joey Galloway 1.50 4.00
X6 Deion Sanders 3.00 8.00
X7 Steve Young 5.00 12.00
X8 Dan Marino 12.50 30.00
X9 Drew Bledsoe 3.00 8.00
X10 Emmitt Smith 10.00 25.00

1996 Classic Promos

NNO Kerry Collins .60 1.50
(back advertises five Classic brands)

2010 Classics

101-200 ROOKIE PRINT RUN 999
201-250 LEGEND PRINT RUN 999
1 Chris Wells .25 .60
2 Larry Fitzgerald .30 .75
3 Matt Leinart .25 .60
4 Matt Ryan .30 .75
5 Michael Turner .20 .50
6 Roddy White .25 .60
7 Anquan Boldin .25 .60
8 Joe Flacco .30 .75
9 Ray Rice .25 .60
10 Fred Jackson .30 .75
11 Lee Evans .25 .60
12 Marshawn Lynch .25 .60
13 DeAngelo Williams .25 .60
14 Jonathan Stewart .25 .60
15 Steve Smith .25 .60
16 Devin Hester .30 .75
17 Jay Cutler .30 .75
18 Matt Forte .25 .60
19 Carson Palmer .25 .60
20 Cedric Benson .25 .60
21 Chad Ochocinco .25 .60
22 Jake Delhomme .25 .60
23 Josh Cribbs .30 .75
24 Jerome Harrison .20 .50
25 Felix Jones .25 .60
26 Jason Witten .30 .75
27 Miles Austin .30 .75
28 Tony Romo .40 1.00
29 Eddie Royal .20 .50
30 Knowshon Moreno .25 .60
31 Kyle Orton .25 .60
32 Calvin Johnson .30 .75
33 Matthew Stafford .30 .75
34 Nate Burleson .20 .50
35 Aaron Rodgers .60 1.50
36 Greg Jennings .25 .60
37 Ryan Grant .25 .60
38 Andre Johnson .25 .60
39 Matt Schaub .25 .60
40 Steve Slaton .20 .50
41 Dallas Clark .25 .60
42 Peyton Manning .50 1.25
43 Pierre Garcon .25 .60
44 Reggie Wayne .25 .60
45 David Garrard .25 .60
46 Maurice Jones-Drew .25 .60
47 Mike Sims-Walker .25 .60
48 Dwayne Bowe .25 .60
49 Jamaal Charles .25 .60
50 Matt Cassel .25 .60
51 Chad Henne .25 .60
52 Ronnie Brown .25 .60
53 Davone Bess .20 .50
54 Adrian Peterson .50 1.25
55 Brett Favre .75 2.00
56 Sidney Rice .25 .60
57 Visanthe Shiancoe .25 .60
58 Randy Moss .30 .75
59 Tom Brady .50 1.25
60 Wes Welker .30 .75
61 Devery Henderson .20 .50
62 Drew Brees .30 .75
63 Pierre Thomas .25 .60
64 Brandon Jacobs .25 .60
65 Eli Manning .30 .75
66 Steve Smith USC .25 .60
67 Braylon Edwards .25 .60
68 Mark Sanchez .30 .75
69 Shonn Greene .25 .60
70 Darren McFadden .25 .60
71 Jason Campbell .25 .60

72 Louis Murphy .25 .60
73 Brent Celek .25 .60
74 DeSean Jackson .25 .60
75 Kevin Kolb .25 .60
76 LeSean McCoy .25 .60
77 Ben Roethlisberger .30 .75
78 Rashard Mendenhall .25 .60
79 Hines Ward .25 .60
80 Antonio Gates .25 .60
81 Darren Sproles .25 .60
82 Philip Rivers .30 .75
83 Alex Smith QB .25 .60
84 Frank Gore .25 .60
85 Vernon Davis .25 .60
86 John Carlson .20 .50
87 Matt Hasselbeck .20 .50
88 T.J. Houshmandzadeh .25 .60
89 Danny Amendola .30 .75
90 Donnie Avery .25 .60
91 Steven Jackson .25 .60
92 Cadillac Williams .25 .60
93 Josh Freeman .30 .75
94 Kellen Winslow Jr. .25 .60
95 Chris Johnson .30 .75
96 Kenny Britt .25 .60
97 Vince Young .20 .50
98 Chris Cooley .25 .60
99 Clinton Portis .25 .60
100 Donovan McNabb .30 .75
101 Aaron Hernandez RC 3.00 8.00
102 Andre Anderson RC 1.50 4.00
103 Andre Dixon RC 2.00 5.00
104 Andre Roberts RC 2.00 5.00
105 Anthony Dixon RC 2.00 5.00
106 Anthony McCoy RC 1.50 4.00
107 Antonio Brown RC 3.00 8.00
108 Armanti Edwards RC 2.00 5.00
109 Arrelious Benn RC 2.00 5.00
110 Ben Tate RC 2.50 6.00
111 Blair White RC 2.00 5.00
112 Brandon Graham RC 1.50 4.00
113 Brandon LaFell RC 2.00 5.00
114 Brandon Spikes RC 2.00 5.00
115 Bryan Bulaga RC 2.00 5.00
116 C.J. Spiller RC 3.00 8.00
117 Carlos Dunlap RC 2.00 5.00
118 Carlton Mitchell RC 1.50 4.00
119 Chad Jones RC 2.00 5.00
120 Charles Scott RC 1.50 4.00
121 Chris Cook RC 2.00 5.00
122 Chris McGaha RC 1.25 3.00
123 Colt McCoy RC 4.00 10.00
124 Corey Wootton RC 1.50 4.00
125 Damian Williams RC 2.00 5.00
126 Dan LeFevour RC 2.00 5.00
127 Daryl Washington RC 1.50 4.00
128 David Gettis RC 2.00 5.00
129 Demaryius Thomas RC 2.50 6.00
130 Derrick Morgan RC 1.50 4.00
131 Devin McCourty RC 2.00 5.00
132 Dexter McCluster RC 2.00 5.00
133 Dez Bryant RC 6.00 15.00
134 Dezmon Briscoe RC 1.50 4.00
135 Dominique Franks RC 1.25 3.00
136 Earl Thomas RC 2.00 5.00
137 Ed Dickson RC 2.00 5.00
138 Emmanuel Sanders RC 2.00 5.00
139 Eric Berry RC 2.00 5.00
140 Eric Decker RC 2.50 6.00
141 Everson Griffen RC 2.00 5.00
142 Freddie Barnes RC 1.50 4.00
143 Garrett Graham RC 1.50 4.00
144 Gerald McCoy RC 2.00 5.00
145 Golden Tate RC 2.00 5.00
146 Jacoby Ford RC 2.00 5.00
147 Jahvid Best RC 3.00 8.00
148 James Starks RC 3.00 8.00
149 Jarrett Brown RC 2.00 5.00
150 Jason Pierre-Paul RC 3.00 8.00
151 Jason Worilds RC 2.00 5.00
152 Jeremy Williams RC 1.25 3.00
153 Jermaine Gresham RC 2.50 6.00
154 Jerry Hughes RC 2.00 5.00
155 Jevan Snead RC 2.00 5.00
156 Jimmy Clausen RC 2.00 5.00
157 Jimmy Graham RC 4.00 10.00
158 Joe Haden RC 2.00 5.00
159 Joe McKnight RC 2.00 5.00
160 John Skelton RC 2.00 5.00
161 Jonathan Crompton RC 1.50 4.00
162 Jonathan Dwyer RC 2.00 5.00
163 Jordan Shipley RC 2.00 5.00
164 Kareem Jackson RC 2.00 5.00
165 Kyle Wilson RC 2.00 5.00
166 LeGarrette Blount RC 3.00 8.00
167 Lonyae Miller RC 1.50 4.00
168 Marcus Easley RC 1.50 4.00
169 Mardy Gilyard RC 2.00 5.00
170 Mike Kafka RC 2.00 5.00
171 Mike Williams RC 3.00 8.00
172 Montario Hardesty RC 2.00 5.00
173 Morgan Burnett RC 2.00 5.00
174 Nate Allen RC 2.00 5.00
175 NaVorro Bowman RC 2.00 5.00
176 Ndamukong Suh RC 4.00 10.00
177 Pat Paschall RC 1.50 4.00
178 Patrick Robinson RC 2.00 5.00
179 Perrish Cox RC 1.50 4.00
180 Ricky Sapp RC 1.50 4.00
181 Riley Cooper RC 2.00 5.00
182 Rob Gronkowski RC 5.00 12.00
183 Rolando McClain RC 2.00 5.00
184 Russell Okung RC 2.00 5.00
185 Ryan Mathews RC 4.00 10.00
186 Sam Bradford RC 8.00 20.00
187 Sean Canfield RC 1.50 4.00
188 Sean Lee RC 2.00 5.00
189 Sean Weatherspoon RC 2.00 5.00
190 Sergio Kindle RC 2.00 5.00
191 Seyi Ajirotutu RC 2.00 5.00
192 Shay Hodge RC 1.50 4.00
193 Taylor Mays RC 2.00 5.00
194 Taylor Price RC 2.00 5.00
195 Tim Tebow RC 8.00 20.00
196 Toby Gerhart RC 2.00 5.00
197 Tony Pike RC 2.00 5.00
198 Trent Williams RC 2.00 5.00
199 Tyson Alualu RC 1.50 4.00
200 Zac Robinson RC 1.50 4.00
201 Art Monk 2.00 5.00
202 Barry Sanders 3.00 8.00
203 Bernie Kosar 1.50 4.00
204 Bob Hayes 2.00 5.00
205 Boomer Esiason 1.50 4.00
206 Brent Jones 1.25 3.00
207 Bruce Smith 1.50 4.00
208 Chuck Howley 1.25 3.00
209 Craig James 1.25 3.00
210 Cris Carter 2.00 5.00
211 Curtis Martin 1.50 4.00
212 Dan Marino 4.00 10.00
213 Darren Woodson 1.50 4.00
214 Deion Sanders 2.00 5.00
215 Derrick Thomas 2.00 5.00
216 Doug Flutie 1.50 4.00
217 Ed Too Tall Jones 1.50 4.00
218 Ed McCaffrey 1.25 3.00
219 Eddie George 1.50 4.00
220 Harvey Martin 1.25 3.00
221 Henry Ellard 1.25 3.00
222 Hank Jordan 1.25 3.00
224 Irving Fryar 1.25 3.00
225 Jackie Slater 1.25 3.00
226 Jim Kelly 2.00 5.00
227 Jim Plunkett 1.50 4.00
228 Joe Montana 4.00 10.00
229 John Elway 3.00 8.00
230 John Taylor 1.25 3.00
231 Junior Seau 1.50 4.00
232 Keyshawn Johnson 1.25 3.00
233 L.C. Greenwood 1.50 4.00
234 Mike Singletary 2.00 5.00
235 Gale Sayers 2.50 6.00
236 Mel Blount 1.50 4.00
237 Michael Strahan 1.50 4.00
238 Mike Alstott 1.25 3.00
239 Priest Holmes 1.25 3.00
240 Randall Cunningham 1.50 4.00
241 Rod Smith 1.25 3.00
242 Rod Woodson 2.00 5.00
245 Terrell Davis 2.00 5.00
246 Terry Bradshaw 2.50 6.00
247 Todd Christensen 1.25 3.00
248 Tom Rathman 1.25 3.00
249 Wayne Chrebet 1.25 3.00
250 William Perry 1.25 3.00

2010 Classics Timeless Tributes Gold

*VETS 1-100: 5X TO 12X BASIC CARDS
*ROOKIES 101-200: .8X TO 2X BASIC CARDS
*LEGENDS 201-250: 1X TO 2.5X BASIC CARDS
STATED PRINT RUN 50 SER.#'d SETS

2010 Classics Timeless Tributes Platinum

*VETS 1-100: 8X TO 20X BASIC CARDS
*ROOKIES 101-200: 1X TO 2.5X BASIC CARDS
*LEGENDS 201-250: 1.5X TO 4X BASIC CARDS
STATED PRINT RUN 25 SER.#'d SETS

2010 Classics Timeless Tributes Silver

*VETS 1-100: 4X TO 10X BASIC CARDS
*ROOKIES 101-200: .6X TO 1.5X BASIC CARDS
*LEGENDS 201-250: .8X TO 2X BASIC CARDS
STATED PRINT RUN 100 SER.#'d SETS

2010 Classics Classic Combos

*GOLD/100: .8X TO 2X BASIC INSERTS
*PLATINUM/25: 1.2X TO 3X BASIC INSERTS
1 Jim Kelly 2.00 5.00
Bruce Smith
2 Derrick Thomas 2.50 6.00
Junior Seau
3 Bob Hayes 2.00 5.00
Chuck Howley
4 Henry Ellard 1.25 3.00
Jackie Slater
5 Todd Christensen 1.50 4.00
Jim Plunkett
6 Dan Marino 3.00 8.00
Irving Fryar
8 Harvey Martin 1.50 4.00
Ed Too Tall Jones
9 Rod Woodson 2.00 5.00
Darren Woodson
10 Mike Singletary 2.00 5.00
Michael Strahan

2010 Classics Classic Combos Jerseys

STATED PRINT RUN 75 SER.#'d SETS
*PRIME/25: .8X TO 2X BASIC JSY/75
1 Jim Kelly 8.00 20.00
Bruce Smith
2 Derrick Thomas 25.00 50.00
Junior Seau
3 Bob Hayes 10.00 25.00
Chuck Howley
4 Henry Ellard 8.00 20.00
Jackie Slater
5 Todd Christensen 8.00 20.00
Jim Plunkett
6 Dan Marino 15.00 40.00
Irving Fryar
8 Harvey Martin 8.00 20.00
Ed Too Tall Jones
9 Rod Woodson 8.00 20.00
Darren Woodson
10 Mike Singletary 12.00 30.00
Michael Strahan

2010 Classics Classic Cuts

STATED PRINT RUN 1-100
SERIAL #'d UNDER 20 NOT PRICED
3 Alex Wojciechowicz/43 30.00 60.00
8 Bert Bell/19 40.00 80.00
9 Bill Dudley/100 25.00 50.00
16 Bulldog Turner/100 30.00 60.00
21 Elroy Hirsch/100 30.00 60.00
23 Dante Lavelli/100 30.00 60.00
25 Don Hutson/50 100.00 175.00
28 Frank Gatski/45 30.00 60.00
30 George Connor/50 25.00 50.00
32 George McAfee/90 25.00 50.00
35 Hank Stram/50 25.00 50.00
36 Jay Berwanger/40 25.00 50.00
39 Jim Ringo/20 40.00 80.00
45 Kyle Rote/45 40.00 80.00
50 Lou Groza/25 40.00 80.00
56 Otto Graham/35 40.00 80.00
58 Paul Brown/50 50.00 100.00
63 Red Badgro/35 30.00 60.00
65 Roosevelt Brown/20 30.00 60.00
72 Tony Canadeo/45 40.00 80.00
73 Walter Payton/25 175.00 300.00
75 Weeb Ewbank/80 25.00 50.00

2010 Classics Classic Quads

*GOLD/100: .8X TO 2X BASIC INSERTS
*PLATINUM/25: 1.2X TO 3X BASIC INSERTS
1 Joe Montana 5.00 12.00
Brent Jones
John Taylor
Tom Rathman
3 Terry Bradshaw 2.50 6.00
Mel Blount
L.C. Greenwood
Rod Woodson
4 Boomer Esiason 1.50 4.00
Wayne Chrebet
Keyshawn Johnson
Curtis Martin
5 Bruce Smith 3.00 8.00
Michael Strahan
Mike Singletary
Derrick Thomas

2010 Classics Classic Quads Jerseys

STATED PRINT RUN 25 SER.#'d SETS
*PRIME15: .5X TO 1.2X QUAD JSY/25
1 Joe Montana 30.00 60.00
Brent Jones
John Taylor
Tom Rathman
4 Boomer Esiason 15.00 30.00
Wayne Chrebet
Keyshawn Johnson
Curtis Martin
5 Bruce Smith 60.00 120.00
Michael Strahan
Mike Singletary
Derrick Thomas

2010 Classics Classic Singles

*GOLD/100: .8X TO 2X BASIC INSERTS
*PLATINUM/25: 1.2X TO 3X BASIC INSERTS
1 Bernie Kosar 1.25 3.00
2 Bob Hayes 1.50 4.00
3 Boomer Esiason 1.25 3.00
4 Brent Jones 1.00 2.50
5 Bruce Smith 1.25 3.00
6 Chuck Howley 1.00 2.50
7 Craig James 1.00 2.50
8 Curtis Martin 1.25 3.00
9 Darren Woodson 1.25 3.00
10 Doug Flutie 1.25 3.00
11 Ed McCaffrey 1.00 2.50
12 Harvey Martin 1.00 2.50
13 Henry Ellard 1.00 2.50
14 Hank Jordan 1.00 2.50
15 Jackie Slater 1.00 2.50
16 John Taylor 1.00 2.50
17 L.C. Greenwood 1.25 3.00
18 Gale Sayers 2.00 5.00
19 Mel Blount 1.25 3.00
20 Rod Smith 1.00 2.50
21 Rod Woodson 1.50 4.00
22 Todd Christensen 1.00 2.50
23 Tom Rathman 1.00 2.50
24 Wayne Chrebet 1.00 2.50
25 William Perry 1.00 2.50

2010 Classics Classic Singles Jerseys

STATED PRINT RUN 100-299
*PRIME/50: .6X TO 1.5X JSY/175-299
*PRIME/50: .5X TO 1.2X JSY/100
*PRIME/25: .8X TO 2X JSY/175-299
1 Bernie Kosar/299 5.00 12.00
2 Bob Hayes/199 10.00 25.00
3 Boomer Esiason/299 5.00 12.00
4 Brent Jones/199 4.00 10.00
5 Bruce Smith/200 5.00 12.00
6 Chuck Howley/299 4.00 10.00
7 Craig James/200 4.00 10.00
8 Curtis Martin/200 5.00 12.00
9 Darren Woodson/100 6.00 15.00
10 Doug Flutie/299 5.00 12.00
11 Ed McCaffrey/200 4.00 10.00
12 Harvey Martin/100 5.00 12.00
13 Henry Ellard/299 4.00 10.00
14 Hank Jordan/299 6.00 15.00
15 Jackie Slater/299 4.00 10.00
16 John Taylor/299 4.00 10.00
17 L.C. Greenwood/100 6.00 15.00
18 Gale Sayers/299 6.00 15.00
19 Mel Blount/299 5.00 12.00
20 Rod Smith/299 4.00 10.00
21 Rod Woodson/299 6.00 15.00
22 Todd Christensen/299 4.00 10.00
23 Tom Rathman/299 4.00 10.00
24 Wayne Chrebet/299 4.00 10.00
25 William Perry/175 4.00 10.00

2010 Classics Classic Singles Jerseys Autographs

STATED PRINT RUN 10-25
EXCH EXPIRATION: 1/28/2012
1 Bernie Kosar/25 25.00 50.00
3 Boomer Esiason/15
4 Brent Jones/10
5 Bruce Smith/15
6 Chuck Howley/20 25.00 50.00
8 Curtis Martin/20 30.00 60.00
11 Ed McCaffrey/15 15.00 40.00
16 John Taylor/15 25.00 50.00
17 L.C. Greenwood/15
20 Rod Smith/15
21 Rod Woodson/10
22 Todd Christensen/10
23 Tom Rathman/15 EXCH
24 Wayne Chrebet/15 EXCH 15.00 40.00
25 William Perry/10

2010 Classics Classic Triples

*GOLD/100: .8X TO 2X BASIC INSERTS
*PLATINUM/25: 1.2X TO 3X BASIC INSERTS
1 John Elway 4.00 10.00
Bernie Kosar
Dan Marino
2 Terry Bradshaw 3.00 8.00
Mel Blount
L.C. Greenwood
3 Wayne Chrebet 1.50 4.00
Keyshawn Johnson
Curtis Martin
4 Brent Jones 1.50 4.00
John Taylor
Tom Rathman
5 Henry Ellard 2.00 5.00
Cris Carter
Irving Fryar
6 Mike Singletary 2.50 6.00
Derrick Thomas
Junior Seau
7 Rod Woodson 2.00 5.00
Deion Sanders
Mel Blount
8 Bernie Kosar 2.00 5.00
Randall Cunningham
Jim Kelly
9 Eddie George 1.50 4.00
Curtis Martin
Priest Holmes

2010 Classics Classic Triples Jerseys

STATED PRINT RUN 50 SER.#'d SETS
*PRIME/25: .6X TO 1.5X BASIC JSY/50
1 John Elway 25.00 60.00
Bernie Kosar
Dan Marino
3 Wayne Chrebet 10.00 25.00
Keyshawn Johnson
Curtis Martin
4 Brent Jones 10.00 25.00
John Taylor
Tom Rathman
5 Henry Ellard 12.00 30.00
Cris Carter
Irving Fryar
6 Mike Singletary 30.00 60.00
Derrick Thomas
Junior Seau
7 Rod Woodson 15.00 40.00
Deion Sanders
Mel Blount
8 Bernie Kosar 12.00 30.00
Randall Cunningham
Jim Kelly
9 Eddie George 10.00 25.00
Curtis Martin
Priest Holmes

2010 Classics Cowboys 50th Anniversary

1 Roger Staubach 3.00 8.00
2 Troy Aikman 3.00 8.00
3 Emmitt Smith 4.00 10.00
4 Tony Dorsett 2.50 6.00
5 Don Perkins 2.00 5.00
6 Michael Irvin 2.50 6.00
7 Bob Hayes 2.50 6.00
8 Jason Witten 2.50 6.00
9 Erik Williams 1.50 4.00
10 Rayfield Wright 1.50 4.00
11 Larry Allen 1.50 4.00
12 John Niland 1.50 4.00
13 Mark Stepnoski 1.50 4.00
14 Harvey Martin 1.50 4.00
15 Ed Too Tall Jones 2.00 5.00
16 Bob Lilly 2.50 6.00
17 Randy White 2.00 5.00
18 DeMarcus Ware 2.00 5.00
19 Chuck Howley 2.00 5.00
20 Lee Roy Jordan 2.00 5.00
21 Everson Walls 1.50 4.00
22 Mel Renfro 2.00 5.00
23 Darren Woodson 2.00 5.00
24 Cliff Harris 2.00 5.00
25 Mat McBriar 1.50 4.00
26 Rafael Septien 1.50 4.00
27 Deion Sanders 2.50 6.00
28 Bill Bates 2.00 5.00
29 Tom Landry 2.50 6.00
30 Jerry Jones 2.00 5.00

2010 Classics Cowboys 50th Anniversary Autographs

STATED PRINT RUN 5-100
EXCH EXPIRATION: 1/28/2012
SERIAL #'d UNDER 25 NOT PRICED
1 Roger Staubach/10
2 Troy Aikman/10
3 Emmitt Smith/5
4 Tony Dorsett/10
5 Don Perkins/10
6 Michael Irvin/10
8 Jason Witten/10
9 Erik Williams/100 20.00 40.00
10 Rayfield Wright/100 25.00 60.00
11 Larry Allen/100 EXCH 20.00 40.00
12 John Niland/100 12.00 30.00
13 Mark Stepnoski/100 12.00 30.00
15 Ed Too Tall Jones/10 EXCH
16 Bob Lilly/10
17 Randy White/10
18 DeMarcus Ware/10
19 Chuck Howley/10
20 Lee Roy Jordan/100 12.00 30.00
21 Everson Walls/100 12.00 30.00
22 Mel Renfro/50 25.00 60.00
24 Cliff Harris/50 20.00 40.00
25 Mat McBriar/100 EXCH 12.00 30.00
27 Deion Sanders/10
28 Bill Bates/10
30 Jerry Jones/25 EXCH 90.00 150.00

2010 Classics Cowboys 50th Anniversary Autographs Triples

TRIPLE AU PRINT RUN 15
1 DeMarcus Ware 40.00 80.00
Chuck Howley
Lee Roy Jordan

2010 Classics Cowboys 50th Anniversary Materials

STATED PRINT RUN 50 SER.#'d SETS
*PRIME/15-25: .6X TO 1.5X BASIC JSY/50
1 Roger Staubach 12.00 30.00
2 Troy Aikman 12.00 30.00
3 Emmitt Smith 15.00 40.00
4 Tony Dorsett 10.00 25.00
6 Michael Irvin 10.00 25.00
7 Bob Hayes 10.00 25.00
8 Jason Witten 10.00 25.00
14 Harvey Martin 8.00 20.00
16 Bob Lilly 8.00 20.00
17 Randy White 8.00 20.00
18 DeMarcus Ware 8.00 20.00
19 Chuck Howley 8.00 20.00
23 Darren Woodson 10.00 25.00
24 Cliff Harris 8.00 20.00
27 Deion Sanders 10.00 25.00
28 Bill Bates 8.00 20.00
29 Tom Landry 20.00 40.00

2010 Classics Cowboys 50th Anniversary Materials Combos

COMBO PRINT RUN 50 SER.#'d SETS
*COMBO PRIME/20: .6X TO 1.5X COMBO JSY
1 Roger Staubach 20.00 50.00
Troy Aikman
2 Bob Lilly 12.00 30.00
Randy White
3 Darren Woodson 12.00 30.00
Cliff Harris
4 Emmitt Smith 15.00 40.00
Tony Dorsett
5 Michael Irvin 15.00 40.00
Bob Hayes

2010 Classics Cowboys 50th Anniversary Materials Quads

QUAD PRINT RUN 25 SER.#'d SETS
1 Tom Landry
Roger Staubach
Tony Dorsett
Randy White
2 Emmitt Smith 50.00 100.00
Tony Dorsett
Michael Irvin
Bob Hayes
3 Roger Staubach 50.00 100.00
Troy Aikman
Emmitt Smith
Tony Dorsett
4 Harvey Martin 30.00 60.00
Bob Lilly
Randy White
Chuck Howley
5 Cliff Harris 25.00 50.00
Bill Bates
Darren Woodson
Deion Sanders

2010 Classics Cowboys 50th Anniversary Materials Triples

STATED PRINT RUN 30 SER.#'d SETS
*PRIME/15: .6X TO 1.5X BASIC TRIPLE/30
1 Tom Landry 40.00 80.00
Randy White
Harvey Martin
2 Michael Irvin 25.00 50.00
Bob Hayes
Jason Witten

2010 Classics Dress Code

*GOLD/100: .6X TO 1.5X BASIC INSERTS
*PLATINUM/25: 1X TO 2.5X BASIC INSERTS
1 Matt Schaub 1.25 3.00
2 Eli Manning 1.50 4.00
3 Jonathan Stewart 1.25 3.00
4 Chad Ochocinco 1.25 3.00
5 Andre Johnson 1.25 3.00
6 Roddy White 1.25 3.00
7 Steven Jackson 1.25 3.00
8 Heath Miller 1.25 3.00
9 Calvin Johnson 1.50 4.00
10 Philip Rivers 1.50 4.00
11 Jason Witten 1.50 4.00
12 Matt Ryan 1.50 4.00
13 Wes Welker 1.50 4.00
14 Dallas Clark 1.25 3.00
15 Troy Polamalu 1.50 4.00
16 Santonio Holmes 1.25 3.00
17 Randy Moss 1.50 4.00
18 Antonio Gates 1.25 3.00
19 Steve Smith 1.25 3.00
20 Greg Jennings 1.25 3.00
21 Brandon Jacobs 1.25 3.00
22 Chris Cooley 1.25 3.00
23 Marques Colston 1.25 3.00
24 Donald Driver 1.25 3.00
25 Cadillac Williams 1.25 3.00

2010 Classics Dress Code Jerseys Prime

PRIME PRINT RUN 25-50
*BASIC JSY/175-299: .25X TO .6X PRIME/50
*BASIC JSY/175-299: .2X TO .5X PRIME/25
*BASIC JSY/90: .3X TO .8X PRIME JSY/35
1 Matt Schaub/35 5.00 12.00
2 Eli Manning/50 6.00 15.00
3 Jonathan Stewart/50 5.00 12.00
4 Chad Ochocinco/50 5.00 12.00
5 Andre Johnson/50 5.00 12.00
6 Roddy White/50 5.00 12.00
7 Steven Jackson/50 5.00 12.00
8 Heath Miller/50 5.00 12.00
9 Calvin Johnson/50 6.00 15.00
10 Philip Rivers/50 6.00 15.00
11 Jason Witten/50 6.00 15.00
12 Matt Ryan/25 8.00 20.00
13 Wes Welker/50 6.00 15.00
14 Dallas Clark/50 5.00 12.00
15 Troy Polamalu/50 6.00 15.00
16 Santonio Holmes/50 5.00 12.00
17 Randy Moss/50 6.00 15.00
18 Antonio Gates/50 5.00 12.00
19 Steve Smith/50 5.00 12.00
20 Greg Jennings/50 6.00 15.00
21 Brandon Jacobs/50 5.00 12.00
22 Chris Cooley/50 6.00 15.00
23 Marques Colston/50 5.00 12.00
24 Donald Driver/50 6.00 15.00
25 Cadillac Williams/50 5.00 12.00

2010 Classics Dress Code Jerseys Autographs

JERSEY AUTO PRINT RUN 10-15
EXCH EXPIRATION: 1/28/2012
1 Matt Schaub/10
2 Eli Manning/10
3 Jonathan Stewart/15 20.00 50.00
4 Chad Ochocinco/15 20.00 50.00
5 Andre Johnson/10 EXCH
6 Roddy White/10
8 Heath Miller/15 20.00 50.00
9 Calvin Johnson/10
10 Philip Rivers/15 25.00 60.00
11 Jason Witten/15 25.00 60.00
12 Matt Ryan/10
18 Antonio Gates/15 20.00 50.00
19 Steve Smith/10
21 Brandon Jacobs/15
22 Chris Cooley/15 20.00 50.00
23 Marques Colston/10
25 Cadillac Williams/10

2010 Classics Flashback Fabrics Jerseys

STATED PRINT RUN 10-500
1 LaDainian Tomlinson/50 5.00 12.00
2 Tony Gonzalez/75 4.00 10.00
3 Ricky Williams/500 2.50 6.00
4 Randy Moss/75 8.00 20.00
6 Kyle Orton/500 2.50 6.00
7 Jay Cutler/500 3.00 8.00
8 Cedric Benson/500 2.50 6.00
9 Terrell Owens/35 6.00 15.00
10 Brian Westbrook/190 3.00 8.00
11 Charles Woodson/160 4.00 10.00
12 Torry Holt/150 3.00 8.00
13 T.J. Houshmandzadeh/15 6.00 15.00
14 Kellen Winslow Jr./10 6.00 15.00
15 Jonathan Vilma/500 2.00 5.00
16 Julius Peppers/260 4.00 10.00
17 Chris Chambers/500 2.50 6.00
18 Nate Burleson/70 3.00 8.00
19 Larry Johnson/80 4.00 10.00
20 Brett Favre/500 8.00 20.00
21 Terrell Owens/190 4.00 10.00
22 Randy Moss/30 6.00 15.00
23 Clinton Portis/130 3.00 8.00
24 Santana Moss/500 2.50 6.00
25 Anquan Boldin/500 2.50 6.00

2010 Classics Flashback Fabrics Jerseys Prime

STATED PRINT RUN 60-200
1 LaDainian Tomlinson/200 5.00 12.00
2 Tony Gonzalez/200 4.00 10.00
3 Ricky Williams/200 4.00 10.00
4 Randy Moss/200 8.00 20.00
5 Jeremy Shockey/200 4.00 10.00
6 Kyle Orton/200 4.00 10.00
8 Cedric Benson/150 4.00 10.00
9 Terrell Owens/200 5.00 12.00
10 Brian Westbrook/200 4.00 10.00
11 Charles Woodson/200 5.00 12.00
12 Torry Holt/200 4.00 10.00
13 T.J. Houshmandzadeh/200 4.00 10.00
14 Kellen Winslow Jr./200 4.00 10.00
15 Jonathan Vilma/175 3.00 8.00
16 Julius Peppers/180 5.00 12.00
17 Chris Chambers/200 4.00 10.00
18 Nate Burleson/100 4.00 10.00
19 Larry Johnson/200 4.00 10.00
21 Terrell Owens/200 5.00 12.00
22 Randy Moss/60 6.00 15.00
23 Clinton Portis/200 4.00 10.00
24 Santana Moss/200 4.00 10.00
25 Anquan Boldin/90 5.00 12.00

2010 Classics Hall of Fame

1 Emmitt Smith 8.00 20.00
2 Jerry Rice 8.00 20.00
3 Russ Grimm 2.00 5.00
4 Rickey Jackson 2.00 5.00
5 Floyd Little 2.00 5.00
6 John Randle 2.00 5.00
7 Dick LeBeau 2.00 5.00

2010 Classics Hall of Fame Autographs

STATED PRINT RUN 50 SER.#'d SETS
EXCH EXPIRATION: 1/28/2012
1 Emmitt Smith 125.00 200.00
2 Jerry Rice 100.00 200.00
3 Russ Grimm 25.00 50.00
4 Rickey Jackson 40.00 80.00
5 Floyd Little 25.00 50.00
6 John Randle 25.00 50.00
7 Dick LeBeau 100.00 175.00

2010 Classics Hall of Fame Materials

STATED PRINT RUN 100 SER.#'d SETS
*PRIME/25: .8X TO 2X BASIC JSY/100
1 Emmitt Smith 12.00 30.00
2 Jerry Rice 10.00 25.00

2010 Classics Membership

*GOLD/100: .6X TO 1.5X BASIC INSERTS
*PLATINUM/25: 1X TO 2.5X BASIC INSERTS
1 Rashard Mendenhall 1.25 3.00
2 Knowshon Moreno 1.25 3.00
3 Mark Sanchez 1.50 4.00
4 Jamaal Charles 1.25 3.00
5 Austin Collie 1.25 3.00
6 Kenny Britt 1.25 3.00
7 LeSean McCoy 1.25 3.00
8 Matt Forte 1.25 3.00
9 Brent Celek 1.25 3.00
10 Darren Sproles 1.25 3.00
11 Felix Jones 1.25 3.00
12 Matthew Stafford 1.50 4.00
13 Visanthe Shiancoe 1.25 3.00
14 Ray Rice 1.25 3.00
15 Miles Austin 1.50 4.00
16 Shonn Greene 1.25 3.00
17 Jeremy Maclin 1.25 3.00
18 Chris Wells 1.25 3.00
19 Pierre Garcon 1.25 3.00
20 Percy Harvin 1.50 4.00
21 Mike Wallace 1.25 3.00
22 Mike Sims-Walker 1.25 3.00
23 Pierre Thomas 1.25 3.00
24 Michael Crabtree 1.50 4.00
25 Kevin Boss 1.25 3.00

2010 Classics Membership VIP Jerseys

STATED PRINT RUN 40-299
*PRIME/50: .6X TO 1.5X BASIC JSY/225-299
*PRIME/50: .4X TO 1X BASIC JSY/40
1 Rashard Mendenhall/299 3.00 8.00
2 Knowshon Moreno/299 3.00 8.00
3 Mark Sanchez/299 4.00 10.00
4 Jamaal Charles/40 5.00 12.00
6 Kenny Britt/299 3.00 8.00
7 LeSean McCoy/299 3.00 8.00
8 Matt Forte/225 3.00 8.00
10 Darren Sproles/299 3.00 8.00
11 Felix Jones/299 3.00 8.00
12 Matthew Stafford/299 4.00 10.00
13 Visanthe Shiancoe/299 3.00 8.00
16 Shonn Greene/299 3.00 8.00
17 Jeremy Maclin/299 3.00 8.00
18 Chris Wells/299 3.00 8.00
20 Percy Harvin/299 4.00 10.00
24 Michael Crabtree/299 4.00 10.00

2010 Classics Monday Night Heroes

*GOLD/100: .6X TO 1.5X BASIC INSERTS
*PLATINUM/25: 1X TO 2.5X BASIC INSERTS
1 Tom Brady 2.50 6.00
2 Dallas Clark 1.25 3.00
3 Ronnie Brown 1.25 3.00
4 Felix Jones 1.25 3.00
5 Aaron Rodgers 3.00 8.00
6 Brett Favre 4.00 10.00
7 Ricky Williams 1.25 3.00
8 Kyle Orton 1.25 3.00
9 DeSean Jackson 1.25 3.00
10 Drew Brees 1.50 4.00
11 Michael Turner 1.00 2.50
12 Ben Roethlisberger 1.50 4.00
13 Rashard Mendenhall 1.25 3.00
14 Ray Rice 1.25 3.00
15 Chris Johnson 1.50 4.00
16 Vince Young 1.00 2.50
17 Drew Brees 1.50 4.00
18 Marques Colston 1.25 3.00
19 Aaron Rodgers 3.00 8.00
20 Jermichael Finley 1.25 3.00
21 Frank Gore 1.25 3.00
22 Eli Manning 1.50 4.00
23 Ahmad Bradshaw 1.25 3.00
24 Jay Cutler 1.50 4.00
25 Adrian Peterson 2.50 6.00

2010 Classics Monday Night Heroes Jerseys

STATED PRINT RUN 100-299
1 Tom Brady/150 6.00 15.00
2 Dallas Clark/299 3.00 8.00
3 Ronnie Brown/150 3.00 8.00
4 Felix Jones/299 3.00 8.00
6 Brett Favre/100 12.00 30.00
7 Ricky Williams/299 3.00 8.00
8 Kyle Orton/299 3.00 8.00
10 Drew Brees/100 5.00 12.00
11 Michael Turner/299 2.50 6.00
12 Ben Roethlisberger/299 4.00 10.00
13 Rashard Mendenhall/100 4.00 10.00
15 Chris Johnson/299 4.00 10.00
16 Vince Young/299 2.50 6.00
17 Drew Brees/250 4.00 10.00
18 Marques Colston/299 3.00 8.00
21 Frank Gore/250 3.00 8.00
22 Eli Manning/299 4.00 10.00
23 Ahmad Bradshaw/299 3.00 8.00
24 Jay Cutler/299 4.00 10.00
25 Adrian Peterson/299 6.00 15.00

2010 Classics Monday Night Heroes Jerseys Prime

STATED PRINT RUN 5-50
SERIAL #'d UNDER 25 NOT PRICED
1 Tom Brady/50 10.00 25.00
2 Dallas Clark/50 5.00 12.00
3 Ronnie Brown/50 5.00 12.00
4 Felix Jones/50 5.00 12.00
5 Aaron Rodgers/25 20.00 50.00
6 Brett Favre/10
7 Ricky Williams/50 5.00 12.00
8 Kyle Orton/50 5.00 12.00
10 Drew Brees/9
11 Michael Turner/50 4.00 10.00
12 Ben Roethlisberger/25 8.00 20.00
13 Rashard Mendenhall/50 5.00 12.00
15 Chris Johnson/50 6.00 15.00
16 Vince Young/50 4.00 10.00
17 Drew Brees/5
18 Marques Colston/50 5.00 12.00
19 Aaron Rodgers/25 10.00 25.00
21 Frank Gore/50 5.00 12.00
22 Eli Manning/50 6.00 15.00
23 Ahmad Bradshaw/50 5.00 12.00
24 Jay Cutler/10
25 Adrian Peterson/50 10.00 25.00

2010 Classics Monday Night Heroes Jerseys Autographs

STATED PRINT RUN 4-15
EXCH EXPIRATION: 1/28/2012
11 Michael Turner/15 12.00 30.00
13 Rashard Mendenhall/15 15.00 40.00
24 Jay Cutler/15 20.00 50.00

2010 Classics Significant Signatures Gold

1-100 VETERAN PRINT RUN 5-50
101-200 ROOKIE PRINT RUN 99-499
201-250 LEGEND PRINT RUN 5-50
EXCH EXPIRATION: 1/28/2012
11 Lee Evans/20
29 Eddie Royal/25 8.00 20.00
30 Knowshon Moreno/20
42 Peyton Manning/18 75.00 150.00
43 Pierre Garcon/25 12.00 30.00
48 Dwayne Bowe/15
57 Visanthe Shiancoe/20 EXCH
63 Pierre Thomas/20 12.00 30.00
67 Braylon Edwards/20
68 Mark Sanchez/15 30.00 60.00
69 Shonn Greene/20 12.00 30.00
72 Louis Murphy/50 8.00 20.00
73 Brent Celek/20 10.00 25.00
96 Kenny Britt/25 10.00 25.00
101 Aaron Hernandez/499 8.00 20.00
102 Andre Anderson/499 4.00 10.00
103 Andre Dixon/499 5.00 12.00
104 Andre Roberts/399 5.00 12.00
105 Anthony Dixon/99 8.00 20.00
106 Anthony McCoy/499 4.00 10.00
107 Antonio Brown/499 6.00 15.00
108 Armanti Edwards/499 6.00 15.00
109 Arrelious Benn/499 5.00 12.00
110 Ben Tate/299 8.00 20.00
111 Blair White/99 8.00 20.00
112 Brandon Graham/499 4.00 10.00
113 Brandon LaFell/399 6.00 15.00
114 Brandon Spikes/99 8.00 20.00
115 Bryan Bulaga/499 5.00 12.00
116 C.J. Spiller/249 20.00 50.00
117 Carlos Dunlap/499 5.00 12.00
118 Carlton Mitchell/499 4.00 10.00
119 Chad Jones/499 5.00 12.00
120 Charles Scott/499 4.00 10.00
121 Chris Cook/499 5.00 12.00
122 Chris McGaha/499 3.00 8.00
123 Colt McCoy/249 12.00 30.00
124 Corey Wootton/499 4.00 10.00
125 Damian Williams/399 5.00 12.00
126 Dan LeFevour/499 6.00 15.00
127 Daryl Washington/99 EXCH 6.00 15.00
128 David Gettis/499 5.00 12.00
129 Demaryius Thomas/399 6.00 15.00
130 Derrick Morgan/299 5.00 12.00
131 Devin McCourty/499 5.00 12.00
132 Dexter McCluster/399 8.00 20.00
133 Dez Bryant/299 40.00 80.00
134 Dezmon Briscoe/99 6.00 15.00
135 Dominique Franks/399 3.00 8.00
136 Earl Thomas/399 5.00 12.00
137 Ed Dickson/499 5.00 12.00
138 Emmanuel Sanders/499 5.00 12.00
139 Eric Berry/99 20.00 50.00
140 Eric Decker/399 8.00 20.00
141 Everson Griffen/499 5.00 12.00
142 Freddie Barnes/99 6.00 15.00
143 Garrett Graham/399 4.00 10.00
144 Gerald McCoy/399 5.00 12.00
145 Golden Tate/299 6.00 15.00
146 Jacoby Ford/499 10.00 20.00
147 Jahvid Best/399 25.00 50.00
148 James Starks/499 10.00 25.00
149 Jarrett Brown/249 6.00 15.00
150 Jason Pierre-Paul/499 8.00 20.00
151 Jason Worilds/499 5.00 12.00
152 Jeremy Williams/99 5.00 12.00
153 Jermaine Gresham/199 8.00 20.00
154 Jerry Hughes/499 5.00 12.00
155 Jevan Snead/499 5.00 12.00
156 Jimmy Clausen/249 6.00 15.00
157 Jimmy Graham/99 15.00 40.00
158 Joe Haden/399 5.00 12.00
159 Joe McKnight/99 8.00 20.00
160 John Skelton/99 8.00 20.00
161 Jonathan Crompton/499 4.00 10.00
162 Jonathan Dwyer/399 5.00 12.00
163 Jordan Shipley/199 6.00 15.00
164 Kareem Jackson/499 6.00 15.00
165 Kyle Wilson/99 8.00 20.00
166 LeGarrette Blount/499 8.00 20.00
167 Lonyae Miller/499 4.00 10.00
168 Marcus Easley/499 4.00 10.00
169 Mardy Gilyard/499 5.00 12.00
170 Mike Kafka/499 5.00 12.00
171 Mike Williams/99 20.00 40.00
172 Montario Hardesty/399 6.00 15.00
173 Morgan Burnett/499 5.00 12.00
174 Nate Allen/499 5.00 12.00
175 NaVorro Bowman/99 8.00 20.00
176 Ndamukong Suh/299 12.00 30.00
177 Pat Paschall/99 6.00 15.00
178 Patrick Robinson/499 5.00 12.00
179 Perrish Cox/499 4.00 10.00
180 Ricky Sapp/99 6.00 15.00
181 Riley Cooper/499 5.00 12.00
182 Rob Gronkowski/499 15.00 40.00
183 Rolando McClain/299 6.00 15.00
184 Russell Okung/99 8.00 20.00
185 Ryan Mathews/299 15.00 40.00
186 Sam Bradford/249 50.00 100.00
187 Sean Canfield/99 6.00 15.00
188 Sean Lee/499 5.00 12.00
189 Sean Weatherspoon/499 5.00 12.00
190 Sergio Kindle/499 5.00 12.00
191 Seyi Ajirotutu/499 5.00 12.00
192 Shay Hodge/499 4.00 10.00
193 Taylor Mays/499 5.00 12.00
194 Taylor Price/399 5.00 12.00
195 Tim Tebow/249 60.00 120.00
196 Toby Gerhart/299 6.00 15.00
197 Tony Pike/499 6.00 15.00

198 Trent Williams/99 EXCH	12.00	30.00
200 Zac Robinson/399	4.00	10.00
201 Art Monk/25	40.00	80.00
202 Barry Sanders/25	60.00	120.00
203 Bernie Kosar/50	25.00	50.00
205 Boomer Esiason/15		
206 Brent Jones/15	10.00	25.00
211 Curtis Martin/50	25.00	50.00
212 Dan Marino/20		
217 Ed Too Tall Jones/25 EXCH	20.00	40.00
219 Eddie George/15		
224 Irving Fryar/25	10.00	25.00
226 Jim Kelly/20	40.00	80.00
228 Joe Montana/15	90.00	150.00
229 John Elway/15	75.00	150.00
234 Mike Singletary/20	20.00	40.00
238 Mike Alstott/20	20.00	40.00
239 Priest Holmes/20	15.00	30.00
240 Randall Cunningham/20	25.00	50.00
245 Terrell Davis/20	20.00	40.00

2010 Classics Significant Signatures Platinum

*VETERAN/25: .5X TO 1.2X GOLD/50
1-100 VET PRINT RUN 1-25
*ROOKIES/24-25: 1X TO 2.5X GOLD/399-499
*ROOKIES/24-25: .8X TO 2X GOLD/199-299
*ROOKIES/24-25: .6X TO 1.5X GOLD/99
101-200 ROOKIE PRINT RUN 1-25
*LEGEND/25: .5X TO 1.2X GOLD/50
201-250 LEGEND PRINT RUN 1-25
SERIAL #'d UNDER 20 NOT PRICED

123 Colt McCoy/25	40.00	100.00
133 Dez Bryant/25	75.00	150.00
156 Jimmy Clausen/25	12.00	30.00
185 Ryan Mathews/25	30.00	80.00
186 Sam Bradford/25	100.00	200.00
195 Tim Tebow/25	125.00	250.00

2010 Classics Sunday's Best

*GOLD/100: .6X TO 1.5X BASIC INSERTS
*PLATINUM/25: 1X TO 2.5X BASIC INSERTS

1 Vernon Davis	1.25	3.00
2 Aaron Rodgers	3.00	8.00
3 Larry Fitzgerald	1.50	4.00
4 Chris Johnson	1.50	4.00
5 DeSean Jackson	1.25	3.00
6 Tony Romo	2.00	5.00
7 Ryan Grant	1.25	3.00
8 Josh Cribbs	1.50	4.00
9 Vince Young	1.00	2.50
10 Sidney Rice	1.25	3.00
11 Vincent Jackson	1.00	2.50
12 DeAngelo Williams	1.25	3.00
13 Carson Palmer	1.25	3.00
14 Maurice Jones-Drew	1.25	3.00
15 Brett Favre	4.00	10.00
16 Drew Brees	1.50	4.00
17 Frank Gore	1.25	3.00
18 Ronnie Brown	1.25	3.00
19 Adrian Peterson	2.50	6.00
20 Peyton Manning	2.50	6.00
21 Reggie Wayne	1.25	3.00
22 Tom Brady	2.50	6.00
23 Devery Henderson	1.00	2.50
24 Ben Roethlisberger	1.50	4.00
25 Marion Barber	1.25	3.00

2010 Classics Sunday's Best Jerseys

STATED PRINT RUN 100-299

1 Vernon Davis/185	3.00	8.00
3 Larry Fitzgerald/299	4.00	10.00
4 Chris Johnson/299	4.00	10.00
6 Tony Romo/299	5.00	12.00
7 Ryan Grant/145	3.00	8.00
8 Josh Cribbs/299	4.00	10.00
9 Vince Young/299	2.50	6.00
10 Sidney Rice/299	3.00	8.00
11 Vincent Jackson/299	2.50	6.00
12 DeAngelo Williams/299	3.00	8.00
13 Carson Palmer/299	3.00	8.00
14 Maurice Jones-Drew/299	3.00	8.00
15 Brett Favre/100	12.00	30.00
16 Drew Brees/100	5.00	12.00
17 Frank Gore/250	3.00	8.00
18 Ronnie Brown/150	3.00	8.00
19 Adrian Peterson/280	6.00	15.00
20 Peyton Manning/299	6.00	15.00
21 Reggie Wayne/299	3.00	8.00
22 Tom Brady/150	6.00	15.00
23 Devery Henderson/299	2.50	6.00
24 Ben Roethlisberger/299	4.00	10.00
25 Marion Barber/299	3.00	8.00

2010 Classics Sunday's Best Jerseys Prime

*PRIME/45-50: .6X TO 1.5X JSY/145-299
*PRIME/25: .8X TO 2X JSY/145-299
PRIME JSY PRINT RUN 9-50

2 Aaron Rodgers/25	15.00	40.00

2010 Classics Sunday's Best Jerseys Autographs

STATED PRINT RUN 5-25
EXCH EXPIRATION: 1/28/2012

1 Vernon Davis/10		
4 Chris Johnson/5		
6 Tony Romo/10		
7 Ryan Grant/25	20.00	50.00
8 Josh Cribbs/15	40.00	80.00
9 Vince Young/10		
10 Sidney Rice/10		
11 Vincent Jackson/15	15.00	40.00
12 DeAngelo Williams/15	20.00	50.00
13 Carson Palmer/10		
14 Maurice Jones-Drew/10		
15 Brett Favre/10		
16 Drew Brees/5		
17 Frank Gore/10		
18 Ronnie Brown/10		
19 Adrian Peterson/10		
20 Peyton Manning/20	60.00	120.00
21 Reggie Wayne/10		
22 Tom Brady/5		
23 Devery Henderson/25	15.00	40.00
24 Ben Roethlisberger/10		

2010 Classics Super Bowl Pigskins

STATED PRINT RUN 4-100

1 Fred Biletnikoff/25	10.00	25.00
2 Bart Starr/24	40.00	80.00
4 Jim Taylor/10		
5 Harvey Martin/25	20.00	40.00
6 Jerry Rice/100	15.00	40.00
7 Thurman Thomas/75	12.00	30.00
8 Troy Aikman/4		

2010 Classics Super Bowl Pigskins Combos

STATED PRINT RUN 5-25

1 Bart Starr/10 Jim Taylor		
2 Roger Staubach/10 Tony Dorsett		
3 Joe Montana/25 Jerry Rice	30.00	80.00
4 Troy Aikman/5 Emmitt Smith		

2010 Classics Team Colors

1 Rob Gronkowski	3.00	8.00
2 Rolando McClain	1.25	3.00
3 Ryan Mathews	2.50	6.00
4 Sam Bradford	5.00	12.00
5 Taylor Price	1.25	3.00
6 Tim Tebow	5.00	12.00
7 Toby Gerhart	1.25	3.00
8 Andre Roberts	1.25	3.00
9 Armanti Edwards	1.25	3.00
10 Arrelious Benn	1.25	3.00
11 Ben Tate	1.50	4.00
12 Brandon LaFell	1.25	3.00
13 C.J. Spiller	2.00	5.00
14 Colt McCoy	2.50	6.00
15 Damian Williams	1.25	3.00
16 Demaryius Thomas	1.50	4.00
17 Dexter McCluster	1.25	3.00
18 Dez Bryant	4.00	10.00
19 Emmanuel Sanders	1.25	3.00
20 Eric Berry	1.25	3.00
21 Eric Decker	1.50	4.00
22 Gerald McCoy	1.25	3.00
23 Golden Tate	1.25	3.00
24 Jahvid Best	2.00	5.00
25 Jermaine Gresham	1.50	4.00
26 Jimmy Clausen	1.25	3.00
27 Joe McKnight	1.25	3.00
28 Jonathan Dwyer	1.25	3.00
29 Jordan Shipley	1.25	3.00
30 Marcus Easley	1.00	2.50
31 Mardy Gilyard	1.25	3.00
32 Mike Kafka	1.25	3.00
33 Mike Williams	2.00	5.00
34 Montario Hardesty	1.25	3.00
35 Ndamukong Suh	2.50	6.00

2010 Classics Team Colors Autographs

STATED PRINT RUN 25 SER.#'d SETS

1 Rob Gronkowski	40.00	80.00
2 Rolando McClain	12.00	30.00
3 Ryan Mathews	75.00	150.00
4 Sam Bradford	100.00	200.00
5 Taylor Price	12.00	30.00
6 Tim Tebow	100.00	200.00
7 Toby Gerhart	12.00	30.00
8 Andre Roberts	12.00	30.00
9 Armanti Edwards	12.00	30.00
10 Arrelious Benn	12.00	30.00
11 Ben Tate	15.00	40.00
12 Brandon LaFell	12.00	30.00
13 C.J. Spiller	20.00	50.00
14 Colt McCoy	50.00	100.00
15 Damian Williams	12.00	30.00
16 Demaryius Thomas	15.00	40.00
17 Dexter McCluster	12.00	30.00
18 Dez Bryant	60.00	120.00
19 Emmanuel Sanders	12.00	30.00
20 Eric Berry	12.00	30.00
21 Eric Decker	15.00	40.00
22 Gerald McCoy	12.00	30.00
23 Golden Tate	12.00	30.00
24 Jahvid Best	50.00	100.00
25 Jermaine Gresham		
26 Jimmy Clausen	15.00	40.00
27 Joe McKnight	12.00	30.00
28 Jonathan Dwyer	12.00	30.00
29 Jordan Shipley	12.00	30.00
30 Marcus Easley		
31 Mardy Gilyard	12.00	30.00
32 Mike Kafka	12.00	30.00
33 Mike Williams	25.00	50.00
34 Montario Hardesty		
35 Ndamukong Suh	25.00	60.00

2010 Classics Team Colors Materials

STATED PRINT RUN 299 SER.#'d SETS
*PRIME/50: .8X TO 2X JSY/299

1 Rob Gronkowski	8.00	20.00
2 Rolando McClain	3.00	8.00
3 Ryan Mathews	6.00	15.00
4 Sam Bradford	10.00	25.00
5 Taylor Price	3.00	8.00
6 Tim Tebow	15.00	40.00
7 Toby Gerhart	3.00	8.00
8 Andre Roberts	3.00	8.00
9 Armanti Edwards	3.00	8.00
10 Arrelious Benn	3.00	8.00
11 Ben Tate	4.00	10.00
12 Brandon LaFell	3.00	8.00
13 C.J. Spiller	5.00	12.00
14 Colt McCoy	6.00	15.00
15 Damian Williams	3.00	8.00
16 Demaryius Thomas	4.00	10.00
17 Dexter McCluster	3.00	8.00
18 Dez Bryant	10.00	25.00
19 Emmanuel Sanders	3.00	8.00
20 Eric Berry	3.00	8.00
21 Eric Decker	4.00	10.00
22 Gerald McCoy	3.00	8.00
23 Golden Tate	3.00	8.00
24 Jahvid Best	5.00	12.00
25 Jermaine Gresham	4.00	10.00
26 Jimmy Clausen	3.00	8.00
27 Joe McKnight	3.00	8.00
28 Jonathan Dwyer	3.00	8.00
29 Jordan Shipley	3.00	8.00
30 Marcus Easley	2.50	6.00
31 Mardy Gilyard	3.00	8.00
32 Mike Kafka	3.00	8.00
33 Mike Williams	5.00	12.00
34 Montario Hardesty	3.00	8.00
35 Ndamukong Suh	6.00	15.00

1995 Cleo Quarterback Club Valentines

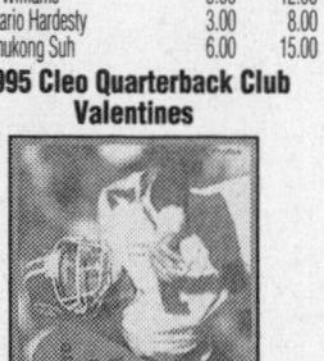

COMPLETE SET (11)	1.20	3.00
1A Troy Aikman Valentine	.15	.40
1B Troy Aikman box bottom card	.20	.50
2 John Elway	.25	.60
3A Brett Favre	.25	.60
3B Brett Favre	.30	.75
4 Jim Kelly	.05	.15
5 Dan Marino	.25	.60
6A Warren Moon Valentine	.05	.15
6B Warren Moon box bottom card	.08	.25
7 Phil Simms	.05	.15
8 Steve Young	.10	.30

1996 Cleo Quarterback Club Valentines

These white-bordered valentine cards came in 40-card boxes with featuring a color action photo of one of eight NFL quarterbacks. The valentines are printed on thin white card stock and each measures approximately 2 1/2" by 5" except Marcus Allen measures 3 3/4" by 5". The back of the box features two bonus cards that are identical to two of the cards inside. We've included those in the complete set price. The cards are unnumbered and checklisted below in alphabetical order.

COMPLETE SET (10)	1.00	2.50
1 Troy Aikman	.15	.40
2 Marcus Allen	.05	.15
3 Drew Bledsoe	.15	.40
4 John Elway	.25	.60
5 Jim Kelly	.08	.25
6A Junior Seau Valentine	.05	.15
6B Junior Seau box bottom card	.08	.25
7A Emmitt Smith Valentine	.25	.60
7B Emmitt Smith box bottom card	.30	.75
8 Steve Young	.10	.30

1997 Cleo Quarterback Club Valentines

COMPLETE SET (8)	1.25	3.00
*WINDOW CLINGS: .4X TO 1X		
1 Troy Aikman Emmitt Smith	.25	.60
2 Drew Bledsoe	.10	.25
3 Mark Brunell	.10	.25
4 Kerry Collins	.10	.25
5 John Elway	.20	.50
6 Brett Favre	.30	.75
7 Dan Marino	.25	.60
8 Jerry Rice	.20	.50

1998 Cleo Quarterback Club Valentines

COMPLETE SET (8)	1.25	3.00
1 Drew Bledsoe	.14	.40
2 Kerry Collins	.08	.25
3 John Elway	.25	.60
4 Brett Favre	.30	.75
5 Dan Marino	.30	.75
6 Steve McNair	.08	.25
7 Kordell Stewart	.08	.25
8 Steve Young	.20	.50

1962 Cleveland Bulldogs UFL Picture Pack

Big League Books produced and distributed this set of 5" by 7" photos for the Cleveland Bulldogs of the United Football League. This semi-pro league was centered in the Midwest and consisted of 7-teams. It's likely that each of the teams had a similar set produced, and any additional information on those would be appreciated.

COMPLETE SET (10)	75.00	150.00
1 Dave Adams Gordon Helms	7.50	15.00
2 Bob Alford Leo Bland	7.50	15.00
3 Bob Brodhead	10.00	20.00
4 John Drew Bill Eyesdom Ed Nemetz	7.50	15.00
5 Clay Hill Gary Hostetler	7.50	15.00
6 Clark Kellogg Bill Slacas	7.50	15.00
7 Dick Louis Frank Mancini	7.50	15.00
8 Dick Newsome Paul Pirrone	7.50	15.00
9 Coaching Staff Ben Barber Ted Livingston Chet Mutryn Lowell Lander Joe Governale	7.50	15.00
10 Officers Dominic LoGalbo Norman McLeod Norman Bash David Kasunic Louis DiVito J.Robert Mylott Paul Schambs	7.50	15.00

1992 Cleveland Thunderbolts Arena

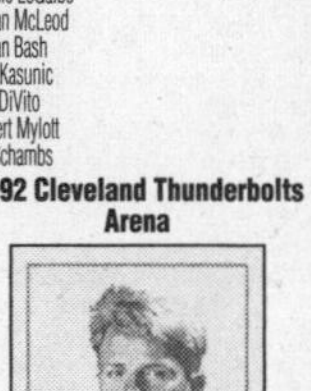

Printed on plain white card stock, these 24 cards are irregularly cut and so vary in size, but are close to standard size. Framed by a purple line, the fronts feature coarsely screened posed black-and-white player photos of the Arena Football League's (AFL) Cleveland Thunderbolts. The player's name and position, along with the logo of the sponsor, Area Temps, appear below the photo. The backs carry the player's name at the top, followed by the team logo, position, jersey number, biography, and career highlights. The cards are unnumbered and checklisted below in alphabetical order.

COMPLETE SET (24)	12.00	30.00
1 Eric Anderson	.50	1.25
2 Robert Banks WR DB	.50	1.25
3 Bobby Bounds	.50	1.25
4 Marvin Bowman	.50	1.25
5 George Cooper	.50	1.25
6 Michael Denbrock ACO	.50	1.25
7 Chris Drennan	.50	1.25
8 Dennis Fitzgerald ACO	.50	1.25
9 John Fletcher	.50	1.25
10 Andre Giles	.50	1.25
11 Chris Harkness	.50	1.25
12 Major Harris	2.00	5.00
13 Luther Johnson	.50	1.25
14 Marvin Mattox	.50	1.25
15 Cedric McKinnon	.50	1.25
16 Cleo Miller ACO	.80	2.00
17 Tony Missick	.50	1.25
18 Anthony Newsom	.50	1.25
19 Phil Poirier	.50	1.25
20 Alvin Powell	.50	1.25
21 Ray Puryear	.50	1.25
22 Dave Whinham CO	.50	1.25
23 Brian Williams DL	.50	1.25
24 Kennedy Wilson	.50	1.25

1963 Coke Caps Chargers

Little is actually known about these recently discovered Coke Caps but they are thought to be a scarce test issue to the more common Coke Cap series released nationally from 1964-1966. Each is similar in format to the 1964 release but coaches were included in this test issue and the player caps include the player's jersey number and position initials below the image. The set includes the earliest known Al Davis football collectible.

1 Lance Alworth	25.00	50.00
2 Frank Buncom	10.00	20.00
3 Reg Carolan	10.00	20.00
4 Al Davis CO	60.00	100.00
5 Wayne Frazier	10.00	20.00
6 Sid Gillman CO	15.00	30.00
7 George Gross	10.00	20.00
8 Sam Gruneisen	10.00	20.00
9 Rufus Guthrie	10.00	20.00
10 John Hadl	15.00	30.00
11 Bob Jackson	10.00	20.00
12 Emil Karas	10.00	20.00
13 Keith Kinderman	10.00	20.00
14 Ernie Ladd	12.50	25.00
15 Keith Lincoln	12.50	25.00
16 Gerry McDougall	10.00	20.00
17 Charlie McNeil	10.00	20.00
18 Ron Mix	15.00	30.00
19 Chuck Noll CO	25.00	50.00
20 Tobin Rote	12.50	25.00
21 Pat Shea	10.00	20.00

1964 Coke Caps All-Stars AFL

These AFL All-Star caps were issued in AFL cities (and a few other cities as well) along with the local team caps as part of the Go with the Pros promotion. The AFL team Cap Saver sheets had separate sections in which to affix the local team's player caps, the AFL team logos, and the All-Stars' caps. The caps measure approximately 1 1/8" in diameter and have the drink logo and a football on the outside, while the inside has the player's face printed in black, with text surrounding the face. The consumer could turn in his completed saver sheet to receive various prizes. The caps are unnumbered, but have been alphabetically listed below. These caps were also produced for 1964 on Sprite and King Size Coke bottles. Sprite caps typically carry a slight premium over the value of the Coke version.

COMPLETE SET (44)	100.00	200.00
1 Tommy Addison	1.75	3.50
2 Dalva Allen	1.75	3.50
3 Lance Alworth	7.50	15.00
4 Houston Antwine	1.75	3.50
5 Fred Arbanas	1.75	3.50
6 Tony Banfield	1.75	3.50
7 Stew Barber	1.75	3.50
8 George Blair	1.75	3.50
9 Mel Branch	1.75	3.50
10 Nick Buoniconti	3.75	7.50
11 Doug Cline	1.75	3.50
12 Eldon Danenhauer	1.75	3.50
13 Clem Daniels	2.00	4.00
14 Larry Eisenhauer	1.75	3.50
15 Earl Faison	1.75	3.50
16 Cookie Gilchrist	2.00	5.00
17 Freddy Glick	1.75	3.50
18 Larry Grantham	2.00	4.00
19 Ron Hall	1.75	3.50
20 Charlie Hennigan	2.00	4.00
21 E.J. Holub	2.00	4.00
22 Ed Husmann	1.75	3.50
23 Jack Kemp	12.50	25.00
24 Dave Kocourek	1.75	3.50
25 Keith Lincoln	2.00	4.00
26 Charles Long	1.75	3.50
27 Paul Lowe	2.00	4.00
28 Archie Matsos	1.75	3.50
29 Jerry Mays	2.00	4.00
30 Ron Mix	3.00	6.00
31 Tom Morrow	1.75	3.50
32 Billy Neighbors	2.00	4.00
33 Jim Otto	3.75	7.50
34 Art Powell	2.00	4.00
35 Johnny Robinson	2.00	4.00
36 Tobin Rote	2.00	4.00
37 Bob Schmidt	1.75	3.50
38 Tom Sestak	1.75	3.50
39 Billy Shaw	2.00	4.00
40 Bob Talamini	1.75	3.50
41 Lionel Taylor	2.00	4.00
42 Jim Tyrer	2.00	4.00
43 Dick Westmoreland	1.75	3.50
44 Fred Williamson	2.00	5.00

1964 Coke Caps All-Stars NFL

These NFL All-Star caps were issued in NFL cities (and a few other cities as well) along with the local team caps as part of the Go with the Pros promotion. The NFL team Cap Saver sheets had separate sections in which to affix the local team's player caps, the NFL team logos, and the All-Stars' caps. The caps measure approximately 1 1/8" in diameter and have the drink logo and a football on the outside, while the inside has the player's face printed in black, with text surrounding the face. The consumer could turn in his completed saver sheet to receive various prizes. The caps are unnumbered, but have been alphabetically listed below. These caps were also produced for 1964 on Sprite and King Size Coke bottles. Sprite caps typically carry a slight premium over the value of the Coke version.

COMPLETE SET (44)	100.00	200.00
1 Doug Atkins	3.00	6.00
2 Terry Barr	1.25	2.50
3 Jim Brown	12.50	25.00
4 Roger Brown	2.00	4.00
5 Roosevelt Brown	2.50	5.00
6 Timmy Brown	2.00	4.00
7 Bobby Joe Conrad	2.00	4.00
8 Willie Davis	3.00	6.00
9 Bob DeMarco	1.25	2.50
10 Darrell Dess	1.25	2.50
11 Mike Ditka	7.50	15.00
12 Bill Forester	1.25	2.50
13 Joe Fortunato	1.25	2.50
14 Bill George	3.00	6.00
15 Ken Gray	1.25	2.50
16 Forrest Gregg	3.00	6.00
17 Roosevelt Grier	2.50	5.00
18 Hank Jordan	3.00	6.00
19 Jim Katcavage	2.00	4.00
20 Jerry Kramer	2.50	5.00
21 Ron Kramer	1.25	2.50
22 Dick Lane	3.00	6.00
23 Dick Lynch	1.25	2.50
24 Gino Marchetti	3.00	6.00
25 Tommy Mason	2.00	4.00
26 Ed Meador	1.25	2.50
27 Bobby Mitchell	3.00	6.00
28 Larry Morris	1.25	2.50
29 Merlin Olsen	4.00	8.00
30 Jim Parker	2.50	5.00
31 Jim Patton	2.00	4.00
32 Myron Pottios	1.25	2.50
33 Jim Ringo	2.50	5.00
34 Dick Schafrath	1.25	2.50
35 Joe Schmidt	3.00	6.00
36 Del Shofner	2.00	4.00
37 Bob St. Clair	2.50	5.00
38 Jim Taylor	4.00	8.00
39 Roosevelt Taylor	2.00	4.00
40 Y.A. Tittle	5.00	10.00
41 Johnny Unitas	7.50	15.00
42 Larry Wilson	3.00	6.00
43 Willie Wood	3.00	6.00
44 Abe Woodson	2.00	4.00

1964 Coke Caps Bears

Coke caps were issued in each NFL city (except for the St.Louis Cardinals) featuring 35-members of that team along with the NFL All-Stars caps as part of the 1964 Go with the Pros promotion. The NFL team Cap Saver sheets had separate sections in which to affix both the local team's caps, the NFL team logos, and the All-Stars' caps. The caps measure approximately 1 1/8" in diameter and have the drink logo and a football on the outside, while the inside has the player's face printed in black with the team name above the photo, the player's name below, his jersey number to the left and his position to the right. Most caps were issued with either a plastic or cork liner on the inside. The consumer could turn in his completed saver sheet (before the expiration date of Nov. 21, 1964) to receive various prizes. The 1964 caps look very similar to those issued in 1965 and 1966 but were numbered only according to the player's jersey number. We've arranged them alphabetically by team for ease in cataloging. Football caps were produced for Coca-Cola, Sprite and King Size Coke bottles. Sprite caps typically carry a slight premium over the value of the Coke version.

COMPLETE SET (35)	75.00	150.00
1 Doug Atkins	4.00	8.00
2 Steve Barnett	1.50	3.00
3 Charlie Bivins	1.50	3.00
4 Rudy Bukich	2.50	4.00
5 Ronnie Bull	2.50	4.00
6 Jim Cadile	1.50	3.00
7 J.C. Caroline	1.50	3.00
8 Rick Casares	2.50	4.00
9 Roger Davis	1.50	3.00
10 Mike Ditka	6.00	12.00
11 John Farrington	1.50	3.00
12 Joe Fortunato	1.50	3.00
13 Willie Galimore	2.50	4.00
14 Bill George	3.50	6.00
15 Larry Glueck	1.50	3.00
16 Bobby Joe Green	1.50	3.00
17 Bob Jencks	1.50	3.00
18 John Johnson	1.50	3.00
19 Stan Jones	3.50	6.00
20 Ted Karras	1.50	3.00
21 Bob Kilcullen	1.50	3.00
22 Roger LeClerc	1.50	3.00
23 Herman Lee	1.50	3.00
24 Earl Leggett	1.50	3.00
25 Joe Marconi	1.50	3.00
26 Bennie McRae	1.50	3.00
27 Johnny Morris	1.50	3.00
28 Larry Morris	1.50	3.00
29 Ed O'Bradovich	1.50	3.00
30 Richie Petitbon	2.50	4.00
31 Mike Pyle	1.50	3.00
32 Roosevelt Taylor	2.50	4.00
33 Bill Wade	2.50	4.00
34 Bob Wetoska	1.50	3.00
35 Dave Whitsell	1.50	3.00
NNO Bears Saver Sheet	15.00	30.00

1964 Coke Caps Browns

Please see the 1964 Coke Caps Bears listing for information on this set.

COMPLETE SET (35)	75.00	150.00
1 Walter Beach	1.50	3.00
2 Larry Benz	1.50	3.00
3 Johnny Brewer	1.50	3.00
4 Jim Brown	15.00	30.00
5 John Brown	1.50	3.00
6 Monte Clark	1.50	3.00
7 Gary Collins	2.50	5.00
8 Vince Costello	1.50	3.00
9 Ross Fichtner	1.50	3.00
10 Galen Fiss	1.50	3.00
11 Bobby Franklin	1.50	3.00
12 Bob Gain	2.00	4.00
13 Bill Glass	2.00	4.00
14 Ernie Green	1.50	3.00
15 Lou Groza	5.00	10.00
16 Gene Hickerson	2.00	4.00
17 Jim Houston	1.50	3.00
18 Tom Hutchinson	1.50	3.00
19 Jim Kanicki	1.50	3.00
20 Mike Lucci	2.00	4.00
21 Dick Modzelewski	2.00	4.00
22 John Morrow	1.50	3.00
23 Jim Ninowski	2.00	4.00
24 Frank Parker	1.50	3.00
25 Bernie Parrish	2.00	4.00
26 Frank Ryan	2.50	5.00
27 Charlie Scales	1.50	3.00
28 Dick Schafrath	2.00	4.00
29 Roger Shoals	1.50	3.00
30 Jim Shorter	1.50	3.00
31 Billy Truax	2.00	4.00
32 Paul Warfield	7.50	15.00
33 Ken Webb	1.50	3.00
34 Paul Wiggin	1.50	3.00
35 John Wooten	2.00	4.00
NNO Browns Saver Sheet Frank Ryan pictured	15.00	30.00

1964 Coke Caps Chargers

Coke caps were issued in each AFL city, except Buffalo, featuring 35-members of that team along with the AFL All-Stars caps as part of the 1964 Go with the Pros promotion. The AFL team Cap Saver sheets had separate sections in which to affix both the local team's caps, all of the AFL team logos, and the AFL All-Star caps. The caps measure approximately 1 1/8" in diameter and have the drink logo and a football on the outside, while the inside has the player's face printed in black with the team name above the photo, the player's name below, his jersey number to the left and his position to the right. Most caps were issued with either a plastic or cork liner on the inside. The consumer could turn in his completed saver sheet (before the expiration date of Nov. 21, 1964) to receive various prizes. The 1964 caps look very similar to those issued in 1965 and 1966 but were numbered only according to the player's jersey number. We've arranged them alphabetically by team for ease in cataloging. Football caps were produced for Coca-Cola, Sprite and King Size Coke bottles. Sprite caps typically carry a slight premium over the value of the Coke version.

COMPLETE SET (35)	100.00	175.00
1 Chuck Allen	2.50	5.00
2 Lance Alworth	10.00	20.00
3 George Blair	2.00	4.00
4 Frank Buncom	2.00	4.00
5 Earl Faison	2.50	5.00
6 Kenny Graham	2.00	4.00
7 George Gross	2.00	4.00
8 Sam Gruneisen	2.00	4.00
9 John Hadl	5.00	10.00
10 Dick Harris	2.50	5.00
11 Bob Jackson	2.00	4.00
12 Emil Karas	2.00	4.00
13 Dave Kocourek	2.00	4.00
14 Ernie Ladd	5.00	10.00
15 Bob Lane	2.00	4.00
16 Keith Lincoln	3.00	6.00
17 Paul Lowe	3.00	6.00
18 Jacque MacKinnon	2.00	4.00
19 Gerry McDougall	2.00	4.00
20 Charlie McNeil	2.50	5.00
21 Bob Mitinger	2.00	4.00
22 Ron Mix	5.00	10.00
23 Don Norton	2.00	4.00
24 Ernie Park	2.00	4.00
25 Bob Petrich	2.00	4.00
26 Jerry Robinson	2.00	4.00
27 Don Rogers	2.00	4.00
28 Tobin Rote	2.50	5.00
29 Henry Schmidt	2.00	4.00
30 Pat Shea	2.00	4.00
31 Walt Sweeney	2.50	5.00
32 Jim Warren	2.00	4.00
33 Dick Westmoreland	2.50	5.00
34 Bud Whitehead	2.00	4.00
35 Ernie Wright	2.50	5.00
NNO Chargers Saver Sheet	15.00	30.00

1964 Coke Caps Eagles

Please see the 1964 Coke Caps Bears listing for information on this set.

COMPLETE SET (35)	75.00	150.00
1 Mickey Babb	2.00	3.00
2 Sam Baker	2.00	3.00
3 Maxie Baughan	2.00	3.00
4 Ed Blaine	2.00	3.00
5 Bob Brown	2.50	4.00
6 Timmy Brown	2.50	4.00
7 Don Burroughs	2.00	3.00
8 Pete Case	2.00	3.00
9 Jack Concannon	2.50	4.00
10 Claude Crabb	2.00	3.00
11 Glenn Glass	2.00	3.00
12 Ron Goodwin	2.00	3.00
13 Dave Graham	2.00	3.00
14 Earl Gros	2.00	3.00
15 Riley Gunnels	2.00	3.00
16 King Hill	2.50	4.00
17 Lynn Hoyem	2.00	3.00
18 Don Hultz	2.00	3.00
19 Terry Kosens	2.00	3.00
20 Chuck Lamson	2.00	3.00
21 Dave Lloyd	2.00	3.00
22 Red Mack	2.00	3.00
23 Ollie Matson	6.00	10.00
24 John Mellekas	2.00	3.00
25 John Meyers	2.00	3.00
26 Floyd Peters	2.50	4.00
27 Ray Poage	2.00	3.00
28 Nate Ramsey	2.00	3.00
29 Pete Retzlaff	2.50	4.00
30 Jim Ringo	5.00	8.00
31 Jim Skaggs	2.00	3.00
32 Ralph Smith	2.00	3.00
33 Norm Snead	3.00	5.00
34 George Tarasovic	2.00	3.00
35 Tom Woodeshick	2.50	4.00
NNO Eagles Saver Sheet	15.00	30.00

1964 Coke Caps 49ers

Please see the 1964 Coke Caps Bears listing for information on this set.

COMPLETE SET (35)	75.00	150.00
1 Kermit Alexander	2.00	3.00
2 Bruce Bosley	2.00	3.00
3 John Brodie	4.00	8.00
4 Vern Burke	2.00	3.00
5 Bernie Casey	2.50	4.00
6 Dan Colchico	2.00	3.00
7 Clyde Conner	2.00	3.00
8 Bill Cooper	2.00	3.00
9 Tommy Davis	2.50	4.00
10 Leon Donohue	2.00	3.00
11 Mike Dowdle	2.00	3.00
12 Matt Hazeltine	2.00	3.00
13 Jim Johnson	3.00	5.00
14 Billy Kilmer	3.60	6.00
15 Elbert Kimbrough	2.00	3.00
16 Charlie Krueger	2.00	3.00
17 Roland Lakes	2.00	3.00
18 Don Lisbon	2.00	3.00
19 Mike Magac	2.00	3.00
20 Jerry Mertens	2.00	3.00
21 Dave Messer	2.00	3.00
22 Clark Miller	2.00	3.00
23 George Mira	2.50	4.00
24 Dave Parks	2.50	4.00
25 Ed Pine	2.00	3.00
26 Walter Rock	2.00	3.00
27 Len Rohde	2.00	3.00
28 Karl Rubke	2.00	3.00
29 Bob St. Clair	3.00	5.00
30 Charlie Sieminski	2.00	3.00
31 J.D. Smith	2.50	4.00
32 Monty Stickles	2.00	3.00
33 John Thomas	2.00	3.00
34 Jim Vollenweider	2.00	3.00
35 Abe Woodson	2.50	4.00
NNO 49ers Saver Sheet	15.00	30.00

1964 Coke Caps Giants

Please see the 1964 Coke Caps Bears listing for information on this set.

COMPLETE SET (38)	75.00	150.00
1 Roger Anderson	1.50	4.00
2 Erich Barnes	1.50	4.00
3 Bookie Bolin UER (name misspelled Bolen)	1.50	4.00
4 Ken Byers	1.50	4.00
5 Roosevelt Brown	2.50	6.00
6 Don Chandler	2.00	5.00
7 Bob Crespino	1.50	4.00
8 Darrell Dess	1.50	4.00
9 Ed Dove	1.50	4.00
10 Frank Gifford	5.00	4.00
11 Glynn Griffing	1.50	4.00
12 Jerry Hillebrand	1.50	4.00
13 Lane Howell	1.50	4.00
14 Dick James	1.50	4.00
15 Jim Katcavage	2.00	5.00
16 Charlie Killett	1.50	4.00
17 Phil King	1.50	4.00
18 Lou Kirouac	1.50	4.00
19 Greg Larson	1.50	4.00
20 Joe Don Looney	2.00	5.00
21 John LoVetere	1.50	4.00
22 Dick Lynch	1.50	4.00
23 Jim Moran	1.50	4.00
24 Joe Morrison	2.00	5.00
25 Jimmy Patton	1.50	4.00
26 Dick Pesonen	1.50	4.00
27 Tom Scott	1.50	4.00
28 Del Shofner	2.00	5.00
29 Jack Stroud	1.50	4.00
30 Andy Stynchula	1.50	4.00
31 Aaron Thomas	1.50	4.00
32 Bob Timberlake	1.50	4.00
33 Y.A. Tittle	6.00	12.00
34 Mickey Walker	1.50	4.00
35 Joe Walton	1.50	4.00
36 Allan Webb	1.50	4.00
37 Alex Webster	2.00	5.00
38 Bill Winter	1.50	4.00

1964 Coke Caps Lions

Please see the 1964 Coke Caps Bears listing for information on this set.

COMPLETE SET (35)	75.00	150.00
1 Terry Barr	1.50	3.00
2 Carl Brettschneider	1.50	3.00
3 Roger Brown	2.00	4.00
4 Mike Bundra	1.50	3.00
5 Ernie Clark	1.50	3.00
6 Gail Cogdill	2.00	4.00
7 Larry Ferguson	1.50	3.00
8 Dennis Gaubatz	1.50	3.00
9 Jim Gibbons	2.00	4.00
10 John Gonzaga	1.50	3.00
11 John Gordy	1.50	3.00
12 Tom Hall	1.50	3.00
13 Alex Karras	5.00	10.00
14 Dick Lane	4.00	8.00
15 Dan LaRose	1.50	3.00
16 Yale Lary	4.00	8.00
17 Dick LeBeau	2.00	4.00
18 Dan Lewis	1.50	3.00
19 Gary Lowe	1.50	3.00
20 Bruce Maher	1.50	3.00
21 Darris McCord	1.50	3.00
22 Max Messner	1.50	3.00
23 Earl Morrall	3.00	6.00
24 Nick Pietrosante	2.00	4.00
25 Milt Plum	2.50	5.00
26 Daryl Sanders	1.50	3.00
27 Joe Schmidt	5.00	10.00
28 Bob Scholtz	1.50	3.00
29 J.D. Smith	2.00	4.00
30 Pat Studstill	2.00	4.00
31 Larry Vargo	1.50	3.00
32 Wayne Walker	2.00	4.00
33 Tom Watkins	1.50	3.00
34 Bob Whitlow	1.50	3.00
35 Sam Williams	1.50	3.00
NNO Lions Saver Sheet	15.00	30.00

1964 Coke Caps National NFL

This set of 68 Coke caps was issued on bottled soft drinks primarily in cities without an NFL team. The caps were issued along with their own Saver Sheet. Each measures approximately 1 1/8" in diameter and has the drink logo and a football on the outside, while the inside has the player's face printed with text surrounding the face. An "NFL ALL STARS" title appears above the player's photo, therefore some players below appear in both this set and the NFL All-Stars set listing. The consumer could turn in his completed saver sheet to receive various prizes. The caps are unnumbered and checklisted below in alphabetical order. Football caps were also produced for Sprite and King Size Coke bottles. Sprite caps typically carry a slight premium over the value of the Coke version.

COMPLETE SET (68)	125.00	250.00
1 Herb Adderley	2.50	5.00
2 Grady Alderman	1.50	3.00
3 Doug Atkins	3.00	6.00
4 Sam Baker	1.50	3.00
5 Erich Barnes	1.50	3.00
6 Terry Barr	1.50	3.00
7 Dick Bass	1.50	3.00
8 Maxie Baughan	1.50	3.00
9 Raymond Berry	3.00	6.00
10 Charley Bradshaw	1.50	3.00
11 Jim Brown	12.50	25.00
12 Roger Brown	1.50	3.00
13 Timmy Brown	1.50	3.00
14 Gail Cogdill	1.50	3.00
15 Tommy Davis	1.50	3.00
16 Willie Davis	1.50	3.00
17 Bob DeMarco	1.50	3.00
18 Darrell Dess	1.50	3.00
19 Buddy Dial	2.00	4.00
20 Mike Ditka	7.50	15.00
21 Galen Fiss	1.50	3.00
22 Lee Folkins	1.50	3.00
23 Joe Fortunato	1.50	3.00
24 Bill Glass	1.50	3.00

25 John Gordy	1.50	3.00
26 Ken Gray	1.50	3.00
27 Forrest Gregg	3.00	6.00
28 Rip Hawkins	1.50	3.00
29 Charley Johnson	2.00	4.00
30 John Henry Johnson	2.50	5.00
31 Hank Jordan	2.50	5.00
32 Jim Katcavage	1.50	3.00
33 Jerry Kramer	2.50	5.00
34 Joe Krupa	1.50	3.00
35 John Lovetere	1.50	3.00
36 Dick Lynch	1.50	3.00
37 John Mackey	3.00	6.00
38 Gino Marchetti	2.50	5.00
39 Joe Marconi	1.50	3.00
40 Tommy Mason	1.50	3.00
41 Dale Meinert	1.50	3.00
42 Lou Michaels	2.00	4.00
43 Bobby Mitchell	3.00	6.00
44 John Morrow	1.50	3.00
45 Merlin Olsen	4.00	8.00
46 Jack Pardee	2.00	4.00
47 Jim Parker	1.50	3.00
48 Bernie Parrish	1.50	3.00
49 Don Perkins	2.00	4.00
50 Richie Petitbon	1.50	3.00
51 Myron Pottios	1.50	3.00
52 Vince Promuto	1.50	3.00
53 Mike Pyle	1.50	3.00
54 Pete Retzlaff	2.00	4.00
55 Jim Ringo	2.50	5.00
56 Joe Rutgens	1.50	3.00
57 Dick Schafrath	1.50	3.00
58 Del Shofner	1.50	3.00
59 Jim Taylor	3.75	7.50
60 Roosevelt Taylor	1.50	3.00
61 Clendon Thomas	1.50	3.00
62 Y.A. Tittle	5.00	10.00
63 John Unitas	7.50	15.00
64 Bill Wade	1.50	3.00
65 Wayne Walker	1.50	3.00
66 Jesse Whittenton	2.00	4.00
67 Larry Wilson	2.50	5.00
68 Abe Woodson	2.00	4.00
NNO NFL All-Star Saver Sheet	15.00	30.00

1964 Coke Caps Oilers

Please see the 1964 Coke Caps Chargers listing for information on this set.

COMPLETE SET (35)	90.00	150.00
1 Scott Appleton	2.00	4.00
2 Johnny Baker	2.00	4.00
3 Tony Banfield	2.00	4.00
4 George Blanda	10.00	20.00
5 Danny Brabham	2.00	4.00
6 Ode Burrell	2.00	4.00
7 Billy Cannon	3.00	6.00
8 Doug Cline	2.00	4.00
9 Bobby Crenshaw	2.00	4.00
10 Gary Cutsinger	2.00	4.00
11 Willard Dewveall	2.00	4.00
12 Mike Dukes	2.00	4.00
13 Staley Faulkner	2.00	4.00
14 Don Floyd	2.00	4.00
15 Freddy Glick	2.00	4.00
16 Tom Goode	2.00	4.00
17 Charlie Hennigan	2.50	5.00
18 Ed Husmann	2.00	4.00
19 Bobby Jancik	2.00	4.00
20 Mark Johnston	2.00	4.00
21 Jacky Lee	2.50	5.00
22 Bob McLeod	2.00	4.00
23 Dudley Meredith	2.00	4.00
24 Rich Michael	2.00	4.00
25 Benny Nelson	2.00	4.00
26 Jim Norton	2.50	5.00
27 Larry Onesti	2.00	4.00
28 Bob Schmidt	2.00	4.00
29 Dave Smith	2.00	4.00
30 Walt Suggs	2.00	4.00
31 Bob Talamini	2.00	4.00
32 Charley Tolar	2.00	4.00
33 Don Trull	2.50	5.00
34 John Varnell	2.00	4.00
35 Hogan Wharton	2.00	4.00

1964 Coke Caps Packers

Please see the 1964 Coke Caps Bears listing for information on this set.

COMPLETE SET (35)	125.00	225.00
1 Herb Adderley	4.00	8.00
2 Lionel Aldridge	3.00	5.00
3 Zeke Bratkowski	3.00	5.00
4 Lee Roy Caffey	2.50	4.00
5 Dennis Claridge	2.50	4.00
6 Dan Currie	2.50	4.00
7 Willie Davis	4.00	8.00
8 Boyd Dowler	3.00	5.00
9 Marv Fleming	3.00	5.00
10 Forrest Gregg	4.00	8.00
11 Hank Gremminger	2.50	4.00
12 Dan Grimm	2.50	4.00
13 Dave Hanner	3.00	5.00
14 Urban Henry	2.50	4.00
15 Paul Hornung	10.00	20.00
16 Bob Jeter	3.00	5.00
17 Hank Jordan	4.00	8.00
18 Ron Kostelnik	2.50	4.00
19 Jerry Kramer	3.00	6.00
20 Ron Kramer	2.50	4.00
21 Norm Masters	2.50	4.00
22 Max McGee	3.00	5.00
23 Frank Mestnik	2.50	4.00
24 Tom Moore	3.00	5.00
25 Ray Nitschke	6.00	12.00
26 Jerry Norton	2.50	4.00
27 Elijah Pitts	3.00	5.00
28 Dave Robinson	3.50	6.00
29 Bob Skoronski	2.50	4.00
30 Bart Starr	12.50	25.00
31 Jim Taylor	6.00	12.00
32 Fuzzy Thurston	4.00	8.00
33 Lloyd Voss	2.50	4.00
34 Jesse Whittenton	2.50	4.00
35 Willie Wood	4.00	8.00
NNO Packers Saver Sheet	20.00	40.00

1964 Coke Caps Patriots

Please see the 1964 Coke Caps Chargers listing for information on this set.

COMPLETE SET (35)	75.00	150.00
1 Tom Addison	2.50	4.00
2 Houston Antwine	2.50	4.00
3 Nick Buoniconti	6.00	10.00
4 Ron Burton	3.00	5.00
5 Gino Cappelletti	3.50	6.00
6 Jim Colclough	2.50	4.00
7 Harry Crump	2.50	4.00
8 Bob Dee	2.50	4.00
9 Bob Dentel	2.50	4.00
10 Larry Eisenhauer	2.50	4.00
11 Dick Felt	2.50	4.00
12 Larry Garron	2.50	4.00
13 Art Graham	3.00	5.00
14 Ron Hall	2.50	4.00
15 Jim Hunt	2.50	4.00
16 Charles Long	2.50	4.00
17 Don McKinnon	2.50	4.00
18 Jon Morris	2.50	4.00
19 Billy Neighbors	2.50	4.00
20 Tom Neumann	2.50	4.00
21 Don Oakes	2.50	4.00
22 Ross O'Hanley	2.50	4.00
23 Babe Parilli	3.00	5.00
24 Jesse Richardson	2.50	4.00
25 Tony Romeo	2.50	4.00
26 Jack Rudolph	2.50	4.00
27 Chuck Shonta	2.50	4.00
28 Al Snyder	2.50	4.00
29 Nick Spinelli	2.50	4.00
30 Bob Suci	2.50	4.00
31 Dave Watson	2.50	4.00
32 Don Webb	2.50	4.00
33 Bob Yates	2.50	4.00
34 Tom Yewcic	2.50	4.00
35 Mack Yoho	2.50	4.00

1964 Coke Caps Raiders

Please see the 1964 Coke Caps Chargers listing for information on this set.

1 Jan Barrett	3.00	6.00
2 Dan Birdwell	3.00	6.00
3 Sonny Bishop	3.00	6.00
4 Bill Budness	3.00	6.00
5 Dave Costa	3.00	6.00
6 Dobie Craig	3.00	6.00
7 Clem Daniels	4.00	8.00
8 Claude Gibson	3.00	6.00
9 Wayne Hawkins	4.00	8.00
10 Ken Herock	3.00	6.00
11 Dick Klein	3.00	6.00
12 Jim McMillin	3.00	6.00
13 Chuck McMurtry	3.00	6.00
14 Mike Mercer	3.00	6.00
15 Al Miller	3.00	6.00
16 Rex Mirich	3.00	6.00
17 Bob Mischak	3.00	6.00
18 Jim Norris	3.00	6.00
19 Jim Otto	7.50	15.00
20 Art Powell	4.00	8.00
21 Warren Powers	3.00	6.00
22 Ken Rice	3.00	6.00
23 Bo Roberson	3.00	6.00
24 Jack Simpson	3.00	6.00
25 Fred Williamson	5.00	10.00
26 Frank Youso	3.00	6.00

1964 Coke Caps Rams

Please see the 1964 Coke Caps Bears listing for information on this set.

COMPLETE SET (35)	75.00	150.00
1 Jon Arnett	2.50	4.00
2 Pervis Atkins	1.50	3.00
3 Terry Baker	3.00	5.00
4 Dick Bass	2.50	4.00
5 Charley Britt	1.50	3.00
6 Willie Brown	2.50	4.00
7 Joe Carollo	1.50	3.00
8 Don Chuy	1.50	3.00
9 Charlie Cowan	1.50	3.00
10 Lindon Crow	1.50	3.00
11 Carroll Dale	2.50	4.00
12 Roman Gabriel	4.00	8.00
13 Roosevelt Grier	3.00	6.00
14 Mike Henry	1.50	3.00
15 Art Hunter	1.50	3.00
16 Ken Iman	1.50	3.00
17 Deacon Jones	5.00	10.00
18 Cliff Livingston	1.50	3.00
19 Lamar Lundy	2.50	4.00
20 Marlin McKeever	1.50	3.00
21 Ed Meador	1.50	3.00
22 Bill Munson	2.50	4.00
23 Merlin Olsen	6.00	12.00
24 Jack Pardee	2.50	4.00
25 Art Perkins	1.50	3.00
26 Jim Phillips	2.50	4.00
27 Roger Pillath	1.50	3.00
28 Mel Profit	1.50	3.00
29 Joe Scibelli	1.50	3.00
30 Carver Shannon	1.50	3.00
31 Bobby Smith	1.50	3.00
32 Bill Swain	1.50	3.00
33 Frank Varrichione	1.50	3.00
34 Danny Villanueva	1.50	3.00
35 Nat Whitmyer	1.50	3.00
NNO Rams Saver Sheet	15.00	30.00

1964 Coke Caps Redskins

Please see the 1964 Coke Caps Bears listing for information on this set.

COMPLETE SET (35)	90.00	150.00
1 Bill Barnes	2.50	4.00
2 Don Bosseler	2.50	4.00
3 Rod Breedlove	2.50	4.00
4 Frank Budd	2.50	4.00
5 Henry Butsko	2.50	4.00
6 Jimmy Carr	2.50	4.00
7 Bill Clay	2.50	4.00
8 Angelo Coia	2.50	4.00
9 Fred Dugan	2.50	4.00
10 Fred Hageman	2.50	4.00
11 Sam Huff	5.00	10.00
12 George Izo	3.00	5.00
13 Sonny Jurgensen	5.00	10.00
14 Carl Kammerer	2.50	4.00
15 Gordon Kelley	2.50	4.00
16 Bob Khayat	2.50	4.00
17 Paul Krause	3.50	6.00
18 J.W. Lockett	2.50	4.00
19 Riley Mattson	2.50	4.00
20 Bobby Mitchell	4.00	8.00
21 John Nisby	2.50	4.00
22 Fran O'Brien	2.50	4.00
23 John Paluck	2.50	4.00
24 Jack Pardee	3.50	6.00
25 Bob Pellegrini	2.50	4.00
26 Vince Promuto	2.50	4.00
27 Pat Richter	3.00	5.00
28 Johnny Sample	3.00	5.00
29 Lonnie Sanders	2.50	4.00
30 Dick Shiner	2.50	4.00
31 Ron Snidow	2.50	4.00
32 Jim Steffen	2.50	4.00
33 Charley Taylor	5.00	10.00
34 Tom Tracy	3.00	5.00
35 Fred Williams	2.50	4.00
NNO Redskins Saver Sheet	15.00	30.00

1964 Coke Caps Steelers

Please see the 1964 Coke Caps Bears listing for information on this set.

COMPLETE SET (35)	75.00	150.00
1 Art Anderson	2.50	4.00
2 Frank Atkinson	2.50	4.00
3 Gary Ballman	2.50	4.00
4 John Baker	2.50	4.00
5 Charley Bradshaw	2.50	4.00
6 Jim Bradshaw	2.50	4.00
7 Ed Brown	3.00	5.00
8 John Burrell	2.50	4.00
9 Preston Carpenter	3.00	5.00
10 Lou Cordileone	2.50	4.00
11 Willie Daniel	2.50	4.00
12 Dick Haley	2.50	4.00
13 Bob Harrison	2.50	4.00
14 Dick Hoak	3.00	5.00
15 Dan James	2.50	4.00
16 Tom Jenkins	2.50	4.00
17 John Henry Johnson	5.00	10.00
18 Jim Kelly	2.50	4.00
19 Brady Keys	2.50	4.00
20 Joe Krupa	2.50	4.00
21 Ray Lemek	2.50	4.00
22 Paul Martha	2.50	4.00
23 Lou Michaels	3.00	5.00
24 Bill Nelsen	3.00	6.00
25 Terry Nofsinger	2.50	4.00
26 Buzz Nutter	2.50	4.00
27 Clarence Peaks	2.50	4.00
28 Myron Pottios	2.50	4.00
29 John Reger	2.50	4.00
30 Mike Sandusky	2.50	4.00
31 Theron Sapp	2.50	4.00
32 Bob Schmitz	2.50	4.00
33 Ron Stehouwer	2.50	4.00
34 Clendon Thomas	2.50	4.00
35 Joe Womack	2.50	4.00

1964 Coke Caps Team Emblems AFL

Each 1964 Coke Caps saver sheet had a section for collecting caps featuring the team emblem for all eight AFL teams. The caps are unnumbered and checklisted below in alphabetical order. These "Coke" caps were also available on Sprite bottles. Sprite caps typically carry a 1.5X-2X premium over the Coke version.

COMPLETE SET (8)	20.00	40.00
1 Boston Patriots	2.50	5.00
2 Buffalo Bills	2.50	5.00
3 Denver Broncos	3.00	6.00
4 Houston Oilers	2.50	5.00
5 Kansas City Chiefs	2.50	5.00
6 New York Jets	2.50	5.00
7 Oakland Raiders	3.00	6.00
8 San Diego Chargers	2.50	5.00

1964 Coke Caps Team Emblems NFL

Each 1964 Coke Caps saver sheet had a section for collecting caps featuring the team emblem for all fourteen NFL teams. The caps are unnumbered and checklisted below in alphabetical order. These "Coke" caps were also available on Sprite bottles. Sprite caps typically carry a 1.5X-2X premium over the Coke version.

COMPLETE SET (14)	30.00	60.00
1 Baltimore Colts	2.50	5.00
2 Chicago Bears	2.50	5.00
3 Cleveland Browns	2.50	5.00
4 Dallas Cowboys	3.00	6.00
5 Detroit Lions	2.50	5.00
6 Green Bay Packers	3.00	6.00
7 Los Angeles Rams	2.50	5.00
8 Minnesota Vikings	2.50	5.00
9 New York Giants	2.50	5.00
10 Philadelphia Eagles	2.50	5.00
11 Pittsburgh Steelers	2.50	5.00
12 San Francisco 49ers	2.50	5.00
13 St. Louis Cardinals	2.50	5.00
14 Washington Redskins	3.00	6.00

1964 Coke Caps Vikings

Please see the 1964 Coke Caps Bears listing for information on this set.

COMPLETE SET (35)	75.00	150.00
1 Grady Alderman	2.50	5.00
2 Hal Bedsole	2.00	4.00
3 Larry Bowie	2.00	4.00
4 Jim Boylan	2.00	4.00
5 Bill Brown	2.50	5.00
6 Bill Butler	2.00	4.00
7 Lee Calland	2.00	4.00
8 John Campbell	2.00	4.00
9 Fred Cox	2.50	5.00
10 Ted Dean	2.00	4.00
11 Bob Denton	2.00	4.00
12 Paul Dickson	2.00	4.00
13 Carl Eller	6.00	10.00
14 Paul Flatley	2.00	4.00
15 Tom Franckhauser	2.00	4.00
16 Rip Hawkins	2.00	4.00
17 Bill Jobko	2.00	4.00
18 Karl Kassulke	2.00	4.00
19 John Kirby	2.00	4.00
20 Bob Lacey	2.00	4.00
21 Errol Linden	2.00	4.00
22 Jim Marshall	6.00	10.00
23 Tommy Mason	2.50	5.00
24 Dave O'Brien	2.00	4.00
25 Palmer Pike	2.00	4.00
26 Jim Prestel	2.00	4.00
27 Jerry Reichow	2.00	4.00
28 George Rose	2.00	4.00
29 Ed Sharockman	2.00	4.00
30 Gordon Smith	2.00	4.00
31 Fran Tarkenton	15.00	25.00
32 Mick Tingelhoff	2.50	5.00
33 Ron Vanderkelen	2.00	4.00
34 Tom Wilson	2.00	4.00
35 Roy Winston	2.50	5.00

1965 Coke Caps All-Stars AFL

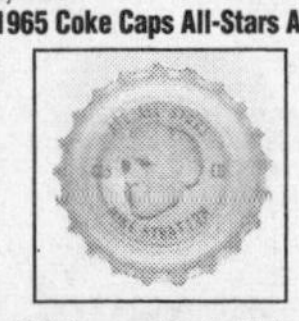

These AFL All-Star caps were issued in AFL cities (and a few other cities as well) along with the local team caps as part of the Go with the Pros promotion. The AFL team Cap Saver sheets had separate sections in which to affix both the local team's caps and the All-Stars' caps. The caps measure approximately 1 1/8" in diameter and have the drink logo and a football on the outside, while the inside has the player's face printed in black or red, with text surrounding the face. The consumer could turn in his completed saver sheet to receive various prizes. The caps are numbered with a "C" prefix. The 1965 caps are very similar to the 1966 issue and many of the players are the same in both years. However, the 1965 caps do not have the words "Caramel Colored" on the outside of the cap as do the 1966 caps. These caps were also produced for 1965 on other Coca-Cola products: TAB, Fanta and Sprite. The other drink caps typically carry a slight premium (1.5-2 times) over the value of the Coke version.

COMPLETE SET (34)	87.50	175.00
C37 Jerry Mays	1.50	3.00
C38 Cookie Gilchrist	2.00	4.00
C39 Lionel Taylor	2.00	4.00
C40 Goose Gonsoulin	2.00	4.00
C41 Gino Cappelletti	2.00	4.00
C42 Nick Buoniconti	2.50	5.00
C43 Larry Eisenhauer	1.50	3.00
C44 Babe Parilli	2.00	4.00
C45 Jack Kemp	12.50	25.00
C46 Billy Shaw	2.00	4.00
C47 Scott Appleton	1.50	3.00
C48 Matt Snell	2.00	4.00
C49 Charlie Hennigan	2.00	4.00
C50 Tom Flores	2.50	5.00
C51 Clem Daniels	2.00	4.00
C52 George Blanda	7.50	15.00
C53 Art Powell	2.00	4.00
C54 Jim Otto	5.00	10.00
C55 Larry Grantham	1.50	3.00
C56 Don Maynard	6.00	12.00
C57 Gerry Philbin	1.50	3.00
C58 E.J. Holub	1.50	3.00
C59 Chris Burford	1.50	3.00
C60 Ron Mix	3.75	7.50
C61 Ernie Ladd	3.75	7.50
C62 Fred Arbanas	1.50	3.00
C63 Tom Sestak	1.50	3.00
C64 Elbert Dubenion	2.00	4.00
C65 Mike Stratton	1.50	3.00
C66 Willie Brown	5.00	10.00
C67 Sid Blanks	1.50	3.00
C68 Len Dawson	6.00	12.00
C69 Lance Alworth	6.00	12.00
C70 Keith Lincoln	2.00	4.00

1965 Coke Caps All-Stars NFL

These NFL All-Star caps were issued in NFL cities (and a few other cities as well) along with the local team caps as part of the Go with the Pros promotion. The NFL team Cap Saver sheets had separate sections in which to affix both the local team's caps and the All-Stars' caps. The caps measure approximately 1 1/8" in diameter and have the drink logo and a football on the outside, while the inside has the player's face printed in black or red with text surrounding the face. The 1965 caps are very similar to the 1966 issue and many of the players are the same in both years. However, the 1965 caps do not have the words "Caramel Colored" on the outside of the cap as do the 1966 caps. The consumer could turn in his completed saver sheet to receive various prizes. The caps are numbered with a "C" prefix. These caps were also produced for 1965 on other Coca-Cola products: TAB, Fanta and Sprite. The other drink caps typically carry a slight premium (1.5-2 times) over the value of the Coke version.

COMPLETE SET (34)	50.00	100.00
C37 Sonny Jurgensen	2.50	6.00
C38 Fran Tarkenton	3.00	8.00
C39 Frank Ryan	1.25	3.00
C40 Johnny Unitas	5.00	12.00
C41 Tommy Mason	1.25	3.00
C42 Mel Renfro	1.50	4.00
C43 Ed Meador	1.00	2.50
C44 Paul Krause	1.50	4.00
C45 Irv Cross	1.25	3.00
C46 Bill Brown	1.25	3.00
C47 Joe Fortunato	1.00	2.50
C48 Jim Taylor	2.50	6.00
C49 John Henry Johnson	1.50	4.00
C50 Pat Fischer	1.00	2.50
C51 Bob Boyd	1.00	2.50
C52 Terry Barr	1.00	2.50
C53 Charley Taylor	1.50	4.00
C54 Paul Warfield	2.50	6.00
C55 Pete Retzlaff	1.25	3.00
C56 Maxie Baughan	1.00	2.50
C57 Matt Hazeltine	1.00	2.50
C58 Ken Gray	1.00	2.50
C59 Ray Nitschke	2.50	6.00
C60 Myron Pottios	1.00	2.50
C61 Charlie Krueger	1.00	2.50
C62 Deacon Jones	2.00	5.00
C63 Bob Lilly	2.50	6.00
C64 Merlin Olsen	2.00	5.00
C65 Jim Parker	1.50	4.00
C66 Roosevelt Brown	1.50	4.00
C67 Jim Gibbons	1.00	2.50
C68 Mike Ditka	3.00	8.00
C69 Willie Davis	1.50	4.00
C70 Aaron Thomas	1.00	2.50

1965 Coke Caps Bears

Coke caps were again issued for each NFL team in 1965 primarily in that team's local area along with the NFL All-Stars caps as part of the Go with the Pros promotion. The NFL team Cap Saver sheets had separate sections in which to affix both the local team's caps and the All-Stars' caps. The caps measure approximately 1 1/8" in diameter and have the drink logo and a football on the outside, while the inside has the player's face printed in red or black, with the team name above the photo, the player's name below, his position to the right and the cap number to the left. Some teams are also known to exist in a version that features a slightly smaller player photo. Cap numbers included a "C" prefix on all NFL teams except the Giants which had two sets using either a "C" or "G" prefix. The consumer could turn in his completed saver sheet to receive various prizes. The 1965 caps are very similar to the 1966 issue and many of the players are the same in both years. However, the 1965 caps do not have the words "Caramel Colored" on the outside of the cap as do the 1966 caps. Football caps were also produced for 1965 on other Coca-Cola products: Coke lift top, TAB (Low-Calorie Beverage), TAB lift top, Fanta Grape, Fanta Grapefruit, Fanta Orange, King Size Coke and Sprite. The other drink caps typically carry a slight premium over the value of the basic Coke version.

C1 Bennie McRae	1.50	3.00
C2 Johnny Morris	1.50	3.00
C3 Roosevelt Taylor	2.50	4.00
C4 Larry Morris	1.50	3.00
C5 Ed O'Bradovich	1.50	3.00
C6 Richie Petitbon	2.50	4.00
C7 Mike Pyle	1.50	3.00
C8 Dave Whitsell	1.50	3.00
C9 Billy Martin	1.50	3.00
C10 John Johnson	1.50	3.00
C11 Stan Jones	3.50	6.00
C12 Ted Karras	1.50	3.00
C13 Bob Kilcullen	1.50	3.00
C14 Roger LeClerc	1.50	3.00
C15 Herman Lee	1.50	3.00
C16 Earl Leggett	1.50	3.00
C17 Joe Marconi	1.50	3.00
C18 Rudy Bukich	2.50	4.00
C19 Mike Reilly	1.50	3.00
C20 Mike Ditka	6.00	12.00
C21 Dick Evey	1.50	3.00
C22 Joe Fortunato	1.50	3.00
C23 Bill Wade	2.50	4.00
C24 Bill George	3.50	6.00
C25 Larry Glueck	1.50	3.00
C26 Bobby Joe Green	1.50	3.00
C27 Bob Wetoska	1.50	3.00
C28 Doug Atkins	4.00	8.00
C29 Jon Arnett	2.50	4.00
C30 Dick Butkus	18.00	30.00
C31 Charlie Bivins	1.50	3.00
C32 Ronnie Bull	2.50	4.00
C33 Jim Cadile	1.50	3.00
C34 J.C. Caroline	1.50	3.00
C35 Gale Sayers	18.00	30.00
C36 Team Logo	1.50	3.00
NNO Saver Sheet	15.00	30.00

1965 Coke Caps Bills B

Coke caps were again issued for each AFL team in 1965 primarily in that team's local area along with the AFL All-Stars caps as part of the Go with the Pros promotion. The AFL team Cap Saver sheets had separate sections in which to affix both the local team's caps and the All-Stars' caps. The caps measure approximately 1 1/8" in diameter and have the drink logo and a football on the outside, while the inside has the player's face printed in red or black, with the team name above the photo, the player's name below, his position to the right and the cap number to the left. Some teams are also known to exist in a version that features a slightly smaller player photo. Cap numbers included a "C" prefix on all AFL teams except the Jets (J prefix) and Bills (B prefix). The consumer could turn in his completed saver sheet to receive various prizes. The 1965 caps are very similar to the 1966 issue and many of the players are the same in both years. However, the 1965 caps do not have the words "Caramel Colored" on the outside of the cap as do the 1966 caps. Football caps were also produced for 1965 on other Coca-Cola products: TAB, Fanta, King Size Coke and Sprite. The other drink caps typically carry a slight premium over the value of the basic Coke version.

COMPLETE SET (35)	75.00	150.00
*C CAPS: .4X TO 1X B CAPS		
B1 Ray Abruzzese	1.50	3.00
B2 Joe Auer	1.50	3.00
B3 Stew Barber	2.00	4.00
B4 Glenn Bass	1.50	3.00
B5 Dave Behrman	1.50	3.00
B6 Al Bemiller	1.50	3.00
B7 George Butch Byrd	2.00	4.00
B8 Wray Carlton	2.00	4.00
B9 Hagood Clarke	1.50	3.00
B10 Jack Kemp	15.00	30.00
B11 Oliver Dobbins	1.50	3.00
B12 Elbert Dubenion	2.00	4.00
B13 Jim Dunaway	2.00	4.00
B14 Booker Edgerson	1.50	3.00
B15 George Flint	1.50	3.00
B16 Pete Gogolak	2.00	4.00
B17 Dick Hudson	2.00	4.00
B18 Harry Jacobs	2.00	4.00
B19 Tom Keating	1.50	3.00
B20 Tom Day	1.50	3.00
B21 Daryle Lamonica	6.00	12.00
B22 Paul Maguire	3.00	6.00
B23 Roland McDole	2.00	4.00
B24 Dudley Meredith	1.50	3.00
B25 Joe O'Donnell	1.50	3.00
B26 Willie Ross	1.50	3.00
B27 Ed Rutkowski	1.50	3.00
B28 George Saimes	2.00	4.00
B29 Tom Sestak	2.00	4.00
B30 Billy Shaw	2.00	4.00
B31 Bob Lee Smith	1.50	3.00
B32 Mike Stratton	2.00	4.00
B33 Gene Sykes	1.50	3.00
B34 John Tracey	1.50	3.00
B35 Ernie Warlick	1.50	3.00
NNO Bills Saver Sheet	15.00	30.00

1965 Coke Caps Broncos

Please see the 1965 Coke Caps Bills listing for information on this set.

COMPLETE SET (36)	125.00	225.00
C1 Odell Barry	3.00	6.00
C2 Willie Brown	6.00	12.00
C3 Bob Scarpitto	3.00	6.00
C4 Ed Cooke	3.00	6.00
C5 Al Denson	3.00	6.00
C6 Tom Erlandson	3.00	6.00
C7 Hewritt Dixon	3.00	6.00
C8 Mickey Slaughter	3.00	6.00
C9 Lionel Taylor	4.00	8.00
C10 Jerry Sturm	3.00	6.00
C11 Jerry Hopkins	3.00	6.00
C12 Charlie Mitchell	3.00	6.00
C13 Ray Jacobs	3.00	6.00
C14 Larry Jordan	3.00	6.00
C15 Charlie Janerette	3.00	6.00
C16 Ray Kubala	3.00	6.00
C17 Leroy Moore	3.00	6.00
C18 Bob Breitenstein	3.00	6.00
C19 Eldon Danenhauer	3.00	6.00
C20 Miller Farr	3.00	6.00
C21 Max Leetzow	3.00	6.00
C22 Gene Jeter	3.00	6.00
C23 Tom Janik	3.00	6.00
C24 Gerry Bussell	3.00	6.00
C25 Bob McCullough	3.00	6.00
C26 Jim McMillin	3.00	6.00
C27 Abner Haynes	4.00	8.00
C28 John McGeever	3.00	6.00
C29 Cookie Gilchrist	4.00	8.00
C30 John McCormick	3.00	6.00
C31 Don Shackelford	3.00	6.00
C32 Goose Gonsoulin	3.00	6.00
C33 Jim Perkins	3.00	6.00
C34 Marv Matuszak	3.00	6.00
C35 Jacky Lee	3.00	6.00
C36 Team Logo	3.00	6.00

1965 Coke Caps Browns

Please see the 1965 Coke Caps Bears listing for information on this set.

COMPLETE SET (36)	75.00	125.00
C1 Jim Ninowski	2.50	4.00
C2 Leroy Kelly	5.00	10.00
C3 Lou Groza	4.00	8.00
C4 Gary Collins	2.50	4.00
C5 Bill Glass	2.50	4.00
C6 Bobby Franklin	1.50	3.00
C7 Galen Fiss	1.50	3.00
C8 Ross Fichtner	1.50	3.00
C9 John Wooten	2.50	4.00
C10 Clifton McNeil	1.50	3.00
C11 Paul Wiggin	2.50	4.00
C12 Gene Hickerson	2.50	4.00
C13 Ernie Green	1.50	3.00
C14 Dale Memmelaar	1.50	3.00
C15 Dick Schafrath	1.50	3.00
C16 Sidney Williams	1.50	3.00
C17 Frank Ryan	2.50	4.00
C18 Bernie Parrish	1.50	3.00
C19 Vince Costello	1.50	3.00
C20 John Brown	1.50	3.00
C21 Monte Clark	1.50	3.00
C22 Walter Roberts	1.50	3.00
C23 Johnny Brewer	1.50	3.00
C24 Walter Beach	1.50	3.00
C25 Dick Modzelewski	1.50	3.00
C26 Larry Benz	1.50	3.00
C27 Jim Houston	1.50	3.00
C28 Mike Lucci	1.50	3.00
C29 Mel Anthony	1.50	3.00
C30 Tom Hutchinson	1.50	3.00
C31 John Morrow	1.50	3.00
C32 Jim Kanicki	1.50	3.00
C33 Paul Warfield	5.00	10.00
C34 Jim Garcia	1.50	3.00
C35 Walter Johnson	1.50	3.00
C36 Team Logo	1.50	3.00

1965 Coke Caps Cardinals

Please see the 1965 Coke Caps Bears listing for information on this set.

C1 Pat Fischer	4.00	8.00
C2 Sonny Randle	3.00	6.00
C3 Joe Childress	3.00	6.00
C4 Dave Meggysey	4.00	8.00
C5 Joe Robb	3.00	6.00
C6 Jerry Stovall	3.00	6.00
C7 Ernie McMillan	3.00	6.00
C8 Dale Meinert	3.00	6.00
C9 Irv Goode	3.00	6.00
C10 Bob DeMarco	3.00	6.00
C11 Mal Hammack	3.00	6.00
C12 Jim Bakken	3.00	6.00
C13 Bill Thornton	3.00	6.00
C14 Buddy Humphrey	3.00	6.00
C15 Bill Koman	3.00	6.00
C16 Larry Wilson	5.00	10.00
C17 Ed Cook	3.00	6.00
C18 Prentice Gautt	3.00	6.00
C19 Charlie Johnson	4.00	8.00
C20 Ken Gray	3.00	6.00
C21 Taz Anderson	3.00	6.00
C22 Sam Silas	3.00	6.00
C23 Larry Stallings	3.00	6.00
C24 Don Brumm	3.00	6.00
C25 Bobby Joe Conrad	3.00	6.00
C26 Bill Triplett	3.00	6.00
C27 Luke Owens	3.00	6.00
C28 Jackie Smith	5.00	10.00
C29 Bob Reynolds	3.00	6.00
C30 Abe Woodson	3.00	6.00
C31 Jim Burson	3.00	6.00
C32 Willis Crenshaw	3.00	6.00
C33 Billy Gambrell	3.00	6.00
C34 Tom Redmond	3.00	6.00
C35 Herschel Turner	3.00	6.00
C36 Team Logo	3.00	6.00

1965 Coke Caps Chiefs

Please see the 1965 Coke Caps Bills listing for information on this set.

COMPLETE SET (36)		
C1 E.J. Holub	4.00	8.00
C2 Al Reynolds	3.00	6.00
C3 Buck Buchanan	5.00	10.00
C4 Curt Merz	3.00	6.00
C5 Dave Hill	3.00	6.00
C6 Bobby Hunt	3.00	6.00
C7 Jerry Mays	3.00	6.00
C8 Jon Gilliam	3.00	6.00
C9 Walt Corey	3.00	6.00
C10 Curt Farrier	3.00	6.00
C11 Jerry Cornelison	3.00	6.00
C12 Bert Coan	3.00	6.00
C13 Ed Budde	3.00	6.00
C14 Tommy Brooker	3.00	6.00
C15 Bobby Bell	5.00	10.00
C16 Smokey Stover	3.00	6.00
C17 Curtis McClinton	4.00	8.00
C18 Jerrel Wilson	3.00	6.00
C19 Jim Fraser	3.00	6.00
C20 Mack Lee Hill	3.00	6.00
C21 Jim Tyrer	3.00	6.00
C22 Johnny Robinson	4.00	8.00
C23 Bobby Ply	3.00	6.00
C24 Frank Jackson	3.00	6.00
C25 Ed Lothamer	3.00	6.00
C26 Sherrill Headrick	3.00	6.00
C27 Fred Williamson	4.00	8.00
C28 Chris Burford	3.00	6.00
C29 Willie Mitchell	3.00	6.00
C30 Mel Branch	3.00	6.00
C31 Fred Arbanas	3.00	6.00
C32 Hatch Rosdahl	3.00	6.00
C33 Reggie Carolan	3.00	6.00
C34 Len Dawson	6.00	12.00
C35 Pete Beathard	3.00	6.00
C36 Team Logo	2.50	5.00

1965 Coke Caps Colts

Please see the 1965 Coke Caps Bears listing for information on this set.

COMPLETE SET (36)	75.00	150.00
C1 Ted Davis	1.50	3.00
C2 Bob Boyd DB	1.50	3.00
C3 Lenny Moore	6.00	12.00
C4 Lou Kirouac	1.50	3.00
C5 Jimmy Orr	2.00	4.00
C6 Wendell Harris	1.50	3.00
C7 Mike Curtis	4.00	8.00
C8 Jerry Logan	1.50	3.00
C9 Steve Stonebreaker	1.50	3.00
C10 John Mackey	5.00	10.00
C11 Dennis Gaubatz	1.50	3.00
C12 Don Shinnick	1.50	3.00
C13 Dick Szymanski	1.50	3.00
C14 Ordell Braase	1.50	3.00
C15 Lonny Lyles	1.50	3.00
C16 John Campbell	1.50	3.00
C17 Dan Sullivan	1.50	3.00
C18 Lou Michaels	2.00	4.00
C19 Gary Cuozzo	2.00	4.00
C20 Butch Wilson	1.50	3.00
C21 Alex Sandusky	1.50	3.00
C22 Jim Welch	1.50	3.00
C23 Tony Lorick	1.50	3.00
C24 Billy Ray Smith	2.00	4.00
C25 Fred Miller	1.50	3.00
C26 Tom Matte	3.00	6.00
C27 Johnny Unitas	10.00	20.00
C28 Glenn Ressler	1.50	3.00
C29 Alex Hawkins	2.00	4.00
C30 Jim Parker	4.00	8.00
C31 Guy Reese	1.50	3.00
C32 Bob Vogel	1.50	3.00
C33 Jerry Hill	1.50	3.00
C34 Raymond Berry	6.00	12.00
C35 George Preas	1.50	3.00
C36 Team Logo	1.50	3.00
NNO Colts Saver Sheet	15.00	30.00

1965 Coke Caps Cowboys

Please see the 1965 Coke Caps Bears listing for information on this set.

COMPLETE SET (36)	100.00	175.00
C1 Mike Connelly	2.50	5.00
C2 Tony Liscio	2.50	5.00
C3 Maury Youmans	2.50	5.00
C4 Larry Stephens	2.50	5.00
C5 Jim Colvin	2.50	5.00
C6 Malcolm Walker	2.50	5.00
C7 Danny Villanueva	2.50	5.00
C8 Frank Clarke	3.00	6.00
C9 Don Meredith	10.00	20.00
C10 George Andrie	2.50	5.00
C11 Mel Renfro	5.00	10.00
C12 Pettis Norman	2.50	5.00
C13 Buddy Dial	3.00	6.00
C14 Lee Folkins	2.50	5.00
C15 Jerry Rhome	2.50	5.00
C16 Bob Hayes	7.50	15.00
C17 Mike Gaechter	2.50	5.00
C18 Joe Bob Isbell	2.50	5.00
C19 Harold Hays	2.50	5.00
C20 Craig Morton	4.00	8.00
C21 Jake Kupp	2.50	5.00
C22 Cornell Green	2.50	5.00
C23 Perry Lee Dunn	2.50	5.00
C24 Don Talbert	2.50	5.00
C25 Dave Manders	2.50	5.00
C26 Warren Livingston	2.50	5.00
C27 Bob Lilly	7.50	15.00
C28 Chuck Howley	4.00	8.00
C29 Don Bishop	2.50	5.00
C30 Don Perkins	3.00	6.00
C31 Jim Boeke	2.50	5.00
C32 Dave Edwards	2.50	5.00
C33 Lee Roy Jordan	3.00	6.00
C34 Jerry Tubbs	2.50	5.00
C35 Amos Marsh	2.50	5.00
C36 Team Logo	2.00	4.00

1965 Coke Caps Eagles

Please see the 1965 Coke Caps Bears listing for information on this set.

COMPLETE SET (36)	80.00	120.00
C1 Norm Snead	2.50	5.00
C2 Al Nelson	1.50	3.00
C3 Jim Skaggs	1.50	3.00
C4 Glenn Glass	1.50	3.00
C5 Pete Retzlaff	2.00	4.00
C6 Bill Mack	1.50	3.00
C7 Ray Rissmiller	1.50	3.00
C8 Lynn Hoyem	1.50	3.00
C9 King Hill	2.00	4.00
C10 Timmy Brown	2.50	5.00
C11 Ollie Matson	5.00	10.00
C12 Dave Lloyd	2.00	4.00
C13 Jim Ringo	3.50	7.00
C14 Floyd Peters	2.00	4.00
C15 Riley Gunnels	1.50	3.00
C16 Claude Crabb	1.50	3.00
C17 Earl Gros	2.00	4.00
C18 Fred Hill	1.50	3.00
C19 Don Hultz	1.50	3.00
C20 Ray Poage	1.50	3.00
C21 Irv Cross	2.50	5.00
C22 Mike Morgan	1.50	3.00
C23 Maxie Baughan	2.00	4.00
C24 Ed Blaine	1.50	3.00
C25 Jack Concannon	2.00	4.00
C26 Sam Baker	1.50	3.00
C27 Tom Woodeshick	2.00	4.00
C28 Joe Scarpati	1.50	3.00
C29 John Meyers	1.50	3.00
C30 Nate Ramsey	1.50	3.00
C31 George Tarasovic	1.50	3.00
C32 Bob Brown T	2.50	5.00
C33 Ralph Smith	1.50	3.00
C34 Ron Goodwin	1.50	3.00
C35 Dave Graham	1.50	3.00
C36 Team Logo	1.50	3.00
NNO Eagles Saver Sheet	15.00	30.00

1965 Coke Caps Giants C

Please see the 1965 Coke Caps Bears listing for information on this set.

COMPLETE SET (36)	75.00	125.00
C1 Ernie Koy	2.50	4.00
C2 Chuck Mercein	2.50	4.00
C3 Bob Timberlake	1.75	3.00
C4 Jim Katcavage	2.50	4.00
C5 Mickey Walker	1.75	3.00
C6 Roger Anderson	1.75	3.00
C7 Jerry Hillebrand	1.75	3.00
C8 Tucker Frederickson	2.50	4.00
C9 Jim Moran	1.75	3.00
C10 Bill Winter	1.75	3.00
C11 Aaron Thomas	2.50	4.00
C12 Clarence Childs	1.75	3.00
C13 Jim Patton	2.50	4.00
C14 Joe Morrison	2.50	4.00
C15 Homer Jones	2.50	4.00
C16 Dick Lynch	2.50	4.00
C17 John Lovetere	1.75	3.00
C18 Greg Larson	2.50	4.00
C19 Lou Slaby	1.75	3.00
C20 Tom Costello	1.75	3.00
C21 Darrell Dess	1.75	3.00
C22 Frank Lasky	1.75	3.00
C23 Dick Pesonen	1.75	3.00
C24 Tom Scott	1.75	3.00
C25 Erich Barnes	2.50	4.00
C26 Roosevelt Brown	3.50	6.00
C27 Del Shofner	2.50	4.00
C28 Dick James	1.75	3.00
C29 Andy Stynchula	1.75	3.00
C30 Tony Dimidio	1.75	3.00
C31 Steve Thurlow	1.75	3.00
C32 Ernie Wheelwright	1.75	3.00
C33 Bookie Bolin	1.75	3.00
C34 Gary Wood	2.50	4.00
C35 John Contoulis	1.75	3.00
C36 Team Logo	1.75	3.00

1965 Coke Caps Giants G

Please see the 1965 Coke Caps Bears listing for information on this set.

COMPLETE SET (35)	75.00	150.00
G1 Joe Morrison	2.00	4.00
G2 Dick Lynch	2.00	4.00
G3 Andy Stynchula	1.50	3.00
G4 Clarence Childs	1.50	3.00
G5 Aaron Thomas	2.00	4.00
G6 Mickey Walker	1.50	3.00

G7 Bill Winter	1.50	3.00
G8 Bookie Bolin	1.50	3.00
G9 Tom Scott	1.50	3.00
G10 John Lovetere	1.50	3.00
G11 Jim Patton	2.00	4.00
G12 Darrell Dess	1.50	3.00
G13 Dick James	1.50	3.00
G14 Jerry Hillebrand	1.50	3.00
G15 Dick Pesonen	1.50	3.00
G16 Del Shofner	2.00	4.00
G17 Erich Barnes	2.00	4.00
G18 Roosevelt Brown	3.00	6.00
G19 Greg Larson	2.00	4.00
G20 Jim Katcavage	2.00	4.00
G21 Frank Lasky	1.50	3.00
G22 Lou Slaby	1.50	3.00
G23 Jim Moran	1.50	3.00
G24 Roger Anderson	1.50	3.00
G25 Steve Thurlow	1.50	3.00
G26 Ernie Wheelwright	1.50	3.00
G27 Gary Wood	2.00	4.00
G28 Tony Dimidio	1.50	3.00
G29 John Contoulis	1.50	3.00
G30 Tucker Frederickson	2.00	4.00
G31 Bob Timberlake	1.50	3.00
G32 Chuck Mercein	2.00	4.00
G33 Ernie Koy	2.00	4.00
G34 Tom Costello	1.50	3.00
G35 Homer Jones	2.00	4.00
NNO Giants Saver Sheet	15.00	30.00

1965 Coke Caps Jets

Please see the 1965 Coke Caps Bills listing for information on this set.

COMPLETE SET (35)	125.00	200.00
J1 Don Maynard	6.00	12.00
J2 George Sauer Jr.	3.00	6.00
J3 Cosmo Iacavazzi	2.00	4.00
J4 Jim O'Mahoney	2.00	4.00
J5 Matt Snell	3.00	6.00
J6 Clyde Washington	2.00	4.00
J7 Jim Turner	2.50	5.00
J8 Mike Taliaferro	2.00	4.00
J9 Marshall Starks	2.00	4.00
J10 Mark Smolinski	2.00	4.00
J11 Bob Schweickert	2.00	4.00
J12 Paul Rochester	2.00	4.00
J13 Sherman Plunkett	2.50	5.00
J14 Gerry Philbin	2.50	5.00
J15 Pete Perreault	2.00	4.00
J16 Dainard Paulson	2.00	4.00
J17 Joe Namath	30.00	50.00
J18 Winston Hill	2.50	5.00
J19 Dee Mackey	2.00	4.00
J20 Curley Johnson	2.00	4.00
J21 Mike Hudock	2.00	4.00
J22 John Huarte	3.00	6.00
J23 Gordy Holz	2.00	4.00
J24 Gene Heeter	2.50	5.00
J25 Larry Grantham	2.50	5.00
J26 Dan Ficca	2.00	4.00
J27 Sam DeLuca	2.50	5.00
J28 Bill Baird	2.00	4.00
J29 Ralph Baker	2.00	4.00
J30 Wahoo McDaniel	6.00	12.00
J31 Jim Evans	2.00	4.00
J32 Dave Herman	2.50	5.00
J33 John Schmitt	2.00	4.00
J34 Jim Harris	2.00	4.00
J35 Bake Turner	2.50	5.00
NNO Jets Saver Sheet	15.00	30.00

1965 Coke Caps Lions

Please see the 1965 Coke Caps Bears listing for information on this set.

COMPLETE SET (36)	75.00	150.00
C1 Pat Studstill	2.00	4.00
C2 Bob Whitlow	1.50	3.00
C3 Wayne Walker	2.00	4.00
C4 Tom Watkins	1.50	3.00
C5 Jim Simon	1.50	3.00
C6 Sam Williams	1.50	3.00
C7 Terry Barr	1.50	3.00
C8 Jerry Rush	1.50	3.00
C9 Roger Brown	2.00	4.00
C10 Tom Nowatzke	2.00	4.00
C11 Dick Lane	4.00	8.00
C12 Dick Compton	1.50	3.00
C13 Yale Lary	4.00	8.00
C14 Dick Lebeau	2.00	4.00
C15 Dan Lewis	2.00	4.00
C16 Wally Hilgenberg	2.00	4.00
C17 Bruce Maher	1.50	3.00
C18 Darris McCord	1.50	3.00
C19 Hugh McInnis	1.50	3.00
C20 Ernie Clark	1.50	3.00
C21 Gail Cogdill	2.00	4.00
C22 Wayne Rasmussen	1.50	3.00
C23 Joe Don Looney	5.00	10.00
C24 Jim Gibbons	2.00	4.00
C25 John Gonzaga	1.50	3.00
C26 John Gordy	1.50	3.00
C27 Bobby Thompson DB	1.50	3.00
C28 J.D. Smith	2.00	4.00
C29 Earl Morrall	2.50	5.00
C30 Alex Karras	5.00	10.00
C31 Nick Pietrosante	2.00	4.00
C32 Milt Plum	2.00	4.00
C33 Daryl Sanders	1.50	3.00
C34 Joe Schmidt	5.00	10.00
C35 Bob Scholtz	1.50	3.00
C36 Team Logo	1.50	3.00
NNO Lions Saver Sheet	15.00	30.00

1965 Coke Caps National NFL

This set of 70 Coke caps was issued on bottled soft drinks primarily in cities without an NFL team. The caps were issued along with their own Saver Sheet. Each measures approximately 1 1/8" in diameter and has the drink logo and a football on the outside, while the inside has the player's face printed in black or red, with NFL ALL STARS above the player image. The 1965 caps are very similar to the 1966 issue and many of the players are the same in both years. However, the 1965 caps do not have the words "Caramel Colored" on the outside of the cap as do the 1966 caps. An "NFL ALL STARS" title appears above the player's photo so some caps were issued with this set and the NFL All-Stars set. The consumer could turn in his completed saver sheet to receive various prizes. These caps were also produced for 1965 on other Coca-Cola products: TAB, Fanta and Sprite. The other drink caps typically carry a slight premium (1.5-2 times) over the value of the Coke version.

COMPLETE SET (70)	112.50	225.00
C1 Herb Adderley	2.50	5.00
C2 Yale Lary	2.50	5.00
C3 Dick LeBeau	1.50	3.00
C4 Bill Brown	2.00	4.00
C5 Jim Taylor	3.75	7.50
C6 Joe Fortunato	1.50	3.00
C7 Bob Boyd DB	1.50	3.00
C8 Terry Barr	1.50	3.00
C9 Dick Szymanski	1.50	3.00
C10 Mick Tingelhoff	2.00	4.00
C11 Wayne Walker	1.50	3.00
C12 Matt Hazeltine	1.50	3.00
C13 Ray Nitschke	3.75	7.50
C14 Grady Alderman	1.50	3.00
C15 Charlie Krueger	1.50	3.00
C16 Tommy Mason	1.50	3.00
C17 Willie Wood	2.50	5.00
C18 John Unitas	6.00	12.00
C19 Lenny Moore	3.00	6.00
C20 Fran Tarkenton	5.00	10.00
C21 Deacon Jones	3.00	6.00
C22 Bob Vogel	1.50	3.00
C23 John Gordy	1.50	3.00
C24 Jim Parker	2.50	5.00
C25 Jim Gibbons	1.50	3.00
C26 Merlin Olsen	3.00	6.00
C27 Forrest Gregg	2.50	5.00
C28 Roger Brown	1.50	3.00
C29 Dave Parks	1.50	3.00
C30 Raymond Berry	3.00	6.00
C31 Mike Ditka	6.00	12.00
C32 Gino Marchetti	3.00	6.00
C33 Willie Davis	3.00	6.00
C34 Ed Meador	1.50	3.00
C35 Browns Logo	1.50	3.00
C36 Colts Logo	1.50	3.00
C37 Sam Baker	1.50	3.00
C38 Irv Cross	2.00	4.00
C39 Maxie Baughan	1.50	3.00
C40 Vince Promuto	1.50	3.00
C41 Paul Krause	1.50	3.00
C42 Charley Taylor	3.00	6.00
C43 John Paluck	1.50	3.00
C44 Paul Warfield	5.00	10.00
C45 Dick Modzelewski	1.50	3.00
C46 Myron Pottios	1.50	3.00
C47 Erich Barnes	1.50	3.00
C48 Bill Koman	1.50	3.00
C49 John Thomas	1.50	3.00
C50 Gary Ballman	1.50	3.00
C51 Sam Huff	3.00	6.00
C52 Ken Gray	1.50	3.00
C53 Roosevelt Brown	2.50	5.00
C54 Bobby Joe Conrad	1.50	3.00
C55 Pat Fischer	1.50	3.00
C56 Irv Goode	1.50	3.00
C57 Floyd Peters	1.50	3.00
C58 Charley Johnson	2.00	4.00
C59 John Henry Johnson	3.00	6.00
C60 Charles Bradshaw	1.50	3.00
C61 Jim Ringo	2.50	5.00
C62 Pete Retzlaff	2.00	4.00
C63 Sonny Jurgensen	3.50	7.00
C64 Don Meredith	6.00	12.00
C65 Bob Lilly	5.00	10.00
C66 Bill Glass	1.50	3.00
C67 Dick Schafrath	1.50	3.00
C68 Mel Renfro	3.00	6.00
C69 Jim Houston	1.50	3.00
C70 Frank Ryan	2.00	4.00
NNO NFL Saver Sheet	15.00	30.00

1965 Coke Caps Packers

Please see the 1965 Coke Caps Bears listing for information on this set.

COMPLETE SET (36)	125.00	200.00
C1 Herb Adderley	4.00	8.00
C2 Lionel Aldridge	3.00	5.00
C3 Hank Gremminger	2.50	4.00
C4 Willie Davis	4.00	8.00
C5 Boyd Dowler	3.00	5.00
C6 Marv Fleming	3.00	5.00
C7 Ken Bowman	3.00	5.00
C8 Tom Brown	2.50	4.00
C9 Doug Hart	2.50	4.00
C10 Steve Wright	2.50	4.00
C11 Dennis Claridge	2.50	4.00
C12 Dave Hanner	3.00	5.00
C13 Tommy Crutcher	2.50	4.00
C14 Fred Thurston	4.00	8.00
C15 Elijah Pitts	3.00	5.00
C16 Lloyd Voss	2.50	4.00
C17 Lee Roy Caffey	2.50	4.00
C18 Dave Robinson	3.50	6.00
C19 Bart Starr	10.00	20.00
C20 Ray Nitschke	6.00	12.00
C21 Max McGee	3.00	5.00
C22 Don Chandler	3.00	5.00
C23 Norman Masters	2.50	4.00
C24 Ron Kostelnik	2.50	4.00
C25 Carroll Dale	3.00	5.00
C26 Hank Jordan	4.00	8.00
C27 Bob Jeter	3.00	5.00
C28 Bob Skoronski	2.50	4.00
C29 Jerry Kramer	3.50	6.00
C30 Willie Wood	4.00	8.00
C31 Paul Hornung	7.50	15.00
C32 Forrest Gregg	4.00	8.00
C33 Zeke Bratkowski	3.00	5.00
C34 Tom Moore	3.00	5.00
C35 Jim Taylor	6.00	12.00
C36 Team Logo	2.50	4.00
NNO Packers Saver Sheet	15.00	30.00

1965 Coke Caps Patriots

Please see the 1965 Coke Caps Bills listing for information on this set.

COMPLETE SET (36)	75.00	135.00
C1 Jon Morris	2.50	4.00
C2 Don Webb	2.50	4.00
C3 Charles Long	2.50	4.00
C4 Tony Romeo	2.50	4.00
C5 Bob Dee	2.50	4.00
C6 Tommy Addison	3.00	5.00
C7 Bob Yates	2.50	4.00
C8 Ron Hall	2.50	4.00
C9 Billy Neighbors	2.50	4.00
C10 Jack Rudolph	2.50	4.00
C11 Don Oakes	2.50	4.00
C12 Tom Yewcic	2.50	4.00
C13 Ron Burton	3.00	5.00
C14 Jim Colclough	2.50	4.00
C15 Larry Garron	2.50	4.00
C16 Dave Watson	2.50	4.00
C17 Art Graham	3.00	5.00
C18 Babe Parilli	3.00	6.00
C19 Jim Hunt	2.50	4.00
C20 Don McKinnon	2.50	4.00
C21 Houston Antwine	2.50	4.00
C22 Nick Buoniconti	5.00	10.00
C23 Ross O'Hanley	2.50	4.00
C24 Gino Cappelletti	3.00	6.00
C25 Chuck Shonta	2.50	4.00
C26 Dick Felt	2.50	4.00
C27 Mike Dukes	2.50	4.00
C28 Larry Eisenhauer	2.50	4.00
C29 Bob Schmidt	2.50	4.00
C30 Len St. Jean	2.50	4.00
C31 J.D. Garrett	2.50	4.00
C32 Jim Whalen	2.50	4.00
C33 Jim Nance	3.00	6.00
C34 Eddie Wilson	2.50	4.00
C35 Lonnie Farmer	2.50	4.00
C36 Boston Patriots Logo	2.50	4.00
NNO Patriots Saver Sheet	15.00	30.00

1965 Coke Caps Raiders

Please see the 1965 Coke Caps Bills listing for information on this set.

COMPLETE SET (36)	100.00	175.00
C1 Fred Biletnikoff	6.00	12.00
C2 Gus Otto	2.50	5.00
C3 Harry Schuh	2.50	5.00
C4 Ken Herock	2.50	5.00
C5 Claude Gibson	2.50	5.00
C6 Cotton Davidson	2.50	5.00
C7 Rich Zecher	2.50	5.00
C8 Ben Davidson	3.00	6.00
C9 Frank Youso	2.50	5.00
C10 Bob Svihus	2.50	5.00
C11 John R. Williamson	2.50	5.00
C12 Dave Grayson	2.50	5.00
C13 Archie Matsos	2.50	5.00
C14 Dave Costa	2.50	5.00
C15 Bo Roberson	2.50	5.00
C16 Alan Miller	2.50	5.00
C17 Billy Cannon	4.00	8.00
C18 Wayne Hawkins	3.00	6.00
C19 Warren Powers	2.50	5.00
C20 Clancy Osborne	2.50	5.00
C21 Dan Conners	2.50	5.00
C22 Jim Otto	5.00	10.00
C23 Clem Daniels	3.00	6.00
C24 Tom Flores	4.00	8.00
C25 Art Powell	3.00	6.00
C26 Rex Mirich	2.50	5.00
C27 Dick Klein	2.50	5.00
C28 Dan Birdwell	2.50	5.00
C29 Dalva Allen	2.50	5.00
C30 Mike Mercer	2.50	5.00
C31 Ken Rice	2.50	5.00
C32 Bill Budness	2.50	5.00
C33 Tommy Morrow	2.50	5.00
C34 Joe Krakoski	2.50	5.00
C35 Bob Mischak	2.50	5.00
C36 Team Logo	2.50	5.00

1965 Coke Caps Rams

Please see the 1965 Coke Caps Bears listing for information on this set.

COMPLETE SET (36)	75.00	125.00
C1 Jerry Richardson	2.50	4.00
C2 Bobby Smith	1.50	3.00
C3 Bill Munson	2.50	4.00
C4 Frank Varrichione	1.50	3.00
C5 Joe Carollo	1.50	3.00
C6 Dick Bass	2.50	4.00
C7 Ken Iman	1.50	3.00
C8 Charlie Cowan	1.50	3.00
C9 Terry Baker	3.00	5.00
C10 Don Chuy	1.50	3.00
C11 Cliff Livingston	1.50	3.00
C12 Lamar Lundy	2.50	4.00
C13 Duane Allen	1.50	3.00
C14 Roman Gabriel	3.00	6.00
C15 Roosevelt Grier	3.00	6.00
C16 Mike Henry	1.50	3.00
C17 Merlin Olsen	5.00	10.00
C18 Deacon Jones	5.00	10.00
C19 Joe Scibelli	1.50	3.00
C20 Marlin McKeever	1.50	3.00
C21 Fred Brown	1.50	3.00
C22 Frank Budka	1.50	3.00
C23 Dan Currie	1.50	3.00
C24 Roger Davis	1.50	3.00
C25 Bruce Gossett	2.50	4.00
C26 Les Josephson	2.50	4.00
C27 Ed Meador	1.50	3.00
C28 Joe Krupa	1.50	3.00
C29 Aaron Martin	1.50	3.00
C30 Tommy McDonald	3.00	5.00
C31 Bucky Pope	1.50	3.00
C32 Jack Snow	2.50	4.00
C33 Joe Wendryhoski	1.50	3.00
C34 Clancy Williams	1.50	3.00
C35 Ben Wilson	1.50	3.00
C36 Team Logo	1.50	3.00

1965 Coke Caps Redskins

Please see the 1965 Coke Caps Bears listing for information on this set.

COMPLETE SET (36)	62.50	125.00
C1 Jimmy Carr	1.50	3.00
C2 Fred Mazurek	1.50	3.00
C3 Lonnie Sanders	1.50	3.00
C4 Jim Steffen	1.50	3.00
C5 John Nisby	1.50	3.00
C6 George Izo	2.50	4.00
C7 Vince Promuto	1.50	3.00
C8 Johnny Sample	2.50	4.00
C9 Pat Richter	2.50	4.00
C10 Preston Carpenter	1.50	3.00
C11 Sam Huff	5.00	10.00
C12 Pervis Atkins	1.50	3.00
C13 Steve Barnett	1.50	3.00
C14 Len Hauss	2.50	4.00
C15 Bill Anderson	1.50	3.00
C16 John Reger	1.50	3.00
C17 George Seals	1.50	3.00
C18 J.W. Lockett	1.50	3.00
C19 Tom Walters	1.50	3.00
C20 Joe Rutgens	1.50	3.00
C21 John Paluck	1.50	3.00
C22 Fran O'Brien	1.50	3.00
C23 Willie Adams	1.50	3.00
C24 Rod Breedlove	1.50	3.00
C25 Bob Pellegrini	1.50	3.00
C26 Bob Jencks	1.50	3.00
C27 Joe Hernandez	1.50	3.00
C28 Sonny Jurgensen	5.00	10.00
C29 Bob Toneff	1.50	3.00
C30 Charley Taylor	5.00	10.00
C31 Dick Shiner	1.50	3.00
C32 Bobby Williams	1.50	3.00
C33 Angelo Coia	1.50	3.00
C34 Ron Snidow	1.50	3.00
C35 Paul Krause	3.00	6.00
C36 Team Logo	1.50	3.00
NNO Redskins Saver Sheet	15.00	30.00

1965 Coke Caps Southern Pros

This set of Coke caps was created for and, apparently, only issued in the south as part of the Go with the Pros promotion. The player selection focused on athletes playing in the south or those who had college careers in the south. Most of the players appear in the various team sets as well but carry a different cap number in this set. The caps measure approximately 1 1/8" in diameter and have the drink logo and a football on the outside, while the inside has the player's face printed in black, with his team name above the photo, the player's name below, his position to the right and the cap number to the left including a "C" prefix. The 1965 caps are very similar to the 1966 issue but the 1965 caps do not have the words "Caramel Colored" on the outside of the cap. Football caps were also produced for 1965 on other Coca-Cola products: TAB (Low-Calorie Beverage), Fanta, King Size Coke and Sprite. The other drink caps typically carry a slight premium over the value of the basic Coke version.

C1 Bart Starr	12.50	25.00
C2 Roman Gabriel	4.00	8.00
C3 Tommy Mason	3.00	6.00
C4 Jim Patton	2.50	5.00
C5 Maxie Baughan	2.50	5.00
C6 Johnny Unitas	12.50	25.00
C7 Richie Petitbon	3.00	6.00
C8 Johnny Brewer	2.50	5.00
C9 Lee Roy Jordan	3.00	6.00
C10 John Gordy	2.50	5.00
C11 Theron Sapp	2.50	5.00
C12 Joe Childress	2.50	5.00
C13 Tommy Davis	2.50	5.00
C14 Sam Huff	4.00	8.00
C15 Clendon Thomas	2.50	5.00
C16 Jerry Stovall	2.50	5.00
C17 George Mira	2.50	5.00
C18 Sonny Jurgensen	6.00	12.00
C19 Jim Taylor	7.50	15.00
C20 Deacon Jones	4.00	8.00
C21 Fran Tarkenton	6.00	12.00
C22 Bookie Bolin	2.50	5.00
C23 Earl Gros	2.50	5.00
C24 Raymond Berry	6.00	12.00
C25 Bill Wade	3.00	6.00
C26 Ernie Green	2.50	5.00
C27 Bob Lilly	6.00	12.00
C28 Yale Lary	4.00	8.00
C29 Jimmy Orr	3.00	6.00
C30 Larry Morris	2.50	5.00
C31 Gene Hickerson	4.00	8.00
C32 Don Meredith	10.00	20.00
C33 Darris McCord	2.50	5.00
C34 Willie Davis	5.00	10.00
C35 Ed Meador	2.50	5.00
C36 Rip Hawkins	2.50	5.00
C37 Clarence Childs	2.50	5.00
C38 Norm Snead	4.00	8.00
C39 Charley Bradshaw	2.50	5.00
C40 Bill Koman	2.50	5.00
C41 J.D. Smith	3.00	6.00
C42 Preston Carpenter	2.50	5.00
C43 Buzz Nutter	2.50	5.00
C44 Sonny Randle	2.50	5.00
C45 John David Crow	3.00	6.00
C46 Tom Tracy	3.00	6.00
C47 Lou Michaels	3.00	6.00
C48 Joe Fortunato	2.50	5.00
C49 Bernie Parrish	2.50	5.00
C50 Harold Hays	2.50	5.00
C51 Pat Studstill	3.00	6.00
C52 Tom Moore	3.00	6.00
C53 Bucky Pope	2.50	5.00
C54 Jim Phillips	2.50	5.00
C55 Darrell Dess	2.50	5.00
C56 Riley Gunnels	2.50	5.00
C57 Don Chandler	2.50	5.00
C58 Tommy McDonald	4.00	8.00
C59 Bobby Walden	2.50	5.00
C60 Frank Lasky	2.50	5.00
C61 Tom Woodeshick	2.50	5.00
C62 Fred Miller	2.50	5.00
C63 Bobby Joe Green	2.50	5.00
C64 Frank Ryan	3.00	6.00
C65 Bob Hayes	7.50	15.00
C66 Hugh McInnis	2.50	5.00
C67 Ben McGee	2.50	5.00
C68 Bobby Joe Conrad	2.50	5.00
C69 Charlie Krueger	2.50	5.00
C70 Rick Casares	3.00	6.00

1965 Coke Caps Steelers

Please see the 1965 Coke Caps Bears listing for information on this set.

COMPLETE SET (36)	75.00	150.00
C1 John Baker	2.00	5.00
C2 Ed Brown	2.00	5.00
C3 Jim Kelly	2.00	5.00
C4 Willie Daniel	2.00	5.00
C5 Bob Harrison	2.00	5.00
C6 Dick Haley	2.00	5.00
C7 Dan James	2.00	5.00
C8 Gary Ballman	2.00	5.00
C9 Brady Keys	2.00	5.00
C10 Charlie Bradshaw	2.00	5.00
C11 Jim Bradshaw	2.00	5.00
C12 Bill Saul	2.00	5.00
C13 Paul Martha	2.00	5.00
C14 Mike Clark	2.00	5.00
C15 Ray Lemek	2.00	5.00
C16 Clarence Peaks	2.00	5.00
C17 Theron Sapp	2.00	5.00
C18 Ray Mansfield	2.00	5.00
C19 Chuck Hinton	2.00	5.00
C20 Bill Nelsen	2.50	6.00
C21 Dan LaRose	2.00	5.00
C22 Buzz Nutter	2.00	5.00
C23 Ben McGee	2.00	5.00
C24 Myron Pottios	2.00	5.00
C25 Max Messner	2.00	5.00
C26 Andy Russell	2.50	6.00
C27 Mike Sandusky	2.00	5.00
C28 Bob Schmitz	2.00	5.00
C29 Ron Stehouwer	2.00	5.00
C30 Clendon Thomas	2.00	5.00
C31 Tommy Wade	2.00	5.00
C32 Dick Hoak	2.00	5.00
C33 Marv Woodson	2.00	5.00
C34 John Burrell	2.00	5.00
C35 John Henry Johnson	4.00	8.00
C36 Team Logo	2.00	5.00

1965 Coke Caps Vikings

Please see the 1965 Coke Caps Bears listing for information on this set.

COMPLETE SET (36)	90.00	150.00
C1 Jerry Reichow	1.25	3.00
C2 Jim Prestel	1.25	3.00
C3 Jim Marshall	3.00	6.00
C4 Errol Linden	1.25	3.00
C5 Bob Lacey	1.25	3.00
C6 Rip Hawkins	1.25	3.00
C7 John Kirby	1.25	3.00
C8 Roy Winston	1.50	4.00
C9 Ron Vanderkelen	1.25	3.00
C10 Gordon Smith	1.25	3.00
C11 Larry Bowie	1.25	3.00
C12 Paul Flatley	1.50	4.00
C13 Grady Alderman	1.50	4.00
C14 Mick Tingelhoff	2.00	5.00
C15 Lee Calland	1.25	3.00
C16 Fred Cox	1.50	4.00
C17 Bill Brown	1.50	4.00
C18 Ed Sharockman	1.25	3.00
C19 George Rose	1.25	3.00
C20 Paul Dickson	1.25	3.00
C21 Tommy Mason	1.50	4.00
C22 Carl Eller	2.00	5.00
C23 Bill Jobko	1.25	3.00
C24 Hal Bedsole	1.25	3.00
C25 Karl Kassulke	1.25	3.00
C26 Fran Tarkenton	7.50	15.00
C27 Tom Hall	1.25	3.00
C28 Archie Sutton	1.25	3.00
C29 Jim Phillips	1.25	3.00
C30 Bill Swain	1.25	3.00
C31 Larry Vargo	1.25	3.00
C32 Bobby Walden	1.25	3.00
C33 Bob Berry	1.50	4.00
C34 Jeff Jordan	1.25	3.00
C35 Lance Rentzel	1.50	4.00
C36 Vikings Logo	1.25	3.00
NNO Vikings Saver Sheet	15.00	30.00

1966 Coke Caps All-Stars AFL

The AFL All-Star caps were issued in AFL cities (and a few other cities as well) along with the local team caps as part of the Score with the Pros promotion. The local team cap saver sheets had separate sections in which to affix both the local team's caps and the All-Stars' caps. The caps measure approximately 1 1/8" in diameter and have the drink logo and a football on the outside, while the inside has the player's face printed in black, with the words "AFL ALL STAR" above the player photo and his name below. The consumer could turn in his completed saver sheet to receive various prizes. The caps are numbered with a "C" prefix. These caps were also produced for 1966 on other Coca-Cola products: Tab, Fanta, Fresca and Sprite. The other drink caps typically carry a slight premium over the value of the basic Coke version.

COMPLETE SET (34)	90.00	150.00
C37 Babe Parilli	1.50	3.00
C38 Mike Stratton	1.00	2.00
C39 Jack Kemp	12.50	25.00
C40 Len Dawson	3.75	7.50
C41 Fred Arbanas	1.00	2.00
C42 Bobby Bell	2.50	5.00
C43 Willie Brown	2.50	5.00
C44 Buck Buchanan	2.50	5.00
C45 Frank Buncom	1.00	2.00
C46 Nick Buoniconti	2.00	4.00
C47 Gino Cappelletti	1.50	3.00
C48 Eldon Danenhauer	1.00	2.00
C49 Clem Daniels	1.50	3.00
C50 Les Speedy Duncan	1.50	3.00
C51 Willie Frazier	1.00	2.00
C52 Cookie Gilchrist	1.50	3.00
C53 Dave Grayson	1.00	2.00
C54 John Hadl	2.00	4.00
C55 Wayne Hawkins	1.00	2.00
C56 Sherrill Headrick	1.00	2.00
C57 Charlie Hennigan	1.50	3.00
C58 E.J. Holub	1.00	2.00
C59 Curley Johnson	1.00	2.00
C60 Keith Lincoln	1.50	3.00
C61 Paul Lowe	1.50	3.00
C62 Don Maynard	3.00	6.00
C63 Jon Morris	1.00	2.00
C64 Joe Namath	15.00	30.00
C65 Jim Otto	2.50	5.00
C66 Dainard Paulson	1.00	2.00
C67 Art Powell	1.50	3.00
C68 Walt Sweeney	1.50	3.00
C69 Bob Talamini	1.00	2.00
C70 Lance Alworth UER (Name misspelled Alsworth)	3.75	7.50

1966 Coke Caps All-Stars NFL

These NFL All-Star caps were issued in NFL cities (and a few other cities as well) along with the local team caps as part of the Score with the Pros promotion. The local team cap saver sheets had separate sections in which to affix both the local team's caps and the All-Stars' caps. The caps measure approximately 1 1/8" in diameter and have the drink logo and a football on the outside, while the inside has the player's face printed in black, with the words "NFL ALL STAR" above the player photo and his name below. The consumer could turn in his completed saver sheet to receive various prizes. The caps are numbered with a "C" prefix. These caps were also produced for 1966 on other Coca-Cola products: Tab, Fanta, Fresca and Sprite. The other drink caps typically carry a slight premium over the value of the basic Coke version.

COMPLETE SET (34)	50.00	100.00
C37 Frank Ryan	1.00	2.50
C38 Timmy Brown	1.00	2.50
C39 Tucker Frederickson	.75	2.00
C40 Cornell Green	1.00	2.50
C41 Bob Hayes	1.50	4.00
C42 Charley Taylor	1.25	3.00
C43 Pete Retzlaff	1.00	2.50
C44 Jim Ringo	1.25	3.00
C45 John Wooten	.75	2.00
C46 Dale Meinert	.75	2.00
C47 Bob Lilly	2.00	5.00
C48 Sam Silas	.75	2.00
C49 Roosevelt Brown	1.25	3.00
C50 Gary Ballman	.75	2.00
C51 Gary Collins	.75	2.00
C52 Sonny Randle	.75	2.00
C53 Charley Johnson UER (spelled Charley)	1.00	2.50
C54 Herb Adderley	1.25	3.00
C55 Doug Atkins	1.25	3.00
C56 Roger Brown	.75	2.00
C57 Dick Butkus	4.00	10.00
C58 Willie Davis	1.25	3.00
C59 Tommy McDonald	1.00	2.50
C60 Alex Karras	1.50	4.00
C61 John Mackey	1.25	3.00
C62 Ed Meador	.75	2.00
C63 Merlin Olsen	1.50	4.00
C64 Dave Parks	.75	2.00
C65 Gale Sayers	4.00	10.00
C66 Fran Tarkenton	2.50	6.00
C67 Mick Tingelhoff	.75	2.00
C68 Ken Willard	.75	2.00
C69 Willie Wood	1.25	3.00
C70 Bill Brown	1.00	2.50

1966 Coke Caps Bears

Coca-Cola issued its final run of football caps in 1966. Each NFL team had a set released in their area along with the NFL All-Stars caps as part of the "Score with the Pros" promotion. Each team's Saver Sheets had separate sections in which to affix both the local team's caps and the All-Stars' caps. The caps measure approximately 1 1/8" in diameter and have the drink logo and a football on the outside, while the inside has the player's face printed in black with the team name above the photo, the player's name below, his position to the right and the cap number to the left. Some teams are also known to exist in a version that features a slightly smaller player photo. Cap numbers included a "C" prefix on all NFL teams except the Giants which had two versions with either "C" or "G" prefixes. The consumer could turn in his completed saver sheet to receive various prizes. The 1966 caps are very similar to the 1965 issue and many of the players are the same in both years. However, the 1966 caps have the words "Caramel Colored" on the outside of the cap while the 1965 caps do not. Most caps were also produced for 1966 on other Coca-Cola products: Tab (Dietary Beverage), Fanta, Fresca, King Size Coke and Sprite. These other drink caps typically carry a slight premium over the value of the Coke version.

COMPLETE SET (36)	75.00	135.00
C1 Bennie McRae	1.25	2.50
C2 Johnny Morris	1.25	2.50
C3 Roosevelt Taylor	2.00	4.00
C4 Doug Buffone	1.25	2.50
C5 Ed O'Bradovich	1.25	2.50
C6 Richie Petitbon	2.00	4.00
C7 Mike Pyle	1.25	2.50
C8 Dave Whitsell	1.25	2.50
C9 Dick Gordon	1.25	2.50
C10 John Johnson DT	1.25	2.50
C11 Jim Jones	1.25	2.50
C12 Andy Livingston	1.25	2.50
C13 Bob Kilcullen	1.25	2.50
C14 Roger LeClerc	1.25	2.50
C15 Herman Lee	1.25	2.50
C16 Earl Leggett	1.25	2.50
C17 Joe Marconi	1.25	2.50
C18 Rudy Bukich	2.00	4.00
C19 Mike Reilly	1.25	2.50
C20 Mike Ditka	5.00	10.00
C21 Dick Evey	1.25	2.50
C22 Joe Fortunato	1.25	2.50
C23 Bill Wade	3.00	5.00
C24 Jim Purnell	1.25	2.50
C25 Larry Glueck	1.25	2.50
C26 Mike Rabold	1.25	2.50
C27 Bob Wetoska	1.25	2.50
C28 Mike Rabold	1.25	2.50
C29 Jon Arnett	2.00	4.00
C30 Dick Butkus	15.00	25.00
C31 Charlie Bivins	1.25	2.50
C32 Ronnie Bull	2.00	4.00
C33 Jim Cadile	1.25	2.50
C34 George Seals	1.25	2.50
C35 Gale Sayers	15.00	25.00
C36 Bears Logo	1.25	2.50

1966 Coke Caps Bills

Coca-Cola issued its final run of football caps in 1966. Each AFL team had a set released in their area along with the AFL All-Stars caps as part of the "Score with the Pros" promotion. Each team's Saver Sheets had separate sections in which to affix both the local team's caps and the All-Stars' caps. The caps measure approximately 1 1/8" in diameter and have the drink logo and a football on the outside, while the inside has the player's face printed in black with the team name above the photo, the player's name below, his position to the right and the cap number to the left. Some teams are also known to exist in a version that features a slightly smaller player photo. Cap numbers included a "C" prefix on all AFL teams except the Jets (J prefix) and Bills (B prefix). The consumer could turn in his completed saver sheet to receive various prizes. The 1966 caps are very similar to the 1965 issue and many of the players are the same in both years. However, the 1966 caps have the words "Caramel Colored" on the outside of the cap while the 1965 caps do not. Most caps were also produced for 1966 on other Coca-Cola products: Tab, Fanta, Fresca, King Size Coke and Sprite. These other drink caps typically carry a slight premium over the value of the Coke version.

COMPLETE SET (35)	90.00	150.00
B1 Bill Laskey	1.25	2.50
B2 Marty Schottenheimer	6.00	12.00
B3 Stew Barber	2.50	4.00
B4 Glenn Bass	1.25	2.50
B5 Remi Prudhomme	1.25	2.50
B6 Al Bemiller	1.25	2.50
B7 George Butch Byrd	2.50	4.00
B8 Wray Carlton	2.50	4.00
B9 Hagood Clarke	1.25	2.50
B10 Jack Kemp	15.00	30.00
B11 Charley Warner	1.25	2.50
B12 Elbert Dubenion	2.50	4.00
B13 Jim Dunaway	2.50	4.00
B14 Booker Edgerson	2.50	4.00
B15 Paul Costa	1.25	2.50
B16 Henry Schmidt	1.25	2.50
B17 Dick Hudson	1.25	2.50
B18 Harry Jacobs	2.50	4.00
B19 Tom Janik	1.25	2.50
B20 Tom Day	2.50	4.00
B21 Daryle Lamonica	4.00	8.00
B22 Paul Maguire	3.00	6.00
B23 Roland McDole	2.50	4.00
B24 Dudley Meredith	1.25	2.50
B25 Joe O'Donnell	1.25	2.50
B26 Charley Ferguson	1.25	2.50
B27 Ed Rutkowski	1.25	2.50
B28 George Saimes	2.50	4.00
B29 Tom Sestak	2.50	4.00
B30 Billy Shaw	2.50	4.00
B31 Bob Lee Smith	1.25	2.50
B32 Mike Stratton	2.50	4.00
B33 Gene Sykes	1.25	2.50
B34 John Tracey	1.25	2.50
B35 Ernie Warlick	1.25	2.50
NNO Bills Saver Sheet	15.00	30.00

1966 Coke Caps Broncos

Please see the 1966 Coke Caps Bills listing for information on this set.

COMPLETE SET (36)	70.00	120.00
C1 Fred Forsberg	1.50	3.00
C2 Willie Brown DB	5.00	10.00
C3 Bob Scarpitto	2.50	4.00
C4 Butch Davis	1.50	3.00
C5 Al Denson	2.50	4.00
C6 Ron Sbranti	1.50	3.00
C7 John Bramlett	1.50	3.00
C8 Mickey Slaughter	1.50	3.00
C9 Lionel Taylor	3.00	5.00
C10 Jerry Sturm	1.50	3.00
C11 Jerry Hopkins	1.50	3.00
C12 Charlie Mitchell	1.50	3.00
C13 Ray Jacobs	1.50	3.00
C14 Lonnie Wright	1.50	3.00
C15 Goldie Sellers	1.50	3.00
C16 Ray Kubala	1.50	3.00
C17 John Griffin	1.50	3.00
C18 Bob Breitenstein	1.50	3.00
C19 Eldon Danenhauer	1.50	3.00
C20 Wendell Hayes	2.50	4.00
C21 Max Leetzow	1.50	3.00
C22 Nemiah Wilson	2.50	4.00
C23 Jim Thibert	1.50	3.00
C24 Gerry Bussell	1.50	3.00
C25 Bob McCullough	1.50	3.00
C26 Jim McMillin	1.50	3.00
C27 Abner Haynes	3.00	5.00
C28 Darrell Lester	1.50	3.00
C29 Cookie Gilchrist	3.00	5.00
C30 John McCormick	2.50	4.00
C31 Lee Bernet	1.50	3.00
C32 Goose Gonsoulin	2.50	4.00
C33 Scotty Glacken	1.50	3.00
C34 Bob Hadrick	1.50	3.00
C35 Archie Matsos	2.50	4.00
C36 Broncos Logo	1.50	3.00

1966 Coke Caps Browns

Please see the 1966 Coke Caps Bears listing for information on this set.

COMPLETE SET (36)	75.00	125.00
C1 Jim Ninowski	2.00	3.50
C2 Leroy Kelly	4.00	8.00
C3 Lou Groza	4.00	8.00
C4 Gary Collins	2.00	3.50
C5 Bill Glass	2.00	3.50
C6 Dale Lindsey	1.25	2.50
C7 Galen Fiss	1.25	2.50
C8 Ross Fichtner	1.25	2.50
C9 John Wooten	2.00	3.50
C10 Clifton McNeil	1.25	2.50
C11 Paul Wiggin	2.00	3.50
C12 Gene Hickerson	2.00	3.50
C13 Ernie Green	1.25	2.50
C14 Mike Howell	1.25	2.50
C15 Dick Schafrath	1.25	2.50
C16 Sidney Williams	1.25	2.50
C17 Frank Ryan	2.00	3.50
C18 Bernie Parrish	1.25	2.50
C19 Vince Costello	1.25	2.50
C20 John Brown OT	1.25	2.50
C21 Monte Clark	1.25	2.50
C22 Walter Roberts	1.25	2.50
C23 Johnny Brewer	1.25	2.50
C24 Walter Beach	1.25	2.50
C25 Dick Modzelewski	1.25	2.50
C26 Gary Lane	1.25	2.50
C27 Jim Houston	1.25	2.50
C28 Milt Morin	1.25	2.50
C29 Erich Barnes	1.25	2.50
C30 Tom Hutchinson	1.25	2.50
C31 John Morrow	1.25	2.50
C32 Jim Kanicki	1.25	2.50
C33 Paul Warfield	4.00	8.00
C34 Jim Garcia	1.25	2.50
C35 Walter Johnson	1.25	2.50
C36 Browns Logo	1.25	2.50
NNO Browns Saver Sheet	15.00	30.00

1966 Coke Caps Cardinals

Please see the 1966 Coke Caps Bears listing for information on this set.

COMPLETE SET (36)	50.00	100.00
C1 Pat Fischer	1.75	3.50
C2 Sonny Randle	1.75	3.50
C3 Joe Childress	1.25	2.50
C4 Dave Meggysey UER (Name misspelled Meggyesy)	2.50	5.00
C5 Joe Robb	1.25	2.50
C6 Jerry Stovall	1.25	2.50
C7 Ernie McMillan	1.75	3.50
C8 Dale Meinert	1.25	2.50
C9 Irv Goode	1.25	2.50
C10 Bob DeMarco	1.25	2.50
C11 Mal Hammack	1.25	2.50
C12 Jim Bakken	1.75	3.50
C13 Bill Thornton	1.25	2.50
C14 Buddy Humphrey	1.25	2.50
C15 Bill Koman	1.25	2.50
C16 Larry Wilson	3.00	6.00
C17 Charles Walker	1.25	2.50
C18 Prentice Gautt	1.25	2.50
C19 Charley Johnson UER (Name misspelled Charley)	2.00	4.00
C20 Ken Gray	1.25	2.50
C21 Dave Simmons	1.25	2.50
C22 Sam Silas	1.25	2.50
C23 Larry Stallings	1.25	2.50
C24 Don Brumm	1.25	2.50
C25 Bobby Joe Conrad	1.75	3.50
C26 Bill Triplett	1.25	2.50
C27 Luke Owens	1.25	2.50
C28 Jackie Smith	3.00	6.00
C29 Bob Reynolds	1.25	2.50
C30 Abe Woodson	1.75	3.50
C31 Jim Burson	1.25	2.50
C32 Willis Crenshaw	1.25	2.50
C33 Billy Gambrell	1.25	2.50
C34 Ray Ogden	1.25	2.50
C35 Herschel Turner	1.25	2.50
C36 Cardinals Logo	1.25	2.50
NNO Cardinals Saver Sheet	15.00	30.00

1966 Coke Caps Chargers

Please see the 1966 Coke Caps Bills listing for information on this set.

COMPLETE SET (36)	70.00	120.00
C1 John Hadl	4.00	8.00
C2 George Gross	1.50	3.00
C3 Frank Buncom	1.50	3.00
C4 Lance Alworth	4.00	8.00
C5 Paul Lowe	3.00	5.00
C6 Herb Travenio	1.50	3.00
C7 Dick Degen	1.50	3.00
C8 Jacque MacKinnon	1.50	3.00
C9 Les Duncan	2.50	4.00
C10 John Farris	1.50	3.00
C11 Willie Frazier	2.50	4.00
C12 Howard Kindig	1.50	3.00
C13 Pat Shea	1.50	3.00
C14 Fred Moore	1.50	3.00
C15 Bob Petrich	1.50	3.00
C16 Ron Mix	3.00	6.00
C17 Miller Farr	1.50	3.00
C18 Keith Lincoln	3.00	5.00
C19 Sam Gruneisen	1.50	3.00
C20 Jim Allison	1.50	3.00
C21 Chuck Allen	1.50	3.00
C22 Gene Foster	1.50	3.00
C23 Rick Redman	1.50	3.00
C24 Steve DeLong	1.50	3.00
C25 Gary Kirner	1.50	3.00
C26 Steve Tensi	1.50	3.00
C27 Kenny Graham	1.50	3.00
C28 Bud Whitehead	1.50	3.00
C29 Walt Sweeney	1.50	3.00
C30 Bob Zeman	1.50	3.00
C31 Gary Garrison	2.50	4.00
C32 Don Norton	1.50	3.00
C33 Ernie Wright	2.50	4.00
C34 Ron Carpenter	1.50	3.00
C35 Pete Jacques	1.50	3.00
C36 Team Logo	1.50	3.00

1966 Coke Caps Chiefs

Please see the 1966 Coke Caps Bills listing for information on this set.

COMPLETE SET (36)	75.00	150.00
C1 E.J. Holub	2.00	4.00
C2 Al Reynolds	1.50	3.00
C3 Buck Buchanan	4.00	8.00
C4 Curt Merz SP	4.00	8.00
C5 Dave Hill	1.50	3.00
C6 Bobby Hunt	1.50	3.00
C7 Jerry Mays	2.00	4.00
C8 Jon Gilliam	1.50	3.00
C9 Walt Corey	2.00	4.00
C10 Solomon Brannan	1.50	3.00
C11 Aaron Brown	1.50	3.00
C12 Bert Coan	1.50	3.00
C13 Ed Budde	2.00	4.00
C14 Tommy Brooker	1.50	3.00
C15 Bobby Bell	4.00	8.00
C16 Smokey Stover	1.50	3.00
C17 Curtis McClinton	2.00	4.00
C18 Jerrel Wilson	2.00	4.00
C19 Ron Burton	2.00	4.00
C20 Mike Garrett	2.50	5.00
C21 Jim Tyrer	2.00	4.00
C22 Johnny Robinson	2.00	4.00
C23 Bobby Ply	1.50	3.00
C24 Frank Pitts	1.50	3.00
C25 Ed Lothamer	1.50	3.00
C26 Sherrill Headrick	2.00	4.00
C27 Fred Williamson	3.00	6.00
C28 Chris Burford	2.00	4.00
C29 Willie Mitchell	1.50	3.00
C30 Otis Taylor	3.00	6.00
C31 Fred Arbanas	2.00	4.00
C32 Hatch Rosdahl	1.50	3.00
C33 Reg Carolan	1.50	3.00
C34 Len Dawson	6.00	12.00
C35 Pete Beathard	2.00	4.00
C36 Chiefs Logo	1.50	3.00
NNO Chiefs Saver Sheet	15.00	30.00

1966 Coke Caps Colts

Please see the 1966 Coke Caps Bears listing for information on this set.

COMPLETE SET (36)	75.00	135.00
C1 Ted Davis	1.25	2.50
C2 Bob Boyd	1.25	2.50
C3 Lenny Moore	5.00	10.00
C4 Jackie Burkett	1.25	2.50
C5 Jimmy Orr	1.50	3.50
C6 Andy Stynchula	1.25	2.50
C7 Mike Curtis	3.00	6.00
C8 Jerry Logan	1.25	2.50
C9 Steve Stonebreaker	1.25	2.50
C10 John Mackey	4.00	8.00
C11 Dennis Gaubatz	1.25	2.50
C12 Don Shinnick	1.25	2.50
C13 Dick Szymanski	1.25	2.50
C14 Urdell Braase	1.25	2.50
C15 Lenny Lyles	1.25	2.50
C16 Rick Kestner	1.25	2.50
C17 Dan Sullivan	1.25	2.50
C18 Lou Michaels	1.50	3.50
C19 Gary Cuozzo	1.50	3.50
C20 Butch Wilson	1.25	2.50
C21 Willie Richardson	1.50	3.50
C22 Jim Welch	1.25	2.50
C23 Tony Lorick	1.25	2.50
C24 Billy Ray Smith	1.50	3.50
C25 Fred Miller	1.25	2.50
C26 Tom Matte	2.50	5.00
C27 Johnny Unitas	7.50	15.00
C28 Glenn Ressler	1.25	2.50
C29 Alvin Haymond	1.50	3.50
C30 Jim Parker	3.00	6.00
C31 Butch Allison	1.25	2.50
C32 Bob Vogel	1.25	2.50
C33 Jerry Hill	1.25	2.50
C34 Raymond Derry	5.00	10.00
C35 Sam Ball	1.25	2.50
C36 Colts Team Logo	1.25	2.50
NNO Colts Saver Sheet	15.00	30.00

1966 Coke Caps Cowboys

Please see the 1966 Coke Caps Bears listing for information on this set.

COMPLETE SET (36)	100.00	175.00
C1 Mike Connelly	2.00	4.00
C2 Tony Liscio	1.50	3.00
C3 Jethro Pugh	2.00	4.00
C4 Larry Stephens	1.50	3.00
C5 Jim Colvin	1.50	3.00
C6 Malcolm Walker	1.50	3.00
C7 Danny Villanueva	1.50	3.00
C8 Frank Clarke	2.00	4.00
C9 Don Meredith	7.50	15.00
C10 George Andrie	2.00	4.00
C11 Mel Renfro	5.00	10.00
C12 Pettis Norman	2.00	4.00
C13 Buddy Dial	2.00	4.00
C14 Pete Gent	2.00	4.00
C15 Jerry Rhome	2.00	4.00
C16 Bob Hayes	7.50	15.00
C17 Mike Gaechter	1.50	3.00
C18 Joe Bob Isbell	1.50	3.00
C19 Harold Hays	1.50	3.00
C20 Craig Morton	4.00	8.00
C21 Jake Kupp	1.50	3.00
C22 Cornell Green	2.00	4.00
C23 Dan Reeves	5.00	10.00
C24 Leon Donohue	1.50	3.00
C25 Dave Manders	1.50	3.00
C26 Warren Livingston	1.50	3.00
C27 Bob Lilly	6.00	12.00
C28 Chuck Howley	3.00	6.00
C29 Don Bishop	2.00	4.00
C30 Don Perkins	2.00	4.00
C31 Jim Boeke	1.50	3.00
C32 Dave Edwards	2.00	4.00
C33 Lee Roy Jordan	3.00	6.00
C34 Obert Logan	1.50	3.00
C35 Ralph Neely	2.00	4.00
C36 Cowboys Logo	1.50	3.00
NNO Cowboys Saver Sheet	15.00	30.00

1966 Coke Caps Eagles

Please see the 1966 Coke Caps Bears listing for information on this set.

COMPLETE SET (36)	75.00	135.00
C1 Norm Snead	2.00	4.00
C2 Al Nelson	1.25	2.50
C3 Jim Skaggs	1.25	2.50
C4 Glenn Glass	1.25	2.50
C5 Pete Retzlaff	1.75	3.50
C6 John Osmond	1.25	2.50
C7 Ray Rissmiller	1.25	2.50
C8 Lynn Hoyem	1.25	2.50
C9 King Hill	1.75	3.50
C10 Timmy Brown	1.75	3.50
C11 Ollie Matson	3.75	7.50
C12 Dave Lloyd	1.75	3.50
C13 Jim Ringo	3.00	6.00
C14 Floyd Peters	1.75	3.50
C15 Gary Pettigrew	1.25	2.50
C16 Frank Molden	1.25	2.50
C17 Earl Gros	1.75	3.50
C18 Fred Hill	1.25	2.50
C19 Don Hultz	1.25	2.50
C20 Ray Poage	1.25	2.50
C21 Aaron Martin	1.25	2.50
C22 Mike Morgan	1.25	2.50
C23 Lane Howell	1.25	2.50
C24 Ed Blaine	1.25	2.50
C25 Jack Concannon	1.75	3.50
C26 Sam Baker	1.25	2.50
C27 Tom Woodeshick	1.75	3.50
C28 Joe Scarpati	1.25	2.50
C29 John Meyers	1.25	2.50
C30 Nate Ramsey	1.75	3.50
C31 Ben Hawkins	1.25	2.50
C32 Bob Brown T	1.75	3.50
C33 Willie Brown	1.25	2.50
C34 Ron Goodwin	1.25	2.50
C35 Randy Beisler	1.25	2.50
C36 Team Logo	1.25	2.50
NNO Eagles Saver Sheet	15.00	30.00

1966 Coke Caps Falcons

Please see the 1966 Coke Caps Bears listing for information on this set.

COMPLETE SET (36)	50.00	100.00
C1 Tommy Nobis	4.00	8.00
C2 Ernie Wheelwright	1.75	3.50
C3 Lee Calland	1.25	2.50
C4 Chuck Sieminski	1.25	2.50
C5 Dennis Claridge	1.75	3.50
C6 Ralph Heck	1.25	2.50
C7 Alex Hawkins	1.75	3.50
C8 Dan Grimm	1.75	3.50
C9 Marion Rushing	1.25	2.50
C10 Bobbie Johnson	1.25	2.50
C11 Bobby Franklin	1.25	2.50
C12 Bill McWatters	1.25	2.50
C13 Billy Lothridge	1.75	3.50
C14 Billy Martin E	1.75	3.50
C15 Tom Wilson	1.25	2.50
C16 Dennis Murphy	1.25	2.50
C17 Randy Johnson	1.75	3.50
C18 Guy Reese	1.25	2.50
C19 Frank Marchlewski	1.25	2.50
C20 Don Talbert	1.25	2.50
C21 Errol Linden	1.25	2.50
C22 Dan Lewis	1.25	2.50
C23 Ed Cook	1.25	2.50
C24 Hugh McInnis	1.25	2.50
C25 Frank Lasky	1.25	2.50
C26 Bob Jencks	1.25	2.50
C27 Bill Jobko	1.25	2.50
C28 Nick Rassas	1.25	2.50
C29 Bob Riggle	1.25	2.50
C30 Ken Reaves	1.75	3.50
C31 Bob Sanders	1.25	2.50
C32 Steve Sloan	1.75	3.50
C33 Ron Smith	1.75	3.50
C34 Bob Whitlow	1.25	2.50
C35 Roger Anderson	1.25	2.50
C36 Falcons Logo	1.25	2.50
NNO Falcons Saver Sheet	15.00	30.00

1966 Coke Caps 49ers

Please see the 1966 Coke Caps Bears listing for information on this set.

COMPLETE SET (36)	75.00	135.00
C1 Bernie Casey	1.75	3.50
C2 Bruce Bosley	1.75	3.50
C3 Kermit Alexander	1.75	3.50
C4 John Brodie	3.75	7.50
C5 Dave Parks	1.75	3.50
C6 Len Rohde	1.75	3.50
C7 Walter Rock	1.75	3.50
C8 George Mira	2.50	5.00
C9 Karl Rubke	1.25	2.50
C10 Ken Willard	1.75	3.50
C11 John David Crow UER (Name misspelled Crowe)	2.00	4.00
C12 George Donnelly	1.25	2.50
C13 Dave Wilcox	2.00	4.00
C14 Vern Burke	1.25	2.50
C15 Wayne Swinford	1.25	2.50
C16 Elbert Kimbrough	1.25	2.50
C17 Clark Miller	1.25	2.50
C18 Dave Kopay	1.75	3.50
C19 Joe Cerne	1.25	2.50
C20 Roland Lakes	1.25	2.50
C21 Charlie Krueger	1.75	3.50
C22 Billy Kilmer	2.50	5.00
C23 Jim Johnson	3.00	6.00
C24 Matt Hazeltine	1.75	3.50
C25 Mike Dowdle	1.25	2.50
C26 Jim Wilson	1.25	2.50
C27 Tommy Davis	1.75	3.50
C28 Jim Norton	1.25	2.50
C29 Jack Chapple	1.25	2.50
C30 Ed Beard	1.25	2.50
C31 John Thomas	1.25	2.50
C32 Monty Stickles	1.25	2.50
C33 Kay McFarland	1.25	2.50
C34 Gary Lewis	1.25	2.50
C35 Howard Mudd	1.25	2.50
C36 49ers Logo	1.25	2.50
NNO 49ers Saver Sheet	15.00	30.00

1966 Coke Caps Giants C

Please see the 1966 Coke Caps Bears listing for information on this set.

COMPLETE SET (36)	60.00	100.00
C1 Joe Morrison	2.00	3.50
C2 Dick Lynch	2.00	3.50
C3 Pete Case	2.00	3.50
C4 Clarence Childs	1.50	2.50
C5 Aaron Thomas	2.00	3.50
C6 Jim Carroll	1.50	2.50
C7 Henry Carr	2.00	3.50
C8 Bookie Bolin	1.50	2.50
C9 Roosevelt Davis	1.50	2.50
C10 John Lovetere	1.50	2.50
C11 Jim Patton	2.00	3.50
C12 Wendell Harris	1.50	2.50
C13 Roger LaLonde	1.50	2.50
C14 Jerry Hillebrand	1.50	2.50
C15 Spider Lockhart	2.00	3.50
C16 Del Shofner	2.00	3.50
C17 Earl Morrall	3.00	5.00
C18 Roosevelt Brown	3.00	5.00
C19 Greg Larson	2.00	3.50
C20 Jim Katcavage	2.00	3.50
C21 Smith Reed	1.50	2.50
C22 Lou Slaby	1.50	2.50
C23 Jim Moran	1.50	2.50
C24 Bill Swain	1.50	2.50
C25 Steve Thurlow	1.50	2.50
C26 Olen Underwood	1.50	2.50
C27 Gary Wood	2.00	3.50
C28 Larry Vargo	1.50	2.50
C29 Jim Prestel	1.50	2.50
C30 Tucker Frederickson	2.00	3.50
C31 Bob Timberlake	1.50	2.50
C32 Chuck Mercein	2.50	4.00
C33 Ernie Koy	2.00	3.50
C34 Tom Costello	1.50	2.50
C35 Homer Jones	2.00	3.50
C36 Team Logo	1.50	2.50

1966 Coke Caps Giants G

Please see the 1966 Coke Caps Bears listing for information on this set.

COMPLETE SET (35)	60.00	100.00
G1 Joe Morrison	2.00	3.50
G2 Dick Lynch	2.00	3.50
G3 Pete Case	2.00	3.50
G4 Clarence Childs	1.50	2.50
G5 Aaron Thomas	2.00	3.50
G6 Jim Carroll	1.50	2.50
G7 Henry Carr	2.00	3.50
G8 Bookie Bolin	1.50	2.50
G9 Roosevelt Davis	1.50	2.50
G10 John Lovetere	1.50	2.50
G11 Jim Patton	2.00	3.50
G12 Wendell Harris	1.50	2.50
G13 Roger LaLonde	1.50	2.50
G14 Jerry Hillebrand	1.50	2.50
G15 Spider Lockhart	2.00	3.50
G16 Del Shofner	2.00	3.50
G17 Earl Morrall	2.50	5.00
G18 Roosevelt Brown	2.50	5.00
G19 Greg Larson	2.00	3.50
G20 Jim Katcavage	2.00	3.50
G21 Smith Reed	1.50	2.50
G22 Lou Slaby	1.50	2.50
G23 Jim Moran	1.50	2.50
G24 Bill Swain	1.50	2.50
G25 Steve Thurlow	1.50	2.50
G26 Olen Underwood	1.50	2.50
G27 Gary Wood	2.00	3.50
G28 Larry Vargo	1.50	2.50
G29 Jim Prestel (Cap saver sheet reads Ed Prestel)	1.50	2.50
G30 Tucker Frederickson	2.00	3.50
G31 Bob Timberlake	1.50	2.50
G32 Chuck Mercein	2.50	4.00
G33 Ernie Koy	2.00	3.50
G34 Tom Costello	1.50	2.50
G35 Homer Jones	2.00	3.50
NNO Giants Saver Sheet	15.00	30.00

1966 Coke Caps Jets

Please see the 1966 Coke Caps Bills listing for information on this set.

COMPLETE SET (35)	75.00	150.00
J1 Don Maynard	5.00	10.00
J2 George Sauer Jr.	2.50	5.00
J3 Paul Crane	1.25	2.50
J4 Jim Colclough	1.25	2.50
J5 Matt Snell	3.00	6.00
J6 Sherman Lewis	3.00	6.00
J7 Jim Turner	1.75	3.50
J8 Mike Taliaferro	1.25	2.50
J9 Cornell Gordon	1.75	3.50
J10 Mark Smolinski	1.25	2.50
J11 Al Atkinson	1.75	3.50
J12 Paul Rochester	1.25	2.50
J13 Sherman Plunkett	1.25	2.50
J14 Gerry Philbin	1.75	3.50
J15 Pete Lammons	1.75	3.50
J16 Dainard Paulson	1.25	2.50
J17 Joe Namath	25.00	50.00
J18 Winston Hill	1.75	3.50
J19 Dee Mackey	1.25	2.50
J20 Curley Johnson	1.25	2.50
J21 Verlon Biggs	1.75	3.50
J22 Bill Mathis	1.75	3.50
J23 Carl McAdams	1.25	2.50
J24 Bert Wilder	1.25	2.50
J25 Larry Grantham	1.75	3.50
J26 Bill Yearby	1.25	2.50
J27 Sam DeLuca	1.25	2.50
J28 Bill Baird	1.25	2.50
J29 Ralph Baker	1.75	3.50
J30 Ray Abruzzese	1.25	2.50
J31 Jim Hudson	1.25	2.50
J32 Dave Herman	1.75	3.50
J33 John Schmitt	1.25	2.50
J34 Jim Harris	1.25	2.50
J35 Bake Turner	1.75	3.50
NNO Jets Saver Sheet	15.00	30.00

1966 Coke Caps Lions

Please see the 1966 Coke Caps Bears listing for information on this set.

COMPLETE SET (36)	50.00	100.00
C1 Pat Studstill	1.75	3.50
C2 Ed Flanagan	1.75	3.50
C3 Wayne Walker	1.75	3.50
C4 Tom Watkins	1.25	2.50
C5 Tommy Vaughn	1.25	2.50
C6 Jim Kearney	1.25	2.50
C7 Larry Hand	1.75	3.50
C8 Jerry Rush	1.25	2.50
C9 Roger Brown	1.75	3.50
C10 Tom Nowatzke	1.75	3.50
C11 John Henderson	1.25	2.50
C12 Tom Myers	1.25	2.50
C13 Ron Kramer	1.75	3.50
C14 Dick LeBeau	1.75	3.50
C15 Amos Marsh	1.75	3.50
C16 Wally Hilgenberg	1.75	3.50
C17 Bruce Maher	1.25	2.50
C18 Darris McCord	1.75	3.50
C19 Ted Karras	1.25	2.50
C20 Ernie Clark	1.25	2.50
C21 Gail Cogdill	1.75	3.50
C22 Wayne Rasmussen	1.25	2.50
C23 Joe Don Looney	4.00	8.00
C24 Jim Gibbons	1.75	3.50
C25 John Gonzaga	1.25	2.50
C26 John Gordy	1.25	2.50
C27 Bobby Thompson	1.25	2.50
C28 J.D. Smith	1.25	2.50
C29 Roger Shoals	1.25	2.50
C30 Alex Karras	3.50	7.00
C31 Nick Pietrosante	1.75	3.50
C32 Milt Plum	2.00	4.00
C33 Daryl Sanders	1.25	2.50
C34 Mike Lucci	1.75	3.50
C35 George Izo	1.75	3.50
C36 Lions Logo	1.25	2.50

1966 Coke Caps National NFL

As part of an advertising promotion, Coca-Cola issued 21 sets of bottle caps, covering the 14 NFL cities, the six AFL cities, and a separate National set for cities not reached by the leagues. This National issue was released primarily in non-NFL cities as part of the Score with the Pros promotion. There was a separate Saver Sheet for the National set. The caps measure approximately 1 1/8" in diameter and have the drink logo and a football on the outside, while the inside has the player's face printed in black, with text surrounding the face. The consumer could turn in his completed saver sheet to receive various prizes. The caps are numbered with a "C" prefix. These caps were also produced for 1966 on other Coca-Cola products: Tab, Fanta, Fresca and Sprite. The other drink caps typically carry a slight premium of 1.5X to 2X the value of the Coke version.

COMPLETE SET (70)	112.50	225.00
C1 Larry Wilson	2.50	5.00
C2 Frank Ryan	1.75	3.50
C3 Norm Snead	1.75	3.50
C4 Mel Renfro	2.50	5.00
C5 Timmy Brown	1.75	3.50
C6 Tucker Frederickson	1.25	2.50
C7 Jim Bakken	1.25	2.50
C8 Paul Krause	2.00	4.00
C9 Irv Cross	1.25	2.50
C10 Cornell Green	1.75	3.50
C11 Pat Fischer	1.25	2.50
C12 Bob Hayes	3.00	6.00
C13 Charley Taylor	2.50	5.00
C14 Pete Retzlaff	1.75	3.50
C15 Jim Ringo	2.50	5.00
C16 Maxie Baughan	1.25	2.50
C17 Chuck Howley	1.50	3.00
C18 John Wooten	1.25	2.50
C19 Bob DeMarco	1.25	2.50
C20 Dale Meinert	1.25	2.50
C21 Gene Hickerson	1.25	2.50
C22 George Andrie	1.25	2.50
C23 Joe Rutgens	1.25	2.50
C24 Bob Lilly	5.00	10.00
C25 Sam Silas	1.25	2.50
C26 Bob Brown OT	1.75	3.50
C27 Dick Schafrath	1.25	2.50
C28 Roosevelt Brown	2.50	5.00
C29 Jim Houston	1.25	2.50
C30 Paul Wiggin	1.25	2.50
C31 Gary Ballman	1.25	2.50
C32 Gary Collins	1.75	3.50
C33 Sonny Randle	1.25	2.50
C34 Charley Johnson	1.75	3.50
C35 Browns Logo	1.25	2.50
C36 Packers Logo	1.25	2.50
C37 Herb Adderley	2.50	5.00
C38 Grady Alderman	1.25	2.50
C39 Doug Atkins	2.50	5.00
C40 Bruce Bosley UER name spelled Bosely	1.25	2.50
C41 John Brodie UER Name spelled Brody	2.50	5.00
C42 Roger Brown	1.25	2.50
C43 Bill Brown	1.25	2.50
C44 Dick Butkus	7.50	15.00
C45 Lee Roy Caffey	1.25	2.50
C46 John David Crow UER name spelled Crowe	1.75	3.50
C47 Willie Davis	2.50	5.00
C48 Mike Ditka	6.00	12.00
C49 Joe Fortunato	1.25	2.50
C50 John Gordy	1.25	2.50
C51 Deacon Jones	2.50	5.00
C52 Alex Karras	3.75	7.50
C53 Dick LeBeau	1.25	2.50
C54 Jerry Logan	1.25	2.50
C55 John Mackey	2.50	5.00
C56 Ed Meador	1.25	2.50
C57 Tommy McDonald	1.75	3.50
C58 Merlin Olsen	3.75	7.50
C59 Jimmy Orr	1.75	3.50
C60 Jim Parker	2.50	5.00
C61 Dave Parks	1.25	2.50
C62 Walter Rock	1.25	2.50
C63 Gale Sayers	7.50	15.00
C64 Pat Studstill	1.25	2.50
C65 Fran Tarkenton	6.00	12.00
C66 Mick Tingelhoff	1.75	3.50
C67 Bob Vogel	1.25	2.50
C68 Wayne Walker	1.25	2.50
C69 Ken Willard	1.25	2.50
C70 Willie Wood	2.50	5.00
NNO National Saver Sheet	7.50	15.00

1966 Coke Caps Oilers

Please see the 1966 Coke Caps Bills listing for information on this set.

COMPLETE SET (36)	62.50	125.00
C1 Scott Appleton	1.50	3.00
C2 George Allen	2.50	4.00
C3 Don Floyd	1.50	3.00
C4 Ronnie Caveness	1.50	3.00
C5 Jim Norton	1.50	3.00
C6 Jacky Lee	2.50	4.00
C7 George Blanda	7.50	15.00
C8 Tony Banfield	2.50	4.00
C9 George Rice	1.50	3.00
C10 Charley Tolar	2.50	4.00
C11 Bobby Jancik	1.50	3.00
C12 Freddy Glick	1.50	3.00
C13 Ode Burrell	2.50	4.00
C14 Walt Suggs	2.50	4.00
C15 Bob McLeod	1.50	3.00
C16 Johnny Baker	1.50	3.00
C17 Danny Brabham	1.50	3.00
C18 Gary Cutsinger	2.50	4.00
C19 Doug Cline	1.50	3.00
C20 Hoyle Granger	2.50	4.00
C21 Bob Talamini	2.50	4.00
C22 Don Trull	2.50	4.00
C23 Charlie Hennigan	2.50	4.00
C24 Sid Blanks	2.50	4.00
C25 Pat Holmes	1.50	3.00
C26 John Frongillo	1.50	3.00
C27 John Wittenborn	1.50	3.00
C28 George Kinney	1.50	3.00
C29 Charles Frazier	1.50	3.00
C30 Ernie Ladd	4.00	8.00
C31 W.K. Hicks	1.50	3.00
C32 Sonny Bishop	2.50	4.00
C33 Larry Elkins	2.50	4.00
C34 Glen Ray Hines	2.50	4.00
C35 Bobby Maples	2.50	4.00
C36 Oilers Logo	1.50	3.00
NNO Oilers Saver Sheet	15.00	30.00

1966 Coke Caps Packers

Please see the 1966 Coke Caps Bears listing for information on this set.

COMPLETE SET (31)	100.00	175.00
C1 Herb Adderley	4.00	8.00
C2 Lionel Aldridge	2.50	4.00
C3 Bob Long	1.50	3.00
C4 Willie Davis	4.00	8.00
C5 Boyd Dowler	2.50	4.00
C6 Marv Fleming	2.50	4.00
C7 Ken Bowman	2.50	4.00
C8 Tom Brown	1.50	3.00
C9 Doug Hart	1.50	3.00
C10 Steve Wright	1.50	3.00
C11 Bill Anderson	1.50	3.00
C12 Bill Curry	2.50	4.00
C13 Tommy Crutcher	1.50	3.00
C14 Fred Thurston	4.00	8.00
C15 Elijah Pitts	2.50	4.00
C16 Lloyd Voss	1.50	3.00
C17 Lee Roy Caffey	1.50	3.00
C18 Dave Robinson	3.00	5.00
C19 Bart Starr	7.50	15.00
C20 Ray Nitschke	5.00	10.00
C21 Max McGee	2.50	4.00
C22 Don Chandler	2.50	4.00
C23 Rich Marshall	1.50	3.00
C24 Ron Kostelnik	1.50	3.00
C25 Carroll Dale	2.50	4.00
C26 Hank Jordan	4.00	8.00
C27 Bob Jeter	2.50	4.00
C28 Bob Skoronski	1.50	3.00
C29 Jerry Kramer	3.00	6.00
C30 Willie Wood	4.00	8.00
C31 Paul Hornung	7.50	15.00
C32 Forrest Gregg	4.00	8.00
C33 Zeke Bratkowski	2.50	4.00
C34 Tom Moore	2.50	4.00
C35 Jim Taylor	5.00	10.00
C36 Packers Team Emblem	1.50	3.00
NNO Packers Saver Sheet	15.00	30.00

1966 Coke Caps Patriots

Please see the 1966 Coke Caps Bills listing for information on this set.

COMPLETE SET (36)	75.00	125.00
C1 Jon Morris	2.50	4.00
C2 Don Webb	1.50	3.00
C3 Charles Long	1.50	3.00
C4 Tony Romeo	1.50	3.00
C5 Bob Dee	2.50	4.00
C6 Tommy Addison	2.50	4.00
C7 Tom Neville	2.50	4.00
C8 Ron Hall	1.50	3.00
C9 White Graves	1.50	3.00
C10 Ellis Johnson	1.50	3.00
C11 Don Oakes	1.50	3.00
C12 Tom Yewcic	1.50	3.00
C13 Tom Hennessey	1.50	3.00
C14 Jay Cunningham	1.50	3.00
C15 Larry Garron	2.50	4.00
C16 Justin Canale	1.50	3.00
C17 Art Graham	2.50	4.00
C18 Babe Parilli	2.50	4.00
C19 Jim Hunt	2.50	4.00
C20 Karl Singer	1.50	3.00
C21 Houston Antwine	2.50	4.00
C22 Nick Buoniconti	3.00	6.00
C23 John Huarte	2.50	5.00
C24 Gino Cappelletti	2.50	4.00
C25 Chuck Shonta	1.50	3.00
C26 Dick Felt	2.50	4.00
C27 Mike Dukes	1.50	3.00
C28 Larry Eisenhauer	2.50	4.00
C29 Jim Fraser	1.50	3.00
C30 Len St. Jean	2.50	4.00
C31 J.D. Garrett	1.50	3.00
C32 Jim Whalen	1.50	3.00
C33 Jim Nance	2.50	5.00
C34 Dick Arrington	1.50	3.00
C35 Lonnie Farmer	1.50	3.00
C36 Patriots Logo	1.50	3.00
NNO Patriots Saver Sheet	15.00	30.00

1966 Coke Caps Raiders

Please see the 1966 Coke Caps Bills listing for information on this set.

COMPLETE SET (36)	70.00	120.00
C1 Fred Biletnikoff	4.00	8.00
C2 Gus Otto	1.50	3.00
C3 Harry Schuh	1.50	3.00
C4 Ken Herock	1.50	3.00
C5 Claude Gibson	1.50	3.00
C6 Cotton Davidson	2.50	4.00
C7 Cliff Kenney	1.50	3.00
C8 Ben Davidson	3.00	5.00
C9 Roger Hagberg	1.50	3.00
C10 Bob Svihus	1.50	3.00
C11 John R. Williamson	1.50	3.00
C12 Dave Grayson	1.50	3.00
C13 Hewritt Dixon	2.50	4.00
C14 Dave Costa	1.50	3.00
C15 Tom Keating	1.50	3.00
C16 Alan Miller	1.50	3.00
C17 Billy Cannon	3.00	5.00
C18 Wayne Hawkins	2.50	4.00
C19 Warren Powers	1.50	3.00
C20 Joe Labruzzo	1.50	3.00
C21 Dan Conners	1.50	3.00
C22 Jim Otto	3.00	6.00
C23 Clem Daniels	2.50	4.00
C24 Tom Flores	3.00	5.00
C25 Art Powell	2.50	4.00
C26 Larry Todd	1.50	3.00
C27 James Harvey	1.50	3.00
C28 Dan Birdwell	1.50	3.00
C29 Carleton Oats	1.50	3.00
C30 Mike Mercer	1.50	3.00
C31 Pete Banaszak	1.50	3.00
C32 Bill Budness	1.50	3.00
C33 Kent McCloughan	1.50	3.00
C34 Howie Williams	1.50	3.00
C35 Rodger Bird	1.50	3.00
C36 Team Logo	1.50	3.00

1966 Coke Caps Rams

Please see the 1966 Coke Caps Bears listing for information on this set.

COMPLETE SET (36)	62.50	125.00
C1 Tom Mack	4.00	8.00
C2 Tom Moore	1.25	2.50
C3 Bill Munson	2.00	3.50
C4 Bill George	3.00	6.00
C5 Joe Carollo	1.25	2.50
C6 Dick Bass	2.00	3.50
C7 Ken Iman	1.25	2.50
C8 Charlie Cowan	2.00	3.50
C9 Terry Baker	3.00	5.00
C10 Don Chuy	1.25	2.50
C11 Jack Pardee	2.00	3.50
C12 Lamar Lundy	2.00	3.50
C13 Bill Anderson	1.25	2.50
C14 Roman Gabriel	3.00	6.00
C15 Roosevelt Grier	3.00	6.00
C16 Billy Truax	2.00	3.50
C17 Merlin Olsen	4.00	8.00
C18 Deacon Jones	4.00	8.00
C19 Joe Scibelli	1.25	2.50
C20 Marlin McKeever	1.25	2.50
C21 Doug Woodlief	1.25	2.50
C22 Chuck Lamson	1.25	2.50
C23 Dan Currie	1.25	2.50
C24 Maxie Baughan	2.00	3.50
C25 Bruce Gossett	2.00	3.50
C26 Les Josephson	2.00	3.50
C27 Ed Meador	1.25	2.50
C28 Anthony Guillory	1.25	2.50
C29 Irv Cross	2.00	3.50
C30 Tommy McDonald	3.00	5.00
C31 Bucky Pope	1.25	2.50
C32 Jack Snow	2.00	3.50
C33 Joe Wendryhoski	1.25	2.50
C34 Clancy Williams	1.25	2.50
C35 Ben Wilson	1.25	2.50
C36 Rams Logo	1.25	2.50
NNO Rams Saver Sheet	15.00	30.00

1966 Coke Caps Redskins

Please see the 1966 Coke Caps Bears listing for information on this set.

COMPLETE SET (36)	75.00	125.00
C1 Don Croftcheck	1.50	3.00
C2 Fred Mazurek	1.50	3.00
C3 Lonnie Sanders	1.50	3.00
C4 Jim Steffen	1.50	3.00
C5 Jim Shofner	2.00	4.00
C6 Bill Hunter	1.50	3.00
C7 Vince Promuto	1.50	3.00
C8 Jerry Smith	1.50	3.00
C9 Pat Richter	1.50	3.00
C10 Preston Carpenter	1.50	3.00
C11 Sam Huff	4.00	8.00
C12 Darrell Dess	1.50	3.00
C13 Jim Snowden	1.50	3.00
C14 Len Hauss	1.50	3.00
C15 Chris Hanburger	2.00	4.00
C16 John Reger	1.50	3.00
C17 George Hughley	1.50	3.00
C18 Rickie Harris	1.50	3.00
C19 Tom Walters	1.50	3.00
C20 Joe Rutgens	1.50	3.00
C21 Carl Kammerer	1.50	3.00
C22 Fran O'Brien	1.50	3.00
C23 Willie Adams	1.50	3.00
C24 Bill Clay	1.50	3.00
C25 Charlie Gogolak	1.50	3.00
C26 Dick Lemay	1.50	3.00
C27 Walter Barnes	1.50	3.00
C28 Sonny Jurgensen	4.00	8.00
C29 John Strohmeyer	1.50	3.00
C30 Charley Taylor	4.00	8.00
C31 Dick Shiner	1.50	3.00
C32 Fred Williams	1.50	3.00
C33 Angelo Coia	1.50	3.00
C34 Ron Snidow	1.50	3.00
C35 Paul Krause	2.50	5.00
C36 Team Logo	1.50	3.00

1966 Coke Caps Steelers

Please see the 1966 Coke Caps Bears listing for information on this set.

COMPLETE SET (36)	70.00	120.00
C1 John Baker	1.50	3.00
C2 Mike Lind	2.50	4.00
C3 Ken Kortas	1.50	3.00
C4 Willie Daniel	1.50	3.00
C5 Roy Jefferson	2.50	4.00
C6 Bob Hohn	1.50	3.00
C7 Dan James	1.50	3.00
C8 Gary Ballman	2.50	4.00
C9 Brady Keys	1.50	3.00
C10 Charley Bradshaw	2.50	4.00
C11 Jim Bradshaw	1.50	3.00
C12 Jim Butler	2.50	4.00
C13 Paul Martha	2.50	4.00
C14 Mike Clark	1.50	3.00
C15 Ray Lemek	1.50	3.00
C16 Clarence Peaks	2.50	4.00
C17 Theron Sapp	1.50	3.00
C18 Ray Mansfield	2.50	4.00
C19 Chuck Hinton	1.50	3.00
C20 Bill Nelsen	2.50	4.00
C21 Rod Breedlove	1.50	3.00
C22 Frank Lambert	1.50	3.00
C23 Ben McGee	1.50	3.00
C24 Myron Pottios	2.50	4.00
C25 John Campbell	1.50	3.00
C26 Andy Russell	2.50	5.00
C27 Mike Sandusky	1.50	3.00
C28 Bob Schmitz	1.50	3.00
C29 Riley Gunnels	1.50	3.00
C30 Clendon Thomas	2.50	4.00
C31 Tommy Wade	1.50	3.00
C32 Dick Hoak	2.50	4.00
C33 Marv Woodson	1.50	3.00
C34 Bob Nichols	1.50	3.00
C35 John Henry Johnson	3.00	6.00
C36 Steelers Logo	1.50	3.00
NNO Steelers Saver Sheet	15.00	30.00

1966 Coke Caps Vikings

Please see the 1966 Coke Caps Bears listing for information on this set.

COMPLETE SET (36)	50.00	100.00
C1 Milt Sunde	1.75	3.50
C2 Don Hansen	1.25	2.50
C3 Jim Marshall	3.00	6.00
C4 Jerry Shay	1.25	2.50
C5 Ken Byers	1.25	2.50
C6 Rip Hawkins	1.25	2.50
C7 John Kirby	1.25	2.50
C8 Roy Winston	1.75	3.50
C9 Ron VanderKelen	1.75	3.50
C10 Jim Lindsey	1.25	2.50
C11 Paul Flatley	1.75	3.50
C12 Larry Bowie	1.25	2.50
C13 Grady Alderman	1.75	3.50
C14 Mick Tingelhoff	2.50	5.00
C15 Lonnie Warwick	1.75	3.50
C16 Fred Cox	1.75	3.50
C17 Bill Brown	1.75	3.50
C18 Ed Sharockman	1.75	3.50
C19 George Rose	1.25	2.50
C20 Paul Dickson	1.25	2.50
C21 Tommy Mason	1.75	3.50
C22 Carl Eller	3.00	6.00
C23 Jim Young	1.25	2.50
C24 Hal Bedsole	1.25	2.50
C25 Karl Kassulke	1.75	3.50
C26 Fran Tarkenton	6.00	12.00
C27 Tom Hall	1.25	2.50
C28 Archie Sutton	1.25	2.50
C29 Jim Phillips	1.25	2.50
C30 Gary Larsen	1.75	3.50
C31 Phil King	1.25	2.50
C32 Bobby Walden	1.25	2.50
C33 Bob Berry	1.75	3.50
C34 Jeff Jordan	1.25	2.50
C35 Lance Rentzel	1.75	3.50
C36 Team Logo	1.25	2.50
NNO Vikings Saver Sheet	15.00	30.00

1971 Coke Caps Packers

This is a 22-player set of Coca-Cola bottle caps featuring members of the Green Bay Packers. They have the Coke logo and a football on the outside, while the inside has the player's face printed in black, with the player's name below the picture. The caps measure approximately 1 1/8" in diameter. A cap-saver sheet was also issued to aid in collecting the bottle caps, and the consumer could turn in his completed sheet to receive various prizes. The caps are unnumbered and therefore listed below alphabetically. The caps were also produced in a twist-off version with red printing.

COMPLETE SET (22)	25.00	50.00
*TWIST-OFF CAPS: .6X TO 1.5X		
1 Ken Bowman	1.00	2.00
2 John Brockington	1.50	3.00
3 Bob Brown DT	.75	1.50
4 Fred Carr	1.00	2.00
5 Jim Carter	.75	1.50
6 Carroll Dale	1.00	2.00
7 Ken Ellis	1.00	2.00
8 Gale Gillingham	1.00	2.00
9 Dave Hampton	.75	1.50
10 Doug Hart	.75	1.50
11 Jim Hill	.75	1.50
12 Dick Himes	.75	1.50
13 Scott Hunter	1.00	2.00
14 MacArthur Lane	1.50	3.00
15 Bill Lueck	.75	1.50
16 Al Matthews	.75	1.50
17 Rich McGeorge	1.00	1.50
18 Ray Nitschke	3.00	8.00
19 Francis Peay	.75	1.50
20 Dave Robinson	1.50	3.00
21 Alden Roche	.75	1.50
22 Bart Starr	7.50	15.00
NNO Saver Sheet	12.50	25.00

1971 Coke Fun Kit Photos

These color photos were released around 1971 with packages of Coca-Cola drinks in packages of four. Each is blankbacked, measures roughly 7" by 10" and includes a color photo of the featured player with his name and team name below the photo. The photos were printed on thin white paper stock. No Coca-Cola logos appear on the photos only that of the NFL Player's Association. Any additions to this list are appreciated.

COMPLETE SET (106)	500.00	800.00
1 Donny Anderson	4.00	8.00
2 Tony Baker	3.00	6.00
3 Pete Barnes	3.00	6.00
4 Lem Barney	4.00	8.00
5 Bill Bergey	4.00	8.00
6 Fred Biletnikoff	10.00	18.00
7 George Blanda	12.00	20.00
8 Lee Bouggess	3.00	6.00
9 Marlin Briscoe	3.00	6.00
10 John Brodie	6.00	12.00
11 Larry Brown	4.00	8.00
12 Willie Brown	4.00	8.00
13 Nick Buoniconti	6.00	12.00
14 Dick Butkus	18.00	30.00
15 Butch Byrd	3.00	6.00
16 Fred Carr	3.00	6.00
17 Virgil Carter	3.00	6.00
18 Gary Collins	3.00	6.00
19 Jack Concannon	3.00	6.00
20 Greg Cook	3.00	6.00
21 Dave Costa	3.00	6.00
22 Paul Costa	3.00	6.00
23 Larry Csonka	15.00	25.00
24 Carroll Dale	3.00	6.00
25 Len Dawson	12.00	20.00
26 Tom Dempsey	3.00	6.00
27 Al Dodd	3.00	6.00
28 Fred Dryer	4.00	8.00
29 Carl Eller	4.00	8.00
30 Mel Farr	3.00	6.00
31 Jim Files	3.00	6.00
32 John Fuqua	3.00	6.00
33 Roman Gabriel	6.00	12.00
34 Gary Garrison	3.00	6.00
35 Walt Garrison	4.00	8.00
36 Joe Greene	12.00	20.00
37 Bob Griese	15.00	25.00
38 John Hadl	6.00	12.00
39 Terry Hanratty	3.00	6.00
40 Jim Hart	6.00	12.00
41 Ben Hawkins	3.00	6.00
42 Alvin Haymond	3.00	6.00
43 Eddie Hinton	3.00	6.00
44 Claude Humphrey	3.00	6.00
45 Rich Jackson	3.00	6.00
46 Charley Johnson	3.00	6.00
47 Ron Johnson	4.00	8.00
48 Walter Johnson	3.00	6.00
49 Deacon Jones	10.00	15.00
50 Lee Roy Jordan	6.00	12.00
51 Joe Kapp	4.00	8.00
52 Leroy Kelly	6.00	12.00
53 Curt Knight	3.00	6.00
54 Charlie Krueger	3.00	6.00
55 Jake Kupp	3.00	6.00
56 MacArthur Lane	3.00	6.00
57 Willie Lanier	6.00	12.00
58 Jerry Levias	3.00	6.00
59 Bob Lilly	10.00	18.00
60 Floyd Little	4.00	8.00
61 Mike Lucci	4.00	8.00
62 Dave Manders	3.00	6.00
62 Jim Marshall	6.00	12.00
63 Tom Matte	4.00	8.00
64 Don Maynard	10.00	18.00
65 Mike McCoy	3.00	6.00
66 Jim Mitchell	3.00	6.00
67 Jon Morris	3.00	6.00

68 Joe Namath	25.00	40.00
69 Jim Nance	4.00	8.00
70 Bill Nelsen	4.00	8.00
72 Tommy Nobis	4.00	8.00
73 Merlin Olsen	10.00	15.00
74 Dave Osborn	3.00	6.00
76 Alan Page	6.00	12.00
77 Preston Pearson	4.00	8.00
78 Mac Percival	3.00	6.00
79 Gerry Philbin	3.00	6.00
80 Jess Phillips	3.00	6.00
81 Tom Regner	3.00	6.00
82 Mel Renfro	6.00	12.00
83 Johnny Robinson	3.00	6.00
84 Tim Rossovich	3.00	6.00
85 Charlie Sanders	3.00	6.00
86 Gale Sayers	18.00	30.00
87 Ron Sellers	3.00	6.00
88 Dennis Shaw	3.00	6.00
89 Bubba Smith	6.00	12.00
90 Charlie Smith	3.00	6.00
91 Jerry Smith	3.00	6.00
92 Matt Snell	4.00	8.00
93 Larry Stallings	3.00	6.00
94 Walt Sweeney	3.00	6.00
95 Fran Tarkenton	12.00	20.00
96 Bruce Taylor	3.00	6.00
97 Charley Taylor	6.00	12.00
98 Otis Taylor	4.00	8.00
99 Bill Thompson	3.00	6.00
100 Johnny Unitas	18.00	30.00
101 Harmon Wages	3.00	6.00
102 Paul Warfield	10.00	18.00
103 Gene Washington 49er	4.00	8.00
104 George Webster	3.00	6.00
104 Gene Washington Vik	3.00	6.00
105 Larry Wilson	6.00	12.00
106 Tom Woodeshick	3.00	6.00

1973 Coke Cap Team Logos

This set of caps were issued in bottles of Coca-Cola in the Milwaukee area in 1973. Each clear plastic liner inside the cap features a black and white NFL team logo. The inside liners were to be attached to a saver sheet that could be partially or completely filled in order to be exchanged for various prizes from Coke.

COMPLETE SET (26)	30.00	60.00
1 Atlanta Falcons	1.00	2.50
2 Baltimore Colts	1.25	3.00
3 Buffalo Bills	1.00	2.50
4 Chicago Bears	1.25	3.00
5 Cincinnati Bengals	1.00	2.50
6 Cleveland Browns	1.25	3.00
7 Dallas Cowboys	2.00	4.00
8 Denver Broncos	1.25	3.00
9 Detroit Lions	1.00	2.50
10 Green Bay Packers	2.00	4.00
11 Houston Oilers	1.00	2.50
12 Kansas City Chiefs	1.00	2.50
13 Los Angeles Rams	1.00	2.50
14 Miami Dolphins	2.00	4.00
15 Minnesota Vikings	1.25	3.00
16 New England Patriots	1.00	2.50
17 New Orleans Saints	1.00	2.50
18 New York Giants	1.00	2.50
19 New York Jets	1.00	2.50
20 Oakland Raiders	2.00	4.00
21 Philadelphia Eagles	1.00	2.50
22 Pittsburgh Steelers	2.00	4.00
23 San Diego Chargers	1.00	2.50
24 San Francisco 49ers	2.00	4.00
25 St. Louis Cardinals	1.00	2.50
26 Washington Redskins	2.00	4.00

1973 Coke Prints

These prints were released around 1973 through retailers as an inducement to their customers to purchase Coke flavored Icee or Frozen Coca-Cola drinks. Each measures roughly 8 1/2" x 11" and features a black and white artist's rendering of the player along with two characatures of football players and a facsimile autograph in blue ink. The backs feature a brief write-up on the player printed in blue ink along with either a large Frozen Coke or Icee ad. Some players were issued with both back versions as noted below. Any additions to this checklist are appreciated.

COMPLETE SET (49)	500.00	800.00
1 Danny Abramowicz	10.00	20.00
(Frozen Coke back)		
2 Julius Adams	10.00	20.00
(Frozen Coke back)		
3 Bobby Anderson	10.00	20.00
(Frozen Coke back)		
4 Dick Anderson	12.50	25.00
(Frozen Coke back)		
5 Terry Bradshaw	40.00	75.00
(Frozen Coke back)		
6 Larry Brown	12.50	25.00
(Frozen Coke back)		
7A Nick Buoniconti	15.00	30.00
(Frozen Coke back)		
7B Nick Buoniconti	15.00	30.00
(Icee back)		
8 Ken Burrow	12.50	25.00
(Frozen Coke back)		
9 Richard Caster	12.50	25.00
(Frozen Coke back)		
10 Larry Csonka	30.00	50.00
(Frozen Coke back)		
11A Mike Curtis	12.50	25.00
(Frozen Coke back)		
11B Mike Curtis	12.50	25.00
(Icee back)		
12 John Elliott	10.00	20.00
(Frozen Coke back)		
13 Manny Fernandez	10.00	20.00
(Frozen Coke back)		
14A John Fuqua	12.50	25.00
(Frozen Coke back)		
14B John Fuqua	12.50	25.00
(Icee back)		
15 Walt Garrison	10.00	20.00
(Frozen Coke back)		
16 Joe Greene	25.00	40.00
(Frozen Coke back)		
17A Bob Griese	30.00	50.00
(Frozen Coke back)		
17B Bob Griese	30.00	50.00
(Icee back)		
18 Paul Guidry	10.00	20.00
(Frozen Coke back)		
19 Don Hansen	10.00	20.00
(Frozen Coke back)		
20A Ted Hendricks	15.00	30.00
(Frozen Coke back)		
20B Ted Hendricks	15.00	30.00
(Icee back)		
21 Dave Herman	10.00	20.00
(Frozen Coke back)		
22 J.D. Hill	10.00	20.00
(Frozen Coke back)		
23 Fred Hoaglin	10.00	20.00
(Frozen Coke back)		
24 Jim Houston	10.00	20.00
(Frozen Coke back)		
25A Rich Jackson	10.00	20.00
(Frozen Coke back)		
25B Rich Jackson	10.00	20.00
(Icee back)		
26 Walter Johnson	10.00	20.00
(Frozen Coke back)		
27A Leroy Kelly	15.00	30.00
(Frozen Coke back)		
27B Leroy Kelly	15.00	30.00
(Icee back)		
28A Jim Kiick	12.50	25.00
(Frozen Coke back)		
28B Jim Kiick	12.50	25.00
(Icee back)		
29 George Kunz	10.00	20.00
(Frozen Coke back)		
30 Floyd Little	12.50	25.00
(Frozen Coke back)		
31 Archie Manning	15.00	30.00
(Frozen Coke back)		
32 Milt Morin	10.00	20.00
(Frozen Coke back)		
33A Earl Morrall	12.50	25.00
(Frozen Coke back)		
33B Earl Morrall	12.50	25.00
(Icee back)		
34 Mercury Morris	15.00	30.00
(Frozen Coke back)		
35 Haven Moses	12.50	25.00
(Frozen Coke back)		
36A John Niland	10.00	20.00
(Frozen Coke back)		
36B John Niland	10.00	20.00
(Icee back)		
37A Walt Patulski	10.00	20.00
(Frozen Coke back)		
37B Walt Patulski	10.00	20.00
(Icee back)		
38A Jim Plunkett	15.00	30.00
(Frozen Coke back)		
38B Jim Plunkett	15.00	30.00
(Icee back)		
39 Andy Russell	12.50	25.00
(Frozen Coke back)		
40 Jake Scott	12.50	25.00
(Frozen Coke back)		
41 Jerry Smith	12.50	25.00
(Frozen Coke back)		
42A Royce Smith	10.00	20.00
(Frozen Coke back)		
42B Royce Smith	10.00	20.00
(Icee back)		
43 Steve Tannen	10.00	20.00
(Frozen Coke back)		
44 Charley Taylor	15.00	30.00
(Frozen Coke back)		
45 Billy Truax	10.00	20.00
(Frozen Coke back)		
46 Randy Vataha	10.00	20.00
(Frozen Coke back)		
47A Rick Volk	10.00	20.00
(Frozen Coke back)		
47B Rick Volk	10.00	20.00
(Icee back)		
48 Paul Warfield	15.00	30.00
(Frozen Coke back)		
49 Garo Yepremian	10.00	20.00
(Frozen Coke back)		

1981 Coke Caps

In 1981 Coca-Cola included player's photos underneath Coke caps as part of a redemption contest. Apparently the contest was released around the country (Atlanta, Miami, Green Bay area and Dallas confirmed) using a variety of players in each area. At least three different cap saver sheets were issued for the game in each area. It required the consumer collect Coke, Sprite and/or TAB bottle caps of certain players and attach them to the saver sheets. Sheets 1-3 measure approximately 6 3/8" by 9 1/8" and were divided into three 2 1/8" columns. The top of each column has a hole so that the offer could hang on a soft drink bottle. The first column included a picture of Joe Greene with the quote "Look for me and my friends under caps from Coke and TAB." If one found all seven caps required to complete the yellow middle column, a cash prize of a thousand dollars was awarded. If one completed the five caps required by the third column on the front, the prize was one "Mean" Joe jersey. Finally, the first column on the back required four caps in order to win a player T-shirt. It appears this group always contained four players from the local NFL team. The back also presented official rules for the game. The more difficult caps to find were Steve Fuller and Gene Upshaw from the top two prize levels and one local player from the t-shirt prize level (for example Ed Jones for Dallas). These SPs have not been priced below since it is thought very few exist. Another saver sheet features a grouping of 28-players that had to be completed to be eligible to purchase an NFL t-shirt or Joe Greene replica jersey. Since there were many different bottlers around the country involved in the program, the caps can be found in a number of varieties. Many of the standard bottle cap style can be found in white and/or silver and most, if not all, were issued as twist-off caps. We have checklisted the caps below according to their skip-number and any confirmed additions are appreciated.

1 Joe Greene	1.50	4.00
3 Steve Grogan	.75	2.00
4 Rich Wingo	.60	1.50
5 Steve Bartkowski	.75	2.00
6 Mike Siani	.60	1.50
7 Drew Pearson	1.50	4.00
10 Ottis Anderson	.75	2.00
11 Dan Fouts	2.00	5.00
12 Wesley Walker	.75	2.00
13 Nat Moore	.75	2.00
14 Rick Upchurch	.75	2.00
17 Craig Morton	.75	2.00
22 John Riggins	2.00	5.00
23 Harold Carmichael	.75	2.00
25 Kim Bokamper	.60	1.50
26 Tommy Kramer	.75	2.00
29 Ken Anderson	1.25	3.00
30 Greg Pruitt	.75	2.00
31 Alfred Jenkins	.60	1.50
32 Curtis Dickey SP		
33 Bob Breunig	.60	1.50
35 Jack Youngblood	.75	2.00
36 Ralph Ortega	.60	1.50
38 Gene Upshaw SP		
47 Steve Fuller SP		
49 Walter Payton	7.50	15.00
50 Pete Johnson	.60	1.50
51 Ozzie Newsome	.75	2.00
53 Ed Too Tall Jones SP		
56 Vagas Ferguson	.60	1.50
57 Herman Edwards	.60	1.50
64 Jerry Robinson	.60	1.50
65 Jimmy Cefalo	.60	1.50
67 Mike Bell	.60	1.50
71 John James	.60	1.50
74 Ezra Johnson	.60	1.50
82 Joe Washington	.75	2.00
86 Harold Jackson	.75	2.00
87 James Lofton	1.50	4.00
91 William Andrews	.75	2.00
92 Roger Carr	.75	2.00
94 Terdell Middleton	.60	1.50
95 A.J. Duhe	.60	1.50
96 Jeff Siemon	.60	1.50
102 Clarence Harmon	.75	2.00
106 Matt Blair	.60	1.50
107 Benny Barnes	.60	1.50
108 Billy Sims	1.25	3.00
109 Lyle Alzado	.75	2.00
111 Jeff Van Note	.60	1.50
112 Bruce Laird	.60	1.50
115 Fred Dryer	.75	2.00
118 Keith Krepfle	.60	1.50
122 Tony Franklin	.60	1.50
124 Ahmad Rashad	.75	2.00
127 Robert Newhouse	.60	1.50
128 Archie Griffin	.75	2.00
130 Alfred Jackson	.60	1.50
131 Mike Barnes	.60	1.50
134 Elvis Peacock	.60	1.50
135 Bob Baumhower	.75	2.00
143 Max Runager	.60	1.50
146 Charlie Waters	.75	2.00
154 Jewerl Thomas	.60	1.50
155 Tim Mazzetti	.60	1.50
164 Andy Johnson	.60	1.50
165 Delvin Williams	.60	1.50
166 Isaac Curtis	.60	1.50
169 Ed Simonini	.60	1.50
172 Pat Thomas	.60	1.50
178 Brad Dusek	.60	1.50
180 Leon Gray	.60	1.50
184 Aundra Thompson	.60	1.50
188 Joe Lavender	.60	1.50
191 Reggie Rucker	.75	2.00
192 Lynn Dickey	.75	2.00
NNO Saver Sheet 3	6.00	15.00
(measures 6 1/4" x 9" bottle hanger, displays/ 16 players in three groups)		
NNO Saver Sheet 28	10.00	20.00
(measures 6 1/2" x 9 1/2" carton insert, displays/ 28 players in one group)		
NNO Saver Sheet 1	6.00	15.00
(measures 6 1/4" x 9 1/4" bottle hanger, displays/ 16 players in three groups)		

1981 Coke

The 1981 Coca-Cola/Topps football set of 84 standard-size cards contains 11 player cards and one header card each from seven National Football League teams. The cards are actually numbered on the back in alphabetical order within team from 1-11; however in the checklist below the cards are numbered 1-77 alphabetically by team. The backs of the header cards carried an offer to receive one (of four) uncut sheet(s) of the 1981 Topps regular series. Similar in design to the Topps cards of that year, these cards contain the Coke logo on both the front and the back. The key cards in the set are Art Monk and Kellen Winslow, both appearing in their "Rookie" year for cards.

COMPLETE SET (84)	25.00	60.00
1 Raymond Butler	.15	.40
2 Roger Carr	.25	.60
3 Curtis Dickey	.25	.60
4 Nesby Glasgow	.15	.40
5 Bert Jones	.30	.75
6 Bruce Laird	.15	.40
7 Greg Landry	.25	.60
8 Reese McCall	.15	.40
9 Don McCauley	.15	.40
10 Herb Orvis	.15	.40
11 Ed Simonini	.15	.40
12 Pat Donovan	.15	.40
13 Tony Dorsett	2.00	5.00
14 Billy Joe DuPree	.25	.60
15 Tony Hill	.25	.60
16 Ed Too Tall Jones	.40	1.00
17 Harvey Martin	.25	.60
18 Robert Newhouse	.15	.40
19 Drew Pearson	.30	.75
20 Charlie Waters	.25	.60
21 Danny White	.30	.75
22 Randy White	.60	1.50
23 Mike Barber	.15	.40
24 Elvin Bethea	.30	.75
25 Gregg Bingham	.15	.40
26 Robert Brazile	.25	.60
27 Ken Burrough	.15	.40
28 Rob Carpenter	.15	.40
29 Leon Gray	.15	.40
30 Vernon Perry	.15	.40
31 Mike Renfro	.15	.40
32 Carl Roaches	.15	.40
33 Morris Towns	.15	.40
34 Harry Carson	.25	.60
35 Mike Dennis	.15	.40
36 Mike Friede	.15	.40
37 Earnest Gray	.15	.40
38 Dave Jennings	.15	.40
39 Gary Jeter	.15	.40
40 George Martin	.15	.40
41 Roy Simmons	.15	.40
42 Phil Simms	1.25	3.00
43 Billy Taylor	.15	.40
44 Brad Van Pelt	.15	.40
45 Ottis Anderson	.40	1.00
46 Rush Brown	.15	.40
47 Theotis Brown	.15	.40
48 Dan Dierdorf	.30	.75
49 Mel Gray	.25	.60
50 Ken Greene	.15	.40
51 Jim Hart	.25	.60
52 Doug Marsh	.15	.40
53 Wayne Morris	.15	.40
54 Pat Tilley	.15	.40
55 Roger Wehrli	.30	.75
56 Rolf Benirschke	.25	.60
57 Fred Dean	.25	.60
58 Dan Fouts	1.00	2.50
59 John Jefferson	.25	.60
60 Gary Johnson	.15	.40
61 Charlie Joiner	.50	1.25
62 Louie Kelcher	.15	.40
63 Chuck Muncie	.25	.60
64 Doug Wilkerson	.15	.40
65 Clarence Williams	.15	.40
66 Kellen Winslow	2.00	5.00
67 Coy Bacon	.15	.40
68 Wilbur Jackson	.15	.40
69 Karl Lorch	.15	.40
70 Rich Milot	.15	.40
71 Art Monk	2.40	6.00
72 Mark Moseley	.15	.40
73 Mike Nelms	.15	.40
74 Lemar Parrish	.15	.40
75 Joe Theismann	.60	1.50
76 Ricky Thompson	.15	.40
77 Joe Washington	.25	.60
NNO Colts Header Card	.15	.40
NNO Cowboys Header Card	.15	.40
NNO Oilers Header Card	.15	.40
NNO Giants Header Card	.15	.40
NNO Cardinals Header Card	.15	.40
NNO Chargers Header Card	.15	.40
NNO Redskins Header Card	.15	.40

1993 Coke Monsters of the Gridiron

Sponsored by Coca-Cola, this 30-card standard-size set was released as a complete set at Super Bowl Card Show V, January 27-30, 1994 in Atlanta. The set was available to the first 10,000 fans at the redemption booth in exchange for ten wrappers from any 1993 NFL-licensed trading card packs. The fronts feature borderless color studio shots of NFL players posed in their uniforms. The players are also dressed in horror costumes and made up to look like "monsters." Three of the cards (10, 19, and 20) feature fanciful color paintings of the players instead of photos. The white back carries the player's name and "monstrous" nickname at the top, followed below by career highlights. The cards are numbered on the back. Television ads featuring Randall Cunningham helped promote this set. The actual in-store promotion consisted of two randomly selected cards included in specially marked multi-packs of Coca-Cola Classic, diet Coke, Caffeine-free diet Coke, and Sprite. An "instant win" scratch-off game piece inside the same multi-packs could entitle the collector to win various prizes, including a gold foil edition of the entire set. Also collectors could obtain a random group of five cards by sending in a proof-of-purchase from any specially marked two-liter bottle. Reportedly more than 100 million collector cards were available nationwide. The promotion ran from Sept. 19 until Halloween, or while supplies lasted. Although the cards carry a 1994 copyright line date, they are considered a 1993 issue.

COMPLETE SET (30)	16.00	40.00
1 Title Card	.30	.75
Checklist		
2 Cornelius Bennett	.50	1.25
Big Bear		
3 Terrell Buckley	.30	.75
Tiger		
4 Tony Casillas	.30	.75
Conde (Count)		
5 Reggie Cobb	.30	.75
Crossbones		
6 Marco Coleman	.30	.75
Cobra		
7 Shane Conlan	.30	.75
Conlan The Barbarian		
8 Randall Cunningham	.75	2.00
Rocket Man		
9 Chris Doleman	.30	.75
Dr. Doomsday		
10 Steve Emtman	.30	.75
Beast-Man		
11 Harold Green	.30	.75
Slime		
12 Michael Haynes	.50	1.25
Moonlight Flyer		
13 Garrison Hearst	1.60	4.00
Hearse		
14 Craig Heyward	.30	.75
Iron Head		
15 Rickey Jackson	.30	.75
The Jackal		
16 Joe Jacoby	.30	.75
Frankenstein		
17 Sean Jones	.30	.75
Ghost		
18 Cortez Kennedy	.50	1.25
Tez Rex		
19 Howie Long	.75	2.00
Howlin'		
20 Ronnie Lott	.75	2.00
The Rattler		
21 Karl Mecklenburg	.30	.75
Midnight Marauder		
22 Neil O'Donnell	.50	1.25
Knight Raider		
23 Tom Rathman	.30	.75
Psycho		
24 Junior Seau	.75	2.00
Stealth		
25 Emmitt Smith	6.00	15.00
26 Pat Swilling	.30	.75
Chillin'		
27 Lawrence Taylor	.75	2.00
Six Gun		
28 Derrick Thomas	.75	2.00
Attack Cat		
29 Andre Tippett	.30	.75
Andre The Terrible		
30 Eric Turner	.30	.75
Bad Bone		

1994 Coke Monsters of the Gridiron

This 31-card set was sponsored by Coca-Cola and features color player photos dressed in horror costumes and made to look like monsters. The backs carry a head photo of the player with player information. The set was primarily distributed at the 1995 Super Bowl Card Show VI in Miami in exchange for 10 wrappers from any 1994 NFL card set. A Gold parallel version of the cards was also distributed.

COMPLETE SET (31)	20.00	40.00
*GOLD CARDS: 1X TO 2.5X BASIC CARDS		
1 Eric Swann	.40	1.00
2 Jessie Tuggle	.25	.60
3 Cornelius Bennett	.40	1.00
4 Carolina Panthers Mascot	.60	1.50
5 Chris Zorich	.25	.60
6 Dan Wilkinson	.25	.60
7 Eric Turner	.25	.60
8 Emmitt Smith	6.00	12.00
9 Steve Atwater	.25	.60
10 Pat Swilling	.25	.60
11 Sean Jones	.25	.60
12 Ray Childress	.25	.60
13 Marshall Faulk	4.00	10.00
14 Jacksonville Jaguars	.60	1.50
Mascot		
15 Derrick Thomas	.60	1.50
16 Chester McGlockton	.25	.60
17 Shane Conlan	.25	.60
18 Marco Coleman	.25	.60
19 John Randle	.40	1.00
20 Bruce Armstrong	.25	.60
21 Renaldo Turnbull	.25	.60
22 Jumbo Elliott	.25	.60
23 Ronnie Lott	.60	1.50
24 Randall Cunningham	.60	1.50
25 Neil O'Donnell	.60	1.50
26 Junior Seau	.60	1.50
27 Tom Rathman	.25	.60
28 Cortez Kennedy	.40	1.00
29 Hardy Nickerson	.25	.60
30 Ken Harvey UER	.25	.60
Name spelled Hen		
NNO Title Card	.25	.60
Checklist		

1994 Collector's Choice

This standard-size 384-card set features color action player photos. Cards were issued in 12, 13 and 20-card packs. One gold or silver parallel card was inserted per pack. Also issued was a 36-card Spanish promo set and a 260-card full Spanish set. Rookie Cards include Derrick Alexander, Marshall Faulk, William Floyd, Greg Hill, Charles Johnson, Errict Rhett, Darnay Scott and Heath Shuler. A Joe Montana Promo card was produced and priced below.

COMPLETE SET (384)	7.50	20.00
1 Antonio Langham RC	.02	.10
2 Aaron Glenn RC	.08	.25
3 Sam Adams RC	.02	.10
4 Dewayne Washington RC	.02	.10
5 Dan Wilkinson RC	.02	.10
6 Bryant Young RC	.15	.40
7 Aaron Taylor RC	.01	.05
8 Willie McGinest RC	.08	.25
9 Trev Alberts RC	.02	.10
10 Jamir Miller RC	.02	.10
11 John Thierry RC	.01	.05
12 Heath Shuler RC	.08	.25
13 Trent Dilfer RC	.50	1.25
14 Marshall Faulk RC	2.00	5.00
15 Greg Hill RC	.08	.25
16 William Floyd RC	.08	.25
17 Chuck Levy RC	.01	.05
18 Charlie Garner RC	.50	1.25
19 Mario Bates RC	.08	.25
20 Donnell Bennett RC	.08	.25
21 LeShon Johnson RC	.02	.10
22 Calvin Jones RC	.01	.05
23 Darnay Scott RC	.20	.50
24 Charles Johnson RC	.08	.25
25 Johnnie Morton RC	.20	.50
26 Shante Carver RC	.01	.05
27 Derrick Alexander WR RC	.08	.25
28 David Palmer RC	.08	.25
29 Ryan Yarborough RC	.01	.05
30 Errict Rhett RC	.08	.25
31 James Washington I93	.01	.05
32 Sterling Sharpe I93	.01	.05
33 Drew Bledsoe I93	.08	.25
34 Eric Allen I93	.01	.05
35 Jerome Bettis I93	.08	.25
36 Joe Montana I93	.25	.60
37 John Carney I93	.01	.05
38 Emmitt Smith I93	.20	.50
39 Chris Warren I93	.08	.25
40 Reggie Brooks I93	.01	.05
41 Gary Brown I93	.01	.05
42 Tim Brown I93	.02	.10
43 Erric Pegram I93	.01	.05
44 Ronald Moore I93	.01	.05
45 Jerry Rice I93	.15	.40
46 Ricky Watters TE	.02	.10
47 Joe Montana TE	.25	.60
48 Reggie Brooks TE	.01	.05
49 Rick Mirer TE	.08	.25
50 Rocket Ismail TE	.02	.10
51 Curtis Conway TE	.02	.10
52 Junior Seau TE	.08	.25
53 Mark Carrier DB TE	.01	.05
54 Ronnie Lott TE	.02	.10
55 Marcus Allen TE	.08	.25
56 Michael Irvin TE	.08	.25
57 Bennie Blades	.01	.05
58 Randal Hill	.01	.05
59 Brian Blades	.02	.10
60 Russell Maryland	.01	.05
61 Jim Kelly	.08	.25
62 Arthur Marshall	.01	.05
63 Webster Slaughter	.01	.05
64 Dave Krieg	.02	.10
65 Steve Jordan	.01	.05
66 Neil O'Donnell	.08	.25
67 Andre Reed	.02	.10
68 Mike Croel	.01	.05
69 Al Smith	.01	.05
70 Joe Montana	.60	1.50
71 Randall McDaniel	.02	.10
72 Greg Lloyd	.02	.10
73 Thomas Smith	.01	.05
74 Glyn Milburn	.02	.10
75 Lorenzo White	.01	.05
76 Neil Smith	.02	.10
77 John Randle	.02	.10
78 Rod Woodson	.02	.10
79 Russell Maryland	.01	.05
80 Rodney Peete	.01	.05
81 Jackie Harris	.01	.05
82 James Jett	.01	.05
83 Rodney Hampton	.02	.10
84 Bill Romanowski	.01	.05
85 Ken Norton Jr.	.02	.10
86 Barry Sanders	.50	1.25
87 Johnny Holland	.01	.05
88 Terry McDaniel	.01	.05
89 Greg Jackson	.01	.05
90 Dana Stubblefield	.02	.10
91 Jay Novacek	.02	.10
92 Chris Spielman	.02	.10
93 Ken Ruettgers	.01	.05
94 Greg Robinson	.01	.05
95 Mark Jackson	.01	.05
96 John Taylor	.02	.10
97 Roger Harper	.01	.05
98 Jerry Ball	.01	.05
99 Keith Byars	.01	.05
100 Morten Andersen	.01	.05
101 Eric Allen	.01	.05
102 Marion Butts	.01	.05
103 Michael Haynes	.02	.10
104 Rob Burnett	.01	.05
105 Marco Coleman	.01	.05
106 Derek Brown RBK	.01	.05
107 Andy Harmon	.01	.05
108 Darren Carrington	.01	.05
109 Bobby Hebert	.01	.05
110 Mark Carrier WR	.02	.10
111 Bryan Cox	.01	.05
112 Toi Cook	.01	.05
113 Tim Harris	.01	.05
114 John Friesz	.02	.10
115 Neal Anderson	.01	.05
116 Jerome Bettis	.15	.40
117 Bruce Armstrong	.01	.05
118 Brad Baxter	.01	.05
119 Johnny Bailey	.01	.05
120 Brian Blades	.02	.10
121 Mark Carrier DB	.01	.05
122 Shane Conlan	.01	.05
123 Drew Bledsoe	.25	.60
124 Chris Burkett	.01	.05
125 Steve Beuerlein	.02	.10
126 Ferrell Edmunds	.01	.05
127 Curtis Conway	.08	.25
128 Troy Drayton	.01	.05
129 Vincent Brown	.01	.05
130 Boomer Esiason	.02	.10
131 Larry Centers	.08	.25
132 Carlton Gray	.01	.05
133 Chris Miller	.01	.05
134 Eric Metcalf	.02	.10
135 Mark Higgs	.01	.05
136 Tyrone Hughes	.02	.10
137 Randall Cunningham	.08	.25
138 Ronnie Harmon	.01	.05
139 Andre Rison	.02	.10
140 Eric Turner	.01	.05
141 Terry Kirby	.08	.25
142 Eric Martin	.01	.05
143 Seth Joyner	.01	.05
144 Stan Humphries	.02	.10
145 Deion Sanders	.15	.40
146 Vinny Testaverde	.02	.10
147 Dan Marino	.60	1.50
148 Renaldo Turnbull	.01	.05
149 Herschel Walker	.02	.10
150 Anthony Miller	.02	.10
151 Richard Dent	.02	.10
152 Jim Everett	.02	.10
153 Ben Coates	.02	.10
154 Jeff Lageman	.01	.05
155 Garrison Hearst	.08	.25
156 Kelvin Martin	.01	.05
157 Dante Jones	.01	.05
158 Sean Gilbert	.01	.05
159 Leonard Russell	.01	.05
160 Ronnie Lott	.02	.10
161 Randal Hill	.01	.05
162 Rick Mirer	.08	.25
163 Alonzo Spellman	.01	.05
164 Todd Lyght	.01	.05
165 Chris Slade	.01	.05
166 Johnny Mitchell	.01	.05
167 Ronald Moore	.01	.05
168 Eugene Robinson	.01	.05
169 Chris Hinton	.01	.05
170 Dan Footman	.01	.05
171 Keith Jackson	.01	.05
172 Rickey Jackson	.01	.05
173 Heath Sherman	.01	.05
174 Chris Mims	.01	.05
175 Erric Pegram	.01	.05
176 Leroy Hoard	.01	.05
177 O.J. McDuffie	.08	.25
178 Wayne Martin	.01	.05
179 Clyde Simmons	.01	.05
180 Leslie O'Neal	.01	.05
181 Mike Pritchard	.01	.05
182 Michael Jackson	.02	.10
183 Scott Mitchell	.02	.10
184 Lorenzo Neal	.01	.05
185 William Thomas	.01	.05
186 Junior Seau UER	.08	.25
(Career tackles 322, but add up to 451)		
187 Chris Gedney	.01	.05
188 Tim Lester	.01	.05
189 Sam Gash	.01	.05
190 Johnny Johnson	.01	.05
191 Chuck Cecil	.01	.05
192 Cortez Kennedy	.02	.10
193 Jim Harbaugh	.08	.25
194 Roman Phifer	.01	.05
195 Pat Harlow	.01	.05
196 Rob Moore	.02	.10
197 Gary Clark	.02	.10
198 Jon Vaughn	.01	.05
199 Craig Heyward	.02	.10
200 Michael Stewart	.01	.05
201 Greg McMurtry	.01	.05
202 Brian Washington	.01	.05
203 Ken Harvey	.01	.05
204 Chris Warren	.02	.10
205 Bruce Smith	.08	.25
206 Tom Rouen	.01	.05
207 Cris Dishman	.01	.05
208 Keith Cash	.01	.05
209 Carlos Jenkins	.01	.05
210 Levon Kirkland	.01	.05
211 Pete Metzelaars	.01	.05
212 Shannon Sharpe	.02	.10
213 Cody Carlson	.01	.05
214 Derrick Thomas	.08	.25
215 Emmitt Smith	.50	1.25
216 Robert Porcher	.01	.05
217 Sterling Sharpe	.02	.10
218 Anthony Smith	.01	.05
219 Mike Sherrard	.01	.05
220 Tom Rathman	.01	.05
221 Nate Newton	.01	.05
222 Pat Swilling	.01	.05
223 George Teague	.01	.05
224 Greg Townsend	.01	.05
225 Eric Guliford RC	.02	.10
226 Leroy Thompson	.01	.05
227 Thurman Thomas	.08	.25
228 Dan Williams	.01	.05
229 Bubba McDowell	.01	.05
230 Tracy Simien	.01	.05
231 Scottie Graham RC	.02	.10
232 Eric Green	.01	.05
233 Phil Simms	.02	.10
234 Ricky Watters	.02	.10
235 Kevin Williams	.02	.10
236 Brett Perriman	.02	.10
237 Reggie White	.08	.25
238 Steve Wisniewski	.01	.05
239 Mark Collins	.01	.05
240 Steve Young	.30	.75
241 Steve Tovar	.01	.05
242 Jason Belser	.01	.05
243 Ray Seals	.01	.05
244 Earnest Byner	.01	.05
245 Ricky Proehl	.01	.05
246 Rich Miano	.01	.05
247 Alfred Williams	.01	.05
248 Ray Buchanan UER	.01	.05
(Buchannan on front)		
249 Hardy Nickerson	.02	.10
250 Brad Edwards	.01	.05
251 Jerrol Williams	.01	.05
252 Marvin Washington	.01	.05
253 Tony McGee	.01	.05
254 Jeff George	.08	.25
255 Ron Hall	.01	.05
256 Tim Johnson	.01	.05
257 Willie Roaf	.01	.05
258 Corwin Brown RC	.01	.05
259 Ricardo McDonald	.01	.05
260 Jeff Herrod	.01	.05
261 Demetrius DuBose	.01	.05
262 Ricky Sanders	.01	.05
263 John L. Williams	.01	.05
264 John Lynch	.08	.25
265 Lance Gunn	.01	.05
266 Jessie Hester	.01	.05
267 Mark Wheeler	.01	.05
268 Chip Lohmiller	.01	.05
269 Eric Swann	.02	.10
270 Byron Evans	.01	.05
271 Gary Plummer	.01	.05
272 Roger Duffy RC	.01	.05
273 Irv Smith	.01	.05
274 Todd Collins	.01	.05
275 Robert Blackmon	.01	.05
276 Reggie Roby	.01	.05
277 Russell Copeland	.01	.05
278 Simon Fletcher	.01	.05
279 Ernest Givins	.02	.10
280 Tim Barnett	.01	.05
281 Chris Doleman	.01	.05
282 Jeff Graham	.01	.05
283 Kenneth Davis	.01	.05
284 Vance Johnson	.01	.05
285 Haywood Jeffires	.02	.10
286 Todd McNair	.01	.05
287 Daryl Johnston	.02	.10
288 Ryan McNeil	.01	.05
289 Terrell Buckley	.01	.05
290 Ethan Horton	.01	.05
291 Corey Miller	.01	.05
292 Marc Logan	.01	.05
293 Lincoln Coleman RC	.01	.05
294 Derrick Moore	.01	.05
295 LeRoy Butler	.01	.05
296 Jeff Hostetler	.02	.10
297 Qadry Ismail	.08	.25
298 Andre Hastings	.02	.10
299 Henry Jones	.01	.05
300 John Elway	.60	1.50
301 Warren Moon	.08	.25
302 Willie Davis	.02	.10
303 Vencie Glenn	.01	.05
304 Kevin Greene	.02	.10
305 Marcus Buckley	.01	.05
306 Tim McDonald	.01	.05
307 Michael Irvin	.08	.25
308 Herman Moore	.08	.25
309 Brett Favre	.60	1.50
310 Rocket Ismail	.02	.10
311 Jarrod Bunch	.01	.05
312 Don Beebe	.01	.05
313 Steve Atwater	.01	.05
314 Gary Brown	.01	.05
315 Marcus Allen	.08	.25
316 Terry Allen	.02	.10
317 Chad Brown	.01	.05
318 Cornelius Bennett	.02	.10
319 Rod Bernstine	.01	.05
320 Greg Montgomery	.01	.05
321 Kimble Anders	.02	.10
322 Charles Haley	.02	.10
323 Mel Gray	.01	.05
324 Edgar Bennett	.08	.25
325 Eddie Anderson	.01	.05
326 Derek Brown TE	.01	.05
327 Steve Bono	.02	.10
328 Alvin Harper	.02	.10

329 Willie Green .01 .05
330 Robert Brooks .08 .25
331 Patrick Bates .01 .05
332 Anthony Carter .02 .10
333 Barry Foster .01 .05
334 Bill Brooks .01 .05
335 Jason Elam .02 .10
336 Ray Childress .01 .05
337 J.J. Birden .01 .05
338 Cris Carter .15 .40
339 Deon Figures .01 .05
340 Carlton Bailey .01 .05
341 Brent Jones .02 .10
342 Troy Aikman UER .30 .75
(Stats on back has 60 Int., should be 66)
343 Rodney Holman .01 .05
344 Tony Bennett .01 .05
345 Tim Brown .08 .25
346 Michael Brooks .01 .05
347 Martin Harrison .01 .05
348 Jerry Rice .30 .75
349 John Copeland .01 .05
350 Kerry Cash .01 .05
351 Reggie Cobb .01 .05
352 Brian Mitchell .01 .05
353 Derrick Fenner .01 .05
354 Roosevelt Potts .01 .05
355 Courtney Hawkins .01 .05
356 Carl Banks .01 .05
357 Harold Green .01 .05
358 Steve Emtman .01 .05
359 Santana Dotson .02 .10
360 Reggie Brooks .02 .10
361 Terry Obee .01 .05
362 David Klingler .01 .05
363 Quentin Coryatt .01 .05
364 Craig Erickson .01 .05
365 Desmond Howard .02 .10
366 Carl Pickens .02 .10
367 Lawrence Dawsey .01 .05
368 Henry Ellard .02 .10
369 Shaun Gayle .01 .05
370 David Lang .01 .05
371 Anthony Johnson .02 .10
372 Darnell Walker RC .01 .05
373 Pepper Johnson .01 .05
374 Kurt Gouveia .01 .05
375 Louis Oliver .01 .05
376 Lincoln Kennedy .01 .05
377 Anthony Pleasant .01 .05
378 Irving Fryar .02 .10
379 Carolina Panthers .08 .25
Expansion Team Card
380 Jacksonville Jaguars .01 .05
Expansion Team Card
381 Checklist UER .02 .10
Sterling Sharpe
(Front has 193-288 and back has Sharp; should be Sharpe)
382 Dan Marino ART .08 .25
Checklist Card
383 Jerry Rice ART UER .08 .25
Checklist Card
(Front has 289-384)
384 Joe Montana ART UER .08 .25
Checklist Card
(Front has 1-96)
Joe Montana
P19 Joe Montana Promo .75 2.00

1994 Collector's Choice Gold

*STARS: 10X TO 25X BASIC CARDS
*RCs: 6X TO 15X BASIC CARDS
ONE GOLD OR SILVER PER PACK

1994 Collector's Choice Silver

COMPLETE SET (384) 35.00 80.00
*STARS: 1.2X TO 3X BASIC CARDS
*RCS: 1X TO 2X BASIC CARDS
ONE GOLD OR SILVER PER FOIL PA
TWO SILV/GOLD PER SPECIAL RETAIL

1994 Collector's Choice Crash the Game

COMP.BLUE SET (30) 15.00 40.00
COMP.GREEN SET (30) 15.00 40.00
BLUE FOIL INSERTED IN HOBBY PA
GREEN FOIL INSERTED IN RETAIL
COMP.BRONZE SET (30) 5.00 12.00
*BRONZES: .1X to .3X BASIC INSERTS
ONE SET PER BRONZE WINNER CARD
COMP.SILVER SET (30) 6.00 15.00
*SILVERS: .15X to .4X BASIC INSERTS
ONE SET PER SILVER WINNER CARD
COMP.GOLD SET (30) 10.00 25.00
*GOLDS: .25X to .6X BASIC INSERTS
ONE SET PER GOLD WINNER CARD
C1B Steve Young WIN 1.00 2.50
C1G Steve Young WIN 1.00 2.50
C2B Troy Aikman WIN S 1.00 2.50
C2G Troy Aikman WIN B 1.00 2.50
C3B Rick Mirer WIN B .30 .75
C3G Rick Mirer WIN B .30 .75
C4B Trent Dilfer WIN B .50 1.25
C4G Trent Dilfer NO WIN .50 1.25
C5B Dan Marino WIN 2.00 5.00
C5G Dan Marino WIN S 2.00 5.00
C6B John Elway WIN S 2.00 5.00
C6G John Elway WIN S 2.00 5.00
C7B Heath Shuler WIN S .08 .25
C7G Heath Shuler NO WIN .08 .25
C8B Joe Montana WIN 2.00 5.00
C8G Joe Montana WIN S 2.00 5.00
C9B Drew Bledsoe .75 2.00
UER WIN G
C9G Drew Bledsoe .75 2.00
UER WIN G
C10B Warren Moon WIN S .30 .75
C10G Warren Moon WIN S .30 .75
C11B Marshall Faulk WIN B 2.00 5.00
C11G Marshall Faulk WIN S 2.00 5.00
C12B Thurman Thomas .30 .75
WIN B
C12G Thurman Thomas .30 .75
WIN B
C13B Barry Foster WIN B .05 .15
C13G Barry Foster WIN B .05 .15
C14B Gary Brown NO WIN .05 .15
C14G Gary Brown NO WIN .05 .15
C15B Emmitt Smith WIN 1.50 4.00
C15G Emmitt Smith WIN 1.50 4.00
C16B Barry Sanders WIN B 1.50 4.00
C16G Barry Sanders WIN B 1.50 4.00
C17B Rodney Hampton .10 .30
WIN B
C17G Rodney Hampton .10 .30
WIN B
C18B Jerome Bettis WIN B .50 1.25
C18G Jerome Bettis NO WIN .50 1.25
C19B Ricky Watters WIN B .10 .30
C19G Ricky Watters NO WIN .10 .30
C20B Ronald Moore WIN B .05 .15
C20G Ronald Moore WIN B .05 .15
C21B Jerry Rice WIN 1.00 2.50
C21G Jerry Rice NO WIN 1.00 2.50
C22B Andre Rison WIN .10 .30
C22G Andre Rison WIN B .10 .30
C23B Michael Irvin NO WIN .30 .75
C23G Michael Irvin WIN S .30 .75
C24B Sterling Sharpe WIN S .10 .30
C24G Sterling Sharpe WIN B .10 .30
C25B Shannon Sharpe .10 .30
NO WIN
C25G Shannon Sharpe .10 .30
NO WIN
C26B Darnay Scott NO WIN .20 .50
C26G Darnay Scott WIN B .20 .50
C27B Andre Reed WIN S .10 .30
C27G Andre Reed WIN B .10 .30
C28B Tim Brown NO WIN .30 .75
C28G Tim Brown WIN S .30 .75
C29B Charles Johnson WIN B .08 .25
C29G Charles Johnson .08 .25
NO WIN
C30B Irving Fryar NO WIN .10 .30
C30G Irving Fryar NO WIN .10 .30

1994 Collector's Choice Then and Now

COMPLETE SET (8) 4.00 10.00
ONE SET PER TRADE CARD BY MAIL
1 Eric Dickerson .50 1.25
Jerome Bettis
2 Fred Biletnikoff .40 1.00
Tim Brown
3 Len Dawson .75 2.00
Joe Montana
4 Joe Montana 1.00 2.50
Steve Young
5 Bob Griese 1.25 3.00
Dan Marino
6 Jim Zorn .30 .75
Rick Mirer
NNO Joe Montana .75 2.00
Header Card
NNO Eric Dickerson .30 .75
Checklist Card

1994 Collector's Choice Spanish Promos NNO

This standard-size set was issued to preview the Collector's Choice Spanish series. The cards are nearly identical to their American counterparts, with the exception that the player profile on the backs have been shortened to create space for the Spanish translation. Also these cards are unnumbered with just a solid black oval where the card number should be. They are checklisted below alphabetically.

COMPLETE SET (36) 36.00 90.00
1 Troy Aikman 6.00 15.00
2 Marcus Allen 2.00 5.00
3 Terry Allen 1.20 3.00
4 Kimble Anders .80 2.00
5 Eddie Anderson .50 1.25
6 Steve Atwater .50 1.25
7 Carlton Bailey .50 1.25
8 Patrick Bates .50 1.25
9 Don Beebe .50 1.25
10 Cornelius Bennett .80 2.00
11 Edgar Bennett .80 2.00
12 Tony Bennett .50 1.25
13 Rod Bernstine .50 1.25
14 J.J.Birden .50 1.25
15 Steve Bono .50 1.25
16 Bill Brooks .50 1.25
17 Michael Brooks .50 1.25
18 Robert Brooks .80 2.00
19 Chad Brown .50 1.25
20 Derek Brown TE .50 1.25
21 Gary Brown .50 1.25
22 Tim Brown 2.00 5.00
23 Anthony Carter .50 1.25
24 Cris Carter 3.00 6.00
25 Ray Childress .50 1.25
26 Jason Elam .50 1.25
27 Deon Figures .50 1.25
28 Barry Foster .50 1.25
29 Mel Gray .50 1.25
30 Willie Green .50 1.25
31 Charles Haley .50 1.25
32 Alvin Harper .50 1.25
33 Martin Harrison .50 1.25
34 Rodney Holman .50 1.25
35 Brent Jones .50 1.25
36 Greg Montgomery .50 1.25

1994 Collector's Choice Spanish

Produced by Upper Deck for sale in Mexico, this 260-card set measures the standard size. The set starts with the subsets Rookie Class 1994 (1-30) and Images of 93 (31-45), followed by 215-regular cards. Each cardback is written in both English and Spanish.

COMPLETE SET (260) 32.00 80.00
1 Antonio Langham .10 .30
2 Aaron Glenn .20 .50
3 Sam Adams .10 .30
4 Dewayne Washington .10 .30
5 Dan Wilkinson .10 .30
6 Bryant Young .10 .30
7 Aaron Taylor .07 .20
8 Willie McGinest .20 .50
9 Trev Alberts .10 .30
10 Jamir Miller .07 .20
11 John Thierry .07 .20
12 Heath Shuler .20 .50
13 Trent Dilfer 2.00 5.00
14 Marshall Faulk 10.00 20.00
15 Greg Hill .10 .30
16 William Floyd .10 .30
17 Chuck Levy .07 .20
18 Charlie Garner .20 .50
19 Mario Bates .10 .30
20 Donnell Bennett .07 .20
21 LeShon Johnson .10 .30
22 Calvin Jones .07 .20
23 Darnay Scott .20 .50
24 Charles Johnson .20 .50
25 Johnnie Morton .20 .50
26 Shante Carver .07 .20
27 Derrick Alexander WR .20 .50
28 David Palmer .10 .30
29 Ryan Yarborough .07 .20
30 Errict Rhett .40 1.00
31 James Washington I93 .07 .20
32 Sterling Sharpe I93 .07 .20
33 Drew Bledsoe I93 1.00 2.50
34 Eric Allen I93 .07 .20
35 Jerome Bettis I93 .50 1.25
36 Joe Montana I93 2.50 5.00
37 John Carney I93 .07 .20
38 Emmitt Smith I93 1.60 4.00
39 Chris Warren I93 .20 .50
40 Reggie Brooks I93 .07 .20
41 Gary Brown I93 .07 .20
42 Tim Brown I93 .20 .50
43 Erric Pegram I93 .07 .20
44 Ronald Moore I93 .07 .20
45 Jerry Rice I93 1.25 3.00
46 Don Beebe .07 .20
47 Steve Atwater .07 .20
48 Gary Brown .07 .20
49 Marcus Allen .20 .50
50 Terry Allen .10 .30
51 Chad Brown .07 .20
52 Cornelius Bennett .10 .30
53 Rod Bernstine .07 .20
54 Greg Montgomery .07 .20
55 Kimble Anders .07 .20
56 Charles Haley .10 .30
57 Mel Gray .07 .20
58 Edgar Bennett .10 .30
59 Eddie Anderson .07 .20
60 Derek Brown TE .07 .20
61 Jim Kelly .20 .50
62 Arthur Marshall .07 .20
63 Webster Slaughter .07 .20
64 Dave Krieg .10 .30
65 Steve Jordan .07 .20
66 Neil O'Donnell .10 .30
67 Andre Reed .10 .30
68 Mike Croel .07 .20
69 Al Smith .07 .20
70 Joe Montana 3.20 8.00
71 Randall McDaniel .07 .20
72 Greg Lloyd .10 .30
73 Thomas Smith .07 .20
74 Glyn Milburn .10 .30
75 Lorenzo White .07 .20
76 Neil Smith .10 .30
77 John Randle .10 .30
78 Rod Woodson .10 .30
79 Russell Maryland .07 .20
80 Rodney Peete .07 .20
81 Jackie Harris .07 .20
82 James Jett .07 .20
83 Rodney Hampton .10 .30
84 Bill Romanowski .07 .20
85 Ken Norton, Jr. .10 .30
86 Barry Sanders 3.20 8.00
87 Johnny Holland .07 .20
88 Terry McDaniel .07 .20
89 Greg Jackson .07 .20
90 Dana Stubblefield .10 .30
91 Jay Novacek .10 .30
92 Chris Spielman .10 .30
93 Ken Ruettgers .07 .20
94 Greg Robinson .07 .20
95 Mark Jackson .07 .20
96 John Taylor .10 .30
97 Roger Harper .07 .20
98 Jerry Ball .07 .20
99 Keith Byars .07 .20
100 Morten Andersen .07 .20
101 Eric Allen .07 .20
102 Marion Butts .07 .20
103 Michael Haynes .10 .30
104 Rob Burnett .07 .20
105 Marco Coleman .07 .20
106 Derek Brown RBK .07 .20
107 Andy Harmon .07 .20
108 Darren Carrington .07 .20
109 Bobby Hebert .07 .20
110 Mark Carrier WR .10 .30
111 Bryan Cox .07 .20
112 Toi Cook .07 .20
113 Tim Harris .07 .20
114 John Friesz .10 .30
115 Neal Anderson .07 .20
116 Jerome Bettis 1.00 2.50
117 Bruce Armstrong .07 .20
118 Brad Baxter .07 .20
119 Johnny Bailey .07 .20
120 Brian Blades .10 .30
121 Mark Carrier DB UER .07 .20
listed as WR on back
122 Shane Conlan .07 .20
123 Drew Bledsoe 2.00 5.00
124 Chris Burkett .07 .20
125 Steve Beuerlein .10 .30
126 Ferrell Edmunds .07 .20
127 Curtis Conway .20 .50
128 Troy Drayton .07 .20
129 Vincent Brown .07 .20
130 Boomer Esiason .10 .30
131 Larry Centers .10 .30
132 Carlton Gray .07 .20
133 Chris Miller .07 .20
134 Eric Metcalf .10 .30
135 Mark Higgs .07 .20
136 Tyrone Hughes .10 .30
137 Randall Cunningham .20 .50
138 Ronnie Harmon .07 .20
139 Andre Rison .10 .30
140 Eric Turner .07 .20
141 Terry Kirby .10 .30
142 Eric Martin .07 .20
143 Seth Joyner .07 .20
144 Stan Humphries .10 .30
145 Deion Sanders 1.00 2.50
146 Vinny Testaverde .10 .30
147 Dan Marino 3.20 8.00
148 Renaldo Turnbull .07 .20
149 Herschel Walker .10 .30
150 Anthony Miller .10 .30
151 Richard Dent .10 .30
152 Jim Everett .10 .30
153 Ben Coates .10 .30
154 Jeff Lageman .07 .20
155 Garrison Hearst .80 2.00
156 Kelvin Martin .07 .20
157 Dante Jones .07 .20
158 Sean Gilbert .07 .20
159 Leonard Russell .07 .20
160 Ronnie Lott .10 .30
161 Randal Hill .07 .20
162 Rick Mirer .20 .50
163 Alonzo Spellman .07 .20
164 Todd Lyght .07 .20
165 Chris Slade .07 .20
166 Johnny Mitchell .07 .20
167 Ronald Moore .07 .20
168 Eugene Robinson .07 .20
169 John Copeland .07 .20
170 Kerry Cash .07 .20
171 Reggie Cobb .07 .20
172 Brian Mitchell .07 .20
173 Derrick Fenner .07 .20
174 Roosevelt Potts .07 .20
175 Courtney Hawkins .07 .20
176 Carl Banks .07 .20
177 Harold Green .07 .20
178 Steve Emtman .07 .20
179 Santana Dotson .10 .30
180 Reggie Brooks .10 .30
181 Terry Obee .07 .20
182 David Klingler .07 .20
183 Quentin Coryatt .07 .20
184 Craig Erickson .07 .20
185 Desmond Howard .10 .30
186 Carl Pickens .10 .30
187 Lawrence Dawsey .07 .20
188 Henry Ellard .07 .20
189 Shaun Gayle .07 .20
190 David Lang .07 .20
191 Anthony Johnson .10 .30
192 Darnell Walker .07 .20
193 Pepper Johnson .07 .20
194 Kurt Gouveia .07 .20
195 Louis Oliver .07 .20
196 Lincoln Kennedy .07 .20
197 Anthony Pleasant .07 .20
198 Irving Fryar .10 .30
199 Steve Bono .10 .30
200 Alvin Harper .10 .30
201 Willie Green .07 .20
202 Robert Brooks .20 .50
203 Patrick Bates .07 .20
204 Anthony Carter .10 .30
205 Bruce Smith .20 .50
206 Tom Rouen .07 .20
207 Cris Dishman .07 .20
208 Keith Cash .07 .20
209 Carlos Jenkins .07 .20
210 Levon Kirkland .07 .20
211 Pete Metzelaars .07 .20
212 Shannon Sharpe .10 .30
213 Cody Carlson .07 .20
214 Derrick Thomas .20 .50
215 Emmitt Smith 2.40 6.00
216 Robert Porcher .07 .20
217 Sterling Sharpe .10 .30
218 Anthony Smith .07 .20
219 Mike Sherrard .07 .20
220 Tom Rathman .07 .20
221 Nate Newton .07 .20
222 Pat Swilling .07 .20
223 George Teague .07 .20
224 Greg Townsend .07 .20
225 Eric Guliford .07 .20
226 Leroy Thompson .07 .20
227 Thurman Thomas .20 .50
228 Dan Williams .07 .20
229 Bubba McDowell .07 .20
230 Tracy Simien .07 .20
231 Scottie Graham .10 .30
232 Eric Green .07 .20
233 Phil Simms .10 .30
234 Ricky Watters .10 .30
235 Kevin Williams WR .10 .30
236 Brett Perriman .10 .30
237 Reggie White .20 .50
238 Steve Wisniewski .07 .20
239 Mark Collins .07 .20
240 Steve Young 1.60 4.00
241 Barry Foster .07 .20
242 Bill Brooks .07 .20
243 Jason Elam .10 .30
244 Ray Childress .07 .20
245 J.J. Birden .07 .20
246 Cris Carter .20 .50
247 Deon Figures .07 .20
248 Carlton Bailey .07 .20
249 Brent Jones .10 .30
250 Troy Aikman 2.00 5.00
251 Rodney Holman .07 .20
252 Tony Bennett .07 .20
253 Tim Brown .20 .50
254 Michael Brooks .07 .20
255 Martin Harrison .07 .20
256 Carolina Panthers Logo .20 .50
257 Jacksonville Jaguars Logo .07 .20
258 Dan Marino ART .50 1.25
Checklist Card
card #170 Kerry not Keith
259 Jerry Rice ART .40 1.00
Checklist Card
260 Joe Montana ART UER .50 1.25
Checklist Card
several incorrect player listings

1994-95 Collector's Choice Crash the Super Bowl XXIX

Upper Deck produced eight standard-size cards specifically for Super Bowl XXIX. These cards were available at the NFL Experience card show in Miami, in various hobby publications and through the nationally-syndicated "Sports Collector's Radio Network." The set features four players from the AFC champion San Diego Chargers (1-4) and four from the NFC San Francisco 49ers (5-8). If the player featured scored a touchdown in the Super Bowl, the card was redeemable for a special nine-card set. The redemption prize set featured the eight players in the set plus a Super Bowl "header" card. The redemption prize cards' text were rewritten to present a summary of that player's Super Bowl performance.

COMPLETE SET (9) 4.00 10.00
*PRIZES: .4X TO 1X BASIC INSERTS
1 Steve Young WIN 1.00 2.50
2 Jerry Rice WIN 1.20 3.00
3 Brent Jones .30 .75
4 Ricky Watters WIN .40 1.00
5 Stan Humphries WIN .30 .75
6 Natrone Means WIN .40 1.00
7 Ronnie Harmon .30 .75
8 Tony Martin WIN .40 1.00
NNO Header Card .30 .75

1995 Collector's Choice

This 348-card standard-size set features color action player photos with white borders on the front. Subsets include 1995 Rookie Class (1-30, sequenced in draft order), Did You Know (31-50), Jacksonville Jaguars expansion selections (331-338) and Carolina Panthers picks (339-346). The 12-card packs had a suggested retail price of .99 cents. Each pack contained a Player's Club parallel insert card. Inserted one per hobby boxes was a Platinum Player's Club card. Hobby dealers ordering cases directly from Upper Deck received 30 silver Crash the Game cards for their first case ordered and 90 silver Crash the Game cards if they ordered two cases. Rookie Cards in this set include Ki-Jana Carter, Kerry Collins, Joey Galloway, Steve McNair, Rashaan Salaam, J.J.Stokes and Michael Westbrook. A Joe Montana Promo card was produced and priced below.

COMPLETE SET (348) 10.00 20.00
1 Ki-Jana Carter RC .08 .25
2 Tony Boselli RC .08 .25
3 Steve McNair RC 1.00 2.50
4 Michael Westbrook RC .08 .25
5 Kerry Collins RC .60 1.50
6 Kevin Carter RC .08 .25
7 Mike Mamula RC .01 .05
8 Joey Galloway RC .50 1.25
9 Kyle Brady RC .08 .25
10 J.J. Stokes RC .08 .25
11 Derrick Alexander DE RC .01 .05
12 Warren Sapp RC .50 1.25
13 Mark Fields RC .08 .25
14 Tyrone Wheatley RC .40 1.00
15 Napoleon Kaufman RC .40 1.00
16 James O. Stewart RC .40 1.00
17 Luther Elliss RC .01 .05
18 Rashaan Salaam RC .02 .10
19 Ty Law RC .50 1.25
20 Mark Bruener RC .02 .10
21 Derrick Brooks RC .50 1.25
22 Christian Fauria RC .02 .10
23 Ray Zellars RC .02 .10
24 Todd Collins RC .30 .75
25 Sherman Williams RC .01 .05
26 Frank Sanders RC .08 .25
27 Rodney Thomas RC .02 .10
28 Rob Johnson RC .30 .75
29 Steve Stenstrom RC .01 .05
30 James A.Stewart RC .01 .05
31 Barry Sanders DYK .25 .60
32 Marshall Faulk DYK .15 .40
33 Darnay Scott DYK .02 .10
34 Joe Montana DYK .25 .60
35 Michael Irvin DYK .02 .10
36 Jerry Rice DYK .15 .40
37 Errict Rhett DYK .02 .10
38 Drew Bledsoe DYK .08 .25
39 Dan Marino DYK .25 .60
40 Terance Mathis DYK .01 .05
41 Natrone Means DYK .02 .10
42 Tim Brown DYK .02 .10
43 Steve Young DYK .10 .30
44 Mel Gray DYK .01 .05
45 Jerome Bettis DYK .08 .25
46 Aeneas Williams DYK .01 .05
47 Charlie Garner DYK .02 .10
48 Deion Sanders DYK .08 .25
49 Ken Harvey DYK .01 .05
50 Emmitt Smith DYK .20 .50
51 Andre Reed .02 .10
52 Sean Dawkins .02 .10
53 Irving Fryar .02 .10
54 Vincent Brisby .01 .05
55 Rob Moore .02 .10
56 Carl Pickens .02 .10
57 Vinny Testaverde .02 .10
58 Webster Slaughter .01 .05
59 Eric Green .01 .05
60 Anthony Miller .02 .10
61 Lake Dawson .02 .10
62 Tim Brown .08 .25
63 Stan Humphries .02 .10
64 Rick Mirer .02 .10
65 Gary Clark .01 .05
66 Troy Aikman .30 .75
67 Mike Sherrard .01 .05
68 Fred Barnett .02 .10
69 Henry Ellard .02 .10
70 Terry Allen .02 .10
71 Jeff Graham .01 .05
72 Herman Moore .08 .25
73 Brett Favre .60 1.50
74 Trent Dilfer .08 .25
75 Derek Brown RBK .01 .05
76 Andre Rison .02 .10
77 Flipper Anderson .01 .05
78 Jerry Rice UER .30 .75
Career totals are all wrong
79 Thurman Thomas .08 .25
80 Marshall Faulk .40 1.00
81 O.J. McDuffie .08 .25
82 Ben Coates .02 .10
83 Johnny Mitchell .01 .05
84 Darnay Scott .02 .10
85 Derrick Alexander WR .08 .25
86 Micheal Barrow UER .01 .05
Name spelled Michael on both sides
87 Charles Johnson .02 .10
88 John Elway .60 1.50
89 Willie Davis .02 .10
90 James Jett .02 .10
91 Mark Seay .02 .10
92 Brian Blades .02 .10
93 Ricky Proehl .01 .05
94 Charles Haley .02 .10
95 Chris Calloway .01 .05
96 Calvin Williams .02 .10
97 Ethan Horton .01 .05
98 Cris Carter .08 .25
99 Curtis Conway .08 .25
100 Lomas Brown .01 .05
101 Edgar Bennett .02 .10
102 Craig Erickson .01 .05
103 Jim Everett .01 .05
104 Terance Mathis .02 .10
105 Wayne Gandy .01 .05
106 Brent Jones .01 .05
107 Bruce Smith .08 .25
108 Roosevelt Potts .01 .05
109 Dan Marino .60 1.50
110 Michael Timpson .01 .05
111 Boomer Esiason .02 .10
112 David Klingler .02 .10
113 Eric Metcalf .02 .10
114 Lorenzo White .01 .05
115 Neil O'Donnell .02 .10
116 Shannon Sharpe .02 .10
117 Joe Montana .60 1.50
118 Jeff Hostetler .02 .10
119 Ronnie Harmon .01 .05
120 Chris Warren .02 .10
121 Randal Hill .01 .05
122 Alvin Harper .01 .05
123 Dave Brown .02 .10
124 Randall Cunningham .08 .25
125 Heath Shuler .02 .10
126 Jake Reed .02 .10
127 Donnell Woolford .01 .05
128 Scott Mitchell .02 .10
129 Reggie White .08 .25
130 Lawrence Dawsey .01 .05
131 Michael Haynes .02 .10
132 Bert Emanuel .08 .25
133 Troy Drayton .01 .05
134 Merton Hanks .01 .05
135 Jim Kelly .08 .25
136 Tony Bennett .01 .05
137 Terry Kirby .02 .10
138 Drew Bledsoe .20 .50
139 Johnny Johnson .01 .05
140 Dan Wilkinson .02 .10
141 Leroy Hoard .01 .05
142 Gary Brown .01 .05
143 Barry Foster .02 .10
144 Shane Dronett .01 .05
145 Marcus Allen .08 .25
146 Harvey Williams .01 .05
147 Tony Martin .02 .10
148 Rod Stephens .01 .05
149 Ronald Moore .01 .05
150 Michael Irvin .08 .25
151 Rodney Hampton .02 .10
152 Herschel Walker .02 .10
153 Reggie Brooks .02 .10
154 Qadry Ismail .02 .10
155 Chris Zorich .01 .05
156 Barry Sanders .50 1.25
157 Sean Jones .01 .05
158 Errict Rhett .02 .10
159 Tyrone Hughes .02 .10
160 Jeff George .02 .10
161 Chris Miller .01 .05
162 Steve Young .25 .60
163 Cornelius Bennett .02 .10
164 Trev Alberts .01 .05
165 J.B. Brown .01 .05
166 Marion Butts .01 .05
167 Aaron Glenn .01 .05
168 James Francis .01 .05
169 Eric Turner .01 .05
170 Darryll Lewis .01 .05
171 John L. Williams .01 .05
172 Simon Fletcher .01 .05
173 Neil Smith .02 .10
174 Chester McGlockton .02 .10
175 Natrone Means .02 .10
176 Michael Sinclair .01 .05
177 Larry Centers .02 .10
178 Daryl Johnston .02 .10
179 Dave Meggett .01 .05
180 Greg Jackson .01 .05
181 Ken Harvey .01 .05
182 Warren Moon .02 .10
183 Steve Walsh .01 .05
184 Chris Spielman .02 .10
185 Bryce Paup .02 .10
186 Courtney Hawkins .01 .05
187 Willie Roaf .01 .05
188 Chris Doleman .01 .05
189 Jerome Bettis .08 .25
190 Ricky Watters .02 .10
191 Henry Jones .01 .05
192 Quentin Coryatt .02 .10
193 Bryan Cox .01 .05
194 Kevin Turner .01 .05
195 Siupeli Malamala .01 .05
196 Louis Oliver .01 .05
197 Rob Burnett .01 .05
198 Cris Dishman .01 .05
199 Byron Bam Morris .01 .05
200 Ray Crockett .01 .05
201 Jon Vaughn .01 .05
202 Nolan Harrison .01 .05
203 Leslie O'Neal .02 .10
204 Sam Adams .01 .05
205 Eric Swann .02 .10
206 Jay Novacek .02 .10
207 Keith Hamilton .01 .05
208 Charlie Garner .08 .25
209 Tom Carter .01 .05
210 Henry Thomas .01 .05
211 Lewis Tillman .01 .05
212 Pat Swilling .01 .05
213 Terrell Buckley .01 .05
214 Hardy Nickerson .01 .05
215 Mario Bates .02 .10
216 D.J. Johnson .01 .05
217 Robert Young .01 .05
218 Dana Stubblefield .02 .10
219 Jeff Burris .01 .05
220 Floyd Turner .01 .05
221 Troy Vincent .01 .05
222 Willie McGinest .02 .10
223 James Hasty .01 .05
224 Jeff Blake RC .25 .60
225 Stevon Moore .01 .05
226 Ernest Givins .01 .05
227 Greg Lloyd .02 .10
228 Steve Atwater .01 .05
229 Dale Carter .02 .10
230 Terry McDaniel .01 .05
231 John Carney .01 .05
232 Cortez Kennedy .02 .10
233 Clyde Simmons .01 .05
234 Emmitt Smith .50 1.25
235 Thomas Lewis .02 .10
236 William Fuller .01 .05
237 Ricky Ervins .01 .05
238 John Randle .02 .10
239 John Thierry .01 .05
240 Mel Gray .01 .05
241 George Teague .01 .05
242 Charles Wilson Bucs .01 .05
see '95 Coll.Choice Update #U170
243 Joe Johnson .01 .05
244 Chuck Smith .01 .05
245 Sean Gilbert .02 .10
246 Bryant Young .02 .10
247 Bucky Brooks .01 .05
248 Ray Buchanan .01 .05
249 Tim Bowens .01 .05
250 Vincent Brown .01 .05
251 Marcus Turner .01 .05
252 Derrick Fenner .01 .05
253 Antonio Langham .01 .05
254 Cody Carlson .01 .05
255 Kevin Greene .02 .10
256 Leonard Russell .01 .05
257 Donnell Bennett .02 .10
258 Rocket Ismail .02 .10
259 Alfred Pupunu RC .01 .05
260 Eugene Robinson .01 .05
261 Seth Joyner .01 .05
262 Darren Woodson .02 .10
263 Phillippi Sparks .01 .05
264 Andy Harmon .01 .05
265 Brian Mitchell .01 .05
266 Fuad Reveiz .01 .05
267 Mark Carrier DB .01 .05
268 Johnnie Morton .02 .10
269 LeShon Johnson .02 .10
270 Eric Curry .01 .05
271 Quinn Early .02 .10
272 Elbert Shelley .01 .05
273 Roman Phifer .01 .05
274 Ken Norton Jr. .02 .10
275 Steve Tasker .02 .10
276 Jim Harbaugh .02 .10
277 Aubrey Beavers .01 .05
278 Chris Slade .01 .05
279 Mo Lewis .01 .05
280 Alfred Williams .01 .05
281 Michael Dean Perry UER .01 .05
misspelled Micheal
282 Marcus Robertson .01 .05
283 Rod Woodson .02 .10
284 Glyn Milburn .01 .05
285 Greg Hill .02 .10
286 Rob Fredrickson .01 .05
287 Junior Seau .08 .25
288 Rick Tuten .01 .05
289 Aeneas Williams .01 .05
290 Darrin Smith .01 .05
291 John Booty .01 .05
292 Eric Allen .01 .05
293 Reggie Roby .01 .05
294 David Palmer .02 .10
295 Trace Armstrong .01 .05
296 Dave Krieg UER .01 .05
misspelled Kreig on front
297 Robert Brooks .08 .25
298 Brad Culpepper .01 .05
299 Wayne Martin .01 .05
300 Craig Heyward .02 .10
301 Isaac Bruce .15 .40
302 Deion Sanders .15 .40
303 Matt Darby .01 .05
304 Kirk Lowdermilk .01 .05
305 Bernie Parmalee .02 .10
306 Leroy Thompson .01 .05
307 Ronnie Lott .02 .10
308 Steve Tovar .01 .05
309 Michael Jackson .02 .10
310 Al Smith .01 .05
311 Chad Brown .02 .10
312 Elijah Alexander .01 .05
313 Kimble Anders .02 .10
314 Anthony Smith .01 .05
315 Andre Coleman .01 .05
316 Terry Wooden .01 .05
317 Garrison Hearst .08 .25
318 Russell Maryland .01 .05
319 Michael Brooks .01 .05
320 Bernard Williams .01 .05
321 Andre Collins .01 .05
322 Dewayne Washington .02 .10
323 Raymont Harris .01 .05
324 Brett Perriman .02 .10
325 LeRoy Butler .01 .05
326 Santana Dotson .01 .05
327 Irv Smith .01 .05
328 Ron George .01 .05
329 Marquez Pope .01 .05
330 William Floyd .02 .10
331 Mickey Washington .01 .05
332 Keith Goganious .01 .05
333 Derek Brown TE .01 .05
334 Steve Beuerlein UER .02 .10
Name spelled Beuerlien on front
335 Reggie Cobb .01 .05
336 Jeff Lageman .01 .05
337 Kelvin Martin .01 .05
338 Darren Carrington .01 .05
339 Mark Carrier WR .02 .10
340 Willie Green .01 .05
341 Frank Reich .01 .05
342 Don Beebe .01 .05
343 Lamar Lathon .01 .05
344 Tim McKyer .01 .05
345 Pete Metzelaars .01 .05
346 Vernon Turner .01 .05
347 Dan Marino .08 .25
Checklist 1-174
348 Joe Montana .08 .25
Checklist 175-348
PC1 Joe Montana Promo .40 1.00
(Crash the Game promo)
P1 Joe Montana Promo .40 1.00

1995 Collector's Choice Player's Club

COMPLETE SET (348) 25.00 50.00
*STARS: 1X TO 2.5X BASIC CARDS
*RCs: .75X TO 2X BASIC CARDS
ONE PER PACK

1995 Collector's Choice Player's Club Platinum

COMPLETE SET (348) 200.00 400.00
*STARS: 8X TO 20X BASIC CARDS
*RCs: 4X TO 10X BASIC CARDS
STATED ODDS 1:35

1995 Collector's Choice Crash The Game

COMPLETE SILVER SET (90) 20.00 50.00
SILVER ODDS 1:5 HOB/RET, 1:1 JUM
*GOLD INSERTS: 1.2X TO 3X SILVER
GOLD STATED ODDS 1:50 HOB/RET
COMP.SILVER REDEMPT.(30) 4.00 8.00
*SILVER SET REDEMPTION: .2X TO .5X
*SILVER TD REDEMPTION: .8X TO 2X
COMP.GOLD REDEMPT.(30) 15.00 40.00
*GOLD SET REDEMPTION: .6X TO 1.5X
*GOLD TD REDEMPTION: 2.5X TO 6X
C1A Dan Marino 9/10 W 1.00 2.00
C1B Dan Marino 10/8 W 1.00 2.00
C1C Dan Marino 11/20 W 1.00 2.00
C2A John Elway 9/3 L 1.00 2.00
C2B John Elway 11/12 W 1.00 2.00
C2C John Elway 11/19 W 1.00 2.00
C3A Kerry Collins 10/1 W .25 .60

C3B Kerry Collins 10/29 W	.25	.60
C3C Kerry Collins 11/12 W	.25	.60
C4A Stan Humphries 9/3 W	.02	.10
C4B Stan Humphries 10/9 W	.02	.10
C4C Stan Humphries 11/5 W	.02	.10
C5A Steve Young 9/10 W	.30	.75
C5B Steve Young 10/15 W	.30	.75
C5C Steve Young 11/5 L	.30	.75
C6A Brett Favre	1.00	2.00
C6B Brett Favre 9/24 W	1.00	2.00
C6C Brett Favre 10/29 W	1.00	2.00
C7A Troy Aikman 9/4 W	.40	1.00
C7B Troy Aikman 10/1 L	.40	1.00
C7C Troy Aikman 11/12 L	.40	1.00
C8A Warren Moon 9/3 W	.02	.10
C8B Warren Moon 10/8 W	.02	.10
C8C Warren Moon 11/23 W	.02	.10
C9A Drew Bledsoe 9/10 L	.25	.60
C9B Drew Bledsoe 9/17 L	.25	.60
C9C Drew Bledsoe 10/23 W	.25	.60
C10A Steve McNair 10/1 L	.60	1.25
C10B Steve McNair 10/29 L	.60	1.25
C10C Steve McNair 11/19 L	.60	1.25
C11A Chris Warren 10/22 W	.02	.10
C11B Chris Warren 11/12 W	.02	.10
C11C Chris Warren 11/26 L	.02	.10
C12A Natrone Means 10/1 W	.02	.10
C12B Natrone Means 10/9 W	.02	.10
C12C Natrone Means 11/27 L	.02	.10
C13A T.Thomas 9/17 W	.10	.30
C13B T.Thomas 10/22 L	.10	.30
C13C T.Thomas 12/3 L	.10	.30
C14A Barry Sanders	.75	1.50
C14B Barry Sanders 10/22 L	.75	1.50
C14C Barry Sanders 11/23 W	.75	1.50
C15A Emmitt Smith 9/10 W	.75	1.50
C15B Emmitt Smith 10/29 W	.75	1.50
C15C Emmitt Smith 11/19 W	.75	1.50
C16A Jerome Bettis 9/10 L	.10	.30
C16B Jerome Bettis 10/22 L	.10	.30
C16C Jerome Bettis 11/19 L	.10	.30
C17A Ki-Jana Carter 9/10 L	.05	.15
C17B Ki-Jana Carter 10/1 L	.05	.15
C17C Ki-Jana Carter 11/12 L	.05	.15
C18A N.Kaufman 10/8 L	.20	.50
C18B N.Kaufman 11/5 L	.20	.50
C18C N.Kaufman 12/3 L	.20	.50
C19A Marshall Faulk 9/3 L	.60	1.25
C19B Marshall Faulk 10/1 W	.60	1.25
C19C Marshall Faulk 11/5 W	.60	1.25
C20A Errict Rhett 10/8 W	.02	.10
C20B Errict Rhett 10/22 W	.02	.10
C20C Errict Rhett 11/19 W	.02	.10
C21A Cris Carter 9/17 W	.10	.30
C21B Cris Carter 10/30 L	.10	.30
C21C Cris Carter 11/19 W	.10	.30
C22A Jerry Rice 9/3 W	.40	1.00
C22B Jerry Rice 10/1 W	.40	1.00
C22C Jerry Rice 11/26 W	.40	1.00
C23A Tim Brown 10/1 W	.10	.30
C23B Tim Brown 10/16 L	.10	.30
C23C Tim Brown 11/27 L	.10	.30
C24A Andre Reed 9/10 L	.02	.10
C24B Andre Reed 10/29 L	.02	.10
C24C Andre Reed 11/26 L	.02	.10
C25A Andre Rison 9/3 L	.02	.10
C25B Andre Rison 10/2 L	.02	.10
C25C Andre Rison 10/22 L	.02	.10
C26A Ben Coates 10/8 L	.02	.10
C26B Ben Coates 10/29 L	.02	.10
C26C Ben Coates 11/19 L	.02	.10
C27A Michael Irvin 9/17 W	.10	.30
C27B Michael Irvin 10/15 L	.10	.30
C27C Michael Irvin 11/6 W	.10	.30
C28B Terance Mathis 10/1 L	.02	.10
C28C Terance Mathis 10/12 L	.02	.10
C29A M.Westbrook 9/24 L	.10	.30
C29B M.Westbrook 10/22 L	.10	.30
C29C M.Westbrook 11/19 W	.10	.30
C30A Herman Moore 9/10 W	.10	.30
C30B Herman Moore 10/15 W	.10	.30
C30C Herman Moore 11/12 L	.10	.30

1995 Collector's Choice Dan Marino Chronicles

COMPLETE SET (10)	6.00	15.00
COMMON CARD (DM1-DM10)	.60	1.50
ONE PER SPECIAL RETAIL PACK		
DM8J Dan Marino Jumbo	1.50	4.00
Marino's Back		

1995 Collector's Choice Joe Montana Chronicles

COMPLETE SET (10)	6.00	15.00
COMMON CARD (JM1-JM10)	.60	1.50
ONE PER SPECIAL RETAIL PACK		
JM8J Joe Montana Jumbo	1.50	4.00
Super Bowl XXIV		

1995 Collector's Choice Update

This 225 card update set was produced late in the 1995 season and the format of the cards are identical to the regular Collector's Choice release. Subsets include Rookie Collection cards featuring first-year players, Expansion cards from Carolina and Jacksonville and The Key cards describing what NFL teams do to stop "key" players on each NFL team. Rookie Cards not included in the first issue include Terrell Davis, Curtis Martin, Kordell Stewart and Tamarick Vanover. Each card has a "U" prefix. Also, a parallel of the cards were randomly inserted in packs as Silver and Gold versions.

COMPLETE SET (225)	7.50	15.00
U111 Mark Brunell UER	.40	1.00
name spelled Brunnell on front		

1995 Collector's Choice Update Gold

COMPLETE SET (90)	200.00	400.00
*STARS: 8X TO 20X BASIC CARDS		
*RCs: 5X TO 12X BASIC CARDS		
U1-U60 STATED ODDS 1:35		
U61-U90 STATED ODDS 1:52		

1995 Collector's Choice Update Silver

COMPLETE SET (90)	30.00	60.00
*STARS: 1.2X TO 3X BASIC CARDS		
*RCs: 1X TO 2.5X BASIC CARDS		
U1-U60 STATED ODDS 1:3		
U61-U90 STATED ODDS 1:5		

1995 Collector's Choice Update Crash the Playoffs

COMPLETE SET (18)	7.50	20.00
SILVER STATED ODDS 1:5		
GOLD STATED ODDS 1:50		
CP1 AFC East QB	1.50	3.00
Drew Bledsoe		
Dan Marino		
Boomer Esiason		
Jim Kelly		
CP2 AFC Central QB	1.00	2.50
Steve Beuerlein		
Jeff Blake		
Steve McNair		
Neil O'Donnell		
Vinny Testaverde		
CP3 AFC West QB	1.00	2.50
Steve Bono		
John Elway		
Jeff Hostetler		
Stan Humphries		
Rick Mirer		
CP4 NFC East QB	.60	1.50
Troy Aikman		
Dave Brown		
Randall Cunningham		
Dave Krieg		
Heath Shuler		
CP5 NFC Central QB	1.50	3.00
Trent Dilfer		
Brett Favre		
Erik Krmaer		
Scott Mitchell		
Warren Moon		
CP6 NFC West QB	.60	1.50
Kerry Collins		
Jim Everett		
Jeff George		
Chris Miller		
Steve Young		
CP7 AFC East RB	1.00	2.50
Brad Baxter		
Marshall Faulk		
Darick Holmes		
Terry Kirby		
Curtis Martin		
CP8 AFC Central RB	.20	.50
Gary Brown		
Harold Green		
Leroy Hoard		
Bam Morris		
James O. Stewart		
CP9 AFC West RB	.75	2.00
Terrell Davis		
Greg Hill		
Napoleon Kaufman		
Natrone Means		
Chris Warren		
CP10 NFC East RB	.30	.75
Terry Allen		
Rodney Hampton		
Garrison Hearst		
Emmitt Smith		
Ricky Watters		
CP11 NFC Central WR	.20	.50
Robert Brooks		
Cris Carter		
Jeff Graham		
Alvin Harper		
Herman Moore		
CP12 NFC West RB	.20	.50
Randy Baldwin		
Mario Bates		
Jerome Bettis		
William Floyd		
Craig Heyward		
CP13 AFC East WR	.20	.50
Kyle Brady		
Ben Coates		
Sean Dawkins		
Irving Fryar		
Andre Reed		
CP14 AFC Central WR	.20	.50
Desmond Howard		
Haywood Jeffires		
Charles Johnson		
Andre Rison		
Darnay Scott		
CP15 AFC West WR	.40	1.00
Tim Brown		
Willie Davis		
Joey Galloway		
Tony Martin		
Shannon Sharpe		
CP16 NFC East WR	.30	.75
Fred Barnett		
Michael Irvin		
Rob Moore		
Mike Sherrard		
Michael Westbrook		
CP17 NFC Central RB	1.50	3.00
Edgar Bennett		
Errict Rhett		
Rashaan Salaam		
Barry Sanders		
Robert Smith		
CP18 NFC West WR	.60	1.50
Isaac Bruce		
Mark Carrier		
Michael Haynes		
Terance Mathis		
Jerry Rice		

1995 Collector's Choice Update Post Season Heroics

COMPLETE SET (20)	5.00	12.00
*GOLDS: 1.2X TO 3X BASIC INSERTS		
1 Stan Humphries	.07	.20
2 Natrone Means	.15	.40
3 Tony Martin	.40	1.00
4 Neil O'Donnell	.15	.40
5 Byron Bam Morris	.07	.20
6 Charles Johnson	.15	.40
7 Jim Harbaugh	.40	1.00
8 Darick Holmes	.15	.40
9 Sean Dawkins	.07	.20
10 Steve Young	.75	1.50
11 Craig Heyward	.07	.20
12 Jerry Rice	1.00	2.00
13 Brett Favre	2.00	4.00
14 Edgar Bennett	.15	.40
15 Robert Brooks	.15	.40
16 Troy Aikman	1.00	2.00
17 Emmitt Smith	1.50	3.00
18 Michael Irvin	.40	1.00
19 Byron Bam Morris	.07	.20
20 Larry Brown	.07	.20

1995 Collector's Choice Update Stick-Ums

COMPLETE SET (90)	6.00	12.00
ONE PER HOB.PACK/TWO PER RET.PACK		
1 Jeff George	.08	.25
2 Kerry Collins	.08	.25
3 Jerome Bettis	.08	.25
4 Mario Bates	.05	.15
5 Steve Young	.15	.40
6 Rashaan Salaam	.08	.25
7 Barry Sanders	.30	.75
8 Brett Favre	.40	1.00
9 Warren Moon	.08	.25
10 Errict Rhett	.05	.15
11 Emmitt Smith	.30	.75
12 Rodney Hampton	.05	.15
13 Ricky Watters	.05	.15
14 Garrison Hearst	.08	.25
15 Michael Westbrook	.08	.25
16 Jim Kelly	.08	.25
17 Marshall Faulk	.25	.60
18 Dan Marino	.40	1.00
19 Drew Bledsoe	.10	.30
20 Kyle Brady	.05	.15
21 Ki-Jana Carter	.05	.15
22 Andre Rison	.05	.15
23 Steve McNair	.25	.60
24 James O. Stewart	.08	.25
25 Byron Bam Morris	.02	.10
26 John Elway	.40	1.00
27 Marcus Allen	.08	.25
28 Tim Brown	.08	.25
29 Natrone Means	.05	.15
30 Chris Warren	.05	.15
31 Terence Mathis	.05	.15
Mark Carrier WR		
Chris Miller		
Jim Everett		
32 Bert Emanuel	.05	.15
Pete Metzelaars		
Isaac Bruce		
Dana Stubblefield		
33 Chris Doleman	.10	.30
Frank Reich		
Derek Brown RBK		
Jerry Rice		
34 Jesse Tuggle	.10	.30
Roman Phifer		
Tyrone Hughes		
Steve Young		
35 Sam Mills	.02	.10
Kevin Carter		
Michael Haynes		
Brent Jones		
36 Falcons Helmet	.08	.25
Eric Metcalf		
Tyrone Poole		
Lovell Pinkney		
37 Panthers Helmet	.02	.10
Morten Andersen UER		
(Morton on front)		
John Kasay		
Troy Drayton		
38 Rams Helmet	.08	.25
Sean Gilbert		
Mark Fields		
J.J.Stokes		
39 Saints Helmet	.02	.10
Bob Christian		
Willie Roaf		
Ken Norton		
40 49ers Helmet	.02	.10
Craig Heyward		
Renaldo Turnbull		
William Floyd		
41 Raymont Harris	.08	.25
Herman Moore		
Edgar Bennett		
Cris Carter		
42 Jeff Graham	.08	.25
Henry Thomas		
Reggie White		
Trent Dilfer		
43 Curtis Conway	.08	.25
Scott Mitchell		
Robert Smith		
Alvin Harper		
44 Steve Walsh	.02	.10
Sean Jones		
Qadry Ismail		
Hardy Nickerson		
45 Bennie Blades	.02	.10
John Jurkovic		
John Randle		
Courtney Hawkins		
46 Bears Helmet	.02	.10
John Thierry		
Luther Elliss		
Leroy Butler		
47 Lions Helmet	.08	.25
Johnnie Morton		
Robert Brooks		
Jake Reed		
48 Packers Helmet	.02	.10
LeShon Johnson		
Dewayne Washington		
Jackie Harris		
49 Vikings Helmet	.02	.10
Donnell Woolford		
James A.Stewart		
Eric Curry		
50 Buccaneers Helmet	.02	.10
Mark Carrier DB		
Chris Spielman		
Warren Sapp		
51 Troy Aikman	.10	.30
Mike Sherrard		
Fred Barnett		
Dave Krieg		
52 Michael Irvin	.05	.15
Chris Calloway		
Calvin Williams		
Henry Ellard		
53 Sherman Williams	.08	.25
Dave Brown		
Rob Moore		
Heath Shuler		
54 Charles Haley	.05	.15
Randall Cunningham		
Eric Swann		
Ken Harvey		
55 Thomas Lewis	.02	.10
Charlie Garner		
Clyde Simmons		
Tom Carter		
56 Cowboys Helmet	.05	.15
Tyrone Wheatley		
Bobby Taylor		
Daryl Johnston		
57 Giants Helmet	.02	.10
Mike Croel		
Byron Evans		
Aeneas Williams		
58 Eagles Helmet	.02	.10
Mike Mamula		
Larry Centers		
Brian Mitchell		
59 Cardinals Helmet	.08	.25
Jay Novacek		
Frank Sanders		
Terry Allen		
60 Redskins Helmet	.08	.25
Deion Sanders		
Herschel Walker		
Sterling Palmer		
61 Henry Jones	.02	.10
Craig Erickson		
Terry Kirby		
Ben Coates		
62 Andre Reed	.05	.15
Flipper Anderson		
Irving Fryar		
Johnny Mitchell		
63 Russell Copeland	.05	.15
Sean Dawkins		
Vincent Brisby		
Boomer Esiason		
64 Bruce Smith	.08	.25
O.J.McDuffie		
Willie McGinest		
Ryan Yarborough		
65 Roosevelt Potts	.25	.60
Keith Byars		
Curtis Martin		
Brad Baxter		
66 Bills Helmet	.02	.10
Cornelius Bennett		
Ray Buchanan		
Marco Coleman		
67 Colts Helmet	.02	.10
Quentin Coryatt		
Bryan Cox		
Chris Slade		
68 Dolphins Helmet	.02	.10
Eric Green		
Ty Law		
Marvin Washington		
69 Patriots Helmet	.25	.60
Todd Collins		
Vincent Brown		
Ronald Moore		
70 Jets Helmet	.02	.10
Jeff Burris		
Floyd Turner		
Aaron Glenn		
71 Carl Pickens	.08	.25
Vinny Testaverde		
Haywood Jeffires		
Desmond Howard		
72 Darnay Scott	.05	.15
Eric Turner		
Gary Brown		
Neil O'Donnell		
73 David Klingler	.08	.25
Leroy Hoard		
Tony Boselli		
Charles Johnson		
74 Steve Tovar	.02	.10
Al Smith		
Derek Brown TE		
John L.Williams		
75 Lorenzo White	.05	.15
Rodney Thomas		
Steve Beuerlein		
Kevin Greene		
76 Bengals Helmet	.08	.25
Jeff Blake		
Derrick Alexander WR		
Ray Childress		
77 Browns Helmet	.02	.10
Eric Zeier		
Mel Gray		
Reggie Cobb		
78 Oilers Helmet	.05	.15
Todd McNair		
Jeff Lageman		
Greg Lloyd		
79 Jaguars Helmet	.08	.25
Dan Wilkinson		
Rob Johnson		
Rod Woodson		
80 Steelers Helmet	.02	.10
Eric Bieniemy		
Antonio Langham		
Mark Bruener		
81 Shannon Sharpe	.08	.25
Willie Davis		
Jeff Hostetler		
Stan Humphries		
82 Rod Bernstine	.05	.15
Ronnie Lott		
Harvey Williams		
Rick Mirer		
83 Anthony Miller	.08	.25
Neil Smith		
Junior Seau		
Brian Blades		
84 Mike Pritchard	.05	.15
Napoleon Kaufman		
Leslie O'Neal		
Sam Adams		
85 Greg Hill	.05	.15
Rocket Ismail		
Alfred Pupunu		
Cortez Kennedy		
86 Broncos Helmet	.05	.15
Steve Atwater		
Tamarick Vanover		
Chester McGlockton		
87 Chiefs Helmet	.05	.15
Steve Bono		
Rob Fredrickson		
Tony Martin		
88 Raiders Helmet	.02	.10
Terry McDaniel		
Jimmy Oliver		
Christian Fauria		
89 Chargers Helmet	.15	.40
Glen Milburn		
John Carney		
Joey Galloway		
90 Seahawks Helmet	.02	.10
Terrell Fletcher		
Keith Cash		
Eugene Robinson		

1996 Collector's Choice

The 1996 Collector's Choice first series containted 375 standard-size cards. The 14-card hobby packs had a suggested retail price of $.99 each. A factory set was produced and sold with ten Stick-Ums inserts and ten Gold foil MVPs inserts. The set features the topical subsets: Rookie Class (1-45) and Season To Remember (46-79). This set has a slightly different design than previous Collector's Choice sets in that the player's name and position was printed either on the side or the bottom. Rookie Cards in this set include Karim Abdul-Jabbar, Tim Biakabutuka, Bobby Engram, Terry Glenn, Eddie George, Keyshawn Johnson and Lawrence Phillips. A Jerry Rice base brand and a Dan Marino unnumbered Promo Crash the Game card were produced to promote the set and are priced below.

COMPLETE SET (375)	10.00	25.00
COMP.FACT.SET (395)	20.00	30.00
1 Keyshawn Johnson RC	.40	1.00
2 Kevin Hardy RC	.15	.40
3 Simeon Rice RC	.30	.75
4 Jonathan Ogden RC	.15	.40
5 Cedric Jones RC	.02	.10
6 Lawrence Phillips RC	.15	.40
7 Tim Biakabutuka RC	.15	.40
8 Terry Glenn RC	.40	1.00
9 Rickey Dudley RC	.15	.40
10 Regan Upshaw RC	.02	.10
11 Walt Harris RC	.02	.10
12 Eddie George RC	.50	1.25
13 John Mobley RC	.02	.10
14 Duane Clemons RC	.02	.10
15 Marvin Harrison RC	1.00	2.50
16 Daryl Gardener RC	.02	.10
17 Pete Kendall RC	.02	.10
18 Marcus Jones RC	.02	.10
19 Eric Moulds RC	.50	1.25
20 Ray Lewis RC	1.00	2.50
21 Alex Van Dyke RC	.07	.20
22 Leeland McElroy RC	.07	.20
23 Mike Alstott RC	.40	1.00
24 Lawyer Milloy RC	.15	.40
25 Marco Battaglia RC	.02	.10
26 Je'rod Cherry RC	.02	.10
27 Israel Ifeanyi RC	.02	.10
28 Bobby Engram RC	.15	.40
29 Jason Dunn RC	.07	.20
30 Derrick Mayes RC	.15	.40
31 Stepfret Williams RC	.07	.20
32 Bobby Hoying RC	.15	.40
33 Karim Abdul-Jabbar RC	.15	.40
34 Danny Kanell RC	.15	.40
35 Chris Darkins RC	.02	.10
36 Charlie Jones RC	.15	.40
37 Tedy Bruschi RC	1.50	4.00
38 Stanley Pritchett RC	.07	.20
39 Donnie Edwards RC	.15	.40
40 Jeff Lewis RC	.07	.20
41 Stephen Davis RC	.60	1.50
42 Winslow Oliver RC	.02	.10
43 Mercury Hayes RC	.02	.10
44 Jon Runyan RC	.02	.10
45 Steve Taneyhill RC	.02	.10
46 Eric Metcalf SR	.02	.10
47 Bryce Paup SR	.02	.10
48 Kerry Collins SR	.07	.20
49 Rashaan Salaam SR	.07	.20
50 Carl Pickens SR	.07	.20
51 Emmitt Smith SR	.20	.50
52 Michael Irvin SR	.07	.20
53 Troy Aikman SR	.15	.40
54 Terrell Davis SR	.07	.20
55 John Elway SR	.30	.75
56 Herman Moore SR	.07	.20
57 Brett Favre SR	.30	.75
58 Rodney Thomas SR	.02	.10
59 Jim Harbaugh SR	.07	.20
60 Mark Brunell SR	.07	.20
61 Marcus Allen SR	.07	.20
62 Tamarick Vanover SR	.07	.20
63 Steve Bono SR	.02	.10
64 Dan Marino SR	.30	.75
65 Warren Moon SR	.02	.10
66 Curtis Martin SR	.07	.20
67 Tyrone Hughes SR	.02	.10
68 Rodney Hampton SR	.02	.10
69 Hugh Douglas SR	.02	.10
70 Tim Brown SR	.07	.20
71 Ricky Watters SR	.07	.20
72 Kordell Stewart SR	.15	.40
73 Andre Coleman SR	.02	.10
74 Jerry Rice SR	.15	.40
75 Joey Galloway SR	.07	.20
76 Isaac Bruce SR	.07	.20
77 Errict Rhett SR	.07	.20
78 Michael Westbrook SR	.02	.10
79 Brian Mitchell SR	.02	.10
80 Aeneas Williams	.02	.10
81 Andre Reed	.07	.20
82 Brett Maxie	.02	.10
83 Jim Flanigan	.02	.10
84 Jeff Blake	.15	.40
85 Mike Frederick	.02	.10
86 Michael Irvin	.15	.40
87 Aaron Craver	.02	.10
88 Barry Sanders	.50	1.25
89 Travis Jervey RC	.15	.40
90 Chris Sanders	.07	.20
91 Marshall Faulk	.15	.40
92 Bryan Schwartz	.02	.10
93 Tamarick Vanover	.07	.20
94 Troy Vincent	.02	.10
95 Robert Smith	.07	.20
96 Drew Bledsoe	.20	.50
97 Quinn Early	.02	.10
98 Wayne Chrebet	.15	.40
99 Tim Brown	.15	.40
100 Charlie Garner	.07	.20
101 Yancey Thigpen	.07	.20
102 Isaac Bruce	.15	.40
103 Natrone Means	.07	.20
104 Jerry Rice	.30	.75
105 Chris Warren	.07	.20
106 Errict Rhett	.07	.20
107 Heath Shuler	.07	.20
108 Eric Swann	.02	.10
109 Jeff George	.07	.20
110 Steve Tasker	.02	.10
111 Sam Mills	.02	.10
112 Jeff Graham	.02	.10
113 Carl Pickens	.07	.20
114 Vinny Testaverde	.07	.20
115 Emmitt Smith	.50	1.25
116 John Elway	.60	1.50
117 Henry Thomas	.02	.10
118 LeRoy Butler	.02	.10
119 Blaine Bishop	.02	.10
120 Floyd Turner	.02	.10
121 Jeff Lageman	.02	.10
122 Kimble Anders	.07	.20
123 Bryan Cox	.02	.10
124 Qadry Ismail	.07	.20
125 Ted Johnson RC	.15	.40
126 Wesley Walls	.07	.20
127 Rodney Hampton	.07	.20
128 Adrian Murrell	.07	.20
129 Daryl Hobbs RC	.02	.10
130 Ricky Watters	.07	.20
131 Carnell Lake	.02	.10
132 Toby Wright	.02	.10
133 Darren Bennett	.02	.10
134 J.J. Stokes	.15	.40
135 Eugene Robinson	.02	.10
136 Eric Curry	.02	.10
137 Tom Carter	.02	.10
138 Dave Krieg	.02	.10
139 Eric Metcalf	.02	.10
140 Bill Brooks	.02	.10
141 Pete Metzelaars	.02	.10
142 Kevin Butler	.02	.10
143 John Copeland	.02	.10
144 Keenan McCardell	.15	.40
145 Larry Brown	.02	.10
146 Jason Elam	.07	.20
147 Willie Clay	.02	.10
148 Robert Brooks	.15	.40
149 Chris Chandler	.07	.20
150 Quentin Coryatt	.02	.10
151 Pete Mitchell	.07	.20
152 Martin Bayless	.02	.10
153 Pete Stoyanovich	.02	.10
154 Cris Carter	.15	.40
155 Jimmy Hitchcock RC	.02	.10
156 Mario Bates	.07	.20
157 Mike Sherrard	.02	.10
158 Boomer Esiason	.07	.20
159 Chester McGlockton	.02	.10
160 Bobby Taylor	.02	.10
161 Kordell Stewart	.15	.40
162 Kevin Carter	.02	.10
163 Junior Seau	.15	.40
164 Derek Loville	.02	.10
165 Brian Blades	.02	.10
166 Jackie Harris	.02	.10
167 Michael Westbrook	.15	.40
168 Rob Moore	.07	.20
169 Jessie Tuggle	.02	.10
170 Darick Holmes	.02	.10
171 Tim McKyer	.02	.10
172 Erik Kramer	.02	.10
173 Harold Green	.02	.10
174 Stevon Moore	.02	.10
175 Deion Sanders	.15	.40
176 Anthony Miller	.07	.20
177 Herman Moore	.07	.20
178 Brett Favre	.60	1.50
179 Rodney Thomas	.02	.10
180 Ken Dilger	.07	.20
181 Mark Brunell	.20	.50
182 Marcus Allen	.15	.40
183 Dan Marino	.60	1.50
184 John Randle	.07	.20
185 Ben Coates	.07	.20
186 Tyrone Hughes	.02	.10
187 Dave Brown	.02	.10
188 Johnny Mitchell	.02	.10
189 Harvey Williams	.02	.10
190 Andy Harmon	.02	.10
191 Kevin Greene	.07	.20
192 D'Marco Farr	.02	.10
193 Andre Coleman	.02	.10
194 Bryant Young	.07	.20
195 Rick Mirer	.07	.20
196 Horace Copeland	.02	.10
197 Leslie Shepherd	.02	.10
198 Jamir Miller	.02	.10
199 Bert Emanuel	.07	.20
200 Steve Christie	.02	.10
201 Kerry Collins	.15	.40
202 Rashaan Salaam	.07	.20
203 Steve Tovar	.02	.10
204 Michael Jackson	.07	.20
205 Kevin Williams	.02	.10
206 Glyn Milburn	.02	.10
207 Johnnie Morton	.07	.20
208 Antonio Freeman	.15	.40
209 Cris Dishman	.02	.10
210 Ellis Johnson	.02	.10
211 Cedric Tillman	.02	.10
212 Steve Bono	.02	.10
213 Eric Green	.02	.10
214 David Palmer	.02	.10
215 Vincent Brisby	.02	.10
216 Michael Haynes	.02	.10
217 Chris Calloway	.02	.10
218 Kyle Brady	.02	.10
219 Terry McDaniel	.02	.10
220 Calvin Williams	.02	.10
221 Greg Lloyd	.07	.20
222 Jerome Bettis	.15	.40
223 Stan Humphries	.07	.20
224 Lee Woodall	.02	.10
225 Robert Blackmon	.02	.10
226 Warren Sapp	.02	.10
227 Brian Mitchell	.02	.10
228 Garrison Hearst	.07	.20
229 Terance Mathis	.02	.10
230 Bryce Paup	.02	.10
231 Derrick Moore	.02	.10
232 Curtis Conway	.15	.40
233 Darnay Scott	.07	.20
234 Andre Rison	.07	.20
235 Jay Novacek	.02	.10
236 Terrell Davis	.20	.50
237 David Sloan	.02	.10
238 Reggie White	.15	.40
239 Todd McNair	.02	.10
240 Ray Buchanan	.02	.10
241 Steve Beuerlein	.07	.20
242 Dan Saleaumua	.02	.10
243 Bernie Parmalee	.02	.10
244 Warren Moon	.07	.20
245 Ty Law	.15	.40
246 Torrance Small	.02	.10
247 Phillippi Sparks	.02	.10
248 Mo Lewis	.02	.10
249 Jeff Hostetler	.02	.10
250 Rodney Peete	.02	.10
251 Byron Bam Morris	.02	.10
252 Chris Miller	.02	.10
253 Tony Martin	.07	.20
254 Eric Davis	.02	.10
255 Joey Galloway	.15	.40
256 Derrick Brooks	.15	.40
257 Ken Harvey	.02	.10
258 Frank Sanders	.07	.20
259 Morten Andersen	.02	.10
260 Marlon Kerner	.02	.10
261 Mark Carrier WR	.02	.10
262 Mark Carrier DB	.02	.10
263 Tony McGee	.02	.10
264 Eric Zeier	.02	.10
265 Darren Woodson	.07	.20
266 Shannon Sharpe	.07	.20
267 Brett Perriman	.02	.10
268 Edgar Bennett	.07	.20
269 Darryll Lewis	.02	.10
270 Jim Harbaugh	.07	.20
271 Desmond Howard	.07	.20
272 Derrick Thomas	.15	.40
273 Irving Fryar	.07	.20
274 Jake Reed	.07	.20
275 Curtis Martin	.20	.50
276 Eric Allen	.02	.10
277 Thomas Lewis	.02	.10
278 Hugh Douglas	.07	.20
279 Pat Swilling	.02	.10
280 William Thomas	.02	.10
281 Norm Johnson	.02	.10
282 Roman Phifer	.02	.10
283 Chris Mims	.02	.10
284 Steve Young	.25	.60
285 Cortez Kennedy	.02	.10
286 Trent Dilfer	.15	.40
287 Terry Allen	.07	.20
288 Clyde Simmons	.02	.10
289 Craig Heyward	.02	.10
290 Jim Kelly	.15	.40
291 Tyrone Poole	.02	.10
292 Chris Zorich	.02	.10
293 Dan Wilkinson	.02	.10
294 Antonio Langham	.02	.10
295 Troy Aikman	.30	.75
296 Steve Atwater	.02	.10
297 Scott Mitchell	.07	.20
298 Mark Chmura	.07	.20
299 Steve McNair	.20	.50
300 Tony Bennett	.02	.10
301 Willie Jackson	.07	.20
302 Neil Smith	.07	.20
303 Terry Kirby	.07	.20
304 Orlando Thomas	.02	.10
305 Willie McGinest	.02	.10
306 Wayne Martin	.02	.10
307 Michael Brooks	.02	.10
308 Marvin Washington	.02	.10
309 Nolan Harrison	.02	.10
310 William Fuller	.02	.10
311 Willie Williams	.02	.10
312 Troy Drayton	.02	.10
313 Shawn Lee	.02	.10
314 Ken Norton	.02	.10
315 Terry Wooden	.02	.10
316 Hardy Nickerson	.02	.10
317 Gus Frerotte	.07	.20
318 Oscar McBride	.02	.10
319 Merton Hanks	.02	.10
320 Justin Armour	.02	.10
321 Willie Green	.02	.10
322 Roger Jones RC	.02	.10
323 Leroy Hoard	.02	.10
324 Chris Boniol	.02	.10
325 Jason Hanson	.02	.10
326 Sean Jones	.02	.10
327 Roosevelt Potts	.02	.10
328 Greg Hill	.07	.20
329 O.J. McDuffie	.07	.20
330 Amp Lee	.02	.10
331 Chris Slade	.02	.10
332 Jim Everett	.02	.10
333 Tyrone Wheatley	.07	.20
334 Charles Wilson	.02	.10
335 Napoleon Kaufman	.15	.40
336 Fred Barnett	.02	.10
337 Neil O'Donnell	.07	.20
338 Sean Gilbert	.02	.10
339 Aaron Hayden RC	.02	.10
340 Brent Jones	.02	.10
341 Christian Fauria	.02	.10
342 Alvin Harper	.02	.10
343 Henry Ellard	.02	.10
344 Willie Davis	.02	.10
345 Charles Haley	.07	.20
346 Chris Jacke	.02	.10
347 Allen Aldridge	.02	.10
348 Jeff Herrod	.02	.10
349 Rocket Ismail	.07	.20
350 Leslie O'Neal	.02	.10
351 Marquez Pope	.02	.10
352 Brock Marion	.02	.10
353 Ernie Mills	.02	.10
354 Larry Centers	.07	.20
355 Chris Doleman	.02	.10
356 Bruce Smith	.07	.20
357 John Kasay	.02	.10
358 Donnell Woolford	.02	.10
359 David Dunn	.02	.10
360 Eric Turner	.02	.10
361 Sherman Williams	.02	.10
362 Chris Spielman	.02	.10
363 Craig Newsome	.02	.10
364 Sean Dawkins	.02	.10
365 James O. Stewart	.07	.20
366 Dale Carter	.02	.10
367 Marco Coleman	.02	.10
368 Dave Meggett	.02	.10
369 Irv Smith	.02	.10
370 Mike Mamula	.02	.10
371 Erric Pegram	.02	.10
372 Dana Stubblefield	.07	.20
373 Terrance Shaw	.02	.10
374 Jerry Rice CL	.15	.40
375 Dan Marino CL	.15	.40
P1 Jerry Rice Promo	.40	1.00
Base brand card #801		
P2 Dan Marino Promo	.40	1.00
Crash the Game April 1		

1996 Collector's Choice A Cut Above

COMPLETE SET (10)	5.00	12.00
ONE PER SPECIAL RETAIL PACK		
*UDA JUMBO's: .4X TO 1X BASIC INSERTS		
1 Troy Aikman	.50	1.25
2 Tim Biakabutuka	.25	.60
3 Drew Bledsoe	.30	.75
4 Emmitt Smith UER	.75	2.00
5 Marshall Faulk	.25	.60
6 Brett Favre	1.00	2.50
7 Keyshawn Johnson	.60	1.50
8 Deion Sanders	.25	.60
9 Lawrence Phillips	.25	.60
10 Jerry Rice	.50	1.25

1996 Collector's Choice Crash The Game

COMPLETE SET (90)	35.00	75.00
SILVER STATED ODDS 1:5		
*GOLD CARDS: 2X TO 4X SILVERS		
GOLD STATED ODDS 1:50		
*GOLD REDEMPTIONS: 5X TO 10X SILV.		
*SILVER REDEMPTIONS: 1.5X TO 3X SILV.		
ONE PRIZE CARD VIA MAIL PER WINNER		
CG1A Dan Marino 9/23 L	1.50	3.00
CG1B Dan Marino 10/27 W	1.50	3.00
CG1C Dan Marino 11/25 W	1.50	3.00
CG2A John Elway 10/6 W	1.50	3.00
CG2B John Elway 10/27 W	1.50	3.00
CG2C John Elway 12/24 W	1.50	3.00
CG3A Jeff Blake 9/29 W	.30	.75

CG3B Jeff Blake 10/20 W .30 .75
CG3C Jeff Blake 12/1 W .30 .75
CG4A Drew Bledsoe 9/22 W .40 1.00
CG4B Drew Bledsoe 10/13 L .40 1.00
CG4C Drew Bledsoe 12/1 W .40 1.00
CG5A Steve Young 9/29 L .60 1.25
CG5B Steve Young 10/14 L .60 1.25
CG5C Steve Young 12/8 W .60 1.25
CG6A Brett Favre 10/6 W 1.50 3.00
CG6B Brett Favre 11/3 W 1.50 3.00
CG6C Brett Favre 11/24 W 1.50 3.00
CG7A Jim Kelly 9/22 L .30 .75
CG7B Jim Kelly 10/27 W .30 .75
CG7C Jim Kelly 11/10 W .30 .75
CG8A Scott Mitchell 10/6 W .15 .40
CG8B Scott Mitchell 10/27 W .15 .40
CG8C Scott Mitchell 11/11 L .15 .40
CG9A Jeff George 9/22 W .15 .40
CG9B Jeff George 10/20 L .15 .40
CG9C Jeff George 11/17 L .15 .40
CG10A Erik Kramer 9/29 L .07 .20
CG10B Erik Kramer 10/28 L .07 .20
CG10C Erik Kramer 11/24 L .07 .20
CG11A Jerry Rice 9/22 L .75 1.50
CG11B Jerry Rice 10/27 L .75 1.50
CG11C Jerry Rice 11/17 W .75 1.50
CG12A Michael Irvin 9/30 L .30 .75
CG12B Michael Irvin 10/13 L .30 .75
CG12C Michael Irvin 11/10 L .30 .75
CG13A Joey Galloway 9/22 L .30 .75
CG13B Joey Galloway 10/27 L .30 .75
CG13C Joey Galloway 11/24 L .30 .75
CG14A Cris Carter 9/29 L .30 .75
CG14B Cris Carter 11/3 W .30 .75
CG14C Cris Carter 12/1 W .30 .75
CG15A Carl Pickens 10/6 L .15 .40
CG15B Carl Pickens 10/27 W .15 .40
CG15C Carl Pickens 11/17 W .15 .40
CG16A Herman Moore 9/22 L .15 .40
CG16B Herman Moore 10/13 W .15 .40
CG16C Herman Moore 11/28 L .15 .40
CG17A Isaac Bruce 10/13 L .30 .75
CG17B Isaac Bruce 11/10 W .30 .75
CG17C Isaac Bruce 11/24 W .30 .75
CG18A Tim Brown 9/22 W .30 .75
CG18B Tim Brown 10/21L .30 .75
CG18C Tim Brown 11/24 L .30 .75
CG19A Keyshawn Johnson 10/6 L .40 1.00
CG19B Keyshawn Johnson 11/10 L .40 1.00
CG19C Keyshawn Johnson 12/1 W .40 1.00
CG20A Terry Glenn 10/13 L .40 1.00
CG20B Terry Glenn 11/10 W .40 1.00
CG20C Terry Glenn 12/1 W .40 1.00
CG21A Emmitt Smith 9/22 W 1.25 2.50
CG21B Emmitt Smith 11/3 W 1.25 2.50
CG21C Emmitt Smith 11/28 W 1.25 2.50
CG22A Edgar Bennett 10/6 L .15 .40
CG22B Edgar Bennett 11/3 L .15 .40
CG22C Edgar Bennett 11/18 L .15 .40
CG23A Chris Warren 10/6 L .15 .40
CG23B Chris Warren 10/27 W .15 .40
CG23C Chris Warren 11/17 L .15 .40
CG24A Marshall Faulk 9/23 L .30 .75
CG24B Marshall Faulk 11/3 L .30 .75
CG24C Marshall Faulk 11/24 L .30 .75
CG25A Curtis Martin 9/22 W .40 1.00
CG25B Curtis Martin 10/20 W .40 1.00
CG25C Curtis Martin 12/1 L .40 1.00
CG26A Barry Sanders 9/29 L 1.25 2.50
CG26B Barry Sanders 10/17 W 1.25 2.50
CG26C Barry Sanders 11/17 W 1.25 2.50
CG27A Rashaan Salaam 9/22 L .15 .40
CG27B Rashaan Salaam 10/28 W .15 .40
CG27C Rashaan Salaam 11/17 L .15 .40
CG28A Leeland McElroy 9/29 L .07 .20
CG28B Leeland McElroy 10/27 L .07 .20
CG28C Leeland McElroy 11/17 L .07 .20
CG29A Tim Biakabutuka 9/22 L .15 .40
CG29B Tim Biakabutuka 10/13 L .15 .40
CG29C Tim Biakabutuka 11/3 L .15 .40
CG30A Lawrence Phillips 9/29 L .15 .40
CG30B Lawrence Phillips 10/20 L .15 .40
CG30C Lawrence Phillips 10/27 L .15 .40

1996 Collector's Choice Jumbos 3x5

COMPLETE SET (9) 12.00 30.00
48 Kerry Collins 1.00 2.50
49 Rashaan Salaam .60 1.50
51 Emmitt Smith 1.60 4.00
57 Brett Favre 2.00 5.00
60 Mark Brunell 1.20 3.00
64 Dan Marino 2.00 5.00
70 Tim Brown 1.00 2.50
72 Kordell Stewart 1.00 2.50
74 Jerry Rice 1.20 3.00

1996 Collector's Choice Dan Marino A Cut Above

COMPLETE SET (10) 6.00 15.00
COMMON CARD (CA1-CA10) .60 1.50
ONE PER SPECIAL RETAIL PACK
*UDA JUMBO CARDS: SAME PRICE

1996 Collector's Choice MVPs

COMPLETE SET (45) 4.00 10.00
STATED ODDS 1:1 HOBBY, 2:1 SPEC.RET
*GOLD STARS: 3X TO 8X BASIC INSERTS
TEN GOLDS PER FACTORY SET
GOLD STATED ODDS 1:35
M1 Larry Centers .10 .30
M2 Jeff George .10 .30
M3 Jim Kelly .25 .60
M4 Bryce Paup .05 .15
M5 Kerry Collins .25 .60
M6 Erik Kramer .05 .15
M7 Rashaan Salaam .10 .30
M8 Jeff Blake .25 .60
M9 Carl Pickens .10 .30
M10 Vinny Testaverde .10 .30
M11 Michael Irvin .25 .60
M12 Emmitt Smith 1.00 2.00
M13 John Elway 1.25 2.50
M14 Terrell Davis .30 .75
M15 Herman Moore .10 .30
M16 Barry Sanders 1.00 2.00
M17 Brett Favre 1.25 2.50
M18 Edgar Bennett .10 .30
M19 Rodney Thomas .05 .15
M20 Jim Harbaugh .10 .30
M21 Marshall Faulk .25 .60
M22 Mark Brunell .30 .75
M23 Steve Bono .05 .15
M24 Marcus Allen .25 .60
M25 Dan Marino 1.25 2.50
M26 Bryan Cox .05 .15
M27 Cris Carter .25 .60
M28 Curtis Martin .30 .75
M29 Drew Bledsoe .30 .75
M30 Jim Everett .05 .15
M31 Rodney Hampton .10 .30
M32 Adrian Murrell .10 .30
M33 Tim Brown .25 .60
M34 Rodney Peete .05 .15
M35 Ricky Watters .10 .30
M36 Yancey Thigpen .10 .30
M37 Greg Lloyd .10 .30
M38 Isaac Bruce .25 .60
M39 Tony Martin .10 .30
M40 Junior Seau .25 .60
M41 Steve Young .40 1.00
M42 Jerry Rice .60 1.25
M43 Chris Warren .10 .30
M44 Errict Rhett .10 .30
M45 Brian Mitchell .05 .15

1996 Collector's Choice Stick-Ums

COMPLETE SET (30) 5.00 12.00
STATED ODDS 1:3
TEN PER FACTORY SET
S1 Dan Marino 1.00 2.50
S2 Mike Mamula .05 .15
S3 Errict Rhett .10 .30
S4 Drew Bledsoe .30 .75
S5 Anthony Smith .05 .15
S6 Brett Favre UER 1.00 2.50
S7 Morten Andersen .05 .15
S8 Deion Sanders .25 .60
S9 Jeff George .10 .30
S10 Erik Kramer .05 .15
S11 Jerry Rice .50 1.25
S12 Michael Irvin .25 .60
S13 Greg Lloyd .10 .30
S14 Cris Carter .25 .60
S15 Ken Norton .05 .15
S16 Natrone Means .10 .30
S17 Robert Brooks .25 .60
S18 Bomb .05 .15
Blitz
S19 Kordell Stewart .25 .60
S20 Referee .05 .15
S21 Emmitt Smith .75 2.00
S22 Reggie White .25 .60
S23 Eric Metcalf .05 .15
S24 Jesse Sapolu .05 .15
S25 Curtis Martin .30 .75
S26 Neil Smith .10 .30
S27 Junior Seau .25 .60
S28 TD .05 .15
S29 Yardmarkers .05 .15
S30 Terry McDaniel .05 .15

1996 Collector's Choice Update

The 1996 Collector's Choice Update set was issued in one series totalling 200 cards. The 12-card packs retail for $.99 each. The set contains the topical subsets: Rookie Collection (1-60), Franchise Playmaker (61-90) and Regular cards (91-200).

COMPLETE SET (200) 7.50 15.00
U1 Zach Thomas RC .25 .60
U2 Simeon Rice .20 .50
U3 Jonathan Ogden .10 .30
U4 Eric Moulds .10 .30
U5 Tim Biakabutuka .10 .30
U6 Walt Harris .02 .10
U7 Willie Anderson .02 .10
U8 Ricky Whittle .02 .10
U9 John Mobley .02 .10
U10 Reggie Brown RC .02 .10
U11 John Michels .02 .10
U12 Eddie George .25 .60
U13 Marvin Harrison .50 1.25
U14 Kevin Hardy .07 .20
U15 Kavika Pittman RC .02 .10
U16 Daryl Gardener .02 .10
U17 Duane Clemons .02 .10
U18 Terry Glenn .10 .30
U19 Alex Molden RC .02 .10
U20 Cedric Jones .02 .10
U21 Keyshawn Johnson .20 .50
U22 Rickey Dudley .10 .30
U23 Jason Dunn .02 .10
U24 Jamain Stephens .02 .10
U25 Lawrence Phillips .02 .10
U26 Bryan Still RC .02 .10
U27 Israel Ifeanyi .02 .10
U28 Pete Kendall .02 .10
U29 Regan Upshaw .02 .10
U30 Andre Johnson RC .02 .10
U31 Leeland McElroy .02 .10
U32 Ray Lewis .50 1.25
U33 Sean Moran RC .02 .10
U34 Muhsin Muhammad RC .40 1.00
U35 Bobby Engram .10 .30
U36 Marco Battaglia .02 .10
U37 Stepfret Williams .02 .10
U38 Jeff Lewis .07 .20
U39 Derrick Mayes .07 .20
U40 Reggie Tongue RC .02 .10
U41 Tony James RC .07 .20
U42 Tony Banks RC .10 .30
U43 Tedy Bruschi 1.25 3.00
U44 Mike Alstott .20 .50
U45 Anthony Dorsett .07 .20
U46 Tony Brackens RC .10 .30
U47 Bryant Mix .02 .10
U48 Karim Abdul-Jabbar .10 .30
U49 Moe Williams RC .30 .75
U50 Lawyer Milloy .07 .20
U51 Je'rod Cherry .02 .10
U52 Amani Toomer RC .40 1.00
U53 Alex Van Dyke .07 .20
U54 Lance Johnstone RC .07 .20
U55 Bobby Hoying .07 .20
U56 Jon Witman RC .07 .20
U57 Eddie Kennison RC .10 .30
U58 Brian Roche RC .02 .10
U59 Terrell Owens RC 1.00 2.50
U60 Stephen Davis .20 .50
U61 Jeff George FP .02 .10
U62 Darick Holmes FP .02 .10
U63 Kerry Collins FP .07 .20
U64 Rashaan Salaam FP .02 .10
U65 Jeff Blake FP .07 .20
U66 Emmitt Smith FP .30 .75
U67 Troy Aikman FP .20 .50
U68 John Elway FP .40 1.00
U69 Terrell Davis FP .15 .40
U70 Barry Sanders FP .30 .75
U71 Herman Moore FP .07 .20
U72 Brett Favre FP .40 1.00
U73 Robert Brooks FP .07 .20
U74 Steve McNair FP .15 .40
U75 Marshall Faulk FP .10 .30
U76 Marcus Allen FP .07 .20
U77 Dan Marino FP .40 1.00
U78 Warren Moon FP .02 .10
U79 Drew Bledsoe FP .10 .30
U80 Curtis Martin FP .10 .30
U81 Mario Bates FP .07 .20
U82 Tim Brown FP .07 .20
U83 Charlie Garner FP .07 .20
U84 Kordell Stewart FP .07 .20
U85 Isaac Bruce FP .10 .30
U86 Tony Martin FP .07 .20
U87 Jerry Rice FP .20 .50
U88 J.J. Stokes FP .10 .30
U89 Joey Galloway FP .10 .30
U90 Errict Rhett FP .07 .20
U91 Mike Pritchard .02 .10
U92 Jerome Bettis .10 .30
U93 Winslow Oliver .02 .10
U94 David Klingler .02 .10
U95 Lawrence Dawsey .02 .10
U96 Charlie Jones .07 .20
U97 Dave Krieg .02 .10
U98 Chris Spielman .02 .10
U99 Stanley Pritchett .02 .10
U100 Sean Gilbert .02 .10
U101 Tommy Vardell .02 .10
U102 DeRon Jenkins .02 .10
U103 Larry Bowie .02 .10
U104 Kyle Wachholtz .02 .10
U105 Brady Smith RC .02 .10
U106 Steve Walsh .02 .10
U107 Wesley Walls .07 .20
U108 Kevin Ross .02 .10
U109 Willie Clay .02 .10
U110 Olanda Truitt .02 .10
U111 Calvin Williams .02 .10
U112 Chris Doleman .02 .10
U113 Irving Fryar .07 .20
U114 Jimmy Spencer .02 .10
U115 Reggie Barlow RC .07 .20
U116 Reggie Brown RBK RC .02 .10
U117 Dixon Edwards .02 .10
U118 Haywood Jeffires .02 .10
U119 Santana Dotson .02 .10
U120 Herschel Walker .07 .20
U121 Darryl Williams .02 .10
U122 Bryan Cox .02 .10
U123 Lamar Thomas .02 .10
U124 Hendrick Lusk .02 .10
U125 Jahine Arnold RC .02 .10
U126 Boomer Esiason .07 .20
U127 Willie Davis .02 .10
U128 Pete Stoyanovich .02 .10
U129 Bill Romanowski .02 .10
U130 Tim McKyer .02 .10
U131 Patrick Sapp .02 .10
U132 Natrone Means .07 .20
U133 Quinn Early .02 .10
U134 Leslie O'Neal .02 .10
U135 Mark Seay .02 .10
U136 Pete Metzelaars .02 .10
U137 Jay Leeuwenburg UER RC .02 .10
name misspelled ...berg
U138 Buster Owens .02 .10
U139 Todd McNair .02 .10
U140 Eugene Robinson .02 .10
U141 Sean Salisbury .02 .10
U142 Eddie Robinson .02 .10
U143 Jerris McPhail .02 .10
U144 Ray Farmer RC .02 .10
U145 Garrison Hearst .07 .20
U146 Leonard Russell .02 .10
U147 Roy Barker .02 .10
U148 Larry Brown .02 .10
U149 Webster Slaughter .02 .10
U150 Roman Oben RC .02 .10
U151 LeShon Johnson .02 .10
U152 Patrick Bates .02 .10
U153 Ifeanyi Uwaezuoke UER .10 .30
Uwaezoke on back
U154 Scott Slutzker .02 .10
U155 John Jurkovic .02 .10
U156 Brian Milne .02 .10
U157 Mike Sherrard .02 .10
U158 Neil O'Donnell .07 .20
U159 Roger Harper .02 .10
U160 Desmond Howard .07 .20
U161 Alfred Williams .02 .10
U162 Ronnie Harmon .02 .10
U163 Sammie Burroughs RC .02 .10
U164 Keenan McCardell .10 .30
U165 Shane Dronett .02 .10
U166 Jeff Graham .02 .10
U167 Bill Brooks .02 .10
U168 Shawn Jefferson .02 .10
U169 Detron Smith .02 .10
U170 Danny Kanell .10 .30
U171 Jevon Langford .02 .10
U172 Russell Maryland .02 .10
U173 Scott Milanovich RC .10 .30
U174 Eric Davis .02 .10
U175 Ernie Conwell .02 .10
U176 Kurt Gouveia .02 .10
U177 Andre Rison .07 .20
U178 Harold Green .02 .10
U179 Frank Reich .02 .10
U180 Glyn Milburn .02 .10
U181 Nilo Silvan .02 .10
U182 Cornelius Bennett .02 .10
U183 Freddie Solomon RC .02 .10
U184 Pat Terrell .02 .10
U185 Miles Macik .02 .10
U186 Bo Orlando .02 .10
U187 Kelvin Martin .02 .10
U188 Todd Kinchen .02 .10
U189 Reggie Brooks .02 .10
U190 Steve Beuerlein UER .07 .20
name misspelled Beurlein
U191 Marco Coleman .02 .10
U192 Johnny Johnson .02 .10
U193 Dedric Mathis .02 .10
U194 Leon Searcy .02 .10
U195 Kevin Greene .07 .20
U196 Daniel Stubbs .02 .10
U197 Ray Mickens .02 .10
U198 Devin Wyman .02 .10
U199 Lorenzo Lynch .02 .10
U200 Checklist Card .10 .30
Jerry Rice and
Dan Marino ghosted images

1996 Collector's Choice Update Record Breaking Trio

COMPLETE SET (4) 25.00 60.00
STATED ODDS 1:100
1 Joe Montana 7.50 15.00
2 Dan Marino 12.50 30.00
3 Jerry Rice 7.50 15.00
4 Joe Montana 12.50 25.00
Dan Marino
Jerry Rice

1996 Collector's Choice Update Stick-Ums

COMPLETE SET (30) 7.50 15.00
STICKER STATED ODDS 1:4
*MYSTERY BASE: .5X TO 1X BASE CARD HI
MYSTERY STATED ODDS 1:4
S1 Jeff George .15 .40
S2 Darren Bennett .07 .20
S3 Marcus Allen .25 .60
S4 Brett Favre 1.00 2.00
S5 Carl Pickens .15 .40
S6 Troy Aikman .40 1.00
S7 John Elway 1.00 2.00
S8 Steve Young .25 .60
S9 Norm Johnson .07 .20
S10 Kordell Stewart .25 .60
S11 Drew Bledsoe .25 .60
S12 Jim Kelly .25 .60
S13 Dan Marino 1.00 2.00
S14 Joey Galloway .25 .60
S15 Lawrence Phillips .25 .60
S16 Reggie White .25 .60
S17 Kevin Hardy .15 .40
S18 Isaac Bruce .25 .60
S19 Keyshawn Johnson .40 1.00
S20 Barry Sanders .75 1.50
S21 Deion Sanders .25 .60
S22 Emmitt Smith .75 1.50
S23 Chris Warren .15 .40
S24 Tim Biakabutuka .25 .60
S25 Terry Glenn .25 .60
S26 Marshall Faulk .25 .60
S27 Tamarick Vanover .07 .20
S28 Curtis Martin .30 .75
S29 Terrell Davis .30 .75
S30 Jerry Rice .40 1.00

1996 Collector's Choice Update You Make The Play

COMPLETE SET (90) 10.00 20.00
ONE PER PACK
Y1 Norm Johnson .07 .20
Kick Good
Y2 Jerry Rice .40 1.00
Touchdown
Y3 Dan Marino/9 Yards 1.00 2.00
Y4 Marshall Faulk/3 Yards .25 .60
Y5 Neil Smith .07 .20
Sack - 5 Yards
Y6 Herman Moore/1st Down .15 .40
Y7 Brett Favre 1.00 2.00
Y8 Curtis Martin/5 Yards .30 .75
Y9 Reggie White .25 .60
Sack - 8 Yards
Y10 Cris Carter/12 Yards .25 .60
Y11 Rick Tuten .07 .20
Kick Good
Y12 Steve Young/6 Yards .30 .75
Y13 Barry Sanders .75 1.50
Y14 Deion Sanders .25 .60
Interception
Y15 Isaac Bruce/11 Yards .25 .60
Y16 Troy Aikman/6 Yards .30 .75
Y17 Emmitt Smith/7 Yards .75 1.50
Y18 Junior Seau .25 .60
Fumble
Y19 Joey Galloway/17 Yards .25 .60
Y20 Drew Bledsoe/4 Yards .25 .60
Y21 Jason Elam .07 .20
Kick No Good
Y22 Edgar Bennett/3 Yards .15 .40
Y23 Greg Lloyd .07 .20
Fumble
Y24 Tamarick Vanover/13 Yards .07 .20
Y25 John Elway/5 Yards 1.00 2.00
Y26 Larry Centers/4 Yards .15 .40
Y27 Derrick Thomas .25 .60
Sack - 7 Yards
Y28 Michael Irvin/12 Yards .25 .60
Y29 Jeff George/3 Yards .15 .40
Y30 Thurman Thomas/3 Yards .25 .60
Y31 Darren Bennett .07 .20
Kick Good
Y32 Ken Norton .07 .20
Fumble
Y33 Carl Pickens/14 Yards .25 .60
Y34 Jeff Blake/10 Yards .15 .40
Y35 Craig Heyward/3 Yards .15 .40
Y36 Aeneas Williams .07 .20
No Gain
Y37 Terance Mathis/10 Yards .15 .40
Y38 Jim Kelly/7 Yards .25 .60
Y39 Marcus Allen/5 Yards .25 .60
Y40 Tim McDonald/1 Yard .07 .20
Y41 Jason Hanson .07 .20
Kick No Good
Y42 Scott Mitchell/4 Yards .15 .40
Y43 Tim Brown/16 Yards .25 .60
Y44 Kordell Stewart/3 Yards .25 .60
Y45 Eric Metcalf/4 Yards .15 .40
Y46 Norm Johnson .07 .20
Kick Good
Y47 Jerry Rice/1st Down .40 1.00
Y48 Dan Marino/1st Down 1.00 2.00
Y49 Marshall Faulk/8 Yards .25 .60
Y50 Neil Smith/2 Yards .07 .20
Y51 Herman Moore/14 Yards .15 .40
Y52 Brett Favre 1.00 2.00
Y53 Curtis Martin/6 Yards .30 .75
Y54 Reggie White/2 Yards .25 .60
Y55 Cris Carter/1st Down .25 .60
Y56 Rick Tuten .07 .20
Kick No Good
Y57 Steve Young/1st Down .30 .75
Y58 Barry Sanders .75 1.50
Y59 Deion Sanders/1 Yard .25 .60
Y60 Isaac Bruce/1st Down .25 .60
Y61 Troy Aikman/1st Down .40 1.00
Y62 Emmitt Smith .75 1.50
Touchdown
Y63 Junior Seau/-2 Yards .25 .60
Y64 Joey Galloway/1st Down .25 .60
Y65 Drew Bledsoe/1st Down .25 .60
Y66 Jason Elam .07 .20
Kick Good
Y67 Edgar Bennett/4 Yards .15 .40
Y68 Greg Lloyd/-4 Yards .07 .20
Y69 Tamarick Vanover/15 Yards .07 .20
Y70 John Elway/1st Down 1.00 2.00
Y71 Larry Centers/7 Yards .15 .40
Y72 Derrick Thomas .25 .60
No Gain
Y73 Michael Irvin/1st Down .25 .60
Y74 Jeff George/12 Yards .15 .40
Y75 Thurman Thomas/5 Yards .25 .60
Y76 Darren Bennett .07 .20
Kick No Good
Y77 Ken Norton/-3 Yards .07 .20
Y78 Carl Pickens/1st Down .25 .60
Y79 Jeff Blake/1st Down .15 .40
Y80 Craig Heyward/5 Yards .15 .40
Y81 Aeneas Williams/-3 Yards .07 .20
Y82 Terance Mathis/14 Yards .15 .40
Y83 Jim Kelly/1st Down .25 .60
Y84 Marcus Allen/6 Yards .25 .60
Y85 Tim McDonald .07 .20
No Gain
Y86 Jason Hanson .07 .20
Kick Good
Y87 Scott Mitchell/7 Yards .15 .40
Y88 Tim Brown/1st Down .25 .60
Y89 Kordell Stewart/7 Yards .25 .60
Y90 Eric Metcalf/7 Yards .15 .40

1997 Collector's Choice

This 565-card set was distributed in two series. The first 310-cards were released in 14-card packs with a suggested retail price of $1.29 and featured color action player photos in white borders. The backs carried player information and statistics along with dual numbering that helps collectors put together cards of their favorite NFL team. There were 220 regular player cards, 45 Rookie Class subset cards (1-45), 40 Names of the Game subset cards (46-85), and five checklists which featured collecting tips for new collectors. Series two included 255 different cards with Rookie Collection and Building Blocks subsets.

COMPLETE SET (565) 12.50 30.00
COMP.SERIES 1 (310) 7.50 20.00
COMP.FACT.SER.1(330) 10.00 25.00
COMP.SERIES 2 (255) 5.00 12.00
1 Orlando Pace RC .20 .50
2 Darrell Russell RC .07 .20
3 Shawn Springs RC .10 .30
4 Peter Boulware RC .20 .50
5 Bryant Westbrook RC .07 .20
6 Tom Knight RC .07 .20
7 Ike Hilliard RC .30 .75
8 James Farrior RC .20 .50
9 Chris Naeole RC .07 .20
10 Michael Booker RC .07 .20
11 Warrick Dunn RC UER .60 1.50
(no card number on back)
12 Tony Gonzalez RC .75 2.00
13 Reinard Wilson RC .10 .30
14 Yatil Green RC .10 .30
15 Reidel Anthony RC .20 .50
16 Kenard Lang RC .10 .30
17 Kenny Holmes RC .20 .50
18 Tarik Glenn RC .20 .50
19 Dwayne Rudd RC .20 .50
20 Renaldo Wynn RC .07 .20
21 David LaFleur RC .07 .20
22 Antowain Smith RC .50 1.25
23 Jim Druckenmiller RC .10 .30
24 Rae Carruth RC .07 .20
25 Jared Tomich RC .07 .20
26 Chris Canty RC .07 .20
27 Jake Plummer RC .75 2.00
28 Troy Davis RC .10 .30
29 Sedrick Shaw RC .10 .30
30 Jamie Sharper RC .10 .30
31 Tiki Barber RC 1.25 3.00
32 Byron Hanspard RC .10 .30
33 Darnell Autry RC .10 .30
34 Corey Dillon RC .75 2.00
35 Joey Kent RC .20 .50
36 Nathan Davis RC .07 .20
37 Will Blackwell RC .10 .30
38 Kim Herring RC .07 .20
39 Pat Barnes RC .20 .50
40 Kevin Lockett RC .10 .30
41 Trevor Pryce RC .20 .50
42 Matt Russell RC .07 .20
43 Greg Jones RC .07 .20
44 Antonio Anderson RC .07 .20
45 George Jones RC .10 .30
46 Steve Young NG .20 .50
47 Jerry Rice NG .20 .50
48 Curtis Conway NG .10 .30
49 Jeff Blake NG .10 .30
50 Carl Pickens NG .10 .30
51 Bruce Smith NG .07 .20
52 John Elway NG .40 1.00
53 Terrell Davis NG .20 .50
54 Shannon Sharpe NG .10 .30
55 Junior Seau NG .10 .30
56 Darren Bennett NG .07 .20
57 Jim Harbaugh NG .07 .20
58 Marshall Faulk NG .20 .50
59 Emmitt Smith NG .30 .75
60 Troy Aikman NG .20 .50
61 Deion Sanders NG .10 .30
62 Dan Marino NG .40 1.00
63 Ricky Watters NG .07 .20
64 Mark Brunell NG .20 .50
65 Keenan McCardell NG .10 .30
66 Keyshawn Johnson NG .10 .30
67 Barry Sanders NG .30 .75
68 Herman Moore NG .10 .30
69 Eddie George NG .10 .30
70 Steve McNair NG .10 .30
71 Brett Favre NG .40 1.00
72 Reggie White NG .10 .30
73 Edgar Bennett NG .07 .20
74 Kerry Collins NG .10 .30
75 Kevin Greene NG .07 .20
76 Drew Bledsoe NG .10 .30
77 Terry Glenn NG .10 .30
78 Curtis Martin NG .10 .30
79 Jeff Hostetler NG .07 .20
80 Napoleon Kaufman NG .10 .30
81 Isaac Bruce NG .10 .30
82 Terry Allen NG .10 .30
83 Joey Galloway NG .10 .30
84 Kordell Stewart NG .10 .30
85 Jerome Bettis NG .10 .30
86 Dana Stubblefield .07 .20
87 Merton Hanks .07 .20
88 Terrell Owens .25 .60
89 Brent Jones .07 .20
90 Ken Norton Jr. .07 .20
91 Jerry Rice .40 1.00
92 Terry Kirby .10 .30
93 Bryant Young .07 .20
94 Raymont Harris .07 .20
95 Jeff Jaeger .07 .20
96 Curtis Conway .10 .30
97 Walt Harris .07 .20
98 Bobby Engram .10 .30
99 Donnell Woolford .07 .20
100 Rashaan Salaam .07 .20
101 Jeff Blake .10 .30
102 Tony McGee .07 .20
103 Ashley Ambrose .07 .20
104 Dan Wilkinson .07 .20
105 Jevon Langford .07 .20
106 Darnay Scott .10 .30
107 David Dunn .07 .20
108 Eric Moulds .25 .60
109 Darick Holmes .07 .20
110 Thurman Thomas .20 .50
111 Quinn Early .07 .20
112 Jim Kelly .20 .50
113 Bryce Paup .07 .20
114 Bruce Smith .10 .30
115 Todd Collins .07 .20
116 Tory James .07 .20
117 Anthony Miller .07 .20
118 Terrell Davis .25 .60
119 Tyrone Braxton .07 .20
120 John Mobley .07 .20
121 Bill Romanowski .07 .20
122 Vaughn Hebron .07 .20
123 Mike Alstott .20 .50
124 Errict Rhett .07 .20
125 Trent Dilfer .20 .50
126 Courtney Hawkins .07 .20
127 Hardy Nickerson .07 .20
128 Donnie Abraham RC .20 .50
129 Regan Upshaw .07 .20
130 Kent Graham .07 .20
131 Rob Moore .10 .30
132 Simeon Rice .10 .30
133 LeShon Johnson .07 .20
134 Frank Sanders .10 .30
135 Leeland McElroy .07 .20
136 Seth Joyner .07 .20
137 Andre Coleman .07 .20
138 Stan Humphries .10 .30
139 Charlie Jones .07 .20
140 Junior Seau .20 .50
141 Rodney Harrison RC .40 1.00
142 Darrien Gordon .07 .20
143 Terrell Fletcher .07 .20
144 Tamarick Vanover .10 .30
145 Greg Hill .07 .20
146 Marcus Allen .20 .50
147 Lake Dawson .07 .20
148 Dale Carter .07 .20
149 Kimble Anders .10 .30
150 Chris Penn .07 .20
151 Sean Dawkins .07 .20
152 Ken Dilger .07 .20
153 Marvin Harrison .20 .50
154 Jeff Herrod .07 .20
155 Jim Harbaugh .10 .30
156 Cary Blanchard .07 .20
157 Aaron Bailey .07 .20
158 Deion Sanders .20 .50
159 Jim Schwantz RC .07 .20
160 Michael Irvin .20 .50
161 Herschel Walker .10 .30
162 Emmitt Smith .60 1.50
163 Chris Boniol .07 .20
164 Eric Bjornson .07 .20
165 Karim Abdul-Jabbar .10 .30
166 O.J. McDuffie .10 .30
167 Troy Drayton .07 .20
168 Zach Thomas .20 .50
169 Irving Spikes .07 .20
170 Shane Burton RC .07 .20
171 Stanley Pritchett .07 .20
172 Ty Detmer .10 .30
173 Chris T. Jones .07 .20
174 Troy Vincent .07 .20
175 Brian Dawkins .20 .50
176 Irving Fryar .10 .30
177 Charlie Garner .10 .30
178 Bobby Taylor .07 .20
179 Jamal Anderson .20 .50
180 Terance Mathis .10 .30
181 Craig Heyward .07 .20
182 Cornelius Bennett .07 .20
183 Jessie Tuggle .07 .20
184 Devin Bush .07 .20
185 Dave Brown .07 .20
186 Danny Kanell .07 .20
187 Rodney Hampton .10 .30
188 Tyrone Wheatley .10 .30
189 Amani Toomer .20 .50
190 Phillippi Sparks .07 .20
191 Thomas Lewis .07 .20
192 Jimmy Smith .10 .30
193 Pete Mitchell .07 .20
194 Natrone Means .10 .30
195 Mark Brunell .25 .60
196 Kevin Hardy .07 .20
197 Tony Brackens .07 .20
198 Aaron Beasley RC .07 .20
199 Chris Hudson .07 .20
200 Wayne Chrebet .20 .50
201 Keyshawn Johnson .20 .50
202 Adrian Murrell .10 .30
203 Neil O'Donnell .10 .30
204 Hugh Douglas .10 .30
205 Mo Lewis .07 .20
206 Glenn Foley .07 .20
207 Aaron Glenn .07 .20
208 Johnnie Morton .10 .30
209 Reggie Brown LB .07 .20
210 Barry Sanders .60 1.50
211 Glyn Milburn .07 .20
212 Bennie Blades .07 .20
213 Steve McNair .25 .60
214 Frank Wycheck .07 .20
215 Chris Sanders .07 .20
216 Blaine Bishop .07 .20
217 Willie Davis .07 .20
218 Darryll Lewis .07 .20
219 Marcus Robertson .07 .20
220 Robert Brooks .10 .30
221 Antonio Freeman .20 .50
222 Keith Jackson .07 .20
223 Mark Chmura .10 .30
224 Brett Favre .75 2.00
225 Sean Jones .07 .20
226 Reggie White .20 .50
227 LeRoy Butler .07 .20
228 Craig Newsome .07 .20
229 Wesley Walls .10 .30
230 Mark Carrier WR .07 .20
231 Muhsin Muhammad .10 .30
232 John Kasay .07 .20
233 Anthony Johnson .07 .20
234 Kerry Collins .20 .50
235 Kevin Greene .10 .30
236 Sam Mills .07 .20
237 Ben Coates .10 .30
238 Terry Glenn .20 .50
239 Willie McGinest .07 .20
240 Ted Johnson .07 .20
241 Lawyer Milloy .07 .20
242 Drew Bledsoe .25 .60
243 Willie Clay .07 .20
244 Chris Slade .07 .20
245 Tim Brown .20 .50
246 Daryl Hobbs .07 .20
247 Rickey Dudley .10 .30
248 Joe Aska .07 .20
249 Chester McGlockton .07 .20
250 Rob Fredrickson .07 .20
251 Terry McDaniel .07 .20
252 Tony Banks .10 .30
253 Lawrence Phillips .07 .20
254 Isaac Bruce .20 .50
255 Eddie Kennison .10 .30
256 Kevin Carter .07 .20
257 Roman Phifer .07 .20
258 Keith Lyle .07 .20
259 Vinny Testaverde .10 .30
260 Derrick Alexander WR .10 .30
261 Ray Lewis .30 .75
262 Jermaine Lewis .20 .50
263 Byron Bam Morris .07 .20
264 Stevon Moore .07 .20
265 Antonio Langham .07 .20
266 Brian Mitchell .07 .20
267 Henry Ellard .07 .20
268 Leslie Shepherd .07 .20
269 Michael Westbrook .10 .30
270 Jamie Asher .07 .20
271 Ken Harvey .07 .20
272 Gus Frerotte .07 .20
273 Michael Haynes .07 .20
274 Ray Zellars .07 .20
275 Jim Everett .07 .20
276 Tyrone Hughes .07 .20
277 Joe Johnson .07 .20
278 Eric Allen .07 .20
279 Brady Smith .07 .20
280 Mario Bates .07 .20
281 Torrance Small .07 .20
282 John Friesz .07 .20
283 Brian Blades .07 .20
284 Chris Warren .10 .30
285 Joey Galloway .10 .30
286 Michael Sinclair .07 .20
287 Lamar Smith .20 .50
288 Mike Pritchard .07 .20
289 Jerome Bettis .20 .50
290 Charles Johnson .10 .30
291 Mike Tomczak .07 .20
292 Levon Kirkland .07 .20
293 Carnell Lake .07 .20
294 Eric Pegram .07 .20
295 Kordell Stewart .20 .50
296 Greg Lloyd .07 .20
297 Dixon Edwards .07 .20
298 Cris Carter .20 .50
299 Brad Johnson .20 .50
300 Qadry Ismail .20 .50
301 John Randle .10 .30
302 Orlando Thomas .07 .20
303 Dewayne Washington .07 .20
304 Jake Reed .10 .30
305 Derrick Alexander DE .07 .20
306 Eddie George CL .20 .50
307 Dan Marino CL .15 .40
308 Curtis Martin CL .10 .30
309 Troy Aikman CL .10 .30
310 Marcus Allen CL .10 .30
311 Jim Druckenmiller .07 .20
312 Greg Clark RC .07 .20
313 Darnell Autry .10 .30
314 Reinard Wilson .07 .20
315 Corey Dillon .30 .75
316 Antowain Smith .20 .50
317 Trevor Pryce .10 .30
318 Warrick Dunn .25 .60
319 Reidel Anthony .10 .30
320 Jake Plummer .30 .75
321 Tom Knight .07 .20
322 Freddie Jones RC .10 .30
323 Tony Gonzalez .30 .75
324 Pat Barnes .10 .30
325 Kevin Lockett .10 .30
326 Tarik Glenn .08 .25
327 David LaFleur .07 .20
328 Antonio Anderson .07 .20
329 Yatil Green .10 .30
330 Jason Taylor RC .40 1.00
331 Brian Manning RC .07 .20
332 Michael Booker .07 .20
333 Byron Hanspard .10 .30
334 Ike Hilliard .20 .50
335 Tiki Barber .50 1.25
336 Renaldo Wynn .07 .20
337 Damon Jones RC .07 .20
338 James Farrior .07 .20
339 Dedric Ward RC .10 .30
340 Bryant Westbrook .07 .20
341 Joey Kent .20 .50
342 Kenny Holmes .20 .50
343 Darren Sharper RC 1.25 3.00
344 Rae Carruth .07 .20
345 Chris Canty .07 .20
346 Darrell Russell .07 .20
347 Orlando Pace .20 .50
348 Peter Boulware .20 .50
349 Kenard Lang .07 .20
350 Danny Wuerffel RC .20 .50
351 Troy Davis .07 .20
352 Shawn Springs .10 .30
353 Walter Jones RC .20 .50
354 Will Blackwell .07 .20
355 Dwayne Rudd .07 .20
356 Jerry Rice .07 .20
Steve Young
Ken Norton
Jim Druckenmiller
Bryant Young
357 Bobby Engram .07 .20
Rick Mirer
Raymont Harris
Curtis Conway
Bryan Cox
358 Ki-Jana Carter .07 .20
Jeff Blake
Carl Pickens
Dan Wilkinson
Darnay Scott
359 Thurman Thomas .07 .20
Todd Collins
Antowain Smith
Bruce Smith
Chris Spielman
360 Terrell Davis .10 .30
John Elway
Shannon Sharpe
Neil Smith
Rod Smith WR
361 Warrick Dunn .07 .20
Trent Dilfer
Errict Rhett
Hardy Nickerson
Reidel Anthony
362 Frank Sanders .10 .30
Eric Swann
Jake Plummer
Kent Graham
Rob Moore
363 Tony Martin .07 .20
Stan Humphries
Junior Seau
Eric Metcalf
Freddie Jones
364 Marcus Allen .10 .30

Kevin Lockett		
Tony Gonzalez		
Pat Barnes		
Elvis Grbac		
Derrick Thomas		
Eric Hill		
365 Marvin Harrison	.10	.30
Jim Harbaugh		
Marshall Faulk		
Quentin Coryatt		
Sean Dawkins		
366 Emmitt Smith	.07	.20
Troy Aikman		
Deion Sanders		
Michael Irvin		
David LaFleur		
367 Dan Marino	.07	.20
Troy Drayton		
Karim Abdul-Jabbar		
Zach Thomas		
O.J. McDuffie		
368 Chris T. Jones	.07	.20
Ricky Watters		
Ty Detmer		
Irving Fryar		
Mike Mamula		
369 Byron Hanspard	.07	.20
Jamal Anderson		
Cornelius Bennett		
Ray Buchanan		
Terence Mathis		
370 Ike Hilliard	.07	.20
Dave Brown		
Rodney Hampton		
Tyrone Wheatley		
Phillippi Sparks		
371 Keenan McCardell	.07	.20
Mark Brunell		
Kevin Hardy		
Renaldo Wynn		
Natrone Means		
372 Keyshawn Johnson	.07	.20
Neil O'Donnell		
James Farrior		
Adrian Murrell		
Wayne Chrebet		
373 Barry Sanders	.07	.20
Bryant Westbrook		
Herman Moore		
Johnnie Morton		
Scott Mitchell		
374 Eddie George	.07	.20
Steve McNair		
Joey Kent		
Chris Sanders		
Blaine Bishop		
375 Robert Brooks	.20	.50
Brett Favre		
Reggie White		
Dorsey Levens		
Derrick Mayes		
376 Tim Biakabutuka	.07	.20
Kerry Collins		
Rae Carruth		
Sam Mills		
Anthony Johnson		
377 Terry Glenn	.07	.20
Drew Bledsoe		
Curtis Martin		
Willie McGinest		
Ben Coates		
378 Tim Brown	.07	.20
Jeff George		
Napoleon Kaufman		
Darrell Russell		
Desmond Howard		
379 Eddie Kennison	.07	.20
Tony Banks		
Isaac Bruce		
Orlando Pace		
Lawrence Phillips		
380 Vinny Testaverde	.07	.20
Peter Boulware		
Michael Jackson		
Byron Bam Morris		
Derrick Alexander WR		
381 Brian Mitchell	.07	.20
Gus Frerotte		
Terry Allen		
Sean Gilbert		
Michael Westbrook		
382 Saints BB	.07	.20
Heath Shuler		
Daryl Hobbs		
Troy Davis		
Wayne Martin		
Mario Bates		
383 Joey Galloway	.07	.20
Chris Warren		
Shawn Springs		
Cortez Kennedy		
Warren Moon		
384 Jerome Bettis	.10	.30
Kordell Stewart		
Greg Lloyd		
Charles Johnson		
Will Blackwell		
385 Jake Reed	.10	.30
Cris Carter		
Brad Johnson		
Robert Smith		
John Randle		
386 William Floyd	.10	.30
387 Steve Young	.25	.60
388 Lee Woodall	.07	.20
389 J.J. Stokes	.10	.30
390 Marc Edwards	.07	.20
391 Rod Woodson	.10	.30
392 Jim Schwantz	.07	.20
393 Garrison Hearst	.10	.30
394 Rick Mirer	.07	.20
395 Alonzo Spellman	.07	.20
396 Tom Carter	.07	.20
397 Bryan Cox	.07	.20
398 John Allred RC	.07	.20
399 Ricky Proehl	.07	.20
400 Tyrone Hughes	.07	.20
401 Carl Pickens	.10	.30
402 Tremain Mack RC	.07	.20
403 Boomer Esiason	.10	.30
404 Ki-Jana Carter	.07	.20
405 Steve Tovar	.07	.20
406 Billy Joe Hobert	.10	.30
407 Andre Reed	.10	.30
408 Marcellus Wiley RC	.10	.30
409 Steve Tasker	.07	.20
410 Chris Spielman	.07	.20
411 Alfred Williams	.07	.20
412 John Elway	.75	2.00
413 Shannon Sharpe	.10	.30
414 Steve Atwater	.07	.20
415 Neil Smith	.10	.30
416 Darrien Gordon	.07	.20
417 Jeff Lewis	.07	.20
418 Flipper Anderson	.07	.20
419 Willie Green	.07	.20
420 Jackie Harris	.07	.20
421 Steve Walsh	.07	.20
422 Anthony Parker	.07	.20
423 Ronde Barber RC	.40	1.00
424 Warren Sapp	.10	.30
425 Aeneas Williams	.07	.20
426 Larry Centers	.10	.30
427 Eric Swann	.07	.20
428 Kevin Williams	.07	.20
429 Darren Bennett	.07	.20
430 Tony Martin	.10	.30
431 John Carney	.07	.20
432 Jim Everett	.07	.20
433 William Fuller	.07	.20
434 Latario Rachal RC	.07	.20
435 Erric Pegram	.07	.20
436 Eric Metcalf	.10	.30
437 Jerome Woods	.07	.20
438 Derrick Thomas	.20	.50
439 Elvis Grbac	.10	.30
440 Terry Wooden	.07	.20
441 Andre Rison	.10	.30
442 Brett Perriman	.07	.20
443 Paul Justin	.07	.20
444 Robert Blackmon	.07	.20
445 Carlton Gray	.07	.20
446 Chris Gardocki	.07	.20
447 Marshall Faulk	.25	.60
448 Sammie Burroughs	.07	.20
449 Quentin Coryatt	.07	.20
450 Troy Aikman	.40	1.00
451 Daryl Johnston	.10	.30
452 Tony Tolbert	.07	.20
453 Brock Marion	.07	.20
454 Billy Davis RC	.07	.20
455 Stepfret Williams	.07	.20
456 Anthony Miller	.07	.20
457 Dan Marino	.75	2.00
458 Jerris McPhail	.07	.20
459 Terrell Buckley	.07	.20
460 Daryl Gardener	.07	.20
461 George Teague	.07	.20
462 Derrick Rodgers RC	.07	.20
463 Fred Barnett	.07	.20
464 Darrin Smith	.07	.20
465 Michael Timpson	.07	.20
466 Jon Harris	.07	.20
467 Jason Dunn	.07	.20
468 Bobby Hoying	.10	.30
469 Ricky Watters	.10	.30
470 Derrick Witherspoon	.07	.20
471 Chris Chandler	.10	.30
472 Ray Buchanan	.07	.20
473 Michael Haynes	.07	.20
474 O.J. Santiago RC	.10	.30
475 Morten Andersen	.07	.20
476 Bert Emanuel	.10	.30
477 Chris Calloway	.07	.20
478 Jason Sehorn	.10	.30
479 John Jurkovic	.07	.20
480 Keenan McCardell	.10	.30
481 James O. Stewart	.10	.30
482 Rob Johnson	.20	.50
483 Mike Logan RC	.07	.20
484 Deon Figures	.07	.20
485 Kyle Brady	.07	.20
486 Alex Van Dyke	.07	.20
487 Jeff Graham	.07	.20
488 Jason Hanson	.07	.20
489 Herman Moore	.10	.30
490 Scott Mitchell	.10	.30
491 Tommy Vardell	.07	.20
492 Derrick Mason RC	.40	1.00
493 Rodney Thomas	.07	.20
494 Ronnie Harmon	.07	.20
495 Eddie George	.20	.50
496 Edgar Bennett	.10	.30
497 William Henderson	.10	.30
498 Dorsey Levens	.20	.50
499 Gilbert Brown	.10	.30
500 Steve Bono	.10	.30
501 Derrick Mayes	.10	.30
502 Fred Lane RC	.10	.30
503 Ernie Mills	.07	.20
504 Tim Biakabutuka	.10	.30
505 Michael Bates	.07	.20
506 Winslow Oliver	.07	.20
507 Ty Law	.10	.30
508 Shawn Jefferson	.07	.20
509 Vincent Brisby	.07	.20
510 Henry Thomas	.07	.20
511 Tedy Bruschi	.40	1.00
512 Curtis Martin	.25	.60
513 Jeff George	.10	.30
514 Desmond Howard	.10	.30
515 Napoleon Kaufman	.20	.50
516 Kenny Shedd RC	.07	.20
517 Russell Maryland	.07	.20
518 Lance Johnstone	.07	.20
519 Eric Turner	.07	.20
520 Dexter McCleon RC	.07	.20
521 Craig Heyward	.07	.20
522 Ryan McNeil	.07	.20
523 Mark Rypien	.07	.20
524 Mike Jones LB	.07	.20
525 Jamie Sharper	.07	.20
526 Tony Siragusa	.07	.20
527 Michael Jackson	.10	.30
528 Floyd Turner	.07	.20
529 Eric Green	.07	.20
530 Michael McCrary	.07	.20
531 Jay Graham RC	.10	.30
532 Terry Allen	.20	.50
533 Sean Gilbert	.07	.20
534 Scott Turner	.07	.20
535 Cris Dishman	.07	.20
536 Darrell Green	.10	.30
537 Stephen Davis	.20	.50
538 Alvin Harper	.07	.20
539 Daryl Hobbs	.07	.20
540 Wayne Martin	.07	.20
541 Heath Shuler	.07	.20
542 Andre Hastings	.07	.20
543 Jared Tomich	.07	.20
544 Nicky Savoie RC	.07	.20
545 Cortez Kennedy	.07	.20
546 Warren Moon	.20	.50
547 Chad Brown	.07	.20
548 Willie Williams	.07	.20
549 Bennie Blades	.07	.20
550 Darren Perry	.07	.20
551 Mark Bruener	.07	.20
552 Yancey Thigpen	.10	.30
553 Courtney Hawkins	.07	.20
554 Chad Scott RC	.10	.30
555 George Jones	.10	.30
556 Robert Tate RC	.07	.20
557 Torrian Gray RC	.07	.20
558 Robert Griffith RC	.07	.20
559 Leroy Hoard	.07	.20
560 Robert Smith	.10	.30
561 Randall Cunningham	.20	.50
562 Darrell Russell CL	.07	.20
563 Troy Aikman CL	.20	.50
564 Dan Marino CL	.15	.40
565 Jim Druckenmiller CL	.07	.20

1997 Collector's Choice Crash the Game

COMPLETE SET (90)	30.00	60.00
COMP.SHORT SET (30)	10.00	20.00
STATED ODDS 1:5 SERIES 1		
COMP.PRIZE SET (19)	15.00	30.00
*PRIZE STARS: 1X TO 2.5X BASE CARD HI		
*PRIZE ROOKIES: .4X TO 1X BASE CARD HI		
1A Troy Aikman 10/13 W	.60	1.50
1B Troy Aikman 11/2 W	.60	1.50
1C Troy Aikman 11/27 W	.60	1.50
2A Dan Marino 9/21 W	1.25	3.00
2B Dan Marino 11/17 W	1.25	3.00
2C Dan Marino 11/30 W	1.25	3.00
3A Steve Young 9/29 W	.40	1.00
3B Steve Young 11/2 L	.40	1.00
3C Steve Young 11/23 W	.40	1.00
4A Brett Favre	1.25	3.00
4B Brett Favre 10/27 W	1.25	3.00
4C Brett Favre 12/1 W	1.25	3.00
5A Drew Bledsoe 10/6 W	.40	1.00
5B Drew Bledsoe 11/9 W	.40	1.00
5C Drew Bledsoe 11/23 L	.40	1.00
6A Jeff Blake 9/28 W	.20	.50
6B Jeff Blake 10/19 L	.20	.50
6C Jeff Blake 11/30 L	.20	.50
7A Mark Brunell 9/22 W	.40	1.00
7B Mark Brunell 10/19 W	.40	1.00
7C Mark Brunell 11/16 W	.40	1.00
8A John Elway 10/6 W	1.25	3.00
8B John Elway 11/9 W	1.25	3.00
8C John Elway 11/30 W	1.25	3.00
9A Vinny Testaverde 9/28 W	.20	.50
9B Vinny Testaverde 10/19 W	.20	.50
9C Vinny Testaverde 11/9 L	.20	.50
10A Steve McNair 10/12 W	.40	1.00
10B Steve McNair 10/26 W	.40	1.00
10C Steve McNair 11/27 W	.40	1.00
11A Jerry Rice 9/29 L	.60	1.50
11B Jerry Rice 10/12 L	.60	1.50
11C Jerry Rice 11/10 L	.60	1.50
12A Terry Glenn 10/12 L	.30	.75
12B Terry Glenn 10/27 L	.30	.75
12C Terry Glenn 11/16 L	.30	.75
13A Michael Jackson 10/5 L	.20	.50
13B Michael Jackson 11/9 L	.20	.50
13C Michael Jackson 11/23 L	.20	.50
14A Tony Martin 9/21 L	.20	.50
14B Tony Martin 10/16 L	.20	.50
14C Tony Martin 11/16 L	.20	.50
15A Isaac Bruce 9/28 L	.30	.75
15B Isaac Bruce 10/12 L	.30	.75
15C Isaac Bruce 11/16 L	.30	.75
16A Cris Carter 9/28 W	.30	.75
16B Cris Carter 11/16 L	.30	.75
16C Cris Carter 12/1 L	.30	.75
17A Shannon Sharpe 10/19 L	.20	.50
17B Shannon Sharpe 11/2 L	.20	.50
17C Shannon Sharpe 11/30 L	.20	.50
18A Rae Carruth 9/29 W	.05	.15
18B Rae Carruth 10/26 L	.05	.15
18C Rae Carruth 11/9 L	.05	.15
19A Ike Hilliard 10/5 L	.25	.60
19B Ike Hilliard 10/19 L	.25	.60
19C Ike Hilliard 11/23 L	.25	.60
20A Yatil Green 9/21 L	.08	.25
20B Yatil Green 10/5 L	.08	.25
20C Yatil Green 11/17 L	.08	.25
21A Terry Allen 10/5 W	.30	.75
21B Terry Allen 10/13 L	.30	.75
21C Terry Allen 11/23 L	.30	.75
22A Emmitt Smith 10/19 W	1.00	2.50
22B Emmitt Smith 11/16 L	1.00	2.50
22C Emmitt Smith 11/23 W	1.00	2.50
23A Karim Abdul-Jabbar/10/12 W	.20	.50
23B Karim Abdul-Jabbar/11/17 W	.20	.50
23C Karim Abdul-Jabbar/11/30 W	.20	.50
24A Barry Sanders	1.00	2.50
24B Barry Sanders 11/9 W	1.00	2.50
24C Barry Sanders 11/27 W	1.00	2.50
25A Terrell Davis 9/21 W	.40	1.00
25B Terrell Davis 11/16 L	.40	1.00
25C Terrell Davis 11/24 W	.40	1.00
26A Jerome Bettis 9/22 L	.30	.75
26B Jerome Bettis 11/3 L	.30	.75
26C Jerome Bettis 11/16 L	.30	.75
27A Ricky Watters 9/28 L	.20	.50
27B Ricky Watters 10/26 L	.20	.50
27C Ricky Watters 11/10 L	.20	.50
28A Curtis Martin 10/12 W	.40	1.00
28B Curtis Martin 10/27 L	.40	1.00
28C Curtis Martin 11/16 L	.40	1.00
29A Byron Hanspard 9/28 L	.08	.25
29B Byron Hanspard 10/26 L	.08	.25
29C Byron Hanspard 11/23 L	.08	.25
30A Warrick Dunn 9/21 W	.40	1.00
30B Warrick Dunn 10/5 W	.40	1.00
30C Warrick Dunn 11/16 L	.40	1.00

1997 Collector's Choice Jumbos

COMPLETE SET (5)	4.00	10.00
1 Troy Aikman	.80	2.00
2 Brett Favre	1.60	4.00
3 Terrell Davis	1.00	2.50
4 Reggie White	.40	1.00
5 Eddie George	.80	2.00

1997 Collector's Choice Mini-Standee

COMPLETE SET (30)	12.50	25.00
STATED ODDS 1:5 SERIES 2		
ST1 Jerry Rice	.60	1.50
ST2 Rashaan Salaam	.10	.30
ST3 Jeff Blake	.20	.50
ST4 Antowain Smith	.75	2.00
ST5 John Elway	1.25	3.00
ST6 Errict Rhett	.10	.30
ST7 Jake Plummer	1.50	4.00
ST8 Junior Seau	.30	.75
ST9 Marcus Allen	.30	.75
ST10 Marvin Harrison	.30	.75
ST11 Emmitt Smith	1.00	2.50
ST12 Dan Marino	1.25	3.00
ST13 Ricky Watters	.20	.50
ST14 Jamal Anderson	.30	.75
ST15 Rodney Hampton	.20	.50
ST16 Mark Brunell	.40	1.00
ST17 Keyshawn Johnson	.30	.75
ST18 Barry Sanders	1.00	2.50
ST19 Eddie George	.30	.75
ST20 Brett Favre	1.25	3.00
ST21 Kerry Collins	.30	.75
ST22 Drew Bledsoe	.40	1.00
ST23 Napoleon Kaufman	.30	.75
ST24 Tony Banks	.20	.50
ST25 Vinny Testaverde	.20	.50
ST26 Terry Allen	.30	.75
ST27 Mario Bates	.10	.30
ST28 Joey Galloway	.20	.50
ST29 Jerome Bettis	.30	.75
ST30 Robert Smith	.20	.50

1997 Collector's Choice Names of the Game Jumbos

COMPLETE SET (10)	5.00	12.00
*5X7 CARDS: SAME PRICE		
1 Brett Favre	1.00	2.50
2 Emmitt Smith	.80	2.00
3 Curtis Martin	.40	1.00
4 Jerome Bettis	.40	1.00
5 Terrell Davis	.80	2.00
6 Troy Aikman	.50	1.25
(number 1 in 5X7 version)		
7 Dan Marino	1.00	2.50
(number 2 in 5X7 version)		
8 Drew Bledsoe	.50	1.25
(number 3 in 5X7 version)		
9 Reggie White	.40	1.00
(number 4 in 5X7 version)		
10 Eddie George	.50	1.25
(number 5 in 5X7 version)		

1997 Collector's Choice Star Quest

COMPLETE SET (90)	150.00	300.00
COMP.SERIES 1 (45)	5.00	10.00
SQ1-SQ45 STATED ODDS 1:1 SERIES 2		
SQ46-SQ65 STATED ODDS 1:21 SER.2		
SQ66-SQ80 STATED ODDS 1:71 SER.2		
SQ81-SQ90 STATED ODDS 1:145 SER.2		
SQ1 Frank Sanders	.25	.60
SQ2 Jamal Anderson	.40	1.00
SQ3 Byron Bam Morris	.15	.40
SQ4 Thurman Thomas	.40	1.00
SQ5 Muhsin Muhammad	.25	.60
SQ6 Bobby Engram	.25	.60
SQ7 Carl Pickens	.25	.60
SQ8 Deion Sanders	.40	1.00
SQ9 Shannon Sharpe	.25	.60
SQ10 Herman Moore	.25	.60
SQ11 Robert Brooks	.25	.60
SQ12 Steve McNair	.40	1.00
SQ13 Marshall Faulk	.40	1.00
SQ14 Keenan McCardell	.25	.60
SQ15 Tamarick Vanover	.25	.60
SQ16 Fred Barnett	.15	.40
SQ17 Orlando Thomas	.15	.40
SQ18 Drew Bledsoe	.40	1.00
SQ19 Mario Bates	.15	.40
SQ20 Keyshawn Johnson	.40	1.00
SQ21 Rodney Hampton	.25	.60
SQ22 Darrell Russell	.15	.40
SQ23 Irving Fryar	.25	.60
SQ24 Charles Johnson	.25	.60
SQ25 Stan Humphries	.25	.60
SQ26 Terrell Owens	.40	1.00
SQ27 Chris Warren	.25	.60
SQ28 Isaac Bruce	.40	1.00
SQ29 Warrick Dunn	.60	1.50
SQ30 Gus Frerotte	.15	.40
SQ31 Rocket Ismail	.25	.60
SQ32 Natrone Means	.25	.60
SQ33 Chris Sanders	.15	.40
SQ34 Vinny Testaverde	.25	.60
SQ35 Ken Norton Jr.	.15	.40
SQ36 Tim Biakabutuka	.25	.60
SQ37 Marcus Allen	.40	1.00
SQ38 Zach Thomas	.40	1.00
SQ39 Derrick Thomas	.40	1.00
SQ40 Tyrone Wheatley	.25	.60
SQ41 Dorsey Levens	.40	1.00
SQ42 Darnay Scott	.25	.60
SQ43 Scott Mitchell	.25	.60
SQ44 Marvin Harrison	.40	1.00
SQ45 Eddie Kennison	.25	.60
SQ46 Jake Reed	1.50	4.00
SQ47 Andre Reed	1.50	4.00
SQ48 Neil Smith	1.50	4.00
SQ49 Anthony Johnson	1.00	2.50
SQ50 Napoleon Kaufman	1.50	4.00
SQ51 Terance Mathis	1.50	4.00
SQ52 Tony Martin	1.50	4.00
SQ53 Adrian Murrell	1.50	4.00
SQ54 Glyn Milburn	1.00	2.50
SQ55 Errict Rhett	1.00	2.50
SQ56 Kerry Collins	1.50	4.00
SQ57 Curtis Conway	1.50	4.00
SQ58 Eric Swann	1.00	2.50
SQ59 Michael Jackson	1.50	4.00
SQ60 Ty Detmer	1.50	4.00
SQ61 Michael Irvin	1.50	4.00
SQ62 Terrell Fletcher	1.00	2.50
SQ63 Brian Mitchell	1.00	2.50
SQ64 Tony Banks	1.50	4.00
SQ65 Eddie George	1.50	4.00
SQ66 Kordell Stewart	4.00	10.00
SQ67 Greg Hill	2.50	6.00
SQ68 Karim Abdul-Jabbar	2.50	6.00
SQ69 Cris Carter	4.00	10.00
SQ70 Terry Glenn	4.00	10.00
SQ71 Emmitt Smith	10.00	25.00
SQ72 Jim Harbaugh	4.00	10.00
SQ73 Jeff Blake	4.00	10.00
SQ74 Rashaan Salaam	2.50	6.00
SQ75 Ricky Watters	4.00	10.00
SQ76 Joey Galloway	4.00	10.00
SQ77 Junior Seau	4.00	10.00
SQ78 Dave Brown	2.50	6.00
SQ79 Tim Brown	4.00	10.00
SQ80 Troy Aikman	7.50	20.00
SQ81 Dan Marino	12.50	30.00
SQ82 Brett Favre	12.50	30.00
SQ83 John Elway	12.50	30.00
SQ84 Steve Young	6.00	15.00
SQ85 Mark Brunell	5.00	12.00
SQ86 Barry Sanders	12.50	30.00
SQ87 Jerome Bettis	5.00	12.00
SQ88 Terrell Davis	5.00	12.00
SQ89 Curtis Martin	5.00	12.00
SQ90 Jerry Rice	7.50	20.00

1997 Collector's Choice Stick-Ums

COMPLETE SET (30)	4.00	10.00
STATED ODDS 1:3 SERIES 1		
S1 Kerry Collins	.15	.40
S2 Troy Aikman	.30	.75
S3 Steve Young	.20	.50
S4 Ricky Watters	.08	.25
S5 Cris Carter	.15	.40
S6 Terry Allen	.15	.40
S7 Bobby Engram	.08	.25
S8 Larry Centers	.08	.25
S9 Mike Alstott	.15	.40
S10 Rodney Hampton	.08	.25
S11 Eddie Kennison	.08	.25
S12 Jamal Anderson	.15	.40
S13 Jim Everett	.05	.15
S14 Curtis Martin	.20	.50
S15 Keenan McCardell	.08	.25
S16 Kordell Stewart	.15	.40
S17 John Elway	.60	1.50
S18 Terrell Davis	.20	.50
S19 Thurman Thomas	.15	.40
S20 Marshall Faulk	.20	.50
S21 Marcus Allen	.15	.40
S22 Tony Martin	.08	.25
S23 Dan Marino	.60	1.50
S24 Karim Abdul-Jabbar	.08	.25
S25 Carl Pickens	.08	.25
S26 Eddie George	.15	.40
S27 Joey Galloway	.08	.25
S28 Napoleon Kaufman	.15	.40
S29 Vinny Testaverde	.08	.25
S30 Keyshawn Johnson	.15	.40

1997 Collector's Choice Turf Champions

COMPLETE SET (90)	175.00	350.00
COMP.SERIES 1 (30)	3.00	6.00
TC1-TC30 STATED ODDS 1:1H, 2:1R SER.1		
TC31-TC60 STATED ODDS 1:21 SER.1		
TC61-TC80 STATED ODDS 1:71 SER.1		
TC81-TC90 STATED ODDS 1:145 SER.1		
TC1 Kerry Collins	.15	.40
TC2 Scott Mitchell	.15	.40
TC3 Jim Schwantz	.08	.25
TC4 Orlando Pace	.25	.60
TC5 Troy Davis	.15	.40
TC6 Vinny Testaverde	.15	.40
TC7 Rocket Ismail	.15	.40
TC8 Henry Ellard	.08	.25
TC9 Kevin Turner	.08	.25
TC10 Bobby Engram	.15	.40
TC11 Keyshawn Johnson	.25	.60
TC12 Trent Dilfer	.25	.60
TC13 Elvis Grbac	.15	.40
TC14 Trev Alberts	.08	.25
TC15 Kevin Hardy	.08	.25
TC16 Warren Sapp	.15	.40
TC17 Chris Hudson	.08	.25
TC18 Antonio Langham	.08	.25
TC19 Jonathan Ogden	.08	.25
TC20 Bruce Smith	.15	.40
TC21 Marcus Allen	.25	.60
TC22 Desmond Howard	.15	.40
TC23 Eric Metcalf	.15	.40
TC24 Terance Mathis	.15	.40
TC25 LeShon Johnson	.08	.25
TC26 Kevin Greene	.15	.40
TC27 Alex Van Dyke	.08	.25
TC28 Jeff Jaeger	.08	.25
TC29 Jason Elam	.08	.25
TC30 Thomas Lewis	.08	.25
TC31 Rick Mirer	1.00	3.00
TC32 Warren Moon	3.00	8.00
TC33 Jim Kelly	3.00	8.00
TC34 Junior Seau	3.00	8.00
TC35 Jeff Hostetler	1.00	3.00
TC36 Neil O'Donnell	2.00	5.00
TC37 Jeff Blake	2.00	5.00
TC38 Kordell Stewart	3.00	8.00
TC39 Terry Glenn	3.00	8.00
TC40 Simeon Rice	2.00	5.00
TC41 Jimmy Smith	2.00	5.00
TC42 Natrone Means	2.00	5.00
TC43 Tony Martin	2.00	5.00
TC44 Charles Johnson	2.00	5.00
TC45 Napoleon Kaufman	3.00	8.00
TC46 Dale Carter	1.00	3.00
TC47 Brett Perriman	1.00	3.00
TC48 Cortez Kennedy	1.00	3.00
TC49 Bryce Paup	1.00	3.00
TC50 Greg Lloyd	1.00	3.00
TC51 Bryant Young	1.00	3.00
TC52 Steve McNair	3.00	8.00
TC53 Garrison Hearst	2.00	5.00
TC54 John Copeland	1.00	3.00
TC55 Eric Curry	1.00	3.00
TC56 Reggie White	3.00	8.00
TC57 Rod Woodson	3.00	8.00
TC58 Andre Rison	2.00	5.00
TC59 Herschel Walker	2.00	5.00
TC60 John Kasay	1.00	3.00
TC61 Emmitt Smith	10.00	25.00
TC62 Dan Marino	12.50	30.00
TC63 Michael Irvin	5.00	12.00
TC64 Drew Bledsoe	5.00	12.00
TC65 Mark Brunell	5.00	12.00
TC66 Jim Harbaugh	3.00	8.00
TC67 Herman Moore	3.00	8.00
TC68 Rashaan Salaam	2.00	5.00
TC69 Ty Detmer	3.00	8.00
TC70 Cris Carter	5.00	12.00
TC71 Chris Warren	3.00	8.00
TC72 Thurman Thomas	5.00	12.00
TC73 Ricky Watters	3.00	8.00
TC74 Tim Brown	5.00	12.00
TC75 Marshall Faulk	5.00	12.00
TC76 Jerome Bettis	5.00	12.00
TC77 Karim Abdul-Jabbar	5.00	12.00
TC78 Deion Sanders	5.00	12.00
TC79 Ben Coates	3.00	8.00
TC80 Andre Reed	3.00	8.00
TC81 Brett Favre	12.50	30.00
TC82 Terrell Davis	5.00	12.00
TC83 Troy Aikman	6.00	15.00
TC84 Carl Pickens	3.00	8.00
TC85 Barry Sanders	10.00	25.00
TC86 Jerry Rice	6.00	15.00
TC87 Curtis Martin	5.00	12.00
TC88 Steve Young	5.00	12.00
TC89 Eddie George	5.00	12.00
TC90 John Elway	12.50	30.00

1997 Collector's Choice Turf Champion Jumbos

COMPLETE SET (8)	6.00	15.00
TC1 Kerry Collins	.40	1.00
TC62 Dan Marino	1.50	4.00
TC65 Mark Brunell	.50	1.25
TC76 Jerome Bettis	.50	1.25
TC81 Brett Favre	1.50	4.00
TC83 Troy Aikman	.75	2.00
TC88 Steve Young	.60	1.50
TC90 John Elway	1.50	4.00

1992 Collector's Edge Prototypes

These six prototype cards were issued before the 1992 regular issue was released to show the design of Collector's Edge cards. The cards were issued in two different styles, with slightly sticky backs with a removable paper protective cover backing or with a non-sticky back. The paper-covered back versions are somewhat more difficult to find. The production figures were reportedly 8,000 for each card.

COMPLETE SET (6)	8.00	20.00
*STICKER BACKS: 1X TO 2X		
1 Jim Kelly	.80	2.00
2 Randall Cunningham	.80	2.00
3 Warren Moon	.80	2.00
4 John Elway	3.20	8.00
5 Dan Marino	3.20	8.00
6 Bernie Kosar	.60	1.50

1992 Collector's Edge

This 250-card standard-size set was issued in two series of 175 and 75 cards, respectively. Cards were issued six per pack. The cards are printed on plastic stock and production quantities were limited to 100,000 of each card; with every card individually numbered on the back. The cards are checklisted alphabetically according to teams. There are a few cards in the set which were apparently late additions as counterparts have been found with a large "X" on the cardfront. We've listed the X-out variation cards below, but they are not considered part of the complete set. It is thought card number 179 was also changed, but has not been confirmed. Two thousand five hundred cards autographed by John Elway and Ken O'Brien were randomly inserted in first series foil packs as well as factory sets. Randomly inserted in second series (Rookies) packs were 2500 signed Ronnie Lott cards. These card do not feature serial number. A second version of the Ronnie Lott signed card was also produced bearing a different photo and card number RL1. These card feature a hand serial numbering of 2542. Two Rookie/Update Prototype cards were produced as well and listed below.

COMPLETE SET (250)	15.00	35.00
COMP.SERIES 1 (175)	8.00	20.00
COMP.FACT.SER.1 (175)	8.00	20.00
COMP.SERIES 2 (75)	6.00	15.00
COMP.FACT.SER.2 (75)	6.00	15.00
1 Chris Miller	.07	.20
2 Steve Broussard	.02	.10
3 Mike Pritchard	.07	.20
4 Tim Green	.02	.10
5 Andre Rison	.07	.20
6 Deion Sanders	.40	1.00
7 Jim Kelly	.15	.40
8 James Lofton	.07	.20
9 Andre Reed	.07	.20
10 Bruce Smith	.15	.40
11 Thurman Thomas	.15	.40
12 Cornelius Bennett	.07	.20
13 Jim Harbaugh	.15	.40
14 William Perry	.07	.20
15 Mike Singletary	.07	.20
16 Mark Carrier DB	.02	.10
17 Kevin Butler	.02	.10
18 Tom Waddle	.02	.10
19 Boomer Esiason	.07	.20
20 David Fulcher	.02	.10
21 Anthony Munoz	.07	.20
22 Tim McGee	.02	.10
23 Harold Green	.02	.10
24 Rickey Dixon	.02	.10
25 Bernie Kosar	.07	.20
26 Michael Dean Perry	.07	.20
27 Mike Baab	.02	.10
28 Brian Brennan	.02	.10
29 Michael Jackson	.07	.20
30 Eric Metcalf	.07	.20
31 Troy Aikman	1.00	2.50
32 Emmitt Smith	2.50	5.00
33 Michael Irvin	.15	.40
34 Jay Novacek	.07	.20
35 Issiac Holt	.02	.10
36 Ken Norton	.07	.20
37 John Elway	1.50	4.00
38 Gaston Green	.02	.10
39 Charles Dimry	.02	.10
40 Vance Johnson	.02	.10
41 Dennis Smith	.02	.10
42 David Treadwell	.02	.10
43 Michael Young	.02	.10
44 Bennie Blades	.02	.10
45 Mel Gray	.07	.20
46 Andre Ware	.02	.10
47 Rodney Peete	.07	.20
48 Toby Caston RC	.02	.10
49 Herman Moore	.15	.40
50 Brian Noble	.02	.10
51 Sterling Sharpe	.15	.40
52 Mike Tomczak	.02	.10
53 Vinnie Clark	.02	.10
54 Tony Mandarich	.02	.10
55 Ed West	.02	.10
56 Warren Moon	.15	.40
57 Ray Childress	.02	.10
58 Haywood Jeffires	.07	.20
59 Al Smith	.02	.10
60 Cris Dishman	.02	.10
61 Ernest Givins	.07	.20
62 Richard Johnson	.02	.10
63 Eric Dickerson	.07	.20
64 Jessie Hester	.02	.10
65 Rohn Stark	.02	.10
66 Clarence Verdin	.02	.10
67 Dean Biasucci	.02	.10
68 Duane Bickett	.02	.10
69 Jeff George	.15	.40
70 Christian Okoye	.02	.10
71 Derrick Thomas	.15	.40
72 Stephone Paige	.02	.10
73 Dan Saleaumua	.02	.10
74 Deron Cherry	.02	.10
75 Kevin Ross	.02	.10
76 Barry Word	.02	.10
77 Ronnie Lott	.07	.20
78 Greg Townsend	.02	.10
79 Willie Gault	.07	.20
80 Howie Long	.15	.40
81 Winston Moss	.02	.10
82 Steve Smith	.02	.10
83 Jay Schroeder	.02	.10
84 Jim Everett	.07	.20
85 Flipper Anderson	.02	.10
86 Henry Ellard	.07	.20
87 Tony Zendejas	.02	.10
88 Robert Delpino	.02	.10
89 Pat Terrell	.02	.10
90 Dan Marino	1.50	4.00
91 Mark Clayton	.07	.20
92 Jim C.Jensen	.02	.10
93 Reggie Roby	.02	.10
94 Sammie Smith	.02	.10
95 Tony Martin	.07	.20
96 Jeff Cross	.02	.10
97 Anthony Carter	.07	.20
98 Chris Doleman	.02	.10
99 Wade Wilson	.02	.10
100 Cris Carter	.30	.75
101 Mike Merriweather	.02	.10
102 Gary Zimmerman	.02	.10
103 Chris Singleton	.02	.10
104 Bruce Armstrong	.02	.10
105 Marv Cook	.02	.10
106 Andre Tippett	.02	.10
107 Tommy Hodson	.02	.10
108 Greg McMurtry	.02	.10
109 Jon Vaughn	.02	.10
110 Vaughan Johnson	.02	.10
111 Craig Heyward	.07	.20
112 Floyd Turner	.02	.10
113 Pat Swilling	.02	.10
114 Rickey Jackson	.02	.10
115 Steve Walsh	.02	.10
116 Phil Simms	.07	.20
117 Carl Banks	.02	.10
118 Mark Ingram	.02	.10
119 Bart Oates	.02	.10
120 Lawrence Taylor	.15	.40
121 Jeff Hostetler	.07	.20
122 Rob Moore	.07	.20
123 Ken O'Brien	.02	.10
124 Bill Pickel	.02	.10
125 Irv Eatman	.02	.10
126 Browning Nagle	.02	.10
127 Al Toon	.07	.20
128 Randall Cunningham	.15	.40
129 Eric Allen	.02	.10
130 Mike Golic	.02	.10
131 Fred Barnett	.15	.40
132 Keith Byars	.02	.10
133 Calvin Williams	.07	.20
134 Randal Hill	.02	.10
135 Ricky Proehl	.02	.10
136 Lance Smith	.02	.10
137 Ernie Jones	.02	.10
138 Timm Rosenbach	.02	.10
139 Anthony Thompson	.02	.10
140 Bubby Brister	.02	.10
141 Merril Hoge	.02	.10
142 Louis Lipps	.02	.10
143 Eric Green	.02	.10
144 Gary Anderson K	.02	.10
145 Neil O'Donnell	.07	.20
146 Rod Bernstine	.02	.10
147 John Friesz	.07	.20
148 Anthony Miller	.07	.20
149 Junior Seau	.15	.40
150 Leslie O'Neal	.07	.20
151 Nate Lewis	.02	.10
152 Steve Young	.75	2.00
153 Kevin Fagan	.02	.10
154 Charles Haley	.07	.20
155 Tom Rathman	.02	.10
156 Jerry Rice	1.00	2.50
157 John Taylor	.07	.20
158 Brian Blades	.07	.20
159 Patrick Hunter	.02	.10
160 Cortez Kennedy	.07	.20
161 Vann McElroy	.02	.10
162 Dan McGwire	.02	.10
163 John L. Williams	.02	.10
164 Gary Anderson RB	.02	.10
165 Broderick Thomas	.02	.10
166 Vinny Testaverde	.07	.20
167 Lawrence Dawsey	.07	.20
168 Paul Gruber	.02	.10
169 Keith McCants	.02	.10
170 Mark Rypien	.02	.10
171 Gary Clark	.15	.40
172 Earnest Byner	.02	.10
173 Brian Mitchell	.07	.20
174 Monte Coleman	.02	.10
175 Joe Jacoby	.02	.10
176 Tommy Vardell RC	.02	.10
177 Troy Vincent RC	.02	.10
178 Robert Jones RC	.02	.10
179 Marc Boutte RC	.02	.10
180 Marco Coleman RC	.02	.10
181 Chris Mims RC	.02	.10
182 Tony Casillas	.02	.10
182X Ray Roberts	30.00	50.00
Large X on front		
183 Shane Dronett RC	.02	.10
184 Sean Gilbert RC	.07	.20
185 Siran Stacy RC	.02	.10
186 Tommy Maddox RC	1.25	3.00
187 Steve Israel RC	.02	.10
188 Brad Muster	.02	.10
188X Casey Weldon	30.00	50.00
large X on front		
189 Shane Collins RC	.02	.10
190 Terrell Buckley RC	.02	.10
191 Eugene Chung RC	.02	.10
192 Leon Searcy RC	.02	.10
193 Chuck Smith RC	.02	.10
194 Patrick Rowe RC	.02	.10
195 Bill Johnson RC	.02	.10
196 Gerald Dixon RC	.02	.10
197 Robert Porcher RC	.15	.40
198 Tracy Scroggins RC	.02	.10
199 Jason Hanson RC	.07	.20
200 Corey Harris RC	.02	.10
201 Eddie Robinson RC	.02	.10
202 Steve Emtman RC	.02	.10
203 Ashley Ambrose RC	.15	.40
204 Greg Skrepenak RC	.02	.10
205 Todd Collins RC	.02	.10
206 Derek Brown TE RC	.02	.10
207 Kurt Barber RC	.02	.10
208 Tony Sacca RC	.02	.10
209 Mark Wheeler RC	.02	.10
210 Kevin Smith RC	.02	.10
211 John Fina RC	.02	.10
212 Johnny Mitchell RC	.02	.10
213 Dale Carter RC	.07	.20
214 Bob Spitulski RC	.02	.10
215 Phillippi Sparks RC	.02	.10
216 Levon Kirkland RC	.02	.10
217 Mike Sherrard	.02	.10
218 Marquez Pope RC	.02	.10
219 Courtney Hawkins RC	.07	.20
220 Tyji Armstrong RC	.02	.10
221 Keith Jackson	.07	.20
222 Clayton Holmes RC	.02	.10
223 Quentin Coryatt RC	.02	.10
224 Troy Auzenne RC	.02	.10
225 David Klingler RC	.02	.10
226 Darryl Williams RC	.02	.10
227 Carl Pickens RC	.15	.40
228 Jimmy Smith RC	2.00	5.00
229 Chester McGlockton RC	.07	.20
230 Robert Brooks RC	.50	1.25
231 Alonzo Spellman RC	.07	.20
232 Darren Woodson RC	.15	.40
233 Lewis Billups	.02	.10
234 Edgar Bennett RC	.15	.40
235 Vaughn Dunbar RC	.02	.10
236 Steve Bono RC	.15	.40
237 Clarence Kay	.02	.10
238 Chris Hinton	.02	.10
239 Jimmie Jones	.02	.10

240 Vai Sikahema .02 .10
241 Russell Maryland .02 .10
242 Neal Anderson .02 .10
242X Mark Bavaro 30.00 50.00
large X on front
243 Charles Mann .02 .10
244 Hugh Millen .02 .10
244X Bobby Humphrey 30.00 50.00
large X on front
245 Roger Craig .07 .20
246 Rich Gannon .15 .40
247 Ricky Ervins .02 .10
247X Marion Butts 30.00 50.00
large X on front
248 Leonard Marshall .02 .10
249 Eric Dickerson .07 .20
250 Joe Montana 1.50 4.00
RL1 Ronnie Lott AU/2542 7.50 15.00
RU1 Terrell Buckley .75 2.00
Prototype
RU2 Tommy Maddox 1.00 2.50
Prototype
AU37 John Elway 25.00 60.00
(2,500 signed)
AU77 Ronnie Lott Bonus AUTO 7.50 15.00
(reportedly 2500 signed)
AU123 Ken O'Brien 3.00 8.00
(2,500 signed)

1992 Collector's Edge Promos

This four-card set was issued to promote the Tuff Stuff Buyer's Club. The Elway card was distributed in all copies of the November issue of Tuff Stuff. More than 250,000 cards were printed; only about 40,000 each of the remaining three cards were printed. One of these was given away with each paid membership in the Buyers Club. The Elway card was also printed with the designations "Proto 1," "Elway Foundation," and "John Elway Dealerships." The number of these additional cards is reportedly less than 50,000 and they are not included in the complete set price. The fronts of these standard-size promo cards have a color action player photo inside a gold frame and dark blue borders. The upper left corner of the picture is cut off. The player's name and position appear in the bottom border, and the team helmet is superimposed at the lower right corner of the picture. Within bright blue borders, the backs carry a color head shot, biography, and statistics on a ghosted version of the front photo. The cards are numbered on the back, and each has a serial number in the bottom border.

COMPLETE SET (4) 4.00 10.00
TS1 John Elway 1.20 3.00
TS2 Ronnie Lott 1.60 4.00
TS3 Jim Everett 1.20 3.00
TS4 Bernie Kosar 1.20 3.00
PROT1 John Elway 3.20 8.00
NNO Elway Foundation 10.00 25.00
NNO Elway Dealerships 10.00 25.00

1993 Collector's Edge Prototypes

COMPLETE SET (6) 1.80 12.00
1 John Elway 2.00 5.00
2 Derrick Thomas .50 1.25
3 Randall Cunningham .50 1.25
4 Thurman Thomas .50 1.25
5 Warren Moon .50 1.25
6 Barry Sanders 2.00 5.00

1993 Collector's Edge RU Prototypes

COMPLETE SET (5) 2.00 5.00
RU1 Garrison Hearst 1.00 2.50
RU2 Reggie White .50 1.25
RU3 Boomer Esiason .30 .75
RU4 Rod Bernstine .30 .75
RU5 Dana Stubblefield .30 .75

1993 Collector's Edge

The 1993 Collector's Edge football set consists of 325 standard-size cards. The production run was limited to 100,000 of each player, with each card serially numbered from 000001 to 100,000. In this year's issue, the cards were printed on heavier, 20-mil, thick plastic stock. Also this year's set added new Team Cards that depict whole-team portraits of the 28 NFL teams. The cards are numbered on the back and checklisted below according to teams. Cards 251-325 comprise the Rookie Update series. Randomly inserted in the foil packs was a factory redemption card that entitled the holder to redeem the card for a factory set, in which every card had the same serial number. The offer expired at noon on February 28, 1994. Two cards commemorating the newest expansion teams in the NFL, the Jacksonville Jaguars and the Carolina Panthers, were produced. The Panthers card, originally numbered 326, was issued very late in the pack production run. Only 4,000 of these cards were issued. The company then produced a second version of the Panthers card as well as a Jaguars card. These are numbered with an "M" prefix. The cards were available by mail and cost $3.95 with a production figure of 25,000. The purple marbleized fronts have a grey granite panel with a welcome to the new expansion team. The team logo appears in the lower right corner. Rookie Cards include Drew Bledsoe, Vincent Brisby, Reggie Brooks, Mark Brunell, Curtis Conway, Garrison Hearst, Billy Jo Hobert, Qadry Ismail, Glyn Milburn, Rick Mirer, Roosevelt Potts, Robert Smith and Dana Stubblefield.

COMPLETE SET (325) 10.00 20.00
COMP.SERIES 1 (250) 5.00 10.00
COMP.SERIES 2 (75) 5.00 10.00
1 Falcons Team Photo .01 .05
2 Michael Haynes .02 .10
3 Chris Miller .02 .10
4 Mike Pritchard .02 .10
5 Andre Rison .02 .10
6 Deion Sanders .20 .50
7 Chuck Smith .01 .05
8 Drew Hill .01 .05
9 Bobby Hebert .01 .05
10 Bills Team Photo .01 .05
11 Matt Darby .01 .05
12 John Fina .01 .05
13 Jim Kelly .08 .25
14 Marvcus Patton RC .02 .10
15 Andre Reed .02 .10
16 Thurman Thomas .08 .25
17 James Lofton .02 .10
18 Bruce Smith .08 .25
19 Bears Team Photo .01 .05
20 Neal Anderson .01 .05
21 Troy Auzenne .01 .05
22 Jim Harbaugh .08 .25
23 Alonzo Spellman .01 .05
24 Tom Waddle .01 .05
25 Darren Lewis .01 .05
26 Wendell Davis .01 .05
27 Will Furrer .01 .05
28 Bengals Team Photo .01 .05
29 David Klingler .01 .05
30 Ricardo McDonald .01 .05
31 Carl Pickens .02 .10
32 Harold Green .01 .05
33 Anthony Munoz .02 .10
34 Darryl Williams .01 .05
35 Browns Team Photo .01 .05
36 Michael Jackson .02 .10
37 Pio Sagapolutele .01 .05
38 Tommy Vardell .01 .05
39 Bernie Kosar .02 .10
40 Michael Dean Perry .02 .10
41 Bill Johnson .01 .05
42 Vinny Testaverde .02 .10
43 Cowboys Team Photo .01 .05
44 Troy Aikman .30 .75
45 Alvin Harper .02 .10
46 Michael Irvin .08 .25
47 Russell Maryland .01 .05
48 Emmitt Smith .60 1.50
49 Kenneth Gant .01 .05
50 Jay Novacek .02 .10
51 Robert Jones .01 .05
52 Clayton Holmes .01 .05
53 Broncos Team Photo .01 .05
54 Mike Croel .01 .05
55 Shane Dronett .01 .05
56 Kenny Walker .01 .05
57 Tommy Maddox .08 .25
58 Dennis Smith .01 .05
59 John Elway .60 1.50
60 Karl Mecklenburg .01 .05
61 Steve Atwater .01 .05
62 Vance Johnson .01 .05
63 Lions Team Photo .01 .05
64 Barry Sanders .50 1.25
65 Andre Ware .01 .05
66 Pat Swilling .01 .05
67 Jason Hanson .01 .05
68 Willie Green .01 .05
69 Herman Moore .08 .25
70 Rodney Peete .01 .05
71 Erik Kramer .02 .10
72 Robert Porcher .01 .05
73 Packers Team Photo .01 .05
74 Terrell Buckley .01 .05
75 Reggie White .08 .25
76 Brett Favre .75 2.00
77 Don Majkowski .01 .05
78 Edgar Bennett .08 .25
79 Ty Detmer .08 .25
80 Sanjay Beach .01 .05
81 Sterling Sharpe .00 .25
82 Oilers Team Photo .01 .05
83 Gary Brown .01 .05
84 Ernest Givins .02 .10
85 Haywood Jeffires .02 .10
86 Corey Harris .01 .05
87 Warren Moon .08 .25
88 Eddie Robinson .01 .05
89 Lorenzo White .01 .05
90 Bo Orlando .01 .05
91 Colts Team Photo .01 .05
92 Quentin Coryatt .02 .10
93 Steve Emtman .01 .05
94 Jeff George .08 .25
95 Jessie Hester .01 .05
96 Rohn Stark .01 .05
97 Ashley Ambrose .01 .05
98 John Baylor .01 .05
99 Chiefs Team Photo .01 .05
100 Tim Barnett .01 .05
101 Derrick Thomas .08 .25
102 Barry Word .01 .05
103 Dale Carter .01 .05
104 Jayice Pearson .01 .05
105 Tracy Simien .01 .05
106 Harvey Williams .02 .10
107 Dave Krieg .02 .10
108 Christian Okoye .01 .05
109 Joe Montana .60 1.50
110 Dolphins Team Photo .01 .05
111 J.B. Brown .01 .05
112 Marco Coleman .01 .05
113 Dan Marino .60 1.50
114 Mark Clayton .01 .05
115 Mark Higgs .01 .05
116 Bryan Cox .01 .05
117 Chuck Klingbeil .01 .05
118 Troy Vincent .01 .05
119 Keith Jackson .02 .10
120 Bruce Alexander .01 .05
121 Vikings Team Photo .01 .05
122 Terry Allen .08 .25
123 Rich Gannon .08 .25
124 Todd Scott .01 .05
125 Cris Carter .08 .25
126 Sean Salisbury .01 .05
127 Jack Del Rio .01 .05
128 Chris Doleman .01 .05
129 Anthony Carter .02 .10
130 Patriots Team Photo .01 .05
131 Eugene Chung .01 .05
132 Todd Collins .01 .05
133 Tommy Hodson .01 .05
134 Leonard Russell .02 .10
135 Jon Vaughn .01 .05
136 Andre Tippett .01 .05
137 Saints Team Photo .01 .05
138 Wesley Carroll .01 .05
139 Richard Cooper .01 .05
140 Vaughn Dunbar .01 .05
141 Fred McAfee .01 .05
142 Torrance Small .01 .05
143 Steve Walsh .01 .05
144 Vaughan Johnson .01 .05
145 Giants Team Photo .01 .05
146 Jarrod Bunch .01 .05
147 Phil Simms .02 .10
148 Carl Banks .01 .05
149 Lawrence Taylor .08 .25
150 Rodney Hampton .02 .10
151 Phillippi Sparks .01 .05
152 Derek Brown TE .01 .05
153 Jets Team Photo .01 .05
154 Boomer Esiason .02 .10
155 Johnny Mitchell .01 .05
156 Rob Moore .02 .10
157 Ronnie Lott .02 .10
158 Browning Nagle .01 .05
159 Johnny Johnson .01 .05
160 Dwayne White .01 .05
161 Blair Thomas .01 .05
162 Eagles Team Photo .01 .05
163 Randall Cunningham .08 .25
164 Fred Barnett .02 .10
165 Siran Stacy .01 .05
166 Keith Byars .01 .05
167 Calvin Williams .02 .10
168 Jeff Sydner .01 .05
169 Tommy Jeter .01 .05
170 Andre Waters .01 .05
171 Phoenix Team Photo .01 .05
172 Steve Beuerlein .02 .10
173 Randal Hill .01 .05
174 Timm Rosenbach .01 .05
175 Ed Cunningham .01 .05
176 Walter Reeves .01 .05
177 Michael Zordich .01 .05
178 Gary Clark .02 .10
179 Ken Harvey .01 .05
180 Steelers Team Photo .01 .05
181 Barry Foster .02 .10
182 Neil O'Donnell .08 .25
183 Leon Searcy .01 .05
184 Bubby Brister .01 .05
185 Merril Hoge .01 .05
186 Joel Steed .01 .05
187 Raiders Team Photo .01 .05
188 Nick Bell .01 .05
189 Eric Dickerson .02 .10
190 Nolan Harrison .01 .05
191 Todd Marinovich .01 .05
192 Greg Skrepenak .01 .05
193 Howie Long .08 .25
194 Jay Schroeder .01 .05
195 Chester McGlockton .02 .10
196 Rams Team Photo .01 .05
197 Jim Everett .02 .10
198 Sean Gilbert .02 .10
199 Steve Israel .01 .05
200 Marc Boutte .01 .05
201 Joe Milinichik .01 .05
202 Henry Ellard .02 .10
203 Jackie Slater .01 .05
204 Chargers Team Photo .01 .05
205 Eric Bieniemy .01 .05
206 Marion Butts .01 .05
207 Nate Lewis .01 .05
208 Junior Seau .08 .25
209 Steve Hendrickson .01 .05
210 Chris Mims .01 .05
211 Harry Swayne .01 .05
212 Marquez Pope .01 .05
213 Donald Frank .01 .05
214 Anthony Miller .02 .10
215 Seahawks Team Photo .01 .05
216 Cortez Kennedy .02 .10
217 Dan McGwire .01 .05
218 Kelly Stouffer .01 .05
219 Chris Warren .02 .10
220 Brian Blades .02 .10
221 Rod Stephens RC .01 .05
222 49ers Team Photo .01 .05
223 Jerry Rice .40 1.00
224 Ricky Watters .08 .25
225 Steve Young .30 .75
226 Tom Rathman .01 .05
227 Dana Hall .01 .05
228 Amp Lee .01 .05
229 Brian Bollinger .01 .05
230 Keith DeLong .01 .05
231 John Taylor .02 .10
232 Buccaneers Team Photo .01 .05
233 Tyji Armstrong .01 .05
234 Lawrence Dawsey .01 .05
235 Mark Wheeler .01 .05
236 Vince Workman .01 .05
237 Reggie Cobb .01 .05
238 Tony Mayberry .01 .05
239 Marty Carter .01 .05
240 Courtney Hawkins .01 .05
241 Ray Seals .01 .05
242 Mark Carrier WR .02 .10
243 Redskins Team Photo .01 .05
244 Mark Rypien .01 .05
245 Ricky Ervins .01 .05
246 Gerald Riggs .01 .05
247 Art Monk .02 .10
248 Mark Schlereth .01 .05
249 Monte Coleman .01 .05
250 Wilber Marshall .01 .05
251 Ben Coleman RC .01 .05
252 Curtis Conway RC .15 .40
253 Ernest Dye RC .01 .05
254 Todd Kelly RC .01 .05
255 Patrick Bates RC .01 .05
256 George Teague RC .02 .10
257 Mark Brunell RC .60 1.50
258 Adrian Hardy .01 .05
259 Dana Stubblefield RC .08 .25
260 Willie Roaf RC .02 .10
261 Irv Smith RC .01 .05
262 Drew Bledsoe RC 1.00 2.50
263 Dan Williams RC .01 .05
264 Jerry Ball .01 .05
265 Mark Clayton .01 .05
266 John Stephens .01 .05
267 Reggie White .08 .25
268 Jeff Hostetler .02 .10
269 Boomer Esiason .02 .10
270 Wade Wilson .01 .05
271 Steve Beuerlein .02 .10
272 Tim McDonald .01 .05
273 Craig Heyward .02 .10
274 Everson Walls .01 .05
275 Stan Humphries .02 .10
276 Carl Banks .01 .05
277 Brad Muster .01 .05
278 Tim Harris .01 .05
279 Gary Clark .02 .10
280 Joe Milinichik .01 .05
281 Leonard Marshall .01 .05
282 Joe Montana .60 1.50
283 Rod Bernstine .01 .05
284 Mark Carrier WR .02 .10
285 Michael Brooks .01 .05
286 Marvin Jones RC .01 .05
287 John Copeland RC .02 .10
288 Eric Curry RC .01 .05
289 Steve Everitt RC .01 .05
290 Tom Carter RC .02 .10
291 Deon Figures RC .01 .05
292A Leonard Renfro ERR RC .01 .05
292B Leonard Renfro COR RC .01 .05
293 Thomas Smith RC .02 .10
294 Carlton Gray RC .01 .05
295 Demetrius DuBose RC .01 .05
296 Coleman Rudolph RC .01 .05
297 John Parrella RC .01 .05
298 Glyn Milburn RC .08 .25
299 Reggie Brooks RC .02 .10
300 Garrison Hearst RC .30 .75
301 John Elway .60 1.50
302 Brad Hopkins RC .01 .05
303 Darrien Gordon RC UER .01 .05
Card states he was drafted 12th instead of 22nd
304 Robert Smith RC .50 1.25
305 Chris Slade RC .02 .10
306 Ryan McNeil RC .08 .25
307 Micheal Barrow RC .08 .25
308 Roosevelt Potts RC .01 .05
309 Qadry Ismail RC .08 .25
310 Reggie Freeman RC .01 .05
311 Vincent Brisby RC .08 .25
312 Rick Mirer RC .08 .25
313 Billy Joe Hobert RC .08 .25
314 Natrone Means RC .08 .25
315 Gary Zimmerman .01 .05
316 Bobby Hebert .01 .05
317 Don Beebe .01 .05
318 Wilber Marshall .01 .05
319 Marcus Allen .08 .25
320 Ronnie Lott .02 .10
321 Ricky Sanders .01 .05
322 Charles Mann .01 .05
323 Simon Fletcher .01 .05
324 Johnny Johnson .01 .05
325 Gary Plummer .01 .05
326 Carolina Panthers 10.00 25.00
Insert
M326 Carolina Panthers 1.50 4.00
Send Away
M327 Jacksonville Jaguars 1.50 4.00
Send Away
PRO1 John Elway 30.00 60.00
AUTO/3000

1993 Collector's Edge Elway Prisms

COMPLETE E SET (5) 2.00 4.00
COMMON ELWAY (E1-E5) .40 1.00
COMMON ELWAY (S1-S5) 1.25 3.00

1993 Collector's Edge Jumbos

These jumbo cards were inserted as case toppers in 1993 Collector's Edge. Each measures 8 1/2" by 11" and is essentially a parallel to the respective regular issue card minus the card number. They are also individually numbered in gold ink on the cardback.

COMPLETE SET (6) 14.00 35.00
1 Randall Cunningham 2.00 5.00
2 John Elway 4.00 10.00
3 Warren Moon 2.00 5.00
4 Barry Sanders 4.00 10.00
5 Derrick Thomas 2.00 5.00
6 Thurman Thomas 1.60 4.00

1993 Collector's Edge Rookies FX

COMPLETE SET (25) 6.00 15.00
ONE PER ROOKIE/UPDATE PACK
*GOLD STARS: 6X TO 15X BASE CARD HI
*GOLD ROOKIES: 3X TO 8X BASE CARD HI
1 Garrison Hearst .30 .75
2 Glyn Milburn .08 .25
3 Demetrius DuBose .01 .05
4 Joe Montana 1.50 3.00
5 Thomas Smith .02 .10
6 Mark Clayton .02 .10
7 Curtis Conway .15 .40
8 Drew Bledsoe 1.25 2.50
9 Todd Kelly .01 .05
10 Stan Humphries .07 .20
11 John Elway 1.50 3.00
12 Troy Aikman .75 1.50
13 Marion Butts .02 .10
14 Alvin Harper .07 .20
15 Drew Hill .02 .10
16 Michael Irvin .20 .50
17 Warren Moon .20 .50
18 Andre Reed .07 .20
19 Andre Rison .07 .20
20 Emmitt Smith UER 1.50 3.00
21 Thurman Thomas .20 .50
22 Ricky Watters .20 .50
23 Calvin Williams .07 .20
24 Steve Young .75 1.50
25 Howie Long .20 .50
P1A Drew Bledsoe Prototype 1.25 2.50
(Gray checkered border)
P1B Drew Bledsoe Prototype 1.25 2.50
Red border
P2 Drew Bledsoe Prototype 1.25 2.50
(Red border)
P3 Drew Bledsoe Prototype 1.25 2.50
(Gray checkered border)
P4 Drew Bledsoe Prototype 1.25 2.50
(Red border)
P5 Drew Bledsoe Prototype 1.25 2.50
(Red border)

1994 Collector's Edge Boss Rookies Update Pop Warner Promos

This six-card set was issued to preview the Boss Rookies Update series. Each card is numbered on the back with P prefix and fronts include the "Pop Warner" notation. A parallel version featuring different cropping on the player photos and an "SRH" prefix on the card numbers was also produced.

COMPLETE SET (6) 3.20 8.00
*SRH PREFIX: .4X TO 1X BASIC CARDS
P1 Trent Dilfer .60 1.50
P2 Marshall Faulk 2.00 4.00
P3 Heath Shuler .20 .50
P4 Errict Rhett .40 1.00
P5 Johnnie Morton .20 .50
P6 Charlie Garner .40 1.00

1994 Collector's Edge

Consisting of 200 cards, this standard size set features full-bleed photos on front with the player's name and team logo at the bottom. The cards are checklisted alphabetically according to teams. There are no key Rookie Cards in this set. A Shannon Sharpe prototype card was produced and is listed at the end of our checklist. It is not considered part of the complete set.

COMPLETE SET (200) 7.50 15.00
1 Mike Pritchard .01 .05
2 Erric Pegram .01 .05
3 Michael Haynes .02 .10
4 Bobby Hebert .01 .05
5 Deion Sanders .20 .50
6 Andre Rison .02 .10
7 Don Beebe .01 .05
8 Mark Kelso .01 .05
9 Darryl Talley .01 .05
10 Cornelius Bennett .02 .10
11 Jim Kelly .08 .25
12 Andre Reed .02 .10
13 Bruce Smith .08 .25
14 Thurman Thomas .08 .25
15 Craig Heyward .02 .10
16 Chris Zorich .01 .05
17 Alonzo Spellman .01 .05
18 Tom Waddle .01 .05
19 Neal Anderson .01 .05
20 Kevin Butler .01 .05
21 Curtis Conway .08 .25
22 Richard Dent .02 .10
23 Jim Harbaugh .08 .25
24 Derrick Fenner .01 .05
25 Harold Green .01 .05
26 David Klingler .01 .05
27 Daniel Stubbs .01 .05
28 Alfred Williams .01 .05
29 John Copeland .01 .05
30 Mark Carrier WR .02 .10
31 Michael Jackson .02 .10
32 Eric Metcalf .02 .10
33 Vinny Testaverde .02 .10
34 Tommy Vardell .01 .05
35 Alvin Harper .02 .10
36 Ken Norton Jr. .02 .10
37 Tony Casillas .01 .05
38 Leon Lett .01 .05
39 Jay Novacek .02 .10
40 Kevin Smith .01 .05
41 Troy Aikman .40 1.00
42 Michael Irvin .08 .25
43 Russell Maryland .01 .05
44 Emmitt Smith .60 1.50
45 Robert Delpino .01 .05
46 Simon Fletcher .01 .05
47 Greg Kragen .01 .05
48 Arthur Marshall .01 .05
49 Steve Atwater .01 .05
50 Rod Bernstine .01 .05
51 John Elway .75 2.00
52 Glyn Milburn .02 .10
53 Shannon Sharpe .02 .10
54 Bennie Blades .01 .05
55 Mel Gray .01 .05
56 Herman Moore .08 .25
57 Pat Swilling .01 .05
58 Chris Spielman .02 .10
59 Rodney Peete .01 .05
60 Andre Ware .01 .05
61 Brett Perriman .02 .10
62 Erik Kramer .02 .10
63 Barry Sanders .60 1.50
64 Mark Clayton .01 .05
65 Chris Jacke .01 .05
66 Terrell Buckley .01 .05
67 Ty Detmer .02 .10
68 Sanjay Beach .01 .05
69 Brian Noble .01 .05
70 Edgar Bennett .08 .25
71 Brett Favre .75 2.00
72 Sterling Sharpe .02 .10
73 Reggie White .08 .25
74 Ernest Givins .02 .10
75 Al Del Greco .01 .05
76 Cris Dishman .01 .05
77 Curtis Duncan .01 .05
78 Webster Slaughter .01 .05
79 Spencer Tillman .01 .05
80 Warren Moon .08 .25
81 Wilber Marshall .01 .05
82 Haywood Jeffires .02 .10
83 Lorenzo White .01 .05
84 Gary Brown .01 .05
85 Reggie Langhorne .01 .05
86 Dean Biasucci .01 .05
87 Steve Emtman .01 .05
88 Jessie Hester .01 .05
89 Quentin Coryatt .01 .05
90 Roosevelt Potts .01 .05
91 Jeff George .08 .25
92 Nick Lowery .01 .05
93 Willie Davis .02 .10
94 Joe Montana .75 2.00
95 Neil Smith .02 .10
96 Marcus Allen .08 .25
97 Derrick Thomas .08 .25
98 Greg Townsend .01 .05
99 Willie Gault .01 .05
100 Ethan Horton .01 .05
101 Jeff Hostetler .02 .10
102 Tim Brown .08 .25
103 Rocket Ismail .02 .10
104 Shane Conlan .01 .05
105 Henry Ellard .02 .10
106 T.J. Rubley .01 .05
107 Sean Gilbert .01 .05
108 Troy Drayton .01 .05
109 Jerome Bettis .15 .40
110 Terry Kirby .08 .25
111 Mark Ingram .01 .05
112 John Offerdahl .01 .05
113 Louis Oliver .01 .05
114 Irving Fryar .02 .10
115 Dan Marino .75 2.00
116 Keith Jackson .01 .05
117 O.J. McDuffie .08 .25
118 Jim McMahon .02 .10
119 Sean Salisbury .01 .05
120 Randall McDaniel .02 .10
121 Jack Del Rio .01 .05
122 Cris Carter .20 .50
123 Chris Doleman .01 .05
124 John Randle .01 .05
125 Vincent Brisby .02 .10
126 Greg McMurtry .01 .05
127 Drew Bledsoe .30 .75
128 Leonard Russell .01 .05
129 Michael Brooks .01 .05
130 Mark Jackson .01 .05
131 Pepper Johnson .01 .05
132 Doug Riesenberg .01 .05
133 Phil Simms .02 .10
134 Rodney Hampton .02 .10
135 Leonard Marshall .01 .05
136 Rob Moore .02 .10
137 Chris Burkett .01 .05
138 Boomer Esiason .02 .10
139 Johnny Johnson .01 .05
140 Ronnie Lott .02 .10
141 Brad Muster .01 .05
142 Renaldo Turnbull .01 .05
143 Willie Roaf .01 .05
144 Rickey Jackson .01 .05
145 Morten Andersen .01 .05
146 Vaughn Dunbar .01 .05
147 Wade Wilson .01 .05
148 Eric Martin .01 .05
149 Seth Joyner .01 .05
150 Calvin Williams .02 .10
151 Vai Sikahema .01 .05
152 Herschel Walker .02 .10
153 Eric Allen .01 .05
154 Fred Barnett .02 .10
155 Randall Cunningham .08 .25
156 Steve Beuerlein .02 .10
157 Gary Clark .02 .10
158 Anthony Edwards .01 .05
159 Randal Hill .01 .05
160 Freddie Joe Nunn .01 .05
161 Garrison Hearst .08 .25
162 Ricky Proehl .01 .05
163 Eric Green .01 .05
164 Levon Kirkland .01 .05
165 Joel Steed .01 .05
166 Deon Figures .01 .05
167 Leroy Thompson .01 .05
168 Barry Foster .01 .05
169 Neil O'Donnell .08 .25
170 Junior Seau .08 .25
171 Leslie O'Neal .01 .05
172 Stan Humphries .02 .10
173 Marion Butts .01 .05
174 Anthony Miller .02 .10
175 Natrone Means .08 .25
176 Odessa Turner .01 .05
177 Dana Stubblefield .02 .10
178 John Taylor .02 .10
179 Ricky Watters .02 .10
180 Steve Young .30 .75
181 Jerry Rice .40 1.00
182 Tom Rathman .01 .05
183 Brian Blades .02 .10
184 Patrick Hunter .01 .05
185 Rick Mirer .08 .25
186 Chris Warren .02 .10
187 Cortez Kennedy .02 .10
188 Reggie Cobb .01 .05
189 Craig Erickson .01 .05
190 Hardy Nickerson .02 .10
191 Lawrence Dawsey .01 .05
192 Broderick Thomas .01 .05
193 Ricky Sanders .01 .05
194 Carl Banks .01 .05
195 Ricky Ervins .01 .05
196 Darrell Green .01 .05
197 Mark Rypien .01 .05
198 Desmond Howard .02 .10
199 Art Monk .02 .10
200 Reggie Brooks .02 .10
P1 Sh.Sharpe Prototype .40 1.00
Numbered 53

1994 Collector's Edge Gold

COMPLETE SET (200) 10.00 25.00
*GOLD CARDS: .75X TO 1.5X BASIC CARDS

1994 Collector's Edge Pop Warner

COMPLETE SET (200) 6.00 15.00
*POP WARNER: .4X TO 1X BASE CARD HI

1994 Collector's Edge Pop Warner 22K Gold

COMPLETE SET (200) 30.00 80.00
*PW 22K GOLDS: 2.5X TO 5X BASIC CARDS

1994 Collector's Edge Silver

COMPLETE SET (200) 7.50 20.00
*SILVER CARDS: .5X TO 1.2X BASIC CARDS

1994 Collector's Edge Boss Rookies

COMPLETE SET (19) 5.00 12.00
RANDOM INSERTS IN ALL EDGE PAC
1 Isaac Bruce 1.50 4.00
2 Jeff Burris .10 .30
3 Shante Carver .10 .30
4 Lake Dawson .20 .50
5 Bert Emanuel .30 .75
6 William Floyd .20 .50
7 Wayne Gandy .10 .30
8 Aaron Glenn .30 .75
9 Chris Maumalanga .10 .30
10 David Palmer .30 .75
11 Errict Rhett .30 .75
12 Heath Shuler .30 .75
13 Dewayne Washington .10 .30
14 Bryant Young .20 .50
15 Dan Wilkinson .20 .50
16 Rob Fredrickson .10 .30
17 Calvin Jones .10 .30
18 James Folston .10 .30
19 Marshall Faulk 1.50 4.00

1994 Collector's Edge Boss Rookies Update

COMPLETE FACT.SET (25) 15.00 30.00
*DIAMOND CARDS: 1.5X to 2.5X BASIC CARDS
ONE SET PER MAIL REDEMPTION CA
COMPLETE GREEN SET (25) 12.50 25.00
*GREEN CARDS: .4X TO .75X BASIC CARDS
STATED ODDS 1:3 POP WARNER
1 Trent Dilfer 1.00 2.50
2 Jeff Burris .30 .75
3 Shante Carver .30 .75
4 Lake Dawson .50 1.25
5 Bert Emanuel .50 1.25
6 Marshall Faulk 3.00 8.00
7 William Floyd .50 1.25
8 Charlie Garner 1.00 2.50
9 Rob Fredrickson .30 .75
10 Wayne Gandy .30 .75
11 Aaron Glenn .75 2.00
12 Greg Hill .50 1.25
13 Isaac Bruce 3.00 8.00
14 Charles Johnson .50 1.25
15 Johnnie Morton 1.25 3.00
16 Calvin Jones .30 .75
17 Tim Bowens .30 .75
18 David Palmer .75 2.00
19 Errict Rhett .50 1.25
20 Darnay Scott .60 1.50
21 Heath Shuler .50 1.25
22 John Thierry .30 .75
23 Bernard Williams .30 .75
24 Dan Wilkinson .30 .75
25 Bryant Young .50 1.25

1994 Collector's Edge Boss Squad

COMPLETE SET (25) 6.00 15.00
RANDOM INSERTS IN ALL EDGE PAC
*SILVERS: .4X TO 1X BASIC INSERTS
RANDOM INSERTS IN CE POP WARNE
*BRONZE EQII: .4X TO 1X BASIC INSERTS
ONE SET PER EDGEQUEST REDEMPTI
*GOLD HELMETS: .4X TO 1X BASIC INSERTS
ONE SET PER POP WARNER EDGEQUE
1 John Elway W-2 1.50 4.00
2 Joe Montana 1.50 4.00
3 Vinny Testaverde .07 .20
4 Boomer Esiason .07 .20
5 Steve Young W-1 .60 1.50
6 Troy Aikman .75 2.00
7 Phil Simms .07 .20
8 Bobby Hebert .02 .10
9 Thurman Thomas .20 .50
10 Leonard Russell .02 .10
11 Chris Warren W-2 .07 .20
12 Gary Brown .02 .10
13 Emmitt Smith 1.25 3.00
14 Jerome Bettis .30 .75
15 Erric Pegram .02 .10
16 Barry Sanders W-1 1.25 3.00
17 Reggie Langhorne .02 .10
18 Anthony Miller .07 .20
19 Shannon Sharpe .07 .20
20 Tim Brown .20 .50
21 Sterling Sharpe W-2 .07 .20
22 Jerry Rice W-1 .75 2.00
23 Michael Irvin .20 .50
24 Andre Rison .07 .20
25 Checklist .02 .10

1994 Collector's Edge Boss Squad Promos

COMPLETE SET (6) 3.20 8.00
1 Marshall Faulk 1.60 4.00
2 Jerome Bettis .60 1.50
3 Erric Pegram .30 .75
4 Sterling Sharpe .50 1.25
5 Shannon Sharpe .50 1.25
6 Leonard Russell .30 .75

1994 Collector's Edge FX

COMPLETE SET (7) 7.50 20.00
RANDOM INSERTS IN CE GOLD PACK
*GOLD SHIELDS: .8X to 2X BASIC INSERTS
STATED ODDS 1:200 GOLD PACKS
*WHITE BACKS: .4X TO 1X BASIC INSERTS
STATED ODDS 1:7 RETAIL/JUMBO
*SILVER SHIELDS: 2X to 5X BASIC INSERTS
STATED ODDS 1:200 RETAIL/JUMBO
*SILVER BACKS: .2X TO .5X BASIC INSERTS
STATED ODDS 1:7 SILVER
*GOLD BACKS: 1.2X to 3X BASIC INSERTS
STATED ODDS 1:200 SILVER
*SILVER LETTERS: .4X TO 1X BASIC INSERTS
STATED ODDS 1:7 POP WARNER
*GOLD LETTERS: .8X to 2X BASIC INSERTS
STATED ODDS 1:200 POP WARNER
*RED LETTERS: .3X to .8X BASIC INSERTS
ONE SET PER EDGEQUEST REDEMPTION
1 John Elway 4.00 8.00
2 Joe Montana 4.00 8.00
3 Troy Aikman 2.00 4.00
4 Emmitt Smith 3.00 6.00
5 Jerome Bettis .75 1.50
6 Anthony Miller .15 .40
7 Sterling Sharpe .15 .40

1995 Collector's Edge

This 205-card standard-size set features full-action color photos on front with the player's name across the left-side. The cards are grouped alphabetically within teams and checklisted below alphabetically according to teams. There are no key Rookie Cards in this set. Many parallels of the basic set exist.

COMPLETE SET (205) 10.00 20.00
1 Anthony Edwards .01 .05
2 Garrison Hearst .08 .25
3 Seth Joyner .01 .05
4 Dave Krieg .01 .05
5 Chuck Levy .01 .05
6 Rob Moore .02 .10
7 J.J. Birden .01 .05
8 Jeff George .02 .10
9 Craig Heyward .02 .10
10 Norm Johnson .01 .05
11 Terance Mathis .02 .10
12 Eric Metcalf .02 .10
13 Chuck Smith .01 .05
14 Darryl Talley .01 .05
15 Cornelius Bennett .02 .10
16 Steve Christie .01 .05
17 Kenneth Davis .01 .05
18 Phil Hansen .01 .05
19 Jim Kelly .08 .25
20 Bryce Paup .02 .10
21 Andre Reed .02 .10
22 Bruce Smith .08 .25
23 Eric Ball .01 .05
24 Don Beebe .01 .05
25 Mark Carrier WR .02 .10
26 Tim McKyer .01 .05
27 Pete Metzelaars .01 .05
28 Sam Mills .02 .10
29 Jack Trudeau .01 .05
30 Mark Carrier DB .01 .05
31 Curtis Conway .08 .25
32 Erik Kramer .01 .05
33 Lewis Tillman .01 .05
34 Michael Timpson .01 .05
35 Steve Walsh .01 .05
36 Chris Zorich .01 .05
37 Jeff Blake RC .25 .60
38 Harold Green .01 .05
39 David Klingler .02 .10
40 Carl Pickens .02 .10
41 Tom Waddle .01 .05
42 Dan Wilkinson .02 .10
43 Leroy Hoard .01 .05
44 Michael Jackson .02 .10
45 Antonio Langham .01 .05
46 Andre Rison .02 .10
47 Vinny Testaverde .02 .10
48 Eric Turner .01 .05
49 Tommy Vardell .01 .05
50 Troy Aikman .40 1.00
51 Charles Haley .02 .10
52 Michael Irvin .08 .25
53 Daryl Johnston .02 .10
54 Leon Lett .01 .05
55 Jay Novacek .02 .10
56 Emmitt Smith .60 1.50

57 Kevin Williams WR .02 .10
58 Steve Atwater .01 .05
59 John Elway .75 2.00
60 Simon Fletcher .01 .05
61 Glyn Milburn .01 .05
62 Anthony Miller .02 .10
63 Leonard Russell .01 .05
64 Shannon Sharpe .02 .10
65 Scott Mitchell .02 .10
66 Herman Moore .08 .25
67 Johnnie Morton .02 .10
68 Brett Perriman .02 .10
69 Barry Sanders .60 1.50
70 Edgar Bennett .02 .10
71 Brett Favre .75 2.00
72 Mark Ingram .01 .05
73 Chris Jacke .01 .05
74 Guy McIntyre .01 .05
75 Reggie White .08 .25
76 Gary Brown .01 .05
77 Ernest Givins .01 .05
78 Mel Gray .01 .05
79 Haywood Jeffires .01 .05
80 Webster Slaughter .01 .05
81 Craig Erickson .01 .05
82 Marshall Faulk .50 1.25
83 Jim Harbaugh .02 .10
84 Roosevelt Potts .01 .05
85 Floyd Turner .01 .05
86 Steve Beuerlein .02 .10
87 Reggie Cobb .01 .05
88 Jeff Lageman .01 .05
89 Mazio Royster .01 .05
90 Marcus Allen .08 .25
91 Steve Bono .02 .10
92 Willie Davis .02 .10
93 Lake Dawson .02 .10
94 Ronnie Lott .02 .10
95 Eric Martin .01 .05
96 Chris Penn .01 .05
97 Tim Brown .08 .25
98 Derrick Fenner .01 .05
99 Rob Fredrickson .01 .05
100 Nolan Harrison .01 .05
101 Jeff Hostetler .02 .10
102 Rocket Ismail .02 .10
103 James Jett .02 .10
104 Chester McGlockton .02 .10
105 Anthony Smith .01 .05
106 Harvey Williams .01 .05
107 Jerome Bettis .08 .25
108 Troy Drayton .01 .05
109 Chris Miller .01 .05
110 Robert Young .01 .05
111 Keith Byars .01 .05
112 Gary Clark .01 .05
113 Bryan Cox .01 .05
114 Jeff Cross .01 .05
115 Irving Fryar .02 .10
116 Randal Hill .01 .05
117 Terry Kirby .02 .10
118 Dan Marino .75 2.00
119 O.J. McDuffie .08 .25
120 Bernie Parmalee .02 .10
121 Terry Allen .02 .10
122 Cris Carter .08 .25
123 Qadry Ismail .02 .10
124 Warren Moon .02 .10
125 John Randle .02 .10
126 Jake Reed .02 .10
127 Fuad Reveiz .01 .05
128 Broderick Thomas .01 .05
129 Drew Bledsoe .25 .60
130 Vincent Brisby .01 .05
131 Ben Coates .02 .10
132 Dave Meggett .01 .05
133 Chris Slade .01 .05
134 Leroy Thompson .01 .05
135 Eric Allen .01 .05
136 Mario Bates .02 .10
137 Quinn Early .01 .05
138 Jim Everett .01 .05
139 Michael Haynes .02 .10
140 Torrance Small .01 .05
141 Dave Brown .02 .10
142 Chris Calloway .01 .05
143 Keith Hamilton .01 .05
144 Rodney Hampton .02 .10
145 Mike Sherrard .01 .05
146 David Treadwell .01 .05
147 Herschel Walker .02 .10
148 Boomer Esiason .02 .10
149 Erik Howard .01 .05
150 Johnny Johnson .01 .05
151 Mo Lewis .01 .05
152 Johnny Mitchell .01 .05
153 Fred Barnett .02 .10
154 Randall Cunningham .08 .25
155 William Fuller .01 .05
156 Charlie Garner .08 .25
157 Greg Jackson .01 .05
158 Ricky Watters .02 .10
159 Calvin Williams .02 .10
160 Barry Foster .02 .10
161 Kevin Greene .02 .10
162 Greg Lloyd .02 .10
163 Byron Bam Morris .01 .05
164 Neil O'Donnell .02 .10
165 Erric Pegram .02 .10
166 John L. Williams .01 .05
167 Rod Woodson .02 .10
168 John Carney .01 .05
169 Stan Humphries .02 .10
170 Natrone Means .02 .10
171 Chris Mims .01 .05
172 Leslie O'Neal .02 .10
173 Alfred Pupunu RC .01 .05
174 Junior Seau .08 .25
175 Mark Seay .02 .10
176 William Floyd .02 .10
177 Jerry Rice .40 1.00
178 Deion Sanders .25 .60
179 Dana Stubblefield .02 .10
180 John Taylor .01 .05
181 Steve Young .30 .75
182 Bryant Young .02 .10
183 Brian Blades .02 .10
184 Cortez Kennedy .02 .10
185 Kelvin Martin .01 .05
186 Rick Mirer .02 .10
187 Ricky Proehl .01 .05
188 Michael Sinclair .01 .05
189 Chris Warren .02 .10
190 Trent Dilfer .08 .25
191 Alvin Harper .01 .05
192 Jackie Harris .01 .05
193 Hardy Nickerson .01 .05
194 Erric Rhett .02 .10
195 Reggie Roby .01 .05
196 Henry Ellard .02 .10
197 Ricky Ervins .01 .05
198 Darrell Green .01 .05
199 Brian Mitchell .01 .05
200 Heath Shuler .02 .10
201 Checklist .01 .05
202 Checklist .01 .05
203 Checklist .01 .05
204 Checklist .01 .05
205 Checklist .01 .05
P1 Natrone Means Promo .20 .50
P2 Chris Warren Promo .20 .50

1995 Collector's Edge Black Label

COMPLETE SET (205) 7.50 20.00
*BLACK LABEL: SAME PRICE AS BASIC CARDS

1995 Collector's Edge Black Label Silver Die Cuts

COMPLETE SET (205) 100.00 200.00
*STARS: 4X TO 10X BASIC CARDS
STATED ODDS 1:24 BLACK LABEL

1995 Collector's Edge Black Label 22K Gold

COMPLETE SET (205) 300.00 600.00
*22K GOLD STARS: 12X TO 30X BASIC CARDS
RANDOM INSERTS IN BLACK LABEL

1995 Collector's Edge Die Cuts

COMPLETE SET (205) 40.00 100.00
*STARS: 2X TO 5X BASIC CARDS

1995 Collector's Edge Gold Logo

COMPLETE SET (205) 7.50 20.00
*GOLD LOGOS: SAME PRICE AS BASIC CARDS

1995 Collector's Edge Nitro 22K

COMPLETE SET (205) 75.00 200.00
*NITRO 22K STARS: 5X TO 12X BASIC CARDS

1995 Collector's Edge 22K Gold

COMPLETE SET (205) 250.00 500.00
*22K GOLD: 10X TO 25X BASIC CARDS
RANDOM INSERTS IN RETAIL PACKS

1995 Collector's Edge 22K Gold Die Cuts

COMPLETE SET (205) 150.00 500.00
*DIE CUT/500: 6X TO 15X BASIC CARDS
STATED PRINT RUN 500 SERIAL #'d SETS

1995 Collector's Edge Black Label Quantum Motion

COMPLETE SET (13) 20.00 40.00
*UNNUMBERED PROMOS: .2X TO .5X
1 Jerome Bettis .20 .50
2 Jeff Blake .20 .50
3 Drew Bledsoe .50 1.25
4 Cris Carter .20 .50
5 John Elway 1.00 2.50
6 Marshall Faulk .20 .50
7 Terance Mathis .10 .30
8 Byron Bam Morris .05 .15
9 Erric Rhett .05 .15
10 Jerry Rice .50 1.25
11 Deion Sanders .30 .75
12 Heath Shuler .05 .15
13 Checklist Card .05 .15
unnumbered card
GTW1 Giant TimeWarp AUTO 25.00 50.00
Dick Butkus
Jeff Blake
Junior Seau

1995 Collector's Edge EdgeTech

COMPLETE SET (37) 15.00 40.00
STATED ODDS 1:12 HOB/RET
*22K GOLDS: 1.2X TO 3X BASIC INSERTS
STATED ODDS 1:120 RETAIL
*BLACK LABEL: .2X TO .5X BASIC INSERTS
STATED ODDS 1:12 BLACK LABEL
*BLACK LABEL 22K: .6X TO 1.5X BASIC INS.
BL 22K STATED ODDS 1:120 BLACK LABEL
*QUANTUMS: 2.5X TO 6X BASIC INSERTS
STATED ODDS 1:120 BLACK LABEL
*QUANT.DIE CUTS: 4X TO 10X BASIC INSERTS
RANDOM INSERTS IN BLACK LABEL PACKS
*CIRCULAR PRISMS: .4X TO 1X BASIC INS.
CIRC.PRISMS: ONE PER JUMBO
1 Dan Marino 3.00 6.00
2 Steve Young 1.25 2.50
3 Rick Mirer .10 .30
4 Emmitt Smith 2.50 5.00
5 John Elway 3.00 6.00
6 Neil O'Donnell .10 .30
7 Marshall Faulk 2.00 4.00
8 Deion Sanders 1.00 2.00
9 Terance Mathis .10 .30
10 Kevin Greene .10 .30
11 Ricky Watters .10 .30
12 Tim Brown .30 .75
13 Antonio Langham .05 .15
14 Lake Dawson .10 .30
15 Jay Novacek .10 .30
16 Herman Moore .30 .75
17 Mark Seay .10 .30
18 Bernie Parmalee .10 .30
19 Drew Bledsoe 1.00 2.00
20 Troy Aikman 1.50 3.00
21 Brett Favre 3.00 6.00
22 Jerry Rice 1.50 3.00
23 Barry Sanders 2.50 5.00
24 Heath Shuler .10 .30
25 Erric Rhett .10 .30
26 Cris Carter .30 .75
27 Jerome Bettis .30 .75
28 Reggie White .30 .75
29 Chris Warren .10 .30
30 Ben Coates .10 .30
31 Bryant Young .10 .30
32 Mel Gray .05 .15
33 Darryl Talley .05 .15
34 Mike Sherrard .05 .15
35 William Floyd .10 .30
36 Alvin Harper .05 .15
37 Checklist (1-36) .05 .15

1995 Collector's Edge Nitro Redemption

COMPLETE SET (25) 20.00 50.00
1 Warren Moon .25 .60
2 Scott Mitchell .25 .60
3 Jeff Blake .75 2.00
4 Emmitt Smith 4.00 10.00
5 Barry Sanders 4.00 10.00
6 Terance Mathis .25 .60
7 Herman Moore .60 1.50
8 Isaac Bruce .60 1.50
9 Cris Carter .60 1.50
10 Ben Coates .25 .60
11 Shannon Sharpe .25 .60
12 Jay Novacek .25 .60
13 Norm Johnson .10 .30
14 Morten Andersen .10 .30
15 Fuad Reveiz .10 .30
16 Bryce Paup .25 .60
17 Jim Flanigan .10 .30
18 Kevin Carter .10 .30
19 Sam Mills .25 .60
20 Willie McGinest .10 .30
21 Orlando Thomas .10 .30
22 Brett Favre 5.00 12.00
23 Dan Marino 5.00 12.00
24 Jerry Rice 2.50 6.00
25 Larry Brown .10 .30

1995 Collector's Edge Junior Seau Promos

COMPLETE SET (5) 2.00 5.00
COMMON CARD (1-5) .40 1.00

1995 Collector's Edge Rookies

COMPLETE SET (25) 20.00 40.00
STATED ODDS 1:4 RETAIL
*22K GOLDS: 1.2X TO 3X BASIC INSERTS
22K GOLD ODDS 1:40 RETAIL
*BLACK LABELS: .4X TO 1X BASIC INSERTS
*BL 22K GOLDS: 1.2X TO 3X BASIC INSERTS
1 Derrick Alexander DE .25 .60
2 Tony Boselli .60 1.50
3 Ki-Jana Carter .60 1.50
4 Kevin Carter .60 1.50
5 Kerry Collins 1.25 3.00
6 Steve McNair 2.50 6.00
7 Billy Milner .25 .60
8 Rashaan Salaam .60 1.50
9 Warren Sapp .40 1.00
10 James O. Stewart 1.00 2.50
11 J.J.Stokes .60 1.50
12 Bobby Taylor .60 1.50
13 Tyrone Wheatley UER 1.00 2.50
14 Derrick Brooks 1.25 3.00
15 Reuben Brown .60 1.50
16 Mark Bruener .40 1.00
17 Joey Galloway 1.25 3.00
18 Napoleon Kaufman 1.00 2.50
19 Ty Law 1.00 2.50
20 Craig Newsome .40 1.00
21 Kordell Stewart 1.25 3.00
22 Korey Stringer .50 1.25
23 Zach Wiegert .25 .60
24 Michael Westbrook .60 1.50
25 Checklist .25 .60

1995 Collector's Edge TimeWarp

COMPLETE SET (21) 25.00 60.00
STATED ODDS 1:400 HOB/RET,1:200 JUM
*22K GOLDS: 2X TO 4X BASIC INSERTS
22K GOLD ODDS 1:4000 HOB/RET
*PRISMS: .4X TO 1X BASIC INSERTS
*BLACK LABEL: .4X TO 1X BASIC INSERTS
BL ODDS 1:200 BLACK LABEL PACKS
*BLACK LABEL 22K: 2X TO 4X BASIC INS.
1 Emmitt Smith 5.00 12.00
Dick Butkus
2 Troy Aikman 3.00 8.00
Gino Marchetti
3 Natrone Means 1.00 2.50
Ray Nitschke
4 Chris Zorich 1.00 2.50
Steve Van Buren
5 Barry Sanders 5.00 12.00
Deacon Jones
6 Kevin Greene 1.50 4.00
Paul Hornung
7 Charles Haley 1.50 4.00
Len Dawson
8 Marshall Faulk 2.50 6.00
Willie Lanier
9 Ronnie Lott 1.50 4.00
Gale Sayers
10 Cris Carter 1.00 2.50
Jack Ham
11 Junior Seau 1.50 4.00
Gale Sayers
12 Reggie White 1.50 4.00
Otto Graham
13 Leslie O'Neal 1.00 2.50
Y.A.Tittle
14 Drew Bledsoe 2.50 6.00
Ted Hendricks
15 Heath Shuler 1.50 4.00
Bob Lilly
16 Ricky Watters 1.50 4.00
Daryl Lamonica
17 Marshall Faulk 2.50 6.00
Dick Butkus
18 Deion Sanders 2.00 5.00
Raymond Berry
19 Steve Young 2.50 6.00
Jack Youngblood
20 Bruce Smith 1.50 4.00
Sammy Baugh
NNO Checklist .20 .50
TW1 Gale Sayers 1.25 3.00
Junior Seau
Dick Butkus
Promo card

1995 Collector's Edge 12th Man Redemption

COMPLETE PRIZE SET (25) 6.00 15.00
COMP.LETTERS SET (7) .30 .75
12TH MAN LETTERS: STATED ODDS 1:9
1 Dan Marino 1.25 3.00
2 Jeff Blake .25 .60
3 Steve Bono .05 .15
4 Brett Favre 1.25 3.00
5 Steve Young .50 1.25
6 Scott Mitchell .05 .15
7 Chris Warren .05 .15
8 Marshall Faulk .75 2.00
9 Byron Bam Morris .02 .10
10 Emmitt Smith 1.00 2.50
11 Barry Sanders 1.00 2.50
12 Rashaan Salaam .15 .40
13 Carl Pickens .05 .15
14 Anthony Miller .05 .15
15 Tim Brown .15 .40
16 Jerry Rice .60 1.50
17 Herman Moore .15 .40
18 Isaac Bruce .15 .40
19 Ben Coates .05 .15
20 Shannon Sharpe .05 .15
21 Alfred Pupunu .02 .10
22 Jackie Harris .02 .10
23 Jay Novacek .05 .15
24 Brent Jones .02 .10
25 Checklist Card .02 .10

1995 Collector's Edge Instant Replay

This 51-card set was produced late in the year by Collector's Edge and replaced last year's Pop Warner set. Rookies included in this set are Kerry Collins, Terrell Davis, Joey Galloway, Steve McNair, J.J. Stokes and Michael Westbrook. In addition to the basic set, there is a Prism parallel set. These cards were inserted approximately one in every two packs. There is also a Micro Mini set, which is an eight card set of Black Label base cards. These cards were inserted at a rate of one in 14 packs. Each card contains 50 total "mini" cards with 25 on each side.

COMPLETE SET (51) 6.00 15.00
1 Jeff George .02 .10
2 Eric Metcalf .02 .10
3 Jim Kelly .07 .20
4 Jeff Blake RC .25 .60
5 Andre Rison .02 .10
6 Troy Aikman .30 .75
7 Michael Irvin .07 .20
8 Emmitt Smith .50 1.25
9 John Elway .60 1.50
10 Terrell Davis RC .75 2.00
11 Herman Moore .07 .20
12 Barry Sanders .50 1.25
13 Brett Favre .60 1.50
14 Marshall Faulk .40 1.00
15 Steve Beuerlein .02 .10
16 Steve Bono .02 .10
17 Tim Brown .07 .20
18 Jeff Hostetler .02 .10
19 Jerome Bettis .07 .20
20 Dan Marino .60 1.50
21 Cris Carter .07 .20
22 Drew Bledsoe .20 .50
23 Ben Coates .02 .10
24 Randall Cunningham .07 .20
25 Terry Kirby .02 .10
26 Ricky Watters .02 .10
27 Kyle Brady .07 .20
28 Byron Bam Morris .01 .05
29 Neil O'Donnell .02 .10
30 Natrone Means .02 .10
31 Junior Seau .07 .20
32 William Floyd .02 .10
33 Jerry Rice .30 .75
34 Deion Sanders .20 .50
35 Steve Young .25 .60
36 Rick Mirer .02 .10
37 Chris Warren .02 .10
38 Trent Dilfer .07 .20
39 Erric Rhett .02 .10
40 Heath Shuler .02 .10
41 Ki-Jana Carter RC .07 .20
42 Kerry Collins RC .60 1.50
43 Steve McNair RC 1.00 2.50
44 Rashaan Salaam RC .02 .10
45 James O. Stewart RC .40 1.00
46 J.J. Stokes RC .07 .20
47 Tyrone Wheatley RC .40 1.00
48 Joey Galloway RC .50 1.25
49 Napoleon Kaufman RC .40 1.00
50 Michael Westbrook RC .07 .20
NNO Checklist Card .01 .05

1995 Collector's Edge Instant Replay Prisms

COMP.PRISM SET (50) 12.00 30.00
*PRISM STARS: 1X TO 2.5X BASIC CARDS
STATED ODDS 1:2
*PRISM RCs: .5X TO 1.2X BASIC CARDS

1995 Collector's Edge Instant Replay EdgeTech Die Cuts

COMPLETE SET (13) 4.00 10.00
STATED ODDS 1:4 RET, 1:1 SPEC.RET
1 Troy Aikman .60 1.50
2 Drew Bledsoe .40 1.00
3 Tim Brown .15 .40
4 Ben Coates .07 .20
5 Marshall Faulk .75 2.00
6 William Floyd .07 .20
7 Dan Marino 1.25 3.00
8 Erric Rhett .07 .20
9 Deion Sanders .40 1.00
10 Emmitt Smith 1.00 2.50
11 Ricky Watters .07 .20
12 Steve Young .50 1.25
NNO Checklist .02 .10

1995 Collector's Edge Instant Replay Quantum Motion

COMPLETE SET (22) 12.50 30.00
COMP.SERIES 1 (11) 7.50 20.00
COMP.SERIES 2 (11) 4.00 10.00
1-10/CL: STATED ODDS 1:12
11-21: AVAIL. VIA MAIL REDEMPTION
1 Troy Aikman 1.25 3.00
2 Drew Bledsoe .75 2.00
3 Marshall Faulk 1.50 4.00
4 Michael Irvin .30 .75
5 Dan Marino 2.50 6.00
6 Jerry Rice 1.25 3.00
7 Rod Smith 2.00 5.00
Barry Sanders in foreground
8 Emmitt Smith 2.00 5.00
9 Michael Westbrook .10 .30
10 Steve Young 1.00 2.50
11 Erik Kramer .07 .20
12 Jeff Blake .40 1.00
13 Eric Metcalf .15 .40
14 Steve Bono .15 .40
15 Carl Pickens .15 .40
16 Isaac Bruce .30 .75
17 Erric Rhett .15 .40
18 Kerry Collins 1.00 2.50
19 Rashaan Salaam .05 .15
20 Gus Frerotte .15 .40
21 Terry Kirby .15 .40
NNO Checklist .07 .20

1995 Collector's Edge TimeWarp Jumbos

This 42-card set features borderless color player photos and measures approximately 8" by 10". The cards are similar to the regular issue 1995 Collector's Edge TimeWarp cards, except in jumbo format. Initially distributed to hobby dealers but offered later direct to collectors (for $11.95 each), 5000 of each card was produced with every card serial numbered. Signed versions of each of the cards were also available autographed by the Hall of Fame player featured for $23.95 each. The cards were also made available through a 1996 Collector's Edge special retail pack redemption offer for $3.95 each with 12-wrappers of product.

COMPLETE SET (42) 150.00 250.00
1 Dick Butkus 5.00 12.00
Emmitt Smith
2 Dick Butkus 5.00 12.00
Emmitt Smith
3 Gino Marchetti 3.00 8.00
Troy Aikman
4 Gino Marchetti 3.00 8.00
Troy Aikman
5 Ray Nitschke 2.00 5.00
Natrone Means
6 Ray Nitschke 2.00 5.00
Natrone Means
7 Steve Van Buren 1.50 4.00
Chris Zorich
8 Steve Van Buren 1.50 4.00
Chris Zorich
9 Deacon Jones 6.00 15.00
Barry Sanders
10 Deacon Jones 6.00 15.00
Barry Sanders
11 Paul Hornung 2.00 5.00
Kevin Greene
12 Paul Hornung 2.00 5.00
Kevin Greene
13 Len Dawson 2.00 5.00
Charles Haley
14 Len Dawson 2.00 5.00
Charles Haley
15 Willie Lanier 2.50 6.00
Marshall Faulk
16 Willie Lanier 2.50 6.00
Marshall Faulk
17 Gale Sayers 2.00 5.00
Ronnie Lott
18 Gale Sayers 2.00 5.00
Ronnie Lott
19 Jack Ham 2.00 5.00
Cris Carter
20 Jack Ham 2.00 5.00
Cris Carter
21 Gale Sayers 2.00 5.00
Junior Seau
22 Gale Sayers 2.00 5.00
Junior Seau
23 Otto Graham 2.00 5.00
Reggie White
24 Otto Graham 2.00 5.00
Reggie White
25 Y.A.Tittle 2.00 5.00
Leslie O'Neal
26 Y.A.Tittle 2.00 5.00
Leslie O'Neal
27 Daryle Lamonica 1.50 4.00
Ricky Watters
28 Daryle Lamonica 1.50 4.00
Ricky Watters
29 Dick Butkus 2.40 6.00
Marshall Faulk
30 Dick Butkus 2.40 6.00
Marshall Faulk
31 Raymond Berry 2.40 6.00
Deion Sanders
32 Raymond Berry 2.40 6.00
Deion Sanders
33 Jack Youngblood 3.20 8.00
Steve Young
34 Jack Youngblood 3.20 8.00
Steve Young
35 Sammy Baugh 2.00 5.00
Bruce Smith
36 Sammy Baugh 2.00 5.00
Bruce Smith
37 Ted Hendricks 6.00 15.00
Dan Marino
38 Bob Lilly 6.00 15.00
Dan Marino
39 Ted Hendricks 3.20 8.00
Drew Bledsoe
40 Bob Lilly 2.00 5.00
Heath Shuler
41 Dick Butkus 2.00 5.00
Jeff Blake
42 Dick Butkus 2.40 6.00
Michael Westbrook

1995 Collector's Edge TimeWarp Jumbos Autographs

These are the autographed parallel version of the 1995 Collector's Edger TimeWarp Jumbos cards (measure roughly 8" x 10"). Each card was issued direct to the hobby as a single card (initially at $23.95 each) or part of a compete set that could have been purchased direct for $1005.90. The cards were signed by the retired player only and were issued with a separate gold foil certificate of authenticity.

COMPLETE SET (42) 600.00 1,000.00
1 Dick Butkus AUTO 20.00 40.00
Emmitt Smith
2 Dick Butkus AUTO 20.00 40.00
Emmitt Smith
3 Gino Marchetti AUTO 12.50 25.00
Troy Aikman
4 Gino Marchetti AUTO 12.50 25.00
Troy Aikman
5 Ray Nitschke AUTO 30.00 60.00
Natrone Means
6 Ray Nitschke AUTO 30.00 60.00
Natrone Means
7 Steve Van Buren AUTO 12.50 25.00
Chris Zorich
8 Steve Van Buren AUTO 12.50 25.00
Chris Zorich
9 Deacon Jones AUTO 12.50 25.00
Barry Sanders
10 Deacon Jones AUTO 12.50 25.00
Barry Sanders
11 Paul Hornung AUTO 20.00 40.00
Kevin Greene
12 Paul Hornung AUTO 20.00 40.00
Kevin Greene
13 Len Dawson AUTO 20.00 40.00
Charles Haley
14 Len Dawson AUTO 20.00 40.00
Charles Haley
15 Willie Lanier AUTO 10.00 20.00
Marshall Faulk
16 Willie Lanier AUTO 10.00 20.00
Marshall Faulk
17 Gale Sayers AUTO 25.00 50.00
Ronnie Lott
18 Gale Sayers AUTO 25.00 50.00
Ronnie Lott
19 Jack Ham AUTO 15.00 30.00
Cris Carter
20 Jack Ham AUTO 15.00 30.00
Cris Carter
21 Gale Sayers AUTO 30.00 60.00
Junior Seau
22 Gale Sayers AUTO 30.00 60.00
Junior Seau
23 Otto Graham AUTO 20.00 40.00
Reggie White
24 Otto Graham AUTO 20.00 40.00
Reggie White
25 Y.A.Tittle AUTO 20.00 40.00
Leslie O'Neal
26 Y.A.Tittle AUTO 20.00 40.00
Leslie O'Neal
27 Daryle Lamonica AUTO 12.50 25.00
Ricky Watters
28 Daryle Lamonica AUTO 12.50 25.00
Ricky Watters
29 Dick Butkus AUTO 20.00 40.00
Marshall Faulk
30 Dick Butkus AUTO 20.00 40.00
Marshall Faulk
31 Raymond Berry AUTO 12.50 25.00
Deion Sanders
32 Raymond Berry AUTO 12.50 25.00
Deion Sanders
33 Jack Youngblood AUTO 10.00 20.00
Steve Young
34 Jack Youngblood AUTO 10.00 20.00
Steve Young
35 Sammy Baugh AUTO 40.00 80.00
Bruce Smith
36 Sammy Baugh AUTO 40.00 80.00
Bruce Smith
37 Ted Hendricks AUTO 12.50 25.00
Dan Marino
38 Bob Lilly AUTO 15.00 30.00
Dan Marino
39 Ted Hendricks AUTO 12.50 25.00
Drew Bledsoe
40 Bob Lilly AUTO 15.00 30.00
Heath Shuler
41 Dick Butkus AUTO 20.00 40.00
Jeff Blake
42 Dick Butkus AUTO 20.00 40.00
Michael Westbrook
GTW1 Dick Butkus AUTO 30.00 60.00
Jeff Blake AUTO
Junior Seau AUTO
(Issued as a Promo)

1995 Collector's Edge TimeWarp Sunday Ticket

Collector's Edge originally released this set through a direct mail order offer at $19.95 per set. Each order also included a group of various free promo and preview cards. The five-card Sunday Ticket set features borderless color action player photos of a current player interacting with a previous player in a fictitious game. The backs carry information about both players on a metallic background with the serial number (of 2500 sets produced). Later a set version numbered of 10,000 was released through a special mail order offer.

COMPLETE SET (5) 4.00 10.00
*NUMBERED OF 10,000: .25X TO .5X
1 Paul Hornung .60 1.50
Chris Zorich
2 Gale Sayers .60 1.50
Kevin Greene
3 Ted Hendricks .60 1.50
Ricky Watters
4 Sammy Baugh .60 1.50
Bruce Smith
5 Dick Butkus 1.60 4.00
Marshall Faulk

1996 Collector's Edge Cowboybilia Promos

DCA20 Daryl Johnston .80 2.00
DCA21 Jay Novacek .60 1.50
DCA22 Charles Haley .60 1.50

1996 Collector's Edge Dolphinbilia Preview

This card was produced as a Preview to a card set that was never released -- Dolphinbilia. The card features Dan Marino printed on a holofoil card with a 24K logo. Each is serial numbered of 250.

DB127 Dan Marino 24K 4.00 10.00

1996 Collector's Edge 49erbilia Preview

These cards were produced as a Preview to a set that was never released -- 49erbilia. The cards feature the player printed on holofoil card stock with a 24K logo. Each was serial numbered of 250.

206 Jerry Rice 3.20 8.00
211 Steve Young 2.40 6.00

1996 Collector's Edge Packerbilia Preview

This card was produced as a Preview to a card set that was never released -- Packerbilia. The card features Brett Favre printed on a holofoil card with a 24K logo. Each is serial numbered of 250.

PB82 Brett Favre 24K 4.00 10.00

1996 Collector's Edge Promos

COMPLETE SET (4) 1.20 3.00
P1 Erric Rhett .60 1.50
P2 Junior Seau .40 1.00
P3 Terry Kirby .20 .50
NNO Cover Card .10 .30

1996 Collector's Edge

The 1996 Collector's Edge set was issued in one series totalling 240 cards. The cards were issued in six card packs with 10 packs per box and 24 boxes per case in retail, hobby, and special retail packaging. The cards are grouped alphabetically within teams and checklisted below alphabetically according to teams. Collector's Edge Cowboybilia packs also contained the base brand and insert cards with the same pack configuration. Draft Redemption cards were also randomly inserted into packs. When redeemed, a collector would receive a card of one of that teams' draft picks selected by the company. A special die cut Crucibles Eddie George promo card was produced, apparently for an insert set never released.

COMPLETE SET (250) 8.00 20.00
1 Larry Centers .07 .20
2 Garrison Hearst .07 .20
3 Dave Krieg .02 .10
4 Rob Moore .07 .20
5 Frank Sanders .07 .20
6 Eric Swann .02 .10
7 Morten Andersen .02 .10
8 Chris Doleman .02 .10
9 Bert Emanuel .07 .20
10 Jeff George .07 .20
11 Craig Heyward .02 .10
12 Terance Mathis .02 .10
13 Clay Matthews .02 .10
14 Eric Metcalf .02 .10
15 Bill Brooks .02 .10
16 Todd Collins .07 .20
17 Russell Copeland .02 .10
18 Jim Kelly .15 .40
19 Bryce Paup .02 .10
20 Andre Reed .07 .20
21 Bruce Smith .07 .20
22 Mark Carrier WR .02 .10
23 Kerry Collins .15 .40
24 Willie Green .02 .10
25 Eric Guliford .02 .10
26 Brett Maxie .02 .10
27 Tim McKyer .02 .10
28 Derrick Moore .02 .10
29 Curtis Conway .15 .40
30 Jim Flanigan .02 .10
31 Jeff Graham .02 .10
32 Robert Green .02 .10
33 Erik Kramer .02 .10
34 Rashaan Salaam .07 .20
35 Alonzo Spellman .02 .10
36 Donnell Woolford .02 .10
37 Chris Zorich .02 .10
38 Eric Bieniemy .02 .10
39 Jeff Blake .15 .40
40 Ki-Jana Carter .07 .20
41 John Copeland .02 .10
42 Harold Green .02 .10
43 Tony McGee .02 .10
44 Carl Pickens .07 .20
45 Darnay Scott .07 .20
46 Bracy Walker RC .02 .10
47 Dan Wilkinson .02 .10
48 Rob Burnett .02 .10
49 Leroy Hoard .02 .10
50 Ernest Hunter .02 .10
51 Michael Jackson .07 .20
52 Stevon Moore .02 .10
53 Anthony Pleasant .02 .10
54 Andre Rison .07 .20
55 Vinny Testaverde .07 .20
56 Eric Zeier .02 .10
57 Troy Aikman .40 1.00
58 Bill Bates .07 .20
59 Shante Carver .02 .10
60 Michael Irvin .15 .40
61 Daryl Johnston .07 .20
62 Jay Novacek .02 .10
63 Deion Sanders .25 .60
64 Emmitt Smith .60 1.50
65 Sherman Williams .02 .10
66 Terrell Davis .30 .75
67 John Elway .75 2.00
68 Ed McCaffrey .07 .20
69 Glyn Milburn .02 .10
70 Anthony Miller .07 .20
71 Michael Dean Perry .02 .10
72 Shannon Sharpe .07 .20
73 Willie Clay .02 .10
74 Scott Mitchell .07 .20
75 Herman Moore .07 .20
76 Johnnie Morton .07 .20
77 Brett Perriman .02 .10
78 Barry Sanders .60 1.50
79 Tracy Scroggins .02 .10
80 Edgar Bennett .07 .20
81 Robert Brooks .15 .40
82 Brett Favre .75 2.00
83 Dorsey Levens .15 .40
84 Craig Newsome .02 .10
85 Wayne Simmons .02 .10
86 Reggie White .15 .40
87 Chris Chandler .07 .20
88 Anthony Cook .02 .10
89 Mel Gray .02 .10
90 Haywood Jeffires .02 .10
91 Darryll Lewis .02 .10
92 Steve McNair .30 .75
93 Todd McNair .02 .10
94 Rodney Thomas .02 .10
95 Trev Alberts .02 .10
96 Tony Bennett .02 .10
97 Quentin Coryatt .02 .10
98 Sean Dawkins .02 .10
99 Ken Dilger .07 .20
100 Marshall Faulk .20 .50
101 Jim Harbaugh .07 .20
102 Ronald Humphrey .02 .10
103 Floyd Turner .02 .10
104 Steve Beuerlein .07 .20
105 Tony Boselli .02 .10
106 Mark Brunell .25 .60
107 Willie Jackson .07 .20
108 Jeff Lageman .02 .10
109 James O. Stewart .07 .20

110 Cedric Tillman	.02	.10
111 Marcus Allen	.15	.40
112 Kimble Anders	.07	.20
113 Steve Bono	.02	.10
114 Dale Carter	.02	.10
115 Willie Davis	.02	.10
116 Lake Dawson	.02	.10
117 Dan Saleaumua	.02	.10
118 Neil Smith	.07	.20
119 Derrick Thomas	.15	.40
120 Tamarick Vanover	.07	.20
121 Marco Coleman	.02	.10
122 Bryan Cox	.02	.10
123 Steve Emtman	.02	.10
124 Irving Fryar	.07	.20
125 Eric Green	.02	.10
126 Terry Kirby	.07	.20
127 Dan Marino	.75	2.00
128 O.J. McDuffie	.07	.20
129 Bernie Parmalee	.02	.10
130 Troy Vincent	.02	.10
131 Cris Carter	.15	.40
132 Jack Del Rio	.02	.10
133 Qadry Ismail	.07	.20
134 Amp Lee	.02	.10
135 Warren Moon	.07	.20
136 John Randle	.07	.20
137 Jake Reed	.07	.20
138 Robert Smith	.07	.20
139 Drew Bledsoe	.25	.60
140 Vincent Brisby	.02	.10
141 Ben Coates	.07	.20
142 Curtis Martin	.30	.75
143 Dave Meggett	.02	.10
144 Will Moore	.02	.10
145 Chris Slade	.02	.10
146 Mario Bates	.07	.20
147 Quinn Early	.02	.10
148 Jim Everett	.02	.10
149 Michael Haynes	.02	.10
150 Tyrone Hughes	.02	.10
151 Wayne Martin	.02	.10
152 Renaldo Turnbull	.02	.10
153 Dave Brown	.02	.10
154 Chris Calloway	.02	.10
155 Rodney Hampton	.07	.20
156 Mike Sherrard	.02	.10
157 Michael Strahan	.07	.20
158 Herschel Walker	.07	.20
159 Tyrone Wheatley	.07	.20
160 Kyle Brady	.02	.10
161 Wayne Chrebet	.25	.60
162 Hugh Douglas	.07	.20
163 Adrian Murrell	.07	.20
164 Todd Scott	.02	.10
165 Charles Wilson	.02	.10
166 Tim Brown	.15	.40
167 Aundray Bruce	.02	.10
168 Andrew Glover	.02	.10
169 Jeff Hostetler	.02	.10
170 Napoleon Kaufman	.15	.40
171 Terry McDaniel	.02	.10
172 Chester McGlockton	.02	.10
173 Pat Swilling	.02	.10
174 Harvey Williams	.02	.10
175 Fred Barnett	.02	.10
176 Randall Cunningham	.15	.40
177 William Fuller	.02	.10
178 Charlie Garner	.07	.20
179 Andy Harmon	.02	.10
180 Rodney Peete	.02	.10
181 Ricky Watters	.07	.20
182 Calvin Williams	.02	.10
183 Chad Brown	.02	.10
184 Kevin Greene	.07	.20
185 Greg Lloyd	.07	.20
186 Byron Bam Morris	.02	.10
187 Neil O'Donnell	.07	.20
188 Erric Pegram	.02	.10
189 Kordell Stewart	.15	.40
190 Yancey Thigpen	.07	.20
191 Rod Woodson	.07	.20
192 Darren Bennett	.02	.10
193 Ronnie Harmon	.02	.10
194 Stan Humphries	.07	.20
195 Tony Martin	.07	.20
196 Natrone Means	.07	.20
197 Leslie O'Neal	.02	.10
198 Junior Seau	.15	.40
199 Mark Seay	.02	.10
200 William Floyd	.07	.20
201 Merton Hanks	.02	.10
202 Brent Jones	.02	.10
203 Derek Loville	.02	.10
204 Ken Norton, Jr.	.02	.10
205 Gary Plummer	.02	.10
206 Jerry Rice	.40	1.00
207 J.J. Stokes	.15	.40
208 Dana Stubblefield	.07	.20
209 John Taylor	.02	.10
210 Bryant Young	.07	.20
211 Steve Young	.30	.75
212 Brian Blades	.02	.10
213 Joey Galloway	.15	.40
214 Carlton Gray	.02	.10
215 Cortez Kennedy	.02	.10
216 Rick Mirer	.07	.20
217 Chris Warren	.07	.20
218 Jerome Bettis	.15	.40
219 Isaac Bruce	.15	.40
220 Troy Drayton	.02	.10
221 D'Marco Farr	.02	.10
222 Sean Gilbert	.02	.10
223 Chris Miller	.02	.10
224 Roman Phifer	.02	.10
225 Trent Dilfer	.15	.40
226 Santana Dotson	.02	.10
227 Alvin Harper	.02	.10
228 Jackie Harris	.02	.10
229 John Lynch	.15	.40
230 Hardy Nickerson	.02	.10
231 Errict Rhett	.07	.20
232 Warren Sapp	.02	.10
233 Terry Allen	.07	.20
234 Henry Ellard	.02	.10
235 Gus Frerotte	.07	.20
236 Ken Harvey	.02	.10
237 Brian Mitchell	.02	.10
238 Heath Shuler	.07	.20
239 James Washington	.02	.10
240 Michael Westbrook	.15	.40
241 Checklist	.02	.10
242 Checklist	.02	.10
243 Checklist	.02	.10
244 Checklist	.02	.10
245 Checklist	.02	.10
246 Checklist	.02	.10
247 Checklist	.02	.10
248 Checklist	.02	.10
249 Checklist	.02	.10
250 Checklist	.02	.10
PR1 Eddie George Promo die cut Crucibles promo	.20	.50

1996 Collector's Edge Die Cuts

*STARS: 1.2X TO 3X BASIC CARDS
ONE PER SPECIAL RETAIL PACK

1996 Collector's Edge Holofoil

*STARS: 12X TO 30X BASIC CARDS
STATED ODDS 1:48

1996 Collector's Edge Big Easy

COMPLETE SET (19)	25.00	60.00

STATED ODDS 1:72
STATED PRINT RUN 2000 SERIAL #'d SETS
*GOLD FOILS: .2X TO .5X BASIC INSERTS
GOLDS PRINT RUN 3100 SERIAL #'d SETS
GOLD FOILS ISSUED VIA DIRECT MAIL OFFER

1 Kerry Collins	1.00	2.50
2 Rashaan Salaam	.50	1.25
3 Troy Aikman	2.50	6.00
4 Deion Sanders	1.50	4.00
5 Emmitt Smith	4.00	10.00
6 Terrell Davis	2.00	5.00
7 Barry Sanders	4.00	10.00
8 Brett Favre	5.00	12.00
9 Marshall Faulk	1.25	3.00
10 Tamarick Vanover	.50	1.25
11 Dan Marino	5.00	12.00
12 Drew Bledsoe	1.50	4.00
13 Curtis Martin	2.00	5.00
14 J.J.Stokes	1.00	2.50
15 Joey Galloway	1.00	2.50
16 Isaac Bruce	1.00	2.50
17 Errict Rhett	.50	1.25
18 Carl Pickens	.50	1.25
NNO Checklist Card	.25	.60
P1 Errict Rhett Promo	.30	.75

1996 Collector's Edge Cowboybilia

COMPLETE SET (25)	10.00	20.00

TWO PER 1997 COWBOYBILIA PLUS

Q1 Chris Boniol	.20	.50
Q2 John Jett	.20	.50
Q3 Sherman Williams	.20	.50
Q4 Chad Hennings	.20	.50
Q5 Larry Allen	.20	.50
Q6 Jason Garrett	.50	1.25
Q7 Tony Tolbert	.20	.50
Q8 Kevin Williams	.20	.50
Q9 Mark Tuinei	.20	.50
Q10 Larry Brown/4000 MVP gold foil	.20	.50
Q11 Kevin Smith	.20	.50
Q12 Darrin Smith	.20	.50
Q13 Robert Jones	.20	.50
Q14 Nate Newton	.20	.50
Q15 Darren Woodson	.30	.75
Q16 Leon Lett	.30	.75
Q17 Russell Maryland	.20	.50
Q18 Erik Williams	.20	.50
Q19 Bill Bates	.30	.75
Q20 Daryl Johnston	.30	.75
Q21 Jay Novacek	.30	.75
Q22 Charles Haley	.30	.75
Q23 Troy Aikman	1.50	3.00
Q24 Michael Irvin	.60	1.50
Q25 Emmitt Smith	2.50	5.00

1996 Collector's Edge Cowboybilia Autographs

STATED ODDS 1:2.5 COWBOYBILIA

STATED PRINT RUN 500-4000	10.00	25.00
DCA1 Chris Boniol/4000	6.00	15.00
DCA2 John Jett/4000	6.00	15.00
DCA3 Sherman Williams/4000	6.00	15.00
DCA4 Chad Hennings/4000	6.00	15.00
DCA5 Larry Allen/4000	15.00	30.00
DCA6 Jason Garrett/4000	10.00	25.00
DCA7 Tony Tolbert/4000	6.00	15.00
DCA8 Kevin Williams/4000	6.00	15.00
DCA9 Mark Tuinei/4000	15.00	30.00
DCA10 Larry Brown/1000	8.00	20.00
DCA11 Kevin Smith/4000	8.00	20.00
DCA12 Darrin Smith/4000	6.00	15.00
DCA13 Robert Jones/4000	6.00	15.00
DCA14 Nate Newton/4000	8.00	20.00
DCA15 D.Woodson/4000	10.00	25.00
DCA16 Leon Lett/4000	10.00	25.00
DCA17 Russell Maryland/4000	8.00	20.00
DCA18 Erik Williams/4000	8.00	20.00
DCA19 Bill Bates/4000	10.00	25.00
DCA20 Daryl Johnston/2300	25.00	40.00
DCA21 Jay Novacek/2300	20.00	50.00
DCA22 Charles Haley/2300	20.00	40.00
DCA23 Troy Aikman/600 all cards unsigned	40.00	80.00
DCA24 Michael Irvin/500	100.00	200.00
DCA25 Emmitt Smith/500	50.00	120.00
NNO Roger Staubach Drew Pearson Hail Mary Pass #'d/1000	50.00	120.00

1996 Collector's Edge Cowboybilia 24K Holofoil

COMPLETE SET (4)	100.00	200.00

STATED ODDS 1:48 1996 COWBOYBILIA

CB57 Troy Aikman	15.00	40.00
CB60 Michael Irvin	6.00	15.00
CB63 Deion Sanders	10.00	25.00
CB64 Emmitt Smith	25.00	60.00

1996 Collector's Edge Draft Day Redemption

STATED ODDS 1:8

1 Arizona Cardinals	.08	.25
2 Atlanta Falcons	.08	.25
3 Buffalo Bills	.08	.25
4 Carolina Panthers	.08	.25
5 Chicago Bears	.08	.25
6 Cincinnati Bengals	.08	.25
7 Cleveland Browns	.08	.25
8 Dallas Cowboys	.08	.25
9 Denver Broncos	.08	.25
10 Detroit Lions	.08	.25
11 Green Bay Packers	.08	.25
12 Houston Oilers	.08	.25
13 Indianapolis Colts	.08	.25
14 Jacksonville Jaguars	.08	.25
15 Kansas City Chiefs	.08	.25
16 Los Angeles Raiders	.08	.25
17 Miami Dolphins	.08	.25
18 Minnesota Vikings	.08	.25
19 New England Patriots	.08	.25
20 New Orleans Saints	.08	.25
21 New York Giants	.08	.25
22 New York Jets	.08	.25
23 Philadelphia Eagles	.08	.25
24 Pittsburgh Steelers	.08	.25
25 San Diego Chargers	.08	.25
26 San Francisco 49ers	.08	.25
27 Seattle Seahawks	.08	.25
28 St.Louis Rams	.08	.25
29 Tampa Bay Buccaneers	.08	.25
30 Washington Redskins	.08	.25

1996 Collector's Edge Draft Day Redemption Prizes

COMPLETE SET (30)	25.00	60.00
1 Simeon Rice	1.50	4.00
2 Richard Huntley	.75	2.00
3 Jonathan Ogden	1.25	3.00
4 Eric Moulds	1.25	3.00
5 Tim Biakabutuka	1.25	3.00
6 Walt Harris	.50	1.25
7 Marco Battaglia	.50	1.25
8 Stepfret Williams	.50	1.25
9 John Mobley	.50	1.25
10 Reggie Brown LB	.50	1.25
11 Derrick Mayes	.75	2.00
12 Eddie George	2.00	5.00
13 Marvin Harrison	4.00	8.00
14 Kevin Hardy	.50	1.25
15 Jerome Woods	.50	1.25
16 Karim Abdul-Jabbar	.75	2.00
17 Duane Clemons	.50	1.25
18 Terry Glenn	1.25	3.00
19 Ricky Whittle	.50	1.25
20 Amani Toomer	1.50	4.00
21 Keyshawn Johnson	1.25	3.00
22 Rickey Dudley	.75	2.00
23 Bobby Hoying	.75	2.00
24 Jahine Arnold	.50	1.25
25 Tony Banks	.75	2.00
26 Bryan Still	.50	1.25
27 Terrell Owens	4.00	8.00
28 Reggie Brown RBK	.50	1.25
29 Mike Alstott	1.25	3.00
30 Stephen Davis	2.50	6.00

1996 Collector's Edge Proteges

COMPLETE SET (13)	30.00	80.00

STATED ODDS 1:164

1 Eric Metcalf Joey Galloway	2.00	5.00
2 Herman Moore Michael Westbrook	2.00	5.00
3 Emmitt Smith Errict Rhett	6.00	15.00
4 Kordell Stewart John Elway	7.50	20.00
5 Terrell Davis Marshall Faulk	7.50	20.00
6 Rashaan Salaam Marcus Allen	2.00	5.00
7 Dan Marino Drew Bledsoe	7.50	20.00
8 Brett Favre Kerry Collins	7.50	20.00
9 Tim Brown Isaac Bruce	2.00	5.00
10 Cris Carter Chris Sanders	1.50	4.00
11 Curtis Martin Chris Warren	3.00	8.00
12 Tamarick Vanover Brian Mitchell	2.00	5.00
PR1 Rashaan Salaam Promo Terry Kirby	.40	1.00
NNO Checklist Card	.75	2.00

1996 Collector's Edge Quantum Motion

COMPLETE SET (25)	30.00	80.00

STATED ODDS 1:36 1996 EDGE PACKS
STATED ODDS 1:50 1997 COWBOYBILIA
*FOIL CARDS: .4X TO 1X BASIC INSERTS

1 Troy Aikman	3.00	8.00
2 Marcus Allen	1.25	3.00
3 Drew Bledsoe	2.00	5.00
4 Tim Brown	1.25	3.00
5 Isaac Bruce	1.25	3.00
6 Mark Brunell	2.00	5.00
7 Kerry Collins	1.25	3.00
8 John Elway	6.00	15.00
9 Marshall Faulk	1.50	4.00
10 Brett Favre	6.00	15.00
11 Jeff George	.60	1.50
12 Terry Kirby	.60	1.50
13 Dan Marino	6.00	15.00
14 Natrone Means	.60	1.50
15 Carl Pickens	.60	1.50
16 Errict Rhett	.60	1.50
17 Rashaan Salaam	.60	1.50
18 Deion Sanders	2.00	5.00
19 Barry Sanders	5.00	12.00
20 Emmitt Smith	5.00	12.00
21 Kordell Stewart	1.25	3.00
22 Tamarick Vanover	.60	1.50
23 Michael Westbrook	1.25	3.00
24 Steve Young	2.50	6.00
NNO Checklist Card	.30	.75
QM1 Rashaan Salaam Promo	.30	.75

1996 Collector's Edge Ripped

COMP.SERIES 1 (19)	15.00	40.00

1-18: RANDOM INSERTS IN PACKS
STATED ODDS 1:6 1997 COWBOYBILIA
*DIE CUTS: .4X TO 1X BASIC INSERTS
DIE CUTS PRINT RUN 500 SERIAL #'d SETS
DIE CUTS: AVAIL.VIA DIRECT MAIL OFFER

1 Jeff Blake	1.00	2.00
2 Steve Bono	.20	.50
3 Terrell Davis	2.00	4.00
4 John Elway	5.00	10.00
6 Brett Favre	5.00	10.00
8 Erik Kramer	.20	.50
9 Dan Marino	5.00	10.00
10 Natrone Means	.40	1.00
11 Eric Metcalf	.20	.50
12 Anthony Miller	.40	1.00
13 Herman Moore	.40	1.00
14 Errict Rhett	.40	1.00
15 Andre Rison	.40	1.00
16 Joey Galloway	1.00	2.00
17 Yancey Thigpen	.40	1.00
18 Michael Westbrook	1.00	2.00
CK1 Checklist Series 1	.20	.50
R1 Jeff Blake Promo	.30	.75

1996 Collector's Edge Too Cool Rookies

COMPLETE SET (25)	25.00	50.00

STATED ODDS 1:8 1996 EDGE PACKS
STATED ODDS 1:5 1997 COWBOYBILIA

1 Tony Boselli	.25	.60
2 Kyle Brady	.25	.60
3 Ki-Jana Carter	.60	1.25
4 Kerry Collins	1.25	2.50
5 Todd Collins	.60	1.25
6 Terrell Davis	2.50	5.00
7 Hugh Douglas	.60	1.25
8 Joey Galloway	1.25	2.50
9 Darius Holland	.25	.60
10 Napoleon Kaufman	1.25	2.50
11 Mike Mamula	1.25	2.50
12 Curtis Martin	2.50	5.00
13 Steve McNair	2.50	5.00
14 Billy Milner	.25	.60
15 Rashaan Salaam	.60	1.25
16 Frank Sanders	.60	1.25
17 Warren Sapp	.25	.60
18 James O. Stewart	.60	1.25
19 J.J. Stokes	1.25	2.50
20 Tamarick Vanover	.60	1.25
21 Michael Westbrook	1.25	2.50
22 Tyrone Wheatley	.60	1.25
23 Kordell Stewart	1.25	2.50
24 Sherman Williams	.25	.60
25 Eric Zeier	.25	.60
TC1 M.Westbrook Promo	.30	.75

1996 Collector's Edge All-Stars

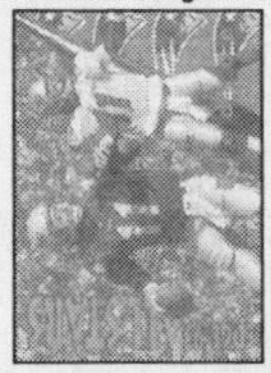

This set was released in late 1996, although the tag "Edge '95" appears on the cardfronts. Each is printed on the typical Edge plastic stock and features two color photos of the player on the front.

COMPLETE SET (13)	8.00	20.00
1 Junior Seau	.40	1.00
2 Drew Bledsoe	1.20	3.00
3 Marshall Faulk	.75	2.00
4 John Elway	2.40	6.00
5 Jerry Rice	1.20	3.00
6 Errict Rhett	.40	1.00
7 Jerome Bettis	.60	1.50
8 Deion Sanders	1.00	2.50
9 Byron Bam Morris	.40	1.00
10 Cris Carter	.60	1.50
11 Terrell Davis	2.40	6.00
12 Terance Mathis	.40	1.00
13 Checklist Card unnumbered	.40	1.00

1998 Collector's Edge Peyton Manning Promos

These unnumbered cards were issued one at a time either as promos to dealers or promos to buyers of card lots from Shop at Home. Several more special cards were issued with one featuring a facsimile silver foil autograph on the front with serial numbering of 6000 cards made. The other also features a facsimile autograph along with a diamond shaped swatch of football. The cards were unnumbered and feature identical cardbacks.

NNO Peyton Manning/6000 (holofoil Facsimile signature)	2.00	5.00
NNO Peyton Manning holding jersey	2.00	5.00
NNO Peyton Manning FB holofoil facsimile signature with football swatch)	4.00	10.00

1998 Collector's Edge Spectrum

This 25-card set features color player photos printed on silver foil stock with shimmering gold foil highlights. The backs carry another player photo and career statistics. The set could be obtained at participating Hobby Direct Shops by redeeming 36-wrappers from the 1998 Supreme Season Review. One random card of the set was received by redeeming three wrappers from Supreme Season Review packs. The cards were also randomly distributed as samples at various card shows throughout the year. An unpriced "Proof" version was also produced for each card.

COMPLETE SET (25)	4.00	10.00
1 Jamal Anderson	.15	.40
2 Antowain Smith	.15	.40
3 Corey Dillon	.40	1.00
4 Emmitt Smith	.40	1.00
5 Terrell Davis	.40	1.00
6 John Elway	.50	1.25
7 Barry Sanders	.50	1.25
8 Brett Favre	.50	1.25
9 Antonio Freeman	.15	.40
10 Marcus Allen	.15	.40
11 Dan Marino	.50	1.25
12 Cris Carter	.15	.40
13 Drew Bledsoe	.25	.60
14 Curtis Martin	.15	.40
15 Ike Hilliard	.05	.15
16 Adrian Murrell	.05	.15
17 Tim Brown	.15	.40
18 Napoleon Kaufman	.08	.25
19 Jerome Bettis	.15	.40
20 Kordell Stewart	.15	.40
21 Jim Druckenmiller	.05	.15
22 Jerry Rice	.25	.60
23 Mike Alstott	.15	.40
24 Warrick Dunn	.30	.75
25 Eddie George	.20	.50

1998 Collector's Edge Super Bowl Card Show

This 25-card set was first distributed at the 1998 Super Bowl Card Show in San Diego. Each card was available via a wrapper redemption program and serial numbered of 1000. Three wrappers from a variety of 1997 Edge football products could be redeemed for one card from this set. Each includes a player photo with the Super Bowl XXXII logo on the cardfront. A parallel set was released a month later via another wrapper redemption involving 1997 Edge Extreme and 1998 Advantage wrappers. Collectors could send in 3-wrappers for a single card, from the parallel set, or 36-wrappers for either the AFC (13-cards) or NFC (12-cards) sets. This parallel includes a gold foil AFC or NFC logo on the cardfronts. Edge also released the cards at various shows across the country during 1998. Finally, third and fourth Proof versions of the cards were issued with one set distributed at the 1998 Hawaii Trade Conference event. Each was numbered of 29-sets produced and designated as "Proof" on the cardfronts. The second Proof set was serial numbered to 500.

COMPLETE SET (25)	12.00	30.00

*GOLD FOIL: .4X TO 1X BASIC CARDS
*PROOF 29: 2X TO 5X BASIC CARDS
*PROOF 500: .5X TO 1.2X BASIC CARDS

1 Jamal Anderson	.50	1.25
2 Antowain Smith	.50	1.25
3 Corey Dillon	1.25	3.00
4 Emmitt Smith	1.20	3.00
5 Terrell Davis	1.20	3.00
6 John Elway	1.60	4.00
7 Barry Sanders	1.60	4.00
8 Brett Favre	1.60	4.00
9 Antonio Freeman	.50	1.25
10 Marcus Allen	.50	1.25
11 Dan Marino	1.60	4.00
12 Cris Carter	.50	1.25
13 Drew Bledsoe	.80	2.00
14 Troy Davis	.20	.50
15 Ike Hilliard	.20	.50
16 Adrian Murrell	.30	.75
17 Tim Brown	.50	1.25
18 Napoleon Kaufman	.50	1.25
19 Jerome Bettis	.50	1.25
20 Kordell Stewart	.50	1.25
21 Jim Druckenmiller	.20	.50
22 Jerry Rice	.80	2.00
23 Mike Alstott	.50	1.25
24 Warrick Dunn	.75	2.00
25 Eddie George	.80	2.00

1998 Collector's Edge Super Bowl XXXII

This set was issued directly to dealers who attended the Super Bowl XXXII Card Show. It features players of the Broncos and Packers the two teams which competed in the game. Each card is highlighted with gold or silver foil printing on the cardfronts.

COMPLETE SET (26)	6.00	15.00

*SILVERS: SAME PRICE

1 John Elway	1.50	4.00
2 Terrell Davis	1.00	2.50
3 Shannon Sharpe	.20	.50
4 Ed McCaffrey	.20	.50
5 Rod Smith WR	.30	.75
6 Ray Crockett	.10	.30
7 Darrien Gordon	.10	.30
8 Bill Romanowski	.10	.30
9 Neil Smith	.20	.50
10 John Mobley	.10	.30
11 Steve Atwater	.10	.30
12 Alfred Williams	.10	.30
13 Vaughn Hebron	.10	.30
14 Brett Favre	1.50	4.00
15 Robert Brooks	.20	.50
16 Antonio Freeman	.30	.75
17 Dorsey Levens	.30	.75
18 Mark Chmura	.10	.30
19 Ross Verba	.10	.30
20 William Henderson	.10	.30
21 Ryan Longwell	.10	.30
22 Reggie White	.30	.75
23 Bernardo Harris	.10	.30
24 LeRoy Butler	.10	.30
25 Eugene Robinson	.10	.30
T1 Score Board Final Score	.10	.30

1999 Collector's Edge Peyton Manning Game Gear Promos

These Game Gear cards were issued one at a time either as promos to dealers or promos to buyers of card lots from Shop at Home. Each includes a diamond shaped swatch of football along with the words "Game Gear" at the top or bottom of the cardfront. The cardbacks are identical for each card and are each numbered simply "PM." We've assigned an additional number below for ease in cataloging.

PM1 Peyton Manning (white jersey, passing to the left)	6.00	15.00
PM2 Peyton Manning (white jersey, passing to the right)	6.00	15.00
PM3 Peyton Manning (blue jersey, dropping back swatch on left side)	6.00	15.00
PM4 Peyton Manning (blue jersey, dropping back swatch in lower right)	6.00	15.00
PM5 Peyton Manning (blue jersey, handing-off ball)	6.00	15.00
PM6 Peyton Manning (1999 Triumph card swatch in lower right)	6.00	15.00
PM7 Peyton Manning (1999 Triumph card swatch on left side)	6.00	15.00

1999 Collector's Edge Super Bowl XXXIII

COMPLETE SET (25)	10.00	20.00
A1 Jamal Anderson	.40	1.00
A1B Scoreboard	.30	.75
A2 Keith Brooking	.30	.75
A3 Chris Chandler	.40	1.00
A4 Tim Dwight	.40	1.00
A5 Jammi German	.30	.75
A6 Cornelius Bennett	.40	1.00
A7 Ken Oxendine	.30	.75
A8 Tony Martin	.40	1.00
A9 Terance Mathis	.40	1.00
A10 O.J. Santiago	.30	.75
A11 Jessie Tuggle	.30	.75
B1 Bubby Brister	.40	1.00
B2 Ray Crockett	.30	.75
B3 Terrell Davis	.75	2.00
B4 John Elway	1.50	4.00
B5 Brian Griese	.50	1.25
B6 Darrien Gordon	.30	.75
B7 Ed McCaffrey	.40	1.00
B8 Bill Romanowski	.40	1.00
B9 Shannon Sharpe	.50	1.25
B10 Howard Griffith	.30	.75
B11 Rod Smith	.40	1.00
R1 Peyton Manning	1.50	4.00
R2 Randy Moss	.75	2.00

2000 Collector's Edge Peyton Manning Destiny

This set was produced in 2000 by Collectors Edge and intended to be released in box set form as well as inserts in various packs at the time. It is thought that some cards did make it into some packs in 2000, but the majority of the cards were released much later after CE suspended their football card operations. Each card in the basic unnumbered set features gold foil highlights on the front. Five additional reprinted cards from other Edge products were also printed along with these 45-cards. Complete sets of all 50-cards in the factory sealed box can often be found. Several numbered parallel versions were also produced with each featuring its own foil color on the front and serial numbering on the back. The most interesting card in the set features a boyhood photo of the three Manning brothers including a very young Eli.

COMPLETE SET (50)	10.00	25.00

*BLUE/75: .8X TO 2X GOLD
BLUE PRINT RUN 75 SER.#'d SETS
*BLUE HOLO/50: .8X TO 2X GOLD
BLUE HOLOFOIL PRINT RUN 50
*GREEN/400: .5X TO 1.2X GOLD
GREEN PRINT RUN 400 SER.#'d SETS
*RED/18: 1.2X TO 3X GOLD
RED PRINT RUN 18 SER.#'d SETS
*RED HOLO/25: 1.2X TO 3X GOLD
RED HOLOFOIL PRINT RUN 25

PM1 Peyton Manning	.40	1.00
PM2 Peyton Manning	.40	1.00
PM3 Peyton Manning	.40	1.00
PM4 Peyton Manning	.40	1.00
PM5 Peyton Manning	.40	1.00
PM6 Peyton Manning	.40	1.00
PM7 Peyton Manning	.40	1.00
PM8 Peyton Manning	.40	1.00
PM9 Peyton Manning	.40	1.00
PM10 Peyton Manning	.40	1.00
PM11 Peyton Manning	.40	1.00
PM12 Peyton Manning	.40	1.00
PM13 Peyton Manning	.40	1.00
PM14 Peyton Manning	.40	1.00
PM15 Peyton Manning	.40	1.00
PM16 Peyton Manning	.40	1.00
PM17 Peyton Manning	.40	1.00
PM18 Peyton Manning	.40	1.00
PM19 Peyton Manning	.40	1.00
PM20 Peyton Manning	.40	1.00
PM21 Peyton Manning	.40	1.00
PM22 Peyton Manning	.40	1.00
PM23 Peyton Manning	.40	1.00
PM24 Peyton Manning	.40	1.00
PM25 Peyton Manning	.40	1.00
PM26 Peyton Manning	.40	1.00
PM27 Peyton Manning	.40	1.00
PM28 Peyton Manning	.40	1.00
PM29 Peyton Manning	.40	1.00
PM30 Peyton Manning	.40	1.00
PM31 Peyton Manning	.40	1.00
PM32 Peyton Manning	.40	1.00
PM33 Peyton Manning	.40	1.00
PM34 Peyton Manning	.40	1.00
PM35 Peyton Manning	.40	1.00
PM36 Peyton Manning	.40	1.00
PM37 Peyton Manning	.40	1.00
PM38 Title Card (NFL Shield)	.08	.25
PM39 Certificate Card	.08	.25
PM40 Peyton Manning 98 REV (1999 CE Fury design)	.40	1.00
PM41 Peyton Manning 98 REV (1999 CE Triumph design)	.40	1.00
PM42 Peyton Manning Archie Manning	.40	1.00
PM43 Peyton Manning Childhood photo with Eli Manning and Cooper Manning	2.00	5.00
PM44 Peyton Manning	.40	1.00
PM45 Peyton Manning	.40	1.00
PM46 Peyton Manning	.40	1.00
53 Peyton Manning (1999 Supreme reprint no Supreme logo on front)	.40	1.00
59 Peyton Manning/2000 Supreme reprint no Supreme logo on front)	.40	1.00
66 Peyton Manning (1999 Odyssey reprint missing Odyssey logo)	.40	1.00
67 Peyton Manning (1999 Advantage reprint no Advantage logo on front)	.40	1.00

2000 Collector's Edge Pro Signature Authentic Unsigned Promos

These unsigned Pro Signature Authentic cards surfaced long after Edge ceased card operations. They follow the style of the 2000 T3 Rookie Ink cards with a different set name at the top of the card and each was printed with gold foil on the fronts. They apparently were samples or promos for veteran signed inserts that were never issued.

AS Akili Smith unsigned	1.50	4.00
DC Daunte Culpepper unsigned	2.00	5.00
GC Germane Crowell unsigned	1.50	4.00
PM Peyton Manning unsigned	3.00	8.00
TC Tim Couch unsigned	1.50	4.00
TH Torry Holt unsigned	2.00	5.00

1996 Collector's Edge Advantage Promos

1 Jeff Blake Base Brand	.60	1.50
2 Steve Bono Game Ball	.80	2.00
3 Rashaan Salaam Crystal Cuts	.60	1.50
4 Michael Westbrook Role Models	.60	1.50

1996 Collector's Edge Advantage

The 1996 Collector's Edge Advantage set was issued in one series totalling 150 cards and features color player photos on front and back embossed gold foil stamped cards. The six-card packs retail for $2.69 each.

COMPLETE SET (150)	10.00	25.00
1 Drew Bledsoe	.30	.75
2 Chris Warren	.08	.25
3 Eddie George RC	.60	1.50
4 Barry Sanders	.75	2.00
5 Scott Mitchell	.08	.25
6 Carl Pickens	.08	.25
7 Tim Brown	.20	.50
8 John Elway	1.00	2.50
9 Michael Westbrook	.20	.50
10 Cris Carter	.20	.50
11 Troy Aikman	.50	1.25
12 Ben Coates	.08	.25
13 Brett Favre	1.25	2.50
14 Marshall Faulk	.25	.60
15 Steve Young	.40	1.00
16 Terrell Davis	.40	1.00
17 Keyshawn Johnson RC	.50	1.25
18 Mario Bates	.08	.25
19 Steve McNair	.40	1.00
20 Kerry Collins	.20	.50
21 Natrone Means	.08	.25
22 Kordell Stewart	.20	.50
23 Jeff George	.08	.25
24 Rick Mirer	.08	.25
25 Herman Moore	.08	.25
26 Rodney Peete	.05	.15
27 Isaac Bruce	.20	.50
28 Errict Rhett	.08	.25
29 Jerry Rice	.50	1.25
30 Rashaan Salaam	.08	.25
31 Eric Metcalf	.05	.15
32 Jim Kelly	.20	.50
33 Jerome Bettis	.20	.50
34 Deion Sanders	.30	.75
35 J.J. Stokes	.20	.50
36 Neil O'Donnell	.08	.25
37 Marcus Allen	.20	.50
38 Thurman Thomas	.20	.50
39 Dan Marino	1.00	2.50
40 Rickey Dudley RC	.20	.50
41 Napoleon Kaufman	.20	.50
42 Kyle Brady	.05	.15
43 Emmitt Smith	.75	2.00
44 Tyrone Wheatley	.08	.25
45 Jeff Blake	.20	.50
46 Reggie White	.20	.50
47 Joey Galloway	.20	.50
48 Antonio Langham	.05	.15
49 Craig Heyward	.05	.15
50 Curtis Martin	.40	1.00
51 Karim Abdul-Jabbar RC	.20	.50
52 Antonio Freeman	.20	.50
53 Ki-Jana Carter	.08	.25
54 Willie Davis	.05	.15
55 Jim Everett	.05	.15
56 Gus Frerotte	.08	.25
57 Daryl Gardener RC	.05	.15
58 Charles Haley	.08	.25
59 Michael Irvin	.20	.50
60 Keith Jackson	.05	.15
61 Cortez Kennedy	.05	.15
62 Greg Lloyd	.08	.25
63 Tony Martin	.08	.25
64 Ken Norton Jr.	.05	.15
65 Bobby Hoying RC	.20	.50
66 Bryce Paup	.05	.15
67 Jake Reed	.08	.25
68 Frank Sanders	.08	.25
69 Vinny Testaverde	.08	.25
70 Regan Upshaw RC	.05	.15
71 Tamarick Vanover	.08	.25
72 Walt Harris RC	.05	.15
73 John Randle	.08	.25
74 Ricky Watters	.08	.25
75 Terry Allen	.08	.25
76 Edgar Bennett	.08	.25
77 Larry Centers	.08	.25
78 Chris Penn	.05	.15
79 Bobby Engram RC	.20	.50
80 Irving Fryar	.08	.25
81 Charlie Garner	.08	.25
82 Rodney Hampton	.08	.25
83 Michael Jackson	.08	.25

84 O.J. McDuffie .08 .25
85 Shannon Sharpe .08 .25
86 Aaron Hayden .05 .15
87 Muhsin Muhammad RC .40 1.00
88 Rod Woodson .08 .25
89 Levon Kirkland .05 .15
90 Chad Brown .05 .15
91 Junior Seau .20 .50
92 Terry Kirby .08 .25
93 Zach Thomas RC .30 .75
94 Harvey Williams .05 .15
95 Robert Brooks .20 .50
96 Darrell Green .05 .15
97 Chester McGlockton .05 .15
98 Neil Smith .08 .25
99 Eric Swann .05 .15
100 Mike Alstott RC .50 1.25
101 Tim Biakabutuka RC .20 .50
102 Mark Brunell .30 .75
103 Chris Doleman .05 .15
104 Sean Gilbert .05 .15
105 Jim Harbaugh .08 .25
106 Chris T. Jones .08 .25
107 Tyrone Hughes .05 .15
108 Amani Toomer RC .50 1.25
109 Larry Brown .05 .15
110 Kevin Greene .08 .25
111 John Mobley .05 .15
112 Danny Kanell RC .20 .50
113 Kevin Hardy RC .20 .50
114 Brett Perriman .05 .15
115 Simeon Rice RC .50 1.25
116 Chris Sanders .08 .25
117 Dave Brown .05 .15
118 Bryan Cox .05 .15
119 Yancey Thigpen .08 .25
120 Terance Mathis .05 .15
121 Warren Moon .08 .25
122 Derrick Thomas .20 .50
123 Trent Dilfer .20 .50
124 Terry Glenn RC .50 1.25
125 Jeff Hostetler .05 .15
126 Leeland McElroy RC .08 .25
127 Hardy Nickerson .05 .15
128 Steve Bono .05 .15
129 Stanley Pritchett RC .08 .25
130 Dana Stubblefield .08 .25
131 Andre Coleman .05 .15
132 Anthony Miller .08 .25
133 Stan Humphries .08 .25
134 Robert Smith .08 .25
135 Curtis Conway .20 .50
136 Darick Holmes .05 .15
137 Pat Swilling .05 .15
138 Andre Rison .08 .25
139 Erik Kramer .05 .15
140 Jason Dunn RC .08 .25
141 Torrance Small .05 .15
142 Cedric Jones RC .05 .15
143 Derek Loville .05 .15
144 Brian Mitchell .05 .15
145 Eric Moulds RC .60 1.50
146 James O.Stewart .08 .25
147 Bruce Smith .08 .25
148 Keenan McCardell .20 .50
149 Warren Sapp .05 .15
150 Marvin Harrison RC 1.25 3.00

1996 Collector's Edge Advantage Perfect Play Foils

COMPLETE SET (150) 40.00 100.00
*STARS: 3X TO 6X BASIC CARDS
*RCs: 1.5X TO 3X BASIC CARDS
STATED ODDS 1:2

1996 Collector's Edge Advantage Crystal Cuts

COMPLETE SET (25) 50.00 100.00
STATED ODDS 1:8
STATED PRINT RUN 5000 SERIAL #'d SETS
*SILVER FOILS: SAME PRICE
SILVERS PRINT RUN 3100 SERIAL #'d SETS
CC1 Barry Sanders 4.00 10.00
CC2 Eddie George 1.50 4.00
CC3 Curtis Martin 2.00 5.00
CC4 J.J. Stokes 1.00 2.50
CC5 Kyle Brady .30 .75
CC6 Chris Warren .50 1.25
CC7 Jerry Rice 2.50 6.00
CC8 Ben Coates .50 1.25
CC9 Terrell Davis 2.00 5.00
CC10 Marcus Allen 1.00 2.50
CC11 John Elway 5.00 12.00
CC12 Joey Galloway 1.00 2.50
CC13 Dan Marino 5.00 12.00
CC14 Napoleon Kaufman 1.00 2.50
CC15 Emmitt Smith 4.00 10.00
CC16 Eric Metcalf .30 .75
CC17 Kerry Collins 1.00 2.50
CC18 Troy Aikman 2.50 6.00
CC19 Rickey Dudley .50 1.25
CC20 Steve McNair 2.00 5.00
CC21 Steve Young 2.00 5.00
CC22 Isaac Bruce 1.00 2.50
CC23 Kordell Stewart 1.00 2.50
CC24 LeShon Johnson .50 1.25
CC25 Scott Mitchell .50 1.25

1996 Collector's Edge Advantage Video

COMPLETE SET (25) 60.00 150.00
STATED ODDS 1:36
STATED PRINT RUN 2000 SERIAL #'d SETS
*DIE CUT/300: 1.2X TO 3X BASIC INSERT/2000
V1 Brett Favre 10.00 25.00
V2 Keyshawn Johnson 2.50 6.00
V3 Deion Sanders 3.00 8.00
V4 Marcus Allen 2.50 6.00
V5 Rashaan Salaam 1.25 3.00
V6 Thurman Thomas 2.50 6.00
V7 Emmitt Smith 8.00 20.00
V8 Isaac Bruce 2.50 6.00
V9 Michael Westbrook 2.50 6.00
V10 Cris Carter 2.50 6.00
V11 Marshall Faulk 3.00 8.00
V12 Jerry Rice 6.00 15.00
V13 Tim Brown 2.50 6.00
V14 Steve Young 4.00 10.00
V15 Eric Metcalf .75 2.00
V16 Chris Warren 1.25 3.00
V17 Drew Bledsoe 2.50 6.00
V18 Barry Sanders 8.00 20.00
V19 Herman Moore 1.25 3.00
V20 Rodney Peete .75 2.00
V21 Troy Aikman 5.00 12.00
V22 Jerome Bettis 2.50 6.00
V23 Errict Rhett 1.25 3.00
V24 Dan Marino 10.00 25.00
V25 Natrone Means 1.25 3.00

1996 Collector's Edge Advantage Game Ball

STATED ODDS 1:72
RICE AUTO ODDS 1:12,000 98 CE MASTERS
G1 Kordell Stewart 4.00 10.00
G2 Emmitt Smith 25.00 60.00
G3 Brett Favre 25.00 60.00
G4 Steve Young 10.00 25.00
G5 Barry Sanders 20.00 50.00
G6 John Elway 25.00 60.00
G7 Drew Bledsoe 6.00 15.00
G8 Dan Marino 25.00 60.00
G9 Keyshawn Johnson 5.00 12.00
G10 Eddie George 5.00 12.00
G11 Kevin Hardy 4.00 10.00
G12 Terry Glenn 5.00 12.00
G13 Michael Westbrook 4.00 10.00
G14 Joey Galloway 5.00 12.00
G15 John Mobley 4.00 10.00
G16 Curtis Martin 7.50 20.00
G17 Rashaan Salaam 4.00 10.00
G18 J.J. Stokes 4.00 10.00
G19 Kerry Collins 5.00 12.00
G20 Deion Sanders 6.00 15.00
G21 Shannon Sharpe 5.00 12.00
G22 Terry Allen 4.00 10.00
G23 Ricky Watters 4.00 10.00
G24 Marshall Faulk 6.00 15.00
G25 Tim Biakabutuka 4.00 10.00
G26 Troy Aikman 12.00 30.00
G27 Jerry Rice 20.00 50.00
G28 Chris Warren 4.00 10.00
G29 Jeff Blake 5.00 12.00
G30 Carl Pickens 4.00 10.00
G31 Isaac Bruce 5.00 12.00
G32 Terrell Davis 6.00 15.00
G33 Mark Brunell 5.00 12.00
G34 Karim Abdul-Jabbar 4.00 10.00
G35 Herman Moore 4.00 10.00
G36 Cris Carter 6.00 15.00
NNO Checklist Card .40 1.00
G27AU Jerry Rice AU/50 150.00 300.00

1996 Collector's Edge Advantage Role Models

COMPLETE SET (13) 25.00 50.00
STATED ODDS 1:12
RM1 John Elway 6.00 12.00
RM2 Dan Marino 6.00 12.00
RM3 Jerry Rice 3.00 6.00
RM4 Emmitt Smith 5.00 10.00
RM5 Chris Warren .60 1.25
RM6 Tim Brown 1.25 2.50
RM7 Jeff George .60 1.25
RM8 Tyrone Wheatley .60 1.25
RM9 Steve Bono .30 .75
RM10 Kerry Collins 1.25 2.50
RM11 Jerome Bettis 1.25 2.50
RM12 Steve Beuerlein 1.25 2.50
NNO Checklist Card .30 .75

1996 Collector's Edge Advantage Super Bowl Game Ball

STATED ODDS 1:164
SB1 Emmitt Smith 30.00 80.00
SB2 Troy Aikman 25.00 50.00
SB3 Michael Irvin 10.00 25.00
SB4 Deion Sanders 12.00 30.00
SB5 John Elway 30.00 80.00
SB6 Dan Marino 30.00 80.00
SB7 Marcus Allen 10.00 25.00
SB8 Kordell Stewart 10.00 25.00
SB9 Steve Young 20.00 40.00
SB10 Ricky Watters 8.00 20.00
SB11 Jerry Rice 25.00 60.00
SB12 Jim Kelly 12.00 30.00
SB13 Thurman Thomas 10.00 25.00
SB14 Bruce Smith 6.00 15.00
SB15 Stan Humphries 6.00 15.00
SB16 Junior Seau 10.00 25.00
SB17 Natrone Means 8.00 20.00
SB18 Neil O'Donnell 8.00 20.00
SB19 Rod Woodson 10.00 25.00
SB20 Andre Reed 10.00 25.00
SB21 Jeff Hostetler 6.00 15.00
SB22 Dave Meggett 6.00 15.00
SB23 Greg Lloyd 6.00 15.00
SB24 Kevin Greene 10.00 25.00
SB25 Yancey Thigpen 6.00 15.00
SB26 Charles Haley 8.00 20.00
SB27 Byron Bam Morris 6.00 15.00
SB28 Alvin Harper 6.00 15.00
SB29 Ken Norton Jr. 6.00 15.00
SB30 William Floyd 6.00 15.00
SB31 Leslie O'Neal 6.00 15.00
SB32 Jay Novacek 10.00 25.00
SB33 Irving Fryar 8.00 20.00
SB34 Leon Lett 6.00 15.00
SB35 Tony Martin 6.00 15.00
SB36 Mark Collins 6.00 15.00

1998 Collector's Edge Advantage

The 1998 Collector's Edge Advantage set was originally issued in one series totaling 180-cards and was distributed in six-card packs with a suggested retail price of $5.99. The fronts feature large player head shots over an action photo with a shadow version of the head photo in the background. The backs carry player information. Twenty "update" and Rookie Cards were inserted in late issue retail boxes as a box topper.

COMPLETE SET (200) 25.00 60.00
COMP.SHORT SET (180) 20.00 50.00
1 Larry Centers .20 .50
2 Kent Graham .20 .50
3 LeShon Johnson .20 .50
4 Leeland McElroy .20 .50
5 Jake Plummer .50 1.25
6 Jamal Anderson .50 1.25
7 Chris Chandler .30 .75
8 Bert Emanuel .30 .75
9 Byron Hanspard .20 .50
10 O.J. Santiago .20 .50
11 Derrick Alexander WR .30 .75
12 Peter Boulware .20 .50
13 Eric Green .20 .50
14 Michael Jackson .20 .50
15 Byron Bam Morris .20 .50
16 Vinny Testaverde .30 .75
17 Todd Collins .20 .50
18 Quinn Early .20 .50
19 Jim Kelly .50 1.25
20 Andre Reed .30 .75
21 Antowain Smith .50 1.25
22 Steve Tasker .20 .50
23 Thurman Thomas .50 1.25
24 Steve Beuerlein .30 .75
25 Rae Carruth .20 .50
26 Kerry Collins .30 .75
27 Anthony Johnson .20 .50
28 Ernie Mills .20 .50
29 Wesley Walls .30 .75
30 Curtis Conway .30 .75
31 Bobby Engram .30 .75
32 Raymont Harris .20 .50
33 Erik Kramer .20 .50
34 Rick Mirer .20 .50
35 Darnay Scott .30 .75
36 Tony McGee .20 .50
37 Jeff Blake .30 .75
38 Corey Dillon .50 1.25
39 Carl Pickens .30 .75
40 Troy Aikman 1.25 2.50
41 Billy Davis .20 .50
42 David LaFleur .20 .50
43 Anthony Miller .20 .50
44 Emmitt Smith 2.00 4.00
45 Herschel Walker .30 .75
46 Sherman Williams .20 .50
47 Flipper Anderson .20 .50
48 Terrell Davis .50 1.25
49 Jason Elam .20 .50
50 John Elway 2.50 5.00
51 Darrien Gordon .20 .50
52 Ed McCaffrey .30 .75
53 Shannon Sharpe .30 .75
54 Neil Smith .30 .75
55 Rod Smith WR .30 .75
56 Maa Tanuvasa .20 .50
57 Glyn Milburn .20 .50
58 Scott Mitchell .30 .75
59 Herman Moore .30 .75
60 Johnnie Morton .30 .75
61 Barry Sanders 1.50 4.00
62 Tommy Vardell .20 .50
63 Bryant Westbrook .20 .50
64 Robert Brooks .30 .75
65 Mark Chmura .30 .75
66 Brett Favre 2.50 5.00
67 Antonio Freeman .50 1.25
68 Dorsey Levens .50 1.25
69 Bill Schroeder RC .75 2.00
70 Marshall Faulk .60 1.50
71 Jim Harbaugh .30 .75
72 Marvin Harrison .50 1.25
73 Derek Brown TE .20 .50
74 Mark Brunell .50 1.25
75 Rob Johnson .30 .75
76 Keenan McCardell .30 .75
77 Natrone Means .30 .75
78 Jimmy Smith .30 .75
79 James O.Stewart .30 .75
80 Marcus Allen .50 1.25
81 Pat Barnes .20 .50
82 Tony Gonzalez .50 1.25
83 Elvis Grbac .30 .75
84 Greg Hill .20 .50
85 Kevin Lockett .20 .50
86 Andre Rison .30 .75
87 Karim Abdul-Jabbar .50 1.25
88 Fred Barnett .20 .50
89 Troy Drayton .20 .50
90 Dan Marino 2.50 5.00
91 Irving Spikes .20 .50
92 Cris Carter .50 1.25
93 Matthew Hatchette .20 .50
94 Brad Johnson .50 1.25
95 Jake Reed .30 .75
96 Robert Smith .50 1.25
97 Drew Bledsoe .75 2.00
98 Keith Byars .20 .50
99 Ben Coates .30 .75
100 Terry Glenn .50 1.25
101 Shawn Jefferson .20 .50
102 Curtis Martin .50 1.25
103 Dave Meggett .20 .50
104 Troy Davis .20 .50
105 Danny Wuerffel .30 .75
106 Ray Zellars .20 .50
107 Tiki Barber .50 1.25
108 Rodney Hampton .30 .75
109 Ike Hilliard .30 .75
110 Danny Kanell .30 .75
111 Tyrone Wheatley .30 .75
112 Kyle Brady .20 .50
113 Wayne Chrebet .50 1.25
114 Aaron Glenn .20 .50
115 Jeff Graham .20 .50
116 Keyshawn Johnson .50 1.25
117 Adrian Murrell .30 .75
118 Neil O'Donnell .30 .75
119 Heath Shuler .20 .50
120 Tim Brown .50 1.25
121 Rickey Dudley .20 .50
122 Jeff George .30 .75
123 Desmond Howard .30 .75
124 James Jett .30 .75
125 Napoleon Kaufman .50 1.25
126 Chad Levitt RC .20 .50
127 Darrell Russell .20 .50
128 Ty Detmer .30 .75
129 Irving Fryar .30 .75
130 Charlie Garner .30 .75
131 Kevin Turner .20 .50
132 Ricky Watters .30 .75
133 Jerome Bettis .50 1.25
134 Will Blackwell .20 .50
135 Mark Bruener .20 .50
136 Charles Johnson .20 .50
137 George Jones .20 .50
138 Kordell Stewart .50 1.25
139 Yancey Thigpen .20 .50
140 Gary Brown .20 .50
141 Jim Everett .20 .50
142 Terrell Fletcher .20 .50
143 Stan Humphries .20 .50
144 Freddie Jones .20 .50
145 Tony Martin .30 .75
146 Jim Druckenmiller .20 .50
147 Garrison Hearst .50 1.25
148 Brent Jones .20 .50
149 Terrell Owens .50 1.25
150 Jerry Rice 1.25 2.50
151 J.J. Stokes .30 .75
152 Steve Young .60 1.50
153 Steve Broussard .20 .50
154 Joey Galloway .30 .75
155 Jon Kitna .50 1.25
156 Warren Moon .50 1.25
157 Shawn Springs .20 .50
158 Chris Warren .30 .75
159 Tony Banks .30 .75
160 Isaac Bruce .50 1.25
161 Eddie Kennison .30 .75
162 Orlando Pace .20 .50
163 Lawrence Phillips .20 .50
164 Mike Alstott .50 1.25
165 Reidel Anthony .30 .75
166 Horace Copeland .20 .50
167 Trent Dilfer .50 1.25
168 Warrick Dunn .50 1.25
169 Hardy Nickerson .20 .50
170 Karl Williams .20 .50
171 Eddie George .50 1.25
172 Ronnie Harmon .20 .50
173 Joey Kent .30 .75
174 Steve McNair .50 1.25
175 Chris Sanders .20 .50
176 Terry Allen .50 1.25
177 Jamie Asher .20 .50
178 Stephen Davis .20 .50
179 Gus Frerotte .20 .50
180 Leslie Shepherd .20 .50
181 Victor Riley RC .20 .50
182 Curtis Enis RC .20 .50
183 Brian Griese RC .75 2.00
184 Eric Brown RC .20 .50
185 Jacquez Green RC .30 .75
186 Andre Wadsworth RC .30 .75
187 Ryan Leaf RC .40 1.00
188 Rashaan Shehee RC .30 .75
189 Peyton Manning RC 5.00 10.00
190 Flozell Adams RC .20 .50
191 Fred Taylor RC .60 1.50
192 Charlie Batch RC .40 1.00
193 Kevin Dyson RC .40 1.00
194 Charles Woodson RC .50 1.25
195 Ahman Green RC 1.00 2.50
196 Randy Moss RC 2.50 6.00
197 Robert Edwards RC .30 .75
198 Reidel Anthony .30 .75
199 Jerome Pathon RC .40 1.00
200 Samari Rolle RC .20 .50

1998 Collector's Edge Advantage Gold

COMPLETE SET (180) 150.00 300.00
*GOLDS: 2X TO 5X BASIC CARDS
STATED ODDS 1:6

1998 Collector's Edge Advantage 50-point

COMPLETE SET (180) 75.00 150.00
*50-POINT: 1X TO 2.5X BASIC CARDS
STATED ODDS 1:1

1998 Collector's Edge Advantage Silver

COMPLETE SET (180) 125.00 250.00
*SILVER VETS: 1.5X TO 4X BASIC CARDS
*SILVER ROOKIES: .8X TO 2X BASIC CARDS
STATED ODDS 1:2

1998 Collector's Edge Advantage Livin' Large

COMPLETE SET (22) 75.00 150.00
STATED ODDS 1:12
*HOLOFOILS: 2X TO 5X BASIC INSERTS
HOLOFOIL STATED PRINT RUN 100 SETS
1 Leeland McElroy 1.00 2.50
2 Jamal Anderson 2.50 6.00
3 Antowain Smith 2.50 6.00
4 Emmitt Smith 8.00 20.00
5 John Elway 10.00 25.00
6 Barry Sanders 8.00 20.00
7 Elvis Grbac 1.50 4.00
8 Dan Marino 10.00 25.00
9 Cris Carter 2.50 6.00
10 Drew Bledsoe 4.00 10.00
11 Curtis Martin 2.50 6.00
12 Troy Davis 1.00 2.50
13 Ike Hilliard 1.50 4.00
14 Adrian Murrell 1.50 4.00
15 Tim Brown 2.50 6.00
16 Kordell Stewart 2.50 6.00
17 Jerry Rice 5.00 12.00
18 Tony Banks 1.50 4.00
19 Mike Alstott 2.50 6.00
20 Trent Dilfer 2.50 6.00
21 Eddie George 2.50 6.00
22 Steve McNair 2.50 6.00

1998 Collector's Edge Advantage Memorable Moments

COMPLETE SET (12) 125.00 300.00
STATED PRINT 200 SERIAL #'d SETS
STATED ODDS 1:360
1 Carl Pickens 7.50 20.00
2 Terrell Davis 15.00 40.00
3 Herman Moore 12.50 30.00
4 Antonio Freeman 15.00 40.00
5 Jimmy Smith 7.50 20.00
6 Marcus Allen 15.00 40.00
7 Cris Carter 15.00 40.00
8 Curtis Martin 15.00 40.00
9 Napoleon Kaufman 12.50 30.00
10 Joey Galloway 12.50 30.00
11 Warrick Dunn 12.50 30.00
12 Eddie George 15.00 40.00

1998 Collector's Edge Advantage Personal Victory

STATED PRINT 200 SETS
STATED ODDS 1:675
1 John Elway 40.00 100.00
2 Barry Sanders 30.00 80.00
3 Brett Favre 60.00 150.00
4 Mark Brunell 15.00 40.00
5 Drew Bledsoe 20.00 50.00
6 Jerry Rice 30.00 80.00

1998 Collector's Edge Advantage Prime Connection

COMPLETE SET (25) 250.00 500.00
STATED ODDS 1:36
1 LeShon Johnson 2.50 6.00
Leeland McElroy
2 Peter Boulware 4.00 10.00
Michael Jackson
3 Andre Reed 6.00 15.00
Antowain Smith
4 Rae Carruth 2.50 6.00
Anthony Johnson
5 Herschel Walker 15.00 40.00
Emmitt Smith
6 Terrell Davis 15.00 40.00
John Elway
7 Ed McCaffrey 4.00 10.00
Shannon Sharpe
8 Herman Moore 25.00 60.00
Barry Sanders
9 Brett Favre 25.00 60.00
Antonio Freeman
10 Mark Brunell 6.00 15.00
James O. Stewart
11 Marcus Allen 6.00 15.00
Elvis Grbac
12 Karim Abdul-Jabbar 25.00 60.00
Dan Marino
13 Drew Bledsoe 10.00 25.00
Ben Coates
14 Terry Glenn 7.50 20.00
Curtis Martin
15 Troy Davis 4.00 10.00
Danny Wuerffel
16 Ike Hilliard 4.00 10.00
Danny Kanell
17 Aaron Glenn 4.00 10.00
Adrian Murrell
18 Tim Brown 6.00 15.00
Napoleon Kaufman
19 Mark Bruener 6.00 15.00
Jerome Bettis
20 Jim Druckenmiller 6.00 15.00
Terrell Owens
21 Garrison Hearst 10.00 25.00
Steve Young
22 Tony Banks 6.00 15.00
Eddie Kennison
23 Mike Alstott 6.00 15.00
Reidel Anthony
24 Hardy Nickerson 6.00 15.00
Warrick Dunn
25 Eddie George 6.00 15.00
Steve McNair

1998 Collector's Edge Advantage Showtime

COMPLETE SET (23) 100.00 200.00
STATED ODDS 1:18
*HOLOFOILS: 2X TO 4X BASIC INSERTS
HOLOFOIL STATED PRINT RUN 100 SETS
1 LeShon Johnson 1.50 4.00
2 Peter Boulware 1.50 4.00
3 Jim Kelly 4.00 10.00
4 Rae Carruth 1.50 4.00
5 Kerry Collins 2.50 6.00
6 Troy Aikman 8.00 20.00
7 Terrell Davis 4.00 10.00
8 Shannon Sharpe 2.50 6.00
9 Brett Favre 15.00 40.00
10 Mark Brunell 4.00 10.00
11 Keenan McCardell 2.50 6.00
12 Marcus Allen 4.00 10.00
13 Terry Glenn 4.00 10.00
14 Danny Wuerffel 2.50 6.00
15 Danny Kanell 2.50 6.00
16 Aaron Glenn 1.50 4.00
17 Napoleon Kaufman 4.00 10.00
18 Mark Bruener 1.50 4.00
19 Jim Druckenmiller 1.50 4.00
20 Terrell Owens 4.00 10.00
21 Steve Young 5.00 12.00
22 Reidel Anthony 2.50 6.00
23 Warrick Dunn 4.00 10.00

1999 Collector's Edge Advantage Previews

This set was released as a Preview to the 1999 Collector's Edge Advantage base set. Each card is essentially a parallel version of the base set card with the player's initials as the card number along with the word "preview" on the cardbacks.

COMPLETE SET (10) 5.00 12.00
CM Curtis Martin .50 1.25
DF Doug Flutie .60 1.50
DM Dan Marino 1.25 3.00
GH Garrison Hearst .30 .75
JA Jamal Anderson .50 1.25
MB Mark Brunell .60 1.50
PM Peyton Manning 1.00 2.50
RE Robert Edwards .30 .75
RM Randy Moss 1.00 2.50
TD Terrell Davis .75 2.00

1999 Collector's Edge Advantage

The 1999 Collector's Edge Advantage set was issued in one series for a total of 190 cards. The rookie subset cards were short printed. The set features color action photos of NFL stars and draft picks printed on 20-point card stock with silver foil stamping. The backs carry season and career statistics, biographical, and other player information.

COMPLETE SET (190) 25.00 50.00
1 Larry Centers .25 .60
2 Rob Moore .20 .50
3 Adrian Murrell .25 .60
4 Jake Plummer .25 .60
5 Frank Sanders .20 .50
6 Jamal Anderson .25 .60
7 Chris Chandler .25 .60
8 Tim Dwight .25 .60
9 Tony Martin .25 .60
10 Terance Mathis .20 .50
11 O.J. Santiago .20 .50
12 Jim Harbaugh .25 .60
13 Priest Holmes .30 .75
14 Jermaine Lewis .20 .50
15 Rod Woodson .30 .75
16 Eric Zeier .20 .50
17 Doug Flutie .30 .75
18 Sam Gash .20 .50
19 Rob Johnson .25 .60
20 Eric Moulds .25 .60
21 Andre Reed .30 .75
22 Antowain Smith .20 .50
23 Bruce Smith .30 .75
24 Thurman Thomas .30 .75
25 Steve Beuerlein .25 .60
26 Kevin Greene .25 .60
27 Rocket Ismail .25 .60
28 Fred Lane .20 .50
29 Muhsin Muhammad .25 .60
30 Edgar Bennett .25 .60
31 Curtis Conway .25 .60
32 Bobby Engram .25 .60
33 Curtis Enis .20 .50
34 Erik Kramer .25 .60
35 Jeff Blake .25 .60
36 Corey Dillon .25 .60
37 Neil O'Donnell .25 .60
38 Carl Pickens .25 .60
39 Takeo Spikes .20 .50
40 Troy Aikman .50 1.25
41 Billy Davis .20 .50
42 Michael Irvin .30 .75
43 Deion Sanders .30 .75
44 Emmitt Smith .75 2.00
45 Darren Woodson .25 .60
46 Bubby Brister .20 .50
47 Terrell Davis .30 .75
48 John Elway 1.00 2.50
49 Ed McCaffrey .25 .60
50 Bill Romanowski .25 .60
51 Shannon Sharpe .30 .75
52 Rod Smith .25 .60
53 Charlie Batch .25 .60
54 Germane Crowell .20 .50
55 Herman Moore .25 .60
56 Johnnie Morton .25 .60
57 Barry Sanders .75 2.00
58 Robert Brooks .25 .60
59 Brett Favre 1.00 2.50
60 Antonio Freeman .25 .60
61 Darick Holmes .20 .50
62 Dorsey Levens .25 .60
63 Roell Preston .20 .50
64 Marshall Faulk .30 .75
65 E.G.Green .20 .50
66 Marvin Harrison .30 .75
67 Peyton Manning 1.00 2.50
68 Jerome Pathon .20 .50
69 Mark Brunell .25 .60
70 Kevin Hardy .20 .50
71 Keenan McCardell .25 .60
72 Jimmy Smith .25 .60
73 Fred Taylor .25 .60
74 Alvis Whitted .20 .50
75 Kimble Anders .20 .50
76 Donnell Bennett .20 .50
77 Rich Gannon .25 .60
78 Elvis Grbac .20 .50
79 Byron Bam Morris .20 .50
80 Andre Rison .25 .60
81 Karim Abdul-Jabbar .25 .60
82 John Avery .20 .50
83 Oronde Gadsden .20 .50
84 Sam Madison .20 .50
85 Dan Marino 1.00 2.50
86 O.J. McDuffie .25 .60
87 Zach Thomas .30 .75
88 Cris Carter .30 .75
89 Randall Cunningham .30 .75
90 Brad Johnson .25 .60
91 Randy Moss .30 .75
92 John Randle .25 .60
93 Jake Reed .25 .60
94 Robert Smith .25 .60
95 Drew Bledsoe .30 .75
96 Ben Coates .25 .60
97 Robert Edwards .20 .50
98 Terry Glenn .25 .60
99 Ty Law .25 .60
100 Cam Cleeland .20 .50
101 Kerry Collins .25 .60
102 Gary Brown .20 .50
103 Kent Graham .20 .50
104 Ike Hilliard .25 .60
105 Joe Jurevicius .20 .50
106 Danny Kanell .20 .50
107 Wayne Chrebet .25 .60
108 Aaron Glenn .20 .50
109 Keyshawn Johnson .25 .60
110 Curtis Martin .30 .75
111 Vinny Testaverde .25 .60
112 Tim Brown .30 .75
113 Jeff George .20 .50
114 James Jett .20 .50
115 Napoleon Kaufman .20 .50
116 Charles Woodson .30 .75
117 Koy Detmer .20 .50
118 Duce Staley .25 .60
119 Jerome Bettis .30 .75
120 Charles Johnson .20 .50
121 Kordell Stewart .25 .60
122 Tony Banks .25 .60
123 Isaac Bruce .30 .75
124 June Henley RC .20 .50
125 Ryan Leaf .25 .60
126 Natrone Means .25 .60
127 Mikhael Ricks .20 .50
128 Craig Whelihan .20 .50
129 Garrison Hearst .25 .60
130 Terrell Owens .30 .75
131 Jerry Rice .60 1.50
132 J.J.Stokes .20 .50
133 Steve Young .40 1.00
134 Joey Galloway .25 .60
135 Ahman Green .25 .60
136 Jon Kitna .25 .60
137 Ricky Watters .25 .60
138 Mike Alstott .30 .75
139 Reidel Anthony .20 .50
140 Trent Dilfer .25 .60
141 Warrick Dunn .25 .60
142 Jacquez Green .20 .50
143 Kevin Dyson .20 .50
144 Eddie George .25 .60
145 Steve McNair .30 .75
146 Yancey Thigpen .20 .50
147 Terry Allen .25 .60
148 Trent Green .25 .60
149 Skip Hicks .20 .50
150 Michael Westbrook .20 .50
151 Rahim Abdullah RC .30 .75
152 Champ Bailey RC 1.00 2.50
153 Marlon Barnes RC .30 .75
154 D'Wayne Bates RC .30 .75
155 Michael Bishop RC .40 1.00
156 Dre Bly RC .50 1.25
157 David Boston RC .40 1.00
158 Chris Claiborne RC .30 .75
159 Tim Couch RC .50 1.25
160 Daunte Culpepper RC .50 1.25
161 Autry Denson RC .30 .75
162 Jared DeVries RC .30 .75
163 Troy Edwards RC .40 1.00
164 Kris Farris RC .30 .75
165 Kevin Faulk RC .50 1.25
166 Martin Gramatica RC .30 .75
167 Torry Holt RC UER .75 2.00
(incorrect college on back)
168 Brock Huard RC .40 1.00
169 Sedrick Irvin RC .30 .75
170 Edgerrin James RC .60 1.50
171 James Johnson RC .30 .75
172 Kevin Johnson RC .40 1.00
173 Andy Katzenmoyer RC .40 1.00
174 Jevon Kearse RC .50 1.25
175 Shaun King RC .40 1.00
176 Rob Konrad RC .30 .75
177 Chris McAlister RC .40 1.00
178 Darnell McDonald RC .30 .75
179 Donovan McNabb RC 2.50 6.00
180 Cade McNown RC .40 1.00
181 Dat Nguyen RC .50 1.25
182 Peerless Price RC .40 1.00
183 Akili Smith RC .40 1.00
184 Tai Streets RC .40 1.00
185 Cuncho Brown RC UER .30 .75
(Photo is actually Courtney Brown)
186 Ricky Williams RC .75 2.00
187 Craig Yeast RC .30 .75
188 Amos Zereoue RC .40 1.00
189 Checklist .10 .30
190 Checklist .10 .30

1999 Collector's Edge Advantage Galvanized

COMPLETE SET (190) 150.00 300.00
*1-190 VETS/500: 2X TO 5X BASIC CARDS
1-190 VETERAN PRINT RUN 500
*151-188 ROOKIES/200: 1.5X TO 4X
151-188 ROOKIE PRINT RUN 200

1999 Collector's Edge Advantage Gold Ingot

COMPLETE SET (190) 40.00 80.00
*1-190 VETS: .8X TO 2X BASIC CARDS
*151-188 ROOKIES: .6X TO 1.5X
ONE PER PACK

1999 Collector's Edge Advantage HoloGold

*1-190 VETS/50: 10X TO 25X BASIC CARDS
1-190 VETERANS PRINT RUN 50
*151-188 ROOKIES/20: 10X TO 25X
151-188 ROOKIES PRINT RUN 20

1999 Collector's Edge Advantage Rookie Autographs

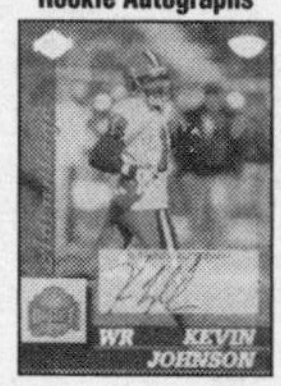

STATED ODDS 1:24
*BLUE INK #'d: 1X TO 2.5X BASIC AU
BLUE INK NUMBERED PRINT RUN 40-80
UNPRICED RED INK PRINT RUN 10-13
151 Rahim Abdullah 4.00 10.00
152 Champ Bailey 6.00 15.00
153 Marlon Barnes 3.00 8.00
154 D'Wayne Bates 4.00 10.00
155 Michael Bishop 5.00 12.00
156 Dre Bly 5.00 12.00
157 David Boston 5.00 12.00
158 Chris Claiborne 3.00 8.00
159 Tim Couch 5.00 12.00
160 Daunte Culpepper 12.00 30.00
162 Jared DeVries 4.00 10.00
163 Troy Edwards 4.00 10.00
164 Kris Farris 3.00 8.00
165 Kevin Faulk 5.00 12.00
166 Martin Gramatica 3.00 8.00
168 Brock Huard 5.00 12.00
169 Sedrick Irvin 3.00 8.00
170 Edgerrin James Blue 12.00 30.00
171 James Johnson 4.00 10.00
172 Kevin Johnson 5.00 12.00
174 Jevon Kearse 6.00 15.00
175 Shaun King 4.00 10.00
176 Rob Konrad 4.00 10.00
177 Chris McAlister 4.00 10.00
178 Darnell McDonald 4.00 10.00
179 Donovan McNabb 15.00 40.00
180 Cade McNown 4.00 10.00
181 Dat Nguyen 5.00 12.00
182 Peerless Price 5.00 12.00
183 Akili Smith 4.00 10.00
184 Tai Streets 5.00 12.00
186 Ricky Williams Blue 10.00 25.00
187 Craig Yeast 4.00 10.00
188 Amos Zereoue 5.00 12.00

1999 Collector's Edge Advantage Jumpstarters

COMPLETE SET (10) 15.00 40.00
STATED PRINT RUN 500 SERIAL #'d SETS
JS1 Champ Bailey 1.50 4.00
JS2 David Boston 1.50 4.00
JS3 Tim Couch 1.50 4.00
JS4 Daunte Culpepper 4.00 10.00
JS5 Torry Holt 2.50 6.00
JS6 Donovan McNabb 4.00 10.00
JS7 Cade McNown 1.50 4.00
JS8 Peerless Price 1.50 4.00
JS9 Brock Huard 1.50 4.00
JS10 Ricky Williams 2.00 5.00

1999 Collector's Edge Advantage Memorable Moments

COMPLETE SET (10) 40.00 80.00
STATED ODDS 1:24
MM1 Terrell Davis 2.00 5.00
MM2 Randy Moss 5.00 12.00
MM3 Peyton Manning 6.00 15.00
MM4 Emmitt Smith 4.00 10.00
MM5 Keyshawn Johnson 2.00 5.00
MM6 Dan Marino 6.00 15.00
MM7 John Elway 6.00 15.00
MM8 Doug Flutie 2.00 5.00

MM9 Jerry Rice 4.00 10.00
MM10 Steve Young 2.50 6.00

1999 Collector's Edge Advantage Overture

COMPLETE SET (10) 50.00 100.00
STATED ODDS 1:24
1 Jamal Anderson 2.00 5.00
2 Terrell Davis 2.00 5.00
3 John Elway 6.00 15.00
4 Brett Favre 6.00 15.00
5 Peyton Manning 6.00 15.00
6 Dan Marino 6.00 15.00
7 Randy Moss 5.00 12.00
8 Jerry Rice 4.00 10.00
9 Barry Sanders 6.00 15.00
10 Emmitt Smith 4.00 10.00

1999 Collector's Edge Advantage Prime Connection

COMPLETE SET (20) 30.00 60.00
STATED ODDS 1:4
PC1 Ricky Williams 1.25 3.00
PC2 Fred Taylor .60 1.50
PC3 Tim Couch .60 1.50
PC4 Peyton Manning 1.50 4.00
PC5 Daunte Culpepper 2.50 6.00
PC6 Drew Bledsoe 1.00 2.50
PC7 Torry Holt 1.50 4.00
PC8 Keyshawn Johnson .60 1.50
PC9 Champ Bailey .60 1.50
PC10 Charles Woodson .60 1.50
PC11 Brock Huard .60 1.50
PC12 Jake Plummer .60 1.50
PC13 Donovan McNabb 3.00 8.00
PC14 Steve Young 1.00 2.50
PC15 Edgerrin James 2.50 6.00
PC16 Jamal Anderson .60 1.50
PC17 Cade McNown .60 1.50
PC18 Mark Brunell .60 1.50
PC19 Peerless Price .60 1.50
PC20 Randy Moss 1.25 3.00

1999 Collector's Edge Advantage Shockwaves

COMPLETE SET (20) 50.00 100.00
STATED ODDS 1:12
SW1 Jamal Anderson 2.00 5.00
SW2 Jake Plummer 1.25 3.00
SW3 Eric Moulds 2.00 5.00
SW4 Troy Aikman 4.00 10.00
SW5 Emmitt Smith 4.00 10.00
SW6 Marshall Faulk 2.50 6.00
SW7 John Elway 6.00 15.00
SW8 Barry Sanders 6.00 15.00
SW9 Brett Favre 6.00 15.00
SW10 Peyton Manning 6.00 15.00
SW11 Mark Brunell 2.00 5.00
SW12 Fred Taylor 2.00 5.00
SW13 Randall Cunningham 2.00 5.00
SW14 Randy Moss 5.00 12.00
SW15 Drew Bledsoe 2.50 6.00
SW16 Keyshawn Johnson 2.00 5.00
SW17 Curtis Martin 2.00 5.00
SW18 Steve Young 2.50 6.00
SW19 Warrick Dunn 2.00 5.00
SW20 Eddie George 2.00 5.00

1999 Collector's Edge Advantage Showtime

COMPLETE SET (15) 50.00 100.00
STATED PRINT RUN 500 SERIAL #'d SETS
ST1 Troy Aikman 4.00 10.00
ST2 Jamal Anderson 2.00 5.00
ST3 Mark Brunell 2.00 5.00
ST4 Terrell Davis 2.00 5.00
ST5 Warrick Dunn 2.00 5.00
ST6 Brett Favre 6.00 15.00
ST7 Doug Flutie 2.00 5.00
ST8 Eddie George 2.00 5.00
ST9 Keyshawn Johnson 2.00 5.00
ST10 Peyton Manning 6.00 15.00
ST11 Dan Marino 6.00 15.00
ST12 Randy Moss 5.00 12.00
ST13 Jake Plummer 1.25 3.00
ST14 Jerry Rice 4.00 10.00
ST15 Barry Sanders 6.00 15.00

2000 Collector's Edge EG Previews

These cards were issued to preview the 2000 Edge Graded product. Each is essentially a parallel to the base set card with a new card number. Cards from this set were also graded by PSA and released as Hawaii XV card show promos in February 2000.

COMPLETE SET (7) 3.00 8.00
EG Eddie George .50 1.25
EJ Edgerrin James .50 1.25
KW Kurt Warner .60 1.50
MB Mark Brunell .40 1.00
MF Marshall Faulk .50 1.25
PM Peyton Manning 1.25 3.00
TC Tim Couch .40 1.00

2000 Collector's Edge EG

Released as a 148-card base set, Collector's Edge EG features cards numbered from 1-150 due to the fact that card #93 and #110 were short printed and intended to not be released. Bill Burke (#93) was included on a very limited basis in packs printed with a red embossed stamp over the front of the card. This stamp was meant to enable the card to be pulled from collation during the packaging process. All other base cards were printed on a gold holofoil card stock with the letters "EG" in gold foil. Collector's Edge EG was packaged in 12-pack boxes with each pack containing ten cards and one PSA Graded card and carried a suggested retail price of $21.99.

COMPLETE SET (148) 60.00 120.00
1 Marcus Robinson .30 .75
2 Adrian Murrell .25 .60
3 Qadry Ismail .30 .75
4 Tim Biakabutuka .30 .75
5 Jamal Anderson .30 .75
6 Dorsey Levens .30 .75
7 Robert Smith .30 .75
8 Tony Banks .25 .60
9 Yancey Thigpen .25 .60
10 Elvis Grbac .25 .60
11 Sedrick Irvin .25 .60
12 Rob Johnson .30 .75
13 Frank Sanders .25 .60
14 Rich Gannon .30 .75
15 Steve Beuerlein .30 .75
16 James Stewart .25 .60
17 Ricky Watters .30 .75
18 Curtis Enis .25 .60
19 Eddie Kennison .25 .60
20 Kerry Collins .30 .75
21 Ray Lucas .25 .60
22 Carl Pickens .30 .75
23 Natrone Means .30 .75
24 Daunte Culpepper .30 .75
25 Karim Abdul-Jabbar .25 .60
26 David Boston .25 .60
27 Rocket Ismail .30 .75
28 Jacquez Green .25 .60
29 Kevin Dyson .30 .75
30 Chris Chandler .30 .75
31 Brian Griese .30 .75
32 Charlie Garner .30 .75
33 Wayne Chrebet .30 .75
34 Mike Alstott .40 1.00
35 Germane Crowell .25 .60
36 Mike Cloud RC .25 .60
37 Antowain Smith .30 .75
38 Jeff George .30 .75
39 Antonio Freeman .30 .75
40 Champ Bailey .30 .75
41 Terrence Wilkins .25 .60
42 Junior Seau .40 1.00
43 Jimmy Smith .30 .75
44 Greg Hill .25 .60
45 Tyrone Wheatley .25 .60
46 Tony Gonzalez .40 1.00
47 Rod Smith .30 .75
48 Damon Huard .30 .75
49 Jerome Bettis .40 1.00
50 Cris Carter .40 1.00
51 Darnay Scott .30 .75
52 Ike Hilliard .30 .75
53 Errict Rhett .30 .75
54 Tim Brown .40 1.00
55 Terry Glenn .30 .75
56 Jeff Blake .30 .75
57 Terance Mathis .25 .60
58 Duce Staley .30 .75
59 Amani Toomer .30 .75
60 Terry Allen .30 .75
61 Corey Dillon .30 .75
62 Kordell Stewart .30 .75
63 Az-Zahir Hakim .25 .60
64 Jim Harbaugh .30 .75
65 Bill Schroeder .30 .75
66 O.J. McDuffie .30 .75
67 Keenan McCardell .30 .75
68 Terrell Owens .40 1.00
69 Joey Galloway .30 .75
70 Derrick Alexander .25 .60
71 Ed McCaffrey .30 .75
72 Reidel Anthony .25 .60
73 Michael Irvin .40 1.00
74 Herman Moore .30 .75
75 Joe Montgomery .25 .60
76 Muhsin Muhammad .30 .75
77 Charles Johnson .25 .60
78 Michael Westbrook .25 .60
79 Jevon Kearse .30 .75
80 Courtney Brown RC .60 1.50
81 Shaun Alexander RC 1.00 2.50
82 R.Jay Soward RC .50 1.25
83 Sylvester Morris RC .50 1.25
84 Giovanni Carmazzi RC .50 1.25
85 J.R. Redmond RC .50 1.25
86 Sherrod Gideon RC .50 1.25
87 Tee Martin RC .75 2.00
88 Dennis Northcutt RC .60 1.50
89 Troy Walters RC .50 1.25
90 Joe Hamilton RC .50 1.25
91 Reuben Droughns RC .75 2.00
92 Trung Canidate RC .60 1.50
93A Bill Burke SP 20.00 40.00
93B Bill Burke Red
94 Tim Rattay RC .60 1.50
95 Jerry Porter RC .75 2.00
96 Michael Wiley RC .50 1.25
97 Anthony Lucas RC .50 1.25
98 Danny Farmer RC .50 1.25
99 Travis Prentice RC .60 1.50
100 Dez White RC .60 1.50
101 Chad Pennington RC 1.25 3.00
102 Chris Redman RC .60 1.50
103 Thomas Jones RC 1.00 2.50
104 Ron Dayne RC .75 2.00
105 Jamal Lewis RC .75 2.00
106 Shyrone Stith RC .50 1.25
107 Peter Warrick RC .75 2.00
108 Plaxico Burress RC .75 2.00
109 Travis Taylor RC .60 1.50
110A LaVar Arrington RC 15.00 40.00
110B LaVar Arrington RC Red 10.00 25.00
111 Terrell Davis .40 1.00
112 Dan Marino 1.25 3.00
113 Brad Johnson .30 .75
114 Isaac Bruce .40 1.00
115 Eric Moulds .30 .75
116 Olandis Gary .30 .75
117 Drew Bledsoe .40 1.00
118 Steve Young .50 1.25
119 Keyshawn Johnson .30 .75
120 Emmitt Smith 1.00 2.50
121 Warrick Dunn .30 .75
122 Doug Flutie .40 1.00
123 Troy Edwards .25 .60
124 Brett Favre 1.25 3.00
125 Charlie Batch .30 .75
126 Curtis Martin .40 1.00
127 Stephen Davis .30 .75
128 Troy Aikman .60 1.50
129 Fred Taylor .40 1.00
130 Jerry Rice .75 2.00
131 Jon Kitna .30 .75
132 Steve McNair .40 1.00
133 Jake Plummer .30 .75
134 Donovan McNabb .40 1.00
135 Ricky Williams .40 1.00
136 Torry Holt .40 1.00
137 James Johnson .25 .60
138 Kevin Johnson .25 .60
139 Akili Smith .25 .60
140 Cade McNown .25 .60
141 Eddie George .30 .75
142 Shaun King .25 .60
143 Marshall Faulk .40 1.00
144 Kurt Warner .60 1.50
145 Randy Moss .40 1.00
146 Mark Brunell .30 .75
147 Marvin Harrison .40 1.00
148 Edgerrin James .40 1.00
149 Tim Couch .30 .75
150 Peyton Manning 1.00 2.50
151 Thomas Jones HN 1.00 2.50
152 Jamal Lewis HN .75 2.00
153 Chris Redman HN .60 1.50
154 Travis Taylor HN .60 1.50
155 Brian Urlacher HN RC 3.00 8.00
156 Dez White HN .60 1.50
157 Ron Dugans HN RC .50 1.25
158 Peter Warrick HN .75 2.00
159 Dennis Northcutt HN .60 1.50
160 Travis Prentice HN .60 1.50
161 Bubba Franks HN RC .75 2.00
162 R.Jay Soward HN .50 1.25
163 Sylvester Morris HN .50 1.25
164 J.R. Redmond HN .50 1.25
165 Ron Dayne HN .75 2.00
166 Anthony Becht HN RC .60 1.50
167 Laveranues Coles HN RC .75 2.00
168 Chad Pennington HN 1.25 3.00
169 Jerry Porter HN .75 2.00
170 Todd Pinkston HN RC .50 1.25
171 Plaxico Burress HN .75 2.00
172 Tee Martin HN .75 2.00
173 Trung Canidate HN .60 1.50
174 Shaun Alexander HN 1.00 2.50
175 Joe Hamilton HN .50 1.25

2000 Collector's Edge EG Brilliant

*VETS 111-150: 2.5X TO 6X BASIC CARDS
*ROOKIES 101-110: 1.2X TO 3X BASIC CARDS
STATED PRINT RUN 500 SERIAL #'d SETS
110 LaVar Arrington 8.00 20.00

2000 Collector's Edge EG Gems Previews

*UNLISTED PREVIEWS: .2X TO .5X BASIC INSERTS
E49 LaVar Arrington 10.00 25.00

2000 Collector's Edge EG Gems

COMPLETE SET (49) 125.00 250.00
STATED PRINT RUN 500 SER.#'d SETS
E1 Doug Flutie 1.50 4.00
E2 Cade McNown 1.00 2.50
E3 Akili Smith 1.00 2.50
E4 Tim Couch 1.25 3.00
E5 Kevin Johnson 1.00 2.50
E6 Troy Aikman 2.50 6.00
E7 Emmitt Smith 4.00 10.00
E8 Terrell Davis 1.50 4.00
E9 Brett Favre 5.00 12.00
E10 Marvin Harrison 1.50 4.00
E11 Edgerrin James 1.50 4.00
E12 Peyton Manning 4.00 10.00
E13 Mark Brunell 1.25 3.00
E14 Dan Marino 5.00 12.00
E15 Randy Moss 1.50 4.00
E16 Drew Bledsoe 1.50 4.00
E17 Ricky Williams 1.50 4.00
E18 Keyshawn Johnson 1.25 3.00
E19 Curtis Martin 1.50 4.00
E20 Donovan McNabb 1.50 4.00
E21 Marshall Faulk 1.50 4.00
E22 Torry Holt 1.50 4.00
E23 Kurt Warner 2.50 6.00
E24 Jerry Rice 3.00 8.00
E25 Steve Young 2.00 5.00
E26 Jon Kitna 1.25 3.00
E27 Shaun King 1.00 2.50
E28 Eddie George 1.25 3.00
E29 Stephen Davis 1.25 3.00
E30 Brad Johnson 1.25 3.00
E31 Chad Pennington 2.50 6.00
E32 Chris Redman 1.25 3.00
E33 Tim Rattay 1.25 3.00
E34 Tee Martin 1.50 4.00
E35 Thomas Jones 2.00 5.00
E36 Ron Dayne 1.50 4.00
E37 Jamal Lewis 1.50 4.00
E38 J.R. Redmond 1.00 2.50
E39 Travis Prentice 1.25 3.00
E40 Shaun Alexander 2.00 5.00
E41 Michael Wiley 1.00 2.50
E42 Quinton Spotwood 1.00 2.50
E43 Peter Warrick 1.50 4.00
E44 Plaxico Burress 1.50 4.00
E45 Travis Taylor 1.25 3.00
E46 Troy Walters 1.00 2.50
E47 R.Jay Soward 1.00 2.50
E48 Dez White 1.25 3.00
E50 Courtney Brown 1.25 3.00

2000 Collector's Edge EG Golden Edge

COMPLETE SET (50) 100.00 200.00
STATED PRINT RUN 2000 SER.#'d SETS
GE1 Jake Plummer .75 2.00
GE2 Qadry Ismail .75 2.00
GE3 Doug Flutie 1.00 2.50
GE4 Muhsin Muhammad .75 2.00
GE5 Cade McNown .60 1.50
GE6 Marcus Robinson .75 2.00
GE7 Akili Smith .60 1.50
GE8 Tim Couch .75 2.00
GE9 Kevin Johnson .60 1.50
GE10 Troy Aikman 1.50 4.00
GE11 Emmitt Smith 2.50 6.00
GE12 Terrell Davis 1.00 2.50
GE13 Charlie Batch .75 2.00
GE14 Brett Favre 3.00 8.00
GE15 Marvin Harrison 1.00 2.50
GE16 Edgerrin James 1.00 2.50
GE17 Peyton Manning 2.50 6.00
GE18 Mark Brunell .75 2.00
GE19 Fred Taylor 1.00 2.50
GE20 Dan Marino 3.00 8.00
GE21 Randy Moss 1.00 2.50
GE22 Drew Bledsoe 1.00 2.50
GE23 Ricky Williams 1.00 2.50
GE24 Curtis Martin 1.00 2.50
GE25 Donovan McNabb 1.00 2.50
GE26 Isaac Bruce 1.00 2.50
GE27 Marshall Faulk 1.00 2.50
GE28 Torry Holt 1.00 2.50
GE29 Kurt Warner 1.50 4.00
GE30 Jerry Rice 2.00 5.00
GE31 Jon Kitna .75 2.00
GE32 Eddie George .75 2.00
GE33 Steve McNair 1.00 2.50
GE34 Stephen Davis .75 2.00
GE35 Brad Johnson .75 2.00
GE36 Travis Prentice .75 2.00
GE37 Dez White .75 2.00
GE38 Chad Pennington 1.50 4.00
GE39 Chris Redman .75 2.00
GE40 Thomas Jones 1.25 3.00
GE41 Ron Dayne 1.00 2.50
GE42 Jamal Lewis 1.00 2.50
GE43 Shyrone Stith .60 1.50
GE44 Peter Warrick 1.00 2.50
GE45 Plaxico Burress 1.00 2.50
GE46 Travis Taylor .75 2.00
GE48 Shaun Alexander 1.25 3.00
GE49 R.Jay Soward .60 1.50
GE50 Sylvester Morris .60 1.50

2000 Collector's Edge EG Impeccable

COMPLETE SET (20) 40.00 80.00
STATED PRINT RUN 2000 SER.#'d SETS
I1 Cade McNown .60 1.50
I2 Tim Couch .75 2.00
I3 Troy Aikman 1.50 4.00
I4 Emmitt Smith 2.50 6.00
I5 Terrell Davis 1.00 2.50
I6 Brett Favre 3.00 8.00
I7 Edgerrin James 1.00 2.50
I8 Peyton Manning 2.50 6.00
I9 Mark Brunell .75 2.00
I10 Fred Taylor 1.00 2.50
I11 Dan Marino 3.00 8.00
I12 Randy Moss 1.00 2.50
I13 Drew Bledsoe 1.00 2.50
I14 Ricky Williams 1.00 2.50
I15 Curtis Martin 1.00 2.50
I16 Marshall Faulk 1.00 2.50
I17 Kurt Warner 1.50 4.00
I18 Eddie George .75 2.00
I19 Steve McNair 1.00 2.50
I20 Stephen Davis .75 2.00

2000 Collector's Edge EG Making the Grade

COMPLETE SET (29) 50.00 100.00
STATED PRINT RUN 2000 SER.#'d SETS
M1 Shaun Alexander 1.50 4.00
M2 R.Jay Soward .75 2.00
M3 Sylvester Morris .75 2.00
M4 Corey Simon 1.00 2.50
M5 J.R. Redmond .75 2.00
M6 Bubba Franks 1.25 3.00
M7 Tee Martin 1.25 3.00
M8 Dennis Northcutt 1.00 2.50
M9 Courtney Brown 1.00 2.50
M10 Joe Hamilton .75 2.00
M11 Reuben Droughns 1.25 3.00
M12 Trung Canidate 1.00 2.50
M13 Laveranues Coles 1.25 3.00
M14 Brian Urlacher 5.00 12.00
M15 Jerry Porter 1.25 3.00
M16 Ron Dugans .75 2.00
M17 Anthony Becht 1.00 2.50
M18 Danny Farmer .75 2.00
M19 Travis Prentice 1.00 2.50
M20 Dez White 1.00 2.50
M21 Chad Pennington 2.00 5.00
M22 Chris Redman 1.00 2.50
M23 Thomas Jones 1.50 4.00
M24 Ron Dayne 1.25 3.00
M25 Jamal Lewis 1.25 3.00
M26 Todd Pinkston .75 2.00
M27 Peter Warrick 1.25 3.00
M28 Plaxico Burress 1.25 3.00
M29 Travis Taylor 1.00 2.50

2000 Collector's Edge EG Rookie Leatherback Autographs

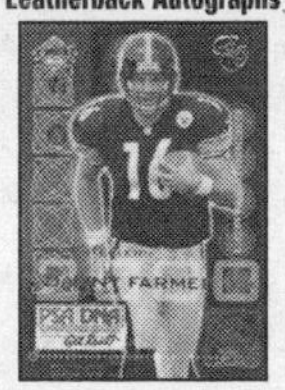

STATED PRINT RUN 12 SER.#'d SETS
AB Anthony Becht 50.00 125.00
BF Bubba Franks 60.00 150.00
BU Brian Urlacher 250.00 400.00
CK Curtis Keaton 40.00 100.00
CP Chad Pennington 125.00 250.00
CR Chris Redman 50.00 120.00
CS Corey Simon 50.00 120.00
DF Danny Farmer 40.00 100.00
DN Dennis Northcutt 50.00 125.00
DW Dez White 50.00 120.00
JH Joe Hamilton 40.00 100.00
JL Jamal Lewis 75.00 200.00
JP Jerry Porter 60.00 150.00
JR J.R. Redmond 40.00 100.00
LC Laveranues Coles 60.00 150.00
PB Plaxico Burress 60.00 150.00
PW Peter Warrick 60.00 150.00
RD Ron Dayne 75.00 200.00
RD Ron Dugans 40.00 100.00
RD Reuben Droughns 60.00 150.00
RS R.Jay Soward 40.00 100.00
SA Shaun Alexander 175.00 300.00
SM Sylvester Morris 40.00 100.00
TC Trung Canidate 50.00 125.00
TJ Thomas Jones 100.00 200.00
TM Tee Martin 60.00 150.00
TP Todd Pinkston 40.00 100.00
TP Travis Prentice 50.00 120.00
TT Travis Taylor 50.00 125.00

2000 Collector's Edge EG Uncirculated

*VETS 111-150: 1.2X TO 3X BASIC CARDS
*ROOKIES 101-109: .6X TO 1.5X BASIC CARDS
STATED PRINT RUN 5000 SER.#'d SETS

1997 Collector's Edge Extreme

This 180-card set was distributed in six-card packs with a suggested retail price of $2.29. The fronts feature color action photos of players from all 30 teams printed on thin glossy card stock. The backs carry complete player historical statistics. A much thicker non-glossy "50-Point" parallel set was also issued which is sometimes confused with the base issue set.

COMPLETE SET (180) 7.50 20.00
1 Larry Centers .10 .30
2 Leeland McElroy .07 .20
3 Jake Plummer RC .75 2.00
4 Simeon Rice .10 .30
5 Eric Swann .07 .20
6 Jamal Anderson .20 .50
7 Bert Emanuel .10 .30
8 Byron Hanspard RC .10 .30
9 Derrick Alexander WR UER .10 .30
(Derek on back)
10 Peter Boulware RC .20 .50
11 Michael Jackson .10 .30
12 Ray Lewis .30 .75
13 Vinny Testaverde .10 .30
14 Todd Collins .07 .20
15 Eric Moulds .20 .50
16 Bryce Paup UER .07 .20
(numbered 122 on back)
17 Andre Reed .10 .30
18 Bruce Smith .10 .30
19 Antowain Smith RC .50 1.25
20 Chris Spielman .07 .20
21 Thurman Thomas .20 .50
22 Tim Biakabutuka .10 .30
23 Rae Carruth RC .07 .20
24 Kerry Collins .20 .50
25 Anthony Johnson .07 .20
26 Lamar Lathon .07 .20
27 Muhsin Muhammad .10 .30
28 Darnell Autry RC .10 .30
29 Curtis Conway .10 .30
30 Bryan Cox .07 .20
31 Bobby Engram .10 .30
32 Walt Harris .07 .20
33 Erik Kramer .07 .20
34 Rashaan Salaam .07 .20
35 Jeff Blake .10 .30
36 Ki-Jana Carter .07 .20
37 Corey Dillon RC .75 2.00
38 Carl Pickens .10 .30
39 Troy Aikman .40 1.00
40 Dexter Coakley RC .20 .50
41 Michael Irvin .20 .50
42 Daryl Johnston .10 .30
43 David LaFleur RC .07 .20
44 Anthony Miller .07 .20
45 Deion Sanders .20 .50
46 Emmitt Smith .60 1.50
47 Broderick Thomas .07 .20
48 Terrell Davis .25 .60
49 John Elway .75 2.00
50 John Mobley .07 .20
51 Shannon Sharpe .10 .30
52 Neil Smith .10 .30
53 Checklist .07 .20
54 Scott Mitchell .10 .30
55 Herman Moore .10 .30
56 Barry Sanders .60 1.50
57 Edgar Bennett .10 .30
58 Robert Brooks .10 .30
59 Mark Chmura .10 .30
60 Brett Favre .75 2.00
61 Antonio Freeman .20 .50
62 Dorsey Levens .20 .50
63 Reggie White .20 .50
64 Eddie George .20 .50
65 Darryll Lewis .07 .20
66 Steve McNair .25 .60
67 Chris Sanders .07 .20
68 Marshall Faulk .25 .60
69 Jim Harbaugh .10 .30
70 Marvin Harrison .20 .50
71 Tony Brackens .07 .20
72 Mark Brunell .25 .60
73 Kevin Hardy .07 .20
74 Rob Johnson .20 .50
75 Keenan McCardell .10 .30
76 Natrone Means .10 .30
77 Jimmy Smith .10 .30
78 Marcus Allen .20 .50
79 Pat Barnes RC .20 .50
80 Tony Gonzalez RC UER .75 2.00
(Gonzalez on back)
81 Elvis Grbac .10 .30
82 Brett Perriman .07 .20
83 Andre Rison .10 .30
84 Derrick Thomas .20 .50
85 Tamarick Vanover .10 .30
86 Karim Abdul-Jabbar .10 .30
87 Fred Barnett .07 .20
88 Terrell Buckley .07 .20
89 Yatil Green RC .10 .30
90 Dan Marino .75 2.00
91 O.J. McDuffie .10 .30
92 Jason Taylor RC .40 1.00
93 Zach Thomas .20 .50
94 Cris Carter .20 .50
95 Brad Johnson .20 .50
96 John Randle .10 .30
97 Jake Reed .10 .30
98 Robert Smith .10 .30
99 Drew Bledsoe .25 .60
100 Chris Canty RC .07 .20
101 Ben Coates .10 .30
102 Terry Glenn .20 .50
103 Ty Law .10 .30
104 Curtis Martin .25 .60
105 Willie McGinest .07 .20
106 Troy Davis RC .10 .30
108 Wayne Martin .07 .20
109 Heath Shuler .07 .20
110 Danny Wuerffel RC .20 .50
111 Ray Zellars .07 .20
112 Tiki Barber RC 1.25 3.00
113A Dave Brown .07 .20
113B Checklist .07 .20
114 Ike Hilliard RC .30 .75
115 Jason Sehorn .10 .30
116 Amani Toomer .10 .30
117 Tyrone Wheatley .10 .30
118 Hugh Douglas .07 .20
119 Aaron Glenn .07 .20
120 Jeff Graham .07 .20
121 Keyshawn Johnson .20 .50
122 Adrian Murrell .10 .30
123 Neil O'Donnell .10 .30
124 Tim Brown .20 .50
125 Jeff George .10 .30
126 Desmond Howard .10 .30
127 Napoleon Kaufman .20 .50
128 Chester McGlockton .07 .20
129 Darrell Russell RC .07 .20
130 Ty Detmer .10 .30
131 Irving Fryar .10 .30
132 Chris T. Jones .07 .20
133 Ricky Watters .10 .30
134 Jerome Bettis .20 .50
135 Charles Johnson .10 .30
136 George Jones RC .10 .30
137 Greg Lloyd .07 .20
138 Kordell Stewart .20 .50
139 Yancey Thigpen .10 .30
140 Jim Everett .07 .20
141 Stan Humphries .10 .30
142 Tony Martin .10 .30
143 Eric Metcalf .10 .30
144 Junior Seau .20 .50
145 Jim Druckenmiller RC .10 .30
146 Kevin Greene .10 .30
147 Garrison Hearst .10 .30
148 Terry Kirby .10 .30
149 Terrell Owens .25 .60
150 Jerry Rice .40 1.00
151 Dana Stubblefield .07 .20
152 Rod Woodson .10 .30
153 Bryant Young .07 .20
154 Steve Young .25 .60
155 Chad Brown .07 .20
156 John Friesz .07 .20
157 Joey Galloway .10 .30
158 Cortez Kennedy .07 .20
159 Warren Moon .20 .50
160 Shawn Springs RC .10 .30
161 Chris Warren .10 .30
162 Tony Banks .10 .30
163 Isaac Bruce .20 .50
164 Eddie Kennison .10 .30
165 Keith Lyle .07 .20
166 Orlando Pace RC .20 .50
167 Lawrence Phillips .07 .20
168 Checklist .07 .20
169 Mike Alstott .20 .50
170 Reidel Anthony RC .20 .50
171 Warrick Dunn RC .60 1.50
172 Hardy Nickerson .07 .20
173 Errict Rhett .07 .20
174 Warren Sapp .10 .30
175 Terry Allen .20 .50
176 Gus Frerotte .07 .20
177 Sean Gilbert .07 .20
178 Ken Harvey .07 .20
179 Jeff Hostetler .07 .20
180 Michael Westbrook .10 .30

1997 Collector's Edge Extreme 50-Point

COMPLETE SET (180) 15.00 30.00
*50-POINT: .5X TO 1.2X BASIC CARDS

1997 Collector's Edge Extreme Foil

*FOIL STARS: 1.25X TO 2.5X BASIC CARDS
*FOIL RCs: .5X TO 1X BASIC CARDS
SILVER STATED ODDS 1:2
*GOLD STARS: 2.5X TO 5X BASIC CARDS
*GOLD RCs: 1X TO 2X BASIC CARDS
GOLD STATED ODDS 1:12
*DIE CUT STARS: 7.5X TO 15X BASIC CARDS
*DIE CUT RCs: 3X TO 6X BASIC CARDS
DIE CUT STATED ODDS 1:36

1997 Collector's Edge Extreme Finesse

COMPLETE SET (25) 40.00 100.00
STATED ODDS 1:60
1 Troy Aikman 5.00 12.00
2 Marcus Allen 2.50 6.00
3 Ben Coates 1.50 4.00
4 Tony Banks 1.50 4.00
5 Jeff Blake 1.50 4.00
6 Tim Brown 2.50 6.00
7 Mark Brunell 2.50 6.00
8 Todd Collins .75 2.00
9 Terrell Davis 3.00 8.00
10 Jim Druckenmiller .75 2.00
11 John Elway 10.00 25.00
12 Marshall Faulk 3.00 8.00
13 Brett Favre 10.00 25.00
14 Antonio Freeman 2.50 6.00
15 Joey Galloway 1.50 4.00
16 Eddie George 2.50 6.00
17 Terry Glenn 2.50 6.00
18 Marvin Harrison 2.50 6.00
19 Garrison Hearst 1.50 4.00
20 Warrick Dunn 4.00 10.00
21 Muhsin Muhammad 1.50 4.00
22 Jerry Rice 5.00 12.00
23 Barry Sanders 8.00 20.00
24 Emmitt Smith 8.00 20.00
25 Shawn Springs .75 2.00

1997 Collector's Edge Extreme Force

COMPLETE SET (25) 25.00 60.00
STATED ODDS 1:8
1 Marcus Allen 1.25 3.00
2 Chris Canty .25 .60
3 Jerome Bettis 1.25 3.00
4 Carl Pickens .75 2.00
5 Drew Bledsoe 1.50 4.00
6 Robert Brooks .75 2.00
7 Shannon Sharpe .75 2.00
8 Tim Brown 1.25 3.00
9 Mark Brunell 1.50 4.00
10 Ben Coates .75 2.00
11 Todd Collins .50 1.25
12 Terrell Davis 1.50 4.00
13 John Elway 5.00 12.00
14 Brett Favre 5.00 12.00
15 Antonio Freeman 1.25 3.00
16 Joey Galloway .75 2.00
17 Warrick Dunn 2.00 5.00
18 Terry Glenn 1.25 3.00
19 Marvin Harrison 1.25 3.00
20 Dan Marino 5.00 12.00
21 Jerry Rice 2.50 6.00
22 Junior Seau 1.25 3.00
23 Tony Banks .75 2.00
24 Emmitt Smith 4.00 10.00
25 Napoleon Kaufman 1.25 3.00

1997 Collector's Edge Extreme Forerunners

COMPLETE SET (25) 40.00 100.00
STATED PRINT RUN 1500 SERIAL #'d SETS
1 Karim Abdul-Jabbar 1.50 4.00
2 Marcus Allen 2.50 6.00
3 Jerome Bettis 2.50 6.00
4 Drew Bledsoe 3.00 8.00
5 Robert Brooks 1.50 4.00
6 Mark Brunell 3.00 8.00
7 Todd Collins 1.00 2.50
8 Terrell Davis 3.00 8.00
9 John Elway 10.00 25.00
10 Brett Favre 10.00 25.00
11 Joey Galloway 1.50 4.00
12 Eddie George 2.50 6.00
13 Terry Glenn 2.50 6.00
14 Marvin Harrison 2.50 6.00
15 Keyshawn Johnson 2.50 6.00
16 Rob Johnson 2.50 6.00
17 Eddie Kennison 1.50 4.00
18 Dorsey Levens 2.50 6.00
19 Dan Marino 10.00 25.00
20 Steve McNair 3.00 8.00
21 Terrell Owens 3.00 8.00
22 Carl Pickens 1.50 4.00
23 Jerry Rice 5.00 12.00
24 Emmitt Smith 8.00 20.00
25 Kordell Stewart 2.50 6.00

1997 Collector's Edge Extreme Fury

COMPLETE SET (18) 50.00 120.00
STATED ODDS 1:48
1 Jerome Bettis 2.50 6.00
2 Terry Glenn 2.50 6.00
3 Drew Bledsoe 3.00 8.00
4 Mark Brunell 2.50 6.00
5 Terrell Davis 3.00 8.00
6 Troy Davis 1.50 4.00
7 Marshall Faulk 3.00 8.00
8 Brett Favre 10.00 25.00
9 Antonio Freeman 2.50 6.00
10 Joey Galloway 1.50 4.00
11 Eddie George 2.50 6.00
12 Eddie Kennison 1.50 4.00
13 Errict Rhett 1.00 2.50
14 Rashaan Salaam 1.00 2.50
15 Emmitt Smith 8.00 20.00
16 Kordell Stewart 2.50 6.00
17 Danny Wuerffel 2.50 6.00
18 Steve Young 3.00 8.00

1997 Collector's Edge Extreme Game Gear Quads

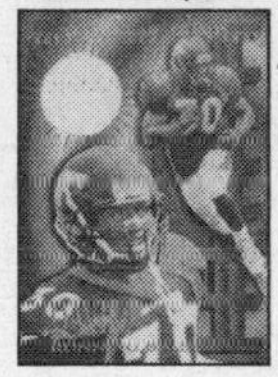

STATED ODDS 1:360
1F Marcus Allen FB 15.00 40.00
1J Marcus Allen JSY 15.00 40.00
2F Mike Alstott FB 15.00 40.00
2J Mike Alstott JSY 15.00 40.00
2P Mike Alstott Pants 15.00 40.00
2S Mike Alstott Shoes 15.00 40.00
3F Drew Bledsoe FB 20.00 50.00
3J Drew Bledsoe JSY 20.00 50.00
4F Tim Brown FB 12.50 30.00
4J Tim Brown JSY 15.00 30.00
5F Mark Brunell FB 20.00 50.00
5J Mark Brunell JSY 20.00 50.00
5P Mark Brunell Pants 20.00 50.00
5S Mark Brunell Shoes 20.00 50.00
6F Kerry Collins FB 10.00 25.00
6J Kerry Collins JSY 10.00 25.00
7F Terrell Davis FB 20.00 50.00
7J Terrell Davis JSY 20.00 50.00
7P Terrell Davis Pants 20.00 50.00
7S Terrell Davis Shoes 20.00 50.00
8F Jim Druckenmiller FB 12.50 30.00
8J Jim Druckenmiller JSY 15.00 30.00
9F Warrick Dunn FB 15.00 40.00
9J Warrick Dunn JSY 15.00 40.00
9P Warrick Dunn Pants 15.00 40.00
9S Warrick Dunn Shoes 15.00 40.00
10F John Elway FB 40.00 100.00
10J John Elway JSY 40.00 100.00
10P John Elway Pants 40.00 100.00
10S John Elway Shoes 40.00 100.00
11F Brett Favre FB 40.00 100.00
11J Brett Favre JSY 40.00 100.00
12F Eddie George FB 15.00 40.00
12J Eddie George JSY 15.00 40.00
12P Eddie George Pants 15.00 40.00
12S Eddie George Shoes 15.00 40.00
13F Terry Glenn FB 12.50 30.00
13J Terry Glenn JSY 15.00 40.00
14F Leeland McElroy FB 10.00 25.00
15F Adrian Murrell FB 10.00 25.00
15J Adrian Murrell JSY 10.00 25.00
15P Adrian Murrell Pants 10.00 25.00
15S Adrian Murrell Shoes 10.00 25.00
16F Carl Pickens FB 12.50 30.00
16J Carl Pickens JSY 15.00 30.00
17F Kordell Stewart FB 15.00 40.00
17J Kordell Stewart JSY 15.00 40.00
18F Danny Wuerffel FB 15.00 40.00
18J Danny Wuerffel JSY 15.00 40.00

1998 Collector's Edge First Place

The 1998 Collector's Edge First Place set was issued in one series with a total of 250 standard size cards. Packs retailed for $4.99 each. The fronts feature large color action shots. The featured player's name, team name, and team position are found along the bottom of the card with the First Place logo in the upper left corner. The checklist cards were numbered CK1, CK2, etc. and are listed after the base player cards. There were two different team logos for each checklist card.

COMPLETE SET (250)	35.00	60.00
1 Karim Abdul-Jabbar	.30	.75
2 Flozell Adams RC	.25	.60
3 Troy Aikman	.60	1.50
4 Robert Smith	.30	.75
5 Stephen Alexander RC	.30	.75
6 Harold Shaw RC	.25	.60
7 Marcus Allen	.30	.75
8 Terry Allen	.30	.75
9 Mike Alstott	.30	.75
10 Jamal Anderson	.30	.75
11 Reidel Anthony	.20	.50
12 Jamie Asher	.10	.30
13 Darnell Autry	.10	.30
14 Phil Savoy RC	.30	.75
15 Jon Ritchie RC	.30	.75
16 Tony Banks	.20	.50
17 Tiki Barber	.30	.75
18 Pat Barnes	.10	.30
19 Charlie Batch RC	.50	1.25
20 Mikhael Ricks RC	.30	.75
21 Jerome Bettis	.30	.75
22 Tim Biakabutuka	.20	.50
23 Roosevelt Blackmon RC	.25	.60
24 Jeff Blake	.20	.50
25 Drew Bledsoe	.50	1.25
26 Tony Boselli	.10	.30
27 Peter Boulware	.10	.30
28 Tony Brackens	.10	.30
29 Corey Bradford RC	.50	1.25
30 Michael Pittman RC	.60	1.50
31 Keith Brooking RC	.50	1.25
32 Robert Brooks	.20	.50
33 Derrick Brooks	.20	.50
34 Ken Oxendine RC	.25	.60
35 R.W. McQuarters RC	.30	.75
36 Tim Brown	.30	.75
37 Chad Brown	.10	.30
38 Isaac Bruce	.30	.75
39 Mark Brunell	.30	.75
40 Chris Canty	.10	.30
41 Mark Carrier	.10	.30
42 Rae Carruth	.10	.30
43 Ki-Jana Carter	.10	.30
44 Cris Carter	.30	.75
45 Larry Centers	.10	.30
46 Corey Chavous RC	.50	1.25
47 Mark Chmura	.20	.50
48 Cameron Cleeland RC	.25	.60
49 Dexter Coakley	.10	.30
50 Ben Coates	.20	.50
51 Jonathan Linton RC	.30	.75
52 Todd Collins	.10	.30
53 Kerry Collins	.20	.50
54 Tebucky Jones RC	.25	.60
55 Curtis Conway	.20	.50
56 Sam Cowart RC	.30	.75
57 Bryan Cox	.10	.30
58 Randall Cunningham	.30	.75
59 Terrell Davis	.30	.75
60 Troy Davis	.10	.30
61 Pat Johnson RC	.30	.75
62 Trent Dilfer	.30	.75
63 Vonnie Holliday RC	.30	.75
64 Corey Dillon	.30	.75
65 Hugh Douglas	.10	.30
66 Jim Druckenmiller	.10	.30
67 Warrick Dunn	.30	.75
68 Robert Edwards RC	.30	.75
69 Greg Ellis RC	.25	.60
70 John Elway	1.25	3.00
71 Bert Emanuel	.20	.50
72 Bobby Engram	.20	.50
73 Curtis Enis RC	.25	.60
74 Marshall Faulk	.40	1.00
75 Brett Favre	1.25	3.00
76 Doug Flutie	.30	.75
77 Glenn Foley	.20	.50
78 Antonio Freeman	.30	.75
79 Gus Frerotte	.10	.30
80 John Friesz	.10	.30
81 Irving Fryar	.20	.50
82 Joey Galloway	.20	.50
83 Rich Gannon	.30	.75
84 Charlie Garner	.20	.50
85 Jeff George	.20	.50
86 Eddie George	.30	.75
87 Sean Gilbert	.10	.30
88 Terry Glenn	.30	.75
89 Aaron Glenn	.10	.30
90 Tony Gonzalez	.30	.75
91 Jeff Graham	.10	.30
92 Elvis Grbac	.20	.50
93 Jacquez Green RC	.30	.75
94 Kevin Greene	.20	.50
95 Brian Griese UER RC	1.00	2.50
96 Byron Hanspard	.10	.30
97 Jim Harbaugh	.20	.50
98 Kevin Hardy	.10	.30
99 Walt Harris	.10	.30
100 Marvin Harrison	.30	.75
101 Rodney Harrison	.20	.50
102 Jeff Hartings	.30	.75
103 Ken Harvey	.10	.30
104 Garrison Hearst	.30	.75
105 Ike Hilliard	.20	.50
106 Jeff Hostetler	.10	.30
107 Bobby Hoying	.20	.50
108 Michael Jackson	.20	.50
109 Anthony Johnson	.10	.30
110 Brad Johnson	.30	.75
111 Keyshawn Johnson	.30	.75
112 Charles Johnson	.10	.30
113 Daryl Johnston	.20	.50
114 Chris Jones	.10	.30
115 George Jones	.10	.30
116 Donald Hayes RC	.30	.75
117 Danny Kanell	.20	.50
118 Napoleon Kaufman	.30	.75
119 Cortez Kennedy	.10	.30
120 Eddie Kennison	.20	.50
121 Levon Kirkland	.10	.30
122 Jon Kitna	.30	.75
123 Erik Kramer	.10	.30
124 David LaFleur	.10	.30
125 Lamar Lathon	.10	.30
126 Ty Law	.20	.50
127 Ryan Leaf RC	.50	1.25
128 Dorsey Levens	.30	.75
129 Ray Lewis	.30	.75
130 Darryll Lewis	.10	.30
131 Matt Hasselbeck RC	10.00	25.00
132 Greg Lloyd	.10	.30
133 Kevin Lockett	.10	.30
134 Keith Lyle	.10	.30
135 Peyton Manning RC	7.50	15.00
136 Dan Marino	1.25	3.00
137 Wayne Martin	.10	.30
138 Ahman Green RC	1.50	4.00
139 Tony Martin	.20	.50
140 E.G. Green RC	.20	.50
141 Derrick Mayes	.20	.50
142 Ed McCaffrey	.20	.50
143 Keenan McCardell	.20	.50
144 O.J. McDuffie	.20	.50
145 Leeland McElroy	.10	.30
146 Willie McGinest	.10	.30
147 Chester McGlockton	.10	.30
148 Steve McNair	.30	.75
149 Natrone Means	.20	.50
150 Eric Metcalf	.10	.30
151 Anthony Miller	.10	.30
152 Rick Mirer	.10	.30
153 Scott Mitchell	.20	.50
154 John Mobley	.10	.30
155 Warren Moon	.30	.75
156 Herman Moore	.20	.50
157 Randy Moss RC	4.00	10.00
158 Eric Moulds	.30	.75
159 Muhsin Muhammad	.20	.50
160 Adrian Murrell	.20	.50
161 Marcus Nash RC	.25	.60
162 Hardy Nickerson	.10	.30
163 Ken Norton	.10	.30
164 Neil O'Donnell	.20	.50
165 Terrell Owens	.30	.75
166 Orlando Pace	.10	.30
167 Jammi German RC	.25	.60
168 Erric Pegram	.10	.30
169 Jason Peter RC	.25	.60
170 Carl Pickens	.20	.50
171 Jake Plummer	.30	.75
172 John Randle	.20	.50
173 Andre Reed	.20	.50
174 Jake Reed	.20	.50
175 Errict Rhett	.20	.50
176 Simeon Rice	.20	.50
177 Jerry Rice	.60	1.50
178 Andre Rison	.20	.50
179 Darrell Russell	.10	.30
180 Rashaan Salaam	.10	.30
181 Deion Sanders	.30	.75
182 Barry Sanders	1.00	2.50
183 Chris Sanders	.10	.30
184 Warren Sapp	.20	.50
185 Junior Seau	.30	.75
186 Jason Sehorn	.20	.50
187 Shannon Sharpe	.20	.50
188 Sedrick Shaw	.10	.30
189 Heath Shuler	.10	.30
190 Chris Floyd RC	.25	.60
191 Terry Fair RC	.30	.75
192 Kevin Dyson RC	.50	1.25
193 Torrance Small	.10	.30
194 Antowain Smith	.30	.75
195 Bruce Smith	.20	.50
196 Tarik Smith RC	.30	.75
197 Emmitt Smith	1.00	2.50
198 Neil Smith	.20	.50
199 Jimmy Smith	.20	.50
200 Chris Spielman	.10	.30
201 Danny Wuerffel	.20	.50
202 Irving Spikes	.10	.30
203 Shawn Springs	.10	.30
204 Duane Starks RC	.25	.60
205 Kordell Stewart	.30	.75
206 J.J. Stokes	.20	.50
207 Eric Swann	.10	.30
208 Steve Tasker	.10	.30
209 Tim Dwight RC	.50	1.25
210 Jason Taylor	.20	.50
211 Vinny Testaverde	.20	.50
212 Thurman Thomas	.30	.75
213 Broderick Thomas	.10	.30
214 Derrick Thomas	.30	.75
215 Zach Thomas	.30	.75
216 Germane Crowell RC	.30	.75
217 Amani Toomer	.20	.50
218 Tamarick Vanover	.10	.30
219 Ross Verba	.10	.30
220 Andre Wadsworth RC	.30	.75
221 Ray Zellars	.10	.30
222 Chris Warren	.20	.50
223 Steve Young	.40	1.00
224 Tyrone Wheatley	.20	.50
225 Reggie White	.30	.75
226 John Avery RC	.30	.75
227 Charles Woodson RC	.60	1.50
228 Takeo Spikes RC	.50	1.25
229 Bryant Young	.10	.30
230 Tavian Banks RC	.20	.50
231 Fred Beasley RC	.25	.60
232 Chris Ruhman RC	.25	.60
CK1A Broncos Logo CL	.02	.10
CK1B Steelers Logo CL	.02	.10
CK2A 49ers Logo CL	.02	.10
CK2B Panthers Logo CL	.02	.10
CK3A Giants Logo CL	.02	.10
CK3B Packers Logo CL	.02	.10
CK4A Colts Logo CL	.02	.10
CK4B Dolphins Logo CL	.02	.10
CK5A Chargers Logo CL	.02	.10
CK5B Vikings Logo Cl	.02	.10
CK6A Patriots Logo Cl	.02	.10
CK6B Raiders Logo CL	.02	.10
CK7A Buccaneers Logo CL	.02	.10
CK7B Cowboys Logo CL	.02	.10
CK8A Bills Logo CL	.02	.10
CK8B Lions Logo CL	.02	.10
CK9A Chiefs Logo CL	.02	.10
CK9B Seahawks Logo CL	.02	.10

1998 Collector's Edge First Place 50-Point

COMPLETE SET (250)	150.00	300.00
*50-POINT STARS: 2X TO 4X BASIC CARDS		
*50-POINT RCs: .8X TO 2X BASIC CARDS		
STATED ODDS 1:1		
131 Matt Hasselbeck	25.00	60.00

1998 Collector's Edge First Place 50-Point Silver

*STARS: 12X TO 30X BASIC CARDS		
*RCs: 3X TO 8X BASIC CARDS		
STATED ODDS 1:24		
131 Matt Hasselbeck	100.00	200.00

1998 Collector's Edge First Place Gold One-of-One

NOT PRICED DUE TO SCARCITY

1998 Collector's Edge First Place Game Gear Jersey

COMPLETE SET (2)	30.00	80.00
STATED ODDS 1:480		
1 Peyton Manning	25.00	50.00
2 Ryan Leaf	10.00	25.00
P1 Peyton Manning Promo (No Jersey Swatch)	3.00	6.00
P2 Ryan Leaf Promo (No Jersey Swatch)	.75	2.00

1998 Collector's Edge First Place Ryan Leaf

COMPLETE SET (5)	1.25	3.00
COMMON CARD (1-5)	.30	.75
*GOLDS: .4X TO 1X BASIC INSERTS		
*SILVERS: .4X TO 1X BASIC INSERTS		

1998 Collector's Edge First Place Peyton Manning

COMPLETE SET (5)	8.00	20.00
COMMON CARD (1-5)	2.00	5.00
*GOLDS: .5X TO 1.2X BASIC INSERTS		
*SILVERS: .5X TO 1.2X BASIC INSERTS		

1998 Collector's Edge First Place Markers

COMPLETE SET (30)	50.00	100.00
STATED ODDS 1:24		
1 Michael Pittman	1.25	3.00
2 Andre Wadsworth	.60	1.50
3 Keith Brooking	1.00	2.50
4 Pat Johnson	.60	1.50
5 Jonathan Linton	.60	1.50
6 Donald Hayes	.60	1.50
7 Mark Chmura	.40	1.00
8 Terry Allen	.60	1.50
9 Brian Griese	2.00	5.00
10 Marcus Nash	.50	1.25
11 Germane Crowell	.60	1.50
12 Roosevelt Blackmon	.50	1.25
13 Peyton Manning	12.50	30.00
14 Tavian Banks	.40	1.00
15 Fred Taylor	3.00	8.00
16 Jim Druckenmiller	.25	.60
17 John Avery	.60	1.50
18 Randy Moss	8.00	20.00
19 Robert Edwards	.60	1.50
20 Cameron Cleeland	.50	1.25
21 Joe Jurevicius	1.00	2.50
22 Charles Woodson	1.25	3.00
23 Terry Allen	.60	1.50
24 Ryan Leaf	1.00	2.50
25 Chris Ruhman	.50	1.25
26 Ahman Green	3.00	8.00
27 Jerome Pathon	1.00	2.50
28 Jacquez Green	.60	1.50
29 Kevin Dyson	1.00	2.50
30 Skip Hicks	1.00	2.50

1998 Collector's Edge First Place Pro Signature Authentics

STATED ODDS 1:600		
1 Jim Druckenmiller		
2 Eddie George		
3 Ryan Leaf/35	50.00	120.00
4 Peyton Manning/50	75.00	150.00
5 Peyton Manning Jumbo (measures 4 1/2" x 6")	75.00	150.00
6 Peyton Manning (Commemorative Limited Edition)	50.00	100.00
7 Emmitt Smith/50	75.00	125.00

1998 Collector's Edge First Place Record Setters

59 Terrell Davis (Super Bowl 33 Champs)	.25	.60
70 John Elway (50,000-yards Passing)	1.00	2.50
135 Peyton Manning (1998 Top Rookie)	2.00	5.00
136 Dan Marino (400-TD Passes)	1.00	2.50
157A Randy Moss (Rookie Record Setter)	1.25	3.00
157B Randy Moss (Rookie of the Year)	1.25	3.00

1998 Collector's Edge First Place Rookie Ink

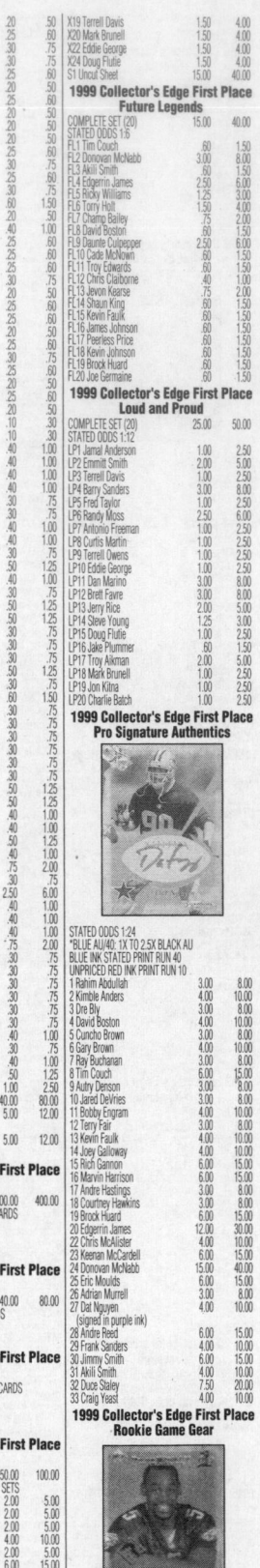

BLUE INK STATED ODDS 1:24		
*RED INK/40-50: 1X TO 2.5X BASIC AU		
RED INK PRINT RUN 40-50		
1 Terry Allen	6.00	15.00
2 Mike Alstott	7.50	20.00
3 Reidel Anthony	6.00	15.00
4 Justin Armour	4.00	10.00
5 Tavian Banks	4.00	10.00
6 Tiki Barber	15.00	30.00
7 Charlie Batch	7.50	20.00
8 Mark Bruener	4.00	10.00
9 Cris Carter	10.00	25.00
10 Stephen Davis	7.50	20.00
11 Jim Druckenmiller	4.00	10.00
12 Tim Dwight	7.50	20.00
13 Ahman Green	12.00	30.00
14 Jacquez Green	6.00	15.00
15 Kevin Greene	6.00	15.00
16 Brian Griese	7.50	20.00
17 Marvin Harrison	15.00	40.00
18 Skip Hicks	6.00	15.00
19 Robert Holcombe	6.00	15.00
20 Joe Jurevicius	7.50	20.00
21 Fred Lane	4.00	10.00
22 Ryan Leaf	6.00	15.00
23A Peyton Manning (Blue Ink)	75.00	150.00
23B Peyton Manning (Black Ink)	75.00	150.00
24 Derrick Mayes	6.00	15.00
25 Randy Moss	60.00	120.00
26 Adrian Murrell	4.00	10.00
27 Marcus Nash	4.00	10.00
28 Jeremy Newberry	4.00	10.00
29 Terrell Owens	15.00	40.00
30 Fred Taylor	7.50	20.00
31 Hines Ward	40.00	80.00

1998 Collector's Edge First Place Successors

COMPLETE SET (25)	25.00	60.00
STATED ODDS 1:8		
1 Troy Aikman	1.50	4.00
2 Jerome Bettis	.75	2.00
3 Drew Bledsoe	1.25	3.00
4 Tim Brown	.75	2.00
5 Mark Brunell	.75	2.00
6 Cris Carter	.75	2.00
7 Terrell Davis	.75	2.00
8 Robert Edwards	.25	.60
9 John Elway	3.00	8.00
10 Brett Favre	3.00	8.00
11 Eddie George	.75	2.00
12 Brian Griese	.75	2.00
13 Napoleon Kaufman	.75	2.00
14 Ryan Leaf	.40	1.00
15 Dorsey Levens	.75	2.00
16 Peyton Manning	6.00	12.00
17 Dan Marino	3.00	8.00
18 Jim Druckenmiller	.30	.75
19 Herman Moore	.50	1.25
20 Randy Moss	3.00	8.00
21 Jake Plummer	.75	2.00
22 Barry Sanders	2.50	6.00
23 Emmitt Smith	2.50	6.00
24 Rod Smith	.50	1.25
25 Fred Taylor	1.00	2.50

1998 Collector's Edge First Place Triple Threat

COMPLETE SET (40)	75.00	150.00
1-15/26-30 BRONZE STATED ODDS 1:12		
16-25 SILVER STATED ODDS 1:24		
31-40 GOLD STATED ODDS 1:36		
1 Robert Brooks	1.00	2.50
2 Troy Aikman	3.00	8.00
3 Randy Moss	5.00	12.00
4 Tim Brown	1.50	4.00
5 Brad Johnson	1.50	4.00
6 Kevin Dyson	1.50	4.00
7 Mark Chmura	1.00	2.50
8 Joey Galloway	1.00	2.50
9 Eddie George	1.50	4.00
10 Napoleon Kaufman	1.50	4.00
11 Dan Marino	6.00	15.00
12 Ed McCaffrey	1.00	2.50
13 Herman Moore	1.00	2.50
14 Carl Pickens	1.00	2.50
15 Emmitt Smith	5.00	12.00
16 Drew Bledsoe	2.50	6.00
17 Keith Brooking	1.50	4.00
18 Mark Brunell	1.50	4.00
19 Terrell Davis	1.50	4.00
20 Antonio Freeman	1.50	4.00
21 Peyton Manning	10.00	20.00
22 Jerry Rice	3.00	8.00
23 Terry Allen	1.50	4.00
24 Danny Wuerffel	1.00	2.50
25 Jerome Bettis	1.50	4.00
26 Fred Taylor	1.25	3.00
27 Andre Wadsworth	1.00	2.50
28 Charles Woodson	1.50	4.00
29 Steve Young	2.00	5.00
30 Mark Chmura	1.00	2.50
31 Cris Carter	2.00	5.00
32 Jim Druckenmiller	2.00	5.00
33 Warrick Dunn	1.50	4.00
34 John Elway	5.00	12.00
35 Brett Favre	7.50	20.00
36 Ryan Leaf	2.00	5.00
37 Dorsey Levens	2.00	5.00
38 Terrell Owens	2.00	5.00
39 Barry Sanders	6.00	15.00
40 Kordell Stewart	2.00	5.00

1998 Collector's Edge First Place Triumph

COMPLETE SET (25)	40.00	80.00
STATED ODDS 1:12		
1 Troy Aikman	2.00	5.00
2 Jerome Bettis	1.00	2.50
3 Drew Bledsoe	1.50	4.00
4 Tim Brown	1.00	2.50
5 Mark Brunell	1.00	2.50
6 Cris Carter	1.00	2.50
7 Terrell Davis	1.00	2.50
8 Jim Druckenmiller	.40	1.00
9 Robert Edwards	.30	.75
10 John Elway	4.00	10.00
11 Brett Favre	4.00	10.00
12 Eddie George	1.00	2.50
13 Brian Griese	1.00	2.50
14 Napoleon Kaufman	1.00	2.50
15 Ryan Leaf	.50	1.25
16 Dorsey Levens	1.00	2.50
17 Peyton Manning	6.00	15.00
18 Dan Marino	4.00	10.00
19 Herman Moore	.60	1.50
20 Randy Moss	4.00	10.00
21 Jake Plummer	1.00	2.50
22 Barry Sanders	3.00	8.00
23 Emmitt Smith	3.00	8.00
24 Rod Smith	.60	1.50
25 Fred Taylor	1.00	2.50

1999 Collector's Edge First Place Previews

These preview cards were issued to promote the 1999 Collector's Edge First Place product. Each card is essentially a parallel of the base card, but printed with gold foil instead of silver along with the word "preview" printed in black on the cardbacks.

COMPLETE SET	3.00	8.00
CB Champ Bailey	.30	.75
CM Cade McNown	.20	.50
DB David Boston	.25	.60
DC Daunte Culpepper	1.00	2.50
EJ Edgerrin James	1.00	2.50
TC Tim Couch	.30	.75
TH Torry Holt	.60	1.50
CMC Chris McAlister	.20	.50

1999 Collector's Edge First Place

Released as a 200-card set, the 1999 Collector's Edge First Place set is comprised of 148 veteran cards, two checklists, and 50 short-printed rookies. Base cards are printed on thick 20 point card stock in full bleed color. This set was packaged in 24-pack boxes containing 12-cards per pack and carried a suggested retail of $3.99. A late addition #201 Kurt Warner card numbered of 500 was included in packs. The card was released later as an unnumbered Promo version through Shop at Home.

COMPLETE SET (200)	20.00	50.00
1 Adrian Murrell	.25	.60
2 Rob Moore	.20	.50
3 Jake Plummer	.25	.60
4 Simeon Rice	.20	.50
5 Frank Sanders	.20	.50
6 Jamal Anderson	.25	.60
7 Chris Calloway	.20	.50
8 Chris Chandler	.25	.60
9 Tim Dwight	.25	.60
10 Terance Mathis	.25	.60
11 Jessie Tuggle	.20	.50
12 Tony Banks	.25	.60
13 Priest Holmes	.30	.75
14 Jermaine Lewis	.20	.50
15 Scott Mitchell	.20	.50
16 Doug Flutie	.30	.75
17 Eric Moulds	.30	.75
18 Andre Reed	.30	.75
19 Antowain Smith	.30	.75
20 Bruce Smith	.30	.75
21 Thurman Thomas	.30	.75
22 Steve Beuerlein	.25	.60
23 Tim Biakabutuka	.25	.60
24 Kevin Greene	.25	.60
25 Muhsin Muhammad	.25	.60
26 Edgar Bennett	.25	.60
27 Curtis Conway	.25	.60
28 Bobby Engram	.25	.60
29 Curtis Enis	.25	.60
30 Erik Kramer	.20	.50
31 Jeff Blake	.25	.60
32 Corey Dillon	.30	.75
33 Carl Pickens	.25	.60
34 Darnay Scott	.25	.60
35 Takeo Spikes	.20	.50
36 Ty Detmer	.25	.60
37 Terry Kirby	.20	.50
38 Leslie Shepherd	.20	.50
39 Chris Spielman	.25	.60
40 Troy Aikman	.50	1.25
41 Michael Irvin	.30	.75
42 Rocket Ismail	.25	.60
43 Ernie Mills	.20	.50
44 Deion Sanders	.30	.75
45 Emmitt Smith	.75	2.00
46 Chris Warren	.25	.60
47 Bubba Brister	.20	.50
48 Terrell Davis	.30	.75
49 Brian Griese	.30	.75
50 Ed McCaffrey	.25	.60
51 Shannon Sharpe	.25	.60
52 Rod Smith	.25	.60
53 Charlie Batch	.30	.75
54 Terry Fair	.20	.50
55 Herman Moore	.25	.60
56 Johnnie Morton	.25	.60
57 Barry Sanders	.75	2.00
58 Santana Dotson	.20	.50
59 Brett Favre	1.00	2.50
60 Mark Chmura	.20	.50
61 Antonio Freeman	.25	.60
62 Dorsey Levens	.25	.60
63 Derrick Mayes	.25	.60
64 Marvin Harrison	.30	.75
65 Peyton Manning	1.00	2.50
66 Jerome Pathon	.20	.50
67 Mark Brunell	.25	.60
68 Keenan McCardell	.25	.60
69 Jimmy Smith	.25	.60
70 Fred Taylor	.30	.75
71 Derrick Alexander WR	.25	.60
72 Kimble Anders	.25	.60
73 Elvis Grbac	.20	.50
74 Warren Moon	.30	.75
75 Byron Bam Morris	.20	.50
76 Andre Rison	.25	.60
77 Karim Abdul-Jabbar	.25	.60
78 Dan Marino	1.00	2.50
79 Tony Martin	.25	.60
80 O.J. McDuffie	.25	.60
81 Zach Thomas	.30	.75
82 Cris Carter	.30	.75
83 Randall Cunningham	.30	.75
84 Jeff George	.20	.50
85 Randy Moss	.30	.75
86 Jake Reed	.25	.60
87 Robert Smith	.30	.75
88 Drew Bledsoe	.30	.75
89 Ben Coates	.25	.60
90 Terry Glenn	.30	.75
91 Ty Law	.25	.60
92 Shawn Jefferson	.20	.50
93 Cameron Cleeland	.20	.50
94 Andre Hastings	.20	.50
95 Billy Joe Hobert	.20	.50
96 Eddie Kennison	.25	.60
97 Gary Brown	.20	.50
98 Kerry Collins	.25	.60
99 Kent Graham	.20	.50
100 Ike Hilliard	.20	.50
101 Joe Jurevicius	.20	.50
102 Wayne Chrebet	.25	.60
103 Aaron Glenn	.20	.50
104 Keyshawn Johnson	.30	.75
105 Mo Lewis	.20	.50
106 Curtis Martin	.30	.75
107 Vinny Testaverde	.25	.60
108 Tim Brown	.30	.75
109 Rich Gannon	.30	.75
110 James Jett	.20	.50
111 Napoleon Kaufman	.25	.60
112 Charles Woodson	.30	.75
113 Koy Detmer	.20	.50
114 Charles Johnson	.20	.50
115 Duce Staley	.25	.60
116 Jerome Bettis	.30	.75
117 Courtney Hawkins	.20	.50
118 Levon Kirkland	.20	.50
119 Kordell Stewart	.25	.60
120 Isaac Bruce	.30	.75
121 Marshall Faulk	.30	.75
122 Trent Green	.25	.60
123 Amp Lee	.20	.50
124 Jim Harbaugh	.25	.60
125 Bryan Still	.20	.50
126 Freddie Jones	.20	.50
127 Mikhael Ricks	.20	.50
128 Natrone Means	.25	.60
129 Junior Seau	.30	.75
130 Lawrence Phillips	.25	.60
131 Terrell Owens	.30	.75
132 Jerry Rice	.60	1.50
133 J.J. Stokes	.20	.50
134 Steve Young	.40	1.00
135 Joey Galloway	.25	.60
136 Jon Kitna	.25	.60
137 Ricky Watters	.25	.60
138 Mike Alstott	.30	.75
139 Reidel Anthony	.25	.60
140 Trent Dilfer	.25	.60
141 Warrick Dunn	.25	.60
142 Kevin Dyson	.20	.50
143 Eddie George	.30	.75
144 Steve McNair	.30	.75
145 Frank Wycheck	.25	.60
146 Skip Hicks	.20	.50
147 Brad Johnson	.25	.60
148 Michael Westbrook	.20	.50
149 Checklist Card	.10	.30
150 Checklist Card	.10	.30
151 David Boston RC	.40	1.00
152 Patrick Kerney RC	.40	1.00
153 Chris McAlister RC	.40	1.00
154 Peerless Price RC	.40	1.00
155 Antoine Winfield RC	.30	.75
156 D'Wayne Bates RC	.30	.75
157 Cade McNown RC	.40	1.00
158 Akili Smith RC	.40	1.00
159 Rahim Abdullah RC	.30	.75
160 Tim Couch RC	.50	1.25
161 Kevin Johnson RC	.40	1.00
162 Ebenezer Ekuban RC	.30	.75
163 Dat Nguyen RC	.50	1.25
164 Al Wilson RC	.50	1.25
165 Chris Claiborne RC	.30	.75
166 Sedrick Irvin RC	.30	.75
167 Antuan Edwards RC	.30	.75
168 Aaron Brooks RC	.50	1.25
169 De'Mond Parker RC	.30	.75
170 Edgerrin James RC	.60	1.50
171 Fernando Bryant RC	.30	.75
172 Mike Cloud RC	.30	.75
173 John Tait RC	.30	.75
174 Cecil Collins RC	.30	.75
175 James Johnson RC	.30	.75
176 Rob Konrad RC	.30	.75
177 Daunte Culpepper RC	.50	1.25
178 Jim Kleinsasser RC	.50	1.25
179 Brock Huard RC	.40	1.00
180 Michael Bishop RC	.40	1.00
181 Kevin Faulk RC	.50	1.25
182 Andy Katzenmoyer RC	.40	1.00
183 Ricky Williams RC	.75	2.00
184 Joe Montgomery RC	.30	.75
185 Donovan McNabb RC	2.50	6.00
186 Troy Edwards RC	.40	1.00
187 Amos Zereoue RC	.40	1.00
188 Joe Germaine RC	.40	1.00
189 Torry Holt RC	.75	2.00
190 Jermaine Fazande RC	.30	.75
191 Reggie McGrew RC	.30	.75
192 Karsten Bailey RC	.30	.75
193 Lamar King RC	.30	.75
194 Autry Denson RC	.30	.75
195 Martin Gramatica RC	.30	.75
196 Shaun King RC	.40	1.00
197 Darnell McDonald RC	.30	.75
198 Anthony McFarland RC	.40	1.00
199 Jevon Kearse RC	.50	1.25
200 Champ Bailey RC	1.00	2.50
201 Kurt Warner/500 RC	40.00	80.00
201PG Kurt Warner Promo (Gold foil on front)	5.00	12.00
201PS Kurt Warner Promo (Silver foil on front)	5.00	12.00

1999 Collector's Edge First Place Galvanized

COMPLETE SET (200)	200.00	400.00
*1-150 VETS/500: 2X TO 5X BASIC CARDS		
1-150 VETERAN PRINT RUN 500		
*151-200 ROOKIES/100: 2.5X TO 6X		
151-200 ROOKIE PRINT RUN 100		

1999 Collector's Edge First Place Gold Ingot

COMPLETE SET (200)	40.00	80.00
*1-150 VETS: .8X TO 2X BASIC CARDS		
*151-200 ROOKIES: .6X TO 1.5X		
ONE GOLD INGOT PER PACK		

1999 Collector's Edge First Place HoloGold

*1-150 VETS/50: 10X TO 25X BASIC CARDS
1-150 VETERAN PRINT RUN 50
*151-200 ROOKIES/10: 15X TO 40X
151-200 ROOKIE PRINT RUN 10

1999 Collector's Edge First Place Adrenalin

COMPLETE SET (20)	50.00	100.00
STATED PRINT RUN 1000 SERIAL #'d SETS		
A1 Jake Plummer	2.00	5.00
A2 Jamal Anderson	2.00	5.00
A3 Eric Moulds	2.00	5.00
A4 Emmitt Smith	4.00	10.00
A5 Terrell Davis	2.00	5.00
A6 Barry Sanders	6.00	15.00
A7 Brett Favre	6.00	15.00
A8 Antonio Freeman	2.00	5.00
A9 Peyton Manning	5.00	12.00
A10 Mark Brunell	2.00	5.00
A11 Fred Taylor	2.00	5.00
A12 Dan Marino	6.00	15.00
A13 Cris Carter	2.00	5.00
A14 Randy Moss	4.00	10.00
A15 Keyshawn Johnson	2.00	5.00
A16 Curtis Martin	2.00	5.00
A17 Jerome Bettis	2.00	5.00
A18 Terrell Owens	2.00	5.00
A19 Joey Galloway	2.00	5.00
A20 Eddie George	2.00	5.00

1999 Collector's Edge First Place Excalibur

COMPLETE SET (9)	25.00	50.00
STATED ODDS 1:24		
X2 Torry Holt	2.50	6.00
X5 Edgerrin James	4.00	10.00
X6 Brett Favre	5.00	12.00
X13 Peyton Manning	4.00	10.00
X17 Randy Moss	3.00	8.00
X19 Terrell Davis	1.50	4.00
X20 Mark Brunell	1.50	4.00
X22 Eddie George	1.50	4.00
X24 Doug Flutie	1.50	4.00
S1 Uncut Sheet	15.00	40.00

1999 Collector's Edge First Place Future Legends

COMPLETE SET (20)	15.00	40.00
STATED ODDS 1:6		
FL1 Tim Couch	.60	1.50
FL2 Donovan McNabb	3.00	8.00
FL3 Akili Smith	.60	1.50
FL4 Edgerrin James	2.50	6.00
FL5 Ricky Williams	1.25	3.00
FL6 Torry Holt	1.50	4.00
FL7 Champ Bailey	.75	2.00
FL8 David Boston	.60	1.50
FL9 Daunte Culpepper	2.50	6.00
FL10 Cade McNown	.60	1.50
FL11 Troy Edwards	.60	1.50
FL12 Chris Claiborne	.40	1.00
FL13 Jevon Kearse	.75	2.00
FL14 Shaun King	.60	1.50
FL15 Kevin Faulk	.60	1.50
FL16 James Johnson	.60	1.50
FL17 Peerless Price	.60	1.50
FL18 Kevin Johnson	.60	1.50
FL19 Brock Huard	.60	1.50
FL20 Joe Germaine	.60	1.50

1999 Collector's Edge First Place Loud and Proud

COMPLETE SET (20)	25.00	50.00
STATED ODDS 1:12		
LP1 Jamal Anderson	1.00	2.50
LP2 Emmitt Smith	2.00	5.00
LP3 Terrell Davis	1.00	2.50
LP4 Barry Sanders	3.00	8.00
LP5 Fred Taylor	1.00	2.50
LP6 Randy Moss	2.50	6.00
LP7 Antonio Freeman	1.00	2.50
LP8 Curtis Martin	1.00	2.50
LP9 Terrell Owens	1.00	2.50
LP10 Eddie George	1.00	2.50
LP11 Dan Marino	3.00	8.00
LP12 Brett Favre	3.00	8.00
LP13 Jerry Rice	2.00	5.00
LP14 Steve Young	1.25	3.00
LP15 Doug Flutie	1.00	2.50
LP16 Jake Plummer	.60	1.50
LP17 Troy Aikman	2.00	5.00
LP18 Mark Brunell	1.00	2.50
LP19 Jon Kitna	1.00	2.50
LP20 Charlie Batch	1.00	2.50

1999 Collector's Edge First Place Pro Signature Authentics

STATED ODDS 1:24		
*BLUE AU/40: 1X TO 2.5X BLACK AU		
BLUE INK STATED PRINT RUN 40		
UNPRICED RED INK PRINT RUN 10		
1 Rahim Abdullah	3.00	8.00
2 Kimble Anders	4.00	10.00
3 Dre Bly	3.00	8.00
4 David Boston	4.00	10.00
5 Cuncho Brown	3.00	8.00
6 Gary Brown	4.00	10.00
7 Ray Buchanan	3.00	8.00
8 Tim Couch	6.00	15.00
9 Autry Denson	3.00	8.00
10 Jared DeVries	3.00	8.00
11 Bobby Engram	4.00	10.00
12 Terry Fair	3.00	8.00
13 Kevin Faulk	4.00	10.00
14 Joey Galloway	4.00	10.00
15 Rich Gannon	6.00	15.00
16 Marvin Harrison	6.00	15.00
17 Andre Hastings	3.00	8.00
18 Courtney Hawkins	3.00	8.00
19 Brock Huard	6.00	15.00
20 Edgerrin James	12.00	30.00
22 Chris McAlister	4.00	10.00
23 Keenan McCardell	6.00	15.00
24 Donovan McNabb	15.00	40.00
25 Eric Moulds	6.00	15.00
26 Adrian Murrell	3.00	8.00
27 Dat Nguyen (signed in purple ink)	4.00	10.00
28 Andre Reed	6.00	15.00
29 Frank Sanders	4.00	10.00
30 Jimmy Smith	6.00	15.00
31 Akili Smith	4.00	10.00
32 Duce Staley	7.50	20.00
33 Craig Yeast	4.00	10.00

1999 Collector's Edge First Place Rookie Game Gear

COMPLETE SET (10)	100.00	200.00
STATED PRINT RUN 500 SERIAL #'d SETS		
*HOLOGOLD: .15X TO .4X BASIC INSERTS		
*PREVIEWS: .2X TO .5X BASIC INSERTS		
RG1 Tim Couch	5.00	12.00
RG2 Donovan McNabb	15.00	40.00
RG3 Akili Smith	5.00	12.00
RG4 Daunte Culpepper	12.50	30.00
RG5 Ricky Williams	6.00	15.00
RG6 Kevin Johnson	5.00	12.00
RG7 Cade McNown	5.00	12.00
RG8 Torry Holt	7.50	20.00
RG9 Champ Bailey	5.00	12.00
RG10 David Boston	5.00	12.00

1999 Collector's Edge First Place Successors

COMPLETE SET (15)	30.00	60.00
STATED ODDS 1:12		
S1 David Boston	1.00	2.50

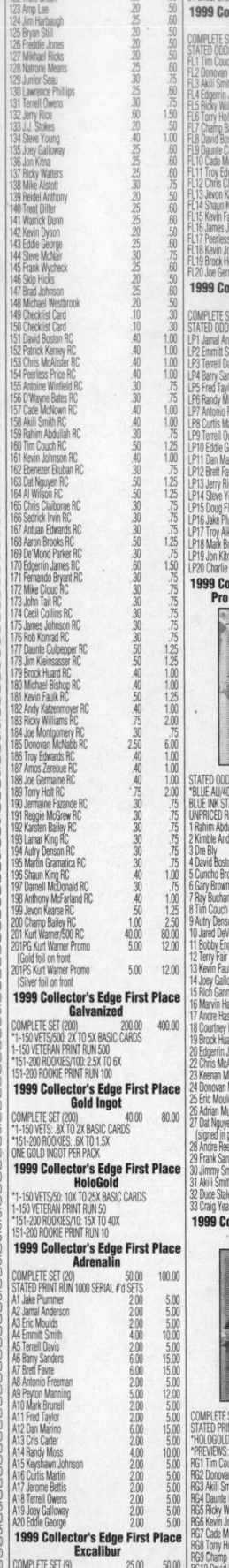

Cris Carter		
S2 Peerless Price	1.25	3.00
Eric Moulds		
S3 Cade McNown	3.00	8.00
Brett Favre		
S4 Akili Smith	1.00	2.50
Charlie Batch		
S5 Tim Couch	4.00	10.00
Peyton Manning		
S6 Kevin Johnson	1.00	2.50
Joey Galloway		
S7 Edgerrin James	4.00	10.00
Emmitt Smith		
S8 James Johnson	1.00	2.50
C.Martin		
S9 Daunte Culpepper	4.00	10.00
Dan Marino		
S10 Kevin Faulk	3.00	8.00
Barry Sanders		
S11 Rickey Williams	1.50	4.00
Marshall Faulk		
S12 Donovan McNabb	3.00	8.00
Steve Young		
S13 Troy Edwards	1.00	2.50
Keyshawn Johnson		
S14 Torry Holt	2.50	6.00
Jerry Rice		
S15 Shaun King	1.00	2.50
Jake Plummer		

1999 Collector's Edge Fury Previews

This set was released as a Preview of the 1999 Collector's Edge Fury base set. Each card is essentially a parallel version of the base set card with the player's initials as the card number along with the word "preview" on the cardbacks.

COMPLETE SET (10)	6.00	15.00
BF Brett Favre	1.20	3.00
CC Cris Carter	.40	1.00
DM Dan Marino	1.20	3.00
JA Jamal Anderson	.40	1.00
JB Jerome Bettis	.40	1.00
PM Peyton Manning	1.20	3.00
RE Robert Edwards	.25	.60
RM Randy Moss	1.20	3.00
TD Terrell Davis	.80	2.00
WD Warrick Dunn	.40	1.00

1999 Collector's Edge Fury

The 1999 Collector's Edge Fury set was issued in one series for a total of 200 cards. The fronts feature color action photos of NFL stars and rookies appearing for the first time in their NFL uniforms. The backs carry player information and career statistics.

COMPLETE SET (200)	15.00	40.00
1 Checklist Card 1	.10	.30
2 Checklist Card 2	.10	.30
3 Karim Abdul-Jabbar	.25	.60
4 Troy Aikman	.50	1.25
5 Derrick Alexander WR	.20	.50
6 Mike Alstott	.30	.75
7 Jamal Anderson	.25	.60
8 Reidel Anthony	.20	.50
9 Tiki Barber	.30	.75
10 Charlie Batch	.25	.60
11 Edgar Bennett	.25	.60
12 Jerome Bettis	.30	.75
13 Steve Beuerlein	.25	.60
14 Tim Biakabutuka	.25	.60
15 Jeff Blake	.25	.60
16 Drew Bledsoe	.30	.75
17 Bubby Brister	.20	.50
18 Robert Brooks	.25	.60
19 Gary Brown	.20	.50
20 Tim Brown	.30	.75
21 Isaac Bruce	.30	.75
22 Mark Brunell	.25	.60
23 Chris Calloway	.20	.50
24 Cris Carter	.30	.75
25 Larry Centers	.25	.60
26 Chris Chandler	.25	.60
27 Wayne Chrebet	.25	.60
28 Cam Cleeland	.20	.50
29 Kerry Collins	.25	.60
30 Curtis Conway	.25	.60
31 Germane Crowell	.20	.50
32 Randall Cunningham	.30	.75
33 Terrell Davis	.30	.75
34 Koy Detmer	.20	.50
35 Ty Detmer	.25	.60
36 Trent Dilfer	.25	.60
37 Corey Dillon	.25	.60
38 Warrick Dunn	.25	.60
39 Tim Dwight	.25	.60
40 Kevin Dyson	.20	.50
41 John Elway	1.00	2.50
42 Bobby Engram	.25	.60
43 Curtis Enis	.20	.50
44 Terry Fair	.20	.50
45 Marshall Faulk	.30	.75
46 Brett Favre	1.00	2.50
47 Doug Flutie	.30	.75
48 Antonio Freeman	.25	.60
49 Joey Galloway	.25	.60
50 Rich Gannon	.25	.60
51 Eddie George	.25	.60
52 Jeff George	.20	.50
53 Terry Glenn	.25	.60
54 Elvis Grbac	.20	.50
55 Ahman Green	.25	.60
56 Jacquez Green	.20	.50
57 Trent Green	.25	.60
58 Kevin Greene	.25	.60
59 Brian Griese	.25	.60
60 Az-Zahir Hakim	.20	.50
61 Jim Harbaugh	.25	.60
62 Marvin Harrison	.30	.75
63 Courtney Hawkins	.20	.50
64 Garrison Hearst	.25	.60
65 Ike Hilliard	.25	.60
66 Billy Joe Hobert	.20	.50
67 Priest Holmes	.30	.75
68 Michael Irvin	.30	.75
69 Rocket Ismail	.25	.60
70 Shawn Jefferson	.20	.50
71 James Jett	.20	.50
72 Brad Johnson	.25	.60
73 Charles Johnson	.20	.50
74 Keyshawn Johnson	.25	.60
75 Pat Johnson	.20	.50
76 Joe Jurevicius	.20	.50
77 Napoleon Kaufman	.20	.50
78 Eddie Kennison	.25	.60
79 Terry Kirby	.20	.50
80 Jon Kitna	.25	.60
81 Erik Kramer	.25	.60
82 Fred Lane	.20	.50
83 Ty Law	.25	.60
84 Ryan Leaf	.25	.60
85 Amp Lee	.20	.50
86 Dorsey Levens	.25	.60
87 Jermaine Lewis	.20	.50
88 Sam Madison	.20	.50
89 Peyton Manning	1.00	2.50
90 Dan Marino	1.00	2.50
91 Curtis Martin	.30	.75
92 Tony Martin	.25	.60
93 Terance Mathis	.20	.50
94 Ed McCaffrey	.25	.60
95 Keenan McCardell	.25	.60
96 O.J. McDuffie	.25	.60
97 Steve McNair	.30	.75
98 Natrone Means	.25	.60
99 Herman Moore	.25	.60
100 Rob Moore	.20	.50
101 Byron Bam Morris	.20	.50
102 Johnnie Morton	.25	.60
103 Randy Moss	.30	.75
104 Eric Moulds	.25	.60
105 Muhsin Muhammad	.25	.60
106 Adrian Murrell	.25	.60
107 Terrell Owens	.30	.75
108 Jerome Pathon	.20	.50
109 Carl Pickens	.25	.60
110 Jake Plummer	.25	.60
111 Andre Reed	.30	.75
112 Jake Reed	.25	.60
113 Jerry Rice	.60	1.50
114 Mikhael Ricks	.20	.50
115 Andre Rison	.25	.60
116 Barry Sanders	.75	2.00
117 Deion Sanders	.30	.75
118 Frank Sanders	.20	.50
119 O.J. Santiago	.20	.50
120 Darnay Scott	.20	.50
121 Junior Seau	.30	.75
122 Shannon Sharpe	.30	.75
123 Leslie Shepherd UER	.20	.50
Back lists him with wrong team		
124 Antowain Smith	.20	.50
125 Bruce Smith	.30	.75
126 Emmitt Smith	.75	2.00
127 Jimmy Smith	.25	.60
128 Robert Smith	.25	.60
129 Rod Smith	.25	.60
130 Chris Spielman	.25	.60
131 Takeo Spikes	.20	.50
132 Duce Staley	.25	.60
133 Kordell Stewart	.25	.60
134 Bryan Still	.20	.50
135 J.J. Stokes	.20	.50
136 Fred Taylor	.25	.60
137 Vinny Testaverde	.25	.60
138 Yancey Thigpen	.20	.50
139 Thurman Thomas	.30	.75
140 Zach Thomas	.30	.75
141 Amani Toomer	.25	.60
142 Hines Ward	.30	.75
143 Chris Warren	.25	.60
144 Ricky Watters	.25	.60
145 Michael Westbrook	.20	.50
146 Alvis Whitted	.20	.50
147 Charles Woodson	.30	.75
148 Rod Woodson	.30	.75
149 Frank Wycheck	.25	.60
150 Steve Young	.40	1.00
151 Rahim Abdullah RC	.30	.75
152 Champ Bailey RC	1.00	2.50
153 D'Wayne Bates RC	.30	.75
154 Michael Bishop RC	.40	1.00
155 Dre Bly RC	.50	1.25
156 David Boston RC	.40	1.00
157 Fernando Bryant RC	.30	.75
158 Chris Claiborne RC	.30	.75
159 Mike Cloud RC	.30	.75
160 Cecil Colliins RC	.30	.75
161 Tim Couch RC	.50	1.25
162 Daunte Culpepper RC	.50	1.25
163 Antuan Edwards RC	.30	.75
164 Troy Edwards RC	.40	1.00
165 Ebenezer Ekuban RC	.30	.75
166 Kevin Faulk RC	.50	1.25
167 Joe Germaine RC	.40	1.00
168 Aaron Gibson RC	.30	.75
169 Martin Gramatica RC	.30	.75
170 Torry Holt RC	.75	2.00
171 Brock Huard RC	.40	1.00
172 Sedrick Irvin RC	.30	.75
173 Edgerrin James RC	.60	1.50
174 James Johnson RC	.30	.75
175 Kevin Johnson RC	.40	1.00
176 Andy Katzenmoyer RC	.40	1.00
177 Jevon Kearse RC	.50	1.25
178 Patrick Kerney RC	.40	1.00
179 Lamar King RC	.30	.75
180 Shaun King RC	.40	1.00
181 Jim Kleinsasser RC	.50	1.25
182 Rob Konrad RC	.30	.75
183 Chris McAlister RC	.40	1.00
184 Anthony McFarland RC	.40	1.00
185 Karsten Bailey RC	.30	.75
186 Donovan McNabb RC	2.50	6.00
187 Cade McNown RC	.40	1.00
188 Joe Montgomery RC	.30	.75
189 Dat Nguyen RC	.50	1.25
190 Luke Petitgout RC	.30	.75
191 Peerless Price RC	.40	1.00
192 Akili Smith RC	.40	1.00
193 Matt Stinchcomb RC	.30	.75
194 John Tait RC	.30	.75
195 Jermaine Fazande RC	.30	.75
196 Ricky Williams RC	.75	2.00
197 Al Wilson RC	.50	1.25
198 Antoine Winfield RC	.30	.75
199 Damien Woody RC	.30	.75
200 Amos Zereoue RC	.40	1.00

1999 Collector's Edge Fury Galvanized

COMPLETE SET (200)	200.00	400.00

*1-150 VETS/500: 2X TO 5X BASIC CARDS
1-150 VETERAN PRINT RUN 500
*151-200 ROOKIES/100: 2.5X TO 6X
151-200 ROOKIE PRINT RUN 100
*PREVIEW VETS: .3X TO .8X BASIC CARDS
*PREVIEW ROOKIES: .2X TO .5X BASIC RC

1999 Collector's Edge Fury Gold Ingot

COMPLETE SET (200)	50.00	100.00

*1-150 VETS: .8X TO 2X BASIC CARDS
*151-200 ROOKIES: .6X TO 1.5X
ONE PER PACK

1999 Collector's Edge Fury HoloGold

*1-150 VETS/50: 10X TO 25X BASIC CARDS
1-150 VETERAN PRINT RUN 50
*151-200 ROOKIES/10: 15X TO 40X
151-200 ROOKIE PRINT RUN 10

1999 Collector's Edge Fury Extreme Team

COMPLETE SET (10)	25.00	60.00
STATED ODDS 1:24		
E1 Keyshawn Johnson	2.00	5.00
E2 Emmitt Smith	4.00	10.00
E3 John Elway	6.00	15.00
E4 Doug Flutie	2.00	5.00
E5 Jamal Anderson	2.00	5.00
E6 Brett Favre	6.00	15.00
E7 Peyton Manning	6.00	15.00
E8 Fred Taylor	2.00	5.00
E9 Dan Marino	6.00	15.00
E10 Randy Moss	5.00	12.00

1999 Collector's Edge Fury Fast and Furious

COMPLETE SET (25)	40.00	100.00
STATED PRINT RUN 500 SERIAL #'d SETS		
1 Jake Plummer	1.25	3.00
2 Jamal Anderson	2.00	5.00
3 Eric Moulds	2.00	5.00
4 Curtis Enis	.75	2.00
5 Emmitt Smith	4.00	10.00
6 Deion Sanders	2.00	5.00
7 Terrell Davis	2.00	5.00
8 Barry Sanders	6.00	15.00
9 Herman Moore	1.25	3.00
10 Charlie Batch	2.00	5.00
11 Marshall Faulk	2.50	6.00
12 Mark Brunell	2.00	5.00
13 Fred Taylor	2.00	5.00
14 Randy Moss	5.00	12.00
15 Cris Carter	2.00	5.00
16 Robert Edwards	.75	2.00
17 Keyshawn Johnson	2.00	5.00
18 Curtis Martin	2.00	5.00
19 Charles Woodson	2.00	5.00
20 Jerome Bettis	2.00	5.00
21 Kordell Stewart	1.25	3.00
22 Steve Young	2.50	6.00
23 Jerry Rice	4.00	10.00
24 Warrick Dunn	2.00	5.00
25 Eddie George	2.00	5.00

1999 Collector's Edge Fury Forerunners

COMPLETE SET (15)	20.00	50.00
STATED ODDS 1:8		
F1 Jamal Anderson	1.50	4.00
F2 Curtis Enis	.60	1.50
F3 Corey Dillon	1.50	4.00
F4 Emmitt Smith	3.00	8.00
F5 Barry Sanders	5.00	12.00
F6 Terrell Davis	1.50	4.00
F7 Marshall Faulk	2.00	5.00
F8 Fred Taylor	1.50	4.00
F9 Robert Smith	1.50	4.00
F10 Curtis Martin	1.50	4.00
F11 Jerome Bettis	1.50	4.00
F12 Garrison Hearst	1.00	2.50
F13 Warrick Dunn	1.50	4.00
F14 Eddie George	1.50	4.00
F15 Ricky Watters	1.00	2.50

1999 Collector's Edge Fury Game Ball

COMPLETE SET (43)	300.00	600.00
STATED ODDS 1:24		
AF Antonio Freeman	6.00	15.00
AM Adrian Murrell	3.00	8.00
AS Antowain Smith	6.00	15.00
BF Brett Favre	20.00	50.00
BS Barry Sanders	20.00	50.00
CB Charlie Batch	6.00	15.00
CC Cris Carter	6.00	15.00
CD Corey Dillon	6.00	15.00
CE Curtis Enis	3.00	8.00
CM Curtis Martin	6.00	15.00
CP Carl Pickens	3.00	8.00
DL Dorsey Levens	6.00	15.00
DS Deion Sanders	6.00	15.00
EG Eddie George	6.00	15.00
ES Emmitt Smith	12.50	30.00
FT Fred Taylor	6.00	15.00
GH Garrison Hearst	3.00	8.00
HM Herman Moore	6.00	15.00
JB Jerome Bettis	6.00	15.00
JE John Elway	20.00	50.00
JG Joey Galloway	6.00	15.00
JP Jake Plummer	6.00	15.00
JR Jerry Rice	12.50	30.00
KS Kordell Stewart	6.00	15.00
MA Mike Alstott	6.00	15.00
MB Mark Brunell	6.00	15.00
MF Marshall Faulk	10.00	25.00
MI Michael Irvin	6.00	15.00
NK Napoleon Kaufman	6.00	15.00
NM Natrone Means	3.00	8.00
PM Peyton Manning	15.00	40.00
RJ Rob Johnson	3.00	8.00
RL Ryan Leaf	6.00	15.00
RM Randy Moss	12.50	30.00
RS Rod Smith	3.00	8.00
SM Steve McNair	6.00	15.00
SS Shannon Sharpe	3.00	8.00
SY Steve Young	7.50	20.00
TA Troy Aikman	12.50	30.00
TD Terrell Davis	6.00	15.00
TO Terrell Owens	6.00	15.00
WD Warrick Dunn	6.00	15.00
WM Warren Moon	6.00	15.00

1999 Collector's Edge Fury Heir Force

COMPLETE SET (20)	20.00	50.00
STATED ODDS 1:6		
HF1 Rahim Abdullah	.50	1.25
HF2 Champ Bailey	.75	2.00
HF3 D'Wayne Bates	.50	1.25
HF4 Michael Bishop	.60	1.50
HF5 David Boston	.60	1.50
HF6 Chris Claiborne	.50	1.25
HF7 Tim Couch	.60	1.50
HF8 Daunte Culpepper	2.50	6.00
HF9 Kevin Faulk	.60	1.50
HF10 Torry Holt	1.50	4.00
HF11 Brock Huard	.60	1.50
HF12 Edgerrin James	2.50	6.00
HF13 Andy Katzenmoyer	.60	1.50
HF14 Shaun King	.60	1.50
HF15 Rob Konrad	.60	1.50
HF16 Donovan McNabb	3.00	8.00
HF17 Cade McNown	.60	1.50
HF18 Peerless Price	.60	1.50
HF19 Akili Smith	.50	1.25
HF20 Ricky Williams	1.25	3.00

1999 Collector's Edge Fury Xplosive

COMPLETE SET (20)	40.00	100.00
STATED ODDS 1:12		
1 Jake Plummer	1.25	3.00
2 Doug Flutie	2.00	5.00
3 Eric Moulds	2.00	5.00
4 Troy Aikman	4.00	10.00
5 John Elway	6.00	15.00
6 Charlie Batch	2.00	5.00
7 Herman Moore	1.25	3.00
8 Brett Favre	6.00	15.00
9 Antonio Freeman	2.00	5.00
10 Peyton Manning	6.00	15.00
11 Mark Brunell	2.00	5.00
12 Dan Marino	6.00	15.00
13 Randy Moss	5.00	12.00
14 Drew Bledsoe	2.50	6.00
15 Keyshawn Johnson	2.00	5.00
16 Vinny Testaverde	1.25	3.00
17 Kordell Stewart	1.25	3.00
18 Terrell Owens	2.00	5.00
19 Jerry Rice	4.00	10.00
20 Steve Young	2.50	6.00

1997 Collector's Edge Masters Promos

COMPLETE SET (3)	1.25	3.00

1997 Collector's Edge Masters

The 1997 Collector's Edge Masters set was issued in one series totaling 270 cards and was distributed in six-card packs with a suggested retail price of $3.49. The set contains color photos of 240 top players in the NFL printed on metalized card stock, for the hobby version, with silver texture or regular white paper stock, for the retail version, plus 30 team flag cards which were inserted randomly at the rate of one every three packs. A collector could send in the Flag Card for either Green Bay or New England plus one Flag Card for each opponent beaten by these teams during the regular and post-season (one Flag Card per game) and receive a foil stamped limited edition team set of the Packers or the Patriots. The card wrappers carried the rules and details for this limited offer.

COMPLETE SET (270)	15.00	40.00
1 Cardinals Flag	.20	.50
2 Larry Centers	.25	.60
3 Rob Moore	.25	.60
4 Frank Sanders	.25	.60
5 Eric Swann	.15	.40
6 Falcons Flag	.20	.50
7 Morten Andersen UER	.15	.40
misspelled Morton		
8 Bert Emanuel	.25	.60
9 Jeff George	.25	.60
10 Craig Heyward	.15	.40
11 Terance Mathis	.25	.60
12 Clay Matthews	.15	.40
13 Eric Metcalf	.25	.60
14 Ravens Flag	.20	.50
15 Rob Burnett	.15	.40
16 Leroy Hoard	.15	.40
17 Ernest Hunter	.15	.40
18 Michael Jackson	.25	.60
19 Stevon Moore	.15	.40
20 Anthony Pleasant	.15	.40
21 Vinny Testaverde	.25	.60
22 Eric Zeier	.25	.60
23 Bills Flag	.20	.50
24 Todd Collins	.15	.40
25 Russell Copeland	.15	.40
26 Quinn Early	.15	.40
27 Jim Kelly	.40	1.00
28 Bryce Paup	.15	.40
29 Andre Reed	.25	.60
30 Bruce Smith	.25	.60
31 Panthers Flag	.20	.50
32 Steve Beuerlein	.25	.60
33 Mark Carrier WR	.15	.40
34 Kerry Collins	.40	1.00
35 Willie Green	.15	.40
36 Kevin Greene	.25	.60
37 Eric Guliford	.15	.40
38 Brett Maxie	.15	.40
39 Tim McKyer	.15	.40
40 Derrick Moore	.15	.40
41 Bears Flag	.20	.50
42 Curtis Conway	.25	.60
43 Bryan Cox	.15	.40
44 Jim Flanigan	.15	.40
45 Robert Green	.15	.40
46 Erik Kramer	.15	.40
47 Dave Krieg	.15	.40
48 Rashaan Salaam	.15	.40
49 Alonzo Spellman	.15	.40
50 Donnell Woolford	.15	.40
51 Chris Zorich	.15	.40
52 Bengals Flag	.20	.50
53 Eric Bieniemy	.15	.40
54 Jeff Blake	.25	.60
55 Ki-Jana Carter	.15	.40
56 John Copeland	.15	.40
57 Garrison Hearst	.25	.60
58 Tony McGee	.15	.40
59 Carl Pickens	.25	.60
60 Darnay Scott	.25	.60
61 Bracy Walker	.15	.40
62 Dan Wilkinson	.15	.40
63 Cowboys Flag	.20	.50
64 Troy Aikman	.75	2.00
65 Bill Bates	.25	.60
66 Shante Carver	.15	.40
67 Michael Irvin	.40	1.00
68 Daryl Johnston	.25	.60
69 Jay Novacek	.15	.40
70 Deion Sanders	.40	1.00
71 Emmitt Smith	1.50	3.00
72 Herschel Walker	.25	.60
73 Sherman Williams	.15	.40
74 Broncos Flag	.20	.50
75 Terrell Davis	.50	1.25
76 John Elway	1.50	4.00
77 Ed McCaffrey	.25	.60
78 Anthony Miller	.15	.40
79 Michael Dean Perry	.15	.40
80 Shannon Sharpe	.25	.60
81 Mike Sherrard	.15	.40
82 Lions Flag	.20	.50
83 Scott Mitchell	.25	.60
84 Glyn Milburn	.15	.40
85 Herman Moore	.25	.60
86 Johnnie Morton	.25	.60
87 Brett Perriman	.15	.40
88 Barry Sanders	1.25	3.00
89 Tracy Scroggins	.15	.40
90 Packers Flag	.20	.50
91 Edgar Bennett	.25	.60
92 Robert Brooks	.25	.60
93 Santana Dotson	.15	.40
94 Brett Favre	2.00	4.00
95 Dorsey Levens	.40	1.00
96 Craig Newsome	.15	.40
97 Wayne Simmons	.15	.40
98 Reggie White	.40	1.00
99 Oilers Flag	.20	.50
100 Chris Chandler	.25	.60
101 Anthony Cook	.15	.40
102 Willie Davis	.15	.40
103 Mel Gray	.15	.40
104 Ronnie Harmon	.15	.40
105 Darryll Lewis	.15	.40
106 Steve McNair	.50	1.25
107 Todd McNair	.15	.40
108 Rodney Thomas	.15	.40
109 Colts Flag	.20	.50
110 Trev Alberts	.15	.40
111 Tony Bennett	.15	.40
112 Quentin Coryatt	.15	.40
113 Sean Dawkins	.15	.40
114 Ken Dilger	.15	.40
115 Marshall Faulk	.50	1.25
116 Jim Harbaugh UER	.25	.60
numbered 115 on back		
117 Ronald Humphrey	.15	.40
118 Floyd Turner	.15	.40
119 Jaguars Flag	.20	.50
120 Tony Boselli	.15	.40
121 Mark Brunell	.50	1.25
122 Willie Jackson	.15	.40
123 Jeff Lageman	.15	.40
124 Natrone Means	.25	.60
125 Andre Rison	.25	.60
126 James O.Stewart	.25	.60
127 Cedric Tillman	.15	.40
128 Chiefs Flag	.20	.50
129 Marcus Allen	.40	1.00
130 Kimble Anders	.25	.60
131 Steve Bono	.25	.60
132 Dale Carter	.15	.40
133 Lake Dawson	.15	.40
134 Dan Saleaumua	.15	.40
135 Neil Smith	.25	.60
136 Derrick Thomas	.40	1.00
137 Tamarick Vanover	.25	.60
138 Dolphins Flag	.20	.50
139 Fred Barnett	.15	.40
140 Steve Emtman	.15	.40
141 Eric Green	.15	.40
142 Dan Marino	1.50	4.00
143 O.J. McDuffie	.25	.60
144 Bernie Parmalee	.15	.40
145 Vikings Flag	.20	.50
146 Cris Carter	.40	1.00
147 Jack Del Rio	.15	.40
148 Qadry Ismail	.25	.60
149 Amp Lee	.15	.40
150 Warren Moon	.40	1.00
151 John Randle	.25	.60
152 Jake Reed	.25	.60
153 Robert Smith	.25	.60
154 Patriots Flag	.20	.50
155 Drew Bledsoe	.50	1.25
156 Vincent Brisby	.15	.40
157 Willie Clay	.15	.40
158 Ben Coates	.25	.60
159 Curtis Martin	.50	1.25
160 Dave Meggett	.15	.40
161 Will Moore	.15	.40
162 Chris Slade	.15	.40
163 Saints Flag	.20	.50
164 Mario Bates	.15	.40
165 Jim Everett	.15	.40
166 Michael Haynes	.15	.40
167 Tyrone Hughes	.15	.40
168 Haywood Jeffires	.15	.40
169 Wayne Martin	.15	.40
170 Renaldo Turnbull	.15	.40
171 Giants Flag	.20	.50
172 Dave Brown	.15	.40
173 Chris Calloway	.15	.40
174 Rodney Hampton	.25	.60
see card 259		
175 Michael Strahan	.25	.60
176 Tyrone Wheatley	.25	.60
177 Jets Flag	.20	.50
178 Kyle Brady	.15	.40
179 Wayne Chrebet	.40	1.00
180 Hugh Douglas	.15	.40
181 Jeff Graham	.15	.40
182 Adrian Murrell	.25	.60
183 Neil O'Donnell	.25	.60
184 Raiders Flag	.20	.50
185 Tim Brown	.40	1.00
186 Aundray Bruce	.15	.40
187 Andrew Glover	.15	.40
188 Jeff Hostetler	.15	.40
189 Napoleon Kaufman	.40	1.00
190 Terry McDaniel	.15	.40
191 Chester McGlockton	.15	.40
192 Pat Swilling	.15	.40
193 Harvey Williams	.15	.40
194 Eagles Flag	.20	.50
195 Randall Cunningham	.40	1.00
196 Irving Fryar	.25	.60
197 William Fuller	.15	.40
198 Charlie Garner	.25	.60
199 Andy Harmon	.15	.40
200 Rodney Peete	.15	.40
201 Mark Seay	.15	.40
202 Troy Vincent	.15	.40
203 Ricky Watters	.25	.60
204 Calvin Williams	.15	.40
205 Steelers Flag	.20	.50
206 Jerome Bettis	.40	1.00
207 Chad Brown	.15	.40
208 Greg Lloyd	.15	.40
209 Byron Bam Morris	.15	.40
210 Erric Pegram	.15	.40
211 Kordell Stewart	.40	1.00
212 Yancey Thigpen	.25	.60
213 Rod Woodson	.25	.60
214 Chargers Flag	.20	.50
215 Darren Bennett	.15	.40
216 Marco Coleman	.15	.40
217 Stan Humphries	.25	.60
218 Tony Martin	.25	.60
219 Junior Seau	.40	1.00
220 49ers Flag	.20	.50
221 Chris Doleman	.15	.40
222 William Floyd	.25	.60
223 Merton Hanks	.15	.40
224 Brent Jones	.15	.40
225 Terry Kirby	.25	.60
226 Derek Loville	.15	.40
227 Ken Norton Jr.	.15	.40
228 Gary Plummer	.15	.40
229 Jerry Rice	.75	2.00
230 J.J. Stokes	.25	.60
231 Dana Stubblefield	.15	.40
232 John Taylor	.15	.40
233 Bryant Young	.15	.40
234 Steve Young	.60	1.50
235 Seahawks Flag	.20	.50
236 Brian Blades	.15	.40
237 Joey Galloway	.25	.60
238 Carlton Gray	.15	.40
239 Cortez Kennedy	.15	.40
240 Rick Mirer	.15	.40
241 Chris Warren	.25	.60
242 Rams Flag	.20	.50
243 Isaac Bruce	.40	1.00
244 Troy Drayton	.15	.40
245 D'Marco Farr	.15	.40
246 Harold Green	.15	.40
247 Chris Miller	.15	.40
248 Leslie O'Neal	.15	.40
249 Roman Phifer	.15	.40
250 Buccaneers Flag	.20	.50
251 Trent Dilfer	.40	1.00
252 Alvin Harper	.15	.40
253 Jackie Harris	.15	.40
254 John Lynch	.25	.60
255 Hardy Nickerson	.15	.40
256 Errict Rhett	.15	.40
257 Warren Sapp	.25	.60
258 Todd Scott	.15	.40
259 Charles Wilson UER	.15	.40
numbered 174 on back		
260 Redskins Flag	.20	.50
261 Terry Allen	.40	1.00
262 Bill Brooks	.15	.40
263 Henry Ellard	.15	.40
264 Gus Frerotte	.15	.40
265 Sean Gilbert	.15	.40
266 Ken Harvey	.15	.40
267 Brian Mitchell	.15	.40
268 Heath Shuler	.15	.40
269 James Washington	.15	.40
270 Michael Westbrook	.25	.60

1997 Collector's Edge Masters Retail

COMPLETE SET (270)	15.00	40.00

*RETAIL: .4X TO 1X BASIC CARDS

1997 Collector's Edge Masters Crucibles

COMPLETE SET (25)	30.00	60.00
STATED ODDS 1:6 HOBBY		
STATED PRINT RUN 3000 SERIAL #'d SETS		
1 Jake Plummer	2.50	6.00
2 Byron Hanspard	.60	1.50
3 Peter Boulware	1.00	2.50
4 Jay Graham	.60	1.50
5 Antowain Smith	1.50	4.00
6 Rae Carruth	.40	1.00
7 Darnell Autry	.60	1.50
8 Corey Dillon	2.50	6.00
9 Bryant Westbrook	.40	1.00
10 Joey Kent	1.00	2.50
11 Kevin Lockett	.60	1.50
12 Pat Barnes	.60	1.50
13 Tony Gonzalez	2.50	6.00
14 Yatil Green	.60	1.50
15 Danny Wuerffel	1.00	2.50
16 Troy Davis	.60	1.50
17 Tiki Barber	4.00	10.00
18 Ike Hilliard	1.00	2.50
19 Leon Johnson	.60	1.50
20 Darrell Russell	.40	1.00
21 Jim Druckenmiller	.60	1.50
22 Shawn Springs	.60	1.50
23 Orlando Pace	1.00	2.50
24 Warrick Dunn	2.00	5.00
25 Reidel Anthony	.60	1.50

1997 Collector's Edge Masters Night Games

COMPLETE SET (25)	125.00	250.00
STATED ODDS 1:20		
STATED PRINT RUN 1500 SERIAL #'d SETS		
*PRISMS: .8X TO 2X BASIC INSERTS		
PRISMS STATED ODDS 1:60		
PRISMS PRINT RUN 250 SERIAL #'d SETS		
1 Terry Glenn	3.00	8.00
2 Eddie George	3.00	8.00
3 Ricky Watters	2.00	5.00
4 Barry Sanders	10.00	25.00
5 Curtis Martin	4.00	10.00
6 Brett Favre	12.50	30.00
7 Emmitt Smith	10.00	25.00
8 John Elway	12.50	30.00
9 Keyshawn Johnson	3.00	8.00
10 Kordell Stewart	3.00	8.00
11 Vinny Testaverde	2.00	5.00
12 Kerry Collins	3.00	8.00
13 Terrell Davis	4.00	10.00
14 Karim Abdul-Jabbar	1.00	2.50
15 Drew Bledsoe	4.00	10.00
16 Antonio Freeman	2.00	5.00
17 Tony Banks	1.00	2.50
18 Jerry Rice	6.00	15.00
19 Mark Brunell	3.00	8.00
20 Mike Alstott	3.00	8.00
21 Napoleon Kaufman	1.00	2.50
22 Herman Moore	1.00	2.50
23 Terry Allen	2.00	5.00
24 Jerome Bettis	3.00	8.00
25 Dorsey Levens	1.00	2.50

1997 Collector's Edge Masters 1996 Rookies

COMPLETE SET (25)	30.00	60.00
STATED ODDS 1:8 RETAIL		
STATED PRINT RUN 2000 SERIAL #'d SETS		
1 Simeon Rice	1.25	3.00
2 Jonathan Ogden	.75	2.00
3 Eric Moulds	1.50	4.00
4 Tim Biakabutuka	1.25	3.00
5 Walt Harris	.75	2.00
6 John Mobley	.75	2.00
7 Stephen Davis	1.50	4.00
8 Derrick Mayes	1.25	3.00
9 Eddie George	2.00	5.00
10 Marvin Harrison	3.00	8.00
11 Kevin Hardy	.75	2.00
12 Jerome Woods	.75	2.00
13 Karim Abdul-Jabbar	1.50	4.00
14 Duane Clemons	.75	2.00
15 Terry Glenn	1.50	4.00
16 Ricky Whittle	.75	2.00
17 Amani Toomer	1.25	3.00
18 Keyshawn Johnson	1.50	4.00
19 Rickey Dudley	1.25	3.00
20 Bobby Hoying	1.25	3.00
21 Tony Banks	1.25	3.00
22 Bryan Still	.75	2.00
23 Terrell Owens	3.00	8.00
24 Reggie Brown RBK	.75	2.00
25 Mike Alstott	1.50	4.00

1997 Collector's Edge Masters Nitro

COMPLETE SET (36)	40.00	80.00
STATED ODDS 1:8		
2 Larry Centers	1.25	2.50
18 Michael Jackson	1.25	2.50
24 Todd Collins	.75	1.50
30 Bruce Smith	1.25	2.50
34 Kerry Collins	2.00	4.00
36 Kevin Greene	1.25	2.50
59 Carl Pickens	1.25	2.50
64 Troy Aikman	4.00	8.00
71 Emmitt Smith	6.00	12.00
75 Terrell Davis	2.50	5.00
76 John Elway	8.00	15.00
85 Herman Moore	1.25	2.50
88 Barry Sanders	6.00	12.00
94 Brett Favre	8.00	15.00
98 Reggie White	2.00	4.00
106 Steve McNair	2.50	5.00
115 Jim Harbaugh	1.25	2.50
121 Mark Brunell	2.50	5.00
136 Derrick Thomas	2.00	4.00
137 Tamarick Vanover	1.25	2.50
142 Dan Marino	8.00	15.00
155 Drew Bledsoe	2.50	5.00
159 Curtis Martin	2.50	5.00
167 Tyrone Hughes	.75	1.50
189 Napoleon Kaufman	2.00	4.00
203 Ricky Watters	1.25	2.50
206 Jerome Bettis	2.00	4.00
207 Chad Brown	.75	1.50
211 Kordell Stewart	2.00	4.00
218 Tony Martin	1.25	2.50
229 Jerry Rice	4.00	8.00
234 Steve Young	3.00	6.00
237 Joey Galloway	1.25	2.50
243 Isaac Bruce	2.00	4.00
261 Terry Allen	2.00	4.00
264 Gus Frerotte	.75	1.50

1997 Collector's Edge Masters Packers Super Bowl XXXI

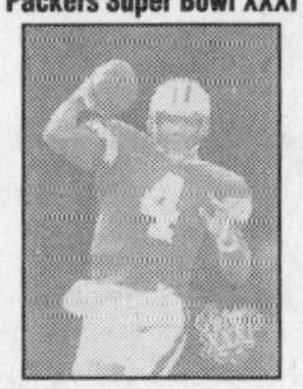

COMPLETE SET (25)	10.00	20.00
SET AVAILABLE VIA MAIL REDEMPTION		
STATED PRINT RUN 5000 SERIAL #'d SETS		
*GOLD FOILS: .6X TO 1.5X BASIC INSERTS		
GOLDS PRINT RUN 1000 SERIAL #'d SETS		
1 Edgar Bennett	.25	.60
2 Mark Chmura	.15	.40
3 Brett Favre	1.50	4.00
4 Dorsey Levens	.40	1.00
5 Wayne Simmons	.15	.40
6 Robert Brooks	.25	.60
7 Sean Jones	.15	.40
8 George Koonce	.15	.40
9 Craig Newsome	.15	.40
10 Reggie White	.40	1.00
11 Desmond Howard	.25	.60
12 Antonio Freeman	.60	1.50
13 Brett Favre	1.50	4.00
14 Keith Jackson	.25	.60
15 Andre Rison	.25	.60
16 Eugene Robinson	.15	.40
17 LeRoy Butler	.15	.40
18 Don Beebe	.25	.60
19 Derrick Mayes	.15	.40
20 Gilbert Brown	.15	.40
21 Santana Dotson	.15	.40
22 Brett Favre	1.50	4.00
23 Reggie White	.40	1.00
24 Desmond Howard	.25	.60
25 Antonio Freeman	.60	1.50

1997 Collector's Edge Masters Playoff Game Ball

COMPLETE SET (19)	300.00	600.00
STATED ODDS 1:72		
*DIAMOND CARDS: .8X TO 2X BASIC INSERTS		
*HOLOFOILS: .4X TO 1X BASIC INSERTS		
*HOLOFOIL PROOFS: .2X TO .5X BASIC INSERTS		
1 Natrone Means	10.00	25.00
Thurman Thomas		
2 Tony Boselli	10.00	25.00
Bruce Smith		
3 Jerome Bettis	12.00	30.00
Marshall Faulk		
4 Kordell Stewart	12.50	30.00
Jim Harbaugh		
5 Natrone Means	12.00	30.00
Terrell Davis		
6 Mark Brunell	30.00	80.00
John Elway		

7 Curtis Martin	12.00	30.00
Jerome Bettis		
8 Drew Bledsoe	12.00	30.00
Mark Brunell		
9 Terry Glenn	10.00	25.00
Keenan McCardell		
10 Ricky Watters	6.00	15.00
Terry Kirby		
11 Kevin Greene	12.50	30.00
Reggie White		
12 Jerry Rice	15.00	40.00
Irving Fryar		
13 Dorsey Levens	10.00	25.00
Terry Kirby		
14 Brett Favre	40.00	100.00
Steve Young		
15 Andre Rison	15.00	40.00
Jerry Rice		
16 Reggie White	6.00	15.00
Ken Norton Jr.		
17 Kerry Collins	15.00	40.00
Troy Aikman		
18 Kerry Collins	30.00	80.00
Brett Favre		
19 Mark Carrier WR	6.00	15.00
Antonio Freeman		

1997 Collector's Edge Masters Radical Rivals

COMPLETE SET (13) 100.00 200.00
STATED ODDS 1:30 HOBBY
STATED PRINT RUN 1000 SERIAL #'d SETS

1 Emmitt Smith	12.50	30.00
Eddie George		
2 Brett Favre	12.50	30.00
Kerry Collins		
3 Jerry Rice	10.00	25.00
Antonio Freeman		
4 Ricky Watters	3.00	8.00
Napoleon Kaufman		
5 Herman Moore	3.00	8.00
Keyshawn Johnson		
6 Dan Marino	12.50	30.00
John Elway		
7 Jerome Bettis	3.00	8.00
Karim Abdul-Jabbar		
8 Isaac Bruce	3.00	8.00
Carl Pickens		
9 Barry Sanders	10.00	25.00
Terry Allen		
10 Terry Glenn	5.00	12.00
Joey Galloway		
11 Mark Brunell	6.00	15.00
Steve Young		
12 Terrell Davis	12.50	30.00
Curtis Martin		
NNO Title Card CL	.40	1.00

1997 Collector's Edge Masters Ripped

COMPLETE SET (19) 75.00 150.00
STATED ODDS 1:24 RET

19 Troy Aikman	6.00	15.00
20 Drew Bledsoe	4.00	10.00
21 Tim Brown	3.00	8.00
22 Mark Brunell	4.00	10.00
23 Cris Carter	3.00	8.00
24 Kerry Collins	3.00	8.00
25 Barry Sanders	10.00	25.00
26 Eddie George	3.00	8.00
27 Karim Abdul-Jabbar	3.00	8.00
28 Curtis Martin	4.00	10.00
29 Carl Pickens	2.00	5.00
30 Marshall Faulk	4.00	10.00
31 Rashaan Salaam	1.25	3.00
32 Deion Sanders	3.00	8.00
33 Emmitt Smith	10.00	25.00
34 Herman Moore	2.00	5.00
35 Ricky Watters	2.00	5.00
36 Terry Allen	3.00	8.00
NNO Checklist Card	1.25	3.00

1997 Collector's Edge Masters Super Bowl Game Ball

COMPLETE SET (6) 150.00 300.00
RANDOM INSERTS IN PACKS
STATED PRINT RUN 250 SETS
*DIAMOND: .8X TO 2X BASIC INSERTS

1 Brett Favre	40.00	100.00
Drew Bledsoe		
2 Dorsey Levens	25.00	60.00
Curtis Martin		
3 Desmond Howard	10.00	25.00
Dave Meggett		
4 Antonio Freeman	25.00	60.00
Terry Glenn		
5 Keith Jackson	10.00	25.00
Ben Coates		
6 Willie McGinest		
Reggie White		

1998 Collector's Edge Masters Previews

14 Priest Holmes GOLD	1.00	2.50
DB David Boston	.40	1.00
148 Jerry Rice	1.50	4.00
183 Peyton Manning	2.50	6.00
S171 Jamal Anderson	.60	1.50
S189 Curtis Martin SM	.75	2.00
S195 Jerry Rice SM	1.50	4.00

1998 Collector's Edge Masters

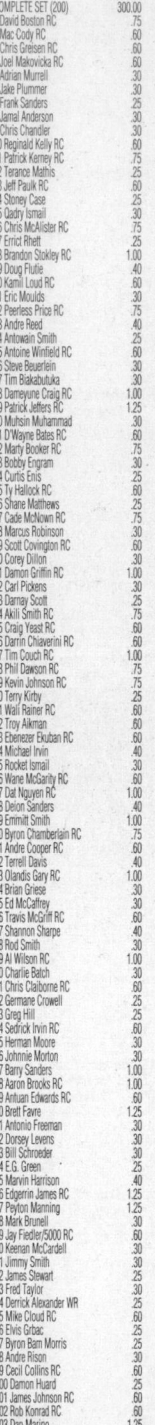

The 1998 Collector's Edge Masters set was issued in one series totalling 199-cards and distributed in three-card packs with a suggested retail price of $6.99. The fronts feature color action player photos printed on micro-etched silver foil and sequentially numbered to 5,000. Card number 28 was never released. Four different limited edition parallel sets were also produced.

COMPLETE SET (199) 75.00 200.00

1 Rob Moore	.40	1.00
2 Adrian Murrell	.40	1.00
3 Jake Plummer	.60	1.50
4 Michael Pittman RC	1.50	3.00
5 Frank Sanders	.40	1.00
6 Andre Wadsworth RC	.75	2.00
7 Jamal Anderson	.60	1.50
8 Chris Chandler	.40	1.00
9 Tim Dwight RC	1.00	2.50
10 Tony Martin	.40	1.00
11 Terance Mathis	.40	1.00
12 Ken Oxendine RC	.50	1.25
13 Jim Harbaugh	.40	1.00
14 Priest Holmes RC	10.00	25.00
15 Michael Jackson	.25	.60
16 Pat Johnson RC	.75	2.00
17 Jermaine Lewis	.40	1.00
18 Eric Zeier	.40	1.00
19 Doug Flutie	.60	1.50
20 Rob Johnson	.40	1.00
21 Eric Moulds	.60	1.50
22 Andre Reed	.40	1.00
23 Antowain Smith	.60	1.50
24 Bruce Smith	.40	1.00
25 Thurman Thomas	.60	1.50
26 Steve Beuerlein	.40	1.00
27 Kevin Greene	.40	1.00
29 Rocket Ismail	.25	.60
30 Fred Lane	.25	.60
31 Muhsin Muhammad	.40	1.00
32 Edgar Bennett	.25	.60
33 Curtis Conway	.40	1.00
34 Bobby Engram	.40	1.00
35 Curtis Enis RC	.50	1.25
36 Erik Kramer	.25	.60
37 Chris Penn	.25	.60
38 Jeff Blake	.40	1.00
39 Corey Dillon	.60	1.50
40 Neil O'Donnell	.40	1.00
41 Carl Pickens	.40	1.00
42 Darnay Scott	.40	1.00
43 Damon Gibson RC	.50	1.25
44 Troy Aikman	1.25	3.00
45 Billy Davis	.25	.60
46 Michael Irvin	.60	1.50
47 Ernie Mills	.25	.60
48 Deion Sanders	.60	1.50
49 Emmitt Smith	2.00	5.00
50 Chris Warren	.40	1.00
51 Bubby Brister	.25	.60
52 Terrell Davis	.60	1.50
53 John Elway	2.50	6.00
54 Brian Griese RC	2.00	5.00
55 Ed McCaffrey	.40	1.00
56 Marcus Nash RC	.50	1.25
57 Shannon Sharpe	.40	1.00
58 Rod Smith	.40	1.00
59 Charlie Batch RC	1.00	2.50
60 Germane Crowell RC	.75	2.00
61 Scott Mitchell	.40	1.00
62 Johnnie Morton	.40	1.00
63 Herman Moore	.40	1.00
64 Barry Sanders	2.00	5.00
65 Robert Brooks	.40	1.00
66 Brett Favre	2.50	6.00
67 Antonio Freeman	.60	1.50
68 Raymont Harris	.25	.60
69 Dorsey Levens	.60	1.50
70 Reggie White	.60	1.50
71 Marshall Faulk	.75	2.00
72 Marvin Harrison	.60	1.50
73 Peyton Manning RC	12.50	25.00
74 Jerome Pathon RC	1.00	2.50
75 Tavian Banks RC	.75	2.00
76 Mark Brunell	.60	1.50
77 Keenan McCardell	.40	1.00
78 Jimmy Smith	.40	1.00
79 Fred Taylor RC	1.50	4.00
80 Derrick Alexander	.40	1.00
81 Donnell Bennett	.25	.60
82 Rich Gannon	.60	1.50
83 Elvis Grbac	.40	1.00
84 Andre Rison	.40	1.00
85 Rashaan Shehee RC	.75	2.00
86 Karim Abdul-Jabbar	.40	1.00
87 John Avery RC	.75	2.00
88 Oronde Gadsden RC	1.00	2.50
89 Dan Marino	2.50	6.00
90 O.J. McDuffie	.40	1.00
91 Zach Thomas	.60	1.50
92 Cris Carter	.60	1.50
93 Randall Cunningham	.60	1.50
94 Brad Johnson	.60	1.50
95 Randy Moss RC	6.00	15.00
96 Jake Reed	.40	1.00
97 Robert Smith	.60	1.50
98 Drew Bledsoe	1.00	2.50
99 Ben Coates	.40	1.00
100 Robert Edwards RC	.75	2.00
101 Terry Glenn	.60	1.50
102 Shawn Jefferson	.25	.60
103 Ty Law	.40	1.00
104 Cameron Cleeland RC	.75	2.00
105 Kerry Collins	.40	1.00
106 Sean Dawkins	.25	.60
107 Andre Hastings	.25	.60
108 Lamar Smith	.40	1.00
109 Danny Wuerffel	.40	1.00
110 Gary Brown	.25	.60
111 Chris Calloway	.25	.60
112 Ike Hilliard	.40	1.00
113 Joe Jurevicius RC	1.00	2.50
114 Danny Kanell	.40	1.00
115 Wayne Chrebet	.60	1.50
116 Glenn Foley	.40	1.00
117 Keyshawn Johnson	.60	1.50
118 Leon Johnson	.25	.60
119 Curtis Martin	.60	1.50
120 Vinny Testaverde	.60	1.50
121 Tim Brown	.60	1.50
122 Jeff George	.40	1.00
123 James Jett	.40	1.00
124 Napoleon Kaufman	.60	1.50
125 Charles Woodson RC	1.25	3.00
126 Irving Fryar	.40	1.00
127 Jeff Graham	.40	1.00
128 Bobby Hoying	.40	1.00
129 Duce Staley	.75	2.00
130 Jerome Bettis	.60	1.50
131 C.Fuamatu-Ma'afala RC	.75	2.00
132 Courtney Hawkins	.25	.60
133 Charles Johnson	.25	.60
134 Kordell Stewart	.60	1.50
135 Hines Ward RC	5.00	10.00
136 Tony Banks	.40	1.00
137 Isaac Bruce	.60	1.50
138 Robert Holcombe RC	.75	2.00
139 Eddie Kennison	.40	1.00
140 Ryan Leaf RC	1.00	2.50
141 Natrone Means	.40	1.00
142 Mikhael Ricks RC	.75	2.00
143 Junior Seau	.60	1.50
144 Bryan Still	.25	.60
145 Garrison Hearst	.60	1.50
146 R.W. McQuarters RC	.75	2.00
147 Terrell Owens	.60	1.50
148 Jerry Rice	1.25	3.00
149 J.J. Stokes	.40	1.00
150 Steve Young	.75	2.00
151 Joey Galloway	.40	1.00
152 Ahman Green RC	2.50	6.00
153 Warren Moon	.60	1.50
154 Shawn Springs	.25	.60
155 Ricky Watters	.40	1.00
156 Mike Alstott	.60	1.50
157 Reidel Anthony	.40	1.00
158 Trent Dilfer	.60	1.50
159 Warrick Dunn	.60	1.50
160 Jacquez Green RC	.75	2.00
161 Kevin Dyson RC	1.00	2.50
162 Eddie George	.60	1.50
163 Steve McNair	.60	1.50
164 Yancey Thigpen	.25	.60
165 Frank Wycheck	.25	.60
166 Terry Allen	.60	1.50
167 Gus Frerotte	.25	.60
168 Trent Green	.60	1.50
169 Skip Hicks RC	.75	2.00
170 Michael Westbrook	.40	1.00
171 Jamal Anderson SM	.60	1.50
172 Carl Pickens SM	.40	1.00
173 Deion Sanders SM	.60	1.50
174 Emmitt Smith SM	1.25	3.00
175 Terrell Davis SM	.60	1.50
176 John Elway SM	1.50	4.00
177 Charlie Batch SM	1.00	2.50
178 Herman Moore SM	.40	1.00
179 Barry Sanders SM	1.25	3.00
180 Brett Favre SM	1.50	4.00
181 Antonio Freeman SM	.40	1.00
182 Marshall Faulk SM	.75	2.00
183 Peyton Manning SM	10.00	20.00
184 Mark Brunell SM	.60	1.50
185 Dan Marino SM	1.50	4.00
186 Randy Moss SM	5.00	12.00
187 Drew Bledsoe SM	.60	1.50
188 Robert Edwards SM	.40	1.00
189 Curtis Martin SM	.60	1.50
190 Charles Woodson SM	1.00	2.50
191 Jerome Bettis SM	.60	1.50
192 Robert Holcombe SM	.40	1.00
193 Ryan Leaf SM	1.00	2.50
194 Natrone Means SM	.40	1.00
195 Jerry Rice SM	.75	2.00
196 Steve Young SM	.60	1.50
197 Warrick Dunn SM	.60	1.50
198 Eddie George SM	.40	1.00
199 Peyton Manning CL	5.00	10.00
200 Ryan Leaf CL	.60	1.50

1998 Collector's Edge Masters 50-point

COMPLETE SET (199) 250.00 400.00
*50-POINT: .5X TO 1.2X BASIC CARD
ONE PER PACK
STATED PRINT RUN 3000 SER.#'d SETS

1998 Collector's Edge Masters 50-point Gold

COMPLETE SET (199) 750.00 1,500.00
*50-PNT GOLD VETS: 4X TO 10X BAS.CARD
*50-POINT GOLD ROOKIES: .8X TO 2X
STATED ODDS 1:20
STATED PRINT RUN 150 SERIAL #'d SETS

1998 Collector's Edge Masters Gold Redemption 500

COMP.FACT SET (199) 150.00 300.00
*VETS: 1.5X TO 4X BASIC CARDS
*ROOKIES: .5X TO 1.2X BASIC CARDS
ISSUED VIA MAIL EXCH IN SET FORM
STATED PRINT RUN 500 SER.#'d SETS

1998 Collector's Edge Masters Gold Redemption 100

COMP. FACT SET (199) 400.00 800.00
*VETS: 2.5X TO 6X BASIC CARDS
*ROOKIES: .8X TO 2X BASIC CARDS
STATED PRINT RUN 100 SER.#'d SETS

1998 Collector's Edge Masters HoloGold

STATED ODDS 1:300
STATED PRINT RUN 10 SERIAL #'d SETS
NOT PRICED DUE TO SCARCITY

1998 Collector's Edge Masters Legends

COMPLETE SET (30) 30.00 80.00
STATED ODDS 1:8
STATED PRINT RUN 2500 SERIAL #'d SETS

ML1 Jake Plummer	1.25	3.00
ML2 Doug Flutie	1.25	3.00
ML3 Corey Dillon	1.25	3.00
ML4 Carl Pickens	.75	2.00
ML5 Troy Aikman	2.50	6.00
ML6 Deion Sanders	1.25	3.00
ML7 Emmitt Smith	4.00	10.00
ML8 Terrell Davis	1.25	3.00
ML9 John Elway	5.00	12.00
ML10 Herman Moore	.75	2.00
ML11 Barry Sanders	4.00	10.00
ML12 Brett Favre	5.00	12.00
ML13 Antonio Freeman	1.25	3.00
ML14 Marshall Faulk	1.50	4.00
ML15 Mark Brunell	1.25	3.00
ML16 Dan Marino	5.00	12.00
ML17 Cris Carter	1.25	3.00
ML18 Drew Bledsoe	2.00	5.00
ML19 Keyshawn Johnson	1.25	3.00
ML20 Curtis Martin	1.25	3.00
ML21 Napoleon Kaufman	1.25	3.00
ML22 Jerome Bettis	1.25	3.00
ML23 Kordell Stewart	1.25	3.00
ML24 Natrone Means	.75	2.00
ML25 Jerry Rice	2.50	6.00
ML26 Steve Young	1.50	4.00
ML27 Joey Galloway	.75	2.00
ML28 Warrick Dunn	1.25	3.00
ML29 Eddie George	1.25	3.00
ML30 Terry Allen	1.25	3.00

1998 Collector's Edge Masters Main Event

COMPLETE SET (20) 60.00 120.00
STATED ODDS 1:16
STATED PRINT RUN 2000 SERIAL #'d SETS

ME1 Troy Aikman	3.00	8.00
ME2 Jamal Anderson	1.50	4.00
ME3 Charlie Batch	1.00	2.50
ME4 Jerome Bettis	1.50	4.00
ME5 Mark Brunell	1.50	4.00
ME6 Terrell Davis	1.50	4.00
ME7 Warrick Dunn	1.50	4.00
ME8 Robert Edwards	.75	2.00
ME9 John Elway	6.00	15.00
ME10 Brett Favre	6.00	15.00
ME11 Doug Flutie	1.50	4.00
ME12 Eddie George	1.50	4.00
ME13 Dan Marino	6.00	15.00
ME14 Curtis Martin	1.50	4.00
ME15 Randy Moss	6.00	15.00
ME16 Carl Pickens	1.00	2.50
ME17 Jake Plummer	1.50	4.00
ME18 Barry Sanders	5.00	12.00
ME19 Emmitt Smith	5.00	12.00
ME20 Fred Taylor	1.50	4.00

1998 Collector's Edge Masters Rookie Masters

COMPLETE SET (30) 50.00 100.00
STATED ODDS 1:8
STATED PRINT RUN 2500 SERIAL #'d SETS
*PREVIEWS: .15X TO .4X BASIC INSERTS

RM1 Peyton Manning	12.50	25.00
RM2 Ryan Leaf	1.00	2.50
RM3 Charlie Batch	1.00	2.50
RM4 Brian Griese	2.00	5.00
RM5 Randy Moss	6.00	15.00
RM6 Jacquez Green	.75	2.00
RM7 Kevin Dyson	1.00	2.50
RM8 Mikhael Ricks	.75	2.00
RM9 Jerome Pathon	1.00	2.50
RM10 Joe Jurevicius	1.00	2.50
RM11 Germane Crowell	.75	2.00
RM12 Tim Dwight	1.00	2.50
RM13 Pat Johnson	.75	2.00
RM14 Hines Ward	4.00	10.00
RM15 Marcus Nash	.50	1.25
RM16 Damon Gibson	.50	1.25
RM17 Robert Edwards	.75	2.00
RM18 Robert Holcombe	.75	2.00
RM19 Tavian Banks	.75	2.00
RM20 Fred Taylor	1.50	4.00
RM21 Skip Hicks	.75	2.00
RM22 Curtis Enis	.50	1.25
RM23 Ahman Green	2.50	6.00
RM24 John Avery	.75	2.00
RM25 C.Fuamatu-Ma'afala	.75	2.00
RM26 Rashaan Shehee	.75	2.00
RM27 Cameron Cleeland	.50	1.25
RM28 Charles Woodson	1.25	3.00
RM29 R.W. McQuarters	.75	2.00
RM30 Andre Wadsworth	.75	2.00

1998 Collector's Edge Masters Sentinels

COMPLETE SET (10) 50.00 120.00
STATED ODDS 1:120
STATED PRINT RUN 500 SERIAL #'d SETS

S1 John Elway	10.00	30.00
S2 Brett Favre	10.00	30.00
S3 Barry Sanders	8.00	25.00
S4 Terrell Davis	2.50	6.00
S5 Dan Marino	10.00	30.00
S6 Emmitt Smith	8.00	25.00
S7 Randy Moss	10.00	25.00
S8 Peyton Manning	20.00	50.00
S9 Robert Edwards	1.50	4.00
S10 Fred Taylor	2.50	6.00

1998 Collector's Edge Masters Super Masters

STATED ODDS 1:10
STATED PRINT RUN 2000 SER.#'d SETS

SM1 Terrell Davis	1.25	3.00
SM2 John Elway	4.00	10.00
SM3 Shannon Sharpe	1.00	2.50
SM4 Rod Smith	.75	2.00
SM5 Brett Favre	5.00	12.00
SM6 Antonio Freeman	1.25	3.00
SM7 Robert Brooks	.75	2.00
SM8 Edgar Bennett	.75	2.00
SM9 Reggie White	1.25	3.00
SM10 Troy Aikman	2.50	6.00
SM11 Michael Irvin	1.25	3.00
SM12 Deion Sanders	1.25	3.00
SM13 Emmitt Smith	4.00	10.00
SM14 Steve Young	1.50	4.00
SM15 Jerry Rice	2.50	6.00
SM16 Bart Starr	3.00	8.00
SM16AU Bart Starr	100.00	175.00
AUTO/50*		
SM17 Johnny Unitas	3.00	8.00
SM17AU Johnny Unitas	125.00	225.00
AUTO/50*		
SM17P John Unitas AU/100	125.00	200.00
(Promo card)		
SM20 Drew Pearson UER	1.00	2.50
(misspelled Pierson)		
SM20 Larry Csonka	1.25	3.00
(not issued in packs)		
SM20AU Drew Pearson AUTO	7.50	20.00
(corrected name)		
SM21 John Riggins	1.25	3.00
(not issued in packs)		
SM22 Marcus Allen	1.25	3.00
(not issued in packs)		
SM23 Dwight Clark	1.00	2.50
SM23AU Dwight Clark	7.50	20.00
AUTO		
SM24 Phil Simms	1.25	3.00
(not issued in packs)		
SM25 Art Monk	1.00	2.50
(not issued in packs)		
SM26 Joe Namath	2.50	6.00
(not issued in packs)		
SM26S Joe Namath	8.00	20.00
(Media Sample)		
SM27 Len Dawson	1.25	3.00
(not issued in packs)		
SM27AU Len Dawson AU	12.00	30.00
SM28 Lynn Swann	1.50	4.00
SM29 John Stallworth	1.00	2.50
SM29AU J.Stallworth AUTO	15.00	30.00
SM30 Butch Johnson AU	6.00	15.00
SM31 Roger Craig	1.00	2.50
SM31AU Roger Craig AU	7.50	20.00
(signed on back of card, inside white box instead of serial numbering)		
SM32 Jack Ham	1.00	2.50
SM32AU Jack Ham AU	20.00	40.00

1999 Collector's Edge Masters Previews

Cards from this set are essentially a parallel version to the player's corresponding base card. The cardbacks contain the word "preview" and each was released primarily to dealers and distributors.

COMPLETE SET (15) 20.00 35.00

AB Aaron Brooks	2.50	6.00
AS Akili Smith	.40	1.00
CB Champ Bailey	.60	1.50
CM Cade McNown	.60	1.50
DB David Boston	1.25	3.00
EJ Edgerrin James	2.50	6.00
JJ J.J. Johnson	.60	1.50
KJ Kevin Johnson	.75	2.00
KW Kurt Warner	3.00	8.00
OG Olandis Gary	.75	2.00
PJ Patrick Jeffers	.75	2.00
PP Peerless Price	1.00	2.50
TC Tim Couch	2.00	5.00
TE Troy Edwards	.75	2.00
TH Torry Holt	1.00	2.50

1999 Collector's Edge Masters

Released as a 200-card set, 1999 Collector's Edge Masters features micro-etched holographic foil cards where each veteran base card is sequentially numbered to 5000. The 1999 Draft Picks cards were serial numbered of 5000 or 2000. Each pack contained three cards and carried a suggested retail price of $5.59. Retail boxes contained one PSA graded Collector's Edge Odessey card.

COMPLETE SET (200) 300.00 500.00

1 David Boston RC	.75	2.00
2 Mac Cody RC	.60	1.50
3 Chris Greisen RC	.60	1.50
4 Joel Makovicka RC	.60	1.50
5 Adrian Murrell	.30	.75
6 Jake Plummer	.30	.75
7 Frank Sanders	.25	.60
8 Jamal Anderson	.30	.75
9 Chris Chandler	.30	.75
10 Reginald Kelly RC	.60	1.50
11 Patrick Kerney RC	.75	2.00
12 Terance Mathis	.25	.60
13 Jeff Paulk RC	.60	1.50
14 Stoney Case	.25	.60
15 Qadry Ismail	.30	.75
16 Chris McAlister RC	.75	2.00
17 Errict Rhett	.25	.60
18 Brandon Stokley RC	1.00	2.50
19 Doug Flutie	.40	1.00
20 Kamil Loud RC	.60	1.50
21 Eric Moulds	.60	1.50
22 Peerless Price RC	.75	2.00
23 Andre Reed	.40	1.00
24 Antowain Smith	.25	.60
25 Antoine Winfield RC	.60	1.50
26 Steve Beuerlein	.30	.75
27 Tim Biakabutuka	.30	.75
28 Dameyune Craig RC	1.00	2.50
29 Patrick Jeffers RC	1.25	3.00
30 Muhsin Muhammad	.30	.75
31 D'Wayne Bates RC	.60	1.50
32 Marty Booker RC	.75	2.00
33 Bobby Engram	.30	.75
34 Curtis Enis	.25	.60
35 Ty Hallock RC	.60	1.50
36 Shane Matthews	.25	.60
37 Cade McNown RC	.75	2.00
38 Marcus Robinson	.30	.75
39 Scott Covington RC	.60	1.50
40 Corey Dillon	.30	.75
41 Damon Griffin RC	1.00	2.50
42 Carl Pickens	.30	.75
43 Darnay Scott	.25	.60
44 Akili Smith RC	.75	2.00
45 Craig Yeast RC	.60	1.50
46 Darrin Chiaverini RC	.60	1.50
47 Tim Couch RC	1.00	2.50
48 Phil Dawson RC	.60	1.50
49 Kevin Johnson RC	.75	2.00
50 Terry Kirby	.25	.60
51 Wali Rainer RC	.60	1.50
52 Troy Aikman	.60	1.50
53 Ebenezer Ekuban RC	.60	1.50
54 Michael Irvin	.40	1.00
55 Rocket Ismail	.30	.75
56 Wane McGarity RC	.60	1.50
57 Dat Nguyen RC	1.00	2.50
58 Deion Sanders	.40	1.00
59 Emmitt Smith	1.00	2.50
60 Byron Chamberlain RC	.75	2.00
61 Andre Cooper RC	.60	1.50
62 Terrell Davis	.40	1.00
63 Olandis Gary RC	1.00	2.50
64 Brian Griese	.30	.75
65 Ed McCaffrey	.30	.75
66 Travis McGriff RC	.60	1.50
67 Shannon Sharpe	.40	1.00
68 Rod Smith	.30	.75
69 Al Wilson RC	1.00	2.50
70 Charlie Batch	.30	.75
71 Chris Claiborne RC	.60	1.50
72 Germane Crowell	.25	.60
73 Greg Hill	.25	.60
74 Sedrick Irvin RC	.60	1.50
75 Herman Moore	.30	.75
76 Johnnie Morton	.30	.75
77 Barry Sanders	1.00	2.50
78 Aaron Brooks RC	1.25	3.00
79 Antuan Edwards RC	.60	1.50
80 Brett Favre	1.25	3.00
81 Antonio Freeman	.30	.75
82 Dorsey Levens	.30	.75
83 Bill Schroeder	.30	.75
84 E.G. Green	.25	.60
85 Marvin Harrison	.40	1.00
86 Edgerrin James RC	1.25	3.00
87 Peyton Manning	1.25	3.00
88 Mark Brunell	.30	.75
89 Jay Fiedler/5000 RC	.60	1.50
90 Keenan McCardell	.30	.75
91 Jimmy Smith	.30	.75
92 James Stewart	.25	.60
93 Fred Taylor	.30	.75
94 Derrick Alexander WR	.25	.60
95 Mike Cloud RC	.60	1.50
96 Elvis Grbac	.25	.60
97 Byron Bam Morris	.25	.60
98 Andre Rison	.30	.75
99 Cecil Collins RC	.60	1.50
100 Damon Huard	.25	.60
101 James Johnson RC	.60	1.50
102 Rob Konrad RC	.60	1.50
103 Dan Marino	1.25	3.00
104 O.J. McDuffie	.30	.75
105 Cris Carter	.40	1.00
106 Daunte Culpepper RC	1.00	2.50
107 Randall Cunningham	.40	1.00
108 Jeff George	.30	.75
109 Jim Kleinsasser RC	1.00	2.50
110 Randy Moss	.40	1.00
111 Robert Smith	.30	.75
112 Terry Allen	.30	.75
113 Michael Bishop RC	.75	2.00
114 Drew Bledsoe	.40	1.00
115 Kevin Faulk RC	1.00	2.50
116 Terry Glenn	.30	.75
117 Andy Katzenmoyer RC	.75	2.00
118 Billy Joe Hobert	.25	.60
119 Eddie Kennison	.30	.75
120 Ricky Williams RC	1.50	4.00
121 Tiki Barber	.40	1.00
122 Sean Bennett RC	.60	1.50
123 Gary Brown	.25	.60
124 Kent Graham	.25	.60
125 Ike Hilliard	.30	.75
126 Joe Montgomery RC	.60	1.50
127 Amani Toomer	.30	.75
128 Wayne Chrebet	.30	.75
129 Keyshawn Johnson	.30	.75
130 Curtis Martin	.40	1.00
131 Ray Lucas RC	.50	1.25
132 Vinny Testaverde	.30	.75
133 Tim Brown	.40	1.00
134 Tony Bryant RC	.60	1.50
135 Scott Dreisbach RC	.60	1.50
136 Rich Gannon	.30	.75
137 Tyrone Wheatley	.30	.75
138 Charles Woodson	.40	1.00
139 Na Brown RC	.60	1.50
140 Charles Johnson	.25	.60
141 Cecil Martin RC	.60	1.50
142 Donovan McNabb RC	5.00	12.00
143 Doug Pederson	.25	.60
144 Duce Staley	.30	.75
145 Jerome Bettis	.40	1.00
146 Kris Brown RC	1.00	2.50
147 Troy Edwards RC	.75	2.00
148 Kordell Stewart	.30	.75
149 Hines Ward	.40	1.00
150 Amos Zereoue RC	.75	2.00
151 Dre Bly RC	1.00	2.50
152 Isaac Bruce	.40	1.00
153 Marshall Faulk	.40	1.00
154 Joe Germaine RC	.75	2.00
155 Az-Zahir Hakim	.25	.60
156 Torry Holt RC	1.50	4.00
157 Kurt Warner RC	6.00	15.00
158 Justin Watson RC	.60	1.50
159 Jermaine Fazande RC	.60	1.50
160 Jeff Graham	.25	.60
161 Jim Harbaugh	.30	.75
162 Steve Heiden RC	.60	1.50
163 Erik Kramer	.30	.75
164 Natrone Means	.30	.75
165 Mikhael Ricks	.25	.60
166 Junior Seau	.40	1.00
167 Jeff Garcia RC	3.00	8.00
168 Charlie Garner	.30	.75
169 Terry Jackson RC	.60	1.50
170 Terrell Owens	.40	1.00
171 Jerry Rice	.75	2.00
172 Steve Young	.50	1.25
173 Karsten Bailey RC	.60	1.50
174 Joey Galloway	.30	.75
175 Brock Huard RC	.75	2.00
176 Jon Kitna	.30	.75
177 Derrick Mayes	.25	.60
178 Charlie Rogers RC	.60	1.50
179 Ricky Watters	.30	.75
180 Rabih Abdullah RC	.60	1.50
181 Mike Alstott	.40	1.00
182 Reidel Anthony	.25	.60
183 Trent Dilfer	.30	.75
184 Warrick Dunn	.30	.75
185 Martin Gramatica RC	.60	1.50
186 Shaun King RC	.75	2.00
187 Darnell McDonald RC	.60	1.50
188 Yo Murphy RC	.60	1.50
189 Kevin Daft RC	.60	1.50
190 Kevin Dyson	.25	.60
191 Eddie George	.30	.75
192 Jevon Kearse RC	1.00	2.50
193 Steve McNair	.40	1.00
194 Yancey Thigpen	.25	.60
195 Champ Bailey RC	2.00	5.00
196 Albert Connell	.25	.60
197 Stephen Davis	.30	.75
198 Skip Hicks	.25	.60
199 Brad Johnson	.30	.75
200 Michael Westbrook	.25	.60

1999 Collector's Edge Masters Galvanized

*VETERANS: 1.2X TO 3X BASIC CARDS
*ROOKIES: .5X TO 1.2X BASIC RC/2000
*ROOKIES: .8X TO 2X BASIC RC/5000
STATED PRINT RUN 1000 SERIAL #'d SETS

1999 Collector's Edge Masters HoloGold

*VETERANS/25: 12X TO 30X BASIC CARDS
*ROOKIES/25: 5X TO 12X BASIC RC/2000
*ROOKIES/25: 8X TO 20X BASIC RC/5000
HOLOGOLD STATED PRINT RUN 25

1999 Collector's Edge Masters HoloSilver

COMPLETE SET (200) 125.00 250.00
*HOLOSILVER STARS: .6X TO 1.5X BASIC CARDS
*ROOKIES: .25X TO .6X BASIC RC/2000
*ROOKIES: .4X TO 1X BASIC RC/5000
HOLOSILVER STATED PRINT RUN 3500

1999 Collector's Edge Masters Excalibur

COMPLETE SET (8) 15.00 40.00
STATED PRINT RUN 5000 SER.#'d SETS

X3 Dan Marino	4.00	10.00
X6 Brett Favre	4.00	10.00
X7 Barry Sanders	4.00	10.00
X10 Champ Bailey	1.25	3.00
X12 Akili Smith	.75	2.00
X14 Tim Couch	.75	2.00
X18 Steve Young	1.50	4.00
X25 Curtis Martin	1.25	3.00

1999 Collector's Edge Masters Legends

COMPLETE SET (20) 75.00 150.00
STATED PRINT RUN 1000 SER.#'d SETS

ML1 Doug Flutie	2.00	5.00
ML2 Troy Aikman	4.00	10.00
ML3 Emmitt Smith	4.00	10.00
ML4 Terrell Davis	2.00	5.00
ML5 Charlie Batch	2.00	5.00
ML6 Barry Sanders	6.00	15.00
ML7 Brett Favre	6.00	15.00
ML8 Antonio Freeman	2.00	5.00
ML9 Peyton Manning	6.00	15.00
ML10 Mark Brunell	2.00	5.00
ML11 Fred Taylor	2.00	5.00
ML12 Dan Marino	6.00	15.00
ML13 Randy Moss	5.00	12.00
ML14 Drew Bledsoe	2.50	6.00
ML15 Kurt Warner	10.00	25.00
ML16 Marshall Faulk	2.50	6.00
ML17 Steve Young	2.50	6.00
ML18 Jerry Rice	4.00	10.00
ML19 Jon Kitna	2.00	5.00
ML20 Eddie George	2.00	5.00

1999 Collector's Edge Masters Main Event

COMPLETE SET (10) 25.00 50.00
STATED PRINT RUN 1000 SER.#'d SETS

ME1 Randy Moss	4.00	10.00
Jamal Anderson		
ME2 Mark Brunell	1.50	4.00
Eddie George		
ME3 Terrell Davis	1.50	4.00
Cecil Collins		
ME4 Rocket Ismail	1.50	4.00
Stephen Davis		
ME5 Troy Edwards	1.50	4.00
Kevin Johnson		
ME6 Antonio Freeman	1.50	4.00
Charlie Batch		
ME7 Terry Glenn	1.50	4.00
Marvin Harrison		
ME8 Keyshawn Johnson	1.50	4.00
Doug Flutie		
ME9 Cade McNown	4.00	10.00
Ricky Williams		
ME10 Steve Young	3.00	8.00
Marshall Faulk		

1999 Collector's Edge Masters Majestic

COMPLETE SET (30) 50.00 100.00
STATED PRINT RUN 3000 SER. #'d SETS

M1 Jake Plummer	.75	2.00
M2 David Boston	1.25	3.00
M3 Doug Flutie	1.25	3.00
M4 Eric Moulds	1.25	3.00
M5 Peerless Price	1.25	3.00
M6 Tim Biakabutuka	.75	2.00
M7 Troy Aikman	2.50	6.00
M8 Olandis Gary	1.25	3.00
M9 Brian Griese	1.25	3.00
M10 Charlie Batch	1.25	3.00
M11 Antonio Freeman	1.25	3.00
M12 Peyton Manning	4.00	10.00
M13 Edgerrin James	3.00	8.00
M14 Marvin Harrison	1.25	3.00
M15 Fred Taylor	1.25	3.00
M16 Daunte Culpepper	3.00	8.00
M17 Terry Glenn	1.25	3.00
M18 Keyshawn Johnson	1.25	3.00
M19 Curtis Martin	1.25	3.00
M20 Donovan McNabb	4.00	10.00
M21 Kordell Stewart	.75	2.00
M22 Torry Holt	2.00	5.00
M23 Marshall Faulk	1.50	4.00
M24 Kurt Warner	7.50	20.00
M25 Jerry Rice	2.50	6.00
M26 Jon Kitna	1.25	3.00
M27 Eddie George	1.25	3.00
M28 Champ Bailey	6.00	15.00
M29 Brad Johnson	1.25	3.00
M30 Stephen Davis	1.25	3.00

1999 Collector's Edge Masters Pro Signature Authentics

COMPLETE SET (2) 125.00 250.00
STATED PRINT RUN 500 SER.#'d SETS
MANNING 1B ISSUED AS MAIL REDEMP.

1A Peyton Manning/500	40.00	80.00
1B Peyton Manning/445	40.00	80.00
1C Peyton Manning/40	100.00	175.00
2 Kurt Warner/500	50.00	100.00

1999 Collector's Edge Masters Quest

COMPLETE SET (20) 20.00 40.00
STATED PRINT RUN 3000 SER.#'d SETS

Q1 Jake Plummer	.75	2.00
Q2 Eric Moulds	1.25	3.00
Q3 Curtis Enis	.50	1.25
Q4 Emmitt Smith	2.50	6.00
Q5 Brian Griese	1.25	3.00
Q6 Dorsey Levens	1.25	3.00
Q7 Marvin Harrison	1.25	3.00
Q8 Mark Brunell	1.25	3.00
Q9 Fred Taylor	1.25	3.00
Q10 Cris Carter	1.25	3.00
Q11 Terry Glenn	1.25	3.00
Q12 Keyshawn Johnson	1.25	3.00
Q13 Isaac Bruce	1.25	3.00
Q14 Terrell Owens	1.25	3.00
Q15 Jon Kitna	1.25	3.00
Q16 Natrone Means	.75	2.00
Q17 Warrick Dunn	1.25	3.00
Q18 Steve McNair	1.25	3.00
Q19 Brad Johnson	1.25	3.00
Q20 Stephen Davis	1.25	3.00

1999 Collector's Edge Masters Rookie Masters

COMPLETE SET (30) 40.00 80.00
STATED PRINT RUN 3000 SER.#'d SETS

RM1 David Boston	.75	2.00
RM2 Chris McAlister	.60	1.50
RM3 Peerless Price	.75	2.00
RM4 D'Wayne Bates	1.25	3.00
RM5 Cade McNown	.75	2.00
RM6 Akili Smith	.75	2.00
RM7 Tim Couch	.75	2.00
RM8 Kevin Johnson	.75	2.00
RM9 Wane McGarity	.60	1.50
RM10 Chris Claiborne	.60	1.50
RM11 Sedrick Irvin	1.00	2.50
RM12 Edgerrin James	3.00	8.00
RM13 Mike Cloud	.75	2.00
RM14 Cecil Collins	.60	1.50
RM15 James Johnson	.75	2.00
RM16 Rob Konrad	.75	2.00
RM17 Daunte Culpepper	3.00	8.00
RM18 Kevin Faulk	.75	2.00
RM19 Andy Katzenmoyer	.75	2.00
RM20 Ricky Williams	1.50	4.00
RM21 Donovan McNabb	4.00	10.00
RM22 Troy Edwards	.75	2.00
RM23 Amos Zereoue	.75	2.00
RM24 Joe Germaine	.75	2.00
RM25 Torry Holt	2.00	5.00
RM26 Karsten Bailey	.75	2.00
RM27 Brock Huard	.75	2.00
RM28 Shaun King	.75	2.00
RM29 Jevon Kearse	1.00	2.50
RM30 Champ Bailey	1.00	2.50

1999 Collector's Edge Masters Sentinels

COMPLETE SET (20)	125.00	250.00
STATED PRINT RUN 500 SER.#'d SETS		
S1 Troy Aikman	6.00	15.00
S2 Emmitt Smith	6.00	15.00
S3 Terrell Davis	3.00	8.00
S4 Barry Sanders	10.00	25.00
S5 Brett Favre	10.00	25.00
S6 Peyton Manning	7.50	20.00
S7 Dan Marino	10.00	25.00
S8 Randy Moss	6.00	15.00
S9 Drew Bledsoe	2.50	10.00
S10 Isaac Bruce	3.00	8.00
S11 Kurt Warner	10.00	25.00
S12 David Boston	3.00	8.00
S13 Cade McNown	3.00	8.00
S14 Akili Smith	3.00	8.00
S15 Tim Couch	3.00	8.00
S16 Edgerrin James	6.00	15.00
S17 Ricky Williams	3.00	8.00
S18 Donovan McNabb	7.50	20.00
S19 Troy Edwards	3.00	8.00
S20 Torry Holt	3.00	8.00
S18P Donovan McNabb PREVIEW	2.00	5.00

2000 Collector's Edge Masters

Released as a 250-card set, Masters features a base card printed on Dot Matrix Hologram card stock divided up into 200 veteran player cards and 50 rookie cards. Veteran cards are sequentially numbered to 2000 and rookies are sequentially numbered to 1000. Masters was packaged in 20-pack boxes with packs containing three cards and carried a suggested retail price of $5.99. Each hobby box contained one PSA 9 or 10 rookie card.

COMP.SET w/o SP's (200)	10.00	25.00
201-250 ROOKIE PRINT RUN 1000		
1 David Boston	.40	1.00
2 Michael Pittman	.40	1.00
3 Jake Plummer	.50	1.25
4 Frank Sanders	.40	1.00
5 Jamal Anderson	.50	1.25
6 Chris Chandler	.50	1.25
7 Tim Dwight	.50	1.25
8 Shawn Jefferson	.40	1.00
9 Terance Mathis	.40	1.00
10 Tony Banks	.40	1.00
11 Trent Dilfer	.50	1.25
12 Priest Holmes	.60	1.50
13 Qadry Ismail	.50	1.25
14 Jermaine Lewis	.40	1.00
15 Shannon Sharpe	.60	1.50
16 Doug Flutie	.60	1.50
17 Rob Johnson	.50	1.25
18 Jeremy McDaniel	.40	1.00
19 Eric Moulds	.50	1.25
20 Peerless Price	.50	1.25
21 Antowain Smith	.50	1.25
22 Steve Beuerlein	.50	1.25
23 Tim Biakabutuka	.50	1.25
24 Dialleo Burks RC	.40	1.00
25 Dameyune Craig	.40	1.00
26 Donald Hayes	.40	1.00
27 Patrick Jeffers	.50	1.25
28 Muhsin Muhammad	.50	1.25
29 Reggie White	.60	1.50
30 Bobby Engram	.50	1.25
31 Curtis Enis	.40	1.00
32 Eddie Kennison	.40	1.00
33 Cade McNown	.40	1.00
34 Marcus Robinson	.50	1.25
35 Corey Dillon	.50	1.25
36 James Hundon	.40	1.00
37 Scott Mitchell	.40	1.00
38 Tony McGee	.40	1.00
39 Akili Smith	.40	1.00
40 Craig Yeast	.40	1.00
41 Darrin Chiaverini	.40	1.00
42 Tim Couch	.50	1.25
43 Kevin Johnson	.40	1.00
44 Errict Rhett	.50	1.25
45 Troy Aikman	1.00	2.50
46 Randall Cunningham	.60	1.50
47 Joey Galloway	.50	1.25
48 Rocket Ismail	.50	1.25
49 James McKnight	.40	1.00
50 Dat Nguyen	.40	1.00
51 Emmitt Smith	1.50	4.00
52 Chris Warren	.40	1.00
53 Robert Brooks	.50	1.25
54 Terrell Davis	.60	1.50
55 Gus Frerotte	.50	1.25
56 Olandis Gary	.50	1.25
57 Brian Griese	.50	1.25
58 Ed McCaffrey	.50	1.25
59 Rod Smith	.50	1.25
60 Charlie Batch	.50	1.25
61 Germane Crowell	.40	1.00
62 Sedrick Irvin	.40	1.00
63 Herman Moore	.50	1.25
64 Johnnie Morton	.50	1.25
65 James Stewart	.40	1.00
66 Corey Bradford	.40	1.00
67 Brett Favre	2.00	5.00
68 Antonio Freeman	.50	1.25
69 Matt Hasselbeck	.60	1.50
70 Dorsey Levens	.50	1.25
71 Bill Schroeder	.50	1.25
72 Ken Dilger	.40	1.00
73 E.G. Green	.40	1.00
74 Marvin Harrison	.60	1.50
75 Edgerrin James	.60	1.50
76 Peyton Manning	1.50	4.00
77 Jerome Pathon	.40	1.00
78 Terrence Wilkins	.40	1.00
79 Kyle Brady	.40	1.00
80 Mark Brunell	.50	1.25
81 Kevin Hardy	.40	1.00
82 Stacey Mack	.40	1.00
83 Keenan McCardell	.50	1.25
84 Jimmy Smith	.50	1.25
85 Fred Taylor	.60	1.50
86 Derrick Alexander	.40	1.00
87 Mike Cloud	.40	1.00
88 Tony Gonzalez	.60	1.50
89 Elvis Grbac	.40	1.00
90 Kevin Lockett	.40	1.00
91 Tony Richardson RC	.50	1.25
92 Jay Fiedler	.50	1.25
93 Oronde Gadsden	.50	1.25
94 Damon Huard	.50	1.25
95 Rob Konrad	.40	1.00
96 James Johnson	.40	1.00
97 Tony Martin	.50	1.25
98 O.J. McDuffie	.50	1.25
99 Lamar Smith	.40	1.00
100 Thurman Thomas	.60	1.50
101 Todd Bouman	.40	1.00
102 Bubby Brister	.50	1.25
103 Cris Carter	.60	1.50
104 Daunte Culpepper	.50	1.25
105 Matthew Hatchette	.40	1.00
106 Randy Moss	.60	1.50
107 Robert Smith	.50	1.25
108 Moe Williams	.40	1.00
109 Michael Bishop	.40	1.00
110 Drew Bledsoe	.60	1.50
111 Troy Brown	.50	1.25
112 Kevin Faulk	.50	1.25
113 Terry Glenn	.50	1.25
114 Andy Katzenmoyer	.40	1.00
115 Tony Simmons	.40	1.00
116 Jeff Blake	.50	1.25
117 Aaron Brooks	.50	1.25
118 Jake Delhomme RC	1.50	4.00
119 Joe Horn	.50	1.25
120 Jake Reed	.50	1.25
121 Ricky Williams	.60	1.50
122 Tiki Barber	.60	1.50
123 Kerry Collins	.50	1.25
124 Ike Hilliard	.50	1.25
125 Amani Toomer	.50	1.25
126 Wayne Chrebet	.50	1.25
127 Ray Lucas	.40	1.00
128 Curtis Martin	.60	1.50
129 Vinny Testaverde	.50	1.25
130 Dedric Ward	.40	1.00
131 Tim Brown	.60	1.50
132 Rickey Dudley	.40	1.00
133 Rich Gannon	.50	1.25
134 James Jett	.50	1.25
135 Napoleon Kaufman	.50	1.25
136 Tyrone Wheatley	.40	1.00
137 Charles Woodson	.60	1.50
138 Charles Johnson	.40	1.00
139 Donovan McNabb	.60	1.50
140 Torrance Small	.40	1.00
141 Duce Staley	.50	1.25
142 Jerome Bettis	.60	1.50
143 Troy Edwards	.40	1.00
144 Kent Graham	.40	1.00
145 Richard Huntley	.40	1.00
146 Kordell Stewart	.50	1.25
147 Amos Zereoue	.40	1.00
148 Isaac Bruce	.60	1.50
149 Kevin Carter	.40	1.00
150 Marshall Faulk	.60	1.50
151 Trent Green	.50	1.25
152 Az-Zahir Hakim	.40	1.00
153 Robert Holcombe	.40	1.00
154 Torry Holt	.60	1.50
155 Kurt Warner	1.00	2.50
156 Kenny Bynum	.40	1.00
157 Robert Chancey	.40	1.00
158 Curtis Conway	.50	1.25
159 Jermaine Fazande	.40	1.00
160 Jeff Graham	.40	1.00
161 Jim Harbaugh	.50	1.25
162 Ryan Leaf	.50	1.25
163 Junior Seau	.60	1.50
164 Jeff Garcia	.50	1.25
165 Charlie Garner	.50	1.25
166 Terrell Owens	.60	1.50
167 Jerry Rice	1.25	3.00
168 J.J. Stokes	.50	1.25
169 Karsten Bailey	.40	1.00
170 Sean Dawkins	.40	1.00
171 Brock Huard	.40	1.00
172 Jon Kitna	.50	1.25
173 Derrick Mayes	.40	1.00
174 Ricky Watters	.50	1.25
175 Rabih Abdullah	.40	1.00
176 Mike Alstott	.60	1.50
177 Reidel Anthony	.40	1.00
178 Warrick Dunn	.50	1.25
179 Jacquez Green	.40	1.00
180 Keyshawn Johnson	.50	1.25
181 Shaun King	.40	1.00
182 Warren Sapp	.50	1.25
183 Kevin Dyson	.50	1.25
184 Eddie George	.50	1.25
185 Jevon Kearse	.50	1.25
186 Steve McNair	.60	1.50
187 Neil O'Donnell	.40	1.00
188 Carl Pickens	.50	1.25
189 Yancey Thigpen	.40	1.00
190 Frank Wycheck	.50	1.25
191 Champ Bailey	.50	1.25
192 Larry Centers	.40	1.00
193 Albert Connell	.40	1.00
194 Stephen Davis	.50	1.25
195 Jeff George	.50	1.25
196 Brad Johnson	.50	1.25
197 Deion Sanders	.60	1.50
198 Bruce Smith	.60	1.50
199 James Thrash	.50	1.25
200 Michael Westbrook	.40	1.00
201 Thomas Jones RC	2.50	6.00
202 Jamal Lewis RC	2.00	5.00
203 Chris Redman RC	1.50	4.00
204 Travis Taylor RC	1.50	4.00
205 Avion Black RC	1.25	3.00
206 Kwame Cavil RC	1.25	3.00
207 Sammy Morris RC	1.50	4.00
208 Brian Urlacher RC	8.00	20.00
209 Dez White RC	1.50	4.00
210 Ron Dugans RC	1.25	3.00
211 Danny Farmer RC	1.25	3.00
212 Curtis Keaton RC	1.25	3.00
213 Peter Warrick RC	2.00	5.00
214 Courtney Brown RC	1.50	4.00
215 JaJuan Dawson RC	1.25	3.00
216 Dennis Northcutt RC	1.50	4.00
217 Travis Prentice RC	1.50	4.00
218 Spergon Wynn RC	1.50	4.00
219 Michael Wiley RC	1.25	3.00
220 Mike Anderson RC	2.00	5.00
221 Chris Cole RC	1.50	4.00
222 Deltha O'Neal RC	1.50	4.00
223 Reuben Droughns RC	2.00	5.00
224 Bubba Franks RC	2.00	5.00
225 Charles Lee RC	1.25	3.00
226 Rob Morris RC	1.50	4.00
227 R.Jay Soward RC	1.25	3.00
228 Shyrone Stith RC	1.25	3.00
229 Frank Moreau RC	1.25	3.00
230 Sylvester Morris RC	1.25	3.00
231 J.R. Redmond RC	1.25	3.00
232 Chad Morton RC	2.00	5.00
233 Ron Dayne RC	2.00	5.00
234 Ron Dixon RC	1.25	3.00
235 Anthony Becht RC	1.50	4.00
236 Laveranues Coles RC	2.00	5.00
237 Chad Pennington RC	3.00	8.00
238 Sebastian Janikowski RC	2.00	5.00
239 Jerry Porter RC	2.00	5.00
240 Todd Pinkston RC	1.25	3.00
241 Gari Scott RC	1.25	3.00
242 Corey Simon RC	1.50	4.00
243 Plaxico Burress RC	2.00	5.00
244 Tee Martin RC	2.00	5.00
245 Trung Canidate RC	1.50	4.00
246 Trevor Gaylor RC	1.25	3.00
247 Giovanni Carmazzi RC	1.25	3.00
248 Tim Rattay RC	1.50	4.00
249 Shaun Alexander RC	2.50	6.00
250 Joe Hamilton RC	1.25	3.00

2000 Collector's Edge Masters HoloGold

*VETS 1-200: 3X TO 8X BASIC CARDS
*ROOKIES 201-250: 1X TO 2.5X
HOLOGOLD PRINT RUN 50 SER.#'d SETS

2000 Collector's Edge Masters HoloSilver

*VETS 1-200: 1.5X TO 4X BASIC CARDS
*ROOKIES 201-250: .5X TO 1.2X
HOLOSILVER PRINT RUN 1000 SER.#'d SETS

2000 Collector's Edge Masters Retail

*VETS 1-200: .1X TO .3X BASIC CARDS
*ROOKIES 201-250: .1X TO .25X

2000 Collector's Edge Masters Domain

COMPLETE SET (20)	10.00	25.00
STATED PRINT RUN 5000 SER.#'d SETS		
D1 Qadry Ismail	.60	1.50
D2 Muhsin Muhammad	.60	1.50
D3 Marcus Robinson	.60	1.50
D4 Akili Smith	.50	1.25
D5 Tim Couch	.60	1.50
D6 Kevin Johnson	.50	1.25
D7 Troy Aikman	1.25	3.00
D8 Brian Griese	.60	1.50
D9 James Stewart	.50	1.25
D10 Dorsey Levens	.60	1.50
D11 Marvin Harrison	.75	2.00
D12 Cris Carter	.75	2.00
D13 Daunte Culpepper	.80	1.50
D14 Donovan McNabb	.75	2.00
D15 Duce Staley	.60	1.50
D16 Isaac Bruce	.75	2.00
D17 Torry Holt	.75	2.00
D18 Kurt Warner	1.25	3.00
D19 Jeff Garcia	.60	1.50
D20 Jerry Rice	1.50	4.00

2000 Collector's Edge Masters Future Masters Gold

COMPLETE SET (30)	25.00	60.00
GOLD PRINT RUN 2000 SER.#'d SETS		
*SILVER/3000: .3X TO .8X GOLD/2000		
SILVER PRINT RUN 3000 SER.#'d SETS		
FM1 Thomas Jones	1.25	3.00
FM2 Jamal Lewis	1.00	2.50
FM3 Chris Redman	.75	2.00
FM4 Travis Taylor	.75	2.00
FM5 Brian Urlacher	4.00	10.00
FM6 Dez White	.75	2.00
FM7 Ron Dugans	.60	1.50
FM8 Danny Farmer	.60	1.50
FM9 Curtis Keaton	.60	1.50
FM10 Peter Warrick	1.00	2.50
FM11 Courtney Brown	.75	2.00
FM12 JaJuan Dawson	.60	1.50
FM13 Dennis Northcutt	.75	2.00
FM14 Travis Prentice	.75	2.00
FM15 Spergon Wynn	.75	2.00
FM16 Reuben Droughns	1.00	2.50
FM17 R.Jay Soward	.60	1.50
FM18 J.R. Redmond	.60	1.50
FM19 Ron Dayne	1.00	2.50
FM20 Anthony Becht	.75	2.00
FM21 Laveranues Coles	1.00	2.50
FM22 Chad Pennington	1.50	4.00
FM23 Jerry Porter	1.00	2.50
FM24 Todd Pinkston	.60	1.50
FM25 Plaxico Burress	1.00	2.50
FM26 Tee Martin	1.00	2.50
FM27 Trung Canidate	.75	2.00
FM28 Giovanni Carmazzi	.60	1.50
FM29 Tim Rattay	.75	2.00
FM30 Joe Hamilton	.60	1.50

2000 Collector's Edge Masters GameGear Leatherbacks

STATED PRINT RUN 12 SER.#'d SETS		
DC Daunte Culpepper	25.00	60.00
KW Kurt Warner	60.00	150.00
PM Peyton Manning	125.00	250.00
PW Peter Warrick	30.00	80.00
RM Randy Moss	125.00	250.00
TC Tim Couch	25.00	60.00

2000 Collector's Edge Masters Hasta La Vista

COMPLETE SET (20)	20.00	50.00
STATED PRINT RUN 2000 SER.#'d SETS		
H1 Eric Moulds	.75	2.00
H2 Cade McNown	.60	1.50
H3 Emmitt Smith	2.50	6.00
H4 Terrell Davis	1.00	2.50
H5 Charlie Batch	.75	2.00
H6 Marvin Harrison	1.00	2.50
H7 Edgerrin James	1.00	2.50
H8 Peyton Manning	2.50	6.00
H9 Mark Brunell	.75	2.00
H10 Fred Taylor	1.00	2.50
H11 Daunte Culpepper	.75	2.00
H12 Torry Holt	1.00	2.50
H13 Marshall Faulk	1.00	2.50
H14 Kurt Warner	1.50	4.00
H15 Ryan Leaf	.75	2.00
H16 Keyshawn Johnson	.75	2.00
H17 Shaun King	.60	1.50
H18 Steve McNair	1.00	2.50
H19 Stephen Davis	.75	2.00
H20 Brad Johnson	.75	2.00

2000 Collector's Edge Masters K-Klub

COMPLETE SET (50)	25.00	60.00
STATED PRINT RUN 3000 SER.#'d SETS		
K1 David Boston	.50	1.25
K2 Frank Sanders	.50	1.25
K3 Jamal Anderson	.60	1.50
K4 Terance Mathis	.50	1.25
K5 Qadry Ismail	.60	1.50
K6 Eric Moulds	.60	1.50
K7 Antowain Smith	.60	1.50
K8 Patrick Jeffers	.60	1.50
K9 Muhsin Muhammad	.60	1.50
K10 Curtis Enis	.50	1.25
K11 Marcus Robinson	.60	1.50
K12 Corey Dillon	.60	1.50
K13 Kevin Johnson	.50	1.25
K14 Joey Galloway	.60	1.50
K15 Rocket Ismail	.60	1.50
K16 Emmitt Smith	2.00	5.00
K17 Olandis Gary	.60	1.50
K18 Ed McCaffrey	.60	1.50
K19 Germane Crowell	.50	1.25
K20 Herman Moore	.60	1.50
K21 Antonio Freeman	.60	1.50
K22 Dorsey Levens	.60	1.50
K23 Marvin Harrison	.75	2.00
K24 Edgerrin James	.75	2.00
K25 Keenan McCardell	.60	1.50
K26 Jimmy Smith	.60	1.50
K27 Fred Taylor	.75	2.00
K28 Cris Carter	.75	2.00
K29 Randy Moss	.75	2.00
K30 Robert Smith	.60	1.50
K31 Terry Glenn	.60	1.50
K32 Ricky Williams	.75	2.00
K33 Curtis Martin	.75	2.00
K34 Tim Brown	.75	2.00
K35 Duce Staley	.60	1.50
K36 Jerome Bettis	.75	2.00
K37 Isaac Bruce	.75	2.00
K38 Marshall Faulk	.75	2.00
K39 Torry Holt	.75	2.00
K40 Charlie Garner	.60	1.50
K41 Terrell Owens	.75	2.00
K42 Ricky Watters	.60	1.50
K43 Warrick Dunn	.60	1.50
K44 Keyshawn Johnson	.60	1.50
K45 Kevin Dyson	.60	1.50
K46 Eddie George	.60	1.50
K47 Carl Pickens	.60	1.50
K48 Albert Connell	.50	1.25
K49 Stephen Davis	.60	1.50
K50 Michael Westbrook	.50	1.25

2000 Collector's Edge Masters Legends

COMPLETE SET (30)	15.00	40.00
STATED PRINT RUN 5000 SER.#'d SETS		
ML1 Jake Plummer	.50	1.25
ML2 Eric Moulds	.50	1.25
ML3 Cade McNown	.40	1.00
ML4 Marcus Robinson	.50	1.25
ML5 Akili Smith	.40	1.00
ML6 Tim Couch	.50	1.25
ML7 Troy Aikman	1.00	2.50
ML8 Emmitt Smith	1.50	4.00
ML9 Terrell Davis	.60	1.50
ML10 Brett Favre	2.00	5.00
ML11 Antonio Freeman	.50	1.25
ML12 Dorsey Levens	.50	1.25
ML13 Mark Brunell	.50	1.25
ML14 Fred Taylor	.60	1.50
ML15 Cris Carter	.60	1.50
ML16 Randy Moss	.60	1.50
ML17 Drew Bledsoe	.60	1.50
ML18 Curtis Martin	.60	1.50
ML19 Donovan McNabb	.60	1.50
ML20 Ricky Williams	.60	1.50
ML21 Jerome Bettis	.60	1.50
ML22 Isaac Bruce	.60	1.50
ML23 Marshall Faulk	.60	1.50
ML24 Jerry Rice	1.25	3.00
ML25 Jon Kitna	.50	1.25
ML26 Keyshawn Johnson	.50	1.25
ML27 Shaun King	.40	1.00
ML28 Steve McNair	.60	1.50
ML29 Stephen Davis	.50	1.25
ML30 Brad Johnson	.50	1.25

2000 Collector's Edge Masters Majestic

COMPLETE SET (30)	15.00	40.00
STATED PRINT RUN 5000 SER.#'d SETS		
M1 Thomas Jones	.75	2.00
M2 Jamal Lewis	.60	1.50
M3 Travis Taylor	.50	1.25
M4 Brian Urlacher	2.50	6.00
M5 Dez White	.50	1.25
M6 Danny Farmer	.40	1.00
M7 Curtis Keaton	.40	1.00
M8 Peter Warrick	.60	1.50
M9 Courtney Brown	.50	1.25
M10 JaJuan Dawson	.40	1.00
M11 Spergon Wynn	.50	1.25
M12 Michael Wiley	.40	1.00
M13 Reuben Droughns	.60	1.50
M14 Bubba Franks	.60	1.50
M15 Rob Morris	.50	1.25
M16 Sylvester Morris	.40	1.00
M17 Ron Dayne	.60	1.50
M18 Ron Dixon	.40	1.00
M19 Anthony Becht	.50	1.25
M20 Chad Pennington	1.00	2.50
M21 Sebastian Janikowski	.60	1.50
M22 Todd Pinkston	.40	1.00
M23 Corey Simon	.50	1.25
M24 Plaxico Burress	.60	1.50
M25 Tee Martin	.60	1.50
M26 Trevor Gaylor	.40	1.00
M27 Giovanni Carmazzi	.40	1.00
M28 Tim Rattay	.50	1.25
M29 Shaun Alexander	.75	2.00
M30 Joe Hamilton	.40	1.00

2000 Collector's Edge Masters Rookie Ink

*BLUE INK/40: 1X TO 2.5X BLACK		
BLUE INK PRINT RUN 40 SER.#'d SETS		
UNPRICED RED INK PRINT RUN 9-10		
CK Curtis Keaton Gold/1130	6.00	15.00
CR Chris Redman/450	8.00	20.00
LC Laveranues Coles/475	10.00	25.00
SA Shaun Alexander Gold No AU	4.00	10.00
TP Travis Prentice Gold/800	8.00	20.00

2000 Collector's Edge Masters Rookie Masters

COMPLETE SET (30)	30.00	80.00
STATED PRINT RUN 2000 SER.#'d SETS		
*PREVIEWS: .4X TO 1X BASIC INSERTS		
MR1 Thomas Jones	1.25	3.00
MR2 Jamal Lewis	1.00	2.50
MR3 Chris Redman	.75	2.00
MR4 Travis Taylor	.75	2.00
MR5 Dez White	.75	2.00
MR6 Ron Dugans	.60	1.50
MR7 Curtis Keaton	.60	1.50
MR8 Peter Warrick	1.00	2.50
MR9 Brian Urlacher	4.00	10.00
MR10 JaJuan Dawson	.60	1.50
MR11 Dennis Northcutt	.75	2.00
MR12 Travis Prentice	.75	2.00
MR13 Spergon Wynn	.75	2.00
MR14 Reuben Droughns	1.00	2.50
MR15 Bubba Franks	1.00	2.50
MR16 Sylvester Morris	.60	1.50
MR17 J.R. Redmond	.60	1.50
MR18 Ron Dayne	1.00	2.50
MR19 Anthony Becht	.75	2.00
MR20 Laveranues Coles	1.00	2.50
MR21 Chad Pennington	1.50	4.00
MR22 Jerry Porter	1.00	2.50
MR23 Todd Pinkston	.60	1.50
MR24 Plaxico Burress	1.00	2.50
MR25 Tee Martin	1.00	2.50
MR26 Trung Canidate	.75	2.00
MR27 Giovanni Carmazzi	.60	1.50
MR28 Tim Rattay	.75	2.00
MR29 Shaun Alexander	1.25	3.00
MR30 Joe Hamilton	.60	1.50

2000 Collector's Edge Masters Sentinel Rookies

COMPLETE SET (30)	40.00	100.00
STATED PRINT RUN 1000 SER.#'d SETS		
RS1 Thomas Jones	1.50	4.00
RS2 Jamal Lewis	1.25	3.00
RS3 Chris Redman	1.00	2.50
RS4 Travis Taylor	1.00	2.50
RS5 Ron Dugans	.75	2.00
RS6 Peter Warrick	1.25	3.00
RS7 Courtney Brown	1.00	2.50
RS8 Dennis Northcutt	1.00	2.50
RS9 Travis Prentice	1.00	2.50
RS10 Bubba Franks	1.25	3.00
RS11 R.Jay Soward	.75	2.00
RS12 Sylvester Morris	.75	2.00
RS13 J.R. Redmond	.75	2.00
RS14 Ron Dayne	1.25	3.00
RS15 Laveranues Coles	1.25	3.00
RS16 Chad Pennington	2.00	5.00
RS17 Jerry Porter	1.25	3.00
RS18 Plaxico Burress	1.25	3.00
RS19 Trung Canidate	1.00	2.50
RS20 Shaun Alexander	1.50	4.00
RS21 Mike Anderson	1.25	3.00
RS22 Danny Farmer	.75	2.00
RS23 Brian Urlacher	5.00	12.00
RS24 Michael Wiley	.75	2.00
RS25 Rob Morris	1.00	2.50
RS26 Corey Simon	1.00	2.50
RS27 Sebastian Janikowski	1.25	3.00
RS28 Sammy Morris	1.00	2.50
RS29 Keith Bulluck	1.00	2.50
RS30 Frank Moreau	.75	2.00

2000 Collector's Edge Masters Sentinels Gold

COMPLETE SET (20)	30.00	80.00
GOLD PRINT RUN 1000 SER.#'d SETS		
*SILVER/2000: .25X TO .6X GOLD/1000		
SILVER PRINT RUN 2000 SER.#'d SETS		
S1 Jake Plummer	1.00	2.50
S2 Eric Moulds	1.00	2.50
S3 Cade McNown	.75	2.00
S4 Akili Smith	.75	2.00
S5 Tim Couch	1.00	2.50
S6 Kevin Johnson	.75	2.00
S7 Troy Aikman	2.00	5.00
S8 Terrell Davis	1.25	3.00
S9 Brett Favre	4.00	10.00
S10 Edgerrin James	1.25	3.00
S11 Peyton Manning	3.00	8.00
S12 Daunte Culpepper	1.00	2.50
S13 Randy Moss	1.25	3.00
S14 Curtis Martin	1.25	3.00
S15 Donovan McNabb	1.25	3.00
S16 Ricky Williams	1.25	3.00
S17 Kurt Warner	2.00	5.00
S18 Jon Kitna	1.00	2.50
S19 Eddie George	1.00	2.50
S20 Brad Johnson	1.00	2.50

1999 Collector's Edge Millennium Collection Advantage

COMPLETE SET (190)	15.00	30.00
*VETERANS 1-190: .2X TO .5X BASIC ADVANT.		
*ROOKIES 151-188 : .12X TO .3X BASIC ADVANT.		
*BLUE FOILS: .4X TO 1X REDS		

1999 Collector's Edge Millennium Collection First Place

*VETERANS 1-150 : .2X TO .5X BASIC ADVANT.
*ROOKIES 151-200 : .1X TO .3X BASIC ADVANT.
*BLUE FOILS: .4X TO 1X REDS

1999 Collector's Edge Millennium Collection Fury

*VETERANS 1-150: .2X TO .5X BASIC FURY
*ROOKIES 151-200: .12X TO .3X BASIC FURY
*BLUE FOILS: .4X TO 1X REDS

1999 Collector's Edge Millennium Collection Odyssey

*1-150 VETERANS: .2X TO .5X BASIC ODYSSEY
*1-150 ROOKIES: .15X TO .4X BASIC ODYSSEY
*151-170 2Q: .1X TO .3X BASIC ODYSSEY 2Q
*171-185 3Q: .08X TO .25X BASIC ODYSSEY 3Q
*186-195 4Q: .06X TO .15X BASIC ODYSSEY 4Q
*BLUE FOILS: .4X TO 1X REDS

1999 Collector's Edge Millennium Collection Triumph

COMPLETE SET (180)	15.00	30.00
*VETERANS: .2X TO .5X BASIC TRIUMPH		
*ROOKIES: .12X TO .3X BASIC TRIUMPH		
*BLUE FOILS: .4X TO 1X REDS		

1998 Collector's Edge Odyssey Previews

This set was released as a Preview of the 1999 Collector's Edge Odyssey base set. Each card is essentially a parallel version of the base set card with the player's initials as the card number along with the word "preview" on the cardfronts.

COMPLETE SET (33)	25.00	60.00
202 Curtis Enis 3Q	.40	1.00
206 Emmitt Smith 3Q	1.50	4.00
207 John Elway 3Q	2.50	6.00
208 Terrell Davis 3Q	1.00	2.50
209 Barry Sanders 3Q	1.50	4.00
210 Brett Favre 3Q	2.50	6.00
211 Antonio Freeman 3Q	.40	1.00
212 Peyton Manning 3Q	2.50	6.00
213 Mark Brunell 3Q	.60	1.50
215 Dan Marino 3Q	2.50	6.00
217 Drew Bledsoe 3Q	.75	2.00
219 Curtis Martin 3Q	.75	2.00
221 Jerome Bettis 3Q	.60	1.50
224 Jerry Rice 3Q	1.25	3.00
225 Steve Young 3Q	.75	2.00
226 Warren Moon 3Q	.60	1.50
227 Trent Dilfer 3Q	.60	1.50
229 Steve McNair 3Q	.60	1.50
230 Eddie George 3Q	.60	1.50
231 Curtis Enis 4Q	.40	1.00
232 Carl Pickens 4Q	.40	1.00
233 Troy Aikman 4Q	1.25	3.00
234 Emmitt Smith 4Q	1.50	4.00
235 John Elway 4Q	2.50	6.00
236 Terrell Davis 4Q	1.00	2.50
237 Barry Sanders 4Q	1.50	4.00
238 Brett Favre 4Q	2.50	6.00
239 Peyton Manning 4Q	2.50	6.00
240 Fred Taylor 4Q	1.25	3.00
241 Dan Marino 4Q	2.50	6.00
242 Randy Moss 4Q	2.00	5.00
243 Drew Bledsoe 4Q	.75	2.00
244 Kordell Stewart 4Q	.60	1.50
245 Jerome Bettis 4Q	.60	1.50
246 Ryan Leaf 4Q	.40	1.00
247 Jerry Rice 4Q	1.25	3.00
248 Steve Young 4Q	.75	2.00
249 Warren Moon 4Q	.60	1.50
250 Eddie George 4Q	.60	1.50

1998 Collector's Edge Odyssey

This 250-card set was distributed in eight-card packs with a suggested retail price of $4.99 and features color action photos of 150 different players. The set is divided into four quarters with the 50 best players pictured on the 2nd Quarter cards. The 30 best of these are on the 3rd Quarter cards, and the 20 best of these are pictured on the 4th Quarter cards. A player that is listed in more than one quarter has a different picture on each of his cards. Cards #1-150 makeup the 1st Quarter which consists of all the players. Cards 151-200 are the 2nd Quarter cards and are shortprinted with an insertion rate of 1:2 packs. Cards 201-230 are the 3rd Quarter cards and are shortprinted even further with an insertion rate of 1:7 packs. Cards 231-250 are shortprinted even further and are available 1:24 packs.

COMPLETE SET (250)	200.00	400.00
1 Terance Mathis	.10	.30
2 Tony Martin	.10	.30
3 Chris Chandler	.10	.30
4 Jamal Anderson	.20	.50
5 Jake Plummer	.20	.50
6 Adrian Murrell	.10	.30
7 Rob Moore	.10	.30
8 Frank Sanders	.10	.30
9 Larry Centers	.07	.20
10 Andre Wadsworth RC	.50	1.25
11 Jim Harbaugh	.10	.30
12 Errict Rhett	.10	.30
13 Jermaine Lewis	.10	.30
14 Michael Jackson	.07	.20
15 Eric Zeier	.10	.30
16 Rob Johnson	.10	.30
17 Antowain Smith	.20	.50
18 Andre Reed	.10	.30
19 Bruce Smith	.10	.30
20 Doug Flutie	.20	.50
21 Thurman Thomas	.20	.50
22 Kerry Collins	.10	.30
23 Fred Lane	.07	.20
24 Muhsin Muhammad	.10	.30
25 Rae Carruth	.07	.20
26 Rocket Ismail	.07	.20
27 Kevin Greene	.10	.30
28 Curtis Enis RC	.30	.75
29 Curtis Conway	.10	.30
30 Erik Kramer	.07	.20
31 Edgar Bennett	.07	.20
32 Neil O'Donnell	.10	.30
33 Jeff Blake	.10	.30
34 Carl Pickens	.10	.30
35 Corey Dillon	.20	.50
36 Troy Aikman	.40	1.00
37 Jason Garrett RC	.30	.75
38 Emmitt Smith	.60	1.50
39 Deion Sanders	.20	.50
40 Michael Irvin	.20	.50
41 Chris Warren	.10	.30
42 John Elway	.75	2.00
43 Terrell Davis	.20	.50
44 Shannon Sharpe	.10	.30
45 Rod Smith WR	.10	.30
46 Marcus Nash RC	.30	.75
47 Brian Griese RC	1.25	3.00
48 Barry Sanders	.60	1.50
49 Herman Moore	.10	.30
50 Scott Mitchell	.10	.30
51 Johnnie Morton	.10	.30
52 Rashaan Shehee RC	.50	1.25
53 Charlie Batch RC	.60	1.50
54 Brett Favre	.75	2.00
55 Dorsey Levens	.20	.50
56 Antonio Freeman	.20	.50
57 Reggie White	.20	.50
58 Robert Brooks	.10	.30
59 Raymont Harris	.07	.20
60 Peyton Manning RC	6.00	15.00
61 Marshall Faulk	.25	.60
62 Jerome Pathon RC	.60	1.50
63 Marvin Harrison	.20	.50
64 Mark Brunell	.20	.50
65 Fred Taylor RC	1.00	2.50
66 Jimmy Smith	.10	.30
67 James Stewart	.10	.30
68 Keenan McCardell	.10	.30
69 Andre Rison	.10	.30
70 Elvis Grbac	.10	.30
71 Donnell Bennett	.07	.20
72 Rich Gannon	.20	.50
73 Derrick Thomas	.20	.50
74 Dan Marino	.75	2.00
75 Karim Abdul-Jabbar UER no first name on cardfront	.20	.50
76 John Avery RC UER photo Karim Abdul-Jabbar	.50	1.25
77 O.J. McDuffie	.10	.30
78 Oronde Gadsden RC	.60	1.50
79 Zach Thomas	.20	.50
80 Randy Moss RC	4.00	10.00
81 Cris Carter	.20	.50
82 Jake Reed	.10	.30
83 Robert Smith	.20	.50
84 Brad Johnson	.20	.50
85 Drew Bledsoe	.30	.75
86 Robert Edwards RC	.50	1.25
87 Terry Glenn	.20	.50
88 Troy Brown	.10	.30
89 Shawn Jefferson	.07	.20
90 Danny Wuerffel	.10	.30
91 Dana Stubblefield	.07	.20
92 Derrick Alexander	.10	.30
93 Ray Zellars	.07	.20
94 Andre Hastings	.07	.20
95 Danny Kanell	.10	.30
96 Tiki Barber	.20	.50
97 Ike Hilliard	.10	.30
98 Charles Way	.07	.20
99 Chris Calloway	.07	.20
100 Curtis Martin	.20	.50
101 Glenn Foley	.10	.30
102 Vinny Testaverde	.10	.30
103 Keyshawn Johnson	.20	.50
104 Wayne Chrebet	.20	.50
105 Leon Johnson	.07	.20
106 Jeff George	.10	.30
107 Charles Woodson RC	1.00	2.50
108 Tim Brown	.20	.50
109 James Jett	.10	.30
110 Napoleon Kaufman	.20	.50
111 Charlie Garner	.10	.30
112 Bobby Hoying	.10	.30
113 Duce Staley	.30	.75
114 Irving Fryar	.10	.30
115 Kordell Stewart	.20	.50
116 Jerome Bettis	.20	.50
117 Charles Johnson	.07	.20
118 Randall Cunningham	.20	.50
119 Courtney Hawkins	.07	.20
120 Tony Banks	.10	.30
121 Isaac Bruce	.20	.50
122 Robert Holcombe RC	.50	1.25
123 Eddie Kennison	.10	.30
124 Ryan Leaf RC	.60	1.50
125 Mikhael Ricks RC	.50	1.25
126 Natrone Means	.10	.30
127 Junior Seau	.20	.50
128 Jerry Rice	.40	1.00
129 Terrell Owens	.20	.50
130 Garrison Hearst	.20	.50
131 Steve Young	.20	.50
132 J.J. Stokes	.10	.30
133 Warren Moon	.20	.50
134 Joey Galloway	.10	.30
135 Ricky Watters	.10	.30
136 Ahman Green RC	1.50	4.00
137 Trent Dilfer	.20	.50
138 Mike Alstott	.20	.50
139 Warrick Dunn	.20	.50
140 Reidel Anthony	.10	.30
141 Jacquez Green RC	.50	1.25
142 Steve McNair	.20	.50
143 Eddie George	.20	.50
144 Yancey Thigpen	.07	.20
145 Kevin Dyson RC	.60	1.50
146 Trent Green	.25	.60
147 Gus Frerotte	.07	.20
148 Terry Allen	.20	.50
149 Michael Westbrook	.10	.30
150 Jim Druckenmiller	.07	.20
151 Jake Plummer 2Q	.30	.75
152 Adrian Murrell 2Q	.20	.50
153 Rob Johnson 2Q	.20	.50
154 Antowain Smith 2Q	.30	.75
155 Kerry Collins 2Q	.20	.50
156 Curtis Enis 2Q	.20	.50
157 Carl Pickens 2Q	.20	.50
158 Corey Dillon 2Q	.30	.75
159 Troy Aikman 2Q	.60	1.50
160 Emmitt Smith 2Q	.75	2.00
161 Deion Sanders 2Q	.30	.75
162 Michael Irvin 2Q	.30	.75
163 John Elway 2Q	1.25	3.00
164 Terrell Davis 2Q	.30	.75
165 Shannon Sharpe 2Q	.20	.50
166 Rod Smith 2Q	.20	.50
167 Barry Sanders 2Q	1.00	2.50
168 Herman Moore 2Q	.20	.50
169 Brett Favre 2Q	1.25	3.00
170 Dorsey Levens 2Q	.30	.75
171 Antonio Freeman 2Q	.30	.75
172 Peyton Manning 2Q	5.00	12.00
173 Marshall Faulk 2Q	.40	1.00
174 Mark Brunell 2Q	.30	.75
175 Fred Taylor 2Q	1.25	3.00
176 Dan Marino 2Q	1.25	3.00
177 Randy Moss 2Q	3.00	8.00
178 Cris Carter 2Q	.30	.75
179 Drew Bledsoe 2Q	.40	1.00
180 Robert Edwards 2Q	.20	.50
181 Curtis Martin 2Q	.30	.75
182 Napoleon Kaufman 2Q	.30	.75
183 Kordell Stewart 2Q	.20	.50
184 Jerome Bettis 2Q	.30	.75
185 Tony Banks 2Q	.20	.50
186 Isaac Bruce 2Q	.30	.75
187 Ryan Leaf 2Q	.30	.75
188 Natrone Means 2Q	.20	.50
189 Jerry Rice 2Q	.60	1.50
190 Terrell Owens 2Q	.30	.75
191 Garrison Hearst 2Q	.30	.75
192 Steve Young 2Q	.30	.75
193 Warren Moon 2Q	.30	.75
194 Joey Galloway 2Q	.20	.50
195 Trent Dilfer 2Q	.30	.75
196 Mike Alstott 2Q	.30	.75
197 Warrick Dunn 2Q	.30	.75
198 Steve McNair 2Q	.30	.75
199 Eddie George 2Q	.30	.75

200 Terry Allen 2Q	.30	.75
201 Jake Plummer 3Q	.40	1.00
202 Curtis Enis 3Q	.25	.60
203 Carl Pickens 3Q	.25	.60
204 Corey Dillon 3Q	.40	1.00
205 Troy Aikman 3Q	.75	2.00
206 Emmitt Smith 3Q	1.25	3.00
207 John Elway 3Q	1.50	4.00
208 Terrell Davis 3Q	.40	1.00
209 Barry Sanders 3Q	1.25	3.00
210 Brett Favre 3Q	1.50	4.00
211 Antonio Freeman 3Q	.40	1.00
212 Peyton Manning 3Q	6.00	15.00
213 Mark Brunell 3Q	.40	1.00
214 Fred Taylor 3Q	1.50	4.00
215 Dan Marino 3Q	1.50	4.00
216 Randy Moss 3Q	4.00	10.00
217 Drew Bledsoe 3Q	.60	1.50
218 Robert Edwards 3Q	.25	.60
219 Curtis Martin 3Q	.40	1.00
220 Kordell Stewart 3Q	.40	1.00
221 Jerome Bettis 3Q	.40	1.00
222 Tony Banks 3Q	.25	.60
223 Ryan Leaf 3Q	.40	1.00
224 Jerry Rice 3Q	.75	2.00
225 Steve Young 3Q	.40	1.00
226 Warren Moon 3Q	.40	1.00
227 Trent Dilfer 3Q	.40	1.00
228 Warrick Dunn 3Q	.40	1.00
229 Steve McNair 3Q	.40	1.00
230 Eddie George 3Q	.40	1.00
231 Curtis Enis 4Q	1.25	3.00
232 Carl Pickens 4Q	1.25	3.00
233 Troy Aikman 4Q	2.50	6.00
234 Emmitt Smith 4Q	4.00	10.00
235 John Elway 4Q	5.00	12.00
236 Terrell Davis 4Q	1.25	3.00
237 Barry Sanders 4Q	4.00	10.00
238 Brett Favre 4Q	5.00	12.00
239 Peyton Manning 4Q	10.00	25.00
240 Fred Taylor 4Q	2.50	6.00
241 Dan Marino 4Q	5.00	12.00
242 Randy Moss 4Q	6.00	15.00
243 Drew Bledsoe 4Q	2.00	5.00
244 Kordell Stewart 4Q	1.25	3.00
245 Jerome Bettis 4Q	1.25	3.00
246 Ryan Leaf 4Q	1.25	3.00
247 Jerry Rice 4Q	2.50	6.00
248 Steve Young 4Q	1.50	4.00
249 Warren Moon 4Q	1.25	3.00
250 Eddie George 4Q	1.25	3.00

1998 Collector's Edge Odyssey Level 1 Galvanized

COMPLETE SET (250) 300.00 600.00
*VETS 1-150: 1.2X TO 3X BASIC CARDS
*ROOKIES 1-150: .6X TO 1.5X
GALVANIZED 1-150 STATED ODDS 1:3
*VETS 151-200: 1.5X TO 4X BASIC CARDS
*ROOKIES 151-200: .8X TO 2X
GALVANIZED 151-200 STATED ODDS 1:15
*VETS 201-230: 1.2X TO 3X BASIC CARDS
*ROOKIES 201-230: .6X TO 1.5X
GALVANIZED 201-230 STATED ODDS 1:29
*VETS 231-250: .8X TO 2X BASIC CARDS
*ROOKIES 231-250: .4X TO 1X
GALVANIZED 231-250 STATED ODDS 1:59

1998 Collector's Edge Odyssey Level 2 HoloGold

*VETS 1-150: 15X TO 40X BASIC CARDS
*ROOKIES 1-150: 3X TO 8X
HOLO.GOLD 1-150 STATED ODDS 1:34
HOLO.GOLD 1-150 PRINT RUN 150 SETS
*VETS 151-200: 10X TO 25X BASIC CARDS
*ROOKIES 151-200: 3X TO 8X
HOLO.GOLD 151-200 STATED ODDS 1:307
HOLO.GOLD 151-200 PRINT RUN 50 SETS
*VETS 201-230: 12X TO 30X BASIC CARDS
*ROOKIES 201-230: 4X TO 10X
HOLO.GOLD 201-230 STATED ODDS 1:840
HOLO.GOLD 201-230 PRINT RUN 30 SETS
*VETS 231-250: 6X TO 15X BASIC CARDS
*ROOKIES 231-250: 2X TO 5X
HOLO.GOLD 231-250 STATED ODDS 1:1920
HOLO.GOLD 231-250 PRINT RUN 20 SETS

1998 Collector's Edge Odyssey Double Edge

COMPLETE SET (12)	25.00	60.00
STATED ODDS 1:15		
1A Jerry Rice F Randy Moss	7.50	15.00
1B Jerry Rice Randy Moss F	7.50	15.00
2A Brett Favre F Ryan Leaf	5.00	12.00
2B B.Favre R.Leaf F	5.00	12.00
3A Dan Marino F Bobby Hoying	5.00	12.00
3B Dan Marino Bobby Hoying F	5.00	12.00
4A Deion Sanders F Charles Woodson	2.00	5.00
4B Deion Sanders Charles Woodson F	2.00	5.00
5A Terrell Davis F Curtis Enis	2.00	5.00
5B Terrell Davis Curtis Enis F	2.00	5.00
6A Barry Sanders F Fred Taylor	3.00	8.00
6B B.Sanders F.Taylor F	3.00	8.00
7A Emmitt Smith F Robert Edwards	4.00	10.00
7B E.Smith R.Edwards F	4.00	10.00
8A John Elway F Brian Griese	5.00	12.00
8B John Elway Brian Griese F	5.00	12.00
9A Reggie White F Andre Wadsworth	1.50	4.00
9B Reggie White Andre Wadsworth F	1.50	4.00
10A Drew Bledsoe F Charlie Batch	2.00	5.00
10B Drew Bledsoe Charlie Batch F	2.00	5.00
11A Doug Flutie F Glenn Foley	1.50	4.00
11B Doug Flutie Glenn Foley F	1.50	4.00
12A Napoleon Kaufman F Warrick Dunn	1.25	3.00
12B Napoleon Kaufman Warrick Dunn F	1.25	3.00

1998 Collector's Edge Odyssey Game Ball

STATED ODDS 1:360		
BS Barry Sanders	10.00	25.00
CC Cris Carter	6.00	15.00
ES Emmitt Smith	10.00	25.00
FT Fred Taylor	5.00	12.00
HM Herman Moore	4.00	10.00
JE John Elway	12.00	30.00
PM Peyton Manning	12.00	30.00
TA Troy Aikman	8.00	20.00
TD Terrell Davis	6.00	15.00
MB Mark Brunell	5.00	12.00
RM Randy Moss	6.00	15.00

1998 Collector's Edge Odyssey Leading Edge

COMPLETE SET (30)	20.00	50.00
STATED ODDS 1:7		
1 Jake Plummer	.60	1.50
2 Rob Johnson	.40	1.00
3 Curtis Enis	.30	.75
4 Carl Pickens	.40	1.00
5 Troy Aikman	1.25	3.00
6 Emmitt Smith	2.00	5.00
7 John Elway	2.50	6.00
8 Terrell Davis	.60	1.50
9 Shannon Sharpe	.40	1.00
10 Barry Sanders	2.00	5.00
11 Brett Favre	2.50	6.00
12 Antonio Freeman	.60	1.50
13 Peyton Manning	6.00	15.00
14 Marshall Faulk	.75	2.00
15 Mark Brunell	.60	1.50
16 Dan Marino	2.50	6.00
17 Randy Moss	4.00	10.00
18 Cris Carter	.60	1.50
19 Robert Edwards	.50	1.25
20 Curtis Martin	.60	1.50
21 Ryan Leaf	.60	1.50
22 Terrell Owens	.60	1.50
23 Garrison Hearst	.60	1.50
24 Steve Young	.60	1.50
25 Joey Galloway	.40	1.00
26 Mike Alstott	.60	1.50
27 Warrick Dunn	.60	1.50
28 Eddie George	.60	1.50
29 Kevin Dyson	.60	1.50
30 Terry Allen	.60	1.50

1998 Collector's Edge Odyssey Prodigies Autographs

STATED ODDS 1:24
*RED INK/50-80: .8X TO 2X BASIC AUT
RED INK PRINT RUN 10-80
ELWAY/T.DAVIS INSERTED IN 1998 MASTERS

1 Tavian Banks	6.00	15.00
2 Charlie Batch	7.50	20.00
3 Blaine Bishop	6.00	15.00
4 Robert Brooks	7.50	20.00
5 Tim Brown	15.00	40.00
6 Mark Brunell	7.50	20.00
7 Wayne Chrebet	7.50	20.00
8 Terrell Davis Blue/40	25.00	60.00
9 Jim Druckenmiller	4.00	10.00
10 Robert Edwards	6.00	15.00
11 John Elway Blue/40	50.00	120.00
12 Doug Flutie	15.00	40.00
13 Glenn Foley	4.00	10.00
14 Oronde Gadsden	6.00	15.00
15 Joey Galloway	6.00	15.00
16 Garrison Hearst	7.50	20.00
17 Robert Holcombe	6.00	15.00
18 Joey Kent	6.00	15.00
19 Jon Kitna	7.50	20.00
20 Ryan Leaf	7.50	20.00
21 Peyton Manning	50.00	100.00
22 Herman Moore	7.50	20.00
23 Randy Moss	40.00	80.00
24 Terrell Owens	15.00	30.00
25 Mikhael Ricks	6.00	15.00
26 Antowain Smith	7.50	20.00
27 Emmitt Smith	50.00	100.00
28 Robert Smith	7.50	20.00
29 Rod Smith	7.50	20.00
30 J.J. Stokes	6.00	15.00
31 Fred Taylor	7.50	20.00
32 Derrick Thomas	40.00	80.00
33 Chris Warren	6.00	15.00
34 Eric Zeier	6.00	15.00
35 Charles Woodson Unsigned	4.00	10.00

1998 Collector's Edge Odyssey Super Limited Edge

COMPLETE SET (12)	50.00	120.00
STATED ODDS 1:99		
1 Emmitt Smith	8.00	20.00
2 Deion Sanders	2.50	6.00
3 John Elway	10.00	25.00
4 Brett Favre	10.00	25.00
5 Antonio Freeman	2.50	6.00
6 Peyton Manning	12.50	30.00
7 Mark Brunell	2.50	6.00
8 Dan Marino	10.00	25.00
9 Randy Moss	8.00	20.00
10 Joey Galloway	1.50	4.00
11 Mike Alstott	2.50	6.00
12 Eddie George	2.50	6.00

1999 Collector's Edge Odyssey Previews

Cards from this set are essentially a parallel version to the player's corresponding base card. The cardbacks contain the word "preview" and each was released primarily to dealers and distributors.

DC Daunte Culpepper 1Q	2.00	5.00
EJ Edgerrin James 1Q	2.00	5.00
PM Peyton Manning 3Q	2.00	5.00
AS Akili Smith 1Q	.60	1.50
DB David Boston 1Q	.40	1.00
TE Troy Edwards 1Q	.40	1.00
KF Kevin Faulk 1Q	.60	1.50

1999 Collector's Edge Odyssey

Released as a 193-card set, 1999 Collector's Edge Odyssey features First through Fourth Quarter cards. First Quarter cards, 1-150, feature both rookies and veterans, Second Quarter cards, 151-170, are found one in four packs and feature top prospects, Third Quarter cards, 171-185, are found one in eight packs and feature veteran stars, and Fourth Quarter cards, 186-195, are found one in 24 packs and feature the 10 top prospects from the 1999 NFL draft. The cards are also distinguishable by the foil stamp along the bottom of the card front which relays what "Quarter" the card belongs to. Note that card numbers 21 and 55 were not released in packs

COMPLETE SET (193)	50.00	120.00
COMP.SET w/o SP's (148)	20.00	40.00
1 Checklist Card	.10	.30
2 Checklist Card	.10	.30
3 David Boston RC	.30	.75
4 Rob Moore	.20	.50
5 Adrian Murrell	.25	.60
6 Jake Plummer	.25	.60
7 Frank Sanders	.20	.50
8 Jamal Anderson	.25	.60
9 Chris Calloway	.20	.50
10 Chris Chandler	.25	.60
11 Tim Dwight	.25	.60
12 Terance Mathis	.20	.50
13 Tony Banks	.25	.60
14 Priest Holmes	.30	.75
15 Jermaine Lewis	.20	.50
16 Chris McAlister RC	.30	.75
17 Scott Mitchell	.20	.50
18 Doug Flutie	.30	.75
19 Eric Moulds	.25	.60
20 Peerless Price RC	.30	.75
21 Antowain Smith (on front) Andre Reed (on back) (was pulled from packout, has embossed player image on front)	30.00	80.00
22 Antowain Smith	.20	.50
23 Antoine Winfield RC	.25	.60
24 Steve Beuerlein	.25	.60
25 Tim Biakabutuka	.25	.60
26 Rae Carruth	.20	.50
27 Muhsin Muhammad	.25	.60
28 D'Wayne Bates RC	.25	.60
29 Bobby Engram	.25	.60
30 Curtis Enis	.20	.50
31 Shane Matthews	.20	.50
32 Cade McNown RC	.30	.75
33 Jeff Blake	.25	.60
34 Corey Dillon	.25	.60
35 Carl Pickens	.25	.60
36 Darnay Scott	.20	.50
37 Akili Smith RC	.30	.75
38 Tim Couch RC	.40	1.00
39 Kevin Johnson RC	.30	.75
40 Terry Kirby	.20	.50
41 Leslie Shepherd	.20	.50
42 Troy Aikman	.50	1.25
43 Michael Irvin	.30	.75
44 Rocket Ismail	.25	.60
45 Deion Sanders	.30	.75
46 Emmitt Smith	.75	2.00
47 Bubby Brister	.20	.50
48 Terrell Davis	.30	.75
49 Brian Griese	.25	.60
50 Ed McCaffrey	.25	.60
51 Shannon Sharpe	.30	.75
52 Rod Smith	.25	.60
53 Charlie Batch	.25	.60
54 Chris Claiborne RC	.25	.60
56 Herman Moore	.25	.60
57 Johnnie Morton	.25	.60
58 Ron Rivers	.20	.50
59 Brett Favre	1.00	2.50
60 Mark Chmura	.20	.50
61 Antonio Freeman	.25	.60
62 Dorsey Levens	.25	.60
63 E.G. Green	.20	.50
64 Marvin Harrison	.30	.75
65 Edgerrin James RC	.50	1.25
66 Peyton Manning	1.00	2.50
67 Mark Brunell	.25	.60
68 Keenan McCardell	.25	.60
69 Jimmy Smith	.25	.60
70 Fred Taylor	.25	.60
71 Derrick Alexander WR	.20	.50
72 Kimble Anders	.20	.50
73 Mike Cloud RC	.25	.60
74 Elvis Grbac	.20	.50
75 Andre Rison	.25	.60
76 Karim Abdul-Jabbar	.25	.60
77 Cecil Collins RC	.25	.60
78 James Johnson RC	.25	.60
79 Rob Konrad RC	.25	.60
80 Dan Marino	1.00	2.50
81 O.J. McDuffie	.25	.60
82 Cris Carter	.30	.75
83 Daunte Culpepper RC	.40	1.00
84 Randall Cunningham	.30	.75
85 Randy Moss	.30	.75
86 Jake Reed	.25	.60
87 Robert Smith	.25	.60
88 Terry Allen	.25	.60
89 Drew Bledsoe	.30	.75
90 Ben Coates	.25	.60
91 Kevin Faulk RC	.40	1.00
92 Terry Glenn	.25	.60
93 Andy Katzenmoyer RC	.30	.75
94 Cameron Cleeland	.20	.50
95 Billy Joe Hobert	.20	.50
96 Eddie Kennison	.25	.60
97 Ricky Williams RC	.60	1.50
98 Sean Bennett RC	.25	.60
99 Gary Brown	.20	.50
100 Kerry Collins	.25	.60
101 Kent Graham	.20	.50
102 Ike Hilliard	.25	.60
103 Wayne Chrebet	.25	.60
104 Keyshawn Johnson	.25	.60
105 Curtis Martin	.30	.75
106 Rick Mirer	.25	.60
107 Tim Brown	.30	.75
108 Rich Gannon	.25	.60
109 Napoleon Kaufman	.20	.50
110 Charles Woodson	.30	.75
111 Charles Johnson	.20	.50
112 Donovan McNabb RC	2.00	5.00
113 Doug Pederson	.20	.50
114 Duce Staley	.25	.60
115 Jerome Bettis	.30	.75
116 Troy Edwards RC	.30	.75
117 Kordell Stewart	.25	.60
118 Amos Zereoue RC	.30	.75
119 Isaac Bruce	.30	.75
120 Marshall Faulk	.30	.75
121 Joe Germaine RC	.30	.75
122 Torry Holt RC	.60	1.50
123 Kurt Warner RC	2.50	6.00
124 Jim Harbaugh	.25	.60
125 Erik Kramer	.25	.60
126 Natrone Means	.25	.60
127 Junior Seau	.30	.75
128 Terrell Owens	.30	.75
129 Lawrence Phillips	.25	.60
130 Jerry Rice	.60	1.50
131 J.J. Stokes	.20	.50
132 Steve Young	.40	1.00
133 Karsten Bailey RC	.25	.60
134 Joey Galloway	.25	.60
135 Brock Huard RC	.30	.75
136 Jon Kitna	.25	.60
137 Ricky Watters	.25	.60
138 Reidel Anthony	.20	.50
139 Trent Dilfer	.25	.60
140 Warrick Dunn	.25	.60
141 Shaun King RC	.30	.75
142 Jevon Kearse RC	.40	1.00
143 Kevin Dyson	.20	.50
144 Eddie George	.25	.60
145 Steve McNair	.30	.75
146 Champ Bailey RC	.75	2.00
147 Stephen Davis	.25	.60
148 Skip Hicks	.20	.50
149 Brad Johnson	.25	.60
150 Michael Westbrook	.20	.50
151 Chris McAlister 2Q	.40	1.00
152 Peerless Price 2Q	.40	1.00
153 Antoine Winfield 2Q	.30	.75
154 D'Wayne Bates 2Q	.30	.75
155 Kevin Johnson 2Q	.40	1.00
156 Chris Claiborne 2Q	.30	.75
157 Sedrick Irvin 2Q	.30	.75
158 Mike Cloud 2Q	.30	.75
159 Cecil Collins 2Q	.30	.75
160 James Johnson 2Q	.30	.75
161 Rob Konrad 2Q	.30	.75
162 Daunte Culpepper 2Q	.50	1.25
163 Andy Katzenmoyer 2Q	.40	1.00
164 Amos Zereoue 2Q	.40	1.00
165 Joe Germaine 2Q	.40	1.00
166 Karsten Bailey 2Q	.30	.75
167 Brock Huard 2Q	.40	1.00
168 Shaun King 2Q	.40	1.00
169 Jevon Kearse 2Q	.50	1.25
170 Champ Bailey 2Q	1.00	2.50
171 Jake Plummer 3Q	.50	1.25
172 Doug Flutie 3Q	.60	1.50
173 Troy Aikman 3Q	1.00	2.50
174 Emmitt Smith 3Q	1.50	4.00
175 Terrell Davis 3Q	.60	1.50
176 Barry Sanders 3Q	1.50	4.00
177 Brett Favre 3Q	2.00	5.00
178 Peyton Manning 3Q	2.00	5.00
179 Mark Brunell 3Q	.50	1.25
180 Fred Taylor 3Q	.50	1.25
181 Dan Marino 3Q	2.00	5.00
182 Randy Moss 3Q	.60	1.50
183 Drew Bledsoe 3Q	.60	1.50
184 Jerry Rice 3Q	1.25	3.00
185 Steve Young 3Q	.75	2.00
186 David Boston 4Q	.75	2.00
187 Cade McNown 4Q	.75	2.00
188 Akili Smith 4Q	.75	2.00
189 Tim Couch 4Q	1.00	2.50
190 Edgerrin James 4Q	1.25	3.00
191 Kevin Faulk 4Q	1.00	2.50
192 Ricky Williams 4Q	1.50	4.00
193 Donovan McNabb 4Q	5.00	12.00
194 Troy Edwards 4Q	.75	2.00
195 Torry Holt 4Q	1.50	4.00

1999 Collector's Edge Odyssey Two Minute Warning

*151-170 2Q/600: 1X TO 2.5X BASIC CARDS
151-170 SECOND QUARTER PRINT RUN 600
*171-185 3Q/300: 1.2X TO 3X BASIC CARDS
171-185 THIRD QUARTER PRINT RUN 300
*186-195 4Q/100: 1.5X TO 4X BASIC CARDS
186-195 FOURTH QUARTER PRINT RUN 100

1999 Collector's Edge Odyssey Overtime

*151-170 ROOKIES: 8X TO 20X BASIC CARD HI
151-170 STATED PRINT RUN 60 SER.#'d SETS
*171-185 STARS: 8X TO 20X BASIC CARD HI
171-185 STATED PRINT RUN 30 SER.#'d SETS
*186-195 ROOKIES: 8X TO 20X BASIC CARD HI.
186-195 STATED PRINT RUN 10 SER.#'d SETS

1999 Collector's Edge Odyssey Cut 'n' Ripped

COMPLETE SET (15)	10.00	20.00
STATED ODDS 1:12		
CR1 Chris McAlister	.40	1.00
CR2 Kevin Johnson	.50	1.25
CR3 Chris Claiborne	.40	1.00
CR4 Sedrick Irvin	.40	1.00
CR5 Edgerrin James	2.50	6.00
CR6 Mike Cloud	.50	1.25
CR7 James Johnson	.50	1.25
CR8 Rob Konrad	.50	1.25
CR9 Daunte Culpepper	2.50	6.00
CR10 Andy Katzenmoyer	.50	1.25
CR11 Amos Zereoue	.50	1.25
CR12 Torry Holt	1.50	4.00
CR13 Shaun King	.50	1.25
CR14 Jevon Kearse	.75	2.00
CR15 Champ Bailey	.60	1.50

1999 Collector's Edge Odyssey Cutting Edge

COMPLETE SET (10)	15.00	30.00
STATED ODDS 1:18		
CE1 Akili Smith	1.00	2.50
CE2 Tim Couch	1.00	2.50
CE3 Brian Griese	1.00	2.50
CE4 Charlie Batch	1.00	2.50
CE5 Brett Favre	3.00	8.00
CE6 Peyton Manning	3.00	8.00
CE7 Mark Brunell	1.00	2.50
CE8 Dan Marino	3.00	8.00
CE9 Drew Bledsoe	1.25	3.00
CE10 Steve Young	1.25	3.00

1999 Collector's Edge Odyssey Excalibur

COMPLETE SET (8)	15.00	30.00
STATED ODDS 1:24		
X1 David Boston	1.50	4.00
X4 Cade McNown	1.50	4.00
X8 Troy Edwards	1.50	4.00
X9 Daunte Culpepper	2.50	6.00
X11 Ricky Williams	1.50	4.00
X15 Donovan McNabb	3.00	8.00
X16 Troy Aikman	3.00	8.00
X21 Emmitt Smith	3.00	8.00
X23 Jake Plummer		

1999 Collector's Edge Odyssey End Zone

COMPLETE SET (20)	15.00	30.00
STATED ODDS 1:9		
EZ1 Jamal Anderson	1.00	2.50
EZ2 Priest Holmes	1.50	4.00
EZ3 Doug Flutie	1.00	2.50
EZ4 Eric Moulds	1.00	2.50
EZ5 Charlie Batch	1.00	2.50
EZ6 Barry Sanders	2.50	6.00
EZ7 Antonio Freeman	1.00	2.50
EZ8 Fred Taylor	1.00	2.50
EZ9 Cris Carter	1.00	2.50
EZ10 Randy Moss	2.50	6.00
EZ11 Keyshawn Johnson	1.00	2.50
EZ12 Curtis Martin	1.00	2.50
EZ13 Vinny Testaverde	.40	1.00
EZ14 Kordell Stewart	.60	1.50
EZ15 Jerry Rice	2.00	5.00
EZ16 Terrell Owens	1.00	2.50
EZ17 Jon Kitna	1.00	2.50
EZ18 Warrick Dunn	1.00	2.50
EZ19 Eddie George	1.00	2.50
EZ20 Steve McNair	1.00	2.50

1999 Collector's Edge Odyssey GameGear

COMPLETE SET (8)	75.00	150.00
STATED ODDS 1:360		
GG1 Terrell Davis/500	4.00	10.00
GG2 Curtis Enis/338	4.00	10.00
GG3 Marshall Faulk/247	7.50	20.00
GG4 Brian Griese/500	6.00	15.00
GG5 Skip Hicks/315	4.00	10.00
GG6 Randy Moss/415	7.50	20.00
GG7 Lawrence Phillips/406	4.00	10.00
GG8 Fred Taylor/85	12.50	30.00
PM Peyton Manning (not serial numbered)	6.00	15.00

1999 Collector's Edge Odyssey GameGear Hologold

COMPLETE SET (8)	15.00	30.00
INSERTED IN SPECIAL RETAIL PACKS		
BG Brian Griese	1.25	3.00
CE Curtis Enis	1.25	3.00
FT Fred Taylor	1.25	3.00
GG1 Terrell Davis	1.25	3.00
GG2 Curtis Enis	1.25	3.00
GG3 Marshall Faulk	1.25	3.00
GG4 Brian Griese	1.25	3.00
GG5 Skip Hicks	1.25	3.00
GG6 Randy Moss	3.00	8.00
GG7 Lawrence Phillips	1.25	3.00
GG8 Fred Taylor	1.25	3.00
LP Lawrence Phillips	1.25	3.00
MF Marshall Faulk	1.25	3.00
PM Peyton Manning	5.00	12.00
RM Randy Moss	4.00	10.00
SH Skip Hicks	1.25	3.00
TD Terrell Davis	1.25	3.00

1999 Collector's Edge Odyssey Old School

COMPLETE SET (25)	25.00	50.00
STATED ODDS 1:8		
OS1 David Boston	.60	1.50
OS2 Chris McAlister	.50	1.25
OS3 Peerless Price	.60	1.50
OS4 D'Wayne Bates	.50	1.25
OS5 Cade McNown	.60	1.50
OS6 Akili Smith	.50	1.25
OS7 Tim Couch	.60	1.50
OS8 Kevin Johnson	.60	1.50
OS9 Chris Claiborne	.50	1.25
OS10 Sedrick Irvin	.50	1.25
OS11 Edgerrin James	2.50	6.00
OS12 Mike Cloud	.60	1.50
OS13 James Johnson	.60	1.50
OS14 Rob Konrad	.60	1.50
OS15 Daunte Culpepper	2.50	6.00
OS16 Kevin Faulk	.60	1.50
OS17 Donovan McNabb	3.00	8.00
OS18 Troy Edwards	.60	1.50
OS19 Amos Zereoue	.60	1.50
OS20 Joe Germaine	.60	1.50
OS21 Torry Holt	1.50	4.00
OS22 Karsten Bailey	.50	1.25
OS23 Shaun King	.60	1.50
OS24 Jevon Kearse	.75	2.00
OS25 Champ Bailey	.75	2.00

1999 Collector's Edge Odyssey Pro Signature Authentics

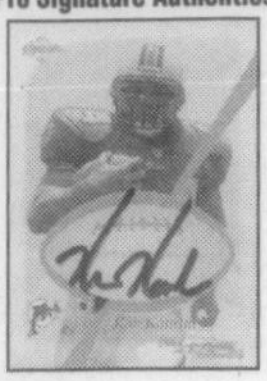

STATED ODDS 1:36
MACHINE SERIAL #'d 111-2435
*BLUE INK/40: 1X TO 2.5X BLACK INK
BLUE INK STATED PRINT RUN 40
UNPRICED RED INK PRINT RUN 10

1 D'Wayne Bates/1450	3.00	8.00
2 Michael Bishop/2200	4.00	10.00
3 Chris Claiborne/1120	3.00	8.00
4 Daunte Culpepper/450	25.00	50.00
5 Jared DeVries/290	4.00	10.00
6 Jeff Garcia/2110 (signed in purple ink)	10.00	25.00
7 Martin Gramatica/1950	4.00	10.00
8 Torry Holt/1115	10.00	25.00
9 Brock Huard/350	6.00	15.00
10 Sedrick Irvin/1240	3.00	8.00
11 Edgerrin James/435	20.00	50.00
12 Kevin Johnson/1920	3.00	8.00
13 Shaun King/920	4.00	10.00
14 Rob Konrad/1420	4.00	10.00
15 Darnell McDonald/2435	3.00	8.00
16 Peerless Price/825	6.00	15.00
17 Akili Smith/111	20.00	50.00
18 Ricky Williams/230	12.50	30.00
19 Amos Zereoue/1450	4.00	10.00

1999 Collector's Edge Odyssey Super Limited Edge

COMPLETE SET (30)	50.00	100.00
STATED PRINT RUN 1000 SER.#'d SETS		
SLE1 Jake Plummer	1.00	2.50
SLE2 Jamal Anderson	1.50	4.00
SLE3 Doug Flutie	1.50	4.00
SLE4 Eric Moulds	1.50	4.00
SLE5 Troy Aikman	3.00	8.00
SLE6 Emmitt Smith	3.00	8.00
SLE7 Terrell Davis	1.50	4.00
SLE8 Charlie Batch	1.50	4.00
SLE9 Herman Moore	1.00	2.50
SLE10 Barry Sanders	15.00	40.00
SLE11 Brett Favre	5.00	12.00
SLE12 Antonio Freeman	1.50	4.00
SLE13 Dorsey Levens	1.50	4.00
SLE14 Peyton Manning	5.00	12.00
SLE15 Mark Brunell	1.50	4.00
SLE16 Fred Taylor	1.50	4.00
SLE17 Dan Marino	5.00	12.00
SLE18 Cris Carter	1.50	4.00
SLE19 Randall Cunningham	1.50	4.00
SLE20 Randy Moss	4.00	10.00
SLE21 Drew Bledsoe	2.00	5.00
SLE22 Ricky Williams	2.00	5.00
SLE23 Keyshawn Johnson	1.50	4.00
SLE24 Curtis Martin	1.50	4.00
SLE25 Jerome Bettis	1.50	4.00
SLE26 Jerry Rice	3.00	8.00
SLE27 Terrell Owens	1.50	4.00
SLE28 Jon Kitna	1.50	4.00
SLE29 Eddie George	1.50	4.00
SLE30 Steve Young	2.00	5.00

2000 Collector's Edge Odyssey Previews

This set was released as a Preview to the 2000 Collector's Edge Odyssey base set. Each card is essentially a parallel version of the base set card along with the phrase "Preview XXX/999" on the cardbacks.

COMPLETE SET (16)	12.50	30.00
101 Thomas Jones	.60	1.50
104 Jamal Lewis	.50	1.25
105 Chris Redman	.40	1.00
106 Travis Taylor	.40	1.00
110 Brian Urlacher	2.00	5.00
111 Dez White	.40	1.00
112 Ron Dugans	.30	.75
113 Curtis Keaton	.30	.75
114 Peter Warrick	.50	1.25
115 Courtney Brown	.40	1.00
117 Dennis Northcutt	.40	1.00
118 Travis Prentice	.40	1.00
124 Reuben Droughns	.50	1.25
125 Bubba Franks	.50	1.25
129 R.Jay Soward	.30	.75
132 Sylvester Morris	.30	.75
134 J.R. Redmond	.30	.75
138 Ron Dayne	.50	1.25
139 Anthony Becht	.40	1.00
140 Laveranues Coles	.50	1.25
142 Chad Pennington	.75	2.00
144 Jerry Porter	.50	1.25
145 Todd Pinkston	.30	.75
148 Plaxico Burress	.50	1.25
149 Danny Farmer	.30	.75
150 Tee Martin	.50	1.25
151 Trung Canidate	.40	1.00
153 Giovanni Carmazzi	.30	.75
157 Shaun Alexander	.60	1.50
158 Joe Hamilton	.30	.75

2000 Collector's Edge Odyssey

Released in early October 2000, Collector's Edge Odyssey features a 190-card base set comprised of 100 veteran cards, 60 rookie cards (numbers 101-160) sequentially numbered to 999, 10 Survivors cards (numbers 161-170) sequentially numbered to 2500, and 20 Last Man Standing cards (numbers 171-190) sequentially numbered to 2500. Base cards feature green and purple foil borders and gold foil highlights. Odyssey was packaged in 20-pack boxes with each pack containing five cards and carried a suggested retail price of $4.99.

COMPLETE SET (190)	250.00	400.00
COMP.SET w/o SP's (100)	6.00	15.00
1 David Boston	.20	.50
2 Jake Plummer	.25	.60
3 Frank Sanders	.20	.50
4 Jamal Anderson	.25	.60
5 Chris Chandler	.25	.60
6 Terance Mathis	.20	.50
7 Tony Banks	.20	.50
8 Qadry Ismail	.25	.60
9 Doug Flutie	.30	.75
10 Rob Johnson	.25	.60
11 Eric Moulds	.25	.60
12 Peerless Price	.25	.60
13 Antowain Smith	.25	.60
14 Steve Beuerlein	.25	.60
15 Tim Biakabutuka	.25	.60
16 Muhsin Muhammad	.25	.60
17 Curtis Enis	.20	.50
18 Cade McNown	.20	.50
19 Marcus Robinson	.25	.60
20 Corey Dillon	.25	.60
21 Akili Smith	.20	.50
22 Tim Couch	.25	.60
23 Kevin Johnson	.20	.50
24 Errict Rhett	.25	.60
25 Troy Aikman	.50	1.25
26 Joey Galloway	.25	.60
27 Rocket Ismail	.25	.60
28 Emmitt Smith	.75	2.00
29 Terrell Davis	.30	.75
30 Olandis Gary	.25	.60
31 Brian Griese	.25	.60
32 Ed McCaffrey	.25	.60
33 Charlie Batch	.25	.60
34 Germane Crowell	.20	.50
35 Herman Moore	.25	.60
36 James Stewart	.20	.50
37 Brett Favre	1.00	2.50
38 Antonio Freeman	.25	.60
39 Dorsey Levens	.25	.60
40 Marvin Harrison	.30	.75
41 Edgerrin James	.30	.75
42 Peyton Manning	.75	2.00
43 Terrence Wilkins	.20	.50
44 Mark Brunell	.25	.60
45 Keenan McCardell	.25	.60
46 Jimmy Smith	.25	.60
47 Fred Taylor	.30	.75
48 Mike Cloud	.20	.50
49 Tony Gonzalez	.30	.75
50 Elvis Grbac	.20	.50
51 Damon Huard	.25	.60
52 James Johnson	.20	.50
53 Tony Martin	.25	.60
54 Cris Carter	.30	.75
55 Daunte Culpepper	.25	.60
56 Randy Moss	.30	.75
57 Robert Smith	.25	.60
58 Drew Bledsoe	.30	.75
59 Terry Glenn	.25	.60
60 Jeff Blake	.25	.60
61 Ricky Williams	.30	.75
62 Kerry Collins	.25	.60
63 Ike Hilliard	.25	.60
64 Amani Toomer	.25	.60
65 Wayne Chrebet	.25	.60
66 Curtis Martin	.30	.75
67 Vinny Testaverde	.25	.60
68 Tim Brown	.30	.75
69 Rich Gannon	.25	.60
70 Donovan McNabb	.30	.75
71 Duce Staley	.25	.60
72 Jerome Bettis	.30	.75
73 Troy Edwards	.20	.50
74 Kordell Stewart	.25	.60
75 Isaac Bruce	.30	.75
76 Marshall Faulk	.30	.75
77 Torry Holt	.30	.75
78 Kurt Warner	.50	1.25
79 Jermaine Fazande	.20	.50
80 Jim Harbaugh	.25	.60
81 Jeff Garcia	.25	.60
82 Charlie Garner	.25	.60
83 Terrell Owens	.30	.75
84 Jerry Rice	.60	1.50
85 Jon Kitna	.25	.60
86 Derrick Mayes	.20	.50
87 Ricky Watters	.25	.60
88 Mike Alstott	.30	.75
89 Warrick Dunn	.25	.60
90 Keyshawn Johnson	.25	.60
91 Shaun King	.20	.50
92 Kevin Dyson	.25	.60
93 Eddie George	.25	.60
94 Jevon Kearse	.25	.60
95 Steve McNair	.30	.75
96 Carl Pickens	.25	.60
97 Champ Bailey	.25	.60
98 Stephen Davis	.25	.60
99 Brad Johnson	.25	.60
100 Michael Westbrook	.20	.50
101 Thomas Jones RC	4.00	10.00
102 Doug Johnson RC	2.50	6.00
103 Mareno Philyaw RC	2.00	5.00
104 Jamal Lewis RC	3.00	8.00
105 Chris Redman RC	2.50	6.00
106 Travis Taylor RC	2.50	6.00
107 Kwame Cavil RC	2.00	5.00
108 Sammy Morris RC	2.50	6.00
109 Frank Murphy RC	2.00	5.00
110 Brian Urlacher RC	12.00	30.00
111 Dez White RC	2.50	6.00
112 Ron Dugans RC	2.00	5.00
113 Curtis Keaton RC	2.00	5.00
114 Peter Warrick RC	3.00	8.00
115 Courtney Brown RC	2.50	6.00
116 JaJuan Dawson RC	2.00	5.00
117 Dennis Northcutt RC	2.50	6.00
118 Travis Prentice RC	2.50	6.00
119 Michael Wiley RC	2.00	5.00
120 Mike Anderson RC	3.00	8.00
121 Chris Cole RC	2.50	6.00
122 Jarious Jackson RC	2.50	6.00
123 Deltha O'Neal RC	2.50	6.00
124 Reuben Droughns RC	3.00	8.00
125 Bubba Franks RC	3.00	8.00
126 Anthony Lucas RC	2.00	5.00
127 Rondell Mealey RC	2.00	5.00
128 Rob Morris RC	2.50	6.00
129 R.Jay Soward RC	2.00	5.00
130 Shyrone Stith RC	2.00	5.00
131 Frank Moreau RC	2.00	5.00
132 Sylvester Morris RC	2.00	5.00
133 Doug Chapman RC	2.00	5.00
134 J.R. Redmond RC	2.00	5.00
135 Marc Bulger RC	3.00	8.00
136 Sherrod Gideon RC	2.00	5.00
137 Terrelle Smith RC	2.00	5.00
138 Ron Dayne RC	3.00	8.00
139 Anthony Becht RC	2.50	6.00

140 Laveranues Coles RC	3.00	8.00
141 Shaun Ellis RC	3.00	8.00
142 Chad Pennington RC	5.00	12.00
143 Sebastian Janikowski RC	3.00	8.00
144 Jerry Porter RC	3.00	8.00
145 Todd Pinkston RC	2.00	5.00
146 Gari Scott RC	2.00	5.00
147 Corey Simon RC	2.50	6.00
148 Plaxico Burress RC	3.00	8.00
149 Danny Farmer RC	2.00	5.00
150 Tee Martin RC	3.00	8.00
151 Trung Canidate RC	2.50	6.00
152 Trevor Gaylor RC	2.00	5.00
153 Giovanni Carmazzi RC	2.00	5.00
154 John Engelberger RC	2.00	5.00
155 Ahmed Plummer RC	2.00	5.00
156 Tim Rattay RC	2.50	6.00
157 Shaun Alexander RC	4.00	10.00
158 Joe Hamilton RC	2.00	5.00
159 Keith Bulluck RC	2.50	6.00
160 Todd Husak RC	2.00	5.00
161 Cade McNown SV	.40	1.00
162 Tim Couch SV	.50	1.25
163 Terrell Davis SV	.60	1.50
164 Brett Favre SV	2.00	5.00
165 Edgerrin James SV	.60	1.50
166 Peyton Manning SV	1.50	4.00
167 Daunte Culpepper SV	.50	1.25
168 Randy Moss SV	.60	1.50
169 Ricky Williams SV	.60	1.50
170 Kurt Warner SV	1.00	2.50
171 Cade McNown LV	.40	1.00
172 Akili Smith LV	.40	1.00
173 Tim Couch LV	.50	1.25
174 Troy Aikman LV	1.00	2.50
175 Emmitt Smith LV	1.50	4.00
176 Terrell Davis LV	.60	1.50
177 Brett Favre LV	2.00	5.00
178 Edgerrin James LV	.60	1.50
179 Peyton Manning LV	1.50	4.00
180 Mark Brunell LV	.50	1.25
181 Daunte Culpepper LV	.50	1.25
182 Randy Moss LV	.60	1.50
183 Drew Bledsoe LV	.60	1.50
184 Ricky Williams LV	.60	1.50
185 Donovan McNabb LV	.60	1.50
186 Torry Holt LV	.60	1.50
187 Kurt Warner LV	1.00	2.50
188 Shaun King LV	.40	1.00
189 Eddie George LV	.50	1.25
190 Steve McNair LV	.60	1.50

2000 Collector's Edge Odyssey Hologold Rookies

*ROOKIES 101-160: .4X TO 1X BASIC CARDS
HOLOGOLD ROOKIE PRINT RUN 500

2000 Collector's Edge Odyssey Retail

*VETS 1-100: .4X TO 1X HOBBY
*ROOKIES 101-160: .08X TO .2X HOBBY
*SV/LS 161-190: .2X TO .5X HOBBY

2000 Collector's Edge Odyssey GameGear Jerseybacks

STATED PRINT RUN 20 SER.#'d SETS

AB Anthony Becht	20.00	50.00
BF Bubba Franks	25.00	60.00
BU Brian Urlacher	100.00	200.00
CK Curtis Keaton	15.00	40.00
CP Chad Pennington	40.00	100.00
CR Chris Redman	20.00	50.00
CS Corey Simon	20.00	50.00
DF Danny Farmer	15.00	40.00
DN Dennis Northcutt	20.00	50.00
JH Joe Hamilton	15.00	40.00
JL Jamal Lewis	25.00	60.00
JP Jerry Porter	25.00	60.00
JR J.R. Redmond	15.00	40.00
LC Laveranues Coles	25.00	60.00
PB Plaxico Burress	25.00	60.00
PW Peter Warrick	25.00	60.00
RD Reuben Droughns	25.00	60.00
RD Ron Dayne	25.00	60.00
RD Ron Dugans	15.00	40.00
RS R.Jay Soward	15.00	40.00
SA Shaun Alexander	50.00	120.00
SM Sylvester Morris	15.00	40.00
TC Trung Canidate	20.00	50.00
TM Tee Martin	25.00	60.00
TP Travis Prentice	20.00	50.00
TP Todd Pinkston	15.00	40.00
TT Travis Taylor	20.00	50.00

2000 Collector's Edge Odyssey GameGear Leatherbacks

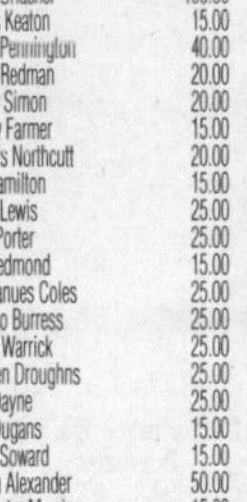

STATED PRINT RUN 12 SER.#'d SETS

AB Anthony Becht	25.00	60.00
BF Bubba Franks	30.00	80.00
BU Brian Urlacher	150.00	250.00
CB Courtney Brown	25.00	60.00
CK Curtis Keaton	20.00	50.00
CP Chad Pennington	50.00	120.00
CR Chris Redman	25.00	60.00
DF Danny Farmer	20.00	50.00
DN Dennis Northcutt	25.00	60.00
DW Dez White	25.00	60.00
JL Jamal Lewis	30.00	80.00
JP Jerry Porter	30.00	80.00
JR J.R. Redmond	20.00	50.00
LC Laveranues Coles	30.00	80.00
PB Plaxico Burress	30.00	80.00
PW Peter Warrick	30.00	80.00
RD1 Ron Dayne	30.00	80.00
RD2 Reuben Droughns	30.00	80.00
RD3 Ron Dugans	20.00	50.00
SA Shaun Alexander	60.00	250.00
SM Sylvester Morris	20.00	50.00
TJ Thomas Jones	40.00	100.00
TP Travis Prentice	25.00	60.00
TP Todd Pinkston	20.00	50.00
TT Travis Taylor	25.00	60.00

2000 Collector's Edge Odyssey Old School

COMPLETE SET (30)	12.00	30.00
STATED ODDS 1:6 HOB, 1:8 RET		
OS1 Thomas Jones	.50	1.25
OS2 Jamal Lewis	.40	1.00
OS3 Chris Redman	.30	.75
OS4 Travis Taylor	.30	.75
OS5 Brian Urlacher	1.50	4.00
OS6 Dez White	.30	.75
OS7 Ron Dugans	.25	.60
OS8 Curtis Keaton	.25	.60
OS9 Peter Warrick	.40	1.00
OS10 Courtney Brown	.30	.75
OS11 Dennis Northcutt	.30	.75
OS12 Travis Prentice	.30	.75
OS13 Reuben Droughns	.40	1.00
OS14 Bubba Franks	.40	1.00
OS15 R.Jay Soward	.25	.60
OS16 Sylvester Morris	.25	.60
OS17 J.R. Redmond	.25	.60
OS18 Ron Dayne	.40	1.00
OS19 Anthony Becht	.30	.75
OS20 Laveranues Coles	.40	1.00
OS21 Chad Pennington	.60	1.50
OS22 Jerry Porter	.40	1.00
OS23 Todd Pinkston	.25	.60
OS24 Corey Simon	.30	.75
OS25 Plaxico Burress	.40	1.00
OS26 Danny Farmer	.25	.60
OS27 Tee Martin	.40	1.00
OS28 Trung Canidate	.30	.75
OS29 Shaun Alexander	.50	1.25
OS30 Joe Hamilton	.25	.60

2000 Collector's Edge Odyssey Restaurant Quality

COMPLETE SET (10)	6.00	15.00
STATED ODDS 1:20 HOB, 1:29 RET		
RQ1 Thomas Jones	.60	1.50
RQ2 Jamal Lewis	.50	1.25
RQ3 Travis Taylor	.40	1.00
RQ4 Peter Warrick	.50	1.25
RQ5 Bubba Franks	.50	1.25
RQ6 Sylvester Morris	.30	.75
RQ7 Ron Dayne	.50	1.25
RQ8 Chad Pennington	.75	2.00
RQ9 Plaxico Burress	.50	1.25
RQ10 Shaun Alexander	.60	1.50

2000 Collector's Edge Odyssey Ripped

R1 Thomas Jones	.40	1.00
R2 Jamal Lewis	.30	.75
R3 Brian Urlacher	1.25	3.00
R4 Dez White	.30	.75
R5 Curtis Keaton	.20	.50
R6 Peter Warrick	.30	.75
R7 Courtney Brown	.25	.60
R8 Travis Prentice	.20	.50
R9 Reuben Droughns	.20	.50
R10 Bubba Franks	.25	.60
R11 J.R. Redmond	.20	.50
R12 Ron Dayne	.30	.75
R13 Anthony Becht	.20	.50
R14 Laveranues Coles	.25	.60
R15 Chad Pennington	.50	1.25
R16 Jerry Porter	.25	.60
R17 Plaxico Burress	.30	.75
R18 Tee Martin	.30	.75
R19 Trung Canidate	.20	.50
R20 Shaun Alexander	.40	1.00

2000 Collector's Edge Odyssey Rookie Ink

STATED ODDS 1:99 HOB, 1:150 RET

BU Brian Urlacher Gold/795	25.00	60.00
CP Chad Pennington Gold/510	20.00	50.00
CR Chris Redman/475	8.00	20.00
DN Dennis Northcutt Gold/800	6.00	15.00
JL Jamal Lewis/540	10.00	25.00
JR J.R. Redmond/1610	5.00	12.00
LC Laveranues Coles Silver/1400	8.00	20.00
PB Plaxico Burress Gold/505	15.00	40.00
RD Ron Dayne/440	10.00	25.00
SM Sylvester Morris Gold/540	6.00	15.00
TJ Thomas Jones Gold/465	12.50	30.00
TP Todd Pinkston Silver/1035	5.00	12.00

2000 Collector's Edge Odyssey Tight

COMPLETE SET (30)	15.00	40.00
STATED ODDS 1:10 HOBBY		
T1 Thomas Jones	.60	1.50
T2 Jamal Lewis	.50	1.25
T3 Chris Redman	.40	1.00
T4 Travis Taylor	.40	1.00
T5 Brian Urlacher	2.00	5.00
T6 Dez White	.40	1.00
T7 Ron Dugans	.30	.75
T8 Curtis Keaton	.30	.75
T9 Peter Warrick	.50	1.25
T10 Courtney Brown	.40	1.00
T11 Dennis Northcutt	.40	1.00
T12 Travis Prentice	.40	1.00
T13 Reuben Droughns	.50	1.25
T14 Bubba Franks	.50	1.25
T15 R.Jay Soward	.30	.75
T16 Sylvester Morris	.30	.75
T17 J.R. Redmond	.30	.75
T18 Ron Dayne	.50	1.25
T19 Anthony Becht	.40	1.00
T20 Laveranues Coles	.50	1.25
T21 Chad Pennington	.75	2.00
T22 Jerry Porter	.50	1.25
T23 Todd Pinkston	.30	.75
T24 Corey Simon	.40	1.00
T25 Plaxico Burress	.50	1.25
T26 Danny Farmer	.30	.75
T27 Tee Martin	.50	1.25
T28 Trung Canidate	.40	1.00
T29 Shaun Alexander	.60	1.50
T30 Joe Hamilton	.30	.75

2000 Collector's Edge Odyssey Wasssuppp

COMPLETE SET (20)	10.00	25.00
STATED ODDS 1:10 HOB, 1:14 RET		
W1 Thomas Jones	.50	1.25
W2 Jamal Lewis	.40	1.00
W3 Travis Taylor	.30	.75
W4 Ron Dugans	.25	.60
W5 Peter Warrick	.40	1.00
W6 Dez White	.30	.75
W7 Dennis Northcutt	.30	.75
W8 Travis Prentice	.30	.75
W9 Bubba Franks	.40	1.00
W10 R.Jay Soward	.25	.60
W11 Sylvester Morris	.25	.60
W12 J.R. Redmond	.25	.60
W13 Ron Dayne	.40	1.00
W14 Laveranues Coles	.40	1.00
W15 Chad Pennington	.60	1.50
W16 Jerry Porter	.40	1.00
W17 Todd Pinkston	.25	.60
W18 Plaxico Burress	.40	1.00
W19 Danny Farmer	.25	.60
W20 Shaun Alexander	.50	1.25

2000 Collector's Edge Awards Promos

R9 Kurt Warner	1.50	4.00
Super Bowl XXXIV		
EJ Edgerrin James/ 1999 Rookie of the Year	1.00	2.50
KW Kurt Warner/ 1999 MVP	1.50	4.00

1996 CE President's Reserve Promos

1 Jeff Blake	.50	1.25
Errict Rhett		
Running Mates		
2 Dick Butkus	1.20	3.00
Steve Bono		
TimeWarp		
3 Philadelphia Eagles	.20	.50
Candidates Rookie Redemption		
4 Rashaan Salaam	.40	1.00
New Regime		
5 Junior Seau	.30	.75
Base Brand		
6 Michael Westbrook	.50	1.25
Air Force One		

1996 CE President's Reserve

The 1996 Collector's Edge President's Reserve set was issued in two series of 200 cards, for a total of 400 cards. A collector could preorder a box (either series) from a dealer for $149.95. Card fronts have a clear plastic background with the card and player's name in gold foil. Card backs contain statistical and biographical information. Reportedly, a total of 20,000 of each card was produced.

COMPLETE SET (400)	30.00	60.00
COMP.SERIES 1 (200)	15.00	30.00
COMP.SERIES 2 (200)	15.00	30.00
1 Larry Centers	.20	.50
2 Frank Sanders	.20	.50
3 Clyde Simmons	.08	.25
4 Eric Swann	.20	.50
5 Morten Andersen	.08	.25
6 Lester Archambeau	.08	.25
7 J.J. Birden	.08	.25
8 Bert Emanuel	.20	.50
9 Jumpy Geathers	.08	.25
10 Jeff George	.20	.50
11 Craig Heyward	.08	.25
12 Bill Brooks	.08	.25
13 Steve Christie	.08	.25
14 Todd Collins	.20	.50
15 Darick Holmes	.08	.25
16 Andre Reed	.20	.50
17 Bryce Paup	.20	.50
18 Bruce Smith	.40	1.00
19 Blake Brockermeyer	.08	.25
20 Mark Carrier	.08	.25
21 Kerry Collins	.40	1.00
22 Darion Conner	.08	.25
23 Eric Guliford	.08	.25
24 Lamar Lathon	.08	.25
25 Derrick Moore	.08	.25
26 Frank Reich	.08	.25
27 Kevin Butler	.08	.25
28 Tony Carter RC	.08	.25
29 Curtis Conway	.40	1.00
30 Robert Green	.08	.25
31 Jay Leeuwenburg RC	.08	.25
32 Alonzo Spellman	.08	.25
33 Chris Zorich	.08	.25
34 Eric Bieniemy	.08	.25
35 Jeff Blake	.40	1.00
36 Tony McGee	.08	.25
37 Carl Pickens	.20	.50
38 Rob Burnett	.08	.25
39 Earnest Byner	.08	.25
40 Michael Jackson	.20	.50
41 Antonio Langham	.08	.25
42 Anthony Pleasant	.08	.25
43 Vinny Testaverde	.20	.50
44 Troy Aikman	1.25	2.50
45 Larry Allen	.08	.25
46 Bill Bates	.20	.50
47 Chris Boniol	.08	.25
48 Charles Haley	.20	.50
49 Michael Irvin	.40	1.00
50 Robert Jones	.08	.25
51 Leon Lett	.08	.25
52 Russell Maryland	.08	.25
53 Nate Newton	.08	.25
54 Deion Sanders	.60	1.50
55 Sherman Williams	.08	.25
56 Darren Woodson	.20	.50
57 Aaron Craver	.08	.25
58 Terrell Davis	.75	2.00
59 Jason Elam	.20	.50
60 Simon Fletcher	.08	.25
61 Anthony Miller	.20	.50
62 Shannon Sharpe	.20	.50
63 Tracy Scroggins	.08	.25
64 Antonio London	.08	.25
65 Scott Mitchell	.20	.50
66 Johnnie Morton	.20	.50
67 Barry Sanders	1.50	4.00
68 Edgar Bennett	.20	.50
69 Mark Chmura	.20	.50
70 Brett Favre	2.50	5.00
71 Mark Ingram	.08	.25
72 Dorsey Levens	.40	1.00
73 Wayne Simmons	.08	.25
74 Gary Brown	.08	.25
75 Anthony Cook	.08	.25
76 Al Del Greco	.08	.25
77 Haywood Jeffires	.08	.25
78 Steve McNair	.75	2.00
79 Rodney Thomas	.08	.25
80 Trev Alberts	.08	.25
81 Quentin Coryatt	.08	.25
82 Ken Dilger	.20	.50
83 Jim Harbaugh	.20	.50
84 Floyd Turner	.08	.25
85 Lamont Warren	.08	.25
86 Steve Beuerlein	.20	.50
87 Mark Brunell	.60	1.50
88 Eugene Chung	.08	.25
89 Jeff Lageman	.08	.25
90 Willie Jackson	.20	.50
91 Kimble Anders	.08	.25
92 Steve Bono	.20	.50
93 Derrick Thomas	.40	1.00
94 Willie Davis	.20	.50
95 Greg Hill	.20	.50
96 Neil Smith	.20	.50
97 Tamarick Vanover	.40	1.00
98 James Hasty	.08	.25
99 Gary Clark	.08	.25
100 Marco Coleman	.08	.25
101 Steve Emtman	.08	.25
102 Irving Fryar	.20	.50
103 Randal Hill	.08	.25
104 Terry Kirby	.20	.50
105 Dan Marino	2.00	5.00
106 Cris Carter	.40	1.00
107 Jack Del Rio	.08	.25
108 David Palmer	.20	.50
109 Jake Reed	.20	.50
110 Robert Smith	.20	.50
111 Korey Stringer	.15	.40
112 Orlando Thomas	.08	.25
113 Drew Bledsoe	.60	1.50
114 Vincent Brisby	.08	.25
115 Ted Johnson RC	.40	1.00
116 Curtis Martin	.75	2.00
117 Chris Slade	.08	.25
118 Jim Dombrowski	.08	.25
119 William Roaf	.08	.25
120 Quinn Early	.08	.25
121 Wesley Walls	.20	.50
122 Wayne Martin	.08	.25
123 Irv Smith	.08	.25
124 Torrance Small	.08	.25
125 Dave Brown	.20	.50
126 Chris Calloway	.08	.25
127 Jumbo Elliott	.08	.25
128 Rodney Hampton	.20	.50
129 Tyrone Wheatley	.20	.50
130 Kyle Brady	.20	.50
131 Hugh Douglas	.20	.50
132 Todd Scott	.08	.25
133 Adrian Murrell	.20	.50
134 Wayne Chrebet	.60	1.50
135 Aundray Bruce	.08	.25
136 Andrew Glover	.08	.25
137 Daryl Hobbs RC	.08	.25
138 Napoleon Kaufman	.40	1.00
139 Chester McGlockton	.08	.25
140 Rob Fredrickson	.08	.25
141 Guy McIntyre	.08	.25
142 Bobby Taylor	.20	.50
143 Fred Barnett	.20	.50
144 William Fuller	.08	.25
145 Rodney Peete	.08	.25
146 Daniel Stubbs	.08	.25
147 Charlie Garner	.20	.50
148 Myron Bell	.08	.25
149 Rod Woodson	.20	.50
150 Charles Johnson	.20	.50
151 Ernie Mills	.08	.25
152 Levon Kirkland	.08	.25
153 Carnell Lake	.08	.25
154 Kevin Greene	.20	.50
155 Neil O'Donnell	.20	.50
156 Erric Pegram	.20	.50
157 Ray Seals	.08	.25
158 Willie Williams	.08	.25
159 Kordell Stewart	.40	1.00
160 Yancey Thigpen	.20	.50
161 Darren Bennett	.20	.50
162 Andre Coleman	.08	.25
163 Aaron Hayden RC	.40	1.00
164 Tony Martin	.20	.50
165 Chris Mims	.08	.25
166 Shawn Lee	.08	.25
167 Junior Seau	.40	1.00
168 Merton Hanks	.08	.25
169 Rickey Jackson	.08	.25
170 Derek Loville	.08	.25
171 Gary Plummer	.08	.25
172 J.J. Stokes	.40	1.00
173 John Taylor	.08	.25
174 Bryant Young	.20	.50
175 Antonio Edwards RC	.20	.50
176 Joey Galloway	.40	1.00
177 Carlton Gray	.08	.25
178 Rick Mirer	.20	.50
179 Winston Moss	.08	.25
180 Jerome Bettis	.40	1.00
181 Troy Drayton	.08	.25
182 Wayne Gandy	.08	.25
183 Sean Gilbert	.08	.25
184 Jessie Hester	.08	.25
185 Sean Landeta	.08	.25
186 Roman Phifer	.08	.25
187 Alberto White	.08	.25
188 Santana Dotson	.08	.25
189 Jerry Ellison RC	.08	.25
190 Jackie Harris	.08	.25
191 Courtney Hawkins	.08	.25
192 Horace Copeland	.08	.25
193 Hardy Nickerson	.08	.25
194 Warren Sapp	.08	.25
195 Terry Allen	.20	.50
196 Henry Ellard	.20	.50
197 Gus Frerotte	.20	.50
198 John Gesek	.08	.25
199 Jim Lachey	.08	.25
200 Brian Mitchell	.08	.25
201 Garrison Hearst	.20	.50
202 Dave Krieg	.08	.25
203 Rob Moore	.20	.50
204 Aeneas Williams	.08	.25
205 Chris Doleman	.08	.25
206 Terance Mathis	.08	.25
207 Clay Matthews	.20	.50
208 Eric Metcalf	.20	.50
209 Jessie Tuggle	.08	.25
210 Cornelius Bennett	.20	.50
211 Ruben Brown	.08	.25
212 Russell Copeland	.08	.25
213 Phil Hansen	.08	.25
214 Jim Kelly	.40	1.00
215 Don Beebe	.08	.25
216 Willie Green	.08	.25
217 Howard Griffith	.08	.25
218 John Kasay	.08	.25
219 Brett Maxie	.08	.25
220 Tim McKyor	.08	.25
221 Sam Mills	.20	.50
222 Jim Flanigan	.08	.25
223 Jeff Graham	.08	.25
224 Erik Kramer	.08	.25
225 Rashaan Salaam	.20	.50
226 Steve Walsh	.08	.25
227 Donnell Woolford	.08	.25
228 Ki-Jana Carter	.20	.50
229 John Copeland	.08	.25
230 Harold Green	.08	.25
231 Doug Pelfrey	.08	.25
232 Darnay Scott	.20	.50
233 Bracy Walker RC	.08	.25
234 Dan Wilkinson	.08	.25
235 Leroy Hoard	.08	.25
236 Ernest Hunter UER	.08	.25
name spelled Earnest		
237 Keenan McCardell	.40	1.00
238 Stevon Moore	.08	.25
239 Andre Rison	.20	.50
240 Eric Zeier	.20	.50
241 Larry Brown	.08	.25
242 Shante Carver	.08	.25
243 Chad Hennings	.20	.50
244 John Jett	.08	.25
245 Daryl Johnston	.20	.50
246 Derek Kennard	.08	.25
247 Brock Marion	.08	.25
248 Jay Novacek	.20	.50
249 Emmitt Smith	2.00	4.00
250 Tony Tolbert	.08	.25
251 Mark Tuinei	.08	.25
252 Erik Williams	.08	.25
253 Kevin Williams	.08	.25
254 John Elway	2.00	5.00
255 Ed McCaffrey	.20	.50
256 Glyn Milburn	.08	.25
257 Michael Dean Perry	.08	.25
258 Mike Pritchard	.08	.25
259 Willie Clay	.08	.25
260 Jason Hanson	.08	.25
261 Herman Moore	.20	.50
262 Brett Perriman	.20	.50
263 Lomas Brown	.08	.25
264 Chris Spielman	.20	.50
265 Henry Thomas	.08	.25
266 Robert Brooks	.40	1.00
267 Sean Jones	.08	.25
268 John Jurkovic	.08	.25
269 Anthony Morgan	.08	.25
270 Craig Newsome	.08	.25
271 Reggie White	.40	1.00
272 Chris Chandler	.20	.50
273 Mel Gray	.08	.25
274 Darryll Lewis	.08	.25
275 Bruce Matthews	.08	.25
276 Todd McNair	.08	.25
277 Chris Sanders	.20	.50
278 Mark Stepnoski	.08	.25
279 Ashley Ambrose	.08	.25
280 Tony Bennett	.08	.25
281 Zack Crockett	.08	.25
282 Sean Dawkins	.08	.25
283 Marshall Faulk	.50	1.25
284 Ronald Humphrey	.08	.25
285 Tony Siragusa	.08	.25
286 Rousevelt Potts	.08	.25
287 Bryan Barker	.08	.25
288 Tony Boselli	.20	.50
289 Keith Goganious	.08	.25
290 Desmond Howard	.20	.50
291 Don Davey	.08	.25
292 Corey Mayfield	.08	.25
293 James O. Stewart	.20	.50
294 Cedric Tillman	.08	.25
295 Marcus Allen	.40	1.00
296 Dale Carter	.08	.25
297 Lake Dawson	.20	.50
298 Darren Mickell	.08	.25
299 Dan Saleaumua	.08	.25
300 Webster Slaughter	.08	.25
301 Keith Cash	.08	.25
302 Bryan Cox	.08	.25
303 Jeff Cross	.08	.25
304 Eric Green	.08	.25
305 O.J. McDuffie	.20	.50
306 Bernie Parmalee	.08	.25
307 Billy Milner	.08	.25
308 Pete Stoyanovich	.08	.25
309 Troy Vincent	.08	.25
310 Qadry Ismail	.20	.50
311 Amp Lee	.08	.25
312 Warren Moon	.20	.50
313 Scottie Graham	.08	.25
314 John Randle	.20	.50
315 Fuad Reveiz	.08	.25
316 Broderick Thomas	.08	.25
317 Ben Coates	.20	.50
318 Willie McGinest	.08	.25
319 Dave Meggett	.08	.25
320 Will Moore	.08	.25
321 Dave Wohlabaugh RC	.08	.25
322 Mario Bates	.20	.50
323 Jim Everett	.08	.25
324 Tyrone Hughes	.08	.25
325 Vaughn Dunbar	.08	.25
326 Renaldo Turnbull	.08	.25
327 Michael Haynes	.20	.50
328 Mike Sherrard	.08	.25
329 Michael Strahan	.20	.50
330 Herschel Walker	.20	.50
331 Charles Wilson	.08	.25
332 Otis Smith RC	.20	.50
333 Mo Lewis	.08	.25
334 Marvin Washington	.08	.25
335 Tim Brown	.40	1.00
336 Greg Skrepenak	.08	.25
337 Kevin Gogan	.08	.25
338 Jeff Hostetler	.20	.50
339 Terry McDaniel	.08	.25
340 Anthony Smith	.08	.25
341 Pat Swilling	.08	.25
342 Harvey Williams	.08	.25
343 Tom Hutton RC	.08	.25
344 Mike Mamula	.08	.25
345 Randall Cunningham	.40	1.00
346 Ricky Watters	.20	.50
347 Andy Harmon	.08	.25
348 William Thomas	.08	.25
349 Calvin Williams	.40	1.00
350 Mark Bruener	.08	.25
351 Dermontti Dawson	.08	.25
352 Greg Lloyd	.20	.50
353 Norm Johnson	.08	.25
354 Byron Bam Morris	.08	.25
355 Thomas Newberry	.08	.25
356 Darren Perry	.08	.25
357 Rohn Stark	.08	.25
358 Joel Steed	.08	.25
359 Brendan Stai UER	.08	.25
name spelled Brenden		
360 Justin Strzelczyk RC	.08	.25
361 Leon Searcy	.08	.25
362 Chad Brown	.20	.50
363 John Carney	.08	.25
364 Rodney Culver	.20	.50
365 Ronnie Harmon	.08	.25
366 Stan Humphries	.20	.50
367 Leslie O'Neal	.08	.25
368 Natrone Means	.20	.50
369 Mark Seay	.08	.25
370 William Floyd	.20	.50
371 Brent Jones	.08	.25
372 Tim McDonald	.08	.25
373 Ken Norton, Jr.	.20	.50
374 Jerry Rice	1.25	2.50
375 Dana Stubblefield	.20	.50
376 Steve Young	.75	2.00
377 Brian Blades	.20	.50
378 Cortez Kennedy	.20	.50
379 Michael Sinclair	.08	.25
380 Lamar Smith	.40	1.00
381 Chris Warren	.20	.50
382 Johnny Bailey	.08	.25
383 Isaac Bruce	.40	1.00
384 Kevin Carter	.20	.50
385 Shane Conlan	.08	.25
386 D'Marco Farr	.08	.25
387 Todd Kinchen	.08	.25
388 Chris Miller	.08	.25
389 Lonnie Marts	.08	.25
390 Trent Dilfer	.20	.50
391 Alvin Harper	.08	.25
392 John Lynch	.40	1.00
393 Errict Rhett	.20	.50
394 Darnell Stephens RC	.08	.25
395 Ken Harvey	.08	.25
396 Eddie Murray	.08	.25
397 Heath Shuler	.20	.50
398 Matt Turk RC	.08	.25
399 Michael Westbrook	.40	1.00
400 James Washington	.08	.25

1996 CE President's Reserve Air Force One

COMPLETE SET (38)	100.00	200.00
COMP.SERIES 1 (19)	50.00	100.00
COMP.SERIES 2 (19)	50.00	100.00
1-18: STATED ODDS 1:16 SER.1 PACKS		
19-36: STATED ODDS 1:16 SER.2 PACKS		
STATED PRINT RUN 2500 SERIAL #'d SETS		
*JUMBOS: .2X TO .5X BASIC INSERTS		
JUMBOS: ONE PER BOX		
STATED PRINT RUN 1300 SERIAL #'d SETS		
*CS/300 CARDS: .4X TO 1X BASIC INSERTS		
1 Brett Favre	12.50	25.00
2 Neil O'Donnell	1.25	2.50
3 Steve Young	5.00	10.00
4 Dan Marino	12.50	25.00
5 Kerry Collins	2.50	5.00
6 Scott Mitchell	1.25	2.50
7 Deion Sanders	4.00	8.00
8 Michael Irvin	2.50	5.00
9 Tim Brown	2.50	5.00
10 Joey Galloway	2.50	5.00
11 Robert Brooks	2.50	5.00
12 Tony Martin	1.25	2.50
13 Michael Westbrook	2.50	5.00
14 Eric Metcalf	1.25	2.50
15 Vincent Brisby	.60	1.25
16 Anthony Miller	1.25	2.50
17 J.J. Stokes	2.50	5.00
18 Kordell Stewart	2.50	5.00
19 Troy Aikman	6.00	12.00
20 Drew Bledsoe	4.00	8.00
21 Jeff Blake	2.50	5.00
22 John Elway	12.50	25.00
23 Jim Harbaugh	1.25	2.50
24 Erik Kramer	.60	1.25
25 Herman Moore	1.25	2.50
26 Carl Pickens	1.25	2.50
27 Michael Irvin	2.50	5.00
28 Jerry Rice	6.00	12.00
29 Isaac Bruce	2.50	5.00
30 Yancey Thigpen	1.25	2.50
31 Brett Perriman	1.25	2.50
32 Ben Coates	1.25	2.50
33 Jay Novacek	1.25	2.50
34 Tamarick Vanover	2.50	5.00
35 Terrell Davis	5.00	10.00
36 Jeff Graham	.60	1.25
NNO Checklist (1-18)	.60	1.25
NNO Checklist (19-36)	.60	1.25

1996 CE President's Reserve Candidates Long Shots

COMPLETE SET (30)	40.00	80.00
SER.1 TRADE CARDS STATED ODDS 1:4		
LS1 Leeland McElroy	.50	1.25
LS2 Richard Huntley	.75	2.00
LS3 Ray Lewis	4.00	10.00
LS4 Eric Moulds	2.00	5.00
LS5 Muhsin Muhammad	2.00	5.00
LS6 Bobby Engram	.75	2.00
LS7 Marco Battaglia	.50	1.25
LS8 Stepfret Williams	.50	1.25
LS9 Jeff Lewis	.75	2.00
LS10 Ryan Stewart	.50	1.25
LS11 Derrick Mayes	1.25	3.00
LS12 Mike Archie	.75	2.00
LS13 Scott Slutzker	.50	1.25
LS14 Kevin Hardy	.75	2.00
LS15 Reggie Tongue	.50	1.25
LS16 Zach Thomas	1.25	3.00
LS17 Duane Clemons	.50	1.25
LS18 Tedy Bruschi	3.00	8.00
LS19 Ricky Whittle	.50	1.25
LS20 Amani Toomer	1.25	3.00
LS21 Alex Van Dyke	.75	2.00
LS22 Lance Johnstone	.75	2.00
LS23 Bobby Hoying	1.25	3.00
LS24 Jahine Arnold	.75	2.00
LS25 Tony Banks	1.25	3.00
LS26 Charlie Jones	.75	2.00
LS27 Terrell Owens	4.00	8.00
LS28 Reggie Brown RBK	.50	1.25
LS29 Mike Alstott	1.50	4.00
LS30 Stephen Davis	2.50	6.00

1996 CE President's Reserve Candidates Top Picks

COMPLETE SET (30)	40.00	80.00
SER.2 TRADE CARDS STATED ODDS 1:4		
1 Simeon Rice	1.50	4.00
inserted in packs		
2 Shannon Brown	.50	1.25
3 Willie Anderson	.50	1.25
4 Tim Biakabutuka	1.25	3.00
inserted in packs		
5 Eric Moulds	2.00	5.00
6 Kavika Pittman	.50	1.25
7 Jonathan Ogden	1.25	3.00
inserted in packs		
8 Reggie Brown LB	.50	1.25
9 John Mobley	.50	1.25
inserted in packs		
10 John Michels	.50	1.25
11 Walt Harris	.50	1.25
12 Eddie George	2.00	5.00
inserted in packs		
13 Marvin Harrison	4.00	8.00
14 Kevin Hardy	.75	2.00
inserted in packs		
15 Jerome Woods	.50	1.25
16 Duane Clemons	.50	1.25
17 Daryl Gardener	.50	1.25
inserted in packs		
18 Terry Glenn	2.00	5.00
19 Alex Molden	.50	1.25
20 Cedric Jones	.50	1.25
21 Rickey Dudley	1.25	3.00
22 Keyshawn Johnson	1.50	4.00
inserted in packs		
23 Jermane Mayberry	.50	1.25
24 Jamain Stephens	.50	1.25
25 Lawrence Phillips	1.25	3.00
26 Bryan Still	.75	2.00
27 Israel Ifeanyi	.75	2.00
28 Pete Kendall	.50	1.25
29 Regan Upshaw	.50	1.25
30 Andre Johnson	.50	1.25

1996 CE President's Reserve Honor Guard

COMPLETE SET (30)	50.00	120.00
EACH CARD NUMBERED OF 1000		
HG1 Troy Aikman	5.00	12.00
HG2 Michael Irvin	2.00	5.00
HG3 Emmitt Smith	8.00	20.00
HG4 Brett Favre	10.00	25.00
HG5 Steve Young	4.00	10.00
HG6 Tim Brown	2.00	5.00
HG7 Errict Rhett	1.00	2.50
HG8 Curtis Martin	4.00	10.00
HG9 Carl Pickens	1.00	2.50
HG10 Herman Moore	1.00	2.50
HG11 Robert Brooks	2.00	5.00
HG12 Michael Westbrook	2.00	5.00
HG13 Leon Lett	.50	1.25
HG14 Russell Maryland	.50	1.25
HG15 Eric Swann	1.00	2.50
HG16 John Elway	10.00	25.00
HG17 Barry Sanders	8.00	20.00
HG18 Dan Marino	10.00	25.00
HG19 Drew Bledsoe	3.00	8.00
HG20 Jerry Rice	5.00	12.00
HG21 Deion Sanders	3.00	8.00
HG22 Rashaan Salaam	1.00	2.50
HG23 Marshall Faulk	2.50	6.00
HG24 Napoleon Kaufman	2.00	5.00
HG25 Ki-Jana Carter	1.00	2.50
HG26 Cris Carter	2.00	5.00
HG27 Joey Galloway	2.00	5.00
HG28 Eric Metcalf	1.00	2.50
HG29 Derrick Thomas	2.00	5.00
HG30 Bruce Smith	2.00	5.00

1996 CE President's Reserve New Regime

COMPLETE SET (26)	25.00	50.00
COMP.SERIES 1 (13)	12.50	25.00
COMP.SERIES 2 (13)	12.50	25.00
1-12: STATED ODDS 1:5 SER.1 PACKS		
13-24: STATED ODDS 1:5 SER.2 PACKS		
STATED PRINT RUN 12,000 SERIAL #'d SETS		
1 Tamarick Vanover	.75	2.00
2 Kerry Collins	.75	2.00
3 J.J. Stokes	.75	2.00
4 Napoleon Kaufman	.75	2.00
5 Steve McNair	1.50	4.00
6 Todd Collins	.40	1.00
7 Frank Sanders	.40	1.00
8 Warren Sapp	.20	.50
9 Tony Boselli	.40	1.00
10 Curtis Martin	1.50	4.00
11 Ki-Jana Carter	.40	1.00
12 Zack Crockett	.20	.50
13 Joey Galloway	.75	2.00
14 Terrell Davis	1.50	4.00
15 Chris Sanders	.40	1.00
16 Rashaan Salaam	.40	1.00
17 Michael Westbrook	.75	2.00
18 Hugh Douglas	.40	1.00
19 Eric Zeier	.40	1.00
20 Kordell Stewart	.75	2.00
21 Ted Johnson	.75	2.00
22 Ken Dilger	.40	1.00
23 Darick Holmes	.20	.50
24 Wayne Chrebet	1.25	3.00
NNO Checklist (1-12)	.20	.50
NNO Checklist (13-24)	.20	.50

1996 CE President's Reserve Running Mates

COMPLETE SET (24)	125.00	250.00
COMP.SERIES 1 (12)	60.00	125.00
COMP.SERIES 2 (12)	60.00	125.00
1-12: STATED ODDS 1:33 SER.1 PACKS		
13-24: STATED ODDS 1:33 SER.2 PACKS		
STATED PRINT RUN 2000 SERIAL #'d SETS		
*GOLD/10: 3X TO 8X SILVER/2000		
*GOLD/100: 1.5X TO 4X SILVER/2000		
*JUMBO SILVER/2000: .25X TO .5X		
JUMBO SILVER PRINT RUN 2000 SER.#'d SETS		
*JUMBO GOLD/200: 1X TO 2X		
JUMBO GOLD PRINT RUN 200 SER.#'d SETS		
RM1 Emmitt Smith	10.00	25.00
Troy Aikman		
RM2 Marshall Faulk	4.00	10.00
Jim Harbaugh		
RM3 Terrell Davis	10.00	25.00
John Elway		
RM4 Stan Humphries	3.00	8.00
Natrone Means		
RM5 Rashaan Salaam	3.00	8.00
Erik Kramer		
RM6 Chris Miller	4.00	10.00
Jerome Bettis		

RM7 Errict Rhett	3.00	8.00
Trent Dilfer		
RM8 Jeff George	2.50	6.00
Craig Heyward		
RM9 Gus Frerotte	3.00	8.00
Terry Allen		
RM10 Curtis Martin	5.00	12.00
Drew Bledsoe		
RM11 Jeff Blake	3.00	8.00
Ki-Jana Carter		
RM12 Rick Mirer	3.00	8.00
Chris Warren		
RM13 Brett Favre	10.00	25.00
Edgar Bennett		
RM14 Neil O'Donnell	2.50	6.00
Byron Bam Morris		
RM15 Scott Mitchell	8.00	20.00
Barry Sanders		
RM16 Steve Young	6.00	15.00
Derek Loville		
RM17 Warren Moon	2.50	6.00
Robert Smith		
RM18 Heath Shuler	3.00	8.00
Brian Mitchell		
RM19 Rodney Peete	3.00	8.00
Ricky Watters		
RM20 Kerry Collins	3.00	8.00
Derrick Moore		
RM21 Dan Marino	10.00	25.00
Terry Kirby		
RM22 Steve Bono	4.00	10.00
Marcus Allen		
RM23 Jim Kelly	4.00	10.00
Darick Holmes		
RM24 Kordell Stewart	4.00	10.00
Eric Pegram		

1996 CE President's Reserve Tanned Rested Ready

COMPLETE SET (27)	40.00	80.00
COMP.SERIES 1 (13)	25.00	50.00
COMP.SERIES 2 (14)	15.00	30.00
1-12: STATED ODDS 1:8 SER.1 PACKS		
13-25: STATED ODDS 1:8 SER.2 PACKS		
1 Jeff Blake	1.50	3.00
2 Warren Moon	.75	1.50
3 Brett Favre	8.00	15.00
4 Steve Young	3.00	6.00
5 Emmitt Smith	6.00	12.00
6 Ricky Watters	.75	1.50
7 Michael Irvin	1.50	3.00
8 Carl Pickens	.75	1.50
9 Tim Brown	1.50	3.00
10 Anthony Miller	.75	1.50
11 Darren Bennett	.75	1.50
12 Yancey Thigpen	.75	1.50
13 Bryce Paup	.75	1.50
14 Jim Harbaugh	.75	1.50
15 Barry Sanders	6.00	12.00
16 Herman Moore	.75	1.50
17 Cris Carter	1.50	3.00
18 Chris Warren	.75	1.50
19 Marshall Faulk	2.00	4.00
20 Curtis Martin	3.00	6.00
21 Ben Coates	.75	1.50
22 Brent Jones	.30	.75
23 Shannon Sharpe	.75	1.50
24 Brian Mitchell	.30	.75
25 Ken Harvey	.30	.75
NNO Checklist (1-12)	.30	.75
NNO Checklist (13-25)	.30	.75

1996 CE President's Reserve TimeWarp

COMPLETE SET (12)	30.00	80.00
1-6: RAND.INS. IN SERIES 1 PACKS		
7-12: RAND.INS. IN SERIES 2 PACKS		
1 Jack Kemp	2.00	5.00
Greg Lloyd		
2 Sonny Jurgensen	3.00	8.00
Marshall Faulk		
3 Fran Tarkenton	2.50	6.00
Bryce Paup		
4 Roger Staubach	8.00	20.00
Emmitt Smith		
4R Emmitt Smith	60.00	100.00
Roger Staubach		
(Ruby on card)		
5 Jack Lambert	4.00	10.00
Curtis Martin		
6 Jack Youngblood	8.00	20.00
Brett Favre		
7 Fran Tarkenton	3.00	8.00
Reggie White		
8 Art Donovan	2.00	5.00
Steve Bono		
9 Bobby Mitchell	5.00	12.00
Troy Aikman		
10 Larry Csonka	2.50	6.00
Kordell Stewart		
11 Dick Butkus	4.00	10.00
Deion Sanders		
12 Deacon Jones	8.00	20.00
Dan Marino		
NNO J.Namath	6.00	15.00
E.Smith		
NNO W.Payton	5.00	12.00
R.White		

1998 CE Supreme Season Review Markers Previews

This set was released to promote the Markers insert in 1998 Edge Supreme Season Review. The cards are identical to the base insert set with the word "Preview" stamped on the cardfronts. The base set features borderless color player photos highlighted with special embossed foil commemorating each player's outstanding achievements.

COMPLETE SET (30)	30.00	60.00
*PREVIEWS: .1X TO .2X BASIC INSERTS		

1998 CE Supreme Season Review

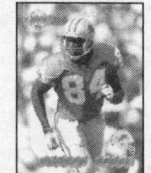

The 200-card set of the 1998 Collector's Edge Supreme Season Review was distributed in six-card packs with a suggested retail price of $3.99 and feature borderless color action player photos. The set includes 170-player cards with 30-redemption cards for top draft picks from each team. The draft pick redemption cards expired March 31, 1999. The draft pick prize cards were numbered as part of the base set with a letter suffix attached to the card number.

COMPLETE SET (200)	30.00	60.00
COMP.SET w/o SPs (200)	12.50	25.00
1 Larry Centers	.20	.50
2 Jake Plummer	.50	1.25
3 Simeon Rice	.20	.50
4 Cardinals Draft Pick	.02	.10
4A Andre Wadsworth RC	.60	1.50
4B Michael Pittman RC	1.25	2.50
5 Jamal Anderson	.20	.50
6 Bert Emanuel	.30	.75
7 Byron Hanspard	.20	.50
8 Falcons Draft Pick	.02	.10
8A Jammi German RC	.60	1.50
8B Keith Brooking RC	.75	2.00
9 Derrick Alexander WR	.30	.75
10 Peter Boulware	.20	.50
11 Michael Jackson	.20	.50
12 Ray Lewis	.50	1.25
13 Vinny Testaverde	.30	.75
14 Ravens Draft Pick	.02	.10
14A Duane Starks RC	.40	1.00
14B Pat Johnson RC	.60	1.50
15 Todd Collins	.20	.50
16 Jim Kelly	.50	1.25
17 Andre Reed	.30	.75
18 Antowain Smith	.50	1.25
19 Bruce Smith	.30	.75
20 Thurman Thomas	.50	1.25
21 Bills Draft Pick	.02	.10
21A Jonathan Linton RC	.60	1.50
22 Tim Biakabutuka	.30	.75
23 Rae Carruth	.20	.50
24 Kerry Collins	.30	.75
25 Anthony Johnson	.20	.50
26 Lamar Lathon	.20	.50
27 Panthers Draft Pick	.02	.10
27A Jason Peters RC	.60	1.50
27B Donald Hayes RC	.60	1.50
28 Curtis Conway	.30	.75
29 Bryan Cox	.20	.50
30 Bobby Engram	.30	.75
31 Erik Kramer	.20	.50
32 Rick Mirer	.20	.50
33 Rashaan Salaam	.20	.50
34 Bears Draft Pick	.02	.10
34A Curtis Enis RC	.40	1.00
35 Jeff Blake	.30	.75
36 Ki-Jana Carter	.20	.50
37 Corey Dillon	.50	1.25
38 Carl Pickens	.30	.75
39 Bengals Draft Pick	.02	.10
39A Takeo Spikes RC	.75	2.00
39B Brian Simmons RC	.60	1.50
40 Troy Aikman	.75	2.00
41 Daryl Johnston	.30	.75
42 David LaFleur	.20	.50
43 Anthony Miller	.20	.50
44 Deion Sanders	.50	1.25
45 Emmitt Smith	1.50	3.00
46 Broderick Thomas	.20	.50
47 Cowboys Draft Pick	.02	.10
47A Greg Ellis RC	.40	1.00
48 Terrell Davis	.50	1.25
49 John Elway	2.00	4.00
50 Ed McCaffrey	.30	.75
51 John Mobley	.20	.50
52 Bill Romanowski	.20	.50
53 Shannon Sharpe	.30	.75
54 Neil Smith	.30	.75
55 Rod Smith WR	.30	.75
56 Maa Tanuvasa	.20	.50
57 Broncos Draft Pick	.02	.10
57A Marcus Nash RC	.40	1.00
57B Brian Griese RC	1.50	4.00
58 Scott Mitchell	.30	.75
59 Herman Moore	.30	.75
60 Barry Sanders	1.25	3.00
61 Lions Draft Pick	.02	.10
61A Jamaal Alexander RC	.40	1.00
61B Chris Liwienski RC	.40	1.00
61C Terry Fair RC	.60	1.50
61D Germane Crowell RC	.60	1.50
61E Charlie Batch RC	.75	2.00
62 Robert Brooks	.30	.75
63 Mark Chmura	.30	.75
64 Brett Favre	2.00	4.00
65 Antonio Freeman	.50	1.25
66 Dorsey Levens	.50	1.25
67 Derrick Mayes	.30	.75
68 Ross Verba	.20	.50
69 Reggie White	.50	1.25
70 Packers Draft Pick	.02	.10
70A Vonnie Holliday RC	.60	1.50
70B Roosevelt Blackmon RC	.40	1.00
71 Marshall Faulk	.60	1.50
72 Jim Harbaugh	.30	.75
73 Marvin Harrison	.50	1.25
74 Colts Draft Pick	.02	.10
74A E.G. Green RC	.60	1.50
74B Peyton Manning RC	10.00	20.00
75 Tony Brackens	.20	.50
76 Mark Brunell	.50	1.25
77 Rob Johnson	.30	.75
78 Keenan McCardell	.30	.75
79 Natrone Means	.30	.75
80 Jimmy Smith	.30	.75
81 Jaguars Draft Pick	.02	.10
81A Tavian Banks RC	.60	1.50
82 Marcus Allen	.50	1.25
83 Tony Gonzalez	.50	1.25
84 Elvis Grbac	.30	.75
85 Derrick Thomas	.50	1.25
86 Tamarick Vanover	.20	.50
87 Chiefs Draft Pick	.02	.10
87A Rashaan Shehee RC	.60	1.50
88 Karim Abdul-Jabbar	.50	1.25
89 Fred Barnett	.20	.50
90 Dan Marino	2.00	4.00
91 O.J. McDuffie	.30	.75
92 Brett Perriman	.20	.50
93 Irving Spikes	.20	.50
94 Zach Thomas	.50	1.25
95 Dolphins Draft Pick	.02	.10
95A John Avery RC	.60	1.50
96 Cris Carter	.50	1.25
97 Brad Johnson	.50	1.25
98 John Randle	.30	.75
99 Jake Reed	.30	.75
100 Robert Smith	.50	1.25
101 Vikings Draft Pick	.02	.10
101A Randy Moss RC	5.00	12.00
102 Drew Bledsoe	.60	1.50
103 Chris Canty	.20	.50
104 Ben Coates	.30	.75
105 Terry Glenn	.50	1.25
106 Curtis Martin	.50	1.25
107 Willie McGinest	.20	.50
108 Sedrick Shaw	.20	.50
109 Patriots Draft Pick	.02	.10
109A Chris Floyd RC	.40	1.00
109B Tebucky Jones RC	.40	1.00
109C Harold Shaw RC	.40	1.00
110 Mario Bates	.30	.75
111 Heath Shuler	.20	.50
112 Danny Wuerffel	.30	.75
113 Saints Draft Pick	.02	.10
113A Cameron Cleeland RC	.40	1.00
114 Ray Zellars	.20	.50
115 Tiki Barber	.50	1.25
116 Dave Brown	.20	.50
117 Ike Hilliard	.30	.75
118 Danny Kanell	.30	.75
119 Jason Sehorn	.30	.75
120 Amani Toomer	.30	.75
121 Giants Draft Pick	.02	.10
121A Shaun Williams RC	.60	1.50
121B Joe Jurevicius RC	.75	2.00
121C Brian Alford RC	.40	1.00
122 Wayne Chrebet	.50	1.25
123 Hugh Douglas	.20	.50
124 Jeff Graham	.20	.50
125 Keyshawn Johnson	.50	1.25
126 Adrian Murrell	.30	.75
127 Neil O'Donnell	.30	.75
128 Jets Draft Pick	.02	.10
128A Scott Frost RC	.40	1.00
129 Tim Brown	.50	1.25
130 Jeff George	.30	.75
131 Desmond Howard	.30	.75
132 Napoleon Kaufman	.50	1.25
133 Darrell Russell	.20	.50
134 Raiders Draft Pick	.02	.10
134A Charles Woodson RC	1.00	2.50
135 Ty Detmer	.30	.75
136 Irving Fryar	.30	.75
137 Bobby Hoying	.30	.75
138 Chris T. Jones	.20	.50
139 Ricky Watters	.30	.75
140 Eagles Draft Pick	.02	.10
140A Allen Rossum RC	.40	1.00
141 Jerome Bettis	.50	1.25
142 Charles Johnson	.20	.50
143 George Jones	.20	.50
144 Greg Lloyd	.20	.50
145 Kordell Stewart	.50	1.25
146 Yancey Thigpen	.20	.50
147 Steelers Draft Pick	.02	.10
147A C.Fuamatu-Ma'afala RC	.60	1.50
148 Stan Humphries	.30	.75
149 Tony Martin	.30	.75
150 Eric Metcalf	.30	.75
151 Junior Seau	.50	1.25
152 Chargers Draft Pick	.02	.10
152A Ryan Leaf RC	.75	2.00
153 Jim Druckenmiller	.20	.50
154 William Floyd	.20	.50
155 Kevin Greene	.30	.75
156 Garrison Hearst	.50	1.25
157 Ken Norton	.20	.50
158 Terrell Owens	.50	1.25
159 Jerry Rice	.75	2.00
160 J.J. Stokes	.30	.75
161 Dana Stubblefield	.20	.50
162 Rod Woodson	.30	.75
163 Bryant Young	.20	.50
164 Steve Young	.50	1.25
165 49ers Draft Pick	.02	.10
165A Fred Beasley RC	.40	1.00
165B R.W. McQuarters RC	.60	1.50
165C Chris Ruhman RC	.40	1.00
166 Steve Broussard	.20	.50
167 Chad Brown	.20	.50
168 Joey Galloway	.30	.75
169 Jon Kitna	.50	1.25
170 Warren Moon	.50	1.25
171 Chris Warren	.30	.75
172 Seahawks Draft Pick	.02	.10
172A Ahman Green RC	2.00	5.00
173 Tony Banks	.30	.75
174 Isaac Bruce	.50	1.25
175 Eddie Kennison	.30	.75
176 Keith Lyle	.20	.50
177 Lawrence Phillips	.20	.50
178 Rams Draft Pick	.02	.10
178A Robert Holcombe RC	.60	1.50
179 Mike Alstott	.50	1.25
180 Reidel Anthony	.30	.75
181 Trent Dilfer	.50	1.25
182 Warrick Dunn	.50	1.25
183 Hardy Nickerson	.20	.50
184 Errict Rhett	.20	.50
185 Warren Sapp	.30	.75
186 Bucs Draft Pick	.02	.10
186A Jacquez Green RC	.60	1.50
187 Eddie George	.50	1.25
188 Darryll Lewis	.20	.50
189 Steve McNair	.50	1.25
190 Chris Sanders	.20	.50
191 Oilers Draft Pick	.02	.10
191A Kevin Dyson RC	.75	2.00
192 Terry Allen	.50	1.25
193 Jamie Asher	.20	.50
194 Stephen Davis	.20	.50
195 Gus Frerotte	.20	.50
196 Sean Gilbert	.20	.50
197 Ken Harvey	.20	.50
198 Jeff Hostetler	.20	.50
199 Michael Westbrook	.30	.75
200 Redskins Draft Pick	.02	.10
200A Stephen Alexander RC	.60	1.50
200B Mike Sellers RC	.40	1.00

1998 CE Supreme Season Review Gold Ingot

COMPLETE SET (200)	200.00	400.00
*STARS: 2X TO 4X BASIC CARDS		
*RCs: .6X TO 1.5X BASIC CARDS		
STATED ODDS 1:1		

1998 CE Supreme Season Review Personal Collection

STATED ODDS 1:4000
STATED PRINT RUN 1 SET

1998 CE Supreme Season Review Markers

COMPLETE SET (30)	125.00	250.00
STATED ODDS 1:24		
1 Jamal Anderson	4.00	10.00
2 Corey Dillon	4.00	10.00
3 Emmitt Smith	10.00	25.00
4 Terrell Davis	4.00	10.00
5 John Elway	12.50	30.00
6 Rod Smith	2.50	6.00
7 Herman Moore	2.50	6.00
8 Barry Sanders	10.00	25.00
9 Robert Brooks	2.50	6.00
10 Brett Favre	12.50	30.00
11 Antonio Freeman	4.00	10.00
12 Dorsey Levens	4.00	10.00
13 Marshall Faulk	5.00	12.00
14 Mark Brunell	4.00	10.00
15 Karim Abdul-Jabbar	4.00	10.00
16 Dan Marino	12.50	30.00
17 Cris Carter	4.00	10.00
18 Drew Bledsoe	5.00	12.00
19 Curtis Martin	4.00	10.00
20 Adrian Murrell	2.50	6.00
21 Tim Brown	4.00	10.00
22 Jeff George	2.50	6.00
23 Napoleon Kaufman	4.00	10.00
24 Jerome Bettis	4.00	10.00
25 Kordell Stewart	4.00	10.00
26 Yancey Thigpen	1.50	4.00
27 Garrison Hearst	4.00	10.00
28 Steve Young	4.00	10.00
29 Joey Galloway	2.50	6.00
30 Eddie George	4.00	10.00

1998 CE Supreme Season Review Pro-Signature Authentic

OVERALL STATED ODDS 1:2300		
VETERANS STATED PRINT RUN 50		
ROOKIE REDEMPTION ODDS 1:800		
EMMITT SMITH INSERTED IN 98 CE MASTERS		
DH Desmond Howard	60.00	150.00
ES Emmitt Smith	150.00	300.00
JR Jerry Rice	125.00	250.00
MA Marcus Allen	60.00	150.00
PM Peyton Manning/500	60.00	120.00
RL Ryan Leaf/500	25.00	60.00
TA Troy Aikman	125.00	250.00
TD Terrell Davis	60.00	150.00
NNO Rookie Redemption	.40	1.00
(Expired; was for Ryan Leaf or Peyton Manning)		

1998 CE Supreme Season Review T3 Previews

This set was released to promote the T3 insert in 1998 Edge Supreme Season Review. The cards are identical to the base insert set with the word "Preview" stamped on the cardfronts. Reportedly, card #18 was not released in the Preview card version.

COMPLETE SET (29)	40.00	100.00
*PROMO CARDS: .2X TO .5X BASE INSERT		

1998 CE Supreme Season Review T3

COMPLETE SET (30)	100.00	200.00
STATED ODDS 1:36 QB/1:24 RB/1:12 WR		
1 Rae Carruth	1.00	2.50
2 Carl Pickens	1.25	3.00
3 Troy Aikman	5.00	12.00
4 Emmitt Smith	5.00	12.00
5 Terrell Davis	1.50	4.00
6 John Elway	12.50	25.00
7 Herman Moore	1.25	3.00
8 Barry Sanders	10.00	20.00
9 Robert Brooks	1.25	3.00
10 Brett Favre	12.50	25.00
11 Antonio Freeman	1.50	4.00
12 Dorsey Levens	1.50	4.00
13 Rob Johnson	2.00	5.00
14 Jerry Rice	4.00	8.00
15 Dan Marino	12.50	25.00
16 Cris Carter	1.50	4.00
17 Drew Bledsoe	5.00	10.00
18 Curtis Martin	1.50	4.00
19 Adrian Murrell	1.50	4.00
20 Tim Brown	1.50	4.00
21 Napoleon Kaufman	1.50	4.00
22 Jerome Bettis	1.50	4.00
23 Kordell Stewart	2.00	5.00
24 Joey Galloway	1.25	3.00
25 Jim Druckenmiller	2.00	5.00
26 Terrell Owens	1.50	4.00
27 Jake Plummer	1.50	4.00
28 Warrick Dunn	1.50	4.00
29 Eddie George	1.50	4.00
30 Steve McNair	2.00	5.00

1999 Collector's Edge Supreme Previews

These cards were released as a preview to the 1999 Edge Supreme card release. Each is very similar to its base set counterpart except for the card number on back and "Preview" printed on the cardbacks.

COMPLETE SET (10)	6.00	15.00
BS Barry Sanders	1.60	4.00
CB Charlie Batch	.80	2.00
ES Emmitt Smith	1.20	3.00
JA Jamal Anderson	.40	1.00
KJ Keyshawn Johnson	.40	1.00
MB Mark Brunell	.80	2.00
PM Peyton Manning	2.00	5.00
RE Robert Edwards	.40	1.00
RM Randy Moss	2.00	5.00
TD Terrell Davis	1.20	3.00

1999 Collector's Edge Supreme Draft Previews

These cards were released as preview or promo cards at various Collector's Edge functions in exchange for product wrappers or through the mail via various redemption cards. Each is essentially identical to the base Supreme card for the player except for the card numbering which is the player's initials in this Preview set. There are two versions of the Couch card with either a 1st Pick or 2nd Pick foil notation on the cardfront.

COMPLETE SET (6)	6.00	15.00
CB Champ Bailey	.40	1.00
CC Chris Claiborne	.30	.75
DC Daunte Culpepper	1.00	2.50
RW Ricky Williams	2.00	5.00
TC1 Tim Couch 1st Pick	2.00	5.00
TC2 Tim Couch 2nd Pick	2.00	5.00
TH Torry Holt	.80	2.00

1999 Collector's Edge Supreme

The 1999 Collector's Edge Supreme set was issued in one series totalling 170-cards. The set features action player photos printed with high definition color and clarity on UV coated, silver foil stamped card stock. The backs carry the player's complete 1999 statistics. Forty short printed rookie cards from the 1999 NFL draft are included in the set along with mail redemption cards for each draft pick including #166. Card #166 Michael Wiley was released in very early packs only and quickly withdrawn with the #166 redemption card exchangeable for an Edgerrin James card.

COMPLETE SET (170)	25.00	60.00
1 Randy Moss CL	.20	.50
2 Peyton Manning CL	.60	1.50
3 Rob Moore	.20	.50
4 Adrian Murrell	.25	.60
5 Jake Plummer	.25	.60
6 Andre Wadsworth	.25	.60
7 Jamal Anderson	.25	.60
8 Chris Chandler	.25	.60
9 Tony Martin	.25	.60
10 Terence Mathis	.25	.60
11 Jim Harbaugh	.25	.60
12 Priest Holmes	.30	.75
13 Jermaine Lewis	.25	.60
14 Eric Zeier	.20	.50
15 Doug Flutie	.30	.75
16 Eric Moulds	.25	.60
17 Andre Reed	.30	.75
18 Antowain Smith	.25	.60
19 Steve Beuerlein	.20	.50
20 Kevin Greene	.20	.50
21 Rocket Ismail	.25	.60
22 Fred Lane	.20	.50
23 Edgar Bennett	.20	.50
24 Curtis Conway	.25	.60
25 Curtis Enis	.20	.50
26 Erik Kramer	.20	.50
27 Corey Dillon	.25	.60
28 Neil O'Donnell	.25	.60
29 Carl Pickens	.25	.60
30 Darnay Scott	.20	.50
31 Troy Aikman	.50	1.25
32 Michael Irvin	.30	.75
33 Deion Sanders	.30	.75
34 Emmitt Smith	.75	2.00
35 Chris Warren	.25	.60
36 Terrell Davis	.30	.75
37 John Elway	1.00	2.50
38 Ed McCaffrey	.25	.60
39 Shannon Sharpe	.30	.75
40 Rod Smith	.25	.60
41 Charlie Batch	.25	.60
42 Herman Moore	.25	.60
43 Johnnie Morton	.25	.60
44 Barry Sanders	.75	2.00
45 Robert Brooks	.25	.60
46 Brett Favre	1.00	2.50
47 Antonio Freeman	.25	.60
48 Darick Holmes	.20	.50
49 Dorsey Levens	.25	.60
50 Reggie White	.30	.75
51 Marshall Faulk	.30	.75
52 Marvin Harrison	.30	.75
53 Peyton Manning	1.00	2.50
54 Jerome Pathon	.20	.50
55 Tavian Banks	.20	.50
56 Mark Brunell	.25	.60
57 Keenan McCardell	.25	.60
58 Fred Taylor	.25	.60
59 Derrick Alexander	.25	.60
60 Donnell Bennett	.20	.50
61 Rich Gannon	.25	.60
62 Andre Rison	.25	.60
63 Karim Abdul-Jabbar	.25	.60
64 John Avery	.20	.50
65 Oronde Gadsden	.25	.60
66 Dan Marino	1.00	2.50
67 O.J. McDuffie	.25	.60
68 Cris Carter	.30	.75
69 Randall Cunningham	.30	.75
70 Brad Johnson	.25	.60
71 Randy Moss	.60	1.50
72 Jake Reed	.25	.60
73 Robert Smith	.25	.60
74 Drew Bledsoe	.30	.75
75 Ben Coates	.25	.60
76 Robert Edwards	.20	.50
77 Terry Glenn	.25	.60
78 Cameron Cleeland	.20	.50
79 Kerry Collins	.25	.60
80 Sean Dawkins	.20	.50
81 Lamar Smith	.25	.60
82 Gary Brown	.20	.50
83 Chris Calloway	.20	.50
84 Danny Kanell	.25	.60
85 Ike Hilliard	.20	.50
86 Wayne Chrebet	.25	.60
87 Keyshawn Johnson	.25	.60
88 Curtis Martin	.30	.75
89 Vinny Testaverde	.25	.60
90 Tim Brown	.25	.60
91 Jeff George	.25	.60
92 Napoleon Kaufman	.25	.60
93 Charles Woodson	.25	.60
94 Irving Fryar	.25	.60
95 Bobby Hoying	.20	.50
96 Duce Staley	.30	.75
97 Jerome Bettis	.30	.75
98 Courtney Hawkins	.20	.50
99 Charles Johnson	.20	.50
100 Kordell Stewart	.25	.60
101 Hines Ward	.30	.75
102 Tony Banks	.25	.60
103 Isaac Bruce	.30	.75
104 Robert Holcombe	.20	.50
105 Ryan Leaf	.25	.60
106 Natrone Means	.25	.60
107 Mikhael Ricks	.20	.50
108 Junior Seau	.30	.75
109 Garrison Hearst	.25	.60
110 Terrell Owens	.30	.75
111 Jerry Rice	.60	1.50
112 J.J. Stokes	.25	.60
113 Steve Young	.40	1.00
114 Joey Galloway	.25	.60
115 Jon Kitna	.25	.60
116 Warren Moon	.30	.75
117 Ricky Watters	.25	.60
118 Mike Alstott	.30	.75
119 Reidel Anthony	.20	.50
120 Warrick Dunn	.25	.60
121 Trent Dilfer	.25	.60
122 Jacquez Green	.20	.50
123 Kevin Dyson	.20	.50
124 Eddie George	.25	.60
125 Steve McNair	.30	.75
126 Frank Wycheck	.25	.60
127 Terry Allen	.25	.60
128 Trent Green	.25	.60
129 Skip Hicks	.20	.50
130 Michael Westbrook	.20	.50
131 Rahim Abdullah RC	.40	1.00
132 Champ Bailey RC	1.25	3.00
133 Marlon Barnes RC	.40	1.00
134 D'Wayne Bates RC	.40	1.00
135 Michael Bishop RC	.50	1.25
136 Dre Bly RC	.60	1.50
137 David Boston RC	.50	1.25
138 Cuncho Brown RC UER	.40	1.00
(Photo is actually Courtney Brown)		
139 Na Brown RC	.40	1.00
140 Tony Bryant RC	.40	1.00
141 Tim Couch RC ERR	25.00	50.00
(text on back reads already sent)		
141TC Tim Couch RC COR	1.00	2.50
(card number reads TC)		
142 Chris Claiborne RC	.40	1.00
143 Daunte Culpepper RC	.60	1.50
144 Jared DeVries RC	.40	1.00
145 Troy Edwards UER RC	.50	1.25
146 Kris Farris RC	.40	1.00
147 Kevin Faulk RC	.60	1.50
148 Joe Germaine RC	.50	1.25
149 Aaron Gibson RC	.40	1.00
150 Torry Holt RC	1.00	2.50
151 Brock Huard RC	.50	1.25
152 Sedrick Irvin RC	.40	1.00
153 James Johnson RC	.40	1.00
154 Kevin Johnson RC	.50	1.25
155 Andy Katzenmoyer RC	.50	1.25
156 Jevon Kearse RC	.60	1.50
157 Shaun King RC	.40	1.00
158 Rob Konrad RC	.40	1.00
159 Chris McAlister RC	.40	1.00
160 Darnell McDonald RC	.40	1.00
161 Donovan McNabb RC	2.50	6.00
162 Cade McNown RC	.50	1.25
163 Peerless Price RC	.50	1.25
164 Akili Smith RC	.50	1.25
165 Matt Stinchcomb RC	.40	1.00
166A Michael Wiley SP	30.00	80.00
(pink tint on cardfront)		
166B Edgerrin James RC	1.50	4.00
167 Ricky Williams RC	1.00	2.50
168 Antoine Winfield RC	.40	1.00
169 Craig Yeast RC	.40	1.00
170 Amos Zereoue RC	.50	1.25

1999 Collector's Edge Supreme Galvanized

COMPLETE SET (167)	400.00	800.00
*VETS 3-130: 2.5X TO 6X BASIC CARDS		
*ROOKIES 131-170: 1.5X TO 4X BASIC CARDS		
*ROOKIE #141: .5X TO 1.2X BASIC CARD		
STATED PRINT RUN 500 SER.#'d SETS		
166A Michael Wiley pink	12.00	30.00
(pink X written on front)		
166B Edgerrin James ERR	50.00	100.00
no Galvanized logo on card		

1999 Collector's Edge Supreme Gold Ingot

*VETS 3-130: .8X TO 2X BASIC CARDS		
*ROOKIES 131-170: .5X TO 1.2X BASIC CARDS		
ONE PER PACK		
141 Tim Couch ERR	20.00	50.00
166B Edgerrin James ERR	10.00	25.00
missing Gold Ingot logo/ not released in packs)		

1999 Collector's Edge Supreme Future

COMPLETE SET (10)	30.00	60.00
STATED ODDS 1:24		
SF1 Ricky Williams	2.00	5.00
SF2 Tim Couch	1.50	4.00
SF3 Daunte Culpepper	3.00	8.00
SF4 Torry Holt	2.50	6.00
SF5 Edgerrin James	4.00	10.00
SF6 Brock Huard	1.50	4.00
SF7 Donovan McNabb	5.00	12.00
SF8 Joe Germaine	1.50	4.00
SF9 Cade McNown	1.50	4.00
SF10 Michael Bishop	1.50	4.00

1999 Collector's Edge Supreme Homecoming

COMPLETE SET (20)	30.00	60.00
STATED ODDS 1:12		
H1 Ricky Williams	2.50	6.00
Priest Holmes		
H2 Andy Katzenmoyer	1.00	2.50
Eddie George		
H3 Daunte Culpepper	2.50	6.00
Shawn Jefferson		
H4 Torry Holt	2.00	5.00
Eric Kramer		
H5 Edgerrin James	3.00	8.00
Vinny Testaverde		
H6 Chris Claiborne	1.00	2.50
Junior Seau		
H7 Brock Huard	1.00	2.50
Mark Brunell		
H8 Champ Bailey	1.00	2.50
Terrell Davis		
H9 Donovan McNabb	4.00	10.00
Rob Moore		
H10 David Boston	1.00	2.50
Joey Galloway		
H11 Cade McNown	3.00	8.00
Troy Aikman		
H12 Kevin Faulk	1.00	2.50
Eddie Kennison		
H13 Sedrick Irvin	1.00	2.50
Andre Rison		
H14 Rob Konrad	.60	1.50
Daryl Johnston		
H15 Amos Zereoue	1.00	2.50
Adrian Murrell		
H16 Peerless Price	3.00	8.00
Peyton Manning		
H17 Kevin Johnson	1.25	3.00
Marvin Harrison		
H18 Jevon Kearse	1.50	4.00
Emmitt Smith		
H19 Antoine Winfield	.60	1.50
Shawn Springs		
H20 Tony Bryant	.60	1.50
Andre Wadsworth		

1999 Collector's Edge Supreme Markers

COMPLETE SET (15)	35.00	70.00
STATED PRINT RUN 5000 SERIAL #'d SETS		
M1 Terrell Davis	1.25	3.00
M2 John Elway	4.00	10.00
M3 Dan Marino	4.00	10.00
M4 Peyton Manning	4.00	10.00
M5 Barry Sanders	4.00	10.00
M6 Emmitt Smith	2.50	6.00
M7 Randy Moss	4.00	10.00
M8 Jake Plummer	.75	2.00
M9 Cris Carter	1.25	3.00
M10 Brett Favre	4.00	10.00
M11 Drew Bledsoe	1.50	4.00
M12 Charlie Batch	1.25	3.00
M13 Curtis Martin	1.25	3.00
M14 Mark Brunell	1.25	3.00
M15 Jamal Anderson	1.25	3.00

1999 Collector's Edge Supreme PSA Series

COMPLETE SET (10)	40.00	80.00
1/2/8/9 ANNOUNCED PRINT RUN 100		
3/4/10 ANNOUNCED PRINT RUN 2000		
5/6/7 ANNOUNCED PRINT RUN 700		
1 Champ Bailey/100*	5.00	12.00
2 David Boston/100*	3.00	8.00
3 Tim Couch/2000*	1.50	4.00
4 Daunte Culpepper/2000*	2.50	6.00
5 Troy Edwards/700*	2.00	5.00
6 Torry Holt/700*	4.00	10.00
7 Edgerrin James/700*	5.00	12.00
8 Donovan McNabb/100*	10.00	25.00
9 Akili Smith/100*	3.00	8.00
10 Ricky Williams/2000*	2.00	5.00

1999 Collector's Edge Supreme Route XXXIII

COMPLETE SET (10)	25.00	50.00
STATED PRINT RUN 1000 SERIAL #'d SETS		
R1 Randy Moss	5.00	12.00
R2 Jamal Anderson	1.50	4.00
R3 Jake Plummer	1.00	2.50
R4 Steve Young	2.00	5.00
R5 Fred Taylor	1.50	4.00
R6 Dan Marino	5.00	12.00
R7 Keyshawn Johnson	1.50	4.00
R8 Curtis Martin	1.50	4.00
R9 John Elway	5.00	12.00
R10 Terrell Davis	1.50	4.00

1999 Collector's Edge Supreme Supremacy

COMPLETE SET (5)	15.00	30.00
STATED PRINT RUN 500 SERIAL #'d SETS		
P2 Terrell Davis PREVIEW	.75	2.00
S1 John Elway	7.50	20.00
S2 Terrell Davis	1.50	4.00
S3 Ed McCaffrey	1.50	4.00
S4 Jamal Anderson	1.50	4.00
S5 Chris Chandler	1.50	4.00

1999 Collector's Edge Supreme T3

COMPLETE SET (30)	50.00	100.00
QB STATED ODDS 1:24		
RB STATED ODDS 1:12		
T1 Doug Flutie	1.50	4.00
T2 Troy Aikman	3.00	8.00
T3 John Elway	5.00	12.00
T4 Jake Plummer	1.50	4.00
T5 Brett Favre	5.00	12.00
T6 Mark Brunell	1.50	4.00
T7 Peyton Manning	5.00	12.00
T8 Dan Marino	5.00	12.00
T9 Drew Bledsoe	2.00	5.00
T10 Steve Young	2.00	5.00
T11 Jamal Anderson	.75	2.00
T12 Emmitt Smith	2.00	5.00
T13 Terrell Davis	1.50	4.00
T14 Barry Sanders	3.00	8.00
T15 Robert Smith	.50	1.25
T16 Robert Edwards	.50	1.25
T17 Curtis Martin	.75	2.00
T18 Jerome Bettis	.75	2.00
T19 Fred Taylor	1.50	4.00
T20 Eddie George	.75	2.00
T21 Michael Irvin	.60	1.50
T22 Eric Moulds	.60	1.50
T23 Herman Moore	.60	1.50
T24 Reidel Anthony	.40	1.00
T25 Randy Moss	2.00	5.00
T26 Cris Carter	1.50	4.00
T27 Keyshawn Johnson	.60	1.50
T28 Jacquez Green	.40	1.00
T29 Jerry Rice	1.25	3.00
T30 Terrell Owens	.60	1.50

2000 Collector's Edge Supreme Previews

This set was issued to preview the 2000 Collector's Edge Supreme release. Each card is essentially a parallel version of the base Supreme card with the word "Preview" on the cardbacks and the player's initials as the card number.

COMPLETE SET (7)	6.00	15.00
EG Eddie George	.40	1.00
EJ Edgerrin James	.50	1.25
KW Kurt Warner	.75	2.00
MB Mark Brunell	.40	1.00
MF Marshall Faulk	.50	1.25
PM Peyton Manning	1.25	3.00
SD Stephen Davis	.40	1.00

2000 Collector's Edge Supreme

Released as a 190-card set, 2000 Collector's Edge Supreme is composed of 150 veteran cards and 40 short-printed rookie cards, which were sequentially numbered to 2000. Several of the rookies were released as redemption cards with an expiration date of 3/31/2001. Supreme was packaged in 24-pack boxes containing 10 cards each, and carried a suggested retail price of $2.99. Card number 151 was initially intended to be LaVar Arrington who was pulled from production and, reportedly, never released in packs. Instead it was replaced by a redemption card that ultimately turned out to be redeemable for Sylvester Morris. However, a number of copies of the Arrington card made their way into the secondary market years later. Also, card #171

Bill Burke (and the HoloGold parallel) surfaced after Edge ceased football card operations.

COMPLETE SET (190) 30.00 60.00
COMP.FACT.SET (190) 30.00 60.00
COMP.SET w/o SP's (150) 7.50 20.00
151-190 ROOKIE PRINT RUN 2000
1 David Boston .15 .40
2 Adrian Murrell .15 .40
3 Michael Pittman .15 .40
4 Jake Plummer .20 .50
5 Frank Sanders .15 .40
6 Jamal Anderson .20 .50
7 Chris Chandler .20 .50
8 Terance Mathis .15 .40
9 Justin Armour .15 .40
10 Tony Banks .15 .40
11 Qadry Ismail .20 .50
12 Errict Rhett .20 .50
13 Doug Flutie .25 .60
14 Eric Moulds .20 .50
15 Peerless Price .20 .50
16 Andre Reed .25 .60
17 Antowain Smith .20 .50
18 Steve Beuerlein .20 .50
19 Tim Biakabutuka .20 .50
20 Muhsin Muhammad .20 .50
21 Wesley Walls .15 .40
22 Bobby Engram .20 .50
23 Curtis Enis .15 .40
24 Shane Matthews .15 .40
25 Cade McNown .15 .40
26 Jim Miller .15 .40
27 Marcus Robinson .20 .50
28 Corey Dillon .20 .50
29 Carl Pickens .20 .50
30 Darnay Scott .20 .50
31 Akili Smith .15 .40
32 Karim Abdul-Jabbar .15 .40
33 Tim Couch .20 .50
34 Kevin Johnson .15 .40
35 Troy Aikman .40 1.00
36 Michael Irvin .25 .60
37 Rocket Ismail .20 .50
38 Deion Sanders .25 .60
39 Emmitt Smith .60 1.50
40 Terrell Davis .25 .60
41 Olandis Gary .20 .50
42 Brian Griese .20 .50
43 Ed McCaffrey .20 .50
44 Rod Smith .20 .50
45 Charlie Batch .20 .50
46 Germane Crowell .15 .40
47 Greg Hill .15 .40
48 Sedrick Irvin .15 .40
49 Herman Moore .20 .50
50 Johnnie Morton .20 .50
51 Corey Bradford .15 .40
52 Brett Favre .75 2.00
53 Antonio Freeman .20 .50
54 Dorsey Levens .20 .50
55 Bill Schroeder .20 .50
56 E.G. Green .15 .40
57 Marvin Harrison .25 .60
58 Edgerrin James .25 .60
59 Peyton Manning .60 1.50
60 Terrence Wilkins .15 .40
61 Mark Brunell .20 .50
62 Keenan McCardell .20 .50
63 Jimmy Smith .20 .50
64 James Stewart .15 .40
65 Fred Taylor .25 .60
66 Derrick Alexander .15 .40
67 Donnell Bennett .15 .40
68 Mike Cloud .15 .40
69 Tony Gonzalez .25 .60
70 Elvis Grbac .15 .40
71 Damon Huard .20 .50
72 James Johnson .15 .40
73 Rob Konrad .15 .40
74 Dan Marino .75 2.00
75 Tony Martin .20 .50
76 O.J. McDuffie .20 .50
77 Cris Carter .25 .60
78 Daunte Culpepper .20 .50
79 Jeff George .20 .50
80 Randy Moss .25 .60
81 Robert Smith .20 .50
82 Terry Allen .20 .50
83 Drew Bledsoe .25 .60
84 Kevin Faulk .20 .50
85 Terry Glenn .20 .50
86 Shawn Jefferson .15 .40
87 Billy Joe Hobert .15 .40
88 Eddie Kennison .15 .40
89 Billy Joe Tolliver .15 .40
90 Ricky Williams .25 .60
91 Tiki Barber .25 .60
92 Gary Brown .15 .40
93 Kent Graham .15 .40
94 Ike Hilliard .20 .50
95 Amani Toomer .20 .50
96 Wayne Chrebet .20 .50
97 Keyshawn Johnson .20 .50
98 Ray Lucas .15 .40
99 Curtis Martin .25 .60
100 Vinny Testaverde .20 .50
101 Tim Brown .25 .60
102 Rich Gannon .20 .50
103 James Jett .20 .50
104 Napoleon Kaufman .20 .50
105 Tyrone Wheatley .15 .40
106 Charles Johnson .15 .40
107 Donovan McNabb .25 .60
108 Duce Staley .20 .50
109 Jerome Bettis .25 .60
110 Troy Edwards .15 .40
111 Kordell Stewart .20 .50
112 Hines Ward .25 .60
113 Isaac Bruce .25 .60
114 Marshall Faulk .25 .60
115 Az-Zahir Hakim .15 .40
116 Torry Holt .25 .60
117 Kurt Warner .40 1.00
118 Jeff Graham .15 .40
119 Jim Harbaugh .20 .50
120 Freddie Jones .15 .40
121 Natrone Means .20 .50
122 Junior Seau .25 .60
123 Jeff Garcia .20 .50
124 Charlie Garner .20 .50
125 Terrell Owens .25 .60
126 Jerry Rice .50 1.25
127 Steve Young .30 .75
128 Sean Dawkins .15 .40
129 Joey Galloway .20 .50
130 Jon Kitna .20 .50
131 Derrick Mayes .15 .40
132 Ricky Watters .20 .50
133 Mike Alstott .25 .60
134 Reidel Anthony .15 .40
135 Trent Dilfer .20 .50
136 Warrick Dunn .20 .50
137 Jacquez Green .15 .40
138 Shaun King .15 .40
139 Kevin Dyson .20 .50
140 Eddie George .20 .50
141 Jevon Kearse .20 .50
142 Steve McNair .25 .60
143 Yancey Thigpen .15 .40
144 Champ Bailey .20 .50
145 Albert Connell .15 .40
146 Stephen Davis .20 .50
147 Brad Johnson .20 .50
148 Michael Westbrook .15 .40
149 Checklist .15 .40
150 Checklist .15 .40
151 Sylvester Morris RC 1.00 2.50
(issued via redemption)
151B LaVar Arrington SP 20.00 50.00
152 Peter Warrick RC 1.50 4.00
153 Chad Pennington RC 2.50 6.00
154 Courtney Brown RC 1.25 3.00
155 Thomas Jones RC 2.00 5.00
156 Chris Redman RC 1.25 3.00
157 R.Jay Soward RC 1.00 2.50
158 Jamal Lewis RC 1.50 4.00
159 Shaun Alexander RC 2.00 5.00
160 Travis Taylor RC 1.25 3.00
161 Ron Dayne RC 1.50 4.00
162 Travis Prentice RC 1.25 3.00
163 Plaxico Burress RC 1.50 4.00
164 J.R. Redmond RC 1.00 2.50
165 Sherrod Gideon RC 1.00 2.50
166 Dez White RC 1.25 3.00
167 Chafie Fields RC 1.00 2.50
168 Brandon Short RC 1.00 2.50
(issued via redemption)
169 Reuben Droughns RC 1.50 4.00
170 Trung Canidate RC 1.25 3.00
171 Keith Bulluck RC 1.25 3.00
(issued via redemption)
171B Bill Burke 2.50 6.00
172 Doug Johnson RC 1.25 3.00
(issued via redemption)
173 Shyrone Stith RC 1.00 2.50
174 Michael Wiley RC 1.00 2.50
175 Bubba Franks RC 1.50 4.00
176 Tom Brady RC 20.00 50.00
177 Anthony Lucas RC 1.00 2.50
178 Danny Farmer RC 1.00 2.50
179 Rob Morris RC 1.25 3.00
180 Dennis Northcutt RC 1.25 3.00
181 Troy Walters RC 1.00 2.50
182 Giovanni Carmazzi RC 1.00 2.50
183 Tee Martin RC 1.50 4.00
184 Joe Hamilton RC 1.00 2.50
185 Tim Rattay RC 1.25 3.00
186 Sebastian Janikowski RC 1.50 4.00
187 Na'il Diggs RC 1.00 2.50
188 Todd Husak RC 1.00 2.50
(issued via redemption)
189 Jerry Porter RC 1.50 4.00
190 Brian Urlacher RC 6.00 15.00
59A P.Manning AUTO/300 50.00 100.00

2000 Collector's Edge Supreme Hologold

*1-150 VETS: 4X TO 10X BASIC CARDS
1-150 VETERAN PRINT RUN 200
*151-290 ROOKIE/20: 2X TO 5X
151-190 ROOKIE PRINT RUN 20
*151-290 ROOKIE NOT #'d: .8X TO 2X
59 Peyton Manning AUTO/200 50.00 100.00
176 Tom Brady 250.00 500.00

2000 Collector's Edge Supreme EdgeTech

COMPLETE SET (50) 300.00 600.00
STATED PRINT RUN 100 SER.#'d SETS
*PREVIEWS: .2X TO .5X BASIC INSERTS
ET1 Doug Flutie 4.00 10.00
ET2 Cade McNown 2.50 6.00
ET3 Akili Smith 2.50 6.00
ET4 Tim Couch 3.00 8.00
ET5 Kevin Johnson 2.50 6.00
ET6 Troy Aikman 6.00 15.00
ET7 Emmitt Smith 10.00 25.00
ET8 Terrell Davis 4.00 10.00
ET9 Brett Favre 12.00 30.00
ET10 Marvin Harrison 4.00 10.00
ET11 Edgerrin James 4.00 10.00
ET12 Peyton Manning 10.00 25.00
ET12AU Peyton Manning AUTO 90.00 150.00
ET13 Mark Brunell 3.00 8.00
ET14 Dan Marino 12.00 30.00
ET15 Randy Moss 4.00 10.00
ET16 Drew Bledsoe 4.00 10.00
ET17 Ricky Williams 4.00 10.00
ET18 Keyshawn Johnson 3.00 8.00
ET19 Curtis Martin 4.00 10.00
ET20 Donovan McNabb 4.00 10.00
ET21 Marshall Faulk 4.00 10.00
ET22 Torry Holt 4.00 10.00
ET23 Kurt Warner 6.00 15.00
ET24 Jerry Rice 8.00 20.00
ET25 Steve Young 5.00 12.00
ET26 Jon Kitna 3.00 8.00
ET27 Shaun King 2.50 6.00
ET28 Eddie George 3.00 8.00
ET29 Stephen Davis 3.00 8.00
ET30 Brad Johnson 3.00 8.00
ET31 Chad Pennington 4.00 10.00
ET32 Chris Redman 3.00 8.00
ET33 Tim Rattay 3.00 8.00
ET34 Tee Martin 4.00 10.00
ET35 Thomas Jones 3.00 8.00
ET36 Ron Dayne 4.00 10.00
ET37 Jamal Lewis 2.50 6.00
ET38 J.R. Redmond 2.50 6.00
ET39 Travis Prentice 3.00 8.00
ET40 Shaun Alexander 3.00 8.00
ET41 Michael Wiley 2.50 6.00
ET42 Shyrone Stith 2.50 6.00
ET43 Peter Warrick 4.00 10.00
ET44 Plaxico Burress 4.00 10.00
ET45 Travis Taylor 3.00 8.00
ET46 Jerry Porter 4.00 10.00
ET47 R.Jay Soward 2.50 6.00
ET48 Dez White 3.00 8.00
ET49 LaVar Arrington SP 40.00 100.00
ET50 Courtney Brown 3.00 8.00

2000 Collector's Edge Supreme Future

STATED PRINT RUN 100 SER.#'d SETS
SF1 Peter Warrick 4.00 10.00
SF2 Plaxico Burress 4.00 10.00
SF3 R.Jay Soward 2.50 6.00
SF4 Ron Dayne 4.00 10.00
SF5 Thomas Jones 5.00 12.00
SF6 Shaun Alexander 5.00 12.00
SF7 Chad Pennington 6.00 15.00
SF8 Chris Redman 3.00 8.00
SF9 Travis Prentice 3.00 8.00
SF10 Lavar Arrington SP 12.00 30.00

2000 Collector's Edge Supreme Monday Knights

COMPLETE SET (20) 10.00 25.00
STATED ODDS 1:8
MK1 Jake Plummer .50 1.25
MK2 Doug Flutie .60 1.50
MK3 Cade McNown .40 1.00
MK4 Akili Smith .40 1.00
MK5 Tim Couch .50 1.25
MK6 Kevin Johnson .40 1.00
MK7 Troy Aikman 1.00 2.50
MK8 Emmitt Smith 1.50 4.00
MK9 Terrell Davis .60 1.50
MK10 Charlie Batch .50 1.25
MK11 Brett Favre 2.00 5.00
MK12 Cris Carter .60 1.60
MK13 Drew Bledsoe .60 1.50
MK14 Ricky Williams .60 1.50
MK15 Curtis Martin .60 1.50
MK16 Jerry Rice 1.25 3.00
MK17 Jon Kitna .50 1.25
MK18 Shaun King .40 1.00
MK19 Eddie George .50 1.25
MK20 Brad Johnson .50 1.25

2000 Collector's Edge Supreme Pro Signature Authentics

STATED ODDS 1:197
STATED PRINT RUN 10-1450
PM Peyton Manning/1000 Black 40.00 80.00
TC Tim Couch/650 Black 8.00 20.00
CM1 Cade McNown/650 Black 6.00 15.00
CM2 Cade McNown/325 Red 8.00 20.00
DM1 Darnell McDonald/230 Black 5.00 12.00
DM2 Darnell McDonald/40 Blue 8.00 20.00
JJ1 James Johnson/1450 Black 5.00 12.00
JJ2 James Johnson/42 Blue 8.00 20.00
RM1 Randy Moss/150 Blue 40.00 80.00
(not wearing helmet)
RM2 Randy Moss/150 Blue 40.00 80.00
(wearing a helmet)
RW1 Ricky Williams/230 Black 15.00 40.00
RW2 Ricky Williams/39 Blue 25.00 60.00

2000 Collector's Edge Supreme Update

COMPLETE SET (40) 20.00 50.00
*ROOKIE U151-U190: .08X TO .25X BASIC RC
ALL 40 ISSUED IN SUPREME FACT.SET

2000 Collector's Edge Supreme Perfect Ten

COMPLETE SET (10) 50.00 120.00
ANNOUNCED EXCH CARD PRINT RUN 100
1 Peter Warrick 2.50 6.00
2 Plaxico Burress 2.50 6.00
3 R.Jay Soward 1.50 4.00
4 Ron Dayne 2.50 6.00
5 Thomas Jones 3.00 8.00
6 Shaun Alexander 3.00 8.00
7 Chad Pennington 4.00 10.00
8 Chris Redman 2.00 5.00
9 Travis Prentice 2.00 5.00
10 LaVar Arrington 8.00 20.00

2000 Collector's Edge Supreme Route XXXIV

COMPLETE SET (10) 7.50 20.00
STATED ODDS 1:16
R1 Peyton Manning 1.50 4.00
R2 Edgerrin James .60 1.50
R3 Warrick Dunn .50 1.25
R4 Dan Marino 2.00 5.00
R5 Steve McNair .60 1.50
R6 Mark Brunell .50 1.25
R7 Kurt Warner 1.00 2.50
R8 Marshall Faulk .60 1.50
R9 Randy Moss .60 1.50
R10 Stephen Davis .50 1.25

2000 Collector's Edge Supreme Team

COMPLETE SET (20) 12.50 30.00
STATED ODDS 1:8
ST1 Peyton Manning 1.50 4.00
ST2 Kurt Warner 1.00 2.50
ST3 Tim Couch .50 1.25
ST4 Cade McNown .40 1.00
ST5 Akili Smith .40 1.00
ST6 Donovan McNabb .60 1.50
ST7 Edgerrin James .60 1.50
ST8 Stephen Davis .50 1.25
ST9 Mark Brunell .50 1.25
ST10 Brett Favre 2.00 5.00
ST11 Marvin Harrison .60 1.50
ST12 Isaac Bruce .60 1.50
ST13 Terrell Davis .60 1.50
ST14 Ricky Williams .60 1.50
ST15 Keyshawn Johnson .50 1.25
ST16 Randy Moss .60 1.50
ST17 Kevin Johnson .40 1.00
ST18 Torry Holt .60 1.50
ST19 Dan Marino 2.00 5.00
ST20 Troy Aikman 1.00 2.50

2000 Collector's Edge T3 Previews

These cards were issued to preview the 2000 Collector's Edge T3 football set. Each is essentially a parallel to it's base set card but has been numbered according to the player's initials. Each is marked on the backs "Preview XXX/999." Two parallels of the Preview cards were also produced: HoloPlatinum numbered of 500 and HoloRed numbered of 50.

COMPLETE SET (34) 30.00 60.00
*HOLOPLATINUM/500: .5X TO 1.2X BASIC PREVIEWS
*HOLORED/50: 1.2X TO 3X BASIC PREVIEWS
AB Anthony Becht .60 1.50
BU Brian Urlacher 3.00 8.00
CB Courtney Brown .60 1.50
CC Chris Cole .60 1.50
CP Chad Pennington 1.25 3.00
CR Chris Redman .60 1.50
DF Danny Farmer .50 1.25
DJ Doug Johnson .60 1.50
DN Dennis Northcutt .60 1.50
JA John Abraham .75 2.00
JH Joe Hamilton .50 1.25
JJ Jarious Jackson .60 1.50
JL Jamal Lewis .75 2.00
JP Jerry Porter .75 2.00
JR J.R. Redmond .50 1.25
KB Keith Bulluck .60 1.50
MW Michael Wiley .50 1.25
NN Tim Rattay .60 1.50
PB Plaxico Burress .75 2.00
PM Peyton Manning 2.00 5.00
RDA Ron Dayne .75 2.00
RDR Reuben Droughns .75 2.00
RDU Ron Dugans .50 1.25
RJS R.Jay Soward .50 1.25
RS R.Jay Soward .50 1.25
SA Shaun Alexander 1.00 2.50
SE Shaun Ellis .75 2.00
SM Sylvester Morris .50 1.25
TH Todd Husak .50 1.25
TJ Thomas Jones 1.00 2.50
TM Tee Martin .75 2.00
TP Travis Prentice .60 1.50
TT Travis Taylor .60 1.50
TW Troy Walters .50 1.25

2000 Collector's Edge T3

This 225-card set features enhanced gold foil printing on the front of white card stock. The left side of the card has a yellow border with blue spots. Prospect cards, 151-225, are sequentially numbered to 999. T3 was packaged in 20-pack boxes with packs containing five cards each.

COMP.SET w/o SP's (150) 12.50 30.00
151-225 ROOKIE PRINT RUN 999
1 David Boston .20 .50
2 Rob Moore .20 .50
3 Michael Pittman .20 .50
4 Jake Plummer .25 .60
5 Frank Sanders .20 .50
6 Jamal Anderson .25 .60
7 Chris Chandler .25 .60
8 Tim Dwight .25 .60
9 Shawn Jefferson .20 .50
10 Terance Mathis .20 .50
11 Tony Banks .20 .50
12 Priest Holmes .30 .75
13 Qadry Ismail .25 .60
14 Shannon Sharpe .30 .75
15 Doug Flutie .30 .75
16 Rob Johnson .25 .60
17 Eric Moulds .25 .00
18 Peerless Price .25 .60
19 Antowain Smith .25 .60
20 Steve Beuerlein .25 .60
21 Tim Biakabutuka .25 .60
22 Muhsin Muhammad .25 .60
23 Patrick Jeffers .25 .80
24 Wesley Walls .20 .50
25 Bobby Engram .25 .60
26 Curtis Enis .20 .50
27 Cade McNown .20 .50
28 Marcus Robinson .25 .60
29 Corey Dillon .25 .60
30 Carl Pickens .25 .60
31 Darnay Scott .25 .60
32 Akili Smith .20 .50
33 Tim Couch .25 .60
34 Kevin Johnson .20 .50
35 Errict Rhett .25 .60
36 Troy Aikman .50 1.25
37 Joey Galloway .25 .60
38 Rocket Ismail .25 .60
39 Emmitt Smith .75 2.00
40 Chris Warren .20 .50
41 Terrell Davis .30 .75
42 Olandis Gary .25 .60
43 Brian Griese .25 .60
44 Ed McCaffrey .25 .60
45 Rod Smith .25 .60
46 Charlie Batch .25 .60
47 Germane Crowell .20 .50
48 Sedrick Irvin .20 .50
49 Herman Moore .25 .60
50 Johnnie Morton .25 .60
51 James Stewart .20 .50
52 Brett Favre 1.00 2.50
53 Antonio Freeman .25 .60
54 Dorsey Levens .25 .60
55 Bill Schroeder .25 .60
56 Ken Dilger .20 .50
57 Marvin Harrison .30 .75
58 Edgerrin James .30 .75
59 Peyton Manning .75 2.00
60 Terrence Wilkins .20 .50
61 Mark Brunell .25 .60
62 Keenan McCardell .25 .60
63 Jimmy Smith .25 .60
64 Fred Taylor .30 .75
65 Derrick Alexander .20 .50
66 Donnell Bennett .20 .50
67 Mike Cloud .20 .50
68 Tony Gonzalez .30 .75
69 Elvis Grbac .20 .50
70 Tony Richardson RC .25 .60
71 Damon Huard .25 .60
72 James Johnson .20 .50
73 Rob Konrad .20 .50
74 Tony Martin .25 .60
75 O.J. McDuffie .25 .60
76 Cris Carter .30 .75
77 Daunte Culpepper .25 .60
78 Randy Moss .30 .75
79 Robert Smith .25 .60
80 Drew Bledsoe .30 .75
81 Kevin Faulk .25 .60
82 Terry Glenn .25 .60
83 Willie McGinest .25 .60
84 Tony Simmons .20 .50
85 Jeff Blake .25 .60
86 Jake Reed .25 .60
87 Ricky Williams .30 .75
88 Kerry Collins .25 .60
89 Ike Hilliard .25 .60
90 Joe Montgomery .20 .50
91 Amani Toomer .25 .60
92 Wayne Chrebet .25 .60
93 Ray Lucas .20 .50
94 Curtis Martin .30 .75
95 Vinny Testaverde .25 .60
96 Tim Brown .30 .75
97 Rich Gannon .25 .60
98 James Jett .25 .60
99 Napoleon Kaufman .25 .60
100 Tyrone Wheatley .20 .50
101 Charles Woodson .30 .75
102 Charles Johnson .20 .50
103 Donovan McNabb .30 .75
104 Duce Staley .25 .60
105 Jerome Bettis .30 .75
106 Troy Edwards .20 .50
107 Kent Graham .20 .50
108 Kordell Stewart .25 .60
109 Hines Ward .30 .75
110 Isaac Bruce .30 .75
111 Kevin Carter .20 .50
112 Marshall Faulk .30 .75
113 Trent Green .25 .60
114 Az-Zahir Hakim .20 .50
115 Torry Holt .30 .75
116 Kurt Warner .50 1.25
117 Curtis Conway .25 .60
118 Jermaine Fazande .20 .50
119 Jeff Graham .20 .50
120 Jim Harbaugh .25 .60
121 Junior Seau .30 .75
122 Jeff Garcia .25 *.60
123 Charlie Garner .25 .60
124 Garrison Hearst .20 .50
125 Terrell Owens .30 .75
126 Jerry Rice .60 1.50
127 Steve Young .40 1.00
128 Sean Dawkins .20 .50
129 Jon Kitna .25 .60
130 Derrick Mayes .20 .50
131 Ricky Watters .25 .60
132 Mike Alstott .30 .75
133 Warrick Dunn .25 .60
134 Jacquez Green .20 .50
135 Keyshawn Johnson .25 .60
136 Shaun King .20 .50
137 Warren Sapp .25 .60
138 Kevin Dyson .25 .60
139 Eddie George .25 .60
140 Jevon Kearse .25 .60
141 Steve McNair .30 .75
142 Yancey Thigpen .20 .50
143 Frank Wycheck .25 .60
144 Champ Bailey .25 .60
145 Larry Centers .20 .50
146 Albert Connell .20 .50
147 Stephen Davis .25 .60
148 Jeff George .25 .60
149 Brad Johnson .25 .60
150 Michael Westbrook .20 .50
151 Thomas Jones RC 3.00 8.00
152 Doug Johnson RC 2.00 5.00
153 Mareno Philyaw RC 1.50 4.00
154 Jamal Lewis RC 2.50 6.00
155 Chris Redman RC 2.00 5.00
156 Travis Taylor RC 2.00 5.00
157 Kwame Cavil RC 1.50 4.00
158 Sammy Morris RC 2.00 5.00
159 Doon Grant RC 1.50 4.00
160 Frank Murphy RC 1.50 4.00
161 Brian Urlacher RC 10.00 25.00
162 Dez White RC 2.00 5.00
163 Ron Dugans RC 1.50 4.00
164 Curtis Keaton RC 1.50 4.00
165 Peter Warrick RC 2.50 6.00
166 Courtney Brown RC 2.00 5.00
167 JaJuan Dawson RC 1.50 4.00
168 Dennis Northcutt RC 2.00 5.00
169 Travis Prentice RC 2.00 5.00
170 Michael Wiley RC 1.50 4.00
171 Mike Anderson RC 2.50 6.00
172 Chris Cole RC 2.00 5.00
173 Jarious Jackson RC 2.00 5.00
174 Deltha O'Neal RC 2.00 5.00
175 Reuben Droughns RC 2.50 6.00
176 Na'il Diggs RC 1.50 4.00
177 Bubba Franks RC 2.50 6.00
178 Anthony Lucas RC 1.50 4.00
179 Rondell Mealey RC 1.50 4.00
180 Dan Kendra RC 1.50 4.00
181 Rob Morris RC 2.00 5.00
182 R.Jay Soward RC 1.50 4.00
183 Shyrone Stith RC 1.50 4.00
184 William Bartee RC 1.50 4.00
185 Frank Moreau RC 1.50 4.00
186 Sylvester Morris RC 1.50 4.00
187 Deon Dyer RC 1.50 4.00
188 Quinton Spotwood RC 1.50 4.00
189 Doug Chapman RC 1.50 4.00
190 Troy Walters RC 1.50 4.00
191 J.R. Redmond RC 1.50 4.00
192 Marc Bulger RC 2.50 6.00
193 Sherrod Gideon RC 1.50 4.00
194 Darren Howard RC 1.50 4.00
195 Chad Morton RC 2.50 6.00
196 Terrelle Smith RC 1.50 4.00
197 Ron Dayne RC 2.50 6.00
198 John Abraham RC 2.50 6.00
199 Anthony Becht RC 2.00 5.00
200 Laveranues Coles RC 2.50 6.00
201 Shaun Ellis RC 2.50 6.00
202 Chad Pennington RC 4.00 10.00
203 Sebastian Janikowski RC 2.50 6.00
204 Jerry Porter RC 2.50 6.00
205 Todd Pinkston RC 1.50 4.00
206 Corey Simon RC 2.00 5.00
207 Plaxico Burress RC 2.50 6.00
208 Danny Farmer RC 1.50 4.00
209 Tee Martin RC 2.50 6.00
210 Hank Poteat RC 1.50 4.00
211 Trung Canidate RC 2.00 5.00
212 Jacoby Shepherd RC 1.50 4.00
213 Trevor Gaylor RC 1.50 4.00
214 Giovanni Carmazzi RC 1.50 4.00
215 John Engelberger RC 1.50 4.00
216 Chafie Fields RC 1.50 4.00
217 Julian Peterson RC 2.50 6.00
218 Ahmed Plummer RC 1.50 4.00
219 Tim Rattay RC 2.00 5.00
220 Shaun Alexander RC 3.00 8.00
221 Joe Hamilton RC 1.50 4.00
222 Keith Bulluck RC 2.00 5.00
223 Erron Kinney RC 1.50 4.00
224 Todd Husak RC 1.50 4.00
225 Chris Samuels RC 2.00 5.00

2000 Collector's Edge T3 HoloPlatinum

*VETS 1-150: 2X TO 5X BASIC CARDS
*ROOKIE 151-225: .25X TO .6X
PLATINUM PRINT RUN 500 SER.#'d SETS

2000 Collector's Edge T3 HoloRed

*VETS 1-150: 6X TO 15X BASIC CARDS
*ROOKIES 151-225: .8X TO 2X
RED PRINT RUN 50 SER.#'d SETS

2000 Collector's Edge T3 Retail

COMPLETE SET (225) 40.00 80.00
*RET.VETS 1-150: .3X TO .8X HOBBY
*RET.ROOKIE 151-225: .08X TO .2X HOB

2000 Collector's Edge T3 Adrenaline

COMPLETE SET (20) 10.00 25.00
STATED ODDS 1:10
A1 Doug Flutie .60 1.50
A2 Troy Aikman 1.00 2.50
A3 Emmitt Smith 1.50 4.00
A4 Terrell Davis .60 1.50
A5 Brett Favre 2.00 5.00
A6 Mark Brunell .50 1.25
A7 Fred Taylor .60 1.50
A8 Daunte Culpepper .50 1.25
A9 Drew Bledsoe .60 1.50
A10 Donovan McNabb .60 1.50
A11 Troy Edwards .40 1.00
A12 Isaac Bruce .60 1.50
A13 Marshall Faulk .60 1.50
A14 Jerry Rice 1.25 3.00
A15 Jon Kitna .50 1.25
A16 Shaun King .40 1.00
A17 Keyshawn Johnson .50 1.25
A18 Eddie George .50 1.25
A19 Steve McNair .60 1.50
A20 Stephen Davis .50 1.25

2000 Collector's Edge T3 EdgeQuest

COMPLETE SET (25) 30.00 60.00
STATED PRINT RUN 1000 SER.#'d SETS
EQ1 Marcus Robinson .75 2.00
EQ2 Kevin Johnson .60 1.50
EQ3 Randy Moss 1.00 2.50
EQ4 Troy Edwards .60 1.50
EQ5 Torry Holt 1.00 2.50
EQ6 Keyshawn Johnson .75 2.00
EQ7 Emmitt Smith 2.50 6.00
EQ8 Terrell Davis 1.00 2.50
EQ9 Edgerrin James 1.00 2.50
EQ10 Fred Taylor 1.00 2.50
EQ11 Ricky Williams 1.00 2.50
EQ12 Curtis Martin 1.00 2.50
EQ13 Marshall Faulk 1.00 2.50
EQ14 Eddie George .75 2.00
EQ15 Stephen Davis .75 2.00
EQ16 Cade McNown .60 1.50
EQ17 Akili Smith .60 1.50
EQ18 Tim Couch .75 2.00
EQ19 Brett Favre 3.00 8.00
EQ20 Peyton Manning 2.50 6.00
EQ21 Daunte Culpepper .75 2.00
EQ22 Donovan McNabb 1.00 2.50
EQ23 Kurt Warner 1.50 4.00
EQ24 Jon Kitna .75 2.00
EQ25 Shaun King .60 1.50

2000 Collector's Edge T3 Future Legends

COMPLETE SET (20) 6.00 15.00
STATED ODDS 1:10
FL1 Thomas Jones .60 1.50
FL2 Jamal Lewis .50 1.25
FL3 Travis Taylor .40 1.00
FL4 Peter Warrick .50 1.25
FL5 Ron Dayne .50 1.25
FL6 Chad Pennington .75 2.00
FL7 Plaxico Burress .50 1.25
FL8 Bubba Franks .50 1.25
FL9 Shaun Alexander .60 1.50
FL10 Sylvester Morris .30 .75
FL11 Laveranues Coles .50 1.25
FL12 Jerry Porter .50 1.25
FL13 Todd Pinkston .30 .75
FL14 Dennis Northcutt .40 1.00
FL15 Travis Prentice .40 1.00
FL16 R.Jay Soward .30 .75
FL17 Chris Redman .40 1.00
FL18 Trung Canidate .40 1.00
FL19 Dez White .40 1.00
FL20 J.R. Redmond .30 .75

2000 Collector's Edge T3 JerseyBacks

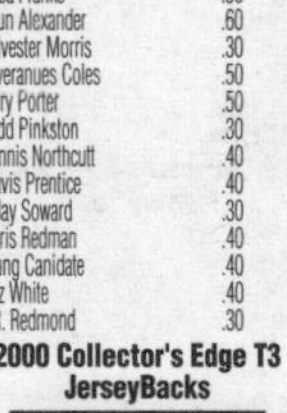

STATED PRINT RUN 20 SER.#'d SETS
CP Chad Pennington 75.00 150.00
JL Jamal Lewis 25.00 60.00
PB Plaxico Burress 25.00 60.00
PW Peter Warrick 25.00 60.00
RD Ron Dayne 25.00 60.00
RS R.Jay Soward
SA Shaun Alexander 50.00 120.00
SM Sylvester Morris 15.00 40.00
TJ Thomas Jones 30.00 80.00
TT Travis Taylor 20.00 50.00

2000 Collector's Edge T3 LeatherBacks

STATED PRINT RUN 12 SER.#'d SETS
AS Akili Smith 20.00 50.00
BF Brett Favre 100.00 200.00
CM Cade McNown
DM Donovan McNabb 40.00 100.00
EG Eddie George 25.00 60.00
EJ Edgerrin James 30.00 80.00
ES Emmitt Smith 75.00 150.00
JK Jon Kitna 25.00 60.00
KW Kurt Warner 40.00 100.00
MR Marcus Robinson 25.00 60.00
PM Peyton Manning 100.00 200.00
RM Randy Moss 50.00 120.00
RW Ricky Williams 30.00 80.00
SD Stephen Davis 25.00 60.00
SK Shaun King 20.00 50.00
SM Steve McNair 30.00 80.00
TA Troy Aikman 50.00 125.00
TC Tim Couch 25.00 60.00
TD Terrell Davis 30.00 80.00
TH Torry Holt 30.00 80.00

2000 Collector's Edge T3 Heir Force

COMPLETE SET (30) 40.00 80.00
STATED PRINT RUN 1000 SER.#'d SETS
HF1 Thomas Jones .75 2.00
HF2 Jamal Lewis .60 1.50
HF3 Chris Redman .50 1.25
HF4 Travis Taylor .50 1.25
HF5 Brian Urlacher 2.50 6.00
HF6 Dez White .50 1.25
HF7 Ron Dugans .40 1.00
HF8 Curtis Keaton .40 1.00
HF9 Peter Warrick .60 1.50
HF10 Courtney Brown .50 1.25
HF11 Dennis Northcutt .50 1.25
HF12 Travis Prentice .75 2.00
HF13 Reuben Droughns .60 1.50
HF14 Bubba Franks .60 1.50
HF15 R.Jay Soward .40 1.00
HF16 Sylvester Morris .40 1.00
HF17 J.R. Redmond .40 1.00
HF18 Ron Dayne .60 1.50
HF19 Anthony Becht .50 1.25
HF20 Laveranues Coles .60 1.50
HF21 Chad Pennington 1.00 2.50
HF22 Jerry Porter .60 1.50
HF23 Todd Pinkston .40 1.00
HF24 Corey Simon .50 1.25
HF25 Plaxico Burress .60 1.50
HF26 Danny Farmer .40 1.00
HF27 Tee Martin .60 1.50
HF28 Trung Canidate .50 1.25
HF29 Shaun Alexander .75 2.00
HF30 Joe Hamilton .40 1.00

2000 Collector's Edge T3 Overture

COMPLETE SET (10) 10.00 20.00
STATED ODDS 1:20
O1 Cade McNown .40 1.00
O2 Akili Smith .40 1.00
O3 Tim Couch .50 1.25
O4 Edgerrin James .60 1.50
O5 Peyton Manning 1.50 4.00
O6 Daunte Culpepper .50 1.25
O7 Randy Moss .60 1.50
O8 Ricky Williams .60 1.50
O9 Torry Holt .60 1.50
O10 Kurt Warner 1.00 2.50

2000 Collector's Edge T3 Rookie Excalibur

COMPLETE SET (20) 30.00 60.00
STATED PRINT RUN 1000 SER.#'d SETS
RE1 Thomas Jones 1.25 3.00
RE2 Jamal Lewis 1.00 2.50
RE3 Chris Redman .75 2.00
RE4 Travis Taylor .75 2.00
RE5 Dez White .75 2.00
RE6 Peter Warrick 1.00 2.50
RE7 Dennis Northcutt .75 2.00
RE8 Travis Prentice .75 2.00
RE9 R.Jay Soward .60 1.50
RE10 Sylvester Morris .60 1.50
RE11 Ron Dayne 1.00 2.50
RE12 Chad Pennington 1.50 4.00
RE13 Laveranues Coles 1.00 2.50
RE14 Jerry Porter 1.00 2.50
RE15 Todd Pinkston .60 1.50
RE16 Plaxico Burress 1.00 2.50
RE17 Trung Canidate .75 2.00
RE18 Bubba Franks 1.00 2.50
RE19 Shaun Alexander 1.25 3.00
RE20 J.R. Redmond .60 1.50

2000 Collector's Edge T3 Rookie Ink

OVERALL STATED ODDS 1:99
BLACK INK PRINT RUN 440-1610
*BLUE/24-40: .8X TO 2X BLACK INK
BLUE INK PRINT RUN 24-40
UNPRICED RED INK PRINT RUN 10
CP Chad Pennington Silver/470 15.00 30.00
CR Chris Redman Silver/470 5.00 12.00
GC Giovanni Carmazzi Silver/1455 4.00 10.00
JL Jamal Lewis Silver/485 6.00 15.00
JR1 J.R. Redmond Gold/1610 4.00 10.00
PB Plaxico Burress Silver/440 8.00 20.00
RS R.Jay Soward Silver/1350 4.00 10.00
SM Sylvester Morris Silver/1000 4.00 10.00
TJ Thomas Jones Silver/915 8.00 20.00
PW Peter Warrick No AU 2.00 5.00
TT Travis Taylor Silver No AU 1.50 4.00
JR2 J.R. Redmond Silver No AU

1999 Collector's Edge Triumph Previews

Released early in the year, this set previews the card stock and design of the 1999 Collector's Edge Triumph set. The card numbers feature the player's initials and the word "preview" is printed on the cardbacks.

COMPLETE SET (39) 15.00 30.00
AD Autry Denson .30 .75
AK Andy Katzenmoyer .50 1.25
AS Akili Smith 1.00 2.50
AW Antoine Winfield .30 .75
AZ Amos Zereoue .50 1.25
BH Brock Huard .30 .75
CC2 Cecil Collins .50 1.25
CC1 Chris Claiborne .30 .75
CM2 Cade McNown .75 2.00
CM1 Chris McAlister .50 1.25
DB David Boston .75 2.00
DC Daunte Culpepper 2.50 6.00
DM Donovan McNabb 1.50 4.00
DN Dat Nguyen .50 1.25
EE Ebeneezer Ekuban .50 1.25
EJ Edgerrin James 2.50 6.00
JF Jermaine Fazande .50 1.25
JG Joe Germaine .50 1.25
JJ James Johnson .50 1.25
JM Joe Montgomery .50 1.25
KB Karsten Bailey .30 .75
KF Kevin Faulk .60 1.50
KJ Kevin Johnson .50 1.25
LP Larry Parker .30 .75
MC Mike Cloud .30 .75
MG Martin Gramatica .30 .75
PK Patrick Kerney .50 1.25
PP Peerless Price .50 1.25
RK Rob Konrad .30 .75
RW Ricky Williams 1.00 2.50
SI Sedrick Irvin .30 .75
SK Shaun King .50 1.25
TC Tim Couch 1.50 4.00
TE Troy Edwards .75 2.00
TH Torry Holt 1.00 2.50
CB1 Champ Bailey .60 1.50
CB2 Cuncho Brown .30 .75
DWB D'Wayne Bates .30 .75
JKE Jevon Kearse .75 2.00

1999 Collector's Edge Triumph

Released as a 180-card set, 1999 Collector's Edge Triumph features a single football team in each pack. Packs contain a shortprinted quarterback, a shortprinted rookie, a running back, two receivers, a defensive player, and a kicker.

COMPLETE SET (180)	20.00	50.00
1 Jamal Anderson	.25	.60
2 Jerome Bettis	.30	.75
3 Terrell Davis	.30	.75
4 Corey Dillon	.25	.60
5 Warrick Dunn	.25	.60
6 Marshall Faulk	.30	.75
7 Eddie George	.25	.60
8 Garrison Hearst	.25	.60
9 Skip Hicks	.20	.50
10 Napoleon Kaufman	.20	.50
11 Dorsey Levens	.25	.60
12 Curtis Martin	.30	.75
13 Natrone Means	.25	.60
14 Adrian Murrell	.25	.60
15 Barry Sanders	.75	2.00
16 Antowain Smith	.20	.50
17 Emmitt Smith	.75	2.00
18 Robert Smith	.25	.60
19 Fred Taylor	.25	.60
20 Ricky Watters	.25	.60
21 Cameron Cleeland	.20	.50
22 Ben Coates	.25	.60
23 Shannon Sharpe	.30	.75
24 Frank Wycheck	.25	.60
25 Derrick Alexander WR	.20	.50
26 Reidel Anthony	.20	.50
27 Robert Brooks	.25	.60
28 Tim Brown	.30	.75
29 Cris Carter	.30	.75
30 Wayne Chrebet	.25	.60
31 Curtis Conway	.25	.60
32 Tim Dwight	.25	.60
33 Kevin Dyson	.20	.50
34 Antonio Freeman	.25	.60
35 Joey Galloway	.25	.60
36 Terry Glenn	.25	.60
37 Marvin Harrison	.30	.75
38 Ike Hilliard	.25	.60
39 Michael Irvin	.30	.75
40 Keyshawn Johnson	.25	.60
41 Jermaine Lewis	.20	.50
42 Terance Mathis	.20	.50
43 Ed McCaffrey	.25	.60
44 Keenan McCardell	.25	.60
45 O.J. McDuffie	.25	.60
46 Herman Moore	.25	.60
47 Rob Moore	.20	.50
48 Randy Moss	.30	.75
49 Eric Moulds	.25	.60
50 Muhsin Muhammad	.25	.60
51 Terrell Owens	.30	.75
52 Jerome Pathon	.20	.50
53 Carl Pickens	.25	.60
54 Andre Reed	.30	.75
55 Jake Reed	.25	.60
56 Jerry Rice	.60	1.50
57 Andre Rison	.25	.60
58 Jimmy Smith	.25	.60
59 Rod Smith WR	.25	.60
60 Michael Westbrook	.20	.50
61 Morten Andersen	.20	.50
62 Gary Anderson	.20	.50
63 Doug Brien	.20	.50
64 Chris Boniol	.20	.50
65 John Carney	.20	.50
66 Steve Christie	.20	.50
67 Richie Cunningham	.20	.50
68 Brad Daluiso	.20	.50
69 AL Del Greco	.20	.50
70 Jason Elam	.20	.50
71 John Hall	.20	.50
72 Jason Hanson	.20	.50
73 Mike Hollis	.20	.50
74 Norm Johnson	.20	.50
75 Olindo Mare	.20	.50
76 Doug Pelfrey	.20	.50
77 Wade Richey	.20	.50
78 Pete Stoyanovich	.20	.50
79 Mike Vanderjagt	.20	.50
80 Adam Vinatieri	.30	.75
81 Ray Buchanan	.20	.50
82 Jim Flanigan	.20	.50
83 Darrell Green	.30	.75
84 Kevin Greene	.25	.60
85 Ty Law	.25	.60
86 Ken Norton Jr.	.20	.50
87 John Randle	.25	.60
88 Bill Romanowski	.25	.60
89 Deion Sanders	.30	.75
90 Junior Seau	.30	.75
91 Michael Sinclair	.20	.50
92 Bruce Smith	.30	.75
93 Takeo Spikes	.20	.50
94 Michael Strahan	.25	.60
95 Derrick Thomas	.30	.75
96 Zach Thomas	.30	.75
97 Andre Wadsworth	.20	.50
98 Charles Woodson	.30	.75
99 Checklist Card	.10	.30
100 Checklist Card	.10	.30
101 Troy Aikman	.50	1.25
102 Tony Banks	.25	.60
103 Charlie Batch	.25	.60
104 Steve Beuerlein	.25	.60
105 Jeff Blake	.25	.60
106 Drew Bledsoe	.30	.75
107 Bubby Brister	.20	.50
108 Mark Brunell	.25	.60
109 Chris Chandler	.25	.60
110 Kerry Collins	.25	.60
111 Randall Cunningham	.30	.75
112 Koy Detmer	.20	.50
113 Ty Detmer	.25	.60
114 Trent Dilfer	.25	.60
115 John Elway	1.00	2.50
116 Brett Favre	1.00	2.50
117 Doug Flutie	.30	.75
118 Rich Gannon	.25	.60
119 Jeff Garcia RC	2.00	5.00
120 Jeff George	.20	.50
121 Jon Kitna	.25	.60
122 Elvis Grbac	.20	.50
123 Brian Griese	.25	.60
124 Trent Green	.25	.60
125 Jim Harbaugh	.25	.60
126 Billy Joe Hobert	.20	.50
127 Brad Johnson	.25	.60
128 Rob Johnson	.25	.60
129 Jon Kitna	.25	.60
130 Erik Kramer	.25	.60
131 Ryan Leaf	.25	.60
132 Peyton Manning	1.00	2.50
133 Dan Marino	1.00	2.50
134 Steve McNair	.30	.75
135 Scott Mitchell	.20	.50
136 Warren Moon	.30	.75
137 Jake Plummer	.25	.60
138 Kordell Stewart	.25	.60
139 Vinny Testaverde	.25	.60
140 Steve Young	.40	1.00
141 Champ Bailey RC	1.00	2.50
142 Karsten Bailey RC	.30	.75
143 D'Wayne Bates RC	.30	.75
144 David Boston RC	.40	1.00
145 Cuncho Brown RC	.30	.75
146 Dat Nguyen RC	.50	1.25
147 Chris Claiborne RC	.30	.75
148 Mike Cloud RC	.30	.75
149 Cecil Collins RC	.30	.75
150 Tim Couch RC	.50	1.25
151 Daunte Culpepper RC	.50	1.25
152 Autry Denson RC	.30	.75
153 Troy Edwards RC	.40	1.00
154 Ebenezer Ekuban RC	.30	.75
155 Kevin Faulk RC	.50	1.25
156 Jermaine Fazande RC	.30	.75
157 Joe Germaine RC	.40	1.00
158 Martin Gramatica RC	.30	.75
159 Torry Holt RC	.75	2.00
160 Brock Huard RC	.40	1.00
161 Sedrick Irvin RC	.30	.75
162 Edgerrin James RC	.60	1.50
163 James Johnson RC	.30	.75
164 Kevin Johnson RC	.40	1.00
165 Andy Katzenmoyer RC	.40	1.00
166 Jevon Kearse RC	.50	1.25
167 Patrick Kerney RC	.40	1.00
168 Shaun King RC	.40	1.00
169 Jim Kleinsasser RC	.50	1.25
170 Rob Konrad RC	.30	.75
171 Chris McAlister RC	.40	1.00
172 Donovan McNabb RC	2.50	6.00
173 Cade McNown RC	.40	1.00
174 Joe Montgomery RC	.30	.75
175 Peerless Price RC	.40	1.00
176 Akili Smith RC	.40	1.00
177 Ricky Williams RC	.75	2.00
178 Larry Parker RC	.40	1.00
179 Antoine Winfield RC	.30	.75
180 Amos Zereoue RC	.40	1.00

1999 Collector's Edge Triumph Galvanized

*VETS 1-140: 2X TO 5X BASIC CARDS
*ROOKIES 141-180: 1.5X TO 4X BASIC CARDS
STATED PRINT RUN 500 SER.#'d SETS

1999 Collector's Edge Triumph Commissioner's Choice

COMPLETE SET (10)	25.00	50.00
STATED ODDS 1:15		
*GOLD/500: .8X TO 2X BASIC INSERTS		
CC1 Tim Couch	1.00	2.50
CC2 Donovan McNabb	4.00	10.00
CC3 Cade McNown	1.00	2.50
CC4 Daunte Culpepper	3.00	8.00
CC5 Akili Smith	1.00	2.50
CC6 Ricky Williams	1.50	4.00
CC7 Edgerrin James	3.00	8.00
CC8 Torry Holt	2.00	5.00
CC9 David Boston	1.00	2.50
CC10 Champ Bailey	1.00	2.50

1999 Collector's Edge Triumph Fantasy Team

COMPLETE SET (10)	20.00	40.00
STATED ODDS 1:10		
FT1 Terrell Davis	1.00	2.50
FT2 John Elway	3.00	8.00
FT3 Brett Favre	3.00	8.00
FT4 Peyton Manning	3.00	8.00
FT5 Dan Marino	3.00	8.00
FT6 Randy Moss	2.50	6.00
FT7 Jake Plummer	.60	1.50
FT8 Barry Sanders	3.00	8.00
FT9 Emmitt Smith	2.00	5.00
FT10 Fred Taylor	1.00	2.50

1999 Collector's Edge Triumph Future Fantasy Team

COMPLETE SET (20)	20.00	40.00
STATED ODDS 1:6		
FFT1 Champ Bailey	.60	1.50
FFT2 D'Wayne Bates	.30	.75
FFT3 David Boston	.60	1.50
FFT4 Tim Couch	.60	1.50
FFT5 Daunte Culpepper	2.00	5.00
FFT6 Troy Edwards	.50	1.25
FFT7 Kevin Faulk	.60	1.50
FFT8 Torry Holt	1.25	3.00
FFT9 Brock Huard	.60	1.50
FFT10 Sedrick Irvin	.30	.75
FFT11 Edgerrin James	2.00	5.00
FFT12 James Johnson	.50	1.25
FFT13 Kevin Johnson	.60	1.50
FFT14 Rob Konrad	.50	1.25
FFT15 Donovan McNabb	2.50	6.00
FFT16 Cade McNown	.50	1.25
FFT17 Peerless Price	.60	1.50
FFT18 Akili Smith	.50	1.25
FFT19 Ricky Williams	1.00	2.50
FFT20 Amos Zereoue	.60	1.50

1999 Collector's Edge Triumph Heir Supply

COMPLETE SET (15)	12.50	30.00
STATED ODDS 1:3		
HS1 Ricky Williams	.75	2.00
HS2 Tim Couch	.50	1.25
HS3 Cade McNown	.40	1.00
HS4 Donovan McNabb	2.00	5.00
HS5 Akili Smith	.30	.75
HS6 Daunte Culpepper	1.50	4.00
HS7 Torry Holt	1.00	2.50
HS8 Edgerrin James	1.50	4.00
HS9 David Boston	.50	1.25
HS10 Troy Edwards	.40	1.00
HS11 Peerless Price	.50	1.25
HS12 Champ Bailey	.50	1.25
HS13 D'Wayne Bates	.30	.75
HS14 Kevin Faulk	.50	1.25
HS15 Amos Zereoue	.50	1.25

1999 Collector's Edge Triumph K-Klub Y3K

COMPLETE SET (50)	60.00	120.00
*PREVIEWS: .4X TO 1X BASIC INSERTS		
STATED PRINT RUN 1000 SER.#'d SETS		
KK1 Karim Abdul-Jabbar	1.00	2.50
KK2 Jamal Anderson	1.50	4.00
KK3 Jerome Bettis	1.50	4.00
KK4 Isaac Bruce	1.50	4.00
KK5 Cris Carter	1.50	4.00
KK6 Terrell Davis	1.50	4.00
KK7 Corey Dillon	1.50	4.00
KK8 Warrick Dunn	1.50	4.00
KK9 Curtis Enis	1.50	4.00
KK10 Marshall Faulk	2.00	5.00
KK11 Antonio Freeman	1.50	4.00
KK12 Joey Galloway	1.00	2.50
KK13 Eddie George	1.50	4.00
KK14 Terry Glenn	1.50	4.00
KK15 Garrison Hearst	1.00	2.50
KK16 Keyshawn Johnson	1.50	4.00
KK17 Napoleon Kaufman	1.50	4.00
KK18 Curtis Martin	1.50	4.00
KK19 Rob Moore	.60	1.50
KK20 Herman Moore	1.00	2.50
KK21 Eric Moulds	1.50	4.00
KK22 Randy Moss	4.00	10.00
KK23 Adrian Murrell	.60	1.50
KK24 Carl Pickens	1.00	2.50
KK25 Jerry Rice	3.00	8.00
KK26 Barry Sanders	5.00	12.00
KK27 Antowain Smith	1.50	4.00
KK28 Emmitt Smith	3.00	8.00
KK29 Fred Taylor	1.50	4.00
KK30 Ricky Watters	1.00	2.50
KK31 Troy Aikman	3.00	8.00
KK32 Charlie Batch	1.50	4.00
KK33 Drew Bledsoe	1.50	4.00
KK34 Mark Brunell	1.50	4.00
KK35 Chris Chandler	1.00	2.50
KK36 Randall Cunningham	1.50	4.00
KK37 Trent Dilfer	1.00	2.50
KK38 John Elway	5.00	12.00
KK39 Brett Favre	5.00	12.00
KK40 Doug Flutie	1.50	4.00
KK41 Brad Johnson	1.50	4.00
KK42 Jon Kitna	1.50	4.00
KK43 Ryan Leaf	1.50	4.00
KK44 Peyton Manning	5.00	12.00
KK45 Dan Marino	5.00	12.00
KK46 Steve McNair	1.50	4.00
KK47 Jake Plummer	1.00	2.50
KK48 Kordell Stewart	1.00	2.50
KK49 Vinny Testaverde	1.00	2.50
KK50 Steve Young	2.00	5.00

1999 Collector's Edge Triumph Pack Warriors

COMPLETE SET (15)	15.00	30.00
STATED ODDS 1:4		
PW1 Jamal Anderson	.60	1.50
PW2 Jake Plummer	.40	1.00
PW3 Emmitt Smith	1.25	3.00
PW4 Troy Aikman	1.25	3.00
PW5 Terrell Davis	.60	1.50
PW6 John Elway	2.00	5.00
PW7 Barry Sanders	2.00	5.00
PW8 Brett Favre	2.00	5.00
PW9 Peyton Manning	2.00	5.00
PW10 Dan Marino	2.00	5.00
PW11 Randy Moss	1.50	4.00
PW12 Keyshawn Johnson	.60	1.50
PW13 Fred Taylor	.60	1.50
PW14 Jerry Rice	1.25	3.00
PW15 Jerome Bettis	.60	1.50

1999 Collector's Edge Triumph Signed, Sealed, Delivered

STATED ODDS 1:32		
*BLUE AU/40-50: 1X TO 2.5X BLACK AU		
BLUE INK AUTO PRINT RUN 40-50		
UNPRICED RED INK PRINT RUN 10		
AD Autry Denson	3.00	8.00
AS Akili Smith	3.00	8.00
AW Antoine Winfield	5.00	12.00
AZ Amos Zereoue	3.00	8.00
BH Brock Huard	5.00	12.00
CB Cuncho Brown	2.50	6.00
CB1 Champ Bailey	7.50	20.00
CC Chris Claiborne	2.50	6.00
CC1 Cecil Collins	2.50	6.00
CM Chris McAlister	3.00	8.00
CMN Cade McNown	3.00	8.00
DB David Boston	5.00	12.00
DC Daunte Culpepper	7.50	20.00
DM Donovan McNabb	20.00	40.00
DN Dat Nguyen	5.00	12.00
EE Ebenezer Ekuban	3.00	8.00
EJ Edgerrin James	10.00	25.00
JF Jermaine Fazande	3.00	8.00
JG Joe Germaine	3.00	8.00
JJ James Johnson	3.00	8.00
JK Jevon Kearse	6.00	15.00
JK1 Jim Kleinsasser	5.00	12.00
JM Joe Montgomery	3.00	8.00
KB Karsten Bailey	3.00	8.00
KF Kevin Faulk	5.00	12.00
KJ Kevin Johnson	3.00	8.00
LP Larry Parker	3.00	8.00
MC Mike Cloud	3.00	8.00
MG Martin Gramatica	2.50	6.00
PK Patrick Kerney	3.00	8.00
PP Peerless Price	5.00	12.00
RK Rob Konrad	5.00	12.00
RW Ricky Williams	10.00	25.00
SI Sedrick Irvin	2.50	6.00
SK Shaun King	3.00	8.00
TC Tim Couch	5.00	12.00
TE Troy Edwards	3.00	8.00
TH Torry Holt	10.00	25.00
DWB D'Wayne Bates	3.00	8.00

1948 Colts Matchbooks

These standard sized (1 1/2" by 4 1/2") matchbooks were thought to have been released during the 1948 season. Each was printed in blue ink with a player head shot on gray card stock. Complete covers with matches intact are valued at approximately 1 1/2 times the prices listed below.

COMPLETE SET (10)	800.00	1,200.00
1 Dick Barwegan	90.00	150.00
2 Lamar Davis	75.00	125.00
3 Spiro Dellerba	75.00	125.00
4 Lou Gambino	75.00	125.00
5 Rex Grossman	75.00	125.00
6 Jake Leicht	75.00	125.00
7 Charlie O'Rourke	75.00	125.00
8 Y.A. Tittle	250.00	500.00
9 Sam Vacanti	75.00	125.00
10 Herman Wedemeyer	90.00	150.00

1949 Colts Silber's Bakery

This rare set of cards was issued by Silber's Bakery only in the Baltimore area in 1949 and featured members of the AAFC Baltimore Colts including future Hall of Famer Y.A. Tittle. Each card measures roughly 2 1/4" by 3 1/4" and features a black and white photo on the front with basic vital statistics for the player below the image. "Silber's Trading Cards" appears above the photo. The cardbacks include brief rules to a contest using a letter printed on the cards to spell SILBER'S in exchange for various prizes. The team's home game schedule is also included on the backs. Any additions to this list are appreciated.

1 Dick Barwegan	800.00	1,200.00
2 Hub Bechtol	600.00	1,000.00
3 Ernie Blandin	600.00	1,000.00
4 Lamar Davis	600.00	1,000.00
5 Barry French	600.00	1,000.00
6 Lou Gambino	600.00	1,000.00
7 Dub Garrett	600.00	1,000.00
8 Rex Grossman	600.00	1,000.00
9 Johnny Mellus	600.00	1,000.00
10 Bus Mertes	600.00	1,000.00
11 John North	600.00	1,000.00
12 Charlie O'Rouke	600.00	1,000.00
13 Paul Page	600.00	1,000.00
14 Bob Pfohl	600.00	1,000.00
15 Billy Stone	600.00	1,000.00
16 Y.A. Tittle	2,000.00	3,500.00
17 Sam Vacanti	600.00	1,000.00
18 Win Williams	600.00	1,000.00

1957 Colts Team Issue

These photos were issued around 1957 by the Baltimore Colts. Each features a black and white player photo with the player's name and team name in a white box near the picture. They measure approximately 8" by 10 1/4" and are blankbacked and unnumbered. Any additions to this list are welcomed.

COMPLETE SET (7)	50.00	100.00
1 Alan Ameche	10.00	20.00
2 L.G. Dupre	7.50	15.00
3 Bill Pellington	7.50	15.00
4 Bert Rechichar	7.50	15.00
5 George Shaw	7.50	15.00
6 Art Spinney	7.50	15.00
7 Carl Taseff	7.50	15.00

1958-60 Colts Team Issue

This set of photos was likely issued over a number of years by the Baltimore Colts. Each card features a black and white player photo with just the player's name and team name below the picture. They measure approximately 8" by 10 1/4" and are blankbacked and unnumbered. There are two known Johnny Unitas photo variations. Any additions to this list are welcomed.

COMPLETE SET (41)	400.00	700.00
1 Alan Ameche	10.00	20.00
2 Raymond Berry	18.00	30.00
3 Ordell Braase	7.50	15.00
4 Ray Brown	7.50	15.00
5 Milt Davis	7.50	15.00
6 Art DeCarlo	7.50	15.00
7 Art Donovan	15.00	25.00
8 L.G. Dupre	7.50	15.00
9 Weeb Ewbank CO	10.00	20.00
10 Alex Hawkins	7.50	15.00
11 Don Joyce	7.50	15.00
12 Ray Krouse	7.50	15.00
13 Harold Lewis	7.50	15.00
14 Gene Lipscomb	10.00	20.00
15 Gino Marchetti	15.00	25.00
16 Marv Matuszak	7.50	15.00
17 Lenny Moore	18.00	30.00
18 Jim Mutscheller	7.50	15.00
19 Steve Myhra	7.50	15.00
20 Andy Nelson	7.50	15.00
21 Buzz Nutter	7.50	15.00
22 Jim Parker	15.00	25.00
23 Bill Pellington	7.50	15.00
24 Sherman Plunkett	7.50	15.00
25 George Preas	7.50	15.00
26 Billy Pricer	7.50	15.00
27 Palmer Pyle	7.50	15.00
28 Bert Rechichar	7.50	15.00
29 Jerry Richardson	7.50	15.00
30 Johnny Sample	7.50	15.00
31 Alex Sandusky	7.50	15.00
32 Dave Sherer	7.50	15.00
33 Don Shinnick	7.50	15.00
34 Jackie Simpson	7.50	15.00
35 Art Spinney	7.50	15.00
36 Dick Szymanski	7.50	15.00
37 Carl Taseff	7.50	15.00
38A Johnny Unitas	40.00	75.00
(jump pass pose)		
38B Johnny Unitas	40.00	75.00
(dropping back to pass)		
39 Jim Welch	7.50	15.00
40 1958 Team Picture	30.00	50.00

1960 Colts Jay Publishing

This 12-card photo set features 5" by 7" black-and-white photos of Baltimore Colts players. The photos show players in traditional posed action shots and were originally packaged 12 to a set. Sets sold primarily through Jay Publishing's Pro Football Yearbook in 1960 and originally sold for 25-cents. The backs are blank. The cards are unnumbered and checklisted below in alphabetical order.

COMPLETE SET (12)	75.00	135.00
1 Alan Ameche	6.00	12.00
2 Raymond Berry	7.50	15.00
3 Art Donovan	6.00	12.00
4 Don Joyce	5.00	10.00
5 Gene Lipscomb	6.00	12.00
6 Gino Marchetti	6.00	12.00
7 Lenny Moore	7.50	15.00
8 Jim Mutscheller	5.00	10.00
9 Steve Myhra	5.00	10.00
10 Jim Parker	6.00	12.00
11 Bill Pellington	5.00	10.00
12 Johnny Unitas	15.00	30.00

1961 Colts Jay Publishing

This 12-card set features (approximately) 5" by 7" black-and-white player photos. The photos show players in traditional poses with the quarterback preparing to throw, the runner heading downfield, and the defenseman ready for the tackle. These cards were packaged 12 to a packet and originally sold for 25 cents. The backs are blank. The cards are unnumbered and checklisted below in alphabetical order.

COMPLETE SET (12)	75.00	135.00
1 Raymond Berry	7.50	15.00
2 Art Donovan	6.00	12.00
3 Weeb Ewbank CO	6.00	12.00
4 Alex Hawkins	5.00	10.00
5 Gino Marchetti	6.00	12.00
6 Lenny Moore	7.50	15.00
7 Jim Mutscheller	5.00	10.00
8 Steve Myhra	5.00	10.00
9 Jimmy Orr	5.00	10.00
10 Jim Parker	6.00	12.00
11 Joe Perry	7.50	15.00
12 Johnny Unitas	15.00	30.00

1963-64 Colts Team Issue

These large photo cards were produced and distributed by the Baltimore Colts. Each photo measures approximately 7 7/8" by 10 1/4" and is black-and-white, blank backed, and printed on glossy heavy paper stock. The player's name appears in bold lettering below the photo with the team name and player's position, height, weight, and college below that. Except for size, these cards are virtually identical to the 1967 and 1968 sets with differences in the photos or text noted below on like players. The cards are unnumbered and checklisted below in alphabetical order. Any additions to this list are appreciated.

COMPLETE SET (34)	250.00	450.00
1 Raymond Berry	12.50	25.00
2 Jackie Burkett	7.50	15.00
(weight listed at 225)		
3 Jim Colvin	7.50	15.00
4 Gary Cuozzo	10.00	20.00
(weight listed at 195)		
5 Wiley Feagin	7.50	15.00
6 Tom Gilburg	7.50	15.00
7 Wendell Harris	7.50	15.00
8 Alex Hawkins	7.50	15.00
(weight 186)		
9 Jerry Hill	7.50	15.00
(position HB)		
10 J.W. Lockett	7.50	15.00
11 Tony Lorick	7.50	15.00
(weight 217, running forward)		
12 Lenny Lyles	7.50	15.00*
(listed as DHB)		
13 Dee Mackey	7.50	15.00
14 John Mackey	10.00	20.00
(weight 217)		
15 Butch Maples	7.50	15.00
16 Lou Michaels	7.50	15.00
17 Fred Miller	7.50	15.00
(hands crossed)		
18 Lenny Moore	12.50	25.00
(listed at 190 lbs.)		
19 Andy Nelson	7.50	15.00
20 Jimmy Orr	7.50	15.00
21 Bill Pellington	7.50	15.00
22 Palmer Pyle	7.50	15.00
23 Alex Sandusky	7.50	15.00
(facing to the side)		
24 Don Shinnick	7.50	15.00
(U.C.L.A. as college)		
25 Don Shula CO	18.00	30.00
26 Billy Ray Smith	7.50	15.00
(weight 235)		
27 Steve Stonebreaker	7.50	15.00
28 Dick Szymanski	7.50	15.00
29 Don Thompson	7.50	15.00
30 Johnny Unitas	25.00	40.00
31 Bob Vogel	7.50	15.00
32 Jim Welch	7.50	15.00
(weight 190)		
33 Butch Wilson	7.50	15.00
(weight 218)		
34 1963 Coaching Staff	10.00	20.00
Don Shula		
Jim Mutscheller		
Charlie Winner		
Bill Pellington		
John Sandusky		
Gino Marchetti		
Don McCafferty		
35 1964 Coaching Staff	10.00	20.00
Don Shula		
Charlie Winner		
Bill Arnsparger		
Dick Bielski		
John Sandusky		
Don McCafferty		

1965 Colts Team Issue

These large photos were produced and distributed by the Baltimore Colts. Each photo measures approximately 7 7/8" by 10" and is black-and-white, blank backed, and printed on heavy glossy stock. The player's name appears in bold lettering below the photo with the team name and player's position, height, weight, and college below that. Except for the slightly smaller size, these photos are virtually identical to the 1963-64 set and exactly the same format as the 1967 and 1968 sets. However, there are noticable differences from one year to the next in terms of the photos or text featured below each photo. We've made note of key changes below on like players from 1965-1968. The cards are unnumbered and checklisted below in alphabetical order.

COMPLETE SET (18)	125.00	250.00
1 Raymond Berry	10.00	20.00
(weight listed at 187)		
2 Bob Boyd	6.00	12.00
(football just touching left hand)		
3 Gary Cuozzo	7.50	15.00
4 Dennis Gaubatz	6.00	12.00
(weight 230)		
5 Jerry Hill	6.00	12.00
(weight 210)		
7 Tony Lorick	6.00	12.00
(weight 215)		
8 John Mackey	7.50	15.00
(weight 217)		
9 Fred Miller	6.00	12.00
(weight 245)		
10 Lenny Moore	10.00	20.00
(weight 190, running forward)		
11 Jimmy Orr	6.00	12.00
(weight 175)		
12 Jim Parker	7.50	15.00
(position listed as T)		
14 Willie Richardson	6.00	12.00
(ball in air, right foot		
over second I in name)		
15 Don Shinnick	6.00	12.00
(weight 235, charging to his		
left, UCLA as college)		
16 Steve Stonebreaker	6.00	12.00
17 Johnny Unitas	25.00	40.00
(dropping back, ball in right hand)		
18 Bob Vogel	6.00	12.00
(cutting to his right)		

1967 Colts Johnny Pro

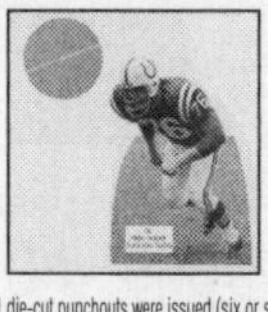

These 41 die-cut punchouts were issued (six or seven per page) in an album which itself measured approximately 11" by 14". Each punchout is approximately 4 1/8" tall and 2 7/8" wide at its base. A stand came with each punchout, and by inserting the punchout in it, the player stood upright. Each punchout consisted of a color player photo against a green grass background. The player's jersey number, name, and position are printed in a white box toward the bottom. The punchouts are unnumbered and checklisted below in alphabetical order.

COMPLETE SET (41)	500.00	850.00
1 Sam Ball	7.50	15.00
2 Raymond Berry	25.00	50.00
3 Bob Boyd	7.50	15.00
4 Ordell Braase	7.50	15.00
5 Barry Brown	7.50	15.00
6 Bill Curry	12.50	25.00
7 Mike Curtis	12.50	25.00
8 Norman Davis	7.50	15.00
9 Jim Detwiler	7.50	15.00
10 Dennis Gaubatz	7.50	15.00
11 Alvin Haymond	7.50	15.00
12 Jerry Hill	7.50	15.00
13 Roy Hilton	10.00	20.00
14 David Lee	7.50	15.00
15 Jerry Logan	10.00	20.00
16 Tony Lorick	10.00	20.00
17 Lenny Lyles	10.00	20.00
18 John Mackey	17.50	35.00
19 Tom Matte	12.50	25.00
20 Lou Michaels	10.00	20.00
21 Fred Miller	7.50	15.00
22 Lenny Moore	25.00	50.00
23 Jimmy Orr	10.00	20.00
24 Jim Parker	17.50	35.00
25 Ray Perkins	10.00	20.00
26 Glenn Ressler	7.50	15.00
27 Willie Richardson	10.00	20.00
28 Don Shinnick	7.50	15.00
29 Billy Ray Smith	10.00	20.00
30 Bubba Smith	20.00	40.00
31 Charlie Stukes	7.50	15.00
32 Andy Stynchula	7.50	15.00
33 Dan Sullivan	7.50	15.00
34 Dick Szymanski	7.50	15.00
35 Johnny Unitas	50.00	100.00
36 Bob Vogel	10.00	20.00
37 Rick Volk	10.00	20.00
38 Bob Wade	7.50	15.00
39 Jim Ward	7.50	15.00
40 Jim Welch	7.50	15.00
41 Butch Wilson	7.50	15.00

1967 Colts Team Issue

These large photos were produced and distributed by the Baltimore Colts in 1967. Each photo measures approximately 7 7/8" by 10" (with a few measuring a slightly larger 10 1/4") and is black-and-white, blank backed, and printed on heavy glossy stock. The player's name appears in bold lettering below the photo with the team name and player's position, height, weight, and college below that. Except for the slightly smaller size on most, these photos are virtually identical to the 1963-64 set and exactly the same format as the 1965 and 1968 sets. However, there are noticable differences from one year to the next in terms of the photos or text featured below each photo. We've made note of key changes below on like players from 1965-1968. The cards are unnumbered and checklisted below in alphabetical order.

COMPLETE SET (44)	200.00	400.00
1 Bob Baldwin	6.00	12.00
2 Sam Ball	6.00	12.00
(small type size)		
3 Raymond Berry	10.00	20.00
(weight listed at 190)		
4 Bob Boyd	6.00	12.00
(football in air)		
5 Jackie Burkett	6.00	12.00
(weight listed at 228)		
6 Gary Cuozzo	6.00	12.00
(weight listed at 198)		
7 Bill Curry	6.00	12.00
(right foot 1/2-inch above		
bottom border)		
8 Mike Curtis	7.50	15.00
(running the ball;		
weight listed at 225)		
9 Norman Davis	6.00	12.00
10 Jim Detwiler	6.00	12.00
11 Dennis Gaubatz	6.00	12.00
(charging to his left;		
weight 232)		
12 Alvin Haymond	6.00	12.00
13 Jerry Hill	6.00	12.00
(weight 215)		
14 Roy Hilton	6.00	12.00
15 David Lee	6.00	12.00
16 Jerry Logan	6.00	12.00
17 Tony Lorick	6.00	12.00
(weight 217, cutting to his right)		
18 Lenny Lyles	6.00	12.00
(DB; right foot on ground)		
19 John Mackey	7.50	15.00
(weight 224; right foot on ground)		
20 Tom Matte	7.50	15.00
(running to his left)		
21 Dale Memmelaar	6.00	12.00
22 Lou Michaels	6.00	12.00
(listed as DE-K)		
23 Fred Miller	6.00	12.00
(charging to his left;		
weight 250)		
24 Lenny Moore	10.00	20.00
(weight 198, catching pass)		
25 Jimmy Orr	6.00	12.00
(weight 185)		
26 Jim Parker	7.50	15.00
(position listed as G)		
27 Ray Perkins	6.00	12.00
28 Glenn Ressler	6.00	12.00
29 Alex Sandusky	6.00	12.00
(facing forward)		
30 Willie Richardson	6.00	12.00
(/(ball in air, right foot		
over E in name)		
31 Don Shinnick	6.00	12.00
(weight 235, charging to his		
right, UCLA as college)		
32 Don Shula CO	15.00	25.00
33 Billy Ray Smith	6.00	12.00
(weight 250; far right tree in		
background slightly cut off)		
34 Bubba Smith	7.50	15.00
(portrait photo)		
35 Andy Stynchula	6.00	12.00
36 Dan Sullivan	6.00	12.00
37 Dick Szymanski	6.00	12.00
(facing left slightly)		
38 Johnny Unitas	18.00	30.00
(set to pass, ball in hands)		
39 Bob Vogel	6.00	12.00
(charging forward)		
40 Rick Volk	6.00	12.00
(portrait photo)		
41 Jim Ward	6.00	12.00
(listed at 190 lbs.)		
42 Jim Welch	6.00	12.00
(weight 196)		
43 Butch Wilson	6.00	12.00
(weight 228)		
44 1967 Coaching Staff	7.50	15.00
Bill Arnsparger		
Don Shula		
Chuck Noll		
Dick Bielski		
John Sandusky		
Ed Rutledge		
Don McCafferty		

1968 Colts Team Issue

These large photos were produced and distributed by the Baltimore Colts in 1968. Each photo measures approximately 8" by 10" and is black-and-white, blank backed, and printed on heavy glossy stock. The player's name appears in bold lettering below the photo with the team name and player's position, height, weight, and college below that. Except for the smaller size, these cards are virtually identical to the 1963-64 set and almost exactly the same format as the 1965 and 1967 sets. However, there are noticable differences from one year to the next in terms of the photos or text featured below each photo. We've made note of key changes below on like players from 1965-1968. The cards are unnumbered and checklisted below in alphabetical order.

COMPLETE SET (30)	200.00	350.00
1 Don Alley	6.00	12.00
2 Ordell Braase	6.00	12.00
3 Timmy Brown	6.00	12.00
4 Terry Cole	6.00	12.00
5 Milo Curtis	7.50	15.00
(weight listed at 232)		
6 Bill Curry	6.00	12.00
(right foot nearly touches bottom border)		
7 Dennis Gaubatz	6.00	12.00
(charging to his right; weight 232)		
8 Alex Hawkins	6.00	12.00
(weight 190)		
9 Jerry Hill	6.00	12.00
(weight 217)		
10 Cornelius Johnson	6.00	12.00
11 Lenny Lyles	6.00	12.00
(DB; left foot on ground)		
12 John Mackey	7.50	15.00
(weight 224; left foot on ground)		
13 Tom Matte	7.50	15.00
(running to his right)		
14 Lou Michaels	6.00	12.00
(listed as DE)		
15 Fred Miller	6.00	12.00
(charging to his right)		
16 Earl Morrall	7.50	15.00
17 Preston Pearson	7.50	15.00
18 Ron Porter	6.00	12.00
19 Willie Richardson	6.00	12.00
(football in hands)		
20 Don Shinnick	6.00	12.00
(listed at 228 lbs.)		
21 Billy Ray Smith	6.00	12.00
(weight 250; far right tree in background fully visible)		
22 Bubba Smith	7.50	15.00
(charging action photo)		
23 Charlie Stukes	6.00	12.00
24 Dick Szymanski	6.00	12.00
(running to his right)		
25 Bob Vogel	6.00	12.00
(cutting to his left)		
26 Rick Volk	6.00	12.00
(running with football)		
27 Jim Ward	6.00	12.00
(listed at 195 lbs.)		
28 John Williams T	6.00	12.00
29 Coaching Staff	7.50	15.00
Bill Arnsparger		
Dick Bielski		
Chuck Noll		
John Sandusky		
Don McCafferty		
Ed Rutledge		
Don Shula		
30 Team Photo	10.00	20.00

1969-70 Colts Team Issue

This set of photos issued by the Colts measure roughly 8" by 10" and feature black and white player images with vital statistics below the photo. Each is blankbacked and features much of the same information as the 1967 and 1968 sets, but presented in much larger text. The player's name can be found with two different sized letters. Unless noted below, all these photos feature a player name with letters that are 3/16" tall. The small names feature letters only 1/8" tall. Any additions to this list are appreciated.

COMPLETE SET (29)	200.00	350.00
1 Ocie Austin	6.00	12.00
2 Sam Ball	6.00	12.00
3 Terry Cole	6.00	12.00
4 Tom Curtis	6.00	12.00
5 Jim Duncan	6.00	12.00
6 Speedy Duncan	6.00	12.00
7 Perry Lee Dunn	6.00	12.00
8 Bob Grant	6.00	12.00
9 Sam Havrilak	6.00	12.00
10 Ted Hendricks	7.50	15.00
11 Jerry Hill	6.00	12.00
12 Ron Kostelnik	6.00	12.00
13 Lenny Lyles	6.00	12.00
14 Tom Matte	7.50	15.00
15 Tom Maxwell	6.00	12.00
16 Lou Michaels	6.00	12.00
17 Fred Miller	6.00	12.00
18 Tom Mitchell	6.00	12.00
19 Earl Morrall	7.50	15.00
20 Jimmy Orr	6.00	12.00
21 Ray Perkins	6.00	12.00
22 Billy Ray Smith	6.00	12.00
23 Bubba Smith	7.50	15.00
24 Charlie Stukes	6.00	12.00
25 Dan Sullivan	6.00	12.00
26A Johnny Unitas Action	15.00	30.00
26B Johnny Unitas Portrait	15.00	30.00
27 Bob Vogel	6.00	12.00
28 Rick Volk	6.00	12.00
29 John Williams	6.00	12.00

1971 Colts Baltimore Sunday Sun Posters

These oversized (roughly 14 1/4" by 21 1/2") posters were to be cut from weekly issues of the Baltimore Sunday Sun newspaper in 1971. Each was printed in color and features typical newsprint pages on the backs. Any additions to this list are appreciated.

COMPLETE SET (17)	100.00	200.00
1 Norm Bulaich	5.00	10.00
2 Mike Curtis	6.00	12.00
3 Jim Duncan	5.00	10.00
4 Ted Hendricks	10.00	20.00
5 Roy Hilton	5.00	10.00
6 Eddie Hinton	5.00	10.00
7 Jerry Logan	5.00	10.00
8 John Mackey	7.50	15.00
9 Tom Matte	6.00	12.00
10 Tom Mitchell	5.00	10.00
11 Earl Morrall	7.50	15.00
12 Jim O'Brien	5.00	10.00
13 Bubba Smith	7.50	15.00
14 Charlie Stukes	5.00	10.00
15 Dan Sullivan	5.00	10.00
16 Bob Vogel	5.00	10.00
17 Rick Volk	5.00	10.00

1971 Colts Jewel Foods

These six color photos are thought to have been released by Jewel Foods in Baltimore. Each measures approximately 7" by 8 3/4" and includes the player's name and team name below the photo. They are blankbacked and unnumbered.

COMPLETE SET (6)	30.00	60.00
1 Norm Bulaich	2.50	5.00
2 Mike Curtis	5.00	10.00
3 Ted Hendricks	6.00	12.00
4 Tom Matte	5.00	10.00
5 Bubba Smith	6.00	12.00
6 Johnny Unitas	12.50	25.00

1971 Colts Team Issue

This set of photos was issued by the Baltimore Colts in 1971. Each photo measures 8" by 10" and includes a black and white player photo on the front with the player's name (printed in large or small letters) and team name below the photo. The photos are blank backed, unnumbered and checklisted below in alphabetical order. Photos in this set are very similar to the 1973 Colts photos except for the smaller font size (measures roughly 1 3/8') used in the team name. They are identical in design to the 1974 set except this year features all players in action photos unless noted below.

COMPLETE SET (10)	50.00	100.00
1 Karl Douglas	5.00	10.00
2 Ted Hendricks	7.50	15.00
(type slightly smaller)		
3 Lonnie Hepburn	5.00	10.00
4 Dennis Nelson	5.00	10.00
(player name in small letters)		
5 Billy Newsome	5.00	10.00
6 Don Nottingham	5.00	10.00
7 Charlie Pittman	5.00	10.00
(portrait)		
8A Bubba Smith	7.50	15.00
(player name in small letters)		
8B Bubba Smith	7.50	15.00
(player name in large letters)		
9 Rick Volk	5.00	10.00

1972 Colts Team Issue

This set of photos was issued by the Baltimore Colts around 1972. Many of these Colts team issue photos were issued over a period of years as players were added to the roster or left the team, therefore the year of issue is an estimate. Each photo in this group is of one of two distinctly different designs or formats. The first style measures 8" by 10" and includes a black and white player photo on the front. Below the photo are: the player's jersey number to the far right, followed by his name and team name printed in large letters. The second style features only the player's name and team name below the photo in small letters resembling that of typewriter type. All of the photos are blank backed, unnumbered and checklisted below in alphabetical order.

COMPLETE SET (20)	100.00	175.00
1 Dick Amman	5.00	10.00
(player's jersey number on left)		
2 Jim Bailey	5.00	10.00
(typewriter style type)		
3 Mike Curtis	6.00	12.00
(typewriter style type)		
4 Marty Domres	5.00	10.00
(player's jersey number on left)		
5 Glenn Doughty	5.00	10.00
(player's jersey number on left)		
6 Tom Drougas	5.00	10.00
(typewriter style type)		
7 Randy Edmunds	5.00	10.00
(player's jersey number on left)		
8 Chuck Hinton	5.00	10.00
(player's jersey number on left)		
9 Conelius Johnson	5.00	10.00
(typewriter style type)		
10 Bruce Laird	5.00	10.00
(typewriter style type)		
11 Don McCauley	5.00	10.00
(typewriter style type)		
12 Ken Mendenhall	5.00	10.00
(typewriter style type)		
13 Jack Mildren	5.00	10.00
(typewriter style type)		
14 Lydell Mitchell	6.00	12.00
(player's jersey number on left)		
15 Nelson Munsey	5.00	10.00
(typewriter style type)		
16 Dennis Nelson	5.00	10.00
(typewriter style type)		
17 Billy Newsome	5.00	10.00
(typewriter style type)		
18 Cotton Speyrer	5.00	10.00
(typewriter style type)		
19 Dan Sullivan	5.00	10.00
(typewriter style type)		
20 Rick Volk	6.00	12.00
(typewriter style type)		

1973 Colts McDonald's

These 11" by 14" color posters were sponsored by and distributed through McDonald's stores. Each includes an artist's rendering of one or two Colts players along with the year and the "McDonald's Superstars Collector's Series" notation below the picture.

COMPLETE SET (4)	50.00	80.00
1 Raymond Chester	10.00	15.00
2 Mike Curtis	12.00	20.00
3 Ted Hendricks	15.00	25.00
Rick Volk		
4 Bert Jones	15.00	25.00

1973 Colts Team Issue B&W

This set of photos was issued by the Baltimore Colts in 1973. Each photo measures 8" by 10" and includes a black and white player photo on the front with the player's name and team below the photo. The photos are blank backed, unnumbered and checklisted below in alphabetical order. Photos in this set are very similar to the 1974 Colts photos except for the larger font size (measures roughly 2') used in the team name.

COMPLETE SET (28)	100.00	175.00
1 Dick Amman	4.00	8.00
2 Mike Barnes	4.00	8.00
3 Stan Cherry	4.00	8.00
4 Raymond Chester	5.00	10.00
5 Larry Christoff	4.00	8.00
6 Elmer Collett	4.00	8.00
7 Glenn Doughty	4.00	8.00
8 Tom Drougas	4.00	8.00
9 Joe Ehrmann	4.00	8.00
10 Hubert Ginn	4.00	8.00
11 Brian Herosian	4.00	8.00
12 Fred Hoaglin	4.00	8.00
13 George Hunt	4.00	8.00
14 Bert Jones	6.00	12.00
15 Mike Kaczmarek	4.00	8.00
16 Ed Mooney	4.00	8.00
17 Nelson Munsey	4.00	8.00
18 Dan Neal	4.00	8.00
19 Ray Oldham	4.00	8.00
20 Bill Olds	4.00	8.00
21 Gery Palmer	4.00	8.00
22 Tom Pierantozzi	4.00	8.00
23 Joe Schmiesing	4.00	8.00
24 Howard Schnellenberger CO	5.00	10.00
25 Ollie Smith	4.00	8.00
26 David Taylor T	4.00	8.00
27 Stan White LB	4.00	8.00
28 Bill Windauer	4.00	8.00

1973 Colts Team Issue Color

The NFLPA worked with many teams in 1973 to issued photo packs to be sold at stadium concession stands. Each measures approximately 7" by 8-5/8" and features a color player photo with a blank back. A small sheet with a player checklist was included in each 6-photo pack. Any additions to this list are appreciated.

1 Norm Bulaich	2.50	5.00
2 Mike Curtis	3.00	6.00
3 Ted Hendricks	4.00	8.00
4 Tom Matte	3.00	6.00
5 Bubba Smith	4.00	8.00

1974 Colts Team Issue

This set of photos was issued by the Baltimore Colts in 1974. Each photo measures 8" by 10" and includes a black and white player photo on the front with the player's name (printed in large letters) and team name below the photo. The players name is oriented to the far left unless noted below. The photos are blank backed, unnumbered and checklisted below in alphabetical order. Photos in this set are very similar to the 1973 Colts photos except for the smaller font size (measures roughly 1 3/8') used in the team name. The photos with the name to the far left are also identical in design to the 1971 set except this year features all players in portrait photos -- no action shots.

COMPLETE SET (34)	125.00	250.00
1 John Andrews	4.00	8.00
2 Jim Bailey	4.00	8.00
(1-inch border on left and right)		
3 Mike Barnes	4.00	8.00
4 Tim Berra	4.00	8.00
5 Tony Bertuca	4.00	8.00
6 Roger Carr	5.00	10.00
7 Fred Cook	4.00	8.00
8 Mike Curtis	5.00	10.00
9 Dan Dickel	4.00	8.00
10 Glenn Doughty	4.00	8.00
11 John Dutton	5.00	10.00
12 Joe Ehrmann	4.00	8.00
13 Randy Hall	4.00	8.00
14 Ted Hendricks	6.00	12.00
(player name indented 3/4-inch)		
15 Bert Jones	6.00	12.00
16 Rex Kern	4.00	8.00
(player name indented 3/4-inch)		
17 Bruce Laird	4.00	8.00
18 Toni Linhart	4.00	8.00
19 Tom MacLeod	4.00	8.00
20 Ted Marchibroda CO	5.00	10.00
21 Jack Mildren	4.00	8.00
(player name indented 3/4-inch)		
22 Nelson Munsey	4.00	8.00
23 Doug Nettles	4.00	8.00
24 Ray Oldham	4.00	8.00
25 Bill Olds	4.00	8.00
26 Joe Orduna	4.00	8.00
27 Robert Pratt	4.00	8.00
28 Danny Rhodes	4.00	8.00
29 Tim Rudnick	4.00	8.00
30 Freddie Scott	5.00	10.00
31 Dave Simonson	4.00	8.00
32 Bob Van Duyne	4.00	8.00
33 Steve Williams	4.00	8.00
34 Bill Windauer	4.00	8.00

1976 Colts Team Issue 5x7

This set of photos was issued by the Baltimore Colts in 1976. Each photo measures approximately 5" by 7". The fronts feature a black and white photo with player's name (on the left in large capital letters) and team name (on the right in slightly smaller letters) below the photo. The photos are blank backed, unnumbered and checklisted below in alphabetical order.

COMPLETE SET (12)	15.00	30.00
1 Roger Carr	2.00	4.00
2 Raymond Chester	2.00	4.00
3 Jim Cheyunski	1.50	3.00
4 Elmer Collett	1.50	3.00
5 Fred Cook	1.50	3.00
6 John Dutton	2.00	4.00
7 Joe Ehrmann	1.50	3.00
8 Bert Jones	2.50	5.00
9 Bruce Laird	1.50	3.00
10 Roosevelt Leaks	2.00	4.00
11 Lydell Mitchell	2.00	4.00
12 Lloyd Mumphord	1.50	3.00

1976 Colts Team Issue 8x10

This set of photos was issued by the Baltimore Colts in 1976. Each photo measures 8" by 10" and includes a black and white player photo on the front with the player's name (printed in bold letters) and team name below the photo. The players name is oriented to the far left and the team name to the far right. The photos are blank backed, unnumbered and checklisted below in alphabetical order. The photo style used in this set is nearly identical to the 1974 Colts photos except for the slightly different font style and size used in the player and team name. All of the photos are close-up portrait shots.

COMPLETE SET (44)	150.00	300.00
1 Mike Barnes	4.00	8.00
2 Tim Baylor	4.00	8.00
3 Forrest Blue	4.00	8.00
4 Roger Carr	5.00	10.00
5 Raymond Chester	5.00	10.00
6 Jim Cheyunski	4.00	8.00
7 Elmer Collett	4.00	8.00
8 Fred Cook	4.00	8.00
9 Dan Dickel	4.00	8.00
10 Glenn Doughty	4.00	8.00
11 John Dutton	5.00	10.00
12 Joe Ehrmann	4.00	8.00
13 Ron Fernandes	4.00	8.00
14 Randy Hall	4.00	8.00
15 Ken Huff	4.00	8.00
16 Bert Jones	6.00	12.00
17 Jimmie Kennedy	4.00	8.00
18 Mike Kirkland	4.00	8.00
19 Bruce Laird	4.00	8.00
20 Roosevelt Leaks	5.00	10.00
21 David Lee	4.00	8.00
22 Ron Lee	4.00	8.00
23 Toni Linhart	4.00	8.00
24 Derrel Luce	4.00	8.00
25 Ted Marchibroda CO	5.00	10.00
26 Don McCauley	4.00	8.00
27 Ken Mendenhall	4.00	8.00
28 Lydell Mitchell	5.00	10.00
29 Lloyd Mumphord	4.00	8.00
30 Nelson Munsey	4.00	8.00
31 Doug Nettles	4.00	8.00
32 Ken Novak	4.00	8.00
33 Ray Oldham	4.00	8.00
34 Robert Pratt	4.00	8.00
35 Freddie Scott	5.00	10.00
36 Sanders Shiver	4.00	8.00
37 Ed Simonini	4.00	8.00
38 Howard Stevens	4.00	8.00
39 David Taylor	4.00	8.00
40 Ricky Thompson	4.00	8.00
41 Bill Troup	4.00	8.00
42 Bob Van Duyne	4.00	8.00
43 Jackie Wallace	4.00	8.00
44 Stan White	4.00	8.00

1977 Colts Book Covers

These book covers were sponsored by Amoco and feature a member of the Baltimore Colts on the front in a black and white photo. The Colts team photo and schedule is printed on the back side once the cover is folded. Each measures roughly 13" by 20".

COMPLETE SET (5)	25.00	50.00
1 Glenn Doughty	4.00	10.00
2 Joe Ehrmann	4.00	10.00
3 Bert Jones	6.00	15.00
4 Ted Marchibroda CO	4.00	10.00
5 Lydell Mitchell	5.00	12.00

1977 Colts Team Issue

This set of photos was issued by the Baltimore Colts in 1977. Each photo measures approximately 5" by 7". The fronts feature a black and white photo with player's name (on the left) and team name (on the right) below the photo in small letters. The date "8/77" is also include just below the team name. The photos are blank backed, unnumbered and checklisted below in alphabetical order.

COMPLETE SET (12)	30.00	60.00
1 Mack Alston	3.00	6.00
2 Mike Barnes	3.00	6.00
3 Lyle Blackwood	3.00	6.00
4 Bert Jones	5.00	10.00
5 Ed Khayat CO	3.00	6.00
6 George Kunz	3.00	6.00
7 Darrell Luce	3.00	6.00
8 Ted Marchibroda CO	4.00	8.00
9 Robert Pratt	3.00	6.00
10 Norm Thompson	3.00	6.00
11 Bob Van Duyne	3.00	6.00
12 Stan White	3.00	6.00

1978-81 Colts Team Issue

This set of photos was issued by the Baltimore Colts. Each photo measures approximately 5" by 7". The fronts display player portrait photos with player name, postion, and team below the photo. The photos are blank backed, unnumbered and checklisted below in alphabetical order. This set listings is likely comprised of photos issued over a number of years. Any additions or confirmed variations on player photos or text styles are appreciated.

1 Mack Alston	2.00	5.00
2 Kim Anderson	2.00	5.00
3 Ron Baker	2.00	5.00
4 Mike Barnes	2.00	5.00
5 Tim Baylor	2.00	5.00
6 Lyle Blackwood	2.00	5.00
7 Mike Bragg	2.00	5.00
8 Larry Braziel	2.00	5.00
9 Randy Burke	2.00	5.00
10 Raymond Butler	2.50	6.00
11 Roger Carr	2.50	6.00
12 Fred Cook	2.00	5.00
13 Brian DeRoo	2.00	5.00
14 Curtis Dickey	2.50	6.00
15 Zachary Dixon	2.00	5.00
16 Ray Donaldson	2.00	5.00
17 Glenn Doughty	2.00	5.00
18 Joe Ehrmann	2.00	5.00
19 Greg Fields	2.00	5.00
20 Ron Fernandes	2.00	5.00
21 Chris Foole	2.00	5.00
22 Cleveland Franklin	2.00	5.00
23 Mike Garrett	2.50	6.00
24 Nesby Glasgow	2.00	5.00
25 Bubba Green	2.00	5.00
26 Wade Griffin	2.00	5.00
27 Lee Gross	2.00	5.00
28 Don Hardeman	2.00	5.00
29 Dwight Harrison	2.00	5.00
30 Jeff Hart	2.00	5.00
31 Derrick Hatchett	2.00	5.00
32 Dallas Hickman	2.00	5.00
33 Ken Huff	2.00	5.00
34 Marshall Johnson	2.00	5.00
35 Bert Jones	3.00	8.00
36 Ricky Jones	2.00	5.00
37 Barry Krauss	2.00	5.00
38 George Kunz	2.00	5.00
39 Bruce Laird	2.00	5.00
40 Greg Landry	3.00	8.00
41 Roosevelt Leaks	2.50	6.00
42 David Lee	2.00	5.00
43 Ron Lee	2.00	5.00
44 Toni Linhart	2.00	5.00
45 Derrel Luce	2.00	5.00
46 Reese McCall	2.00	5.00
47 Don McCauley	2.00	5.00
48 Randy McMillan	2.00	5.00
49 Ken Mendenhall	2.00	5.00
50 Steve Mike-Mayer	2.00	5.00
51 Jim Moore	2.00	5.00
52 Don Morrison	2.00	5.00
53 Lloyd Mumphord	2.00	5.00
54 Doug Nettles	2.00	5.00
55 Calvin O'Neal	2.00	5.00
56 Herb Orvis	2.00	5.00
57 Mike Ozdowski	2.00	5.00
58 Reggie Pinkney	2.00	5.00
59 Robert Pratt	2.00	5.00
60 Dave Rowe	2.00	5.00
61 Tim Sherwin	2.00	5.00
62A Sanders Shiver ERR	2.00	5.00
(name spelled Shriver)		
62B Sanders Shiver COR	2.00	5.00
63 David Shula	2.50	6.00
64 Mike Siani	2.00	5.00
65 Ed Simonini	2.00	5.00
66 Marvin Sims	2.00	5.00
67 Ed Smith	2.00	5.00
68 Hosea Taylor	2.00	5.00
69 Donnell Thompson	2.00	5.00
70 Norm Thompson	2.00	5.00
71 Bill Troup	2.00	5.00
72 Randy Van Diver	2.00	5.00
73 Bob Van Duyne	2.00	5.00
74 Joe Washington	2.50	6.00
75 Stan White	2.00	5.00
76 Mike Wood	2.00	5.00
77 Mike Woods	2.00	5.00
78 Steve Zabel	2.00	5.00

1981 Colts Coke Photos

This set of photos was sponsored by Coca-Cola with each measuring approximately 5" by 6 3/4". The fronts display color action player photos with white borders. Player identification is given below the photo between the Colts' helmet on the left and the Coke logo on the right. The photos are unnumbered and checklisted below in alphabetical order.

COMPLETE SET (24)	50.00	100.00
1 Mike Barnes	2.00	5.00
2 Larry Braziel	2.00	5.00
3 Randy Burke	2.00	5.00
4 Raymond Butler	2.50	6.00
5 Roger Carr	2.50	6.00
6 Curtis Dickey	2.50	6.00
7 Zachary Dixon	2.00	5.00
8 Nesby Glasgow	2.00	5.00
9 Bubba Green	2.00	5.00
10 Ken Huff	2.00	5.00
11 Ricky Jones	2.00	5.00
12 Greg Landry	3.00	8.00
13 Reese McCall	2.00	5.00
14 Randy McMillan	2.00	5.00
15 Jim Moore	2.00	5.00
16 Mike Ozdowski	2.00	5.00
17 Reggie Pinkney	2.00	5.00
18 Tim Sherwin	2.00	5.00
19 Sanders Shiver	2.00	5.00
20 Ed Simonini	2.00	5.00
21 Marvin Sims	2.00	5.00
22 Donnell Thompson	2.00	5.00
23 Randy Van Diver	2.00	5.00
24 Mike Wood	2.00	5.00

1985 Colts Kroger

This set of photos was sponsored by Kroger. Each photo measures approximately 5 1/2" by 8 1/2". The fronts display color action player photos with white borders. Player identification is given below the photo between the Colts' helmet on the left and the Kroger logo on the right. In navy blue print on a white background, the backs carry biographical information, the NFL logo, and the Kroger emblem. The photos are unnumbered and checklisted below in alphabetical order.

COMPLETE SET (33)	60.00	120.00
1 Dave Ahrens	1.50	4.00
2 Raul Allegre	1.50	4.00
3 Karl Baldischwiler	1.50	4.00
4 Pat Beach	1.50	4.00
5 Albert Bentley	2.00	5.00
6 Duane Bickett	2.00	5.00
7 Matt Bouza	1.50	4.00
8 Willie Broughton	1.50	4.00
9 Johnie Cooks	1.50	4.00
10 Eugene Daniel	2.00	5.00
11 Preston Davis	1.50	4.00
12 Ray Donaldson	1.50	4.00
13 Rod Dowhower	1.50	4.00
14 Owen Gill	1.50	4.00
15 Nesby Glasgow	1.50	4.00
16 Chris Hinton	1.50	4.00
17 Lamonte Hunley	1.50	4.00
18 Matt Kofler	1.50	4.00
19 Barry Krauss	1.50	4.00
20 Orlando Lowry	1.50	4.00
21 Robbie Martin	1.50	4.00
22 Randy McMillan	1.50	4.00
23 Cliff Odom	1.50	4.00
24 Tate Randle	1.50	4.00
25 Tim Sherwin	1.50	4.00
26 Byron Smith	1.50	4.00
27 Ron Solt	1.50	4.00
28 Rohn Stark	1.50	4.00
29 Donnell Thompson	1.50	4.00
30 Ben Utt	1.50	4.00
31 Brad White	1.50	4.00
32 George Wonsley	1.50	4.00
33 Anthony Young	1.50	4.00

1988 Colts Kroger

This set of photos was sponsored by Kroger and the Indianapolis Colts and very closely resembles the 1985 Colts Kroger issue. Each photo measures approximately 5 1/2" by 8 1/2" and features a black and white action photo, as opposed to color for the 1985 release. Player identification is given below the photo between the Colts' helmet on the left and the Kroger logo on the right. The black and white printed backs carry a short biographical section, the NFL logo, and the Kroger emblem. The photos are unnumbered and checklisted below in alphabetical order.

COMPLETE SET (26)	50.00	100.00
1 O'Brien Alston	1.50	4.00
2 Harvey Armstrong	1.50	4.00
3 Brian Baldinger	1.50	4.00
4 Michael Ball	1.50	4.00
5 John Baylor	1.50	4.00
6 Albert Bentley	2.00	5.00
7 Mark Boyer	1.50	4.00
(blankbacked)		
8 John Brandes	1.50	4.00
9 Bill Brooks	1.50	4.00
10 Donnie Dee	1.50	4.00
11 Eric Dickerson	4.00	10.00
12 Randy Dixon	1.50	4.00
13 Ray Donaldson	1.50	4.00
14 Chris Goode	1.50	4.00
15 Jon Hand	1.50	4.00
16 Jeff Herrod	1.50	4.00
17 Chris Hinton	1.50	4.00
18 Gary Hogeboom	1.50	4.00
19 Barry Krauss	1.50	4.00
20 Orlando Lowry	1.50	4.00
21 Rohn Stark	1.50	4.00
22 Craig Swoope	1.50	4.00
23 Jack Trudeau	1.50	4.00
24 Ben Utt	1.50	4.00
25 Clarence Verdin	1.50	4.00
26 Fredd Young	2.00	5.00

1988 Colts Police

The 1988 Police Indianapolis Colts set contains eight numbered cards measuring approximately 2 5/8" by 4 1/8". There are seven player cards and one coach card. The backs have one "Colts Tip" and one "Crime Tip."

COMPLETE SET (8)	3.00	8.00
1 Eric Dickerson	1.00	2.50
2 Barry Krauss	.40	1.00
3 Bill Brooks	.50	1.25
4 Duane Bickett	.40	1.00
5 Chris Hinton	.40	1.00
6 Eugene Daniel	.30	.75
7 Jack Trudeau	.50	1.25
8 Ron Meyer CO	.40	1.00

1989 Colts Police

The 1989 Police Indianapolis Colts set contains nine numbered cards measuring approximately 2 5/8" by 4 1/8". The fronts have white borders and color action photos; the horizontally-oriented backs have safety tips. These cards were printed on very thin stock. The set was also sponsored by Louis Rich Co. and WTHR-TV-13. According to sources, at least 50,000 sets were given away. One card was given to young persons each week during the season.

COMPLETE SET (9)	3.00	8.00
1 Colts Team Card	.25	.60
2 Dean Biasucci	.25	.60
3 Andre Rison	1.00	2.50
4 Chris Chandler	.75	2.00
5 O'Brien Alston	.25	.60
6 Ray Donaldson	.20	.50
7 Donnell Thompson	.25	.60
8 Fredd Young	.25	.60
9 Eric Dickerson	.60	1.50

1990 Colts Police

This eight-card set features members of the 1990 Indianapolis Colts. The cards in the set measure approximately 2 5/8" by 4 1/8" and have full-color action shots of the featured players on the front along with safety and crime-prevention tips on the back. The set was sponsored by Region Central Indiana Crime Stoppers, Louis Rich, and Station 13 WTHR.

COMPLETE SET (8)	2.00	5.00
1 Harvey Armstrong	.25	.60
2 Pat Beach	.25	.60
3 Albert Bentley	.30	.75
4 Kevin Call	.25	.60
5 Jeff George	1.20	3.00
6 Mike Prior	.25	.60
7 Rohn Stark	.30	.75
8 Clarence Verdin	.30	.75

1991 Colts Police

Sponsored by 13 WTHR and Coke, this eight-card measure 2 5/8" by 4 1/4". The fronts feature color action player photos inside white borders. The player's name, team name, and two logos occupy the lower white border. The backs carry biography, a Colts Quiz feature (with four questions and their answers), an anti-drug or alcohol message, and sponsor logos. The cards are numbered in the lower right corner; a message encourages the holder to contact his local police officer to collect the other cards in the set.

COMPLETE SET (8)	2.80	7.00
1 Jeff George	1.00	2.50
2 Jack Trudeau	.40	1.00
3 Jeff Herrod	.30	.75
4 Eric Dickerson	.60	1.50
5 Bill Brooks	.50	1.25
6 Jon Hand	.40	1.00
7 Keith Taylor	.30	.75
8 Randy Dixon	.30	.75

1994 Colts NIE

The set of cards measures standard size and were issued by the team with sponsorship from the NIE (Newspaper in Education) group: the Indianapolis Star and Indianapolis News. Each unnumbered card includes a color player photo on the front against a tectured border with a brief player bio printed in blue on the back.

COMPLETE SET (12)	7.50	15.00
1 Ray Buchanan	.60	1.50

2 Quentin Coryatt	.60	1.50
3 Eugene Daniel	.60	1.50
4 Sean Dawkins	.60	1.50
5 Marshall Faulk	1.50	4.00
6 Stephen Grant	.50	1.25
7 Derwin Gray	.50	1.25
8 Kirk Lowdermilk	.50	1.25
9 Roosevelt Potts	.50	1.25
10 Joe Staysniak	.50	1.25
11 Floyd Turner	.50	1.25
12 Will Wolford	.50	1.25

2005 Colts Activa Medallions

COMPLETE SET (22)	30.00	60.00
1 Raheem Brock	1.25	3.00
2 Dallas Clark	1.25	3.00
3 Ryan Diem	1.25	3.00
4 Dwight Freeney	1.25	3.00
5 Tarik Glenn	1.25	3.00
6 Nick Harper	1.25	3.00
7 Marvin Harrison	1.50	4.00
8 Edgerrin James	1.50	4.00
9 Cato June	1.25	3.00
10 Peyton Manning	2.00	5.00
11 Robert Mathis	1.25	3.00
12 Rob Morris	1.25	3.00
13 Montae Reagor	1.25	3.00
14 Dominic Rhodes	1.25	3.00
15 Bob Sanders	1.50	4.00
16 Jeff Saturday	1.25	3.00
17 Brandon Stokley	1.25	3.00
18 David Thornton	1.25	3.00
19 Mike Vanderjagt	1.25	3.00
20 Reggie Wayne	1.25	3.00
21 Josh Williams	1.25	3.00
22 Colts Logo	1.00	2.50

2006 Colts Score Indianapolis Star Jumbos

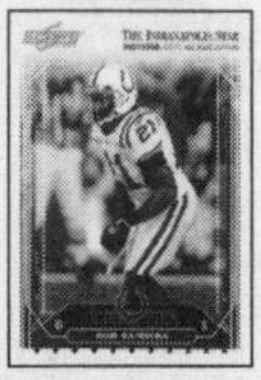

This set was produced by Donruss/Playoff with their Score brand and distributed by the Colts one card at a time at 2006 home games. One card was distributed at each home game starting August 20th and going through December. The over-sized cards measure 5x7 and feature an advertisement for the Indianapolis Star newspaper.

COMPLETE SET (10)	20.00	40.00
1 Jeff Saturday	1.25	3.00
2 Bob Sanders	2.00	5.00
3 Marvin Harrison	2.50	6.00
4 Reggie Wayne	2.00	5.00
5 Peyton Manning	4.00	10.00
6 Brandon Stokley	2.00	5.00
7 Dominic Rhodes	2.00	5.00
8 Dwight Freeney	2.00	5.00
9 Mike Doss	1.50	4.00
10 Dallas Clark	2.00	5.00

2006 Colts Topps

COMPLETE SET (12)	3.00	6.00
IND1 Peyton Manning	.50	1.25
IND2 Dwight Freeney	.25	.60
IND3 Reggie Wayne	.25	.60
IND4 Bob Sanders	.25	.60
IND5 Dallas Clark	.25	.60
IND6 Dominic Rhodes	.25	.60
IND7 Cato June	.25	.60
IND8 Brandon Stokley	.25	.60
IND9 Marvin Harrison	.30	.75
IND10 Adam Vinatieri	.25	.60
IND11 Joseph Addai	.30	.75
IND12 Bryan Fletcher	.20	.50

2007 Colts Donruss Indianapolis Star Jumbos

COMPLETE SET (10)	15.00	30.00
1 Dallas Clark	1.25	3.00
2 Anthony Gonzalez	2.50	6.00
3 Marvin Harrison	2.50	6.00
4 Dwight Freeney	1.50	4.00
5 Tony Dungy CO	1.50	4.00
6 Peyton Manning	4.00	10.00
7 Reggie Wayne	1.50	4.00
8 Joseph Addai	2.50	6.00
9 Bob Sanders	1.50	4.00
10 Adam Vinatieri	1.50	4.00

2007 Colts Topps

COMPLETE SET (12)	3.00	6.00
1 Peyton Manning	.50	1.25
2 Joseph Addai	.25	.60
3 Marvin Harrison	.30	.75
4 Dwight Freeney	.25	.60
5 Dallas Clark	.20	.50
6 Reggie Wayne	.25	.60
7 Adam Vinatieri	.25	.60
8 Ben Utecht	.20	.50
9 Bob Sanders	.25	.60
10 Robert Mathis	.20	.50
11 Anthony Gonzalez	.30	.75
12 Gary Brackett	.20	.50

2007 Colts Upper Deck Super Bowl XLI

COMPLETE SET (50)	10.00	20.00
1 Joseph Addai	.50	1.25
2 Antoine Bethea	.20	.50
3 Rocky Boiman	.20	.50
4 Gary Brackett	.20	.50
5 Raheem Brock	.20	.50
6 Dallas Clark	.20	.50
7 Jason David	.20	.50
8 Ryan Diem	.20	.50
9 Bryan Fletcher	.20	.50
10 Dwight Freeney	.30	.75
11 Gilbert Gardner	.20	.50
12 Matt Giordano	.20	.50
13 Tarik Glenn	.20	.50
14 Nick Harper	.20	.50
15 Marvin Harrison	.40	1.00
16 Kelvin Hayden	.20	.50
17 Marlin Jackson	.20	.50
18 Cato June	.20	.50
19 Ryan Lilja	.20	.50
20 Peyton Manning	.60	1.50
21 Robert Mathis	.20	.50
22 Anthony McFarland	.20	.50
23 Aaron Moorehead	.20	.50
24 Rob Morris	.20	.50
25 Darrell Reid	.20	.50
26 Dominic Rhodes	.30	.75
27 Bob Sanders	.30	.75
28 Jeff Saturday	.20	.50
29 Bo Schobel	.20	.50
30 Jake Scott	.20	.50
31 Hunter Smith	.25	.60
32 Charlie Johnson	.20	.50
33 Jim Sorgi	.30	.75
34 John Standeford	.20	.50
35 Josh Thomas	.20	.50
36 Matt Ulrich	.20	.50
37 Ben Utecht	.20	.50
38 Adam Vinatieri	.30	.75
39 Reggie Wayne	.30	.75
40 Terrence Wilkins	.20	.50
MM1 Reggie Wayne MM	.30	.75
MM2 Kelvin Hayden MM	.20	.50
MM3 Bob Sanders MM	.30	.75
MM4 Dominic Rhodes MM	.30	.75
NNO Jumbo Team Photo	.50	1.25
SH1 Peyton Manning SH	.60	1.50
SH2 Reggie Wayne SH	.30	.75
SH3 Adam Vinatieri SH	.30	.75
SH4 Joseph Addai SH	.50	1.25
SH5 Marvin Harrison SH	.40	1.00
MVP1 Peyton Manning MVP	1.00	2.50

2008 Colts Topps

COMPLETE SET (12)	2.50	5.00
1 Peyton Manning	.50	1.25
2 Reggie Wayne	.25	.60
3 Joseph Addai	.25	.60
4 Dallas Clark	.25	.60
5 Bob Sanders	.25	.60
6 Kenton Keith	.20	.50
7 Antoine Bethea	.20	.50
8 Anthony Gonzalez	.20	.50
9 Marvin Harrison	.30	.75
10 Gary Brackett	.20	.50
11 Mike Hart	.40	1.00
12 Dwight Freeney	.25	.60

1959 Comet Sweets Olympic Achievements

Celebrating various Olympic events, ceremonies, and their history, this 25-card set was issued by Comet Sweets. The cards are printed on thin cardboard stock and measure 1 7/16" by 2 9/16". Inside white borders, the fronts display water color paintings of various Olympic events. Some cards are horizontally oriented; others are vertically oriented. The set title "Olympic Achievements" appears at the top on the backs, with a discussion of the event below. This set is the first series; the cards are numbered "X to 25."

COMPLETE SET (25)	30.00	60.00
18 Football	1.50	3.00

1995 Connecticut Coyotes AFL

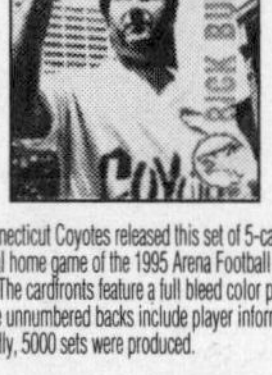

The Connecticut Coyotes released this set of 5-cards at their final home game of the 1995 Arena Football League season. The cardfronts feature a full bleed color photo while the unnumbered backs include player information. Reportedly, 5000 sets were produced.

COMPLETE SET (5)	3.20	8.00
1 Rick Buffington CO	.80	2.00
2 Mike Hold	.80	2.00
3 Merv Mosley	.80	2.00
4 Tyrone Thurman	.80	2.00
5 Team Photo	.80	2.00

2005 Corpus Christi Hammerheads NIFL

COMPLETE SET (25)	6.00	12.00
1 Terrance Bennett	.30	.75
2 Shomari Buchanan	.30	.75
3 Chris Chambers	.30	.75
4 Martin Dossett	.30	.75
5 Brian Gaines	.30	.75
6 Devin Green	.30	.75
7 Mike Green	.30	.75
8 Carl Greenwood	.30	.75
9 Matt Hardison	.30	.75
10 Chris Harrington	.30	.75
11 Jonathan Hayhurst Asst.CO	.30	.75
12 Anthony Hood	.30	.75
13 Estus Hood	.30	.75
14 Chester Jones Jr.	.30	.75
15 David Lose	.30	.75
16 LeDaniel Marshall	.30	.75
17 Hershall McCurn	.30	.75
18 Jason McKinley CO	.30	.75
19 Eddie Miller	.30	.75
20 Oscar Moreno	.30	.75
21 Roy Salas	.30	.75
22 Fred Wallace	.30	.75
23 Derrick Watson	.30	.75
24 Robert Watson	.30	.75
25 Hank-Hammerhead (Mascot)	.30	.75

1993-94 Costacos Brothers Poster Cards

COMPLETE SET (18)	10.00	20.00
1 Troy Aikman	1.25	3.00
2 Troy Aikman	1.25	3.00
Silver Bullet		
8 Michael Irvin	.20	.50
Playmaker		
12 Rick Mirer	.20	.50
Natural Wonder		
16 Jerry Rice	.75	2.00
Speed of Light		
17 Emmitt Smith	1.25	3.00
Catch 22		

1994 Costacos Brothers Poster Cards NFL

COMPLETE SET (12)	6.00	15.00
1 Troy Aikman	.60	1.50
Strong Arm of the Law		
2 Barry Sanders	1.20	3.00
3 Steve Young	.50	1.25
Run and Gun		
4 Rick Mirer	.20	.50
Natural Wonder		
5 John Elway	1.20	3.00
The Rifleman		
6 Dan Marino	1.20	3.00
Tropical Storm		
7 Drew Bledsoe	.60	1.50
Patriot Games		
8 Emmitt Smith	1.00	2.50
Catch 22		
9 Warren Moon	.30	.75
Moonshine		
10 Jerry Rice	.60	1.50
Elite		
11 Michael Irvin	.30	.75
Playmaker		
12 Jim Kelly	.30	.75
Machine Gun Kelly		

1960 Cowboys Team Sheets

This set of press photo sheets was released to publicize players signed early to the first Cowboys' team. Each sheet includes four black and white photos, measures roughly 8 1/2" X 11" and is blankbacked. Some of these player images were also issued as separate 8 x 10 photos as well.

COMPLETE SET (10)	150.00	250.00
1 Tom Braatz	15.00	25.00
L.G. Dupre		
Jack Patera		
Bill Butler DB		
2 Gene Babb	15.00	25.00
Duane Putnam		
Nate Borden		
Don Heinrich		
3 Frank Clarke	15.00	25.00
Dave Sherer		
Don McIlhenny		
Byron Bradfute		
4 Mike Falls	15.00	25.00
Don Bishop		
Paul Dickson		
Bob Bercich		
5 Bob Fry	15.00	25.00
Jim Doran		
Fred Dugan		
Fred Cone and		
Don Heinrich		
6 Wayne Hansen	15.00	25.00
Walt Kowalczyk		
Dick Klein		
John Houser		
7 Don Healy	15.00	25.00
Dick Bielski		
Bill Herchman		
Jerry Tubbs		
8 Don Meredith	35.00	60.00
John Gonzaga		
Buzz Guy		
Tom Franckhouser		
9 Ed Husmann	20.00	35.00
Ray Mathews		
Eddie LeBaron		
Gene Cronin		
10 Woodley Lewis	18.00	30.00
Billy Howton		
Mike Connelly		
Jim Mooty		

1960-62 Cowboys Team Issue 5x7

These team issued photos feature black-and-white player images taken of just head-and-shoulders. Each measures approximately 5" by 7" and was printed on glossy photographic paper stock. Most feature four white borders around the player image but some were created with just one white border at the bottom: noted below. Each photo is a portrait with the player wearing a blue early 1960s era stars-on-the-shoulder Cowboys jersey. The white border at the bottom contains just the player's name and team name printed in all capital letters. These cards are blankbacked and unnumbered. Any additions to the below list are appreciated.

COMPLETE SET (22)	125.00	250.00
1 Dick Bielski	6.00	12.00
2 Frank Clarke	7.50	15.00
3 Donnie Davis	6.00	12.00
4 Jim Doran	6.00	12.00
5 Ken Frost	6.00	12.00
6 Bob Fry	6.00	12.00
7 Mike Gaechter	6.00	12.00
8 John Gonzaga	6.00	12.00
9 Don Healy	6.00	12.00
10 Bill Herchman	6.00	12.00
(first name initial only)		
11 Billy Howton	7.50	15.00
12 Lynn Hoyem	6.00	12.00
13 Walt Kowalczyk	6.00	12.00
14 Eddie LeBaron	7.50	15.00
15 Bob Lilly	12.50	25.00
16 Don McIlhenny	6.00	12.00
17 Don Meredith	18.00	30.00
18 Don Perkins	7.50	15.00
19 Duane Putnam	6.00	12.00
20 Guy Reese	6.00	12.00
21 Lorenzo Stanford	6.00	12.00
22 Don Talbert	6.00	12.00

1960-63 Cowboys Team Issue 8x10

The Dallas Cowboys issued these black-and-white photos and all feature the player wearing the original stars-on-the-sleeves blue jersey. Each measures 8" by 10" and was printed on glossy stock with white borders. Each photo features a posed action shot with the border below the photo containing just the player's name and team name. The type style and size may vary slightly on some photos, and some players have more than one pose, so this may indicate that they were released over a period of years. The photos are blankbacked and unnumbered. Any additions to the below list are appreciated.

1 Gene Babb	7.50	15.00
2 Bob Bercich	7.50	15.00
3A Dick Bielski	7.50	15.00
(cutting to his right)		
3B Dick Bielski	7.50	15.00
(cutting to his left)		
4 Don Bishop	7.50	15.00
5 Nate Borden	7.50	15.00
6 Amos Bullocks	7.50	15.00
7A Frank Clarke	10.00	20.00
(catching pose, horizontal photo)		
7B Frank Clarke	10.00	20.00
(running forward, vertical photo)		
8 Mike Connelly	7.50	15.00
9 Andy Cvercko	7.50	15.00
10 Gerry DeLucca	7.50	15.00
11 Jim Doran	7.50	15.00
12 L.G. Dupre	7.50	15.00
13 Ken Frost	7.50	15.00
14 Don Healy	7.50	15.00
15 Don Heinrich	7.50	15.00
16 Bill Herchman	7.50	15.00
17 John Houser	7.50	15.00
18A Billy Howton	10.00	20.00
(diving for the football)		
18B Billy Howton	10.00	20.00
(cutting to his left)		
18C Billy Howton	10.00	20.00
(falling to his right)		
19 Lee Roy Jordan	12.50	25.00
20A Eddie LeBaron	10.00	20.00
(set to pass; ball in right hand)		
20B Eddie LeBaron	10.00	20.00
(dropping back to pass)		
20C Eddie LeBaron	10.00	20.00
(faking handoff)		
20D Eddie LeBaron	10.00	20.00
(set to pass; ball in both hands)		
20E Eddie LeBaron portrait	10.00	20.00
21 Bob Lilly portrait	15.00	30.00
22 Warren Livingston	7.50	15.00
23 J.W. Lockett	7.50	15.00
24 Amos Marsh	7.50	15.00
25A Don Meredith	25.00	40.00
(dropping back to pass)		
25B Don Meredith	25.00	40.00
(set to pass; standing upright)		
25C Don Meredith	25.00	40.00
(set to pass; crouched)		
25D Don Meredith portrait	25.00	40.00
26 Dick Nolan	7.50	15.00
27 Don Perkins	10.00	20.00
28 Larry Stephens	7.50	15.00
29A Jerry Tubbs	7.50	15.00
(trees in background; running left)		
29B Jerry Tubbs	7.50	15.00
(no trees in background)		
29C Jerry Tubbs	7.50	15.00
(trees in background; legs crisscrossed)		

1961 Cowboys Team Issue 7x9

These team issued photos feature black-and-white player images taken of just head-and-shoulders. They were most likely issued as set in "photo pack" style but that has yet to be confirmed. Each measures approximately 7 1/2" by 9 1/2" and was printed on thin matte finish paper stock. They have four wide white borders and the bottom contains just the player's name and team name, unless noted below. These photos are blankbacked and unnumbered. They look very similar to the 1962 7x9 set but feature a much wider white border around the photos as well as unique images.

COMPLETE SET (8)	75.00	125.00
1 Dick Bielski	6.00	12.00
2 Frank Clarke	7.50	15.00
3 Billy Howton	7.50	15.00
(position initials included)		
4 Eddie LeBaron	7.50	15.00
5 Bob Lilly	10.00	20.00
6 Amos Marsh	6.00	12.00
7 Don Meredith	20.00	35.00
8 Jerry Tubbs	6.00	12.00

1961-62 Cowboys Team Issue 5x6

These team issued photos feature black-and-white player portraits taken of just head-and-shoulders. Each measures approximately 5" by 6 1/2" and was printed on thin matte-finish paper stock with four white borders. The bottom border contains just the player's name and team name with both oriented near the outside edges of the player images. This style, very similar to the Jay Publishing issues of the period, would be used by the Cowboys well into the 1980s. The photos are blankbacked and unnumbered.

COMPLETE SET (6)	40.00	80.00
1 L.G. Dupre	6.00	12.00
2 Don Healy	6.00	12.00
3 Eddie LeBaron	7.50	15.00
4 Don McIlhenny	6.00	12.00
5 Don Meredith	18.00	30.00
6 Jerry Tubbs	6.00	12.00

1962 Cowboys Team Issue 7x9 Photo Pack

These team issued photos feature black-and-white player images taken of just head-and-shoulders. They were issued as set in "photo pack" style. Each measures approximately 7 1/2" by 9 1/2" and was printed on thin matte finish paper stock. They have four white borders and the bottom contains just the player's name and team name, unless noted below. These cards are blankbacked and unnumbered. They look very similar to the 1961 7x9 set but feature a much thinner white border around the photos.

COMPLETE SET (10)	75.00	150.00
1 Don Bishop	6.00	12.00
2 Frank Clarke	7.50	15.00
3 Mike Gaechter	6.00	12.00
4 Sonny Gibbs	6.00	12.00
(position initials included)		
5 Billy Howton	7.50	15.00
6 Eddie LeBaron	7.50	15.00
7 Amos Marsh	6.00	12.00
8 Don Meredith	20.00	35.00
9 Don Perkins	7.50	15.00
10 Jerry Tubbs	6.00	12.00

1962-63 Cowboys Team Issue Sepia

These photos were issued by the Cowboys most likely over the course of the 1962 and 1963 seasons. Each features a sepia-toned posed action photo, measures approximately 4 7/8" by 6 1/2" and was printed on thin paper stock. A wide border at the bottom contains the player's name, position spelled out, and team name. The photos are blankbacked and unnumbered. Any additions to the below list are appreciated.

COMPLETE SET (17)	125.00	250.00
1 Bob Bercich	7.50	15.00
2 Mike Connelly	7.50	15.00
3 L.G. Dupre	7.50	15.00
4 Sonny Gibbs	7.50	15.00
5 Don Healy	7.50	15.00
6 Bill Herchman	7.50	15.00
7 Eddie LeBaron	10.00	20.00
8 Bob Lilly	15.00	30.00
9 Don Meredith	25.00	40.00
10 Bobby Plummer	7.50	15.00
11 Guy Reese Act	7.50	15.00
(action photo in Cowboy jersey)		
12 Guy Reese Port	7.50	15.00
(close up portrait)		
13 Ray Schoenke	7.50	15.00
14 Jim Ray Smith	7.50	15.00
15 Don Talbert	7.50	15.00
(college photo)		
16 Jerry Tubbs	7.50	15.00
17 Team Photo	12.50	25.00

1963-64 Cowboys Team Issue 7x9

These team issued photos feature black-and-white player images taken of just head-and-shoulders. They may have been issued as a set in "photo pack" style but that has not been confirmed. Each measures approximately 7 1/2" by 9 1/2" and was printed on glossy stock. They have four white borders and the bottom contains the player's name, position initals, and team name. These cards are blankbacked and unnumbered. They look very similar to the 1962 7x9 set with the thinner white border but these also include the player's position on every photo. The Clarke and Tubbs photos are virtually identical to the 1962 issue except for this position addition.

1 Frank Clarke	7.50	15.00
2 Buddy Dial	6.00	12.00
3 Cornell Green	6.00	12.00
4 Lee Roy Jordan	7.50	15.00
5 Tommy McDonald	7.50	15.00
6 Don Perkins	7.50	15.00
7 Jerry Tubbs	6.00	12.00

1964-66 Cowboys Team Issue 5x7

These team issued photos feature black-and-white images with roughly the player's chest up to his head in view. The player's are wearing the new solid white or solid blue 1964 era Cowboys jersey unless noted below. Each photo measures approximately 5" by 7" and was printed on glossy photographic paper stock with four white borders unless noted below. The bottom border contains just the player's name and team name. These cards are blankbacked and unnumbered. Any additions to the below list are appreciated.

COMPLETE SET (31)	200.00	350.00
1 George Andrie	6.00	12.00
(borderless on three sides)		
2 Don Bishop	6.00	12.00
(borderless on three sides)		
3 Jim Boeke	6.00	12.00
4 Frank Clarke	7.50	15.00
5 Jim Colvin	6.00	12.00
(borderless on three sides)		
6 Dick Daniels	6.00	12.00
(borderless on three sides)		
7 Austin Denney	6.00	12.00
(wearing t-shirt, borderless on three sides)		
8A Buddy Dial	7.50	15.00
(Steelers jersey, one border)		
8B Buddy Dial	7.50	15.00
(Cowboys jersey, four borders)		
8C Buddy Dial	7.50	15.00
(Cowboys jersey, one border)		
9 Leon Donohue	6.00	12.00
10 Lee Folkins	6.00	12.00
11 Cornell Green	7.50	15.00
12 Bob Hayes	15.00	25.00
13 Harold Hays	6.00	12.00
14 Chuck Howley	7.50	15.00
15 Jake Kupp	6.00	12.00
16 Tom Landry CO	15.00	25.00
(wearing Cowboys t-shirt)		
17 Obert Logan	6.00	12.00
18 Billy Lothridge	6.00	12.00
19 Don Meredith	20.00	35.00
20 Ralph Neely	6.00	12.00
21 Don Perkins	7.50	15.00
22 Dan Reeves	10.00	20.00
23 Mel Renfro	10.00	20.00
24 Jerry Rhome	6.00	12.00
(borderless on three sides)		
25 Ray Schoenke	6.00	12.00
26 Jim Ray Smith	6.00	12.00
27 Willie Townes	6.00	12.00
28 Danny Villanueva	6.00	12.00
29 Malcolm Walker	6.00	12.00
(wearing college jersey; borderless on three sides)		

1965 Cowboys Team Issue 5x6

This team-issued set features black-and-white head-to-foot posed action player photos with white borders. Each photo measures approximately 5 1/2" by 6 1/2" but the exact width is known to vary due to inconsistent cutting. The player's name and team name appear below the image. Most players appear in their white jersey, but a few have been found with the road blue as noted below. The photos were printed on thick card stock with a dull matte finish and have unnumbered blankbacks.

COMPLETE SET (43)	300.00	500.00
1 George Andrie	6.00	12.00
2 Don Bishop	6.00	12.00
3 Jim Boeke	6.00	12.00
4A Frank Clarke	7.50	15.00
(wearing blue jersey)		
4B Frank Clarke	7.50	15.00
(wearing white jersey)		
5 Jim Colvin	6.00	12.00
6 Mike Connelly	6.00	12.00
7 Buddy Dial	7.50	15.00
8 Leon Donohue Blue	6.00	12.00
9 Perry Lee Dunn	6.00	12.00
10A Dave Edwards	6.00	12.00
(wearing blue jersey)		
10B Dave Edwards	6.00	12.00
(wearing white jersey)		
11 Mike Gaechter	6.00	12.00
12 Pete Gent	6.00	12.00
13 Cornell Green	6.00	12.00
14 Bob Hayes	12.50	25.00
15 Harold Hays	6.00	12.00
16 Chuck Howley	10.00	20.00
17 Joe Bob Isbell	6.00	12.00
18 Mitch Johnson Blue	6.00	12.00
19 Lee Roy Jordan	10.00	20.00
20 Jake Kupp	6.00	12.00
21 Bob Lilly	12.50	25.00
22 Tony Liscio	6.00	12.00
23 Warren Livingston	6.00	12.00
24 Obert Logan Blue	6.00	12.00
25 Dave Manders	6.00	12.00
26A Don Meredith	18.00	30.00
(wearing blue jersey)		
26B Don Meredith	18.00	30.00
(wearing white jersey)		
27 Craig Morton Blue	10.00	20.00
28 Ralph Neely Blue	6.00	12.00
29 Pettis Norman	6.00	12.00
30 Don Perkins	7.50	15.00
31 Jethro Pugh Blue	6.00	12.00
32 Dan Reeves Blue	10.00	20.00
33 Mel Renfro	10.00	20.00
34 Jerry Rhome Blue	6.00	12.00
35 Colin Ridgway Blue	6.00	12.00
36 J.D. Smith Blue	6.00	12.00
37 Larry Stephens	6.00	12.00
38 Jim Stiger	6.00	12.00
39 Don Talbert Blue	6.00	12.00
40 Jerry Tubbs	6.00	12.00
41 Danny Villanueva Blue	6.00	12.00
42 Russell Wayt Blue	6.00	12.00
43 Maury Youmans	6.00	12.00

1965-66 Cowboys Team Issue 5-1/4x7 Position

These team issued photos feature black-and-white images with roughly the player's chest up to his head in view. The player's are pictured wearing the solid white Cowboys jersey unless noted below. Each photo measures approximately 5 1/4" by 7" and was printed on matte-finish paper stock with four white borders. The bottom border contains the player's name, position intials, and team name in all caps. These photos are blankbacked and unnumbered. Any additions to the below list are appreciated.

1 Frank Clarke	7.50	15.00
2 Buddy Dial	6.00	12.00
3 Lee Roy Jordan	7.50	15.00
4 Bob Lilly	10.00	20.00
5 Ralph Neely Blue	6.00	12.00
6 Pettis Norman	6.00	12.00
7 Don Perkins	7.50	15.00
8 Jerry Tubbs	6.00	12.00

1966-67 Cowboys Team Issue 5x7

These team issued photos feature black-and-white images, measure approximately 5" by 7" and were printed on matte-finish thin paper stock with four white borders. The bottom border contains the player's name, position spelled out, and team name in uppre and lower case letters - making these unique to most Cowboys issues of the era. These photos are blankbacked and unnumbered. Any additions to the below list are appreciated.

1 George Andrie	6.00	12.00
2 Frank Clarke	7.50	15.00
3 Pete Gent	6.00	12.00
4 Bob Hayes	10.00	20.00
5 Lee Roy Jordan	7.50	15.00
6 Bob Lilly	10.00	20.00
7 Dave Manders	6.00	12.00
8 Don Meredith	18.00	30.00
9 Mel Renfro	7.50	15.00

1966-67 Cowboys Team Issue 8x10

The Dallas Cowboys issued these black-and-white player photos printed on glossy photographic paper. Each measures 8" by 10" and was printed on glossy stock with white borders. Each player photo is a posed action shot head-to-foot and features the player in the blue jersey unless noted below. The border below the photo contains just the player's name and team name in all caps. The type style and size varies slightly on some photos so this may indicate that they were released over a period of years. The photos are blankbacked and unnumbered but can often be found with a photographer's imprint on the backs along with a date. Any additions to the below list are appreciated.

COMPLETE SET (33)	300.00	500.00
1 George Andrie Wht	7.50	15.00
2 Don Bishop	7.50	15.00
3 Phil Clark Wht	7.50	15.00
4 Frank Clarke Wht	10.00	20.00
5 Buddy Dial	7.50	15.00
6 Ron East Wht	7.50	15.00
7 Walt Garrison	7.50	15.00
8 Bob Hayes	15.00	30.00
9 Harold Hays	7.50	15.00
10 Chuck Howley	10.00	20.00
11 Mitch Johnson	7.50	15.00
12 Lee Roy Jordan	10.00	20.00
13 Jake Kupp	7.50	15.00
14 Bob Lilly	15.00	25.00
15 Don Meredith	25.00	40.00
16 Craig Morton Wht	10.00	20.00
17 Ralph Neely	7.50	15.00
18 John Niland	7.50	15.00
19 Pettis Norman	7.50	15.00
20 Brig Owens	7.50	15.00
21 Don Perkins	10.00	20.00
22 Jethro Pugh Wht	7.50	15.00
23 Dan Reeves	10.00	20.00
24 Mel Renfro	10.00	20.00
25A Jerry Rhome Blue	7.50	15.00
25B Jerry Rhome Wht	7.50	15.00
26 Ernie Stautner ACO	10.00	20.00
(wearing dark Cowboys jacket)		
27 Don Talbert	7.50	15.00
28 Willie Townes	7.50	15.00
29 Malcolm Walker	7.50	15.00
30 A.D. Whitfield	7.50	15.00
31 John Wilbur	7.50	15.00
32 Rayfield Wright	10.00	20.00
(wearing jersey #85)		
33 Maury Youmans	7.50	15.00

1968 Cowboys Team Issue 8x10

The Dallas Cowboys issued these black-and-white player photos printed on glossy photographic paper stock. Each measures 8" by 10" and was printed with four white borders with the player's image as a posed action shot. The border below the photo contains the player's name, his position initials, and team name. The type style and size varies slightly on some photos so this may indicate that they were released over a period of years. The photos are blankbacked and unnumbered. Any additions to the below list are appreciated.

1 Raymond Berry ACO	10.00	20.00
(wearing white Cowboys shirt)		
2 Larry Cole	7.50	15.00
3 Dennis Homan	7.50	15.00
4 Tom Landry CO	15.00	25.00
(kneeling pose, hand on football)		
5 Obert Logan	7.50	15.00
6 David McDaniels	7.50	15.00
7 Blaine Nye	7.50	15.00
8 Ron Widby	7.50	15.00
(wearing jersey #12)		

1969 Cowboys Tasco Prints

Tasco Associates produced this set of samll Dallas Cowboys posters. The fronts feature a color artist's rendering of the player along with the player's name and position. The backs are blank. The prints measure approximately 11 1/2" by 16."

1 Chuck Howley	12.50	25.00
2 Ralph Neely	10.00	20.00
3 Dan Reeves	15.00	30.00

1969 Cowboys Team Issue 5x6

These team-issued photos feature black-and-white posed action player photos with white borders. Each measures approximately 5" by 6 1/2" and are virtually identical in style to the 1970 and 1971 listings. We've noted specific differences below (identified by the poses) for players that appear in more than one of the sets. Many of these photos were issued for more than one year but we've cataloged them just one time within the set listing that seems to fit best in terms of the pose style and the years the players were on the roster. A wide white border at the bottom contains only the player's name and team name. These cards are printed on thin card stock, have blankbacks and are unnumbered.

COMPLETE SET (25)	150.00	300.00
1 George Andrie	6.00	12.00
(cutting to his right)		
2 Craig Baynham	6.00	12.00
3 Ron East	6.00	12.00
4 Walt Garrison	6.00	12.00
(blue jersey)		
5 Pete Gent	6.00	12.00
6 Bob Hayes	12.50	25.00
(blue jersey)		
7 Chuck Howley	7.50	15.00
(blue jersey)		
8 Lee Roy Jordan	7.50	15.00
(blue jersey)		
9 Bob Lilly	12.50	25.00
(cutting to his left)		
10 Tony Liscio	6.00	12.00
11 Dave Manders	6.00	12.00
(right foot off ground)		
12 Don Meredith	20.00	35.00
13 Craig Morton	7.50	15.00
(blue jersey)		
14 Ralph Neely	6.00	12.00
(blue jersey)		
15 John Niland	6.00	12.00
(blue jersey)		
16 Pettis Norman	6.00	12.00
17 Don Perkins	7.50	15.00
18A Dan Reeves	10.00	20.00
(blue jersey, no facsimile)		
18B Dan Reeves	10.00	20.00
(blue jersey, facsimile auto)		
19 Mel Renfro	7.50	15.00
(blue jersey)		
20 Lance Rentzel	6.00	12.00
21A Roger Staubach	25.00	40.00
(dropping back to pass; facsimile auto on front)		

21B Roger Staubach (dropping back to pass; no facsimile on front)	25.00	40.00
22 Malcolm Walker	6.00	12.00
23 Ron Widby (wearing jersey #12)	6.00	12.00
24 John Wilbur	6.00	12.00
25 Rayfield Wright (wearing jersey #85)	7.50	15.00

1969-72 Cowboys Team Issue 5x7

These team-issued photos feature black-and-white player images with white borders on four sides, unless otherwise noted below. Each photo measures approximately 5" by 7" and was printed on glossy photographic paper stock. Each photo is a portrait showing the player wearing a white jersey with just half of his jersey number showing. A thick white border at the bottom contains only the player's name and team name except for a few that also include initials for the player's position. They were issued over a period of years and feature a variety of type styles and type sizes for the lettering within the bottom border. We've noted differences in the player The photos are blankbacked and unnumbered.

1 Margene Adkins	6.00	12.00
2 George Andrie	6.00	12.00
3 Bob Asher	6.00	12.00
4 Mike Clark (position initial included)	6.00	12.00
5 Phil Clark	6.00	12.00
6 Ralph Coleman	6.00	12.00
7 Mike Ditka	10.00	20.00
8 Ron East	6.00	12.00
9 John Fitzgerald	6.00	12.00
10 Richmond Flowers	6.00	12.00
11 Walt Garrison (borderless on three sides)	7.50	15.00
12 Cornell Green	6.00	15.00
13 Halvor Hagen	6.00	12.00
14A Bob Hayes (jersey #'s on shoulders)	10.00	20.00
14B Bob Hayes (no jersey #'s on shoulders)	10.00	20.00
15A Calvin Hill (borderless on three sides)	7.50	15.00
15B Calvin Hill (four white borders)	7.50	15.00
16 Dennis Homan	6.00	12.00
17 Mike Johnson (borderless on three sides)	6.00	12.00
18A Lee Roy Jordan (borderless on three sides)	7.50	15.00
18B Lee Roy Jordan (four white borders)	7.50	15.00
19 Tom Landry CO (wearing silver jacket)	12.50	25.00
20 D.D. Lewis	6.00	12.00
21 Bob Lilly	12.50	25.00
22 Dave Manders	6.00	12.00
23A Craig Morton (no jersey #'s on shoulder)	7.50	15.00
23B Craig Morton (jersey #'s on shoulder)	7.50	15.00
24A Ralph Neely (jersey #7 above team name)	6.00	12.00
24B Ralph Neely (jersey #7 above player name)	6.00	12.00
25A John Niland (large player and team names)	6.00	12.00
25B John Niland (small player and team names)	6.00	12.00
26 Pettis Norman	6.00	12.00
27 Blaine Nye	6.00	12.00
28 Billy Parks	6.00	12.00
29 Dan Reeves	7.50	15.00
30A Mel Renfro (no jersey #'s on shoulders)	7.50	15.00
30B Mel Renfro (jersey #'s on shoulders)	7.50	15.00
31 Lance Rentzel (borderless on three sides)	6.00	12.00
32 Reggie Rucker (borderless on three sides)	6.00	12.00
33 Les Shy	6.00	12.00
34 Tody Smith (borderless on three sides)	6.00	12.00
35A Roger Staubach (borderless on three sides)	20.00	35.00
35B Roger Staubach (late 1960s image; smiling)	20.00	35.00
35C Roger Staubach (early 1970s image; smiling slightly)	20.00	35.00
35D Roger Staubach (early 1970s image; not smiling)	20.00	35.00
36 Ernie Stautner ACO (wearing silver jacket)	6.00	12.00
37 Tom Stincic	6.00	12.00
38 Bill Thomas	6.00	12.00
39 Duane Thomas	6.00	12.00
40 Isaac Thomas (borderless on three sides)	6.00	12.00
41 Willie Townes (borderless on three sides)	6.00	12.00
42 Mark Washington	6.00	12.00
43 Claxton Welch (borderless on three sides)	6.00	12.00
44 Fred Whittingham (borderless on three sides)	6.00	12.00
45 Ron Widby	6.00	12.00
46A Rayfield Wright (borderless on three sides)	7.50	15.00
46B Rayfield Wright (four white borders)	7.50	15.00

1970 Cowboys Team Issue 5x6

These team-issued photos feature black-and-white posed action player photos with white borders. Each measures approximately 5" by 6 1/2" and are virtually identical in style to the 1969 and 1971 listings. We've noted specific differences below (identified by the poses) for players that appear in more than one of the sets. Many of these photos were issued for more than one year but we've cataloged them just one time within the set listing that seems to fit best in terms of the pose style and the years the players were on the roster. A wide white border at the bottom contains only the player's name and team name. These cards are printed on thin card stock, have blankbacks and are unnumbered.

COMPLETE SET (30)	200.00	350.00
1 Herb Adderley	7.50	15.00
2 Margene Adkins	6.00	12.00
3 George Andrie (facing forward)	6.00	12.00
4 Bob Asher	6.00	12.00
5 Mike Clark	6.00	12.00
6 Mike Ditka (no mustache)	6.00	12.00
7 Dave Edwards	6.00	12.00
8 Walt Garrison (white jersey)	6.00	12.00
9 Cornell Green	6.00	12.00
10 Cliff Harris	7.50	15.00
11 Bob Hayes (white jersey; ball in air)	10.00	20.00
12 Calvin Hill	7.50	15.00
13 Chuck Howley (white jersey; right foot near ground)	7.50	15.00
14 Lee Roy Jordan (white jersey; clouds in background)	7.50	15.00
15 D.D. Lewis (no mustache)	6.00	12.00
16 Bob Lilly (charging forward)	10.00	20.00
17 Craig Morton (white jersey)	7.50	15.00
18 Ralph Neely (white jersey)	6.00	12.00
19 John Niland (white jersey; charging forward)	6.00	12.00
20 Blaine Nye	6.00	12.00
21 Jethro Pugh	6.00	12.00
22 Dan Reeves (white jersey)	7.50	15.00
23 Mel Renfro (white jersey)	10.00	20.00
24 Roger Staubach (feet are set)	25.00	40.00
25 Duane Thomas	6.00	12.00
26 Pat Toomay (left foot raised)	6.00	12.00
27 Mark Washington	6.00	12.00
28 Claxton Welch	6.00	12.00
29 Ron Widby (wearing jersey #10)	6.00	12.00
30 Rayfield Wright (wearing jersey #70)	7.50	15.00

1970 Cowboys Team Issue 8x10

The Dallas Cowboys issued these black-and-white player photos, measuring 8" by 10," and printed on glossy stock with white borders. Each player photo is a posed action shot. The border below the photo contains just the player's name and team name. The type style and size varies slightly on some photos so this may indicate that they were released over a period of years. The photos are blankbacked and unnumbered. Any additions to the below list are appreciated.

1 Ron Fast	7.50	15.00
2 Halvor Hagen	7.50	15.00
3 Calvin Hill	10.00	20.00
4 Bob Lilly (left foot off of the ground)	12.50	25.00
5 Blaine Nye	7.50	15.00
6 Tom Stincic	7.50	15.00

1971 Cowboys Team Issue 5x6

These team-issued photos feature black-and-white posed action player photos with white borders. Each measures approximately 5" by 6 1/2" and are virtually identical in style to the 1969 and 1970 listings. We've noted specific differences below (identified by the poses) for players that appear in more than one of the sets. Many of these photos were issued for more than one year but we've cataloged them just one time within the set listing that seems to fit best in terms of the pose style and the years the players were on the roster. A wide white border at the bottom contains only the player's name and team name. These cards are printed on thin card stock, have blankbacks and are unnumbered.

COMPLETE SET (23)	150.00	300.00
1 Lance Alworth	7.50	15.00
2 George Andrie (cutting right, right foot raised)	6.00	12.00
3 Larry Cole	6.00	12.00
4 Mike Ditka (with mustache)	10.00	20.00
5 John Fitzgerald	6.00	12.00
6 Toni Fritsch	6.00	12.00
7 Forrest Gregg	7.50	15.00
8 Bill Gregory	6.00	12.00
9 Bob Hayes (white jersey; football in hands)	7.50	15.00
10 Chuck Howley (white jersey; right foot raised)	7.50	15.00
11 Lee Roy Jordan (white jersey; no clouds in background)	7.50	15.00
12 Tom Landry CO	12.50	25.00
13 D.D. Lewis (with mustache)	6.00	12.00
14 Dave Manders (both feet on ground)	6.00	12.00
15 John Niland (white jersey; running to his left)	6.00	12.00
16 Gloster Richardson	6.00	12.00
17 Tody Smith	6.00	12.00
18 Don Talbert	6.00	12.00
19 Isaac Thomas	6.00	12.00
20 Pat Toomay (right foot raised)	6.00	12.00
21 Billy Truax	6.00	12.00
22 Rodney Wallace	6.00	12.00
23 Charlie Waters	6.00	12.00

1972 Cowboys Team Issue 4x5-1/2

These team issued photos feature black-and-white posed action player photos with white borders. Many of the photos are identical to the larger sized pictures from 1971, but this series measures approximately 4 1/4" by 5 1/2" and was likely issued over a period of years. Each features the player's facsimile autograph on the front with a white border at the bottom containing the player's name and team name. These cards are printed on thin card stock and have unnumbered blank backs. They closely resemble the 1975-76 Team Issue set so we've noted differences below on players common to both sets.

COMPLETE SET (43)	200.00	400.00
1 Herb Adderley	6.00	12.00
2 Lance Alworth	7.50	15.00
3 George Andrie	5.00	10.00
4 John Babinecz	5.00	10.00
5 Benny Barnes	5.00	10.00
6 Marv Bateman	5.00	10.00
7 Larry Cole (cutting to his right)	5.00	10.00
8 Jack Concannon	5.00	10.00
9 Mike Ditka	7.50	15.00
10 Dave Edwards	5.00	10.00
11 John Fitzgerald	5.00	10.00
12 Toni Fritsch	5.00	10.00
13 Jean Fugett	5.00	10.00
14 Walt Garrison	5.00	10.00
15 Cornell Green	6.00	12.00
16 Bill Gregory	5.00	10.00
17 Cliff Harris (no mustache)	6.00	12.00
18 Bob Hayes	7.50	15.00
19 Calvin Hill	6.00	12.00
20 Chuck Howley	6.00	12.00
21 Lee Roy Jordan (left foot raised)	6.00	12.00
22 Mike Keller	5.00	10.00
23 Tom Landry CO	10.00	20.00
24 D.D. Lewis (with mustache)	5.00	10.00
25 Bob Lilly	10.00	20.00
26 Dave Manders	5.00	10.00
27 Mike Montgomery,	5.00	10.00
28 Craig Morton	6.00	12.00
29 Ralph Neely	5.00	10.00
30 Robert Newhouse	5.00	10.00
31 John Niland	5.00	10.00
32 Blaine Nye	5.00	10.00
33 Billy Parks	5.00	10.00
34 Jethro Pugh (left foot raised)	5.00	10.00
35 Dan Reeves	6.00	12.00
36 Mel Renfro (left foot raised)	6.00	12.00
37 Roger Staubach (jersey #12 on shoulder)	15.00	30.00
38 Pat Toomay	5.00	10.00
39 Billy Truax	5.00	10.00
40 Rodney Wallace	5.00	10.00
41 Mark Washington	5.00	10.00
42 Charlie Waters (left foot raised)	6.00	12.00
43 Rayfield Wright (charging forward)	6.00	12.00

1973 Cowboys McDonald's

This set of photos was sponsored by McDonald's. Each photo measures approximately 8" by 10" and features a posed color close-up photo bordered in white. The player's name and team name are printed in black in the bottom white border. The top portion of the back has biographical information, career summary, and career statistics. The bottom portion carries the Cowboys 1973 game schedule. The photos are unnumbered and are checklisted below alphabetically.

COMPLETE SET (4)	45.00	90.00
1 Walt Garrison	5.00	10.00
2 Calvin Hill	7.50	15.00
3 Bob Lilly	12.50	25.00
4 Roger Staubach	25.00	50.00

1973 Cowboys Team Issue 4x5-1/2

These team issued photos feature black-and-white posed player photos with white borders. Each photo measures approximately 4 1/4" by 5 1/2" and features the player's name and team name below the player image. Every player is shown in his white jersey and the images were cropped to show no more than half of the jersey number. Some Images were also used to create the 5x7-1/2 version. Each photo was printed on thin paper stock, has a blankback and was not numbered. We've listed all known subjects; any additions to this list are appreciated.

COMPLETE SET (15)	60.00	120.00
1 Jim Arneson	4.00	8.00
2 Rodrigo Barnes	4.00	8.00
3 Marv Bateman	4.00	8.00
4 Jack Concannon	4.00	8.00
5 Billy Joe Dupree	5.00	10.00
6 Harvey Martin	5.00	10.00
7 Robert Newhouse	4.00	8.00
8 Billy Parks	4.00	8.00
9 Drew Pearson	7.50	15.00
10 Cyril Pinder	4.00	8.00
11 Golden Richards	4.00	8.00
12 Larry Robinson	4.00	8.00
13 Otto Stowe	4.00	8.00
14 Les Strayhorn	4.00	8.00
15 Bruce Walton	4.00	8.00

1973 Cowboys Team Issue 5x7-1/2

These team-issued photos feature black-and-white player pictures with a blank back. Each measures approximately 5 1/8" by 7 1/2" and was printed on glossy stock. A thick (3/8") white border surrounds the photo with the player's name and team name below. They are nearly identical to our list for 1974-76 except for the slightly larger overall size and different player photos. The 1973 photos typically show the player waist up with his full jersey number in view while the 1974-76 photos were taken more close-up. Any additions to the below list are appreciated.

COMPLETE SET (24)	75.00	150.00
1 Jim Arneson	4.00	8.00
2 John Babinecz	4.00	8.00
3 Gil Brandt PD	4.00	8.00
4 Larry Cole	4.00	8.00
5 Billy Joe DuPree	5.00	10.00
6 Walt Garrison	4.00	8.00
7 Bob Hayes	6.00	12.00
8 Calvin Hill	5.00	10.00
9 Ed Hughes ACO	4.00	8.00
10 Lee Roy Jordan	5.00	10.00
11 Tom Landry CO	7.50	15.00
12 Dave Manders	4.00	8.00
13 Harvey Martin	5.00	10.00
14 Robert Newhouse	4.00	8.00
15 John Niland	4.00	8.00
16 Blaine Nye	4.00	8.00
17 Jethro Pugh	4.00	8.00
18 Mel Renfro	6.00	12.00
19 John Smith	4.00	8.00
20 Otto Stowe	4.00	8.00
21 Pat Toomay	4.00	8.00
22 Bruce Walton	4.00	8.00
23 Charlie Waters	5.00	10.00
24 Rayfield Wright	5.00	10.00

1974-76 Cowboys Team Issue 5x7

These team-issued photos feature black-and-white player pictures with a blank back. Each measures approximately 5" by 7" and was printed on glossy photo paper stock. A thick (3/8") white border surrounds the photo with the player's name and team name below. They closely resemble the 1973 set but are generally cropped more closely with only a partial jersey number showing versus the 1973 photos. These were likely issued over a number of years as many variations can be found in the photos, but the text size is very close to the same on all of the photos. Any additions to the below list are appreciated.

1 Jim Arneson	4.00	8.00
2A Benny Barnes (slight smile)	4.00	8.00
2B Benny Barnes (no smile)	4.00	8.00
3 Bob Breunig	4.00	8.00
4 Warren Capone	4.00	8.00
5A Larry Cole (jersey number barely shows)	4.00	8.00
5B Larry Cole (half of jersey number shows)	4.00	8.00
6 Kyle Davis	4.00	8.00
7A Doug Dennison (Jersey # to the right)	4.00	8.00
7B Doug Dennison (Jersey # to the left)	4.00	8.00
8 Mike Ditka ACO	6.00	12.00
9 Pat Donovan	4.00	8.00
10A Billy Joe DuPree (slight smile)	5.00	10.00
10B Billy Joe DuPree (no smile)	5.00	10.00
11A Dave Edwards (jersey # barely shows)	4.00	8.00
11B Dave Edwards (half of jersey # shows)	4.00	0.00
12A John Fitzgerald (jersey # barely shows)	4.00	8.00
12B John Fitzgerald (half of jersey # shows)	4.00	8.00
13 Toni Fritsch	4.00	8.00
14A Jean Fugett (smiling)	4.00	8.00
14B Jean Fugett (not smiling)	4.00	8.00
15A Walt Garrison (facing straight)	4.00	8.00
15B Walt Garrison (looking slightly to his left)	4.00	8.00
16A Cornell Green (4 on shoulder visible)	4.00	8.00
16B Cornell Green (4 on shoulder not visible)	4.00	8.00
17A Bill Gregory (1/2 of jersey number shows)	4.00	8.00
17B Bill Gregory (1/3 of jersey number shows)	4.00	8.00
18A Cliff Harris (smiling)	5.00	10.00
18B Cliff Harris (not smiling)	5.00	10.00
19 Bob Hayes	6.00	12.00
20 Thomas Henderson	5.00	10.00
21 Efren Herrera	4.00	8.00
22 Calvin Hill	5.00	10.00
23 Mitch Hoopes	4.00	8.00
24 Bill Houston	4.00	8.00
25 Percy Howard	4.00	8.00
26A Ron Howard (smiling)	4.00	8.00
26B Ron Howard (not smiling)	4.00	8.00
27 Randy Hughes	4.00	8.00
28 Ken Hutcherson	4.00	8.00
29 Ed Too Tall Jones	5.00	10.00
30A Lee Roy Jordan (half of jersey # shows)	5.00	10.00
30B Lee Roy Jordan (3/4 of jersey # shows)	5.00	10.00
31 Gene Killian	4.00	8.00
32 Burton Lawless	4.00	8.00
33A D.D. Lewis (no mustache)	4.00	8.00
33B D.D. Lewis (with mustache)	4.00	8.00
34 Bob Lilly	7.50	15.00
35 Clint Longley	4.00	8.00
36 Dave Manders	4.00	8.00
37A Harvey Martin (facing to his left)	5.00	10.00
37B Harvey Martin (facing to his right)	5.00	10.00
38 Dennis Morgan	4.00	8.00
39A Ralph Neely (facing slightly to his right)	4.00	8.00
39B Ralph Neely (facing slightly to his left)	4.00	8.00
40A Robert Newhouse (half of jersey # shows)	5.00	10.00
40B Robert Newhouse (jersey # not visible)	5.00	10.00
41A Blaine Nye (1/2 of jersey number showing)	4.00	8.00
41B Blaine Nye (1/4 of jersey number showing)	4.00	8.00
42 Drew Pearson	6.00	12.00
43A Cal Peterson (name listed Calvin)	4.00	8.00
43B Cal Peterson (name listed Cal)	4.00	8.00
44A Jethro Pugh (jersey number touches left border)	4.00	8.00
44B Jethro Pugh (jersey # not touching left border)	4.00	8.00
45 Dan Reeves ACO	5.00	10.00
46A Mel Renfro (2 on shoulder fully visible)	5.00	10.00
46B Mel Renfro (2 on shoulder partially visible)	5.00	10.00
47A Golden Richards (looking to his right)	4.00	8.00
47B Golden Richards (facing straight)	4.00	8.00
48 Herb Scott	4.00	8.00
49 Ron Sellers	4.00	8.00
50A Roger Staubach (turned slightly to his left)	12.50	25.00
50B Roger Staubach (turned slightly to his right)	12.50	25.00
51 Les Strayhorn	4.00	8.00
52 Pat Toomay	4.00	8.00
53 Louie Walker	4.00	8.00
54A Bruce Walton (half jersey # visible)	4.00	8.00
54B Bruce Walton (full jersey # visible)	4.00	8.00
55A Mark Washington (not smiling)	4.00	8.00
55B Mark Washington (smiling)	4.00	8.00
56A Charlie Waters (no shoulder #'s visible)	5.00	10.00
56B Charlie Waters (1 on shoulder visible)	5.00	10.00
57 Randy White	7.50	15.00
58 Rollie Woolsey	4.00	8.00
59 Rayfield Wright	5.00	10.00
60A Charlie Young (half jersey # shows)	4.00	8.00
60B Charlie Young (jersey # shows slightly)	4.00	8.00

1975-76 Cowboys Team Issue 4x5-1/2

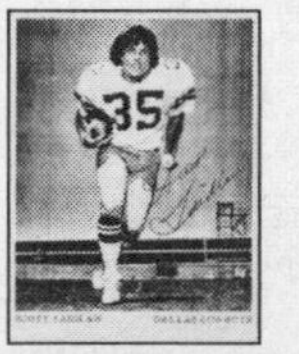

This team issued photo set features black-and-white posed action player photos with white borders. Each photo measures approximately 4 1/2" by 5 1/2" and features a facsimile autograph on the front unless noted below. A wider (1/2") white border at the bottom contains the player's name and team. These cards are printed on thin card stock and have unnumbered blank backs. They closely resemble the 1972 Team Issue set so we've noted differences below on players common to both sets.

COMPLETE SET (28)	100.00	200.00
1 Benny Barnes (no facsimile)	4.00	8.00
2 Bob Breunig	4.00	8.00
3 Larry Cole (charging forward)	4.00	8.00
4 Kyle Davis	4.00	8.00
5 Pat Donovan	4.00	8.00
6 Cliff Harris (with mustache, no facsimile)	5.00	10.00
7 Thomas Henderson	5.00	10.00
8 Efren Herrera	4.00	8.00
9 Mitch Hoopes	4.00	8.00
10 Ed Too Tall Jones	5.00	10.00
11 Lee Roy Jordan (right foot raised)	5.00	10.00
12 Scott Laidlaw	4.00	8.00
13 Burton Lawless	4.00	8.00
14 D.D. Lewis (no mustache)	4.00	8.00
15 Clint Longley	4.00	8.00
16 Harvey Martin (no facsimile)	5.00	10.00
17 Robert Newhouse (no facsimile)	4.00	8.00
18 Drew Pearson (no facsimile)	5.00	10.00
19 Preston Pearson	5.00	10.00
20 Jethro Pugh (right foot raised)	4.00	8.00
21 Mel Renfro (right foot raised)	6.00	12.00
22 Golden Richards	4.00	8.00
23 Herb Scott	4.00	8.00
24 Roger Staubach (no jersey number on shoulder)	10.00	20.00
25 Charlie Waters (right foot raised)	4.00	8.00
26 Randy White	7.50	15.00
27 Rayfield Wright (cutting to his left)	5.00	10.00
28 Charles Young	4.00	8.00

1976-78 Cowboys Team Issue 8x10

These photos were released by the Cowboys for player appearances and fan mail requests from roughly 1976-78. Each measures approximately 8" by 10" and fetures a black and white player photo. The player's name and team name appear immediately below the photo with slightly different font size and style used on the text for some of the photos. Many players were issued in more than one pose with some featuring only slight differences. Each is unnumbered and checklisted below alphabetically.

1A Bob Breunig (charging forward)	5.00	10.00
1B Bob Breunig (cutting to his right; right arm by his side)	5.00	10.00
1C Bob Breunig (cutting to his right; arm over jersey numbers)	5.00	10.00
1D Bob Breunig (cutting to his right; right arm over jerey #5)	5.00	10.00
2 Glenn Carano	5.00	10.00
3 Larry Cole (left foot off of the ground)	5.00	10.00
4 Jim Cooper	5.00	10.00
5A Doug Dennison (right foot raised)	5.00	10.00
5B Doug Dennison (left foot raised)	5.00	10.00
6 Pat Donovan	5.00	10.00
7 Tony Dorsett	10.00	20.00
8 Billy Joe DuPree	5.00	10.00
9 Jim Eidson	5.00	10.00
10 John Fitzgerald	5.00	10.00
11A Bill Gregory (charging forward)	5.00	10.00
11B Bill Gregory (running to his left)	5.00	10.00
12A Cliff Harris (left foot raised)	6.00	12.00
12B Cliff Harris (right foot raised; running sideways)	6.00	12.00
12C Cliff Harris (right foot raised; running forward)	6.00	12.00
13 Mike Hegman	5.00	10.00
14A Thomas Henderson (left foot raised)	6.00	12.00
14B Thomas Henderson (right foot raised; left hand just above head)	6.00	12.00
14C Thomas Henderson (right foot raised; left hand next to head)	6.00	12.00
15A Efren Herrera (facing to his left)	5.00	10.00
15B Efren Herrera (facing camera)	5.00	10.00
16A Tony Hill (four stripe socks)	6.00	12.00
16B Tony Hill (solid white socks)	6.00	12.00
17 Randy Hughes	5.00	10.00
18A Bruce Huther (jersey numbers fully visible)	5.00	10.00
18B Bruce Huther (left arm covering jersey #7)	5.00	10.00
19 Jim Jensen	5.00	10.00
20A Butch Johnson (football at shoulder)	5.00	10.00
20B Butch Johnson (football at waist)	5.00	10.00
21A Ed Too Tall Jones (running straight ahead)	6.00	12.00
21B Ed Too Tall Jones (running to his left)	6.00	12.00
21C Ed Too Tall Jones (running slightly to the right; left foot off of the ground)	6.00	12.00
21D Ed Too Tall Jones (running slightly to the right; right foot off of the ground)	6.00	12.00
22 Lee Roy Jordan	6.00	12.00
23A Aaron Kyle (full jersey number in view)	5.00	10.00
23B Aaron Kyle (#5 on jersey partially obscured)	5.00	10.00
24 Scott Laidlaw	5.00	10.00
25 Burton Lawless	5.00	10.00
26A D.D. Lewis (with mustache)	5.00	10.00
26B D.D. Lewis (without mustache)	5.00	10.00
27A Harvey Martin (left foot off of the ground)	6.00	12.00
27B Harvey Martin (right foot off of the ground)	5.00	10.00
28A Ralph Neely (73 showing on left shoulder)	5.00	10.00
28B Ralph Neely (7 showing on left shoulder)	5.00	10.00
29A Robert Newhouse (right foot off of the ground)	5.00	10.00
29B Robert Newhouse (left foot off of the ground)	5.00	10.00
30 Blaine Nye	5.00	10.00
31A Drew Pearson (football in hands; big hair)	6.00	12.00
31B Drew Pearson (football just entering hands)	6.00	12.00
31C Drew Pearson (football in front of hands)	6.00	12.00
32A Preston Pearson (football in left hand)	6.00	12.00
32B Preston Pearson (football in right hand)	6.00	12.00
33A Jethro Pugh (cutting to his right)	5.00	10.00
33B Jethro Pugh (running forward; left arm on chest)	5.00	10.00
33C Jethro Pugh (running forward; left arm near cheek)	5.00	10.00
34 Tom Rafferty	5.00	10.00
35 Tom Randall	5.00	10.00
36A Mel Renfro (three stripes on sock)	7.50	15.00
36B Mel Renfro (one large stripe on sock)	7.50	15.00
37A Golden Richards (right foot waist high)	5.00	10.00
37B Golden Richards (right foot near ground)	5.00	10.00
38 Jay Saldi	5.00	10.00
39 Rafael Septien	5.00	10.00
40A Roger Staubach (facing to his left)	10.00	20.00
40B Roger Staubach (facing forward)	10.00	20.00
41A Mark Washington (three stripes on sock)	5.00	10.00
41B Mark Washington (one large stripe on sock)	5.00	10.00
42A Charlie Waters (jersey number fully visible)	6.00	12.00
42B Charlie Waters (jersey number #4 obscured)	6.00	12.00
43A Randy White (charging to his left)	10.00	20.00
43B Randy White (charging to his right)	10.00	20.00
44 Rayfield Wright	6.00	12.00
45 Charlie Young	5.00	10.00

1977 Cowboys Burger King Glasses

Burger King restaurants in conjunction with Dr. Pepper released this set of 6-drinking glasses during the 1977 NFL season in Dallas area stores. Each features a black and white photo of a Cowboys player with his name and team name below the picture. This set can be differentiated from the 1978 Burger King due to the row of stars that encircle the glass, as well as the different player selection.

COMPLETE SET (6)	25.00	50.00
1 Billy Joe DuPree	5.00	10.00
2 Efren Herrera	3.75	7.50
3 Harvey Martin	6.00	12.00
4 Drew Pearson	6.00	12.00
5 Charlie Waters	5.00	10.00
6 Randy White	7.50	15.00

1978 Cowboys Burger King Glasses

Burger King restaurants in conjunction with Dr. Pepper released this set of 6-drinking glasses during the 1978 NFL season in Dallas area stores. Each features a black and white photo of a Cowboys player with his name and team name below the picture.

COMPLETE SET (6)	20.00	40.00
1 Bob Breunig	3.00	6.00
2 Pat Donovan	3.00	6.00
3 Cliff Harris	4.00	8.00
4 D.D. Lewis	4.00	8.00
5 Robert Newhouse	4.00	8.00
6 Golden Richards	3.00	6.00

1978 Cowboys Team Sheets

These 8" by 10" sheets were issued primarily to media outlets in need of player photos. Each sheet includes small photos for 8-players (except for the final sheet) with the player's name and position below each image. The "Dallas Cowboys" name is at the top of each sheet. The backs are blank

COMPLETE SET (6)	40.00	80.00
1 Benny Barnes, Bob Breunig, Larry Brinson, Guy Brown, Glenn Carano, Larry Cole, Jim Cooper, Doug Dennison	5.00	10.00
2 Pat Donovan, Tony Dorsett, Billy Jo DuPree, John Fitzgerald, Andy Frederick, Bill Gregory, Cliff Harris, Mike Hegman	10.00	20.00
3 Thomas Henderson, Efren Herrera, Tony Hill, Randy Hughes, Bruce Huther, Butch Johnson, Ed Jones, Aaron Kyle	6.00	12.00
4 Scott Laidlaw, Burton Lawless, D.D. Lewis, Harvey Martin, Ralph Neely, Robert Newhouse, Drew Pearson, Preston Pearson	6.00	12.00
5 Jethro Pugh, Tom Rafferty, Mel Renfro, Goldon Richards, Jay Saldi, Herbert Scott, David Stalls, Roger Staubach	12.50	25.00
6 Mark Washington, Charlie Waters, Danny White, Randy White, Rayfield Wright	7.50	15.00

1979 Cowboys Police

The 1979 Dallas Cowboy Police set consists of 15 cards sponsored by the Kiwanis Clubs, the Dallas Cowboys Weekly (the official fan newspaper), and the local law enforcement agency. The cards measure approximately 2 5/8" by 4 1/8". The cards are unnumbered but have been numbered in the checklist below by the player's uniform number which appears on the fronts of the cards. The backs contain "Cowboys Tips" which draw analogies between action on the football field and law abiding action in real life. D.D. Lewis replaced Thomas (Hollywóod) Henderson midway through the season; hence, both of these cards are available in lesser quantities than the other cards in this set.

COMPLETE SET (15)	10.00	20.00
12 Roger Staubach	4.00	8.00
33 Tony Dorsett	2.50	5.00
41 Charlie Waters	.50	1.00
43 Cliff Harris	.50	1.00
44 Robert Newhouse	.25	.50
50 D.D. Lewis SP	1.50	3.00
53 Bob Breunig	.25	.50
54 Randy White	1.25	2.50
56 Thomas Henderson SP	1.50	3.00
67 Pat Donovan	.25	.50
79 Harvey Martin	.50	1.00
80 Tony Hill	.50	1.00
88 Drew Pearson	.60	1.50
89 Billy Joe DuPree	.50	1.00
NNO Tom Landry CO	2.00	4.00

1979 Cowboys Team Issue Bios

These photos were released by the Cowboys for player appearances and fan mail requests. This style and format was used for a number of years (from roughly 1979-1985) so we've included descriptions below to differentiate players released in more than one year. Each measures approximately 4" by 5 1/2" and was printed on thick paper stock. The white-bordered fronts display black-and-white player photos. The player's name and jersey number appear immediately below the photo with his position, height, weight, and college below that. The Cowboys helmet logo on included on the left. The backs are blank are unnumbered.

COMPLETE SET (47)	150.00	300.00
1 Benny Barnes	4.00	8.00
2 Larry Bethea	4.00	8.00
3 Alois Blackwell	4.00	8.00
4 Bob Breunig (running to his left)	4.00	8.00
5 Guy Brown	4.00	8.00
6 Glenn Carano (right foot raised)	4.00	8.00
7 Larry Cole	4.00	8.00
8 Jim Cooper (no mustache; offensive tackle)	4.00	8.00
9 Doug Cosbie (football in hands)	4.00	8.00
10 Anthony Dickerson (left leg straight)	4.00	8.00
11 Pat Donovan (jersey #7 obscured)	4.00	8.00
12 Tony Dorsett (football in right hand)	7.50	15.00
13 Billy Joe Dupree	5.00	10.00
14 John Dutton (cutting to his left slightly)	4.00	8.00
15 John Fitzgerald (snapping the ball)	4.00	8.00
16 Andy Frederick	4.00	8.00
17 Richard Grimmett	4.00	8.00
18 Cliff Harris	5.00	10.00
19 Mike Hegman (left hand at left shoulder)	4.00	8.00
20 Thomas Henderson	5.00	10.00
21 Tony Hill (football up by shoulder)	5.00	10.00
22 Randy Hughes	4.00	8.00
23 Bruce Huther	4.00	8.00
24 Butch Johnson (football up near head)	4.00	8.00
25 Ed Too Tall Jones (cutting to his right)	5.00	10.00
26 Tom Landry CO (star next to helmet logo)	6.00	12.00
27 D.D. Lewis	4.00	8.00
28 Harvey Martin (jersey #7 partially obscured)	5.00	10.00
29 Aaron Mitchell	4.00	8.00
30 Robert Newhouse (football in left arm)	5.00	10.00
31 Drew Pearson (jersey #8 obscured; weight:183)	6.00	12.00
32 Preston Pearson	5.00	10.00
33 Tom Rafferty	4.00	8.00
34 Jay Saldi	4.00	8.00
35 Tex Schramm GM	5.00	10.00
36 Herb Scott	4.00	8.00
37 Rafael Septien (right foot at left knee)	4.00	8.00
38 Robert Shaw	4.00	8.00
39 Ron Springs (right foot at left knee)	4.00	8.00
40 Dave Stalls	4.00	8.00
41 Roger Staubach	15.00	25.00
42 Bruce Thornton	4.00	8.00
43 Dennis Thurman (left leg raised)	4.00	8.00
44 Charlie Waters	5.00	10.00
45 Danny White (feet planted)	6.00	12.00
46 Randy White (running to his right)	7.50	15.00
47 Steve Wilson (wearing jersey #81)	4.00	8.00

1979 Cowboys Team Sheets

These 8" by 10" sheets were issued primarily to media outlets in need of player photos. Each sheet includes small photos for 8-players with the player's jersey number, name and position below each image. The "Dallas Cowboys" name is at the top of each sheet. The backs are blank

COMPLETE SET (6)	40.00	80.00
1 Larry Bethea, Benny Barnes, Alois Blackwell, Bob Breunig, Larry Brinson, Guy Brown, Glenn Carano, Larry Cole	5.00	10.00
2 Jim Cooper, Doug Cosbie, Pat Donovan, Tony Dorsett, Billy Joe Dupree, John Fitzgerald, Andy Frederick, Richard Grimmett	7.50	15.00
3 Cliff Harris, Mike Hegman, Thomas Henderson, Tony Hill, Randy Hughes, Bruce Huther, Butch Johnson, Aaron Kyle	5.00	10.00
4 Scott Laidlaw, Burton Lawless, D.D. Lewis, Wade Manning, Harvey Martin, Aaron Mitchell, Robert Newhouse, Drew Pearson	6.00	12.00
5 Preston Pearson, Tom Rafferty, Jay Saldi, Herb Scott, Rafael Septien, Robert Shaw, Ron Springs, Dave Stalls	5.00	10.00
6 Roger Staubach, Bruce Thornton, Dennis Thurman, Charlie Waters, Danny White, Randy White, Steve Wilson, Rayfield Wright	12.50	25.00

1979-80 Cowboys Team Issue 4x5-1/2

These team issued photos feature black-and-white posed action player photos with white borders. Each photo measures approximately 4 1/4" by 5 1/2" and features the player's name and team name below the player image. Every player is shown in his white jersey and each photo was printed on thin paper matte-finish stock, has a blankback and was not numbered. We've listed all known subjects; any additions to this list are appreciated.

1 Tony Dorsett	6.00	12.00
2 Billy Joe DuPree	4.00	8.00
3 James Jones	4.00	8.00
4 D.D. Lewis	4.00	8.00
5 Drew Pearson	5.00	10.00
6 Roger Staubach	10.00	20.00
7 Danny White	6.00	12.00
8 Randy White	6.00	12.00

1980 Cowboys McDonald's

These cards were issued two per box on three different Happy Meal type boxes numbered "Super Box I" through "Super Box III." The individual cards, meant to be cut from the boxes, are unnumbered and blankbacked. We've listed prices for single cards, neatly cut from the box, below alphabetically according to the box on which the player appears. Complete Happy Meal Boxes carry a premium of 1.5X to 2X the prices listed below.

COMPLETE SET (6)	125.00	200.00
1 Chuck Howley	15.00	25.00
2 Don Perkins	10.00	25.00
3 Bob Lilly	15.00	30.00
4 Don Meredith	20.00	35.00
5 Walt Garrison	10.00	20.00
6 Roger Staubach	50.00	100.00

1980 Cowboys Police

Quite similar to the 1979 set, the 1980 Dallas Cowboys police set is unnumbered other than the player's uniform number (as is listed in the checklist below). The cards in this 14-card set measure approximately 2 5/8" by 4 1/8". The sponsors are the same as those of the 1979 issue and the section entitled "Cowboys Tips" is contained on the back. The Kiwanis and Cowboys helmet logos appear on the fronts of the cards.

COMPLETE SET (14)	6.00	12.00
1 Rafael Septien	.40	1.00
11 Danny White	1.25	2.50
25 Aaron Kyle	.25	.60
26 Preston Pearson	.60	1.50
31 Benny Barnes	.40	1.00
35 Scott Laidlaw	.25	.60
42 Randy Hughes	.25	.60
62 John Fitzgerald	.40	1.00
63 Larry Cole	.40	1.00
64 Tom Rafferty	.40	1.00
68 Herb Scott	.25	.60
70 Rayfield Wright	.40	1.00
78 John Dutton	.40	1.00
87 Jay Saldi	.40	1.00

1980 Cowboys Team Issue Bios

These photos were released by the Cowboys for player appearances and fan mail requests. This style and format was used for a number of years (from roughly 1979-1985) so we've included descriptions below to differentiate players released in more than one year. Each measures approximately 4" by 5 1/2" and was printed on thick paper stock. The white-bordered fronts display black-and-white player photos. The player's name and jersey number appear immediately below the photo with his position, height, weight, and college below that. The Cowboys helmet logo on included on the left. The backs are blank are unnumbered.

COMPLETE SET (27)	100.00	200.00
1 Bob Breunig (running to his right; weight: 225)	4.00	8.00
2 Glenn Carano (both feet planted)	4.00	8.00
3 Dextor Clinkscale (jersey #'s hidden)	4.00	8.00
4 Jim Cooper (mustache; tackle)	4.00	8.00
5 Doug Cosbie (football in air; left hand over jersey #4)	4.00	8.00
6 Anthony Dickerson (left leg slightly bent)	4.00	8.00
7 Pat Donovan (full jersey #'s visible)	4.00	8.00
8 Tony Dorsett (ball in left hand; right knee down)	7.50	15.00
9 John Dutton (charging straight ahead)	4.00	8.00
12 Tony Hill (football down near waist)	5.00	10.00
10 John Fitzgerald (charging forward)	4.00	8.00
13 Gary Hogeboom	4.00	8.00
11 Mike Hegman (left hand on jersey #5)	4.00	8.00
14 Butch Johnson (football down at waist)	4.00	8.00
16 James Jones	4.00	8.00
15 Ed Too Tall Jones (cutting to his left)	5.00	10.00
17 Tom Landry CO (no star next to helmet logo)	6.00	12.00
18 Harvey Martin (jersey #7 fully visible; weight: 250)	5.00	10.00
19 Robert Newhouse (football in right arm)	4.00	8.00
20 Timmy Newsome (feet close together)	4.00	8.00
21 Drew Pearson (jersey #8 fully visible; Weight: 183)	5.00	10.00
22 Kurt Petersen (clouds in background)	4.00	8.00
23 Bill Roe	4.00	8.00
24 Rafael Septien (right foot waist high; left heel up)	4.00	8.00
25 Roland Solomon	4.00	8.00
26 Ron Springs (right foot just below left knee)	4.00	8.00
27 Dennis Thurman (right leg raised)	4.00	8.00
28 Norm Wells	4.00	8.00
29 Danny White (dropping back; jersey #'s visible)	6.00	12.00
30 Randy White (running to his left)	7.50	15.00
31 Steve Wilson (wearing jersey #45)	4.00	8.00

1980 Cowboys Team Sheets

These 8" by 10" sheets were issued primarily to media outlets in need of player photos. Each sheet includes small photos for 8-players with the player's jersey number, name and position below each image. "The Dallas Cowboys Football Club" is printed at the top of each sheet and the backs are blank

COMPLETE SET (7)	40.00	80.00
1 Benny Barnes, Larry Bethea, Bob Breunig, Guy Brown, Glenn Carano, Dextor Clinkscale, Larry Cole, Jim Cooper	5.00	10.00
2 Doug Cosbie, Anthony Dickerson, Pat Donovan, Tony Dorsett, Billy Joe Dupree, John Dutton, John Fitzgerald, Andy Frederick	7.50	15.00
3 Mike Hegman, Tony Hill, Gary Hogeboom, Randy Hughes, Eric Hurt, Bruce Huther, Butch Johnson, Ed Jones	6.00	12.00
4 James Jones, Aaron Kyle, D.D. Lewis, Harvey Martin, Aaron Mitchell, Robert Newhouse, Timmy Newsome, Drew Pearson	6.00	12.00
5 Preston Pearson, Kurt Petersen, Tom Rafferty, Bill Roe, Jay Saldi, Herb Scott, Rafael Septien, Robert Shaw	5.00	10.00
6 Roland Soloman, Ron Springs, Bruce Thornton, Dennis Thurman, Charlie Waters, Norm Wells, Danny White, Randy White, Steve Wilson	7.50	15.00
7 Coaching Staff, Tom Landry, Ermal Allen, Mike Ditka, Al Lavan, Jim Myers, Dan Reeves, Gene Stallings, Ernie Stautner, Jerry Tubbs, Bob Ward	7.50	15.00

1981 Cowboys Police

The 1981 Dallas Cowboys set of 14 cards is quite similar to sets of the previous two years. Since the cards are unnumbered, except for uniform number, the players have been listed by uniform number in the checklist below. The cards measure approximately 2 5/8" by 4 1/8". The set is sponsored by the Kiwanis Club, the local law enforcement agency, and the Dallas Cowboys Weekly. Appearing on the back along with a Cowboys helmet logo are "Cowboys Tips". A Kiwanis logo and Cowboys helmet logo appear on the front.

COMPLETE SET (14)	5.00	12.00
18 Glenn Carano	.40	1.00
20 Ron Springs	.40	1.00
23 James Jones	.25	.60
26 Michael Downs	.40	1.00
32 Dennis Thurman	.40	1.00
45 Steve Wilson	.25	.60
51 Anthony Dickerson	.25	.60
52 Robert Shaw	.25	.60
58 Mike Hegman	.40	1.00
59 Guy Brown	.25	.60
61 Jim Cooper	.25	.60
72 Ed Too Tall Jones	1.00	2.50
84 Doug Cosbie	.50	1.25
86 Butch Johnson	.50	1.25

1981 Cowboys Thousand Oaks Police

This 14-card set was issued in Thousand Oaks, California, where the Cowboys conduct their summer pre-season workouts. These unnumbered cards measure approximately 2 5/8" by 4 1/8". Similar to other Cowboys sets, the distinguishing factors of this set are the Thousand Oaks Kiwanis Club and Thousand Oaks Police Department names printed on the backs in the place where other sets had the Kiwanis Club and law enforcement agency printed. The 14 players in this set are different from those in the regular set above. The cards are listed below by uniform number.

COMPLETE SET (14)	20.00	50.00
11 Danny White	1.40	3.50
31 Benny Barnes	.60	1.50
33 Tony Dorsett	4.00	10.00
41 Charlie Waters	1.40	3.50
42 Randy Hughes	.60	1.50
44 Robert Newhouse	1.00	2.50
54 Randy White	2.50	6.00
55 D.D. Lewis	.60	1.50
78 John Dutton	.60	1.50
79 Harvey Martin	1.00	2.50
80 Tony Hill	1.00	2.50
88 Drew Pearson	2.00	5.00
89 Billy Joe DuPree	1.00	2.50
NNO Tom Landry CO	3.00	8.00

1982 Cowboys Carrollton Park

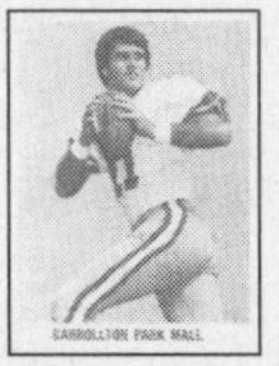

The 1982 Carrollton Park Mall Cowboys set contains six photo cards in black and white with the words "Carrollton Park Mall" in blue at the bottom of the card front. The cards measure approximately 3" by 4". The backs contain the 1982 Cowboys schedule and brief career statistics of the player portrayed. The cards are numbered on the back and the set is available as an uncut sheet with no difference in value.

COMPLETE SET (6)	3.00	8.00
1 Roger Staubach	1.25	3.00
2 Danny White	.30	.75
3 Tony Dorsett	.60	1.50
4 Randy White	.40	1.00
5 Charlie Waters	.20	.50
6 Billy Joe DuPree	.20	.50

1983 Cowboys Marketcom

In 1983 Marketcom issued a separate team set for the Cowboys. These 5 1/2" by 8 1/2" cards feature a large full color picture of each player with a white border. Similar to the 1982 regular 48-card issue, the Cowboys cards have the player's name on front at top and a facsimile autograph on the picture. The cards are unnumbered and the cardbacks carry biographical information, player profile, and statistics. The lower right corner of the card back indicates "St. Louis - Marketcom."

COMPLETE SET (10)	35.00	60.00
1 Bob Breunig	2.00	5.00
2 Pat Donovan	2.00	5.00
3 Tony Dorsett	7.50	20.00
4 Michael Downs	2.00	5.00
5 Butch Johnson	2.00	5.00
6 Harvey Martin	2.50	6.00
7 Timmy Newsome	2.00	5.00
8 Drew Pearson	3.00	8.00
9 Danny White	3.00	8.00
10 Randy White	4.00	10.00

1983 Cowboys Police

This unnumbered set of 28 cards was sponsored by the Kiwannis Club, Law Enforcement Agency, and the Dallas Cowboys Weekly. Cards are approximately 2 5/8" by 4 1/8" and have a white border around the photo on the front of the cards. The backs each contain a safety tip. Cards are listed in the checklist below in uniform number order. Four cheerleaders are included in the set and are so indicated by CHEER.

COMPLETE SET (28)	6.00	15.00
1 Rafael Septien	.20	.50
11 Danny White	.40	1.00
20 Ron Springs	.20	.50
24 Everson Walls	.20	.50
26 Michael Downs	.10	.30
30 Timmy Newsome	.10	.30
32 Dennis Thurman	.20	.50
33 Tony Dorsett	1.00	2.50
47 Dextor Clinkscale	.10	.30
53 Bob Breunig	.20	.50
54 Randy White	.75	2.00
65 Kurt Petersen	.10	.30
67 Pat Donovan	.10	.30
70 Howard Richards	.10	.30
72 Ed Too Tall Jones	.60	1.50
78 John Dutton	.20	.50
79 Harvey Martin	.20	.50
80 Tony Hill	.20	.50
83 Doug Donley	.10	.30
84 Doug Cosbie	.20	.50
86 Butch Johnson	.20	.50
88 Drew Pearson	.60	1.50
89 Billy Joe DuPree	.20	.50
NNO Tom Landry CO	.75	2.00
NNO Melinda May CHEER	.10	.30
NNO Dana Presley CHEER	.10	.30
NNO Judy Trammell CHEER	.10	.30
NNO Toni Washington CHEER	.10	.30

1983-84 Cowboys Team Issue

These photos were released by the Cowboys for player appearances and fan mail requests. This style and format was used for a number of years (from roughly 1979-1985) so we've included descriptions below to differentiate players released in more than one year. Each measures approximately 4" by 5 1/2" and was printed on thick paper stock. The white-bordered fronts display black-and-white player photos. The player's name and jersey number appear immediately below the photo with his position, height, weight, and college below that. The Cowboys helmet logo on included on the left. The backs are blank are unnumbered.

COMPLETE SET (34)	100.00	200.00
1 Brian Baldinger	3.00	6.00
2 Bill Bates	4.00	8.00
3 Bob Breunig (running to his right; weight: 227)	3.00	6.00
4 Dextor Clinkscale (jersey #'s visible)	3.00	6.00
5 Fred Cornwell	3.00	6.00
6 Doug Cosbie (football in air; left hand over jersey #8)	3.00	6.00
7 Anthony Dickerson	3.00	6.00
8A Doug Donley (left hand down at waist)	3.00	6.00
8B Doug Donley (left hand up at neck)	3.00	6.00
9A Tony Dorsett (ball in left hand; right knee up at waist)	6.00	12.00
9B Tony Dorsett (ball in right hand; cutting to his right)	6.00	12.00
10A Michael Downs (right arm down by side)	3.00	6.00
10B Michael Downs (right arm fully extended)	3.00	6.00
11 Ron Fellows	3.00	6.00
12 Rod Hill	3.00	6.00
13 Gary Hogeboom	3.00	6.00
14 Jim Jeffcoat	3.00	6.00
15 Ed Jones	4.00	8.00
16 Eugene Lockhart	3.00	6.00
17 Harvey Martin (jersey #7 fully visible; weight: 255)	4.00	8.00
18 Timmy Newsome (feet far apart)	3.00	6.00
19 Drew Pearson (jersey #8 fully visible; Weight: 190)	4.00	8.00
20 Kurt Petersen (clear sky in background)	3.00	6.00
21 Phil Pozderac	3.00	6.00
22 Mike Renfro	3.00	6.00
23 Howard Richards	3.00	6.00
24 Jeff Rohrer	3.00	6.00
25 Chris Schultz	3.00	6.00
26 Rafael Septien (right foot waist high; left heel on ground)	3.00	6.00
27A Don Smerek (charging forward)	3.00	6.00
27B Don Smerek (cutting to his left slightly)	3.00	6.00
28 Danny Spradlin	3.00	6.00
29 Ron Springs (wrist bands on elbows)	3.00	6.00
30 Mark Tuinei	4.00	8.00
31A Everson Walls (jersey #'s half visible)	4.00	8.00
31B Everson Walls (jersey #'s obscured)	4.00	8.00
32 John Warren	3.00	6.00
33 Danny White (dropping back; jersey #'s hidden)	5.00	10.00
34 Randy White	5.00	10.00

1984 Cowboys Team Sheets

These 8" by 10" sheets were issued primarily to the media for use as player images for print. Each features 8-players or coaches with the player's jersey number, name, and position beneath his picture. The sheets are blankbacked and unnumbered.

COMPLETE SET (8)	20.00	50.00
1 Vince Albritton, Gary Allen, Dowe Aughtman, Brian Baldinger, Bill Bates, Bob Breunig, Billy Cannon Jr., Harold Carmichael	2.50	6.00
2 Dextor Clinkscale, Jim Cooper, Fred Cornwell, Doug Cosbie, Steve DeOssie, Anthony Dickerson, Doug Donley, Tony Dorsett	3.00	8.00
3 Michael Downs, John Dutton, Ron Fellows, Norm Granger, Mike Hegman, Tony Hill, Gary Hogeboom, Carl Howard	2.00	5.00
4 John Hunt, Jim Jeffcoat, Ed Too Tall Jones, Eugene Lockhart, Chuck McSwain, Timmy Newsome, Steve Pelluer, Kurt Petersen	2.50	6.00
5 Kirk Phillips, Phil Pozderac, Tom Rafferty, Mike Renfro, Howard Richards, Jeff Rohrer, Brian Salonen, Herb Scott	2.00	5.00
6 Victor Scott, Rafael Septien, Dom Smerek, Waddell Smith, Ron Springs, Dennis Thurman, Glen Titensor, Mark Tuinei	2.00	5.00
7 Everson Walls, Danny White, Randy White, Tom Landry, Neill Armstrong, Al Lavan, Alan Lowry, Jim Myers	4.00	10.00
8 Dick Nolan, Jim Shofner, Gene Stallings, Ernie Stautner, Jerry Tubbs, Bob Ward, Bum Bright, Tex Schramm	2.00	5.00

1985-86 Cowboys Frito Lay

The Cowboys Frito Lay photos were issued over a number of years in the mid 1980s. The cards measure approximately 4" by 5 1/2" and are printed on photographic quality paper stock. The white-bordered fronts display black-and-white player photos with the Cowboys helmet logo below the image in the lower left corner. The player's jersey number and name appear below the photo with his position, vital stats and college noted below that. The Frito Lay logo in the lower right corner rounds out the front. The backs are blank and unnumbered. Roger Staubach is included in the set even though he retired in 1979.

COMPLETE SET (53)	200.00	400.00
1 Vince Albritton	4.00	8.00
2 Brian Baldinger	4.00	8.00
3 Gordon Banks	4.00	8.00
4A Bill Bates (running to the right)	5.00	10.00
5 Dextor Clinkscale	4.00	8.00
6 Reggie Collier	4.00	8.00
7 Jim Cooper	4.00	8.00
8 Fred Cornwell	4.00	8.00
9 Doug Cosbie	4.00	8.00
10 Steve DeOssie	4.00	8.00
11A Tony Dorsett (ball down by waist)	10.00	20.00
12 Michael Downs	4.00	8.00
13 John Dutton	4.00	8.00
14 Ricky Easmon	4.00	8.00
15 Ron Fellows	4.00	8.00
16 Leon Gonzalez	4.00	8.00
17 Mike Hegman	4.00	8.00
18 Gary Hogeboom	4.00	8.00
19 Jim Jeffcoat	4.00	8.00
20 Ed Too Tall Jones	7.50	15.00
21 James Jones	4.00	8.00
22 Crawford Ker	4.00	8.00
23 Tom Landry CO	10.00	20.00
24 Robert Lavette	4.00	8.00
25 Eugene Lockhart	4.00	8.00
26 Timmy Newsome	4.00	8.00
27 Drew Pearson ACO	6.00	12.00
28 Steve Pelluer	4.00	8.00
29 Jesse Penn	4.00	8.00
30 Kurt Petersen	4.00	8.00
31 Karl Powe	4.00	8.00
32 Phil Pozderac UER (college listed as Notre Name)	4.00	8.00
33 Tom Rafferty	4.00	8.00
34 Mike Renfro	4.00	8.00
35 Howard Richards	4.00	8.00
36 Jeff Rohrer	4.00	8.00
37 Mike Saxon	4.00	8.00
38 Victor Scott	4.00	8.00
39 Rafael Septien	4.00	8.00
40 Don Smerek	4.00	8.00
41 Roger Staubach	20.00	40.00
42 Broderick Thompson	4.00	8.00
43 Dennis Thurman	4.00	8.00
44 Glen Titensor	4.00	8.00
45 Mark Tuinei	5.00	10.00
46 Herschel Walker	7.50	15.00
47A Everson Walls	5.00	10.00
47B Everson Walls	5.00	10.00
48A Danny White (dropping back to pass)	6.00	12.00
49 Randy White	7.50	15.00
50 John Williams	4.00	8.00
51 1985 Team Photo	5.00	10.00
52 1986 Team Photo	5.00	10.00
53 Valley Ranch Offices	4.00	8.00

1987 Cowboys Ace Fact Pack

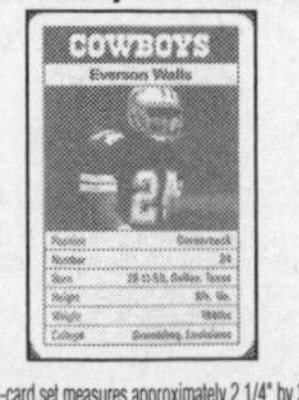

This 33-card set measures approximately 2 1/4" by 3 5/8". This set, which was printed in West Germany (by Ace Fact Pack) for release in Great Britain, has rounded corners and a playing type card back. There were 22 players in this set which we have checklisted alphabetically.

COMPLETE SET (33)	100.00	200.00
1 Bill Bates	3.00	8.00
2 Doug Cosbie	2.00	5.00
3 Tony Dorsett	20.00	50.00
4 Michael Downs	1.25	3.00
5 John Dutton	2.00	5.00
6 Ron Fellows	1.25	3.00
7 Mike Hegman	1.25	3.00
8 Tony Hill	2.00	5.00
9 Jim Jeffcoat	2.00	5.00
10 Ed Too Tall Jones	6.00	15.00
11 Crawford Ker	1.25	3.00
12 Eugene Lockhart	1.25	3.00
13 Phil Pozderac	1.25	3.00
14 Tom Rafferty	1.25	3.00
15 Jeff Rohrer	1.25	3.00
16 Mike Sherrard	2.00	5.00
17 Glen Titensor	1.25	3.00
18 Mark Tuinei	2.00	5.00
19 Herschel Walker	7.50	20.00
20 Everson Walls	1.25	3.00
21 Danny White	5.00	12.00
22 Randy White	7.50	20.00
23 Cowboys Helmet	1.25	3.00
24 Cowboys Information	1.25	3.00
25 Cowboys Uniform	1.25	3.00
26 Game Record Holders	1.25	3.00
27 Season Record Holders	1.25	3.00
28 Career Record Holders	1.25	3.00
29 Record 1967-86	1.25	3.00
30 1986 Team Statistics	1.25	3.00
31 All-Time Greats	1.25	3.00
32 Roll of Honour	1.25	3.00
33 Texas Stadium	1.25	3.00

1974 Cowboys Team Issue 8x10

The Dallas Cowboys issued these black-and-white player photos, measuring 8" by 10," and printed on glossy stock with white borders. Each player photo is a posed action shot. The border below the photo contains just the player's name and team name. The type style and size varies slightly on some photos so this may indicate that they were released over a period of years. The photos are blankbacked and unnumbered. Any additions to the below list are appreciated.

1 Larry Cole (right foot off of the ground)	6.00	12.00
2 Bob Hayes	7.50	15.00
3 Ron Howard	6.00	12.00
4 Cornell Green	6.00	12.00
5 Bob Lilly (left foot off of the ground)	10.00	20.00
6 Ralph Neely	6.00	12.00
7 Mel Renfro (wearing a beard)	7.50	15.00

1990 Cowboys Team Issue

The Cowboys issued these 5" by 7" black and white photos in 1990. Each includes a portrait or action shot of the featured player with his name and team name below the photo in all capital letters. The photo backs are blank.

COMPLETE SET (10)	25.00	50.00
1 Troy Aikman	7.50	15.00
2 Darren Benson	2.50	5.00
3 Louis Cheek	2.50	5.00
4 Dean Hamel	2.50	5.00
5 Issiac Holt	2.50	5.00
6 Babe Laufenberg	2.50	5.00
7 Eugene Lockhart	2.50	5.00
8 Randy Shannon	2.50	5.00
9 Derrick Shepard	2.50	5.00
10 Stan Smagala	2.50	5.00

1993 Cowboys Taco Bell Cups

These cups were issued at Dallas area Taco Bell restaurants during the 1993 season. Each cup contains 2 players on each side, and caricatures the players featured.

1 Bill Bates, Alvin Harper	.80	2.00
2 Jay Novacek, Emmitt Smith	1.60	4.00

1994 Cowboys Pro Line Live Kroger Stickers

COMPLETE SET (7)	2.40	6.00
1 Troy Aikman, Darren Woodson, Erik Williams	.60	1.50
2 Emmitt Smith, James Washington, Mark Stepnoski	1.00	2.50
3 Michael Irvin, Kenneth Gant, Tony Tolbert	.30	.75
4 Daryl Johnston, Kevin Williams WR, Leon Lett	.30	.75
5 Nate Newton, Shante Carver, Charles Haley	.20	.50
6 Russell Maryland, Mark Tuinei, Kevin Smith	.20	.50
7 Alvin Harper, Willie Jackson, Jay Novacek	.20	.50

1997 Cowboys Collector's Choice

Upper Deck released several team sets in 1997 in a blister pack wrapper. Each of the 14-cards in this set are very similar to the base Collector's Choice cards except for the card numbering on the cardback. A

cover/checklist card was added featuring the team helmet.

COMPLETE SET (14)	1.50	4.00
DA1 Deion Sanders	.20	.50
DA2 Jim Schwantz	.02	.10
DA3 Michael Irvin	.10	.30
DA4 Herschel Walker	.07	.20
DA5 Emmitt Smith	.60	1.50
DA6 Troy Aikman	.40	1.00
DA7 Eric Bjornson	.02	.10
DA8 David LaFleur	.02	.10
DA9 Antonio Anderson	.02	.10
DA10 Daryl Johnston	.07	.20
DA11 Tony Tolbert	.02	.10
DA12 Brock Marion	.02	.10
DA13 Anthony Miller	.07	.20
DA14 Checklist	.20	.50
(Troy Aikman on back)		

1997 Cowboys Score

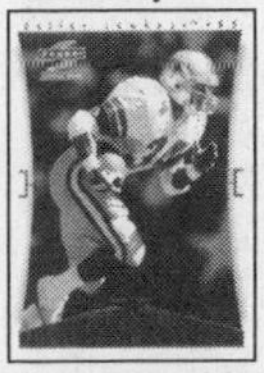

This 15-card set of the Dallas Cowboys was distributed in five-card packs with a suggested retail price of $1.99. The fronts feature color action player photos with white borders and the player's name and team logo printed in team color foil at the bottom. The backs carry player information and career statistics. Platinum Team parallel cards were randomly seeded in packs featuring all foil cardfronts.

COMPLETE SET (15)	3.20	8.00
*PLATINUM TEAMS: 1X TO 2X		
1 Emmitt Smith	1.20	3.00
2 Troy Aikman	.80	2.00
3 Darren Woodson	.15	.40
4 Michael Irvin	.30	.75
5 Sherman Williams	.08	.25
6 Daryl Johnston	.15	.40
7 Deion Sanders	.50	1.25
8 Kevin Williams	.08	.25
9 Jim Schwantz	.08	.25
10 Darrin Smith	.08	.25
11 Kevin Smith	.08	.25
12 Billy Davis	.08	.25
13 Herschel Walker	.15	.40
14 Fred Strickland	.08	.25
15 Tony Tolbert	.08	.25
PC1 Emmitt Smith PC	4.00	10.00

2005 Cowboys Activa Medallions

COMPLETE SET (22)	30.00	60.00
1 Troy Aikman	1.50	4.00
2 Tony Dorsett	1.50	4.00
3 Charles Haley	1.25	3.00
4 Cliff Harris	1.25	3.00
5 Chuck Howley	1.25	3.00
6 Michael Irvin	1.50	4.00
7 Daryl Johnston	1.25	3.00
8 Lee Roy Jordan	1.25	3.00
9 Bob Lilly	1.25	3.00
10 Harvey Martin	1.25	3.00
11 Don Meredith	1.50	4.00
12 Jay Novacek	1.25	3.00
13 Drew Pearson	1.25	3.00
14 Don Perkins	1.25	3.00
15 Mel Renfro	1.25	3.00
16 Emmitt Smith	2.00	5.00
17 Roger Staubach	1.50	4.00
18 Charlie Waters	1.25	3.00
19 Randy White	1.50	4.00
20 Darren Woodson	1.25	3.00
21 Rayfield Wright	1.25	3.00
22 Cowboys Logo	1.00	2.50

2006 Cowboys Donruss Thanksgiving Classic

COMPLETE SET (8)	4.00	10.00
DL1 Terry Glenn	.60	1.50
DL2 Julius Jones	.50	1.25
DL3 Roy Williams S	.60	1.50
DL4 Jason Witten	.75	2.00
DL5 Terrell Owens	.75	2.00
DL6 Tony Dorsett	1.25	3.00
NNO DeMarcus Ware	.60	1.50
(Salvation Army promotion)		
NNO Cover Card CL	.20	.50

2006 Cowboys Topps

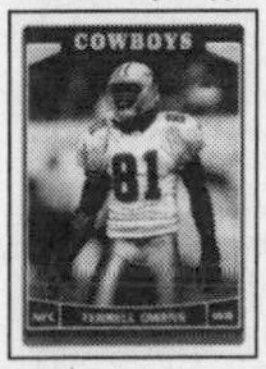

COMPLETE SET (12)	3.00	6.00
DAL1 Drew Bledsoe	.30	.75
DAL2 Roy Williams S	.25	.60
DAL3 Julius Jones	.20	.50
DAL4 Marion Barber	.25	.60
DAL5 Terry Glenn	.25	.60
DAL6 Jason Witten	.30	.75
DAL7 DeMarcus Ware	.25	.60
DAL8 Terence Newman	.20	.50
DAL9 Terrell Owens	.30	.75
DAL10 Mike Vanderjagt	.20	.50
DAL11 Bobby Carpenter	.20	.50
DAL12 Anthony Fasano	.30	.75

2007 Cowboys Donruss Rowdy Rookies

This set of 6-cards was issued for the official kid's fan club of the Cowboys - Rowdy Rookies. Each includes the club's logo on the front.

COMPLETE SET (6)	4.00	10.00
1 Tony Romo	1.00	2.50
2 Terry Glenn	.60	1.50
3 Jason Witten	.75	2.00
4 DeMarcus Ware	.60	1.50
5 Roy Williams S	.60	1.50
6 Terence Newman	.50	1.25

2007 Cowboys Donruss Thanksgiving Classic

COMPLETE SET (5)	4.00	8.00
1 Tony Romo	1.00	2.50
2 Terry Glenn	.60	1.50
3 Roy Williams S	.60	1.50
4 Troy Aikman	1.25	3.00
NNO Roy Williams S	.60	1.50
Salvation Army		

2007 Cowboys Topps

COMPLETE SET (12)	3.00	6.00
1 Marion Barber	.25	.60
2 Roy Williams S	.25	.60
3 Tony Romo	.40	1.00
4 Julius Jones	.20	.50
5 DeMarcus Ware	.25	.60
6 Jason Witten	.30	.75
7 Terence Newman	.20	.50
8 Terrell Owens	.30	.75
9 Patrick Crayton	.20	.50
10 Bradie James	.20	.50
11 Terry Glenn	.25	.60
12 Anthony Spencer	.30	.75

2008 Cowboys Donruss Rowdy Rookies

This set of 6-cards was issued for the official kid's fan club of the Cowboys - Rowdy Rookies. Each includes the club's logo on the front.

COMPLETE SET (6)	5.00	10.00
1 Tony Romo	1.00	2.50
2 Terrell Owens	.75	2.00
3 Marion Barber	.60	1.50
4 Terence Newman	.50	1.25
5 DeMarcus Ware	.60	1.50
6 Jason Witten	.75	2.00

2008 Cowboys Donruss Thanksgiving Classic

Many fans who attended the 2008 Thanksgiving game in Dallas were treated to this complete set. Donruss reported that more than 120,000 cards were given away to fans at both the Dallas and Philadelphia games. Each team set also included one card from the NFL Network broadcasters set.

COMPLETE SET (6)	6.00	12.00
1 Tony Romo	1.00	2.50
2 DeMarcus Ware	.60	1.50
3 Terrell Owens	.75	2.00
4 Randy White	.75	2.00
5 Felix Jones	.60	1.50
NNO Marion Barber	.60	1.50
Salvation Army		

2008 Cowboys Merrick Mint Quartoro

COMPLETE SET (12)	60.00	120.00
1 Marion Barber	5.00	10.00
2 Patrick Crayton	5.00	10.00
3 Leonard Davis	5.00	10.00
4 Adam Jones	5.00	10.00
5 Terence Newman	5.00	10.00
6 Terrell Owens	5.00	10.00
7 Tony Romo	6.00	12.00
8 Tony Romo half dollar	7.50	15.00
9 Zach Thomas	5.00	10.00
10 DeMarcus Ware	6.00	12.00
11 Roy Williams S	5.00	10.00
12 Jason Witten	6.00	12.00

2008 Cowboys Topps

COMPLETE SET (12)	3.00	6.00
1 Terrell Owens	.30	.75
2 DeMarcus Ware	.25	.60
3 Tony Romo	.40	1.00
4 Marion Barber	.25	.60
5 Jason Witten	.30	.75
6 Ken Hamlin	.20	.50
7 Roy Williams S	.25	.60
8 Greg Ellis	.20	.50
9 Anthony Henry	.20	.50
10 Terence Newman	.20	.50
11 Patrick Crayton	.25	.60
12 Felix Jones	.60	1.50

2011 Cowboys Panini Super Bowl XLV

This set was sold exclusively at the 2011 Super Bowl Card Show in Dallas. The cards feature the Super Bowl XLV logo on the fronts and the backs are numbered.

COMPLETE SET (10)	8.00	20.00
SB1 Miles Austin	1.00	2.50
SB2 Marion Barber	1.00	2.50
SB3 Dez Bryant	1.25	3.00
SB4 Tashard Choice	.75	2.00
SB5 Felix Jones	1.00	2.50
SB6 Jay Ratliff	1.00	2.50
SB7 Tony Romo	1.25	3.00
SB8 DeMarcus Ware	1.00	2.50
SB9 Jason Witten	1.25	3.00
SB10 Mat McBriar	.75	2.00

1994 CPC/Enviromint Medallions

To commemorate Joe Montana's career, Chicagoland Processing Corporation/Enviromint issued a silver medallion, a silver collector card and a gold medallion. Each one-troy ounce medallion is stamped with Montana's likeness, his team name, and his jersey number on the front while the words "Player of the Decade 1980's" are stamped on the reverse. Each 3.5 ounce silver collector card is stamped with a collage of Montana in both 49ers and Chiefs uniforms on the front. Its back carries team logos and the words "All-Time NFL Leader in QB Rating" and "Athlete of the Decade 1980's." The medallions and the card each have their own serial number. The production figures are as follows: silver medallion (7,000); silver collector card (10,000); silver medallion and card set (500); and gold medallion (100). Except for the serial number, the collectibles are unnumbered.

1 Joe Montana	24.00	60.00
Silver medallion		
2 Joe Montana	24.00	60.00
Silver card		
3 Joe Montana	50.00	125.00
Gold overlay medallion		
4 Joe Montana	50.00	125.00
Gold overlay medallion		

1976 Crane Discs

The 1976 Crane football disc set of 30 cards contains a black and white photo of the player surrounded by a colored border. These circular cards measure 3 3/8" in diameter. The word Crane completes the circle of the border. The backs contain a Crane (Potato Chips) advertisement and the letters MSA, signifying Michael Schechter Associates. A recently discovered version of the discs was apparently inserted into potato chip packages as several players have been found printed without the "National Football League Players" notation around the small football logo on the fronts. Known discs from this version also feature food product stains as would be expected. Franco Harris can only be found in this "product inserted" version of the discs. None of the second version of the discs are considered part of the complete set price below due to their scarcity. Any additions to the checklist of this version of the discs is appreciated. These discs were also available as a complete set via a mail-in offer on the potato chip wrappers; consequently they are commonly found in nice condition. Of these, there are 12 discs that were produced in shorter supply than the other 18 and are noted by SP in the checklist below. These extras found their way into the hobby when Crane sold their leftovers to a major midwestern dealer. Since the cards are unnumbered, they are ordered below alphabetically. The discs can also be found with the sponsor Saga Philadelphia School District on the cardback. The Saga discs are much more difficult to find and are listed as a separate release.

COMPLETE SET (30)	12.50	25.00
1 Ken Anderson	.30	.60
2 Otis Armstrong	.20	.40
3 Steve Bartkowski	.20	.40
4 Terry Bradshaw	1.50	3.00
5 John Brockington SP	.18	.35
6 Doug Buffone	.13	.25
7 Wally Chambers	.13	.25
8 Isaac Curtis SP	.25	.50
9 Chuck Foreman	.20	.40
10 Roman Gabriel SP	.25	.50
11 Mel Gray	.20	.40
12 Joe Greene	.50	1.00
13 Franco Harris SP	7.50	15.00
(missing 'NFL Players' notation,		
inserted in Potato Chip bags only)		
14 James Harris SP	.18	.35
15 Jim Hart	.20	.40
16 Billy Kilmer	.20	.40
17 Greg Landry SP	.25	.50
18 Ed Marinaro SP	.25	.50
19 Lawrence McCutcheon SP	.25	.50
20 Terry Metcalf	.20	.40
21 Lydell Mitchell SP	.25	.50
22 Jim Otis	.13	.25
23 Alan Page	.30	.60
24 Walter Payton SP	7.50	15.00
25A Greg Pruitt SP	.25	.50
25B Greg Pruitt SP	2.50	5.00
(missing 'NFL Players' notation,		
inserted in Potato Chip bags)		
26 Charlie Sanders SP	.30	.75
27 Ron Shanklin SP	.18	.35
28 Roger Staubach	2.00	4.00
29 Jan Stenerud	.20	.40
30 Charley Taylor	.30	.60
31 Roger Wehrli	.20	.50

1997 Crown Pro Stickers

COMPLETE SET (12)	8.00	20.00
R1 Tony Banks	.40	1.00
R2 Keyshawn Johnson	.60	1.50
R3 Joey Galloway	.60	1.50
R4 Terry Glenn	.60	1.50
R5 Eddie George	.60	1.50
R6 Emmitt Smith	1.50	4.00
R7 Dan Marino	1.50	4.00
R8 Barry Sanders	1.25	3.00
R9 Kerry Collins	.50	1.25
R10 Drew Bledsoe	.60	1.50
R11 Tim Brown	.60	1.50
R12 Brett Favre	2.00	5.00

1999 Crown Pro Key Chains

This set was issued by Crown Pro and distributed primarily through mass retailers. Each package contained a small player statue with an attached key ring. A small (1 1/8" by 2") Dog Tag was also included with the statue. The prices below are for complete unopened packages.

COMPLETE SET (6)	8.00	20.00
1 Troy Aikman	1.20	3.00
2 Terrell Davis	1.20	3.00
3 Brett Favre	1.60	4.00
4 Peyton Manning	1.60	4.00
5 Dan Marino	1.60	4.00
6 Randy Moss	1.60	4.00

1999 Crown Pro Self Inking Stampers

This set was issued by Crown Pro and distributed primarily through mass retailers. Each package contained a small player statue with a self inking stamp at the base of the statue. A standard sized (2 1/2" by 3 1/2") Pro Stamp was also included with the statue. The prices below are for complete unopened packages.

COMPLETE SET (9)	16.00	40.00
1 Troy Aikman	1.60	4.00
2 Terrell Davis	1.60	4.00
3 John Elway	2.00	5.00
4 Brett Favre	2.00	5.00
5 Peyton Manning	2.00	5.00
6 Dan Marino	2.00	5.00
7 Randy Moss	2.00	5.00
8 Barry Sanders	2.00	5.00
9 Steve Young	1.60	4.00

1995 Crown Royale

This set is actually a spin-off of the popular Gold Crown Die Cuts insert from the regular Pacific product. It contains 144 cards and was issued in four card packs. Some boxes of Crown Royale also contained one instant win card redeemable for a trip to Super Bowl XXX.

COMPLETE SET (144)	20.00	50.00
1 Lake Dawson	.20	.50
2 Steve Beuerlein	.20	.50
3 Jake Reed	.20	.50
4 Jim Everett	.08	.25
5 Sean Dawkins	.20	.50
6 Jeff Hostetler	.20	.50
7 Marshall Faulk	1.25	3.00
8 Jeff Blake RC	.75	2.00
9 Dave Brown	.20	.50
10 Frank Reich	.08	.25
11 Rocket Ismail	.20	.50
12 Jerry Jones OWN UER	.40	1.00
Built is spelled bulit		
13 Dan Marino	2.00	5.00
14 Ricky Watters	.20	.50
15 Herman Moore	.40	1.00
16 Daryl Johnston	.20	.50
17 Craig Erickson	.08	.25
18 Alexander Wright	.08	.25
19 Reggie White	.40	1.00
20 Andre Rison	.20	.50
21 Fred Barnett	.20	.50
22 Tyrone Wheatley RC	1.25	3.00
23 Charles Johnson	.20	.50
24 Rashaan Salaam RC	.20	.50
25 Mark Brunell	.60	1.50
26 Derek Loville	.08	.25
27 Garrison Hearst	.40	1.00
28 Ken Norton Jr.	.20	.50
29 Kerry Collins RC	1.50	4.00
30 Isaac Bruce	.60	1.50
31 Andre Reed	.20	.50
32 Leon Lett	.08	.25
33 Deion Sanders	.60	1.50
34 Terance Mathis	.20	.50
35 Tim Bowens	.08	.25
36 Shannon Sharpe	.20	.50
37 Quinn Early	.20	.50
38 Jerry Rice	1.00	2.50
39 Bruce Smith	.40	1.00
40 Drew Bledsoe	.60	1.50
41 Alvin Harper	.08	.25
42 Jim Kelly	.40	1.00
43 Napoleon Kaufman RC	1.25	3.00
44 Errict Rhett	.20	.50
45 Henry Ellard	.20	.50
46 Barry Sanders	1.50	4.00
47 Vincent Brisby	.08	.25
48 Chris Zorich	.08	.25
49 Zack Crockett RC	.20	.50
50 Haywood Jeffires	.08	.25
51 Byron Bam Morris	.08	.25
52 John Kasay	.08	.25
53 Scott Mitchell	.20	.50
54 Boomer Esiason	.20	.50
55 Eric Metcalf	.20	.50
56 Kevin Greene	.20	.50
57 Courtney Hawkins	.08	.25
58 Johnny Johnson	.08	.25
59 Larry Centers	.20	.50
60 Leroy Hoard	.08	.25
61 Lorenzo White	.08	.25
62 Chris Spielman	.20	.50
63 Carl Pickens	.20	.50
64 Steve Young	.75	2.00
65 Trent Dilfer	.40	1.00
66 Erik Kramer	.08	.25
67 Cortez Kennedy	.20	.50
68 Ray Childress	.08	.25
69 Rick Mirer	.20	.50
70 Kevin Williams WR	.20	.50
71 Joey Galloway RC	1.50	4.00
72 Dan Wilkinson	.20	.50
73 Antonio Freeman RC	1.25	3.00
74 Curtis Conway	.40	1.00
75 Troy Aikman	1.00	2.50
76 Natrone Means	.20	.50
77 Jeff George	.20	.50
78 Curtis Martin RC	3.00	8.00
79 William Floyd	.20	.50
80 Anthony Miller	.20	.50
81 Greg Hill	.20	.50
82 Craig Heyward	.20	.50
83 Brian Mitchell	.08	.25
84 Anthony Carter	.20	.50
85 Jerome Bettis	.40	1.00
86 Jim Harbaugh	.20	.50
87 Harvey Williams	.08	.25
88 Tony Martin	.20	.50
89 Rob Moore	.20	.50
90 Neil O'Donnell	.20	.50
91 Cris Carter	.40	1.00
92 Warren Sapp RC	1.50	4.00
93 Terry Allen	.20	.50
94 Michael Irvin	.40	1.00
95 Heath Shuler	.20	.50
96 Cornelius Bennett	.20	.50
97 Randy Baldwin	.08	.25
98 Vince Workman	.08	.25
99 Irving Fryar	.20	.50
100 Randall Cunningham	.40	1.00
101 James O. Stewart RC	1.25	3.00
102 Stan Humphries	.20	.50
103 Mario Bates	.20	.50
104 Ben Coates	.20	.50
105 Charlie Garner	.40	1.00
106 Todd Collins RC	1.25	3.00
107 Tim Brown	.40	1.00
108 Edgar Bennett	.20	.50
109 J.J. Stokes RC	.40	1.00
110 Michael Timpson	.08	.25
111 Junior Seau	.40	1.00
112 Bernie Parmalee	.20	.50
113 Willie McGinest	.20	.50
114 David Dunn RC	.08	.25
115 Kyle Brady RC	.40	1.00
116 Vinny Testaverde	.20	.50
117 Ernest Givins	.08	.25
118 Eric Zeier RC	.40	1.00
119 Michael Jackson	.20	.50
120 Chad May RC	.08	.25
121 Dave Krieg	.08	.25
122 Rodney Hampton	.20	.50
123 Darnay Scott	.20	.50
124 Chris Miller	.08	.25
125 Emmitt Smith	1.50	4.00
126 Steve McNair RC	3.00	8.00
127 Warren Moon	.20	.50
128 Robert Brooks	.40	1.00
129 Bert Emanuel	.40	1.00
130 John Elway	2.00	5.00
131 Chris Warren	.20	.50
132 Herschel Walker	.20	.50
133 Terry Kirby	.20	.50
134 Michael Westbrook RC	.40	1.00
135 Kordell Stewart RC	1.50	4.00
136 Terrell Davis RC	2.50	6.00
137 Desmond Howard	.20	.50
138 Rodney Thomas RC	.20	.50
139 Brett Favre	2.00	5.00
140 Ray Zellars RC	.20	.50
141 Marcus Allen	.40	1.00
142 Gus Frerotte	.20	.50
143 Steve Bono	.20	.50
144 Aaron Craver	.08	.25
P144 Natrone Means Promo	.75	2.00
Jumbo card 7-in by 9 3/4-in		

1995 Crown Royale Blue Holofoil

COMPLETE SET (144)	200.00	400.00
*STARS: 2.5X TO 6X BASIC CARDS		
*RCs: 1.5X TO 4X BASIC CARDS		
STATED ODDS 4:25 RETAIL		

1995 Crown Royale Copper

COMPLETE SET (144)	150.00	300.00
*STARS: 2X TO 5X BASIC CARDS		
*RCs: 1.25X TO 3X BASIC CARDS		
STATED ODDS 4:25 HOBBY		

1995 Crown Royale Cramer's Choice Jumbos

COMPLETE SET (6)	25.00	60.00
RANDOM INSERTS IN PACKS		
CC1 Rashaan Salaam	1.25	3.00
CC2 Emmitt Smith	10.00	25.00
CC3 Marshall Faulk	8.00	20.00
CC4 Jerry Rice	6.00	15.00
CC5 Deion Sanders	4.00	10.00
CC6 Steve Young	5.00	12.00

1995 Crown Royale Pride of the NFL

COMPLETE SET (36)	30.00	80.00
STATED ODDS 3:25		
PN1 Jim Kelly	.75	2.00
PN2 Kerry Collins	2.00	5.00
PN3 Darnay Scott	.40	1.00
PN4 Jeff Blake	1.00	2.50
PN5 Terry Allen	.40	1.00
PN6 Emmitt Smith	3.00	8.00
PN7 Michael Irvin	.75	2.00
PN8 Troy Aikman	2.00	5.00
PN9 John Elway	4.00	10.00
PN10 Napoleon Kaufman	1.50	4.00
PN11 Barry Sanders	3.00	8.00
PN12 Brett Favre	4.00	10.00
PN13 Michael Westbrook	.50	1.25
PN14 Marcus Allen	.75	2.00
PN15 Tim Brown	.75	2.00
PN16 Bernie Parmalee	.40	1.00
PN17 Dan Marino	4.00	10.00
PN18 Cris Carter	.75	2.00
PN19 Drew Bledsoe	1.25	3.00
PN20 Mario Bates	.40	1.00
PN21 Rodney Hampton	.40	1.00
PN22 Ben Coates	.40	1.00
PN23 Charles Johnson	.40	1.00
PN24 Byron Bam Morris	.20	.50
PN25 Stan Humphries	.40	1.00
PN26 Rashaan Salaam	.25	.60
PN27 Jerry Rice	2.00	5.00
PN28 Ricky Watters	.40	1.00
PN29 Steve Young	1.50	4.00
PN30 Natrone Means	.40	1.00
PN31 William Floyd	.40	1.00
PN32 Chris Warren	.40	1.00
PN33 Rick Mirer	.40	1.00
PN34 Jerome Bettis	.75	2.00
PN35 Errict Rhett	.40	1.00
PN36 Heath Shuler	.40	1.00

1995 Crown Royale Pro Bowl Die Cuts

COMPLETE SET (20)	50.00	120.00
STATED ODDS 1:25		
PB1 Drew Bledsoe	2.00	5.00
PB2 Ben Coates	1.00	2.50
PB3 John Elway	10.00	25.00
PB4 Marshall Faulk	4.00	10.00
PB5 Dan Marino	10.00	25.00
PB6 Natrone Means	1.00	2.50
PB7 Junior Seau	2.00	5.00
PB8 Chris Warren	1.00	2.50
PB9 Rod Woodson	1.50	4.00
PB10 Tim Brown	2.00	5.00
PB11 Troy Aikman	5.00	12.00
PB12 Jerome Bettis	2.00	5.00
PB13 Michael Irvin	2.00	5.00
PB14 Jerry Rice	5.00	12.00
PB15 Barry Sanders	8.00	20.00
PB16 Deion Sanders	3.00	8.00
PB17 Emmitt Smith	8.00	20.00
PB18 Steve Young	4.00	10.00
PB19 Reggie White	2.00	5.00
PB20 Cris Carter	2.00	5.00

1996 Crown Royale

The 1996 Pacific Crown Royale set was issued in one series totalling 144 cards and was distributed in five-card packs. The set features color player images on an etched die cut gold crown background with the player's name and position printed at the bottom beside the team logo.

COMPLETE SET (144)	20.00	50.00
1 Dan Marino	2.00	5.00
2 Frank Sanders	.25	.60
3 Bobby Engram RC	.40	1.00
4 Cornelius Bennett	.15	.40
5 Steve Bono	.15	.40
6 Aaron Hayden RC	.15	.40
7 Leroy Hoard	.15	.40
8 Brett Perriman	.15	.40
9 Irv Smith	.15	.40
10 Jim Kelly	.40	1.00
11 Rodney Thomas	.15	.40
12 Eric Bieniemy	.15	.40
13 Darnay Scott	.25	.60
14 Ki-Jana Carter	.25	.60
15 Kerry Collins	.40	1.00
16 Shannon Sharpe	.25	.60
17 Michael Westbrook	.40	1.00
18 Steve McNair	.75	2.00
19 Tony Banks RC	.75	2.00
20 Rashaan Salaam	.25	.60
21 Terrell Fletcher	.15	.40
22 Michael Timpson	.15	.40
23 Bobby Hoying RC	.40	1.00
24 Quinn Early	.15	.40
25 Warren Moon	.25	.60
26 Tommy Vardell	.15	.40
27 Marvin Harrison RC	6.00	12.00
28 Lake Dawson	.15	.40
29 Karim Abdul-Jabbar RC	.75	2.00
30 Chris Warren	.25	.60
31 Heath Shuler	.25	.60
32 Bert Emanuel	.25	.60
33 Howard Griffith RC	.25	.60
34 Alex Van Dyke RC	.25	.60
35 Isaac Bruce	.40	1.00
36 Mark Brunell	.60	1.50
37 Winslow Oliver RC	.25	.60
38 O.J. McDuffie	.25	.60
39 Terrell Owens RC	6.00	12.00
40 Jerry Rice	1.00	2.50
41 Henry Ellard	.15	.40
42 Chris Sanders	.25	.60
43 Craig Heyward	.15	.40
44 Eddie Kennison RC	.75	2.00
45 Terrell Davis	.75	2.00
46 Rodney Hampton	.25	.60
47 Bryan Still RC	.25	.60
48 Tim Brown	.40	1.00
49 Keyshawn Johnson RC	2.50	6.00
50 Barry Sanders	1.50	4.00
51 Terry Allen	.25	.60
52 Sean Dawkins	.15	.40
53 Bryce Paup	.15	.40
54 Brett Favre	2.00	5.00
55 Deion Sanders	.60	1.50
56 Kevin Hardy RC	.75	2.00
57 Kevin Williams	.15	.40
58 Jeff George	.25	.60
59 Tim Biakabutuka RC	.75	2.00
60 Drew Bledsoe	.60	1.50
61 Michael Jackson	.25	.60
62 James O. Stewart	.25	.60
63 Mario Bates	.25	.60
64 Daryl Johnston	.25	.60
65 Herman Moore	.25	.60
66 Ben Coates	.25	.60
67 Terry Glenn RC	2.50	6.00
68 Robert Smith	.25	.60
69 Irving Fryar	.25	.60
70 Napoleon Kaufman	.40	1.00
71 Rickey Dudley RC	.75	2.00
72 Bernie Parmalee	.15	.40
73 Kyle Brady	.15	.40
74 Neil O'Donnell	.25	.60
75 Lawrence Phillips RC	.75	2.00
76 Hardy Nickerson	.15	.40
77 John Elway	2.00	5.00
78 Pete Mitchell	.25	.60
79 Jason Dunn RC	.50	1.25
80 Reggie White	.40	1.00
81 J.J. Stokes	.40	1.00
82 Jake Reed	.25	.60
83 Yancey Thigpen	.25	.60
84 Jonathan Ogden RC	.75	2.00
85 Larry Centers	.25	.60
86 Scott Mitchell	.25	.60
87 Eric Zeier	.15	.40
88 Anthony Miller	.25	.60
89 Brian Blades	.15	.40
90 Cris Carter	.40	1.00
91 Kordell Stewart	.40	1.00
92 Charles Way RC	.50	1.25
93 Jeff Hostetler	.15	.40
94 Brad Johnson	.75	2.00
95 Marcus Allen	.40	1.00
96 Errict Rhett	.25	.60
97 Stan Humphries	.25	.60
98 Michael Haynes	.15	.40
99 Curtis Martin	.75	2.00
100 Troy Aikman	.75	2.50
101 Earnest Byner	.15	.40
102 Vincent Brisby	.15	.40
103 Zack Crockett	.15	.40
104 Haywood Jeffires	.15	.40
105 Joey Galloway	.40	1.00
106 Carl Pickens	.25	.60
107 Leeland McElroy RC	.50	1.25
108 Adrian Murrell	.25	.60
109 Joe Horn RC	5.00	10.00
110 Steve Young	.75	2.00
111 Andre Rison	.25	.60
112 Jim Everett	.15	.40
113 Jamie Asher RC	.50	1.25
114 Steve Walsh	.15	.40
115 Robert Brooks	.40	1.00
110 Eric Moulds RC	3.00	0.00
117 Edgar Bennett	.25	.60
118 Greg Lloyd	.25	.60
119 Jerris McPhail RC	.25	.60
120 Marshall Faulk	.60	1.50
121 Dave Brown	.15	.40
122 Harvey Williams	.15	.40
123 Trent Dilfer	.40	1.00
124 Eddie George RC	3.00	8.00
125 Jeff Blake	.40	1.00
126 Mark Chmura	.25	.60
127 Boomer Esiason	.25	.60
128 Jim Harbaugh	.25	.60
129 Bryan Cox	.15	.40
130 Ricky Watters	.25	.60
131 Amani Toomer RC	2.50	6.00
132 Jim Miller	.40	1.00
133 Cortez Kennedy	.15	.40
134 Courtney Hawkins	.15	.40
135 Junior Seau	.40	1.00
136 Tamarick Vanover	.25	.60
137 Jerome Bettis	.40	1.00
138 Chris Calloway	.15	.40
139 Rick Mirer	.25	.60
140 Thurman Thomas	.40	1.00
141 Sheddrick Wilson RC	.25	.60
142 Charlie Garner	.25	.60
143 Erik Kramer	.15	.40
144 Emmitt Smith	1.50	4.00

1996 Crown Royale Blue

COMPLETE SET (144)	200.00	400.00
*STARS: 1.5X TO 4X BASIC CARDS		
*RCs: 1X TO 2.5X BASIC CARDS		
STATED ODDS 4:25 HOBBY		

1996 Crown Royale Silver

COMPLETE SET (144)	250.00	500.00
*STARS: 2X TO 5X BASIC CARDS		
*RCs: 1.2X TO 3X BASIC CARDS		
STATED ODDS 4:25 RETAIL		

1996 Crown Royale Cramer's Choice Jumbos

COMPLETE SET (10)	125.00	300.00
STATED ODDS 1:385		
1 John Elway	15.00	40.00
2 Brett Favre	15.00	40.00
3 Keyshawn Johnson *	20.00	50.00
4 Dan Marino	15.00	40.00
5 Curtis Martin *	6.00	15.00
6 Jerry Rice	8.00	20.00
7 Barry Sanders	12.50	30.00
8 Emmitt Smith	12.50	30.00
9 Kordell Stewart *	3.00	8.00
10 Reggie White *	3.00	8.00

1996 Crown Royale Field Force

COMPLETE SET (20)	100.00	250.00
STATED ODDS 1:49		
1 Troy Aikman	4.00	10.00
2 Karim Abdul-Jabbar	2.00	5.00
3 Jeff Blake	1.50	4.00
4 Drew Bledsoe	2.50	6.00
5 Lawrence Phillips	2.00	5.00
6 Kerry Collins	1.50	4.00
7 Terrell Davis	3.00	8.00
8 John Elway	8.00	20.00
9 Brett Favre	8.00	20.00
10 Eddie George	8.00	20.00
11 Dan Marino	8.00	20.00
12 Curtis Martin	3.00	8.00
13 Jerry Rice	4.00	10.00
14 Rashaan Salaam	1.00	2.50
15 Barry Sanders	6.00	15.00
16 Deion Sanders	2.50	6.00
17 Emmitt Smith	6.00	15.00
18 Kordell Stewart	1.50	4.00
19 Chris Warren	1.00	2.50
20 Steve Young	3.00	8.00

1996 Crown Royale NFL Regime

COMPLETE SET (110)	12.50	25.00
ONE PER PACK		

1 Steve Young	.40	1.00
2 Jamir Miller	.05	.15
3 Tyrone Brown	.05	.15
4 Chris Shelling	.05	.15
5 Warren Moon	.07	.20
6 Shane Bonham	.05	.15
7 Gary Brown T	.05	.15
8 Chris Chandler	.07	.20
9 Bradford Banta	.05	.15
10 John Elway	1.00	2.50
11 Tom McManus	.05	.15
12 Alfred Jackson	.05	.15
13 Jay Barker	.05	.15
14 Kirk Botkin	.05	.15
15 Jim Kelly	.15	.40
16 Lou Benfatti	.05	.15
17 Billy Joe Hobert	.07	.20
18 John Jackson	.05	.15
19 Torin Dorn	.05	.15
20 Drew Bledsoe	.30	.75
21 Gale Gilbert	.05	.15
22 James Atkins	.05	.15
23 John Lynch	.15	.40
24 James Jenkins	.05	.15
25 Kerry Collins	.15	.40
26 Eric Swann	.05	.15
27 Dan Stryzinski	.05	.15
28 Mike Groh	.05	.15
29 Tim Tindale	.05	.15
30 Kordell Stewart	.30	.75
31 Frank Garcia	.05	.15
32 Mill Coleman	.05	.15
33 Bracy Walker	.05	.15
34 Ryan McNeil	.05	.15
35 Rodney Hampton	.07	.20
36 John Mobley	.05	.15
37 Derek Russell	.05	.15
38 Jeff George	.07	.20
39 Steve Morrison	.05	.15
40 Rashaan Salaam	.07	.20
41 Ryan Christopherson	.05	.15
42 Darren Anderson	.05	.15
43 Ronnie Williams	.05	.15
44 Scottie Graham	.05	.15
45 Thurman Thomas	.15	.40
46 Corwin Brown	.05	.15
47 Lee DeRamus	.05	.15
48 Ray Agnew	.05	.15
49 Erik Howard	.05	.15
50 Emmitt Smith	.75	2.00
51 Dan Land	.05	.15
52 Vinny Testaverde	.07	.20
53 Myron Bell	.05	.15
54 Keith Lyle	.05	.15
55 Aaron Hayden	.05	.15
56 Jeff Brohm	.05	.15
57 Ronnie Harris	.05	.15
58 Trent Dilfer	.15	.40
59 Browning Nagle	.05	.15
60 Jeff Blake	.15	.40
61 Rich Owens	.05	.15
62 Anthony Edwards	.05	.15
63 Orlando Brown	.05	.15
64 Matthew Campbell	.05	.15
65 Ricky Watters	.07	.20
66 Travis Hannah	.05	.15
67 Melvin Tuten	.05	.15
68 Aaron Taylor	.05	.15
69 Dale Hellestrae	.05	.15
70 Marshall Faulk	.20	.50
71 Gary Anderson	.05	.15
72 David Williams	.05	.15
73 Jim Harbaugh	.07	.20
74 Ray Hall	.05	.15
75 Dan Marino	1.00	2.50
76 Chris Mims	.05	.15
77 Matt Blundin	.05	.15
78 Roy Barker	.05	.15
79 John Burke	.05	.15
80 Troy Aikman	.50	1.25
81 Ed King	.05	.15
82 Stan White	.05	.15
83 Vance Joseph	.05	.15
84 David Klingler	.05	.15
85 Terrell Davis	.40	1.00
86 Bobby Hoying	.15	.40
87 Lethon Flowers	.05	.15
88 Dwayne White	.05	.15
89 Vaughn Parker	.05	.15
90 Jerry Rice	.50	1.25
91 Casey Weldon	.05	.15
92 Rick Mirer	.07	.20
93 Jim Pyne	.05	.15
94 Matt Turk	.05	.15
95 Marcus Allen	.15	.40
96 Rob Moore	.07	.20
97 Ruben Brown	.05	.15
98 Zach Thomas	.30	.75
99 Carwell Gardner	.05	.15
100 Barry Sanders	.75	2.00
101 Ben Coleman	.05	.15
102 Steve Rhem	.05	.15
103 Everett McIver	.05	.15
104 Cole Ford	.05	.15
105 Dave Krieg	.05	.15
106 Anthony Parker	.05	.15
107 Michael Brandon	.05	.15
108 Michael McCrary	.05	.15
109 Chad Fann	.05	.15
110 Brett Favre	1.00	2.50

1996 Crown Royale Pro Bowl Die Cuts

COMPLETE SET (20)	30.00	80.00
STATED ODDS 1:25		
1 Jeff Blake	1.25	3.00
2 Mark Chmura	.75	2.00
3 Marshall Faulk	2.00	5.00
4 Brett Favre	6.00	15.00
5 Charles Haley	.50	1.25
6 Merton Hanks	.50	1.25
7 Greg Lloyd	.75	2.00
8 Dan Marino	6.00	15.00
9 Curtis Martin	2.50	6.00
10 Anthony Miller	.75	2.00
11 Herman Moore	.75	2.00
12 Bryce Paup	.50	1.25
13 Jerry Rice	3.00	8.00
14 Barry Sanders	5.00	12.00
15 Junior Seau	1.25	3.00
16 Emmitt Smith	5.00	12.00
17 Yancey Thigpen	.75	2.00
18 Chris Warren	.75	2.00
19 Ricky Watters	.75	2.00
20 Steve Young	2.50	6.00

1996 Crown Royale Triple Crown Die Cuts

COMPLETE SET (10)	40.00	100.00
STATED ODDS 1:73		
1 Troy Aikman	3.00	8.00
2 John Elway	6.00	15.00
3 Brett Favre	6.00	15.00
4 Keyshawn Johnson	4.00	10.00
5 Dan Marino	6.00	15.00
6 Curtis Martin	2.50	6.00
7 Jerry Rice	3.00	8.00
8 Barry Sanders	5.00	12.00
9 Emmitt Smith	5.00	12.00
10 Steve Young	2.50	6.00

1997 Crown Royale

This hobby exclusive set was issued in one series totalling 144-cards and was distributed in four-card packs. The set features color action player images printed on double-foiled double-etched cards with a die-cut gold crown background. The backs carry a paragraph about the player.

COMPLETE SET (144)	30.00	80.00
1 Larry Centers	.30	.75
2 Kent Graham	.20	.50
3 LeShon Johnson	.20	.50
4 Leeland McElroy	.20	.50
5 Jake Plummer RC	3.00	8.00
6 Jamal Anderson	.50	1.25
7 Chris Chandler	.30	.75
8 Byron Hanspard RC	.30	.75
9 O.J. Santiago RC	.30	.75
10 Derrick Alexander WR	.30	.75
11 Jay Graham RC	.30	.75
12 Michael Jackson	.30	.75
13 Vinny Testaverde	.30	.75
14 Todd Collins	.20	.50
15 Jay Riemersma RC	.20	.50
16 Antowain Smith RC	2.00	5.00
17 Steve Tasker	.20	.50
18 Thurman Thomas	.50	1.25
19 Rae Carruth RC	.20	.50
20 Kerry Collins	.50	1.25
21 Anthony Johnson	.20	.50
22 Fred Lane RC	.30	.75
23 Muhsin Muhammad	.30	.75
24 Wesley Walls	.30	.75
25 Darnell Autry RC	.30	.75
26 Raymont Harris	.20	.50
27 Erik Kramer	.20	.50
28 Rick Mirer	.20	.50
29 Rashaan Salaam	.20	.50
30 Jeff Blake	.30	.75
31 Ki-Jana Carter	.20	.50
32 Corey Dillon RC	3.00	8.00
33 Carl Pickens	.30	.75
34 Troy Aikman	1.00	2.50
35 Michael Irvin	.50	1.25
36 Daryl Johnston	.30	.75
37 David LaFleur RC	.50	1.25
38 Deion Sanders	.50	1.25
39 Emmitt Smith	1.50	4.00
40 Terrell Davis	.60	1.50
41 John Elway	2.00	5.00
42 Ed McCaffrey	.30	.75
43 Shannon Sharpe	.30	.75
44 Neil Smith	.30	.75
45 Scott Mitchell	.30	.75
46 Herman Moore	.30	.75
47 Johnnie Morton	.30	.75
48 Barry Sanders	1.50	4.00
49 Robert Brooks	.30	.75
50 Mark Chmura	.30	.75
51 Brett Favre	2.00	5.00
52 Antonio Freeman	.50	1.25
53 Dorsey Levens	.50	1.25
54 Reggie White	.50	1.25
55 Ken Dilger	.20	.50
56 Marshall Faulk	.60	1.50
57 Jim Harbaugh	.30	.75
58 Marvin Harrison	.50	1.25
59 Mark Brunell	.60	1.50
60 Rob Johnson	.50	1.25
61 Keenan McCardell	.30	.75
62 Natrone Means	.30	.75
63 Jimmy Smith	.30	.75
64 Marcus Allen	.50	1.25
65 Tony Gonzalez RC	3.00	8.00
66 Elvis Grbac	.30	.75
67 Greg Hill	.20	.50
68 Tamarick Vanover	.30	.75
69 Karim Abdul-Jabbar	.30	.75
70 Fred Barnett	.20	.50
71 Dan Marino	2.00	5.00
72 O.J. McDuffie	.30	.75
73 Jerris McPhail	.20	.50
74 Cris Carter	.50	1.25
75 Randall Cunningham	.50	1.25
76 Brad Johnson	.50	1.25
77 Jake Reed	.30	.75
78 Robert Smith	.30	.75
79 Drew Bledsoe	.60	1.50
80 Ben Coates	.30	.75
81 Terry Glenn	.50	1.25
82 Curtis Martin	.60	1.50
83 Troy Davis RC	.30	.75
84 Heath Shuler	.20	.50
85 Irv Smith	.20	.50
86 Danny Wuerffel RC	.50	1.25
87 Tiki Barber RC	5.00	12.00
88 Dave Brown	.20	.50
89 Rodney Hampton	.30	.75
90 Ike Hilliard RC	1.25	3.00
91 Amani Toomer	.30	.75
92 Wayne Chrebet	.50	1.25
93 Keyshawn Johnson	.50	1.25
94 Adrian Murrell	.30	.75
95 Neil O'Donnell	.30	.75
96 Dedric Ward RC	.30	.75
97 Tim Brown	.50	1.25
98 Jeff George	.30	.75
99 Desmond Howard	.30	.75
100 Napoleon Kaufman	.50	1.25
101 Ty Detmer	.30	.75
102 Irving Fryar	.30	.75
103 Bobby Hoying	.30	.75
104 Ricky Watters	.30	.75
105 Jerome Bettis	.50	1.25
106 Will Blackwell RC	.30	.75
107 Charles Johnson	.30	.75
108 George Jones RC	.30	.75
109 Kordell Stewart	.50	1.25
110 Tony Banks	.30	.75
111 Isaac Bruce	.50	1.25
112 Eddie Kennison	.30	.75
113 Lawrence Phillips	.20	.50
114 Jim Everett	.20	.50
115 Stan Humphries	.30	.75
116 Freddie Jones	.30	.75
117 Tony Martin	.30	.75
118 Junior Seau	.50	1.25
119 Jim Druckenmiller RC	.30	.75
120 Garrison Hearst	.30	.75
121 Brent Jones	.20	.50
122 Terrell Owens	.60	1.50
123 Jerry Rice	1.00	2.50
124 Steve Young	.60	1.50
125 Chad Brown	.20	.50
126 Joey Galloway	.30	.75
127 Jon Kitna RC	5.00	10.00
128 Warren Moon	.50	1.25
129 Chris Warren	.30	.75
130 Mike Alstott	.50	1.25
131 Reidel Anthony RC	.50	1.25
132 Trent Dilfer	.50	1.25
133 Warrick Dunn RC	2.50	6.00
134 Karl Williams RC	.30	.75
135 Willie Davis	.20	.50
136 Eddie George	.50	1.25
137 Joey Kent RC	.50	1.25
138 Steve McNair	.60	1.50
139 Chris Sanders	.20	.50
140 Terry Allen	.50	1.25
141 Jamie Asher	.20	.50
142 Stephen Davis	.50	1.25
143 Henry Ellard	.20	.50
144 Gus Frerotte	.20	.50
S1 Mark Brunell Sample	.40	1.00

1997 Crown Royale Blue Holofoil

*BLUE HOLO.STARS: 6X TO 15X BASIC CARDS
*BLUE HOLO.RCs: 2.5X TO 6X BASIC CARDS
STATED ODDS 1:25

1997 Crown Royale Gold Holofoil

*GOLD HOLO.STARS: 2X TO 5X BASIC CARDS
*ROOKIES: 1X TO 2.5X BASIC CARDS
STATED ODDS 4:25

1997 Crown Royale Silver

*SILVER STARS: 2X TO 4X HI COL.
*SILVER RCs: 1X TO 2X
SILVERS INSERTED IN SPECIAL RETAIL

1997 Crown Royale Cel-Fusion

COMPLETE SET (20)	50.00	120.00
STATED ODDS 1:49		
1 Antowain Smith	4.00	10.00
2 Troy Aikman	4.00	10.00
3 Emmitt Smith	6.00	15.00
4 Terrell Davis	2.50	6.00
5 John Elway	8.00	20.00
6 Barry Sanders	6.00	15.00
7 Brett Favre	8.00	20.00
8 Mark Brunell	2.50	6.00
9 Elvis Grbac	1.25	3.00
10 Karim Abdul-Jabbar	1.25	3.00
11 Dan Marino	8.00	20.00
12 Drew Bledsoe	2.50	6.00
13 Curtis Martin	2.50	6.00
14 Danny Wuerffel	1.00	2.50
15 Tiki Barber	10.00	25.00
16 Jeff George	1.25	3.00
17 Kordell Stewart	2.00	5.00
18 Tony Banks	1.25	3.00
19 Jerry Rice	4.00	10.00
20 Steve Young	2.50	6.00

1997 Crown Royale Chalk Talk

COMPLETE SET (20)	50.00	120.00
STATED ODDS 1:73		
1 Kerry Collins	2.00	5.00
2 Troy Aikman	4.00	10.00
3 Emmitt Smith	6.00	15.00
4 Terrell Davis	2.50	6.00
5 John Elway	8.00	20.00
6 Barry Sanders	6.00	15.00
7 Brett Favre	8.00	20.00
8 Mark Brunell	2.00	5.00
9 Marcus Allen	2.00	5.00
10 Dan Marino	8.00	20.00
11 Drew Bledsoe	2.50	6.00
12 Curtis Martin	2.50	6.00
13 Troy Davis	.50	1.25
14 Napoleon Kaufman	1.00	2.50
15 Jerome Bettis	2.00	5.00
16 Jim Druckenmiller	.50	1.25
17 Jerry Rice	4.00	10.00
18 Steve Young	2.50	6.00
19 Warrick Dunn	4.00	10.00
20 Eddie George	2.00	5.00

1997 Crown Royale Cramer's Choice Jumbos

COMPLETE SET (10)	25.00	60.00
ONE PER BOX		
PURPLES/10 TOO SCARCE TO PRICE		
*UNNUM.PURPLE: .6X TO 1.5X BASIC INSERTS		
1 Deion Sanders	1.25	3.00
2 Emmitt Smith	4.00	10.00
3 Terrell Davis	1.50	4.00
4 John Elway	5.00	12.00
5 Barry Sanders	4.00	10.00
6 Brett Favre	5.00	12.00
7 Mark Brunell	1.25	3.00
8 Drew Bledsoe	1.50	4.00
9 Jim Druckenmiller	.75	2.00
10 Eddie George	1.25	3.00

1997 Crown Royale Firestone on Football

COMPLETE SET (21)	30.00	80.00
STATED ODDS 1:25		
1 Kerry Collins	2.00	5.00
2 Troy Aikman	4.00	10.00
3 Deion Sanders	2.00	5.00
4 Emmitt Smith	6.00	15.00
5 Terrell Davis	2.50	6.00
6 John Elway	8.00	20.00
7 Barry Sanders	6.00	15.00
8 Brett Favre	8.00	20.00
9 Reggie White	2.00	5.00
10 Mark Brunell	2.00	5.00
11 Marcus Allen	2.00	5.00
12 Dan Marino	8.00	20.00
13 Drew Bledsoe	2.50	6.00
14 Terry Glenn	2.00	5.00
15 Curtis Martin	2.50	6.00
16 Jerome Bettis	2.00	5.00
17 Jerry Rice	4.00	10.00
18 Steve Young	2.50	6.00
19 Eddie George	2.00	5.00
20 Gus Frerotte	.75	2.00
21 Roy Firestone	.75	2.00

1997 Crown Royale Pro Bowl Die Cuts

COMPLETE SET (20)	40.00	100.00
STATED ODDS 1:25		
1 Kerry Collins	1.50	4.00
2 Troy Aikman	3.00	8.00
3 Deion Sanders	1.50	4.00
4 Terrell Davis	2.00	5.00
5 John Elway	6.00	15.00
6 Shannon Sharpe	1.00	2.50
7 Barry Sanders	5.00	12.00
8 Brett Favre	6.00	15.00
9 Reggie White	1.50	4.00
10 Mark Brunell	1.50	4.00
11 Derrick Thomas	1.50	4.00
12 Drew Bledsoe	2.00	5.00
13 Ben Coates	1.00	2.50
14 Curtis Martin	2.00	5.00
15 Jerome Bettis	1.50	4.00
16 Isaac Bruce	1.50	4.00
17 Jerry Rice	3.00	8.00
18 Steve Young	2.00	5.00
19 Terry Allen	1.50	4.00
20 Gus Frerotte	.60	1.50

1998 Crown Royale

The 1998 Pacific Crown Royale was issued in one series totalling 144 cards and distributed in six-card packs with a suggested retail price of $5.99. The set features color action player images printed on double-foiled, double-etched, all die-cut crown-shaped cards.

COMPLETE SET (144)	40.00	100.00
1 Larry Centers	.20	.50
2 Rob Moore	.30	.75
3 Adrian Murrell	.30	.75
4 Jake Plummer	.50	1.25
5 Jamal Anderson	.50	1.25
6 Chris Chandler	.30	.75
7 Tim Dwight RC	1.25	3.00
8 Tony Martin	.30	.75
9 Jay Graham	.20	.50
10 Pat Johnson RC	1.00	2.50
11 Jermaine Lewis	.30	.75
12 Eric Zeier	.30	.75
13 Rob Johnson	.30	.75
14 Eric Moulds	.50	1.25
15 Antowain Smith	.50	1.25
16 Bruce Smith	.30	.75
17 Steve Beuerlein	.30	.75
18 Anthony Johnson	.20	.50
19 Fred Lane	.20	.50
20 Muhsin Muhammad	.30	.75
21 Curtis Conway	.30	.75
22 Curtis Enis RC	.60	1.50
23 Erik Kramer	.20	.50
24 Tony Parrish RC	1.25	3.00
25 Corey Dillon	.50	1.25
26 Neil O'Donnell	.30	.75
27 Carl Pickens	.30	.75
28 Takeo Spikes RC	1.25	3.00
29 Troy Aikman	1.00	2.50
30 Michael Irvin	.50	1.25
31 Deion Sanders	.50	1.25
32 Emmitt Smith	1.50	4.00
33 Chris Warren	.30	.75
34 Terrell Davis	.50	1.25
35 John Elway	2.00	5.00
36 Brian Griese RC	2.50	6.00
37 Ed McCaffrey	.30	.75
38 Shannon Sharpe	.30	.75
39 Rod Smith WR	.30	.75
40 Charlie Batch RC	1.25	3.00
41 Herman Moore	.30	.75
42 Johnnie Morton	.30	.75
43 Barry Sanders	1.50	4.00
44 Bryant Westbrook	.20	.50
45 Robert Brooks	.30	.75
46 Brett Favre	2.00	5.00
47 Antonio Freeman	.50	1.25
48 Raymont Harris	.20	.50
49 Vonnie Holliday RC	1.00	2.50
50 Reggie White	.50	1.25
51 Marshall Faulk	.60	1.50
52 E.G. Green RC	1.00	2.50
53 Marvin Harrison	.50	1.25
54 Peyton Manning RC	10.00	25.00
55 Jerome Pathon RC	1.25	3.00
56 Tavian Banks RC	.30	.75
57 Mark Brunell	.50	1.25
58 Keenan McCardell	.30	.75
59 Jimmy Smith	.30	.75
60 Fred Taylor RC	2.00	5.00
61 Derrick Alexander WR	.30	.75
62 Tony Gonzalez	.50	1.25
63 Elvis Grbac	.30	.75
64 Andre Rison	.30	.75
65 Rashaan Shehee RC	1.00	2.50
66 Derrick Thomas	.50	1.25
67 Karim Abdul-Jabbar	.50	1.25
68 John Avery RC	1.00	2.50
69 Oronde Gadsden RC	1.25	3.00
70 Dan Marino	2.00	5.00
71 O.J. McDuffie	.30	.75
72 Cris Carter	.50	1.25
73 Randall Cunningham	.50	1.25
74 Brad Johnson	.50	1.25
75 Randy Moss RC	5.00	12.00
76 John Randle	.30	.75
77 Jake Reed	.30	.75
78 Robert Smith	.50	1.25
79 Drew Bledsoe	.75	2.00
80 Robert Edwards RC	1.00	2.50
81 Terry Glenn	.50	1.25
82 Tebucky Jones RC	.60	1.50
83 Tony Simmons RC	1.00	2.50
84 Mark Fields	.20	.50
85 Andre Hastings	.20	.50
86 Danny Wuerffel	.30	.75
87 Ray Zellars	.20	.50
88 Tiki Barber	.50	1.25
89 Ike Hilliard	.30	.75
90 Joe Jurevicius RC	1.25	3.00
91 Danny Kanell	.30	.75
92 Wayne Chrebet	.50	1.25
93 Glenn Foley	.30	.75
94 Keyshawn Johnson	.50	1.25
95 Leon Johnson	.20	.50
96 Curtis Martin	.50	1.25
97 Tim Brown	.50	1.25
98 Jeff George	.30	.75
99 Napoleon Kaufman	.50	1.25
100 Jon Ritchie RC	1.00	2.50
101 Charles Woodson RC	1.50	4.00
102 Irving Fryar	.30	.75
103 Bobby Hoying	.30	.75
104 Allen Rossum RC	.60	1.50
105 Duce Staley	.60	1.50
106 Jerome Bettis	.50	1.25
107 C.Fuamatu-Ma'afala RC	1.00	2.50
108 Charles Johnson	.20	.50
109 Levon Kirkland	.20	.50
110 Kordell Stewart	.50	1.25
111 Hines Ward RC	5.00	10.00
112 Tony Banks	.30	.75
113 Tony Horne RC	.60	1.50
114 Eddie Kennison	.30	.75
115 Amp Lee	.20	.50
116 Freddie Jones	.20	.50
117 Ryan Leaf RC	1.25	3.00
118 Natrone Means	.30	.75
119 Mikhael Ricks RC	1.00	2.50
120 Bryan Still	.20	.50
121 Marc Edwards	.20	.50
122 Garrison Hearst	.50	1.25
123 Terrell Owens	.50	1.25
124 Jerry Rice	1.00	2.50
125 J.J. Stokes	.30	.75
126 Steve Young	.60	1.50
127 Joey Galloway	.30	.75
128 Ahman Green RC	2.50	6.00
129 Warren Moon	.50	1.25
130 Ricky Watters	.30	.75
131 Mike Alstott	.50	1.25
132 Trent Dilfer	.50	1.25
133 Warrick Dunn	.50	1.25
134 Jacquez Green RC	1.00	2.50
135 Warren Sapp	.30	.75
136 Kevin Dyson RC	1.25	3.00
137 Eddie George	.50	1.25
138 Steve McNair	.50	1.25
139 Yancey Thigpen	.20	.50
140 Stephen Alexander RC	1.00	2.50
141 Terry Allen	.50	1.25
142 Trent Green	.60	1.50
143 Skip Hicks RC	1.00	2.50
144 Michael Westbrook	.30	.75

1998 Crown Royale Limited Series

*VETS: 5X TO 12X BASIC CARDS
*ROOKIES: 2X TO 5X BASIC CARDS
STATED PRINT RUN 99 SER.#'d SETS

1998 Crown Royale Cramer's Choice Jumbos

COMPLETE SET (10)	60.00	120.00
OVERALL STATED ODDS 1 PER BOX		
*DARK BLUES: 4X TO 10X BASIC INSERTS		
DARK BLUE PRINT RUN 35 SERIAL #'d SETS		
*GOLDS: 8X TO 20X BASIC INSERTS		
GOLD PRINT RUN 10 SERIAL #'d SETS		
*GREENS: 4X TO 10X BASIC INSERTS		
GREEN PRINT RUN 30 SERIAL #'d SETS		
*LIGHT BLUE: 5X TO 12X BASIC INSERTS		
LIGHT BLUE PRINT RUN 20 SERIAL #'d SETS		
*REDS: 5X TO 12X BASIC INSERTS		
RED PRINT RUN 25 SERIAL #'d SETS		
1 Terrell Davis	1.50	4.00
2 John Elway	6.00	15.00
3 Barry Sanders	5.00	12.00
4 Brett Favre	6.00	15.00
5 Peyton Manning	8.00	20.00
6 Mark Brunell	1.50	4.00
7 Dan Marino	6.00	15.00
8 Randy Moss	5.00	12.00
9 Jerry Rice	3.00	8.00
10 Warrick Dunn	1.50	4.00

1998 Crown Royale Living Legends

COMPLETE SET (10)	100.00	200.00
STATED PRINT RUN 375 SERIAL #'d SETS		
1 Troy Aikman	5.00	12.00
2 Emmitt Smith	8.00	20.00
3 Terrell Davis	2.50	6.00
4 John Elway	10.00	25.00
5 Barry Sanders	8.00	20.00
6 Brett Favre	10.00	25.00
7 Mark Brunell	2.50	6.00
8 Dan Marino	10.00	25.00
9 Drew Bledsoe	4.00	10.00
10 Jerry Rice	5.00	12.00

1998 Crown Royale Master Performers

COMPLETE SET (20)	40.00	80.00
STATED ODDS 2:25 HOBBY		
1 Corey Dillon	.75	2.00
2 Troy Aikman	1.50	4.00
3 Emmitt Smith	2.50	6.00
4 Terrell Davis	.75	2.00
5 John Elway	3.00	8.00
6 Charlie Batch	.50	1.25
7 Barry Sanders	2.50	6.00
8 Brett Favre	3.00	8.00
9 Peyton Manning	6.00	15.00
10 Mark Brunell	.75	2.00
11 Fred Taylor	1.25	3.00
12 Dan Marino	3.00	8.00
13 Randy Moss	4.00	10.00
14 Drew Bledsoe	1.25	3.00
15 Curtis Martin	.75	2.00
16 Kordell Stewart	.75	2.00
17 Ryan Leaf	.50	1.25
18 Jerry Rice	1.50	4.00
19 Steve Young	1.00	2.50
20 Warrick Dunn	.75	2.00

1998 Crown Royale Pillars of the Game

COMPLETE SET (25)	12.50	30.00
STATED ODDS 1:1 HOBBY		
1 Antowain Smith	.15	.40
2 Corey Dillon	.15	.40
3 Troy Aikman	.30	.75
4 Emmitt Smith	.40	1.25
5 Terrell Davis	.15	.40
6 John Elway	.50	1.50
7 Charlie Batch	.05	.15
8 Barry Sanders	.40	1.25
9 Brett Favre	.50	1.50
10 Antonio Freeman	.08	.25
11 Peyton Manning	3.00	8.00
12 Mark Brunell	.15	.40
13 Dan Marino	.50	1.50
14 Randy Moss	2.00	5.00
15 Drew Bledsoe	.25	.60
16 Curtis Martin	.15	.40
17 Napoleon Kaufman	.08	.25
18 Jerome Bettis	.15	.40
19 Kordell Stewart	.15	.40
20 Ryan Leaf	.05	.15
21 Jerry Rice	.30	.75
22 Steve Young	.20	.50
23 Ricky Watters	.08	.25
24 Eddie George	.08	.25
25 Warrick Dunn	.15	.40

1998 Crown Royale Pivotal Players

COMPLETE SET (25)	12.50	30.00
STATED ODDS 1:1 HOBBY		
1 Jake Plummer	.15	.40
2 Antowain Smith	.15	.40
3 Corey Dillon	.15	.40
4 Troy Aikman	.30	.75
5 Deion Sanders	.15	.40
6 Emmitt Smith	.40	1.25
7 Terrell Davis	.15	.40
8 John Elway	.50	1.50
9 Charlie Batch	.40	1.00
10 Barry Sanders	.40	1.25
11 Brett Favre	.50	1.50
12 Peyton Manning	3.00	8.00
13 Mark Brunell	.15	.40
14 Fred Taylor	.50	1.50
15 Dan Marino	.50	1.50
16 Randy Moss	2.00	5.00
17 Drew Bledsoe	.25	.60
18 Curtis Martin	.15	.40
19 Napoleon Kaufman	.15	.40
20 Jerome Bettis	.15	.40
21 Kordell Stewart	.15	.40
22 Ryan Leaf	.40	1.00
23 Jerry Rice	.30	.75
24 Eddie George	.15	.40
25 Warrick Dunn	.15	.40

1998 Crown Royale Rookie Paydirt

COMPLETE SET (20)	75.00	150.00
STATED ODDS 1:25 HOBBY		
1 Curtis Enis	.60	1.50
2 Marcus Nash	.60	1.50
3 Charlie Batch	1.50	4.00
4 Vonnie Holliday	1.25	3.00
5 E.G. Green	.60	1.50
6 Peyton Manning	12.00	30.00
7 Jerome Pathon	1.50	4.00
8 Tavian Banks	.60	1.50
9 Fred Taylor	2.50	6.00
10 Rashaan Shehee	.60	1.50
11 John Avery	.60	1.50
12 Randy Moss	8.00	20.00
13 Robert Edwards	1.25	3.00
14 Charles Woodson	2.00	5.00
15 Hines Ward	5.00	12.00
16 Ryan Leaf	1.25	3.00
17 Mikhael Ricks	.60	1.50
18 Ahman Green	3.00	8.00
19 Jacquez Green	1.25	3.00
20 Kevin Dyson	1.25	3.00

1999 Crown Royale

Released as a 144-card set, 1999 Crown Royale football features "crown" die-cut cards where veteran crowns where backgrounds are highlighted with silver foil and crown borders are highlighted with gold foil, and prospect crowns where backgrounds are highlighted with gold foil and crown borders are highlighted with silver foil. Crown Royale was packaged in 24-pack boxes with packs containing six cards and carried a suggested retail price of $5.99.

COMPLETE SET (144)	50.00	120.00
1 David Boston RC	.60	1.50
2 Chris Greisen RC	.50	1.25
3 Rob Moore	.25	.60
4 Jake Plummer	.30	.75
5 Frank Sanders	.25	.60
6 Jamal Anderson	.30	.75
7 Chris Chandler	.30	.75
8 Tim Dwight	.30	.75
9 Byron Hanspard	.25	.60
10 Stoney Case	.25	.60
11 Priest Holmes	.40	1.00
12 Jermaine Lewis	.25	.60
13 Chris McAlister RC	.60	1.50
14 Brandon Stokley RC	.75	2.00
15 Doug Flutie	.40	1.00
16 Eric Moulds	.30	.75
17 Peerless Price RC	.60	1.50
18 Antowain Smith	.25	.60
19 Steve Beuerlein	.30	.75
20 Tim Biakabutuka	.30	.75
21 Muhsin Muhammad	.30	.75
22 Curtis Conway	.30	.75
23 Curtis Enis	.25	.60
24 Shane Matthews	.25	.60
25 Cade McNown RC	.60	1.50
26 Marcus Robinson	.30	.75
27 Jeff Blake	.30	.75
28 Scott Covington RC	.50	1.25
29 Corey Dillon	.30	.75
30 Damon Griffin RC	.75	2.00
31 Carl Pickens	.30	.75
32 Akili Smith RC	.60	1.50
33 Tim Couch RC	.75	2.00
34 Kevin Johnson RC	.60	1.50
35 Terry Kirby	.25	.60
36 Leslie Shepherd	.25	.60
37 Troy Aikman	.60	1.50
38 Rocket Ismail	.30	.75
39 Wane McGarity RC	.50	1.25
40 Deion Sanders	.40	1.00
41 Emmitt Smith	1.00	2.50
42 Terrell Davis	.40	1.00
43 Brian Griese	.30	.75
44 Ed McCaffrey	.30	.75
45 Shannon Sharpe	.40	1.00
46 Rod Smith	.30	.75
47 Charlie Batch	.30	.75
48 Germane Crowell	.25	.60
49 Sedrick Irvin RC	.50	1.25
50 Herman Moore	.30	.75
51 Barry Sanders	1.00	2.50
52 Brett Favre	1.25	3.00
53 Antonio Freeman	.30	.75
54 Matt Hasselbeck	.40	1.00
55 Dorsey Levens	.30	.75
56 Basil Mitchell RC	.50	1.25
57 E.G. Green	.25	.60
58 Marvin Harrison	.40	1.00
59 Edgerrin James RC	1.00	2.50
60 Peyton Manning	1.25	3.00
61 Terrence Wilkins RC	.60	1.50
62 Mark Brunell	.30	.75
63 Keenan McCardell	.30	.75
64 Jimmy Smith	.30	.75
65 Fred Taylor	.30	.75
66 Derrick Alexander WR	.25	.60
67 Elvis Grbac	.25	.60
68 Warren Moon	.40	1.00
69 Larry Parker RC	.60	1.50
70 Andre Rison	.30	.75
71 Cecil Collins RC	.50	1.25
72 Damon Huard	.25	.60
73 James Johnson RC	.50	1.25
74 Rob Konrad RC	.50	1.25
75 Dan Marino	1.25	3.00
76 O.J. McDuffie	.30	.75
77 Cris Carter	.40	1.00
78 Daunte Culpepper RC	.75	2.00
79 Randall Cunningham	.40	1.00
80 Randy Moss UER (card actually #81)	.40	1.00
81 Robert Smith	.30	.75
82 Michael Bishop RC	.60	1.50
83 Drew Bledsoe	.40	1.00
84 Ben Coates	.30	.75
85 Kevin Faulk RC	.75	2.00
86 Terry Glenn	.30	.75
87 Billy Joe Hobert	.25	.60
88 Eddie Kennison	.30	.75
89 Keith Poole	.25	.60
90 Ricky Williams RC	1.25	3.00
91 Sean Bennett RC	.50	1.25
92 Kerry Collins	.30	.75
93 Pete Mitchell	.25	.60
94 Amani Toomer	.30	.75
95 Wayne Chrebet	.30	.75
96 Keyshawn Johnson	.30	.75
97 Curtis Martin	.40	1.00
98 Tim Brown	.40	1.00
99 Scott Dreisbach RC	.50	1.25
100 Rich Gannon	.30	.75
101 Napoleon Kaufman	.25	.60
102 Tyrone Wheatley	.30	.75
103 Duce Staley	.30	.75
104 Charles Johnson	.25	.60
105 Donovan McNabb RC	4.00	10.00
106 Torrance Small	.25	.60
107 Jed Weaver RC	.50	1.25
108 Jerome Bettis	.40	1.00
109 Troy Edwards RC	.60	1.50
110 Kordell Stewart	.30	.75
111 Amos Zereoue RC	.60	1.50
112 Isaac Bruce	.40	1.00
113 Marshall Faulk	.40	1.00
114 Joe Germaine RC	.60	1.50
115 Torry Holt RC	1.25	3.00
116 Kurt Warner RC	5.00	12.00
117 Jim Harbaugh	.30	.75
118 Erik Kramer	.30	.75
119 Natrone Means	.30	.75
120 Junior Seau	.40	1.00
121 Jeff Garcia RC	3.00	8.00
122 Terrell Owens	.40	1.00
123 Jerry Rice	.75	2.00
124 J.J. Stokes	.25	.60
125 Steve Young	.50	1.25
126 Sean Dawkins	.25	.60
127 Brock Huard RC	.60	1.50
128 Jon Kitna	.30	.75
129 Derrick Mayes	.25	.60
130 Charlie Rogers RC	.50	1.25
131 Ricky Watters	.30	.75
132 Mike Alstott	.40	1.00
133 Trent Dilfer	.30	.75
134 Warrick Dunn	.30	.75
135 Eric Zeier	.25	.60
136 Kevin Daft RC	.50	1.25
137 Kevin Dyson	.25	.60
138 Eddie George	.30	.75
139 Steve McNair	.40	1.00
140 Neil O'Donnell	.30	.75
141 Champ Bailey RC	1.50	4.00
142 Albert Connell	.25	.60
143 Stephen Davis	.30	.75
144 Brad Johnson	.30	.75

1999 Crown Royale Limited Series

*VETERANS: 2.5X TO 6X BASIC CARDS
*ROOKIES: 1.2X TO 3X BASIC CARDS
STATED PRINT RUN 99 SER.#'d SETS

1999 Crown Royale Premiere Date

*VETERANS: 3X TO 8X BASIC CARDS
*ROOKIES: 1.5X TO 4X BASIC CARDS
PREMIERE DATE/68 ODDS 1:25

1999 Crown Royale Card Supials

COMPLETE SET (20)	50.00	100.00
*SMALL CARDS: .3X TO .8X LARGE		
STATED ODDS 2:25		
1 Cade McNown	.60	1.50
2 Tim Couch	.75	2.00
3 Troy Aikman	2.00	5.00
4 Emmitt Smith	2.50	6.00
5 Barry Sanders	3.00	8.00
6 Brett Favre	3.00	8.00
7 Edgerrin James	2.50	6.00
8 Peyton Manning	3.00	8.00
9 Mark Brunell	.75	2.00
10 Fred Taylor	.75	2.00
11 Damon Huard	.75	2.00
12 Dan Marino	3.00	8.00
13 Randy Moss	2.50	6.00
14 Drew Bledsoe	1.25	3.00
15 Ricky Williams	1.25	3.00
16 Jerome Bettis	.75	2.00
17 Kurt Warner	4.00	10.00
18 Terrell Owens	.75	2.00
19 Jerry Rice	2.50	6.00
20 Jon Kitna	.75	2.00

1999 Crown Royale Century 21

COMPLETE SET (10)	50.00	100.00
STATED PRINT RUN 375 SER.#'d SETS		
1 Jake Plummer	1.00	2.50
2 Tim Couch	1.00	2.50
3 Terrell Davis	1.50	4.00
4 Peyton Manning	6.00	15.00
5 Mark Brunell	1.50	4.00
6 Fred Taylor	1.50	4.00
7 Randy Moss	5.00	12.00
8 Drew Bledsoe	2.50	6.00
9 Ricky Williams	2.00	5.00
10 Kurt Warner	10.00	25.00

1999 Crown Royale Cramer's Choice Jumbos

COMPLETE SET (10)	30.00	60.00
OVERALL STATED ODDS ONE PER BOX		
*DARK BLUE/35: 2X TO 5X BASIC INSERTS		

*GOLD/10: 6X TO 15X BASIC INSERTS
*GREEN/30: 2X TO 5X BASIC INSERTS
*LIGHT BLUE/20: 3X TO 8X BASIC INSERTS
UNPRICED PURPLE PRINT RUN 1
*RED/25: 2.5X TO 6X BASIC INSERTS
1 Cade McNown 1.50 4.00
2 Tim Couch 2.50 6.00
3 Emmitt Smith 5.00 12.00
4 Edgerrin James 3.00 8.00
5 Mark Brunell 1.50 4.00
6 Fred Taylor 1.50 4.00
7 Randy Moss 3.00 8.00
8 Kurt Warner 4.00 10.00
9 Jon Kitna 1.50 4.00
10 Eddie George 1.50 4.00

1999 Crown Royale Franchise Glory

COMPLETE SET (25) 20.00 40.00
ONE PER PACK
1 Doug Flutie .40 1.00
2 Corey Dillon .40 1.00
3 Troy Aikman 1.00 2.50
4 Emmitt Smith 1.25 3.00
5 Terrell Davis .40 1.00
6 Herman Moore .25 .60
7 Barry Sanders 1.50 4.00
8 Brett Favre 1.50 4.00
9 Antonio Freeman .40 1.00
10 Peyton Manning 1.50 4.00
11 Mark Brunell .40 1.00
12 Fred Taylor .40 1.00
13 Dan Marino 1.50 4.00
14 Randy Moss 1.25 3.00
15 Drew Bledsoe .60 1.50
16 Keyshawn Johnson .40 1.00
17 Jerome Bettis .40 1.00
18 Marshall Faulk .60 1.50
19 Kurt Warner 5.00 12.00
20 Terrell Owens .40 1.00
21 Jerry Rice 1.25 3.00
22 Steve Young .60 1.50
23 Warrick Dunn .40 1.00
24 Eddie George .40 1.00
25 Brad Johnson .40 1.00

1999 Crown Royale Franchise Glory Super Bowl XXXIV

This parallel set to the base Franchise Glory inserts was distributed at the 2000 Super Bowl Card Show in Atlanta to all attendees who opened 1-box of any Pacific product at the Pacific booth. Each card features a silver foil Super Bowl XXXIV logo with the dates of the card show on the fronts. Hand serial numbering of 25-sets was also applied to each card with red ink on the fronts.

COMPLETE SET (25) 160.00 400.00
*SUPER BOWL CARDS: 4X TO 10X BASIC INSERTS

1999 Crown Royale Gold Crown Die Cuts

COMPLETE SET (6) 30.00 60.00
STATED PRINT RUN 976 SER.#'d SETS
1 Tim Couch 1.25 3.00
2 Troy Aikman 3.00 8.00
3 Emmitt Smith 4.00 10.00
4 Damon Huard 1.25 3.00
5 Randy Moss 4.00 10.00
6 Kurt Warner 6.00 15.00

1999 Crown Royale Rookie Gold

COMPLETE SET (25) 25.00 50.00
ONE PER PACK
*DIE CUT/10: 15X TO 40X BASIC INSERTS
1 David Boston .50 1.25
2 Brandon Stokley .60 1.50
3 Cade McNown .40 1.00
4 Akili Smith .40 1.00
5 Tim Couch .50 1.25
6 Kevin Johnson .50 1.25
7 Wane McGarity .25 .60
8 Edgerrin James 1.50 4.00
9 Terrence Wilkins .40 1.00
10 Cecil Collins .25 .60
11 Rob Konrad .40 1.00
12 James Johnson .40 1.00
13 Daunte Culpepper 1.50 4.00
14 Michael Bishop .50 1.25
15 Kevin Faulk .50 1.25
16 Ricky Williams .75 2.00
17 Scott Dreisbach .40 1.00
18 Donovan McNabb 2.00 5.00
19 Troy Edwards .40 1.00
20 Amos Zereoue .50 1.25
21 Joe Germaine .40 1.00
22 Torry Holt 1.25 3.00
23 Brock Huard .50 1.25
24 Charlie Rogers .25 .60
25 Champ Bailey .60 1.50

1999 Crown Royale Test of Time

COMPLETE SET (10) 30.00 60.00
STATED ODDS 1:25
1 Tim Couch 1.25 3.00
2 Emmitt Smith 3.00 8.00
3 Terrell Davis 1.00 2.50
4 Barry Sanders 4.00 10.00
5 Brett Favre 4.00 10.00
6 Antonio Freeman 1.00 2.50
7 Edgerrin James 4.00 10.00
8 Mark Brunell 1.00 2.50
9 Dan Marino 4.00 10.00
10 Jerry Rice 3.00 8.00

2000 Crown Royale

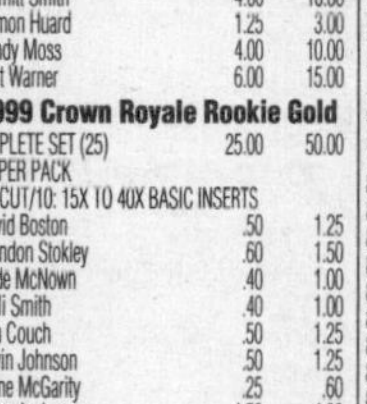

Crown Royale was released as a 144-card die cut base set with 36 short printed draft pick cards. Hobby versions feature a gold crown with silver background for veterans, and a silver crown with gold background for rookies. The retail version features a burgandy background with gold and silver foil on the crown die cut.

COMPLETE SET (144) 40.00 100.00
1 Rob Moore .25 .60
2 Jake Plummer .30 .75
3 Frank Sanders .25 .60
4 Jamal Anderson .30 .75
5 Chris Chandler .30 .75
6 Tim Dwight .30 .75
7 Tony Banks .25 .60
8 Priest Holmes .40 1.00
9 Qadry Ismail .30 .75
10 Doug Flutie .40 1.00
11 Rob Johnson .30 .75
12 Eric Moulds .30 .75
13 Peerless Price .30 .75
14 Steve Beuerlein .30 .75
15 Patrick Jeffers .30 .75
16 Muhsin Muhammad .30 .75
17 Curtis Enis .25 .60
18 Cade McNown .25 .60
19 Marcus Robinson .30 .75
20 Corey Dillon .30 .75
21 Darnay Scott .30 .75
22 Akili Smith .25 .60
23 Karim Abdul-Jabbar .25 .60
24 Tim Couch .30 .75
25 Kevin Johnson .25 .60
26 Troy Aikman .60 1.50
27 Joey Galloway .30 .75
28 Emmitt Smith 1.00 2.50
29 Terrell Davis .40 1.00
30 Olandis Gary .30 .75
31 Brian Griese .30 .75
32 Ed McCaffrey .30 .75
33 Charlie Batch .30 .75
34 Herman Moore .30 .75
35 Barry Sanders .75 2.00
36 James Stewart .25 .60
37 Brett Favre 1.25 3.00
38 Antonio Freeman .30 .75
39 Dorsey Levens .30 .75
40 Marvin Harrison .40 1.00
41 Edgerrin James .40 1.00
42 Peyton Manning 1.00 2.50
43 Mark Brunell .30 .75
44 Keenan McCardell .30 .75
45 Jimmy Smith .30 .75
46 Fred Taylor .40 1.00
47 Derrick Alexander .25 .60
48 Tony Gonzalez .40 1.00
49 Elvis Grbac .25 .60
50 Damon Huard .30 .75
51 James Johnson .25 .60
52 Dan Marino 1.25 3.00
53 O.J. McDuffie .30 .75
54 Cris Carter .40 1.00
55 Daunte Culpepper .30 .75
56 Jeff George .30 .75
57 Randy Moss .40 1.00
58 Robert Smith .30 .75
59 Drew Bledsoe .40 1.00
60 Terry Glenn .30 .75
61 Lawyer Milloy .25 .60
62 Jeff Blake .30 .75
63 Keith Poole .25 .60
64 Ricky Williams .40 1.00
65 Kerry Collins .30 .75
66 Ike Hilliard .30 .75
67 Amani Toomer .30 .75
68 Wayne Chrebet .30 .75
69 Keyshawn Johnson .30 .75
70 Ray Lucas .25 .60
71 Curtis Martin .40 1.00
72 Vinny Testaverde .30 .75
73 Tim Brown .40 1.00
74 Rich Gannon .30 .75
75 Napoleon Kaufman .30 .75
76 Tyrone Wheatley .25 .60
77 Donovan McNabb .40 1.00
78 Torrance Small .25 .60
79 Duce Staley .30 .75
80 Jerome Bettis .40 1.00
81 Troy Edwards .25 .60
82 Kordell Stewart .30 .75
83 Isaac Bruce .40 1.00
84 Marshall Faulk .40 1.00
85 Torry Holt .40 1.00
86 Kurt Warner .60 1.50
87 Jim Harbaugh .30 .75
88 Jermaine Fazande .25 .60
89 Junior Seau .40 1.00
90 Charlie Garner .30 .75
91 Terrell Owens .40 1.00
92 Jerry Rice .75 2.00
93 Steve Young .50 1.25
94 Sean Dawkins .25 .60
95 Jon Kitna .30 .75
96 Derrick Mayes .25 .60
97 Ricky Watters .30 .75
98 Mike Alstott .40 1.00
99 Warrick Dunn .30 .75
100 Jacquez Green .25 .60
101 Shaun King .25 .60
102 Kevin Dyson .30 .75
103 Eddie George .30 .75
104 Jevon Kearse .30 .75
105 Steve McNair .40 1.00
106 Stephen Davis .30 .75
107 Brad Johnson .30 .75
108 Michael Westbrook .25 .60
109 Shaun Alexander RC 1.25 3.00
110 Tom Brady RC 30.00 60.00
111 Marc Bulger RC 1.00 2.50
112 Plaxico Burress RC 1.00 2.50
113 Giovanni Carmazzi RC .60 1.50
114 Kwame Cavil RC .60 1.50
115 Chris Cole RC .75 2.00
116 Chris Coleman RC .60 1.50
117 Laveranues Coles RC 1.00 2.50
118 Ron Dayne RC 1.00 2.50
119 Reuben Droughns RC 1.00 2.50
120 Ron Dugans RC .60 1.50
121 Danny Farmer RC .60 1.50
122 Chafie Fields RC .60 1.50
123 Joe Hamilton RC .60 1.50
124 Todd Husak RC .60 1.50
125 Darrell Jackson RC .75 2.00
126 Thomas Jones RC 1.25 3.00
127 Jamal Lewis RC 1.00 2.50
128 Tee Martin RC 1.00 2.50
129 Rondell Mealey RC .60 1.50
130 Sylvester Morris RC .60 1.50
131 Chad Morton RC 1.00 2.50
132 Dennis Northcutt RC .75 2.00
133 Chad Pennington RC 1.50 4.00
134 Travis Prentice RC .75 2.00
135 Tim Rattay RC .75 2.00
136 Chris Redman RC .75 2.00
137 J.R. Redmond RC .60 1.50
138 R.Jay Soward RC .60 1.50
139 Shyrone Stith RC .60 1.50
140 Travis Taylor RC .75 2.00
141 Troy Walters RC .60 1.50
142 Peter Warrick RC 1.00 2.50
143 Dez White RC .75 2.00
144 Michael Wiley RC .60 1.50
S1 Jon Kitna Sample .60 1.50

2000 Crown Royale Draft Picks 499

*ROOKIES/499: .8X TO 2X BASE RC
STATED PRINT RUN 499 SER.#'d SETS
110 Tom Brady 60.00 120.00

2000 Crown Royale Limited Series

*VETS 1-108: 4X TO 10X BASIC CARDS
*ROOKIES 109-144: 1.5X TO 4X
STATED PRINT RUN 144 SER.#'d SETS
110 Tom Brady 75.00 150.00

2000 Crown Royale Premiere Date

*VETS 1-108: 4X TO 10X BASIC CARDS
*ROOKIES 109-144: 1.5X TO 4X
STATED PRINT RUN 145 SER.#'d SETS
110 Tom Brady 75.00 150.00

2000 Crown Royale Retail

COMPLETE SET (144) 60.00 120.00
*RETAIL CARDS: .4X TO 1X HOBBY
110 Tom Brady RC 25.00 50.00

2000 Crown Royale Cramer's Choice Jumbos

COMPLETE SET (10) 12.50 30.00
STATED ODDS ONE PER HOBBY BOX
*DARK BLUE/35: 2.5X TO 6X BASIC INSERT
DARK BLUE PRINT RUN 35 SER.#'d SETS
*GOLD/10: 6X TO 15X BASIC INSERTS
GOLD PRINT RUN 10 SER.#'d SETS
*GREEN/30: 2.5X TO 6X BASIC INSERT
GREEN PRINT RUN 30 SER.#'d SETS
*LIGHT BLUE/20: 3X TO 8X BASIC INSERT
LIGHT BLUE PRINT RUN 20 SER.#'d SETS
UNPRICED PURPLE PRINT RUN 1
*RED/25: 3X TO 8X BASIC INSERT
RED PRINT RUN 25 SER.#'d SETS
1 Tim Couch 1.00 2.50
2 Emmitt Smith 3.00 8.00
3 Edgerrin James 1.25 3.00
4 Damon Huard 1.00 2.50
5 Randy Moss 1.25 3.00
6 Kurt Warner 2.00 5.00
7 Jon Kitna 1.00 2.50
8 Eddie George 1.00 2.50
9 Chad Pennington 1.50 4.00
10 Peter Warrick 1.25 3.00

2000 Crown Royale Fifth Anniversary Jumbos

COMPLETE SET (6) 7.50 20.00
STATED ODDS 6:10 BOXES
1 Terrell Davis 1.25 3.00
2 Eddie George 1.00 2.60
3 Jon Kitna 1.00 2.50
4 Randy Moss 1.25 3.00
5 Kurt Warner 2.00 5.00
6 Peter Warrick 1.25 3.00

2000 Crown Royale First and Ten

COMPLETE SET (10) 30.00 60.00
STATED PRINT RUN 375 SER.#'d SETS
*RETAIL: .1X TO .3X BASIC INSERTS
1 Tim Couch 1.25 3.00
2 Troy Aikman 2.50 6.00
3 Emmitt Smith 4.00 10.00
4 Terrell Davis 1.50 4.00
5 Brett Favre 5.00 12.00
6 Edgerrin James 1.50 4.00
7 Peyton Manning 4.00 10.00
8 Randy Moss 1.50 4.00
9 Kurt Warner 2.50 6.00
10 Jerry Rice 3.00 8.00

2000 Crown Royale Game Worn Jerseys

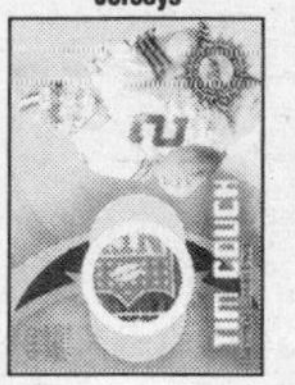

COMPLETE SET (9) 60.00 150.00
1 Eric Moulds 5.00 12.00
2 Brett Favre 20.00 50.00
3 Antonio Freeman 5.00 12.00
4 Ricky Williams 6.00 15.00
5 Tiki Barber 6.00 15.00
6 Charles Woodson 6.00 15.00
7 Isaac Bruce 6.00 15.00
8 Kurt Warner 10.00 25.00
9 Tim Couch 5.00 12.00

2000 Crown Royale In the Pocket

COMPLETE SET (20) 40.00 80.00
STATED ODDS 2:25
*MINI: .25X TO .6X BASIC INSERTS
1 Tim Couch .75 2.00
2 Troy Aikman 1.50 4.00
3 Emmitt Smith 2.50 6.00
4 Charlie Batch .75 2.00
5 Edgerrin James 1.00 2.50
6 Peyton Manning 2.50 6.00
7 Mark Brunell .75 2.00
8 Randy Moss 1.00 2.50
9 Drew Bledsoe 1.00 2.50
10 Donovan McNabb 1.00 2.50
11 Kurt Warner 1.50 4.00
12 Jon Kitna .75 2.00
13 Eddie George .75 2.00
14 Steve McNair 1.00 2.50
15 Brad Johnson .75 2.00
16 Plaxico Burress 1.00 2.50
17 Ron Dayne 1.00 2.50
18 Thomas Jones 1.25 3.00
19 Chad Pennington 1.50 4.00
20 Peter Warrick 1.00 2.50

2000 Crown Royale In Your Face

COMPLETE SET (25) 7.50 20.00
STATED ODDS 1:1H/1:2R
*RAINBOW/20: 15X TO 40X BASIC INSERTS
RAINBOW PRINT RUN 20 SER.#'d SETS
RAINBOW FOUND ONLY IN HOBBY PACKS
1 Jake Plummer .25 .60
2 Cade McNown .20 .50
3 Marcus Robinson .25 .60
4 Corey Dillon .25 .60
5 Tim Couch .25 .60
6 Emmitt Smith .75 2.00
7 Terrell Davis .30 .75
8 Barry Sanders .60 1.50
9 Marvin Harrison .30 .75
10 Edgerrin James .30 .75
11 Mark Brunell .25 .60
12 Fred Taylor .30 .75
13 Dan Marino 1.00 2.50
14 Randy Moss .30 .75
15 Drew Bledsoe .30 .75
16 Ricky Williams .30 .75
17 Curtis Martin .30 .75
18 Isaac Bruce .30 .75
19 Marshall Faulk .30 .75
20 Kurt Warner .50 1.25
21 Jerry Rice .60 1.50
22 Jon Kitna .25 .60
23 Shaun King .20 .50
24 Eddie George .25 .60
25 Stephen Davis .25 .60

2000 Crown Royale Productions

COMPLETE SET (20) 20.00 50.00
STATED ODDS 1:25
1 Cade McNown .60 1.50
2 Tim Couch .75 2.00
3 Emmitt Smith 3.00 8.00
4 Olandis Gary .75 2.00
5 Barry Sanders 2.00 5.00
6 Brett Favre 3.00 8.00
7 Edgerrin James 1.00 2.50
8 Peyton Manning 2.50 6.00
9 Fred Taylor 1.00 2.50
10 Damon Huard .75 2.00
11 Dan Marino 3.00 8.00
12 Randy Moss 1.00 2.50
13 Drew Bledsoe 1.00 2.50
14 Ricky Williams 1.00 2.50
15 Marshall Faulk 1.00 2.50
16 Kurt Warner 1.50 4.00
17 Jerry Rice 2.00 5.00
18 Shaun King .60 1.50
19 Eddie George .75 2.00
20 Stephen Davis .75 2.00

2000 Crown Royale Rookie Autographs

PACIFIC ANNOUNCED SOME PRINT RUNS
109 Shaun Alexander 12.00 30.00
110 Tom Brady 350.00 600.00
111 Marc Bulger 8.00 20.00
112 Plaxico Burress 15.00 30.00
113 Giovanni Carmazzi 5.00 12.00
114 Kwame Cavil 5.00 12.00
115 Chris Cole 6.00 15.00
116 Chris Coleman 5.00 12.00
117 Laveranues Coles 8.00 20.00
118 Ron Dayne/100* 12.00 30.00
119 Reuben Droughns 8.00 20.00
120 Ron Dugans 5.00 12.00
121 Danny Farmer 5.00 12.00
122 Chafie Fields 5.00 12.00
123 Joe Hamilton 5.00 12.00
124 Todd Husak 5.00 12.00
125 Darrell Jackson 6.00 15.00
126 Thomas Jones 10.00 25.00
127 Jamal Lewis 8.00 20.00
128 Tee Martin 8.00 20.00
129 Rondell Mealey 5.00 12.00
130 Sylvester Morris 5.00 12.00
131 Chad Morton 8.00 20.00
132 Dennis Northcutt 6.00 15.00
133 Chad Pennington/100* 15.00 40.00
134 Travis Prentice 6.00 15.00
135 Tim Rattay 6.00 15.00
136 Chris Redman/100* 6.00 15.00
137 J.R. Redmond 5.00 12.00
138 R.Jay Soward 5.00 12.00
139 Shyrone Stith 5.00 12.00
140 Travis Taylor 6.00 15.00
141 Troy Walters
142 Peter Warrick/100* 8.00 20.00
143 Dez White 6.00 15.00
144 Michael Wiley 5.00 12.00

2000 Crown Royale Rookie Royalty

COMPLETE SET (25) 20.00 40.00
STATED ODDS 1:1H/1:2R
UNPRICED HOBBY DIE CUT PRINT RUN 1
1 Shaun Alexander .50 1.25
2 Tom Brady 12.00 30.00
3 Plaxico Burress .40 1.00
4 Ron Dayne .40 1.00
5 Reuben Droughns .40 1.00
6 Danny Farmer .25 .60
7 Chafie Fields .25 .60
8 Joe Hamilton .25 .60
9 Todd Husak .25 .60
10 Thomas Jones .50 1.25
11 Jamal Lewis .40 1.00
12 Tee Martin .40 1.00
13 Sylvester Morris .25 .60
14 Dennis Northcutt .30 .75
15 Chad Pennington .60 1.50
16 Travis Prentice .30 .75
17 Tim Rattay .30 .75
18 Chris Redman .30 .75
19 J.R. Redmond .25 .60
20 R.Jay Soward .25 .60
21 Shyrone Stith .25 .60
22 Travis Taylor .30 .75
23 Troy Walters .25 .60
24 Peter Warrick .40 1.00
25 Dez White .30 .75

2001 Crown Royale

Crown Royale was released as a 218-card die cut base set with 72 serial numbered draft pick cards. Hobby versions feature a gold crown with silver background for veterans, and a gold crown with gold background for rookies. The print runs for rookies varies for different positions, QB's are numbered to 500, RB's are numbered to 750, WR's are numbered to 1000, and all others are numbered to 1750. The Exchange card expired on December 31, 2001.

COMP.SET w/o SP's (144) 10.00 25.00
1 David Boston .20 .50
2 Thomas Jones .25 .60
3 Rob Moore .20 .50
4 Michael Pittman .25 .60
5 Jake Plummer .25 .60
6 Jamal Anderson .25 .60
7 Chris Chandler .25 .60
8 Tim Dwight .25 .60
9 Shawn Jefferson .20 .50
10 Doug Johnson .20 .50
11 Terance Mathis .20 .50
12 Tony Banks .20 .50
13 Trent Dilfer .25 .60
14 Elvis Grbac .25 .60
15 Priest Holmes .30 .75
16 Qadry Ismail .25 .60
17 Jamal Lewis .30 .75
18 Ray Lewis .30 .75
19 Shannon Sharpe .30 .75
20 Shawn Bryson .20 .50
21 Rob Johnson .25 .60
22 Eric Moulds .25 .60
23 Peerless Price .20 .50
24 Antowain Smith .25 .60
25 Steve Beuerlein .25 .60
26 Tim Biakabutuka .20 .50
27 Patrick Jeffers .20 .50
28 Muhsin Muhammad .25 .60
29 James Allen .20 .50
30 Bobby Engram .25 .60
31 Cade McNown .25 .60
32 Marcus Robinson .25 .60
33 Brian Urlacher .40 1.00
34 Corey Dillon .25 .60
35 Jon Kitna .25 .60
36 Akili Smith .20 .50
37 Peter Warrick .25 .60
38 Tim Couch .20 .50
39 Kevin Johnson .20 .50
40 Travis Prentice .20 .50
41 Troy Aikman .50 1.25
42 Rocket Ismail .25 .60
43 Emmitt Smith .75 2.00
44 Mike Anderson .25 .60
45 Terrell Davis .30 .75
46 Olandis Gary .20 .50
47 Brian Griese .25 .60
48 Ed McCaffrey .25 .60
49 Rod Smith .25 .60
50 Charlie Batch .25 .60
51 Herman Moore .25 .60
52 Johnnie Morton .25 .60
53 James Stewart .20 .50
54 Brett Favre 1.00 2.50
55 Antonio Freeman .30 .75
56 Ahman Green .30 .75
57 Dorsey Levens .25 .60
58 Bill Schroeder .25 .60
59 Marvin Harrison .30 .75
60 Edgerrin James .30 .75
61 Peyton Manning .75 2.00
62 Jerome Pathon .20 .50
63 Mark Brunell .25 .60
64 Keenan McCardell .25 .60
65 Jimmy Smith .25 .60
66 Fred Taylor .30 .75
67 Derrick Alexander .20 .50
68 Tony Gonzalez .30 .75
69 Sylvester Morris .20 .50
70 Tony Richardson .20 .50
71 Jay Fiedler .25 .60
72 Oronde Gadsden .20 .50
73 Tony Martin .25 .60
74 James McKnight .20 .50
75 Lamar Smith .25 .60
76 Cris Carter .30 .75
77 Daunte Culpepper .25 .60
78 Randy Moss .30 .75
79 Robert Smith .25 .60
80 Drew Bledsoe .30 .75
81 Troy Brown .25 .60
82 Kevin Faulk .25 .60
83 Terry Glenn .25 .60
84 J.R. Redmond .20 .50
85 Jeff Blake .25 .60
86 Aaron Brooks .25 .60
87 Joe Horn .25 .60
88 Ricky Williams .30 .75
89 Tiki Barber .30 .75
90 Kerry Collins .25 .60
91 Ron Dayne .25 .60
92 Ike Hilliard .25 .60
93 Amani Toomer .25 .60
94 Wayne Chrebet .25 .60
95 Curtis Martin .30 .75
96 Chad Pennington .30 .75
97 Vinny Testaverde .25 .60
98 Dedric Ward .20 .50
99 Tim Brown .30 .75
100 Rich Gannon .25 .60
101 Napoleon Kaufman .20 .50
102 Andre Rison .25 .60
103 Tyrone Wheatley .25 .60
104 Charles Johnson .20 .50
105 Donovan McNabb .30 .75
106 Torrance Small .20 .50
107 Duce Staley .25 .60
108 Jerome Bettis .30 .75
109 Plaxico Burress .25 .60
110 Kordell Stewart .25 .60
111 Hines Ward .30 .75
112 Isaac Bruce .30 .75
113 Marshall Faulk .30 .75
114 Trent Green .30 .75
115 Az-Zahir Hakim .20 .50
116 Torry Holt .25 .60
117 Kurt Warner .50 1.25
118 Curtis Conway .25 .60
119 Doug Flutie .30 .75
120 Jeff Graham .20 .50
121 Junior Seau .30 .75
122 Jeff Garcia .25 .60
123 Charlie Garner .25 .60
124 Terrell Owens .30 .75
125 Jerry Rice .60 1.50
126 Shaun Alexander .30 .75
127 Darrell Jackson .25 .60
128 Ricky Watters .25 .60
129 Mike Alstott .25 .60
130 Warrick Dunn .30 .75
131 Brad Johnson .25 .60
132 Keyshawn Johnson .25 .60
133 Shaun King .20 .50
134 Ryan Leaf .20 .50
135 Warren Sapp .25 .60
136 Kevin Dyson .20 .50
137 Eddie George .30 .75
138 Jevon Kearse .25 .60
139 Derrick Mason .25 .60
140 Steve McNair .30 .75
141 Stephen Davis .25 .60
142 Jeff George .25 .60
143 Deion Sanders .30 .75
144 Michael Westbrook .20 .50
145 Anthony Thomas AU/250 RC 10.00 25.00
146 Michael Vick AU/250 RC 100.00 200.00
147 Chris Chambers AU/250 RC 15.00 40.00
148 Michael Bennett AU/250 RC 8.00 20.00
149 Chris Weinke AU/250 RC 8.00 20.00
150 Drew Brees AU/250 RC 100.00 175.00
151 LaDainian Tomlinson AU/250 RC 75.00 150.00
152 Marques Tuiasosopo AU RC/250 8.00 20.00
153 David Terrell AU/250 RC 8.00 20.00
154 Rod Gardner AU/250 RC 8.00 20.00
155 Dan Alexander/1750 RC 2.00 5.00
156 Brian Allen/1750 RC 1.50 4.00
157 David Allen/750 RC 1.50 4.00
158 Will Allen/1750 RC 2.50 6.00
159 Scotty Anderson/1000 RC 2.50 6.00
160 Adam Archuleta/1750 RC 2.00 5.00
161 Jeff Backus/1750 RC 1.50 4.00
162 Alex Bannister/1000 RC 2.50 6.00
163 Kevan Barlow/750 RC 4.00 10.00
164 Gary Baxter/1750 RC 1.50 4.00
165 Josh Booty/500 RC 5.00 12.00
166 Larry Casher/1750 RC 1.50 4.00
167 Tay Cody/1750 RC 1.50 4.00
168 Jarrod Cooper/1750 RC 2.00 5.00
169 Ennis Davis/1750 RC 1.50 4.00
170 Leonard Davis/1750 RC 2.50 6.00
171 Tony Dixon/1750 RC 1.50 4.00
172 Tony Driver/1750 RC 2.00 5.00
173 Heath Evans/1750 RC 2.00 5.00
174 Jamar Fletcher/1750 RC 1.50 4.00
175 Derrick Gibson/1750 RC 1.50 4.00
176 Morlon Greenwood/1750 RC 1.50 4.00
177 Edgerton Hartwell/1750 RC 1.50 4.00
178 Tim Hasselbeck/500 RC 5.00 12.00
179 Todd Heap/1750 RC 2.50 6.00
180 Travis Henry/750 RC 4.00 10.00
181 Josh Heupel/500 RC 6.00 15.00
182 Sedrick Hodge/1750 RC 1.50 4.00
183 Jabari Holloway/1750 RC 1.50 4.00
184 Willie Howard/1750 RC 1.50 4.00
185 Steve Hutchinson/1750 RC 4.00 10.00
186 James Jackson/750 RC 3.00 8.00
187 Chad Johnson/1000 RC 6.00 15.00
188 Rudi Johnson/750 RC 5.00 12.00
189 LaMont Jordan/750 RC 5.00 12.00
190 Ben Leard/500 RC 4.00 10.00
191 Alex Lincoln/1750 RC 1.50 4.00
192 Torrance Marshall/1750 RC 1.50 4.00
193 Deuce McAllister/750 RC 5.00 12.00
194 Jason McKinley/500 RC 4.00 10.00
195 Mike McMahon/500 RC 5.00 12.00
196 Snoop Minnis/1000 RC 2.50 6.00
197 Travis Minor/750 RC 4.00 10.00
198 Freddie Mitchell/1000 RC 2.50 6.00
199 Zeke Moreno/1750 RC 2.00 5.00
200 Quincy Morgan/1000 RC 3.00 8.00
201 Santana Moss/1000 RC 5.00 12.00
202 Bobby Newcombe/1000 RC 3.00 8.00
203 Moran Norris/1750 RC 1.50 4.00
204 Tommy Polley/1750 RC 1.50 4.00
205 Ken-Yon Rambo/1000 RC 2.50 6.00
206 Koren Robinson/1000 RC 3.00 8.00
207 Sage Rosenfels/500 RC 6.00 15.00
208 John Schlecht/1750 RC 1.50 4.00
209 Brandon Spoon/1750 RC 2.00 5.00
210 Michael Stone/1750 RC 1.50 4.00
211 Marcus Stroud/1750 RC 2.00 5.00
212 Vinny Sutherland/1000 RC 2.50 6.00
213 Joe Tafoya/1750 RC 1.50 4.00
214 Clevan Thomas/1750 RC 1.50 4.00
215 Ja'Mar Toombs/1750 RC 1.50 4.00
216 Fred Wakefield/1750 RC 1.50 4.00
217 Reggie Wayne/1000 RC 8.00 20.00
218 Reggie White/750 RC 3.00 8.00

2001 Crown Royale Limited Series

*VETS: 10X TO 25X BASIC CARDS
STATED PRINT RUN 25 SER.#'d SETS

2001 Crown Royale Platinum Blue

*VETS: 5X TO 12X BASIC CARDS
STATED PRINT RUN 75 SER.#'d SETS

2001 Crown Royale Premiere Date

*VETS/99: 5X TO 12X BASIC CARDS
STATED PRINT RUN 99 SER.#'d SETS

2001 Crown Royale Retail

COMPLETE SET (144) 10.00 25.00
*RETAIL VETS: .4X TO 1X HOBBY

2001 Crown Royale 21st Century Rookies

COMPLETE SET (25) 12.50 30.00
STATED ODDS 1:1 HOB, 1:2 RET
1 Kevan Barlow .50 1.25
2 Michael Bennett .50 1.25
3 Josh Booty .50 1.25
4 Drew Brees 4.00 10.00
5 Chris Chambers .60 1.50
6 Rod Gardner .50 1.25
7 Tim Hasselbeck .50 1.25
8 Todd Heap .60 1.50
9 Travis Henry .50 1.25
10 Chad Johnson 1.00 2.50
11 Rudi Johnson .60 1.50
12 LaMont Jordan .60 1.50
13 Ben Leard .40 1.00
14 Deuce McAllister .60 1.50
15 Mike McMahon .50 1.25
16 Freddie Mitchell .40 1.00
17 Quincy Morgan .50 1.25
18 Sage Rosenfels .60 1.50
19 David Terrell .50 1.25
20 Anthony Thomas .60 1.50
21 LaDainian Tomlinson 2.00 5.00
22 Marques Tuiasosopo .50 1.25
23 Michael Vick 2.50 6.00
24 Reggie Wayne 1.25 3.00
25 Chris Weinke .50 1.25

2001 Crown Royale Coming Soon

COMPLETE SET (10) 20.00 50.00
STATED PRINT RUN 500 SER.#'d SETS
1 Drew Brees 10.00 25.00
2 Chris Chambers 1.50 4.00
3 Rod Gardner 1.25 3.00
4 Travis Henry 1.25 3.00
5 Deuce McAllister 1.50 4.00
6 David Terrell 1.25 3.00
7 Anthony Thomas 1.50 4.00
8 LaDainian Tomlinson 5.00 12.00
9 Michael Vick 6.00 15.00
10 Chris Weinke 1.25 3.00

2001 Crown Royale Cramers Choice Jumbos Footballs

COMPLETE SET (10) 60.00 120.00
ONE PER HOBBY BOX
1 Jamal Lewis 5.00 12.00
2 Corey Dillon 4.00 10.00
3 Peter Warrick 4.00 10.00
4 Brett Favre 15.00 40.00
5 Fred Taylor 5.00 12.00
6 Daunte Culpepper 4.00 10.00
7 Randy Moss 5.00 12.00
8 Ricky Williams 5.00 12.00
9 Marshall Faulk 5.00 12.00
10 Kurt Warner 8.00 20.00

2001 Crown Royale Cramers Choice Jumbos Jerseys

STATED PRINT RUN 50-150
2 Corey Dillon/150 6.00 15.00
3 Peter Warrick/150 6.00 15.00
4 Brett Favre/50 30.00 80.00
5 Fred Taylor/150 8.00 20.00
6 Daunte Culpepper/150 6.00 15.00
7 Randy Moss/150 8.00 20.00
8 Ricky Williams/150 8.00 20.00
9 Marshall Faulk/150 8.00 20.00
10 Kurt Warner/150 12.00 30.00

2001 Crown Royale Crown Rookies

ONE PER SPECIAL RETAIL PACK
STATED PRINT RUN 2500 SER.#'d SETS
1 Kevan Barlow .50 1.25
2 Drew Brees 4.00 10.00
3 Travis Henry .50 1.25
4 Chad Johnson 1.00 2.50
5 Freddie Mitchell .40 1.00
6 Sage Rosenfels .60 1.50
7 Anthony Thomas .60 1.50
8 LaDainian Tomlinson 2.00 5.00
9 Marques Tuiasosopo .50 1.25
10 Chris Weinke .50 1.25

2001 Crown Royale Game Worn Jerseys

STATED PRINT RUN 276-523
1 Thomas Jones/277 5.00 12.00
2 Rob Johnson/277 5.00 12.00
3 Thurman Thomas/276 6.00 15.00
4 Corey Dillon/277 5.00 12.00
5 Peter Warrick/277 5.00 12.00
6 Brett Favre/277 20.00 50.00
7 Jay Fiedler/521 4.00 10.00
8 Lamar Smith/506 4.00 10.00
9 Aaron Brooks/523 4.00 10.00
10 Joe Horn/522 4.00 10.00
11 Ricky Williams/519 5.00 12.00
12 Marshall Faulk/277 6.00 15.00
13 Az-Zahir Hakim/519 3.00 8.00
14 Torry Holt/523 4.00 10.00
15 Kurt Warner/277 10.00 25.00

2001 Crown Royale Jewels of the Crown

COMPLETE SET (25) 5.00 12.00
STATED ODDS 1:1 HOB,1:2 RET
1 Trent Dilfer .25 .60
2 Brian Urlacher .40 1.00
3 Corey Dillon .25 .60
4 Peter Warrick .25 .60
5 Tim Couch .20 .50
6 Emmitt Smith .75 2.00
7 Mike Anderson .25 .60
8 Brian Griese .25 .60
9 Marvin Harrison .30 .75
10 Edgerrin James .30 .75
11 Mark Brunell .25 .60
12 Fred Taylor .30 .75
13 Daunte Culpepper .25 .60
14 Randy Moss .30 .75
15 Drew Bledsoe .30 .75
16 Ron Dayne .25 .60
17 Curtis Martin .30 .75
18 Rich Gannon .25 .60
19 Jerome Bettis .30 .75
20 Marshall Faulk .30 .75
21 Kurt Warner .50 1.25
22 Jeff Garcia .25 .60
23 Eddie George .30 .75
24 Steve McNair .30 .75
25 Stephen Davis .25 .60

2001 Crown Royale Landmarks

COMPLETE SET (10) 40.00 100.00
STATED PRINT RUN 99 SER.#'d SETS
1 Emmitt Smith 10.00 25.00
2 Brian Griese 3.00 8.00
3 Edgerrin James 4.00 10.00
4 Brett Favre 12.00 30.00
5 Peyton Manning 10.00 25.00
6 Ricky Williams 4.00 10.00
7 Marshall Faulk 4.00 10.00
8 Kurt Warner 6.00 15.00
9 Jerry Rice 8.00 20.00
10 Eddie George 4.00 10.00

2001 Crown Royale Living Legends

COMPLETE SET (20) 20.00 50.00
STATED PRINT RUN 950 SER.#'d SETS
1 Tim Couch .75 2.00
2 Troy Aikman 2.00 5.00
3 Emmitt Smith 3.00 8.00
4 Terrell Davis 1.25 3.00
5 Brian Griese 1.00 2.50
6 Brett Favre 4.00 10.00
7 Edgerrin James 1.25 3.00
8 Mark Brunell 1.00 2.50
9 Daunte Culpepper 1.00 2.50
10 Cris Carter 1.25 3.00
11 Randy Moss 1.25 3.00
12 Drew Bledsoe 1.25 3.00
13 Ricky Williams 1.25 3.00
14 Marshall Faulk 1.25 3.00
15 Kurt Warner 2.00 5.00
16 Junior Seau 1.25 3.00
17 Jerry Rice 2.50 6.00
18 Eddie George 1.25 3.00
19 Steve McNair 1.25 3.00
20 Stephen Davis 1.00 2.50

2001 Crown Royale Now Playing

COMPLETE SET (20) 20.00 50.00
STATED PRINT RUN 1000 SER.#'d SETS
1 Peter Warrick 1.00 2.50
2 Tim Couch .75 2.00
3 Troy Aikman 2.00 5.00
4 Emmitt Smith 3.00 8.00
5 Terrell Davis 1.25 3.00

6 Brian Griese 1.00 2.50
7 Edgerrin James 1.25 3.00
8 Mark Brunell 1.00 2.50
9 Daunte Culpepper 1.00 2.50
10 Randy Moss 1.25 3.00
11 Drew Bledsoe 1.25 3.00
12 Ricky Williams 1.25 3.00
13 Ron Dayne 1.00 2.50
14 Donovan McNabb 1.25 3.00
15 Marshall Faulk 1.25 3.00
16 Kurt Warner 2.00 5.00
17 Jeff Garcia 1.00 2.50
18 Jerry Rice 2.50 6.00
19 Eddie George 1.25 3.00
20 Steve McNair 1.25 3.00

2001 Crown Royale Pro Bowl Honors

COMPLETE SET (20) 15.00 40.00
STATED PRINT RUN 850 SER.#'d SETS
1 Eric Moulds 1.00 2.50
2 Corey Dillon 1.00 2.50
3 Brian Griese 1.00 2.50
4 Marvin Harrison 1.25 3.00
5 Peyton Manning 3.00 8.00
6 Edgerrin James 1.25 3.00
7 Jimmy Smith 1.00 2.50
8 Tony Gonzalez 1.25 3.00
9 Elvis Grbac 1.00 2.50
10 Cris Carter 1.25 3.00
11 Daunte Culpepper 1.00 2.50
12 Randy Moss 1.25 3.00
13 Rich Gannon 1.00 2.50
14 Marshall Faulk 1.25 3.00
15 Torry Holt 1.00 2.50
16 Kurt Warner 2.00 5.00
17 Jeff Garcia 1.00 2.50
18 Terrell Owens 1.25 3.00
19 Warrick Dunn 1.25 3.00
20 Eddie George 1.25 3.00

2001 Crown Royale Rookie Jumbos

COMPLETE SET (25) 40.00 100.00
STATED PRINT RUN 499 SER.#'d SETS
1 Dan Alexander 1.50 4.00
2 Alex Bannister 1.25 3.00
3 Kevan Barlow 1.50 4.00
4 Michael Bennett 1.50 4.00
5 Drew Brees 12.00 30.00
6 Chris Chambers 2.00 5.00
7 Rod Gardner 1.50 4.00
8 Travis Henry 1.50 4.00
9 Chad Johnson 3.00 8.00
10 Rudi Johnson 2.00 5.00
11 LaMont Jordan 2.00 5.00
12 Ben Leard 1.25 3.00
13 Deuce McAllister 2.00 5.00
14 Mike McMahon 1.50 4.00
15 Freddie Mitchell 1.25 3.00
16 Quincy Morgan 1.50 4.00
17 Koren Robinson 1.50 4.00
18 Sage Rosenfels 2.00 5.00
19 David Terrell 1.50 4.00
20 Anthony Thomas 2.00 5.00
21 LaDainian Tomlinson 6.00 15.00
22 Marques Tuiasosopo 1.50 4.00
23 Michael Vick 8.00 20.00
24 Reggie Wayne 4.00 10.00
25 Chris Weinke 1.50 4.00

2001 Crown Royale Rookie Royalty

COMPLETE SET (20) 20.00 50.00
STATED PRINT RUN 1250 SER. #'d SETS
1 Alex Bannister .60 1.50
2 Kevan Barlow .75 2.00
3 Michael Bennett .75 2.00
4 Drew Brees 6.00 15.00
5 Rod Gardner .75 2.00
6 Travis Henry .75 2.00
7 Chad Johnson 1.50 4.00
8 Rudi Johnson 1.00 2.50
9 Mike McMahon .75 2.00
10 Freddie Mitchell .60 1.50
11 Quincy Morgan .75 2.00
12 Koren Robinson .75 2.00
13 Sage Rosenfels 1.00 2.50
14 David Terrell .75 2.00
15 Anthony Thomas 1.00 2.50
16 LaDainian Tomlinson 3.00 8.00
17 Marques Tuiasosopo .75 2.00
18 Michael Vick 4.00 10.00
19 Reggie Wayne 2.00 5.00
20 Chris Weinke .75 2.00

2001 Crown Royale Rookie Signatures

PRINT RUN 500 UNLESS NOTED BELOW
1 Scotty Anderson/500 4.00 10.00
2 Alex Bannister/500 4.00 10.00
3 Kevan Barlow/500 5.00 12.00
4 Michael Bennett/100 8.00 20.00
5 Josh Booty/500 5.00 12.00
6 Drew Brees/100 100.00 175.00
7 Chris Chambers/250 8.00 20.00
8 Heath Evans/500 5.00 12.00
11 Tim Hasselbeck/500 5.00 12.00
12 Todd Heap/500 6.00 15.00
15 James Jackson/500 4.00 10.00
16 Chad Johnson/500 15.00 40.00
17 Rudi Johnson/500 6.00 15.00
18 Ben Leard/500 4.00 10.00
19 Jason McKinley/500 4.00 10.00
20 Mike McMahon/500 5.00 12.00
21 Snoop Minnis/500 4.00 10.00
22 Freddie Mitchell/500 4.00 10.00
23 Quincy Morgan/500 5.00 12.00
24 Bobby Newcombe/500 5.00 12.00
25 Moran Norris/500 4.00 10.00
26 Sage Rosenfels/500 6.00 15.00
27 Vinny Sutherland/500 4.00 10.00
28 David Terrell/250 6.00 15.00
29 Anthony Thomas/250 8.00 20.00
30 LaDainian Tomlinson/100 60.00 120.00
32 Marques Tuiasosopo/250 6.00 15.00
33 Michael Vick/100 75.00 150.00
34 Reggie Wayne/500 20.00 50.00
35 Chris Weinke/100 8.00 20.00
36 Reggie White/500 4.00 10.00

2002 Crown Royale

Released in August 2002, this 216-card set includes 144 veterans and 72 rookies. The S.R.P. per hobby pack is $5.99. The rookies were inserted one per hobby pack or at a stated rate of one in four retail packs.

COMPLETE SET (216) 100.00 200.00
COMP.SET w/o RCs (144) 20.00 50.00
145-216 ROOKIE ODDS 1:1 H, 1:4 R
1 David Boston .25 .60
2 Thomas Jones .40 1.00
3 Jake Plummer .30 .75
4 Frank Sanders .25 .60
5 Jamal Anderson .30 .75
6 Warrick Dunn .30 .75
7 Brian Finneran .25 .60
8 Shawn Jefferson .25 .60
9 Michael Vick .60 1.50
10 Jeff Blake .30 .75
11 Jamal Lewis .30 .75
12 Ray Lewis .40 1.00
13 Chris Redman .25 .60
14 Travis Taylor .25 .60
15 Drew Bledsoe .40 1.00
16 Travis Henry .25 .60
17 Eric Moulds .30 .75
18 Peerless Price .25 .60
19 Isaac Byrd .25 .60
20 Muhsin Muhammad .30 .75
21 Lamar Smith .30 .75
22 Chris Weinke .25 .60
23 Marty Booker .30 .75
24 Jim Miller .25 .60
25 Marcus Robinson .30 .75
26 Anthony Thomas .30 .75
27 Brian Urlacher .40 1.00
28 Corey Dillon .30 .75
29 Gus Frerotte .30 .75
30 Jon Kitna .30 .75
31 Darnay Scott .30 .75
32 Peter Warrick .30 .75
33 Tim Couch .25 .60
34 James Jackson .25 .60
35 Kevin Johnson .25 .60
36 Quincy Morgan .25 .60
37 Quincy Carter .25 .60
38 Joey Galloway .30 .75
39 Rocket Ismail .30 .75
40 Emmitt Smith 1.00 2.50
41 Mike Anderson .30 .75
42 Terrell Davis .40 1.00
43 Brian Griese .30 .75
44 Ed McCaffrey .30 .75
45 Rod Smith .30 .75
46 Germane Crowell .25 .60
47 Az-Zahir Hakim .25 .60
48 Mike McMahon .25 .60
49 Bill Schroeder .25 .60
50 Brett Favre 1.00 2.50
51 Bubba Franks .30 .75
52 Antonio Freeman .40 1.00
53 Terry Glenn .30 .75
54 Ahman Green .30 .75
55 James Allen .25 .60
56 Corey Bradford .25 .60
57 Kent Graham .25 .60
58 Jermaine Lewis .25 .60
59 Marvin Harrison .40 1.00
60 Edgerrin James .30 .75
61 Peyton Manning .75 2.00
62 Dominic Rhodes .30 .75
63 Reggie Wayne .40 1.00
64 Mark Brunell .30 .75
65 Patrick Johnson .25 .60
66 Jimmy Smith .30 .75
67 Fred Taylor .30 .75
68 Tony Gonzalez .40 1.00
69 Trent Green .30 .75
70 Priest Holmes .40 1.00
71 Johnnie Morton .30 .75
72 Chris Chambers .30 .75
73 Jay Fiedler .30 .75
74 James McKnight .25 .60
75 Ricky Williams .30 .75
76 Derrick Alexander .25 .60
77 Michael Bennett .30 .75
78 Daunte Culpepper .30 .75
79 Randy Moss .40 1.00
80 Tom Brady 1.00 2.50
81 Troy Brown .30 .75
82 Kevin Faulk .30 .75
83 David Patten .25 .60
84 Antowain Smith .30 .75
85 Aaron Brooks .30 .75
86 Joe Horn .30 .75
87 Deuce McAllister .30 .75
88 Jerome Pathon .25 .60
89 Tiki Barber .40 1.00
90 Kerry Collins .30 .75
91 Ron Dayne .30 .75
92 Ike Hilliard .30 .75
93 Michael Strahan .40 1.00
94 Amani Toomer .30 .75
95 Wayne Chrebet .30 .75
96 Laveranues Coles .30 .75
97 Curtis Martin .40 1.00
98 Vinny Testaverde .30 .75
99 Tim Brown .40 1.00
100 Rich Gannon .30 .75
101 Charlie Garner .30 .75
102 Jerry Rice .75 2.00
103 Tyrone Wheatley .30 .75
104 Charles Woodson .40 1.00
105 Donovan McNabb .40 1.00
106 Todd Pinkston .25 .60
107 Duce Staley .30 .75
108 James Thrash .30 .75
109 Jerome Bettis .40 1.00
110 Plaxico Burress .30 .75
111 Kordell Stewart .30 .75
112 Hines Ward .40 1.00
113 Isaac Bruce .40 1.00
114 Marshall Faulk .40 1.00
115 Torry Holt .40 1.00
116 Kurt Warner .40 1.00
117 Drew Brees .60 1.50
118 Curtis Conway .30 .75
119 Tim Dwight .25 .60
120 Doug Flutie .40 1.00
121 Junior Seau .40 1.00
122 LaDainian Tomlinson .50 1.25
123 Jeff Garcia .30 .75
124 Garrison Hearst .30 .75
125 Terrell Owens .40 1.00
126 J.J. Stokes .25 .60
127 Shaun Alexander .30 .75
128 Trent Dilfer .30 .75
129 Darrell Jackson .30 .75
130 Koren Robinson .25 .60
131 Mike Alstott .30 .75
132 Brad Johnson .30 .75
133 Keyshawn Johnson .30 .75
134 Keenan McCardell .30 .75
135 Michael Pittman .30 .75
136 Warren Sapp .30 .75
137 Kevin Dyson .30 .75
138 Eddie George .30 .75
139 Derrick Mason .30 .75
140 Steve McNair .40 1.00
141 Stephen Davis .30 .75
142 Rod Gardner .25 .60
143 Jacquez Green .25 .60
144 Shane Matthews .25 .60
145 Jason McAddley RC 1.00 2.50
146 Josh McCown RC 1.25 3.00
147 Josh Scobey RC 1.00 2.50
148 T.J. Duckett RC 1.25 3.00
149 Kahlil Hill RC .75 2.00
150 Kurt Kittner RC .75 2.00
151 Ron Johnson RC 1.00 2.50
152 Tellis Redmon RC .75 2.00
153 Chester Taylor RC 1.25 3.00
154 Josh Reed RC 1.00 2.50
155 Randy Fasani RC 1.00 2.50
156 DeShaun Foster RC 1.25 3.00
157 Julius Peppers RC 2.50 6.00
158 Adrian Peterson RC 1.25 3.00
159 Andre Davis RC 1.00 2.50
160 William Green RC 1.00 2.50
161 Antonio Bryant RC 1.25 3.00
162 Woody Dantzler RC 1.00 2.50
163 Ennis Haywood RC .75 2.00
164 Chad Hutchinson RC .75 2.00
165 Jamar Martin RC 1.00 2.50
166 Roy Williams RC 1.25 3.00
167 Herb Haygood RC .75 2.00
168 Ashley Lelie RC 1.00 2.50
169 Clinton Portis RC 1.50 4.00
170 Eddie Drummond RC .75 2.00
171 Joey Harrington RC 1.25 3.00
172 Luke Staley RC .75 2.00
173 Craig Nall RC 1.00 2.50
174 Javon Walker RC 1.25 3.00
175 Jarrod Baxter RC .75 2.00
176 David Carr RC 1.25 3.00
177 Delvon Flowers RC .75 2.00
178 Jabar Gaffney RC 1.25 3.00
179 Jonathan Wells RC 1.25 3.00
180 David Garrard RC 1.50 4.00
181 John Henderson RC 1.00 2.50
182 Omar Easy RC 1.00 2.50
183 Leonard Henry RC .75 2.00
184 Atrews Bell RC .75 2.00
185 Deion Branch RC 1.25 3.00
186 Rohan Davey RC 1.25 3.00
187 Daniel Graham RC 1.00 2.50
188 Antwoine Womack RC .75 2.00
189 J.T. O'Sullivan RC 1.00 2.50
190 Donte Stallworth RC 1.25 3.00
191 Tim Carter RC 1.00 2.50
192 Daryl Jones RC .75 2.00
193 Jeremy Shockey RC 2.00 5.00
194 Ronald Curry RC 1.00 2.50
195 Napoleon Harris RC 1.00 2.50
196 Larry Ned RC .75 2.00
197 Freddie Milons RC .75 2.00
198 Lito Sheppard RC 1.25 3.00
199 Brian Westbrook RC 2.00 5.00
200 Lee Mays RC .75 2.00
201 Antwaan Randle El RC 1.25 3.00
202 Eric Crouch RC 1.25 3.00
203 Lamar Gordon RC 1.00 2.50
204 Robert Thomas RC .75 2.00
205 Seth Burford RC .75 2.00
206 Reche Caldwell RC 1.25 3.00
207 Quentin Jammer RC 1.25 3.00
208 Brandon Doman RC .75 2.00
209 Maurice Morris RC 1.00 2.50
210 Jerramy Stevens RC 1.25 3.00
211 Travis Stephens RC .75 2.00
212 Marquise Walker RC .75 2.00
213 Jake Schifino RC .75 2.00
214 Ladell Betts RC 1.25 3.00
215 Patrick Ramsey RC 1.25 3.00
216 Cliff Russell RC .75 2.00

2002 Crown Royale Blue

*BLUE VETS/175: 3X TO 8X BASIC CARDS
1-144 VETERAN/175 ODDS 1:15 HOB/RET
1-144 VETERAN PRINT RUN 175
*BLUE ROOKIES/99: 2X TO 5X
145-216 ROOKIE/99 ODDS 1:25 HOB
145-216 ROOKIE PRINT RUN 99

2002 Crown Royale Red

COMPLETE SET (144) 40.00 100.00
*RED VETS: 1X TO 2.5X BASIC CARDS
RED/525 ODDS 1:3 HOBBY
STATED PRINT RUN 525 SER.#'d SETS

2002 Crown Royale Crowning Glory

COMPLETE SET (20) 40.00 100.00
1-10 STATED ODDS 1:25 HOBBY
11-20 STATED ODDS 1:25 RETAIL
1 T.J. Duckett 1.50 4.00
2 DeShaun Foster 1.50 4.00
3 William Green 1.25 3.00
4 Ashley Lelie 1.25 3.00
5 Clinton Portis 2.00 5.00
6 Joey Harrington 1.50 4.00
7 David Carr 1.50 4.00
8 Jabar Gaffney 1.50 4.00
9 Donte Stallworth 1.50 4.00
10 Patrick Ramsey 1.50 4.00
11 Michael Vick 3.00 8.00
12 Anthony Thomas 1.50 4.00
13 Emmitt Smith 5.00 12.00
14 Brett Favre 5.00 12.00
15 Peyton Manning 4.00 10.00
16 Randy Moss 2.00 5.00
17 Tom Brady 5.00 12.00
18 Jerry Rice 4.00 10.00
19 Kurt Warner 2.00 5.00
20 LaDainian Tomlinson 2.50 6.00

2002 Crown Royale Legendary Heroes

LEG. HERO/80 ODDS 1:392 HOB, 1:968 RET
STATED PRINT RUN 80 SER.#'d SETS
1 Emmitt Smith 15.00 40.00
2 Terrell Davis 6.00 15.00
3 Brett Favre 15.00 40.00
4 Peyton Manning 12.00 30.00
5 Ricky Williams 5.00 12.00
6 Randy Moss 6.00 15.00
7 Jerry Rice 12.00 30.00
8 Donovan McNabb 6.00 15.00
9 Marshall Faulk 6.00 15.00
10 Kurt Warner 6.00 15.00

2002 Crown Royale Majestic Motion

COMPLETE SET (10) 25.00 60.00
STATED ODDS 1:25 HOB, 1:49 RET
1 Michael Vick 3.00 8.00
2 Anthony Thomas 1.50 4.00
3 Emmitt Smith 5.00 12.00
4 Brett Favre 5.00 12.00
5 Peyton Manning 4.00 10.00
6 Randy Moss 2.00 5.00
7 Jerry Rice 4.00 10.00
8 Marshall Faulk 2.00 5.00
9 Kurt Warner 2.00 5.00
10 LaDainian Tomlinson 2.50 6.00

2002 Crown Royale Pro Bowl Honors

COMPLETE SET (20) 15.00 40.00
STATED ODDS 1:6 HOB, 1:13 RET
1 Brian Urlacher 1.25 3.00
2 Corey Dillon .75 2.00
3 Emmitt Smith 3.00 8.00
4 Terrell Davis 1.00 2.50
5 Ahman Green .75 2.00
6 Marvin Harrison 1.00 2.50
7 Edgerrin James .75 2.00
8 Peyton Manning 2.00 5.00
9 Daunte Culpepper .75 2.00
10 Randy Moss 1.00 2.50
11 Tom Brady 2.50 6.00
12 Curtis Martin 1.00 2.50
13 Rich Gannon .75 2.00
14 Jerry Rice 2.00 5.00
15 Donovan McNabb 1.00 2.50
16 Kordell Stewart .75 2.00
17 Marshall Faulk 1.00 2.50
18 Kurt Warner 1.00 2.50
19 Junior Seau 1.00 2.50
20 Eddie George .75 2.00

2002 Crown Royale Sunday Soldiers

COMPLETE SET (20) 30.00 80.00
STATED ODDS 1:15 HOB. 1:25 RET
1 T.J. Duckett 2.00 5.00
2 Michael Vick 3.00 8.00
3 Drew Bledsoe 2.00 5.00
4 DeShaun Foster 2.00 5.00
5 William Green 1.50 4.00
6 Emmitt Smith 5.00 12.00
7 Ashley Lelie 1.50 4.00
8 Joey Harrington 2.00 5.00
9 Brett Favre 5.00 12.00
10 David Carr 2.00 5.00
11 Peyton Manning 4.00 10.00
12 Randy Moss 2.00 5.00
13 Tom Brady 5.00 12.00
14 Donte Stallworth 2.00 5.00
15 Donovan McNabb 2.00 5.00
16 Marshall Faulk 2.00 5.00
17 Kurt Warner 2.00 5.00
18 LaDainian Tomlinson 2.50 6.00
19 Shaun Alexander 1.50 4.00
20 Patrick Ramsey 2.00 5.00

2002 Crown Royale Triple Threads Jerseys

STATED ODDS 2:25 HOB, 1:97 RET
*GOLD/25: .8X TO 2X BASIC TRIPLE
GOLD SERIAL #'d TO 25
1 David Boston 8.00 20.00
Thomas Jones
Jake Plummer/535
2 MarTay Jenkins 5.00 12.00
Tywan Mitchell
Frank Sanders/1079
3 Ray Lewis 8.00 20.00
Chris Redman
Travis Taylor/326
4 Reggie Germany 6.00 15.00
Eric Moulds
Peerless Price/256
5 Shawn Bryson 6.00 15.00
Sammy Morris
Jay Riemersma/731
6 Jim Miller 8.00 20.00
David Terrell
Brian Urlacher/216
7 T.J. Houshmanzadeh 8.00 20.00
Chad Johnson
Peter Warrick/480
8 JaJuan Dawson 5.00 12.00
Dennis Northcutt
Jamel White/606
9 Mike Anderson 6.00 15.00
Ed McCaffrey
Rod Smith/100
10 Scotty Anderson 6.00 15.00
Germane Crowell
Desmond Howard/956
11 Mark Brunell 6.00 15.00
Jimmy Smith
Fred Taylor/355
12 Derrick Blaylock 6.00 15.00
Trent Green
Tony Richardson/776
13 Richie Anderson 8.00 20.00
Chad Pennington
Vinny Testaverde/500
14 Tim Brown 8.00 20.00
James Jett
Randy Jordan/1265
15 Chad Lewis 5.00 12.00
Cecil Martin
Todd Pinkston/728
16 Mark Bruener 8.00 20.00
Hines Ward
Amos Zereoue/900
17 Chris Fuamatu-Ma'afala 5.00 12.00
Dan Kreider
Tee Martin/1063
18 Doug Flutie 8.00 20.00
Ronney Jenkins
Junior Seau/1043
19 Champ Bailey 8.00 20.00
Stephen Davis
Darnerian McCants/1640
20 Terrell Davis 10.00 25.00
Edgerrin James
Ricky Williams/215
21 Daunte Culpepper 20.00 50.00
Tom Brady
Donovan McNabb/281
22 Corey Dillon 6.00 15.00
Shaun Alexander
Eddie George/983
23 Emmitt Smith 15.00 40.00
Marshall Faulk
LaDainian Tomlinson/820
24 Michael Vick 12.00 30.00
Chris Weinke
Drew Brees/246
25 Brett Favre 20.00 50.00
Peyton Manning
Kurt Warner/480
26 Ahman Green 8.00 20.00
Curtis Martin
Jerome Bettis/727
27 Drew Bledsoe 8.00 20.00
Tim Couch
Brian Griese/716
28 Aaron Brooks 8.00 20.00
Kordell Stewart
Steve McNair/1217
29 Randy Moss 15.00 40.00
Jerry Rice
Isaac Bruce/886
30 Marvin Harrison 8.00 20.00
Cris Carter
Terrell Owens/361
31 Jamal Anderson 6.00 15.00
Bob Christian
Reggie Kelly/650
32 Joey Galloway 6.00 15.00
Troy Hambrick
Darren Woodson/730
33 Matt Hasselbeck 8.00 20.00
Itula Mili
Mack Strong/606
34 Bryan Gilmore 5.00 12.00
Chris Greisen
Arnold Jackson/486
35 Todd Heap 6.00 15.00
Chris Redman
Brandon Stokley/606
36 Donald Hayes 6.00 15.00
Patrick Pass
Antowain Smith/892
37 Derrick Alexander 5.00 12.00
D'Wayne Bates
Chris Walsh/544
38 Emmitt Smith 15.00 40.00
Ahman Green
Ricky Williams/232
39 Brett Favre 20.00 50.00
Mark Brunell
Donovan McNabb/558
40 Drew Brees 12.00 30.00
Anthony Thomas
Chris Weinke/554

2010 Crown Royale

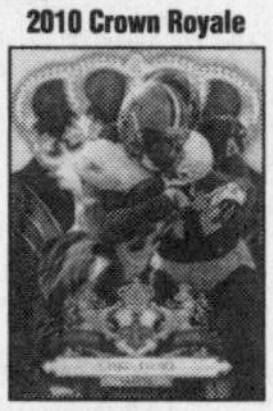

201-235 ROOKIE AU PRINT RUN 199-499
1 Chris Wells .50 1.25
2 Larry Fitzgerald .60 1.50
3 Steve Breaston .40 1.00
4 Matt Ryan .60 1.50
5 Michael Turner .40 1.00
6 Roddy White .50 1.25
7 Anquan Boldin .50 1.25
8 Joe Flacco .60 1.50
9 Ray Rice .50 1.25
10 Lee Evans .50 1.25
11 Marshawn Lynch .50 1.25
12 Ryan Fitzpatrick .60 1.50
13 DeAngelo Williams .50 1.25
14 Matt Moore .50 1.25
15 Steve Smith .50 1.25
16 Devin Hester .60 1.50
17 Jay Cutler .60 1.50
18 Matt Forte .50 1.25
19 Carson Palmer .50 1.25
20 Cedric Benson .50 1.25
21 Chad Ochocinco .50 1.25
22 Terrell Owens .60 1.50
23 Jake Delhomme .50 1.25
24 Josh Cribbs .60 1.50
25 Mohamed Massaquoi .50 1.25
26 Felix Jones .50 1.25
27 Jason Witten .60 1.50
28 Miles Austin .60 1.50
29 Tony Romo .75 2.00
30 Eddie Royal .40 1.00
31 Knowshon Moreno .50 1.25
32 Kyle Orton .50 1.25
33 Brandon Pettigrew .40 1.00
34 Calvin Johnson .60 1.50
35 Matthew Stafford .60 1.50
36 Aaron Rodgers 1.25 3.00
37 Greg Jennings .50 1.25
38 Ryan Grant .50 1.25
39 Andre Johnson .50 1.25
40 Matt Schaub .50 1.25
41 Steve Slaton .40 1.00
42 Dallas Clark .50 1.25
43 Peyton Manning 1.00 2.50
44 Reggie Wayne .50 1.25
45 David Garrard .50 1.25
46 Maurice Jones-Drew .50 1.25
47 Mike Sims-Walker .50 1.25
48 Dwayne Bowe .50 1.25
49 Jamaal Charles .50 1.25
50 Matt Cassel .50 1.25
51 Brandon Marshall .50 1.25
52 Chad Henne .50 1.25
53 Ronnie Brown .50 1.25
54 Adrian Peterson 1.00 2.50
55 Brett Favre 1.50 4.00
56 Percy Harvin .60 1.50
57 Sidney Rice .50 1.25
58 Randy Moss .60 1.50
59 Tom Brady 1.00 2.50
60 Wes Welker .60 1.50
61 Drew Brees .60 1.50
62 Marques Colston .50 1.25
63 Pierre Thomas .50 1.25
64 Brandon Jacobs .50 1.25
65 Eli Manning .60 1.50
66 Steve Smith USC .50 1.25
67 Braylon Edwards .50 1.25
68 LaDainian Tomlinson .60 1.50
69 Mark Sanchez .60 1.50
70 Shonn Greene .50 1.25
71 Darren McFadden .50 1.25
72 Jason Campbell .50 1.25
73 Louis Murphy .50 1.25
74 DeSean Jackson .50 1.25
75 Kevin Kolb .50 1.25
76 LeSean McCoy .50 1.25
77 Ben Roethlisberger .60 1.50
78 Rashard Mendenhall .50 1.25
79 Troy Polamalu .60 1.50
80 Antonio Gates .50 1.25
81 Darren Sproles .50 1.25
82 Philip Rivers .60 1.50
83 Frank Gore .50 1.25
84 Michael Crabtree .60 1.50
85 Vernon Davis .50 1.25
86 Julius Jones .40 1.00
87 Matt Hasselbeck .40 1.00
88 T.J. Houshmandzadeh .50 1.25
89 Donnie Avery .50 1.25
90 James Laurinaitis .50 1.25
91 Steven Jackson .50 1.25
92 Cadillac Williams .50 1.25
93 Josh Freeman .60 1.50
94 Kellen Winslow Jr. .50 1.25
95 Chris Johnson .60 1.50
96 Kenny Britt .50 1.25
97 Vince Young .40 1.00
98 Chris Cooley .50 1.25
99 Clinton Portis .50 1.25
100 Donovan McNabb .60 1.50
101 Aaron Hernandez RC 2.50 6.00
102 Amari Spievey RC 1.50 4.00
103 Andrew Quarless RC 1.50 4.00
104 Anthony Davis RC 1.25 3.00
105 Anthony Dixon RC 1.50 4.00
106 Anthony McCoy RC 1.25 3.00
107 Antonio Brown RC 2.50 6.00
108 Blair White RC 1.50 4.00
109 Stephen Williams RC 1.50 4.00
110 Brandon Graham RC 1.25 3.00
111 Brandon Spikes RC 1.50 4.00
112 Brian Price RC 1.50 4.00
113 Bryan Bulaga RC 1.50 4.00
114 Carlos Dunlap RC 1.50 4.00
115 Carlton Mitchell RC 1.25 3.00
116 Chad Jones RC 1.50 4.00
117 Keith Toston RC 1.50 4.00
118 Chris Cook RC 1.50 4.00
119 Victor Cruz RC 5.00 12.00
120 Corey Wootton RC 1.25 3.00
121 Dan LeFevour RC 1.50 4.00
122 Dan Williams RC 1.25 3.00
123 Daryl Washington RC 1.25 3.00
124 David Gettis RC 1.50 4.00
125 David Reed RC 1.25 3.00
126 Deji Karim RC 1.50 4.00
127 Dennis Pitta RC 1.50 4.00
128 Derrick Morgan RC 1.25 3.00
129 Devin McCourty RC 1.50 4.00
130 Dezmon Briscoe RC 1.25 3.00
131 Dominique Franks RC 1.00 2.50
132 Michael Hoomanawanui RC 1.50 4.00
133 Earl Thomas RC 1.50 4.00
134 Ed Dickson RC 1.50 4.00
135 Everson Griffen RC 1.50 4.00
136 Johnathan Haggerty RC 1.25 3.00
137 Garrett Graham RC 1.25 3.00
138 Jacoby Ford RC 1.50 4.00
139 James Starks RC 2.50 6.00
140 Jared Odrick RC 1.50 4.00
141 Jarrett Brown RC 1.50 4.00
142 Jason Pierre-Paul RC 2.50 6.00
143 Jason Worilds RC 1.50 4.00
144 Javier Arenas RC 1.50 4.00
145 Jeremy Williams RC 1.00 2.50
146 Jermaine Cunningham RC 1.50 4.00
147 Jerome Murphy RC 1.25 3.00
148 Jerry Hughes RC 1.50 4.00
149 Matt Willis RC 1.50 4.00
150 Jimmy Graham RC 3.00 8.00
151 Joe Haden RC 1.50 4.00
152 Joe Webb RC 1.50 4.00
153 John Conner RC 1.50 4.00
154 John Skelton RC 1.50 4.00
155 Joique Bell RC 1.25 3.00
156 Jonathan Crompton RC 1.25 3.00
157 Kareem Jackson RC 1.50 4.00
158 Kerry Meier RC 1.25 3.00
159 Koa Misi RC 1.50 4.00
160 Kyle Williams RC 1.50 4.00
161 Kyle Wilson RC 1.50 4.00
162 Lamarr Houston RC 1.50 4.00
163 LeGarrette Blount RC 2.50 6.00
164 Brody Eldridge RC 1.50 4.00
165 Linval Joseph RC 1.25 3.00
166 Lonyae Miller RC 1.25 3.00
167 Major Wright RC 1.50 4.00
168 Marc Mariani RC 1.50 4.00
169 Maurkice Pouncey RC 1.50 4.00
170 Mike Iupati RC 1.50 4.00
171 Mike Neal RC 1.50 4.00
172 Morgan Burnett RC 1.50 4.00
173 Myron Lewis RC 1.25 3.00
174 Nate Allen RC 1.50 4.00
175 NaVorro Bowman RC 1.50 4.00
176 Pat Angerer RC 1.50 4.00
177 Patrick Robinson RC 1.50 4.00
178 Perrish Cox RC 1.25 3.00
179 Ricky Sapp RC 1.25 3.00
180 Riley Cooper RC 1.50 4.00
181 Russell Okung RC 1.50 4.00
182 Rusty Smith RC 1.50 4.00
183 Sean Canfield RC 1.25 3.00
184 Sean Lee RC 1.50 4.00
185 Sean Weatherspoon RC 1.50 4.00
186 Sergio Kindle RC 1.50 4.00
187 Seyi Ajirotutu RC 1.50 4.00
188 Tervaris Johnson RC 1.25 3.00
189 T.J. Ward RC 1.50 4.00
190 Taylor Mays RC 1.50 4.00
191 Chris Ivory RC 2.00 5.00
192 Terrence Cody RC 1.25 3.00
193 Thaddeus Lewis RC 1.25 3.00
194 Tony Moeaki RC 1.50 4.00
195 Tony Pike RC 1.50 4.00
196 Torell Troup RC 1.25 3.00
197 Trent Williams RC 1.50 4.00
198 Max Hall RC 1.50 4.00
199 Tyson Alualu RC 1.25 3.00
200 Zac Robinson RC 1.25 3.00
201 Armanti Edwards AU/499 RC 5.00 12.00
202 C.J. Spiller AU/299 RC 10.00 25.00
203 Demaryius Thomas AU/399 RC 8.00 20.00
204 Emmanuel Sanders AU/499 RC 5.00 12.00
205 Gerald McCoy AU/199 RC 6.00 15.00
206 Jermaine Gresham AU/499 RC 6.00 15.00
207 Jonathan Dwyer AU/499 RC 5.00 12.00
208 Ryan Mathews AU/299 RC 20.00 50.00
209 Mardy Gilyard AU/499 RC 5.00 12.00
210 Mike Williams AU/499 RC 8.00 20.00
211 Tim Tebow AU/299 RC 75.00 150.00
212 Toby Gerhart AU/449 RC 5.00 12.00
213 Rolando McClain AU/499 RC 5.00 12.00
214 Montario Hardesty AU/499 RC 5.00 12.00
215 Ben Tate AU/499 RC 6.00 15.00
216 Damian Williams AU/449 RC 5.00 12.00
217 Eric Berry AU/499 RC 5.00 12.00
218 Marcus Easley AU/499 RC 4.00 10.00
219 Jahvid Best AU/299 RC 10.00 25.00
220 Joe McKnight AU/499 RC 5.00 12.00
221 Jordan Shipley AU/499 RC 5.00 12.00
222 Eric Decker AU/499 RC 8.00 20.00
223 Brandon LaFell AU/499 RC 5.00 12.00
224 Golden Tate AU/299 RC 6.00 15.00
225 Colt McCoy AU/299 RC 12.00 30.00
226 Sam Bradford AU/299 RC 50.00 100.00
227 Dez Bryant AU/299 RC 20.00 50.00
228 Jimmy Clausen AU/299 RC 6.00 15.00
229 Arrelious Benn AU/399 RC 5.00 12.00
230 Rob Gronkowski AU/499 RC 15.00 40.00
231 Mike Kafka AU/499 RC 5.00 12.00
232 Taylor Price AU/499 RC 5.00 12.00
233 Andre Roberts AU/499 RC 5.00 12.00
234 Ndamukong Suh AU/399 RC 20.00 40.00
235 Dexter McCluster AU/499 RC 5.00 12.00

2010 Crown Royale Blue

*VETS: 2X TO 5X BASIC CARDS
*ROOKIES: .8X TO 2X BASIC CARDS
BLUE PRINT RUN 100 SER.#'d SETS

2010 Crown Royale Gold

*VETS: 4X TO 10X BASIC CARDS
*ROOKIES: 1.5X TO 4X BASIC CARDS
GOLD PRINT RUN 25 SER.#'d SETS

2010 Crown Royale All Pros

1 Austin Collie 1.50 4.00
2 Chris Wells 1.50 4.00
3 Brent Celek 1.50 4.00
4 Chris Cooley 1.50 4.00
5 DeSean Jackson 1.50 4.00
6 Donald Driver 1.50 4.00
7 Heath Miller 1.50 4.00
8 Jeremy Maclin 1.50 4.00
9 Joe Flacco 2.00 5.00
10 Jonathan Stewart 1.50 4.00
11 Knowshon Moreno 1.50 4.00
12 LeSean McCoy 1.50 4.00
13 Marques Colston 1.50 4.00
14 Miles Austin 2.00 5.00
15 Percy Harvin 2.00 5.00
16 Rashard Mendenhall 1.50 4.00
17 Santana Moss 1.50 4.00
18 Vince Young 1.25 3.00
19 Vincent Jackson 1.25 3.00
20 Ed Reed 1.50 4.00
21 Greg Olsen 1.25 3.00
22 Joseph Addai 1.50 4.00
23 Ronnie Brown 1.50 4.00
24 Jamaal Charles 1.50 4.00
25 Derrick Mason 1.50 4.00

2010 Crown Royale All Pros Materials

STATED PRINT RUN 80-299
*PRIME/50: .6X TO 1.5X BASIC JSY/160-299
*PRIME/15-25: .8X TO 2X BASIC JSY/160-299
*PRIME/50: .5X TO 1.2X BASIC JSY/80
PRIME STATED PRINT RUN 5-50
2 Chris Wells/250 3.00 8.00
3 Brent Celek/299 3.00 8.00
4 Chris Cooley/250 4.00 10.00
6 Donald Driver/80 4.00 10.00
7 Heath Miller/299 3.00 8.00
8 Jeremy Maclin/299 3.00 8.00
9 Joe Flacco/299 4.00 10.00
10 Jonathan Stewart/299 3.00 8.00
11 Knowshon Moreno/220 3.00 8.00
12 LeSean McCoy/299 3.00 8.00
13 Marques Colston/299 3.00 8.00
15 Percy Harvin/299 4.00 10.00
16 Rashard Mendenhall/299 4.00 10.00
17 Santana Moss/299 3.00 8.00
18 Vince Young/299 2.50 6.00
19 Vincent Jackson/299 2.50 6.00
20 Ed Reed/299 4.00 10.00
21 Greg Olsen/299 2.50 6.00
22 Joseph Addai/299 3.00 8.00
23 Ronnie Brown/160 3.00 8.00
24 Jamaal Charles/299 3.00 8.00
25 Derrick Mason/299 3.00 8.00

2010 Crown Royale Autographs Blue

101-200 STATED PRINT RUN 50
201-235 STATED PRINT RUN 25-50
*101-200 BSE AU/199-249: .3X TO .8X BLU/50
*101-200 BASE AU/99: .4X TO 1X BLU AU/50
EXCH EXPIRATION: 4/27/2012
101 Aaron Hernandez 12.00 30.00
105 Anthony Dixon 8.00 20.00
106 Anthony McCoy 6.00 15.00
107 Antonio Brown 20.00 40.00
108 Blair White 8.00 20.00
110 Brandon Graham 6.00 15.00
111 Brandon Spikes 8.00 20.00
113 Bryan Bulaga 8.00 20.00
114 Carlos Dunlap 8.00 20.00
115 Carlton Mitchell 6.00 15.00
116 Chad Jones 8.00 20.00
118 Chris Cook 8.00 20.00
120 Corey Wootton 6.00 15.00
121 Dan LeFevour 8.00 20.00
123 Daryl Washington EXCH 6.00 15.00
124 David Gettis 8.00 20.00
128 Derrick Morgan 6.00 15.00
129 Devin McCourty 8.00 20.00
130 Dezmon Briscoe 6.00 15.00
131 Dominique Franks 5.00 12.00
133 Earl Thomas 8.00 20.00
134 Ed Dickson 8.00 20.00
135 Everson Griffen 8.00 20.00
137 Garrett Graham 6.00 15.00
138 Jacoby Ford 15.00 30.00
139 James Starks 15.00 40.00
141 Jarrett Brown 8.00 20.00
142 Jason Pierre-Paul 20.00 40.00
143 Jason Worilds 8.00 20.00
145 Jeremy Williams 5.00 12.00
148 Jerry Hughes 8.00 20.00
150 Jimmy Graham 20.00 40.00
151 Joe Haden 8.00 20.00
154 John Skelton 8.00 20.00
155 Joique Bell 6.00 15.00

156 Jonathan Crompton 6.00 15.00
157 Kareem Jackson 8.00 20.00
161 Kyle Wilson 10.00 25.00
163 LeGarrette Blount 12.00 30.00
166 Lonyae Miller 6.00 15.00
172 Morgan Burnett 8.00 20.00
174 Nate Allen 8.00 20.00
175 NaVorro Bowman 8.00 20.00
177 Patrick Robinson 8.00 20.00
178 Perrish Cox 6.00 15.00
179 Ricky Sapp 6.00 15.00
180 Riley Cooper 8.00 20.00
181 Russell Okung 8.00 20.00
183 Sean Canfield 6.00 15.00
184 Sean Lee 8.00 20.00
185 Sean Weatherspoon 8.00 20.00
186 Sergio Kindle 8.00 20.00
187 Seyi Ajirotutu 8.00 20.00
190 Taylor Mays 8.00 20.00
195 Tony Pike 8.00 20.00
197 Trent Williams EXCH 8.00 20.00
200 Zac Robinson 6.00 15.00
201 Armanti Edwards/50 8.00 20.00
202 C.J. Spiller/25 30.00 80.00
203 Demaryius Thomas/50 10.00 25.00
204 Emmanuel Sanders/50 8.00 20.00
205 Gerald McCoy/50 8.00 20.00
206 Jermaine Gresham/50 10.00 25.00
207 Jonathan Dwyer/50 8.00 20.00
208 Ryan Mathews/25 30.00 80.00
209 Mardy Gilyard/50 8.00 20.00
210 Mike Williams/50 15.00 40.00
211 Tim Tebow/25 125.00 200.00
212 Toby Gerhart/50 12.00 30.00
213 Rolando McClain/50 8.00 20.00
214 Montario Hardesty/50 8.00 20.00
215 Ben Tate/50 10.00 25.00
216 Damian Williams/50 8.00 20.00
217 Eric Berry/50 20.00 50.00
218 Marcus Easley/50 6.00 15.00
219 Jahvid Best/25 40.00 80.00
220 Joe McKnight/50 8.00 20.00
221 Jordan Shipley/50 8.00 20.00
222 Eric Decker/50 10.00 25.00
223 Brandon LaFell/50 8.00 20.00
224 Golden Tate/50 8.00 20.00
225 Colt McCoy/25 50.00 100.00
226 Sam Bradford/25 75.00 150.00
227 Dez Bryant/25 75.00 150.00
228 Jimmy Clausen/25 20.00 50.00
229 Arrelious Benn/50 8.00 20.00
230 Rob Gronkowski/50 30.00 60.00
231 Mike Kafka/50 8.00 20.00
232 Taylor Price/50 8.00 20.00
233 Andre Roberts/50 8.00 20.00
234 Ndamukong Suh/50 30.00 60.00
235 Dexter McCluster/50 8.00 20.00

2010 Crown Royale Autographs Gold

1-100 VETERAN PRINT RUN 1-25
*GOLD ROOKIE/25: .5X TO 1.2X BLUE AU/50
101-235 ROOKIE PRINT RUN 10-25
EXCH EXPIRATION: 4/27/2012
8 Joe Flacco/15
9 Ray Rice/25 12.00 30.00
17 Jay Cutler/15 15.00 40.00
20 Cedric Benson/25 12.00 30.00
24 Josh Cribbs/15
26 Felix Jones/15 12.00 30.00
32 Kyle Orton/15 12.00 30.00
35 Matthew Stafford/15 30.00 60.00
38 Ryan Grant/25 15.00 40.00
43 Peyton Manning/25 100.00 175.00
48 Dwayne Bowe/20 12.00 30.00
49 Jamaal Charles/15 12.00 30.00
53 Ronnie Brown/25 15.00 40.00
56 Percy Harvin/25
65 Eli Manning/15 40.00 80.00
67 Braylon Edwards/15 12.00 30.00
69 Mark Sanchez/25 30.00 60.00
70 Shonn Greene/25 12.00 30.00
73 Louis Murphy/25 12.00 30.00
74 DeSean Jackson/20 15.00 40.00
75 Kevin Kolb/25 12.00 30.00
76 LeSean McCoy/15 12.00 30.00
78 Rashard Mendenhall/25 12.00 30.00
81 Darren Sproles/20 12.00 30.00
84 Michael Crabtree/25 15.00 40.00
96 Kenny Britt/20 12.00 30.00
98 Chris Cooley/20 30.00 60.00
100 Donovan McNabb/15

2010 Crown Royale Kings of the NFL

1 Peyton Manning 3.00 8.00
2 Adrian Peterson 3.00 8.00
3 Aaron Rodgers 4.00 10.00
4 Ben Roethlisberger 2.00 5.00
5 Calvin Johnson 2.00 5.00
6 Cadillac Williams 1.50 4.00
7 Chris Johnson 2.00 5.00
8 Frank Gore 1.50 4.00
9 Matt Ryan 2.00 5.00
10 Wes Welker 2.00 5.00
11 Ryan Grant 1.50 4.00
12 Matt Schaub 1.50 4.00
13 Vernon Davis 1.50 4.00
14 Greg Jennings 1.50 4.00
15 Lee Evans 1.50 4.00
16 Devery Henderson 1.25 3.00
17 Brandon Jacobs 1.50 4.00
18 Dallas Clark 1.50 4.00
19 Josh Cribbs 2.00 5.00
20 Matt Forte 1.50 4.00
21 Mark Sanchez 2.00 5.00
22 Roddy White 1.50 4.00
23 Pierre Thomas 1.50 4.00
24 Ray Rice 1.50 4.00
25 Sidney Rice 1.50 4.00

2010 Crown Royale Kings of the NFL Materials

STATED PRINT RUN 10-299
1 Peyton Manning/299 6.00 15.00
2 Adrian Peterson/299 6.00 15.00
4 Ben Roethlisberger/299 4.00 10.00
5 Calvin Johnson/299 4.00 10.00
6 Cadillac Williams/200 3.00 8.00
7 Chris Johnson/299 4.00 10.00
8 Frank Gore/299 3.00 8.00
9 Matt Ryan/299 4.00 10.00
10 Wes Welker/299 4.00 10.00
13 Vernon Davis/299 3.00 8.00
14 Greg Jennings/175 3.00 8.00
15 Lee Evans/299 3.00 8.00
16 Devery Henderson/299 2.50 6.00
18 Dallas Clark/299 3.00 8.00
19 Josh Cribbs/10
20 Matt Forte/299 3.00 8.00
21 Mark Sanchez/299 4.00 10.00
22 Roddy White/245 3.00 8.00
24 Ray Rice/299 3.00 8.00
25 Sidney Rice/299 3.00 8.00

2010 Crown Royale Kings of the NFL Materials Prime

*PRIME/50: .6X TO 1.5X BASIC JSY/175-299
*PRIME/15: .8X TO 2X BASIC JSY/175
PRIME PRINT RUN 15-50
17 Brandon Jacobs/50 5.00 12.00

2010 Crown Royale Kings of the NFL Materials Autographs

STATED PRINT RUN 15-25
1 Peyton Manning/20 60.00 120.00
2 Adrian Peterson/25 75.00 150.00
4 Ben Roethlisberger/20 60.00 120.00
5 Calvin Johnson/25 20.00 50.00
6 Cadillac Williams/25
8 Frank Gore/25 15.00 40.00
9 Matt Ryan/25 30.00 60.00
13 Vernon Davis/25 15.00 40.00
15 Lee Evans/20 15.00 40.00
16 Devery Henderson/15
18 Dallas Clark/25 20.00 50.00
19 Josh Cribbs/25
20 Matt Forte/25
21 Mark Sanchez/25 40.00 80.00
22 Roddy White/25 15.00 40.00
24 Ray Rice/25 15.00 40.00
25 Sidney Rice/25 15.00 40.00

2010 Crown Royale Living Legends

1 Barry Sanders 4.00 10.00
2 Bruce Smith 2.00 5.00
3 Charley Taylor 1.50 4.00
4 Charlie Joiner 1.50 4.00
5 Chuck Bednarik 2.00 5.00
6 Daryle Lamonica 1.50 4.00
7 Deacon Jones 2.00 5.00
8 Del Shofner 1.50 4.00
9 Joe Namath 3.00 8.00
10 Floyd Little 1.50 4.00
11 Frank Gifford 2.00 5.00
12 Henry Ellard 1.50 4.00
13 Jim Brown 3.00 8.00
14 Jim Otto 1.50 4.00
15 Jimmy Orr 1.50 4.00
16 Joe Greene 2.50 6.00
17 Joe Montana 5.00 12.00
18 John Elway 4.00 10.00
19 John Randle 1.50 4.00
20 Ozzie Newsome 2.00 5.00
21 Paul Warfield 2.00 5.00
22 Pete Retzlaff 1.50 4.00
23 Rickey Jackson 1.50 4.00
24 Sonny Jurgensen 2.00 5.00
25 Willie Lanier 1.50 4.00

2010 Crown Royale Living Legends Materials

STATED PRINT RUN 49-299
*PRIME/50: .6X TO 1.5X BASIC JSY/190-299
*PRIME/25: .8X TO 2X BASIC JSY/190-299
1 Barry Sanders/190 10.00 25.00
2 Bruce Smith/299 5.00 12.00
3 Charley Taylor/299 4.00 10.00
4 Charlie Joiner/299 4.00 10.00
5 Chuck Bednarik/230 5.00 12.00
6 Daryle Lamonica/299 4.00 10.00
7 Deacon Jones/299 5.00 12.00
9 Joe Namath/299 8.00 20.00
11 Frank Gifford/219 5.00 12.00
12 Henry Ellard/299 4.00 10.00
13 Jim Brown/49 10.00 25.00
14 Jim Otto/299 4.00 10.00
16 Joe Greene/299 6.00 15.00
17 Joe Montana/299 12.00 30.00
18 John Elway/299 10.00 25.00
19 John Randle/299 4.00 10.00
20 Ozzie Newsome/266 5.00 12.00
21 Paul Warfield/299 5.00 12.00
23 Rickey Jackson/299 4.00 10.00
24 Sonny Jurgensen/299 5.00 12.00
25 Willie Lanier/299 4.00 10.00

2010 Crown Royale Majestic

1 Alan Page 2.00 5.00
2 Alex Karras 2.00 5.00
3 Andre Reed 2.00 5.00
4 Archie Manning 2.50 6.00
5 Billy Howton 1.50 4.00
6 Boyd Dowler 1.50 4.00
7 Charley Trippi 1.50 4.00
8 Dante Lavelli 1.50 4.00
9 Dave Casper 1.50 4.00
10 Forrest Gregg 1.50 4.00
11 Fred Williamson 1.50 4.00
12 Harlon Hill 1.50 4.00
13 Howie Long 2.50 6.00
14 Jan Stenerud 1.50 4.00
15 Joe Klecko 1.50 4.00
16 Johnny Morris 1.50 4.00
17 Kellen Winslow 2.00 5.00
18 Larry Little 1.50 4.00
19 Lee Roy Selmon 1.50 4.00
20 Lem Barney 1.50 4.00
21 Len Dawson 2.50 6.00
22 Lenny Moore 2.00 5.00
23 Leroy Kelly 2.00 5.00
24 Lydell Mitchell 1.50 4.00
25 Mike Alstott 1.50 4.00
26 Mike Curtis 1.50 4.00
27 Paul Krause 1.50 4.00
28 Phil Simms 2.00 5.00
29 Raymond Berry 2.00 5.00
30 Rick Casares 1.50 4.00
31 Ron Mix 1.50 4.00
32 Sammy Baugh 2.50 6.00
33 Tiki Barber 2.00 5.00
34 Tom Rathman 1.50 4.00
35 Walter Payton 5.00 12.00
36 Wayne Chrebet 1.50 4.00
37 Willie Brown 1.50 4.00
38 Willie Davis 1.50 4.00
39 Willie Wood 1.50 4.00
40 Y.A. Tittle 2.50 6.00

2010 Crown Royale Majestic Materials

STATED PRINT RUN 25-299
1 Alan Page/299 5.00 12.00
2 Alex Karras/299 5.00 12.00
3 Andre Reed/40 6.00 15.00
4 Archie Manning/135 8.00 20.00
9 Dave Casper/165 4.00 10.00
10 Forrest Gregg/299 4.00 10.00
13 Howie Long/201 6.00 15.00
14 Jan Stenerud/43 5.00 12.00
15 Joe Klecko/299 4.00 10.00
18 Larry Little/299 4.00 10.00
19 Lee Roy Selmon/299 4.00 10.00
20 Lem Barney/200 4.00 10.00
21 Len Dawson/299 6.00 15.00
22 Lenny Moore/299 5.00 12.00
23 Leroy Kelly/25 8.00 20.00
28 Phil Simms/299 5.00 12.00
29 Raymond Berry/299 5.00 12.00
31 Ron Mix/95 5.00 12.00
32 Sammy Baugh/299 10.00 25.00
33 Tiki Barber/299 5.00 12.00
34 Tom Rathman/299 5.00 12.00
35 Walter Payton/299 12.00 30.00
36 Wayne Chrebet/115 5.00 12.00
37 Willie Brown/299 4.00 10.00
40 Y.A. Tittle/299 6.00 15.00

2010 Crown Royale Majestic Materials Prime

PRIME PRINT RUN 1-50
3 Andre Reed/25 6.00 15.00
13 Howie Long/25 8.00 20.00
18 Larry Little/25 5.00 12.00
19 Lee Roy Selmon/25 5.00 12.00
21 Len Dawson/25 8.00 20.00
25 Mike Alstott/30 4.00 10.00
29 Raymond Berry/25 6.00 15.00
31 Ron Mix/25 5.00 12.00
33 Tiki Barber/50 5.00 12.00
34 Tom Rathman/25 6.00 15.00
35 Walter Payton/25 15.00 40.00
36 Wayne Chrebet/50 4.00 10.00
40 Y.A. Tittle/25 8.00 20.00

2010 Crown Royale Rookie Die Cut Material Autographs

STATED PRINT RUN 50 SER.#'d SETS
EXCH EXPIRATION: 4/27/2012
1 Andre Roberts 10.00 25.00
2 Armanti Edwards 10.00 25.00
3 Arrelious Benn 10.00 25.00
4 Ben Tate 12.00 30.00
5 Brandon LaFell 10.00 25.00
6 C.J. Spiller 15.00 40.00
7 Colt McCoy 20.00 50.00
8 Damian Williams 10.00 25.00
9 Demaryius Thomas 12.00 30.00
10 Dexter McCluster 10.00 25.00
11 Dez Bryant 40.00 100.00
12 Emmanuel Sanders 10.00 25.00
13 Eric Berry 10.00 25.00
14 Eric Decker 12.00 30.00
15 Gerald McCoy 10.00 25.00
16 Golden Tate 10.00 25.00
17 Jahvid Best 15.00 40.00
18 Jermaine Gresham 12.00 30.00
19 Jimmy Clausen 10.00 25.00
20 Joe McKnight 10.00 25.00
21 Jonathan Dwyer 10.00 25.00
22 Jordan Shipley 10.00 25.00
23 Marcus Easley 8.00 20.00
24 Mardy Gilyard 10.00 25.00
25 Mike Kafka 10.00 25.00
26 Mike Williams 30.00 50.00
27 Montario Hardesty 10.00 25.00
28 Ndamukong Suh 30.00 60.00
29 Rob Gronkowski 30.00 60.00
30 Rolando McClain 10.00 25.00
31 Ryan Mathews 20.00 50.00
32 Sam Bradford 75.00 150.00
33 Taylor Price 10.00 25.00
34 Tim Tebow 100.00 175.00
35 Toby Gerhart 10.00 25.00

2010 Crown Royale Rookie Royalty

1 Armanti Edwards 1.50 4.00
2 Brandon LaFell 1.50 4.00
3 Toby Gerhart 1.50 4.00
4 Andre Roberts 1.50 4.00
5 Golden Tate 1.50 4.00
6 Emmanuel Sanders 1.50 4.00
7 Jimmy Clausen 1.50 4.00
8 Mardy Gilyard 1.50 4.00
9 Joe McKnight 1.50 4.00
10 Mike Kafka 1.50 4.00
11 Tim Tebow 6.00 15.00
12 Taylor Price 1.50 4.00
13 Rob Gronkowski 4.00 10.00
14 Mike Williams 2.50 6.00
15 Colt McCoy 3.00 8.00
16 Arrelious Benn 1.50 4.00
17 Damian Williams 1.50 4.00
18 Jermaine Gresham 2.00 5.00
19 Jahvid Best 2.50 6.00
20 Sam Bradford 6.00 15.00
21 Ndamukong Suh 3.00 8.00
22 C.J. Spiller 2.50 6.00
23 Demaryius Thomas 2.00 5.00
24 Dez Bryant 5.00 12.00
25 Jonathan Dwyer 1.50 4.00
26 Montario Hardesty 1.50 4.00
27 Ryan Mathews 3.00 8.00
28 Marcus Easley 1.25 3.00
29 Ben Tate 2.00 5.00
30 Jordan Shipley 1.50 4.00
31 Dexter McCluster 1.50 4.00
32 Eric Berry 1.50 4.00
33 Eric Decker 2.00 5.00
34 Rolando McClain 1.50 4.00
35 Gerald McCoy 1.50 4.00

2010 Crown Royale Rookie Royalty Autographs

STATED PRINT RUN 10-25
EXCH EXPIRATION: 4/27/2012
1 Armanti Edwards/25 8.00 20.00
2 Brandon LaFell/25 8.00 20.00
3 Toby Gerhart/25 8.00 20.00
4 Andre Roberts/25 8.00 20.00
5 Golden Tate/10
6 Emmanuel Sanders/25 8.00 20.00
7 Jimmy Clausen/10
8 Mardy Gilyard/25 8.00 20.00
9 Joe McKnight/25 8.00 20.00
10 Mike Kafka/25 8.00 20.00
11 Tim Tebow/10
12 Taylor Price/25 8.00 20.00
13 Rob Gronkowski/25 30.00 60.00
14 Mike Williams/25 12.00 30.00
15 Colt McCoy/10
16 Arrelious Benn/25 8.00 20.00
17 Damian Williams/25 8.00 20.00
18 Jermaine Gresham/25 10.00 25.00
19 Jahvid Best/10
20 Sam Bradford/10
21 Ndamukong Suh/25 25.00 50.00
22 C.J. Spiller/10
23 Demaryius Thomas/25 10.00 25.00
24 Dez Bryant/10
25 Jonathan Dwyer/25 8.00 20.00
26 Montario Hardesty/25 8.00 20.00
27 Ryan Mathews/10
28 Marcus Easley/25 6.00 15.00
29 Ben Tate/25 10.00 25.00
30 Jordan Shipley/25 8.00 20.00
31 Dexter McCluster/25 8.00 20.00
32 Eric Berry/25 8.00 20.00
33 Eric Decker/25 10.00 25.00
34 Rolando McClain/25 8.00 20.00
35 Gerald McCoy/25 8.00 20.00

2010 Crown Royale Rookie Royalty Materials

STATED PRINT RUN 299 SER.#'d SETS
*PRIME/50: .8X TO 2X BASIC JSY/299
1 Armanti Edwards 2.50 6.00
2 Brandon LaFell 2.50 6.00
3 Toby Gerhart 2.50 6.00
4 Andre Roberts 2.50 6.00
5 Golden Tate 2.50 6.00
6 Emmanuel Sanders 2.50 6.00
7 Jimmy Clausen 2.50 6.00
8 Mardy Gilyard 2.50 6.00
9 Joe McKnight 2.50 6.00
10 Mike Kafka 2.50 6.00
11 Tim Tebow 10.00 25.00
12 Taylor Price 2.50 6.00
13 Rob Gronkowski 6.00 15.00
14 Mike Williams 4.00 10.00
15 Colt McCoy 5.00 12.00
16 Arrelious Benn 2.50 6.00
17 Damian Williams 2.50 6.00
18 Jermaine Gresham 3.00 8.00
19 Jahvid Best 4.00 10.00
20 Sam Bradford 10.00 25.00
21 Ndamukong Suh 5.00 12.00
22 C.J. Spiller 4.00 10.00
23 Demaryius Thomas 3.00 8.00
24 Dez Bryant 8.00 20.00
25 Jonathan Dwyer 2.50 6.00
26 Montario Hardesty 2.50 6.00
27 Ryan Mathews 5.00 12.00
28 Marcus Easley 2.00 5.00
29 Ben Tate 3.00 8.00
30 Jordan Shipley 2.50 6.00
31 Dexter McCluster 2.50 6.00
32 Eric Berry 2.50 6.00
33 Eric Decker 3.00 8.00
34 Rolando McClain 2.50 6.00
35 Gerald McCoy 2.50 6.00

2010 Crown Royale Rookie Royalty Materials Autographs

STATED PRINT RUN 25-50
*PRIME/25: .5X TO 1.2X BASIC JSY AU/50
EXCH EXPIRATION: 4/27/2012
1 Armanti Edwards/50 8.00 20.00
2 Brandon LaFell/50 8.00 20.00
3 Toby Gerhart/50 8.00 20.00
4 Andre Roberts/50 8.00 20.00
5 Golden Tate/50 8.00 20.00
6 Emmanuel Sanders/50 8.00 20.00
7 Jimmy Clausen/25 10.00 25.00
8 Mardy Gilyard/50 8.00 20.00
9 Joe McKnight/50 8.00 20.00
10 Mike Kafka/50 8.00 20.00
11 Tim Tebow/25 60.00 120.00
12 Taylor Price/50 8.00 20.00
13 Rob Gronkowski/50 30.00 60.00
14 Mike Williams/50 12.00 30.00
15 Colt McCoy/25 20.00 50.00
16 Arrelious Benn/50 8.00 20.00
17 Damian Williams/50 8.00 20.00
18 Jermaine Gresham/50 10.00 25.00
19 Jahvid Best/50 12.00 30.00
20 Sam Bradford/25 50.00 120.00
21 Ndamukong Suh/50 30.00 60.00
22 C.J. Spiller/25 15.00 40.00
23 Demaryius Thomas/50 10.00 25.00
24 Dez Bryant/50 40.00 100.00
25 Jonathan Dwyer/50 8.00 20.00
26 Montario Hardesty/50 8.00 20.00
27 Ryan Mathews/50 25.00 60.00
28 Marcus Easley/50 6.00 15.00
29 Ben Tate/50 10.00 25.00
30 Jordan Shipley/50 8.00 20.00
31 Dexter McCluster/50 8.00 20.00
32 Eric Berry/50 8.00 20.00
33 Eric Decker/50 10.00 25.00
34 Rolando McClain/50 8.00 20.00
35 Gerald McCoy/50 8.00 20.00

2010 Crown Royale Royalty

1 Brett Favre 5.00 12.00
2 Tom Brady 3.00 8.00
3 Larry Fitzgerald 2.00 5.00
4 Randy Moss 2.00 5.00
5 Reggie Wayne 1.50 4.00
6 Tony Romo 2.50 6.00
7 DeAngelo Williams 1.50 4.00
8 Drew Brees 2.00 5.00
9 Antonio Gates 1.50 4.00
10 Maurice Jones-Drew 1.50 4.00
11 Steve Smith 1.50 4.00
12 Tony Gonzalez 1.50 4.00
13 Ray Lewis 2.00 5.00
14 Troy Polamalu 2.00 5.00
15 Brian Urlacher 2.00 5.00
16 Steven Jackson 1.50 4.00
17 Jason Witten 2.00 5.00
18 Hines Ward 1.50 4.00
19 Eli Manning 2.00 5.00
20 Michael Turner 1.25 3.00
21 Chad Ochocinco 1.50 4.00
22 Andre Johnson 1.50 4.00
23 Carson Palmer 1.50 4.00
24 Darrelle Revis 1.50 4.00
25 Philip Rivers 2.00 5.00

2010 Crown Royale Royalty Materials

STATED PRINT RUN 245-299
1 Brett Favre/299 10.00 25.00
2 Tom Brady/299 6.00 15.00
3 Larry Fitzgerald/299 4.00 10.00
4 Randy Moss/299 4.00 10.00
5 Reggie Wayne/299 3.00 8.00
6 Tony Romo/299 5.00 12.00
7 DeAngelo Williams/290 3.00 8.00
9 Antonio Gates/299 3.00 8.00
10 Maurice Jones-Drew/299 3.00 8.00
12 Tony Gonzalez/270 3.00 8.00
13 Ray Lewis/299 4.00 10.00
14 Troy Polamalu/299 8.00 20.00
15 Brian Urlacher/299 4.00 10.00
16 Steven Jackson/290 3.00 8.00
17 Jason Witten/299 4.00 10.00
18 Hines Ward/299 3.00 8.00
19 Eli Manning/299 4.00 10.00
21 Chad Ochocinco/299 3.00 8.00
22 Andre Johnson/245 3.00 8.00
23 Carson Palmer/299 3.00 8.00
24 Darrelle Revis/290 3.00 8.00
25 Philip Rivers/299 4.00 10.00

2010 Crown Royale Royalty Materials Prime

*PRIME/40-50: .6X TO 1.5X BASIC JSY
*PRIME/15: .8X TO 2X BASIC JSY
PRIME STATED PRINT RUN 15-50
11 Steve Smith/50 5.00 12.00

2010 Crown Royale Royalty Materials Autographs

STATED PRINT RUN 5-25
EXCH EXPIRATION: 4/27/2012
1 Brett Favre/20 125.00 250.00
2 Tom Brady/20 125.00 250.00
5 Reggie Wayne/25 15.00 40.00
6 Tony Romo/25 40.00 80.00
7 DeAngelo Williams/25 15.00 40.00
9 Antonio Gates/20 15.00 40.00
10 Maurice Jones-Drew/25 15.00 40.00
11 Steve Smith/5
12 Tony Gonzalez/25 15.00 40.00
14 Troy Polamalu/25 100.00 175.00
17 Jason Witten/25 20.00 50.00
19 Eli Manning/25 40.00 80.00
21 Chad Ochocinco/20 15.00 40.00
22 Andre Johnson/25 EXCH 15.00 40.00
23 Carson Palmer/20 15.00 40.00
25 Philip Rivers/25

2010 Crown Royale The Zone

RAMDON INSERTS IN PACKS
1 Bernard Berrian 1.25 3.00
2 Braylon Edwards 1.50 4.00
3 Darren Sproles 1.50 4.00
4 Darren McFadden 1.50 4.00
5 Clinton Portis 1.50 4.00
6 Devin Hester 2.00 5.00
7 Dustin Keller 1.50 4.00
8 Johnny Knox 1.50 4.00
9 Jerricho Cotchery 1.50 4.00
10 Ladell Betts 1.25 3.00
11 Laurence Maroney 1.50 4.00
12 Marion Barber 1.50 4.00
13 Matthew Stafford 2.00 5.00
14 Michael Crabtree 2.00 5.00
15 Reggie Bush 2.00 5.00
16 Robert Meachem 1.50 4.00
17 Shonn Greene 1.50 4.00
18 T.J. Houshmandzadeh 1.50 4.00
19 Visanthe Shiancoe 1.50 4.00
20 Felix Jones 1.50 4.00
21 Matt Hasselbeck 1.25 3.00
22 Owen Daniels 1.25 3.00
23 Steve Smith USC 1.50 4.00
24 Todd Heap 1.25 3.00
25 Pierre Garcon 1.50 4.00

2010 Crown Royale The Zone Materials Prime

STATED PRINT RUN 15-50
1 Bernard Berrian/50 4.00 10.00
2 Braylon Edwards/50 5.00 12.00
3 Darren Sproles/50 5.00 12.00
4 Darren McFadden/50 5.00 12.00
5 Clinton Portis/50 5.00 12.00
6 Devin Hester/50 6.00 15.00
7 Dustin Keller/50 5.00 12.00
8 Johnny Knox/50 5.00 12.00
9 Jerricho Cotchery/50 5.00 12.00
10 Ladell Betts/50 4.00 10.00
11 Laurence Maroney/50 5.00 12.00
12 Marion Barber/50 5.00 12.00
13 Matthew Stafford/50 6.00 15.00
15 Reggie Bush/50 6.00 15.00
16 Robert Meachem/50 5.00 12.00
19 Visanthe Shiancoe/50 5.00 12.00
20 Felix Jones/50 5.00 12.00
21 Matt Hasselbeck/40 4.00 10.00
22 Owen Daniels/50 4.00 10.00
23 Steve Smith USC/20 6.00 15.00
24 Todd Heap/15 5.00 12.00

2011 Crown Royale

101-200 ROOKIES ONE PER HOBBY PACK
201-236 JSY AU RC PRINT RUN 199-299
EXCH EXPIRATION: 4/26/2013
1 Aaron Rodgers 1.25 3.00
2 Adrian Peterson 1.00 2.50
3 Ahmad Bradshaw .60 1.50
4 Andre Johnson .60 1.50
5 Anquan Boldin .60 1.50
6 Antonio Gates .60 1.50
7 Arian Foster .60 1.50
8 Beanie Wells .60 1.50
9 Ben Roethlisberger .75 2.00
10 Brandon Lloyd .60 1.50
11 Braylon Edwards .60 1.50
12 Calvin Johnson .75 2.00
13 Carson Palmer .60 1.50
14 Cedric Benson .60 1.50
15 Chad Henne .60 1.50
16 Chad Ochocinco .60 1.50
17 Chris Cooley .60 1.50
18 Chris Johnson .60 1.50
19 Colt McCoy .60 1.50
20 Danny Amendola .60 1.50
21 Danny Woodhead .75 2.00
22 Darren McFadden .60 1.50
23 David Garrard .60 1.50
24 Davone Bess .50 1.25
25 DeSean Jackson .60 1.50
26 Devin Hester .75 2.00
27 Donald Driver .60 1.50
28 Donovan McNabb .75 2.00
29 Drew Brees .75 2.00
30 Dwayne Bowe .60 1.50
31 Eli Manning .75 2.00
32 Felix Jones .60 1.50
33 Frank Gore .60 1.50
34 Greg Jennings .60 1.50
35 Hakeem Nicks .60 1.50
36 Jahvid Best .60 1.50
37 Jamaal Charles .60 1.50
38 Jason Witten .75 2.00
39 Jay Cutler .60 1.50
40 Joromy Maclin .60 1.60
41 Joe Flacco .75 2.00
42 John Carlson .50 1.25
43 Johnny Knox .60 1.50
44 Jonathan Stewart .60 1.50
45 Josh Cribbs .60 1.50
46 Josh Freeman .75 2.00
47 Justin Forsett .60 1.50
48 Bo Scaife .50 1.25
49 Knowshon Moreno .60 1.50
50 LaDainian Tomlinson .75 2.00
51 Larry Fitzgerald .60 1.50
52 Lee Evans .60 1.50
53 LeGarrette Blount .60 1.50
54 LeSean McCoy .60 1.50
55 Marcedes Lewis .50 1.25
56 Mario Manningham .60 1.50
57 Mark Sanchez .75 2.00
58 Marques Colston .60 1.50
59 Matt Cassel .60 1.50
60 Matt Forte .60 1.50
61 Matt Ryan .75 2.00
62 Matt Schaub .60 1.50
63 Matthew Stafford .75 2.00
64 Maurice Jones-Drew .60 1.50
65 Michael Crabtree .60 1.50
66 Michael Turner .60 1.50
67 Michael Vick .75 2.00
68 Mike Goodson .50 1.25
69 Mike Tolbert .60 1.50
70 Mike Wallace .75 2.00
71 Mike Williams USC .60 1.50
72 Mike Williams .60 1.50
73 Miles Austin .60 1.50
74 Nate Washington .50 1.25
75 Nnamdi Asomugha .60 1.50
76 Percy Harvin .60 1.50
77 Peyton Hillis .60 1.50
78 Peyton Manning 1.25 3.00
79 Philip Rivers .75 2.00
80 Pierre Garcon .60 1.50
81 Rashard Mendenhall .60 1.50
82 Ray Rice .60 1.50
83 Reggie Bush .60 1.50
84 Reggie Wayne .60 1.50
85 Roddy White .60 1.50
86 Ronnie Brown .60 1.50
87 Ryan Fitzpatrick .60 1.50
88 Ryan Torain .50 1.25
89 Sam Bradford .75 2.00
90 Sidney Rice .60 1.50
91 Steve Breaston .50 1.25
92 Steve Johnson .60 1.50
93 Steve Smith .60 1.50
94 Steven Jackson .60 1.50
95 Tim Tebow 1.50 4.00
96 Tom Brady 1.25 3.00
97 Tony Romo .75 2.00
98 Vernon Davis .60 1.50
99 Wes Welker .75 2.00
100 Zach Miller .60 1.50
101 Aaron Williams RC 1.50 4.00
102 Adrian Clayborn RC 2.00 5.00
103 Ahmad Black RC 1.50 4.00
104 Akeem Ayers RC 1.50 4.00
105 Aldon Smith RC 3.00 8.00
106 Aldrick Robinson RC 1.25 3.00
107 Allen Bradford RC 1.50 4.00
108 Anthony Allen RC 1.25 3.00
109 Anthony Castonzo RC 1.25 3.00
110 Baron Batch RC 2.00 5.00
111 Brandon Harris RC 1.25 3.00
112 Brooks Reed RC 2.00 5.00
113 Bruce Carter RC 2.00 5.00
114 Cameron Heyward RC 2.00 5.00
115 Cameron Jordan RC 1.50 4.00
116 Cecil Shorts RC 1.50 4.00
117 Chris Culliver RC 1.50 4.00
118 Corey Liuget RC 1.25 3.00
119 D.J. Williams RC 2.00 5.00
120 Da'Quan Bowers RC 2.00 5.00
121 Da'Rel Scott RC 1.50 4.00
122 Daniel Hardy RC 1.50 4.00
123 Danny Watkins RC 1.50 4.00
124 David Ausberry RC 1.50 4.00
125 DeMarco Sampson RC 1.25 3.00
126 DeMarcus Van Dyke RC 1.50 4.00
127 Denarius Moore RC 2.50 6.00
128 Derek Sherrod RC 2.00 5.00
129 Dion Lewis RC 2.00 5.00
130 Dontay Moch RC 1.25 3.00
131 Dwayne Harris RC 2.00 5.00
132 Evan Royster RC 2.00 5.00
133 Gabe Carimi RC 2.00 5.00
134 Greg Jones RC 1.50 4.00
135 Greg McElroy RC 2.00 5.00
136 Greg Salas RC 2.00 5.00
137 J.J. Watt RC 2.50 6.00
138 Jabaal Sheard RC 2.00 5.00
139 Jacquizz Rodgers RC 2.00 5.00
140 Jaiquawn Jarrett RC 1.50 4.00
141 James Carpenter RC 2.00 5.00
142 Jarvis Jenkins RC 1.25 3.00
143 Jay Finley RC 1.50 4.00
144 Jeremy Kerley RC 2.00 5.00
145 Jimmy Smith RC 2.00 5.00
146 Johnny White RC 1.50 4.00
147 Jonas Mouton RC 1.50 4.00
148 Jordan Cameron RC 1.50 4.00
149 Julius Thomas RC 1.50 4.00
150 Jurrell Casey RC 1.25 3.00
151 Justin Houston RC 2.00 5.00
152 Kealoha Pilares RC 2.00 5.00
153 Kelvin Sheppard RC 2.00 5.00
154 Kris Durham RC 1.50 4.00
155 Lance Kendricks RC 1.50 4.00
156 Lee Smith RC 1.50 4.00
157 Luke Stocker RC 1.50 4.00
158 Marcus Cannon RC 1.25 3.00
159 Marcus Gilbert RC 2.00 5.00
160 Marcus Gilchrist RC 1.25 3.00
161 Martez Wilson RC 2.00 5.00
162 Marvin Austin RC 1.50 4.00
163 Mason Foster RC 2.00 5.00
164 Mike Pouncey RC 2.00 5.00
165 Muhammad Wilkerson RC 2.00 5.00
166 Nate Irving RC 1.50 4.00
167 Nate Solder RC 2.00 5.00
168 Nathan Enderle RC 2.00 5.00
169 Nick Fairley RC 2.50 6.00
170 Niles Paul RC 2.00 5.00
171 Orlando Franklin RC 1.50 4.00
172 Owen Marecic RC 2.00 5.00
173 Patrick Peterson RC 3.00 8.00
174 Phil Taylor RC 1.50 4.00
175 Prince Amukamara RC 2.00 5.00
176 Quinton Carter RC 1.25 3.00
177 Rahim Moore RC 1.50 4.00
178 Ras-I Dowling RC 2.00 5.00
179 Richard Gordon RC 1.50 4.00
180 Ricky Stanzi RC 2.50 6.00
181 Robert Housler RC 1.50 4.00
182 Robert Quinn RC 2.00 5.00
183 Rodney Hudson RC 1.25 3.00
184 Ronald Johnson RC 1.50 4.00
185 Roy Helu RC 4.00 10.00
186 Ryan Kerrigan RC 2.00 5.00
187 Ryan Whalen RC 1.50 4.00
188 Scotty McKnight RC 1.50 4.00
189 Shane Bannon RC 1.25 3.00
190 Stanley Havili RC 1.25 3.00
191 Stefen Wisniewski RC 2.00 5.00
192 Stephen Burton RC 1.25 3.00
193 Stephen Paea RC 2.00 5.00
194 T.J. Yates RC 2.50 6.00
195 Tandon Doss RC 1.50 4.00
196 Terrell McClain RC 1.50 4.00
197 Tyler Sash RC 2.00 5.00
198 Tyrod Taylor RC 2.00 5.00
199 Tyron Smith RC 2.50 6.00
200 Virgil Green RC 1.50 4.00
201 Greg Little JSY AU/299 RC 15.00 40.00
202 Colin Kaepernick JSY AU/299 RC 15.00 40.00
203 Taiwan Jones JSY AU/299 RC 12.00 30.00
204 Kendall Hunter JSY AU/299 RC 15.00 40.00
205 Christian Ponder JSY AU/199 RC 40.00 100.00
206 Ryan Mallett JSY AU/199 RC 30.00 60.00
207 Randall Cobb JSY AU/299 RC 30.00 60.00
208 Kyle Rudolph JSY AU/299 RC 15.00 40.00
209 Jerrel Jernigan JSY AU/299 RC 8.00 20.00
210 Andy Dalton JSY AU/299 RC 60.00 150.00
211 Torrey Smith JSY AU/299 RC 15.00 40.00
212 Titus Young JSY AU/299 RC 15.00 40.00
213 Delone Carter JSY AU/299 RC 12.00 30.00
214 Von Miller JSY AU/299 RC 15.00 40.00
215 Shane Vereen JSY AU/299 RC 12.00 30.00
216 Alex Green JSY AU/299 RC 10.00 25.00
217 Mark Ingram JSY AU/199 RC 50.00 120.00
218 DeMarco Murray JSY AU/299 RC EXCH 40.00 80.00
219 Jordan Todman JSY AU/299 RC 6.00 15.00
220 Julio Jones JSY AU/299 RC 40.00 80.00
221 Leonard Hankerson JSY AU/299 RC 10.00 25.00
222 Jamie Harper JSY AU/299 RC 10.00 25.00
223 Vincent Brown JSY AU/299 RC 10.00 25.00
224 Daniel Thomas JSY AU/299 RC 15.00 40.00
225 Marcell Dareus JSY AU/299 RC EXCH 10.00 25.00
226 Jake Locker JSY AU/199 RC 60.00 120.00
227 Blaine Gabbert JSY AU/199 RC 30.00 80.00
228 Cam Newton JSY AU/199 RC 175.00 300.00
229 Bilal Powell JSY AU/299 RC 6.00 15.00
230 Clyde Gates JSY AU/299 RC 8.00 20.00
231 Ryan Williams JSY AU/299 RC 12.00 30.00
232 Mikel Leshoure JSY AU/299 RC 15.00 40.00
233 Stevan Ridley JSY AU/299 RC 10.00 25.00
234 Jonathan Baldwin JSY AU/299 RC 15.00 40.00
235 Austin Pettis JSY AU/299 RC 8.00 20.00
236 A.J. Green JSY AU/199 RC 50.00 100.00

2011 Crown Royale Blue

*1-100 VETS/100: 2X TO 5X BASIC CARDS
*101-200 ROOK/100: .6X TO 1.5X BASIC CARDS
BLUE PRINT RUN 100 SER.#'d SETS

2011 Crown Royale Gold

*1-100 VETS/25: 4X TO 10X BASIC CARDS
*101-200 ROOK/25: 1.2X TO 3X BASIC CARDS
GOLD PRINT RUN 25 SER.#'d SETS

2011 Crown Royale All Pros

1 Arian Foster 1.50 4.00
2 Jamaal Charles 1.50 4.00
3 Roddy White 1.50 4.00
4 Reggie Wayne 1.50 4.00
5 Devin Hester 2.00 5.00
6 Tom Brady 3.00 8.00
7 Julius Peppers 1.50 4.00
8 Haloti Ngata 1.25 3.00
9 Ndamukong Suh 2.00 5.00
10 Clay Matthews 2.00 5.00
11 James Harrison 2.00 5.00
12 Patrick Willis 1.50 4.00
13 Jerod Mayo 1.25 3.00
14 Nnamdi Asomugha 1.50 4.00
15 Darrelle Revis 1.50 4.00
16 Ed Reed 1.50 4.00
17 Troy Polamalu 2.00 5.00
18 Shane Lechler 1.25 3.00
19 Billy Cundiff 1.25 3.00
20 Vonta Leach 1.25 3.00

2011 Crown Royale All Pros Materials

STATED PRINT RUN 75-299
*PRIME/50: .6X TO 1.5X JSY/199-299
*PRIME/50: .5X TO 1.2X JSY/75-99
1 Arian Foster/99 5.00 12.00
2 Jamaal Charles/75 4.00 10.00
3 Roddy White/199 3.00 8.00
4 Reggie Wayne/299 3.00 8.00
5 Devin Hester/99 5.00 12.00
6 Tom Brady/99 8.00 20.00
7 Julius Peppers/99 5.00 12.00
9 Ndamukong Suh/299 4.00 10.00
10 Clay Matthews/299 6.00 15.00
11 James Harrison/299 6.00 15.00
12 Patrick Willis/299 3.00 8.00
15 Darrelle Revis/299 3.00 8.00
16 Ed Reed/299 3.00 8.00
17 Troy Polamalu/99 6.00 15.00

2011 Crown Royale All Pros Materials Autographs

STATED PRINT RUN 5-25
1 Arian Foster/15
10 Clay Matthews/25 30.00 60.00
12 Patrick Willis/25 15.00 40.00
15 Darrelle Revis/25 15.00 40.00

2011 Crown Royale Autographs Gold

UNPRICED GOLD VET AU PRINT RUN 1
ROOKIE PRINT RUN 299-499
*ROOKIE BLUE/50: .6X TO 1.5X GOLD/499
*ROOKIE BLUE/50: .5X TO 1.2X GOLD/299
101 Aaron Williams/499 4.00 10.00
102 Adrian Clayborn/499 6.00 15.00
103 Ahmad Black/499 5.00 12.00
104 Akeem Ayers/499 4.00 10.00
105 Aldon Smith/499 12.00 30.00
106 Aldrick Robinson/499 3.00 8.00
107 Allen Bradford/499 4.00 10.00
108 Anthony Allen/499 3.00 8.00
109 Anthony Castonzo/499 3.00 8.00
111 Brandon Harris/499 3.00 8.00
114 Cameron Heyward/499 5.00 12.00
115 Cameron Jordan/499 4.00 10.00
116 Cecil Shorts/499 4.00 10.00
118 Corey Liuget/499 3.00 8.00
119 D.J. Williams/499 5.00 12.00
120 Da'Quan Bowers/499 5.00 12.00
121 Da'Rel Scott/499 4.00 10.00
127 Denarius Moore/499 8.00 20.00
129 Dion Lewis/499 5.00 12.00
131 Dwayne Harris/499 5.00 12.00
132 Evan Royster/499 6.00 15.00
134 Greg Jones/499 4.00 10.00
135 Greg McElroy/499 6.00 15.00
136 Greg Salas/499 5.00 12.00
137 J.J. Watt/499 6.00 15.00
139 Jacquizz Rodgers/499 5.00 12.00
144 Jeremy Kerley/499 5.00 12.00
145 Jimmy Smith/499 5.00 12.00
146 Johnny White/499 4.00 10.00
148 Jordan Cameron/499 4.00 10.00
149 Julius Thomas/499 4.00 10.00
151 Justin Houston/499 4.00 10.00
152 Kealoha Pilares/499 8.00 20.00
154 Kris Durham/499 4.00 10.00
155 Lance Kendricks/499 4.00 10.00
157 Luke Stocker/499 4.00 10.00
158 Marcus Cannon/499 3.00 8.00
161 Martez Wilson/499 5.00 12.00
168 Nathan Enderle/499 EXCH 5.00 12.00
170 Niles Paul/499 5.00 12.00
172 Owen Marecic/499 EXCH 5.00 12.00
174 Phil Taylor/499 5.00 12.00

175 Prince Amukamara/499 6.00 15.00
176 Quinton Carter/499 3.00 8.00
177 Rahim Moore/499 4.00 10.00
180 Ricky Stanzi/299 8.00 20.00
181 Robert Housler/499 4.00 10.00
184 Ronald Johnson/499 4.00 10.00
185 Roy Helu/499 10.00 25.00
186 Ryan Kerrigan/499 8.00 20.00
187 Ryan Whalen/499 4.00 10.00
188 Scotty McKnight/499 4.00 10.00
189 Shane Bannon/499 3.00 8.00
190 Stanley Havili/499 3.00 8.00
192 Stephen Burton/499 3.00 8.00
193 Stephen Paea/499 5.00 12.00
194 T.J. Yates/499 12.00 30.00
195 Tandon Doss/499 4.00 10.00
197 Tyler Sash/499 5.00 12.00
198 Tyrod Taylor/499 5.00 12.00
199 Tyron Smith/499 8.00 20.00

2011 Crown Royale Calling All Captains

1 Tony Gonzalez 1.50 4.00
2 Ray Lewis 2.00 5.00
3 Ryan Fitzpatrick 1.50 4.00
4 Steve Smith 1.50 4.00
5 Dhani Jones 1.25 3.00
6 Jason Witten 2.00 5.00
7 Brandon Lloyd 1.50 4.00
8 Calvin Johnson 2.00 5.00
9 Greg Jennings 1.50 4.00
10 Matt Schaub 1.50 4.00
11 Maurice Jones-Drew 1.50 4.00
12 David Garrard 1.50 4.00
13 Adrian Peterson 2.50 6.00
14 Will Smith 1.25 3.00
15 Mark Sanchez 2.00 5.00
16 Peyton Manning 3.00 8.00
17 Asante Samuel 1.25 3.00
18 Antonio Gates 1.50 4.00
19 Vernon Davis 1.50 4.00
20 Steven Jackson 1.50 4.00
21 Josh Freeman 2.00 5.00
22 Tom Brady 3.00 8.00
23 London Fletcher 1.25 3.00
24 Hines Ward 1.50 4.00

2011 Crown Royale Calling All Captains Materials

STATED PRINT RUN 99-299
1 Tony Gonzalez/299 3.00 8.00
2 Ray Lewis/299 4.00 10.00
3 Ryan Fitzpatrick/299 6.00 15.00
6 Jason Witten/299 4.00 10.00
8 Calvin Johnson/299 4.00 10.00
10 Matt Schaub/299 3.00 8.00
11 Maurice Jones-Drew/99 4.00 10.00
12 David Garrard/299 3.00 8.00
13 Adrian Peterson/299 5.00 12.00
14 Will Smith/200 2.50 6.00
15 Mark Sanchez/299 4.00 10.00
16 Peyton Manning/299 6.00 15.00
18 Antonio Gates/299 3.00 8.00
19 Vernon Davis/299 3.00 8.00
20 Steven Jackson/299 3.00 8.00
22 Tom Brady/99 8.00 20.00
24 Hines Ward/299 4.00 10.00

2011 Crown Royale Calling All Captains Materials Prime

STATED PRINT RUN 8-50
1 Tony Gonzalez/50 5.00 12.00
2 Ray Lewis/50 6.00 15.00
3 Ryan Fitzpatrick/50 10.00 25.00
4 Steve Smith/50 5.00 12.00
6 Jason Witten/50 6.00 15.00
7 Brandon Lloyd/50 5.00 12.00
8 Calvin Johnson/50 6.00 15.00
11 Maurice Jones-Drew/50 5.00 12.00
12 David Garrard/50 5.00 12.00
13 Adrian Peterson/50 8.00 20.00
15 Mark Sanchez/50 6.00 15.00
17 Asante Samuel/50 4.00 10.00
18 Antonio Gates/50 5.00 12.00
19 Vernon Davis/50 5.00 12.00
20 Steven Jackson/50 5.00 12.00
23 London Fletcher/50 6.00 15.00

2011 Crown Royale Calling All Captains Materials Autographs

STATED PRINT RUN 5-15
4 Steve Smith/15
6 Jason Witten/15 15.00 40.00
10 Matt Schaub/15 12.00 30.00
12 David Garrard/15 12.00 30.00
23 London Fletcher/15 25.00 50.00

2011 Crown Royale Crown Jewel Rookies

1 Christian Ponder 4.00 10.00
2 Julio Jones 4.00 10.00
3 Jerrel Jernigan 1.50 4.00
4 Kyle Rudolph 2.00 5.00
5 Greg Little 2.00 5.00
6 Clyde Gates 1.50 4.00
7 Cam Newton 15.00 30.00
8 Shane Vereen 2.00 5.00
9 Titus Young 2.50 6.00
10 Mikel Leshoure 2.00 5.00
11 Ryan Mallett 4.00 10.00
12 DeMarco Murray 4.00 10.00
13 Colin Kaepernick 2.50 6.00
14 Ryan Williams 2.50 6.00
15 Daniel Thomas 2.00 5.00
16 Bilal Powell 1.25 3.00
17 Stevan Ridley 2.00 5.00
18 Andy Dalton 5.00 12.00
19 Torrey Smith 2.50 6.00
20 Taiwan Jones 1.50 4.00
21 Von Miller 2.50 6.00
22 Vincent Brown 2.00 5.00
23 Mark Ingram 4.00 10.00
24 Jake Locker 5.00 12.00
25 Blaine Gabbert 3.00 8.00
26 A.J. Green 4.00 10.00
27 Randall Cobb 2.50 6.00
28 Leonard Hankerson 2.00 5.00
29 Delone Carter 1.50 4.00
30 Alex Green 2.00 5.00
31 Marcell Dareus 2.00 5.00
32 Jamie Harper 2.00 5.00
33 Kendall Hunter 2.00 5.00
34 Jonathan Baldwin 2.00 5.00
35 Jordan Todman 1.25 3.00
36 Austin Pettis 1.50 4.00

2011 Crown Royale Crown Jewel Rookies Autographs Sapphire

AUTO STATED PRINT RUN 1-25
1 Christian Ponder/25 40.00 100.00
2 Julio Jones/25 30.00 80.00
3 Jerrel Jernigan/25
4 Kyle Rudolph/25 10.00 25.00
5 Greg Little/25 10.00 25.00
6 Clyde Gates/25 12.00 30.00
8 Shane Vereen/25 10.00 25.00
9 Titus Young/25 12.00 30.00
10 Mikel Leshoure/25 10.00 25.00
11 Ryan Mallett/25 30.00 80.00
12 DeMarco Murray/25 50.00 100.00
13 Colin Kaepernick/25 20.00 40.00
14 Ryan Williams/25 15.00 40.00
15 Daniel Thomas/25 10.00 25.00
18 Andy Dalton/25 60.00 120.00
19 Torrey Smith/25 12.00 30.00
21 Von Miller/25 12.00 30.00
22 Vincent Brown/25 10.00 25.00
23 Mark Ingram/25 30.00 80.00
24 Jake Locker/25 50.00 100.00
25 Blaine Gabbert/25 40.00 80.00
26 A.J. Green/25 40.00 80.00
27 Randall Cobb/25 25.00 50.00
28 Leonard Hankerson/25 10.00 25.00
31 Marcell Dareus/25 10.00 25.00
32 Jamie Harper/25 10.00 25.00
33 Kendall Hunter/25 10.00 25.00
34 Jonathan Baldwin/25 25.00 50.00
35 Jordan Todman/25 6.00 15.00

2011 Crown Royale Jersey Number Materials

STATED PRINT RUN 50 SER.#'d SETS
1 Adrian Peterson 8.00 20.00
2 Pierre Thomas
3 Jeremy Maclin 5.00 12.00
4 Ray Rice 5.00 12.00
5 DeAngelo Hall 4.00 10.00
6 Matt Cassel 4.00 10.00
7 Marques Colston 5.00 12.00
8 Philip Rivers 6.00 15.00
9 Devin Hester 6.00 15.00
10 Ben Roethlisberger 6.00 15.00
11 C.J. Spiller 5.00 12.00
12 Anquan Boldin 5.00 12.00
13 Steven Jackson 5.00 12.00
14 Tom Brady 10.00 25.00
15 Patrick Willis 5.00 12.00
16 Louis Murphy 5.00 12.00
17 Julius Peppers 6.00 15.00
18 Shonn Greene 5.00 12.00
19 Vernon Davis 5.00 12.00
20 Brent Celek 5.00 12.00

2011 Crown Royale Kings of the NFL

1 Aaron Rodgers 2.50 6.00
2 Reggie Wayne 1.25 3.00
3 Wes Welker 1.50 4.00
4 DeSean Jackson 1.25 3.00
5 Larry Fitzgerald 1.25 3.00
6 Calvin Johnson 1.50 4.00
7 Greg Jennings 1.25 3.00
8 Chris Johnson 1.25 3.00
9 Tom Brady 2.50 6.00
10 Mark Sanchez 1.50 4.00
11 Arian Foster 1.25 3.00
12 Adrian Peterson 2.00 5.00
13 Matt Ryan 1.50 4.00
14 Brandon Lloyd 1.25 3.00
15 LeSean McCoy 1.25 3.00
16 Hines Ward 1.25 3.00
17 Roddy White 1.25 3.00
18 Peyton Manning 2.50 6.00
19 Brian Urlacher 1.50 4.00
20 Michael Turner 1.25 3.00

2011 Crown Royale Kings of the NFL Materials

STATED PRINT RUN 99-299
1 Aaron Rodgers/299 10.00 25.00
2 Reggie Wayne/299 3.00 8.00
3 Wes Welker/99 5.00 12.00
4 DeSean Jackson/299 3.00 8.00
5 Larry Fitzgerald/99 4.00 10.00
6 Calvin Johnson/299 4.00 10.00
8 Chris Johnson/299 3.00 8.00
9 Tom Brady/99 8.00 20.00
10 Mark Sanchez/299 4.00 10.00
11 Arian Foster/299 4.00 10.00
12 Adrian Peterson/299 5.00 12.00
13 Matt Ryan/299 4.00 10.00
15 LeSean McCoy/299 3.00 8.00
16 Hines Ward/299 4.00 10.00
17 Roddy White/199 3.00 8.00
18 Peyton Manning/299 6.00 15.00
19 Brian Urlacher/299 4.00 10.00
20 Michael Turner/99 4.00 10.00

2011 Crown Royale Kings of the NFL Materials Prime

STATED PRINT RUN 5-50
1 Aaron Rodgers/50 15.00 40.00
2 Reggie Wayne/50 4.00 10.00
3 Wes Welker/50 5.00 12.00
4 DeSean Jackson/50 4.00 10.00
5 Larry Fitzgerald/50 4.00 10.00
6 Calvin Johnson/50 5.00 12.00
8 Chris Johnson/50 4.00 10.00
10 Mark Sanchez/50 5.00 12.00
12 Adrian Peterson/50 6.00 15.00
13 Matt Ryan/50 5.00 12.00
14 Brandon Lloyd/50 4.00 10.00
15 LeSean McCoy/50 4.00 10.00
16 Hines Ward/50 5.00 12.00
17 Roddy White/50 4.00 10.00
19 Brian Urlacher/50 5.00 12.00
20 Michael Turner/50 4.00 10.00

2011 Crown Royale Kings of the NFL Materials Autographs

AUTO STATED PRINT RUN 5-25
1 Aaron Rodgers/20 200.00 350.00
4 DeSean Jackson/25 12.00 30.00
5 Larry Fitzgerald/20
10 Mark Sanchez/15 25.00 50.00
11 Arian Foster/15 25.00 50.00
13 Matt Ryan/20
15 LeSean McCoy/20 15.00 40.00
18 Peyton Manning/15 75.00 150.00
20 Michael Turner/20

2011 Crown Royale Knights of the Gridiron

*GOLD/100: .6X TO 1.5X BASIC INSERTS
*BLACK/25: 1.5X TO 4X BASIC INSERTS
1 Jared Allen 2.00 5.00
2 Clay Matthews 2.50 6.00
3 Brian Cushing 1.50 4.00
4 Jerod Mayo 1.50 4.00
5 Brian Urlacher 2.50 6.00
6 Charles Woodson 2.50 6.00
7 Nnamdi Asomugha 2.00 5.00
8 Dhani Jones 1.50 4.00
9 Patrick Willis 2.00 5.00
10 Darrelle Revis 2.00 5.00

2011 Crown Royale Living Legends

1 Alex Karras 2.00 5.00
2 Art Monk 2.00 5.00
3 Bart Starr 4.00 10.00
4 Billy Howton 1.50 4.00
5 Bobby Bell 1.50 4.00
6 Boomer Esiason 2.00 5.00
7 Boyd Dowler 1.50 4.00
8 Charley Trippi 1.50 4.00
9 Craig James 1.50 4.00
10 Deacon Jones 2.00 5.00
11 Doug Flutie 2.00 5.00
12 Doug Williams 1.50 4.00
13 Dub Jones 1.50 4.00
14 Frank Gifford 2.00 5.00
15 Harlon Hill 1.50 4.00
16 Jack Lambert 2.50 6.00
17 Ozzie Newsome 2.00 5.00
18 Sterling Sharpe 2.00 5.00
19 Wayne Chrebet 1.50 4.00
20 Willie Brown 1.50 4.00

2011 Crown Royale Living Legends Autographs

AUTO STATED PRINT RUN 1-25
1 Alex Karras/25 10.00 25.00
4 Billy Howton/25
5 Bobby Bell/25 8.00 20.00
7 Boyd Dowler/25 10.00 25.00
8 Charley Trippi/25 8.00 20.00
13 Dub Jones/25 8.00 20.00
15 Harlon Hill/25
17 Ozzie Newsome/25
20 Willie Brown/25 8.00 20.00

2011 Crown Royale Living Legends Materials Prime

PRIME PRINT RUN 25 SER.#'d SETS
*BASE JSY/199-299: .2X TO .5X PRIME/25
*BASE JSY/99: .25X TO .6X PRIME/25
1 Alex Karras 10.00 25.00
3 Bart Starr 15.00 40.00
6 Boomer Esiason 10.00 25.00
11 Doug Flutie 10.00 25.00
16 Jack Lambert 12.00 30.00
17 Ozzie Newsome 10.00 25.00
18 Sterling Sharpe 10.00 25.00
19 Wayne Chrebet 8.00 20.00
20 Willie Brown 8.00 20.00

2011 Crown Royale Living Legends Materials Autographs

STATED PRINT RUN 20-25
*PRIME/15: .6X TO 1.5X BASIC JSY AU/20-25
1 Alex Karras/25 12.00 30.00
3 Bart Starr/20 60.00 120.00
6 Boomer Esiason/25* 15.00 40.00
9 Craig James/25 15.00 40.00
11 Doug Flutie/25 15.00 40.00
16 Jack Lambert/25 30.00 60.00
17 Ozzie Newsome/25 12.00 30.00
18 Sterling Sharpe/25 12.00 30.00
19 Wayne Chrebet/25 10.00 25.00
20 Willie Brown/25 10.00 25.00

2011 Crown Royale Majestic

1 Johnny Knox 1.50 4.00
2 Andre Johnson 1.50 4.00
3 Josh Freeman 2.00 5.00
4 Danny Woodhead 2.00 5.00
5 Tim Tebow 4.00 10.00
6 Michael Vick 2.00 5.00
7 Visanthe Shiancoe 1.50 4.00
8 Eli Manning 2.00 5.00
9 Heath Miller 1.50 4.00
10 Peyton Hillis 1.50 4.00
11 Maurice Jones-Drew 1.50 4.00
12 Shonn Greene 1.50 4.00
13 DeMarcus Ware 1.50 4.00
14 Miles Austin 1.50 4.00
15 Drew Brees 2.00 5.00
16 Bo Scaife 1.25 3.00
17 Joe Flacco 2.00 5.00
18 Jamaal Charles 1.50 4.00
19 Jay Cutler 1.50 4.00
20 Ryan Mathews 1.50 4.00

2011 Crown Royale Majestic Materials

STATED PRINT RUN 50-299
*PRIME/50: .6X TO 1.5X BASIC JSY/199-299
*PRIME/50: .5X TO 1.2X BASIC JSY/75-99
*PRIME/25: .6X TO 1.5X BASIC JSY/50
1 Johnny Knox 4.00 10.00
2 Andre Johnson 3.00 8.00
3 Josh Freeman 4.00 10.00
4 Danny Woodhead 4.00 10.00
5 Tim Tebow 10.00 25.00
6 Michael Vick 4.00 10.00
7 Visanthe Shiancoe 3.00 8.00
8 Eli Manning 5.00 12.00
9 Heath Miller 3.00 8.00
10 Peyton Hillis 3.00 8.00
11 Maurice Jones-Drew 4.00 10.00
12 Shonn Greene 3.00 8.00
13 DeMarcus Ware 3.00 8.00
14 Miles Austin 3.00 8.00
15 Drew Brees 5.00 12.00
16 Bo Scaife 2.50 6.00
17 Joe Flacco 4.00 10.00
18 Jamaal Charles 4.00 10.00
19 Jay Cutler 3.00 8.00
20 Ryan Mathews 3.00 8.00

2011 Crown Royale Majestic Materials Autographs

JSY AU STATED PRINT RUN 10-25
1 Johnny Knox EXCH/25 12.00 30.00
5 Tim Tebow/15 60.00 100.00
9 Heath Miller/25 12.00 30.00
10 Peyton Hillis/20 30.00 60.00
11 Maurice Jones-Drew/15 15.00 40.00
12 Shonn Greene/20 15.00 40.00
14 Miles Austin/20 20.00 50.00
15 Drew Brees/20 50.00 100.00
16 Bo Scaife/20 8.00 20.00
17 Joe Flacco/15 25.00 50.00
19 Jay Cutler/15 15.00 40.00
20 Ryan Mathews EXCH/25 12.00 30.00

2011 Crown Royale Net Fusion

1 Sebastian Janikowski 8.00 20.00
2 David Akers 6.00 15.00
3 Billy Cundiff 6.00 15.00
4 Robbie Gould 6.00 15.00
5 Adam Vinatieri 6.00 15.00
6 Jay Feely 6.00 15.00
7 Rob Bironas 6.00 15.00
8 Nate Kaeding 6.00 15.00
9 Mason Crosby 8.00 20.00
10 Josh Scobee 6.00 15.00
11 Garrett Hartley 6.00 15.00
12 Ryan Succop 6.00 15.00
13 Nick Folk 6.00 15.00
14 Neil Rackers 6.00 15.00
15 Stephen Gostkowski 8.00 20.00
16 Olindo Mare 6.00 15.00
17 David Buehler 6.00 15.00
18 Ryan Longwell 6.00 15.00
19 Matt Prater 6.00 15.00
20 Graham Gano 6.00 15.00

2011 Crown Royale Player Die Cut Materials

STATED PRINT RUN 3-100
1 David Harris/100 4.00 10.00
2 Dallas Clark/100 5.00 12.00
3 Tony Romo/100 6.00 15.00
4 Ahmad Bradshaw/16 10.00 25.00
5 Troy Polamalu/49 8.00 20.00
6 Vincent Jackson/100 5.00 12.00
7 Frank Gore/100 5.00 12.00
8 Felix Jones/100 5.00 12.00
9 Darren McFadden/49
10 Jonathan Stewart/25 8.00 20.00
12 Tashard Choice/100 4.00 10.00
13 James Laurinaitis/49
14 Chris Cooley/100 5.00 12.00
15 Santana Moss/25 8.00 20.00
16 Malcom Floyd/25 8.00 20.00
17 LaDainian Tomlinson/100 6.00 15.00
18 Michael Vick/100 6.00 15.00
19 Matt Schaub/100 5.00 12.00
20 LaRon Landry/100 4.00 10.00

2011 Crown Royale Player Die Cut Materials Autographs

STATED PRINT RUN 5-25
EXCH EXPIRATION: 4/26/2013
1 David Harris/15 10.00 25.00
2 Dallas Clark/25 EXCH
3 Tony Romo/20
6 Vincent Jackson/25 12.00 30.00
7 Frank Gore/25
13 James Laurinaitis/25 10.00 25.00
14 Chris Cooley/20 12.00 30.00
16 Malcom Floyd/25 EXCH 12.00 30.00
17 LaDainian Tomlinson/20 25.00

2011 Crown Royale Rookie Die Cut Material Autographs Blue

*BLUE AU/50: .5X TO 1.2X JSY AU/299
*BLUE AU/50: .4X TO 1X JSY AU/199
BLUE JSY AU PRINT RUN 50
205 Christian Ponder 75.00 150.00
210 Andy Dalton 125.00 200.00
228 Cam Newton 175.00 300.00

2011 Crown Royale Rookie Royalty

1 Jamie Harper 1.25 3.00
2 Ryan Williams 1.50 4.00
3 Titus Young 1.50 4.00
4 Mark Ingram 2.50 6.00
5 Greg Little 1.25 3.00
6 Torrey Smith 1.50 4.00
7 Marcell Dareus 1.25 3.00
8 Mikel Leshoure 1.25 3.00
9 Jake Locker 3.00 8.00
10 Leonard Hankerson 1.25 3.00
11 Christian Ponder 2.50 6.00
12 Julio Jones 2.50 6.00
13 Andy Dalton 3.00 8.00
14 Kendall Hunter 1.25 3.00
15 Colin Kaepernick 1.50 4.00
16 Austin Pettis 1.00 2.50
17 Delone Carter 1.00 2.50
18 Clyde Gates 1.00 2.50
19 Stevan Ridley 1.25 3.00
20 Jonathan Baldwin 1.25 3.00
21 Shane Vereen 1.25 3.00
22 Jordan Todman .75 2.00
23 Daniel Thomas 1.25 3.00
24 Blaine Gabbert 2.50 6.00
25 Taiwan Jones 1.25 3.00
26 Vincent Brown 1.25 3.00
27 Cam Newton 6.00 15.00
28 Randall Cobb 1.50 4.00
29 DeMarco Murray 2.50 6.00
30 Bilal Powell .75 2.00
31 A.J. Green 2.50 6.00
32 Kyle Rudolph 1.25 3.00
33 Jerrel Jernigan 1.00 2.50
34 Von Miller 1.50 4.00
35 Alex Green 1.25 3.00
36 Ryan Mallett 2.50 6.00

2011 Crown Royale Rookie Royalty Materials

STATED PRINT RUN 299 SER.#'d SETS
*PRIME/50: .8X TO 2X BASIC JSY/299
1 Jamie Harper 2.50 6.00
2 Ryan Williams 3.00 8.00
3 Titus Young 3.00 8.00
4 Mark Ingram 5.00 12.00
5 Greg Little 2.50 6.00
6 Torrey Smith 3.00 8.00
7 Marcell Dareus 2.50 6.00
8 Mikel Leshoure 2.50 6.00
9 Jake Locker 6.00 15.00
10 Leonard Hankerson 2.50 6.00
11 Christian Ponder 5.00 12.00
12 Julio Jones 5.00 12.00
13 Andy Dalton 6.00 15.00
14 Kendall Hunter 2.50 6.00
15 Colin Kaepernick 3.00 8.00
16 Austin Pettis 2.00 5.00
17 Delone Carter 2.00 5.00
18 Clyde Gates 2.00 5.00
19 Stevan Ridley 2.50 6.00
20 Jonathan Baldwin 2.50 6.00
21 Shane Vereen 2.50 6.00
22 Jordan Todman 1.50 4.00
23 Daniel Thomas 2.50 6.00
24 Blaine Gabbert 4.00 10.00
25 Taiwan Jones 2.50 6.00
26 Vincent Brown 2.50 6.00
27 Cam Newton 12.00 30.00
28 Randall Cobb 3.00 8.00
29 DeMarco Murray 5.00 12.00
30 Bilal Powell 1.50 4.00
31 A.J. Green 5.00 12.00
32 Kyle Rudolph 2.50 6.00
33 Jerrel Jernigan 2.00 5.00
34 Von Miller 3.00 8.00
35 Alex Green 2.50 6.00
36 Ryan Mallett 5.00 12.00

2011 Crown Royale Rookie Royalty Materials Autographs

JSY AUTO PRINT RUN 25-100
*PRIME AU/25: .6X TO 1.5X JSY AU/100
*PRIME AU/25: .5X TO 1.2X JSY AU/50
EXCH EXPIRATION: 4/26/2013
1 Jamie Harper/100 8.00 20.00
2 Ryan Williams/100 10.00 25.00
3 Titus Young/100 8.00 20.00
4 Mark Ingram/50 50.00 100.00
5 Greg Little/100 8.00 20.00
6 Torrey Smith/100 15.00 40.00
7 Marcell Dareus/100 EXCH 8.00 20.00
8 Mikel Leshoure/100 10.00 25.00
9 Jake Locker/50 50.00 100.00
10 Leonard Hankerson/100 8.00 20.00
11 Christian Ponder/50 30.00 80.00
12 Julio Jones/100 30.00 60.00
13 Andy Dalton/100 50.00 100.00
14 Kendall Hunter/100 10.00 25.00
15 Colin Kaepernick/100 15.00 40.00
16 Austin Pettis/100 6.00 15.00
17 Delone Carter/100 6.00 15.00
18 Clyde Gates/100 6.00 15.00
19 Stevan Ridley/100 8.00 20.00
20 Jonathan Baldwin/100 8.00 20.00
21 Shane Vereen/100 8.00 20.00
22 Jordan Todman/100 5.00 12.00
23 Daniel Thomas/100 15.00 40.00
24 Blaine Gabbert/100 25.00 60.00
25 Taiwan Jones/100 12.00 30.00
26 Vincent Brown/100 8.00 20.00
27 Cam Newton/25 125.00 200.00
28 Randall Cobb/100 15.00 40.00
29 DeMarco Murray/100 40.00 80.00
30 Bilal Powell/100 5.00 12.00
31 A.J. Green/50 40.00 80.00
32 Kyle Rudolph/100 8.00 20.00
33 Jerrel Jernigan/100 6.00 15.00
34 Von Miller/100 12.00 30.00
35 Alex Green/100 8.00 20.00
36 Ryan Mallett/50 20.00 50.00

2011 Crown Royale Royalty

1 Keith Jackson 1.50 4.00
2 Jan Stenerud 1.50 4.00
3 Forrest Gregg 1.50 4.00
4 Don Meredith 2.50 6.00
5 Richard Dent 1.50 4.00
6 Franco Harris 2.50 6.00
7 Fran Tarkenton 2.50 6.00
8 Steve Bartkowski 2.00 5.00
9 Bob Lilly 2.00 5.00
10 George Blanda 2.00 5.00
11 Dick Butkus 3.00 8.00
12 Mark Carrier 1.50 4.00
13 John Hadl 1.50 4.00
14 John Fuqua 1.50 4.00
15 John Brodie 1.50 4.00
16 Fred Biletnikoff 2.00 5.00
17 Emmitt Smith 4.00 10.00
18 Dan Marino 5.00 12.00
19 Ken Anderson 2.00 5.00
20 Bernie Kosar 2.00 5.00

2011 Crown Royale Royalty Materials

STATED PRINT RUN 99-299
*PRIME/25: .8X TO 2X BASIC JSY/299
*PRIME/25: .6X TO 1.5X BASIC JSY/99
1 Keith Jackson/99 5.00 12.00
2 Jan Stenerud/299 4.00 10.00
3 Forrest Gregg/99 5.00 12.00
4 Don Meredith/99 15.00 40.00
5 Richard Dent/299 4.00 10.00
6 Franco Harris/99 8.00 20.00
7 Fran Tarkenton/99 8.00 20.00
8 Steve Bartkowski/299 5.00 12.00
9 Bob Lilly/99 6.00 15.00
10 George Blanda/299 6.00 15.00
11 Dick Butkus/99 10.00 25.00
12 Mark Carrier/299 4.00 10.00
13 John Hadl/99 4.00 10.00
14 John Fuqua/99 8.00 20.00
15 John Brodie/99
16 Fred Biletnikoff/299 5.00 12.00
17 Emmitt Smith/99 10.00 25.00
18 Dan Marino/299 10.00 25.00
19 Ken Anderson/99 6.00 15.00
20 Bernie Kosar/299 6.00 15.00

2011 Crown Royale Royalty Materials Autographs

STATED PRINT RUN 20-25
EXCH EXPIRATION: 4/26/2013
1 Keith Jackson/25 EXCH 12.00 30.00
2 Jan Stenerud/25 20.00 50.00
3 Forrest Gregg/25 12.00 30.00
5 Richard Dent/25
6 Franco Harris/25 30.00 60.00
7 Fran Tarkenton/25 20.00 50.00
8 Steve Bartkowski/25 15.00 40.00
9 Bob Lilly/25 20.00 50.00
11 Dick Butkus/25 EXCH 30.00 60.00
12 Mark Carrier/25 20.00 50.00
13 John Hadl/25 EXCH 12.00 30.00
14 John Fuqua/25 EXCH
15 John Brodie/25 30.00 60.00
16 Fred Biletnikoff/25 20.00 50.00
17 Emmitt Smith/20
18 Dan Marino/25 75.00 150.00
19 Ken Anderson/25 EXCH 15.00 40.00
20 Bernie Kosar/25 15.00 40.00

2011 Crown Royale The Zone

1 Darren McFadden 1.50 4.00
2 Lee Evans 1.50 4.00
3 Jahvid Best 1.50 4.00
4 Jacoby Ford 1.50 4.00
5 Michael Crabtree 1.50 4.00
6 Percy Harvin 1.50 4.00
7 Matt Forte 1.50 4.00
8 Steve Smith 1.50 4.00
9 DeAngelo Williams 1.50 4.00
10 Braylon Edwards 1.50 4.00
11 Colt McCoy 1.50 4.00
12 Rashard Mendenhall 1.50 4.00
13 Santonio Holmes 1.50 4.00
14 Mike Wallace 2.00 5.00
15 Sam Bradford 2.00 5.00
16 Felix Jones 1.50 4.00
17 Knowshon Moreno 1.50 4.00
18 Dwayne Bowe 1.50 4.00
19 Antonio Gates 1.50 4.00
20 Mike Thomas 1.50 4.00

2011 Crown Royale The Zone Materials

STATED PRINT RUN 94-299
*PRIME/50: .6X TO 1.5X BASIC JSY/199-299
*PRIME/50: .5X TO 1.2X BASIC JSY/94-99
*PRIME/25: .6X TO 1.5X BASIC JSY/99
1 Darren McFadden/99 4.00 10.00
2 Lee Evans/299 3.00 8.00
3 Jahvid Best/99 4.00 10.00
4 Jacoby Ford/99 3.00 8.00
5 Michael Crabtree/199 3.00 8.00
6 Percy Harvin/99 4.00 10.00
7 Matt Forte/99 4.00 10.00
8 Steve Smith/299 3.00 8.00
9 DeAngelo Williams/299 3.00 8.00
11 Colt McCoy/299 4.00 10.00
12 Rashard Mendenhall/99 4.00 10.00
13 Santonio Holmes/99 4.00 10.00
14 Mike Wallace/99 5.00 12.00
15 Sam Bradford/99 5.00 12.00
16 Felix Jones/299 3.00 8.00
17 Knowshon Moreno/299 3.00 8.00
18 Dwayne Bowe/94 4.00 10.00
19 Antonio Gates/299 3.00 8.00
20 Mike Thomas/99 4.00 10.00

2011 Crown Royale The Zone Materials Autographs

STATED PRINT RUN 10-25
EXCH EXPIRATION: 4/26/2013
1 Darren McFadden/25 15.00 40.00
2 Lee Evans/20 12.00 30.00
3 Jahvid Best/25 12.00 30.00
4 Jacoby Ford/25 EXCH
5 Michael Crabtree/25 12.00 30.00
6 Percy Harvin/20 15.00 40.00
7 Matt Forte/20
9 DeAngelo Williams/25 12.00 30.00
11 Colt McCoy/25 12.00 30.00
12 Rashard Mendenhall/20 EXCH 12.00 30.00
13 Santonio Holmes/25 12.00 30.00
14 Mike Wallace/20 25.00 50.00
15 Sam Bradford/20 30.00 60.00
16 Felix Jones/20 12.00 30.00
17 Knowshon Moreno/20 12.00 30.00
18 Dwayne Bowe/25 12.00 30.00

1986 DairyPak Cartons

This set of 24 numbered cards was issued as the side panel on half-gallon cartons of various brands of milk all over the country. Depending on the sponsoring milk company, the cards can be found in a large number of printing colors including: black, blue/red, brown, green, olive green, lime green, dark blue, lavender, light blue, aqua, orange, pink, purple, red, salmon or yellow. The actual pictures of the players on the cards are in black and white. Each player's card also contains a facsimile autograph above or to the side of his head. The prices listed below are for cards cut from the carton. Complete carton prices are 50 percent greater than the prices listed below. The cards, when cut on the dotted line, measure approximately 3 1/4" by 4 7/16". The set was only licensed by the NFL Players Association and hence team logos are not shown, i.e., the players are pictured without helmets. The bottom of the panel details an offer to receive a 24" by 32" poster (featuring the card fronts of the 24 NFL Superstars featured in this set) for 1.95 and two proofs-of-purchase. The Lofton card was supposedly withdrawn at some time during the promotion; however there does not appear to be any drastic shortage of Lofton cards needed for complete sets.

COMPLETE SET (24) 40.00 80.00
1 Joe Montana 10.00 20.00
2 Marcus Allen 1.25 3.00
3 Art Monk 1.00 2.50
4 Mike Quick .75 2.00
5 John Elway 7.50 15.00
6 Eric Hipple .60 1.50
7 Louis Lipps .75 2.00
8 Dan Fouts 1.25 3.00
9 Phil Simms 1.00 2.50
10 Mike Rozier .60 1.50
11 Greg Bell .60 1.50
12 Ottis Anderson 1.00 2.50
13 Dave Krieg .75 2.00
14 Anthony Carter .75 2.00
15 Freeman McNeil .75 2.00
16 Doug Cosbie .60 1.50
17 James Lofton 1.25 3.00
18 Dan Marino 7.50 15.00
19 James Wilder .60 1.50
20 Cris Collinsworth UER .75 2.00
(Name misspelled Chris)
21 Eric Dickerson 1.25 3.00
22 Walter Payton 10.00 20.00
23 Ozzie Newsome 1.00 2.50
24 Chris Hinton .60 1.50

2007 Dallas Desperados AFL Donruss

This set was produced by Donruss and issued at a regular season Desperados game in 2007.

COMPLETE SET (15) 5.00 10.00
ANNOUNCED PRINT RUN 5000 SETS
1 Clint Dolezel .50 1.25
2 Will Pettis .40 1.00
3 Colston Weatherington .30 .75
4 Devin Wyman .30 .75
5 Duke Pettijohn .30 .75
6 Marcus Nash .50 1.25
7 Jeff Chase .30 .75
8 Terrance Dotsy .30 .75
9 Josh White .30 .75
10 Bobby Keyes .30 .75
11 Jermaine Jones .30 .75
12 Rickie Simpkins .30 .75
13 Will McClay CO .30 .75
PL1 Clint Dolezel .50 1.25
PL2 Will Pettis .40 1.00

2008 Dallas Desperados AFL Donruss

This set was produced by Donruss, sponsored by Pepsi, and issued at a regular season Desperados game in 2008.

D1 Clint Dolezel .50 1.25
D2 Colston Weatherington .30 .75
D3 Jermaine Jones .30 .75
D4 Rickie Simpkins .30 .75
D5 Bobby Keyes .30 .75
D6 Josh White .30 .75
D7 Andrae Thurman .30 .75
D8 Duke Pettijohn .30 .75
D9 Marcus Nash .50 1.25
D10 Jeff Chase .30 .75
D11 Terrance Dotsy .30 .75
D12 Will Pettis .40 1.00
D16 Anthony Armstong 1.00 2.50

1999 Danbury Mint 22K Gold

The Danbury Mint issued these 22K Gold cards in 1999. Each card was produced with an all-gold foil cardfront and back and carried an initial retail sales price of $9.99. An album complete with matching plastic pages was issued for the set as well.

1 Troy Aikman 5.00 12.00
2 Morten Andersen 2.50 6.00
3 Jamal Anderson 3.00 8.00
4 Jessie Armstead 3.00 8.00
5 Drew Bledsoe 4.00 10.00
6 Tony Boselli 2.50 6.00
7 Tim Brown 4.00 10.00
8 Mark Brunell 3.00 8.00
9 Cris Carter 4.00 10.00
10 Ben Coates 2.50 6.00
11 Randall Cunningham 3.00 8.00
12 Terrell Davis 4.00 10.00
13 Dermontti Dawson 2.50 6.00
14 Corey Dillon 4.00 10.00
15 John Elway 7.50 20.00
16 Marshall Faulk 4.00 10.00
17 Brett Favre 7.50 20.00
18 Eddie George 3.00 8.00
19 Darrell Green 3.00 8.00
20 Michael Irvin 4.00 10.00
21 Cortez Kennedy 2.50 6.00
22 Levon Kirkland 2.50 6.00
23 Peyton Manning 6.00 15.00
24 Dan Marino 7.50 20.00
25 Curtis Martin 4.00 10.00
26 Bruce Matthews 2.50 6.00
27 Herman Moore 2.50 6.00
28 Randy Moss 5.00 12.00
29 Hardy Nickerson 2.50 6.00
30 Jonathan Ogden 2.50 6.00
31 Carl Pickens 3.00 8.00
32 Jake Plummer 3.00 8.00
33 Jerry Rice 6.00 15.00
34 Willie Roaf 2.50 6.00
35 Barry Sanders 7.50 20.00
36 Warren Sapp 3.00 8.00
37 Junior Seau 4.00 10.00
38 Bruce Smith 4.00 10.00
39 Emmitt Smith 6.00 15.00
40 Michael Strahan 3.00 8.00
41 Dana Stubblefield 2.50 6.00
42 Dave Szott 2.50 6.00
43 Bobby Taylor 2.50 6.00
44 Derrick Thomas 4.00 10.00
45 Zach Thomas 4.00 10.00
46 Wesley Walls 2.50 6.00
47 Reggie White 4.00 10.00
48 Aeneas Williams 2.50 6.00
49 Rod Woodson 3.00 8.00
50 Steve Young 5.00 12.00

1999-01 Danbury Mint 22K Gold Legends

The Danbury Mint issued these 22K Gold cards at the rate of 2-per month from 1999-2001. Each card was produced with an all-gold foil cardfront and back and carried an initial retail sales price of $9.99. The cards are sealed individually in clear plastic holders. There is no year designations on the cards and the copyright line simply reads "ISM-MBI." Complete sets could have been purchased for $599.99 and an album complete with matching plastic sheets was issued for the set as well.

COMPLETE SET (50) 150.00 400.00
1 Jerry Kramer 3.00 8.00
2 Matt Snell 3.00 8.00
3 Franco Harris 6.00 15.00
4 Jim Hart 2.50 6.00
5 Paul Krause 2.50 6.00
6 Otto Graham 4.00 10.00
7 Bert Jones 2.50 6.00
8 Joe Jacoby 2.50 6.00
9 Billy Kilmer 2.50 6.00
10 Ben Davidson 2.50 6.00
11 Bart Starr 7.50 20.00
12 Garo Yepremian 2.50 6.00
13 Floyd Little 2.50 6.00
14 Andre Tippett 2.50 6.00
15 Gale Sayers 6.00 15.00
16 Ken Riley 2.50 6.00
17 Bob Lilly 4.00 10.00
18 Lee Roy Jordan 3.00 8.00
19 Chuck Bednarik 4.00 10.00
20 Steve Bartkowski 2.50 6.00
21 Dan Hampton 3.00 8.00
22 Paul Hornung 5.00 12.00
23 Kyle Rote 2.50 6.00
24 Carl Eller 3.00 8.00
25 Joe Ferguson 2.50 6.00
26 Daryle Lamonica 3.00 8.00
27 James Lofton 3.00 8.00
28 Y.A. Tittle 4.00 10.00
29 Bobby Bell 3.00 8.00
30 Len Dawson 5.00 12.00
31 John Stallworth 4.00 10.00
32 Steve Largent 4.00 10.00
33 Mike Singletary 4.00 10.00
34 Tommy Nobis 3.00 8.00
35 Lenny Moore 3.00 8.00
36 John Hadl 3.00 8.00
37 Harry Carson 3.00 8.00
38 Joe Washington 2.50 6.00
39 Drew Pearson 3.00 8.00
40 Ron Jaworski 3.00 8.00
41 Mark Moseley 2.50 6.00
42 John Mackey 2.50 6.00
43 Jan Stenerud 2.50 6.00
44 Jim Plunkett 3.00 8.00
45 Jim Taylor 3.00 8.00
46 George Blanda 5.00 12.00

47 Tom Matte	3.00	8.00
48 Harold Carmichael	3.00	8.00
49 Jackie Smith	2.50	6.00
50 Ottis Anderson	2.50	6.00

2001-02 Danbury Mint 22K Gold Super Bowl XXXVI

This set was issued by the Danbury Mint in a special binder with each card wiithin a plastic holder mounted to a page. It commemorates the Patriots Super Bowl win following the 2001 season.

COMPLETE SET (8)	40.00	80.00
1 Drew Bledsoe	4.00	10.00
2 Tom Brady	15.00	30.00
3 Troy Brown	2.50	6.00
4 Tedy Bruschi	3.00	8.00
5 Ty Law	2.50	6.00
6 Lawyer Milloy	2.50	6.00
7 Antowain Smith	2.50	6.00
8 Adam Vinatieri	4.00	10.00

1970 Dayton Daily News

Each of these "bubble gum-less cards" are actually a cut-out photo from The Dayton Daily News newspaper. Each card measures approximately 3 1/2" by 4" when properly cut. The checklist below is incomplete, any additions to it would be appreciated.

1 Herb Adderley	5.00	10.00
2 Virgil Carter	2.50	5.00
4 Gary Cuozzo	3.00	6.00
6 Ken Dyer	2.50	5.00
7 Walt Garrison	3.00	6.00
8 Bob Hayes	4.00	8.00
9 Bob Lilly	6.00	12.00
13 Joe Morrison	3.00	6.00
14 Craig Morton	4.00	8.00
16 Bart Starr	15.00	30.00
17 Fran Tarkenton	10.00	20.00
161 Bill Bergey	3.00	6.00
172 Don Cockroft UER	2.50	5.00
(wrong player photo)		
174 John DeMarie	2.50	5.00
176A Dale Lindsey ERR	2.50	5.00
(wrong player bio)		
176B Dale Lindsey COR	2.50	5.00
(corrected bio)		
182 Fred Hoaglin	2.50	5.00
190 Mike Howell	2.50	5.00
191 Al Jenkins	2.50	5.00
194 Milt Morin	2.50	5.00
200 Donny Anderson	3.00	6.00
201 Fred Carr	2.50	5.00
209 Pete Case	2.50	5.00
214 Tuckor Frodorickson	3.00	6.00
217 Mike Wilson	2.50	5.00
220 Bill Munson	3.00	6.00
221 Bennie McRae	2.50	5.00
224 Bubba Smith	4.00	8.00
226 John Brodie	4.00	8.00
229 Ken Willard	3.00	6.00
234 John Mackey	5.00	10.00
236 Mike Curtis	3.00	6.00
241 Earl Morrall	3.00	6.00
242 Jim O'Brien	2.50	5.00

1971-72 Dell Photos

Measuring approximately 8 1/4" by 10 3/4", the 1971-72 Dell Pro Football Guide features a center insert that unfolds to display 48 color player photos that are framed by black and yellow border stripes. Each picture measures approximately 1 3/4" by 3" and is not perforated. The player's name and team name are printed beneath the picture. The backs have various color action shots that are framed by a black-and-white film type pattern. Biographies on the NFL stars featured on the insert are found throughout the guide. The uncut set still in the book brings up to a 25 percent premium over the complete set price. The pictures are unnumbered and checklisted below in alphabetical order.

COMPLETE SET (48)	40.00	80.00
1 Dan Abramowicz	.40	1.00
2 Herb Adderley	1.00	2.00
3 Lem Barney	.60	1.50
4 Bobby Bell	.60	1.50
5 George Blanda	2.00	4.00
6 Terry Bradshaw	5.00	10.00
7 John Brodie	1.00	2.00
8 Larry Brown	.50	1.25
9 Dick Butkus	4.00	8.00
10 Fred Carr	.40	1.00
11 Virgil Carter	.40	1.00
12 Mike Curtis	.50	1.25
13 Len Dawson	1.25	3.00
14 Carl Eller	.60	1.50
15 Mel Farr	.40	1.00
16 Roman Gabriel	.60	1.50
17 Gary Garrison	.40	1.00
18 Dick Gordon	.40	1.00
19 Bob Griese	3.00	6.00
20 Bob Hayes	1.00	2.00
21 Rich Jackson	.40	1.00
22 Charley Johnson	.50	1.25
23 Ron Johnson	.40	1.00
24 Deacon Jones	.60	1.50
25 Sonny Jurgensen	1.00	2.00
26 Leroy Kelly	1.00	2.00
27 Daryle Lamonica	.60	1.50
28 MacArthur Lane	.40	1.00
29 Willie Lanier	.60	1.50
30 Bob Lilly	1.00	2.50
31 Floyd Little	.50	1.25
32 Mike Lucci	.40	1.00
33 Don Maynard	1.00	2.50
34 Joe Namath	5.00	10.00
35 Tommy Nobis	.60	1.50
36 Merlin Olsen	1.00	2.00
37 Alan Page	1.00	2.00
38 Gerry Philbin	.40	1.00
39 Jim Plunkett	.60	1.50
40 Tim Rossovich	.40	1.00
41 Gale Sayers	4.00	8.00
42 Dennis Shaw	.40	1.00
43 O.J. Simpson	3.00	8.00
44 Fran Tarkenton	2.00	5.00
45 Johnny Unitas	5.00	12.00
46 Paul Warfield	1.25	3.00
47 Gene Washington 49er	.50	1.25
48 Larry Wilson	.60	1.50

1995 Destiny Tom Landry Phone Cards

This set of phone cards was released to highlight the career of Tom Landry. Each color card follows the typical phone card style and size and includes the card number on the front. Each was also numbered of 2000 sets produced.

COMPLETE SET (5)	14.00	35.00
COMMON CARD (1-5)	3.20	8.00

1933 Diamond Matchbooks Silver

Diamond Match Co. produced their first football matchbook set in 1933. Many covers appear with both a green and pink background on the text area surrounded by a silver border, although a few cards appear in only one color. This set is clearly the most difficult to complete of all the football Diamond Matchbooks. Each cover measures approximately 1 1/2" by 4 1/2" (when completely folded out) and is priced below as unfolded with the matches removed. Complete covers with matches intact sometimes sell for as much as 1-1/2 ttimes the prices listed below. Although the covers are not numbered, we've assigned numbers alphabetically with the white bordered All-American Seal leading off and the color variations listed with a G (green) and P (pink) suffix. Several covers are thought to be much more difficult to find; we've labeled those as SP below.

1 All-American Board	30.00	60.00
of Football Seal		
(on white cardboard stock)		
2G Gene Alford	40.00	75.00
2P Gene Alford	40.00	75.00
3G Marger Apsit	40.00	75.00
3P Marger Apsit	40.00	75.00
4G Red Badgro	75.00	125.00
4P Red Badgro	75.00	125.00
5G Cliff Battles	100.00	175.00
5P Cliff Battles	100.00	175.00
6P Maury Bodenger	40.00	75.00
7P Jim Bowdoin	40.00	75.00
8G John Boylan	40.00	75.00
8P John Boylan	40.00	75.00
9G Hank Bruder	60.00	100.00
9P Hank Bruder	60.00	100.00
10G Carl Brumbaugh	40.00	75.00
10P Carl Brumbaugh	40.00	75.00
11P Bill Buckler	40.00	75.00
12G Jerome Buckley	40.00	75.00
12P Jerome Buckley	40.00	75.00
13G Dale Burnett	40.00	75.00
13P Dale Burnett	40.00	75.00
14P Ernie Caddel	60.00	100.00
15G1 Chris Cagle OFB	60.00	100.00
(orange football in photo)		
15G2 Chris Cagle WFB	75.00	150.00
(black and white football in photo)		
15P Chris Cagle	60.00	100.00
16G Glen Campbell	40.00	75.00
16P Glen Campbell	40.00	75.00
17G John Cannella	40.00	75.00
18P Zuck Carlson	40.00	75.00
19P George Christensen	75.00	125.00
20G Stu Clancy	40.00	75.00
21G Paul(Rip) Collins	40.00	75.00
21P Paul(Rip) Collins	40.00	75.00
22P Jack Connell	40.00	75.00
23P George Corbett	40.00	75.00
24G Orien Crow	40.00	75.00
24P Orien Crow	40.00	75.00
25G Ed Danowski	40.00	75.00
25P Ed Danowski	40.00	75.00
26G Sylvester(Red) Davis	40.00	75.00
26P Sylvester(Red) Davis	40.00	75.00
27G Johnny Dell Isola	60.00	100.00
27P Johnny Dell Isola	60.00	100.00
28P John Doehring	40.00	75.00
29G Turk Edwards	175.00	300.00
29P Turk Edwards	175.00	300.00
30G Earl Elser	40.00	75.00
30P Earl Elser	40.00	75.00
31G Ox Emerson	60.00	100.00
31P Ox Emerson	60.00	100.00
32G Tiny Feather	75.00	125.00
33G Ray Flaherty	75.00	125.00
33P Ray Flaherty	75.00	125.00
34G Ike Frankian	40.00	75.00
34P Ike Frankian	40.00	75.00
35G Red Grange	300.00	500.00
35P Red Grange	300.00	500.00
36G Len Grant	40.00	75.00
37G Ace Gutowsky	75.00	125.00
37P Ace Gutowsky	75.00	125.00
38G Mel Hein	300.00	500.00
39P Arnie Herber	500.00	800.00
40G Bill Hewitt	350.00	600.00
40P Bill Hewitt	350.00	600.00
41G Herman Hickman	60.00	100.00
41P Herman Hickman	60.00	100.00
42G Clarke Hinkle	350.00	600.00
42P Clarke Hinkle	350.00	600.00
43G Cal Hubbard	600.00	1,000.00
43P Cal Hubbard	600.00	1,000.00
44G George Hurley	40.00	75.00
44P George Hurley	40.00	75.00
45P Herman Hussey	75.00	125.00
46G Cecil(Tex) Irvin	40.00	75.00
47G Luke Johnsos	75.00	125.00
47P Luke Johnsos	75.00	125.00
48G Bruce Jones	40.00	75.00
48P Bruce Jones	40.00	75.00
49G Potsy Jones	40.00	75.00
50P Thacker Kaye SP	75.00	125.00
51G Shipwreck Kelly	60.00	100.00
51P Shipwreck Kelly	60.00	100.00
52P Joe Doc Kopcha	60.00	100.00
53G Joe Kurth	90.00	150.00
53P Joe Kurth	90.00	150.00
54G Milo Lubratevich	40.00	75.00
54P Milo Lubratevich	40.00	75.00
55G Father Lumpkin	60.00	100.00
55P Father Lumpkin	60.00	100.00
56G Jim MacMurdo	40.00	75.00
56P Jim MacMurdo	40.00	75.00
57P Joe Maniaci	40.00	75.00
58G Jack McBride	40.00	75.00
59G Ookie Miller	40.00	75.00
59P Ookie Miller	40.00	75.00
60P Buster Mitchell	40.00	75.00
61P Keith Molesworth	40.00	75.00
62P Bob Monnett	90.00	150.00
63G Hap Moran	40.00	75.00
63P Hap Moran	40.00	75.00
64G Bill Morgan	40.00	75.00
65P Maynard Morrison	75.00	125.00
66P Mathew Murray	40.00	75.00
67G Jim Musick	40.00	75.00
67P Jim Musick	40.00	75.00
68P Bronko Nagurski	600.00	1,000.00
69P Dick Nesbitt	40.00	75.00
70G Harry Newman	60.00	100.00
71G1 Bill Owen ERR	75.00	125.00
bio for Bill Owen but photo		
is Steve Owen (standing pose)		
71G2 Bill Owen COR	40.00	75.00
(pose in 3-point stance)		
72G Steve Owen SP	150.00	250.00
(Correct bio and photo)		
73P Andy Pavlicovic	60.00	100.00
74P Bert Pearson	40.00	75.00
75G William Pendergast	40.00	75.00
75P William Pendergast	40.00	75.00
76P Jerry Pepper	40.00	75.00
77P Stan Piawlock	40.00	75.00
78G Erny Pinckert	60.00	100.00
78P Erny Pinckert	60.00	100.00
79G Glenn Presnell	40.00	75.00
79P Glenn Presnell	40.00	75.00
80P Jess Quatse	90.00	150.00
81G Hank Reese	40.00	75.00
82G Dick Richards	40.00	75.00
82P Dick Richards	40.00	75.00
83P Tony Sarausky	40.00	75.00
84G Elmer Schaake	40.00	75.00
84P Elmer Schaake	40.00	75.00
85G John Schneller	40.00	75.00
85P John Schneller	40.00	75.00
86P Johnny Sisk	40.00	75.00
87G Mike Steponovich	40.00	75.00
87P Mike Steponovich	40.00	75.00
88G Ken Strong	250.00	400.00
89P Charles Tackwell	60.00	100.00
90G Harry Thayer	40.00	75.00
90P Harry Thayer	40.00	75.00
91P Walt Uzdavinis	40.00	75.00
92P John Welch	40.00	75.00
93P William Whalen	40.00	75.00
94G Mule Wilson	60.00	100.00
94P Mule Wilson	60.00	100.00
95G Frank Babe Wright	40.00	75.00
95P Frank Babe Wright	40.00	75.00

1934 Diamond Matchbooks

The 1934 Diamond Matchbook set is the first of many issues from the company printed with colorful borders. Four border colors were used for this set: blue, green, red, and tan. Many players appear with three border color variations, while some only appear with one, two or four different border colors. We've noted below known border colors for each matchbook. It is thought that a complete checklist with all color variations is still unknown. A Tan colored Bronko Nagurski matchbook was recently discovered as was a Green Clarke Hinkle. There is no player position included nor picture frame border shown on the player photo. The text printing is in black ink and each cover measures approximately 1 1/2" by 4 1/2" when completely unfolded. The set is very similar in appearance to the 1935 issues, but can be distinguished by the single lined manufacturer's identification "The Diamond Match Co., N.Y.C." Complete covers with matches intact sometimes sell for as much as 1-1/2 ttimes the prices listed below. Although the covers are not numbered, we've assigned numbers alphabetically. Several covers are thought to be much more difficult to find; we've labeled those as SP below.

1 Arvo Antilla	18.00	30.00
2 Red Badgro	35.00	60.00
3 Norbert Bartell	150.00	300.00
4 Cliff Battles	50.00	80.00
5 Chuck Bennis	18.00	30.00
6 Jack Beynon	18.00	30.00
7 Maury Bodenger	18.00	30.00
(misspelled Morry)		
8 John Bond	18.00	30.00
9 John Brown	18.00	30.00
10 Carl Brumbaugh	150.00	300.00
11 Dale Burnett	18.00	30.00
12 Ernie Caddel	50.00	100.00
13 Chris Red Cagle	50.00	100.00
14 Glen Campbell	18.00	30.00
15 John Cannella	18.00	30.00
16 Joe Carter	150.00	300.00
17 Les Caywood B SP	50.00	100.00
18 George Buck Chapman	18.00	30.00
19 Frank Christensen	18.00	30.00
20 Stu Clancy	18.00	30.00
21 Myers Algy Clark	18.00	30.00
22 Paul Rip Collins	18.00	30.00
23 Jack Connell	50.00	100.00
24 Orien Crow	18.00	30.00
25 Lone Star Dietz CO	50.00	100.00
26 John Doehring	150.00	300.00
27 Jimmie Downey	150.00	300.00
28 Turk Edwards	50.00	80.00
29 Ox Emerson	20.00	35.00
30 Tiny Feather	18.00	30.00
31 Ray Flaherty	35.00	60.00
32 Frank Froschauer	18.00	30.00
33 Chuck Galbreath	18.00	30.00
34 Red Gragg	18.00	30.00
35 Red Grange	800.00	1,200.00
36 Cy Grant	18.00	30.00
37 Leonard Grant	18.00	30.00
38 Ross Grant	18.00	30.00
39 Jack Griffith	18.00	30.00
40 Ed Gryboski	18.00	30.00
41 Ace Gutowsky	25.00	40.00
42 Swede Hanson	18.00	30.00
43 Mel Hein	35.00	60.00
44 Warren Heller	18.00	30.00
45 Bill Hewitt	500.00	800.00
46 Clarke Hinkle	500.00	800.00
47 Cecil Tex Irvin	18.00	30.00
48 Frank Johnson	18.00	30.00
49 Jack Johnson	18.00	30.00
50 Robert Jones	150.00	300.00
51 Potsy Jones	18.00	30.00
52 Carl Jorgensen	150.00	300.00
53 John Karcis	18.00	30.00
54 Eddie Kawal	50.00	100.00
55 Shipwreck Kelly	150.00	300.00
56 George Kenneally	150.00	300.00
57 Walt Kiesling	1,000.00	1,500.00
58 Jack Knapper	150.00	300.00
59 Frank Knox	50.00	100.00
60 Joe Doc Kopcha	150.00	300.00
61 Joe Kresky	150.00	300.00
62 Joe Laws	150.00	300.00
63 Russ Lay	18.00	30.00
64 Hilary Biff Lee	18.00	30.00
65 Gil LeFebvre	18.00	30.00
66 Jim Leonard	18.00	30.00
67 Les Lindberg	18.00	30.00
68 John Lipski T	18.00	30.00
69 Milo Lubratevich	18.00	30.00
70 Father Lumpkin	50.00	100.00
71 Link Lyman	500.00	800.00
72 Jim MacMurdo	18.00	30.00
73 Ed Matesic	150.00	300.00
74 Dave McCollough	18.00	30.00
75 John McKnight	18.00	30.00
76 Johnny Blood McNally	250.00	400.00
77 Al Minot	18.00	30.00
78 Keith Molesworth	35.00	60.00
79 Jim Mooney	18.00	30.00
80 Leroy Morehead	18.00	30.00
81 Bill Morgan	18.00	30.00
82 Bob Moser	50.00	100.00
83 Lee Mulleneaux	18.00	30.00
84 George Munday	18.00	30.00
85 George Musso	1,000.00	1,500.00
86 Bronko Nagurski	500.00	800.00
87 Harry Newman	20.00	35.00
88 Al Norgard	150.00	300.00
89 John Oehler	18.00	30.00
90 Charlie Opper	18.00	30.00
91 Bill Owen	18.00	30.00
92 Steve Owen	35.00	60.00
93 Bert Pearson	150.00	300.00
94 Tom Perkinson	18.00	30.00
95 Mace Pike	35.00	60.00
96 Joe Pilconis	150.00	300.00
97 Lew Pope	18.00	30.00
98 Crain Portman	18.00	30.00
99 Glenn Presnell	18.00	30.00
100 Jess Quatse	50.00	100.00
101 Clare Randolph	50.00	100.00
102 Hank Reese	18.00	30.00
103 Paul Riblett	150.00	300.00
104 Dick Richards	150.00	300.00
105 Jack Roberts	18.00	30.00
106 John Lee Rogers	18.00	30.00
107 Gene Ronzani	150.00	300.00
108 Bob Rowe	35.00	60.00
109 John Schneller	35.00	60.00
110 Adolph Schwammel	150.00	300.00
111 Earl Red Seick	150.00	300.00
112 Allen Shi	18.00	30.00
113 Ben Smith	18.00	30.00
114 Ken Strong	60.00	100.00
115 Elmer Taber	50.00	100.00
116 Charles Tackwell	18.00	30.00
117 Ray Tesser	18.00	30.00
118 John Thomason	18.00	30.00
119 Charlie Turbyville	18.00	30.00
(misspelled Turbeyville)		
120 Claude Urevig	50.00	100.00
121 John Harp Vaughan	18.00	30.00
122 Henry Wagnon	18.00	30.00
123 John West	18.00	30.00
124 Lee Woodruff	18.00	30.00
125 Jim Zyntell	18.00	30.00

1934 Diamond Matchbooks College Rivals

Diamond Match Co. produced this set issued in 1934. Each cover features a top college rivalry with a short write-up about the latest games between the two teams. The covers contain a single line manufacturer's identification "The Diamond Match Co. N.Y.C." This set is very similar to the 1935 issue, but can be distinguished by the last line of type in the text as indicated below. Each of the twelve unnumbered covers was produced with either a black or tan colored border. Some collectors attempt to assemble a complete 24-card set with all variations. Complete covers with matches intact sometimes sell for as much as 1-1/2 times the prices listed below.

COMPLETE SET (12)	175.00	300.00
1 Alabama vs. Fordham SP/1933	75.00	125.00
2 Army vs. Navy	12.50	25.00
start to finish		
3 Fordham vs. St. Mary's	10.00	20.00
lose by a 13-6 score		
4 Georgia vs. Georgia Tech	10.00	20.00
Bulldog Alumni and followers		
5 Holy Cross vs. Boston Coll.	10.00	20.00
in atoning for this one defeat		
6 Lafayette vs. Lehigh	10.00	20.00
victory for Lafayette		
7 Michigan vs. Ohio State	12.50	25.00
Champions		
8 Notre Dame vs. Army	12.50	25.00
leader of men, Knute Rockne		
9 Penn vs. Cornell	10.00	20.00
pass		
10 USC vs. Notre Dame	12.50	25.00
year		
11 Yale vs. Harvard	10.00	20.00
Harvard		
12 Yale vs. Princeton	10.00	20.00
scoring 27.		

1935 Diamond Matchbooks

The 1935 Diamond Matchbook set is very similar in design to the 1934 set, but can be distinguished by the double lined manufacturer's identification "Made in U.S.A./The Diamond Match Co., N.Y.C." Only three border colors were used for this set: green, red, and tan and each player appears with only one border color. There is no player position included nor picture frame border shown on the player photo. The text printing is in black ink and each cover measures approximately 1 1/2" by 4 1/2" when completely unfolded. Complete covers with matches intact sometimes sell for as much as 1-1/2 ttimes the prices listed below. Although the covers are not numbered, we've assigned numbers alphabetically.

1 Alf Anderson	15.00	25.00
2 Alec Ashford	15.00	25.00
3 Gene Augusterfer SP	30.00	60.00
4 Red Badgro	20.00	35.00
5 Cliff Battles	35.00	60.00
6 Harry Benson	15.00	25.00
7 Tony Blazine	15.00	25.00
8 John Bond	15.00	25.00
9 Maurice (Mule) Bray	15.00	25.00
10 Dale Burnett	15.00	25.00
11 Charles(Cocky) Bush	15.00	25.00
12 Ernie Caddel	18.00	30.00
13 Zuck Carlson	15.00	25.00
14 Joe Carter	15.00	25.00
15 Cy Casper	15.00	25.00
16 Paul Causey	15.00	25.00
17 Frank Christensen	15.00	25.00
18 Stu Clancy	15.00	25.00
19 Dutch Clark	90.00	150.00
20 Paul(Rip) Collins	15.00	25.00
21 Dave Cook	15.00	25.00
22 Fred Crawford	15.00	25.00
23 Paul Cuba	15.00	25.00
24 Harry Ebding	15.00	25.00
25 Turk Edwards	35.00	60.00
26 Marvin(Swede) Ellstrom	15.00	25.00
27 Beattie Feathers	25.00	40.00
28 Ray Flaherty	20.00	35.00
29 John Gildea	15.00	25.00
30 Tom Graham	15.00	25.00
31 Len Grant	15.00	25.00
32 Maurice Green	15.00	25.00
33 Norman Greeney	15.00	25.00
34 Ace Gutowsky	18.00	30.00
35 Julius Hall	15.00	25.00
36 Swede Hanson	15.00	25.00
37 Charles Harold	15.00	25.00
38 Tom Haywood	15.00	25.00
39 Mel Hein	75.00	125.00
40 Bill Hewitt	90.00	150.00
41 Cecil(Tex) Irvin	15.00	25.00
42 Frank Johnson	15.00	25.00
43 Jack Johnson	15.00	25.00
44 Luke Johnsos	18.00	30.00
45 Potsy Jones	15.00	25.00
46 Carl Jorgensen	25.00	40.00
47 George Kenneally	15.00	25.00
48 Roger(Reds) Kirkman	15.00	25.00
49 Frank Knox	15.00	25.00
50 Joe Doc Kopcha	18.00	30.00
51 Rick Lackman	15.00	25.00
52 Jim Leonard	15.00	25.00
53 Joe(Hunk) Malkovich	15.00	25.00
54 Ed Manske	15.00	25.00
55 Bernie Masterson	18.00	30.00
56 James McMillen	15.00	25.00
57 Mike Mikulak	15.00	25.00
58 Ookie Miller	15.00	25.00
59 Milford(Dub) Miller	15.00	25.00
60 Al Minot	15.00	25.00
61 Buster Mitchell	15.00	25.00
62 Bill Morgan	15.00	25.00
63 George Musso	35.00	60.00
64 Harry Newman	18.00	30.00
65 Al Nichelini	15.00	25.00
66 Bill(Red) Owen	15.00	25.00
67 Steve Owen	20.00	35.00
68 Max Padlow	15.00	25.00
69 Hal Pangle	15.00	25.00
70 Melvin(Swede) Pittman	15.00	25.00
71 William(Red) Pollock	15.00	25.00
72 Glenn Presnell	15.00	25.00
73 George(Mousie) Rado	15.00	25.00
74 Clare Randolph	15.00	25.00
75 Hank Reese	15.00	25.00
76 Ray Richards	15.00	25.00
77 Doug Russell	15.00	25.00
78 Sandy Sandberg	15.00	25.00
79 Phil Sarboe	15.00	25.00
80 Big John Schneller	15.00	25.00
81 Michael Sebastian	15.00	25.00
82 Allen Shi	15.00	25.00
83 Johnny Sisk	15.00	25.00
84 James(Red) Stacy	15.00	25.00
85 Ed Storm	15.00	25.00
86 Ken Strong	35.00	60.00
87 Art Strutt	15.00	25.00
88 Frank Sullivan	15.00	25.00
89 Charles Treadaway	15.00	25.00
90 John Turley	15.00	25.00
91 Claude Urevig	15.00	25.00
92 Charles(Pug) Vaughan	15.00	25.00
93 Izzy Weinstock	15.00	25.00
94 Henry Wiesenbaugh	15.00	25.00
95 Joe Zeller	15.00	25.00
96 Vince Zizak	15.00	25.00

1935 Diamond Matchbooks College Rivals

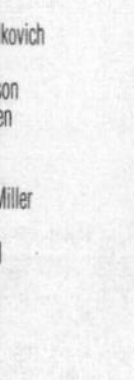

Diamond Match Co. produced this set issued in 1935. Each cover features a top college rivalry with a short write-up about the latest games between the two teams. The covers contain either a single line or a double line manufacturer's identification "Made in U.S.A./The Diamond Match Co. N.Y.C." This set is very similar to the 1934 issue but can be distinguished by the last line of type in the text as indicated below. Each of the unnumbered covers was produced with three versions. The manufacturer's name can be found as a single line with either a black or a tan colored border and the covers can be found in tan with a double lined manufacturer's name. Some collectors attempt to assemble a complete 36-book set with all variations. Complete covers with matches intact sometimes sell for as much as 1-1/2 times the prices listed below.

COMPLETE SET (11)	125.00	200.00
1 Alabama vs. Fordham	20.00	40.00
once championship		
2 Army vs. Navy	12.50	25.00
over the Cadets since 1921		
3 Fordham vs. St. Mary's	10.00	20.00
the gamely fighting "Rams"		
4 Georgia vs. Georgia Tech/7-0 defeat.	10.00	20.00
5 Holy Cross vs. Boston Coll.	10.00	20.00
defeat.		
6 Lafayette vs. Lehigh	10.00	20.00
in a 13-7 victory for Lehigh.		
7 Michigan vs. Ohio State	12.50	25.00
tory for State.		
8 Notre Dame vs. Army	12.50	25.00
Cadets 12-6.		
9 Penn vs. Cornell	10.00	20.00
from start to finish.		
10 USC vs. Notre Dame	12.50	25.00
carriers of Elmer Layden.		
11 Yale vs. Harvard	10.00	20.00
set back.		
12 Yale vs. Princeton	10.00	20.00
ed still led 7-0.		

1936 Diamond Matchbooks

The Diamond Match Co. produced these matchbook covers featuring players of the Chicago Bears and Philadelphia Eagles. They measure approximately 1 1/2" by 4 1/2" (when completely folded out). We've listed below the players alphabetically by team with the Bears first. Each of the covers was produced with either black or brown ink on the text. Three border colors (green, red and tan) were used on the covers, but each player appears with only one border color in black ink and one border color in brown ink. The only exception is Ray Nolting who appears with two border colors with both black and brown ink versions. A picture frame design is included on the left and right sides of the player photo. Don Jackson's and all of the Bears' players' positions are included before the bio. Some collectors consider these two or more separate issues due to the variations and assemble "sets" with either the brown or black printing. Since no price differences are seen between variations and the text and photos are identical for each version, we've listed them together. With all variations, a total of 96-covers were produced. A few of the players are included in the 1937 set as well with only slight differences between the two issues. For those players, we've included the first or last lines of text to help identify the year. Complete covers with matches intact sometimes sell for as much as 1-1/2 ttimes the prices listed below.

COMPLETE SET (47)	500.00	800.00
1 Carl Brumbaugh	10.00	20.00
2 Zuck Carlson	10.00	20.00
3 George Corbett	10.00	20.00
last line (Sigma Alpha Epsilon.)		
4 John Doehring	10.00	20.00
last line (is a bachelor.)		
5 Beattie Feathers	12.50	25.00
first line (...will be 28 years)		
6 Dan Fortmann	12.50	25.00
first line (...April 11, 1916, at)		
7 George Grosvenor	10.00	20.00
8 Bill Hewitt	18.00	30.00
9 Luke Johnsos	10.00	20.00
10 William Karr	10.00	20.00
first line (... in Ripley,)		
11 Eddie Kawal	10.00	20.00
12 Jack Manders	10.00	20.00
last line (200, Height 6 ft. 1 in.)		
13 Bernie Masterson	10.00	20.00
last line (Alpha Epsilon. Single.)		
14 Eddie Michaels	10.00	20.00
15 Ookie Miller	10.00	20.00
16 Keith Molesworth	10.00	20.00
last line (5 ft. 9 1/2 in. Weight 168.)		
17 George Musso	12.50	25.00
last line (Science degree. Is single.)		
18 Bronko Nagurski	150.00	250.00
19 Ray Nolting	10.00	20.00
first line (...three years for Cin-)		
20 Vernon Oech	10.00	20.00
21 William(Red) Pollock	10.00	20.00
22 Gene Ronzani	10.00	20.00
last line (is married.)		
23 Ted Rosequist	10.00	20.00
24 Johnny Sisk	10.00	20.00
25 Joe Stydahar	12.50	25.00
last line (Is single.)		
26 Frank Sullivan	10.00	20.00
first line (...Loyola U. (New)		
27 Russell Thompson	10.00	20.00
last line (Sigma Nu fraternity.)		
28 Milt Trost	10.00	20.00
last line (Is single.)		
29 Joe Zeller	10.00	20.00
last line (and is single. Sigma Nu.)		
30 Bill Brian	7.50	15.00
31 Art Buss	7.50	15.00
32 Joe Carter	7.50	15.00
33 Swede Hanson	7.50	15.00
34 Don Jackson	7.50	15.00
35 John Kusko	7.50	15.00
36 Jim Leonard	7.50	15.00
37 Jim MacMurdo	7.50	15.00
38 Ed Manske	7.50	15.00
39 Forrest McPherson	7.50	15.00
40 George Mulligan	7.50	15.00
41 Joe Pilconis	7.50	15.00
42 Hank Reese	7.50	15.00
43 Jim Russell	7.50	15.00
44 Dave Smukler	7.50	15.00
45 Pete Stevens	7.50	15.00
46 John Thomason	7.50	15.00
47 Vince Zizak	7.50	15.00

1937 Diamond Matchbooks

The Diamond Match Co. produced these matchbook covers featuring players of the Chicago Bears. They measure approximately 1 1/2" by 4 1/2" (when completely folded out). The covers look very similar to the 1936 set, but use a slightly smaller print type. Each of the 24-covers was produced with either black or brown ink on the text. Three border colors (green, red and tan) were used on the covers, with all three used for each of the brown ink varieties. Only one border color was used for each cover printed in black ink. Similar to the 1936 issue, a picture frame design is included on the left and right sides of the player photo. Some collectors consider these two separate issues due to the variations and assemble "sets" with either the brown or black printing. Since no price differences are seen between variations and the text and photos are identical for each version, we've listed them together. With all variations, a total of 96-covers were produced. Several of the players are included in the 1936 set as well with only slight differences between the two issues. For those players, we've included the first or last lines of text to help identify the year. Complete covers with matches intact sometimes sell for as much as 1-1/2 ttimes the prices listed below. Although the covers are not numbered, we've assigned numbers alphabetically.

COMPLETE SET (24)	200.00	350.00
1 Frank Bausch	7.50	15.00
2 Delbert Bjork	7.50	15.00
3 William(Red) Conkright	7.50	15.00
4 George Corbett	7.50	15.00
last line (ion.)		
5 John Doehring	7.50	15.00
last line (baseball.)		
6 Beattie Feathers	10.00	20.00
first line (...turned 29 years)		
7 Dan Fortmann	10.00	20.00
first line (April 11, 1916, in)		
8 Sam Francis	7.50	15.00
9 Henry Hammond	7.50	15.00
10 William Karr	7.50	15.00
first line (in Ripley, W.)		
11 Jack Manders	7.50	15.00
last line (height 6 ft. 1 in.)		
12 Ed Manske	7.50	15.00
13 Bernie Masterson	7.50	15.00
last line (single.)		
14 Keith Molesworth	7.50	15.00
last line (9 1/2 in. Weight 168.)		
15 George Musso	10.00	20.00
last line (married.)		
16 Ray Nolting	7.50	15.00
first line (...three years for)		
17 Richard Plasman	7.50	15.00
18 Gene Ronzani	7.50	15.00
last line (married.)		
19 Joe Stydahar	10.00	20.00
last line (ing. Is single.)		
20 Frank Sullivan	7.50	15.00
first line (Loyola U. New)		
21 Russell Thompson	7.50	15.00
last line (year.)		
22 Milt Trost	7.50	15.00
last line (pounds. Is single.)		
23 George Wilson	7.50	15.00
24 Joe Zeller	7.50	15.00
last line (Nu.)		

1938 Diamond Matchbooks

Diamond Match Co. again produced a matchcover set for 1938 featuring players from the Bears and Lions. They measure approximately 1 1/2" by 4 1/2" (when completely folded out). The overall border color is silver with the bio background color being red for the Bears (1-12) and blue for the Lions (13-24). The Lions players seem to be much tougher to find than the Bears. We've assigned card numbers below alphabetically by the two teams included. There are no known variations. Complete covers with matches intact sometimes sell for as much as 1-1/2 ttimes the prices listed below.

COMPLETE SET (24)	600.00	1,000.00
1 Delbert Bjork	15.00	25.00
2 Raymond Buivid	15.00	25.00
3 Gary Famiglietti	15.00	25.00
4 Dan Fortmann	20.00	35.00
5 Bert Johnson	15.00	25.00
6 Jack Manders	15.00	25.00
7 Joe Maniaci	15.00	25.00
8 Lester McDonald	15.00	25.00
9 Frank Sullivan	15.00	25.00
10 Robert Swisher	15.00	25.00
11 Russell Thompson	15.00	25.00
12 Gust Zarnas	15.00	25.00
13 Ernie Caddel	35.00	60.00
14 Lloyd Cardwell	30.00	50.00
15 Dutch Clark	175.00	300.00
16 Jack Johnson	30.00	50.00
17 Ed Klewicki	30.00	50.00
18 James McDonald	30.00	50.00
19 James(Monk) Moscrip	30.00	50.00
20 Maurice (Babe) Patt	30.00	50.00
21 Bob Reynolds	30.00	50.00
22 Kent Ryan	30.00	50.00
23 Fred Vanzo	30.00	50.00
24 Alex Wojciechowicz	125.00	200.00

1992 Diamond Stickers

Produced by Diamond Publishing Inc., the first series of NFL Superstar stickers consists of 160 stickers, each measuring approximately 1 15/16" by 2 15/16". The stickers were sold in six-sticker packets and could be pasted in a 36-page sticker album. Eight hundred autographed stickers were randomly inserted throughout the packs; apparently, each of the featured stars (Mark Carrier, Cornelius Bennett, Chris Miller, and Rob Moore) signed 200 each. The fronts feature action color player photos framed by a team-color coded inner border and a white outer border. The team name appears in the team's accent color within the top border. The horizontally oriented backs are white with purple print and carry biographical and statistical information. The stickers are numbered on the back and checklisted alphabetically according to teams in the AFC and NFC.

COMPLETE SET (160)	15.00	40.00
1 Super Bowl XXVI logo (Top portion)	.10	.30
2 Super Bowl XXVI logo (Bottom portion)	.10	.30
3 Jim Kelly	.30	.75
4 Thurman Thomas	.20	.50
5 Andre Reed	.15	.40
6 James Lofton	.15	.40
7 Cornelius Bennett	.10	.30
8 Boomer Esiason	.15	.40
9 Harold Green	.07	.20
10 Anthony Munoz	.15	.40
11 Mitchell Price	.07	.20
12 Lewis Billups	.07	.20
13 Bernie Kosar	.10	.30
14 Eric Metcalf	.10	.30
15 Michael Dean Perry	.10	.30
16 Van Waiters	.07	.20
17 Brian Brennan	.07	.20
18 John Elway	1.50	4.00
19 Gaston Green	.07	.20
20 Vance Johnson	.08	.25
21 Dennis Smith	.07	.20
22 Clarence Kay	.07	.20
23 Warren Moon	.15	.40
24 Haywood Jeffires	.10	.30
25 Cris Dishman	.07	.20
26 Bubba McDowell	.07	.20
27 Ray Childress	.15	.40
28 Eric Dickerson	.15	.40
29 Jessie Hester	.07	.20
30 Clarence Verdin	.07	.20
31 Bill Brooks	.10	.30
32 Albert Bentley	.07	.20
33 Christian Okoye	.10	.30
34 Derrick Thomas	.15	.40
35 Dino Hackett	.07	.20
36 Deron Cherry	.07	.20
37 Bill Maas	.07	.20
38 Todd Marinovich	.07	.20
39 Roger Craig	.15	.40
40 Greg Townsend	.07	.20
41 Ronnie Lott	.20	.50
42 Howie Long	.15	.40
43 Dan Marino	1.50	4.00
44 Mark Clayton	.10	.30
45 Sammie Smith	.07	.20
46 Jim Jensen	.07	.20
47 Reggie Roby	.07	.20
48 Brent Williams	.07	.20
49 Andre Tippett	.15	.40
50 John Stephens	.07	.20
51 Johnny Rembert	.07	.20
52 Irving Fryar	.10	.30
53 Ken O'Brien	.08	.25
54 Al Toon	.10	.30
55 Brad Baxter	.08	.25
56 James Hasty	.07	.20
57 Rob Moore	.10	.30
58 Neil O'Donnell	.10	.30
59 Bubby Brister	.10	.30
60 Louis Lipps	.07	.20
61 Merril Hoge	.08	.25
62 Gary Anderson K	.08	.25
63 John Friesz	.08	.25
64 Junior Seau	.15	.40
65 Leslie O'Neal	.08	.25
66 Rod Bernstine	.07	.20
67 Burt Grossman	.07	.20
68 Brian Blades	.08	.25
69 Cortez Kennedy	.10	.30
70 David Wyman	.07	.20
71 John L. Williams	.07	.20
72 Robert Blackmon	.07	.20
73 Checklist 33-48 Jim Kelly	.10	.30
74 Checklist 49-64 Ronnie Lott	.07	.20
75 Jerry Rice Andre Reed	.75	2.00
76 Jay Novacek Dennis Smith	.15	.40
77 Mark Rypien Jim Kelly	.10	.30
78 Pat Swilling Derrick Thomas	.20	.50
79 Deion Sanders Cris Dishman	.50	1.25
80 Mel Gray Gaston Green	.07	.20
81 Earnest Byner Christian Okoye	.08	.25
82 Eric Allen Ronnie Lott	.08	.25
83 Mike Singletary	.20	.50
84 Andre Rison Haywood Jeffires	.15	.40
85 Checklist 65-80 Steve Young	.08	.25
86 Checklist 81-96 Pat Swilling	.07	.20
87 Chris Miller	.10	.30
88 Andre Rison	.15	.40
89 Deion Sanders	.50	1.25
90 Michael Haynes	.07	.20
91 Tim Green	.07	.20
92 Jim Harbaugh	.15	.40
93 Mark Carrier DB	.07	.20
94 Mike Singletary	.20	.50
95 William Perry	.10	.30
96 Donnell Woolford	.07	.20
97 Troy Aikman	.75	2.00
98 Michael Irvin	.30	.75
99 Russell Maryland	.08	.25
100 Jay Novacek	.15	.40
101 Ken Norton Jr.	.08	.25
102 Mel Gray	.07	.20
103 Bennie Blades	.07	.20
104 Rodney Peete	.08	.25
105 Brett Perriman	.08	.25
106 William White	.07	.20
107 Vai Sikahema	.07	.20
108 Vince Workman	.07	.20
109 Jeff Query	.07	.20
110 Sterling Sharpe	.15	.40
111 Tony Mandarich	.07	.20
112 Jim Everett	.10	.30
113 Flipper Anderson	.08	.25
114 Robert Delpino	.07	.20
115 Darryl Henley	.07	.20
116 Henry Ellard	.10	.30
117 Wade Wilson	.08	.25
118 Anthony Carter	.10	.30
119 Chris Doleman	.10	.30
120 Cris Carter	.20	.50
121 Henry Thomas	.07	.20
122 Steve Walsh	.08	.25
123 Pat Swilling	.10	.30
124 Dalton Hilliard	.07	.20
125 Floyd Turner	.07	.20
126 Craig Heyward	.10	.30
127 Jeff Hostetler	.10	.30
128 Phil Simms	.20	.50
129 Lawrence Taylor	.20	.50
130 Mark Ingram	.08	.25
131 Leonard Marshall	.08	.25
132 Randall Cunningham	.15	.40
133 Eric Allen	.08	.25
134 Keith Byars	.08	.25
135 Fred Barnett	.10	.30
136 Wes Hopkins	.07	.20
137 Ernie Jones	.07	.20
138 Johnny Johnson	.07	.20
139 Anthony Thompson	.07	.20
140 Timm Rosenbach	.07	.20
141 Randal Hill	.07	.20
142 Steve Young	.60	1.50
143 Jerry Rice	.75	2.00
144 Tom Rathman	.08	.25
145 Charles Haley	.15	.40
146 John Taylor	.15	.40
147 Vinny Testaverde	.15	.40
148 Gary Anderson RB	.08	.25
149 Broderick Thomas	.07	.20
150 Mark Carrier WR	.10	.30
151 Ian Beckles	.07	.20
152 Mark Rypien	.10	.30
153 Earnest Byner	.08	.25
154 Gary Clark	.10	.30
155 Monte Coleman	.07	.20
156 Ricky Ervins	.07	.20
157 Earnest Byner	.08	.25
158 Jim Kelly Fred Stokes Jumpy Geathers	.30	.75
159 Checklist 129-144 Mark Rypien	.07	.20
160 Mark Rypien	.10	.30

1938 Dixie Lids Small

This unnumbered set of lids is actually a combined sport and non-sport set with 24 different lids. The lids are found in more than one size, approximately 2 11/16" in diameter as well as 2 5/16" in diameter. The catalog designation is F7-1. The 1938 lids are distinguished from the 1937 Dixie Lids by the fact that the 1938 lids are printed in blue ink whereas the 1938 lids are printed in black or wine-colored ink. In the checklist below only the sports subjects are checklisted; non-sport subjects (celebrities) included in this 24 card set are Don Ameche, Annabella, Gene Autry, Warner Baxter, William Boyd, Bobby Breen, Gary Cooper, Alice Fay, Sonja Henie, Tommy Kelly, June Lang, Colonel Tim McCoy, Tyrone Power, Tex Ritter, Simone Simon, Bob Steele, The Three Musquiteers and Jane Withers.

COMPLETE SPORT SET (6)	250.00	500.00
*LARGE: .6X TO 1.5X SMALL		
1 Sam Baugh	75.00	125.00
6 Bronko Nagurski	90.00	150.00

1938 Dixie Premiums

COMPLETE SET (6)	375.00	750.00
1 Sam Baugh	150.00	250.00
6 Bronko Nagurski	150.00	250.00

1999 Doak Walker Award Banquet

This set of three cards was released to attendees of the 1998 Dr.Pepper Doak Walker Award Banquet in January 1999. Each card features a photo of the player on the cardfront and career highlights on the back. The unnumbered cards are listed alphabetically below.

COMPLETE SET (3)	14.00	35.00
1 Gale Sayers	2.40	6.00
2 Doak Walker	2.40	6.00
3 Ricky Williams	10.00	25.00

1992 Dog Tags

Produced by Chris Martin Enterprises, Inc., this boxed set consists of 81 dog tags. Made of durable plastic, each tag measures approximately 2 1/8" by 3 3/8" and, with its rounded corners, resembles a credit card. The set subdivides into three groups: team tags (1-28), regular player tags (29-76), and rookie tags (R1-R5). The cards are numbered on both sides. Tag number 42 (Emmitt Smith) was also issued as a promo, stamped "PROMO TAG" on its back. Also produced was a Chris Martin dog tag that was personally autographed.

COMPLETE SET (81)	40.00	100.00
1 Atlanta Falcons	.20	.50
2 Buffalo Bills	.20	.50
3 Chicago Bears	.20	.50
4 Cincinnati Bengals	.20	.50
5 Cleveland Browns	.20	.50
6 Dallas Cowboys	.30	.75
7 Denver Broncos	.20	.50
8 Detroit Lions	.20	.50
9 Green Bay Packers	.20	.50
10 Houston Oilers	.20	.50
11 Indianapolis Colts	.20	.50
12 Kansas City Chiefs	.20	.50
13 Los Angeles Raiders	.30	.75
14 Los Angeles Rams	.20	.50
15 Miami Dolphins	.30	.75
16 Minnesota Vikings	.20	.50
17 New England Patriots	.20	.50
18 New Orleans Saints	.20	.50
19 New York Giants	.20	.50
20 New York Jets	.20	.50
21 Philadelphia Eagles	.20	.50
22 Phoenix Cardinals	.20	.50
23 Pittsburgh Steelers	.20	.50
24 San Diego Chargers	.20	.50
25 San Francisco 49ers	.20	.50
26 Seattle Seahawks	.20	.50
27 Tampa Bay Buccaneers	.20	.50
28 Washington Redskins	.20	.50
29 Chris Martin	.30	.75
30 Dan Marino	4.80	12.00
31 Chris Miller	.40	1.00
32 Deion Sanders	1.20	3.00
33 Jim Kelly	.60	1.50
34 Thurman Thomas	.60	1.50
35 Jim Harbaugh	.60	1.50
36 Mike Singletary	.40	1.00
37 Boomer Esiason	.40	1.00
38 Anthony Munoz	.60	1.50
39 Bernie Kosar	.40	1.00
40 Troy Aikman	2.40	6.00
41 Michael Irvin	.60	1.50
42 Emmitt Smith	4.80	12.00
43 John Elway	4.80	12.00
44 Rodney Peete	.40	1.00
45 Sterling Sharpe	.40	1.00
46 Haywood Jeffires	.40	1.00
47 Warren Moon	.60	1.50
48 Jeff George	.40	1.00
49 Christian Okoye	.40	1.00
50 Derrick Thomas	.60	1.50
51 Howie Long	.60	1.50
52 Ronnie Lott	.40	1.00
53 Jim Everett	.40	1.00
54 Mark Clayton	.40	1.00
55 Anthony Carter	.40	1.00
56 Chris Doleman	.40	1.00
57 Andre Tippett	.30	.75
58 Pat Swilling	.40	1.00
59 Jeff Hostetler	.40	1.00
60 Lawrence Taylor	.60	1.50
61 Rob Moore	.40	1.00
62 Ken O'Brien	.30	.75
63 Keith Byars	.40	1.00
64 Randall Cunningham	.60	1.50
65 Johnny Johnson	.30	.75
66 Timm Rosenbach	.40	1.00
67 Bubby Brister	.40	1.00
68 John Friesz	.40	1.00
69 Jerry Rice	2.40	6.00
70 Steve Young	2.00	5.00
71 Dan McGwire	.40	1.00
72 Broderick Thomas	.30	.75
73 Vinny Testaverde	.40	1.00
74 Gary Clark	.40	1.00
75 Mark Rypien	.40	1.00
76 Neil Smith	.40	1.00
R1 Dale Carter	.40	1.00
R2 Steve Emtman	.40	1.00
R3 David Klingler	.40	1.00
R4 Tommy Maddox	.40	1.00
R5 Vaughn Dunbar	.40	1.00
29AU Chris Martin AUTO signed card	4.00	10.00
P1 Chris Martin Promo	.40	1.00
P2 Emmitt Smith Promo	2.40	6.00

1993 Dog Tags

Produced by Chris Martin Enterprises, Inc., this set of "Dog Tags Plus" consists of 110 individual player tags and 28 team tags. Two tags, numbers 48 and 138, were not produced. The dog tags were originally distributed in random assortments but later as complete team sets. The only two teams not included in the team set packaging were the Atlanta Falcons and the Los Angeles Raiders. There were also 25,000 sequentially numbered Joe Montana limited edition bonus tags. The collector could obtain one of these Montana tags through a mail-in offer for 5.00 and three proofs of purchase. Reportedly 50,000 of each base set tag were produced, with each one sequentially numbered. Autographed tags were randomly inserted throughout the cases. The players with randomly-inserted autograph tags were Dale Carter, Chris Martin, Emmitt Smith, and Harvey Williams. Also collectors could enter a contest to win a seven-point diamond tag and a 14K gold bead chain. Made of durable plastic, each tag measures approximately 2 1/8" by 3 3/8" and, with its rounded corners, resembles a credit card. After team logo tags (1-28), the set is arranged alphabetically within teams.

COMPLETE SET (138)	50.00	125.00
1 Atlanta Falcons	.20	.50
2 Buffalo Bills	.20	.50
3 Chicago Bears	.20	.50
4 Cincinnati Bengals	.20	.50
5 Cleveland Browns	.20	.50
6 Dallas Cowboys	.30	.75
7 Denver Broncos	.20	.50
8 Detroit Lions	.20	.50
9 Green Bay Packers	.20	.50
10 Houston Oilers	.20	.50
11 Indianapolis Colts	.20	.50
12 Kansas City Chiefs	.20	.50
13 Los Angeles Raiders	.30	.75
14 Los Angeles Rams	.20	.50
15 Miami Dolphins	.30	.75
16 Minnesota Vikings	.20	.50
17 New England Patriots	.20	.50
18 New Orleans Saints	.20	.50
19 New York Giants	.20	.50
20 New York Jets	.20	.50
21 Philadelphia Eagles	.20	.50
22 Phoenix Cardinals	.20	.50
23 Pittsburgh Steelers	.20	.50
24 San Diego Chargers	.20	.50
25 San Francisco 49ers	.20	.50
26 Seattle Seahawks	.20	.50
27 Tampa Bay Buccaneers	.20	.50
28 Washington Redskins	.20	.50
29 Steve Broussard	.30	.75
30 Chris Miller	.30	.75
31 Andre Rison	.60	1.50
32 Deion Sanders	1.20	3.00
33 Cornelius Bennett	.40	1.00
34 Jim Kelly	.60	1.50
35 Bruce Smith	.60	1.50
36 Thurman Thomas	.60	1.50
37 Neal Anderson	.30	.75
38 Mark Carrier DB	.30	.75
39 Jim Harbaugh	.60	1.50
40 Alonzo Spellman	.30	.75
41 David Fulcher	.30	.75
42 Harold Green	.30	.75
43 David Klingler	.30	.75
44 Carl Pickens	.40	1.00
45 Bernie Kosar	.30	.75
46 Clay Matthews	.40	1.00
47 Eric Metcalf	.40	1.00
49 Troy Aikman	2.00	5.00
50 Michael Irvin	.60	1.50
51 Russell Maryland	.40	1.00
52 Emmitt Smith	3.20	8.00
53 Steve Atwater	.30	.75
54 John Elway	4.00	10.00
55 Tommy Maddox	.60	1.50
56 Shannon Sharpe	.60	1.50
57 Herman Moore	.60	1.50
58 Rodney Peete	.40	1.00
59 Barry Sanders	4.00	10.00
60 Andre Ware	.40	1.00
61 Terrell Buckley	.30	.75
62 Brett Favre	4.80	12.00
63 Sterling Sharpe	.40	1.00
64 Reggie White	.60	1.50
65 Ray Childress	.40	1.00
66 Haywood Jeffires	.40	1.00
67 Warren Moon	.60	1.50
68 Lorenzo White	.30	.75
69 Duane Bickett	.30	.75
70 Quentin Coryatt	.40	1.00
71 Steve Emtman	.30	.75
72 Jeff George	.60	1.50
73 Dale Carter	.40	1.00
74 Neil Smith	.40	1.00
75 Derrick Thomas	.60	1.50
76 Harvey Williams	.40	1.00
77 Eric Dickerson	.40	1.00
78 Howie Long	.60	1.50
79 Todd Marinovich	.30	.75
80 Alexander Wright	.30	.75
81 Flipper Anderson	.30	.75
82 Jim Everett	.30	.75
83 Cleveland Gary	.30	.75
84 Chris Martin	.30	.75
85 Irving Fryar	.40	1.00
86 Keith Jackson	.40	1.00
87 Dan Marino	4.00	10.00
88 Louis Oliver	.30	.75
89 Terry Allen	.60	1.50
90 Anthony Carter	.30	.75
91 Chris Doleman	.40	1.00
92 Rich Gannon	.60	1.50
93 Eugene Chung	.30	.75
94 Marv Cook	.30	.75
95 Leonard Russell	.40	1.00
96 Andre Tippett	.30	.75
97 Morten Andersen	.30	.75
98 Vaughn Dunbar	.30	.75
99 Rickey Jackson	.30	.75
100 Sam Mills	.30	.75
101 Derek Brown TE	.30	.75
102 Lawrence Taylor	.60	1.50
103 Rodney Hampton	.40	1.00
104 Phil Simms	.40	1.00
105 Johnny Mitchell	.40	1.00
106 Rob Moore	.40	1.00
107 Blair Thomas	.30	.75
108 Browning Nagle	.30	.75
109 Eric Allen	.30	.75
110 Fred Barnett	.40	1.00
111 Randall Cunningham	.60	1.50
112 Herschel Walker	.40	1.00
113 Chris Chandler	.40	1.00
114 Randal Hill	.30	.75
115 Ricky Proehl	.30	.75
116 Eric Swann	.40	1.00
117 Barry Foster	.40	1.00
118 Eric Green	.30	.75
119 Neil O'Donnell	.40	1.00
120 Rod Woodson	.40	1.00
121 Marion Butts	.40	1.00
122 Stan Humphries	.40	1.00
123 Anthony Miller	.40	1.00
124 Junior Seau	.60	1.50
125 Amp Lee	.30	.75
126 Jerry Rice	2.00	5.00
127 Ricky Watters	.40	1.00
128 Steve Young	1.60	4.00
129 Brian Blades	.40	1.00
130 Cortez Kennedy	.40	1.00
131 Dan McGwire	.30	.75
132 John L. Williams	.30	.75
133 Reggie Cobb	.30	.75
134 Steve DeBerg	.40	1.00
135 Keith McCants	.30	.75
136 Broderick Thomas	.30	.75
137 Earnest Byner	.30	.75
139 Mark Rypien	.30	.75
140 Ricky Sanders	.30	.75
LE1 Joe Montana Bonus numbered of 25,000	3.20	8.00
P1 Chris Martin Promo	.20	.50
P2 Super Bowl XXVII Promo	.75	2.00

1967 Dolphins Royal Castle

This 27-card set was issued by Royal Castle, a south Florida hamburger stand, at a rate of two new cards every week during the season. These unnumbered cards measure approximately 3" by 4 3/8". The front features a black and white (almost sepia-toned) posed photo of the player enframed by an orange border, with the player's signature below the photo. Biographical information is given on the back (including player's nickname where appropriate), along with the logos for the Miami Dolphins and Royal Castle. This set features a card of Bob Griese during his rookie season. There may be a 28th card of George Wilson Jr., but it has never been substantiated. There are 17-cards that are easier than the others; rather than calling these double prints, the other ten cards are marked as SP's in the checklist below.

COMPLETE SET (27)	4,500.00	7,000.00
1 Joe Auer SP	175.00	300.00
2 Tom Beier	75.00	125.00
3 Mel Branch	75.00	125.00
4 Jon Brittenum	75.00	125.00
5 George Chesser	75.00	125.00
6 Edward Cooke	75.00	125.00
7 Frank Emanuel SP	175.00	300.00
8 Tom Erlandson SP	175.00	300.00
9 Norm Evans SP	200.00	350.00
10 Bob Griese SP	1,800.00	3,000.00
11 Abner Haynes SP	250.00	400.00
12 Jerry Hopkins SP	175.00	300.00
13 Frank Jackson	75.00	125.00
14 Billy Joe	75.00	125.00
15 Wahoo McDaniel	150.00	250.00
16 Robert Neff	75.00	125.00
17 Billy Neighbors	75.00	125.00
18 Rick Norton	75.00	125.00
19 Bob Petrich	75.00	125.00
20 Jim Riley	75.00	125.00
21 John Stofa SP	175.00	300.00
22 Laverne Torczon	75.00	125.00
23 Howard Twilley	75.00	125.00
24 Jim Warren SP	175.00	300.00
25 Dick Westmoreland	75.00	125.00
26 Maxie Williams	75.00	125.00
27 George Wilson Sr. SP (Head Coach)	200.00	350.00

1970 Dolphins Team Issue

The Miami Dolphins likely issued this series of player photos over a two or three year period around 1970. The format is the same for each photo with only subtle differences in the type (size and style) and player position (some spelled out and others initials only). Each of these black-and-white photos measures approximately 5" by 7" and is blankbacked and unnumbered.

COMPLETE SET (12)	60.00	120.00
1 Dean Brown	6.00	12.00
2 Frank Cornish	6.00	12.00
3 Ted Davis	6.00	12.00
4 Norm Evans	6.00	12.00
5 Hubert Ginn	6.00	12.00
6 Mike Kolen	6.00	12.00
7 Bob Kuechenberg	7.50	15.00
8 Stan Mitchell	6.00	12.00
9 Lloyd Mumphord	6.00	12.00
10 Dick Palmer	6.00	12.00
11 Barry Pryor	6.00	12.00
12 Bill Stanfill	6.00	12.00

1970-71 Dolphins Team Issue

The Miami Dolphins likely issued this series of player photos over a two or three year period around 1970. The format is the same for each photo with only subtle differences in the type (size and style) and player position (some are included while others are not). Each of these black-and-white photos measures approximately 8" by 10" and is blankbacked and unnumbered.

COMPLETE SET (22)	125.00	250.00
1 Dick Anderson (SS in small print)	6.00	12.00
2 Dick Anderson (SS in large print)	6.00	12.00
3 Nick Buoniconti	7.50	15.00
4 Larry Csonka	10.00	18.00
5 Manny Fernandez	6.00	12.00
6 Tom Goode	6.00	12.00
7 Bob Griese	12.00	20.00
8 Jimmy Hines	6.00	12.00
9 Jim Kiick	7.50	15.00
10 Mike Kolen	6.00	12.00
11 Larry Little	7.50	15.00
12 Bob Matheson	6.00	12.00
13 Mercury Morris	7.50	15.00
14 Bob Petrella	6.00	12.00
15 Larry Seiple	6.00	12.00
16 Don Shula CO	12.00	20.00
18 Otto Stowe	6.00	12.00
19 Howard Twilley	6.00	12.00
20 Paul Warfield (WR initials)	7.50	15.00
21 Paul Warfield (Wide Receiver spelled out)	7.50	15.00
22 Garo Yepremian	6.00	12.00

1972 Dolphins Glasses

This set of player glasses was thought to have been issued in 1972. Each features a color artist's rendition of a Dolphins player against a background of white. The reverse includes a short bio of the player. The glasses stand roughly 5 1/2" tall with a diameter of 2 3/4."

COMPLETE SET (8)	50.00	100.00
1 Larry Csonka	15.00	25.00
2 Larry Little	6.00	12.00
2 Jim Kiick	6.00	12.00
2 Nick Buoniconti	7.50	15.00
3 Bob Griese	15.00	25.00
4 Mercury Morris	6.00	12.00
5 Paul Warfield	10.00	20.00
6 Manny Fernandez	6.00	12.00

1972 Dolphins Koole Frozen Cups

This set of plastic cups was sponsored by Koole Frozen Foods and Coca-Cola. Each looks very similar to the 1972 7-11 cups with a color artist's rendering of the featured player along with a cup number of 20 in the set. Each cup measures roughly 5 1/4" tall with a diameter at the top of 3 1/4."

COMPLETE SET (20)	100.00	200.00
1 Dick Anderson	6.00	12.00
2 Nick Buoniconti	7.50	15.00
3 Bob Griese	15.00	25.00
4 Bob Kuechenberg	6.00	12.00
5 Bill Stanfill	4.00	8.00
6 Jake Scott	6.00	12.00
7 Manny Fernandez	6.00	12.00
8 Earl Morrall	7.50	15.00
9 Larry Csonka	15.00	25.00
10 Jim Kiick	7.50	15.00
11 Bob Heinz	4.00	8.00
12 Jim Langer	7.50	15.00
13 Bob Matheson	4.00	8.00
14 Vern Den Herder	4.00	8.00
15 Larry Little	7.50	15.00
16 Curtis Johnson	4.00	8.00
17 Mercury Morris	6.00	12.00
18 Paul Warfield	12.00	20.00
19 Marv Fleming	6.00	12.00
20 Lloyd Mumphord	4.00	8.00

1972 Dolphins Team Issue

These large (approximately 8 1/2" by 11") black and white photos were issued by the Dolphins around 1972. Each features the player's name, position initals and team name below the photo with a facsimile autograph on the image.

COMPLETE SET (12)	60.00	120.00
1 Dick Anderson	5.00	10.00
2 Marlin Briscoe	5.00	10.00
3 Nick Buoniconti	6.00	12.00
4 Larry Csonka	7.50	15.00
5 Manny Fernandez	5.00	10.00
6 Bob Griese	10.00	20.00
7 Jim Kiick	6.00	12.00
8 Larry Little	6.00	12.00
9 Earl Morrall	5.00	10.00
10 Mercury Morris	6.00	12.00
11 Don Shula CO	10.00	20.00
12 Garo Yepremian	5.00	10.00

1972 Dolphins Team Issue Color

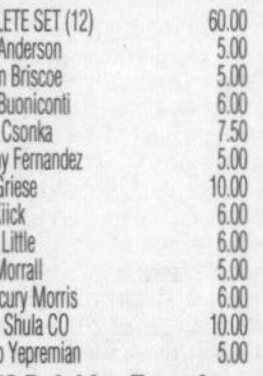

These color photos, issued in 1972, measure roughly 8 3/8" by 10 1/2" and feature a player photo surrounded by a white border with the player's name and position in the upper border. The photo backs include a detailed player bio and statistics as well as the name "Dolphins Graphics, Miami Florida" at the bottom.

COMPLETE SET (6)	40.00	80.00
1 Nick Buoniconti	7.50	15.00
2 Larry Csonka	10.00	20.00
3 Manny Fernandez	5.00	10.00
4 Bob Griese	12.50	25.00
5 Jim Kiick	6.00	12.00
6 Paul Warfield	10.00	20.00

1974 Dolphins All-Pro Graphics

Each of these ten photos measures approximately 8 1/4" by 10 3/4". The fronts feature color action photos bordered in white. The player's name, position, and team name appear in the top border, while the copyright year (1974) and the manufacturer "All Pro Graphics, Inc." are printed in the bottom white border at the left. It is reported that several of these photos do not have the tagline in the lower left corner. The backs are blank. The photos are unnumbered and checklisted below in alphabetical order.

COMPLETE SET (10)	62.50	125.00
1 Dick Anderson	6.00	12.00
2 Nick Buoniconti	7.50	15.00
3 Larry Csonka	10.00	20.00
4 Manny Fernandez	4.00	8.00
5 Bob Griese	12.50	25.00
6 Jim Kiick	6.00	12.00
7 Earl Morrall	7.50	15.00
8 Mercury Morris	6.00	12.00
9 Jake Scott	5.00	10.00
10 Garo Yepremian	4.00	8.00

1974 Dolphins Team Issue

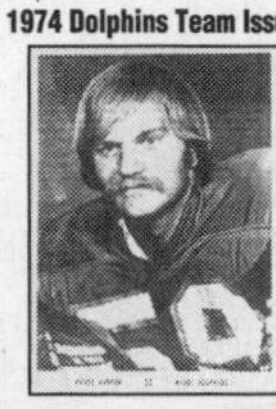

The Miami Dolphins likely issued this series of player photos over a two or three year period around 1974. The format is the same for each photo with only subtle differences in the type size and style. The photos are similar to the 1970 release but feature a distinctly different type style. Each of these black-and-white photos measures approximately 5" by 7" and is blankbacked and unnumbered.

COMPLETE SET (21)	75.00	150.00
1 Charlie Babb	4.00	8.00
2 Mel Baker	4.00	8.00
3 Bruce Bannon	4.00	8.00
4 Randy Crowder	4.00	8.00
5 Norm Evans	4.00	8.00
6 Hubert Ginn	4.00	8.00
7 Irv Goode	4.00	8.00
8 Bob Heinz	4.00	8.00
9 Curtis Johnson	4.00	8.00
10 Bob Kuechenberg	5.00	10.00
11 Nat Moore	5.00	10.00
12 Wayne Moore	4.00	8.00
13 Lloyd Mumphord	4.00	8.00
14 Ed Newman	4.00	8.00
15 Don Reese	4.00	8.00
16 Larry Seiple	4.00	8.00
17 Bill Stanfill	5.00	10.00
18 Henry Stuckey	4.00	8.00
19 Doug Swift	4.00	8.00
20 Jeris White	4.00	8.00
21 Tom Wickert	4.00	8.00

1976 Dolphins McDonald's

This set of photos was sponsored by McDonald's. Each photo measures approximately 8" by 10" and features a posed color close-up photo bordered in white. The player's name and team name are printed in black below the player's photo with the Dolphin's 1976 regular season schedule below it. The top portion of the back has a black and white photo and biographical information on the player. The bottom portion carries an ad for McDonald's. The photos are unnumbered and are checklisted below alphabetically.

COMPLETE SET (4)	15.00	30.00
1 Dick Anderson	5.00	10.00
2 Vern Den Herder	4.00	8.00
3 Nat Moore	5.00	10.00
4 Don Nottingham	4.00	8.00

1980 Dolphins Police

The 1980 Miami Dolphins set contains 16 unnumbered cards, which have been listed by player uniform number in the checklist below. The cards measure approximately 2 5/8" by 4 1/8". The set was sponsored by the Kiwanis Club, the local law enforcement agency, and the Miami Dolphins. The backs contain "Dolphins Tips" and the Miami Dolphins logo. The backs are printed in black with blue accent on white card stock. The fronts contain the Kiwanis logo, but not the Dolphins logo as in the following year. The card of Larry Little is reportedly more difficult to obtain than other cards in this set.

COMPLETE SET (16)	50.00	100.00
5 Uwe Von Schamann	1.50	3.00
10 Don Strock	3.00	6.00
12 Bob Griese	7.50	15.00
22 Tony Nathan	3.00	6.00
24 Delvin Williams	3.00	6.00
25 Tim Foley	2.00	4.00
50 Larry Gordon	1.50	3.00
58 Kim Bokamper	1.50	3.00
64 Ed Newman	1.50	3.00
66 Larry Little SP	10.00	20.00
67 Bob Kuechenberg	3.00	6.00
73 Bob Baumhower	2.00	4.00
77 A.J. Duhe	3.00	6.00
82 Duriel Harris	2.00	4.00
89 Nat Moore	3.00	6.00
NNO Don Shula CO	7.50	15.00

1981 Dolphins Police

The 1981 Miami Dolphins police set consists of 16 numbered cards. The cards measure approximately 2 5/8" by 4 1/8". Player uniform numbers also appear on the fronts of the cards, as does a Kiwanis and blue Dolphins logo. The set is sponsored by the local Kiwanis Club, the local law enforcement agency, and the Dolphins. The backs feature the Dolphins logo and "Dolphins Tips". Card backs are printed in black with gold and blue accent on thin white card stock.

COMPLETE SET (16)	8.00	20.00
1 Duriel Harris	.60	1.50
2 Bob Kuechenberg	.60	1.50
3 Don Bessillieu	.40	1.00
4 Gerald Small	.40	1.00
5 David Woodley	.60	1.50
6 Don McNeal	.40	1.00
7 Nat Moore	.75	2.00
8 A.J. Duhe	.60	1.50
9 Glenn Blackwood	.40	1.00
10 Don Strock	.75	2.00
11 Doug Betters	.40	1.00
12 George Roberts	.40	1.00
13 Bob Baumhower	.60	1.50
14 Kim Bokamper	.40	1.00
15 Tony Nathan	.75	2.00
16 Don Shula CO	2.50	6.00

1981 Dolphins Team Issue

The Dolphins likely issued this series of player photos over a period of years in the early 1980s. The format is the same for each photo with only subtle differences in the type size and style. Each photo features a black and white game action shot of the player and measures approximately 5" by 7." The photos are also blankbacked and unnumbered.

COMPLETE SET (16)	25.00	50.00
1 Bill Barnett	1.50	3.00
2 Glenn Blackwood	1.50	3.00
3 Bob Brudzinski	1.50	3.00
4 A.J. Duhe	2.50	4.00
5 Nick Giaquinto	1.50	3.00
6 Bruce Hardy	1.50	3.00

7 Jim Jensen 1.50 3.00
8 Mike Kozlowski 1.50 3.00
9 Bob Kuechenberg 2.50 4.00
10 Eric Laakso 1.50 3.00
11A Don McNeal 1.50 3.00
(feet close together)
11B Don McNeal 1.50 3.00
(feet far apart)
12 Tom Orosz 1.50 3.00
13 Steve Potter 1.50 3.00
14 Steve Shull 1.50 3.00
15 Tommy Vigorito 1.50 3.00
16 David Woodley 2.50 4.00

1982 Dolphins Police

The 1982 Miami Dolphins set of 16 numbered cards is one of the most attractive of the police sets. The cards measure approximately 2 5/8" by 4 1/8". The orange and greenish-blue frame line on the front contains the player's number and name. The Kiwanis logo is also contained on the front. The backs are printed in black, orange, greenish-blue, and blue and feature "Dolphins Tips," the Dolphins logo, and the Kiwanis logo. The set is sponsored by the Kiwanis Club, the local law enforcement agency, and the Dolphins. Shula and Von Schamann are supposedly a little tougher to find than the other cards in the set.

COMPLETE SET (16) 12.00 30.00
1 Don Shula CO SP 4.00 10.00
2 Uwe Von Schamann SP 1.50 4.00
3 Jimmy Cefalo .60 1.50
4 Andra Franklin .60 1.50
5 Larry Gordon .40 1.00
6 Nat Moore .75 2.00
7 Bob Baumhower .60 1.50
8 A.J. Duhe .60 1.50
9 Tony Nathan .75 2.00
10 Glenn Blackwood .40 1.00
11 Don Strock .75 2.00
12 David Woodley .60 1.50
13 Kim Bokamper .40 1.00
14 Bob Kuechenberg .60 1.50
15 Duriel Harris .60 1.50
16 Ed Newman .40 1.00

1983 Dolphins Police

This numbered set of 16 cards features the Miami Dolphins. Cards measure approximately 2 5/8" by 4 1/8". The cards are numbered on the back in the bottom right corner. The cards look very similar to the 1982 Police Dolphins set. Card backs feature black print with orange and aquamarine accent on white card stock. The cards were sponsored by Kiwanis, Law Enforcement Agencies, Burger King, and the Miami Dolphins. The Burger King and Kiwanis logos both appear on the fronts of the cards.

COMPLETE SET (16) 7.50 15.00
1 Earnie Rhone .40 1.00
2 Andra Franklin .40 1.00
3 Eric Laakso .40 1.00
4 Joe Rose .40 1.00
5 David Woodley .50 1.25
6 Uwe Von Schamann .40 1.00
7 Eddie Hill .40 1.00
8 Bruce Hardy .40 1.00
9 Woody Bennett .40 1.00
10 Fulton Walker .40 1.00
11 Lyle Blackwood .40 1.00
12 A.J. Duhe .50 1.25
13 Don Shula CO 1.50 4.00
14 Duriel Harris .50 1.25
15 Bob Brudzinski .40 1.00
16 Bob Baumhower .40 1.00

1984 Dolphins Police

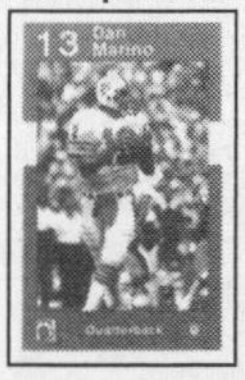

This unnumbered 17-card set features the Miami Dolphins. The Mark Clayton card was added to the set after the first sixteen cards had been distributed. Cards measure approximately 2 5/8" by 4 1/8". Cards are listed below alphabetically by player's name. The Dan Marino card is noteworthy in that it features Marino during his rookie year for cards. Cards are known to exist with the glossy sheen on the back due to a printing error. It is unknown what percent of the print run was reversed in that fashion.

COMPLETE SET (17) 20.00 40.00
1 Bob Baumhower .30 .75
2 Doug Betters .30 .75
3 Glenn Blackwood .20 .50
4 Kim Bokamper .20 .50
5 Dolfan Denny (Mascot) .20 .50
6 A.J. Duhe .30 .75
7 Mark Duper .75 2.00
8 Jim Jensen .30 .75
9 Dan Marino 10.00 25.00
10 Don McNeal .20 .50
11 Nat Moore .40 1.00
12 Tony Nathan .40 1.00
13 Ed Newman .20 .50
14 Don Shula CO 1.25 3.00
15 Dwight Stephenson .30 .75
16 Fulton Walker .20 .50
17 Mark Clayton SP 1.50 4.00

1985 Dolphins Police

This 16-card set is numbered on the back. The card backs are printed in black ink on white card stock. Cards measure 2 5/8" by 4 1/8". The set was sponsored by Kiwanis, Hospital Corporation of America, the Dolphins, and area law enforcement agencies. Uniform numbers are printed on the card front above the player's name. Cards are known to exist with the glossy sheen on the back due to a printing error. It is unknown what percent of the print run was reversed in that fashion.

COMPLETE SET (16) 10.00 25.00
1 William Judson .15 .40
2 Fulton Walker .20 .50
3 Mark Clayton .60 1.50
4 Lyle Blackwood and .20 .50
Glenn Blackwood
(Bruise Brothers)
5 Dan Marino 6.00 15.00
6 Reggie Roby .30 .75
7 Doug Betters .20 .50
8 Jay Brophy .15 .40
9 Dolfan Denny (Mascot) .15 .40
10 Kim Bokamper .15 .40
11 Mark Duper .50 1.25
12 Nat Moore .30 .75
13 Mike Kozlowski .15 .40
14 Don Shula CO .60 1.50
15 Don McNeal .15 .40
16 Tony Nathan .30 .75

1985 Dolphins Posters

These small posters (measuring roughly 18" by 25") feature a color photo of a Dolphins' player on the front with a facsimile autograph and a blank back. Each was sponsored by Eckerd Drug and Kodak and includes a strip of coupons at the bottom. The title "Dolphins 20 Years" appears below each photo.

COMPLETE SET (9) 75.00 125.00
1 Reggie Roby 5.00 10.00
2 Tony Nathan 5.00 10.00
3 Don Shula 10.00 20.00
4 Bob Baumhower 6.00 12.00
5 Lyle Blackwood and 5.00 10.00
Glenn Blackwood
6 Mark Duper 7.50 15.00
7 Dan Marino 20.00 40.00
8 Mark Clayton 7.50 15.00
9 Doug Betters 5.00 10.00

1986 Dolphins Police

This 16-card set is numbered on the card backs, which are printed in black ink on white card stock. Cards measure approximately 2 5/8" by 4 1/8". The set was sponsored by Kiwanis, Anon Anew, the Dolphins, and area law enforcement agencies. Uniform numbers are printed on the front of the card.

COMPLETE SET (16) 6.00 15.00
1 Dwight Stephenson .30 .75
2 Bob Baumhower .20 .50
3 Dolfan Denny (Mascot) .15 .40
4 Don Shula CO .60 1.50
5 Dan Marino 3.00 8.00
6 Tony Nathan .30 .75
7 Mark Duper .50 1.25
8 John Offerdahl .40 1.00
9 Fuad Reveiz .15 .40
10 Hugh Green .20 .50
11 Lorenzo Hampton .20 .50
12 Mark Clayton .60 1.50
13 Nat Moore .30 .75
14 Bob Brudzinski .15 .40
15 Reggie Roby .20 .50
16 T.J. Turner .20 .50

1987 Dolphins Ace Fact Pack

This 33-card set measures approximately 2 1/4" by 3 5/8". The set was printed in West Germany (by Ace Fact Pack) for release in Great Britain. This set features members of the Miami Dolphins and the set has rounded corners on the front and a design for Ace (looks like a playing card) on the back. We have checklisted the set in alphabetical order.

COMPLETE SET (33) 250.00 500.00
1 Bob Baumhower 2.50 6.00
2 Woody Bennett 2.00 5.00
3 Doug Betters 2.50 6.00
4 Glenn Blackwood 2.50 6.00
5 Bud Brown 2.00 5.00
6 Bob Brudzinski 2.00 5.00
7 Mark Clayton 4.00 10.00
8 Mark Duper 4.00 10.00
9 Roy Foster 2.00 5.00
10 Jon Giesler 2.00 5.00
11 Hugh Green 2.50 6.00
12 Lorenzo Hampton 2.00 5.00
13 Bruce Hardy 2.00 5.00
14 William Judson 2.00 5.00
15 Greg Koch 2.00 5.00
16 Paul Lankford 2.00 5.00
17 George Little 2.00 5.00
18 Dan Marino 200.00 350.00
19 John Offerdahl 2.50 6.00
20 Dwight Stephenson 2.50 6.00
21 Don Strock 2.50 6.00
22 T.J. Turner 2.00 5.00
23 Dolphins Helmet 2.00 5.00
24 Dolphins Information 2.00 5.00
25 Dolphins Uniform 2.00 5.00
26 Game Record Holders 2.00 5.00
27 Season Record Holders 2.00 5.00
28 Career Record Holders 2.00 5.00
29 Record 1967-86 2.00 5.00
30 1986 Team Statistics 2.00 5.00
31 All-Time Greats 2.00 5.00
32 Roll of Honour 2.00 5.00
33 Joe Robbie Stadium 2.00 5.00

1987 Dolphins Holsum

This 22-card set features players of the Miami Dolphins; cards were available only in Holsum Bread packages. The set was co-produced by Mike Schechter Associates on behalf of the NFL Players Association. The cards are standard size, 2 1/2" by 3 1/2", and are done in full color. Card fronts have a color photo within a green border and the backs are printed in black ink on white card stock.

COMPLETE SET (22) 60.00 120.00
1 Bob Baumhower 2.00 4.00
2 Mark Brown 2.00 4.00
3 Mark Clayton 2.50 5.00
4 Mark Duper 2.50 5.00
5 Roy Foster 2.00 4.00
6 Hugh Green 2.00 4.00
7 Lorenzo Hampton 2.00 4.00
8 William Judson 2.00 4.00
9 George Little 2.00 4.00
10 Dan Marino 20.00 40.00
11 Nat Moore 2.00 4.00
12 Tony Nathan 2.00 4.00
13 John Offerdahl 2.00 4.00
14 James Pruitt 2.00 4.00
15 Fuad Reveiz 2.00 4.00
16 Dwight Stephenson 2.50 6.00
17 Glenn Blackwood 2.00 4.00
18 Bruce Hardy 2.00 4.00
19 Reggie Roby 2.00 4.00
20 Bob Brudzinski 2.00 4.00
21 Ron Jaworski 2.00 4.00
22 T.J. Turner 2.00 4.00

1987 Dolphins Police

This 16-card set is numbered on the back and measures approximately 2 5/8" by 4 1/8". The set was sponsored by Kiwanis, Children's Center of Fair Oaks Hospital at Boca/Delray, the Dolphins, and area law enforcement agencies. Uniform numbers are printed on the front of the card. Reportedly approximately three million cards were produced for this promotion. The Dwight Stephenson card is considered more difficult to find than the other cards in the set.

COMPLETE SET (16) 25.00 40.00
1 Joe Robbie OWN .50 1.25
2 Glenn Blackwood .50 1.25
3 Mark Duper .60 1.50
4 Fuad Reveiz .50 1.25
5 Dolfan Denny (Mascot) .50 1.25
6 Dwight Stephenson SP 3.00 6.00
7 Hugh Green .60 1.50
8 Larry Csonka 1.00 2.50
(All-Time Great)
9 Bud Brown .50 1.25
10 Don Shula CO 1.00 2.50
11 T.J. Turner .50 1.25
12 Reggie Roby .50 1.25
13 Dan Marino 12.00 20.00
14 John Offerdahl .50 1.25
15 Bruce Hardy .50 1.25
16 Lorenzo Hampton .50 1.25

1988 Dolphins Holsum

This 12-card set features players of the Miami Dolphins; cards were available only in Holsum Bread packages. The set was co-produced by Mike Schechter Associates on behalf of the NFL Players Association. The cards are standard size, 2 1/2" by 3 1/2", and are done in full color. Card fronts have a color photo within a green border and the backs are printed in black ink on white card stock.

COMPLETE SET (12) 15.00 30.00
1 Mark Clayton 1.25 3.00
2 Dwight Stephenson 1.50 4.00
3 Mark Duper 1.25 3.00
4 John Offerdahl .75 2.00
5 Dan Marino 7.50 15.00
6 T.J. Turner .60 1.50
7 Lorenzo Hampton .60 1.50
8 Bruce Hardy .60 1.50
9 Fuad Reveiz .60 1.50
10 Reggie Roby .60 1.50
11 William Judson .60 1.50
12 Bob Brudzinski .60 1.50

1995 Dolphins Chevron Pin Cards

Chevron released these 8-cards as a promotion throughout the 1995 season. The cards themselves are unnumbered, but have been arranged below in accordance with the checklist printed on each cardback. A lapel pin was included with and attached to each card in the lower right hand corner. Each card measures approximately 3" by 5" and includes a color photo on front and text on back along with a checklist.

COMPLETE SET (8) 8.00 20.00
1 Miami Dolphins .80 2.00
2 Dan Marino 4.00 10.00
3 Bryan Cox .80 2.00
4 Troy Vincent .80 2.00
5 Irving Fryar 1.20 3.00
6 Eric Green .80 2.00
7 Team '95 1.20 3.00
8 Hall of Famers 1.60 4.00

1996 Dolphins AT&T

This set was issued in 1996 on a large perforated sheet. Each card when separated measures roughly 2 1/2" by 3" and includes a color photo of the player along with the AT&T sponsor logo on the cardfronts. The cardbacks feature the typical player statistics and bio.

COMPLETE SET (24) 15.00 30.00
1 Karim Abdul-Jabbar .50 1.25
2 Trace Armstrong .40 1.00
3 Fred Barnett .50 1.25
4 Tim Bowens .40 1.00
5 James Brown .40 1.00
6 Terrell Buckley .50 1.25
7 Troy Drayton .40 1.00
8 Daryl Gardener .40 1.00
9 Chris Gray .40 1.00
10 Dwight Hollier .40 1.00
11 Calvin Jackson .40 1.00
12 Jimmy Johnson CO .40 1.00
13 John Kidd .40 1.00
14 Dan Marino 2.50 6.00
15 O.J. McDuffie .50 1.25
16 Louis Oliver .40 1.00
17 Stanley Pritchett .40 1.00
18 Tim Ruddy .40 1.00
19 Keith Sims .40 1.00
20 Chris Singleton .40 1.00
21 Daniel Stubbs .40 1.00
22 Zach Thomas .75 2.00
23 Richmond Webb .40 1.00
24 Shawn Wooden .40 1.00

1996 Dolphins Miami Subs Cards/Coins

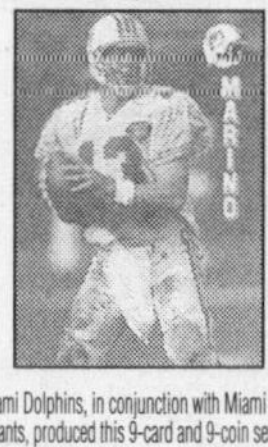

The Miami Dolphins, in conjunction with Miami Subs Restaurants, produced this 9-card and 9-coin set commemorating the 1972 Super Bowl VII team and the present Miami Dolphins. The card fronts feature color action player photos with the player's name printed diagonally on the right side on the card. The backs display the complete 9-card checklist and individual card numbers. We've listed the cards below using a "CA" prefix. The coin fronts feature a player likeness with the player's name and jersey number. The backs display the Dolphins team logo. The coins are unnumbered but have been listed below alphabetically using a "CO" prefix. A cardboard holder featuring Dan Marino, Bernie Kosar, Jimmy Johnson, Fred Barnett, and Mark Clayton was produced to house the set.

COMP.CARD/COIN SET (18) 15.00 30.00
COMPLETE CARD SET (9) 10.00 18.00
COMPLETE COIN SET (9) 5.00 12.00
CA1 Dan Marino 3.00 8.00
CA2 Larry Csonka 1.00 2.50
CA3 Pete Stoyanovich .60 1.50
CA4 Paul Warfield 1.00 2.50
CA5 Bernie Kosar .60 1.50
CA6 Mark Clayton .60 1.50
CA7 Fred Barnett .60 1.50
CA8 Nat Moore .75 2.00
CA9 Don Shula 1.50 4.00
George Allen
Super Bowl VII
CO1 Fred Barnett .40 1.00
CO2 Mark Clayton .40 1.00
CO3 Larry Csonka .60 1.50
CO4 Bernie Kosar .40 1.00
CO5 Dan Marino 2.00 5.00
CO6 Nat Moore .50 1.25
CO7 Pete Stoyanovich .40 1.00
CO8 Paul Warfield .60 1.50
CO9 Super Bowl VII Trophy .50 1.25
gold coin
NNO Display Holder .60 1.50
Dan Marino
Jimmy Johnson
Bernie Kosar
Mark Clayton
Fred Barnett
Pete Stoyanovich

1997 Dolphins Collector's Choice

Upper Deck released several team sets in 1997 in a blister pack wrapper. Each of the 14-cards in this set are very similar to the base Collector's Choice cards except for the card numbering on the cardback. A cover/checklist card was added featuring the team helmet.

COMPLETE SET (14) 1.50 4.00
MI1 Karim Abdul-Jabbar .10 .30
MI2 O.J. McDuffie .07 .20
MI3 Troy Drayton .02 .10
MI4 Zach Thomas .20 .50
MI5 Irving Spikes .02 .10
MI6 Shane Burton .07 .20
MI7 Stanley Pritchett .02 .10
MI8 Yatil Green .10 .30
MI9 Dan Marino .75 2.00
MI10 Jerris McPhail .02 .10
MI11 Daryl Gardener .02 .10
MI12 Fred Barnett .07 .20
MI13 Terrell Buckley .02 .10
MI14 Checklist .30 .75
(Dan Marino on back)

1997 Dolphins NCL

This set was issued in 1997 on a large perforated sheet. Each card when separated measures roughly 2 1/2" by 3" and includes a color photo of the player along with the NCL (Norwegian Cruise Lines) sponsor logo on the cardfronts. The cardbacks feature the typical player statistics and bio.

COMPLETE SET (24) 15.00 30.00
1 Karim Abdul-Jabbar .50 1.25
2 Trace Armstrong .40 1.00
3 Tim Bowens .50 1.25
4 James Brown .40 1.00
5 Terrell Buckley .50 1.25
6 Troy Drayton .40 1.00
7 Daryl Gardener .40 1.00
8 Anthony Harris .40 1.00
9 Calvin Jackson .40 1.00
10 Jimmy Johnson CO .50 1.25
11 Olindo Mare .40 1.00
12 Dan Marino 3.00 6.00
13 O.J. McDuffie .50 1.25
14 Everett McIver .40 1.00
15 Stanley Pritchett .40 1.00
16 Derrick Rodgers .40 1.00
17 Tim Ruddy .40 1.00
18 Keith Sims .40 1.00
19 Jason Taylor .75 2.00
20 George Teague .40 1.00
21 Lamar Thomas .40 1.00
22 Zach Thomas .75 2.00
23 Richmond Webb .50 1.25
24 Shawn Wooden .40 1.00

1997 Dolphins Score

This 15-card set of the Miami Dolphins was distributed in five-card packs with a suggested retail price of $1.99. The fronts feature color action player photos with white borders and the player's name and team logo printed in team color foil at the bottom. The backs carry player information and career statistics. Platinum Team parallel cards were randomly seeded in packs featuring all foil cardfronts.

COMPLETE SET (15) 3.20 8.00
*PLATINUM TEAMS: 1X TO 2X
1 Dan Marino 1.60 4.00
2 Troy Drayton .08 .25
3 O.J. McDuffie .15 .40
4 Karim Abdul-Jabbar .30 .75
5 Terrell Buckley .08 .25
6 Stanley Pritchett .08 .25
7 Jerris McPhail .08 .25
8 Fred Barnett .15 .40
9 Zach Thomas .15 .40
10 Daryl Gardener .08 .25
11 Tim Bowens .08 .25
12 Shawn Wooden .08 .25
13 Richmond Webb .08 .25
14 Lamar Thomas .08 .25
15 Craig Erickson .08 .25

1999 Dolphins NCL

This set was issued in 1999 on a large perforated sheet. Each card when separated measures roughly 2 1/2" by 3" and includes a color photo of the player along with the NCL (Norwegian Cruise Lines) sponsor logo on the cardfronts. The cardbacks feature the typical player statistics and bio.

COMPLETE SET (24) 15.00 30.00
1 Tim Bowens .40 1.00
2 James Brown .40 1.00
3 Terrell Buckley .50 1.25
4 Cecil Collins .40 1.00
5 Mark Dixon .40 1.00
6 Kevin Donnalley .40 1.00
7 Troy Drayton .40 1.00
8 Daryl Gardener .40 1.00
9 Calvin Jackson .40 1.00
10 Jimmy Johnson CO .50 1.25
11 Robert Jones LB .40 1.00
12 Rob Konrad .40 1.00
13 Sam Madison .50 1.25
14 Olindo Mare .40 1.00
15 Dan Marino 3.00 6.00
16 Brock Marion .40 1.00
17 Tony Martin .50 1.25
18 O.J. McDuffie .50 1.25
19 Kenny Mixon .40 1.00
20 Derrick Rodgers .40 1.00
21 Tim Ruddy .40 1.00
22 Jason Taylor .50 1.25
23 Zach Thomas .75 2.00
24 Richmond Webb .50 1.25

2000 Dolphins NCL

This set was issued in 2000 on a large perforated sheet. Each card when separated measures roughly 2 1/2" by 3" and includes a color photo of the player along with the NCL (Norwegian Cruise Lines) sponsor logo on the cardfronts. The cardbacks feature the typical player statistics and bio.

COMPLETE SET (30) 12.50 25.00
1 Trace Armstrong .40 1.00
2 Tim Bowens .40 1.00
3 Mark Dixon .40 1.00
4 Kevin Donnalley .40 1.00
5 Jay Fiedler .50 1.25
6 Oronde Gadsden .40 1.00
7 Daryl Gardener .40 1.00
8 Hunter Goodwin .40 1.00
9 Larry Izzo .40 1.00
10 Robert Jones .40 1.00
11 Rob Konrad .40 1.00
12 Sam Madison .40 1.00
13 Olindo Mare .40 1.00
14 Brock Marion .40 1.00
15 Tony Martin .50 1.25
16 O.J. McDuffie .50 1.25
17 Kenny Mixon .40 1.00
18 Derrick Rodgers .40 1.00
19 Tim Ruddy .40 1.00
20 Brent Smith .40 1.00
21 Lamar Smith .40 1.00
22 Patrick Surtain .40 1.00
23 Jason Taylor .60 1.50
24 Thurman Thomas .75 2.00
25 Zach Thomas .60 1.50
26 Matt Turk .40 1.00
27 Todd Wade .40 1.00
28 Brian Walker .40 1.00
29 Dave Wannstedt CO .40 1.00
30 Richmond Webb .40 1.00

2001 Dolphins Bookmarks

This set of bookmarks was issued in the Miami area by local libraries. Each card measures roughly 2" by 8" and features a color image of the player on the front and vital statistics, two more photos, and reading public service notes on the back.

COMPLETE SET (3) 4.00 8.00
1 Sam Madison .75 2.00
2 O.J. McDuffie 1.25 3.00
3 Zach Thomas 1.50 4.00

2001 Dolphins NCL

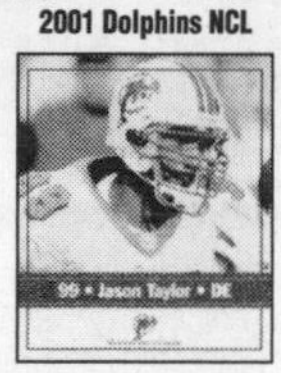

This set was issued in 2001 as six different 5-card perforated sheets stapled together as a booklet. Each card when separated measures roughly 2 1/2" by 3" and includes a color photo of the player along with his name and team name below the photo. The NCL (Norwegian Cruise Lines) sponsor logo appears on the unnumbered cardbacks as well as player statistics and a brief bio.

COMPLETE SET (30) 10.00 20.00
1 Tim Bowens .30 .75
2 Lorenzo Bromell .30 .75
3 Nick Buoniconti .60 1.50
4 Chris Chambers .40 1.00
5 Mark Dixon .30 .75
6 Deon Dyer .30 .75
7 Jay Fiedler .50 1.25
8 Spencer Folau .30 .75
9 Oronde Gadsden .30 .75
10 Daryl Gardener .30 .75
11 Hunter Goodwin .30 .75
12 Morlon Greenwood .30 .75
13 Rob Konrad .30 .75
14 Sam Madison .30 .75
15 Olindo Mare .30 .75
16 Brock Marion .30 .75
17 James McKnight .30 .75
18 Kenny Mixon .30 .75
19 Tom Perry .30 .75
20 Derrick Rodgers .30 .75
21 Tim Ruddy .30 .75
22 Twan Russell .30 .75
23 Lamar Smith .30 .75
24 Patrick Surtain .30 .75
25 Jason Taylor .50 1.25
26 Zach Thomas .60 1.50
27 Matt Turk .30 .75
28 Todd Wade .30 .75
29 Brian Walker .30 .75
30 Dave Wannstedt CO .30 .75

2005 Dolphins Greats DHL

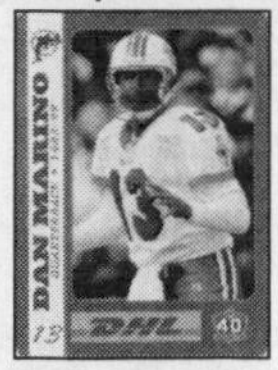

This set, sponsored by DHL, was distributed at a Dolphins home game during the 2005 season. Each unnumbered card measures standard size but features rounded corners similar to a standard playing card. The set includes 40 of the greatest Dolphins players in history to celebrate the team's 40th season.

COMPLETE SET (40) 12.50 25.00
1 Dick Anderson .30 .75
2 Trace Armstrong .30 .75
3 Bob Baumhower .30 .75
4 Kim Bokamper .30 .75
5 Tim Bowens .30 .75
6 Nick Buoniconti .40 1.00
7 Mark Clayton .40 1.00
8 Bryan Cox .30 .75
9 Larry Csonka .50 1.25
10 A.J. Duhe .30 .75
11 Mark Duper .40 1.00
12 Manny Fernandez .30 .75
13 Bob Griese .60 1.50
14 Larry Izzo .30 .75
15 Keith Jackson .30 .75
16 Jim Kiick .40 1.00
17 Bob Kuechenberg .30 .75
18 Jim Langer .40 1.00
19 Larry Little .40 1.00
20 Sam Madison .30 .75
21 Olindo Mare .30 .75
22 Dan Marino 2.00 5.00
23 Brock Marion .30 .75
24 O.J. McDuffie .30 .75
25 Nat Moore .30 .75
26 Mercury Morris .40 1.00
27 John Offerdahl .30 .75
28 Reggie Roby .30 .75
29 Tim Ruddy .30 .75
30 Jake Scott .30 .75
31 Keith Sims .30 .75
32 Dwight Stephenson .30 .75
33 Pete Stoyanovich .30 .75
34 Patrick Surtain .30 .75
35 Jason Taylor .30 .75
36 Zach Thomas .50 1.25
37 Paul Warfield .50 1.25
38 Richmond Webb .30 .75
39 Ricky Williams .40 1.00
40 Garo Yepremian .30 .75

2006 Dolphins Topps

COMPLETE SET (12) 3.00 6.00
MIA1 Jason Taylor .25 .60
MIA2 Chris Chambers .25 .60
MIA3 Zach Thomas .30 .75
MIA4 Randy McMichael .20 .50
MIA5 Ronnie Brown .30 .75
MIA6 Marty Booker .20 .50
MIA7 Travis Minor .20 .50
MIA8 Kevin Carter .20 .50
MIA9 Travis Daniels .20 .50
MIA10 Daunte Culpepper .25 .60
MIA11 Jason Allen .25 .60
MIA12 Derek Hagan .25 .60

2007 Dolphins Donruss Playoff Super Bowl XLI Card Show

These cards were issued via a wrapper redemption program at the Donruss booth at the 2007 Super Bowl XLI Card Show in Miami. Each card features the Super Bowl XLI logo on the front and was issued one card at a time in exchange for the collector opening three packs of 2006 Topps football products at the booth.

SB9 Dan Marino 2.50 6.00
SB10 Chris Chambers .60 1.50
SB11 Jason Taylor .50 1.25
SB12 Marty Booker .50 1.25

2007 Dolphins Topps

COMPLETE SET (12) 2.50 5.00
1 Jason Taylor .25 .60
2 Ronnie Brown .25 .60
3 Chris Chambers .25 .60
4 Zach Thomas .25 .60
5 David Martin .20 .50
6 Marty Booker .20 .50
7 Derek Hagan .20 .50
8 Joey Porter .20 .50
9 Daunte Culpepper .25 .60
10 Channing Crowder .20 .50
11 Ted Ginn Jr. .25 .60
12 John Beck .30 .75

2007 Dolphins Topps Super Bowl XLI Card Show

These cards were issued via a wrapper redemption program at the Topps booth at the 2007 Super Bowl XLI Card Show in Miami. Each card features the Super Bowl XLI logo on the front and was issued one card at a time in exchange for the collector opening three packs of 2006 Topps football products at the booth.

1 Dan Marino	2.50	6.00
2 Zach Thomas	.50	1.25
3 Ronnie Brown	.75	2.00
4 Joey Harrington	.50	1.25

2007 Dolphins Upper Deck Super Bowl XLI Card Show

These cards were issued via a wrapper redemption program at the Upper Deck booth at the 2007 Super Bowl XLI Card Show in Miami. Each card was serial numbered to 2006 and features the Super Bowl XLI logo on the front.

5 Dan Marino	2.50	6.00
6 Bob Griese	.75	2.00
7 Wes Welker	.50	1.25
8 Jason Allen	.50	1.25

2008 Dolphins Topps

COMPLETE SET (12)	2.50	5.00
1 Josh McCown	.20	.50
2 John Beck	.20	.50
3 Ted Ginn Jr.	.25	.60
4 Ronnie Brown	.25	.60
5 Jason Taylor	.25	.60
6 Derek Hagan	.20	.50
7 David Martin	.20	.50
8 Channing Crowder	.20	.50
9 Joey Porter	.20	.50
10 Lorenzo Booker	.20	.50
11 Chad Henne	.40	1.00
12 Jake Long	.40	1.00

1991 Domino's Quarterbacks

This 50-card NFL quarterback set was produced by Upper Deck and sponsored by Domino's Pizza in conjunction with Coca-Cola and NFL Properties. These standard-size cards were part of a national promotion that was kicked off during the August 3, 1991, "NBC Sportsworld" telecast of "NFL Quarterback Challenge". The cards were distributed through the 5,000 Domino's restaurants across the country. During August, or while supplies lasted, customers who ordered the Domino's Pizza NFL Kick-off Deal received two medium cheese pizzas, four cans of Coke, Diet Coke, or Coke Classic, and one free foil pack with four NFL Quarterback cards, all for 9.99. The first 32 cards in the set were active quarterbacks arranged in alphabetical order by teams. Cards 33-46 feature retired quarterbacks in alphabetical order by player name and cards 47-49 depict quarterback duos from the same team but different eras.

COMPLETE SET (50)	2.40	6.00
1 Chris Miller	.02	.10
2 Jim Kelly	.08	.25
3 Jim Harbaugh	.08	.25
4 Boomer Esiason	.05	.15
5 Bernie Kosar	.05	.15
6 Troy Aikman	.20	.50
7 John Elway	.40	1.00
8 Rodney Peete	.02	.10
9 Andre Ware	.02	.10
10 Anthony Dilweg	.02	.10
11 Warren Moon	.08	.25
12 Jeff George	.05	.15
13 Jim Everett	.02	.10
14 Jay Schroeder	.02	.10
15 Wade Wilson	.02	.10
16 Dan Marino	.40	1.00
17 Phil Simms	.05	.15
18 Jeff Hostetler	.02	.10
19 Ken O'Brien	.02	.10
20 Timm Rosenbach	.02	.10
21 Bubby Brister	.02	.10
22 Steve DeBerg	.05	.15
23 Randall Cunningham	.08	.25
24 Steve Walsh	.02	.10
25 Billy Joe Tolliver	.02	.10
26 Steve Young	.15	.40
27 Dave Krieg	.02	.10
28 Dan McGwire	.02	.10
29 Vinny Testaverde	.05	.15
30 Stan Humphries	.02	.10
31 Mark Rypien	.02	.10
32 Terry Bradshaw	.20	.50
33 John Brodie	.05	.15
34 Len Dawson	.05	.15
35 Dan Fouts	.05	.15
36 Otto Graham	.15	.40
37 Bob Griese	.08	.25
38 Sonny Jurgensen	.08	.25
39 Daryle Lamonica	.05	.15
40 Archie Manning	.05	.15
41 Jim Plunkett	.05	.15
42 Bart Starr	.20	.50
43 Roger Staubach	.20	.50
44 Joe Theismann	.08	.25
45 Y.A. Tittle	.08	.25
46 Johnny Unitas	.20	.50
47 Cowboy Gunslingers Troy Aikman Roger Staubach	.20	.50
48 Cajun Connection Bubby Brister Terry Bradshaw	.15	.40
49 Dolphin Duo Dan Marino Bob Griese	.30	.75
50 Checklist Card	.02	.10

1996 Donruss

The 1996 Donruss set was issued in one series totalling 240 cards. The only subset included was Rookies (208-237). The fronts feature color action player photos. The backs carry a small player photo with biographical information and career statistics.

COMPLETE SET (240)	7.50	20.00
1 Barry Sanders	.60	1.50
2 Flipper Anderson	.02	.10
3 Ben Coates	.07	.20
4 Rob Johnson	.15	.40
5 Rodney Hampton	.07	.20
6 Desmond Howard	.07	.20
7 Craig Heyward	.02	.10
8 Alvin Harper	.02	.10
9 Todd Collins	.07	.20
10 Ken Norton Jr.	.02	.10
11 Stan Humphries	.07	.20
12 Aeneas Williams	.02	.10
13 Jeff Hostetler	.02	.10
14 Frank Sanders	.07	.20
15 J.J. Birden	.02	.10
16 Bryce Paup	.02	.10
17 Bill Brooks	.02	.10
18 Kevin Williams	.02	.10
19 Boomer Esiason	.07	.20
20 O.J. McDuffie	.07	.20
21 Eric Swann	.02	.10
22 Neil Smith	.07	.20
23 Charlie Garner	.07	.20
24 Greg Lloyd	.07	.20
25 Willie Jackson	.07	.20
26 Shawn Jefferson	.02	.10
27 Rodney Peete	.02	.10
28 Michael Westbrook	.15	.40
29 J.J. Stokes	.15	.40
30 Troy Aikman	.40	1.00
31 Sean Dawkins	.02	.10
32 Larry Centers	.07	.20
33 Herschel Walker	.07	.20
34 Stoney Case	.02	.10
35 Kevin Greene	.07	.20
36 Quinn Early	.02	.10
37 Fred Barnett	.02	.10
38 Andre Coleman	.02	.10
39 Mark Chmura	.07	.20
40 Adrian Murrell	.07	.20
41 Roosevelt Potts	.02	.10
42 Jay Novacek	.02	.10
43 Derrick Alexander WR	.07	.20
44 Ken Dilger	.07	.20
45 Rob Moore	.07	.20
46 Cris Carter	.15	.40
47 Jeff Blake	.15	.40
48 Derek Loville	.02	.10
49 Tyrone Wheatley	.07	.20
50 Terrell Fletcher	.02	.10
51 Sherman Williams	.02	.10
52 Justin Armour	.02	.10
53 Kordell Stewart	.15	.40
54 Tim Brown	.15	.40
55 Kevin Carter	.02	.10
56 Andre Rison	.07	.20
57 James O.Stewart	.07	.20
58 Brent Jones	.02	.10
59 Erik Kramer	.02	.10
60 Floyd Turner	.02	.10
61 Ricky Watters	.07	.20
62 Hardy Nickerson	.02	.10
63 Aaron Craver	.02	.10
64 Dave Krieg	.02	.10
65 Warren Moon	.07	.20
66 Wayne Chrebet	.20	.50
67 Napoleon Kaufman	.15	.40
68 Terance Mathis	.02	.10
69 Chad May	.02	.10
70 Andre Reed	.07	.20
71 Reggie White	.15	.40
72 Brett Favre	.75	2.00
73 Chris Zorich	.02	.10
74 Kerry Collins	.15	.40
75 Herman Moore	.07	.20
76 Yancey Thigpen	.07	.20
77 Glenn Foley	.07	.20
78 Quentin Coryatt	.02	.10
79 Terry Kirby	.07	.20
80 Edgar Bennett	.07	.20
81 Mark Brunell	.25	.60
82 Heath Shuler	.07	.20
83 Gus Frerotte	.07	.20
84 Deion Sanders	.25	.60
85 Calvin Williams	.02	.10
86 Junior Seau	.15	.40
87 Jim Kelly	.15	.40
88 Daryl Johnston	.07	.20
89 Irving Fryar	.07	.20
90 Brian Blades	.02	.10
91 Willie Davis	.02	.10
92 Jerome Bettis	.15	.40
93 Marcus Allen	.15	.40
94 Jeff Graham	.02	.10
95 Rick Mirer	.07	.20
96 Harvey Williams	.02	.10
97 Steve Atwater	.02	.10
98 Carl Pickens	.07	.20
99 Darick Holmes	.02	.10
100 Bruce Smith	.07	.20
101 Vinny Testaverde	.07	.20
102 Thurman Thomas	.15	.40
103 Drew Bledsoe	.25	.60
104 Bernie Parmalee	.02	.10
105 Greg Hill	.07	.20
106 Steve McNair	.30	.75
107 Andre Hastings	.02	.10
108 Eric Metcalf	.02	.10
109 Kimble Anders	.07	.20
110 Steve Tasker	.02	.10
111 Mark Carrier WR	.02	.10
112 Jerry Rice	.40	1.00
113 Joey Galloway	.15	.40
114 Robert Smith	.07	.20
115 Hugh Douglas	.07	.20
116 Willie McGinest	.02	.10
117 Terrell Davis	.30	.75
118 Cortez Kennedy	.02	.10
119 Marshall Faulk	.20	.50
120 Michael Haynes	.02	.10
121 Isaac Bruce	.15	.40
122 Brian Mitchell	.02	.10
123 Bryan Cox	.02	.10
124 Tamarick Vanover	.07	.20
125 William Floyd	.07	.20
126 Chris Chandler	.07	.20
127 Carnell Lake	.02	.10
128 Aaron Bailey	.02	.10
129 Darnay Scott	.07	.20
130 Darren Woodson	.07	.20
131 Ernie Mills	.02	.10
132 Charles Haley	.07	.20
133 Rocket Ismail	.02	.10
134 Bert Emanuel	.07	.20
135 Lake Dawson	.02	.10
136 Jake Reed	.07	.20
137 Dave Brown	.02	.10
138 Steve Bono	.02	.10
139 Terry Allen	.07	.20
140 Errict Rhett	.07	.20
141 Rod Woodson	.07	.20
142 Charles Johnson	.02	.10
143 Emmitt Smith	.60	1.50
144 Ki-Jana Carter	.07	.20
145 Garrison Hearst	.07	.20
146 Rashaan Salaam	.07	.20
147 Tony Boselli	.02	.10
148 Derrick Thomas	.15	.40
149 Mark Seay	.02	.10
150 Derrick Alexander DE	.02	.10
151 Christian Fauria	.02	.10
152 Aaron Hayden	.02	.10
153 Chris Warren	.07	.20
154 Dave Meggett	.02	.10
155 Jeff George	.07	.20
156 Jackie Harris	.02	.10
157 Michael Irvin	.15	.40
158 Scott Mitchell	.07	.20
159 Trent Dilfer	.15	.40
160 Kyle Brady	.02	.10
161 Dan Marino	.75	2.00
162 Curtis Martin	.30	.75
163 Mario Bates	.07	.20
164 Erric Pegram	.02	.10
165 Eric Zeier	.02	.10
166 Rodney Thomas	.02	.10
167 Neil O'Donnell	.07	.20
168 Warren Sapp	.02	.10
169 Jim Harbaugh	.07	.20
170 Henry Ellard	.02	.10
171 Anthony Miller	.07	.20
172 Derrick Moore	.02	.10
173 John Elway	.75	2.00
174 Vincent Brisby	.02	.10
175 Antonio Freeman	.15	.40
176 Chris Sanders	.07	.20
177 Steve Young	.30	.75
178 Shannon Sharpe	.07	.20
179 Brett Perriman	.02	.10
180 Orlando Thomas	.02	.10
181 Eric Bjornson	.02	.10
182 Natrone Means	.07	.20
183 Jim Everett	.02	.10
184 Curtis Conway	.15	.40
185 Robert Brooks	.15	.40
186 Tony Martin	.07	.20
187 Mark Carrier DB	.02	.10
188 LeShon Johnson	.02	.10
189 Bernie Kosar	.02	.10
190 Ray Zellars	.02	.10
191 Steve Walsh	.02	.10
192 Craig Erickson	.02	.10
193 Tommy Maddox	.15	.40
194 Leslie O'Neal	.02	.10
195 Harold Green	.02	.10
196 Steve Beuerlein	.07	.20
197 Ronald Moore	.02	.10
198 Leslie Shepherd	.02	.10
199 Leroy Hoard	.02	.10
200 Michael Jackson	.07	.20
201 Will Moore	.02	.10
202 Ricky Ervins	.02	.10
203 Keith Jennings	.02	.10
204 Eric Green	.02	.10
205 Mark Rypien	.02	.10
206 Torrance Small	.02	.10
207 Sean Gilbert	.02	.10
208 Mike Alstott RC	.40	1.00
209 Willie Anderson RC	.02	.10
210 Alex Molden RC	.02	.10
211 Jonathan Ogden RC	.15	.40
212 Stepfret Williams RC	.07	.20
213 Jeff Lewis RC	.07	.20
214 Regan Upshaw RC	.02	.10
215 Daryl Gardener RC	.02	.10
216 Danny Kanell RC	.15	.40
217 John Mobley RC	.02	.10
218 Reggie Brown LB RC	.02	.10
219 Muhsin Muhammad RC	.40	1.00
220 Kevin Hardy RC	.15	.40
221 Stanley Pritchett RC	.07	.20
222 Cedric Jones RC	.02	.10
223 Marco Battaglia RC	.02	.10
224 Duane Clemons RC	.02	.10
225 Jerald Moore RC	.07	.20
226 Simeon Rice RC	.40	1.00
227 Chris Darkins RC	.02	.10
228 Bobby Hoying RC	.15	.40
229 Stephen Davis RC	.60	1.50
230 Walt Harris RC	.02	.10
231 Jermane Mayberry RC	.02	.10
232 Tony Brackens RC	.15	.40
233 Eric Moulds RC	.50	1.25
234 Alex Van Dyke RC	.07	.20
235 Marvin Harrison RC	1.00	2.50
236 Rickey Dudley RC	.15	.40
237 Terrell Owens RC	1.00	2.50
238 Jerry Rice Checklist Card	.15	.40
239 Dan Marino Checklist Card	.15	.40
240 Emmitt Smith Checklist Card	.15	.40

1996 Donruss Press Proofs

COMPLETE SET (240)	125.00	250.00
*STARS: 5X TO 12X BASIC CARDS		
*RCs: 2.5X TO 6X BASIC CARDS		
STATED ODDS 1:5		
ANNOUNCED PRINT RUN 2000 SETS		

1996 Donruss Elite

COMPLETE SET (20)	40.00	100.00
STAT.PRINT RUN 10,000 SER.#'d SETS		
*GOLD STARS: .8X TO 2X SILVERS		
GOLD STAT.PRINT RUN 2000 SER.#'d SETS		
1 Emmitt Smith	5.00	12.00
2 Barry Sanders	5.00	12.00
3 Marshall Faulk	1.50	4.00
4 Curtis Martin	2.50	6.00
5 Junior Seau	1.25	3.00
6 Troy Aikman	3.00	8.00
7 Steve Young	2.50	6.00
8 Dan Marino	6.00	15.00
9 Brett Favre	6.00	15.00
10 John Elway	6.00	15.00
11 Kerry Collins	1.25	3.00
12 Drew Bledsoe	2.00	5.00
13 Jerry Rice	3.00	8.00
14 Keyshawn Johnson	1.50	4.00
15 Deion Sanders	2.00	5.00
16 Isaac Bruce	1.25	3.00
17 Rashaan Salaam	.60	1.50
18 Tim Biakabutuka	.75	2.00
19 Lawrence Phillips	.75	2.00
20 Robert Brooks	1.25	3.00

1996 Donruss Hit List

COMPLETE SET (20)	40.00	100.00
STATED PRINT RUN 10,000 SERIAL #'d SETS		
*PROMOS: .4X TO 1X BASIC INSERTS		
1 Bruce Smith	.50	1.25
2 Barry Sanders	4.00	10.00
3 Kevin Hardy	1.00	2.50
4 Greg Lloyd	.50	1.25
5 Brett Favre	5.00	12.00
6 Emmitt Smith	4.00	10.00
7 Kerry Collins	1.00	2.50
8 Ken Norton Jr.	.25	.60
9 Steve Atwater	.25	.60
10 Curtis Martin	2.00	5.00
11 Chris Warren	.50	1.25
12 Steve Young	2.00	5.00
13 Marshall Faulk	1.25	3.00
14 Junior Seau	1.00	2.50
15 Lawrence Phillips	2.50	6.00
16 Troy Aikman	2.50	6.00
17 Jerry Rice	2.50	6.00
18 Dan Marino	5.00	12.00
19 Reggie White	1.00	2.50
20 John Elway	5.00	12.00

1996 Donruss Rated Rookies

COMPLETE SET (10)	10.00	25.00
1 Keyshawn Johnson	1.25	3.00
2 Terry Glenn	1.25	3.00
3 Tim Biakabutuka	1.25	3.00
4 Bobby Engram	.75	2.00
5 Leeland McElroy	.75	2.00
6 Eddie George	1.50	4.00
7 Lawrence Phillips	1.25	3.00
8 Derrick Mayes	.75	2.00
9 Karim Abdul-Jabbar	1.25	3.00
10 Eddie Kennison		

1996 Donruss Stop Action

COMPLETE SET (10)	25.00	60.00
STATED PRINT RUN 4000 SERIAL #'d SETS		
RANDOM INSERTS IN JUMBO PACKS		
1 Deion Sanders	2.00	5.00
2 Troy Aikman	3.00	8.00
3 Brett Favre	6.00	15.00
4 Steve Young	2.50	6.00
5 Joey Galloway	1.25	3.00
6 Dan Marino	6.00	15.00
7 Jerry Rice	3.00	8.00
8 Emmitt Smith	5.00	12.00
9 Isaac Bruce	1.25	3.00
10 Barry Sanders	5.00	12.00

1996 Donruss What If?

COMPLETE SET (10)	25.00	60.00
RANDOM INSERTS IN HOBBY PACKS		
STATED PRINT RUN 5000 SERIAL #'d SETS		
1 Troy Aikman	3.00	8.00
2 Jerry Rice	3.00	8.00
3 Barry Sanders	5.00	12.00
4 Drew Bledsoe	2.00	5.00
5 Deion Sanders	2.00	5.00
6 Brett Favre	6.00	15.00
7 Dan Marino	6.00	15.00
8 Steve Young	2.50	6.00
9 Emmitt Smith	5.00	12.00
10 John Elway	6.00	15.00

1996 Donruss Will To Win

COMPLETE SET (10)	30.00	80.00
RANDOM INSERTS IN RETAIL PACKS		
STATED PRINT RUN 5000 SERIAL #'d SETS		
1 Emmitt Smith	5.00	12.00
2 Brett Favre	6.00	15.00
3 Curtis Martin	2.50	6.00
4 Jerry Rice	3.00	8.00
5 Barry Sanders	5.00	12.00
6 Errict Rhett	.60	1.50
7 Troy Aikman	3.00	8.00
8 Dan Marino	6.00	15.00
9 Steve Young	2.50	6.00
10 John Elway	6.00	15.00

1997 Donruss

The 1997 Donruss set was issued in one series totaling 230 cards.The cards were distributed in 10-card hobby packs with a suggested retail price of $1.99 and 14-card blister packs with a suggested retail of $2.99. Blister packs also contained one ad/cover promo card as listed below. Cardfronts feature color action player photos with foil treatment, while the backs carry player information.

COMPLETE SET (230)	7.50	20.00
1 Dan Marino	.75	2.00
2 Brett Favre	.75	2.00
3 Emmitt Smith	.60	1.50
4 Eddie George	.20	.50
5 Karim Abdul-Jabbar	.10	.30
6 Terrell Davis	.25	.60
7 Curtis Martin	.25	.60
8 Drew Bledsoe	.25	.60
9 Jerry Rice	.40	1.00
10 Troy Aikman	.40	1.00
11 Barry Sanders	.60	1.50
12 Mark Brunell	.25	.60
13 Kerry Collins	.20	.50
14 Steve Young	.25	.60
15 Kordell Stewart	.20	.50
16 Eddie Kennison	.10	.30
17 Terry Glenn	.20	.50
18 John Elway	.75	2.00
19 Joey Galloway	.10	.30
20 Deion Sanders	.20	.50
21 Keyshawn Johnson	.20	.50
22 Lawrence Phillips	.07	.20
23 Ricky Watters	.10	.30
24 Marvin Harrison	.20	.50
25 Bobby Engram	.10	.30
26 Marshall Faulk	.25	.60
27 Carl Pickens	.10	.30
28 Isaac Bruce	.20	.50
29 Herman Moore	.10	.30
30 Jerome Bettis	.20	.50
31 Rashaan Salaam	.07	.20
32 Errict Rhett	.07	.20
33 Tim Biakabutuka	.10	.30
34 Robert Brooks	.10	.30
35 Antonio Freeman	.20	.50
36 Steve McNair	.25	.60
37 Jeff Blake	.10	.30
38 Tony Banks	.10	.30
39 Terrell Owens	.25	.60
40 Eric Moulds	.20	.50
41 Leeland McElroy	.07	.20
42 Chris Sanders	.07	.20
43 Thurman Thomas	.20	.50
44 Bruce Smith	.10	.30
45 Reggie White	.20	.50
46 Chris Warren	.10	.30
47 J.J. Stokes	.10	.30
48 Ben Coates	.10	.30
49 Tim Brown	.20	.50
50 Marcus Allen	.20	.50
51 Michael Irvin	.20	.50
52 William Floyd	.10	.30
53 Ken Dilger	.07	.20
54 Bobby Taylor	.07	.20
55 Keenan McCardell	.10	.30
56 Raymont Harris	.07	.20
57 Keith Byars	.07	.20
58 O.J. McDuffie	.10	.30
59 Robert Smith	.10	.30
60 Bert Emanuel	.10	.30
61 Rick Mirer	.07	.20
62 Vinny Testaverde	.10	.30
63 Kyle Brady	.07	.20
64 Mark Bruener	.07	.20
65 Neil O'Donnell	.10	.30
66 Anthony Johnson	.07	.20
67 Ken Norton	.07	.20
68 Warren Sapp	.10	.30
69 Amani Toomer	.10	.30
70 Simeon Rice	.10	.30
71 Kevin Hardy	.07	.20
72 Junior Seau	.20	.50
73 Neil Smith	.10	.30
74 LeShon Johnson	.07	.20
75 Quinn Early	.07	.20
76 Andre Reed	.10	.30
77 Jake Reed	.10	.30
78 Elvis Grbac	.10	.30
79 Tyrone Wheatley	.10	.30
80 Adrian Murrell	.10	.30
81 Fred Barnett	.07	.20
82 Darrell Green	.10	.30
83 Stan Humphries	.10	.30
84 Troy Drayton	.07	.20
85 Steve Atwater	.07	.20
86 Quentin Coryatt	.07	.20
87 Dan Wilkinson	.07	.20
88 Scott Mitchell	.10	.30
89 Willie McGinest	.07	.20
90 Kevin Smith	.07	.20
91 Gus Frerotte	.07	.20
92 Byron Bam Morris	.07	.20
93 Darick Holmes	.07	.20
94 Zach Thomas	.20	.50
95 Tom Carter	.07	.20
96 Cortez Kennedy	.07	.20
97 Kevin Williams	.07	.20
98 Michael Haynes	.07	.20
99 Lamont Warren	.07	.20
100 Jeff Graham	.07	.20
101 Alex Van Dyke	.07	.20
102 Jim Everett	.07	.20
103 Chris Chandler	.10	.30
104 Qadry Ismail	.10	.30
105 Ray Zellars	.07	.20
106 Chris T. Jones	.07	.20
107 Charlie Garner	.10	.30
108 Bobby Hoying	.10	.30
109 Mark Chmura	.10	.30
110 Cris Carter	.20	.50
111 Darnay Scott	.10	.30
112 Anthony Miller	.07	.20
113 Desmond Howard	.10	.30
114 Terance Mathis	.10	.30
115 Rodney Hampton	.10	.30
116 Napoleon Kaufman	.20	.50
117 Jim Harbaugh	.10	.30
118 Shannon Sharpe	.10	.30
119 Irving Fryar	.10	.30
120 Garrison Hearst	.10	.30
121 Terry Allen	.20	.50
122 Larry Centers	.10	.30
123 Sean Dawkins	.07	.20
124 Jeff George	.10	.30
125 Tony Martin	.10	.30
126 Mike Alstott	.20	.50
127 Rickey Dudley	.10	.30
128 Kevin Carter	.07	.20
129 Derrick Alexander WR	.10	.30
130 Greg Lloyd	.07	.20
131 Bryce Paup	.07	.20
132 Derrick Thomas	.20	.50
133 Greg Hill	.07	.20
134 Jamal Anderson	.20	.50
135 Curtis Conway	.10	.30
136 Frank Sanders	.10	.30
137 Brett Perriman	.07	.20
138 Edgar Bennett	.10	.30
139 Wayne Chrebet	.20	.50
140 Natrone Means	.10	.30
141 Eric Metcalf	.10	.30
142 Trent Dilfer	.20	.50
143 Terry Kirby	.10	.30
144 Johnnie Morton	.10	.30
145 Dale Carter	.07	.20
146 Michael Westbrook	.10	.30
147 Stanley Pritchett	.07	.20
148 Todd Collins	.07	.20
149 Tamarick Vanover	.10	.30
150 Kevin Greene	.10	.30
151 Lamar Lathon	.07	.20
152 Muhsin Muhammad	.10	.30
153 Dorsey Levens	.20	.50
154 Rod Woodson	.10	.30
155 Brent Jones	.07	.20
156 Michael Jackson	.10	.30
157 Shawn Jefferson	.07	.20
158 Kimble Anders	.10	.30
159 Sean Gilbert	.07	.20
160 Carnell Lake	.07	.20
161 Darren Woodson	.07	.20
162 Dave Meggett	.07	.20
163 Henry Ellard	.07	.20
164 Eric Swann	.07	.20
165 Tony Boselli	.07	.20
166 Daryl Johnston	.10	.30
167 Willie Jackson	.07	.20
168 Wesley Walls	.10	.30
169 Mario Bates	.07	.20
170 Lake Dawson	.07	.20
171 Mike Mamula	.07	.20
172 Ed McCaffrey	.10	.30
173 Tony Brackens	.07	.20
174 Craig Heyward	.07	.20
175 Harvey Williams	.07	.20
176 Dave Brown	.07	.20
177 Aaron Glenn	.07	.20
178 Jeff Hostetler	.07	.20
179 Alvin Harper	.07	.20
180 Ty Detmer	.10	.30
181 James Jett	.10	.30
182 James O.Stewart	.10	.30
183 Warren Moon	.20	.50
184 Herschel Walker	.10	.30
185 Ki-Jana Carter	.07	.20
186 Leslie O'Neal	.07	.20
187 Danny Kanell	.07	.20
188 Eric Bjornson	.07	.20
189 Alex Molden	.07	.20
190 Bryant Young	.07	.20
191 Merton Hanks	.07	.20
192 Heath Shuler	.07	.20
193 Brian Blades	.07	.20
194 Steve Bono	.10	.30
195 Wayne Simmons	.07	.20
196 Warrick Dunn RC	.60	1.50
197 Peter Boulware RC	.20	.50
198 David LaFleur RC	.07	.20
199 Shawn Springs RC	.10	.30
200 Reidel Anthony RC	.20	.50
201 Jim Druckenmiller RC	.10	.30
202 Orlando Pace RC	.20	.50
203 Yatil Green RC	.10	.30
204 Bryant Westbrook RC	.07	.20
205 Tiki Barber RC	1.25	3.00
206 James Farrior RC	.20	.50
207 Rae Carruth RC	.07	.20
208 Danny Wuerffel RC	.20	.50
209 Corey Dillon RC	.75	2.00
210 Ike Hilliard RC	.30	.75
211 Tony Gonzalez RC	.75	2.00
212 Antowain Smith RC	.50	1.25
213 Pat Barnes RC	.20	.50
214 Troy Davis RC	.10	.30
215 Byron Hanspard RC	.10	.30
216 Joey Kent RC	.20	.50
217 Jake Plummer RC	.75	2.00
218 Kenny Holmes RC	.20	.50
219 Darnell Autry RC	.10	.30
220 Darrell Russell RC	.07	.20
221 Walter Jones RC	.20	.50
222 Dwayne Rudd RC	.20	.50
223 Tom Knight RC	.07	.20
224 Kevin Lockett RC	.10	.30
225 Will Blackwell RC	.10	.30
226 Dan Marino Checklist back	.15	.40
227 Brett Favre CL	.15	.40
228 Emmitt Smith Checklist back	.20	.50
229 Barry Sanders CL	.20	.50
230 Jerry Rice Checklist back	.08	.25
P1 Drew Bledsoe (Ad back promo)	.40	1.00
P2 Mark Brunell (Ad back promo)	.40	1.00
P3 Barry Sanders Promo	.60	1.50

1997 Donruss Press Proofs Gold Die Cuts

COMPLETE SET (230)	200.00	400.00
*STARS: 8X TO 20X BASIC CARDS		
*RCs: 5X TO 12X BASIC CARDS		
GOLD STATED PRINT RUN 500 SETS		

1997 Donruss Press Proofs Silver

COMPLETE SET (230)	75.00	150.00
*STARS: 3X TO 8X BASIC CARDS		
*RCs: 2.5X TO 6X BASIC CARDS		
STATED PRINT RUN 1500 SER.#'d SETS		

1997 Donruss Elite

COMPLETE SET (20)	40.00	100.00
SILVER STATED PRINT RUN 5000 #'d SETS		
*GOLD CARDS: .8X TO 2X SILVERS		
GOLD STATED PRINT RUN 2000 #'d SETS		
1 Emmitt Smith	5.00	12.00
2 Dan Marino	6.00	15.00
3 Brett Favre	6.00	15.00
4 Curtis Martin	2.00	5.00
5 Terrell Davis	2.00	5.00
6 Barry Sanders	5.00	12.00
7 Drew Bledsoe	2.00	5.00
8 Mark Brunell	2.00	5.00
9 Troy Aikman	3.00	8.00
10 Jerry Rice	3.00	8.00
11 Steve McNair	2.00	5.00
12 Kerry Collins	1.50	4.00
13 John Elway	6.00	15.00
14 Eddie George	1.50	4.00
15 Karim Abdul-Jabbar	1.00	2.50
16 Kordell Stewart	1.50	4.00
17 Jerome Bettis	1.50	4.00
18 Terry Glenn	1.50	4.00
19 Errict Rhett	.60	1.50
20 Carl Pickens	1.00	2.50

1997 Donruss Legends of the Fall

COMPLETE SET (10)	30.00	80.00
STATED PRINT RUN 10,000 #'d SETS		
*CANVAS CARDS: .6X TO 1.5X BASIC INSERTS		
CANVAS PRINT RUN FIRST 500 SETS		
1 Troy Aikman	3.00	8.00
2 Barry Sanders	5.00	12.00
3 John Elway	6.00	15.00
4 Dan Marino	6.00	15.00
5 Emmitt Smith	5.00	12.00
6 Jerry Rice	3.00	8.00
7 Deion Sanders	1.50	4.00
8 Brett Favre	6.00	15.00
9 Marcus Allen	1.50	4.00
10 Steve Young	2.00	5.00

1997 Donruss Passing Grade

COMPLETE SET (16)	60.00	120.00
STATED PRINT RUN 3000 #'d SETS		
RANDOM INSERTS IN HOBBY PACKS		
1 Steve Young	2.50	6.00
2 Drew Bledsoe	2.50	6.00
3 Mark Brunell	2.50	6.00
4 Kerry Collins	2.00	5.00
5 Steve McNair	2.50	6.00
6 John Elway	8.00	20.00
7 Ty Detmer	1.25	3.00
8 Jeff Blake	1.25	3.00
9 Dan Marino	8.00	20.00
10 Kordell Stewart	2.00	5.00
11 Tony Banks	1.25	3.00
12 Brett Favre	8.00	20.00
13 Gus Frerotte	.75	2.00
14 Troy Aikman	4.00	10.00
15 Jeff George	1.25	3.00
16 Brad Johnson	2.00	5.00

1997 Donruss Rated Rookies

COMPLETE SET (10)	20.00	40.00
*MEDALISTS: 1.2X TO 3X BASIC INSERTS		
*PRESS PROOF: 1.5X TO 4X BASIC INSERTS		
1 Ike Hilliard	1.50	4.00
2 Warrick Dunn	2.50	6.00
3 Yatil Green	.60	1.50
4 Jim Druckenmiller	.60	1.50
5 Rae Carruth	.50	1.25
6 Antowain Smith	1.50	4.00
7 Tiki Barber	5.00	12.00
8 Byron Hanspard	.60	1.50
9 Reidel Anthony	1.00	2.50
10 Jake Plummer	3.00	8.00

1997 Donruss Zoning Commission

COMPLETE SET (20)	60.00	120.00
RANDOM INSERTS IN RETAIL PACKS		
STATED PRINT RUN 5000 #'d SETS		
1 Brett Favre	6.00	15.00
2 Jerry Rice	3.00	8.00
3 Jerome Bettis	1.50	4.00
4 Troy Aikman	3.00	8.00
5 Drew Bledsoe	2.00	5.00
6 Natrone Means	1.00	2.50
7 Steve Young	2.00	5.00
8 John Elway	6.00	15.00
9 Barry Sanders	5.00	12.00
10 Emmitt Smith	5.00	12.00
11 Curtis Martin	2.00	5.00
12 Terry Allen	1.50	4.00
13 Dan Marino	6.00	15.00
14 Mark Brunell	2.00	5.00
15 Terry Glenn	1.50	4.00
16 Herman Moore	1.00	2.50
17 Ricky Watters	1.00	2.50
18 Terrell Davis	2.00	5.00
19 Isaac Bruce	1.50	4.00
20 Curtis Conway	1.00	2.50

1998 Donruss Elite Promos

These cards were released in 1998 as a preview to the Donruss product which was never printed due to the bankruptcy of Pinnacle Brands. Each card was serial numbered of 2500 but it is unknown how many cards actually made it out into the secondary market.

1 Brett Favre	3.00	8.00
6 Drew Bledsoe	1.25	3.00
7 Troy Aikman	2.00	5.00
13 Steve McNair	1.25	3.00
15 Steve Young	1.50	4.00
16 Terry Glenn	1.00	2.50
17 Deion Sanders	1.25	3.00
20 Jake Plummer	1.00	2.50

1999 Donruss

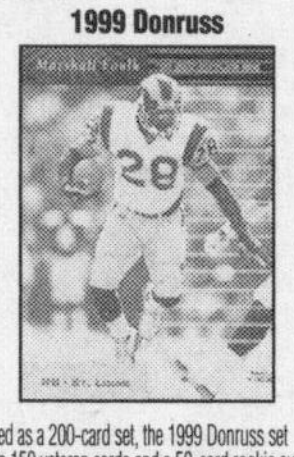

Released as a 200-card set, the 1999 Donruss set features 150 veteran cards and a 50-card rookie subset inserted at one in four packs. Two parallel sets were released also, each numbered to a specifc season stat, or a career stat. Donurss was packaged in 24-pack boxes containing seven cards each.

COMPLETE SET (200)	40.00	100.00
COMP.SET w/o SP's (150)	10.00	20.00
1 Jake Plummer	.20	.50
2 Rob Moore	.15	.40
3 Adrian Murrell	.20	.50
4 Frank Sanders	.15	.40
5 Jamal Anderson	.20	.50
6 Tim Dwight	.20	.50
7 Terance Mathis	.15	.40
8 Chris Chandler	.20	.50
9 Byron Hanspard	.15	.40
10 Priest Holmes	.25	.60
11 Jermaine Lewis	.15	.40
12 Errict Rhett	.15	.40
13 Doug Flutie	.25	.60
14 Eric Moulds	.20	.50
15 Antowain Smith	.15	.40
16 Thurman Thomas	.25	.60
17 Andre Reed	.25	.60
18 Bruce Smith	.25	.60
19 Tim Biakabutuka	.20	.50
20 Rae Carruth UER (photo actually Mark Carrier)	.15	.40
21 Muhsin Muhammad	.20	.50
22 Curtis Enis	.15	.40
23 Curtis Conway	.20	.50
24 Bobby Engram	.20	.50
25 Corey Dillon	.20	.50
26 Carl Pickens	.20	.50
27 Jeff Blake	.20	.50
28 Darnay Scott	.15	.40
29 Ty Detmer	.20	.50
30 Leslie Shepherd	.15	.40
31 Emmitt Smith	.60	1.50
32 Troy Aikman	.40	1.00
33 Michael Irvin	.25	.60
34 Deion Sanders	.25	.60
35 Rocket Ismail	.20	.50
36 John Elway	.75	2.00
37 Terrell Davis	.25	.60
38 Ed McCaffrey	.20	.50
39 Shannon Sharpe	.25	.60
40 Rod Smith	.20	.50
41 Bubby Brister	.15	.40
42 Brian Griese	.20	.50
43 Barry Sanders	.60	1.50
44 Charlie Batch	.20	.50
45 Herman Moore	.20	.50
46 Germane Crowell	.15	.40
47 Johnnie Morton	.20	.50
48 Ron Rivers	.15	.40
49 Brett Favre	.75	2.00
50 Antonio Freeman	.20	.50
51 Dorsey Levens	.20	.50
52 Mark Chmura	.15	.40
53 Corey Bradford	.20	.50
54 Bill Schroeder	.20	.50
55 Peyton Manning ERR (stats date listed on back '88)	.75	2.00
56 Marvin Harrison	.25	.60
57 E.G. Green	.15	.40
58 Fred Taylor	.20	.50
59 Mark Brunell	.20	.50
60 Tavian Banks	.15	.40
61 Jimmy Smith	.20	.50
62 Keenan McCardell	.20	.50

63 Warren Moon	.25	.60
64 Derrick Alexander WR	.15	.40
65 Byron Bam Morris	.15	.40
66 Elvis Grbac	.15	.40
67 Andre Rison	.20	.50
68 Dan Marino	.75	2.00
69 Karim Abdul-Jabbar	.20	.50
70 O.J. McDuffie	.20	.50
71 Tony Martin	.20	.50
72 Randy Moss	.25	.60
73 Cris Carter	.25	.60
74 Randall Cunningham	.25	.60
75 Robert Smith	.20	.50
76 Jeff George	.15	.40
77 Jake Reed	.20	.50
78 Terry Allen	.20	.50
79 Drew Bledsoe	.25	.60
80 Terry Glenn	.20	.50
81 Ben Coates	.20	.50
82 Tony Simmons	.15	.40
83 Cam Cleeland	.15	.40
84 Eddie Kennison	.20	.50
85 Kerry Collins	.20	.50
86 Ike Hilliard	.20	.50
87 Gary Brown	.15	.40
88 Joe Jurevicius	.15	.40
89 Kent Graham	.15	.40
90 Wayne Chrebet	.20	.50
91 Keyshawn Johnson	.20	.50
92 Curtis Martin	.25	.60
93 Vinny Testaverde	.20	.50
94 Tim Brown	.25	.60
95 Napoleon Kaufman	.15	.40
96 Charles Woodson	.25	.60
97 Tyrone Wheatley	.20	.50
98 Rich Gannon	.20	.50
99 Charles Johnson	.15	.40
100 Duce Staley	.20	.50
101 Kordell Stewart	.20	.50
102 Jerome Bettis	.25	.60
103 Hines Ward	.25	.60
104 Ryan Leaf	.20	.50
105 Natrone Means	.20	.50
106 Jim Harbaugh	.20	.50
107 Junior Seau	.25	.60
108 Mikhael Ricks	.15	.40
109 Jerry Rice	.50	1.25
110 Steve Young	.30	.75
111 Garrison Hearst	.20	.50
112 Terrell Owens	.25	.60
113 Lawrence Phillips	.20	.50
114 J.J. Stokes	.15	.40
115 Sean Dawkins	.15	.40
116 Derrick Mayes	.15	.40
117 Joey Galloway	.20	.50
118 Jon Kitna	.20	.50
119 Ahman Green	.20	.50
120 Ricky Watters	.20	.50
121 Isaac Bruce	.25	.60
122 Marshall Faulk	.25	.60
123 Az-Zahir Hakim	.15	.40
124 Warrick Dunn	.20	.50
125 Mike Alstott	.25	.60
126 Trent Dilfer	.20	.50
127 Reidel Anthony	.15	.40
128 Jacquez Green	.15	.40
129 Warren Sapp	.20	.50
130 Eddie George	.20	.50
131 Steve McNair	.25	.60
132 Kevin Dyson	.15	.40
133 Yancey Thigpen	.15	.40
134 Frank Wycheck	.20	.50
135 Stephen Davis	.20	.50
136 Brad Johnson	.20	.50
137 Skip Hicks	.15	.40
138 Michael Westbrook	.15	.40
139 Darrell Green	.25	.60
140 Albert Connell	.15	.40
141 Tim Couch RC	.60	1.50
142 Donovan McNabb RC	3.00	8.00
143 Akili Smith RC	.50	1.25
144 Edgerrin James RC	.75	2.00
145 Ricky Williams RC	1.00	2.50
146 Torry Holt RC	1.00	2.50
147 Champ Bailey RC	1.25	3.00
148 David Boston RC	.50	1.25
149 Andy Katzenmoyer RC	.50	1.25
150 Chris McAlister RC	.50	1.25
151 Daunte Culpepper RC	.60	1.50
152 Cade McNown RC	.50	1.25
153 Troy Edwards RC	.50	1.25
154 Kevin Johnson RC	.50	1.25
155 James Johnson RC	.40	1.00
156 Rob Konrad RC	.40	1.00
157 Jim Kleinsasser RC	.60	1.50
158 Kevin Faulk RC	.60	1.50
159 Joe Montgomery RC	.40	1.00
160 Shaun King RC	.50	1.25
161 Peerless Price RC	.50	1.25
162 Mike Cloud RC	.40	1.00
163 Jermaine Fazande RC	.40	1.00
164 D'Wayne Bates RC	.40	1.00
165 Brock Huard RC	.50	1.25
166 Marty Booker RC	.50	1.25
167 Karsten Bailey RC	.40	1.00
168 Shawn Bryson RC	.40	1.00
169 Jeff Paulk RC	.40	1.00
170 Travis McGriff RC	.40	1.00
171 Amos Zereoue RC	.50	1.25
172 Craig Yeast RC	.40	1.00
173 Joe Germaine RC	.50	1.25
174 Dameane Douglas RC	.40	1.00
175 Brandon Stokley RC	.60	1.50
176 Larry Parker RC	.50	1.25
177 Joel Makovicka RC	.40	1.00
178 Wane McGarity RC	.40	1.00
179 Na Brown RC	.40	1.00
180 Cecil Collins RC	.40	1.00
181 Nick Williams RC	.40	1.00
182 Charlie Rogers RC	.40	1.00
183 Darrin Chiaverini RC	.40	1.00
184 Terry Jackson RC	.40	1.00
185 De'Mond Parker RC	.40	1.00
186 Sedrick Irvin RC	.40	1.00
187 MarTay Jenkins RC	.50	1.25
188 Kurt Warner RC	4.00	10.00
189 Michael Bishop RC UER (name misspelled on front Biship)	.50	1.25
190 Sean Bennett RC	.40	1.00
191 Jamal Anderson CL	.15	.40
192 Eric Moulds CL	.15	.40
193 Terrell Davis CL	.20	.50
194 John Elway CL	.40	1.00
195 Barry Sanders CL	.40	1.00
196 Peyton Manning CL	.40	1.00
197 Fred Taylor CL	.15	.40
198 Dan Marino CL	.40	1.00
199 Randy Moss CL	.20	.50
200 Terrell Owens CL	.20	.50

1999 Donruss Stat Line Career

*STARS/400-589: 5X TO 12X BASIC CARDS
*ROOKIES/400-589: .8X TO 2X BASIC CARDS
*STARS/300-399: 4X TO 10X BASIC CARDS
*ROOKIES/300-399: 1.2X TO 3X BASIC CARDS
*STARS/200-299: 5X TO 12X BASIC CARDS
*ROOKIES/200-299: 1.5X TO 4X BASIC CARDS
*STARS/140-199: 8X TO 20X BASIC CARDS
*ROOKIES/140-199: 2X TO 5X BASIC CARDS
*STARS/100-139: 10X TO 25X BASIC CARDS
*ROOKIES/100-139: 2.5X TO 6X BASIC CARDS
*STARS/70-99: 15X TO 40X BASIC CARDS
*ROOKIES/70-99: 3X TO 8X BASIC CARDS
*STARS/45-69: 20X TO 50X BASIC CARDS
*STARS/30-44: 25X TO 60X BASIC
*STARS/20-29: 30X TO 80X BASIC
*STARS/10-19: 50X TO 100X BASIC

1999 Donruss Stat Line Season

*ROOKIES/200-299: 1.5X TO 4X BASIC CARDS
*ROOKIES/140-199: 2X TO 5X BASIC CARDS
*ROOKIES/100-139: 2.5X TO 6X BASIC CARDS
*ROOKIES/70-99: 3X TO 8X BASIC CARDS
*STARS/45-69: 20X TO 50X BASIC CARDS
*ROOKIES/45-69: 4X TO 10X BASIC CARDS
*STARS/30-44: 30X TO 80X BASIC CARDS
*ROOKIES/30-44: 5X TO 12X BASIC CARDS
*STARS/20-29: 40X TO 100X BASIC CARDS
*STARS/10-19: 50X TO 120X BASIC CARDS
*ROOKIES/10-19: 8X TO 20X BASIC CARDS

1999 Donruss All-Time Gridiron Kings

COMPLETE SET (5)	30.00	60.00

STATED PRINT RUN 1000 SER.#'d SETS
FIRST 500 CARDS SIGNED ON CANVAS STOCK

AGK1 Bart Starr	7.50	20.00
AGK2 Johnny Unitas	7.50	20.00
AGK3 Earl Campbell	5.00	12.00
AGK4 Walter Payton	10.00	25.00
AGK5 Jim Brown	7.50	20.00

1999 Donruss All-Time Gridiron Kings Autographs

FIRST 500 CARDS SIGNED ON CANVAS STOCK

AGK1 Bart Starr	75.00	125.00
AGK2 Johnny Unitas	175.00	250.00
AGK3 Earl Campbell	30.00	60.00
AGK4 Walter Payton	350.00	600.00
AGK5 Jim Brown	50.00	100.00

1999 Donruss Elite Inserts

COMPLETE SET (20)	40.00	80.00

STATED PRINT RUN 2500 SER.#'d SETS

EL1 Cris Carter	1.25	3.00
EL2 Jerry Rice	2.50	6.00
EL3 Mark Brunell	1.25	3.00
EL4 Brett Favre	4.00	10.00
EL5 Keyshawn Johnson	1.25	3.00
EL6 Eddie George	1.25	3.00
EL7 John Elway	4.00	10.00
EL8 Troy Aikman	2.50	6.00
EL9 Marshall Faulk	1.50	4.00
EL10 Antonio Freeman	1.25	3.00
EL11 Drew Bledsoe	1.50	4.00
EL12 Steve Young	1.50	4.00
EL13 Dan Marino	4.00	10.00
EL14 Emmitt Smith	2.50	6.00
EL15 Fred Taylor	1.25	3.00
EL16 Jake Plummer	.75	2.00
EL17 Terrell Davis	1.25	3.00
EL18 Peyton Manning	4.00	10.00
EL19 Randy Moss	3.00	8.00
EL20 Barry Sanders	4.00	10.00

1999 Donruss Executive Producers

COMPLETE SET (45)	50.00	100.00
EP1 Dan Marino/3497	2.50	6.00
EP2 John Elway/2806	3.00	8.00
EP3 Kordell Stewart/2560	.60	1.50
EP4 Troy Aikman/2330	2.00	5.00
EP5 Steve Young/4170	1.00	2.50
EP6 Doug Flutie/2711	.75	2.00
EP7 Drew Bledsoe/3633	1.00	2.50
EP8 Jon Kitna/1177	.75	2.00
EP9 Steve McNair/3228	.75	2.00
EP10 Mark Brunell/2601	.75	2.00
EP11 R.Cunningham/3704	.75	2.00
EP12 Jake Plummer/3737	.60	1.50
EP13 Charlie Batch/2178	.75	2.00
EP14 Peyton Manning/3739	2.00	5.00
EP15 Brett Favre/4212	2.50	6.00
EP16 Terrell Davis/2008	1.25	3.00
EP17 Fred Taylor/1223	1.25	3.00
EP18 Eddie George/1294	.75	2.00
EP19 Corey Dillon/1130	1.00	2.50
EP20 Jamal Anderson/1846	1.00	2.50
EP21 Curtis Martin/1287	1.00	2.50
EP22 Dorsey Levens/378	1.25	3.00
EP23 Karim Abdul-Jabbar/960	1.00	2.50
EP24 Curtis Enis/497	1.00	2.50
EP25 Mike Alstott/846	1.00	2.50
EP26 Natrone Means/883	1.00	2.50
EP27 Jerome Bettis/1185	1.00	2.50
EP28 Warrick Dunn/1026	1.00	2.50
EP29 Emmitt Smith/1332	2.50	6.00
EP30 Barry Sanders/1491	4.00	10.00
EP31 Jerry Rice/1157	2.50	6.00
EP32 Randy Moss/1313	2.50	6.00
EP33 K.Johnson/1131	1.00	2.50
EP34 Isaac Bruce/457	1.25	3.00
EP35 Antonio Freeman/1424	1.00	2.50
EP36 Eric Moulds/1368	1.00	2.50
EP37 Tim Dwight/94	2.50	6.00
EP38 Herman Moore/983	1.00	2.50
EP39 Tim Brown/1012	1.00	2.50
EP40 Marshall Faulk/1319	1.50	4.00
EP41 Terry Glenn/792	1.00	2.50
EP42 Joey Galloway/1047	1.00	2.50
EP43 Carl Pickens/1023	.75	2.00
EP44 Terrell Owens/1097	1.00	2.50
EP45 Cris Carter/1011	1.00	2.50

1999 Donruss Fan Club Gold

COMPLETE SET (20)	25.00	50.00

GOLD PRINT RUN 5000 SER.#'d SETS
*SILVER: .3X TO .8X GOLD
SILVERS INSERTED IN RETAIL PACKS

FC1 Troy Aikman	2.00	5.00
FC2 Ricky Williams	1.25	3.00
FC3 Jerry Rice	2.00	5.00
FC4 Brett Favre	3.00	8.00
FC5 Terrell Davis	1.00	2.50
FC6 Doug Flutie	1.00	2.50
FC7 John Elway	3.00	8.00
FC8 Steve Young	1.25	3.00
FC9 Steve McNair	1.00	2.50
FC10 Kordell Stewart	.60	1.50
FC11 Drew Bledsoe	1.25	3.00
FC12 Donovan McNabb	3.00	8.00
FC13 Dan Marino	3.00	8.00
FC14 Cade McNown	.60	1.50
FC15 Vinny Testaverde	.60	1.50
FC16 Jake Plummer	.60	1.50
FC17 Randall Cunningham	1.00	2.50
FC18 Peyton Manning	3.00	8.00
FC19 Keyshawn Johnson	1.00	2.50
FC20 Barry Sanders	3.00	8.00

1999 Donruss Gridiron Kings

COMPLETE SET (20)	50.00	100.00

STATED PRINT RUN 5000 SER.#'d SETS
*CANVAS CARDS: 1X TO 2.5X BASIC INSERTS
FIRST 500 CARDS ON CANVAS STOCK

GK1 Randy Moss	4.00	10.00
GK2 Fred Taylor	1.50	4.00
GK3 Doug Flutie	1.50	4.00
GK4 Brett Favre	5.00	12.00
GK5 Mark Brunell	1.50	4.00
GK6 Troy Aikman	3.00	8.00
GK7 John Elway	5.00	12.00
GK8 Jerry Rice	3.00	8.00
GK9 Drew Bledsoe	2.00	5.00
GK10 Eddie George	1.50	4.00
GK11 Randall Cunningham	1.50	4.00
GK12 Emmitt Smith	3.00	8.00
GK13 Dan Marino	5.00	12.00
GK14 Jake Plummer	1.00	2.50
GK15 Jamal Anderson	1.50	4.00
GK16 Terrell Davis	1.50	4.00
GK17 Steve Young	2.00	5.00
GK18 Peyton Manning	5.00	12.00
GK19 Jerome Bettis	1.50	4.00
GK20 Barry Sanders	5.00	12.00

1999 Donruss Private Signings

1 Mike Alstott/600	12.50	30.00
2 Jerome Bettis/500	40.00	80.00
3 Tim Brown/500	12.50	30.00
4 Isaac Bruce/500	12.50	30.00
5 Cris Carter/600	12.50	30.00
6 Randall Cunningham/150	12.50	30.00
7 Terrell Davis/475	12.50	30.00
8 Corey Dillon/500	12.50	30.00
9 Curtis Enis/500	6.00	15.00
10 Doug Flutie/275	12.50	30.00
11 Antonio Freeman/500	12.50	30.00
12 Eddie George/300	12.50	30.00
13 Brian Griese/1500	12.50	30.00
14 Skip Hicks/500	6.00	15.00
15 Priest Holmes/500	12.50	30.00
16 Natrone Means/500	7.50	20.00
17 Randy Moss/250	40.00	80.00
18 Eric Moulds/800	12.50	30.00
19 Terrell Owens/500	20.00	40.00
20 Jerry Rice	75.00	150.00
21 Barry Sanders/50	100.00	200.00
22 Neil Smith/350	6.00	15.00
23 Duce Staley/500	12.50	30.00
24 Kordell Stewart/300	7.50	20.00
25 Fred Taylor/175	12.50	30.00
26 Vinny Testaverde/500	7.50	20.00
27 Derrick Thomas/350	75.00	125.00
28 Thurman Thomas/500	15.00	40.00
29 Wesley Walls/500	6.00	15.00
30 Ricky Williams/150	12.50	30.00
31 Steve Young/150	40.00	80.00

1999 Donruss Rated Rookies

COMPLETE SET (20)	40.00	80.00

STATED PRINT RUN 5000 SER.#'d SETS
*MEDALISTS: 1X TO 2.5X BASIC INSERTS
MEDALISTS PRINT RUN FIRST 250 CARDS

RR1 Tim Couch	1.25	3.00
RR2 Peerless Price	1.25	3.00
RR3 Ricky Williams	2.00	5.00
RR4 Torry Holt	2.50	6.00
RR5 Champ Bailey	1.50	4.00
RR6 Rob Konrad	1.00	2.50
RR7 Donovan McNabb	5.00	12.00
RR8 Edgerrin James	4.00	10.00
RR9 David Boston	1.25	3.00
RR10 Akili Smith	1.00	2.50
RR11 Cecil Collins	.60	1.50
RR12 Troy Edwards	1.00	2.50
RR13 Daunte Culpepper	4.00	10.00
RR14 Kevin Faulk	1.25	3.00
RR15 Kevin Johnson	1.25	3.00
RR16 Cade McNown	1.00	2.50
RR17 Shaun King	1.00	2.50
RR18 Brock Huard	1.25	3.00
RR19 James Johnson	1.00	2.50
RR20 Sedrick Irvin	.60	1.50

1999 Donruss Rookie Gridiron Kings

COMPLETE SET (10)	30.00	60.00

STATED PRINT RUN 5000 SER.#'d SETS
*CANVAS CARDS: 1X TO 2.5X BASIC INSERTS
FIRST 500 CARDS PRINTED ON CANVAS STOCK

RGK1 Ricky Williams	2.00	5.00
RGK2 Donovan McNabb	5.00	12.00
RGK3 Daunte Culpepper	4.00	10.00
RGK4 Edgerrin James	4.00	10.00
RGK5 David Boston	1.25	3.00
RGK6 Champ Bailey	1.50	4.00
RGK7 Torry Holt	2.50	6.00
RGK8 Cade McNown	1.00	2.50
RGK9 Akili Smith	1.00	2.50
RGK10 Tim Couch	1.25	3.00

1999 Donruss Zoning Commission

COMPLETE SET (25)	30.00	60.00

STATED PRINT RUN 1000 SER.#'d SETS

1 Eric Moulds	1.00	2.50
2 Steve Young	1.25	3.00
3 Brad Johnson	1.00	2.50
4 Peyton Manning	3.00	8.00
5 Randy Moss	2.50	6.00
6 Brett Favre	3.00	8.00
7 Emmitt Smith	2.00	5.00
8 Mark Brunell	1.00	2.50
9 Keyshawn Johnson	1.00	2.50
10 Dan Marino	3.00	8.00
11 Eddie George	1.00	2.50
12 Drew Bledsoe	1.25	3.00
13 Terrell Davis	1.00	2.50
14 Terrell Owens	1.00	2.50
15 Barry Sanders	3.00	8.00
16 Curtis Martin	1.00	2.50
17 John Elway	3.00	8.00
18 Jake Plummer	.60	1.50
19 Jerry Rice	2.00	5.00
20 Fred Taylor	1.00	2.50
21 Antonio Freeman	1.00	2.50
22 Marshall Faulk	1.25	3.00
23 Dorsey Levens	1.00	2.50
24 Steve McNair	1.00	2.50
25 Cris Carter	1.00	2.50

1999 Donruss Zoning Commission Red

2 Steve Young/36	20.00	50.00
4 Peyton Manning/26	60.00	150.00
6 Brett Favre/31	60.00	150.00
8 Mark Brunell/20	30.00	80.00
10 Dan Marino/23	60.00	150.00
12 Drew Bledsoe/20	30.00	80.00
13 Terrell Davis/21	30.00	80.00
17 John Elway/22	75.00	200.00

2000 Donruss

Released in early October, Donruss features a 250-card base set comprised of 150 veteran cards and 100 rookie cards. Each shortprinted rookie card is sequentially numbered to 1325. Donruss was packaged differently for both Hobby and Retail. Retail boxes contained 24 packs of seven cards each and carried a suggested retail price of $1.99, and Hobby boxes contained 18 packs of 16 cards each and carried a suggested retail price of $3.99.

COMPLETE SET (250)	150.00	400.00
COMP.SET w/o RC's (150)	7.50	20.00

151-250 ROOKIE PRINT RUN 1325

1 Jake Plummer	.15	.40
2 Frank Sanders	.12	.30
3 Rob Moore	.12	.30
4 David Boston	.12	.30
5 Tim Dwight	.15	.40
6 Jamal Anderson	.15	.40
7 Chris Chandler	.15	.40
8 Terance Mathis	.12	.30
9 Tony Banks	.12	.30
10 Jermaine Lewis	.12	.30
11 Shannon Sharpe	.20	.50
12 Trent Dilfer	.15	.40
13 Qadry Ismail	.15	.40
14 Eric Moulds	.15	.40
15 Doug Flutie	.20	.50
16 Antowain Smith	.15	.40
17 Jonathan Linton	.12	.30
18 Peerless Price	.15	.40
19 Rob Johnson	.15	.40
20 Natrone Means	.15	.40
21 Muhsin Muhammad	.15	.40
22 Wesley Walls	.12	.30
23 Tim Biakabutuka	.15	.40
24 Steve Beuerlein	.15	.40
25 Patrick Jeffers	.15	.40
26 Curtis Enis	.12	.30
27 Cade McNown	.12	.30
28 Bobby Engram	.15	.40
29 Marcus Robinson	.15	.40
30 Marty Booker	.15	.40
31 Corey Dillon	.15	.40
32 Darnay Scott	.15	.40
33 Carl Pickens	.15	.40
34 Akili Smith	.12	.30
35 Michael Basnight	.12	.30
36 Tim Couch	.15	.40
37 Kevin Johnson	.12	.30
38 Karim Abdul Jabbar	.12	.30
39 Errict Rhett	.15	.40
40 Darrin Chiaverini	.12	.30
41 Emmitt Smith	.50	1.25
42 Troy Aikman	.30	.75
43 Joey Galloway	.15	.40
44 Randall Cunningham	.20	.50
45 Michael Irvin	.20	.50
46 Rocket Ismail	.15	.40
47 Jason Tucker	.12	.30
48 Terrell Davis	.20	.50
49 John Elway	.50	1.25
50 Olandis Gary	.15	.40
51 Ed McCaffrey	.15	.40
52 Rod Smith	.15	.40
53 Brian Griese	.15	.40
54 Charlie Batch	.15	.40
55 Barry Sanders	.40	1.00
56 Herman Moore	.15	.40
57 Johnnie Morton	.15	.40
58 Germane Crowell	.12	.30
59 James Stewart	.12	.30
60 Brett Favre	.60	1.50
61 Dorsey Levens	.15	.40
62 Antonio Freeman	.15	.40
63 Corey Bradford	.12	.30
64 Bill Schroeder	.15	.40
65 E.G. Green	.12	.30
66 Peyton Manning	.50	1.25
67 Edgerrin James	.20	.50
68 Marvin Harrison	.20	.50
69 Terrence Wilkins	.12	.30
70 Mark Brunell	.15	.40
71 Fred Taylor	.20	.50
72 Keenan McCardell	.15	.40
73 Jimmy Smith	.15	.40
74 Warren Moon	.20	.50
75 Elvis Grbac	.12	.30
76 Tony Gonzalez	.20	.50
77 Dan Marino	.60	1.50
78 O.J. McDuffie	.15	.40
79 Tony Martin	.15	.40
80 James Johnson	.12	.30
81 Thurman Thomas	.20	.50
82 Randy Moss	.20	.50
83 Daunte Culpepper	.15	.40
84 Cris Carter	.20	.50
85 Robert Smith	.15	.40
86 John Randle	.15	.40
87 Drew Bledsoe	.20	.50
88 Terry Glenn	.15	.40
89 Kevin Faulk	.15	.40
90 Ricky Williams	.20	.50
91 Jeff Blake	.15	.40
92 Jake Reed	.15	.40
93 Amani Toomer	.15	.40
94 Kerry Collins	.15	.40
95 Tiki Barber	.20	.50
96 Ike Hilliard	.15	.40
97 Curtis Martin	.20	.50
98 Vinny Testaverde	.15	.40
99 Wayne Chrebet	.15	.40
100 Ray Lucas	.12	.30
101 Charles Woodson	.20	.50
102 Napoleon Kaufman	.15	.40
103 Tim Brown	.20	.50
104 Tyrone Wheatley	.12	.30
105 Rich Gannon	.15	.40
106 Duce Staley	.15	.40
107 Donovan McNabb	.20	.50
108 Amos Zereoue	.12	.30
109 Kordell Stewart	.15	.40
110 Jerome Bettis	.20	.50
111 Troy Edwards	.12	.30
112 Ryan Leaf	.15	.40
113 Junior Seau	.20	.50
114 Jim Harbaugh	.15	.40
115 Jermaine Fazande	.12	.30
116 Curtis Conway	.15	.40
117 Steve Young	.25	.60
118 Jerry Rice	.40	1.00
119 Terrell Owens	.20	.50
120 Charlie Garner	.15	.40
121 Jeff Garcia	.15	.40
122 Jon Kitna	.15	.40
123 Derrick Mayes	.12	.30
124 Ricky Watters	.15	.40
125 Kurt Warner	.30	.75
126 Marshall Faulk	.20	.50
127 Torry Holt	.20	.50
128 Az-Zahir Hakim	.12	.30
129 Isaac Bruce	.20	.50
130 Mike Alstott	.20	.50
131 Warrick Dunn	.15	.40
132 Shaun King	.12	.30
133 Keyshawn Johnson	.15	.40
134 Jacquez Green	.12	.30
135 Reidel Anthony	.12	.30
136 Warren Sapp	.15	.40
137 Eddie George	.15	.40
138 Steve McNair	.20	.50
139 Yancey Thigpen	.12	.30
140 Kevin Dyson	.15	.40
141 Frank Wycheck	.15	.40
142 Jevon Kearse	.15	.40
143 Stephen Davis	.15	.40
144 Skip Hicks	.12	.30
145 Brad Johnson	.15	.40
146 Bruce Smith	.20	.50
147 Michael Westbrook	.12	.30
148 Albert Connell	.12	.30
149 Jeff George	.15	.40
150 Deion Sanders	.20	.50
151 Courtney Brown RC	2.00	5.00
152 Corey Simon RC	2.00	5.00
153 Brian Urlacher RC	10.00	25.00
154 Shaun Ellis RC	2.50	6.00
155 John Abraham RC	2.50	6.00
156 Deltha O'Neal RC	2.00	5.00
157 Ahmed Plummer RC	1.50	4.00
158 Chris Hovan RC	2.00	5.00
159 Rob Morris RC	2.00	5.00
160 Keith Bulluck RC	2.00	5.00
161 Darren Howard RC	1.50	4.00
162 John Engelberger RC	1.50	4.00
163 Raynoch Thompson RC	1.50	4.00
164 Cornelius Griffin RC	1.50	4.00
165 William Bartee RC	1.50	4.00
166 Fred Robbins RC	1.50	4.00
167 Micheal Boireau RC	1.50	4.00
168 Brandon Short RC	1.50	4.00
169 Jacoby Shepherd RC	1.50	4.00
170 Peter Warrick RC	2.50	6.00
171 Jamal Lewis RC	2.50	6.00
172 Thomas Jones RC	3.00	8.00
173 Plaxico Burress RC	2.50	6.00
174 Travis Taylor RC	2.00	5.00
175 Ron Dayne RC	2.50	6.00
176 Bubba Franks RC	2.50	6.00
177 Sebastian Janikowski RC	2.50	6.00
178 Chad Pennington RC	4.00	10.00
179 Shaun Alexander RC	3.00	8.00
180 Sylvester Morris RC	1.50	4.00
181 Anthony Becht RC	2.00	5.00
182 R.Jay Soward RC	1.50	4.00
183 Trung Canidate RC	2.00	5.00
184 Dennis Northcutt RC	2.00	5.00
185 Todd Pinkston RC	1.50	4.00
186 Jerry Porter RC	2.50	6.00
187 Travis Prentice RC	2.00	5.00
188 Giovanni Carmazzi RC	1.50	4.00
189 Ron Dugans RC	1.50	4.00
190 Erron Kinney RC	1.50	4.00
191 Dez White RC	2.00	5.00
192 Chris Cole RC	2.00	5.00
193 Ron Dixon RC	1.50	4.00
194 Chris Redman RC	2.00	5.00
195 J.R. Redmond RC	1.50	4.00
196 Laveranues Coles RC	2.50	6.00
197 JaJuan Dawson RC	1.50	4.00
198 Darrell Jackson RC	2.00	5.00
199 Reuben Droughns RC	2.50	6.00
200 Doug Chapman RC	1.50	4.00
201 Terrelle Smith RC	1.50	4.00
202 Curtis Keaton RC	1.50	4.00
203 Gari Scott RC	1.50	4.00
204 Danny Farmer RC	1.50	4.00
205 Hank Poteat RC	1.50	4.00
206 Ben Kelly RC	1.50	4.00
207 Corey Moore RC	1.50	4.00
208 Na'il Diggs RC	1.50	4.00
209 Aaron Shea RC	2.00	5.00
210 Trevor Gaylor RC	1.50	4.00
211 Julian Peterson RC	2.50	6.00
212 Frank Moreau RC	1.50	4.00
213 Deon Dyer RC	1.50	4.00
214 Avion Black RC	1.50	4.00
215 Paul Smith RC	1.50	4.00
216 Michael Wiley RC	1.50	4.00
217 Dante Hall RC	2.50	6.00
218 Mike Brown RC	2.50	6.00
219 Sammy Morris RC	2.00	5.00
220 Billy Volek RC	2.50	6.00
221 Tee Martin RC	2.50	6.00
222 Troy Walters RC	1.50	4.00
223 Chad Morton RC	2.50	6.00
224 Erik Flowers RC	1.50	4.00
225 Ronney Jenkins RC	1.50	4.00
226 Thomas Hamner RC	1.50	4.00
227 Mareno Philyaw RC	1.50	4.00
228 James Williams RC	1.50	4.00
229 Mike Anderson RC	2.50	6.00
230 Tom Brady RC	90.00	150.00
231 Mike Green RC	2.50	6.00
232 Todd Husak RC	1.50	4.00
233 Tim Rattay RC	2.00	5.00
234 Jarious Jackson RC	2.00	5.00
235 Joe Hamilton RC	1.50	4.00
236 Shyrone Stith RC	1.50	4.00
237 Rondell Mealey RC	1.50	4.00
238 Demario Brown RC	1.50	4.00
239 Chris Coleman RC	1.50	4.00
240 Dwayne Goodrich RC	1.50	4.00
241 Drew Haddad RC	1.50	4.00
242 Doug Johnson RC	2.00	5.00
243 Windrell Hayes RC	1.50	4.00
244 Charles Lee RC	1.50	4.00
245 Kevin McDougal RC	1.50	4.00
246 Spergon Wynn RC	2.00	5.00
247 Shockmain Davis RC	1.50	4.00
248 Jamel White RC	1.50	4.00
249 Bashir Yamini RC	1.50	4.00
250 Kwame Cavil RC	1.50	4.00

2000 Donruss Stat Line Career

*VETS/200-300: 5X TO 12X BASIC CARDS
*ROOKIES/200-300: .4X TO 1X
*VETS/140-199: 6X TO 15X BASIC CARDS
*ROOKIES/140-199: .5X TO 1.2X
*VETS/100-139: 8X TO 20X BASIC CARDS
*ROOKIES/100-139: .6X TO 1.5X
*VETS/70-99: 10X TO 25X BASIC CARDS
*ROOKIES/70-99: .8X TO 2X
*VETS/40-69: 12X TO 30X BASIC CARDS
*ROOKIES/40-69: 1X TO 2.5X
*VETS/30-39: 15X TO 40X BASIC CARDS
*ROOKIES/30-39: 1.2X TO 3X
*VETS/20-29: 20X TO 50X BASIC
*ROOKIES/20-29: 1.5X TO 4X
*ROOKIES/10-19: 2X TO 5X
CAREER/2-300 ODDS 1:25 HOB, 1:48 RET
CARDS SER.#'d TO A CAREER STAT

230 Tom Brady/214	125.00	200.00

2000 Donruss Stat Line Season

*VETS/70-99: 10X TO 25X BASIC CARDS
*ROOKIES/70-99: .8X TO 2X
*VETS/40-69: 12X TO 30X BASIC CARDS
*ROOKIES/40-69: 1X TO 2.5X
*VETS/30-39: 15X TO 40X BASIC CARDS
*ROOKIES/30-39: 1.2X TO 3X
*VETS/20-29: 20X TO 50X BASIC CARDS
*ROOKIES/20-29: 1.5X TO 4X
*VETS/10-19: 25X TO 60X BASIC CARDS
*ROOKIES/10-19: 2X TO 5X
SEASON/1-99 ODDS 1:192 H, 1:396 R

230 Tom Brady/20	500.00	800.00

2000 Donruss All-Time Gridiron Kings

COMPLETE SET (10)	12.50	30.00

STATED PRINT RUN 2500 SER.#'d SETS

1 Joe Montana	4.00	10.00
2 Terry Bradshaw	3.00	8.00
3 Fran Tarkenton	1.50	4.00
4 Dan Fouts	1.25	3.00
5 Sammy Baugh	1.25	3.00
6 Eric Dickerson	1.00	2.50
7 Bob Griese	1.25	3.00
8 Ken Stabler	1.50	4.00
9 Joe Namath	2.50	6.00
10 Lawrence Taylor	1.25	3.00

2000 Donruss All-Time Gridiron Kings Studio Autographs

STAT.PRINT RUN 250 SER.#'d SETS

1 Joe Montana	60.00	120.00
2 Terry Bradshaw	30.00	80.00
3 Fran Tarkenton	20.00	50.00
5 Sammy Baugh	100.00	175.00
6 Eric Dickerson	15.00	40.00
7 Bob Griese	15.00	40.00
8 Ken Stabler	25.00	60.00
9 Joe Namath	50.00	100.00
10 Lawrence Taylor	20.00	50.00

2000 Donruss Dominators

COMPLETE SET (60)	12.50	30.00

STATED PRINT RUN 5000 SER.#'d SETS

1 Jake Plummer	.30	.75
2 Tim Couch	.30	.75
3 Emmitt Smith	1.00	2.50
4 Troy Aikman	.60	1.50
5 John Elway	1.00	2.50
6 Terrell Davis	.40	1.00
7 Charlie Batch	.30	.75
8 Barry Sanders	.75	2.00
9 Brett Favre	1.25	3.00
10 Peyton Manning	1.00	2.50
11 Edgerrin James	.40	1.00
12 Mark Brunell	.30	.75
13 Fred Taylor	.40	1.00
14 Dan Marino	1.25	3.00
15 Randy Moss	.40	1.00
16 Drew Bledsoe	.40	1.00
17 Ricky Williams	.40	1.00
18 Jerry Rice	.75	2.00
19 Steve Young	.50	1.25
20 Kurt Warner	.60	1.50
21 Eddie George	.30	.75
22 Jamal Anderson	.30	.75
23 Eric Moulds	.30	.75
24 Cade McNown	.25	.60
25 Corey Dillon	.30	.75
26 Kevin Johnson	.25	.60
27 Joey Galloway	.30	.75
28 Olandis Gary	.30	.75
29 Dorsey Levens	.30	.75
30 Antonio Freeman	.30	.75
31 Marvin Harrison	.40	1.00
32 Daunte Culpepper	.30	.75
33 Cris Carter	.40	1.00
34 Robert Smith	.30	.75
35 Curtis Martin	.40	1.00
36 Tim Brown	.40	1.00
37 Duce Staley	.30	.75
38 Donovan McNabb	.40	1.00
39 Jerome Bettis	.40	1.00
40 Terrell Owens	.40	1.00
41 Jon Kitna	.30	.75
42 Marshall Faulk	.40	1.00
43 Warrick Dunn	.30	.75
44 Shaun King	.25	.60
45 Keyshawn Johnson	.30	.75
46 Steve McNair	.40	1.00
47 Stephen Davis	.30	.75
48 Brad Johnson	.30	.75
49 Muhsin Muhammad	.30	.75
50 Marcus Robinson	.30	.75
51 Akili Smith	.25	.60
52 Brian Griese	.30	.75
53 Germane Crowell	.25	.60
54 Jimmy Smith	.30	.75
55 Ricky Watters	.30	.75
56 Isaac Bruce	.40	1.00
57 Warren Sapp	.30	.75
58 Jevon Kearse	.30	.75
59 Michael Westbrook	.25	.60
60 Ed McCaffrey	.30	.75

2000 Donruss Elite Series

COMPLETE SET (40)	25.00	60.00

STATED PRINT RUN 2500 SER.#'d SETS

ES1 Jake Plummer	.60	1.50
ES2 Emmitt Smith	2.00	5.00
ES3 Tim Couch	.60	1.50
ES4 Troy Aikman	1.25	3.00
ES5 John Elway	2.00	5.00
ES6 Terrell Davis	.75	2.00
ES7 Barry Sanders	1.50	4.00
ES8 Brett Favre	2.50	6.00
ES9 Peyton Manning	2.00	5.00
ES10 Mark Brunell	.60	1.50
ES11 Edgerrin James	.75	2.00
ES12 Fred Taylor	.75	2.00
ES13 Dan Marino	2.50	6.00
ES14 Randy Moss	.75	2.00
ES15 Drew Bledsoe	.75	2.00
ES16 Ricky Williams	.75	2.00
ES17 Jerry Rice	1.50	4.00
ES18 Steve Young	1.00	2.50
ES19 Kurt Warner	1.25	3.00
ES20 Eddie George	.60	1.50
ES21 Deion Sanders	.75	2.00
ES22 Cade McNown	.50	1.25
ES23 Joey Galloway	.60	1.50
ES24 Dorsey Levens	.60	1.50
ES25 Antonio Freeman	.60	1.50
ES26 Marvin Harrison	.75	2.00
ES27 Daunte Culpepper	.60	1.50
ES28 Cris Carter	.75	2.00
ES29 Curtis Martin	.75	2.00
ES30 Tim Brown	.75	2.00
ES31 Donovan McNabb	.75	2.00
ES32 Jerome Bettis	.75	2.00
ES33 Marshall Faulk	.75	2.00
ES34 Jon Kitna	.60	1.50
ES35 Keyshawn Johnson	.60	1.50
ES36 Steve McNair	.75	2.00
ES37 Stephen Davis	.60	1.50
ES38 Jimmy Smith	.60	1.50
ES39 Brad Johnson	.60	1.50
ES40 Isaac Bruce	.75	2.00

2000 Donruss Gridiron Kings

COMPLETE SET (10)	12.50	30.00

STATED PRINT RUN 2500 SER.#'d SETS
*STUDIO/250: 1.2X TO 3X BASIC INSERTS
STUDIO PRINT RUN 250 SER.#'d SETS

GK1 Emmitt Smith	2.50	6.00
GK2 John Elway	2.50	6.00
GK3 Barry Sanders	2.00	5.00
GK4 Brett Favre	3.00	8.00
GK5 Peyton Manning	2.50	6.00
GK6 Dan Marino	3.00	8.00
GK7 Randy Moss	1.00	2.50
GK8 Jerry Rice	2.00	5.00
GK9 Steve Young	1.25	3.00
GK10 Kurt Warner	1.50	4.00

2000 Donruss Gridiron Kings Studio Autographs

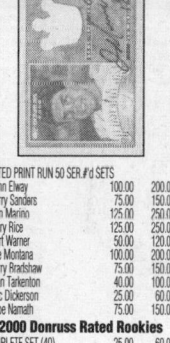

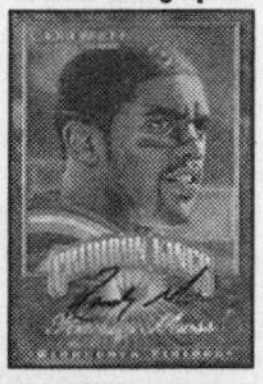

STATED PRINT RUN 19-50

GK1 Emmitt Smith	125.00	250.00
GK2 John Elway	100.00	200.00
GK3 Barry Sanders	75.00	150.00
GK4 Brett Favre	125.00	250.00
GK5 Peyton Manning	100.00	200.00
GK6 Dan Marino	125.00	250.00
GK7 Randy Moss/19	100.00	200.00
GK8 Jerry Rice	75.00	150.00
GK9 Steve Young	40.00	80.00
GK10 Kurt Warner	35.00	60.00

2000 Donruss Jersey King Autographs

STATED PRINT RUN 50 SER.#'d SETS

1 John Elway	100.00	200.00
2 Barry Sanders	75.00	150.00
3 Dan Marino	125.00	250.00
4 Jerry Rice	125.00	250.00
5 Kurt Warner	50.00	120.00
6 Joe Montana	100.00	200.00
7 Terry Bradshaw	75.00	150.00
8 Fran Tarkenton	40.00	100.00
9 Eric Dickerson	25.00	60.00
10 Joe Namath	75.00	150.00

2000 Donruss Rated Rookies

COMPLETE SET (40)	25.00	60.00

STATED PRINT RUN 2500 SER.#'d SETS
*MEDALIST/100: 1.2X TO 3X BASIC INSERTS
MEDALIST PRINT RUN 100 SER.#'d SETS

1 Peter Warrick	.75	2.00
2 Jamal Lewis	.75	2.00
3 Thomas Jones	1.00	2.50
4 Plaxico Burress	.75	2.00
5 Travis Taylor	.60	1.50
6 Ron Dayne	.75	2.00
7 Bubba Franks	.75	2.00
8 Chad Pennington	1.25	3.00
9 Shaun Alexander	1.00	2.50
10 Sylvester Morris	.50	1.25
11 R.Jay Soward	.50	1.25
12 Trung Canidate	.60	1.50
13 Dennis Northcutt	.60	1.50
14 Todd Pinkston	.50	1.25
15 Jerry Porter	.75	2.00
16 Travis Prentice	.60	1.50
17 Giovanni Carmazzi	.50	1.25
18 Ron Dugans	.50	1.25
19 Dez White	.60	1.50
20 Chris Cole	.60	1.50
21 Ron Dixon	.50	1.25
22 Chris Redman	.60	1.50
23 J.R. Redmond	.50	1.25
24 Laveranues Coles	.75	2.00
25 JaJuan Dawson	.50	1.25
26 Darrell Jackson	.60	1.50
27 Reuben Droughns	.75	2.00
28 Doug Chapman	.50	1.25
29 Curtis Keaton	.50	1.25
30 Gari Scott	.50	1.25
31 Danny Farmer	.50	1.25
32 Trevor Gaylor	.50	1.25
33 Anthony Becht	.60	1.50
34 Frank Moreau	.50	1.25
35 Avion Black	.50	1.25
36 Michael Wiley	.50	1.25
37 Dante Hall	.75	2.00
38 Tim Rattay	.60	1.50
39 Tee Martin	.75	2.00
40 Courtney Brown	.60	1.50

2000 Donruss Rookie Gridiron Kings

COMPLETE SET (10)	10.00	25.00

STATED PRINT RUN 2500 SER.#'d SETS

*STUDIO/250: 1.2X TO 3X BASIC INSERTS
STUDIO PRINT RUN 250 SER.#'d SETS

1 Peter Warrick	.75	2.00
2 Jamal Lewis	.75	2.00
3 Thomas Jones	1.00	2.50
4 Plaxico Burress	.75	2.00
5 Travis Taylor	.60	1.50
6 Ron Dayne	.75	2.00
7 Chad Pennington	1.25	3.00
8 Shaun Alexander	1.00	2.50
9 Sylvester Morris	.50	1.25
10 Chris Redman	.60	1.50

2000 Donruss Rookie Gridiron Kings Studio Autographs

ANNOUNCED PRINT RUN 50 SETS

1 Peter Warrick	15.00	40.00
2 Jamal Lewis	15.00	40.00
3 Thomas Jones	20.00	50.00
4 Plaxico Burress	25.00	60.00
5 Travis Taylor	12.00	30.00
6 Ron Dayne	15.00	40.00
7 Chad Pennington	25.00	60.00
8 Shaun Alexander	20.00	50.00
10 Chris Redman	12.00	30.00

2000 Donruss Signature Series Red

PLAYOFF ANNC'D PRINT RUNS 25-750

1 Troy Aikman/25*	50.00	100.00
2 Tony Banks/325*	3.00	8.00
3 Jeff Blake/125*	5.00	12.00
4 Drew Bledsoe/35*	20.00	50.00
5 Isaac Bruce/25*	15.00	40.00
6 Trung Canidate/75*	6.00	15.00
7 Giovanni Carmazzi/175*	4.00	10.00
8 Kwame Cavil/375*	3.00	8.00
9 Doug Chapman/375*	4.00	10.00
11 Kerry Collins/125*	7.50	20.00
12 Albert Connell/750*	3.00	8.00
13 Tim Couch/25*	15.00	40.00
14 Germane Crowell/350*	3.00	8.00
16 Reuben Droughns/375*	6.00	15.00
17 Ron Dugans/175*	4.00	10.00
18 Tim Dwight/350*	5.00	12.00
19 Troy Edwards/350*	3.00	8.00
20 Danny Farmer/175*	5.00	12.00
21 Kevin Faulk/750*	3.00	8.00
22 Marshall Faulk/25*	25.00	60.00
23 Jermaine Fazande/750*	3.00	8.00
24 Antonio Freeman/175*	6.00	15.00
26 Olandis Gary/350*	5.00	12.00
28 Eddie George/25*	15.00	40.00
29 Marvin Harrison/75*	15.00	40.00
30 Torry Holt/75*	12.50	30.00
32 Edgerrin James/25*	25.00	60.00
33 Patrick Jeffers/750*	3.00	8.00
34 Brad Johnson/25*	15.00	40.00
35 Kevin Johnson/350*	4.00	10.00
37 Tee Martin/275*	5.00	12.00
38 Derrick Mayes/750*	3.00	8.00
39 Cade McNown/75*	6.00	15.00
40 Sylvester Morris/125*	5.00	12.00
41 Randy Moss/75*	40.00	80.00
42 Eric Moulds/100*	7.50	20.00
43 Dennis Northcutt/175*	5.00	12.00
44 Todd Pinkston/175*	5.00	12.00
45 Jake Plummer/25*	15.00	40.00
46 Jerry Porter/175*	6.00	15.00
47 Travis Prentice/175*	5.00	12.00
48 Tim Rattay/375*	5.00	12.00
49 J.R. Redmond/175*	5.00	12.00
50 Corey Simon/175*	6.00	15.00
51 Akili Smith/75*	6.00	15.00
52 Antowain Smith/75*	7.50	20.00
53 Jimmy Smith/75*	7.50	20.00
55 Shyrone Stith/175*	4.00	10.00
56 Fred Taylor/75*	7.50	20.00
57 Thurman Thomas/75*	15.00	40.00
58 Kurt Warner/75*	25.00	50.00
59 Ricky Williams/25*	20.00	50.00
60 Tyrone Wheatley/350*	4.00	10.00

2000 Donruss Signature Series Blue

STATED PRINT RUN 100 SER.#'d SETS

2 Tony Banks	6.00	15.00
3 Jeff Blake		
7 Giovanni Carmazzi	6.00	15.00
8 Kwame Cavil	6.00	15.00
9 Doug Chapman	6.00	15.00
11 Kerry Collins	8.00	20.00
12 Albert Connell	6.00	15.00
14 Germane Crowell	6.00	15.00
16 Reuben Droughns	10.00	25.00
17 Ron Dugans	6.00	15.00
18 Tim Dwight	8.00	20.00
19 Troy Edwards	6.00	15.00
20 Danny Farmer	6.00	15.00
21 Kevin Faulk	8.00	20.00
23 Jermaine Fazande	6.00	15.00
24 Antonio Freeman	8.00	20.00
26 Olandis Gary	8.00	20.00
33 Patrick Jeffers	8.00	20.00
35 Kevin Johnson	6.00	15.00
37 Tee Martin	10.00	25.00
38 Derrick Mayes	6.00	15.00
40 Sylvester Morris	6.00	15.00
43 Dennis Northcutt	8.00	20.00
44 Todd Pinkston	6.00	15.00
46 Jerry Porter	10.00	25.00
47 Travis Prentice	8.00	20.00
48 Tim Rattay	8.00	20.00
49 J.R. Redmond	6.00	15.00
50 Corey Simon	8.00	20.00
55 Shyrone Stith	6.00	15.00
60 Tyrone Wheatley	6.00	15.00

2000 Donruss Signature Series Gold

STATED PRINT RUN 25 SER.#'d SETS

1 Troy Aikman	50.00	100.00
2 Tony Banks	10.00	25.00
3 Jeff Blake	12.00	30.00
4 Drew Bledsoe		
5 Isaac Bruce	15.00	40.00
6 Trung Canidate	12.00	30.00
7 Giovanni Carmazzi	10.00	25.00
8 Kwame Cavil	10.00	25.00
9 Doug Chapman	10.00	25.00
11 Kerry Collins	12.00	30.00
12 Albert Connell	10.00	25.00
13 Tim Couch	12.00	30.00
14 Germane Crowell	10.00	25.00
16 Reuben Droughns	15.00	40.00
17 Ron Dugans		
18 Tim Dwight	12.00	30.00
19 Troy Edwards	10.00	25.00
20 Kevin Faulk	12.00	30.00
21 Danny Farmer		
22 Marshall Faulk	15.00	40.00
23 Jermaine Fazande		
24 Antonio Freeman	12.00	30.00
26 Olandis Gary	12.00	30.00
28 Eddie George	12.00	30.00
29 Marvin Harrison	15.00	40.00
30 Torry Holt	15.00	40.00
32 Edgerrin James		
33 Patrick Jeffers	12.00	30.00
34 Brad Johnson	12.00	30.00
35 Kevin Johnson	10.00	25.00
37 Tee Martin	15.00	40.00
38 Derrick Mayes	10.00	25.00
39 Cade McNown	10.00	25.00
40 Sylvester Morris	10.00	25.00
41 Randy Moss	50.00	100.00
42 Eric Moulds	12.00	30.00
43 Dennis Northcutt	12.00	30.00
44 Todd Pinkston	10.00	25.00
45 Jake Plummer	12.00	30.00
46 Jerry Porter	15.00	40.00
47 Travis Prentice		
48 Tim Rattay	12.00	30.00
49 J.R. Redmond	10.00	25.00
50 Corey Simon	12.00	30.00
51 Akili Smith	10.00	25.00
52 Antowain Smith	12.00	30.00
53 Jimmy Smith	12.00	30.00
55 Shyrone Stith	10.00	25.00
56 Fred Taylor	15.00	40.00
57 Thurman Thomas	15.00	40.00
58 Kurt Warner	40.00	80.00
59 Ricky Williams	15.00	40.00
60 Tyrone Wheatley	10.00	25.00

2000 Donruss Zoning Commission

COMPLETE SET (60)	30.00	80.00

STATED PRINT RUN 1000 SER.#'d SETS
*RED/41: 4X TO 10X BASIC INSERTS
*RED/22-26: 5X TO 12X BASIC INSERTS
*RED/11-19: 6X TO 15X BASIC INSERTS
RED STATED PRINT RUN 8-41

1 Jake Plummer	.75	2.00
2 Tim Couch	.75	2.00
3 Emmitt Smith	2.50	6.00
4 Troy Aikman	1.50	4.00
5 Charlie Batch	.75	2.00
6 Brett Favre	3.00	8.00
7 Peyton Manning	2.50	6.00
8 Edgerrin James	1.00	2.50
9 Mark Brunell	.75	2.00
10 Fred Taylor	1.00	2.50
11 Dan Marino	3.00	8.00
12 Randy Moss	1.00	2.50
13 Drew Bledsoe	1.00	2.50
14 Ricky Williams	1.00	2.50
15 Jerry Rice	2.00	5.00
16 Steve Young	1.25	3.00
17 Kurt Warner	1.50	4.00
18 Eddie George	.75	2.00
19 Eric Moulds	.75	2.00
20 Doug Flutie	1.00	2.50
21 Antowain Smith	.75	2.00
22 Cade McNown	.60	1.50
23 Corey Dillon	.75	2.00
24 Kevin Johnson	.60	1.50
25 Joey Galloway	.75	2.00
26 Olandis Gary	.75	2.00
27 Dorsey Levens	.75	2.00
28 Antonio Freeman	.75	2.00
29 Marvin Harrison	1.00	2.50
30 Cris Carter	1.00	2.50
31 Robert Smith	.75	2.00
32 Curtis Martin	1.00	2.50
33 Tim Brown	1.00	2.50
34 Duce Staley	.75	2.00
35 Donovan McNabb	1.00	2.50
36 Kordell Stewart	.75	2.00
37 Jerome Bettis	1.00	2.50
38 Terrell Owens	1.00	2.50
39 Jon Kitna	.75	2.00
40 Marshall Faulk	1.00	2.50
41 Torry Holt	1.00	2.50
42 Mike Alstott	1.00	2.50
43 Shaun King	.60	1.50
44 Keyshawn Johnson	.75	2.00
45 Steve McNair	1.00	2.50
46 Stephen Davis	.75	2.00
47 Brad Johnson	.75	2.00
48 Qadry Ismail	.75	2.00
49 Muhsin Muhammad	.75	2.00
50 Patrick Jeffers	.75	2.00
51 Marcus Robinson	.75	2.00
52 Akili Smith	.60	1.50
53 Germane Crowell	.60	1.50
54 James Stewart	.60	1.50
55 Jimmy Smith	.75	2.00
56 Amani Toomer	.75	2.00
57 Charlie Garner	.75	2.00
58 Isaac Bruce	1.00	2.50
59 Albert Connell	.60	1.50
60 Jeff George	.75	2.00

2002 Donruss Samples

*SILVER SAMPLES: 1X TO 2.5X BASIC CARDS
*GOLD SAMPLES: 1.5X TO 4X BASIC CARDS

2002 Donruss

Released in August 2002, this 300-card set includes 200 veterans and 100 rookies. Pack SRP was $2.99. Boxes contained 24 packs of 5 cards.

COMPLETE SET (300)	60.00	120.00
COMP.SET w/o SP's (200)	7.50	20.00
1 Jake Plummer	.15	.40
2 David Boston	.12	.30
3 MarTay Jenkins	.12	.30
4 Thomas Jones	.20	.50
5 Frank Sanders	.12	.30
6 Shawn Jefferson	.12	.30
7 Alge Crumpler	.15	.40
8 Michael Vick	.30	.75
9 Jamal Anderson	.15	.40
10 Warrick Dunn	.15	.40
11 Peter Boulware	.12	.30
12 Jamal Lewis	.15	.40
13 Jeff Blake	.15	.40
14 Travis Taylor	.12	.30
15 Ray Lewis	.20	.50
16 Todd Heap	.15	.40
17 Nate Clements	.12	.30
18 Alex Van Pelt	.12	.30
19 Reggie Germany	.12	.30
20 Larry Centers	.15	.40
21 Eric Moulds	.15	.40
22 Travis Henry	.12	.30
23 Wesley Walls	.15	.40
24 Steve Smith	.20	.50
25 Lamar Smith	.15	.40
26 Patrick Jeffers	.15	.40
27 Chris Weinke	.12	.30
28 Muhsin Muhammad	.15	.40
29 Marcus Robinson	.15	.40
30 Jim Miller	.12	.30
31 Anthony Thomas	.15	.40
32 David Terrell	.12	.30
33 Brian Urlacher	.20	.50
34 Marty Booker	.15	.40
35 Darnay Scott	.15	.40
36 Jon Kitna	.15	.40
37 Chad Johnson	.20	.50
38 T.J. Houshmandzadeh	.20	.50
39 Corey Dillon	.15	.40
40 Peter Warrick	.15	.40
41 Gerard Warren	.12	.30
42 Anthony Henry	.12	.30
43 Quincy Morgan	.12	.30
44 JaJuan Dawson	.12	.30
45 Tim Couch	.12	.30
46 Kevin Johnson	.12	.30
47 James Jackson	.12	.30
48 La'Roi Glover	.12	.30
49 Anthony Wright	.12	.30
50 Rocket Ismail	.15	.40
51 Troy Hambrick	.12	.30
52 Emmitt Smith	.50	1.25
53 Quincy Carter	.12	.30
54 Joey Galloway	.15	.40
55 Shannon Sharpe	.20	.50
56 Kevin Kasper	.12	.30
57 Olandis Gary	.15	.40
58 Brian Griese	.15	.40
59 Rod Smith	.15	.40
60 Terrell Davis	.20	.50
61 Ed McCaffrey	.15	.40
62 Mike Anderson	.15	.40
63 Bill Schroeder	.12	.30
64 Scotty Anderson	.12	.30
65 Mike McMahon	.12	.30
66 James Stewart	.12	.30
67 Az-Zahir Hakim	.12	.30
68 Germane Crowell	.12	.30
69 Kabeer Gbaja-Biamila	.15	.40
70 LeRoy Butler	.15	.40
71 Antonio Freeman	.20	.50
72 Bubba Franks	.15	.40
73 Brett Favre	.50	1.25
74 Ahman Green	.15	.40
75 Terry Glenn	.15	.40
76 Jamie Sharper	.15	.40
77 Tony Simmons	.12	.30
78 James Allen	.12	.30
79 Terrence Wilkins	.12	.30
80 Dominic Rhodes	.15	.40
81 Qadry Ismail	.15	.40
82 Peyton Manning	.40	1.00
83 Edgerrin James	.15	.40
84 Marvin Harrison	.20	.50
85 Reggie Wayne	.20	.50
86 Fred Taylor	.15	.40
87 Elvis Joseph	.12	.30
88 Mark Brunell	.15	.40
89 Keenan McCardell	.15	.40
90 Jimmy Smith	.15	.40
91 Kyle Brady	.12	.30
92 Derrick Alexander	.12	.30
93 Johnnie Morton	.15	.40
94 Trent Green	.15	.40
95 Priest Holmes	.20	.50
96 Tony Gonzalez	.20	.50
97 Snoop Minnis	.12	.30
98 Travis Minor	.12	.30
99 Oronde Gadsden	.12	.30
100 Jay Fiedler	.15	.40
101 Chris Chambers	.15	.40
102 Ricky Williams	.15	.40
103 Zach Thomas	.20	.50
104 Byron Chamberlain	.12	.30
105 Todd Bouman	.12	.30
106 Daunte Culpepper	.15	.40
107 Michael Bennett	.15	.40
108 Randy Moss	.20	.50
109 Cris Carter	.20	.50
110 David Patten	.12	.30
111 Donald Hayes	.12	.30
112 Tom Brady	.50	1.25
113 Antowain Smith	.15	.40
114 Troy Brown	.15	.40
115 Drew Bledsoe	.20	.50
116 Bryan Cox	.15	.40
117 Boo Williams	.12	.30
118 Aaron Brooks	.15	.40
119 Deuce McAllister	.15	.40
120 Joe Horn	.15	.40
121 Amani Toomer	.15	.40
122 Ron Dayne	.15	.40
123 Kerry Collins	.15	.40
124 Ike Hilliard	.15	.40
125 Tiki Barber	.20	.50
126 Michael Strahan	.20	.50
127 Chad Pennington	.20	.50
128 Santana Moss	.15	.40
129 LaMont Jordan	.15	.40
130 Curtis Martin	.20	.50
131 Wayne Chrebet	.15	.40
132 Laveranues Coles	.15	.40
133 Vinny Testaverde	.15	.40
134 Charles Woodson	.20	.50
135 Tyrone Wheatley	.15	.40
136 Jerry Porter	.12	.30
137 Rich Gannon	.15	.40
138 Charlie Garner	.15	.40
139 Tim Brown	.20	.50
140 Jerry Rice	.40	1.00
141 James Thrash	.15	.40
142 Todd Pinkston	.12	.30
143 A.J. Feeley	.12	.30
144 Donovan McNabb	.20	.50
145 Duce Staley	.15	.40
146 Freddie Mitchell	.12	.30
147 Correll Buckhalter	.15	.40
148 Casey Hampton	.12	.30
149 Hines Ward	.20	.50
150 Chris Fuamatu-Ma'afala	.12	.30
151 Jerome Bettis	.20	.50
152 Kordell Stewart	.15	.40
153 Plaxico Burress	.15	.40
154 Kendrell Bell	.12	.30
155 Trevor Gaylor	.12	.30
156 Curtis Conway	.15	.40
157 Doug Flutie	.20	.50
158 Drew Brees	.30	.75
159 LaDainian Tomlinson	.25	.60
160 Junior Seau	.20	.50
161 Bryant Young	.12	.30
162 Andre Carter	.12	.30
163 Eric Johnson	.12	.30
164 Jeff Garcia	.15	.40
165 Garrison Hearst	.15	.40
166 Terrell Owens	.20	.50
167 Kevan Barlow	.12	.30
168 Levon Kirkland	.12	.30
169 Ricky Watters	.15	.40
170 Trent Dilfer	.15	.40
171 Shaun Alexander	.15	.40
172 Koren Robinson	.12	.30
173 Darrell Jackson	.15	.40
174 Adam Archuleta	.12	.30
175 Aeneas Williams	.15	.40
176 Trung Canidate	.12	.30
177 Kurt Warner	.20	.50
178 Marshall Faulk	.20	.50
179 Torry Holt	.20	.50
180 Isaac Bruce	.20	.50
181 John Lynch	.15	.40
182 Joe Jurevicius	.12	.30
183 Brad Johnson	.15	.40
184 Rob Johnson	.15	.40
185 Keyshawn Johnson	.15	.40
186 Mike Alstott	.15	.40
187 Warren Sapp	.15	.40
188 Drew Bennett	.15	.40
189 Frank Wycheck	.12	.30
190 Kevin Dyson	.15	.40
191 Steve McNair	.20	.50
192 Eddie George	.15	.40
193 Jevon Kearse	.15	.40
194 Derrick Mason	.15	.40
195 Champ Bailey	.20	.50
196 Darrell Green	.20	.50
197 Bruce Smith	.20	.50
198 Jacquez Green	.12	.30
199 Stephen Davis	.15	.40
200 Rod Gardner	.12	.30
201 David Carr RC	1.00	2.50
202 Joey Harrington RC	1.00	2.50
203 Patrick Ramsey RC	1.00	2.50
204 Kurt Kittner RC	.60	1.50
205 Rohan Davey RC	1.00	2.50
206 Josh McCown RC	1.00	2.50
207 David Garrard RC	1.25	3.00
208 Randy Fasani RC	.75	2.00
209 Atrews Bell RC	.60	1.50
210 Brandon Doman RC	.60	1.50
211 Eric Crouch RC	1.00	2.50
212 Woody Dantzler RC	.75	2.00
213 Chad Hutchinson RC	.60	1.50
214 Zak Kustok RC	.60	1.50
215 Ronald Curry RC	.75	2.00
216 William Green RC	.75	2.00
217 T.J. Duckett RC	1.00	2.50
218 Clinton Portis RC	1.25	3.00
219 DeShaun Foster RC	1.00	2.50
220 Lamar Gordon RC	.75	2.00
221 Jonathan Wells RC	1.00	2.50
222 Adrian Peterson RC	1.00	2.50
223 Ladell Betts RC	1.00	2.50
224 Maurice Morris RC	.75	2.00
225 Brian Westbrook RC	1.50	4.00
226 Luke Staley RC	.60	1.50
227 Travis Stephens RC	.60	1.50
228 Craig Nall RC	.75	2.00
229 Chester Taylor RC	1.00	2.50
230 Ken Simonton RC	.60	1.50
231 Verron Haynes RC	.60	1.50
232 Tellis Redmon RC	.60	1.50
233 J.T. O'Sullivan RC	.75	2.00
234 Major Applewhite RC	1.00	2.50
235 Ricky Williams RC	.75	2.00
236 James Mungro RC	1.00	2.50
237 Josh Scobey RC	.75	2.00
238 Najeh Davenport RC	1.00	2.50
239 Dicenzo Miller RC	.60	1.50
240 Ennis Haywood RC	.60	1.50
241 Jabar Gaffney RC	1.00	2.50
242 Antonio Bryant RC	1.00	2.50
243 Donte Stallworth RC	1.00	2.50
244 Josh Reed RC	.75	2.00
245 Ashley Lelie RC	.75	2.00
246 Reche Caldwell RC	1.00	2.50
247 Marquise Walker RC	.60	1.50
248 Javon Walker RC	1.00	2.50
249 Andre Davis RC	.75	2.00
250 Antwaan Randle El RC	1.00	2.50
251 Kelly Campbell RC	.75	2.00
252 Cliff Russell RC	.60	1.50
253 Kahlil Hill RC	.60	1.50
254 Ron Johnson RC	.75	2.00
255 Deion Branch RC	1.00	2.50
256 Brian Poli-Dixon RC	.60	1.50
257 Freddie Milons RC	.60	1.50
258 Lee Mays RC	.60	1.50
259 Tim Carter RC	.75	2.00
260 Terry Charles RC	.60	1.50
261 Jamar Martin RC	.75	2.00
262 Jason McAddley RC	.75	2.00
263 Chris Hope RC	1.00	2.50
264 Howard Green RC	.60	1.50
265 Jeremy Shockey RC	1.50	4.00
266 Daniel Graham RC	.75	2.00
267 Eddie Freeman RC	.60	1.50
268 Julius Peppers RC	2.00	5.00
269 Kalimba Edwards RC	.75	2.00
270 Dwight Freeney RC	1.25	3.00
271 Dennis Johnson RC	.60	1.50
272 Alex Brown RC	1.00	2.50
273 Bryan Thomas RC	.60	1.50
274 Bryan Fletcher RC	.60	1.50
275 Will Overstreet RC	.60	1.50
276 Ryan Denney RC	.60	1.50
277 Charles Grant RC	1.00	2.50
278 John Henderson RC	.75	2.00
279 Albert Haynesworth RC	1.00	2.50
280 Wendell Bryant RC	.60	1.50
281 Ryan Sims RC	1.00	2.50
282 Anthony Weaver RC	.60	1.50
283 Larry Tripplett RC	.60	1.50
284 Alan Harper RC	.60	1.50
285 Napoleon Harris RC	.75	2.00
286 Robert Thomas RC	.60	1.50
287 Levar Fisher RC	.60	1.50
288 Andra Davis RC	.60	1.50
289 Quentin Jammer RC	1.00	2.50
290 Phillip Buchanon RC	1.00	2.50
291 Keyuo Craver RC	.60	1.50
292 Lito Sheppard RC	1.00	2.50
293 Rocky Calmus RC	.75	2.00
294 Mike Rumph RC	.60	1.50
295 Mike Echols RC	.60	1.50
296 Joseph Jefferson RC	.60	1.50
297 Roy Williams RC	1.00	2.50
298 Ed Reed RC	4.00	10.00
299 Michael Lewis RC	1.00	2.50
300 Eddie Drummond RC	.60	1.50

2002 Donruss Statline Career

*STARS/300-430: 3X TO 8X
*ROOKIES/300-430: .6X TO 1.5X
*STARS/200-299: 4X TO 10X
*ROOKIES/200-299: .8X TO 2X
*STARS/150-199: 5X TO 12X
*ROOKIES/150-199: 1X TO 2.5X
*VETS/101-149: 6X TO 15X
*ROOKIES/101-149: 1.2X TO 3X
*VETS/70-99: 10X TO 25X
*ROOKIES/70-99: 2X TO 5X
*VETS/45-69: 12X TO 30X
*ROOKIES/45-69: 2.5X TO 6X
*VETS/30-44: 20X TO 50X
*ROOKIES/30-44: 4X TO 10X
*ROOKIES/20-29: 5X TO 12X
*ROOKIES/10-19: 6X TO 15X
CAREER STATED PRINT RUN 17-430

2002 Donruss Statline Season

*ROOKIES/379: .6X TO 1.5X
*VETS/150-196: 5X TO 12X
*ROOKIES/150-196: 1X TO 2.5X
*VETS/101-149: 6X TO 15X
*ROOKIES/101-149: 1.2X TO 3X
*VETS/70-99: 10X TO 25X
*ROOKIES/70-99: 2X TO 5X
*VETS/45-69: 12X TO 30X
*ROOKIES/45-69: 2.5X TO 6X
*VETS/30-44: 20X TO 50X
*ROOKIES/30-44: 4X TO 10X
*VETS/20-29: 25X TO 60X
*ROOKIES/20-29: 5X TO 12X
*VETS/10-19: 30X TO 80X
*ROOKIES/10-19: 6X TO 15X
SEASON STATED PRINT RUN 3-379
SERIAL #'d UNDER 10 NOT PRICED

2002 Donruss All-Time Gridiron Kings

COMPLETE SET (10)	15.00	40.00

STATED PRINT RUN 2000 SER.#'d SETS
*STUDIO/250: 1X TO 2.5X BASIC INSERTS
STUDIO PRINT RUN 250 SER.#'d SETS

AT1 Dan Marino	4.00	10.00
AT2 Jim Kelly	2.00	5.00
AT3 Earl Campbell	1.50	4.00
AT4 John Elway	3.00	8.00
AT5 Dick Butkus	2.50	6.00
AT6 Troy Aikman	2.50	6.00
AT7 Barry Sanders	2.50	6.00
AT8 Roger Staubach	2.50	6.00
AT9 John Riggins	1.50	4.00
AT10 Steve Young	2.00	5.00

2002 Donruss Elite Series

COMPLETE SET (20)	20.00	50.00

STATED PRINT RUN 1500 SER.#'d SETS

ES1 Brett Favre	3.00	8.00
ES2 Kordell Stewart	1.00	2.50
ES3 Jevon Kearse	1.00	2.50
ES4 Ahman Green	1.00	2.50
ES5 Anthony Thomas	1.00	2.50
ES6 Cris Carter	1.25	3.00
ES7 Tim Brown	1.25	3.00
ES8 Ray Lewis	1.25	3.00
ES9 Aaron Brooks	1.00	2.50
ES10 Isaac Bruce	1.25	3.00
ES11 Chris Chambers	1.00	2.50
ES12 David Boston	.75	2.00
ES13 Jimmy Smith	1.00	2.50
ES14 Brian Urlacher	1.25	3.00
ES15 Edgerrin James	1.00	2.50
ES16 Dan Marino	3.00	8.00
ES17 Barry Sanders	2.00	5.00
ES18 Steve Young	1.50	4.00
ES19 Troy Aikman	2.00	5.00
ES20 Thurman Thomas	1.25	3.00

2002 Donruss Elite Series Autographs

STATED PRINT RUN 50 SER.#'d SETS

ES1 Brett Favre	100.00	175.00
ES2 Kordell Stewart	12.00	30.00
ES3 Jevon Kearse	12.00	30.00
ES4 Ahman Green	12.00	30.00
ES5 Anthony Thomas	12.00	30.00
ES6 Cris Carter	25.00	50.00
ES7 Tim Brown	25.00	50.00
ES8 Ray Lewis	30.00	60.00
ES9 Aaron Brooks	12.00	30.00
ES10 Isaac Bruce	15.00	40.00
ES11 Chris Chambers	12.00	30.00
ES12 David Boston	10.00	25.00
ES13 Jimmy Smith	12.00	30.00
ES14 Brian Urlacher	40.00	80.00
ES15 Edgerrin James	12.00	30.00
ES16 Dan Marino	75.00	150.00
ES17 Barry Sanders	60.00	120.00
ES18 Steve Young	40.00	80.00
ES19 Troy Aikman	50.00	100.00
ES20 Thurman Thomas	15.00	40.00

2002 Donruss Executive Producers

COMPLETE SET (20)	30.00	80.00

STATED PRINT RUN 1000 SER.#'d SETS

EP1 Randy Moss	1.50	4.00
EP2 Emmitt Smith	4.00	10.00
EP3 Kurt Warner	1.50	4.00
EP4 Jerry Rice	3.00	8.00
EP5 Edgerrin James	1.25	3.00
EP6 Anthony Thomas	1.25	3.00
EP7 Jerome Bettis	1.50	4.00
EP8 Daunte Culpepper	1.25	3.00
EP9 Brian Griese	1.25	3.00
EP10 Steve McNair	1.50	4.00
EP11 Marshall Faulk	1.50	4.00
EP12 Ahman Green	1.25	3.00
EP13 Peyton Manning	3.00	8.00
EP14 Shaun Alexander	1.25	3.00
EP15 Donovan McNabb	1.50	4.00
EP16 Jeff Garcia	1.25	3.00
EP17 Eddie George	1.25	3.00
EP18 Tim Brown	1.50	4.00
EP19 Brett Favre	4.00	10.00
EP20 Curtis Martin	1.50	4.00

2002 Donruss Gridiron Kings Inserts

COMPLETE SET (20)	25.00	60.00

STATED PRINT RUN 2000 SER.#'d SETS
*STUDIO/250: 1X TO 2.5X BASIC INSERT
STUDIO PRINT RUN 250 SER.#'d SETS

GK1 Emmitt Smith	3.00	8.00
GK2 Jerome Bettis	1.25	3.00
GK3 Jerry Rice	2.50	6.00
GK4 Brett Favre	3.00	8.00
GK5 Tom Brady	3.00	8.00
GK6 Anthony Thomas	1.00	2.50
GK7 Kurt Warner	1.25	3.00
GK8 Daunte Culpepper	1.00	2.50
GK9 Brian Griese	1.00	2.50
GK10 Cris Carter	1.25	3.00
GK11 Peyton Manning	2.50	6.00
GK12 Donovan McNabb	1.25	3.00
GK13 LaDainian Tomlinson	1.50	4.00
GK14 Eddie George	1.00	2.50
GK15 Edgerrin James	1.00	2.50
GK16 Randy Moss	1.25	3.00
GK17 Tim Brown	1.25	3.00
GK18 Brian Urlacher	1.25	3.00
GK19 Marshall Faulk	1.25	3.00
GK20 Michael Vick	2.00	5.00

2002 Donruss Jersey Kings

STATED PRINT RUN 125 SER.#'d SETS
*STUDIO/25: .8X TO 2X BASIC JSY/125
STUDIO PRINT RUN 25 SER.#'d SETS

JK1 Emmitt Smith	15.00	40.00
JK2 Jerome Bettis	6.00	15.00
JK3 Jerry Rice	12.00	30.00
JK4 Brett Favre	15.00	40.00
JK5 Tom Brady	15.00	40.00
JK6 Anthony Thomas	5.00	12.00
JK7 Kurt Warner	6.00	15.00
JK8 Daunte Culpepper	5.00	12.00
JK9 Brian Griese	5.00	12.00
JK10 Cris Carter	6.00	15.00
JK11 Peyton Manning	12.00	30.00
JK12 Donovan McNabb	6.00	15.00
JK13 LaDainian Tomlinson	8.00	20.00
JK14 Eddie George	5.00	12.00
JK15 Edgerrin James	5.00	12.00
JK16 Randy Moss	6.00	15.00
JK17 Tim Brown	6.00	15.00
JK18 Brian Urlacher	6.00	15.00
JK19 Marshall Faulk	6.00	15.00
JK20 Michael Vick	10.00	25.00

2002 Donruss Leather Kings

STATED PRINT RUN 250 SER.#'d SETS
*STUDIO/25: 1.2X TO 3X BASIC JSY/250
STUDIO PRINT RUN 25 SER.#'d SETS

LK1 Emmitt Smith	15.00	40.00
LK2 Jerome Bettis	6.00	15.00
LK3 Jerry Rice	12.00	30.00
LK4 Brett Favre	15.00	40.00
LK5 Tom Brady	15.00	40.00
LK6 Anthony Thomas	5.00	12.00
LK7 Kurt Warner	6.00	15.00
LK8 Daunte Culpepper	5.00	12.00
LK9 Brian Griese	5.00	12.00
LK10 Cris Carter	6.00	15.00
LK11 Peyton Manning	12.00	30.00
LK12 Donovan McNabb	6.00	15.00
LK13 LaDainian Tomlinson	8.00	20.00
LK14 Eddie George	5.00	12.00
LK15 Edgerrin James	5.00	12.00
LK16 Randy Moss	6.00	15.00
LK17 Tim Brown	6.00	15.00
LK18 Brian Urlacher	6.00	15.00
LK19 Marshall Faulk	6.00	16.00
LK20 Michael Vick	10.00	25.00

2002 Donruss Private Signings

STATED ODDS 1:160

PS1 Adrian Peterson	6.00	15.00
PS2 Alex Brown	6.00	15.00
PS3 Andra Davis	4.00	10.00
PS4 Andre Davis	5.00	12.00
PS5 Andre Lott	4.00	10.00
PS6 Antonio Bryant	6.00	15.00
PS7 Brian Poli-Dixon	4.00	10.00
PS8 Bryant McKinnie	4.00	10.00
PS9 Chad Hutchinson	4.00	10.00
PS10 Chester Taylor	10.00	25.00
PS11 Clinton Portis/50*	30.00	80.00
PS12 Cortlen Johnson	4.00	10.00
PS13 Damien Anderson	4.00	10.00
PS14 David Carr/50*	10.00	25.00
PS15 David Garrard	20.00	50.00
PS16 Demontray Carter	4.00	10.00
PS17 Dwight Freeney	15.00	30.00
PS18 Ed Reed	40.00	80.00
PS19 Eric Crouch/63*	10.00	25.00
PS20 Freddie Milons	4.00	10.00
PS21 Javon Walker NO AUTO	6.00	15.00
PS22 Ron Johnson	5.00	12.00
PS23 Jerramy Stevens/50*	10.00	25.00
PS24 Joey Harrington/75*	10.00	25.00
PS25 Josh Reed/50*	8.00	20.00
PS26 Julius Peppers/15*		
PS27 Kalimba Edwards	5.00	12.00
PS28 Kelly Campbell	5.00	12.00
PS29 Ken Simonton	4.00	10.00
PS30 Keyuo Craver		
PS31 Kurt Kittner/50*	6.00	15.00
PS32 Lito Sheppard	6.00	15.00
PS33 Luke Staley	4.00	10.00
PS34 Maurice Morris	5.00	12.00
PS35 Najeh Davenport	6.00	15.00
PS36 Quentin Jammer	6.00	15.00
PS37 Reche Caldwell/50*	10.00	25.00
PS38 Rocky Calmus	5.00	12.00
PS39 Tavon Mason	4.00	10.00
PS40 Woody Dantzler/25*	12.00	30.00
PS41 John Riggins/100*	20.00	50.00
PS42 Deuce McAllister/50*	8.00	20.00
PS43 Drew Brees/50*	40.00	80.00
PS44 Edgerrin James/27*	15.00	40.00
PS45 Emmitt Smith/25*	175.00	300.00
PS46 Kurt Warner/35*	20.00	50.00
PS47 Marshall Faulk/50*	15.00	40.00
PS48 Quincy Carter/50*	6.00	15.00
PS49 Tim Brown/50*	15.00	40.00
PS50 Brett Favre/25*	150.00	250.00

2002 Donruss Rookie Year Materials

STATED PRINT RUN 100 SER.#'d SETS

RY1 John Riggins	15.00	40.00
RY2 Joe Montana	50.00	120.00
RY3 Randy Moss	10.00	25.00
RY4 Ricky Williams	8.00	20.00
RY5 Tim Couch	6.00	15.00
RY6 Peyton Manning	20.00	50.00
RY7 Mark Brunell	8.00	20.00
RY8 Keyshawn Johnson	8.00	20.00
RY9 LaDainian Tomlinson	12.00	30.00
RY10 Michael Vick	15.00	40.00

2002 Donruss Rookie Year Materials Numbers

STATED PRINT RUN 2-84
SERIAL #'d UNDER 25 NOT PRICED

RY1 John Riggins/44	25.00	60.00
RY3 Randy Moss/84	15.00	40.00
RY4 Ricky Williams/34	20.00	50.00
RY9 LaDainian Tomlinson/21	25.00	60.00

2002 Donruss Zoning Commission

COMPLETE SET (8)	15.00	40.00

STATED PRINT RUN 500 SER.#'d SETS

ZC1 Marshall Faulk	2.50	6.00
ZC2 Terrell Owens	2.50	6.00
ZC3 Shaun Alexander	2.00	5.00
ZC4 Marvin Harrison	2.50	6.00
ZC5 Antowain Smith	2.00	5.00
ZC6 Kurt Warner	2.50	6.00
ZC7 Jeff Garcia	2.00	5.00
ZC8 Brett Favre	6.00	15.00

2003 Donruss AFL Star Standouts

These cards were issued in one 9-card panel that included one cover/advertising card in the middle. Each features a star Arena Football League player with a typical all-color cardback. The cards are commonly found in uncut sheet form but can be separated at the perforations.

COMPLETE SET (9)	4.00	8.00
1 Greg Hopkins	.40	1.00
2 Aaron Garcia	.50	1.25
3 Jay Gruden	.75	2.00
4 Chris Jackson	.40	1.00
5 Jim Kubiak	.50	1.25
6 Freddie Solomon	.50	1.25
7 Clevan Thomas	.40	1.00
8 Hunkie Cooper	.40	1.00
NNO Cover Card	.40	1.00

2006 Donruss Frito Lay

These cards were issued four at a time in specially marked packages of Frito Lay products in January 2007. Each card was produced in the design of the 2006 Score set but included a Donruss logo at the top of the card along with a Frito Lay logo. Two partial parallel sets were also issued with the cards featuring either a Doritos or Cheetos Brand logo on the front. The Doritos version is slightly tougher to find than the base Frito Lay with the Cheetos version being the most difficult to pull.

COMPLETE SET (28)	25.00	50.00
1 Brett Favre	1.50	4.00
2 Ben Roethlisberger	1.00	2.50
3 Peyton Manning	1.25	3.00
4 LaDainian Tomlinson	.75	2.00
5 Larry Johnson	.60	1.50
6 Tom Brady	1.25	3.00
7 Shaun Alexander	.60	1.50
8 Ronnie Brown	.75	2.00
9 Eli Manning	1.00	2.50
10 Cadillac Williams	.60	1.50
11 Michael Vick	.75	2.00
12 Brian Urlacher	.75	2.00
13 Carson Palmer	.75	2.00
14 Roy Williams S	.60	1.50

15 Troy Polamalu	1.00	2.50
16 Donovan McNabb	.75	2.00
17 Clinton Portis	.75	2.00
18 DeAngelo Williams	.75	2.00
19 A.J. Hawk	.60	1.50
20 Laurence Maroney	.50	1.25
21 Greg Jennings	1.25	3.00
22 Matt Leinart	.60	1.50
23 Jay Cutler	1.25	3.00
24 Reggie Bush	1.25	3.00
25 Vince Young	.75	2.00
CL1 Matt Leinart	.75	2.00
Reggie Bush		
(Checklist Card)		
CL2 Kellen Clemens	.30	.75
Leon Washington		
(Checklist Card)		
CL3 Maurice Drew	.60	1.50
Marcedes Lewis		
(Checklist Card)		

2006 Donruss Frito Lay Cheetos

COMPLETE SET (16)	30.00	60.00
*CHEETOS: .6X TO 1.5X FRITO LAY		
CL5 LenDale White	1.25	3.00
Matt Leinart		
Reggie Bush		
(Checklist Card)		

2006 Donruss Frito Lay Doritos

COMPLETE SET (16)	25.00	50.00
*DORITOS: .5X TO 1.2X FRITO LAY		
CL4 Matt Leinart	.50	1.25
Vince Young		
(Checklist Card)		

2006 Donruss Playoff Orlando Auto Auction Association

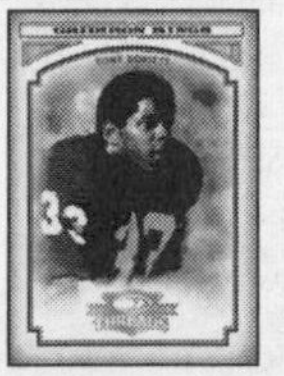

COMPLETE SET (11)	15.00	30.00
H03 Jason White	1.50	4.00
2006 Donruss Threads Gridiron Kings)		
H51 Dick Kazmaier	1.50	4.00
2006 Donruss Threads Gridiron Kings)		
H58 Pete Dawkins	1.50	4.00
2006 Donruss Threads Gridiron Kings)		
H60 Joe Bellino	1.50	4.00
2006 Donruss Threads Gridiron Kings)		
H67 Gary Beban	1.50	4.00
2006 Donruss Threads Gridiron Kings)		
H72 Johnny Rodgers	2.00	5.00
2006 Donruss Threads Gridiron Kings)		
H74 Archie Griffin	2.00	5.00
2006 Donruss Threads Gridiron Kings)		
H76 Tony Dorsett	2.50	6.00
2006 Donruss Threads Gridiron Kings)		
H70 Billy Sims	2.00	5.00
2006 Donruss Threads Gridiron Kings)		
H92 Gino Torretta	1.50	4.00
2005 Playoff Honors Award Winners)		
H96 Danny Wuerffel	1.50	4.00
2005 Playoff Honors Award Winners)		

2006 Donruss Thanksgiving Classic Beckett Inserts

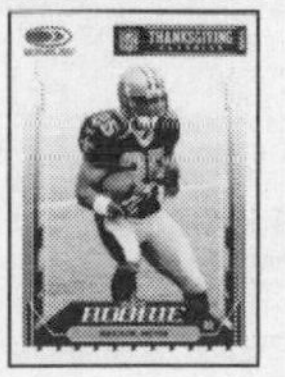

COMPLETE SET (6)	6.00	12.00
DN1 Jay Cutler	1.00	2.50
DN2 Mike Bell	.50	1.25
MI1 Ronnie Brown	.50	1.25
NO1 Reggie Bush	1.00	2.50
TB1 Cadillac Williams	.40	1.00
TN1 Vince Young	.60	1.50

2006 Donruss Tom Landry

This single card was given away at the event of the memorial of the Texas State Cemetery in the name of Tom Landry.

NNO Tom Landry	2.00	5.00
(Dedication of Texas State Cemetery)/(March 24, 2006)		

2007 Donruss Frito Lay

COMPLETE SET (25)	20.00	40.00
1 Adrian Peterson	3.00	8.00
2 Brady Quinn	.75	2.00
3 Calvin Johnson	2.50	6.00
4 Gaines Adams	.75	2.00
5 Marshawn Lynch	.75	2.00
6 Ted Ginn	.60	1.50
7 JaMarcus Russell	.50	1.25
8 Donald Driver	.50	1.25
9 Champ Bailey	.40	1.00
10 DeAngelo Hall	.40	1.00
11 Frank Gore	.50	1.25
12 Jonathan Vilma	.40	1.00
13 Larry Johnson	.30	.75
14 Drew Brees	.50	1.25
15 Torry Holt	.40	1.00
16 Vince Young	.40	1.00
17 Antonio Gates	.50	1.25
18 Andre Johnson	.40	1.00
19 Anquan Boldin	.40	1.00
20 Carson Palmer	.40	1.00
21 Maurice Jones-Drew	.50	1.25
22 Michael Strahan	.40	1.00
23 Shaun Alexander	.40	1.00
24 Steve Smith	.40	1.00
25 Tedy Bruschi	.50	1.25
C1 Brian Westbrook	.60	1.50
(Cheetos)		
C2 Steve McNair	.60	1.50
(Cheetos)		
D1 Tony Romo	1.00	2.50
(Doritos)		
D2 Marvin Harrison	.75	2.00
(Doritos)		
D3 LaRon Landry	.75	2.00
(Doritos)		
L1 Devin Hester	.75	2.00
(Lay's)		
L2 Hines Ward	.75	2.00
(Lay's)		

2007 Donruss London Game

Many fans who attended the 2007 international game in London were treated to this complete set. The set features three cards from each of the two teams that matched up.

COMPLETE SET (6)	6.00	12.00
1 Eli Manning	1.00	2.50
2 Jason Taylor	.75	2.00
3 Jeremy Shockey	.75	2.00
4 Ronnie Brown	.75	2.00
5 Steve Smith USC	.60	1.50
6 Ted Ginn	.50	1.25

2007 Donruss National Convention

COMPLETE SET (7)	15.00	40.00
1 JaMarcus Russell	.60	1.50
2 Calvin Johnson	3.00	8.00
3 Joe Thomas	1.00	2.50
4 Adrian Peterson	4.00	10.00
5 Ted Ginn Jr.	.75	2.00
6 Troy Smith	1.00	2.50
7 Brady Quinn	1.00	2.50
(issued at show booth only)		

2007 Donruss Pepsi National Convention

This set was issued at the 2007 National Sports Collector's Convention in Cleveland. Collectors who presented a special coupon at the Donruss Playoff booth at the event received a complete set. Each card features the Pepsi logo on the front.

COMPLETE SET (6)	5.00	12.00
1 Brady Quinn	.50	1.25
2 Torry Holt	.40	1.00
3 Adrian Peterson	2.00	5.00
4 Calvin Johnson	1.50	4.00
5 Tony Romo	.60	1.50
6 Dwayne Jarrett	.40	1.00

2007 Donruss Playoff Award Winner Promos

These cards were issued at the 2007 Super Bowl XLI Card Show in Miami and feature players who won 2006 NFL season awards. Each card, except Reggie Bush, was issued one card at a time in exchange for the collector opening three packs of 2006 Donruss Playoff football products at their card show booth. The Reggie Bush card was issued as part of the wrapper redemption program at the Beckett Media booth.

MVPLT LaDainian Tomlinson	1.00	2.50
(Offensive Player of the Year)		
CPOYCP Chad Pennington	.60	1.50
(Comeback Player of the Year)		
DPOYJT Jason Taylor	.50	1.25
(Defensive Player of the Year)		
DROYDR DeMeco Ryans	.60	1.50
(Defensive Rookie of the Year)		
OPOYLT LaDainian Tomlinson	1.00	2.50
OROYVY Vince Young	3.00	8.00
(Offensive Rookie of the Year)		
SPEDRB Reggie Bush	5.00	12.00
(Special Edition)		

2007 Donruss Thanksgiving Classic NFL Network

COMPLETE SET (4)	2.50	6.00
1 Rich Eisen	.60	1.50
2 Marshall Faulk	.75	2.00
3 Steve Mariucci	.60	1.50
4 Deion Sanders	.75	2.00

2008 Donruss London Game

Many fans who attended the 2008 international game in London were treated to this complete set. The set features three cards from each of the two teams that matched up.

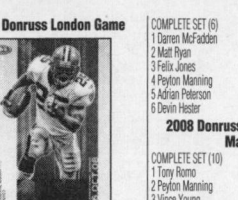

COMPLETE SET (6)	6.00	12.00
1 Reggie Bush	.75	2.00
2 Drew Brees	.75	2.00
3 Sedrick Ellis	.75	2.00
4 LaDainian Tomlinson	.75	2.00
5 Shawne Merriman	.60	1.50
6 Antoine Cason	.75	2.00

2008 Donruss National Convention VIP Crown

V1 Darren McFadden	3.00	8.00
V2 Matt Forte	2.00	5.00
V3 Matt Ryan	5.00	12.00
V4 Jonathan Stewart	2.00	5.00
V5 Joe Flacco	4.00	10.00
V6 Felix Jones	2.00	5.00

2008 Donruss National Convention VIP Crown Autographs

RANDOM INSERTS IN 2009 LIMITED PACKS		
V3 Matt Ryan	100.00	200.00

2008 Donruss Playoff Award Winner Promos

Cards from this set were issued at the 2008 NFL Experience Super Bowl Card Show in Glendale Arizona. Most were released as complete sets for winners of the "Spin the Wheel" game at the Donruss Playoff booth at the show. The Greg Ellis card was short-printed and the Adrian Peterson RB foil card was released at the Beckett booth at the show.

COMPLETE SET (7)	5.00	12.00
AP Adrian Peterson OROY	1.00	2.50
BS Bob Sanders DPOY	.50	1.25
GE Greg Ellis CPOY SP	.40	1.00
PW Patrick Willis DROY	.50	1.25
TB1 Tom Brady MVP	1.00	2.50
TB2 Tom Brady OPOY	1.00	2.50
APRB Adrian Peterson RB foil	1.00	2.50
NE16 Tom Brady	1.00	2.50
Wes Welker		
Randy Moss		

2008 Donruss Playoff Silver Signatures

Cards from this set were issued via mail as replacement cards for various unfulfilled redemptions from Donruss Playoff football products. The company also released some for promotional purposes at shows. Each features a sticker autograph of the featured player. Although the cards are not serial numbered, Donruss Playoff did announce print runs for most of the cards.

AJ Andre Johnson/104*	6.00	15.00
AM Art Monk/122*	20.00	40.00
AR Andre Reed/160*	12.00	30.00
AY Ashton Youboty/54*	5.00	12.00
CB Cedric Benson/64*	6.00	15.00
CH Chris Henry/146*	6.00	15.00
CR Carlos Rogers/548*	5.00	12.00
DB Derrick Brooks/577*	6.00	15.00
DM Dan Marino/64*	100.00	200.00
HE Herman Edwards/628*	10.00	25.00
JA Jared Allen	30.00	60.00
JE John Elway	60.00	120.00
JK Jevon Kearse/261*	6.00	15.00
JL Johnny Lujack/230*	12.00	30.00
KJ Kevin Jones/42*	5.00	12.00
LB Lance Briggs/825*	5.00	12.00
LS Lee Roy Selmon/34*	12.00	30.00
PD Pete Dawkins/47*	10.00	25.00
RB Reggie Brown/37*	5.00	12.00
TB Terry Bradshaw/31*	50.00	100.00
TJ Tarvaris Jackson/101*	6.00	15.00
TR Tony Romo/10*		
APJ Adam Jones/185*	5.00	12.00
AR2 Antrel Rolle/168*	5.00	12.00
JT2 Joe Theismann/1050*	8.00	20.00

2008 Donruss Pop Warner

This set was issued at the 2008 Pop Warner Super Bowl. Each card features the Pop Warner logo at the top.

COMPLETE SET (6)	6.00	12.00
1 Darren McFadden	.75	2.00
2 Matt Ryan	1.25	3.00
3 Felix Jones	.50	1.25
4 Peyton Manning	1.00	2.50
5 Adrian Peterson	1.00	2.50
6 Devin Hester	.60	1.50

2008 Donruss 7-11 EA Sports Madden

COMPLETE SET (10)	15.00	40.00
1 Tony Romo	1.50	4.00
2 Peyton Manning	2.00	5.00
3 Vince Young	1.00	2.50
4 LaDainian Tomlinson	1.25	3.00
5 Adrian Peterson	2.00	5.00
6 Ben Roethlisberger	1.25	3.00
7 Darren McFadden	3.00	8.00
8 Matt Ryan	5.00	12.00
9 Maurice Jones-Drew	1.00	2.50
10 Matt Hasselbeck	1.00	2.50

2008 Donruss Thanksgiving Classic NFL Network

Cards from this set were issued one per team set with either the Dallas Cowboys or Philadelphia Eagles Thanksgiving day sets. Each features an NFL Network commentator on the front and a brief NFL Network schedule on the back.

COMPLETE SET (7)	3.00	8.00
1 Terrell Davis	.60	1.50
2 Rich Eisen	.40	1.00
3 Marshall Faulk	.60	1.50
4 Steve Mariucci	.40	1.00
5 Deion Sanders	.60	1.50
6 Warren Sapp	.50	1.25
7 Rod Woodson	.50	1.25

2008 Donruss Toronto Game

Many fans who attended the 2008 international game in Toronto were treated to this complete set. The set features three cards from each of the two teams that matched up.

COMPLETE SET (6)	4.00	8.00
1 Marshawn Lynch	.60	1.50
2 Lee Evans	.60	1.50
3 James Hardy	.30	.75
4 Ronnie Brown	.60	1.50
5 Ted Ginn	.60	1.50
6 Chad Henne	.40	1.00

2009 Donruss Draft NFL Patch Promos

Cards from this set were released at the Hawaii Trade Conference Mainland Edition in April 2009. Each includes a manufactured swatch featuring an NFL logo.

CW Chris Wells SP	6.00	15.00
MC Michael Crabtree	8.00	20.00
MS1 Mark Sanchez	12.00	30.00
MS2 Matthew Stafford	20.00	50.00

2009 Donruss Draft Team Logo Promos

Cards from this promo set were issued at the NFL Draft in April 2009. Each features a sticker of the player's new NFL team helmet logo attached to the cardfront.

CW Chris Wells	15.00	40.00
JM Jeremy Maclin	15.00	40.00
KM Knowshon Moreno	10.00	25.00
MC Michael Crabtree	20.00	50.00
PH Percy Harvin	15.00	40.00
MS1 Mark Sanchez	30.00	80.00
MS2 Matthew Stafford	50.00	120.00

2009 Donruss Playoff Award Winner Promos

This set was issued at the Donruss/Playoff booth during the 2009 Super Bowl Card Show in Tampa, Florida. Single cards were given to collectors as prizes for a spin-the-wheel contest. The features former Super Bowl MVP Award winners and top 2008 NFL rookies.

COMPLETE SET (12)	7.50	15.00
SBAP Adrian Peterson	1.00	2.50
SBBF Brett Favre Jets	1.50	4.00
SBCJ Chris Johnson	.60	1.50
SBDJ Dexter Jackson SBMVP	.40	1.00
SBDM Darren McFadden	.60	1.50
SBEM Eli Manning SBMVP	.60	1.50
SBHW Hines Ward SBMVP	.50	1.25
SBMR Matt Ryan	.60	1.50
SBPM Peyton Manning SBMVP	1.00	2.50
SBRL Ray Lewis SBMVP	.60	1.50
SBTB Tom Brady SBMVP	1.00	2.50
OROYMR Matt Ryan ROY	.60	1.50

2009 Donruss Pro Bowl Promos

As part of their sponsorship of the 2009 NFL Pro Bowl, Donruss created this set of 10-cards issued around that weekend's events.

COMPLETE SET (10)	6.00	15.00
AJ Andre Johnson	.60	1.50
AP Adrian Peterson	1.25	3.00
CJ Chris Johnson	.75	2.00
DB Drew Brees	.75	2.00
JF Joe Flacco	.75	2.00
LF Larry Fitzgerald	.75	2.00
LT LaDainian Tomlinson	.75	2.00
MF Matt Forte	.75	2.00
MR Matt Ryan	.75	2.00
PM Peyton Manning	1.25	3.00

2009 Donruss Super Bowl XLIII Jersey Promos

Cards from this set were issued at the Donruss/Playoff booth during the 2009 Super Bowl Card Show in Tampa, Florida. A single card was given to any collector that purchased a Score Super Bowl XLIII Glossy factory set at the booth during the show.

AP Adrian Peterson	15.00	40.00
DM Darren McFadden	10.00	25.00
FJ Felix Jones	10.00	25.00
JA Joseph Addai	10.00	25.00
LT LaDainian Tomlinson	10.00	25.00
PR Philip Rivers	10.00	25.00
RM Randy Moss	10.00	25.00
RM Rashard Mendenhall	8.00	20.00
TB Tom Brady	15.00	40.00
TO Terrell Owens	10.00	25.00

2009 Donruss Super Bowl XLIII VIP Promos

COMPLETE SET (11)	12.00	30.00
AP Adrian Peterson	1.50	4.00
BF Brett Favre	2.50	6.00
CJ Chris Johnson	1.00	2.50
DJ Dexter Jackson	.60	1.50
DM Darren McFadden	1.00	2.50
EM Eli Manning	1.00	2.50
HW Hines Ward	.75	2.00
MR Matt Ryan	1.00	2.50
PM Peyton Manning	1.50	4.00
RL Ray Lewis	1.00	2.50
TB Tom Brady	1.50	4.00

2001 Donruss Classics

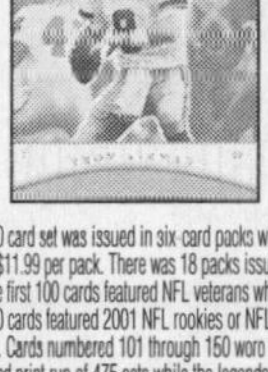

This 200 card set was issued in six-card packs with an SRP of $11.99 per pack. There was 18 packs issued per box. The first 100 cards featured NFL veterans while the final 100 cards featured 2001 NFL rookies or NFL legends. Cards numbered 101 through 150 were issued at a stated print run of 475 sets while the legends were issued at a stated print run of 1425 sets.

COMP.SET w/o SPs (100)	7.50	20.00
1 David Boston	.20	.50
2 Jake Plummer	.25	.60
3 Thomas Jones	.25	.60
4 Jamal Anderson	.25	.60
5 Chris Redman	.30	.75
6 Elvis Grbac	.25	.60
7 Jamal Lewis	.30	.75
8 Qadry Ismail	.25	.60
9 Ray Lewis	.30	.75
10 Shannon Sharpe	.30	.75
11 Travis Taylor	.20	.50
12 Eric Moulds	.25	.60
13 Rob Johnson	.25	.60
14 Muhsin Muhammad	.25	.60
15 Brian Urlacher	.40	1.00
16 Cade McNown	.25	.60
17 Marcus Robinson	.25	.60
18 Akili Smith	.20	.50
19 Corey Dillon	.25	.60
20 Peter Warrick	.25	.60
21 Courtney Brown	.20	.50
22 Tim Couch	.20	.50
23 Emmitt Smith	.75	2.00
24 Brian Griese	.25	.60
25 Ed McCaffery	.25	.60
26 Olandis Gary	.20	.50
27 Mike Anderson	.25	.60
28 Rod Smith	.25	.60
29 Terrell Davis	.30	.75
30 Charlie Batch	.25	.60
31 James Stewart	.20	.50
32 Ahman Green	.30	.75
33 Antonio Freeman	.30	.75
34 Brett Favre	1.00	2.50
35 Edgerrin James	.30	.75
36 Marvin Harrison	.30	.75
37 Peyton Manning	.75	2.00
38 Fred Taylor	.30	.75
39 Jimmy Smith	.25	.60
40 Keenan McCardell	.25	.60
41 Mark Brunell	.25	.60
42 Sylvester Morris	.20	.50
43 Tony Gonzalez	.30	.75
44 Zach Thomas	.30	.75
45 Jay Fiedler	.25	.60
46 Lamar Smith	.25	.60
47 Cris Carter	.30	.75
48 Daunte Culpepper	.25	.60
49 Randy Moss	.30	.75
50 Drew Bledsoe	.30	.75
51 Terry Glenn	.25	.60
52 Aaron Brooks	.25	.60
53 Joe Horn	.25	.60
54 Ricky Williams	.30	.75
55 Amani Toomer	.25	.60
56 Ike Hilliard	.25	.60
57 Kerry Collins	.25	.60
58 Ron Dayne	.25	.60
59 Tiki Barber	.30	.75
60 Chad Pennington	.30	.75
61 Curtis Martin	.30	.75
62 Laveranues Coles	.25	.60
63 Vinny Testaverde	.25	.60
64 Wayne Chrebet	.25	.60
65 Charles Woodson	.30	.75
66 Rich Gannon	.25	.60
67 Tim Brown	.30	.75
68 Tyrone Wheatley	.25	.60
69 Corey Simon	.20	.50
70 Donovan McNabb	.30	.75
71 Duce Staley	.25	.60
72 Jerome Bettis	.30	.75
73 Plaxico Burress	.25	.60
74 Doug Flutie	.30	.75
75 Junior Seau	.30	.75
76 Jeff Garcia	.25	.60
77 Jerry Rice	.60	1.50
78 Giovanni Carmazzi	.20	.50
79 Terrell Owens	.30	.75
80 Darrell Jackson	.25	.60
81 Ricky Watters	.25	.60
82 Shaun Alexander	.30	.75
83 Isaac Bruce	.30	.75
84 Kurt Warner	.50	1.25
85 Marshall Faulk	.30	.75
86 Torry Holt	.25	.60
87 Brad Johnson	.25	.60
88 Keyshawn Johnson	.25	.60
89 Mike Alstott	.25	.60
90 Shaun King	.20	.50
91 Warren Sapp	.25	.60
92 Warrick Dunn	.30	.75
93 Eddie George	.30	.75
94 Jevon Kearse	.25	.60
95 Steve McNair	.30	.75
96 Jeff George	.25	.60
97 Stephen Davis	.25	.60
98 Charlie Garner	.25	.60
99 Trent Dilfer	.25	.60
100 Troy Aikman	.50	1.25
101 Michael Vick RC	10.00	25.00
102 Drew Brees RC	20.00	40.00
103 Chris Weinke RC	2.00	5.00
104 Mike McMahon RC	2.00	5.00
105 Jesse Palmer RC	2.00	5.00
106 Quincy Carter RC	2.00	5.00
107 Josh Heupel RC	2.50	6.00
108 Tim Hasselbeck RC	2.00	5.00
109 LaDainian Tomlinson RC	8.00	20.00
110 Deuce McAllister RC	2.50	6.00
111 Michael Bennett RC	2.00	5.00
112 Anthony Thomas RC	2.50	6.00
113 LaMont Jordan RC	2.50	6.00
114 Travis Henry RC	2.00	5.00
115 Kevan Barlow RC	2.00	5.00
116 Travis Minor RC	2.00	5.00
117 Rudi Johnson RC	2.50	6.00
118 David Allen RC	1.50	4.00
119 Heath Evans RC	2.00	5.00
120 Moran Norris RC	1.50	4.00
121 David Terrell RC	2.00	5.00
122 Koren Robinson RC	2.00	5.00
123 Rod Gardner RC	2.00	5.00
124 Santana Moss RC	3.00	8.00
125 Freddie Mitchell RC	1.50	4.00
126 Reggie Wayne RC	5.00	12.00
127 Quincy Morgan RC	2.00	5.00
128 Chad Johnson RC	4.00	10.00
129 Robert Ferguson RC	2.50	6.00
130 Chris Chambers RC	2.50	6.00
131 Snoop Minnis RC	1.50	4.00
132 Eddie Berlin RC	1.50	4.00
133 Alex Bannister RC	1.50	4.00
134 Todd Heap RC	2.50	6.00
135 Alge Crumpler RC	2.50	6.00
136 Justin Smith RC	2.50	6.00
137 Andre Carter RC	2.00	5.00
138 Jamal Reynolds RC	1.50	4.00
139 Richard Seymour RC	2.50	6.00
140 Marcus Stroud RC	2.00	5.00
141 Casey Hampton RC	2.50	6.00
142 Gerard Warren RC	2.00	5.00
143 Torrance Marshall RC	1.50	4.00
144 Brian Allen RC	1.50	4.00
145 Morlon Greenwood RC	1.50	4.00
146 Keith Adams RC	1.50	4.00
147 Will Allen RC	2.50	6.00
148 Nate Clements RC	2.00	5.00
149 Adam Archuleta RC	2.00	5.00
150 Hakim Akbar RC	1.50	4.00
151 James Lofton	.50	1.25
152 Jim Kelly	1.00	2.50
153 Gale Sayers	1.00	2.50
154 Mike Singletary	.75	2.00
155 Boomer Esiason	.60	1.50
156 Charlie Joiner	.50	1.25
157 Ken Anderson	.60	1.50
158 Y.A. Tittle	.75	2.00
159 Jim Brown	1.25	3.00
160 Otto Graham	.60	1.50
161 Ozzie Newsome	.50	1.25
162 Drew Pearson	.60	1.50
163 Lance Alworth	.60	1.50
164 Roger Staubach	1.25	3.00
165 Tony Dorsett	.75	2.00
166 John Elway	2.00	5.00
167 Barry Sanders	2.00	5.00
168 Bart Starr	1.50	4.00
169 Paul Hornung	.75	2.00
170 Earl Campbell	.75	2.00
171 Warren Moon	.75	2.00
172 Johnny Unitas	1.50	4.00
173 Deacon Jones	.60	1.50
174 Eric Dickerson	.60	1.50
175 Bob Griese	.75	2.00
176 Dan Marino	2.00	5.00
177 Larry Csonka	.75	2.00
178 Paul Warfield	.60	1.50
179 Fran Tarkenton	1.00	2.50
180 Archie Manning	.60	1.50
181 Frank Gifford	.75	2.00
182 Lawrence Taylor	.75	2.00
183 Dan Fouts	.75	2.00
184 Don Maynard	.60	1.50
185 Joe Namath	1.25	3.00
186 Fred Biletnikoff	.75	2.00
187 Marcus Allen	.75	2.00
188 Jim Plunkett	.60	1.50
189 Franco Harris	.75	2.00
190 Terry Bradshaw	1.25	3.00
191 Joe Montana	2.00	5.00
192 Roger Craig	.60	1.50
193 Steve Young	1.00	2.50
194 Dwight Clark	.60	1.50
195 Steve Largent	.75	2.00
196 Art Monk	.60	1.50
197 Charley Taylor	.60	1.50
198 Joe Theismann	.75	2.00
199 Sammy Baugh	.75	2.00
200 Sonny Jurgensen	.75	2.00

2001 Donruss Classics Significant Signatures

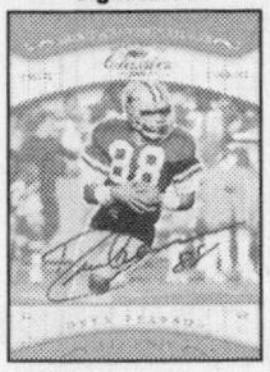

STATED ODDS 1:18		
ANNOUNCED PRINT RUNS LISTED BELOW		
101 Michael Vick/25*	150.00	300.00
102 Drew Brees/30*	175.00	300.00
103 Chris Weinke/30*	12.00	30.00
104 Mike McMahon/125*	6.00	15.00
105 Jesse Palmer/150*	6.00	15.00
106 Quincy Carter/50*	8.00	20.00
107 Josh Heupel/100*	8.00	20.00
108 Tim Hasselbeck/150*	6.00	15.00
109 LaDainian Tomlinson/50*	125.00	250.00
110 Deuce McAllister/25*	15.00	40.00
111 Michael Bennett/30*	12.00	30.00
112 Anthony Thomas/50*	10.00	25.00
113 LaMont Jordan/50*	10.00	25.00
114 Travis Henry/100*	6.00	15.00
115 Kevan Barlow/125*	6.00	15.00
116 Travis Minor/150*	6.00	15.00
117 Rudi Johnson/75*	10.00	25.00
118 David Allen/150*	5.00	12.00
119 Heath Evans/150*	6.00	15.00
120 Moran Norris/150*	5.00	12.00
121 David Terrell/25*	12.00	30.00
122 Koren Robinson/25*	12.00	30.00
123 Rod Gardner/25*	12.00	30.00
124 Santana Moss/30*	25.00	50.00
125 Freddie Mitchell/30*	10.00	25.00
126 Reggie Wayne/30*	50.00	100.00
127 Quincy Morgan/75*	8.00	20.00
128 Chad Johnson/75*	15.00	40.00
129 Robert Ferguson/85*	8.00	20.00
130 Chris Chambers/75*	10.00	25.00
131 Snoop Minnis/100*	5.00	12.00
132 Eddie Berlin/190*	5.00	12.00
133 Alex Bannister/100*	5.00	12.00
134 Todd Heap/100*	8.00	20.00
135 Alge Crumpler/200*	8.00	20.00
136 Justin Smith/75*	10.00	25.00
137 Andre Carter/50*	8.00	20.00
138 Jamal Reynolds/55*	6.00	15.00
139 Richard Seymour No Auto	5.00	12.00
140 Marcus Stroud/200*	6.00	15.00
141 Casey Hampton No Auto	5.00	12.00
142 Gerard Warren/50*	8.00	20.00
143 Torrance Marshall	5.00	12.00
144 Brian Allen	5.00	12.00
145 Morlon Greenwood	5.00	12.00
146 Keith Adams No Auto	3.00	8.00
147 Will Allen/150*	8.00	20.00
148 Nate Clements No Auto	4.00	10.00
149 Adam Archuleta No Auto	4.00	10.00
150 Hakim Akbar	5.00	12.00
151 James Lofton	8.00	20.00
152 Jim Kelly/175*	20.00	50.00
153 Gale Sayers/175*	30.00	50.00
154 Mike Singletary	12.00	30.00
155 Boomer Esiason/100*	10.00	25.00
156 Charlie Joiner	8.00	20.00
157 Ken Anderson	10.00	25.00
158 Y.A. Tittle	20.00	40.00
159 Jim Brown	40.00	80.00
160 Otto Graham	30.00	60.00
161 Ozzie Newsome	8.00	20.00
162 Drew Pearson	10.00	25.00
163 Lance Alworth/100*	30.00	60.00
164 Roger Staubach/50*	60.00	120.00
165 Tony Dorsett/100*	30.00	60.00
166 John Elway/50*	100.00	200.00
167 Barry Sanders/75*	60.00	120.00
168 Bart Starr/125*	75.00	150.00
169 Paul Hornung	12.00	30.00
170 Earl Campbell/100*	20.00	40.00
171 Warren Moon/142*	12.50	30.00
172 Johnny Unitas/125*	200.00	350.00
173 Deacon Jones	12.00	30.00
174 Eric Dickerson/100*	15.00	40.00
175 Bob Griese	12.00	30.00
176 Dan Marino/50*	100.00	200.00
177 Larry Csonka	15.00	40.00
178 Paul Warfield	10.00	25.00
179 Fran Tarkenton	15.00	40.00
180 Archie Manning	10.00	25.00
181 Frank Gifford	25.00	50.00
182 Lawrence Taylor/50*	25.00	50.00
183 Dan Fouts	12.00	30.00
184 Don Maynard	10.00	25.00
185 Joe Namath	50.00	100.00
186 Fred Biletnikoff	12.00	30.00
187 Marcus Allen/50*	25.00	50.00
188 Jim Plunkett	10.00	25.00
189 Franco Harris	30.00	60.00
190 Terry Bradshaw/150*	50.00	100.00
191 Joe Montana	50.00	100.00
192 Roger Craig	10.00	25.00
193 Steve Young/75*	35.00	60.00
194 Dwight Clark	10.00	25.00
195 Steve Largent	12.00	30.00
196 Art Monk	15.00	40.00
197 Charley Taylor	10.00	25.00
198 Joe Theismann/100*	12.00	30.00
199 Sammy Baugh/100*	100.00	200.00
200 Sonny Jurgensen/100*	12.00	30.00

2001 Donruss Classics Timeless Tributes

*VET 1-100: 5X TO 12X BASIC CARDS
*ROOKIES 101-150: .8X TO 2X
*LEGENDS 151-200: 2X TO 5X
STATED PRINT RUN 100 SER.#'d SETS

2001 Donruss Classics Classic Combos

DUALS PRINT RUN 100 SERIAL #'d SETS		
QUADS PRINT RUN 25 SERIAL #'d SETS		
1 Walter Payton	40.00	100.00
Gale Sayers/75 unsigned		
1A Walter Payton	100.00	200.00
Gale Sayers AU/25		
2 Cade McNown	30.00	80.00
Jim McMahon		
(all 100 signed by McMahon only)		
3 Roger Staubach JER	25.00	60.00
Tony Dorsett HEL		
4 Troy Aikman	40.00	100.00
Emmitt Smith		
5 Terry Bradshaw	25.00	60.00
Franco Harris		

6 Joe Greene HEL AU 75.00 150.00
Jack Ham HEL AU
7 Joe Montana 40.00 100.00
Jerry Rice
8 Steve Young 20.00 50.00
Terrell Owens
9 Jim Kelly 20.00 50.00
Thurman Thomas
10 Doug Flutie 15.00 40.00
Eric Moulds
11 Joe Namath JER 25.00 60.00
Don Maynard HEL
11A Joe Namath JER AU 60.00 150.00
Maynard HEL/25
12 Vinny Testaverde 12.00 30.00
Curtis Martin
13A Deacon Jones 12.00 30.00
Fred Dryer AU
13B Deacon Jones AU 50.00 100.00
Fred Dryer AU/100
14 Kurt Warner 25.00 60.00
Isaac Bruce
15 Joe Montana HEL 40.00 100.00
Marcus Allen JER
16 Tony Gonzalez 15.00 40.00
Sylvester Morris
17 Phil Simms JER AU 15.00 40.00
Lawrence Taylor HEL
(signed by Simms only)
18 Kerry Collins 12.00 30.00
Ron Dayne
19 Jim Plunkett 15.00 40.00
George Blanda
20 Ken Stabler AU 75.00 150.00
Daryle Lamonica AU
21 Earl Campbell HEL 15.00 40.00
Warren Moon JER
22 Eddie George JER 15.00 40.00
Steve McNair HEL
23 Dan Marino 40.00 100.00
John Elway
25 Barry Sanders 40.00 100.00
Eric Dickerson
26 Marshall Faulk 15.00 40.00
Terrell Davis
27 Peyton Manning 40.00 100.00
Edgerrin James
28 Mark Brunell 15.00 40.00
Fred Taylor
29 Daunte Culpepper 15.00 40.00
Randy Moss
30 Brett Favre 50.00 120.00
Antonio Freeman
31 Walter Payton 175.00 300.00
Gale Sayers
Cade McNown
Jim McMahon
32 Roger Staubach JER 150.00 250.00
Tony Dorsett HEL
Troy Aikman JER
Emmitt Smith JER
33 Terry Bradshaw JER 175.00 300.00
Franco Harris JER
Joe Greene HEL
Jack Ham HEL
34 Joe Montana 200.00 350.00
Jerry Rice
Steve Young
Terrell Owens
35 Jim Kelly
Thurman Thomas
Doug Flutie
Eric Moulds
36 Joe Namath JER 60.00 120.00
Don Maynard HEL
Vinny Testaverde JER
Curtis Martin JER
37 Deacon Jones 30.00 80.00
Kurt Warner
Isaac Bruce
Fred Dryer
38 Joe Montana HEL 175.00 300.00
Marcus Allen JER
Tony Gonzalez JER
Sylvester Morris JER
39 Phil Simms JER
Lawrence Taylor HEL
Kerry Collins JER
Ron Dayne JER
40 Jim Plunkett 100.00 200.00
George Blanda
Ken Stabler
Jack Lambert
41 Earl Campbell HEL 50.00 100.00
Warren Moon JER
Eddie George JER
Steve McNair HEL
43 Barry Sanders 100.00 200.00
Eric Dickerson
Marshall Faulk
Terrell Davis
44 Peyton Manning 50.00 120.00
Edgerrin James
Mark Brunell
Fred Taylor
45 Daunte Culpepper 60.00 150.00
Randy Moss
Brett Favre
Antonio Freeman

2001 Donruss Classics Hash Marks

STATED ODDS ONE PER BOX
HM1 Jamal Lewis 5.00 12.00
HM2 Jim Kelly 8.00 20.00
HM3 Archie Griffin 4.00 10.00
HM4 Walter Payton 15.00 40.00
HM5 Emmitt Smith 10.00 25.00
HM6 Troy Aikman 8.00 20.00
HM7 John Elway 12.50 30.00
HM8 Barry Sanders 8.00 20.00
HM9 Bart Starr 10.00 25.00
HM10 Brett Favre 15.00 40.00
HM11 Reggie White 10.00 25.00
HM12 Edgerrin James 5.00 12.00
HM13 Dan Marino 15.00 30.00
HM14 Fran Tarkenton 8.00 20.00
HM15 Cris Carter 6.00 15.00
HM16 Cris Collinsworth 4.00 10.00
HM17 Fred Biletnikoff 6.00 15.00
HM18 George Blanda 6.00 15.00
HM19 Donovan McNabb 5.00 12.00
HM20 Jerry Rice 12.00 30.00
HM21 Steve Young 8.00 20.00
HM22 Steve Largent 6.00 15.00
HM23 Marshall Faulk 5.00 12.00
HM24 Eddie George 5.00 12.00
HM25 Joe Theismann 6.00 15.00

2001 Donruss Classics Hash Marks Autographs

ANNOUNCED PRINT RUNS BELOW
HM2 Jim Kelly/25* 60.00 120.00
HM3 Archie Griffin/100* 10.00 25.00
HM7 John Elway/25* 75.00 150.00
HM8 Barry Sanders/25* 60.00 120.00
HM9 Bart Starr/25* 60.00 120.00
HM14 Fran Tarkenton/25* 40.00 80.00
HM16 Cris Collinsworth/100* 10.00 25.00
HM18 George Blanda/100* 25.00 50.00

2001 Donruss Classics Stadium Stars

STATED ODDS 1:18
SS1 Johnny Unitas 10.00 25.00
SS2 Raymond Berry 5.00 12.00
SS3 Jamal Lewis 5.00 12.00
SS4 Ray Lewis 5.00 12.00
SS5 Eddie George 5.00 12.00
SS6 Jim Brown 8.00 20.00
SS7 Ozzie Newsome 4.00 10.00
SS8 Paul Warfield 5.00 12.00
SS9 Tim Couch 3.00 8.00
SS10 John Elway 12.50 30.00
SS11 Rocky Bleier 5.00 12.00
SS13 Jack Lambert 10.00 25.00
SS14 John Stallworth 6.00 15.00
SS15 Bernie Kosar 5.00 12.00
SS16 Jerome Bettis 6.00 15.00
SS17 Emmitt Smith 12.00 30.00
SS18 Troy Aikman 8.00 20.00
SS19 Barry Sanders 10.00 25.00
SS20 Brett Favre 12.50 30.00
SS21 Donovan McNabb 5.00 12.00
SS22 Corey Dillon 4.00 10.00
SS23 Jerry Rice 10.00 25.00
SS24 Steve Young 8.00 20.00
SS25 Dan Marino 12.50 30.00

2001 Donruss Classics Stadium Stars Autographs

ANNOUNCED PRINT RUNS BELOW
SS1 Johnny Unitas/25* 200.00 350.00
SS2 Raymond Berry/200* 12.50 30.00
SS6 Jim Brown/25* 60.00 120.00
SS7 Ozzie Newsome/75* 10.00 25.00
SS8 Paul Warfield/25* 20.00 40.00
SS11 Rocky Bleier/100* 30.00 80.00
SS13 Jack Lambert/100* 75.00 150.00
SS14 John Stallworth/200* 20.00 50.00
SS24 Steve Young/25* 50.00 100.00

2001 Donruss Classics Team Colors

STATED ODDS 1:18
TC1 John Elway Pants 20.00 50.00
TC2 Brian Griese 5.00 12.00
TC3 Terrell Davis 6.00 15.00
TC4 Olandis Gary 4.00 10.00
TC5 Rod Smith P 5.00 12.00
TC6 Ed McCaffrey 5.00 12.00
TC7 Allen Aldridge P 10.00 25.00
Bill Romanowski P
John Mobley P
Keith Traylor P
Neil Smith P
Trevor Pryce P
TC8 Dan Neil P 8.00 20.00
Gary Zimmerman P
Mark Schlereth P
TC9 Kurt Warner Pants 10.00 25.00
TC10 Marshall Faulk Pants 6.00 15.00
TC11 Isaac Bruce Pants 6.00 15.00
TC12 London Fletcher P 8.00 20.00
Mike Jones LB P
Todd Lyght P
TC13 Az-Zahir Hakim 15.00 40.00
Isaac Bruce
Torry Holt
TC14 Marshall Faulk 15.00 40.00
Justin Watson
Robert Holcombe
TC15 Eddie George Pants 6.00 15.00
TC16 Eddie George 6.00 15.00
TC17 Jevon Kearse Pants 5.00 12.00
TC18 Jevon Kearse 5.00 12.00
TC19 Steve McNair 6.00 15.00
TC20 Brett Favre 20.00 50.00
TC21 Antonio Freeman 6.00 15.00
TC22 Dorsey Levens 5.00 12.00
TC23 LeRoy Butler 5.00 12.00
TC24 Daunte Culpepper 5.00 12.00
TC25 Warren Moon 8.00 20.00
TC26 Randy Moss 15.00 40.00
Cris Carter
Jake Reed
TC27 Mark Brunell 5.00 12.00
TC28 Fred Taylor 6.00 15.00
TC29 Jimmy Smith 8.00 20.00
Keenan McCardell
R.Jay Soward
TC30 Hardy Nickerson 4.00 10.00
TC31 Tony Boselli 5.00 12.00
TC32 Troy Aikman 12.00 30.00
TC33 Emmitt Smith 15.00 40.00
TC34 Daryl Johnston 8.00 20.00
TC35 Deion Sanders 10.00 25.00
TC36 Bill Bates 6.00 15.00
TC37 Michael Irvin 8.00 20.00
TC38 Barry Sanders 20.00 50.00
TC39 Sedrick Irvin 4.00 10.00
TC40 Charlie Batch 5.00 12.00
TC41 Herman Moore 5.00 12.00
TC42 Johnnie Morton 5.00 12.00
TC43 Donovan McNabb 6.00 15.00
TC44 Irving Fryar 5.00 12.00
TC45 Charles Johnson 4.00 10.00
TC46 Duce Staley 5.00 12.00
TC47 Curtis Martin 6.00 15.00
TC48 Bryan Cox 5.00 12.00
TC49 Vinny Testaverde 5.00 12.00
TC50 Ray Lucas 8.00 20.00
Keyshawn Johnson
Wayne Chrebet

2001 Donruss Classics Team Colors Autographs

ANNOUNCED PRINT RUNS 25-100
TC9 Kurt Warner/25* 30.00 80.00
TC25 Warren Moon/25* 40.00 80.00
TC34 Daryl Johnston/100* 15.00 40.00
TC36 Bill Bates/100* 15.00 40.00
TC44 Irving Fryar/100* 10.00 25.00

2001 Donruss Classics Timeless Treasures

STATED ODDS 1:340
1 Mike Anderson FB SP 20.00 40.00
2 John Fuqua JSY 10.00 25.00
3 Corey Dillon JSY 12.50 25.00
4 Jamal Lewis PYLON 10.00 20.00
5 Drew Bledsoe JSY SP 25.00 50.00

2001 Donruss Classics Chicago Collection

NOT PRICED DUE TO SCARCITY

2002 Donruss Classics Samples

*SILVER SAMPLES: 1X TO 2.5X BASIC CARDS
*GOLD SAMPLES: 1.5X TO 4X BASIC CARDS

2002 Donruss Classics

Released in July 2002. The set contains 100 veterans, 50 rookies, and 49 retired players. The retired players and the rookies are sequentially #'d to 1000. Some cards were issued only via redemption. The EXCH expiration date is 2/1/2004. Boxes included 9 packs of 6 cards.

COMP.SET w/o SP's (100) 7.50 20.00
151-200 ROOKIE PRINT RUN 1000
1 David Boston .20 .50
2 Jake Plummer .25 .60
3 Jamal Anderson .25 .60
4 Michael Vick .50 1.25
5 Chris Weinke .20 .50
6 Muhsin Muhammad .25 .60
7 Steve Smith .30 .75
8 Anthony Thomas .25 .60
9 David Terrell .20 .50
10 Brian Urlacher .30 .75
11 Marty Booker .25 .60
12 Quincy Carter .20 .50
13 Emmitt Smith .75 2.00
14 Mike McMahon .20 .50
15 James Stewart .20 .50
16 Brett Favre .75 2.00
17 Ahman Green .25 .60
18 Antonio Freeman .30 .75
19 Michael Bennett .25 .60
20 Randy Moss .30 .75
21 Cris Carter .30 .75
22 Daunte Culpepper .25 .60
23 Aaron Brooks .25 .60
24 Ricky Williams .25 .60
25 Deuce McAllister .25 .60
26 Kerry Collins .25 .60
27 Michael Strahan .30 .75
28 Donovan McNabb .30 .75
29 Duce Staley .25 .60
30 Freddie Mitchell .20 .50
31 Correll Buckhalter .25 .60
32 Jeff Garcia .25 .60
33 Terrell Owens .30 .75
34 Garrison Hearst .25 .60
35 Marshall Faulk .30 .75
36 Isaac Bruce .30 .75
37 Kurt Warner .30 .75
38 Torry Holt .30 .75
39 Brad Johnson .25 .60
40 Keyshawn Johnson .25 .60
41 Mike Alstott .25 .60
42 Warrick Dunn .25 .60
43 Stephen Davis .25 .60
44 Rod Gardner .20 .50
45 Bruce Smith .30 .75
46 Elvis Grbac .20 .50
47 Ray Lewis .30 .75
48 Jamal Lewis .25 .60
49 Rob Johnson .25 .60
50 Eric Moulds .25 .60
51 Travis Henry .20 .50
52 Corey Dillon .25 .60
53 Peter Warrick .25 .60
54 Tim Couch .20 .50
55 James Jackson .20 .50
56 Kevin Johnson .20 .50
57 Brian Griese .25 .60
58 Terrell Davis .30 .75
59 Rod Smith .25 .60
60 Mike Anderson .25 .60
61 Peyton Manning .60 1.50
62 Marvin Harrison .30 .75
63 Edgerrin James .25 .60
64 Dominic Rhodes .25 .60
65 Mark Brunell .25 .60
66 Fred Taylor .25 .60
67 Jimmy Smith .25 .60
68 Tony Gonzalez .30 .75
69 Trent Green .25 .60
70 Priest Holmes .30 .75
71 Snoop Minnis .20 .50
72 Jay Fiedler .25 .60
73 Lamar Smith .25 .60
74 Chris Chambers .25 .60
75 Tom Brady .75 2.00
76 Drew Bledsoe .30 .75
77 Antowain Smith .25 .60
78 Troy Brown .25 .60
79 Vinny Testaverde .25 .60
80 Curtis Martin .30 .75
81 Wayne Chrebet .25 .60
82 Laveranues Coles .25 .60
83 Tim Brown .30 .75
84 Jerry Rice .60 1.50
85 Rich Gannon .25 .60
86 Charlie Garner .25 .60
87 Kordell Stewart .25 .60
88 Jerome Bettis .30 .75
89 Kendrell Bell .20 .50
90 Plaxico Burress .25 .60
91 Drew Brees .50 1.25
92 LaDainian Tomlinson .40 1.00
93 Doug Flutie .30 .75
94 Shaun Alexander .25 .60
95 Matt Hasselbeck .30 .75
96 Koren Robinson .20 .50
97 Steve McNair .30 .75
98 Eddie George .25 .60
99 Derrick Mason .25 .60
100 Jevon Kearse .25 .60
101 Joe Montana 3.00 8.00
102 Joe Namath 2.00 5.00
103 Warren Moon 1.25 3.00
104 Dan Marino 3.00 8.00
105 Steve Bartkowski 1.00 2.50
106 John Elway 2.50 6.00
107 Troy Aikman 2.00 5.00
108 Steve Young 1.50 4.00
109 Terry Bradshaw 2.00 5.00
110 Bart Starr 2.50 6.00
111 Bert Jones .75 2.00
112 Craig Morton 1.00 2.50
113 Bob Griese 1.25 3.00
114 Dan Fouts 1.25 3.00
115 Phil Simms 1.00 2.50
116 Jim McMahon 1.25 3.00
117 Joe Theismann 1.25 3.00
118 Ken Stabler 1.50 4.00
119 Johnny Unitas 2.00 5.00
120 Roger Staubach 2.00 5.00
121 Len Dawson 1.25 3.00
122 Tony Dorsett 1.25 3.00
123 Gale Sayers 1.50 4.00
124 Jim Kelly 1.50 4.00
125 Herschel Walker 1.00 2.50
126 John Riggins 1.25 3.00
127 Eric Dickerson 1.00 2.50
128 Franco Harris 1.25 3.00
129 Earl Campbell 1.25 3.00
130 Thurman Thomas 1.25 3.00
131 Barry Sanders 2.00 5.00
132 Marcus Allen 1.25 3.00
134 Natrone Means .75 2.00
135 Steve Largent 1.25 3.00
136 Don Maynard 1.00 2.50
137 Henry Ellard .75 2.00
138 Sterling Sharpe 1.00 2.50
139 Art Monk 1.00 2.50
140 Andre Reed 1.00 2.50
141 Raymond Berry 1.00 2.50
142 Ozzie Newsome 1.00 2.50
143 William Perry 1.00 2.50
144 Deacon Jones 1.00 2.50
145 Howie Long 1.25 3.00
146 L.C. Greenwood 1.00 2.50
147 Ronnie Lott 1.25 3.00
148 Dick Butkus 2.00 5.00
149 Fran Tarkenton 1.25 3.00
150 Mike Singletary 1.25 3.00
151 David Carr RC 2.00 5.00
152 Joey Harrington RC 2.00 5.00
153 Patrick Ramsey RC 2.00 5.00
154 Kurt Kittner RC 1.25 3.00
155 DeShaun Foster RC 2.00 5.00
156 William Green RC 1.50 4.00
157 Clinton Portis RC 2.50 6.00
158 T.J. Duckett RC 2.00 5.00
159 Cliff Russell RC 1.25 3.00
160 Antonio Bryant RC 2.00 5.00
161 Donte Stallworth RC 2.00 5.00
162 Reche Caldwell RC 2.00 5.00
163 Jabar Gaffney RC 2.00 5.00
164 Ashley Lelie RC 1.50 4.00
165 Andre Davis RC 1.50 4.00
166 Josh Reed RC 1.50 4.00
167 Ron Johnson RC 1.50 4.00
168 Kelly Campbell RC 1.50 4.00
169 Javon Walker RC 2.00 5.00
170 Antwaan Randle El RC 2.00 5.00
171 Marquise Walker RC 1.25 3.00
172 Jeremy Shockey RC 3.00 8.00
173 Jerramy Stevens RC 2.00 5.00
174 Daniel Graham RC 1.50 4.00
175 Julius Peppers RC 4.00 10.00
176 Kalimba Edwards RC 1.50 4.00
177 Alex Brown RC 2.00 5.00
178 Will Overstreet RC 1.25 3.00
179 Dwight Freeney RC 2.50 6.00
180 John Henderson RC 1.50 4.00
181 Ryan Sims RC 2.00 5.00
182 Albert Haynesworth RC 2.00 5.00
183 Wendell Bryant RC 1.25 3.00
184 Anthony Weaver RC 1.25 3.00
185 Napoleon Harris RC 1.50 4.00
186 Robert Thomas RC 1.25 3.00
187 Quentin Jammer RC 2.00 5.00
188 Ed Reed RC 8.00 20.00
189 Roy Williams RC 2.00 5.00
190 Phillip Buchanon RC 2.00 5.00
191 Lito Sheppard RC 2.00 5.00
192 Mike Rumph RC 1.25 3.00
193 Keyuo Craver RC 1.25 3.00
194 Randy Fasani RC 1.50 4.00
195 Rohan Davey RC 2.00 5.00
196 Chad Hutchinson RC 1.25 3.00
197 Eric Crouch RC 2.00 5.00
198 Lamar Gordon RC 1.50 4.00
199 Brian Westbrook RC 3.00 8.00
200 Adrian Peterson RC 2.00 5.00

2002 Donruss Classics Timeless Tributes

*VETS 1-100: 4X TO 10X BASIC CARDS
1-100 VETERAN PRINT RUN 150
*LEGENDS 101-150: 2X TO 5X
*ROOKIES 151-200: .8X TO 2X
101-200 PRINT RUN 100

2002 Donruss Classics Classic Materials

STATED PRINT RUN 50-350
CM1 Bart Starr/50 30.00 80.00
CM2 William Perry Helmet/100 10.00 25.00
CM3 L.C. Greenwood Shoe/100 10.00 25.00
CM4 Len Dawson Helmet/100 12.00 30.00
CM5 Terry Bradshaw/100 20.00 50.00
CM6 Bob Griese/100 12.00 30.00
CM7 Ken Stabler/150 12.00 30.00
CM8 Steve Largent/250 8.00 20.00
CM9 Earl Campbell/150 10.00 25.00
CM10 Warren Moon/300 8.00 20.00
CM11 Fran Tarkenton/250 8.00 20.00
CM12 Barry Sanders/100 20.00 50.00
CM13 Dan Marino/250 20.00 50.00
CM14 John Elway/250 15.00 40.00
CM15 Marcus Allen/300 8.00 20.00
CM16 Ozzie Newsome/300 6.00 15.00
CM17 Howie Long/300 12.00 30.00
CM18 Deacon Jones/300 6.00 15.00
CM19 Jerry Rice/250 15.00 40.00
CM20 Bert Jones/300 5.00 12.00
CM21 Brett Favre/100 30.00 80.00
Sterling Sharpe
CM22 Johnny Unitas/100 40.00 100.00
Raymond Berry
CM23 Emmitt Smith/100 30.00 80.00
Herschel Walker Shoe
CM24 Joe Montana/100 75.00 200.00
Steve Young
CM25 Joe Theismann/100 20.00 50.00
Art Monk
CM26 Joe Namath/100 30.00 80.00
Don Maynard
CM27 Eric Dickerson/100 10.00 25.00
Henry Ellard
CM28 Jim Kelly/100 20.00 50.00
Andre Reed
CM29 Walter Payton/50 50.00 120.00
Gale Sayers
Anthony Thomas
CM30 Roger Staubach/50 40.00 100.00
Craig Morton
Troy Aikman
CM31 Dick Butkus 125.00 250.00
Mike Singletary
Brian Urlacher/50

2002 Donruss Classics Classic Materials Autographs

STATED PRINT RUN 10-25
CM2 William Perry/25 30.00 80.00
CM3 L.C. Greenwood/25 30.00 80.00
CM7 Ken Stabler/25 40.00 100.00
CM10 Warren Moon/25 40.00 100.00
CM12 Barry Sanders/25 100.00 200.00
CM13 Dan Marino/25 125.00 250.00
CM18 Deacon Jones/25 30.00 80.00
CM19 Jerry Rice/25 125.00 250.00
CM20 Bert Jones/50 15.00 40.00

2002 Donruss Classics Classic Pigskin

STATED PRINT RUN 250 SER.#'d SETS
*DOUBLE/25: 1.2X TO 3X BASIC INSERTS
DOUBLES PRINT RUN 25 SER.#'d SETS
CP1 Jerry Rice 15.00 40.00
CP2 Joe Montana 20.00 50.00
CP3 Troy Aikman 12.00 30.00
CP4 Emmitt Smith 20.00 50.00
CP5 Ray Lewis 8.00 20.00
CP6 Jamal Lewis 6.00 15.00

2002 Donruss Classics New Millennium Classics Jerseys

STATED PRINT RUN 400-500
NM1 Ahman Green/400 5.00 12.00
NM2 Brian Griese/400 5.00 12.00
NM3 Chris Chambers/400 5.00 12.00
NM4 Curtis Martin/400 6.00 15.00
NM5 Daunte Culpepper/400 5.00 12.00
NM6 Edgerrin James/400 5.00 12.00
NM7 Emmitt Smith/400 15.00 40.00
NM8 Kurt Warner/400 6.00 15.00
NM9 Marshall Faulk/400 6.00 15.00
NM10 Randy Moss/400 6.00 15.00
NM11 Antonio Freeman/500 6.00 15.00
NM12 Charles Woodson/500 6.00 15.00
NM13 Corey Dillon/400 5.00 12.00
NM14 Cris Carter/400 6.00 15.00
NM15 David Boston/400 4.00 10.00
NM16 Donovan McNabb/400 6.00 15.00
NM17 Drew Bledsoe/400 6.00 15.00
NM18 Champ Bailey/500 6.00 15.00
NM19 Eric Moulds/400 5.00 12.00
NM20 Germane Crowell/500 4.00 10.00
NM21 Jake Plummer/400 5.00 12.00
NM22 Jeff Garcia/400 5.00 12.00
NM23 Jerome Bettis/500 6.00 15.00
NM24 Jevon Kearse/500 5.00 12.00
NM25 Keyshawn Johnson/400 5.00 12.00
NM26 Kordell Stewart/500 5.00 12.00
NM27 Warren Sapp/400 5.00 12.00
NM28 Marvin Harrison/500 6.00 15.00
NM29 Zach Thomas/400 6.00 15.00
NM30 Rod Smith/500 5.00 12.00
NM31 Steve McNair/400 6.00 15.00
NM32 Terrell Owens/400 6.00 15.00

2002 Donruss Classics Past and Present Jerseys

SINGLES PRINT RUN 400 SER.#'d SETS
PP1 Donovan McNabb 6.00 15.00
PP2 Kurt Warner 6.00 15.00
PP3 Mark Brunell 5.00 12.00
PP4 Jeff Garcia 5.00 12.00
PP5 Brett Favre 15.00 40.00
PP6 LaDainian Tomlinson 8.00 20.00
PP7 Jamal Anderson 5.00 12.00
PP8 Mike Anderson 5.00 12.00
PP9 Terrell Davis 6.00 15.00
PP10 Ricky Watters 5.00 12.00
PP11 Stephen Davis 5.00 12.00
PP12 Eddie George 5.00 12.00
PP13 Marshall Faulk 6.00 15.00
PP14 Edgerrin James 5.00 12.00
PP15 Jerome Bettis 6.00 15.00
PP16 Emmitt Smith 15.00 40.00
PP18 Tony Dorsett 12.00 30.00
PP19 Thurman Thomas 8.00 20.00
PP20 Marcus Allen 10.00 25.00
PP21 Earl Campbell 25.00 50.00
Franco Harris
PP22 Eric Dickerson 30.00 60.00
Barry Sanders
PP23 Gale Sayers 60.00 120.00
John Riggins
PP24 Dan Marino 75.00 150.00
John Elway
PP25 Troy Aikman 25.00 60.00
Steve Young

2002 Donruss Classics Past and Present Jersey Autographs

STATED PRINT RUN 25 SER.#'d SETS
PP7 Jamal Anderson 15.00 40.00
PP8 Mike Anderson 15.00 40.00
PP9 Terrell Davis 20.00 50.00
PP10 Ricky Watters
PP11 Stephen Davis
PP13 Marshall Faulk 20.00 50.00
PP14 Edgerrin James 15.00 40.00

2002 Donruss Classics Significant Signatures

STATED PRINT RUN 20-250
1 David Boston/50 8.00 20.00
5 Chris Weinke/100 6.00 15.00
8 Anthony Thomas/150 8.00 20.00
9 David Terrell/100 6.00 15.00
10 Brian Urlacher/224 12.00 30.00
12 Quincy Carter/250 6.00 15.00
14 Mike McMahon/250 6.00 15.00
16 Brett Favre/25 175.00 300.00
17 Ahman Green/50 40.00 80.00
19 Michael Bennett/150 8.00 20.00
22 Daunte Culpepper/50 10.00 25.00
23 Aaron Brooks/150 8.00 20.00
24 Ricky Williams/35 20.00 50.00
25 Deuce McAllister/150 8.00 20.00
26 Kerry Collins/142 10.00 25.00
27 Michael Strahan/50 15.00 40.00
31 Correll Buckhalter/250 8.00 20.00
32 Jeff Garcia/25 15.00 40.00
33 Terrell Owens/100 15.00 40.00
35 Marshall Faulk/25 20.00 50.00
36 Isaac Bruce/125 12.50 30.00
37 Kurt Warner/40 30.00 80.00
38 Torry Holt/150 10.00 25.00
43 Stephen Davis/100 12.50 30.00
44 Rod Gardner/25 12.00 30.00
46 Elvis Grbac/75 8.00 20.00
47 Ray Lewis/100 20.00 40.00
48 Jamal Lewis/100 15.00 40.00
50 Eric Moulds/150 8.00 20.00
51 Travis Henry No Auto/100 7.50 20.00
53 Peter Warrick/100 7.50 20.00
55 James Jackson/200 6.00 15.00
58 Terrell Davis/50 15.00 40.00
60 Mike Anderson/75 10.00 25.00
62 Marvin Harrison/75 25.00 50.00
63 Edgerrin James/50 10.00 25.00
65 Mark Brunell/75 10.00 25.00
67 Jimmy Smith/150 8.00 20.00
68 Tony Gonzalez/75 12.00 30.00
71 Snoop Minnis No Auto/200 6.00 15.00
74 Chris Chambers/75 10.00 25.00
76 Drew Bledsoe/75 30.00 60.00
79 Vinny Testaverde/100 12.50 30.00
82 Laveranues Coles/200 8.00 20.00
83 Tim Brown/75 25.00 50.00
87 Kordell Stewart/50 10.00 25.00
91 Drew Brees/150 30.00 60.00
96 Koren Robinson/200 6.00 15.00
100 Jevon Kearse/100 7.50 20.00
101 Joe Montana/100 90.00 175.00
102 Joe Namath/50 60.00 120.00
104 Dan Marino/25 175.00 300.00
105 Steve Bartkowski/97 8.00 20.00
106 John Elway/25 125.00 250.00
107 Troy Aikman/40 75.00 125.00
108 Steve Young/50 40.00 80.00
109 Terry Bradshaw/78 60.00 120.00
110 Bart Starr/40 90.00 150.00
111 Bert Jones/243 6.00 15.00
112 Craig Morton/250 8.00 20.00
113 Bob Griese/50 30.00 50.00
114 Dan Fouts/25 20.00 50.00
115 Phil Simms/50 30.00 60.00
116 Jim McMahon/66 15.00 40.00
117 Joe Theismann/93 15.00 40.00
118 Ken Stabler/63 20.00 50.00
119 Johnny Unitas/75 175.00 300.00
120 Roger Staubach/55 50.00 100.00
121 Len Dawson/50 25.00 50.00
122 Tony Dorsett/50 25.00 50.00
123 Gale Sayers/25 50.00 120.00
125 Herschel Walker/50 20.00 40.00
126 John Riggins/125 30.00 60.00
127 Eric Dickerson/25 15.00 40.00
128 Franco Harris/25 20.00 50.00
129 Earl Campbell/50 25.00 50.00
130 Thurman Thomas/150 15.00 40.00
131 Barry Sanders/50 75.00 150.00
132 Marcus Allen/25 20.00 50.00
134 Natrone Means/170 6.00 15.00
135 Steve Largent/20 50.00 100.00
136 Don Maynard/112 8.00 20.00
137 Henry Ellard/20 12.00 30.00
138 Sterling Sharpe/116 12.50 30.00
139 Art Monk/25 30.00 60.00
140 Andre Reed/117 7.50 20.00
141 Raymond Berry/68 12.00 30.00
142 Ozzie Newsome/43 12.00 30.00
143 William Perry/75 12.00 30.00
144 Deacon Jones/50 12.00 30.00
145 Howie Long/25 60.00 120.00
146 L.C. Greenwood/75 25.00 60.00
147 Ronnie Lott/75 20.00 40.00
148 Dick Butkus/24 75.00 150.00
149 Fran Tarkenton/50 30.00 60.00
150 Mike Singletary/50 15.00 40.00
151 David Carr/50 12.00 30.00
152 Joey Harrington/50 12.00 30.00
156 William Green/43 12.00 30.00
157 Clinton Portis/150 12.00 30.00
160 Antonio Bryant/100 12.50 30.00
161 Donte Stallworth/33 40.00 100.00
164 Ashley Lelie/100 12.50 30.00
165 Andre Davis/150 8.00 20.00
166 Josh Reed/75 10.00 25.00
168 Kelly Campbell/250 8.00 20.00
176 Kalimba Edwards/250 8.00 20.00
177 Alex Brown/250 10.00 25.00
181 Ryan Sims/250 No Auto 10.00 25.00
186 Robert Thomas/250 6.00 15.00
189 Roy Williams/150 10.00 25.00
192 Mike Rumph/200 6.00 15.00
200 Adrian Peterson/200 10.00 25.00

2002 Donruss Classics Timeless Treasures

STATED PRINT RUN 25-375
TT1 Red Grange HEL/25 200.00 350.00
TT2 Jim Thorpe/100 100.00 200.00
TT3 Brett Favre/375 15.00 40.00
TT4 Terrell Davis/375 8.00 20.00
TT5 Barry Sanders/300 12.00 30.00
TT6 Jerry Rice/375 12.00 30.00

2003 Donruss Classics Samples

*SAMPLES: .8X TO 2X BASIC CARDS

2003 Donruss Classics Samples Gold

*GOLD: .8X TO 2X SILVER SAMPLES

2003 Donruss Classics

Released in July of 2003, this set consists of 250 cards, including 100 veterans, 50 retired players, and 100 rookies. The retired players were serial numbered to 1000, and the rookies were serial numbered to 900. Please note that several rookies were issued in packs as exchange cards with an expiration date of 1/7/2005. Please note that the EXCH cards are listed with a quantity of 100, due to Playoff destroying the remainder of the print run. Boxes contained two 9-pack mini-boxes. Pack SRP was $6.

COMP.SET w/o SP's (100) 7.50 20.00
151-250 PRINT RUN 900 SER.#'d SETS
1 Jake Plummer .25 .60
2 Marcel Shipp .20 .50
3 David Boston .20 .50
4 Michael Vick .40 1.00
5 T.J. Duckett .25 .60
6 Warrick Dunn .25 .60
7 Ray Lewis .30 .75
8 Jamal Lewis .25 .60
9 Todd Heap .25 .60
10 Drew Bledsoe .30 .75
11 Travis Henry .20 .50
12 Peerless Price .20 .50
13 Eric Moulds .25 .60
14 Julius Peppers .30 .75
15 Steve Smith .30 .75
16 Lamar Smith .25 .60
17 Anthony Thomas .25 .60
18 Marty Booker .25 .60
19 Brian Urlacher .30 .75
20 Corey Dillon .25 .60
21 Chad Johnson .30 .75
22 Tim Couch .20 .50
23 William Green .20 .50
24 Quincy Morgan .20 .50
25 Chad Hutchinson .20 .50
26 Emmitt Smith .75 2.00
27 Antonio Bryant .20 .50
28 Roy Williams .25 .60
29 Brian Griese .25 .60
30 Clinton Portis .25 .60
31 Rod Smith .25 .60
32 Ashley Lelie .20 .50
33 Joey Harrington .20 .50
34 James Stewart .20 .50
35 Bill Schroeder .20 .50
36 Brett Favre .75 2.00
37 Ahman Green .25 .60
38 Donald Driver .30 .75
39 David Carr .25 .60
40 Jonathan Wells .20 .50
41 Corey Bradford .20 .50
42 Peyton Manning .60 1.50
43 Edgerrin James .30 .75
44 Marvin Harrison .30 .75
45 Mark Brunell .25 .60
46 Fred Taylor .25 .60
47 Jimmy Smith .25 .60
48 Trent Green .25 .60
49 Priest Holmes .30 .75
50 Tony Gonzalez .30 .75
51 Ricky Williams .25 .60
52 Chris Chambers .25 .60
53 Zach Thomas .30 .75
54 Daunte Culpepper .25 .60
55 Michael Bennett .25 .60
56 Randy Moss .30 .75
57 Tom Brady .75 2.00
58 Antowain Smith .25 .60
59 Troy Brown .25 .60
60 Aaron Brooks .25 .60
61 Deuce McAllister .25 .60
62 Donte Stallworth .20 .50
63 Kerry Collins .25 .60
64 Jeremy Shockey .30 .75
65 Amani Toomer .25 .60
66 Chad Pennington .30 .75
67 Curtis Martin .30 .75
68 Laveranues Coles .20 .50
69 Rich Gannon .25 .60
70 Charlie Garner .25 .60
71 Jerry Rice .60 1.50
72 Tim Brown .30 .75
73 Donovan McNabb .30 .75
74 Duce Staley .25 .60
75 Todd Pinkston .20 .50
76 Tommy Maddox .25 .60
77 Jerome Bettis .30 .75
78 Plaxico Burress .25 .60
79 Hines Ward .30 .75
80 Drew Brees .30 .75
81 LaDainian Tomlinson .30 .75
82 Junior Seau .30 .75
83 Jeff Garcia .25 .60
84 Garrison Hearst .25 .60
85 Terrell Owens .30 .75
86 Matt Hasselbeck .25 .60
87 Shaun Alexander .25 .60
88 Koren Robinson .25 .60
89 Kurt Warner .30 .75
90 Marshall Faulk .30 .75
91 Isaac Bruce .30 .75
92 Brad Johnson .25 .60
93 Mike Alstott .30 .75
94 Keyshawn Johnson .30 .75
95 Steve McNair .30 .75
96 Eddie George .25 .60
97 Derrick Mason .25 .60
98 Patrick Ramsey .25 .60
99 Stephen Davis .25 .60
100 Rod Gardner .20 .50
101 Archie Manning 1.25 3.00
102 Bo Jackson 2.00 5.00
103 Bob Griese 1.25 3.00
104 Bob Lilly 1.00 2.50
105 Craig James 1.00 2.50
106 Cliff Branch 1.00 2.50
107 Dan Fouts 1.25 3.00
108 Daryl Johnston 1.25 3.00
109 Daryle Lamonica .75 2.00
110 Dick Butkus 2.00 5.00
111 Don Maynard 1.00 2.50

112 Ed Too Tall Jones 1.00 2.50
113 Franco Harris 1.50 4.00
114 Frank Gifford 1.25 3.00
115 Fred Biletnikoff 1.25 3.00
116 Gale Sayers 2.00 5.00
117 George Blanda 1.25 3.00
118 Herman Edwards 1.00 2.50
119 Herschel Walker 1.00 2.50
120 Jack Ham 1.00 2.50
121 Jack Tatum .75 2.00
122 Jack Youngblood .75 2.00
123 James Lofton 1.00 2.50
124 Jay Novacek 1.00 2.50
125 Jim Brown 2.00 5.00
126 Jim McMahon/100* 20.00 40.00
127 Jim Plunkett 1.00 2.50
129 Joe Greene 1.25 3.00
130 Joe Montana 3.00 8.00
131 John Riggins 1.25 3.00
132 John Stallworth 1.00 2.50
133 John Taylor/100* 2.00 5.00
134 Ken Stabler 1.50 4.00
135 L.C. Greenwood 1.00 2.50
136 Lance Alworth 1.00 2.50
137 Mel Blount 1.00 2.50
138 Mike Ditka/100* 3.00 8.00
139 Paul Hornung 1.25 3.00
140 Randy White 1.00 2.50
141 Raymond Berry 1.00 2.50
142 Roger Craig 1.00 2.50
143 Roger Staubach 2.00 5.00
144 Ron Jaworski 1.00 2.50
145 Sammy Baugh 1.25 3.00
146 Sonny Jurgenson 1.00 2.50
147 Steve Young 1.50 4.00
148 Ted Hendricks 1.00 2.50
149 Thurman Thomas 1.25 3.00
150 Tom Jackson/100* 2.00 5.00
151 Brian St.Pierre RC 1.50 4.00
152 Byron Leftwich RC 2.00 5.00
153 Carson Palmer RC 4.00 10.00
154 Chris Simms RC 2.00 5.00
155 Dave Ragone RC 1.25 3.00
156 Ken Dorsey RC 1.50 4.00
157 Kliff Kingsbury RC 1.50 4.00
158 Kyle Boller RC 2.00 5.00
159 Rex Grossman RC 2.00 5.00
160 Seneca Wallace RC 2.00 5.00
161 Jason Gesser RC 1.50 4.00
162 Artose Pinner RC 1.25 3.00
163 Avon Cobourne RC 1.25 3.00
164 Cecil Sapp RC 1.25 3.00
165 Chris Brown RC 1.25 3.00
166 Derek Watson RC 1.25 3.00
167 Domanick Davis RC 1.50 4.00
168 Dwone Hicks RC 1.25 3.00
169 Earnest Graham RC 2.00 5.00
170 Justin Fargas RC 2.00 5.00
171 Larry Johnson RC 2.00 5.00
172 Lee Suggs RC 1.50 4.00
173 Musa Smith RC 1.25 3.00
174 Onterrio Smith RC 1.25 3.00
175 Quentin Griffin RC 1.50 4.00
176 Willis McGahee RC 2.50 6.00
177 Sultan McCullough RC 1.25 3.00
178 LaBrandon Toefield RC 1.50 4.00
179 B.J. Askew RC 1.50 4.00
180 Andre Johnson RC 5.00 12.00
181 Anquan Boldin RC 3.00 8.00
182 Arnaz Battle RC 2.00 5.00
183 Bethel Johnson RC 1.25 3.00
184 Billy McMullen RC 1.25 3.00
185 Bobby Wade RC 1.50 4.00
186 Brandon Lloyd RC 3.00 8.00
187 Bryant Johnson RC 2.00 5.00
188 Charles Rogers RC 1.50 4.00
189 Doug Gabriel RC 1.50 4.00
190 Justin Gage RC 1.50 4.00
191 Kareem Kelly RC 1.25 3.00
192 Kelley Washington RC 1.25 3.00
193 Kevin Curtis RC 2.00 5.00
194 Nate Burleson RC 1.50 4.00
195 Sam Aiken RC 1.50 4.00
196 Shaun McDonald RC 1.50 4.00
197 Talman Gardner RC 1.25 3.00
198 Taylor Jacobs RC 1.25 3.00
199 Terrence Edwards RC 1.25 3.00
200 Tyrone Calico RC 1.50 4.00
201 Walter Young RC 1.25 3.00
202 Ryan Hoag/100 RC 4.00 10.00
203 Paul Arnold RC 1.25 3.00
204 Bennie Joppru RC 1.25 3.00
205 Dallas Clark RC 3.00 8.00
206 George Wrighster RC 1.25 3.00
207 Jason Witten RC 5.00 12.00
208 Mike Pinkard RC 1.25 3.00
209 Robert Johnson RC 1.25 3.00
210 Teyo Johnson RC 1.50 4.00
211 Calvin Pace RC 1.50 4.00
212 Chris Kelsay RC 1.50 4.00
213 Cory Redding RC 1.50 4.00
214 DeWayne Robertson RC 1.50 4.00
215 DeWayne White RC 1.25 3.00
216 Jerome McDougle RC 1.25 3.00
217 Kenny Peterson RC 1.50 4.00
218 Kindal Moorehead RC 1.50 4.00
219 Michael Haynes RC 1.25 3.00
220 Terrell Suggs RC 2.00 5.00
221 Tully Banta-Cain RC 2.00 5.00
222 Jimmy Kennedy RC 1.50 4.00
223 Johnathan Sullivan RC 1.25 3.00
224 Kevin Williams RC 2.00 5.00
225 Nick Eason/100 RC 4.00 10.00
226 Rien Long RC 1.25 3.00
227 Ty Warren RC 1.50 4.00
228 William Joseph RC 1.25 3.00
229 Boss Bailey RC 1.50 4.00
230 Bradie James RC 2.00 5.00
231 Victor Hobson RC 1.25 3.00
232 Clifton Smith RC 1.25 3.00
233 E.J. Henderson/100 RC 5.00 12.00
234 Gerald Hayes/100 RC 5.00 12.00
235 LaMarcus McDonald RC 1.25 3.00
236 Nick Barnett RC 2.00 5.00
237 Terry Pierce RC 1.25 3.00
238 Andre Woolfolk RC 1.50 4.00
239 Dennis Weathersby RC 1.25 3.00
240 Drayton Florence RC 2.00 5.00
241 Eugene Wilson RC 2.00 5.00
242 Marcus Trufant RC 1.50 4.00
243 Rashean Mathis RC 1.50 4.00
244 Ricky Manning RC 1.50 4.00
245 Sammy Davis/100 RC 5.00 12.00
246 Terence Newman RC 1.50 4.00
247 Julian Battle RC 1.50 4.00
248 Ken Hamlin RC 2.00 5.00
249 Mike Doss RC 2.00 5.00
250 Troy Polamalu RC 15.00 25.00

2003 Donruss Classics Timeless Tributes

*VETS 1-100: 4X TO 10X BASIC CARDS
*STARS 101-150: 1.5X TO 4X BASIC CARDS
*LEGENDS 101-150: .8X TO 2X BASE/100
1-149 PRINT RUN 150 SER. #'d SETS
*ROOKIES 151-250: .8X TO 2X
150-250 PRINT RUN 100 SER. #'d SETS
250 Troy Polamalu 40.00 100.00

2003 Donruss Classics Classic Pigskin

STATED PRINT RUN 250 SER.#'d SETS
*DOUBLE/25: .8X TO 2X SINGLE FB
PS1 Marcus Allen 8.00 20.00
PS2 John Elway 20.00 50.00
PS3 Jim Kelly 10.00 25.00
PS4 Emmitt Smith 20.00 50.00
PS5 Trent Dilfer 6.00 15.00
PS6 Tom Brady 20.00 50.00

2003 Donruss Classics Classic Materials

STATED PRINT RUN 10-400
#'d/10 NOT PRICED DUE TO SCARCITY
CM1 Alan Page/100 8.00 20.00
CM2 Andre Reed/400 5.00 12.00
CM3 Art Monk/400 6.00 15.00
CM4 Bart Starr/50 50.00 80.00
CM5 Earl Campbell/300 6.00 15.00
CM6 Eric Dickerson/400 5.00 12.00
CM7 Irving Fryar/400 4.00 10.00
CM8 Jim Kelly/400 8.00 20.00
CM9 Larry Csonka/100 10.00 25.00
CM11 Marcus Allen/400 6.00 15.00
CM12 Ray Nitschke/75 30.00 50.00
CM13 Terry Bradshaw/300 10.00 25.00
CM14 Tony Dorsett/100 10.00 25.00
CM15 Troy Aikman/300 8.00 20.00
CM16 Barry Sanders/200 15.00 40.00
CM17 Craig James/400 5.00 12.00
CM18 Dan Fouts/300 6.00 15.00
CM19 Dan Marino/400 15.00 40.00
CM20 Daryl Johnston/400 6.00 15.00
CM21 Frank Gifford/100 10.00 25.00
CM22 Steve Young/400 8.00 20.00
CM23 Herman Edwards/400 5.00 12.00
CM24 Jack Youngblood/100 6.00 15.00
CM25 Jim Brown/50 30.00 80.00
CM26 Warren Moon/400 5.00 12.00
CM27 Jimmy Johnson/400 5.00 12.00
CM28 Randy White/125 8.00 20.00
CM29 Ron Jaworski/100 8.00 20.00
CM30 Cris Carter/400 6.00 15.00
CM31 Dick Butkus 60.00 120.00
Walter Payton/100
CM32 Jim McMahon 25.00 50.00
Gale Sayers/100
CM33 Earl Campbell 10.00 25.00
Warren Moon/100
CM34 Franco Harris 30.00 80.00
Terry Bradshaw/100
CM35 Daryle Lamonica 20.00 50.00
Fred Biletnikoff/100
CM36 Ted Hendricks 20.00 50.00
Jack Tatum/100
CM37 Troy Aikman 25.00 50.00
Jay Novacek/100
CM38 Roger Staubach 25.00 60.00
Tony Dorsett/100
CM39 Johnny Unitas 30.00 80.00
Raymond Berry/100
CM40 Peyton Manning 15.00 40.00
Edgerrin James/100

2003 Donruss Classics Classic Materials Autographs

STATED PRINT RUN 50-100
CM1 Alan Page/100 30.00 60.00
CM2 Andre Reed/50 15.00 40.00
CM3 Art Monk/50 40.00 80.00
CM4 Bart Starr/50 100.00 250.00
CM5 Earl Campbell/50 30.00 60.00
CM6 Eric Dickerson/50 40.00 80.00
CM7 Irving Fryar/100 15.00 40.00
CM8 Jim Kelly/50 40.00 100.00
CM9 Larry Csonka/65 30.00 60.00
CM10 Leonard Marshall/100 25.00 50.00
CM11 Marcus Allen/50 35.00 60.00
CM13 Terry Bradshaw/50 100.00 175.00
CM14 Tony Dorsett/50 40.00 80.00
CM15 Troy Aikman/75 75.00 150.00

2003 Donruss Classics Dress Code Jerseys

STATED PRINT RUN 550 SER.#'d SETS
DC1 Dennis Northcutt 3.00 8.00
DC2 Jason Taylor 4.00 10.00
DC3 Donovan McNabb 5.00 12.00
DC4 Jerome Bettis 5.00 12.00
DC5 Joey Harrington 3.00 8.00
DC6 Duce Staley 4.00 10.00
DC7 Keyshawn Johnson 5.00 12.00
DC8 Kurt Warner 5.00 12.00
DC9 Santana Moss 4.00 10.00
DC10 Marvin Harrison 5.00 12.00
DC11 Michael Strahan 5.00 12.00
DC12 Mike Alstott 5.00 12.00
DC13 Rod Gardner 3.00 8.00
DC14 Rod Smith 4.00 10.00
DC15 Stephen Davis 4.00 10.00
DC16 Charles Woodson 5.00 12.00
DC17 Eric Moulds 4.00 10.00
DC18 Jeff Garcia 4.00 10.00
DC19 Anthony Thomas 4.00 10.00

2003 Donruss Classics Membership

STATED PRINT RUN 1500 SER.#'d SETS
M1 Warren Moon .75 2.00
M2 Dan Marino 2.50 6.00
M3 John Elway 2.50 6.00
M4 Jerry Rice 2.00 5.00
M5 Cris Carter 1.00 2.50
M6 Tim Brown 1.00 2.50
M7 Emmitt Smith 2.50 6.00
M8 John Riggins 1.00 2.50
M9 Priest Holmes 1.00 2.50
M10 Lawrence Taylor 1.00 2.50
M11 Reggie White 1.00 2.50
M12 Bruce Smith .75 2.00
M13 Jerry Rice 2.00 5.00
M14 Emmitt Smith 2.50 6.00
M15 Marcus Allen 1.00 2.50
M16 Walter Payton 3.00 8.00
M17 Emmitt Smith 2.50 6.00
M18 Barry Sanders 2.00 5.00
M19 Eric Dickerson .75 2.00
M20 Tony Dorsett 1.00 2.50

2003 Donruss Classics Membership VIP Jerseys

STATED PRINT RUN 75-400
M1 Warren Moon/400 5.00 12.00
M2 Dan Marino/250 15.00 40.00
M3 John Elway/250 15.00 40.00
M4 Jerry Rice/250 12.00 30.00
M5 Cris Carter/200 6.00 15.00
M6 Tim Brown/200 6.00 15.00
M7 Emmitt Smith/75 20.00 50.00
M8 John Riggins/100 8.00 20.00
M9 Priest Holmes/300 6.00 15.00
M10 Lawrence Taylor/200 6.00 15.00
M11 Reggie White/300 6.00 15.00
M12 Bruce Smith/400 5.00 12.00
M13 Jerry Rice/75 15.00 40.00
M14 Emmitt Smith/100 20.00 50.00
M15 Marcus Allen/150 6.00 15.00
M16 Walter Payton/100 50.00 100.00
M17 Emmitt Smith/250 15.00 40.00
M19 Eric Dickerson/250 5.00 12.00
M20 Tony Dorsett/100 8.00 20.00

2003 Donruss Classics Membership VIP Jerseys Autographs

PLAYOFF ANNOUNCED PRINT RUNS BELOW
M1 Warren Moon/50* 25.00 50.00
M2 Dan Marino/50* 125.00 250.00
M3 John Elway/15* 150.00 300.00
M10 Lawrence Taylor/50* 30.00 80.00
M11 Reggie White/50* 150.00 250.00
M18 Barry Sanders/50 100.00 200.00

2003 Donruss Classics Significant Signatures

RANDOM INSERTS IN PACKS
#'d/15 NOT PRICED DUE TO SCARCITY
4 Michael Vick/25 50.00 100.00
8 Jamal Lewis/25 15.00 40.00
13 Eric Moulds/50 12.00 30.00
17 Anthony Thomas/25 15.00 40.00
18 Marty Booker/50 12.00 30.00
19 Brian Urlacher/25 60.00 120.00
20 Corey Dillon No Auto 6.00 15.00
30 Clinton Portis/25 15.00 40.00
31 Rod Smith/50 12.00 30.00
33 Joey Harrington/25 12.00 30.00
37 Ahman Green/25 15.00 40.00
38 Donald Driver/50 25.00 50.00
44 Marvin Harrison/25 20.00 50.00
47 Jimmy Smith/50 12.00 30.00
49 Priest Holmes/25 20.00 50.00
52 Chris Chambers/25 15.00 40.00
53 Zach Thomas/25 20.00 50.00
56 Randy Moss/25 40.00 80.00
58 Antowain Smith/50 12.00 30.00
68 Laveranues Coles/50 10.00 25.00
76 Tommy Maddox/50 12.00 30.00
83 Jeff Garcia/25 15.00 40.00
84 Garrison Hearst/25 15.00 40.00
85 Terrell Owens/25 20.00 50.00
89 Kurt Warner/50 25.00 50.00
91 Isaac Bruce/25 20.00 50.00
93 Mike Alstott/25 20.00 50.00
95 Steve McNair/25 20.00 50.00
97 Derrick Mason/25 15.00 40.00
101 Archie Manning/150 12.00 30.00
102 Bo Jackson/100 40.00 80.00
103 Bob Griese/100 12.00 30.00
104 Bob Lilly/200 10.00 25.00
105 Craig James/200 10.00 25.00
106 Cliff Branch/200 10.00 25.00
107 Dan Fouts/100 20.00 40.00
108 Daryl Johnston/200 20.00 40.00
109 Daryle Lamonica/150 8.00 20.00
110 Dick Butkus/100 50.00 80.00
111 Don Maynard/100 10.00 25.00
112 Ed Too Tall Jones/200 10.00 25.00
113 Franco Harris/100 20.00 40.00
114 Frank Gifford/100 25.00 50.00
115 Fred Biletnikoff/100 15.00 40.00
116 Gale Sayers/100 30.00 60.00
117 George Blanda/100 20.00 40.00
118 Herman Edwards/150 10.00 25.00
119 Herschel Walker/200 15.00 40.00
120 Jack Ham/150 15.00 30.00
121 Jack Tatum/150 30.00 60.00
122 Jack Youngblood/150 8.00 20.00
123 James Lofton/100 10.00 25.00
124 Jay Novacek/200 30.00 80.00
125 Jim Brown/250 30.00 60.00
127 Jim Plunkett/200 10.00 25.00
128 Jimmy Johnson/100 30.00 60.00
129 Joe Greene/100 25.00 50.00
130 Joe Montana/200 50.00 120.00
131 John Riggins/200 20.00 50.00
132 John Stallworth/250 15.00 40.00
133 John Taylor/250 10.00 25.00
134 Ken Stabler/150 40.00 80.00
135 L.C. Greenwood/150 15.00 40.00
136 Lance Alworth/150 20.00 40.00
137 Mel Blount/253 10.00 25.00
138 Mike Ditka/100 20.00 50.00
139 Paul Hornung/200 25.00 50.00
140 Randy White/200 10.00 25.00
141 Raymond Berry/150 10.00 25.00
142 Roger Craig/150 10.00 25.00
143 Roger Staubach/117 40.00 80.00
144 Ron Jaworski/150 10.00 25.00
145 Sammy Baugh/200 90.00 150.00
146 Sonny Jurgenson/150 10.00 25.00
147 Steve Young/100 40.00 80.00
148 Ted Hendricks/150 10.00 25.00
150 Tom Jackson/250 10.00 25.00
152 Byron Leftwich/100 15.00 40.00
153 Carson Palmer/100 40.00 80.00
154 Chris Simms/125 12.00 30.00
155 Dave Ragone/200 6.00 15.00
164 Cecil Sapp/225 6.00 15.00
176 Willis McGahee/125 30.00 60.00
189 Doug Gabriel/250 8.00 20.00
190 Justin Gage/220 8.00 20.00
204 Bennie Joppru/200 6.00 15.00
210 Teyo Johnson/250 8.00 20.00
214 DeW Robertson/250 No AU 4.00 10.00
215 DeWayne White/250 6.00 15.00
216 Jerome McDougle/250 6.00 15.00
217 Kenny Peterson/300 No AU 4.00 10.00
223 John Sullivan/300 No AU 3.00 8.00
224 Kevin Williams/250 10.00 25.00
226 Rien Long/250 6.00 15.00
228 William Joseph/250 6.00 15.00
233 E.J. Henderson/200 8.00 20.00
239 Dennis Weathersby/250 6.00 15.00
242 Marcus Trufant/250 8.00 20.00
246 Terence Newman/250 8.00 20.00
249 Mike Doss/200 10.00 25.00

2003 Donruss Classics Timeless Triples Jerseys

STATED PRINT RUN 50-150
TT1 Doak Walker 200.00 400.00
Jim Thorpe
Red Grange/50
TT2 Jim Kelly 20.00 50.00
Thurman Thomas
Andre Reed/150
TT3 Troy Aikman 30.00 80.00
Emmitt Smith
Daryl Johnston/100
TT4 Joe Montana 30.00 80.00
John Taylor
Jerry Rice/150
TT5 Dan Marino 40.00 100.00
Bob Griese
Jay Fiedler/100
TT6 Terrell Davis 15.00 40.00
Mike Anderson
Clinton Portis/50
TT7 Fred Biletnikoff 25.00 60.00
Jerry Rice
Tim Brown/100
TT8 Kurt Warner 12.00 30.00
Marshall Faulk
Isaac Bruce/100
TT9 Joe Greene 25.00 60.00
Mel Blount
L.C. Greenwood/100
TT10 Steve McNair 12.00 30.00
Eddie George
Derrick Mason/100

2004 Donruss Classics

Donruss Classics initially released in mid-July 2004. The base set consists of 250-cards including 50-Legends subset cards serial numbered to 2000 and 100-rookies with print runs ranging from 500 to 1850. Hobby boxes contained 18-packs of 6-cards and carried an S.R.P. of $5.99 per pack. Three parallel sets and a variety of inserts can be found seeded in hobby and retail packs highlighted by the Timeless Triples Jerseys inserts and the multi-tiered Significant Signatures autograph inserts.

COMP.SET w/o SP's (100) 7.50 20.00
151-175 RC PRINT RUN 1850 SER.#'d SETS
176-200 RC PRINT RUN 1250 SER.#'d SETS
201-225 RC PRINT RUN 925 SER.#'d SETS
226-250 RC PRINT RUN 500 SER.#'d SETS
1 Anquan Boldin .30 .75
2 Emmitt Smith .75 2.00
3 Michael Vick .40 1.00
4 Peerless Price .20 .50
5 Warrick Dunn .25 .60
6 Jamal Lewis .25 .60
7 Kyle Boller .25 .60
8 Terrell Suggs .25 .60
9 Todd Heap .25 .60
10 Drew Bledsoe .30 .75
11 Travis Henry .20 .50
12 DeShaun Foster .25 .60
13 Jake Delhomme .25 .60
14 Stephen Davis .25 .60
15 Steve Smith .30 .75
16 Anthony Thomas .25 .60
17 Brian Urlacher .30 .75
18 Rex Grossman .25 .60
19 Chad Johnson .30 .75
20 Carson Palmer .30 .75
21 Rudi Johnson .25 .60
22 Andre Davis .20 .50
23 Lee Suggs .25 .60
24 Quincy Carter .20 .50
25 Roy Williams S .25 .60
26 Clinton Portis .30 .75
27 Jake Plummer .25 .60
28 Rod Smith .25 .60
29 Charles Rogers .20 .50
30 Joey Harrington .25 .60
31 Ahman Green .25 .60
32 Brett Favre .75 2.00
33 Javon Walker .20 .50
34 Andre Johnson .30 .75
35 David Carr .20 .50
36 Domanick Davis .20 .50
37 Edgerrin James .25 .60
38 Marvin Harrison .30 .75
39 Peyton Manning .60 1.50
40 Reggie Wayne .30 .75
41 Byron Leftwich .25 .60
42 Fred Taylor .25 .60
43 Jimmy Smith .25 .60
44 Priest Holmes .30 .75
45 Dante Hall .25 .60
46 Tony Gonzalez .30 .75
47 Trent Green .25 .60
48 Chris Chambers .25 .60
49 Ricky Williams .25 .60
50 Zach Thomas .30 .75
51 Daunte Culpepper .25 .60
52 Michael Bennett .25 .60
53 Randy Moss .30 .75
54 Deion Branch .25 .60
55 Adam Vinatieri .30 .75
56 Tedy Bruschi .30 .75
57 Tom Brady .60 1.50
58 Aaron Brooks .25 .60
59 Deuce McAllister .25 .60
60 Donte' Stallworth .20 .50
61 Joe Horn .25 .60
62 Jeremy Shockey .25 .60
63 Kerry Collins .25 .60
64 Michael Strahan .30 .75
65 Tiki Barber .30 .75
66 Chad Pennington .30 .75
67 Curtis Martin .30 .75
68 Santana Moss .25 .60
69 Jerry Rice .60 1.50
70 Charles Woodson .30 .75
71 Rod Woodson .25 .60
72 Tim Brown .30 .75
73 Brian Westbrook .30 .75
74 Correll Buckhalter .25 .60
75 Donovan McNabb .30 .75
76 Antwaan Randle El .25 .60
77 Hines Ward .30 .75
78 Kendrell Bell .20 .50
79 David Boston .20 .50
80 Drew Brees .30 .75
81 LaDainian Tomlinson .30 .75
82 Jeff Garcia .25 .60
83 Kevan Barlow .20 .50
84 Terrell Owens .30 .75
85 Koren Robinson .20 .50
86 Matt Hasselbeck .25 .60
87 Shaun Alexander .25 .60
88 Isaac Bruce .25 .60
89 Marc Bulger .25 .60
90 Marshall Faulk .30 .75
91 Torry Holt .25 .60
92 Brad Johnson .25 .60
93 Keenan McCardell .20 .50
94 Keyshawn Johnson .25 .60
95 Derrick Mason .25 .60
96 Eddie George .25 .60
97 Steve McNair .30 .75
98 LaVar Arrington .25 .60
99 Laveranues Coles .20 .50
100 Patrick Ramsey .25 .60
101 Archie Manning .75 2.00
102 Bart Starr 2.00 5.00
103 Bo Jackson 1.25 3.00
104 Bob Griese .75 2.00
105 Christian Okoye .50 1.25
106 Daryl Johnston .75 2.00
107 Deacon Jones .60 1.50
108 Deion Sanders .75 2.00
109 Dick Butkus 1.25 3.00
110 Lynn Swann 1.00 2.50
111 Don Maynard .60 1.50
112 Don Shula .75 2.00
113 Franco Harris 1.00 2.50
114 Fred Biletnikoff .75 2.00
115 Gale Sayers 1.00 2.50
116 George Blanda .75 2.00
117 Herman Edwards .60 1.50
118 Herschel Walker .60 1.50
119 Jack Lambert 1.00 2.50
120 James Lofton .50 1.25
121 Jim Plunkett .60 1.50
122 Jim Thorpe .75 2.00
123 Joe Greene .75 2.00
124 John Riggins .75 2.00
125 L.C. Greenwood .60 1.50
126 Larry Csonka .75 2.00
127 Leroy Kelly .60 1.50
128 Walter Payton 3.00 8.00
129 Marcus Allen .75 2.00
130 Mark Bavaro .50 1.25
131 Mel Blount .60 1.50
132 Michael Irvin .75 2.00
133 Mike Ditka .75 2.00
134 Mike Singletary .75 2.00
135 Ozzie Newsome .60 1.50
136 Paul Hornung .75 2.00
137 Paul Warfield .60 1.50
138 Randall Cunningham .60 1.50
139 Ray Nitschke .75 2.00
140 Reggie White .75 2.00
141 Richard Dent .50 1.25
142 Sammy Baugh .75 2.00
143 Sonny Jurgensen .60 1.50
144 Sterling Sharpe .60 1.50
145 Steve Largent .75 2.00
146 Terrell Davis .75 2.00
147 Terry Bradshaw 1.25 3.00
148 Thurman Thomas .60 1.50
149 Tony Dorsett .75 2.00
150 Warren Moon .60 1.50
151 John Navarre RC 1.00 2.50
152 Derek Abney RC 1.00 2.50
153 Ryan Dinwiddie RC 1.00 2.50
154 Bruce Perry/100 RC 7.50 20.00
155 Adimchinobe Echemandu RC 1.25 3.00
156 Troy Fleming RC 1.00 2.50
157 Brandon Miree RC 1.00 2.50
158 Jarrett Payton RC 1.25 3.00
159 Ben Hartsock RC 1.00 2.50
160 Chris Cooley RC 1.50 4.00
161 Derrick Ward RC 1.50 4.00
162 Triandos Luke RC 1.00 2.50
163 Clarence Moore RC 1.00 2.50
164 D.J. Hackett RC 1.25 3.00
165 Mark Jones RC 1.00 2.50
166 Sloan Thomas RC 1.25 3.00
167 Jamaar Taylor RC 1.00 2.50
168 Casey Bramlet RC 1.00 2.50
169 Drew Carter RC 1.25 3.00
170 Antwan Odom RC 1.25 3.00
171 Marquise Hill RC 1.00 2.50
172 Ricardo Colclough RC 1.25 3.00
173 Keith Smith RC 1.00 2.50
174 Joey Thomas RC 1.00 2.50
175 Stuart Schweigert RC 1.25 3.00
176 Cody Pickett RC 1.50 4.00
177 B.J. Symons RC 1.25 3.00
178 Matt Mauck RC 1.25 3.00
179 Bradlee Van Pelt RC 1.50 4.00
180 Jim Sorgi RC 1.50 4.00
181 Ernest Wilford RC 1.50 4.00
182 Bernard Berrian RC 2.00 5.00
183 Darius Watts RC 1.25 3.00
184 Derrick Hamilton RC 1.25 3.00
185 Jerricho Cotchery RC 1.50 4.00
186 Jeris McIntyre RC 1.25 3.00
187 Carlos Francis RC 1.25 3.00
188 Maurice Mann RC 1.25 3.00
189 Randy Starks RC 1.25 3.00
190 Darnell Dockett RC 1.25 3.00
191 Marcus Tubbs RC 1.25 3.00
192 Daryl Smith RC 1.25 3.00
193 Karlos Dansby RC 2.00 5.00
194 Michael Boulware RC 2.00 5.00
195 Teddy Lehman RC 1.25 3.00
196 Will Poole RC 2.00 5.00
197 Derrick Strait RC 1.25 3.00
198 Ahmad Carroll RC 1.25 3.00
199 Jeremy LeSueur RC 1.25 3.00
200 Bob Sanders RC 5.00 12.00
201 J.P. Losman RC 1.50 4.00
202 Matt Schaub RC 4.00 10.00
203 Josh Harris RC 1.25 3.00
204 Luke McCown RC 1.50 4.00
205 Quincy Wilson RC 1.50 4.00
206 Michael Turner RC 2.50 6.00
207 Mewelde Moore RC 1.50 4.00
208 Cedric Cobbs RC 1.25 3.00
209 Ben Watson RC 2.00 5.00
210 Michael Jenkins RC 2.00 5.00
211 Devery Henderson RC 2.00 5.00
212 Johnnie Morant RC 1.25 3.00
213 Keary Colbert RC 1.25 3.00
214 Devard Darling RC 1.25 3.00
215 P.K. Sam RC 1.25 3.00
216 Samie Parker RC 1.25 3.00
217 Jason Babin RC 2.00 5.00
218 Tommie Harris RC 2.00 5.00
219 Vince Wilfork RC 2.00 5.00
220 Jonathan Vilma RC 2.00 5.00
221 D.J. Williams RC 2.00 5.00
222 Chris Gamble RC 1.50 4.00
223 Matt Ware RC 2.00 5.00
224 Shawntae Spencer RC 1.25 3.00
225 Sean Jones RC 1.50 4.00
226 Drew Henson RC 1.50 4.00
227 Ben Roethlisberger RC 15.00 40.00
228 Eli Manning RC 15.00 40.00
229 Philip Rivers RC 10.00 25.00
230 Steven Jackson RC 4.00 10.00
231 Kevin Jones RC 2.00 5.00
232 Chris Perry RC 2.00 5.00
233 Greg Jones RC 1.50 4.00
234 Tatum Bell RC 2.00 5.00
235 Jeff Smoker RC 2.00 5.00
236 Julius Jones RC 2.00 5.00
237 Kellen Winslow RC 2.50 6.00
238 Ben Troupe RC 2.00 5.00
239 Larry Fitzgerald RC 6.00 15.00
240 Craig Krenzel RC 2.00 5.00
241 Roy Williams RC 2.50 6.00
242 Reggie Williams RC 2.00 5.00
243 Michael Clayton RC 2.00 5.00
244 Lee Evans RC 2.50 6.00
245 Rashaun Woods RC 1.50 4.00
246 Kenechi Udeze RC 2.00 5.00
247 Will Smith RC 2.00 5.00
248 DeAngelo Hall RC 2.50 6.00
249 Dunta Robinson RC 1.50 4.00
250 Sean Taylor RC 5.00 12.00

2004 Donruss Classics Timeless Tributes Green

*STARS 1-100: 8X TO 20X BASE CARD HI
*LEGENDS 101-150: 2.5X TO 6X BASIC CARDS
*ROOKIES 151-175: 1.5X TO 4X BASE CARD HI
*ROOKIES 176-200: 1.2X TO 3X BASE CARD HI
*ROOKIES 201-225: 1.2X TO 3X BASE CARD HI
*ROOKIES 226-250: 1X TO 2.5X BASE CARD HI
STATED PRINT RUN 50 SER.#'d SETS
UNPRICED PLATINUM PRINT RUN 1 SET

2004 Donruss Classics Timeless Tributes Platinum

UNPRICED PLATINUM PRINT RUN 1 SET

2004 Donruss Classics Timeless Tributes Red

*STARS 1-100: 4X TO 10X BAIC CARDS
*LEGENDS 101-150: 1.2X TO 3X
*ROOKIES 151-175: 1X TO 2.5X BASIC CARD
*ROOKIES 176-200: .8X TO 2X
*ROOKIES 201-225: .8X TO 2X
*ROOKIES 226-250: .6X TO 1.5X
STATED PRINT RUN 100 SER.#'d SETS

2004 Donruss Classics Classic

C1-C30 PRINT RUN 1000 SER.#'d SETS
C31-C45 PRINT RUN 750 SER.#'d SETS
C46-C50 PRINT RUN 500 SER.#'d SETS
C1 Barry Sanders 2.00 5.00
C2 Bart Starr 2.50 6.00
C3 Bob Griese 1.00 2.50
C4 Dan Marino 2.50 6.00
C5 Doak Walker 1.00 2.50
C6 Don Shula 1.00 2.50
C7 Emmitt Smith 2.50 6.00
C8 Franco Harris 1.25 3.00
C9 Jerry Rice 2.00 5.00
C10 Jim Brown 1.50 4.00
C11 Jim Kelly 1.00 2.50
C12 Jim Thorpe 1.00 2.50
C13 Joe Montana 2.50 6.00
C14 Joe Namath 1.50 4.00
C15 John Elway 2.50 6.00
C16 John Riggins 1.00 2.50
C17 Johnny Unitas 2.50 6.00
C19 Lawrence Taylor 1.00 2.50
C20 Mark Bavaro .60 1.50
C21 Michael Irvin 1.00 2.50
C22 Mike Singletary 1.00 2.50
C23 Paul Warfield .75 2.00
C24 Ray Nitschke 1.00 2.50
C25 Roger Staubach 1.50 4.00
C26 Terrell Davis 1.00 2.50
C27 Terry Bradshaw 1.50 4.00
C28 Tom Brady 2.00 5.00
C29 Troy Aikman 1.50 4.00
C30 Walter Payton 5.00 12.00
C31 Bart Starr 3.00 8.00
Ray Nitschke
C32 Bob Griese 3.00 8.00
Dan Marino
C33 Walter Payton 5.00 12.00
Mike Singletary
C34 Doak Walker 2.50 6.00
Barry Sanders
C35 Don Shula 3.00 8.00
Johnny Unitas
C36 Roger Staubach 2.00 5.00
Troy Aikman
C37 Michael Irvin 3.00 8.00
Emmitt Smith
C38 Joe Montana 3.00 8.00
Jerry Rice
C39 Jim Brown 2.00 5.00
Paul Warfield
C40 Jim Kelly 1.25 3.00
Thurman Thomas
C41 Joe Namath 2.00 5.00
John Riggins
C42 John Elway 3.00 8.00
Terrell Davis
C43 Lawrence Taylor 1.25 3.00
Mark Bavaro
C44 Terry Bradshaw 2.00 5.00
Franco Harris
C45 Doak Walker 2.50 6.00
Jim Thorpe
C46 Dan Marino 6.00 15.00
John Elway
Jim Kelly
C47 Johnny Unitas 5.00 12.00
Joe Namath
Bart Starr
C48 Walter Payton 7.50 20.00
Barry Sanders
Emmitt Smith
C49 Jim Thorpe 5.00 12.00
Doak Walker
Jim Brown
C50 Troy Aikman 7.50 20.00
Joe Montana
Tom Brady

2004 Donruss Classics Classic Materials

C1-C30 PRINT RUN 150 SER.#'d SETS
C31-C45 PRINT RUN 75 SER.#'d SETS
C46-C50 PRINT RUN 25 SER.#'d SETS
C1 Barry Sanders 12.00 30.00
C2 Bart Starr 12.50 30.00
C3 Bob Griese 6.00 15.00
C4 Dan Marino 15.00 40.00
C5 Doak Walker 10.00 25.00
C6 Don Shula 6.00 15.00
C7 Emmitt Smith 12.00 30.00
C8 Franco Harris 8.00 20.00
C9 Jerry Rice 10.00 25.00
C10 Jim Brown 10.00 25.00
C11 Jim Kelly 7.50 20.00
C12 Jim Thorpe 60.00 120.00
C13 Joe Montana 15.00 40.00
C14 Joe Namath 15.00 30.00
C15 John Elway 12.50 30.00
C16 John Riggins 7.50 20.00
C17 Johnny Unitas 15.00 30.00
C18 Larry Csonka 6.00 15.00
C19 Lawrence Taylor 6.00 15.00
C20 Mark Bavaro 4.00 10.00
C21 Michael Irvin 6.00 15.00
C22 Mike Singletary 6.00 15.00
C23 Paul Warfield 5.00 12.00
C24 Ray Nitschke 15.00 30.00
C25 Roger Staubach 12.50 30.00
C26 Terrell Davis 6.00 15.00
C27 Terry Bradshaw 12.50 30.00
C28 Tom Brady 10.00 25.00
C29 Troy Aikman 10.00 25.00
C30 Walter Payton 20.00 50.00
C31 Bart Starr 30.00 60.00
Ray Nitschke
C32 Bob Griese 40.00 80.00
Dan Marino
C33 Walter Payton 40.00 100.00
Mike Singletary
C34 Doak Walker 25.00 50.00
Barry Sanders
C35 Don Shula 25.00 50.00
Johnny Unitas
C36 Roger Staubach 25.00 50.00
Troy Aikman
C37 Michael Irvin 20.00 50.00
Emmitt Smith
C38 Joe Montana 40.00 100.00
Jerry Rice
C39 Jim Brown 15.00 40.00
Paul Warfield
C40 Jim Kelly 15.00 40.00
Thurman Thomas
C41 Joe Namath 25.00 60.00
John Riggins
C42 John Elway 20.00 50.00
Terrell Davis
C43 Lawrence Taylor 20.00 50.00
Mark Bavaro
C44 Terry Bradshaw 25.00 50.00
Franco Harris
C45 Doak Walker 75.00 150.00
Jim Thorpe
C46 Dan Marino 60.00 120.00
John Elway
Jim Kelly
C47 Johnny Unitas 50.00 120.00
Joe Namath
Bart Starr
C48 Walter Payton 100.00 200.00
Barry Sanders
Emmitt Smith
C49 Jim Thorpe 125.00 250.00
Doak Walker
Jim Brown
C50 Troy Aikman 50.00 120.00
Joe Montana
Tom Brady

2004 Donruss Classics Classic Pigskin

SINGLES PRINT RUN 250 SER.#'d SETS
*DOUBLE/25: 1.2X TO 3X BASIC INSERT/250
DOUBLES PRINT RUN 25 SER.#'d SETS
CP1 Roger Staubach 12.50 30.00
CP2 Lawrence Taylor 12.50 25.00
CP3 Joe Montana 20.00 50.00
CP4 Emmitt Smith 15.00 30.00
CP5 Troy Aikman 10.00 25.00
CP6 Tom Brady 15.00 40.00

2004 Donruss Classics Dress Code Jerseys

STATED PRINT RUN 250 SER.#'d SETS
DC1 Aaron Brooks 3.00 8.00
DC2 Ahman Green 3.00 8.00
DC3 Brian Urlacher 4.00 10.00
DC4 Byron Leftwich 3.00 8.00
DC5 Chad Johnson 4.00 10.00
DC6 Chris Chambers 3.00 8.00
DC7 Curtis Martin 4.00 10.00
DC8 Daunte Culpepper 3.00 8.00
DC9 David Carr 2.50 6.00
DC10 Donovan McNabb 4.00 10.00
DC11 Drew Bledsoe 4.00 10.00
DC12 Drew Brees 4.00 10.00
DC13 Eddie George 3.00 8.00
DC14 Isaac Bruce 3.00 8.00
DC15 Jake Plummer 3.00 8.00
DC16 Jeff Garcia 3.00 8.00
DC17 Jerome Bettis 4.00 10.00
DC18 Jevon Kearse 3.00 8.00
DC19 Joey Harrington 3.00 8.00

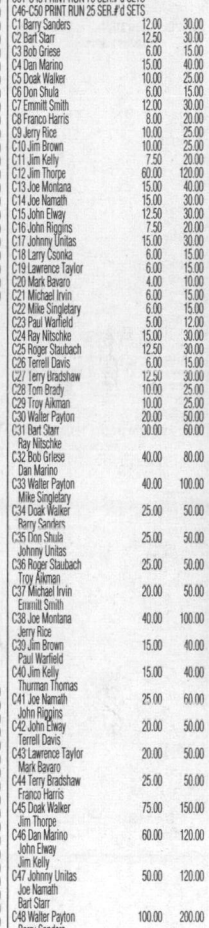

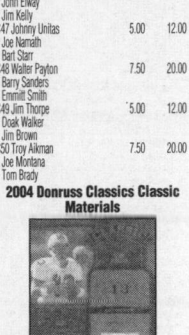

DC20 Kurt Warner 4.00 10.00
DC21 LaVar Arrington 10.00 25.00
DC22 Laveranues Coles 2.50 6.00
DC23 Marc Bulger 3.00 8.00
DC24 Stephen Davis 3.00 8.00
DC25 Terrell Owens 4.00 10.00

2004 Donruss Classics Legendary Players

STATED PRINT RUN 1000 SER.#'d SETS
LP1 Barry Sanders 2.00 5.00
LP2 Bart Starr 2.50 6.00
LP3 Bruce Smith 1.00 2.50
LP4 Dan Marino 2.50 6.00
LP5 Deion Sanders 1.00 2.50
LP6 Earl Campbell 1.00 2.50
LP7 Franco Harris 1.25 3.00
LP8 Fred Biletnikoff 1.00 2.50
LP9 Jim Brown 1.50 4.00
LP10 Joe Montana 2.50 6.00
LP11 Joe Namath 1.50 4.00
LP12 Johnny Unitas 2.50 6.00
LP14 Lawrence Taylor 1.00 2.50
LP15 Mark Bavaro .60 1.50
LP16 Mike Singletary 1.00 2.50
LP17 Ozzie Newsome .75 2.00
LP18 Sterling Sharpe .75 2.00
LP19 Steve Largent 1.00 2.50
LP20 Terry Bradshaw 1.50 4.00
LP21 Thurman Thomas .75 2.00
LP22 Walter Payton 4.00 10.00
LP23 Warren Moon .75 2.00
LP24 Jim Thorpe 1.00 2.50
LP25 Reggie White 1.00 2.50

2004 Donruss Classics Legendary Players Jerseys

STATED PRINT RUN 100 SER.#'d SETS
PRIME/5 NOT PRICED DUE TO SCARCITY
LP1 Barry Sanders 15.00 30.00
LP2 Bart Starr 15.00 40.00
LP3 Bruce Smith 8.00 20.00
LP4 Dan Marino 25.00 50.00
LP5 Deion Sanders 8.00 20.00
LP6 Earl Campbell 8.00 20.00
LP7 Franco Harris 10.00 25.00
LP8 Fred Biletnikoff 8.00 20.00
LP9 Jim Brown 12.50 30.00
LP10 Joe Montana 20.00 50.00
LP11 Joe Namath 15.00 40.00
LP12 Johnny Unitas 20.00 50.00
LP13 Larry Csonka 8.00 20.00
LP14 Lawrence Taylor 12.50 30.00
LP15 Mark Bavaro 5.00 12.00
LP16 Mike Singletary 8.00 20.00
LP17 Ozzie Newsome 6.00 15.00
LP18 Sterling Sharpe 6.00 15.00
LP19 Steve Largent 12.50 30.00
LP20 Terry Bradshaw 15.00 40.00
LP21 Thurman Thomas 6.00 15.00
LP22 Walter Payton 30.00 60.00
LP23 Warren Moon 6.00 15.00
LP24 Jim Thorpe 75.00 150.00
LP25 Reggie White 8.00 20.00

2004 Donruss Classics Membership

STATED PRINT RUN 1000 SER.#'d SETS
M1 Anquan Boldin 1.25 3.00
M2 Barry Sanders 2.50 6.00
M3 Brett Favre 3.00 8.00
M4 Chad Pennington 1.25 3.00
M5 Clinton Portis 1.25 3.00
M6 Dan Marino 3.00 8.00
M7 Earl Campbell 1.25 3.00
M8 Jamal Lewis 1.00 2.50
M9 Jim Brown 2.00 5.00
M10 Jim Kelly 1.25 3.00
M11 Joe Montana 3.00 8.00
M12 Joe Namath 2.00 5.00
M13 John Elway 3.00 8.00
M14 Johnny Unitas 3.00 8.00
M15 LaDainian Tomlinson 1.25 3.00
M16 Lawrence Taylor 1.25 3.00
M17 Marcus Allen 1.25 3.00
M18 Marshall Faulk 1.25 3.00
M19 Michael Vick 1.50 4.00
M20 Peyton Manning 2.50 6.00
M21 Ricky Williams 1.00 2.50
M22 Roger Staubach 2.00 5.00
M23 Steve McNair 1.25 3.00
M24 Tom Brady 2.50 6.00
M25 Troy Aikman 2.00 5.00

2004 Donruss Classics Membership VIP Jerseys

STATED PRINT RUN 250 SER.#'d SETS
M1 Anquan Boldin 4.00 10.00
M2 Barry Sanders 12.50 25.00
M3 Brett Favre 10.00 25.00
M4 Chad Pennington 4.00 10.00
M5 Clinton Portis 4.00 10.00
M6 Dan Marino 15.00 30.00
M7 Earl Campbell 5.00 12.00
M8 Jamal Lewis 3.00 8.00
M9 Jim Brown 8.00 20.00
M10 Jim Kelly 5.00 12.00
M11 Joe Montana 20.00 40.00
M12 Joe Namath 10.00 25.00
M13 John Elway 12.50 25.00
M14 Johnny Unitas 12.50 30.00
M15 LaDainian Tomlinson 4.00 10.00
M16 Lawrence Taylor 5.00 12.00
M17 Marcus Allen 6.00 15.00
M18 Marshall Faulk 4.00 10.00
M19 Michael Vick 5.00 12.00
M20 Peyton Manning 8.00 20.00
M21 Ricky Williams 3.00 8.00
M22 Roger Staubach 10.00 25.00
M23 Steve McNair 4.00 10.00
M24 Tom Brady 10.00 25.00
M25 Troy Aikman 7.50 20.00

2004 Donruss Classics Membership VIP Jerseys Autographs

FIRST 25 JERSEY CARDS SIGNED
M2 Barry Sanders 75.00 150.00
M6 Dan Marino 100.00 200.00
M7 Earl Campbell 30.00 60.00

M9 Jim Brown 50.00 100.00
M10 Jim Kelly 40.00 80.00
M11 Joe Montana 100.00 200.00
M12 Joe Namath 75.00 150.00
M13 John Elway 100.00 200.00
M16 Lawrence Taylor 40.00 80.00
M22 Roger Staubach 60.00 120.00
M25 Troy Aikman 50.00 100.00

2004 Donruss Classics Sideline Generals

STATED PRINT RUN 2000 SER.#'d SETS
SG1 Barry Switzer 2.50 6.00
Jimmy Johnson
SG2 Bill Walsh 2.00 5.00
Bill Belichick
SG3 Chuck Noll 3.00 8.00
Bill Cowher
SG4 Don Shula 1.25 3.00
Tony Dungy
SG5 Dick Vermeil 1.25 3.00
Andy Reid

2004 Donruss Classics Sideline Generals Autographs

STATED PRINT RUN 250 SER.#'d SETS
SG1 Barry Switzer 40.00 80.00
Jimmy Johnson
SG2 Bill Walsh 200.00 400.00
Bill Belichick
SG3 Chuck Noll 125.00 225.00
Bill Cowher
SG4 Don Shula 40.00 80.00
Tony Dungy
SG5 Dick Vermeil 25.00 50.00
Andy Reid

2004 Donruss Classics Significant Signatures Green

*GREEN: .2X TO .5X PLATINUM
STATED PRINT RUN 75 SER.#'d SETS
110 Lynn Swann 125.00 225.00
140 Reggie White 150.00 250.00
142 Sammy Baugh No Auto 15.00 40.00

2004 Donruss Classics Significant Signatures Platinum

STATED PRINT RUN 25 SER.#'d SETS
1 Anquan Boldin 20.00 50.00
3 Michael Vick 50.00 80.00
6 Jamal Lewis 15.00 40.00
7 Kyle Boller 15.00 40.00
9 Todd Heap 15.00 40.00
13 Jake Delhomme 15.00 40.00
14 Stephen Davis 15.00 40.00
15 Steve Smith 20.00 50.00
17 Brian Urlacher 20.00 50.00
18 Rex Grossman 15.00 40.00
19 Chad Johnson 20.00 50.00
21 Rudi Johnson 15.00 40.00
25 Roy Williams S 15.00 40.00
30 Joey Harrington 15.00 40.00
32 Brett Favre 125.00 250.00
33 Javon Walker 12.00 30.00
35 David Carr 12.00 30.00
36 Domanick Davis 12.00 30.00
43 Jimmy Smith 15.00 40.00
44 Priest Holmes 20.00 50.00
45 Dante Hall 15.00 40.00
48 Chris Chambers 15.00 40.00
55 Adam Vinatieri 20.00 50.00
57 Tom Brady 175.00 300.00
58 Aaron Brooks 15.00 40.00
59 Deuce McAllister 15.00 40.00
61 Joe Horn
64 Michael Strahan 20.00 50.00
65 Tiki Barber 25.00 60.00
66 Chad Pennington 20.00 50.00
68 Santana Moss 15.00 40.00
75 Donovan McNabb 40.00 100.00
76 Antwaan Randle El 15.00 40.00
77 Hines Ward 20.00 50.00
78 Kendrell Bell 12.00 30.00
86 Matt Hasselbeck 15.00 40.00
87 Shaun Alexander 15.00 40.00
91 Torry Holt 15.00 40.00
94 Keyshawn Johnson 15.00 40.00
95 Derrick Mason 15.00 40.00
96 Eddie George 20.00 50.00
97 Steve McNair 20.00 50.00
99 Laveranues Coles 12.00 30.00
100 Patrick Ramsey 15.00 40.00
101 Archie Manning 25.00 60.00
102 Bart Starr 100.00 200.00
103 Bo Jackson 40.00 100.00
104 Bob Griese 25.00 60.00
105 Christian Okoye 15.00 40.00
106 Daryl Johnston 30.00 80.00
107 Deacon Jones 20.00 50.00
108 Deion Sanders 40.00 100.00
109 Dick Butkus 40.00 100.00
110 Lynn Swann 150.00 225.00
111 Don Maynard 20.00 50.00
112 Don Shula 25.00 60.00
113 Franco Harris 30.00 80.00
114 Fred Biletnikoff 25.00 60.00
115 Gale Sayers 30.00 80.00
116 George Blanda 40.00 80.00
117 Herman Edwards 20.00 50.00
118 Herschel Walker 20.00 50.00
119 Jack Lambert 75.00 150.00
120 James Lofton 15.00 40.00
121 Jim Plunkett 20.00 50.00
123 Joe Greene 25.00 60.00
124 John Riggins 25.00 60.00
125 L.C. Greenwood 20.00 50.00
127 Leroy Kelly 20.00 50.00
129 Marcus Allen 25.00 60.00
130 Mark Bavaro 15.00 40.00
131 Mel Blount 20.00 50.00
132 Michael Irvin 30.00 80.00
133 Mike Ditka 25.00 60.00
134 Mike Singletary 25.00 60.00
135 Ozzie Newsome 20.00 50.00
136 Paul Hornung 25.00 60.00
137 Paul Warfield 20.00 50.00
138 Randall Cunningham 20.00 50.00
140 Reggie White 175.00 300.00
141 Richard Dent 15.00 40.00
142 Sammy Baugh No Auto 25.00 50.00
143 Sonny Jurgensen 20.00 50.00
144 Sterling Sharpe 20.00 50.00
145 Steve Largent 25.00 60.00
146 Terrell Davis 25.00 60.00
147 Terry Bradshaw 75.00 150.00
148 Thurman Thomas 20.00 50.00
149 Tony Dorsett 25.00 60.00
150 Warren Moon 25.00 60.00
164 D.J. Hackett 12.00 30.00
172 Ricardo Colclough 12.00 30.00
181 Ernest Wilford 12.00 30.00
182 Bernard Berrian 15.00 40.00
183 Darius Watts 10.00 25.00
184 Derrick Hamilton 10.00 25.00
185 Jerricho Cotchery 12.00 30.00
198 Ahmad Carroll 10.00 25.00
201 J.P. Losman 12.00 30.00
202 Matt Schaub 30.00 80.00
203 Josh Harris 10.00 25.00
204 Luke McCown 12.00 30.00
205 Quincy Wilson 12.00 30.00
206 Michael Turner 25.00 60.00
207 Mewelde Moore 12.00 30.00
208 Cedric Cobbs 10.00 25.00
209 Ben Watson 15.00 40.00
210 Michael Jenkins 15.00 40.00
211 Devery Henderson 15.00 40.00
212 Johnnie Morant 10.00 25.00
213 Keary Colbert 10.00 25.00
214 Devard Darling 10.00 25.00
215 P.K. Sam 10.00 25.00
216 Samie Parker 10.00 25.00
218 Tommie Harris 15.00 40.00
219 Vince Wilfork 15.00 40.00
220 Jonathan Vilma 15.00 40.00
222 Chris Gamble 12.00 30.00
225 Sean Jones 12.00 30.00
226 Drew Henson 10.00 25.00
227 Ben Roethlisberger 200.00 350.00
228 Eli Manning 200.00 350.00
229 Philip Rivers 60.00 150.00
230 Steven Jackson 50.00 120.00
231 Kevin Jones 12.00 30.00
232 Chris Perry 12.00 30.00
233 Greg Jones 10.00 25.00
234 Tatum Bell 12.00 30.00
236 Julius Jones 12.00 30.00
238 Ben Troupe 12.00 30.00
241 Roy Williams WR 15.00 40.00
242 Reggie Williams 12.00 30.00
243 Michael Clayton 12.00 30.00
244 Lee Evans 15.00 40.00
245 Rashaun Woods 10.00 25.00
246 Kenechi Udeze 12.00 30.00
247 Will Smith
248 DeAngelo Hall 15.00 40.00
249 Dunta Robinson 10.00 25.00

2004 Donruss Classics Significant Signatures Red

PLAYOFF ANNOUNCED PRINT RUNS BELOW
7 Kyle Boller/50* 10.00 25.00
9 Todd Heap/50* 12.00 25.00
15 Steve Smith 12.00 30.00
21 Rudi Johnson 10.00 25.00
33 Javon Walker/50* 12.00 30.00
36 Domanick Davis 12.00 25.00
45 Dante Hall/25* 12.00 30.00
48 Chris Chambers/25* 12.50 30.00
55 Adam Vinatieri/75* 20.00 40.00
68 Santana Moss 10.00 25.00
95 Derrick Mason/90* 10.00 25.00
99 Laveranues Coles/25* 12.00 30.00
101 Archie Manning/75* 12.00 30.00
103 Bo Jackson/50* 50.00 120.00
105 Christian Okoye 10.00 25.00
106 Daryl Johnston 12.00 30.00
107 Deacon Jones 8.00 20.00
110 Lynn Swann/62* 100.00 175.00
111 Don Maynard 8.00 20.00
114 Fred Biletnikoff 12.00 30.00
116 George Blanda/84* 25.00 50.00
117 Herman Edwards 12.00 30.00
118 Herschel Walker 12.00 30.00
120 James Lofton 8.00 20.00
121 Jim Plunkett 10.00 25.00
123 Joe Greene/75* 25.00 50.00
124 John Riggins 12.00 30.00
125 L.C. Greenwood 10.00 25.00
127 Leroy Kelly 10.00 25.00
130 Mark Bavaro/50* 12.00 30.00
131 Mel Blount 12.00 30.00
133 Mike Ditka/75 20.00 40.00
136 Paul Hornung 12.00 30.00
137 Paul Warfield 10.00 25.00
138 Randall Cunningham 10.00 25.00
141 Richard Dent/50* 10.00 25.00
142 Sammy Baugh No Auto 12.00 30.00
143 Sonny Jurgensen 10.00 25.00
144 Sterling Sharpe/66* 20.00 40.00
145 Steve Largent/75* 12.00 30.00
148 Thurman Thomas 12.00 30.00
150 Warren Moon/50* 15.00 40.00
164 D.J. Hackett 8.00 20.00
182 Bernard Berrian 10.00 25.00
184 Derrick Hamilton 6.00 15.00
185 Jerricho Cotchery 8.00 20.00
207 Mewelde Moore 8.00 20.00
208 Cedric Cobbs 6.00 15.00
211 Devery Henderson/75* 12.00 30.00
212 Johnnie Morant 6.00 15.00
213 Keary Colbert 6.00 15.00
215 P.K. Sam 6.00 15.00
233 Greg Jones/75* 10.00 25.00

2004 Donruss Classics Team Colors Jerseys Away

AWAY PRINT RUN 150 SER.#'d SETS
*HOME/75: .6X TO 1.5X AWAY JSY/150
HOME PRINT RUN 75 SER.#'d SETS
*PRIME/25: 1.2X TO 3X AWAY JSY/150
PRIME PRINT RUN 25 SER.#'d SETS
TC1 Anquan Boldin 4.00 10.00
TC2 Barry Sanders 10.00 25.00
TC3 Brian Urlacher 4.00 10.00
TC4 Daunte Culpepper 3.00 8.00
TC5 Deuce McAllister 3.00 8.00
TC6 Donovan McNabb 4.00 10.00
TC7 Drew Bledsoe 4.00 10.00
TC8 Earl Campbell 5.00 12.00
TC9 Edgerrin James 3.00 8.00
TC10 Jeremy Shockey 3.00 8.00
TC11 Jerry Rice 8.00 20.00
TC12 Jim Kelly 6.00 15.00
TC13 Brett Favre 10.00 25.00
TC14 John Elway 12.00 30.00
TC15 Kurt Warner 4.00 10.00
TC16 LaDainian Tomlinson 4.00 10.00
TC17 Marshall Faulk 4.00 10.00
TC18 Marvin Harrison 4.00 10.00
TC19 Peyton Manning 8.00 20.00
TC20 Plaxico Burress 3.00 8.00
TC21 Priest Holmes 4.00 10.00
TC22 Randy Moss 4.00 10.00
TC23 Steve McNair 4.00 10.00
TC24 Torry Holt 3.00 8.00
TC25 Walter Payton 20.00 50.00

2004 Donruss Classics Timeless Triples Jerseys

STATED PRINT RUN 100 SER.#'d SETS
UNPRICED PRIME SER.#'d TO 10
TT1 Fred Biletnikoff 15.00 40.00
Jim Plunkett
Marcus Allen
TT2 Dick Butkus 40.00 100.00
Walter Payton
Mike Singletary
TT3 Terry Bradshaw 30.00 80.00
Franco Harris
Lynn Swann
TT4 Bart Starr 40.00 100.00
Ray Nitschke
Brett Favre
TT5 Bob Griese 40.00 80.00
Larry Csonka
Dan Marino
TT6 Don Shula 40.00 80.00
Johnny Unitas
Peyton Manning
TT7 Joe Montana 30.00 80.00
Jerry Rice
Terrell Owens
TT8 Troy Aikman 30.00 80.00
Emmitt Smith
Michael Irvin
TT9 Jim Brown 25.00 60.00
Paul Warfield
Leroy Kelly
TT10 Joe Namath 25.00 60.00
John Riggins
Don Maynard
TT11 John Elway 25.00 60.00
Terrell Davis
Rod Smith
TT12 Jim Kelly 15.00 40.00
Bruce Smith
Thurman Thomas
TT13 Joe Greene 20.00 50.00
L.C. Greenwood
Mel Blount
TT14 Roger Staubach 25.00 60.00
Tony Dorsett
Deion Sanders

2005 Donruss Classics

This 250-card set was released in August, 2005. The set was issued in the hobby in five-card packs with an $6 SRP which came 18 packs to a box. Cards numbered 1-100 feature active veterans basically in team alphabetical order while cards numbered 101-150 feature retired greats also in team alphabetica order and cards 151-250 feature 2005 rookies In the rookie section, cards numbered 226-250 were all signed by the player as well. Cards numbered 101-150 have a stated print run of 1000 serial numbered sets, cards numbered 151-175 have a stated print run of 1999 serial numbered sets, cards numbered 176-200 have a stated print ruf of 1499 serial numbered sets, cards numbered 201-225 have a stated print run of 999 serial numbered sets and the signed rookie cards (226-250) have a stated print run of 499 serial numbered sets.

COMP.SET w/o SP's (100) 7.50 20.00
101-150 LEG PRINT RUN 1000 SER.#'d SETS
151-175 PRINT RUN 1999 SER.#'d SETS
176-200 PRINT RUN 1499 SER.#'d SETS
201-225 PRINT RUN 999 SER.#'d SETS
226-250 AU PRINT RUN 499 SER.#'d SETS
1 Kurt Warner .30 .75
2 Josh McCown .25 .60
3 Larry Fitzgerald .30 .75
4 Alge Crumpler .25 .60
5 Michael Vick .30 .75
6 Warrick Dunn .25 .60
7 Todd Heap .25 .60
8 Jamal Lewis .25 .60
9 Kyle Boller .25 .60
10 Drew Bledsoe .30 .75
11 Lee Evans .25 .60
12 Willis McGahee .30 .75
13 Steve Smith .30 .75
14 Jake Delhomme .25 .60
15 Muhsin Muhammad .25 .60
16 Brian Urlacher .30 .75
17 Rex Grossman .25 .60
18 Thomas Jones .30 .75
19 Carson Palmer .30 .75
20 Chad Johnson .25 .60
21 Rudi Johnson .25 .60
22 Antonio Bryant .20 .50
23 Kellen Winslow Jr. .25 .60
24 Lee Suggs .20 .50
25 Julius Jones .20 .50
26 Keyshawn Johnson .25 .60
27 Roy Williams S .20 .50
28 Jake Plummer .25 .60
29 Rod Smith .25 .60
30 Tatum Bell .20 .50
31 Joey Harrington .25 .60
32 Kevin Jones .20 .50
33 Roy Williams WR .25 .60
34 Ahman Green .25 .60
35 Brett Favre .75 2.00
36 Javon Walker .20 .50
37 Andre Johnson .30 .75
38 David Carr .20 .50
39 Domanick Davis .20 .50
40 Edgerrin James .25 .60
41 Marvin Harrison .30 .75
42 Peyton Manning .60 1.50
43 Reggie Wayne .30 .75
44 Byron Leftwich .25 .60
45 Fred Taylor .25 .60
46 Jimmy Smith .25 .60
47 Priest Holmes .25 .60
48 Tony Gonzalez .25 .60
49 Trent Green .25 .60
50 A.J. Feeley .20 .50
51 Chris Chambers .25 .60
52 Zach Thomas .30 .75
53 Daunte Culpepper .25 .60
54 Michael Bennett .25 .60
55 Randy Moss .30 .75
56 Corey Dillon .25 .60
57 David Givens .20 .50
58 Tom Brady .60 1.50
59 Aaron Brooks .20 .50
60 Deuce McAllister .25 .60
61 Joe Horn .25 .60
62 Eli Manning .50 1.25
63 Jeremy Shockey .30 .75
64 Tiki Barber .30 .75
65 Chad Pennington .30 .75
66 Curtis Martin .30 .75
67 Santana Moss .25 .60
68 Jerry Porter .20 .50
69 Kerry Collins .25 .60
70 J.P. Losman .20 .50
71 Brian Westbrook .25 .60
72 Donovan McNabb .30 .75
73 Terrell Owens .30 .75
74 Ben Roethlisberger .50 1.25
75 Duce Staley .25 .60
76 Hines Ward .30 .75
77 Jerome Bettis .30 .75
78 Antonio Gates .30 .75
79 Drew Brees .30 .75
80 LaDainian Tomlinson .30 .75
81 Brandon Lloyd .20 .50
82 Kevan Barlow .20 .50
83 Laveranues Coles .20 .50
84 Darrell Jackson .20 .50
85 Jerry Rice .60 1.50
86 Matt Hasselbeck .25 .60
87 Shaun Alexander .25 .60
88 Isaac Bruce .25 .60
89 Marc Bulger .25 .60
90 Steven Jackson .30 .75
91 Torry Holt .25 .60
92 Brian Griese .25 .60
93 Michael Clayton .20 .50
94 Mike Alstott .25 .60
95 Chris Brown .20 .50
96 Drew Bennett .25 .60
97 Steve McNair .30 .75
98 Clinton Portis .25 .60
99 LaVar Arrington .25 .60
100 Patrick Ramsey .25 .60
101 Don Shula 1.25 3.00
102 James Lofton 1.00 2.50
103 Thurman Thomas 1.50 4.00
104 Gale Sayers 2.00 5.00
105 Mike Singletary 1.50 4.00
106 Boomer Esiason 1.25 3.00
107 Cris Collinsworth 1.25 3.00
108 Ickey Woods 1.00 2.50
109 Jim Brown 2.00 5.00
110 Leroy Kelly 1.25 3.00
111 Ozzie Newsome 1.25 3.00
112 Paul Warfield 1.25 3.00
113 Deion Sanders 2.00 5.00
114 Herschel Walker 1.25 3.00
115 Mike Ditka 1.50 4.00
116 Michael Irvin 1.50 4.00
117 Roger Staubach 2.50 6.00
118 Tony Dorsett 1.25 3.00
119 Troy Aikman 2.00 5.00
120 John Elway 3.00 8.00
121 Barry Sanders 2.50 6.00
122 Bart Starr 2.50 6.00
123 Paul Hornung 1.50 4.00
124 Sterling Sharpe 1.25 3.00
125 Warren Moon 1.50 4.00
126 Christian Okoye 1.00 2.50
127 Marcus Allen 1.50 4.00
128 Deacon Jones 1.25 3.00
129 Bob Griese 1.50 4.00
130 Dan Marino 4.00 10.00
131 Fran Tarkenton 1.50 4.00
132 Y.A. Tittle 1.50 4.00
133 Don Maynard 1.25 3.00
134 Joe Namath 2.50 6.00
135 Jim Plunkett 1.25 3.00
136 Bo Jackson 2.00 5.00
137 Herman Edwards 1.00 2.50
138 Randall Cunningham 1.25 3.00
139 Franco Harris 1.50 4.00
140 Jack Lambert 1.50 4.00
141 Joe Greene 1.50 4.00
142 L.C. Greenwood 1.25 3.00
143 Terry Bradshaw 2.50 6.00
144 Dan Fouts 1.50 4.00
145 Joe Montana 4.00 10.00
146 John Taylor 1.25 3.00
147 Roger Craig 1.50 4.00
148 Steve Young 2.00 5.00
149 Steve Largent 1.50 4.00
150 Sonny Jurgensen 1.25 3.00
151 Adam Jones RC 1.25 3.00
152 Antrel Rolle RC 2.00 5.00
153 Carlos Rogers RC 2.00 5.00
154 DeMarcus Ware RC 4.00 10.00
155 Shawne Merriman RC 2.00 5.00
156 Thomas Davis RC 1.25 3.00
157 Derrick Johnson RC 1.50 4.00
158 Travis Johnson RC 1.25 3.00
159 David Pollack RC 1.50 4.00
160 Erasmus James RC 1.50 4.00
161 Marcus Spears RC 1.50 4.00
162 Fabian Washington RC 1.50 4.00
163 Luis Castillo RC 1.50 4.00
164 Marlin Jackson RC 1.25 3.00
165 Mike Patterson RC 1.25 3.00
166 Brodney Pool RC 1.50 4.00
167 Barrett Ruud RC 2.00 5.00
168 Shaun Cody RC 1.50 4.00
169 Stanford Routt RC 1.50 4.00
170 Josh Bullocks RC 1.50 4.00
171 Kevin Burnett RC 1.50 4.00
172 Corey Webster RC 1.50 4.00
173 Lofa Tatupu RC 2.00 5.00
174 Justin Miller RC 1.50 4.00
175 Odell Thurman RC 2.00 5.00
176 Heath Miller RC 3.00 8.00
177 Vernand Morency RC 1.50 4.00
178 Ryan Moats RC 1.50 4.00
179 Courtney Roby RC 2.00 5.00
180 Alex Smith TE RC 1.50 4.00
181 Kevin Everett RC 2.50 6.00
182 Brandon Jones RC 2.00 5.00
183 Maurice Clarett 1.50 4.00
184 Marion Barber RC 2.50 6.00
185 Brandon Jacobs RC 3.00 8.00
186 Matt Cassel RC 5.00 12.00
187 Stefan LeFors RC 1.50 4.00
188 Alvin Pearman RC 1.50 4.00
189 James Kilian RC 1.50 4.00
190 Airese Currie RC 1.50 4.00
191 Damien Nash RC 2.00 5.00
192 Dan Orlovsky RC 2.50 6.00
193 Larry Brackins RC 1.50 4.00
194 Rasheed Marshall RC 2.00 5.00
195 Marcus Maxwell RC 1.50 4.00
196 LeRon McCoy RC 1.50 4.00
197 Harry Williams RC 2.00 5.00
198 Noah Herron RC 1.50 4.00
199 Tab Perry RC 1.50 4.00
200 Chad Owens RC 2.00 5.00
201 Alex Smith QB RC 4.00 10.00
202 Ronnie Brown RC 3.00 8.00
203 Braylon Edwards RC 3.00 8.00
204 Cedric Benson RC 2.50 6.00
205 Cadillac Williams RC 2.50 6.00
206 Troy Williamson RC 2.00 5.00
207 Mike Williams 2.50 6.00
208 Matt Jones RC 2.00 5.00
209 Mark Clayton RC 2.00 5.00
210 Aaron Rodgers RC 25.00 50.00
211 Jason Campbell RC 3.00 8.00
212 Roddy White RC 3.00 8.00
213 Reggie Brown RC 1.50 4.00
214 Mark Bradley RC 1.50 4.00
215 J.J. Arrington RC 2.00 5.00
216 Eric Shelton RC 1.50 4.00
217 Roscoe Parrish RC 1.50 4.00
218 Terrence Murphy RC 1.50 4.00
219 Vincent Jackson RC 3.00 8.00
220 Frank Gore RC 4.00 10.00
221 Charlie Frye RC 2.50 6.00
222 Andrew Walter RC 2.00 5.00
223 David Greene RC 1.50 4.00
224 Kyle Orton RC 2.50 6.00
225 Ciatrick Fason RC 1.50 4.00
226 Cedric Houston AU RC 6.00 15.00
227 Dante Ridgeway AU RC 4.00 10.00
228 Craig Bragg AU RC 4.00 10.00
229 Deandra Cobb AU RC 4.00 10.00
230 Derek Anderson AU RC 5.00 12.00
231 Paris Warren AU RC 5.00 12.00
232 Lionel Gates AU RC 4.00 10.00
233 Anthony Davis AU RC 4.00 10.00
234 Ryan Fitzpatrick AU RC 15.00 40.00
235 J.R. Russell AU RC 4.00 10.00
236 Dan Cody AU RC 5.00 12.00
237 Bryant McFadden AU RC 5.00 12.00
238 Adrian McPherson AU RC 4.00 10.00
239 Chris Henry AU RC 6.00 15.00
240 Craphonso Thorpe AU RC 4.00 10.00
241 Darren Sproles AU RC 10.00 25.00
242 Fred Gibson AU RC 5.00 12.00
243 Jerome Mathis AU RC 6.00 15.00
244 Josh Davis AU RC 4.00 10.00
245 Kay-Jay Harris AU RC 4.00 10.00
246 Matt Roth AU RC 5.00 12.00
247 Roydell Williams AU RC 5.00 12.00
248 Steve Savoy AU RC 4.00 10.00
249 T.A. McLendon AU RC 4.00 10.00
250 Taylor Stubblefield AU RC 4.00 10.00

2005 Donruss Classics Timeless Tributes Bronze

*VETERANS 1-100: 4X TO 10X BASIC CARDS
*LEGENDS 101-150: 1X TO 2.5X
*ROOKIES 151-175: .8X TO 2X BASIC CARDS
*ROOKIES 176-200: .6X TO 1.5X
*ROOKIES 201-225: .6X TO 1.5X
COMMON ROOKIE 226-250 2.50 6.00
ROOKIE SEMISTARS 226-250 3.00 8.00
ROOKIE UNL.STARS 226-250 4.00 10.00
STATED PRINT RUN 100 SER.#'d SETS
230 Derek Anderson 3.00 8.00

2005 Donruss Classics Timeless Tributes Gold

*VETERANS 1-100: 10X TO 25X BASIC CARDS
*LEGENDS 101-150: 2X TO 5X BASIC CARDS
*ROOKIES 151-175: 2.5X TO 6X BASIC RC
*ROOKIES 176-200: 2X TO 5X BASIC RC
*ROOKIES 201-225: 2X TO 5X BASIC RC
COMMON ROOKIE 226-250 8.00 20.00
ROOKIE SEMISTARS 226-250 10.00 25.00
ROOKIE UNL.STARS 226-250 12.50 30.00
STATED PRINT RUN 25 SER.#'d SETS
230 Derek Anderson 10.00 25.00

2005 Donruss Classics Timeless Tributes Platinum

UNPRICED PLATINUM SER.#'d OF 10

2005 Donruss Classics Timeless Tributes Silver

*VETERANS 1-100: 6X TO 15X BASIC CARDS
*LEGENDS 101-150: 1.2X TO 3X
*ROOKIES 151-175: 1.2X TO 3X BASIC CARDS
*ROOKIES 176-200: 1X TO 2.5X BASIC CARDS
*ROOKIES 201-225: 1X TO 2.5X BASIC CARDS
COMMON ROOKIE 226-250 4.00 10.00
ROOKIE SEMISTARS 226-250 5.00 12.00
ROOKIE UNL.STARS 226-250 6.00 15.00
STATED PRINT RUN 50 SER.#'d SETS
230 Derek Anderson 5.00 12.00

2005 Donruss Classics Classic Combos Bronze

BRONZE PRINT RUN 500 SER.#'d SETS
*GOLD/100: .8X TO 2X BRONZE/500
*SILVER/250: .5X TO 1.2X BRONZE/500
1 Jim Brown 3.00 8.00
Barry Sanders
2 Mike Ditka 5.00 12.00
Walter Payton
3 Earl Campbell 2.50 6.00
Bo Jackson
4 Gale Sayers 2.50 6.00
Terrell Davis
5 Bob Griese 5.00 12.00
Dan Marino
6 Joe Montana 5.00 12.00
John Elway
7 Bart Starr 3.00 8.00
Terry Bradshaw
8 Roger Staubach 3.00 8.00
Troy Aikman
9 Joe Namath 3.00 8.00
Jim Kelly
10 Steve Young 2.50 6.00
Michael Vick
11 Don Maynard 2.00 5.00
Steve Largent
12 Jerry Rice 4.00 10.00
Michael Irvin

2005 Donruss Classics Classic Combos Jerseys

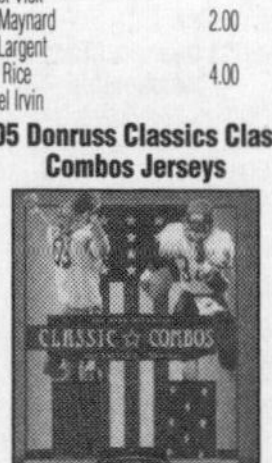

STATED PRINT RUN 75 SER.#'d SETS
*PRIME/15: 1X TO 2.5X BASIC DUAL/75
1 Jim Brown 15.00 40.00
Barry Sanders
2 Mike Ditka 25.00 60.00
Walter Payton
3 Earl Campbell 12.00 30.00
Bo Jackson
4 Gale Sayers 12.00 30.00
Terrell Davis
5 Bob Griese 25.00 60.00
Dan Marino
6 Joe Montana 25.00 60.00
John Elway
7 Bart Starr 15.00 40.00
Terry Bradshaw
8 Roger Staubach 15.00 40.00
Troy Aikman
9 Joe Namath 15.00 40.00
Jim Kelly
10 Steve Young 12.00 30.00
Michael Vick
11 Don Maynard 10.00 25.00
Steve Largent
12 Jerry Rice 20.00 50.00
Michael Irvin

2005 Donruss Classics Classic Pigskin

STATED PRINT RUN 250 SER.#'d SETS
*DOUBLE/25: 1X TO 2.5X BASIC INSERT
1 Bart Starr 30.00 80.00
2 John Elway 25.00 60.00
3 Bob Griese 20.00 40.00
4 Tony Dorsett 20.00 40.00
5 Walter Payton 40.00 100.00
6 Joe Montana 30.00 80.00

2005 Donruss Classics Classic Quads Bronze

BRONZE PRINT RUN 100 SER.#'d SETS
*GOLD/25: .8X TO 2X BRONZE/100
*SILVER/50: .5X TO 1.2X BRONZE/100
1 Jim Thorpe 10.00 25.00
Jim Brown
Walter Payton
Barry Sanders
2 Earl Campbell 5.00 12.00
Marcus Allen
Bo Jackson
Terrell Davis
3 Terry Bradshaw 10.00 25.00
Joe Montana
Troy Aikman
Tom Brady
4 Bart Starr 10.00 25.00
Joe Namath
John Elway
Brett Favre
5 Dan Marino 10.00 25.00
Peyton Manning
Steve Young
Michael Vick
6 Roger Staubach 8.00 20.00
Bob Griese
Jerry Rice
Michael Irvin

2005 Donruss Classics Classic Quads Jerseys

STATED PRINT RUN 25 SER.#'d SETS
UNPRICED PRIME PRINT RUN 5
1 Jim Thorpe 300.00 400.00
Jim Brown
Walter Payton
Barry Sanders
2 Earl Campbell 40.00 100.00
Marcus Allen
Bo Jackson
Terrell Davis
3 Terry Bradshaw 75.00 150.00
Joe Montana
Troy Aikman
Tom Brady
4 Bart Starr 75.00 150.00
Joe Namath
John Elway
Brett Favre
5 Dan Marino 75.00 150.00
Peyton Manning
Steve Young
Michael Vick
6 Roger Staubach 50.00 100.00
Bob Griese
Jerry Rice
Michael Irvin

2005 Donruss Classics Classic Singles Bronze

BRONZE PRINT RUN 1000 SER.#'d SETS
*GOLD/250: .8X TO 2X BRONZE/1000
*SILVER/500: .5X TO 1.2X BRONZE/1000
SILVER PRINT RUN 500 SER.#'d SETS
1 Barry Sanders 2.50 6.00
2 Bo Jackson 2.00 5.00
3 Bob Griese 1.50 4.00
4 Brett Favre 3.00 8.00
5 Dan Marino 4.00 10.00
6 Deion Sanders 2.00 5.00
7 Don Maynard 1.25 3.00
8 Earl Campbell 1.50 4.00
9 Gale Sayers 2.00 5.00
10 Jerry Rice 2.50 6.00
11 Jim Kelly 2.00 5.00
12 Joe Montana 4.00 10.00
13 Joe Namath 2.50 6.00
14 John Elway 3.00 8.00
15 Michael Irvin 1.50 4.00
16 Mike Ditka 1.50 4.00
17 Randall Cunningham 1.25 3.00
18 Roger Staubach 2.50 6.00
19 Steve Largent 1.50 4.00
20 Steve Young 2.00 5.00
21 Terrell Davis 1.50 4.00
22 Terry Bradshaw 2.50 6.00
23 Troy Aikman 2.00 5.00
24 Walter Payton 4.00 10.00

2005 Donruss Classics Classic Singles Jerseys

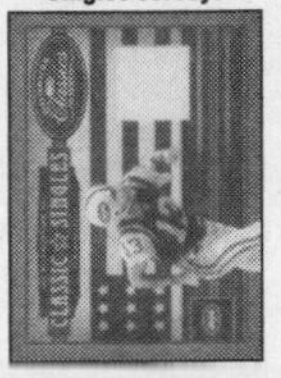

STATED PRINT RUN 150 SER.#'d SETS
*PRIME/25: 1X TO 2.5X BASIC JSY/150
PRIME PRINT RUN 25 SER.#'d SETS

CS1 Barry Sanders	8.00	20.00
CS2 Bo Jackson	6.00	15.00
CS3 Bob Griese	5.00	12.00
CS4 Brett Favre	10.00	25.00
CS5 Dan Marino	12.00	30.00
CS6 Deion Sanders	6.00	15.00
CS7 Don Maynard	4.00	10.00
CS8 Earl Campbell	5.00	12.00
CS9 Gale Sayers	6.00	15.00
CS10 Jerry Rice	8.00	20.00
CS11 Jim Kelly	6.00	15.00
CS12 Joe Montana	12.00	30.00
CS13 Joe Namath	8.00	20.00
CS14 John Elway	10.00	25.00
CS15 Michael Irvin	5.00	12.00
CS16 Mike Ditka	6.00	15.00
CS17 Randall Cunningham	4.00	10.00
CS18 Roger Staubach	8.00	20.00
CS19 Steve Largent	5.00	12.00
CS20 Steve Young	6.00	15.00
CS21 Terrell Davis	5.00	12.00
CS22 Terry Bradshaw	8.00	20.00
CS23 Troy Aikman	6.00	15.00
CS24 Walter Payton	12.00	30.00

2005 Donruss Classics Classic Triples Bronze

BRONZE PRINT RUN 250 SER.#'d SETS
*GOLD/75: .8X TO 2X BRONZE/250
*SILVER/150: .5X TO 1.2X BRONZE/250

1 Jim Brown	8.00	20.00
Walter Payton		
Barry Sanders		
2 Earl Campbell	4.00	10.00
Marcus Allen		
Bo Jackson		
3 Terry Bradshaw	8.00	20.00
Joe Montana		
Tom Brady		
4 Bart Starr	8.00	20.00
John Elway		
Brott Favro		
5 Joe Namath	8.00	20.00
Dan Marino		
Peyton Manning		
6 Roger Staubach	5.00	12.00
Bob Griese		
Troy Aikman		
7 Steve Young	4.00	10.00
Randall Cunningham		
Michael Vick		
8 Steve Largent	6.00	15.00
Jerry Rice		
Michael Irvin		

2005 Donruss Classics Classic Triples Jerseys

STATED PRINT RUN 50 SER.#'d SETS
UNPRICED PRIME PRINT RUN 10

1 Jim Brown	50.00	120.00
Walter Payton		
Barry Sanders		
2 Earl Campbell	20.00	50.00
Marcus Allen		
Bo Jackson		
3 Terry Bradshaw	50.00	100.00
Joe Montana		
Tom Brady		
4 Bart Starr	50.00	100.00
John Elway		
Brett Favre		
5 Joe Namath	40.00	100.00
Dan Marino		
Peyton Manning		
6 Roger Staubach	20.00	50.00
Bob Griese		
Troy Aikman		
7 Steve Young	20.00	50.00
Randall Cunningham		
Michael Vick		
8 Steve Largent	25.00	60.00
Jerry Rice		
Michael Irvin		

2005 Donruss Classics Dress Code Jerseys

STATED PRINT RUN 250 SER.#'d SETS
*PRIME/25: 1.2X TO 3X BASIC JSY/250

1 Alex Smith QB	5.00	12.00
2 Adam Jones	2.50	6.00
3 Andrew Walter	2.50	6.00
4 Braylon Edwards	4.00	10.00
5 Cadillac Williams	3.00	8.00
6 Carlos Rogers	3.00	8.00
7 Charlie Frye	3.00	8.00
8 Ciatrick Fason	2.00	5.00
9 Eric Shelton	2.00	5.00
10 Frank Gore	5.00	12.00
11 J.J. Arrington	2.50	6.00
12 Jason Campbell	4.00	10.00
13 Kyle Orton	3.00	8.00
14 Mark Bradley	2.00	5.00
15 Mark Clayton	3.00	8.00
16 Maurice Clarett	2.50	6.00
17 Matt Jones	3.00	8.00
18 Reggie Brown	2.00	5.00
19 Roddy White	4.00	10.00
20 Ronnie Brown	4.00	10.00
21 Roscoe Parrish	2.00	5.00
22 Stefan LeFors	2.00	5.00
23 Terrence Murphy	2.00	5.00
24 Troy Williamson	2.50	6.00
25 Vincent Jackson	4.00	10.00

2005 Donruss Classics Legendary Players Bronze

BRONZE PRINT RUN 1000 SER.#'d SETS
*GOLD/250: .8X TO 2X BRONZE/1000
*SILVER/500: .5X TO 1.2X BRONZE/1000

L1 Barry Sanders	2.50	6.00
L2 Bart Starr	2.50	6.00
L3 Bo Jackson	2.00	5.00
L4 Bob Griese	1.50	4.00
L5 Boomer Esiason	1.25	3.00
L6 Brett Favre	3.00	8.00
L7 Dan Marino	4.00	10.00
L8 Deacon Jones	1.25	3.00
L9 Deion Sanders	1.50	4.00
L10 Don Maynard	1.25	3.00
L11 Don Meredith	1.50	4.00
L12 Gale Sayers	2.00	5.00
L13 Jerry Rice	2.50	6.00
L14 Jim Brown	2.00	5.00
L15 Jim Kelly	2.00	5.00
L16 Jim Thorpe	2.00	5.00
L17 Joe Greene	1.50	4.00
L18 Joe Montana	4.00	10.00
L19 Joe Namath	2.50	6.00
L20 John Elway	3.00	8.00
L21 Jack Lambert	1.50	4.00
L22 Michael Irvin	1.50	4.00
L23 Randall Cunningham	1.25	3.00
L24 Sterling Sharpe	1.25	3.00
L25 Steve Largent	1.50	4.00
L26 Steve Young	2.00	5.00
L27 Troy Aikman	2.00	5.00
L28 Walter Payton	4.00	10.00
L29 Lawrence Taylor	1.50	4.00
L30 Mike Ditka	1.50	4.00

2005 Donruss Classics Legendary Players Jerseys

STATED PRINT RUN 150 SER.#'d SETS
*PRIME/25: 1X TO 2.5X BASIC JSY/150

1 Barry Sanders	10.00	25.00
2 Bart Starr	10.00	25.00
3 Bo Jackson	8.00	20.00
4 Bob Griese	6.00	15.00
5 Boomer Esiason	5.00	12.00
6 Brett Favre	12.00	30.00
7 Dan Marino	15.00	40.00
8 Deacon Jones	5.00	12.00
9 Deion Sanders	6.00	15.00
10 Don Maynard	5.00	12.00
11 Don Meredith	12.00	30.00
12 Gale Sayers	8.00	20.00
13 Jerry Rice	10.00	25.00
14 Jim Brown	8.00	20.00
15 Jim Kelly	8.00	20.00
16 Jim Thorpe	60.00	120.00
17 Joo Groone	6.00	15.00
18 Joe Montana	15.00	40.00
19 Joe Namath	10.00	25.00
20 John Elway	12.00	30.00
21 Jack Lambert	6.00	15.00
22 Michael Irvin	6.00	15.00
23 Randall Cunningham	5.00	12.00
24 Sterling Sharpe	5.00	12.00
25 Steve Largent	6.00	15.00
26 Steve Young	8.00	20.00
27 Troy Aikman	8.00	20.00
28 Walter Payton	15.00	40.00
29 Lawrence Taylor	6.00	15.00
30 Mike Ditka	6.00	15.00

2005 Donruss Classics Membership Bronze

BRONZE PRINT RUN 1000 SER.#'d SETS
*GOLD/250: .8X TO 2X BRONZE/1000
*SILVER/500: .5X TO 1.2X BRONZE/1000

MS1 Barry Sanders	2.50	6.00
MS2 Ben Roethlisberger	2.00	5.00
MS3 Brett Favre	3.00	8.00
MS4 Brian Urlacher	1.25	3.00
MS5 Dan Marino	4.00	10.00
MS6 Daunte Culpepper	1.00	2.50
MS7 Deion Sanders	2.00	5.00
MS8 Donovan McNabb	1.25	3.00
MS9 Earl Campbell	1.50	4.00
MS10 Gale Sayers	2.00	5.00
MS11 Jamal Lewis	1.00	2.50
MS12 Jerry Rice	2.50	6.00
MS13 Jim Kelly	2.00	5.00
MS14 Joe Montana	4.00	10.00
MS15 Joe Namath	2.50	6.00
MS16 John Elway	3.00	8.00
MS17 LaDainian Tomlinson	1.25	3.00
MS18 Lawrence Taylor	1.50	4.00
MS19 Marshall Faulk	1.25	3.00
MS20 Marvin Harrison	1.25	3.00
MS21 Michael Irvin	1.50	4.00
MS22 Michael Strahan	1.25	3.00
MS23 Michael Vick	1.25	3.00
MS24 Peyton Manning	2.50	6.00
MS25 Randall Cunningham	1.25	3.00
MS26 Randy Moss	1.25	3.00
MS27 Steve Young	2.00	5.00
MS28 Terrell Davis	1.50	4.00
MS29 Troy Aikman	2.00	5.00
MS30 Walter Payton	4.00	10.00

2005 Donruss Classics Membership VIP Jerseys

STATED PRINT RUN 150 SER.#'d SETS
*PRIME/25: 1X TO 2.5X BASIC JSY/150

1 Barry Sanders	8.00	20.00
2 Ben Roethlisberger	6.00	15.00
3 Brett Favre	10.00	25.00
4 Brian Urlacher	4.00	10.00
5 Dan Marino	12.00	30.00
6 Daunte Culpepper	3.00	8.00
7 Deion Sanders	6.00	15.00
8 Donovan McNabb	4.00	10.00
9 Earl Campbell	5.00	12.00
10 Gale Sayers	6.00	15.00
11 Jamal Lewis	3.00	8.00
12 Jerry Rice	8.00	20.00
13 Jim Kolly	6.00	16.00
14 Joe Montana	12.00	30.00
15 Joe Namath	8.00	20.00
16 John Elway	10.00	25.00
17 LaDainian Tomlinson	4.00	10.00
18 Lawrence Taylor	5.00	12.00
19 Marshall Faulk	4.00	10.00
20 Marvin Harrison	4.00	10.00
21 Michael Irvin	5.00	12.00
22 Michael Strahan	4.00	10.00
23 Michael Vick	4.00	10.00
24 Peyton Manning	8.00	20.00
25 Randall Cunningham	4.00	10.00
26 Randy Moss	4.00	10.00
27 Steve Young	6.00	15.00
28 Terrell Davis	5.00	12.00
29 Troy Aikman	6.00	15.00
30 Walter Payton	12.00	30.00

2005 Donruss Classics Past and Present Bronze

BRONZE PRINT RUN 1000 SER.#'d SETS
*GOLD/250: .8X TO 2X BRONZE/1000
*SILVER/500: .5X TO 1.2X BRONZE/1000

PP1 Jim Kelly	2.00	5.00
Drew Bledsoe		
PP2 Thurman Thomas	1.50	4.00
Willis McGahee		
PP3 Gale Sayers	4.00	10.00
Walter Payton		
PP4 Mike Singletary	1.50	4.00
Brian Urlacher		
PP5 Cris Collinsworth	1.25	3.00
Chad Johnson		
PP6 Jim Brown	2.00	5.00
Jamal Lewis		
PP7 Tony Dorsett	1.25	3.00
Julius Jones		
PP8 Michael Irvin	1.50	4.00
Keyshawn Johnson		
PP9 John Elway	3.00	8.00
Jake Plummer		
PP10 Barry Sanders	2.50	6.00
Kevin Jones		
PP11 Bart Starr	4.00	10.00
Brett Favre		
PP12 Earl Campbell	1.50	4.00
Chris Brown		
PP13 Warren Moon	1.50	4.00
Steve McNair		
PP14 Bob Griese	4.00	10.00
Dan Marino		
PP15 Fran Tarkenton	1.50	4.00
Daunte Culpepper		
PP16 Drew Bledsoe	2.50	6.00
Tom Brady		
PP17 Curtis Martin	1.25	3.00
Corey Dillon		
PP18 Fran Tarkenton	2.50	6.00
Eli Manning		
PP19 Joe Namath	2.50	6.00
Chad Pennington		
PP20 Randall Cunningham	1.50	4.00
Donovan McNabb		
PP21 Terry Bradshaw	2.50	6.00
Ben Roethlisberger		
PP22 Franco Harris	1.50	4.00
Jerome Bettis		
PP23 Steve Largent	1.50	4.00
Darrell Jackson		
PP24 Marshall Faulk	1.25	3.00
Steven Jackson		

2005 Donruss Classics Past and Present Jerseys

STATED PRINT RUN 50 SER.#'d SETS
UNPRICED PRIME PRINT RUN 10

1 Jim Kelly	12.00	30.00
Drew Bledsoe		
2 Thurman Thomas	10.00	25.00
Willis McGahee		
3 Gale Sayers	40.00	100.00
Walter Payton		
4 Mike Singletary	12.00	30.00
Brian Urlacher		
5 Cris Collinsworth	8.00	20.00
Chad Johnson		
6 Jim Brown	12.00	30.00
Jamal Lewis		
7 Tony Dorsett	10.00	20.00
Julius Jones		
8 Michael Irvin	10.00	25.00
Keyshawn Johnson		
9 John Elway	20.00	50.00
Jake Plummer		
10 Barry Sanders	15.00	40.00
Kevin Jones		
11 Bart Starr	30.00	80.00
Brett Favre		
12 Earl Campbell	10.00	25.00
Chris Brown		
13 Warren Moon	10.00	25.00
Steve McNair		
14 Bob Griese	25.00	60.00
Dan Marino		
15 Fran Tarkenton	10.00	25.00
Daunte Culpepper		
16 Drew Bledsoe	20.00	50.00
Tom Brady		
17 Curtis Martin	10.00	25.00
Corey Dillon		
18 Fran Tarkenton	12.00	30.00
Eli Manning		
19 Joe Namath	15.00	40.00
Chad Pennington		
20 Randall Cunningham	10.00	25.00
Donovan McNabb		
21 Terry Bradshaw	50.00	100.00
Ben Roethlisberger		
22 Franco Harris	15.00	40.00
Jerome Bettis		
23 Steve Largent	10.00	25.00
Darrell Jackson		
24 Marshall Faulk	10.00	25.00
Steven Jackson		

2005 Donruss Classics Significant Signatures Bronze

BRONZE STATED PRINT RUN 15-150
CARDS SER.#'d UNDER 25 NOT PRICED

4 Alge Crumpler/75	8.00	20.00
5 Michael Vick/25	40.00	80.00
7 Todd Heap/75	8.00	20.00
9 Kyle Boller/75	8.00	20.00
10 Drew Bledsoe/25	15.00	40.00
11 Lee Evans/75	8.00	20.00
12 Willis McGahee/50	10.00	25.00
13 Steve Smith/75	10.00	25.00
14 Jake Delhomme/15	12.00	30.00
16 Brian Urlacher/15	15.00	40.00
17 Rex Grossman/75	8.00	20.00
19 Carson Palmer/15	15.00	40.00
20 Chad Johnson/75	10.00	25.00
21 Rudi Johnson/100	6.00	15.00
25 Julius Jones/25	10.00	25.00
26 Keyshawn Johnson/25	12.00	30.00
27 Roy Williams S/50	6.00	15.00
30 Tatum Bell/100	5.00	12.00
31 Joey Harrington/15	12.00	30.00
33 Roy Williams WR/15	12.00	30.00
34 Ahman Green/15	12.00	30.00
35 Brett Favre/15	100.00	200.00
37 Andre Johnson/50	10.00	25.00
38 David Carr/15	10.00	25.00
39 Domanick Davis/75	6.00	15.00
41 Marvin Harrison/15	15.00	40.00
42 Peyton Manning/15	75.00	150.00
43 Reggie Wayne/25	15.00	40.00
44 Byron Leftwich/15	12.00	30.00
46 Jimmy Smith/50	8.00	20.00
47 Priest Holmes/15	12.00	30.00
49 Trent Green/15	12.00	30.00
51 Chris Chambers/50	8.00	20.00
50 Corey Dillon/25	12.00	30.00
58 Tom Brady/15	125.00	250.00
59 Aaron Brooks/25	10.00	25.00
60 Deuce McAllister/25	12.00	30.00
61 Joe Horn/50	8.00	20.00
62 Eli Manning/25	75.00	135.00
64 Tiki Barber/25	25.00	50.00
65 Chad Pennington/15	15.00	40.00
70 J.P. Losman/100	5.00	12.00
71 Brian Westbrook/50	8.00	20.00
72 Donovan McNabb/15	30.00	60.00
74 Ben Roethlisberger/15	75.00	150.00
75 Duce Staley/75	8.00	20.00
76 Hines Ward/75	25.00	50.00
78 Antonio Gates/100	15.00	30.00
83 Laveranues Coles/75	6.00	15.00
84 Darrell Jackson/75	6.00	15.00
85 Jerry Rice/15	100.00	175.00
86 Matt Hasselbeck/50	8.00	20.00
90 Steven Jackson/50	10.00	25.00
93 Michael Clayton/75	6.00	15.00
95 Chris Brown/75	6.00	15.00
98 Clinton Portis/25	12.00	30.00
100 Patrick Ramsey/25	12.00	30.00
101 Don Shula/25	15.00	40.00
102 James Lofton/100	6.00	15.00
103 Thurman Thomas/75	12.00	30.00
104 Gale Sayers/15	30.00	60.00
105 Mike Singletary/50	12.00	30.00
106 Boomer Esiason/50	12.00	30.00
107 Cris Collinsworth/50	10.00	25.00
108 Ickey Woods/150	6.00	15.00
109 Jim Brown/15	50.00	100.00
110 Leroy Kelly/100	10.00	25.00
111 Ozzie Newsome/75	10.00	25.00
112 Paul Warfield/50	10.00	25.00
113 Deion Sanders/15 EXCH		
114 Herschel Walker/100	12.00	30.00
115 Mike Ditka/50	30.00	60.00
116 Michael Irvin/25	20.00	50.00
117 Roger Staubach/15	30.00	80.00
118 Tony Dorsett/15	20.00	50.00
119 Troy Aikman/15	40.00	80.00
120 John Elway/15	100.00	200.00
121 Barry Sanders/15	75.00	150.00
122 Bart Starr/15	100.00	175.00
123 Paul Hornung/100	10.00	25.00
124 Sterling Sharpe/25	15.00	40.00
125 Warren Moon/25	20.00	50.00
126 Christian Okoye/150	6.00	15.00
127 Marcus Allen/25	30.00	60.00
128 Deacon Jones/100	8.00	20.00
129 Bob Griese/50	15.00	30.00
130 Dan Marino/15	100.00	200.00
131 Fran Tarkenton/50	15.00	30.00
132 Y.A. Tittle/75	15.00	40.00
133 Don Maynard/75	10.00	25.00
134 Joe Namath/15	50.00	100.00
135 Jim Plunkett/100	8.00	20.00
136 Bo Jackson/50	40.00	80.00
137 Herman Edwards/100	6.00	15.00
138 Randall Cunningham/50	12.50	30.00
139 Franco Harris/25	20.00	50.00
140 Jack Lambert/25	25.00	50.00
141 Joe Greene/50	12.00	30.00
142 L.C. Greenwood/100	12.50	30.00
143 Terry Bradshaw/15	50.00	100.00
144 Dan Fouts/15	20.00	50.00
145 Joe Montana/15	100.00	200.00
146 John Taylor/100	6.00	15.00
147 Roger Craig/50	12.00	30.00
148 Steve Young/15	40.00	80.00
149 Steve Largent/50	15.00	40.00
150 Sonny Jurgensen/50	10.00	25.00
151 Adam Jones/25	10.00	25.00
155 Shawne Merriman/75	10.00	25.00
157 Derrick Johnson/75	8.00	20.00
159 David Pollack/50	8.00	20.00
176 Heath Miller/75	20.00	50.00
178 Ryan Moats/75	6.00	15.00
179 Courtney Roby/25	12.00	30.00
183 Maurice Clarett/15	10.00	25.00
184 Marion Barber/75	10.00	25.00
201 Alex Smith QB/15	30.00	80.00
202 Ronnie Brown/75	12.00	30.00
203 Braylon Edwards/25	20.00	50.00
204 Cedric Benson/15	15.00	40.00
205 Cadillac Williams/15	15.00	40.00
206 Troy Williamson/15	12.00	30.00
207 Mike Williams/15	15.00	40.00
208 Matt Jones/15	12.00	30.00
209 Mark Clayton/25	12.00	30.00
210 Aaron Rodgers/25	300.00	450.00
211 Jason Campbell/15	20.00	50.00
212 Roddy White/15	20.00	50.00
213 Reggie Brown/25	10.00	25.00
214 Mark Bradley/75	6.00	15.00
215 J.J. Arrington/15	12.00	30.00
216 Eric Shelton/75	6.00	15.00
217 Roscoe Parrish/75	6.00	15.00
218 Terrence Murphy/75	6.00	15.00
219 Vincent Jackson/75	12.00	30.00
220 Frank Gore/75	20.00	50.00
221 Charlie Frye/50	10.00	25.00
222 Andrew Walter/15	12.00	30.00
223 David Greene/75	6.00	15.00
224 Kyle Orton/75	10.00	25.00
225 Ciatrick Fason/75	6.00	15.00

2005 Donruss Classics Significant Signatures Gold

*GOLD/15-25: .6X TO 1.5X BRONZE AU
GOLD STATED PRINT RUN
CARDS SER.#'d UNDER 15 NOT PRICED

2005 Donruss Classics Significant Signatures Platinum

*PLATINUM/25: 1X TO 2.5X BRONZE
PLATINUM STATED PRINT RUN 1-25
CARDS SER.#'d UNDER 25 NOT PRICED

2005 Donruss Classics Significant Signatures Silver

*SILVER/50-100: .5X TO 1.2X BRONZE AU
*SILVER/25: .6X TO 1.5X BRONZE AU
SILVER STATED PRINT RUN 10-100
CARDS SER.#'d UNDER 25 NOT PRICED

212 Roddy White/50	20.00	50.00

2005 Donruss Classics Stadium Stars Goal Line Bronze

BRONZE PRINT RUN 750 SER.#'d SETS
*GOLD/250: .6X TO 1.5X BRONZE/750
*SILVER/500: .4X TO 1X BRONZE/750

1 Michael Vick	1.50	4.00
2 Jamal Lewis	1.25	3.00
3 Kyle Boller	1.25	3.00
4 Drew Bledsoe	1.50	4.00
5 Lee Evans	1.25	3.00
6 Jake Delhomme	1.25	3.00
7 Julius Peppers	1.25	3.00
8 Brian Urlacher	1.50	4.00
9 Carson Palmer	1.50	4.00
10 Jeff Garcia	1.25	3.00
11 Julius Jones	1.00	2.50
12 Joey Harrington	1.25	3.00
13 Andre Johnson	1.50	4.00
14 David Carr	1.00	2.50
15 Domanick Davis	1.00	2.50
16 Marvin Harrison	1.50	4.00
17 Peyton Manning	3.00	8.00
18 Byron Leftwich	1.25	3.00
19 Tony Gonzalez	1.25	3.00
20 Junior Seau	1.50	4.00
21 Jason Taylor	1.25	3.00
22 Michael Bennett	1.25	3.00
23 Aaron Brooks	1.00	2.50
24 Larry Fitzgerald	1.50	4.00
25 Eli Manning	2.50	6.00
26 Jeremy Shockey	1.50	4.00
27 Michael Strahan	1.50	4.00
28 Chad Pennington	1.50	4.00
29 Justin McCareins	1.00	2.50
30 John Abraham	1.00	2.50
31 Charles Woodson	1.50	4.00
32 Brian Westbrook	1.25	3.00
33 Donovan McNabb	1.50	4.00
34 Freddie Mitchell	1.00	2.50
35 Ben Roethlisberger	2.50	6.00
36 Duce Staley	1.25	3.00
37 Hines Ward	1.50	4.00
38 Koren Robinson	1.00	2.50
39 Matt Hasselbeck	1.25	3.00
40 Isaac Bruce	1.25	3.00
41 Marc Bulger	1.25	3.00
42 Torry Holt	1.25	3.00
43 Steven Jackson	1.50	4.00
44 Mike Alstott	1.25	3.00
45 Chris Brown	1.00	2.50
46 Derrick Mason	1.25	3.00
47 Drew Bennett	1.25	3.00
48 LaVar Arrington	1.25	3.00
49 Patrick Ramsey	1.25	3.00
50 Rod Gardner	1.00	2.50

2005 Donruss Classics Stadium Stars 30 Yard Line Jerseys

30-YARD PRINT RUN 199 SER.#'d SETS
*40-YARD/150: .4X TO 1X 30-YRD/199
*50-YARD/25: 1X TO 2.5X 30-YRD/199

1 Michael Vick	4.00	10.00
2 Jamal Lewis	3.00	8.00
3 Kyle Boller	3.00	8.00
4 Drew Bledsoe	4.00	10.00
5 Lee Evans	3.00	8.00
6 Jake Delhomme	3.00	8.00
7 Julius Peppers	3.00	8.00
8 Brian Urlacher	4.00	10.00
9 Carson Palmer	4.00	10.00
10 Jeff Garcia	3.00	8.00
11 Julius Jones	2.50	6.00
12 Joey Harrington	3.00	8.00
13 Andre Johnson	4.00	10.00
14 David Carr	2.50	6.00
15 Domanick Davis	2.50	6.00
16 Marvin Harrison	4.00	10.00
17 Peyton Manning	8.00	20.00
18 Byron Leftwich	3.00	8.00
19 Tony Gonzalez	3.00	8.00
20 Junior Seau	4.00	10.00
21 Jason Taylor	3.00	8.00
22 Michael Bennett	3.00	8.00
23 Aaron Brooks	2.50	6.00
24 Larry Fitzgerald	4.00	10.00
25 Eli Manning	6.00	15.00
26 Jeremy Shockey	4.00	10.00
27 Michael Strahan	4.00	10.00
28 Chad Pennington	4.00	10.00
29 Justin McCareins	2.50	6.00
30 John Abraham	2.50	6.00
31 Charles Woodson	4.00	10.00
32 Brian Westbrook	3.00	8.00
33 Donovan McNabb	4.00	10.00
34 Freddie Mitchell	2.50	6.00
35 Ben Roethlisberger	6.00	15.00
36 Duce Staley	3.00	8.00
37 Hines Ward	4.00	10.00
38 Koren Robinson	2.50	6.00
39 Matt Hasselbeck	3.00	8.00
40 Isaac Bruce	3.00	8.00
41 Marc Bulger	3.00	8.00
42 Torry Holt	3.00	8.00
43 Steven Jackson	4.00	10.00
44 Mike Alstott	3.00	8.00
45 Chris Brown	2.50	6.00
46 Derrick Mason	3.00	8.00
47 Drew Bennett	3.00	8.00
48 LaVar Arrington	3.00	8.00
49 Patrick Ramsey	3.00	8.00
50 Rod Gardner	2.50	6.00

2005 Donruss Classics Team Colors Bronze

BRONZE PRINT RUN 1000 SER.#'d SETS
*GOLD/250: .8X TO 2X BRONZE/1000
*SILVER/500: .5X TO 1.2X BRONZE/1000

TC1 Aaron Brooks	.75	2.00
TC2 Dan Marino	4.00	10.00
TC3 David Carr	.75	2.00
TC4 Deion Sanders	2.00	5.00
TC5 Donovan McNabb	1.25	3.00
TC6 Hines Ward	1.25	3.00
TC7 Jake Delhomme	1.00	2.50
TC8 Jerry Rice	2.50	6.00
TC9 John Elway	3.00	8.00
TC10 Marc Bulger	1.00	2.50
TC11 Matt Hasselbeck	1.00	2.50
TC12 Michael Irvin	1.50	4.00
TC13 Peyton Manning	2.50	6.00
TC14 Michael Vick	1.25	3.00
TC15 Steve Young	2.00	5.00
TC16 Tony Gonzalez	1.00	2.50
TC17 Torry Holt	1.00	2.50
TC18 Troy Aikman	2.00	5.00
TC19 Walter Payton	4.00	10.00
TC20 Isaac Bruce	1.00	2.50
TC21 Anquan Boldin	1.00	2.50
TC22 Larry Fitzgerald	1.25	3.00
TC23 Stephen Davis	1.00	2.50
TC24 Drew Bledsoe	1.25	3.00
TC25 LaDainian Tomlinson	1.25	3.00

2005 Donruss Classics Team Colors Jerseys Away

AWAY PRINT RUN 199 SER.#'d SETS
*HOME/99: .5X TO 1.2X AWAY JSY/199
*PRIME/25: 1X TO 2.5X AWAY JSY/199

1 Aaron Brooks	2.50	6.00
2 Dan Marino	12.00	30.00
3 David Carr	2.50	6.00
4 Deion Sanders	6.00	15.00
5 Donovan McNabb	4.00	10.00
6 Hines Ward	4.00	10.00
7 Jake Delhomme	3.00	8.00
8 Jerry Rice	8.00	20.00
9 John Elway	10.00	25.00
10 Marc Bulger	3.00	8.00
11 Matt Hasselbeck	3.00	8.00
12 Michael Irvin	5.00	12.00
13 Peyton Manning	8.00	20.00
14 Michael Vick	4.00	10.00
15 Steve Young	6.00	15.00
16 Tony Gonzalez	3.00	8.00
17 Torry Holt	3.00	8.00
18 Troy Aikman	6.00	15.00
19 Walter Payton	12.00	30.00
20 Isaac Bruce	3.00	8.00
21 Anquan Boldin	3.00	8.00
22 Larry Fitzgerald	4.00	10.00
23 Stephen Davis	3.00	8.00
24 Drew Bledsoe	4.00	10.00
25 LaDainian Tomlinson	4.00	10.00

2005 Donruss Classics Timeless Triples Bronze

BRONZE PRINT RUN 1000 SER.#'d SETS
*GOLD/250: .8X TO 2X BRONZE/1000
*SILVER/500: .5X TO 1.2X BRONZE/1000

1 Jim Kelly	2.00	5.00
Thurman Thomas		
Drew Bledsoe		
2 Walter Payton	4.00	10.00
Gale Sayers		
Richard Dent		
3 Jim Brown	2.00	5.00
Paul Warfield		
Leroy Kelly		
4 Roger Staubach	2.50	6.00
Troy Aikman		
Michael Irvin		
5 Earl Campbell	1.50	4.00
Warren Moon		
Steve McNair		
6 Johnny Unitas	3.00	8.00
Peyton Manning		
Don Shula		
7 Joe Namath	2.50	6.00
Don Maynard		
Chad Pennington		
8 Fran Tarkenton	2.50	6.00
Eli Manning		
Lawrence Taylor		
9 Jerry Rice	3.00	8.00
Do Jackson		
Marcus Allen		
10 Joe Montana	4.00	10.00
Marcus Allen		
Priest Holmes		

2005 Donruss Classics Timeless Triples Jerseys

STATED PRINT RUN 100 SER.#'d SETS
UNPRICED PRIME PRINT RUN 10

1 Jim Kelly	12.00	30.00
Thurman Thomas		
Drew Bledsoe		
2 Walter Payton	25.00	60.00
Gale Sayers		
Richard Dent		
3 Jim Brown	12.00	30.00
Paul Warfield		
Leroy Kelly		
4 Roger Staubach	15.00	40.00
Troy Aikman		
Michael Irvin		
5 Earl Campbell	10.00	25.00
Warren Moon		
Steve McNair		
6 Johnny Unitas	20.00	50.00
Peyton Manning		
Don Shula		
7 Joe Namath	15.00	40.00
Don Maynard		
Chad Pennington		
8 Fran Tarkenton	15.00	40.00
Eli Manning		
Lawrence Taylor		
9 Jerry Rice	20.00	50.00
Bo Jackson		
Marcus Allen		
10 Joe Montana	25.00	60.00
Marcus Allen		
Priest Holmes		

2006 Donruss Classics

This 274-card set was released in July, 2006. Cards numbered 1-100 feature veterans in alphabetical team order, while cards numbered 101-160 are rookies printed to different serial numbering, cards 161-225 feature signed rookies (again to differing serial numbering) and the set concludes with retired greats (226-274) most of which were sequenced in first name alphabetical order. All the retired greats were issued to a stated print run of 1000 serial numbered copies.

COMP.SET w/o SP's (100)	7.50	20.00
LEGEND PRINT RUN 1000 SER.#'d SETS		
1 Anquan Boldin	.25	.60
2 Kurt Warner	.30	.75
3 Larry Fitzgerald	.30	.75
4 Marcel Shipp	.20	.50
5 Alge Crumpler	.25	.60
6 Michael Vick	.30	.75
7 Warrick Dunn	.25	.60
8 Jamal Lewis	.25	.60
9 Kyle Boller	.25	.60
10 Eric Moulds	.20	.50
11 J.P. Losman	.25	.60
12 Willis McGahee	.25	.60
13 Jake Delhomme	.25	.60
14 Stephen Davis	.25	.60
15 Steve Smith	.30	.75
16 Cedric Benson	.25	.60
17 Kyle Orton	.30	.75
18 Muhsin Muhammad	.25	.60
19 Thomas Jones	.25	.60
20 Carson Palmer	.30	.75
21 Chad Johnson	.25	.60
22 Rudi Johnson	.25	.60
23 T.J. Houshmandzadeh	.25	.60
24 Braylon Edwards	.25	.60
25 Reuben Droughns	.25	.60
26 Trent Dilfer	.25	.60
27 Drew Bledsoe	.30	.75
28 Julius Jones	.20	.50
29 Keyshawn Johnson	.25	.60
30 Terry Glenn	.25	.60
31 Ashley Lelie	.20	.50
32 Jake Plummer	.25	.60
33 Tatum Bell	.20	.50
34 Joey Harrington	.20	.50
35 Kevin Jones	.20	.50
36 Roy Williams WR	.25	.60
37 Aaron Rodgers	.60	1.50
38 Brett Favre	.60	1.50
39 Samkon Gado	.25	.60
40 Andre Johnson	.30	.75
41 David Carr	.20	.50
42 Domanick Davis	.20	.50
43 Edgerrin James	.25	.60
44 Marvin Harrison	.30	.75
45 Peyton Manning	.50	1.25
46 Reggie Wayne	.25	.60
47 Byron Leftwich	.25	.60
48 Fred Taylor	.25	.60
49 Jimmy Smith	.25	.60
50 Matt Jones	.20	.50
51 Larry Johnson	.25	.60
52 Tony Gonzalez	.25	.60
53 Trent Green	.25	.60
54 Chris Chambers	.25	.60
55 Ricky Williams	.20	.50
56 Ronnie Brown	.30	.75
57 Daunte Culpepper	.25	.60
58 Mewelde Moore	.20	.50
59 Nate Burleson	.20	.50
60 Corey Dillon	.25	.60
61 Deion Branch	.25	.60
62 Tom Brady	.50	1.25
63 Aaron Brooks	.25	.60
64 Deuce McAllister	.25	.60
65 Donte Stallworth	.20	.50
66 Eli Manning	.40	1.00
67 Plaxico Burress	.25	.60
68 Tiki Barber	.30	.75
69 Chad Pennington	.25	.60
70 Curtis Martin	.30	.75
71 Laveranues Coles	.20	.50
72 Kerry Collins	.25	.60
73 LaMont Jordan	.25	.60
74 Randy Moss	.30	.75
75 Brian Westbrook	.25	.60
76 Donovan McNabb	.30	.75
77 Reggie Brown	.20	.50
78 Ben Roethlisberger	.40	1.00
79 Hines Ward	.30	.75
80 Willie Parker	.25	.60
81 Antonio Gates	.30	.75
82 Drew Brees	.30	.75
83 LaDainian Tomlinson	.30	.75
84 Alex Smith QB	.30	.75
85 Frank Gore	.30	.75
86 Darrell Jackson	.25	.60
87 Matt Hasselbeck	.25	.60
88 Shaun Alexander	.25	.60
89 Marc Bulger	.25	.60
90 Steven Jackson	.30	.75
91 Torry Holt	.25	.60
92 Cadillac Williams	.25	.60
93 Joey Galloway	.25	.60
94 Michael Clayton	.20	.50
95 Chris Brown	.20	.50
96 Steve McNair	.25	.60
97 Drew Bennett	.25	.60
98 Clinton Portis	.30	.75
99 Mark Brunell	.25	.60
100 Santana Moss	.25	.60
101 Brodie Croyle/999 RC	2.50	6.00
102 Omar Jacobs/1499 RC	1.50	4.00
103 Charlie Whitehurst/999 RC	2.50	6.00
104 Tarvaris Jackson/999 RC	2.50	6.00
105 Kellen Clemens/999 RC	2.00	5.00
106 Vince Young/599 RC	4.00	10.00
107 Reggie McNeal/1499 RC	2.00	5.00
108 Marcus Vick/1499 RC	1.50	4.00
109 DonTrell Moore/1499 RC	2.00	5.00
110 Willie Reid/1499 RC	2.00	5.00
111 Matt Leinart/599 RC	3.00	8.00
112 Jay Cutler/599 RC	6.00	15.00
113 Brad Smith/1499 RC	2.50	6.00
114 Joseph Addai/599 RC	3.00	8.00
115 DeAngelo Williams/599 RC	4.00	10.00
116 Laurence Maroney/599 RC	2.50	6.00
117 Jerious Norwood/999 RC	2.00	5.00
118 Claude Wroten/1499 RC	1.50	4.00
119 Antonio Cromartie/1499 RC	2.50	6.00
120 Maurice Drew/999 RC	4.00	10.00
121 Anwar Phillips/1499 RC	2.00	5.00
122 LenDale White/599 RC	2.50	6.00
123 Reggie Bush/599 RC	6.00	15.00
124 Cedric Humes/1499 RC	1.50	4.00
125 Jerome Harrison/1499 RC	2.50	6.00
126 Brian Calhoun/999 RC	1.50	4.00
127 Joe Klopfenstein/999 RC	1.50	4.00
128 Leonard Pope/1499 RC	2.50	6.00
129 Vernon Davis/599 RC	4.00	10.00
130 Anthony Fasano/999 RC	2.50	6.00
131 Marcedes Lewis/999 RC	2.50	6.00
132 Dominique Byrd/1499 RC	2.00	5.00
133 Derek Hagan/1499 RC	2.00	5.00
134 Pat Watkins/1499 RC	2.00	5.00
135 Todd Watkins/1499 RC	1.50	4.00
136 Jeremy Bloom/1499 RC	2.00	5.00
137 Chad Jackson/599 RC	2.00	5.00
138 Devin Hester/1499 RC	5.00	12.00
139 Sinorice Moss/599 RC	3.00	8.00
140 Jason Avant/1499 RC	1.50	4.00
141 Maurice Stovall/1499 RC	1.50	4.00
142 Santonio Holmes/599 RC	4.00	10.00
143 Travis Wilson/999 RC	1.50	4.00
144 Demetrius Williams/1499 RC	2.00	5.00
145 Bernard Pollard/1499 RC	2.00	5.00
146 Michael Robinson/1499 RC	2.00	5.00
147 Brandon Marshall/1499 RC	2.50	6.00
148 Greg Jennings/999 RC	5.00	12.00
149 Brandon Williams/1499 RC	1.50	4.00
150 Jonathan Orr/1499 RC	2.00	5.00
151 David Thomas/1499 RC	2.00	5.00
152 Skyler Green/1499 RC	1.50	4.00
153 Mario Williams/499 RC	3.00	8.00
154 Ernie Sims/999 RC	2.00	5.00
155 A.J. Hawk/599 RC	3.00	8.00
156 Donte Whitner/1499 RC	2.50	6.00
157 Michael Huff/999 RC	2.00	5.00
158 Leon Washington/1499 RC	2.00	5.00

159 P.J. Daniels/1499 RC 1.50 4.00
160 Cory Rodgers/1499 RC 2.00 5.00
161 Tony Scheffler AU/499 RC 8.00 20.00
162 Paul Pinegar AU/999 RC 3.00 8.00
163 D.J. Shockley AU/599 RC 5.00 12.00
164 Ben Obomanu AU/899 RC 5.00 12.00
165 Adam Jennings AU/599 RC 5.00 12.00
166 Brandon Kirsch AU/999 RC 4.00 10.00
167 Mike Bell AU/999 RC 5.00 12.00
168 De'Arrius Howard AU/999 RC 5.00 12.00
169 Martin Nance AU/999 RC 4.00 10.00
170 Miles Austin AU/999 RC 25.00 50.00
171 Wendell Mathis AU/999 RC 4.00 10.00
172 Gerald Riggs AU/995 RC 4.00 10.00
173 Hank Baskett AU/999 RC 5.00 12.00
174 Greg Lee AU/999 RC 3.00 8.00
175 Quinton Ganther AU/799 RC 3.00 8.00
176 Garrett Mills/1499 RC 2.50 6.00
177 Jeff Webb AU/599 RC 5.00 12.00
178 Delanie Walker AU/599 RC 6.00 15.00
179 D'Brickashaw Ferguson AU/599 RC 6.00 15.00
180 Mathias Kiwanuka AU/499 RC 6.00 15.00
181 Kamerion Wimbley AU/499 RC 6.00 15.00
182 Tamba Hali AU/499 RC 6.00 15.00
183 Brodrick Bunkley AU/499 RC 5.00 12.00
184 Gabe Watson/1499 RC 1.50 4.00
185 Haloti Ngata AU/499 RC 6.00 15.00
186 DeMeco Ryans AU/599 RC 6.00 15.00
187 A.J. Nicholson/1499 RC 1.50 4.00
188 Abdul Hodge AU/999 RC 5.00 12.00
189 Chad Greenway AU/499 RC 6.00 15.00
190 D'Qwell Jackson AU/599 RC 5.00 12.00
191 Manny Lawson AU/499 RC 5.00 12.00
192 Bobby Carpenter AU/499 RC 4.00 10.00
193 Jon Alston AU/999 RC 3.00 8.00
194 Thomas Howard AU/599 RC 5.00 12.00
195 Tye Hill AU/499 RC 4.00 10.00
196 Kelly Jennings AU/499 RC 5.00 12.00
197 Ashton Youboty AU/999 RC 3.00 8.00
198 Alan Zemaitis AU/999 RC 5.00 12.00
199 Johnathan Joseph AU/499 RC 5.00 12.00
200 Jimmy Williams AU/599 RC 6.00 15.00
201 Ko Simpson AU/999 RC 4.00 10.00
202 Jason Allen AU/499 RC 5.00 12.00
203 Darnell Bing AU/999 RC 4.00 10.00
204 Erik Meyer AU/999 RC 4.00 10.00
205 Bruce Gradkowski AU/499 RC 6.00 15.00
206 Darrell Hackney AU/999 RC 4.00 10.00
207 Derrick Ross AU/799 RC 4.00 10.00
207 Drew Olson AU/999 RC 3.00 8.00
209 Taurean Henderson AU/999 RC 5.00 12.00
210 Andre Hall AU/999 RC 4.00 10.00
211 Devin Aromashodu AU/899 RC 6.00 15.00
212 Mike Hass AU/599 RC 5.00 12.00
213 Ingle Martin AU/499 RC 5.00 12.00
214 Marques Hagans AU/499 RC 4.00 10.00
215 Wali Lundy AU/499 RC 5.00 12.00
216 Domenik Hixon AU/499 RC 6.00 15.00
217 Ethan Kilmer AU/899 RC 4.00 10.00
218 Bennie Brazell/1499 RC 2.00 5.00
219 David Anderson/1499 RC 2.00 5.00
220 Marques Colston AU/770 RC 15.00 40.00
221 Kevin McMahan AU/999 RC 4.00 10.00
222 Anthony Mix/1499 RC 2.00 5.00
223 John McCargo AU/499 RC 4.00 10.00
224 Rocky McIntosh/1499 RC 2.00 5.00
225 Cedric Griffin AU/599 RC 5.00 12.00
226 Barry Sanders 2.50 6.00
227 Bart Starr 2.50 6.00
228 Bo Jackson 2.00 5.00
229 Bob Griese 1.50 4.00
230 Bobby Layne 1.50 4.00
231 Boomer Esiason 1.25 3.00
232 Bulldog Turner 1.25 3.00
233 Dan Marino 3.00 8.00
234 Deacon Jones 1.25 3.00
235 Derrick Thomas 2.50 6.00
236 Dick Butkus 2.00 5.00
237 Don Meredith 1.50 4.00
238 Eric Dickerson 1.25 3.00
239 Fran Tarkenton 2.00 5.00
240 Fred Biletnikoff 1.50 4.00
241 Gale Sayers 2.00 5.00
242 Harvey Martin 1.00 2.50
243 Herman Edwards 1.25 3.00
244 Jack Lambert 1.50 4.00
245 Jim Brown 2.00 5.00
246 Jim Kelly 2.00 5.00
247 Jim Plunkett 1.25 3.00
248 Jim Thorpe 2.00 5.00
249 Joe Montana 3.00 8.00
250 John Elway 2.50 6.00
251 John Riggins 1.50 4.00
252 Johnny Unitas 2.50 6.00
253 Len Dawson 1.50 4.00
254 Marcus Allen 1.50 4.00
255 Mike Singletary 1.50 4.00
256 Ozzie Newsome 1.25 3.00
257 Phil Simms 1.25 3.00
258 Ray Nitschke 1.50 4.00
259 Red Grange 2.00 5.00
260 Roger Staubach 2.50 6.00
261 Ronnie Lott 1.25 3.00
262 Steve Largent 1.50 4.00
263 Terry Bradshaw 2.50 6.00
264 Troy Aikman 2.00 5.00
265 Walter Payton 3.00 8.00
266 Bill Dudley 1.25 3.00
267 Joe Perry 1.25 3.00
268 Charley Trippi 1.00 2.50
269 Paul Lowe 1.00 2.50
270 Clem Daniels 1.00 2.50
271 Ken Kavanaugh 1.00 2.50
272 Andre Reed 1.25 3.00
273 Steve Van Buren 1.25 3.00
274 Jim Taylor 1.50 4.00

2006 Donruss Classics Timeless Tributes Bronze

*VETERANS: 4X TO 10X BASIC CARDS
COMMON ROOKIE 2.50 6.00
ROOKIE SEMISTARS 4.00 10.00
ROOKIE UNL.STARS 5.00 12.00
*LEGENDS: 1X TO 2.5X BASIC CARDS
STATED PRINT RUN 100 SER.#'d SETS
106 Vince Young 6.00 15.00
112 Jay Cutler 10.00 25.00
115 DeAngelo Williams 6.00 15.00
120 Maurice Drew 8.00 20.00
123 Reggie Bush 10.00 25.00
138 Devin Hester 10.00 25.00
142 Santonio Holmes 6.00 15.00
148 Greg Jennings 10.00 25.00
154 Ernie Sims 4.00 10.00
155 A.J. Hawk 5.00 12.00
220 Marques Colston 10.00 25.00

2006 Donruss Classics Timeless Tributes Gold

*VETERANS: 8X TO 20X BASIC CARDS
*ROOKIES: .6X TO 1.5X BRONZE ROOKIES
*LEGENDS: 2X TO 5X BASIC CARDS
GOLD PRINT RUN 25 SER.#'d SETS

2006 Donruss Classics Timeless Tributes Platinum

UNPRICED PLAT.PRINT RUN 10 SER.#'d SETS

2006 Donruss Classics Timeless Tributes Silver

*VETERANS: 6X TO 15X BASIC CARDS
*ROOKIES: .5X TO 1.2X BRONZE ROOKIES
*LEGENDS: 1.5X TO 4X BASIC CARDS
STATED PRINT RUN 50 SER.#'d SETS

2006 Donruss Classics Classic Combos Bronze

BRONZE PRINT RUN 500 SER.#'d SETS
*GOLD: .6X TO 1.5X BRONZE INSERTS
GOLD PRINT RUN 100 SER.#'d SETS
*PLATINUM: 1.2X TO 3X BRONZE INSERTS
PLATINUM PRINT RUN 25 SER.#'d SETS
*SILVER: .5X TO 1.2X BRONZE INSERTS
SILVER PRINT RUN 250 SER.#'d SETS
1 Barry Sanders 3.00 8.00
Gale Sayers
2 Bob Griese 2.00 5.00
Len Dawson
3 Dan Marino 4.00 10.00
Joe Montana
4 Don Meredith 2.50 6.00
Troy Aikman
5 Dick Butkus 2.50 6.00
Deacon Jones
6 Jim Brown 2.50 6.00
Jim Thorpe
7 Jack Lambert 2.00 5.00
Harvey Martin
8 Jim Kelly 3.00 8.00
John Elway
9 Mike Singletary 2.00 5.00
Bulldog Turner
10 Johnny Unitas 3.00 8.00
Peyton Manning
11 Ozzie Newsome 2.00 5.00
Steve Largent
12 Eric Dickerson 4.00 10.00
Walter Payton
13 Boomer Esiason 1.50 4.00
Phil Simms
14 Doak Walker 2.00 5.00
Dutch Clark
15 Steve Young 2.50 6.00
Y.A. Tittle
16 Jim Plunkett 2.00 5.00
Fred Biletnikoff

2006 Donruss Classics Classic Combos Jerseys

STATED PRINT RUN 50-250
UNPRICED PRIME PRINT RUN 1-10
1 Barry Sanders 12.00 30.00
Gale Sayers/207
2 Bob Griese 8.00 20.00
Len Dawson/163
3 Dan Marino 15.00 40.00
Joe Montana/250
4 Don Meredith 20.00 50.00
Troy Aikman/50
5 Dick Butkus 10.00 25.00
Deacon Jones/150
6 Jim Brown 150.00 250.00
Jim Thorpe/25
7 Jack Lambert 6.00 15.00
Harvey Martin/250
8 Jim Kelly 12.00 30.00
John Elway/250
9 Mike Singletary 10.00 25.00
Bulldog Turner/163
10 Johnny Unitas 12.00 30.00
Peyton Manning/215
11 Ozzie Newsome 6.00 15.00
Steve Largent/163
12 Eric Dickerson 15.00 40.00
Walter Payton/163
13 Boomer Esiason 6.00 15.00
Phil Simms/250
14 Doak Walker 60.00 100.00
Dutch Clark/50
15 Steve Young 10.00 25.00
Y.A. Tittle/215
16 Jim Plunkett 6.00 15.00
Fred Biletnikoff/215

2006 Donruss Classics Classic Pigskin

STATED PRINT RUN 250 SER.#'d SETS
*DOUBLES: 1X TO 2.5X BASIC INSERTS
DOUBLES PRINT RUN 25 SER.#'d SETS
1 Bart Starr 30.00 60.00
2 Andre Reed 6.00 15.00
3 Fred Biletnikoff 8.00 20.00
4 John Elway 12.00 30.00
5 Jim Kelly 10.00 25.00
6 Thurman Thomas 8.00 20.00

2006 Donruss Classics Classic Quads Bronze

BRONZE PRINT RUN 100 SER.#'d SETS
*GOLD: .6X TO 1.5X BRONZE INSERTS
GOLD PRINT RUN 25 SER.#'d SETS
UNPRICED PLATINUM PRINT RUN 10
*SILVER: .5X TO 1.2X BRONZE INSERTS
SILVER PRINT RUN 50 SER.#'d SETS
1 Bart Starr 10.00 25.00
Johnny Unitas
Y.A. Tittle
Don Meredith
2 Deacon Jones 6.00 15.00
Bulldog Turner
Harvey Martin
Jack Lambert
3 Jim Brown 10.00 25.00
Barry Sanders
Eric Dickerson
Walter Payton
4 Joe Montana 12.50 30.00
Len Dawson
Peyton Manning
Brett Favre
5 Jim Kelly 10.00 25.00
Troy Aikman
John Elway
Dan Marino
6 Boomer Esiason 8.00 20.00
Bob Griese
Phil Simms
Steve Young
7 Steve Largent 8.00 20.00
Ozzie Newsome
Fred Biletnikoff
Henry Ellard
8 Dick Butkus 8.00 20.00
Mike Singletary
Ronnie Lott
Derrick Thomas

2006 Donruss Classics Classic Quads Materials

STATED PRINT RUN 50 SER.#'d SETS
UNPRICED PRIME PRINT RUN 1-5 SETS
2 Deacon Jones 15.00 40.00
Bulldog Turner
Harvey Martin
Jack Lambert
3 Jim Brown 60.00 150.00
Barry Sanders
Eric Dickerson
Walter Payton
4 Joe Montana 50.00 120.00
Len Dawson
Peyton Manning
Brett Favre
5 Jim Kelly 40.00 100.00
Troy Aikman
John Elway
Dan Marino
6 Boomer Esiason 30.00 80.00
Bob Griese
Phil Simms
Steve Young
7 Steve Largent 20.00 50.00
Ozzie Newsome
Fred Biletnikoff
Henry Ellard
8 Dick Butkus 25.00 60.00
Mike Singletary
Ronnie Lott
Derrick Thomas

2006 Donruss Classics Classic Singles Bronze

BRONZE PRINT RUN 1000 SER.#'d SETS
*GOLD: .8X TO 2X BRONZE INSERTS
GOLD PRINT RUN 100 SER.#'d SETS
*PLATINUM: 1.2X TO 3X BRONZE INSERTS
PLATINUM PRINT RUN 25 SER.#'d SETS
*SILVER: .6X TO 1.5X BRONZE INSERTS
SILVER PRINT RUN 250 SER.#'d SETS
1 Barry Sanders 2.50 6.00
2 Bob Griese 1.50 4.00
3 Dan Marino 3.00 8.00
4 Eric Dickerson 1.25 3.00
5 Don Meredith 1.50 4.00
6 Herman Edwards 1.25 3.00
7 Jim Brown 2.00 5.00
8 Jack Lambert 1.50 4.00
9 Jim Kelly 2.00 5.00
10 Joe Montana 3.00 8.00
11 Jim Thorpe 2.00 5.00
12 John Elway 2.50 6.00
13 Peyton Manning 2.50 6.00
14 Marcus Allen 1.50 4.00
15 Len Dawson 1.50 4.00
16 Jim Plunkett 1.25 3.00
17 Mike Singletary 1.50 4.00
18 Ozzie Newsome 1.25 3.00
19 Ronnie Lott 1.25 3.00
20 Steve Largent 1.50 4.00
21 Walter Payton 3.00 8.00
22 Dick Butkus 2.00 5.00
23 Deacon Jones 1.25 3.00
24 Gale Sayers 2.00 5.00
25 Harvey Martin 1.00 2.50
26 Johnny Unitas 2.50 6.00
27 Troy Aikman 2.00 5.00
28 Ray Nitschke 1.50 4.00
29 Boomer Esiason 1.25 3.00
30 Phil Simms 1.25 3.00

2006 Donruss Classics Classic Singles Jerseys

STATED PRINT RUN 75-250 SETS
*PRIME/25: 1.2X TO 3X BASIC JERSEYS
PRIME STATED PRINT RUN 1-25
1 Barry Sanders/250 8.00 20.00
2 Bob Griese/189 4.00 10.00
3 Dan Marino/250 10.00 25.00
4 Eric Dickerson/250 4.00 10.00
5 Don Meredith/75 10.00 25.00
6 Herman Edwards/250 3.00 8.00
7 Jim Brown/175 6.00 15.00
8 Jack Lambert/250 5.00 12.00
9 Jim Kelly/250 5.00 12.00
10 Joe Montana/250 10.00 25.00
11 Jim Thorpe/100 60.00 120.00
12 John Elway/250 8.00 20.00
13 Peyton Manning/250 8.00 20.00
14 Marcus Allen/250 4.00 10.00
15 Len Dawson/250 4.00 10.00
16 Jim Plunkett/250 4.00 10.00
17 Mike Singletary/200 4.00 10.00
18 Ozzie Newsome/250 4.00 10.00
19 Ronnie Lott/250 4.00 10.00
20 Steve Largent/215 4.00 10.00
21 Walter Payton/163 10.00 25.00
22 Dick Butkus/250 6.00 15.00
23 Deacon Jones/250 4.00 10.00
24 Gale Sayers/250 6.00 15.00
25 Harvey Martin/250 5.00 12.00
26 Johnny Unitas/250 10.00 25.00
27 Troy Aikman/250 6.00 15.00
28 Ray Nitschke/250 6.00 15.00
29 Boomer Esiason/250 3.00 8.00
30 Phil Simms/250 4.00 10.00

2006 Donruss Classics Classic Triples Bronze

BRONZE PRINT RUN 250 SER.#'d SETS
*GOLD: .6X TO 1.5X BRONZE INSERTS
GOLD PRINT RUN 50 SER.#'d SETS
UNPRICED PLATINUM PRINT RUN 10 SETS
*SILVER: .5X TO 1.2X BRONZE INSERTS
SILVER PRINT RUN 100 SER.#'d SETS
1 Mike Singletary 5.00 12.00
Bulldog Turner
Dick Butkus
2 Jim Thorpe 8.00 20.00
Gale Sayers
Walter Payton
3 Derrick Thomas 4.00 10.00
Deacon Jones
Harvey Martin
4 Barry Sanders 6.00 15.00
Eric Dickerson
Marcus Allen
5 Steve Young 8.00 20.00
Dan Marino
Phil Simms
6 Don Meredith 8.00 20.00
Joe Montana
Johnny Unitas
7 Troy Aikman 6.00 15.00
Jim Kelly
John Elway
8 Bob Griese 6.00 15.00
Len Dawson
Bart Starr
9 Fred Biletnikoff 4.00 10.00
Steve Largent
Ozzie Newsome
10 Y.A. Tittle 5.00 12.00
Peyton Manning
Jim Plunkett

2006 Donruss Classics Classic Triples Materials

STATED PRINT RUN 100 SER.#'d SETS
UNPRICED PRIME PRINT RUN 1-10
1 Mike Singletary 20.00 50.00
Bulldog Turner
Dick Butkus
2 Jim Thorpe 250.00 350.00
Gale Sayers
Walter Payton/50
3 Derrick Thomas 25.00 60.00
Deacon Jones
Harvey Martin
4 Barry Sanders 15.00 40.00
Eric Dickerson
Marcus Allen
5 Steve Young 25.00 60.00
Dan Marino
Phil Simms
6 Don Meredith 75.00 125.00
Joe Montana
Johnny Unitas/25
7 Troy Aikman 15.00 40.00
Jim Kelly
John Elway
8 Bob Griese 25.00 60.00
Len Dawson
Bart Starr/55
9 Fred Biletnikoff 15.00 40.00
Steve Largent
Ozzie Newsome
10 Y.A. Tittle 15.00 40.00
Peyton Manning
Jim Plunkett

2006 Donruss Classics Legendary Players Bronze

BRONZE PRINT RUN 1000 SER.#'d SETS
*GOLD: .8X TO 2X BRONZE INSERTS
GOLD PRINT RUN 100 SER.#'d SETS
*PLATINUM: 1.2X TO 3X BRONZE INSERTS
PLATINUM PRINT RUN 25 SER.#'d SETS
*SILVER: .6X TO 1.5X BRONZE INSERTS
SILVER PRINT RUN 250 SER.#'d SETS
1 Barry Sanders 2.50 6.00
2 Bobby Layne 1.50 4.00
3 Bulldog Turner 1.25 3.00
4 Dan Marino 3.00 8.00
5 Y.A. Tittle 1.50 4.00
7 Yale Lary 1.00 2.50
8 Lance Alworth 1.25 3.00
9 John Elway 2.50 6.00
10 Troy Aikman 2.00 5.00
11 Daryle Lamonica 1.00 2.50
12 Henry Ellard 1.00 2.50
13 Jerry Rice 2.50 6.00
14 Fred Biletnikoff 1.50 4.00
15 Deacon Jones 1.25 3.00
16 Jim Brown 2.00 5.00
17 Joe Montana 3.00 8.00
18 Johnny Unitas 2.50 6.00
19 Roger Staubach 2.50 6.00
20 John Riggins 1.50 4.00
21 Steve Largent 1.50 4.00
22 Ozzie Newsome 1.25 3.00
23 Terry Bradshaw 2.50 6.00
24 Jim Plunkett 1.25 3.00
25 Gale Sayers 2.00 5.00
26 Phil Simms 1.25 3.00
27 Jack Lambert 1.50 4.00
28 Walter Payton 3.00 8.00
29 Ray Nitschke 1.50 4.00
30 Don Meredith 1.50 4.00

2006 Donruss Classics Legendary Players Jerseys

STATED PRINT RUN 50-250 SETS
*PRIME/25: 1.2X TO 3X BASIC JERSEYS
PRIME PRINT RUN 2-25 SETS
1 Barry Sanders/250 8.00 20.00
2 Bobby Layne/50 20.00 50.00
3 Bulldog Turner/250 8.00 20.00
4 Dan Marino/250 10.00 25.00
5 Y.A. Tittle/250 8.00 20.00
7 Yale Lary/250 5.00 12.00
8 Lance Alworth/250 6.00 15.00
9 John Elway/250 8.00 20.00
10 Troy Aikman/250 6.00 15.00
11 Daryle Lamonica/250 5.00 12.00
12 Henry Ellard/250 4.00 10.00
13 Jerry Rice/250 6.00 15.00
14 Fred Biletnikoff/250 5.00 12.00
15 Deacon Jones/250 4.00 10.00
16 Jim Brown/100 8.00 20.00
17 Joe Montana/250 10.00 25.00
18 Johnny Unitas/250 10.00 25.00
19 Roger Staubach/215 8.00 20.00
20 John Riggins/150 4.00 10.00
21 Steve Largent/215 4.00 10.00
22 Ozzie Newsome/175 4.00 10.00
23 Terry Bradshaw/189 8.00 20.00
24 Jim Plunkett/250 4.00 10.00
25 Gale Sayers/215 6.00 15.00
26 Phil Simms/250 4.00 10.00
27 Jack Lambert/250 6.00 15.00
28 Walter Payton/189 10.00 25.00
29 Ray Nitschke/250 8.00 20.00
30 Don Meredith/107 10.00 25.00

2006 Donruss Classics Membership Bronze

BRONZE PRINT RUN 1000 SER.#'d SETS
*GOLD: .8X TO 2X BRONZE INSERTS
GOLD PRINT RUN 100 SER.#'d SETS
*PLATINUM: 1.2X TO 3X BRONZE INSERTS
PLATINUM PRINT RUN 25 SER.#'d SETS
*SILVER: .6X TO 1.5X BRONZE INSERTS
SILVER PRINT RUN 250 SER.#'d SETS
1 Aaron Brooks 1.00 2.50
2 Alex Smith QB 1.25 3.00
3 Alge Crumpler 1.00 2.50
4 Ben Roethlisberger 1.50 4.00
5 Braylon Edwards 1.00 2.50
6 Cadillac Williams 1.00 2.50
7 Carson Palmer 1.25 3.00
8 Chad Pennington 1.00 2.50
9 Clinton Portis 1.25 3.00
10 Deuce McAllister 1.00 2.50
11 Edgerrin James 1.00 2.50
12 Jimmy Smith 1.00 2.50
13 Marvin Harrison 1.25 3.00
14 Michael Vick 1.25 3.00
15 Randy Moss 1.25 3.00
16 Ronnie Brown 1.25 3.00
17 T.J. Houshmandzadeh 1.00 2.50
18 Terrell Owens 1.25 3.00
19 Thomas Jones 1.00 2.50
20 Warrick Dunn 1.00 2.50

2006 Donruss Classics Membership VIP Jerseys

STATED PRINT RUN 250 SER.#'d SETS
*PRIME: 1X TO 2.5X BASIC JERSEYS
PRIME PRINT RUN 25 SER.#'d SETS
1 Aaron Brooks 3.00 8.00
2 Alex Smith QB 4.00 10.00
3 Alge Crumpler 2.50 6.00
4 Ben Roethlisberger 10.00 25.00
5 Braylon Edwards 4.00 10.00
6 Cadillac Williams 4.00 10.00
7 Carson Palmer 4.00 10.00
8 Chad Pennington 3.00 8.00
9 Clinton Portis 4.00 10.00
10 Deuce McAllister 3.00 8.00
11 Edgerrin James 4.00 10.00
12 Jimmy Smith 3.00 8.00
13 Marvin Harrison 4.00 10.00
14 Michael Vick 4.00 10.00
15 Randy Moss 4.00 10.00
16 Ronnie Brown 4.00 10.00
17 T.J. Houshmandzadeh 2.50 6.00
18 Terrell Owens 4.00 10.00
19 Thomas Jones 3.00 8.00
20 Warrick Dunn 3.00 8.00

2006 Donruss Classics Monday Night Heroes Bronze

BRONZE PRINT RUN 1000 SER.#'d SETS
*GOLD: .8X TO 2X BRONZE INSERTS
GOLD PRINT RUN 100 SER.#'d SETS
*PLATINUM: 1.2X TO 3X BRONZE INSERTS
PLATINUM PRINT RUN 25 SER.#'d SETS
*SILVER: .6X TO 1.5X BRONZE INSERTS
SILVER PRINT RUN 250 SER.#'d SETS
1 Antonio Gates 1.25 3.00
2 Antwaan Randle El 1.00 2.50
3 Ben Roethlisberger 1.50 4.00
4 Brian Westbrook 1.00 2.50
5 Cadillac Williams 1.00 2.50
6 Carson Palmer 1.25 3.00
7 Chad Johnson 1.00 2.50
8 Clinton Portis 1.25 3.00
9 Corey Dillon 1.00 2.50
10 Curtis Martin 1.25 3.00
11 Daunte Culpepper 1.00 2.50
12 Donovan McNabb 1.25 3.00
13 Drew Bledsoe 1.25 3.00
14 Drew Brees 1.25 3.00
15 Edgerrin James 1.00 2.50
16 Eli Manning 1.50 4.00
17 Jake Plummer 1.00 2.50
18 Jimmy Smith 1.00 2.50
19 Julius Jones .75 2.00
20 LaDainian Tomlinson 1.25 3.00
21 Marvin Harrison 1.25 3.00
22 Matt Hasselbeck 1.00 2.50
23 Michael Vick 1.25 3.00
24 Peyton Manning 2.00 5.00
25 Randy Moss 1.25 3.00
26 Willis McGahee 1.00 2.50
27 Shaun Alexander 1.00 2.50
28 Steven Jackson 1.25 3.00
29 Tom Brady 2.00 5.00
30 Trent Green 1.00 2.50

2006 Donruss Classics Monday Night Heroes Jerseys

STATED PRINT RUN 250 SER.#'d SETS
*PRIME: 1X TO 2.5X BASIC JERSEYS
PRIME PRINT RUN 25 SER.#'d SETS
1 Antonio Gates 4.00 10.00
2 Antwaan Randle El 3.00 8.00
3 Ben Roethlisberger 10.00 25.00
4 Brian Westbrook 3.00 8.00
5 Cadillac Williams 4.00 10.00
6 Carson Palmer 4.00 10.00
7 Chad Johnson 3.00 8.00
8 Clinton Portis 4.00 10.00
9 Corey Dillon 3.00 8.00
10 Curtis Martin 4.00 10.00
11 Daunte Culpepper 4.00 10.00
12 Donovan McNabb 4.00 10.00
13 Drew Bledsoe 4.00 10.00
14 Drew Brees 4.00 10.00
15 Edgerrin James 4.00 10.00
16 Eli Manning 6.00 15.00
17 Jake Plummer 3.00 8.00
18 Jimmy Smith/230 3.00 8.00
19 Julius Jones 4.00 10.00
20 LaDainian Tomlinson 4.00 10.00
21 Marvin Harrison 4.00 10.00
22 Matt Hasselbeck 4.00 10.00
23 Michael Vick 4.00 10.00
24 Peyton Manning 8.00 20.00
25 Randy Moss 4.00 10.00
26 Willis McGahee 3.00 8.00
27 Shaun Alexander 5.00 12.00
28 Steven Jackson 4.00 10.00
29 Tom Brady 6.00 15.00
30 Trent Green 3.00 8.00

2006 Donruss Classics Monday Night Heroes Jerseys Autographs

STATED PRINT RUN 5-25
UNPRICED PRIME AUTO PRINT RUN 5
1 Antonio Gates/25 10.00 25.00
16 Eli Manning/25 60.00 120.00
22 Matt Hasselbeck/25 30.00 60.00
28 Steven Jackson/25 10.00 25.00

2006 Donruss Classics Saturday Stars Bronze

BRONZE PRINT RUN 1000 SER.#'d SETS
*GOLD: .8X TO 2X BRONZE INSERTS
GOLD PRINT RUN 100 SER.#'d SETS
*PLATINUM: 1.2X TO 3X BRONZE INSERTS
PLATINUM PRINT RUN 25 SER.#'d SETS
*SILVER: .6X TO 1.5X BRONZE INSERTS
SILVER PRINT RUN 250 SER.#'d SETS
1 Cadillac Williams 1.00 2.50
2 Ronnie Brown 1.25 3.00
3 Mike Singletary 1.25 3.00
4 Fred Taylor 1.00 2.50
5 Jevon Kearse 1.00 2.50
6 Anquan Boldin 1.00 2.50
7 Laveranues Coles .75 2.00
8 Hines Ward 1.25 3.00
9 Michael Clayton .75 2.00
10 Clinton Portis 1.25 3.00
11 Edgerrin James 1.00 2.50
12 Jeremy Shockey 1.25 3.00
13 Kellen Winslow 1.00 2.50
14 Reggie Wayne 1.00 2.50
15 Sean Taylor 1.25 3.00
16 Willis McGahee 1.00 2.50
17 Braylon Edwards 1.00 2.50
18 Ahman Green 1.00 2.50
19 Barry Sanders 2.00 5.00
20 Curtis Martin 1.25 3.00
21 Dan Marino 2.50 6.00
22 Terry Bradshaw 2.00 5.00
23 Eric Dickerson 1.00 2.50
24 John Elway 2.00 5.00
25 Peyton Manning 2.00 5.00
26 Cedric Benson 1.00 2.50
27 Carson Palmer 1.25 3.00
28 Michael Vick 1.25 3.00
29 Drew Bledsoe 1.25 3.00
30 Lee Evans 1.00 2.50

2006 Donruss Classics Saturday Stars Autographs

STATED PRINT RUN 5-25
14 Reggie Wayne/25 15.00 30.00

2006 Donruss Classics Saturday Stars Jerseys

STATED PRINT RUN 18-250
*PRIME/16-28: 1X TO 2.5X BASIC JERSEYS
PRIME PRINT RUN 6-28
1 Cadillac Williams 5.00 12.00
2 Ronnie Brown 6.00 15.00
3 Mike Singletary/236 6.00 15.00
5 Jevon Kearse/88 5.00 12.00
6 Anquan Boldin/164 5.00 12.00
7 Laveranues Coles 4.00 10.00
8 Hines Ward 6.00 15.00
9 Michael Clayton 4.00 10.00
10 Clinton Portis/102 6.00 15.00
11 Edgerrin James 5.00 12.00
12 Jeremy Shockey/139 6.00 15.00
13 Kellen Winslow 5.00 12.00
14 Reggie Wayne 5.00 12.00
15 Sean Taylor 10.00 25.00
16 Willis McGahee 5.00 12.00
17 Braylon Edwards 5.00 12.00
18 Ahman Green 5.00 12.00
19 Barry Sanders 10.00 25.00
20 Curtis Martin 6.00 15.00
21 Dan Marino 12.00 30.00
22 Terry Bradshaw 10.00 25.00
23 Eric Dickerson 5.00 12.00
24 John Elway 10.00 25.00
25 Peyton Manning 10.00 25.00
26 Cedric Benson 5.00 12.00
27 Carson Palmer 6.00 15.00
28 Michael Vick 6.00 15.00
29 Drew Bledsoe 6.00 15.00
30 Lee Evans 5.00 12.00

2006 Donruss Classics Saturday Stars Jerseys Autographs

UNPRICED AUTO PRINT RUN 4-15
UNPRICED PRIME AU PRINT RUN 2-5

2006 Donruss Classics School Colors

ONE PER CASE
1 Vince Young 3.00 8.00
2 Reggie Bush 5.00 12.00
3 Matt Leinart 2.50 6.00
4 Jay Cutler 5.00 12.00
5 Laurence Maroney 2.00 5.00
6 DeAngelo Williams 3.00 8.00
7 Vernon Davis 3.00 8.00
8 Chad Jackson 1.50 4.00
9 Santonio Holmes 3.00 8.00
10 Sinorice Moss 2.50 6.00
11 Charlie Whitehurst 2.50 6.00
12 Erik Meyer 2.00 5.00
13 Joseph Addai 2.50 6.00
14 Brodie Croyle 2.50 6.00
15 Maurice Drew 4.00 10.00
16 Jerious Norwood 2.00 5.00
17 Demetrius Williams 2.00 5.00
18 Todd Watkins 1.50 4.00
19 Travis Wilson 1.50 4.00
20 Marcedes Lewis 2.50 6.00

2006 Donruss Classics School Colors Autographs

STATED PRINT RUN 25 SER.#'d SETS
1 Vince Young 60.00 120.00
2 Reggie Bush 75.00 150.00
3 Matt Leinart 40.00 100.00
4 Jay Cutler 60.00 120.00
5 Laurence Maroney 15.00 40.00
6 DeAngelo Williams 50.00 100.00
7 Vernon Davis 25.00 60.00
8 Chad Jackson 12.00 30.00
9 Santonio Holmes 50.00 100.00
10 Sinorice Moss 20.00 50.00
11 Charlie Whitehurst 20.00 50.00
12 Erik Meyer 15.00 40.00
13 Joseph Addai 20.00 50.00
14 Brodie Croyle 20.00 50.00
15 Maurice Drew 50.00 100.00
16 Jerious Norwood 15.00 40.00
17 Demetrius Williams 15.00 40.00
18 Todd Watkins 12.00 30.00
19 Travis Wilson 12.00 30.00
20 Marcedes Lewis 20.00 50.00

2006 Donruss Classics Significant Signatures Gold

ROOKIE PRINT RUN 100 SER.#'d SETS
LEGEND PRINT RUN 5-100
SERIAL #'d UNDER 25 NOT PRICED
101 Brodie Croyle 12.00 30.00
102 Omar Jacobs 8.00 20.00
103 Charlie Whitehurst 12.00 30.00
104 Tarvaris Jackson 12.00 30.00
105 Kellen Clemens 10.00 25.00
106 Vince Young 15.00 40.00
107 Reggie McNeal ?á 10.00 25.00
110 Willie Reid 10.00 25.00
111 Matt Leinart 12.00 30.00
112 Jay Cutler 25.00 60.00
113 Brad Smith 12.00 30.00
114 Joseph Addai 12.00 30.00
115 DeAngelo Williams 15.00 40.00
116 Laurence Maroney 10.00 25.00
117 Jerious Norwood 10.00 25.00
118 Claude Wroten 8.00 20.00
120 Maurice Drew 20.00 50.00
121 Anwar Phillips 10.00 25.00
122 LenDale White 10.00 25.00
123 Reggie Bush 25.00 60.00
124 Cedric Humes 8.00 20.00
126 Brian Calhoun 8.00 20.00
127 Joe Klopfenstein 8.00 20.00
128 Leonard Pope 12.00 30.00
129 Vernon Davis 15.00 40.00
130 Anthony Fasano 12.00 30.00
131 Marcedes Lewis 12.00 30.00
132 Dominique Byrd 10.00 25.00
133 Derek Hagan 10.00 25.00
134 Pat Watkins 10.00 25.00
135 Todd Watkins 8.00 20.00
136 Jeremy Bloom 10.00 25.00
137 Chad Jackson 8.00 20.00
138 Devin Hester 25.00 60.00
139 Sinorice Moss 12.00 30.00
140 Jason Avant 8.00 20.00
141 Maurice Stovall 8.00 20.00
142 Santonio Holmes 15.00 40.00
143 Travis Wilson 8.00 20.00
144 Demetrius Williams 10.00 25.00
145 Bernard Pollard 10.00 25.00
146 Michael Robinson 10.00 25.00
147 Brandon Marshall 20.00 40.00
148 Greg Jennings 25.00 60.00
149 Brandon Williams 8.00 20.00
150 Jonathan Orr 10.00 25.00
151 David Thomas 10.00 25.00
152 Skyler Green 8.00 20.00
153 Mario Williams 12.00 30.00
155 A.J. Hawk 12.00 30.00
156 Donte Whitner 12.00 30.00
157 Michael Huff 10.00 25.00
158 Leon Washington 15.00 40.00
159 P.J. Daniels 8.00 20.00
241 Gale Sayers/40 30.00 80.00
243 Herman Edwards/100 8.00 20.00
245 Jim Brown/32 50.00 100.00
251 John Riggins/44 25.00 50.00
255 Mike Singletary/50 15.00 40.00
256 Ozzie Newsome/50 8.00 20.00
266 Bill Dudley/100 25.00 50.00
267 Joe Perry/34 25.00 50.00
268 Charley Trippi/100 15.00 40.00
269 Paul Lowe/100 8.00 20.00
271 Ken Kavanaugh/100 12.00 30.00
272 Andre Reed/100 10.00 25.00
274 Jim Taylor/31 30.00 80.00

2006 Donruss Classics Significant Signatures Platinum

*PLAT/25: .6X TO 1.5X GOLD AUTOS
PLAT.ROOKIE PRINT RUN 25 SER.#'d SETS
PLATINUM LEGEND PRINT RUN 1-25
SERIAL #'d UNDER 25 NOT PRICED

2006 Donruss Classics Sunday's Best Bronze

BRONZE PRINT RUN 1000 SER.#'d SETS
*GOLD: .8X TO 2X BRONZE INSERTS
GOLD PRINT RUN 100 SER.#'d SETS
*PLATINUM: 1.2X TO 3X BRONZE INSERTS
PLATINUM PRINT RUN 25 SER.#'d SETS
*SILVER: .6X TO 1.5X BRONZE INSERTS
SILVER PRINT RUN 250 SER.#'d SETS
1 Willis McGahee 1.00 2.50
2 Alge Crumpler 1.00 2.50
3 Antonio Gates 1.25 3.00
4 Antwaan Randle El 1.00 2.50
5 Ben Roethlisberger 1.50 4.00
6 Warrick Dunn 1.00 2.50
7 Brian Westbrook 1.00 2.50
8 Cadillac Williams 1.00 2.50
9 Carson Palmer 1.25 3.00
10 Chad Johnson 1.00 2.50
11 Chad Pennington 1.00 2.50
12 Clinton Portis 1.25 3.00
13 Corey Dillon 1.00 2.50
14 Curtis Martin 1.25 3.00
15 Deion Branch 1.00 2.50
16 Deuce McAllister 1.00 2.50
17 Domanick Davis .75 2.00
18 Donovan McNabb 1.25 3.00
19 Drew Bledsoe 1.25 3.00
20 Drew Brees 1.25 3.00
21 Edgerrin James 1.00 2.50
22 Eli Manning 1.50 4.00
23 Jake Plummer 1.00 2.50
24 Jimmy Smith 1.00 2.50
25 Julius Jones .75 2.00
26 LaDainian Tomlinson 1.25 3.00
27 Marvin Harrison 1.25 3.00
28 Matt Hasselbeck 1.00 2.50
29 Michael Vick 1.25 3.00
30 Peyton Manning 2.00 5.00

31 Randy Moss 1.25 3.00
32 Ronnie Brown 1.25 3.00
33 Shaun Alexander 1.00 2.50
34 Steve Smith 1.25 3.00
35 Steven Jackson 1.25 3.00
36 T.J. Houshmandzadeh 1.00 2.50
37 Tatum Bell .75 2.00
38 Thomas Jones 1.00 2.50
39 Tom Brady 2.00 5.00
40 Trent Green 1.00 2.50

2006 Donruss Classics Sunday's Best Jerseys

STATED PRINT RUN 250 SER.#'d SETS
*PRIME: 1X TO 2.5X BASIC JERSEYS
PRIME PRINT RUN 25 SER.#'d SETS
1 Willis McGahee 3.00 8.00
2 Alge Crumpler 2.50 6.00
3 Antonio Gates 4.00 10.00
4 Antwaan Randle El 3.00 8.00
5 Ben Roethlisberger 10.00 25.00
6 Warrick Dunn 3.00 8.00
7 Brian Westbrook 3.00 8.00
8 Cadillac Williams 5.00 10.00
9 Carson Palmer 4.00 10.00
10 Chad Johnson 3.00 8.00
11 Chad Pennington 3.00 8.00
12 Clinton Portis 4.00 10.00
13 Corey Dillon 3.00 8.00
14 Curtis Martin 4.00 10.00
15 Deion Branch 3.00 8.00
16 Deuce McAllister 3.00 8.00
17 Domanick Davis 3.00 8.00
18 Donovan McNabb 4.00 10.00
19 Drew Bledsoe 4.00 10.00
20 Drew Brees 4.00 10.00
21 Edgerrin James 4.00 10.00
22 Eli Manning 6.00 15.00
23 Jake Plummer 3.00 8.00
24 Jimmy Smith 3.00 8.00
25 Julius Jones 4.00 10.00
26 LaDainian Tomlinson 4.00 10.00
27 Marvin Harrison 4.00 10.00
28 Matt Hasselbeck 4.00 10.00
29 Michael Vick 4.00 10.00
30 Peyton Manning 8.00 20.00
31 Randy Moss 4.00 10.00
32 Ronnie Brown 4.00 10.00
33 Shaun Alexander 5.00 12.00
34 Steve Smith 4.00 10.00
35 Steven Jackson 4.00 10.00
36 T.J. Houshmandzadeh 2.50 6.00
37 Tatum Bell 3.00 8.00
38 Thomas Jones 3.00 8.00
39 Tom Brady 6.00 15.00
40 Trent Green 3.00 8.00

2006 Donruss Classics Sunday's Best Jerseys Autographs

STATED PRINT RUN 10-25
UNPRICED PRIME PRINT RUN 5 SETS
2 Alge Crumpler/25 10.00 25.00
17 Domanick Davis/25 10.00 25.00
28 Matt Hasselbeck/25 30.00 60.00
32 Ronnie Brown/25 30.00 80.00

2006 Donruss Classics Timeless Triples Bronze

BRONZE PRINT RUN 1000 SER.#'d SETS
*GOLD: .8X TO 2X BRONZE INSERTS
GOLD PRINT RUN 100 SER.#'d SETS
*PLATINUM: 1.2X TO 3X BRONZE INSERTS
PLATINUM PRINT RUN 25 SER.#'d SETS
*SILVER: .6X TO 1.5X BRONZE INSERTS
SILVER PRINT RUN 250 SER.#'d SETS
1 Joe Montana 3.00 8.00
Steve Young
Alex Smith QB
2 Warrick Dunn 1.50 4.00
Michael Vick
Alge Crumpler
3 Gale Sayers 4.00 10.00
Walter Payton
Cedric Benson
4 Boomer Esiason 1.50 4.00
Chad Johnson
Carson Palmer
5 Roger Staubach 2.50 6.00
Troy Aikman
Drew Bledsoe
6 Bobby Layne 2.50 6.00
Yale Lary
Barry Sanders
7 Marcus Allen 2.00 5.00
Priest Holmes
Larry Johnson
8 Jim Thorpe 3.00 8.00
Dutch Clark
Red Grange
9 LaDainian Tomlinson 2.00 5.00
Drew Brees
Antonio Gates
10 Bart Starr 4.00 10.00
Brett Favre
Aaron Rodgers

2006 Donruss Classics Timeless Triples Materials

STATED PRINT RUN 100 SER.#'d SETS
UNPRICED PRIME PRINT RUN 10 SETS
1 Joe Montana 40.00 80.00
Steve Young
Alex Smith QB
2 Warrick Dunn 10.00 25.00
Michael Vick
Alge Crumpler
3 Gale Sayers 25.00 60.00
Walter Payton
Cedric Benson
4 Boomer Esiason 10.00 25.00
Chad Johnson
Carson Palmer
5 Roger Staubach 15.00 40.00
Troy Aikman
Drew Bledsoe
6 Bobby Layne 40.00 80.00
Yale Lary
Barry Sanders/50
7 Marcus Allen 12.00 30.00
Priest Holmes
Larry Johnson
8 Jim Thorpe 300.00 450.00
Dutch Clark
Red Grange/50
9 LaDainian Tomlinson 10.00 25.00
Drew Brees
Antonio Gates
10 Bart Starr 40.00 80.00
Brett Favre
Aaron Rodgers

2007 Donruss Classics

This 271-card set was released in July, 2007. The set was issued into the hobby five-card packs, with a $6 SRP, which came 18 packs to a box. Cards numbered 1-100 feature active veterans sequenced in their 2006 team alphabetical order, while cards numbered 101-150 feature retired greats in first name alphabetical order which were issued to a stated print run of 999 serial numbered copies. The set concludes with Rookie Cards from 151-275 of which cards numbered 221-275 were signed by the player. The cards between 151-220 were issued to stated print runs of between 599 and 1499 serial numbered cards while the cards between 221 and 275 were issued to stated print runs of between 499 and 999 serial numbered cards. Cards numbers 102, 107, 119 and 132 were not made for this set.

COMP.SET w/o SP's (100) 7.50 20.00
LEGEND PRINT RUN 999 SER.#'d SETS
ROOKIE PRINT RUN 499-1499
1 Anquan Boldin .25 .60
2 Edgerrin James .25 .60
3 Larry Fitzgerald .30 .75
4 Matt Leinart .25 .60
5 Alge Crumpler .25 .60
6 Michael Vick .30 .75
7 Warrick Dunn .25 .60
8 Todd Heap .20 .50
9 Mark Clayton .25 .60
10 Steve McNair .25 .60
11 J.P. Losman .20 .50
12 Lee Evans .25 .60
13 Willis McGahee .25 .60
14 DeAngelo Williams .30 .75
15 Jake Delhomme .25 .60
16 Steve Smith .25 .60
17 Brian Urlacher .30 .75
18 Muhsin Muhammad .25 .60
19 Rex Grossman .25 .60
20 Thomas Jones .25 .60
21 Carson Palmer .25 .60
22 Chad Johnson .25 .60
23 Rudi Johnson .25 .60
24 T.J. Houshmandzadeh .25 .60
25 Braylon Edwards .25 .60
26 Charlie Frye .25 .60
27 Julius Jones .20 .50
28 Terrell Owens .30 .75
29 Tony Romo .40 1.00
30 Javon Walker .25 .60
31 Jay Cutler .30 .75
32 Mike Bell .25 .60
33 Jon Kitna .20 .50
34 Kevin Jones .20 .50
35 Roy Williams WR .25 .60
36 Brett Favre .60 1.50
37 Donald Driver .30 .75
38 Ahman Green .25 .60
39 Andre Johnson .25 .60
40 Matt Schaub .25 .60
41 Eric Moulds .25 .60
42 Joseph Addai .25 .60
43 Marvin Harrison .30 .75
44 Peyton Manning .50 1.25
45 Reggie Wayne .25 .60
46 Byron Leftwich .25 .60
47 Fred Taylor .25 .60
48 Maurice Jones-Drew .30 .75
49 Larry Johnson .20 .50
50 Tony Gonzalez .25 .60
51 Trent Green .25 .60
52 Chris Chambers .25 .60
53 Daunte Culpepper .25 .60
54 Ronnie Brown .25 .60
55 Chester Taylor .20 .50
56 Tarvaris Jackson .20 .50
57 Travis Taylor .20 .50
58 Tom Brady .50 1.25
59 Corey Dillon .25 .60
60 Laurence Maroney .25 .60
61 Deuce McAllister .25 .60
62 Drew Brees .30 .75
63 Marques Colston .30 .75
64 Reggie Bush .30 .75
65 Eli Manning .30 .75
66 Jeremy Shockey .25 .60
67 Plaxico Burress .25 .60
68 Chad Pennington .25 .60
69 Laveranues Coles .20 .50
70 Leon Washington .25 .60
71 LaMont Jordan .25 .60
72 Michael Huff .25 .60
73 Randy Moss .30 .75
74 Brian Westbrook .25 .60
75 Donovan McNabb .30 .75
76 Reggie Brown .20 .50
77 Ben Roethlisberger .30 .75
78 Hines Ward .30 .75
79 Willie Parker .25 .60
80 Antonio Gates .30 .75
81 LaDainian Tomlinson .30 .75
82 Philip Rivers .30 .75
83 Alex Smith QB .30 .75
84 Frank Gore .30 .75
85 Vernon Davis .25 .60
86 Darrell Jackson .20 .50
87 Matt Hasselbeck .25 .60
88 Shaun Alexander .25 .60
89 Marc Bulger .25 .60
90 Steven Jackson .30 .75
91 Torry Holt .25 .60
92 Bruce Gradkowski .20 .50
93 Cadillac Williams .25 .60
94 Joey Galloway .25 .60
95 Drew Bennett .20 .50
96 Vince Young .25 .60
97 Travis Henry .25 .60
98 Clinton Portis .25 .60
99 Jason Campbell .25 .60
100 Santana Moss .25 .60
101 Archie Manning 2.00 5.00
103 Bill Bates 1.50 4.00
104 Bob Hayes 2.50 6.00
105 Bob Lilly 1.50 4.00
106 Bobby Mitchell 1.50 4.00
108 Charley Taylor 1.50 4.00
109 Charlie Joiner 1.50 4.00
110 Cliff Harris 1.25 3.00
111 Cris Collinsworth 1.50 4.00
112 Dan Fouts 2.00 5.00
113 Daryle Lamonica 1.25 3.00
114 Dave Casper 1.50 4.00
115 Don Maynard 1.50 4.00
116 Earl Campbell 2.00 5.00
117 Forrest Gregg 1.25 3.00
118 Franco Harris 2.00 5.00
120 Gale Sayers 2.50 6.00
121 Gene Upshaw 1.25 3.00
122 George Blanda 1.50 4.00
123 Hugh McElhenny 1.50 4.00
124 Jack Youngblood 1.50 4.00
125 Boyd Dowler 1.25 3.00
126 Jan Stenerud 1.25 3.00
127 Jim McMahon 2.50 6.00
128 Harlon Hill 1.25 3.00
129 Joe Namath 2.50 6.00
130 Joe Theismann 2.00 5.00
131 John Mackey 1.50 4.00
133 Kellen Winslow 1.50 4.00
134 Ken Stabler 2.50 6.00
135 Lenny Moore 1.50 4.00
136 Lou Groza 1.50 4.00
137 Mark Duper 1.25 3.00
138 Michael Irvin 1.50 4.00
139 Paul Warfield 1.50 4.00
140 Randall Cunningham 1.50 4.00
141 Roger Craig 1.50 4.00
142 Ron Mix 1.25 3.00
143 Roosevelt Brown 1.25 3.00
144 Roosevelt Grier 1.25 3.00
145 Sam Huff 1.50 4.00
146 Sammy Baugh 2.00 5.00
147 Sterling Sharpe 1.50 4.00
148 Tim Brown 2.00 5.00
149 Y.A. Tittle 2.00 5.00
150 Yale Lary 1.25 3.00
151 JaMarcus Russell/599 RC 2.50 6.00
152 Brady Quinn/599 RC 4.00 10.00
153 Kevin Kolb/1499 RC 4.00 10.00
154 John Beck/1499 RC 2.50 6.00
155 Drew Stanton/1499 RC 1.50 4.00
156 Trent Edwards/1499 RC 2.50 6.00
157 Isaiah Stanback/1499 RC 1.50 4.00
158 Troy Smith/1499 RC 2.50 6.00
159 Adrian Peterson/599 RC 15.00 40.00
160 Marshawn Lynch/599 RC 4.00 10.00
161 Kenny Irons/599 RC 2.50 6.00
162 Chris Henry/599 RC 2.50 6.00
163 Brian Leonard/599 RC 3.00 8.00
164 Brandon Jackson/599 RC 3.00 8.00
165 Lorenzo Booker/599 RC 3.00 8.00
166 Tony Hunt/599 RC 2.50 6.00
167 Garrett Wolfe/599 RC 2.50 6.00
168 Michael Bush/599 RC 4.00 10.00
169 Antonio Pittman/1499 RC 1.50 4.00
170 Kolby Smith/1499 RC 2.00 5.00
171 DeShawn Wynn/1499 RC 2.00 5.00
172 Calvin Johnson/599 RC 12.00 30.00
173 Ted Ginn Jr.RC/599 RC 3.00 8.00
174 Dwayne Bowe/599 RC 5.00 12.00
175 Robert Meachem/599 RC 4.00 10.00
176 Craig Buster Davis/599 RC 3.00 8.00
177 Anthony Gonzalez/599 RC 4.00 10.00
178 Sidney Rice/1499 RC 3.00 8.00
179 Dwayne Jarrett/1499 RC 2.00 5.00
180 Steve Smith USC/1499 RC 2.50 6.00
181 Jacoby Jones/1499 RC 2.50 6.00
182 Yamon Figurs/1499 RC 1.50 4.00
183 Laurent Robinson/1499 RC 2.50 6.00
184 Jason Hill/1499 RC 2.50 6.00
185 James Jones/1499 RC 2.50 6.00
186 Mike Walker/1499 RC 2.50 6.00
187 Paul Williams/1499 RC 1.50 4.00
188 Johnnie Lee Higgins/1499 RC 2.00 5.00
189 Chris Davis/1499 RC 1.50 4.00
190 Aundrae Allison/1499 RC 1.50 4.00
191 David Clowney/1499 RC 2.00 5.00
192 Courtney Taylor/1499 RC 2.00 5.00
193 Dallas Baker/1499 RC 1.50 4.00
194 Greg Olsen/1499 RC 2.00 5.00
195 Zach Miller/1499 RC 2.50 6.00
196 Amobi Okoye/1499 RC 2.50 6.00
197 Alan Branch/1499 RC 2.00 5.00
198 Gaines Adams/1499 RC 2.50 6.00
199 Jamaal Anderson/1499 RC 2.00 5.00
200 Adam Carriker/1499 RC 2.00 5.00
201 Jarvis Moss/1499 RC 2.00 5.00
202 Anthony Spencer/1499 RC 2.50 6.00
203 LaMarr Woodley/1499 RC 2.50 6.00
204 Tim Crowder/1499 RC 2.50 6.00
205 Victor Abiamiri/1499 RC 2.50 6.00
206 Patrick Willis/1499 RC 5.00 12.00
207 David Harris/1499 RC 2.00 5.00
208 Lawrence Timmons/1499 RC 2.50 6.00
209 Jon Beason/1499 RC 2.00 5.00
210 Paul Posluszny/1499 RC 2.50 6.00
211 Leon Hall/1499 RC 2.00 5.00
212 Aaron Ross/1499 RC 2.50 6.00
213 Chris Houston/1499 RC 2.00 5.00
214 Eric Wright/1499 RC 2.50 6.00
215 Josh Wilson/1499 RC 2.00 5.00
216 LaRon Landry/1499 RC 2.50 6.00
217 Michael Griffin/1499 RC 2.50 6.00
218 Reggie Nelson/1499 RC 2.00 5.00
219 Brandon Meriweather/1499 RC 2.50 6.00
220 Sabby Piscitelli/1499 RC 2.50 6.00
221 Jordan Palmer AU/499 RC 6.00 15.00
222 Jon Cornish AU/999 RC 4.00 10.00
223 Jared Zabransky AU/499 RC 6.00 15.00
224 Jarrett Hicks AU/999 RC 4.00 10.00
225 Kenneth Darby AU/499 RC 6.00 15.00
226 Steve Breaston AU/499 RC 8.00 20.00
227 Matt Spaeth AU/499 RC 8.00 20.00
228 Stewart Bradley AU/499 RC 6.00 15.00
229 Tymere Zimmerman AU/999 RC 4.00 10.00
230 Kenny Scott AU/999 RC 3.00 8.00
231 Chris Leak AU/499 RC 6.00 15.00
232 Ronnie McGill AU/999 RC 4.00 10.00
234 Syndric Steptoe AU/499 RC 6.00 15.00
236 Chansi Stuckey AU/499 RC 8.00 20.00
237 Nate Ilaoa AU/499 RC 6.00 15.00
239 Aaron Fairooz AU/999 RC 4.00 10.00
240 Jeff Rowe AU/499 RC 5.00 12.00
241 Rhema McKnight AU/999 RC 3.00 8.00
242 Danny Ware AU/999 RC 5.00 12.00
243 Tyler Palko AU/999 RC 4.00 10.00
244 Syvelle Newton AU/999 RC 4.00 10.00
245 Michael Okwo AU/499 RC 6.00 15.00
246 Brandon Siler AU/999 RC 3.00 8.00
247 Ryan McBean AU/999 RC 5.00 12.00
248 Ray McDonald AU/499 RC 6.00 15.00
249 David Ball AU/999 RC 4.00 10.00
250 Alonzo Coleman AU/999 RC 4.00 10.00
251 H.B. Blades AU/999 RC 3.00 8.00
252 Thomas Clayton AU/499 RC 6.00 15.00
253 Darius Walker AU/499 RC 5.00 12.00
255 Dwayne Wright AU/499 RC 6.00 15.00
256 Rufus Alexander AU/999 RC 4.00 10.00
257 Gary Russell AU/999 RC 4.00 10.00
258 Aaron Rouse AU/499 RC 6.00 15.00
259 Joel Filani AU/499 RC 6.00 15.00
260 Zak DeOssie AU/999 RC 4.00 10.00
261 Scott Chandler AU/499 RC 8.00 20.00
263 Tim Shaw AU/999 RC 4.00 10.00
264 Jemalle Cornelius AU/999 RC 4.00 10.00
265 Ahmad Bradshaw AU/499 RC 12.00 30.00
266 Earl Everett AU/999 RC 4.00 10.00
267 D'Juan Woods AU/999 RC 3.00 8.00
268 Toby Korrodi AU/999 RC 4.00 10.00
269 Ryne Robinson AU/499 RC 6.00 15.00
270 Selvin Young AU/999 RC 4.00 10.00
271 Marcus McCauley AU/499 RC 6.00 15.00
272 Daymeion Hughes AU/499 RC 6.00 15.00
273 A.J. Davis AU/999 RC 3.00 8.00
274 David Irons AU/999 RC 3.00 8.00
275 Josh Gattis AU/999 RC 3.00 8.00

2007 Donruss Classics Timeless Tributes Bronze

*VETERANS 1-100: 4X TO 10X BASIC CARDS
*LEGENDS 101-150: 1X TO 2.5X BASIC CARDS
COMMON ROOKIE (151-275) 4.00 10.00
ROOKIE SEMISTARS 5.00 12.00
ROOKIE UNL.STARS 6.00 15.00
STATED PRINT RUN 100 SER.#'d SETS
151 JaMarcus Russell 4.00 10.00
152 Brady Quinn 6.00 15.00
153 Kevin Kolb 10.00 25.00
156 Trent Edwards 6.00 15.00
158 Troy Smith 6.00 15.00
159 Adrian Peterson 25.00 60.00
160 Marshawn Lynch 6.00 15.00
164 Brandon Jackson 5.00 12.00
168 Michael Bush 6.00 15.00
169 Antonio Pittman 4.00 10.00
170 Kolby Smith 5.00 12.00
171 DeShawn Wynn 5.00 12.00
172 Calvin Johnson 20.00 50.00
173 Ted Ginn Jr. 5.00 12.00
174 Dwayne Bowe 8.00 20.00
177 Anthony Gonzalez 6.00 15.00
178 Sidney Rice 8.00 20.00
180 Steve Smith USC 6.00 15.00
181 Jacoby Jones 6.00 15.00
194 Greg Olsen 5.00 12.00
199 Jamaal Anderson 5.00 12.00
200 Adam Carriker 5.00 12.00
206 Patrick Willis 12.00 30.00
208 Lawrence Timmons 6.00 15.00
210 Paul Posluszny 6.00 15.00
216 LaRon Landry 6.00 15.00
218 Reggie Nelson 5.00 12.00
223 Jared Zabransky 5.00 12.00
231 Chris Leak 5.00 12.00

2007 Donruss Classics Timeless Tributes Gold

*VETS 1-100: 8X TO 20X BASIC CARDS
*LEGENDS 101-150: 2X TO 5X BASIC CARDS
*ROOKIES: .6X TO 1.5X TRIBUTE BRONZE
STATED PRINT RUN 25 SER.#'d SETS

2007 Donruss Classics Timeless Tributes Platinum

*VETS 1-100: 12X TO 30X BASIC CARDS
*LEGENDS 101-150: 3X TO 8X BASIC CARDS
*ROOKIES: 1X TO 2.5X TRIBUTE BRONZE
STATED PRINT RUN 10 SER.#'d SETS

2007 Donruss Classics Timeless Tributes Silver

*VETS 1-100: 6X TO 15X BASIC CARDS
*LEGENDS 101-150: 1.5X TO 4X BASIC CARDS
*ROOKIES: .5X TO 1.2X TRIBUTE BRONZE
STATED PRINT RUN 50 SER.#'d SETS

2007 Donruss Classics Classic Combos Bronze

BRONZE PRINT RUN 1000 SER.#'d SETS
*GOLD/100: .8X TO 2X BRONZE/1000
GOLD PRINT RUN 100 SER.#'d SETS
*PLATINUM/25: 1.5X TO 4X BRONZE/1000
PLATINUM PRINT RUN 25 SER.#'d SETS
*SILVER/250: .6X TO 1.5X BRONZE/1000
SILVER PRINT RUN 250 SER.#'d SETS
1 Deacon Jones 1.25 3.00
Jack Youngblood
2 Jim McMahon 3.00 8.00
Walter Payton
3 Joe Montana 3.00 8.00
Roger Craig
5 Len Dawson 1.50 4.00
Jan Stenerud
7 Dan Fouts 1.50 4.00
Kellen Winslow
8 Thurman Thomas 2.00 5.00
Jim Kelly
9 Joe Theismann 1.50 4.00
John Riggins
10 Dan Marino 3.00 8.00
Mark Duper
11 Troy Aikman 2.00 5.00
Michael Irvin
12 Terrell Davis 2.50 6.00
John Elway
13 Roger Staubach 3.00 8.00
Bob Hayes
14 Jerry Rice 2.50 6.00
Steve Young
15 Don Maynard 2.00 5.00
Joe Namath

2007 Donruss Classics Classic Combos Jerseys

STATED PRINT RUN 250 SER.#'d SETS
*PRIME/16-25: 1X TO 2.5X BASIC JSYs
PRIME PRINT RUN 16-25
1 Deacon Jones 6.00 15.00
Jack Youngblood
2 Jim McMahon 20.00 50.00
Walter Payton
3 Joe Montana 15.00 40.00
Roger Craig
5 Len Dawson 8.00 20.00
Jan Stenerud
7 Dan Fouts 8.00 20.00
Kellen Winslow
8 Thurman Thomas 10.00 25.00
Jim Kelly
9 Joe Theismann 8.00 20.00
John Riggins
10 Dan Marino 15.00 40.00
Mark Duper
11 Troy Aikman 10.00 25.00
Michael Irvin
12 Terrell Davis 12.00 30.00
John Elway
13 Roger Staubach 12.00 30.00
Bob Hayes
14 Jerry Rice 12.00 30.00
Steve Young
15 Don Maynard 10.00 25.00
Joe Namath

2007 Donruss Classics Classic Quads Bronze

BRONZE PRINT RUN 250 SER.#'d SETS
*GOLD/25: .8X TO 2X BRONZE/250
GOLD PRINT RUN 25 SER.#'d SETS
*PLATINUM/10: 1.5X TO 4X BRONZE/250
PLATINUM PRINT RUN 10 SER.#'d SETS
*SILVER/50: .6X TO 1.5X BRONZE/250
SILVER PRINT RUN 50 SER.#'d SETS
1 Joe Montana 8.00 20.00
Sammy Baugh
Otto Graham
Johnny Unitas
2 Gale Sayers 8.00 20.00
Jim McMahon
Walter Payton
Mike Singletary
3 Dan Fouts 4.00 10.00
Ron Mix
Kellen Winslow
Lance Alworth
4 Troy Aikman 6.00 15.00
Michael Irvin
Bob Hayes
Roger Staubach
5 Johnny Unitas 8.00 20.00
Jerry Rice
Joe Montana
Raymond Berry
6 Dan Marino 8.00 20.00
Jerry Rice
Tim Brown
John Elway
7 Dan Marino 8.00 20.00
Fran Tarkenton
Brett Favre
John Elway
8 Ozzie Newsome 5.00 12.00
Lou Groza
Jim Brown
Paul Warfield
10 Jim Kelly 5.00 12.00
Michael Irvin
Thurman Thomas
Troy Aikman

2007 Donruss Classics Classic Quads Jerseys

STATED PRINT RUN 100 SER.#'d SETS
*PRIME/20-25: .8X TO 2X BASIC JSYs
PRIME PRINT RUN 5-25
1 Joe Montana 75.00 150.00
Sammy Baugh
Otto Graham
Johnny Unitas
2 Gale Sayers 40.00 100.00
Jim McMahon
Walter Payton
Mike Singletary
3 Dan Fouts 25.00 50.00
Ron Mix
Kellen Winslow
Lance Alworth
4 Troy Aikman 40.00 80.00
Michael Irvin
Bob Hayes
Roger Staubach
5 Johnny Unitas 50.00 100.00
Jerry Rice
Joe Montana
Raymond Berry
6 Dan Marino 50.00 100.00
Jerry Rice
Tim Brown
John Elway
7 Dan Marino 50.00 100.00
Fran Tarkenton
Brett Favre
John Elway
8 Ozzie Newsome/85 30.00 60.00
Lou Groza
Jim Brown
Paul Warfield
10 Jim Kelly 25.00 50.00
Michael Irvin
Thurman Thomas
Troy Aikman

2007 Donruss Classics Classic Singles Bronze

BRONZE PRINT RUN 1000 SER.#'d SETS
*GOLD/100: .8X TO 2X BRONZE/1000
GOLD PRINT RUN 100 SER.#'d SETS
*PLATINUM/25: 1.2X TO 3X BRONZE/1000
PLATINUM PRINT RUN 25 SER.#'d SETS
*SILVER/250: .6X TO 1.5X BRONZE/1000
SILVER PRINT RUN 250 SER.#'d SETS
1 Bob Lilly 1.25 3.00
2 Charlie Joiner 1.25 3.00
3 Earl Campbell 1.50 4.00
5 Gale Sayers 2.00 5.00
6 Joe Theismann 1.50 4.00
7 Ken Stabler 2.00 5.00
8 Larry Csonka 1.50 4.00
9 Lawrence Taylor 1.50 4.00
10 Marcus Allen 1.50 4.00
11 Mike Singletary 1.50 4.00
12 Randall Cunningham 1.25 3.00
13 Thurman Thomas 1.25 3.00
14 Barry Sanders 2.50 6.00
15 Bo Jackson 2.00 5.00
16 Dan Marino 3.00 8.00
17 Deacon Jones 1.25 3.00
18 Fran Tarkenton 2.00 5.00
19 Jerry Rice 2.50 6.00
20 Jim Kelly 2.00 5.00
21 John Riggins 1.25 3.00
22 Len Dawson 1.50 4.00
23 Ronnie Lott 1.25 3.00
24 Steve Young 2.00 5.00
25 Terrell Davis 1.50 4.00
26 Troy Aikman 2.00 5.00
27 Walter Payton 3.00 8.00
28 Johnny Unitas 2.50 6.00
29 Lance Alworth 1.25 3.00
30 Lenny Moore 1.25 3.00

2007 Donruss Classics Classic Singles Jerseys

STATED PRINT RUN 250 SER.#'d SETS
*PRIME/25: 1X TO 2.5X BASIC JSYs
PRIME PRINT RUN 2-25
*JSY.NUM./50-80: .6X TO 1.5X BASIC JSYs
*JSY.NUM./30-44: .8X TO 2X BASIC JSYs
*JSY.NUM./20-24: 1X TO 2.5X BASIC JSYs
JERSEY NUMBER PRINT RUN 7-80
1 Bob Lilly/250 6.00 15.00
2 Charlie Joiner/250 6.00 15.00
3 Earl Campbell/250 8.00 20.00
5 Gale Sayers/125 10.00 25.00
6 Joe Theismann/250 8.00 20.00
7 Ken Stabler/150 10.00 25.00
8 Larry Csonka/250 8.00 20.00
9 Lawrence Taylor/250 8.00 20.00
10 Marcus Allen/250 8.00 20.00
11 Mike Singletary/250 8.00 20.00
12 Randall Cunningham/250 6.00 15.00
13 Thurman Thomas/175 6.00 15.00
14 Barry Sanders/250 12.00 30.00
15 Bo Jackson/250 10.00 25.00
16 Dan Marino/250 15.00 40.00
17 Deacon Jones/120 6.00 15.00
18 Fran Tarkenton/250 10.00 25.00
19 Jerry Rice/250 12.00 30.00
20 Jim Kelly/250 10.00 25.00
21 John Riggins/250 6.00 15.00
22 Len Dawson/175 8.00 20.00
23 Ronnie Lott/250 6.00 15.00
24 Steve Young/250 10.00 25.00
25 Terrell Davis/175 8.00 20.00
26 Troy Aikman/250 10.00 25.00
27 Walter Payton/175 15.00 40.00
28 Johnny Unitas/175 15.00 40.00
29 Lance Alworth/175 8.00 20.00
30 Lenny Moore/250 6.00 15.00

2007 Donruss Classics Classic Triples Bronze

BRONZE PRINT RUN 500 SER.#'d SETS
*GOLD/50: .6X TO 1.5X BRONZE/500
GOLD PRINT RUN 50 SER.#'d SETS
*PLATINUM/10: 1X TO 2.5X BRONZE/500
PLATINUM PRINT RUN 10 SER.#'d SETS
*SILVER/250: .5X TO 1.2X BRONZE/500
SILVER PRINT RUN 250 SER.#'d SETS
1 Jim Brown 4.00 10.00
Lou Groza
Otto Graham
2 Bob Lilly 5.00 12.00
Bob Hayes
Roger Staubach
3 Joe Montana 6.00 15.00
Jerry Rice
Roger Craig
4 Jim McMahon 6.00 15.00
Walter Payton
Mike Singletary
7 Dan Fouts 3.00 8.00
Kellen Winslow
Lance Alworth
8 Johnny Unitas 6.00 15.00
Raymond Berry
Lenny Moore
9 Troy Aikman 5.00 12.00
John Elway
Steve Young
10 Deacon Jones 2.50 6.00
Jack Youngblood
Bob Lilly

2007 Donruss Classics Classic Triples Jerseys

STATED PRINT RUN 250 SER.#'d SETS
*PRIME/16-25: .8X TO 2X BASIC JSYs
PRIME PRINT RUN 2-25
1 Jim Brown 15.00 40.00
Lou Groza
Otto Graham
2 Bob Lilly 20.00 50.00
Bob Hayes
Roger Staubach
3 Joe Montana 25.00 60.00
Jerry Rice
Roger Craig
4 Jim McMahon 25.00 60.00
Walter Payton
Mike Singletary
7 Dan Fouts 12.00 30.00
Kellen Winslow
Lance Alworth
8 Johnny Unitas 20.00 50.00
Raymond Berry
Lenny Moore
9 Troy Aikman 20.00 50.00
John Elway
Steve Young
10 Deacon Jones 10.00 25.00
Jack Youngblood
Bob Lilly

2007 Donruss Classics Legendary Players Bronze

BRONZE PRINT RUN 1000 SER.#'d SETS
*GOLD/100: .8X TO 2X BRONZE/1000
GOLD PRINT RUN 100 SER.#'d SETS
*PLATINUM/25: 1.2X TO 3X BRONZE/1000
PLATINUM PRINT RUN 25 SER.#'d SETS
*SILVER/250: .6X TO 1.5X BRONZE/1000
SILVER PRINT RUN 250 SER.#'d SETS
2 Bill Bates 1.25 3.00
3 Bob Hayes 2.00 5.00
4 Cris Collinsworth 1.25 3.00
5 Dan Fouts 1.50 4.00
6 Forrest Gregg 1.00 2.50
7 Franco Harris 1.50 4.00
8 Jack Youngblood 1.25 3.00
9 Jan Stenerud 1.00 2.50
10 Jim McMahon 2.00 5.00
11 Joe Namath 2.00 5.00
12 John Hannah 1.00 2.50
14 Lou Groza 1.25 3.00
15 Mark Duper 1.00 2.50
16 Michael Irvin 1.25 3.00
17 Randall Cunningham 1.25 3.00
18 Roger Craig 1.25 3.00
19 Sterling Sharpe 1.25 3.00
20 Tim Brown 1.50 4.00
21 Sammy Baugh 1.50 4.00
22 Y.A. Tittle 1.50 4.00
23 Sam Huff 1.25 3.00
24 Ron Mix 1.00 2.50
25 Roosevelt Brown 1.00 2.50
26 Kellen Winslow 1.25 3.00
27 Joe Montana 3.00 8.00
28 John Elway 2.50 6.00
29 Jim Brown 2.00 5.00
30 Roger Staubach 2.50 6.00

2007 Donruss Classics Legendary Players Jerseys

STATED PRINT RUN 250 SER.#'d SETS
*PRIME/25: 1X TO 2.5X BASIC JSYs
PRIME PRINT RUN 25 SER.#'d SETS
*TEAM LOGO/70-88: .6X TO 1.5X BASIC JSYs
*TEAM LOGO/32-40: .8X TO 2X BASIC JSYs
*TEAM LOGO/22: 1X TO 2.5X BASIC JSYs
TEAM LOGO PRINT RUN 3-88
2 Bill Bates 5.00 12.00
3 Bob Hayes 10.00 25.00
4 Cris Collinsworth 5.00 12.00
5 Dan Fouts 6.00 15.00
6 Forrest Gregg 4.00 10.00
7 Franco Harris/185 6.00 15.00
8 Jack Youngblood 5.00 12.00
9 Jan Stenerud 4.00 10.00
10 Jim McMahon/175 8.00 20.00
11 Joe Namath/175 8.00 20.00
12 John Hannah 5.00 12.00
14 Lou Groza/175 8.00 20.00
15 Mark Duper 4.00 10.00
16 Michael Irvin 5.00 12.00
17 Randall Cunningham 5.00 12.00
18 Roger Craig/175 5.00 12.00
19 Sterling Sharpe 5.00 12.00
20 Tim Brown 6.00 15.00
21 Sammy Baugh/175 30.00 60.00
22 Y.A. Tittle 8.00 20.00
23 Sam Huff 5.00 12.00
24 Ron Mix 4.00 10.00
25 Roosevelt Brown 4.00 10.00
26 Kellen Winslow/175 5.00 12.00
27 Joe Montana 12.00 30.00
28 John Elway 10.00 25.00
29 Jim Brown 8.00 20.00
30 Roger Staubach/175 10.00 25.00

2007 Donruss Classics Membership Bronze

BRONZE PRINT RUN 1000 SER.#'d SETS
*GOLD/100: .6X TO 1.5X BRONZE/1000
GOLD PRINT RUN 100 SER.#'d SETS
*PLATINUM/25: 1.2X TO 3X BRONZE/1000
PLATINUM PRINT RUN 25 SER.#'d SETS
*SILVER/250: .5X TO 1.2X BRONZE/1000
SILVER PRINT RUN 250 SER.#'d SETS
1 Alex Smith QB 1.00 2.50
2 Leon Washington .75 2.00
3 Reggie Bush 1.00 2.50
4 Joseph Addai .75 2.00
5 Marques Colston 1.00 2.50
6 Cadillac Williams .75 2.00
7 Ronnie Brown .75 2.00
8 Vince Young .75 2.00
9 Laurence Maroney .75 2.00
10 Jerious Norwood .75 2.00
11 Mike Bell .75 2.00
12 Vernon Davis .75 2.00
13 Maurice Jones-Drew 1.00 2.50
14 Jay Cutler 1.00 2.50
15 DeAngelo Williams 1.00 2.50
16 Matt Leinart .75 2.00
17 Sinorice Moss .75 2.00
18 LenDale White .75 2.00
19 Devin Hester 1.00 2.50
20 Santonio Holmes .75 2.00

2007 Donruss Classics Membership VIP Jerseys

JERSEY PRINT RUN 170-250
*PRIME/20-25: 1X TO 2.5X BASIC JSYs
PRIME PRINT RUN 6-25
*TEAM LOGO/83-85: .6X TO 1.5X BASIC JSYs
*TEAM LOGO/32-39: .8X TO 2X BASIC JSYs
*TEAM LOGO/20-29: 1X TO 2.5X BASIC JSYs
TEAM LOGO PRINT RUN 6-85
1 Alex Smith QB 4.00 10.00
2 Leon Washington 3.00 8.00
3 Reggie Bush/170 4.00 10.00
4 Joseph Addai 3.00 8.00
5 Marques Colston 4.00 10.00
6 Cadillac Williams 3.00 8.00
7 Ronnie Brown 3.00 8.00
8 Vince Young 3.00 8.00
9 Laurence Maroney 3.00 8.00
10 Jerious Norwood 3.00 8.00
11 Mike Bell 3.00 8.00
12 Vernon Davis 3.00 8.00
13 Maurice Jones-Drew 4.00 10.00
14 Jay Cutler 4.00 10.00
15 DeAngelo Williams 4.00 10.00
16 Matt Leinart 3.00 8.00
17 Sinorice Moss 3.00 8.00
18 LenDale White 3.00 8.00
19 Devin Hester 4.00 10.00
20 Santonio Holmes 3.00 8.00

2007 Donruss Classics Monday Night Heroes Bronze

BRONZE PRINT RUN 1000 SER.#'d SETS
*GOLD/100: .6X TO 1.5X BRONZE/1000
GOLD PRINT RUN 100 SER.#'d SETS
*PLATINUM/25: 1.2X TO 3X BRONZE/1000
PLATINUM PRINT RUN 25 SER.#'d SETS
*SILVER/250: .5X TO 1.2X BRONZE/1000
SILVER PRINT RUN 250 SER.#'d SETS
1 Chester Taylor .60 1.50
2 Fred Taylor .75 2.00
3 Donovan McNabb 1.00 2.50
4 Greg Lewis .60 1.50
5 Brett Favre 2.00 5.00

6 Matt Leinart .75 2.00
7 Anquan Boldin .75 2.00
8 Eli Manning 1.00 2.50
9 Tony Romo 1.25 3.00
10 Terrell Owens 1.00 2.50
11 Tiki Barber 1.00 2.50
12 Plaxico Burress .75 2.00
13 Tom Brady 1.50 4.00
14 Ben Watson .60 1.50
15 Mewelde Moore .60 1.50
16 Deion Branch .75 2.00
17 Jake Delhomme .75 2.00
18 Steve Smith .75 2.00
19 Maurice Jones-Drew 1.00 2.50
20 Shaun Alexander .75 2.00
21 Donald Driver 1.00 2.50
22 Donte Stallworth .75 2.00
23 DeAngelo Williams 1.00 2.50
24 Steven Jackson 1.00 2.50
25 Marc Bulger .75 2.00
26 Thomas Jones .75 2.00
27 Peyton Manning 1.50 4.00
28 Marvin Harrison 1.00 2.50
29 Rudi Johnson .75 2.00
30 Brian Westbrook .75 2.00

2007 Donruss Classics Monday Night Heroes Jerseys

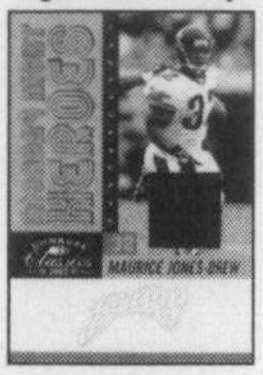

JERSEY STATED PRINT RUN 175-250
*PRIME/25: 1X TO 2.5X BASIC JSYs
PRIME PRINT RUN 25 SER.#'d SETS
UNPRICED PRIME AUTOS SER.#'d TO 10
*JSY.NUM/80-89: .6X TO 1.5X BASIC JSYs
*JSY.NUM/30-39: .8X TO 2X BASIC JSYs
*JSY.NUM/20-29: 1X TO 2.5X BASIC JSYs
JERSEY NUMBER PRINT RUN 4-89
1 Chester Taylor 2.50 6.00
2 Fred Taylor/240 3.00 8.00
3 Donovan McNabb 4.00 10.00
4 Greg Lewis 2.50 6.00
5 Brett Favre 8.00 20.00
6 Matt Leinart/200 3.00 8.00
7 Anquan Boldin 3.00 8.00
8 Eli Manning 4.00 10.00
9 Tony Romo 5.00 12.00
10 Terrell Owens 4.00 10.00
11 Tiki Barber 4.00 10.00
12 Plaxico Burress 3.00 8.00
13 Tom Brady 6.00 15.00
14 Ben Watson 2.50 6.00
15 Mewelde Moore 2.50 6.00
16 Deion Branch 3.00 8.00
17 Jake Delhomme 3.00 8.00
18 Steve Smith 3.00 8.00
19 Maurice Jones-Drew/225 4.00 10.00
20 Shaun Alexander 3.00 8.00
21 Donald Driver 4.00 10.00
22 Donte Stallworth 3.00 8.00
23 DeAngelo Williams 4.00 10.00
24 Steven Jackson/240 4.00 10.00
25 Marc Bulger 3.00 8.00
26 Thomas Jones 3.00 8.00
27 Peyton Manning 6.00 15.00
28 Marvin Harrison 4.00 10.00
29 Rudi Johnson 3.00 8.00
30 Brian Westbrook/175 3.00 8.00

2007 Donruss Classics Monday Night Heroes Jerseys Jersey Numbers Autographs

STATED PRINT RUN 4-39
1 Chester Taylor/29 15.00 30.00
2 Fred Taylor/28 12.50 25.00
11 Tiki Barber/21
23 DeAngelo Williams/34 20.00 40.00
24 Steven Jackson/39 20.00 40.00
29 Rudi Johnson/32
30 Brian Westbrook/36

2007 Donruss Classics Saturday Stars Bronze

BRONZE PRINT RUN 1000 SER.#'d SETS
*GOLD/100 .6X TO 1.5X BRONZE/1000
GOLD PRINT RUN 100 SER.#'d SETS
*PLATINUM/25: 1.2X TO 3X BRONZE/1000
PLATINUM PRINT RUN 25 SER.#'d SETS
*SILVER/250: .5X TO 1.2X BRONZE/1000
SILVER PRINT RUN 250 SER.#'d SETS
UNPRICED AUTO PRINT RUN 5
1 A.J. Hawk 1.00 2.50
2 Joseph Addai 1.00 2.50
3 Demetrius Williams .75 2.00
4 Marcedes Lewis .75 2.00
5 Jay Cutler 1.25 3.00
6 Matt Leinart 1.00 2.50
7 Reggie Bush 1.25 3.00
8 LenDale White 1.00 2.50
9 Laurence Maroney 1.00 2.50
10 Maurice Jones-Drew 1.25 3.00
11 Maurice Stovall .75 2.00
12 Travis Wilson .75 2.00
13 Mario Williams 1.00 2.50
14 Vince Young 1.00 2.50
15 Larry Fitzgerald 1.25 3.00
16 Devery Henderson .75 2.00
17 Andre Johnson 1.00 2.50
18 Santana Moss 1.00 2.50
19 Roger Staubach 2.50 6.00
20 Lawrence Taylor 1.50 4.00
21 Thurman Thomas 1.25 3.00
22 Steven Jackson 1.25 3.00
23 Frank Gore 1.25 3.00
24 Roy Williams WR 1.00 2.50
25 Marcus Allen 1.50 4.00
26 Julius Jones .75 2.00
27 Larry Csonka 1.50 4.00
28 Antonio Bryant .75 2.00
29 Sinorice Moss 1.00 2.50
30 Tony Dorsett 1.50 4.00

2007 Donruss Classics Saturday Stars Jerseys

JERSEY PRINT RUN 150-250
*PRIME/25: 1X TO 2.5X BASIC JSYs
PRIME PRINT RUN 25 SER.#'d SETS
UNPRICED PRIME AUTO PRINT RUN 1-10
*JSY.NUM/80-98: .6X TO 1.5X BASIC JSYs
*JSY.NUM/33-47: .8X TO 2X BASIC JSYs
*JSY.NUM/21-22: 1X TO 2.5X BASIC JSYs
JERSEY NUMBERS PRINT RUN 1-98
1 A.J. Hawk 4.00 10.00
2 Joseph Addai 4.00 10.00
3 Demetrius Williams 3.00 8.00
4 Marcedes Lewis 3.00 8.00
5 Jay Cutler 5.00 12.00
6 Matt Leinart 4.00 10.00
7 Reggie Bush 5.00 12.00
8 LenDale White 4.00 10.00
9 Laurence Maroney 4.00 10.00
10 Maurice Jones-Drew 5.00 12.00
11 Maurice Stovall 3.00 8.00
12 Travis Wilson 3.00 8.00
13 Mario Williams 4.00 10.00
14 Vince Young 4.00 10.00
15 Larry Fitzgerald 5.00 12.00
16 Devery Henderson 3.00 8.00
17 Andre Johnson 4.00 10.00
18 Santana Moss/185 4.00 10.00
19 Roger Staubach 12.00 30.00
20 Lawrence Taylor 8.00 20.00
21 Thurman Thomas 6.00 15.00
22 Steven Jackson/150 5.00 12.00
23 Frank Gore 5.00 12.00
24 Roy Williams WR 4.00 10.00
25 Marcus Allen 8.00 20.00
26 Julius Jones 6.00 15.00
27 Larry Csonka 8.00 20.00
28 Antonio Bryant 3.00 8.00
29 Sinorice Moss 4.00 10.00
30 Tony Dorsett 8.00 20.00

2007 Donruss Classics Saturday Stars Jerseys Jersey Numbers Autographs

STATED PRINT RUN 1-34
22 Steven Jackson/34 20.00 40.00
25 Marcus Allen/33 25.00 50.00

2007 Donruss Classics School Colors

1 Brady Quinn 12.00 30.00
2 JaMarcus Russell 2.00 5.00
3 Troy Smith 3.00 8.00
4 Adrian Peterson 12.00 30.00
5 Marshawn Lynch 3.00 8.00
6 Kenny Irons 5.00 12.00
7 Calvin Johnson 12.00 30.00
8 Ted Ginn Jr. 5.00 12.00
9 Dwayne Jarrett 4.00 10.00
10 Sidney Rice 6.00 15.00
11 Robert Meachem 3.00 8.00
12 Chris Leak 3.00 8.00
13 Craig Buster Davis 3.00 8.00
14 Darrelle Revis 5.00 12.00
15 Paul Posluszny 3.00 8.00
16 Reggie Nelson 3.00 8.00
17 Trent Edwards 3.00 8.00
18 Brandon Jackson 4.00 10.00
19 Paul Williams 3.00 8.00
20 Johnnie Lee Higgins 3.00 8.00
21 Jordan Palmer 4.00 10.00
22 Garrett Wolfe 4.00 10.00
23 Gary Russell 3.00 8.00
24 Steve Smith USC 3.00 8.00
25 Aaron Ross 3.00 8.00
26 Michael Bush 4.00 10.00
27 Tony Hunt 4.00 10.00
28 Drew Stanton 2.00 5.00
29 LaRon Landry 3.00 8.00
30 Lawrence Timmons 4.00 10.00

2007 Donruss Classics School Colors Autographs

STATED PRINT RUN 25 SER.#'d SETS
1 Brady Quinn 50.00 100.00
2 JaMarcus Russell 12.00 30.00
3 Troy Smith 20.00 50.00
4 Adrian Peterson 125.00 250.00
5 Marshawn Lynch 30.00 60.00
6 Kenny Irons 12.00 30.00
7 Calvin Johnson 75.00 150.00
8 Ted Ginn Jr. 15.00 40.00
9 Dwayne Jarrett 15.00 40.00
10 Sidney Rice 25.00 60.00
11 Robert Meachem 20.00 50.00
12 Chris Leak 15.00 40.00
13 Craig Buster Davis 15.00 40.00
14 Darrelle Revis 30.00 80.00
15 Paul Posluszny 20.00 50.00
16 Reggie Nelson 15.00 40.00
17 Trent Edwards 20.00 50.00
18 Brandon Jackson 15.00 40.00
19 Paul Williams 12.00 30.00
20 Johnnie Lee Higgins 15.00 40.00
21 Jordan Palmer 15.00 40.00
22 Garrett Wolfe 12.00 30.00
23 Gary Russell 15.00 40.00
24 Steve Smith USC 20.00 50.00
25 Aaron Ross 20.00 50.00
26 Michael Bush 20.00 50.00
27 Tony Hunt 12.00 30.00
28 Drew Stanton 12.00 30.00
29 LaRon Landry 20.00 50.00
30 Lawrence Timmons 20.00 50.00

2007 Donruss Classics Significant Signatures Gold

GOLD PRINT RUN 10-100
1 Anquan Boldin/25 12.00 30.00
10 Steve McNair/50 15.00 40.00
49 Larry Johnson/25 15.00 40.00
54 Ronnie Brown/25 15.00 40.00
90 Steven Jackson/100 15.00 30.00
103 Bill Bates/100 25.00 50.00
105 Bob Lilly/25 12.00 30.00
109 Charlie Joiner/25
110 Cliff Harris/100 20.00 40.00
112 Dan Fouts/100 20.00 40.00
113 Daryle Lamonica/25 15.00 40.00
114 Dave Casper/100 15.00 30.00
115 Don Maynard/25 12.00 30.00
120 Gale Sayers/25 30.00 60.00
123 Hugh McElhenny/100 12.50 30.00
124 Jack Youngblood/25 15.00 40.00
125 Boyd Dowler/100 15.00 40.00
127 Jim McMahon/50 25.00 50.00
128 Harlon Hill/100 12.50 30.00
131 John Mackey/100 12.50 30.00
135 Lenny Moore/25 15.00 40.00
139 Paul Warfield/75 12.00 30.00
141 Roger Craig/25 25.00 50.00
144 Rosey Grier/100 12.50 30.00
147 Sterling Sharpe/25
150 Yale Lary/25 12.00 30.00
151 JaMarcus Russell 20.00 50.00
152 Brady Quinn 25.00 60.00
153 Kevin Kolb 20.00 50.00
154 John Beck 12.00 30.00
155 Drew Stanton 8.00 20.00
156 Trent Edwards 12.00 30.00
157 Isaiah Stanback 8.00 20.00
158 Troy Smith 12.00 30.00
159 Adrian Peterson 100.00 200.00
160 Marshawn Lynch 25.00 50.00
161 Kenny Irons 8.00 20.00
162 Chris Henry 8.00 20.00
163 Brian Leonard 10.00 25.00
164 Brandon Jackson 10.00 25.00
165 Lorenzo Booker 10.00 25.00
166 Tony Hunt 8.00 20.00
167 Garrett Wolfe 8.00 20.00
168 Michael Bush 12.00 30.00
169 Antonio Pittman 8.00 20.00
170 Kolby Smith 10.00 25.00
171 DeShawn Wynn 10.00 25.00
172 Calvin Johnson 60.00 120.00
173 Ted Ginn Jr. 20.00 50.00
174 Dwayne Bowe 30.00 60.00
175 Robert Meachem 12.00 30.00
177 Anthony Gonzalez 12.00 30.00
178 Sidney Rice 15.00 40.00
179 Dwayne Jarrett 10.00 25.00
180 Steve Smith USC 12.00 30.00
181 Jacoby Jones 12.00 30.00
182 Yamon Figurs 8.00 20.00
183 Laurent Robinson 12.00 30.00
184 Jason Hill 12.00 30.00
185 James Jones 12.00 30.00
186 Mike Walker 12.00 30.00
187 Paul Williams 8.00 20.00
188 Johnnie Lee Higgins 10.00 25.00
189 Chris Davis 8.00 20.00
190 Aundrae Allison 8.00 20.00
191 David Clowney 10.00 25.00
193 Dallas Baker 8.00 20.00
194 Greg Olsen 10.00 25.00
195 Zach Miller 12.00 30.00
196 Amobi Okoye 12.00 30.00
198 Gaines Adams 12.00 30.00
199 Jamaal Anderson 10.00 25.00
200 Adam Carriker 10.00 25.00
202 Anthony Spencer 12.00 30.00
203 LaMarr Woodley 12.00 30.00
204 Tim Crowder 12.00 30.00
205 Victor Abiamiri 12.00 30.00
206 Patrick Willis 20.00 50.00
207 David Harris 10.00 25.00
208 Lawrence Timmons 12.00 30.00
209 Jon Beason 10.00 25.00
210 Paul Posluszny 12.00 30.00
211 Leon Hall 10.00 25.00
212 Aaron Ross 12.00 30.00
213 Chris Houston 10.00 25.00
215 Josh Wilson 10.00 25.00
216 LaRon Landry 12.00 30.00
217 Michael Griffin 12.00 30.00
218 Reggie Nelson 10.00 25.00
219 Brandon Meriweather 12.00 30.00
220 Sabby Piscitelli 12.00 30.00

2007 Donruss Classics Significant Signatures Platinum

*PLATINUM ROOKIES/25: .6X TO 1.5X GOLD
PLATINUM PRINT RUN 5-25
SER.#'d UNDER 25 NOT PRICED
151 JaMarcus Russell 40.00 100.00
152 Brady Quinn 50.00 120.00
159 Adrian Peterson 200.00 400.00
172 Calvin Johnson 125.00 250.00

2007 Donruss Classics Sunday's Best Bronze

BRONZE PRINT RUN 1000 SER.#'d SETS
*GOLD/100: .6X TO 1.5X BRONZE/1000
GOLD PRINT RUN 100 SER.#'d SETS
*PLATINUM/25: 1.2X TO 3X BRONZE/1000
PLATINUM PRINT RUN 25 SER.#'d SETS
*SILVER/250: .5X TO 1.2X BRONZE/1000
SILVER PRINT RUN 250 SER.#'d SETS
1 LaDainian Tomlinson 1.00 2.50
2 Drew Brees 1.00 2.50
3 Michael Vick 1.00 2.50
4 Frank Gore 1.00 2.50
5 Carson Palmer .75 2.00
6 Willie Parker .75 2.00
7 T.J. Houshmandzadeh .75 2.00
8 Alge Crumpler .75 2.00
9 Tony Gonzalez .75 2.00
10 Larry Fitzgerald 1.00 2.50
11 Roy Williams WR .75 2.00
12 Reggie Wayne .75 2.00
13 Muhsin Muhammad .75 2.00
14 Steve McNair .75 2.00
15 Larry Johnson .60 1.50
16 Mark Clayton .75 2.00
17 Philip Rivers 1.00 2.50
18 Deuce McAllister .75 2.00
19 Darrell Jackson .60 1.50
20 Tatum Bell .60 1.50
21 Joe Horn .75 2.00
22 Chris Chambers .75 2.00
23 Santana Moss .75 2.00
24 Laveranues Coles .60 1.50
25 Chad Pennington .75 2.00
26 Andre Johnson .75 2.00
27 Trent Green .75 2.00
28 Randy McMichael .60 1.50
29 Ben Roethlisberger 1.00 2.50
30 Rex Grossman .75 2.00
31 Torry Holt .75 2.00
32 Jerricho Cotchery .75 2.00
33 Matt Hasselbeck .75 2.00
34 Julius Jones .60 1.50
35 Todd Heap .60 1.50
36 Javon Walker .75 2.00
37 Willis McGahee .75 2.00
38 Chad Johnson .75 2.00
39 Hines Ward 1.00 2.50
40 Ahman Green .75 2.00

2007 Donruss Classics Sunday's Best Jerseys

JERSEY PRINT RUN 45-250
*PRIME/25: 1X TO 2.5X BASIC JSYs
PRIME PRINT RUN 25 SER.#'d SETS
UNPRICED PRIME AUTOS PRINT RUN 10
*JSY.NUM/80-89: .6X TO 1.5X BASIC JSYs
*JSY.NUM/30-39: .8X TO 2X BASIC JSYs
*JSY.NUM/21-27: 1X TO 2.5X BASIC JSYs
JERSEY NUMBERS PRINT RUN 7-89
1 LaDainian Tomlinson 4.00 10.00
2 Drew Brees 4.00 10.00
3 Michael Vick 4.00 10.00
4 Frank Gore/188 4.00 10.00
5 Carson Palmer 3.00 8.00
6 Willie Parker 3.00 8.00
7 T.J. Houshmandzadeh 3.00 8.00
8 Alge Crumpler 3.00 8.00
9 Tony Gonzalez 3.00 8.00
10 Larry Fitzgerald 4.00 10.00
11 Roy Williams WR 3.00 8.00
12 Reggie Wayne/180 3.00 8.00
13 Muhsin Muhammad 3.00 8.00
14 Steve McNair 3.00 8.00
15 Larry Johnson 2.50 6.00
16 Mark Clayton 3.00 8.00
17 Philip Rivers/240 4.00 10.00
18 Deuce McAllister 3.00 8.00
19 Darrell Jackson 2.50 6.00
20 Tatum Bell 2.50 6.00
21 Joe Horn 3.00 8.00
22 Chris Chambers 3.00 8.00
23 Santana Moss 3.00 8.00
24 Laveranues Coles 2.50 6.00
25 Chad Pennington 3.00 8.00
26 Andre Johnson 3.00 8.00
27 Trent Green 3.00 8.00
28 Randy McMichael/45 3.00 8.00
29 Ben Roethlisberger 4.00 10.00
30 Rex Grossman 3.00 8.00
31 Torry Holt 3.00 8.00
32 Jerricho Cotchery 3.00 8.00
33 Matt Hasselbeck 3.00 8.00
34 Julius Jones 2.50 6.00
35 Todd Heap 2.50 6.00
36 Javon Walker 3.00 8.00
37 Willis McGahee 3.00 8.00
38 Chad Johnson 3.00 8.00
39 Hines Ward 4.00 10.00
40 Ahman Green 3.00 8.00

2007 Donruss Classics Sunday's Best Jerseys Jersey Numbers Autographs

STATED PRINT RUN 7-89
1 LaDainian Tomlinson/21 50.00 100.00
4 Frank Gore/21
6 Willie Parker/39 20.00 40.00
7 T.J. Houshmandzadeh/84 12.00 30.00
15 Larry Johnson/27 20.00 50.00
18 Deuce McAllister/26
32 Jerricho Cotchery/89 10.00 25.00

2007 Donruss Classics Timeless Triples Bronze

BRONZE PRINT RUN 1000 SER.#'d SETS
*GOLD/100: .6X TO 1.5X BRONZE/1000
GOLD PRINT RUN 100 SER.#'d SETS
*PLATINUM/25: 1X TO 2.5X BRONZE/1000
PLATINUM PRINT RUN 25 SER.#'d SETS
*SILVER/250: .5X TO 1.2X BRONZE/1000
SILVER PRINT RUN 250 SER.#'d SETS
1 Terrell Owens 2.50 6.00
Tony Romo
Terry Glenn
2 Antonio Gates 2.00 5.00
Philip Rivers
LaDainian Tomlinson
3 Javon Walker 2.00 5.00
Mike Bell
Jay Cutler
4 Drew Brees 2.00 5.00
Deuce McAllister
Reggie Bush
5 Willie Parker 2.00 5.00
Hines Ward
Ben Roethlisberger
6 T.J. Houshmandzadeh 1.50 4.00
Carson Palmer
Chad Johnson
7 Donald Driver 1.50 4.00
Brett Favre
AJ Hawk
8 Trent Green 1.50 4.00
Larry Johnson
Tony Gonzalez
9 Tom Brady 3.00 8.00
Corey Dillon
Laurence Maroney
10 Peyton Manning 3.00 8.00
Reggie Wayne
Marvin Harrison

2007 Donruss Classics Timeless Triples Jerseys

JERSEY PRINT RUN 250 SER.#'d SETS
*PRIME/25: .8X TO 2X BASIC JSYs
PRIME PRINT RUN 25 SER.#'d SETS
1 Terrell Owens 15.00 40.00
Tony Romo
Terry Glenn
2 Antonio Gates 8.00 20.00
Philip Rivers
LaDainian Tomlinson
3 Javon Walker 6.00 15.00
Mike Bell
Jay Cutler
4 Drew Brees 12.00 30.00
Deuce McAllister
Reggie Bush
5 Willie Parker 12.00 30.00
Hines Ward
Ben Roethlisberger
6 T.J. Houshmandzadeh 10.00 25.00
Carson Palmer
Chad Johnson
7 Donald Driver 20.00 50.00
Brett Favre
AJ Hawk
8 Trent Green 8.00 20.00
Larry Johnson
Tony Gonzalez
9 Tom Brady 10.00 25.00
Corey Dillon
Laurence Maroney
10 Peyton Manning 15.00 40.00
Reggie Wayne
Marvin Harrison

2008 Donruss Classics

This set was released on July 2, 2008. The base set consists of 248 cards. Cards 1-100 feature veterans, cards 101-150 are Legends serial numbered of 999, and cards 151-250 are rookies. Most are standard rookie cards serial numbered to 999, while others are autographed rookie cards serial numbered from 375 to 499.

COMP.SET w/o SP's (100) 7.50 20.00
LEGEND PRINT RUN 999 SER.#'d SETS
ROOKIE PRINT RUN 999 SER.#'d SETS
AU ROOKIE PRINT RUN 99-499 SER.#'d SETS
1 Edgerrin James .25 .60
2 Larry Fitzgerald .30 .75
3 Matt Leinart .30 .75
4 Warrick Dunn .25 .60
5 Roddy White .25 .60
6 Alge Crumpler .25 .60
7 Willis McGahee .25 .60
8 Mark Clayton .25 .60
9 Derrick Mason .25 .60
10 Trent Edwards .20 .50
11 Marshawn Lynch .25 .60
12 Lee Evans .25 .60
13 DeAngelo Williams .25 .60
14 DeShaun Foster .25 .60
15 Steve Smith .25 .60
16 Cedric Benson .25 .60
17 Bernard Berrian .25 .60
18 Greg Olsen .25 .60
19 Carson Palmer .30 .75
20 Chad Johnson .25 .60
21 T.J. Houshmandzadeh .25 .60
22 Rudi Johnson .25 .60
23 Brady Quinn .25 .60
24 Jamal Lewis .25 .60
25 Braylon Edwards .25 .60
26 Tony Romo .40 1.00
27 Terrell Owens .30 .75
28 Jason Witten .30 .75
29 Marion Barber .25 .60
30 Jay Cutler .30 .75
31 Brandon Marshall .25 .60
32 Brandon Stokley .25 .60
33 Jon Kitna .25 .60
34 Roy Williams WR .25 .60
35 Shaun McDonald .20 .50
36 Aaron Rodgers .60 1.50
37 Greg Jennings .30 .75
38 Ryan Grant .30 .75
39 Matt Schaub .25 .60
40 Andre Johnson .25 .60
41 Kevin Walter .25 .60
42 Peyton Manning .50 1.25
43 Reggie Wayne .25 .60
44 Joseph Addai .25 .60
45 Dallas Clark .25 .60
46 David Garrard .25 .60
47 Fred Taylor .25 .60
48 Maurice Jones-Drew .25 .60
49 Larry Johnson .25 .60
50 Tony Gonzalez .25 .60
51 Dwayne Bowe .25 .60
52 Ronnie Brown .25 .60
53 Ted Ginn Jr. .25 .60
54 John Beck .20 .50
55 Tarvaris Jackson .25 .60
56 Adrian Peterson .50 1.25
57 Chester Taylor .20 .50
58 Tom Brady .50 1.25
59 Randy Moss .30 .75
60 Wes Welker .30 .75
61 Laurence Maroney .25 .60
62 Drew Brees .30 .75
63 Marques Colston .25 .60
64 Reggie Bush .30 .75
65 Eli Manning .30 .75
66 Plaxico Burress .25 .60
67 Brandon Jacobs .25 .60
68 Kellen Clemens .25 .60
69 Jerricho Cotchery .25 .60
70 Thomas Jones .25 .60
71 Justin Fargas .20 .50
72 Jerry Porter .20 .50
73 JaMarcus Russell .25 .60
74 Donovan McNabb .30 .75
75 Brian Westbrook .25 .60
76 Kevin Curtis .20 .50
77 Ben Roethlisberger .30 .75
78 Willie Parker .25 .60
79 Hines Ward .25 .60
80 Philip Rivers .30 .75
81 LaDainian Tomlinson .30 .75
82 Antonio Gates .30 .75
83 Frank Gore .25 .60
84 Vernon Davis .25 .60
85 Devin Hester .30 .75
86 Matt Hasselbeck .25 .60
87 Julius Jones .20 .50
88 Deion Branch .25 .60
89 Marc Bulger .25 .60
90 Steven Jackson .30 .75
91 Torry Holt .25 .60
92 Jeff Garcia .25 .60
93 Earnest Graham .20 .50
94 Joey Galloway .25 .60
95 Vince Young .25 .60
96 LenDale White .25 .60
97 Roydell Williams .20 .50
98 Jason Campbell .25 .60
99 Chris Cooley .25 .60
100 Clinton Portis .25 .60
101 Jay Novacek 1.50 4.00
102 Knute Rockne 3.00 8.00
103 Tom Landry 2.50 6.00
104 Sammy Baugh 2.00 5.00
105 Willie Lanier 1.25 3.00
106 Ken Strong 1.25 3.00
107 Marion Motley 1.50 4.00
108 Tom Fears 1.25 3.00
109 Bob Waterfield 1.50 4.00
110 Hank Stram 1.50 4.00
111 Elroy Hirsch 1.50 4.00
112 Dick Lane 1.25 3.00
113 Jim Parker 1.25 3.00
114 Red Grange 2.50 6.00
115 Bobby Layne 2.00 5.00
116 Norm Van Brocklin 1.50 4.00
117 Michael Irvin 1.50 4.00
118 Steve Largent 2.00 5.00
119 Dick Butkus 2.50 6.00
120 Ray Nitschke 2.00 5.00
121 Lawrence Taylor 2.00 5.00
122 Bob Lilly 1.50 4.00
123 Mike Singletary 2.00 5.00
124 Y.A. Tittle 2.00 5.00
125 Steve Young 2.50 6.00
126 Tim Brown 2.00 5.00
127 Joe Greene 2.00 5.00
128 Paul Krause 1.25 3.00
129 Troy Aikman 2.50 6.00
130 Bo Jackson 2.50 6.00
131 George Blanda 2.00 5.00
132 Charlie Joiner 1.25 3.00
133 Walter Payton 4.00 10.00
134 Jack Youngblood 1.25 3.00
135 Ozzie Newsome 1.50 4.00
136 Dan Marino 4.00 10.00
137 John Elway 3.00 8.00
138 Joe Montana 4.00 10.00
139 Barry Sanders 3.00 8.00
140 Doak Walker 2.00 5.00
141 Lem Barney 1.25 3.00
142 Bert Bell 1.25 3.00
143 Bulldog Turner 1.50 4.00
144 Greasy Neale 1.25 3.00
145 Ernie Stautner 1.25 3.00
146 Frank Gatski 1.25 3.00
148 Leo Nomellini 1.25 3.00
150 Otto Graham 2.00 5.00
151 Brandon Flowers AU/499 RC 6.00 15.00
152 Tracy Porter AU/499 RC 6.00 15.00
153 Terrell Thomas RC 2.00 5.00
154 Chevis Jackson AU/375 RC 4.00 10.00
155 Reggie Smith AU/499 RC 5.00 12.00
156 Phillip Merling RC 2.00 5.00
157 Calais Campbell RC 2.00 5.00
158 Quentin Groves RC 2.00 5.00
159 Pat Sims RC 2.00 5.00
160 Dan Connor RC 2.50 6.00
161 Shawn Crable AU/436 RC 4.00 10.00
162 Xavier Adibi RC 1.50 4.00
163 Jerod Mayo RC 2.50 6.00
164 Jordon Dizon RC 2.50 6.00
165 Jake Long RC 2.50 6.00
166 Matt Ryan RC 10.00 25.00
167 Brian Brohm RC 2.50 6.00
168 Chad Henne RC 2.50 6.00
169 Dennis Dixon RC 2.50 6.00
170 Erik Ainge RC 2.50 6.00
171 Colt Brennan RC 2.50 6.00
172 Andre Woodson RC 2.50 6.00
173 Marcus Thomas RC 2.00 5.00
174 Darren McFadden RC 6.00 15.00
175 Jonathan Stewart RC 4.00 10.00
176 Felix Jones RC 4.00 10.00
177 Rashard Mendenhall RC 5.00 12.00
178 Tashard Choice RC 2.00 5.00
179 Ryan Torain AU/499 RC 6.00 15.00
180 Tim Hightower RC 2.50 6.00
181 Craig Steltz AU/499 RC 5.00 12.00
182 Caleb Campbell RC 2.50 6.00
183 Dustin Keller RC 2.50 6.00
184 John Carlson RC 2.50 6.00
185 Fred Davis RC 2.50 6.00
186 Martellus Bennett AU/499 RC 5.00 12.00
187 Donnie Avery RC 2.00 5.00
188 Devin Thomas RC 2.00 5.00
189 Jordy Nelson RC 3.00 8.00
190 James Hardy RC 2.00 5.00
191 Eddie Royal RC 2.50 6.00
192 Jerome Simpson RC 2.50 6.00
193 DeSean Jackson RC 5.00 12.00
194 Malcolm Kelly RC 2.00 5.00
195 Limas Sweed RC 2.50 6.00
196 Earl Bennett RC 2.50 6.00
197 Early Doucet RC 2.00 5.00
198 Harry Douglas RC 2.00 5.00
199 Mario Manningham RC 2.50 6.00
200 Andre Caldwell RC 2.00 5.00
201 Leodis McKelvin AU/499 RC 5.00 12.00
202 Antoine Cason AU/499 RC 6.00 15.00
203 Dominique Rodgers-Cromartie AU/499 RC 6.00 15.00
204 Aqib Talib RC 2.50 6.00
205 Mike Jenkins RC 2.50 6.00
206 Vernon Gholston AU/499 RC 5.00 12.00
207 Derfick Harvey AU/499 RC 4.00 10.00
208 Lawrence Jackson AU/499 RC 5.00 12.00
209 Chris Long AU/499 RC 6.00 15.00
210 Kentwan Balmer AU/499 RC 5.00 12.00
211 Glenn Dorsey RC 2.50 6.00
212 Sedrick Ellis RC 2.50 6.00
213 Jacob Hester AU/499 RC 6.00 15.00
214 Owen Schmitt AU/499 RC 6.00 15.00
215 Peyton Hillis AU/499 RC 8.00 20.00
216 Kenny Phillips RC 2.50 6.00
217 Curtis Lofton AU/499 RC 5.00 12.00
218 Keith Rivers AU/499 RC 6.00 15.00
219 Joe Flacco AU/399 RC 30.00 60.00
220 Matt Flynn AU/499 RC 15.00 40.00
221 Kevin O'Connell AU/499 RC 5.00 12.00
222 John David Booty AU/349 RC 5.00 12.00
223 Josh Johnson AU/399 RC 6.00 15.00
224 Matt Forte AU/499 RC 15.00 40.00
225 Thomas Brown AU/499 RC 5.00 12.00
226 Chauncey Washington AU/499 RC 5.00 12.00
227 Justin Forsett AU/499 RC 6.00 15.00
228 Cory Boyd AU/499 RC 4.00 10.00
229 Allen Patrick AU/499 RC 5.00 12.00
230 Chris Johnson AU/499 RC 20.00 50.00
231 Ray Rice AU/499 RC 15.00 30.00
232 Kevin Smith AU/99 RC 12.00 30.00
233 Mike Hart AU/499 RC 6.00 15.00
234 Jamaal Charles AU/499 RC 10.00 25.00
235 Steve Slaton AU/99 RC 15.00 40.00
236 Brad Cottam AU/499 RC 5.00 12.00
237 Jermichael Finley AU/499 RC 10.00 25.00
238 Martin Rucker AU/499 RC 5.00 12.00
239 Jacob Tamme AU/499 RC 6.00 15.00
240 Kellen Davis AU/499 RC 4.00 10.00
241 Will Franklin AU/499 RC 5.00 12.00
242 Marcus Smith AU/499 RC 5.00 12.00
243 Keenan Burton RC 1.50 4.00
244 Josh Morgan AU/499 RC 6.00 15.00
245 Kevin Robinson RC 1.50 4.00
246 Paul Hubbard AU/499 RC 5.00 12.00
247 Adrian Arrington RC 2.00 5.00
248 Marcus Monk AU/499 RC 5.00 12.00
249 Lavelle Hawkins AU/499 RC 4.00 10.00
250 Dexter Jackson AU/499 RC 5.00 12.00

2008 Donruss Classics Timeless Tributes Bronze

*VETS 1-100: 3X TO 8X BASIC CARDS
*LEGENDS 101-150: .6X TO 1.5X BASIC CARDS
COMMON ROOKIE (151-250) 2.00 5.00
ROOKIE SEMISTARS 2.50 6.00
ROOKIE UNL.STARS 3.00 8.00
STATED PRINT RUN 250 SER.#'d SETS
163 Jerod Mayo 3.00 8.00
165 Jake Long 3.00 8.00
166 Matt Ryan 12.00 30.00
167 Brian Brohm 3.00 8.00
168 Chad Henne 3.00 8.00
169 Dennis Dixon 3.00 8.00
170 Erik Ainge 3.00 8.00
171 Colt Brennan 3.00 8.00
172 Andre Woodson 3.00 8.00
174 Darren McFadden 8.00 20.00
175 Jonathan Stewart 5.00 12.00
176 Felix Jones 5.00 12.00
177 Rashard Mendenhall 6.00 15.00
180 Tim Hightower 3.00 8.00
188 Devin Thomas 2.50 6.00
189 Jordy Nelson 4.00 10.00
190 James Hardy 2.50 6.00
193 DeSean Jackson 6.00 15.00
194 Malcolm Kelly 2.50 6.00
195 Limas Sweed 3.00 8.00
197 Early Doucet 2.50 6.00
199 Mario Manningham 3.00 8.00
205 Mike Jenkins 3.00 8.00
206 Vernon Gholston 2.50 6.00
209 Chris Long 3.00 8.00
211 Glenn Dorsey 3.00 8.00
213 Jacob Hester 3.00 8.00
214 Owen Schmitt 3.00 8.00
215 Peyton Hillis 4.00 10.00
218 Keith Rivers 3.00 8.00
219 Joe Flacco 10.00 25.00
220 Matt Flynn 6.00 15.00
221 Kevin O'Connell 2.50 6.00
222 John David Booty 2.50 6.00
223 Josh Johnson 3.00 8.00
224 Matt Forte 5.00 12.00
230 Chris Johnson 8.00 20.00
231 Ray Rice 6.00 15.00
232 Kevin Smith 3.00 8.00
233 Mike Hart 3.00 8.00
234 Jamaal Charles 5.00 12.00
235 Steve Slaton 3.00 8.00
250 Dexter Jackson 2.50 6.00

2008 Donruss Classics Timeless Tributes Gold

*VETS 1-100: 5X TO 12X BASIC CARDS
*LEGENDS 101-150: 1X TO 2.5X BASIC CARDS
*ROOKIES: .6X TO 1.5X TRIBUTE BRONZE
STATED PRINT RUN 50 SER.#'d SETS

2008 Donruss Classics Timeless Tributes Platinum

*VETS 1-100: 10X TO 25X BASIC CARDS
*LEGENDS 101-150: 2X TO 5X BASIC CARDS
*ROOKIES: 1X TO 2.5X TRIBUTE BRONZE
STATED PRINT RUN 25 SER.#'d SETS

2008 Donruss Classics Timeless Tributes Silver

*VETS 1-100: 4X TO 10X BASIC CARDS
*LEGENDS 101-150: .8X TO 2X BASIC CARDS
*ROOKIES: .5X TO 1.2X TRIBUTE BRONZE
STATED PRINT RUN 100 SER.#'d SETS

2008 Donruss Classics Classic Combos

STATED PRINT RUN 1000 SER.#'d SETS
*SILVER/250: .6X TO 1.5X BASIC INSERTS
SILVER PRINT RUN 250 SER.#'d SETS
*GOLD/100: .8X TO 2X BASIC INSERTS
GOLD PRINT RUN 100 SER.#'d SETS
*PLATINUM/25: 1.5X TO 4X BASIC INSERTS
PLATINUM PRINT RUN 25 SER.#'d SETS
1 Hank Stram 1.50 4.00
Willie Lanier
2 Tom Landry 2.50 6.00
Roger Staubach
3 Gene Upshaw 1.50 4.00
Merlin Olsen
4 Emmitt Smith 4.00 10.00
Michael Irvin
5 Bobby Layne 2.00 5.00
Dick Lane
6 Leroy Kelly 2.50 6.00
Jim Brown
7 Jim Parker 1.50 4.00
Raymond Berry
8 Elroy Hirsch 1.50 4.00
Tom Fears
9 Troy Aikman 2.50 6.00
Jay Novacek
10 Joe Montana 4.00 10.00
Jerry Rice
11 Steve Young 3.00 8.00
John Elway
12 Bob Lilly 2.00 5.00
Joe Greene
13 Dan Marino 4.00 10.00
Joe Montana
14 Hank Stram 2.50 6.00
Tom Landry
15 Jim Thorpe 2.50 6.00
Sammy Baugh

2008 Donruss Classics Classic Combos Jerseys

STATED PRINT RUN 10-250
*PRIME/25: 1X TO 2.5X BASIC JSY/250
PRIME PRINT RUN 4-25
SER.#'d UNDER 25 NOT PRICED
1 Hank Stram 8.00 20.00
Willie Lanier
2 Tom Landry 20.00 40.00
Roger Staubach
3 Gene Upshaw 6.00 15.00
Merlin Olsen
4 Emmitt Smith 12.00 30.00
Michael Irvin
5 Bobby Layne 8.00 20.00
Dick Lane
6 Leroy Kelly 12.00 30.00
Jim Brown/85
7 Jim Parker 6.00 15.00
Raymond Berry
8 Elroy Hirsch 6.00 15.00
Tom Fears
9 Troy Aikman 10.00 25.00
Jay Novacek
10 Joe Montana 12.00 30.00
Jerry Rice
11 Steve Young 10.00 25.00
John Elway
12 Bob Lilly 6.00 15.00
Joe Greene
13 Dan Marino 15.00 40.00

Joe Montana
14 Hank Stram 12.00 30.00
Tom Landry

2008 Donruss Classics Classic Cuts

STATED PRINT RUN 1-50
SERIAL #'d UNDER 25 NOT PRICED
8 Bob Waterfield/25 60.00 120.00
9 Hank Stram/25 50.00 120.00
16 Doak Walker/25 125.00 250.00
17 Bert Bell/50 50.00 100.00
20 Ernie Stautner/50 40.00 80.00
21 Frank Gatski/25 60.00 120.00
28 Bulldog Turner/50 50.00 100.00
32 Walter Payton/34 200.00 400.00
33 Weeb Ewbank/50 40.00 80.00

2008 Donruss Classics Classic Quads

STATED PRINT RUN 1000 SER.#'d SETS
*SILVER/250: .6X TO 1.5X BASIC INSERTS
SILVER PRINT RUN 250 SER.#'d SETS
*GOLD/100: .8X TO 2X BASIC INSERTS
GOLD PRINT RUN 100 SER.#'d SETS
*PLATINUM/25: 1.5X TO 4X BASIC INSERTS
PLATINUM PRINT RUN 25 SER.#'d SETS
1 Troy Aikman 4.00 10.00
Emmitt Smith
Michael Irvin
Jay Novacek
2 Bobby Layne 3.00 8.00
Barry Sanders
Doak Walker
Lem Barney
3 Chad Johnson 2.00 5.00
Randy Moss
Terrell Owens
Torry Holt
4 Terrell Owens 2.00 5.00
LaDainian Tomlinson
Randy Moss
Marvin Harrison
5 Edgerrin James 2.00 5.00
Fred Taylor
LaDainian Tomlinson
Warrick Dunn
6 Brett Favre 5.00 12.00
Tom Brady
Peyton Manning
Ben Roethlisberger
7 Barry Sanders 4.00 10.00
LaDainian Tomlinson
Walter Payton
Emmitt Smith
8 Troy Aikman 4.00 10.00
John Elway
Dan Marino
Steve Young
9 Emmitt Smith 4.00 10.00
Walter Payton
Barry Sanders
Eric Dickerson
10 Jerry Rice 3.00 8.00
Steve Largent
Michael Irvin
Tim Brown

2008 Donruss Classics Classic Quads Jerseys

STATED PRINT RUN 100 SER.#'d SETS
*PRIME/25: .8X TO 2X BASIC QUAD/100
PRIME PRINT RUN 2-25
SER.#'d UNDER 25 NOT PRICED
1 Troy Aikman 30.00 80.00
Emmitt Smith
Michael Irvin
Jay Novacek
2 Bobby Layne 25.00 60.00
Barry Sanders
Doak Walker
Lem Barney
3 Chad Johnson 12.00 30.00
Randy Moss
Terrell Owens
Torry Holt
4 Terrell Owens 12.00 30.00
LaDainian Tomlinson
Randy Moss
Marvin Harrison
5 Edgerrin James 12.00 30.00
Fred Taylor
LaDainian Tomlinson
Warrick Dunn
6 Brett Favre 40.00 100.00
Tom Brady
Peyton Manning
Ben Roethlisberger
7 Barry Sanders 40.00 100.00
LaDainian Tomlinson
Walter Payton
Emmitt Smith
8 Troy Aikman 40.00 100.00
John Elway
Dan Marino
Steve Young
9 Emmitt Smith 50.00 120.00
Walter Payton
Barry Sanders
Eric Dickerson
10 Jerry Rice 15.00 40.00
Steve Largent
Michael Irvin
Tim Brown

2008 Donruss Classics Classic Singles

STATED PRINT RUN 1000 SER.#'d SETS
*SILVER/250: .6X TO 1.5X BASIC INSERTS
SILVER PRINT RUN 250 SER.#'d SETS
*GOLD/100: .8X TO 2X BASIC INSERTS
GOLD PRINT RUN 100 SER.#'d SETS
*PLATINUM/25: 1.5X TO 4X BASIC INSERTS
PLATINUM PRINT RUN 25 SER.#'d SETS
1 Emmitt Smith 3.00 8.00
2 Joe Montana 3.00 8.00
3 John Elway 2.50 6.00
4 Dan Marino 3.00 8.00
5 Gene Upshaw 1.00 2.50
6 John Mackey 1.00 2.50
7 Knute Rockne 2.50 6.00
8 Tom Landry 2.00 5.00
9 Sammy Baugh 1.50 4.00
10 Willie Lanier 1.00 2.50
11 Ken Strong 1.00 2.50
12 Marion Motley 1.25 3.00
13 Tom Fears 1.00 2.50
14 Bob Waterfield 1.25 3.00
15 Hank Stram 1.25 3.00
16 Elroy Hirsch 1.25 3.00
17 Dick Lane 1.00 2.50
18 Jim Parker 1.00 2.50
19 Jim Thorpe 2.00 5.00
20 Bobby Layne 1.50 4.00
21 Norm Van Brocklin 1.25 3.00
22 Merlin Olsen 1.25 3.00
23 Jim Brown 2.00 5.00
24 Bob Lilly 1.25 3.00
25 Chuck Bednarik 1.25 3.00
26 Leroy Kelly 1.25 3.00
27 Raymond Berry 1.25 3.00
28 Roger Staubach 2.00 5.00
29 Dan Fouts 1.50 4.00
30 Eric Dickerson 1.25 3.00

2008 Donruss Classics Classic Singles Jerseys

STATED PRINT RUN 10-50
*PRIME/15-25: .6X TO 1.5X BASIC JSY/50
*PRIME/15-25: .5X TO 1.2X BASIC JSY/25
PRIME PRINT RUN 1-25
*JERSEY #'s/50-88: .4X TO 1X BASIC JSY/50
*JERSEY #'s/32-40: .5X TO 1.2X BASIC JSY/50
*JERSEY #'s/14-29: .6X TO 1.5X BASIC JSY/50
JERSEY NUMBERS PRINT RUN 1-88
*JERSEY #'s PRIME/25: .6X TO 1.5X BASIC JSY/50
JERSEY NUMBERS PRIME PRINT RUN 1-25
SERIAL #'d UNDER 20 NOT PRICED
1 Emmitt Smith 20.00 50.00
2 Joe Montana 20.00 50.00
3 John Elway 15.00 40.00
4 Dan Marino 20.00 50.00
5 Gene Upshaw 6.00 15.00
6 John Mackey 6.00 15.00
7 Knute Rockne Jkt 30.00 60.00
8 Tom Landry 20.00 50.00
9 Sammy Baugh 12.00 30.00
10 Willie Lanier 6.00 15.00
11 Ken Strong 6.00 15.00
12 Marion Motley 10.00 25.00
13 Tom Fears 6.00 15.00
14 Bob Waterfield 10.00 25.00
15 Hank Stram 8.00 20.00
16 Elroy Hirsch 8.00 20.00
17 Dick Lane 6.00 15.00
18 Jim Parker 6.00 15.00
20 Bobby Layne 10.00 25.00
21 Norm Van Brocklin 10.00 25.00
22 Merlin Olsen 8.00 20.00
23 Jim Brown 12.00 30.00
24 Bob Lilly 8.00 20.00
25 Chuck Bednarik 8.00 20.00
26 Leroy Kelly/25 10.00 25.00
27 Raymond Berry 8.00 20.00
28 Roger Staubach 12.00 30.00
29 Dan Fouts 10.00 25.00
30 Eric Dickerson 8.00 20.00

2008 Donruss Classics Classic Singles Jerseys Autographs

STATED PRINT RUN 10-25
2 Joe Montana/20 100.00 175.00
3 John Elway/15 60.00 120.00
4 Dan Marino/25 100.00 200.00
5 Gene Upshaw/25 10.00 25.00
6 John Mackey/25 10.00 25.00
23 Jim Brown/20 50.00 100.00
24 Bob Lilly/25 12.00 30.00
25 Chuck Bednarik/25 12.00 30.00
27 Raymond Berry/25 15.00 40.00
29 Dan Fouts/25 30.00 60.00

2008 Donruss Classics Classic Singles Jerseys Jersey Numbers Autographs

SERIAL #'d UNDER 15 NOT PRICED
JERSEY NUMBERS PRINT RUN 5-25
ANNC'D EXCH EXPIRATION: 1/2/2010
5 Gene Upshaw/15 30.00 60.00
6 John Mackey /15 15.00 40.00
27 Raymond Berry/25 15.00 40.00
29 Dan Fouts/25 25.00 60.00

2008 Donruss Classics Classic Singles Jerseys Jersey Numbers Prime Autographs

SERIAL #'d UNDER 25 NOT PRICED
JERSEY NUMBERS PRIME PRINT RUN 1-25
27 Raymond Berry/25 20.00 50.00

2008 Donruss Classics Classic Singles Jerseys Prime Autographs

PRIME PRINT RUN 5-25
SERIAL #'d UNDER 20 NOT PRICED
5 Gene Upshaw/20 12.00 30.00
6 John Mackey/20 12.00 30.00
27 Raymond Berry/25 20.00 50.00

2008 Donruss Classics Classic Triples

STATED PRINT RUN 1000 SER.#'d SETS
*SILVER/250: .6X TO 1.5X BASIC INSERTS
SILVER PRINT RUN 250 SER.#'d SETS
*GOLD/100: .8X TO 2X BASIC INSERTS
GOLD PRINT RUN 100 SER.#'d SETS
*PLATINUM/25: 1.5X TO 4X BASIC INSERTS
PLATINUM PRINT RUN 25 SER.#'d SETS
1 Knute Rockne 3.00 8.00
Hank Stram
Tom Landry
2 Leroy Kelly 2.50 6.00
Jim Brown
Marion Motley
3 Willie Lanier 2.50 6.00
Dick Butkus
Ray Nitschke
4 Bob Lilly 2.00 5.00
Joe Greene
Gene Upshaw
5 Bobby Layne 2.00 5.00
Norm Van Brocklin
Bob Waterfield
6 Merlin Olsen 2.00 5.00
Joe Greene
Jack Youngblood
7 Chuck Bednarik 1.50 4.00
Marion Motley
Dick Lane
8 Jim Thorpe 2.50 6.00
Sammy Baugh
Ken Strong
9 Jerry Rice 3.00 8.00
Steve Largent
Ozzie Newsome
10 Joe Montana 4.00 10.00
Troy Aikman
Tom Brady

2008 Donruss Classics Classic Triples Jerseys

STATED PRINT RUN 75-250
*PRIME/25: .8X TO 2X BASIC JSY/250
PRIME PRINT RUN 1-25
1 Knute Rockne Jkt 25.00 60.00
Hank Stram
Tom Landry
2 Leroy Kelly 15.00 40.00
Jim Brown
Marion Motley/75
3 Willie Lanier 12.00 30.00
Dick Butkus
Ray Nitschke
4 Bob Lilly 6.00 15.00
Joe Greene
Gene Upshaw
5 Bobby Layne 10.00 25.00
Norm Van Brocklin
Bob Waterfield
6 Merlin Olsen 6.00 15.00
Joe Greene
Jack Youngblood
7 Chuck Bednarik 10.00 25.00
Marion Motley
Dick Lane
8 Jim Thorpe 50.00 100.00
Sammy Baugh
Ken Strong/100
9 Jerry Rice 10.00 25.00
Steve Largent
Ozzie Newsome
10 Joe Montana 15.00 40.00
Troy Aikman
Tom Brady

2008 Donruss Classics Membership

STATED PRINT RUN 1000 SER.#'d SETS
*SILVER/250: .6X TO 1.5X BASIC INSERTS
SILVER PRINT RUN 250 SER.#'d SETS
*GOLD/100: .8X TO 2X BASIC INSERTS
GOLD PRINT RUN 100 SER.#'d SETS
*PLATINUM/25: 1.5X TO 4X BASIC INSERTS
PLATINUM PRINT RUN 25 SER.#'d SETS
1 Adrian Peterson 2.50 6.00
2 Wes Welker 1.50 4.00
3 Dwayne Bowe 1.25 3.00
4 Marshawn Lynch 1.25 3.00
5 Steven Jackson 1.50 4.00
6 Santana Moss 1.00 2.50
7 Braylon Edwards 1.25 3.00
8 Jason Witten 1.50 4.00
9 Derek Anderson 1.00 2.50
10 Marion Barber 1.25 3.00
11 Ryan Grant 1.50 4.00
12 David Garrard 1.25 3.00
13 Matt Schaub 1.25 3.00
14 Justin Fargas 1.00 2.50
15 LaRon Landry 1.25 3.00
16 Tarvaris Jackson 1.25 3.00
17 Roddy White 1.25 3.00
18 Brandon Marshall 1.25 3.00
19 Patrick Willis 1.25 3.00
20 Calvin Johnson 1.50 4.00

2008 Donruss Classics Membership VIP Jerseys

STATED PRINT RUN 250 SER.#'d SETS
*PRIME/25: 1X TO 2.5X BASIC JSY/250
PRIME PRINT RUN 25 SER.#'d SETS
*DIE CUT/100: .6X TO 1.5X BASIC JSY/250
DIE CUT PRINT RUN 100 SER.#'d SETS
*DC PRIME/25: 1.2X TO 3X BASIC JSY/250
DIE CUT PRIME PRINT RUN 25 SER.#'d SETS
1 Adrian Peterson 6.00 15.00
2 Wes Welker 4.00 10.00
3 Dwayne Bowe 3.00 8.00
4 Marshawn Lynch 3.00 8.00
5 Steven Jackson 4.00 10.00
6 Santana Moss 2.50 6.00
7 Braylon Edwards 3.00 8.00
8 Jason Witten 4.00 10.00
9 Derek Anderson 2.50 6.00
10 Marion Barber 3.00 8.00
11 Ryan Grant 4.00 10.00
12 David Garrard 3.00 8.00
13 Matt Schaub 3.00 8.00
14 Justin Fargas 2.50 6.00
15 LaRon Landry 3.00 8.00
16 Tarvaris Jackson 3.00 8.00
17 Roddy White 3.00 8.00
18 Brandon Marshall 3.00 8.00
19 Patrick Willis 3.00 8.00
20 Calvin Johnson 4.00 10.00

2008 Donruss Classics Monday Night Heroes

STATED PRINT RUN 1000 SER.#'d SETS
*SILVER/250: .6X TO 1.5X BASIC INSERTS
SILVER PRINT RUN 250 SER.#'d SETS
*GOLD/100: .8X TO 2X BASIC INSERTS
GOLD PRINT RUN 100 SER.#'d SETS
*PLATINUM/25: 1.5X TO 4X BASIC INSERTS
PLATINUM PRINT RUN 25 SER.#'d SETS
1 Carson Palmer 1.50 4.00
2 Chad Johnson 1.25 3.00
3 Edgerrin James 1.25 3.00
4 Donovan McNabb 1.50 4.00
5 Brian Westbrook 1.25 3.00
6 Tom Brady 2.50 6.00
7 Randy Moss 1.50 4.00
8 T.J. Houshmandzadeh 1.25 3.00
9 Brandon Jones 1.00 2.50
10 Jason Witten 1.50 4.00
11 Eli Manning 1.50 4.00
12 Plaxico Burress 1.25 3.00
13 Peyton Manning 2.50 6.00
14 Brett Favre 4.00 10.00
15 Jay Cutler 1.50 4.00
16 Ryan Grant 1.50 4.00
17 Greg Jennings 1.50 4.00
18 Ben Roethlisberger 1.50 4.00
19 Santonio Holmes 1.25 3.00
20 Matt Hasselbeck 1.25 3.00
21 Vince Young 1.25 3.00
22 Brandon Stokley 1.25 3.00
23 Hines Ward 1.25 3.00
24 Willis McGahee 1.25 3.00
25 Derrick Mason 1.25 3.00
26 Drew Brees 1.50 4.00
27 Tarvaris Jackson 1.25 3.00
28 Adrian Peterson 2.50 6.00
29 LaDainian Tomlinson 1.50 4.00
30 Brandon Marshall 1.25 3.00

2008 Donruss Classics Monday Night Heroes Jerseys

STATED PRINT RUN 210-250
*PRIME/25: 1X TO 2.5X BASIC JSY/210-250
PRIME PRINT RUN 25 SER.#'d SETS
*JSY #'s/81-86: .6X TO 1.5X BASIC JSY/210-250
*JSY #'s/32-36: .8X TO 2X BASIC JSY/210-250
*JSY #'s/21-28: 1X TO 2.5X BASIC JSY/210-250
JERSEY NUMBERS PRINT RUN 4-86
1 Carson Palmer 4.00 10.00
2 Chad Johnson 3.00 8.00
3 Edgerrin James 3.00 8.00
4 Donovan McNabb 4.00 10.00
5 Brian Westbrook 3.00 8.00
6 Tom Brady 6.00 15.00
7 Randy Moss 4.00 10.00
8 T.J. Houshmandzadeh 3.00 8.00
9 Brandon Jones 2.50 6.00
10 Jason Witten 4.00 10.00
11 Eli Manning 4.00 10.00
12 Plaxico Burress 3.00 8.00
13 Peyton Manning 6.00 15.00
14 Brett Favre 10.00 25.00
15 Jay Cutler 4.00 10.00
16 Ryan Grant 4.00 10.00
17 Greg Jennings 4.00 10.00
18 Ben Roethlisberger 4.00 10.00
19 Santonio Holmes 3.00 8.00
20 Matt Hasselbeck 3.00 8.00
21 Vince Young 3.00 8.00
22 Brandon Stokley 3.00 8.00
23 Hines Ward 3.00 8.00
24 Willis McGahee 3.00 8.00
25 Derrick Mason 3.00 8.00
26 Drew Brees 4.00 10.00
27 Tarvaris Jackson 3.00 8.00
28 Adrian Peterson/210 6.00 15.00
29 LaDainian Tomlinson 4.00 10.00
30 Brandon Marshall 3.00 8.00

2008 Donruss Classics Monday Night Heroes Jerseys Jersey Numbers Autographs

STATED PRINT RUN 4-25
SERIAL #'d UNDER 20 NOT PRICED
ANNC'D EXCH EXPIRATION: 1/2/2010
2 Chad Johnson/25 15.00 40.00
5 Brian Westbrook/20 15.00 40.00
8 T.J. Houshmandzadeh/15 12.00 30.00
10 Jason Witten/20 25.00 50.00
17 Greg Jennings/20 15.00 40.00
18 Ben Roethlisberger/19 60.00 120.00
19 Santonio Holmes/15 15.00 40.00
26 Drew Brees/20 40.00 80.00
27 Tarvaris Jackson/15 12.00 30.00
28 Adrian Peterson/25 100.00 200.00
30 Brandon Marshall/25 15.00 40.00

2008 Donruss Classics Monday Night Heroes Jerseys Prime Autographs

PRIME PRINT RUN 1-20
SERIAL #'d UNDER 20 NOT PRICED
ANNC'D EXCH EXPIRATION: 1/2/2010
17 Greg Jennings/20 20.00 50.00
20 Drew Drees/15 30.00 80.00

2008 Donruss Classics Old School Colors

STATED PRINT RUN 1000 SER.#'d SETS
1 Dan Marino 4.00 10.00
2 Braylon Edwards 1.50 4.00
3 Roger Staubach 2.50 6.00
4 Thurman Thomas 1.50 4.00
5 Barry Sanders 3.00 8.00
6 Tony Dorsett 2.00 5.00
7 Eric Dickerson 1.50 4.00
8 John Elway 3.00 8.00
9 Peyton Manning 3.00 8.00
10 Carson Palmer 2.00 5.00
11 Steve Largent 2.00 5.00
12 Laveranues Coles 1.25 3.00
13 Willis McGahee 1.50 4.00
14 Fred Taylor 1.50 4.00
15 Mike Singletary 2.00 5.00
16 Reggie Wayne 1.50 4.00
17 Lawrence Taylor 2.00 5.00
18 Hines Ward 1.50 4.00
19 Roy Williams WR 1.50 4.00
20 Lee Evans 1.50 4.00
21 Reggie Williams 1.50 4.00
22 Andre Johnson 1.50 4.00
24 Marcus Allen 2.00 5.00
25 Kellen Winslow 1.50 4.00

2008 Donruss Classics Old School Colors Autographs

STATED PRINT RUN 4-25
SERIAL #'d UNDER 20 NOT PRICED
ANNC'D EXCH EXPIRATION: 1/2/2010
1 Dan Marino/20 125.00 200.00
2 Braylon Edwards/20 EXCH 20.00 40.00
4 Thurman Thomas/25 25.00 50.00
5 Barry Sanders/20 60.00 120.00
6 Tony Dorsett/25 25.00 50.00
7 Eric Dickerson/25 25.00 50.00
11 Steve Largent/25 20.00 40.00
13 Willis McGahee/20 12.00 30.00
15 Mike Singletary/20 EXCH 25.00 50.00
16 Reggie Wayne/20 EXCH 15.00 40.00
17 Lawrence Taylor/25 25.00 50.00
24 Marcus Allen/25 20.00 50.00

2008 Donruss Classics Old School Colors Jerseys

STATED PRINT RUN 40-100
*PRIME/25: .8X TO 2X BASIC JSY/40-100
PRIME PRINT RUN 25 SER.#'d SETS
1 Dan Marino/68 15.00 40.00
2 Braylon Edwards 6.00 15.00
3 Roger Staubach 12.00 30.00
4 Thurman Thomas 8.00 20.00
5 Barry Sanders 12.00 30.00
6 Tony Dorsett/66 10.00 25.00
7 Eric Dickerson 8.00 20.00
8 John Elway 15.00 40.00
9 Peyton Manning 15.00 40.00
10 Carson Palmer
11 Steve Largent 10.00 25.00
12 Laveranues Coles 5.00 12.00
13 Willis McGahee 6.00 15.00
15 Mike Singletary 10.00 25.00
17 Lawrence Taylor 10.00 25.00
18 Hines Ward 6.00 15.00
19 Roy Williams WR/66 6.00 15.00
20 Lee Evans 6.00 15.00
21 Reggie Williams 6.00 15.00
22 Andre Johnson/40 6.00 15.00
24 Marcus Allen 10.00 25.00
25 Kellen Winslow Jr. 8.00 20.00

2008 Donruss Classics Saturday Stars

STATED PRINT RUN 1000 SER.#'d SETS
*SILVER/250: .6X TO 1.5X BASIC INSERTS
SILVER PRINT RUN 250 SER.#'d SETS
*GOLD/100: .8X TO 2X BASIC INSERTS
GOLD PRINT RUN 100 SER.#'d SETS
*PLATINUM/25: 1.5X TO 4X BASIC INSERTS
PLATINUM PRINT RUN 25 SER.#'d SETS
1 Allen Patrick .75 2.00
2 Antoine Cason 1.00 2.50
3 Brian Brohm 1.00 2.50
4 Chad Henne 1.00 2.50
5 Chris Long 1.00 2.50
6 Colt Brennan 1.00 2.50
7 Dan Connor 1.00 2.50
8 Dennis Dixon 1.00 2.50
9 Early Doucet .75 2.00
10 Eddie Royal 1.00 2.50
11 Erik Ainge 1.00 2.50
12 DJ Hall .75 2.00
13 Glenn Dorsey 1.00 2.50
14 John David Booty .75 2.00
15 Keith Rivers 1.00 2.50
16 Kenny Phillips 1.00 2.50
17 Limas Sweed 1.00 2.50
18 Matt Ryan 4.00 10.00
19 Matt Flynn 2.00 5.00
20 Mike Hart 1.00 2.50
21 Malcolm Kelly .75 2.00
22 Mario Manningham 1.00 2.50
23 Adrian Arrington .75 2.00
24 Darren McFadden 2.50 6.00
25 DeSean Jackson 2.00 5.00
26 Felix Jones 1.50 4.00
27 Jamaal Charles 1.50 4.00
28 Jonathan Stewart 1.50 4.00
29 Rashard Mendenhall 2.00 5.00
30 Steve Slaton 1.00 2.50

2008 Donruss Classics Saturday Stars Autographs

STATED PRINT RUN 25 SER.#'d SETS
1 Allen Patrick 10.00 25.00
2 Antoine Cason 12.00 30.00
3 Brian Brohm 12.00 30.00
4 Chad Henne 12.00 30.00
5 Chris Long 12.00 30.00
6 Colt Brennan 12.00 30.00
7 Dan Connor 12.00 30.00
8 Dennis Dixon 12.00 30.00
9 Early Doucet 10.00 25.00
11 Erik Ainge 12.00 30.00
14 John David Booty 10.00 25.00
15 Keith Rivers 12.00 30.00
17 Limas Sweed 12.00 30.00
18 Matt Ryan 50.00 120.00
19 Matt Flynn 30.00 80.00
20 Mike Hart 12.00 30.00
21 Malcolm Kelly 10.00 25.00
22 Mario Manningham 12.00 30.00
23 Adrian Arrington 10.00 25.00
24 Darren McFadden 40.00 80.00
25 DeSean Jackson 15.00 40.00
26 Felix Jones 30.00 80.00
27 Jamaal Charles 20.00 50.00
28 Jonathan Stewart 20.00 50.00
29 Rashard Mendenhall 25.00 60.00
30 Steve Slaton 12.00 30.00

2008 Donruss Classics Saturday Stars Jerseys

STATED PRINT RUN 55-250
*PRIME/25: 1X TO 2.5X BASIC JSY/230-250
*PRIME/25: .8X TO 2X BASIC JSY/55
PRIME PRINT RUN 25 SER.#'d SETS
*JSY #'s/55-91: .5X TO 1.2X BASIC JSY/230-250
*JSY #'s/40: .6X TO 1.5X BASIC JSY/230-250
*JSY #'s/20-28: .8X TO 2X BASIC JSY/230-250
JERSEY NUMBERS PRINT RUN 1-91 SER.#'d SETS
UNPRICED JSY #'s AU PRINT RUN 10
UNPRICED PRIME AU PRINT RUN 5
1 Allen Patrick 3.00 8.00
2 Antoine Cason/230 4.00 10.00
3 Brian Brohm 4.00 10.00
4 Chad Henne 8.00 20.00
5 Chris Long 4.00 10.00
6 Colt Brennan 4.00 10.00
7 Dan Connor 4.00 10.00
8 Dennis Dixon 4.00 10.00
9 Early Doucet 3.00 8.00
10 Eddie Royal 4.00 10.00
11 Erik Ainge 4.00 10.00
12 DJ Hall 3.00 8.00
13 Glenn Dorsey 4.00 10.00
14 John David Booty 3.00 8.00
15 Keith Rivers 4.00 10.00
16 Kenny Phillips 4.00 10.00
17 Limas Sweed 4.00 10.00
18 Matt Ryan 10.00 25.00
19 Matt Flynn 8.00 20.00
20 Mike Hart 4.00 10.00
21 Malcolm Kelly 3.00 8.00
23 Adrian Arrington/55 4.00 10.00
24 Darren McFadden 10.00 25.00
25 DeSean Jackson 8.00 20.00
26 Felix Jones 10.00 25.00
27 Jamaal Charles 6.00 15.00
28 Jonathan Stewart 8.00 20.00
29 Rashard Mendenhall 8.00 20.00
30 Steve Slaton 4.00 10.00

2008 Donruss Classics School Colors

STATED PRINT RUN 1000 SER.#'d SETS
1 Ali Highsmith .75 2.00
2 Allen Patrick 1.00 2.50
3 Antoine Cason 1.25 3.00
4 Brian Brohm 1.25 3.00
5 Chad Henne 1.25 3.00
6 Chevis Jackson .75 2.00
7 Chris Long 1.25 3.00
8 Colt Brennan 1.25 3.00
9 DJ Hall 1.00 2.50
10 Dan Connor 1.25 3.00
11 Dennis Dixon 1.25 3.00
12 Early Doucet 1.00 2.50
13 Eddie Royal 1.25 3.00
14 Erik Ainge 1.25 3.00
15 Ernie Wheelwright 1.00 2.50
16 Fred Davis 1.25 3.00
17 Glenn Dorsey 1.25 3.00
18 Harry Douglas 1.00 2.50
19 Jamar Adams 1.00 2.50
20 John David Booty 1.00 2.50
21 Jonathan Hefney 1.00 2.50
22 Keith Rivers 1.25 3.00
23 Kenny Phillips 1.25 3.00
24 Lawrence Jackson 1.00 2.50
25 Limas Sweed 1.25 3.00
26 Marcus Monk 1.00 2.50
27 Matt Ryan 5.00 12.00
28 Matt Flynn 2.50 6.00
29 Mike Hart 1.25 3.00
30 Malcolm Kelly 1.00 2.50
31 Mario Manningham 1.25 3.00
32 Owen Schmitt 1.25 3.00
33 Quentin Groves 1.00 2.50
34 Robert Killebrew 1.00 2.50
35 Sedrick Ellis 1.25 3.00
36 Shawn Crable .75 2.00
37 Terrell Thomas 1.00 2.50
38 Xavier Adibi .75 2.00
39 Adrian Arrington 1.00 2.50
40 Aqib Talib 1.25 3.00
41 Brandon Flowers 1.25 3.00
42 Calais Campbell 1.00 2.50
43 Darren McFadden 3.00 8.00
44 DeSean Jackson 2.50 6.00
45 Felix Jones 2.00 5.00
46 Jamaal Charles 2.00 5.00
47 Jonathan Stewart 2.00 5.00
48 Rashard Mendenhall 2.50 6.00
49 Steve Slaton 1.25 3.00
50 Vernon Gholston 1.00 2.50

2008 Donruss Classics School Colors Autographs

STATED PRINT RUN 50 SER.#'d SETS
2 Allen Patrick 10.00 25.00
3 Antoine Cason 12.00 30.00
4 Brian Brohm 12.00 30.00
5 Chad Henne 20.00 50.00
6 Chevis Jackson 8.00 20.00
7 Chris Long 12.00 30.00
8 Colt Brennan 15.00 40.00
9 DJ Hall 10.00 25.00
10 Dan Connor 12.00 30.00
11 Dennis Dixon 15.00 40.00
14 Erik Ainge 15.00 40.00
15 Ernie Wheelwright 10.00 25.00
16 Fred Davis 12.00 30.00
17 Glenn Dorsey 12.00 30.00
18 Harry Douglas 10.00 25.00
19 Jamar Adams 10.00 25.00
20 John David Booty 10.00 25.00
22 Keith Rivers 12.00 30.00
24 Lawrence Jackson 10.00 25.00
25 Limas Sweed 12.00 30.00
26 Marcus Monk 10.00 25.00
27 Matt Ryan 40.00 100.00
28 Matt Flynn 30.00 60.00
29 Mike Hart 12.00 30.00
30 Malcolm Kelly 10.00 25.00
31 Mario Manningham 12.00 30.00
32 Owen Schmitt 12.00 30.00
33 Quentin Groves 10.00 25.00
34 Robert Killebrew 10.00 25.00
36 Shawn Crable 8.00 20.00
37 Terrell Thomas 10.00 25.00
38 Xavier Adibi 8.00 20.00
39 Adrian Arrington 10.00 25.00
41 Brandon Flowers 12.00 30.00
42 Calais Campbell 10.00 25.00
43 Darren McFadden 30.00 60.00
44 DeSean Jackson 15.00 40.00
45 Felix Jones 20.00 50.00
46 Jamaal Charles 15.00 40.00
47 Jonathan Stewart 20.00 50.00
48 Rashard Mendenhall 25.00 60.00
49 Steve Slaton 12.00 30.00
50 Vernon Gholston 10.00 25.00

2008 Donruss Classics School Colors Jerseys

STATED PRINT RUN 60-100
*PRIME/25: .8X TO 2X BASIC JSY/60-100
PRIME PRINT RUN 10-25
1 Ali Highsmith 3.00 8.00
2 Allen Patrick 4.00 10.00
3 Antoine Cason 5.00 12.00
4 Brian Brohm 5.00 12.00
5 Chad Henne 10.00 25.00
6 Chevis Jackson 3.00 8.00
7 Chris Long 5.00 12.00
8 Colt Brennan 5.00 12.00
9 DJ Hall 4.00 10.00
10 Dan Connor 5.00 12.00
11 Dennis Dixon 5.00 12.00
12 Early Doucet 4.00 10.00
13 Eddie Royal 5.00 12.00
14 Erik Ainge 10.00 25.00
15 Ernie Wheelwright 4.00 10.00
16 Fred Davis 5.00 12.00
17 Glenn Dorsey 5.00 12.00
18 Harry Douglas 4.00 10.00
19 Jamar Adams/94 4.00 10.00
20 John David Booty 4.00 10.00
21 Jonathan Hefney 4.00 10.00
22 Keith Rivers 5.00 12.00
23 Kenny Phillips 5.00 12.00
24 Lawrence Jackson 4.00 10.00
25 Limas Sweed 5.00 12.00
26 Marcus Monk 4.00 10.00
27 Matt Ryan 10.00 25.00
28 Matt Flynn 10.00 25.00
29 Mike Hart 5.00 12.00
30 Malcolm Kelly 4.00 10.00
31 Mario Manningham 5.00 12.00
32 Owen Schmitt 5.00 12.00
33 Quentin Groves/60 4.00 10.00
34 Robert Killebrew 4.00 10.00
35 Sedrick Ellis 5.00 12.00
36 Shawn Crable 3.00 8.00
37 Terrell Thomas 4.00 10.00
38 Xavier Adibi 3.00 8.00
39 Adrian Arrington 4.00 10.00
40 Aqib Talib 5.00 12.00
41 Brandon Flowers 5.00 12.00
42 Calais Campbell 4.00 10.00
43 Darren McFadden 10.00 25.00
44 DeSean Jackson 10.00 25.00
45 Felix Jones 10.00 25.00
46 Jamaal Charles 8.00 20.00
47 Jonathan Stewart 10.00 25.00
48 Rashard Mendenhall 10.00 25.00
49 Steve Slaton 5.00 12.00
50 Vernon Gholston 4.00 10.00

2008 Donruss Classics Significant Signatures Gold

STATED PRINT RUN 25-125
153 Terrell Thomas/125 6.00 15.00
157 Calais Campbell/125 6.00 15.00
158 Quentin Groves/125 6.00 15.00
159 Pat Sims/25 12.00 30.00
160 Dan Connor/125 8.00 20.00
162 Xavier Adibi/125 5.00 12.00
163 Jerod Mayo/125 8.00 20.00
164 Jordon Dizon/25 15.00 40.00
165 Jake Long/25 15.00 40.00
166 Matt Ryan/125 50.00 120.00
167 Brian Brohm/125 8.00 20.00
168 Chad Henne/125 8.00 20.00
169 Dennis Dixon/125 10.00 25.00
170 Erik Ainge/125 8.00 20.00
171 Colt Brennan/125 8.00 20.00
172 Andre Woodson/125 8.00 20.00
173 Marcus Thomas/50 10.00 25.00
174 Darren McFadden/125 30.00 60.00
175 Jonathan Stewart/125 12.00 30.00
176 Felix Jones/125 30.00 60.00
177 Rashard Mendenhall/125 15.00 40.00
178 Tashard Choice/125 6.00 15.00
180 Tim Hightower/50 15.00 40.00
182 Caleb Campbell/125 8.00 20.00
183 Dustin Keller/125 8.00 20.00
184 John Carlson/125 8.00 20.00
185 Fred Davis/125 8.00 20.00
187 Donnie Avery/125 6.00 15.00
188 Devin Thomas/125 6.00 15.00
189 Jordy Nelson/50 25.00 50.00
190 James Hardy/125 6.00 15.00
191 Eddie Royal/50 12.00 30.00
192 Jerome Simpson/125 8.00 20.00
193 DeSean Jackson/125 15.00 40.00
194 Malcolm Kelly/125 6.00 15.00
195 Limas Sweed/125 8.00 20.00
196 Earl Bennett/125 8.00 20.00
197 Early Doucet/50 10.00 25.00
198 Harry Douglas/50 10.00 25.00
199 Mario Manningham/125 12.50 25.00
200 Andre Caldwell/125 6.00 15.00
205 Mike Jenkins/50
211 Glenn Dorsey/25 15.00 40.00
245 Kevin Robinson/50 8.00 20.00
247 Adrian Arrington/25

2008 Donruss Classics Significant Signatures Platinum

*PLATINUM/25: .6X TO 1.5X GOLD AU/125
PLATINUM PRINT RUN 5-25
166 Matt Ryan/25 75.00 150.00
174 Darren McFadden/25 50.00 120.00
176 Felix Jones/25 50.00 120.00
177 Rashard Mendenhall/25 40.00 100.00

2008 Donruss Classics Sunday's Best

STATED PRINT RUN 1000 SER.#'d SETS
*SILVER/250: .6X TO 1.5X BASIC INSERTS
SILVER PRINT RUN 250 SER.#'d SETS
*GOLD/100: .8X TO 2X BASIC INSERTS
GOLD PRINT RUN 100 SER.#'d SETS
*PLATINUM/25: 1.5X TO 4X BASIC INSERTS
PLATINUM PRINT RUN 25 SER.#'d SETS
1 Wes Welker 1.50 4.00
2 Jamal Lewis 1.25 3.00
3 Joseph Addai 1.25 3.00
4 Dwayne Bowe 1.25 3.00
5 Philip Rivers 1.50 4.00
6 Larry Fitzgerald 1.50 4.00
7 Larry Johnson 1.25 3.00
8 Willie Parker 1.25 3.00
9 Adrian Peterson 2.50 6.00
10 Terrell Owens 1.50 4.00
11 Reggie Wayne 1.25 3.00
12 Jason Campbell 1.25 3.00
13 Frank Gore 1.25 3.00
14 Antonio Gates 1.50 4.00
15 Braylon Edwards 1.25 3.00
16 Derek Anderson 1.00 2.50
17 Plaxico Burress 1.25 3.00
18 Steve Smith 1.25 3.00
19 Tony Gonzalez 1.25 3.00
20 Tom Brady 2.50 6.00
21 Peyton Manning 2.50 6.00
22 Laurence Maroney 1.25 3.00
23 Clinton Portis 1.25 3.00
24 Donald Driver 1.25 3.00
25 Marshawn Lynch 1.25 3.00
26 Brett Favre 4.00 10.00
27 Reggie Bush 1.50 4.00
28 Marion Barber 1.25 3.00
29 Vince Young 1.25 3.00
30 Steven Jackson 1.50 4.00
31 Ryan Grant 1.50 4.00
32 Marques Colston 1.25 3.00
33 Tony Romo 2.00 5.00
34 Torry Holt 1.25 3.00
35 Eli Manning 1.50 4.00
36 Matt Hasselbeck 1.25 3.00
37 Brandon Jacobs 1.25 3.00
38 Maurice Jones-Drew 1.25 3.00
39 Deion Branch 1.25 3.00
40 Devin Hester 1.50 4.00

2008 Donruss Classics Sunday's Best Jerseys

STATED PRINT RUN 250 SER.#'d SETS
*PRIME/25: 1X TO 2.5X BASIC JSY/250
PRIME PRINT RUN 25 SER.#'d SETS
*JERSEY #'s/80-89: .5X TO 1.2X BASIC INSERTS
*JERSEY #'s/31-39: .6X TO 1.5X BASIC INSERTS
*JERSEY #'s/21-29: .8X TO 2X BASIC INSERTS
JERSEY NUMBERS PRINT RUN 3-89
1 Wes Welker 4.00 10.00
2 Jamal Lewis 3.00 8.00
3 Joseph Addai 3.00 8.00
4 Dwayne Bowe 3.00 8.00
5 Philip Rivers 4.00 10.00
6 Larry Fitzgerald 4.00 10.00
7 Larry Johnson 3.00 8.00
8 Willie Parker 3.00 8.00
9 Adrian Peterson 6.00 15.00
10 Terrell Owens 4.00 10.00
11 Reggie Wayne 3.00 8.00
12 Jason Campbell 3.00 8.00
13 Frank Gore 3.00 8.00
14 Antonio Gates 4.00 10.00
15 Braylon Edwards 3.00 8.00
16 Derek Anderson 2.50 6.00
17 Plaxico Burress 3.00 8.00
18 Steve Smith 3.00 8.00
19 Tony Gonzalez 3.00 8.00
20 Tom Brady 6.00 15.00
21 Peyton Manning 6.00 15.00
22 Laurence Maroney 3.00 8.00
23 Clinton Portis 3.00 8.00
24 Donald Driver 3.00 8.00
25 Marshawn Lynch 3.00 8.00
26 Brett Favre 10.00 25.00
27 Reggie Bush 4.00 10.00

28 Marion Barber 3.00 8.00
29 Vince Young 3.00 8.00
30 Steven Jackson 4.00 10.00
31 Ryan Grant 4.00 10.00
32 Marques Colston 3.00 8.00
33 Tony Romo 5.00 12.00
34 Torry Holt 3.00 8.00
35 Eli Manning 4.00 10.00
36 Matt Hasselbeck 3.00 8.00
37 Brandon Jacobs 3.00 8.00
38 Maurice Jones-Drew 3.00 8.00
39 Deion Branch 3.00 8.00
40 Devin Hester 4.00 10.00

2008 Donruss Classics Sunday's Best Jerseys Jersey Numbers Autographs

STATED PRINT RUN 5-25
SERIAL #'d UNDER 20 NOT PRICED
7 Larry Johnson/25 12.00 30.00
9 Adrian Peterson/25 100.00 200.00
13 Frank Gore/15 15.00 40.00
24 Donald Driver/25 15.00 40.00
25 Marshawn Lynch/25 15.00 40.00
28 Marion Barber/15 15.00 40.00
32 Marques Colston/25 15.00 40.00
33 Tony Romo/20 50.00 100.00
37 Brandon Jacobs/20 15.00 40.00
38 Maurice Jones-Drew/20 15.00 40.00

2008 Donruss Classics Sunday's Best Jerseys Prime Autographs

PRIME PRINT RUN 1-25
SERIAL #'d UNDER 20 NOT PRICED
7 Larry Johnson/25 20.00 50.00
25 Marshawn Lynch/20 20.00 50.00
32 Marques Colston/25 20.00 50.00

2008 Donruss Classics Team Colors

RANDOM INSERTS IN RETAIL PACKS
1 Darren McFadden 5.00 12.00
2 Felix Jones 3.00 8.00
3 Jonathan Stewart 3.00 8.00
4 Rashard Mendenhall 4.00 10.00
5 Matt Ryan 8.00 20.00
6 Brian Brohm 2.00 5.00
7 Chad Henne 2.00 5.00
8 Joe Flacco 6.00 15.00
9 Donnie Avery 1.50 4.00
10 Devin Thomas 1.50 4.00

2008 Donruss Classics Timeless Treasures

STATED PRINT RUN 1000 SER.#'d SETS
*SILVER/250: .6X TO 1.5X BASIC INSERTS
SILVER PRINT RUN 250 SER.#'d SETS
*GOLD/100: .8X TO 2X BASIC INSERTS
GOLD PRINT RUN 100 SER.#'d SETS
*PLATINUM/25: 1.5X TO 4X BASIC INSERTS
PLATINUM PRINT RUN 25 SER.#'d SETS
1 Y.A. Tittle 2.00 5.00
2 Tony Dorsett 2.00 5.00
3 Tom Landry 2.50 6.00
4 Knute Rockne 3.00 8.00
5 Peyton Manning 3.00 8.00
6 Paul Krause 1.25 3.00
7 Jim Brown 2.50 6.00
8 Hank Stram 1.50 4.00
9 John Elway 3.00 8.00
10 George Blanda 2.00 5.00
11 Emmitt Smith 4.00 10.00
12 Dan Marino 4.00 10.00
13 Charlie Joiner 1.25 3.00
14 Sammy Baugh 2.00 5.00
15 Bo Jackson 2.50 6.00

2008 Donruss Classics Timeless Treasures Cuts

STATED PRINT RUN 1-25
SERIAL #'d UNDER 25 NOT PRICED
8 Hank Stram/25 75.00 150.00
10 George Blanda/25 30.00 60.00

2008 Donruss Classics Timeless Treasures Material

STATED PRINT RUN 250 SER.#'d SETS
*PRIME/25: 1X TO 2.5X BASIC JSY/250
PRIME PRINT RUN 1-25
1 Y.A. Tittle 6.00 15.00
2 Tony Dorsett 6.00 15.00
3 Tom Landry 15.00 40.00
4 Knute Rockne Jkt 25.00 50.00
5 Peyton Manning 6.00 15.00
7 Jim Brown 8.00 20.00
8 Hank Stram 6.00 15.00
9 John Elway 10.00 25.00
10 George Blanda 6.00 15.00
11 Emmitt Smith 12.00 30.00
12 Dan Marino 12.00 30.00
13 Charlie Joiner 4.00 10.00
14 Sammy Baugh/100 10.00 25.00
15 Bo Jackson 8.00 20.00

2008 Donruss Classics Timeless Treasures Material Autographs

STATED PRINT RUN 10-25
SERIAL #'d UNDER 20 NOT PRICED
2 Tony Dorsett/25 30.00 60.00
7 Jim Brown/20 50.00 100.00
10 George Blanda/25 25.00 50.00
12 Dan Marino/25 100.00 200.00
13 Charlie Joiner/25 20.00 40.00
15 Bo Jackson/25 40.00 80.00

2008 Donruss Classics Timeless Treasures Material Prime Autographs

PRIME PRINT RUN 5-25 SER.#'d SETS
SERIAL #'d UNDER 25 NOT PRICED
2 Tony Dorsett/25 40.00 80.00
15 Bo Jackson/25 40.00 80.00

2009 Donruss Classics

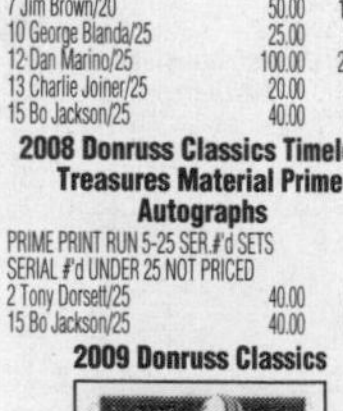

COMP.SET w/o SP's (100) 7.50 20.00
101-150 LEGEND PRINT RUN 999
ROOKIE UNSIGNED PRINT RUN 999
ROOKIE AUTO PRINT RUN 299-999
1 Anquan Boldin .25 .60
2 Kurt Warner .30 .75
3 Larry Fitzgerald .30 .75
4 Steve Breaston .25 .60
5 Matt Ryan .30 .75
6 Michael Turner .25 .60
7 Roddy White .25 .60
8 Joe Flacco .30 .75
9 Willis McGahee .25 .60
10 Derrick Mason .25 .60
11 Lee Evans .25 .60
12 Marshawn Lynch .25 .60
13 DeAngelo Williams .30 .75
14 Jake Delhomme .25 .60
15 Jonathan Stewart .25 .60
16 Steve Smith .25 .60
17 Greg Olsen .20 .50
18 Kyle Orton .25 .60
19 Matt Forte .30 .75
20 Carson Palmer .30 .75
21 Chad Ochocinco .25 .60
22 T.J. Houshmandzadeh .25 .60
23 Brady Quinn .25 .60
24 Braylon Edwards .25 .60
25 Jamal Lewis .25 .60
26 Kellen Winslow Jr. .25 .60
27 Felix Jones .30 .75
28 Roy Williams WR .25 .60
29 Marion Barber .25 .60
30 Tony Romo .50 1.25
31 Brandon Marshall .25 .60
32 Eddie Royal .25 .60
33 Jay Cutler .30 .75
34 Calvin Johnson .30 .75
35 Kevin Smith .25 .60
36 Aaron Rodgers .60 1.50
37 Donald Driver .25 .60
38 Ryan Grant .25 .60
39 Andre Johnson .25 .60
40 Matt Schaub .25 .60
41 Steve Slaton .25 .60
42 Anthony Gonzalez .20 .50
43 Joseph Addai .30 .75
44 Peyton Manning .50 1.25
45 Reggie Wayne .25 .60
46 David Garrard .25 .60
47 Maurice Jones-Drew .25 .60
48 Marcedes Lewis .20 .50
49 Dwayne Bowe .25 .60
50 Larry Johnson .25 .60
51 Chad Pennington .25 .60
52 Ronnie Brown .25 .60
53 Ricky Williams .25 .60
54 Adrian Peterson .50 1.25
55 Bernard Berrian .25 .60
56 Chester Taylor .20 .50
57 Laurence Maroney .25 .60
58 Randy Moss .30 .75
59 Tom Brady .50 1.25
60 Drew Brees .30 .75
61 Marques Colston .25 .60
62 Reggie Bush .30 .75
63 Brandon Jacobs .25 .60
64 Kevin Boss .25 .60
65 Eli Manning .30 .75
66 Kellen Clemens .20 .50
67 Jerricho Cotchery .25 .60
68 Laveranues Coles .20 .50
69 Thomas Jones .25 .60
70 JaMarcus Russell .20 .50
71 Justin Fargas .20 .50
72 Darren McFadden .30 .75
73 Brian Westbrook .25 .60
74 Donovan McNabb .30 .75
75 Kevin Curtis .20 .50
76 Ben Roethlisberger .30 .75
77 Heath Miller .25 .60
78 Santonio Holmes .25 .60
79 Willie Parker .20 .50
80 Antonio Gates .25 .60
81 LaDainian Tomlinson .30 .75
82 Philip Rivers .30 .75
83 Frank Gore .25 .60
84 Isaac Bruce .25 .60
85 Deion Branch .25 .60
86 Julius Jones .20 .50
87 Matt Hasselbeck .25 .60
88 Marc Bulger .25 .60
89 Steven Jackson .25 .60
90 Donnie Avery .25 .60
91 Antonio Bryant .20 .50
92 Earnest Graham .20 .50
93 Derrick Ward .20 .50
94 Chris Johnson .30 .75
95 Justin Gage .20 .50
96 LenDale White .25 .60
97 Chris Cooley .25 .60
98 Clinton Portis .25 .60
99 Jason Campbell .20 .50
100 Santana Moss .25 .60
101 Alan Page 1.50 4.00
102 Andre Reed 1.50 4.00
103 Barry Sanders 3.00 8.00
104 Billy Sims 1.50 4.00
105 Bo Jackson 2.50 6.00
106 Bob Lilly 1.50 4.00
107 Bobby Layne 2.00 5.00
108 Carl Eller 1.25 3.00
109 Chuck Bednarik 1.50 4.00
110 Ace Parker 1.25 3.00
111 Cliff Harris 1.50 4.00
112 Danny White 1.50 4.00
113 Daryl Johnston 2.00 5.00
114 Dave Casper 1.25 3.00
115 Earl Campbell 2.00 5.00
116 Emmitt Smith 3.00 8.00
117 Eric Dickerson 1.50 4.00
118 Franco Harris 2.00 5.00
119 Gale Sayers 2.50 6.00
121 Jack Youngblood 1.25 3.00
122 Jay Novacek 1.50 4.00
123 Jerry Rice 3.00 8.00
124 Jim Brown 2.50 6.00
125 Jim Kelly 2.00 5.00
126 Jim McMahon 1.50 4.00
127 Joe Greene 2.00 5.00
128 Joe Montana 4.00 10.00
129 John Stallworth 1.50 4.00
130 Lawrence Taylor 2.00 5.00
131 Lou Groza 1.50 4.00
132 Marion Motley 1.50 4.00
133 Merlin Olsen 1.50 4.00
134 Michael Irvin 1.50 4.00
135 Mike Singletary 2.00 5.00
136 Phil Simms 1.50 4.00
137 Reggie White 2.00 5.00
138 Roger Craig 1.50 4.00
139 Roger Staubach 2.50 6.00
140 Sid Luckman 1.50 4.00
141 Steve Young 2.50 6.00
142 Ted Hendricks 1.25 3.00
143 Thurman Thomas 2.00 5.00
144 Tim Brown 2.00 5.00
145 Tom Landry 2.50 6.00
146 Tony Dorsett 2.00 5.00
147 Troy Aikman 2.50 6.00
148 Walter Payton 4.00 10.00
149 William Perry 1.50 4.00
150 Y.A. Tittle 2.00 5.00
151 Aaron Curry RC 2.00 5.00
152 Aaron Kelly AU/999 RC 4.00 10.00
153 Aaron Maybin RC 1.50 4.00
154 Alphonso Smith RC 1.50 4.00
155 Andre Brown AU/299 RC 4.00 10.00
156 Andre Smith RC 1.50 4.00
157 Arian Foster RC 4.00 10.00
158 Austin Collie AU/399 RC 8.00 20.00
159 B.J. Raji RC 2.00 5.00
160 Brandon Gibson AU/499 RC 6.00 15.00
161 Brandon Pettigrew RC 2.00 5.00
162 Brandon Tate AU/399 RC 6.00 15.00
163 Brian Cushing RC 2.00 5.00
164 Brian Hartline RC 2.00 5.00
165 Brian Orakpo RC 2.00 5.00
166 Brian Robiskie RC 2.00 5.00
167 Brooks Foster AU/399 RC 4.00 10.00
168 Cameron Morrah RC 1.25 3.00
169 Cedric Peerman AU/499 RC 5.00 12.00
170 Chase Coffman AU/299 RC 5.00 12.00
171 Chris Wells RC 3.00 8.00
172 Clay Matthews RC 5.00 12.00
173 Clint Sintim AU/299 RC 6.00 15.00
174 Cody Brown RC 1.25 3.00
175 Cornelius Ingram AU/399 RC 4.00 10.00
176 Darcel McBath RC 1.50 4.00
177 Darius Butler RC 2.00 5.00
178 Darius Passmore AU/999 RC 4.00 10.00
179 Darrius Heyward-Bey RC 2.00 5.00
180 Demetrius Byrd RC 1.50 4.00
181 Deon Butler AU/399 RC 5.00 12.00
182 Derrick Williams AU/299 RC 5.00 12.00
183 Devin Moore AU/999 RC 4.00 10.00
184 Dominique Edison AU/499 RC 4.00 10.00
185 Donald Brown RC 2.00 5.00
186 Eugene Monroe RC 1.25 3.00
187 Everette Brown RC 1.50 4.00
188 Gartrell Johnson RC 1.25 3.00
189 Glen Coffee RC 1.50 4.00
190 Graham Harrell AU/999 RC 8.00 20.00
191 Hakeem Nicks RC 3.00 8.00
192 Hunter Cantwell AU/999 RC 5.00 12.00
193 Ian Johnson RC 2.00 5.00
194 Jairus Byrd RC 2.00 5.00
195 James Casey AU/299 RC 5.00 12.00
196 James Davis RC 2.00 5.00
197 James Laurinaitis RC 2.00 5.00
198 Jared Cook AU/299 RC 6.00 15.00
199 Jarett Dillard AU/299 RC 6.00 15.00
200 Jason Smith RC 1.50 4.00
201 Javon Ringer RC 2.00 5.00
202 Jeremiah Johnson AU/999 RC 5.00 12.00
203 Jeremy Childs RC 1.50 4.00
204 Jeremy Maclin RC 3.00 8.00
205 John Parker Wilson AU/999 RC 5.00 12.00
206 Johnny Knox AU/399 RC 10.00 20.00
207 Josh Freeman RC 4.00 10.00
208 Juaquin Iglesias AU/399 RC 5.00 12.00
209 Kenny Britt RC 2.50 6.00
210 Kenny McKinley AU/399 RC 6.00 15.00
211 Kevin Ogletree AU/999 RC 6.00 15.00
212 Knowshon Moreno RC 2.00 5.00
213 Kory Sheets AU/999 RC 4.00 10.00
214 Larry English RC 2.00 5.00
215 LeSean McCoy RC 4.00 10.00
216 Louis Delmas RC 2.00 5.00
217 Louis Murphy RC 2.00 5.00
218 Malcolm Jenkins RC 2.00 5.00
219 Mark Sanchez RC 6.00 15.00
220 Matthew Stafford RC 10.00 25.00
221 Michael Crabtree RC 4.00 10.00
222 Michael Mitchell RC 1.50 4.00
223 Mike Goodson AU/299 RC 6.00 15.00
224 Mike Thomas AU/299 RC 6.00 15.00
225 Mike Wallace AU/299 RC 15.00 30.00
226 Mohamed Massaquoi RC 1.50 4.00
227 Nate Davis AU/299 RC 12.50 25.00
228 Nathan Brown AU/999 RC 4.00 10.00
229 Pat White RC 2.00 5.00
230 Patrick Chung RC 2.00 5.00
231 Patrick Turner AU/399 RC 5.00 12.00
232 Percy Harvin RC 3.00 8.00
233 Peria Jerry RC 1.50 4.00
234 Quan Cosby AU/999 RC 4.00 10.00
235 Quinten Lawrence RC 1.25 3.00
236 Quinn Johnson AU/699 RC 4.00 10.00
237 Ramses Barden AU/299 RC 4.00 10.00
238 Rashad Jennings AU/499 RC 6.00 15.00
239 Rey Maualuga AU/299 RC 6.00 15.00
240 Rhett Bomar AU/299 RC 5.00 12.00
241 Richard Quinn RC 1.50 4.00
242 Shawn Nelson AU/499 RC 5.00 12.00
243 Shonn Greene RC 3.00 8.00
244 Stephen McGee AU/299 RC 12.50 25.00
245 Tom Brandstater AU/299 RC 6.00 15.00
246 Tony Fiammetta AU/699 RC 4.00 10.00
247 Travis Beckum AU/499 RC 5.00 12.00
248 Tyrell Sutton AU/999 RC 4.00 10.00
249 Tyson Jackson RC 1.50 4.00
250 Vontae Davis RC 2.00 5.00

2009 Donruss Classics Timeless Tributes Gold

*VETS 1-100: 5X TO 12X BASIC CARDS
*LEGENDS 101-150: 1X TO 2.5X BASIC CARDS
*ROOKIES 151-250: .5X TO 1.2X TT SILVER
STATED PRINT RUN 50 SER.#'d SETS

2009 Donruss Classics Timeless Tributes Platinum

*VETS 1-100: 8X TO 20X BASIC CARDS
*LEGENDS 101-150: 1.5X TO 4X BASIC CARDS
*ROOKIES 151-250: .8X TO 2X TT SILVER
STATED PRINT RUN 25 SER.#'d SETS

2009 Donruss Classics Timeless Tributes Silver

*VETS 1-100: 4X TO 10X BASIC CARDS
*LEGENDS 101-150: .8X TO 2X BASIC CARDS
STATED PRINT RUN 100 SER.#'d SETS
151 Aaron Curry 2.50 6.00
152 Aaron Kelly 2.00 5.00
153 Aaron Maybin 2.00 5.00
154 Alphonso Smith 2.00 5.00
155 Andre Brown 1.50 4.00
156 Andre Smith 2.00 5.00
157 Arian Foster 5.00 12.00
158 Austin Collie 2.50 6.00
159 B.J. Raji 2.50 6.00
160 Brandon Gibson 2.50 6.00
161 Brandon Pettigrew 2.50 6.00
162 Brandon Tate 2.50 6.00
163 Brian Cushing 2.50 6.00
164 Brian Hartline 2.50 6.00
165 Brian Orakpo 2.50 6.00
166 Brian Robiskie 2.50 6.00
167 Brooks Foster 1.50 4.00
168 Cameron Morrah 1.50 4.00
169 Cedric Peerman 2.00 5.00
170 Chase Coffman 2.00 5.00
171 Chris Wells 4.00 10.00
172 Clay Matthews 6.00 15.00
173 Clint Sintim 2.50 6.00
174 Cody Brown 1.50 4.00
175 Cornelius Ingram 1.50 4.00
176 Darcel McBath 2.00 5.00
177 Darius Butler 2.50 6.00
178 Darius Passmore 2.00 5.00
179 Darrius Heyward-Bey 2.50 6.00
180 Demetrius Byrd 2.00 5.00
181 Deon Butler 2.00 5.00
182 Derrick Williams 2.00 5.00
183 Devin Moore 2.00 5.00
184 Dominique Edison 1.50 4.00
185 Donald Brown 2.50 6.00
186 Eugene Monroe 1.50 4.00
187 Everette Brown 2.00 5.00
188 Gartrell Johnson 1.50 4.00
189 Glen Coffee 2.00 5.00
190 Graham Harrell 2.50 6.00
191 Hakeem Nicks 4.00 10.00
192 Hunter Cantwell 2.50 6.00
193 Ian Johnson 2.50 6.00
194 Jairus Byrd 2.50 6.00
195 James Casey 2.00 5.00
196 James Davis 2.50 6.00
197 James Laurinaitis 2.50 6.00
198 Jared Cook 2.50 6.00
199 Jarett Dillard 2.50 6.00
200 Jason Smith 2.00 5.00
201 Javon Ringer 2.50 6.00
202 Jeremiah Johnson 2.50 6.00
203 Jeremy Childs 2.00 5.00
204 Jeremy Maclin 4.00 10.00
205 John Parker Wilson 2.50 6.00
206 Johnny Knox 4.00 10.00
207 Josh Freeman 5.00 12.00
208 Juaquin Iglesias 2.00 5.00
209 Kenny Britt 3.00 8.00
210 Kenny McKinley 2.50 6.00
211 Kevin Ogletree 2.50 6.00
212 Knowshon Moreno 2.50 6.00
213 Kory Sheets 2.00 5.00
214 Larry English 2.50 6.00
215 LeSean McCoy 5.00 12.00
216 Louis Delmas 2.50 6.00
217 Louis Murphy 2.50 6.00
218 Malcolm Jenkins 2.50 6.00
219 Mark Sanchez 8.00 20.00
220 Matthew Stafford 12.00 30.00
221 Michael Crabtree 5.00 12.00
222 Michael Mitchell 2.00 5.00
223 Mike Goodson 2.50 6.00
224 Mike Thomas 2.50 6.00
225 Mike Wallace 5.00 12.00
226 Mohamed Massaquoi 2.00 5.00
227 Nate Davis 2.00 5.00
228 Nathan Brown 2.00 5.00
229 Pat White 2.50 6.00
230 Patrick Chung 2.50 6.00
231 Patrick Turner 2.00 5.00
232 Percy Harvin 4.00 10.00
233 Peria Jerry 2.00 5.00
234 Quan Cosby 2.00 5.00
235 Quinten Lawrence 1.50 4.00
236 Quinn Johnson 2.00 5.00
237 Ramses Barden 1.50 4.00
238 Rashad Jennings 2.50 6.00
239 Rey Maualuga 2.50 6.00
240 Rhett Bomar 2.00 5.00
241 Richard Quinn 2.00 5.00
242 Shawn Nelson 2.00 5.00
243 Shonn Greene 4.00 10.00
244 Stephen McGee 2.50 6.00
245 Tom Brandstater 2.50 6.00
246 Tony Fiammetta 2.00 5.00
247 Travis Beckum 2.00 5.00
248 Tyrell Sutton 2.00 5.00
249 Tyson Jackson 2.00 5.00
250 Vontae Davis 2.50 6.00

2009 Donruss Classics Classic Combos

*GOLD/100: .8X TO 2X BASIC INSERTS
GOLD PRINT RUN 100 SER.#'d SETS
*PLATINUM/25: 1.2X TO 3X BASIC INSERTS
PLATINUM PRINT RUN 25 SER.#'d SETS
*SILVER/250: .6X TO 1.5X BASIC INSERTS
SILVER PRINT RUN 250
1 Alan Page 1.50 4.00
Carl Eller
2 Y.A. Tittle 2.50 6.00
Steve Young
3 Jim Brown 2.50 6.00
Lou Groza
4 Dave Casper 2.00 5.00
Tim Brown
5 Jack Youngblood 1.50 4.00
Merlin Olsen
6 Emmitt Smith 3.00 8.00
Daryl Johnston
7 Eric Dickerson 2.50 6.00
Bo Jackson
8 Phil Simms 2.00 5.00
Lawrence Taylor
9 John Stallworth 2.00 5.00
Franco Harris
10 Chuck Bednarik 2.00 5.00
Reggie White
11 Joe Montana 4.00 10.00
Roger Craig
12 Tom Landry 2.50 6.00
Tony Dorsett
13 Andre Reed 2.00 5.00
Thurman Thomas
14 Cliff Harris 1.50 4.00
Bob Lilly
15 Walter Payton 4.00 10.00
William Perry

2009 Donruss Classics Classic Combos Jerseys

STATED PRINT RUN 30-50
*PRIME/25: .8X TO 2X DUAL JSY/25
PRIME PRINT RUN 5-25
1 Alan Page 6.00 15.00
Carl Eller
2 Y.A. Tittle 10.00 25.00
Steve Young
3 Jim Brown 10.00 25.00
Lou Groza
4 Dave Casper 8.00 20.00
Tim Brown
5 Jack Youngblood 6.00 15.00
Merlin Olsen
6 Emmitt Smith/30 15.00 40.00
Daryl Johnston
7 Eric Dickerson 10.00 25.00
Bo Jackson
8 Phil Simms 8.00 20.00
Lawrence Taylor
9 John Stallworth 8.00 20.00
Franco Harris
10 Chuck Bednarik 8.00 20.00
Reggie White
11 Joe Montana 15.00 40.00
Roger Craig
12 Tom Landry 15.00 30.00
Tony Dorsett
13 Andre Reed 8.00 20.00
Thurman Thomas
14 Cliff Harris 8.00 20.00
Bob Lilly

2009 Donruss Classics Classic Cuts

STATED PRINT RUN 1-100
SERIAL #'d UNDER 15 NOT PRICED
4 Arnie Weinmeister/27 40.00 80.00
14 Bill Willis/18 40.00 80.00
27 Ace Parker/55 30.00 60.00
28 Clark Shaughnessy/62 40.00 80.00
31 Bulldog Turner/23 50.00 100.00
34 Dante Lavelli/21 30.00 80.00
35 Dick Night Train Lane/21 50.00 100.00
45 Ernie Stautner/77 30.00 60.00
47 Frank Gatski/28 50.00 100.00
49 Gene Upshaw/20 30.00 60.00
51 George Connor/34 30.00 60.00
53 George McAfee/16 40.00 80.00
54 George Musso/15 40.00 80.00
56 Glenn Davis/23 40.00 80.00
57 Hank Stram/66 30.00 80.00
64 Jim Ringo/21 50.00 100.00
78 Lamar Hunt/17 60.00 120.00
84 Lou Groza/25 30.00 80.00
91 Red Badgro/46 30.00 60.00
92 Otto Graham/23 50.00 100.00
97 Pete Pihos/25 40.00 80.00
100 Ray Flaherty/18 50.00 80.00
106 Roosevelt Brown/100 20.00 40.00
107 Sammy Baugh/28 75.00 150.00
108 Sid Gillman/32 40.00 80.00
114 Tom Fears/26 40.00 80.00
115 Tony Canadeo/55 30.00 80.00
117 Walter Payton/25 200.00 350.00
119 Weeb Ewbank/53 30.00 80.00

2009 Donruss Classics Classic Quads

*GOLD/100: .8X TO 2X BASIC INSERTS
GOLD PRINT RUN 100 SER.#'d SETS
*PLATINUM/25: 1.2X TO 3X BASIC INSERTS
PLATINUM PRINT RUN 25 SER.#'d SETS
*SILVER HOLO/250: .6X TO 1.5X BASIC INSERTS
SILVER HOLOFOIL PRINT RUN 250
1 Andre Reed 3.00 8.00
Michael Irvin
Jerry Rice
Tim Brown
2 Joe Montana 5.00 12.00
Roger Craig
Jerry Rice
Steve Young
3 Barry Sanders 4.00 10.00
Earl Campbell
Emmitt Smith
Walter Payton
5 Sid Luckman 4.00 10.00
Jim McMahon
Gale Sayers
Walter Payton
6 Tom Landry 2.50 6.00
Roger Staubach
Bob Lilly
Cliff Harris
7 Emmitt Smith 4.00 10.00
Michael Irvin
Daryl Johnston
Jay Novacek
9 Eric Dickerson 2.50 6.00
Bo Jackson
Dave Casper
Ted Hendricks
10 Merlin Olsen 1.50 4.00
Alan Page
Carl Eller
Jack Youngblood

2009 Donruss Classics Classic Singles

*GOLD/100: .8X TO 2X BASIC INSERTS
GOLD PRINT RUN 100 SER.#'d SETS
*PLATINUM/25: 1.2X TO 3X BASIC INSERTS
PLATINUM PRINT RUN 25 SER.#'d SETS
*SILVER HOL/250: .6X TO 1.5X BASIC INSERTS
SILVER HOLOFOIL PRINT RUN 250
1 Alan Page 1.25 3.00
2 Andre Reed 1.25 3.00
3 Barry Sanders 2.50 6.00
4 Bo Jackson 2.00 5.00
5 Bob Lilly 1.25 3.00
6 Carl Eller 1.00 2.50
7 Chuck Bednarik 1.25 3.00
8 Daryl Johnston 1.50 4.00
9 Dave Casper 1.00 2.50
10 Emmitt Smith 2.50 6.00
11 Eric Dickerson 1.25 3.00
12 Franco Harris 1.50 4.00
13 Jack Youngblood 1.00 2.50
14 Jim Brown 2.00 5.00
15 Joe Montana 3.00 8.00
16 John Stallworth 1.25 3.00
17 Lawrence Taylor 1.50 4.00
18 Lou Groza 1.25 3.00
19 Merlin Olsen 1.25 3.00
20 Phil Simms 1.25 3.00
21 Reggie White 1.50 4.00
22 Roger Craig 1.25 3.00
23 Steve Young 2.00 5.00
24 Thurman Thomas 1.50 4.00
25 Tim Brown 1.50 4.00
26 Tom Landry 2.00 5.00
27 Tony Dorsett 1.50 4.00
28 Walter Payton 3.00 8.00
29 William Perry 1.25 3.00
30 Y.A. Tittle 1.50 4.00

2009 Donruss Classics Classic Singles Jerseys

STATED PRINT RUN 42-250
*PRIME/32-50: .8X TO 2X BASIC JSY/250
*PRIME/15-25: 1X TO 2.5X BASIC JSY/250
PRIME PRINT RUN 2-50
1 Alan Page 5.00 12.00
2 Andre Reed 5.00 12.00
3 Barry Sanders 10.00 25.00
4 Bo Jackson 8.00 20.00
5 Bob Lilly 5.00 12.00
6 Carl Eller 4.00 10.00
7 Chuck Bednarik 5.00 12.00
9 Dave Casper 4.00 10.00
10 Emmitt Smith 10.00 25.00
11 Eric Dickerson 5.00 12.00
12 Franco Harris 6.00 15.00
13 Jack Youngblood 4.00 10.00
14 Jim Brown 8.00 20.00
15 Joe Montana 12.00 30.00
16 John Stallworth 5.00 12.00
17 Lawrence Taylor 6.00 15.00
18 Lou Groza 5.00 12.00
19 Merlin Olsen 5.00 12.00
20 Phil Simms 5.00 12.00
21 Reggie White 8.00 20.00
22 Roger Craig 5.00 12.00
23 Steve Young 8.00 20.00
24 Thurman Thomas 6.00 15.00
25 Tim Brown 6.00 15.00
26 Tom Landry Jkt 15.00 30.00
27 Tony Dorsett 6.00 15.00
28 Walter Payton 12.00 30.00
30 Y.A. Tittle/42 8.00 20.00

2009 Donruss Classics Classic Singles Jerseys Autographs

STATED PRINT RUN 25 SER.#'d SETS
*PRIME/25: .5X TO 1.2X BASIC JSY AU/25
PRIME PRINT RUN 1-25
1 Alan Page 15.00 40.00
2 Andre Reed 15.00 40.00
3 Barry Sanders 60.00 120.00
4 Bo Jackson 50.00 100.00
5 Bob Lilly 15.00 40.00
6 Carl Eller 12.00 30.00
7 Chuck Bednarik 15.00 40.00
9 Dave Casper 15.00 40.00
10 Emmitt Smith 100.00 200.00
11 Eric Dickerson 25.00 50.00
12 Franco Harris 25.00 50.00
13 Jack Youngblood 15.00 40.00
14 Jim Brown 40.00 80.00
15 Joe Montana 75.00 150.00
16 John Stallworth 25.00 50.00
17 Lawrence Taylor 40.00 80.00
19 Merlin Olsen 20.00 50.00
20 Phil Simms 15.00 40.00
22 Roger Craig 15.00 40.00
23 Steve Young 40.00 80.00
24 Thurman Thomas 25.00 50.00
25 Tim Brown 20.00 50.00
27 Tony Dorsett 25.00 50.00
30 Y.A. Tittle 30.00 60.00

2009 Donruss Classics Classic Triples

*GOLD/100: .8X TO 2X BASIC INSERTS
GOLD PRINT RUN 100 SER.#'d SETS
*PLATINUM/25: 1.5X TO 4X BASIC INSERTS
PLATINUM PRINT RUN 25 SER.#'d SETS
*SILVER/250: .6X TO 1.5X BASIC INSERTS
SILVER PRINT RUN 250
1 Roger Staubach 2.50 6.00
Danny White
Troy Aikman
2 Jim Kelly 2.00 5.00
Andre Reed
Thurman Thomas
3 Joe Greene 2.00 5.00
Reggie White
Jack Youngblood
4 Emmitt Smith 3.00 8.00
Michael Irvin
Jay Novacek
5 Joe Montana 4.00 10.00
Jerry Rice
Roger Craig
7 Jim Brown 2.50 6.00
Lou Groza
Marion Motley
8 Sid Luckman 4.00 10.00
Gale Sayers
Walter Payton
9 Bobby Layne 3.00 8.00
Billy Sims
Barry Sanders
10 Y.A. Tittle 4.00 10.00
Joe Montana
Steve Young

2009 Donruss Classics Classic Triples Jerseys

STATED PRINT RUN 25 SER.#'d SETS
1 Roger Staubach 15.00 40.00
Danny White
Troy Aikman
2 Jim Kelly 12.00 30.00
Andre Reed
Thurman Thomas
3 Joe Greene 12.00 30.00
Reggie White
Jack Youngblood
4 Emmitt Smith 25.00 60.00
Michael Irvin
Jay Novacek
5 Joe Montana 25.00 60.00
Jerry Rice
Roger Craig
7 Jim Brown 15.00 40.00
Lou Groza
Marion Motley
8 Sid Luckman 25.00 60.00
Gale Sayers
Walter Payton
9 Bobby Layne 20.00 50.00
Billy Sims
Barry Sanders
10 Y.A. Tittle 25.00 60.00
Joe Montana
Steve Young

2009 Donruss Classics Dress Code

*GOLD/100: .8X TO 2X BASIC INSERTS
GOLD PRINT RUN 100 SER.#'d SETS
*PLATINUM/25: 1.5X TO 4X BASIC INSERTS
PLATINUM PRINT RUN 25 SER.#'d SETS
*SILVER/250: .6X TO 1.5X BASIC INSERTS
SILVER PRINT RUN 250
1 Antonio Gates 1.25 3.00
2 Ben Roethlisberger 1.50 4.00
3 Cadillac Williams 1.25 3.00
4 Chad Ochocinco 1.25 3.00
5 Deuce McAllister 1.25 3.00
6 Frank Gore 1.25 3.00
7 Jason Witten 1.50 4.00
8 Jerricho Cotchery 1.25 3.00
9 Joseph Addai 1.50 4.00
10 Justin McCareins 1.00 2.50
11 Kevin Curtis 1.00 2.50
12 Ladell Betts 1.00 2.50
13 Larry Johnson 1.25 3.00
14 Lee Evans 1.25 3.00
15 Marion Barber 1.25 3.00
16 Marques Colston 1.25 3.00
17 Matt Hasselbeck 1.25 3.00
18 Maurice Jones-Drew 1.25 3.00
19 Reggie Wayne 1.25 3.00
20 Steven Jackson 1.25 3.00
21 Tarvaris Jackson 1.25 3.00
22 T.J. Houshmandzadeh 1.25 3.00
23 Tony Gonzalez 1.25 3.00
24 Tony Romo 2.50 6.00
25 Vincent Jackson 1.25 3.00

2009 Donruss Classics Dress Code Jerseys

STATED PRINT RUN 15-299
*PRIME/50: .6X TO 1.5X BASE JSY/290-299
*PRIME/50: .8X TO 2X BASE JSY/80-108
*PRIME/50: 1X TO 2.5X BASE JSY/15
*PRIME/18-25: 1X TO 2.5X BASE JSY/290-299
PRIME PRINT RUN 18-50
1 Antonio Gates/299 3.00 8.00
2 Ben Roethlisberger/299 4.00 10.00
3 Cadillac Williams/299 3.00 8.00
4 Chad Ochocinco/299 3.00 8.00
5 Deuce McAllister/80 4.00 10.00
6 Frank Gore/299 3.00 8.00
7 Jason Witten/299 4.00 10.00
8 Jerricho Cotchery/299 3.00 8.00
9 Joseph Addai/299 4.00 10.00
10 Justin McCareins/299 2.50 6.00
11 Kevin Curtis/299 2.50 6.00
12 Ladell Betts/108 3.00 8.00
13 Larry Johnson/299 3.00 8.00
14 Lee Evans/299 3.00 8.00
15 Marion Barber/299 3.00 8.00
16 Marques Colston/299 3.00 8.00
17 Matt Hasselbeck/299 3.00 8.00
18 Maurice Jones-Drew/299 3.00 8.00
19 Reggie Wayne/299 3.00 8.00
20 Steven Jackson/299 3.00 8.00
21 Tarvaris Jackson/299 3.00 8.00
22 T.J. Houshmandzadeh/15 5.00 12.00
23 Tony Gonzalez/299 3.00 8.00
24 Tony Romo/299 6.00 15.00
25 Vincent Jackson/299 3.00 8.00

2009 Donruss Classics Dress Code Jerseys Autographs

STATED PRINT RUN 5-25
SERIAL #'d UNDER 15 NOT PRICED
5 Deuce McAllister/25 12.00 30.00
22 T.J. Houshmandzadeh/15 12.00 30.00

2009 Donruss Classics Dress Code Jerseys Prime Autographs

STATED PRINT RUN 5-25
5 Deuce McAllister/25 15.00 40.00
11 Kevin Curtis/25 15.00 40.00
13 Larry Johnson/25 15.00 40.00
16 Marques Colston/25 15.00 40.00
21 Tarvaris Jackson/25 15.00 40.00
25 Vincent Jackson/25 15.00 40.00

2009 Donruss Classics Membership

*GOLD/100: .8X TO 2X BASIC INSERTS
GOLD PRINT RUN 100 SER.#'d SETS
*PLATINUM/25: 1.2X TO 3X BASIC INSERTS
PLATINUM PRINT RUN 25 SER.#'d SETS
*SILVER/250: .6X TO 1.5X BASIC INSERTS
SILVER PRINT RUN 250
1 Aaron Rodgers 3.00 8.00
2 Chris Cooley 1.25 3.00
3 Chris Johnson 1.50 4.00
4 David Garrard 1.25 3.00
5 Derrick Ward 1.00 2.50
6 DeSean Jackson 1.25 3.00
7 Devin Hester 1.50 4.00
8 Dwayne Bowe 1.25 3.00
9 Earnest Graham 1.00 2.50
10 Eddie Royal 1.25 3.00
11 Heath Miller 1.25 3.00
12 Jason Campbell 1.00 2.50
13 Joe Flacco 1.50 4.00
14 Jonathan Stewart 1.25 3.00
15 Justin Fargas 1.00 2.50
16 Kellen Winslow Jr. 1.25 3.00
17 Leon Washington 1.25 3.00
18 Matt Forte 1.50 4.00
19 Matt Ryan 1.50 4.00
20 Michael Turner 1.25 3.00
21 Roddy White 1.25 3.00
22 Selvin Young 1.00 2.50
23 Kyle Orton 1.25 3.00
24 Trent Edwards 1.00 2.50
25 Vernon Davis 1.25 3.00

2009 Donruss Classics Membership VIP Jerseys

STATED PRINT RUN 285-299
*PRIME/30-50: .6X TO 1.5X BASIC JSY/285-299
*PRIME/25: 1X TO 2.5X BASIC JSY/299
PRIME PRINT RUN 25-50
1 Aaron Rodgers 8.00 20.00
2 Chris Cooley 3.00 8.00
4 David Garrard 3.00 8.00
7 Devin Hester 4.00 10.00
8 Dwayne Bowe 3.00 8.00
12 Jason Campbell 2.50 6.00
13 Joe Flacco 4.00 10.00
14 Jonathan Stewart 3.00 8.00
15 Justin Fargas 2.50 6.00
17 Leon Washington 3.00 8.00
19 Matt Ryan 4.00 10.00
20 Michael Turner 3.00 8.00
21 Roddy White 3.00 8.00
22 Selvin Young 2.50 6.00
24 Trent Edwards 2.50 6.00
25 Vernon Davis 3.00 8.00

2009 Donruss Classics Monday Night Heroes

*GOLD/100: .8X TO 2X BASIC INSERTS
GOLD PRINT RUN 100 SER.#'d SETS
*PLATINUM/25: 1.2X TO 3X BASIC INSERTS
PLATINUM PRINT RUN 25 SER.#'d SETS
*SILVER/250: .6X TO 1.5X BASIC INSERTS
SILVER PRINT RUN 250 SER.#'d SETS
1 Adrian Peterson 2.50 6.00
2 Jay Cutler 1.50 4.00
3 Tony Romo 2.50 6.00
4 Brian Westbrook 1.25 3.00
5 Brett Favre 4.00 10.00
6 Philip Rivers 1.50 4.00
7 Derrick Mason 1.25 3.00
8 Santonio Holmes 1.25 3.00
9 Drew Brees 1.50 4.00
10 Bernard Berrian 1.25 3.00
11 Derrick Ward 1.00 2.50
12 Braylon Edwards 1.25 3.00
13 Randy Moss 1.50 4.00
14 Wes Welker 1.50 4.00
15 Dallas Clark 1.25 3.00
16 LenDale White 1.25 3.00
17 Willie Parker 1.00 2.50
18 Clinton Portis 1.25 3.00
19 Kurt Warner 1.50 4.00
20 Anquan Boldin 1.25 3.00
21 Marshawn Lynch 1.25 3.00
22 Greg Jennings 1.50 4.00
23 Steve Slaton 1.25 3.00
24 Andre Johnson 1.25 3.00
25 DeAngelo Williams 1.50 4.00
26 Jonathan Stewart 1.25 3.00
27 Steve Smith 1.25 3.00
28 Donovan McNabb 1.50 4.00

29 Aaron Rodgers	3.00	8.00
30 Matt Forte	1.50	4.00

2009 Donruss Classics Monday Night Heroes Jerseys

JERSEY PRINT RUN 175-299
*PRIME/50: .6X TO 1.5X BASIC JSY/175-299
*PRIME/19-25: 1X TO 2.5X BASIC JSY/175-299
PRIME STATED PRINT RUN 19-50

1 Adrian Peterson/299	6.00	15.00
2 Jay Cutler/299	4.00	10.00
3 Tony Romo/299	6.00	15.00
4 Brian Westbrook/299	3.00	8.00
5 Brett Favre/250	10.00	25.00
6 Philip Rivers/299	4.00	10.00
7 Derrick Mason/299	3.00	8.00
8 Santonio Holmes/299	3.00	8.00
9 Drew Brees/299	4.00	10.00
10 Bernard Berrian/299	3.00	8.00
11 Derrick Ward/175	2.50	6.00
12 Braylon Edwards/299	3.00	8.00
13 Randy Moss/299	4.00	10.00
14 Wes Welker/299	4.00	10.00
15 Dallas Clark/299	3.00	8.00
16 LenDale White/299	3.00	8.00
17 Willie Parker/299	2.50	6.00
18 Clinton Portis/299	3.00	8.00
20 Anquan Boldin/294	3.00	8.00
21 Marshawn Lynch/299	3.00	8.00
22 Greg Jennings/299	4.00	10.00
23 Steve Slaton/299	3.00	8.00
24 Andre Johnson/299	3.00	8.00
25 DeAngelo Williams/299	4.00	10.00
26 Jonathan Stewart/299	3.00	8.00
27 Steve Smith/299	3.00	8.00
28 Donovan McNabb/299	4.00	10.00
29 Aaron Rodgers/299	8.00	20.00

2009 Donruss Classics Saturday Stars

*GOLD/100: .8X TO 2X BASIC INSERTS
GOLD PRINT RUN 100 SER.#'d SETS
*PLATINUM/25: 1.2X TO 3X BASIC INSRTS
PLATINUM PRINT RUN 25 SER.#'d SETS
*SILVER/250: .6X TO 1.5X BASIC INSERTS
SILVER PRINT RUN 250 SER.#'d SETS

1 Andre Smith	.75	2.00
2 Nate Davis	.75	2.00
3 Brandon Pettigrew	1.00	2.50
4 Brian Cushing	1.00	2.50
5 Brian Orakpo	1.00	2.50
6 Brian Robiskie	1.00	2.50
7 Chase Coffman	.75	2.00
8 Chris Wells	1.50	4.00
9 Clint Sintim	1.00	2.50
10 Derrick Williams	.75	2.00
11 Donald Brown	1.00	2.50
12 Graham Harrell	1.00	2.50
13 Hakeem Nicks	1.50	4.00
14 James Laurinaitis	1.00	2.50
15 Javon Ringer	1.00	2.50
16 Jeremiah Johnson	1.00	2.50
17 Jeremy Maclin	1.50	4.00
18 Juaquin Iglesias	.75	2.00
19 Knowshon Moreno	1.00	2.50
20 LeSean McCoy	2.00	5.00
21 Louis Murphy	1.00	2.50
22 Malcolm Jenkins	1.00	2.50
23 Mark Sanchez	3.00	8.00
24 Matthew Stafford	5.00	12.00
25 Michael Crabtree	2.00	5.00
26 Pat White	1.00	2.50
27 Percy Harvin	1.50	4.00
28 Quan Cosby	.75	2.00
29 Rey Maualuga	1.00	2.50
30 Shonn Greene	1.50	4.00

2009 Donruss Classics Saturday Stars Autographs

STATED PRINT RUN 25-100

2 Nate Davis/50	6.00	15.00
4 Brian Cushing/50	8.00	20.00
5 Brian Orakpo/50	8.00	20.00
6 Brian Robiskie/50	8.00	20.00
7 Chase Coffman/50	6.00	15.00
8 Chris Wells/50	12.00	30.00
9 Clint Sintim/100	8.00	20.00
10 Derrick Williams/50	6.00	15.00
11 Donald Brown/25	8.00	20.00
12 Graham Harrell/100	12.00	30.00
13 Hakeem Nicks/50	12.00	30.00
14 James Laurinaitis/50	8.00	20.00
16 Jeremiah Johnson/100	8.00	20.00
17 Jeremy Maclin/50	12.00	30.00
18 Juaquin Iglesias/50	6.00	15.00
19 Knowshon Moreno/50	30.00	60.00
20 LeSean McCoy/25	15.00	40.00
22 Malcolm Jenkins/100	8.00	20.00
23 Mark Sanchez/25	50.00	100.00
24 Matthew Stafford/25	50.00	100.00
25 Michael Crabtree/50	30.00	60.00
26 Pat White/50	8.00	20.00
27 Percy Harvin/50	30.00	60.00
28 Quan Cosby/100	6.00	15.00
29 Rey Maualuga/50	8.00	20.00
30 Shonn Greene/50	12.00	30.00

2009 Donruss Classics Saturday Stars Jerseys

JERSEY PRINT RUN 50-299
*PRIME/50: .8X TO 2X BASIC JSY/150-299
*PRIME/50: .5X TO 1.2X BASIC JSY/50
*PRIME/25: .8X TO 2X BASIC JSY/150-299
PRIME PRINT RUN 25-50

4 Brian Cushing/299	3.00	8.00
5 Brian Orakpo/50	4.00	10.00
10 Derrick Williams/200	2.50	6.00
11 Donald Brown/150	3.00	8.00
12 Graham Harrell/299	3.00	8.00
14 James Laurinaitis/299	3.00	8.00
16 Jeremiah Johnson/299	3.00	8.00
18 Juaquin Iglesias/299	2.50	6.00
20 LeSean McCoy/299	5.00	12.00
23 Mark Sanchez/299	6.00	15.00
24 Matthew Stafford/150	8.00	20.00
28 Quan Cosby/299	2.50	6.00
29 Rey Maualuga/299	3.00	8.00

2009 Donruss Classics Saturday Stars Jerseys Autographs

JSY AU PRINT RUN 25 SER.#'d SETS

4 Brian Cushing	10.00	25.00
5 Brian Orakpo	10.00	25.00
10 Derrick Williams	8.00	20.00
11 Donald Brown	10.00	25.00
12 Graham Harrell	15.00	40.00
14 James Laurinaitis	10.00	25.00
16 Jeremiah Johnson	10.00	25.00
18 Juaquin Iglesias	8.00	20.00
20 LeSean McCoy	20.00	50.00
23 Mark Sanchez	50.00	100.00
24 Matthew Stafford	75.00	150.00
28 Quan Cosby	8.00	20.00
29 Rey Maualuga	20.00	50.00

2009 Donruss Classics School Colors

1 Aaron Curry	1.25	3.00
2 Aaron Maybin	1.00	2.50
3 B.J. Raji	1.25	3.00
4 Mohamed Massaquoi	1.00	2.50
5 Brandon Pettigrew	1.25	3.00
6 Brian Cushing	1.25	3.00
7 Brian Orakpo	1.25	3.00
8 Brian Robiskie	1.25	3.00
9 Chase Coffman	1.00	2.50
10 Chris Wells	2.00	5.00
11 Clint Sintim	1.25	3.00
12 Darrius Heyward-Bey	1.25	3.00
13 Derrick Williams	1.00	2.50
14 Donald Brown	1.25	3.00
15 Hakeem Nicks	2.00	5.00
16 James Casey	1.00	2.50
17 James Laurinaitis	1.25	3.00
18 Javon Ringer	1.25	3.00
19 Jeremiah Johnson	1.25	3.00
20 Jeremy Maclin	2.00	5.00
21 Josh Freeman	2.50	6.00
22 Juaquin Iglesias	1.00	2.50
23 Kenny Britt	1.50	4.00
24 Knowshon Moreno	1.25	3.00
25 Larry English	1.25	3.00
26 LeSean McCoy	2.50	6.00
27 Malcolm Jenkins	1.25	3.00
28 Mark Sanchez	4.00	10.00
29 Matthew Stafford	6.00	15.00
30 Michael Crabtree	2.50	6.00
31 Nate Davis	1.00	2.50
32 Pat White	1.25	3.00
33 Percy Harvin	2.00	5.00
34 Rashad Jennings	1.25	3.00
35 Rey Maualuga	1.25	3.00
36 Shonn Greene	2.00	5.00

2009 Donruss Classics School Colors Autographs

1 Aaron Curry	10.00	25.00
5 Brandon Pettigrew	10.00	25.00
8 Brian Robiskie	10.00	25.00
10 Chris Wells	15.00	40.00
12 Darrius Heyward-Bey	10.00	25.00
13 Derrick Williams	8.00	20.00
14 Donald Brown	10.00	25.00
15 Hakeem Nicks	15.00	40.00
16 James Casey	8.00	20.00
18 Javon Ringer	10.00	25.00
20 Jeremy Maclin	15.00	40.00
21 Josh Freeman	20.00	50.00
22 Juaquin Iglesias	8.00	20.00
23 Kenny Britt	12.00	30.00
24 Knowshon Moreno	10.00	25.00
26 LeSean McCoy	20.00	50.00
28 Mark Sanchez	40.00	100.00
29 Matthew Stafford	50.00	100.00
30 Michael Crabtree	20.00	50.00
31 Nate Davis	8.00	20.00
32 Pat White	10.00	25.00
33 Percy Harvin	25.00	60.00
36 Shonn Greene	15.00	40.00

2009 Donruss Classics Significant Signatures Gold

32-90 VET PRINT RUN 10-20
*GOLD LEGEND/50-126: .3X TO .8X PLAT.AU/25
101-50 LEGEND PRINT RUN 26-126
*GOLD ROOKIE/250: .2X TO .5X PLAT.AU/25
151-250 ROOKIE PRINT RUN 150-250

32 Eddie Royal/20	12.00	30.00
35 Kevin Smith/20	12.00	30.00
42 Anthony Gonzalez/20	10.00	25.00
90 Donnie Avery/20	12.00	30.00
101 Alan Page/91	10.00	25.00
102 Andre Reed/75	10.00	25.00
104 Billy Sims/76	10.00	25.00
106 Bob Lilly/76	10.00	25.00
108 Carl Eller/95	8.00	20.00
109 Chuck Bednarik/101	10.00	25.00
110 Ace Parker/51	20.00	40.00
111 Cliff Harris/76	10.00	25.00
112 Danny White/51	12.00	30.00
113 Daryl Johnston/126	20.00	50.00
114 Dave Casper/101	8.00	20.00
115 Earl Campbell/51	12.00	30.00
116 Emmitt Smith/26	75.00	150.00
117 Eric Dickerson/51	12.00	30.00
118 Franco Harris/51	25.00	50.00
119 Gale Sayers/51	25.00	50.00
121 Jack Youngblood/76	10.00	25.00
122 Jay Novacek/126	15.00	40.00
123 Jerry Rice/26	75.00	150.00
124 Jim Brown/50	30.00	60.00
125 Jim Kelly/51	30.00	60.00
126 Jim McMahon/51	12.00	30.00
127 Joe Greene/51	25.00	50.00
128 Joe Montana/26	60.00	120.00
129 John Stallworth/51	15.00	40.00
130 Lawrence Taylor/50	20.00	40.00
133 Merlin Olsen/76	15.00	40.00
134 Michael Irvin/26	25.00	50.00
135 Mike Singletary/51	20.00	40.00
136 Phil Simms/51	15.00	30.00
138 Roger Craig/101	10.00	25.00
139 Roger Staubach/26	40.00	80.00
141 Steve Young/51	25.00	50.00
142 Ted Hendricks/51	8.00	20.00
143 Thurman Thomas/51	15.00	40.00
144 Tim Brown/66	20.00	40.00
146 Tony Dorsett/32	25.00	50.00
147 Troy Aikman/26	40.00	80.00
149 William Perry/126	10.00	25.00
150 Y.A. Tittle/59	12.00	30.00
151 Aaron Curry/250	6.00	15.00
159 B.J. Raji/250	6.00	15.00
163 Brian Cushing/250	6.00	15.00
165 Brian Orakpo/250	6.00	15.00
166 Brian Robiskie/250	6.00	15.00
171 Chris Wells/150	20.00	50.00
172 Clay Matthews/250	25.00	50.00
179 Darrius Heyward-Bey/250	6.00	15.00
185 Donald Brown/250	6.00	15.00
187 Everette Brown/250	5.00	12.00
191 Hakeem Nicks/250	10.00	25.00
197 James Laurinaitis/250	8.00	20.00
200 Jason Smith/250	5.00	12.00
204 Jeremy Maclin/250	10.00	25.00
207 Josh Freeman/250	12.00	30.00
212 Knowshon Moreno/150	20.00	50.00
214 Larry English/250	6.00	15.00
215 LeSean McCoy/250	12.00	30.00
218 Malcolm Jenkins/250	6.00	15.00
219 Mark Sanchez/250	40.00	80.00
220 Matthew Stafford/150	60.00	120.00
221 Michael Crabtree/250	25.00	60.00
226 Mohamed Massaquoi/250	8.00	20.00
229 Pat White/250	6.00	15.00
232 Percy Harvin/250	25.00	60.00
249 Tyson Jackson/250	5.00	12.00
250 Vontae Davis/250	6.00	15.00

2009 Donruss Classics Significant Signatures Platinum

101-150 LEGEND PRINT RUN 15-25
151-250 ROOKIE PRINT RUN 25

101 Alan Page/25	12.00	30.00
102 Andre Reed/25	12.00	30.00
103 Barry Sanders/15	75.00	150.00
104 Billy Sims/25	12.00	30.00
106 Bob Lilly/25	12.00	30.00
108 Carl Eller/25	10.00	25.00
109 Chuck Bednarik/25	12.00	30.00
110 Ace Parker/25	25.00	50.00
111 Cliff Harris/25	12.00	30.00
112 Danny White/25	15.00	40.00
113 Daryl Johnston/25	30.00	60.00
114 Dave Casper/25	10.00	25.00
115 Earl Campbell/25	15.00	40.00
116 Emmitt Smith/15	100.00	175.00
117 Eric Dickerson/25	15.00	40.00
118 Franco Harris/25	25.00	60.00
119 Gale Sayers/25	25.00	60.00
121 Jack Youngblood/25	12.00	30.00
122 Jay Novacek/25	20.00	50.00
123 Jerry Rice/15	90.00	150.00
124 Jim Brown/15	40.00	80.00
125 Jim Kelly/25	30.00	80.00
126 Jim McMahon/25	20.00	40.00
127 Joe Greene/25	25.00	60.00
128 Joe Montana/15	50.00	10.00
129 John Stallworth/25	20.00	50.00
130 Lawrence Taylor/15	25.00	50.00
133 Merlin Olsen/25	20.00	50.00
134 Michael Irvin/15	30.00	60.00
135 Mike Singletary/25	20.00	50.00
136 Phil Simms/25	15.00	40.00
138 Roger Craig/25	12.00	30.00
139 Roger Staubach/15	50.00	100.00
141 Steve Young/25	30.00	60.00
142 Ted Hendricks/25	10.00	25.00
143 Thurman Thomas/25	20.00	50.00
144 Tim Brown/25	20.00	50.00
146 Tony Dorsett/15	30.00	60.00
147 Troy Aikman/15	50.00	100.00
149 William Perry/25	12.00	30.00
150 Y.A. Tittle/25	15.00	40.00
151 Aaron Curry/25	12.00	30.00
152 Aaron Kelly/25	10.00	25.00
155 Andre Brown/25	8.00	20.00
158 Austin Collie/25	15.00	40.00
159 B.J. Raji/25	12.00	30.00
160 Brandon Gibson/25	12.00	30.00
162 Brandon Tate/25	12.00	30.00
163 Brian Cushing/25	12.00	30.00
165 Brian Orakpo/25	12.00	30.00
166 Brian Robiskie/25	12.00	30.00
167 Brooks Foster/25	8.00	20.00
169 Cedric Peerman/25	10.00	25.00
170 Chase Coffman/25	10.00	25.00
171 Chris Wells/25	40.00	80.00
172 Clay Matthews/25	40.00	80.00
173 Clint Sintim/25	12.00	30.00
175 Cornelius Ingram/25	8.00	20.00
178 Darius Passmore/25	10.00	25.00
179 Darrius Heyward-Bey/25	12.00	30.00
181 Deon Butler/25	10.00	25.00
182 Derrick Williams/25	10.00	25.00
183 Devin Moore/25	10.00	25.00
184 Dominique Edison/25	8.00	20.00
185 Donald Brown/25	12.00	30.00
187 Everette Brown/25	10.00	25.00
189 Glen Coffee/25	10.00	25.00
190 Graham Harrell/25	20.00	59.00
191 Hakeem Nicks/25	20.00	50.00
192 Hunter Cantwell/25 EXCH	12.00	30.00
195 James Casey/25	10.00	25.00
197 James Laurinaitis/25	15.00	40.00
198 Jared Cook/25	12.00	30.00
199 Jarett Dillard/25	12.00	30.00
200 Jason Smith/25	10.00	25.00
202 Jeremiah Johnson/25	12.00	30.00
204 Jeremy Maclin/25	20.00	50.00
205 John Parker Wilson/25	12.00	30.00
206 Johnny Knox/25	20.00	50.00
207 Josh Freeman/25	25.00	60.00
208 Juaquin Iglesias/25	10.00	25.00
210 Kenny McKinley/25	12.00	30.00
211 Kevin Ogletree/25	12.00	30.00
212 Knowshon Moreno/25	50.00	100.00
213 Kory Sheets/25	10.00	25.00
214 Larry English/25	12.00	30.00
215 LeSean McCoy/25	25.00	60.00
218 Malcolm Jenkins/25	12.00	30.00
219 Mark Sanchez/25	75.00	150.00
220 Matthew Stafford/25	75.00	150.00
221 Michael Crabtree/25	50.00	100.00
223 Mike Goodson/25	12.00	30.00
224 Mike Thomas/25	12.00	30.00
225 Mike Wallace/25	25.00	60.00
226 Mohamed Massaquoi/25	10.00	25.00
227 Nate Davis/25	10.00	25.00
228 Nathan Brown/25	10.00	25.00
229 Pat White/25	12.00	30.00
231 Patrick Turner/25	10.00	25.00
232 Percy Harvin/25	40.00	100.00
234 Quan Cosby/25	10.00	25.00
236 Quinn Johnson/25	10.00	25.00
237 Ramses Barden/25	8.00	20.00
238 Rashad Jennings/25	12.00	30.00
239 Rey Maualuga/25	12.00	30.00
240 Rhett Bomar/25	10.00	25.00
242 Shawn Nelson/25	10.00	25.00
243 Shonn Greene/25	20.00	50.00
244 Stephen McGee/25	12.00	30.00
245 Tom Brandstater/25	12.00	30.00
246 Tony Fiammetta/25	10.00	25.00
247 Travis Beckum/25	10.00	25.00
248 Tyrell Sutton/25	10.00	25.00
249 Tyson Jackson/25	10.00	25.00
250 Vontae Davis/25	12.00	30.00

2009 Donruss Classics Sunday's Best

*GOLD/100: .8X TO 2X BASIC INSERTS
GOLD PRINT RUN 100 SER.#'d SETS
*PLATINUM/25: 1.5X TO 4X BASIC INSERTS
PLATINUM PRINT RUN 25 SER.#'d SETS
*SILVER/250: .6X TO 1.5X BASIC INSERTS
SILVER PRINT RUN 250 SER.#'d SETS

1 Aaron Rodgers	3.00	8.00
2 Adrian Peterson	2.50	6.00
3 Andre Johnson	1.25	3.00
4 Anquan Boldin	1.25	3.00
5 Anthony Gonzalez	1.00	2.50
6 Ben Roethlisberger	1.50	4.00
7 Brandon Jacobs	1.25	3.00
8 Brandon Marshall	1.25	3.00
9 Braylon Edwards	1.25	3.00
10 Brian Westbrook	1.25	3.00
11 Calvin Johnson	1.50	4.00
12 Clinton Portis	1.25	3.00
13 Dallas Clark	1.25	3.00
14 DeAngelo Williams	1.50	4.00
15 Donald Driver	1.25	3.00
16 Drew Brees	1.50	4.00
17 Eli Manning	1.50	4.00
18 Greg Jennings	1.50	4.00
19 Hines Ward	1.25	3.00
20 Jake Delhomme	1.25	3.00
21 Jay Cutler	1.50	4.00
22 Joseph Addai	1.50	4.00
23 Kurt Warner	1.50	4.00
24 Larry Fitzgerald	1.50	4.00
25 Lee Evans	1.25	3.00
26 LenDale White	1.25	3.00
27 Marshawn Lynch	1.25	3.00
28 Marvin Harrison	1.50	4.00
29 Matt Schaub	1.25	3.00
30 Maurice Jones-Drew	1.25	3.00
31 Peyton Manning	2.50	6.00
32 Philip Rivers	1.50	4.00
33 Reggie Wayne	1.25	3.00
34 Ronnie Brown	1.25	3.00
35 Ryan Grant	1.25	3.00
36 Santonio Holmes	1.25	3.00
37 Terrell Owens	1.50	4.00
38 Torry Holt	1.25	3.00
39 Vincent Jackson	1.25	3.00
40 Willie Parker	1.00	2.50

2009 Donruss Classics Sunday's Best Jerseys

JERSEY PRINT RUN 288-299
*PRIME/50: .6X TO 1.5X BASIC JSY/288-299
*PRIME/20-25: 1X TO 2.5X BASIC JSY/288-299
PRIME JERSEY PRINT RUN 20-50

1 Aaron Rodgers	8.00	20.00
2 Adrian Peterson	6.00	15.00
3 Andre Johnson	3.00	8.00
4 Anquan Boldin	3.00	8.00
5 Anthony Gonzalez	2.50	6.00
6 Ben Roethlisberger	4.00	10.00
7 Brandon Jacobs	3.00	8.00
8 Brandon Marshall	3.00	8.00
9 Braylon Edwards	3.00	8.00
10 Brian Westbrook	3.00	8.00
11 Calvin Johnson	4.00	10.00
12 Clinton Portis	3.00	8.00
13 Dallas Clark	3.00	8.00
14 DeAngelo Williams	4.00	10.00
15 Donald Driver	3.00	8.00
16 Drew Brees	4.00	10.00
17 Eli Manning	4.00	10.00
18 Greg Jennings	4.00	10.00
19 Hines Ward	3.00	8.00
20 Jake Delhomme	3.00	8.00
21 Jay Cutler	4.00	10.00
22 Joseph Addai	4.00	10.00
24 Larry Fitzgerald	4.00	10.00
25 Lee Evans	3.00	8.00
26 LenDale White	3.00	8.00
27 Marshawn Lynch	3.00	8.00
29 Matt Schaub	3.00	8.00
30 Maurice Jones-Drew	3.00	8.00
31 Peyton Manning	6.00	15.00
32 Philip Rivers	4.00	10.00
33 Reggie Wayne/288	3.00	8.00
34 Ronnie Brown	3.00	8.00
35 Ryan Grant	3.00	8.00
36 Santonio Holmes	3.00	8.00
37 Terrell Owens	4.00	10.00
38 Torry Holt	3.00	8.00
39 Vincent Jackson	3.00	8.00
40 Willie Parker	2.50	6.00

2009 Donruss Classics Sunday's Best Jerseys Autographs

JERSEY AUTO PRINT RUN 5-25
5 Anthony Gonzalez/25

2009 Donruss Classics Team Colors

RANDOM INSERTS IN RETAIL PACKS

1 Aaron Curry	1.50	4.00
2 Andre Brown	1.00	2.50
3 Brandon Pettigrew	1.50	4.00
4 Tyson Jackson	1.25	3.00
5 Brian Robiskie	1.50	4.00
6 Chris Wells	2.50	6.00
7 Darrius Heyward-Bey	1.50	4.00
8 Deon Butler	1.25	3.00
9 Derrick Williams	1.25	3.00
10 Donald Brown	1.50	4.00
11 Glen Coffee	1.25	3.00
12 Hakeem Nicks	2.50	6.00
13 Jason Smith	1.25	3.00
14 Javon Ringer	1.50	4.00
15 Jeremy Maclin	2.50	6.00
16 Josh Freeman	3.00	8.00
17 Juaquin Iglesias	1.25	3.00
18 Kenny Britt	2.00	5.00
19 Knowshon Moreno	1.50	4.00
20 LeSean McCoy	3.00	8.00
21 Mark Sanchez	5.00	12.00
22 Matthew Stafford	8.00	20.00
23 Michael Crabtree	3.00	8.00
24 Mike Thomas	1.50	4.00
25 Mike Wallace	3.00	8.00
26 Mohamed Massaquoi	1.25	3.00
27 Nate Davis	1.25	3.00
28 Pat White	1.50	4.00
29 Patrick Turner	1.25	3.00
30 Percy Harvin	2.50	6.00
31 Ramses Barden	1.00	2.50
32 Rhett Bomar	1.25	3.00
33 Shonn Greene	2.50	6.00
34 Stephen McGee	1.50	4.00

1999 Donruss Elite

The 1999 Donruss Elite set was issued in one series totalling 200 cards. The fronts feature action color player photos with player information on the backs. Cards 1-100 were printed on foil board and were inserted four cards per pack. Cards 101-200, which includes 40 short-printed rookies, were printed on micro-etched foil cards and inserted one per pack. Two die-cut parallel sets were produced. Donruss Elite Status cards were sequentially numbered to the featured player's jersey number, and the Donruss Elite Aspirations cards were sequentially numbered to the remaining number out of 100.

COMPLETE SET (200)	30.00	80.00
COMP.SET w/o SP's (160)	15.00	30.00
1 Warren Moon	.40	1.00
2 Terry Allen UER	.30	.75
(1990 stat line missing on back)		
3 Jeff George	.25	.60
4 Brett Favre	1.25	3.00
5 Rob Moore	.25	.60
6 Bubby Brister	.25	.60
7 John Elway	1.25	3.00
8 Troy Aikman	.60	1.50
9 Steve McNair	.40	1.00
10 Charlie Batch	.30	.75
11 Elvis Grbac	.25	.60
12 Trent Dilfer	.30	.75
13 Kerry Collins	.30	.75
14 Neil O'Donnell	.30	.75
15 Tony Simmons	.25	.60
16 Ryan Leaf	.30	.75
17 Bobby Hoying	.25	.60
18 Marvin Harrison	.40	1.00
19 Keyshawn Johnson	.30	.75
20 Cris Carter	.40	1.00
21 Deion Sanders	.40	1.00
22 Emmitt Smith UER	1.00	2.50
(career TD total incorrect)		
23 Antowain Smith	.25	.60
24 Terry Fair	.25	.60
25 Robert Holcombe	.25	.60
26 Napoleon Kaufman	.25	.60
27 Eddie George	.30	.75
28 Corey Dillon	.30	.75
29 Adrian Murrell	.30	.75
30 Charles Way	.25	.60
31 Amp Lee	.25	.60
32 Ricky Watters	.30	.75
33 Gary Brown	.25	.60
34 Thurman Thomas	.40	1.00
35 Pat Johnson	.25	.60
36 Jerome Bettis	.40	1.00
37 Muhsin Muhammad	.30	.75
38 Kimble Anders	.25	.60
39 Curtis Enis	.25	.60
40 Mike Alstott	.40	1.00
41 Charles Johnson	.25	.60
42 Chris Warren	.30	.75
43 Tony Banks	.30	.75
44 Leroy Hoard	.25	.60
45 Chris Fuamatu-Ma'afala	.25	.60
46 Michael Irvin	.40	1.00
47 Robert Edwards	.25	.60
48 Hines Ward	.40	1.00
49 Trent Green	.30	.75
50 Eric Zeier	.25	.60
51 Sean Dawkins	.25	.60
52 Yancey Thigpen	.25	.60
53 Jacquez Green	.25	.60
54 Zach Thomas	.40	1.00
55 Junior Seau	.40	1.00
56 Darnay Scott	.25	.60
57 Kent Graham	.25	.60
58 O.J. Santiago	.25	.60
59 Tony Gonzalez	.40	1.00
60 Ty Detmer	.30	.75
61 Albert Connell	.25	.60
62 James Jett	.25	.60
63 Bert Emanuel	.30	.75
64 Derrick Alexander WR	.25	.60
65 Wesley Walls	.30	.75
66 Jake Reed	.30	.75
67 Randall Cunningham	.40	1.00
68 Leslie Shepherd	.25	.60
69 Mark Chmura	.25	.60
70 Bobby Engram	.30	.75
71 Rickey Dudley	.25	.60
72 Darick Holmes	.25	.60
73 Andre Reed	.40	1.00
74 Az-Zahir Hakim	.25	.60
75 Cameron Cleeland	.25	.60
76 Lamar Thomas	.25	.60
77 Oronde Gadsden	.25	.60
78 Ben Coates	.30	.75
79 Bruce Smith	.40	1.00
80 Jerry Rice	.75	2.00
81 Tim Brown	.40	1.00
82 Michael Westbrook	.25	.60
83 J.J. Stokes	.25	.60
84 Shannon Sharpe	.40	1.00
85 Reidel Anthony	.25	.60
86 Antonio Freeman	.30	.75
87 Keenan McCardell	.30	.75
88 Terry Glenn	.30	.75
89 Andre Rison	.30	.75
90 Neil Smith	.25	.60
91 Terrance Mathis	.25	.60
92 Rocket Ismail	.30	.75
93 Byron Bam Morris	.25	.60
94 Ike Hilliard	.30	.75
95 Eddie Kennison	.30	.75
96 Tavian Banks	.25	.60
97 Yatil Green	.25	.60
98 Frank Wycheck	.30	.75
99 Warren Sapp UER	.30	.75
(tackle total incorrect on back)		
100 Germane Crowell	.25	.60
101 Curtis Martin	.75	2.00
102 John Avery	.50	1.25
103 Eric Moulds	.60	1.50
104 Randy Moss	.75	2.00
105 Terrell Owens	.75	2.00
106 Vinny Testaverde	.60	1.50
107 Doug Flutie	.75	2.00
108 Mark Brunell	.60	1.50
109 Isaac Bruce UER	.75	2.00
(Raiders listed on back for 1994)		
110 Kordell Stewart	.60	1.50
111 Drew Bledsoe	.75	2.00
112 Chris Chandler	.60	1.50
113 Dan Marino	2.50	6.00
114 Brian Griese	.60	1.50
115 Carl Pickens	.60	1.50
116 Jake Plummer	.60	1.50
117 Natrone Means	.60	1.50
118 Peyton Manning	2.50	6.00
119 Garrison Hearst	.60	1.50
120 Barry Sanders	2.00	5.00
121 Steve Young	1.00	2.50
122 Rashaan Shehee	.50	1.25
123 Ed McCaffrey	.60	1.50
124 Charles Woodson	.75	2.00
125 Dorsey Levens	.60	1.50
126 Robert Smith	.60	1.50
127 Greg Hill	.50	1.25
128 Fred Taylor	.60	1.50
129 Marcus Nash	.50	1.25
130 Terrell Davis	.75	2.00
131 Ahman Green	.60	1.50
132 Jamal Anderson	.60	1.50
133 Karim Abdul-Jabbar	.60	1.50
134 Jermaine Lewis	.50	1.25
135 Jerome Pathon	.50	1.25
136 Brad Johnson	.60	1.50
137 Herman Moore	.60	1.50
138 Tim Dwight	.60	1.50
139 Johnnie Morton	.60	1.50
140 Marshall Faulk	.75	2.00
141 Frank Sanders	.50	1.25
142 Kevin Dyson	.50	1.25
143 Curtis Conway	.60	1.50
144 Derrick Mayes	.50	1.25
145 O.J. McDuffie	.60	1.50
146 Joe Jurevicius	.50	1.25
147 Jon Kitna	.60	1.50
148 Joey Galloway	.60	1.50
149 Jimmy Smith	.60	1.50
150 Skip Hicks	.50	1.25
151 Rod Smith	.60	1.50
152 Duce Staley	.60	1.50
153 James Stewart	.50	1.25
154 Rob Johnson	.60	1.50
155 Mikhael Ricks	.50	1.25
156 Wayne Chrebet	.60	1.50
157 Robert Brooks	.60	1.50
158 Tim Biakabutuka	.60	1.50
159 Priest Holmes	.75	2.00
160 Warrick Dunn	.60	1.50
161 Champ Bailey RC	2.50	6.00
162 D'Wayne Bates RC	.75	2.00
163 Michael Bishop RC	1.00	2.50
164 David Boston RC	1.00	2.50
165 Na Brown RC	.75	2.00
166 Chris Claiborne RC	.75	2.00
167 Joe Montgomery RC	.75	2.00
168 Mike Cloud RC	.75	2.00
169 Travis McGriff RC	.75	2.00
170 Tim Couch RC	1.25	3.00
171 Daunte Culpepper RC	1.25	3.00
172 Autry Denson RC	.75	2.00
173 Jermaine Fazande RC	.75	2.00
174 Troy Edwards RC	1.00	2.50
175 Kevin Faulk RC	1.25	3.00
176 Dee Miller RC UER	.75	2.00
(Mississippi listed incorrectly on back)		
177 Brock Huard RC	1.00	2.50
178 Torry Holt RC	2.00	5.00
179 Sedrick Irvin RC	.75	2.00
180 Edgerrin James RC	1.50	4.00
181 Joe Germaine RC	1.00	2.50
182 James Johnson RC	.75	2.00
183 Kevin Johnson RC	1.00	2.50
184 Andy Katzenmoyer RC	1.00	2.50
185 Jevon Kearse RC	1.25	3.00
186 Shaun King RC	1.00	2.50
187 Rob Konrad RC	.75	2.00
188 Jim Kleinsasser RC	1.25	3.00
189 Chris McAlister RC	1.00	2.50
190 Donovan McNabb RC	6.00	15.00
191 Cade McNown RC	1.00	2.50
192 De'Mond Parker RC	.75	2.00
193 Craig Yeast RC	.75	2.00
194 Shawn Bryson RC	.75	2.00
195 Peerless Price RC	1.00	2.50
196 Darnell McDonald RC	.75	2.00
197 Akili Smith RC	1.00	2.50
198 Tai Streets RC	1.00	2.50
199 Ricky Williams RC	2.00	5.00
200 Amos Zereoue RC	1.00	2.50

1999 Donruss Elite Aspirations

CARDS #'d UNDER 20 NOT PRICED

1 Warren Moon/99	5.00	12.00
2 Terry Allen/79	4.00	10.00
3 Jeff George/97	3.00	8.00
4 Brett Favre/96	25.00	60.00
6 Bubby Brister/94	3.00	8.00
7 John Elway/93	25.00	60.00
8 Troy Aikman/92	15.00	40.00
9 Steve McNair/91	5.00	12.00
10 Charlie Batch/90	5.00	12.00
11 Elvis Grbac/89	3.00	8.00
12 Trent Dilfer/88	3.00	8.00
13 Kerry Collins/87	3.00	8.00
14 Neil O'Donnell/88	3.00	8.00
16 Ryan Leaf/84	5.00	12.00
17 Bobby Hoying/93	3.00	8.00
19 Keyshawn Johnson/81	5.00	12.00
20 Cris Carter/20	20.00	50.00
21 Deion Sanders/79	7.50	20.00
22 Emmitt Smith/78	25.00	60.00
23 Antowain Smith/77	7.50	20.00
24 Terry Fair/77	2.50	6.00
25 Robert Holcombe/75	2.50	6.00
26 Napoleon Kaufman/74	7.50	20.00
27 Eddie George/73	7.50	20.00
28 Corey Dillon/72	7.50	20.00
29 Adrian Murrell/71	4.00	10.00
30 Charles Way/70	2.50	6.00
31 Amp Lee/69	2.50	6.00
32 Ricky Watters/68	4.00	10.00
33 Gary Brown/67	2.50	6.00
34 Thurman Thomas/66	7.50	20.00
36 Jerome Bettis/64	10.00	25.00
38 Kimble Anders/62	5.00	12.00
39 Curtis Enis/61	3.00	8.00
40 Mike Alstott/60	10.00	25.00
42 Chris Warren/58	3.00	8.00
43 Tony Banks/88	3.00	8.00
44 Leroy Hoard/56	3.00	8.00
45 Chris Fuamatu-Ma'afala/55	3.00	8.00
47 Robert Edwards/53	3.00	8.00
49 Trent Green/90	3.00	8.00
50 Eric Zeier/90	3.00	8.00
54 Zach Thomas/46	10.00	25.00
55 Junior Seau/45	10.00	25.00
57 Kent Graham/90	2.00	5.00
60 Ty Detmer/89	2.00	5.00
67 Randall Cunningham/93	5.00	12.00
72 Darick Holmes/78	2.50	6.00
79 Bruce Smith/22	20.00	50.00
80 Jerry Rice/20	75.00	150.00
93 Byron Bam Morris/61	3.00	8.00
96 Tavian Banks/78	2.50	6.00
101 Curtis Martin/72	7.50	20.00
102 John Avery/80	2.00	5.00
103 Eric Moulds/20	20.00	50.00
106 Vinny Testaverde/84	3.00	8.00
107 Doug Flutie/93	5.00	12.00
108 Mark Brunell/92	5.00	12.00
109 Isaac Bruce/20	20.00	50.00
110 Kordell Stewart/90	5.00	12.00
111 Drew Bledsoe/89	12.50	30.00
112 Chris Chandler/88	3.00	8.00
113 Dan Marino/87	25.00	60.00
114 Brian Griese/86	5.00	12.00
116 Jake Plummer/84	3.00	8.00
117 Natrone Means/80	3.00	8.00
118 Peyton Manning/82	25.00	60.00
119 Garrison Hearst/80	5.00	12.00
120 Barry Sanders/80	25.00	60.00
121 Steve Young/92	12.50	30.00
122 Rashaan Shehee/78	2.50	6.00
124 Charles Woodson/76	7.50	20.00
125 Dorsey Levens/75	7.50	20.00
126 Robert Smith/74	7.50	20.00
127 Greg Hill/73	2.50	6.00
128 Fred Taylor/72	7.50	20.00
130 Terrell Davis/70	7.50	20.00
131 Ahman Green/70	7.50	20.00
132 Jamal Anderson/68	7.50	20.00
133 Karim Abdul-Jabbar/67	4.00	10.00
136 Brad Johnson/86	5.00	12.00
140 Marshall Faulk/72	12.50	30.00
144 Derrick Mayes/20	20.00	50.00
147 Jon Kitna/93	5.00	12.00
150 Skip Hicks/80	2.00	5.00
151 Rod Smith/20	20.00	50.00
152 Duce Staley/78	7.50	20.00
153 James Stewart/67	4.00	10.00
154 Rob Johnson/89	3.00	8.00
155 Mikhael Ricks/90	2.00	5.00
156 Wayne Chrebet/20	20.00	50.00
158 Tim Biakabutuka/79	4.00	10.00
159 Priest Holmes/67	12.50	25.00
160 Warrick Dunn/72	7.50	20.00
161 Champ Bailey/96	7.50	20.00
162 D'Wayne Bates/95	5.00	12.00
163 Michael Bishop/93	5.00	12.00
164 David Boston/91	5.00	12.00
165 Na Brown/81	3.00	8.00
166 Chris Claiborne/45	3.00	8.00
167 Joe Montgomery/67	4.00	10.00
168 Mike Cloud/79	4.00	10.00
169 Travis McGriff/97	2.00	5.00
170 Tim Couch/98	5.00	12.00
171 Daunte Culpepper/92	25.00	60.00
172 Autry Denson/67	4.00	10.00
173 Jermaine Fazande/70	4.00	10.00
174 Troy Edwards/84	3.00	8.00
175 Kevin Faulk/97	5.00	12.00
176 Dee Miller/85	2.00	5.00
177 Brock Huard/93	5.00	12.00
179 Sedrick Irvin/67	12.50	25.00
180 Edgerrin James/95	25.00	60.00
181 Joe Germaine/93	3.00	8.00
182 James Johnson/78	4.00	10.00
183 Kevin Johnson/88	5.00	12.00
184 Andy Katzenmoyer/55	5.00	12.00
185 Jevon Kearse/58	12.00	30.00
186 Shaun King/90	3.00	8.00
187 Rob Konrad/56	10.00	25.00
188 Jim Kleinsasser/78	4.00	10.00
189 Chris McAlister/89	4.00	10.00
190 Donovan McNabb/95	30.00	80.00
191 Cade McNown/82	3.00	8.00
192 De'Mond Parker/67	2.50	6.00
193 Craig Yeast/97	5.00	12.00
194 Shawn Bryson/76	7.50	20.00
195 Peerless Price/63	7.50	20.00
196 Darnell McDonald/20	20.00	50.00
197 Akili Smith/89	2.00	5.00
199 Ricky Williams/66	15.00	40.00
200 Amos Zereoue/80	5.00	12.00

1999 Donruss Elite Status

CARDS #'d UNDER 20 NOT PRICED

2 Terry Allen/21	12.50	30.00
5 Rob Moore/85	3.00	8.00
15 Tony Simmons/81	2.00	5.00
18 Marvin Harrison/88	5.00	12.00
20 Cris Carter/80	5.00	12.00
21 Deion Sanders/21	20.00	50.00
22 Emmitt Smith/22	75.00	150.00
23 Antowain Smith/23	20.00	50.00
24 Terry Fair/23	6.00	15.00
25 Robert Holcombe/25	6.00	15.00
26 Napoleon Kaufman/26	20.00	50.00
27 Eddie George/27	25.00	60.00
28 Corey Dillon/28	20.00	50.00
29 Adrian Murrell/29	12.50	30.00
30 Charles Way/30	4.00	10.00
31 Amp Lee/31	4.00	10.00
32 Ricky Watters/32	7.50	20.00
33 Gary Brown/33	4.00	10.00
34 Thurman Thomas/34	15.00	40.00
35 Patrick Johnson/85	2.00	5.00
36 Jerome Bettis/36	15.00	40.00
37 Muhsin Muhammad/87	3.00	8.00
38 Kimble Anders/38	4.00	10.00
39 Curtis Enis/39	4.00	10.00
40 Mike Alstott/40	15.00	40.00
41 Charles Johnson/81	3.00	8.00
42 Chris Warren/42	4.00	10.00
44 Leroy Hoard/44	4.00	10.00
45 Chris Fuamatu-Ma'afala/45	3.00	8.00
46 Michael Irvin/88	5.00	12.00
47 Robert Edwards/47	3.00	8.00
48 Hines Ward/86	5.00	12.00
51 Sean Dawkins/86	2.00	5.00
52 Yancey Thigpen/82	2.00	5.00
53 Jacquez Green/81	2.00	5.00
54 Zach Thomas/54	10.00	25.00
55 Junior Seau/55	10.00	25.00
56 Darnay Scott/86	3.00	8.00
58 O.J. Santiago/88	2.00	5.00
59 Tony Gonzalez/88	5.00	12.00
61 Albert Connell/83	2.00	5.00
62 James Jett/82	3.00	8.00
63 Bert Emanuel/87	2.00	5.00
64 Derrick Alexander WR/82	3.00	8.00
65 Wesley Walls/85	3.00	8.00
66 Jake Reed/86	3.00	8.00
68 Leslie Shepherd/86	2.00	5.00
69 Mark Chmura/89	2.00	5.00
70 Bobby Engram/81	2.00	5.00
71 Rickey Dudley/83	2.00	5.00
72 Darick Holmes/22	6.00	15.00
73 Andre Reed/83	3.00	8.00
74 Az-Zahir Hakim/81	3.00	8.00
75 Cameron Cleeland/85	2.00	5.00
76 Lamar Thomas/85	2.00	5.00
77 Oronde Gadsden/86	2.00	5.00
78 Ben Coates/87	3.00	8.00
79 Bruce Smith/78	2.50	6.00
80 Jerry Rice/80	20.00	50.00
81 Tim Brown/81	5.00	12.00
82 Michael Westbrook/82	3.00	8.00
83 J.J. Stokes/83	3.00	8.00
84 Shannon Sharpe/84	3.00	8.00
85 Reidel Anthony/85	3.00	8.00
86 Antonio Freeman/86	5.00	12.00
87 Keenan McCardell/87	3.00	8.00
88 Terry Glenn/88	5.00	12.00
89 Andre Rison/89	3.00	8.00
90 Neil Smith/90	2.00	5.00
91 Terrance Mathis/81	3.00	8.00
92 Rocket Ismail/81	3.00	8.00
93 Byron Bam Morris/39	4.00	10.00
94 Ike Hilliard/88	3.00	8.00
95 Eddie Kennison/88	3.00	8.00
96 Tavian Banks/22	6.00	15.00
97 Yatil Green/87	2.00	5.00
98 Frank Wycheck/89	2.00	5.00
99 Warren Sapp/99	2.00	5.00
100 Germane Crowell/82	2.00	5.00
101 Curtis Martin/28	20.00	50.00
102 John Avery/20	6.00	15.00
103 Eric Moulds/80	5.00	12.00
104 Randy Moss/84	25.00	60.00
105 Terrell Owens/81	5.00	12.00
109 Isaac Bruce/80	5.00	12.00
115 Carl Pickens/81	3.00	8.00
117 Natrone Means/20	12.50	30.00
119 Garrison Hearst/20	20.00	50.00
120 Barry Sanders/20	125.00	250.00

122 Rashaan Shehee/22	6.00	15.00
123 Ed McCaffrey/87	3.00	8.00
124 Charles Woodson/24	20.00	50.00
125 Dorsey Levens/25	20.00	50.00
126 Robert Smith/26	20.00	50.00
127 Greg Hill/27	6.00	15.00
128 Fred Taylor/28	25.00	60.00
129 Marcus Nash/82	2.00	5.00
130 Terrell Davis/30	30.00	80.00
131 Ahman Green/30	15.00	40.00
132 Jamal Anderson/32	15.00	40.00
133 Karim Abdul-Jabbar/33	7.50	20.00
134 Jermaine Lewis/84	3.00	8.00
135 Jerome Pathon/86	2.00	5.00
137 Herman Moore/84	3.00	8.00
138 Tim Dwight/83	5.00	12.00
139 Johnnie Morton/87	3.00	8.00
140 Marshall Faulk/28	30.00	80.00
141 Frank Sanders/81	3.00	8.00
142 Kevin Dyson/87	3.00	8.00
143 Curtis Conway/83	3.00	8.00
144 Derrick Mayes/80	3.00	8.00
145 O.J. McDuffie/81	3.00	8.00
146 Joe Jurevicius/86	3.00	8.00
148 Joey Galloway/84	3.00	8.00
149 Jimmy Smith/82	3.00	8.00
150 Skip Hicks/20	6.00	15.00
151 Rod Smith/80	3.00	8.00
152 Duce Staley/22	20.00	50.00
153 James Stewart/33	7.50	20.00
156 Wayne Chrebet/80	5.00	12.00
157 Robert Brooks/87	3.00	8.00
158 Tim Biakabutuka/21	12.50	30.00
159 Priest Holmes/33	30.00	60.00
160 Warrick Dunn/28	20.00	50.00
166 Chris Claiborne/55	3.00	8.00
167 Joe Montgomery/33	7.50	20.00
168 Mike Cloud/21	12.50	30.00
172 Autry Denson/23	12.50	30.00
173 Jermaine Fazande/30	7.50	20.00
178 Torry Holt/81	12.50	30.00
179 Sedrick Irvin/33	20.00	50.00
182 James Johnson/22	12.50	30.00
184 Andy Katzenmoyer/45	12.50	30.00
185 Jevon Kearse/42	15.00	40.00
187 Rob Konrad/44	15.00	40.00
188 Jim Kleinsasser/82	5.00	12.00
192 De'Mond Parker/33	4.00	10.00
194 Shawn Bryson/24	20.00	50.00
195 Peerless Price/37	15.00	40.00
196 Darnell McDonald/80	7.50	20.00
198 Tai Streets/86	5.00	12.00
199 Ricky Williams/34	40.00	100.00
200 Amos Zereoue/20	20.00	50.00

1999 Donruss Elite Common Threads

MULTI-COLORED SWATCHES: .6X TO 1.5X
STATED PRINT RUN 150 SERIAL #'d SETS

1 Randy Moss	30.00	80.00
Randall Cunningham		
2 Randy Moss	30.00	80.00
3 Randall Cunningham	15.00	40.00
4 John Elway	40.00	100.00
Terrell Davis		
5 John Elway	30.00	80.00
6 Terrell Davis	15.00	40.00
7 Jerry Rice	40.00	100.00
Steve Young		
8 Jerry Rice	30.00	80.00
9 Steve Young	25.00	60.00
10 Mark Brunell	20.00	50.00
Fred Taylor		
11 Mark Brunell	15.00	40.00
12 Fred Taylor	15.00	40.00
13 Kordell Stewart	15.00	40.00
Jerome Bettis		
14 Kordell Stewart	12.50	30.00
15 Jerome Bettis	15.00	40.00
16 Dan Marino	50.00	120.00
Karim Abdul-Jabbar		
17 Dan Marino	40.00	100.00
18 Karim Abdul-Jabbar	10.00	25.00

1999 Donruss Elite Field of Vision

1A Dan Marino/1712	4.00	10.00
1B Dan Marino/834	6.00	15.00
1C Dan Marino/951	6.00	15.00
2A Emmitt Smith/640	5.00	12.00
2B Emmitt Smith/202	7.50	20.00
2C Emmitt Smith/490	5.00	12.00
3A Jake Plummer/1165	2.00	5.00
3B Jake Plummer/624	3.00	8.00
3C Jake Plummer/1948	2.00	5.00
4A Brett Favre/1409	4.00	10.00
4B Brett Favre/983	6.00	15.00
4C Brett Favre/1820	4.00	10.00
5A Fred Taylor/486	2.00	5.00
5B Fred Taylor/400	2.00	5.00
5C Fred Taylor/337	2.50	6.00
6A Drew Bledsoe/1355	2.00	5.00
6B Drew Bledsoe/689	3.00	8.00
6C Drew Bledsoe/1589	2.00	5.00
7A Terrell Davis/1283	2.00	5.00
7B Terrell Davis/306	4.00	10.00
7C Terrell Davis/419	3.00	8.00
8A Jerry Rice/611	4.00	10.00
8B Jerry Rice/234	7.50	20.00
8C Jerry Rice/312	6.00	15.00
9A Randy Moss/639	6.00	15.00
9B Randy Moss/16	50.00	120.00
9C Randy Moss/658	6.00	15.00
10A John Elway/1320	5.00	12.00
10B John Elway/615	6.00	15.00
10C John Elway/871	6.00	15.00
11A Peyton Manning/1141	5.00	12.00
11B Peyton Manning/1020	5.00	12.00
11C Peyton Manning/1578	4.00	10.00
12A Barry Sanders/556	6.00	15.00
12B Barry Sanders/373	7.50	20.00
12C Barry Sanders/562	6.00	15.00

1999 Donruss Elite Field of Vision Die Cuts

1A Dan Marino/164	15.00	40.00
1B Dan Marino/56	40.00	100.00
1C Dan Marino/90	25.00	60.00
2A Emmitt Smith/158	7.50	20.00
2B Emmitt Smith/64	25.00	60.00
2C Emmitt Smith/97	12.50	30.00
3A Jake Plummer/89	7.50	20.00
3B Jake Plummer/44	15.00	40.00
3C Jake Plummer/191	3.00	8.00
4A Brett Favre/112	20.00	50.00
4B Brett Favre/67	40.00	100.00
4C Brett Favre/168	15.00	40.00
5A Fred Taylor/103	7.50	20.00
5B Fred Taylor/79	10.00	25.00
5C Fred Taylor/82	10.00	25.00
6A Drew Bledsoe/90	7.50	20.00
6B Drew Bledsoe/48	12.50	30.00
6C Drew Bledsoe/125	3.00	8.00
7A Terrell Davis/217	4.00	10.00
7B Terrell Davis/66	10.00	25.00
7C Terrell Davis/109	5.00	12.00
8A Jerry Rice/50	25.00	60.00
8C Jerry Rice/21	60.00	120.00
9A Randy Moss/34	30.00	80.00
9C Randy Moss/33	30.00	80.00
10A John Elway/98	25.00	60.00
10B John Elway/35	50.00	120.00
10C John Elway/77	30.00	80.00
11A Peyton Manning/110	15.00	40.00
11B Peyton Manning/79	20.00	50.00
11C Peyton Manning/137	10.00	25.00
12A Barry Sanders/137	15.00	40.00
12B Barry Sanders/83	30.00	80.00
12C Barry Sanders/123	20.00	50.00

1999 Donruss Elite Passing the Torch

COMPLETE SET (18)	75.00	150.00
TOTAL PRINT RUN 1500 SERIAL #'d SETS		
FIRST 100-CARDS WERE SIGNED		
1 Johnny Unitas	6.00	15.00
Peyton Manning		
2 Johnny Unitas	4.00	10.00
3 Peyton Manning	6.00	15.00
4A Walter Payton	10.00	25.00
Barry Sanders		
4B Emmitt Smith	5.00	12.00
Fred Taylor		
5A Walter Payton	6.00	15.00
5B Emmitt Smith	4.00	10.00
6A Barry Sanders	7.50	15.00
6B Fred Taylor	2.00	5.00
7A Earl Campbell	6.00	15.00
Ricky Williams COR		
7B Earl Campbell ERR	30.00	50.00
Ricky Williams ERR		
(Rams listed as Williams' team)		
7C Earl Campbell ERR	30.00	50.00
Ricky Williams ERR		
(Redskins listed as Williams' team)		
8 Earl Campbell	2.00	5.00
9A Ricky Williams COR	2.50	6.00
9B Ricky Williams ERR	30.00	50.00
(Rams listed as team)		
9C Ricky Williams ERR	30.00	50.00
(Redskins listed as team)		
10 Jim Brown	3.00	8.00
Terrell Davis		
11 Jim Brown	4.00	10.00
12 Terrell Davis	2.00	5.00
16 Cris Carter	5.00	12.00
Randy Moss		
17 Cris Carter	2.00	5.00
18 Randy Moss	5.00	12.00

1999 Donruss Elite Passing the Torch Autographs

FIRST 100-CARDS OF PRINT RUN SIGNED		
1 Johnny Unitas	750.00	1,500.00
Peyton Manning		
2 Johnny Unitas	350.00	600.00
3 Peyton Manning	150.00	300.00
4A Walter Payton	1,500.00	2,500.00
Barry Sanders		
4B Emmitt Smith	200.00	400.00
Fred Taylor		
5A Walter Payton	600.00	900.00
5B Emmitt Smith	175.00	300.00
6A Barry Sanders	100.00	200.00
6B Fred Taylor	30.00	60.00
7 Earl Campbell	60.00	120.00
Ricky Williams		
8 Earl Campbell	50.00	100.00
9 Ricky Williams	30.00	60.00
10 Jim Brown	125.00	250.00
Terrell Davis		
11 Jim Brown	100.00	200.00
12 Terrell Davis	50.00	100.00
16 Cris Carter	150.00	300.00
Randy Moss		
17 Cris Carter	60.00	120.00
18 Randy Moss	125.00	200.00

1999 Donruss Elite Power Formulas

COMPLETE SET (30)	50.00	100.00
STATED PRINT RUN 3500 SERIAL #'d SETS		
1 Randy Moss	3.00	8.00
2 Terrell Davis	1.25	3.00
3 Brett Favre	4.00	10.00
4 Dan Marino	4.00	10.00
5 Barry Sanders	4.00	10.00
6 Peyton Manning	4.00	10.00
7 John Elway	4.00	10.00
8 Fred Taylor	1.25	3.00
9 Emmitt Smith	2.50	6.00
10 Steve Young	1.50	4.00
11 Jerry Rice	2.50	6.00
12 Jake Plummer	1.25	3.00
13 Kordell Stewart	1.25	3.00
14 Mark Brunell	1.25	3.00
15 Drew Bledsoe	1.50	4.00
16 Eddie George	1.25	3.00
17 Troy Aikman	2.50	6.00
18 Warrick Dunn	1.25	3.00
19 Keyshawn Johnson	1.25	3.00
20 Jamal Anderson	1.25	3.00
21 Randall Cunningham	1.25	3.00
22 Doug Flutie	1.25	3.00
23 Jerome Bettis	1.25	3.00
24 Garrison Hearst	1.25	3.00
25 Curtis Martin	1.25	3.00
26 Corey Dillion	1.25	3.00
27 Antowain Smith	1.25	3.00
28 Antonio Freeman	1.25	3.00
29 Terrell Owens	1.25	3.00
30 Carl Pickens	1.25	3.00

1999 Donruss Elite Primary Colors Yellow

COMPLETE SET (40)	75.00	150.00
YELLOW PRINT RUN 1875 SER.#'d SETS		
*BLUE CARDS: .6X TO 1.5X YELLOW		
BLUE PRINT RUN 950 SERIAL #'d SET		
*RED STARS: 8X TO 20X YELLOWS		
*RED ROOKIES: 5X TO 12X YELLOWS		
RED PRINT RUN 25 SERIAL #'d SET		
*BLUE DIE CUT STARS: 4X TO 10X YELLOWS		
*BLUE DIE CUT ROOKIES: 3X TO 8X		
BLUE DIE CUT PRINT RUN 50 SER.#'d SETS		
*RED DIE CUT STARS: 4X TO 10X YELLOWS		
*RED DIE CUT ROOKIES: 2.5X TO 6X		
RED DIE CUT PRINT RUN 75 SER.#'d SETS		
*YELLOW DIE CUT STARS: 6X TO 15X		
*YELLOW DIE CUT ROOKIES: 4X TO 10X		
YELLOW DIE CUT PRINT RUN 25 SER.#'d SETS		
1 Herman Moore	1.25	3.00
2 Marshall Faulk	2.00	5.00
3 Dorsey Levens	1.25	3.00
4 Napoleon Kaufman	1.25	3.00
5 Jamal Anderson	1.25	3.00
6 Edgerrin James	4.00	10.00
7 Troy Aikman	2.50	6.00
8 Cris Carter	1.25	3.00
9 Eddie George	1.25	3.00
10 Donovan McNabb	5.00	12.00
11 Drew Bledsoe	1.50	4.00
12 Daunte Culpepper	4.00	10.00
13 Mark Brunell	1.25	3.00
14 Corey Dillon	1.25	3.00
15 Kordell Stewart	1.25	3.00
16 Curtis Martin	1.25	3.00
17 Jake Plummer	1.25	3.00
18 Charlie Batch	1.25	3.00
19 Jerry Rice	2.50	6.00
20 Antonio Freeman	1.25	3.00
21 Steve Young	1.50	4.00
22 Steve McNair	1.25	3.00
23 Emmitt Smith	2.50	6.00
24 Terrell Owens	1.25	3.00
25 Fred Taylor	1.25	3.00
26 Joey Galloway	1.25	3.00
27 John Elway	4.00	10.00
28 Ryan Leaf	1.25	3.00
29 Barry Sanders	4.00	10.00
30 Ricky Williams	2.00	5.00
31 Dan Marino	4.00	10.00
32 Tim Couch	1.25	3.00
33 Brett Favre	4.00	10.00
34 Eric Moulds	1.25	3.00
35 Peyton Manning	4.00	10.00
36 Deion Sanders	1.25	3.00
37 Terrell Davis	1.25	3.00
38 Tim Brown	1.25	3.00
39 Randy Moss	3.00	8.00
40 Mike Alstott	1.25	3.00

2000 Donruss Elite

Released as a 200-card set, 2000 Donruss Elite is comprised of 100 base cards, 25 short-printed veteran cards, and 75 prospect cards which are sequentially numbered to 2000 with the first 500 of each die-cut. Some Rookie Cards were issued via mail redemptions that carried an expiration date of 5/31/2001. Base cards are printed on foil board with red foil highlights. Elite was packaged in 18-pack boxes containing five cards each and carried a suggested retail price of $3.99.

COMPLETE SET (200)	300.00	500.00
COMP.SET w/o SP's (100)	6.00	15.00
126-200 ROOKIE PRINT RUN 2000		
1 Jake Plummer	.20	.50
2 David Boston	.15	.40
3 Rob Moore	.15	.40
4 Chris Chandler	.20	.50
5 Tim Dwight	.20	.50
6 Terance Mathis	.15	.40
7 Jamal Anderson	.20	.50
8 Priest Holmes	.25	.60
9 Tony Banks	.15	.40
10 Shannon Sharpe	.25	.60
11 Qadry Ismail	.20	.50
12 Eric Moulds	.20	.50
13 Doug Flutie	.25	.60
14 Antowain Smith	.20	.50
15 Peerless Price	.20	.50
16 Muhsin Muhammad	.20	.50
17 Tim Biakabutuka	.20	.50
18 Patrick Jeffers	.20	.50
19 Steve Beuerlein	.20	.50
20 Wesley Walls	.15	.40
21 Curtis Enis	.15	.40
22 Marcus Robinson	.20	.50
23 Carl Pickens	.20	.50
24 Corey Dillon	.20	.50
25 Akili Smith	.15	.40
26 Darnay Scott	.20	.50
27 Kevin Johnson	.15	.40
28 Errict Rhett	.20	.50
29 Emmitt Smith	.60	1.50
30 Deion Sanders	.25	.60
31 Troy Aikman	.40	1.00
32 Joey Galloway	.20	.50
33 Michael Irvin	.25	.60
34 Rocket Ismail	.20	.50
35 Jason Tucker	.15	.40
36 Ed McCaffrey	.20	.50
37 Rod Smith	.20	.50
38 Brian Griese	.20	.50
39 Terrell Davis	.25	.60
40 Olandis Gary	.20	.50
41 Charlie Batch	.20	.50
42 Johnnie Morton	.20	.50
43 Herman Moore	.20	.50
44 James Stewart	.15	.40
45 Dorsey Levens	.20	.50
46 Antonio Freeman	.20	.50
47 Brett Favre	.75	2.00
48 Bill Schroeder	.20	.50
49 Peyton Manning	.60	1.50
50 Keenan McCardell	.20	.50
51 Fred Taylor	.25	.60
52 Jimmy Smith	.20	.50
53 Elvis Grbac	.15	.40
54 Tony Gonzalez	.25	.60
55 Derrick Alexander	.15	.40
56 Dan Marino	.75	2.00
57 Tony Martin	.20	.50
58 James Johnson	.15	.40
59 Damon Huard	.20	.50
60 Thurman Thomas	.25	.60
61 Robert Smith	.20	.50
62 Randall Cunningham	.25	.60
63 Jeff George	.20	.50
64 Terry Glenn	.20	.50
65 Drew Bledsoe	.25	.60
66 Jeff Blake	.20	.50
67 Amani Toomer	.20	.50
68 Kerry Collins	.20	.50
69 Joe Montgomery	.15	.40
70 Vinny Testaverde	.20	.50
71 Ray Lucas	.15	.40
72 Keyshawn Johnson	.20	.50
73 Wayne Chrebet	.20	.50
74 Napoleon Kaufman	.20	.50
75 Tim Brown	.25	.60
76 Rich Gannon	.20	.50
77 Duce Staley	.20	.50
78 Kordell Stewart	.20	.50
79 Jerome Bettis	.25	.60
80 Troy Edwards	.15	.40
81 Natrone Means	.20	.50
82 Curtis Conway	.20	.50
83 Jim Harbaugh	.20	.50
84 Junior Seau	.25	.60
85 Jermaine Fazande	.15	.40
86 Terrell Owens	.25	.60
87 Charlie Garner	.20	.50
88 Steve Young	.30	.75
89 Jeff Garcia	.20	.50
90 Derrick Mayes	.15	.40
91 Ricky Watters	.20	.50
92 Az-Zahir Hakim	.15	.40
93 Torry Holt	.25	.60
94 Warren Sapp	.20	.50
95 Mike Alstott	.25	.60
96 Warrick Dunn	.20	.50
97 Kevin Dyson	.20	.50
98 Bruce Smith	.25	.60
99 Albert Connell	.15	.40
100 Michael Westbrook	.15	.40
101 Cade McNown	.50	1.25
102 Tim Couch	.60	1.50
103 John Elway	2.00	5.00
104 Barry Sanders	1.50	4.00
105 Germane Crowell	.50	1.25
106 Marvin Harrison	.75	2.00
107 Edgerrin James	.75	2.00
108 Mark Brunell	.60	1.50
109 Randy Moss	.75	2.00
110 Cris Carter	.75	2.00
111 Daunte Culpepper	.60	1.50
112 Ricky Williams	.75	2.00
113 Curtis Martin	.75	2.00
114 Donovan McNabb	.75	2.00
115 Jerry Rice	1.50	4.00
116 Jon Kitna	.60	1.50
117 Isaac Bruce	.75	2.00
118 Marshall Faulk	.75	2.00
119 Kurt Warner	1.25	3.00
120 Shaun King	.50	1.25
121 Eddie George	.60	1.50
122 Steve McNair	.75	2.00
123 Jevon Kearse	.60	1.50
124 Stephen Davis	.60	1.50
125 Brad Johnson	.60	1.50
126 Mike Anderson RC	2.00	5.00
127 Peter Warrick RC	2.00	5.00
128 Courtney Brown RC	1.50	4.00
129 Plaxico Burress RC	2.00	5.00
130 Corey Simon RC	1.50	4.00
131 Thomas Jones RC	2.50	6.00
132 Travis Taylor RC	1.50	4.00
133 Shaun Alexander RC	2.50	6.00
134 Deon Grant RC	1.25	3.00
135 Chris Redman RC	1.50	4.00
136 Chad Pennington RC	3.00	8.00
137 Jamal Lewis RC	2.00	5.00
138 Brian Urlacher RC	8.00	20.00
139 Keith Bulluck RC	1.50	4.00
140 Bubba Franks RC	2.00	5.00
141 Dez White RC	1.50	4.00
142 Na'il Diggs RC	1.25	3.00
143 Ahmed Plummer RC	1.25	3.00
144 Ron Dayne RC	2.00	5.00
145 Shaun Ellis RC	2.00	5.00
146 Sylvester Morris RC	1.25	3.00
147 Deltha O'Neal RC	1.50	4.00
148 Raynoch Thompson RC	1.25	3.00
149 R.Jay Soward RC	1.25	3.00
150 Mario Edwards RC	1.25	3.00
151 John Engelberger RC	1.25	3.00
152 D.Goodrich RC	1.25	3.00
153 Sherrod Gideon RC	1.25	3.00
154 John Abraham RC	2.00	5.00
155 Ben Kelly RC	1.25	3.00
156 Travis Prentice RC	1.50	4.00
157 Darrell Jackson RC	1.50	4.00
158 Giovanni Carmazzi RC	1.25	3.00
159 Anthony Lucas RC	1.25	3.00
160 Danny Farmer RC	1.25	3.00
161 Dennis Northcutt RC	1.50	4.00
162 Troy Walters RC	1.25	3.00
163 Laveranues Coles RC	2.00	5.00
164 Tee Martin RC	2.00	5.00
165 J.R. Redmond RC	1.25	3.00
166 Tim Rattay RC	1.50	4.00
167 Jerry Porter RC	2.00	5.00
168 Sebastian Janikowski RC	2.00	5.00
169 Michael Wiley RC	1.25	3.00
170 Reuben Droughns RC	2.00	5.00
171 Trung Canidate RC	1.50	4.00
172 Shyrone Stith RC	1.25	3.00
173 Chris Hovan RC	1.50	4.00
174 Brandon Short RC	1.25	3.00
175 Mark Roman RC	1.25	3.00
176 Trevor Gaylor RC	1.25	3.00
177 Chris Cole RC	1.50	4.00
178 Hank Poteat RC	1.25	3.00
179 Darren Howard RC	1.25	3.00
180 Rob Morris RC	1.50	4.00
181 Spergon Wynn RC	1.50	4.00
182 Marc Bulger RC	2.00	5.00
183 Tom Brady RC	90.00	150.00
184 Todd Husak RC	1.25	3.00
185 Gari Scott RC	1.25	3.00
186 Erron Kinney RC	1.25	3.00
187 Julian Peterson RC	2.00	5.00
188 Sammy Morris RC	1.50	4.00
189 Rondell Mealey RC	1.25	3.00
190 Doug Chapman RC	1.25	3.00
191 Ron Dugans RC	1.25	3.00
192 Deon Dyer RC	1.25	3.00
193 Fred Robbins RC	1.25	3.00
194 Ike Charlton RC	1.25	3.00
195 Mareno Philyaw RC	1.25	3.00
196 Thomas Hamner RC	1.25	3.00
197 Jarious Jackson RC	1.50	4.00
198 Anthony Becht RC	1.50	4.00
199 Joe Hamilton RC	1.25	3.00
200 Todd Pinkston RC	1.25	3.00

2000 Donruss Elite Aspirations

*VETS/70-99: 8X TO 20X BASE 1-100		
*VETS/70-99: 2.5X TO 6X BASE 101-125		
*ROOKIES/70-99: 1X TO 2.5X		
*VETS/45-69: 10X TO 25X BASE 1-100		
*VETS/45-69: 3X TO 8X BASE 101-125		
*ROOKIE/45-69: 1.2X TO 3X BASIC CARD		
*VETS/20-29: 20X TO 50X BASE 1-100		
*VETS/20-29: 6X TO 15X BASE 101-125		
*ROOKIE/20-29: 2.5X TO 6X BASIC CARD		
*VETS/10-19: 25X TO 60X BASE 1-100		
*VETS/10-19: 8X TO 20X BASE 101-125		
*ROOKIE/10-19: 3X TO 8X BASIC CARD		
STATED PRINT RUN 1-99		
183 Tom Brady/90	350.00	600.00

2000 Donruss Elite Rookie Die Cuts

*DIE CUTS: .6X TO 1.5X BASE RCs		
FIRST 500 SER.#'d RC's WERE DIE CUT		
183 Tom Brady	125.00	250.00

2000 Donruss Elite Status

*VETS/78-99: 8X TO 20X BASE 1-100
*VETS/78-99: 2.5X TO 6X BASE 101-125
*ROOKIES/78-99: 1X TO 2.5X
*VETS/40-55: 10X TO 25X BASE 1-100
*VETS/40-55: 3X TO 8X BASE 101-125
*ROOKIE/40-55: 1.2X TO 3X BASIC CARD
*VETS/30-39: 12X TO 30X BASE 1-100
*VETS/30-39: 4X TO 10X BASE 101-125
*ROOKIE/30-39: 1.5X TO 4X BASIC CARD
*VETS/20-29: 20X TO 50X BASE 1-100
*VETS/20-29: 6X TO 15X BASE 101-125
*ROOKIE/20-29: 2.5X TO 6X BASIC CARD
*VETS/10-19: 25X TO 60X BASE 1-100
*VETS/10-19: 8X TO 20X BASE 101-125
*ROOKIE/11-19: 3X TO 8X BASIC CARD
STATED PRINT RUN 1-99

2000 Donruss Elite Craftsmen

COMPLETE SET (40)	40.00	80.00
STATED PRINT RUN 2500 SER.#'d SETS		
*MASTERS/50: 3X TO 8X BASIC INSERTS		
MASTERS PRINT RUN 50 SER.#'d SETS		
C1 Dan Marino	2.50	6.00
C2 Edgerrin James	.75	2.00
C3 Peyton Manning	2.00	5.00
C4 Drew Bledsoe	.75	2.00
C5 Doug Flutie	.75	2.00
C6 Curtis Martin	.75	2.00
C7 Eddie George	.60	1.50
C8 Steve McNair	.75	2.00
C9 Fred Taylor	.75	2.00
C10 Mark Brunell	.60	1.50
C11 Tim Couch	.60	1.50
C12 Corey Dillon	.60	1.50
C13 Terrell Davis	.75	2.00
C14 Jon Kitna	.60	1.50
C15 Emmitt Smith	2.00	5.00
C16 Troy Aikman	1.25	3.00
C17 Stephen Davis	.60	1.50
C18 Brad Johnson	.60	1.50
C19 Jake Plummer	.60	1.50
C20 Brett Favre	2.50	6.00
C21 Barry Sanders	1.50	4.00
C22 Marshall Faulk	.75	2.00
C23 Kurt Warner	1.25	3.00
C24 Ricky Williams	.75	2.00
C25 Steve Young	1.00	2.50
C26 Randy Moss	.75	2.00
C27 John Elway	2.00	5.00
C28 Jerry Rice	1.50	4.00
C29 Tim Brown	.75	2.00
C30 Cris Carter	.75	2.00
C31 Antonio Freeman	.60	1.50
C32 Joey Galloway	.60	1.50
C33 Terry Glenn	.60	1.50
C34 Marvin Harrison	.75	2.00
C35 Keyshawn Johnson	.60	1.50
C36 Eric Moulds	.60	1.50
C37 Isaac Bruce	.75	2.00
C38 Peter Warrick	.75	2.00
C39 Plaxico Burress	.75	2.00
C40 Thomas Jones	1.00	2.50

2000 Donruss Elite Down and Distance

STATED PRINT RUN 2-1857		
CARDS SER.#'d TO A 1999 SEASON STAT		
1D1 Randy Moss/611	1.25	3.00
1D2 Randy Moss/493	1.25	3.00
1D3 Randy Moss/263	1.50	4.00
1D4 Randy Moss/46	3.00	8.00
2D1 Brett Favre/1386	3.00	8.00
2D2 Brett Favre/1543	3.00	8.00
2D3 Brett Favre/1139	3.00	8.00
2D4 Brett Favre/23	15.00	40.00
3D1 Dan Marino/1023	3.00	8.00
3D2 Dan Marino/855	4.00	10.00
3D3 Dan Marino/505	4.00	10.00
3D4 Dan Marino/65	6.00	15.00
4D1 Peyton Manning/1857	2.50	6.00
4D2 Peyton Manning/1219	2.50	6.00
4D3 Peyton Manning/1029	2.50	6.00
4D4 Peyton Manning/30	8.00	20.00
5D1 Emmitt Smith/832	3.00	8.00
5D2 Emmitt Smith/506	3.00	8.00
5D3 Emmitt Smith/55	5.00	12.00
6D1 Jerry Rice/391	2.50	6.00
6D2 Jerry Rice/238	3.00	8.00
6D3 Jerry Rice/176	3.00	8.00
6D4 Jerry Rice/25	10.00	25.00
7D1 Mark Brunell/1066	.75	2.00
7D2 Mark Brunell/1112	.75	2.00
7D3 Mark Brunell/878	1.00	2.50
8D1 Eddie George/716	1.00	2.50
8D2 Eddie George/487	1.00	2.50
8D3 Eddie George/98	1.50	4.00
9D1 Marshall Faulk/762	1.25	3.00
9D2 Marshall Faulk/512	1.25	3.00
9D3 Marshall Faulk/101	2.00	5.00
10D1 Kurt Warner/1682	1.50	4.00
10D2 Kurt Warner/1336	1.50	4.00
10D3 Kurt Warner/1307	1.50	4.00
10D4 Kurt Warner/28	8.00	20.00
11D1 Edgerrin James/894	1.25	3.00
11D2 Edgerrin James/531	1.25	3.00
11D3 Edgerrin James/126	1.50	4.00
12D1 Tim Couch/940	1.00	2.50
12D2 Tim Couch/908	1.00	2.50
12D3 Tim Couch/564	1.00	2.50
12D4 Tim Couch/35	2.50	6.00

2000 Donruss Elite Down and Distance Die Cuts

STATED PRINT RUN 1-220		
1D1 Randy Moss/34	3.00	8.00
1D2 Randy Moss/30	3.00	8.00
1D3 Randy Moss/14	6.00	15.00
2D1 Brett Favre/133	5.00	12.00
2D2 Brett Favre/119	5.00	12.00
2D3 Brett Favre/88	6.00	15.00
3D1 Dan Marino/82	6.00	15.00
3D2 Dan Marino/77	6.00	15.00
3D3 Dan Marino/42	10.00	25.00
4D1 Peyton Manning/121	4.00	10.00
4D2 Peyton Manning/118	4.00	10.00
4D3 Peyton Manning/91	5.00	12.00
5D1 Emmitt Smith/175	4.00	10.00
5D2 Emmitt Smith/121	4.00	10.00
5D3 Emmitt Smith/29	12.00	30.00
6D1 Jerry Rice/24	10.00	25.00
6D2 Jerry Rice/24	10.00	25.00
6D3 Jerry Rice/16	12.00	30.00
7D1 Mark Brunell/81	1.50	4.00
7D2 Mark Brunell/100	1.50	4.00
7D3 Mark Brunell/77	1.50	4.00
8D1 Eddie George/171	1.25	3.00
8D2 Eddie George/119	1.25	3.00
8D3 Eddie George/29	4.00	10.00
9D1 Marshall Faulk/138	1.50	4.00
9D2 Marshall Faulk/94	2.00	5.00
9D3 Marshall Faulk/20	5.00	12.00
10D1 Kurt Warner/129	2.50	6.00
10D2 Kurt Warner/106	2.50	6.00
10D3 Kurt Warner/87	3.00	8.00
11D1 Edgerrin James/220	1.50	4.00
11D2 Edgerrin James/130	1.50	4.00
11D3 Edgerrin James/17	6.00	15.00
12D1 Tim Couch/83	1.50	4.00
12D2 Tim Couch/81	1.50	4.00
12D3 Tim Couch/56	1.50	4.00

2000 Donruss Elite Passing the Torch

COMPLETE SET (18)	100.00	200.00
PT1-PT12 STATED PRINT RUN 1500		
PT1-PT12 FIRST 100 CARDS SIGNED		
PT13-PT18 STATED PRINT RUN 500		
PT13-PT18 FIRST 50 CARDS SIGNED		
PT1 Jerry Rice	3.00	8.00
PT2 Randy Moss	1.50	4.00
PT3 Dan Marino	5.00	12.00
PT4 Kurt Warner	2.50	6.00
PT5 Joe Montana	5.00	12.00
PT6 Steve Young	2.00	5.00
PT7 Bart Starr	4.00	10.00
PT8 Brett Favre	5.00	12.00
PT9 Roger Staubach	3.00	8.00
PT10 Troy Aikman	2.50	6.00
PT11 Gale Sayers	2.50	6.00
PT12 Edgerrin James	1.50	4.00
PT13 Jerry Rice	5.00	12.00
Randy Moss		
PT14 Dan Marino	8.00	20.00
Kurt Warner		
PT15 Joe Montana	8.00	20.00
Steve Young		
PT16 Bart Starr	8.00	20.00
Brett Favre		
PT17 Roger Staubach	5.00	12.00
Troy Aikman		
PT18 Gale Sayers	4.00	10.00
Edgerrin James		

2000 Donruss Elite Passing the Torch Autographs

PT1-PT12 FIRST 100-CARDS SIGNED		
PT13-PT18 FIRST 50-CARDS SIGNED		
PT1 Jerry Rice	90.00	150.00
PT2 Randy Moss	50.00	100.00
PT3 Dan Marino	100.00	200.00
PT4 Kurt Warner	35.00	60.00
PT5 Joe Montana	100.00	200.00
PT6 Steve Young	50.00	100.00
PT7 Bart Starr	100.00	200.00
PT8 Brett Favre	125.00	250.00
PT9 Roger Staubach	50.00	100.00
PT10 Troy Aikman	60.00	120.00
PT11 Gale Sayers	40.00	80.00
PT12 Edgerrin James	30.00	60.00
PT13 Jerry Rice	200.00	350.00
Randy Moss		
PT14 Dan Marino	125.00	250.00
Kurt Warner		
PT15 Joe Montana	250.00	400.00
Steve Young		
PT16 Bart Starr	250.00	400.00
Brett Favre		
PT17 Roger Staubach	100.00	200.00
Troy Aikman		
PT18 Gale Sayers	100.00	200.00
Edgerrin James		

2000 Donruss Elite Throwback Threads

TT1-TT30 SINGLE JSY PRINT RUN 100		
TT31-TT45 DUAL JSY PRINT RUN 50		
TT1 Joe Namath AU/100	100.00	200.00
TT2 Dan Marino	30.00	80.00
TT3 Walter Payton	30.00	80.00
TT4 Barry Sanders	20.00	50.00
TT5 Joe Montana/50*	30.00	80.00
TT5A Joe Montana AU/50*	125.00	250.00
TT6 Steve Young	25.00	50.00
TT7 Eric Dickerson/50*	15.00	40.00
TT7A Eric Dickerson AU/50*	40.00	100.00
TT8 Edgerrin James	10.00	25.00
TT9 Johnny Unitas/75*	40.00	80.00
TT9A Johnny Unitas AU/25*	300.00	450.00
TT10 Peyton Manning	25.00	60.00
TT11 Bart Starr/75*	30.00	80.00
TT11A Bart Starr AU/25*	200.00	400.00
TT12 Brett Favre	30.00	80.00
TT13 Terry Bradshaw/50*	30.00	80.00
TT13A Terry Bradshaw AU/50*	125.00	250.00
TT14 Kurt Warner	15.00	40.00
TT15 Dan Fouts/50*	25.00	60.00
TT15A Dan Fouts AU/50*	50.00	100.00
TT16 Drew Bledsoe	10.00	25.00
TT17 Earl Campbell/75*	30.00	60.00
TT17A Earl Campbell AU/25*	75.00	150.00
TT18 Eddie George	8.00	20.00
TT19 Jim Brown	25.00	60.00
TT20 Terrell Davis	10.00	25.00
TT21 Marcus Allen	20.00	50.00
TT22 Emmitt Smith	25.00	60.00
TT23 Bob Griese/75*	25.00	50.00
TT23A Bob Griese AU/25*	60.00	120.00
TT24 Brian Griese	8.00	20.00
TT25 Roger Staubach AU/100	60.00	120.00
TT26 Troy Aikman	25.00	50.00
TT27 Ken Stabler AU/25*	125.00	250.00
TT27 Ken Stabler/75*	25.00	60.00
TT28 Jake Plummer	8.00	20.00
TT29 Fran Tarkenton AU/25*	75.00	150.00
TT29 Fran Tarkenton/75*	25.00	50.00
TT30 Mark Brunell	8.00	20.00
TT31 Joe Namath AU	300.00	500.00
Dan Marino AU		
TT32 Walter Payton	60.00	120.00
Barry Sanders		
TT33 Joe Montana	30.00	80.00
Steve Young		
TT34 Eric Dickerson	20.00	50.00
Edgerrin James		
TT35 Johnny Unitas	40.00	100.00
Peyton Manning		
TT36 Bart Starr	60.00	120.00
Brett Favre		
TT37 Terry Bradshaw	25.00	60.00
Kurt Warner		
TT38 Dan Fouts	20.00	50.00
Drew Bledsoe		
TT39 Earl Campbell	20.00	50.00
Eddie George		
TT40 Jim Brown	25.00	60.00
Terrell Davis		
TT41 Marcus Allen	30.00	80.00
Emmitt Smith		
TT42 Bob Griese	20.00	50.00
Brian Griese		
TT43 Roger Staubach AU	125.00	250.00
Troy Aikman AU		
TT44 Ken Stabler	20.00	50.00
Jake Plummer		
TT45 Fran Tarkenton	20.00	50.00
Mark Brunell		

2000 Donruss Elite Turn of the Century

COMPLETE SET (60)	100.00	200.00
STATED PRINT RUN 1000 SER.#'d SETS		
*GOLD DIE CUT/21: 4X TO 10X BASIC INSERTS		
GOLD DIE CUT PRINT RUN 21		
TC1 Dan Marino	3.00	8.00
TC2 Edgerrin James	1.00	2.50
TC3 Peyton Manning	2.50	6.00
TC4 Drew Bledsoe	1.00	2.50
TC5 Doug Flutie	1.00	2.50
TC6 Curtis Martin	1.00	2.50
TC7 Eddie George	.75	2.00
TC8 Steve McNair	1.00	2.50
TC9 Fred Taylor	1.00	2.50
TC10 Mark Brunell	.75	2.00
TC11 Tim Couch	.75	2.00
TC12 Peter Warrick	1.00	2.50
TC13 Terrell Davis	1.00	2.50
TC14 Jon Kitna	.75	2.00
TC15 Emmitt Smith	2.50	6.00
TC16 Troy Aikman	1.50	4.00
TC17 Stephen Davis	.75	2.00
TC18 Brad Johnson	.75	2.00
TC19 Jake Plummer	.75	2.00
TC20 Brett Favre	3.00	8.00
TC21 Barry Sanders	2.00	5.00
TC22 Marshall Faulk	1.00	2.50
TC23 Kurt Warner	1.50	4.00
TC24 Ricky Williams	1.00	2.50
TC25 Steve Young	1.25	3.00
TC26 Randy Moss	1.00	2.50
TC27 John Elway	2.50	6.00
TC28 Jerry Rice	2.00	5.00
TC29 Plaxico Burress	1.00	2.50
TC30 Cris Carter	1.00	2.50
TC31 Antonio Freeman	.75	2.00
TC32 Thomas Jones	1.25	3.00
TC33 Travis Taylor	.75	2.00
TC34 Marvin Harrison	1.00	2.50
TC35 Keyshawn Johnson	.75	2.00
TC36 Shaun Alexander	1.25	3.00
TC37 Isaac Bruce	1.00	2.50
TC38 Ricky Watters	.75	2.00
TC39 Ron Dayne	1.00	2.50
TC40 Brian Griese	.75	2.00
TC41 Charlie Batch	.75	2.00
TC42 Jamal Lewis	1.00	2.50
TC43 Jamal Anderson	.75	2.00
TC44 Dorsey Levens	.75	2.00
TC45 Chris Redman	.75	2.00
TC46 Robert Smith	.75	2.00
TC47 Chad Pennington	1.50	4.00
TC48 Terrell Owens	1.00	2.50
TC49 Deion Sanders	1.00	2.50
TC50 Duce Staley	.75	2.00
TC51 Dez White	.75	2.00
TC52 Jimmy Smith	.75	2.00
TC53 Cade McNown	.60	1.50
TC54 Daunte Culpepper	.75	2.00
TC55 Akili Smith	.60	1.50
TC56 Torry Holt	1.00	2.50
TC57 Kevin Johnson	.60	1.50
TC58 Shaun King	.60	1.50
TC59 Olandis Gary	.75	2.00
TC60 Donovan McNabb	1.00	2.50

2001 Donruss Elite

Released as a 200-card set, 2001 Donruss Elite is comprised of 100 base cards, 100 rookie cards which are sequentially numbered to 500 with the first 50 of each autographed. Please note that some of the Rookie Cards were short printed and some were issued as redemption cards to be mailed in. Base cards are printed on foil board with team color highlights foil highlights. Elite was packaged in 18-pack boxes containing five cards each and carried a suggested retail price of $3.99.

COMP.SET w/o SP's (100)	7.50	20.00
ROOKIE PRINT RUN 250-500		
1 David Boston	.15	.40
2 Jake Plummer	.20	.50
3 Thomas Jones	.20	.50
4 Jamal Anderson	.20	.50
5 Chris Redman	.25	.60
6 Jamal Lewis	.25	.60
7 Shannon Sharpe	.25	.60
8 Travis Taylor	.15	.40
9 Trent Dilfer	.20	.50
10 Doug Flutie	.25	.60
11 Eric Moulds	.20	.50
12 Rob Johnson	.20	.50

13 Muhsin Muhammad	.20	.50
14 Steve Beuerlein	.20	.50
15 Brian Urlacher	.30	.75
16 Cade McNown	.20	.50
17 Marcus Robinson	.20	.50
18 Akili Smith	.15	.40
19 Corey Dillon	.20	.50
20 Peter Warrick	.20	.50
21 Kevin Johnson	.15	.40
22 Tim Couch	.15	.40
23 Emmitt Smith	.60	1.50
24 Troy Aikman	.40	1.00
25 Brian Griese	.20	.50
26 John Elway	.60	1.50
27 Mike Anderson	.20	.50
28 Rod Smith	.20	.50
29 Terrell Davis	.25	.60
30 Barry Sanders	.60	1.50
31 Charlie Batch	.20	.50
32 James Stewart	.15	.40
33 Ahman Green	.25	.60
34 Antonio Freeman	.25	.60
35 Brett Favre	.75	2.00
36 Edgerrin James	.25	.60
37 Marvin Harrison	.25	.60
38 Peyton Manning	.60	1.50
39 Fred Taylor	.25	.60
40 Jimmy Smith	.20	.50
41 Keenan McCardell	.20	.50
42 Mark Brunell	.20	.50
43 Derrick Alexander	.15	.40
44 Elvis Grbac	.20	.50
45 Sylvester Morris	.15	.40
46 Tony Gonzalez	.25	.60
47 Dan Marino	.60	1.50
48 Jay Fiedler	.20	.50
49 Lamar Smith	.20	.50
50 Oronde Gadsden	.15	.40
51 Cris Carter	.25	.60
52 Daunte Culpepper	.20	.50
53 Randy Moss	.25	.60
54 Robert Smith	.20	.50
55 Drew Bledsoe	.25	.60
56 Terry Glenn	.20	.50
57 Aaron Brooks	.20	.50
58 Joe Horn	.20	.50
59 Ricky Williams	.25	.60
60 Amani Toomer	.20	.50
61 Ike Hilliard	.20	.50
62 Kerry Collins	.20	.50
63 Ron Dayne	.20	.50
64 Tiki Barber	.25	.60
65 Chad Pennington	.25	.60
66 Curtis Martin	.25	.60
67 Vinny Testaverde	.20	.50
68 Wayne Chrebet	.20	.50
69 Rich Gannon	.20	.50
70 Tim Brown	.25	.60
71 Tyrone Wheatley	.20	.50
72 Donovan McNabb	.25	.60
73 Jerome Bettis	.25	.60
74 Plaxico Burress	.20	.50
75 Junior Seau	.25	.60
76 Charlie Garner	.20	.50
77 Jeff Garcia	.20	.50
78 Jerry Rice	.50	1.25
79 Terrell Owens	.25	.60
80 Darrell Jackson	.20	.50
81 Ricky Watters	.20	.50
82 Shaun Alexander	.25	.60
83 Isaac Bruce	.25	.60
84 Kurt Warner	.40	1.00
85 Marshall Faulk	.25	.60
86 Torry Holt	.20	.50
87 Trent Green	.25	.60
88 Keyshawn Johnson	.20	.50
89 Shaun King	.15	.40
90 Warren Sapp	.20	.50
91 Warrick Dunn	.25	.60
92 Eddie George	.25	.60
93 Jevon Kearse	.20	.50
94 Steve McNair	.25	.60
95 Albert Connell	.15	.40
96 Jeff George	.20	.50
97 Brad Johnson	.20	.50
98 Bruce Smith	.25	.60
99 Michael Westbrook	.15	.40
100 Stephen Davis	.20	.50
101 Michael Vick RC	15.00	40.00
102 Drew Brees RC	50.00	80.00
103 Chris Weinke RC	3.00	8.00
104 Quincy Carter RC	3.00	8.00
105 Sage Rosenfels RC	4.00	10.00
106 Josh Heupel RC	4.00	10.00
107 Tony Driver RC	3.00	8.00
108 Ben Leard RC	2.50	6.00
109 Marques Tuiasosopo RC	3.00	8.00
110 Tim Hasselbeck RC	3.00	8.00
111 Mike McMahon RC	3.00	8.00
112 Deuce McAllister RC	4.00	10.00
113 LaMont Jordan RC	4.00	10.00
114 LaDainian Tomlinson RC	12.00	30.00
115 James Jackson RC	2.50	6.00
116 Anthony Thomas RC	4.00	10.00
117 Travis Henry RC	3.00	8.00
118 DeAngelo Evans RC	3.00	8.00
119 Travis Minor RC	3.00	8.00
120 Rudi Johnson RC	4.00	10.00
121 Michael Bennett RC	3.00	8.00
122 Kevan Barlow RC	3.00	8.00
123 Dan Alexander RC	3.00	8.00
124 David Allen RC	2.50	6.00
125 Correll Buckhalter RC	4.00	10.00
126 David Rivers RC	2.50	6.00
127 Reggie White RC	2.50	6.00
128 Moran Norris RC	2.50	6.00
129 Ja'Mar Toombs RC	2.50	6.00
130 Jason McKinley RC	2.50	6.00
131 Scotty Anderson RC	2.50	6.00
132 Dustin McClintock RC	3.00	8.00
133 Heath Evans RC	3.00	8.00
134 David Terrell RC	3.00	8.00
135 Santana Moss RC	5.00	12.00
136 Rod Gardner RC	3.00	8.00
137 Quincy Morgan RC	3.00	8.00
138 Freddie Mitchell RC	2.50	6.00
139 Boo Williams RC	2.50	6.00
140 Reggie Wayne RC	8.00	20.00
141 Ronney Daniels RC	2.50	6.00
142 Bobby Newcombe RC	3.00	8.00
143 Reggie Germany/250 RC	3.00	8.00
144 Jesse Palmer RC	3.00	8.00
145 Robert Ferguson RC	4.00	10.00
146 Ken-Yon Rambo RC	2.50	6.00
147 Alex Bannister RC	2.50	6.00
148 Koren Robinson RC	3.00	8.00
149 Chad Johnson RC	6.00	15.00
150 Chris Chambers RC	4.00	10.00
151 Javon Green RC	2.50	6.00
152 Snoop Minnis RC	2.50	6.00
153 Vinny Sutherland RC	2.50	6.00
154 Cedrick Wilson RC	3.00	8.00
155 John Capel/250 RC	3.00	8.00
156 T.J. Houshmandzadeh RC	5.00	12.00
157 Todd Heap RC	4.00	10.00
158 Alge Crumpler RC	4.00	10.00
159 Jabari Holloway RC	2.50	6.00
160 Marcellus Rivers RC	2.50	6.00
161 Rashon Burns RC	2.50	6.00
162 Tony Stewart RC	3.00	8.00
163 Jevaris Johnson RC	2.50	6.00
164 Jamal Reynolds RC	2.50	6.00
165 Andre Carter RC	3.00	8.00
166 David Warren RC	2.50	6.00
167 Justin Smith RC	4.00	10.00
168 Josh Booty RC	3.00	8.00
169 Karon Riley RC	2.50	6.00
170 Cedric Scott RC	2.50	6.00
171 Kenny Smith RC	2.50	6.00
172 Richard Seymour RC	4.00	10.00
173 Willie Howard RC	2.50	6.00
174 Markus Steele RC	2.50	6.00
175 Marcus Stroud RC	3.00	8.00
176 Damione Lewis RC	3.00	8.00
177 Casey Hampton RC	6.00	15.00
178 Ennis Davis RC	2.50	6.00
179 Gerard Warren RC	3.00	8.00
180 Tommy Polley RC	2.50	6.00
181 Kendrell Bell/250 RC	5.00	12.00
182 Dan Morgan RC	3.00	8.00
183 Morlon Greenwood RC	2.50	6.00
184 Quinton Caver/250	3.00	8.00
185 Keith Adams RC	2.50	6.00
186 Brian Allen RC	2.50	6.00
187 Carlos Polk RC	2.50	6.00
188 Torrance Marshall RC	2.50	6.00
189 Jamie Winborn RC	3.00	8.00
190 Jamar Fletcher RC	2.50	6.00
191 Ken Lucas RC	3.00	8.00
192 Fred Smoot RC	4.00	10.00
193 Nate Clements RC	3.00	8.00
194 Will Allen RC	4.00	10.00
195 Willie Middlebrooks/250 RC	4.00	10.00
196 Gary Baxter RC	2.50	6.00
197 Derrick Gibson RC	2.50	6.00
198 Robert Carswell/250 RC	3.00	8.00
199 Hakim Akbar RC	2.50	6.00
200 Adam Archuleta RC	3.00	8.00

2001 Donruss Elite Aspirations

*VETS/70-99: 8X TO 20X BASIC CARDS		
*ROOKIE/70-99: .3X TO .8X RC/500		
*ROOKIE/70-99: .25X TO .6X RC/250		
*VETS/45-69: 10X TO 25X BASIC CARDS		
*ROOKIES/45-69: .4X TO 1X RC/500		
*ROOKIES/45-69: .3X TO .8X RC/250		
*ROOKIES/30-44: .5X TO 1.2X RC/500		
*ROOKIES/30-44: .4X TO 1X RC/250		
*VETS/20-29: 20X TO 50X BASIC CARDS		
*ROOKIES/20-29: 1X TO 2.5X RC/500		
*ROOKIES/20-29: .8X TO 2X RC/250		
*VETS/10-19: 25X TO 60X BASIC CARDS		
*ROOKIES/10-19: 1.2X TO 3X RC/500		
101 Michael Vick/93	30.00	60.00
102 Drew Brees/85	75.00	125.00
114 LaDainian Tomlinson/95	25.00	60.00

2001 Donruss Elite Status

*VETS/70-99: 8X TO 20X BASIC CARDS		
*ROOKIES/70-99: .3X TO .8X RC/500		
*VETS/45-69: 10X TO 25X BASIC CARDS		
*ROOKIES/45-69: .4X TO 1X RC/500		
*VETS/30-44: 12X TO 30X BASIC CARDS		
*ROOKIES/30-44: .5X TO 1.2X RC/500		
*VETS/20-29: 20X TO 50X BASIC CARDS		
*ROOKIES/20-29: 1X TO 2.5X RC/500		
*STARS/10-19: 25X TO 60X BASIC CARDS		
*ROOKIES/10-19: 1.2X TO 3X RC/500		
102 Drew Brees/15	175.00	300.00
181 Kendrell Bell/37	5.00	12.00
195 Willie Middlebrooks/42	4.00	10.00

2001 Donruss Elite Turn of the Century Autographs

STATED PRINT RUN 50 SER.#'d SETS		
101 Michael Vick unsigned	30.00	80.00
102 Drew Brees	150.00	250.00
103 Chris Weinke	10.00	25.00
104 Quincy Carter	10.00	25.00
105 Sage Rosenfels	12.00	30.00
106 Josh Heupel	12.00	30.00
107 Tony Driver No Auto	6.00	15.00
108 Ben Leard	8.00	20.00
109 Marques Tuiasosopo	10.00	25.00
110 Tim Hasselbeck	10.00	25.00
111 Mike McMahon	10.00	25.00
112 Deuce McAllister	25.00	60.00
113 LaMont Jordan	12.00	30.00
114 LaDainian Tomlinson	100.00	200.00
115 James Jackson	8.00	20.00
116 Anthony Thomas	12.00	30.00
117 Travis Henry	10.00	25.00
118 DeAngelo Evans	10.00	25.00
119 Travis Minor	10.00	25.00
120 Rudi Johnson	12.00	30.00
121 Michael Bennett	10.00	25.00
122 Kevan Barlow	10.00	25.00
123 Dan Alexander	10.00	25.00
124 David Allen	8.00	20.00
125 Correll Buckhalter	12.00	30.00
126 David Rivers No Auto	5.00	12.00
127 Reggie White	8.00	20.00
128 Moran Norris	8.00	20.00
129 Ja'Mar Toombs No Auto	5.00	12.00
130 Jason McKinley No Auto	5.00	12.00
131 Scotty Anderson	8.00	20.00
132 Dustin McClintock No Auto	6.00	15.00
133 Heath Evans	10.00	25.00
134 David Terrell	10.00	25.00
135 Santana Moss	15.00	40.00
136 Rod Gardner	10.00	25.00
137 Quincy Morgan	10.00	25.00
138 Freddie Mitchell	8.00	20.00
139 Boo Williams	8.00	20.00
140 Reggie Wayne	60.00	100.00
141 Ronney Daniels	8.00	20.00
142 Bobby Newcombe	10.00	25.00
143 Reggie Germany	8.00	20.00
144 Jesse Palmer	10.00	25.00
145 Robert Ferguson	12.00	30.00
146 Ken-Yon Rambo	8.00	20.00
147 Alex Bannister	8.00	20.00
148 Koren Robinson	10.00	25.00
149 Chad Johnson	40.00	100.00
150 Chris Chambers	30.00	60.00
151 Javon Green	8.00	20.00
152 Snoop Minnis	8.00	20.00
153 Vinny Sutherland	8.00	20.00
154 Cedrick Wilson	10.00	25.00
155 John Capel No Auto	5.00	12.00
156 T.J. Houshmandzadeh	15.00	40.00
157 Todd Heap	12.00	30.00
158 Alge Crumpler	12.00	30.00
159 Jabari Holloway	8.00	20.00
160 Marcellus Rivers No Auto	5.00	12.00
161 Rashon Burns	8.00	20.00
162 Tony Stewart	10.00	25.00
163 Jevaris Johnson No Auto	5.00	12.00
164 Jamal Reynolds	8.00	20.00
165 Andre Carter	10.00	25.00
166 David Warren No Auto	5.00	12.00
167 Justin Smith	12.00	30.00
168 Josh Booty	10.00	25.00
169 Karon Riley	8.00	20.00
170 Cedric Scott	8.00	20.00
171 Kenny Smith	8.00	20.00
172 Richard Seymour No Auto	8.00	20.00
173 Willie Howard	8.00	20.00
174 Markus Steele	8.00	20.00
175 Marcus Stroud	10.00	25.00
176 Damione Lewis	10.00	25.00
177 Casey Hampton No Auto	8.00	20.00
178 Ennis Davis	8.00	20.00
179 Gerard Warren	10.00	25.00
180 Tommy Polley	8.00	20.00
181 Kendrell Bell	12.00	30.00
182 Dan Morgan	10.00	25.00
183 Morlon Greenwood	8.00	20.00
184 Quinton Caver No Auto	5.00	12.00
185 Keith Adams No Auto	5.00	12.00
186 Brian Allen	8.00	20.00
187 Carlos Polk	8.00	20.00
188 Torrance Marshall	8.00	20.00
189 Jamie Winborn	10.00	25.00
190 Jamar Fletcher No Auto	5.00	12.00
191 Ken Lucas	10.00	25.00
192 Fred Smoot No Auto	8.00	20.00
193 Nate Clements No Auto	6.00	15.00
194 Will Allen	12.00	30.00
195 Willie Middlebrooks No Auto	6.00	15.00
196 Gary Baxter	8.00	20.00
197 Derrick Gibson No Auto	5.00	12.00
198 Robert Carswell No Auto	5.00	12.00
199 Hakim Akbar	8.00	20.00
200 Adam Archuleta No Auto	6.00	15.00

2001 Donruss Elite Face To Face

FF1-FF30 SINGLE MASK PRINT RUN 100		
FF31-FF45 DUAL MASK PRINT RUN 50		
FF1 John Elway	30.00	80.00
FF2 Dan Marino	30.00	80.00
FF3 Brett Favre	30.00	80.00
FF4 Barry Sanders	30.00	80.00
FF5 Marshall Faulk	10.00	25.00
FF6 Edgerrin James	10.00	25.00
FF7 Troy Aikman	20.00	50.00
FF8 Steve Young	15.00	40.00
FF9 Jamal Anderson	8.00	20.00
FF10 Terrell Davis	10.00	25.00
FF11 Tim Brown	12.00	30.00
FF12 Jerry Rice	25.00	60.00
FF13 Isaac Bruce	10.00	25.00
FF14 Torry Holt	8.00	20.00
FF15 Reggie White DE	12.00	30.00
FF16 Warren Sapp	8.00	20.00
FF17 Jerome Bettis	10.00	25.00
FF18 Fred Taylor	10.00	25.00
FF19 Ray Lewis	10.00	25.00
FF20 Eddie George	10.00	25.00
FF21 Ryan Leaf	6.00	15.00
FF22 Peyton Manning	25.00	60.00
FF23 Lawrence Taylor	12.00	30.00
FF24 Phil Simms	10.00	25.00
FF25 Joe Montana	30.00	80.00
FF26 Marcus Allen	12.00	30.00
FF27 Keyshawn Johnson	8.00	20.00
FF28 Wayne Chrebet	8.00	20.00
FF29 Shaun King	6.00	15.00
FF30 Donovan McNabb	10.00	25.00
FF31 Dan Marino	125.00	250.00
John Elway		
FF32 Brett Favre	60.00	150.00
Barry Sanders		
FF33 Edgerrin James	20.00	50.00
Marshall Faulk		
FF34 Troy Aikman	30.00	80.00
Steve Young		
FF35 Jamal Anderson	20.00	50.00
Terrell Davis		
FF36 Jerry Rice	40.00	100.00
Tim Brown		
FF37 Isaac Bruce	20.00	50.00
Torry Holt		
FF38 Reggie White	20.00	50.00
Warren Sapp		
FF39 Fred Taylor	20.00	50.00
Jerome Bettis		
FF40 Ray Lewis	20.00	50.00
Eddie George		
FF41 Peyton Manning	50.00	120.00
Ryan Leaf		
FF42 Phil Simms	20.00	50.00
Lawrence Taylor		
FF43 Joe Montana	90.00	175.00
Marcus Allen		
FF44 Wayne Chrebet	15.00	40.00
Keyshawn Johnson		
FF45 Donoan McNabb	20.00	50.00
Shaun King		

2001 Donruss Elite Face To Face Autographs

ANNOUNCED PRINT RUN 15-55		
1 John Elway/55*	125.00	250.00
2 Dan Marino/35*	175.00	300.00
4 Barry Sanders/50*	125.00	200.00
8 Steve Young/35*	75.00	135.00
10 Terrell Davis/15*		
23 Lawrence Taylor/25*	75.00	125.00
31 John Elway/15		
Dan Marino		
33 Edgerrin James/15		
Marshall Faulk		
34 Troy Aikman/15		
Steve Young		
42 Phil Simms/15		
Lawrence Taylor		

2001 Donruss Elite Passing the Torch

COMPLETE SET (24)	50.00	100.00
PT1-PT16 SINGLE PLAYER PRINT RUN 1000		
PT17-PT24 DUAL PLAYER PRINT RUN 500		
PT1 John Elway	4.00	10.00
PT2 Brian Griese	1.00	2.50
PT3 Dick Butkus	2.00	5.00
PT4 Brian Urlacher	1.50	4.00
PT5 Fran Tarkenton	2.00	5.00
PT6 Daunte Culpepper	1.00	2.50
PT7 Jim Brown	2.50	6.00
PT8 Jamal Lewis	1.25	3.00
PT9 Larry Csonka	1.50	4.00
PT10 Ron Dayne	1.00	2.50
PT11 Tony Dorsett	1.50	4.00
PT12 Emmitt Smith	3.00	8.00
PT13 Eric Dickerson	1.25	3.00
PT14 Marshall Faulk	1.25	3.00
PT15 Joe Namath	2.50	6.00
PT16 Chad Pennington	1.25	3.00
PT17 John Elway	6.00	15.00
Brian Griese		
PT18 Brian Urlacher	3.00	8.00
Dick Butkus		
PT19 Fran Tarkenton	3.00	8.00
Daunte Culpepper		
PT20 Jamal Lewis	4.00	10.00
Jim Brown		
PT21 Larry Csonka	2.50	6.00
Ron Dayne		
PT22 Tony Dorsett	6.00	15.00
Emmitt Smith		
PT23 Marshall Faulk	2.50	6.00
Eric Dickerson		
PT24 Joe Namath	4.00	10.00
Chad Pennington		

2001 Donruss Elite Passing the Torch Autographs

PT1-PT16 SINGLE PRINT RUN 100		
PT17-PT24 DUAL PRINT RUN 50		
PT1 John Elway	90.00	150.00
PT2 Brian Griese	25.00	60.00
PT3 Dick Butkus	35.00	80.00
PT4 Brian Urlacher	30.00	80.00
PT5 Fran Tarkenton	25.00	60.00
PT6 Daunte Culpepper	25.00	60.00
PT7 Jim Brown	75.00	135.00
PT8 Jamal Lewis	15.00	40.00
PT9 Larry Csonka	30.00	80.00
PT10 Ron Dayne	15.00	40.00
PT11 Tony Dorsett	40.00	80.00
PT12 Emmitt Smith	150.00	225.00
PT13 Eric Dickerson	20.00	50.00
PT14 Marshall Faulk	40.00	80.00
PT15 Joe Namath	60.00	150.00
PT16 Chad Pennington	25.00	60.00
PT17 John Elway	125.00	250.00
Brian Griese		
PT18 Brian Urlacher	125.00	200.00
Dick Butkus		
PT19 Fran Tarkenton	40.00	100.00
Daunte Culpepper		
PT20 Jamal Lewis	75.00	135.00
Jim Brown		
PT21 Larry Csonka	40.00	100.00
Ron Dayne		
PT22 Tony Dorsett	150.00	250.00
Emmitt Smith		
PT23 Marshall Faulk	75.00	135.00
Eric Dickerson		
PT24 Joe Namath	100.00	200.00
Chad Pennington		

2001 Donruss Elite Primary Colors

COMPLETE SET (40)	50.00	100.00
STATED PRINT RUN 975 SER.#'d SETS		
*RED DIE CUT/25: 5X TO 12X		
RED DIE CUT PRINT RUN 25		
*BLUE/200: .8X TO 2X BASIC INSERTS		
BLUE PRINT RUN 200		
*BLUE DIE CUT/50: 3X TO 8X		
BLUE DIE CUT PRINT RUN 50		
*YELLOW/25: 5X TO 12X BASIC INSERTS		
YELLOW PRINT RUN 25		
*YELLOW DIE CUT/75: 2X TO 5X		
YELLOW DIE CUT PRINT RUN 75		
PC1 Peyton Manning	2.50	6.00
PC2 Edgerrin James	1.00	2.50
PC3 Marvin Harrison	1.00	2.50
PC4 Curtis Martin	1.00	2.50
PC5 Eric Moulds	.75	2.00
PC6 Dan Marino	2.50	6.00
PC7 Drew Bledsoe	1.00	2.50
PC8 Drew Brees	8.00	20.00
PC9 Jamal Lewis	1.00	2.50
PC10 Michael Vick	4.00	10.00
PC11 Eddie George	1.00	2.50
PC12 Steve McNair	1.00	2.50
PC13 Jerome Bettis	1.00	2.50
PC14 Koren Robinson	.75	2.00
PC15 Mark Brunell	.75	2.00
PC16 Fred Taylor	1.00	2.50
PC17 Michael Bennett	.75	2.00
PC18 David Terrell	.75	2.00
PC19 Brian Griese	.75	2.00
PC20 Mike Anderson	.75	2.00
PC21 John Elway	2.50	6.00
PC22 Terrell Owens	1.00	2.50
PC23 Rudi Johnson	1.00	2.50
PC24 Jerry Rice	2.00	5.00
PC25 Ricky Williams	1.00	2.50
PC26 Aaron Brooks	.75	2.00
PC27 Kurt Warner	1.50	4.00
PC28 Marshall Faulk	1.00	2.50
PC29 Isaac Bruce	1.00	2.50
PC30 Brett Favre	3.00	8.00
PC31 Santana Moss	1.25	3.00
PC32 Daunte Culpepper	.75	2.00
PC33 Randy Moss	1.00	2.50
PC34 Cris Carter	1.00	2.50
PC35 Barry Sanders	2.50	6.00
PC36 Emmitt Smith	2.50	6.00
PC37 Stephen Davis	.75	2.00
PC38 Ron Dayne	.75	2.00
PC39 Donovan McNabb	1.00	2.50
PC40 Deuce McAllister	1.00	2.50

2001 Donruss Elite Prime Numbers

STATED PRINT RUN 1-400		
PN1A Dan Marino/300	4.00	10.00
PN1B Dan Marino/80	8.00	20.00
PN2A John Elway/300	4.00	10.00
PN2B John Elway/40	12.00	30.00
PN3A Mike Anderson/200	2.00	5.00
PN3B Mike Anderson/50	4.00	10.00
PN4A Randy Moss/200	2.50	6.00
PN5A Daunte Culpepper/300	1.25	3.00
PN5B Daunte Culpepper/50	4.00	10.00
PN6A Kurt Warner/400	2.50	6.00
PN6B Kurt Warner/40	8.00	20.00
PN7A Jerry Rice/100	6.00	15.00
PN7B Jerry Rice/80	6.00	15.00
PN8A Edgerrin James/200	2.50	6.00
PN9A Peyton Manning/300	4.00	10.00
PN9B Peyton Manning/20	20.00	50.00
PN10A Brett Favre/100	10.00	25.00
PN10B Brett Favre/40	15.00	40.00

2001 Donruss Elite Prime Numbers Die Cuts

STATED PRINT RUN 12-440		
PN1A Dan Marino/85	8.00	20.00
PN1B Dan Marino/305	4.00	10.00
PN1C Dan Marino/380	4.00	10.00
PN2A John Elway/48	12.00	30.00
PN2B John Elway/308	4.00	10.00
PN2C John Elway/340	4.00	10.00
PN3A Mike Anderson/51	4.00	10.00
PN3B Mike Anderson/201	2.00	5.00
PN3C Mike Anderson/250	1.25	3.00
PN4A Randy Moss/12	8.00	20.00
PN4B Randy Moss/202	2.50	6.00
PN4C Randy Moss/210	2.50	6.00
PN5A Daunte Culpepper/57	4.00	10.00
PN5B Daunte Culpepper/307	1.25	3.00
PN5C Daunte Culpepper/350	1.25	3.00
PN6A Kurt Warner/41	8.00	20.00
PN6B Kurt Warner/401	2.50	6.00
PN6C Kurt Warner/440	2.50	6.00
PN7A Jerry Rice/87	6.00	15.00
PN7B Jerry Rice/107	6.00	15.00
PN7C Jerry Rice/180	5.00	12.00
PN8A Edgerrin James/19	8.00	20.00
PN8B Edgerrin James/209	2.50	6.00
PN8C Edgerrin James/210	2.50	6.00
PN9A Peyton Manning/26	20.00	50.00
PN9B Peyton Manning/306	4.00	10.00
PN9C Peyton Manning/320	4.00	10.00
PN10A Brett Favre/41	15.00	40.00
PN10B Brett Favre/101	10.00	25.00
PN10C Brett Favre/140	8.00	20.00

2001 Donruss Elite Throwback Threads

TT1-TT30 SINGLE JSY PRINT RUN 100		
TT31-TT45 DUAL JSY PRINT RUN 50		
TT1 Art Monk	10.00	25.00
TT2 Joe Theismann	12.00	30.00
TT3 Jim Kelly	15.00	40.00
TT4 Thurman Thomas	12.00	30.00
TT5 Joe Namath	20.00	50.00
TT6 Don Maynard	10.00	25.00
TT7 Bob Griese	12.00	30.00
TT8 Larry Csonka	12.00	30.00
TT9 Joe Montana	30.00	80.00
TT10 Jerry Rice	25.00	60.00
TT11 Raymond Berry	10.00	25.00
TT12 Marvin Harrison	10.00	25.00
TT13 Warren Moon	12.00	30.00
TT14 Steve McNair	10.00	25.00
TT15 Terrell Davis	12.00	30.00
TT16 Mike Anderson	8.00	20.00
TT17 Frank Gifford	12.00	30.00
TT18 Ron Dayne	8.00	20.00
TT19 Walter Payton	50.00	120.00
TT20 Gale Sayers	15.00	40.00
TT21 Terry Bradshaw	20.00	50.00
TT22 Franco Harris	12.00	30.00
TT23 Troy Aikman	20.00	50.00
TT24 Emmitt Smith	25.00	60.00
TT25 Fran Tarkenton	15.00	40.00
TT26 Daunte Culpepper	8.00	20.00
TT27 John Elway	30.00	80.00
TT28 Brian Griese	8.00	20.00
TT29 Eric Dickerson	10.00	25.00
TT30 Marshall Faulk	10.00	25.00
TT31 Joe Theismann	25.00	60.00
Art Monk		
TT32 Thurman Thomas	30.00	80.00
Jim Kelly		
TT33 Joe Namath	40.00	100.00
Don Maynard		
TT34 Bob Griese	25.00	60.00
Larry Csonka		
TT35 Joe Montana	100.00	200.00
Jerry Rice		
TT36 Raymond Berry	25.00	60.00
Marvin Harrison		
TT37 Warren Moon	25.00	60.00
Steve McNair		
TT38 Terrell Davis	25.00	60.00
Mike Anderson		
TT39 Frank Gifford	25.00	60.00
Ron Dayne		
TT40 Walter Payton	75.00	200.00
Gale Sayers		
TT41 Franco Harris	40.00	100.00
Terry Bradshaw		
TT42 Troy Aikman	60.00	150.00
Emmitt Smith		
TT43 Fran Tarkenton	30.00	80.00
Daunte Culpepper		
TT44 John Elway	60.00	150.00
Brian Griese		
TT45 Eric Dickerson	25.00	60.00
Marshall Faulk		

2001 Donruss Elite Throwback Threads Autographs

ANNOUNCED PRINT RUNS LISTED BELOW		
TT1 Art Monk/25*	40.00	80.00
TT2 Joe Theismann/25*	40.00	80.00
TT3 Jim Kelly/39*	40.00	100.00
TT5 Joe Namath/25*	100.00	200.00
TT6 Don Maynard/25*	25.00	60.00
TT8 Larry Csonka/35*	40.00	80.00
TT9 Joe Montana/16*	100.00	225.00
TT11 Raymond Berry/15*		
TT12 Marvin Harrison/50*	40.00	80.00
TT13 Warren Moon/25*	40.00	80.00
TT16 Mike Anderson/50*	20.00	50.00
TT17 Frank Gifford/15*		
TT20 Gale Sayers/15*	75.00	150.00
TT21 Terry Bradshaw/25*	100.00	200.00
TT23 Troy Aikman/25*	75.00	150.00
TT24 Emmitt Smith/15*	125.00	250.00
TT26 Daunte Culpepper/50*	25.00	60.00
TT27 John Elway/15*	125.00	250.00
TT33 Joe Namath	125.00	200.00
Don Maynard/25*		
TT34 Bob Griese		
Larry Csonka/15*		
TT35 Joe Montana		
Jerry Rice/15*		
TT43 Fran Tarkenton		
Daunte Culpepper/15*		
TT44 Brian Griese		
John Elway/15*		
TT45 Eric Dickerson		
Marshall Faulk/15*		

2001 Donruss Elite Title Waves

COMPLETE SET (30)	20.00	50.00
*HOLOFOIL/100: 2.5X TO 6X BASIC INSERTS		
HOLOFOIL PRINT RUN 100 SER.#'d SETS		
TW1 Kurt Warner/1999	1.00	2.50
TW2 Dan Marino/1994	1.50	4.00
TW3 Brett Favre/1995	2.00	5.00
TW4 Peyton Manning/2000	1.50	4.00
TW5 John Elway/1996	1.50	4.00
TW6 Steve Young/1997	.75	2.00
TW7 Barry Sanders/1997	1.50	4.00
TW8 Emmitt Smith/1993	1.50	4.00
TW9 Terrell Davis/1998	.60	1.50
TW10 Edgerrin James/2000	.60	1.50
TW11 Stephen Davis/1999	.50	1.25
TW12 Curtis Martin/1995	.60	1.50
TW13 Marvin Harrison/1999	.60	1.50
TW14 Antonio Freeman/1998	.60	1.50
TW15 Jerry Rice/1995	1.25	3.00
TW16 Randy Moss/1999	.60	1.50
TW17 Tim Brown/1997	.60	1.50
TW18 Isaac Bruce/1996	.60	1.50
TW19 Ricky Williams/2000	.60	1.50
TW20 Peyton Manning/1999	1.50	4.00
TW21 Eddie George/2000	.60	1.50
TW22 Barry Sanders/1993	1.50	4.00
TW23 Daunte Culpepper/2000	.50	1.25
TW24 Dan Marino/1994	1.50	4.00
TW25 John Elway/1999	1.50	4.00
TW26 Marshall Faulk/2000	.60	1.50
TW27 Brett Favre/1997	2.00	5.00
TW28 Steve Young/1995	.75	2.00
TW29 Troy Aikman/1993	1.00	2.50
TW30 Jerry Rice/1990	1.25	3.00

2001 Donruss Elite Chicago Collection

NOT PRICED DUE TO SCARCITY

2002 Donruss Elite Samples

*SILVER SAMPLE: .8X TO 2X BASIC CARDS
*GOLD SAMPLE: 1.5X TO 4X BASIC CARDS

2002 Donruss Elite

This 200-card set was released in June, 2002. The first 100-cards in this set feature veterans while cards #101-200 feature rookies. The rookie cards were sequentially numbered to 400.

COMP.SET w/o SP's (100)	7.50	20.00
1 Elvis Grbac	.15	.40
2 Jamal Lewis	.20	.50
3 Ray Lewis	.25	.60
4 Travis Henry	.15	.40
5 Eric Moulds	.20	.50
6 Corey Dillon	.20	.50
7 Peter Warrick	.20	.50
8 Tim Couch	.15	.40
9 James Jackson	.15	.40
10 Kevin Johnson	.15	.40
11 Mike Anderson	.20	.50
12 Terrell Davis	.25	.60
13 Brian Griese	.20	.50
14 Rod Smith	.20	.50
15 Marvin Harrison	.25	.60
16 Reggie Wayne	.25	.60
17 Dominic Rhodes	.20	.50
18 Edgerrin James	.20	.50
19 Mark Brunell	.20	.50
20 Keenan McCardell	.20	.50
21 Jimmy Smith	.20	.50
22 Tony Gonzalez	.25	.60
23 Trent Green	.20	.50
24 Priest Holmes	.25	.60
25 Snoop Minnis	.15	.40
26 Chris Chambers	.20	.50
27 Jay Fiedler	.20	.50
28 Travis Minor	.15	.40
29 Lamar Smith	.20	.50
30 Tom Brady	.60	1.50
31 Troy Brown	.20	.50
32 Antowain Smith	.20	.50
33 Laveranues Coles	.20	.50
34 Curtis Martin	.25	.60
35 Vinny Testaverde	.20	.50
36 Wayne Chrebet	.20	.50
37 Tim Brown	.25	.60
38 Rich Gannon	.20	.50
39 Jerry Rice	.50	1.25
40 Charlie Garner	.20	.50
41 Jerome Bettis	.25	.60
42 Plaxico Burress	.20	.50
43 Kordell Stewart	.20	.50
44 Kendrell Bell	.15	.40
45 Doug Flutie	.25	.60
46 LaDainian Tomlinson	.30	.75
47 Junior Seau	.25	.60
48 Drew Brees	.40	1.00
49 Shaun Alexander	.20	.50
50 Koren Robinson	.15	.40
51 Ricky Watters	.20	.50
52 Eddie George	.20	.50
53 Derrick Mason	.20	.50
54 Steve McNair	.25	.60
55 David Boston	.15	.40
56 Jake Plummer	.20	.50
57 Chris Chandler	.20	.50
58 Jamal Anderson	.20	.50
59 Michael Vick	.40	1.00
60 Wesley Walls	.20	.50
61 Chris Weinke	.15	.40
62 David Terrell	.15	.40
63 Anthony Thomas	.20	.50
64 Brian Urlacher	.25	.60
65 Quincy Carter	.15	.40
66 Rocket Ismail	.20	.50
67 Emmitt Smith	.60	1.50
68 James Stewart	.15	.40
69 Germane Crowell	.15	.40
70 Mike McMahon	.15	.40
71 Brett Favre	.60	1.50
72 Ahman Green	.20	.50
73 Antonio Freeman	.25	.60
74 Michael Bennett	.20	.50
75 Cris Carter	.25	.60
76 Daunte Culpepper	.20	.50
77 Randy Moss	.25	.60
78 Aaron Brooks	.20	.50
79 Deuce McAllister	.20	.50
80 Ricky Williams	.20	.50
81 Kerry Collins	.20	.50
82 Ron Dayne	.20	.50
83 Amani Toomer	.20	.50
84 Correll Buckhalter	.20	.50
85 James Thrash	.20	.50
86 Freddie Mitchell	.15	.40
87 Duce Staley	.20	.50
88 Jeff Garcia	.20	.50
89 Garrison Hearst	.20	.50
90 Terrell Owens	.25	.60
91 Isaac Bruce	.25	.60
92 Marshall Faulk	.25	.60
93 Torry Holt	.25	.60
94 Kurt Warner	.25	.60
95 Mike Alstott	.20	.50
96 Brad Johnson	.20	.50
97 Keyshawn Johnson	.20	.50
98 Stephen Davis	.20	.50
99 Rod Gardner	.15	.40
100 Tony Banks	.15	.40
101 David Carr RC	5.00	12.00
102 Joey Harrington RC	5.00	12.00
103 Rohan Davey RC	5.00	12.00
104 Chad Hutchinson RC	3.00	8.00
105 Patrick Ramsey RC	5.00	12.00
106 Kurt Kittner RC	3.00	8.00
107 Eric Crouch RC	5.00	12.00
108 David Garrard RC	6.00	15.00
109 Ronald Curry RC	4.00	10.00
110 Zak Kustok RC	3.00	8.00
111 Woody Dantzler RC	4.00	10.00
112 Wes Pate RC	3.00	8.00
113 Brian Westbrook RC	8.00	20.00
114 Josh McCown RC	5.00	12.00
115 Travis Stephens RC	3.00	8.00
116 Luke Staley RC	3.00	8.00
117 William Green RC	4.00	10.00
118 Clinton Portis RC	6.00	15.00
119 DeShaun Foster RC	5.00	12.00
120 Verron Haynes RC	3.00	8.00
121 T.J. Duckett RC	5.00	12.00
122 Antwoine Womack RC	3.00	8.00
123 Leonard Henry RC	3.00	8.00
124 Lamar Gordon RC	4.00	10.00
125 Adrian Peterson RC	5.00	12.00
126 Chester Taylor RC	5.00	12.00
127 Damien Anderson RC	3.00	8.00
128 Maurice Morris RC	4.00	10.00
129 Ricky Williams RC	4.00	10.00
130 Terry Charles RC	3.00	8.00
131 Demontray Carter RC	3.00	8.00
132 Jason McAddley RC	4.00	10.00
133 Ladell Betts RC	5.00	12.00
134 Cortlen Johnson RC	3.00	8.00
135 James Mungro RC	5.00	12.00
136 Atrews Bell RC	3.00	8.00
137 Josh Scobey RC	4.00	10.00
138 Justin Peelle RC	3.00	8.00
139 Najeh Davenport RC	5.00	12.00
140 Josh Reed RC	4.00	10.00
141 Marquise Walker RC	3.00	8.00
142 Jabar Gaffney RC	5.00	12.00
143 Antwaan Randle El RC	5.00	12.00
144 Ashley Lelie RC	4.00	10.00
145 Tavon Mason RC	3.00	8.00
146 Antonio Bryant RC	5.00	12.00
147 Javon Walker RC	5.00	12.00
148 Kelly Campbell RC	4.00	10.00
149 Ron Johnson RC	4.00	10.00
150 Andre Davis RC	4.00	10.00
151 Cliff Russell RC	3.00	8.00
152 Reche Caldwell RC	5.00	12.00
153 Kyle Johnson RC	3.00	8.00
154 Freddie Milons RC	3.00	8.00
155 Brian Poli-Dixon RC	3.00	8.00
156 David Thornton RC	3.00	8.00
157 Bryan Thomas RC	3.00	8.00
158 Kahlil Hill RC	3.00	8.00
159 Deion Branch RC	5.00	12.00
160 Akin Ayodele RC	4.00	10.00
161 Donte Stallworth RC	5.00	12.00
162 Tim Carter RC	4.00	10.00
163 Kenyon Coleman RC	3.00	8.00
164 Jeremy Shockey RC	8.00	20.00
165 Eddie Freeman RC	3.00	8.00
166 Tracey Wistrom RC	4.00	10.00
167 Daniel Graham RC	4.00	10.00
168 Julius Peppers RC	10.00	25.00
169 Alex Brown RC	5.00	12.00
170 Dwight Freeney RC	6.00	15.00
171 Kalimba Edwards RC	4.00	10.00
172 Dennis Johnson RC	3.00	8.00
173 Travis Fisher RC	4.00	10.00
174 John Henderson RC	4.00	10.00
175 Anthony Weaver RC	3.00	8.00
176 Ryan Sims RC	5.00	12.00
177 Alan Harper RC	3.00	8.00
178 Larry Tripplett RC	3.00	8.00
179 Wendell Bryant RC	3.00	8.00
180 Albert Haynesworth RC	5.00	12.00
181 Levar Fisher RC	3.00	8.00
182 Andra Davis RC	3.00	8.00
183 Joseph Jefferson RC	3.00	8.00
184 Lamont Thompson RC	4.00	10.00
185 Robert Thomas RC	3.00	8.00
186 Michael Lewis RC	5.00	12.00
187 Rocky Calmus RC	4.00	10.00
188 Napoleon Harris RC	4.00	10.00
189 Lito Sheppard RC	5.00	12.00
190 Quentin Jammer RC	5.00	12.00
191 Roy Williams RC	5.00	12.00
192 Marques Anderson RC	4.00	10.00
193 Chris Hope RC	5.00	12.00
194 Raonall Smith RC	3.00	8.00
195 Mike Rumph RC	3.00	8.00
196 James Allen RC	3.00	8.00
197 Ed Reed RC	20.00	50.00
198 Mike Williams RC	3.00	8.00
199 Phillip Buchanon RC	5.00	12.00
200 Bryant McKinnie RC	3.00	8.00

2002 Donruss Elite Aspirations

*VETS/70-99: 8X TO 20X BASIC CARDS
*ROOKIES/70-99: .4X TO 1X
*VETS/45-69: 10X TO 25X
*ROOKIES/45-69: .5X TO 1.2X
*VETS/30-44: 15X TO 40X
*ROOKIES/30-44: .8X TO 2X
*VETS/20-29: 20X TO 50X
*ROOKIES/20-29: 1X TO 2.5X
*VETS/10-19: 25X TO 60X
*ROOKIES/10-19: 1.2X TO 3X
ASPIRATIONS PRINT RUN 1-98
SERIAL #'d UNDER 10 NOT PRICED

2002 Donruss Elite Status

*VETS/70-99: 8X TO 20X BASIC CARDS
*ROOKIES/70-99: .4X TO 1X
*VETS/45-69: 10X TO 25X

*ROOKIES/45-69: .5X TO 1.2X
*ROOKIES/30-44: .8X TO 2X
*VETS/20-29: 20X TO 50X
*ROOKIES/20-29: 1X TO 2.5X
*VETS/10-19: 25X TO 60X
*ROOKIES/10-19: 1.2X TO 3X
STATUS STATED PRINT RUN 2-99
SERIAL #'d UNDER 10 NOT PRICED

2002 Donruss Elite Turn of the Century Autographs

STATED PRINT RUN 40 SER.#'d SETS
FIRST 40 CARDS OF PRINT RUN SIGNED
101 David Carr 15.00 40.00
102 Joey Harrington 15.00 40.00
103 Rohan Davey 15.00 40.00
106 Kurt Kittner 10.00 25.00
107 Eric Crouch 15.00 40.00
111 Woody Dantzler 12.00 30.00
115 Travis Stephens 10.00 25.00
116 Luke Staley 10.00 25.00
117 William Green 12.00 30.00
118 Clinton Portis 20.00 50.00
119 DeShaun Foster 15.00 40.00
121 T.J. Duckett 15.00 40.00
125 Adrian Peterson 15.00 40.00
127 Damien Anderson 10.00 25.00
128 Maurice Morris 12.00 30.00
131 Demontray Carter 10.00 25.00
134 Cortlen Johnson 10.00 25.00
139 Najeh Davenport 15.00 40.00
140 Josh Reed 12.00 30.00
141 Marquise Walker 10.00 25.00
142 Jabar Gaffney 15.00 40.00
143 Antwaan Randle El 15.00 40.00
144 Ashley Lelie 12.00 30.00
146 Antonio Bryant 15.00 40.00
147 Javon Walker 15.00 40.00
148 Kelly Campbell 12.00 30.00
149 Ron Johnson 12.00 30.00
150 Andre Davis 12.00 30.00
152 Reche Caldwell 15.00 40.00
154 Freddie Milons 10.00 25.00
155 Brian Poli-Dixon 10.00 25.00
161 Donte Stallworth 15.00 40.00
164 Jeremy Shockey 25.00 60.00
167 Daniel Graham 12.00 30.00
168 Julius Peppers 75.00 135.00
169 Alex Brown 15.00 40.00
170 Dwight Freeney 30.00 60.00
171 Kalimba Edwards 12.00 30.00
174 John Henderson 12.00 30.00
176 Ryan Sims No Auto 15.00 40.00
179 Wendell Bryant 10.00 25.00
181 Levar Fisher 10.00 25.00
182 Andra Davis 10.00 25.00
185 Robert Thomas 10.00 25.00
187 Rocky Calmus 12.00 30.00
189 Lito Sheppard 15.00 40.00
190 Quentin Jammer 15.00 40.00
191 Roy Williams 15.00 40.00
195 Mike Rumph 10.00 25.00
199 Phillip Buchanon No Auto 15.00 40.00

2002 Donruss Elite Back to the Future

COMPLETE SET (24) 40.00 100.00
BF1-BF16 SINGLE PRINT RUN 800
BF17-BF24 DUAL PRINT RUN 400
BF1 Walter Payton 5.00 12.00
BF2 Anthony Thomas 1.00 2.50
BF3 Bernie Kosar 1.00 2.50
BF4 James Jackson .75 2.00
BF5 Troy Aikman 2.00 5.00
BF6 Quincy Carter .75 2.00
BF7 Steve Bartkowski 1.00 2.50
BF8 Michael Vick 2.00 5.00
BF9 Natrone Means .75 2.00
BF10 LaDainian Tomlinson 1.50 4.00
BF11 Earl Campbell 1.25 3.00
BF12 Eddie George 1.00 2.50
BF13 Eric Dickerson 1.00 2.50
BF14 Edgerrin James 1.00 2.50
BF15 John Elway 2.50 6.00
BF16 Brian Griese 1.00 2.50
BF17 Walter Payton / Anthony Thomas 8.00 20.00
BF18 Bernie Kosar / James Jackson 1.50 4.00
BF19 Troy Aikman / Quincy Carter 3.00 8.00
BF20 Steve Bartkowski / Michael Vick 3.00 8.00
BF21 Natrone Means / LaDainian Tomlinson 2.50 6.00
BF22 Earl Campbell / Eddie George 2.00 5.00
BF23 Eric Dickerson / Edgerrin James 1.50 4.00
BF24 John Elway / Brian Griese 4.00 10.00

2002 Donruss Elite Back to the Future Threads

BF1-BF16 SINGLES PRINT RUN 75
BF17-BF24 DUAL PRINT RUN 25
BF1 Walter Payton 50.00 120.00
BF2 Anthony Thomas 6.00 15.00
BF4 James Jackson 5.00 12.00
BF5 Troy Aikman 20.00 40.00
BF6 Quincy Carter 5.00 12.00
BF7 Steve Bartkowski 8.00 20.00
BF8 Michael Vick 12.00 30.00
BF9 Natrone Means 6.00 15.00
BF10 LaDainian Tomlinson 10.00 25.00
BF11 Earl Campbell 12.00 30.00
BF12 Eddie George 6.00 15.00
BF13 Eric Dickerson 8.00 20.00
BF14 Edgerrin James 6.00 15.00
BF15 John Elway 20.00 50.00
BF16 Brian Griese 6.00 15.00
BF17 Walter Payton / Anthony Thomas 100.00 200.00
BF19 Troy Aikman / Quincy Carter 40.00 100.00
BF20 Steve Bartkowski / Michael Vick 40.00 100.00
BF21 Natrone Means / LaDainian Tomlinson 30.00 80.00
BF22 Earl Campbell / Eddie George 25.00 60.00
BF23 Eric Dickerson / Edgerrin James 20.00 50.00
BF24 John Elway / Brian Griese 100.00 200.00

2002 Donruss Elite College Ties

COMPLETE SET (25) 20.00 50.00
STATED PRINT RUN 1600 SER.#'d SETS
CT1 David Terrell / Marquise Walker .60 1.50
CT2 Travis Henry / Travis Stephens .60 1.50
CT3 Trent Dilfer / David Carr 1.00 2.50
CT4 Jevon Kearse / Alex Brown 1.00 2.50
CT5 Ahman Green / Eric Crouch 1.00 2.50
CT6 Edgerrin James / Clinton Portis 1.25 3.00
CT7 Plaxico Burress / T.J. Duckett 1.00 2.50
CT8 Snoop Minnis / Javon Walker 1.00 2.50
CT9 Kevin Dyson / Cliff Russell .75 2.00
CT10 Michael Vick / Andre Davis 1.50 4.00
CT11 Chad Johnson / Ken Simonton 1.00 2.50
CT12 Freddie Mitchell / DeShaun Foster 1.00 2.50
CT13 Qadry Ismail / Marvin Harrison 1.00 2.50
CT14 Quincy Carter / Kendrell Bell .60 1.50
CT15 Brian Griese / Tom Brady 2.50 6.00
CT16 Jerome Bettis / Tim Brown 1.00 2.50
CT17 Eddie George / Cris Carter 1.00 2.50
CT18 Mike Alstott / Drew Brees 1.50 4.00
CT19 Curtis Martin / Kevan Barlow 1.00 2.50
CT20 Ricky Williams / Priest Holmes 1.00 2.50
CT21 Charlie Garner / Jamal Lewis .75 2.00
CT22 Keyshawn Johnson / Junior Seau 1.00 2.50
CT23 Mark Brunell / Corey Dillon .75 2.00
CT24 Emmitt Smith / Fred Taylor 2.50 6.00
CT25 Edgerrin James / James Jackson .75 2.00

2002 Donruss Elite Face to Face

STATED PRINT RUN 350 SER.#'d SETS
FF1 Eddie George / Zach Thomas 8.00 20.00
FF2 Michael Irvin / Darrell Green 8.00 20.00
FF3 Mike Anderson / Junior Seau 8.00 20.00
FF4 Jake Plummer / Jason Sehorn 6.00 15.00
FF5 Mark Brunell / Jevon Kearse 6.00 15.00
FF6 Randy Moss / Brett Favre 20.00 50.00
FF7 Kerry Collins / Ray Lewis 8.00 20.00
FF8 Steve McNair / Kurt Warner 8.00 20.00
FF9 John Elway / Steve Young 15.00 40.00
FF10 Cris Carter / Jerry Rice 15.00 40.00
FF11 Tim Couch / Daunte Culpepper 6.00 15.00
FF12 Dan Marino / Barry Sanders 20.00 50.00
FF13 Michael Vick / LaDainian Tomlinson 12.00 30.00
FF14 Troy Aikman / Warren Moon 12.00 30.00
FF15 Curtis Martin / Lamar Smith 8.00 20.00

2002 Donruss Elite Passing the Torch

COMPLETE SET (24) 25.00 60.00
PT1-PT16 SINGLE PRINT RUN 800
PT17-PT24 DUAL PRINT RUN 400 SER.#'d SETS
PT1 Thurman Thomas 1.25 3.00
PT2 Travis Henry .75 2.00
PT3 Gale Sayers 1.50 4.00
PT4 Anthony Thomas 1.00 2.50
PT5 Dan Fouts 1.25 3.00
PT6 Drew Brees 2.00 5.00
PT7 Bernie Kosar 1.00 2.50
PT8 Tim Couch .75 2.00
PT9 Steve Young 1.50 4.00
PT10 Jeff Garcia 1.00 2.50
PT11 Ricky Watters 1.00 2.50
PT12 Shaun Alexander 1.00 2.50
PT13A Robert Smith 1.00 2.50
PT13B Herschel Walker 1.00 2.50
PT14 Michael Bennett 1.00 2.50
PT15 Jerry Rice 2.50 6.00
PT16 Terrell Owens 1.25 3.00
PT17 Thurman Thomas / Travis Henry 2.00 5.00
PT18 Gale Sayers / Anthony Thomas 2.50 6.00
PT19 Dan Fouts / Drew Brees 3.00 8.00
PT20 Bernie Kosar / Tim Couch 1.50 4.00
PT21 Steve Young / Jeff Garcia 2.50 6.00
PT22 Ricky Watters / Stephen Alexander 1.50 4.00
PT23A Robert Smith / Michael Bennett 1.50 4.00
PT23B Herchel Walker / Michael Bennett 1.50 4.00
PT24 Jerry Rice / Terrell Owens 4.00 10.00

2002 Donruss Elite Passing the Torch Autographs

PT1-PT16 SINGLE AU PRINT RUN 100
PT17-PT24 DUAL AU PRINT RUN 50
PT1 Thurman Thomas 15.00 40.00
PT2 Travis Henry 10.00 25.00
PT3 Gale Sayers 25.00 60.00
PT4 Anthony Thomas 12.00 30.00
PT5 Dan Fouts 15.00 40.00
PT6 Drew Brees 40.00 80.00
PT7 Bernie Kosar 12.00 30.00
PT8 Tim Couch 10.00 25.00
PT9 Steve Young 30.00 60.00
PT10 Jeff Garcia 12.00 30.00
PT11 Ricky Watters 12.00 30.00
PT12 Shaun Alexander 15.00 40.00
PT13 Herschel Walker 20.00 50.00
PT14 Michael Bennett 12.00 30.00
PT15 Jerry Rice 60.00 120.00
PT16 Terrell Owens 20.00 50.00
PT17 Thurman Thomas / Travis Henry 30.00 80.00
PT18 Gale Sayers / Anthony Thomas 30.00 80.00
PT19 Dan Fouts / Drew Brees 50.00 120.00
PT20 Bernie Kosar / Tim Couch 25.00 60.00
PT21 Steve Young / Jeff Garcia 50.00 120.00
PT22 Ricky Watters / Stephen Alexander 25.00 60.00
PT23 Herschel Walker / Michael Bennett 25.00 60.00
PT24 Jerry Rice / Terrell Owens 75.00 150.00

2002 Donruss Elite Prime Numbers

COMPLETE SET (10) 7.50 20.00
STATED PRINT RUN 1600 SER.#'d SETS
PN1 Brian Urlacher / Zach Thomas 1.00 2.50
PN2 Chris Weinke / Jake Plummer .75 2.00
PN3 Drew Brees / Steve McNair 1.50 4.00
PN4 Jeff Garcia / Kerry Collins .75 2.00
PN5 Emmitt Smith / Duce Staley 2.50 6.00
PN6 Eddie George / Ron Dayne .75 2.00
PN7 Curtis Martin / Marshall Faulk 1.00 2.50
PN8 Randy Moss / Chris Chambers 1.00 2.50
PN9 Tim Brown / Terrell Owens 1.00 2.50
PN10 Jerry Rice / Isaac Bruce 2.00 5.00

2002 Donruss Elite Recollection Autographs

STATED PRINT RUN 25-75
1 Jeff Garcia/25 40.00 80.00
2 Jeff Garcia/75 20.00 50.00

2002 Donruss Elite Throwback Threads

TT1-TT20 SINGLES PRINT RUN 75
TT21-TT30 DUAL PRINT RUN 25
TT1 Jim Thorpe 125.00 250.00
TT2 Red Grange HEL 125.00 250.00
TT3 Bart Starr 25.00 60.00
TT4 Brett Favre 20.00 50.00
TT5 Joe Namath 20.00 50.00
TT6 John Riggins 15.00 40.00
TT7 Dan Marino 25.00 60.00
TT8 Bob Griese 12.50 30.00
TT9 Roger Staubach 15.00 40.00
TT10 Troy Aikman 15.00 40.00
TT11 Bernie Kosar 12.50 30.00
TT12 Ozzie Newsome 10.00 25.00
TT13 John Elway 20.00 50.00
TT14 Craig Morton 10.00 25.00
TT15 Jim McMahon 15.00 40.00
TT16 Walter Payton 30.00 80.00
TT17 Franco Harris 15.00 40.00
TT18 Jerome Bettis 12.50 30.00
TT19 Brian Urlacher 12.50 30.00
TT20 Dick Butkus 20.00 50.00
TT21 Jim Thorpe / Red Grange HEL 800.00 1,200.00
TT22 Bart Starr / Brett Favre 50.00 100.00
TT23 Joe Namath / John Riggins 30.00 80.00
TT24 Dan Marino / Bob Griese 50.00 120.00
TT25 Roger Staubach / Troy Aikman 30.00 80.00
TT26 Bernie Kosar / Ozzie Newsome 20.00 50.00
TT27 John Elway / Craig Morton 30.00 80.00
TT28 Jim McMahon / Walter Payton 60.00 120.00
TT29 Franco Harris / Jerome Bettis 25.00 60.00
TT30 Brian Urlacher / Dick Butkus 25.00 60.00

2002 Donruss Elite Throwback Threads Autographs

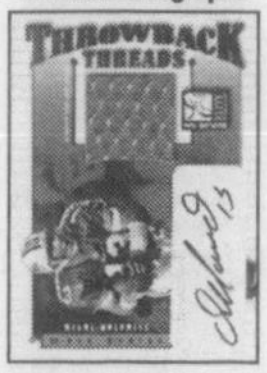

STATED PRINT RUN 25 SER.#'d SETS
TT3 Bart Starr 150.00 300.00
TT4 Brett Favre 200.00 400.00
TT5 Joe Namath 100.00 200.00
TT6 John Riggins 60.00 120.00
TT7 Dan Marino 150.00 300.00
TT8 Bob Griese 50.00 100.00
TT10 Troy Aikman 75.00 150.00
TT15 Jim McMahon 90.00 175.00

2003 Donruss Elite Samples

*SAMPLES: .8X TO 2X BASIC CARDS
*GOLD: .8X TO 2X SILVER

2003 Donruss Elite

Released in June 2003, this set is composed of 100 veterans and 100 rookies, which were serial numbered to 500. Each box contained 20 packs of 5 cards, and carried an SRP of $3. Please note that several cards were originally issued in packs as redemptions with an exchange deadline of 12/1/2004.

COMP.SET w/o SP's (100) 7.50 20.00
ROOKIE PRINT RUN 500 SERIAL #'d SETS
1 Jamal Lewis .20 .50
2 Ray Lewis .25 .60
3 Todd Heap .20 .50
4 Drew Bledsoe .25 .60
5 Travis Henry .15 .40
6 Eric Moulds .20 .50
7 Peerless Price .15 .40
8 Jon Kitna .20 .50
9 Corey Dillon .20 .50
10 Chad Johnson .25 .60
11 Tim Couch .15 .40
12 William Green .15 .40
13 Andre Davis .15 .40
14 Brian Griese .20 .50
15 Ashley Lelie .15 .40
16 Clinton Portis .20 .50
17 Rod Smith .20 .50
18 David Carr .20 .50
19 Jonathan Wells .15 .40
20 Jabar Gaffney .15 .40
21 Peyton Manning .50 1.25
22 Edgerrin James .25 .60
23 Marvin Harrison .25 .60
24 Mark Brunell .20 .50
25 Jimmy Smith .20 .50
26 Fred Taylor .20 .50
27 Priest Holmes .25 .60
28 Trent Green .20 .50
29 Tony Gonzalez .25 .60
30 Chris Chambers .20 .50
31 Zach Thomas .25 .60
32 Ricky Williams .20 .50
33 Tom Brady .60 1.50
34 Antowain Smith .20 .50
35 Troy Brown .20 .50
36 Chad Pennington .25 .60
37 Curtis Martin .25 .60
38 Laveranues Coles .15 .40
39 Tim Brown .25 .60
40 Rich Gannon .20 .50
41 Jerry Rice .50 1.25
42 Charlie Garner .20 .50
43 Antwaan Randle El .20 .50
44 Plaxico Burress .20 .50
45 Tommy Maddox .20 .50
46 Jerome Bettis .25 .60
47 Drew Brees .25 .60
48 LaDainian Tomlinson .25 .60
49 Junior Seau .25 .60
50 Eddie George .20 .50
51 Steve McNair .25 .60
52 Derrick Mason .20 .50
53 David Boston .15 .40
54 Jake Plummer .20 .50
55 Marcel Shipp .15 .40
56 Michael Vick .30 .75
57 T.J. Duckett .20 .50
58 Warrick Dunn .20 .50
59 Julius Peppers .25 .60
60 Steve Smith .25 .60
61 Muhsin Muhammad .20 .50
62 Anthony Thomas .20 .50
63 Brian Urlacher .25 .60
64 Marty Booker .20 .50
65 Chad Hutchinson .15 .40
66 Antonio Bryant .15 .40
67 Emmitt Smith .60 1.50
68 Joey Harrington .15 .40
69 Germane Crowell .15 .40
70 James Stewart .15 .40
71 Brett Favre .60 1.50
72 Donald Driver .25 .60
73 Ahman Green .20 .50
74 Randy Moss .25 .60
75 Michael Bennett .20 .50
76 Daunte Culpepper .20 .50
77 Aaron Brooks .20 .50
78 Deuce McAllister .20 .50
79 Donte Stallworth .15 .40
80 Tiki Barber .25 .60
81 Jeremy Shockey .25 .60
82 Kerry Collins .20 .50
83 Donovan McNabb .25 .60
84 James Thrash .15 .40
85 Duce Staley .20 .50
86 Jeff Garcia .20 .50
87 Terrell Owens .25 .60
88 Garrison Hearst .20 .50
89 Shaun Alexander .20 .50
90 Darrell Jackson .20 .50
91 Koren Robinson .20 .50
92 Marshall Faulk .25 .60
93 Kurt Warner .25 .60
94 Isaac Bruce .25 .60
95 Keyshawn Johnson .25 .60
96 Brad Johnson .20 .50
97 Warren Sapp .20 .50
98 Patrick Ramsey .20 .50
99 Rod Gardner .15 .40
100 Stephen Davis .20 .50
101 Brian St.Pierre RC 3.00 8.00
102 Byron Leftwich RC 4.00 10.00
103 Carson Palmer RC 8.00 20.00
104 Chris Simms RC 4.00 10.00
105 Dave Ragone RC 2.50 6.00
106 Ken Dorsey RC 3.00 8.00
107 Kliff Kingsbury RC 3.00 8.00
108 Kyle Boller RC 4.00 10.00
109 Rex Grossman RC 4.00 10.00
110 Seneca Wallace RC 4.00 10.00
111 Jason Gesser RC 3.00 8.00
112 Artose Pinner RC 2.50 6.00
113 Avon Cobourne RC 2.50 6.00
114 Cecil Sapp RC 2.50 6.00
115 Chris Brown RC 2.50 6.00
116 Derek Watson RC 2.50 6.00
117 Domanick Davis RC 3.00 8.00
118 Dwone Hicks/100 RC 10.00 25.00
119 Earnest Graham RC 4.00 10.00
120 Justin Fargas RC 4.00 10.00
121 Larry Johnson RC 4.00 10.00
122 Lee Suggs RC 3.00 8.00
123 Musa Smith RC 2.50 6.00
124 Onterrio Smith RC 2.50 6.00
125 Quentin Griffin RC 3.00 8.00
126 Willis McGahee RC 5.00 12.00
127 Sultan McCullough RC 2.50 6.00
128 LaBrandon Toefield RC 3.00 8.00
129 B.J. Askew RC 3.00 8.00
130 Andre Johnson RC 10.00 25.00
131 Anquan Boldin RC 6.00 15.00
132 Arnaz Battle RC 4.00 10.00
133 Bethel Johnson RC 2.50 6.00
134 Billy McMullen RC 2.50 6.00
135 Bobby Wade RC 3.00 8.00
136 Brandon Lloyd RC 6.00 15.00
137 Bryant Johnson RC 4.00 10.00
138 Charles Rogers RC 3.00 8.00
139 Doug Gabriel RC 3.00 8.00
140 Justin Gage RC 3.00 8.00
141 Kareem Kelly RC 2.50 6.00
142 Kelley Washington RC 2.50 6.00
143 Kevin Curtis RC 4.00 10.00
144 Nate Burleson RC 3.00 8.00
145 Sam Aiken RC 3.00 8.00
146 Shaun McDonald RC 3.00 8.00
147 Talman Gardner RC 2.50 6.00
148 Taylor Jacobs RC 2.50 6.00
149 Terrence Edwards RC 2.50 6.00
150 Tyrone Calico RC 3.00 8.00
151 Walter Young RC 2.50 6.00
152 Ryan Hoag/100 RC 10.00 25.00
153 Paul Arnold/100 RC 10.00 25.00
154 Bennie Joppru RC 2.50 6.00
155 Dallas Clark RC 6.00 15.00
156 George Wrighster RC 2.50 6.00
157 Jason Witten RC 10.00 25.00
158 Mike Pinkard RC 2.50 6.00
159 Robert Johnson/100 RC 10.00 25.00
160 Teyo Johnson RC 3.00 8.00
161 Andrew Williams RC 2.50 6.00
162 Chris Kelsay RC 3.00 8.00
163 Cory Redding RC 3.00 8.00
164 DeWayne Robertson RC 3.00 8.00
165 DeWayne White RC 2.50 6.00
166 Jerome McDougle RC 2.50 6.00
167 Kenny Peterson RC 3.00 8.00
168 Kindal Moorehead RC 3.00 8.00
169 Michael Haynes RC 2.50 6.00
170 Terrell Suggs RC 4.00 10.00
171 Tully Banta-Cain RC 4.00 10.00
172 Jimmy Kennedy RC 3.00 8.00
173 Johnathan Sullivan RC 2.50 6.00
174 Kevin Williams RC 4.00 10.00
175 Nick Eason/100 RC 10.00 25.00
176 Rien Long RC 2.50 6.00
177 Ty Warren RC 3.00 8.00
178 William Joseph RC 2.50 6.00
179 Boss Bailey RC 3.00 8.00
180 Bradie James RC 4.00 10.00
181 Victor Hobson RC 2.50 6.00
182 Clifton Smith/100 RC 10.00 25.00
183 E.J. Henderson/100 RC 12.00 30.00
184 Gerald Hayes/100 RC 12.00 30.00
185 LaMarcus McDonald/100 RC 10.00 25.00
186 Nick Barnett RC 4.00 10.00
187 Terry Pierce RC 2.50 6.00
188 Andre Woolfolk RC 3.00 8.00
189 Dennis Weathersby RC 2.50 6.00
190 Drayton Florence/100 RC 15.00 40.00
191 Eugene Wilson RC 4.00 10.00
192 Marcus Trufant RC 3.00 8.00
193 Rashean Mathis RC 3.00 8.00
194 Ricky Manning RC 3.00 8.00
195 Sammy Davis/100 RC 12.00 30.00
196 Terence Newman RC 3.00 8.00
197 Julian Battle RC 3.00 8.00
198 Ken Hamlin RC 4.00 10.00
199 Mike Doss RC 4.00 10.00
200 Troy Polamalu/100 RC 90.00 150.00

2003 Donruss Elite Aspirations

*VETS/70-99: 8X TO 20X BASIC CARD
*ROOKIES/70-99: .4X TO 1X SP/100 RC
*ROOKIES/70-99: .5X TO 1.2X
*VETS/45-69: 10X TO 25X
*ROOKIES/45-69: .4X TO 1X SP/100 RC
*ROOKIES/45-69: .6X TO 1.5X BASIC RC
*ROOKIES/30-44: .5X TO 1.2X SP/100 RC
*ROOKIES/30-44: .8X TO 2X
*VETS/20-29: 15X TO 40X
*ROOKIES/20-29: 1X TO 2.5X
*VETS/10-19: 20X TO 50X
*ROOKIES/10-19: 1.2X TO 3X
STATED PRINT RUN 1-98
UNPRICED GOLD ASPIRATIONS #'d OF 1
200 Troy Polamalu/57 90.00 150.00

2003 Donruss Elite Status

*VETS/70-99: 8X TO 20X BASIC CARD
*ROOKIES/70-99: .4X TO 1X SP/100 RC
*ROOKIES/70-99: .5X TO 1.2X
*VETS/45-69: 10X TO 25X
*ROOKIES/45-69: .4X TO 1X SP/100 RC
*ROOKIES/45-69: .6X TO 1.5X
*VETS/30-44: 12X TO 30X
*ROOKIES/30-44: .8X TO 2X
*VETS/20-29: 15X TO 40X
*ROOKIES/20-29: .6X TO 1.5X SP/100 RC
*ROOKIES/20-29: 1X TO 2.5X
*VETS/10-19: 20X TO 50X
*ROOKIES/10-19: 1.2X TO 3X
STATED PRINT RUN 2-99
200 Troy Polamalu/43 90.00 150.00

2003 Donruss Elite Turn of the Century Autographs

STATED PRINT RUN 125 SER.#'d SETS
101 Brian St.Pierre 10.00 25.00
102 Byron Leftwich 12.00 30.00
103 Carson Palmer 100.00 175.00
104 Chris Simms 12.00 30.00
105 Dave Ragone 8.00 20.00
108 Kyle Boller 12.00 30.00
109 Rex Grossman 50.00 120.00
112 Artose Pinner 8.00 20.00
114 Cecil Sapp 8.00 20.00
115 Chris Brown 8.00 20.00
120 Justin Fargas 12.00 30.00
121 Larry Johnson 12.00 30.00
122 Lee Suggs 10.00 25.00
123 Musa Smith 8.00 20.00
124 Onterrio Smith 8.00 20.00
126 Willis McGahee 40.00 100.00
130 Andre Johnson 30.00 80.00
136 Brandon Lloyd 20.00 50.00
137 Bryant Johnson 12.00 30.00
138 Charles Rogers 10.00 25.00
139 Doug Gabriel 10.00 25.00
140 Justin Gage 10.00 25.00
142 Kelley Washington 8.00 20.00
143 Kevin Curtis 12.00 30.00
145 Sam Aiken 10.00 25.00
148 Taylor Jacobs 8.00 20.00
149 Terrence Edwards 8.00 20.00
150 Tyrone Calico 10.00 25.00
154 Bennie Joppru 8.00 20.00
155 Dallas Clark 30.00 60.00
157 Jason Witten 30.00 60.00
158 Mike Pinkard 8.00 20.00
160 Teyo Johnson 10.00 25.00
162 Chris Kelsay 10.00 25.00
164 DeWayne Robertson No AU 6.00 15.00
165 DeWayne White 8.00 20.00
166 Jerome McDougle 8.00 20.00
167 Kenny Peterson No AU 6.00 15.00
170 Terrell Suggs 25.00 50.00
172 Jimmy Kennedy 10.00 25.00
173 Johnathon Sullivan No AU 5.00 12.00
174 Kevin Williams 20.00 50.00
176 Rien Long 8.00 20.00
178 William Joseph 8.00 20.00
179 Boss Bailey 10.00 25.00
183 E.J. Henderson 10.00 25.00
189 Dennis Weathersby 8.00 20.00
192 Marcus Trufant 10.00 25.00
196 Terence Newman 10.00 25.00
199 Mike Doss 12.00 30.00

2003 Donruss Elite Back to the Future

BF1-BF12 PRINT RUN 1000
BF13-BF18 PRINT RUN 500
BF1 Drew Brees 1.50 4.00
BF2 Dan Fouts 1.50 4.00
BF3 Marvin Harrison 1.50 4.00
BF4 Raymond Berry 1.25 3.00
BF5 Rod Gardner 1.00 2.50
BF6 Art Monk 1.25 3.00
BF7 Daunte Culpepper 1.25 3.00
BF8 Warren Moon 1.25 3.00
BF9 Kerry Collins 1.25 3.00
BF10 Frank Gifford 1.50 4.00
BF11 Tom Brady 4.00 10.00
BF12 Drew Bledsoe 1.50 4.00
BF13 Drew Brees / Dan Fouts 2.00 5.00
BF14 Marvin Harrison / Raymond Berry 2.00 5.00
BF15 Rod Gardner / Art Monk 1.50 4.00
BF16 Daunte Culpepper / Warren Moon 1.50 4.00
BF17 Kerry Collins / Frank Gifford 2.00 5.00
BF18 Tom Brady / Drew Bledsoe 5.00 12.00

2003 Donruss Elite Back to the Future Threads

1-12 PRINT RUN 250 SER.#'d SETS
13-18 PRINT RUN 100 SER.#'d SETS
BF1 Drew Brees 6.00 15.00
BF2 Dan Fouts 8.00 20.00
BF3 Marvin Harrison 6.00 15.00
BF4 Raymond Berry 6.00 15.00
BF5 Rod Gardner 4.00 10.00
BF6 Art Monk 6.00 15.00
BF7 Daunte Culpepper 5.00 12.00
BF8 Warren Moon 6.00 15.00
BF9 Kerry Collins 5.00 12.00
BF10 Frank Gifford 8.00 20.00
BF11 Tom Brady 15.00 40.00
BF12 Drew Bledsoe 6.00 15.00
BF13 Drew Brees / Dan Fouts 10.00 25.00
BF14 Marvin Harrison / Raymond Berry 10.00 25.00
BF15 Rod Gardner / Art Monk 8.00 20.00
BF16 Daunte Culpepper / Warren Moon 8.00 20.00
BF17 Kerry Collins / Frank Gifford 10.00 25.00
BF18 Tom Brady / Drew Bledsoe 20.00 50.00

2003 Donruss Elite College Ties

COMPLETE SET (15) 15.00 40.00
STATED PRINT RUN 2000 SER.#'d SETS
CT1 Ricky Williams / Chris Simms 1.25 3.00
CT2 Chad Pennington / Byron Leftwich .75 2.00
CT3 Keyshawn Johnson / Carson Palmer 1.50 4.00
CT4 Deion Branch / Dave Ragone 1.00 2.50
CT5 Drew Bledsoe / Jason Gesser 1.25 3.00
CT6 Jeremy Shockey / Ken Dorsey 1.25 3.00
CT7 Michael Vick / LeeSuggs 1.50 4.00
CT8 Clinton Portis / Willis McGahee 1.00 2.50
CT9 Emmitt Smith / Rex Grossman 3.00 8.00
CT10 Plaxico Burress / Charlie Rogers 1.00 2.50
CT11 Santana Moss / Andre Johnson 2.00 5.00
CT12 Kerry Collins / Larry Johnson .75 2.00
CT13 Donte Stallworth / Kelley Washington .75 2.00
CT14 Warren Sapp / William Joseph 1.00 2.50
CT15 Nate Clements / Mike Doss 1.25 3.00

2003 Donruss Elite Masks of Steel

1-25 PRINT RUN 400 SER.#'d SETS
26-30 PRINT RUN 50 SER.#'d SETS
MS31-MS35 PRINT RUN 25
MS1 Michael Vick 5.00 12.00
MS2 Marvin Harrison 4.00 10.00
MS3 Jeff Garcia 3.00 8.00
MS4 Eddie George 3.00 8.00
MS5 Tom Brady 10.00 25.00
MS6 Jerry Rice/350 8.00 20.00
MS7 Aaron Brooks 3.00 8.00
MS8 Chris Chambers 3.00 8.00
MS9 Kordell Stewart 3.00 8.00
MS10 Koren Robinson 3.00 8.00
MS11 Quincy Morgan 2.50 6.00
MS12 Deuce McAllister 3.00 8.00
MS13 LaDainian Tomlinson 4.00 10.00
MS14 Travis Henry 2.50 6.00
MS15 Mark Brunell 3.00 8.00
MS16 Quincy Carter 2.50 6.00
MS17 Chad Johnson 4.00 10.00
MS18 Chad Pennington 4.00 10.00
MS19 Drew Brees 4.00 10.00
MS20 Santana Moss 3.00 8.00
MS21 Kevan Barlow 2.50 6.00
MS22 Reggie Wayne 4.00 10.00
MS23 Anthony Thomas 3.00 8.00
MS24 Todd Heap 3.00 8.00
MS25 Michael Bennett 3.00 8.00
MS26 Michael Vick / Aaron Brooks 12.00 30.00
MS27 Eddie George / Anthony Thomas 8.00 20.00
MS28 Deuce McAllister / Travis Henry 8.00 20.00
MS29 Jeff Garcia / Jerry Rice 20.00 50.00
MS30 LaDainian Tomlinson / Drew Brees 10.00 25.00
MS31 Drew Brees / Mark Brunell / Quincy Carter 15.00 40.00
MS32 Travis Henry / Michael Bennett / Anthony Thomas 12.00 30.00
MS33 Jerry Rice / Marvin Harrison / Chris Chambers 30.00 80.00
MS34 Eddie George / Deuce McAllister / LaDainian Tomlinson 15.00 40.00
MS35 Michael Vick / Aaron Brooks / Jeff Garcia 20.00 50.00

2003 Donruss Elite Passing the Torch

COMPLETE SET (27) 30.00 80.00
PT1-PT20 PRINT RUN 1000 SER.#'d SETS
PT21-PT27 PRINT RUN 500 SER.#'d SETS
PT1 David Carr 1.25 3.00
PT2 Warren Moon 1.50 4.00
PT3 Patrick Ramsey 1.25 3.00
PT4 Joe Theismann 2.00 5.00
PT5 Clinton Portis 1.25 3.00
PT6 Terrell Davis 2.00 5.00
PT7 Roy Williams 1.25 3.00
PT8 Deion Sanders 2.00 5.00
PT9 Deuce McAllister 1.25 3.00
PT10 Ricky Williams 1.25 3.00
PT11 Drew Bledsoe 1.50 4.00
PT12 Jim Kelly 2.50 6.00
PT13 Jerome Bettis 1.50 4.00
PT14 Franco Harris 2.50 6.00
PT15 Priest Holmes 1.50 4.00
PT16 Marcus Allen 2.00 5.00
PT19 Kendrell Bell 1.00 2.50
PT20 Jack Lambert 2.00 5.00
PT21 David Carr / Warren Moon 2.00 5.00
PT22 Patrick Ramsey / Joe Theisman 2.50 6.00
PT23 Clinton Portis / Terrell Davis 2.50 6.00
PT24 Deion Sanders / Roy Williams 2.50 6.00
PT25 Deuce McAllister / Ricky Williams 2.00 5.00
PT26 Drew Bledsoe / Jim Kelly 2.50 6.00
PT27 Jerome Bettis / Franco Harris 3.00 8.00
PT28 Priest Holmes / Marcus Allen 2.50 6.00
PT30 Kendrell Bell / Jack Lambert 2.50 6.00

2003 Donruss Elite Passing the Torch Autographs

PT1-PT20 SINGLE AU PRINT RUN 100
PT21-PT30 DUAL AU PRINT RUN 50
PT1 David Carr 12.00 30.00
PT2 Warren Moon 15.00 40.00
PT3 Patrick Ramsey 12.00 30.00
PT4 Joe Theismann 20.00 50.00
PT5 Clinton Portis 12.00 30.00
PT6 Terrell Davis 20.00 50.00
PT7 Roy Williams 12.00 30.00
PT8 Deion Sanders 40.00 100.00

PT9 Deuce McAllister	12.00	30.00
PT10 Ricky Williams	12.00	30.00
PT11 Drew Bledsoe	15.00	40.00
PT12 Jim Kelly	30.00	80.00
PT13 Jerome Bettis	50.00	80.00
PT14 Franco Harris	25.00	60.00
PT15 Priest Holmes	15.00	40.00
PT16 Marcus Allen	20.00	50.00
PT19 Kendrell Bell	10.00	25.00
PT20 Jack Lambert	50.00	80.00
PT21 David Carr	30.00	80.00
Warren Moon		
PT22 Patrick Ramsey	40.00	100.00
Joe Theismann		
PT23 Clinton Portis	40.00	100.00
Terrell Davis		
PT24 Deion Sanders	75.00	150.00
Roy Williams		
PT25 Deuce McAllister	30.00	80.00
Ricky Williams		
PT26 Drew Bledsoe	50.00	120.00
Jim Kelly		
PT27 Jerome Bettis	100.00	175.00
Franco Harris		
PT28 Priest Holmes	40.00	100.00
Marcus Allen		
PT30 Kendrell Bell	40.00	100.00
Jack Lambert		

2003 Donruss Elite Prime Patches

STATED PRINT RUN 50 SER.#'d SETS

PP1 Emmitt Smith	30.00	80.00
PP2 William Green	8.00	20.00
PP3 Travis Henry	8.00	20.00
PP4 Tim Brown	12.00	30.00
PP5 Steve McNair	12.00	30.00
PP6 Jerry Rice	25.00	60.00
PP7 Michael Vick	15.00	40.00
PP8 Jamal Lewis	10.00	25.00
PP9 Brett Favre	30.00	80.00
PP10 Randy Moss	12.00	30.00
PP11 Joey Harrington	8.00	20.00
PP12 Peyton Manning	25.00	60.00
PP13 Garrison Hearst	10.00	25.00
PP14 Junior Seau	12.00	30.00
PP15 Priest Holmes	12.00	30.00
PP16 Deuce McAllister	10.00	25.00
PP17 Terrell Owens	12.00	30.00
PP18 LaDainian Tomlinson	12.00	30.00
PP19 Donovan McNabb	12.00	30.00
PP20 Eddie George	10.00	25.00
PP7P Michael Vick Promo	5.00	12.00

2003 Donruss Elite Pro Bowl Standouts

COMPLETE SET (20)	15.00	40.00
STATED PRINT RUN 2002 SER.#'d SETS		
PB1 Donovan McNabb	1.25	3.00
PB2 Mike Alstott	1.25	3.00
PB3 Jeff Garcia	1.00	2.50
PB4 Deuce McAllister	1.00	2.50
PB5 Michael Bennett	1.00	2.50
PB6 Marshall Faulk	1.25	3.00
PB7 Jeremy Shockey	1.25	3.00
PB8 Terrell Owens	1.25	3.00
PB9 Joe Horn	1.00	2.50
PB10 Brian Urlacher	1.25	3.00
PB11 Rich Gannon	1.00	2.50
PB12 Drew Bledsoe	1.25	3.00
PB13 Peyton Manning	2.50	6.00
PB14 Ricky Williams	1.00	2.50
PB15 Travis Henry	.75	2.00
PB16 LaDainian Tomlinson	1.25	3.00
PB17 Marvin Harrison	1.25	3.00
PB18 Jerry Rice	2.50	6.00
PB19 Eric Moulds	1.00	2.50
PB20 Zach Thomas	1.25	3.00

2003 Donruss Elite Throwback Threads

1-30 PRINT RUN 250 SER.#'d SETS
31-45 PRINT RUN 75 SER.#'d SETS

TT1 Joe Montana	20.00	50.00
TT2 Jeff Garcia	6.00	15.00
TT3 Walter Payton	25.00	60.00
TT4 Red Grange	75.00	150.00
TT5 Jim Kelly	12.00	30.00
TT6 Thurman Thomas	10.00	25.00
TT7 Jim Brown	15.00	40.00
TT8 Jim Thorpe	75.00	150.00
TT9 Bob Griese	10.00	25.00
TT10 Larry Csonka	10.00	25.00
TT11 Barry Sanders	15.00	40.00
TT12 Doak Walker	20.00	50.00
TT13 Warren Moon	8.00	20.00
TT14 Earl Campbell	10.00	25.00
TT15 Eric Dickerson	8.00	20.00
TT16 Marshall Faulk	8.00	20.00
TT17 Joe Theismann	10.00	25.00
TT18 John Riggins	10.00	25.00
TT19 Fred Biletnikoff	10.00	25.00
TT20 Jerry Rice	15.00	40.00
TT21 Joe Greene	10.00	25.00
TT22 L.C. Greenwood	8.00	20.00
TT23 Sterling Sharpe	10.00	25.00
TT24 James Lofton	8.00	20.00
TT25 Tony Dorsett	10.00	25.00
TT26 Emmitt Smith	20.00	50.00
TT27 Bart Starr	15.00	40.00
TT28 Ray Nitschke	12.00	30.00
TT29 Sonny Jurgensen	8.00	20.00
TT30 Charley Taylor	8.00	20.00
TT31 Joe Montana	30.00	80.00
Jeff Garcia		
TT32 Walter Payton	100.00	250.00
Red Grange		
TT33 Jim Kelly	25.00	60.00
Thurman Thomas		
TT34 Jim Brown	125.00	250.00
Jim Thorpe		
TT35 Bob Griese	20.00	50.00
Larry Csonka		
TT36 Barry Sanders	40.00	100.00
Doak Walker		
TT37 Warren Moon	20.00	50.00
Earl Campbell		
TT38 Eric Dickerson	20.00	50.00
Marshall Faulk		
TT39 Joe Theismann	20.00	50.00
John Riggins		
TT40 Fred Biletnikoff	40.00	100.00
Jerry Rice		
TT41 Joe Greene	20.00	50.00
L.C. Greenwood		
TT42 Sterling Sharpe	20.00	50.00
James Lofton		
TT43 Tony Dorsett	30.00	80.00
Emmitt Smith		
TT44 Bart Starr	50.00	120.00
Ray Nitschke		
TT45 Sonny Jurgensen	15.00	40.00
Charley Taylor		

2003 Donruss Elite Throwback Threads Autographs

STATED PRINT RUN 25 SER.#'d SETS

TT1 Joe Montana	175.00	300.00
TT7 Jim Brown	60.00	150.00
TT9 Bob Griese	30.00	80.00
TT10 Larry Csonka	30.00	80.00
TT11 Barry Sanders	125.00	250.00
TT14 Earl Campbell	30.00	80.00
TT18 John Riggins	30.00	80.00
TT23 Sterling Sharpe	30.00	80.00

2004 Donruss Elite

Donruss Elite was released in late June 2004. The base set consists of 200-cards including 100-veterans and 100-rookies. The rookie subset featured cards serial numbered to 500. Hobby boxes contained 20-packs of 5-cards each at an SRP of $5. Included in the product was an extensive selection of inserts and memorabilia sets highlighted by the Turn of the Century Autographs set and the very first Lynn Swann game-used memorabilia card in Throwback Threads.

COMP.SET w/o SP's (100)	7.50	20.00
ROOKIE PRINT RUN 500 SER.#'d SETS		
1 Emmitt Smith	.75	2.00
2 Anquan Boldin	.30	.75
3 Michael Vick	.40	1.00
4 Peerless Price	.20	.50
5 T.J. Duckett	.25	.60
6 Warrick Dunn	.25	.60
7 Jamal Lewis	.25	.60
8 Kyle Boller	.25	.60
9 Todd Heap	.25	.60
10 Ray Lewis	.30	.75
11 Drew Bledsoe	.30	.75
12 Eric Moulds	.25	.60
13 Travis Henry	.20	.50
14 Jake Delhomme	.25	.60
15 Stephen Davis	.25	.60
16 Steve Smith	.30	.75
17 Anthony Thomas	.25	.60
18 Brian Urlacher	.30	.75
19 Rex Grossman	.25	.60
20 Chad Johnson	.30	.75
21 Carson Palmer	.30	.75
22 Rudi Johnson	.25	.60
23 Peter Warrick	.25	.60
24 Andre Davis	.20	.50
25 Tim Couch	.25	.60
26 Quincy Carter	.20	.50
27 Roy Williams S	.25	.60
28 Terence Newman	.25	.60
29 Clinton Portis	.30	.75
30 Jake Plummer	.25	.60
31 Rod Smith	.25	.60
32 Charles Rogers	.20	.50
33 Joey Harrington	.25	.60
34 Ahman Green	.25	.60
35 Brett Favre	.75	2.00
36 Javon Walker	.20	.50
37 Andre Johnson	.30	.75
38 David Carr	.20	.50
39 Domanick Davis	.20	.50
40 Edgerrin James	.25	.60
41 Marvin Harrison	.30	.75
42 Peyton Manning	.60	1.50
43 Reggie Wayne	.30	.75
44 Byron Leftwich	.25	.60
45 Fred Taylor	.25	.60
46 Jimmy Smith	.25	.60
47 Priest Holmes	.30	.75
48 Tony Gonzalez	.30	.75
49 Trent Green	.25	.60
50 Chris Chambers	.25	.60
51 Ricky Williams	.25	.60
52 Zach Thomas	.30	.75
53 Daunte Culpepper	.25	.60
54 Michael Bennett	.25	.60
55 Moe Williams	.20	.50
56 Randy Moss	.30	.75
57 Deion Branch	.25	.60
58 Tom Brady	.60	1.50
59 Tedy Bruschi	.30	.75
60 Aaron Brooks	.25	.60
61 Deuce McAllister	.25	.60
62 Joe Horn	.25	.60
63 Jeremy Shockey	.25	.60
64 Kerry Collins	.25	.60
65 Michael Strahan	.30	.75
66 Tiki Barber	.30	.75
67 Chad Pennington	.30	.75
68 Curtis Martin	.30	.75
69 Santana Moss	.25	.60
70 Jerry Porter	.20	.50
71 Jerry Rice	.60	1.50
72 Tim Brown	.30	.75
73 Brian Westbrook	.30	.75
74 Correll Buckhalter	.25	.60
75 Donovan McNabb	.30	.75
76 Hines Ward	.30	.75
77 Kendrell Bell	.20	.50
78 Plaxico Burress	.25	.60
79 David Boston	.20	.50
80 Drew Brees	.30	.75
81 LaDainian Tomlinson	.30	.75
82 Jeff Garcia	.25	.60
83 Kevan Barlow	.20	.50
84 Terrell Owens	.30	.75
85 Koren Robinson	.20	.50
86 Matt Hasselbeck	.25	.60
87 Shaun Alexander	.25	.60
88 Isaac Bruce	.25	.60
89 Marc Bulger	.25	.60
90 Marshall Faulk	.30	.75
91 Torry Holt	.25	.60
92 Brad Johnson	.25	.60
93 Derrick Brooks	.25	.60
94 Keenan McCardell	.20	.50
95 Derrick Mason	.25	.60
96 Eddie George	.25	.60
97 Steve McNair	.30	.75
98 Jevon Kearse	.25	.60
99 Laveranues Coles	.20	.50
100 Patrick Ramsey	.25	.60
101 Adimchinobe Echemandu RC	2.50	6.00
102 Ahmad Carroll RC	2.00	5.00
103 Antwan Odom RC	2.50	6.00
104 B.J. Johnson RC	2.00	5.00
105 Ben Roethlisberger RC	25.00	50.00
106 Ben Troupe RC	2.50	6.00
107 Ben Watson RC	3.00	8.00
108 Bernard Berrian RC	3.00	8.00
109 Bob Sanders RC	8.00	20.00
110 Brandon Everage RC	2.00	5.00
111 Brandon Miree RC	2.00	5.00
112 Carlos Francis RC	2.00	5.00
113 Cedric Cobbs RC	2.00	5.00
114 Chad Lavalais RC	2.00	5.00
115 Chris Collins RC	2.00	5.00
116 Chris Gamble RC	2.50	6.00
117 Chris Perry RC	2.50	6.00
118 Cody Pickett RC	2.50	6.00
119 Craig Krenzel RC	2.50	6.00
120 D.J. Hackett RC	2.50	6.00
121 D.J. Williams RC	3.00	8.00
122 Darius Watts RC	2.00	5.00
123 Darnell Dockett RC	2.00	5.00
124 DeAngelo Hall RC	3.00	8.00
125 Derek Abney RC	2.00	5.00
126 Derrick Hamilton RC	2.00	5.00
127 Derrick Strait RC	2.00	5.00
128 Devard Darling RC	2.00	5.00
129 Devery Henderson RC	3.00	8.00
130 Dontarrious Thomas RC	2.50	6.00
131 Drew Henson RC	2.00	5.00
132 Dunta Robinson RC	2.00	5.00
133 Dwan Edwards RC	2.00	5.00
134 Eli Manning RC	25.00	50.00
135 Ernest Wilford RC	2.50	6.00
136 Fred Russell RC	2.50	6.00
137 Greg Jones RC	2.00	5.00
138 Igor Olshansky RC	2.50	6.00
139 J.P. Losman RC	2.50	6.00
140 Jared Lorenzen RC	2.50	6.00
141 Jarrett Payton RC	2.50	6.00
142 Jason Babin RC	3.00	8.00
143 Jason Fife RC	2.00	5.00
144 Jeff Smoker RC	2.50	6.00
145 Jeremy LeSueur RC	2.00	5.00
146 Jerricho Cotchery RC	2.50	6.00
147 John Navarre RC	2.00	5.00
148 John Standeford RC	2.00	5.00
149 Johnnie Morant RC	2.00	5.00
150 Jonathan Vilma RC	3.00	8.00
151 Josh Davis RC	2.50	6.00
152 Josh Harris RC	2.00	5.00
153 Julius Jones RC	2.50	6.00
154 Justin Jenkins RC	2.00	5.00
155 Karlos Dansby RC	3.00	8.00
156 Keary Colbert RC	2.00	5.00
157 Keith Smith RC	2.00	5.00
158 Keiwan Ratliff RC	2.00	5.00
159 Kellen Winslow RC	3.00	8.00
160 Kendrick Starling RC	2.00	5.00
161 Kenechi Udeze RC	2.50	6.00
162 Kevin Jones RC	2.50	6.00
163 Larry Fitzgerald RC	8.00	20.00
164 Lee Evans RC	3.00	8.00
165 Luke McCown RC	2.50	6.00
166 Marquise Hill RC	2.00	5.00
167 Matt Schaub RC	6.00	15.00
168 Matt Ware RC	3.00	8.00
169 Matt Mauck RC	2.00	5.00
170 Maurice Mann RC	2.00	5.00
171 Mewelde Moore RC	2.50	6.00
172 Michael Boulware RC	3.00	8.00
173 Michael Clayton RC	2.50	6.00
174 Michael Jenkins RC	3.00	8.00
175 Michael Turner RC	4.00	10.00
176 B.J. Symons RC	2.00	5.00
177 Nathan Vasher RC	3.00	8.00
178 P.K. Sam RC	2.00	5.00
179 Philip Rivers RC	12.00	30.00
180 Quincy Wilson RC	2.50	6.00
181 Ran Carthon RC	2.00	5.00
182 Randy Starks RC	2.00	5.00
183 Rashaun Woods RC	2.00	5.00
184 Reggie Williams RC	2.50	6.00
185 Ricardo Colclough RC	2.50	6.00
186 Robert Kent RC	2.00	5.00
187 Roy Williams RC	3.00	8.00
188 Samie Parker RC	2.00	5.00
189 Scott Rislov RC	2.00	5.00
190 Sean Jones RC	2.50	6.00
191 Sean Taylor RC	6.00	15.00
192 Steven Jackson RC	5.00	12.00
193 Stuart Schweigert RC	2.50	6.00
194 Tatum Bell RC	2.50	6.00
195 Teddy Lehman RC	2.00	5.00
196 Tommie Harris RC	3.00	8.00
197 Troy Fleming RC	2.00	5.00
198 Vince Wilfork RC	3.00	8.00
199 Will Poole RC	3.00	8.00
200 Will Smith RC	2.50	6.00

2004 Donruss Elite Aspirations

*VETS/70-99: 6X TO 15X BASIC CARDS
*ROOKIES/70-99: .6X TO 1.5X
*VETS/45-69: 8X TO 20X
*ROOKIES/45-69: .8X TO 2X
*ROOKIES/30-44: 1X TO 2.5X
*VETS/20-29: 12X TO 30X
*ROOKIES/20-29: 1.2X TO 3X
*VETS/10-19: 15X TO 40X
*ROOKIES/10-19: 1.5X TO 4X
STATED PRINT RUN 2-99

2004 Donruss Elite Status

*VETS/70-99: 6X TO 15X BASIC CARDS
*ROOKIES/70-99: .6X TO 1.5X
*VETS/45-69: 8X TO 20X
*ROOKIES/45-69: .8X TO 2X
*VETS/30-44: 6X TO 15X
*ROOKIES/30-44: 1X TO 2.5X
*VETS/20-29: 12X TO 30X
*ROOKIES/20-29: 1.2X TO 3X
*VETS/10-19: 15X TO 40X
*ROOKIES/10-19: 1.5X TO 4X
STATED PRINT RUN 1-98

2004 Donruss Elite Career Best

COMPLETE SET (15)	20.00	50.00
STATED PRINT RUN 1650 SER.#'d SETS		
CB1 Barry Sanders	2.50	6.00
CB2 Brett Favre	3.00	8.00
CB3 Chad Pennington	1.25	3.00
CB4 Clinton Portis	1.25	3.00
CB5 Dan Marino	3.00	8.00
CB6 Priest Holmes	1.25	3.00
CB7 Deuce McAllister	1.00	2.50
CB8 Jerry Rice	2.50	6.00
CB9 John Elway	3.00	8.00
CB10 Marshall Faulk	1.25	3.00
CB11 Emmitt Smith	3.00	8.00
CB12 Marvin Harrison	1.25	3.00
CB13 Peyton Manning	2.50	6.00
CB14 Ricky Williams	1.00	2.50
CB15 Steve McNair	1.25	3.00

2004 Donruss Elite Career Best Jerseys

STATED PRINT RUN 250 SER. #'d SETS
*PRIME/25: 1.2X TO 3X BASIC JSY/250
PRIME PRINT RUN 25 SER. #'d SETS
*YEAR: .6X TO 1.5X BASIC JSY/250
YEAR STATED PRINT RUN 84-103

CB1 Barry Sanders	8.00	20.00
CB2 Brett Favre	10.00	25.00
CB3 Chad Pennington	4.00	10.00
CB4 Clinton Portis	4.00	10.00
CB5 Dan Marino	10.00	25.00
CB6 Priest Holmes	4.00	10.00
CB7 Deuce McAllister	3.00	8.00
CB8 Jerry Rice	8.00	20.00
CB9 John Elway	10.00	25.00
CB10 Marshall Faulk	4.00	10.00
CB11 Emmitt Smith	10.00	25.00
CB12 Marvin Harrison	4.00	10.00
CB13 Peyton Manning	8.00	20.00
CB14 Ricky Williams	3.00	8.00
CB15 Steve McNair	4.00	10.00

2004 Donruss Elite College Ties

COMPLETE SET (15)	15.00	40.00
STATED PRINT RUN 2000 SER.#'d SETS		
CT1 Deuce McAllister	3.00	8.00
Eli Manning		
CT2 Torry Holt	2.00	5.00
Philip Rivers		
CT3 Patrick Ramsey	.75	2.00
J.P. Losman		
CT4 Chad Johnson	1.25	3.00
Steven Jackson		
CT5 Michael Vick	1.25	3.00
Kevin Jones		
CT6 Ricky Williams	1.00	3.00
Roy Williams WR		
CT7 Corey Dillon	.75	2.00
Reggie Williams		
CT8 Domanick Davis	.75	2.00
Michael Clayton		
CT9 Jeremy Shockey	1.00	2.50
Kellen Winslow		
CT10 Anthony Thomas	.75	2.00
Chris Perry		
CT11 Antonio Bryant	1.25	3.00
Larry Fitzgerald		
CT12 Eddie George	1.00	2.50
Michael Jenkins		
CT13 Warrick Dunn	.75	2.00
Greg Jones		
CT14 Michael Bennett	1.00	2.50
Lee Evans		
CT15 Jerry Porter	.75	2.00
Quincy Wilson		

2004 Donruss Elite Face to Face Face Masks

STATED PRINT RUN 125 SER.#'d SETS

FF1 Jim Kelly	12.00	30.00
Troy Aikman		
FF2 Brett Favre	20.00	40.00
Randy Moss		
FF3 Ricky Williams	6.00	15.00
Deuce McAllister		
FF4 Brian Urlacher	10.00	25.00
Michael Bennett		
FF5 John Elway	5.00	60.00
Dan Marino		
FF6 Zach Thomas	8.00	20.00
Travis Henry		
FF7 Peyton Manning	15.00	40.00
Champ Bailey		
FF8 Marshall Faulk	8.00	20.00
Shaun Alexander		
FF9 Barry Sanders	15.00	40.00
Mike Singletary		
FF10 Emmitt Smith	15.00	40.00
Terrell Owens		
FF11 Priest Holmes	8.00	20.00
Rich Gannon		
FF12 Peyton Manning	15.00	40.00
Steve McNair		
FF13 Jeremy Shockey	6.00	15.00
Todd Heap		
FF14 Chad Pennington	15.00	40.00
Tom Brady		
FF15 Chad Johnson	8.00	20.00
Marvin Harrison		
FF16 Jeff Garcia	6.00	15.00
Marc Bulger		
FF17 Ray Lewis	8.00	20.00
Eddie George		
FF18 Torry Holt	6.00	15.00
Koren Robinson		
FF19 Jerry Rice Dual	15.00	30.00
FF20 Matt Hasselbeck	8.00	20.00
Anquan Boldin		
FF21 Jake Plummer	6.00	15.00
Trent Green		
FF22 Chris Chambers	6.00	15.00.
Santana Moss		
FF23 Peter Warrick	6.00	15.00
Ed Reed		
FF24 Kevin Faulk	6.00	15.00
Corey Dillon		
FF25 Ahman Green	6.00	15.00
Duce Staley		

2004 Donruss Elite Gridiron Gear Bronze

BRONZE STATED PRINT RUN 250
*GOLD/25: 1.2X TO 3X BRONZE/250
GOLD STATED PRINT RUN 25
*PLATINUM/10: 2X TO 5X BASIC INSERTS
PLATINUM PRINT RUN 10
*SILVER/150: .5X TO 1.2X BRONZE/250
SILVER STATED PRINT RUN 150

GG1 Ashley Lelie	2.50	6.00
GG2 Chris Chambers	3.00	8.00
GG3 Correll Buckhalter	3.00	8.00
GG4 Donovan McNabb	4.00	10.00
GG5 Drew Brees	4.00	10.00
GG6 Fred Taylor	3.00	8.00
GG7 Hines Ward	4.00	10.00
GG8 Isaac Bruce	3.00	8.00
GG9 Jeff Garcia	3.00	8.00
GG10 Jerome Bettis	4.00	10.00
GG11 Jevon Kearse	3.00	8.00
GG12 Jimmy Smith	3.00	8.00
GG13 Joey Harrington	3.00	8.00
GG14 Josh Reed	2.50	6.00
GG15 LaDainian Tomlinson	4.00	10.00
GG16 Marc Bulger	3.00	8.00
GG17 Steve McNair	4.00	10.00
GG18 Peyton Manning	8.00	20.00
GG19 Randy Moss	4.00	10.00
GG20 Santana Moss	3.00	8.00
GG21 Tim Brown	4.00	10.00
GG22 Dan Marino	10.00	25.00
GG23 John Elway	10.00	25.00
GG24 Barry Sanders	8.00	20.00
GG25 Troy Aikman	6.00	15.00

2004 Donruss Elite Lineage

COMPLETE SET (5)	10.00	25.00
STATED ODDS 1:24		
L1 Aaron Brooks	2.00	5.00
Michael Vick		
L2 Ronde Barber	1.50	4.00
Tiki Barber		
L3 Archie Manning	6.00	15.00
Eli Manning		
Peyton Manning		
L4 Chad Johnson	1.50	4.00
Keyshawn Johnson		
L5 Anthony Dorsett	1.50	4.00
Tony Dorsett		

2004 Donruss Elite Lineage Autographs

STATED PRINT RUN 100 SER.#'d SETS

L1 Aaron Brooks	30.00	80.00
Michael Vick		
L2 Ronde Barber	25.00	60.00
Tiki Barber		
L3 Archie Manning	300.00	500.00
Eli Manning		
Peyton Manning		
L4 Chad Johnson	20.00	50.00
Keyshawn Johnson		
L5 Anthony Dorsett	25.00	60.00
Tony Dorsett		

2004 Donruss Elite Passing the Torch

PT1-PT20 PRINT RUN 1000 SER.#'d SETS
PT21-PT30 PRINT RUN 500 SER.#'d SETS

PT1 Earl Campbell	1.50	4.00
PT2 Domanick Davis	1.00	2.50
PT3 Ricky Williams	1.25	3.00
PT4 Larry Csonka	1.50	4.00
PT5 John Elway	4.00	10.00
PT6 Jake Plummer	1.25	3.00
PT7 Mike Singletary	1.50	4.00
PT8 Brian Urlacher	1.50	4.00
PT9 Drew Bledsoe	1.50	4.00
PT10 Tom Brady	3.00	8.00
PT11 Paul Hornung	1.50	4.00
PT12 Ahman Green	1.25	3.00
PT13 Randall Cunningham	1.25	3.00
PT14 Donovan McNabb	1.50	4.00
PT15 Christian Okoye	1.00	2.50
PT16 Priest Holmes	1.50	4.00
PT17 Warren Moon	1.25	3.00
PT18 Steve McNair	1.50	4.00
PT19 Archie Manning	1.50	4.00
PT20 Eli Manning	4.00	10.00
PT21 Domanick Davis	2.50	6.00
Earl Campbell		
PT22 Larry Csonka	2.50	6.00
Ricky Williams		
PT23 Jake Plummer	6.00	15.00
John Elway		
PT24 Brian Urlacher	2.50	6.00
Mike Singletary		
PT25 Drew Bledsoe	5.00	12.00
Tom Brady		
PT26 Ahman Green	2.50	6.00
Paul Hornung		
PT27 Donovan McNabb	2.50	6.00
Randall Cunningham		
PT28 Christian Okoye	2.50	6.00
Priest Holmes		
PT29 Steve McNair	2.50	6.00
Warren Moon		
PT30 Archie Manning	6.00	15.00
Eli Manning		

2004 Donruss Elite Passing the Torch Autographs

PT1-PT20 PRINT RUN 100 SER.#'d SETS
PT21-PT30 PRINT RUN 50 SER.#'d SETS

PT1 Earl Campbell	20.00	50.00
PT2 Domanick Davis	12.00	30.00
PT3 Bob Griese	20.00	50.00
PT4 Larry Csonka	20.00	50.00
PT5 John Elway	75.00	150.00
PT6 Jake Plummer	15.00	40.00
PT7 Mike Singletary	20.00	50.00
PT8 Brian Urlacher	20.00	50.00
PT9 Drew Bledsoe	20.00	50.00
PT10 Tom Brady	150.00	250.00
PT11 Paul Hornung	30.00	60.00
PT12 Ahman Green	15.00	40.00
PT13 Randall Cunningham	15.00	40.00
PT14 Donovan McNabb	25.00	60.00
PT15 Christian Okoye	12.00	30.00
PT16 Priest Holmes	20.00	50.00
PT17 Warren Moon	15.00	40.00
PT18 Steve McNair	20.00	50.00
PT19 Archie Manning	20.00	50.00
PT20 Eli Manning	75.00	150.00
PT21 Domanick Davis	30.00	80.00
Earl Campbell		
PT22 Larry Csonka	40.00	80.00
Bob Griese		
PT23 Jake Plummer	100.00	200.00
John Elway		
PT24 Brian Urlacher	75.00	135.00
Mike Singletary		
PT25 Drew Bledsoe	150.00	250.00
Tom Brady		
PT26 Ahman Green	30.00	80.00
Paul Hornung		
PT27 Donovan McNabb	60.00	120.00
Randall Cunningham		
PT28 Christian Okoye	25.00	60.00
Priest Holmes		
PT29 Steve McNair	30.00	80.00
Warren Moon		
PT30 Archie Manning	150.00	250.00
Eli Manning		

2004 Donruss Elite Series

STATED PRINT RUN 850 SER.#'d SETS

ES1 Aaron Brooks	1.25	3.00
ES2 Ahman Green	1.25	3.00
ES3 Anquan Boldin	1.50	4.00
ES4 Brett Favre	4.00	10.00
ES5 Brian Urlacher	1.50	4.00
ES6 Byron Leftwich	1.25	3.00
ES7 Chad Johnson	1.50	4.00
ES8 Chad Pennington	1.50	4.00
ES9 Chris Chambers	1.25	3.00
ES10 Clinton Portis	1.50	4.00
ES11 David Carr	1.00	2.50
ES12 Deuce McAllister	1.25	3.00
ES13 Drew Bledsoe	1.50	4.00
ES14 Edgerrin James	1.25	3.00
ES15 Jamal Lewis	1.25	3.00
ES16 Jerry Rice	3.00	8.00
ES17 Jimmy Smith	1.25	3.00
ES18 LaDainian Tomlinson	1.50	4.00
ES19 Michael Vick	2.00	5.00
ES20 Donovan McNabb	1.50	4.00
ES21 Peyton Manning	3.00	8.00
ES22 Priest Holmes	1.50	4.00
ES23 Randy Moss	1.50	4.00
ES24 Ricky Williams	1.25	3.00
ES25 Steve McNair	1.50	4.00
ES26 Terrell Owens	1.50	4.00
ES27 Tom Brady	3.00	8.00
ES28 Emmitt Smith	4.00	10.00
ES29 Daunte Culpepper	1.25	3.00
ES30 Joey Harrington	1.25	3.00

2004 Donruss Elite Series Jerseys Bronze

BRONZE PRINT RUN 250 SER.#'d SETS
*GOLD/25: 1X TO 2.5X BRONZE
GOLD PRINT RUN 25 SER.#'d SETS
*PLATINUM/10: 2X TO 5X BRONZE
PLATINUM PRINT RUN 10
*SILVER/150: .5X TO 1.2X BRONZE
SILVER PRINT RUN 150 SER.#'d SETS

ES1 Aaron Brooks	3.00	8.00
ES2 Ahman Green	3.00	8.00
ES3 Anquan Boldin	4.00	10.00
ES4 Brett Favre	10.00	25.00
ES5 Brian Urlacher	4.00	10.00
ES6 Byron Leftwich	3.00	8.00
ES7 Chad Johnson	4.00	10.00
ES8 Chad Pennington	4.00	10.00
ES9 Chris Chambers	3.00	8.00
ES10 Clinton Portis	4.00	10.00
ES11 David Carr	2.50	6.00
ES12 Deuce McAllister	3.00	8.00
ES13 Drew Bledsoe	4.00	10.00
ES14 Edgerrin James	3.00	8.00
ES15 Jamal Lewis	3.00	8.00
ES16 Jerry Rice	8.00	20.00
ES17 Jimmy Smith	3.00	8.00
ES18 LaDainian Tomlinson	4.00	10.00
ES19 Michael Vick	5.00	12.00
ES20 Donovan McNabb	4.00	10.00
ES21 Peyton Manning	8.00	20.00
ES22 Priest Holmes	4.00	10.00
ES23 Randy Moss	4.00	10.00
ES24 Ricky Williams	3.00	8.00
ES25 Steve McNair	4.00	10.00
ES26 Terrell Owens	4.00	10.00
ES27 Tom Brady	8.00	20.00
ES28 Emmitt Smith	10.00	25.00
ES29 Daunte Culpepper	3.00	8.00
ES30 Joey Harrington	3.00	8.00

2004 Donruss Elite Throwback Threads

TT1-TT30 PRINT RUN 150 SER. #'d SETS
TT31-TT45 PRINT RUN 75 SER. #'d SETS

TT1 Mark Bavaro	6.00	15.00
TT2 Jeremy Shockey	3.00	8.00
TT3 Tony Dorsett	8.00	20.00
TT4 Clinton Portis	4.00	10.00
TT5 Lynn Swann	20.00	50.00
TT6 Hines Ward	4.00	10.00
TT7 Larry Csonka	8.00	20.00
TT8 Ricky Williams	3.00	8.00
TT9 Troy Aikman	10.00	25.00
TT10 Quincy Carter	2.50	6.00
TT11 Jim Kelly	8.00	20.00
TT12 Drew Bledsoe	4.00	10.00
TT13 Mike Singletary	8.00	20.00
TT14 Brian Urlacher	6.00	15.00
TT15 Warren Moon	8.00	20.00
TT16 David Carr	2.50	6.00
TT17 Thurman Thomas	8.00	20.00
TT18 Travis Henry	2.50	6.00
TT19 Marcus Allen	5.00	12.00
TT20 Priest Holmes	4.00	10.00
TT21 Randall Cunningham	6.00	15.00
TT22 Donovan McNabb	4.00	10.00
TT23 Joe Namath	15.00	40.00
TT24 Chad Pennington	4.00	10.00
TT25 Jim Brown	12.00	30.00
TT26 Jamal Lewis	3.00	8.00
TT27 Walter Payton	20.00	50.00
TT28 LaDainian Tomlinson	4.00	10.00
TT29 Johnny Unitas	20.00	50.00
TT30 Peyton Manning	8.00	20.00
TT31 Mark Bavaro	10.00	25.00
Jeremy Shockey		
TT32 Tony Dorsett	12.50	30.00
Clinton Portis		
TT33 Lynn Swann	30.00	60.00
Hines Ward		
TT34 Larry Csonka	10.00	25.00
Ricky Williams		
TT35 Troy Aikman	15.00	40.00
Quincy Carter		
TT36 Jim Kelly	12.50	30.00
Drew Bledsoe		
TT37 Mike Singletary	15.00	40.00
Brian Urlacher		
TT38 Warren Moon	12.50	30.00
David Carr		
TT39 Thurman Thomas	12.50	30.00
Travis Henry		
TT40 Marcus Allen	12.50	30.00
Priest Holmes		
TT41 Randall Cunningham	15.00	40.00
Donovan McNabb		
TT42 Joe Namath	30.00	60.00
Chad Pennington		
TT43 Jim Brown	15.00	40.00
Jamal Lewis		
TT44 Walter Payton	40.00	80.00
LaDainian Tomlinson		
TT45 Johnny Unitas	30.00	60.00
Peyton Manning		

2004 Donruss Elite Throwback Threads Prime

*PRIME TT1-TT30: 1X TO 2.5X BASIC INSERTS
*PRIME TT31-TT45: .8X TO 2X
STATED PRINT RUN 25 SER.#'d SETS

2004 Donruss Elite Turn of the Century Autographs

STATED PRINT RUN 125 SER.#'d SETS

105 Ben Roethlisberger	100.00	200.00
108 Bernard Berrian	12.00	30.00
116 Chris Gamble	10.00	25.00
117 Chris Perry	10.00	25.00
120 D.J. Hackett	10.00	25.00
124 DeAngelo Hall	12.00	30.00
126 Derrick Hamilton	8.00	20.00
128 Devard Darling	8.00	20.00
129 Devery Henderson	12.00	30.00
131 Drew Henson	8.00	20.00
132 Dunta Robinson	8.00	20.00
134 Eli Manning	100.00	200.00
135 Ernest Wilford	10.00	25.00
137 Greg Jones	8.00	20.00
139 J.P. Losman	10.00	25.00
146 Jerricho Cotchery	10.00	25.00
149 Johnnie Morant	8.00	20.00
150 Jonathan Vilma	12.00	30.00
152 Josh Harris	8.00	20.00
153 Julius Jones	10.00	25.00
156 Keary Colbert	8.00	20.00
159 Kellen Winslow Jr.	12.00	30.00
162 Kevin Jones	10.00	25.00
163 Larry Fitzgerald	60.00	120.00
164 Lee Evans	12.00	30.00
165 Luke McCown	10.00	25.00
167 Matt Schaub	25.00	60.00
173 Michael Clayton	10.00	25.00
174 Michael Jenkins	12.00	30.00
175 Michael Turner	15.00	40.00
179 Philip Rivers	50.00	100.00
180 Quincy Wilson	10.00	25.00
183 Rashaun Woods	8.00	20.00
184 Reggie Williams	10.00	25.00
185 Ricardo Colclough	10.00	25.00
187 Roy Williams WR	12.00	30.00
188 Samie Parker	8.00	20.00
192 Steven Jackson	20.00	50.00
194 Tatum Bell	10.00	25.00
196 Tommie Harris	12.00	30.00
198 Vince Wilfork	12.00	30.00
200 Will Smith	10.00	25.00

2005 Donruss Elite

Donruss Elite was initially released in late-June 2005. The base set consists of 200-cards including 100-rookies serial numbered to 499. Hobby boxes contained 20-packs of 5-cards and carried an S.R.P. of $5 per pack. Three parallel sets and a variety of inserts can be found seeded in packs highlighted by the Turn of the Century Autographs and Passing the Torch Autographs inserts.

COMP.SET w/o SP's (100)	7.50	20.00
101-200 PRINT RUN 499 SER.#'d SETS		
1 Kurt Warner	.30	.75
2 Larry Fitzgerald	.30	.75
3 Anquan Boldin	.25	.60
4 Emmitt Smith	.60	1.50
5 Michael Vick	.30	.75
6 Warrick Dunn	.25	.60
7 Alge Crumpler	.25	.60
8 Jamal Lewis	.25	.60
9 Kyle Boller	.25	.60
10 Ray Lewis	.30	.75
11 Drew Bledsoe	.30	.75
12 Willis McGahee	.30	.75
13 Travis Henry	.20	.50
14 Eric Moulds	.20	.50
15 Rex Grossman	.25	.60
16 Brian Urlacher	.30	.75
17 Thomas Jones	.30	.75
18 Carson Palmer	.30	.75
19 Rudi Johnson	.25	.60
20 Chad Johnson	.25	.60
21 J.P. Losman	.20	.50
22 Lee Suggs	.20	.50

2005 Donruss Elite

23 Antonio Bryant	.20	.50
24 Julius Jones	.20	.50
25 Roy Williams S	.20	.50
26 Keyshawn Johnson	.25	.60
27 Jake Plummer	.25	.60
28 Tatum Bell	.20	.50
29 Rod Smith	.25	.60
30 Joey Harrington	.25	.60
31 Kevin Jones	.20	.50
32 Roy Williams WR	.25	.60
33 Brett Favre	.75	2.00
34 Ahman Green	.25	.60
35 Javon Walker	.20	.50
36 David Carr	.20	.50
37 Andre Johnson	.30	.75
38 Domanick Davis	.20	.50
39 Peyton Manning	.60	1.50
40 Edgerrin James	.25	.60
41 Brandon Stokley	.20	.50
42 Reggie Wayne	.30	.75
43 Marvin Harrison	.30	.75
44 Byron Leftwich	.25	.60
45 Jimmy Smith	.25	.60
46 Fred Taylor	.25	.60
47 Trent Green	.25	.60
48 Priest Holmes	.25	.60
49 Tony Gonzalez	.25	.60
50 A.J. Feeley	.20	.50
51 Chris Chambers	.25	.60
52 Daunte Culpepper	.25	.60
53 Randy Moss	.30	.75
54 Onterrio Smith	.20	.50
55 Corey Dillon	.25	.60
56 Tom Brady	.60	1.50
57 David Givens	.20	.50
58 Aaron Brooks	.20	.50
59 Deuce McAllister	.25	.60
60 Joe Horn	.25	.60
61 Eli Manning	.50	1.25
62 Tiki Barber	.30	.75
63 Jeremy Shockey	.30	.75
64 Chad Pennington	.30	.75
65 Curtis Martin	.30	.75
66 Santana Moss	.25	.60
67 Kerry Collins	.25	.60
68 Jerry Porter	.20	.50
69 Donovan McNabb	.30	.75
70 Terrell Owens	.30	.75
71 Brian Westbrook	.25	.60
72 Ben Roethlisberger	.50	1.25
73 Plaxico Burress	.25	.60
74 Hines Ward	.30	.75
75 Jerome Bettis	.30	.75
76 Duce Staley	.25	.60
77 Antonio Gates	.30	.75
78 Drew Brees	.30	.75
79 LaDainian Tomlinson	.30	.75
80 Brandon Lloyd	.20	.50
81 Kevan Barlow	.20	.50
82 Matt Hasselbeck	.25	.60
83 Shaun Alexander	.25	.60
84 Darrell Jackson	.20	.50
85 Jerry Rice	.60	1.50
86 Marc Bulger	.25	.60
87 Marshall Faulk	.30	.75
88 Steven Jackson	.30	.75
89 Isaac Bruce	.25	.60
90 Torry Holt	.25	.60
91 Michael Clayton	.20	.50
92 Brian Griese	.25	.60
93 Mike Alstott	.25	.60
94 Steve McNair	.30	.75
95 Derrick Mason	.25	.60
96 Chris Brown	.20	.50
97 Drew Bennett	.25	.60
98 Patrick Ramsey	.25	.60
99 Clinton Portis	.25	.60
100 LaVar Arrington	.25	.60
101 Aaron Rodgers RC	60.00	120.00
102 Adam Jones RC	3.00	8.00
103 Adrian McPherson RC	2.50	6.00
104A Alex Smith TE ERR RC	2.50	6.00
(49ers logo on front)		
104B Alex Smith TE COR RC	2.50	6.00
(Buccaneers logo on front)		
105A Alex Smith QB ERR RC	6.00	15.00
(Buccaneers logo on front)		
105B Alex Smith QB COR RC	6.00	15.00
(49ers logo on front)		
106 Alvin Pearman RC	2.50	6.00
107 Andrew Walter RC	3.00	8.00
108 Anthony Davis RC	2.50	6.00
109 Antrel Rolle RC	4.00	10.00
110 Anttaj Hawthorne RC	2.50	6.00
111 Brandon Browner RC	4.00	10.00
112 Brandon Jacobs RC	5.00	12.00
113 Braylon Edwards RC	5.00	12.00
114 Brock Berlin RC	3.00	8.00
115 Brandon Jones RC	3.00	8.00
116 Bryant McFadden RC	3.00	8.00
117 Carlos Rogers RC	4.00	10.00
118 Cadillac Williams RC	4.00	10.00
119 Cedric Benson RC	4.00	10.00
120 Cedric Houston RC	4.00	10.00
121 Channing Crowder RC	3.00	8.00
122 Charles Frederick RC	2.50	6.00
123 Charlie Frye RC	4.00	10.00
124 Chase Lyman RC	2.50	6.00
125 Chris Henry RC	4.00	10.00
126 Chris Rix RC	3.00	8.00
127 Ciatrick Fason RC	2.50	6.00
128 Corey Webster RC	3.00	8.00
129 Courtney Roby RC	3.00	8.00
130 Craig Bragg RC	2.50	6.00
131 Craphonso Thorpe RC	2.50	6.00
132 Damien Nash RC	3.00	8.00
133 Dan Cody RC	3.00	8.00
134 Dan Orlovsky RC	4.00	10.00
135 Dante Ridgeway RC	2.50	6.00
136 Darian Durant RC	2.50	6.00
137 Darren Sproles RC	4.00	10.00
138 Darryl Blackstock RC	2.50	6.00
139 David Greene RC	2.50	6.00
140 David Pollack RC	3.00	8.00
141 DeMarcus Ware RC	8.00	20.00
142 Derek Anderson RC	3.00	8.00
143 Derrick Johnson RC	3.00	8.00
144 Erasmus James RC	3.00	8.00
145 Eric Shelton RC	2.50	6.00
146 Ernest Shazor RC	3.00	8.00
147 Fabian Washington RC	3.00	8.00
148 Frank Gore UER RC	6.00	15.00
149 Fred Amey RC	3.00	8.00
150 Fred Gibson RC	3.00	8.00
151 Maurice Clarett	3.00	8.00
152 Gino Guidugli RC	2.50	6.00
153 Heath Miller RC	5.00	12.00
154 J.J. Arrington RC	3.00	8.00
155 J.R. Russell RC	2.50	6.00
156 Jason Campbell RC	5.00	12.00
157 Jason White RC	4.00	10.00
158 Jerome Mathis RC	4.00	10.00
159 Josh Bullocks RC	3.00	8.00
160 Josh Davis RC	2.50	6.00
161 Justin Miller RC	3.00	8.00
162 Justin Tuck RC	5.00	12.00
163 Kay-Jay Harris RC	2.50	6.00
164 Kevin Burnett RC	3.00	8.00
165 Kyle Orton RC	4.00	10.00
166 Larry Brackins RC	2.50	6.00
167 Marcus Spears RC	3.00	8.00
168 Marion Barber RC	4.00	10.00
169 Mark Bradley RC	2.50	6.00
170 Mark Clayton RC	4.00	10.00
171 Marlin Jackson RC	2.50	6.00
172 Matt Jones RC	4.00	10.00
173 Matt Roth RC	3.00	8.00
174 Mike Patterson RC	2.50	6.00
175 Mike Williams	4.00	10.00
176 Airese Currie RC	2.50	6.00
177 Reggie Brown RC	2.50	6.00
178 Roddy White RC	5.00	12.00
179 Ronnie Brown RC	5.00	12.00
180 Roscoe Parrish RC	2.50	6.00
181 Roydell Williams RC	3.00	8.00
182 Ryan Fitzpatrick RC	6.00	15.00
183 Rasheed Marshall RC	3.00	8.00
184 Ryan Moats RC	3.00	8.00
185 Shaun Cody RC	3.00	8.00
186 Shawne Merriman RC	4.00	10.00
187 Chad Owens RC	3.00	8.00
188 Stefan LeFors RC	2.50	6.00
189 Steve Savoy RC	2.50	6.00
190 T.A. McLendon RC	2.50	6.00
191 Tab Perry RC	2.50	6.00
192 Taylor Stubblefield RC	2.50	6.00
193 Terrence Murphy RC	2.50	6.00
194 Thomas Davis RC	2.50	6.00
195 Timmy Chang RC	3.00	8.00
196 Travis Johnson RC	2.50	6.00
197 Troy Williamson RC	3.00	8.00
198 Vernand Morency RC	3.00	8.00
199 Vincent Jackson RC	5.00	12.00
200 Walter Reyes RC	2.50	6.00

2005 Donruss Elite Aspirations

*VETS/70-99: 5X TO 12X BASIC CARDS
*ROOKIES/70-99: .6X TO 1.5X
*VETS/44-69: 6X TO 15X
*ROOKIES/44-69: .8X TO 2X
*VETS/20-29: 10X TO 25X
*ROOKIES/20-29: 1.2X TO 3X
STATED PRINT RUN 1-99
#'d UNDER 20 TOO SCARCE TO PRICE

101 Aaron Rodgers/92	75.00	135.00
105A Alex Smith QB ERR/89	10.00	25.00
(Buccaneers logo on front)		

2005 Donruss Elite Status Gold

*VETS: 10X TO 25X BASIC CARDS
*ROOKIES: 1.2X TO 3X BASIC CARDS
STATED PRINT RUN 24 SER.#'d SETS

101 Aaron Rodgers	150.00	300.00

2005 Donruss Elite Status Red

*VETS/70-99: 5X TO 12X BASIC CARDS
*ROOKIES/70-99: .6X TO 1.5X
*VETS/45-69: 6X TO 15X
*ROOKIES/45-69: .8X TO 2X
*VETS/30-44: 8X TO 20X
*ROOKIES/30-44: 1X TO 2.5X
*VETS/20-29: 10X TO 25X
*ROOKIES/20-29: 1.2X TO 3X
STATED PRINT RUN 1-99
#'d/19 or LESS TOO SCARCE TO PRICE

2005 Donruss Elite Back to the Future Green

COMPLETE SET (15)	20.00	50.00

STATED PRINT RUN 1000 SER.#'d SETS
*BLUE/500: .5X TO 1.2X GREEN/1000
*RED/250: .6X TO 1.5X GREEN/1000

BF1 Randall Cunningham	1.50	4.00
Donovan McNabb		
BF2 Dan Fouts	1.50	4.00
Drew Brees		
BF3 Marcus Allen	1.50	4.00
Priest Holmes		
BF4 Sterling Sharpe	1.25	3.00
Javon Walker		
BF5 Steve Largent	1.50	4.00
Darrell Jackson		
BF6 Jerome Bettis	1.50	4.00
Duce Staley		
BF7 Michael Irvin	1.50	4.00
Keyshawn Johnson		
BF8 Eric Moulds	1.25	3.00
Lee Evans		
BF9 Jimmy Smith	1.25	3.00
Reggie Williams		
BF10 Walter Payton	4.00	10.00
Thomas Jones		
BF11 Marshall Faulk	1.50	4.00
Steven Jackson		
BF12 Warren Moon	1.50	4.00
Steve McNair		
BF13 Curtis Martin	1.50	4.00
Corey Dillon		
BF14 Keyshawn Johnson	1.25	3.00
Michael Clayton		
BF15 Corey Dillon	1.25	3.00
Rudi Johnson		

2005 Donruss Elite Back to the Future Jerseys

STATED PRINT RUN 100 SER.#'d SETS
UNPRICED PRIME PRINT RUN 10

BF1 Randall Cunningham	8.00	20.00
Donovan McNabb		
BF2 Dan Fouts	8.00	20.00
Drew Brees		
BF3 Marcus Allen	8.00	20.00
Priest Holmes		
BF4 Sterling Sharpe	6.00	15.00
Javon Walker		
BF5 Steve Largent	8.00	20.00
Darrell Jackson		
BF6 Jerome Bettis	8.00	20.00
Duce Staley		
BF7 Michael Irvin	8.00	20.00
Keyshawn Johnson		
BF8 Eric Moulds	6.00	15.00
Lee Evans		
BF9 Jimmy Smith	6.00	15.00
Reggie Williams		
BF10 Walter Payton	20.00	50.00
Thomas Jones		
BF11 Marshall Faulk	8.00	20.00
Steven Jackson		
BF12 Warren Moon	8.00	20.00
Steve McNair		
BF13 Curtis Martin	8.00	20.00
Corey Dillon		
BF14 Keyshawn Johnson	6.00	15.00
Michael Clayton		
BF15 Corey Dillon	6.00	15.00
Rudi Johnson		

2005 Donruss Elite Career Best Red

RED STATED PRINT RUN 1000
*BLACK/250: .6X TO 1.5X RED/1000
*GOLD/500: .5X TO 1.2X RED/1000

CB1 Andre Johnson	1.25	3.00
CB2 Barry Sanders	2.50	6.00
CB3 Ben Roethlisberger	2.00	5.00
CB4 Brett Favre	3.00	8.00
CB5 Brian Urlacher	1.25	3.00
CB6 Brian Westbrook	1.00	2.50
CB7 Byron Leftwich	1.00	2.50
CB8 Carson Palmer	1.25	3.00
CB9 Chad Johnson	1.00	2.50
CB10 Chad Pennington	1.25	3.00
CB11 Corey Dillon	1.00	2.50
CB12 Dan Marino	4.00	10.00
CB13 Daunte Culpepper	1.00	2.50
CB14 David Carr	.75	2.00
CB15 Deuce McAllister	1.00	2.50
CB16 Donovan McNabb	1.25	3.00
CB17 Drew Bledsoe	1.25	3.00
CB18 Edgerrin James	1.00	2.50
CB19 Jake Delhomme	1.00	2.50
CB20 Jake Plummer	1.00	2.50
CB21 Jamal Lewis	1.00	2.50
CB22 Javon Walker	.75	2.00
CB23 Jerry Rice	2.50	6.00
CB24 Joe Montana	4.00	10.00
CB25 Joey Harrington	1.00	2.50
CB26 John Elway	3.00	8.00
CB27 Julius Jones	.75	2.00
CB28 Kevin Jones	.75	2.00
CB29 LaDainian Tomlinson	1.25	3.00
CB30 Marc Bulger	1.00	2.50
CB31 Marshall Faulk	1.25	3.00
CB32 Marvin Harrison	1.25	3.00
CB33 Matt Hasselbeck	1.00	2.50
CB34 Michael Clayton	.75	2.00
CB35 Michael Vick	1.25	3.00
CB36 Peyton Manning	2.50	6.00
CB37 Priest Holmes	1.00	2.50
CB38 Randy Moss	1.25	3.00
CB39 Larry Fitzgerald	1.25	3.00
CB40 Rudi Johnson	1.00	2.50
CB41 Shaun Alexander	1.00	2.50
CB42 Steve McNair	1.25	3.00
CB43 Steve Young	2.00	5.00
CB44 Terrell Owens	1.25	3.00
CB45 Tom Brady	2.50	6.00
CB46 Torry Holt	1.00	2.50
CB47 Trent Green	1.00	2.50
CB48 Troy Aikman	2.00	5.00
CB49 Walter Payton	4.00	10.00
CB50 Willis McGahee	1.25	3.00

2005 Donruss Elite Career Best Jerseys

STATED PRINT RUN 175 SER.#'d SETS
*YEAR/77-104: .5X TO 1.2X BASIC JSY/175

CB1 Andre Johnson	4.00	10.00
CB2 Barry Sanders	8.00	20.00
CB3 Ben Roethlisberger	6.00	15.00
CB4 Brett Favre	10.00	25.00
CB5 Brian Urlacher	4.00	10.00
CB6 Brian Westbrook	3.00	8.00
CB7 Byron Leftwich	3.00	8.00
CB8 Carson Palmer	4.00	10.00
CB9 Chad Johnson	3.00	8.00
CB10 Chad Pennington	4.00	10.00
CB11 Corey Dillon	3.00	8.00
CB12 Dan Marino	12.00	30.00
CB13 Daunte Culpepper	3.00	8.00
CB14 David Carr	2.50	6.00
CB15 Deuce McAllister	3.00	8.00
CB16 Donovan McNabb	4.00	10.00
CB17 Drew Bledsoe	4.00	10.00
CB18 Edgerrin James	3.00	8.00
CB19 Jake Delhomme	3.00	8.00
CB20 Jake Plummer	3.00	8.00
CB21 Jamal Lewis	3.00	8.00
CB22 Javon Walker	2.50	6.00
CB23 Jerry Rice	8.00	20.00
CB24 Joe Montana	12.00	30.00
CB25 Joey Harrington	3.00	8.00
CB26 John Elway	8.00	20.00
CB27 Julius Jones	2.50	6.00
CB28 Kevin Jones	2.50	6.00
CB29 LaDainian Tomlinson	4.00	10.00
CB30 Marc Bulger	3.00	8.00
CB31 Marshall Faulk	4.00	10.00
CB32 Marvin Harrison	4.00	10.00
CB33 Matt Hasselbeck	3.00	8.00
CB34 Michael Clayton	2.50	6.00
CB35 Michael Vick	4.00	10.00
CB36 Peyton Manning	8.00	20.00
CB37 Priest Holmes	3.00	8.00
CB38 Randy Moss	4.00	10.00
CB39 Larry Fitzgerald	4.00	10.00
CB40 Rudi Johnson	3.00	8.00
CB41 Shaun Alexander	3.00	8.00
CB42 Steve McNair	4.00	10.00
CB43 Steve Young	6.00	15.00
CB44 Terrell Owens	4.00	10.00
CB45 Tom Brady	8.00	20.00
CB46 Torry Holt	3.00	8.00
CB47 Trent Green	3.00	8.00
CB48 Troy Aikman	6.00	15.00
CB49 Walter Payton	12.00	30.00
CB50 Willis McGahee	4.00	10.00

2005 Donruss Elite College Ties

STATED ODDS 1:20

CT1 Kyle Boller	8.00	20.00
Aaron Rodgers		
CT2 Steve Smith	2.50	6.00
Alex Smith QB		
CT3 Roy Williams WR	1.50	4.00
Cedric Benson		
CT4 Bo Jackson	1.25	3.00
Ronnie Brown		
CT5 Rudi Johnson	1.00	2.50
Cadillac Williams		
CT6 Tom Brady	3.00	8.00
Braylon Edwards		
CT7 Dunta Robinson	1.25	3.00
Troy Williamson		
CT8 Tatum Bell	1.00	2.50
Vernand Morency		
CT9 Rex Grossman	1.25	3.00
Ciatrick Fason		
CT10 Clinton Portis	1.25	3.00
Roscoe Parrish		

2005 Donruss Elite College Ties Autographs

STATED PRINT RUN 50 SER.#'d SETS

CT1 Kyle Boller	125.00	250.00
Aaron Rodgers		
CT2 Steve Smith	40.00	80.00
Alex Smith QB		
CT3 Roy Williams WR	30.00	80.00
Cedric Benson		
CT4 Bo Jackson	60.00	120.00
Ronnie Brown		
CT5 Rudi Johnson	40.00	80.00
Cadillac Williams		
CT6 Tom Brady	100.00	200.00
Braylon Edwards		
CT7 Dunta Robinson	15.00	40.00
Troy Williamson		
CT8 Tatum Bell AU	15.00	40.00
Vernand Morency No AU		
CT9 Rex Grossman	20.00	50.00
Ciatrick Fason		
CT10 Clinton Portis	20.00	50.00
Roscoe Parrish		

2005 Donruss Elite Elite Teams Silver

SILVER STATED PRINT RUN 1000
*GOLD/250: .6X TO 1.5X SILVER/1000
*RED/500: .5X TO 1.2X SILVER/1000

ET1 Anquan Boldin	1.50	4.00
Larry Fitzgerald		
Josh McCown		
ET2 Michael Vick	1.50	4.00
T.J. Duckett		
Peerless Price		
ET3 Jamal Lewis	1.25	3.00
Kyle Boller		
Todd Heap		
ET4 Willis McGahee	1.50	4.00
Drew Bledsoe		
Eric Moulds		
ET5 Jake Delhomme	1.25	3.00
Steve Smith		
Stephen Davis		
ET6 Carson Palmer	1.50	4.00
Chad Johnson		
Rudi Johnson		
ET7 Julius Jones	1.25	3.00
Keyshawn Johnson		
Roy Williams S		
ET8 Kevin Jones	1.25	3.00
Joey Harrington		
Roy Williams WR		
ET9 Brett Favre	4.00	10.00
Ahman Green		
Javon Walker		
ET10 David Carr	1.50	4.00
Domanick Davis		
Andre Johnson		
ET11 Peyton Manning	3.00	8.00
Marvin Harrison		
Edgerrin James		
ET12 Byron Leftwich	1.25	3.00
Fred Taylor		
Jimmy Smith		
ET13 Priest Holmes	1.25	3.00
Trent Green		
Dante Hall		
ET14 Randy Moss	1.50	4.00
Daunte Culpepper		
Michael Bennett		
ET15 Tom Brady	3.00	8.00
Corey Dillon		
Ty Law		
ET16 Deuce McAllister	1.25	3.00
Aaron Brooks		
Donte Stallworth		
ET17 Eli Manning	2.50	6.00
Jeremy Shockey		
Amani Toomer		
ET18 Chad Pennington	1.50	4.00
Curtis Martin		
Santana Moss		
ET19 Donovan McNabb	1.25	3.00
Terrell Owens		
Brian Westbrook		
ET20 Ben Roethlisberger	2.50	6.00
Plaxico Burress		
Duce Staley		
ET21 Shaun Alexander	1.25	3.00
Matt Hasselbeck		
Darrell Jackson		
ET22 Marc Bulger	1.50	4.00
Marshall Faulk		
Isaac Bruce		
ET23 Michael Clayton	1.25	3.00
Mike Alstott		
Brad Johnson		
ET24 Chris Brown	1.50	4.00
Steve McNair		
Derrick Mason		
ET25 Clinton Portis	1.50	4.00
LaVar Arrington		
Laveranues Coles		

2005 Donruss Elite Elite Teams Jerseys

STATED PRINT RUN 100 SER.#'d SETS
*PRIME/25: .8X TO 2X BASIC JSY/100

ET1 Anquan Boldin	8.00	20.00
Larry Fitzgerald		
Josh McCown		
ET2 Michael Vick	8.00	20.00
T.J. Duckett		
Peerless Price		
ET3 Jamal Lewis	6.00	15.00
Kyle Boller		
Todd Heap		
ET4 Willis McGahee	8.00	20.00
Drew Bledsoe		
Eric Moulds		
ET5 Jake Delhomme	6.00	15.00
Steve Smith		
Stephen Davis		
ET6 Carson Palmer	8.00	20.00
Chad Johnson		
Rudi Johnson		
ET7 Julius Jones	6.00	15.00
Keyshawn Johnson		
Roy Williams S		
ET8 Kevin Jones	6.00	15.00
Joey Harrington		
Roy Williams WR		
ET9 Brett Favre	20.00	50.00
Ahman Green		
Javon Walker		
ET10 David Carr	8.00	20.00
Domanick Davis		
Andre Johnson		
ET11 Peyton Manning	15.00	40.00
Marvin Harrison		
Edgerrin James		
ET12 Byron Leftwich	6.00	15.00
Fred Taylor		
Jimmy Smith		
ET13 Priest Holmes	6.00	15.00
Trent Green		
Dante Hall		
ET14 Randy Moss	8.00	20.00
Daunte Culpepper		
Michael Bennett		
ET15 Tom Brady	15.00	40.00
Corey Dillon		
Ty Law		
ET16 Deuce McAllister	6.00	15.00
Aaron Brooks		
Donte Stallworth		
ET17 Eli Manning	12.00	30.00
Jeremy Shockey		
Amani Toomer		
ET18 Chad Pennington	8.00	20.00
Curtis Martin		
Santana Moss		
ET19 Donovan McNabb	6.00	15.00
Terrell Owens		
Brian Westbrook		
ET20 Ben Roethlisberger	12.00	30.00
Plaxico Burress		
Duce Staley		
ET21 Shaun Alexander	6.00	15.00
Matt Hasselbeck		
Darrell Jackson		
ET22 Marc Bulger	8.00	20.00
Marshall Faulk		
Isaac Bruce		
ET23 Michael Clayton	6.00	15.00
Mike Alstott		
Brad Johnson		
ET24 Chris Brown	8.00	20.00
Steve McNair		
Derrick Mason		
ET25 Clinton Portis	6.00	15.00
LaVar Arrington		
Laveranues Coles		

2005 Donruss Elite Face 2 Face Gold

GOLD STATED PRINT RUN 1000
*BLACK/500: .5X TO 1.2X GOLD/1000
*RED/250: .6X TO 1.5X GOLD/1000

CB1 Andre Johnson	1.25	3.00
Anquan Boldin		
CB2 David Carr	1.00	2.50
Byron Leftwich		
CB3 Daunte Culpepper	1.00	2.50
Joey Harrington		
CB4 Tom Brady	2.50	6.00
Chad Pennington		
CB5 John Elway	4.00	10.00
Brett Favre		
CB6 Dan Marino	4.00	10.00
Peyton Manning		
CB7 Troy Aikman	2.00	5.00
Donovan McNabb		
CB8 Deuce McAllister	1.00	2.50
Stephen Davis		
CB9 Randy Moss	1.25	3.00
Ahman Green		
CB10 Jamal Lewis	1.00	2.50
Kendrell Bell		
CB11 Priest Holmes	1.25	3.00
LaDainian Tomlinson		
CB12 Hines Ward	1.25	3.00
Chad Johnson		
CB13 Torry Holt	1.00	2.50
Koren Robinson		
CB14 Matt Hasselbeck	1.00	2.50
Marc Bulger		
CB15 Jerry Rice	2.50	6.00
Marvin Harrison		
CB16 Marshall Faulk	1.25	3.00
Shaun Alexander		
CB17 Ray Lewis	1.25	3.00
Brian Urlacher		
CB18 Jeremy Shockey	1.25	3.00
Todd Heap		
CB19 Jake Plummer	1.00	2.50
Trent Green		
CB20 Barry Sanders	3.00	8.00
Emmitt Smith		
CB21 Santana Moss	1.00	2.50
Chris Chambers		
CB22 Terrell Owens	1.25	3.00
Jeff Garcia		
CB23 Peyton Manning	2.50	6.00
Steve McNair		
CB24 Jake Delhomme	1.00	2.50
Steve Smith		
CB25 Joe Montana	4.00	10.00
Steve Young		

2005 Donruss Elite Face 2 Face Jerseys

JERSEY STATED PRINT RUN 250
*FACEMASK/125: .6X TO 1.5X JSY/250

CB1 Andre Johnson	5.00	12.00
Anquan Boldin		
CB2 David Carr	4.00	10.00
Byron Leftwich		
CB3 Daunte Culpepper	4.00	10.00
Joey Harrington		
CB4 Tom Brady	10.00	25.00
Chad Pennington		
CB5 John Elway	15.00	40.00
Brett Favre		
CB6 Dan Marino	15.00	40.00
Peyton Manning		
CB7 Troy Aikman	8.00	20.00
Donovan McNabb		
CB8 Deuce McAllister	4.00	10.00
Stephen Davis		
CB9 Randy Moss	5.00	12.00
Ahman Green		
CB10 Jamal Lewis	4.00	10.00
Kendrell Bell		
CB11 Priest Holmes	5.00	12.00
LaDainian Tomlinson		
CB12 Hines Ward	5.00	12.00
Chad Johnson		
CB13 Torry Holt	4.00	10.00
Koren Robinson		
CB14 Matt Hasselbeck	4.00	10.00
Marc Bulger		
CB15 Jerry Rice	10.00	25.00
Marvin Harrison		
CB16 Marshall Faulk	5.00	12.00
Shaun Alexander		
CB17 Ray Lewis	5.00	12.00
Brian Urlacher		
CB18 Jeremy Shockey	5.00	12.00
Todd Heap		
CB19 Jake Plummer	4.00	10.00
Trent Green		
CB20 Barry Sanders	12.00	30.00
Emmitt Smith		
CB21 Santana Moss	4.00	10.00
Chris Chambers		
CB22 Terrell Owens	5.00	12.00
Jeff Garcia		
CB23 Peyton Manning	10.00	25.00
Steve McNair		
CB24 Jake Delhomme	4.00	10.00
Steve Smith		
CB25 Joe Montana	15.00	40.00
Steve Young		

2005 Donruss Elite Passing the Torch Red

RED PT1-PT20 PRINT RUN 1000
RED PT21-PT30 PRINT RUN 750
*BLUE: .6X TO 1.5X RED/750-1000
BLUE PT1-PT20 PRINT RUN 250
BLUE PT21-PT30 PRINT RUN 100
*GREEN: .5X TO 1.2X RED/750-1000
GREEN PT1-PT20 PRINT RUN 500
GREEN PT21-PT30 PRINT RUN 250

PT1 Eric Dickerson	1.50	4.00
PT2 Steven Jackson	1.50	4.00
PT3 Thurman Thomas	2.00	5.00
PT4 Willis McGahee	1.50	4.00
PT5 Len Dawson	2.00	5.00
PT6 Trent Green	1.25	3.00
PT7 Terry Bradshaw	3.00	8.00
PT8 Ben Roethlisberger	2.50	6.00
PT9 Terrell Davis	2.00	5.00
PT10 Tatum Bell	1.00	2.50
PT11 Boomer Esiason	1.50	4.00
PT12 Carson Palmer	1.50	4.00
PT13 Cris Collinsworth	1.50	4.00
PT14 Chad Johnson	1.25	3.00
PT15 John Riggins	2.00	5.00
PT16 Clinton Portis	1.25	3.00
PT17 Dan Marino	5.00	12.00
PT18 Peyton Manning	3.00	8.00
PT19 Joe Montana	5.00	12.00
PT20 Tom Brady	3.00	8.00
PT21 Eric Dickerson	2.00	5.00
Steven Jackson		
PT22 Thurman Thomas	2.00	5.00
Willis McGahee		
PT23 Len Dawson	2.00	5.00
Trent Green		
PT24 Terry Bradshaw	3.00	8.00
Ben Roethlisberger		
PT25 Terrell Davis	2.00	5.00
Tatum Bell		
PT26 Boomer Esiason	2.00	5.00
Carson Palmer		
PT27 Cris Collinsworth	1.50	4.00
Chad Johnson		
PT28 John Riggins	2.00	5.00
Clinton Portis		
PT29 Dan Marino	5.00	12.00
Peyton Manning		
PT30 Joe Montana	5.00	12.00
Tom Brady		

2005 Donruss Elite Passing the Torch Autographs

PT1-PT20 AUTO PRINT RUN 100
PT21-PT30 DUAL AU PRINT RUN 50

PT1 Eric Dickerson	15.00	40.00
PT2 Steven Jackson	15.00	40.00
PT3 Thurman Thomas	20.00	50.00
PT4 Willis McGahee	15.00	40.00
PT5 Len Dawson	20.00	50.00
PT6 Trent Green	12.00	30.00
PT7 Terry Bradshaw	50.00	100.00
PT8 Ben Roethlisberger	60.00	120.00
PT9 Terrell Davis	20.00	50.00
PT10 Tatum Bell	10.00	25.00
PT11 Boomer Esiason	15.00	40.00
PT12 Carson Palmer	15.00	40.00
PT13 Cris Collinsworth	15.00	40.00
PT14 Chad Johnson	12.00	30.00
PT15 John Riggins	20.00	50.00
PT16 Clinton Portis	12.00	30.00
PT17 Dan Marino	75.00	150.00
PT18 Peyton Manning	60.00	100.00
PT19 Joe Montana	75.00	150.00
PT20 Tom Brady	125.00	200.00
PT21 Eric Dickerson	30.00	80.00
Steven Jackson		
PT22 Thurman Thomas	30.00	80.00
Willis McGahee		
PT23 Len Dawson	30.00	80.00
Trent Green		
PT24 Terry Bradshaw	175.00	350.00
Ben Roethlisberger		
PT25 Terrell Davis	30.00	80.00
Tatum Bell		
PT26 Boomer Esiason	30.00	80.00
Carson Palmer		
PT27 Cris Collinsworth	25.00	60.00
Chad Johnson		
PT28 John Riggins	30.00	80.00
Clinton Portis		
PT29 Dan Marino	175.00	300.00
Peyton Manning		
PT30 Joe Montana	250.00	400.00
Tom Brady		

2005 Donruss Elite Series

COMPLETE SET (25)	25.00	60.00

STATED PRINT RUN 1000 SER.#'d SETS

ES1 Ben Roethlisberger	2.00	5.00
ES2 Brett Favre	3.00	8.00
ES3 Brian Urlacher	1.25	3.00
ES4 Byron Leftwich	1.00	2.50
ES5 Carson Palmer	1.25	3.00
ES6 Chad Pennington	1.25	3.00
ES7 Clinton Portis	1.00	2.50
ES8 Corey Dillon	1.00	2.50
ES9 Daunte Culpepper	1.00	2.50
ES10 David Carr	.75	2.00
ES11 Donovan McNabb	1.25	3.00
ES12 Jerry Rice	2.50	6.00
ES13 Julius Jones	.75	2.00
ES14 Kevin Jones	.75	2.00
ES15 LaDainian Tomlinson	1.25	3.00
ES16 Marvin Harrison	1.25	3.00
ES17 Michael Vick	1.25	3.00
ES18 Peyton Manning	2.50	6.00
ES19 Priest Holmes	1.00	2.50
ES20 Randy Moss	1.25	3.00
ES21 Ray Lewis	1.25	3.00
ES22 Shaun Alexander	1.00	2.50
ES23 Terrell Owens	1.25	3.00
ES24 Tom Brady	2.50	6.00
ES25 Willis McGahee	1.25	3.00

2005 Donruss Elite Series Jerseys

STATED PRINT RUN 199 SER.#'d SETS
*PRIME/25: 1X TO 2.5X BASIC JSY/199

ES1 Ben Roethlisberger	6.00	15.00
ES2 Brett Favre	10.00	25.00
ES3 Brian Urlacher	4.00	10.00
ES4 Byron Leftwich	3.00	8.00
ES5 Carson Palmer	4.00	10.00
ES6 Chad Pennington	4.00	10.00
ES7 Clinton Portis	3.00	8.00
ES8 Corey Dillon	3.00	8.00
ES9 Daunte Culpepper	3.00	8.00
ES10 David Carr	2.50	6.00
ES11 Donovan McNabb	4.00	10.00
ES12 Jerry Rice	8.00	20.00
ES13 Julius Jones	2.50	6.00
ES14 Kevin Jones	2.50	6.00
ES15 LaDainian Tomlinson	4.00	10.00
ES16 Marvin Harrison	4.00	10.00
ES17 Michael Vick	4.00	10.00
ES18 Peyton Manning	8.00	20.00
ES19 Priest Holmes	3.00	8.00
ES20 Randy Moss	4.00	10.00
ES21 Ray Lewis	4.00	10.00
ES22 Shaun Alexander	3.00	8.00
ES23 Terrell Owens	4.00	10.00
ES24 Tom Brady	8.00	20.00
ES25 Willis McGahee	4.00	10.00

2005 Donruss Elite Throwback Threads

TT1-TT30 STATED PRINT RUN 150
TT31-TT45 STATED PRINT RUN 75
*PRIME TT1-TT30: .8X TO 2X BASIC JSY
PRIME TT1-TT30 PRINT RUN 25
UNPRICED PRIME TT31-TT45 PRINT RUN 10

TT1 Joe Montana 49ers	15.00	40.00
TT2 Tom Brady	10.00	25.00
TT3 Joe Montana Chiefs	15.00	40.00
TT4 Trent Green	4.00	10.00
TT5 Joe Namath	10.00	25.00
TT6 Chad Pennington	5.00	12.00
TT7 John Elway	12.00	30.00
TT8 Jake Plummer	4.00	10.00
TT9 John Riggins	6.00	15.00
TT10 Clinton Portis	4.00	10.00
TT11 Tony Dorsett	5.00	12.00
TT12 Julius Jones	3.00	8.00
TT13 Thurman Thomas	6.00	15.00
TT14 Willis McGahee	5.00	12.00
TT15 Terry Bradshaw	10.00	25.00
TT16 Ben Roethlisberger	8.00	20.00
TT17 Fran Tarkenton Vikings	6.00	15.00
TT18 Daunte Culpepper	4.00	10.00
TT19 Dan Marino	15.00	40.00
TT20 Peyton Manning	10.00	25.00
TT21 Barry Sanders	10.00	25.00
TT22 Kevin Jones	3.00	8.00
TT23 Fran Tarkenton Giants	6.00	15.00
TT24 Eli Manning	8.00	20.00
TT25 Steve Young	8.00	20.00
TT26 Michael Vick	5.00	12.00
TT27 Earl Campbell	6.00	15.00
TT28 Domanick Davis	3.00	8.00
TT29 Boomer Esiason	5.00	12.00
TT30 Carson Palmer	5.00	12.00
TT31 Joe Montana	30.00	80.00
Tom Brady		
TT32 Joe Montana	30.00	60.00
Trent Green		
TT33 Joe Namath	12.50	30.00
Chad Pennington		
TT34 John Elway	20.00	50.00
Jake Plummer		
TT35 John Riggins	15.00	40.00
Clinton Portis		
TT36 Tony Dorsett	10.00	25.00
Julius Jones		
TT37 Thurman Thomas	10.00	25.00
Willis McGahee		
TT38 Terry Bradshaw	40.00	100.00
Ben Roethlisberger		
TT39 Fran Tarkenton	10.00	25.00
Daunte Culpepper		
TT40 Dan Marino	30.00	80.00
Peyton Manning		
TT41 Barry Sanders	25.00	60.00
Kevin Jones		
TT42 Fran Tarkenton	12.50	30.00
Eli Manning		
TT43 Steve Young	12.50	30.00
Michael Vick		
TT44 Earl Campbell	7.50	20.00
Domanick Davis		
TT45 Boomer Esiason	10.00	25.00
Carson Palmer		

2005 Donruss Elite Turn of the Century Autographs

STATED PRINT RUN 125 SER.#'d SETS
101 Aaron Rodgers 250.00 400.00
102 Adam Jones 8.00 20.00
103 Adrian McPherson 8.00 20.00
105 Alex Smith QB ERR 40.00 80.00
108 Anthony Davis 8.00 20.00
109 Antrel Rolle 12.00 30.00
113 Braylon Edwards 30.00 80.00
116 Bryant McFadden 10.00 25.00
117 Carlos Rogers 12.00 30.00
118 Cadillac Williams 12.00 30.00
119 Cedric Benson 15.00 40.00
123 Charlie Frye 12.00 30.00
127 Ciatrick Fason 8.00 20.00
129 Courtney Roby 10.00 25.00
130 Craig Bragg 8.00 20.00
131 Craphonso Thorpe 8.00 20.00
133 Dan Cody 10.00 25.00
139 David Greene 8.00 20.00
140 David Pollack 10.00 25.00
143 Derrick Johnson 10.00 25.00
145 Eric Shelton 8.00 20.00
148 Frank Gore 20.00 50.00
151 Maurice Clarett 8.00 20.00
153 Heath Miller 15.00 40.00
154 J.J. Arrington 10.00 25.00
156 Jason Campbell 15.00 40.00
157 Jason White 12.00 30.00
158 Jerome Mathis 12.00 30.00
160 Josh Davis 8.00 20.00
163 Kay-Jay Harris 8.00 20.00
165 Kyle Orton 12.00 30.00
168 Marion Barber 12.00 30.00
169 Mark Bradley 8.00 20.00
170 Mark Clayton 12.00 30.00
172 Matt Jones 12.00 30.00
175 Mike Williams 12.00 30.00
177 Reggie Brown 8.00 20.00
178 Roddy White 15.00 40.00
179 Ronnie Brown 40.00 100.00
180 Roscoe Parrish 8.00 20.00
184 Ryan Moats 10.00 25.00
186 Shawne Merriman 12.00 30.00
188 Stefan LeFors 8.00 20.00
189 Steve Savoy 8.00 20.00
192 Taylor Stubblefield 8.00 20.00
193 Terrence Murphy 8.00 20.00
196 Travis Johnson 8.00 20.00
197 Troy Williamson 10.00 25.00
198 Vernand Morency 10.00 25.00
199 Vincent Jackson 15.00 40.00

2006 Donruss Elite

This 225-card set was released in June, 2008. The set was issued into the hobby in five card packs, with an $5 SRP, which came 20 packs to a box. The first 100 cards in this set are veterans sequenced in team alphabetical order while cards numbered 101-225 feature rookies sequenced in first name order. The Rookie Cards were all printed to a stated print run of 599 serial numbered sets.

COMP.SET w/o RC's (100) 7.50 20.00
ROOKIE PRINT RUN 599 SER.#'d SETS
1 Anquan Boldin .30 .75
2 Kurt Warner .40 1.00
3 Larry Fitzgerald .40 1.00
4 Marcel Shipp .25 .60
5 Alge Crumpler .30 .75
6 Michael Vick .40 1.00
7 Warrick Dunn .30 .75
8 Derrick Mason .30 .75
9 Jamal Lewis .30 .75
10 Kyle Boller .30 .75
11 J.P. Losman .30 .75
12 Lee Evans .30 .75
13 Willis McGahee .30 .75
14 Jake Delhomme .30 .75
15 Stephen Davis .30 .75
16 Steve Smith .40 1.00
17 Cedric Benson .30 .75
18 Kyle Orton .40 1.00
19 Thomas Jones .30 .75
20 Carson Palmer .40 1.00
21 Chad Johnson .30 .75
22 Rudi Johnson .30 .75
23 Braylon Edwards .30 .75
24 Reuben Droughns .30 .75
25 Trent Dilfer .30 .75
26 Drew Bledsoe .40 1.00
27 Julius Jones .25 .60
28 Keyshawn Johnson .30 .75
29 Jake Plummer .30 .75
30 Rod Smith .30 .75
31 Tatum Bell .25 .60
32 Joey Harrington .25 .60
33 Kevin Jones .25 .60
34 Roy Williams WR .30 .75
35 Aaron Rodgers .75 2.00
36 Brett Favre .75 2.00
37 Ahman Green .30 .75
38 Andre Johnson .40 1.00
39 David Carr .25 .60
40 Domanick Davis .25 .60
41 Edgerrin James .30 .75
42 Marvin Harrison .40 1.00
43 Peyton Manning .60 1.50
44 Byron Leftwich .30 .75
45 Fred Taylor .30 .75
46 Jimmy Smith .30 .75
47 Matt Jones .25 .60
48 Larry Johnson .30 .75
49 Tony Gonzalez .30 .75
50 Trent Green .30 .75
51 Chris Chambers .30 .75
52 Ricky Williams .25 .60
53 Ronnie Brown .40 1.00
54 Randy McMichael .25 .60
55 Daunte Culpepper .30 .75
56 Mewelde Moore .25 .60
57 Nate Burleson .25 .60
58 Corey Dillon .30 .75
59 Deion Branch .30 .75
60 Tom Brady .60 1.50
61 Aaron Brooks .30 .75
62 Deuce McAllister .30 .75
63 Donte Stallworth .25 .60
64 Eli Manning .50 1.25
65 Jeremy Shockey .40 1.00
66 Plaxico Burress .30 .75
67 Tiki Barber .40 1.00
68 Chad Pennington .30 .75
69 Curtis Martin .40 1.00
70 Laveranues Coles .25 .60
71 Kerry Collins .30 .75
72 LaMont Jordan .30 .75
73 Randy Moss .40 1.00
74 Donovan McNabb .40 1.00
75 Reggie Brown .25 .60
76 Brian Westbrook .30 .75
77 Ben Roethlisberger .50 1.25
78 Duce Staley .25 .60
79 Hines Ward .40 1.00
80 Antonio Gates .40 1.00
81 Drew Brees .40 1.00
82 LaDainian Tomlinson .40 1.00
83 Alex Smith QB .40 1.00
84 Kevan Barlow .25 .60
85 Brandon Lloyd .25 .60
86 Darrell Jackson .30 .75
87 Matt Hasselbeck .30 .75
88 Shaun Alexander .30 .75
89 Marc Bulger .30 .75
90 Steven Jackson .40 1.00
91 Torry Holt .30 .75
92 Cadillac Williams .30 .75
93 Joey Galloway .30 .75
94 Michael Clayton .25 .60
95 Chris Brown .25 .60
96 Drew Bennett .30 .75
97 Steve McNair .30 .75
98 Clinton Portis .40 1.00
99 Mark Brunell .30 .75
100 Santana Moss .30 .75
101 A.J. Hawk RC 5.00 12.00
102 Abdul Hodge RC 3.00 8.00
103 Adam Jennings RC 4.00 10.00
104 Alan Zemaitis RC 5.00 12.00
105 Andre Hall RC 4.00 10.00
106 Anthony Fasano RC 5.00 12.00
107 Anthony Mix RC 4.00 10.00
108 Ashton Youboty RC 3.00 8.00
109 Miles Austin RC 12.00 30.00
110 Barrick Nealy RC 4.00 10.00
111 Ben Obomanu RC 5.00 12.00
112 Bobby Carpenter RC 3.00 8.00
113 Brad Smith RC 5.00 12.00
114 Brandon Kirsch RC 4.00 10.00
115 Brandon Marshall RC 5.00 12.00
116 Brandon Williams RC 5.00 12.00
117 Brett Elliott RC 5.00 12.00
118 Brian Calhoun RC 3.00 8.00
119 Brodie Croyle RC 5.00 12.00
120 Brodrick Bunkley RC 4.00 10.00
121 Bruce Gradkowski RC 5.00 12.00
122 Cedric Griffin RC 4.00 10.00
123 Cedric Humes RC 3.00 8.00
124 Chad Greenway RC 5.00 12.00
125 Chad Jackson RC 3.00 8.00
126 Charlie Whitehurst RC 5.00 12.00
127 Cory Rodgers RC 4.00 10.00
128 D.J. Shockley RC 4.00 10.00
129 Darnell Bing RC 4.00 10.00
130 Darrell Hackney RC 4.00 10.00
131 David Thomas RC 4.00 10.00
132 D'Brickashaw Ferguson RC 5.00 12.00
133 DeAngelo Williams RC 6.00 15.00
134 De'Arrius Howard RC 5.00 12.00
135 Dee Webb RC 4.00 10.00
136 Delanie Walker RC 5.00 12.00
137 DeMeco Ryans RC 5.00 12.00
138 Demetrius Williams RC 4.00 10.00
139 Derek Hagan RC 4.00 10.00
140 Derrick Ross RC 4.00 10.00
141 Devin Aromashodu RC 5.00 12.00
142 Devin Hester RC 10.00 25.00
143 Dominique Byrd RC 4.00 10.00
144 Donte Whitner RC 5.00 12.00
145 DonTrell Moore RC 4.00 10.00
146 D'Qwell Jackson RC 4.00 10.00
147 Drew Olson RC 3.00 8.00
148 Eric Winston RC 3.00 8.00
149 Erik Meyer RC 4.00 10.00
150 Ernie Sims RC 4.00 10.00
151 Gabe Watson RC 3.00 8.00
152 Gerald Riggs RC 4.00 10.00
153 Ryan Gilbert RC 4.00 10.00
154 Greg Jennings RC 10.00 25.00
155 Greg Lee RC 3.00 8.00
156 Haloti Ngata RC 5.00 12.00
157 Hank Baskett RC 5.00 12.00
158 Ingle Martin RC 4.00 10.00
159 Jason Allen RC 4.00 10.00
160 Jason Avant RC 3.00 8.00
161 Jason Carter RC 4.00 10.00
162 Jay Cutler RC 10.00 25.00
163 Jeff King RC 4.00 10.00
164 Jeff Webb RC 4.00 10.00
165 Jeremy Bloom RC 4.00 10.00
166 Jerious Norwood RC 4.00 10.00
167 Jerome Harrison RC 5.00 12.00
168 Jimmy Williams RC 5.00 12.00
169 Joe Klopfenstein RC 3.00 8.00
170 Jon Alston RC 3.00 8.00
171 Johnathan Joseph RC 4.00 10.00
172 Jonathan Orr RC 4.00 10.00
173 Joseph Addai RC 5.00 12.00
174 Kai Parham RC 5.00 12.00
175 Kamerion Wimbley RC 5.00 12.00
176 Kellen Clemens RC 4.00 10.00
177 Kelly Jennings RC 4.00 10.00
178 Kent Smith RC 5.00 12.00
179 Ko Simpson RC 4.00 10.00
180 Laurence Maroney RC 4.00 10.00
181 Lawrence Vickers RC 4.00 10.00
182 LenDale White RC 4.00 10.00
183 Leon Washington RC 4.00 10.00
184 Leonard Pope RC 5.00 12.00
185 Manny Lawson RC 4.00 10.00
186 Marcedes Lewis RC 5.00 12.00
187 Marcus Vick RC 3.00 8.00
188 Mario Williams RC 5.00 12.00
189 Marques Colston RC 10.00 25.00
190 Martin Nance RC 4.00 10.00
191 Mathias Kiwanuka RC 5.00 12.00
192 Matt Leinart RC 5.00 12.00
193 Maurice Drew RC 8.00 20.00
194 Maurice Stovall RC 3.00 8.00
195 Michael Huff RC 4.00 10.00
196 Michael Robinson RC 4.00 10.00
197 Mike Bell RC 5.00 12.00
198 Mike Hass RC 4.00 10.00
199 Omar Jacobs RC 3.00 8.00
200 Owen Daniels RC 5.00 12.00
201 P.J. Daniels RC 3.00 8.00
202 Paul Pinegar RC 3.00 8.00
203 Quinton Ganther RC 3.00 8.00
204 Reggie Bush RC 10.00 25.00
205 Reggie McNeal RC 4.00 10.00
206 Rodrique Wright RC 3.00 8.00
207 Santonio Holmes RC 6.00 15.00
208 Sinorice Moss RC 5.00 12.00
209 Skyler Green RC 3.00 8.00
210 Tamba Hali RC 5.00 12.00
211 Tarvaris Jackson RC 5.00 12.00
212 Taurean Henderson RC 5.00 12.00
213 Terrence Whitehead RC 4.00 10.00
214 Tim Day RC 4.00 10.00
215 Todd Watkins RC 3.00 8.00
216 Tony Scheffler RC 5.00 12.00
217 Travis Lulay RC 4.00 10.00
218 Travis Wilson RC 3.00 8.00
219 Tye Hill RC 3.00 8.00
220 Vernon Davis RC 6.00 15.00
221 Vince Young RC 6.00 15.00
222 Wali Lundy RC 4.00 10.00
223 Wendell Mathis RC 4.00 10.00
224 Willie Reid RC 4.00 10.00
225 Winston Justice RC 4.00 10.00

2006 Donruss Elite Aspirations

*VETS/70-99: 5X TO 12X BASIC CARDS
*ROOKIES/70-99: .6X TO 1.5X BAS.CARDS
*VETS/45-69: 6X TO 15X BASIC CARDS
*ROOKIES/45-69: .8X TO 2X BAS.CARDS
*ROOKIES/30-44: 1X TO 2.5X BAS.CARDS
*VETS/20-29: 10X TO 25X BASIC CARDS
*ROOKIES/20-29: 1.2X TO 3X BAS.CARDS
SER.#'d UNDER 20 NOT PRICED

2006 Donruss Elite Status

*VETS/70-99: 5X TO 12X BASIC CARDS
*ROOKIES/70-99: .6X TO 1.5X BAS.CARDS
*VETS/45-69: 6X TO 15X BASIC CARDS
*ROOKIES/45-69: .8X TO 2X BAS.CARDS
*VETS/30-44: 8X TO 20X BASIC CARDS
*ROOKIES/30-44: 1X TO 2.5X BAS.CARDS
*VETS/20-29: 10X TO 25X BASIC CARDS
*ROOKIES/20-29: 1.2X TO 3X BAS.CARDS
SER.#'d UNDER 20 NOT PRICED

2006 Donruss Elite Status Gold

*VETERANS: 10X TO 25X BASIC CARDS
*ROOKIES: 1.2X TO 3X BASIC CARDS
STATED PRINT RUN 24 SER.#'d SETS

2006 Donruss Elite Back to the Future Green

GREEN PRINT RUN 1000 SER.#'d SETS
*BLUE: .5X TO 1.2X GREEN
BLUE PRINT RUN 500 SER.#'d SETS
*RED: .6X TO 1.5X GREEN
RED PRINT RUN 250 SER.#'d SETS
1 Jake Plummer 1.00 2.50
Josh McCown
2 Andre Reed 1.00 2.50
Lee Evans
3 Steve Smith 1.50 4.00
Keary Colbert
4 Gale Sayers 2.00 5.00
Thomas Jones
5 Len Dawson 1.50 4.00
Trent Green
6 Barry Sanders 2.50 6.00
Kevin Jones
7 Bob Griese 1.00 2.50
Jay Fiedler
8 Boomer Esiason 1.50 4.00
Carson Palmer
9 Randy Moss 1.50 4.00
Nate Burleson
10 Terry Bradshaw 3.00 8.00
Ben Roethlisberger
11 Marcus Allen 1.50 4.00
LaMont Jordan
12 John Elway 2.50 6.00
Jake Plummer
13 Roger Staubach 2.50 6.00
Drew Bledsoe
14 Jerome Bettis 1.50 4.00
Willie Parker
15 Dan Marino 3.00 8.00
Ronnie Brown
16 Mike Singletary 1.50 4.00
Brian Urlacher
17 Deacon Jones 1.50 4.00
Fran Tarkenton
18 Earl Campbell 1.50 4.00
Chris Brown
19 Deion Sanders 1.50 4.00
Roy Williams S
20 Ickey Woods 1.00 2.50
Rudi Johnson
21 Kurt Warner 1.00 2.50
Marc Bulger
22 Priest Holmes 1.50 4.00
Larry Johnson
23 Mark Brunell 1.00 2.50
Byron Leftwich
24 Marshall Faulk 1.50 4.00
Edgerrin James
25 Ricky Williams 1.00 2.50
Deuce McAllister

2006 Donruss Elite Back to the Future Jerseys

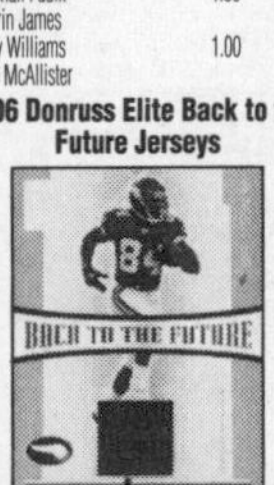

STATED PRINT RUN 299 SER.#'d SETS
*PRIME: 1X TO 2.5X BASIC INSERTS
PRIME PRINT RUN 25 SER.#'d SETS
1 Jake Plummer 4.00 10.00
Josh McCown
2 Andre Reed 4.00 10.00
Lee Evans
3 Steve Smith 4.00 10.00
Keary Colbert
4 Gale Sayers 8.00 20.00
Thomas Jones
5 Len Dawson 5.00 12.00
Trent Green
6 Barry Sanders 10.00 25.00
Kevin Jones
7 Bob Griese 4.00 10.00
Jay Fiedler
8 Boomer Esiason 6.00 15.00
Carson Palmer
9 Randy Moss 4.00 10.00
Nate Burleson
10 Terry Bradshaw 15.00 40.00
Ben Roethlisberger
11 Marcus Allen 6.00 15.00
LaMont Jordan
12 John Elway 10.00 25.00
Jake Plummer
13 Roger Staubach 8.00 20.00
Drew Bledsoe
14 Jerome Bettis 12.50 30.00
Willie Parker
15 Dan Marino 12.50 30.00
Ronnie Brown
16 Mike Singletary 8.00 20.00
Brian Urlacher
17 Deacon Jones 5.00 12.00
Fran Tarkenton
18 Earl Campbell 5.00 12.00
Chris Brown
19 Deion Sanders 5.00 12.00
Roy Williams
20 Ickey Woods 4.00 10.00
Rudi Johnson
21 Kurt Warner 4.00 10.00
Marc Bulger
22 Priest Holmes 6.00 15.00
Larry Johnson
23 Mark Brunell 4.00 10.00
Byron Leftwich
24 Marshall Faulk 5.00 12.00
Edgerrin James
25 Ricky Williams 4.00 10.00
Deuce McAllister

2006 Donruss Elite Chain Reaction Gold

GOLD PRINT RUN 1000 SER.#'d SETS
*BLACK: .5X TO 1.2X GOLD INSERTS
BLACK PRINT RUN 500 SER.#'d SETS
*RED: .6X TO 1.5X GOLD INSERTS
RED PRINT RUN 250 SER.#'d SETS
1 Darrell Jackson 1.00 2.50
2 Aaron Brooks 1.00 2.50
3 Daunte Culpepper 1.00 2.50
4 Joey Harrington .75 2.00
5 David Carr .75 2.00
6 Steve McNair 1.00 2.50
7 Matt Hasselbeck 1.00 2.50
8 Jake Plummer 1.00 2.50
9 Byron Leftwich 1.00 2.50
10 Randy Moss 1.25 3.00
11 Hines Ward 1.25 3.00
12 Chris Chambers 1.00 2.50
13 Anquan Boldin 1.00 2.50
14 Rod Smith 1.00 2.50
15 Shaun Alexander 1.00 2.50
16 Michael Vick 1.25 3.00
17 Ronnie Brown 1.25 3.00
18 Domanick Davis .75 2.00
19 Priest Holmes 1.00 2.50
20 Matt Jones .75 2.00
21 Brett Favre 2.50 6.00
22 Willie Parker 1.00 2.50
23 Fred Taylor 1.00 2.50
24 Edgerrin James 1.00 2.50
25 Steve Smith 1.25 3.00

2006 Donruss Elite Chain Reaction Jerseys

STATED PRINT RUN 299 SER.#'d SETS
*PRIME: .6X TO 1.5X BASIC INSERTS
PRIME PRINT RUN 99 SER.#'d SETS
1 Darrell Jackson 2.50 6.00
2 Aaron Brooks/54 4.00 10.00
3 Daunte Culpepper 4.00 10.00
4 Joey Harrington 3.00 8.00
5 David Carr 3.00 8.00
6 Steve McNair 4.00 10.00
7 Matt Hasselbeck 3.00 8.00
8 Jake Plummer 4.00 10.00
9 Byron Leftwich 3.00 8.00
10 Randy Moss 4.00 10.00
11 Hines Ward 4.00 10.00
12 Chris Chambers 3.00 8.00
13 Anquan Boldin 3.00 8.00
14 Rod Smith 3.00 8.00
15 Shaun Alexander 5.00 12.00
16 Michael Vick 4.00 10.00
17 Ronnie Brown/200 4.00 10.00
18 Domanick Davis 2.50 6.00
19 Priest Holmes 3.00 8.00
20 Matt Jones 2.50 6.00
21 Brett Favre 10.00 25.00
22 Willie Parker/200 5.00 12.00
23 Fred Taylor 3.00 8.00
24 Edgerrin James 4.00 10.00
25 Steve Smith 4.00 10.00

2006 Donruss Elite College Ties Green

GREEN PRINT RUN 1000 SER.#'d SETS
*BLACK: .6X TO 1.5X GREEN INSERTS
BLACK PRINT RUN 250 SER.#'d SETS
*GOLD: .5X TO 1.2X GREEN INSERTS
GOLD PRINT RUN 500 SER.#'d SETS
1 Carson Palmer 2.00 5.00
Matt Leinart
2 Peyton Manning 2.50 6.00
Gerald Riggs
3 Anquan Boldin 1.50 4.00
Leon Washington
4 Roger Staubach 2.00 5.00
Joe Bellino
5 Drew Bledsoe 1.50 4.00
Jerome Harrison
6 Julius Jones 1.50 4.00
Anthony Fasano
7 Braylon Edwards 1.50 4.00
Jason Avant
8 Matt Leinart 4.00 10.00
Reggie Bush
9 Cedric Benson 3.00 8.00
Vince Young
10 Michael Vick 1.50 4.00
Marcus Vick
11 Matt Leinart 2.00 5.00
12 Gerald Riggs 1.00 2.50
13 Leon Washington 1.50 4.00
14 Maurice Drew 2.00 5.00
15 Jerome Harrison 1.00 2.50
16 Anthony Fasano 1.00 2.50
17 Jason Avant 1.00 2.50
18 Reggie Bush 4.00 10.00
19 Vince Young 3.00 8.00
20 Marcus Vick 1.50 4.00

2006 Donruss Elite College Ties Autographs

STATED PRINT RUN 25-50 SER.#'d SETS
1 Carson Palmer/50 40.00 100.00
Matt Leinart
2 Peyton Manning/30 125.00 200.00
Gerald Riggs
3 Anquan Boldin/25 25.00 50.00
Leon Washington
4 Roger Staubach/25 100.00 200.00
Joe Bellino
6 Julius Jones/50 25.00 60.00
Anthony Fasano
7 Braylon Edwards/50 30.00 80.00
Jason Avant
8 Matt Leinart/50 30.00 80.00
Reggie Bush
9 Cedric Benson/50 40.00 100.00
Vince Young
11 Matt Leinart/25 40.00 100.00
12 Gerald Riggs/25 20.00 40.00
13 Leon Washington/25 20.00 40.00
14 Maurice Drew/25 50.00 100.00
15 Jerome Harrison/25 20.00 50.00
16 Anthony Fasano/25 20.00 50.00
17 Jason Avant/25 20.00 40.00
18 Reggie Bush/25 75.00 150.00
19 Vince Young/25 50.00 120.00

2006 Donruss Elite College Ties Jerseys

PRINT RUN 17-250 SER.#'d SETS
1 Carson Palmer/250 8.00 20.00
Matt Leinart
2 Peyton Manning/250 15.00 40.00
Gerald Riggs
3 Anquan Boldin/250 6.00 15.00
Leon Washington
4 Roger Staubach 10.00 25.00
Joe Bellino/200
6 Julius Jones 12.50 30.00
Anthony Fasano/49
7 Braylon Edwards/250 8.00 20.00
Jason Avant
8 Matt Leinart/250 15.00 40.00
Reggie Bush
9 Cedric Benson/250 8.00 20.00
Vince Young
10 Michael Vick 6.00 15.00
Marcus Vick/225
11 Matt Leinart/100 8.00 20.00
18 Reggie Bush/100 15.00 40.00

2006 Donruss Elite College Ties Jerseys Prime

*PRIME/99: .6X TO 1.5X BASIC INSERTS
*PRIME/25-50: .8X TO 2X BASIC INSERTS
PRIME PRINT RUN 5-99 SER.#'d SETS
5 Drew Bledsoe/99 15.00 40.00
Jerome Harrison

2006 Donruss Elite Elite Teams Black

BLACK PRINT RUN 1000 SER.#'d SETS
*GOLD: .6X TO 1.5X BLACK INSERTS
GOLD PRINT RUN 250 SER.#'d SETS
*RED: .5X TO 1.2X BLACK INSERTS
RED PRINT RUN 500 SER.#'d SETS
1 Alge Crumpler 1.25 3.00
Michael Vick
Warrick Dunn
2 Lee Evans 1.00 2.50
J.P. Losman
Willis McGahee
3 Stephen Davis 1.25 3.00
Jake Delhomme
Steve Smith
4 Cedric Benson 1.25 3.00
Kyle Orton
Thomas Jones
5 Chad Johnson 1.25 3.00
Carson Palmer
Rudi Johnson
6 Keyshawn Johnson 1.25 3.00
Drew Bledsoe
Julius Jones
7 Ashley Lelie 1.00 2.50
Jake Plummer
Tatum Bell
8 Ahman Green 2.50 6.00
Brett Favre
Robert Ferguson
9 Reggie Wayne 2.00 5.00
Peyton Manning
Edgerrin James
10 Jimmy Smith 1.00 2.50
Byron Leftwich
Matt Jones
11 Larry Johnson 1.00 2.50
Trent Green
Tony Gonzalez
12 Troy Williamson 1.00 2.50
Daunte Culpepper
Nate Burleson
13 Corey Dillon 2.00 5.00
Tom Brady
Deion Branch
14 Deuce McAllister 1.00 2.50
Aaron Brooks
Joe Horn
15 Plaxico Burress 1.50 4.00
Eli Manning
Tiki Barber
16 Curtis Martin 1.25 3.00
Chad Pennington
Laveranues Coles
17 Randy Moss 1.25 3.00
Kerry Collins
LaMont Jordan
18 Brian Westbrook 1.25 3.00
Donovan McNabb
Reggie Brown
19 Hines Ward 3.00 8.00
Ben Roethlisberger
Willie Parker
20 Antonio Gates 1.25 3.00
Drew Brees
LaDainian Tomlinson
21 Brandon Lloyd 1.25 3.00
Alex Smith
Kevan Barlow
22 Darrell Jackson 1.00 2.50
Matt Hasselbeck
Shaun Alexander
23 Steven Jackson 1.25 3.00
Marc Bulger
Torry Holt
24 Cadillac Williams 1.00 2.50
Michael Clayton
Mike Alstott
25 Chris Brown 1.00 2.50
Steve McNair
Brandon Jones

2006 Donruss Elite Elite Teams Jerseys

STATED PRINT RUN 99 SER.#'d SETS
*PRIME/25: .8X TO 2X BASIC JSY/99
PRIME PRINT RUN 25 SER.#'d SETS
1 Alge Crumpler 10.00 25.00
Michael Vick
Warrick Dunn
2 Lee Evans 8.00 20.00
J.P. Losman
Willis McGahee
3 Stephen Davis 10.00 25.00
Jake Delhomme
Steve Smith
4 Cedric Benson 10.00 25.00
Kyle Orton
Thomas Jones
5 Chad Johnson 10.00 25.00
Carson Palmer
Rudi Johnson
6 Keyshawn Johnson 10.00 25.00
Drew Bledsoe
Julius Jones
7 Ashley Lelie 8.00 20.00
Jake Plummer
Tatum Bell
8 Ahman Green 20.00 50.00
Brett Favre
Robert Ferguson
9 Reggie Wayne 15.00 40.00
Peyton Manning
Edgerrin James
10 Jimmy Smith 8.00 20.00
Byron Leftwich
Matt Jones
11 Larry Johnson 8.00 20.00
Trent Green
Tony Gonzalez
12 Troy Williamson 8.00 20.00
Daunte Culpepper
Nate Burleson
13 Corey Dillon 15.00 40.00
Tom Brady
Deion Branch
14 Deuce McAllister 8.00 20.00
Aaron Brooks
Joe Horn
15 Plaxico Burress 12.00 30.00
Eli Manning
Tiki Barber
16 Curtis Martin 10.00 25.00
Chad Pennington
Laveranues Coles
17 Randy Moss 10.00 25.00
Kerry Collins
LaMont Jordan
18 Brian Westbrook 10.00 25.00
Donovan McNabb
Reggie Brown
19 Hines Ward 12.00 30.00
Ben Roethlisberger
Willie Parker
20 Antonio Gates 10.00 25.00
Drew Brees
LaDainian Tomlinson
21 Brandon Lloyd 10.00 25.00
Alex Smith
Kevan Barlow
22 Darrell Jackson 8.00 20.00
Matt Hasselbeck
Shaun Alexander
23 Steven Jackson 10.00 25.00
Marc Bulger
Torry Holt
24 Cadillac Williams 8.00 20.00
Michael Clayton
Mike Alstott
25 Chris Brown 8.00 20.00
Steve McNair
Brandon Jones

2006 Donruss Elite Passing the Torch Red

RED PRINT RUN 1000 SER.#'d SETS
*BLUE: .6X TO 1.5X RED INSERTS
BLUE PRINT RUN 250 SER.#'d SETS
*GREEN: .5X TO 1.2X RED INSERTS
GREEN PRINT RUN 500 SER.#'d SETS
1 Alex Smith QB 1.50 4.00
2 Steve Young 2.00 5.00
3 Braylon Edwards 1.50 4.00
4 Paul Warfield 1.50 4.00
5 Cedric Benson 1.50 4.00
6 Gale Sayers 1.50 4.00
7 Eli Manning 2.00 5.00
8 Phil Simms 1.50 4.00
9 Willie Parker 1.50 4.00
10 Jerome Bettis 1.50 4.00
11 Julius Jones 1.50 4.00
12 Tony Dorsett 1.50 4.00
13 Kevin Jones 1.50 4.00
14 Barry Sanders 2.50 6.00
15 LaMont Jordan 1.00 2.50
16 Bo Jackson 1.50 4.00
17 Nate Burleson 1.00 2.50
18 Cris Carter 1.50 4.00
19 Antonio Gates 1.50 4.00
20 Lance Alworth 1.00 2.50
21 Alex Smith QB 2.00 5.00
Steve Young
22 Braylon Edwards 1.50 4.00
Paul Warfield
23 Cedric Benson 1.50 4.00
Gale Sayers
24 Eli Manning 2.00 5.00
Phil Simms
25 Willie Parker 1.50 4.00
Jerome Bettis
26 Julius Jones 1.50 4.00
Tony Dorsett
27 Kevin Jones 2.50 6.00
Barry Sanders
28 LaMont Jordan 1.50 4.00
Bo Jackson
29 Nate Burleson 1.50 4.00
Cris Carter
30 Antonio Gates 1.50 4.00
Lance Alworth

2006 Donruss Elite Passing the Torch Autographs

STATED PRINT RUN 49-99
1 Alex Smith QB/99 25.00 50.00
2 Steve Young/49 40.00 80.00
3 Braylon Edwards/99 12.00 30.00
4 Paul Warfield/99 10.00 25.00
5 Cedric Benson/99 12.00 30.00
6 Gale Sayers/49 25.00 50.00
7 Eli Manning/49 50.00 100.00
8 Phil Simms/99 15.00 40.00
9 Willie Parker/99 10.00 25.00
10 Jerome Bettis/49 30.00 60.00
11 Julius Jones/49 10.00 25.00
12 Tony Dorsett/49 25.00 50.00
13 Kevin Jones/99 8.00 20.00
14 Barry Sanders/49 60.00 120.00
15 LaMont Jordan/99 10.00 25.00
16 Bo Jackson/99 40.00 80.00
17 Nate Burleson/99 8.00 20.00
18 Cris Carter/99 12.00 30.00
19 Antonio Gates/99 12.00 30.00
20 Lance Alworth/99 15.00 40.00
21 Alex Smith QB/49 50.00 100.00
Steve Young
22 Braylon Edwards/49 25.00 60.00
Paul Warfield
23 Cedric Benson/49 30.00 80.00
Gale Sayers
24 Eli Manning/49 50.00 120.00
Phil Simms
25 Willie Parker/49 50.00 120.00
Jerome Bettis
26 Julius Jones/49 30.00 80.00
Tony Dorsett
27 Kevin Jones/49 50.00 120.00
Barry Sanders
28 LaMont Jordan/49 40.00 100.00
Bo Jackson
29 Nate Burleson/49 30.00 80.00
Cris Carter
30 Antonio Gates/49 30.00 80.00
Lance Alworth

2006 Donruss Elite Prime Targets Gold

GOLD PRINT RUN 1000 SER.#'d SETS
*BLACK: .5X TO 1.2X GOLD INSERTS
BLACK PRINT RUN 500 SER.#'d SETS
*RED: .6X TO 1.5X GOLD INSERTS
RED PRINT RUN 250 SER.#'d SETS
1 LaDainian Tomlinson 1.25 3.00
2 Shaun Alexander 1.00 2.50
3 Edgerrin James 1.00 2.50
4 Steven Jackson 1.25 3.00
5 Stephen Davis 1.00 2.50
6 Steve Smith 1.25 3.00
7 Marvin Harrison 1.25 3.00
8 Antonio Gates 1.25 3.00
9 Chad Johnson 1.00 2.50
10 Larry Fitzgerald 1.25 3.00

2006 Donruss Elite Prime Targets Jerseys

STATED PRINT RUN 299 SER.#'d SETS
*PRIME: .6X TO 1.5X BASIC INSERTS
PRIME PRINT RUN 50 SER.#'d SETS
1 LaDainian Tomlinson 4.00 10.00
2 Shaun Alexander 4.00 10.00
3 Edgerrin James 4.00 10.00
4 Steven Jackson 4.00 10.00
5 Stephen Davis 3.00 8.00
6 Steve Smith 4.00 10.00
7 Marvin Harrison 4.00 10.00
8 Antonio Gates 4.00 10.00
9 Chad Johnson 3.00 8.00
10 Larry Fitzgerald 3.00 8.00

2006 Donruss Elite Series Gold

GOLD PRINT RUN 1000 SER.#'d SETS
*BLACK: .5X TO 1.2X GOLD INSERTS
BLACK PRINT RUN 500 SER.#'d SETS
*RED: .6X TO 1.5X GOLD INSERTS
RED PRINT RUN 250 SER.#'d SETS
1 Aaron Brooks 1.00 2.50
2 Kyle Orton 1.25 3.00
3 Michael Vick 1.25 3.00
4 Troy Williamson .75 2.00
5 Jason Campbell 1.00 2.50
6 Antonio Gates 1.25 3.00
7 Jerry Porter .75 2.00
8 Amani Toomer 1.00 2.50
9 Andre Johnson 1.25 3.00
9AU Andre Johnson AU/25 12.50 30.00
10 Alex Smith QB 1.25 3.00
11 Aaron Rodgers 2.50 6.00
12 Bethel Johnson .75 2.00
13 Brandon Lloyd .75 2.00
14 Bryant Johnson .75 2.00
15 Cedric Benson 1.00 2.50
16 Clinton Portis 1.25 3.00
17 Torry Holt 1.00 2.50
18 Chad Johnson 1.00 2.50
19 Tom Brady 2.00 5.00
20 Warrick Dunn 1.00 2.50
21 Willis McGahee 1.00 2.50
22 Kevin Jones .75 2.00
23 Corey Dillon 1.00 2.50
24 LaMont Jordan 1.00 2.50
25 Steven Jackson 1.25 3.00

2006 Donruss Elite Series Jerseys

STATED PRINT RUN 299 SER.#'d SETS
*PRIME: .6X TO 1.5X BASIC INSERTS
PRIME PRINT RUN 50 SER.#'d SETS
1 Aaron Brooks/54 4.00 10.00
2 Kyle Orton 3.00 8.00
3 Michael Vick 3.00 8.00
4 Troy Williamson 2.50 6.00
5 Jason Campbell 3.00 8.00
6 Antonio Gates 4.00 10.00
7 Jerry Porter 3.00 8.00
8 Amani Toomer 3.00 8.00
9 Andre Johnson 2.50 6.00
10 Alex Smith QB 4.00 10.00
11 Aaron Rodgers 15.00 40.00
12 Bethel Johnson/150 2.50 6.00
13 Brandon Lloyd 2.50 6.00
14 Bryant Johnson 2.50 6.00
15 Cedric Benson 4.00 10.00

16 Clinton Portis 4.00 10.00
17 Torry Holt 3.00 8.00
18 Chad Johnson 3.00 8.00
19 Tom Brady 6.00 15.00
20 Warrick Dunn 3.00 8.00
21 Willis McGahee 3.00 8.00
22 Kevin Jones 4.00 10.00
23 Corey Dillon 3.00 8.00
24 LaMont Jordan 3.00 8.00
25 Steven Jackson 4.00 10.00

2006 Donruss Elite Status Autographs Gold

STATED PRINT RUN 24 SER.#'d SETS
UNPRICED BLACK AUs SER.#'d TO 1
101 A.J. Hawk 20.00 50.00
102 Abdul Hodge 12.00 30.00
103 Adam Jennings 15.00 40.00
104 Alan Zemaitis 20.00 50.00
105 Andre Hall 15.00 40.00
106 Anthony Fasano 20.00 50.00
109 Miles Austin 125.00 200.00
111 Ben Obomanu 20.00 50.00
112 Bobby Carpenter 12.00 30.00
113 Brad Smith 20.00 50.00
114 Brandon Kirsch 15.00 40.00
115 Brandon Marshall 20.00 50.00
116 Brandon Williams 12.00 30.00
118 Brian Calhoun 12.00 30.00
121 Bruce Gradkowski 20.00 50.00
123 Cedric Humes 12.00 30.00
124 Chad Greenway 20.00 50.00
125 Chad Jackson 12.00 30.00
126 Charlie Whitehurst 20.00 50.00
128 D.J. Shockley 15.00 40.00
129 Darnell Bing 15.00 40.00
132 D'Brickashaw Ferguson 20.00 50.00
133 DeAngelo Williams 50.00 120.00
136 Delanie Walker 20.00 50.00
137 DeMeco Ryans 20.00 50.00
138 Demetrius Williams 15.00 40.00
139 Derek Hagan 15.00 40.00
140 Derrick Ross 15.00 40.00
141 Devin Aromashodu 20.00 50.00
143 Dominique Byrd 15.00 40.00
146 D'Qwell Jackson 15.00 40.00
147 Drew Olson 12.00 30.00
149 Erik Meyer 15.00 40.00
152 Gerald Riggs 15.00 40.00
154 Greg Jennings 40.00 100.00
155 Greg Lee 12.00 30.00
156 Haloti Ngata 20.00 50.00
157 Hank Baskett 20.00 50.00
160 Jason Avant 12.00 30.00
162 Jay Cutler 100.00 200.00
164 Jeff Webb 15.00 40.00
166 Jerious Norwood 15.00 40.00
168 Jimmy Williams 20.00 50.00
169 Joe Klopfenstein 12.00 30.00
170 Jon Alston 12.00 30.00
172 Jonathan Orr 15.00 40.00
173 Joseph Addai 20.00 50.00
175 Kamerion Wimbley 20.00 50.00
176 Kellen Clemens 15.00 40.00
177 Kelly Jennings 15.00 40.00
179 Ko Simpson 15.00 40.00
180 Laurence Maroney 15.00 40.00
182 LenDale White 15.00 40.00
183 Leon Washington 40.00 80.00
184 Leonard Pope 20.00 50.00
186 Marcedes Lewis 20.00 50.00
188 Mario Williams 20.00 50.00
190 Martin Nance 15.00 40.00
192 Matt Leinart 50.00 120.00
193 Maurice Drew 30.00 80.00
194 Maurice Stovall 12.00 30.00
195 Michael Huff 15.00 40.00
196 Michael Robinson 15.00 40.00
198 Mike Hass 15.00 40.00
199 Omar Jacobs 12.00 30.00
202 Paul Pinegar 12.00 30.00
203 Quinton Ganther 12.00 30.00
204 Reggie Bush 60.00 150.00
205 Reggie McNeal 15.00 40.00
207 Santonio Holmes 40.00 100.00
208 Sinorice Moss 20.00 50.00
209 Skyler Green 12.00 30.00
210 Tamba Hali 20.00 50.00
211 Tarvaris Jackson 20.00 50.00
215 Todd Watkins 12.00 30.00
218 Travis Wilson 12.00 30.00
219 Tye Hill 12.00 30.00
220 Vernon Davis 25.00 60.00
221 Vince Young 60.00 120.00
223 Wendell Mathis 15.00 40.00

2006 Donruss Elite Throwback Threads

STATED PRINT RUN 20-249 SER.#'d SETS
*PRIME/30: .8X TO 2X BASIC INSERTS
PRIME PRINT RUN 5-30 SER.#'d SETS
1 Johnny Unitas 12.50 30.00
2 Peyton Manning 8.00 20.00
3 Don Meredith 8.00 20.00
4 Troy Aikman 8.00 20.00
5 Bobby Layne 15.00 40.00
6 Barry Sanders 10.00 25.00
7 Joe Montana 12.50 30.00
8 Alex Smith QB 5.00 12.00
9 Fred Biletnikoff 6.00 15.00
10 Randy Moss 4.00 10.00
11 Walter Payton 12.50 30.00
12 Cedric Benson 4.00 10.00
13 Ozzie Newsome 3.00 8.00
14 Braylon Edwards 4.00 10.00
15 Jim Brown/100 8.00 20.00
16 Reuben Droughns 3.00 8.00
17 Steve Largent 4.00 10.00
18 Darrell Jackson 3.00 8.00
19 Jim Kelly 5.00 12.00
20 J.P. Losman 3.00 8.00
21 Marcus Allen 4.00 10.00
22 Larry Johnson 5.00 12.00
23 Ronnie Lott 4.00 10.00
24 Lawrence Taylor 4.00 10.00
25 Red Grange/75 90.00 150.00
26 Ray Nitschke 10.00 25.00
28 Curtis Martin 4.00 10.00
29 Herschel Walker 4.00 10.00
30 Daunte Culpepper 4.00 10.00
31 Johnny Unitas 20.00 40.00
Peyton Manning/249
32 Don Meredith 20.00 40.00
Troy Aikman/162
33 Bobby Layne 20.00 40.00
Barry Sanders/149
34 Joe Montana 20.00 40.00
Alex Smith QB/249
35 Fred Biletnikoff 8.00 20.00
Randy Moss/249
36 Walter Payton 20.00 40.00
Cedric Benson/162
37 Ozzie Newsome 6.00 15.00
Braylon Edwards/249
38 Jim Brown 8.00 20.00
Reuben Droughns/162
39 Steve Largent 6.00 15.00
Darrell Jackson/162
40 Jim Kelly 8.00 20.00
J.P. Losman/249
41 Marcus Allen 10.00 25.00
Larry Johnson/200
42 Ronnie Lott 8.00 20.00
Lawrence Taylor/249
43 Red Grange 125.00 225.00
Ray Nitschke/25
44 John Riggins 8.00 20.00
Curtis Martin/44
45 Herschel Walker 8.00 20.00
Daunte Culpepper/248

2006 Donruss Elite Throwback Threads Autographs

NOT PRICED DUE TO SCARCITY
UNPRICED PRIME PRINT RUN 1-5 SETS

2006 Donruss Elite Turn of the Century Autographs

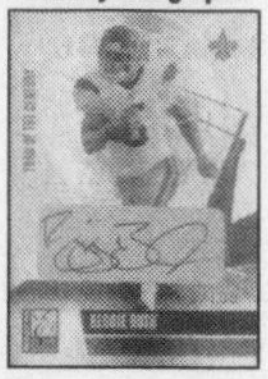

STATED PRINT RUN 50-100
101 A.J. Hawk/50 40.00 80.00
102 Abdul Hodge 8.00 20.00
103 Adam Jennings 10.00 25.00
104 Alan Zemaitis 12.00 30.00
105 Andre Hall 10.00 25.00
106 Anthony Fasano 12.00 30.00
109 Miles Austin 75.00 150.00
111 Ben Obomanu 12.00 30.00
112 Bobby Carpenter/50 8.00 20.00
113 Brad Smith 12.00 30.00
114 Brandon Kirsch 10.00 25.00
115 Brandon Marshall 20.00 40.00
116 Brandon Williams 8.00 20.00
118 Brian Calhoun 8.00 20.00
121 Bruce Gradkowski 12.00 30.00
123 Cedric Humes 8.00 20.00
124 Chad Greenway/50 12.00 30.00
125 Chad Jackson 8.00 20.00
126 Charlie Whitehurst 12.00 30.00
128 D.J. Shockley 10.00 25.00
129 Darnell Bing 10.00 25.00
132 D'Brickashaw Ferguson 12.00 30.00
133 DeAngelo Williams 30.00 60.00
136 Delanie Walker 12.00 30.00
137 DeMeco Ryans 12.00 30.00
138 Demetrius Williams 10.00 25.00
139 Derek Hagan 10.00 25.00
140 Derrick Ross 10.00 25.00
141 Devin Aromashodu 12.00 30.00
143 Dominique Byrd 10.00 25.00
146 D'Qwell Jackson 10.00 25.00
147 Drew Olson 8.00 20.00
149 Erik Meyer 10.00 25.00
152 Gerald Riggs 10.00 25.00
154 Greg Jennings 30.00 60.00
155 Greg Lee 8.00 20.00
156 Haloti Ngata 12.00 30.00
157 Hank Baskett 12.00 30.00
160 Jason Avant 8.00 20.00
162 Jay Cutler 60.00 120.00
164 Jeff Webb 10.00 25.00
166 Jerious Norwood 10.00 25.00
168 Jimmy Williams 12.00 30.00
169 Joe Klopfenstein 8.00 20.00
170 Jon Alston 8.00 20.00
172 Jonathan Orr 10.00 25.00
173 Joseph Addai 12.00 30.00
175 Kamerion Wimbley/50 12.00 30.00
176 Kellen Clemens 10.00 25.00
177 Kelly Jennings/50 10.00 25.00
179 Ko Simpson 10.00 25.00
180 Laurence Maroney 10.00 25.00
182 LenDale White 20.00 50.00
183 Leon Washington 20.00 50.00
184 Leonard Pope 12.00 30.00
186 Marcedes Lewis 12.00 30.00
188 Mario Williams/50 15.00 40.00
190 Martin Nance
192 Matt Leinart 25.00 60.00
193 Maurice Drew 50.00 80.00
194 Maurice Stovall 8.00 20.00
195 Michael Huff/50 10.00 25.00
196 Michael Robinson 10.00 25.00
198 Mike Hass 10.00 25.00
199 Omar Jacobs 8.00 20.00
202 Paul Pinegar 8.00 20.00
203 Quinton Ganther 8.00 20.00
204 Reggie Bush 75.00 150.00
205 Reggie McNeal 10.00 25.00
207 Santonio Holmes 30.00 60.00
208 Sinorice Moss 12.00 30.00
209 Skyler Green 8.00 20.00
210 Tamba Hali/50 12.00 30.00
211 Tarvaris Jackson/50 12.00 30.00
215 Todd Watkins 8.00 20.00
218 Travis Wilson 8.00 20.00
219 Tye Hill/50 8.00 20.00
220 Vernon Davis 15.00 40.00
221 Vince Young 30.00 60.00
223 Wendell Mathis 10.00 25.00

2006 Donruss Elite Zoning Commission Gold

GOLD PRINT RUN 1000 SER.#'d SETS
*BLACK: .5X TO 1.2X GOLD INSERTS
BLACK PRINT RUN 500 SER.#'d SETS
*RED: .6X TO 1.5X GOLD INSERTS
RED PRINT RUN 250 SER.#'d SETS
1 Tom Brady 2.00 5.00
2 Donovan McNabb 1.25 3.00
3 Brett Favre 2.50 6.00
4 Carson Palmer 1.25 3.00
5 Peyton Manning 2.00 5.00
6 Drew Brees 1.25 3.00
7 Drew Bledsoe 1.25 3.00
8 Eli Manning 1.50 4.00
9 Trent Green 1.00 2.50
10 Kerry Collins 1.00 2.50
11 Jake Delhomme 1.00 2.50
12 Marc Bulger 1.00 2.50
13 Ben Roethlisberger 1.50 4.00
14 Michael Vick 1.25 3.00
15 Steve Smith 1.25 3.00
16 Santana Moss 1.00 2.50
17 Chad Johnson 1.00 2.50
18 Terrell Owens 1.25 3.00
19 Plaxico Burress 1.00 2.50
20 Torry Holt 1.00 2.50
21 Reggie Wayne 1.00 2.50
22 Jeremy Shockey 1.25 3.00
23 Jimmy Smith 1.00 2.50
24 Donte Stallworth .75 2.00
25 Alge Crumpler 1.00 2.50
26 Deion Branch 1.00 2.50
27 Keyshawn Johnson 1.00 2.50
28 Warrick Dunn 1.00 2.50
29 Willis McGahee 1.00 2.50
30 Tiki Barber 1.25 3.00
31 Clinton Portis 1.25 3.00
32 Rudi Johnson 1.00 2.50
33 Cadillac Williams 1.00 2.50
34 Thomas Jones 1.00 2.50
35 Larry Johnson 1.00 2.50
36 Kevin Jones .75 2.00
37 Corey Dillon 1.00 2.50
38 Julius Jones .75 2.00
39 Brian Westbrook 1.00 2.50
40 Curtis Martin 1.25 3.00

2006 Donruss Elite Zoning Commission Jerseys

STATED PRINT RUN 399 SER.#'d SETS
*PRIME: .6X TO 1.5X BASIC INSERTS
PRIME PRINT RUN 50 SER.#'d SETS
1 Tom Brady 6.00 15.00
2 Donovan McNabb 4.00 10.00
3 Brett Favre 10.00 25.00
4 Carson Palmer 4.00 10.00
5 Peyton Manning 6.00 15.00
6 Drew Brees 4.00 10.00
7 Drew Bledsoe 4.00 10.00
8 Eli Manning 5.00 12.00
9 Trent Green 3.00 8.00
10 Kerry Collins 3.00 8.00
11 Jake Delhomme 3.00 8.00
12 Marc Bulger 3.00 8.00
13 Ben Roethlisberger 8.00 20.00
14 Michael Vick 4.00 10.00
15 Steve Smith 4.00 10.00
16 Santana Moss 3.00 8.00
17 Chad Johnson 3.00 8.00
18 Terrell Owens 4.00 10.00
19 Plaxico Burress 3.00 8.00
20 Torry Holt 3.00 8.00
21 Reggie Wayne 3.00 8.00
22 Jeremy Shockey 4.00 10.00
23 Jimmy Smith 3.00 8.00
24 Donte Stallworth 3.00 8.00
25 Alge Crumpler 2.50 6.00
26 Deion Branch 2.50 6.00
27 Keyshawn Johnson/54 4.00 10.00
28 Warrick Dunn 3.00 8.00
29 Willis McGahee 3.00 8.00
30 Tiki Barber 4.00 10.00
31 Clinton Portis 4.00 10.00
32 Rudi Johnson 3.00 8.00
33 Cadillac Williams/321 4.00 10.00
34 Thomas Jones 3.00 8.00
35 Larry Johnson 4.00 10.00
36 Kevin Jones 4.00 10.00
37 Corey Dillon 3.00 8.00
38 Julius Jones 4.00 10.00
39 Brian Westbrook 3.00 8.00
40 Curtis Martin 4.00 10.00

2007 Donruss Elite

This 200-card set was released in June, 2007. The set was issued into the hobby in five-card packs, with a $5 SRP, which came 20 packs to a box. Cards numbered 1-100 feature veterans in their 2006 team alphabetical order while cards 101-200 feature 2007 NFL rookies. Those Rookie Cards were issued to a stated print run of 599 serial numbered sets.

COMP.SET w/o RC's (100) 7.50 20.00
ROOKIE PRINT RUN 599 SER.#'d SETS
1 Anquan Boldin .30 .75
2 Edgerrin James .30 .75
3 Matt Leinart .30 .75
4 Alge Crumpler .30 .75
5 Michael Vick .40 1.00
6 Jerious Norwood .30 .75
7 Warrick Dunn .30 .75
8 Jamal Lewis .30 .75
9 Mark Clayton .30 .75
10 Steve McNair .30 .75
11 J.P. Losman .25 .60
12 Lee Evans .30 .75
13 Willis McGahee .30 .75
14 DeAngelo Williams .40 1.00
15 Jake Delhomme .30 .75
16 Steve Smith .30 .75
17 Bernard Berrian .25 .60
18 Rex Grossman .30 .75
19 Thomas Jones .30 .75
20 Carson Palmer .30 .75
21 Chad Johnson .30 .75
22 Rudi Johnson .30 .75
23 T.J. Houshmandzadeh .30 .75
24 Braylon Edwards .30 .75
25 Charlie Frye .30 .75
26 Reuben Droughns .30 .75
27 Julius Jones .25 .60
28 Terrell Owens .40 1.00
29 Tony Romo .50 1.25
30 Javon Walker .30 .75
31 Jay Cutler .40 1.00
32 Mike Bell .30 .75
33 Jon Kitna .25 .60
34 Kevin Jones .25 .60
35 Roy Williams WR .30 .75
36 Brett Favre .75 2.00
37 Donald Driver .40 1.00
38 Ahman Green .30 .75
39 Andre Johnson .30 .75
40 Matt Schaub .30 .75
41 Wali Lundy .25 .60
42 Joseph Addai .30 .75
43 Marvin Harrison .40 1.00
44 Peyton Manning .60 1.50
45 Reggie Wayne .30 .75
46 Byron Leftwich .30 .75
47 Fred Taylor .30 .75
48 Maurice Jones-Drew .40 1.00
49 Larry Johnson .25 .60
50 Tony Gonzalez .30 .75
51 Trent Green .30 .75
52 Chris Chambers .30 .75
53 Daunte Culpepper .30 .75
54 Ronnie Brown .30 .75
55 Chester Taylor .25 .60
56 Tarvaris Jackson .25 .60
57 Travis Taylor .25 .60
58 Tom Brady .60 1.50
59 Corey Dillon .30 .75
60 Laurence Maroney .30 .75
61 Deuce McAllister .30 .75
62 Drew Brees .40 1.00
63 Marques Colston .40 1.00
64 Reggie Bush .40 1.00
65 Brandon Jacobs .30 .75
66 Eli Manning .40 1.00
67 Jeremy Shockey .30 .75
68 Chad Pennington .30 .75
69 Laveranues Coles .25 .60
70 Leon Washington .30 .75
71 Ronald Curry .30 .75
72 LaMont Jordan .30 .75
73 Randy Moss .40 1.00
74 Brian Westbrook .30 .75
75 Donovan McNabb .40 1.00
76 Reggie Brown .25 .60
77 Ben Roethlisberger .40 1.00
78 Hines Ward .40 1.00
79 Willie Parker .30 .75
80 Antonio Gates .40 1.00
81 LaDainian Tomlinson .40 1.00
82 Philip Rivers .40 1.00
83 Alex Smith QB .40 1.00
84 Frank Gore .40 1.00
85 Vernon Davis .30 .75
86 Darrell Jackson .25 .60
87 Matt Hasselbeck .30 .75
88 Shaun Alexander .30 .75
89 Marc Bulger .30 .75
90 Steven Jackson .40 1.00
91 Torry Holt .30 .75
92 Chris Simms .25 .60
93 Cadillac Williams .30 .75
94 Joey Galloway .30 .75
95 Drew Bennett .25 .60
96 LenDale White .30 .75
97 Vince Young .30 .75
98 Clinton Portis .30 .75
99 Jason Campbell .30 .75
100 Santana Moss .30 .75
101 A.J. Davis RC 2.50 6.00
102 Aaron Ross RC 4.00 10.00
103 Aaron Rouse RC 3.00 8.00
104 Adam Carriker RC 3.00 8.00
105 Adrian Peterson RC 15.00 40.00
106 Ahmad Bradshaw RC 6.00 15.00
107 Alan Branch RC 3.00 8.00
108 Amobi Okoye RC 4.00 10.00
109 Anthony Gonzalez RC 4.00 10.00
110 Anthony Spencer RC 4.00 10.00
111 Antonio Pittman RC 2.50 6.00
112 Aundrae Allison RC 2.50 6.00
113 Brady Quinn RC 4.00 10.00
114 Brandon Jackson RC 3.00 8.00
115 Brandon Meriweather RC 4.00 10.00
116 Brandon Siler RC 2.50 6.00
117 Brian Leonard RC 3.00 8.00
118 Calvin Johnson RC 12.00 30.00
119 Chansi Stuckey RC 4.00 10.00
120 Chris Davis RC 2.50 6.00
121 Chris Henry RC 2.50 6.00
122 Chris Houston RC 3.00 8.00
123 Chris Leak RC 3.00 8.00
124 Courtney Taylor RC 3.00 8.00
125 Craig Buster Davis RC 3.00 8.00
126 Dallas Baker RC 2.50 6.00
127 Darius Walker RC 2.50 6.00
128 Darrelle Revis RC 6.00 15.00
129 David Ball RC 3.00 8.00
130 David Clowney RC 3.00 8.00
131 David Harris RC 3.00 8.00
132 DeShawn Wynn RC 3.00 8.00
133 D'Juan Woods RC 2.50 6.00
134 Drew Stanton RC 2.50 6.00
135 Dwayne Bowe RC 5.00 12.00
136 Dwayne Jarrett RC 3.00 8.00
137 Dwayne Wright RC 3.00 8.00
138 Eric Weddle RC 4.00 10.00
139 Gaines Adams RC 4.00 10.00
140 Garrett Wolfe RC 2.50 6.00
141 Gary Russell RC 3.00 8.00
142 Greg Olsen RC 3.00 8.00
143 H.B. Blades RC 2.50 6.00
144 Isaiah Stanback RC 2.50 6.00
145 Jacoby Jones RC 4.00 10.00
146 Jamaal Anderson RC 3.00 8.00
147 JaMarcus Russell RC 2.50 6.00
148 James Jones RC 4.00 10.00
149 Jared Zabransky RC 3.00 8.00
150 Jarrett Hicks RC 3.00 8.00
151 Jarvis Moss RC 3.00 8.00
152 Jason Hill RC 4.00 10.00
153 Jason Snelling RC 4.00 10.00
154 Jeff Rowe RC 2.50 6.00
155 Joel Filani RC 3.00 8.00
156 John Beck RC 4.00 10.00
157 Johnnie Lee Higgins RC 3.00 8.00
158 Jon Beason RC 3.00 8.00
159 Jon Cornish RC 3.00 8.00
160 Jonathan Wade RC 3.00 8.00
161 Jordan Kent RC 3.00 8.00
162 Jordan Palmer RC 3.00 8.00
163 Kenneth Darby RC 3.00 8.00
164 Kenny Irons RC 2.50 6.00
165 Kevin Kolb RC 6.00 15.00
166 Kolby Smith RC 3.00 8.00
167 LaRon Landry RC 4.00 10.00
168 Laurent Robinson RC 4.00 10.00
169 Lawrence Timmons RC 4.00 10.00
170 Leon Hall RC 3.00 8.00
171 Lorenzo Booker RC 3.00 8.00
172 Marshawn Lynch RC 4.00 10.00
173 Matt Trannon RC 2.50 6.00
174 Michael Bush RC 4.00 10.00
175 Michael Griffin RC 4.00 10.00
176 Mike Walker RC 4.00 10.00
177 Nate Ilaoa RC 3.00 8.00
178 Patrick Willis RC 8.00 20.00
179 Paul Posluszny RC 4.00 10.00
180 Paul Williams RC 2.50 6.00
181 Reggie Nelson RC 3.00 8.00
182 Rhema McKnight RC 2.50 6.00
183 Robert Meachem RC 4.00 10.00
184 Rufus Alexander RC 3.00 8.00
185 Ryan Moore RC 3.00 8.00
186 Selvin Young RC 3.00 8.00
187 Sidney Rice RC 5.00 12.00
188 Steve Breaston RC 4.00 10.00
189 Steve Smith USC RC 4.00 10.00
190 Syvelle Newton RC 3.00 8.00
191 DeMarcus Tank Tyler RC 2.50 6.00
192 Ted Ginn Jr. RC 3.00 8.00
193 Tony Hunt RC 2.50 6.00
194 Trent Edwards RC 4.00 10.00
195 Troy Smith RC 4.00 10.00
196 Tyler Palko RC 3.00 8.00
197 Tymere Zimmerman RC 3.00 8.00
198 Yamon Figurs RC 2.50 6.00
199 Zac Taylor RC 3.00 8.00
200 Zach Miller RC 4.00 10.00

2007 Donruss Elite Aspirations

*VETS/70-99: 5X TO 12X BASIC CARDS
*ROOKIES/70-99: .6X TO 1.5X BASIC CARDS
*VETS/45-69: 6X TO 15X BASIC CARDS
*ROOKIES/45-69: .8X TO 2X BASIC CARDS
*VETS/20-29: 10X TO 25X BASIC CARDS
*ROOKIES/20-29: 1.2X TO 3X BASIC CARDS
*VETS/10-19: 12X TO 30X BASIC CARDS
*ROOKIES/10-19: 1.5X TO 4X BASIC CARDS
SERIAL #'d UNDER 20 NOT PRICED
STATED PRINT RUN 6-99 SER.#'d SETS

2007 Donruss Elite Status

*VETS/70-99: 5X TO 12X BASIC CARDS
*ROOKIES/70-99: .6X TO 1.5X BASIC CARDS
*ROOKIES/45-69: .8X TO 2X BASIC CARDS
*VETS/30-44: 8X TO 20X BASIC CARDS
*ROOKIES/30-44: 1X TO 2.5X BASIC CARDS
*VETS/20-29: 10X TO 25X BASIC CARDS
*ROOKIES/20-29: 1.2X TO 3X BASIC CARDS
*VETS/10-19: 12X TO 30X BASIC CARDS
*ROOKIES/10-19: 1.5X TO 4X BASIC CARDS
STATED PRINT RUN 1-93
SERIAL #'d UNDER 20 NOT PRICED

2007 Donruss Elite Status Gold

*VETS 1-100: 10X TO 25X BASIC CARDS
*ROOKIES 101-200: 1.2X TO 3X BASIC CARDS
STATED PRINT RUN 24 SER.#'d SETS

2007 Donruss Elite Back to the Future Green

GREEN PRINT RUN 800 SER.#'d SETS
*BLUE/400: .6X TO 1.2X GREEN/800
BLUE PRINT RUN 400 SER.#'d SETS
*RED/200: .6X TO 1.5X GREEN/800
RED PRINT RUN 200 SER.#'d SETS
1 Hines Ward 1.50 4.00
Santonio Holmes
2 Fred Taylor 1.50 4.00
Maurice Jones-Drew
3 Warrick Dunn 1.25 3.00
Jerious Norwood
4 Steve McNair 1.25 3.00
Vince Young
5 Troy Aikman 4.00 10.00
Tony Romo
6 Dan Fouts 1.50 4.00
Philip Rivers
7 John Elway 2.00 5.00
Jay Cutler
8 Eric Dickerson 2.00 5.00
Joseph Addai
10 Gale Sayers 2.00 5.00
Reggie Bush
11 Jim Brown 2.00 5.00
LaDainian Tomlinson
12 Lawrence Taylor 1.50 4.00
Shawne Merriman
13 Matt Leinart 2.00 5.00
Steve Young
14 Tim Brown 1.50 4.00
Marques Colston
15 Brian Urlacher 1.25 3.00
A.J. Hawk
16 Roger Craig 1.50 4.00
Frank Gore
17 Randall Cunningham 1.50 4.00
Michael Vick
18 Michael Irvin 1.50 4.00
Terrell Owens
19 Marcus Allen 1.50 4.00
Steven Jackson
20 Dave Casper 1.25 3.00
Tony Gonzalez
21 Jerry Rice 2.50 6.00
Marvin Harrison
22 Rod Smith 1.25 3.00
Brandon Marshall
23 Mark Duper 1.25 3.00
Chris Chambers
24 Bill Bates 1.25 3.00
Roy Williams S
25 Joe Theismann 1.50 4.00
Jason Campbell

2007 Donruss Elite Back to the Future Jerseys

STATED PRINT RUN 46-299
*PRIME/25: .8X TO 2X JSY/150-299
*PRIME/25: .5X TO 1.2X JSY/46
PRIME PRINT RUN 25 SER.#'d SETS
1 Hines Ward 5.00 12.00
Santonio Holmes
2 Fred Taylor 5.00 12.00
Maurice Jones-Drew
3 Warrick Dunn 4.00 10.00
Jerious Norwood
4 Steve McNair 4.00 10.00
Vince Young
5 Troy Aikman 6.00 15.00
Tony Romo/150
6 Dan Fouts 5.00 12.00
Philip Rivers
7 John Elway 12.00 30.00
Jay Cutler
8 Eric Dickerson 4.00 10.00
Joseph Addai
10 Gale Sayers 12.00 30.00
Reggie Bush
11 Jim Brown 8.00 20.00
LaDainian Tomlinson
12 Lawrence Taylor 5.00 12.00
Shawne Merriman/150
13 Matt Leinart 8.00 20.00
Steve Young
14 Tim Brown 5.00 12.00
Marques Colston/150
15 Brian Urlacher 4.00 10.00
A.J. Hawk
16 Roger Craig 5.00 12.00
Frank Gore
17 Randall Cunningham 5.00 12.00
Michael Vick
18 Michael Irvin 5.00 12.00
Terrell Owens/150
19 Marcus Allen 5.00 12.00
Steven Jackson
20 Dave Casper 4.00 10.00
Tony Gonzalez
21 Jerry Rice 8.00 20.00
Marvin Harrison
22 Rod Smith 4.00 10.00
Brandon Marshall/150
23 Mark Duper 4.00 10.00
Chris Chambers
24 Bill Bates 4.00 10.00
Roy Williams S
25 Joe Theismann 8.00 20.00
Jason Campbell/46

2007 Donruss Elite Chain Reaction Gold

GOLD PRINT RUN 1000 SER.#'d SETS
*BLACK/400: .5X TO 1.2X GOLD/1000
BLACK PRINT RUN 400 SER.#'d SETS
*RED/200: .6X TO 1.5X GOLD/1000
RED PRINT RUN 200 SER.#'d SETS
1 Plaxico Burress 1.00 2.50
2 Chris Henry .75 2.00
3 Antonio Gates 1.25 3.00
4 Lee Evans 1.00 2.50
5 Reggie Brown .75 2.00
6 Marques Colston 1.25 3.00
7 Alge Crumpler 1.00 2.50
8 Jeremy Shockey 1.00 2.50
9 Roy Williams WR 1.00 2.50
10 Andre Johnson 1.00 2.50
11 Laveranues Coles .75 2.00
12 Terry Glenn 1.00 2.50
13 LaDainian Tomlinson 1.25 3.00
14 Larry Johnson .75 2.00
15 Rudi Johnson 1.00 2.50
16 Edgerrin James 1.00 2.50
17 Jamal Lewis 1.00 2.50
18 Willis McGahee 1.00 2.50
19 Drew Brees 1.25 3.00
20 Peyton Manning 2.00 5.00
21 Donovan McNabb 1.25 3.00
22 Carson Palmer 1.00 2.50
23 Tom Brady 2.00 5.00
24 Marc Bulger 1.00 2.50
25 Philip Rivers 1.25 3.00

2007 Donruss Elite Chain Reaction Jerseys

STATED PRINT RUN 150 SER.#'d SETS
*PRIME/99: .6X TO 1.5X BASIC JSY/150
*PRIME/30: .8X TO 2X BASIC JSY/150
PRIME PRINT RUN 30-99
1 Plaxico Burress 4.00 10.00
2 Chris Henry 3.00 8.00
3 Antonio Gates 5.00 12.00
4 Lee Evans 4.00 10.00
5 Reggie Brown 3.00 8.00
6 Marques Colston 5.00 12.00
7 Alge Crumpler 4.00 10.00
8 Jeremy Shockey 4.00 10.00
9 Roy Williams WR 4.00 10.00
10 Andre Johnson 4.00 10.00
11 Laveranues Coles 3.00 8.00
12 Terry Glenn 4.00 10.00
13 LaDainian Tomlinson 5.00 12.00
14 Larry Johnson 3.00 8.00
15 Rudi Johnson 4.00 10.00
16 Edgerrin James 4.00 10.00
17 Jamal Lewis 4.00 10.00
18 Willis McGahee 4.00 10.00
19 Drew Brees 5.00 12.00
20 Peyton Manning 10.00 25.00
21 Donovan McNabb 5.00 12.00
22 Carson Palmer 4.00 10.00
23 Tom Brady 8.00 20.00
24 Marc Bulger 4.00 10.00
25 Philip Rivers 5.00 12.00

2007 Donruss Elite College Ties Green

GREEN PRINT RUN 800 SER.#'d SETS
*GOLD/400: .5X TO 1.2X GREEN/800
GOLD PRINT RUN 400 SER.#'d SETS
*BLACK/200: .6X TO 1.5X GREEN/800
BLACK PRINT RUN 200 SER.#'d SETS
1 Cadillac Williams 1.50 4.00
Kenny Irons
2 Roy Williams S 4.00 10.00
Adrian Peterson
3 Derek Hagan 1.25 3.00
Zach Miller
4 Matt Leinart 1.50 4.00
Steve Smith USC
5 Maurice Stovall 3.00 8.00
Brady Quinn
6 Joseph Addai 2.00 5.00
Dwayne Bowe
7 Michael Clayton 1.50 4.00
Craig Buster Davis
8 Robert Meachem 1.25 3.00
Jayson Swain
9 Reggie Bush 3.00 8.00
Dwayne Jarrett
10 Ahman Green 3.00 8.00
Zac Taylor
11 Devery Henderson 1.00 2.50
JaMarcus Russell
12 A.J. Hawk 2.50 6.00
Troy Smith
13 Frank Gore 1.50 4.00
Tyrone Moss
14 Tiki Barber 1.50 4.00
Jason Snelling
15 Ronnie Brown 1.25 3.00
Courtney Taylor
16 Anquan Boldin 1.50 4.00
Lorenzo Booker
17 Cedric Benson 1.25 3.00
Selvin Young
18 Michael Bush 2.00 5.00
Amobi Okoye
19 Aaron Rodgers 3.00 8.00
Marshawn Lynch
20 Larry Johnson 2.50 6.00
Paul Posluszny

2007 Donruss Elite College Ties Autographs

STATED PRINT RUN 10-25
SERIAL #'d UNDER 25 NOT PRICED
1 Cadillac Williams 15.00 40.00
Kenny Irons AU/25
2 Roy Williams S 200.00 350.00
Adrian Peterson AU/10
3 Derek Hagan 15.00 40.00
Zach Miller AU/25
6 Joseph Addai 20.00 50.00
Dwayne Bowe AU/25
8 Robert Meachem
Jayson Swain/25
9 Reggie Bush 150.00 300.00
Dwayne Jarrett/10
12 A.J. Hawk 30.00 80.00
Troy Smith AU/25
17 Cedric Benson AU 20.00 50.00
Selvin Young AU/25
18 Michael Bush AU 30.00 80.00
Amobi Okoye AU/25
19 Aaron Rodgers 125.00 200.00
Marshawn Lynch AU/25
20 Larry Johnson AU 60.00 120.00
Paul Posluszny AU/25

2007 Donruss Elite College Ties Jerseys

STATED PRINT RUN 120-250
*PRIME/50-99: .6X TO 1.5X BASIC JSYs
*PRIME/25-35: .8X TO 2X BASIC JSYs
PRIME PRINT RUN 25-99
1 Cadillac Williams 6.00 15.00
Kenny Irons/250
2 Roy Williams S 25.00 60.00
Adrian Peterson/200
3 Derek Hagan 5.00 12.00
Zach Miller/120
4 Matt Leinart 8.00 20.00
Steve Smith USC/250
5 Maurice Stovall 12.00 30.00
Brady Quinn/250
6 Joseph Addai 8.00 20.00
Dwayne Bowe/250
7 Michael Clayton 6.00 15.00
Craig Buster Davis/250
8 Robert Meachem 10.00 25.00
Jayson Swain/250
9 Reggie Bush 12.00 30.00
Dwayne Jarrett/250
10 Ahman Green 12.00 30.00
Zac Taylor/120
11 Devery Henderson 4.00 10.00
JaMarcus Russell/250
12 A.J. Hawk 10.00 25.00
Troy Smith/120
13 Frank Gore 5.00 12.00
Tyrone Moss/120
15 Ronnie Brown 5.00 12.00
Courtney Taylor/250
16 Anquan Boldin 5.00 12.00
Lorenzo Booker/120
17 Cedric Benson 5.00 12.00
Selvin Young/120

2007 Donruss Elite Passing the Torch Red

RED PRINT RUN 800 SER.#'d SETS
*GREEN/400: .5X TO 1.2X RED/800
GREEN PRINT RUN 400 SER.#'d SETS
*BLUE/200: .6X TO 1.5X RED/800
BLUE PRINT RUN 200 SER.#'d SETS
1 Steve McNair 1.00 2.50
2 Vince Young 1.00 2.50
3 Troy Aikman 1.50 4.00
4 Tony Romo 1.50 4.00
5 Dan Fouts 1.25 3.00
6 Philip Rivers 1.25 3.00
7 Archie Manning 1.25 3.00
8 Drew Brees 1.25 3.00
9 Curtis Martin 1.25 3.00
10 Leon Washington 1.00 2.50
11 Corey Dillon 1.00 2.50
12 Laurence Maroney 1.00 2.50
13 John Elway 2.00 5.00
14 Jay Cutler 1.25 3.00
15 Eric Dickerson 1.00 2.50
16 Joseph Addai 1.00 2.50
17 Terrell Davis 1.25 3.00
18 Mike Bell 1.00 2.50
19 Sterling Sharpe 1.00 2.50
20 Greg Jennings 1.25 3.00
21 Steve McNair 1.25 3.00
Vince Young
22 Troy Aikman 2.00 5.00
Tony Romo
23 Dan Fouts 1.50 4.00
Philip Rivers
24 Archie Manning 1.50 4.00
Drew Brees
25 Curtis Martin 1.50 4.00
Leon Washington
26 Corey Dillon 1.25 3.00
Laurence Maroney
27 John Elway 2.50 6.00
Jay Cutler
28 Eric Dickerson 1.25 3.00

Joseph Addai
29 Terrell Davis 1.50 4.00
Mike Bell
30 Sterling Sharpe 1.50 4.00
Greg Jennings

2007 Donruss Elite Passing the Torch Autographs

1-20 SINGLE AU STATED PRINT RUN 99
21-30 DUAL AU STATED PRINT RUN 49
1 Steve McNair 20.00 40.00
2 Vince Young 15.00 40.00
3 Troy Aikman 40.00 80.00
4 Tony Romo 50.00 100.00
5 Dan Fouts 25.00 50.00
6 Philip Rivers 15.00 40.00
8 Drew Brees 30.00 60.00
9 Curtis Martin 35.00 60.00
10 Leon Washington 12.00 30.00
11 Corey Dillon 10.00 25.00
12 Laurence Maroney 12.00 30.00
13 John Elway 60.00 120.00
14 Jay Cutler 30.00 60.00
15 Eric Dickerson 15.00 40.00
16 Joseph Addai 12.00 30.00
17 Terrell Davis 15.00 40.00
18 Mike Bell 10.00 25.00
19 Sterling Sharpe 15.00 40.00
20 Greg Jennings 15.00 40.00
21 Steve McNair 60.00 120.00
Vince Young
22 Troy Aikman 75.00 150.00
Tony Romo
24 Archie Manning 60.00 120.00
Drew Brees
27 John Elway 100.00 200.00
Jay Cutler
28 Eric Dickerson 50.00 100.00
Joseph Addai
29 Terrell Davis 30.00 60.00
Mike Bell
30 Sterling Sharpe 50.00 100.00
Greg Jennings

2007 Donruss Elite Prime Targets Gold

GOLD PRINT RUN 1000 SER.#'d SETS
*BLACK/400: .5X TO 1.2X GOLD/1000
BLACK PRINT RUN 400 SER.#'d SETS
*RED/200: .6X TO 1.5X GOLD/1000
RED PRINT RUN 200 SER.#'d SETS
1 Reggie Bush 1.25 3.00
2 Terrell Owens 1.25 3.00
3 LaDainian Tomlinson 1.25 3.00
4 Chad Johnson 1.00 2.50
5 Steven Jackson 1.25 3.00
6 Maurice Jones-Drew 1.25 3.00
7 Marvin Harrison 1.25 3.00
8 Donald Driver 1.25 3.00
9 Darrell Jackson .75 2.00
10 Torry Holt 1.00 2.50

2007 Donruss Elite Prime Targets Jerseys

STATED PRINT RUN 175-299
*PRIME/50: .6X TO 1.5X BASIC JSYs
PRIME PRINT RUN 50 SER.#'d SETS
1 Reggie Bush 5.00 12.00
2 Terrell Owens/175 5.00 12.00
3 LaDainian Tomlinson/250 5.00 12.00
4 Chad Johnson 4.00 10.00
5 Steven Jackson 5.00 12.00
6 Maurice Jones-Drew 5.00 12.00
7 Marvin Harrison 5.00 12.00
8 Donald Driver 5.00 12.00
9 Darrell Jackson 3.00 8.00
10 Torry Holt 4.00 10.00

2007 Donruss Elite Series Gold

GOLD PRINT RUN 1000 SER.#'d SETS
*BLACK/400: .5X TO 1.2X GOLD/1000
BLACK PRINT RUN 400 SER.#'d SETS
*RED/200: .6X TO 1.5X GOLD/1000
RED PRINT RUN 200 SER.#'d SETS
1 Hines Ward 1.25 3.00
2 Peyton Manning 2.00 5.00
3 Drew Brees 1.25 3.00
4 Vince Young 1.00 2.50
5 Reggie Bush 1.25 3.00
6 Matt Leinart 1.00 2.50
7 Maurice Jones-Drew 1.25 3.00
8 Joseph Addai 1.00 2.50
9 Tony Romo 1.50 4.00
10 Philip Rivers 1.25 3.00
11 LaDainian Tomlinson 1.25 3.00
12 Vernon Davis 1.00 2.50
13 Frank Gore 1.25 3.00
14 Willie Parker 1.00 2.50
15 Steven Jackson 1.25 3.00
16 Cadillac Williams 1.00 2.50
17 Ronnie Brown 1.00 2.50
18 Chris Chambers 1.00 2.50
19 Larry Fitzgerald 1.25 3.00
20 Mark Clayton 1.00 2.50
21 Braylon Edwards 1.00 2.50
22 Matt Hasselbeck 1.00 2.50
23 J.P. Losman .75 2.00
24 Thomas Jones 1.00 2.50
25 Shaun Alexander 1.00 2.50

2007 Donruss Elite Series Autographs

UNPRICED AUTO PRINT RUN 1-10

2007 Donruss Elite Series Jerseys

STATED PRINT RUN 30-299
*PRIME/50-99: .6X TO 1.5X JSY/150-299
*PRIME/99: .4X TO 1X JSY/30
*PRIME/25: .8X TO 2X JSY/175
PRIME PRINT RUN 25-99
1 Hines Ward/30 8.00 20.00
2 Peyton Manning/170 10.00 25.00
3 Drew Brees/175 5.00 12.00
4 Vince Young/175 4.00 10.00
5 Reggie Bush/175 5.00 12.00
6 Matt Leinart/175 4.00 10.00
7 Maurice Jones-Drew/175 5.00 12.00
8 Joseph Addai/175 4.00 10.00
9 Tony Romo/150 6.00 15.00
10 Philip Rivers/175 5.00 12.00
11 LaDainian Tomlinson/175 5.00 12.00
12 Vernon Davis/175 4.00 10.00
13 Frank Gore/115 5.00 12.00
14 Willie Parker/175 4.00 10.00
15 Steven Jackson/175 5.00 12.00
16 Cadillac Williams/175 4.00 10.00
17 Ronnie Brown/299 4.00 10.00
18 Chris Chambers/299 4.00 10.00
19 Larry Fitzgerald/299 5.00 12.00
20 Mark Clayton/299 4.00 10.00
21 Braylon Edwards/175 4.00 10.00
22 Matt Hasselbeck/299 4.00 10.00
23 J.P. Losman/299 3.00 8.00
24 Thomas Jones/299 4.00 10.00
25 Shaun Alexander/175 4.00 10.00

2007 Donruss Elite Status Autographs Gold

GOLD PRINT RUN 24 SER.#'d SETS
UNPRICED BLACK PRINT RUN 1
101 A.J. Davis 12.00 30.00
102 Aaron Ross 20.00 50.00
103 Aaron Rouse 15.00 40.00
104 Adam Carriker 15.00 40.00
105 Adrian Peterson 250.00 400.00
106 Ahmad Bradshaw 30.00 80.00
108 Amobi Okoye 20.00 50.00
109 Anthony Gonzalez 20.00 50.00
110 Anthony Spencer 20.00 50.00
111 Antonio Pittman 12.00 30.00
112 Aundrae Allison 12.00 30.00
113 Brady Quinn 40.00 100.00
114 Brandon Jackson 15.00 40.00
116 Brandon Siler 12.00 30.00
117 Brian Leonard 15.00 40.00
118 Calvin Johnson 125.00 250.00
119 Chansi Stuckey 20.00 50.00
120 Chris Davis 12.00 30.00
121 Chris Henry 12.00 30.00
122 Chris Houston 15.00 40.00
123 Chris Leak 15.00 40.00
124 Courtney Taylor 15.00 40.00
126 Dallas Baker 12.00 30.00
127 Darius Walker 12.00 30.00
128 Darrelle Revis 30.00 80.00
129 David Ball 15.00 40.00
130 David Clowney 15.00 40.00
131 David Harris 15.00 40.00
132 DeShawn Wynn 15.00 40.00
133 D'Juan Woods 12.00 30.00
134 Drew Stanton 12.00 30.00
135 Dwayne Bowe 25.00 60.00
136 Dwayne Jarrett 15.00 40.00
137 Dwayne Wright 15.00 40.00
139 Gaines Adams 20.00 50.00
140 Garrett Wolfe 12.00 30.00
141 Gary Russell 15.00 40.00
142 Greg Olsen 15.00 40.00
143 H.B. Blades 12.00 30.00
144 Isaiah Stanback 12.00 30.00
146 Jamaal Anderson 15.00 40.00
147 JaMarcus Russell 12.00 30.00
148 James Jones 20.00 50.00
149 Jared Zabransky 15.00 40.00
150 Jarrett Hicks 15.00 40.00
151 Jarvis Moss 15.00 40.00
152 Jason Hill 20.00 50.00
153 Jason Snelling 20.00 50.00
154 Jeff Rowe 12.00 30.00
155 Joel Filani 15.00 40.00
156 John Beck 20.00 50.00
157 Johnnie Lee Higgins 15.00 40.00
158 Jon Beason 15.00 40.00
159 Jon Cornish 15.00 40.00
162 Jordan Palmer 15.00 40.00
163 Kenneth Darby 15.00 40.00
164 Kenny Irons 12.00 30.00
165 Kevin Kolb 30.00 80.00
166 Kolby Smith 15.00 40.00
167 LaRon Landry 20.00 50.00
168 Laurent Robinson 20.00 50.00
169 Lawrence Timmons 20.00 50.00
170 Leon Hall 15.00 40.00
171 Lorenzo Booker 15.00 40.00
172 Marshawn Lynch 25.00 60.00
174 Michael Bush 20.00 50.00
175 Michael Griffin 20.00 50.00
176 Mike Walker 20.00 50.00
177 Nate Ilaoa 15.00 40.00
178 Patrick Willis 50.00 100.00
179 Paul Posluszny 20.00 50.00
180 Paul Williams 12.00 30.00
181 Reggie Nelson 15.00 40.00
182 Rhema McKnight 12.00 30.00
183 Robert Meachem 20.00 50.00
184 Rufus Alexander 15.00 40.00
186 Selvin Young 15.00 40.00
187 Sidney Rice 25.00 60.00
188 Steve Breaston 20.00 50.00
189 Steve Smith USC 20.00 50.00
190 Syvelle Newton 15.00 40.00
192 Ted Ginn Jr. 15.00 40.00
193 Tony Hunt 12.00 30.00
194 Trent Edwards 20.00 50.00
195 Troy Smith 20.00 50.00
196 Tyler Palko 15.00 40.00
197 Tymere Zimmerman 15.00 40.00
198 Yamon Figurs 12.00 30.00
200 Zach Miller 20.00 50.00

2007 Donruss Elite Teams Black

BLACK PRINT RUN 800 SER.#'d SETS
*RED/400: .5X TO 1.2X BLACK/800
RED PRINT RUN 400 SER.#'d SETS
*GOLD/200: .6X TO 1.5X BLACK/800
GOLD PRINT RUN 200 SER.#'d SETS
1 Matt Leinart 1.25 3.00
Edgerrin James
Anquan Boldin
2 Michael Vick 1.50 4.00
Alge Crumpler
Jerious Norwood
3 Steve McNair 1.25 3.00
Derrick Mason
Mark Clayton
4 J.P. Losman 1.25 3.00
Willis McGahee
Lee Evans
5 Jake Delhomme 1.50 4.00
Steve Smith
DeAngelo Williams
6 Rex Grossman 1.25 3.00
Bernard Berrian
Cedric Benson
7 Carson Palmer 1.25 3.00
Chad Johnson
T.J. Houshmandzadeh
8 Tony Romo 2.00 5.00
Julius Jones
Terrell Owens
9 Jay Cutler 1.50 4.00
Mike Bell
Javon Walker
10 Brett Favre 1.25 3.00
A.J. Hawk
Donald Driver
11 Peyton Manning 2.50 6.00
Marvin Harrison
Joseph Addai
12 Byron Leftwich 1.50 4.00
Fred Taylor
Maurice Jones-Drew
13 Tom Brady 2.50 6.00
Corey Dillon
Laurence Maroney
14 Drew Brees 1.50 4.00
Deuce McAllister
Reggie Bush
15 Eli Manning 1.50 4.00
Jeremy Shockey
Brandon Jacobs
16 Donovan McNabb 1.50 4.00
Brian Westbrook
Donte Stallworth
17 Ben Roethlisberger 1.50 4.00
Willie Parker
Hines Ward
18 Philip Rivers 1.50 4.00
LaDainian Tomlinson
Antonio Gates
19 Alex Smith QB 1.50 4.00
Frank Gore
Vernon Davis
20 Matt Hasselbeck 1.25 3.00
Shaun Alexander
Darrell Jackson
21 Marc Bulger 1.50 4.00
Steven Jackson
Torry Holt
22 Vince Young 1.25 3.00
Brandon Jones
LenDale White
23 Jason Campbell 1.25 3.00
Clinton Portis
Santana Moss
24 Trent Green 1.25 3.00
Larry Johnson
Tony Gonzalez
25 Chad Pennington 1.25 3.00
Leon Washington
Laveranues Coles

2007 Donruss Elite Teams Jerseys

STATED PRINT RUN 50-99
*PRIME/25: .8X TO 2X BASIC JSY
PRIME PRINT RUN 25 SER.#'d SETS
1 Matt Leinart 8.00 20.00
Edgerrin James
Anquan Boldin
2 Michael Vick 10.00 25.00
Alge Crumpler
Jerious Norwood
3 Steve McNair 8.00 20.00
Derrick Mason
Mark Clayton
4 J.P. Losman 8.00 20.00
Willis McGahee
Lee Evans
5 Jake Delhomme 10.00 25.00
Steve Smith
DeAngelo Williams
6 Rex Grossman 8.00 20.00
Bernard Berrian
Cedric Benson
7 Carson Palmer 8.00 20.00
Chad Johnson
T.J. Houshmandzadeh
8 Tony Romo 12.00 30.00
Julius Jones
Terrell Owens/50
9 Jay Cutler 10.00 25.00
Mike Bell
Javon Walker
10 Brett Favre 8.00 20.00
A.J. Hawk
Donald Driver
11 Peyton Manning 15.00 40.00
Marvin Harrison
Joseph Addai
12 Byron Leftwich 10.00 25.00
Fred Taylor
Maurice Jones-Drew
13 Tom Brady 15.00 40.00
Corey Dillon
Laurence Maroney
14 Drew Brees 10.00 25.00
Deuce McAllister
Reggie Bush
15 Eli Manning 10.00 25.00
Jeremy Shockey
Brandon Jacobs
16 Donovan McNabb 10.00 25.00
Brian Westbrook
Donte Stallworth
17 Ben Roethlisberger 10.00 25.00
Willie Parker
Hines Ward
18 Philip Rivers 10.00 25.00
LaDainian Tomlinson
Antonio Gates
19 Alex Smith QB 10.00 25.00
Frank Gore
Vernon Davis
20 Matt Hasselbeck 8.00 20.00
Shaun Alexander
Darrell Jackson
21 Marc Bulger 10.00 25.00
Steven Jackson
Torry Holt
22 Vince Young 8.00 20.00
Brandon Jones
LenDale White
23 Jason Campbell 8.00 20.00
Clinton Portis
Santana Moss/50
24 Trent Green 8.00 20.00
Larry Johnson
Tony Gonzalez
25 Chad Pennington 8.00 20.00
Leon Washington
Laveranues Coles

2007 Donruss Elite Throwback Threads

1-30 PRINT RUN 175-249
31-45 PRINT RUN 100 SER.#'d SETS
*PRIME/20-30: .8X TO 2X BASIC JSYs
PRIME PRINT RUN 6-30
1 Joe Namath/175 8.00 20.00
2 Chad Pennington 4.00 10.00
3 Ozzie Newsome 5.00 12.00
4 Kellen Winslow/245 4.00 10.00
5 Dick Butkus 8.00 20.00
6 Brian Urlacher 5.00 12.00
7 Cris Collinsworth 5.00 12.00
8 Chad Johnson 4.00 10.00
9 Barry Sanders 10.00 25.00
10 Reggie Bush 10.00 25.00
11 Earl Campbell 5.00 12.00
12 Jamal Lewis 4.00 10.00
13 Dan Marino 12.00 30.00
14 Daunte Culpepper 4.00 10.00
16 Terry Glenn 4.00 10.00
17 Roger Staubach 8.00 20.00
18 Tony Romo/175 12.00 30.00
19 Gale Sayers 8.00 20.00
20 Devin Hester 4.00 10.00
21 Warren Moon 5.00 12.00
22 Vince Young 8.00 20.00
23 Jim Brown 8.00 20.00
24 LaDainian Tomlinson 5.00 12.00
25 Dan Fouts 5.00 12.00
26 Philip Rivers 5.00 12.00
27 Tom Brady 6.00 15.00
28 Matt Leinart 6.00 15.00
29 Jim McMahon 6.00 15.00
30 Rex Grossman 4.00 10.00
31 Joe Namath 12.00 30.00
Chad Pennington
32 Ozzie Newsome 6.00 15.00
Kellen Winslow
33 Dick Butkus 12.00 30.00
Brian Urlacher
34 Cris Collinsworth 6.00 15.00
Chad Johnson
35 Barry Sanders 15.00 40.00
Reggie Bush
36 Earl Campbell 6.00 15.00
Jamal Lewis
37 Dan Marino 15.00 40.00
Daunte Culpepper
39 Roger Staubach 20.00 50.00
Tony Romo
40 Gale Sayers 10.00 25.00
Devin Hester
41 Warren Moon 12.00 30.00
Vince Young
42 Jim Brown 12.00 30.00
LaDainian Tomlinson
43 Dan Fouts 8.00 20.00
Philip Rivers
44 Tom Brady 10.00 25.00
Matt Leinart
45 Jim McMahon 10.00 25.00
Rex Grossman

2007 Donruss Elite Throwback Threads Autographs

UNPRICED AUTO PRINT RUN 1-10
UNPRICED AU PRIME PRINT RUN 1-5

2007 Donruss Elite Turn of the Century Autographs

STATED PRINT RUN 50-100
101 A.J. Davis/100 8.00 20.00
103 Aaron Rouse/100 10.00 25.00
104 Adam Carriker/100 10.00 25.00
105 Adrian Peterson/100 100.00 200.00
106 Ahmad Bradshaw/100 20.00 50.00
108 Amobi Okoye/50 15.00 40.00
109 Anthony Gonzalez/100 12.00 30.00
111 Antonio Pittman/50 10.00 25.00
112 Aundrae Allison/50 10.00 25.00
113 Brady Quinn/100 20.00 50.00
114 Brandon Jackson/100 10.00 25.00
115 Brandon Meriweather/50 15.00 40.00
116 Brandon Siler/100 8.00 20.00
117 Brian Leonard/100 10.00 25.00
118 Calvin Johnson/100 60.00 120.00
119 Chansi Stuckey/100 12.00 30.00
120 Chris Davis/50 10.00 25.00
121 Chris Henry/100 8.00 20.00
122 Chris Houston/50 12.00 30.00
123 Chris Leak/50 12.00 30.00
124 Courtney Taylor/50 12.00 30.00
126 Dallas Baker/100 8.00 20.00
127 Darius Walker/100 8.00 20.00
128 Darrelle Revis/50 25.00 60.00
129 David Ball/100 10.00 25.00
130 David Clowney/100 10.00 25.00
131 David Harris/100 10.00 25.00
132 DeShawn Wynn/100 10.00 25.00
133 D'Juan Woods/100 8.00 20.00
134 Drew Stanton/100 8.00 20.00
135 Dwayne Bowe/100 15.00 40.00
136 Dwayne Jarrett/100 10.00 25.00
137 Dwayne Wright/50 12.00 30.00
139 Gaines Adams/100 12.00 30.00
140 Garrett Wolfe/50 10.00 25.00
142 Greg Olsen/100 10.00 25.00
144 Isaiah Stanback/50 10.00 25.00
145 Jacoby Jones/50 15.00 40.00
146 Jamaal Anderson/50 12.00 30.00
147 JaMarcus Russell/100 8.00 20.00
149 Jared Zabransky/100 10.00 25.00
152 Jason Hill/100 12.00 30.00
153 Jason Snelling/50 15.00 40.00
154 Jeff Rowe/100 8.00 20.00
155 Joel Filani/100 10.00 25.00
156 John Beck/100 12.00 30.00
157 Johnnie Lee Higgins/50 12.00 30.00
158 Jon Beason/100 10.00 25.00
159 Jon Cornish/100 10.00 25.00
163 Kenneth Darby/100 10.00 25.00
164 Kenny Irons/100 8.00 20.00
165 Kevin Kolb/100 20.00 50.00
166 Kolby Smith/100 10.00 25.00
167 LaRon Landry/100 12.00 30.00
168 Laurent Robinson/50 15.00 40.00
169 Lawrence Timmons/100 12.00 30.00
170 Leon Hall/100 10.00 25.00
171 Lorenzo Booker/100 10.00 25.00
172 Marshawn Lynch/100 15.00 40.00
174 Michael Bush/50 15.00 40.00
175 Michael Griffin/50 15.00 40.00
176 Mike Walker/100 12.00 30.00
177 Nate Ilaoa/50 12.00 30.00
178 Patrick Willis/50 40.00 80.00
179 Paul Posluszny/50 15.00 40.00
180 Paul Williams/100 8.00 20.00
181 Reggie Nelson/100 10.00 25.00
182 Rhema McKnight/50 10.00 25.00
183 Robert Meachem/100 12.00 30.00
184 Rufus Alexander/100 10.00 25.00
186 Selvin Young/50 12.00 30.00
187 Sidney Rice/100 15.00 40.00
188 Steve Breaston/50 15.00 40.00
189 Steve Smith USC/100 12.00 30.00
190 Syvelle Newton/50 12.00 30.00
192 Ted Ginn Jr./100 10.00 25.00
193 Tony Hunt/50 10.00 25.00
194 Trent Edwards/50 15.00 40.00
195 Troy Smith/50 15.00 40.00
196 Tyler Palko/100 10.00 25.00
197 Tymere Zimmerman/100 10.00 25.00
198 Yamon Figurs/100 8.00 20.00
200 Zach Miller/50 15.00 40.00

2007 Donruss Elite Zoning Commission Gold

GOLD PRINT RUN 1000 SER.#'d SETS
*BLACK/400: .5X TO 1.2X GOLD/1000
BLACK PRINT RUN 400 SER.#'d SETS
*RED/200: .6X TO 1.5X GOLD/1000
RED PRINT RUN 200 SER.#'d SETS
1 Vince Young 1.00 2.50
2 Drew Brees 1.25 3.00
3 Peyton Manning 2.00 5.00
4 Matt Leinart 1.00 2.50
5 Jay Cutler 1.25 3.00
6 Carson Palmer 1.00 2.50
7 Marc Bulger 1.00 2.50
8 Jon Kitna .75 2.00
9 Tom Brady 2.00 5.00
10 Philip Rivers 1.25 3.00
11 Michael Vick 1.25 3.00
12 Eli Manning 1.25 3.00
13 Rex Grossman 1.00 2.50
14 Steve McNair 1.00 2.50
15 Tony Romo 1.50 4.00
16 Chad Johnson 1.00 2.50
17 Marvin Harrison 1.25 3.00
18 Reggie Wayne 1.00 2.50
19 Roy Williams WR 1.00 2.50
20 Anquan Boldin 1.00 2.50
21 Donald Driver 1.25 3.00
22 Torry Holt 1.00 2.50
23 Steve Smith 1.00 2.50
24 Javon Walker 1.00 2.50
25 T.J. Houshmandzadeh 1.00 2.50
26 Tony Gonzalez 1.00 2.50
27 LaDainian Tomlinson 1.25 3.00
28 Larry Johnson .75 2.00
29 Frank Gore 1.25 3.00
30 Tiki Barber 1.25 3.00
31 Steven Jackson 1.25 3.00
32 Willie Parker 1.00 2.50
33 Brian Westbrook 1.00 2.50
34 Rudi Johnson 1.00 2.50
35 Chester Taylor .75 2.00
36 Joseph Addai 1.00 2.50
37 Deuce McAllister 1.00 2.50
38 Julius Jones .75 2.00
39 Ahman Green 1.00 2.50
40 Thomas Jones 1.00 2.50

2007 Donruss Elite Zoning Commission Jerseys

STATED PRINT RUN 150-175
*PRIME/50: .6X TO 1.5X BASIC JSY
PRIME PRINT RUN 50 SER.#'d SETS
1 Vince Young 4.00 10.00
2 Drew Brees 5.00 12.00
3 Peyton Manning 10.00 25.00
4 Matt Leinart 4.00 10.00
5 Jay Cutler 5.00 12.00
6 Carson Palmer 4.00 10.00
7 Marc Bulger 4.00 10.00
8 Jon Kitna/150 3.00 8.00
9 Tom Brady 8.00 20.00
10 Philip Rivers 5.00 12.00
11 Michael Vick 5.00 12.00
12 Eli Manning 5.00 12.00
13 Rex Grossman 4.00 10.00
14 Steve McNair 4.00 10.00
15 Tony Romo/150 6.00 15.00
16 Chad Johnson 4.00 10.00
17 Marvin Harrison 5.00 12.00
18 Reggie Wayne 4.00 10.00
19 Roy Williams WR 4.00 10.00
20 Anquan Boldin 4.00 10.00
21 Donald Driver 5.00 12.00
22 Torry Holt 4.00 10.00
23 Steve Smith 4.00 10.00
24 Javon Walker 4.00 10.00
25 T.J. Houshmandzadeh 4.00 10.00
26 Tony Gonzalez 4.00 10.00
27 LaDainian Tomlinson 5.00 12.00
28 Larry Johnson/170 3.00 8.00
29 Frank Gore 5.00 12.00
30 Tiki Barber 5.00 12.00
31 Steven Jackson 5.00 12.00
32 Willie Parker 4.00 10.00
33 Brian Westbrook 4.00 10.00
34 Rudi Johnson 4.00 10.00
35 Chester Taylor 3.00 8.00
36 Joseph Addai 4.00 10.00
37 Deuce McAllister 4.00 10.00
38 Julius Jones 3.00 8.00
39 Ahman Green 4.00 10.00
40 Thomas Jones 4.00 10.00

2007 Donruss Elite National Convention

COMPLETE SET (20) 40.00 80.00
STATED PRINT RUN 599 SER.#'d SETS
*STATUS GOLD/25: 1.2X TO 3X
*STATUS RED/50: .8X TO 2X
UNPRICED AUTO PRINT RUN 6-10
PHOTOS ARE UPDATED NFL IMAGES
105 Adrian Peterson 6.00 15.00
109 Anthony Gonzalez 1.50 4.00
113 Brady Quinn 1.50 4.00
114 Brandon Jackson 1.25 3.00
118 Calvin Johnson 5.00 12.00
121 Chris Henry 1.00 2.50
134 Drew Stanton 1.00 2.50
135 Dwayne Bowe 2.00 5.00
136 Dwayne Jarrett 1.25 3.00
142 Greg Olsen 1.25 3.00
147 JaMarcus Russell 1.00 2.50
156 John Beck 1.50 4.00
164 Kenny Irons 1.00 2.50
165 Kevin Kolb 2.50 6.00
172 Marshawn Lynch 1.50 4.00
174 Michael Bush 1.50 4.00
183 Robert Meachem 1.50 4.00
189 Steve Smith USC 1.50 4.00
192 Ted Ginn Jr. 1.25 3.00
195 Troy Smith 1.50 4.00

2008 Donruss Elite

This set was released on June 11, 2008. The base set consists of 200 cards. Cards 1-100 feature veterans, and cards 101-200 are rookies serial numbered of 199, 249, 299, and 999. The rookies serial numbered of 199, 249, and 299 are autographed.

COMP.SET w/o RC's (100) 7.50 20.00
ROOKIE PRINT RUN 199-999
1 Anquan Boldin .30 .75
2 Edgerrin James .30 .75
3 Larry Fitzgerald .40 1.00
4 Matt Leinart .40 1.00
5 Alge Crumpler .30 .75
6 Warrick Dunn .30 .75
7 Roddy White .30 .75
8 Willis McGahee .30 .75
9 Todd Heap .25 .60
10 Derrick Mason .30 .75
11 Marshawn Lynch .30 .75
12 Trent Edwards .25 .60
13 Lee Evans .30 .75
14 Steve Smith .30 .75
15 DeShaun Foster .30 .75
16 DeAngelo Williams .30 .75
17 Cedric Benson .30 .75
18 Bernard Berrian .30 .75
19 Devin Hester .40 1.00
20 Carson Palmer .40 1.00
21 T.J. Houshmandzadeh .30 .75
22 Chad Johnson .30 .75
23 Jamal Lewis .30 .75
24 Braylon Edwards .30 .75
25 Kellen Winslow .30 .75
26 Tony Romo .50 1.25
27 Terrell Owens .40 1.00
28 Jason Witten .40 1.00
29 Jay Cutler .40 1.00
30 Travis Henry .25 .60
31 Brandon Marshall .30 .75
32 Jon Kitna .30 .75
33 Roy Williams WR .30 .75
34 Calvin Johnson .40 1.00
35 Brett Favre 1.00 2.50
36 Greg Jennings .40 1.00
37 Ryan Grant .40 1.00
38 Matt Schaub .30 .75
39 Ahman Green .30 .75
40 Andre Johnson .30 .75
41 Peyton Manning .60 1.50
42 Reggie Wayne .30 .75
43 Marvin Harrison .40 1.00
44 Joseph Addai .30 .75
45 David Garrard .30 .75
46 Fred Taylor .30 .75
47 Reggie Williams .30 .75
48 Larry Johnson .30 .75
49 Tony Gonzalez .30 .75
50 Dwayne Bowe .30 .75
51 Derek Hagan .25 .60
52 Ronnie Brown .30 .75
53 Ted Ginn Jr. .30 .75
54 Tarvaris Jackson .30 .75
55 Chester Taylor .25 .60
56 Adrian Peterson .60 1.50
57 Tom Brady .60 1.50
58 Laurence Maroney .30 .75
59 Randy Moss .40 1.00
60 Wes Welker .40 1.00
61 Drew Brees .40 1.00
62 Reggie Bush .40 1.00
63 Marques Colston .30 .75
64 Eli Manning .40 1.00
65 Brandon Jacobs .30 .75
66 Plaxico Burress .30 .75
67 Thomas Jones .30 .75
68 Jerricho Cotchery .30 .75
69 Laveranues Coles .25 .60
70 JaMarcus Russell .30 .75
71 Justin Fargas .25 .60
72 Jerry Porter .25 .60
73 Donovan McNabb .40 1.00
74 Brian Westbrook .30 .75
75 Kevin Curtis .25 .60
76 Ben Roethlisberger .40 1.00
77 Willie Parker .30 .75
78 Santonio Holmes .30 .75
79 Hines Ward .30 .75
80 Philip Rivers .40 1.00
81 LaDainian Tomlinson .40 1.00
82 Antonio Gates .40 1.00
83 Frank Gore .30 .75
84 Arnaz Battle .25 .60
85 Vernon Davis .30 .75
86 Matt Hasselbeck .30 .75
87 Shaun Alexander .30 .75
88 Deion Branch .30 .75
89 Marc Bulger .30 .75
90 Torry Holt .30 .75
91 Steven Jackson .40 1.00
92 Jeff Garcia .30 .75
93 Joey Galloway .30 .75
94 Earnest Graham .25 .60
95 Vince Young .30 .75
96 LenDale White .30 .75
97 Roydell Williams .25 .60
98 Clinton Portis .30 .75
99 Chris Cooley .30 .75
100 Santana Moss .25 .60
101 Matt Ryan AU/199 RC 40.00 100.00
102 Brian Brohm AU/199 RC 10.00 25.00
103 Chad Henne AU/199 RC 30.00 60.00
104 Andre Woodson AU/249 RC 8.00 20.00
105 Joe Flacco AU/299 RC 25.00 60.00
106 John David Booty/999 RC 2.00 5.00
107 Josh Johnson/999 RC 2.50 6.00
108 Erik Ainge AU/299 RC 8.00 20.00
109 Colt Brennan AU/249 RC 10.00 25.00
110 Dennis Dixon AU/299 RC 10.00 25.00
111 Kevin O'Connell/999 RC 2.00 5.00
112 Matt Flynn/999 RC 5.00 12.00
113 Bernard Morris/999 RC 2.00 5.00
114 Sam Keller/999 RC 2.00 5.00
115 Paul Smith/999 RC 2.50 6.00
116 Darren McFadden/ AU/199 RC 25.00 60.00
117 Jonathan Stewart/ AU/199 RC 20.00 50.00
118 Rashard Mendenhall AU/199 RC 25.00 60.00
119 Felix Jones AU/199 RC 25.00 50.00
120 Chris Johnson/999 RC 6.00 15.00
121 Jamaal Charles/999 RC 4.00 10.00
122 Ray Rice/999 RC 5.00 12.00
123 Steve Slaton/999 RC 2.50 6.00
124 Mike Hart/999 RC 2.50 6.00
125 Matt Forte AU/299 RC 20.00 50.00
126 Tashard Choice AU/299 RC 6.00 15.00
127 Kevin Smith/999 RC 2.50 6.00
128 Allen Patrick/999 RC 2.00 5.00
129 Thomas Brown/999 RC 2.00 5.00
130 Justin Forsett AU/299 RC 8.00 20.00
131 Cory Boyd AU/299 RC 5.00 12.00
132 Dantrell Savage/999 RC 2.00 5.00
133 Kalvin McRae/999 RC 1.50 4.00
134 Darrell Strong AU/299 RC 6.00 15.00
135 Owen Schmitt AU/299 RC 8.00 20.00
136 Peyton Hillis AU/299 RC 15.00 40.00
137 Jacob Hester AU/299 RC 8.00 20.00
138 Fred Davis/999 RC 2.50 6.00
139 Martellus Bennett AU/299 RC 6.00 15.00
140 John Carlson AU/299 RC 8.00 20.00
141 Martin Rucker/999 RC 2.00 5.00
142 Brad Cottam AU/299 RC 6.00 15.00
143 Jermichael Finley/999 RC 2.50 6.00
144 Jacob Tamme/999 RC 2.50 6.00
145 Dustin Keller AU/299 RC 10.00 25.00
146 Kellen Davis/999 RC 1.50 4.00
147 DeSean Jackson AU/249 RC 20.00 40.00
148 James Hardy AU/299 RC 6.00 15.00
149 Malcolm Kelly AU/249 RC 6.00 15.00
150 Early Doucet AU/199 RC 6.00 15.00
151 Limas Sweed AU/249 RC 8.00 20.00
152 Andre Caldwell AU/299 RC 6.00 15.00
153 Mario Manningham/ AU/299 RC 12.50 25.00
154 Devin Thomas AU/299 RC 6.00 15.00
155 Donnie Avery AU/299 RC 6.00 15.00
156 Earl Bennett AU/299 RC 8.00 20.00
157 Eddie Royal AU/249 RC 8.00 20.00
158 Lavelle Hawkins AU/299 RC 5.00 12.00
159 DJ Hall/999 RC 2.00 5.00
160 Adarius Bowman/999 RC 2.00 5.00
161 Jordy Nelson AU/249 RC 20.00 40.00
162 Harry Douglas AU/299 RC 6.00 15.00
163 Jerome Simpson AU/299 RC 8.00 20.00
164 Dorien Bryant/999 RC 2.00 5.00
165 Will Franklin/999 RC 2.00 5.00
166 Keenan Burton/999 RC 1.50 4.00
167 Kevin Robinson/999 RC 1.50 4.00
168 Paul Hubbard AU/299 RC 6.00 15.00
169 Davone Bess/999 RC 2.50 6.00
170 Adrian Arrington/999 RC 2.00 5.00
171 Dexter Jackson AU/299 RC 6.00 15.00
172 Ryan Grice-Mullen/999 RC 1.50 4.00
173 Darius Reynaud/999 RC 1.50 4.00
174 Josh Morgan AU/299 RC 8.00 20.00
175 Anthony Alridge/999 RC 2.00 5.00
176 Jason Rivers/999 RC 2.00 5.00
177 Marcus Smith AU/299 RC 6.00 15.00
178 Mark Bradford/999 RC 1.50 4.00
179 Marcus Monk AU/299 RC 6.00 15.00
180 Chris Long/999 RC 2.50 6.00
181 Vernon Gholston/999 RC 2.00 5.00
182 Derrick Harvey/999 RC 1.50 4.00
183 Glenn Dorsey/999 RC 2.50 6.00
184 Sedrick Ellis/999 RC 2.50 6.00
185 Dan Connor AU/299 RC 8.00 20.00
186 Curtis Lofton/999 RC 2.00 5.00
187 Keith Rivers AU/299 RC 8.00 20.00
188 Xavier Adibi/999 RC 1.50 4.00
189 Ali Highsmith/999 RC 1.50 4.00
190 Quentin Groves AU/299 RC 6.00 15.00
191 Erin Henderson/999 RC 2.50 6.00
192 Mike Jenkins/999 RC 2.50 6.00
193 Antoine Cason AU/299 RC 8.00 20.00
194 Dominique Rodgers-Cromartie RC/900 2.50 6.00
195 Leodis McKelvin/999 RC 2.00 5.00
196 Aqib Talib/999 RC 2.50 6.00
197 Reggie Smith/999 RC 2.00 5.00
198 Tracy Porter AU/299 RC 8.00 20.00
199 Terrell Thomas AU/299 RC 6.00 15.00
200 Kenny Phillips/999 RC 2.50 6.00

2008 Donruss Elite 10th Anniversary

*VETS/10: 8X TO 20X BASIC CARDS
STATED PRINT RUN 10 SER.#'d SETS

2008 Donruss Elite Aspirations

*VETS/70-98: 4X TO 10X BASIC CARDS
*VETS/53-69: 5X TO 12X BASIC CARDS
*VETS/20: 8X TO 20X BASIC CARDS
*VETS/10-19: 10X TO 25X BASIC CARDS
COMMON ROOKIE/72-99 2.50 6.00
ROOKIE SEMIS/72-99 3.00 8.00
ROOKIE UNL.STAR/72-99 4.00 10.00
COMMON ROOKIE/45-66 5.00 12.00
COMMON ROOKIE/20-28 6.00 15.00
COMMON ROOKIE/10-19 8.00 20.00
ROOKIE SEMIS/10-19 10.00 25.00
ROOKIE UNL.STAR/10-19 12.00 30.00
STATED PRINT RUN 9-99
101 Matt Ryan/88 15.00 40.00
102 Brian Brohm/88 4.00 10.00
103 Chad Henne/93 4.00 10.00
104 Andre Woodson/97 4.00 10.00
105 Joe Flacco/95 12.00 30.00
106 John David Booty/90 3.00 8.00
107 Josh Johnson/89 4.00 10.00
108 Erik Ainge/90 4.00 10.00
109 Colt Brennan/85 4.00 10.00
110 Dennis Dixon/90 4.00 10.00
111 Kevin O'Connell/93 3.00 8.00
112 Matt Flynn/85 8.00 20.00
116 Darren McFadden/95 10.00 25.00
117 Jonathan Stewart/72 6.00 15.00
118 Rashard Mendenhall/95 8.00 20.00
119 Felix Jones/75 6.00 15.00
120 Chris Johnson/95 10.00 25.00
121 Jamaal Charles/75 6.00 15.00
122 Ray Rice/73 8.00 20.00
123 Steve Slaton/90 4.00 10.00
124 Mike Hart/80 4.00 10.00
125 Matt Forte/75 6.00 15.00
127 Kevin Smith/76 4.00 10.00
135 Owen Schmitt/65 5.00 12.00
136 Peyton Hillis/78 8.00 20.00
137 Jacob Hester/82 4.00 10.00
139 Martellus Bennett/87 3.00 8.00
147 DeSean Jackson/99 8.00 20.00
148 James Hardy/18 10.00 25.00
149 Malcolm Kelly/96 3.00 8.00
150 Early Doucet/91 3.00 8.00
151 Limas Sweed/96 4.00 10.00
153 Mario Manningham/14 12.00 30.00
154 Devin Thomas/95 3.00 8.00
161 Jordy Nelson/73 5.00 12.00
169 Davone Bess/93 4.00 10.00
171 Dexter Jackson/98 3.00 8.00
174 Josh Morgan/98 4.00 10.00
181 Vernon Gholston/50 4.00 10.00
183 Glenn Dorsey/28 8.00 20.00
187 Keith Rivers/45 5.00 12.00
192 Mike Jenkins/96 4.00 10.00

2008 Donruss Elite Status

*VETS/80-89: 4X TO 10X BASIC CARDS
*VETS/30-47: 6X TO 15X BASIC CARDS
*VETS/20-29: 8X TO 20X BASIC CARDS
*VETS/10-19: 10X TO 25X BASIC CARDS
COMMON ROOKIE/72-91 2.50 6.00
ROOKIE SEMIS/72-91 3.00 8.00
ROOKIE UNL.STAR/72-91 4.00 10.00
COMMON ROOKIE/49-55 5.00 12.00
COMMON ROOKIE/34-45 6.00 15.00
COMMON ROOKIE/20-29 5.00 12.00
ROOKIE SEMIS/20-29 6.00 15.00
ROOKIE UNL.STAR/20-29 8.00 20.00
COMMON ROOKIE/10-19 10.00 25.00
ROOKIE UNL.STAR/10-19 12.00 30.00
STATED PRINT RUN 1-91
101 Matt Ryan/12 50.00 125.00
102 Brian Brohm/12 12.00 30.00
106 John David Booty/10 10.00 25.00
107 Josh Johnson/11 12.00 30.00
108 Erik Ainge/10 12.00 30.00
109 Colt Brennan/15 12.00 30.00
110 Dennis Dixon/10 12.00 30.00
112 Matt Flynn/15 25.00 60.00
117 Jonathan Stewart/28 12.00 30.00
119 Felix Jones/25 12.00 30.00
121 Jamaal Charles/25 12.00 30.00
122 Ray Rice/27 15.00 40.00
123 Steve Slaton/10 12.00 30.00
124 Mike Hart/20 8.00 20.00
125 Matt Forte/25 12.00 30.00
127 Kevin Smith/24 8.00 20.00
135 Owen Schmitt/35 6.00 15.00
136 Peyton Hillis/22 15.00 40.00
137 Jacob Hester/18 12.00 30.00
139 Martellus Bennett/13 10.00 25.00
148 James Hardy/82 3.00 8.00
153 Mario Manningham/86 4.00 10.00
161 Jordy Nelson/27 10.00 25.00
180 Chris Long/91 4.00 10.00
181 Vernon Gholston/50 4.00 10.00
183 Glenn Dorsey/72 4.00 10.00
187 Keith Rivers/55 5.00 12.00

2008 Donruss Elite Status Gold

*VETS 1-100: 6X TO 15X BASIC CARDS
COMMON ROOKIE (101-200) 5.00 12.00
ROOKIE SEMISTARS 6.00 15.00
ROOKIE UNL.STARS 8.00 20.00
GOLD PRINT RUN 24 SER.#'d SETS
101 Matt Ryan 30.00 80.00
102 Brian Brohm 8.00 20.00
103 Chad Henne 8.00 20.00
104 Andre Woodson 8.00 20.00
105 Joe Flacco 25.00 60.00
106 John David Booty 6.00 15.00
107 Josh Johnson 8.00 20.00
108 Erik Ainge 8.00 20.00
109 Colt Brennan 8.00 20.00
110 Dennis Dixon 8.00 20.00
111 Kevin O'Connell 6.00 15.00
112 Matt Flynn 15.00 40.00
116 Darren McFadden 20.00 50.00
117 Jonathan Stewart 12.00 30.00
118 Rashard Mendenhall 15.00 40.00
119 Felix Jones 12.00 30.00
120 Chris Johnson 20.00 50.00
121 Jamaal Charles 12.00 30.00
122 Ray Rice 15.00 40.00
123 Steve Slaton 8.00 20.00
124 Mike Hart 8.00 20.00
125 Matt Forte 12.00 30.00
127 Kevin Smith 8.00 20.00
136 Peyton Hillis 10.00 25.00
139 Martellus Bennett 6.00 15.00
147 DeSean Jackson 15.00 40.00
148 James Hardy 6.00 15.00
149 Malcolm Kelly 6.00 15.00
150 Early Doucet 6.00 15.00
151 Limas Sweed 8.00 20.00
153 Mario Manningham 8.00 20.00
154 Devin Thomas 6.00 15.00
161 Jordy Nelson 10.00 25.00
169 Davone Bess 8.00 20.00
171 Dexter Jackson 6.00 15.00
174 Josh Morgan 8.00 20.00
180 Chris Long 8.00 20.00
181 Vernon Gholston 6.00 15.00
183 Glenn Dorsey 8.00 20.00
187 Keith Rivers 8.00 20.00
192 Mike Jenkins 8.00 20.00

2008 Donruss Elite Chain Reaction Gold

GOLD PRINT RUN 800 SER.#'d SETS
*BLACK/400: .5X TO 1.2X GOLD/800
BLACK PRINT RUN 400 SER.#'d SETS
*RED/200: .6X TO 1.5X GOLD/800
RED PRINT RUN 200 SER.#'d SETS
1 Adrian Peterson 2.00 5.00
2 Willie Parker 1.00 2.50
3 Brian Westbrook 1.00 2.50
4 Marshawn Lynch 1.00 2.50
5 Willis McGahee 1.00 2.50
6 Brandon Jacobs 1.00 2.50
7 Joseph Addai 1.00 2.50
8 Marvin Harrison 1.25 3.00
9 Tom Brady 2.00 5.00
10 Tony Romo 1.50 4.00
11 Peyton Manning 2.00 5.00
12 Brett Favre 3.00 8.00
13 Carson Palmer 1.25 3.00
14 Jay Cutler 1.25 3.00
15 Donovan McNabb 1.25 3.00
16 Marion Barber 1.00 2.50
17 Reggie Bush 1.25 3.00
18 Roy Williams WR 1.00 2.50
19 Hines Ward 1.00 2.50
20 Dwayne Bowe 1.00 2.50
21 Anthony Gonzalez .75 2.00
22 Ted Ginn Jr. 1.00 2.50
23 Larry Johnson 1.00 2.50
24 Maurice Jones-Drew 1.00 2.50
25 Donald Driver 1.00 2.50

2008 Donruss Elite Chain Reaction Jerseys

STATED PRINT RUN 199 SER.#'d SETS
*PRIME/50: .6X TO 1.5X BASIC JSY/199
PRIME PRINT RUN 50 SER.#'d SETS
1 Adrian Peterson 6.00 15.00
2 Willie Parker 3.00 8.00
3 Brian Westbrook 3.00 8.00
4 Marshawn Lynch 3.00 8.00
5 Willis McGahee 3.00 8.00
6 Brandon Jacobs 3.00 8.00
7 Joseph Addai 3.00 8.00
8 Marvin Harrison 4.00 10.00
9 Tom Brady 6.00 15.00
10 Tony Romo 5.00 12.00
11 Peyton Manning 6.00 15.00
12 Brett Favre 10.00 25.00
13 Carson Palmer 4.00 10.00
14 Jay Cutler 4.00 10.00
15 Donovan McNabb 4.00 10.00
16 Marion Barber 3.00 8.00
17 Reggie Bush 4.00 10.00
18 Roy Williams WR 3.00 8.00
19 Hines Ward 3.00 8.00
20 Dwayne Bowe 3.00 8.00
21 Anthony Gonzalez 2.50 6.00
22 Ted Ginn Jr. 3.00 8.00
23 Larry Johnson 3.00 8.00
24 Maurice Jones-Drew 3.00 8.00
25 Donald Driver 3.00 8.00

2008 Donruss Elite College Ties Autographs

STATED PRINT RUN 50 SER.#'d SETS
1 Simeon Castille 6.00 15.00
2 Chris Long 8.00 20.00
4 Antoine Cason 8.00 20.00
5 Marcus Monk 6.00 15.00
6 Quentin Groves 6.00 15.00
7 Matt Ryan 60.00 120.00
8 DeSean Jackson 15.00 40.00
9 Colt Brennan 15.00 40.00
10 Rashard Mendenhall 25.00 50.00
13 Vernon Gholston 6.00 15.00
14 Dan Connor 10.00 25.00
15 Robert Killebrew 6.00 15.00
17 Darren McFadden 25.00 60.00
18 Early Doucet 6.00 15.00
19 Mario Manningham 12.50 25.00
20 Malcolm Kelly 6.00 15.00
21 Jonathan Stewart 20.00 50.00
22 Brian Brohm 8.00 20.00
23 Chad Henne 15.00 40.00
24 Steve Slaton 8.00 20.00
25 Mike Hart 8.00 20.00

2008 Donruss Elite College Ties Green

GREEN PRINT RUN 800 SER.#'d SETS
*GOLD/400: .5X TO 1.2X GREEN/800
GOLD PRINT RUN 400 SER.#'d SETS
*BLACK/200: .6X TO 1.5X GREEN/800
BLACK PRINT RUN 200 SER.#'d SETS
1 Simeon Castille .60 1.50
2 Chris Long .75 2.00
3 DJ Hall .60 1.50
4 Antoine Cason .75 2.00
5 Marcus Monk .60 1.50
6 Quentin Groves .60 1.50
7 Matt Ryan 3.00 8.00
8 DeSean Jackson 1.50 4.00
9 Colt Brennan .75 2.00
10 Rashard Mendenhall 1.50 4.00
11 Aqib Talib .75 2.00
12 Ernie Wheelwright .60 1.50
13 Vernon Gholston .60 1.50
14 Dan Connor .75 2.00
15 Robert Killebrew .60 1.50
16 Xavier Adibi .50 1.25
17 Darren McFadden 2.00 5.00
18 Early Doucet .60 1.50
19 Mario Manningham .75 2.00
20 Malcolm Kelly .60 1.50
21 Jonathan Stewart 1.25 3.00
22 Brian Brohm .75 2.00
23 Chad Henne .75 2.00
24 Steve Slaton .75 2.00
25 Mike Hart .75 2.00

2008 Donruss Elite College Ties Jerseys

STATED PRINT RUN 150 SER.#'d SETS
*PRIME/50: .8X TO 2X BASIC JSY/150
*PRIME/25: 1X TO 2.5X BASIC JSY/150
PRIME PRINT RUN 25-50
1 Simeon Castille 4.00 10.00
2 Chris Long 4.00 10.00
3 DJ Hall 4.00 10.00
4 Antoine Cason 3.00 8.00
5 Marcus Monk 4.00 10.00
6 Quentin Groves 3.00 8.00
7 Matt Ryan 10.00 25.00
8 DeSean Jackson 5.00 12.00
9 Colt Brennan 4.00 10.00
10 Rashard Mendenhall 8.00 20.00
11 Aqib Talib 4.00 10.00
12 Ernie Wheelwright 3.00 8.00
13 Vernon Gholston 4.00 10.00
14 Dan Connor 4.00 10.00
15 Robert Killebrew 3.00 8.00
16 Xavier Adibi 3.00 8.00
17 Darren McFadden 10.00 25.00
18 Early Doucet 4.00 10.00
19 Mario Manningham 4.00 10.00
20 Malcolm Kelly 6.00 15.00
21 Jonathan Stewart 6.00 15.00
22 Brian Brohm 4.00 10.00
23 Chad Henne 6.00 15.00
24 Steve Slaton 4.00 10.00
25 Mike Hart 6.00 15.00

2008 Donruss Elite College Ties Combos Autographs

STATED PRINT RUN 50 SER.#'d SETS
2 Malcolm Kelly 15.00 40.00
Allen Patrick
3 Jonathan Stewart 30.00 60.00
Dennis Dixon
4 Darren McFadden 40.00 100.00
Felix Jones
5 Brian Brohm 10.00 25.00
Harry Douglas
6 Mike Hart 25.00 60.00
Chad Henne
9 Matt Flynn 30.00 60.00
Early Doucet
10 Steve Slaton 25.00 60.00
Owen Schmitt
11 Shawn Crable 10.00 25.00
Jamar Adams
12 Jamaal Charles 15.00 40.00
Limas Sweed
13 Eddie Royal 10.00 25.00
Brandon Flowers
16 Keith Rivers 15.00 40.00
Terrell Thomas

2008 Donruss Elite College Ties Combos Green

GREEN PRINT RUN 800 SER.#'d SETS
*GOLD/400: .5X TO 1.2X GREEN/800
GOLD PRINT RUN 400 SER.#'d SETS
*BLACK/200: .6X TO 1.5X GREEN/800
BLACK PRINT RUN 200 SER.#'d SETS
1 Erik Ainge 1.50 4.00
Jonathan Hefney
2 Malcolm Kelly 1.25 3.00
Allen Patrick
3 Jonathan Stewart 2.00 5.00
Dennis Dixon
4 Darren McFadden 4.00 10.00
Felix Jones
5 Brian Brohm 1.00 2.50
Harry Douglas
6 Mike Hart 2.00 5.00
Chad Henne
7 Sedrick Ellis 1.00 2.50
Lawrence Jackson
8 Kenny Phillips 1.00 2.50
Calais Campbell
9 Matt Flynn 2.00 5.00
Early Doucet
10 Steve Slaton 1.00 2.50
Owen Schmitt
11 Shawn Crable 1.00 2.50
Jamar Adams
12 Jamaal Charles 1.50 4.00
Limas Sweed
13 Eddie Royal 1.00 2.50
Brandon Flowers
14 Ali Highsmith 1.00 2.50
Craig Steltz
15 John David Booty .75 2.00
Fred Davis
16 Keith Rivers 1.25 3.00
Terrell Thomas
17 Mario Manningham 1.00 2.50
Adrian Arrington
18 Chevis Jackson 1.25 3.00
Glenn Dorsey
19 DJ Hall 1.00 2.50
Simeon Castille
20 Quentin Groves 1.00 2.50
Ronnie Brown

2008 Donruss Elite College Ties Combos Jerseys

STATED PRINT RUN 100 SER.#'d SETS
*PRIME/25: .6X TO 1.5X BASIC JSY/100
PRIME PRINT RUN 25 SER.#'d SETS
1 Erik Ainge 10.00 25.00
Jonathan Hefney
2 Malcolm Kelly 10.00 25.00
Allen Patrick
3 Jonathan Stewart 10.00 25.00
Dennis Dixon
4 Darren McFadden 20.00 50.00
Felix Jones
5 Brian Brohm 6.00 15.00
Harry Douglas
6 Mike Hart 10.00 25.00
Chad Henne
7 Sedrick Ellis 5.00 12.00
Lawrence Jackson
8 Kenny Phillips 5.00 12.00
Calais Campbell
9 Matt Flynn 12.00 30.00
Early Doucet
10 Steve Slaton 6.00 15.00
Owen Schmitt
11 Shawn Crable 5.00 12.00
Jamar Adams
12 Jamaal Charles 10.00 25.00
Limas Sweed
13 Eddie Royal 6.00 15.00
Brandon Flowers
14 Ali Highsmith 5.00 12.00
Craig Steltz
15 John David Booty 5.00 12.00
Fred Davis
16 Keith Rivers 5.00 12.00
Terrell Thomas
17 Mario Manningham 8.00 20.00
Adrian Arrington
18 Chevis Jackson 5.00 12.00
Glenn Dorsey
19 DJ Hall 5.00 12.00
Simeon Castille
20 Quentin Groves 5.00 12.00
Ronnie Brown

2008 Donruss Elite National Convention

COMPLETE SET (20) 20.00 50.00
ASPIRATIONS/50: .6X TO 1.5X BASE/499
ASPIRATIONS/50: .5X TO 1.2X BASE/299
STATUS GOLD/25: 1.2X TO 3X BASE/499
STATUS GOLD/25: 1X TO 2.5X BASE/299
STATUS RED/50: .6X TO 1.5X BASE/499
STATUS RED/50: .5X TO 1.2X BASE/299
UNPRICED AUTO PRINT RUN 5-10
101 Matt Ryan/499 4.00 10.00
102 Brian Brohm/499 1.00 2.50
103 Chad Henne/499 1.00 2.50
105 Joe Flacco/499 3.00 8.00
116 Darren McFadden/499 2.50 6.00
117 Jonathan Stewart/499 1.50 4.00
118 Rashard Mendenhall/499 2.00 5.00
119 Felix Jones/499 1.50 4.00
120 Chris Johnson/499 2.50 6.00
121 Jamaal Charles/499 1.50 4.00
125 Matt Forte/499 1.50 4.00
148 James Hardy/499 .75 2.00
149 Malcom Kelly/499 .75 2.00
151 Limas Sweed/499 1.00 2.50
153 Mario Manningham/499 1.00 2.50
154 Devin Thomas/299 1.00 2.50
155 Donnie Avery/299 1.00 2.50
157 Eddie Royal/299 1.25 3.00
161 Jordy Nelson/299 1.50 4.00
201 Jake Long/499 1.00 2.50

2008 Donruss Elite Passing the Torch Autographs

STATED PRINT RUN 25 SER.#'d SETS
1 Gale Sayers 250.00 400.00
Devin Hester/10
2 Emmitt Smith 125.00 250.00
Marion Barber
3 Barry Sanders 250.00 500.00
Adrian Peterson
4 Thurman Thomas 50.00 100.00
Marshawn Lynch
5 Jim Kelly 60.00 120.00
Trent Edwards
7 Fran Tarkenton 40.00 80.00
Tarvaris Jackson
8 Roger Craig 40.00 80.00
Frank Gore
9 DeMeco Ryans 50.00 100.00
Patrick Willis
10 Earl Campbell 40.00 80.00
LenDale White
11 Dan Marino 250.00 450.00
Brett Favre
12 Frank Gifford 75.00 150.00
Eli Manning
14 Jerry Rice 150.00 250.00
Calvin Johnson
15 Dave Casper 25.00 50.00
Zach Miller

2008 Donruss Elite Passing the Torch Red

RED PRINT RUN 800 SER.#'d SETS
*GREEN/400: .5X TO 1.2X RED/800
GREEN PRINT RUN 400 SER.#'d SETS
*BLUE/200: .6X TO 1.5X RED/800
BLUE PRINT RUN 200 SER.#'d SETS
1 Gale Sayers 2.00 5.00
Devin Hester
2 Emmitt Smith 3.00 8.00
Marion Barber
3 Barry Sanders 2.50 6.00
Adrian Peterson
4 Thurman Thomas 1.25 3.00
Marshawn Lynch
5 Jim Kelly 1.50 4.00
Trent Edwards
6 Franco Harris 1.50 4.00
Willie Parker
7 Fran Tarkenton 1.50 4.00
Tarvaris Jackson
8 Roger Craig 1.25 3.00
Frank Gore
9 DeMeco Ryans 1.25 3.00
Patrick Willis
10 Earl Campbell 1.50 4.00
LenDale White
11 Dan Marino 4.00 10.00
Brett Favre
12 Frank Gifford 1.50 4.00
Eli Manning
13 Jay Novacek 1.50 4.00
Jason Witten
14 Jerry Rice 2.50 6.00
Calvin Johnson
15 Dave Casper 1.25 3.00
Zach Miller

2008 Donruss Elite Prime Targets Gold

GOLD PRINT RUN 800 SER.#'d SETS
*BLACK/400: .5X TO 1.2X GOLD/800
BLACK PRINT RUN 400 SER.#'d SETS
*RED/200: .6X TO 1.5X GOLD/800
RED PRINT RUN 200 SER.#'d SETS
1 Terrell Owens 1.25 3.00
2 Randy Moss 1.25 3.00
3 Chad Johnson 1.00 2.50
4 Reggie Wayne 1.00 2.50
5 Larry Fitzgerald 1.25 3.00
6 Braylon Edwards 1.00 2.50
7 Torry Holt 1.00 2.50
8 Brandon Marshall 1.00 2.50
9 Joey Galloway 1.00 2.50
10 T.J. Houshmandzadeh 1.00 2.50
11 Jason Witten 1.25 3.00
12 Tony Gonzalez 1.00 2.50
13 Greg Jennings 1.25 3.00
14 Plaxico Burress 1.00 2.50
15 Antonio Gates 1.25 3.00
16 Marques Colston 1.00 2.50
17 Lee Evans 1.00 2.50
18 Steve Smith 1.00 2.50
19 Calvin Johnson 1.25 3.00
20 Dwayne Bowe 1.00 2.50
21 Santonio Holmes 1.00 2.50
22 Andre Johnson 1.00 2.50
23 Jeremy Shockey 1.00 2.50
24 Bernard Berrian 1.00 2.50
25 Jerricho Cotchery 1.00 2.50

2008 Donruss Elite Prime Targets Jerseys

STATED PRINT RUN 199 SER.#'d SETS
*PRIME/50: .6X TO 1.5X BASIC JSY/199
PRIME PRINT RUN 50 SER.#'d SETS
1 Terrell Owens 4.00 10.00
2 Randy Moss 4.00 10.00
3 Chad Johnson 3.00 8.00
4 Reggie Wayne 3.00 8.00
5 Larry Fitzgerald 4.00 10.00
6 Braylon Edwards 3.00 8.00
7 Torry Holt 3.00 8.00
8 Brandon Marshall 3.00 8.00
9 Joey Galloway 3.00 8.00
10 T.J. Houshmandzadeh 3.00 8.00
11 Jason Witten 4.00 10.00
12 Tony Gonzalez 3.00 8.00
13 Greg Jennings 4.00 10.00
14 Plaxico Burress 3.00 8.00
15 Antonio Gates 4.00 10.00
16 Marques Colston 3.00 8.00
17 Lee Evans 3.00 8.00
18 Steve Smith 3.00 8.00
19 Calvin Johnson 4.00 10.00
20 Dwayne Bowe 3.00 8.00
21 Santonio Holmes 3.00 8.00
22 Andre Johnson 3.00 8.00
23 Jeremy Shockey 3.00 8.00
24 Bernard Berrian 3.00 8.00
25 Jerricho Cotchery 3.00 8.00

2008 Donruss Elite Stars Red

RED PRINT RUN 800 SER.#'d SETS
*GOLD/400: .5X TO 1.2X RED/800
GOLD PRINT RUN 400 SER.#'d SETS
*BLACK/200: .6X TO 1.5X RED/800
BLACK PRINT RUN 200 SER.#'d SETS
1 Brett Favre 3.00 8.00
2 T.J. Houshmandzadeh 1.00 2.50
3 Reggie Wayne 1.00 2.50
4 Warrick Dunn 1.00 2.50
5 Matt Hasselbeck 1.00 2.50
6 Terrell Owens 1.25 3.00
7 Drew Brees 1.25 3.00
8 Eli Manning 1.25 3.00
9 Ben Roethlisberger 1.25 3.00
10 Vince Young 1.00 2.50
11 Peyton Manning 2.00 5.00
12 Wes Welker 1.25 3.00
13 Derrick Mason 1.00 2.50
14 Jerry Porter .75 2.00
15 Donald Driver 1.00 2.50
16 Derek Anderson .75 2.00
17 Jay Cutler 1.25 3.00
18 Philip Rivers 1.25 3.00
19 Donovan McNabb 1.25 3.00
20 Derrick Ward .75 2.00
21 LaDainian Tomlinson 1.25 3.00
22 Adrian Peterson 2.00 5.00
23 Frank Gore 1.00 2.50
24 Tom Brady 2.00 5.00
25 Tony Romo 1.50 4.00

2008 Donruss Elite Stars Jerseys Silver

SILVER PRINT RUN 199 SER.#'d SETS
*GOLD/100: .5X TO 1.2X SLVR JSY/199
GOLD PRINT RUN 100 SER.#'d SETS
*BLACK PRIME/50: .6X TO 1.5X SLVR/199
BLACK PRIME PRINT RUN 50 SER.#'d SETS
1 Brett Favre 10.00 25.00
2 T.J. Houshmandzadeh 3.00 8.00
3 Reggie Wayne 3.00 8.00
4 Warrick Dunn 3.00 8.00
5 Matt Hasselbeck 3.00 8.00
6 Terrell Owens 4.00 10.00
7 Drew Brees 4.00 10.00
8 Eli Manning 4.00 10.00
9 Ben Roethlisberger 4.00 10.00
10 Vince Young 3.00 8.00
11 Peyton Manning 6.00 15.00
12 Wes Welker 4.00 10.00
13 Derrick Mason 3.00 8.00
14 Jerry Porter 2.50 6.00
15 Donald Driver 3.00 8.00
16 Derek Anderson 2.50 6.00
17 Jay Cutler 4.00 10.00
18 Philip Rivers 4.00 10.00
19 Donovan McNabb 4.00 10.00
20 Derrick Ward 2.50 6.00
21 LaDainian Tomlinson 4.00 10.00
22 Adrian Peterson 6.00 15.00
23 Frank Gore 3.00 8.00
24 Tom Brady 6.00 15.00
25 Tony Romo 5.00 12.00

2008 Donruss Elite Status Autographs Gold

COMMON CARD 12.00 30.00
SEMISTARS 15.00 40.00
UNLISTED STARS 20.00 50.00
GOLD PRINT RUN 24 SER.#'d SETS
UNPRICED AUTO BLACK PRINT RUN 1
101 Matt Ryan 125.00 250.00
102 Brian Brohm 20.00 50.00
103 Chad Henne 20.00 50.00
105 Joe Flacco 100.00 175.00
106 John David Booty 15.00 40.00
109 Colt Brennan 30.00 80.00
111 Kevin O'Connell 15.00 40.00
112 Matt Flynn 50.00 100.00
116 Darren McFadden 40.00 100.00
117 Jonathan Stewart 40.00 100.00
118 Rashard Mendenhall 40.00 100.00
119 Felix Jones 40.00 100.00
120 Chris Johnson 50.00 120.00
121 Jamaal Charles 30.00 80.00
122 Ray Rice 40.00 80.00
123 Steve Slaton 20.00 50.00
124 Mike Hart 20.00 50.00
125 Matt Forte 40.00 100.00
126 Tashard Choice 15.00 40.00
136 Peyton Hillis 25.00 60.00
147 DeSean Jackson 40.00 100.00
151 Limas Sweed 20.00 50.00
155 Donnie Avery 15.00 40.00
157 Eddie Royal 20.00 50.00
161 Jordy Nelson 40.00 80.00
169 Davone Bess 20.00 50.00
180 Chris Long 20.00 50.00

2008 Donruss Elite Teams Black

BLACK PRINT RUN 800 SER.#'d SETS
*RED/400: .5X TO 1.2X BLACK/800TS
RED PRINT RUN 400 SER.#'d SETS
*GOLD/200: .6X TO 1.5X BLACK/800TS
GOLD PRINT RUN 200 SER.#'d SETS
1 Tony Romo 1.50 4.00
Terrell Owens
Jason Witten
2 Tom Brady 2.00 5.00
Randy Moss
Laurence Maroney
3 Carson Palmer 1.25 3.00
Chad Johnson
T.J. Houshmandzadeh
4 Ben Roethlisberger 2.00 5.00
Willie Parker
Hines Ward
5 Kurt Warner 1.25 3.00
Larry Fitzgerald
Anquan Boldin
6 Trent Edwards 1.00 2.50
Marshawn Lynch
Lee Evans
7 Brett Favre 3.00 8.00
Greg Jennings
Ryan Grant
8 Peyton Manning 2.00 5.00
Reggie Wayne
Joseph Addai
9 Tarvaris Jackson 2.00 5.00
Adrian Peterson
Chester Taylor
10 Eli Manning 1.25 3.00
Brandon Jacobs
Plaxico Burress
11 Derek Anderson 1.00 2.50
Braylon Edwards
Kellen Winslow
12 Jon Kitna 1.25 3.00
Roy Williams WR
Calvin Johnson
13 David Garrard 1.00 2.50
Fred Taylor
Maurice Jones-Drew
14 Larry Johnson 1.00 2.50
Tony Gonzalez
Dwayne Bowe
15 Drew Brees 1.25 3.00
Reggie Bush
Marques Colston
16 Thomas Jones 1.00 2.50
Jerricho Cotchery
Laveranues Coles
17 Donovan McNabb 1.25 3.00
Brian Westbrook
Kevin Curtis
18 Philip Rivers 1.25 3.00
LaDainian Tomlinson
Antonio Gates
19 Matt Hasselbeck 1.00 2.50
Shaun Alexander
Deion Branch
20 Marc Bulger 1.25 3.00
Steven Jackson
Torry Holt
21 Vince Young 1.00 2.50
LenDale White
Brandon Jones
22 Jason Campbell 1.00 2.50
Clinton Portis
Chris Cooley
23 Willis McGahee 1.25 3.00
Derrick Mason
Ray Lewis
24 DeShaun Foster 1.00 2.50
Steve Smith
DeAngelo Williams
25 Cedric Benson 1.25 3.00
Bernard Berrian
Devin Hester

2008 Donruss Elite Teams Jerseys

STATED PRINT RUN 199 SER.#'d SETS
*PRIME/50: .6X TO 1.5X BASIC JSY/199
PRIME PRINT RUN 50 SER.#'d SETS
1 Tony Romo 12.00 30.00
Terrell Owens
Jason Witten
2 Tom Brady 15.00 40.00
Randy Moss
Laurence Maroney
3 Carson Palmer 6.00 15.00
Chad Johnson
T.J. Houshmandzadeh
4 Ben Roethlisberger 12.00 30.00
Willie Parker
Hines Ward
5 Kurt Warner 6.00 15.00
Larry Fitzgerald
Anquan Boldin
6 Trent Edwards 6.00 15.00
Marshawn Lynch
Lee Evans
7 Brett Favre 15.00 40.00
Greg Jennings
Ryan Grant
8 Peyton Manning 12.00 30.00
Reggie Wayne
Joseph Addai
9 Tarvaris Jackson 12.00 30.00
Adrian Peterson
Chester Taylor
10 Eli Manning 8.00 20.00
Brandon Jacobs
Plaxico Burress
11 Derek Anderson 6.00 15.00
Braylon Edwards
Kellen Winslow
12 Jon Kitna 5.00 12.00
Roy Williams WR
Calvin Johnson
13 David Garrard 6.00 15.00
Fred Taylor
Maurice Jones-Drew
14 Larry Johnson 6.00 15.00
Tony Gonzalez
Dwayne Bowe
15 Drew Brees 10.00 25.00
Reggie Bush
Marques Colston
16 Thomas Jones 5.00 12.00
Jerricho Cotchery
Laveranues Coles
17 Donovan McNabb 6.00 15.00
Brian Westbrook
Kevin Curtis
18 Philip Rivers 8.00 20.00
LaDainian Tomlinson
Antonio Gates
19 Matt Hasselbeck 5.00 12.00
Shaun Alexander
Deion Branch
20 Marc Bulger 5.00 12.00
Steven Jackson
Torry Holt
21 Vince Young 6.00 15.00
LenDale White
Brandon Jones
22 Jason Campbell 6.00 15.00
Clinton Portis
Chris Cooley
23 Willis McGahee 5.00 12.00
Derrick Mason
Ray Lewis
24 DeShaun Foster 5.00 12.00
Steve Smith
DeAngelo Williams/190
25 Cedric Benson 8.00 20.00
Bernard Berrian
Devin Hester

2008 Donruss Elite Throwback Threads

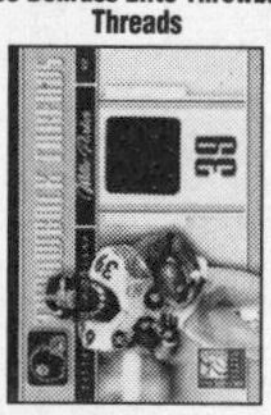

STATED PRINT RUN 199 SER.#'d SETS
*PRIME/50: .6X TO 1.5X BASIC JSY/199
*PRIME/20-30: .8X TO 2X BASIC JSY/199
PRIME PRINT RUN 50 SER.#'d SETS
UNPRICED AUTO PRINT RUN 4-10
UNPRICED PRIME AUTO PRINT RUN 2-5
1 Emmitt Smith 12.00 30.00
2 Marion Barber 3.00 8.00
3 Barry Sanders 10.00 25.00
4 Adrian Peterson 6.00 15.00
5 Thurman Thomas 5.00 12.00
6 Marshawn Lynch 3.00 8.00
7 Jim Kelly 6.00 15.00
8 Trent Edwards 2.50 6.00
9 Franco Harris 6.00 15.00
10 Willie Parker 3.00 8.00
11 Fran Tarkenton 6.00 15.00
12 Tarvaris Jackson 3.00 8.00
13 Roger Craig 5.00 12.00
14 Frank Gore 3.00 8.00
15 Earl Campbell 6.00 15.00
16 LenDale White 3.00 8.00
17 Dan Marino 12.00 30.00
18 Brett Favre 10.00 25.00
19 Lawrence Taylor 6.00 15.00
20 Shawne Merriman 3.00 8.00
21 Archie Manning 6.00 15.00
22 Peyton Manning 6.00 15.00
23 Elroy Hirsch 6.00 15.00
24 Torry Holt 3.00 8.00
25 Tom Landry 20.00 40.00
26 Hank Stram 6.00 15.00
27 Frank Gifford 6.00 15.00
28 Eli Manning 5.00 12.00
29 Ken Strong 5.00 12.00
30 Sid Luckman 8.00 20.00
31 Emmitt Smith 15.00 40.00
Marion Barber
32 Barry Sanders 20.00 40.00
Adrian Peterson
33 Thurman Thomas 6.00 15.00
Marshawn Lynch
34 Jim Kelly 8.00 20.00
Trent Edwards
35 Franco Harris 8.00 20.00
Willie Parker
36 Fran Tarkenton 6.00 15.00
Tarvaris Jackson
37 Roger Craig 5.00 12.00
Frank Gore
38 Earl Campbell 6.00 15.00
LenDale White
39 Dan Marino 25.00 60.00
Brett Favre
40 Lawrence Taylor 8.00 20.00
Shawne Merriman
41 Archie Manning 15.00 40.00
Peyton Manning
42 Elroy Hirsch 10.00 25.00
Torry Holt
43 Tom Landry 20.00 50.00
Hank Stram
44 Frank Gifford 8.00 20.00
Eli Manning
45 Ken Strong 10.00 25.00
Sid Luckman

2008 Donruss Elite Throwback Threads Autographs

UNPRICED AUTO PRINT RUN 4-10
UNPRICED PRIME AUTO PRINT RUN 2-5

2008 Donruss Elite Turn of the Century Autographs

COMMON CARD 6.00 15.00
SEMISTARS 8.00 20.00
UNLISTED STARS 10.00 25.00
STATED PRINT RUN 10-100
SERIAL #'d TO 10 NOT PRICED
105 Joe Flacco/50 60.00 120.00
106 John David Booty/100 8.00 20.00
107 Josh Johnson/100 10.00 25.00
108 Erik Ainge/50 10.00 25.00
110 Dennis Dixon/50 10.00 25.00
111 Kevin O'Connell/100 8.00 20.00
112 Matt Flynn/100 30.00 60.00
113 Bernard Morris/50 8.00 20.00
114 Sam Keller/50 8.00 20.00
115 Paul Smith/100 10.00 25.00
120 Chris Johnson/100 40.00 80.00
121 Jamaal Charles/100 20.00 40.00
122 Ray Rice/100 20.00 50.00
123 Steve Slaton/100 10.00 25.00
124 Mike Hart/100 10.00 25.00
125 Matt Forte/50 30.00 80.00
126 Tashard Choice/50 8.00 20.00
128 Allen Patrick/100 8.00 20.00
130 Justin Forsett/50 10.00 25.00
131 Cory Boyd/50 6.00 15.00
132 Dantrell Savage/50 8.00 20.00
133 Kalvin McRae/100 6.00 15.00
134 Darrell Strong/50 8.00 20.00
135 Owen Schmitt/50 10.00 25.00
136 Peyton Hillis/50 25.00 60.00
137 Jacob Hester/50 10.00 25.00
139 Martellus Bennett/50 8.00 20.00
140 John Carlson/50 10.00 25.00
141 Martin Rucker/100 8.00 20.00
142 Brad Cottam/50 8.00 20.00
143 Jermichael Finley/100 15.00 40.00
144 Jacob Tamme/100 10.00 25.00
145 Dustin Keller/50 10.00 25.00
146 Kellen Davis/100 6.00 15.00
148 James Hardy/50 8.00 20.00
152 Andre Caldwell/50 8.00 20.00
153 Mario Manningham/50 15.00 30.00
154 Devin Thomas/50 8.00 20.00
155 Donnie Avery/50 8.00 20.00
156 Earl Bennett/50 10.00 25.00
157 Eddie Royal/50 10.00 25.00
158 Lavelle Hawkins/50 6.00 15.00
159 DJ Hall/50 8.00 20.00
160 Adarius Bowman/100 8.00 20.00
161 Jordy Nelson/50 25.00 50.00
162 Harry Douglas/50 8.00 20.00
163 Jerome Simpson/50 10.00 25.00
164 Dorien Bryant/100 8.00 20.00
165 Will Franklin/100 8.00 20.00
168 Paul Hubbard/50 8.00 20.00
169 Davone Bess/100 10.00 25.00
171 Dexter Jackson/50 8.00 20.00
173 Darius Reynaud/100 6.00 15.00
174 Josh Morgan/50 10.00 25.00
175 Anthony Alridge/100 8.00 20.00
177 Marcus Smith/50 8.00 20.00
178 Mark Bradford/100 6.00 15.00
179 Marcus Monk/50 8.00 20.00
180 Chris Long/100 10.00 25.00
181 Vernon Gholston/100 8.00 20.00
182 Derrick Harvey/100 6.00 15.00
185 Dan Connor/50 10.00 25.00
186 Curtis Lofton/100 8.00 20.00
187 Keith Rivers/50 10.00 25.00
190 Quentin Groves/50 8.00 20.00
191 Erin Henderson/100 10.00 25.00
193 Antoine Cason/50 10.00 25.00
194 Dominique Rodgers-Cromartie/100 10.00 25.00
195 Leodis McKelvin/100 8.00 20.00
198 Tracy Porter/50 10.00 25.00
199 Terrell Thomas/50 8.00 20.00

2008 Donruss Elite Zoning Commission Gold

GOLD PRINT RUN 800 SER.#'d SETS
*BLACK/400: .5X TO 1.2X GOLD/800
BLACK PRINT RUN 400 SER.#'d SETS
*RED/200: .6X TO 1.5X GOLD/800
RED PRINT RUN 200 SER.#'d SETS
1 Plaxico Burress 1.00 2.50
2 Peyton Manning 2.00 5.00
3 Carson Palmer 1.25 3.00
4 Joseph Addai 1.00 2.50
5 Ted Ginn Jr. 1.00 2.50
6 Steve Smith USC 1.00 2.50
7 Sidney Rice 1.25 3.00
8 Vince Young 1.00 2.50
9 Chester Taylor .75 2.00
10 Marion Barber 1.00 2.50
11 Rudi Johnson 1.00 2.50
12 LenDale White 1.00 2.50
13 Deion Branch 1.00 2.50
14 Laurence Maroney 1.00 2.50
15 Tedy Bruschi 1.25 3.00
16 Kevin Jones .75 2.00
17 Fred Taylor 1.00 2.50
18 Clinton Portis 1.00 2.50

19 Zach Thomas 1.00 2.50
20 Shaun Alexander 1.00 2.50
21 Thomas Jones 1.00 2.50
22 DeShaun Foster 1.00 2.50
23 Ed Reed 1.00 2.50
24 Jason Witten 1.25 3.00
25 Deuce McAllister 1.00 2.50
26 Edgerrin James 1.00 2.50
27 Jon Kitna 1.00 2.50
28 Kevin Curtis .75 2.00
29 Brian Urlacher 1.25 3.00
30 Brandon Marshall 1.00 2.50
31 Marc Bulger 1.00 2.50
32 Jamal Lewis 1.00 2.50
33 Darrelle Revis 1.00 2.50
34 Jeremy Shockey 1.00 2.50
35 Santonio Holmes 1.00 2.50
36 Steven Jackson 1.25 3.00
37 Laveranues Coles .75 2.00
38 Ronnie Brown 1.00 2.50
39 Cadillac Williams 1.00 2.50
40 Antonio Gates 1.25 3.00

2008 Donruss Elite Zoning Commission Jerseys

STATED PRINT RUN 45-299
*PRIME/50: .6X TO 1.5X BASIC JSY/299
*PRIME/50: .5X TO 1.2X BASIC JSY/45-71
PRIME PRINT RUN 50 SER.#'d SETS
1 Plaxico Burress 3.00 8.00
2 Peyton Manning 6.00 15.00
3 Carson Palmer 4.00 10.00
4 Joseph Addai 3.00 8.00
5 Ted Ginn Jr. 3.00 8.00
6 Steve Smith USC 3.00 8.00
7 Sidney Rice 4.00 10.00
8 Vince Young 3.00 8.00
9 Chester Taylor 2.50 6.00
10 Marion Barber 3.00 8.00
11 Rudi Johnson 3.00 8.00
12 LenDale White 3.00 8.00
13 Deion Branch 3.00 8.00
14 Laurence Maroney 3.00 8.00
15 Tedy Bruschi 4.00 10.00
16 Kevin Jones 2.50 6.00
17 Fred Taylor 3.00 8.00
18 Clinton Portis 3.00 8.00
19 Zach Thomas 3.00 8.00
20 Shaun Alexander 3.00 8.00
21 Thomas Jones 3.00 8.00
22 DeShaun Foster/45 4.00 10.00
23 Ed Reed 3.00 8.00
24 Jason Witten 4.00 10.00
25 Deuce McAllister 3.00 8.00
26 Edgerrin James 3.00 8.00
27 Jon Kitna 3.00 8.00
28 Kevin Curtis 2.50 6.00
29 Brian Urlacher 4.00 10.00
30 Brandon Marshall 3.00 8.00
31 Marc Bulger 3.00 8.00
32 Jamal Lewis 3.00 8.00
33 Darrelle Revis 3.00 8.00
34 Jeremy Shockey 3.00 8.00
35 Santonio Holmes 3.00 8.00
36 Steven Jackson 4.00 10.00
37 Laveranues Coles 2.50 6.00
38 Ronnie Brown 3.00 8.00
39 Cadillac Williams/71 4.00 10.00
40 Antonio Gates 4.00 10.00

2009 Donruss Elite

COMP.SET w/o RC's (100) 7.50 20.00
ROOKIE AUTO PRINT RUN 299-999
200-250 INSERTED IN RETAIL PACKS
1 Kurt Warner .40 1.00
2 Larry Fitzgerald .40 1.00
3 Anquan Boldin .30 .75
4 Tim Hightower .25 .60
5 Roddy White .30 .75
6 Michael Turner .30 .75
7 Matt Ryan .40 1.00
8 Willis McGahee .30 .75
9 Joe Flacco .40 1.00
10 Trent Edwards .25 .60
11 Marshawn Lynch .30 .75
12 Lee Evans .30 .75
13 Steve Smith .30 .75
14 DeAngelo Williams .40 1.00
15 Jake Delhomme .30 .75
16 Jonathan Stewart .30 .75
17 Devin Hester .40 1.00
18 Kyle Orton .30 .75
19 Matt Forte .40 1.00
20 Carson Palmer .40 1.00
21 Chad Ochocinco .30 .75
22 T.J. Houshmandzadeh .30 .75
23 Brady Quinn .30 .75
24 Jamal Lewis .30 .75
25 Kellen Winslow .30 .75
26 Braylon Edwards .30 .75
27 Tony Romo .60 1.50
28 Terrell Owens .40 1.00
29 Marion Barber .30 .75
30 Jason Witten .40 1.00
31 Jay Cutler .40 1.00
32 Brandon Marshall .30 .75
33 Eddie Royal .30 .75
34 Calvin Johnson .40 1.00
35 Kevin Smith .30 .75
36 Aaron Rodgers .75 2.00
37 Ryan Grant .30 .75
38 Greg Jennings .40 1.00
39 Matt Schaub .30 .75
40 Andre Johnson .30 .75
41 Steve Slaton .30 .75
42 Peyton Manning .60 1.50
43 Joseph Addai .40 1.00
44 Reggie Wayne .30 .75
45 Dallas Clark .30 .75
46 David Garrard .30 .75
47 Marcedes Lewis .25 .60
48 Maurice Jones-Drew .30 .75
49 Larry Johnson .30 .75
50 Dwayne Bowe .30 .75
51 Chad Pennington .30 .75
52 Ronnie Brown .30 .75
53 Greg Camarillo .30 .75
54 Bernard Berrian .30 .75
55 Adrian Peterson .60 1.50
56 Chester Taylor .25 .60
57 Tom Brady .60 1.50
58 Randy Moss .40 1.00
59 Wes Welker .40 1.00
60 Drew Brees .40 1.00
61 Reggie Bush .40 1.00
62 Jeremy Shockey .25 .60
63 Eli Manning .40 1.00
64 Amani Toomer .30 .75
65 Brandon Jacobs .30 .75
66 Kellen Clemens .25 .60
67 Jerricho Cotchery .30 .75
68 Laveranues Coles .25 .60
69 Thomas Jones .30 .75
70 JaMarcus Russell .25 .60
71 Justin Fargas .25 .60
72 Zach Miller .25 .60
73 Donovan McNabb .40 1.00
74 Brian Westbrook .30 .75
75 DeSean Jackson .30 .75
76 Ben Roethlisberger .40 1.00
77 Willie Parker .25 .60
78 Hines Ward .30 .75
79 Heath Miller .30 .75
80 Philip Rivers .40 1.00
81 LaDainian Tomlinson .40 1.00
82 Vincent Jackson .30 .75
83 Frank Gore .30 .75
84 Isaac Bruce .30 .75
85 Matt Hasselbeck .30 .75
86 Deion Branch .30 .75
87 John Carlson .30 .75
88 Marc Bulger .30 .75
89 Steven Jackson .30 .75
90 Donnie Avery .30 .75
91 Derrick Ward .25 .60
92 Earnest Graham .25 .60
93 Antonio Bryant .25 .60
94 Kerry Collins .30 .75
95 Justin Gage .25 .60
96 Chris Johnson .40 1.00
97 Jason Campbell .25 .60
98 Clinton Portis .30 .75
99 Santana Moss .30 .75
100 Chris Cooley .30 .75
101 Aaron Curry RC 2.50 6.00
102 Aaron Kelly AU/999 RC 4.00 10.00
103 Aaron Maybin RC 2.00 5.00
104 Alphonso Smith RC 2.00 5.00
105 Andre Brown AU/299 RC 4.00 10.00
106 Arian Foster RC 5.00 12.00
107 Austin Collie AU/299 RC 8.00 20.00
108 B.J. Raji RC 2.50 6.00
109 Brandon Gibson AU/499 RC 5.00 12.00
110 Brandon Pettigrew RC 2.50 6.00
111 Brandon Tate AU/299 RC 6.00 15.00
112 Brian Cushing AU/299 RC 6.00 15.00
113 Brian Hartline RC 2.50 6.00
114 Brian Orakpo AU/299 RC 6.00 15.00
115 Brian Robiskie RC 2.50 6.00
116 Brooks Foster AU/499 RC 3.00 8.00
117 Cameron Morrah RC 1.50 4.00
118 Cedric Peerman AU/499 RC 4.00 10.00
119 Chase Coffman AU/299 RC 5.00 12.00
120 Chip Vaughn RC 1.50 4.00
121 Chris Wells RC 4.00 10.00
122 Clay Matthews AU/299 RC 35.00 60.00
123 Clint Sintim AU/299 RC 6.00 15.00
124 Connor Barwin RC 2.50 6.00
125 Cornelius Ingram AU/499 RC 3.00 8.00
126 D.J. Moore RC 2.00 5.00
127 Darius Passmore RC 2.00 5.00
128 Darrius Heyward-Bey RC 2.50 6.00
129 Demetrius Byrd RC 2.00 5.00
130 Deon Butler AU/299 RC 5.00 12.00
131 Derrick Williams RC 2.00 5.00
132 Devin Moore AU/999 RC 4.00 10.00
133 Dominique Edison AU/499 RC 3.00 8.00
134 Donald Brown RC 2.50 6.00
135 Everette Brown AU/299 RC 5.00 12.00
136 Glen Coffee RC 2.00 5.00
137 Graham Harrell AU/999 RC 8.00 20.00
138 Hakeem Nicks RC 4.00 10.00
139 Hunter Cantwell RC 2.50 6.00
140 Ian Johnson RC 2.50 6.00
141 James Casey AU/499 RC 4.00 10.00
142 James Davis RC 2.50 6.00
143 James Laurinaitis AU/299 RC 6.00 15.00
144 Jared Cook AU/299 RC 6.00 15.00
145 Jarett Dillard RC 2.50 6.00
146 Javon Ringer RC 2.50 6.00
147 Jeremiah Johnson AU/999 RC 5.00 12.00
148 Jeremy Childs RC 2.00 5.00
149 Jeremy Maclin RC 4.00 10.00
150 John Parker Wilson AU/999 RC 5.00 12.00
151 Johnny Knox AU/499 RC 8.00 20.00
152 Josh Freeman RC 5.00 12.00
153 Juaquin Iglesias RC 2.00 5.00
154 Kenny Britt RC 3.00 8.00
155 Kenny McKinley AU/499 RC 5.00 12.00
156 Kevin Ogletree AU/999 RC 5.00 12.00
157 Knowshon Moreno RC 2.50 6.00
158 Kory Sheets AU/999 RC 4.00 10.00
159 Larry English AU/299 RC 10.00 20.00
160 LeSean McCoy RC 5.00 12.00
161 Louis Delmas RC 2.50 6.00
162 Louis Murphy RC 2.50 6.00
163 Malcolm Jenkins RC 2.50 6.00
164 Mark Sanchez RC 8.00 20.00
165 Matthew Stafford RC 12.00 30.00
166 Bear Pascoe RC 2.00 5.00
167 Michael Crabtree RC 5.00 12.00
168 Michael Johnson RC 1.50 4.00
169 Mike Goodson AU/299 RC 6.00 15.00
170 Mike Thomas RC 2.50 6.00
171 Mike Wallace RC 5.00 12.00
172 Mohamed Massaquoi RC 2.00 5.00
173 Nate Davis AU/299 RC 5.00 12.00
174 Nathan Brown AU/999 RC 4.00 10.00
175 P.J. Hill AU/999 RC 4.00 10.00
176 Pat White RC 2.50 6.00
177 Patrick Chung RC 2.50 6.00
178 Patrick Turner AU/299 RC 5.00 12.00
179 Percy Harvin RC 4.00 10.00
180 Peria Jerry RC 2.00 5.00
181 Quan Cosby AU/999 RC 4.00 10.00
182 Quinn Johnson AU/499 RC 4.00 10.00
183 Ramses Barden AU/299 RC 4.00 10.00
184 Rashad Jennings AU/499 RC 5.00 12.00
185 Rashad Johnson RC 2.00 5.00
186 Rey Maualuga RC 2.50 6.00
187 Rhett Bomar RC 2.00 5.00
188 Gartrell Johnson RC 1.50 4.00
189 Sammie Stroughter RC 2.50 6.00
190 Sean Smith RC 2.50 6.00
191 Shawn Nelson AU/499 RC 4.00 10.00
192 Shonn Greene RC 4.00 10.00
193 Stephen McGee RC 2.50 6.00
194 Tom Brandstater AU/299 RC 6.00 15.00
195 Tony Fiammetta AU/499 RC 4.00 10.00
196 Travis Beckum AU/299 RC 5.00 12.00
197 Tyrell Sutton RC 2.00 5.00
198 Tyson Jackson RC 2.00 5.00
199 Vontae Davis AU/299 RC 6.00 15.00
200 William Moore RC 2.50 6.00
201 Andre Smith RC 1.25 3.00
202 Asher Allen RC 1.25 3.00
203 Brandon Underwood RC 1.50 4.00
204 Alex Mack RC 1.25 3.00
205 Captain Munnerlyn RC 1.25 3.00
206 Chris Clemons RC 1.00 2.50
207 Cody Brown RC 1.00 2.50
208 Coye Francies RC 1.00 2.50
209 Eric Wood RC 1.25 3.00
210 Darcel McBath RC 1.25 3.00
211 Darius Butler RC 1.50 4.00
212 Darry Beckwith RC 1.25 3.00
213 David Bruton RC 1.25 3.00
214 Sherrod Martin RC 1.25 3.00
215 Eben Britton RC 1.25 3.00
216 Richard Quinn RC 1.25 3.00
217 Eugene Monroe RC 1.00 2.50
218 Evander Hood RC 2.00 5.00
219 Fili Moala RC 1.25 3.00
220 Duke Robinson RC 1.00 2.50
221 Gerald McRath RC 1.25 3.00
222 Herman Johnson RC 1.25 3.00
223 Jairus Byrd RC 1.50 4.00
224 Jamon Meredith RC 1.25 3.00
225 Jarron Gilbert RC 1.25 3.00
226 Jason Phillips RC 1.25 3.00
227 Jason Smith RC 1.25 3.00
228 Jason Williams RC 1.50 4.00
229 Jasper Brinkley RC 1.25 3.00
230 Anthony Hill RC 1.00 2.50
231 Kaluka Maiava RC 1.50 4.00
232 Keenan Lewis RC 1.50 4.00
233 Kraig Urbik RC 1.25 3.00
234 Lawrence Sidbury RC 1.00 2.50
235 Marcus Freeman RC 1.50 4.00
236 Michael Hamlin RC 1.25 3.00
237 Michael Oher RC 2.50 6.00
238 Mike Mickens RC 1.25 3.00
239 Nic Harris RC 1.25 3.00
240 Paul Kruger RC 1.25 3.00
241 Phil Loadholt RC 1.25 3.00
242 Robert Ayers RC 1.50 4.00
243 Ron Brace RC 1.25 3.00
244 Scott McKillop RC 1.25 3.00
245 Sen'Derrick Marks RC 1.00 2.50
246 Troy Kropog RC 1.00 2.50
247 Tyrone McKenzie RC 1.25 3.00
248 Victor Harris RC 1.50 4.00
249 William Beatty RC 1.00 2.50
250 Zack Follett RC 1.00 2.50

2009 Donruss Elite Aspirations

*VETS/70-99: 4X TO 10X BASIC CARDS
*VETS/46-69: 5X TO 12X BASIC CARDS
*VETS/20-29: 8X TO 20X BASIC CARDS
*VETS/10-19: 10X TO 25X BASIC CARDS
*ROOK/70-99: .2X TO .5X STATUS GOLD
*ROOK/46-69: .25X TO .6X STATUS GOLD
*ROOK/30-45: .3X TO .8X STATUS GOLD
*ROOK/20-29: .4X TO 1X STATUS GOLD
*ROOK/10-19: .6X TO 1.5X STATUS GOLD
STATED PRINT RUN 1-99
SERIAL #'d UNDER 10 NOT PRICED

2009 Donruss Elite Retail

COMPLETE SET (100) 7.50 20.00
*VETS: .4X TO 1X BASIC CARDS
RETAIL PRINTED ON WHITE STOCK

2009 Donruss Elite Status

*VETS/70-99: 4X TO 10X BASIC CARDS
*ROOK/70-99: .2X TO .5X STATUS GOLD
*VETS/46-69: 5X TO 12X BASIC CARDS
*ROOK/46-69: .25X TO .6X STATUS GOLD
*VETS/30-45: 6X TO 15X BASIC CARDS
*ROOK/30-45: .3X TO .8X STATUS GOLD
*VETS/20-29: 8X TO 20X BASIC CARDS
*ROOK/20-29: .4X TO 1X STATUS GOLD
*VETS/10-19: 10X TO 25X BASIC CARDS
*ROOK/10-19: .6X TO 1.5X STATUS GOLD
STATED PRINT RUN 1-99
SERIAL #'d UNDER 10 NOT PRICED

2009 Donruss Elite Status Gold

*VETS: 8X TO 20X BASIC CARDS
COMMON ROOKIE 5.00 12.00
ROOKIE SEMISTARS 6.00 15.00
ROOKIE UNL.STARS 8.00 20.00
STATED PRINT RUN 24 SER.#'d SETS
101 Aaron Curry 8.00 20.00
103 Aaron Maybin 6.00 15.00
108 B.J. Raji 8.00 20.00
110 Brandon Pettigrew 8.00 20.00
111 Brandon Tate 8.00 20.00
112 Brian Cushing 8.00 20.00
114 Brian Orakpo 8.00 20.00
115 Brian Robiskie 8.00 20.00
121 Chris Wells 12.00 30.00
122 Clay Matthews 20.00 50.00
128 Darrius Heyward-Bey 8.00 20.00
131 Derrick Williams 6.00 15.00
134 Donald Brown 8.00 20.00
136 Glen Coffee 6.00 15.00
137 Graham Harrell 8.00 20.00
138 Hakeem Nicks 12.00 30.00
143 James Laurinaitis 10.00 25.00
149 Jeremy Maclin 12.00 30.00
152 Josh Freeman 15.00 40.00
153 Juaquin Iglesias 6.00 15.00
154 Kenny Britt 10.00 25.00
157 Knowshon Moreno 8.00 20.00
160 LeSean McCoy 15.00 40.00
163 Malcolm Jenkins 8.00 20.00
164 Mark Sanchez 25.00 60.00
165 Matthew Stafford 40.00 100.00
167 Michael Crabtree 15.00 40.00
172 Mohamed Massaquoi 6.00 15.00
173 Nate Davis 6.00 15.00
176 Pat White 8.00 20.00
179 Percy Harvin 12.00 30.00
182 Quinn Johnson 6.00 15.00
186 Rey Maualuga 8.00 20.00
192 Shonn Greene 12.00 30.00

2009 Donruss Elite Chain Reaction Gold

GOLD PRINT RUN 899 SER.#'d SETS
*BLACK/399: .5X TO 1.2X GOLD/899
BLACK PRINT RUN 399 SER.#'d SETS
*RED/199: .6X TO 1.5X GOLD/899
RED PRINT RUN 199 SER.#'d SETS
1 Ryan Grant 1.00 2.50
2 Willie Parker .75 2.00
3 Chris Johnson 1.25 3.00
4 Ricky Williams 1.00 2.50
5 Steven Jackson 1.00 2.50
6 Santana Moss 1.00 2.50
7 T.J. Houshmandzadeh 1.00 2.50
8 Steve Slaton 1.00 2.50
9 DeSean Jackson 1.00 2.50
10 Anthony Gonzalez .75 2.00
11 Derrick Mason 1.00 2.50
12 Bernard Berrian 1.00 2.50
13 Devin Hester 1.25 3.00
14 Laveranues Coles .75 2.00
15 Justin Gage .75 2.00
16 Laurence Maroney 1.00 2.50
17 Kevin Curtis .75 2.00
18 Vernon Davis 1.00 2.50
19 Brandon Jacobs 1.00 2.50
20 Chris Cooley 1.00 2.50
21 Antonio Gates 1.00 2.50
22 Thomas Jones 1.00 2.50
23 Marion Barber 1.00 2.50
24 Reggie Bush 1.25 3.00
25 Larry Johnson 1.00 2.50

2009 Donruss Elite Chain Reaction Jerseys

STATED PRINT RUN 175-299
*PRIME/33-50: .8X TO 2X BASIC JSY
PRIME PRINT RUN 33-50
1 Ryan Grant/299 2.50 6.00
2 Willie Parker/299 2.00 5.00
3 Chris Johnson/299 3.00 8.00
4 Ricky Williams/299 2.50 6.00
5 Steven Jackson/299 2.50 6.00
6 Santana Moss/299 2.50 6.00
7 T.J. Houshmandzadeh/175 2.50 6.00
8 Steve Slaton/299 2.50 6.00
9 DeSean Jackson/299 2.50 6.00
10 Anthony Gonzalez/299 2.00 5.00
11 Derrick Mason/299 2.50 6.00
12 Bernard Berrian/299 2.50 6.00
13 Devin Hester/299 3.00 8.00
14 Laveranues Coles/299 2.00 5.00
15 Justin Gage/299 2.00 5.00
16 Laurence Maroney/299 2.50 6.00
17 Kevin Curtis/299 2.00 5.00
18 Vernon Davis/299 2.50 6.00
19 Brandon Jacobs/299 2.50 6.00
20 Chris Cooley/299 2.50 6.00
21 Antonio Gates/299 2.50 6.00
22 Thomas Jones/299 2.50 6.00
23 Marion Barber/299 2.50 6.00
24 Reggie Bush/299 3.00 8.00
25 Larry Johnson/299 2.50 6.00

2009 Donruss Elite College Ties Green

GREEN PRINT RUN 899 SER.#'d SETS
*BLACK/199: .6X TO 1.5X GREEN/899
BLACK PRINT RUN 199 SER.#'d SETS
*GOLD/399: .5X TO 1.2X GREEN/899
GOLD PRINT RUN 399 SER.#'d SETS
1 Brandon Pettigrew .75 2.00
2 Brian Robiskie .75 2.00
3 Chase Coffman .60 1.50
4 Chris Wells 1.25 3.00
5 Darrius Heyward-Bey .75 2.00
6 Derrick Williams .60 1.50
7 Donald Brown .75 2.00
8 Hakeem Nicks 1.25 3.00
9 Javon Ringer .75 2.00
10 Jeremy Maclin 1.25 3.00
11 Josh Freeman 1.50 4.00
12 Juaquin Iglesias .60 1.50
13 Kenny Britt 1.00 2.50
14 Knowshon Moreno .75 2.00
15 LeSean McCoy 1.50 4.00
16 Mark Sanchez 2.50 6.00
17 Matthew Stafford 4.00 10.00
18 Michael Crabtree 1.50 4.00
19 Mohamed Massaquoi .60 1.50
20 Nate Davis .60 1.50
21 Pat White .75 2.00
22 Percy Harvin 1.25 3.00
23 Rashad Jennings .75 2.00
24 Rhett Bomar .60 1.50
25 Shonn Greene 1.25 3.00

2009 Donruss Elite College Ties Autographs

STATED PRINT RUN 50 SER.#'d SETS
1 Brandon Pettigrew 8.00 20.00
3 Chase Coffman 6.00 15.00
4 Chris Wells 12.00 30.00
5 Darrius Heyward-Bey 8.00 20.00
6 Derrick Williams 6.00 15.00
7 Donald Brown 8.00 20.00
8 Hakeem Nicks 12.00 30.00
9 Javon Ringer 10.00 25.00
10 Jeremy Maclin 12.00 30.00
11 Josh Freeman 15.00 40.00
12 Juaquin Iglesias 6.00 15.00
13 Kenny Britt 10.00 25.00
14 Knowshon Moreno 25.00 60.00
15 LeSean McCoy 15.00 40.00
16 Mark Sanchez 40.00 100.00
17 Matthew Stafford 50.00 100.00
18 Michael Crabtree 25.00 60.00
19 Mohamed Massaquoi 6.00 15.00
20 Nate Davis 6.00 15.00
21 Pat White 8.00 20.00
22 Percy Harvin 30.00 80.00
23 Rashad Jennings 8.00 20.00
24 Rhett Bomar 6.00 15.00
25 Shonn Greene 12.00 30.00

2009 Donruss Elite College Ties Combos Green

GREEN PRINT RUN 899 SER.#'d SETS
*BLACK/199: .6X TO 1.5X GREEN/899
BLACK PRINT RUN 199 SER.#'d SETS
*GOLD/399: .5X TO 1.2X GREEN/899
GOLD PRINT RUN 399 SER.#'d SETS
1 Glen Coffee .75 2.00
John Parker Wilson
2 Aaron Kelly .75 2.00
James Davis
3 Louis Murphy 1.25 3.00
Percy Harvin
4 Bear Pascoe .75 2.00
Tom Brandstater
5 Knowshon Moreno 4.00 10.00
Matthew Stafford
6 Demetrius Byrd .60 1.50
Quinn Johnson
7 Chase Coffman 1.25 3.00
Jeremy Maclin
8 Brandon Tate 1.25 3.00
Hakeem Nicks
9 Malcolm Jenkins 1.25 3.00
Chris Wells
10 James Laurinaitis .75 2.00
Brian Robiskie
11 Aaron Maybin .60 1.50
Derrick Williams
12 Greg Orton .60 1.50
Kory Sheets
13 James Casey .75 2.00
Jarett Dillard
14 Jared Cook .75 2.00
Kenny McKinley
15 Brian Orakpo .75 2.00
Quan Cosby
16 Michael Crabtree 1.50 4.00
Graham Harrell
17 Mark Sanchez 2.50 6.00
Patrick Turner
18 Rey Maualuga .75 2.00
Brian Cushing
19 Cedric Peerman .75 2.00
Kevin Ogletree
20 P.J. Hill .60 1.50
Travis Beckum
21 Javon Ringer .75 2.00
Devin Thomas
22 Shonn Greene 1.25 3.00
Dallas Clark
23 Darrius Heyward-Bey .75 2.00
LaMont Jordan
24 Josh Freeman 1.50 4.00
Jordy Nelson
25 Kenny Britt 1.00 2.50
Ray Rice

2009 Donruss Elite College Ties Combos Autographs

STATED PRINT RUN 50 SER.#'d SETS
1 Glen Coffee 25.00 50.00
John Parker Wilson
5 Knowshon Moreno 40.00 80.00
Matthew Stafford
7 Chase Coffman 20.00 50.00
Jeremy Maclin
8 Brandon Tate 15.00 40.00
Hakeem Nicks
9 Malcolm Jenkins 30.00 60.00
Chris Wells
14 Jared Cook 12.00 30.00
Kenny McKinley
15 Brian Orakpo 12.00 30.00
Quan Cosby
16 Michael Crabtree 30.00 60.00
Graham Harrell
17 Mark Sanchez 40.00 100.00
Patrick Turner
18 Rey Maualuga 10.00 25.00
Brian Cushing
19 Cedric Peerman 12.00 30.00
Kevin Ogletree
21 Javon Ringer 20.00 40.00
Devin Thomas
22 Shonn Greene 25.00 60.00
Dallas Clark
23 Darrius Heyward-Bey 12.00 30.00
LaMont Jordan
24 Josh Freeman 20.00 50.00
Jordy Nelson
25 Kenny Britt 15.00 40.00
Ray Rice

2009 Donruss Elite Passing the Torch Red

RED PRINT RUN 999 SER.#'d SETS
*BLUE/199: .6X TO 1.5X RED/999
BLUE PRINT RUN 199 SER.#'d SETS
*GREEN/499: .5X TO 1.2X RED/999
GREEN PRINT RUN 499 SER.#'d SETS
1 Gale Sayers 2.00 5.00
Matt Forte
2 Barry Sanders 2.50 6.00
Kevin Smith
3 Joe Namath 4.00 10.00
Brett Favre
4 Bo Jackson 2.00 5.00
Darren McFadden
5 Tony Dorsett 1.50 4.00
Felix Jones
6 Don Maynard 1.25 3.00
Dustin Keller
7 Marcus Allen 1.50 4.00
Jamaal Charles
8 Earl Campbell 1.50 4.00
Chris Johnson
9 Michael Irvin 1.25 3.00
Andre Johnson
10 Raymond Berry 1.25 3.00
Reggie Wayne
11 Andre Reed 1.25 3.00
Lee Evans
12 Roger Craig 1.25 3.00
Frank Gore
13 John Stallworth 1.25 3.00
Santonio Holmes
14 Tiki Barber 1.25 3.00
Brandon Jacobs
15 John Mackey 1.25 3.00
Dallas Clark

2009 Donruss Elite Passing the Torch Autographs

STATED PRINT RUN 25 SER.#'d SETS
1 Gale Sayers 40.00 80.00
Matt Forte
2 Barry Sanders 75.00 150.00
Kevin Smith
3 Joe Namath 200.00 350.00
Brett Favre
4 Bo Jackson 75.00 150.00
Darren McFadden
5 Tony Dorsett 50.00 100.00
Felix Jones
6 Don Maynard 25.00 50.00
Dustin Keller
7 Marcus Allen 30.00 60.00
Jamaal Charles
8 Earl Campbell 30.00 60.00
Chris Johnson
9 Michael Irvin 50.00 100.00
Andre Johnson
10 Raymond Berry 30.00 60.00
Reggie Wayne
11 Andre Reed
Lee Evans
12 Roger Craig 30.00 60.00
Frank Gore
13 John Stallworth 40.00 80.00
Santonio Holmes
14 Tiki Barber 40.00 80.00
Brandon Jacobs
15 John Mackey 30.00 60.00
Dallas Clark

2009 Donruss Elite Prime Targets Gold

GOLD PRINT RUN 899 SER.#'d SETS
*BLACK/399: .5X TO 1.2X GOLD/899
BLACK PRINT RUN 399 SER.#'d SETS
*RED/199: .6X TO 1.5X GOLD/899
RED PRINT RUN 199 SER.#'d SETS
1 Andre Johnson 1.00 2.50
2 Roddy White 1.00 2.50
3 Calvin Johnson 1.25 3.00
4 Anquan Boldin 1.00 2.50
5 Reggie Wayne 1.00 2.50
6 Lee Evans 1.00 2.50
7 Dwayne Bowe 1.00 2.50
8 Hines Ward 1.00 2.50
9 Braylon Edwards 1.00 2.50
10 Torry Holt 1.00 2.50
11 Donald Driver 1.00 2.50
12 Marques Colston 1.00 2.50
13 Eddie Royal 1.00 2.50
14 Justin McCareins .75 2.00
15 Tony Gonzalez 1.00 2.50
16 Dallas Clark 1.00 2.50
17 Adrian Peterson 2.00 5.00
18 Brian Westbrook 1.00 2.50
19 Maurice Jones-Drew 1.00 2.50
20 Marshawn Lynch 1.00 2.50
21 LaDainian Tomlinson 1.25 3.00
22 Derrick Ward .75 2.00
23 Joseph Addai 1.25 3.00
24 Randy Moss 1.25 3.00
25 Jason Witten 1.25 3.00

2009 Donruss Elite Prime Targets Jerseys

JERSEY PRINT RUN 150-299
*PRIME/50: .8X TO 2X BASIC JSY/260-299
*PRIME/50: .6X TO 1.5X BASIC JSY/150
PRIME PRINT RUN 50 SER.#'d SETS
1 Andre Johnson/299 2.50 6.00
2 Roddy White/299 2.50 6.00
3 Calvin Johnson/299 3.00 8.00
4 Anquan Boldin/299 2.50 6.00
5 Reggie Wayne/150 3.00 8.00
6 Lee Evans/299 2.50 6.00
7 Dwayne Bowe/299 2.50 6.00
8 Hines Ward/299 2.50 6.00
9 Braylon Edwards/299 2.50 6.00
10 Torry Holt/299 2.50 6.00
11 Donald Driver/299 2.50 6.00
12 Marques Colston/299 2.50 6.00
13 Eddie Royal/299 2.50 6.00
14 Justin McCareins/299 2.00 5.00
15 Tony Gonzalez/299 2.50 6.00
16 Dallas Clark/299 2.50 6.00
17 Adrian Peterson/299 5.00 12.00
18 Brian Westbrook/299 2.50 6.00
19 Maurice Jones-Drew/299 2.50 6.00
20 Marshawn Lynch/299 2.50 6.00
21 LaDainian Tomlinson/299 3.00 8.00
22 Derrick Ward/260 2.00 5.00
23 Joseph Addai/299 3.00 8.00
24 Randy Moss/299 3.00 8.00
25 Jason Witten/299 3.00 8.00

2009 Donruss Elite Series Red

RED PRINT RUN 999 SER.#'d SETS
*BLUE/199: .6X TO 1.5X RED/999
BLUE PRINT RUN 199 SER.#'d SETS
*GREEN/499: .5X TO 1.2X RED/999
GREEN PRINT RUN 499 SER.#'d SETS
1 LaDainian Tomlinson 1.25 3.00
2 Peyton Manning 2.00 5.00
3 Jake Delhomme 1.00 2.50
4 Tom Brady 2.00 5.00
5 Donovan McNabb 1.25 3.00
6 Ray Lewis 1.25 3.00
7 Vincent Jackson 1.00 2.50
8 Jason Campbell .75 2.00
9 Kellen Winslow 1.00 2.50
10 Kyle Orton 1.00 2.50
11 Joe Flacco 1.25 3.00
12 Correll Buckhalter .75 2.00
13 Matt Ryan 1.25 3.00
14 Aaron Rodgers 2.50 6.00
15 Bob Sanders 1.00 2.50
16 Deuce McAllister 1.00 2.50
17 Joey Galloway 1.00 2.50
18 Roddy White 1.00 2.50
19 Jonathan Stewart 1.00 2.50
20 Matt Hasselbeck 1.00 2.50
21 Jamal Lewis 1.00 2.50
22 Willis McGahee 1.00 2.50
23 Marc Bulger 1.00 2.50
24 Warrick Dunn 1.00 2.50
25 Leon Washington 1.00 2.50
26 Matt Schaub 1.00 2.50
27 Justin Fargas .75 2.00
28 David Garrard 1.00 2.50
29 Jeff Garcia 1.00 2.50
30 Trent Edwards .75 2.00
31 DeMeco Ryans 1.00 2.50
32 Fred Taylor 1.00 2.50
33 Chester Taylor .75 2.00
34 Patrick Willis 1.00 2.50
35 Tony Romo 2.00 5.00

2009 Donruss Elite Series Jerseys

JERSEY PRINT RUN 5-299
*PRIME/35-50: .8X TO 2X BASIC JSY/299
*PRIME/35-50: .6X TO 1.5X BASIC JSY/150
PRIME PRINT RUN 1-50
1 LaDainian Tomlinson/299 3.00 8.00
2 Peyton Manning/299 5.00 12.00
4 Tom Brady/299 5.00 12.00
5 Donovan McNabb/299 3.00 8.00
6 Ray Lewis/299 3.00 8.00
7 Vincent Jackson/299 2.50 6.00
8 Jason Campbell/299 2.00 5.00
9 Kellen Winslow/299 2.50 6.00
11 Joe Flacco/299 3.00 8.00
12 Correll Buckhalter/299 2.00 5.00
15 Bob Sanders/299 2.50 6.00
16 Deuce McAllister/299 2.50 6.00
17 Joey Galloway/299 2.50 6.00
18 Roddy White/150 3.00 8.00
19 Jonathan Stewart/299 2.50 6.00
20 Matt Hasselbeck/299 2.50 6.00
21 Jamal Lewis/299 2.50 6.00
22 Willis McGahee/299 2.50 6.00
23 Marc Bulger/299 2.50 6.00
25 Leon Washington/299 2.50 6.00
26 Matt Schaub/299 2.50 6.00
27 Justin Fargas/299 2.00 5.00
28 David Garrard/299 2.50 6.00
29 Jeff Garcia/299 2.50 6.00
30 Trent Edwards/299 2.00 5.00
31 DeMeco Ryans/299 2.50 6.00
32 Fred Taylor/299 2.50 6.00
33 Chester Taylor/299 2.00 5.00
34 Patrick Willis/299 2.50 6.00
35 Tony Romo/299 5.00 12.00

2009 Donruss Elite Stars Gold

GOLD PRINT RUN 899 SER.#'d SETS
*BLACK/399: .5X TO 1.2X GOLD/899
BLACK PRINT RUN 399 SER.#'d SETS
*RED/199: .6X TO 1.5X GOLD/899
RED PRINT RUN 199 SER.#'d SETS
1 Drew Brees 1.25 3.00
2 Jay Cutler 1.25 3.00
3 Peyton Manning 2.00 5.00
4 Philip Rivers 1.25 3.00
5 Brandon Jacobs 1.00 2.50
6 Frank Gore 1.00 2.50
7 Terrell Owens 1.25 3.00
8 Brian Westbrook 1.00 2.50
9 Tony Romo 2.00 5.00
10 Maurice Jones-Drew 1.00 2.50
11 Adrian Peterson 2.00 5.00
12 Brett Favre 3.00 8.00
13 LaDainian Tomlinson 1.25 3.00
14 DeAngelo Williams 1.25 3.00
15 Eli Manning 1.25 3.00
16 Anquan Boldin 1.00 2.50
17 Clinton Portis 1.00 2.50
18 Brian Urlacher 1.25 3.00
19 Greg Jennings 1.25 3.00
20 Randy Moss 1.25 3.00
21 Steve Smith 1.00 2.50
22 Tom Brady 2.00 5.00
23 T.J. Houshmandzadeh 1.00 2.50
24 Ben Roethlisberger 1.25 3.00
25 Reggie Wayne 1.00 2.50

2009 Donruss Elite Stars Jerseys Gold

JERSEY PRINT RUN 100-299
*PRIME/40-50: .8X TO 2X BASIC JSY/299
*PRIME/40-50: .6X TO 1.5X BASIC JSY/100-150
PRIME PRINT RUN 40-50
1 Drew Brees/299 3.00 8.00
2 Jay Cutler/299 3.00 8.00
3 Peyton Manning/299 5.00 12.00
4 Philip Rivers/299 3.00 8.00
5 Brandon Jacobs/299 2.50 6.00
6 Frank Gore/299 2.50 6.00
7 Terrell Owens/299 3.00 8.00
8 Brian Westbrook/299 2.50 6.00
9 Tony Romo/299 5.00 12.00
10 Maurice Jones-Drew/299 2.50 6.00
11 Adrian Peterson/299 5.00 12.00
12 Brett Favre/299 8.00 20.00
13 LaDainian Tomlinson/299 3.00 8.00
14 DeAngelo Williams/299 3.00 8.00
15 Eli Manning/299 3.00 8.00
16 Anquan Boldin/299 2.50 6.00
17 Clinton Portis/100 3.00 8.00
18 Brian Urlacher/299 3.00 8.00
19 Greg Jennings/299 3.00 8.00
20 Randy Moss/299 3.00 8.00
21 Steve Smith/299 2.50 6.00
22 Tom Brady/299 5.00 12.00
23 T.J. Houshmandzadeh/150 3.00 8.00
24 Ben Roethlisberger/299 3.00 8.00
25 Reggie Wayne/299 2.50 6.00

2009 Donruss Elite Status Autographs Gold

GOLD PRINT RUN 24 SER.#'d SETS
101 Aaron Curry 15.00 40.00
102 Aaron Kelly 12.00 30.00
105 Andre Brown 10.00 25.00
107 Austin Collie 20.00 50.00
108 B.J. Raji 15.00 40.00
109 Brandon Gibson 15.00 40.00
110 Brandon Pettigrew 15.00 40.00
111 Brandon Tate 15.00 40.00
112 Brian Cushing 15.00 40.00
114 Brian Orakpo 15.00 40.00
115 Brian Robiskie 15.00 40.00
116 Brooks Foster 10.00 25.00
118 Cedric Peerman 12.00 30.00
119 Chase Coffman 12.00 30.00
121 Chris Wells 25.00 60.00
122 Clay Matthews 60.00 120.00
123 Clint Sintim 15.00 40.00
125 Cornelius Ingram 10.00 25.00
128 Darrius Heyward-Bey 15.00 40.00
130 Deon Butler 12.00 30.00
131 Derrick Williams 12.00 30.00
132 Devin Moore 12.00 30.00
133 Dominique Edison 10.00 25.00
134 Donald Brown 15.00 40.00
135 Everette Brown 12.00 30.00
136 Glen Coffee 12.00 30.00
137 Graham Harrell 25.00 60.00
138 Hakeem Nicks 25.00 60.00
141 James Casey 12.00 30.00
143 James Laurinaitis 20.00 50.00
144 Jared Cook 15.00 40.00
146 Javon Ringer 15.00 40.00
147 Jeremiah Johnson 15.00 40.00
149 Jeremy Maclin 25.00 60.00
150 John Parker Wilson 15.00 40.00
151 Johnny Knox 25.00 60.00
152 Josh Freeman 60.00 120.00
153 Juaquin Iglesias 12.00 30.00
154 Kenny Britt 20.00 50.00
155 Kenny McKinley 15.00 40.00
156 Kevin Ogletree 15.00 40.00
157 Knowshon Moreno 50.00 120.00
158 Kory Sheets 12.00 30.00
159 Larry English 15.00 40.00
160 LeSean McCoy 30.00 80.00
163 Malcolm Jenkins 15.00 40.00
164 Mark Sanchez 125.00 200.00
165 Matthew Stafford 125.00 200.00
167 Michael Crabtree 60.00 120.00
169 Mike Goodson 15.00 40.00
170 Mike Thomas 15.00 40.00
171 Mike Wallace 30.00 80.00
172 Mohamed Massaquoi 12.00 30.00
173 Nate Davis 12.00 30.00
174 Nathan Brown 12.00 30.00
175 P.J. Hill 12.00 30.00
176 Pat White 15.00 40.00
178 Patrick Turner 12.00 30.00
179 Percy Harvin 75.00 150.00
181 Quan Cosby 12.00 30.00
182 Quinn Johnson 12.00 30.00
183 Ramses Barden 10.00 25.00
184 Rashad Jennings 15.00 40.00
186 Rey Maualuga 15.00 40.00
187 Rhett Bomar 12.00 30.00
191 Shawn Nelson 12.00 30.00
192 Shonn Greene 25.00 60.00
193 Stephen McGee 15.00 40.00
194 Tom Brandstater 15.00 40.00
195 Tony Fiammetta 12.00 30.00
196 Travis Beckum 12.00 30.00
198 Tyson Jackson 12.00 30.00
199 Vontae Davis 15.00 40.00

2009 Donruss Elite Throwback Threads

DUAL JERSEY PRINT RUN 30-299
1 Willis McGahee/65
3 Jamal Lewis/130 5.00 12.00
5 Deion Branch/299 4.00 10.00
6 Terrell Owens/299
7 Randy Moss/299 5.00 12.00
8 Laveranues Coles/299 3.00 8.00
9 Thomas Jones/299 4.00 10.00
10 Clinton Portis/299 4.00 10.00
11 Warrick Dunn/30 6.00 15.00
12 Drew Brees/299 5.00 12.00
13 Edgerrin James/299 4.00 10.00
14 Santana Moss/299 4.00 10.00
15 Jeff Garcia/285 4.00 10.00
16 Alge Crumpler/299 3.00 8.00
17 Early Doucet/299 5.00 12.00
JaMarcus Russell
18 Brian Brohm/299 5.00 12.00
Michael Bush
19 Brady Quinn/100 12.00 30.00
Julius Jones
20 Cedric Benson/280 6.00 15.00
Jamaal Charles
21 John David Booty/299 5.00 12.00
Matt Leinart
22 Gale Sayers/140 10.00 25.00
Matt Forte
23 Joe Namath/100 20.00 50.00
Brett Favre
24 Eric Dickerson/250 6.00 15.00
Darren McFadden
25 Earl Campbell/200 6.00 15.00
LenDale White

26 Deion Sanders/299 10.00 25.00
28 Devery Henderson/299 3.00 8.00
29 Frank Gore/214 4.00 10.00
30 Reggie Williams/149
31 Lee Evans/299 4.00 10.00
32 Jay Cutler/275 5.00 12.00
33 Carson Palmer/299 5.00 12.00
34 Matt Leinart/299 4.00 10.00
35 Reggie Bush/299 5.00 12.00
36 Willis McGahee/299 4.00 10.00
37 Jeremy Shockey/299 3.00 8.00
38 Cadillac Williams/50
39 Peyton Manning/180 20.00 40.00
40 Larry Fitzgerald/299 5.00 12.00
41 Mario Williams/299 4.00 10.00
42 Kellen Winslow/275 4.00 10.00
43 Braylon Edwards/299 4.00 10.00
44 Ronnie Brown/130 5.00 12.00
45 Jevon Kearse/299 4.00 10.00
46 Anquan Boldin/299 4.00 10.00
47 Felix Jones/299 6.00 15.00
48 Vince Young/80 5.00 12.00
49 Adrian Peterson/299 15.00 30.00
50 Dwayne Bowe/299 4.00 10.00

2009 Donruss Elite Throwback Threads Prime

*PRIME/35-50: .8X TO 2X BASE JSY/214-299
*PRIME/20-29: 1X TO 2.5X BASE JSY/214-299
*PRIME/45-50: .6X TO 1.5X BASE JSY/65-180
*PRIME/45-50: .5X TO 1.2X BASE JSY/30-50
PRIME PRINT RUN 1-50
SERIAL #'d UNDER 20 NOT PRICED
2 Michael Turner/45 8.00 20.00

2009 Donruss Elite Throwback Threads Autographs

STATED PRINT RUN 5-25
SERIAL #'d UNDER 15 NOT PRICED
12 Drew Brees/25 50.00 100.00
18 Brian Brohm/25 15.00 40.00
Michael Bush
20 Cedric Benson/25 25.00 50.00
Jamaal Charles
21 John David Booty/25 30.00 60.00
Matt Leinart
22 Gale Sayers/25 50.00 100.00
Matt Forte
23 Joe Namath/25 250.00 400.00
Brett Favre
24 Eric Dickerson/25 40.00 80.00
Darren McFadden
25 Earl Campbell/25 30.00 80.00
LenDale White
26 Deion Sanders/25 60.00 120.00
27 Eddie Royal/25 15.00 40.00
28 Devery Henderson/15 15.00 40.00
29 Frank Gore/25 15.00 40.00
34 Matt Leinart/25 25.00 50.00
38 Cadillac Williams/25 15.00 40.00
39 Peyton Manning/25 100.00 175.00
43 Braylon Edwards/25 15.00 40.00
44 Ronnie Brown/25 15.00 40.00
49 Adrian Peterson/25 100.00 175.00

2009 Donruss Elite Turn of the Century Autographs

STATED PRINT RUN 25-250
101 Aaron Curry/250 8.00 20.00
108 B.J. Raji/250 8.00 20.00
110 Brandon Pettigrew/25 15.00 40.00
115 Brian Robiskie/75 10.00 25.00
121 Chris Wells/200 12.00 30.00
128 Darrius Heyward-Bey/200 8.00 20.00
131 Derrick Williams/25 12.00 30.00
134 Donald Brown/200 8.00 20.00
136 Glen Coffee/50 8.00 20.00
138 Hakeem Nicks/200 12.00 30.00
146 Javon Ringer/25 15.00 40.00
149 Jeremy Maclin/200 12.00 30.00
152 Josh Freeman/200 15.00 40.00
153 Juaquin Iglesias/200 6.00 15.00
154 Kenny Britt/25 30.00 60.00
157 Knowshon Moreno/200 8.00 20.00
160 LeSean McCoy/200 15.00 40.00
163 Malcolm Jenkins/250 8.00 20.00
164 Mark Sanchez/250 30.00 80.00
165 Matthew Stafford/200 60.00 120.00
167 Michael Crabtree/250 20.00 50.00
170 Mike Thomas/250 8.00 20.00
171 Mike Wallace/100 20.00 50.00
172 Mohamed Massaquoi/200 6.00 15.00
176 Pat White/200 8.00 20.00
179 Percy Harvin/200 20.00 50.00
186 Rey Maualuga/250 8.00 20.00
187 Rhett Bomar/50 8.00 20.00
192 Shonn Greene/25 25.00 60.00
193 Stephen McGee/50 10.00 25.00
198 Tyson Jackson/250 6.00 15.00

2009 Donruss Elite Zoning Commission Gold

GOLD PRINT RUN 899 SER.#'d SETS
*BLACK/399: .5X TO 1.2X GOLD/899
BLACK PRINT RUN 399 SER.#'d SETS
*RED/199: .6X TO 1.5X GOLD/899
RED PRINT RUN 199 SER.#'d SETS
1 Larry Fitzgerald 1.25 3.00
2 Greg Jennings 1.25 3.00
3 Brandon Marshall 1.00 2.50
4 Steve Smith 1.00 2.50
5 Wes Welker 1.25 3.00
6 Jerricho Cotchery 1.00 2.50
7 Santonio Holmes 1.00 2.50
8 Randy Moss 1.25 3.00
9 Vincent Jackson 1.00 2.50
10 Marvin Harrison 1.25 3.00
11 Chad Ochocinco 1.00 2.50
12 Amani Toomer 1.00 2.50
13 Terrell Owens 1.25 3.00
14 Justin Gage .75 2.00
15 Reggie Brown .75 2.00
16 Patrick Crayton .75 2.00
17 Josh Reed .75 2.00
18 Selvin Young .75 2.00
19 Clinton Portis 1.00 2.50
20 Michael Turner 1.00 2.50
21 DeAngelo Williams 1.25 3.00
22 Frank Gore 1.00 2.50
23 Ronnie Brown 1.00 2.50
24 Matt Forte 1.25 3.00
25 LenDale White 1.00 2.50

2009 Donruss Elite Zoning Commission Jerseys

JERSEY PRINT RUN 20-299
*PRIME/41-50: .8X TO 2X BASE JSY/260-299
*PRIME/50: .6X TO 1.5X BASE JSY/99-100
*PRIME/50: .5X TO 1.2X BASE JSY/20
PRIME STATED PRINT RUN 41-50
1 Larry Fitzgerald/299 3.00 8.00
2 Greg Jennings/260 3.00 8.00
3 Brandon Marshall/299 2.50 6.00
4 Steve Smith/299 2.50 6.00
5 Wes Welker/299 3.00 8.00
6 Jerricho Cotchery/299 2.50 6.00
7 Santonio Holmes/299 2.50 6.00
8 Randy Moss/299 3.00 8.00
9 Vincent Jackson/299 2.50 6.00
11 Chad Ochocinco/299 2.50 6.00
12 Amani Toomer/299 2.50 6.00
13 Terrell Owens/299 3.00 8.00
14 Justin Gage/299 2.00 5.00
15 Reggie Brown/299 2.00 5.00
16 Patrick Crayton/299 2.00 5.00
17 Josh Reed/299 2.00 5.00
18 Selvin Young/299 2.00 5.00
19 Clinton Portis/99 3.00 8.00
20 Michael Turner/100 3.00 8.00
21 DeAngelo Williams/299 3.00 8.00
22 Frank Gore/299 2.50 6.00
23 Ronnie Brown/20 4.00 10.00
24 Matt Forte/299 3.00 8.00
25 LenDale White/299 2.50 6.00

2009 Donruss Elite National Convention

STATED PRINT RUN 499-999
*ASPIR.RED/50: .6X TO 1.5X BASIC CARD/999
*ASPIR.RED/50: .5X TO 1.2X BASIC CARD/499
*STATUS BLUE/50: .6X TO 1.5X BASIC CARD/999
*STATUS BLUE/50: .5X TO 1.2X BASIC CARD/499
*STATUS GOLD/25: .8X TO 2X BASIC CARD/999
*STATUS GOLD/25: .6X TO 1.5X BASIC CARD/499
101 Aaron Curry/999 1.00 2.50
110 Brandon Pettigrew/999 1.00 2.50
115 Brian Robiskie/999 1.00 2.50
121 Chris Wells/999 1.50 4.00
128 Darrius Heyward-Bey/499 1.25 3.00
134 Donald Brown/999 1.00 2.50
136 Glen Coffee/499 1.00 2.50
138 Hakeem Nicks/999 1.50 4.00
149 Jeremy Maclin/999 1.50 4.00
152 Josh Freeman/999 2.00 5.00
154 Kenny Britt/999 1.25 3.00
157 Knowshon Moreno/999 1.00 2.50
160 LeSean McCoy/499 2.50 6.00
163 Malcolm Jenkins/499 1.25 3.00
164 Mark Sanchez/999 3.00 8.00
165 Matthew Stafford/999 5.00 12.00
167 Michael Crabtree/499 2.50 6.00
171 Mike Wallace/999 2.00 5.00
172 Mohamed Massaquoi/999 .75 2.00
179 Percy Harvin/999 1.50 4.00
227 Jason Smith/499 1.00 2.50

2009 Donruss Elite National Convention Insert Promos

STATED PRINT RUN 499 SER.#'d SETS
*BLUE/50: .5X TO 1.2X BASIC CARD/499
*GOLD/25: .6X TO 1.5X BASIC CARD/499
*RED/50: .5X TO 1.2X BASIC CARD/499
KM Knowshon Moreno 1.00 2.50
(Zoning Commission)
MC Michael Crabtree 2.00 5.00
Prime Targets)
CBW Chris Wells 1.50 4.00
(Chain Reaction)
DHB Darrius Heyward-Bey 1.00 2.50
(Prime Targets)
MS1 Matthew Stafford 5.00 12.00
(Elite Series)
MS2 Mark Sanchez 3.00 8.00
(Elite Series)

2009 Donruss Elite National Convention Insert Promos Autographs

NOT PRICED DUE TO SCARCITY

2010 Donruss Elite

COMP.SET w/o RC's (100) 7.50 20.00
101-200 ROOKIE PRINT RUN 999
1 Anquan Boldin .25 .60
2 Chris Wells .25 .60
3 Larry Fitzgerald .30 .75
4 Matt Ryan .30 .75
5 Michael Turner .20 .50
6 Roddy White .25 .60
7 Joe Flacco .30 .75
8 Ray Rice .25 .60
9 Todd Heap .20 .50
10 Lee Evans .25 .60
11 Marshawn Lynch .25 .60
12 Ryan Fitzpatrick .30 .75
13 DeAngelo Williams .25 .60
14 Jonathan Stewart .25 .60
15 Steve Smith .25 .60
16 Greg Olsen .20 .50
17 Jay Cutler .30 .75
18 Matt Forte .25 .60
19 Carson Palmer .25 .60
20 Cedric Benson .25 .60
21 Chad Ochocinco .25 .60
22 Jake Delhomme .25 .60
23 Jerome Harrison .20 .50
24 Josh Cribbs .30 .75
25 Jason Witten .30 .75
26 Marion Barber .25 .60
27 Miles Austin .30 .75
28 Tony Romo .40 1.00
29 Brandon Marshall .25 .60
30 Knowshon Moreno .25 .60
31 Kyle Orton .25 .60
32 Calvin Johnson .30 .75
33 Kevin Smith .25 .60
34 Matthew Stafford .30 .75
35 Aaron Rodgers .60 1.50
36 Greg Jennings .25 .60
37 Ryan Grant .25 .60
38 Andre Johnson .25 .60
39 Matt Schaub .25 .60
40 Steve Slaton .20 .50
41 Dallas Clark .25 .60
42 Pierre Garcon .25 .60
43 Peyton Manning .50 1.25
44 Reggie Wayne .25 .60
45 David Garrard .25 .60
46 Maurice Jones-Drew .25 .60
47 Mike Sims-Walker .25 .60
48 Dwayne Bowe .25 .60
49 Jamaal Charles .25 .60
50 Matt Cassel .25 .60
51 Chad Henne .25 .60
52 Davone Bess .20 .50
53 Ronnie Brown .25 .60
54 Adrian Peterson .50 1.25
55 Brett Favre .75 2.00
56 Sidney Rice .25 .60
57 Visanthe Shiancoe .25 .60
58 Laurence Maroney .25 .60
59 Tom Brady .50 1.25
60 Wes Welker .30 .75
61 Devery Henderson .20 .50
62 Drew Brees .30 .75
63 Pierre Thomas .25 .60
64 Brandon Jacobs .25 .60
65 Eli Manning .30 .75
66 Steve Smith USC .25 .60
67 Mark Sanchez .30 .75
68 Shonn Greene .25 .60
69 Jerricho Cotchery .25 .60
70 Chaz Schilens .20 .50
71 Darren McFadden .25 .60
72 Zach Miller .25 .60
73 Brent Celek .25 .60
74 DeSean Jackson .25 .60
75 Kevin Kolb .25 .60
76 Ben Roethlisberger .30 .75
77 Rashard Mendenhall .25 .60
78 Santonio Holmes .25 .60
79 Antonio Gates .25 .60
80 Darren Sproles .25 .60
81 Philip Rivers .30 .75
82 Vincent Jackson .20 .50
83 Frank Gore .25 .60
84 Michael Crabtree .30 .75
85 Vernon Davis .25 .60
86 Julius Jones .20 .50
87 Nate Burleson .20 .50
88 T.J. Houshmandzadeh .25 .60
89 Donnie Avery .25 .60
90 Kyle Boller .20 .50
91 Steven Jackson .25 .60
92 Cadillac Williams .25 .60
93 Josh Freeman .30 .75
94 Kellen Winslow Jr. .25 .60
95 Bo Scaife .20 .50
96 Chris Johnson .30 .75
97 Vince Young .20 .50
98 Chris Cooley .25 .60
99 Clinton Portis .25 .60
100 Donovan McNabb .30 .75
101 Kareem Jackson RC 2.50 6.00
102 Rolando McClain RC 2.50 6.00
103 Rob Gronkowski RC 6.00 15.00
104 Chris McGaha RC 1.50 4.00
105 Ben Tate RC 3.00 8.00
106 David Gettis RC 2.50 6.00
107 Kyle Wilson RC 2.50 6.00
108 Freddie Barnes RC 2.00 5.00
109 James Starks RC 4.00 10.00
110 Jahvid Best RC 4.00 10.00
111 Antonio Brown RC 4.00 10.00
112 Dan LeFevour RC 2.50 6.00
113 Mardy Gilyard RC 2.50 6.00
114 Tony Pike RC 2.50 6.00
115 Andre Roberts RC 2.50 6.00
116 C.J. Spiller RC 4.00 10.00
117 Jacoby Ford RC 2.50 6.00
118 Ricky Sapp RC 2.00 5.00
119 Andre Dixon RC 2.50 6.00
120 Marcus Easley RC 2.00 5.00
121 Aaron Hernandez RC 4.00 10.00
122 Brandon Spikes RC 2.50 6.00
123 Carlos Dunlap RC 2.50 6.00
124 Joe Haden RC 2.50 6.00
125 Riley Cooper RC 2.50 6.00
126 Tim Tebow RC 10.00 25.00
127 Patrick Robinson RC 2.50 6.00
128 John Skelton RC 2.50 6.00
129 Lonyae Miller RC 2.00 5.00
130 Ryan Mathews RC 5.00 12.00
131 Seyi Ajirotutu RC 2.50 6.00
132 Demaryius Thomas RC 3.00 8.00
133 Derrick Morgan RC 2.00 5.00
134 Jonathan Dwyer RC 2.50 6.00
135 Morgan Burnett RC 2.50 6.00
136 Arrelious Benn RC 2.50 6.00
137 Bryan Bulaga RC 2.50 6.00
138 Dezmon Briscoe RC 2.00 5.00
139 Brandon LaFell RC 2.50 6.00
140 Chad Jones RC 2.50 6.00
141 Charles Scott RC 2.00 5.00
142 Jimmy Graham RC 5.00 12.00
143 Brandon Graham RC 2.00 5.00
144 Blair White RC 2.50 6.00
145 Eric Decker RC 3.00 8.00
146 Dexter McCluster RC 2.50 6.00
147 Jevan Snead RC 2.50 6.00
148 Shay Hodge RC 2.00 5.00
149 Anthony Dixon RC 2.50 6.00
150 Armanti Edwards RC 2.50 6.00
151 Sean Weatherspoon RC 2.50 6.00
152 Ndamukong Suh RC 5.00 12.00
153 Pat Paschall RC 2.00 5.00
154 Corey Wootton RC 2.00 5.00
155 Mike Kafka RC 2.50 6.00
156 Golden Tate RC 2.50 6.00
157 Jimmy Clausen RC 2.50 6.00
158 Taylor Price RC 2.50 6.00
159 Emmanual Sanders RC 2.50 6.00
160 Dominique Franks RC 1.50 4.00
161 Gerald McCoy RC 2.50 6.00
162 Jermaine Gresham RC 3.00 8.00
163 Sam Bradford RC 10.00 25.00
164 Trent Williams RC 2.50 6.00
165 Dez Bryant RC 8.00 20.00
166 Perrish Cox RC 2.00 5.00
167 Russell Okung RC 2.50 6.00
168 Zac Robinson RC 2.00 5.00
169 Ed Dickson RC 2.50 6.00
170 LeGarrette Blount RC 4.00 10.00
171 Sean Canfield RC 2.00 5.00
172 NaVorro Bowman RC 2.50 6.00
173 Sean Lee RC 2.50 6.00
174 Devin McCourty RC 2.50 6.00
175 Carlton Mitchell RC 2.00 5.00
176 Jason Pierre-Paul RC 4.00 10.00
177 Nate Allen RC 2.50 6.00
178 Anthony McCoy RC 2.00 5.00
179 Damian Williams RC 2.50 6.00
180 Everson Griffen RC 2.50 6.00
181 Joe McKnight RC 2.50 6.00
182 Taylor Mays RC 2.50 6.00
183 Toby Gerhart RC 2.50 6.00
184 Mike Williams RC 4.00 10.00
185 Daryl Washington RC 2.00 5.00
186 Jerry Hughes RC 2.50 6.00
187 Eric Berry RC 2.50 6.00
188 Jonathan Crompton RC 2.00 5.00
189 Montario Hardesty RC 2.50 6.00
190 Colt McCoy RC 5.00 12.00
191 Earl Thomas RC 2.50 6.00
192 Jordan Shipley RC 2.50 6.00
193 Sergio Kindle RC 2.50 6.00
194 Andre Anderson RC 2.00 5.00
195 Jeremy Williams RC 1.50 4.00
196 Chris Cook RC 2.50 6.00
197 Jason Worilds RC 2.50 6.00
198 Joique Bell RC 2.00 5.00
199 Jarrett Brown RC 2.50 6.00
200 Garrett Graham RC 2.00 5.00

2010 Donruss Elite Aspirations

*VETS/70-99: 5X TO 12X BASIC CARDS
*ROOK/70-99: .6X TO 1.5X BASIC CARDS
*VETS/46-69: 6X TO 15X BASIC CARDS
*ROOK/46-69: .8X TO 2X BASIC CARDS
*VETS/30-45: 8X TO 20X BASIC CARDS
*ROOK/30-45: 1X TO 2.5X BASIC CARDS
*VETS/20-29: 10X TO 25X BASIC CARDS
*ROOK/20-29: 1.2X TO 3X BASIC CARDS
*VETS/10-19: 12X TO 30X BASIC CARDS
*ROOK/10-19: 2X TO 5X BASIC CARDS
STATED PRINT RUN 1-99

2010 Donruss Elite Status

*VETS/70-99: 5X TO 12X BASIC CARDS
*ROOK/70-99: .6X TO 1.5X BASIC CARDS
*VETS/46-69: 6X TO 15X BASIC CARDS
*ROOK/46-69: .8X TO 2X BASIC CARDS
*VETS/30-45: 8X TO 20X BASIC CARDS
*ROOK/30-45: 1X TO 2.5X BASIC CARDS
*VETS/20-29: 10X TO 25X BASIC CARDS
*ROOK/20-29: 1.2X TO 3X BASIC CARDS
*VETS/10-19: 12X TO 30X BASIC CARDS
*ROOK/10-19: 2X TO 5X BASIC CARDS
STATED PRINT RUN 1-99

2010 Donruss Elite Status Black

*VETS 1-100: 10X TO 25X BASIC CARDS
*ROOKIES 101-200: 1.2X TO 3X BASIC CARDS
STATUS PRINT RUN 24 SER.#'d SETS

2010 Donruss Elite Aspirations Autographs

7-67 VETERAN PRINT RUN 10-24
102-200 ROOKIE PRINT RUN 49
7 Joe Flacco/10
31 Kyle Orton/15
39 Matt Schaub/15
48 Dwayne Bowe/15
59 Tom Brady/10
67 Mark Sanchez/24 50.00 100.00
102 Rolando McClain/49 10.00 25.00
103 Rob Gronkowski/49 40.00 80.00
104 Chris McGaha/49 6.00 15.00
105 Ben Tate/49 12.00 30.00
106 David Gettis/49 10.00 25.00
108 Freddie Barnes/49 8.00 20.00
109 James Starks/49 30.00 60.00
110 Jahvid Best/49 40.00 100.00
111 Antonio Brown/49 15.00 40.00
112 Dan LeFevour/49 10.00 25.00
114 Tony Pike/49 10.00 25.00
115 Andre Roberts/49 10.00 25.00
116 C.J. Spiller/49 30.00 80.00
117 Jacoby Ford/49 15.00 30.00
120 Marcus Easley/49 8.00 20.00
*121 Aaron Hernandez/49 15.00 40.00
124 Joe Haden/49 10.00 25.00
125 Riley Cooper/49 12.00 30.00
126 Tim Tebow/49 100.00 200.00
127 Patrick Robinson/49 10.00 25.00
129 Lonyae Miller/49 8.00 20.00
130 Ryan Mathews/49 60.00 120.00
131 Seyi Ajirotutu/49 10.00 25.00
132 Demaryius Thomas/49 12.00 30.00
133 Derrick Morgan/49 8.00 20.00
134 Jonathan Dwyer/49 10.00 25.00
135 Morgan Burnett/49 10.00 25.00
136 Arrelious Benn/49 10.00 25.00
137 Bryan Bulaga/49 10.00 25.00
138 Dezmon Briscoe/49 8.00 20.00
139 Brandon LaFell/49 10.00 25.00
140 Chad Jones/49 10.00 25.00
141 Charles Scott/49 8.00 20.00
143 Brandon Graham/49 8.00 20.00
144 Blair White/49 10.00 25.00
145 Eric Decker/49 12.00 30.00
146 Dexter McCluster/49 10.00 25.00
147 Jevan Snead/49 10.00 25.00
148 Shay Hodge/49 8.00 20.00
150 Armanti Edwards/49 10.00 25.00
151 Sean Weatherspoon/49 10.00 25.00
152 Ndamukong Suh/49 50.00 100.00
153 Pat Paschall/49 8.00 20.00
154 Corey Wootton/49 8.00 20.00
155 Mike Kafka/49 10.00 25.00
156 Golden Tate/49 10.00 25.00
157 Jimmy Clausen/49 15.00 40.00
158 Taylor Price/49 10.00 25.00
159 Emmanuel Sanders/49 10.00 25.00
160 Dominique Franks/49 6.00 15.00
161 Gerald McCoy/49 10.00 25.00
162 Jermaine Gresham/49 12.00 30.00
163 Sam Bradford/49 100.00 200.00
165 Dez Bryant/49 75.00 125.00
166 Perrish Cox/49 8.00 20.00
168 Zac Robinson/49 8.00 20.00
169 Ed Dickson/49 10.00 25.00
170 LeGarrette Blount/49 25.00 50.00
171 Sean Canfield/49 8.00 20.00
173 Sean Lee/49 15.00 30.00
174 Devin McCourty/49 10.00 25.00
175 Carlton Mitchell/49 8.00 20.00
176 Jason Pierre-Paul/49 15.00 40.00
177 Nate Allen/49 10.00 25.00
178 Anthony McCoy/49 8.00 20.00
179 Damian Williams/49 10.00 25.00
180 Everson Griffen/49 10.00 25.00
182 Taylor Mays/49 10.00 25.00
183 Toby Gerhart/49 10.00 25.00
186 Jerry Hughes/49 10.00 25.00
188 Jonathan Crompton/49 8.00 20.00
189 Montario Hardesty/49 10.00 25.00
190 Colt McCoy/49 50.00 100.00
191 Earl Thomas/49 10.00 25.00
192 Jordan Shipley/49 10.00 25.00
193 Sergio Kindle/49 10.00 25.00
194 Andre Anderson/49 8.00 20.00
195 Jeremy Williams/49 6.00 15.00
196 Chris Cook/49 10.00 25.00
197 Jason Worilds/49 10.00 25.00
198 Joique Bell/49 8.00 20.00
199 Jarrett Brown/49 10.00 25.00
200 Garrett Graham/49 8.00 20.00

2010 Donruss Elite Chain Reaction Gold

GOLD PRINT RUN 999 SER.#'d SETS
*BLACK/99: .8X TO 2X GOLD/999
*RED/49: 1X TO 2.5X GOLD/999
1 Aaron Rodgers 2.50 6.00
2 Josh Cribbs 1.25 3.00
3 Austin Collie 1.00 2.50
4 Ben Roethlisberger 1.25 3.00
5 Brandon Jacobs 1.00 2.50
6 Calvin Johnson 1.25 3.00
7 Cadillac Williams 1.00 2.50
8 Carson Palmer 1.00 2.50
9 Chris Johnson 1.25 3.00
10 Donald Driver 1.00 2.50
11 Donovan McNabb 1.25 3.00
12 Drew Brees 1.25 3.00
13 Eli Manning 1.25 3.00
14 Hines Ward 1.00 2.50
15 Joe Flacco 1.25 3.00
16 Percy Harvin 1.25 3.00
17 Peyton Manning 2.00 5.00
18 Pierre Garcon 1.00 2.50
19 Rashard Mendenhall 1.00 2.50
20 Steve Smith 1.00 2.50

2010 Donruss Elite Chain Reaction Jerseys

STATED PRINT RUN 196-299
*PRIME/50: .8X TO 2X BASIC JSY
1 Aaron Rodgers/299 6.00 15.00
2 Josh Cribbs/299 3.00 8.00
4 Ben Roethlisberger/299 3.00 8.00
5 Brandon Jacobs/299 2.50 6.00
6 Calvin Johnson/299 3.00 8.00
7 Cadillac Williams/299 2.50 6.00
8 Carson Palmer/299 2.50 6.00
10 Donald Driver/196 2.50 6.00
11 Donovan McNabb/299 3.00 8.00
12 Drew Brees/299 3.00 8.00
13 Eli Manning/299 3.00 8.00
14 Hines Ward/299 2.50 6.00
15 Joe Flacco/299 3.00 8.00
16 Percy Harvin/299 3.00 8.00
17 Peyton Manning/299 5.00 12.00
19 Rashard Mendenhall/299 2.50 6.00
20 Steve Smith/299 2.50 6.00

2010 Donruss Elite Down and Distance Jerseys

STATED PRINT RUN 3-299
1 Aaron Rodgers/299 6.00 15.00
2 Calvin Johnson/299 3.00 8.00
3 Antonio Gates/299 2.50 6.00
4 Anthony Gonzalez/299 2.00 5.00
6 Chris Cooley/299 2.50 6.00
7 LaDainian Tomlinson/299 3.00 8.00
8 Jonathan Stewart/299 2.50 6.00
9 Frank Gore/299 2.50 6.00
10 Jason Witten/299 3.00 8.00
11 Justin Gage/299 2.00 5.00
13 Jamaal Charles/299 2.50 6.00
14 Vernon Davis/299 2.50 6.00
16 Ryan Grant/299 2.50 6.00
17 Hakeem Nicks/299 2.50 6.00
19 Antwaan Randle El/225 2.00 5.00
20 Leon Washington/3
21 Ben Roethlisberger/299 3.00 8.00
22 Marques Colston/299 2.50 6.00
23 Eli Manning/299 3.00 8.00
24 Ben Watson/200 2.00 5.00
25 Rashard Mendenhall/299 2.50 6.00
26 Sidney Rice/34 5.00 12.00
27 Reggie Wayne/299 2.50 6.00
29 Randy Moss/299 3.00 8.00
30 Steven Jackson/299 2.50 6.00
31 Santonio Holmes/55 4.00 10.00
32 Marion Barber/299 2.50 6.00
33 Mike Wallace/299 2.50 6.00
34 Vincent Jackson/299 2.00 5.00
35 Cadillac Williams/299 2.50 6.00
36 Owen Daniels/299 2.00 5.00
37 Philip Rivers/299 3.00 8.00
38 Patrick Crayton/299 2.00 5.00
39 Dallas Clark/299 2.50 6.00
40 Donald Driver/299 2.50 6.00
41 Matt Forte/299 2.50 6.00
42 Muhsin Muhammad/299 2.50 6.00
43 Adrian Peterson/299 5.00 12.00
44 Darren Sproles/299 2.50 6.00
45 Larry Fitzgerald/299 3.00 8.00
46 Steve Smith/299 2.50 6.00
47 Todd Heap/299 2.00 5.00
48 Steve Slaton/299 2.00 5.00
49 Peyton Manning/299 5.00 12.00
50 Wes Welker/299 3.00 8.00

2010 Donruss Elite Down and Distance Jerseys Red Zone Prime

*PRIME/50: .8X TO 2X BASIC JSY/200-299
*PRIME/50: .5X TO 1.2X BASIC JSY/34-55
*PRIME/15: 1.2X TO 3X BASIC JSY/299
PRIME PRINT RUN 15-50
12 Miles Austin/50 10.00 25.00

2010 Donruss Elite Down and Distance Jerseys Autographs

STATED PRINT RUN 5-25
3 Antonio Gates/10
21 Ben Roethlisberger/5
23 Eli Manning/10
33 Mike Wallace/25 20.00 40.00
34 Vincent Jackson/10
41 Matt Forte/10
46 Steve Smith/10

2010 Donruss Elite Passing the Torch Red

RED PRINT RUN 999 SER.#'d SETS
*BLUE/49: 1X TO 2.5X RED/999
*GREEN/99: .8X TO 2X RED/999
1 Joe Namath 2.00 5.00
Mark Sanchez
2 Brett Favre 4.00 10.00
Fran Tarkenton
3 Brent Jones 1.25 3.00
Vernon Davis
4 DeMarcus Ware 1.25 3.00
Ed Too Tall Jones
5 Jamaal Charles 1.25 3.00
Priest Holmes
6 Cris Carter 1.50 4.00
Sidney Rice
7 Knowshon Moreno 1.50 4.00
Terrell Davis
8 Emmitt Smith 2.50 6.00
Felix Jones
9 John Taylor 2.00 5.00
Michael Crabtree
10 Curtis Martin 1.50 4.00
Shonn Greene
11 Brent Celek 1.25 3.00
Pete Retzlaff
12 Darrelle Revis 2.00 5.00
Deion Sanders
13 Steve Largent 1.50 4.00
Wes Welker
14 Jack Lambert 2.00 5.00
James Harrison
15 Michael Irvin 2.00 5.00
Miles Austin

2010 Donruss Elite Passing the Torch Autographs

STATED PRINT RUN 25 SER.#'d SETS
EXCH EXPIRATION: 12/16/2011
1 Joe Namath 125.00 200.00
Mark Sanchez
2 Brett Favre 150.00 300.00
Fran Tarkenton
3 Brent Jones 30.00 60.00
Vernon Davis
4 DeMarcus Ware 40.00 80.00
Ed Too Tall Jones
5 Jamaal Charles 40.00 80.00
Priest Holmes
7 Knowshon Moreno 60.00 120.00
Terrell Davis
8 Emmitt Smith 125.00 200.00
Felix Jones
9 John Taylor 40.00 80.00
Michael Crabtree
10 Curtis Martin 40.00 80.00
Shonn Greene
11 Brent Celek EXCH 30.00 60.00
Pete Retzlaff
12 Darrelle Revis 60.00 120.00
Deion Sanders

2010 Donruss Elite Prime Targets Gold

GOLD PRINT RUN 999 SER.#'d SETS
*BLACK/99: .8X TO 2X GOLD/999
*RED/49: 1X TO 2.5X GOLD/999
1 Adrian Peterson 2.00 5.00
2 Andre Johnson 1.00 2.50
3 Antonio Gates 1.00 2.50
4 Brandon Marshall 1.00 2.50
5 Chris Johnson 1.25 3.00
6 Dallas Clark 1.00 2.50
7 DeSean Jackson 1.00 2.50
8 Frank Gore 1.00 2.50
9 Jamaal Charles 1.00 2.50
10 Larry Fitzgerald 1.25 3.00
11 Miles Austin 1.25 3.00
12 Randy Moss 1.25 3.00
13 Darren Sproles 1.00 2.50
14 Reggie Wayne 1.00 2.50
15 Ricky Williams 1.00 2.50
16 Ryan Grant 1.00 2.50
17 Sidney Rice 1.00 2.50
18 DeAngelo Williams 1.00 2.50
19 Vincent Jackson .75 2.00
20 Wes Welker 1.25 3.00

2010 Donruss Elite Prime Targets Jerseys

STATED PRINT RUN 299 SER.#'d SETS
1 Adrian Peterson 5.00 12.00
2 Andre Johnson 2.50 6.00
3 Antonio Gates 2.50 6.00
4 Brandon Marshall 2.50 6.00
6 Dallas Clark 2.50 6.00
8 Frank Gore 2.50 6.00
9 Jamaal Charles 2.50 6.00
10 Larry Fitzgerald 3.00 8.00
12 Randy Moss 3.00 8.00
13 Darren Sproles 2.50 6.00
14 Reggie Wayne 2.50 6.00
15 Ricky Williams 2.50 6.00
16 Ryan Grant 2.50 6.00
17 Sidney Rice 3.00 8.00
18 DeAngelo Williams 2.50 6.00
19 Vincent Jackson 2.00 5.00
20 Wes Welker 3.00 8.00

2010 Donruss Elite Prime Targets Jerseys Prime

*PRIME/50: .8X TO 2X BASIC JSY/299
PRIME PRINT RUN 2-50
5 Chris Johnson/50 6.00 15.00

2010 Donruss Elite Rookie NFL Shield

NLF SHIELD PRINT RUN 999 SER.#'d SETS
*TEAM LOGO/999: .4X TO 1X NFL SHIELD/999
1 Andre Roberts 1.25 3.00
2 Armanti Edwards 1.25 3.00
3 Arrelious Benn 1.25 3.00
4 Ben Tate 1.50 4.00
5 Brandon LaFell 1.25 3.00
6 C.J. Spiller 2.00 5.00
7 Colt McCoy 2.50 6.00
8 Damian Williams 1.25 3.00
9 Demaryius Thomas 1.50 4.00
10 Dexter McCluster 1.25 3.00
11 Dez Bryant 4.00 10.00
12 Emmanuel Sanders 1.25 3.00
13 Eric Berry 1.25 3.00
14 Eric Decker 1.50 4.00
15 Gerald McCoy 1.25 3.00
16 Golden Tate 1.25 3.00
17 Jahvid Best 2.00 5.00
18 Jermaine Gresham 1.50 4.00
19 Jimmy Clausen 1.25 3.00
20 Joe McKnight 1.25 3.00
21 Jonathan Dwyer 1.25 3.00
22 Jordan Shipley 1.25 3.00
23 Marcus Easley 1.00 2.50
24 Mardy Gilyard 1.25 3.00
25 Mike Kafka 1.25 3.00
26 Mike Williams 2.00 5.00
27 Montario Hardesty 1.25 3.00
28 Ndamukong Suh 2.50 6.00
29 Rob Gronkowski 3.00 8.00
30 Rolando McClain 1.25 3.00
31 Ryan Mathews 2.50 6.00
32 Sam Bradford 5.00 12.00
33 Taylor Price 1.25 3.00
34 Tim Tebow 8.00 20.00
35 Toby Gerhart 1.25 3.00

2010 Donruss Elite Rookie NFL Shield Autographs

1 Andre Roberts 6.00 15.00
2 Armanti Edwards 6.00 15.00
3 Arrelious Benn 6.00 15.00
4 Ben Tate 8.00 20.00
5 Brandon LaFell 6.00 15.00
6 C.J. Spiller 15.00 40.00
7 Colt McCoy 25.00 50.00
8 Damian Williams 6.00 15.00
9 Demaryius Thomas 8.00 20.00
10 Dexter McCluster 10.00 25.00
11 Dez Bryant 30.00 80.00
12 Emmanuel Sanders 6.00 15.00
13 Eric Berry 15.00 40.00
14 Eric Decker 8.00 20.00
15 Gerald McCoy 6.00 15.00
16 Golden Tate 6.00 15.00
17 Jahvid Best 15.00 40.00
18 Jermaine Gresham 8.00 20.00
19 Jimmy Clausen 6.00 15.00
20 Joe McKnight 6.00 15.00
21 Jonathan Dwyer 6.00 15.00
22 Jordan Shipley 6.00 15.00
23 Marcus Easley 5.00 12.00
24 Mardy Gilyard 6.00 15.00
25 Mike Kafka 6.00 15.00
26 Mike Williams 8.00 20.00
27 Montario Hardesty 6.00 15.00
28 Ndamukong Suh 25.00 50.00
29 Rob Gronkowski 20.00 40.00
30 Rolando McClain 6.00 15.00
31 Ryan Mathews 15.00 40.00
32 Sam Bradford 50.00 120.00
33 Taylor Price 6.00 15.00
34 Tim Tebow 75.00 150.00
35 Toby Gerhart 6.00 15.00

2010 Donruss Elite Rookie NFL Team Logo Autographs

1 Andre Roberts 6.00 15.00
2 Armanti Edwards 6.00 15.00
3 Arrelious Benn 6.00 15.00
4 Ben Tate 8.00 20.00
5 Brandon LaFell 8.00 20.00
6 C.J. Spiller 20.00 50.00
7 Colt McCoy 25.00 50.00
8 Damian Williams 6.00 15.00
9 Demaryius Thomas 8.00 20.00
10 Dexter McCluster 10.00 25.00
11 Dez Bryant 30.00 80.00
12 Emmanuel Sanders 6.00 15.00
13 Eric Berry 25.00 50.00
14 Eric Decker 8.00 20.00
15 Gerald McCoy 6.00 15.00
16 Golden Tate 6.00 15.00
17 Jahvid Best 15.00 40.00
18 Jermaine Gresham 8.00 20.00
19 Jimmy Clausen 6.00 15.00
20 Joe McKnight 6.00 15.00
21 Jonathan Dwyer 6.00 15.00
22 Jordan Shipley 6.00 15.00
23 Marcus Easley 5.00 12.00
24 Mardy Gilyard 6.00 15.00
25 Mike Kafka 6.00 15.00
26 Mike Williams 8.00 20.00
27 Montario Hardesty 8.00 20.00
28 Ndamukong Suh 25.00 50.00
29 Rob Gronkowski 20.00 50.00
30 Rolando McClain 6.00 15.00
31 Ryan Mathews 15.00 40.00
32 Sam Bradford 40.00 100.00
33 Taylor Price 6.00 15.00
34 Tim Tebow 60.00 120.00
35 Toby Gerhart 6.00 15.00

2010 Donruss Elite Series Red

RED PRINT RUN 999 SER.#'d SETS
*BLUE/49: 1X TO 2.5X RED/999
*GREEN/99: .8X TO 2X RED/999
1 Adrian Peterson 2.00 5.00
2 Andre Johnson 1.00 2.50
3 Ben Roethlisberger 1.25 3.00
4 Bob Sanders 1.00 2.50
5 Brian Urlacher 1.25 3.00
6 Calvin Johnson 1.25 3.00
7 Dallas Clark 1.00 2.50
8 Darrelle Revis 1.00 2.50
9 Ed Reed 1.00 2.50
10 Felix Jones 1.00 2.50
11 Greg Jennings 1.00 2.50
12 Jason Witten 1.25 3.00
13 Jay Cutler 1.25 3.00
14 Joseph Addai 1.00 2.50
15 LaDainian Tomlinson 1.25 3.00
16 LaRon Landry .75 2.00
17 Marshawn Lynch 1.00 2.50
18 Patrick Willis 1.00 2.50
19 Philip Rivers 1.25 3.00
20 Pierre Thomas 1.00 2.50
21 Ray Lewis 1.25 3.00
22 Sidney Rice 1.00 2.50
23 Terrell Suggs .75 2.00
24 Vince Young .75 2.00
25 Willis McGahee 1.00 2.50

2010 Donruss Elite Series Jerseys

STATED PRINT RUN 38-299
*PRIME/50: .8X TO 2X BASIC JSY/216-299
*PRIME/34: .5X TO 1.2X BASIC JSY/38
*PRIME/25: 1X TO 2.5X BASIC JSY/299
1 Adrian Peterson/299 5.00 12.00
2 Andre Johnson/299 2.50 6.00
3 Ben Roethlisberger/299 3.00 8.00
4 Bob Sanders/299 2.50 6.00
5 Brian Urlacher/299 3.00 8.00
6 Calvin Johnson/299 3.00 8.00
7 Dallas Clark/299 2.50 6.00
8 Darrelle Revis/299 3.00 6.00
9 Ed Reed/299 2.50 6.00
10 Felix Jones/299 2.50 6.00
11 Greg Jennings/299 2.50 6.00
12 Jason Witten/299 3.00 8.00
13 Jay Cutler/39 5.00 12.00
14 Joseph Addai/299 2.50 6.00
15 LaDainian Tomlinson/299 3.00 8.00
16 LaRon Landry/299 2.00 5.00
17 Marshawn Lynch/299 2.50 6.00
18 Patrick Willis/38 4.00 10.00
19 Philip Rivers/299 3.00 8.00
21 Ray Lewis/299 4.00 10.00
22 Sidney Rice/216 3.00 8.00
23 Terrell Suggs/299 2.00 5.00
24 Vince Young/299 2.00 5.00
25 Willis McGahee/299 2.50 6.00

2010 Donruss Elite Stars Gold

GOLD PRINT RUN 999 SER.#'d SETS
*BLACK/99: .8X TO 2X GOLD/999
*RED/49: 1X TO 2.5X GOLD/999
1 Bernard Berrian .75 2.00
2 Brian Westbrook 1.00 2.50
3 Chris Cooley 1.00 2.50
4 David Garrard 1.00 2.50
5 DeAngelo Williams 1.00 2.50
6 Devery Henderson .75 2.00
7 Devin Hester 1.25 3.00
8 Jerricho Cotchery 1.00 2.50
9 Marion Barber 1.00 2.50
10 Laurence Maroney 1.00 2.50
11 Mark Sanchez 1.25 3.00
12 Matt Forte 1.00 2.50
13 Matt Ryan 1.25 3.00
14 Michael Turner .75 2.00
15 Nate Burleson .75 2.00
16 Reggie Bush 1.25 3.00
17 Ronnie Brown 1.00 2.50
18 T.J. Houshmandzadeh 1.00 2.50
19 Tony Gonzalez 1.00 2.50
20 Torry Holt 1.00 2.50

2010 Donruss Elite Stars Jerseys Gold

STATED PRINT RUN 100-299
*PRIME/50: .8X TO 2X BASIC JSY/261-299
*PRIME/50: .6X TO 1.5X BASIC JSY/100
1 Bernard Berrian/299 2.00 5.00
2 Brian Westbrook/299 2.50 6.00
3 Chris Cooley/299 2.50 6.00
4 David Garrard/299 2.50 6.00
5 DeAngelo Williams/299 2.50 6.00
6 Devery Henderson/299 2.00 5.00
7 Devin Hester/299 3.00 8.00

8 Jerricho Cotchery/299 2.50 6.00
9 Marion Barber/299 2.50 6.00
10 Laurence Maroney/299 2.50 6.00
11 Mark Sanchez/299 3.00 8.00
12 Matt Forte/299 2.50 6.00
13 Matt Ryan/299 3.00 8.00
14 Michael Turner/261 2.00 5.00
15 Nate Burleson/299 2.00 5.00
16 Reggie Bush/299 3.00 8.00
17 Ronnie Brown/299 2.50 6.00
19 Tony Gonzalez/299 2.50 6.00
20 Torry Holt/100 3.00 8.00

2010 Donruss Elite Status Autographs

102-200 ROOKIE PRINT RUN 24
7 Joe Flacco/5
13 DeAngelo Williams/15
15 Steve Smith/5
18 Matt Forte/5
28 Tony Romo/5
31 Kyle Orton/5
39 Matt Schaub/10
48 Dwayne Bowe/5
59 Tom Brady/5
67 Mark Sanchez/10
102 Rolando McClain/24 15.00 40.00
103 Rob Gronkowski/24 50.00 100.00
104 Chris McGaha/24 10.00 25.00
105 Ben Tate/24 20.00 50.00
106 David Gettis/24 15.00 40.00
108 Freddie Barnes/24 12.00 30.00
109 James Starks/24 40.00 80.00
110 Jahvid Best/24 60.00 120.00
111 Antonio Brown/24 30.00 60.00
112 Dan LeFevour/24 15.00 40.00
114 Tony Pike/24 15.00 40.00
115 Andre Roberts/24 15.00 40.00
116 C.J. Spiller/24 50.00 120.00
117 Jacoby Ford/24 25.00 50.00
120 Marcus Easley/24 12.00 30.00
121 Aaron Hernandez/24 25.00 60.00
123 Carlos Dunlap/24 15.00 40.00
124 Joe Haden/24 15.00 40.00
125 Riley Cooper/24 15.00 40.00
126 Tim Tebow/24 150.00 250.00
127 Patrick Robinson/24 15.00 40.00
129 Lonyae Miller/24 12.00 30.00
130 Ryan Mathews/24 75.00 150.00
131 Seyi Ajirotutu/24 15.00 40.00
132 Demaryius Thomas/24 20.00 50.00
133 Derrick Morgan/24 12.00 30.00
134 Jonathan Dwyer/24 15.00 40.00
135 Morgan Burnett/24 15.00 40.00
136 Arrelious Benn/24 15.00 40.00
137 Bryan Bulaga/24 15.00 40.00
138 Dezmon Briscoe/24 12.00 30.00
139 Brandon LaFell/24 15.00 40.00
140 Chad Jones/24 15.00 40.00
141 Charles Scott/24 12.00 30.00
143 Brandon Graham/24 12.00 30.00
144 Blair White/24 15.00 40.00
145 Eric Decker/24 20.00 50.00
146 Dexter McCluster/24 15.00 40.00
147 Jevan Snead/24 15.00 40.00
148 Shay Hodge/24 12.00 30.00
150 Armanti Edwards/24 15.00 40.00
151 Sean Weatherspoon/24 15.00 40.00
152 Ndamukong Suh/24 60.00 120.00
153 Pat Paschall/24 12.00 30.00
154 Corey Wootton/24 12.00 30.00
155 Mike Kafka/24 15.00 40.00
156 Golden Tate/24 15.00 40.00
157 Jimmy Clausen/24 25.00 60.00
158 Taylor Price/24 15.00 40.00
159 Emmanuel Sanders/24 15.00 40.00
160 Dominique Franks/24 10.00 25.00
161 Gerald McCoy/24 15.00 40.00
162 Jermaine Gresham/24 20.00 50.00
163 Sam Bradford/24 125.00 250.00
165 Dez Bryant/24 100.00 175.00
166 Perrish Cox/24 12.00 30.00
168 Zac Robinson/24 12.00 30.00
169 Ed Dickson/24 15.00 40.00
170 LeGarrette Blount/24 50.00 100.00
171 Sean Canfield/24 12.00 30.00
173 Sean Lee/24 25.00 50.00
174 Devin McCourty/24 15.00 40.00
175 Carlton Mitchell/24 12.00 30.00
176 Jason Pierre-Paul/24 25.00 60.00
177 Nate Allen/24 15.00 40.00
178 Anthony McCoy/24 12.00 30.00
179 Damian Williams/24 15.00 40.00
180 Everson Griffen/24 15.00 40.00
182 Taylor Mays/24 15.00 40.00
183 Toby Gerhart/24 15.00 40.00
186 Jerry Hughes/24 15.00 40.00
188 Jonathan Crompton/24 12.00 30.00
189 Montario Hardesty/24 15.00 40.00
190 Colt McCoy/24 75.00 150.00
191 Earl Thomas/24 15.00 40.00
192 Jordan Shipley/24 15.00 40.00
193 Sergio Kindle/24 15.00 40.00
194 Andre Anderson/24 12.00 30.00
195 Jeremy Williams/24 10.00 25.00
196 Chris Cook/24 15.00 40.00
197 Jason Worilds/24 15.00 40.00
198 Joique Bell/24 12.00 30.00
199 Jarrett Brown/24 15.00 40.00
200 Garrett Graham/24 12.00 30.00

2010 Donruss Elite Super Bowl XLIV

STATED PRINT RUN 999 SER.#'d SETS
1 Garrett Hartley 1.50 4.00
2 Reggie Bush 2.50 6.00
3 Darren Sharper 2.00 5.00
4 Robert Meachem 2.00 5.00
5 Tracy Porter 1.50 4.00
6 Drew Brees 2.50 6.00
7 Devery Henderson 1.50 4.00
8 Pierre Thomas 2.00 5.00
9 Jeremy Shockey 2.00 5.00
10 Marques Colston 2.00 5.00

2010 Donruss Elite Super Bowl XLIV Autographs

STATED PRINT RUN 4-44
4 Robert Meachem/7
5 Tracy Porter/8
6 Drew Brees/7
7 Devery Henderson/44 15.00 30.00
8 Pierre Thomas/4
10 Marques Colston/5

2010 Donruss Elite Super Bowl XLIV Materials

STATED PRINT RUN 264-299
*PRIME/44: .8X TO 2X BASIC JSY/264-299
2 Reggie Bush/299 6.00 15.00
6 Drew Brees/299 8.00 20.00
7 Devery Henderson/299 5.00 12.00
9 Jeremy Shockey/264 6.00 15.00
10 Marques Colston/299 5.00 12.00

2010 Donruss Elite Throwback Threads

1-10 SINGLE PRINT RUN 200-299
11-20 DUAL PRINT RUN 50-150
1 Deion Sanders/299 6.00 15.00
2 Cris Carter/299 6.00 15.00
3 Rod Woodson/299 6.00 15.00
4 Brent Jones/299 4.00 10.00
5 Brett Favre/299 8.00 20.00
7 Bernie Kosar/299 5.00 12.00
8 Harvey Martin/200 6.00 15.00
9 John Taylor/299 4.00 10.00
10 Curtis Martin/299 5.00 12.00
11 DeMarcus Ware/150 6.00 15.00
Harvey Martin
12 Ricky Williams Dual/150 6.00 16.00
14 Darrelle Revis/150 10.00 25.00
Deion Sanders
15 Brent Jones/150 6.00 15.00
Vernon Davis
16 Rod Woodson/150 10.00 25.00
Troy Polamalu
17 Jamaal Charles/80 6.00 15.00
Priest Holmes
18 Emmitt Smith/150 15.00 40.00
Felix Jones
19 Drew Brees Dual/50 8.00 20.00
20 Cris Carter/150 8.00 20.00
Sidney Rice

2010 Donruss Elite Throwback Threads Prime

*PRIME 1-10: .6X TO 1.5X BASIC JSY/200-299
1-10 PRIME SINGLE PRINT RUN 10-50
*PRIME 11-20: .6X TO 1.5X BASIC DUAL/50-150
11-20 PRIME DUAL PRINT RUN 2-25
6 Priest Holmes/50 6.00 15.00

2010 Donruss Elite Throwback Threads Autographs

1 Deion Sanders/15 40.00 80.00

2010 Donruss Elite Turn of the Century Autographs

STATED PRINT RUN 199-499
102 Rolando McClain/399 6.00 15.00
103 Rob Gronkowski/299 30.00 60.00
104 Chris McGaha/499 4.00 10.00
105 Ben Tate/399 8.00 20.00
106 David Gettis/499 6.00 15.00
108 Freddie Barnes/499 5.00 12.00
109 James Starks/499 12.00 30.00
110 Jahvid Best/249 20.00 50.00
111 Antonio Brown/499 10.00 25.00
112 Dan LeFevour/499 6.00 15.00
114 Tony Pike/499 6.00 15.00
115 Andre Roberts/399 6.00 15.00
116 C.J. Spiller/199 20.00 50.00
117 Jacoby Ford/499 8.00 20.00
120 Marcus Easley/399 5.00 12.00
121 Aaron Hernandez/399 10.00 25.00
123 Carlos Dunlap/299 8.00 20.00
124 Joe Haden/399 6.00 15.00
125 Riley Cooper/499 6.00 15.00
126 Tim Tebow/199 60.00 150.00
127 Patrick Robinson/399 6.00 15.00
129 Lonyae Miller/499 5.00 12.00
130 Ryan Mathews/199 20.00 50.00
131 Seyi Ajirotutu/499 6.00 15.00
132 Demaryius Thomas/249 10.00 25.00
133 Derrick Morgan/499 5.00 12.00
134 Jonathan Dwyer/399 6.00 15.00
135 Morgan Burnett/399 6.00 15.00
136 Arrelious Benn/299 8.00 20.00
137 Bryan Bulaga/399 6.00 15.00
138 Dezmon Briscoe/499 5.00 12.00
139 Brandon LaFell/399 6.00 15.00
140 Chad Jones/499 6.00 15.00
141 Charles Scott/499 5.00 12.00
143 Brandon Graham/499 5.00 12.00
144 Blair White/499 6.00 15.00
145 Eric Decker/399 8.00 20.00
146 Dexter McCluster/299 8.00 20.00
147 Jevan Snead/399 6.00 15.00
148 Shay Hodge/499 5.00 12.00
150 Armanti Edwards/399 8.00 20.00
151 Sean Weatherspoon/499 6.00 15.00
152 Ndamukong Suh/399 25.00 50.00
153 Pat Paschall/499 5.00 12.00
154 Corey Wootton/399 5.00 12.00
155 Mike Kafka/299 8.00 20.00
156 Golden Tate/249 8.00 20.00
157 Jimmy Clausen/249 10.00 25.00
158 Taylor Price/399 6.00 15.00
159 Emmanuel Sanders/399 8.00 20.00
160 Dominique Franks/499 4.00 10.00
161 Gerald McCoy/399 6.00 15.00
162 Jermaine Gresham/299 10.00 25.00
163 Sam Bradford/199 75.00 150.00
165 Dez Bryant/249 50.00 80.00
166 Perrish Cox/499 5.00 12.00
168 Zac Robinson/499 5.00 12.00
169 Ed Dickson/399 6.00 15.00
170 LeGarrette Blount/499 12.00 30.00
171 Sean Canfield/499 5.00 12.00
173 Sean Lee/399 8.00 20.00
174 Devin McCourty/499 8.00 20.00
175 Carlton Mitchell/499 5.00 12.00
176 Jason Pierre-Paul/399 10.00 25.00
177 Nate Allen/499 6.00 15.00
178 Anthony McCoy/399 5.00 12.00
179 Damian Williams/299 8.00 20.00
180 Everson Griffen/399 6.00 15.00
182 Taylor Mays/399 6.00 15.00
183 Toby Gerhart/299 10.00 25.00
186 Jerry Hughes/399 6.00 15.00
188 Jonathan Crompton/399 5.00 12.00
189 Montario Hardesty/299 8.00 20.00
190 Colt McCoy/249 40.00 80.00
191 Earl Thomas/399 6.00 15.00
192 Jordan Shipley/299 8.00 20.00
193 Sergio Kindle/499 6.00 15.00
194 Andre Anderson/499 5.00 12.00
195 Jeremy Williams/499 4.00 10.00
196 Chris Cook/499 6.00 15.00
197 Jason Worilds/499 6.00 15.00
198 Joique Bell/499 5.00 12.00
199 Jarrett Brown/399 6.00 15.00
200 Garrett Graham/499 5.00 12.00

2010 Donruss Elite Zoning Commission Gold

GOLD PRINT RUN 999 SER.#'d SETS
*BLACK/99: .8X TO 2X GOLD/999
*RED/49: 1X TO 2.5X GOLD/999
1 Brent Celek 1.00 2.50
2 Chad Ochocinco 1.00 2.50
3 Drew Brees 1.25 3.00
4 Frank Gore 1.00 2.50
5 Greg Jennings 1.00 2.50
6 Heath Miller 1.00 2.50
7 Jason Witten 1.25 3.00
8 Lee Evans 1.00 2.50
9 Marques Colston 1.00 2.50
10 Matt Schaub 1.00 2.50
11 Maurice Jones-Drew 1.00 2.50
12 Mike Sims-Walker 1.00 2.50
13 Philip Rivers 1.25 3.00
14 Ray Rice 1.00 2.50
15 Santonio Holmes 1.00 2.50
16 Steven Jackson 1.00 2.50
17 Tom Brady 2.00 5.00
18 Tony Romo 1.50 4.00
19 Vernon Davis 1.00 2.50
20 Visanthe Shiancoe 1.00 2.50

2010 Donruss Elite Zoning Commission Jerseys

STATED PRINT RUN 135-299
*PRIME/50: .8X TO 2X BASIC JSY/237-299
*PRIME/50: .6X TO 1.5X BASIC JSY/135
2 Chad Ochocinco/299 2.50 6.00
3 Drew Brees/299 3.00 8.00
4 Frank Gore/299 2.50 6.00
5 Greg Jennings/299 2.50 6.00
6 Heath Miller/299 2.50 6.00
7 Jason Witten/299 3.00 8.00
8 Lee Evans/237 2.50 6.00
9 Marques Colston/299 2.50 6.00
10 Matt Schaub/299 2.50 6.00
11 Maurice Jones-Drew/299 2.50 6.00
13 Philip Rivers/299 3.00 8.00
15 Santonio Holmes/135 3.00 8.00
16 Steven Jackson/290 2.50 6.00
17 Tom Brady/299 5.00 12.00
18 Tony Romo/299 4.00 10.00
19 Vernon Davis/299 2.50 6.00
20 Visanthe Shiancoe/299 3.00 8.00

2010 Donruss Elite National Convention

ANNOUNCED PRINT RUN 499 SETS
1 Aaron Rodgers 1.50 4.00
2 Adrian Peterson 1.50 4.00
3 Brett Favre 6.00 15.00
4 Chris Johnson 1.25 3.00
5 C.J. Spiller 5.00 12.00
6 Colt McCoy 5.00 12.00
7 Dez Bryant 6.00 15.00
8 Drew Brees 1.25 3.00
9 Jahvid Best 3.00 8.00
10 Jimmy Clausen 3.00 8.00
11 Joe Flacco 1.25 3.00
12 Larry Fitzgerald 1.25 3.00
13 Mark Sanchez 1.50 4.00
14 Peyton Manning 1.50 4.00
15 Ray Rice 1.25 3.00
16 Ryan Matthews UER 5.00 12.00
(last name misspelled on front)
17 Sam Bradford 6.00 15.00
18 Tim Tebow 10.00 25.00
19 Tom Brady 1.50 4.00
20 Tony Romo 1.25 3.00

2010 Donruss Elite National Convention Aspirations

*ASPIRATIONS: .8X TO 2X BASIC CARDS
ANNOUNCED PRINT RUN 50

2010 Donruss Elite National Convention Green

STATED PRINT RUN 10 SER. #'d SETS
UNPRICED DUE TO SCARCITY

2010 Donruss Elite National Convention Status

*STATUS: .8X TO 2X BASIC CARDS
ANNOUNCED PRINT RUN 25

2010 Donruss Elite National Convention Autographs

STATED PRINT RUN 1-25
1 Aaron Rodgers/1
3 Brett Favre/1
5 C.J. Spiller/25 60.00 100.00
6 Colt McCoy/5
7 Dez Bryant/5
10 Jimmy Clausen/25 30.00 80.00
11 Joe Flacco/5
13 Mark Sanchez/5
14 Peyton Manning/1
15 Ray Rice/20 25.00 50.00
16 Ryan Matthews/25 UER/ (last name misspelled on front) 75.00 150.00
17 Sam Bradford/25 100.00 175.00
18 Tim Tebow/10
19 Tom Brady/1
20 Tony Romo/10

2010 Donruss Elite National Convention Status Autographs

STATED PRINT RUN 5-15
UNPRICED DUE TO SCARCITY
5 C.J. Spiller/10
16 Ryan Matthews/10 UER/ (last name misspelled on front)
17 Sam Bradford/5

2011 Donruss Elite

COMP.SET w/o RC's (100) 8.00 20.00
101-200 ROOKIE PRINT RUN 999
BF INSERTS IN BLACK FRIDAY PACKS
UNPRICED PRINT PLATE #'d TO 1
1 Chris Wells .25 .60
2 Larry Fitzgerald .25 .60
3 Steve Breaston .20 .50
4 Matt Ryan .30 .75
5 Michael Turner .25 .60
6 Roddy White .25 .60
7 Anquan Boldin .25 .60
8 Joe Flacco .30 .75
9 Ray Rice .25 .60
10 Fred Jackson .30 .75
11 Ryan Fitzpatrick .25 .60
12 Steve Johnson .25 .60
13 DeAngelo Williams .25 .60
14 Jonathan Stewart .25 .60
15 Steve Smith .25 .60
16 Devin Hester .30 .75
17 Jay Cutler .25 .60
18 Johnny Knox .25 .60
19 Matt Forte .25 .60
20 Carson Palmer .25 .60
21 Cedric Benson .25 .60
22 Chad Johnson .25 .60
23 Colt McCoy .25 .60
24 Josh Cribbs .25 .60
25 Peyton Hillis .25 .60
26 Felix Jones .25 .60
27 Jason Witten .30 .75
28 Miles Austin .25 .60
29 Tony Romo .30 .75
30 Brandon Lloyd .25 .60
31 Knowshon Moreno .25 .60
32 Tim Tebow .60 1.50
33 Calvin Johnson .30 .75
34 Jahvid Best .25 .60
35 Matthew Stafford .30 .75
36 Aaron Rodgers .60 1.50
37 Donald Driver .25 .60
38 Greg Jennings .25 .60
39 Andre Johnson .25 .60
40 Arian Foster .25 .60
41 Matt Schaub .25 .60
42 Peyton Manning .50 1.25
43 Pierre Garcon .25 .60
44 Reggie Wayne .25 .60
45 David Garrard .25 .60
46 Marcedes Lewis .20 .50
47 Maurice Jones-Drew .25 .60
48 Dwayne Bowe .25 .60
49 Jamaal Charles .25 .60
50 Matt Cassel .25 .60
51 Brandon Marshall .25 .60
52 Chad Henne .25 .60
53 Ronnie Brown .25 .60
54 Adrian Peterson .40 1.00
55 Percy Harvin .25 .60
56 Tarvaris Jackson .20 .50
57 Tom Brady .50 1.25
58 Danny Woodhead .30 .75
59 Wes Welker .30 .75
60 Drew Brees .30 .75
61 Marques Colston .25 .60
62 Reggie Bush .25 .60
63 Ahmad Bradshaw .25 .60
64 Eli Manning .30 .75
65 Hakeem Nicks .25 .60
66 Mario Manningham .25 .60
67 Braylon Edwards .25 .60
68 LaDainian Tomlinson .30 .75
69 Mark Sanchez .30 .75
70 Darren McFadden .25 .60
71 Jason Campbell .25 .60
72 Zach Miller .25 .60
73 DeSean Jackson .25 .60
74 Jeremy Maclin .25 .60
75 LeSean McCoy .25 .60
76 Michael Vick .30 .75
77 Ben Roethlisberger .30 .75
78 Mike Wallace .30 .75
79 Rashard Mendenhall .25 .60
80 Antonio Gates .25 .60
81 Mike Tolbert .25 .60
82 Philip Rivers .30 .75
83 Frank Gore .25 .60
84 Michael Crabtree .25 .60
85 Vernon Davis .25 .60
86 John Carlson .20 .50
87 Justin Forsett .25 .60
88 Mike Williams .25 .60
89 Danny Amendola .25 .60
90 Sam Bradford .30 .75
91 Steven Jackson .25 .60
92 Josh Freeman .30 .75
93 LeGarrette Blount .25 .60
94 Mike Williams .25 .60
95 Chris Johnson .25 .60
96 Kenny Britt .25 .60
97 Nate Washington .20 .50
98 Chris Cooley .25 .60
99 Donovan McNabb .30 .75
100 Ryan Torain .20 .50
101 A.J. Green RC 5.00 12.00
102 Aaron Williams RC 2.00 5.00
103 Adrian Clayborn RC 2.50 6.00
104 Ahmad Black RC 2.00 5.00
105 Akeem Ayers RC 2.00 5.00
106 Aldon Smith RC 4.00 10.00
106B Aldon Smith BF 2.00 5.00
(inserted in Black Friday packs)
107 Alex Green RC 2.50 6.00
108 Andy Dalton RC 6.00 15.00
109 Austin Pettis RC 2.00 5.00
110 Bilal Powell RC 1.50 4.00
111 Blaine Gabbert RC 4.00 10.00
112 Brandon Harris RC 1.50 4.00
113 Brooks Reed RC 2.50 6.00
114 Bruce Carter RC 2.50 6.00
115 Cam Newton RC 12.00 30.00
115B Cam Newton BF UER 6.00 15.00
(inserted in Black Friday packs; incorrectly lists TCU in stats line)
116 Cameron Heyward RC 2.50 6.00
117 Cameron Jordan RC 2.00 5.00
118 Cecil Shorts RC 2.00 5.00
119 Christian Ponder RC 5.00 12.00
120 Colin Kaepernick RC 3.00 8.00
121 Colin McCarthy RC 2.00 5.00
122 Corey Liuget RC 1.50 4.00
123 Tyron Smith RC 3.00 8.00
123B Tyron Smith BF 1.50 4.00
(inserted in Black Friday packs)
124 Curtis Brown RC 2.50 6.00
125 D.J. Williams RC 2.50 6.00
126 Daniel Thomas RC 2.50 6.00
127 Da'Quan Bowers RC 2.50 6.00
128 Darvin Adams RC 2.00 5.00
129 Davon House RC 2.00 5.00
130 Jordan Cameron RC 2.00 5.00
131 DeAndre McDaniel RC 2.00 5.00
132 Delone Carter RC 2.00 5.00
133 DeMarco Murray RC 5.00 12.00
134 Denarius Moore RC 3.00 8.00
135 Derrick Locke RC 2.00 5.00
136 Dion Lewis RC 2.50 6.00
137 Drake Nevis RC 2.50 6.00
138 Dwayne Harris RC 2.50 6.00
139 Edmond Gates RC 2.00 5.00
140 Evan Royster RC 2.50 6.00
141 Greg Jones RC 2.00 5.00
142 Greg Little RC 2.50 6.00
143 Greg McElroy RC 2.50 6.00
143B Greg McElroy BF 1.25 3.00
(inserted in Black Friday packs)
144 Greg Salas RC 2.50 6.00
145 J.J. Watt RC 3.00 8.00
145B J.J. Watt BF 1.50 4.00
(inserted in Black Friday packs)
146 Jabaal Sheard RC 2.50 6.00
147 Jacquizz Rodgers RC 2.50 6.00
147B Jacquizz Rodgers BF 1.25 3.00
(inserted in Black Friday packs)
148 Jake Locker RC 6.00 15.00
149 Jamie Harper RC 2.50 6.00
150 Jeremy Kerley RC 2.50 6.00
151 Jerrel Jernigan RC 2.00 5.00
152 Jimmy Smith RC 2.50 6.00
153 John Clay RC 2.50 6.00
154 Jonathan Baldwin RC 2.50 6.00
155 Jordan Todman RC 1.50 4.00
156 Roy Helu RC 5.00 12.00
156B Roy Helu BF 2.50 6.00
(inserted in Black Friday packs)
157 Julio Jones RC 5.00 12.00
158 Justin Houston RC 2.50 6.00
159 Kendall Hunter RC 2.50 6.00
160 Kyle Rudolph RC 2.50 6.00
161 Lance Kendricks RC 2.00 5.00
162 Leonard Hankerson RC 2.50 6.00
163 Luke Stocker RC 2.00 5.00
164 Marcell Dareus RC 2.50 6.00
165 Mark Ingram RC 5.00 12.00
165B Mark Ingram BF 2.50 6.00
(inserted in Black Friday packs)
166 Martez Wilson RC 2.50 6.00
167 Mike Pouncey RC 2.50 6.00
168 Mikel Leshoure RC 2.50 6.00
169 Nick Fairley RC 3.00 8.00
169B Nick Fairley BF 1.50 4.00
(inserted in Black Friday packs)
170 Niles Paul RC 2.50 6.00
170B Niles Paul BF 1.25 3.00
(inserted in Black Friday packs)
171 Muhammad Wilkerson RC 2.50 6.00
172 Owen Marecic RC 2.50 6.00
173 Pat Devlin RC 2.50 6.00
174 Patrick Peterson RC 4.00 10.00
174B Patrick Peterson BF 2.00 5.00
(inserted in Black Friday packs)
175 Phil Taylor RC 2.00 5.00
176 Prince Amukamara RC 2.50 6.00
177 Quan Sturdivant RC 2.50 6.00
178 Quinton Carter RC 1.50 4.00
179 Rahim Moore RC 2.00 5.00
180 Randall Cobb RC 3.00 8.00
181 Ricky Stanzi RC 3.00 8.00
181B Ricky Stanzi BF 1.50 4.00
(inserted in Black Friday packs)
182 Rob Housler RC 2.00 5.00
183 Robert Quinn RC 2.50 6.00
184 Ronald Johnson RC 2.00 5.00
185 Ryan Kerrigan RC 2.50 6.00
186 Ryan Mallett RC 5.00 12.00
187 Ryan Whalen RC 2.00 5.00
188 Ryan Williams RC 3.00 8.00
189 Shane Vereen RC 2.50 6.00
190 Stanley Havili RC 1.50 4.00
191 Stephen Paea RC 2.50 6.00
192 Stevan Ridley RC 2.50 6.00
193 Taiwan Jones RC 2.50 6.00
194 Tandon Doss RC 2.00 5.00
195 Ras-I Dowling RC 2.50 6.00
196 Titus Young RC 3.00 8.00
197 Torrey Smith RC 3.00 8.00
198 Tyler Sash RC 2.50 6.00
199 Vincent Brown RC 2.50 6.00
200 Von Miller RC 3.00 8.00
201 Terrelle Pryor BF 1.50 4.00
(inserted in Black Friday packs)

2011 Donruss Elite Aspirations

*VETS/71-99: 5X TO 12X BASIC CARDS
*ROOKIES/71-99: .6X TO 1.5X BASIC CARDS
*VETS/46-69: 6X TO 15X BASIC CARDS
*ROOKIES/46-69: .8X TO 2X BASIC CARDS
*ROOKIES/30-45: 1X TO 2.5X BASIC CARDS
*VETS/20: 10X TO 25X BASIC CARDS
*ROOKIES/20: 1.2X TO 3X BASIC CARDS
*VETS/10-19: 12X TO 30X BASIC CARDS
*ROOKIES/10-19: 1.5X TO 4X BASIC CARDS
STATED PRINT RUN 1-99
115 Cam Newton/98 30.00 60.00

2011 Donruss Elite Status

*VETS/70-99: 5X TO 12X BASIC CARDS
*ROOKIES/70-99: .6X TO 1.5X BASIC CARDS
*VETS/46-57: 6X TO 15X BASIC CARDS
*ROOKIES/46-57: .8X TO 2X BASIC CARDS
*VETS/31-45: 8X TO 20X BASIC CARDS
*ROOKIES/31-45: 1X TO 2.5X BASIC CARDS
*VETS/20-29: 10X TO 25X BASIC CARDS
*ROOKIES/20-29: 1.2X TO 3X BASIC CARDS
*VETS/10-19: 12X TO 30X BASIC CARDS
*ROOKIES/10-19: 1.5X TO 4X BASIC CARDS
STATED PRINT RUN 1-99

2011 Donruss Elite Status Black

*VETS 1-100: 10X TO 25X BASIC CARDS
*ROOKIES 101-200: 1.2X TO 3X
STATED PRINT RUN 24 SER.#'d SETS
115 Cam Newton 60.00 120.00

2011 Donruss Elite Aspirations Autographs

1-100 VETERAN PRINT RUN 5-25
ROOKIE STATED PRINT RUN 49
SERIAL #'d UNDER 16 NOT PRICED
5 Michael Turner/17 15.00 40.00
14 Jonathan Stewart/25 15.00 40.00
23 Colt McCoy/25 15.00 40.00
24 Josh Cribbs/25 15.00 40.00
37 Donald Driver/25 15.00 40.00
43 Pierre Garcon/16 20.00 50.00
55 Percy Harvin/25 15.00 40.00
69 Mark Sanchez/25 40.00 80.00
74 Jeremy Maclin/25 15.00 40.00
81 Mike Tolbert/25 15.00 40.00
90 Sam Bradford/25 50.00 100.00
94 Mike Williams/25 15.00 40.00
101 A.J. Green 30.00 60.00
102 Aaron Williams 8.00 20.00
103 Adrian Clayborn 10.00 25.00
104 Ahmad Black 8.00 20.00
105 Akeem Ayers 8.00 20.00
106 Aldon Smith 15.00 40.00
107 Alex Green 10.00 25.00
108 Andy Dalton 40.00 80.00
109 Austin Pettis 8.00 20.00
110 Bilal Powell 6.00 15.00
111 Blaine Gabbert 40.00 80.00
112 Brandon Harris 6.00 15.00
115 Cam Newton 100.00 175.00
116 Cameron Heyward 10.00 25.00
117 Cameron Jordan 8.00 20.00
118 Cecil Shorts 8.00 20.00
119 Christian Ponder 30.00 80.00
120 Colin Kaepernick 25.00 50.00
122 Corey Liuget 8.00 20.00
125 D.J. Williams 10.00 25.00
126 Daniel Thomas 10.00 25.00
127 Da'Quan Bowers 10.00 25.00
131 DeAndre McDaniel 8.00 20.00
132 Delone Carter 8.00 20.00
133 DeMarco Murray 40.00 80.00
134 Denarius Moore 40.00 80.00
135 Derrick Locke 8.00 20.00
136 Dion Lewis 10.00 25.00
138 Dwayne Harris 10.00 25.00
139 Edmond Gates 8.00 20.00
140 Evan Royster 10.00 25.00
141 Greg Jones 8.00 20.00
142 Greg Little 10.00 25.00
144 Greg Salas 10.00 25.00
145 J.J. Watt 12.00 30.00
148 Jake Locker 60.00 100.00
149 Jamie Harper 10.00 25.00
150 Jeremy Kerley 10.00 25.00
151 Jerrel Jernigan 8.00 20.00
152 Jimmy Smith 10.00 25.00
153 John Clay 8.00 20.00
154 Jonathan Baldwin 10.00 25.00
155 Jordan Todman 6.00 15.00
157 Julio Jones 40.00 80.00
159 Kendall Hunter 10.00 25.00
160 Kyle Rudolph 10.00 25.00
161 Lance Kendricks 8.00 20.00
162 Leonard Hankerson 10.00 25.00
163 Luke Stocker 8.00 20.00
164 Marcell Dareus 10.00 25.00
165 Mark Ingram 50.00 100.00
166 Martez Wilson 8.00 20.00
168 Mikel Leshoure 10.00 25.00
170 Niles Paul 10.00 25.00
173 Pat Devlin 8.00 20.00
175 Phil Taylor 8.00 20.00
176 Prince Amukamara 10.00 25.00
178 Quinton Carter 6.00 15.00
179 Rahim Moore 8.00 20.00
180 Randall Cobb 25.00 50.00
181 Ricky Stanzi 12.00 30.00
184 Ronald Johnson 8.00 20.00
185 Ryan Kerrigan 10.00 25.00
186 Ryan Mallett 30.00 60.00
187 Ryan Whalen 8.00 20.00
188 Ryan Williams 20.00 50.00
189 Shane Vereen 10.00 25.00
190 Stanley Havili 6.00 15.00
191 Stephen Paea 10.00 25.00
192 Stevan Ridley 10.00 25.00
193 Taiwan Jones 10.00 25.00
194 Tandon Doss 8.00 20.00
196 Titus Young 12.00 30.00
197 Torrey Smith 12.00 30.00
198 Tyler Sash 10.00 25.00
199 Vincent Brown 10.00 25.00
200 Von Miller 12.00 30.00

2011 Donruss Elite Craftsmen Gold

GOLD PRINT RUN 999 SER.#'d SETS
*BLACK/99: .8X TO 2X GOLD/999
*RED/49: 1X TO 2.5X GOLD/999
1 Aaron Rodgers 2.00 5.00
2 Andre Johnson 1.00 2.50
3 Antonio Gates 1.00 2.50
4 Braylon Edwards 1.00 2.50
5 Calvin Johnson 1.25 3.00
6 Carson Palmer 1.00 2.50
7 Darren McFadden 1.00 2.50
8 David Garrard 1.00 2.50
9 Devery Henderson .75 2.00
10 Devin Hester 1.25 3.00
11 Drew Brees 1.25 3.00
12 Heath Miller 1.00 2.50
13 Jamaal Charles 1.00 2.50
14 Jason Witten 1.25 3.00
15 Jeremy Maclin 1.00 2.50
16 Joe Flacco 1.25 3.00
17 Lee Evans 1.00 2.50
18 Matt Schaub 1.00 2.50
19 Michael Turner 1.00 2.50
20 Mike Wallace 1.25 3.00
21 Peyton Manning 2.00 5.00
22 Sam Bradford 1.25 3.00
23 Santonio Holmes 1.00 2.50
24 Steven Jackson 1.00 2.50
25 Vincent Jackson 1.00 2.50
26 Andy Dalton BF 1.25 3.00
(inserted in Black Friday packs)

2011 Donruss Elite Craftsmen Jerseys

STATED PRINT RUN 299 SER.#'d SETS
*PRIME/50: .8X TO 2X BASIC JSY/299
1 Aaron Rodgers 5.00 12.00
2 Andre Johnson 2.50 6.00
3 Antonio Gates 2.50 6.00
4 Braylon Edwards 2.50 6.00
5 Calvin Johnson 3.00 8.00
6 Carson Palmer 2.50 6.00
7 Darren McFadden 2.50 6.00
8 David Garrard 2.50 6.00
9 Devery Henderson 2.00 5.00
10 Devin Hester 3.00 8.00
11 Drew Brees 3.00 8.00
12 Heath Miller 2.50 6.00
13 Jamaal Charles 2.50 6.00
14 Jason Witten 3.00 8.00
15 Jeremy Maclin 2.50 6.00
16 Joe Flacco 3.00 8.00
17 Lee Evans 2.50 6.00
18 Matt Schaub 2.50 6.00
19 Michael Turner 2.50 6.00
20 Mike Wallace 3.00 8.00
21 Peyton Manning 5.00 12.00
22 Sam Bradford 3.00 8.00
23 Santonio Holmes 2.50 6.00
24 Steven Jackson 2.50 6.00
25 Vincent Jackson 2.50 6.00

2011 Donruss Elite Down and Distance Black Friday

INSERTED IN BLACK FRIDAY PACKS
52 Julio Jones .60 1.50
53 A.J. Green .60 1.50

2011 Donruss Elite Down and Distance Jerseys

STATED PRINT RUN 30-299
*PRIME/35-50: .8X TO 2X BASIC JSY/214-299
*PRIME/40: .4X TO 1X BASIC JSY/30
2 Chris Wells/299 2.50 6.00
3 Bernard Berrian/299 2.00 5.00
4 Bo Scaife/225 2.00 5.00
5 Brandon Jacobs/299 2.50 6.00
6 Brandon Marshall/299 2.50 6.00
7 Cadillac Williams/299 2.00 5.00
8 Dallas Clark/299 2.50 6.00
9 Darren Sproles/299 2.50 6.00
10 Donald Driver/299 2.50 6.00
11 Dustin Keller/299 2.50 6.00
12 Eddie Royal/299 2.00 5.00
13 Felix Jones/299 2.50 6.00
14 Frank Gore/299 2.50 6.00
15 Greg Olsen/299 2.00 5.00
16 James Jones/30 5.00 12.00
17 Jeremy Shockey/299 2.50 6.00
18 Johnny Knox/299 2.50 6.00
19 Jonathan Stewart/299 2.50 6.00
20 Joseph Addai/299 2.50 6.00
21 Kenny Britt/275 2.50 6.00
22 Kevin Boss/299 2.50 6.00
23 Louis Murphy/299 2.50 6.00
24 Malcom Floyd/299 2.50 6.00
25 Marion Barber/299 2.50 6.00
26 Matt Cassel/299 2.50 6.00
27 Matthew Stafford/299 3.00 8.00
28 Mike Sims-Walker/299 2.50 6.00
29 Sam Hurd/299 2.00 5.00
30 Miles Austin/299 3.00 8.00
31 Willis McGahee/299 2.00 5.00
32 Nate Washington/299 2.00 5.00
33 Owen Daniels/299 2.00 5.00
34 Pierre Garcon/299 2.50 6.00
35 Randy Moss/299 2.50 6.00
36 Robert Meachem/214 2.50 6.00
37 Ronnie Brown/299 2.50 6.00
38 Ryan Fitzpatrick/299 4.00 10.00
40 Ryan Mathews/299 2.50 6.00
41 Santana Moss/299 2.50 6.00
42 Shonn Greene/299 2.50 6.00
43 Sidney Rice/299 2.50 6.00
44 Steve Smith/299 2.50 6.00
45 Tarvaris Jackson/299 2.00 5.00
46 Tashard Choice/299 2.00 5.00
47 Todd Heap/299 2.00 5.00
48 Tony Gonzalez/299 2.50 6.00
49 Wes Welker/299 3.00 8.00

2011 Donruss Elite Down and Distance Jerseys Autographs

JERSEY AUTO PRINT RUN 6-25
UNPRICED PRIME AU PRINT RUN 9-10
3 Bernard Berrian/25 12.00 30.00
8 Dallas Clark/25 15.00 40.00
16 James Jones/15 12.00 30.00
19 Jonathan Stewart/25 15.00 40.00
22 Kevin Boss/25 15.00 40.00
23 Louis Murphy/19 15.00 40.00
40 Ryan Mathews/25 15.00 40.00
42 Shonn Greene/25 15.00 40.00

2011 Donruss Elite Hit List Gold

STATED PRINT RUN 999 SER.#'d SETS
*BLACK/99: .8X TO 2X GOLD/999
*RED/49: 1X TO 2.5X GOLD/999
1 Barrett Ruud .75 2.00
2 Brian Cushing .75 2.00
3 Brian Urlacher 1.25 3.00
4 Chad Greenway 1.00 2.50
5 Clay Matthews 1.25 3.00
6 Curtis Lofton .75 2.00
7 Darrelle Revis 1.00 2.50
8 DeMarcus Ware 1.00 2.50
9 Dwight Freeney 1.00 2.50
10 Ed Reed 1.00 2.50
11 James Harrison 1.25 3.00
12 James Laurinaitis .75 2.00
13 Jared Allen 1.00 2.50
14 Jerod Mayo .75 2.00
15 Jon Beason .75 2.00
16 Julius Peppers 1.00 2.50
17 LaRon Landry .75 2.00
18 London Fletcher .75 2.00
19 Ndamukong Suh 1.25 3.00
20 Patrick Willis 1.00 2.50
21 Ray Lewis 1.25 3.00
22 Stephen Tulloch .75 2.00
23 Tamba Hali .75 2.00
24 Troy Polamalu 1.25 3.00
25 Asante Samuel .75 2.00
26 Von Miller BF .60 1.50
(inserted in Black Friday packs)

2011 Donruss Elite Hit List Jerseys

STATED PRINT RUN 299 SER.#'d SETS
*PRIME/50: .8X TO 2X BASIC JSY/299
1 Barrett Ruud 2.50 6.00
3 Brian Urlacher 4.00 10.00
4 Chad Greenway 3.00 8.00
5 Clay Matthews 6.00 15.00
7 Darrelle Revis 3.00 8.00
8 DeMarcus Ware 3.00 8.00
9 Dwight Freeney 3.00 8.00
10 Ed Reed 3.00 8.00
11 James Harrison 4.00 10.00
12 James Laurinaitis 2.50 6.00
13 Jared Allen 3.00 8.00
15 Jon Beason 2.50 6.00
17 LaRon Landry 2.50 6.00
18 London Fletcher 2.50 6.00
20 Patrick Willis 3.00 8.00
21 Ray Lewis 4.00 10.00
23 Tamba Hali 3.00 8.00
24 Troy Polamalu 4.00 10.00
25 Asante Samuel 2.50 6.00

2011 Donruss Elite Legends of the Fall Gold

GOLD PRINT RUN 999 SER.#'d SETS
*BLACK/99: .8X TO 2X GOLD/999
*RED/49: 1X TO 2.5X GOLD/999
1 Adrian Peterson 1.50 4.00
2 Ben Roethlisberger 1.25 3.00
3 Chad Johnson 1.00 2.50
4 Chris Johnson 1.00 2.50
5 DeSean Jackson 1.00 2.50
6 Donovan McNabb 1.25 3.00
7 Dwayne Bowe 1.00 2.50
8 Eli Manning 1.25 3.00
9 Greg Jennings 1.00 2.50
10 Jay Cutler 1.00 2.50
11 LaDainian Tomlinson 1.25 3.00
12 Larry Fitzgerald 1.00 2.50
13 LeSean McCoy 1.00 2.50
14 Mark Sanchez 1.25 3.00
15 Matt Ryan 1.25 3.00
16 Maurice Jones-Drew 1.00 2.50
17 Michael Vick 1.25 3.00
18 Percy Harvin 1.00 2.50
19 Philip Rivers 1.25 3.00
20 Ray Rice 1.00 2.50
21 Roddy White 1.00 2.50
22 Reggie Wayne 1.00 2.50
23 Tony Romo 1.25 3.00
24 Tom Brady 2.00 5.00
25 Vernon Davis 1.00 2.50

2011 Donruss Elite Legends of the Fall Jerseys

STATED PRINT RUN 76-299
*PRIME/50: .8X TO 2X BASIC JSY/299
*PRIME/50: .6X TO 1.5X BASIC JSY/76
1 Adrian Peterson/299 4.00 10.00
3 Chad Johnson/299 2.50 6.00
4 Chris Johnson/299 2.50 6.00
5 DeSean Jackson/299 2.50 6.00
6 Donovan McNabb/299 3.00 8.00
7 Dwayne Bowe/299 2.50 6.00
8 Eli Manning/299 3.00 8.00
9 Greg Jennings/76 3.00 8.00
10 Jay Cutler/299 2.50 6.00
11 LaDainian Tomlinson/299 3.00 8.00

12 Larry Fitzgerald/299 2.50 6.00
13 LeSean McCoy/299 2.50 6.00
14 Mark Sanchez/299 3.00 8.00
15 Matt Ryan/299 3.00 8.00
16 Maurice Jones-Drew/299 2.50 6.00
17 Michael Vick/299 3.00 8.00
18 Percy Harvin/299 2.50 6.00
19 Philip Rivers/299 3.00 8.00
20 Ray Rice/299 3.00 8.00
21 Roddy White/299 2.50 6.00
22 Reggie Wayne/299 2.50 6.00
23 Tony Romo/299 3.00 8.00
24 Tom Brady/299 5.00 12.00
25 Vernon Davis/299 2.50 6.00

2011 Donruss Elite New Breed Jersey

STATED PRINT RUN 299 SER.#'d SETS
*PRIME/50: .8X TO 2X BASIC JSY/299
1 A.J. Green 5.00 12.00
2 Alex Green 2.50 6.00
3 Andy Dalton 6.00 15.00
4 Austin Pettis 2.00 5.00
5 Bilal Powell 1.50 4.00
6 Blaine Gabbert 4.00 10.00
7 Cam Newton 12.00 30.00
8 Christian Ponder 5.00 12.00
9 Colin Kaepernick 3.00 8.00
10 Daniel Thomas 2.50 6.00
11 Delone Carter 2.00 5.00
12 DeMarco Murray 5.00 12.00
13 Greg Little 2.50 6.00
14 Jake Locker 6.00 15.00
15 Jamie Harper 2.50 6.00
16 Jerrel Jernigan 2.00 5.00
17 Jonathan Baldwin 2.50 6.00
18 Jordan Todman 1.50 4.00
19 Julio Jones 5.00 12.00
20 Kendall Hunter 2.50 6.00
21 Kyle Rudolph 2.50 6.00
22 Leonard Hankerson 2.50 6.00
23 Marcell Dareus 2.50 6.00
24 Mark Ingram 5.00 12.00
25 Mikel Leshoure 2.50 6.00
26 Randall Cobb 3.00 8.00
27 Ryan Mallett 5.00 12.00
28 Ryan Williams 3.00 8.00
29 Shane Vereen 2.50 6.00
30 Stevan Ridley 2.50 6.00
31 Taiwan Jones 2.50 6.00
32 Titus Young 3.00 8.00
33 Torrey Smith 3.00 8.00
34 Vincent Brown 2.50 6.00
35 Von Miller 3.00 8.00
36 Edmond Gates 2.00 5.00

2011 Donruss Elite New Breed Jersey Autographs

STATED PRINT RUN 25 SER.#'d SETS
UNPRICED PRIME AU PRINT RUN 10
1 A.J. Green 40.00 80.00
2 Alex Green 12.00 30.00
3 Andy Dalton 50.00 100.00
4 Austin Pettis 10.00 25.00
5 Bilal Powell 8.00 20.00
6 Blaine Gabbert 40.00 80.00
7 Cam Newton 125.00 250.00
8 Christian Ponder 40.00 80.00
9 Colin Kaepernick 30.00 60.00
10 Daniel Thomas 12.00 30.00
11 Delone Carter 10.00 25.00
12 DeMarco Murray 40.00 80.00
13 Greg Little 12.00 30.00
14 Jake Locker 75.00 135.00
15 Jamie Harper 12.00 30.00
16 Jerrel Jernigan 10.00 25.00
17 Jonathan Baldwin 12.00 30.00
18 Jordan Todman 8.00 20.00
19 Julio Jones 40.00 80.00
20 Kendall Hunter 12.00 30.00
21 Kyle Rudolph 12.00 30.00
22 Leonard Hankerson 12.00 30.00
23 Marcell Dareus 12.00 30.00
24 Mark Ingram 60.00 120.00
25 Mikel Leshoure 12.00 30.00
26 Randall Cobb
27 Ryan Mallett 40.00 80.00
28 Ryan Williams 15.00 40.00
29 Shane Vereen 12.00 30.00
30 Stevan Ridley 12.00 30.00
31 Taiwan Jones 12.00 30.00
32 Titus Young 15.00 40.00
33 Torrey Smith 15.00 40.00
34 Vincent Brown 12.00 30.00
35 Von Miller 15.00 40.00
36 Edmond Gates 10.00 25.00

2011 Donruss Elite Passing the Torch Autographs

STATED PRINT RUN 19-25
EXCH EXPIRATION: 12/22/2012
1 Peyton Manning/25 150.00 300.00
Sam Bradford
2 LaDainian Tomlinson/25 60.00 120.00
Ryan Mathews
3 John Elway/25 150.00 300.00
Tim Tebow
4 Michael Irvin/25 50.00 120.00
Dez Bryant
5 Tony Gonzalez/25 50.00 100.00
Tony Moeaki
6 Keyshawn Johnson/19 40.00 80.00
Mike Williams
7 Randall Cunningham/25 75.00 150.00
Michael Vick
8 Franco Harris/25 40.00 80.00
Rashard Mendenhall
9 Priest Holmes/25 50.00 100.00
Arian Foster
10 Percy Harvin/25 60.00 120.00
Sam Bradford
11 Bart Starr/25 175.00 300.00
Joe Namath
12 Santonio Holmes/25 50.00 100.00
Eli Manning
13 Drew Brees/25 200.00 350.00
Aaron Rodgers
14 Curtis Martin/25 50.00 100.00
LaDainian Tomlinson
15 Mark Ingram/25 125.00 250.00
Cam Newton

2011 Donruss Elite Power Formulas Gold

STATED PRINT RUN 999 SER.#'d SETS
*BLACK/99: .8X TO 2X GOLD/999
*RED/49: 1X TO 2.5X GOLD/999
1 Ahmad Bradshaw 1.00 2.50
2 Anquan Boldin 1.00 2.50
3 Anthony Gonzalez .75 2.00
4 Arian Foster 1.00 2.50
5 Brent Celek 1.00 2.50
6 C.J. Spiller 1.00 2.50
7 Chad Henne 1.00 2.50
8 Chris Cooley 1.00 2.50
9 DeAngelo Williams 1.00 2.50
10 Dez Bryant 1.25 3.00
11 Hakeem Nicks 1.00 2.50
12 Hines Ward 1.00 2.50
13 Jahvid Best 1.00 2.50
14 Josh Cribbs 1.00 2.50
15 Josh Freeman 1.25 3.00
16 Knowshon Moreno 1.00 2.50
17 Marques Colston 1.00 2.50
18 Matt Forte 1.00 2.50
19 Michael Crabtree 1.00 2.50
20 Mike Williams 1.00 2.50
21 Rashard Mendenhall 1.00 2.50
22 Reggie Bush 1.00 2.50
23 Rob Gronkowski 1.25 3.00
24 Tim Tebow 2.50 6.00
25 Visanthe Shiancoe 1.00 2.50
26 Mark Ingram BF 1.00 2.50
(inserted in Black Friday packs)
27 Cam Newton BF 2.50 6.00
(inserted in Black Friday packs

2011 Donruss Elite Power Formulas Jerseys Prime

PRIME PRINT RUN 50 SER.#'d SETS
*BASE JSY/299: .2X TO .5X PRIME/50
1 Ahmad Bradshaw 5.00 12.00
2 Anquan Boldin 5.00 12.00
3 Anthony Gonzalez 4.00 10.00
4 Arian Foster 6.00 15.00
5 Brent Celek 5.00 12.00
6 C.J. Spiller 5.00 12.00
7 Chad Henne 5.00 12.00
8 Chris Cooley 5.00 12.00
9 DeAngelo Williams 5.00 12.00
10 Dez Bryant 6.00 15.00
11 Hakeem Nicks 5.00 12.00
12 Hines Ward 6.00 15.00
13 Jahvid Best 5.00 12.00
14 Josh Cribbs 5.00 12.00
15 Josh Freeman 6.00 15.00
16 Knowshon Moreno 5.00 12.00
17 Marques Colston 5.00 12.00
18 Matt Forte 5.00 12.00
19 Michael Crabtree 5.00 12.00
21 Rashard Mendenhall 5.00 12.00
22 Reggie Bush 5.00 12.00
24 Tim Tebow 12.00 30.00
25 Visanthe Shiancoe 5.00 12.00

2011 Donruss Elite Rookie NFL Shield

STATED PRINT RUN 999 SER.#'d SETS
*TEAM LOGO/999: .4X TO 1X NFL SHIELD/999
1 A.J. Green 2.50 6.00
2 Austin Pettis 1.00 2.50
3 Greg Little 1.25 3.00
4 Jerrel Jernigan 1.00 2.50
5 Jonathan Baldwin 1.25 3.00
6 Julio Jones 2.50 6.00
7 Leonard Hankerson 1.25 3.00
8 Randall Cobb 1.50 4.00
9 Titus Young 1.50 4.00
10 Torrey Smith 1.50 4.00
11 Vincent Brown 1.25 3.00
12 Von Miller 1.50 4.00
13 Marcell Dareus 1.25 3.00
14 Alex Green 1.25 3.00
15 Bilal Powell .75 2.00
16 Daniel Thomas 1.25 3.00
17 Delone Carter 1.00 2.50
18 DeMarco Murray 2.50 6.00
19 Jamie Harper 1.25 3.00
20 Jordan Todman .75 2.00
21 Kendall Hunter 1.25 3.00
22 Mark Ingram 2.50 6.00
23 Mikel Leshoure 1.25 3.00
24 Ryan Williams 1.50 4.00
25 Shane Vereen 1.25 3.00
26 Stevan Ridley 1.25 3.00
27 Taiwan Jones 1.25 3.00
28 Andy Dalton 3.00 8.00
29 Blaine Gabbert 2.00 5.00
30 Cam Newton 6.00 15.00
31 Christian Ponder 2.50 6.00
32 Colin Kaepernick 1.50 4.00
33 Jake Locker 3.00 8.00
34 Kyle Rudolph 1.25 3.00
35 Ryan Mallett 2.50 6.00
36 Edmond Gates 1.00 2.50

2011 Donruss Elite Rookie NFL Shield Autographs

RANDOM INSERTS IN PACKS
1 A.J. Green 25.00 50.00
2 Austin Pettis 5.00 12.00
3 Greg Little 6.00 15.00
4 Jerrel Jernigan 5.00 12.00
5 Jonathan Baldwin 8.00 20.00
6 Julio Jones 25.00 50.00
7 Leonard Hankerson 6.00 15.00
8 Randall Cobb 15.00 30.00
9 Titus Young 8.00 20.00
10 Torrey Smith 8.00 20.00
11 Vincent Brown 6.00 15.00
12 Von Miller 10.00 25.00
13 Marcell Dareus 12.00 30.00
14 Alex Green 15.00 30.00
15 Bilal Powell 4.00 10.00
16 Daniel Thomas 6.00 15.00
17 Delone Carter 5.00 12.00
18 DeMarco Murray 25.00 50.00
19 Jamie Harper 6.00 15.00
20 Jordan Todman 4.00 10.00
21 Kendall Hunter 6.00 15.00
22 Mark Ingram 25.00 60.00
23 Mikel Leshoure 6.00 15.00
24 Ryan Williams 8.00 20.00
25 Shane Vereen 6.00 15.00
26 Stevan Ridley 6.00 15.00
27 Taiwan Jones 6.00 15.00
28 Andy Dalton 30.00 60.00
29 Blaine Gabbert 25.00 50.00
30 Cam Newton 90.00 150.00
31 Christian Ponder 25.00 50.00
32 Colin Kaepernick 20.00 40.00
33 Jake Locker 25.00 60.00
34 Kyle Rudolph 6.00 15.00
35 Ryan Mallett 20.00 40.00
36 Edmond Gates 5.00 12.00

2011 Donruss Elite Rookie NFL Team Logo Autographs

RANDOM INSERTS IN PACKS
1 A.J. Green 25.00 50.00
2 Austin Pettis 5.00 12.00
3 Greg Little 6.00 15.00
4 Jerrel Jernigan 5.00 12.00
5 Jonathan Baldwin 8.00 20.00
6 Julio Jones 25.00 50.00
7 Leonard Hankerson 6.00 15.00
8 Randall Cobb 15.00 30.00
9 Titus Young 8.00 20.00
10 Torrey Smith 8.00 20.00
11 Vincent Brown 6.00 15.00
12 Von Miller 10.00 25.00
13 Marcell Dareus 12.00 30.00
14 Alex Green 15.00 30.00
15 Bilal Powell 4.00 10.00
16 Daniel Thomas 10.00 25.00
17 Delone Carter 5.00 12.00
18 DeMarco Murray 30.00 60.00
19 Jamie Harper 6.00 15.00
20 Jordan Todman 4.00 10.00
21 Kendall Hunter 6.00 15.00
22 Mark Ingram 25.00 60.00
23 Mikel Leshoure 6.00 15.00
24 Ryan Williams 8.00 20.00
25 Shane Vereen 6.00 15.00
26 Stevan Ridley 6.00 15.00
27 Taiwan Jones 6.00 15.00
28 Andy Dalton 30.00 60.00
29 Blaine Gabbert 25.00 50.00
30 Cam Newton 90.00 150.00
31 Christian Ponder 20.00 40.00
32 Colin Kaepernick 20.00 40.00
33 Jake Locker 25.00 60.00
34 Kyle Rudolph 6.00 15.00
35 Ryan Mallett 20.00 40.00
36 Edmond Gates 5.00 12.00

2011 Donruss Elite Status Autographs

UNPRICED VET PRINT RUN 3-10
*ROOKIES/24: .6X TO 1.5X ASPIR.AU/49
101-200 ROOKIE PRINT RUN 24
UNPRICED STATUS BLACK PRINT RUN 1
108 Andy Dalton 60.00 120.00
111 Blaine Gabbert 75.00 135.00
115 Cam Newton 175.00 300.00
119 Christian Ponder 50.00 120.00
120 Colin Kaepernick 50.00 100.00
148 Jake Locker 100.00 200.00
157 Julio Jones 50.00 100.00
165 Mark Ingram 75.00 135.00

2011 Donruss Elite Throwback Threads

STATED PRINT RUN 66-99
*PRIME/25: .8X TO 2X BASIC JSY/66-99
1 Otto Graham/99 25.00 50.00
Sammy Baugh
2 Deion Sanders/99 15.00 40.00
Bo Jackson
3 Randall Cunningham/99 15.00 40.00
Michael Vick
4 Joe Montana/99 30.00 60.00
Tom Brady
5 Jim Plunkett/99 12.00 30.00
Marcus Allen
6 Danny White/99 12.00 30.00
Ed Too Tall Jones
7 Raymond Berry/99 10.00 25.00
Lenny Moore
8 Emmitt Smith/99 15.00 40.00
Eric Dickerson
9 Richard Dent/99 10.00 25.00
Jim McMahon
10 Bob Griese/66 10.00 25.00
Paul Warfield
11 Paul Hornung/99 12.00 30.00
Forrest Gregg
12 Dan Marino/99 20.00 50.00
Mark Duper
13 George Blanda/99 10.00 25.00
Jan Stenerud
14 Boomer Esiason/99 12.00 30.00
Jim Kelly
15 Joe Greene/99 12.00 30.00
Roger Staubach

2011 Donruss Elite Throwback Threads Autographs

DUAL AU STATED PRINT RUN 3-25
UNPRICED PRIME AU PRINT RUN 10
2 Deion Sanders/25 90.00 150.00
Bo Jackson
3 Randall Cunningham/25 75.00 150.00
Michael Vick
4 Joe Montana/25 EXCH
Tom Brady
5 Jim Plunkett/25 60.00 120.00
Marcus Allen
6 Danny White/25 50.00 100.00
Ed Too Tall Jones
7 Raymond Berry/25 40.00 80.00
Lenny Moore
8 Emmitt Smith/25 125.00 200.00
Eric Dickerson
9 Richard Dent/25 60.00 120.00
Jim McMahon
10 Bob Griese/25 50.00 100.00
Paul Warfield
11 Paul Hornung/25 50.00 100.00
Forrest Gregg
12 Dan Marino/25 125.00 250.00
Mark Duper
14 Boomer Esiason/25 50.00 100.00
Jim Kelly
15 Joe Greene/25 EXCH 60.00 120.00
Roger Staubach

2011 Donruss Elite Turn of the Century Autographs

STATED PRINT RUN 14-499
UNPRICED PRINT PLATE #'d TO 1
101 A.J. Green/199 30.00 60.00
102 Aaron Williams/499 5.00 12.00
103 Adrian Clayborn/499 6.00 15.00
104 Ahmad Black/499 5.00 12.00
105 Akeem Ayers/499 5.00 12.00
106 Aldon Smith/499 10.00 25.00
107 Alex Green/499 6.00 15.00
108 Andy Dalton/199 30.00 60.00
109 Austin Pettis/499 5.00 12.00
110 Bilal Powell/399 4.00 10.00
111 Blaine Gabbert/199 20.00 50.00
112 Brandon Harris/499 5.00 12.00
115 Cam Newton/199 100.00 175.00
116 Cameron Heyward/499 6.00 15.00
117 Cameron Jordan/499 5.00 12.00
118 Cecil Shorts/499 5.00 12.00
119 Christian Ponder/199 30.00 60.00
120 Colin Kaepernick/199 10.00 25.00
122 Corey Liuget/499 5.00 12.00
125 D.J. Williams/299 8.00 20.00
126 Daniel Thomas/299 8.00 20.00
127 Da'Quan Bowers/299 8.00 20.00
131 DeAndre McDaniel/499 5.00 12.00
132 Delone Carter/299 6.00 15.00
133 DeMarco Murray/299 25.00 60.00
135 Derrick Locke/199 6.00 15.00
136 Dion Lewis/499 5.00 12.00
138 Dwayne Harris/499 6.00 15.00
139 Edmond Gates/299 6.00 15.00
140 Evan Royster/499 6.00 15.00
141 Greg Jones/499 5.00 12.00
142 Greg Little/299 8.00 20.00
144 Greg Salas/499 6.00 15.00
145 J.J. Watt/499 8.00 20.00
148 Jake Locker/199 40.00 80.00
149 Jamie Harper/299 6.00 15.00
150 Jeremy Kerley/499 6.00 15.00
151 Jerrel Jernigan/299 6.00 15.00
152 Jimmy Smith/499 5.00 12.00
153 John Clay/499 5.00 12.00
154 Jonathan Baldwin/299 8.00 20.00
155 Jordan Todman/299 6.00 15.00
157 Julio Jones/199 25.00 60.00
159 Kendall Hunter/299 8.00 20.00
160 Kyle Rudolph/299 8.00 20.00
161 Lance Kendricks/499 5.00 12.00
162 Leonard Hankerson/299 8.00 20.00
163 Luke Stocker/499 5.00 12.00
164 Marcell Dareus/499 6.00 15.00
165 Mark Ingram/199 30.00 60.00
166 Martez Wilson/499 5.00 12.00
168 Mikel Leshoure/299 8.00 20.00
170 Niles Paul/499 6.00 15.00
173 Pat Devlin/14
175 Phil Taylor/499 5.00 12.00
176 Prince Amukamara/399 6.00 15.00
178 Quinton Carter/499 4.00 10.00
179 Rahim Moore/499 5.00 12.00
180 Randall Cobb/299 15.00 30.00
181 Ricky Stanzi/299 10.00 25.00
184 Ronald Johnson/499 5.00 12.00
185 Ryan Kerrigan/499 6.00 15.00
186 Ryan Mallett/199 20.00 50.00
187 Ryan Whalen/499 5.00 12.00
188 Ryan Williams/299 10.00 25.00
189 Shane Vereen/299 8.00 20.00
190 Stanley Havili/499 4.00 10.00
191 Stephen Paea/499 6.00 15.00
192 Stevan Ridley/399 6.00 15.00
193 Taiwan Jones/499 6.00 15.00
194 Tandon Doss/499 5.00 12.00
196 Titus Young/299 10.00 25.00
197 Torrey Smith/299 10.00 25.00
198 Tyler Sash/499 6.00 15.00
199 Vincent Brown/99 10.00 25.00
200 Von Miller/299 10.00 25.00

2011 Donruss Elite National Convention

ANNOUNCED PRINT RUN 500 SETS
*BLUE/10: 2X TO 5X BASIC CARDS
*RED/25: 1.5X TO 4X BASIC CARDS
1 Aaron Rodgers 1.50 4.00
2 Adrian Peterson 1.50 4.00
3 Peyton Manning 2.00 5.00
4 Sam Bradford 1.50 4.00
5 Tim Tebow 1.50 4.00
6 Tom Brady 1.50 4.00
7 Terrelle Pryor 2.50 6.00

2011 Donruss Elite National Convention VIP

*BLUE/10: 2X TO 5X BASIC CARDS
*RED/25: 1.5X TO 4X BASIC CARDS
VIP1 Cam Newton 4.00 10.00
VIP2 Mark Ingram 1.50 4.00
VIP3 Terrelle Pryor 2.00 5.00
VIP4 A.J. Green 1.50 4.00
VIP5 Jake Locker 2.00 5.00
VIP6 Blaine Gabbert 1.25 3.00

2007 Donruss Elite Extra Edition

COMPLETE SET (142)
COMP.SET w/o AU's (92) 8.00 20.00
COMMON CARD (1-92) .20 .50
COMMON AU (92-142) 4.00 10.00
OVERALL AUTO/MEM ODDS 1:5
AU PRINT RUNS B/WN 374-999 COPIES PER
EXCHANGE DEADLINE 07/01/2009
66 Ara Parseghian .20 .50
70 Frank Broyles .20 .50
74 Steve Spurrier .20 .50
75 Tom Osborne .20 .50
76 Vince Dooley .20 .50
82 Clint Dolezel .20 .50

2007 Donruss Elite Extra Edition Aspirations

*ASP 1-92: 3X TO 8X BASIC
OVERALL INSERT ODDS 1:4
STATED PRINT RUN 100 SER.#'d SETS

2007 Donruss Elite Extra Edition Status

*STATUS 1-92: 4X TO 10X BASIC
OVERALL INSERT ODDS 1:4
STATED PRINT RUN 50 SER.#'d SETS

2007 Donruss Elite Extra Edition Status Gold

OVERALL INSERT ODDS 1:4
STATED PRINT RUN 25 SER.#'d SETS
NO PRICING DUE TO SCARCITY

2007 Donruss Elite Extra Edition Collegiate Patches

OVERALL AUTO/MEM ODDS 1:5
PRINT RUNS B/WN 25-250 COPIES PER
NO PRICING ON QTY 25 OR LESS
2 Ara Parseghian/250 15.00 40.00
4 Burt Reynolds/25
8 Frank Broyles/250 6.00 15.00
15 Ron Howard/25
16 Steve Spurrier/100
17 Tom Osborne/249 20.00 50.00
18 Vince Dooley/250 6.00 15.00
24 Steve Spurrier/100

2007 Donruss Elite Extra Edition School Colors

OVERALL INSERT ODDS 1:4
STATED PRINT RUN 1500 SER.#'d SETS
12 Steve Spurrier .75 2.00
13 Tom Osborne .75 2.00
18 Ara Parseghian .75 2.00
20 Frank Broyles .75 2.00
24 Vince Dooley .75 2.00
27 Burt Reynolds .75 2.00
28 Ron Howard .75 2.00

2007 Donruss Elite Extra Edition School Colors Autographs

OVERALL AUTO/MEM ODDS 1:5
PRINT RUNS B/WN 10-50 COPIES PER
NO PRICING ON QTY 25 OR LESS
EXCHANGE DEADLINE 07/01/2009
12 Steve Spurrier/25
13 Tom Osborne/25
18 Ara Parseghian/25
20 Frank Broyles/25
24 Vince Dooley/25
27 Burt Reynolds/10
28 Ron Howard/10

2007 Donruss Elite Extra Edition Signature Aspirations

OVERALL AU/MEM ODDS 1:5
PRINT RUNS B/WN 5-100 COPIES PER
NO PRICING ON QTY 25 OR LESS
EXCHANGE DEADLINE 07/01/2007
66 Ara Parseghian/100 12.50 30.00
70 Frank Broyles/100 5.00 12.00
74 Steve Spurrier/25
75 Tom Osborne/100 12.50 30.00
76 Vince Dooley/50 10.00 25.00
82 Clint Dolezel/100 4.00 10.00

2007 Donruss Elite Extra Edition Signature Status

OVERALL AU/MEM ODDS 1:5
PRINT RUNS B/WN 1-50 COPIES PER
NO PRICING ON QTY 25 OR LESS
EXCHANGE DEADLINE 07/01/2007
66 Ara Parseghian/50 20.00 50.00
70 Frank Broyles/50 8.00 20.00
74 Steve Spurrier/10
75 Tom Osborne/50 20.00 50.00
76 Vince Dooley/25
82 Clint Dolezel/50 6.00 15.00

2007 Donruss Elite Extra Edition Signature Status Black

OVERALL AUTO/MEM ODDS 1:5
STATED PRINT RUN 1 SER.#'d SET
NO PRICING DUE TO SCARCITY
EXCHANGE DEADLINE 07/01/2009

2007 Donruss Elite Extra Edition Signature Status Gold

OVERALL AUTO/MEM ODDS 1:5
STATED PRINT RUN 5 SER.#'d SETS
NO PRICING DUE TO SCARCITY
EXCHANGE DEADLINE 07/01/2009

2007 Donruss Elite Extra Edition Signature Turn of the Century

OVERALL AU/MEM ODDS 1:5
PRINT RUNS B/WN 10-500 COPIES PER
NO PRICING ON QTY 25 OR LESS
EXCHANGE DEADLINE 07/01/2007
66 Ara Parseghian/69 10.00 25.00
70 Frank Broyles/69 6.00 15.00
74 Steve Spurrier/59 30.00 60.00
75 Tom Osborne/320 10.00 25.00
76 Vince Dooley/91 6.00 15.00
82 Clint Dolezel/243 4.00 10.00

2007 Donruss Elite Extra Edition Throwback Threads

OVERALL AUTO/MEM ODDS 1:5
PRINT RUNS B/WN 44-500 COPIES PER
5 Clint Dolezel/500 3.00 8.00
8 Vince Dooley/500 3.00 8.00
20 Steve Spurrier/500 4.00 10.00

2007 Donruss Elite Extra Edition Throwback Threads Prime

*PRIME: .75X TO 2X BASIC
OVERALL AUTO/MEM ODDS 1:5
PRINT RUNS B/WN 3-50 COPIES PER
NO PRICING ON QTY 25 OR LESS
8 Vince Dooley/7

2007 Donruss Elite Extra Edition Throwback Threads Autographs

OVERALL AUTO/MEM ODDS 1:5
PRINT RUNS B/WN 50-100 COPIES PER
EXCHANGE DEADLINE 07/01/2009
5 Clint Dolezel/100 6.00 15.00
8 Vince Dooley/50 10.00 25.00
20 Steve Spurrier/50 30.00 60.00

2007 Donruss Elite Extra Edition Throwback Threads Autographs Prime

OVERALL AUTO/MEM ODDS 1:5
PRINT RUNS B/WN 1-25 COPIES PER
NO PRICING DUE TO SCARCITY
EXCHANGE DEADLINE 07/01/2009

2005 Donruss Gridiron Gear

This 150-card set was relased in February, 2007. This set was issued in the hobby through five-card packs which came 18 packs to a box. Cards numbered 1-100 feature veterans sequenced in first name alphabetical order while cards numbered 101-150 feature rookies. The rookie cards were all issued to a stated print run of 399 serial numbered sets.

COMP.SET w/o RC's (100) 10.00 25.00
101-150 PRINT RUN 399 SER.#'d SETS
1 Aaron Brooks .25 .60
2 Ahman Green .30 .75
3 Alge Crumpler .30 .75
4 Amani Toomer .30 .75
5 Andre Johnson .40 1.00
6 Anquan Boldin .30 .75
7 Antonio Gates .40 1.00
8 Antwaan Randle El .30 .75
9 Ashley Lelie .25 .60
10 Barry Sanders 1.50 4.00
11 Ben Roethlisberger .60 1.50
12 Bob Griese 1.00 2.50
13 Brandon Lloyd .25 .60
14 Brett Favre 1.00 2.50
15 Brian Urlacher .40 1.00
16 Brian Westbrook .30 .75
17 Byron Leftwich .30 .75
18 Carson Palmer .40 1.00
19 Chad Johnson .30 .75
20 Chad Pennington .40 1.00
21 Champ Bailey .30 .75
22 Chris Brown .25 .60
23 Chris Chambers .30 .75
24 Clinton Portis .30 .75
25 Corey Dillon .30 .75
26 Curtis Martin .40 1.00
27 Daunte Culpepper .30 .75
28 David Carr .25 .60
29 Deion Sanders .50 1.25
30 Derrick Brooks .30 .75
31 Deuce McAllister .30 .75
32 Domanick Davis .25 .60
33 Don Maynard .75 2.00
34 Donovan McNabb .40 1.00
35 Drew Bledsoe .40 1.00
36 Drew Brees .40 1.00
37 Edgerrin James .30 .75
38 Eli Manning .60 1.50
39 Eric Moulds .25 .60
40 Fred Taylor .30 .75
41 Hines Ward .40 1.00
42 Ickey Woods .60 1.50
43 Isaac Bruce .30 .75
44 J.P. Losman .25 .60
45 Jake Delhomme .30 .75
46 Jake Plummer .30 .75
47 Jamal Lewis .30 .75
48 Javon Walker .25 .60
49 Jeremy Shockey .40 1.00
50 Jerome Bettis .40 1.00
51 Jerry Porter .25 .60
52 Jevon Kearse .30 .75
53 Jimmy Smith .30 .75
54 Joe Namath 1.50 4.00
55 Joey Harrington .30 .75
56 Josh McCown .30 .75
57 Josh Reed .25 .60
58 Julius Jones .25 .60
59 Julius Peppers .30 .75
60 Keary Colbert .25 .60
61 Kerry Collins .30 .75
62 Kevin Jones .25 .60
63 Kyle Boller .30 .75
64 LaDainian Tomlinson .40 1.00
65 LaMont Jordan .30 .75
66 Larry Fitzgerald .40 1.00
67 Lee Evans .30 .75
68 Marc Bulger .30 .75
69 Marvin Harrison .40 1.00
70 Matt Hasselbeck .30 .75
71 Michael Clayton .25 .60
72 Michael Vick .40 1.00
73 Mike Alstott .30 .75
74 Muhsin Muhammad .30 .75
75 Nate Burleson .25 .60
76 Peyton Manning .75 2.00
77 Plaxico Burress .30 .75
78 Priest Holmes .30 .75
79 Randy Moss .40 1.00
80 Ray Lewis .40 1.00
81 Reggie Wayne .40 1.00
82 Rex Grossman .30 .75
83 Rod Smith .30 .75
84 Roy Williams S .25 .60
85 Roy Williams WR .30 .75
86 Rudi Johnson .30 .75
87 Shaun Alexander .30 .75
88 Sonny Jurgensen .75 2.00
89 Stephen Davis .30 .75
90 Steve McNair .40 1.00
91 Steve Smith .40 1.00
92 Steven Jackson .40 1.00
93 Terrell Owens .40 1.00
94 Tiki Barber .40 1.00
95 Todd Heap .30 .75
96 Tom Brady .75 2.00
97 Tony Gonzalez .30 .75
98 Torry Holt .30 .75
99 Trent Green .30 .75
100 Willis McGahee .40 1.00
101 Alex Smith QB RC 3.00 8.00
102 Ronnie Brown RC 2.50 6.00
103 Braylon Edwards RC 2.50 6.00
104 Cedric Benson RC 2.00 5.00
105 Cadillac Williams RC 2.00 5.00
106 Adam Jones RC 1.50 4.00
107 Troy Williamson RC 1.50 4.00
108 Mike Williams 2.00 5.00
109 Derrick Johnson RC 1.50 4.00
110 Demarcus Ware RC 4.00 10.00
111 Matt Jones RC 2.00 5.00
112 Mark Clayton RC 2.00 5.00
113 Aaron Rodgers RC 25.00 50.00
114 Jason Campbell RC 2.50 6.00
115 Roddy White RC 2.50 6.00
116 Heath Miller RC 2.50 6.00
117 Reggie Brown RC 1.25 3.00
118 Mark Bradley RC 1.25 3.00
119 J.J. Arrington RC 1.50 4.00
120 Odell Thurman RC 2.00 5.00
121 Roscoe Parrish RC 1.25 3.00
122 Terrence Murphy RC 1.25 3.00
123 Vincent Jackson RC 2.50 6.00
124 Frank Gore RC 3.00 8.00
125 Charlie Frye RC 2.00 5.00
126 Courtney Roby RC 1.50 4.00
127 Andrew Walter RC 1.50 4.00
128 Vernand Morency RC 1.50 4.00
129 Ryan Moats RC 1.50 4.00
130 Chris Henry RC 2.00 5.00
131 David Greene RC 1.25 3.00
132 Brandon Jones RC 1.50 4.00
133 Kyle Orton RC 2.00 5.00
134 Marion Barber RC 2.00 5.00
135 Brandon Jacobs RC 2.50 6.00
136 Ciatrick Fason RC 1.25 3.00
137 Lofa Tatupu RC 2.00 5.00
138 Stefan LeFors RC 1.25 3.00
139 Alvin Pearman RC 1.25 3.00
140 Darren Sproles RC 2.00 5.00
141 Samkon Gado RC 2.00 5.00
142 Antrel Rolle RC 2.00 5.00
143 Maurice Clarett 1.50 4.00
144 Adrian McPherson RC 1.25 3.00
145 Eric Shelton RC 1.25 3.00
146 Bo Scaife RC 1.50 4.00
147 Carlos Rogers RC 2.00 5.00
148 Otis Amey RC 1.50 4.00
149 Alex Smith TE RC 1.25 3.00
150 Jerome Mathis RC 2.00 5.00

2005 Donruss Gridiron Gear Gold Holofoil

*VETS: 3X TO 8X BASIC CARDS
*RETIRED: 2X TO 5X BASIC CARDS
*ROOKIES: .6X TO 1.5X BASIC CARDS
STATED PRINT RUN 100 SER.#'d SETS

2005 Donruss Gridiron Gear Platinum Holofoil

*VETS: 8X TO 20X BASIC CARDS
*RETIRED: 5X TO 12X BASIC CARDS
*ROOKIES: 1X TO 2.5X BASIC CARDS
STATED PRINT RUN 25 SER.#'d SETS
113 Aaron Rodgers 100.00 175.00

2005 Donruss Gridiron Gear Silver Holofoil

*VETS: 2X TO 5X BASIC CARDS
*RETIRED: 1.2X TO 3X BASIC CARDS
STATED PRINT RUN 250 SER.#'d SETS

2005 Donruss Gridiron Gear Autographs Silver

SILVER STATED PRINT RUN 1-250
#'d UNDER 20 NOT PRICED DUE TO SCARCITY
UNPRICED PLATINUM PRINT RUN 1-10
1 Aaron Brooks/49 6.00 15.00
3 Alge Crumpler/80 6.00 15.00
6 Anquan Boldin/46 8.00 20.00
11 Ben Roethlisberger/23 100.00 200.00
30 Derrick Brooks/250 5.00 12.00
31 Deuce McAllister/26 10.00 25.00
32 Domanick Davis/250 4.00 10.00
38 Eli Manning/71 40.00 80.00
44 J.P. Losman/61 5.00 12.00
45 Jake Delhomme/100 10.00 25.00
52 Jevon Kearse/250 5.00 12.00
54 Joe Namath/67 30.00 60.00
58 Julius Jones/50 8.00 20.00
60 Keary Colbert/125 4.00 10.00
63 Kyle Boller/33 10.00 25.00
65 LaMont Jordan/250 5.00 12.00
67 Lee Evans/62 6.00 15.00
69 Marvin Harrison/28 12.00 30.00
70 Matt Hasselbeck/45 10.00 25.00
75 Nate Burleson/51 5.00 12.00
81 Reggie Wayne/30 12.00 30.00
82 Rex Grossman/63 8.00 20.00
84 Roy Williams S/75 8.00 20.00
86 Rudi Johnson/40 8.00 20.00
88 Sonny Jurgensen/63 8.00 20.00
91 Steve Smith/50 8.00 20.00
94 Tiki Barber/72 15.00 30.00
95 Todd Heap/79 6.00 15.00
99 Trent Green/56 6.00 15.00

2005 Donruss Gridiron Gear Autographs Gold Holofoil

STATED PRINT RUN 25 SER.#'d SETS
1 Aaron Brooks 8.00 20.00
3 Alge Crumpler 10.00 25.00
5 Andre Johnson 12.00 30.00
6 Anquan Boldin 10.00 25.00
7 Antonio Gates 12.00 30.00
11 Ben Roethlisberger 100.00 200.00
15 Brian Urlacher 25.00 50.00
17 Byron Leftwich 10.00 25.00
22 Chris Brown 8.00 20.00
28 David Carr 8.00 20.00
29 Deion Sanders 30.00 60.00
30 Derrick Brooks 15.00 40.00
32 Domanick Davis 8.00 20.00
33 Don Maynard 10.00 25.00
35 Drew Bledsoe 12.00 30.00
38 Eli Manning 50.00 100.00
41 Hines Ward 35.00 60.00
44 J.P. Losman 8.00 20.00
45 Jake Delhomme 10.00 25.00
52 Jevon Kearse 10.00 25.00
53 Jimmy Smith 10.00 25.00
54 Joe Namath 40.00 80.00
58 Julius Jones 8.00 20.00
60 Keary Colbert 8.00 20.00
61 Kerry Collins 10.00 25.00
63 Kyle Boller 10.00 25.00
65 LaMont Jordan 10.00 25.00
67 Lee Evans 10.00 25.00
69 Marvin Harrison 12.00 30.00
70 Matt Hasselbeck 15.00 40.00
71 Michael Clayton 8.00 20.00
75 Nate Burleson 8.00 20.00
76 Peyton Manning 60.00 100.00
81 Reggie Wayne 12.00 30.00
82 Rex Grossman 12.00 30.00
84 Roy Williams S 8.00 20.00
85 Roy Williams WR 10.00 25.00
86 Rudi Johnson 10.00 25.00
87 Shaun Alexander 15.00 40.00
88 Sonny Jurgensen 10.00 25.00
91 Steve Smith 12.00 30.00
94 Tiki Barber 20.00 50.00
95 Todd Heap 10.00 25.00
99 Trent Green 10.00 25.00
100 Willis McGahee 12.00 30.00

2005 Donruss Gridiron Gear Autographs Silver Holofoil

PRINT RUN 100 SER.#'d SETS UNLESS NOTED
5 Andre Johnson/100 10.00 25.00
6 Anquan Boldin/100 8.00 20.00
30 Derrick Brooks/100 8.00 20.00
31 Deuce McAllister/31 10.00 25.00
32 Domanick Davis/100 6.00 15.00
33 Don Maynard/100 8.00 20.00
45 Jake Delhomme/50 12.00 30.00
52 Jevon Kearse/100 8.00 20.00
53 Jimmy Smith/100 8.00 20.00
60 Keary Colbert/100 6.00 15.00
65 LaMont Jordan/100 8.00 20.00
67 Lee Evans/100 8.00 20.00
84 Roy Williams S/100 6.00 15.00
87 Shaun Alexander/100 12.00 30.00
95 Todd Heap/100 8.00 20.00

2005 Donruss Gridiron Gear Jerseys

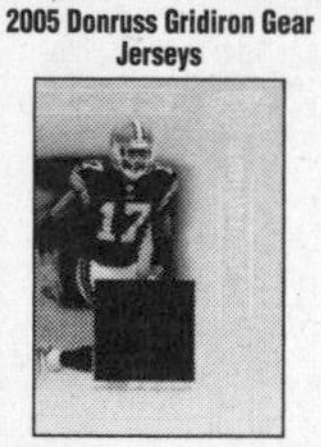

STATED PRINT RUN 1-150
SERIAL #'d UNDER 10 NOT PRICED
3 Alge Crumpler 3.00 8.00
4 Amani Toomer 3.00 8.00
5 Andre Johnson/50 5.00 12.00
6 Anquan Boldin 3.00 8.00
8 Antwaan Randle El/80 4.00 10.00
9 Ashley Lelie/55 3.00 8.00
11 Ben Roethlisberger 6.00 15.00
12 Bob Griese 4.00 10.00
13 Brandon Lloyd 2.50 6.00
14 Brett Favre 10.00 25.00
15 Brian Urlacher/65 5.00 12.00
16 Brian Westbrook 3.00 8.00
17 Byron Leftwich 3.00 8.00
18 Carson Palmer 4.00 10.00
20 Chad Pennington 4.00 10.00
21 Champ Bailey/15 10.00 25.00
24 Clinton Portis/15 8.00 20.00
25 Corey Dillon 3.00 8.00
26 Curtis Martin 4.00 10.00
27 Daunte Culpepper/35 6.00 15.00
28 David Carr 2.50 6.00
29 Deion Sanders 5.00 12.00
30 Derrick Brooks 5.00 12.00
31 Deuce McAllister 3.00 8.00
33 Don Maynard 3.00 8.00
34 Donovan McNabb/85 5.00 12.00
35 Drew Bledsoe 4.00 10.00
36 Drew Brees 4.00 10.00
38 Eli Manning 6.00 15.00
41 Hines Ward/75 6.00 15.00
42 Ickey Woods 3.00 8.00

43 Isaac Bruce 3.00 8.00
44 J.P. Losman 2.50 6.00
45 Jake Delhomme/120 3.00 8.00
46 Jake Plummer 3.00 8.00
47 Jamal Lewis 3.00 8.00
48 Javon Walker/35 5.00 12.00
50 Jerome Bettis 8.00 20.00
51 Jerry Porter 2.50 6.00
52 Jevon Kearse 3.00 8.00
53 Jimmy Smith/11 8.00 20.00
54 Joe Namath/50 15.00 30.00
55 Joey Harrington 3.00 8.00
56 Josh McCown 3.00 8.00
57 Josh Reed 2.50 6.00
58 Julius Jones 2.50 6.00
59 Julius Peppers 3.00 8.00
60 Keary Colbert 2.50 6.00
62 Kevin Jones/31 5.00 12.00
63 Kyle Boller 3.00 8.00
64 LaDainian Tomlinson 4.00 10.00
66 Larry Fitzgerald 4.00 10.00
67 Lee Evans 3.00 8.00
68 Marc Bulger 3.00 8.00
69 Marvin Harrison 4.00 10.00
70 Matt Hasselbeck/107 3.00 8.00
71 Michael Clayton/93 3.00 8.00
72 Michael Vick 5.00 12.00
73 Mike Alstott/90 4.00 10.00
75 Nate Burleson 2.50 6.00
76 Peyton Manning/100 8.00 20.00
78 Priest Holmes 3.00 8.00
79 Randy Moss 4.00 10.00
80 Ray Lewis/21 15.00 30.00
81 Reggie Wayne 4.00 10.00
82 Rex Grossman 3.00 8.00
84 Roy Williams S/45 3.00 8.00
85 Roy Williams WR/75 4.00 10.00
86 Rudi Johnson/26 6.00 15.00
87 Shaun Alexander/100 3.00 8.00
88 Sonny Jurgensen/55 6.00 15.00
90 Steve McNair/17 10.00 25.00
92 Steven Jackson 4.00 10.00
94 Tiki Barber/13 10.00 25.00
95 Todd Heap 3.00 8.00
96 Tom Brady 8.00 20.00
97 Tony Gonzalez 3.00 8.00
98 Torry Holt 3.00 8.00
99 Trent Green/25 6.00 15.00
100 Willis McGahee/69 5.00 12.00
101 Alex Smith QB 5.00 12.00
102 Ronnie Brown 4.00 10.00
103 Braylon Edwards 4.00 10.00
105 Cadillac Williams 3.00 8.00
106 Adam Jones 2.50 6.00
107 Troy Williamson 2.50 6.00
111 Matt Jones 3.00 8.00
112 Mark Clayton 3.00 8.00
114 Jason Campbell 4.00 10.00
115 Roddy White 4.00 10.00
117 Reggie Brown 2.00 5.00
118 Mark Bradley 2.00 5.00
119 J.J. Arrington 2.50 6.00
121 Roscoe Parrish 2.00 5.00
122 Terrence Murphy 2.00 5.00
123 Vincent Jackson 4.00 10.00
124 Frank Gore 5.00 12.00
125 Charlie Frye 3.00 8.00
126 Courtney Roby 2.50 6.00
127 Andrew Walter 2.50 6.00
128 Vernand Morency 2.50 6.00
129 Ryan Moats 2.50 6.00
133 Kyle Orton 3.00 8.00
136 Ciatrick Fason 2.00 5.00
138 Stefan LeFors 2.00 5.00
142 Antrel Rolle 3.00 8.00
143 Maurice Clarett 2.50 6.00
145 Eric Shelton 2.00 5.00
147 Carlos Rogers 3.00 8.00

2005 Donruss Gridiron Gear Jerseys Name Plate

*ROOKIES/50: .8X TO 2X BASIC JSY/150
*ROOKIES/31: 1X TO 2.5X BASIC JSY/150
NAME PLATE PRINT RUN 1-60
SERIAL #'d UNDER 10 NOT PRICED
3 Alge Crumpler/20 10.00 25.00
4 Amani Toomer/40 8.00 20.00
5 Andre Johnson/10 15.00 40.00
6 Anquan Boldin/50 8.00 20.00
8 Antwaan Randle El/60 8.00 20.00
9 Ashley Lelie/19 10.00 25.00
10 Barry Sanders/20 60.00 100.00
11 Ben Roethlisberger/30 30.00 80.00
12 Bob Griese/10 15.00 40.00
13 Brandon Lloyd/15 10.00 25.00
15 Brian Urlacher/50 10.00 25.00
17 Byron Leftwich/24 10.00 25.00
19 Chad Johnson/35 10.00 25.00
20 Chad Pennington/24 12.00 30.00
21 Champ Bailey/15 12.00 30.00
22 Chris Brown/19 10.00 25.00
23 Chris Chambers/50 8.00 20.00
24 Clinton Portis/10 12.00 30.00
25 Corey Dillon/20 10.00 25.00
26 Curtis Martin/50 10.00 25.00
27 Daunte Culpepper/38 10.00 25.00
28 David Carr/11 10.00 25.00
29 Deion Sanders/35 15.00 40.00
31 Deuce McAllister/50 8.00 20.00
32 Domanick Davis/33 8.00 20.00
33 Don Maynard/25 12.00 30.00
35 Drew Bledsoe/17 15.00 40.00
37 Edgerrin James/25 10.00 25.00
38 Eli Manning/25 20.00 50.00
40 Fred Taylor/19 12.00 30.00
44 J.P. Losman/21 8.00 20.00
45 Jake Delhomme/43 8.00 20.00
46 Jake Plummer/50 8.00 20.00
47 Jamal Lewis/50 8.00 20.00
52 Jevon Kearse/29 10.00 25.00
53 Jimmy Smith/50 8.00 20.00
56 Josh McCown/13 12.00 30.00
58 Julius Jones/15 10.00 25.00
59 Julius Peppers/50 8.00 20.00
62 Kevin Jones/26 8.00 20.00
63 Kyle Boller/36 10.00 25.00
64 LaDainian Tomlinson/50 10.00 25.00
66 Larry Fitzgerald/21 12.00 30.00
67 Lee Evans/12 12.00 30.00
69 Marvin Harrison/50 10.00 25.00
73 Mike Alstott/16 12.00 30.00
76 Peyton Manning/50 20.00 50.00
78 Priest Holmes/20 10.00 25.00
79 Randy Moss/12 15.00 40.00
80 Ray Lewis/30 12.00 30.00
81 Reggie Wayne/25 12.00 30.00
82 Rex Grossman/50 8.00 20.00
83 Rod Smith/36 10.00 25.00
84 Roy Williams S/50 6.00 15.00
86 Rudi Johnson/50 8.00 20.00
87 Shaun Alexander/50 8.00 20.00
89 Stephen Davis/14 12.00 30.00
92 Steven Jackson/28 12.00 30.00
95 Todd Heap/21 10.00 25.00
96 Tom Brady/34 25.00 60.00
98 Torry Holt/21 10.00 25.00
100 Willis McGahee/18 15.00 40.00

2005 Donruss Gridiron Gear Jerseys Numbers

*ROOKIES/100: .6X TO 1.5X BASIC JSY/150
STATED PRINT RUN 1-100
SERIAL #'d UNDER 10 NOT PRICED
2 Ahman Green/50 8.00 20.00
3 Alge Crumpler/50 8.00 20.00
4 Amani Toomer/50 8.00 20.00
5 Andre Johnson/50 10.00 25.00
6 Anquan Boldin/50 8.00 20.00
7 Antonio Gates/50 10.00 25.00
8 Antwaan Randle El/50 8.00 20.00
9 Ashley Lelie/50 6.00 15.00
10 Barry Sanders/50 15.00 40.00
12 Bob Griese/25 15.00 40.00
13 Brandon Lloyd/50 6.00 15.00
15 Brian Urlacher/50 10.00 25.00
16 Brian Westbrook/50 8.00 20.00
17 Byron Leftwich/46 8.00 20.00
19 Chad Johnson/50 8.00 20.00
21 Champ Bailey/50 8.00 20.00
22 Chris Brown/40 6.00 15.00
23 Chris Chambers/50 8.00 20.00
24 Clinton Portis/50 8.00 20.00
25 Corey Dillon/50 8.00 20.00
26 Curtis Martin/50 10.00 25.00
27 Daunte Culpepper/50 8.00 20.00
28 David Carr/50 6.00 15.00
29 Deion Sanders/50 12.00 30.00
30 Derrick Brooks/50 10.00 25.00
31 Deuce McAllister/50 8.00 20.00
33 Don Maynard/50 10.00 25.00
35 Drew Bledsoe/40 10.00 25.00
36 Drew Brees/50 10.00 25.00
37 Edgerrin James/50 8.00 20.00
38 Eli Manning/50 15.00 40.00
39 Eric Moulds/50 6.00 15.00
40 Fred Taylor/50 8.00 20.00
41 Hines Ward/50 10.00 25.00
42 Ickey Woods/50 8.00 20.00
43 Isaac Bruce/50 8.00 20.00
44 J.P. Losman/12 10.00 25.00
45 Jake Delhomme/27 10.00 25.00
46 Jake Plummer/50 8.00 20.00
47 Jamal Lewis/50 8.00 20.00
48 Javon Walker/50 6.00 15.00
49 Jeremy Shockey/50 10.00 25.00
50 Jerome Bettis/50 15.00 40.00
51 Jerry Porter/50 6.00 15.00
52 Jevon Kearse/50 8.00 20.00
53 Jimmy Smith/50 8.00 20.00
56 Josh McCown/50 8.00 20.00
57 Josh Reed/50 6.00 15.00
58 Julius Jones/30 8.00 20.00
59 Julius Peppers/50 8.00 20.00
60 Keary Colbert/50 6.00 15.00
62 Kevin Jones/35 8.00 20.00
63 Kyle Boller/41 8.00 20.00
64 LaDainian Tomlinson/50 10.00 25.00
66 Larry Fitzgerald/50 10.00 25.00
67 Lee Evans/50 8.00 20.00
69 Marvin Harrison/50 10.00 25.00
70 Matt Hasselbeck/25 10.00 25.00
71 Michael Clayton/50 6.00 15.00
72 Michael Vick/10 20.00 50.00
73 Mike Alstott/23 10.00 25.00
75 Nate Burleson/50 6.00 15.00
76 Peyton Manning/50 20.00 50.00
78 Priest Holmes/50 8.00 20.00
79 Randy Moss/50 10.00 25.00
80 Ray Lewis/42 10.00 25.00
82 Rex Grossman/28 10.00 25.00
83 Rod Smith/32 10.00 25.00
84 Roy Williams S/25 8.00 20.00
86 Rudi Johnson/50 8.00 20.00
87 Shaun Alexander/50 8.00 20.00
89 Stephen Davis/50 8.00 20.00
91 Steve Smith/50 10.00 25.00
92 Steven Jackson/33 12.00 30.00
94 Tiki Barber/11 15.00 40.00
95 Todd Heap/50 8.00 20.00
96 Tom Brady/50 20.00 50.00
97 Tony Gonzalez/50 8.00 20.00
98 Torry Holt/50 8.00 20.00
99 Trent Green/50 8.00 20.00

2005 Donruss Gridiron Gear Jerseys Team Logo

*ROOKIES/20-25: 1.5X TO 4X BASIC JSY/150
*ROOKIES/14-18: 2X TO 5X BASIC JSY/150
STATED PRINT RUN 1-25
SERIAL #'d UNDER 10 NOT PRICED
8 Antwaan Randle El/15 15.00 40.00
19 Chad Johnson/25 12.00 30.00
22 Chris Brown/12 12.00 30.00
23 Chris Chambers/25 12.00 30.00
25 Corey Dillon/20 12.00 30.00
26 Curtis Martin/10 20.00 50.00
29 Deion Sanders/25 25.00 60.00
31 Deuce McAllister/25 12.00 30.00
40 Fred Taylor/25 12.00 30.00
45 Jake Delhomme/25 12.00 30.00
50 Jerome Bettis/23 50.00 120.00
52 Jevon Kearse/25 12.00 30.00
59 Julius Peppers/25 12.00 30.00
60 Keary Colbert/15 12.00 30.00
63 Kyle Boller/25 12.00 30.00
73 Mike Alstott/22 12.00 30.00
75 Nate Burleson/13 12.00 30.00
86 Rudi Johnson/13 15.00 40.00
89 Stephen Davis/14 15.00 40.00
95 Todd Heap/18 15.00 40.00
96 Tom Brady/17 40.00 100.00
98 Torry Holt/25 12.00 30.00

2005 Donruss Gridiron Gear Next Generation Gold

COMPLETE SET (10) 6.00 15.00
STATED PRINT RUN 1000 SER.#'d SETS
*GOLD HOLO/100: .8X TO 2X GOLD/1000
*PLAT.HOLO/25: 1.2X TO 3X GOLD/1000
*SILVER HOLO/250: .5X TO 1.2X GOLD/1000
1 Andre Johnson 1.25 3.00
2 Bryant Johnson .75 2.00
3 Charles Rogers .75 2.00
4 Darius Watts .75 2.00
5 Josh McCown 1.00 2.50
6 Keary Colbert .75 2.00
7 Larry Fitzgerald 1.25 3.00
8 Michael Clayton .75 2.00
9 Nate Burleson .75 2.00
10 Reggie Williams .75 2.00

2005 Donruss Gridiron Gear Next Generation Autographs

SERIAL #'d UNDER 20 NOT PRICED
1 Andre Johnson/50 12.00 30.00
6 Keary Colbert/50 6.00 15.00

2005 Donruss Gridiron Gear Next Generation Jersey Autographs

COMMON CARD/15-35 8.00 20.00
UNL.STARS/15-35 12.00 30.00
SERIAL #'d UNDER 20 NOT PRICED
UNPRICED TEAM LOGO AU PRINT RUN 1-2
UNPRICED DBL PATCH AU PRINT RUN 1-10
UNPRICED NAME PLATE AU PRINT RUN 1-2
*JSY NUMB AU/25: .4X TO 1X AU/35
6 Keary Colbert/35 8.00 20.00
8 Michael Clayton/15 12.00 30.00

2005 Donruss Gridiron Gear Next Generation Jerseys

STATED PRINT RUN 90-150
*DBL PATCH/30-50: .8X TO 2X JSY/90-150
*DBL PATCH/17-25: 1X TO 2.5X JSY/90-150
*JUMBO/56-100: .6X TO 1.5X JSY/90-150
*JUMBO/10-21: 1X TO 2.5X JSY/90-150
*JUM.PTCH/44-50: 1X TO 2.5X JSY/90-150
*JUM.PTCH/21-29: 1.2X TO 3X JSY/90-150
*NAME PLATE/35-50: .8X TO 2X JSY/90-150
*NAME PLATE/10-25: 1.2X TO 3X JSY/90-150
*JSY NO/50-100: .8X TO 2X JSY/90-150
*JSY NO/11: 1.2X TO 3X JSY/90-150
UNPRICED TEAM LOGO PRINT RUN 1-10
1 Andre Johnson/150 4.00 10.00
2 Bryant Johnson/150 2.50 6.00
3 Charles Rogers/90 2.50 6.00
4 Darius Watts/150 2.50 6.00
5 Josh McCown/150 3.00 8.00
6 Keary Colbert/150 2.50 6.00
7 Larry Fitzgerald/150 4.00 10.00
8 Michael Clayton/100 2.50 6.00
9 Nate Burleson/150 2.50 6.00
10 Reggie Williams/150 2.50 6.00

2005 Donruss Gridiron Gear Past and Present Gold

COMPLETE SET (20) 20.00 50.00
STATED PRINT RUN 750 SER.#'d SETS
*GOLD HOLOFOIL: .8X TO 2X BASIC CARDS
GOLD HOLOFOIL PRINT RUN 100 SER.#'d SETS
*PLATINUM HOLO: 1.2X TO 3X BASIC CARDS
PLATINUM HOLOFOIL PRINT RUN 25 SETS
*SILVER HOLO: .5X TO 1.2X BASIC CARDS
SILVER HOLOFOIL PRINT RUN 250 SETS
1 Aaron Brooks 1.00 2.50
2 Ahman Green 1.25 3.00
3 Carson Palmer 1.50 4.00
4 Clinton Portis 1.25 3.00
5 Corey Dillon 1.25 3.00
6 Curtis Martin 1.50 4.00
7 DeShaun Foster 1.25 3.00
8 Duce Staley 1.25 3.00
9 Hines Ward 1.50 4.00
10 Jake Plummer 1.25 3.00
11 Jeremy Shockey 1.50 4.00
12 Jerome Bettis 1.50 4.00
13 Jevon Kearse 1.25 3.00
14 Julius Jones 1.00 2.50
15 Marshall Faulk 1.50 4.00
16 Ricky Williams 1.25 3.00
17 Roy Williams S 1.00 2.50
18 Stephen Davis 1.25 3.00
19 Steven Jackson 1.50 4.00
20 Terrell Owens 1.50 4.00

2005 Donruss Gridiron Gear Past and Present Autographs

AUTO STATED PRINT RUN 2-250
SERIAL #'d UNDER 24 NOT PRICED
1 Aaron Brooks/25 10.00 25.00
8 Duce Staley/24 10.00 25.00
13 Jevon Kearse/250 5.00 12.00
14 Julius Jones/25 10.00 25.00

2005 Donruss Gridiron Gear Past and Present Jerseys Double

STATED PRINT RUN 5-75
SERIAL #'d UNDER 15 NOT PRICED
*DBL NME PLTE/15-25: 1X TO 2.5X DBL/75
1 Aaron Brooks/75 4.00 10.00
2 Ahman Green/15 8.00 20.00
3 Carson Palmer/75 6.00 15.00
4 Clinton Portis/75 5.00 12.00
5 Corey Dillon/75 5.00 12.00
6 Curtis Martin/75 6.00 15.00
8 Duce Staley/75 5.00 12.00
10 Jake Plummer/75 5.00 12.00
13 Jevon Kearse/75 5.00 12.00
14 Julius Jones/50 4.00 10.00
15 Marshall Faulk/65 6.00 15.00
16 Ricky Williams/75 5.00 12.00
17 Roy Williams S/26 6.00 15.00
18 Stephen Davis/75 5.00 12.00
19 Steven Jackson/40 8.00 20.00
20 Terrell Owens/30 8.00 20.00

2005 Donruss Gridiron Gear Past and Present Jerseys Jumbo Swatch

STATED PRINT RUN 3-100
SERIAL #'d UNDER 20 NOT PRICED
1 Aaron Brooks/30 6.00 15.00
3 Carson Palmer/67 8.00 20.00
5 Corey Dillon/35 8.00 20.00
6 Curtis Martin/30 10.00 25.00
8 Duce Staley/100 6.00 15.00
9 Hines Ward/100 8.00 20.00
10 Jake Plummer/100 6.00 15.00
12 Jerome Bettis/100 15.00 40.00
14 Julius Jones/40 6.00 15.00
15 Marshall Faulk/27 12.00 30.00
16 Ricky Williams/100 6.00 15.00
17 Roy Williams S/23 8.00 20.00
18 Stephen Davis/100 6.00 15.00
19 Steven Jackson/30 10.00 25.00

2005 Donruss Gridiron Gear Past and Present Jerseys Jumbo Swatch Prime

STATED PRINT RUN 6-50
#'d UNDER 20 NOT PRICED DUE TO SCARCITY
2 Ahman Green/48 10.00 25.00
5 Corey Dillon/50 10.00 25.00
6 Curtis Martin/50 12.00 30.00
7 DeShaun Foster/50 10.00 25.00
8 Duce Staley/50 10.00 25.00
9 Hines Ward/50 12.00 30.00
10 Jake Plummer/23 15.00 40.00
11 Jeremy Shockey/50 12.00 30.00
12 Jerome Bettis/46 25.00 60.00
13 Jevon Kearse/50 10.00 25.00
14 Julius Jones/29 12.00 30.00
16 Ricky Williams/50 10.00 25.00
17 Roy Williams S/50 8.00 20.00
18 Stephen Davis/50 10.00 25.00
19 Steven Jackson/20 20.00 50.00

2005 Donruss Gridiron Gear Past and Present Jerseys Name Plate Single

STATED PRINT RUN 1-50
SERIAL #'d UNDER 15 NOT PRICED
2 Ahman Green/25 15.00 40.00
3 Carson Palmer/20 20.00 50.00
4 Clinton Portis/25 15.00 40.00
5 Corey Dillon/50 12.00 30.00
6 Curtis Martin/28 20.00 50.00
8 Duce Staley/35 12.00 30.00
9 Hines Ward/50 15.00 40.00
10 Jake Plummer/50 12.00 30.00
11 Jeremy Shockey/31 15.00 40.00
12 Jerome Bettis/50 30.00 60.00
13 Jevon Kearse/36 12.00 30.00
16 Ricky Williams/50 12.00 30.00
17 Roy Williams S/19 12.00 30.00
18 Stephen Davis/18 15.00 40.00
20 Terrell Owens/15 20.00 50.00

2005 Donruss Gridiron Gear Past and Present Jerseys Name Plate Single Autographs

STATED PRINT RUN 5-25
SERIAL #'d UNDER 20 NOT PRICED
1 Aaron Brooks/25 12.00 30.00
14 Julius Jones/21 12.00 30.00
19 Steven Jackson/24 20.00 50.00

2005 Donruss Gridiron Gear Past and Present Jerseys Numbers Single

PRINT RUN 100 SER.#'d SETS UNLESS NOTED
#'d UNDER 20 NOT PRICED DUE TO SCARCITY
*DOUBLE/30-50: .6X TO 1.5X SNGL/100
*DOUBLE/25: .8X TO 2X SNGL/100
*DOUBLE/22-25: .6X TO 1.5X SNGL/40-50
*DOUBLE/15-25: .5X TO 1.2X SNGL/20-25
1 Aaron Brooks/20 8.00 20.00
2 Ahman Green/30 8.00 20.00
3 Carson Palmer/40 10.00 25.00
4 Clinton Portis/100 6.00 15.00
5 Corey Dillon/100 6.00 15.00
6 Curtis Martin/100 8.00 20.00
7 DeShaun Foster/100 6.00 15.00
8 Duce Staley/100 6.00 15.00
9 Hines Ward/100 8.00 20.00
10 Jake Plummer/100 6.00 15.00
11 Jeremy Shockey/93 8.00 20.00
12 Jerome Bettis/100 15.00 40.00
13 Jevon Kearse/89 6.00 15.00
14 Julius Jones/50 6.00 15.00
15 Marshall Faulk/100 8.00 20.00
16 Ricky Williams/100 6.00 15.00
17 Roy Williams S/25 8.00 20.00
18 Stephen Davis/100 6.00 15.00
19 Steven Jackson/20 12.00 30.00

2005 Donruss Gridiron Gear Past and Present Jerseys Numbers Single Autographs

STATED PRINT RUN 2-50
SERIAL #'d UNDER 25 NOT PRICED
1 Aaron Brooks/50 10.00 25.00
2 Ahman Green/25 15.00 40.00
9 Hines Ward/45 40.00 100.00
17 Roy Williams S/25 12.00 30.00

2005 Donruss Gridiron Gear Past and Present Jerseys Single

SERIAL #'d UNDER 20 NOT PRICED
1 Aaron Brooks/50 3.00 8.00
2 Ahman Green/35 5.00 12.00
3 Carson Palmer/150 4.00 10.00
4 Clinton Portis/15 6.00 15.00
5 Corey Dillon/150 3.00 8.00
6 Curtis Martin/150 4.00 10.00
8 Duce Staley/85 4.00 10.00
9 Hines Ward/150 4.00 10.00
10 Jake Plummer/150 3.00 8.00
12 Jerome Bettis/150 8.00 20.00
13 Jevon Kearse/150 3.00 8.00
14 Julius Jones/22 5.00 12.00
15 Marshall Faulk/150 4.00 10.00
16 Ricky Williams/150 3.00 8.00
17 Roy Williams S/30 4.00 10.00
18 Stephen Davis/150 3.00 8.00
19 Steven Jackson/55 5.00 12.00
20 Terrell Owens/25 8.00 20.00

2005 Donruss Gridiron Gear Past and Present Jerseys Single Autographs

STATED PRINT RUN 1-50
*DBL JSY AU/25: .5X TO 1.2X JSY AU/50
UNPRICED JSY NUM AU PRINT RUN 1-10
UNPRICED NME PLTE DBL PRINT RUN 1-15
UNPRICED TM LOGO DBL PRINT RUN 1-5
UNPRICED TM LOGO SINGL PRINT RUN 1-10
SERIAL #'d UNDER 20 NOT PRICED
1 Aaron Brooks/50 8.00 20.00
9 Hines Ward/50 40.00 80.00
13 Jevon Kearse/50 10.00 25.00
17 Roy Williams S/50 12.00 30.00
19 Steven Jackson/50 12.00 30.00

2005 Donruss Gridiron Gear Past and Present Jerseys Team Logo Single

TEAM LOGO SINGLE PRINT RUN 1-25
SERIAL #'d UNDER 15 NOT PRICED
*TEAM LOGO DBL/15: .5X TO 1.2X SNGL
5 Corey Dillon/25 10.00 25.00
6 Curtis Martin/25 12.00 30.00
7 DeShaun Foster/16 10.00 25.00
8 Duce Staley/25 10.00 25.00
13 Jevon Kearse/25 10.00 25.00
16 Ricky Williams/25 10.00 25.00
18 Stephen Davis/16 10.00 25.00
19 Steven Jackson/15 12.00 30.00
20 Terrell Owens/20 12.00 30.00

2005 Donruss Gridiron Gear Performers Gold

GOLD STATED PRINT RUN 500
*GOLD HOLO/100: .8X TO 2X GOLD/500
*PLATINUM/25: 1.2X TO 3X GOLD/500
*SILVER HOLO/250: .5X TO 1.2X GOLD/500
1 Tatum Bell 1.00 2.50
2 Antonio Gates 1.50 4.00
3 Barry Sanders 2.50 6.00
4 Brett Favre 4.00 10.00
5 Brian Westbrook 1.25 3.00
6 Chad Johnson 1.25 3.00
7 Chris Chambers 1.25 3.00
8 Corey Simon 1.00 2.50
9 Deion Branch 1.00 2.50
10 Deion Sanders 2.00 5.00
11 Deuce McAllister 1.25 3.00
12 Donte Stallworth 1.00 2.50
13 Doug Flutie 1.50 4.00
14 Drew Bledsoe 1.50 4.00
15 Drew Brees 1.50 4.00
16 Earl Campbell 1.50 4.00
17 Eddie George 1.25 3.00
18 Edgerrin James 1.25 3.00
19 Eric Moulds 1.00 2.50
20 Fred Taylor 1.25 3.00
21 Andre Johnson 1.50 4.00
22 Ickey Woods 1.00 2.50
23 Isaac Bruce 1.25 3.00
24 Javon Walker 1.00 2.50
25 Jerry Rice 3.00 8.00
26 Joey Harrington 1.25 3.00
27 John Taylor 1.00 2.50
28 Junior Seau 1.50 4.00
29 Ken Stabler 2.00 5.00
30 L.C. Greenwood 1.25 3.00
31 LaDainian Tomlinson 1.50 4.00
32 Larry Fitzgerald 1.50 4.00
33 Leroy Kelly 1.25 3.00
34 Mark Brunell 1.25 3.00
35 Michael Vick 1.50 4.00
36 Mike Singletary 1.50 4.00
37 Paul Warfield 1.25 3.00
38 Peyton Manning 3.00 8.00
39 Plaxico Burress 1.25 3.00
40 Randy Moss 1.50 4.00
41 Jake Plummer 1.25 3.00
42 Ricky Williams 1.25 3.00
43 Roger Craig 1.50 4.00
44 Shaun Alexander 1.25 3.00
45 Steve Smith 1.50 4.00
46 Terence Newman 1.00 2.50
47 Tom Brady 3.00 8.00
48 Tony Gonzalez 1.25 3.00
49 Warren Sapp 1.25 3.00
50 Willis McGahee 1.50 4.00

2005 Donruss Gridiron Gear Performers Autographs

STATED PRINT RUN 1-250
1 Tatum Bell/90 12.50 30.00
3 Barry Sanders/25 75.00 150.00
9 Deion Branch/14 12.00 30.00
16 Earl Campbell/25 15.00 40.00
21 Andre Johnson/25 15.00 40.00
27 John Taylor/89 8.00 20.00
29 Ken Stabler/250 15.00 40.00
35 Michael Vick/40 40.00 80.00
43 Roger Craig/98 12.50 30.00
44 Shaun Alexander/25 15.00 40.00
45 Steve Smith/15 15.00 40.00

2005 Donruss Gridiron Gear Performers Jersey Autographs

STATED PRINT RUN 1-50
*DBL PATCH/22-25: .6X TO 1.5X JSY AU
*TEAM LOGO/25: .6X TO 1.5X JSY AU
2 Antonio Gates/50 15.00 40.00
6 Chad Johnson/50 12.00 30.00
9 Deion Branch/50 10.00 25.00
16 Earl Campbell/50 15.00 40.00
26 Joey Harrington/20 15.00 40.00
27 John Taylor/30 12.00 30.00
30 L.C. Greenwood/16 15.00 40.00
35 Michael Vick/50 40.00 80.00
36 Mike Singletary/50 15.00 40.00
43 Roger Craig/15 20.00 50.00
44 Shaun Alexander/50 15.00 40.00
46 Terence Newman/25 12.00 30.00
50 Willis McGahee/50 15.00 40.00

2005 Donruss Gridiron Gear Performers Jerseys

STATED PRINT RUN 1-150
*JUMBO/50-100: .6X TO 1.5X JSY
*JUMBO/30 41: .8X TO 2X JSY
*JUMBO/20-25: 1X TO 2.5X JSY
1 Tatum Bell/150 2.50 6.00
2 Antonio Gates/80 5.00 12.00
4 Brett Favre/150 10.00 25.00
5 Brian Westbrook/150 3.00 8.00
6 Chad Johnson/50 4.00 10.00
7 Chris Chambers/25 6.00 15.00
8 Corey Simon/150 2.50 6.00
9 Deion Branch/70 3.00 8.00
10 Deion Sanders/150 6.00 15.00
11 Deuce McAllister/150 3.00 8.00
12 Donte Stallworth/120 2.50 6.00
13 Doug Flutie/150 5.00 12.00
14 Drew Bledsoe/150 4.00 10.00
15 Drew Brees/150 4.00 10.00
16 Earl Campbell/150 5.00 12.00
17 Eddie George/22 6.00 15.00
18 Edgerrin James/15 6.00 15.00
22 Ickey Woods/150 3.00 8.00
23 Isaac Bruce/150 3.00 8.00
24 Javon Walker/150 2.50 6.00
25 Jerry Rice/150 8.00 20.00
26 Joey Harrington/150 3.00 8.00
27 John Taylor/100 3.00 8.00
28 Junior Seau/150 4.00 10.00
30 L.C. Greenwood/100 4.00 10.00
31 LaDainian Tomlinson/150 4.00 10.00
32 Larry Fitzgerald/150 4.00 10.00
33 Leroy Kelly/75 5.00 12.00
34 Mark Brunell/150 3.00 8.00
35 Michael Vick/150 5.00 12.00
36 Mike Singletary/75 6.00 15.00
37 Paul Warfield/25 6.00 15.00
38 Peyton Manning/150 8.00 20.00
40 Randy Moss/150 4.00 10.00
41 Jake Plummer/150 3.00 8.00
42 Ricky Williams/150 3.00 8.00
43 Roger Craig/150 5.00 12.00
44 Shaun Alexander/75 4.00 10.00
46 Terence Newman/125 2.50 6.00
47 Tom Brady/150 8.00 20.00
48 Tony Gonzalez/150 3.00 8.00
49 Warren Sapp/118 3.00 8.00
50 Willis McGahee/125 4.00 10.00

2005 Donruss Gridiron Gear Performers Jerseys Jumbo Swatch Prime

STATED PRINT RUN 2-50
2 Antonio Gates/27 20.00 50.00
3 Barry Sanders/20 50.00 120.00
4 Brett Favre/42 60.00 120.00
5 Brian Westbrook/50 12.00 30.00
6 Chad Johnson/50 12.00 30.00
7 Chris Chambers/50 12.00 30.00
8 Corey Simon/50 10.00 25.00
11 Deuce McAllister/50 12.00 30.00
12 Donte Stallworth/50 10.00 25.00
13 Doug Flutie/33 20.00 50.00
15 Drew Brees/50 15.00 40.00
17 Eddie George/23 15.00 40.00
18 Edgerrin James/50 12.00 30.00
19 Eric Moulds/38 10.00 25.00
20 Fred Taylor/50 12.00 30.00
22 Ickey Woods/20 15.00 40.00
23 Isaac Bruce/50 12.00 30.00
24 Javon Walker/50 10.00 25.00
25 Jerry Rice/50 30.00 80.00
26 Joey Harrington/50 12.00 30.00
27 John Taylor/25 15.00 40.00
28 Junior Seau/50 15.00 40.00
31 LaDainian Tomlinson/15 20.00 50.00
34 Mark Brunell/27 15.00 40.00
36 Mike Singletary/25 25.00 60.00
38 Peyton Manning/50 30.00 80.00
39 Plaxico Burress/16 15.00 40.00
40 Randy Moss/50 15.00 40.00
41 Jake Plummer/41 12.00 30.00
42 Ricky Williams/50 12.00 30.00
44 Shaun Alexander/28 15.00 40.00
45 Steve Smith/15 20.00 50.00
46 Terence Newman/46 10.00 25.00
48 Tony Gonzalez/50 12.00 30.00
49 Warren Sapp/50 12.00 30.00
50 Willis McGahee/50 15.00 40.00

2005 Donruss Gridiron Gear Performers Jerseys Name Plate

STATED PRINT RUN 1-50
3 Barry Sanders/50 25.00 60.00
5 Brian Westbrook/50 12.00 30.00
6 Chad Johnson/50 12.00 30.00
7 Chris Chambers/50 10.00 25.00
8 Corey Simon/50 10.00 25.00
10 Deion Sanders/20 25.00 60.00
11 Deuce McAllister/50 12.00 30.00
12 Donte Stallworth/29 12.00 30.00
13 Doug Flutie/25 25.00 60.00
14 Drew Bledsoe/16 20.00 50.00
15 Drew Brees/19 20.00 50.00
16 Earl Campbell/25 25.00 60.00
17 Eddie George/45 12.00 30.00
18 Edgerrin James/50 12.00 30.00
19 Eric Moulds/48 10.00 25.00
20 Fred Taylor/50 12.00 30.00
22 Ickey Woods/36 12.00 30.00
23 Isaac Bruce/50 12.00 30.00
24 Javon Walker/45 10.00 25.00
25 Jerry Rice/50 30.00 80.00
26 Joey Harrington/50 12.00 30.00
31 LaDainian Tomlinson/26 20.00 50.00
34 Mark Brunell/50 12.00 30.00
38 Peyton Manning/25 30.00 80.00
40 Randy Moss/36 15.00 40.00
41 Jake Plummer/16 15.00 40.00
42 Ricky Williams/48 12.00 30.00
44 Shaun Alexander/25 15.00 40.00
46 Terence Newman/35 10.00 25.00
47 Tom Brady/23 30.00 80.00
48 Tony Gonzalez/36 12.00 30.00
49 Warren Sapp/20 15.00 40.00

2005 Donruss Gridiron Gear Performers Jerseys Numbers

STATED PRINT RUN 1-100
2 Antonio Gates/100 10.00 25.00
3 Barry Sanders/100 15.00 40.00
4 Brett Favre/80 25.00 60.00
5 Brian Westbrook/100 8.00 20.00
6 Chad Johnson/100 8.00 20.00
7 Chris Chambers/100 8.00 20.00
8 Corey Simon/100 6.00 15.00
9 Deion Branch/55 8.00 20.00
10 Deion Sanders/100 12.00 30.00
11 Deuce McAllister/100 8.00 20.00
12 Donte Stallworth/100 6.00 15.00
13 Doug Flutie/80 12.00 30.00
14 Drew Bledsoe/15 15.00 40.00
15 Drew Brees/100 10.00 25.00
16 Earl Campbell/100 12.00 30.00
17 Eddie George/100 8.00 20.00
18 Edgerrin James/100 8.00 20.00
19 Eric Moulds/100 6.00 15.00
20 Fred Taylor/100 8.00 20.00
21 Andre Johnson/20 15.00 40.00
22 Ickey Woods/100 8.00 20.00
23 Isaac Bruce/100 8.00 20.00
24 Javon Walker/100 6.00 15.00
25 Jerry Rice/100 20.00 50.00
26 Joey Harrington/25 12.00 30.00
27 John Taylor/25 12.00 30.00
28 Junior Seau/100 10.00 25.00
31 LaDainian Tomlinson/100 10.00 25.00
32 Larry Fitzgerald/100 10.00 25.00
34 Mark Brunell/100 8.00 20.00
36 Mike Singletary/50 15.00 40.00
37 Paul Warfield/50 12.00 30.00
38 Peyton Manning/50 25.00 60.00
39 Plaxico Burress/26 12.00 30.00
40 Randy Moss/100 10.00 25.00
41 Jake Plummer/99 8.00 20.00
42 Ricky Williams/100 8.00 20.00
43 Roger Craig/73 12.00 30.00
44 Shaun Alexander/37 10.00 25.00
45 Steve Smith/35 12.00 30.00
46 Terence Newman/75 6.00 15.00
47 Tom Brady/64 20.00 50.00
48 Tony Gonzalez/100 8.00 20.00
49 Warren Sapp/100 8.00 20.00

2005 Donruss Gridiron Gear Performers Jerseys Numbers Autographs

STATED PRINT RUN 1-50
*NAME PLATE/25: .4X TO 1X JSY NUM/25
*NAME PLATE/25: .5X TO 1.2X JSY NUM/50
2 Antonio Gates/50 20.00 50.00
3 Barry Sanders/25 125.00 200.00
6 Chad Johnson/50 20.00 50.00
9 Deion Branch/50 15.00 40.00
16 Earl Campbell/25 30.00 80.00
21 Andre Johnson/25 15.00 40.00
26 Joey Harrington/25 15.00 40.00
35 Michael Vick/25 50.00 100.00
43 Roger Craig/35 25.00 60.00
44 Shaun Alexander/25 20.00 50.00
46 Terence Newman/25 15.00 40.00
50 Willis McGahee/25 20.00 50.00

2005 Donruss Gridiron Gear Performers Jerseys Patch Double

STATED PRINT RUN 1-50
3 Barry Sanders/50 25.00 60.00
4 Brett Favre/25 30.00 80.00
7 Chris Chambers/50 10.00 25.00
8 Corey Simon/50 8.00 20.00
11 Deuce McAllister/50 10.00 25.00
16 Earl Campbell/25 20.00 50.00
17 Eddie George/25 12.00 30.00
18 Edgerrin James/25 12.00 30.00
19 Eric Moulds/30 8.00 20.00
20 Fred Taylor/50 10.00 25.00
23 Isaac Bruce/25 12.00 30.00
25 Jerry Rice/15 30.00 80.00
28 Junior Seau/28 15.00 40.00
31 LaDainian Tomlinson/50 12.00 30.00
32 Larry Fitzgerald/50 12.00 30.00
34 Mark Brunell/50 10.00 25.00
36 Mike Singletary/30 15.00 40.00
38 Peyton Manning/25 25.00 60.00
39 Plaxico Burress/50 10.00 25.00
40 Randy Moss/50 12.00 30.00
42 Ricky Williams/50 10.00 25.00
44 Shaun Alexander/15 12.00 30.00
48 Tony Gonzalez/50 10.00 25.00
49 Warren Sapp/30 10.00 25.00

2005 Donruss Gridiron Gear Performers Jerseys Team Logo

STATED PRINT RUN 2-25
5 Brian Westbrook/25 12.00 30.00
6 Chad Johnson/25 12.00 30.00
7 Chris Chambers/25 12.00 30.00
8 Corey Simon/25 10.00 25.00
11 Deuce McAllister/25 12.00 30.00
12 Donte Stallworth/20 10.00 25.00
14 Drew Bledsoe/25 15.00 40.00
17 Eddie George/25 12.00 30.00
20 Fred Taylor/25 12.00 30.00
28 Junior Seau/16 15.00 40.00
34 Mark Brunell/25 12.00 30.00
40 Randy Moss/17 15.00 40.00
42 Ricky Williams/25 12.00 30.00
47 Tom Brady/24 30.00 80.00
49 Warren Sapp/25 12.00 30.00

2005 Donruss Gridiron Gear Pro Bowl Squad Gold

COMPLETE SET (5) 8.00 20.00
GOLD STATED PRINT RUN 1000
*GOLD HOLO/100: .6X TO 1.5X GOLD/1000
*PLATINUM/25: 1X TO 2.5X GOLD/1000
*SILVER HOLO/250.: .5X TO 1.2X GOLD/1000
1 Daunte Culpepper 1.25 3.00
2 Fran Tarkenton 1.50 4.00
3 Jamal Lewis 1.25 3.00
4 Jeff Garcia 1.25 3.00
5 Tom Brady 3.00 8.00

2005 Donruss Gridiron Gear Pro Bowl Squad Jerseys

STATED PRINT RUN 100 SER.#'d SETS
*DBL PATCH/19-25: 1.2X TO 3X JSY/100
*NAME PLATE/15-22: 1.2X TO 3X JSY/100
*JSY NUM/100: .6X TO 1.5X JSY/100
*JSY NUM/42: .8X TO 2X JSY/100
*TEAM LOGO/15-18: 1.2X TO 3X JSY/100
1 Daunte Culpepper 4.00 10.00
2 Fran Tarkenton 5.00 12.00
3 Jamal Lewis 4.00 10.00
4 Jeff Garcia 4.00 10.00
5 Tom Brady 10.00 25.00

2005 Donruss Gridiron Gear Rookie Jerseys Jumbo Swatch

STATED PRINT RUN 52-150
*PRIME/75: 1X TO 2.5X BASIC JSY/52-150
101 Alex Smith QB/139 6.00 15.00
102 Ronnie Brown/150 5.00 12.00
103 Braylon Edwards/150 5.00 12.00
105 Cadillac Williams/150 4.00 10.00
106 Adam Jones/150 3.00 8.00
107 Troy Williamson/150 3.00 8.00
111 Matt Jones/150 4.00 10.00
112 Mark Clayton/150 4.00 10.00
114 Jason Campbell/150 5.00 12.00
115 Roddy White/150 5.00 12.00
118 Mark Bradley/150 2.50 6.00
121 Roscoe Parrish/150 2.50 6.00
122 Terrence Murphy/150 2.50 6.00
123 Vincent Jackson/150 5.00 12.00
124 Frank Gore/92 6.00 15.00
125 Charlie Frye/150 4.00 10.00
126 Courtney Roby/150 3.00 8.00
127 Andrew Walter/150 3.00 8.00
128 Vernand Morency/150 3.00 8.00
129 Ryan Moats/150 3.00 8.00
133 Kyle Orton/52 4.00 10.00
136 Ciatrick Fason/150 2.50 6.00
138 Stefan LeFors/150 2.50 6.00
142 Antrel Rolle/150 4.00 10.00
143 Maurice Clarett/150 3.00 8.00
145 Eric Shelton/150 2.50 6.00
147 Carlos Rogers/150 4.00 10.00

2005 Donruss Gridiron Gear Triplets Gold

STATED PRINT RUN 1000 SER.#'d SETS
*GOLD HOLO/100: .6X TO 1.5X GOLD/1000
*PLATINUM/25: 1X TO 2.5X GOLD/1000
*SILVER HOLO/250: .5X TO 1.2X GOLD/1000
1 Terry Glenn 1.50 4.00
John Abraham
Jonathan Vilma
2 Amani Toomer 1.50 4.00
Ike Hilliard
Ron Dayne
3 Antwaan Randle El 2.00 5.00
Hines Ward
Jerome Bettis
4 Richard Seymour 1.25 3.00
David Givens
Deion Branch
5 Byron Leftwich 1.50 4.00
Fred Taylor
Jimmy Smith
6 Chris Brown 1.50 4.00
Drew Bennett
Jevon Kearse
7 Chris Chambers 2.00 5.00
Jason Taylor
Junior Seau
8 Donovan McNabb 2.00 5.00
Correll Buckhalter
Duce Staley
9 Dante Hall 1.50 4.00
Tony Gonzalez
Trent Green
10 Aaron Brooks 1.50 4.00
Michael Clayton
Mike Alstott
11 Deuce McAllister 1.50 4.00
Donte Stallworth
Joe Horn
12 Donald Driver 2.00 5.00
Javon Walker
Robert Ferguson

13 Drew Brees 2.00 5.00
Junior Seau
LaDainian Tomlinson
14 Eric Moulds 1.50 4.00
Josh Reed
Lee Evans
15 Keyshawn Johnson 2.00 5.00
Drew Bledsoe
Roy Williams

2005 Donruss Gridiron Gear Triplets Jerseys

STATED PRINT RUN 25-100
*NME PLTE/41-50: 1X TO 2.5X JSY/55-100
*JSY NUM/50-100: .8X TO 2X JSY/55-100
*JSY NUM/100: .5X TO 1.2X JSY/25
*JSY NUM/17-25: 1.2X TO 3X JSY/55-100
*JSY NUM/25: 1X TO 2.5X JSY/33
*TEAM LOGO/25: 1.2X TO 3X JSY/100
1 Terry Glenn/100 6.00 15.00
John Abraham
Jonathan Vilma
2 Amani Toomer/100 6.00 15.00
Ike Hilliard
Ron Dayne
3 Antwaan Randle El/100 12.00 30.00
Hines Ward
Jerome Bettis
4 Richard Seymour/100 5.00 12.00
David Givens
Deion Branch
5 Byron Leftwich/100 6.00 15.00
Fred Taylor
Jimmy Smith
6 Chris Brown/55 6.00 15.00
Drew Bennett
Jevon Kearse
7 Chris Chambers/100 8.00 20.00
Jason Taylor
Junior Seau
8 Donovan McNabb/33 10.00 25.00
Correll Buckhalter
Duce Staley
9 Dante Hall/25 10.00 25.00
Tony Gonzalez
Trent Green
10 Aaron Brooks/100 6.00 15.00
Michael Clayton
Mike Alstott
11 Deuce McAllister/100 6.00 15.00
Donte Stallworth
Joe Horn
12 Donald Driver/75 8.00 20.00
Javon Walker
Robert Ferguson
13 Drew Brees/100 8.00 20.00
Junior Seau
LaDainian Tomlinson
14 Eric Moulds/100 6.00 15.00
Josh Reed
Lee Evans
15 Keyshawn Johnson/100 8.00 20.00
Drew Bledsoe
Roy Williams

2006 Donruss Gridiron Gear

This 231-card set was released in October, 2006. The set is broken down into veterans in team alphabetical order (1-100) and 2006 rookies (101-231). Within the rookies, cards numbered 101-200 were issued to a stated print run of 599 serial numbered sets and cards numbered 201-231 were issued to a stated production run of 50 sets and those cards also featured a player-worn swatch.

COMP.SET w/o RC's (100) 10.00 25.00
ROOKIE PRINT RUN 599 SER.#'d SETS
201-231 ANNOUNCED PRINT RUN 50
201-231 JSY RCs FEATURE JUMBO SWATCH
1 Edgerrin James .30 .75
2 Kurt Warner .40 1.00
3 Larry Fitzgerald .40 1.00
4 Alge Crumpler .30 .75
5 Michael Vick .40 1.00
6 Warrick Dunn .30 .75
7 Jamal Lewis .30 .75
8 Mike Anderson .30 .75
9 Neil Rackers .25 .60
10 Derrick Mason .30 .75
11 J.P. Losman .30 .75
12 Lee Evans .30 .75
13 Willis McGahee .30 .75
14 DeShaun Foster .30 .75
15 Jake Delhomme .30 .75
16 Josh Brown .25 .60
17 Steve Smith .40 1.00
18 Cedric Benson .30 .75
19 Rex Grossman .30 .75
20 Shayne Graham .25 .60
21 Carson Palmer .40 1.00
22 Chad Johnson .30 .75
23 Rudi Johnson .30 .75
24 T.J. Houshmandzadeh .30 .75
25 Charlie Frye .30 .75
26 Lance Briggs .30 .75
27 Reuben Droughns .30 .75
28 Drew Bledsoe .40 1.00
29 Julius Jones .25 .60
30 Terrell Owens .40 1.00
31 Terry Glenn .30 .75
32 Jake Plummer .30 .75
33 Rod Smith .30 .75
34 Tatum Bell .25 .60
35 Robert Mathis .25 .60
36 Kevin Jones .25 .60
37 Roy Williams WR .30 .75
38 Ahman Green .30 .75
39 Brett Favre .75 2.00
40 Scottie Vines .25 .60
41 Samkon Gado .30 .75
42 Andre Johnson .40 1.00
43 David Carr .25 .60
44 Domanick Davis .25 .60
45 Marvin Harrison .40 1.00
46 Peyton Manning .60 1.50
47 Reggie Wayne .30 .75
48 Byron Leftwich .30 .75
49 Fred Taylor .30 .75
50 Jimmy Smith .30 .75
51 Matt Jones .25 .60
52 Larry Johnson .30 .75
53 Tony Gonzalez .30 .75
54 Trent Green .30 .75
55 Chris Chambers .30 .75
56 Daunte Culpepper .30 .75
57 Ronnie Brown .40 1.00
58 Robert Pollard .25 .60
59 Mewelde Moore .25 .60
60 Chester Taylor .30 .75
61 Corey Dillon .30 .75
62 Deion Branch .30 .75
63 Tom Brady .60 1.50
64 Deuce McAllister .30 .75
65 Drew Brees .40 1.00
66 Donte Stallworth .25 .60
67 Eli Manning .50 1.25
68 Jeremy Shockey .40 1.00
69 Plaxico Burress .30 .75
70 Tiki Barber .40 1.00
71 Chad Pennington .30 .75
72 Curtis Martin .40 1.00
73 Laveranues Coles .25 .60
74 LaMont Jordan .30 .75
75 Randy Moss .40 1.00
76 Aaron Brooks .30 .75
77 Brian Westbrook .30 .75
78 Donovan McNabb .40 1.00
79 Jabar Gaffney .25 .60
80 Ben Roethlisberger .50 1.25
81 Hines Ward .40 1.00
82 Willie Parker .30 .75
83 Antonio Gates .40 1.00
84 LaDainian Tomlinson .40 1.00
85 Philip Rivers .40 1.00
86 Alex Smith QB .40 1.00
87 Edell Shepherd RC .25 .60
88 Kevan Barlow .25 .60
89 Darrell Jackson .30 .75
90 Matt Hasselbeck .30 .75
91 Shaun Alexander .30 .75
92 Marc Bulger .30 .75
93 Torry Holt .30 .75
94 Steven Jackson .40 1.00
95 Chris Simms .30 .75
96 Cadillac Williams .30 .75
97 Joey Galloway .30 .75
98 Chris Brown .25 .60
99 Clinton Portis .40 1.00
100 Santana Moss .30 .75
101 A.J. Nicholson RC 1.25 3.00
102 Abdul Hodge RC 1.25 3.00
103 Adam Jennings RC 1.50 4.00
104 Andre Hall RC 1.50 4.00
105 Anthony Fasano RC 2.00 5.00
106 Anthony Mix RC 1.50 4.00
107 Anthony Smith RC 2.00 5.00
108 Antonio Cromartie RC 2.00 5.00
109 Ashton Youboty RC 1.25 3.00
110 Ben Obomanu RC 2.00 5.00
111 Bennie Brazell RC 1.50 4.00
112 Bernard Pollard RC 1.50 4.00
113 Bobby Carpenter RC 1.25 3.00
114 Brad Smith RC 2.00 5.00
115 Brodie Croyle RC 2.00 5.00
116 Brodrick Bunkley RC 1.50 4.00
117 Bruce Gradkowski RC 2.00 5.00
118 Calvin Lowry RC 2.00 5.00
119 Cedric Griffin RC 1.50 4.00
120 Cedric Humes RC 1.25 3.00
121 Chad Greenway RC 2.00 5.00
122 Claude Wroten RC 1.25 3.00
123 Cory Rodgers RC 1.50 4.00
124 D.J. Shockley RC 1.50 4.00
125 Danieal Manning RC 2.00 5.00
126 Daniel Bullocks RC 2.00 5.00
127 Darryl Tapp RC 1.50 4.00
128 David Anderson RC 1.50 4.00
129 David Kirtman RC 1.50 4.00
130 David Pittman RC 1.50 4.00
131 David Thomas RC 1.50 4.00
132 Dawan Landry RC 2.00 5.00
133 D'Brickashaw Ferguson RC 2.00 5.00
134 Delanie Walker RC 2.00 5.00
135 DeMario Minter RC 1.50 4.00
136 DeMeco Ryans RC 2.00 5.00
137 Derrick Ross RC 1.50 4.00
138 Devin Aromashodu RC 2.00 5.00
139 Devin Hester RC 3.00 8.00
140 Domenik Hixon RC 2.00 5.00
141 Dominique Byrd RC 1.50 4.00
142 Donte Whitner RC 2.00 5.00
143 D'Qwell Jackson RC 1.50 4.00
144 Dusty Dvoracek RC 2.00 5.00
145 Erik Meyer RC 1.50 4.00
146 Ernie Sims RC 1.50 4.00
147 Ethan Kilmer RC 1.50 4.00
148 Gabe Watson RC 1.25 3.00
149 Garrett Mills RC 2.00 5.00
150 Greg Blue RC 1.50 4.00
151 Greg Jennings RC 4.00 10.00
152 Greg Lee RC 1.25 3.00
153 Haloti Ngata RC 2.00 5.00
154 Ingle Martin RC 1.50 4.00
155 Jai Lewis RC 1.50 4.00
156 Jason Allen RC 1.50 4.00
157 Jay Cutler RC 4.00 10.00
158 Jeffrey Webb RC 1.50 4.00
159 Jeremy Bloom RC 1.50 4.00
160 Jerome Harrison RC 2.00 5.00
161 Jimmy Williams RC 2.00 5.00
162 John David Washington RC 1.50 4.00
163 John McCargo RC 1.25 3.00
164 Johnathan Joseph RC 1.50 4.00
165 Jon Alston RC 1.25 3.00
166 Jonathan Orr RC 1.50 4.00
167 Joseph Addai RC 2.00 5.00
168 Kamerion Wimbley RC 2.00 5.00
169 Kelly Jennings RC 1.50 4.00
170 Ko Simpson RC 1.50 4.00
171 Leonard Pope RC 2.00 5.00
172 Manny Lawson RC 1.50 4.00
173 Marcus Maxey RC 1.50 4.00
174 Marcus Vick RC 1.25 3.00
175 Marques Hagans RC 1.25 3.00
176 Martin Nance RC 1.50 4.00
177 Mathias Kiwanuka RC 2.00 5.00
178 Mike Bell RC 2.00 5.00
179 Mike Hass RC 1.50 4.00
180 Nate Salley RC 1.50 4.00
181 Owen Daniels RC 2.00 5.00
182 P.J. Daniels RC 1.25 3.00
183 Pat Watkins RC 1.50 4.00
184 Paul Pinegar RC 1.25 3.00
185 Quinton Ganther RC 1.25 3.00
186 Reggie McNeal RC 1.50 4.00
187 Richard Marshall RC 1.50 4.00
188 Rocky McIntosh RC 1.50 4.00
189 Roman Harper RC 1.50 4.00
190 Skyler Green RC 1.25 3.00
191 Tamba Hali RC 2.00 5.00
192 Thomas Howard RC 1.50 4.00
193 Tim Jennings RC 1.50 4.00
194 Todd Watkins RC 1.25 3.00
195 Tony Scheffler RC 2.00 5.00
196 Tye Hill RC 1.25 3.00
197 Wali Lundy RC 1.50 4.00
198 Wendell Mathis RC 1.50 4.00
199 Will Blackmon RC 1.50 4.00
200 Willie Reid RC 1.50 4.00
201 Brian Calhoun JSY RC 2.00 5.00
202 Joe Klopfenstein JSY RC 2.00 5.00
203 Travis Wilson JSY RC 2.00 5.00
204 Charlie Whitehurst JSY RC 3.00 8.00
205 DeAngelo Williams JSY RC 4.00 10.00
206 Maurice Stovall JSY RC 2.00 5.00
207 A.J. Hawk JSY RC 3.00 8.00
208 Kellen Clemens JSY RC 2.50 6.00
209 Leon Washington JSY RC 2.50 6.00
210 Sinorice Moss JSY RC 3.00 8.00
211 Demetrius Williams JSY RC 2.50 6.00
212 Jerious Norwood JSY RC 2.50 6.00
213 Santonio Holmes JSY RC 4.00 10.00
214 Omar Jacobs JSY RC 2.00 5.00
215 Brandon Marshall JSY RC 3.00 8.00
216 Jason Avant JSY RC 2.00 5.00
217 Derek Hagan JSY RC 2.50 6.00
218 Brandon Williams JSY RC 2.00 5.00
219 Vernon Davis JSY RC 4.00 10.00
220 Michael Robinson JSY RC 2.50 6.00
221 Matt Leinart JSY RC 3.00 8.00
222 Reggie Bush JSY RC 6.00 15.00
223 LenDale White JSY RC 2.50 6.00
224 Vince Young JSY RC 4.00 10.00
225 Maurice Drew JSY RC 5.00 12.00
226 Marcedes Lewis JSY RC 3.00 8.00
227 Mario Williams JSY RC 3.00 8.00
228 Michael Huff JSY RC 2.50 6.00
229 Tarvaris Jackson JSY RC 3.00 8.00
230 Laurence Maroney JSY RC 2.50 6.00
231 Chad Jackson JSY RC 2.00 5.00

2006 Donruss Gridiron Gear Gold Holofoil

*VETERANS: 1.5X TO 4X BASIC CARDS
RANDOM INSERTS IN RETAIL PACKS

2006 Donruss Gridiron Gear Gold Holofoil O's

*VETS 1-100: 2.5X TO 6X BASIC CARDS
*ROOKIES 101-200: .6X TO 1.5X BASIC CARDS
RANDOM INSERTS IN RETAIL PACKS
STATED PRINT RUN 100 SER.#'d SETS

2006 Donruss Gridiron Gear Gold Holofoil X's

*VETS 1-100: 2.5X TO 6X BASIC CARDS
*ROOKIES 101-200: .6X TO 1.5X BASIC CARDS
RANDOM INSERTS IN HOBBY PACKS
STATED PRINT RUN 100 SER.#'d SETS

2006 Donruss Gridiron Gear Platinum Holofoil

*VETERANS: 4X TO 10X BASIC CARDS
RANDOM INSERTS IN RETIAL PACKS

2006 Donruss Gridiron Gear Platinum Holofoil O's

*VETS 1-100: 6X TO 15X BASIC CARDS
*ROOKIES 101-200: 1X TO 2.5X BASIC CARDS
RANDOM INSERTS IN RETAIL PACKS
STATED PRINT RUN 25 SER.#'d SETS

2006 Donruss Gridiron Gear Platinum Holofoil X's

*VETS 1-100: 6X TO 15X BASIC CARDS
*ROOKIES 101-200: 1X TO 2.5X BASIC CARDS
RANDOM INSERTS IN HOBBY PACKS
STATED PRINT RUN 25 SER.#'d SETS

2006 Donruss Gridiron Gear Retail

*ROOKIES 101-200: .4X TO 1X BASIC CARDS
STATED PRINT RUN 599 SER.#'d SETS

2006 Donruss Gridiron Gear Silver Holofoil

*VETERANS: 1X TO 2.5X BASIC CARDS
RANDOM INSERTS IN RETAIL PACKS

2006 Donruss Gridiron Gear Silver Holofoil O's

*VETS 1-100: 1.5X TO 4X BASIC CARDS
RANDOM INSERTS IN RETAIL PACKS
STATED PRINT RUN 250 SER.#'d SETS

2006 Donruss Gridiron Gear Silver Holofoil X's

*VETS 1-100: 1.5X TO 4X BASIC CARDS
RANDOM INSERTS IN HOBBY PACKS
STATED PRINT RUN 250 SER.#'d SETS

2006 Donruss Gridiron Gear Autographs Gold Holofoil

STATED PRINT RUN 5-250 SER.#'d SETS
SERIAL #'d UNDER 25 NOT PRICED
1 Edgerrin James/25 15.00 40.00
3 Larry Fitzgerald/35 25.00 50.00
9 Neil Rackers/100 5.00 12.00
12 Lee Evans/35 8.00 20.00
13 Willis McGahee/35 10.00 25.00
15 Jake Delhomme/35 10.00 25.00
16 Josh Brown/100 8.00 20.00
20 Shayne Graham/100 6.00 15.00
25 Charlie Frye/25
26 Lance Briggs/100 30.00 60.00
34 Tatum Bell/50 8.00 20.00
35 Robert Mathis/100 8.00 20.00
37 Roy Williams WR/25 15.00 40.00
40 Scottie Vines/100 5.00 12.00
41 Samkon Gado/25 10.00 25.00
48 Byron Leftwich/50 10.00 25.00
50 Jimmy Smith/35 8.00 20.00
51 Matt Jones/50 8.00 20.00
52 Larry Johnson/25 15.00 40.00
55 Chris Chambers/25 10.00 25.00
57 Ronnie Brown/25 15.00 40.00
58 Robert Pollard/100 6.00 12.00
74 LaMont Jordan/35 8.00 20.00
78 Donovan McNabb/25 35.00 60.00
82 Willie Parker/75 8.00 20.00
84 LaDainian Tomlinson/25 50.00 100.00
87 Edell Shepherd/100 5.00 12.00
89 Darrell Jackson/35
90 Matt Hasselbeck/35 15.00 40.00
93 Torry Holt/25 15.00 40.00
94 Steven Jackson/25 15.00 40.00
98 Chris Brown/25 8.00 20.00
99 Clinton Portis/25 15.00 40.00
101 A.J. Nicholson/225 4.00 10.00
102 Abdul Hodge/250 6.00 15.00
103 Adam Jennings/250 5.00 12.00
104 Andre Hall/70 10.00 25.00
105 Anthony Fasano/75 8.00 20.00
106 Anthony Mix/250 5.00 12.00
108 Antonio Cromartie/100 8.00 20.00
109 Ashton Youboty/208 6.00 15.00
110 Ben Obomanu/165 5.00 12.00
111 Bennie Brazell/250 5.00 12.00
112 Bernard Pollard/250 5.00 12.00
113 Bobby Carpenter/175 6.00 15.00
114 Brad Smith/250 6.00 15.00
115 Brodie Croyle/225 6.00 15.00
116 Brodrick Bunkley/75 8.00 20.00
117 Bruce Gradkowski/75 10.00 25.00
119 Cedric Griffin/250 5.00 12.00
120 Cedric Humes/175 6.00 15.00
121 Chad Greenway/250 6.00 15.00
122 Claude Wroten/250 4.00 10.00
123 Cory Rodgers/250 6.00 15.00
124 D.J. Shockley/75 8.00 20.00
128 David Anderson/250 5.00 12.00
131 David Thomas/250 6.00 15.00
133 D'Brickashaw Ferguson/250 6.00 15.00
134 Delanie Walker/250 5.00 12.00
136 DeMeco Ryans/125 12.00 30.00
139 Devin Hester/100 30.00 60.00
140 Domenik Hixon/250 6.00 15.00
141 Dominique Byrd/75 8.00 20.00
142 Donte Whitner/250 6.00 15.00
143 D'Qwell Jackson/25 8.00 20.00
145 Erik Meyer/250 5.00 12.00
147 Ethan Kilmer/250 6.00 15.00
148 Gabe Watson/175 5.00 12.00
149 Garrett Mills/250 6.00 15.00
151 Greg Jennings/100 15.00 40.00
152 Greg Lee/30 8.00 20.00
153 Haloti Ngata/225 8.00 20.00
154 Ingle Martin/75 6.00 15.00
156 Jason Allen/250 6.00 15.00
157 Jay Cutler/225 30.00 80.00
158 Jeffrey Webb/250 5.00 12.00
160 Jerome Harrison/75 8.00 20.00
161 Jimmy Williams/250 6.00 15.00
163 John McCargo/250 5.00 12.00
164 Johnathan Joseph/25 8.00 20.00
165 Jon Alston/219 6.00 15.00
166 Jonathan Orr/250 5.00 12.00
167 Joseph Addai/225 10.00 25.00
168 Kamerion Wimbley/25 10.00 25.00
169 Kelly Jennings/75 8.00 20.00
170 Ko Simpson/250 5.00 12.00
171 Leonard Pope/75 8.00 20.00
172 Manny Lawson/250 6.00 15.00
175 Marques Hagans/250 5.00 12.00
176 Martin Nance/30 8.00 20.00
177 Mathias Kiwanuka/25 10.00 25.00
178 Mike Bell/94 10.00 25.00
179 Mike Hass/250 6.00 15.00
181 Owen Daniels/81 8.00 20.00
182 P.J. Daniels/75 6.00 15.00
183 Pat Watkins/250 6.00 15.00
184 Paul Pinegar/219 5.00 12.00
185 Quinton Ganther/250 5.00 12.00
186 Reggie McNeal/75 6.00 15.00
188 Rocky McIntosh/250 6.00 15.00
190 Skyler Green/250 6.00 15.00
191 Tamba Hali/175 8.00 20.00
192 Thomas Howard/219 6.00 15.00
194 Todd Watkins/250 5.00 12.00
195 Tony Scheffler/250 8.00 20.00
196 Tye Hill/100 8.00 20.00
197 Wali Lundy/250 6.00 15.00
198 Wendell Mathis/70 6.00 15.00
200 Willie Reid/250 6.00 15.00

2006 Donruss Gridiron Gear Autographs Platinum Holofoil

*VETERANS/25: .8X TO 2X GOLD/100
*ROOKIES/25: .4X TO 1X GOLD/25-35
*ROOKIES/25: .6X TO 1.5X GOLD/165-250
*ROOKIES/25: .5X TO 1.2X GOLD/70-125
PLATINUM PRINT RUN 1-25 SER.#'d SETS
SERIAL #'d UNDER NOT PRICED
26 Lance Briggs/25 40.00 80.00
139 Devin Hester/25 40.00 80.00
157 Jay Cutler/25 100.00 200.00
167 Joseph Addai/25 15.00 40.00

2006 Donruss Gridiron Gear Jerseys

STATED PRINT RUN 89-250
*O's/50: .5X TO 1.2X BASIC INSERTS
O's PRINT RUN 50 SER.#'d SETS
*PRIME/25: .8X TO 2X BASIC INSERTS
PRIME PRINT RUN 25 SER.#'d SETS
*X's/86-100: .5X TO 1.2X BASIC INSERTS
*X's/25-60: .6X TO 1.5X BASIC INSERTS
X's PRINT RUN 25-100 SER.#'d SETS
*RETAIL: .4X TO 1X BASIC INSERTS
RETAIL PRINTED ON WHITE STOCK
1 Edgerrin James/89 3.00 8.00
3 Larry Fitzgerald/250 4.00 10.00
4 Alge Crumpler/125 3.00 8.00
5 Michael Vick/250 4.00 10.00
6 Warrick Dunn/125 3.00 8.00
7 Jamal Lewis/250 3.00 8.00
11 J.P. Losman/150 3.00 8.00
12 Lee Evans/125 3.00 8.00
13 Willis McGahee/97 3.00 8.00
14 DeShaun Foster/125 3.00 8.00
15 Jake Delhomme/125 3.00 8.00
17 Steve Smith/125 4.00 10.00
18 Cedric Benson/100 3.00 8.00
19 Rex Grossman/97 3.00 8.00
21 Carson Palmer/125 4.00 10.00
22 Chad Johnson/125 3.00 8.00
23 Rudi Johnson/250 3.00 8.00
24 T.J. Houshmandzadeh/125 3.00 8.00
25 Charlie Frye/125 3.00 8.00
27 Reuben Droughns/125 3.00 8.00
28 Drew Bledsoe/150 4.00 10.00
29 Julius Jones/125 2.50 6.00
31 Terry Glenn/125 3.00 8.00
32 Jake Plummer/250 3.00 8.00
33 Rod Smith/100 3.00 8.00
34 Tatum Bell/125 2.50 6.00
36 Kevin Jones/125 2.50 6.00
37 Roy Williams WR/150 3.00 8.00
38 Ahman Green/125 3.00 8.00
39 Brett Favre/125 8.00 20.00
41 Samkon Gado/100 3.00 8.00
42 Andre Johnson/125 4.00 10.00
43 David Carr/250 2.50 6.00
44 Domanick Davis/150 2.50 6.00
45 Marvin Harrison/125 4.00 10.00
46 Peyton Manning/125 6.00 15.00
47 Reggie Wayne/250 3.00 8.00
48 Byron Leftwich/250 3.00 8.00
49 Fred Taylor/150 3.00 8.00
50 Jimmy Smith/125 3.00 8.00
51 Matt Jones/125 2.50 6.00
52 Larry Johnson/125 3.00 8.00
53 Tony Gonzalez/125 3.00 8.00
54 Trent Green/200 3.00 8.00
55 Chris Chambers/125 3.00 8.00
56 Daunte Culpepper/250 3.00 8.00
57 Ronnie Brown/125 4.00 10.00
59 Mewelde Moore/125 2.50 6.00
61 Corey Dillon/125 3.00 8.00
62 Deion Branch/125 3.00 8.00
63 Tom Brady/200 6.00 15.00
64 Deuce McAllister/250 3.00 8.00
66 Donte Stallworth/125 2.50 6.00
67 Eli Manning/125 5.00 12.00
68 Jeremy Shockey/250 4.00 10.00
69 Plaxico Burress/150 3.00 8.00
70 Tiki Barber/150 4.00 10.00
71 Chad Pennington/250 3.00 8.00
72 Curtis Martin/125 4.00 10.00
73 Laveranues Coles/125 2.50 6.00
74 LaMont Jordan/130 3.00 8.00
75 Randy Moss/125 4.00 10.00
77 Brian Westbrook/125 3.00 8.00
78 Donovan McNabb/250 4.00 10.00
80 Ben Roethlisberger/125 5.00 12.00
81 Hines Ward/125 4.00 10.00
82 Willie Parker/125 3.00 8.00
83 Antonio Gates/125 4.00 10.00
84 LaDainian Tomlinson/125 4.00 10.00
85 Philip Rivers/125 4.00 10.00
86 Alex Smith QB/125 4.00 10.00
88 Kevan Barlow/250 2.50 6.00
89 Darrell Jackson/125 3.00 8.00
90 Matt Hasselbeck/125 3.00 8.00
91 Shaun Alexander/100 3.00 8.00
92 Marc Bulger/150 3.00 8.00
93 Torry Holt/125 3.00 8.00
94 Steven Jackson/125 4.00 10.00
95 Chris Simms/150 3.00 8.00
96 Cadillac Williams/125 3.00 8.00
97 Joey Galloway/150 3.00 8.00
98 Chris Brown/250 2.50 6.00
99 Clinton Portis/200 4.00 10.00
100 Santana Moss/100 3.00 8.00

2006 Donruss Gridiron Gear Next Generation Gold

GOLD PRINT RUN 500 SER.#'d SETS
*RED: .4X TO 1X GOLD/500
*SILVER/250: .5X TO 1.2X GOLD/500
SILVER PRINT RUN 250 SER.#'d SETS
*HOLOGOLD/100: .6X TO 1.5X GOLD/500
HOLOGOLD PRINT RUN 100 SER.#'d SETS
*PLATINUM/25: 1X TO 2.5X GOLD/500
PLATINUM PRINT RUN 25 SER.#'d SETS
1 Alex Smith QB 1.25 3.00
2 Braylon Edwards 1.00 2.50
3 Cadillac Williams 1.00 2.50
4 Cedric Benson 1.00 2.50
5 Charlie Frye 1.00 2.50
6 Dallas Clark 1.00 2.50
7 Matt Jones .75 2.00
8 Philip Rivers 1.25 3.00
9 Samkon Gado 1.00 2.50
10 Willie Parker 1.00 2.50
11 Anquan Boldin 1.00 2.50
12 Antonio Gates 1.25 3.00
13 Chris Brown .75 2.00
14 Eli Manning 1.50 4.00
15 Julius Jones .75 2.00
16 Kevin Jones .75 2.00
17 Larry Fitzgerald 1.25 3.00
18 Lee Evans 1.00 2.50
19 Mark Clayton 1.00 2.50
20 Reggie Brown .75 2.00
21 Ronnie Brown 1.25 3.00
22 Roy Williams WR 1.00 2.50
23 Steven Jackson 1.25 3.00
24 T.J. Houshmandzadeh 1.00 2.50
25 Willis McGahee 1.00 2.50

2006 Donruss Gridiron Gear Next Generation Autographs

STATED PRINT RUN 5-50 SER.#'d SETS
SERIAL #'d UNDER 25 NOT PRICED
6 Dallas Clark/35 10.00 25.00
7 Matt Jones/25
10 Willie Parker/40 12.00 30.00
17 Larry Fitzgerald/25 25.00 50.00
19 Mark Clayton/50 10.00 25.00

2006 Donruss Gridiron Gear Next Generation Jerseys

STATED PRINT RUN 150-250
*COMBO PRIME/25-50: .8X TO 2X
*JUMBO/25-50: .6X TO 1.5X BASIC INSERTS
*JUMBO PRIME/15-25: 1X TO 2.5X
*PRIME/25-50: .8X TO 2X BASIC INSERTS
COMBO JSY AUTOS/1-10 NOT PRICED
PRIME AUTOS/1-10 NOT PRICED
1 Alex Smith QB/200 4.00 10.00
2 Braylon Edwards/250 3.00 8.00
3 Cadillac Williams/200 3.00 8.00
4 Cedric Benson/200 3.00 8.00
5 Charlie Frye/200 3.00 8.00
6 Dallas Clark/200 3.00 8.00
7 Matt Jones/200 2.50 6.00
8 Philip Rivers/200 4.00 10.00
9 Samkon Gado/150 3.00 8.00
10 Willie Parker/200 3.00 8.00
11 Anquan Boldin/250 3.00 8.00
12 Antonio Gates/250 4.00 10.00
13 Chris Brown/250 2.50 6.00
14 Eli Manning/250 5.00 12.00
15 Julius Jones/250 2.50 6.00
16 Kevin Jones/250 2.50 6.00
17 Larry Fitzgerald/250 4.00 10.00
18 Lee Evans/250 3.00 8.00
19 Mark Clayton/150 3.00 8.00
20 Reggie Brown/250 2.50 6.00
21 Ronnie Brown/250 4.00 10.00
22 Roy Williams WR/250 3.00 8.00
23 Steven Jackson/250 4.00 10.00
24 T.J. Houshmandzadeh/250 3.00 8.00
25 Willis McGahee/250 3.00 8.00

2006 Donruss Gridiron Gear Next Generation Jerseys Autographs

STATED PRINT RUN 2-40 SER.#'d SETS
SERIAL #'d UNDER 25 NOT PRICED
10 Willie Parker/25 15.00 40.00
19 Mark Clayton/40 12.00 30.00

2006 Donruss Gridiron Gear Performers Gold

GOLD PRINT RUN 500 SER.#'d SETS
*RED: .3X TO .8X GOLD/500
*SILVER/250: .5X TO 1.2X GOLD/500
SILVER PRINT RUN 250 SER.#'d SETS
*HOLOGOLD/100: .6X TO 1.5X GOLD/500
HOLOGOLD PRINT RUN 100 SER.#'d SETS
*PLATINUM/25: 1X TO 2.5X GOLD/500
PLATINUM PRINT RUN 25 SER.#'d SETS
1 Jim Otto 1.00 2.50
2 Paul Warfield 1.25 3.00
3 Craig Morton 1.00 2.50
4 Paul Krause 1.00 2.50
5 Joe Greene 1.50 4.00
6 Thurman Thomas 1.25 3.00
7 Lee Roy Selmon 1.00 2.50
8 Lester Hayes 1.00 2.50
9 Ozzie Newsome 1.25 3.00
10 Jim Plunkett 1.25 3.00
11 Mark Gastineau 1.00 2.50
12 Henry Ellard 1.00 2.50
13 Boomer Esiason 1.25 3.00
14 Herschel Walker 1.25 3.00
15 Eric Dickerson 1.25 3.00
16 Dan Marino 3.00 8.00
17 Barry Sanders 2.50 6.00
18 Jim Kelly 2.00 5.00
19 Julius Peppers .75 2.00
20 Tedy Bruschi 1.25 3.00
21 T.J. Houshmandzadeh .75 2.00
22 Rudi Johnson .75 2.00
23 Steve Smith 1.25 3.00
24 Peyton Manning 2.00 5.00
25 Brett Favre 2.50 6.00
26 Torry Holt .75 2.00
27 Donovan McNabb 1.25 3.00
28 Marc Bulger .75 2.00
29 Alge Crumpler .75 2.00
30 Larry Johnson 1.25 3.00
31 Nate Burleson .75 2.00
32 Charlie Frye 1.25 3.00
33 Carson Palmer 1.25 3.00
34 Samkon Gado 1.25 3.00
35 Javon Walker .75 2.00
36 Tiki Barber 1.25 3.00
37 Reuben Droughns .75 2.00
38 Darrell Jackson .75 2.00
39 Chris Chambers .75 2.00
40 Ben Roethlisberger 2.50 6.00
41 Dallas Clark .75 2.00
42 Reggie Brown .75 2.00
43 LaDainian Tomlinson 1.25 3.00
44 Shaun Alexander 1.25 3.00
45 Marvin Harrison 1.25 3.00
46 Robert Ferguson .75 2.00
47 Michael Vick 1.25 3.00
48 Clinton Portis 1.25 3.00
49 Curtis Martin 1.25 3.00
50 Philip Rivers 1.25 3.00

2006 Donruss Gridiron Gear Performers Autographs

STATED PRINT RUN 1-250 SER.#'d SETS
SERIAL #'d UNDER 25 NOT PRICED
1 Jim Otto/35 10.00 25.00
3 Craig Morton/25 10.00 25.00
4 Paul Krause/50 8.00 20.00
5 Joe Greene/25
6 Thurman Thomas/35 12.00 30.00
7 Lee Roy Selmon/40 12.00 30.00
8 Lester Hayes/250 8.00 20.00
9 Ozzie Newsome/40 8.00 20.00
10 Jim Plunkett/35 10.00 25.00
11 Mark Gastineau/35 10.00 25.00
13 Boomer Esiason/35 15.00 40.00
14 Herschel Walker/35 15.00 40.00
18 Jim Kelly/25 20.00 50.00
20 Tedy Bruschi/250 25.00 50.00
28 Marc Bulger/45 10.00 25.00
38 Darrell Jackson/25 10.00 25.00
41 Dallas Clark/25 10.00 25.00
43 LaDainian Tomlinson/25 50.00 100.00
44 Shaun Alexander/25 25.00 50.00

2006 Donruss Gridiron Gear Performers Jerseys

STATED PRINT RUN 43-200 SER.#'d SETS
*COMBOS/25-50: .5X TO 1.2X BASIC INSERTS
COMBO AUTOS/1-10 NOT PRICED
*COMBO PRM/25: .8X TO 2X BASIC INSERTS
COMBO PRIME AUTOS/1-25 NOT PRICED
*JUMBO SWATCH/25-30: .6X TO 1.5X BASIC INSERTS
UNPRICED JUMBO PRIME PRINT RUN 10
*PRIME/25: .8X TO 2X BASIC INSERTS
PRIME AUTOS/1-25 NOT PRICED
*RED: .4X TO 1X BASIC INSERTS
1 Jim Otto/100 4.00 10.00
2 Paul Warfield/100 4.00 10.00
3 Craig Morton/100 3.00 8.00
4 Paul Krause/200 3.00 8.00
5 Joe Greene/43 6.00 15.00
6 Thurman Thomas/100 4.00 10.00
7 Lee Roy Selmon/200 4.00 10.00
9 Ozzie Newsome/100 4.00 10.00
10 Jim Plunkett/150 3.00 8.00
11 Mark Gastineau/100 4.00 10.00
12 Henry Ellard/200 3.00 8.00
13 Boomer Esiason/200 3.00 8.00
14 Herschel Walker/75 3.00 8.00
15 Eric Dickerson/100 3.00 8.00
16 Dan Marino/100 10.00 25.00
17 Barry Sanders/100 8.00 20.00
18 Jim Kelly/100 5.00 12.00
21 T.J. Houshmandzadeh/100 3.00 8.00
22 Rudi Johnson/100 3.00 8.00
23 Steve Smith/100 4.00 10.00
24 Peyton Manning/100 6.00 15.00
25 Brett Favre/100 8.00 20.00
26 Torry Holt/100 3.00 8.00
27 Donovan McNabb/100 4.00 10.00
28 Marc Bulger/100 3.00 8.00
29 Alge Crumpler/100 3.00 8.00
30 Larry Johnson/100 4.00 10.00
32 Charlie Frye/100 4.00 10.00
33 Carson Palmer/94 4.00 10.00
34 Samkon Gado/100 4.00 10.00
35 Javon Walker/100 3.00 8.00
36 Tiki Barber/100 4.00 10.00
37 Reuben Droughns/100 2.50 6.00
38 Darrell Jackson/100 3.00 8.00
39 Chris Chambers/100 3.00 8.00
40 Ben Roethlisberger/100 8.00 20.00
41 Dallas Clark/100 2.50 6.00
42 Reggie Brown/100 2.50 6.00
43 LaDainian Tomlinson/100 4.00 10.00
44 Shaun Alexander/100 4.00 10.00
45 Marvin Harrison/100 4.00 10.00
46 Robert Ferguson/100 2.50 6.00
47 Michael Vick/100 4.00 10.00
48 Clinton Portis/100 4.00 10.00
49 Curtis Martin/100 4.00 10.00
50 Philip Rivers/100 4.00 10.00

2006 Donruss Gridiron Gear Performers Jerseys Autographs

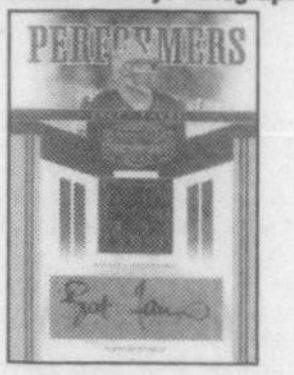

STATED PRINT RUN 1-30 SER.#'d SETS
SERIAL #'d UNDER 25 NOT PRICED
1 Jim Otto/25
4 Paul Krause/30 10.00 25.00
7 Lee Roy Selmon/25 25.00 50.00
9 Ozzie Newsome/25 10.00 25.00
10 Jim Plunkett/25 12.00 30.00
11 Mark Gastineau/25 12.00 30.00
18 Jim Kelly/25 25.00 60.00
28 Marc Bulger/25 12.00 30.00

2006 Donruss Gridiron Gear Plates and Patches

STATED PRINT RUN 25-100 SER.#'d SETS
1 Tom Brady/100 12.00 30.00
2 LaDainian Tomlinson/47 10.00 25.00
3 Hines Ward/50 10.00 25.00
4 Matt Hasselbeck/50 8.00 20.00
5 Willis McGahee/100 8.00 20.00
6 Carson Palmer/50 10.00 25.00
7 Shaun Alexander/25 10.00 25.00
8 Ben Roethlisberger/25 20.00 50.00
9 Steve Smith/50 8.00 20.00
10 Tiki Barber/50 8.00 20.00
11 Peyton Manning/50 15.00 40.00
12 Torry Holt/90 6.00 15.00
13 Michael Vick/80 8.00 20.00
14 Ahman Green/100 6.00 15.00

2006 Donruss Gridiron Gear Playbook Gold

GOLD PRINT RUN 500 SER.#'d SETS
*RED: .3X TO .8X GOLD/500
*SILVER/250: .5X TO 1.2X GOLD/500
SILVER PRINT RUN 250 SER.#'d SETS
*HOLOGOLD/100: .6X TO 1.5X GOLD/500
HOLOGOLD PRINT RUN 100 SER.#'d SETS
*PLATINUM/25: 1X TO 2.5X GOLD/500
PLATINUM PRINT RUN 25 SER.#'d SETS
1 Steve Smith 1.25 3.00
2 Chad Johnson 1.00 2.50
3 Julius Jones .75 2.00
4 Brett Favre 2.50 6.00
5 Peyton Manning 2.00 5.00
6 Marvin Harrison 1.25 3.00
7 Larry Johnson 1.00 2.50
8 Tiki Barber 1.25 3.00
9 Ben Roethlisberger 1.50 4.00
10 Antonio Gates 1.25 3.00
11 Carson Palmer 1.25 3.00
12 Shaun Alexander 1.00 2.50
13 Hines Ward 1.25 3.00
14 Donte Stallworth .75 2.00
15 Anquan Boldin 1.00 2.50
16 Curtis Martin 1.25 3.00
17 Willis McGahee 1.00 2.50
18 Clinton Portis 1.25 3.00
19 Donovan McNabb 1.25 3.00
20 Tom Brady 2.00 5.00
21 Tatum Bell .75 2.00
22 Tony Gonzalez 1.00 2.50
23 Michael Vick 1.25 3.00
24 Byron Leftwich 1.00 2.50
25 Randy Moss 1.25 3.00

2006 Donruss Gridiron Gear Playbook Jerseys O's

O's PRINT RUN 250 SER.#'d SETS
*X's/250: .4X TO 1X O's JERSEYS
*PATCHES/25: 1X TO 2.5X JSY O's
1 Steve Smith 3.00 8.00
2 Chad Johnson 2.50 6.00
3 Julius Jones 2.00 5.00
4 Brett Favre 6.00 15.00
5 Peyton Manning 5.00 12.00
6 Marvin Harrison 3.00 8.00
7 Larry Johnson 2.50 6.00
8 Tiki Barber 3.00 8.00
9 Ben Roethlisberger 4.00 10.00
10 Antonio Gates 3.00 8.00
11 Carson Palmer 3.00 8.00
12 Shaun Alexander 2.50 6.00
13 Hines Ward 3.00 8.00
14 Donte Stallworth 2.00 5.00
15 Anquan Boldin 2.50 6.00
16 Curtis Martin 3.00 8.00
17 Willis McGahee 2.50 6.00
18 Clinton Portis 3.00 8.00
19 Donovan McNabb 3.00 8.00
20 Tom Brady 5.00 12.00
21 Tatum Bell 2.00 5.00
22 Tony Gonzalez 2.50 6.00
23 Michael Vick 3.00 8.00
24 Byron Leftwich 2.50 6.00
25 Randy Moss 3.00 8.00

2006 Donruss Gridiron Gear Player Timeline Gold

GOLD PRINT RUN 500 SER.#'d SETS
*RED: .3X TO .8X GOLD/500
*SILVER/250: .5X TO 1.2X GOLD/500
SILVER PRINT RUN 250 SER.#'d SETS
*HOLOGOLD/100: .6X TO 1.5X GOLD/500
HOLOGOLD PRINT RUN 100 SER.#'d SETS
*PLATINUM/25: 1X TO 2.5X GOLD/500
PLATINUM PRINT RUN 25 SER.#'d SETS
1 Barry Sanders 2.50 6.00
2 Ronnie Brown 1.25 3.00
3 Laveranues Coles .75 2.00
4 Lee Evans 1.00 2.50
5 Andre Johnson 1.25 3.00
6 Drew Bledsoe 1.25 3.00
7 Santana Moss 1.00 2.50
8 Willis McGahee 1.00 2.50
9 Braylon Edwards 1.00 2.50
10 Ahman Green 1.00 2.50
11 Julius Jones .75 2.00
12 Roy Williams S 1.00 2.50
13 Thurman Thomas 1.25 3.00
14 Dan Marino 3.00 8.00
15 Tony Dorsett 1.50 4.00
16 Joe Greene 1.50 4.00
17 Eric Dickerson 1.25 3.00
18 Lawrence Taylor 1.50 4.00
19 Kevin Jones .75 2.00
20 Peyton Manning 2.00 5.00
21 Cadillac Williams 1.00 2.50
22 Mike Hass .60 1.50

23 Joseph Addai .75 2.00
24 Mario Williams .75 2.00
25 Demetrius Williams .60 1.50
26 Marcedes Lewis .75 2.00
27 Sinorice Moss .75 2.00
28 Jay Cutler 1.50 4.00
29 LenDale White .60 1.50
30 A.J. Hawk .75 2.00
31 Laurence Maroney .60 1.50
32 Maurice Drew 1.25 3.00
33 Maurice Stovall .50 1.25
34 Travis Wilson .50 1.25
35 Curtis Martin 1.25 3.00
36 Jeremy Shockey 1.25 3.00
37 Paul Warfield 1.25 3.00
38 Michael Clayton .75 2.00
39 Roy Williams WR 1.00 2.50
40 Deion Sanders 1.50 4.00

2006 Donruss Gridiron Gear Player Timeline Autographs

STATED PRINT RUN 5-50 SER.#'d SETS
4 Lee Evans/20 10.00 25.00
13 Thurman Thomas/25 15.00 40.00
15 Tony Dorsett/20 25.00 50.00
16 Joe Greene/25
17 Eric Dickerson/25 15.00 40.00
18 Lawrence Taylor/50 20.00 50.00
24 Mario Williams/25 12.00 30.00
25 Demetrius Williams/25 10.00 25.00
26 Marcedes Lewis/35 8.00 20.00
27 Sinorice Moss/25 10.00 25.00
28 Jay Cutler/35 50.00 120.00
29 LenDale White/30 10.00 25.00
30 A.J. Hawk/30 30.00 80.00
31 Laurence Maroney/35 12.00 30.00
32 Maurice Drew/30 25.00 60.00
33 Maurice Stovall/35 6.00 15.00
34 Travis Wilson/35 6.00 15.00
39 Roy Williams WR/25 10.00 25.00
40 Deion Sanders/50 20.00 40.00

2006 Donruss Gridiron Gear Player Timeline Jerseys

STATED PRINT RUN 75-250 SER.#'d SETS
*COMBOS/75-100: .5X TO 1.2X BASIC JSYs
*COMBOS/40 59: .6X TO 1.5X BASIC JSYs
*COMBO PRIME/37-50: .8X TO 2X
*JUMBO SWATCH/25-50: .6X TO 1.5X
*PRIME/25-50: .8X TO 2X BASIC JSYs
*JUMBO SWATCH PRIME/25: 1X TO 2.5X
*RED: .4X TO 1X BASIC JSYs
1 Barry Sanders/100 10.00 25.00
2 Ronnie Brown/250 4.00 10.00
3 Laveranues Coles/139 2.50 6.00
4 Lee Evans/250 3.00 8.00
5 Andre Johnson/200 3.00 8.00
6 Drew Bledsoe/175 4.00 10.00
7 Santana Moss/200 3.00 8.00
8 Willis McGahee/250 3.00 8.00
9 Braylon Edwards/200 3.00 8.00
10 Ahman Green/200 3.00 8.00
11 Julius Jones/200 2.50 6.00
12 Roy Williams S/200 3.00 8.00
13 Thurman Thomas/250 5.00 12.00
14 Dan Marino/150 12.00 30.00
15 Tony Dorsett/250 6.00 15.00
16 Joe Greene/250 6.00 15.00
17 Eric Dickerson/150 5.00 12.00
18 Lawrence Taylor/200 6.00 15.00
19 Kevin Jones/200 2.50 6.00
20 Peyton Manning/150 6.00 15.00
21 Cadillac Williams/200 3.00 8.00
22 Mike Hass/250 1.50 4.00
23 Joseph Addai/250 2.00 5.00
24 Mario Williams/250 2.00 5.00
25 Demetrius Williams/250 1.50 4.00
26 Marcedes Lewis/250 2.00 5.00
27 Sinorice Moss/250 2.00 5.00
28 Jay Cutler/250 4.00 10.00
29 LenDale White/250 1.50 4.00
30 A.J. Hawk/250 4.00 10.00
31 Laurence Maroney/250 1.50 4.00
32 Maurice Drew/250 3.00 8.00
33 Maurice Stovall/250 1.25 3.00
34 Travis Wilson/250 1.25 3.00
35 Curtis Martin/75 4.00 10.00
36 Jeremy Shockey/250 4.00 10.00
37 Paul Warfield/75 5.00 12.00
38 Michael Clayton/250 2.50 6.00
39 Roy Williams WR/250 3.00 8.00
40 Deion Sanders/250 5.00 12.00

2006 Donruss Gridiron Gear Player Timeline Jerseys Autographs

STATED PRINT RUN 1-50
UNPRICED JSY COMBO AU PRINT RUN 1-20
UNPRICED COMBO PRIME PRINT RUN 1-15
UNPRICED PRIME PRINT RUN 1-25
16 Joe Greene/25 30.00 60.00
18 Lawrence Taylor/30 30.00 60.00
20 Peyton Manning/25 75.00 135.00
23 Joseph Addai/25 25.00 60.00
26 Marcedes Lewis/25 10.00 25.00
28 Jay Cutler/25 60.00 150.00
29 LenDale White/25 12.00 30.00
30 A.J. Hawk/25 30.00 80.00
31 Laurence Maroney/25
32 Maurice Drew/25 30.00 80.00
33 Maurice Stovall/30 8.00 20.00
34 Travis Wilson/30 8.00 20.00
40 Deion Sanders/50 30.00 60.00

2006 Donruss Gridiron Gear Rivals Gold

GOLD PRINT RUN 500 SER.#'d SETS
*RED: .3X TO .8X GOLD/500
*SILVER/250: .5X TO 1.2X GOLD/500
SILVER PRINT RUN 250 SER.#'d SETS
*HOLOGOLD/100: .6X TO 1.5X GOLD/500
HOLOGOLD PRINT RUN 100 SER.#'d SETS
*PLATINUM/25: 1X TO 2.5X GOLD/500
PLATINUM PRINT RUN 25 SER.#'d SETS
1 Lawrence Taylor 2.00 5.00
Joe Theismann
2 Peyton Manning 3.00 8.00
Ben Roethlisberger
3 Curtis Martin 2.00 5.00
Shaun Alexander
4 Y.A. Tittle 2.00 5.00
Yale Lary
5 Dan Marino 4.00 10.00
Jim Kelly
6 Walter Payton 4.00 10.00
Tony Dorsett
7 Barry Sanders 3.00 8.00
Thurman Thomas
8 Clinton Portis 2.00 5.00
Roy Williams S
9 Brian Urlacher 2.00 5.00
Ahman Green
10 Terry Glenn 1.50 4.00
Santana Moss
11 Daryle Lamonica 1.50 4.00
Lance Alworth
12 Paul Warfield 1.50 4.00
Cliff Branch
13 LaDainian Tomlinson 2.00 5.00
Larry Johnson
14 Julius Jones 1.50 4.00
Thomas Jones
15 Chad Johnson 2.50 6.00
Troy Polamalu

2006 Donruss Gridiron Gear Rivals Jerseys

STATED PRINT RUN 100 SER.#'d SETS
*PRIME/25-30: .8X TO 2X BASIC JSYs
PRIME PRINT RUN 10-30 SER.#'d SETS
1 Lawrence Taylor 8.00 20.00
Joe Theismann
2 Peyton Manning 10.00 25.00
Ben Roethlisberger
3 Curtis Martin 6.00 15.00
Shaun Alexander
4 Y.A. Tittle 8.00 20.00
Yale Lary
5 Dan Marino 12.00 30.00
Jim Kelly
6 Walter Payton 15.00 40.00
Tony Dorsett
7 Barry Sanders 12.00 30.00
Thurman Thomas
8 Clinton Portis 6.00 15.00
Roy Williams S
9 Brian Urlacher 6.00 15.00
Ahman Green
10 Terry Glenn 6.00 15.00
Santana Moss
11 Daryle Lamonica 8.00 20.00
Lance Alworth
12 Paul Warfield 8.00 20.00
Cliff Branch
13 LaDainian Tomlinson 8.00 20.00
Larry Johnson
14 Julius Jones 6.00 15.00
Thomas Jones
15 Chad Johnson 8.00 20.00
Troy Polamalu

2006 Donruss Gridiron Gear Rookie Jerseys

*SINGLES/50: .3X TO .8X BASIC RCs
STATED PRINT RUN 50 SER.#'d SETS

2006 Donruss Gridiron Gear Rookie Jerseys Combos

*COMBOS/50: .4X TO 1X BASIC RCs
STATED PRINT RUN 50 SER.#'d SETS

2006 Donruss Gridiron Gear Rookie Jerseys Combos Prime

*COMBO PRIME/50: .6X TO 1.5X BASIC RCs
PRIME PRINT RUN 50 SER.#'d SETS

2006 Donruss Gridiron Gear Rookie Jerseys Jumbo Swatch Prime

*JUMBO PRIME: .5X TO 1.2X BASIC RCs
PRIME/150 ANNOUNCED PRINT RUN 50

2006 Donruss Gridiron Gear Rookie Jerseys Prime

*PRIME/50: .4X TO 1X BASIC RCs
PRIME PRINT RUN 50 SER.#'d SETS

2006 Donruss Gridiron Gear Rookie Jerseys Retail Red

*RETAIL/50: .3X TO .8X BASIC RCs
RETAIL PRINT RUN 50 SER.#'d SETS

2006 Donruss Gridiron Gear Rookie Jerseys Trios

*TRIOS/50: .6X TO 1.5X BASIC RCs
STATED PRINT RUN 50 SER.#'d SETS

2006 Donruss Gridiron Gear Rookie Jerseys Trios Prime

*TRIO PRIME/50: .8X TO 2X BASIC RCs
TRIO PRIME PRINT RUN 50 SER.#'d SETS

2006 Donruss Gridiron Gear Rookie Jerseys Autographs

AUTO PRINT RUN 50 SER.#'d SETS
*COMBO AU/50: .4X TO 1X BASIC INSERTS
*PRIME: .5X TO 1.2X BASIC INSERTS
*COMBO PRIME AU/50: .5X TO 1.2X
201 Brian Calhoun 6.00 15.00
202 Joe Klopfenstein 6.00 15.00
203 Travis Wilson 6.00 15.00
204 Charlie Whitehurst 10.00 25.00
205 DeAngelo Williams 12.00 30.00
206 Maurice Stovall 6.00 15.00
207 A.J. Hawk 10.00 25.00
208 Kellen Clemens 8.00 20.00
209 Leon Washington 8.00 20.00
210 Sinorice Moss 10.00 25.00
211 Demetrius Williams 8.00 20.00
212 Jerious Norwood 8.00 20.00
213 Santonio Holmes 12.00 30.00
214 Omar Jacobs 6.00 15.00
215 Brandon Marshall 10.00 25.00
216 Jason Avant 6.00 15.00
217 Derek Hagan 8.00 20.00
218 Brandon Williams 6.00 15.00
219 Vernon Davis 12.00 30.00
220 Michael Robinson 8.00 20.00
221 Matt Leinart 10.00 25.00
222 Reggie Bush 40.00 80.00
223 LenDale White 8.00 20.00
224 Vince Young 12.00 30.00
225 Maurice Drew 15.00 40.00
226 Marcedes Lewis 10.00 25.00
227 Mario Williams 10.00 25.00
228 Michael Huff 8.00 20.00
229 Tarvaris Jackson 10.00 25.00
230 Laurence Maroney 8.00 20.00
231 Chad Jackson 6.00 15.00

2006 Donruss Gridiron Gear Rookie Jerseys Jumbo Swatch Autographs

AUTO/150 ANNOUNCED PRINT RUN 50
201 Brian Calhoun 8.00 20.00
202 Joe Klopfenstein 8.00 20.00
203 Travis Wilson 8.00 20.00
204 Charlie Whitehurst 12.00 30.00
205 DeAngelo Williams 15.00 40.00
206 Maurice Stovall 8.00 20.00
207 A.J. Hawk 12.00 30.00
208 Kellen Clemens 10.00 25.00
209 Leon Washington 10.00 25.00
210 Sinorice Moss 12.00 30.00
211 Demetrius Williams 10.00 25.00
212 Jerious Norwood 10.00 25.00
213 Santonio Holmes 15.00 40.00
214 Omar Jacobs 8.00 20.00
215 Brandon Marshall 12.00 30.00
216 Jason Avant 8.00 20.00
217 Derek Hagan 10.00 25.00
218 Brandon Williams 8.00 20.00
219 Vernon Davis 15.00 40.00
220 Michael Robinson 10.00 25.00
221 Matt Leinart 12.00 30.00
222 Reggie Bush 40.00 100.00
223 LenDale White 10.00 25.00
224 Vince Young 15.00 40.00
225 Maurice Drew 20.00 50.00
226 Marcedes Lewis 12.00 30.00
227 Mario Williams 12.00 30.00
228 Michael Huff 10.00 25.00
229 Tarvaris Jackson 12.00 30.00
230 Laurence Maroney 10.00 25.00
231 Chad Jackson 8.00 20.00

2007 Donruss Gridiron Gear

This 234-card set was released in October, 2007. The set was issued into the hobby in five-card packs, with a $6 SRP, which came 18 packs to a box. The set is divided into veterans (1-100) and 2007 NFL rookies (101-234). Within the Rookie Card grouping there are two subsets: Cards numbered 101-200 were issued to a stated print run of 599 serial numbered sets and cards numbered 201-234 which were signed by the player were issued to a stated print run of 100 serial numbered sets.

COMP.SET w/o RC's (100) 10.00 25.00
101-200 ROOKIE PRINT RUN 599
201-234 AU ROOKIE PRINT RUN 100
1 Tony Romo .50 1.25
2 Julius Jones .25 .60
3 Terrell Owens .40 1.00
4 Eli Manning .40 1.00
5 Plaxico Burress .30 .75
6 Jeremy Shockey .30 .75
7 Brandon Jacobs .30 .75
8 Donovan McNabb .40 1.00
9 Brian Westbrook .30 .75
10 Reggie Brown .25 .60
11 Jason Campbell .30 .75
12 Clinton Portis .30 .75
13 Santana Moss .30 .75
14 Rex Grossman .30 .75
15 Cedric Benson .30 .75
16 Muhsin Muhammad .30 .75
17 Jon Kitna .25 .60
18 Roy Williams WR .30 .75
19 Tatum Bell .25 .60
20 Brett Favre .75 2.00
21 Donald Driver .40 1.00
22 Greg Jennings .40 1.00
23 Tarvaris Jackson .25 .60
24 Chester Taylor .25 .60
25 Joe Horn .30 .75
26 Warrick Dunn .30 .75
27 Alge Crumpler .30 .75
28 Jake Delhomme .30 .75
29 Steve Smith .30 .75
30 DeAngelo Williams .40 1.00
31 Drew Brees .40 1.00
32 Deuce McAllister .30 .75
33 Reggie Bush .40 1.00
34 Jeff Garcia .30 .75
35 Cadillac Williams .30 .75
36 Joey Galloway .30 .75
37 Matt Leinart .30 .75
38 Edgerrin James .30 .75
39 Anquan Boldin .30 .75
40 Larry Fitzgerald .40 1.00
41 Marc Bulger .30 .75
42 Steven Jackson .40 1.00
43 Torry Holt .30 .75
44 Alex Smith QB .40 1.00
45 Frank Gore .40 1.00
46 Vernon Davis .30 .75
47 Darrell Jackson .25 .60
48 Matt Hasselbeck .30 .75
49 Shaun Alexander .30 .75
50 Deion Branch .30 .75
51 J.P. Losman .25 .60
52 Lee Evans .30 .75
53 Josh Reed .25 .60
54 Trent Green .30 .75
55 Ronnie Brown .30 .75
56 Chris Chambers .30 .75
57 Tom Brady .60 1.50
58 Laurence Maroney .30 .75
59 Randy Moss .40 1.00
60 Chad Pennington .30 .75
61 Laveranues Coles .25 .60
62 Leon Washington .30 .75
63 Steve McNair .30 .75
64 Willis McGahee .30 .75
65 Mark Clayton .30 .75
66 Carson Palmer .30 .75
67 Rudi Johnson .30 .75
68 Chad Johnson .30 .75
69 T.J. Houshmandzadeh .30 .75
70 Charlie Frye .30 .75
71 Braylon Edwards .30 .75
72 Jamal Lewis .30 .75
73 Ben Roethlisberger .40 1.00
74 Willie Parker .30 .75
75 Hines Ward .40 1.00
76 Ahman Green .30 .75
77 Andre Johnson .30 .75
78 Matt Schaub .30 .75
79 Peyton Manning .60 1.50
80 Joseph Addai .30 .75
81 Marvin Harrison .40 1.00
82 Reggie Wayne .30 .75
83 Byron Leftwich .30 .75
84 Fred Taylor .30 .75
85 Maurice Jones-Drew .40 1.00
86 Vince Young .30 .75
87 LenDale White .30 .75
88 Brandon Jones .25 .60
89 Jay Cutler .40 1.00
90 Javon Walker .30 .75
91 Mike Bell .30 .75
92 Larry Johnson .25 .60
93 Tony Gonzalez .30 .75
94 Brodie Croyle .30 .75
95 Andrew Walter .25 .60
96 LaMont Jordan .30 .75
97 Philip Rivers .40 1.00
98 LaDainian Tomlinson .40 1.00
99 Vincent Jackson .30 .75
100 Antonio Gates .40 1.00
101 A.J. Davis RC 1.50 4.00
102 Aaron Ross RC 2.50 6.00
103 Aaron Rouse RC 2.00 5.00
104 Adam Carriker RC 2.00 5.00
105 Ahmad Bradshaw RC 4.00 10.00
106 Alan Branch RC 2.00 5.00
107 Alonzo Coleman RC 2.00 5.00
108 Amobi Okoye RC 2.50 6.00
109 Anthony Spencer RC 2.50 6.00
110 Aundrae Allison RC 1.50 4.00
111 Ben Patrick RC 2.00 5.00
112 Brandon Meriweather RC 2.50 6.00
113 Buster Davis RC 2.00 5.00
114 Chansi Stuckey RC 2.50 6.00
115 Charles Johnson RC 1.50 4.00
116 Chris Davis RC 1.50 4.00
117 Chris Houston RC 2.00 5.00
118 Chris Leak RC 2.00 5.00
119 Courtney Taylor RC 2.00 5.00
120 Craig Buster Davis RC 2.00 5.00
121 Dallas Baker RC 1.50 4.00
122 Dan Bazuin RC 2.00 5.00
123 Darius Walker RC 1.50 4.00
124 Darrelle Revis RC 4.00 10.00
125 David Ball RC 2.00 5.00
126 David Clowney RC 2.00 5.00
127 David Harris RC 2.00 5.00
128 David Irons RC 1.50 4.00
129 Daymeion Hughes RC 2.00 5.00
130 DeShawn Wynn RC 2.00 5.00
131 Dwayne Wright RC 2.00 5.00
132 Earl Everett RC 2.00 5.00
133 Eric Frampton RC 2.00 5.00
134 Eric Weddle RC 2.50 6.00
135 Eric Wright RC 2.50 6.00
136 Fred Bennett RC 1.50 4.00
137 Zak DeOssie RC 2.00 5.00
138 Gary Russell RC 2.00 5.00
139 H.B. Blades RC 1.50 4.00
140 Ikaika Alama-Francis RC 2.50 6.00
141 Isaiah Stanback RC 1.50 4.00
142 Jacoby Jones RC 2.50 6.00
143 Jamaal Anderson RC 2.00 5.00
144 James Jones RC 2.50 6.00
145 Jared Zabransky RC 2.00 5.00
146 Jarrett Hicks RC 2.00 5.00
147 Jarvis Moss RC 2.00 5.00
148 Jason Snelling RC 2.50 6.00
149 Jeff Rowe RC 1.50 4.00
150 Joel Filani RC 2.00 5.00
151 Jon Beason RC 2.00 5.00
152 Jonathan Wade RC 2.00 5.00
153 Jordan Kent RC 2.00 5.00
154 Jordan Palmer RC 2.00 5.00
155 Josh Gattis RC 1.50 4.00
156 Josh Wilson RC 2.00 5.00
157 Kenneth Darby RC 2.00 5.00
158 Kenny Scott RC 1.50 4.00
159 Kolby Smith RC 2.00 5.00
160 LaMarr Woodley RC 2.50 6.00
161 LaRon Landry RC 2.50 6.00
162 Laurent Robinson RC 2.50 6.00
163 Lawrence Timmons RC 2.50 6.00
164 Legedu Naanee RC 2.50 6.00
165 Leon Hall RC 2.00 5.00
166 Levi Brown RC 2.50 6.00
167 Marcus McCauley RC 2.00 5.00
168 Matt Spaeth RC 2.50 6.00
169 Michael Griffin RC 2.50 6.00
170 Michael Okwo RC 2.00 5.00
171 Mike Walker RC 2.50 6.00
172 Nate Ilaoa RC 2.00 5.00
173 Paul Posluszny RC 2.50 6.00
174 Quentin Moses RC 2.00 5.00
175 Ray McDonald RC 2.00 5.00
176 Reggie Ball RC 2.00 5.00
177 Reggie Nelson RC 2.00 5.00
178 Rhema McKnight RC 1.50 4.00
179 Jerard Rabb RC 2.00 5.00
180 Roy Hall RC 2.50 6.00
181 Rufus Alexander RC 2.00 5.00
182 Ryan McBean RC 2.50 6.00
183 Ryne Robinson RC 2.00 5.00
184 Sabby Piscitelli RC 2.50 6.00
185 Scott Chandler RC 2.50 6.00
186 Selvin Young RC 2.00 5.00
187 Steve Breaston RC 2.50 6.00
188 Stewart Bradley RC 2.00 5.00
189 Syndric Steptoe RC 2.00 5.00
190 Mason Crosby RC 2.00 5.00
191 Demarcus Tank Tyler RC 1.50 4.00
192 Thomas Clayton RC 2.00 5.00
193 Tim Crowder RC 2.50 6.00
194 Tim Shaw RC 2.00 5.00
195 Toby Korrodi RC 2.00 5.00
196 Tyler Palko RC 2.00 5.00
197 Tyler Thigpen RC 2.50 6.00
198 Daniel Sepulveda RC 2.50 6.00
199 Victor Abiamiri RC 2.50 6.00
200 Zach Miller RC 2.50 6.00
201 Marshawn Lynch AU RC 20.00 40.00
202 Yamon Figurs AU RC 8.00 20.00
203 Joe Thomas AU RC 12.00 30.00
204 Brandon Jackson AU RC 10.00 25.00
205 Steve Smith USC AU RC 12.00 30.00
206 Ted Ginn AU RC 10.00 25.00
207 Dwayne Bowe AU RC 15.00 40.00
208 Anthony Gonzalez AU RC 12.00 30.00
209 Sidney Rice AU RC 15.00 40.00
210 Chris Henry RB AU RC 8.00 20.00
211 Trent Edwards AU RC 12.00 30.00
212 Calvin Johnson AU RC 60.00 120.00
213 Greg Olsen AU RC 10.00 25.00
214 Antonio Pittman AU RC 8.00 20.00
215 Kevin Kolb AU RC 20.00 50.00
216 Adrian Peterson AU RC 125.00 250.00
217 Brian Leonard AU RC 10.00 25.00
218 Patrick Willis AU RC 25.00 60.00
219 Jason Hill AU RC 12.00 30.00
220 Robert Meachem AU RC 12.00 30.00
221 Michael Bush AU RC 12.00 30.00
222 Tony Hunt AU RC 8.00 20.00
223 Garrett Wolfe AU RC 8.00 20.00
224 Paul Williams AU RC 8.00 20.00
225 Brady Quinn AU RC 12.00 30.00
226 Gaines Adams AU RC 12.00 30.00
227 JaMarcus Russell AU RC 8.00 20.00
228 Dwayne Jarrett AU RC 10.00 25.00
229 Johnnie Lee Higgins AU RC 10.00 25.00
230 Drew Stanton AU RC 8.00 20.00
231 Troy Smith AU RC 12.00 30.00
232 Lorenzo Booker AU RC 10.00 25.00
233 Kenny Irons AU RC 8.00 20.00
234 John Beck AU RC 12.00 30.00

2007 Donruss Gridiron Gear Gold Holofoil

*VETS 1-100: 1.5X TO 4X BASIC CARDS
STATED PRINT RUN 200 SER.#'d SETS

2007 Donruss Gridiron Gear Gold Holofoil O's

*VETS 1-100: 2.5X TO 6X BASIC CARDS
*ROOKIES 101-200: .6X TO 1.5X BASIC CARDS
STATED PRINT RUN 100 SER.#'d SETS

2007 Donruss Gridiron Gear Gold Holofoil X's

*VETS 1-100: 2.5X TO 6X BASIC CARDS
*ROOKIES 101-200: .6X TO 1.5X BASIC CARDS
STATED PRINT RUN 100 SER.#'d SETS

2007 Donruss Gridiron Gear Platinum Holofoil

*VETS 1-100: 3X TO 8X BASIC CARDS
STATED PRINT RUN 50 SER.#'d SETS

2007 Donruss Gridiron Gear Platinum Holofoil O's

*VETS 1-100: 5X TO 12X BASIC CARDS
*ROOKIES 101-200: 1X TO 2.5X BASIC CARDS
STATED PRINT RUN 25 SER.#'d SETS

2007 Donruss Gridiron Gear Platinum Holofoil X's

*VETS 1-100: 5X TO 12X BASIC CARDS
*ROOKIES 101-200: 1X TO 2.5X BASIC CARDS
STATED PRINT RUN 25 SER.#'d SETS

2007 Donruss Gridiron Gear Red Holofoil

*VETS 1-100: .8X TO 2X BASIC CARDS

2007 Donruss Gridiron Gear Silver Holofoil

*VETS 1-100: 1X TO 2.5X BASIC CARDS

2007 Donruss Gridiron Gear Silver Holofoil O's

*VETS 1-100: 1.5X TO 4X BASIC CARDS
STATED PRINT RUN 250 SER.#'d SETS

2007 Donruss Gridiron Gear Silver Holofoil X's

*VETS 1-100: 1.5X TO 4X BASIC CARDS
STATED PRINT RUN 250 SER.#'d SETS

2007 Donruss Gridiron Gear Autographs Gold Holofoil

GOLD HOLOFOIL PRINT RUN 5-250
SERIAL #'d UNDER 25 NOT PRICED
102 Aaron Ross/250 4.00 10.00
104 Adam Carriker/100 4.00 10.00
108 Amobi Okoye/100 5.00 12.00
111 Ben Patrick/250 3.00 8.00
112 Brandon Meriweather/250 4.00 10.00
114 Chansi Stuckey/100 5.00 12.00
116 Chris Davis/100 3.00 8.00
118 Chris Leak/100 4.00 10.00
119 Courtney Taylor/100 4.00 10.00
122 Dan Bazuin/250 3.00 8.00
123 Darius Walker/250 2.50 6.00
124 Darrelle Revis/100 8.00 20.00
126 David Clowney/100 4.00 10.00
127 David Harris/250 3.00 8.00
130 DeShawn Wynn/100 4.00 10.00
131 Dwayne Wright/100 4.00 10.00
133 Eric Frampton/250 3.00 8.00
136 Fred Bennett/250 2.50 6.00
141 Isaiah Stanback/100 3.00 8.00
142 Jacoby Jones/100 5.00 12.00
143 Jamaal Anderson/100 4.00 10.00
144 James Jones/100 5.00 12.00
148 Jason Snelling/250 4.00 10.00
149 Jeff Rowe/100 3.00 8.00
150 Joel Filani/100 4.00 10.00
159 Kolby Smith/100 4.00 10.00
160 LaMarr Woodley/250 8.00 20.00
161 LaRon Landry/100 5.00 12.00
162 Laurent Robinson/100 5.00 12.00
163 Lawrence Timmons/100 5.00 12.00
165 Leon Hall/100 4.00 10.00
166 Levi Brown/250 4.00 10.00
169 Michael Griffin/250 4.00 10.00
173 Paul Posluszny/100 5.00 12.00
174 Quentin Moses/250 3.00 8.00
175 Ray McDonald/250 3.00 8.00
176 Reggie Ball/250 3.00 8.00
177 Reggie Nelson/100 4.00 10.00
184 Sabby Piscitelli/250 4.00 10.00
185 Scott Chandler/100 5.00 12.00
193 Tim Crowder/250 4.00 10.00
199 Victor Abiamiri/250 4.00 10.00
200 Zach Miller/100 5.00 12.00

2007 Donruss Gridiron Gear Autographs Platinum Holofoil

102 Aaron Ross/25 8.00 20.00
103 Aaron Rouse/25 6.00 15.00
104 Adam Carriker/25 6.00 15.00
105 Ahmad Bradshaw/25 15.00 40.00
108 Amobi Okoye/25 8.00 20.00
109 Anthony Spencer/25 8.00 20.00
111 Ben Patrick/25 6.00 15.00
112 Brandon Meriweather/25 8.00 20.00
114 Chansi Stuckey/25 8.00 20.00
116 Chris Davis/25 5.00 12.00
117 Chris Houston/25 6.00 15.00
118 Chris Leak/25 6.00 15.00
119 Courtney Taylor/25 6.00 15.00
121 Dallas Baker/25 5.00 12.00
122 Dan Bazuin/25 6.00 15.00
123 Darius Walker/25 5.00 12.00
124 Darrelle Revis/25 12.00 30.00
126 David Clowney/25 6.00 15.00
127 David Harris/25 6.00 15.00
128 David Irons/25 5.00 12.00
129 Daymeion Hughes/25 6.00 15.00
130 DeShawn Wynn/25 6.00 15.00
131 Dwayne Wright/25 6.00 15.00
132 Earl Everett/25 6.00 16.00
133 Eric Frampton/25 6.00 15.00
136 Fred Bennett/25 5.00 12.00
139 H.B. Blades/25 5.00 12.00
140 Ikaika Alama-Francis/25 8.00 20.00
141 Isaiah Stanback/25 5.00 12.00
142 Jacoby Jones/25 8.00 20.00
143 Jamaal Anderson/25 6.00 15.00
144 James Jones/25 8.00 20.00
145 Jared Zabransky/25 6.00 15.00
146 Jarrett Hicks/25 6.00 15.00
148 Jason Snelling/25 8.00 20.00
149 Jeff Rowe/25 5.00 12.00
150 Joel Filani/25 6.00 15.00
151 Jon Beason/25 6.00 15.00
152 Jonathan Wade/25 6.00 15.00
153 Jordan Kent/25 6.00 15.00
154 Jordan Palmer/25 6.00 15.00
155 Josh Gattis/25 5.00 12.00
156 Josh Wilson/25 6.00 15.00
157 Kenneth Darby/25 6.00 15.00
158 Kenny Scott/25 5.00 12.00
159 Kolby Smith/25 15.00 40.00
160 LaMarr Woodley/25 15.00 40.00
161 LaRon Landry/25 8.00 20.00
162 Laurent Robinson/25 8.00 20.00
163 Lawrence Timmons/25 8.00 20.00
165 Leon Hall/25 6.00 15.00
166 Levi Brown/25 8.00 20.00
167 Marcus McCauley/25 6.00 15.00
168 Matt Spaeth/25 8.00 20.00
169 Michael Griffin/25 8.00 20.00
170 Michael Okwo/25 6.00 15.00
171 Mike Walker/25 8.00 20.00
172 Nate Ilaoa/25 6.00 15.00
173 Paul Posluszny/25 8.00 20.00
174 Quentin Moses/25 6.00 15.00
175 Ray McDonald/25 6.00 15.00
176 Reggie Ball/25 6.00 15.00
177 Reggie Nelson/25 6.00 15.00
178 Rhema McKnight/25 5.00 12.00
182 Ryan McBean/25 8.00 20.00
183 Ryne Robinson/25 6.00 15.00
184 Sabby Piscitelli/25 8.00 20.00
185 Scott Chandler/25 8.00 20.00
186 Selvin Young/25 20.00 60.00
188 Stewart Bradley/25 6.00 15.00
193 Tim Crowder/25 8.00 20.00
194 Tim Shaw/25 6.00 15.00
195 Toby Korrodi/25 6.00 15.00
196 Tyler Palko/25 6.00 15.00
199 Victor Abiamiri/25 8.00 20.00
200 Zach Miller/25 8.00 20.00

2007 Donruss Gridiron Gear EA Sports Madden

1 Peyton Manning 1.25 3.00
2 Jason Elam .50 1.25
3 Patrick Willis 1.50 4.00
4 LaRon Landry .75 2.00
5 Ray Lewis .75 2.00
6 JaMarcus Russell .50 1.25
7 Adam Vinatieri .60 1.50
8 Alan Faneca .50 1.25
9 LaDainian Tomlinson .75 2.00
10 Jason Taylor .60 1.50
11 Reggie Bush .75 2.00
12 Marcus McNeill .50 1.25
13 Marvin Harrison .75 2.00
14 Shaun Alexander .60 1.50
15 Shawne Merriman .60 1.50
16 Champ Bailey .60 1.50
17 Chad Johnson .60 1.50
18 Chris McAlister .50 1.25
19 Ty Law .60 1.50
20 Brian Urlacher .75 2.00
21 Tom Brady 1.25 3.00
22 Troy Polamalu .75 2.00
23 Calvin Johnson 2.50 6.00
24 Dwayne Jarrett .60 1.50
25 Ted Ginn Jr. .60 1.50
26 Yamon Figurs .50 1.25
27 Vince Young .60 1.50
28 Larry Johnson .50 1.25

2007 Donruss Gridiron Gear Jerseys O's

O's PRINT RUN 100 SER.#'d SETS
*X's/100-175: .4X TO 1X O's JSYs
X's PRINT RUN 100-175
*PRIME/50: .6X TO 1.5X X's JSYs
PRIME PRINT RUN 50 SER.#'d SETS
1 Tony Romo 5.00 12.00
2 Julius Jones 2.50 6.00
3 Terrell Owens 4.00 10.00
4 Eli Manning 4.00 10.00
5 Plaxico Burress 3.00 8.00
6 Jeremy Shockey 3.00 8.00
7 Brandon Jacobs 3.00 8.00
8 Donovan McNabb 4.00 10.00
9 Brian Westbrook 3.00 8.00
10 Reggie Brown 2.50 6.00
11 Jason Campbell 3.00 8.00
12 Clinton Portis 3.00 8.00
13 Santana Moss 3.00 8.00
14 Rex Grossman 3.00 8.00
15 Cedric Benson 3.00 8.00
16 Muhsin Muhammad 3.00 8.00
17 Jon Kitna 2.50 6.00
18 Roy Williams WR 3.00 8.00
20 Brett Favre 8.00 20.00
21 Donald Driver 4.00 10.00
22 Greg Jennings 4.00 10.00
23 Tarvaris Jackson 2.50 6.00
24 Chester Taylor 2.50 6.00
26 Warrick Dunn 3.00 8.00
27 Alge Crumpler 3.00 8.00
28 Jake Delhomme 3.00 8.00
29 Steve Smith 3.00 8.00
30 DeAngelo Williams 4.00 10.00
31 Drew Brees 4.00 10.00
32 Deuce McAllister 3.00 8.00
33 Reggie Bush 4.00 10.00
34 Jeff Garcia 3.00 8.00
35 Cadillac Williams 3.00 8.00
36 Joey Galloway 3.00 8.00
37 Matt Leinart 3.00 8.00
38 Edgerrin James 3.00 8.00
39 Anquan Boldin 3.00 8.00
40 Larry Fitzgerald 4.00 10.00
41 Marc Bulger 3.00 8.00
42 Steven Jackson 4.00 10.00
43 Torry Holt 3.00 8.00
44 Alex Smith QB 4.00 10.00
45 Frank Gore 4.00 10.00
46 Vernon Davis 3.00 8.00
48 Matt Hasselbeck 3.00 8.00
49 Shaun Alexander 3.00 8.00
50 Deion Branch 3.00 8.00
51 J.P. Losman 2.50 6.00
52 Lee Evans 3.00 8.00
53 Josh Reed 2.50 6.00
54 Trent Green 3.00 8.00
55 Ronnie Brown 3.00 8.00
56 Chris Chambers 3.00 8.00
57 Tom Brady 6.00 15.00
58 Laurence Maroney 3.00 8.00
59 Randy Moss 4.00 10.00
60 Chad Pennington 3.00 8.00
61 Laveranues Coles 2.50 6.00
62 Leon Washington 3.00 8.00
63 Steve McNair 3.00 8.00
65 Mark Clayton/66 3.00 8.00
66 Carson Palmer 3.00 8.00
67 Rudi Johnson 3.00 8.00
68 Chad Johnson 3.00 8.00
69 T.J. Houshmandzadeh 3.00 8.00
70 Charlie Frye 3.00 8.00
71 Braylon Edwards 3.00 8.00
72 Jamal Lewis 3.00 8.00
73 Ben Roethlisberger 4.00 10.00
74 Willie Parker 3.00 8.00
75 Hines Ward 4.00 10.00
77 Andre Johnson 3.00 8.00
79 Peyton Manning 6.00 15.00
80 Joseph Addai 3.00 8.00
81 Marvin Harrison 4.00 10.00
82 Reggie Wayne 3.00 8.00
83 Byron Leftwich 3.00 8.00
84 Fred Taylor 3.00 8.00
85 Maurice Jones-Drew 4.00 10.00
86 Vince Young 3.00 8.00
87 LenDale White 3.00 8.00
88 Brandon Jones 2.50 6.00
89 Jay Cutler 4.00 10.00
90 Javon Walker 3.00 8.00
91 Mike Bell 3.00 8.00
92 Larry Johnson 2.50 6.00
93 Tony Gonzalez 3.00 8.00
94 Brodie Croyle 3.00 8.00
96 LaMont Jordan 3.00 8.00
97 Philip Rivers 4.00 10.00
98 LaDainian Tomlinson 4.00 10.00
99 Vincent Jackson 3.00 8.00
100 Antonio Gates 4.00 10.00

2007 Donruss Gridiron Gear Next Generation Gold

GOLD PRINT RUN 500 SER.#'d SETS
*RED: .3X TO .8X GOLD/500
*SILVER/250: .5X TO 1.2X GOLD/500
SILVER PRINT RUN 250 SER.#'d SETS
*GOLD HOLO/100: .6X TO 1.5X GOLD/500
GOLD HOLOFOIL PRINT RUN 100 SER.#'d SETS
*PLATINUM/25: 1X TO 2.5X GOLD/500
PLATINUM PRINT RUN 25 SER.#'d SETS
1 Aaron Rodgers 3.00 8.00
2 A.J. Hawk 1.00 2.50
3 Anthony Fasano .75 2.00
4 Bernard Berrian .75 2.00
5 Brandon Jacobs 1.00 2.50
6 Brandon Marshall 1.00 2.50
7 Brodie Croyle 1.00 2.50
8 DeAngelo Williams 1.25 3.00
9 DeMeco Ryans 1.00 2.50
10 Demetrius Williams .75 2.00
11 Devin Hester 1.25 3.00
12 Frank Gore 1.25 3.00
13 Hank Baskett 1.00 2.50
14 Jay Cutler 1.25 3.00
15 Jerricho Cotchery 1.00 2.50
16 Jerious Norwood 1.00 2.50
17 Joseph Addai 1.00 2.50
18 Ladell Betts .75 2.00
19 LenDale White 1.00 2.50
20 Marion Barber 1.25 3.00
21 Marques Colston 1.25 3.00
22 Matt Leinart 1.00 2.50
23 Michael Turner 1.25 3.00
24 Mike Furrey 1.00 2.50
25 Mike Bell 1.00 2.50
26 Reggie Bush 1.25 3.00
27 Santonio Holmes 1.00 2.50
28 Shawne Merriman 1.00 2.50
29 Vince Young 1.00 2.50
30 Vincent Jackson 1.00 2.50
31 Maurice Jones-Drew 1.25 3.00
32 Greg Jennings 1.25 3.00
33 Devery Henderson .75 2.00
34 Chester Taylor .75 2.00
35 Patrick Crayton .75 2.00
36 Tony Romo 1.50 4.00
37 Vernon Davis 1.00 2.50
38 Todd Heap .75 2.00
39 Reggie Williams 1.00 2.50
40 Nate Burleson .75 2.00

2007 Donruss Gridiron Gear Next Generation Autographs

STATED PRINT RUN 25 SER.#'d SETS
UNPRICED JSY AUTO PRINT RUN 6-13
UNPRICED JSY COMBO AUTO PRINT RUN 3-5
UNPRICED JSY PRIME AUTO PRINT RUN 5
13 Hank Baskett 6.00 15.00
15 Jerricho Cotchery 6.00 15.00
27 Santonio Holmes 6.00 15.00
32 Greg Jennings 8.00 20.00

2007 Donruss Gridiron Gear Next Generation Jerseys

STATED PRINT RUN 77-250
*COMBO PRIME/50: .8X TO 2X BASIC JSYs
COMBO PRIME PRINT RUN 50
*JUMBO/32-50: .6X TO 1.5X BASIC JSYs
JUMBO SWATCH PRINT RUN 32-50
*JUMBO PRIME/15-25: 1X TO 2.5X BASIC JSYs
JUMBO PRIME PRINT RUN 2-25
*PRIME/25-50: .8X TO 2X BASIC JSYs
PRIME PRINT RUN 25-50
1 Aaron Rodgers 12.00 30.00
2 A.J. Hawk 3.00 8.00
3 Anthony Fasano 2.50 6.00
4 Bernard Berrian 2.50 6.00
5 Brandon Jacobs 3.00 8.00
6 Brandon Marshall/77 3.00 8.00
7 Brodie Croyle 3.00 8.00
8 DeAngelo Williams 4.00 10.00
9 DeMeco Ryans 3.00 8.00
10 Demetrius Williams 2.50 6.00
11 Devin Hester 4.00 10.00
12 Frank Gore 4.00 10.00

13 Hank Baskett 3.00 8.00
14 Jay Cutler 4.00 10.00
15 Jerricho Cotchery 3.00 8.00
16 Jerious Norwood 3.00 8.00
17 Joseph Addai 3.00 8.00
18 Ladell Betts 2.50 6.00
19 LenDale White 3.00 8.00
20 Marion Barber 4.00 10.00
21 Marques Colston 4.00 10.00
22 Matt Leinart 3.00 8.00
23 Michael Turner 4.00 10.00
24 Mike Furrey 3.00 8.00
25 Mike Bell 3.00 8.00
26 Reggie Bush 4.00 10.00
27 Santonio Holmes 3.00 8.00
28 Shawne Merriman 3.00 8.00
29 Vince Young 3.00 8.00
30 Vincent Jackson 3.00 8.00
31 Maurice Jones-Drew 4.00 10.00
32 Greg Jennings 4.00 10.00
33 Devery Henderson 2.50 6.00
34 Chester Taylor 2.50 6.00
35 Patrick Crayton 2.50 6.00
36 Tony Romo 5.00 12.00
37 Vernon Davis 3.00 8.00
38 Todd Heap 2.50 6.00
39 Reggie Williams 3.00 8.00
40 Nate Burleson 2.50 6.00

2007 Donruss Gridiron Gear NFL Gridiron Rookie Signatures

STATED PRINT RUN 25-30
1 John Beck/26 12.00 30.00
2 Kenny Irons/30 8.00 20.00
3 Lorenzo Booker/25 10.00 25.00
4 Troy Smith/25 12.00 30.00
5 Drew Stanton/30 8.00 20.00
6 Johnnie Lee Higgins/25 10.00 25.00
7 Dwayne Jarrett/30 10.00 25.00
8 JaMarcus Russell/25 8.00 20.00
9 Gaines Adams/25 12.00 30.00
10 Brady Quinn/30 12.00 30.00
11 Paul Williams/25 8.00 20.00
12 Garrett Wolfe/30 8.00 20.00
13 Tony Hunt/30 8.00 20.00
14 Michael Bush/25 12.00 30.00
15 Robert Meachem/25 12.00 30.00
16 Jason Hill/25 12.00 30.00
17 Patrick Willis/25 25.00 60.00
18 Brian Leonard/30 10.00 25.00
19 Adrian Peterson/30 150.00 300.00
20 Kevin Kolb/25 20.00 50.00
21 Antonio Pittman/25 8.00 20.00
22 Greg Olsen/25 10.00 25.00
23 Calvin Johnson/30 50.00 120.00
24 Trent Edwards/30 12.00 30.00
25 Chris Henry RB/30 8.00 20.00
26 Sidney Rice/25 15.00 40.00
27 Anthony Gonzalez/30 12.00 30.00
28 Dwayne Bowe/25 15.00 40.00
29 Ted Ginn Jr./25 10.00 25.00
30 Steve Smith USC/25 12.00 30.00
31 Brandon Jackson/25 10.00 25.00
32 Joe Thomas/30 12.00 30.00
33 Yamon Figurs/30 8.00 20.00
34 Marshawn Lynch/30 15.00 40.00

2007 Donruss Gridiron Gear NFL Teams Veteran Signatures

STATED PRINT RUN 6-32
SERIAL #'d UNDER 22 NOT PRICED
1 Andre Johnson/22 12.50 25.00
2 Ben Roethlisberger 50.00 100.00
3 Brett Favre 125.00 200.00
5 Eli Manning 50.00 80.00
6 Donovan McNabb
7 Drew Brees 40.00 80.00
8 LaDainian Tomlinson 40.00 80.00
9 Larry Johnson 25.00 50.00
10 Marvin Harrison 20.00 40.00
12 Maurice Jones-Drew 12.50 25.00
13 A.J. Hawk 20.00 40.00
14 Cedric Benson 20.00 40.00
15 Peyton Manning 75.00 150.00
16 Reggie Bush 40.00 80.00
17 Reggie Wayne 20.00 40.00
18 Rex Grossman 12.50 25.00
19 Ronnie Brown 20.00 40.00
20 Cadillac Williams 20.00 40.00
22 Rudi Johnson 12.50 25.00
23 Steve Smith 20.00 40.00
24 Steven Jackson 20.00 40.00
26 T.J. Houshmandzadeh 12.50 25.00
28 Torry Holt 20.00 40.00
29 Vince Young 30.00 60.00
30 Willie Parker 25.00 50.00
31 Willis McGahee 12.50 25.00

2007 Donruss Gridiron Gear NFL Teams Rookie Signatures

STATED PRINT RUN 30 SER.#'d SETS
1 John Beck 12.00 30.00
2 Kenny Irons 8.00 20.00
3 Lorenzo Booker 10.00 25.00
4 Troy Smith 12.00 30.00
5 Drew Stanton 8.00 20.00
6 Johnnie Lee Higgins 10.00 25.00
7 Dwayne Jarrett 10.00 25.00
8 JaMarcus Russell 8.00 20.00
9 Gaines Adams 12.00 30.00
10 Brady Quinn 12.00 30.00
11 Paul Williams 8.00 20.00
12 Garrett Wolfe 8.00 20.00
13 Tony Hunt 8.00 20.00
14 Michael Bush 12.00 30.00
15 Robert Meachem 12.00 30.00
16 Jason Hill 12.00 30.00
17 Patrick Willis 25.00 60.00
18 Brian Leonard 10.00 25.00
19 Adrian Peterson 150.00 300.00
20 Kevin Kolb 20.00 50.00
21 Antonio Pittman 8.00 20.00
22 Greg Olsen 10.00 25.00
23 Calvin Johnson 50.00 120.00
24 Trent Edwards 12.00 30.00
26 Sidney Rice 15.00 40.00
27 Anthony Gonzalez 12.00 30.00
28 Dwayne Bowe 15.00 40.00
29 Ted Ginn Jr. 10.00 25.00
30 Steve Smith USC 12.00 30.00
32 Joe Thomas 12.00 30.00
33 Yamon Figurs 8.00 20.00
34 Marshawn Lynch 15.00 40.00

2007 Donruss Gridiron Gear Performers Gold

GOLD PRINT RUN 500 SER.#'d SETS
*RED: .3X TO .8X GOLD/500
*SILVER/250: .5X TO 1.2X GOLD/500
SILVER PRINT RUN 250 SER.#'d SETS
*GOLD HOLO/100: .6X TO 1.5X GOLD/500
GOLD HOLOFOIL PRINT RUN 100 SER.#'d SETS
*PLATINUM/25: 1X TO 2.5X GOLD/500
PLATINUM PRINT RUN 25 SER.#'d SETS
1 Alan Page 1.25 3.00
2 Archie Manning 2.00 5.00
3 Barry Sanders 3.00 8.00
4 Bart Starr 3.00 8.00
5 Bill Bates 1.50 4.00
6 Billy Howton 1.25 3.00
7 Bob Griese 2.00 5.00
8 Boyd Dowler 1.25 3.00
9 Charley Taylor 1.50 4.00
10 Chuck Bednarik 1.50 4.00
11 Cris Collinsworth 1.50 4.00
12 Dan Marino 4.00 10.00
13 Dante Lavelli 1.25 3.00
14 Daryle Lamonica 1.25 3.00
15 Deacon Jones 1.50 4.00
16 Eric Dickerson 1.50 4.00
17 Fred Biletnikoff 2.00 5.00
18 Gale Sayers 2.50 6.00
19 Harlon Hill 1.25 3.00
20 Jack Youngblood 1.50 4.00
21 Jethro Pugh 1.25 3.00
22 Jimmy Orr 1.25 3.00
23 Joe Namath 2.50 6.00
24 Johnny Morris 1.25 3.00
25 Larry Little 1.25 3.00
26 Lydell Mitchell 1.25 3.00
27 Merlin Olsen 1.50 4.00
28 Rick Casares 1.25 3.00
29 Rosey Grier 1.25 3.00
30 Sonny Jurgensen 1.50 4.00
31 Sterling Sharpe 1.50 4.00
32 Steve Largent 2.00 5.00
33 Tony Dorsett 2.00 5.00
34 Willie Brown 1.50 4.00
35 Willie Lanier 1.25 3.00
36 Yale Lary 1.25 3.00
37 Marvin Harrison 1.25 3.00
38 Matt Hasselbeck 1.00 2.50
39 J.P. Losman .75 2.00
40 Carson Palmer 1.00 2.50
41 Steve McNair 1.00 2.50
42 Lee Evans 1.00 2.50
43 Donald Driver 1.25 3.00
44 Hines Ward 1.25 3.00
45 Antonio Gates 1.25 3.00
46 Frank Gore 1.25 3.00
47 Rudi Johnson 1.00 2.50
48 Fred Taylor 1.00 2.50
49 Joseph Addai 1.00 2.50
50 Larry Fitzgerald 1.25 3.00

2007 Donruss Gridiron Gear Performers Autographs

STATED PRINT RUN 75-250 SER.#'d SETS
22 Jimmy Orr/250 5.00 12.00
27 Merlin Olsen/75 15.00 30.00

2007 Donruss Gridiron Gear Performers Jerseys

STATED PRINT RUN 90-250
*COMBOS/50-100: .5X TO 1.2X BASIC JSYs
COMBOS PRINT RUN 50-100
*COMBO PRIME/25-50: .8X TO 2X BASIC JSYs
COMBOS PRIME PRINT RUN 5-50
*JUM.SWATCH/19-50: .8X TO 2X BASIC JSYs
JUMBO SWATCH PRINT RUN 19-50
*JUMBO PRIME/15-25: 1.2X TO 3X BASIC JSYs
JUMBO SWATCH PRIME PRINT RUN 10-25
*PRIME/25-50: .6X TO 1.5X BASIC JSYs
PRIME PRINT RUN 5-50
3 Barry Sanders/240 10.00 25.00
4 Bart Starr 10.00 25.00
5 Bill Bates/150 5.00 12.00
7 Bob Griese/150 6.00 15.00
9 Charley Taylor/150 5.00 12.00
11 Cris Collinsworth/150 5.00 12.00
12 Dan Marino 12.00 30.00
14 Daryle Lamonica/150 4.00 10.00
15 Deacon Jones/150 5.00 12.00
16 Eric Dickerson 5.00 12.00
17 Fred Biletnikoff 6.00 15.00
18 Gale Sayers 8.00 20.00
20 Jack Youngblood 5.00 12.00
23 Joe Namath 8.00 20.00
25 Larry Little 4.00 10.00
27 Merlin Olsen 5.00 12.00
30 Sonny Jurgensen/90 5.00 12.00
31 Sterling Sharpe 5.00 12.00
32 Steve Largent 6.00 15.00
33 Tony Dorsett 6.00 15.00
34 Willie Brown 5.00 12.00
36 Yale Lary/235 4.00 10.00
37 Marvin Harrison 4.00 10.00
38 Matt Hasselbeck 3.00 8.00
39 J.P. Losman 2.50 6.00
40 Carson Palmer 3.00 8.00
41 Steve McNair 3.00 8.00
42 Lee Evans 3.00 8.00
43 Donald Driver 4.00 10.00
44 Hines Ward 4.00 10.00
45 Antonio Gates 4.00 10.00
46 Frank Gore 4.00 10.00
47 Rudi Johnson 3.00 8.00
48 Fred Taylor 3.00 8.00
49 Joseph Addai 3.00 8.00
50 Larry Fitzgerald 4.00 10.00

2007 Donruss Gridiron Gear Performers Jerseys Autographs

STATED PRINT RUN 10-25
*JSY COMBO AUTO/25: .5X TO 1.2X JSY AU/25
JSY COMBO AUTO PRINT RUN 3-25
UNPRICED JSY COMBO PRIME PRINT RUN 5
UNPRICED PRIME AUTO PRINT RUN 5-15
SERIAL #'d UNDER 25 NOT PRICED
27 Merlin Olsen/25 15.00 40.00

2007 Donruss Gridiron Gear Plates and Patches

STATED PRINT RUN 100 SER.#'d SETS
1 Donovan McNabb 8.00 20.00
2 Tom Brady 20.00 50.00
3 Peyton Manning 15.00 40.00
4 LaDainian Tomlinson 8.00 20.00
5 Tony Romo 25.00 60.00
6 Shaun Alexander 6.00 15.00
7 Carson Palmer 6.00 15.00
8 Vince Young 6.00 15.00
9 Reggie Bush 8.00 20.00
10 Terrell Owens 8.00 20.00

2007 Donruss Gridiron Gear Playbook Gold

GOLD PRINT RUN 500 SER.#'d SETS
*RED: .3X TO .8X GOLD/500
*SILVER/250: .5X TO 1.2X GOLD/500
SILVER PRINT RUN 250 SER.#'d SETS
*GOLD HOLO/100: .6X TO 1.5X GOLD/500
GOLD HOLOFOIL PRINT RUN 100 SER.#'d SETS
*PLATINUM/25: 1X TO 2.5X GOLD/500
PLATINUM PRINT RUN 25 SER.#'d SETS
1 Eli Manning 1.25 3.00
2 Chad Pennington 1.00 2.50
3 Drew Brees 1.25 3.00
4 Marc Bulger 1.00 2.50
5 Brett Favre 2.50 6.00
6 Ben Roethlisberger 1.25 3.00
7 Philip Rivers 1.25 3.00
8 Matt Leinart 1.00 2.50
9 Reggie Wayne 1.00 2.50
10 Chad Johnson 1.00 2.50
11 Roy Williams WR 1.00 2.50
12 Anquan Boldin 1.00 2.50
13 Torry Holt 1.00 2.50
14 Andre Johnson 1.00 2.50
15 T.J. Houshmandzadeh 1.00 2.50
16 Larry Johnson .75 2.00
17 Steven Jackson 1.25 3.00
18 Willie Parker 1.00 2.50
19 Brian Westbrook 1.00 2.50
20 Edgerrin James 1.00 2.50
21 Warrick Dunn 1.00 2.50
22 Julius Jones .75 2.00
23 Deuce McAllister 1.00 2.50
24 Ronnie Brown 1.00 2.50
25 Cadillac Williams 1.00 2.50

2007 Donruss Gridiron Gear Playbook Jerseys X's

X's PRINT RUN 250 SER.#'d SETS
*O's: .4X TO 1X X's JSYs
O's PRINT RUN 250 SER.#'d SETS
*PATCH/25: .8X TO 2X X's JSYs
PATCH PRINT RUN 25 SER.#'d SETS
1 Eli Manning 4.00 10.00
2 Chad Pennington 3.00 8.00
3 Drew Brees 4.00 10.00
4 Marc Bulger 3.00 8.00
5 Brett Favre 8.00 20.00
6 Ben Roethlisberger 4.00 10.00
7 Philip Rivers 4.00 10.00
8 Matt Leinart 3.00 8.00
9 Reggie Wayne 3.00 8.00
10 Chad Johnson 3.00 8.00
11 Roy Williams WR 3.00 8.00
12 Anquan Boldin 3.00 8.00
13 Torry Holt 3.00 8.00
14 Andre Johnson 3.00 8.00
15 T.J. Houshmandzadeh 3.00 8.00
16 Larry Johnson 2.50 6.00
17 Steven Jackson 4.00 10.00
18 Willie Parker 3.00 8.00
19 Brian Westbrook 3.00 8.00
20 Edgerrin James 3.00 8.00
21 Warrick Dunn 3.00 8.00
22 Julius Jones 2.50 6.00
23 Deuce McAllister 3.00 8.00
24 Ronnie Brown 3.00 8.00
25 Cadillac Williams 3.00 8.00

2007 Donruss Gridiron Gear Player Timeline Gold

GOLD PRINT RUN 500 SER.#'d SETS
*RED: .3X TO .8X GOLD/500
*SILVER/250: .5X TO 1.2X GOLD/500
SILVER PRINT RUN 250 SER.#'d SETS
*GOLD HOLO/100: .6X TO 1.5X GOLD/500
GOLD HOLOFOIL PRINT RUN 100 SER.#'d SETS
*PLATINUM/25: 1X TO 2.5X GOLD/500
PLATINUM PRINT RUN 25 SER.#'d SETS
1 Carson Palmer 1.00 2.50
2 Larry Fitzgerald 1.25 3.00
3 Cedric Benson 1.00 2.50
4 Reggie Williams 1.00 2.50
5 Matt Leinart 1.00 2.50
6 Reggie Bush 1.25 3.00
7 Vince Young 1.00 2.50
8 Devery Henderson .75 2.00
9 Frank Gore 1.25 3.00
10 Kenny Irons .60 1.50
11 Dwayne Jarrett .75 2.00
12 Steve Smith USC 1.00 2.50
13 Greg Olsen .75 2.00
14 Brady Quinn 1.00 2.50
15 Adrian Peterson 4.00 10.00
16 JaMarcus Russell .60 1.50
17 Dwayne Bowe 1.25 3.00
18 Johnnie Lee Higgins .75 2.00
19 Robert Meachem 1.00 2.50
20 Michael Bush 1.00 2.50
21 Steven Jackson 1.25 3.00
22 Steve McNair 1.00 2.50
23 Terrell Owens 1.25 3.00
24 Edgerrin James 1.00 2.50
25 Deion Branch 1.00 2.50

2007 Donruss Gridiron Gear Player Timeline Autographs

STATED PRINT RUN 7-100
3 Cedric Benson/100 6.00 15.00
6 Reggie Bush/25 40.00 100.00
8 Devery Henderson/100 6.00 15.00
9 Frank Gore/50 8.00 20.00
10 Kenny Irons/25 10.00 25.00
11 Dwayne Jarrett/25 10.00 25.00
12 Steve Smith USC/25 12.00 30.00
13 Greg Olsen/25 10.00 25.00
15 Adrian Peterson/28 150.00 250.00
16 JaMarcus Russell/18 20.00 50.00
17 Dwayne Bowe/25 20.00 50.00
18 Johnnie Lee Higgins/25 8.00 20.00
19 Robert Meachem/25 10.00 25.00
20 Michael Bush/25 10.00 25.00
21 Steven Jackson/50 10.00 25.00

2007 Donruss Gridiron Gear Player Timeline Jerseys

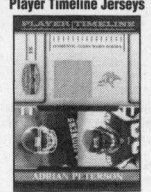

STATED PRINT RUN 50-250
*COMBOS/80-100: .5X TO 1.2X BASIC JSYs
*COMBOS/30: .8X TO 2X BASIC JSYs
COMBOS PRINT RUN 30-100
*CMBO PRME/25-50: 1X TO 2.5X BASIC JSY
COMBOS PRIME PRINT RUN 5-50
*JUM.SWATCH/40-50: .6X TO 1.5X BASIC JSY
JUMBO SWATCH PRIME PRINT RUN 40-50
*JUMBO PRIME/15-25: 1X TO 2.5X BASIC JSYs
JUMBO SWATCH PRIME PRINT RUN 5-25
*PRIME/25-50: .8X TO 2X BASIC JSYs
PRIME PRINT RUN 10-50
1 Carson Palmer 3.00 8.00
2 Larry Fitzgerald 4.00 10.00
3 Cedric Benson 3.00 8.00
4 Reggie Williams 3.00 8.00
5 Matt Leinart 3.00 8.00
6 Reggie Bush 4.00 10.00
7 Vince Young 3.00 8.00
8 Devery Henderson 2.50 6.00
9 Frank Gore 4.00 10.00
10 Kenny Irons 1.50 4.00
11 Dwayne Jarrett 2.00 5.00
12 Steve Smith USC 2.50 6.00
13 Greg Olsen 2.00 5.00
14 Brady Quinn 2.50 6.00
15 Adrian Peterson 10.00 25.00
16 JaMarcus Russell 1.50 4.00
17 Dwayne Bowe 3.00 8.00
18 Johnnie Lee Higgins 2.00 5.00
19 Robert Meachem 2.50 6.00
20 Michael Bush 2.50 6.00
21 Steven Jackson 4.00 10.00
22 Steve McNair 3.00 8.00
23 Terrell Owens/50 4.00 10.00
24 Edgerrin James 3.00 8.00
25 Deion Branch 3.00 8.00

2007 Donruss Gridiron Gear Player Timeline Jerseys Autographs

STATED PRINT RUN 5-25 SER.#'d SETS
*COMBO/25: .5X TO 1.2X BASIC JSY AUTO/25
COMBO JSY AUTO PRINT RUN 5-25
*CMBO PRIM/25: .5X TO 1.2X BSC.JSY AU/25
COMBO JSY PRIME PRINT RUN 1-25
*PRIME/20-25: .5X TO 1.2X BASIC JSY AU/25
PRIME PRINT RUN 2-25
3 Cedric Benson/25 10.00 25.00
8 Devery Henderson/25 10.00 25.00
9 Frank Gore/25 15.00 40.00
10 Kenny Irons/25 12.00 30.00
11 Dwayne Jarrett/25 10.00 25.00
12 Steve Smith USC/25 12.00 30.00
13 Greg Olsen/25 15.00 40.00
14 Brady Quinn/25 30.00 80.00
16 JaMarcus Russell/25 20.00 50.00
21 Steven Jackson/25 15.00 40.00

2007 Donruss Gridiron Gear Rivals Gold

GOLD PRINT RUN 500 SER.#'d SETS
*RED: .3X TO .8X GOLD/500
*SILVER/250: .5X TO 1.2X GOLD/500
SILVER PRINT RUN 250 SER.#'d SETS
*GOLD HOLO/100: .6X TO 1.5X GOLD/500
GOLD HOLOFOIL PRINT RUN 100 SER.#'d SETS
*PLATINUM/25: 1X TO 2.5X GOLD/500
PLATINUM PRINT RUN 25 SER.#'d SETS
1 Peyton Manning 2.50 6.00
Brian Urlacher
2 Donovan McNabb 1.50 4.00
Terrell Owens
3 LaDainian Tomlinson 1.50 4.00
Shaun Alexander
4 Torry Holt 1.25 3.00
Anquan Boldin
5 Marvin Harrison 1.50 4.00
Chad Johnson
6 Brett Favre 3.00 8.00
Rex Grossman
7 Roy Williams S 1.25 3.00
Roy Williams WR
8 Vince Young 1.25 3.00
Matt Leinart
9 Matt Hasselbeck 2.00 5.00
Tony Romo
10 Carson Palmer 1.50 4.00
Ben Roethlisberger
11 Clinton Portis 1.25 3.00
Julius Jones
12 Larry Johnson 1.25 3.00
LaMont Jordan
13 Braylon Edwards 1.50 4.00
Hines Ward
14 Reggie Wayne 1.50 4.00
Ray Lewis
15 Eli Manning 1.50 4.00
Chad Pennington
16 Tom Brady 2.50 6.00
Philip Rivers

2007 Donruss Gridiron Gear Rivals Jerseys

STATED PRINT RUN 100 SER.#'d SETS
*PRIME/25: .8X TO 2X BASIC JSYs
PRIME PRINT RUN 25 SER.#'d SETS
1 Peyton Manning 8.00 20.00
Brian Urlacher
2 Donovan McNabb 5.00 12.00
Terrell Owens
3 LaDainian Tomlinson 5.00 12.00
Shaun Alexander
4 Torry Holt 4.00 10.00
Anquan Boldin
5 Marvin Harrison 5.00 12.00
Chad Johnson
6 Brett Favre 8.00 20.00
Rex Grossman
7 Roy Williams S 4.00 10.00
Roy Williams WR
8 Vince Young 4.00 10.00
Matt Leinart
9 Matt Hasselbeck 6.00 15.00
Tony Romo
10 Carson Palmer 5.00 12.00
Ben Roethlisberger
11 Clinton Portis 4.00 10.00
Julius Jones
12 Larry Johnson 4.00 10.00
LaMont Jordan
13 Braylon Edwards 5.00 12.00
Hines Ward
14 Reggie Wayne 5.00 12.00
Ray Lewis
15 Eli Manning 5.00 12.00
Chad Pennington
16 Tom Brady 8.00 20.00
Philip Rivers

2007 Donruss Gridiron Gear Rookie Jerseys

STATED PRINT RUN 50 SER.#'d SETS
*COMBOS/50: .5X TO 1.2X BASIC JSYs
COMBOS PRINT RUN 50 SER.#'d SETS
*CMBO PRIME/25-50: .6X TO 1.5X BASIC JSY
COMBOS PRIME PRINT RUN 25-50
*JUMBO SWATCH/50: .6X TO 1.5X BASIC JSYs
JUMBO SWATCH PRINT RUN 50
*JUMBO PRIME/50: 1X TO 2.5X BASIC JSYs
JUMBO SWATCH PRIME PRINT RUN 2-50
*PRIME/50: .6X TO 1.5X BASIC JSYs
PRIME PRINT RUN 10-50
*RETAIL RED/50: .4X TO 1X BASIC JSYs
RETAIL RED PRINT RUN 50
*TRIOS/50: .8X TO 2X BASIC JSYs
TRIOS PRINT RUN 50
*TRIOS PRIME/25-50: 1.2X TO 3X BASIC JSYs
TRIOS PRIME PRINT RUN 25-50
201 Marshawn Lynch 2.50 6.00
202 Yamon Figurs 1.50 4.00
203 Joe Thomas 2.50 6.00
204 Brandon Jackson 2.00 5.00
205 Steve Smith USC 2.50 6.00
206 Ted Ginn Jr. 2.00 5.00
207 Dwayne Bowe 3.00 8.00
208 Anthony Gonzalez 2.50 6.00
209 Sidney Rice 3.00 8.00
210 Chris Henry RB 1.50 4.00
211 Trent Edwards 2.50 6.00
212 Calvin Johnson 8.00 20.00
213 Greg Olsen 2.00 5.00
214 Antonio Pittman 1.50 4.00
215 Kevin Kolb 4.00 10.00
216 Adrian Peterson 10.00 25.00
217 Brian Leonard 2.00 5.00
218 Patrick Willis 5.00 12.00
219 Jason Hill 2.50 6.00
220 Robert Meachem 2.50 6.00
221 Michael Bush 2.50 6.00
222 Tony Hunt 1.50 4.00
223 Garrett Wolfe 1.50 4.00
224 Paul Williams 1.50 4.00
225 Brady Quinn 2.50 6.00
226 Gaines Adams 2.50 6.00
227 JaMarcus Russell 1.50 4.00
228 Dwayne Jarrett 2.00 5.00
229 Johnnie Lee Higgins 2.00 5.00
230 Drew Stanton 1.50 4.00
231 Troy Smith 2.50 6.00
232 Lorenzo Booker 2.00 5.00
233 Kenny Irons 1.50 4.00
234 John Beck 2.50 6.00

2007 Donruss Gridiron Gear Rookie Jerseys Combos Prime Autographs

*COMBO PRIME AU/50: .4X TO 1X BASE RC/100
COMBOS PRIME AUTO PRINT RUN 10-50

2007 Donruss Gridiron Gear Rookie Jerseys Prime Autographs

*JSY PRIME AU/50: .4X TO 1X BASE RC/100
JERSEY PRIME AUTO PRINT RUN 5-50

2007 Donruss Gridiron Gear Rookie Jerseys Trios Prime Autographs

*TRIOS PRIME/50: .5X TO 1.2X BASE RC/100
TRIOS PRIME PRINT RUN 10-50
216 Adrian Peterson 150.00 300.00

2007 Donruss Gridiron Gear Retail

*RETAIL ROOKIE: .4X TO 1X BASIC CARDS
STATED PRINT RUN 599 SER.#'d SETS
RETAIL PRINTED ON WHITE CARD STOCK

2008 Donruss Gridiron Gear

COMP.SET w/o RC's (100) 7.50 20.00
101-200 ROOKIE PRINT RUN 999
ROOKIE AUTO PRINT RUN 100
1 Matt Leinart .40 1.00
2 Larry Fitzgerald .40 1.00
3 Anquan Boldin .30 .75
4 Edgerrin James .30 .75
5 Jerious Norwood .30 .75
6 Roddy White .30 .75
7 Michael Turner .40 1.00
8 Willis McGahee .30 .75
9 Derrick Mason .30 .75
10 Mark Clayton .30 .75
11 Trent Edwards .25 .60
12 Marshawn Lynch .30 .75
13 Lee Evans .30 .75
14 Steve Smith .30 .75
15 DeAngelo Williams .30 .75
16 Jake Delhomme .30 .75
17 Brian Urlacher .40 1.00
18 Devin Hester .40 1.00
19 Rex Grossman .30 .75
20 Carson Palmer .40 1.00
21 T.J. Houshmandzadeh .30 .75
22 Rudi Johnson .30 .75
23 Derek Anderson .25 .60
24 Kellen Winslow .30 .75
25 Braylon Edwards .30 .75
26 Tony Romo .50 1.25
27 Terrell Owens .40 1.00
28 Marion Barber .30 .75
29 Jason Witten .40 1.00
30 Jay Cutler .40 1.00
31 Selvin Young .25 .60
32 Brandon Marshall .30 .75
33 Jon Kitna .30 .75
34 Roy Williams WR .30 .75
35 Calvin Johnson .40 1.00
36 Aaron Rodgers .75 2.00
37 Ryan Grant .40 1.00
38 Greg Jennings .40 1.00
39 Matt Schaub .30 .75
40 Ahman Green .30 .75
41 Andre Johnson .30 .75
42 Peyton Manning .60 1.50
43 Joseph Addai .30 .75
44 Reggie Wayne .30 .75
45 Anthony Gonzalez .25 .60
46 David Garrard .30 .75
47 Fred Taylor .30 .75
48 Maurice Jones-Drew .30 .75
49 Brodie Croyle .30 .75
50 Larry Johnson .30 .75
51 Tony Gonzalez .30 .75
52 John Beck .25 .60
53 Ronnie Brown .30 .75
54 Ted Ginn Jr. .30 .75
55 Tarvaris Jackson .30 .75
56 Adrian Peterson .60 1.50
57 Chester Taylor .25 .60
58 Tom Brady .60 1.50
59 Randy Moss .40 1.00
60 Laurence Maroney .30 .75
61 Drew Brees .40 1.00
62 Reggie Bush .40 1.00
63 Marques Colston .30 .75
64 Eli Manning .40 1.00
65 Plaxico Burress .30 .75
66 Brandon Jacobs .30 .75
67 Brett Favre 2.00 5.00
68 Jerricho Cotchery .30 .75
69 Laveranues Coles .25 .60
70 JaMarcus Russell .30 .75
71 Justin Fargas .25 .60
72 Zach Miller .30 .75
73 Donovan McNabb .40 1.00
74 Brian Westbrook .30 .75
75 Kevin Curtis .25 .60
76 Ben Roethlisberger .40 1.00
77 Willie Parker .30 .75
78 Hines Ward .30 .75
79 Santonio Holmes .30 .75
80 Philip Rivers .40 1.00
81 LaDainian Tomlinson .40 1.00
82 Antonio Gates .40 1.00
83 Alex Smith QB .40 1.00
84 Frank Gore .30 .75
85 Vernon Davis .30 .75
86 Matt Hasselbeck .30 .75
87 Deion Branch .30 .75
88 Julius Jones .25 .60
89 Marc Bulger .30 .75
90 Steven Jackson .40 1.00
91 Torry Holt .30 .75
92 Jeff Garcia .30 .75
93 Cadillac Williams .30 .75
94 Joey Galloway .30 .75
95 Vince Young .30 .75
96 LenDale White .30 .75
97 Roydell Williams .25 .60
98 Jason Campbell .30 .75
99 Clinton Portis .30 .75
100 Chris Cooley .30 .75
101 Adrian Arrington RC 1.50 4.00
102 Alex Brink RC 2.00 5.00
103 Ali Highsmith RC 1.25 3.00
104 Allen Patrick RC 1.50 4.00
105 Andre Woodson RC 2.00 5.00
106 Anthony Alridge RC 1.50 4.00
107 Antoine Cason RC 2.00 5.00
108 Aqib Talib RC 2.00 5.00
109 Arman Shields RC 1.50 4.00
110 Brad Cottam RC 1.50 4.00
111 Brandon Flowers RC 2.00 5.00
112 Calais Campbell RC 1.50 4.00
113 Caleb Campbell RC 2.00 5.00
114 Chauncey Washington RC 1.50 4.00
115 Chevis Jackson RC 1.25 3.00
116 Colt Brennan RC 2.00 5.00
117 Cory Boyd RC 1.25 3.00
118 Craig Steltz RC 1.50 4.00
119 Curtis Lofton RC 1.50 4.00
120 DJ Hall RC 1.50 4.00
121 Dan Connor RC 2.00 5.00
122 Dantrell Savage RC 1.50 4.00
123 Darius Reynaud RC 1.25 3.00
124 Darrell Strong RC 1.50 4.00
125 David Vobora RC 1.25 3.00
126 Davone Bess RC 2.00 5.00
127 Dennis Dixon RC 2.00 5.00
128 Derrick Harvey RC 1.25 3.00
129 Dominique Rodgers-Cromartie RC 2.00 5.00
130 Erik Ainge RC 2.00 5.00
131 Erin Henderson RC 2.00 5.00
132 Ernie Wheelwright RC 1.50 4.00
133 Fred Davis RC 2.00 5.00
134 Joe Jon Finley RC 1.50 4.00
135 Jacob Hester RC 2.00 5.00
136 Jacob Tamme RC 2.00 5.00
137 Jalen Parmele RC 1.50 4.00
138 Jamar Adams RC 1.50 4.00
139 Jason Rivers RC 1.50 4.00
140 Jaymar Johnson RC 1.25 3.00
141 Jed Collins RC 1.50 4.00
142 Jerod Mayo RC 2.00 5.00
143 Jermichael Finley RC 2.00 5.00
144 Jerome Felton RC 1.25 3.00
145 John Carlson RC 2.00 5.00
146 Jonathan Hefney RC 1.50 4.00
147 Jordon Dizon RC 2.00 5.00
148 Josh Johnson RC 2.00 5.00
149 Josh Morgan RC 2.00 5.00
150 Justin Forsett RC 2.00 5.00
151 Justin Harper RC 1.50 4.00
152 Kalvin McRae RC 1.25 3.00
153 Keenan Burton RC 1.25 3.00
154 Keith Rivers RC 2.00 5.00
155 Kellen Davis RC 1.25 3.00
156 Kenneth Moore RC 1.50 4.00
157 Kenny Phillips RC 2.00 5.00
158 Kentwan Balmer RC 1.50 4.00
159 Kevin Robinson RC 1.25 3.00
160 Lavelle Hawkins RC 1.25 3.00
161 Lawrence Jackson RC 1.50 4.00
162 Leodis McKelvin RC 1.50 4.00
163 Marcus Monk RC 1.50 4.00
164 Marcus Smith RC 1.50 4.00
165 Marcus Thomas RC 1.50 4.00
166 Marcus Henry RC 1.50 4.00
167 Mario Urrutia RC 1.25 3.00
168 Mark Bradford RC 1.25 3.00
169 Martellus Bennett RC 1.50 4.00
170 Martin Rucker RC 1.50 4.00
171 Matt Flynn RC 4.00 10.00
172 Mike Hart RC 2.00 5.00
173 Mike Jenkins RC 2.00 5.00
174 Owen Schmitt RC 2.00 5.00
175 Pat Sims RC 1.50 4.00
176 Patrick Lee RC 1.50 4.00
177 Paul Hubbard RC 1.50 4.00
178 Paul Smith RC 2.00 5.00
179 Peyton Hillis RC 2.50 6.00
180 Phillip Merling RC 1.50 4.00
181 Pierre Garcon RC 2.50 6.00
182 Quentin Groves RC 1.50 4.00
183 Reggie Smith RC 1.50 4.00
184 Ryan Grice-Mullen RC 1.25 3.00
185 Ryan Torain RC 2.00 5.00
186 Sam Keller RC 1.50 4.00
187 Sedrick Ellis RC 2.00 5.00
188 Shawn Crable RC 1.25 3.00
189 Simeon Castille RC 1.50 4.00
190 Steve Johnson RC 3.00 8.00
191 Tashard Choice RC 1.50 4.00
192 Terrell Thomas RC 1.50 4.00
193 Terrence Wheatley RC 1.25 3.00
194 Thomas Brown RC 1.50 4.00
195 Tim Hightower RC 2.00 5.00
196 Tracy Porter RC 2.00 5.00
197 Vernon Gholston RC 1.50 4.00
198 Will Franklin RC 1.50 4.00
199 Xavier Adibi RC 1.25 3.00
200 Xavier Omon RC 2.00 5.00
201 Andre Caldwell JSY AU RC 8.00 20.00
202 Brian Brohm JSY AU RC 10.00 25.00
203 Chad Henne JSY AU RC 10.00 25.00
204 Chris Johnson JSY AU RC 25.00 60.00
205 Darren McFadden JSY AU RC 25.00 60.00
206 DeSean Jackson JSY AU RC 30.00 60.00
207 Devin Thomas JSY AU RC 8.00 20.00
208 Dexter Jackson JSY AU RC 8.00 20.00
209 Donnie Avery JSY AU RC 8.00 20.00
210 Dustin Keller JSY AU RC 10.00 25.00
211 Earl Bennett JSY AU RC 10.00 25.00
212 Early Doucet JSY AU RC 8.00 20.00
213 Eddie Royal JSY AU RC 10.00 25.00
214 Felix Jones JSY AU RC 25.00 60.00
215 Glenn Dorsey JSY AU RC 10.00 25.00
216 Harry Douglas JSY AU RC 8.00 20.00
217 Jamaal Charles JSY AU RC 15.00 40.00
218 James Hardy JSY AU RC 8.00 20.00
219 Jerome Simpson JSY AU RC 10.00 25.00
220 Joe Flacco JSY AU RC 40.00 100.00
221 John David Booty JSY AU RC 8.00 20.00
222 Jonathan Stewart JSY AU RC 15.00 40.00
223 Jordy Nelson JSY AU RC 20.00 40.00
224 Kevin O'Connell JSY AU RC 8.00 20.00
225 Kevin Smith JSY AU RC 10.00 25.00
226 Limas Sweed JSY AU RC 10.00 25.00
227 Malcolm Kelly JSY AU RC 8.00 20.00
228 Mario Manningham JSY AU RC 10.00 25.00
229 Matt Forte JSY AU RC 30.00 80.00
230 Matt Ryan JSY AU RC 50.00 120.00
231 Rashard Mendenhall JSY AU RC 20.00 50.00
232 Ray Rice JSY AU RC 20.00 50.00
233 Steve Slaton JSY AU RC 10.00 25.00
234 Jake Long JSY AU RC 10.00 25.00

2008 Donruss Gridiron Gear Gold Holofoil

*VETS 1-100: 1.5X TO 4X BASIC CARDS
STATED PRINT RUN 200 SER.#'d SETS
67 Brett Favre 4.00 10.00

2008 Donruss Gridiron Gear Gold Holofoil O's

*VETS 1-100: 2.5X TO 6X BASIC CARDS
*ROOKIES 101-200: .6X TO 1.5X BASIC CARDS
STATED PRINT RUN 100 SER.#'d SETS
67 Brett Favre 6.00 15.00

2008 Donruss Gridiron Gear Gold Holofoil X's

*VETS 1-100: 2.5X TO 6X BASIC CARDS
*ROOKIES 101-200: .6X TO 1.5X BASIC CARDS
STATED PRINT RUN 100 SER.#'d SETS
67 Brett Favre 6.00 15.00

2008 Donruss Gridiron Gear Platinum Holofoil

*VETS 1-100: 3X TO 8X BASIC CARDS
STATED PRINT RUN 50 SER.#'d SETS

2008 Donruss Gridiron Gear Platinum Holofoil O's

*VETS 1-100: 5X TO 12X BASIC CARDS
*ROOKIES 101-200: 1X TO 2.5X BASIC CARDS
STATED PRINT RUN 25 SER.#'d SETS

2008 Donruss Gridiron Gear Platinum Holofoil X's

*VETS 1-100: 5X TO 12X BASIC CARDS
*ROOKIES 101-200: 1X TO 2.5X BASIC CARDS
STATED PRINT RUN 25 SER.#'d SETS

2008 Donruss Gridiron Gear Red Holofoil

*VETS 1-100: .8X TO 2X BASIC CARDS
67 Brett Favre 2.50 6.00

2008 Donruss Gridiron Gear Retail

*VETERANS 1-100: .3X TO .8X BASIC CARDS
*ROOKIES 101-200: .4X TO 1X BASIC CARDS
ROOKIES PRINT RUN 999 SER.#'d SETS

2008 Donruss Gridiron Gear Silver Holofoil

*VETS 1-100: 1X TO 2.5X BASIC CARDS
67 Brett Favre 2.50 6.00

2008 Donruss Gridiron Gear Silver Holofoil O's

*VETS: 1.5X TO 4X BASIC CARDS
STATED PRINT RUN 250 SER.#'d SETS
67 Brett Favre 4.00 10.00

2008 Donruss Gridiron Gear Silver Holofoil X's

*VETS: 1.5X TO 4X BASIC CARDS
STATED PRINT RUN 250 SER.#'d SETS
67 Brett Favre 4.00 10.00

2008 Donruss Gridiron Gear Autographs Gold Holofoil

STATED PRINT RUN 5-250
*PLATINUM/25: .6X TO 1.5X GOLD/250
*PLATINUM/25: .5X TO 1.2X GOLD/50-100
*PLATINUM/25: .4X TO 1X GOLD/25-35
PLATINUM HOLOFOIL PRINT RUN 1-25
101 Adrian Arrington 4.00 10.00
103 Ali Highsmith 3.00 8.00
104 Allen Patrick/100 5.00 12.00
105 Andre Woodson/100 6.00 15.00
106 Anthony Alridge/25 6.00 15.00
107 Antoine Cason/100 6.00 15.00
108 Aqib Talib/100 6.00 15.00
110 Brad Cottam/100 5.00 12.00
112 Calais Campbell 4.00 10.00
113 Caleb Campbell/100 6.00 15.00
116 Colt Brennan/100 15.00 40.00
117 Cory Boyd 3.00 8.00
119 Curtis Lofton 4.00 10.00
121 Dan Connor 5.00 12.00
122 Dantrell Savage 4.00 10.00
123 Darius Reynaud 3.00 8.00
124 Darrell Strong/35 6.00 15.00
126 Davone Bess 5.00 12.00
127 Dennis Dixon/100 8.00 20.00
128 Derrick Harvey 3.00 8.00
129 Dominique Rodgers-Cromartie 5.00 12.00
130 Erik Ainge 5.00 12.00
131 Erin Henderson 5.00 12.00
133 Fred Davis 5.00 12.00
135 Jacob Hester/100 6.00 15.00
136 Jacob Tamme 5.00 12.00
139 Jason Rivers 4.00 10.00
142 Jerod Mayo 5.00 12.00
143 Jermichael Finley 8.00 20.00
145 John Carlson 5.00 12.00
147 Jordon Dizon/25 8.00 20.00
148 Josh Johnson 5.00 12.00
149 Josh Morgan/25 8.00 20.00
150 Justin Forsett/25 8.00 20.00
153 Keenan Burton 3.00 8.00
154 Keith Rivers 5.00 12.00
155 Kellen Davis 3.00 8.00
157 Kenny Phillips 5.00 12.00
158 Kentwan Balmer 4.00 10.00
159 Kevin Robinson/25 5.00 12.00
160 Lavelle Hawkins 3.00 8.00
161 Lawrence Jackson 4.00 10.00
162 Leodis McKelvin 4.00 10.00

164 Marcus Smith/50 5.00 12.00
165 Marcus Thomas/25 6.00 15.00
168 Mark Bradford 3.00 8.00
169 Martellus Bennett 4.00 10.00
170 Martin Rucker 4.00 10.00
171 Matt Flynn 30.00 60.00
172 Mike Hart/100 6.00 15.00
173 Mike Jenkins 5.00 12.00
175 Pat Sims 4.00 10.00
178 Paul Smith 5.00 12.00
179 Peyton Hillis/25 25.00 60.00
180 Phillip Merling 4.00 10.00
183 Reggie Smith 4.00 10.00
184 Ryan Grice-Mullen 3.00 8.00
185 Ryan Torain/25 8.00 20.00
186 Sam Keller 4.00 10.00
187 Sedrick Ellis 5.00 12.00
191 Tashard Choice/100 5.00 12.00
192 Terrell Thomas 4.00 10.00
194 Thomas Brown/25 6.00 15.00
195 Tim Hightower/25 15.00 40.00
197 Vernon Gholston 4.00 10.00
198 Will Franklin/25 6.00 15.00
199 Xavier Adibi 3.00 8.00

2008 Donruss Gridiron Gear Jerseys

BASIC JERSEY PRINT RUN 32-250
*O/92-100: .5X TO 1.2X BASIC JSY/145-250
*O/92-100: .4X TO 1X BASIC JSY/80-125
*O/92-100: .3X TO .8X BASIC JSY/80-125
*O/27-34: .6X TO 1.5X BASIC JSY/250
O's PRINT RUN 15-100
*X/98-100: .5X TO 1.2X BASIC JSY/145-250
*X/98-100: .4X TO 1X BASIC JSY/80-125
*X/98-100: .3X TO .8X BASIC JSY/32-65
X's PRINT RUN 100 SER.#'d SETS
1 Matt Leinart 3.00 8.00
2 Larry Fitzgerald 3.00 8.00
3 Anquan Boldin 2.50 6.00
4 Edgerrin James/125 3.00 8.00
8 Willis McGahee/80 3.00 8.00
10 Mark Clayton/240 2.50 6.00
11 Trent Edwards 2.00 5.00
12 Marshawn Lynch 2.50 6.00
13 Lee Evans/50 4.00 10.00
14 Steve Smith/58 4.00 10.00
17 Brian Urlacher 3.00 8.00
18 Devin Hester 3.00 8.00
19 Rex Grossman 2.50 6.00
20 Carson Palmer 3.00 8.00
21 T.J. Houshmandzadeh 2.50 6.00
22 Rudi Johnson 2.50 6.00
23 Derek Anderson 2.00 5.00
25 Braylon Edwards 2.50 6.00
26 Tony Romo 4.00 10.00
27 Terrell Owens 3.00 8.00
28 Marion Barber 2.50 6.00
29 Jason Witten 3.00 8.00
30 Jay Cutler 3.00 0.00
32 Brandon Marshall 2.50 6.00
33 Jon Kitna/160 2.50 6.00
34 Roy Williams WR 2.50 6.00
36 Aaron Rodgers/100 10.00 25.00
37 Ryan Grant 3.00 8.00
38 Greg Jennings 3.00 8.00
41 Andre Johnson 2.50 6.00
42 Peyton Manning 5.00 12.00
43 Joseph Addai 2.50 6.00
44 Reggie Wayne 2.50 6.00
46 David Garrard/90 3.00 8.00
47 Fred Taylor 2.50 6.00
48 Maurice Jones-Drew 2.50 6.00
49 Brodie Croyle 2.50 6.00
50 Larry Johnson/145 2.50 6.00
51 Tony Gonzalez 2.50 6.00
53 Ronnie Brown 2.50 6.00
55 Tarvaris Jackson/200 2.50 6.00
56 Adrian Peterson 5.00 12.00
57 Chester Taylor 2.00 5.00
58 Tom Brady 5.00 12.00
59 Randy Moss 3.00 8.00
60 Laurence Maroney 2.50 6.00
61 Drew Brees/51 5.00 12.00
62 Reggie Bush/35 5.00 12.00
63 Marques Colston 2.50 6.00
64 Eli Manning 3.00 8.00
65 Plaxico Burress 2.50 6.00
66 Brandon Jacobs/32 4.00 10.00
68 Jerricho Cotchery/65 4.00 10.00
73 Donovan McNabb/45 5.00 12.00
74 Brian Westbrook 2.50 6.00
76 Ben Roethlisberger 3.00 8.00
77 Willie Parker 2.50 6.00
78 Hines Ward/83 3.00 8.00
79 Santonio Holmes 2.50 6.00
80 Philip Rivers/125 4.00 10.00
81 LaDainian Tomlinson 3.00 8.00
82 Antonio Gates 3.00 8.00
83 Alex Smith QB/230 3.00 8.00
84 Frank Gore 2.50 6.00
85 Vernon Davis/35 4.00 10.00
86 Matt Hasselbeck 2.50 6.00
88 Julius Jones 2.00 5.00
89 Marc Bulger 2.50 6.00
90 Steven Jackson 3.00 8.00
91 Torry Holt 2.50 6.00
92 Jeff Garcia 2.50 6.00
93 Cadillac Williams/230 2.50 6.00
95 Vince Young/240 2.50 6.00
96 LenDale White 2.50 6.00
97 Roydell Williams 2.00 5.00
98 Jason Campbell 2.50 6.00
99 Clinton Portis 2.50 6.00
100 Chris Cooley/110 3.00 8.00

2008 Donruss Gridiron Gear Jerseys Prime

PRIME PRINT RUN 2-50
2 Larry Fitzgerald 6.00 15.00
3 Anquan Boldin 5.00 12.00
4 Edgerrin James 5.00 12.00
8 Willis McGahee 5.00 12.00
10 Mark Clayton 5.00 12.00
11 Trent Edwards/40 4.00 10.00
12 Marshawn Lynch 5.00 12.00
13 Lee Evans 5.00 12.00
14 Steve Smith 5.00 12.00
16 Jake Delhomme 5.00 12.00
17 Brian Urlacher 6.00 15.00
19 Rex Grossman 5.00 12.00
20 Carson Palmer 6.00 15.00
21 T.J. Houshmandzadeh 5.00 12.00
22 Rudi Johnson 5.00 12.00
23 Derek Anderson 4.00 10.00
25 Braylon Edwards 5.00 12.00
26 Tony Romo 8.00 20.00
27 Terrell Owens 6.00 15.00
28 Marion Barber 5.00 12.00
29 Jason Witten 6.00 15.00
30 Jay Cutler 6.00 15.00
33 Jon Kitna 5.00 12.00
34 Roy Williams WR 5.00 12.00
35 Calvin Johnson 6.00 15.00
36 Aaron Rodgers 15.00 40.00
37 Ryan Grant/19 6.00 15.00
38 Greg Jennings 6.00 15.00
41 Andre Johnson 5.00 12.00
42 Peyton Manning/56 10.00 25.00
43 Joseph Addai 5.00 12.00
44 Reggie Wayne 5.00 12.00
45 Anthony Gonzalez 4.00 10.00
46 David Garrard 5.00 12.00
47 Fred Taylor 5.00 12.00
48 Maurice Jones-Drew 5.00 12.00
49 Brodie Croyle/25 5.00 12.00
50 Larry Johnson 5.00 12.00
51 Tony Gonzalez 5.00 12.00
53 Ronnie Brown 5.00 12.00
54 Ted Ginn Jr. 5.00 12.00
56 Adrian Peterson 10.00 25.00
57 Chester Taylor/45 4.00 10.00
58 Tom Brady 10.00 25.00
59 Randy Moss 6.00 15.00
60 Laurence Maroney 5.00 12.00
61 Drew Brees 6.00 15.00
62 Reggie Bush 6.00 15.00
63 Marques Colston 5.00 12.00
64 Eli Manning/25 6.00 15.00
65 Plaxico Burress 5.00 12.00
66 Brandon Jacobs 5.00 12.00
68 Jerricho Cotchery/45 5.00 12.00
69 Laveranues Coles 4.00 10.00
73 Donovan McNabb 6.00 15.00
74 Brian Westbrook 5.00 12.00
76 Ben Roethlisberger 6.00 15.00
77 Willie Parker 5.00 12.00
78 Hines Ward 5.00 12.00
79 Santonio Holmes 5.00 12.00
80 Philip Rivers/36 6.00 15.00
81 LaDainian Tomlinson 6.00 15.00
82 Antonio Gates 6.00 15.00
83 Alex Smith QB 6.00 15.00
84 Frank Gore 5.00 12.00
85 Vernon Davis 5.00 12.00
86 Matt Hasselbeck 5.00 12.00
87 Deion Branch 5.00 12.00
89 Marc Bulger 5.00 12.00
90 Steven Jackson 6.00 15.00
91 Torry Holt 5.00 12.00
92 Jeff Garcia/40 5.00 12.00
93 Cadillac Williams 5.00 12.00
95 Vince Young 5.00 12.00
96 LenDale White/45 5.00 12.00
97 Roydell Williams 4.00 10.00
98 Jason Campbell 5.00 12.00
99 Clinton Portis 5.00 12.00
100 Chris Cooley/25 5.00 12.00

2008 Donruss Gridiron Gear Next Generation Gold

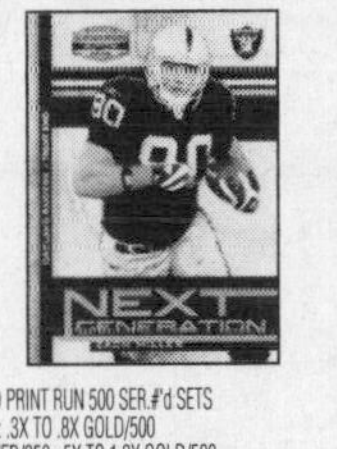

GOLD PRINT RUN 500 SER.#'d SETS
*RED: .3X TO .8X GOLD/500
*SILVER/250: .5X TO 1.2X GOLD/500
SILVER PRINT RUN 250 SER.#'d SETS
*GOLD HOLO/100: .6X TO 1.5X GOLD/500
GOLD HOLO PRINT RUN 100 SER.#'d SETS
*PLATINUM/25: 1X TO 2.5X GOLD/500
PLATINUM PRINT RUN 25 SER.#'d SETS
1 James Hardy .60 1.50
2 Malcolm Kelly .60 1.50
3 Jake Long .75 2.00
4 Matt Ryan 3.00 8.00
5 Dexter Jackson .60 1.50
6 Jerome Simpson .75 2.00
7 Jordy Nelson 1.00 2.50
8 Kevin O'Connell .60 1.50
9 Chad Henne .75 2.00
10 Mario Manningham .75 2.00
11 Jonathan Stewart 1.25 3.00
12 Devin Thomas .60 1.50
13 Limas Sweed .75 2.00
14 Kevin Smith .75 2.00
15 Glenn Dorsey .75 2.00
16 Darren McFadden 2.00 5.00
17 Dustin Keller .75 2.00
18 Earl Bennett .75 2.00
19 Joe Flacco 2.50 6.00
20 Ray Rice 1.50 4.00
21 Steve Slaton .75 2.00
22 Eddie Royal .75 2.00
23 Early Doucet .60 1.50
24 John David Booty .60 1.50
25 Jamaal Charles 1.25 3.00
26 Matt Forte 1.25 3.00
27 Felix Jones 1.25 3.00
28 Rashard Mendenhall 1.50 4.00
29 Chris Johnson 2.00 5.00
30 DeSean Jackson 1.50 4.00
31 Brian Brohm .75 2.00
32 Andre Caldwell .75 2.00
33 Donnie Avery .60 1.50
34 Harry Douglas .60 1.50
35 Calvin Johnson 1.25 3.00
36 Anthony Gonzalez .75 2.00
37 Zach Miller 1.00 2.50
38 James Jones .75 2.00
39 Ryan Grant 1.25 3.00
40 Kenny Watson .75 2.00

2008 Donruss Gridiron Gear Next Generation Jerseys

STATED PRINT RUN 250 SER.#'d SETS
*PRIME/50: .8X TO 2X BASIC JSY/250
PRIME PRINT RUN 2-50
*COMBO PRIME/20-50: .8X TO 2X JSY/250
COMBO PRIME PRINT RUN 10-50
*JUMBO/19-50: .6X TO 1.5X BASIC JSY/250
JUMBO SWATCH PRINT RUN 19-50
*JUMBO PRIME/25: .8X TO 2X BASIC JSY/250
JUMBO PRIME PRINT RUN 1-25
1 James Hardy 2.00 5.00
2 Malcolm Kelly 2.00 5.00
3 Jake Long 2.50 6.00
4 Matt Ryan 8.00 20.00
5 Dexter Jackson 2.00 5.00
6 Jerome Simpson 2.50 6.00
7 Jordy Nelson 3.00 8.00
8 Kevin O'Connell 2.00 5.00
9 Chad Henne 2.50 6.00
10 Mario Manningham 2.50 6.00
11 Jonathan Stewart 4.00 10.00
12 Devin Thomas 2.00 5.00
13 Limas Sweed 2.50 6.00
14 Kevin Smith 2.50 6.00
15 Glenn Dorsey 2.50 6.00
16 Darren McFadden 6.00 15.00
17 Dustin Keller 2.50 6.00
18 Earl Bennett 2.50 6.00
19 Joe Flacco 8.00 20.00
20 Ray Rice 5.00 12.00
21 Steve Slaton 2.50 6.00
22 Eddie Royal 2.50 6.00
23 Early Doucet 2.00 5.00
24 John David Booty 2.00 5.00
25 Jamaal Charles 4.00 10.00
26 Matt Forte 4.00 10.00
27 Felix Jones 4.00 10.00
28 Rashard Mendenhall 5.00 12.00
29 Chris Johnson 6.00 15.00
30 DeSean Jackson 5.00 12.00
31 Brian Brohm 2.50 6.00
32 Andre Caldwell 2.00 5.00
33 Donnie Avery 2.00 5.00
34 Harry Douglas 2.00 5.00
38 James Jones 2.00 5.00
39 Ryan Grant 3.00 8.00

2008 Donruss Gridiron Gear Next Generation Jerseys Autographs

STATED PRINT RUN 50 SER.#'d SETS
*PRIME/25: .5X TO 1.2X BASIC JSY AU/50
PRIME PRINT RUN 1-25
1 James Hardy 5.00 12.00
2 Malcolm Kelly 5.00 12.00
3 Jake Long 6.00 15.00
4 Matt Ryan 50.00 100.00
5 Dexter Jackson 5.00 12.00
6 Jerome Simpson 6.00 15.00
7 Jordy Nelson 12.00 30.00
8 Kevin O'Connell 5.00 12.00
9 Chad Henne 6.00 15.00
10 Mario Manningham 6.00 15.00
11 Jonathan Stewart 10.00 25.00
12 Devin Thomas 5.00 12.00
13 Limas Sweed 6.00 15.00
14 Kevin Smith
16 Darren McFadden 20.00 50.00
17 Dustin Keller 6.00 15.00
18 Earl Bennett 6.00 15.00
19 Joe Flacco 40.00 80.00
20 Ray Rice 12.00 30.00
21 Steve Slaton 6.00 15.00
22 Eddie Royal 6.00 15.00
23 Early Doucet 5.00 12.00
24 John David Booty 5.00 12.00
25 Jamaal Charles 10.00 25.00
26 Matt Forte 25.00 50.00
27 Felix Jones 20.00 50.00
28 Rashard Mendenhall 12.00 30.00
29 Chris Johnson 30.00 60.00
30 DeSean Jackson 15.00 40.00
31 Brian Brohm 6.00 15.00
32 Andre Caldwell 5.00 12.00
33 Donnie Avery 5.00 12.00
38 James Jones/25 6.00 15.00
39 Ryan Grant/25 25.00 50.00

2008 Donruss Gridiron Gear NFL Gridiron Rookie Signatures

STATED PRINT RUN 40 SER.#'d SETS
1 Chris Johnson 30.00 80.00
2 Darren McFadden 25.00 60.00
3 DeSean Jackson 15.00 40.00
4 Eddie Royal 8.00 20.00
5 Dustin Keller 8.00 20.00
6 Jamaal Charles 12.00 30.00
7 Jerome Simpson 8.00 20.00
8 John David Booty 6.00 15.00
9 Jordy Nelson 15.00 40.00
10 Kevin Smith 8.00 20.00
11 Malcolm Kelly 6.00 15.00
12 Matt Forte 15.00 40.00
13 Rashard Mendenhall 15.00 40.00
14 Steve Slaton 8.00 20.00
15 Dexter Jackson 6.00 15.00
16 Andre Caldwell 6.00 15.00
17 Joe Flacco 40.00 100.00
18 Brian Brohm 8.00 20.00
19 Felix Jones 15.00 40.00
20 Limas Sweed 8.00 20.00
21 Early Doucet 6.00 15.00
22 Donnie Avery 6.00 15.00
23 Chad Henne 8.00 20.00
24 Glenn Dorsey 8.00 20.00
25 Jonathan Stewart 12.00 30.00
26 Ray Rice 15.00 40.00
27 Matt Ryan 60.00 150.00
28 Mario Manningham 8.00 20.00
29 Kevin O'Connell 6.00 15.00
30 James Hardy 6.00 15.00
31 Devin Thomas 6.00 15.00
32 Harry Douglas 6.00 15.00
33 Jake Long 8.00 20.00
34 Earl Bennett 8.00 20.00

2008 Donruss Gridiron Gear NFL Teams Rookie Signatures

STATED PRINT RUN 30 SER.#'d SETS
1 Devin Thomas 6.00 15.00
2 Dexter Jackson 6.00 15.00
3 Donnie Avery 6.00 15.00
4 Dustin Keller 8.00 20.00
5 Earl Bennett 8.00 20.00
7 Eddie Royal 8.00 20.00
8 Felix Jones 25.00 60.00
9 Glenn Dorsey EXCH
10 Andre Caldwell 6.00 15.00
11 Brian Brohm 8.00 20.00
12 Chad Henne 25.00 50.00
13 Chris Johnson 40.00 80.00
14 Darren McFadden 25.00 60.00
15 Jamaal Charles 12.00 30.00
16 James Hardy 6.00 15.00
17 Jerome Simpson 8.00 20.00
18 Mario Manningham 8.00 20.00
19 Matt Forte 30.00 60.00
20 Matt Ryan 60.00 120.00
21 Rashard Mendenhall 15.00 40.00
22 Ray Rice 15.00 40.00
23 Steve Slaton 8.00 20.00
24 Jake Long 8.00 20.00
25 Chris Long 8.00 20.00
26 John David Booty 6.00 15.00
27 Jonathan Stewart 12.00 30.00
28 Jordy Nelson 15.00 40.00
29 Kevin O'Connell 6.00 15.00
30 Kevin Smith 8.00 20.00
31 Limas Sweed 8.00 20.00
32 Malcolm Kelly 6.00 15.00
33 Joe Flacco 50.00 100.00
34 Harry Douglas EXCH
35 DeSean Jackson 20.00 50.00

2008 Donruss Gridiron Gear NFL Teams Veteran Signatures

STATED PRINT RUN 25 SER.#'d SETS
1 Peyton Manning 60.00 120.00
2 Ben Roethlisberger 60.00 120.00
3 Braylon Edwards 10.00 25.00
4 Donald Driver 10.00 25.00
5 Frank Gore 10.00 25.00
7 Reggie Wayne 12.00 30.00
8 Roddy White 10.00 25.00
9 T.J. Houshmandzadeh 10.00 25.00
10 Trent Edwards 8.00 20.00
11 Vincent Jackson 8.00 20.00
12 Willie Parker 10.00 25.00
13 Ryan Grant 20.00 40.00
14 Tony Romo 40.00 100.00
15 Brandon Jacobs 10.00 25.00
16 Josh Cribbs 20.00 40.00
17 DeAngelo Williams 10.00 25.00
18 Drew Brees 40.00 80.00
19 Greg Lewis 8.00 20.00
21 Justin Fargas 8.00 20.00
22 Larry Johnson 10.00 25.00
23 Ladell Betts 8.00 20.00
24 Marques Colston 10.00 25.00
25 Patrick Willis 10.00 25.00
26 Santonio Holmes 10.00 25.00
27 Selvin Young 8.00 20.00
28 Sidney Rice 12.00 30.00
29 Wes Welker 30.00 60.00
30 Zach Miller 10.00 25.00
31 Adrian Peterson 90.00 150.00

2008 Donruss Gridiron Gear Performers Gold

GOLD PRINT RUN 500 SER.#'d SETS
*RED: .3X TO .8X GOLD/500
*SILVER/250: .5X TO 1.2X GOLD/500
SILVER PRINT RUN 250 SER.#'d SETS
*GOLD HOLO/100: .6X TO 1.5X GOLD/500
GOLD HOLO PRINT RUN 100 SER.#'d SETS
*PLATINUM/25: 1X TO 2.5X GOLD/500
PLATINUM PRINT RUN 25 SER.#'d SETS
1 Alex Karras 1.50 4.00
2 Barry Sanders 3.00 8.00
3 Bert Jones 1.25 3.00
4 Bill Dudley 1.25 3.00
5 Billy Howton 1.25 3.00
6 Dante Lavelli 1.25 3.00
7 Bob Griese 2.00 5.00
8 Brett Favre 5.00 12.00
9 Carl Eller 1.25 3.00
10 Charley Trippi 1.25 3.00
11 Cliff Harris 1.25 3.00
12 Dan Marino 4.00 10.00
13 Danny White 1.25 3.00
14 Daryl Johnston 2.00 5.00
15 Daryle Lamonica 1.50 4.00
16 Del Shofner 1.25 3.00
17 Don Perkins 1.25 3.00
18 Fred Dryer 1.25 3.00
19 Fred Williamson 1.25 3.00
20 Gary Collins 1.25 3.00
21 Cris Collinsworth 1.50 4.00
22 Jan Stenerud 1.25 3.00
23 Joe Montana 4.00 10.00
24 John Riggins 1.50 4.00
25 Ken Stabler 2.00 5.00
26 Lance Alworth 1.50 4.00
27 Len Dawson 2.00 5.00
28 Lenny Moore 1.50 4.00
29 Leroy Kelly 1.50 4.00
30 Lydell Mitchell 1.25 3.00
31 Marcus Allen 2.00 5.00
32 Mark Duper 1.25 3.00
33 Mike Curtis 1.25 3.00
34 Ozzie Newsome 1.50 4.00
35 Paul Warfield 1.50 4.00
36 Pete Retzlaff 1.25 3.00
37 Randall Cunningham 2.00 5.00
38 Raymond Berry 1.50 4.00
39 Reggie White 2.00 5.00
40 Rosey Grier 1.25 3.00
41 Sammy Baugh 2.00 5.00
42 Steve Young 2.50 6.00
43 Ted Hendricks 1.25 3.00
44 Tommy McDonald 1.50 4.00
45 Troy Aikman 2.50 6.00
46 William Perry 1.25 3.00
47 Willie Davis 1.25 3.00
48 Willie Wood 1.25 3.00
49 Y.A. Tittle 2.00 5.00
50 Yale Lary 1.25 3.00

2008 Donruss Gridiron Gear Performers Autographs

STATED PRINT RUN 1-250
SERIAL #'d TO 1 NOT PRICED
1 Alex Karras/25 12.00 30.00
3 Bert Jones/50 8.00 20.00
4 Bill Dudley/96 8.00 20.00
5 Billy Howton/250 8.00 20.00
6 Dante Lavelli/50 8.00 20.00
10 Charley Trippi/100 8.00 20.00
15 Daryle Lamonica/50 10.00 25.00
16 Del Shofner/250 8.00 20.00
17 Don Perkins/100 8.00 20.00
19 Fred Williamson/100 20.00 40.00
20 Gary Collins/175 8.00 20.00
21 Cris Collinsworth/25 12.00 30.00
22 Jan Stenerud/100 8.00 20.00
28 Lenny Moore/100 10.00 25.00
29 Leroy Kelly/100 10.00 25.00
30 Lydell Mitchell/250 8.00 20.00
33 Mike Curtis/100 8.00 20.00
34 Ozzie Newsome/25 12.00 30.00
36 Pete Retzlaff/100 8.00 20.00
37 Randall Cunningham/75 15.00 40.00
38 Raymond Berry/100 10.00 25.00
40 Rosey Grier/75 8.00 20.00
44 Tommy McDonald/25 12.00 30.00
46 William Perry/150 8.00 20.00
47 Willie Davis/100 12.00 30.00
48 Willie Wood/100 12.00 30.00
50 Yale Lary/50 8.00 20.00

2008 Donruss Gridiron Gear Performers Jerseys

STATED PRINT RUN 250 SER.#'d SETS
*PRIME/50: .6X TO 1.5X BASIC JSY
*PRIME/15-25: .8X TO 2X BASIC JSY
PRIME PRINT RUN 5-50
1 Alex Karras 3.00 8.00
3 Bert Jones 2.50 6.00
8 Brett Favre 10.00 25.00
11 Cliff Harris/240 2.50 6.00
12 Dan Marino 8.00 20.00
13 Danny White 2.50 6.00
15 Daryle Lamonica/175 3.00 8.00
18 Fred Dryer 2.50 6.00
21 Cris Collinsworth/150 3.00 8.00
23 Joe Montana 8.00 20.00
24 John Riggins 3.00 8.00
25 Ken Stabler/90 4.00 10.00
28 Lenny Moore 3.00 8.00
31 Marcus Allen 4.00 10.00
32 Mark Duper/145 2.50 6.00
34 Ozzie Newsome 3.00 8.00
35 Paul Warfield 3.00 8.00
38 Raymond Berry 3.00 8.00
39 Reggie White 6.00 15.00
40 Rosey Grier 2.50 6.00
41 Sammy Baugh 8.00 20.00
42 Steve Young 5.00 12.00
43 Ted Hendricks 2.50 6.00
44 Tommy McDonald 3.00 8.00
45 Troy Aikman 5.00 12.00

2008 Donruss Gridiron Gear Performers Jerseys Autographs

STATED PRINT RUN 2-50
*PRIME/25: .6X TO 1.5X BASE JSY/50
*PRIME/25: .5X TO 1.2X BASE JSY/25
PRIME PRINT RUN 2-25
SERIAL #'d UNDER 25 NOT PRICED
1 Alex Karras/50 12.00 30.00
2 Barry Sanders/25 60.00 120.00
3 Bert Jones/25 12.00 30.00
7 Bob Griese/50 15.00 40.00
11 Cliff Harris/50 10.00 25.00
13 Danny White/25 15.00 40.00
15 Daryle Lamonica/25 15.00 40.00
18 Fred Dryer/25 12.00 30.00
23 Joe Montana/25 60.00 120.00
24 John Riggins/50 15.00 40.00
25 Ken Stabler/25 20.00 50.00
28 Lenny Moore/50 12.00 30.00
31 Marcus Allen/25 20.00 50.00
32 Mark Duper/25 12.00 30.00
34 Ozzie Newsome/25 15.00 40.00
35 Paul Warfield/25 15.00 40.00
37 Randall Cunningham/25 40.00 80.00
38 Raymond Berry/50 12.00 30.00
40 Rosey Grier/50 10.00 25.00
42 Steve Young/25 40.00 80.00
43 Ted Hendricks/25 12.00 30.00
44 Tommy McDonald/25 15.00 40.00

2008 Donruss Gridiron Gear Performers Jerseys Combos

*COMBOS/50-100: .5X TO 1.2X BASIC JSY
COMBOS PRINT RUN 1-100
*COMBO PRIME/50: .6X TO 1.5X BASIC JSY
*COMBO PRIME/25-30: .8X TO 2X BASIC JSY
COMBO PRIME PRINT RUN 5-50
2 Barry Sanders 8.00 20.00
7 Bob Griese 5.00 12.00

2008 Donruss Gridiron Gear Performers Jerseys Combos Autographs

STATED PRINT RUN 25 SER.#'d SETS
*PRIME/25: .4X TO 1X JSY COMBO/25
PRIME PRINT RUN 1-25
SERIAL #'d UNDER 25 NOT PRICED
1 Alex Karras 15.00 40.00
3 Bert Jones 12.00 30.00
7 Bob Griese 20.00 50.00
11 Cliff Harris 12.00 30.00
13 Danny White 12.00 30.00
14 Daryl Johnston 20.00 50.00
15 Daryle Lamonica 15.00 40.00
18 Fred Dryer 12.00 30.00
23 Joe Montana/19
24 John Riggins 20.00 50.00
25 Ken Stabler 20.00 50.00
28 Lenny Moore 15.00 40.00
31 Marcus Allen 20.00 50.00
32 Mark Duper 12.00 30.00
34 Ozzie Newsome 15.00 40.00
37 Randall Cunningham 40.00 80.00
38 Raymond Berry 15.00 40.00
40 Rosey Grier 12.00 30.00
42 Steve Young 40.00 80.00
44 Tommy McDonald 15.00 40.00
49 Y.A. Tittle 20.00 50.00

2008 Donruss Gridiron Gear Performers Jerseys Jumbo Swatch

*JUMBO/50: .6X TO 1.5X BASIC JSY
*JUMBO/15-25: .8X TO 2X BASIC JSY
JUMBO PRINT RUN 5-50
*JUMBO PRIME/25: 1X TO 2.5X BASIC JSY
JUMBO PRIME PRINT RUN 1-25
2 Barry Sanders/45 10.00 25.00

2008 Donruss Gridiron Gear Plates and Patches

STATED PRINT RUN 100 SER.#'d SETS
1 Adrian Peterson 10.00 25.00
2 Marshawn Lynch 5.00 12.00
3 Antonio Gates 6.00 15.00
4 Fred Taylor 5.00 12.00
5 Tony Romo 8.00 20.00
6 Joseph Addai 5.00 12.00
7 Tony Gonzalez 5.00 12.00
8 Torry Holt 5.00 12.00
9 Brandon Jacobs 5.00 12.00
10 Brian Westbrook 5.00 12.00
11 Randy Moss 6.00 15.00
12 Marques Colston 5.00 12.00
13 Willis McGahee 5.00 12.00
14 Reggie Wayne 5.00 12.00
15 Clinton Portis 5.00 12.00

2008 Donruss Gridiron Gear Plates and Patches Autographs

STATED PRINT RUN 25 SER.#'d SETS
1 Adrian Peterson 75.00 150.00
4 Fred Taylor 15.00 40.00
5 Tony Romo 75.00 150.00
9 Brandon Jacobs 15.00 40.00
10 Brian Westbrook 15.00 40.00
12 Marques Colston 15.00 40.00
14 Reggie Wayne 15.00 40.00

2008 Donruss Gridiron Gear Playbook Gold

GOLD PRINT RUN 500 SER.#'d SETS
*RED: .3X TO .8X GOLD/500
*SILVER/250: .5X TO 1.2X GOLD/500
SILVER PRINT RUN 250 SER.#'d SETS
*GOLD HOLO/100: .6X TO 1.5X GOLD/500
GOLD HOLO PRINT RUN 100 SER.#'d SETS
*PLATINUM/25: 1X TO 2.5X GOLD/500
PLATINUM PRINT RUN 25 SER.#'d SETS
1 Adrian Peterson 2.00 5.00
2 Peyton Manning 2.00 5.00
3 Tom Brady 2.00 5.00
4 Tony Romo 1.50 4.00
5 Carson Palmer 1.25 3.00
6 Torry Holt 1.00 2.50
7 David Garrard 1.00 2.50
8 Braylon Edwards 1.00 2.50
9 Eli Manning 1.25 3.00
10 Willie Parker 1.00 2.50
11 T.J. Houshmandzadeh 1.00 2.50
12 Jay Cutler 1.25 3.00
13 Steve Smith 1.00 2.50
14 Larry Fitzgerald 1.25 3.00
15 Plaxico Burress 1.00 2.50
16 Greg Jennings 1.25 3.00
17 Ben Roethlisberger 1.25 3.00
18 Reggie Wayne 1.00 2.50
19 LaDainian Tomlinson 1.25 3.00
20 Santonio Holmes 1.00 2.50
21 Philip Rivers 1.25 3.00
22 Marshawn Lynch 1.00 2.50
23 Brian Westbrook 1.00 2.50
24 Maurice Jones-Drew 1.00 2.50
25 Edgerrin James 1.00 2.50

2008 Donruss Gridiron Gear Playbook Jerseys O's

O's PRINT RUN 125-250
*X's/90-250: .4X TO 1X O'S/125-250
X's STATED PRINT RUN 9-250
*PATCH/25: .8X TO 2X O'S/125-250
PATCHES STATED PRINT RUN 25
1 Adrian Peterson 5.00 12.00
2 Peyton Manning 5.00 12.00
3 Tom Brady 5.00 12.00
4 Tony Romo 4.00 10.00
5 Carson Palmer 3.00 8.00
6 Torry Holt 2.50 6.00
7 David Garrard 2.50 6.00
8 Braylon Edwards 2.50 6.00
9 Eli Manning 3.00 8.00
10 Willie Parker 2.50 6.00
11 T.J. Houshmandzadeh 2.50 6.00
12 Jay Cutler 3.00 8.00
13 Steve Smith 2.50 6.00
14 Larry Fitzgerald 3.00 8.00
15 Plaxico Burress 2.50 6.00
16 Greg Jennings 3.00 8.00
17 Ben Roethlisberger 3.00 8.00
18 Reggie Wayne 2.50 6.00
19 LaDainian Tomlinson 3.00 8.00
20 Santonio Holmes 2.50 6.00
21 Philip Rivers 3.00 8.00
22 Marshawn Lynch 2.50 6.00
23 Brian Westbrook/125 2.50 6.00
24 Maurice Jones-Drew 2.50 6.00
25 Edgerrin James 2.50 6.00

2008 Donruss Gridiron Gear Player Timeline Gold

GOLD PRINT RUN 500 SER.#'d SETS
*RED: .3X TO .8X GOLD/500
*SILVER/250: .5X TO 1.2X GOLD/500
SILVER PRINT RUN 250 SER.#'d SETS
*GOLD HOLO/100: .6X TO 1.5X GOLD/500
GOLD HOLO PRINT RUN 100 SER.#'d SETS
*PLATINUM/25: 1X TO 2.5X GOLD/500
PLATINUM PRINT RUN 25 SER.#'d SETS
1 Reggie White 2.00 5.00
2 Joe Montana 4.00 10.00
3 Warren Moon 2.00 5.00
4 John Riggins 1.50 4.00
5 Randy Moss 1.25 3.00
6 Julius Jones .75 2.00
7 Isaac Bruce 1.00 2.50
8 Alge Crumpler 1.00 2.50
9 Bernard Berrian 1.00 2.50
10 Clinton Portis 1.00 2.50
11 Brandon Stokley 1.00 2.50
12 Zach Thomas 1.00 2.50
13 Santana Moss .75 2.00
14 Ahman Green 1.00 2.50
15 Jamal Lewis 1.00 2.50
16 Plaxico Burress 1.00 2.50
17 Derrick Mason 1.00 2.50
18 Nate Burleson .75 2.00
19 DeShaun Foster 1.00 2.50
20 Michael Turner 1.25 3.00
21 Warrick Dunn 1.00 2.50
22 Jeff Garcia 1.00 2.50
23 Drew Brees 1.25 3.00
24 Darren McFadden 2.00 5.00
25 Willis McGahee 1.00 2.50

2008 Donruss Gridiron Gear Player Timeline Autographs

STATED PRINT RUN 1-100
4 John Riggins/25 12.00 30.00
9 Bernard Berrian/53 10.00 25.00
17 Derrick Mason/100 10.00 25.00
20 Michael Turner/25 15.00 40.00

2008 Donruss Gridiron Gear Player Timeline Jerseys Prime

PRIME PRINT RUN 25-50
*BASIC JSY/70-250: .2X TO .5X PRIME/25-50
*BASIC JSY/25: .3X TO .8X PRIME/25-50
BASIC JERSEY PRINT RUN 2-250
*COMBO JSY/60-100: .3X TO .8X PRIME/25-50
*COMBO JSY/20-30: .4X TO 1X PRIME/25-50
COMBO JERSEY PRINT RUN 10-100
*COMBO JSY PRIME/25-50: .4X TO 1X PRIME
COMBO JERSEY PRIME PRINT RUN 1-50
*JUMBO JSY/25-50: .3X TO .8X PRIME
JUMBO JERSEY PRINT RUN 10-50
*JUMBO PRIME/20-25: .5X TO 1.2X PRIME
JUMBO PRIME PRINT RUN 12-25
1 Reggie White/25 12.00 30.00
2 Joe Montana 15.00 40.00
3 Warren Moon 8.00 20.00
4 John Riggins/25 6.00 15.00
5 Randy Moss 6.00 15.00
6 Julius Jones 4.00 10.00
7 Isaac Bruce 5.00 12.00
8 Alge Crumpler 5.00 12.00
9 Bernard Berrian 5.00 12.00
10 Clinton Portis/30 5.00 12.00
11 Brandon Stokley/25 5.00 12.00
12 Zach Thomas 5.00 12.00
13 Santana Moss 4.00 10.00
14 Ahman Green 5.00 12.00
15 Jamal Lewis 5.00 12.00
16 Plaxico Burress 5.00 12.00
17 Derrick Mason 5.00 12.00
18 Nate Burleson 4.00 10.00
19 DeShaun Foster 5.00 12.00
20 Michael Turner 6.00 15.00
21 Warrick Dunn 5.00 12.00
22 Jeff Garcia 5.00 12.00
23 Drew Brees 6.00 15.00
24 Darren McFadden 8.00 20.00
25 Willis McGahee 5.00 12.00

2008 Donruss Gridiron Gear Player Timeline Jerseys Autographs

BASIC JSY AUTO PRINT RUN 10-50
*PRIME/15-25: .5X TO 1.2X BASIC JSY AU
PRIME PRINT RUN 3-25
*JSY COMBO AU/20-25: .4X TO 1X
JSY COMBO AUTO PRINT RUN 5-25
UNPRICED COMBO AU PRIME PRINT RUN 15-20
SERIAL #'d UNDER 25 NOT PRICED
2 Joe Montana/15 75.00 150.00
4 John Riggins/50 15.00 40.00
9 Bernard Berrian/25 15.00 40.00
17 Derrick Mason/25 15.00 40.00
20 Michael Turner/50 20.00 50.00
24 Darren McFadden/25 30.00 80.00

2008 Donruss Gridiron Gear Rivals Gold

GOLD PRINT RUN 500 SER.#'d SETS
*RED: .3X TO .8X GOLD/500
*SILVER/250: .5X TO 1.2X GOLD/500
SILVER PRINT RUN 250 SER.#'d SETS
*GOLD HOLO/100: .6X TO 1.5X GOLD/500
GOLD HOLO PRINT RUN 100 SER.#'d SETS
*PLATINUM/25: 1X TO 2.5X GOLD/500
PLATINUM PRINT RUN 25 SER.#'d SETS
1 Randy Moss 1.25 3.00
Terrell Owens
2 Peyton Manning 2.00 5.00
Tom Brady
3 Eli Manning 1.50 4.00
Tony Romo
4 Laurence Maroney 1.00 2.50
Shawne Merriman
5 Carson Palmer 1.25 3.00
Ray Lewis
6 Troy Aikman 2.50 6.00
Steve Young
7 Brett Favre 3.00 8.00
Michael Strahan
8 T.J. Houshmandzadeh 1.00 2.50
Braylon Edwards
9 Clinton Portis 1.00 2.50
Marion Barber
10 Jay Cutler 1.25 3.00
Tony Gonzalez

2008 Donruss Gridiron Gear Rivals Jerseys

STATED PRINT RUN 10-100
*PRIME/25: .8X TO 2X BASIC DUAL
PRIME PRINT RUN 2-25
1 Randy Moss 5.00 12.00
Terrell Owens
3 Eli Manning 6.00 15.00
Tony Romo/65
4 Laurence Maroney 4.00 10.00
Shawne Merriman
5 Carson Palmer 5.00 12.00
Ray Lewis/50
6 Troy Aikman 10.00 25.00
Steve Young
7 Brett Favre 12.00 30.00
Michael Strahan
8 T.J. Houshmandzadeh 4.00 10.00
Braylon Edwards
9 Clinton Portis 4.00 10.00
Marion Barber
10 Jay Cutler 5.00 12.00
Tony Gonzalez

2008 Donruss Gridiron Gear Rookie Gridiron Gems Jerseys

BASIC JSY PRINT RUN 50 SER.#'d SETS
*COMBO/50: .5X TO 1.2X BASIC JSY/50
*COMBO PRIME/25: .6X TO 1.5X BASIC JSY/50
*JUMBO/50: .5X TO 1.2X BASIC JSY/50
*JUMBO PRIME/25: .8X TO 2X BASIC JSY/50
*PRIME/50: .5X TO 1.2X BASIC JSY/50
*RETAIL RED/50: .4X TO 1X BASIC JSY/50
*TRIOS/50: .6X TO 1.5X BASIC JSY/50
*TRIOS PRIME/25: .8X TO 2X BASIC JSY/50
201 Andre Caldwell 2.00 5.00
202 Brian Brohm 2.50 6.00
203 Chad Henne 2.50 6.00
204 Chris Johnson 6.00 15.00
205 Darren McFadden 6.00 15.00
206 DeSean Jackson 5.00 12.00
207 Devin Thomas 2.00 5.00
208 Dexter Jackson 2.00 5.00
209 Donnie Avery 2.00 5.00
210 Dustin Keller 2.50 6.00
211 Earl Bennett 2.50 6.00
212 Early Doucet 2.00 5.00
213 Eddie Royal 2.50 6.00
214 Felix Jones 4.00 10.00
215 Glenn Dorsey 2.50 6.00
216 Harry Douglas 2.00 5.00
217 Jamaal Charles 4.00 10.00
218 James Hardy 2.00 5.00
219 Jerome Simpson 2.50 6.00
220 Joe Flacco 5.00 12.00
221 John David Booty 2.00 5.00
222 Jonathan Stewart 5.00 12.00
223 Jordy Nelson 3.00 8.00
224 Kevin O'Connell 2.00 5.00
225 Kevin Smith 2.50 6.00
226 Limas Sweed 2.50 6.00
227 Malcolm Kelly 2.00 5.00
228 Mario Manningham 2.50 6.00
229 Matt Forte 5.00 12.00
230 Matt Ryan 8.00 20.00
231 Rashard Mendenhall 5.00 12.00
232 Ray Rice 5.00 12.00
233 Steve Slaton 2.50 6.00
234 Jake Long 2.50 6.00

2008 Donruss Gridiron Gear Rookie Gridiron Gems Jerseys Autographs Prime

*PRIME JSY AU/50: .4X TO 1X BASE JSY AU
STATED PRINT RUN 50 SER.#'d SETS

2008 Donruss Gridiron Gear Rookie Gridiron Gems Jerseys Combos Autographs Prime

*PRIME JSY AU/50: .4X TO 1X BASE JSY AU
STATED PRINT RUN 50 SER.#'d SETS

2008 Donruss Gridiron Gear Rookie Gridiron Gems Jerseys Trios Autographs Prime

*TRIO JSY AU/50: .5X TO 1.2X BASE JSY AU
STATED PRINT RUN 50 SER.#'d SETS

2009 Donruss Gridiron Gear

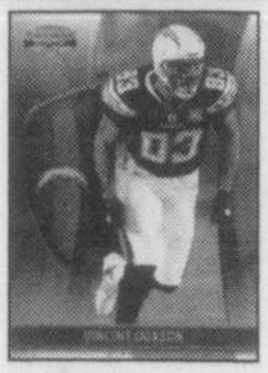

COMP.SET w/o RC's (100) 10.00 25.00
101-200 ROOKIE PRINT RUN 999
201-234 ROOKIE AU PRINT RUN 98-100
1 Aaron Rodgers .60 1.50
2 Adrian Peterson .50 1.25
3 Andre Johnson .25 .60
4 Anthony Gonzalez .20 .50
5 Antonio Bryant .20 .50
6 Antonio Gates .25 .60
7 Ben Roethlisberger .30 .75
8 Bernard Berrian .25 .60
9 Brady Quinn .25 .60
10 Brandon Jacobs .25 .60
11 Brandon Marshall .25 .60
12 Braylon Edwards .25 .60
13 Brian Urlacher .30 .75
14 Brian Westbrook .25 .60
15 Calvin Johnson .30 .75
16 Carson Palmer .30 .75
17 Chad Ochocinco .25 .60
18 Chad Pennington .25 .60
19 Chris Cooley .25 .60
20 Chris Johnson .30 .75
21 Clinton Portis .25 .60
22 Darren McFadden .30 .75
23 Daunte Culpepper .25 .60
24 David Garrard .25 .60
25 DeAngelo Williams .30 .75
26 Derrick Ward .20 .50
27 DeSean Jackson .25 .60
28 Donnie Avery .25 .60
29 Donovan McNabb .30 .75
30 Drew Brees .30 .75
31 Dwayne Bowe .25 .60
32 Eddie Royal .25 .60
33 Eli Manning .30 .75
34 Frank Gore .25 .60
35 Greg Olsen .20 .50
36 Greg Jennings .30 .75
37 Jake Delhomme .25 .60
38 Jamal Lewis .25 .60
39 JaMarcus Russell .20 .50
40 Jason Campbell .20 .50
41 Jason Witten .30 .75
42 Jay Cutler .30 .75
43 Jerricho Cotchery .25 .60
44 Joe Flacco .30 .75
45 Joseph Addai .30 .75
46 Josh Morgan .20 .50
47 Julius Jones .20 .50
48 Kellen Winslow Jr. .25 .60
49 Kerry Collins .25 .60
50 Kevin Boss .25 .60
51 Kevin Smith .25 .60
52 Kurt Warner .30 .75
53 Kyle Orton .25 .60
54 LaDainian Tomlinson .30 .75
55 Larry Fitzgerald .30 .75
56 Larry Johnson .25 .60
57 Laurence Maroney .25 .60
58 Laveranues Coles .20 .50
59 Lee Evans .25 .60
60 LenDale White .25 .60
61 Leon Washington .25 .60
62 Marc Bulger .25 .60
63 Marion Barber .25 .60
64 Marques Colston .25 .60
65 Marshawn Lynch .25 .60
66 Matt Cassel .25 .60
67 Matt Forte .30 .75
68 Matt Hasselbeck .25 .60
69 Matt Ryan .30 .75
70 Matt Schaub .25 .60
71 Maurice Jones-Drew .25 .60
72 Michael Turner .25 .60
73 Peyton Manning .50 1.25
74 Philip Rivers .30 .75
75 Randy Moss .30 .75
76 Ray Rice .30 .75
77 Reggie Bush .30 .75
78 Reggie Wayne .25 .60
79 Ricky Williams .25 .60
80 Roddy White .25 .60
81 Ronnie Brown .25 .60
82 Ryan Grant .25 .60
83 Santonio Holmes .25 .60
84 Steve Breaston .25 .60
85 Steve Slaton .25 .60
86 Steve Smith .25 .60
87 Steven Jackson .25 .60
88 T.J. Houshmandzadeh .25 .60
89 Brett Favre 5.00 12.00
90 Terrell Owens .30 .75
91 Tom Brady .50 1.25
92 Tony Gonzalez .25 .60
93 Tony Romo .50 1.25
94 Torry Holt .25 .60
95 Vernon Davis .25 .60
96 Vincent Jackson .25 .60
97 Wes Welker .30 .75
98 Willie Parker .20 .50
99 Willis McGahee .25 .60
100 Zach Miller .20 .50
101 Aaron Brown RC 2.00 5.00
102 Aaron Kelly RC 1.50 4.00
103 Aaron Maybin RC 1.50 4.00
104 Alex Mack RC 1.50 4.00
105 Alphonso Smith RC 1.50 4.00
106 Andre Smith RC 1.50 4.00
107 Anthony Hill RC 1.25 3.00
108 Arian Foster RC 4.00 10.00
109 Austin Collie RC 2.00 5.00
110 B.J. Raji RC 2.00 5.00
111 Bear Pascoe RC 1.50 4.00
112 Bernard Scott RC 2.00 5.00
113 Bradley Fletcher RC 1.50 4.00
114 Brandon Gibson RC 2.00 5.00
115 Brandon Tate RC 2.00 5.00
116 Brian Cushing RC 2.00 5.00
117 Brian Hartline RC 2.00 5.00
118 Brian Orakpo RC 2.00 5.00
119 Brooks Foster RC 1.25 3.00
120 Cameron Morrah RC 1.25 3.00
121 Cedric Peerman RC 1.50 4.00
122 Chase Coffman RC 1.50 4.00
123 Chase Daniel RC 2.00 5.00
124 Chris Ogbonnaya RC 1.50 4.00
125 Clay Matthews RC 5.00 12.00
126 Clint Sintim RC 2.00 5.00
127 Cody Brown RC 1.25 3.00
128 Connor Barwin RC 2.00 5.00
129 Cornelius Ingram RC 1.25 3.00
130 Curtis Painter RC 2.00 5.00
131 Dan Gronkowski RC 1.25 3.00
132 Darcel McBath RC 1.50 4.00
133 Darius Butler RC 2.00 5.00
134 David Johnson RC 1.50 4.00
135 David Veikune RC 1.50 4.00
136 Davon Drew RC 1.50 4.00
137 DeAndre Levy RC 2.00 5.00
138 Demetrius Byrd RC 1.50 4.00
139 Derek Cox RC 2.00 5.00
140 Devin Moore RC 1.50 4.00
141 Dominique Edison RC 1.25 3.00
142 Eddie Williams RC 1.50 4.00
143 Eric Wood RC 1.50 4.00
144 Eugene Monroe RC 1.25 3.00
145 Evander Hood RC 2.50 6.00
146 Everette Brown RC 1.50 4.00
147 Frank Summers RC 2.00 5.00
148 Fui Vakapuna RC 1.50 4.00
149 Gartrell Johnson RC 1.25 3.00
150 Hunter Cantwell RC 2.00 5.00
151 James Casey RC 1.50 4.00
152 James Davis RC 2.00 5.00
153 James Laurinaitis RC 2.00 5.00
154 Jared Cook RC 2.00 5.00
155 Jarett Dillard RC 2.00 5.00
156 Jairus Byrd RC 2.00 5.00
157 Jason Williams RC 2.00 5.00
158 Javarris Williams RC 1.50 4.00
159 Jeremy Childs RC 1.50 4.00
160 John Nalbone RC 1.25 3.00
161 John Phillips RC 2.00 5.00
162 Johnny Knox RC 3.00 8.00
163 Julian Edelman RC 2.00 5.00
164 Keith Null RC 1.50 4.00
165 Kenny McKinley RC 2.00 5.00
166 Kevin Ogletree RC 2.00 5.00
167 Kory Sheets RC 1.50 4.00
168 Lardarius Webb RC 2.00 5.00
169 Larry English RC 2.00 5.00
170 Louis Delmas RC 2.00 5.00
171 Louis Murphy RC 2.00 5.00
172 Malcolm Jenkins RC 2.00 5.00
173 Manuel Johnson RC 1.50 4.00
174 Marko Mitchell RC 1.50 4.00
175 Michael Mitchell RC 1.50 4.00
176 Michael Oher RC 3.00 8.00
177 Mike Goodson RC 2.00 5.00
178 Mike Teel RC 2.00 5.00
179 P.J. Hill RC 1.50 4.00
180 Patrick Chung RC 2.00 5.00
181 Peria Jerry RC 1.50 4.00
182 Quan Cosby RC 1.50 4.00
183 Quinn Johnson RC 1.50 4.00
184 Quinten Lawrence RC 1.25 3.00
185 Rashad Jennings RC 2.00 5.00
186 Rey Maualuga RC 2.00 5.00
187 Richard Quinn RC 1.50 4.00
188 Robert Ayers RC 2.00 5.00
189 Ron Brace RC 1.50 4.00
190 Sammie Stroughter RC 2.00 5.00
191 Sean Smith RC 2.00 5.00
192 Shawn Nelson RC 1.50 4.00
193 Sherrod Martin RC 1.50 4.00
194 Tiquan Underwood RC 1.50 4.00
195 Tom Brandstater RC 2.00 5.00
196 Tony Fiammetta RC 1.50 4.00
197 Travis Beckum RC 1.50 4.00
198 Tyrell Sutton RC 1.50 4.00
199 Vontae Davis RC 2.00 5.00
200 William Moore RC 2.00 5.00
201 Mark Sanchez JSY AU RC 30.00 80.00
202 Chris Wells JSY AU RC 12.00 30.00
203 Matthew Stafford JSY AU RC 50.00 100.00
204 Donald Brown JSY AU RC 10.00 25.00
205 Hakeem Nicks JSY AU RC 15.00 40.00
206 Michael Crabtree JSY AU RC 20.00 50.00
207 Brandon Pettigrew JSY AU RC 10.00 25.00
208 Ramses Barden JSY AU RC 6.00 15.00
209 Kenny Britt JSY AU RC 12.00 30.00
210 Deon Butler JSY AU RC 8.00 20.00
211 Juaquin Iglesias JSY AU RC 8.00 20.00
212 Jeremy Maclin JSY AU RC 15.00 40.00
213 Glen Coffee JSY AU/99 RC 8.00 20.00
214 Jason Smith JSY AU RC 8.00 20.00
215 Patrick Turner JSY AU RC 8.00 20.00
216 Knowshon Moreno JSY AU RC 10.00 25.00
217 Mohamed Massaquoi JSY AU RC 8.00 20.00
218 Shonn Greene JSY AU RC 15.00 40.00
219 Nate Davis JSY AU RC 8.00 20.00
220 LeSean McCoy JSY AU RC 20.00 50.00
221 Pat White JSY AU RC 10.00 25.00
222 Percy Harvin JSY AU RC 15.00 40.00
223 Tyson Jackson JSY AU RC 8.00 20.00
224 Javon Ringer JSY AU RC 10.00 25.00
225 Mike Wallace JSY AU RC 20.00 50.00
226 Josh Freeman JSY AU/98 RC 20.00 50.00
227 Stephen McGee JSY AU RC 10.00 25.00
228 Mike Thomas JSY AU RC 10.00 25.00
229 Brian Robiskie JSY AU RC 10.00 25.00
230 Aaron Curry JSY AU RC 10.00 25.00
231 Andre Brown JSY AU RC 6.00 15.00
232 Derrick Williams JSY AU RC 8.00 20.00
233 Darrius Heyward-Bey JSY AU RC 10.00 25.00
234 Rhett Bomar JSY AU RC 8.00 20.00

2009 Donruss Gridiron Gear Gold O's

*VETS 1-100: 3X TO 8X BASIC CARDS
*ROOKIES 101-200: .6X TO 1.5X BASIC CARDS
STATED PRINT RUN 100 SER.#'d SETS
89 Brett Favre 12.00 30.00

2009 Donruss Gridiron Gear Gold X's

*VETS 1-100: 3X TO 8X BASIC CARDS
*ROOKIES 101-200: .6X TO 1.5X BASIC CARDS
STATED PRINT RUN 100 SER.#'d SETS
89 Brett Favre 12.00 30.00

2009 Donruss Gridiron Gear Platinum O's

*VETS 1-100: 6X TO 15X BASIC CARDS
*ROOKIES 101-200: 1X TO 2.5X BASIC CARDS
STATED PRINT RUN 25 SER.#'d SETS
89 Brett Favre 25.00 60.00

2009 Donruss Gridiron Gear Platinum X's

*VETS 1-100: 6X TO 15X BASIC CARDS
*ROOKIES 101-200: 1X TO 2.5X BASIC CARDS
STATED PRINT RUN 25 SER.#'d SETS
89 Brett Favre 25.00 60.00

2009 Donruss Gridiron Gear Silver O's

*VETS 1-100: 2X TO 5X BASIC CARDS
*ROOKIES 101-200: .4X TO 1X BASIC CARDS
STATED PRINT RUN 250 SER.#'d SETS
89 Brett Favre 8.00 20.00

2009 Donruss Gridiron Gear Silver X's

*VETS 1-100: 2X TO 5X BASIC CARDS
*ROOKIES 101-200: .4X TO 1X BASIC CARDS
STATED PRINT RUN 250 SER.#'d SETS
89 Brett Favre 8.00 20.00

2009 Donruss Gridiron Gear Autographs Gold

VET STATED PRINT RUN 4-75
ROOKIE STATED PRINT RUN 25-250
30 Drew Brees/50 40.00 80.00
59 Lee Evans/50 6.00 15.00
67 Matt Forte/50 8.00 20.00
69 Matt Ryan/25 40.00 80.00
82 Ryan Grant/75 8.00 20.00
85 Steve Slaton/40 6.00 15.00
102 Aaron Kelly/250 4.00 10.00
103 Aaron Maybin/25 6.00 15.00
109 Austin Collie/100 6.00 15.00
110 B.J. Raji/100 5.00 12.00
114 Brandon Gibson/100 5.00 12.00
115 Brandon Tate/100 5.00 12.00
116 Brian Cushing/100 5.00 12.00
118 Brian Orakpo/100 5.00 12.00
119 Brooks Foster/100 3.00 8.00
120 Cameron Morrah/100 3.00 8.00
121 Cedric Peerman/100 4.00 10.00
122 Chase Coffman/100 4.00 10.00
125 Clay Matthews/100 30.00 60.00
126 Clint Sintim/100 5.00 12.00
129 Cornelius Ingram/100 3.00 8.00
138 Demetrius Byrd/100 4.00 10.00
140 Devin Moore/25 6.00 15.00
141 Dominique Edison/250 3.00 8.00
146 Everette Brown/100 4.00 10.00
150 Hunter Cantwell/100 5.00 12.00
151 James Casey/100 4.00 10.00
153 James Laurinaitis/100 5.00 12.00
154 Jared Cook/100 5.00 12.00
155 Jarett Dillard/100 5.00 12.00
162 Johnny Knox/250 8.00 20.00
165 Kenny McKinley/100 5.00 12.00
166 Kevin Ogletree/25 15.00 30.00
169 Larry English/100 5.00 12.00
171 Louis Murphy/100 8.00 20.00
172 Malcolm Jenkins/100 5.00 12.00
177 Mike Goodson/100 No AU 2.00 5.00
179 P.J. Hill/100 4.00 10.00
182 Quan Cosby/25 6.00 15.00
183 Quinn Johnson/100 4.00 10.00
185 Rashad Jennings/100 5.00 12.00
186 Rey Maualuga/100 5.00 12.00
192 Shawn Nelson/100 EXCH 4.00 10.00
195 Tom Brandstater/100 5.00 12.00
196 Tony Fiammetta/100 4.00 10.00
197 Travis Beckum/250 4.00 10.00
198 Tyrell Sutton/25 6.00 15.00
199 Vontae Davis/100 5.00 12.00

2009 Donruss Gridiron Gear Autographs Platinum

STATED PRINT RUN 1-25
SER.#'d UNDER 16 NOT PRICED
30 Drew Brees/25 50.00 100.00
59 Lee Evans/25 8.00 20.00
67 Matt Forte/25 10.00 25.00
76 Ray Rice/16 10.00 25.00
82 Ryan Grant/25 10.00 25.00
85 Steve Slaton/25 8.00 20.00
102 Aaron Kelly/25 6.00 15.00
109 Austin Collie/25 10.00 25.00
110 B.J. Raji/25 8.00 20.00
114 Brandon Gibson/25 8.00 20.00
115 Brandon Tate/25 8.00 20.00
116 Brian Cushing/25 8.00 20.00
118 Brian Orakpo/25 8.00 20.00
119 Brooks Foster/25 5.00 12.00
120 Cameron Morrah/25 5.00 12.00
121 Cedric Peerman/25 6.00 15.00
122 Chase Coffman/25 6.00 15.00
125 Clay Matthews/25 50.00 100.00
126 Clint Sintim/25 8.00 20.00
129 Cornelius Ingram/25 5.00 12.00
138 Demetrius Byrd/25 6.00 15.00
141 Dominique Edison/25 5.00 12.00
146 Everette Brown/25 6.00 15.00
150 Hunter Cantwell/25 8.00 20.00
151 James Casey/25 6.00 15.00
153 James Laurinaitis/25 8.00 20.00
154 Jared Cook/25 8.00 20.00
155 Jarett Dillard/25 8.00 20.00
162 Johnny Knox/25 12.00 30.00
165 Kenny McKinley/25 8.00 20.00
169 Larry English/25 8.00 20.00
171 Louis Murphy EXCH/25 12.00 30.00
172 Malcolm Jenkins/25 8.00 20.00
177 Mike Goodson/25 No AU 3.00 8.00
179 P.J. Hill/25 6.00 15.00
183 Quinn Johnson/25 6.00 15.00
185 Rashad Jennings/25 8.00 20.00
186 Rey Maualuga/25 8.00 20.00
192 Shawn Nelson/25 EXCH 6.00 15.00
195 Tom Brandstater/25 8.00 20.00
196 Tony Fiammetta/25 6.00 15.00
197 Travis Beckum/25 6.00 15.00
199 Vontae Davis/25 8.00 20.00

2009 Donruss Gridiron Gear Jerseys

STATED PRINT RUN 9-250
8 Bernard Berrian/60 3.00 8.00
16 Carson Palmer/250 3.00 8.00
29 Donovan McNabb/250 3.00 8.00
30 Drew Brees/250 3.00 8.00
31 Dwayne Bowe/90 3.00 8.00
34 Frank Gore/225 2.50 6.00
39 JaMarcus Russell/210 2.00 5.00
40 Jason Campbell/40 3.00 8.00
42 Jay Cutler/250 3.00 8.00
59 Lee Evans/35 4.00 10.00
62 Marc Bulger/250 2.50 6.00
65 Marshawn Lynch/225 2.50 6.00
73 Peyton Manning/250 5.00 12.00
79 Ricky Williams/250 2.50 6.00
100 Zach Miller/45 3.00 8.00

2009 Donruss Gridiron Gear Jerseys Prime

PRIME PRINT RUN 1-50
SERIAL #'d UNDER 30 NOT PRICED
6 Antonio Gates/50 5.00 12.00
9 Brady Quinn/45 5.00 12.00
12 Braylon Edwards/30 5.00 12.00
14 Brian Westbrook/50 5.00 12.00
17 Chad Ochocinco/50 5.00 12.00
19 Chris Cooley/50 5.00 12.00
21 Clinton Portis/50 5.00 12.00
25 DeAngelo Williams/50 6.00 15.00
31 Dwayne Bowe/30 5.00 12.00
34 Frank Gore/50 5.00 12.00
40 Jason Campbell/30 4.00 10.00
56 Larry Johnson/50 5.00 12.00
57 Laurence Maroney/50 5.00 12.00
59 Lee Evans/35 5.00 12.00
62 Marc Bulger/50 5.00 12.00
63 Marion Barber/50 5.00 12.00
65 Marshawn Lynch/50 5.00 12.00
68 Matt Hasselbeck/50 5.00 12.00
71 Maurice Jones-Drew/50 5.00 12.00
79 Ricky Williams/50 5.00 12.00
81 Ronnie Brown/50 5.00 12.00
82 Ryan Grant/50 5.00 12.00
83 Santonio Holmes/50 5.00 12.00
86 Steve Smith/50 5.00 12.00
87 Steven Jackson/50 5.00 12.00
91 Tom Brady/50 10.00 25.00
96 Vincent Jackson/50 5.00 12.00
98 Willie Parker/50 4.00 10.00

2009 Donruss Gridiron Gear Jerseys X's

X's HOBBY PRINT RUN 2-100
*RET.O's/80-100: .4X TO 1X HOB X's
*RET.O's/40-65: .5X TO 1.2X HOB X's
*RET.O's/19-30: .6X TO 1.5X HOB X's
O's RETAIL PRINT RUN 10-100
7 Ben Roethlisberger/100 4.00 10.00
8 Bernard Berrian/100 3.00 8.00
10 Brandon Jacobs/100 3.00 8.00
11 Brandon Marshall/100 3.00 8.00
12 Braylon Edwards/100 3.00 8.00
16 Carson Palmer/100 4.00 10.00
25 DeAngelo Williams/100 4.00 10.00
29 Donovan McNabb/100 4.00 10.00
30 Drew Brees/100 4.00 10.00
31 Dwayne Bowe/100 3.00 8.00
34 Frank Gore/100 3.00 8.00
35 Greg Olsen/100 2.50 6.00
36 Greg Jennings/100 4.00 10.00
39 JaMarcus Russell/100 2.50 6.00
40 Jason Campbell/100 2.50 6.00
42 Jay Cutler/100 4.00 10.00
45 Joseph Addai/100 4.00 10.00
54 LaDainian Tomlinson/25 6.00 15.00
56 Larry Johnson/100 3.00 8.00
59 Lee Evans/100 3.00 8.00
60 LenDale White/100 3.00 8.00
61 Leon Washington/100 3.00 8.00
62 Marc Bulger/100 3.00 8.00
65 Marshawn Lynch/100 3.00 8.00
69 Matt Ryan/100 4.00 10.00
73 Peyton Manning/100 6.00 15.00
74 Philip Rivers/65 5.00 12.00
75 Randy Moss/90 4.00 10.00
78 Reggie Wayne/100 3.00 8.00
79 Ricky Williams/100 3.00 8.00
99 Willis McGahee/55 4.00 10.00

2009 Donruss Gridiron Gear Next Generation

*GOLD/100: .6X TO 1.5X BASIC INSERTS
*PLATINUM/25: .8X TO 2X BASIC INSERTS
*SILVER/250: .5X TO 1.2X BASIC INSERTS
1 Matthew Stafford 5.00 12.00
2 Mark Sanchez 3.00 8.00
3 Michael Crabtree 2.00 5.00
4 LeSean McCoy 2.00 5.00
5 Donald Brown 1.00 2.50
6 Kenny Britt 1.25 3.00
7 Josh Freeman 2.00 5.00
8 Deon Butler .75 2.00
9 Juaquin Iglesias .75 2.00
10 Ramses Barden .60 1.50
11 Patrick Turner .75 2.00
12 Knowshon Moreno 1.00 2.50
13 Pat White 1.00 2.50
14 Hakeem Nicks 1.50 4.00
15 Jason Smith .75 2.00
16 Darrius Heyward-Bey 1.00 2.50
17 Mike Thomas 1.00 2.50
18 Nate Davis .75 2.00
19 Mohamed Massaquoi .75 2.00
20 Aaron Curry 1.00 2.50
21 Percy Harvin 1.50 4.00
22 Tyson Jackson .75 2.00
23 Mike Wallace 2.00 5.00
24 Javon Ringer 1.00 2.50
25 Glen Coffee .75 2.00
26 Chris Wells 1.50 4.00
27 Brandon Pettigrew 1.00 2.50
28 Rhett Bomar .75 2.00
29 Shonn Greene 1.50 4.00
30 Brian Robiskie 1.00 2.50
31 Derrick Williams .75 2.00
32 Jeremy Maclin 1.50 4.00
33 Andre Brown .60 1.50
34 Stephen McGee 1.00 2.50

2009 Donruss Gridiron Gear Next Generation Jerseys

STATED PRINT RUN 250 SER.#'d SETS
*COMBOS PRIME/50: .8X TO 2X BASIC JSY
*JUMBO PRIME/25: 1X TO 2.5X BASIC JSY
*PRIME/50: .6X TO 1.5X BASIC JSY
1 Matthew Stafford 6.00 15.00
2 Mark Sanchez 8.00 20.00
3 Michael Crabtree 4.00 10.00
4 LeSean McCoy 4.00 10.00
5 Donald Brown 2.00 5.00
6 Kenny Britt 2.50 6,00
7 Josh Freeman 4.00 10.00
8 Deon Butler 1.50 4.00
9 Juaquin Iglesias 1.50 4.00
10 Ramses Barden 1.25 3.00
11 Patrick Turner 1.50 4.00
12 Knowshon Moreno 2.00 5.00
13 Pat White 2.00 5.00
14 Hakeem Nicks 3.00 8.00
15 Jason Smith 1.50 4.00
16 Darrius Heyward-Bey 2.00 5.00
17 Mike Thomas 2.00 5.00
18 Nate Davis 1.50 4.00
19 Mohamed Massaquoi 1.50 4.00
20 Aaron Curry 2.00 5.00
21 Percy Harvin 3.00 8.00
22 Tyson Jackson 1.50 4.00
23 Mike Wallace 4.00 10.00
24 Javon Ringer 2.00 5.00
25 Glen Coffee 1.50 4.00
26 Chris Wells 3.00 8.00
27 Brandon Pettigrew 2.00 5.00
28 Rhett Bomar 1.50 4.00
29 Shonn Greene 3.00 8.00
30 Brian Robiskie 2.00 5.00
31 Derrick Williams 1.50 4.00
32 Jeremy Maclin 3.00 8.00
33 Andre Brown 1.25 3.00
34 Stephen McGee 2.00 5.00

2009 Donruss Gridiron Gear Next Generation Jerseys Combos Autographs Prime

STATED PRINT RUN 25 SER.#'d SETS
1 Matthew Stafford 60.00 120.00
2 Mark Sanchez 40.00 100.00
3 Michael Crabtree 30.00 60.00
4 LeSean McCoy 15.00 40.00
5 Donald Brown 8.00 20.00
6 Kenny Britt 10.00 25.00
7 Josh Freeman 15.00 40.00
8 Deon Butler 6.00 15.00
9 Juaquin Iglesias 6.00 15.00
10 Ramses Barden 5.00 12.00
11 Patrick Turner 6.00 15.00
12 Knowshon Moreno 8.00 20.00
13 Pat White 8.00 20.00
14 Hakeem Nicks 12.00 30.00
15 Jason Smith 6.00 15.00
16 Darrius Heyward-Bey 8.00 20.00
17 Mike Thomas 8.00 20.00
18 Nate Davis 6.00 15.00
19 Mohamed Massaquoi 6.00 15.00
20 Aaron Curry 8.00 20.00
21 Percy Harvin 40.00 80.00
22 Tyson Jackson 6.00 15.00
23 Mike Wallace 15.00 40.00
24 Javon Ringer 8.00 20.00
25 Glen Coffee 6.00 15.00
26 Chris Wells 12.00 30.00
27 Brandon Pettigrew 8.00 20.00
28 Rhett Bomar 6.00 15.00
29 Shonn Greene 12.00 30.00
30 Brian Robiskie 8.00 20.00
31 Derrick Williams 6.00 15.00
32 Jeremy Maclin 12.00 30.00
33 Andre Brown 5.00 12.00
34 Stephen McGee 8.00 20.00

2009 Donruss Gridiron Gear Next Generation Materials Combos

STATED PRINT RUN 250 SER.#'d SETS
*PRIME/25: .6X TO 1.5X BASIC COMBO
1 Darrius Heyward-Bey 4.00 10.00
Hakeem Nicks
2 Shonn Greene 4.00 10.00
Javon Ringer
3 Brian Robiskie 2.50 6.00
Derrick Williams
4 Jeremy Maclin 4.00 10.00
Brandon Pettigrew
5 Donald Brown 5.00 12.00
LeSean McCoy
6 Mike Thomas 2.50 6.00
Patrick Turner
7 Percy Harvin 4.00 10.00
Mohamed Massaquoi
8 Michael Crabtree 5.00 12.00
Juaquin Iglesias
9 Donald Brown 4.00 10.00
Shonn Greene
10 Andre Brown 2.50 6.00
Aaron Curry

2009 Donruss Gridiron Gear Next Generation Materials Triple

STATED PRINT RUN 250 SER.#'d SETS
*PRIME/25: .6X TO 1.5X BASIC TRIPLE
1 Matthew Stafford 8.00 20.00
Mark Sanchez
Josh Freeman
2 Tyson Jackson 2.50 6.00
Aaron Curry
Jason Smith
3 Knowshon Moreno 4.00 10.00
Donald Brown
Chris Wells
4 LeSean McCoy 5.00 12.00
Shonn Greene
Glen Coffee
5 Darrius Heyward-Bey 4.00 10.00
Michael Crabtree
Jeremy Maclin
6 Pat White 2.50 6.00
Stephen McGee
Rhett Bomar
7 Brandon Pettigrew 2.50 6.00
Brian Robiskie
Mohamed Massaquoi
8 Percy Harvin 6.00 15.00
Hakeem Nicks
Kenny Britt
9 Derrick Williams 5.00 12.00
Mike Wallace
Ramses Barden
10 Mike Thomas 6.00 15.00
Patrick Turner
Mark Sanchez

2009 Donruss Gridiron Gear NFL Gridiron Rookie Signatures

*GRIDIRON/42-45: .5X TO 1.2X TEAMS AU/50
STATED PRINT RUN 42-45

2009 Donruss Gridiron Gear NFL Teams Rookie Signatures

STATED PRINT RUN 50 SER.#'d SETS
1 Glen Coffee 6.00 15.00
2 Michael Crabtree 30.00 60.00
3 Nate Davis 6.00 15.00
4 Javon Ringer 8.00 20.00
5 Kenny Britt 10.00 25.00
6 Mike Wallace 15.00 40.00
7 Jeremy Maclin 10.00 25.00
8 LeSean McCoy 15.00 40.00
9 Donald Brown 8.00 20.00
10 Mike Thomas 8.00 20.00
11 Tyson Jackson 6.00 15.00
12 Josh Freeman 15.00 40.00
13 Darrius Heyward-Bey 8.00 20.00
14 Aaron Curry 8.00 20.00
15 Deon Butler 6.00 15.00
16 Jason Smith 6.00 15.00
17 Juaquin Iglesias 6.00 15.00
18 Stephen McGee 8.00 20.00
19 Andre Brown 5.00 12.00
20 Hakeem Nicks 12.00 30.00
21 Ramses Barden 5.00 12.00
22 Rhett Bomar 6.00 15.00
23 Percy Harvin 30.00 60.00
24 Pat White 8.00 20.00
25 Patrick Turner 6.00 15.00
26 Chris Wells 12.00 30.00
27 Mark Sanchez 40.00 80.00
28 Shonn Greene 12.00 30.00
29 Brian Robiskie 8.00 20.00
30 Mohamed Massaquoi 6.00 15.00
31 Brandon Pettigrew 8.00 20.00
32 Derrick Williams 6.00 15.00
33 Matthew Stafford 40.00 80.00
34 Knowshon Moreno 8.00 20.00

2009 Donruss Gridiron Gear NFL Teams Veteran Signatures

STATED PRINT RUN 25-500
1 Yale Lary/75 10.00 25.00
2 Pete Retzlaff/74 8.00 20.00
3 Lee Roy Selmon/100 15.00 40.00
4 Don Perkins/125 12.00 30.00
5 Willie Lanier/150 8.00 20.00
6 Willie Davis/98 15.00 40.00
7 Mark Gastineau/102 8.00 20.00
8 Lydell Mitchell/200 8.00 20.00
9 Joe Klecko/119 8.00 20.00
10 Archie Manning/175 15.00 40.00
11 Fred Williamson/123 10.00 25.00
12 Dan Marino/100 60.00 120.00
13 Gene Upshaw/150 12.00 30.00
14 Cliff Harris/137 10.00 25.00
15 Chuck Bednarik/25 40.00 80.00
16 Mark Duper/162 10.00 25.00
17 Dan Fouts/150 20.00 40.00
18 Charlie Joiner/200 8.00 20.00
19 Deacon Jones/140 10.00 25.00
20 Don Maynard/200 8.00 20.00
21 Jethro Pugh/250 8.00 20.00
22 Billy Howton/250 8.00 20.00
23 Darrell Green/250 15.00 40.00
24 Charley Taylor/250 8.00 20.00
25 Willie Brown/350 8.00 20.00
26 Larry Little/367 6.00 15.00
27 Lem Barney/400 8.00 20.00
28 Paul Krause/450 8.00 20.00
29 Rick Casares/500 6.00 15.00
30 Joe Namath/50 50.00 100.00
31 Jim Brown/100 30.00 60.00

2009 Donruss Gridiron Gear Performers

*GOLD/100: .6X TO 1.5X BASIC INSERTS
*PLATINUM/25: .8X TO 2X BASIC INSERTS
*SILVER/250: .5X TO 1.2X BASIC INSERTS
1 Knowshon Moreno 1.00 2.50
2 Matthew Stafford 5.00 12.00
3 Derrick Williams .75 2.00
4 Brandon Pettigrew 1.00 2.50
5 Mohamed Massaquoi .75 2.00
6 Brian Robiskie 1.00 2.50
7 Shonn Greene 1.50 4.00
8 Mark Sanchez 3.00 8.00
9 Chris Wells 1.50 4.00
10 Patrick Turner .75 2.00
11 Pat White 1.00 2.50
12 Glen Coffee .75 2.00
13 Michael Crabtree 2.00 5.00
14 Nate Davis .75 2.00
15 Javon Ringer 1.00 2.50
16 Kenny Britt 1.25 3.00
17 Mike Wallace 2.00 5.00
18 Jeremy Maclin 1.50 4.00
19 LeSean McCoy 2.00 5.00
20 Donald Brown 1.00 2.50
21 Mike Thomas 1.00 2.50
22 Tyson Jackson .75 2.00
23 Josh Freeman 2.00 5.00
24 Percy Harvin 1.50 4.00
25 Ramses Barden .60 1.50
26 Andre Brown .60 1.50
27 Juaquin Iglesias .75 2.00
28 Deon Butler .75 2.00
29 Darrius Heyward-Bey 1.00 2.50
30 Aaron Curry 1.00 2.50
31 Jason Smith .75 2.00
32 Stephen McGee 1.00 2.50
33 Hakeem Nicks 1.50 4.00
34 Rhett Bomar .75 2.00

2009 Donruss Gridiron Gear Performers Jerseys

STATED PRINT RUN 250 SER.#'d SETS
*COMBOS/100: .5X TO 1.2X BASIC JSY
*COMBOS PRIME/50: .8X TO 2X BASIC JSY
*JUMBO PRIME/25: 1X TO 2.5X BASIC JSY
*PRIME/50: .6X TO 1.5X BASIC JSY
1 Knowshon Moreno 2.00 5.00
2 Matthew Stafford 6.00 15.00
3 Derrick Williams 1.50 4.00
4 Brandon Pettigrew 2.00 5.00
5 Mohamed Massaquoi 1.50 4.00
6 Brian Robiskie 2.00 5.00
7 Shonn Greene 3.00 8.00
8 Mark Sanchez 8.00 20.00
9 Chris Wells 3.00 8.00
10 Patrick Turner 1.50 4.00
11 Pat White 2.00 5.00
12 Glen Coffee 1.50 4.00
13 Michael Crabtree 4.00 10.00
14 Nate Davis 1.50 4.00
15 Javon Ringer 2.00 5.00
16 Kenny Britt 2.50 6.00
17 Mike Wallace 4.00 10.00
18 Jeremy Maclin 3.00 8.00
19 LeSean McCoy 4.00 10.00
20 Donald Brown 2.00 5.00
21 Mike Thomas 2.00 5.00
22 Tyson Jackson 1.50 4.00
23 Josh Freeman 4.00 10.00
24 Percy Harvin 3.00 8.00
25 Ramses Barden 1.25 3.00
26 Andre Brown 1.25 3.00
27 Juaquin Iglesias 1.50 4.00
28 Deon Butler 1.50 4.00
29 Darrius Heyward-Bey 2.00 5.00
30 Aaron Curry 2.00 5.00
31 Jason Smith 1.50 4.00
32 Stephen McGee 2.00 5.00
33 Hakeem Nicks 3.00 8.00
34 Rhett Bomar 1.50 4.00

2009 Donruss Gridiron Gear Performers Materials Combos Autographs Prime

COMBO PRIME AU PRINT RUN 25
1 Knowshon Moreno 8.00 20.00
2 Matthew Stafford 50.00 100.00
3 Derrick Williams EXCH 6.00 15.00
4 Brandon Pettigrew 8.00 20.00
5 Mohamed Massaquoi 6.00 15.00
6 Brian Robiskie 8.00 20.00
7 Shonn Greene 12.00 30.00
8 Mark Sanchez 50.00 100.00
9 Chris Wells 12.00 30.00
10 Patrick Turner 6.00 15.00
11 Pat White 8.00 20.00
12 Glen Coffee 6.00 15.00
13 Michael Crabtree 15.00 40.00
14 Nate Davis 6.00 15.00
15 Javon Ringer 8.00 20.00
16 Kenny Britt 10.00 25.00
17 Mike Wallace 15.00 40.00
18 Jeremy Maclin 12.00 30.00
19 LeSean McCoy 15.00 40.00
20 Donald Brown 8.00 20.00
21 Mike Thomas 8.00 20.00
22 Tyson Jackson 6.00 15.00
23 Josh Freeman 15.00 40.00
24 Percy Harvin 40.00 80.00
25 Ramses Barden 5.00 12.00
26 Andre Brown 5.00 12.00
27 Juaquin Iglesias 6.00 15.00
28 Deon Butler 6.00 15.00
29 Darrius Heyward-Bey 8.00 20.00
30 Aaron Curry 8.00 20.00
31 Jason Smith 6.00 15.00
32 Stephen McGee 8.00 20.00
33 Hakeem Nicks 12.00 30.00
34 Rhett Bomar 6.00 15.00

2009 Donruss Gridiron Gear Plates and Patches

STATED PRINT RUN 35-100
1 Andre Johnson/100 5.00 12.00
2 Antonio Gates/100 5.00 12.00
3 Brian Westbrook/100 5.00 12.00
6 Chad Ochocinco/100 5.00 12.00
8 Frank Gore/100 5.00 12.00
10 Jason Campbell/100 4.00 10.00
11 Lee Evans/35 6.00 15.00
13 Maurice Jones-Drew/100 5.00 12.00
15 Steve Smith/100 5.00 12.00

2009 Donruss Gridiron Gear Plates and Patches Autographs

STATED PRINT RUN 25 SER.#'d SETS
1 Andre Johnson 20.00 50.00
11 Lee Evans 12.00 30.00

2009 Donruss Gridiron Gear Playbook

*GOLD/100: .6X TO 1.5X BASIC INSERTS
*PLATINUM/25: .8X TO 2X BASIC INSERTS
*SILVER/250: .5X TO 1.2X BASIC INSERTS
1 DeAngelo Williams 1.00 2.50
2 Willie Parker .60 1.50
3 Philip Rivers 1.00 2.50
4 Joseph Addai 1.00 2.50
5 Aaron Rodgers 2.00 5.00
6 LaDainian Tomlinson 1.00 2.50
7 Tony Romo 1.50 4.00
8 Reggie Bush 1.00 2.50
9 Michael Turner .75 2.00
10 Adrian Peterson 1.50 4.00
11 Clinton Portis .75 2.00
12 Matt Hasselbeck .75 2.00
13 Matt Ryan 1.00 2.50
14 Wes Welker 1.00 2.50
15 Anthony Gonzalez .60 1.50
16 Larry Fitzgerald 1.00 2.50
17 Peyton Manning 1.50 4.00
18 Randy Moss 1.00 2.50
19 Ben Roethlisberger 1.00 2.50
20 Kurt Warner 1.00 2.50
21 Drew Brees 1.00 2.50
22 Marion Barber .75 2.00
23 Steven Jackson .75 2.00
24 Santonio Holmes .75 2.00
25 Maurice Jones-Drew .75 2.00

2009 Donruss Gridiron Gear Playbook Jerseys Patch

STATED PRINT RUN 8-50
1 DeAngelo Williams/50 6.00 15.00
2 Willie Parker/50 4.00 10.00
5 Aaron Rodgers/20 15.00 40.00
10 Adrian Peterson/50 10.00 25.00
11 Clinton Portis/50 5.00 12.00
15 Anthony Gonzalez/25 5.00 12.00
19 Ben Roethlisberger/20 8.00 20.00
22 Marion Barber/50 5.00 12.00
23 Steven Jackson/50 5.00 12.00
24 Santonio Holmes/50 5.00 12.00
25 Maurice Jones-Drew/50 5.00 12.00

2009 Donruss Gridiron Gear Playbook Jerseys X's

STATED PRINT RUN 40-250
*RET.O's/195-250: .4X TO 1X HOB X's/250
4 Joseph Addai/250 3.00 8.00
10 Adrian Peterson/40 8.00 20.00
13 Matt Ryan/225 3.00 8.00
17 Peyton Manning/250 5.00 12.00
21 Drew Brees/250 3.00 8.00

2009 Donruss Gridiron Gear Player Timeline

*GOLD/100: .6X TO 1.5X BASIC INSERTS
*PLATINUM/25: .8X TO 2X BASIC INSERTS
*SILVER/250: .5X TO 1.2X BASIC INSERTS
1 Jimmy Orr 1.00 2.50
2 Steve Largent 1.50 4.00
3 Antoine Cason .60 1.50
4 Brandon Meriweather .60 1.50
5 Chad Henne .75 2.00
6 DeSean Jackson .75 2.00
7 Early Doucet .75 2.00
8 Jamaal Charles 1.00 2.50
9 Malcolm Kelly .60 1.50
10 Vernon Gholston .60 1.50
11 Limas Sweed .75 2.00
12 Aqib Talib .60 1.50
13 LaRon Landry .60 1.50
14 Laveranues Coles .60 1.50
15 Terrell Owens 1.00 2.50
16 Kellen Winslow Jr. .75 2.00
17 Roy Williams WR .75 2.00
18 Torry Holt .75 2.00
19 Cedric Benson .75 2.00
20 Joe Namath 2.00 5.00
21 Jim Brown 2.00 5.00
22 Jay Cutler 1.00 2.50
23 Kyle Orton .75 2.00
24 Tony Gonzalez .75 2.00
25 Thomas Jones .75 2.00

2009 Donruss Gridiron Gear Player Timeline Autographs

STATED PRINT RUN 3-250
1 Jimmy Orr/250 4.00 10.00
2 Steve Largent/22 15.00 40.00
3 Antoine Cason/250 4.00 10.00
4 Brandon Meriweather/77 5.00 12.00
6 DeSean Jackson/100 8.00 20.00
7 Early Doucet/114 5.00 12.00
11 Limas Sweed/250 5.00 12.00
13 LaRon Landry/250 4.00 10.00
20 Joe Namath/50 40.00 80.00
21 Jim Brown/32 50.00 100.00

2009 Donruss Gridiron Gear Player Timeline Jerseys

STATED PRINT RUN 1-250
2 Steve Largent/250 5.00 12.00
3 Antoine Cason/55 2.50 6.00
4 Brandon Meriweather/200 2.00 5.00

5 Chad Henne/250 2.50 6.00
6 DeSean Jackson/20 5.00 12.00
8 Jamaal Charles/250 3.00 8.00
9 Malcolm Kelly/250 2.00 5.00
11 Limas Sweed/250 2.50 6.00
12 Aqib Talib/250 2.00 5.00
13 LaRon Landry/250 2.00 5.00
14 Laveranues Coles/250 2.00 5.00
15 Terrell Owens/250 3.00 8.00
17 Roy Williams WR/250 2.50 6.00
18 Torry Holt/250 2.50 6.00
19 Cedric Benson/250 2.50 6.00
21 Jim Brown/25 10.00 25.00
22 Jay Cutler/250 3.00 8.00
23 Kyle Orton/250 2.50 6.00
24 Tony Gonzalez/65 3.00 0.00
25 Thomas Jones/250 2.50 6.00

2009 Donruss Gridiron Gear Player Timeline Jerseys Jumbo Swatch

STATED PRINT RUN 1-50
2 Steve Largent/50 8.00 20.00
3 Antoine Cason/50 3.00 8.00
4 Brandon Meriweather/50 3.00 8.00
5 Chad Henne/50 4.00 10.00
7 Early Doucet/50 4.00 10.00
8 Jamaal Charles/50 5.00 12.00
9 Malcolm Kelly/50 3.00 8.00
11 Limas Sweed/50 4.00 10.00
12 Aqib Talib/50 3.00 8.00
13 LaRon Landry/50 3.00 8.00
14 Laveranues Coles/50 3.00 8.00
15 Terrell Owens/45 5.00 12.00
17 Roy Williams WR/25 5.00 12.00
18 Torry Holt/50 4.00 10.00
19 Cedric Benson/50 4.00 10.00
22 Jay Cutler/50 5.00 12.00
23 Kyle Orton/50 4.00 10.00
24 Tony Gonzalez/50 4.00 10.00
25 Thomas Jones/50 4.00 10.00

2009 Donruss Gridiron Gear Player Timeline Jerseys Jumbo Swatch Prime

STATED PRINT RUN 1-25
2 Steve Largent/25 12.00 30.00
4 Brandon Meriweather/25 5.00 12.00
8 Jamaal Charles/25 8.00 20.00
11 Limas Sweed/25 6.00 15.00
12 Aqib Talib/25 5.00 12.00
14 Laveranues Coles/25 5.00 12.00
15 Terrell Owens/25 8.00 20.00
16 Kellen Winslow Jr./25 6.00 15.00
17 Roy Williams WR/25 6.00 15.00
18 Torry Holt/25 6.00 15.00
19 Cedric Benson/25 6.00 15.00
23 Kyle Orton/25 6.00 15.00
24 Tony Gonzalez/25 6.00 15.00
25 Thomas Jones/25 6.00 15.00

2009 Donruss Gridiron Gear Player Timeline Jerseys Prime

STATED PRINT RUN 1-50
2 Steve Largent/50 8.00 20.00
4 Brandon Meriweather/40 3.00 8.00
7 Early Doucet/20 5.00 12.00
8 Jamaal Charles/50 5.00 12.00
9 Malcolm Kelly/30 3.00 8.00
10 Vernon Gholston /50 3.00 8.00
11 Limas Sweed/50 4.00 10.00
12 Aqib Talib/50 3.00 8.00
14 Laveranues Coles/50 3.00 8.00
15 Terrell Owens/50 5.00 12.00
16 Kellen Winslow Jr./50 4.00 10.00
17 Roy Williams WR/50 4.00 10.00
18 Torry Holt/50 4.00 10.00
19 Cedric Benson/50 4.00 10.00
23 Kyle Orton/50 4.00 10.00
24 Tony Gonzalez/50 4.00 10.00
25 Thomas Jones/50 4.00 10.00

2009 Donruss Gridiron Gear Player Timeline Jerseys Autographs

STATED PRINT RUN 5-50
2 Steve Largent/25
3 Antoine Cason/50 6.00 15.00
4 Brandon Meriweather/50 6.00 15.00
5 Chad Henne/25 10.00 25.00
6 DeSean Jackson/25 15.00 40.00
7 Early Doucet/50 8.00 20.00
11 Limas Sweed/50 8.00 20.00
13 LaRon Landry/50 6.00 15.00

2009 Donruss Gridiron Gear Player Timeline Jerseys Autographs Prime

STATED PRINT RUN 5-30
3 Antoine Cason/25 10.00 25.00
4 Brandon Meriweather/25 10.00 25.00
5 Chad Henne/22 12.00 30.00
7 Early Doucet/25 12.00 30.00
10 Vernon Gholston /30 10.00 25.00
11 Limas Sweed/25 12.00 30.00
13 LaRon Landry/25 10.00 25.00
21 Jim Brown/25 40.00 80.00

2009 Donruss Gridiron Gear Rivals

*GOLD/100: .6X TO 1.5X BASIC INSERTS
*PLATINUM/25: .8X TO 2X BASIC INSERTS
*SILVER/250: .5X TO 1.2X BASIC INSERTS
1 Ronnie Brown .75 2.00
Marshawn Lynch
2 Randy Moss 1.00 2.50
Thomas Jones
3 Ryan Grant 1.00 2.50
Brian Urlacher
4 Donovan McNabb 1.00 2.50
Eli Manning
5 Hines Ward .75 2.00
LenDale White
6 Terence Newman .75 2.00
Clinton Portis
7 Greg Jennings 1.50 4.00
Adrian Peterson
8 Peyton Manning 1.50 4.00
Tom Brady
9 Jason Witten 1.00 2.50
Brandon Jacobs
10 Willie Parker 1.00 2.50
Ray Lewis

2009 Donruss Gridiron Gear Rivals Jerseys

STATED PRINT RUN 5-250
2 Randy Moss 6.00 15.00
Thomas Jones
8 Peyton Manning 10.00 25.00
Tom Brady

2009 Donruss Gridiron Gear Rivals Jerseys Prime

STATED PRINT RUN 1-50
1 Ronnie Brown 8.00 20.00
Marshawn Lynch
6 Terence Newman 8.00 20.00
Clinton Portis
8 Peyton Manning 12.00 30.00
Tom Brady

2009 Donruss Gridiron Gear Rookie Gridiron Gems Jerseys Prime

STATED PRINT RUN 50 SER.#'d SETS
*COMBO PRM/50: .6X TO 1.5X PRIME/50
*JUMBO PRM/50: .6X TO 1.5X PRIME/50
*JSY TRIO/50: .6X TO 1.5X PRIME/50
*PRIME TRIO/50: .6X TO 1.5X PRIME/50
*RETAIL/50: .4X TO 1X PRIME/50
201 Mark Sanchez 6.00 15.00
202 Chris Wells 0.00 0.00
203 Matthew Stafford 10.00 25.00
204 Donald Brown 2.00 5.00
205 Hakeem Nicks 3.00 8.00
206 Michael Crabtree 4.00 10.00
207 Brandon Pettigrew 2.00 5.00
208 Ramses Barden 1.25 3.00
209 Kenny Britt 2.50 6.00
210 Deon Butler 1.50 4.00
211 Juaquin Iglesias 1.50 4.00
212 Jeremy Maclin 3.00 8.00
213 Glen Coffee 1.50 4.00
214 Jason Smith 1.50 4.00
215 Patrick Turner 1.50 4.00
216 Knowshon Moreno 2.00 5.00
217 Mohamed Massaquoi 1.50 4.00
218 Shonn Greene 3.00 8.00
219 Nate Davis 1.50 4.00
220 LeSean McCoy 4.00 10.00
221 Pat White 2.00 5.00
222 Percy Harvin 3.00 8.00
223 Tyson Jackson 1.50 4.00
224 Javon Ringer 2.00 5.00
225 Mike Wallace 4.00 10.00
226 Josh Freeman 4.00 10.00
227 Stephen McGee 2.00 5.00
228 Mike Thomas 2.00 5.00
229 Brian Robiskie 2.00 5.00
230 Aaron Curry 2.00 5.00
231 Andre Brown 1.25 3.00
232 Derrick Williams 1.50 4.00
233 Darrius Heyward-Bey 2.00 5.00
234 Rhett Bomar 1.50 4.00

2009 Donruss Gridiron Gear Rookie Gridiron Gems Jerseys Trios Autographs Prime

*TRIO AU/25: .5X TO 1.2X BASIC JSY AU
STATED PRINT RUN 25 SER.#'d SETS

2003 Donruss Kickoff Magazine

Cards from this set were issued in 8-card sheets in two different issues of Kickoff magazine. They were produced by Donruss/Playoff and came perforated on each sheet.

COMPLETE SET (16) 5.00 10.00
1 Marcellus Wiley .20 .50
2 Sam Adams .20 .50
3 Eddie George .30 .75
4 Jeff Garcia .40 1.00
5 Keith Brooking .20 .50
6 Drew Bledsoe .50 1.25
7 Edgerrin James .50 1.25
8 Zach Thomas .40 1.00
9 Shaun O'Hara .20 .50
10 Tiki Barber .30 .75
11 Ronde Barber .30 .75
12 Ricky Williams .60 1.50
13 Hines Ward .40 1.00
14 Eddie Mason .20 .50
15 Billy Conaty .20 .50
16 Gerald McBurrows .20 .50

2006 Donruss/Playoff Hawaii Rookie Autographs

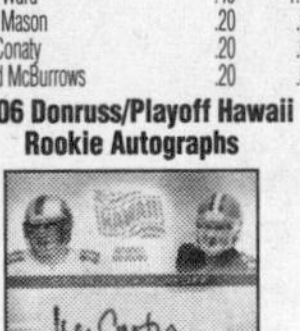

AUTOGRAPHS TOO SCARCE TO PRICE

1997 Donruss Preferred

The 1997 Donruss Preferred set was issued in one series totalling 150 cards. The fronts feature color player photos on all-foil, micro-etched card stock with micro-etched borders. The set is divided into 80 bronze (5:1 insert odds), 40 silver (1:5), 20 gold (1:17), and 10 platinum cards (1:48) cards. The set contains the topical subset: National Treasure (118-147).

COMPLETE SET (150) 150.00 300.00
COMP.BRONZE SET (80) 10.00 25.00
1 Emmitt Smith P 7.50 20.00
2 Steve Young G 3.00 8.00
3 Cris Carter S 2.50 6.00
4 Tim Biakabutuka B .25 .60
5 Brett Favre P 10.00 25.00
6 Troy Aikman G 4.00 10.00
7 Eddie Kennison S 1.50 4.00
8 Ben Coates B .25 .60
9 Dan Marino P 10.00 25.00
10 Deion Sanders G 2.50 6.00
11 Curtis Conway S 1.50 4.00
12 Jeff George B .25 .60
13 Barry Sanders P 7.50 20.00
14 Kerry Collins G 2.50 6.00
15 Marvin Harrison S 2.50 6.00
16 Bobby Engram B .25 .60
17 Jerry Rice P 5.00 12.00
18 Kordell Stewart G 2.50 6.00
19 Tony Banks S 2.50 6.00
20 Jim Harbaugh B .25 .60
21 Mark Brunell P 2.50 6.00
22 Steve McNair G 3.00 8.00
23 Terrell Owens S 3.00 8.00
24 Raymont Harris B .15 .40
25 Curtis Martin P 3.00 8.00
26 Karim Abdul-Jabbar G 2.50 6.00
27 Joey Galloway S 1.50 4.00
28 Bobby Hoying B .25 .60
29 Terrell Davis P 3.00 8.00
30 Terry Glenn G 1.50 4.00
31 Antonio Freeman S 2.50 6.00
32 Brad Johnson B .40 1.00
33 Drew Bledsoe P 2.50 6.00
34 John Elway G 8.00 20.00
35 Herman Moore G 1.50 4.00
36 Robert Brooks S 1.50 4.00
37 Rod Smith B .40 1.00
38 Eddie George P 2.50 6.00
39 Keyshawn Johnson G 2.50 6.00
40 Greg Hill S 1.00 2.50
41 Scott Mitchell B .25 .60
42 Muhsin Muhammad B .25 .60
43 Isaac Bruce G 2.50 6.00
44 Jeff Blake S 1.50 4.00
45 Neil O'Donnell B .25 .60
46 Jimmy Smith B .25 .60
47 Jerome Bettis G 2.50 6.00
48 Terry Allen S 1.50 4.00
49 Andre Reed B .25 .60
50 Frank Sanders B .25 .60
51 Tim Brown G 2.50 6.00
52 Thurman Thomas S 1.50 4.00
53 Heath Shuler B .15 .40
54 Vinny Testaverde B .25 .60
55 Marcus Allen S 2.50 6.00
56 Napoleon Kaufman B .40 1.00
57 Derrick Alexander WR B .25 .60
58 Carl Pickens G 1.50 4.00
59 Marshall Faulk S 3.00 8.00
60 Mike Alstott B .40 1.00
61 Jamal Anderson B .40 1.00
62 Ricky Watters G 1.50 4.00
63 Dorsey Levens S 2.50 6.00
64 Todd Collins B .15 .40
65 Trent Dilfer B .40 1.00
66 Natrone Means S 1.50 4.00
67 Gus Frerotte B .15 .40
68 Irving Fryar B .25 .60
69 Adrian Murrell S 1.50 4.00
70 Rodney Hampton B .25 .60
71 Garrison Hearst B .25 .60
72 Reggie White S 2.50 6.00
73 Anthony Johnson B .15 .40
74 Tony Martin B .25 .60
75 Chris Sanders S 1.00 2.50
76 O.J. McDuffie B .25 .60
77 Leeland McElroy B .15 .40
78 Ki-Jana Carter S 1.50 4.00
79 Anthony Miller B .15 .40
80 Johnnie Morton B .25 .60
81 Robert Smith S .25 .60
82 Brett Perriman B .15 .40
83 Errict Rhett B .15 .40
84 Michael Irvin S 1.50 4.00
85 Darnay Scott B .25 .60
86 Shannon Sharpe B .25 .60
87 Lawrence Phillips S 1.50 4.00
88 Bruce Smith B .25 .60
89 James O.Stewart B .25 .60
90 J.J. Stokes B .25 .60
91 Chris Warren B .25 .60
92 Daryl Johnston B .25 .60
93 Andre Rison B .25 .60
94 Rashaan Salaam B .15 .40
95 Amani Toomer B .25 .60
96 Warrick Dunn G RC 6.00 15.00
97 Tiki Barber S RC 6.00 15.00
98 Peter Boulware B RC .40 1.00
99 Ike Hilliard G RC 4.00 10.00
100 Antowain Smith S RC 4.00 10.00
101 Yatil Green S RC 1.50 4.00
102 Tony Gonzalez B RC 3.00 8.00
103 Reidel Anthony G RC 2.50 6.00
104 Troy Davis S RC 1.50 4.00
105 Rae Carruth S RC 1.00 2.50
106 David LaFleur B RC .15 .40
107 Jim Druckenmiller G RC 1.50 4.00
108 Joey Kent S RC 1.50 4.00
109 Byron Hanspard S RC 1.50 4.00
110 Darrell Russell B RC .15 .40
111 Danny Wuerffel S RC 2.50 6.00
112 Jake Plummer S RC 4.00 10.00
113 Jay Graham B RC .25 .60
114 Corey Dillon S RC 4.00 10.00
115 Orlando Pace B RC .40 1.00
116 Pat Barnes S RC 1.50 4.00
117 Shawn Springs B RC .25 .60
118 Troy Aikman NT B .75 2.00
119 Drew Bledsoe NT B .40 1.00
120 Mark Brunell NT B .40 1.00
121 Kerry Collins NT B .40 1.00
122 Terrell Davis NT B .50 1.25
123 Jerome Bettis NT B .40 1.00
124 Brett Favre NT B 2.00 4.00
125 Eddie George NT B .40 1.00
126 Terry Glenn NT B .40 1.00
127 Karim Abdul-Jabbar NT B .25 .60
128 Keyshawn Johnson NT B .40 1.00
129 Dan Marino NT B 2.00 4.00
130 Curtis Martin NT B .50 1.25
131 Natrone Means NT B .25 .60
132 Herman Moore NT S 1.50 4.00
133 Jerry Rice NT B .75 2.00
134 Barry Sanders NT B 1.25 3.00
135 Deion Sanders NT B .40 1.00
136 Emmitt Smith NT B 1.50 3.00
137 Kordell Stewart NT B .40 1.00
138 Steve Young NT B .50 1.25
139 Carl Pickens NT S 1.50 4.00
140 Isaac Bruce NT S 2.50 6.00
141 Steve McNair NT S 2.00 5.00
142 John Elway NT S 5.00 10.00
143 Cris Carter NT B .25 .60
144 Tim Brown NT B .25 .60
145 Ricky Watters NT B .15 .40
146 Robert Brooks NT B .25 .60
147 Jeff Blake NT B .25 .60
148 Tiki Barber CL B .60 1.50
149 Jim Druckenmiller CL B .15 .40
150 Warrick Dunn CL B .50 1.25

1997 Donruss Preferred Cut To The Chase

COMP.BRONZE SET (80) 150.00 300.00
*BRONZE STARS: 2X TO 5X BASIC CARDS
*BRONZE RCs: 2X TO 4X
BRONZE STATED ODDS 1:7
*SILVER STARS: 1X TO 2.5X BASIC CARDS
*SILVER RCs: 1.25X TO 2.5X
SILVER STATED ODDS 1:63
*GOLD STARS: .6X TO 1.5X BASIC CARDS
*GOLD RCs: .8X TO 2X
GOLD STATED ODDS 1:189
*PLATINUM STARS: .6X TO 1.5X BASIC CARDS
PLATINUM STATED ODDS 1:756

1997 Donruss Preferred Chain Reaction

COMPLETE SET (24) 100.00 200.00
STATED PRINT RUN 3000 SERIAL #'d SETS
1A Dan Marino 8.00 20.00
1B Karim Abdul-Jabbar 2.00 5.00
2A Troy Aikman 4.00 10.00
2B Emmitt Smith 6.00 15.00
3A Steve McNair 3.00 8.00
3B Eddie George 2.50 6.00
4A Brett Favre 10.00 25.00
4B Robert Brooks 2.00 5.00
5A John Elway 8.00 20.00
5B Terrell Davis 3.00 8.00
6A Drew Bledsoe 3.00 8.00
6B Curtis Martin 3.00 8.00
7A Steve Young 4.00 10.00
7B Jerry Rice 5.00 12.00
8A Mark Brunell 3.00 8.00
8B Natrone Means 2.00 5.00
9A Barry Sanders 6.00 15.00
9B Herman Moore 2.50 6.00
10A Kordell Stewart 2.50 6.00
10B Jerome Bettis 3.00 8.00
11A Jeff Blake 2.00 5.00
11B Carl Pickens 2.50 6.00
12A Lawrence Phillips 2.00 5.00
12B Isaac Bruce 2.50 6.00

1997 Donruss Preferred Double-Wide Tins

COMPLETE SET (12) 5.00 12.00
1 Emmitt Smith .40 1.50
Terrell Davis
2 Troy Aikman .40 1.00
Kerry Collins
3 Herman Moore .20 .50
Carl Pickens
4 Brett Favre .75 2.00
Mark Brunell
5 Deion Sanders .40 1.00
Kordell Stewart
6 Barry Sanders .60 1.50
Karim Abdul-Jabbar
7 Jerry Rice .40 1.00
Terry Glenn
8 Dan Marino .75 2.00
Drew Bledsoe
9 John Elway .75 2.00
Steve Young
10 Curtis Martin .40 1.00
Warrick Dunn
11 Eddie George .40 1.00
Tim Brown
12 Keyshawn Johnson .20 .50
Ike Hilliard

1997 Donruss Preferred Precious Metals

ANNOUNCED PRINT RUN 100 SETS
ONE GRAM (.032 Troy Oz) METAL PER CARD
1 Drew Bledsoe Plat 50.00 100.00
2 Curtis Martin Plat. 50.00 100.00
3 Troy Aikman Gold 60.00 120.00
4 Eddie George Plat 40.00 80.00
5 Warrick Dunn Gold 50.00 100.00
6 Brett Favre Plat 100.00 200.00
7 John Elway Gold 75.00 150.00
8 Barry Sanders Plat 75.00 150.00
9 Emmitt Smith Plat 75.00 150.00
10 Terrell Davis Plat 50.00 100.00
11 Mark Brunell 40.00 80.00
12 Jerry Rice Plat 60.00 120.00
13 Dan Marino Plat 100.00 200.00
14 Terry Glenn 40.00 80.00
15 Tiki Barber 50.00 100.00

1997 Donruss Preferred Staremasters

COMPLETE SET (24) 100.00 250.00
STATED PRINT RUN 1500 SERIAL #'d SETS
1 Tim Brown 2.00 5.00
2 Mark Brunell 4.00 10.00
3 Kerry Collins 3.00 8.00
4 Brett Favre 12.50 30.00
5 Eddie George 3.00 8.00
6 Terry Glenn 3.00 8.00
7 Dan Marino 12.50 30.00
8 Curtis Martin 4.00 10.00
9 Jerry Rice 6.00 15.00
10 Barry Sanders 10.00 25.00
11 Deion Sanders 3.00 8.00
12 Emmitt Smith 10.00 25.00
13 Drew Bledsoe 4.00 10.00
14 Troy Aikman 6.00 15.00
15 Tiki Barber 5.00 12.00
16 Terrell Davis 4.00 10.00
17 Karim Abdul-Jabbar 2.00 5.00
18 Warrick Dunn 5.00 12.00
19 John Elway 15.00 40.00
20 Yatil Green 2.00 5.00
21 Ike Hilliard 2.00 5.00
22 Kordell Stewart 3.00 8.00
23 Ricky Watters 1.25 3.00
24 Steve Young 4.00 10.00

1997 Donruss Preferred Tins

COMP.BLUE PACK SET (24) 10.00 20.00
COMP.SILVER PACK SET (24) 100.00 200.00
*SILVER PACK TINS: 5X TO 10X BLUES
STATED PRINT RUN 1200 SETS
*BLUE BOX TINS: 3X TO 6X BLUE PACKS
STATED PRINT RUN 1200 SETS
*GOLD PACK TINS: 10X TO 20X BLUE PACKS
STATED PRINT RUN 300 SETS
*GOLD BOX TINS: 8X TO 16X BLUE PACKS
STATED PRINT RUN 300 SETS
1 Mark Brunell .25 .60
2 Karim Abdul-Jabbar .10 .30
3 Terry Glenn .20 .50
4 Brett Favre .75 2.00
5 Troy Aikman .40 1.00
6 Eddie George .20 .50
7 John Elway .75 2.00
8 Steve Young .25 .60
9 Terrell Davis .25 .60
10 Kordell Stewart .20 .50
11 Drew Bledsoe .25 .60
12 Kerry Collins .20 .50
13 Dan Marino .75 2.00
14 Tim Brown .10 .30
15 Carl Pickens .20 .50
16 Warrick Dunn .25 .60
17 Herman Moore .20 .50
18 Curtis Martin .25 .60
19 Ike Hilliard .20 .50
20 Barry Sanders .60 1.50
21 Deion Sanders .20 .50
22 Emmitt Smith .60 1.50
23 Keyshawn Johnson .20 .50
24 Jerry Rice .40 1.00

1999 Donruss Preferred QBC

Released as a 120-card set, 1999 Donruss Preferred QBC features only members of the Quarterback Club and is divided up into four tiers. Tier one, Bronze, are found three in every pack, tier two, Silver, are found one per pack, tier three, Gold, are found one in four, and tier four, Platinum, are found one in eight. Base cards feature action photos and a "fleck" foil border.

COMPLETE SET (120) 75.00 150.00
COMP.BRONZE SET (45) 12.50 25.00
1 Troy Aikman B .50 1.25
2 Tony Banks B .25 .60
3 Jeff Blake B .25 .60
4 Drew Bledsoe B .30 .75
5 Bubby Brister B .20 .50
6 Chris Chandler B .25 .60
7 Kerry Collins B .25 .60
8 Randall Cunningham B .30 .75
9 Terrell Davis B .30 .75
10 Trent Dilfer B .25 .60
11 John Elway B 1.00 2.50
12 Boomer Esiason B .30 .75
13 Jim Everett B .20 .50
14 Brett Favre B 1.00 2.50
15 Doug Flutie B .30 .75
16 Gus Frerotte B .20 .50
17 Jeff George B .20 .50
18 Elvis Grbac B .20 .50
19 Jim Harbaugh B .25 .60
20 Michael Irvin B .30 .75
21 Brad Johnson B .25 .60
22 Keyshawn Johnson B .25 .60
23 Danny Kanell B .20 .60
24 Jim Kelly B .40 1.00
25 Bernie Kosar B .25 .60
26 Erik Kramer B .25 .60
27 Ryan Leaf B .25 .60
28 Peyton Manning B 1.00 2.50
29 Dan Marino B 1.00 2.50
30 Donovan McNabb B RC 1.00 2.50
31 Steve McNair B .30 .75
32 Cade McNown B RC .30 .75
33 Scott Mitchell B .20 .50
34 Warren Moon B .30 .75
35 Neil O'Donnell B .25 .60
36 Jake Plummer B .25 .60
37 Jerry Rice B .60 1.50
38 Barry Sanders B .75 2.00
39 Junior Seau B .30 .75
40 Phil Simms B .30 .75
41 Kordell Stewart B .25 .60
42 Vinny Testaverde B .25 .60
43 Ricky Williams B RC .60 1.50
44 Steve Young B .40 1.00
45 Dan Marino B 1.00 2.50
Brett Favre B
John Elway B
46 Troy Aikman S .60 1.50
47 Tony Banks S .30 .75
48 Drew Bledsoe S .40 1.00
49 Bubby Brister S .25 .60
50 Chris Chandler S .30 .75
51 Kerry Collins S .30 .75
52 Randall Cunningham S .40 1.00
53 Terrell Davis S .40 1.00
54 Trent Dilfer S .30 .75
55 John Elway S 1.25 3.00
56 Boomer Esiason S .40 1.00
57 Brett Favre S 1.25 3.00
58 Doug Flutie S .40 1.00
59 Elvis Grbac S .25 .60
60 Jim Harbaugh S .30 .75
61 Michael Irvin S .40 1.00
62 Brad Johnson S .30 .75
63 Keyshawn Johnson S .30 .75
64 Jim Kelly S .50 1.25
65 Ryan Leaf S .30 .75
66 Peyton Manning S 1.25 3.00
67 Dan Marino S 1.25 3.00
68 Donovan McNabb S 1.25 3.00
69 Steve McNair S .40 1.00
70 Cade McNown S .40 1.00
71 Warren Moon S .40 1.00
72 Jake Plummer S .30 .75
73 Jerry Rice S .75 2.00
74 Barry Sanders S 1.00 2.50
75 Junior Seau S .40 1.00
76 Phil Simms S .40 1.00
77 Kordell Stewart S .30 .75
78 Vinny Testaverde S .30 .75
79 Ricky Williams S .75 2.00
80 Steve Young S .50 1.25
81 Troy Aikman G 1.25 3.00
82 Drew Bledsoe G .75 2.00
83 Bubby Brister G .50 1.25
84 Chris Chandler G .60 1.50
85 Randall Cunningham G .75 2.00
86 Terrell Davis G .75 2.00
87 John Elway G 2.50 6.00
88 Brett Favre G 2.50 6.00
89 Doug Flutie G .75 2.00
90 Brad Johnson G .60 1.50
91 Keyshawn Johnson G .60 1.50
92 Ryan Leaf G .60 1.50
93 Peyton Manning G 2.50 6.00
94 Dan Marino G 2.50 6.00
95 Donovan McNabb G 2.50 6.00
96 Steve McNair G .75 2.00
97 Cade McNown G .75 2.00
98 Warren Moon G .75 2.00
99 Jake Plummer G .60 1.50
100 Jerry Rice G 1.50 4.00
101 Barry Sanders G 2.00 5.00
102 Kordell Stewart G .60 1.50
103 Vinny Testaverde G .60 1.50
104 Ricky Williams G 1.50 4.00
105 Steve Young G 1.00 2.50
106 Troy Aikman P 2.00 5.00
107 Drew Bledsoe P 1.25 3.00
108 Terrell Davis P 1.25 3.00
109 John Elway P 4.00 10.00
110 Brett Favre P 4.00 10.00
111 Keyshawn Johnson P 1.00 2.50
112 Peyton Manning P 4.00 10.00
113 Dan Marino P 4.00 10.00
114 Donovan McNabb P 4.00 10.00
115 Cade McNown P 1.25 3.00
116 Jake Plummer P 1.00 2.50
117 Jerry Rice P 2.50 6.00
118 Barry Sanders P 3.00 8.00
119 Kordell Stewart P 1.00 2.50
120 Ricky Williams P 2.50 6.00

1999 Donruss Preferred QBC Power

*POWER BRONZE STARS: 2X TO 5X
*POWER BRONZE RCs: 1.2X TO 3X
POWER BRONZE PRINT RUN 500 SER.#'d SETS
*POWER SILVER STARS: 2X TO 5X
*POWER SILVER ROOKIES: 1.2X TO 3X
POWER SILVER PRINT RUN 300 SER.#'d SETS
*POWER GOLD STARS: 2.5X TO 6X
*POWER GOLD ROOKIES: 1.2X TO 3X
POWER GOLD PRINT RUN 150 SER.#'d SETS
*POWER PLATINUM STARS: 3X TO 8X
*POWER PLATINUM ROOKIES: 1.5X TO 4X
POWER PLAT.PRINT RUN 50 SER.#'d SETS

1999 Donruss Preferred QBC Autographs

1 Steve Young 25.00 60.00
2 Ricky Williams 15.00 40.00
3 Jerry Rice 60.00 100.00
4 Jake Plummer 12.50 30.00
5 Peyton Manning 50.00 100.00
6 Michael Irvin 15.00 40.00
7 Dan Marino 60.00 120.00
8 Randall Cunningham 15.00 40.00
9 Troy Aikman 40.00 80.00
10 Terrell Davis 15.00 40.00
11 Vinny Testaverde 12.50 30.00
12 Chris Chandler 10.00 25.00
13 Kordell Stewart 10.00 26.00
14 Bubby Brister 10.00 25.00
15 Steve McNair 15.00 40.00

1999 Donruss Preferred QBC Chain Reaction

COMPLETE SET (20) 30.00 60.00
STATED PRINT RUN 5000 SERIAL #'d SETS
1A Terrell Davis 1.00 2.50
1B Ricky Williams 1.25 3.00
2A Donovan McNabb 3.00 8.00
2B Cade McNown .50 1.25
3A Brett Favre 3.00 8.00
3B Barry Sanders 3.00 8.00
4A Jerry Rice 2.00 5.00
4B Steve Young 1.25 3.00
5A John Elway 3.00 8.00
5B Chris Chandler .60 1.50
6A Dan Marino 3.00 8.00
6B Drew Bledsoe 1.25 3.00
7A Keyshawn Johnson 1.00 2.50
7B Vinny Testaverde .60 1.50
8A Warren Moon 1.00 2.50
8B Steve McNair 1.00 2.50
9A Jake Plummer .60 1.50
9B Kordell Stewart .60 1.50
10A Troy Aikman 2.00 5.00
10B Peyton Manning 3.00 8.00

1999 Donruss Preferred QBC Hard Hats

COMPLETE SET (30) 60.00 120.00
STATED PRINT RUN 3000 SER.#'d SETS
1 Brett Favre 6.00 15.00
2 Keyshawn Johnson 2.00 5.00
3 John Elway 6.00 15.00
4 Drew Bledsoe 2.50 6.00
5 Chris Chandler 1.25 3.00
6 Terrell Davis 2.00 5.00
7 Ryan Leaf 2.00 5.00
8 Ricky Williams 2.00 5.00
9 Cade McNown .75 2.00
10 Barry Sanders 6.00 15.00
11 Donovan McNabb 5.00 12.00
12 Peyton Manning 6.00 15.00
13 Troy Aikman 4.00 10.00
14 Steve Young 2.50 6.00
15 Vinny Testaverde 1.25 3.00
16 Dan Marino 6.00 15.00
17 Steve McNair 2.00 5.00
18 Kordell Stewart 1.25 3.00
19 Michael Irvin 1.25 3.00
20 Jake Plummer 1.25 3.00
21 Jerry Rice 4.00 10.00
22 Brad Johnson 2.00 5.00
23 Phil Simms .75 2.00
24 Jim Kelly .75 2.00
25 Trent Dilfer 1.25 3.00
26 Kerry Collins 1.25 3.00
27 Warren Moon 2.00 5.00
28 Bubby Brister .75 2.00
29 Randall Cunningham 2.00 5.00
30 Doug Flutie 2.00 5.00

1999 Donruss Preferred QBC Materials

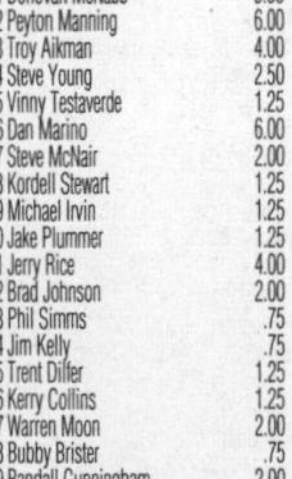

JERSEY PRINT RUN 300 SER. #'d SETS
SHOE PRINT RUN 300 SER. #'d SETS
HELMET PRINT RUN 120 SER. #'d SETS
1 Dan Marino J 25.00 60.00
2 John Elway J 25.00 60.00
3 Drew Bledsoe J 10.00 25.00
4 Jake Plummer J 8.00 20.00
5A Doug Flutie White 10.00 25.00
5H Doug Flutie Blue 10.00 25.00
6 Peyton Manning J 25.00 60.00
7A Jerry Rice White/150 30.00 80.00
7H Jerry Rice Red 20.00 50.00
8 Brett Favre J 25.00 60.00
9 Jim Kelly J 12.00 30.00
10 Barry Sanders J 20.00 50.00
11 Keyshawn Johnson S 8.00 20.00
12 Brett Favre S 25.00 60.00
14 Troy Aikman S 15.00 40.00
15 Terrell Davis S 10.00 25.00
16 Dan Marino H 40.00 100.00
17 Troy Aikman H 25.00 60.00
18 Brett Favre H 40.00 100.00
19 Jerry Rice H 30.00 80.00
20 Terrell Davis H 15.00 40.00

1999 Donruss Preferred QBC National Treasures

COMPLETE SET (44) 75.00 150.00
STATED PRINT RUN 2000 SERIAL #'d SETS
1 Jake Plummer 1.25 3.00
2 Chris Chandler 1.25 3.00
3 Danny Kanell .75 2.00
4 Tony Banks 1.25 3.00
5 Scott Mitchell .75 2.00
6 Doug Flutie 2.00 5.00
7 Jim Kelly .75 2.00
8 Erik Kramer .75 2.00
9 Cade McNown 1.00 2.50
10 Jeff Blake 1.25 3.00
11 Boomer Esiason .75 2.00
12 Bernie Kosar .75 2.00
13 Troy Aikman 4.00 10.00
14 Michael Irvin 1.25 3.00
15 Bubby Brister .75 2.00
16 Terrell Davis 2.00 5.00
17 John Elway 6.00 15.00
18 Gus Frerotte .75 2.00
19 Barry Sanders 6.00 15.00
20 Brett Favre 6.00 15.00
21 Peyton Manning 6.00 15.00
22 Elvis Grbac 1.25 3.00
23 Warren Moon 2.00 5.00
24 Dan Marino 6.00 15.00
25 Randall Cunningham 2.00 5.00
26 Jeff George 1.25 3.00
27 Drew Bledsoe 2.50 6.00
28 Ricky Williams 2.50 6.00
29 Kerry Collins 1.25 3.00
30 Phil Simms .75 2.00
31 Keyshawn Johnson 2.00 5.00
32 Vinny Testaverde 1.25 3.00
33 Donovan McNabb 6.00 15.00
34 Kordell Stewart 1.25 3.00
35 Jim Harbaugh 1.25 3.00
36 Ryan Leaf 2.00 5.00
37 Junior Seau 2.00 5.00
38 Jerry Rice 4.00 10.00
39 Steve Young 2.50 6.00
40 Jim Everett .75 2.00
41 Trent Dilfer 1.25 3.00
42 Steve McNair 2.00 5.00
43 Brad Johnson 2.00 5.00
44 Neil O'Donnell 1.25 3.00

1999 Donruss Preferred QBC Passing Grade

COMPLETE SET (20) 75.00 150.00
STATED PRINT RUN 1500 SERIAL #'d SETS
1 Steve Young 3.00 8.00
2 Dan Marino 8.00 20.00
3 Kordell Stewart 1.50 4.00
4 Trent Dilfer 1.50 4.00
5 Doug Flutie 2.50 6.00
6 Vinny Testaverde 1.50 4.00
7 Donovan McNabb 6.00 15.00
8 Brad Johnson 2.50 6.00
9 Troy Aikman 5.00 12.00
10 Brett Favre 8.00 20.00
11 Steve McNair 2.50 6.00
12 Peyton Manning 8.00 20.00
13 John Elway 8.00 20.00
14 Chris Chandler 1.50 4.00
15 Randall Cunningham 2.50 6.00
16 Cade McNown 1.00 2.50
17 Ryan Leaf 2.50 6.00
18 Drew Bledsoe 3.00 8.00
19 Jake Plummer 1.50 4.00
20 Warren Moon 2.50 6.00

1999 Donruss Preferred QBC Precious Metals

STATED PRINT RUN 25 SER.#'d SETS
1 Troy Aikman G 50.00 120.00
2 Drew Bledsoe G 40.00 100.00
3 Terrell Davis G 30.00 80.00
4 John Elway P 75.00 200.00
5 Brett Favre P 75.00 200.00
6 Keyshawn Johnson G 25.00 60.00
7 Peyton Manning G 60.00 150.00
8 Dan Marino P 75.00 200.00
9 Donovan McNabb G 75.00 150.00
10 Cade McNown G 20.00 50.00
11 Jake Plummer G 25.00 60.00
12 Jerry Rice P 60.00 150.00
13 Barry Sanders P 60.00 150.00
14 Kordell Stewart G 20.00 50.00
15 Ricky Williams P 30.00 80.00
16 Bubby Brister S 20.00 50.00
17 Chris Chandler S 20.00 50.00
18 Randall Cunningham S 30.00 80.00
19 Doug Flutie S 30.00 80.00
20 Brad Johnson S 25.00 60.00
21 Ryan Leaf S 20.00 50.00
22 Steve McNair S 30.00 80.00
23 Warren Moon S 30.00 80.00
24 Vinny Testaverde S 20.00 50.00
25 Steve Young S 40.00 100.00
26 Kerry Collins S 20.00 50.00
27 Trent Dilfer S 20.00 50.00
28 Boomer Esiason S 30.00 80.00
29 Jim Kelly S 30.00 80.00
30 Phil Simms S 30.00 80.00

1999 Donruss Preferred QBC Staremasters

COMPLETE SET (20) 100.00 200.00
STATED PRINT RUN 1000 SERIAL #'d SETS
1 Jake Plummer 1.50 4.00
2 Doug Flutie 2.50 6.00
3 Cade McNown 1.00 2.50
4 Troy Aikman 5.00 12.00
5 Michael Irvin 1.50 4.00
6 Terrell Davis 2.50 6.00
7 John Elway 8.00 20.00
8 Barry Sanders 8.00 20.00

9 Brett Favre 8.00 20.00
10 Peyton Manning 8.00 20.00
11 Dan Marino 8.00 20.00
12 Randall Cunningham 2.50 6.00
13 Drew Bledsoe 3.00 8.00
14 Ricky Williams 2.50 6.00
15 Keyshawn Johnson 2.50 6.00
16 Donovan McNabb 6.00 15.00
17 Kordell Stewart 1.50 4.00
18 Ryan Leaf 2.50 6.00
19 Steve Young 3.00 8.00
20 Jerry Rice 5.00 12.00

1999 Donruss Preferred QBC X-Ponential Power

COMPLETE SET (20) 75.00 150.00
STATED PRINT RUN 2500 SERIAL #'d SETS
1A Troy Aikman 3.00 8.00
1B Cade McNown 1.00 2.50
2A Kordell Stewart 1.00 2.50
2B Steve McNair 1.50 4.00
3A Donovan McNabb 6.00 15.00
3B Ricky Williams 2.50 6.00
4A Barry Sanders 5.00 12.00
4B Terrell Davis 1.50 4.00
5A Dan Marino 5.00 12.00
5B Peyton Manning 5.00 12.00
6A Jerry Rice 3.00 8.00
6B Keyshawn Johnson 1.50 4.00
7A Doug Flutie 1.50 4.00
7B Jim Kelly .60 1.50
8A Brett Favre 5.00 12.00
8B Steve Young 2.00 5.00
9A Drew Bledsoe 2.00 5.00
9B Ryan Leaf 1.50 4.00
10A John Elway 5.00 12.00
10B Jake Plummer 1.00 2.50

2000 Donruss Preferred

Released as a 103-card set, Donruss Preferred cards feature the members of the NFL's Quarterback Club. Base cards are white bordered on the top and feature player action photography centered on an orange, red, or purple border on the left and right sides of the card with silver foil highlights. Preferred was packaged in 10-pack boxes with four cards plus one Beckett Grading Services graded card per pack and carried a suggested retail price of $18.99.

COMPLETE SET (103) 8.00 20.00
1 Jake Plummer .15 .40
2 Chris Chandler .15 .40
3 Trent Dilfer .15 .40
4 Doug Flutie .20 .50
5 Cade McNown .12 .30
6 Michael Irvin .20 .50
7 Troy Aikman .30 .75
8 Terrell Davis .20 .50
9 John Elway .50 1.25
10 Brett Favre .60 1.50
11 Peyton Manning .50 1.25
12 Warren Moon .20 .50
13 Randall Cunningham .20 .50
14 Drew Bledsoe .20 .50
15 Ricky Williams .20 .50
16 Kerry Collins .15 .40
17 Vinny Testaverde .15 .40
18 Donovan McNabb .20 .50
19 Jim Harbaugh .15 .40
20 Jerry Rice .40 1.00
21 Steve Young .25 .60
22 Keyshawn Johnson .15 .40
23 Neil O'Donnell .12 .30
24 Steve McNair .20 .50
25 Brad Johnson .15 .40
26 Jeff George .15 .40
27 Dan Marino .60 1.50
28 Jim Kelly .25 .60
29 Barry Sanders .40 1.00
30 Phil Simms .20 .50
31 Gus Frerotte .15 .40
32 Elvis Grbac .12 .30
33 Jeff Blake .15 .40
34 Kordell Stewart .15 .40
35 Tony Banks .12 .30
36 Doug Flutie C .20 .50
37 Cade McNown C .12 .30
38 Troy Aikman C .30 .75
39 Terrell Davis C .20 .50
40 John Elway C .50 1.25
41 Brett Favre C .60 1.50
42 Peyton Manning C .50 1.25
43 Drew Bledsoe C .20 .50
44 Ricky Williams C .20 .50
45 Kerry Collins C .15 .40
46 Vinny Testaverde C .15 .40
47 Donovan McNabb C .20 .50
48 Kordell Stewart C .15 .40
49 Ryan Leaf C .15 .40
50 Jerry Rice C .40 1.00
51 Steve Young C .25 .60
52 Keyshawn Johnson C .15 .40
53 Steve McNair C .20 .50
54 Jeff George C .15 .40
55 Dan Marino C .60 1.50
56 Jim Kelly C .25 .60
57 Barry Sanders C .40 1.00
58 Bernie Kosar C .15 .40
59 Chris Chandler C .15 .40
60 Jim Everett C .15 .40
61 Jake Plummer HS .15 .40
62 Cade McNown HS .12 .30
63 Troy Aikman HS .30 .75
64 Ricky Williams HS .20 .50
65 Donovan McNabb HS .20 .50
66 Steve Young HS .25 .60
67 Brad Johnson HS .15 .40
68 Kerry Collins HS .15 .40
69 Ryan Leaf HS .15 .40
70 Drew Bledsoe HS .20 .50
71 Jake Plummer PS .15 .40
72 Chris Chandler PS .15 .40
73 Michael Irvin PS .20 .50
74 Troy Aikman PS .30 .75
75 Terrell Davis PS .20 .50
76 John Elway PS .50 1.25
77 Brett Favre PS .60 1.50
78 Peyton Manning PS .50 1.25
79 Drew Bledsoe PS .20 .50
80 Junior Seau PS .20 .50
81 Jerry Rice PS .40 1.00
82 Steve Young PS .25 .60
83 Keyshawn Johnson PS .15 .40
84 Steve McNair PS .20 .50
85 Brad Johnson PS .15 .40
86 Dan Marino PS .60 1.50
87 Jim Kelly PS .25 .60
88 Barry Sanders PS .40 1.00
89 Phil Simms PS .20 .50
90 Boomer Esiason PS .20 .50
91 Jake Plummer OF .15 .40
92 Chris Chandler OF .15 .40
93 Bubby Brister OF .15 .40
94 Cade McNown OF .12 .30
95 Jim Harbaugh OF .15 .40
96 Peyton Manning OF .50 1.25
97 Donovan McNabb OF .20 .50
98 Jim Kelly OF .25 .60
99 Brad Johnson OF .15 .40
100 Kordell Stewart OF .15 .40
101 Rob Johnson SP .40 1.00
102 Jevon Kearse SP .40 1.00
103 Rich Gannon SP .40 1.00

2000 Donruss Preferred Power

*VETS 1-20: 2X TO 5X BASIC CARDS
1-20 VETERAN PRINT RUN 750
*VETS 21-40: 2.5X TO 6X BASIC CARDS
21-40 VETERAN PRINT RUN 500
*VETS 41-60: 3X TO 8X BASIC CARDS
41-60 VETERAN PRINT RUN 300
*VETS 61-80: 5X TO 12X BASIC CARDS
61-80 VETERAN PRINT RUN 150
*VETS 81-100: 10X TO 25X BASIC CARD
*VETS 101-103: 4X TO 10X BASIC CARD
81-103 VETERAN PRINT RUN 50

2000 Donruss Preferred Lettermen

STATED ODDS 1:9
STATED PRINT RUN 50-1000
LM1 Peyton Manning/1000 2.50 6.00
LM2 Peyton Manning/750 2.50 6.00
LM3 Peyton Manning/500 3.00 8.00
LM4 Peyton Manning/350 3.00 8.00
LM5 Peyton Manning/250 4.00 10.00
LM6 Peyton Manning/125 5.00 12.00
LM7 Peyton Manning/75 6.00 15.00
LM8 Dan Marino/1000 3.00 8.00
LM9 Dan Marino/750 3.00 8.00
LM10 Dan Marino/500 4.00 10.00
LM11 Dan Marino/350 4.00 10.00
LM12 Dan Marino/250 5.00 12.00
LM13 Dan Marino/125 6.00 15.00
LM14 John Elway/1000 2.50 6.00
LM15 John Elway/750 2.50 6.00
LM16 John Elway/500 3.00 8.00
LM17 John Elway/350 3.00 8.00
LM18 John Elway/250 4.00 10.00
LM19 Terrell Davis/1000 1.00 2.50
LM20 Terrell Davis/750 1.00 2.50
LM21 Terrell Davis/500 1.25 3.00
LM22 Terrell Davis/350 1.25 3.00
LM23 Terrell Davis/250 1.50 4.00
LM24 Jerry Rice/1000 2.00 5.00
LM25 Jerry Rice/750 2.00 5.00
LM26 Jerry Rice/500 2.50 6.00
LM27 Jerry Rice/350 2.50 6.00
LM28 Cade McNown/1000 .60 1.50
LM29 Cade McNown/750 .60 1.50
LM30 Cade McNown/500 .75 2.00
LM31 Cade McNown/350 .75 2.00
LM32 Cade McNown/250 1.00 2.50
LM33 Cade McNown/125 1.25 3.00
LM34 Ricky Williams/1000 1.00 2.50
LM35 Ricky Williams/750 1.00 2.50
LM36 Ricky Williams/500 1.25 3.00
LM37 Ricky Williams/350 1.25 3.00
LM38 Ricky Williams/250 1.50 4.00
LM39 Ricky Williams/125 2.00 5.00
LM40 Ricky Williams/75 2.50 6.00
LM41 Ricky Williams/50 2.50 6.00
LM42 Drew Bledsoe/1000 1.00 2.50
LM43 Drew Bledsoe/750 1.00 2.50
LM44 Drew Bledsoe/500 1.25 3.00
LM45 Drew Bledsoe/350 1.25 3.00
LM46 Drew Bledsoe/250 1.50 4.00
LM47 Drew Bledsoe/125 2.00 5.00
LM48 Drew Bledsoe/75 2.50 6.00
LM49 Steve McNair/1000 1.00 2.50
LM50 Steve McNair/750 1.00 2.50
LM51 Steve McNair/500 1.25 3.00
LM52 Steve McNair/350 1.25 3.00
LM53 Steve McNair/250 1.50 4.00
LM54 Steve McNair/125 2.00 5.00
LM55 Troy Aikman/1000 1.50 4.00
LM56 Troy Aikman/750 1.50 4.00
LM57 Troy Aikman/500 2.00 5.00
LM58 Troy Aikman/350 2.00 5.00
LM59 Troy Aikman/250 2.50 6.00
LM60 Troy Aikman/125 3.00 8.00
LM61 Jake Plummer/1000 .75 2.00
LM62 Jake Plummer/750 .75 2.00
LM63 Jake Plummer/500 1.00 2.50
LM64 Jake Plummer/350 1.00 2.50
LM65 Jake Plummer/250 1.25 3.00
LM66 Jake Plummer/125 1.50 4.00
LM67 Jake Plummer/75 2.00 5.00
LM68 Steve Young/1000 1.25 3.00
LM69 Steve Young/750 1.25 3.00
LM70 Steve Young/500 1.50 4.00
LM71 Steve Young/350 1.50 4.00
LM72 Steve Young/250 2.00 5.00
LM73 Barry Sanders/1000 2.00 5.00
LM74 Barry Sanders/750 2.00 5.00
LM75 Barry Sanders/500 2.50 6.00
LM76 Barry Sanders/350 2.50 6.00
LM77 Barry Sanders/250 3.00 8.00
LM78 Barry Sanders/125 4.00 10.00
LM79 Barry Sanders/75 5.00 12.00
LM80 Brett Favre/1000 3.00 8.00
LM81 Brett Favre/750 3.00 8.00
LM82 Brett Favre/500 4.00 10.00
LM83 Brett Favre/350 4.00 10.00
LM84 Brett Favre/250 5.00 12.00
LM85 Donovan McNabb/1000 1.00 2.50
LM86 Donovan McNabb/750 1.00 2.50
LM87 Donovan McNabb/500 1.25 3.00
LM88 Donovan McNabb/350 1.25 3.00
LM89 Donovan McNabb/250 1.50 4.00
LM90 Donovan McNabb/125 2.00 5.00
LM91 Brad Johnson/1000 .75 2.00
LM92 Brad Johnson/750 .75 2.00
LM93 Brad Johnson/500 1.00 2.50
LM94 Brad Johnson/350 1.00 2.50
LM95 Brad Johnson/250 1.25 3.00
LM96 Brad Johnson/125 1.50 4.00
LM97 Brad Johnson/75 2.00 5.00

2000 Donruss Preferred Materials

STATED ODDS 1:34
PM1 Jerry Rice H/125 15.00 40.00
PM2 John Elway H/125 20.00 50.00
PM3 Doug Flutie H/125 8.00 20.00
PM4 Barry Sanders H/125 15.00 40.00
PM5 Dan Marino P/250 20.00 50.00
PM6 Jerry Rice P/250 12.00 30.00
PM7 Steve McNair S/50 10.00 25.00
PM8 Keyshawn Johnson S/125 6.00 15.00
PM9 Peyton Manning S/125 20.00 50.00
PM10 Steve Young S/125 10.00 25.00
PM11 John Elway S/125 20.00 50.00
PM12 Dan Marino S/125 25.00 60.00
PM13 Warren Moon S/125 8.00 20.00
PM14 Kordell Stewart S/125 6.00 15.00
PM15 Brett Favre S/125 25.00 60.00
PM16 Barry Sanders S/125 15.00 40.00
PM17 Randall Cunningham S/125 8.00 20.00
PM18 Bernie Kosar J/300 5.00 12.00
PM19 Boomer Esiason J/300 6.00 15.00
PM20 Brett Favre J/100 25.00 60.00
PM21 Barry Sanders J/200 12.00 30.00
PM22 Cade McNown J/300 4.00 10.00
PM23 Dan Marino J/300 20.00 50.00
PM24 Drew Bledsoe J/100 8.00 20.00
PM25 Doug Flutie J W/300 6.00 15.00
PM26 Doug Flutie J B/300 6.00 15.00
PM27 Donovan McNabb J/300 6.00 15.00
PM28 Jerry Rice J/300 12.00 30.00
PM29 Jim Harbaugh J/300 5.00 12.00
PM30 Jim Kelly J/300 8.00 20.00
PM31 John Elway J/100 20.00 50.00
PM32 Jake Plummer J/300 5.00 12.00
PM33 Junior Seau J/300 6.00 15.00
PM34 Kordell Stewart J/300 5.00 12.00
PM35 Phil Simms J/200 6.00 15.00
PM36 Peyton Manning J/100 20.00 50.00
PM37 Randall Cunningham J/300 6.00 15.00
PM38 Ricky Williams J W/100 8.00 20.00
PM39 Ricky Williams J B/100 8.00 20.00
PM40 Steve McNair J/100 8.00 20.00
PM41 Steve Young J/300 8.00 20.00
PM42 Troy Aikman J/100 12.00 30.00
PM43 Vinny Testaverde J/300 5.00 12.00
PM44 Warren Moon J/300 6.00 15.00

2000 Donruss Preferred National Treasures

COMPLETE SET (41) 30.00 80.00
STATED ODDS 1:8
STATED PRINT RUN 1000 SER.#'d SETS
NT1 Warren Moon 1.25 3.00
NT2 Steve Young 1.50 4.00
NT3 Jeff Blake 1.00 2.50
NT4 Brett Favre 4.00 10.00
NT5 Donovan McNabb 1.25 3.00
NT6 Bubby Brister 1.00 2.50
NT7 John Elway 3.00 8.00
NT8 Troy Aikman 2.00 5.00
NT9 Steve McNair 1.25 3.00
NT10 Kordell Stewart 1.00 2.50
NT11 Drew Bledsoe 1.25 3.00
NT12 Chris Chandler 1.00 2.50
NT13 Dan Marino 4.00 10.00
NT14 Brad Johnson 1.00 2.50
NT15 Jim Kelly 1.50 4.00
NT16 Jake Plummer 1.00 2.50
NT17 Boomer Esiason 1.25 3.00
NT18 Peyton Manning 3.00 8.00
NT19 Keyshawn Johnson 1.00 2.50
NT20 Barry Sanders 2.50 6.00
NT21 Bernie Kosar 1.00 2.50
NT22 Cade McNown .75 2.00
NT23 Elvis Grbac .75 2.00
NT24 Junior Seau 1.25 3.00
NT25 Phil Simms 1.25 3.00
NT26 Jim Everett 1.00 2.50
NT27 Vinny Testaverde 1.00 2.50
NT28 Jerry Rice 2.50 6.00
NT29 Terrell Davis 1.25 3.00
NT30 Ryan Leaf 1.00 2.50
NT31 Neil O'Donnell .75 2.00
NT32 Ricky Williams 1.25 3.00
NT33 Michael Irvin 1.25 3.00
NT34 Jim Harbaugh 1.00 2.50
NT35 Jeff George 1.00 2.50
NT36 Gus Frerotte 1.00 2.50
NT37 Doug Flutie 1.25 3.00
NT38 Trent Dilfer 1.00 2.50
NT39 Randall Cunningham 1.25 3.00
NT40 Kerry Collins 1.00 2.50
NT41 Tony Banks .75 2.00

2000 Donruss Preferred Pass Time

COMPLETE SET (20) 30.00 60.00
STATED ODDS 1:31
STATED PRINT RUN 500 SER.#'d SETS
PT1 John Elway 4.00 10.00
PT2 Jim Kelly 2.00 5.00
PT3 Steve McNair 1.50 4.00
PT4 Doug Flutie 1.50 4.00
PT5 Dan Marino 5.00 12.00
PT6 Brett Favre 5.00 12.00
PT7 Cade McNown 1.00 2.50
PT8 Elvis Grbac 1.00 2.50
PT9 Vinny Testaverde 1.25 3.00
PT10 Kordell Stewart 1.25 3.00
PT11 Donovan McNabb 1.50 4.00
PT12 Jake Plummer 1.25 3.00
PT13 Troy Aikman 2.50 6.00
PT14 Chris Chandler 1.25 3.00
PT15 Kerry Collins 1.25 3.00
PT16 Peyton Manning 4.00 10.00
PT17 Steve Young 2.00 5.00
PT18 Brad Johnson 1.25 3.00
PT19 Jeff Blake 1.25 3.00
PT20 Drew Bledsoe 1.50 4.00

2000 Donruss Preferred Pen Pals

PP1-PP41 ANNC'D PRINT RUN 50
PP42-PP76 ANNC'D PRINT RUN 40
PP77-PP91 ANNC'D PRINT RUN 20
PP92-PP96 ANNC'D PRINT RUN 10
OVERALL STATED ODDS 1:43
PP1 Warren Moon 12.50 30.00
PP2 Steve Young 20.00 50.00
PP3 Jeff Blake 6.00 15.00
PP4 Brett Favre 100.00 200.00
PP5 Donovan McNabb 20.00 40.00
PP6 Bubby Brister 6.00 15.00
PP7 John Elway 75.00 150.00
PP8 Troy Aikman 40.00 80.00
PP9 Steve McNair 20.00 40.00
PP10 Kordell Stewart 7.50 20.00
PP11 Drew Bledsoe 30.00 60.00
PP12 Chris Chandler 6.00 15.00
PP13 Dan Marino 75.00 150.00
PP14 Brad Johnson 7.50 20.00
PP15 Jim Kelly 20.00 50.00
PP16 Jake Plummer 7.50 20.00
PP17 Boomer Esiason 7.50 20.00
PP18 Peyton Manning 75.00 125.00
PP19 Keyshawn Johnson 7.50 20.00
PP20 Barry Sanders 75.00 125.00
PP21 Bernie Kosar 7.50 20.00
PP22 Cade McNown 6.00 15.00
PP23 Elvis Grbac 6.00 15.00
PP24 Junior Seau 30.00 60.00
PP25 Phil Simms 20.00 40.00
PP26 Jim Everett 6.00 15.00
PP27 Vinny Testaverde 7.50 20.00
PP28 Jerry Rice 60.00 120.00
PP29 Terrell Davis 15.00 30.00
PP30 Ryan Leaf 6.00 15.00
PP31 Neil O'Donnell 6.00 15.00
PP32 Ricky Williams 12.50 30.00
PP33 Michael Irvin 15.00 30.00
PP34 Jim Harbaugh 15.00 30.00
PP35 Jeff George 6.00 15.00
PP36 Gus Frerotte 6.00 15.00
PP37 Doug Flutie 12.50 30.00
PP38 Trent Dilfer 6.00 15.00
PP39 Randall Cunningham 12.50 30.00
PP40 Kerry Collins 7.50 20.00
PP41 Tony Banks 6.00 15.00
PP42 Jerry Rice / Steve Young 150.00 300.00
PP43 Jim Kelly / Doug Flutie 60.00 120.00
PP44 Troy Aikman / Michael Irvin 60.00 120.00
PP45 Jeff Blake / Ricky Williams 25.00 50.00
PP46 John Elway / Terrell Davis 125.00 250.00
PP47 Keyshawn Johnson / Vinny Testaverde 25.00 50.00
PP48 Warren Moon / Elvis Grbac 30.00 80.00
PP49 Bubby Brister / John Elway 75.00 150.00
PP50 Peyotn Manning / Ryan Leaf 60.00 120.00
PP51 Steve Young / Vinny Testaverde 40.00 80.00
PP52 Ryan Leaf / Junior Seau 30.00 60.00
PP53 John Elway / Dan Marino 300.00 500.00
PP54 Jim Kelly / Troy Aikman 75.00 150.00
PP55 Jim Kelly / Phil Simms 60.00 100.00
PP56 Brett Favre / Troy Aikman 200.00 350.00
PP57 Jake Plummer / Brad Johnson 25.00 50.00
PP58 Barry Sanders / Jerry Rice 300.00 450.00
PP59 Dan Marino / Peyotn Manning 300.00 500.00
PP60 Chris Simms / Kerry Collins 25.00 50.00
PP61 Cade McNown / Donovan McNabb 35.00 60.00
PP62 Terrell Davis / Ricky Williams 60.00 120.00
PP63 Peyton Manning / John Elway 200.00 350.00
PP64 Troy Aikman / Jake Plummer 40.00 80.00
PP65 Steve McNair / Donovan McNabb 40.00 80.00
PP66 Steve Young / Cade McNown 25.00 50.00
PP67 Barry Sanders / Terrell Davis 125.00 250.00
PP68 Drew Bledsoe / Ryan Leaf 25.00 50.00
PP69 Cade McNown / Troy Aikman 40.00 80.00
PP70 Randall Cunningham / Chris Chandler 25.00 50.00
PP71 Brett Favre / Jerry Rice 200.00 350.00
PP72 Peyton Manning / Brad Johnson 75.00 150.00
PP73 Jake Plummer / Steve Young 25.00 50.00
PP74 Brett Favre / John Elway 200.00 400.00
PP75 Steve McNair / Kordell Stewart 20.00 40.00
PP76 Barry Sanders / Ricky Williams 100.00 175.00
PP77 Jim Kelly / Boomer Esiason / Phil Simms 90.00 150.00
PP78 Michael Irvin / Jerry Rice / Keyshawn Johnson 150.00 300.00
PP79 Terrell Davis / Jerry Rice / Peyton Manning 250.00 400.00
PP81 Jake Plummer / Troy Aikman / Brad Johnson 75.00 150.00
PP82 Ricky Williams / Donovan McNabb / Cade McNown 75.00 150.00
PP83 Troy Aikman / Drew Bledsoe / Chris Chandler 75.00 150.00
PP84 Doug Flutie / Jake Plummer / Steve Young 75.00 125.00
PP85 Steve McNair / Randall Cunningham / Donovan McNabb 75.00 150.00
PP86 John Elway / Troy Aikman / Steve Young 250.00 400.00
PP87 Ricky Williams / Brett Favre / Terrell Davis 175.00 300.00
PP88 Dan Marino / Barry Sanders / Jerry Rice 400.00 600.00
PP89 Troy Aikman / Chris Chandler / Barry Sanders 175.00 300.00
PP90 Dan Marino / John Elway / Brett Favre 500.00 800.00
PP91 Barry Sanders / Ricky Williams / Terrell Davis 125.00 250.00
PP92 Dan Marino / John Elway / Brett Favre / Peyton Manning
PP93 Jerry Rice / Keyshawn Johnson / Terrell Davis / Ricky Williams
PP94 Troy Aikman / Steve Young / Jerry Rice / Michael Irvin
PP95 Steve McNair / Donovan McNabb / Steve Young / Cade McNown

2000 Donruss Preferred QB Challenge Materials

STATED PRINT RUN 220-500
CM1 Donovan McNabb J/500 5.00 12.00
CM2 Jake Plummer J/500 4.00 10.00
CM3 Cade McNown J/500 3.00 8.00
CM4 Tony Banks J/500 3.00 8.00
CM5 Peyton Manning F/250 15.00 40.00
CM6 Donovan McNabb F/250 6.00 15.00
CM7 Brad Johnson F/250 5.00 12.00
CM8 Chris Chandler F/250 5.00 12.00
CM9 Jake Plummer F/250 5.00 12.00
CM10 Cade McNown F/250 4.00 10.00
CM11 Donovan McNabb T/225 6.00 15.00
CM12 Chris Chandler T/225 5.00 12.00
CM13 Cade McNown T/225 4.00 10.00
CM14 Jake Plummer T/225 5.00 12.00
CM15 Peyton Manning T/225 15.00 40.00
CM16 Brad Johnson T/225 5.00 12.00

2000 Donruss Preferred Signatures

STATED ODDS 1:51
PLAYOFF ANNC'D PRINT RUNS 20-450
PS1 Brett Favre/20* 125.00 250.00
PS2 Drew Bledsoe/20* 30.00 80.00
PS3 Peyton Manning/20* 75.00 200.00
PS4 Terrell Davis/20* 30.00 80.00
PS5 Cade McNown/300* 5.00 12.00
PS6 Donovan McNabb/20* 60.00 120.00
PS7 Brad Johnson/340* 8.00 20.00
PS8 Dan Marino/20* 125.00 250.00
PS9 John Elway/50* 75.00 150.00
PS10 Troy Aikman/20* 75.00 150.00
PS11 Jeff Blake/410* 6.00 15.00
PS12 Vinny Testaverde/350* 6.00 15.00
PS13 Steve Young/20* 50.00 100.00
PS14 Steve McNair/20* 50.00 100.00
PS15 Jake Plummer/280* 5.00 12.00
PS16 Jim Harbaugh/450* 10.00 25.00
PS17 Kordell Stewart/410* 5.00 12.00
PS18 Junior Seau/410* 25.00 50.00
PS19 Ricky Williams/20* 25.00 60.00
PS20 Rob Johnson/100* 10.00 25.00
PS21 Jevon Kearse/200* 6.00 15.00
PS22 Rich Gannon/200* 8.00 20.00

2000 Donruss Preferred Staremasters

COMPLETE SET (20) 15.00 40.00
STATED ODDS 1:8
STATED PRINT RUN 1500 SER.#'d SETS
SM1 Steve Young 1.25 3.00
SM2 Brad Johnson .75 2.00
SM3 Brett Favre 3.00 8.00
SM4 Junior Seau 1.00 2.50
SM5 Donovan McNabb 1.00 2.50
SM6 Jake Plummer .75 2.00
SM7 John Elway 2.50 6.00
SM8 Peyton Manning 2.50 6.00
SM9 Troy Aikman 1.50 4.00
SM10 Keyshawn Johnson .75 2.00
SM11 Steve McNair 1.00 2.50
SM12 Barry Sanders 2.00 5.00
SM13 Kordell Stewart .75 2.00
SM14 Cade McNown .60 1.50
SM15 Drew Bledsoe 1.00 2.50
SM16 Ricky Williams 1.00 2.50
SM17 Doug Flutie 1.00 2.50
SM18 Jerry Rice 2.00 5.00
SM19 Dan Marino 3.00 8.00
SM20 Terrell Davis 1.00 2.50

2010 Donruss Rated Rookies

COMPLETE SET (100) 6.00 15.00
COMP.FACT.SET (101) 15.00 25.00
1 Aaron Hernandez .50 1.25
2 Andre Roberts .30 .75
3 Andrew Quarless .30 .75
4 Anthony Dixon .30 .75
5 Anthony McCoy .25 .60
6 Antonio Brown .50 1.25
7 Armanti Edwards .30 .75
8 Arrelious Benn .30 .75
9 Ben Tate .40 1.00
10 Brandon Graham .25 .60
11 Brandon LaFell .30 .75
12 Brandon Spikes .30 .75
13 Brody Eldridge .30 .75
14 Bryan Bulaga .30 .75
15 C.J. Spiller .50 1.25
16 Carlton Mitchell .25 .60
17 Chris Cook .30 .75
18 Chris Ivory .40 1.00
19 Colt McCoy .60 1.50
20 Corey Wootton .25 .60
21 Damian Williams .30 .75
22 Dan LeFevour .30 .75
23 David Gettis .30 .75
24 David Nelson .30 .75
25 David Reed .25 .60
26 Deji Karim .30 .75
27 Demaryius Thomas .40 1.00
28 Dennis Pitta .30 .75
29 Derrick Morgan .25 .60
30 Devin McCourty .30 .75
31 Dexter McCluster .30 .75
32 Dez Bryant 1.00 2.50
33 Donald Jones .30 .75
34 Earl Thomas .30 .75
35 Ed Dickson .30 .75
36 Emmanuel Sanders .30 .75
37 Eric Berry .30 .75
38 Eric Decker .40 1.00
39 Fendi Onobun .25 .60
40 Garrett Graham .25 .60
41 Gerald McCoy .30 .75
42 Golden Tate .30 .75
43 Jacoby Ford .30 .75
44 Jahvid Best .50 1.25
45 Jason Pierre-Paul .50 1.25
46 Jason Worilds .30 .75
47 Javier Arenas .30 .75
48 Jeremy Horne .25 .60
49 Jermaine Gresham .40 1.00
50 Jerry Hughes .30 .75
51 Jimmy Clausen .30 .75
52 Jimmy Graham .60 1.50
53 Joe Haden .30 .75
54 Joe McKnight .30 .75
55 Joe Webb .30 .75
56 John Conner .30 .75
57 John Skelton .30 .75
58 Jonathan Dwyer .30 .75
59 Jordan Shipley .30 .75
60 Kareem Jackson .30 .75
61 Keiland Williams .30 .75
62 Keith Toston .30 .75
63 Kerry Meier .25 .60
64 Kyle Williams .30 .75
65 Marc Mariani .30 .75
66 Marcus Easley .25 .60
67 Mardy Gilyard .30 .75
68 Marlon Moore .30 .75
69 Max Hall .30 .75
70 Max Komar .30 .75
71 Michael Hoomanawanui .30 .75
72 Mickey Shuler .30 .75
73 Mike Kafka .30 .75
74 Mike Williams .50 1.25
75 Montario Hardesty .30 .75
76 Morgan Burnett .30 .75
77 Nate Allen .30 .75
78 NaVorro Bowman .30 .75
79 Ndamukong Suh .60 1.50
80 Patrick Robinson .30 .75
81 Perrish Cox .25 .60
82 Ricky Sapp .25 .60
83 Riley Cooper .30 .75
84 Rob Gronkowski .75 2.00
85 Roberto Wallace .25 .60
86 Rolando McClain .30 .75
87 Russell Okung .30 .75
88 Ryan Mathews .60 1.50
89 Sam Bradford 2.00 5.00
90 Sean Lee .30 .75
91 Sean Weatherspoon .30 .75
92 Stephen Williams .30 .75
93 Taylor Mays .30 .75
94 Taylor Price .30 .75
95 Tim Tebow 2.00 5.00
96 Toby Gerhart .30 .75
97 Tony Moeaki .30 .75
98 Tony Pike .30 .75
99 Trent Williams .30 .75
100 Victor Cruz 1.00 2.50

2010 Donruss Rated Rookies Autographs

ONE AUTO PER FACTORY SET
EXCH EXPIRATION: 7/5/2012
1 Aaron Hernandez/125* 10.00 25.00
2 Andre Roberts/25* 12.00 30.00
3 Andrew Quarless 6.00 15.00
4 Anthony Dixon/25* 12.00 30.00
5 Anthony McCoy/125* 5.00 12.00
6 Antonio Brown/25* 30.00 60.00
7 Armanti Edwards/25* 12.00 30.00
8 Arrelious Benn/25* 12.00 30.00
9 Ben Tate/25* 15.00 40.00
10 Brandon Graham/25* 10.00 25.00
11 Brandon LaFell/25*
12 Brandon Spikes/125* 6.00 15.00
13 Brody Eldridge 6.00 15.00
14 Bryan Bulaga/125* 8.00 20.00
15 C.J. Spiller/25* 30.00 60.00
16 Carlton Mitchell/25* 10.00 25.00
17 Chris Cook/125* 6.00 15.00
18 Chris Ivory 12.00 30.00
19 Colt McCoy/25* 60.00 120.00
20 Corey Wootton/425* 5.00 12.00
21 Damian Williams/25* 12.00 30.00
22 Dan LeFevour/25* 12.00 30.00
23 David Gettis/125* 6.00 15.00
24 David Nelson 8.00 20.00
25 David Reed 5.00 12.00
26 Deji Karim 5.00 12.00
27 Demaryius Thomas/25* 15.00 40.00
28 Dennis Pitta 6.00 15.00
29 Derrick Morgan/25* 10.00 25.00
30 Devin McCourty/25* 12.00 30.00
32 Dez Bryant/25* 40.00 80.00
33 Donald Jones 6.00 15.00
34 Earl Thomas/125* 6.00 15.00
35 Ed Dickson 6.00 15.00
36 Emmanuel Sanders/25* 6.00 15.00
37 Eric Berry/25* 20.00 50.00
38 Eric Decker/25* 15.00 40.00
39 Fendi Onobun 4.00 10.00
40 Garrett Graham/25* 10.00 25.00
41 Gerald McCoy/25* 12.00 30.00
42 Golden Tate/25*
43 Jacoby Ford/125* 6.00 15.00
44 Jahvid Best/25* 30.00 80.00
45 Jason Pierre-Paul/125* 12.00 30.00
46 Jason Worilds/125* 5.00 12.00
47 Javier Arenas 6.00 15.00
48 Jeremy Horne 4.00 10.00
49 Jermaine Gresham/25* 40.00 80.00
50 Jerry Hughes 5.00 12.00
51 Jimmy Clausen/25* 25.00 60.00
52 Jimmy Graham/125* 20.00 40.00
53 Joe Haden/125* 6.00 15.00
54 Joe McKnight/25* 10.00 25.00
55 Joe Webb 6.00 15.00
56 John Conner 5.00 12.00
57 John Skelton/500* 6.00 15.00
59 Jordan Shipley/25* 12.00 30.00
60 Kareem Jackson/125* 5.00 12.00
61 Keiland Williams 8.00 20.00
62 Keith Toston 6.00 15.00
63 Kerry Meier 5.00 12.00
64 Kyle Williams 5.00 12.00
65 Marc Mariani 6.00 15.00
66 Marcus Easley/25* 10.00 25.00
67 Mardy Gilyard/25*
68 Marlon Moore 5.00 12.00
69 Max Hall/500* 6.00 15.00
70 Max Komar EXCH 6.00 15.00
71 Michael Hoomanawanui 5.00 12.00
72 Mickey Shuler 6.00 15.00
73 Mike Kafka/25* 12.00 30.00
74 Mike Williams/25*
75 Montario Hardesty/25* 12.00 30.00
76 Morgan Burnett/300* 6.00 15.00
77 Nate Allen/125* 6.00 15.00
78 NaVorro Bowman/125* 6.00 15.00
79 Ndamukong Suh/25* 50.00 100.00
80 Patrick Robinson/300* 5.00 12.00
81 Perrish Cox/250* 5.00 12.00
82 Ricky Sapp/125* 4.00 10.00
83 Riley Cooper/25* 12.00 30.00
84 Rob Gronkowski/25* 60.00 120.00
85 Roberto Wallace 5.00 12.00
86 Rolando McClain/25* 12.00 30.00
87 Russell Okung 6.00 15.00
88 Ryan Mathews/25* 50.00 100.00
89 Sam Bradford/25* 100.00 200.00
90 Sean Lee/125* 10.00 25.00
91 Sean Weatherspoon/25* 12.00 30.00
92 Stephen Williams 5.00 12.00
93 Taylor Mays/125* 6.00 15.00
94 Taylor Price/25* 12.00 30.00
95 Tim Tebow/25* 150.00 250.00
96 Toby Gerhart/25*
97 Tony Moeaki 6.00 15.00
98 Tony Pike/25* 12.00 30.00
99 Trent Williams/125* EXCH 6.00 15.00
100 Victor Cruz 30.00 60.00

2011 Donruss Rated Rookies National Convention

RR1 Cam Newton 4.00 10.00
RR2 Jake Locker 3.00 8.00
RR3 Mark Ingram 2.50 6.00
RR4 Julio Jones 2.50 6.00
RR5 A.J. Green 2.00 5.00

1995 Donruss Red Zone

The 1995 Donruss Red Zone series consists of 336 cards. The standard-sized rounded-corner playing cards were distributed as part of a football game. The cards were available in both 80-card starter decks and 12-card booster packs. A Deluxe Double Deck Game Set was distributed as well that contained two 80-card decks and one 12-card pack. The red backs carry the game logo. The cards were unnumbered and are checklisted in alphabetical order within each team below. All cards were available in both issues, but some cards were printed in greater supply than others, and those are noted with the designation DP below. Conversely, there are cards that were produced in smaller quantities than the others, and those are listed with the designation SP below. A 98-card expansion Update set was released later in foil packs.

COMPLETE SET (336) 100.00 250.00
1 Michael Bankston .10 .30
2 Larry Centers .20 .50
3 Ben Coleman DP .01 .05
4 Ed Cunningham DP .01 .05
5 Garrison Hearst .60 1.50
6 Eric Hill .10 .30
7 Lorenzo Lynch DP .01 .05
8 Clyde Simmons DP .01 .05
9 Eric Swann .20 .50
10 Aeneas Williams SP .80 2.00
11 Chris Doleman .10 .30
12 Bert Emanuel DP .20 .50
13 Roman Fortin DP .01 .05
14 Jeff George SP 1.20 3.00
15 Craig Heyward DP .02 .10
16 D.J. Johnson SP .80 2.00
17 Terance Mathis SP 1.20 3.00
18 Clay Matthews DP .01 .05
19 Kevin Ross DP .01 .05
20 Jessie Tuggle DP .01 .05
21 Bob Whitfield SP .80 2.00
22 Cornelius Bennett SP .80 2.00
23 Russell Copeland DP .10 .30
24 John Fina SP .80 2.00
25 Carwell Gardner DP .01 .05
26 Henry Jones DP .01 .05
27 Jim Kelly SP 3.00 8.00
28 Mark Maddox DP .01 .05
29 Glenn Parker .10 .30
30 Andre Reed SP 1.20 3.00
31 Bruce Smith SP 1.20 3.00
32 Thomas Smith DP .01 .05
33 Joe Cain DP .01 .05
34 Mark Carrier DB .20 .50
35 Curtis Conway DP .20 .50
36 Al Fontenot DP .01 .05
37 Jeff Graham DP .02 .10
38 Raymont Harris DP .01 .05
39 Andy Heck .10 .30
40 Erik Kramer DP .02 .10
41 Vinson Smith .10 .30
42 Lewis Tillman DP .01 .05
43 Steve Walsh .10 .30
44 James Williams DP .01 .05
45 Donnell Woolford SP .80 2.00
46 Mike Brim DP .01 .05
47 Tony McGee DP .01 .05
48 Carl Pickens .30 .75
49 Keith Rucker DP .01 .05
50 Darnay Scott SP 1.20 3.00
51 Dan Wilkinson DP .02 .10
52 Darryl Williams DP .01 .05
53 Derrick Alexander WR .20 .50
54 Carl Banks DP .01 .05
55 Rob Burnett SP .80 2.00
56 Earnest Byner .10 .30
57 Steve Everitt DP .01 .05

58 Leroy Hoard SP .80 2.00
59 Michael Jackson DP .01 .05
60 Pepper Johnson .10 .30
61 Tony Jones .10 .30
62 Antonio Langham .10 .30
63 Anthony Pleasant DP .01 .05
64 Vinny Testaverde DP .02 .10
65 Eric Turner SP .80 2.00
66 Tommy Vardell .10 .30
67 Troy Aikman SP 5.00 12.00
68 Larry Brown .10 .30
69 Dixon Edwards DP .10 .30
70 Charles Haley SP .80 2.00
71 Michael Irvin SP 2.00 5.00
72 Daryl Johnston DP .02 .10
73 Leon Lett .10 .30
74 Nate Newton .10 .30
75 Jay Novacek SP .80 2.00
76 Darrin Smith .10 .30
77 Kevin Smith .10 .30
78 Tony Tolbert DP .01 .05
79 Mark Tuinei SP .80 2.00
80 Kevin Williams DP .02 .10
81 Darren Woodson .10 .30
82 Elijah Alexander .10 .30
83 Steve Atwater .10 .30
84 Rod Bernstine SP .80 2.00
85 Ray Crockett .10 .30
86 Shane Dronett DP .01 .05
87 John Elway SP 10.00 20.00
88 Simon Fletcher .10 .30
89 Brian Habib DP .01 .05
90 Glyn Milburn .10 .30
91 Anthony Miller SP .80 2.00
92 Mike Pritchard DP .02 .10
93 Shannon Sharpe .20 .50
94 Gary Zimmerman DP .01 .05
95 Bennie Blades .10 .30
96 Lomas Brown SP .80 2.00
97 Mike Johnson DP .01 .05
98 Robert Massey DP .01 .05
99 Scott Mitchell DP .02 .10
100 Herman Moore SP 1.20 3.00
101 Brett Perriman .20 .50
102 Barry Sanders SP 10.00 20.00
103 Tracy Scroggins DP .01 .05
104 Chris Spielman .10 .30
105 Doug Widell SP .80 2.00
106 Edgar Bennett SP 1.20 3.00
107 LeRoy Butler DP .01 .05
108 Harry Galbreath DP .01 .05
109 Sean Jones SP .80 2.00
110 George Koonce DP .01 .05
111 Anthony Morgan DP .01 .05
112 Ken Ruettgers DP .01 .05
113 Fred Strickland DP .01 .05
114 George Teague .10 .30
115 Reggie White SP 2.00 5.00
116 Micheal Barrow .10 .30
117 Blaine Bishop DP .01 .05
118 Gary Brown .10 .30
119 Ray Childress .10 .30
120 Kenny Davidson SP .80 2.00
121 Cris Dishman SP .80 2.00
122 Brad Hopkins SP .80 2.00
123 Haywood Jeffires DP .01 .05
124 Eddie Robinson DP .01 .05
125 Al Smith DP .01 .05
126 David Williams SP .80 2.00
127 Tony Bennett SP .80 2.00
128 Ray Buchanan SP .80 2.00
129 Quentin Coryatt DP .02 .10
130 Eugene Daniel DP .01 .05
131 Sean Dawkins DP .02 .10
132 Marshall Faulk SP 4.00 10.00
133 Jim Harbaugh .20 .50
134 Jeff Herrod DP .01 .05
135 Kirk Lowdermilk DP .01 .05
136 Tony Siragusa DP .01 .05
137 Floyd Turner DP .01 .05
138 Will Wolford SP .80 2.00
139 Marcus Allen .20 .50
140 Kimble Anders SP .80 2.00
141 Steve Bono DP .10 .30
142 Dale Carter DP .01 .05
143 Mark Collins DP .01 .05
144 Willie Davis .20 .50
145 Lake Dawson DP .02 .10
146 Tim Grunhard DP .01 .05
147 Greg Hill DP .02 .10
148 George Jamison DP .01 .05
149 Darren Mickell DP .01 .05
150 Will Shields DP .01 .05
151 Tracy Simien DP .01 .05
152 Neil Smith SP .80 2.00
153 Tim Bowens DP .01 .05
154 J.B. Brown DP .01 .05
155 Keith Byars .10 .30
156 Bryan Cox .10 .30
157 Jeff Cross .10 .30
158 Irving Fryar SP .80 2.00
159 Ron Heller .10 .30
160 Terry Kirby SP .80 2.00
161 Dan Marino SP 10.00 20.00
162 O.J. McDuffie .30 .75
163 Bernie Parmalee DP .02 .10
164 Chris Singleton DP .01 .05
165 Troy Vincent SP .80 2.00
166 Richmond Webb SP .80 2.00
167 Roy Barker DP .01 .05
168 Cris Carter DP .08 .25
169 Jack Del Rio SP .80 2.00
170 Chris Hinton DP .01 .05
171 Qadry Ismail .20 .50
172 Amp Lee .10 .30
173 Ed McDaniel .10 .30
174 Randall McDaniel DP .02 .10
175 Warren Moon SP 2.00 5.00
176 John Randle SP 1.20 3.00
177 Jake Reed DP .02 .10
178 Robert Smith DP .02 .10
179 Todd Steussie DP .01 .05
180 Dewayne Washington DP .01 .05
181 Bruce Armstrong DP .01 .05
182 Drew Bledsoe 1.00 2.50
183 Vincent Brisby DP .01 .05
184 Vincent Brown DP .01 .05
185 Ben Coates SP 1.20 3.00
186 Sam Gash DP .01 .05
187 Myron Guyton DP .01 .05
188 Maurice Hurst SP .80 2.00
189 Mike Jones DP .01 .05
190 Bob Kratch DP .01 .05
191 Chris Slade SP .80 2.00
192 Derek Brown .10 .30
193 Vince Buck DP .01 .05
194 Jim Dombrowski DP .01 .05
195 Quinn Early DP .02 .10
196 Jim Everett .20 .50
197 Michael Haynes DP .02 .10
198 Wayne Martin SP .80 2.00
199 Lorenzo Neal DP .01 .05
200 William Roaf SP .80 2.00
201 Irv Smith DP .01 .05
202 Jimmy Spencer DP .01 .05
203 Winfred Tubbs DP .01 .05
204 Renaldo Turnbull SP .80 2.00
205 Michael Brooks DP .01 .05
206 Dave Brown DP .02 .10
207 Chris Calloway .10 .30
208 Jesse Campbell DP .01 .05
209 Jumbo Elliott DP .01 .05
210 Keith Hamilton DP .01 .05
211 Rodney Hampton DP .02 .10
212 Corey Miller DP .01 .05
213 Doug Riesenberg DP .01 .05
214 Mike Sherrard .10 .30
215 Phillippi Sparks .10 .30
216 Michael Strahan DP .80 2.00
217 Richie Anderson DP .80 2.00
218 Brad Baxter DP .01 .05
219 Tony Casillas DP .01 .05
220 Roger Duffy .10 .30
221 Boomer Esiason DP .02 .10
222 Aaron Glenn DP .01 .05
223 Bobby Houston DP .01 .05
224 Mo Lewis SP .80 2.00
225 Siupeli Malamala DP .01 .05
226 Johnny Mitchell DP .01 .05
227 Eddie Anderson DP .01 .05
228 Jerry Ball DP .01 .05
229 Greg Biekert .10 .30
230 Tim Brown SP 2.00 5.00
231 Rob Fredrickson DP .01 .05
232 Nolan Harrison .10 .30
233 Jeff Hostetler DP .02 .10
234 Rocket Ismail SP 1.20 3.00
235 Terry McDaniel SP .80 2.00
236 Chester McGlockton SP .80 2.00
237 Don Mosebar .10 .30
238 Anthony Smith .10 .30
239 Harvey Williams DP .02 .10
240 Steve Wisniewski DP .01 .05
241 Fred Barnett .20 .50
242 Randall Cunningham .40 1.00
243 William Fuller SP .80 2.00
244 Charlie Garner .80 2.00
245 Vaughn Hebron DP .01 .05
246 Lester Holmes .10 .30
247 Greg Jackson SP .80 2.00
248 Bill Romanowski DP .01 .05
249 William Thomas SP .80 2.00
250 Bernard Williams .10 .30
251 Calvin Williams DP .01 .05
252 Michael Zordich SP .80 2.00
253 Chad Brown SP .80 2.00
254 Dermontti Dawson DP .01 .05
255 Kevin Greene SP 1.20 3.00
256 Charles Johnson .20 .50
257 Carnell Lake .10 .30
258 Greg Lloyd SP .80 2.00
259 Neil O'Donnell DP .10 .30
260 Ray Seals DP .01 .05
261 Leon Searcy SP .80 2.00
262 Yancey Thigpen DP .40 1.00
263 John L. Williams DP .01 .05
264 Rod Woodson SP .80 2.00
265 Stan Brock .10 .30
266 Courtney Hall .10 .30
267 Ronnie Harmon .10 .30
268 Dwayne Harper DP .01 .05
269 Rodney Harrison DP .40 1.00
270 Stan Humphries DP .20 .50
271 Shawn Jefferson .10 .30
272 Shawn Lee .10 .30
273 Tony Martin .20 .50
274 Natrone Means SP 1.20 3.00
275 Chris Mims SP .80 2.00
276 Leslie O'Neal SP .80 2.00
277 Junior Seau SP 1.20 3.00
278 Mark Seay DP .02 .10
279 Harry Swayne DP .01 .05
280 Eric Davis .10 .30
281 William Floyd .20 .50
282 Merton Hanks SP .80 2.00
283 Brent Jones .20 .50
284 Tim McDonald DP .01 .05
285 Ken Norton SP .80 2.00
286 Gary Plummer DP .01 .05
287 Jerry Rice SP 5.00 12.00
288 Dana Stubblefield SP .10 .30
289 John Taylor SP .80 2.00
290 Bryant Young DP .02 .10
291 Steve Young SP 4.00 10.00
292 Steve Wallace SP .80 2.00
293 Sam Adams DP .01 .05
294 Robert Blackmon DP .01 .05
295 Jeff Blackshear DP .01 .05
296 Brian Blades .20 .50
297 Howard Ballard SP .80 2.00
298 Cortez Kennedy DP .01 .05
299 Rick Mirer .20 .50
300 Eugene Robinson DP .01 .05
301 Chris Warren SP 1.20 3.00
302 Terry Wooden SP .80 2.00
303 Johnny Bailey .10 .30
304 Isaac Bruce DP .30 .75
305 Shane Conlan DP .01 .05
306 Troy Drayton DP .01 .05
307 Sean Gilbert DP .01 .05
308 Leo Goeas DP .01 .05
309 Jessie Hester .10 .30
310 Clarence Jones .10 .30
311 Todd Lyght .10 .30
312 Chris Miller DP .02 .10
313 Toby Wright DP .01 .05
314 Robert Young DP .01 .05
315 Eric Curry DP .01 .05
316 Trent Dilfer .20 .50
317 Thomas Everett DP .01 .05
318 Paul Gruber DP .01 .05
319 Jackie Harris DP .01 .05
320 Courtney Hawkins DP .01 .05
321 Lonnie Marts DP .01 .05
322 Tony Mayberry DP .01 .05
323 Martin Mayhew DP .01 .05
324 Hardy Nickerson DP .01 .05
325 Errict Rhett DP .30 .75
326 Reggie Brooks DP .01 .05
327 Tom Carter DP .01 .05
328 Henry Ellard SP .80 2.00
329 Darrell Green SP .80 2.00
330 Ken Harvey SP .80 2.00
331 James Jenkins DP .01 .05
332 Tim Johnson DP .01 .05
333 Jim Lachey .10 .30
334 Brian Mitchell .10 .30
335 Heath Shuler .30 .75
336 Tony Woods DP .01 .05

1995 Donruss Red Zone Update

This 98-card Update (expansion) set to the Red Zone release was distributed in foil pack form in late 1995. The cards essentially follow the design of the first series and include many of the star players not included in the first release. We've designated the short-printed cards below as SP. The Emmitt Smith, Brett Favre, Deion Sanders, and Kordell Stewart cards appear to be the most difficult to find.

COMPLETE SET (98) 75.00 150.00
1 Seth Joyner SP .50 1.25
2 Dave Krieg .40 1.00
3 Rob Moore .75 2.00
4 Frank Sanders SP 2.00 5.00
5 J.J. Birden .40 1.00
6 Moe Gardner .40 1.00
7 Eric Metcalf .40 1.00
8 Bill Brooks .40 1.00
9 Phil Hansen .40 1.00
10 Darick Holmes .50 1.25
11 Bryce Paup SP .50 1.25
12 Blake Brockermeyer .40 1.00
13 Mark Carrier WR SP .50 1.25
14 Kerry Collins 2.00 5.00
15 Mike Fox .40 1.00
16 Derrick Graham .40 1.00
17 Howard Griffith .40 1.00
18 Lamar Lathon .40 1.00
19 Bubba McDowell .40 1.00
20 Pete Metzelaars .40 1.00
21 Sam Mills .40 1.00
22 Derrick Moore .40 1.00
23 Rod Smith .40 1.00
24 Gerald Williams .40 1.00
25 Rashaan Salaam SP .75 2.00
26 Chris Zorich .40 1.00
27 Eric Bieniemy .40 1.00
28 Jeff Blake .75 2.00
29 Ki-Jana Carter SP .75 2.00
30 James Francis .40 1.00
31 Bruce Kozerski .40 1.00
32 Kevin Sargent SP .50 1.25
33 Steve Tovar .40 1.00
34 Andre Rison SP .75 2.00
35 Deion Sanders SP 3.20 8.00
36 Emmitt Smith SP 6.00 15.00
37 Terrell Davis 5.00 12.00
38 Michael Dean Perry .40 1.00
39 Ron Rivers .50 1.25
40 Henry Thomas SP .50 1.25
41 Robert Brooks .50 1.25
42 Mark Chmura .75 2.00
43 Brett Favre SP 8.00 20.00
44 Dorsey Levens .75 2.00
45 Chris Chandler .75 2.00
46 Chris Sanders .75 2.00
47 Rodney Thomas .40 1.00
48 Roosevelt Potts SP .50 1.25
49 Tony Boselli .40 1.00
50 Mark Brunell 1.60 4.00
51 Vinnie Clark SP .50 1.25
52 Don Davey .40 1.00
53 Vaughn Dunbar .40 1.00
54 Keith Goganious .40 1.00
55 Desmond Howard SP .75 2.00
56 Willie Jackson .50 1.25
57 Jeff Lageman .40 1.00
58 James O. Stewart 2.00 5.00
59 Mickey Washington .40 1.00
60 Dave Widell .40 1.00
61 James Williams .40 1.00
62 Keith Cash .40 1.00
63 Eric Green SP .50 1.25
64 Charles Mincy .40 1.00
65 Curtis Martin 4.00 10.00
66 Dave Meggett .40 1.00
67 Tim Roberts .40 1.00
68 Mario Bates .50 1.25
69 Rufus Porter .40 1.00
70 Tyrone Wheatley 1.60 4.00
71 Wayne Chrebet 2.40 6.00
72 Todd Scott .40 1.00
73 Marvin Washington .40 1.00
74 Napoleon Kaufman 2.40 6.00
75 Pat Swilling .40 1.00
76 Andy Harmon .40 1.00
77 Mike Mamula .40 1.00
78 Ricky Watters SP .75 2.00
79 Byron Bam Morris .40 1.00
80 Erric Pegram .40 1.00
81 Joel Steed .40 1.00
82 Kordell Stewart SP 4.00 10.00
83 Dennis Gibson .40 1.00
84 Derek Loville .40 1.00
85 Jesse Sapolu .40 1.00
86 Joey Galloway SP 4.00 10.00
87 Winston Moss .40 1.00
88 Steve Smith .40 1.00
89 Jerome Bettis 1.00 2.50
90 Carlos Jenkins .40 1.00
91 Jerry Ellison .40 1.00
92 Alvin Harper SP .50 1.25
93 Warren Sapp .40 1.00
94 Terry Allen SP .75 2.00
95 Gus Frerotte .50 1.25
96 Marvcus Patton .40 1.00
97 Ed Simmons .40 1.00
98 Michael Westbrook 1.20 3.00

2009 Donruss Rookies and Stars

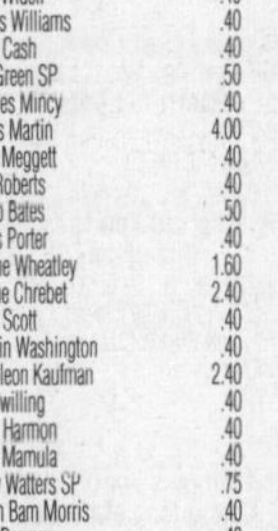

COMP.SET w/o SP's (100) 8.00 20.00
116-200 ROOKIE PRINT RUN 999
201-234 ROOK.AU PRINT RUN 139-142
1 Kurt Warner .30 .75
2 Larry Fitzgerald .30 .75
3 Steve Breaston .25 .60
4 Matt Ryan .30 .75
5 Michael Turner .25 .60
6 Roddy White .25 .60
7 Derrick Mason .25 .60
8 Joe Flacco .30 .75
9 Willis McGahee .25 .60
10 Lee Evans .25 .60
11 Marshawn Lynch .25 .60
12 Trent Edwards .20 .50
13 DeAngelo Williams .30 .75
14 Jake Delhomme .25 .60
15 Jonathan Stewart .25 .60
16 Steve Smith .25 .60
17 Greg Olsen .20 .50
18 Kyle Orton .25 .60
19 Matt Forte .30 .75
20 Carson Palmer .30 .75
21 Chad Ochocinco .25 .60
22 T.J. Houshmandzadeh .25 .60
23 Brady Quinn .25 .60
24 Braylon Edwards .25 .60
25 Jamal Lewis .25 .60
26 Jason Witten .30 .75
27 Marion Barber .25 .60
28 Tony Romo .50 1.25
29 Brandon Marshall .25 .60
30 Jay Cutler .30 .75
31 Eddie Royal .25 .60
32 Calvin Johnson .30 .75
33 Daunte Culpepper .25 .60
34 Kevin Smith .25 .60
35 Aaron Rodgers .60 1.50
36 Greg Jennings .30 .75
37 Ryan Grant .25 .60
38 Andre Johnson .25 .60
39 Matt Schaub .25 .60
40 Owen Daniels .20 .50
41 Steve Slaton .25 .60
42 Anthony Gonzalez .20 .50
43 Joseph Addai .30 .75
44 Peyton Manning .50 1.25
45 Reggie Wayne .25 .60
46 David Garrard .25 .60
47 Marcedes Lewis .20 .50
48 Maurice Jones-Drew .25 .60
49 Dwayne Bowe .25 .60
50 Larry Johnson .25 .60
51 Tony Gonzalez .25 .60
52 Chad Pennington .25 .60
53 Ricky Williams .25 .60
54 Ronnie Brown .25 .60
55 Adrian Peterson .50 1.25
56 Bernard Berrian .25 .60
57 Tarvaris Jackson .25 .60
58 Laurence Maroney .25 .60
59 Tom Brady .50 1.25
60 Wes Welker .30 .75
61 Drew Brees .30 .75
62 Marques Colston .25 .60
63 Reggie Bush .30 .75
64 Brandon Jacobs .25 .60
65 Eli Manning .30 .75
66 Kevin Boss .25 .60
67 Thomas Jones .25 .60
68 Jerricho Cotchery .25 .60
69 Leon Washington .25 .60
70 Darren McFadden .30 .75
71 JaMarcus Russell .20 .50
72 Zach Miller .20 .50
73 Brian Westbrook .25 .60
74 DeSean Jackson .25 .60
75 Donovan McNabb .30 .75
76 Ben Roethlisberger .30 .75
77 Heath Miller .25 .60
78 Santonio Holmes .25 .60
79 Willie Parker .20 .50
80 LaDainian Tomlinson .30 .75
81 Philip Rivers .30 .75
82 Vincent Jackson .25 .60
83 Frank Gore .25 .60
84 Shaun Hill .20 .50
85 Vernon Davis .25 .60
86 John Carlson .25 .60
87 Julius Jones .20 .50
88 Matt Hasselbeck .25 .60
89 Marc Bulger .25 .60
90 Steven Jackson .25 .60
91 Torry Holt .25 .60
92 Antonio Bryant .20 .50
93 Cadillac Williams .25 .60
94 Kellen Winslow .25 .60
95 Chris Johnson .30 .75
96 Kerry Collins .25 .60
97 LenDale White .25 .60
98 Chris Cooley .25 .60
99 Clinton Portis .25 .60
100 Jason Campbell .20 .50
101 Santonio Holmes ELE 1.25 3.00
102 Willie Parker ELE 1.00 2.50
103 Kurt Warner ELE 1.50 4.00
104 Brian Westbrook ELE 1.25 3.00
105 Tim Hightower ELE 1.00 2.50
106 Donovan McNabb ELE 1.50 4.00
107 Wes Welker ELE 1.50 4.00
108 Randy Moss ELE 1.50 4.00
109 Philip Rivers ELE 1.50 4.00
110 Antonio Gates ELE 1.25 3.00
111 Thomas Jones ELE 1.25 3.00
112 Brandon Marshall ELE 1.25 3.00
113 Nate Burleson ELE 1.00 2.50
114 Leon Washington ELE 1.25 3.00
115 Brandon Jacobs ELE 1.25 3.00
116 Aaron Kelly RC 1.50 4.00
117 Aaron Maybin RC 1.50 4.00
118 Alphonso Smith RC 1.50 4.00
119 Andre Smith RC 1.50 4.00
120 Arian Foster RC 4.00 10.00
121 Asher Allen RC 1.50 4.00
122 Austin Collie RC 2.00 5.00
123 B.J. Raji RC 2.00 5.00
124 Bradley Fletcher RC 1.50 4.00
125 Brandon Gibson RC 2.00 5.00
126 Brian Cushing RC 2.00 5.00
127 Brian Hartline RC 2.00 5.00
128 Brian Orakpo RC 2.00 5.00
129 Brooks Foster RC 1.25 3.00
130 Cameron Morrah RC 1.25 3.00
131 Cedric Peerman RC 1.50 4.00
132 Chase Coffman RC 1.50 4.00
133 Chip Vaughn RC 1.25 3.00
134 Chris Owens RC 1.50 4.00
135 Clay Matthews RC 5.00 12.00
136 Clint Sintim RC 2.00 5.00
137 Cody Brown RC 1.25 3.00
138 Connor Barwin RC 2.00 5.00
139 Cornelius Ingram RC 1.25 3.00
140 Darcel McBath RC 1.50 4.00
141 Darius Butler RC 2.00 5.00
142 Darius Passmore RC 1.50 4.00
143 David Bruton RC 1.50 4.00
144 DeAndre Levy RC 2.00 5.00
145 Demetrius Byrd RC 1.50 4.00
146 Devin Moore RC 1.50 4.00
147 Dominique Edison RC 1.25 3.00
148 Eugene Monroe RC 1.25 3.00
149 Evander Hood RC 2.50 6.00
150 Everette Brown RC 1.50 4.00
151 Brandon Tate RC 2.00 5.00
152 Graham Harrell RC 2.00 5.00
153 Hunter Cantwell RC 2.00 5.00
154 Jairus Byrd RC 2.00 5.00
155 James Casey RC 1.50 4.00
156 James Laurinaitis RC 2.00 5.00
157 Jared Cook RC 2.00 5.00
158 Jarett Dillard RC 2.00 5.00
159 Jason Williams RC 2.00 5.00
160 Jeremiah Johnson RC 2.00 5.00
161 Jeremy Childs RC 1.50 4.00
162 Jerraud Powers RC 1.50 4.00
163 John Parker Wilson RC 2.00 5.00
164 Johnny Knox RC 3.00 8.00
165 Kaluka Maiava RC 2.00 5.00
166 Keenan Lewis RC 2.00 5.00
167 Kenny McKinley RC 2.00 5.00
168 Kevin Barnes RC 1.50 4.00
169 Kevin Ogletree RC 2.00 5.00
170 Kory Sheets RC 1.50 4.00
171 Lardarius Webb RC 2.00 5.00
172 Larry English RC 2.00 5.00
173 Louis Delmas RC 2.00 5.00
174 Louis Murphy RC 2.00 5.00
175 Malcolm Jenkins RC 2.00 5.00
176 Michael Mitchell RC 1.50 4.00
177 Mike Goodson RC 2.00 5.00
178 Nathan Brown RC 1.50 4.00
179 P.J. Hill RC 1.50 4.00
180 Patrick Chung RC 2.00 5.00
181 Peria Jerry RC 1.50 4.00
182 Quan Cosby RC 1.50 4.00
183 Quinn Johnson RC 1.50 4.00
184 Rashad Jennings RC 2.00 5.00
185 Rashad Johnson RC 1.50 4.00
186 Rey Maualuga RC 2.00 5.00
187 Richard Quinn RC 1.50 4.00
188 Robert Ayers RC 2.00 5.00
189 Ryan Mouton RC 1.50 4.00
190 Sean Smith RC 2.00 5.00
191 Sen'Derrick Marks RC 1.25 3.00
192 Shawn Nelson RC 1.50 4.00
193 Sherrod Martin RC 1.50 4.00
194 Tom Brandstater RC 2.00 5.00
195 Tony Fiammetta RC 1.50 4.00
196 Travis Beckum RC 1.50 4.00
197 Tyrell Sutton RC 1.50 4.00
198 Tyrone McKenzie RC 1.50 4.00
199 Vontae Davis RC 2.00 5.00
200 William Moore RC 2.00 5.00
201 Matthew Stafford AU RC 60.00 120.00
202 Jason Smith AU RC 8.00 20.00
203 Tyson Jackson AU RC 8.00 20.00
204 Aaron Curry AU RC 10.00 25.00
205 Mark Sanchez AU RC 40.00 100.00
206 Darrius Heyward-Bey AU RC 10.00 25.00
207 Michael Crabtree AU RC 20.00 50.00
208 Knowshon Moreno AU RC 12.00 30.00
209 Josh Freeman AU RC 20.00 50.00
210 Jeremy Maclin AU RC 15.00 40.00
211 Brandon Pettigrew AU RC 10.00 25.00
212 Percy Harvin AU RC 15.00 40.00
213 Donald Brown AU RC 10.00 25.00
214 Hakeem Nicks AU RC 15.00 40.00
215 Kenny Britt AU RC 12.00 30.00
216 Chris Wells AU RC 15.00 40.00
217 Brian Robiskie AU RC 10.00 25.00
218 Pat White AU RC 10.00 25.00
219 Mohamed Massaquoi AU RC 8.00 20.00
220 LeSean McCoy AU RC 20.00 50.00
221 Shonn Greene AU RC 15.00 40.00
222 Glen Coffee AU RC 8.00 20.00
223 Derrick Williams AU RC 8.00 20.00
224 Javon Ringer AU RC 10.00 25.00
225 Mike Wallace AU RC 20.00 50.00
226 Ramses Barden AU RC 6.00 15.00
227 Patrick Turner AU RC 8.00 20.00
228 Deon Butler AU RC 8.00 20.00
229 Juaquin Iglesias AU RC 8.00 20.00
230 Stephen McGee AU RC 10.00 25.00
231 Mike Thomas AU RC 10.00 25.00
232 Andre Brown AU RC 6.00 15.00
233 Rhett Bomar AU RC 8.00 20.00
234 Nate Davis AU RC 8.00 20.00

2009 Donruss Rookies and Stars Gold Retail

*VETS 1-100: .6X TO 1.5X BASIC R&S
*ELEM 101-115: .3X TO .8X BASIC R&S
*ROOKIES 116-200: .4X TO 1X BASIC R&S
RANDOM INSERTS IN RETAIL PACKS

2009 Donruss Rookies and Stars Longevity Parallel Gold

*VETS 1-100: 4X TO 10X BASIC CARDS
*ELEMENT 101-115: 1X TO 2.5X BASIC CARDS
*ROOKIE 116-200: 1X TO 2.5X BASIC CARDS
STATED PRINT RUN 49 SER.#'d SETS

2009 Donruss Rookies and Stars Longevity Parallel Platinum

*VETS 1-100: 5X TO 12X BASIC CARDS
*ELEMENT 101-115: 1.2X TO 3X BASIC CARDS
*ROOKIE 116-200: 1.2X TO 3X BASIC CARDS
STATED PRINT RUN 25 SER.#'d SETS

2009 Donruss Rookies and Stars Longevity Parallel Silver

*VETS 1-100: 2X TO 5X BASIC CARDS
*ELEMENT 101-115: .5X TO 1.2X BASIC CARDS
*ROOKIE 116-200: .6X TO 1.5X BASIC CARDS
STATED PRINT RUN 249 SER.#'d SETS

2009 Donruss Rookies and Stars Longevity Parallel Silver Holofoil

*VETS 1-100: 3X TO 8X BASIC CARDS
*ELEMENT 101-115: .8X TO 2X BASIC CARDS
*ROOKIE 116-200: .8X TO 2X BASIC CARDS
STATED PRINT RUN 99 SER.#'d SETS

2009 Donruss Rookies and Stars Autographs

STATED PRINT RUN 1-100
SERIAL #'d UNDER 20 NOT PRICED
12 Trent Edwards/30 6.00 15.00
15 Jonathan Stewart/25 10.00 25.00
22 T.J. Houshmandzadeh/25 10.00 25.00
34 Kevin Smith/100 6.00 15.00
36 Greg Jennings/20 10.00 25.00
41 Steve Slaton/100 6.00 15.00
42 Anthony Gonzalez/65 5.00 12.00
43 Joseph Addai/30 10.00 25.00
57 Tarvaris Jackson/25 10.00 25.00
62 Marques Colston/100 6.00 15.00
72 Zach Miller/100 5.00 12.00
74 DeSean Jackson/50 8.00 20.00
82 Vincent Jackson/50 6.00 15.00
83 Frank Gore/20 10.00 25.00
86 John Carlson/35 8.00 20.00

2009 Donruss Rookies and Stars Crosstraining

*BLACK/100: .6X TO 1.5X BASIC INSERTS
*GOLD/500: .5X TO 1.2X BASIC INSERTS
1 Matthew Stafford 4.00 10.00
2 Mark Sanchez 2.50 6.00
3 Josh Freeman 1.50 4.00
4 Pat White .75 2.00
5 Stephen McGee .75 2.00
6 Rhett Bomar .60 1.50
7 Nate Davis .60 1.50
8 Mike Thomas .75 2.00
9 Mohamed Massaquoi .60 1.50
10 Derrick Williams .60 1.50
11 Aaron Curry .75 2.00
12 Mike Wallace 1.50 4.00
13 Ramses Barden .50 1.25
14 Patrick Turner .60 1.50
15 Deon Butler .60 1.50
16 Juaquin Iglesias .60 1.50
17 Jeremy Maclin 1.25 3.00
18 Percy Harvin 1.25 3.00
19 Hakeem Nicks 1.25 3.00
20 Kenny Britt 1.00 2.50
21 Darrius Heyward-Bey .75 2.00
22 Michael Crabtree 1.50 4.00
23 Brian Robiskie .75 2.00
24 Brandon Pettigrew .75 2.00
25 Donald Brown .75 2.00
26 Chris Wells 1.25 3.00
27 Knowshon Moreno .75 2.00
28 LeSean McCoy 1.50 4.00
29 Shonn Greene 1.25 3.00
30 Glen Coffee .60 1.50
31 Andre Brown .50 1.25
32 Javon Ringer .75 2.00
33 Jason Smith .60 1.50
34 Tyson Jackson .60 1.50

2009 Donruss Rookies and Stars Crosstraining Materials

STATED PRINT RUN 299 SER.#'d SETS
*PRIME/50: .6X TO 1.5X BASIC JSY/299
1 Matthew Stafford 8.00 20.00
2 Mark Sanchez 8.00 20.00
3 Josh Freeman 5.00 12.00
4 Pat White 2.50 6.00
5 Stephen McGee 2.50 6.00
6 Rhett Bomar 2.00 5.00
7 Nate Davis 2.00 5.00
8 Mike Thomas 2.50 6.00
9 Mohamed Massaquoi 2.00 5.00
10 Derrick Williams 2.00 5.00
11 Aaron Curry 2.50 6.00
12 Mike Wallace 5.00 12.00
13 Ramses Barden 1.50 4.00
14 Patrick Turner 2.00 5.00
15 Deon Butler 2.00 5.00
16 Juaquin Iglesias 2.00 5.00
17 Jeremy Maclin 4.00 10.00
18 Percy Harvin 4.00 10.00
19 Hakeem Nicks 4.00 10.00
20 Kenny Britt 3.00 8.00
21 Darrius Heyward-Bey 2.50 6.00
22 Michael Crabtree 6.00 15.00
23 Brian Robiskie 2.50 6.00
24 Brandon Pettigrew 2.50 6.00
25 Donald Brown 2.50 6.00
26 Chris Wells 4.00 10.00
27 Knowshon Moreno 6.00 15.00
28 LeSean McCoy 5.00 12.00
29 Shonn Greene 4.00 10.00
30 Glen Coffee 2.00 5.00
31 Andre Brown 1.50 4.00
32 Javon Ringer 2.50 6.00
33 Jason Smith 2.00 5.00
34 Tyson Jackson 2.00 5.00

2009 Donruss Rookies and Stars Dress for Success Jerseys

STATED PRINT RUN 299 SER.#'d SETS
*PRIME/50: .6X TO 1.5X BASIC JSY/299
*LONG/100: .5X TO 1.2X BASIC JSY/299
1 Mohamed Massaquoi 1.50 4.00
2 Aaron Curry 2.00 5.00
3 Mark Sanchez 6.00 15.00
4 Stephen McGee 2.00 5.00
5 Deon Butler 1.50 4.00
6 Michael Crabtree 4.00 10.00
7 Kenny Britt 2.50 6.00
8 Tyson Jackson 1.50 4.00
9 Donald Brown 2.00 5.00
10 Nate Davis 1.50 4.00
11 Rhett Bomar 1.50 4.00
12 Javon Ringer 2.00 5.00
13 LeSean McCoy 4.00 10.00
14 Darrius Heyward-Bey 2.00 5.00
15 Glen Coffee 1.50 4.00
16 Josh Freeman 4.00 10.00
17 Hakeem Nicks 3.00 8.00
18 Shonn Greene 3.00 8.00
19 Chris Wells 3.00 8.00
20 Jeremy Maclin 3.00 8.00
21 Brian Robiskie 2.00 5.00
22 Matthew Stafford 10.00 25.00
23 Jason Smith 1.50 4.00
24 Percy Harvin 3.00 8.00
25 Patrick Turner 1.50 4.00
26 Pat White 2.00 5.00
27 Juaquin Iglesias 1.50 4.00
28 Mike Wallace 4.00 10.00
29 Derrick Williams 1.50 4.00
30 Mike Thomas 2.00 5.00
31 Brandon Pettigrew 2.00 5.00
32 Knowshon Moreno 2.00 5.00
33 Andre Brown 1.25 3.00
34 Ramses Barden 1.25 3.00

2009 Donruss Rookies and Stars Dress for Success Jerseys Autographs

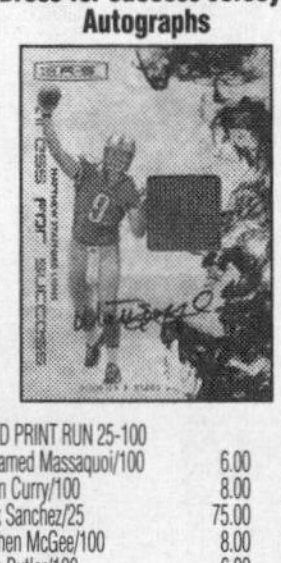

STATED PRINT RUN 25-100
1 Mohamed Massaquoi/100 6.00 15.00
2 Aaron Curry/100 8.00 20.00
3 Mark Sanchez/25 75.00 150.00
4 Stephen McGee/100 8.00 20.00
5 Deon Butler/100 6.00 15.00
6 Michael Crabtree/100 30.00 60.00
7 Kenny Britt/25 15.00 40.00
8 Tyson Jackson/100 6.00 15.00
9 Donald Brown/100 8.00 20.00
10 Nate Davis/100 6.00 15.00
11 Rhett Bomar/100 6.00 15.00
12 Javon Ringer/100 8.00 20.00
13 LeSean McCoy/100 20.00 50.00
14 Darrius Heyward-Bey/100 8.00 20.00
15 Glen Coffee/100 6.00 15.00
16 Josh Freeman/100 15.00 40.00
17 Hakeem Nicks/100 12.00 30.00
18 Shonn Greene/25 EXCH 20.00 50.00
19 Chris Wells/100 20.00 50.00
20 Jeremy Maclin/100 12.00 30.00
21 Brian Robiskie/100 8.00 20.00
22 Matthew Stafford/15 75.00 150.00
23 Jason Smith/100 6.00 15.00
24 Percy Harvin/100 40.00 80.00
25 Patrick Turner/100 6.00 15.00
26 Pat White/50 10.00 25.00
27 Juaquin Iglesias/100 6.00 15.00
28 Mike Wallace/100 15.00 40.00
29 Derrick Williams/100 6.00 15.00
30 Mike Thomas/100 8.00 20.00
31 Brandon Pettigrew/25 12.00 30.00
32 Knowshon Moreno/100 8.00 20.00
33 Andre Brown/100 5.00 12.00
34 Ramses Barden/100 5.00 12.00

2009 Donruss Rookies and Stars Elements Materials Holofoil

HOLOFOIL PRINT RUN 30-50
*FOIL/80-100: .3X TO .8X HOLOFOIL/30-50
*BASE JSY/299: .25X TO .6X HOLO/30-50
*BASE JSY/75-135: .3X TO .8X HOLO/30-50

2009 Donruss Rookies and Stars Freshman Orientation Materials Jerseys

STATED PRINT RUN 299 SER.#'d SETS
*PRIME/50: .6X TO 1.5X BASIC JSY/299
*LONG/100: .5X TO 1.2X BASIC JSY/299
1 Jason Smith 1.50 4.00
2 Tyson Jackson 1.50 4.00
3 Aaron Curry 2.00 5.00
4 Knowshon Moreno 2.00 5.00
5 Donald Brown 2.00 5.00
6 Chris Wells 3.00 8.00
7 LeSean McCoy 4.00 10.00
8 Shonn Greene 3.00 8.00
9 Glen Coffee 1.50 4.00
10 Andre Brown 1.25 3.00
11 Mike Thomas 2.00 5.00
12 Derrick Williams 1.50 4.00
13 Javon Ringer 2.00 5.00
14 Mike Wallace 4.00 10.00
15 Ramses Barden 1.25 3.00
16 Patrick Turner 1.50 4.00
17 Deon Butler 1.50 4.00
18 Juaquin Iglesias 1.50 4.00
19 Brian Robiskie 2.00 5.00
20 Mohamed Massaquoi 1.50 4.00
21 Hakeem Nicks 3.00 8.00
22 Kenny Britt 2.50 6.00
23 Jeremy Maclin 3.00 8.00
24 Brandon Pettigrew 2.00 5.00
25 Percy Harvin 3.00 8.00
26 Darrius Heyward-Bey 2.00 5.00
27 Michael Crabtree 4.00 10.00
28 Josh Freeman 4.00 10.00
29 Mark Sanchez 6.00 15.00
30 Matthew Stafford 10.00 25.00
31 Pat White 2.00 5.00
32 Stephen McGee 2.00 5.00
33 Rhett Bomar 1.50 4.00
34 Nate Davis 1.50 4.00

2009 Donruss Rookies and Stars Freshman Orientation Materials Jerseys Autographs

STATED PRINT RUN 1-100
SERIAL #'d UNDER 25 NOT PRICED
1 Jason Smith/100 6.00 15.00
2 Tyson Jackson/100 6.00 15.00
3 Aaron Curry/100 8.00 20.00
4 Knowshon Moreno/100 8.00 20.00
5 Donald Brown/100 8.00 20.00
6 Chris Wells/100 25.00 50.00
7 LeSean McCoy/100 15.00 40.00
8 Shonn Greene/25 25.00 60.00
9 Glen Coffee/100 6.00 15.00
10 Andre Brown/100 5.00 12.00
11 Mike Thomas/100 8.00 20.00
12 Derrick Williams/100 6.00 15.00
13 Javon Ringer/100 8.00 20.00
14 Mike Wallace/100 15.00 40.00
15 Ramses Barden/100 5.00 12.00
16 Patrick Turner/100 6.00 15.00
17 Deon Butler/100 6.00 15.00
19 Brian Robiskie/100 8.00 20.00
20 Mohamed Massaquoi/100 6.00 15.00
21 Hakeem Nicks/100 12.00 30.00
22 Kenny Britt/25 15.00 40.00
23 Jeremy Maclin/100 12.00 30.00
24 Brandon Pettigrew/25 12.00 30.00
25 Percy Harvin/100 25.00 60.00
26 Darrius Heyward-Bey/100 8.00 20.00
27 Michael Crabtree/100 25.00 60.00
28 Josh Freeman/100 15.00 40.00
29 Mark Sanchez/25 50.00 100.00
30 Matthew Stafford/25 60.00 120.00
31 Pat White/50 10.00 25.00
32 Stephen McGee/100 8.00 20.00
33 Rhett Bomar/100 6.00 15.00
34 Nate Davis/100 6.00 15.00

2009 Donruss Rookies and Stars Gold Stars

*BLACK/50: .8X TO 2X BASIC INSERTS
*GOLD/500: .5X TO 1.2X BASIC INSERTS
*HOLOFOIL/100: .6X TO 1.5X BASIC INSERTS
1 Ben Roethlisberger 1.00 2.50
2 Wes Welker 1.00 2.50
3 Chris Johnson 1.00 2.50
4 Larry Johnson .75 2.00
5 Tony Romo 1.50 4.00
6 Matt Ryan 1.00 2.50
7 Tony Gonzalez .75 2.00
8 Marques Colston .75 2.00
9 Frank Gore .75 2.00
10 Marshawn Lynch .75 2.00
11 Brandon Marshall .75 2.00
12 Jake Delhomme .75 2.00
13 Maurice Jones-Drew .75 2.00
14 Antonio Gates .75 2.00
15 Joe Flacco 1.00 2.50
16 Willie Parker .60 1.50
17 Steve Smith .75 2.00
18 Torry Holt .75 2.00
19 Vincent Jackson .75 2.00
20 Lee Evans .75 2.00

2009 Donruss Rookies and Stars Gold Stars Autographs

STATED PRINT RUN 1-50
SERIAL #'d UNDER 15 NOT PRICED
4 Larry Johnson/25 10.00 25.00
6 Matt Ryan/15 40.00 80.00
8 Marques Colston/50 6.00 15.00
13 Maurice Jones-Drew/15 12.00 30.00
15 Joe Flacco/25 12.00 30.00
19 Vincent Jackson/50 6.00 15.00

2009 Donruss Rookies and Stars Gold Stars Materials Prime

PRIME JSY PRINT RUN 15-50
*BASE/299: .25X TO .6X PRIME/50
*BASE/299: .2X TO .5X PRIME/25
*BASE/100: .3X TO .8X PRIME/50
*BASE/100: .25X TO .6X PRIME/15-25
BASE JSY PRINT RUN 100-299
1 Ben Roethlisberger/50 6.00 15.00
2 Wes Welker/50 6.00 15.00

3 Chris Johnson/15 8.00 20.00
4 Larry Johnson/50 5.00 12.00
5 Tony Romo/50 10.00 25.00
6 Matt Ryan/25 8.00 20.00
8 Marques Colston/50 5.00 12.00
9 Frank Gore/50 5.00 12.00
10 Marshawn Lynch/50 5.00 12.00
11 Brandon Marshall/50 5.00 12.00
12 Jake Delhomme/25 6.00 15.00
13 Maurice Jones-Drew/50 5.00 12.00
14 Antonio Gates/50 5.00 12.00
15 Joe Flacco/25 8.00 20.00
16 Willie Parker/50 4.00 10.00
17 Steve Smith/50 5.00 12.00
19 Vincent Jackson/50 5.00 12.00
20 Lee Evans/50 5.00 12.00

2009 Donruss Rookies and Stars Materials Emerald Prime Longevity

STATED PRINT RUN 25-50
*BLACK PRM/25: .5X TO 1.2X EMERALD/50
*BLACK PRM/25: .4X TO 1X EMRLD/28-30
BLACK PRIME PRINT RUN 1-25
*GOLD RETAIL: .25X TO .6X EMERALD/50
*GOLD RETAIL: .2X TO .5X EMERALD/25
2 Larry Fitzgerald/50 6.00 15.00
4 Matt Ryan/50 6.00 15.00
5 Michael Turner/50 5.00 12.00
6 Roddy White/50 5.00 12.00
7 Derrick Mason/50 5.00 12.00
8 Joe Flacco/50 6.00 15.00
9 Willis McGahee/50 5.00 12.00
10 Lee Evans/50 5.00 12.00
11 Marshawn Lynch/50 5.00 12.00
12 Trent Edwards/50 4.00 10.00
13 DeAngelo Williams/50 6.00 15.00
14 Jake Delhomme/25 6.00 15.00
15 Jonathan Stewart/50 5.00 12.00
16 Steve Smith/50 5.00 12.00
17 Greg Olsen/50 4.00 10.00
20 Carson Palmer/50 6.00 15.00
21 Chad Ochocinco/50 5.00 12.00
23 Brady Quinn/50 5.00 12.00
24 Braylon Edwards/50 5.00 12.00
26 Jason Witten/50 6.00 15.00
27 Marion Barber/50 5.00 12.00
28 Tony Romo/25 12.00 30.00
29 Brandon Marshall/50 5.00 12.00
32 Calvin Johnson/50 6.00 15.00
33 Daunte Culpepper/50 5.00 12.00
35 Aaron Rodgers/50 12.00 30.00
36 Greg Jennings/50 6.00 15.00
37 Ryan Grant/50 5.00 12.00
38 Andre Johnson/50 5.00 12.00
41 Steve Slaton/50 5.00 12.00
42 Anthony Gonzalez/28 5.00 12.00
43 Joseph Addai/50 6.00 15.00
44 Peyton Manning/50 10.00 25.00
45 Reggie Wayne/50 5.00 12.00
46 David Garrard/50 5.00 12.00
48 Maurice Jones-Drew/50 5.00 12.00
49 Dwayne Bowe/50 5.00 12.00
50 Larry Johnson/50 5.00 12.00
53 Ricky Williams/50 5.00 12.00
54 Ronnie Brown/50 5.00 12.00
55 Adrian Peterson/50 10.00 25.00
56 Bernard Berrian/50 5.00 12.00
58 Laurence Maroney/50 5.00 12.00
59 Tom Brady/50 10.00 25.00
60 Wes Welker/50 6.00 15.00
61 Drew Brees/30 8.00 20.00
62 Marques Colston/50 5.00 12.00
63 Reggie Bush/50 6.00 15.00
64 Brandon Jacobs/50 5.00 12.00
65 Eli Manning/50 6.00 15.00
68 Jerricho Cotchery/50 5.00 12.00
69 Leon Washington/50 5.00 12.00
70 Darren McFadden/50 6.00 15.00
71 JaMarcus Russell/25 5.00 12.00
73 Brian Westbrook/50 5.00 12.00
75 Donovan McNabb/50 6.00 15.00
76 Ben Roethlisberger/50 6.00 15.00
78 Santonio Holmes/50 5.00 12.00
79 Willie Parker/50 4.00 10.00
80 LaDainian Tomlinson/50 6.00 15.00
81 Philip Rivers/50 6.00 15.00
82 Vincent Jackson/50 5.00 12.00
83 Frank Gore/50 5.00 12.00
85 Vernon Davis/50 5.00 12.00
88 Matt Hasselbeck/50 5.00 12.00
89 Marc Bulger/50 5.00 12.00
90 Steven Jackson/50 5.00 12.00
93 Cadillac Williams/50 5.00 12.00
95 Chris Johnson/25 8.00 20.00
97 LenDale White/50 5.00 12.00
98 Chris Cooley/50 5.00 12.00
99 Clinton Portis/50 5.00 12.00
100 Jason Campbell/50 4.00 10.00

2009 Donruss Rookies and Stars NFL Draft Patch Autographs

STATED PRINT RUN 88-100
1 Josh Freeman/100 20.00 40.00
2 Brian Cushing/100 10.00 25.00
3 LeSean McCoy/88 20.00 50.00
4 Malcolm Jenkins/100 10.00 25.00

2009 Donruss Rookies and Stars Prime Cuts Combos

PRIMT CUT COMBO PRINT RUN 30-50
*BASE PRM CUT/50: .3X TO .8X COMBO/50
1 Jay Cutler/30 8.00 20.00
2 Thomas Jones/50 6.00 15.00
3 Greg Jennings/50 8.00 20.00
4 Jason Witten/50 8.00 20.00
5 Steve Smith/50 6.00 15.00
6 Ronnie Brown/50 6.00 15.00
7 LaDainian Tomlinson/50 8.00 20.00
8 Eli Manning/50 8.00 20.00
9 Brian Westbrook/50 6.00 15.00
10 Braylon Edwards/50 6.00 15.00
11 Santonio Holmes/50 6.00 15.00
12 Marion Barber/50 6.00 15.00
13 Jason Campbell/50 5.00 12.00
14 Tom Brady/50 12.00 30.00
15 Reggie Wayne/50 6.00 15.00

2009 Donruss Rookies and Stars Rookie Autographs Holofoil

STATED PRINT RUN 83-250
116 Aaron Kelly/250 3.00 8.00

122 Austin Collie/150 5.00 12.00
123 B.J. Raji/100 6.00 15.00
125 Brandon Gibson/125 4.00 10.00
126 Brian Cushing/100 5.00 12.00
128 Brian Orakpo/100 5.00 12.00
129 Brooks Foster/150 2.50 6.00
130 Cameron Morrah/250 2.50 6.00
131 Cedric Peerman/100 4.00 10.00
132 Chase Coffman/125 3.00 8.00
135 Clay Matthews/100 25.00 50.00
136 Clint Sintim/100 5.00 12.00
139 Cornelius Ingram/125 2.50 6.00
142 Darius Passmore/250 3.00 8.00
146 Devin Moore/250 3.00 8.00
147 Dominique Edison/100 3.00 8.00
150 Everette Brown/250 3.00 8.00
151 Brandon Tate/125 4.00 10.00
152 Graham Harrell/250 6.00 15.00
153 Hunter Cantwell/250 4.00 10.00
155 James Casey/125 3.00 8.00
156 James Laurinaitis/125 4.00 10.00
157 Jared Cook/125 4.00 10.00
158 Jarett Dillard/125 4.00 10.00
163 John Parker Wilson/250 4.00 10.00
164 Johnny Knox/200 6.00 15.00
167 Kenny McKinley/125 4.00 10.00
169 Kevin Ogletree/250 4.00 10.00
170 Kory Sheets/250 3.00 8.00
175 Malcolm Jenkins/83 5.00 12.00
177 Mike Goodson/200 4.00 10.00
179 P.J. Hill/250 3.00 8.00
182 Quan Cosby/250 3.00 8.00
183 Quinn Johnson/250 3.00 8.00
184 Rashad Jennings/180 4.00 10.00
186 Rey Maualuga/100 5.00 12.00
192 Shawn Nelson/100 4.00 10.00
194 Tom Brandstater/100 5.00 12.00
195 Tony Fiammetta/250 3.00 8.00
196 Travis Beckum/125 3.00 8.00
199 Vontae Davis/150 4.00 10.00

2009 Donruss Rookies and Stars Rookie Patch Autographs Gold

*GOLD/25: .5X TO 1.2X BASE AU/139-142
GOLD PRINT RUN 25 SER.#'d SETS
201 Matthew Stafford 100.00 200.00
205 Mark Sanchez 60.00 150.00

2009 Donruss Rookies and Stars Rookie Jersey Jumbo Swatch

STATED PRINT RUN 50 SER.#'d SETS
*EMERALD/10: 1X TO 2.5X BASIC JSY/50
*GOLD/25: .6X TO 1.5X BASIC JSY/50
*LONGEVITY/50: .4X TO 1X BASIC JSY
201 Matthew Stafford 20.00 50.00
202 Jason Smith 3.00 8.00
203 Tyson Jackson 3.00 8.00
204 Aaron Curry 4.00 10.00
205 Mark Sanchez 12.00 30.00
206 Darrius Heyward-Bey 4.00 10.00
207 Michael Crabtree 8.00 20.00
208 Knowshon Moreno 4.00 10.00
209 Josh Freeman 8.00 20.00
210 Jeremy Maclin 6.00 15.00
211 Brandon Pettigrew 4.00 10.00
212 Percy Harvin 6.00 15.00
213 Donald Brown 4.00 10.00
214 Hakeem Nicks 6.00 15.00
215 Kenny Britt 5.00 12.00
216 Chris Wells 6.00 15.00
217 Brian Robiskie 4.00 10.00
218 Pat White 4.00 10.00
219 Mohamed Massaquoi 3.00 8.00
220 LeSean McCoy 8.00 20.00
221 Shonn Greene 6.00 15.00
222 Glen Coffee 3.00 8.00
223 Derrick Williams 3.00 8.00
224 Javon Ringer 4.00 10.00
225 Mike Wallace 8.00 20.00
226 Ramses Barden 2.50 6.00
227 Patrick Turner 3.00 8.00
228 Deon Butler 3.00 8.00
229 Juaquin Iglesias 3.00 8.00
230 Stephen McGee 4.00 10.00
231 Mike Thomas 4.00 10.00
232 Andre Brown 2.50 6.00
233 Rhett Bomar 3.00 8.00
234 Nate Davis 3.00 8.00

2009 Donruss Rookies and Stars Rookie Patch Autographs College

STATED PRINT RUN 19-70
201 Matthew Stafford/22 90.00 150.00
203 Tyson Jackson/20 10.00 25.00
204 Aaron Curry/20 12.00 30.00
205 Mark Sanchez/20 75.00 150.00
206 Darrius Heyward-Bey/19 12.00 30.00
207 Michael Crabtree/21 50.00 100.00
208 Knowshon Moreno/20 50.00 100.00
209 Josh Freeman/70 20.00 50.00
210 Jeremy Maclin/20 20.00 50.00
211 Brandon Pettigrew/20 12.00 30.00
212 Percy Harvin/19 60.00 120.00
213 Donald Brown/20 12.00 30.00
214 Hakeem Nicks/19 20.00 50.00
215 Kenny Britt/20 15.00 40.00
216 Chris Wells/19 40.00 80.00
217 Brian Robiskie/20 12.00 30.00
218 Pat White/20 40.00 80.00
219 Mohamed Massaquoi/20 10.00 25.00
220 LeSean McCoy/68 20.00 50.00
221 Shonn Greene/20 20.00 50.00
222 Glen Coffee/20 10.00 25.00
223 Derrick Williams/19 10.00 25.00
224 Javon Ringer/20 12.00 30.00
225 Mike Wallace/19 25.00 60.00
226 Ramses Barden/20 8.00 20.00
227 Patrick Turner/20 10.00 25.00
228 Deon Butler/20 10.00 25.00
229 Juaquin Iglesias/20 20.00 50.00
230 Stephen McGee/20 12.00 30.00
231 Mike Thomas/19 12.00 30.00
232 Andre Brown/19 8.00 20.00

2009 Donruss Rookies and Stars Statistical Standouts Materials Prime

PRIME PRINT RUN 25-50
*BASE JSY/240-299: .25X TO .6X PRIME/50
*BASE JSY/240-299: .2X TO .5X PRIME/25
*BASE JSY/95: .3X TO .8X PRIME/50
*BASE JSY/25: .3X TO .8X PRIME/25
BASE JSY PRINT RUN 25-299
1 Aaron Rodgers/50 10.00 25.00
2 Drew Brees/50 5.00 12.00
4 Peyton Manning/50 8.00 20.00
5 Philip Rivers/50 5.00 12.00
6 Brandon Jacobs/50 4.00 10.00
7 Clinton Portis/50 4.00 10.00
8 DeAngelo Williams/50 5.00 12.00
9 Michael Turner/25 5.00 12.00
10 Adrian Peterson/50 8.00 20.00
11 Andre Johnson/50 4.00 10.00
12 Calvin Johnson/50 5.00 12.00
13 Larry Fitzgerald/25 6.00 15.00
14 Randy Moss/50 5.00 12.00
15 Roddy White/50 4.00 10.00

2009 Donruss Rookies and Stars Statistical Standouts Materials Autographs

STATED PRINT RUN 1-25
SERIAL #'d UNDER 15 NOT PRICED
8 DeAngelo Williams/25 15.00 30.00
9 Michael Turner/15 20.00 40.00

2009 Donruss Rookies and Stars Studio Rookies

*BLACK/100: .6X TO 1.5X BASIC INSERTS
GOLD/500: .5X TO 1.2X BASIC INSERTS
1 Jason Smith .60 1.50
2 Tyson Jackson .60 1.50
3 Aaron Curry .75 2.00
4 Darrius Heyward-Bey .75 2.00
5 Michael Crabtree 1.50 4.00
6 Percy Harvin 1.25 3.00
7 Hakeem Nicks 1.25 3.00
8 Kenny Britt 1.00 2.50
9 Brian Robiskie .75 2.00
10 Derrick Williams .60 1.50
11 Jeremy Maclin 1.25 3.00
12 Mike Wallace 1.50 4.00
13 Ramses Barden .50 1.25
14 Patrick Turner .60 1.50
15 Deon Butler .60 1.50
16 Juaquin Iglesias .60 1.50
17 Mohamed Massaquoi .60 1.50
18 Mike Thomas .75 2.00
19 Andre Brown .50 1.25
20 LeSean McCoy 1.50 4.00
21 Shonn Greene 1.25 3.00
22 Glen Coffee .60 1.50
23 Chris Wells 1.25 3.00
24 Donald Brown .75 2.00
25 Knowshon Moreno .75 2.00
26 Javon Ringer .75 2.00
27 Brandon Pettigrew .75 2.00
28 Matthew Stafford 4.00 10.00
29 Pat White .75 2.00
30 Mark Sanchez 2.50 6.00
31 Josh Freeman 1.50 4.00
32 Rhett Bomar .60 1.50
33 Nate Davis .60 1.50
34 Stephen McGee .75 2.00

2009 Donruss Rookies and Stars Studio Rookies Materials

STATED PRINT RUN 299 SER.#'d SETS
*PRIME/50: .6X TO 1.5X BASIC JSY/299
PRIME PRINT RUN 50 SER.#'d SETS
1 Jason Smith 2.00 5.00
2 Tyson Jackson 2.00 5.00
3 Aaron Curry 2.50 6.00
4 Darrius Heyward-Bey 2.50 6.00
5 Michael Crabtree 5.00 12.00
6 Percy Harvin 4.00 10.00
7 Hakeem Nicks 4.00 10.00
8 Kenny Britt 3.00 8.00
9 Brian Robiskie 2.50 6.00
10 Derrick Williams 2.00 5.00
11 Jeremy Maclin 4.00 10.00
12 Mike Wallace 5.00 12.00
13 Ramses Barden 1.50 4.00
14 Patrick Turner 2.00 5.00
15 Deon Butler 2.00 5.00
16 Juaquin Iglesias 2.00 5.00
17 Mohamed Massaquoi 2.00 5.00
18 Mike Thomas 2.50 6.00
19 Andre Brown 1.50 4.00
20 LeSean McCoy 5.00 12.00
21 Shonn Greene 4.00 10.00
22 Glen Coffee 2.00 5.00
23 Chris Wells 4.00 10.00
24 Donald Brown 2.50 6.00
25 Knowshon Moreno 2.50 6.00
26 Javon Ringer 2.50 6.00
27 Brandon Pettigrew 2.50 6.00
28 Matthew Stafford 12.00 30.00
29 Pat White 2.50 6.00
30 Mark Sanchez 8.00 20.00
31 Josh Freeman 5.00 12.00
32 Rhett Bomar 2.00 5.00
33 Nate Davis 2.00 5.00
34 Stephen McGee 2.50 6.00

2009 Donruss Rookies and Stars Studio Rookies Combos

*BLACK/100: .6X TO 1.5X BASIC INSERTS
*GOLD/500: .5X TO 1.2X BASIC INSERTS
1 Jeremy Maclin 1.25 3.00
LeSean McCoy
2 Aaron Curry .75 2.00
Deon Butler
3 Michael Crabtree 1.50 4.00
Nate Davis
4 Matthew Stafford 4.00 10.00
Brandon Pettigrew
5 Hakeem Nicks 1.25 3.00
Rhett Bomar
6 Mark Sanchez 2.50 6.00
Shonn Greene
7 Javon Ringer 1.00 2.50
Kenny Britt
8 Patrick Turner .75 2.00
Pat White
9 Mohamed Massaquoi .75 2.00
Brian Robiskie
10 Matthew Stafford 4.00 10.00
Mark Sanchez

2009 Donruss Rookies and Stars Studio Rookies Combos Materials

STATED PRINT RUN 299 SER.#'d SETS
*PRIME/50: .6X TO 1.5X DUAL JSY/50
1 Jeremy Maclin 4.00 10.00
LeSean McCoy
2 Aaron Curry 5.00 12.00
Deon Butler
3 Michael Crabtree 5.00 12.00
Nate Davis
4 Matthew Stafford 12.00 30.00
Brandon Pettigrew
5 Hakeem Nicks 4.00 10.00
Rhett Bomar
6 Mark Sanchez 8.00 20.00
Shonn Greene
7 Javon Ringer 5.00 12.00
Kenny Britt
8 Patrick Turner 2.50 6.00
Pat White
9 Mohamed Massaquoi 5.00 12.00
Brian Robiskie
10 Matthew Stafford 12.00 30.00
Mark Sanchez

2009 Donruss Rookies and Stars Longevity

COMP.SET w/o RC's (100) 8.00 20.00
*VETS 1-100: .4X TO 1X BASIC R&S
*ELEM 101-115: .25X TO .6X BASIC R&S
*ROOKIES 116-200: .4X TO 1X BASIC R&S
116-200 ROOKIE PRINT RUN 999
201-234 UNPRICED AUTO PRINT RUN 10

2009 Donruss Rookies and Stars Longevity Emerald

*VETS 1-100: 5X TO 12X BASIC R&S
*ELEMENT 101-115: 1.2X TO 3X BASIC R&S
*ROOKIES 116-200: 1.2X TO 3X BASIC R&S
STATED PRINT RUN 25 SER.#'d SETS

2009 Donruss Rookies and Stars Longevity Ruby

*VETS 1-100: 2.5X TO 6X BASIC R&S
*ELEMENT 101-115: .6X TO 1.5X BASIC R&S
*ROOKIES 116-200: .6X TO 1.5X BASIC R&S
1-200 STATED PRINT RUN 150 SER.#'d SETS

2009 Donruss Rookies and Stars Longevity Sapphire

*VETS 1-100: 3X TO 8X BASIC R&S
*ELEMENT 101-115: .8X TO 2X BASIC R&S
*ROOKIES 116-200: .8X TO 2X BASIC R&S
1-200 STATED PRINT RUN 75

2009 Donruss Rookies and Stars Longevity Autographs

VET STATED PRINT RUN 5-100
34 Kevin Smith/100 6.00 15.00
41 Steve Slaton/100 8.00 20.00
42 Anthony Gonzalez/30 8.00 20.00
57 Tarvaris Jackson/25 10.00 25.00
62 Marques Colston/100 6.00 15.00
72 Zach Miller/30 8.00 20.00
74 DeSean Jackson/35 8.00 20.00
82 Vincent Jackson/20 8.00 20.00
86 John Carlson/27 8.00 20.00
116 Aaron Kelly/250 3.00 8.00
122 Austin Collie/150 5.00 12.00
123 B.J. Raji/100 5.00 12.00
125 Brandon Gibson/125 4.00 10.00
126 Brian Cushing/100 5.00 12.00
128 Brian Orakpo/100 5.00 12.00
129 Brooks Foster/150 2.50 6.00
130 Cameron Morrah/250 2.50 6.00
131 Cedric Peerman/100 4.00 10.00
132 Chase Coffman/125 3.00 8.00
135 Clay Matthews/100 30.00 60.00
136 Clint Sintim/100 5.00 12.00
139 Cornelius Ingram/125 2.50 6.00
142 Darius Passmore/250 3.00 8.00
146 Devin Moore/250 3.00 8.00
147 Dominique Edison/100 3.00 8.00
150 Everette Brown/250 3.00 8.00
151 Brandon Tate/125 4.00 10.00
152 Graham Harrell/250 6.00 15.00
153 Hunter Cantwell/250 4.00 10.00
155 James Casey/125 3.00 8.00
156 James Laurinaitis/125 4.00 10.00
157 Jared Cook/125 4.00 10.00
158 Jarett Dillard/125 4.00 10.00
163 John Parker Wilson/28 8.00 20.00
164 Johnny Knox/200 6.00 15.00
167 Kenny McKinley/125 4.00 10.00
169 Kevin Ogletree/250 4.00 10.00
170 Kory Sheets/250 3.00 8.00
172 Larry English/100 5.00 12.00
177 Mike Goodson/200 4.00 10.00
179 P.J. Hill/250 3.00 8.00
182 Quan Cosby/250 3.00 8.00
183 Quinn Johnson/250 3.00 8.00
186 Rey Maualuga/100 5.00 12.00
192 Shawn Nelson/100 4.00 10.00
194 Tom Brandstater/100 5.00 12.00
195 Tony Fiammetta/250 3.00 8.00
196 Travis Beckum/125 3.00 8.00
199 Vontae Davis/150 4.00 10.00

2009 Donruss Rookies and Stars Longevity Materials Sapphire

SAPPHIRE PRINT RUN 20-100
*RUBY JSY/155-299: .3X TO .8X SAPP/100
*RUBY JSY/70-115: .4X TO 1X SAPP/100
*RUBY JSY/70-115: .3X TO .8X SAPP/50
*RUBY JSY/40: .5X TO 1.2X SAPP/100
*RUBY JSY/25: .6X TO 1.5X SAPP/100
RUBY STATED PRINT RUN 25-299
2 Larry Fitzgerald/100 5.00 12.00
4 Matt Ryan/100 5.00 12.00
5 Michael Turner/75 4.00 10.00
6 Roddy White/100 4.00 10.00
7 Derrick Mason/100 4.00 10.00
8 Joe Flacco/100 5.00 12.00
9 Willis McGahee/100 4.00 10.00
10 Lee Evans/20 6.00 15.00
11 Marshawn Lynch/100 4.00 10.00
12 Trent Edwards/100 3.00 8.00
13 DeAngelo Williams/100 5.00 12.00
14 Jake Delhomme/50 5.00 12.00
15 Jonathan Stewart/35 6.00 15.00
16 Steve Smith/100 4.00 10.00
17 Greg Olsen/100 3.00 8.00
20 Carson Palmer/100 5.00 12.00
21 Chad Ochocinco/100 4.00 10.00
23 Brady Quinn/100 4.00 10.00
24 Braylon Edwards/100 4.00 10.00
26 Jason Witten/100 5.00 12.00
27 Marion Barber/100 4.00 10.00
28 Tony Romo/100 8.00 20.00
29 Brandon Marshall/100 4.00 10.00
32 Calvin Johnson/100 5.00 12.00
33 Daunte Culpepper/100 4.00 10.00
36 Greg Jennings/100 5.00 12.00
37 Ryan Grant/100 4.00 10.00
38 Andre Johnson/100 4.00 10.00
39 Matt Schaub/100 4.00 10.00
41 Steve Slaton/100 4.00 10.00
42 Anthony Gonzalez/100 3.00 8.00
43 Joseph Addai/100 5.00 12.00
44 Peyton Manning/100 8.00 20.00
46 David Garrard/100 4.00 10.00
48 Maurice Jones-Drew/100 4.00 10.00
49 Dwayne Bowe/100 4.00 10.00
50 Larry Johnson/100 4.00 10.00
52 Chad Pennington/100 4.00 10.00
53 Ricky Williams/100 4.00 10.00
54 Ronnie Brown/100 4.00 10.00
55 Adrian Peterson/100 8.00 20.00
56 Bernard Berrian/100 4.00 10.00
57 Tarvaris Jackson/100 4.00 10.00
58 Laurence Maroney/100 4.00 10.00
59 Tom Brady/100 8.00 20.00
60 Wes Welker/100 5.00 12.00
61 Drew Brees/100 5.00 12.00
62 Marques Colston/100 4.00 10.00
63 Reggie Bush/100 5.00 12.00
64 Brandon Jacobs/100 4.00 10.00
65 Eli Manning/100 5.00 12.00
68 Jerricho Cotchery/100 4.00 10.00
69 Leon Washington/100 4.00 10.00
70 Darren McFadden/100 5.00 12.00
71 JaMarcus Russell/50 4.00 10.00
73 Brian Westbrook/100 4.00 10.00
75 Donovan McNabb/100 5.00 12.00
76 Ben Roethlisberger/100 5.00 12.00
78 Santonio Holmes/100 4.00 10.00
79 Willie Parker/65 4.00 10.00
80 LaDainian Tomlinson/100 5.00 12.00
81 Philip Rivers/100 5.00 12.00
82 Vincent Jackson/100 4.00 10.00
83 Frank Gore/100 4.00 10.00
85 Vernon Davis/60 5.00 12.00
88 Matt Hasselbeck/100 4.00 10.00
89 Marc Bulger/100 4.00 10.00
90 Steven Jackson/100 4.00 10.00
93 Cadillac Williams/100 4.00 10.00
95 Chris Johnson/50 6.00 15.00
96 Kerry Collins/100 4.00 10.00
97 LenDale White/100 4.00 10.00
98 Chris Cooley/100 4.00 10.00
99 Clinton Portis/100 4.00 10.00
100 Jason Campbell/100 3.00 8.00

2008 Donruss Sports Legends

This set was released on December 10, 2008. The base set consists of 144 cards and features cards of players from various sports.

COMPLETE SET (144) 40.00 100.00
2 Jim Brown .75 2.00
9 Joe Montana 1.25 3.00
16 John Elway 1.00 2.50
21 Troy Aikman .75 2.00
29 John Riggins .50 1.25
36 Frank Gifford .50 1.25
41 Roger Staubach .75 2.00
53 Steve Young .75 2.00
59 Earl Campbell .50 1.25
64 Jim Kelly .60 1.50
69 Lance Alworth .50 1.25
73 Dan Marino 1.25 3.00
78 Tony Dorsett .60 1.50
82 Vince Dooley .40 1.00
83 Bob Griese .50 1.25
88 Jim Taylor .50 1.25
96 Eric Dickerson .50 1.25
104 Dan Fouts .60 1.50
108 Michael Irvin .50 1.25
113 Dick Butkus .75 2.00
118 Gale Sayers .75 2.00
131 Lawrence Taylor .60 1.50
138 Raymond Berry .50 1.25
142 Lenny Moore .50 1.25
148 Knute Rockne 1.00 2.50

2008 Donruss Sports Legends Mirror Black

UNPRICED MIRROR BLACK PRINT RUN 1

2008 Donruss Sports Legends Mirror Blue

*BLUE/100: 2X TO 5X BASIC CARDS
STATED PRINT RUN 100 SER.#'d SETS

2008 Donruss Sports Legends Mirror Emerald

UNPRICED MIRROR EMERALD PRINT RUN 5

2008 Donruss Sports Legends Mirror Gold

*GOLD/25: 3X TO 8X BASIC CARDS
STATED PRINT RUN 25 SER.#'d SETS

2008 Donruss Sports Legends Mirror Red

*RED/250: 1.5X TO 4X BASIC CARDS
STATED PRINT RUN 250 SER.#'d SETS

2008 Donruss Sports Legends Certified Cuts

STATED PRINT RUN 1-100
SERIAL #'d TO 1 NOT PRICED
2 Bo Schembechler/1

2008 Donruss Sports Legends Champions

SILVER PRINT RUN 1000 SER.#'d SETS
*GOLD/100: .6X TO 1.5X SILVER/1000
GOLD PRINT RUN 100 SER.#'d SETS
2 Joe Montana 3.00 8.00
5 John Riggins 1.50 4.00
8 Roger Staubach 2.00 5.00
12 John Elway 2.50 6.00

2008 Donruss Sports Legends Champions Materials

STATED PRINT RUN 10-250
2 Joe Montana Jsy/250 8.00 20.00
5 John Riggins Jsy/250 6.00 15.00
8 Roger Staubach Jsy/250 6.00 15.00
12 John Elway Jsy/250 6.00 15.00

2008 Donruss Sports Legends Champions Signatures

STATED PRINT RUN 1-100
SERIAL #'d UNDER 25 NOT PRICED
2 Joe Montana/10
5 John Riggins/5
8 Roger Staubach/10
12 John Elway/10

2008 Donruss Sports Legends College Heroes

SILVER PRINT RUN 1000 SER.#'d SETS
*GOLD/100: .6X TO 1.5X SILVER/1000
GOLD PRINT RUN 100 SER.#'d SETS
3 Adrian Peterson 3.00 8.00
4 Bo Jackson 2.00 5.00

2008 Donruss Sports Legends College Heroes Materials

STATED PRINT RUN 50-250
3 Adrian Peterson Jsy/250 8.00 20.00
4 Bo Jackson Jsy/250 8.00 20.00

2008 Donruss Sports Legends College Heroes Signatures

STATED PRINT RUN 25-100
3 Adrian Peterson/25 60.00 100.00
4 Bo Jackson/25 60.00 100.00

2008 Donruss Sports Legends Collegiate Legends Patch Autographs

STATED PRINT RUN 25-250
7 Steve Spurrier/75 30.00 60.00
12 Steve Spurrier/65 30.00 60.00
24 Bo Jackson/25 60.00 100.00
25 Deion Sanders/50 50.00 100.00

2008 Donruss Sports Legends Legends of the Game Combos

STATED PRINT RUN 25-100
UNPRICED PRIME PRINT RUN 1-10
1 Knute Rockne Jkt 40.00 80.00
Pat O'Brien/25
3 Joe Montana Jsy 30.00 60.00
Knute Rockne Jkt
5 Dan Fouts Jsy 12.00 30.00
Tony Gwynn Jsy
7 Nolan Ryan Jsy 20.00 50.00
Troy Aikman Jsy
8 Earl Campbell Jsyll 6.00 15.00
Elvin Hayes Jsy
11 Nolan Ryan Jsy 12.00 30.00
Earl Campbell Jsy
12 Willie Mays Jsy 30.00 60.00
Joe Montana Jsy/50
15 Cal Ripken Jr. Bat 25.00 50.00
Raymond Berry Jsy

2008 Donruss Sports Legends Materials Mirror Blue

*MIRROR BLUE: .5X TO 1.2X MIRROR RED
MIRROR BLUE PRINT RUN 5-250
SERIAL #'d UNDER 15 NOT PRICED
29 John Riggins/25 6.00 15.00

2008 Donruss Sports Legends Materials Mirror Gold

*GOLD/25: .8X TO 2X MIRROR RED
GOLD PRINT RUN 1-25 SER.#'d SETS
SERIAL #'d UNDER 20 NOT PRICED
21 Troy Aikman/1
118 Gale Sayers/1
131 Lawrence Taylor/1

2008 Donruss Sports Legends Materials Mirror Red

MIRROR RED PRINT RUN 10-500
SERIAL #'d UNDER 25 NOT PRICED
*GOLD/25: .8X TO 2X MIRROR RED
UNPRICED MIRROR EMERALD PRINT RUN 1-5
UNPRICED MIRROR BLACK PRINT RUN 1
9 Joe Montana Jsy/100 8.00 20.00
16 John Elway Jsy/100 6.00 15.00
21 Troy Aikman Jsy/10
29 John Riggins Jsy/100 4.00 10.00
41 Roger Staubach Jsy/100 5.00 12.00
53 Steve Young Jsy/100 5.00 12.00
59 Earl Campbell Jsy/50 4.00 10.00
64 Jim Kelly Jsy/100 5.00 12.00
73 Dan Marino Jsy/100 8.00 20.00
78 Tony Dorsett Jsy/100 5.00 12.00
82 Vince Dooley Sweater/500 3.00 8.00
83 Bob Griese Jsy/50 5.00 12.00
96 Eric Dickerson Jsy/100 4.00 10.00
104 Dan Fouts Jsy/100 5.00 12.00
108 Michael Irvin Jsy/25 4.00 10.00
113 Dick Butkus Jsy/25 8.00 20.00
131 Lawrence Taylor Jsy/10
138 Raymond Berry Jsy/100 3.00 8.00
142 Lenny Moore Jsy/100 3.00 8.00
148 Knute Rockne Jkt/500 10.00 25.00

2008 Donruss Sports Legends Museum Collection

SILVER PRINT RUN 1000 SER.#'d SETS
*GOLD/100: .6X TO 1.5X SILVER/1000
GOLD PRINT RUN 100 SER.#'d SETS
2 Joe Montana 3.00 8.00
6 John Elway 2.50 6.00
8 Raymond Berry 1.25 3.00
10 Roger Staubach 2.00 5.00
14 Steve Young 2.00 5.00
15 Tony Dorsett 1.50 4.00
16 Knute Rockne 2.50 6.00
18 Dan Marino 3.00 8.00
20 Lenny Moore 1.25 3.00
24 Dan Fouts 1.50 4.00
26 Eric Dickerson 1.25 3.00

2008 Donruss Sports Legends Museum Collection Materials

STATED PRINT RUN 25-250
*PRIME/25: .6X TO 1.5X BASIC MATERIAL
PRIME PRINT RUN 1-25
SERIAL #'d UNDER 25 NOT PRICED
2 Joe Montana/100 10.00 25.00
6 John Elway/100 8.00 20.00
8 Raymond Berry/250 4.00 10.00
10 Roger Staubach/100 6.00 15.00
14 Steve Young/250 6.00 15.00
15 Tony Dorsett/250 6.00 15.00
16 Knute Rockne Jkt/250 12.00 30.00
18 Dan Marino/100 10.00 25.00
20 Lenny Moore/250 4.00 10.00
24 Dan Fouts/250 6.00 15.00
26 Eric Dickerson/250 5.00 12.00

2008 Donruss Sports Legends Museum Collection Signatures

STATED PRINT RUN 1-250
SERIAL #'d UNDER 25 NOT PRICED
2 Joe Montana/10
6 John Elway/10
8 Raymond Berry/10
10 Roger Staubach/10
14 Steve Young/10
15 Tony Dorsett/10
18 Dan Marino/10
20 Lenny Moore/10
24 Dan Fouts/10
26 Eric Dickerson/1

2008 Donruss Sports Legends Museum Collection Signatures Materials

STATED PRINT RUN 1-50
SERIAL #'d UNDER 25 NOT PRICED
2 Joe Montana/5
6 John Elway/5
8 Raymond Berry/5
10 Roger Staubach/5
14 Steve Young/5
15 Tony Dorsett/5
18 Dan Marino/5
20 Lenny Moore/5
24 Dan Fouts/5
26 Eric Dickerson/1

2008 Donruss Sports Legends Museum Curator Collection Materials

STATED PRINT RUN 10-100
*PRIME/25: .6X TO 1.5X BASIC MATERIAL
PRIME PRINT RUN 1-25
SERIAL #'d UNDER 25 NOT PRICED
2 Joe Montana/10
6 John Elway/10
8 Raymond Berry/100 5.00 12.00
10 Roger Staubach/10
14 Steve Young/100 8.00 20.00
15 Tony Dorsett/100 8.00 20.00
16 Knute Rockne Jkt/100 15.00 40.00
18 Dan Marino/25 15.00 40.00
20 Lenny Moore/100 5.00 12.00
24 Dan Fouts/100 8.00 20.00
26 Eric Dickerson/100 6.00 15.00

2008 Donruss Sports Legends Museum Curator Collection Signatures Materials

STATED PRINT RUN 1-25
SERIAL #'d UNDER 25 NOT PRICED
2 Joe Montana
6 John Elway
8 Raymond Berry
10 Roger Staubach
14 Steve Young
15 Tony Dorsett
18 Dan Marino
20 Lenny Moore
24 Dan Fouts
26 Eric Dickerson

2008 Donruss Sports Legends Signature Connection Combos

STATED PRINT RUN 25-100
2 Cal Ripken Jr. 150.00 250.00
John Riggins
3 Dan Fouts 60.00 100.00
Tony Gwynn
4 Nolan Ryan 100.00 175.00
Troy Aikman
5 Elvin Hayes 20.00 40.00
Earl Campbell
6 Gale Sayers 20.00 40.00
Lynette Woodard
7 Bob Feller 40.00 80.00
Jim Brown
8 Lance Alworth 90.00 150.00
Sidney Moncrief/10
10 Jim Brown
Mike Powell
11 Bo Jackson 100.00 175.00
Deion Sanders
12 Troy Aikman 60.00 100.00
Bill Walton

2008 Donruss Sports Legends Signatures Mirror Blue

MIRROR BLUE PRINT RUN 2-250
SERIAL #'d UNDER 10 NOT PRICED
UNPRICED MIRROR EMERALD PRINT RUN 1-5
UNPRICED MIRROR BLACK PRINT RUN 1
2 Jim Brown/25
9 Joe Montana/25 75.00 150.00
16 John Elway/25 75.00 150.00
21 Troy Aikman/25 40.00 80.00
29 John Riggins/25 15.00 40.00
36 Frank Gifford/25 20.00 50.00
41 Roger Staubach/25
59 Earl Campbell/25
64 Jim Kelly/15 30.00 60.00
83 Bob Griese/25 12.00 30.00
88 Jim Taylor/15 30.00 60.00
104 Dan Fouts/25 15.00 40.00
108 Michael Irvin/25 15.00 40.00
113 Dick Butkus/15 50.00 100.00
131 Lawrence Taylor/25 15.00 40.00
142 Lenny Moore/25 10.00 25.00

2008 Donruss Sports Legends Signatures Mirror Gold

MIRROR GOLD PRINT RUN 4-25
SERIAL #'d UNDER 10 NOT PRICED
2 Jim Brown/10
9 Joe Montana/10 100.00 175.00
16 John Elway/10 100.00 175.00
21 Troy Aikman/10 50.00 100.00
29 John Riggins/10 20.00 50.00
36 Frank Gifford/10 25.00 60.00
41 Roger Staubach/10
53 Steve Young/10
59 Earl Campbell/10
64 Jim Kelly/10 30.00 80.00
69 Lance Alworth/10
73 Dan Marino/10
78 Tony Dorsett/25 15.00 40.00
83 Bob Griese/10 15.00 40.00
88 Jim Taylor/10 30.00 80.00
104 Dan Fouts/15 20.00 50.00
108 Michael Irvin/10 20.00 50.00
113 Dick Butkus/10 60.00 120.00
118 Gale Sayers/10
131 Lawrence Taylor/20 20.00 50.00
138 Raymond Berry/25 15.00 40.00
142 Lenny Moore/20 12.00 30.00

2008 Donruss Sports Legends Signatures Mirror Red

*MIRROR RED: .3X TO .8X MIRROR BLUE
MIRROR RED PRINT RUN 25-1370
36 Frank Gifford/25 20.00 50.00
83 Bob Griese/55 10.00 25.00
88 Jim Taylor/25 20.00 50.00
108 Michael Irvin/25 15.00 40.00
113 Dick Butkus/25 30.00 80.00
131 Lawrence Taylor/50 12.00 30.00
142 Lenny Moore/50 8.00 20.00

2006 Donruss Threads

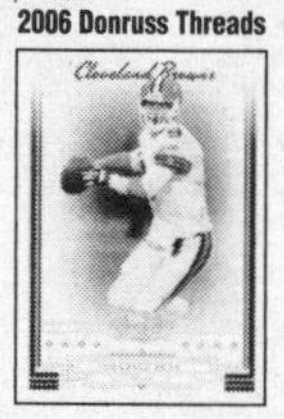

This 285-card set was released in August, 2006. The set was issued into the hobby in five-card packs, with an $3.99 SRP, which came 24 packs to a box. Cards numbered 1-150 feature veterans; while cards numbered 151-285 all feature rookies. Cards numbered 151-225 were issued to a stated print run of 999 serial numbered sets while cards numbered 226-260 were all signed by the featured player and were issued to a stated print run of between 100 and 240 serial numbered copies.

COMP.SET w/o RC's (150) 10.00 25.00
151-225 ROOKIES SER. #'d TO 999
226-260 ROOKIE AU PRINT RUN 100-240
261-285 ROOK. AUs SER. #'d TO 999
1 Braylon Edwards .30 .75
2 Jason Witten .40 1.00
3 Julius Jones .25 .60
4 Roy Williams S .30 .75
5 Terry Glenn .30 .75
6 Ashley Lelie .25 .60
7 Kevin Jones .25 .60
8 Mike Williams .25 .60
9 Roy Williams WR .30 .75
10 Aaron Rodgers .75 2.00
11 Tatum Bell .25 .60
12 Samkon Gado .30 .75
13 Corey Bradford .25 .60
14 Dallas Clark .30 .75
15 Matt Jones .25 .60
16 Larry Johnson .30 .75
17 Byron Leftwich .30 .75
18 Fred Taylor .30 .75
19 Anquan Boldin .30 .75
20 Kurt Warner .40 1.00
21 Larry Fitzgerald .40 1.00
22 Alge Crumpler .30 .75
23 Michael Vick .40 1.00
24 Warrick Dunn .30 .75

25 Jamal Lewis .30 .75
26 Ray Lewis .40 1.00
27 Eric Moulds .25 .60
28 Josh Reed .25 .60
29 Lee Evans .30 .75
30 Steve Smith .40 1.00
31 Brian Urlacher .40 1.00
32 Thomas Jones .30 .75
33 Chad Johnson .30 .75
34 Rudi Johnson .30 .75
35 T.J. Houshmandzadeh .30 .75
36 Reuben Droughns .30 .75
37 Drew Bledsoe .40 1.00
38 Keyshawn Johnson .30 .75
39 Jake Plummer .30 .75
40 Rod Smith .30 .75
41 Mike Anderson .30 .75
42 Joey Harrington .25 .60
43 Brett Favre .75 2.00
44 Donald Driver .40 1.00
45 Javon Walker .30 .75
46 Andre Johnson .40 1.00
47 David Carr .25 .60
48 Domanick Davis .25 .60
49 Edgerrin James .30 .75
50 Marvin Harrison .40 1.00
51 Peyton Manning .60 1.50
52 Reggie Wayne .30 .75
53 Jimmy Smith .30 .75
54 Tony Gonzalez .30 .75
55 Trent Green .30 .75
56 Eddie Kennison .25 .60
57 Chris Chambers .30 .75
58 Zach Thomas .40 1.00
59 Daunte Culpepper .30 .75
60 Corey Dillon .30 .75
61 Deion Branch .30 .75
62 Tedy Bruschi .40 1.00
63 Tom Brady .60 1.50
64 Deuce McAllister .30 .75
65 Donte Stallworth .30 .75
66 Jeremy Shockey .40 1.00
67 Tiki Barber .40 1.00
68 Chad Pennington .30 .75
69 Curtis Martin .40 1.00
70 Donovan McNabb .40 1.00
71 Antwaan Randle El .40 1.00
72 Hines Ward .40 1.00
73 Antonio Gates .40 1.00
74 Drew Brees .40 1.00
75 Keenan McCardell .30 .75
76 LaDainian Tomlinson .40 1.00
77 Alex Smith QB .40 1.00
78 Brandon Lloyd .25 .60
79 Frank Gore .40 1.00
80 Kevan Barlow .25 .60
81 Darrell Jackson .30 .75
82 Joe Jurevicius .25 .60
83 Matt Hasselbeck .30 .75
84 Shaun Alexander .30 .75
85 Shaun McDonald .25 .60
86 Marc Bulger .30 .75
87 Steven Jackson .40 1.00
88 Torry Holt .30 .75
89 Cadillac Williams .30 .75
90 Chris Simms .30 .75
91 Joey Galloway .30 .75
92 Michael Clayton .25 .60
93 Chris Brown .25 .60
94 Drew Bennett .30 .75
95 Steve McNair .30 .75
96 Tyrone Calico .25 .60
97 Clinton Portis .40 1.00
98 David Patten .25 .60
99 Mark Brunell .30 .75
100 Santana Moss .30 .75
101 Randy McMichael .25 .60
102 Ronnie Brown .40 1.00
103 Mewelde Moore .25 .60
104 Nate Burleson .25 .60
105 Troy Williamson .25 .60
106 David Givens .25 .60
107 Aaron Brooks .30 .75
108 Laveranues Coles .25 .60
109 Justin McCareins .25 .60
110 Kerry Collins .30 .75
111 LaMont Jordan .30 .75
112 Randy Moss .40 1.00
113 Jerry Porter .25 .60
114 Brian Westbrook .30 .75
115 Plaxico Burress .30 .75
116 Joe Horn .30 .75
117 Eli Manning .50 1.25
118 Reggie Brown .25 .60
119 Ryan Moats .25 .60
120 Ben Roethlisberger .50 1.25
121 Willie Parker .30 .75
122 Marcus Pollard .25 .60
123 Bubba Franks .25 .60
124 Jabar Gaffney .25 .60
125 Brandon Stokley .30 .75
126 Ernest Wilford .25 .60
127 Dante Hall .30 .75
128 Marty Booker .25 .60
129 Samie Parker .25 .60
130 J.J. Arrington .25 .60
131 Marcel Shipp .25 .60
132 Michael Jenkins .25 .60
133 T.J. Duckett .25 .60
134 Derrick Mason .30 .75
135 Kyle Boller .30 .75
136 Mark Clayton .30 .75
137 Willis McGahee .30 .75
138 DeShaun Foster .30 .75
139 Jake Delhomme .30 .75
140 Julius Peppers .30 .75
141 Keary Colbert .25 .60
142 Stephen Davis .30 .75
143 Todd Heap .30 .75
144 J.P. Losman .30 .75
145 Muhsin Muhammad .30 .75
146 Carson Palmer .40 1.00
147 Cedric Benson .30 .75
148 Rex Grossman .30 .75
149 Charlie Frye .30 .75
150 Dennis Northcutt .25 .60
151 Mathias Kiwanuka RC 2.50 6.00
152 Reggie McNeal RC 2.00 5.00
153 Ingle Martin RC 2.00 5.00
154 Bruce Gradkowski RC 2.50 6.00
155 D.J. Shockley RC 2.00 5.00
156 Paul Pinegar RC 1.50 4.00
157 Brandon Kirsch RC 2.00 5.00
158 P.J. Daniels RC 1.50 4.00
159 Marques Hagans RC 1.50 4.00
160 Jerome Harrison RC 2.50 6.00
161 Wali Lundy RC 2.00 5.00
162 Cedric Humes RC 1.50 4.00
163 Quinton Ganther RC 1.50 4.00
164 Mike Bell RC 2.50 6.00
165 John David Washington RC 2.00 5.00
166 Anthony Fasano RC 2.50 6.00
167 Tony Scheffler RC 2.50 6.00
168 Leonard Pope RC 2.50 6.00
169 David Thomas RC 2.00 5.00
170 Dominique Byrd RC 2.00 5.00
171 Devin Hester RC 5.00 12.00
172 Willie Reid RC 2.00 5.00
173 Brad Smith RC 2.50 6.00
174 Cory Rodgers RC 2.00 5.00
175 Domenik Hixon RC 2.50 6.00
176 Jeremy Bloom RC 2.00 5.00
177 Jonathan Orr RC 2.00 5.00
178 Jeff Webb RC 2.00 5.00
179 Ethan Kilmer RC 2.00 5.00
180 Bennie Brazell RC 2.00 5.00
181 David Anderson RC 2.00 5.00
182 Kevin McMahan RC 2.00 5.00
183 Anthony Mix RC 2.00 5.00
184 D'Brickashaw Ferguson RC 2.50 6.00
185 Kamerion Wimbley RC 2.50 6.00
186 Tamba Hali RC 2.50 6.00
187 Haloti Ngata RC 2.50 6.00
188 Brodrick Bunkley RC 2.00 5.00
189 John McCargo RC 1.50 4.00
190 Claude Wroten RC 1.50 4.00
191 Gabe Watson RC 1.50 4.00
192 D'Qwell Jackson RC 2.00 5.00
193 Abdul Hodge RC 1.50 4.00
194 Ernie Sims RC 2.00 5.00
195 Chad Greenway RC 2.50 6.00
196 Bobby Carpenter RC 1.50 4.00
197 Manny Lawson RC 2.00 5.00
198 DeMeco Ryans RC 2.50 6.00
199 Rocky McIntosh RC 2.00 5.00
200 Thomas Howard RC 2.00 5.00
201 Jon Alston RC 1.50 4.00
202 A.J. Nicholson RC 1.50 4.00
203 Tye Hill RC 1.50 4.00
204 Antonio Cromartie RC 2.50 6.00
205 Johnathan Joseph RC 2.00 5.00
206 Kelly Jennings RC 2.00 5.00
207 Ashton Youboty RC 1.50 4.00
208 Alan Zemaitis RC 2.50 6.00
209 Jason Allen RC 2.00 5.00
210 Cedric Griffin RC 2.00 5.00
211 Ko Simpson RC 2.00 5.00
212 Pat Watkins RC 2.00 5.00
213 Donte Whitner RC 2.50 6.00
214 Bernard Pollard RC 2.00 5.00
215 Darnell Bing RC 2.00 5.00
216 Marcus Vick RC 1.50 4.00
217 Roman Harper RC 2.00 5.00
218 Anthony Smith RC 2.00 5.00
219 Daniel Bullocks RC 2.50 6.00
220 Eric Smith RC 2.00 5.00
221 Danieal Manning RC 2.50 6.00
222 Anthony Schlegel RC 2.00 5.00
223 Dusty Dvoracek RC 2.50 6.00
224 Darryl Tapp RC 2.00 5.00
225 Chris Gocong RC 2.00 5.00
226 Brandon Williams AU/240 RC 8.00 20.00
227 Michael Robinson AU/240 RC 10.00 25.00
228 Vernon Davis AU/100 RC 25.00 50.00
229 Brandon Marshall AU/240 RC 10.00 25.00
230 Travis Wilson AU/100 RC 8.00 20.00
231 Maurice Stovall AU/140 RC 8.00 20.00
232 Matt Leinart AU/140 RC 12.00 30.00
233 Charlie Whitehurst AU/200 RC 12.00 30.00
234 Derek Hagan AU/100 RC 10.00 25.00
235 Jason Avant AU/150 RC 8.00 20.00
236 Jerious Norwood AU/210 RC 10.00 25.00
237 Sinorice Moss AU/100 RC 12.00 30.00
238 Mercedes Lewis AU/100 RC 12.00 30.00
239 Maurice Drew AU/100 RC 20.00 50.00
240 Kellen Clemens AU/210 RC 10.00 25.00
241 Leon Washington AU/200 RC 10.00 25.00
242 Brian Calhoun AU/140 RC 8.00 20.00
243 A.J. Hawk AU/100 RC 20.00 50.00
244 DeAngelo Williams AU/160 RC 15.00 40.00
245 Chad Jackson AU/140 RC 8.00 20.00
246 Laurence Maroney AU/140 RC 10.00 25.00
247 Michael Huff AU/100 RC 10.00 25.00
248 Joe Klopfenstein AU/240 RC 8.00 20.00
249 Demetrius Williams AU/160 RC 10.00 25.00
250 Reggie Bush AU/100 RC 30.00 80.00
251 Omar Jacobs AU/120 RC 8.00 20.00
252 Santonio Holmes AU/120 RC 15.00 40.00
253 Mario Williams AU/160 RC 12.00 30.00
254 LenDale White AU/100 RC 12.00 30.00
255 Vince Young AU/100 RC 15.00 40.00
256 Tarvaris Jackson AU/210 RC 12.00 30.00
257 Jay Cutler AU/120 RC 50.00 120.00
258 Joseph Addai AU/100 RC 12.00 30.00
259 Brodie Croyle AU/120 RC 12.00 30.00
260 Greg Jennings AU/240 RC 25.00 60.00
261 Erik Meyer AU RC 4.00 10.00
262 Drew Olson AU RC 3.00 8.00
263 Darrell Hackney AU RC 3.00 8.00
264 Andre Hall AU RC 4.00 10.00
265 Taurean Henderson AU RC 5.00 12.00
266 Derrick Ross AU RC 4.00 10.00
267 De'Arrius Howard AU RC 5.00 12.00
268 Wendell Mathis AU RC 4.00 10.00
269 Gerald Riggs AU RC 4.00 10.00
270 Garrett Mills AU RC 3.00 8.00
271 Jai Lewis AU RC 4.00 10.00
272 Skyler Green AU RC 4.00 10.00
273 Mike Hass AU RC 3.00 8.00
274 Delanie Walker AU RC 5.00 12.00
275 Adam Jennings AU RC 4.00 10.00
276 Todd Watkins AU RC 3.00 8.00
277 Devin Aromashodu AU RC 5.00 12.00
278 Ben Obomanu AU RC 4.00 10.00
279 Marques Colston AU RC 15.00 40.00
280 Miles Austin AU RC 25.00 60.00
281 Martin Nance AU RC 4.00 10.00
282 Greg Lee AU RC 3.00 8.00
283 Hank Baskett AU RC 5.00 12.00
284 Jimmy Williams AU RC 5.00 12.00
285 Anwar Phillips AU RC 4.00 10.00

2006 Donruss Threads Bronze Holofoil

*VETERANS 1-150: 2X TO 5X BASIC CARDS
*ROOKIES 151-225: .5X TO 1.2X
STATED PRINT RUN 250 SER.#'d SETS

2006 Donruss Threads Gold Holofoil

*VETERANS 1-150: 4X TO 10X BASIC CARDS
*ROOKIES 151-225: 1X TO 2.5X BASIC CARDS
STATED PRINT RUN 50 SER.#'d SETS

2006 Donruss Threads Platinum Holofoil

*VETERANS 1-150: 6X TO 15X BASIC CARDS
*ROOKIES 151-225: 1.5X TO 4X BASIC CARDS
STATED PRINT RUN 25 SER.#'d SETS

2006 Donruss Threads Retail Blue

*VETERANS 1-150: 2X TO 5X BASIC CARDS
*ROOKIES 151-225: .5X TO 1.2X
STATED PRINT RUN 200 SER.#'d SETS

2006 Donruss Threads Retail Rookies

*ROOKIES: .4X TO 1X BASIC CARDS
RETAIL/999 PRINTED ON WHITE STOCK

2006 Donruss Threads Retail Green

*VETERANS 1-150: 3X TO 8X BASIC CARDS
*ROOKIES 151-225: .8X TO 2X BASIC CARDS
STATED PRINT RUN 100 SER.#'d SETS

2006 Donruss Threads Retail Red

*VETERANS 1-150: 4X TO 10X BASIC CARDS
*ROOKIES 151-225: 1X TO 2.5X BASIC CARDS
1-150 PRINT RUN 150 SER.#'d SETS
151-225 PRINT RUN 50 SER.#'d SETS

2006 Donruss Threads Retail Pewter

*VETERANS 1-150: 2X TO 5X BASIC CARDS
*ROOKIES: 151-225: .5X TO 1.2X
STATED PRINT RUN 250 SER.#'d SETS

2006 Donruss Threads Silver Holofoil

*VETERANS 1-150: 3X TO 8X BASIC CARDS
*ROOKIES 151-225: .8X TO 2X BASIC CARDS
STATED PRINT RUN 100 SER.#'d SETS

2006 Donruss Threads Century Collection Materials

STATED PRINT RUN 250 SER.#'d SETS
*PRIME/25: .8X TO 2X BASIC INSERTS
PRIME PRINT RUN 25 SER.#'d SETS
1 Jim Brown 8.00 20.00
2 Forrest Gregg 6.00 15.00
3 Yale Lary 6.00 15.00
4 Charley Taylor 4.00 10.00
5 Lance Alworth 6.00 15.00
6 Cliff Branch 5.00 12.00
7 Bob Griese 4.00 10.00
8 Daryle Lamonica 5.00 12.00
9 Fred Biletnikoff 5.00 12.00
10 Paul Warfield 4.00 10.00
11 Earl Campbell 5.00 12.00
12 Joe Montana 10.00 25.00
13 John Riggins 4.00 10.00
14 Mark Gastineau 4.00 10.00
15 Ozzie Newsome 4.00 10.00
16 Tom Brady 6.00 15.00
17 Peyton Manning 6.00 15.00
18 Jerry Rice 6.00 15.00
19 Brett Favre 10.00 25.00
20 Curtis Martin 5.00 12.00

2006 Donruss Threads Century Legends Gold

GOLD ODDS 1:18 HOB, 1:81 RET
*BLUE/100: .8X TO 2X BASIC INSERTS
BLUE PRINT RUN 100 SER.#'d SETS
1 Lance Alworth 1.25 3.00
2 Fred Biletnikoff 1.50 4.00
3 Earl Campbell 1.50 4.00
4 Joe Montana 3.00 8.00
5 John Elway 2.50 6.00
6 Jim Kelly 1.50 4.00
7 Jim Brown 2.00 5.00
8 Tom Brady 2.00 5.00
9 Jerry Rice 2.50 6.00
10 Peyton Manning 2.00 5.00
11 Brett Favre 2.50 6.00
12 Jim Plunkett 1.25 3.00
13 Phil Simms 1.25 3.00
14 Thurman Thomas 1.25 3.00

2006 Donruss Threads Century Legends Materials

STATED PRINT RUN 250 SER.#'d SETS
*PRIME/25: .8X TO 2X BASIC INSERTS
PRIME PRINT RUN 25 SER.#'d SETS
1 Lance Alworth 6.00 15.00
2 Fred Biletnikoff 5.00 12.00
3 Earl Campbell 5.00 12.00
4 Joe Montana 10.00 25.00
5 John Elway 8.00 20.00
6 Jim Kelly 6.00 15.00
7 Jim Brown/100 10.00 25.00
8 Tom Brady 6.00 15.00
9 Jerry Rice 6.00 15.00
10 Peyton Manning 6.00 15.00
11 Brett Favre 10.00 25.00
12 Jim Plunkett 4.00 10.00
13 Phil Simms 4.00 10.00
14 Thurman Thomas 4.00 10.00

2006 Donruss Threads Century Stars Gold

GOLD ODDS 1:18 HOB, 1:81 RET
*BLUE/100: .8X TO 2X BASIC INSERTS
BLUE PRINT RUN 100 SER.#'d SETS
1 Carson Palmer 1.00 2.50
2 Ben Roethlisberger 2.50 6.00
3 Brett Favre 2.50 6.00
4 Isaac Bruce .60 1.50
5 Jerome Bettis 1.00 2.50
6 Jerry Rice 2.50 6.00
7 LaDainian Tomlinson 1.00 2.50
8 Steve Smith 1.00 2.50
9 Marvin Harrison 1.00 2.50
10 Matt Hasselbeck .60 1.50
11 Michael Vick 1.00 2.50
12 Peyton Manning 2.00 5.00
13 Randy Moss 1.00 2.50
14 Shaun Alexander 1.25 3.00
15 Tom Brady 2.00 5.00

2006 Donruss Threads Century Stars Materials

STATED PRINT RUN 250 SER.#'d SETS
*PRIME/25: .8X TO 2X BASIC INSERTS
PRIME PRINT RUN 25 SER.#'d SETS
1 Carson Palmer 4.00 10.00
2 Ben Roethlisberger 5.00 12.00
3 Brett Favre 8.00 20.00
4 Isaac Bruce 4.00 10.00
5 Jerome Bettis 6.00 15.00
6 Jerry Rice 6.00 15.00
7 LaDainian Tomlinson 6.00 15.00
8 Steve Smith 4.00 10.00
9 Marvin Harrison 4.00 10.00
10 Matt Hasselbeck 3.00 8.00
11 Michael Vick 4.00 10.00
12 Peyton Manning 6.00 15.00
13 Randy Moss 4.00 10.00
14 Shaun Alexander 5.00 12.00
15 Tom Brady 6.00 15.00

2006 Donruss Threads College Greats

STATED ODDS 1:989 RET
1 Peyton Manning 3.00 8.00
2 Carson Palmer 1.50 4.00
3 Ronnie Brown 1.50 4.00
4 Cadillac Williams 1.50 4.00
5 LaDainian Tomlinson 1.50 4.00
6 Cedric Benson 1.50 4.00
7 Hines Ward 1.50 4.00
8 Larry Johnson 1.50 4.00
9 Michael Vick 1.50 4.00
10 Willis McGahee 1.50 4.00
11 Reggie Bush 3.00 8.00
12 Matt Leinart 1.50 4.00
13 Vince Young 2.00 5.00
14 Jim Brown 2.50 6.00
15 Anquan Boldin 1.00 2.50
16 Chad Johnson 1.00 2.50
17 Ben Roethlisberger 4.00 10.00
18 Ken Kavanaugh 1.50 4.00
19 Jack Cloud 1.00 2.50
20 Doc Blanchard 1.50 4.00

2006 Donruss Threads College Greats Autographs

UNPRICED DUAL AUs SER.#'d TO 5
1 Peyton Manning SP 60.00 120.00
2 Carson Palmer SP 15.00 40.00
4 Cadillac Williams SP 15.00 40.00
6 Cedric Benson SP 15.00 40.00
7 Hines Ward SP 20.00 50.00
8 Larry Johnson SP 15.00 40.00
9 Michael Vick SP 30.00 60.00
10 Willis McGahee SP 15.00 40.00
11 Reggie Bush SP 40.00 100.00
12 Matt Leinart SP 25.00 60.00
13 Vince Young SP 30.00 80.00
14 Jim Brown SP 60.00 120.00
15 Anquan Boldin SP 15.00 40.00
16 Chad Johnson SP 15.00 40.00
17 Ben Roethlisberger SP 50.00 100.00
18 Ken Kavanaugh 10.00 25.00

2006 Donruss Threads College Greats Autographs Dual

STATED PRINT RUN 5 SER.#'d SETS
3 John Elway
Joe Montana EXCH
4 Herschel Walker
Shaun Alexander EXCH

2006 Donruss Threads College Gridiron Kings Gold

GOLD ODDS 1:19 HOB, 1:24 RET
UNPRICED FRAMED BLACK SER.#'d TO 10
*FRAMED BLUE/50: 1.2X TO 3X
FRAMED BLUE PRINT RUN 50 SER.#'d SETS
*FRAMED GREEN/25: 1.5X TO 4X
FRAMED GREEN PRINT RUN 25 SER.#'d SETS
*FRAMED RED/100: 1X TO 2.5X
FRAMED RED PRINT RUN 100 SER.#'d SETS
*GOLD HOLOFOIL/100: 1X TO 2.5X
GOLD HOLO.PRINT RUN 100 SER.#'d SETS
*PLATINUM/25: 1.5X TO 4X BASIC INSERTS
PLATINUM PRINT RUN 25 SER.#'d SETS
*SILVER HOLOFOIL/250: .6X TO 1.5X
SILVER HOLO.PRINT RUN 250 SER.#'d SETS
1 Marcus Allen 1.25 3.00
2 Terry Baker .75 2.00
3 Joe Bellino .75 2.00
4 Billy Cannon .75 2.00
5 John Cappelletti .75 2.00
6 Howard Cassady 1.25 3.00
7 Eric Crouch 1.25 3.00
8 John David Crow .75 2.00
9 Tony Dorsett 1.50 4.00
10 Doug Flutie 1.25 3.00
11 Paul Hornung 1.25 3.00
12 John Huarte .75 2.00
13 Dick Kazmaier .75 2.00
14 John Lattner .75 2.00
15 John Lujack 1.25 3.00
16 Steve Owens 1.25 3.00
17 Johnny Rodgers 1.25 3.00
18 Billy Sims 1.25 3.00
19 Roger Staubach 2.50 6.00
20 Matt Leinart 1.25 3.00
21 Reggie Bush 2.50 6.00
22 Eddie George 1.25 3.00
23 Jason White 1.25 3.00
24 Doak Walker 1.25 3.00
25 Jim Plunkett .75 2.00
26 Bo Jackson 1.50 4.00
27 Carson Palmer 1.25 3.00
28 Gary Beban .75 2.00
29 Glenn Davis .75 2.00
30 Pete Dawkins 1.25 3.00
31 Archie Griffin 1.25 3.00
32 Jay Berwanger .75 2.00
33 Nile Kinnick 1.25 3.00
34 Tom Harmon .75 2.00
35 Angelo Bertelli .75 2.00
36 Les Horvath .75 2.00
37 Leon Hart .75 2.00
38 Vic Janowicz .75 2.00
39 Doc Blanchard 1.25 3.00
40 Larry Kelley .75 2.00

2006 Donruss Threads College Gridiron Kings Autographs

1 Marcus Allen 15.00 40.00
2 Terry Baker 8.00 20.00
3 Joe Bellino 10.00 25.00
4 Billy Cannon 8.00 20.00
5 John Cappelletti 6.00 15.00
6 Howard Cassady 10.00 25.00
7 Eric Crouch 8.00 20.00
8 John David Crow 12.00 30.00
9 Tony Dorsett 15.00 40.00
10 Doug Flutie SP 25.00 60.00
11 Paul Hornung 15.00 40.00
12 John Huarte 12.00 30.00
13 Dick Kazmaier 15.00 40.00
14 John Lattner 10.00 25.00
15 John Lujack 15.00 40.00
16 Steve Owens 10.00 25.00
17 Johnny Rodgers 8.00 20.00
18 Billy Sims 10.00 25.00
19 Roger Staubach SP 75.00 135.00
20 Matt Leinart SP 25.00 60.00
21 Reggie Bush SP 30.00 80.00
22 Eddie George 25.00 50.00
23 Jason White 10.00 25.00
25 Jim Plunkett SP 10.00 25.00
26 Bo Jackson SP 50.00 80.00
27 Carson Palmer SP 40.00 80.00
28 Gary Beban SP 25.00 40.00
29 Glenn Davis SP 25.00 50.00
30 Pete Dawkins SP 25.00 40.00
31 Archie Griffin SP 25.00 40.00
39 Doc Blanchard SP No AU 3.00 8.00

2006 Donruss Threads Dynasty Gold

GOLD ODDS 1:24 HOB, 1:212 RET
*BLUE/100: .8X TO 2X BASIC INSERTS
BLUE PRINT RUN 100 SER.#'d SETS
1 Jim Plunkett 1.25 3.00
Cliff Branch
Fred Biletnikoff
2 Joe Montana 3.00 8.00
Jerry Rice
Steve Young
3 Ben Roethlisberger 3.00 8.00
Jerome Bettis
Hines Ward
4 Peyton Manning 2.50 6.00
Edgerrin James
Marvin Harrison
5 Drew Brees 1.50 4.00
LaDainian Tomlinson
Antonio Gates
6 Matt Hasselbeck 1.50 4.00
Shaun Alexander
Darrell Jackson
7 Jake Delhomme 1.25 3.00
Stephen Davis
Steve Smith
8 John Elway 2.50 6.00
Terrell Davis
Rod Smith
9 Brett Favre 3.00 8.00
Ahman Green
Javon Walker
10 Jim Kelly 1.50 4.00
Thurman Thomas
Andre Reed

2006 Donruss Threads Dynasty Materials

STATED PRINT RUN 250 SER.#'d SETS
*PRIME/25: .8X TO 2X BASIC INSERTS
PRIME PRINT RUN 25 SER.#'d SETS
1 Jim Plunkett 10.00 25.00
Cliff Branch
Fred Biletnikoff
2 Joe Montana 25.00 60.00
Jerry Rice
Steve Young
3 Ben Roethlisberger 20.00 50.00
Jerome Bettis
Hines Ward
4 Peyton Manning 10.00 25.00
Edgerrin James
Marvin Harrison
5 Drew Brees 8.00 20.00
LaDainian Tomlinson
Antonio Gates
6 Matt Hasselbeck 8.00 20.00
Shaun Alexander
Darrell Jackson
7 Jake Delhomme 8.00 20.00
Stephen Davis
Steve Smith
8 John Elway 15.00 40.00
Terrell Davis
Rod Smith
9 Brett Favre 12.00 30.00
Ahman Green
Javon Walker
10 Jim Kelly 12.00 30.00
Thurman Thomas
Andre Reed

2006 Donruss Threads Footballs

PRINT RUN 250 UNLESS NOTED
19 Anquan Boldin 3.00 8.00
20 Kurt Warner 4.00 10.00
21 Larry Fitzgerald 3.00 8.00
22 Alge Crumpler 3.00 8.00
23 Michael Vick 4.00 10.00
24 Warrick Dunn 3.00 8.00
25 Jamal Lewis/240 4.00 10.00
26 Ray Lewis/175 4.00 10.00
27 Eric Moulds/200 3.00 8.00
28 Josh Reed 2.50 6.00
30 Steve Smith 4.00 10.00
31 Brian Urlacher 4.00 10.00
32 Thomas Jones 3.00 8.00
33 Chad Johnson 3.00 8.00
34 Rudi Johnson 3.00 8.00
35 T.J. Houshmandzadeh 3.00 8.00
36 Reuben Droughns 2.50 6.00
37 Drew Bledsoe 4.00 10.00
38 Keyshawn Johnson 3.00 8.00
39 Jake Plummer 3.00 8.00
40 Rod Smith 3.00 8.00
41 Mike Anderson 3.00 8.00
42 Joey Harrington 3.00 8.00
43 Brett Favre 10.00 25.00
44 Donald Driver/60 4.00 10.00
46 Andre Johnson/140 5.00 12.00
47 David Carr/75 5.00 12.00
48 Domanick Davis/100 5.00 12.00
49 Edgerrin James/200 4.00 10.00
50 Marvin Harrison 4.00 10.00
51 Peyton Manning 8.00 20.00
52 Reggie Wayne/176 4.00 10.00
53 Jimmy Smith 3.00 8.00
54 Tony Gonzalez 3.00 8.00
55 Trent Green 3.00 8.00
56 Eddie Kennison 2.50 6.00
57 Chris Chambers 3.00 8.00
58 Zach Thomas 4.00 10.00
59 Daunte Culpepper/248 4.00 10.00
60 Corey Dillon/115 4.00 10.00
61 Deion Branch 3.00 8.00
62 Tedy Bruschi/88 6.00 15.00
63 Tom Brady 6.00 15.00
64 Deuce McAllister 3.00 8.00
65 Donte Stallworth 3.00 8.00
66 Jeremy Shockey 4.00 10.00
67 Tiki Barber 4.00 10.00
68 Chad Pennington 3.00 8.00
69 Curtis Martin 4.00 10.00
70 Donovan McNabb 4.00 10.00
71 Antwaan Randle El 4.00 10.00
72 Hines Ward 4.00 10.00
75 Keenan McCardell 2.50 6.00
76 LaDainian Tomlinson 4.00 10.00
81 Darrell Jackson 3.00 8.00
82 Joe Jurevicius 2.50 6.00
83 Matt Hasselbeck 4.00 10.00
84 Shaun Alexander 5.00 12.00
86 Marc Bulger 3.00 8.00
87 Steven Jackson 4.00 10.00
88 Torry Holt 3.00 8.00
91 Joey Galloway 3.00 8.00
95 Steve McNair 4.00 10.00

2006 Donruss Threads Generations Gold

GOLD ODDS 1:17 HOB, 1:40 RET
*BLUE/100: .8X TO 2X BASIC INSERTS
BLUE PRINT RUN 100 SER.#'d SETS
1 Earl Campbell 1.00 2.50
Chris Brown
2 Phil Simms 1.00 2.50
Chris Simms
3 Brett Favre 2.50 6.00
Aaron Rodgers
4 Ozzie Newsome 1.00 2.50
Braylon Edwards
5 Boomer Esiason 1.25 3.00
Carson Palmer
6 Ronnie Lott 1.00 2.50
Roy Williams S
7 Jerry Rice 1.50 4.00
Marvin Harrison
8 Curtis Martin 1.00 2.50
Edgerrin James
9 Shaun Alexander 1.25 3.00
Julius Jones
10 Paul Warfield 1.00 2.50
Ronnie Brown
11 Thurman Thomas 1.00 2.50
Tatum Bell
12 Steve Young 1.25 3.00
Alex Smith QB
13 Jerome Bettis 1.50 4.00
Willie Parker
14 Randy Moss 1.00 2.50
Chad Johnson
15 Jim Plunkett 1.00 2.50
Chad Pennington
16 Peyton Manning 2.00 5.00
Eli Manning
17 Mike Singletary 1.00 2.50
Junior Seau
18 Paul Warfield 1.00 2.50
Chris Chambers
19 John Elway 3.00 8.00
Ben Roethlisberger
20 Warren Moon 1.00 2.50
Donovan McNabb

2006 Donruss Threads Generations Materials

STATED PRINT RUN 250 SER.#'d SETS
*PRIME/25: 1X TO 2.5X BASIC INSERTS
PRIME PRINT RUN 25 SER.#'d SETS
1 Earl Campbell 5.00 12.00
Chris Brown
2 Phil Simms 6.00 15.00
Chris Simms
3 Brett Favre 20.00 50.00
Aaron Rodgers
4 Ozzie Newsome 5.00 12.00
Braylon Edwards
5 Boomer Esiason 6.00 15.00
Carson Palmer
6 Ronnie Lott 5.00 12.00
Roy Williams S
7 Jerry Rice 8.00 20.00
Marvin Harrison
8 Curtis Martin 5.00 12.00
Edgerrin James
9 Shaun Alexander 6.00 15.00
Julius Jones
10 Paul Warfield 5.00 12.00
Ronnie Brown
11 Thurman Thomas 5.00 12.00
Tatum Bell
12 Steve Young 6.00 15.00
Alex Smith QB
13 Jerome Bettis 8.00 20.00
Willie Parker
14 Randy Moss 5.00 12.00
Chad Johnson
15 Jim Plunkett 5.00 12.00
Chad Pennington
16 Peyton Manning 10.00 25.00
Eli Manning
17 Mike Singletary 5.00 12.00
Junior Seau
18 Paul Warfield 5.00 12.00
Chris Chambers
19 John Elway 12.00 30.00
Ben Roethlisberger
20 Warren Moon 5.00 12.00
Donovan McNabb

2006 Donruss Threads Jerseys

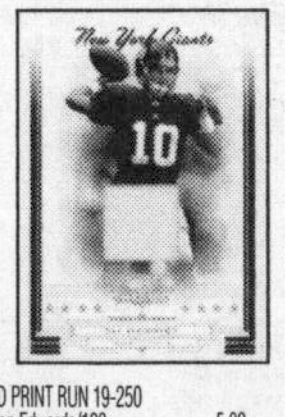

STATED PRINT RUN 19-250
1 Braylon Edwards/100 5.00 12.00
3 Julius Jones/80 5.00 12.00
4 Roy Williams S/250 4.00 10.00
5 Terry Glenn/200 4.00 10.00
6 Ashley Lelie/75 3.00 8.00
7 Kevin Jones/54 6.00 15.00
9 Roy Williams WR/244 4.00 10.00
10 Aaron Rodgers/50 20.00 50.00
11 Tatum Bell/200 3.00 8.00
12 Samkon Gado/25 8.00 20.00
13 Matt Jones/100 4.00 10.00
16 Larry Johnson/200 4.00 10.00
17 Byron Leftwich/250 4.00 10.00
18 Fred Taylor/250 2.50 6.00
19 Anquan Boldin/250 3.00 8.00
20 Kurt Warner/28 6.00 15.00
21 Larry Fitzgerald/250 4.00 10.00
22 Alge Crumpler/55 4.00 10.00
23 Michael Vick/250 4.00 10.00
24 Warrick Dunn/250 3.00 8.00
25 Jamal Lewis/250 3.00 8.00
26 Ray Lewis/75 4.00 10.00
28 Josh Reed/250 2.50 6.00
29 Lee Evans/50 4.00 10.00
30 Steve Smith/225 4.00 10.00
31 Brian Urlacher/250 4.00 10.00
32 Thomas Jones/250 3.00 8.00
33 Chad Johnson/150 4.00 10.00
34 Rudi Johnson/200 3.00 8.00
35 T.J. Houshmandzadeh/50 4.00 10.00
37 Drew Bledsoe/50 6.00 15.00
39 Jake Plummer/250 3.00 8.00
43 Brett Favre/155 12.00 30.00
46 Andre Johnson/182 3.00 8.00
47 David Carr/250 4.00 10.00
48 Domanick Davis/150 4.00 10.00
50 Marvin Harrison/200 4.00 10.00
51 Peyton Manning/92 10.00 25.00
52 Reggie Wayne/125 4.00 10.00
53 Jimmy Smith/115 4.00 10.00
55 Trent Green/50 5.00 12.00
57 Chris Chambers/35 5.00 12.00
58 Zach Thomas/19 6.00 15.00
60 Corey Dillon/43 5.00 12.00
61 Deion Branch/40 5.00 12.00
63 Tom Brady/45 10.00 25.00
64 Deuce McAllister/250 3.00 8.00
65 Donte Stallworth/55 4.00 10.00
66 Jeremy Shockey/250 4.00 10.00
67 Tiki Barber/45 6.00 15.00
68 Chad Pennington/250 3.00 8.00
69 Curtis Martin/190 4.00 10.00
70 Donovan McNabb/250 4.00 10.00
72 Hines Ward/215 4.00 10.00
73 Antonio Gates/200 4.00 10.00
75 Keenan McCardell/250 3.00 8.00
76 LaDainian Tomlinson/50 6.00 15.00
77 Alex Smith QB/55 6.00 15.00
81 Darrell Jackson/200 3.00 8.00
83 Matt Hasselbeck/43 6.00 15.00
84 Shaun Alexander/200 5.00 12.00
86 Marc Bulger/215 3.00 8.00
87 Steven Jackson/200 4.00 10.00
88 Torry Holt/45 5.00 12.00
89 Cadillac Williams/45 5.00 12.00
92 Michael Clayton/250 3.00 8.00
93 Chris Brown/45 4.00 10.00
94 Drew Bennett/250 3.00 8.00
95 Steve McNair/250 4.00 10.00
97 Clinton Portis/150 5.00 12.00
102 Ronnie Brown/150 4.00 10.00
105 Troy Williamson/107 4.00 10.00
111 LaMont Jordan/45 5.00 12.00
112 Randy Moss/55 6.00 15.00
113 Jerry Porter/163 3.00 8.00
114 Brian Westbrook/215 3.00 8.00
116 Joe Horn/250 3.00 8.00
117 Eli Manning/137 8.00 20.00
120 Ben Roethlisberger/40 15.00 40.00
121 Willie Parker/35 6.00 15.00
127 Dante Hall/68 4.00 10.00
135 Kyle Boller/29 4.00 10.00
137 Willis McGahee/107 5.00 12.00
139 Jake Delhomme/65 6.00 15.00
141 Keary Colbert/244 2.50 6.00
142 Stephen Davis/45 5.00 12.00
143 Todd Heap/250 3.00 8.00
144 J.P. Losman/37 4.00 10.00
145 Muhsin Muhammad/250 3.00 8.00
146 Carson Palmer/189 4.00 10.00
147 Cedric Benson/55 6.00 15.00
148 Rex Grossman/215 3.00 8.00

2006 Donruss Threads Jerseys Prime

COMMON CARD 5.00 12.00
SEMISTARS 6.00 15.00
UNLISTED STARS 8.00 20.00
PRIME PRINT RUN 5-25
SERIAL #'d UNDER 25 NOT PRICED
16 Larry Johnson 8.00 20.00
43 Brett Favre 20.00 50.00
51 Peyton Manning 15.00 40.00
63 Tom Brady 12.00 30.00
76 LaDainian Tomlinson 8.00 20.00
120 Ben Roethlisberger/24 30.00 80.00

2006 Donruss Threads Pro Gridiron Kings Gold

GOLD ODDS 1:12 HOB, 1:17 RET
UNPRICED FRAMED BLACK SER.#'d TO 10
*FRAMED BLUE/50: 1.2X TO 3X
FRAMED BLUE PRINT RUN 50 SER.#'d SETS
*FRAMED GREEN/25: 1.5X TO 4X
FRAMED GREEN PRINT RUN 25 SER.#'d SETS
*FRAMED RED/100: 1X TO 2.5X
FRAMED RED PRINT RUN 100 SER.#'d SETS
*GOLD HOLOFOIL/100: 1X TO 2.5X
GOLD HOLO.PRINT RUN 100 SER.#'d SETS
*PLATINUM/25: 1.5X TO 4X
PLATINUM PRINT RUN 25 SER.#'d SETS
*SILVER HOLOFOIL/250 .6X TO 1.5X
SILVER HOLO.PRINT RUN 250 SER.#'d SETS
1 Alex Smith QB 1.00 2.50
2 Andre Johnson 1.00 2.50
3 Ben Roethlisberger 1.25 3.00
4 Brett Favre 2.00 5.00
5 Cadillac Williams .75 2.00
6 Carson Palmer 1.00 2.50
7 Cedric Benson .75 2.00
8 Chad Johnson .75 2.00
9 Clinton Portis .75 2.00
10 Corey Dillon .75 2.00
11 Curtis Martin 1.00 2.50
12 Darrell Jackson .75 2.00
13 Domanick Davis .60 1.50
14 Donovan McNabb .75 2.00
15 Drew Bledsoe 1.00 2.50
16 Edgerrin James .75 2.00
17 Eli Manning 1.25 3.00
18 Hines Ward 1.00 2.50
19 Isaac Bruce .75 2.00
20 J.P. Losman .75 2.00
21 Jake Delhomme .75 2.00
22 Javon Walker .75 2.00
23 Jeremy Shockey 1.00 2.50
24 Jerome Bettis 1.00 2.50
25 Jimmy Smith .75 2.00
26 Julius Jones .60 1.50
27 Kevin Jones .60 1.50
28 Keyshawn Johnson .75 2.00
29 LaDainian Tomlinson 1.00 2.50
30 Larry Fitzgerald 1.00 2.50
31 Larry Johnson .75 2.00
32 Lee Evans .75 2.00
33 Marshall Faulk .75 2.00
34 Marvin Harrison 1.00 2.50
35 Matt Hasselbeck .75 2.00
36 Matt Jones .60 1.50
37 Michael Vick 1.00 2.50
38 Peyton Manning 1.50 4.00
39 Randy Moss 1.00 2.50
40 Reggie Brown .60 1.50
41 Reggie Wayne .75 2.00
42 Antonio Gates 1.00 2.50
43 Rod Smith .75 2.00
44 Ronnie Brown 1.00 2.50

45 Roy Williams WR	.75	2.00
46 Rudi Johnson	.75	2.00
47 Samkon Gado	.75	2.00
48 Shaun Alexander	.75	2.00
49 Stephen Davis	.75	2.00
50 Steve Smith	1.00	2.50
51 Steven Jackson	1.00	2.50
52 T.J. Houshmandzadeh	.75	2.00
53 Tatum Bell	.60	1.50
54 Tiki Barber	1.00	2.50
55 Tom Brady	1.50	4.00
56 Tony Gonzalez	.75	2.00
57 Torry Holt	.75	2.00
58 Trent Green	.75	2.00
59 Willie Parker	.75	2.00
60 Willis McGahee	.75	2.00

2006 Donruss Threads Pro Gridiron Kings Autographs

STATED PRINT RUN 5-25
UNPRICED MATERIAL AU PRINT RUN 5-20
UNPRICED MAT.PRIME AU PRINT RUN 2-10

13 Domanick Davis/25	10.00	25.00
40 Reggie Brown/25	10.00	25.00
46 Rudi Johnson/25	10.00	25.00
52 T.J. Houshmandzadeh/25	10.00	25.00
59 Willie Parker/25	20.00	50.00

2006 Donruss Threads Pro Gridiron Kings Materials

STATED PRINT RUN 90-250
*PRIME/25: 1X TO 2.5X BASIC JSY/175-250
*PRIME/25: .8X TO 2X BASIC JSY/90-155
PRIME SER.#'d UNDER 25 NOT PRICED

1 Alex Smith QB/125	5.00	12.00
2 Andre Johnson/137	3.00	8.00
3 Ben Roethlisberger/125	12.00	30.00
4 Brett Favre/250	10.00	25.00
5 Cadillac Williams/125	5.00	12.00
6 Carson Palmer/137	5.00	12.00
7 Cedric Benson/137	4.00	10.00
8 Chad Johnson/147	3.00	8.00
9 Clinton Portis/115	4.00	10.00
10 Corey Dillon/175	3.00	8.00
11 Curtis Martin/137	5.00	12.00
12 Darrell Jackson/175	3.00	8.00
13 Domanick Davis/137	4.00	10.00
14 Donovan McNabb/137	5.00	12.00
15 Drew Bledsoe/125	5.00	12.00
16 Edgerrin James/250	4.00	10.00
17 Eli Manning/155	8.00	20.00
18 Hines Ward/137	5.00	12.00
19 Isaac Bruce/250	3.00	8.00
20 J.P. Losman/90	4.00	10.00
21 Jake Delhomme/125	5.00	12.00
22 Javon Walker/230	4.00	10.00
23 Jeremy Shockey/250	4.00	10.00
24 Jerome Bettis/200	4.00	10.00
25 Jimmy Smith/137	4.00	10.00
26 Julius Jones/125	5.00	12.00
27 Kevin Jones/137	5.00	12.00
28 Keyshawn Johnson/230	3.00	8.00
29 LaDainian Tomlinson/137	5.00	12.00
30 Larry Fitzgerald/250	4.00	10.00
31 Larry Johnson/125	5.00	12.00
32 Lee Evans/125	3.00	8.00
33 Marshall Faulk/250	4.00	10.00
34 Marvin Harrison/250	4.00	10.00
35 Matt Hasselbeck/137	5.00	12.00
36 Matt Jones/125	5.00	12.00
37 Michael Vick/250	3.00	8.00
38 Peyton Manning/250	8.00	15.00
39 Randy Moss/125	5.00	12.00
40 Reggie Brown/125	4.00	10.00
41 Reggie Wayne/137	4.00	10.00
42 Antonio Gates/250	4.00	10.00
43 Rod Smith/250	3.00	8.00
44 Ronnie Brown/125	5.00	12.00
45 Roy Williams WR/225	4.00	10.00
46 Rudi Johnson/125	4.00	10.00
47 Samkon Gado/125	6.00	15.00
48 Shaun Alexander/125	6.00	15.00
49 Stephen Davis/137	4.00	10.00
50 Steve Smith/125	5.00	12.00
51 Steven Jackson/125	5.00	12.00
52 T.J. Houshmandzadeh/125	4.00	10.00
53 Tatum Bell/125	4.00	10.00
54 Tiki Barber/125	5.00	12.00
55 Tom Brady/250	6.00	15.00
56 Tony Gonzalez/137	5.00	12.00
57 Torry Holt/137	4.00	10.00
58 Trent Green/150	4.00	10.00
59 Willie Parker/125	5.00	12.00
60 Willis McGahee/137	5.00	12.00

2006 Donruss Threads Rookie Autographs

STATED PRINT RUN 100 UNLESS NOTED

151 Mathias Kiwanuka/50	10.00	25.00
153 Reggie McNeal ?á	8.00	20.00
152 Ingle Martin	8.00	20.00
154 Bruce Gradkowski	10.00	25.00
155 D.J. Shockley	8.00	20.00
156 Paul Pinegar	6.00	15.00
157 Brandon Kirsch	8.00	20.00
158 P.J. Daniels	6.00	15.00
159 Marques Hagans	6.00	15.00
160 Jerome Harrison	10.00	25.00
161 Wali Lundy	8.00	20.00
162 Cedric Humes	6.00	15.00
163 Quinton Ganther	6.00	15.00
164 Mike Bell	10.00	25.00
166 Anthony Fasano	10.00	25.00
167 Tony Scheffler	10.00	25.00
168 Leonard Pope	10.00	25.00
169 David Thomas	8.00	20.00
170 Dominique Byrd	8.00	20.00
171 Devin Hester	30.00	50.00
172 Willie Reid	8.00	20.00
173 Brad Smith	10.00	25.00
174 Cory Rodgers	8.00	20.00
175 Domenik Hixon	10.00	25.00
176 Jeremy Bloom	8.00	20.00
177 Jonathan Orr	8.00	20.00
178 Jeff Webb	8.00	20.00
179 Ethan Kilmer	8.00	20.00
180 Bennie Brazell	8.00	20.00
181 David Anderson	8.00	20.00
182 Kevin McMahan	8.00	20.00
183 Anthony Mix	8.00	20.00
184 D'Brickashaw Ferguson	10.00	25.00
185 Kamerion Wimbley	10.00	25.00
186 Tamba Hali	10.00	25.00
187 Haloti Ngata	10.00	25.00
188 Brodrick Bunkley	8.00	20.00
189 John McCargo	6.00	15.00
190 Claude Wroten	6.00	15.00
191 Gabe Watson	6.00	15.00
192 D'Qwell Jackson	8.00	20.00
193 Abdul Hodge	6.00	15.00
194 Ernie Sims	8.00	20.00
195 Chad Greenway	10.00	25.00
196 Bobby Carpenter	6.00	15.00
197 Manny Lawson	8.00	20.00
198 DeMeco Ryans	10.00	25.00
199 Rocky McIntosh	8.00	20.00
200 Thomas Howard	8.00	20.00
201 Jon Alston	6.00	15.00
202 A.J. Nicholson	6.00	15.00
203 Tye Hill	6.00	15.00
205 Johnathan Joseph	8.00	20.00
206 Kelly Jennings	8.00	20.00
207 Ashton Youboty	6.00	15.00
208 Alan Zemaitis	10.00	25.00
209 Jason Allen	8.00	20.00
210 Cedric Griffin	8.00	20.00
211 Ko Simpson	8.00	20.00
212 Pat Watkins	8.00	20.00
213 Donte Whitner	10.00	25.00
214 Bernard Pollard	8.00	20.00
215 Darnell Bing	8.00	20.00

2006 Donruss Threads Rookie Collection Materials

STATED PRINT RUN 500 SER.#'d SETS
*PRIME/25: 1X TO 2.5X BASIC INSERTS
PRIME PRINT RUN 25 SER.#'d SETS

1 Chad Jackson	2.00	5.00
2 Laurence Maroney	2.50	6.00
3 Tarvaris Jackson	3.00	8.00
4 Michael Huff	2.50	6.00
5 Mario Williams	3.00	8.00
6 Marcedes Lewis	3.00	8.00
7 Maurice Drew	5.00	12.00
8 Vince Young	4.00	10.00
9 LenDale White	2.50	6.00
10 Reggie Bush	6.00	15.00
11 Matt Leinart	3.00	8.00
12 Michael Robinson	2.50	6.00
13 Vernon Davis	4.00	10.00
14 Brandon Williams	2.00	5.00
15 Derek Hagan	2.50	6.00
16 Jason Avant	2.00	5.00
17 Brandon Marshall	3.00	8.00
18 Omar Jacobs	2.00	5.00
19 Santonio Holmes	4.00	10.00
20 Jerious Norwood	2.50	6.00
21 Demetrius Williams	2.50	6.00
22 Sinorice Moss	3.00	8.00
23 Leon Washington	2.50	6.00
24 Kellen Clemens	2.50	6.00
25 A.J. Hawk	3.00	8.00
26 Maurice Stovall	2.00	5.00
27 DeAngelo Williams	4.00	10.00
28 Charlie Whitehurst	3.00	8.00
29 Travis Wilson	2.00	5.00
30 Joe Klopfenstein	2.00	5.00
31 Brian Calhoun	2.00	5.00

2006 Donruss Threads Rookie Collection Material Autographs

STATED PRINT RUN 5-25
UNPRICED PRIME AU PRINT RUN 3-5
SERIAL #'d UNDER 25 NOT PRICED

3 Tarvaris Jackson/25	25.00	60.00
6 Marcedes Lewis/25	12.00	30.00
12 Michael Robinson/25	15.00	40.00

2006 Donruss Threads Rookie Collection Materials Combo

STATED PRINT RUN 500 SER.#'d SETS
*PRIME/25: 1X TO 2.5X BASIC INSERTS
PRIME PRINT RUN 25 SER.#'d SETS

1 Vince Young LenDale White	5.00	12.00
2 Marcedes Lewis Maurice Drew	6.00	15.00
3 Chad Jackson Laurence Maroney	3.00	8.00
4 Omar Jacobs Santonio Holmes	5.00	12.00
5 Sinorice Moss Demetrius Williams	4.00	10.00
6 Michael Robinson Brandon Williams	3.00	8.00
7 Reggie Bush Matt Leinart	8.00	20.00
8 Vernon Davis Joe Klopfenstein	5.00	12.00
9 Mario Williams A.J. Hawk	4.00	10.00
10 Brandon Marshall Maurice Stovall	4.00	10.00
11 Tarvaris Jackson Charlie Whitehurst	4.00	10.00
12 Derek Hagan Jason Avant	3.00	8.00
13 Michael Huff Travis Wilson	3.00	8.00
14 Kellen Clemens Leon Washington	3.00	8.00
15 DeAngelo Williams Brian Calhoun	5.00	12.00

2006 Donruss Threads Rookie Collection Materials Triple

STATED PRINT RUN 500 SER.#'d SETS
*PRIME/25: .8X TO 2X BASIC INSERTS
PRIME PRINT RUN 25 SER.#'d SETS

1 Reggie Bush Matt Leinart LenDale White	12.00	30.00
2 Michael Robinson Vernon Davis Brandon Williams	8.00	20.00
3 Vince Young Michael Huff Travis Wilson	8.00	20.00
4 Sinorice Moss Leon Washington Kellen Clemens	5.00	12.00
5 Marcedes Lewis Maurice Stovall Joe Klopfenstein	6.00	15.00
6 Santonio Holmes Brandon Marshall Demetrius Williams	8.00	20.00
7 Tarvaris Jackson Charlie Whitehurst Omar Jacobs	6.00	15.00
8 Maurice Drew DeAngelo Williams Jerious Norwood	10.00	25.00
9 Chad Jackson Jason Avant Laurence Maroney	5.00	12.00
10 Mario Williams A.J. Hawk Derek Hagan	6.00	15.00

2006 Donruss Threads Rookie Collection Materials Quad

STATED PRINT RUN 100 SER.#'d SETS
*PRIME: .8X TO 2X BASIC INSERTS
PRIME PRINT RUN 25 SER.#'d SETS

1 Vince Young LenDale White Reggie Bush Matt Leinart	20.00	50.00
2 Vernon Davis Santonio Holmes Chad Jackson Sinorice Moss	10.00	25.00
3 Maurice Drew DeAngelo Williams Laurence Maroney Brian Calhoun	15.00	40.00
4 Tarvaris Jackson Omar Jacobs Kellen Clemens Charlie Whitehurst	12.00	30.00

2007 Donruss Threads

This 294-card set was released in August, 2007. The set was issued into the hobby in five-card packs, with a $4 SRP, which came 24 packs to a box. Cards numbered 1-150 feature veterans while cards numbered 151-294 feature 2007 NFL rookies. The Rookie Cards numbered 151-225 were all issued to a stated print run of 999 serial numbered sets and cards 226-294 were signed by the player and were issued to stated print runs between 100 and 999 serial numbered copies. A few players did not return their signatures in time for pack out and we have notated those cards with an EXCH in our checklist.

COMP.SET w/o RC's (150)	10.00	25.00
226-250 AU ROOKIE PRINT RUN 198-999		
251-294 AU ROOKIE PRINT RUN 100-210		
1 Anquan Boldin	.30	.75
2 Larry Fitzgerald	.40	1.00
3 Alge Crumpler	.30	.75
4 Michael Vick	.40	1.00
5 Steve McNair	.30	.75
6 Ray Lewis	.40	1.00
7 Keyshawn Johnson	.30	.75
8 Steve Smith	.30	.75
9 Brian Urlacher	.40	1.00
10 Muhsin Muhammad	.30	.75
11 Chad Johnson	.30	.75
12 Rudi Johnson	.30	.75
13 T.J. Houshmandzadeh	.30	.75
14 Terry Glenn	.30	.75
15 Terrell Owens	.40	1.00
16 Jon Kitna	.25	.60
17 Brett Favre	.75	2.00
18 Peyton Manning	.60	1.50
19 Fred Taylor	.30	.75
20 Eddie Kennison	.25	.60
21 Larry Johnson	.25	.60
22 Tony Gonzalez	.30	.75
23 Trent Green	.30	.75
24 Chris Chambers	.30	.75
25 Marty Booker	.25	.60
26 Tom Brady	.60	1.50
27 Donte Stallworth	.30	.75
28 Deuce McAllister	.30	.75
29 Drew Brees	.40	1.00
30 Reuben Droughns	.30	.75
31 Jeremy Shockey	.30	.75
32 Plaxico Burress	.30	.75
33 Chad Pennington	.30	.75
34 Jerricho Cotchery	.30	.75
35 Laveranues Coles	.25	.60
36 LaMont Jordan	.30	.75
37 Brian Westbrook UER (last named misspelled Westbr on front)	.30	.75
38 Donovan McNabb	.40	1.00
39 Hines Ward	.40	1.00
40 Antonio Gates	.40	1.00
41 LaDainian Tomlinson	.40	1.00
42 Arnaz Battle	.25	.60
43 Darrell Jackson	.25	.60
44 Deion Branch	.30	.75
45 Matt Hasselbeck	.30	.75
46 Jerramy Stevens	.25	.60
47 Shaun Alexander	.30	.75
48 Isaac Bruce	.30	.75
49 Marc Bulger	.30	.75
50 Drew Bennett	.25	.60
51 Torry Holt	.30	.75
52 Joey Galloway	.30	.75
53 Mike Alstott	.30	.75
54 Travis Henry	.30	.75
55 Clinton Portis	.30	.75
56 Santana Moss	.30	.75
57 Edgerrin James	.30	.75
58 Matt Leinart	.30	.75
59 Jerious Norwood	.30	.75
60 Warrick Dunn	.30	.75
61 Mark Clayton	.30	.75
62 J.P. Losman	.25	.60
63 Josh Reed	.25	.60
64 Lee Evans	.30	.75
65 DeAngelo Williams	.40	1.00
66 DeShaun Foster	.30	.75
67 Jake Delhomme	.30	.75
68 Bernard Berrian	.25	.60
69 Cedric Benson	.30	.75
70 Rex Grossman	.30	.75
71 Carson Palmer	.30	.75
72 Braylon Edwards	.30	.75
73 Kellen Winslow	.30	.75
74 Charlie Frye	.30	.75
75 Julius Jones	.25	.60
76 Marion Barber	.30	.75
77 Javon Walker	.30	.75
78 Jay Cutler	.40	1.00
79 Mike Bell	.30	.75
80 Donald Driver	.40	1.00
81 Greg Jennings	.40	1.00
82 Andre Johnson	.30	.75
83 Matt Schaub	.30	.75
84 Wali Lundy	.25	.60
85 Joseph Addai	.30	.75
86 Marvin Harrison	.40	1.00
87 Kevin Jones	.25	.60
88 Roy Williams WR	.30	.75
89 Mike Furrey	.30	.75
90 A.J. Hawk	.30	.75
91 Reggie Wayne	.30	.75
92 Dallas Clark	.25	.60
93 Byron Leftwich	.30	.75
94 Maurice Jones-Drew	.40	1.00
95 Reggie Williams	.30	.75
96 Tony Romo	.50	1.25
97 Daunte Culpepper	.30	.75
98 Ronnie Brown	.30	.75
99 Chester Taylor	.25	.60
100 Travis Taylor	.25	.60
101 Ben Watson	.25	.60
102 Laurence Maroney	.30	.75
103 Bo Scaife	.25	.60
104 Peerless Price	.25	.60
105 Marques Colston	.40	1.00
106 Reggie Bush	.40	1.00
107 Brandon Jacobs	.30	.75
108 Eli Manning	.40	1.00
109 Leon Washington	.30	.75
110 Kevan Barlow	.30	.75
111 Randy Moss	.40	1.00
112 Troy Polamalu	.40	1.00
113 Willie Parker	.30	.75
114 Santonio Holmes	.30	.75
115 Philip Rivers	.40	1.00
116 Shawne Merriman	.30	.75
117 Alex Smith QB	.40	1.00
118 Frank Gore	.40	1.00
119 Vernon Davis	.30	.75
120 Reggie Brown	.25	.60
121 Ben Roethlisberger	.40	1.00
122 Steven Jackson	.40	1.00
123 Bruce Gradkowski	.25	.60
124 Cadillac Williams	.30	.75
125 Chris Cooley	.30	.75
126 Michael Jenkins	.30	.75
127 Demetrius Williams	.25	.60
128 Roy Williams S	.30	.75
129 Owen Daniels	.25	.60
130 Hank Baskett	.30	.75
131 Marcedes Lewis	.25	.60
132 Brandon Marshall	.30	.75
133 John Madsen	.25	.60
134 Michael Huff	.30	.75
135 Joe Klopfenstein	.25	.60
136 Vincent Jackson	.30	.75
137 Todd Heap	.25	.60
138 Tarvaris Jackson	.25	.60
139 Troy Williamson	.25	.60
140 Ronald Curry	.30	.75
141 Ahman Green	.30	.75
142 LenDale White	.30	.75
143 Vince Young	.30	.75
144 Thomas Jones	.30	.75
145 Jamal Lewis	.30	.75
146 Joe Horn	.30	.75
147 Tatum Bell	.25	.60
148 Willis McGahee	.30	.75
149 Jason Campbell	.30	.75
150 Ladell Betts	.25	.60
151 John Broussard RC	2.00	5.00
152 Michael Allan RC	1.50	4.00
153 Tyler Thigpen RC	2.50	6.00
154 Chandler Williams RC	2.00	5.00
155 Eric Weddle RC	2.50	6.00
156 Derek Stanley RC	2.00	5.00
157 Justise Hairston RC	2.00	5.00
158 Johnathan Holland RC	2.00	5.00
159 Legedu Naanee RC	2.50	6.00
160 Courtney Taylor RC	2.00	5.00
161 David Irons RC	1.50	4.00
162 Joel Filani RC	2.00	5.00
163 H.B. Blades RC	1.50	4.00
164 Rufus Alexander RC	2.00	5.00
165 Roy Hall RC	2.50	6.00
166 Eric Frampton RC	2.00	5.00
167 Tim Shaw RC	2.00	5.00
168 Tymere Zimmerman RC	2.00	5.00
169 Jeff Rowe RC	1.50	4.00
170 Josh Gattis RC	1.50	4.00
171 Brandon Myles RC	2.00	5.00
172 Earl Everett RC	2.00	5.00
173 Steve Breaston RC	2.50	6.00
174 Ryan McBean RC	2.50	6.00
175 Scott Chandler RC	2.50	6.00
176 Chris Davis RC	1.50	4.00
177 Fred Bennett RC	1.50	4.00
178 Ryne Robinson RC	2.00	5.00
179 Zak DeOssie RC	2.00	5.00
180 Dwayne Wright RC	2.00	5.00
181 A.J. Davis RC	1.50	4.00
182 Ray McDonald RC	2.00	5.00
183 Daymeion Hughes RC	2.00	5.00
184 Michael Okwo RC	2.00	5.00
185 Aaron Rouse RC	2.00	5.00
186 Stewart Bradley RC	2.00	5.00
187 Jonathan Wade RC	2.00	5.00
188 Charles Johnson RC	1.50	4.00
189 Demarcus Tank Tyler RC	1.50	4.00
190 Mike Walker RC	2.50	6.00
191 James Jones RC	2.50	6.00
192 Matt Spaeth RC	2.50	6.00
193 Laurent Robinson RC	2.50	6.00
194 Jacoby Jones RC	2.50	6.00
195 Marcus McCauley RC	2.00	5.00
196 Buster Davis RC	2.00	5.00
197 Quentin Moses RC	2.00	5.00
198 Sabby Piscitelli RC	2.50	6.00
199 Dan Bazuin RC	2.00	5.00
200 Ikaika Alama-Francis RC	2.50	6.00
201 Victor Abiamiri RC	2.50	6.00
202 Tim Crowder RC	2.50	6.00
203 Josh Wilson RC	2.00	5.00
204 Eric Wright RC	2.50	6.00
205 David Harris RC	2.00	5.00
206 LaMarr Woodley RC	2.50	6.00
207 Chris Houston RC	2.00	5.00
208 Zach Miller RC	2.50	6.00
209 Aaron Fairooz RC	2.00	5.00
210 Alan Branch RC	2.00	5.00
211 Anthony Spencer RC	2.50	6.00
212 Jon Beason RC	2.00	5.00
213 Brandon Meriweather RC	2.50	6.00
214 Reggie Nelson RC	2.00	5.00
215 Aaron Ross RC	2.50	6.00
216 Michael Griffin RC	2.50	6.00
217 Ronnie McGill RC	2.00	5.00
218 Jarvis Moss RC	2.00	5.00
219 Darrelle Revis RC	4.00	10.00
220 Lawrence Timmons RC	2.50	6.00
221 Adam Carriker RC	2.00	5.00
222 Amobi Okoye RC	2.50	6.00
223 Jamaal Anderson RC	2.00	5.00
224 Syvelle Newton RC	2.00	5.00
225 Levi Brown RC	2.50	6.00
226 Chansi Stuckey AU/499 RC	6.00	15.00
227 Nate Ilaoa AU/999 RC	4.00	10.00
228 Brandon Siler AU/198 RC	4.00	10.00
229 Jason Snelling AU/999 RC	6.00	15.00
230 Kenneth Darby AU/999 RC	4.00	10.00
231 Ahmad Bradshaw AU/999 RC	12.00	30.00
232 Thomas Clayton AU/763 RC	4.00	10.00
233 Dallas Baker AU/499 RC UER#(photo not Baker)		
4.00	10.00	
234 Ben Patrick AU/849 RC	4.00	10.00
235 Jordan Kent AU/999 RC	4.00	10.00
236 Jordan Palmer AU/299 RC	5.00	12.00
237 Chris Leak AU/299 RC	5.00	12.00
238 Jon Cornish AU/876 RC	4.00	10.00
239 Jared Zabransky AU/299 RC	5.00	12.00
240 Rhema McKnight AU/999 RC	3.00	8.00
241 Selvin Young AU/999 RC	8.00	20.00
242 Gary Russell AU/981 RC	4.00	10.00
243 Jerard Rabb AU/999 RC	4.00	10.00
244 Jemalle Cornelius AU/581 RC	5.00	12.00
245 Alonzo Coleman AU/781 RC	4.00	10.00
246 Danny Ware AU/999 RC	5.00	12.00
247 David Ball AU/999 RC	4.00	10.00
248 D'Juan Woods AU/456 RC	4.00	10.00
249 Syndric Steptoe AU/676 RC	4.00	10.00
250 Jarrett Hicks AU/999 RC	4.00	10.00
251 Trent Edwards/140 AU RC	20.00	50.00
252 Marshawn Lynch/100 AU RC	40.00	80.00
253 Chris Henry/105 AU RC	12.00	30.00
254 Paul Williams/200 AU RC	12.00	30.00
255 Sidney Rice/100 AU RC	25.00	60.00
256 Adrian Peterson/120 AU RC	175.00	300.00
257 Drew Stanton/140 AU RC	12.00	30.00
258 Calvin Johnson/105 AU RC	75.00	150.00
259 Yamon Figurs/150 AU RC	12.00	30.00
260 Troy Smith/100 AU RC	20.00	50.00
261 Brian Leonard/210 AU RC	15.00	40.00
262 Greg Olsen/125 AU RC	15.00	40.00
263 Kenny Irons/100 AU RC	12.00	30.00
264 Joe Thomas/120 AU RC	20.00	50.00
265 Brady Quinn/125 AU RC	20.00	50.00
266 Brandon Jackson/140 AU RC	15.00	40.00
267 Steve Smith/150 AU RC	25.00	60.00
268 Dwayne Jarrett/140 AU RC	15.00	40.00
269 Ted Ginn/100 AU RC	15.00	40.00
270 John Beck/120 AU RC	20.00	50.00
271 Lorenzo Booker/150 AU RC	15.00	40.00
272 Antonio Pittman/105 AU RC	12.00	30.00
273 Robert Meachem/140 AU RC	20.00	50.00
274 Dwayne Bowe/100 AU RC	25.00	60.00
275 Anthony Gonzalez/160 AU RC	20.00	50.00
276 JaMarcus Russell/140 AU RC	25.00	60.00
277 Michael Bush/120 AU RC	20.00	50.00
278 J.Lee Higgins/175 AU RC	15.00	40.00
279 Kevin Kolb/100 AU RC	30.00	80.00
280 Gaines Adams/150 AU RC	20.00	50.00
281 Patrick Willis/150 AU RC	40.00	100.00
282 Jason Hill/120 AU RC	20.00	50.00
283 Isaiah Stanback/200 AU RC	12.00	30.00
284 Kolby Smith/125 AU RC	15.00	40.00
285 Leon Hall/120 AU RC	15.00	40.00
286 Darius Walker/180 AU RC	12.00	30.00
287 David Clowney/175 AU RC	15.00	40.00
288 LaRon Landry/150 AU RC	20.00	50.00
289 Paul Posluszny/180 AU RC	20.00	50.00
290 Garrett Wolfe/125 AU RC	12.00	30.00
291 Tony Hunt/120 AU RC		
293 DeShawn Wynn/120 AU RC	15.00	40.00
294 Aundrae Allison/175 AU RC	12.00	30.00

2007 Donruss Threads Bronze Holofoil

*VETS 1-150: 2X TO 5X BASIC CARDS
*ROOKIES 151-225: .5X TO 1.2X BASIC CARDS
STATED PRINT RUN 250 SER.#'d SETS

2007 Donruss Threads Gold Holofoil

*VETS 1-150: 4X TO 10X BASIC CARDS
*ROOKIES 151-225: 1X TO 2.5X BASIC CARDS
STATED PRINT RUN 50 SER.#'d SETS

2007 Donruss Threads Platinum Holofoil

*VETS 1-150: 6X TO 15X BASIC CARDS
*ROOKIES 151-225: 1.5X TO 4X BASIC CARDS
STATED PRINT RUN 25 SER.#'d SETS

2007 Donruss Threads Retail Blue

*VETS 1-150: 2X TO 5X BASIC CARDS
*ROOKIES 151-225: .5X TO 1.2X BASIC CARDS
STATED PRINT RUN 350 SER.#'d SETS

2007 Donruss Threads Retail Rookies

*ROOKIES 151-225: .4X TO 1X BASIC CARDS
STATED PRINT RUN 999 SER.#'d SETS
PRODUCED ON WHITE CARD STOCK

2007 Donruss Threads Retail Green

*VETS 1-150: 2.5X TO 6X BASIC CARDS
*ROOKIES 151-225: .6X TO 1.5X BASIC CARDS
STATED PRINT RUN 200 SER.#'d SETS

2007 Donruss Threads Retail Red

*VETS 1-150: 1.5X TO 4X BASIC CARDS
*ROOKIES 151-225: .4X TO 1X BASIC CARDS

2007 Donruss Threads Silver Holofoil

*VETS 1-150: 3X TO 8X BASIC CARDS
*ROOKIES 151-225: .8X TO 2X BASIC CARDS
STATED PRINT RUN 100 SER.#'d SETS

2007 Donruss Threads Century Collection Materials

STATED PRINT RUN 16-250 SER.#'d SETS
*PRIME/25: .8X TO 2X JSY/190-250
*PRIME/25: .6X TO 1.5X JSY/16-77
*PRIME/10: .8X TO 2X JSY/100
PRIME PRINT RUN 10-25

1 Jerry Rice/250	6.00	15.00
2 Roger Craig Shoe/77	8.00	20.00
3 Dan Hampton/250	8.00	20.00
4 Jim McMahon/16	8.00	20.00
5 Walter Payton/200	12.50	30.00
6 John Elway/250	8.00	20.00
7 Dan Fouts/100	5.00	12.00
8 Jan Stenerud/250	6.00	15.00
9 Roger Staubach/250	8.00	20.00
10 Mark Duper/190	4.00	10.00
11 Lawrence Taylor/200	5.00	12.00
12 John Hannah/100	6.00	15.00
13 Tim Brown/250	4.00	10.00
14 Jack Youngblood/250	4.00	10.00
15 John Riggins/250	5.00	12.00

2007 Donruss Threads Century Legends Gold

GOLD STATED ODDS 1:18
*BLUE: .6X TO 1.5X GOLD
BLUE PRINT RUN 100 SER.#'d SETS

1 Brett Favre	2.50	6.00
2 Tom Brady	2.00	5.00
3 Peyton Manning	2.00	5.00
4 LaDainian Tomlinson	1.25	3.00
5 Gale Sayers	2.50	6.00
6 Jim Kelly	2.50	6.00
7 Jim Brown	2.50	6.00
8 Lance Alworth	1.50	4.00
9 Troy Aikman	2.50	6.00
10 Sam Huff	1.50	4.00
11 Warren Moon	2.00	5.00
12 Bo Jackson	2.50	6.00
13 Marcus Allen	2.00	5.00
14 Eric Dickerson	1.50	4.00
15 Fran Tarkenton	2.50	6.00

2007 Donruss Threads Century Legends Materials

STATED PRINT RUN 250 SER.#'d SETS
*PRIME/25: 1X TO 2.5X BASIC INSERTS
*PRIME/10-15: 1.2X TO 3X BASIC INSERTS
PRIME PRINT RUN 6-25

1 Brett Favre	8.00	20.00
2 Tom Brady	6.00	15.00
3 Peyton Manning	6.00	15.00
4 LaDainian Tomlinson	4.00	10.00
5 Gale Sayers	6.00	15.00
6 Jim Kelly	6.00	15.00
7 Jim Brown	6.00	15.00
8 Lance Alworth/175	6.00	15.00
9 Troy Aikman	6.00	15.00
10 Sam Huff	4.00	10.00
11 Warren Moon	5.00	12.00
12 Bo Jackson	6.00	15.00
13 Marcus Allen	5.00	12.00
14 Eric Dickerson	4.00	10.00
15 Fran Tarkenton	6.00	15.00

2007 Donruss Threads Century Stars Gold

GOLD STATED ODDS 1:13
*BLUE: .8X TO 2X BASIC INSERTS
BLUE PRINT RUN 100 SER.#'d SETS

1 Chad Johnson	.75	2.00
2 Brian Westbrook	.75	2.00
3 Tom Brady	1.50	4.00
4 Ben Roethlisberger	1.00	2.50
5 Reggie Wayne	.75	2.00
6 Torry Holt	.75	2.00
7 Steven Jackson	1.00	2.50
8 Eli Manning	1.00	2.50
9 Willie Parker	.75	2.00
10 Matt Hasselbeck	.75	2.00
11 Michael Vick	1.00	2.50
12 Terrell Owens	1.00	2.50
13 Steve Smith	.75	2.00
14 Steve McNair	.75	2.00
15 Shaun Alexander	.75	2.00
16 Peyton Manning	1.50	4.00
17 Marvin Harrison	1.00	2.50
18 Warrick Dunn	.75	2.00
19 Hines Ward	1.00	2.50
20 Donovan McNabb	1.00	2.50

2007 Donruss Threads Century Stars Materials

STATED PRINT RUN 250 SER.#'d SETS
*PRIME/25: .8X TO 2X BASIC JSY/170-250
*PRIME/25: .4X TO 1X BASIC JSY/12-32
PRIME PRINT RUN 25 SER.#'d SETS

1 Chad Johnson	3.00	8.00
2 Brian Westbrook/170	3.00	8.00
3 Tom Brady	6.00	15.00
4 Ben Roethlisberger	4.00	10.00
5 Reggie Wayne	3.00	8.00
6 Torry Holt	3.00	8.00
7 Steven Jackson/12	8.00	20.00
8 Eli Manning	4.00	10.00
9 Willie Parker/32	6.00	15.00
10 Matt Hasselbeck	3.00	8.00
11 Michael Vick	4.00	10.00
12 Terrell Owens	4.00	10.00
13 Steve Smith	3.00	8.00
14 Steve McNair	3.00	8.00
15 Shaun Alexander	3.00	8.00
16 Peyton Manning	6.00	15.00
17 Marvin Harrison	4.00	10.00
18 Warrick Dunn	3.00	8.00
19 Hines Ward	4.00	10.00
20 Donovan McNabb	4.00	10.00

2007 Donruss Threads College Greats

STATED ODDS 1:151

1 Barry Sanders	8.00	20.00
2 Tony Dorsett	5.00	12.00
3 Marcus Allen	5.00	12.00
4 Adrian Peterson	8.00	20.00
5 JaMarcus Russell	1.25	3.00
6 Brady Quinn	2.00	5.00
7 Tim Brown	5.00	12.00
8 Bo Jackson	6.00	15.00
9 Dan Marino	10.00	25.00
10 Mike Singletary	5.00	12.00
11 Roger Staubach	8.00	20.00
12 Lydell Mitchell	3.00	8.00
13 Raymond Berry	4.00	10.00
14 Lance Alworth	4.00	10.00
15 Lenny Moore	4.00	10.00
16 Ronnie Lott	4.00	10.00
17 Jim McMahon	6.00	15.00
18 Fran Tarkenton	6.00	15.00
19 Jack Youngblood	4.00	10.00
20 Kellen Winslow	4.00	10.00

2007 Donruss Threads College Greats Autographs

STATED ODDS 1:958
STATED PRINT RUN 2-500
SERIAL #'d UNDER 15 NOT PRICED
UNPRICED COMBO AUTO PRINT RUN 10

1 Barry Sanders/21	125.00	200.00
2 Tony Dorsett/33	25.00	50.00
3 Marcus Allen/33	30.00	60.00
4 Adrian Peterson/28	100.00	200.00
7 Tim Brown/20	30.00	60.00
8 Bo Jackson/20	75.00	150.00
10 Mike Singletary/20	15.00	40.00
12 Lydell Mitchell/500	5.00	12.00
14 Lance Alworth/15	60.00	120.00
16 Ronnie Lott/20	50.00	100.00
19 Jack Youngblood/20	15.00	40.00
20 Kellen Winslow/20	15.00	40.00

2007 Donruss Threads College Greats Autographs Combos

STATED ODDS 1:958
UNPRICED COMBO PRINT RUN 10

2007 Donruss Threads College Gridiron Kings Gold

GOLD STATED ODDS 1:17
*SLVR HOLO/250: .5X TO 1.2X BASIC INSERTS
SILVER HOLOFOIL PRINT RUN 250 SER.#'d SETS
*FRAMED RED/100: .8X TO 2X BASIC INSERTS
FRAMED RED PRINT RUN 100 SER.#'d SETS
*GOLD HOLO/100: .8X TO 2X BASIC INSERTS
GOLD HOLOFOIL PRINT RUN 100 SER.#'d SETS
*FRAMED BLUE/50: 1X TO 2.5X BASIC INSERTS
FRAMED BLUE PRINT RUN 50 SER.#'d SETS
*FRAMED GREEN/25: 1.2X TO 3X
FRAMED GREEN PRINT RUN 25 SER.#'d SETS
*PLATINUM/25: 1.2X TO 3X BASIC INSERTS
PLATINUM PRINT RUN 25 SER.#'d SETS
*FRAMED BLACK/10: 2X TO 5X BASIC INSERTS
FRAMED BLACK PRINT RUN 10 SER.#'d SETS

1 Vince Young	.75	2.00
2 Dan Marino	3.00	8.00
3 Tony Dorsett	1.50	4.00
4 Frank Gore	1.00	2.50
5 Kenny Irons	.50	1.25
6 Robert Meachem	.75	2.00
7 Courtney Taylor	.60	1.50
8 Jayson Swain	.60	1.50
9 Dwayne Jarrett	.60	1.50
10 Steve Smith USC	.75	2.00
11 Adrian Peterson	3.00	8.00
12 Brandon Meriweather	.75	2.00
13 Greg Olsen	.60	1.50
14 Brady Quinn	.75	2.00
15 Jon Beason	.60	1.50
16 JaMarcus Russell	.50	1.25
17 Dwayne Bowe	1.00	2.50
18 Craig Buster Davis	.60	1.50
19 LaRon Landry	.75	2.00
20 Devery Henderson	.60	1.50
21 Zach Miller	.75	2.00
22 Jordan Palmer	.60	1.50
23 Johnnie Lee Higgins	.60	1.50
24 Cadillac Williams	.75	2.00
25 Ronnie Brown	.75	2.00
26 Jay Cutler	1.00	2.50
27 LenDale White	.75	2.00
28 Joseph Addai	.75	2.00
29 Mario Williams	.75	2.00
30 Mike Hass	.60	1.50
31 A.J. Hawk	.75	2.00
32 Demetrius Williams	.60	1.50
33 Marcedes Lewis	.60	1.50
34 Laurence Maroney	.75	2.00
35 Maurice Jones-Drew	1.00	2.50
36 Maurice Stovall	.60	1.50
37 Travis Wilson	.60	1.50
38 Peyton Manning	1.50	4.00
39 Larry Fitzgerald	1.00	2.50
40 Sinorice Moss	.75	2.00

2007 Donruss Threads College Gridiron Kings Autographs

STATED PRINT RUN 3-25

22 Jordan Palmer/25	15.00	30.00
23 Johnnie Lee Higgins/21	12.50	25.00
32 Demetrius Williams/25	10.00	25.00

2007 Donruss Threads College Gridiron Kings Materials

STATED PRINT RUN 25-250
*PRIME/25: .8X TO 2X BASIC JSY/175-250
*PRIME/25: .5X TO 1.2X BASIC JSY/25
*PRIME/10: 1X TO 2.5X BASIC JSY/175-250
PRIME PRINT RUN 5-25

1 Vince Young/100	4.00	10.00
2 Dan Marino	10.00	25.00
3 Tony Dorsett/25	8.00	20.00
4 Frank Gore	4.00	10.00
5 Kenny Irons	2.50	6.00
6 Robert Meachem	4.00	10.00
7 Courtney Taylor	3.00	8.00
8 Jayson Swain	3.00	8.00
9 Dwayne Jarrett/100	4.00	10.00
10 Steve Smith USC/100	5.00	12.00
11 Adrian Peterson	15.00	40.00
12 Brandon Meriweather	4.00	10.00
13 Greg Olsen	3.00	8.00
14 Brady Quinn	4.00	10.00
15 Jon Beason	3.00	8.00
16 JaMarcus Russell/100	3.00	8.00
17 Dwayne Bowe/100	6.00	15.00
18 Craig Buster Davis/100	4.00	10.00
19 LaRon Landry/100	5.00	12.00
20 Devery Henderson	2.50	6.00
21 Zach Miller	4.00	10.00
22 Jordan Palmer	3.00	8.00
23 Johnnie Lee Higgins	3.00	8.00
24 Cadillac Williams/175	3.00	8.00
25 Ronnie Brown	3.00	8.00
26 Jay Cutler	4.00	10.00
27 LenDale White/100	4.00	10.00
28 Joseph Addai/75	4.00	10.00
29 Mario Williams	3.00	8.00
30 Mike Hass	2.50	6.00
31 A.J. Hawk	3.00	8.00
32 Demetrius Williams/75	3.00	8.00
33 Marcedes Lewis	2.50	6.00
34 Laurence Maroney/200	3.00	8.00
35 Maurice Jones-Drew	4.00	10.00
36 Maurice Stovall	2.50	6.00
37 Travis Wilson	2.50	6.00
38 Peyton Manning	10.00	25.00
39 Larry Fitzgerald	4.00	10.00
40 Sinorice Moss	3.00	8.00

2007 Donruss Threads College Gridiron Kings Material Autographs

STATED PRINT RUN 12-25
UNPRICED PRIME PRINT RUN 5-10
SERIAL #'d UNDER 25 NOT PRICED

1 Vince Young	20.00	50.00
2 Dan Marino	150.00	250.00
3 Tony Dorsett	30.00	60.00
4 Frank Gore	15.00	40.00
6 Robert Meachem	15.00	40.00
7 Courtney Taylor	12.00	30.00
9 Dwayne Jarrett	12.00	30.00
10 Steve Smith USC	15.00	40.00
11 Adrian Peterson	175.00	350.00
12 Brandon Meriweather	15.00	40.00
13 Greg Olsen	30.00	60.00
14 Brady Quinn	40.00	100.00
15 Jon Beason	12.00	30.00
16 JaMarcus Russell	10.00	25.00
17 Dwayne Bowe	40.00	80.00
19 LaRon Landry	15.00	40.00
20 Devery Henderson	10.00	25.00
21 Zach Miller	15.00	40.00
22 Jordan Palmer	12.00	30.00
23 Johnnie Lee Higgins	12.00	30.00
24 Cadillac Williams	12.00	30.00
25 Ronnie Brown	12.00	30.00
31 A.J. Hawk	12.00	30.00
32 Demetrius Williams	10.00	25.00
35 Maurice Jones-Drew	15.00	40.00
38 Peyton Manning	125.00	200.00
39 Larry Fitzgerald	25.00	50.00

2007 Donruss Threads Dynasty Gold

GOLD STATED ODDS 1:31
*BLUE: .8X TO 2X BASIC INSERTS
BLUE PRINT RUN 100 SER.#'d SETS

1 Carson Palmer	1.50	4.00
Chad Johnson		
T.J. Houshmandzadeh		
2 Tony Romo	2.50	6.00
Terrell Owens		
Terry Glenn		
3 Peyton Manning	3.00	8.00
Marvin Harrison		
Reggie Wayne		
4 Byron Leftwich	2.00	5.00
Fred Taylor		
Maurice Jones-Drew		
5 Trent Green	1.50	4.00
Larry Johnson		
Tony Gonzalez		
6 Tom Brady	3.00	8.00
Laurence Maroney		
Troy Brown		
7 Drew Brees	2.00	5.00
Deuce McAllister		
Reggie Bush		
8 Eli Manning	2.00	5.00
Jeremy Shockey		
Plaxico Burress		
9 Philip Rivers	2.00	5.00
LaDainian Tomlinson		
Antonio Gates		
10 Alex Smith QB	2.00	5.00
Frank Gore		
Vernon Davis		

2007 Donruss Threads Dynasty Materials

STATED PRINT RUN 250 SER.#'d SETS
*PRIME: .8X TO 2X BASIC INSERTS
PRIME PRINT RUN 25 SER.#'d SETS

1 Carson Palmer	6.00	15.00
Chad Johnson		
T.J. Houshmandzadeh		
2 Tony Romo	15.00	40.00
Terrell Owens		
Terry Glenn		
3 Peyton Manning	12.00	30.00
Marvin Harrison		
Reggie Wayne		
4 Byron Leftwich	6.00	15.00
Fred Taylor		
Maurice Jones-Drew		
5 Trent Green	6.00	15.00
Larry Johnson		
Tony Gonzalez		
6 Tom Brady	8.00	20.00
Laurence Maroney		
Troy Brown		
7 Drew Brees	12.50	30.00
Deuce McAllister		
Reggie Bush		
8 Eli Manning	8.00	20.00
Jeremy Shockey		
Plaxico Burress		
9 Philip Rivers	8.00	20.00
LaDainian Tomlinson		
Antonio Gates		
10 Alex Smith QB	8.00	20.00
Frank Gore		
Vernon Davis		

2007 Donruss Threads Footballs

RANDOM INSERTS IN RETAIL PACKS
STATED PRINT RUN 10-250
SERIAL #'d UNDER 40 NOT PRICED

1 Anquan Boldin	3.00	8.00
2 Larry Fitzgerald	4.00	10.00
3 Alge Crumpler	3.00	8.00
4 Michael Vick/40	6.00	15.00
5 Steve McNair	3.00	8.00
7 Keyshawn Johnson	3.00	8.00
8 Steve Smith	3.00	8.00
9 Brian Urlacher	4.00	10.00
10 Muhsin Muhammad	3.00	8.00
11 Chad Johnson	3.00	8.00
12 Rudi Johnson	3.00	8.00
13 T.J. Houshmandzadeh	3.00	8.00
14 Terry Glenn	3.00	8.00
15 Terrell Owens	4.00	10.00
16 Jon Kitna	2.50	6.00
18 Peyton Manning/55	10.00	25.00
19 Fred Taylor/125	4.00	10.00
20 Eddie Kennison	2.50	6.00
21 Larry Johnson/200	2.50	6.00
22 Tony Gonzalez	3.00	8.00
23 Trent Green	3.00	8.00
24 Chris Chambers	3.00	8.00
25 Marty Booker	2.50	6.00
26 Tom Brady	6.00	15.00
27 Donte Stallworth	3.00	8.00
28 Deuce McAllister	3.00	8.00
29 Drew Brees/65	6.00	15.00
30 Reuben Droughns	3.00	8.00
31 Jeremy Shockey	3.00	8.00
32 Plaxico Burress/75	5.00	12.00
33 Chad Pennington	3.00	8.00
34 Jerricho Cotchery	3.00	8.00
35 Laveranues Coles	2.50	6.00
36 LaMont Jordan	3.00	8.00
37 Brian Westbrook	3.00	8.00
38 Donovan McNabb	4.00	10.00
39 Hines Ward	4.00	10.00
40 Antonio Gates	4.00	10.00
41 LaDainian Tomlinson	4.00	10.00
42 Arnaz Battle	2.50	6.00
43 Darrell Jackson	2.50	6.00
44 Deion Branch	3.00	8.00
45 Matt Hasselbeck	3.00	8.00
46 Jerramy Stevens	2.50	6.00
47 Shaun Alexander	3.00	8.00
48 Isaac Bruce	3.00	8.00
49 Marc Bulger	3.00	8.00
50 Drew Bennett	2.50	6.00
51 Torry Holt	3.00	8.00
52 Joey Galloway	3.00	8.00
53 Mike Alstott	3.00	8.00
54 Travis Henry	3.00	8.00
55 Clinton Portis	3.00	8.00
56 Santana Moss	3.00	8.00

2007 Donruss Threads Generations Gold

GOLD STATED ODDS 1:18
*BLUE: .8X TO 2X BASIC INSERTS
BLUE PRINT RUN 100 SER.#'d SETS

1 Dan Marino	3.00	8.00
Drew Brees		
2 Deion Sanders	2.00	5.00
Devin Hester		
3 Barry Sanders	2.50	6.00
LaDainian Tomlinson		
4 Randall Cunningham	1.25	3.00
Vince Young		
5 Michael Irvin	1.50	4.00
Marvin Harrison		
6 Troy Aikman	3.00	8.00
Tony Romo		
7 Kellen Winslow	1.25	3.00
Jeremy Shockey		
8 Joe Montana	3.00	8.00
Peyton Manning		
9 Eric Dickerson	1.25	3.00
Joseph Addai		
10 Tony Dorsett	1.50	4.00
Julius Jones		
11 Mike Singletary	1.50	4.00
Shawne Merriman		
12 Shaun Alexander	1.50	4.00
Maurice Jones-Drew		
13 Steve Largent	1.50	4.00
Darrell Jackson		
14 Eli Manning	1.50	4.00
Philip Rivers		
15 Ronnie Lott	1.50	4.00
Troy Polamalu		

2007 Donruss Threads Generations Materials

STATED PRINT RUN 250 SER.#'d SETS
*PRIME/25: .8X TO 2X BASIC INSERTS
PRIME PRINT RUN 25 SER.#'d SETS

1 Dan Marino	10.00	25.00
Drew Brees		
2 Deion Sanders	8.00	20.00
Devin Hester		
3 Barry Sanders	10.00	25.00
LaDainian Tomlinson		
4 Randall Cunningham	8.00	20.00
Vince Young		
5 Michael Irvin	6.00	15.00
Marvin Harrison		
6 Troy Aikman	12.00	30.00
Tony Romo		
7 Kellen Winslow	5.00	12.00
Jeremy Shockey		
8 Joe Montana	12.00	30.00
Peyton Manning		
9 Eric Dickerson	6.00	15.00
Joseph Addai		
10 Tony Dorsett	6.00	15.00
Julius Jones		
11 Mike Singletary	6.00	15.00
Shawne Merriman		
12 Shaun Alexander	6.00	15.00
Maurice Jones-Drew		
13 Steve Largent	5.00	12.00
Darrell Jackson		
14 Eli Manning	6.00	15.00
Philip Rivers		
15 Ronnie Lott	6.00	15.00
Troy Polamalu		

2007 Donruss Threads Jerseys

STATED PRINT RUN 50-250
*PRIME/25: .8X TO 2X BASIC JSY/200-250
*PRIME/25: .6X TO 1.5X BASIC JSY/100-125
*PRIME/25: .5X TO 1.2X BASIC JSY/50
*PRIME/10: 1X TO 2.5X BASIC JSY/250
*PRIME/9: .8X TO 2X BASIC JSY/100
PRIME PRINT RUN 5-25

1 Anquan Boldin	3.00	8.00
2 Larry Fitzgerald	4.00	10.00
3 Alge Crumpler/100	4.00	10.00
4 Michael Vick	4.00	10.00
5 Steve McNair	3.00	8.00
6 Ray Lewis	4.00	10.00
7 Keyshawn Johnson	3.00	8.00
8 Steve Smith	3.00	8.00
9 Brian Urlacher	4.00	10.00
10 Muhsin Muhammad	3.00	8.00
11 Chad Johnson	3.00	8.00
12 Rudi Johnson	3.00	8.00
14 Terry Glenn	3.00	8.00
15 Terrell Owens	4.00	10.00
16 Jon Kitna	2.50	6.00
17 Brett Favre	8.00	20.00
18 Peyton Manning/100	8.00	20.00
20 Eddie Kennison	2.50	6.00
21 Larry Johnson	2.50	6.00
22 Tony Gonzalez	3.00	8.00
23 Trent Green	3.00	8.00
24 Chris Chambers	3.00	8.00
26 Tom Brady	6.00	15.00
27 Donte Stallworth/125	4.00	10.00
28 Deuce McAllister	3.00	8.00
29 Drew Brees/100	5.00	12.00
30 Reuben Droughns	3.00	8.00
31 Jeremy Shockey	3.00	8.00
32 Plaxico Burress/115	4.00	10.00
33 Chad Pennington	3.00	8.00
34 Jerricho Cotchery/100	4.00	10.00
35 Laveranues Coles	2.50	6.00
36 LaMont Jordan	3.00	8.00
38 Donovan McNabb	4.00	10.00
39 Hines Ward/200	4.00	10.00
40 Antonio Gates	4.00	10.00
41 LaDainian Tomlinson	4.00	10.00
43 Darrell Jackson	2.50	6.00
44 Deion Branch	3.00	8.00
45 Matt Hasselbeck	3.00	8.00
47 Shaun Alexander	3.00	8.00
48 Isaac Bruce	3.00	8.00
49 Marc Bulger	3.00	8.00
50 Drew Bennett/120	3.00	8.00
51 Torry Holt	3.00	8.00
52 Joey Galloway	3.00	8.00
53 Mike Alstott	3.00	8.00
54 Travis Henry	3.00	8.00
55 Clinton Portis	3.00	8.00
56 Santana Moss	3.00	8.00
57 Edgerrin James	3.00	8.00
58 Matt Leinart	3.00	8.00
59 Jerious Norwood	3.00	8.00
60 Warrick Dunn	3.00	8.00
61 Mark Clayton	3.00	8.00
62 J.P. Losman	2.50	6.00
63 Josh Reed	2.50	6.00
64 Lee Evans	3.00	8.00
65 DeAngelo Williams	4.00	10.00
66 DeShaun Foster	3.00	8.00
67 Jake Delhomme	3.00	8.00
68 Bernard Berrian	2.50	6.00
69 Cedric Benson	3.00	8.00
70 Rex Grossman	3.00	8.00
71 Carson Palmer	3.00	8.00
72 Braylon Edwards	3.00	8.00
74 Charlie Frye	3.00	8.00
75 Julius Jones	2.50	6.00
76 Marion Barber	4.00	10.00
77 Javon Walker	3.00	8.00
78 Jay Cutler	4.00	10.00
79 Mike Bell	3.00	8.00
80 Donald Driver	4.00	10.00
82 Andre Johnson	3.00	8.00
85 Joseph Addai	3.00	8.00
86 Marvin Harrison	4.00	10.00
87 Kevin Jones	2.50	6.00
88 Roy Williams WR	3.00	8.00
90 A.J. Hawk	3.00	8.00
91 Reggie Wayne/50	5.00	12.00
92 Dallas Clark	2.50	6.00
93 Byron Leftwich	3.00	8.00
95 Reggie Williams/245	3.00	8.00
96 Tony Romo	5.00	12.00
97 Daunte Culpepper	3.00	8.00
98 Ronnie Brown	3.00	8.00
99 Chester Taylor	2.50	6.00
101 Ben Watson/100	3.00	8.00
102 Laurence Maroney	3.00	8.00
104 Peerless Price	2.50	6.00
105 Marques Colston/100	5.00	12.00
107 Brandon Jacobs	3.00	8.00
108 Eli Manning	4.00	10.00
109 Leon Washington	3.00	8.00
110 Kevan Barlow	3.00	8.00
111 Randy Moss	4.00	10.00
112 Troy Polamalu	4.00	10.00
114 Santonio Holmes/125	4.00	10.00
115 Philip Rivers	4.00	10.00
116 Shawne Merriman	3.00	8.00
117 Alex Smith QB	4.00	10.00
118 Frank Gore	4.00	10.00
119 Vernon Davis	3.00	8.00
120 Reggie Brown	2.50	6.00
121 Ben Roethlisberger	4.00	10.00
123 Bruce Gradkowski	2.50	6.00
124 Cadillac Williams	3.00	8.00
126 Michael Jenkins	3.00	8.00
127 Demetrius Williams	2.50	6.00
128 Roy Williams S	3.00	8.00
130 Hank Baskett	3.00	8.00
132 Brandon Marshall	3.00	8.00
135 Joe Klopfenstein	2.50	6.00
137 Todd Heap	2.50	6.00
139 Troy Williamson	2.50	6.00
141 Ahman Green	3.00	8.00
142 LenDale White	3.00	8.00
143 Vince Young	3.00	8.00
145 Jamal Lewis	3.00	8.00
146 Joe Horn	3.00	8.00
147 Tatum Bell	2.50	6.00
148 Willis McGahee	3.00	8.00
149 Jason Campbell	3.00	8.00

2007 Donruss Threads Pro Gridiron Kings Gold

GOLD STATED ODDS 1:11
*SILVER HOLO/250: .5X TO 1.2X
SILVER HOLOFOIL PRINT RUN 250 SER.#'d SETS
*FRAMED RED: .8X TO 2X BASIC INSERTS
FRAMED RED PRINT RUN 100 SER.#'d SETS
*GOLD HOLO/100: .8X TO 2X BASIC INSERTS
GOLD HOLOFOIL PRINT RUN 100 SER.#'d SETS
*FRAMED BLUE/50: 1X TO 2.5X
FRAMED BLUE PRINT RUN 50 SER.#'d SETS
*FRAMED GREEN/25: 1.2X TO 3X
FRAMED GREEN PRINT RUN 25 SER.#'d SETS
*PLATINUM/25: 1.2X TO 3X BASIC INSERTS
PLATINUM PRINT RUN 25 SER.#'d SETS
*FRAMED BLACK: 2X TO 5X BASIC INSERTS
FRAMED BLACK PRINT RUN 10 SER.#'d SETS

1 Andre Johnson	.75	2.00
2 Bernard Berrian	.60	1.50
3 Brandon Jacobs	.75	2.00
4 Brandon Marshall	.75	2.00
5 Brian Urlacher	1.00	2.50
6 Cedric Benson	.75	2.00
7 Chester Taylor	.60	1.50
8 Chris Henry WR	.60	1.50
9 Corey Dillon	.75	2.00
10 Curtis Martin	1.00	2.50
11 DeAngelo Williams	1.00	2.50
12 DeMeco Ryans	.75	2.00
13 Demetrius Williams	.60	1.50
14 Devery Henderson	.60	1.50
15 Devin Hester	1.00	2.50
16 Donald Driver	1.00	2.50
17 Donovan McNabb	1.00	2.50
18 Drew Brees	1.00	2.50
19 Eli Manning	1.00	2.50
20 Fred Taylor	.75	2.00
21 Greg Jennings	1.00	2.50
22 Hank Baskett	.75	2.00
23 Jerricho Cotchery	.75	2.00
24 LaMont Jordan	.75	2.00
25 Larry Johnson	.60	1.50
26 LenDale White	.75	2.00
27 Leon Washington	.75	2.00
28 Marion Barber	1.00	2.50
29 Matt Leinart	.75	2.00
30 Michael Turner	1.00	2.50
31 Mike Furrey	.75	2.00
32 Mike Bell	.75	2.00
33 Patrick Crayton	.60	1.50
34 Reggie Bush	1.00	2.50
35 Rex Grossman	.75	2.00
36 Ronnie Brown	.75	2.00
37 Santonio Holmes	.75	2.00
38 Shawne Merriman	.75	2.00
39 Steve Smith	.75	2.00
40 Thomas Jones	.75	2.00
41 T.J. Houshmandzadeh	.75	2.00
42 Tony Romo	1.25	3.00
43 Tony Scheffler	.75	2.00
44 Vernon Davis	.75	2.00
45 Vince Young	.75	2.00
46 Vincent Jackson	.75	2.00
47 Willie Parker	.75	2.00
48 Willis McGahee	.75	2.00
49 Cliff Harris	1.00	2.50
50 Larry Little	1.00	2.50
51 Rick Casares	1.00	2.50
52 Billy Howton	1.00	2.50
53 Boyd Dowler	1.00	2.50
54 Jim Brown	2.00	5.00
55 Don Perkins	1.00	2.50
56 Harlon Hill	1.00	2.50
57 Jethro Pugh	1.00	2.50
58 Jimmy Orr	1.00	2.50
59 Johnny Morris	1.00	2.50
60 Rosey Grier	1.00	2.50

2007 Donruss Threads Pro Gridiron Kings Autographs

STATED PRINT RUN 25-500 SER.#'d SETS

12 DeMeco Ryans/100	5.00	12.00
14 Devery Henderson/25	8.00	20.00
33 Patrick Crayton/25	10.00	25.00
46 Vincent Jackson/25	8.00	20.00
49 Cliff Harris/25	15.00	40.00
51 Rick Casares/25	15.00	40.00
52 Billy Howton/500	6.00	15.00
53 Boyd Dowler/500	8.00	20.00
56 Harlon Hill/500	6.00	15.00
57 Jethro Pugh/25	10.00	25.00
60 Rosey Grier/25	10.00	25.00

2007 Donruss Threads Pro Gridiron Kings Materials

STATED PRINT RUN 250 SER.#'d SETS
*PRIME/10-25: .8X TO 2X BASIC JSY
PRIME PRINT RUN 10-25

1 Andre Johnson	3.00	8.00
2 Bernard Berrian	2.50	6.00
3 Brandon Jacobs	3.00	8.00
4 Brandon Marshall	3.00	8.00
5 Brian Urlacher	4.00	10.00
6 Cedric Benson	3.00	8.00
7 Chester Taylor	2.50	6.00
8 Chris Henry WR	2.50	6.00
9 Corey Dillon	3.00	8.00
10 Curtis Martin	4.00	10.00
11 DeAngelo Williams	4.00	10.00
13 Demetrius Williams	2.50	6.00
15 Devin Hester	4.00	10.00
16 Donald Driver	4.00	10.00
17 Donovan McNabb	4.00	10.00
18 Drew Brees/50	6.00	15.00
19 Eli Manning	4.00	10.00
20 Fred Taylor/165	3.00	8.00
22 Hank Baskett	3.00	8.00
23 Jerricho Cotchery	3.00	8.00
24 LaMont Jordan	3.00	8.00
25 Larry Johnson	2.50	6.00
26 LenDale White	3.00	8.00
27 Leon Washington	3.00	8.00
28 Marion Barber	4.00	10.00
29 Matt Leinart	3.00	8.00
32 Mike Bell	3.00	8.00
34 Reggie Bush/100	4.00	10.00
35 Rex Grossman	3.00	8.00
36 Ronnie Brown	3.00	8.00
37 Santonio Holmes/200	3.00	8.00
38 Shawne Merriman	3.00	8.00
39 Steve Smith	3.00	8.00
40 Thomas Jones	3.00	8.00
41 T.J. Houshmandzadeh/150	3.00	8.00
42 Tony Romo	5.00	12.00
44 Vernon Davis	3.00	8.00
45 Vince Young	3.00	8.00
47 Willie Parker	3.00	8.00
48 Willis McGahee	3.00	8.00
50 Larry Little	3.00	8.00
54 Jim Brown	6.00	15.00

2007 Donruss Threads Pro Gridiron Kings Material Autographs

STATED PRINT RUN 25 SER.#'d SETS
UNPRICED PRIME PRINT RUN 2-10

1 Andre Johnson	15.00	40.00
2 Bernard Berrian	12.00	30.00
3 Brandon Jacobs	15.00	40.00
4 Brandon Marshall	15.00	40.00
6 Cedric Benson	15.00	40.00
7 Chester Taylor	12.00	30.00
10 Curtis Martin	30.00	60.00
11 DeAngelo Williams	20.00	50.00
13 Demetrius Williams	12.00	30.00
16 Donald Driver	30.00	60.00
18 Drew Brees	50.00	100.00
20 Fred Taylor	15.00	40.00
22 Hank Baskett	15.00	40.00
23 Jerricho Cotchery	15.00	40.00
25 Larry Johnson	12.00	30.00
28 Marion Barber	15.00	40.00
34 Reggie Bush	30.00	80.00
35 Rex Grossman	15.00	40.00
36 Ronnie Brown	15.00	40.00
37 Santonio Holmes	15.00	40.00
39 Steve Smith	15.00	40.00
42 Tony Romo	75.00	150.00
44 Vernon Davis	15.00	40.00
48 Willis McGahee	15.00	40.00
50 Larry Little	30.00	60.00

2007 Donruss Threads Rookie Autographs

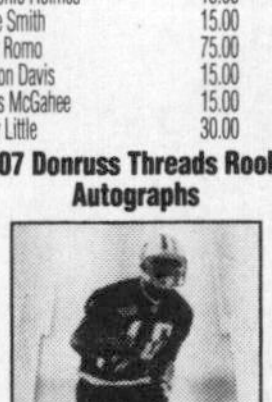

STATED PRINT RUN 100-250

160 Courtney Taylor/200	5.00	12.00
161 David Irons/250	4.00	10.00
162 Joel Filani/200	6.00	15.00
163 H.B. Blades/250	5.00	12.00
164 Rufus Alexander/250	6.00	15.00
166 Eric Frampton/250	5.00	12.00
167 Tim Shaw/250	5.00	12.00
168 Tymere Zimmerman/250	5.00	12.00
169 Jeff Rowe/100	8.00	20.00
170 Josh Gattis/250	4.00	10.00
171 Brandon Myles/250	5.00	12.00
172 Earl Everett/200	5.00	12.00
173 Steve Breaston/200	5.00	12.00
174 Ryan McBean/250	6.00	15.00
175 Scott Chandler/200	6.00	15.00
176 Chris Davis/100	8.00	20.00
177 Fred Bennett/250	4.00	10.00
178 Ryne Robinson/250	5.00	12.00
179 Zak DeOssie/250	5.00	12.00
180 Dwayne Wright/250	4.00	10.00
181 A.J. Davis/250	4.00	10.00
182 Ray McDonald/200	5.00	12.00
183 Daymeion Hughes/250	4.00	10.00
184 Michael Okwo/250	5.00	12.00
185 Aaron Rouse/250	5.00	12.00
186 Stewart Bradley/250	6.00	15.00
187 Jonathan Wade/250	5.00	12.00
190 Mike Walker/250	5.00	12.00
191 James Jones/100	15.00	40.00
192 Matt Spaeth/100	10.00	25.00
193 Laurent Robinson/200	8.00	20.00
194 Jacoby Jones/100	25.00	50.00
195 Marcus McCauley/250	4.00	10.00
196 Buster Davis/250	5.00	12.00
197 Quentin Moses/250	5.00	12.00
198 Sabby Piscitelli/250	6.00	15.00
199 Dan Bazuin/250	6.00	15.00
200 Ikaika Alama-Francis/250	8.00	20.00
201 Victor Abiamiri/200	6.00	15.00
202 Tim Crowder/250	5.00	12.00
203 Josh Wilson/200	5.00	12.00
204 Eric Wright/250	4.00	10.00
205 David Harris/250	5.00	12.00
206 LaMarr Woodley/200	8.00	20.00
207 Chris Houston/200	4.00	10.00
208 Zach Miller/100	8.00	20.00
209 Aaron Fairooz/250	5.00	12.00
211 Anthony Spencer/200	10.00	25.00
212 Jon Beason/100	8.00	20.00
213 Brandon Meriweather/200	6.00	15.00
214 Reggie Nelson/100	10.00	25.00
215 Aaron Ross/200	6.00	15.00
216 Michael Griffin/200	6.00	15.00
217 Ronnie McGill/250	5.00	12.00
219 Darrelle Revis/100	15.00	40.00
220 Lawrence Timmons/100	12.00	30.00
221 Adam Carriker/100	12.00	30.00
222 Amobi Okoye/100	10.00	25.00
223 Jamaal Anderson/100	10.00	25.00
224 Syvelle Newton/250	6.00	15.00
225 Levi Brown/250	6.00	15.00

2007 Donruss Threads Rookie Collection Materials

STATED PRINT RUN 500 SER.#'d SETS
*PRIME: .8X TO 2X BASIC INSERTS
PRIME PRINT RUN 25 SER.#'d SETS

1 Trent Edwards	2.50	6.00
2 Marshawn Lynch	2.50	6.00
3 Chris Henry RB	4.00	10.00
4 Paul Williams	3.00	8.00
5 Sidney Rice	6.00	15.00
6 Adrian Peterson	10.00	25.00
7 Drew Stanton	4.00	10.00
8 Calvin Johnson	8.00	20.00
9 Yamon Figurs	3.00	8.00
10 Troy Smith	4.00	10.00
11 Brian Leonard	4.00	10.00
12 Greg Olsen	2.00	5.00
13 Garrett Wolfe	3.00	8.00
14 Kenny Irons	3.00	8.00
15 Joe Thomas	3.00	8.00
16 Brady Quinn	2.50	6.00
17 Brandon Jackson	4.00	10.00
18 Steve Smith USC	2.50	6.00
19 Dwayne Jarrett	4.00	10.00
20 Ted Ginn Jr	2.00	5.00
21 John Beck	4.00	10.00
22 Lorenzo Booker	3.00	8.00
23 Antonio Pittman	3.00	8.00
24 Robert Meachem	4.00	10.00
25 Dwayne Bowe	4.00	10.00
26 Anthony Gonzalez	2.50	6.00
27 JaMarcus Russell	1.50	4.00
28 Michael Bush	4.00	10.00
29 Johnnie Lee Higgins	3.00	8.00
30 Kevin Kolb	4.00	10.00
31 Tony Hunt	4.00	10.00
32 Patrick Willis	4.00	10.00
33 Jason Hill	3.00	8.00
34 Gaines Adams	4.00	10.00

2007 Donruss Threads Rookie Collection Material Autographs

STATED PRINT RUN 25 SER.#'d SETS
UNPRICED PRIME PRINT RUN 10

1 Trent Edwards	20.00	50.00
2 Marshawn Lynch	40.00	80.00
3 Chris Henry RB	12.00	30.00
4 Paul Williams	12.00	30.00
5 Sidney Rice	25.00	60.00
6 Adrian Peterson	175.00	350.00
7 Drew Stanton	12.00	30.00
8 Calvin Johnson	60.00	150.00
9 Yamon Figurs	12.00	30.00
10 Troy Smith	20.00	50.00
11 Brian Leonard	15.00	40.00
12 Greg Olsen	15.00	40.00
13 Garrett Wolfe	12.00	30.00
14 Kenny Irons	12.00	30.00
15 Joe Thomas		
16 Brady Quinn	50.00	120.00
17 Brandon Jackson	15.00	40.00
18 Steve Smith USC	20.00	50.00
19 Dwayne Jarrett	15.00	40.00
20 Ted Ginn Jr.	15.00	40.00
21 John Beck	20.00	50.00
22 Lorenzo Booker	15.00	40.00
23 Antonio Pittman	12.00	30.00
24 Robert Meachem	20.00	50.00
25 Dwayne Bowe	25.00	60.00
26 Anthony Gonzalez	20.00	50.00
27 JaMarcus Russell	20.00	50.00
28 Michael Bush	20.00	50.00
29 Johnnie Lee Higgins	15.00	40.00
30 Kevin Kolb	30.00	80.00
31 Tony Hunt	12.00	30.00
32 Patrick Willis	40.00	80.00
33 Jason Hill	20.00	50.00
34 Gaines Adams	20.00	50.00

2007 Donruss Threads Rookie Collection Materials Combo

STATED PRINT RUN 500 SER.#'d SETS
*PRIME/25: .8X TO 2X BASIC COMBO
PRIME PRINT RUN 25 SER.#'d SETS

1 Trent Edwards	3.00	8.00
Marshawn Lynch		
2 Chris Henry RB	4.00	10.00
Paul Williams		
3 Sidney Rice	12.00	30.00
Adrian Peterson		
4 Drew Stanton	10.00	25.00
Calvin Johnson		
5 Robert Meachem	5.00	12.00
Antonio Pittman		
6 JaMarcus Russell	3.00	8.00
Michael Bush		
7 Kevin Kolb	5.00	12.00
Tony Hunt		
8 Brady Quinn	3.00	8.00
Joe Thomas		
9 John Beck	3.00	8.00
Ted Ginn Jr.		
10 Troy Smith	3.00	8.00
Yamon Figurs		
11 Greg Olsen	2.50	6.00
Garrett Wolfe		
12 Patrick Willis	5.00	12.00
Jason Hill		
13 Dwayne Bowe	6.00	15.00
Anthony Gonzalez		
14 Steve Smith USC	3.00	8.00
Dwayne Jarrett		
15 Brandon Jackson	5.00	12.00
Kenny Irons		

2007 Donruss Threads Rookie Collection Materials Triple

STATED PRINT RUN 500 SER.#'d SETS
*PRIME/25: .8X TO 2X BASIC INSERTS
PRIME PRINT RUN 25 SER.#'d SETS

1 Adrian Peterson	15.00	40.00
Marshawn Lynch		
Michael Bush		
2 Brady Quinn	8.00	20.00
Drew Stanton		
JaMarcus Russell		
3 Calvin Johnson	10.00	25.00
Dwayne Bowe		
Anthony Gonzalez		
4 Robert Meachem	6.00	15.00
Steve Smith USC		
Dwayne Jarrett		

2007 Donruss Threads Rookie Collection Materials Quad

STATED PRINT RUN 100 SER.#'d SETS
*PRIME/25: .8X TO 2X BASIC QUAD
PRIME PRINT RUN 25 SER.#'d SETS

1 JaMarcus Russell	15.00	40.00
Calvin Johnson		
Anthony Gonzalez		
Dwayne Jarrett		
2 Adrian Peterson	25.00	60.00
Ted Ginn Jr.		
Patrick Willis		
Marshawn Lynch		
3 Brady Quinn	10.00	25.00
Dwayne Bowe		
Robert Meachem		
Greg Olsen		

2008 Donruss Threads

COMP.SET w/o RC's (150)	10.00	25.00

UNSIGNED ROOKIE PRINT RUN 999
251-300 AU ROOKIE PRINT RUN 100-999

1 Anquan Boldin	.25	.60
2 Larry Fitzgerald	.30	.75
3 Warrick Dunn	.25	.60
4 Derrick Mason	.25	.60
5 Steve Smith	.25	.60
6 Brian Urlacher	.30	.75
7 Chad Johnson	.25	.60
8 Terrell Owens	.30	.75
9 Tony Gonzalez	.25	.60
10 Rex Grossman	.25	.60
11 Torry Holt	.25	.60
12 Isaac Bruce	.25	.60
13 Jeff Garcia	.25	.60
14 Santana Moss	.20	.50
15 LaDainian Tomlinson	.30	.75
16 Matt Hasselbeck	.25	.60
17 Julius Jones	.20	.50
18 Earnest Graham	.20	.50
19 Joey Galloway	.25	.60
20 Ike Hilliard	.20	.50
21 Vince Young	.25	.60
22 Jason Taylor	.25	.60
23 Tom Brady	.50	1.25
24 Randy Moss	.30	.75
25 Donte Stallworth	.20	.50
26 Deuce McAllister	.25	.60
27 Eli Manning	.30	.75
28 Michael Strahan	.25	.60
29 Thomas Jones	.25	.60
30 Laveranues Coles	.20	.50
31 Jerry Porter	.20	.50
32 Correll Buckhalter	.25	.60
33 Donovan McNabb	.30	.75
34 Hines Ward	.25	.60
35 Tony Scheffler	.20	.50
36 Jason Witten	.30	.75
37 DeMarcus Ware	.25	.60
38 Jay Cutler	.30	.75
39 Brandon Marshall	.25	.60
40 Brandon Stokley	.25	.60
41 Selvin Young	.20	.50
42 Jon Kitna	.25	.60
43 Roy Williams WR	.25	.60
44 Shaun McDonald	.20	.50
45 Calvin Johnson	.30	.75
46 Aaron Rodgers	.60	1.50
47 Ryan Grant	.30	.75
48 Donald Driver	.25	.60
49 Greg Jennings	.30	.75
50 James Jones	.20	.50
51 Matt Schaub	.25	.60
52 Owen Daniels	.20	.50
53 Andre Johnson	.25	.60
54 Kevin Walter	.25	.60
55 Ahman Green	.25	.60
56 Peyton Manning	.50	1.25
57 Marvin Harrison	.30	.75
58 Joseph Addai	.25	.60
59 Reggie Wayne	.25	.60
60 Dallas Clark	.25	.60
61 David Garrard	.25	.60
62 Fred Taylor	.25	.60
63 Maurice Jones-Drew	.25	.60
64 Reggie Williams	.25	.60
65 Larry Johnson	.25	.60
66 Kolby Smith	.20	.50
67 Dwayne Bowe	.25	.60
68 Ted Ginn Jr.	.25	.60
69 Ronnie Brown	.25	.60
70 John Beck	.20	.50
71 Tarvaris Jackson	.25	.60
72 Adrian Peterson	.50	1.25
73 Chester Taylor	.20	.50
74 Sidney Rice	.30	.75
75 Wes Welker	.30	.75
76 Laurence Maroney	.25	.60
77 Drew Brees	.30	.75
78 Reggie Bush	.30	.75
79 Marques Colston	.25	.60
80 Brandon Jacobs	.25	.60
81 Plaxico Burress	.25	.60
82 Derrick Ward	.20	.50
83 Kellen Clemens	.25	.60
84 Leon Washington	.25	.60
85 Jerricho Cotchery	.25	.60
86 Matt Leinart	.30	.75
87 Edgerrin James	.25	.60
88 JaMarcus Russell	.25	.60
89 Justin Fargas	.20	.50
90 Alge Crumpler	.25	.60
91 Jerious Norwood	.25	.60
92 Roddy White	.25	.60
93 Ronald Curry	.25	.60
94 Willis McGahee	.25	.60
95 Mark Clayton	.25	.60
96 Brian Westbrook	.25	.60
97 Kevin Curtis	.20	.50
98 Ed Reed	.25	.60
99 Ray Lewis	.30	.75
100 Reggie Brown	.20	.50
101 Trent Edwards	.20	.50
102 Marshawn Lynch	.25	.60
103 Ben Roethlisberger	.30	.75
104 Willie Parker	.25	.60
105 Lee Evans	.25	.60
106 Josh Reed	.20	.50
107 Santonio Holmes	.25	.60
108 Jake Delhomme	.25	.60
109 DeShaun Foster	.25	.60
110 Heath Miller	.20	.50
111 Philip Rivers	.30	.75
112 DeAngelo Williams	.25	.60
113 Drew Carter	.20	.50
114 Adrian Peterson Bears	.20	.50
115 Antonio Gates	.30	.75
116 Shawne Merriman	.25	.60
117 Bernard Berrian	.25	.60
118 Cedric Benson	.25	.60
119 Vincent Jackson	.20	.50
120 Alex Smith QB	.30	.75
121 Devin Hester	.30	.75
122 Carson Palmer	.30	.75
123 Frank Gore	.25	.60
124 T.J. Houshmandzadeh	.25	.60
125 Rudi Johnson	.25	.60
126 Vernon Davis	.25	.60
127 Patrick Willis	.25	.60
128 Kenny Watson	.20	.50
129 Derek Anderson	.20	.50
130 Jamal Lewis	.25	.60
131 Kellen Winslow	.25	.60
132 Maurice Morris	.20	.50
133 Nate Burleson	.20	.50
134 Braylon Edwards	.25	.60
135 Josh Cribbs	.30	.75
136 Deion Branch	.25	.60
137 Marc Bulger	.25	.60
138 Tony Romo	.40	1.00
139 Marion Barber	.25	.60
140 Steven Jackson	.30	.75
141 Randy McMichael	.20	.50
142 Cadillac Williams	.25	.60
143 LenDale White	.25	.60
144 Chris Brown	.20	.50
145 Roydell Williams	.20	.50
146 Justin Gage	.20	.50
147 Jason Campbell	.25	.60
148 Clinton Portis	.25	.60
149 Chris Cooley	.25	.60
150 Ladell Betts	.20	.50
151 Adrian Arrington AU/299 RC	4.00	10.00
152 Alex Brink/999 RC	2.50	6.00
153 Ali Highsmith AU/999 RC	3.00	8.00
154 Anthony Alridge AU/999 RC	4.00	10.00
155 Antoine Cason/999 RC	2.50	6.00
156 Antwaun Molden/999 RC	2.00	5.00
157 Aqib Talib/999 RC	2.50	6.00
158 Arman Shields/999 RC	2.00	5.00
159 Brad Cottam AU/299 RC	4.00	10.00
160 Brandon Flowers/999 RC	2.50	6.00
161 Bruce Davis/999 RC	2.00	5.00
162 Calais Campbell AU/299 RC	4.00	10.00
163 Caleb Campbell AU/299 RC	6.00	15.00
164 Charles Godfrey/999 RC	2.50	6.00
165 Chauncey Washington AU/299 RC	4.00	10.00
166 Chevis Jackson AU/299 RC	3.00	8.00
167 Cory Boyd AU/299 RC	3.00	8.00
168 Craig Steltz AU/299 RC	4.00	10.00
169 Craig Stevens/999 RC	1.50	4.00
170 Curtis Lofton AU/299 RC	4.00	10.00
171 DaJuan Morgan/999 RC	2.00	5.00
172 Dantrell Savage AU/999 RC	4.00	10.00
173 Darius Reynaud AU/999 RC	3.00	8.00
174 Darrell Strong AU/999 RC	4.00	10.00
175 Davone Bess AU/999 RC	5.00	12.00
176 Derek Fine/999 RC	2.00	5.00
177 Derrick Harvey/999 RC	1.50	4.00
178 DJ Hall AU/999 RC	4.00	10.00
179 Dominique Rodgers-Cromartie RC/900	2.50	6.00
180 Erin Henderson AU/999 RC	5.00	12.00
181 Ernie Wheelwright AU/755 RC	4.00	10.00
182 Fred Davis/999 RC	2.50	6.00
183 Gary Barnidge/999 RC	1.50	4.00
184 Joe Jon Finley/999 RC	2.00	5.00
185 Jacob Hester AU/299 RC	5.00	12.00
186 Jacob Tamme/999 RC	2.50	6.00
187 Jalen Parmele/999 RC	2.00	5.00
188 Jamar Adams AU/775 RC	4.00	10.00
189 Jason Rivers AU/999 RC	4.00	10.00
190 Jaymar Johnson/999 RC	1.50	4.00
191 Jed Collins AU/999 RC	4.00	10.00
192 Jermichael Finley/999 RC	2.50	6.00
193 Jerod Mayo/999 RC	2.50	6.00
194 John Carlson/999 RC	2.50	6.00
195 Jonathan Hefney AU/928 RC	4.00	10.00
196 Jordon Dizon AU/299 RC	6.00	15.00
197 Josh Morgan AU/499 RC	8.00	20.00
198 Justin Forsett AU/299 RC	5.00	12.00
199 Justin Harper/999 RC	2.00	5.00
200 Kalvin McRae AU/999 RC	3.00	8.00
201 Keenan Burton/999 RC	1.50	4.00
202 Kellen Davis AU/299 RC	3.00	8.00
203 Kenneth Moore/999 RC	2.00	5.00
204 Kentwan Balmer/999 RC	2.00	5.00
205 Kevin Robinson AU/299 RC	3.00	8.00
206 Lawrence Jackson/999 RC	2.00	5.00
207 Leodis McKelvin/999 RC	2.00	5.00
208 Marcus Henry/999 RC	2.00	5.00
209 Marcus Monk AU/350 RC	4.00	10.00
210 Marcus Smith AU/299 RC	4.00	10.00
211 Marcus Thomas AU/299 RC	4.00	10.00
212 Mario Urrutia/999 RC	1.50	4.00
213 Mark Bradford AU/999 RC	3.00	8.00
214 Martellus Bennett/999 RC	2.00	5.00
215 Martin Rucker AU/299 RC	4.00	10.00

216 Matt Sherry/999 RC 2.00 5.00
217 Owen Schmitt AU/199 RC 5.00 12.00
218 Pat Sims/999 RC 2.00 5.00
219 Patrick Lee/999 RC 2.00 5.00
220 Paul Hubbard AU/699 RC 4.00 10.00
221 Paul Smith AU/999 RC 5.00 12.00
222 Peyton Hillis AU/299 RC 20.00 50.00
223 Phillip Merling/999 RC 2.00 5.00
224 Philip Wheeler/999 RC 2.00 5.00
225 Pierre Garcon/999 RC 3.00 8.00
226 Quentin Groves AU/299 RC 4.00 10.00
227 Reggie Smith/999 RC 2.00 5.00
228 Ryan Grice-Mullen AU/999 RC 3.00 8.00
229 Ryan Torain AU/199 RC 6.00 15.00
230 Sam Keller AU/999 RC 4.00 10.00
231 Sedrick Ellis/999 RC 2.50 6.00
232 Shawn Crable AU/299 RC 6.00 15.00
233 Adarius Bowman AU/999 RC 4.00 10.00
234 Simeon Castille AU/805 RC 4.00 10.00
235 Steve Johnson/999 RC 4.00 10.00
236 Tavares Gooden/999 RC 2.00 5.00
237 Terrell Thomas/999 RC 2.00 5.00
238 Terrence Wheatley/999 RC 1.50 4.00
239 Robert Killebrew AU/830 RC 4.00 10.00
240 Thomas Brown/999 RC 2.00 5.00
241 Tim Hightower AU/299 RC 15.00 30.00
242 Tom Zbikowski/999 RC 2.50 6.00
243 Tom Santi/999 RC 2.00 5.00
244 Bernard Morris AU/999 RC 4.00 10.00
245 Tracy Porter AU/299 RC 10.00 25.00
246 Vernon Gholston/999 RC 2.00 5.00
247 Will Franklin AU/199 RC 4.00 10.00
248 Xavier Adibi/999 RC 1.50 4.00
249 Xavier Omon/999 RC 2.50 6.00
250 Zackary Bowman/999 RC 2.00 5.00
251 Brian Brohm AU/100 RC 12.00 30.00
252 Chad Henne AU/100 RC 12.00 30.00
253 Chris Long AU/100 RC 12.00 30.00
254 Donnie Avery AU/100 RC 10.00 25.00
255 Eddie Royal AU/100 RC 12.00 30.00
256 Felix Jones AU/100 RC 20.00 50.00
257 James Hardy AU/100 RC 10.00 25.00
258 John David Booty AU/100 RC 10.00 25.00
259 Kevin Smith AU/100 RC 12.00 30.00
260 Malcolm Kelly AU/100 RC 10.00 25.00
261 Matt Forte AU/100 RC 20.00 50.00
262 Matt Ryan AU/100 RC 50.00 120.00
263 Ray Rice AU/100 RC 25.00 60.00
264 DeSean Jackson AU/105 RC 25.00 60.00
265 Andre Caldwell AU/120 RC 10.00 25.00
266 Darren McFadden AU/120 RC 30.00 80.00
267 Dustin Keller AU/120 RC 12.00 30.00
268 Early Doucet AU/120 RC 10.00 25.00
269 Glenn Dorsey AU/120 RC 12.00 30.00
270 Jake Long AU/120 RC 12.00 30.00
271 Joe Flacco AU/120 RC 40.00 100.00
272 Kevin O'Connell AU/120 RC 10.00 25.00
273 Steve Slaton AU/120 RC 12.00 30.00
274 Limas Sweed AU/125 RC 12.00 30.00
275 Earl Bennett AU/140 RC 12.00 30.00
276 Chris Johnson AU/140 RC 30.00 80.00
277 Dexter Jackson AU/140 RC 10.00 25.00
278 Harry Douglas AU/140 RC 10.00 25.00
279 Jamaal Charles AU/140 RC 25.00 60.00
280 Jerome Simpson AU/140 RC 12.00 30.00
281 Jonathan Stewart AU/140 RC 20.00 50.00
282 Devin Thomas AU/150 RC 10.00 25.00
283 Jordy Nelson AU/150 RC 25.00 50.00
284 Mario Manningham AU/150 RC 15.00 40.00
285 Rashard Mendenhall AU/150 RC 25.00 60.00
286 Dennis Dixon AU/100 RC 12.00 30.00
287 Erik Ainge AU/100 RC EXCH 12.00 30.00
288 Mike Hart AU/100 RC 12.00 30.00
289 Mike Jenkins AU/105 RC EXCH 12.00 30.00
290 Dan Connor AU/120 RC 12.00 30.00
291 Dorien Bryant AU/120 RC 10.00 25.00
292 Keith Rivers AU/120 RC 12.00 30.00
293 Kenny Phillips AU/120 RC 12.00 30.00
294 Matt Flynn AU/125 RC 40.00 80.00
295 Lavelle Hawkins AU/140 RC 8.00 20.00
296 Allen Patrick AU/140 RC 10.00 25.00
297 Andre Woodson AU/140 RC 12.00 30.00
298 Colt Brennan AU/140 RC 12.00 30.00
299 Josh Johnson AU/140 RC 12.00 30.00
300 Tashard Choice AU/150 RC 10.00 25.00

2008 Donruss Threads Bronze Holofoil

*VETS 1-150: 2X TO 5X BASIC CARDS
*ROOKIES 151-250: .5X TO 1.2X RETAIL RED
STATED PRINT RUN 250 SER.#'d SETS

2008 Donruss Threads Gold Holofoil

*VETS 1-150: 4X TO 10X BASIC CARDS
*ROOKIES 151-250: 1X TO 2.5X RETAIL RED
STATED PRINT RUN 50 SER.#'d SETS

2008 Donruss Threads Platinum Holofoil

*VETS 1-150: 6X TO 15X BASIC CARDS
*ROOKIES 151-250: 1.2X TO 3X RETAIL RED
STATED PRINT RUN 25 SER.#'d SETS

2008 Donruss Threads Retail Blue

*VETS 1-150: 2X TO 5X BASIC CARDS
*ROOKIES 151-250: .5X TO 1.2X RETAIL RED
RETAIL BLUE PRINT RUN 350

2008 Donruss Threads Retail Green

*VETS 1-150: 2.5X TO 6X BASIC CARDS
*ROOKIES 151-250: .6X TO 1.5X RETAIL RED
STATED PRINT RUN 200 SER.#'d SETS

2008 Donruss Threads Retail Red

*VETS 1-150: 1.5X TO 4X BASIC CARDS
COMMON ROOKIE (151-250) 1.25 3.00
ROOKIE SEMISTARS 1.50 4.00
ROOKIE UNL.STARS 2.00 5.00
RANDOM INSERTS IN RETAIL PACKS
152 Alex Brink 2.00 5.00
161 Bruce Davis 1.50 4.00
185 Jacob Hester 2.00 5.00
193 Jerod Mayo 2.00 5.00
217 Owen Schmitt 2.00 5.00
222 Peyton Hillis 2.50 6.00
242 Tom Zbikowski 2.00 5.00
246 Vernon Gholston 1.50 4.00

2008 Donruss Threads Retail Rookies

*ROOKIES: .4X TO 1X HOBBY RC
STATED PRINT RUN 999 SER.#'d SETS
PRINTED ON WHITE CARD STOCK

2008 Donruss Threads Silver Holofoil

*VETS 1-150: 3X TO 8X BASIC CARDS
*ROOKIES 151-250: .8X TO 2X RETAIL RED
STATED PRINT RUN 100 SER.#'d SETS

2008 Donruss Threads Century Collection Materials

STATED PRINT RUN 250 SER.#'d SETS
*PRIME/25-50: .8X TO 2X BASIC JSY
PRIME PRINT RUN 25-50
1 Mark Gastineau 3.00 8.00
2 Joe Klecko 3.00 8.00
3 Thurman Thomas 3.00 8.00
4 John Matuszak 4.00 10.00
5 Steve Largent 4.00 10.00
6 Jay Novacek 5.00 12.00
7 Jim Kelly 4.00 10.00
8 Dan Marino 8.00 20.00
9 Andre Reed 3.00 8.00
10 John Elway 6.00 15.00
11 Troy Aikman 5.00 12.00
12 Mike Singletary 4.00 10.00
13 Garo Yepremian 3.00 8.00
14 Jim McMahon 4.00 10.00
15 Chuck Foreman 5.00 12.00

2008 Donruss Threads Century Legends

*CENT.PROOF/100: .6X TO 1.5X BASIC INSERTS
CENTURY PROOF PRINT RUN 100 SER.#'d SETS
1 Emmitt Smith 2.50 6.00
2 Peyton Manning 2.00 5.00
3 Brett Favre 3.00 8.00
4 Walter Payton 2.50 6.00
5 Reggie White 1.25 3.00
6 Dan Marino 2.50 6.00
7 Tom Brady 2.00 5.00
8 Joe Montana 2.50 6.00
9 Roger Craig 1.00 2.50
10 Jim Kelly 1.25 3.00
11 Randy White 1.00 2.50
12 Tony Dorsett 1.25 3.00
13 Barry Sanders 2.00 5.00
14 John Elway 2.00 5.00
15 Otto Graham 1.25 3.00

2008 Donruss Threads Century Legends Materials

STATED PRINT RUN 250 SER.#'d SETS
*PRIME/25-50: .8X TO 2X BASIC INSERTS
PRIME PRINT RUN 10-50
1 Emmitt Smith 8.00 20.00
2 Peyton Manning 5.00 12.00
3 Brett Favre 8.00 20.00
4 Walter Payton 12.00 30.00
5 Reggie White 5.00 12.00
6 Dan Marino 8.00 20.00
7 Tom Brady 6.00 15.00
8 Joe Montana 8.00 20.00
9 Roger Craig 3.00 8.00
10 Jim Kelly 4.00 10.00
11 Randy White 4.00 10.00
12 Tony Dorsett 4.00 10.00
13 Barry Sanders 6.00 15.00
14 John Elway 6.00 15.00
15 Otto Graham 6.00 15.00

2008 Donruss Threads Century Stars

*CENT.PROOF/100: .8X TO 2X BASIC INSERTS
CENTURY PROOF PRINT RUN 100 SER.#'d SETS
1 Randy Moss 1.00 2.50
2 LaDainian Tomlinson 1.00 2.50
3 Peyton Manning 1.50 4.00
4 Torry Holt .75 2.00
5 Ben Roethlisberger 1.00 2.50
6 Chad Johnson .75 2.00
7 Brett Favre 2.50 6.00
8 Larry Johnson .75 2.00
9 Brian Westbrook .75 2.00
10 Devin Hester 1.00 2.50
11 Eli Manning 1.00 2.50
12 Fred Taylor .75 2.00
13 Terrell Owens 1.00 2.50
14 Tony Gonzalez .75 2.00
15 Tony Romo 1.25 3.00
16 Shaun Alexander .75 2.00
17 Marvin Harrison 1.00 2.50
18 Michael Strahan .75 2.00
19 Donald Driver .75 2.00
20 Tom Brady 1.50 4.00

2008 Donruss Threads Century Stars Materials

STATED PRINT RUN 250 SER.#'d SETS
*PRIME/50: .8X TO 2X BASIC JSYs
PRIME PRINT RUN 50 SER.#'d SETS
1 Randy Moss 3.00 8.00
2 LaDainian Tomlinson 3.00 8.00
3 Peyton Manning 5.00 12.00
4 Torry Holt 2.50 6.00
5 Ben Roethlisberger 3.00 8.00
6 Chad Johnson 2.50 6.00
7 Brett Favre 8.00 20.00
8 Larry Johnson 2.50 6.00
9 Brian Westbrook 2.50 6.00
10 Devin Hester 4.00 10.00
11 Eli Manning 3.00 8.00
12 Fred Taylor 2.50 6.00
13 Terrell Owens/135 3.00 8.00
14 Tony Gonzalez 2.50 6.00
15 Tony Romo 4.00 10.00
16 Shaun Alexander 2.50 6.00
17 Marvin Harrison 3.00 8.00
18 Michael Strahan 2.50 6.00
19 Donald Driver 3.00 8.00
20 Tom Brady 5.00 12.00

2008 Donruss Threads College Greats

1 Dave Casper 1.25 3.00
2 Joe Greene 1.50 4.00
3 Gale Sayers 2.00 5.00
4 John Elway 2.50 6.00
5 Emmitt Smith 3.00 8.00
6 Troy Aikman 2.00 5.00
7 Charlie Joiner 1.00 2.50
8 Y.A. Tittle 1.50 4.00
9 Roger Craig 1.25 3.00
10 Darren McFadden 1.25 3.00
11 Matt Ryan 2.00 5.00
12 Steve Slaton .50 1.25
13 Brian Brohm .50 1.25
14 Jonathan Stewart .75 2.00
15 Malcolm Kelly .40 1.00

2008 Donruss Threads College Greats Autographs

STATED PRINT RUN 25-100 SER.#'d SETS
1 Dave Casper/75 8.00 20.00
2 Joe Greene/40 15.00 30.00
3 Gale Sayers/50 40.00 80.00
4 John Elway/25 100.00 175.00
5 Emmitt Smith/22
6 Troy Aikman/20 60.00 120.00
7 Charlie Joiner/100 8.00 20.00
8 Y.A. Tittle/100 15.00 40.00
9 Roger Craig/75 12.00 30.00
10 Darren McFadden/25 30.00 80.00
11 Matt Ryan/25 100.00 175.00
12 Steve Slaton/25 10.00 25.00
13 Brian Brohm/25 12.00 30.00
14 Jonathan Stewart/25 15.00 40.00
15 Malcolm Kelly/25 8.00 20.00

2008 Donruss Threads College Greats Autographs Combo

STATED PRINT RUN 25 SER.#'d SETS
1 Cedric Benson 15.00 40.00
Jamaal Charles
2 Marshawn Lynch 25.00 50.00
DeSean Jackson
3 Dennis Dixon 25.00 50.00
Jonathan Stewart
4 Adrian Peterson 90.00 150.00
Malcolm Kelly
5 Darren McFadden 75.00 150.00
Felix Jones

2008 Donruss Threads College Gridiron Kings

*SILVER/250: .8X TO 2X BASIC INSERTS
SILVER PRINT RUN 250 SER.#'d SETS
*GOLD/100: 1X TO 2.5X BASIC INSERTS
GOLD PRINT RUN 100 SER.#'d SETS
*FRAMED RED/100: 1X TO 2.5X
FRAMED RED PRINT RUN 100 SER.#'d SETS
*FRAMED BLUE/50: 1.2X TO 3X
FRAMED BLUE PRINT RUN 50 SER.#'d SETS
*PLATINUM/25: 2X TO 5X BASIC INSERTS
PLATINUM PRINT RUN 25 SER.#'d SETS
*FRAMED GREEN/25: 2X TO 5X
FRAMED GREEN PRINT RUN 25 SER.#'d SETS
*FRAMED BLACK/10: 3X TO 8X
FRAMED BLACK PRINT RUN 10 SER.#'d SETS
1 Ali Highsmith .30 .75
2 Allen Patrick .40 1.00
3 Antoine Cason .50 1.25
4 Brian Brohm .50 1.25
5 Chad Henne .50 1.25
6 Chevis Jackson .30 .75
7 Chris Long .50 1.25
8 Colt Brennan .50 1.25
9 DJ Hall .40 1.00
10 Dan Connor .50 1.25
11 Dennis Dixon .50 1.25
12 Early Doucet .40 1.00
13 Eddie Royal .50 1.25
14 Erik Ainge .50 1.25
15 Ernie Wheelwright .40 1.00
16 Fred Davis .50 1.25
17 Glenn Dorsey .50 1.25
18 Harry Douglas .40 1.00
19 Jamar Adams .40 1.00
20 John David Booty .40 1.00
21 Jonathan Hefney .40 1.00
22 Keith Rivers .50 1.25
23 Kenny Phillips .50 1.25
24 Lawrence Jackson .40 1.00
25 Limas Sweed .50 1.25
26 Marcus Monk .40 1.00
27 Matt Ryan 2.00 5.00
28 Mike Hart .50 1.25
29 Quentin Groves .40 1.00
30 Robert Killebrew .40 1.00
31 Sedrick Ellis .50 1.25
32 Shawn Crable .30 .75
33 Simeon Castille .40 1.00
34 Terrell Thomas .40 1.00
35 Xavier Adibi .30 .75
36 Adrian Arrington .40 1.00
37 Aqib Talib .50 1.25
38 Brandon Flowers .50 1.25
39 Steve Largent .50 1.25
40 Darren McFadden 1.25 3.00
41 DeSean Jackson 1.00 2.50
42 Felix Jones .75 2.00
43 Jamaal Charles .75 2.00
44 Jonathan Stewart .75 2.00
45 Malcolm Kelly .40 1.00
46 Mario Manningham .50 1.25
47 Matt Flynn 1.00 2.50
48 Rashard Mendenhall 1.00 2.50
49 Steve Slaton .50 1.25
50 Vernon Gholston .40 1.00

2008 Donruss Threads College Gridiron Kings Autographs

STATED PRINT RUN 25 SER.#'d SETS
1 Ali Highsmith 6.00 15.00
2 Allen Patrick 8.00 20.00
3 Antoine Cason 10.00 25.00
4 Brian Brohm 10.00 25.00
5 Chad Henne 20.00 50.00
6 Chevis Jackson 6.00 15.00
7 Chris Long 10.00 25.00
8 Colt Brennan 15.00 40.00
9 DJ Hall 8.00 20.00
10 Dan Connor 10.00 25.00
11 Dennis Dixon 12.00 30.00
12 Early Doucet 8.00 20.00
13 Eddie Royal 10.00 25.00
14 Erik Ainge 10.00 25.00
15 Ernie Wheelwright 8.00 20.00
16 Fred Davis 10.00 25.00
17 Glenn Dorsey 10.00 25.00
18 Harry Douglas EXCH 8.00 20.00
19 Jamar Adams 8.00 20.00
20 John David Booty 8.00 20.00
21 Jonathan Hefney 8.00 20.00
22 Keith Rivers 10.00 25.00
23 Kenny Phillips EXCH 10.00 25.00
24 Lawrence Jackson 8.00 20.00
25 Limas Sweed 10.00 25.00
26 Marcus Monk 8.00 20.00
27 Matt Ryan 60.00 120.00
28 Mike Hart 10.00 25.00
29 Quentin Groves 8.00 20.00
30 Robert Killebrew 8.00 20.00
31 Sedrick Ellis 10.00 25.00
32 Shawn Crable 6.00 15.00
33 Simeon Castille 8.00 20.00
34 Terrell Thomas 8.00 20.00
35 Xavier Adibi 6.00 15.00
36 Adrian Arrington 8.00 20.00
37 Aqib Talib 10.00 25.00
38 Brandon Flowers 10.00 25.00
39 Steve Largent 12.00 30.00
40 Darren McFadden 25.00 60.00
41 DeSean Jackson 20.00 50.00
42 Felix Jones 15.00 40.00
43 Jamaal Charles 15.00 40.00
44 Jonathan Stewart 15.00 40.00
45 Malcolm Kelly 8.00 20.00
46 Mario Manningham 15.00 30.00
47 Matt Flynn 40.00 100.00
48 Rashard Mendenhall 20.00 50.00
49 Steve Slaton 10.00 25.00
50 Vernon Gholston 8.00 20.00

2008 Donruss Threads College Gridiron Kings Material Autographs

STATED PRINT RUN 30 SER.#'d SETS
1 Ali Highsmith 6.00 15.00
2 Allen Patrick 8.00 20.00
4 Brian Brohm 10.00 25.00
5 Chad Henne 20.00 50.00
6 Chevis Jackson 6.00 15.00
7 Chris Long 10.00 25.00
8 Colt Brennan 20.00 50.00
9 DJ Hall 8.00 20.00
10 Dan Connor 10.00 25.00
12 Early Doucet 8.00 20.00
13 Eddie Royal 10.00 25.00
14 Erik Ainge 20.00 40.00
15 Ernie Wheelwright 8.00 20.00
16 Fred Davis 10.00 25.00
17 Glenn Dorsey 10.00 25.00
18 Harry Douglas 10.00 25.00
20 John David Booty 8.00 20.00
21 Jonathan Hefney 8.00 20.00
22 Keith Rivers 10.00 25.00
23 Kenny Phillips EXCH 10.00 25.00
24 Lawrence Jackson 8.00 20.00
25 Limas Sweed 10.00 25.00
26 Marcus Monk 8.00 20.00
27 Matt Ryan 60.00 120.00
28 Mike Hart 10.00 25.00
30 Robert Killebrew 8.00 20.00
31 Sedrick Ellis 10.00 25.00
32 Shawn Crable 6.00 15.00
33 Simeon Castille 8.00 20.00
34 Terrell Thomas 8.00 20.00
35 Xavier Adibi 6.00 15.00
37 Aqib Talib 10.00 25.00
38 Brandon Flowers 10.00 25.00
39 Steve Largent 15.00 40.00
40 Darren McFadden 30.00 80.00
41 DeSean Jackson 20.00 50.00
42 Felix Jones 30.00 80.00
43 Jamaal Charles 15.00 40.00
44 Jonathan Stewart 15.00 40.00
45 Malcolm Kelly 8.00 20.00
48 Rashard Mendenhall 40.00 80.00
49 Steve Slaton 10.00 25.00

2008 Donruss Threads College Gridiron Kings Material Autographs Prime

*PRIME/15: .6X TO 1.5X BASIC INSERTS
PRIME PRINT RUN 10-15
8 Colt Brennan 30.00 80.00
11 Dennis Dixon 25.00 60.00
19 Jamar Adams 20.00 40.00
27 Matt Ryan 100.00 200.00
29 Quentin Groves 12.00 30.00
36 Adrian Arrington 12.00 30.00
46 Mario Manningham 20.00 50.00
47 Matt Flynn 50.00 125.00
50 Vernon Gholston 12.00 30.00

2008 Donruss Threads College Gridiron Kings Materials

STATED PRINT RUN 110-250
*PRIME/15-25: .8X TO 2X BASIC INSERTS
PRIME PRINT RUN 9-25
1 Ali Highsmith 2.00 5.00
2 Allen Patrick 2.50 6.00
4 Brian Brohm 3.00 8.00
5 Chad Henne 5.00 12.00
6 Chevis Jackson 2.00 5.00
7 Chris Long 3.00 8.00
8 Colt Brennan 6.00 15.00
9 DJ Hall 2.50 6.00
10 Dan Connor 5.00 12.00
12 Early Doucet 2.50 6.00
13 Eddie Royal 3.00 8.00
14 Erik Ainge 5.00 12.00
15 Ernie Wheelwright 2.50 6.00
16 Fred Davis 3.00 8.00
17 Glenn Dorsey 3.00 8.00
18 Harry Douglas/110 2.50 6.00
20 John David Booty 2.50 6.00
21 Jonathan Hefney 2.50 6.00
22 Keith Rivers 3.00 8.00
23 Kenny Phillips 3.00 8.00
24 Lawrence Jackson 2.50 6.00
25 Limas Sweed 3.00 8.00
26 Marcus Monk 2.50 6.00
27 Matt Ryan 8.00 20.00
28 Mike Hart 3.00 8.00
30 Robert Killebrew 2.50 6.00
31 Sedrick Ellis 3.00 8.00
32 Shawn Crable 2.00 5.00
33 Simeon Castille 4.00 10.00
34 Terrell Thomas 2.50 6.00
35 Xavier Adibi 3.00 8.00
37 Aqib Talib 3.00 8.00
38 Brandon Flowers 3.00 8.00
39 Steve Largent 4.00 10.00
40 Darren McFadden 8.00 20.00
41 DeSean Jackson 6.00 15.00
42 Felix Jones 5.00 12.00
43 Jamaal Charles 5.00 12.00
44 Jonathan Stewart/220 5.00 12.00
45 Malcolm Kelly 2.50 6.00
48 Rashard Mendenhall 6.00 15.00
49 Steve Slaton/165 3.00 8.00
50 Vernon Gholston/190 2.50 6.00

2008 Donruss Threads Crown Autographs

RANDOM INSERTS IN 2009 LIMITED PACKS
1 Brian Brohm 10.00 25.00
3 Darren McFadden 25.00 60.00
4 Dexter Jackson 8.00 20.00
5 Donnie Avery 8.00 20.00
6 Earl Bennett 10.00 25.00
7 Eddie Royal 10.00 25.00
8 Harry Douglas 8.00 20.00
9 Jamaal Charles 15.00 40.00
10 Jerome Simpson 10.00 25.00
11 John David Booty 8.00 20.00
12 Jordy Nelson 20.00 40.00
13 Kevin Smith 10.00 25.00
15 Matt Forte 15.00 40.00
17 Steve Slaton 10.00 25.00
19 Ray Rice 20.00 50.00
20 Matt Ryan 60.00 120.00
21 Mario Manningham 15.00 30.00
23 Kevin O'Connell 8.00 20.00
24 Jonathan Stewart 15.00 40.00
25 Joe Flacco 30.00 80.00
26 James Hardy 8.00 20.00
27 Jake Long 10.00 25.00
28 Felix Jones 15.00 40.00
29 Early Doucet 8.00 20.00
30 Dustin Keller 10.00 25.00
32 DeSean Jackson 20.00 50.00
33 Chad Henne 10.00 25.00

2008 Donruss Threads Crown Retail

RANDOM INSERTS IN RETAIL PACKS
1 Brian Brohm .60 1.50
2 Chris Johnson 1.50 4.00
3 Darren McFadden 1.50 4.00
4 Devin Thomas .50 1.25
5 Donnie Avery .50 1.25
6 Earl Bennett .60 1.50
7 Eddie Royal .60 1.50
8 Harry Douglas .50 1.25
9 Jamaal Charles 1.00 2.50
10 Jerome Simpson .60 1.50
11 John David Booty .50 1.25
12 Jordy Nelson .75 2.00
13 Kevin Smith 1.00 2.50
14 Malcolm Kelly .50 1.25
15 Matt Forte 1.00 2.50
16 Rashard Mendenhall 1.25 3.00
17 Steve Slaton .60 1.50
18 Glenn Dorsey .60 1.50
19 Ray Rice 1.25 3.00
20 Matt Ryan 2.50 6.00
21 Mario Manningham .60 1.50
22 Limas Sweed .60 1.50
23 Kevin O'Connell .50 1.25
24 Jonathan Stewart 1.00 2.50
25 Joe Flacco 2.00 5.00
26 James Hardy .50 1.25
27 Jake Long .60 1.50
28 Felix Jones 1.00 2.50
29 Early Doucet .50 1.25
30 Dustin Keller .60 1.50
31 Dexter Jackson .50 1.25
32 DeSean Jackson 1.25 3.00
33 Chad Henne .60 1.50
34 Andre Caldwell .50 1.25

2008 Donruss Threads Crowns

ONE PER DICK'S SPORT.GOODS BOX
1 Darren McFadden 1.50 4.00
2 Rashard Mendenhall 1.25 3.00
3 Matt Ryan 2.50 6.00
4 Jonathan Stewart 1.00 2.50
5 Joe Flacco 2.00 5.00
6 Felix Jones 1.00 2.50

2008 Donruss Threads Dynasty

*CENT.PROOF/100: .8X TO 2X BASIC INSERTS
CENTURY PROOF PRINT RUN 100 SER.#'d SETS
1 Tom Brady 2.00 5.00
Randy Moss
Tedy Bruschi
2 Jack Lambert 1.50 4.00
John Stallworth
Joe Greene
3 Bart Starr 2.50 6.00
Paul Hornung
Forrest Gregg
4 Bob Griese 1.50 4.00
Paul Warfield
Garo Yepremian
5 Troy Aikman 3.00 8.00
Emmitt Smith
Michael Irvin
6 Joe Montana 3.00 8.00
Jerry Rice
Roger Craig
7 Jim McMahon 3.00 8.00
Walter Payton
Mike Singletary
8 Jim Kelly 1.50 4.00
Thurman Thomas
Andre Reed
9 Jim Brown 2.00 5.00
Otto Graham
Lou Groza
10 Roger Staubach 2.00 5.00
Tony Dorsett
Randy White

2008 Donruss Threads Dynasty Materials

STATED PRINT RUN 180-250
*PRIME/25-50: .6X TO 1.5X BASIC JSYs
*PRIME/15: .8X TO 2X BASIC JSYs
PRIME PRINT RUN 15-50
1 Tom Brady 12.00 30.00
Randy Moss
Tedy Bruschi
2 Jack Lambert 12.00 30.00
John Stallworth
Joe Greene
3 Bart Starr 15.00 40.00
Paul Hornung
Forrest Gregg
4 Bob Griese 8.00 20.00
Paul Warfield
Garo Yepremian/180
5 Troy Aikman 20.00 50.00
Emmitt Smith
Michael Irvin
6 Joe Montana 15.00 40.00
Jerry Rice
Roger Craig
7 Jim McMahon 20.00 50.00
Walter Payton
Mike Singletary
8 Jim Kelly 8.00 20.00
Thurman Thomas
Andre Reed
9 Jim Brown 10.00 25.00
Otto Graham
Lou Groza/235
10 Roger Staubach 12.00 30.00
Tony Dorsett
Randy White

2008 Donruss Threads Footballs

RANDOM INSERTS IN RETAIL PACKS
STATED PRINT RUN 9-250
1 Anquan Boldin 3.00 8.00
2 Larry Fitzgerald 4.00 10.00
3 Warrick Dunn 3.00 8.00
4 Derrick Mason 3.00 8.00
5 Steve Smith 3.00 8.00
6 Brian Urlacher 4.00 10.00
7 Chad Johnson/139 3.00 8.00
8 Terrell Owens/165 4.00 10.00
9 Tony Gonzalez 3.00 8.00
11 Torry Holt/165 3.00 8.00
12 Isaac Bruce 3.00 8.00
13 Jeff Garcia/190 3.00 8.00
14 Santana Moss 2.50 6.00
15 LaDainian Tomlinson 4.00 10.00
16 Matt Hasselbeck/50 4.00 10.00
18 Earnest Graham 2.50 6.00
19 Joey Galloway 3.00 8.00
20 Ike Hilliard 2.50 6.00
21 Vince Young 3.00 8.00
22 Jason Taylor 3.00 8.00
23 Tom Brady 6.00 15.00
24 Randy Moss 4.00 10.00
25 Donte Stallworth/23 4.00 10.00
26 Deuce McAllister 3.00 8.00
27 Eli Manning 4.00 10.00
28 Michael Strahan 3.00 8.00
29 Thomas Jones 3.00 8.00
30 Laveranues Coles 2.50 6.00
31 Jerry Porter 2.50 6.00
32 Correll Buckhalter 3.00 8.00
33 Donovan McNabb 4.00 10.00

2008 Donruss Threads Generations

*CENT.PROOF/100: .8X TO 2X BASIC INSERTS
CENTURY PROOF PRINT RUN 100 SER.#'d SETS
1 Peyton Manning 1.50 4.00
Eli Manning
2 Thurman Thomas .75 2.00
Marshawn Lynch
3 Dan Marino 2.50 6.00
Brett Favre
4 Steve Largent 1.00 2.50
Deion Branch
5 Roger Craig .75 2.00
Frank Gore
6 John Stallworth .75 2.00
Santonio Holmes
7 Chuck Foreman 1.50 4.00
Adrian Peterson
8 Sterling Sharpe 1.00 2.50
Greg Jennings
9 Dan Fouts 1.00 2.50
Philip Rivers
10 Gale Sayers 1.50 4.00
Devin Hester
11 Jay Novacek 1.25 3.00
Jason Witten
12 Marvin Harrison 1.00 2.50
Anthony Gonzalez
13 Jerry Rice 1.50 4.00
Randy Moss
14 Michael Irvin 1.25 3.00
Terrell Owens
15 Reggie White 1.00 2.50
Michael Strahan

2008 Donruss Threads Generations Materials

STATED PRINT RUN 250 SER.#'d SETS
*PRIME/35-50: .8X TO 2X BASIC JSYs
PRIME PRINT RUN 35-50
1 Peyton Manning 8.00 20.00
Eli Manning
2 Thurman Thomas 4.00 10.00
Marshawn Lynch
3 Dan Marino 15.00 40.00
Brett Favre
4 Steve Largent 5.00 12.00
Deion Branch
5 Roger Craig 5.00 12.00
Frank Gore
6 John Stallworth 5.00 12.00
Santonio Holmes
7 Chuck Foreman 8.00 20.00
Adrian Peterson
8 Sterling Sharpe 5.00 12.00
Greg Jennings
9 Dan Fouts 5.00 12.00
Philip Rivers
10 Gale Sayers 8.00 20.00
Devin Hester
11 Jay Novacek 6.00 15.00
Jason Witten
12 Marvin Harrison 5.00 12.00
Anthony Gonzalez
13 Jerry Rice 8.00 20.00
Randy Moss
14 Michael Irvin 6.00 15.00
Terrell Owens
15 Reggie White 5.00 12.00
Michael Strahan

2008 Donruss Threads Jerseys

STATED PRINT RUN 9-250
1 Anquan Boldin 2.50 6.00
2 Larry Fitzgerald 3.00 8.00
4 Derrick Mason/20 5.00 12.00
5 Steve Smith/200 2.50 6.00
6 Brian Urlacher 3.00 8.00
7 Chad Johnson 2.50 6.00
9 Tony Gonzalez 2.50 6.00
10 Rex Grossman 2.50 6.00
11 Torry Holt 2.50 6.00
13 Jeff Garcia 2.50 6.00
14 Santana Moss 2.00 5.00
15 LaDainian Tomlinson 3.00 8.00
16 Matt Hasselbeck 2.50 6.00
19 Joey Galloway/50 3.00 8.00
20 Ike Hilliard 2.00 5.00
21 Vince Young 2.50 6.00
22 Jason Taylor 3.00 8.00
23 Tom Brady 5.00 12.00
24 Randy Moss 3.00 8.00
26 Deuce McAllister 2.50 6.00
27 Eli Manning 3.00 8.00
28 Michael Strahan 2.50 6.00
30 Laveranues Coles 2.00 5.00
32 Correll Buckhalter 2.50 6.00
33 Donovan McNabb 3.00 8.00
34 Hines Ward 2.50 6.00
36 Jason Witten 3.00 8.00
38 Jay Cutler 3.00 8.00
39 Brandon Marshall 2.50 6.00
42 Jon Kitna 2.50 6.00
43 Roy Williams WR 2.50 6.00
45 Calvin Johnson 3.00 8.00
46 Aaron Rodgers 10.00 25.00
47 Ryan Grant 3.00 8.00
48 Donald Driver 2.50 6.00
49 Greg Jennings 3.00 8.00
50 James Jones 2.00 5.00
51 Matt Schaub 2.50 6.00
53 Andre Johnson 2.50 6.00
55 Ahman Green/110 2.50 6.00
56 Peyton Manning 5.00 12.00
57 Marvin Harrison 3.00 8.00
58 Joseph Addai 2.50 6.00
59 Reggie Wayne 2.50 6.00
60 Dallas Clark 2.50 6.00
61 David Garrard 2.50 6.00
62 Fred Taylor 2.50 6.00
63 Maurice Jones-Drew 2.50 6.00
64 Reggie Williams 2.50 6.00
65 Larry Johnson 2.50 6.00
67 Dwayne Bowe 2.50 6.00
68 Ted Ginn Jr./125 2.50 6.00
69 Ronnie Brown 2.50 6.00
71 Tarvaris Jackson 2.50 6.00
72 Adrian Peterson 5.00 12.00
73 Chester Taylor 2.00 5.00
74 Sidney Rice 3.00 8.00
75 Wes Welker 3.00 8.00
76 Laurence Maroney 2.50 6.00
77 Drew Brees 3.00 8.00
78 Reggie Bush 3.00 8.00
79 Marques Colston 2.50 6.00
80 Brandon Jacobs 2.50 6.00
81 Plaxico Burress 2.50 6.00
84 Leon Washington 2.50 6.00
85 Jerricho Cotchery 2.50 6.00
86 Matt Leinart 3.00 8.00
87 Edgerrin James/30 4.00 10.00
89 Justin Fargas/200 2.00 5.00
90 Alge Crumpler 2.50 6.00
91 Jerious Norwood 2.50 6.00
92 Roddy White/225 2.50 6.00
94 Willis McGahee 2.50 6.00
95 Mark Clayton 2.50 6.00
96 Brian Westbrook 3.00 8.00
97 Kevin Curtis 2.00 5.00
99 Ray Lewis 3.00 8.00
100 Reggie Brown/60 2.50 6.00
101 Trent Edwards/140 2.00 5.00
102 Marshawn Lynch 2.50 6.00
103 Ben Roethlisberger 3.00 8.00
104 Willie Parker 2.50 6.00
105 Lee Evans 2.50 6.00
106 Josh Reed 2.00 5.00
107 Santonio Holmes 2.50 6.00
108 Jake Delhomme/105 2.50 6.00
110 Heath Miller 2.00 5.00
111 Philip Rivers 3.00 8.00
112 DeAngelo Williams 2.50 6.00
115 Antonio Gates 3.00 8.00
116 Shawne Merriman/160 2.50 6.00
118 Cedric Benson 2.50 6.00
119 Vincent Jackson 2.00 5.00
120 Alex Smith QB/70 4.00 10.00
121 Devin Hester 3.00 8.00
122 Carson Palmer 3.00 8.00
123 Frank Gore 2.50 6.00
124 T.J. Houshmandzadeh 2.50 6.00
125 Rudi Johnson 2.50 6.00
126 Vernon Davis 2.50 6.00
127 Patrick Willis 2.50 6.00
129 Derek Anderson 2.00 5.00
131 Kellen Winslow 2.50 6.00
133 Nate Burleson 2.00 5.00
134 Braylon Edwards 2.50 6.00
136 Deion Branch 2.50 6.00
137 Marc Bulger 2.50 6.00
138 Tony Romo 4.00 10.00
139 Marion Barber 2.50 6.00
140 Steven Jackson 3.00 8.00
141 Randy McMichael/15 4.00 10.00
142 Cadillac Williams 2.50 6.00
143 LenDale White/150 2.50 6.00
144 Chris Brown 2.00 5.00
147 Jason Campbell 2.50 6.00
148 Clinton Portis 2.50 6.00
149 Chris Cooley/155 3.00 8.00
150 Ladell Betts 2.00 5.00

2008 Donruss Threads Jerseys Prime

*PRIME/25-50: .8X TO 2X JSY/105-250
*PRIME/25-50: .6X TO 1.5X JSY/50-70
*PRIME/25-50: .5X TO 1.2X JSY/15-30
PRIME PRINT RUN 4-50
3 Warrick Dunn/25 5.00 12.00
8 Terrell Owens 6.00 15.00

2008 Donruss Threads Pro Gridiron Kings

*SILVER/250: .5X TO 1.2X BASIC INSERTS
SILVER PRINT RUN 250 SER.#'d SETS
*GOLD/100: .6X TO 1.5X BASIC INSERTS
GOLD PRINT RUN 100 SER.#'d SETS
*FRAMED RED/100: .6X TO 1.5X
FRAMED RED PRINT RUN 100 SER.#'d SETS
*FRAMED BLUE/50: .8X TO 2X
FRAMED BLUE PRINT RUN 50 SER.#'d SETS
*PLATINUM/25: 1.2X TO 3X BASIC INSERTS
PLATINUM PRINT RUN 25 SER.#'d SETS
*FRAMED GREEN/25: 1.2X TO 3X
FRAMED GREEN PRINT RUN 25 SER.#'d SETS
*FRAMED BLACK/10: 2X TO 5X
FRAMED BLACK PRINT RUN 10 SER.#'d SETS
1 Chad Johnson .75 2.00
2 Brian Westbrook .75 2.00
3 Willie Parker .75 2.00
4 Clinton Portis .75 2.00
5 Edgerrin James .75 2.00
6 Willis McGahee .75 2.00
7 Joseph Addai .75 2.00
8 Steven Jackson 1.00 2.50
9 Emmitt Smith 2.50 6.00
10 Randy White 1.00 2.50
11 Mark Gastineau .75 2.00
12 Joe Klecko .75 2.00
13 Chuck Foreman .75 2.00
14 John Matuszak 1.25 3.00
15 Vince Young .75 2.00
16 Drew Brees 1.00 2.50
17 Jon Kitna .75 2.00
18 Carson Palmer 1.00 2.50
19 Eli Manning 1.00 2.50
20 Reggie Wayne .75 2.00
21 Larry Fitzgerald 1.00 2.50
22 Torry Holt .75 2.00
23 Tony Gonzalez .75 2.00
24 Jason Witten 1.00 2.50
25 Wes Welker 1.00 2.50
26 Plaxico Burress .75 2.00

27 Greg Jennings 1.00 2.50
28 Antonio Gates 1.00 2.50
29 Adrian Peterson 1.50 4.00
30 Dwayne Bowe .75 2.00
31 Marshawn Lynch .75 2.00
32 Laurence Maroney .75 2.00
33 Randy Moss 1.00 2.50
34 Terrell Owens 1.00 2.50
35 Chris Cooley .75 2.00
36 Fred Taylor .75 2.00
37 Derek Anderson .60 1.50
38 Braylon Edwards .75 2.00
39 Marques Colston .75 2.00
40 T.J. Houshmandzadeh .75 2.00
41 Steve Smith .75 2.00
42 Lee Evans .75 2.00
43 Reggie Bush 1.00 2.50
44 Marion Barber .75 2.00
45 Jay Cutler 1.00 2.50
46 Donovan McNabb 1.00 2.50
47 Kurt Warner 1.00 2.50
48 Brandon Jacobs .75 2.00
49 Shaun Alexander .75 2.00
50 Maurice Jones-Drew .75 2.00
51A Brett Favre 3.00 8.00
dropping back
(inserted in 2008 Leaf Rookies and Stars)
51B Brett Favre 3.00 8.00
towel in hands
(inserted in 2008 Leaf Rookies and Stars)
DM Darren McFadden 1.50 4.00
(inserted in Donruss Threads baseball)
NNO Brett Favre Promo 3.00 8.00
(inserted in 2008 Donruss threads baseball)

2008 Donruss Threads Pro Gridiron Kings Autographs

STATED PRINT RUN 10-25
SERIAL #'d UNDER 25 NOT PRICED
3 Willie Parker/25 EXCH 15.00 40.00
10 Randy White/25 40.00 80.00
11 Mark Gastineau/25 EXCH 12.00 30.00
39 Marques Colston/25

2008 Donruss Threads Pro Gridiron Kings Materials

STATED PRINT RUN 250 SER.#'d SETS
*PRIME/20-50: .8X TO 2X BASIC INSERTS
PRIME PRINT RUN 20-50
1 Chad Johnson 3.00 8.00
2 Brian Westbrook 3.00 8.00
3 Willie Parker 3.00 8.00
4 Clinton Portis 3.00 8.00
5 Edgerrin James 3.00 8.00
6 Willis McGahee 3.00 8.00
7 Joseph Addai 3.00 8.00
8 Steven Jackson 4.00 10.00
9 Emmitt Smith 10.00 25.00
10 Randy White 4.00 10.00
11 Mark Gastineau 3.00 8.00
12 Joe Klecko 3.00 8.00
13 Chuck Foreman 5.00 12.00
14 John Matuszak 5.00 12.00
15 Vince Young 3.00 8.00
16 Drew Brees 4.00 10.00
17 Jon Kitna 3.00 8.00
18 Carson Palmer 4.00 10.00
19 Eli Manning 4.00 10.00
20 Reggie Wayne 3.00 8.00
21 Larry Fitzgerald 4.00 10.00
22 Torry Holt 3.00 8.00
23 Tony Gonzalez 3.00 8.00
24 Jason Witten 4.00 10.00
25 Wes Welker 4.00 10.00
26 Plaxico Burress 3.00 8.00
27 Greg Jennings 4.00 10.00
28 Antonio Gates 4.00 10.00
29 Adrian Peterson 6.00 15.00
30 Dwayne Bowe 3.00 8.00
31 Marshawn Lynch 3.00 8.00
32 Laurence Maroney 3.00 8.00
33 Randy Moss 4.00 10.00
34 Terrell Owens 4.00 10.00
35 Chris Cooley 4.00 10.00
36 Fred Taylor 3.00 8.00
37 Derek Anderson 2.50 6.00
38 Braylon Edwards 3.00 8.00
39 Marques Colston 3.00 8.00
40 T.J. Houshmandzadeh 3.00 8.00
41 Steve Smith 3.00 8.00
42 Lee Evans 3.00 8.00
43 Reggie Bush 4.00 10.00
44 Marion Barber 3.00 8.00
45 Jay Cutler 4.00 10.00
46 Donovan McNabb 4.00 10.00
47 Kurt Warner 4.00 10.00
48 Brandon Jacobs 3.00 8.00
49 Shaun Alexander 3.00 8.00
50 Maurice Jones-Drew 3.00 8.00

2008 Donruss Threads Rookie Autographs Silver

STATED PRINT RUN 50 SER.#'d SETS
155 Antoine Cason 8.00 20.00
157 Aqib Talib 8.00 20.00
160 Brandon Flowers 8.00 20.00
177 Derrick Harvey 5.00 12.00
179 Dominique Rodgers-Cromartie 8.00 20.00
182 Fred Davis 8.00 20.00
186 Jacob Tamme 8.00 20.00
192 Jermichael Finley 12.00 30.00
193 Jerod Mayo 8.00 20.00
194 John Carlson 8.00 20.00
201 Keenan Burton 5.00 12.00
204 Kentwan Balmer 6.00 15.00
206 Lawrence Jackson 6.00 15.00
207 Leodis McKelvin 6.00 15.00
214 Martellus Bennett 6.00 15.00
218 Pat Sims 6.00 15.00
223 Phillip Merling 6.00 15.00
227 Reggie Smith 6.00 15.00
231 Sedrick Ellis 8.00 20.00
237 Terrell Thomas 6.00 15.00
240 Thomas Brown 6.00 15.00
246 Vernon Gholston 6.00 15.00
248 Xavier Adibi 5.00 12.00

2008 Donruss Threads Rookie Collection Materials

STATED PRINT RUN 500 SER.#'d SETS
*PRIME/25: .8X TO 2X BASIC JSYs
PRIME PRINT RUN 25 SER.#'d SETS
1 Rashard Mendenhall 5.00 12.00
2 Mario Manningham 2.50 6.00
3 Jordy Nelson 3.00 8.00
4 Devin Thomas 2.00 5.00
5 Jonathan Stewart 4.00 10.00
6 Jerome Simpson 2.50 6.00
7 Jamaal Charles 4.00 10.00
8 Harry Douglas 2.00 5.00
9 Dexter Jackson 2.00 5.00
10 Chris Johnson 6.00 15.00
11 Earl Bennett 2.50 6.00
12 Limas Sweed 2.50 6.00
13 Steve Slaton 2.50 6.00
14 Kevin O'Connell 2.00 5.00
15 Joe Flacco 8.00 20.00
16 Jake Long 2.50 6.00
17 Glenn Dorsey 2.50 6.00
18 Early Doucet 2.00 5.00
19 Dustin Keller 2.50 6.00
20 Darren McFadden 6.00 15.00
21 Andre Caldwell 2.00 5.00
22 DeSean Jackson 5.00 12.00
23 Ray Rice 5.00 12.00
24 Matt Ryan 8.00 20.00
25 Matt Forte 4.00 10.00
26 Malcolm Kelly 2.00 5.00
27 Kevin Smith 2.50 6.00
28 John David Booty 2.00 5.00
29 James Hardy 2.00 5.00
30 Felix Jones 4.00 10.00
31 Eddie Royal 2.50 6.00
32 Donnie Avery 2.00 5.00
33 Chad Henne 5.00 12.00
34 Brian Brohm 2.50 6.00

2008 Donruss Threads Rookie Collection Materials Autographs

STATED PRINT RUN 25 SER.#'d SETS
UNPRICED PRIME PRINT RUN 10
1 Rashard Mendenhall 40.00 80.00
2 Mario Manningham 20.00 40.00
3 Jordy Nelson 25.00 50.00
4 Devin Thomas 10.00 25.00
5 Jonathan Stewart 20.00 50.00
6 Jerome Simpson 12.00 30.00
7 Jamaal Charles 20.00 50.00
8 Harry Douglas 10.00 25.00
9 Dexter Jackson 10.00 25.00
10 Chris Johnson 50.00 100.00
11 Earl Bennett 12.00 30.00
12 Limas Sweed 12.00 30.00
13 Steve Slaton 12.00 30.00
14 Kevin O'Connell 10.00 25.00
15 Joe Flacco 60.00 120.00
16 Jake Long EXCH 12.00 30.00
17 Glenn Dorsey 12.00 30.00
18 Early Doucet EXCH 10.00 25.00
19 Dustin Keller 12.00 30.00
20 Darren McFadden 30.00 80.00
21 Andre Caldwell 10.00 25.00
22 DeSean Jackson 25.00 60.00
23 Ray Rice 25.00 60.00
24 Matt Ryan 100.00 175.00
25 Matt Forte 50.00 80.00
26 Malcolm Kelly 10.00 25.00
27 Kevin Smith 12.00 30.00
28 John David Booty 10.00 25.00
29 James Hardy 10.00 25.00
30 Felix Jones 30.00 80.00
31 Eddie Royal 12.00 30.00
32 Donnie Avery 10.00 25.00
33 Chad Henne 12.00 30.00
34 Brian Brohm 12.00 30.00

2008 Donruss Threads Rookie Collection Materials Combo

STATED PRINT RUN 500 SER.#'d SETS
*PRIME/25: .8X TO 2X BASIC DUAL
PRIME PRINT RUN 25 SER.#'d SETS
1 Matt Ryan 6.00 15.00
Harry Douglas
2 Joe Flacco 8.00 20.00
Ray Rice
3 Earl Bennett 5.00 12.00
Matt Forte
4 Andre Caldwell 3.00 8.00
Jerome Simpson
5 Brian Brohm 4.00 10.00
Jordy Nelson
6 Jamaal Charles 4.00 10.00
Glenn Dorsey
7 Chad Henne 5.00 12.00
Jake Long
8 Rashard Mendenhall 8.00 20.00
Limas Sweed
9 Jonathan Stewart 5.00 12.00
DeSean Jackson
10 Devin Thomas 5.00 12.00
Malcolm Kelly
11 Matt Ryan 12.00 30.00
Darren McFadden
12 Mario Manningham 5.00 12.00
Chad Henne
13 Brian Brohm 3.00 8.00
Harry Douglas
14 Darren McFadden 10.00 25.00
Felix Jones
15 Limas Sweed 5.00 12.00
Jamaal Charles

2008 Donruss Threads Rookie Collection Materials Quad

STATED PRINT RUN 100 SER.#'d SETS
*PRIME/25: .8X TO 2X BASIC QUAD
PRIME PRINT RUN 25 SER.#'d SETS
1 Matt Ryan 15.00 40.00
Joe Flacco
Darren McFadden
Jonathan Stewart
2 Chris Johnson 10.00 25.00
Matt Forte
Malcolm Kelly
Limas Sweed
3 Darren McFadden 10.00 25.00
Jonathan Stewart
Felix Jones
Rashard Mendenhall
4 Matt Ryan 15.00 40.00
Joe Flacco
Brian Brohm
Chad Henne
5 Donnie Avery 5.00 12.00
Devin Thomas
Jordy Nelson
James Hardy

2008 Donruss Threads National Convention

COMPLETE SET (6) 12.00 30.00
72 Adrian Peterson 1.00 2.50
121 Devin Hester .60 1.50
256 Felix Jones 1.50 4.00
262 Matt Ryan 4.00 10.00
266 Darren McFadden 2.50 6.00
281 Jonathan Stewart 1.50 4.00

2009 Donruss Threads

COMP.SET w/o RC's (100) 8.00 20.00
ROOKIE STICKER AU PRINT RUN 99-499
ROOKIE PATCH AU PRINT RUN 99-396
1 Kurt Warner .30 .75
2 Larry Fitzgerald .30 .75
3 Tim Hightower .20 .50
4 Matt Ryan .30 .75
5 Michael Turner .25 .60
6 Roddy White .25 .60
7 Derrick Mason .25 .60
8 Joe Flacco .30 .75
9 Willis McGahee .25 .60
10 Lee Evans .25 .60
11 Marshawn Lynch .25 .60
12 Terrell Owens .30 .75
13 DeAngelo Williams .30 .75
14 Jake Delhomme .25 .60
15 Jonathan Stewart .25 .60
16 Steve Smith .25 .60
17 Greg Olsen .20 .50
18 Kyle Orton .25 .60
19 Matt Forte .30 .75
20 Carson Palmer .30 .75
21 Cedric Benson .25 .60
22 Chad Ochocinco .25 .60
23 Brady Quinn .25 .60
24 Braylon Edwards .25 .60
25 Jamal Lewis .25 .60
26 Marion Barber .25 .60
27 Roy Williams WR .25 .60
28 Tony Romo .50 1.25
29 Brandon Marshall .25 .60
30 Jay Cutler .30 .75
31 Correll Buckhalter .20 .50
32 Calvin Johnson .30 .75
33 Daunte Culpepper .25 .60
34 Kevin Smith .25 .60
35 Aaron Rodgers .60 1.50
36 Greg Jennings .30 .75
37 Ryan Grant .25 .60
38 Andre Johnson .25 .60
39 Matt Schaub .25 .60
40 Steve Slaton .25 .60
41 Anthony Gonzalez .20 .50
42 Joseph Addai .30 .75
43 Peyton Manning .50 1.25
44 Reggie Wayne .25 .60
45 David Garrard .25 .60
46 Marcedes Lewis .20 .50
47 Maurice Jones-Drew .25 .60
48 Dwayne Bowe .25 .60
49 Larry Johnson .25 .60
50 Matt Cassel .25 .60
51 Tony Gonzalez .25 .60
52 Chad Pennington .25 .60
53 Ricky Williams .25 .60
54 Ronnie Brown .25 .60
55 Adrian Peterson .50 1.25
56 Bernard Berrian .25 .60
57 Visanthe Shiancoe .25 .60
58 Laurence Maroney .25 .60
59 Tom Brady .50 1.25
60 Wes Welker .30 .75
61 Randy Moss .30 .75
62 Drew Brees .30 .75
63 Marques Colston .25 .60
64 Reggie Bush .30 .75
65 Brandon Jacobs .25 .60
66 Eli Manning .30 .75
67 Kevin Boss .25 .60
68 Thomas Jones .25 .60
69 Jerricho Cotchery .25 .60
70 Leon Washington .25 .60
71 Darren McFadden .30 .75
72 JaMarcus Russell .20 .50
73 Zach Miller .20 .50
74 Brian Westbrook .25 .60
75 DeSean Jackson .25 .60
76 Donovan McNabb .30 .75
77 Ben Roethlisberger .30 .75
78 Santonio Holmes .25 .60
79 Willie Parker .20 .50
80 LaDainian Tomlinson .30 .75
81 Philip Rivers .30 .75
82 Vincent Jackson .25 .60
83 Frank Gore .25 .60
84 Shaun Hill .20 .50
85 Vernon Davis .25 .60
86 Julius Jones .20 .50
87 Matt Hasselbeck .25 .60
88 T.J. Houshmandzadeh .25 .60
89 Marc Bulger .25 .60
90 Steven Jackson .25 .60
91 Torry Holt .25 .60
92 Antonio Bryant .20 .50
93 Derrick Ward .20 .50
94 Kellen Winslow Jr. .25 .60
95 Chris Johnson .30 .75
96 Kerry Collins .25 .60
97 LenDale White .25 .60
98 Chris Cooley .25 .60
99 Clinton Portis .25 .60
100 Jason Campbell .20 .50
101 Aaron Brown RC 2.50 6.00
102 Aaron Kelly AU/199 RC 4.00 10.00
103 Aaron Maybin RC 2.00 5.00
104 Alphonso Smith RC 2.00 5.00
105 Andre Smith RC 2.00 5.00
106 Anthony Hill RC 1.50 4.00
107 Arian Foster RC 5.00 12.00
108 Asher Allen RC 2.00 5.00
109 Austin Collie AU/149 RC 8.00 20.00
110 Bernard Scott RC 2.50 6.00
111 Bradley Fletcher RC 2.00 5.00
112 Brandon Gibson AU/199 RC 5.00 12.00
113 Brian Hartline RC 2.50 6.00
114 Brooks Foster AU/199 RC 3.00 8.00
115 Cameron Morrah AU/499 RC 3.00 8.00
116 Chase Daniel RC 2.00 5.00
117 Chip Vaughn RC 1.50 4.00
118 Chris Ogbonnaya RC 2.00 5.00
119 Chris Owens RC 2.00 5.00
120 Clay Matthews AU/199 RC 35.00 60.00
121 Clint Sintim AU/99 RC 6.00 15.00
122 Cody Brown RC 1.50 4.00
123 Connor Barwin RC 2.50 6.00
124 Cornelius Ingram AU/199 RC 3.00 8.00
125 Curtis Painter RC 2.50 6.00
126 Darcel McBath RC 2.00 5.00
127 Darius Butler RC 2.50 6.00
128 Darius Passmore AU/199 RC 4.00 10.00
129 David Bruton RC 2.00 5.00
130 David Johnson RC 2.00 5.00
131 DeAndre Levy RC 2.50 6.00
132 Demetrius Byrd AU/499 RC 4.00 10.00
133 Devin Moore AU/249 RC 4.00 10.00
134 Davon Drew RC 2.00 5.00
135 Dominique Edison AU/199 RC 3.00 8.00
136 Eddie Williams RC 2.00 5.00
137 Eugene Monroe RC 1.50 4.00
138 Evander Hood RC 3.00 8.00
139 Gartrell Johnson RC 1.50 4.00
140 Gerald McRath RC 2.00 5.00
141 Glover Quin RC 2.00 5.00
142 Graham Harrell RC 2.50 6.00
143 Hunter Cantwell RC 2.50 6.00
144 Ian Johnson RC 2.50 6.00
145 Jairus Byrd RC 2.50 6.00
146 James Casey AU/199 RC 4.00 10.00
147 James Davis RC 2.50 6.00
148 James Laurinaitis AU/199 RC 5.00 12.00
149 Jarett Dillard AU/499 RC 5.00 12.00
150 Jason Phillips RC 2.00 5.00
151 Jason Williams RC 2.50 6.00
152 Jasper Brinkley RC 2.00 5.00
153 Javarris Williams RC 2.00 5.00
154 Jeremy Childs RC 2.00 5.00
155 Jerraud Powers RC 2.00 5.00
156 John Phillips RC 2.50 6.00
157 Johnny Knox AU/199 RC 15.00 30.00
158 Kaluka Maiava RC 2.50 6.00
160 Keenan Lewis RC 2.50 6.00
160 Keith Null RC 2.00 5.00
161 Kenny McKinley AU/199 RC 5.00 12.00
162 Kevin Barnes RC 2.00 5.00
163 Kevin Huber RC 1.50 4.00
164 Kevin Ogletree AU/199 RC 8.00 20.00
165 Lardarius Webb RC 2.50 6.00
166 Larry English AU/199 RC 5.00 12.00
167 Louis Delmas RC 2.50 6.00
168 Louis Murphy AU/299 RC 8.00 20.00
169 Manuel Johnson RC 2.00 5.00
170 Marcus Freeman RC 2.50 6.00
171 Marko Mitchell RC 2.00 5.00
172 Bear Pascoe RC 2.00 5.00
173 Michael Mitchell RC 2.00 5.00
174 Mike Goodson AU/399 RC 5.00 12.00
175 Nathan Brown AU/149 RC 5.00 12.00
176 Nic Harris RC 2.00 5.00
177 P.J. Hill AU/199 RC 4.00 10.00
178 Patrick Chung RC 2.50 6.00
179 Peria Jerry RC 2.00 5.00
180 Quan Cosby AU/149 RC 5.00 12.00
181 Quinn Johnson AU/149 RC 5.00 12.00
182 Quinten Lawrence RC 1.50 4.00
183 Rashad Johnson RC 2.00 5.00
184 Richard Quinn RC 2.00 5.00
185 Robert Ayers RC 2.50 6.00
186 Ryan Mouton RC 2.00 5.00
187 Sammie Stroughter RC 2.50 6.00
188 Scott McKillop RC 2.00 5.00
189 Sean Smith RC 2.50 6.00
190 Sen'Derrick Marks RC 1.50 4.00
191 Shawn Nelson No AU/149 RC 2.00 5.00
192 Sherrod Martin RC 2.00 5.00
193 Stanley Arnoux RC 2.00 5.00
194 Tiquan Underwood RC 2.00 5.00
195 Tony Fiammetta AU/199 RC 4.00 10.00
196 Travis Beckum AU/249 RC 4.00 10.00
197 Tyrell Sutton AU/499 RC 6.00 15.00
198 Tyrone McKenzie RC 2.00 5.00
199 Victor Butler RC 2.00 5.00
200 William Moore RC 2.50 6.00
201 Aaron Curry AU/275 RC 10.00 25.00
202 Andre Brown AU/175 RC 6.00 15.00
203 B.J. Raji AU/392 RC 12.00 30.00
204 Brandon Pettigrew AU/180 RC 10.00 25.00
205 Brandon Tate AU/200 RC 10.00 25.00
206 Brian Cushing AU/280 RC 10.00 25.00
207 Brian Orakpo AU/258 RC 10.00 25.00
208 Brian Robiskie AU/200 RC 10.00 25.00
209 Cedric Peerman AU/385 RC 8.00 20.00
210 Chase Coffman AU/385 RC 8.00 20.00
211 Chris Wells AU/175 RC 15.00 40.00
212 Darrius Heyward-Bey AU/250 RC 10.00 25.00
213 Derrick Williams AU/200 RC 8.00 20.00
214 Donald Brown AU/175 RC 10.00 25.00
215 Everette Brown AU/275 RC 8.00 20.00
216 Glen Coffee AU/270 RC 8.00 20.00
217 Hakeem Nicks AU/175 RC 15.00 40.00
218 Tyson Jackson AU/350 RC 8.00 20.00
219 Deon Butler AU/300 RC 8.00 20.00
220 Jared Cook AU/396 RC 10.00 25.00
221 Javon Ringer AU/180 RC 10.00 25.00
222 Jeremiah Johnson AU/175 RC 10.00 25.00
223 Jeremy Maclin AU/180 RC 15.00 40.00
224 John Parker Wilson AU/180 RC 10.00 25.00
225 Josh Freeman AU/175 RC 30.00 60.00
226 Juaquin Iglesias AU/200 RC 8.00 20.00
227 Kenny Britt AU/175 RC 12.00 30.00
228 Knowshon Moreno AU/180 RC 20.00 50.00
229 Kory Sheets AU/390 RC 8.00 20.00
230 LeSean McCoy AU/175 RC 20.00 50.00
231 Malcolm Jenkins AU/280 RC 10.00 25.00
232 Mark Sanchez AU/175 RC 60.00 100.00
233 Matthew Stafford AU/160 RC 60.00 100.00
234 Michael Crabtree AU/160 RC 20.00 50.00
235 Jason Smith AU/250 RC 8.00 20.00
236 Mike Thomas AU/390 RC 10.00 25.00
237 Mike Wallace AU/350 RC 20.00 50.00
238 Mohamed Massaquoi AU/180 RC 8.00 20.00
239 Nate Davis AU/125 RC 8.00 20.00
240 Pat White AU/125 RC 12.00 30.00
241 Patrick Turner AU/300 RC 8.00 20.00
242 Percy Harvin AU/180 RC 25.00 60.00
243 Ramses Barden AU/300 RC 6.00 15.00
244 Rashad Jennings AU/160 RC 10.00 25.00
245 Rey Maualuga AU/280 RC 10.00 25.00
246 Rhett Bomar AU/175 RC 8.00 20.00
247 Shonn Greene AU/180 RC 15.00 40.00
248 Stephen McGee AU/200 RC 10.00 25.00
249 Tom Brandstater AU/385 RC 10.00 25.00
250 Vontae Davis AU/275 RC 10.00 25.00
251 Brett Favre 12.00 30.00

2009 Donruss Threads Gold Holofoil

*VETS 1-100: 4X TO 10X BASIC CARDS
*ROOKIE 101-200: 1X TO 2.5X RETAIL RED
STATED PRINT RUN 50 SER.#'d SETS

2009 Donruss Threads Platinum Holofoil

*VETS 1-100: 5X TO 12X BASIC INSERTS
*ROOKIE 101-200: 1.2X TO 3X RETAIL RED
STATED PRINT RUN 25 SER.#'d SETS

2009 Donruss Threads Retail Green

*VETS 1-100: 3X TO 8X BASIC CARDS
*ROOKIE 101-200: .8X TO 2X RETAIL RED
STATED PRINT RUN 100 SER.#'d SETS

2009 Donruss Threads Retail Red

*VETS 1-100: 1.5X TO 4X BASIC CARDS
COMMON ROOKIE (101-200) 1.25 3.00
ROOKIE SEMISTARS 1.50 4.00
ROOKIE UNL.STARS 2.00 5.00
RANDOM INSERTS IN RETAIL PACKS
103 Aaron Maybin 1.50 4.00
116 Chase Daniel 2.00 5.00
120 Clay Matthews 5.00 12.00
138 Evander Hood 2.50 6.00
142 Graham Harrell 2.00 5.00
148 James Laurinaitis 2.00 5.00
157 Johnny Knox 3.00 8.00
185 Robert Ayers 2.00 5.00

2009 Donruss Threads Retail Rookies

*ROOKIES: .4X TO 1X BASIC CARDS
STATED PRINT RUN 999 SER.#'d SETS

2009 Donruss Threads Silver Holofoil

*VETS 1-100: 2X TO 5X BASIC CARDS
*ROOKIE 101-200: .5X TO 1.2X RETAIL RED
STATED PRINT RUN 250 SER.#'d SETS

2009 Donruss Threads Autographs Silver

STATED PRINT RUN 1-50
SERIAL #'d UNDER 20 NOT PRICED
3 Tim Hightower/25 6.00 15.00
5 Michael Turner/20 8.00 20.00
21 Cedric Benson/25 8.00 20.00
34 Kevin Smith/50 6.00 15.00
36 Greg Jennings/25 10.00 25.00
40 Steve Slaton/50 6.00 15.00
42 Joseph Addai/25 10.00 25.00
49 Larry Johnson/25 8.00 20.00
63 Marques Colston/50 6.00 15.00
73 Zach Miller/50 5.00 12.00
75 DeSean Jackson/40 6.00 15.00
93 Derrick Ward/30 6.00 15.00
109 Austin Collie/25 10.00 25.00
112 Brandon Gibson/25 8.00 20.00
114 Brooks Foster/25 5.00 12.00
115 Cameron Morrah/50 4.00 10.00
128 Darius Passmore/42 5.00 12.00
132 Demetrius Byrd/50 5.00 12.00
133 Devin Moore/25 6.00 15.00
135 Dominique Edison/25 5.00 12.00
146 James Casey/25 6.00 15.00
149 Jarett Dillard/50 6.00 15.00
157 Johnny Knox/25 15.00 30.00
161 Kenny McKinley/25 8.00 20.00
164 Kevin Ogletree/25 8.00 20.00
168 Louis Murphy/25 10.00 25.00
174 Mike Goodson/25 8.00 20.00
175 Nathan Brown/25 6.00 15.00
177 P.J. Hill/25 6.00 15.00
181 Quinn Johnson/25 6.00 15.00
191 Shawn Nelson/25 No AU 2.50 6.00
196 Travis Beckum/25 6.00 15.00
197 Tyrell Sutton/50 5.00 12.00

2009 Donruss Threads Century Collection Materials Prime

STATED PRINT RUN 18-50
*BASE JSY/250: .25X TO .6X PRIME/35-50
*BASE JSY/250: .2X TO .5X PRIME/18
*BASE JSY/100: .3X TO .8X PRIME/35-50
1 Antonio Gates/50 5.00 12.00
2 Ben Roethlisberger/50 6.00 15.00
3 Brandon Jacobs/50 5.00 12.00
4 Brian Westbrook/50 5.00 12.00
5 Clinton Portis/50 5.00 12.00
6 Donald Driver/50 5.00 12.00
7 Donovan McNabb/50 6.00 15.00
8 Eli Manning/35 6.00 15.00
9 Joseph Addai/50 6.00 15.00
10 LaDainian Tomlinson/50 6.00 15.00
11 Peyton Manning/18 12.00 30.00
12 Randy Moss/50 6.00 15.00
13 Ricky Williams/50 5.00 12.00
14 Tom Brady/50 10.00 25.00
15 Tony Gonzalez/50 5.00 12.00

2009 Donruss Threads Century Legends

*CENT.PROOF/100: .6X TO 1.5X BASIC INSERT
1 Archie Manning 1.50 4.00
2 Chuck Bednarik 1.25 3.00
3 Danny White 1.25 3.00
4 Dick Butkus 2.00 5.00
5 Frank Gifford 1.50 4.00
6 Jerry Rice 2.50 6.00
7 Jim Brown 2.00 5.00
8 Joe Montana 3.00 8.00
9 Joe Namath 2.00 5.00
10 Ozzie Newsome 1.25 3.00
11 Paul Hornung 1.50 4.00
12 Randy White 1.50 4.00
13 Steve Young 2.00 5.00
14 Thurman Thomas 1.50 4.00
15 Tommy McDonald 1.00 2.50

2009 Donruss Threads Century Legends Materials

STATED PRINT RUN 50-250
*PRIME/50: .8X TO 2X BASIC JSY/200-250
*PRIME/50: .6X TO 1.5X BASIC JSY/125
*PRIME/25-30: 1X TO 2.5X BASIC JSY/200-250
*PRIME/15: 1.2X TO 3X BASIC JSY/200-250
*PRIME/15: .8X TO 2X BASIC JSY/50
PRIME PRINT RUN 4-50
1 Archie Manning/250 6.00 15.00
2 Chuck Bednarik/200 5.00 12.00
3 Danny White/200 5.00 12.00
4 Dick Butkus/250 8.00 20.00
5 Frank Gifford/95 8.00 20.00
6 Jerry Rice/125 12.00 30.00
7 Jim Brown/100 10.00 25.00
8 Joe Montana/250 12.00 30.00
9 Joe Namath/50 12.00 30.00
10 Ozzie Newsome/250 5.00 12.00
11 Paul Hornung/250 6.00 15.00
12 Randy White/250 6.00 15.00
13 Steve Young/250 8.00 20.00
14 Thurman Thomas/250 6.00 15.00
15 Tommy McDonald/250 4.00 10.00

2009 Donruss Threads Century Stars

*CENT.PROOF/100: .6X TO 1.5X BASIC INSERT
1 Adrian Peterson 2.00 5.00
2 Ben Roethlisberger 1.25 3.00
3 Braylon Edwards 1.00 2.50
4 Chad Ochocinco 1.00 2.50
5 Clinton Portis 1.00 2.50
6 Donovan McNabb 1.25 3.00
7 Eli Manning 1.25 3.00
8 Frank Gore 1.00 2.50
9 Hines Ward 1.00 2.50
10 Larry Fitzgerald 1.25 3.00
11 Lee Evans 1.00 2.50
12 Marion Barber 1.00 2.50
13 Maurice Jones-Drew 1.00 2.50
14 Philip Rivers 1.25 3.00
15 Randy Moss 1.25 3.00
16 Reggie Wayne 1.00 2.50
17 Tom Brady 2.00 5.00
18 Tony Gonzalez 1.00 2.50
19 Tony Romo 2.00 5.00
20 Torry Holt 1.00 2.50

2009 Donruss Threads Century Stars Materials

STATED PRINT RUN 20-250
*PRIME/50: .8X TO 2X BASE JSY/250
*PRIME/50: .6X TO 1.5X BASE JSY/100
*PRIME/50: .5X TO 1.2X BASE JSY/65
*PRIME/50: .3X TO .8X BASE JSY/20
*PRIME/25: .8X TO 2X BASE JSY/100
PRIME PRINT RUN 5-50
1 Adrian Peterson/100 6.00 15.00
2 Ben Roethlisberger/100 4.00 10.00
3 Braylon Edwards/250 2.50 6.00
4 Chad Ochocinco/20 6.00 15.00
5 Clinton Portis/100 3.00 8.00
6 Donovan McNabb/250 3.00 8.00
7 Eli Manning/100 4.00 10.00
8 Frank Gore/100 3.00 8.00
9 Hines Ward/65 4.00 10.00
10 Larry Fitzgerald/100 4.00 10.00
11 Lee Evans/100 3.00 8.00
12 Marion Barber/100 3.00 8.00
13 Maurice Jones-Drew/100 3.00 8.00
14 Philip Rivers/100 4.00 10.00
15 Randy Moss/100 4.00 10.00
16 Reggie Wayne/100 3.00 8.00
17 Tom Brady/250 5.00 12.00
19 Tony Romo/250 5.00 12.00
20 Torry Holt/250 2.50 6.00

2009 Donruss Threads College Greats

1 Bob Lilly 1.25 3.00
2 Brandon Pettigrew .60 1.50
3 Carl Eller 1.00 2.50
4 Chris Wells 1.00 2.50
5 Ace Parker 1.00 2.50
6 Donald Brown .60 1.50
7 Earl Campbell 1.50 4.00
8 Graham Harrell .60 1.50
9 Hugh McElhenny 1.00 2.50
10 James Casey .50 1.25
11 Javon Ringer .60 1.50
12 Jeremy Maclin 1.00 2.50
13 Knowshon Moreno .60 1.50
14 LeSean McCoy 1.25 3.00
15 Mark Sanchez 2.00 5.00
16 Matthew Stafford 3.00 8.00
17 Michael Crabtree 1.25 3.00
18 Nate Davis .50 1.25
19 Percy Harvin 1.00 2.50
20 Shonn Greene 1.00 2.50

2009 Donruss Threads College Greats Autographs

STATED PRINT RUN 25-100
1 Bob Lilly/20 12.00 30.00
2 Brandon Pettigrew/50 8.00 20.00
3 Carl Eller/50 8.00 20.00
4 Chris Wells/25 15.00 40.00
5 Ace Parker/75 15.00 30.00
6 Donald Brown/25 10.00 25.00
7 Earl Campbell/25 15.00 40.00
8 Graham Harrell/50 12.00 30.00
9 Hugh McElhenny/100 8.00 20.00
10 James Casey/50 6.00 15.00
11 Javon Ringer/50 8.00 20.00
12 Jeremy Maclin/25 15.00 40.00
13 Knowshon Moreno/25 10.00 25.00
14 LeSean McCoy/25 20.00 50.00
15 Mark Sanchez/25 50.00 100.00
16 Matthew Stafford/25 50.00 100.00
17 Michael Crabtree/25 30.00 60.00
18 Nate Davis/50 6.00 15.00
19 Percy Harvin/25 30.00 60.00
20 Shonn Greene/50 12.00 30.00

2009 Donruss Threads College Gridiron Kings

*FRAMED BLACK/10: 2X TO 5X
*FRAMED BLUE/50: 1X TO 2.5X
*FRAMED GREEN/25: 1.2X TO 3X
*FRAMED RED/100: .8X TO 2X
1 Aaron Curry .75 2.00
2 Aaron Maybin .60 1.50
3 Andre Brown .50 1.25
4 B.J. Raji .75 2.00
5 Brandon Gibson .75 2.00
6 Brandon Pettigrew .75 2.00
7 Brandon Tate .75 2.00
8 Brian Cushing .75 2.00
9 Brian Orakpo .75 2.00
10 Brian Robiskie .75 2.00
11 Chase Coffman .60 1.50
12 Chris Wells 1.25 3.00
13 Darrius Heyward-Bey .75 2.00
14 Deon Butler .60 1.50
15 Derrick Williams .60 1.50
16 Donald Brown .75 2.00
17 Glen Coffee .60 1.50
18 Graham Harrell .75 2.00
19 Hakeem Nicks 1.25 3.00
20 James Casey .60 1.50
21 James Laurinaitis .75 2.00
22 Jared Cook .75 2.00
23 Jason Smith .60 1.50
24 Javon Ringer .75 2.00
25 Jeremiah Johnson .75 2.00
26 Jeremy Maclin 1.25 3.00
27 John Parker Wilson .75 2.00
28 Josh Freeman 1.50 4.00
29 Juaquin Iglesias .60 1.50
30 Kenny Britt 1.00 2.50
31 Kenny McKinley .75 2.00
32 Knowshon Moreno .75 2.00
33 LeSean McCoy 1.50 4.00
34 Malcolm Jenkins .75 2.00
35 Mark Sanchez 2.50 6.00
36 Matthew Stafford 4.00 10.00
37 Michael Crabtree 1.50 4.00
38 Mike Thomas .75 2.00
39 Mike Wallace 1.50 4.00
40 Mohamed Massaquoi .60 1.50
41 Pat White .75 2.00
42 Patrick Turner .60 1.50
43 Percy Harvin 1.25 3.00
44 Quan Cosby .60 1.50
45 Ramses Barden .50 1.25
46 Rey Maualuga .75 2.00
47 Rhett Bomar .60 1.50
48 Shonn Greene 1.25 3.00
49 Tyson Jackson .60 1.50
50 Vontae Davis .75 2.00

2009 Donruss Threads College Gridiron Kings Autographs

STATED PRINT RUN 25-163
1 Aaron Curry/50 8.00 20.00
3 Andre Brown/50 5.00 12.00
5 Brandon Gibson/25 10.00 25.00
6 Brandon Pettigrew/50 8.00 20.00
7 Brandon Tate/25 10.00 25.00
8 Brian Cushing/25 10.00 25.00
9 Brian Orakpo/25 10.00 25.00
10 Brian Robiskie/50 8.00 20.00
11 Chase Coffman/25 8.00 20.00
12 Chris Wells/25 15.00 40.00
13 Darrius Heyward-Bey/25 10.00 25.00
14 Deon Butler/50 6.00 15.00
15 Derrick Williams/25 8.00 20.00
16 Donald Brown/25 10.00 25.00
17 Glen Coffee/50 6.00 15.00
18 Graham Harrell/163 10.00 25.00
19 Hakeem Nicks/25 15.00 40.00
20 James Casey/50 6.00 15.00
21 James Laurinaitis/25 10.00 25.00
23 Jason Smith/50 6.00 15.00
24 Javon Ringer/50 8.00 20.00
26 Jeremy Maclin/25 15.00 40.00
28 Josh Freeman/25 20.00 50.00
31 Kenny McKinley/25 10.00 25.00
32 Knowshon Moreno/25 10.00 25.00
33 LeSean McCoy/25 20.00 50.00
35 Mark Sanchez/25 30.00 80.00
36 Matthew Stafford/25 50.00 120.00
37 Michael Crabtree/25 20.00 50.00
38 Mike Thomas/25 10.00 25.00
39 Mike Wallace/50 15.00 40.00
40 Mohamed Massaquoi/25 8.00 20.00
42 Patrick Turner/50 6.00 15.00
43 Percy Harvin/25 15.00 40.00
44 Quan Cosby/25 8.00 20.00
45 Ramses Barden/25 6.00 15.00
46 Rey Maualuga/25 10.00 25.00
47 Rhett Bomar/25 8.00 20.00
48 Shonn Greene/50 12.00 30.00
49 Tyson Jackson/25 8.00 20.00

2009 Donruss Threads College Gridiron Kings Materials

STATED PRINT RUN 25-250
5 Brandon Gibson/250 3.00 8.00
8 Brian Cushing/175 3.00 8.00
9 Brian Orakpo/30 6.00 15.00
11 Chase Coffman/250 2.50 6.00
12 Chris Wells/100 6.00 15.00
15 Derrick Williams/45 4.00 10.00
18 Graham Harrell/25 6.00 15.00
21 James Laurinaitis/85 4.00 10.00
25 Jeremiah Johnson/250 3.00 8.00
26 Jeremy Maclin/250 5.00 12.00
28 Josh Freeman/250 6.00 15.00
29 Juaquin Iglesias/25 5.00 12.00
31 Kenny McKinley/250 3.00 8.00
33 LeSean McCoy/250 6.00 15.00
35 Mark Sanchez/75 12.00 30.00
40 Mohamed Massaquoi/250 2.50 6.00
44 Quan Cosby/80 3.00 8.00
45 Ramses Barden/250 2.00 5.00
46 Rey Maualuga/95 4.00 10.00
47 Rhett Bomar/250 2.50 6.00
49 Tyson Jackson/250 2.50 6.00

2009 Donruss Threads College Gridiron Kings Materials Prime

PRIME PRINT RUN 5-50
5 Brandon Gibson/50 6.00 15.00
7 Brandon Tate/50 6.00 15.00
8 Brian Cushing/15 10.00 25.00
9 Brian Orakpo/50 6.00 15.00
11 Chase Coffman/50 5.00 12.00
12 Chris Wells/50 10.00 25.00
16 Donald Brown/50 6.00 15.00
18 Graham Harrell/50 6.00 15.00
21 James Laurinaitis/50 6.00 15.00
25 Jeremiah Johnson/50 6.00 15.00
26 Jeremy Maclin/25 12.00 30.00
28 Josh Freeman/50 12.00 30.00
29 Juaquin Iglesias/30 6.00 15.00
31 Kenny McKinley/50 6.00 15.00
33 LeSean McCoy/50 12.00 30.00
35 Mark Sanchez/15 30.00 80.00
40 Mohamed Massaquoi/25 6.00 15.00
44 Quan Cosby/50 5.00 12.00
45 Ramses Barden/30 5.00 12.00
46 Rey Maualuga/50 6.00 15.00
47 Rhett Bomar/50 5.00 12.00
49 Tyson Jackson/50 5.00 12.00

2009 Donruss Threads College Gridiron Kings Material Autographs

JSY AUTO PRINT RUN 9-25
SERIAL #'d UNDER 25 NOT PRICED
5 Brandon Gibson/25 12.00 30.00
8 Brian Cushing/25 12.00 30.00
9 Brian Orakpo/25 12.00 30.00
11 Chase Coffman/25 10.00 25.00
12 Chris Wells/25 20.00 50.00
18 Graham Harrell/25 20.00 50.00
21 James Laurinaitis/25 12.00 30.00
26 Jeremy Maclin/25 20.00 50.00
28 Josh Freeman/25 25.00 60.00
31 Kenny McKinley/25 12.00 30.00
33 LeSean McCoy/25 25.00 60.00
35 Mark Sanchez/25 60.00 120.00
36 Matthew Stafford/25 60.00 120.00
40 Mohamed Massaquoi/25 10.00 25.00
44 Quan Cosby/25 10.00 25.00
45 Ramses Barden/25 8.00 20.00
46 Rey Maualuga/25 12.00 30.00
47 Rhett Bomar/25 10.00 25.00
49 Tyson Jackson/25 10.00 25.00

2009 Donruss Threads Generations

*CENT.PROOF/100: .6X TO 1.5X BASE INSERTS
1 Ozzie Newsome 1.00 2.50
Braylon Edwards
2 Tommy McDonald 1.00 2.50
DeSean Jackson
3 Earl Campbell 1.25 3.00
Chris Johnson
4 Paul Hornung 1.25 3.00
Ryan Grant
5 Archie Manning 1.25 3.00
Drew Brees
6 Jerry Rice 2.00 5.00
Calvin Johnson
7 Hines Ward .75 2.00
Santonio Holmes
8 LaDainian Tomlinson 1.50 4.00
Adrian Peterson
9 Chad Ochocinco .75 2.00
Andre Johnson
10 Tony Gonzalez .75 2.00
Dwayne Bowe
11 Randy Moss 1.00 2.50
Wes Welker
12 Dick Butkus 1.50 4.00
Brian Urlacher
13 DeAngelo Williams 1.00 2.50
Jonathan Stewart
14 Larry Johnson 1.00 2.50
Jamaal Charles
15 Brian Westbrook .75 2.00
Marion Barber

2009 Donruss Threads Generations Materials Prime

PRIME PRINT RUN 50 SER.#'d SETS
*BASE JSY/250: .25X TO .6X PRIME/50
*BASE JSY/80-130: .3X TO .8X PRIME/50
*BASE JSY/20: .6X TO 1.5X PRIME/50
1 Ozzie Newsome 5.00 12.00
Braylon Edwards

3 Earl Campbell	6.00	15.00
Chris Johnson		
4 Paul Hornung	6.00	15.00
Ryan Grant		
5 Archie Manning	6.00	15.00
Drew Brees		
6 Jerry Rice	12.00	30.00
Calvin Johnson		
7 Hines Ward	4.00	10.00
Santonio Holmes		
8 LaDainian Tomlinson	8.00	20.00
Adrian Peterson		
9 Chad Ochocinco	4.00	10.00
Andre Johnson		
10 Tony Gonzalez	4.00	10.00
Dwayne Bowe		
11 Randy Moss	8.00	20.00
Wes Welker		
12 Dick Butkus	8.00	20.00
Brian Urlacher		
13 DeAngelo Williams	5.00	12.00
Jonathan Stewart		
15 Brian Westbrook	4.00	10.00
Marion Barber		

2009 Donruss Threads Jerseys

STATED PRINT RUN 2-250

2 Larry Fitzgerald/100	4.00	10.00
4 Matt Ryan/100	4.00	10.00
5 Michael Turner/100	3.00	8.00
6 Roddy White/100	3.00	8.00
7 Derrick Mason/250	2.50	6.00
8 Joe Flacco/160	4.00	10.00
9 Willis McGahee/250	2.50	6.00
10 Lee Evans/100	3.00	8.00
12 Terrell Owens/250	3.00	8.00
13 DeAngelo Williams/250	3.00	8.00
14 Jake Delhomme/250	2.50	6.00
16 Steve Smith/100	3.00	8.00
17 Greg Olsen/100	2.50	6.00
20 Carson Palmer/250	3.00	8.00
23 Brady Quinn/100	3.00	8.00
24 Braylon Edwards/100	3.00	8.00
26 Marion Barber/100	3.00	8.00
27 Roy Williams WR/119	3.00	8.00
28 Tony Romo/250	5.00	12.00
29 Brandon Marshall/100	3.00	8.00
32 Calvin Johnson/100	4.00	10.00
33 Daunte Culpepper/120	3.00	8.00
35 Aaron Rodgers/250	6.00	15.00
36 Greg Jennings/100	4.00	10.00
38 Andre Johnson/250	2.50	6.00
40 Steve Slaton/100	3.00	8.00
41 Anthony Gonzalez/250	2.00	5.00
42 Joseph Addai/250	3.00	8.00
43 Peyton Manning/250	5.00	12.00
44 Reggie Wayne/100	3.00	8.00
45 David Garrard/250	2.50	6.00
47 Maurice Jones-Drew/100	3.00	8.00
48 Dwayne Bowe/250	2.50	6.00
49 Larry Johnson/60	4.00	10.00
53 Ricky Williams/250	2.50	6.00
55 Adrian Peterson/100	6.00	15.00
58 Laurence Maroney/160	3.00	8.00
59 Tom Brady/250	5.00	12.00
62 Drew Brees/250	3.00	8.00
63 Marques Colston/250	2.50	6.00
64 Reggie Bush/130	4.00	10.00
65 Brandon Jacobs/100	3.00	8.00
66 Eli Manning/100	4.00	10.00
69 Jerricho Cotchery/250	2.50	6.00
71 Darren McFadden/100	4.00	10.00
72 JaMarcus Russell/250	2.00	5.00
74 Brian Westbrook/100	3.00	8.00
76 Donovan McNabb/250	3.00	8.00
77 Ben Roethlisberger/100	4.00	10.00
78 Santonio Holmes/100	3.00	8.00
80 LaDainian Tomlinson/250	3.00	8.00
81 Philip Rivers/100	4.00	10.00
83 Frank Gore/100	3.00	8.00
87 Matt Hasselbeck/250	2.50	6.00
89 Marc Bulger/250	2.50	6.00
92 Antonio Bryant/230	2.00	5.00
95 Chris Johnson/250	3.00	8.00
97 LenDale White/55	4.00	10.00
98 Chris Cooley/100	3.00	8.00
99 Clinton Portis/100	3.00	8.00
100 Jason Campbell/110	2.50	6.00

2009 Donruss Threads Jerseys Prime

PRIME PRINT RUN 2-50

2 Larry Fitzgerald/25	10.00	25.00
4 Matt Ryan/25	10.00	25.00
5 Michael Turner/50	6.00	15.00
6 Roddy White/50	6.00	15.00
7 Derrick Mason/50	6.00	15.00
9 Willis McGahee/50	6.00	15.00
10 Lee Evans/50	6.00	15.00
11 Marshawn Lynch/50	6.00	15.00
13 DeAngelo Williams/50	8.00	20.00
14 Jake Delhomme/50	6.00	15.00
15 Jonathan Stewart/50	6.00	15.00
16 Steve Smith/50	6.00	15.00
17 Greg Olsen/25	6.00	15.00
20 Carson Palmer/50	8.00	20.00
22 Chad Ochocinco/50	6.00	15.00
23 Brady Quinn/25	8.00	20.00
24 Braylon Edwards/50	6.00	15.00
26 Marion Barber/50	6.00	15.00
28 Tony Romo/50	12.00	30.00
29 Brandon Marshall/44	6.00	15.00
32 Calvin Johnson/50	8.00	20.00
35 Aaron Rodgers/50	15.00	40.00
36 Greg Jennings/50	8.00	20.00
37 Ryan Grant/50	6.00	15.00
38 Andre Johnson/50	6.00	15.00
40 Steve Slaton/50	6.00	15.00
42 Joseph Addai/50	8.00	20.00
43 Peyton Manning/25	15.00	40.00
44 Reggie Wayne/25	8.00	20.00
45 David Garrard/50	6.00	15.00
47 Maurice Jones-Drew/50	6.00	15.00
48 Dwayne Bowe/50	6.00	15.00
49 Larry Johnson/50	6.00	15.00
53 Ricky Williams/50	6.00	15.00
54 Ronnie Brown/50	6.00	15.00
55 Adrian Peterson/50	12.00	30.00
56 Bernard Berrian/50	6.00	15.00
58 Laurence Maroney/50	6.00	15.00
59 Tom Brady/50	12.00	30.00
60 Wes Welker/50	8.00	20.00
62 Drew Brees/50	8.00	20.00
63 Marques Colston/50	6.00	15.00
64 Reggie Bush/50	8.00	20.00
65 Brandon Jacobs/50	6.00	15.00
66 Eli Manning/25	10.00	25.00
69 Jerricho Cotchery/50	6.00	15.00
70 Leon Washington/30	8.00	20.00
71 Darren McFadden/25	10.00	25.00
72 JaMarcus Russell/50	5.00	12.00
74 Brian Westbrook/50	6.00	15.00
76 Donovan McNabb/50	8.00	20.00
77 Ben Roethlisberger/50	8.00	20.00
78 Santonio Holmes/50	6.00	15.00
79 Willie Parker/50	5.00	12.00
80 LaDainian Tomlinson/50	8.00	20.00
81 Philip Rivers/50	8.00	20.00
82 Vincent Jackson/20	8.00	20.00
83 Frank Gore/50	6.00	15.00
85 Vernon Davis/50	6.00	15.00
87 Matt Hasselbeck/50	6.00	15.00
89 Marc Bulger/40	6.00	15.00
90 Steven Jackson/50	6.00	15.00
95 Chris Johnson/50	8.00	20.00
97 LenDale White/50	6.00	15.00
98 Chris Cooley/50	6.00	15.00
99 Clinton Portis/50	6.00	15.00
100 Jason Campbell/50	5.00	12.00

2009 Donruss Threads Pro Gridiron Kings

*FRAMED BLACK/10: 1.5X TO 4X
*FRAMED BLUE/50: .8X TO 2X
*FRAMED GREEN/25: 1X TO 2.5X
*FRAMED RED/100: .6X TO 1.5X
1-50 RANDOM INSERTS IN PACKS
51-56 INSERTED INTO RETAIL PACKS

1 Adrian Arrington	.75	2.00
2 A.J. Hawk	1.00	2.50
3 Andre Caldwell	.75	2.00
4 Antoine Cason	.75	2.00
5 Aqib Talib	.75	2.00
6 Archie Manning	1.50	4.00
7 Brandon Flowers	.75	2.00
8 Brandon Meriweather	.75	2.00
9 Brian Brohm	.75	2.00
10 Chad Henne	1.00	2.50
11 Charles Godfrey	.75	2.00
12 Chuck Bednarik	1.25	3.00
13 Danny White	1.25	3.00
14 Davone Bess	.75	2.00
15 Dick Butkus	2.00	5.00
16 Dominique Rodgers-Cromartie	.75	2.00
17 Donnie Avery	1.00	2.50
18 Dustin Keller	.75	2.00
19 Eddie Royal	1.00	2.50
20 Frank Gifford	1.50	4.00
21 Jacob Hester	.75	2.00
22 Jamaal Charles	1.25	3.00
23 James Hardy	1.00	2.50
24 Jerious Norwood	1.00	2.50
25 Jerry Rice	2.50	6.00
26 Jim Brown	2.00	5.00
27 Joe Namath	2.00	5.00
28 John David Booty	1.00	2.50
29 Josh Morgan	.75	2.00
30 Justin Fargas	.75	2.00
31 Keith Rivers	.75	2.00
32 Kevin Curtis	.75	2.00
33 Kevin Smith	1.00	2.50
34 Leodis McKelvin	.75	2.00
35 Marques Colston	1.00	2.50
36 Matt Leinart	1.00	2.50
37 Michael Bush	1.00	2.50
38 Mike Hart	1.00	2.50
39 Ozzie Newsome	1.25	3.00
40 Patrick Crayton	.75	2.00
41 Patrick Willis	1.00	2.50
42 Paul Hornung	1.50	4.00
43 Randy White	1.50	4.00
44 Rashard Mendenhall	1.00	2.50
45 Ray Rice	1.25	3.00
46 Shawne Merriman	1.00	2.50
47 Steve Young	2.00	5.00
48 Ted Ginn, Jr.	1.00	2.50
49 Thurman Thomas	1.50	4.00
50 Tommy McDonald	1.00	2.50
51 Matthew Stafford	3.00	8.00
52 Mark Sanchez	2.00	5.00
53 Michael Crabtree	1.25	3.00
54 Knowhson Moreno	.60	1.50
55 Darrius Heyward-Bey	.60	1.50
56 LeSean McCoy	1.25	3.00

2009 Donruss Threads Pro Gridiron Kings Autographs

AUTO PRINT RUN 5-400
SERIAL #'d UNDER 25 NOT PRICED

1 Adrian Arrington/100	3.00	8.00
2 A.J. Hawk/100	4.00	10.00
3 Andre Caldwell/67	3.00	8.00
4 Antoine Cason/250	2.50	6.00
5 Aqib Talib/125	3.00	8.00
7 Brandon Flowers/80	3.00	8.00
8 Brandon Meriweather/400	2.50	6.00
9 Brian Brohm/40	4.00	10.00
10 Chad Henne/50	5.00	12.00
11 Charles Godfrey/300	2.50	6.00
14 Davone Bess/200	6.00	15.00
16 Dominique Rodgers-Cromartie/300	2.50	6.00
17 Donnie Avery/90	4.00	10.00
18 Dustin Keller/70	3.00	8.00
20 Eddie Royal/90	8.00	20.00
20 Frank Gifford/30	15.00	40.00
21 Jacob Hester/300	2.50	6.00
22 Jamaal Charles/70	5.00	12.00
23 James Hardy/90	4.00	10.00
24 Jerious Norwood/100	4.00	10.00
28 John David Booty/250	3.00	8.00
29 Josh Morgan/175	2.50	6.00
31 Keith Rivers/68	3.00	8.00
33 Kevin Smith/100	4.00	10.00
34 Leodis McKelvin/100	3.00	8.00
37 Michael Bush/125	4.00	10.00
38 Mike Hart/250	5.00	12.00
40 Patrick Crayton/250	2.50	6.00
41 Patrick Willis/75	4.00	10.00
42 Paul Hornung/25	12.00	30.00
43 Randy White/50	12.00	30.00
44 Rashard Mendenhall/50	5.00	12.00
45 Ray Rice/250	6.00	15.00
50 Tommy McDonald/60	10.00	25.00

2009 Donruss Threads Pro Gridiron Kings Materials

BASE JSY PRINT RUN 25-250
*PRIME/50: .6X TO 1.5X JSY/250
*PRIME/50: .5X TO 1.2X JSY/80
*PRIME/25: .8X TO 2X JSY/250
*PRIME/15: 1X TO 2.5X JSY/250
PRIME PRINT RUN 5-50

2 A.J. Hawk/250	3.00	8.00
6 Archie Manning/250	6.00	15.00
12 Chuck Bednarik/200	5.00	12.00
13 Danny White/200	5.00	12.00
15 Dick Butkus/250	8.00	20.00
20 Frank Gifford/25	12.00	30.00
24 Jerious Norwood/80	4.00	10.00
25 Jerry Rice/165	10.00	25.00
26 Jim Brown/50	12.00	30.00
27 Joe Namath/50	12.00	30.00
30 Justin Fargas/250	2.50	6.00
32 Kevin Curtis/250	2.50	6.00
35 Marques Colston/250	3.00	8.00
36 Matt Leinart/250	3.00	8.00
39 Ozzie Newsome/250	5.00	12.00
41 Patrick Willis/250	3.00	8.00
42 Paul Hornung/100	8.00	20.00
43 Randy White/100	8.00	20.00
46 Shawne Merriman/165	3.00	8.00
47 Steve Young/250	8.00	20.00
49 Thurman Thomas/250	6.00	15.00
50 Tommy McDonald/50	6.00	15.00

2009 Donruss Threads Pro Gridiron Kings Materials Autographs

JSY AUTO PRINT RUN 5-25

2 A.J. Hawk/25	10.00	25.00
6 Archie Manning/25	20.00	50.00
12 Chuck Bednarik/25	15.00	40.00
13 Danny White/20	15.00	40.00
15 Dick Butkus/25	25.00	60.00
20 Frank Gifford/25	20.00	50.00
24 Jerious Norwood/25	10.00	25.00
30 Justin Fargas/25	8.00	20.00
32 Kevin Curtis/25	8.00	20.00
35 Marques Colston/25	10.00	25.00
36 Matt Leinart/25	10.00	25.00
39 Ozzie Newsome/25	10.00	25.00
41 Patrick Willis/25	10.00	25.00
42 Paul Hornung/25	20.00	50.00
43 Randy White/25	20.00	50.00
47 Steve Young/25	25.00	60.00
49 Thurman Thomas/25	20.00	50.00
50 Tommy McDonald/25	12.00	30.00

2009 Donruss Threads Rookie Collection Materials

BASE JSY PRINT RUN 500 SER.#'d SETS
*PRIME/25: .8X TO 2X BASIC JSY

1 Andre Brown	1.50	4.00
2 Tyson Jackson	2.00	5.00
3 Chris Wells	4.00	10.00
4 Derrick Williams	2.00	5.00
5 Glen Coffee	2.00	5.00
6 Javon Ringer	2.50	6.00
7 Josh Freeman	5.00	12.00
8 Kenny Britt	3.00	8.00
9 LeSean McCoy	5.00	12.00
10 Matthew Stafford	12.00	30.00
11 Deon Butler	2.00	5.00
12 Mike Thomas	2.50	6.00
13 Mohamed Massaquoi	2.00	5.00
14 Pat White	2.50	6.00
15 Percy Harvin	4.00	10.00
16 Rhett Bomar	2.00	5.00
17 Stephen McGee	2.50	6.00
18 Jason Smith	2.00	5.00
19 Aaron Curry	2.50	6.00
20 Brandon Pettigrew	2.50	6.00
21 Brian Robiskie	2.50	6.00
22 Darrius Heyward-Bey	2.50	6.00
23 Donald Brown	2.50	6.00
24 Hakeem Nicks	4.00	10.00
25 Jeremy Maclin	4.00	10.00
26 Juaquin Iglesias	2.00	5.00
27 Knowshon Moreno	2.50	6.00
28 Mark Sanchez	8.00	20.00
29 Michael Crabtree	5.00	12.00
30 Mike Wallace	5.00	12.00
31 Nate Davis	2.00	5.00
32 Patrick Turner	2.00	5.00
33 Ramses Barden	1.50	4.00
34 Shonn Greene	4.00	10.00

2009 Donruss Threads Rookie Collection Materials Autographs

JSY AUTO PRINT RUN 50 SER.#'d SETS
*AU PRIME/25: .5X TO 1.2X BASIC JSY AU

1 Andre Brown	6.00	15.00
2 Tyson Jackson	8.00	20.00
3 Chris Wells	15.00	40.00
4 Derrick Williams	8.00	20.00
5 Glen Coffee	8.00	20.00
6 Javon Ringer	10.00	25.00
7 Josh Freeman	20.00	50.00
9 LeSean McCoy	20.00	50.00
10 Matthew Stafford	50.00	120.00
11 Deon Butler	8.00	20.00
12 Mike Thomas	10.00	25.00
13 Mohamed Massaquoi	8.00	20.00
15 Percy Harvin	15.00	40.00
16 Rhett Bomar	8.00	20.00
17 Stephen McGee	10.00	25.00
18 Jason Smith	8.00	20.00
19 Aaron Curry	10.00	25.00
20 Brandon Pettigrew	10.00	25.00
21 Brian Robiskie	10.00	25.00
22 Darrius Heyward-Bey	10.00	25.00
23 Donald Brown	10.00	25.00
24 Hakeem Nicks	15.00	40.00
25 Jeremy Maclin	15.00	40.00
27 Knowshon Moreno	10.00	25.00
28 Mark Sanchez	30.00	80.00
29 Michael Crabtree	20.00	50.00
30 Mike Wallace	20.00	50.00
31 Nate Davis	8.00	20.00
32 Patrick Turner	8.00	20.00
33 Ramses Barden	6.00	15.00
34 Shonn Greene	15.00	40.00

2009 Donruss Threads Rookie Collection Materials Combo

COMBO JSY PRINT RUN 500
*COMBO PRIME/25: .8X TO 2X BASIC CMBO

1 Mohamed Massaquoi	2.50	6.00
Brian Robiskie		
2 Matthew Stafford	12.00	30.00
Brandon Pettigrew		
3 Knowshon Moreno	2.50	6.00
Donald Brown		
4 Patrick Turner	2.50	6.00
Pat White		
5 Darrius Heyward-Bey	5.00	12.00
Michael Crabtree		
6 Rhett Bomar	2.00	5.00
Andre Brown		
7 Michael Crabtree	5.00	12.00
Nate Davis		
8 Chris Wells	4.00	10.00
Brian Robiskie		
9 Kenny Britt	3.00	8.00
Javon Ringer		
10 Mark Sanchez	8.00	20.00
Shonn Greene		
11 Matthew Stafford	12.00	30.00
Knowshon Moreno		
12 Hakeem Nicks	4.00	10.00
Ramses Barden		
13 Matthew Stafford	12.00	30.00
Mark Sanchez		
14 Brandon Pettigrew	2.50	6.00
Derrick Williams		
15 Rhett Bomar	4.00	10.00
Hakeem Nicks		

2009 Donruss Threads Rookie Collection Materials Quad

QUAD JSY PRINT RUN 100 SER.#'d SETS
*PRIME/25: .8X TO 2X BASIC QUAD

1 Matthew Stafford	12.00	30.00
Jason Smith		
Tyson Jackson		
Aaron Curry		
2 Darrius Heyward-Bey	10.00	25.00
Michael Crabtree		
Jeremy Maclin		
Percy Harvin		
3 Matthew Stafford	15.00	40.00
Mark Sanchez		
Knowshon Moreno		
Donald Brown		
4 Matthew Stafford	15.00	40.00
Mark Sanchez		
Josh Freeman		
Pat White		
5 Matthew Stafford	12.00	30.00
Knowshon Moreno		
Darrius Heyward-Bey		
Brandon Pettigrew		

2009 Donruss Threads Triple Threat

*CENT.PROOF/100: .6X TO 1.5X BASE INSERTS

1 Jake Delhomme	1.25	3.00
Steve Smith		
DeAngelo Williams		
2 Ben Roethlisberger	1.25	3.00
Santonio Holmes		
Willie Parker		
3 Matt Schaub	1.00	2.50
Andre Johnson		
Steve Slaton		
4 Tom Brady	2.00	5.00
Randy Moss		
Laurence Maroney		
5 Donovan McNabb	1.25	3.00
DeSean Jackson		
Brian Westbrook		
6 Joe Flacco	1.25	3.00
Derrick Mason		
Willis McGahee		
7 Matt Ryan	1.25	3.00
Roddy White		
Michael Turner		
8 Jason Campbell	1.00	2.50
Chris Cooley		
Clinton Portis		
9 Drew Brees	1.25	3.00
Marques Colston		
Reggie Bush		
10 Aaron Rodgers	2.50	6.00
Greg Jennings		
Ryan Grant		

2009 Donruss Threads Triple Threat Materials

BASE JSY PRINT RUN 100-250
*PRIME/50: .8X TO 2X TRIPLE/230-250
*PRIME/50: .6X TO 1.5X TRIPLE/100

1 Jake Delhomme/250	6.00	15.00
Steve Smith		
DeAngelo Williams		
2 Ben Roethlisberger/100	8.00	20.00
Santonio Holmes		
Willie Parker		
3 Matt Schaub/100	6.00	15.00
Andre Johnson		
Steve Slaton		
4 Tom Brady/230	10.00	25.00
Randy Moss		
Laurence Maroney		
6 Joe Flacco/250	6.00	15.00
Derrick Mason		
Willis McGahee		
7 Matt Ryan/100	8.00	20.00
Roddy White		
Michael Turner		
8 Jason Campbell/250	5.00	12.00
Chris Cooley		
Clinton Portis		
9 Drew Brees/250	6.00	15.00
Marques Colston		
Reggie Bush		
10 Aaron Rodgers/250	8.00	20.00
Greg Jennings		
Ryan Grant		

2003 Donruss/Playoff Holiday Cards Doubles

COMPLETE SET (14)	30.00	60.00
HH1 Carson Palmer	7.50	20.00
Kelley Washington		
HH2 Kyle Boller	3.00	8.00
Musa Smith		
HH3 Dave Ragone	5.00	12.00
Andre Johnson		
HH4 Byron Leftwich	5.00	12.00
Dallas Clark		
HH5 Kliff Kingsbury	2.50	6.00
Bethel Johnson		
HH6 Terence Newman	4.00	10.00
Terrell Suggs		
HH7 Brian St.Pierre	2.50	6.00
Taylor Jacobs		
HH8 Onterrio Smith	3.00	8.00
Nate Burleson		
HH9 Seneca Wallace	3.00	8.00
Kevin Curtis		
HH10 Marcus Trufant	4.00	10.00
Willis McGahee		
HH11 Chris Brown	3.00	8.00
Tyrone Calico		
HH12 Bryant Johnson	5.00	12.00
Anquan Boldin		
HH13 Artose Pinner	5.00	12.00
Larry Johnson		
HH14 Teyo Johnson	4.00	10.00
Justin Fargas		

2003 Donruss/Playoff Holiday Cards Triples

COMPLETE SET (6)	20.00	50.00
HH1 Carson Palmer	6.00	15.00
Bryant Johnson		
Bethel Johnson		
HH2 Byron Leftwich	6.00	15.00
Anquan Boldin		
Kelly Washington		
HH3 Kyle Boller	4.00	10.00
Taylor Jacobs		
Kevin Curtis		
HH4 Willis McGahee	4.00	10.00
Onterrio Smith		
Teyo Johnson		
HH5 Larry Johnson	6.00	15.00
Justin Fargas		
Nate Burleson		
HH6 Andre Johnson	4.00	10.00
Tyrone Calico		
Dallas Clark		

2003 Donruss/Playoff Holiday Cards Quads

COMPLETE SET (5)	20.00	50.00
HH1 Carson Palmer	7.50	20.00
Kyle Boller		
Byron Leftwich		
Seneca Wallace		
HH2 Bryant Johnson	4.00	10.00
Tyrone Calico		
Dallas Clark		
Teyo Johnson		
HH3 Justin Fargas	6.00	15.00
Larry Johnson		
Willis McGahee		
Onterrio Smith		
HH4 Andre Johnson	4.00	10.00
Anquan Boldin		
Taylor Jacobs		
Nate Burleson		
HH5 Terence Newman	4.00	10.00
Terrell Suggs		
DeWayne Robertson		
Marcus Trufant		

2005 Donruss/Playoff Hawaii Trade Conference Autographs

Cards from this set were distributed at the February 2005 hobby Trade Conference in Hawaii. Each features autographs from two or more 2004 NFL rookies along with serial numbered print runs of either 10 or 5. The following card numbers were not produced: #12, 14, 22, and 27.

STATED PRINT RUN 10 SER.#'d SETS
NOT PRICED DUE TO SCARCITY

1 Ben Roethlisberger
 Eli Manning
2 J.P. Losman
 Philip Rivers
3 Luke McCown
 Matt Schaub
4 Michael Clayton
 Roy Williams
5 Julius Jones
 Mewelde Moore
6 Robert Gallery
 DeAngelo Hall
7 Steven Jackson
 Tatum Bell
8 Lee Evans
 Reggie Williams
9 Ben Troupe
 Ben Watson
10 Kellen Winslow Jr.
 Dunta Robinson
11 Chris Perry
 Cedric Cobbs
13 Rashaun Woods
 Bernard Berrian
15 Kevin Jones
 Greg Jones
16 Michael Jenkins
 Devard Darling
17 Ben Roethlisberger
 Eli Manning
 J.P. Losman
 Philip Rivers
18 Roy Williams
 Michael Clayton
 Lee Evans
 Reggie Williams
19 Kellen Winslow Jr.
 Dunta Robinson
 Ben Troupe
 Ben Watson
20 Kevin Jones
 Greg Jones
 Steven Jackson
 Tatum Bell
21 Julius Jones
 Mewelde Moore
 Rashaun Woods
 Bernard Berrian
23 Chris Perry
 Cedric Cobbs
 Michael Jenkins
 Devard Darling
24 Robert Gallery
 DeAngelo Hall
 Luke McCown
 Matt Schaub
25 Ben Roethlisberger/5
 Eli Manning
 J.P. Losman
 Philip Rivers
 Luke McCown
 Matt Schaub
26 Kevin Jones/5
 Julius Jones
 Steven Jackson
 Tatum Bell
 Mewelde Moore
 Greg Jones
28 Lee Evans/5
 Michael Jenkins
 Rashaun Woods
 Bernard Berrian
 Darius Watts
 Reggie Williams
29 Chris Perry/5
 Cedric Cobbs
 Robert Gallery
 DeAngelo Hall
 Devard Darling
 Devery Henderson

2007 Donruss/Playoff Hawaii Trade Conference

COMPLETE SET (6)	8.00	20.00
1 Vince Young	.75	2.00
2 Brett Favre	2.00	5.00
3 Reggie Bush	1.00	2.50
4 Peyton Manning	1.50	4.00
5 JaMarcus Russell	.40	1.00
6 Adrian Peterson	2.50	6.00

2000 Dorling Kindersley QB Club Stickers

The book publisher Dorling Kindersley issued these stickers along with a book in which to paste them into. The stickers were printed in groups on 4-different page sized sheets within the book. To exist in single sticker form they actually would have had to be cut out by hand. We've included prices below for single stickers and listed them alphabetically beginning with the player subjects.

COMPLETE SET (50)	4.00	8.00
1 Troy Aikman	.25	.60
2 Troy Aikman	.25	.60
(in race car)		
3 Jeff Blake	.07	.20
4 Drew Bledsoe	.15	.40
5 Drew Bledsoe	.15	.40
(red Pro Bowl jersey)		
6 Terrell Davis	.25	.60
7 John Elway	.40	1.00
8 John Elway	.40	1.00
(running the bal)		
9 John Elway	.40	1.00
(holding Super Bowl Trophy)		
10 Boomer Esiason	.07	.20
(Jets photo)		
11 Boomer Esiason	.07	.20
(Bengals photo)		
12 Jim Everett	.07	.20
13 Brett Favre	.40	1.00
14 Brett Favre	.40	1.00
15 Doug Flutie	.15	.40
16 Gus Frerotte	.07	.20
17 Jeff George	.07	.20
18 Elvis Grbac	.07	.20
19 Michael Irvin	.07	.20
20 Brad Johnson	.10	.30
21 Keyshawn Johnson	.10	.30
22 Jim Kelly	.10	.30
23 Bernie Kosar	.07	.20
(Browns jersey)		
24 Bernie Kosar	.07	.20
(wearing Indians baseball jersey)		
25 Bernie Kosar	.07	.20
(signing autographs)		
26 Peyton Manning	.40	1.00
27 Dan Marino	.40	1.00
28 Dan Marino	.40	1.00
(golfing)		
29 Donovan McNabb	.20	.50
(dropping back)		
30 Donovan McNabb	.20	.50
(standing pose)		
31 Steve McNair	.10	.30
32 Neil O'Donnell	.07	.20
33 Jake Plummer	.10	.30
34 Jerry Rice	.25	.60
35 Jerry Rice	.25	.60
Steve Young		
36 Barry Sanders	.30	.75
37 Barry Sanders	.30	.75
38 Junior Seau	.07	.20
39 Junior Seau	.07	.20
(in swimming trunks)		
40 Phil Simms	.07	.20
41 Kordell Stewart	.07	.20
42 Vinny Testaverde	.07	.20
43 Ricky Williams	.20	.50
(running the ball)		
44 Ricky Williams	.20	.50
(standing pose)		
45 Steve Young	.15	.40
46 Cowboys Helmet	.05	.15
47 Super Bowl Football	.05	.15
48 Super Bowl Trophy	.05	.15
49 Super Bowl XXXIII Program	.05	.15
50 Super Bowl XXI Patch	.05	.15

1949 Eagles Team Issue

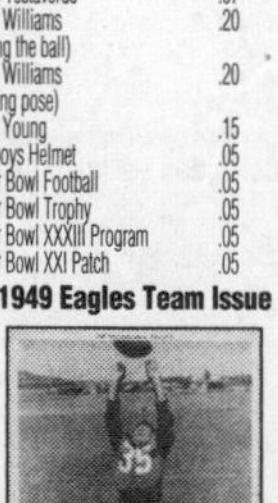

This set of black and white photos was issued in 1949 by the Eagles in celebration of their 1948 NFL Championship team. Each photo measures roughly 8 3/4" by 10 1/2" and includes a facsimile autograph, the player's position, weight, height, and college below the photo. The photos are blankbacked and unnumbered.

COMPLETE SET (20)	250.00	400.00
1 Neill Armstrong	12.00	20.00
2 Russ Craft	12.00	20.00
3 Jack Ferrante	12.00	20.00
4 Noble Doss	12.00	20.00
4 Bucko Kilroy	15.00	25.00
5 Vic Lindskog	12.00	20.00
5 Mario Giannelli	12.00	20.00
6 Pat McHugh	12.00	20.00
7 Joe Muha	12.00	20.00
8 Jack Myers	12.00	20.00
9 Pete Pihos	25.00	40.00
10 Bosh Pritchard	15.00	25.00
11 George Savitsky	12.00	20.00
12 Vic Sears	12.00	20.00
13 Ernie Steele	12.00	20.00
14 Tommy Thompson	18.00	30.00
15 Steve Van Buren	35.00	60.00
(weight is 198 lbs.)		
16 Al Wistert	15.00	25.00
17 Alex Wojciechowicz	18.00	30.00
18 Team Photo	18.00	30.00

1950 Eagles Bulletin Pin-ups

These black and white premium photos measure roughly 8" x 10" and were issued by The Bulletin newspaper in the Philadelphia area. The photos are blankbacked and feature the newspaper's logo in the upper left corner, the team name in the lower left corner and the player's facsimile autograph in the lower right corner.

1 Greasy Neale CO	10.00	20.00
2 Bosh Pritchard	10.00	20.00
3 Steve Van Buren	15.00	30.00

1950 Eagles Team Issue

This set of black and white photos was issued around 1950 by the Eagles. Each photo is very similar to the 1949 issue with the differences being found in the text included below the player image. Some players were featured with the same photo in both years with only the difference in text. Each photo measures roughly 8 3/4" by 11" and includes a printed player name on a top row, followed by the player's position, height, weight, and college on a bottom row of type below the photo. The photos are blankbacked and unnumbered.

COMPLETE SET (10)		
1 Neill Armstrong	12.00	20.00
2 Russ Craft	12.00	20.00
3 Bucko Kilroy	15.00	25.00
4 Pat McHugh	12.00	20.00
5 Joe Muha	12.00	20.00
6 Pete Pihos	25.00	40.00
7 Bosh Pritchard	15.00	25.00
8 Vic Sears	12.00	20.00
9 Steve Van Buren	35.00	60.00
10 Whitey Wistert	15.00	25.00

1956 Eagles Team Issue

The Philadelphia Eagles issued and distributed this set of player photos. Each measures approximately 8" by 10" and features a black and white photo on the cardfront with a blank cardback. The player's name, position (abbreviated), height, weight, and college affiliation appear below the photo with the team name above the picture. The checklist is thought to be incomplete. Any additions to this list are greatly appreciated.

1 Bibbles Bawel	10.00	20.00
2 Eddie Bell	10.00	20.00
3 Ken Keller	10.00	20.00
4 Bob Kelley	10.00	20.00
5 Bob Pellegrini	10.00	20.00
6 Rocky Ryan	10.00	20.00
7 Bill Stribling	10.00	20.00
8 Neil Worden	10.00	20.00

1959 Eagles Jay Publishing

This set features (approximately) 5" by 7" black-and-white player photos with the players in traditional football poses. The photos were packaged 12-per set and originally sold for 25-cents. The fronts include the player's name and team name (Philadelphia Eagles) below the player image. The backs are blank, unnumbered, and checklisted below in alphabetical order.

COMPLETE SET (11)	50.00	100.00
1 Bill Barnes	4.00	8.00
2 Chuck Bednarik	10.00	20.00
3 Tom Brookshier	5.00	10.00
4 Marion Campbell	4.00	8.00
5 Tommy McDonald	6.00	12.00
6 Clarence Peaks	4.00	8.00
7 Pete Retzlaff	5.00	10.00
8 Jesse Richardson	4.00	8.00
9 Norm Van Brocklin	10.00	20.00
10 Bobby Walston	4.00	8.00
11 Chuck Weber	4.00	8.00

1959 Eagles San Giorgio Flipbooks

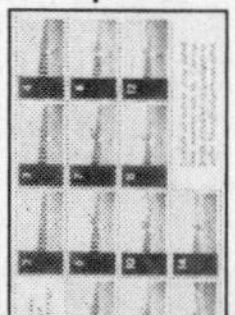

This set features members of the Philadelphia Eagles printed on velum type paper stock created in a multi-image action sequence. The set is commonly referenced as the San Giorgio Macaroni Football Flipbooks. Members of the Philadelphia Eagles, Pittsburgh Steelers, and Washington Redskins were produced regionally with 15-players, reportedly, issued per team. Some players were produced in more than one sequence of poses with different captions and/or slightly different photos used. When the flipbooks are still in uncut form (which is most desirable), they measure approximately 5 3/4" by 3 9/16". The sheets are blank backed, in black and white, and provide 14-small numbered pages when cut apart. Collectors were encouraged to cut out each photo and stack them in such a way as to create a moving image of the player when flipped with the fingers. Any additions to this list are appreciated.

1A Bill Barnes	90.00	150.00
(Grab and Run)		
1B Bill Barnes	90.00	150.00
(Power Runner)		
2 Chuck Bednarik	250.00	400.00
(Blasts Thru)		
3 Proverb Jacobs	90.00	150.00
(Hard Charging)		
4 Tommy McDonald	175.00	300.00
(Stretches For One)		
5A Ed Meadows	90.00	150.00
(Snags One)		
5B Ed Meadows	90.00	150.00
(Up, Down, and Away)		

6A Clarence Peaks (Hard Running)	90.00	150.00
6B Clarence Peaks (Punts)	90.00	150.00
7 Bob Pellegrini (Breaks Thru)	90.00	150.00
8A Pete Retzlaff (One Hands It)	100.00	175.00
8B Pete Retzlaff Reaches High (stretching for the ball)	100.00	175.00
8C Pete Retzlaff Reaches High (catching the football)	100.00	175.00
9 Bobby Walston (Place-Kicker)	90.00	150.00
10 Chuck Weber (Snags One)	90.00	150.00

1960 Eagles Team Issue

This 11-card team issued set measures approximately 5" by 7" and is printed on thin, slick card stock. The fronts feature black-and-white posed action player photos with white borders. The player's name is printed in black below the picture along with the team name "Eagles." The backs are blank. The cards are unnumbered and checklisted below in alphabetical order. Any additions to this list are appreciated.

COMPLETE SET (11)	60.00	120.00
1 Maxie Baughan	6.00	12.00
2 Chuck Bednarik	12.50	25.00
3 Don Burroughs	5.00	10.00
4 Jimmy Carr	6.00	12.00
5 Howard Keys	5.00	10.00
6 Ed Khayat	5.00	10.00
7 Jim McCusker	5.00	10.00
8 John Nocera	5.00	10.00
9 Nick Skorich CO	5.00	10.00
10 J.D. Smith	6.00	12.00
11 John Wittenborn	5.00	10.00

1961 Eagles Jay Publishing

This 12-card set features (approximately) 5" by 7" black-and-white player photos. The photos show players in traditional poses with the quarterback preparing to throw, the runner heading downfield, and the defenseman ready for the tackle. These cards were packaged 12 to a packet and originally sold for 25 cents. The backs are blank. The cards are unnumbered and checklisted below in alphabetical order.

COMPLETE SET (12)	40.00	80.00
1 Maxie Baughan	4.00	8.00
2 Jim McCusker	4.00	8.00
3 Tommy McDonald	6.00	12.00
4 Bob Pellegrini	4.00	8.00
5 Pete Retzlaff	5.00	10.00
6 Jesse Richardson	4.00	8.00
7 Joe Robb	4.00	8.00
8 Theron Sapp	4.00	8.00
9 J.D. Smith T	4.00	8.00
10 Bobby Walston	4.00	8.00
11 Jerry Williams ACO	4.00	8.00
12 John Wittenborn	4.00	8.00

1960-62 Eagles Team Issue

The Eagles issued this set of black and white player photos. Each measures approximately 8" by 10" and features the team name above the player photo with his name, vital statistics and college below. The backs are blank and unnumbered. The checklist below includes the known photos at this time. It's likely there were more produced. Any additions to this list would be appreciated.

COMPLETE SET (25)	150.00	300.00
1 Timmy Brown	7.50	15.00
2 Don Burroughs	7.50	15.00
3 Jimmy Carr	7.50	15.00
4 Irv Cross	7.50	15.00
5 Gene Gossage	7.50	15.00
6 Riley Gunnels	7.50	15.00
7 Bob Harrison	7.50	15.00
8 King Hill	7.50	15.00
9 Sonny Jurgensen	15.00	30.00
10 Jim McCusker	7.50	15.00
11 Alan Miller	7.50	15.00
12 John Nocera	7.50	15.00
13 Don Oakes	7.50	15.00
14 Clarence Peaks	7.50	15.00
15 Will Renfro	7.50	15.00
16 Theron Sapp	7.50	15.00
17 Buck Shaw CO	7.50	15.00
18 Nick Skorich CO	7.50	15.00
19 J.D. Smith T	7.50	15.00
20 Leo Sugar	7.50	15.00
21 Carl Taseff	7.50	15.00
22 John Tracey	7.50	1500
23 Bobby Walston	7.50	15.00
24 Chuck Weber	7.50	15.00
25 John Wittenborn	7.50	15.00

1961 Eagles Team Issue 5x7

This team issued set measures approximately 5" by 7" and is printed on thin, slick card stock. The fronts feature black-and-white posed action player photos with white borders. The player's name is printed in black below the picture along with the team name "Philadelphia Eagles." The backs are blank. The cards are unnumbered and checklisted below in alphabetical order. Any additions to this list are appreciated.

COMPLETE SET (12)	75.00	150.00
1 Bill Barnes	6.00	12.00
2 Chuck Bednarik	10.00	20.00
3 Tom Brookshier	7.50	15.00
4 Timmy Brown	7.50	15.00
5 Marion Campbell	7.50	15.00
6 Stan Campbell	6.00	12.00
7 Jimmy Carr	6.00	12.00
8 Irv Cross	7.50	15.00
9 Sonny Jurgensen	15.00	25.00
10 Clarence Peaks	6.00	12.00
11 Jesse Richardson	6.00	12.00
12 Nick Skorich CO	6.00	12.00

1963 Eagles Phillies' Cigars

This attractive color football photo was part of a premium promotion for Phillies Cigars. It measures 6 1/2" by 9" and features a facsimile autograph on the cardfront. The cardback is blank.

1 Tommy McDonald	15.00	25.00

1964-66 Eagles Program Inserts

These photos were actually bound into Philadelphia Eagles game programs from 1964-66. Each one when cleanly cut from the program measures roughly 8 3/8" by 11" and features a black and white photo of an Eagles player (except for the photo of Giants Y.A. Tittle) on one side and a bio on the back along with two small photos. A facsimile autograph is included on the photo and the first 43-pictures in the series are numbered within the left side border while the remaining were issued without numbers. Early photos include a white border around all sides of the photo while later issues are borderless on three sides.

COMPLETE SET (53)	150.00	300.00
1 Timmy Brown	4.00	8.00
2 Ron Goodwin	3.00	6.00
3 Pete Retzlaff	4.00	8.00
4 Maxie Baughan	4.00	8.00
5 Y.A. Tittle	10.00	20.00
6 Don Burroughs	3.00	6.00
7 Norm Snead	6.00	12.00
8 Jim Ringo	6.00	12.00
9 Riley Gunnels	3.00	6.00
10 George Tarasovic	3.00	6.00
11 Earl Gros	3.00	6.00
12 Bob Brown	4.00	8.00
13 Irv Cross	4.00	8.00
14 Sam Baker	3.00	6.00
15 Ed Blaine	3.00	6.00
16 Nate Ramsey	3.00	6.00
17 Dave Lloyd	3.00	6.00
18 Ollie Matson	7.50	15.00
19 Pete Case	3.00	6.00
20 Mike Morgan	3.00	6.00
21 Bob Richards	3.00	6.00
22 Ray Poage	3.00	6.00
23 Don Hultz	3.00	6.00
24 Dave Graham	3.00	6.00
25 Floyd Peters	3.00	6.00
26 King Hill	4.00	8.00
27 John Meyers	3.00	6.00
28 Lynn Hoyem	3.00	6.00
29 Joe Scarpati	3.00	6.00
30 Jack Concannon	4.00	8.00
31 Jim Skaggs	3.00	6.00
32 Glenn Glass	3.00	6.00
33 Ralph Heck	3.00	6.00
34 Claude Crabb	3.00	6.00
35 Israel Lang	3.00	6.00
36 Tom Woodeshick	4.00	8.00
37 Ed Khayat	3.00	6.00
38 Roger Gill	3.00	6.00
39 Harold Wells	3.00	6.00
40 Lane Howell	3.00	6.00
41 Dave Recher	3.00	6.00
42 Fred Hill	3.00	6.00
43 Al Nelson	3.00	6.00
NNO Randy Beisler	3.00	6.00
NNO Dave Cahill	3.00	6.00
NNO Ben Hawkins	3.00	6.00
NNO Ike Kelley	3.00	6.00
NNO Aaron Martin	3.00	6.00
NNO Ron Medved	3.00	6.00
NNO Jim Nettles	3.00	6.00
NNO Gary Pettigrew	3.00	6.00
NNO Arunas Vasys	3.00	6.00
NNO Fred Whittingham	3.00	6.00

1965-66 Eagles Team Issue

The Eagles issued these black and white glossy player photos likely over a period of years. Each measures approximately 8" by 10" and features the player's name, position (spelled out in full) and team name below the photo. The backs are blank and unnumbered. The checklist below includes the known photos at this time. Any additions to this list would be appreciated.

COMPLETE SET (16)	125.00	250.00
1 Sam Baker (kicking pose, stripes on shoulder)	5.00	10.00
2 Sam Baker (kicking pose, no stripes on shoulder)	5.00	10.00
3 Ed Blaine	5.00	10.00
4 Bob Brown T (action pose)	6.00	12.00
5 Bob Brown T (portrait)	6.00	12.00
6 Timmy Brown	6.00	12.00
7 Jack Concannon	5.00	10.00
8 Dave Graham	5.00	10.00
9 Earl Gros	5.00	10.00
10 Fred Hill	5.00	10.00
11 Lynn Hoyem	5.00	10.00
12 Dwight Kelley	5.00	10.00
13 Ed Khayat	5.00	10.00
14 Israel Lang	5.00	10.00
15 Dave Lloyd	5.00	10.00
16 Aaron Martin	5.00	10.00
17 Mike Morgan LB	5.00	10.00
18 Al Nelson	5.00	10.00
19 Jim Nettles	5.00	10.00
20 Floyd Peters	5.00	10.00
21 Ray Poage	5.00	10.00
22 Pete Retzlaff	6.00	12.00
23 Jim Ringo	6.00	12.00
24 Jim Skaggs	5.00	10.00
25 Norm Snead (dropped back to pass)	6.00	12.00
26 Norm Snead (lateraling the ball)	6.00	12.00
27 Norm Snead (portrait)	6.00	12.00

1967 Eagles Program Inserts

These photos were actually bound into Philadelphia Eagles game programs from 1967 and are entitled "Eagles Portraits." Each one when cleanly cut from the program measures roughly 8 3/8" by 11" and features a black and white photo of an Eagles player on one side and a bio on the back along with two small photos. A facsimile autograph is included on the photo and each photo is numbered within the left side border. Each photo is borderless on three sides.

COMPLETE SET (14)	40.00	80.00
1 Timmy Brown	4.00	8.00
2 Dave Lloyd	3.00	6.00
3 Joe Scarpati	3.00	6.00
4 Bob Brown	4.00	8.00
5 Jim Ringo	6.00	12.00
6 Nate Ramsey	3.00	6.00
7 Israel Lang	3.00	6.00
8 Jim Skaggs	3.00	6.00
9 Norm Snead	6.00	12.00
10 Sam Baker	3.00	6.00
11 Floyd Peters	3.00	6.00
12 Tom Woodeshick	4.00	8.00
13 Don Hultz	3.00	6.00
14 Harold Wells	3.00	6.00

1968 Eagles Postcards

These photos measure approximately 4 1/4" by 5 1/2" and feature posed action black-and-white player photos with white borders. Each photo was taken outside unless noted below. The player's name and team name (measuring either 1 9/16" or 1 3/8") are printed in the bottom border. The Eagles issued Postcards over a number of years and this set is differentiated by the lack of a facsimile autograph on the cardfronts. Since the set is nearly identical to the 1969 issue, we've noted differences of like players below. Unless noted below, the backs include a postcard style format. The cards are unnumbered and checklisted below in alphabetical order.

COMPLETE SET (40)	150.00	300.00
1 Sam Baker (right foot is 1-inch from border)	4.00	8.00
2 Gary Ballman (ball is in air)	4.00	8.00
3 Randy Beisler	4.00	8.00
4 Bob Brown	6.00	12.00
5 Fred Brown	4.00	8.00
6 Gene Ceppetelli	4.00	8.00
7 Wayne Colman	4.00	8.00
8 Mike Ditka	10.00	20.00
9 Rick Duncan	4.00	8.00
10 Ron Goodwin	4.00	8.00
11 Ben Hawkins	4.00	8.00
12 Alvin Haymond	4.00	8.00
13 King Hill	4.00	8.00
14 John Huarte	4.00	8.00
15 Don Hultz (no mustache)	4.00	8.00
16 Ike Kelley (right arm is to side)	4.00	8.00
17 Jim Kelly	4.00	8.00
18 Izzy Lang	4.00	8.00
19 Dave Lloyd (left hand covers part of jersey number)	4.00	8.00
20 John Mallory	4.00	8.00
21 Ron Medved (5 on right shoulder hidden)	4.00	8.00
22 Frank Molden	4.00	8.00
23 Al Nelson (running to the left)	4.00	8.00
24 Jim Nettles	4.00	8.00
25 Mark Nordquist (posed in set position)	4.00	8.00
26 Floyd Peters (running to the right)	4.00	8.00
27 Gary Pettigrew (blocking pose)	4.00	8.00
28 Cyril Pinder (running forward)	4.00	8.00
29 Nate Ramsey (4 visible on right shoulder)	4.00	8.00
30 Dave Recher	4.00	8.00
31 Tim Rossovich (stands in background)	4.00	8.00
32 Joe Scarpati (not smiling)	4.00	8.00
33 Norm Snead (posed photo)	5.00	10.00
34 Mel Tom (green jersey)	4.00	8.00
35 Arunas Vasys	4.00	8.00
36 Harold Wells	4.00	8.00
37 Harry Wilson	4.00	8.00
38 Tom Woodeshick (running to the left)	4.00	8.00
39 Adrian Young (#41 visible on right in background)	4.00	8.00
40 Coaching Staff	4.00	8.00

1969 Eagles Postcards

These photos measure approximately 4 1/4" by 5 1/2" and feature posed action black-and-white player photos with white borders. Each photo was taken outside unless noted below. The player's name and team name (measuring either 1 9/16" or 1 3/8") are printed in the bottom border. The Eagles issued Postcards over a number of years and this set is differentiated by the lack of a facsimile autograph on the cardfronts. Since the set is nearly identical to the 1968 issue, we've noted differences of like players below. Unless noted below, the backs include a postcard style format. The cards are unnumbered and checklisted below in alphabetical order.

COMPLETE SET (41)	150.00	300.00
1 Sam Baker (right foot touching border)	4.00	8.00
2 Gary Ballman (ball between hands)	4.00	8.00
3 Ronnie Blye	4.00	8.00
4 Bill Bradley	5.00	10.00
5 Ernest Calloway	4.00	8.00
6 Joe Carollo	4.00	8.00
7 Irv Cross	4.00	8.00
8 Mike Dirks	4.00	8.00
9 Mike Evans	4.00	8.00
10 Dave Graham	4.00	8.00
11 Tony Guillory	4.00	8.00
12 Dick Hart	4.00	8.00
13 Fred Hill	4.00	8.00
14 William Hobbs	4.00	8.00
15 Lane Howell	4.00	8.00
16 Chuck Hughes	4.00	8.00
17 Don Hultz (with mustache)	4.00	8.00
18 Harold Jackson	6.00	12.00
19 Harry Jones	4.00	8.00
20 Ike Kelley (right arm across body)	4.00	8.00
21 Wade Key	4.00	8.00
22 Leroy Keyes	4.00	8.00
23 Kent Lawrence	4.00	8.00
24 Dave Lloyd (left arm extended)	4.00	8.00
25 Ron Medved (5 on right shoulder visible)	4.00	8.00
26 George Mira	4.00	8.00
27 Al Nelson (running to the right)	4.00	8.00
28 Mark Nordquist (running pose)	4.00	8.00
29 Floyd Peters (running to the left)	4.00	8.00
30 Gary Pettigrew (running pose)	4.00	8.00
31 Cyril Pinder (running to the left)	4.00	8.00
32 Ron Porter	4.00	8.00
33 Nate Ramsey (24 on left shoulder visible)	4.00	8.00
34 Jimmy Raye	4.00	8.00
35 Tim Rossovich (running to the right)	4.00	8.00
36 Joe Scarpati (smiling)	4.00	8.00
37 Jim Skaggs	4.00	8.00
38 Norm Snead (game action photo)	5.00	10.00
39 Mel Tom (white jersey)	4.00	8.00
40 Tom Woodeshick (running to the right)	4.00	8.00
41 Adrian Young (#41 not visible in background)	4.00	8.00

1970-71 Eagles Postcards

These postcards measure approximately 4 1/4" by 5 1/2" and feature posed action black-and-white player photos with white borders. Each photo was taken outside unless noted below. The player's name and team name (measuring either 1 9/16" or 1 3/8") are printed in the bottom border. The Eagles issued Postcards over a number of years and this set is differentiated by the facsimile autograph on the cardfronts. It is likely that our listing combines postcards that were released in 1970 and 1971. Several have been found with a Boy Scouts "BSA" logo near the photo. Unless noted below, the backs include a postcard style format. The cards are unnumbered and checklisted below in alphabetical order.

COMPLETE SET (53)	125.00	250.00
1 Henry Allison	3.00	6.00
2 Rick Arrington	3.00	6.00
3 Tom Bailey	3.00	6.00
4 Gary Ballman	3.00	6.00
5 Lee Bouggess	3.00	6.00
6 Lee Bouggess BSA	3.00	6.00
7 Bill Bradley	4.00	8.00
8 Ernie Calloway	3.00	6.00
9 Harold Carmichael	8.00	12.00
10 Joe Carollo	3.00	6.00
11 Bob Creech	3.00	6.00
12 Norm Davis	3.00	6.00
13 Tom Dempsey	3.00	6.00
14 Tom Dempsey BSA	3.00	6.00
15 Mike Dirks	3.00	6.00
16 Mike Evans	3.00	6.00
17 Happy Feller	3.00	6.00
18 Carl Gersbach	3.00	6.00
19 Dave Graham	3.00	6.00
20 Richard Harris	3.00	6.00
21 Dick Hart	3.00	6.00
22 Ben Hawkins	3.00	6.00
23 Fred Hill	3.00	6.00
24 Bill Hobbs	3.00	6.00
25 Don Hultz	3.00	6.00
26 Harold Jackson	4.00	8.00
27 Jay Johnson	3.00	6.00
28 Harry Jones	3.00	6.00
29 Ray Jones	3.00	6.00
30 Ike Kelley	3.00	6.00
31 Wade Key	3.00	6.00
32 Leroy Keyes	3.00	6.00
33 Pete Liske	3.00	6.00
34 Pete Liske BSA	3.00	6.00
35 Dave Lloyd	3.00	6.00
36 Ron Medved	3.00	6.00
37 Tom McNeill BSA	3.00	6.00
38 Mark Moseley	4.00	8.00
39 Al Nelson	3.00	6.00
40 Mark Nordquist	3.00	6.00
41 Gary Pettigrew	3.00	6.00
42 Steve Preece	3.00	6.00
43 Ron Porter	3.00	6.00
44 Nate Ramsey	3.00	6.00
45 Tim Rossovich	3.00	6.00
46 Jim Skaggs	3.00	6.00
47 Steve Smith T	3.00	6.00
48 Richard Stevens	3.00	6.00
49 Bill Walik	3.00	6.00
50 Jim Ward (photo taken in stadium)	3.00	6.00
51 Larry Watkins	3.00	6.00
52 Adrian Young	3.00	6.00
53 Coaching Staff Irv Cross Marv Levy	8.00	12.00

1972 Eagles Postcards

These photos measure approximately 4 1/4" by 5 1/2" and feature posed action black-and-white player photos with white borders. Each photo was taken outside unless noted below. The player's name and team name (measuring about 1 9/16") are printed in the bottom border. The Eagles issued Postcards over a number of years and this set is differentiated from the 1970-71 list by the lack of a facsimile autograph on the cardfronts. Unless noted below, the backs include a postcard style format. The cards are unnumbered and checklisted below in alphabetical order.

COMPLETE SET (6)	20.00	35.00
1 Henry Allison	3.00	6.00
2 Houston Antwine	3.00	6.00
3 Tony Baker	3.00	6.00
4 Larry Crowe	3.00	6.00
5 Harold Jackson	4.00	8.00
6 Jim Thrower	3.00	6.00

1972-73 Eagles Team Issue

These Philadelphia Eagles team issued photos measure approximately 8" by 10" and feature a black and white player photo on a glossy blankbacked card stock. The photos were likely issued over a number of years with many players issued in both a portrait and posed action format. Just the player's name and team name appear below the photo. The checklist is likely incomplete; any additions to this list would be appreciated.

COMPLETE SET (29)	75.00	150.00
1 Tom Bailey Portrait	3.00	6.00
2 Herman Ball Director of Personnel	3.00	6.00
3 Bill Bradley Posed Action	4.00	8.00
4 Ron Bull	3.00	6.00
5 John Bunting Portrait	3.00	6.00
6 John Bunting Posed Action	3.00	6.00
7 Bill Cody Portrait	3.00	6.00
8 Larry Crowe Portrait	3.00	6.00
9 Larry Crowe Posed action	3.00	6.00
10 Albert Davis Portrait	3.00	6.00
11 Albert Davis Posed action	3.00	6.00
12 Stanley Davis Portrait	3.00	6.00
13 Stanley Davis Posed action	3.00	6.00
14 Bill Dunstan Portrait	3.00	6.00
15 Bill Dunstan Posed action	3.00	6.00
16 Lawrence Estes Portrait	3.00	6.00
17 Mike Evans	3.00	6.00
18 Pat Gibbs Posed Action	3.00	6.00
19 Harold Jackson Posed Action	4.00	8.00
20 Wade Key Posed Action	3.00	6.00
21 Kent Kramer Portrait	3.00	6.00
22 Randy Logan Posed Action	3.00	6.00
23 Tom Luken Posed Action	3.00	6.00
24 Tom McNeill Jersey 12	3.00	6.00
25 Tom McNeill Jersey 36	3.00	6.00
26 Gary Pettigrew Posed Action	3.00	6.00
27 Bob Picard Posed Action	3.00	6.00
28 Ron Porter Posed Action	3.00	6.00
29 Jerry Wampfler CO	3.00	6.00
30 Vern Winfield Posed Action	3.00	6.00
31 Steve Zabel Posed Action	3.00	6.00

1974 Eagles Postcards

These photos measure approximately 4 1/4" by 5 1/2" and feature posed action or portrait style black-and-white player photos with white borders. The player's name and team name (measuring about 1 9/16") are printed in the bottom border. The Eagles issued Postcards over a number of years and this set is very similar to the 1972 issue. The backs include a postcard style format. The photos are unnumbered and checklisted below in alphabetical order.

COMPLETE SET (45)	125.00	250.00
1 Tom Bailey	3.00	6.00
2 Bill Bergey	4.00	8.00
3 Mike Boryla	3.00	6.00
4 Bill Bradley	3.00	6.00
5 Norm Bulaich	3.00	6.00
6 John Bunting	3.00	6.00
7 Jim Cagle	3.00	6.00
8 Harold Carmichael	6.00	12.00
9 Wes Chesson	3.00	6.00
10 Tom Dempsey	3.00	6.00
11 Bill Dunstan	3.00	6.00
12 Charlie Ford	3.00	6.00
13 Roman Gabriel	5.00	10.00
14 Dean Halverson	3.00	6.00
15 Randy Jackson	3.00	6.00
16 Po James	3.00	6.00
17 Joe Jones	3.00	6.00
18 Roy Kirksey	3.00	6.00
19 Merritt Kersey	3.00	6.00
20 Wade Key	3.00	6.00
21 Kent Kramer	3.00	6.00
22 Joe Lavender	3.00	6.00
23 Frank LeMaster	3.00	6.00
24 Tom Luken	3.00	6.00
25 Larry Marshall	3.00	6.00
26 Guy Morriss	3.00	6.00
27 Mark Nordquist	3.00	6.00
28 Greg Oliver	3.00	6.00
29 John Outlaw	3.00	6.00
30 Artimus Parker	3.00	6.00
31 Jerry Patton	3.00	6.00
32 Bob Picard	3.00	6.00
33 John Reaves	3.00	6.00
34 Marion Reeves	3.00	6.00
35 Kevin Reilly	3.00	6.00
36 Charles Smith	3.00	6.00
37 Steve Smith	3.00	6.00
38 Jerry Sisemore	3.00	6.00
39 Richard Stevens	3.00	6.00
40 Mitch Sutton	3.00	6.00
41 Tom Sullivan	3.00	6.00
42 Will Wynn	3.00	6.00
43 Charlie Young	3.00	6.00
44 Steve Zabel	3.00	6.00
45 Don Zimmerman	3.00	6.00

1975 Eagles Postcards

Cards from this set measure approximately 4 1/4" by 5 1/2" and feature game action black-and-white player photos with white borders. The player's name, position (initials), Eagles logo and team name are printed in the bottom white margin. The backs include a postcard style format. The cards are unnumbered and checklisted below in alphabetical order. Any additions to the list below are appreciated.

COMPLETE SET (26)	75.00	135.00
1 George Amundson	3.00	6.00
2 Mike Boryla	3.00	6.00
3 Bill Bradley	3.00	6.00
4 Cliff Brooks	3.00	6.00
5 John Bunting	3.00	6.00
6 Tom Ehler	3.00	6.00
7 Roman Gabriel	6.00	10.00
8 Spike Jones	3.00	6.00
9 Keith Krepfle	3.00	6.00
10 Joe Lavender	3.00	6.00
11 Ron Lou	3.00	6.00
12 Art Malone	3.00	6.00
13 Rosie Manning	3.00	6.00
14 James McAlister	3.00	6.00
15 Guy Morriss	3.00	6.00
16 Horst Muhlmann	3.00	6.00
17 John Niland	3.00	6.00
18 John Outlaw	3.00	6.00
19 Artimus Parker	3.00	6.00
20 Don Ratliff	3.00	6.00
21 Jerry Sisemore	3.00	6.00
22 Charles Smith	3.00	6.00
23 Tom Sullivan	3.00	6.00
24 Stan Walters	3.00	6.00
25 Will Wynn	3.00	6.00
26 Don Zimmerman	3.00	6.00

1976 Eagles Team Issue

The Eagles issued these black and white glossy player photos in 1976. Each measures approximately 5" by 7" and features the player's name and position (initials) below the photo. The team name and year appear above the photo. The backs are blank and unnumbered. The checklist below includes the known photos at this time. Any additions to this list would be appreciated.

COMPLETE SET (7)	20.00	40.00
1 John Bunting	3.00	6.00
2 Harold Carmichael	4.00	8.00
3 Pete Lazetich	3.00	6.00
4 Guy Morriss	3.00	6.00
5 Jerry Sisemore	3.00	6.00
6 Charles Smith	3.00	6.00
7 Dick Vermeil CO	6.00	12.00

1977 Eagles Frito Lay

Cards from this set measure approximately 4 1/4" by 5 1/2" and feature portrait player photos on the fronts. The photo type differentiates this set from the 1978 set which otherwise follows the same type style and printing. It's likely that some of these player photos were released during both years. The team name and logo appear in the top border while the player's name, position, and Frito Lay (FL) logo appear in the bottom border. Most feature postcard style cardbacks. This release can be identified by the shorter "FL" Frito Lay logo in the lower right corner and the 1/8" left and right borders. Because this set is unnumbered, the cards are listed alphabetically.

COMPLETE SET (34)	100.00	200.00
1 Bill Bergey	4.00	8.00
2 John Bunting	3.00	6.00
3 Lem Burnham	3.00	6.00
4 Harold Carmichael	5.00	10.00
5 Mike Cordova	3.00	6.00
6 Herman Edwards	4.00	8.00
7 Tom Ehler	3.00	6.00
8 Cleveland Franklin	3.00	6.00
9 Dennis Franks	3.00	6.00
10 Roman Gabriel	5.00	10.00
11 Carl Hairston	3.00	6.00
12 Mike Hogan	3.00	6.00
13 Charlie Johnson	3.00	6.00
14 Eric Johnson	3.00	6.00
15 Wade Key	3.00	6.00
16 Pete Lazetich	3.00	6.00
17 Randy Logan	3.00	6.00
18 Herb Lusk	3.00	6.00
19 Larry Marshall	3.00	6.00
20 Wilbert Montgomery	4.00	8.00
21 Rocco Moore	3.00	6.00
22 Guy Morriss	3.00	6.00
23 Horst Muhlmann	3.00	6.00
24 John Outlaw	3.00	6.00
25 Vince Papale	7.50	15.00
26 James Reed	3.00	6.00
27 Kevin Russell	3.00	6.00
28 Jerry Sisemore	3.00	6.00
29 Manny Sistrunk	3.00	6.00
30 Charles Smith	3.00	6.00
31 Terry Tautolo	3.00	6.00
32 Art Thoms	3.00	6.00
33 Stan Walters	4.00	8.00
34 John Walton	3.00	6.00

1978 Eagles Frito Lay

Cards from this set measure approximately 4 1/4" by 5 1/2" and feature an action player photo on the fronts. The photo type differentiates this set from the 1977 set which otherwise follows the same type style and printing. It's likely that some of these player photos were released during both years. The team name and logo appear in the top border while the player's name, position, and Frito Lay (FL) logo appear in the bottom border. Most feature postcard style cardbacks. This release can be identified by the shorter "FL" Frito Lay logo in the lower right corner and the 1/8" left and right borders. Because this set is unnumbered, the cards are listed alphabetically.

COMPLETE SET (11)	30.00	60.00
1 Bill Bergey	4.00	8.00
2 Ken Clarke	3.00	6.00
3 Bob Howard	3.00	6.00
4 Keith Krepfle	3.00	6.00
5 Frank LeMaster	3.00	6.00
6 Mike Michel	3.00	6.00
7 Oren Middlebrook	3.00	6.00
8 Wilbert Montgomery	4.00	8.00
9 Mike Osborn	3.00	6.00
10 Reggie Wilkes	3.00	6.00
11 Charles Williams	3.00	6.00

1978 Eagles Team Issue

The Eagles issued these black and white glossy player photos in 1976. Each measures approximately 5" by 7" and features the player's name and position (initials) below the photo. The team name and year appear above the photo. The backs are blank and unnumbered. The checklist below includes the known photos at this time. Any additions to this list would be appreciated.

COMPLETE SET (15)	40.00	80.00
1 Rick Engles	3.00	6.00
2 Cleveland Franklin	3.00	6.00
3 Dennis Franks	3.00	6.00

4 Ed George 3.00 6.00
5 Eric Johnson 3.00 6.00
6 Oren Middlebrook 3.00 6.00
7 Mike Osborn 3.00 6.00
8 Richard Osborne 3.00 6.00
(no year on front)
9 John Outlaw 3.00 6.00
10 Ken Payne 3.00 6.00
11 John Sanders 3.00 6.00
12 Manny Sistrunk 3.00 6.00
13 Terry Tautolo 3.00 6.00
14 John Walton 3.00 6.00
15 Charles Williams 3.00 6.00
(no year on front)

1979 Eagles Frito Lay

The 1979 Frito Lay Eagles cards measure approximately 4 1/4" by 5 1/2" and feature an action player shot enclosed within a white border. The team name and mascot appear in the top border while the player's name, position, and "Lay's Brand Potato Chips" logo appear in the bottom border. Most feature postcard style cardbacks. Frito Lay sponsored several Eagles sets throughout the 1970s and '80s and it is likely that photos from this set were released over a period of years. This release can be specifically identified by the unique "Lay's Potato Chips" logo in the lower right corner. Because this set is unnumbered, the cards are listed alphabetically.

COMPLETE SET (30) 90.00 150.00
1 Larry Barnes 3.00 6.00
2 John Bunting 3.00 6.00
3 Lem Burnham 3.00 6.00
4 Billy Campfield 3.00 6.00
5 Harold Carmichael 5.00 10.00
6 Ken Clarke 3.00 6.00
7 Scott Fritzkee 3.00 6.00
8 Louie Giammona 3.00 6.00
9 Leroy Harris 3.00 6.00
10 Wally Henry 3.00 6.00
11 Bobby Lee Howard 3.00 6.00
12 Claude Humphrey 4.00 8.00
13 Charlie Johnson 3.00 6.00
14 Wade Key 3.00 6.00
15 Keith Krepfle 4.00 8.00
16 Frank LeMaster 3.00 6.00
17 Randy Logan 3.00 6.00
18 Rufus Mayes 3.00 6.00
19 Jerrold McRae 3.00 6.00
20 Wilbert Montgomery 4.00 8.00
21 Woody Peoples 3.00 6.00
22 Petey Perot 3.00 6.00
23 John Sanders 3.00 6.00
24 John Sciarra 3.00 6.00
25 Manny Sistrunk 3.00 6.00
26 Mark Slater 3.00 6.00
27 John Spagnola 3.00 6.00
28 Stan Walters 3.00 6.00
29 Reggie Wilkes 3.00 6.00
30 Brenard Wilson 3.00 6.00

1979 Eagles Team Sheets

This set consists of six 8" by 10" sheets that display five or eight glossy black-and-white player/coaches photos each. Each individual photo on the sheets measures approximately 2 1/4" by 3 1/4". An Eagles logo, team name and year appear above the photos at the top of each sheet and the backs are blank. The sheets are unnumbered and checklisted below alphabetically according to the player featured in the upper left corner.

COMPLETE SET (6) 20.00 40.00
1 Ken Clarke 3.00 6.00
Herman Edwards
Scott Fritzkee
Carl Hairston
Louie Giammona
Tony Franklin
Leroy Harris
Wally Henry
2 Coaches: 4.00 8.00
Sid Gillman
George Hill
Ken Iman
Billy Joe
Lynn Stiles
Jerry Wampfler
Otho Davis
Ron O'Neil
3 Randy Logan 4.00 8.00
Rufus Mayes
Jerrold McRae
Wilbert Montgomery
Guy Morriss
Woody Peoples
Petey Perot
Ray Phillips
4 Jerry Robinson 3.00 6.00
Max Runager
John Sciarra
Jerry Sisemore
Manny Sistrunk
Mark Slater
Charles Smith
John Spagnola
5 Terry Tautolo 3.00 6.00
Stan Walters
Johnnie Walton
Reggie Wilkes
Brenard Wilson
6 Leonard Tose Pres. 5.00 10.00
Jim Murray GM
Carl Peterson Dir.
Dick Vermeil HC
Dick Coury Asst.
Chuck Clausen Asst.
Marion Campbell Asst.
Fred Bruney Asst.

1980 Eagles Frito Lay

Cards from this set measure approximately 4 1/4" by 5 1/2" and feature an action player shot and facsimile autograph (unless noted below) enclosed in a white border. The team name and mascot appear in the top border while the player's name, position, and "Frito Lay" logo appear in the bottom border. The format for these cards is nearly identical to the 1983 Eagles Frito Lay set except that all cards in this set were produced with the postcard format cardback, while most of the 1983 cards were blankbacked. Frito Lay sponsored several Eagles sets throughout the 1970s and '80s. This release can be differentiated by the full "Frito Lay" logo in the lower right corner, the postcard style backs, and the 1/8" left and right borders. Because this set is unnumbered, the cards are listed alphabetically.

COMPLETE SET (48) 125.00 250.00
1 Bill Bergey 4.00 8.00
2 Richard Blackmore 3.00 6.00
3 Thomas Brown 3.00 6.00
(no facsimile autograph)
4 John Bunting 3.00 6.00
5 Lem Burnham 3.00 6.00
6 Billy Campfield 3.00 6.00
7 Harold Carmichael 5.00 10.00
8 Al Chesley 3.00 6.00
9 Ken Clarke 3.00 6.00
10 Ken Dunek 3.00 6.00
(no facsimile autograph)
11 Herman Edwards 3.00 6.00
12 Scott Fitzkee 3.00 6.00
13 Tony Franklin 4.00 8.00
14 Louie Giammona 3.00 6.00
15 Carl Hairston 4.00 8.00
16 Perry Harrington 3.00 6.00
(no facsimile autograph)
17 Leroy Harris 3.00 6.00
18 Dennis Harrison 3.00 6.00
19 Zac Henderson 3.00 6.00
(no facsimile autograph)
20 Wally Henry 3.00 6.00
21 Rob Hertel 3.00 6.00
(no facsimile autograph)
22 Claude Humphrey 4.00 8.00
23 Ron Jaworski 6.00 12.00
(full length photo, postcard back)
24 Charlie Johnson 3.00 6.00
25 Steve Kenney 3.00 6.00
(no facsimile autograph)
26 Keith Krepfle 4.00 8.00
27 Frank LeMaster 3.00 6.00
28 Randy Logan 3.00 6.00
29 Wilbert Montgomery 4.00 8.00
30 Guy Morriss 3.00 6.00
31 Rodney Parker 3.00 6.00
(no facsimile autograph)
32 Woody Peoples 3.00 6.00
33 Pete Perot 3.00 6.00
34 Ray Phillips 3.00 6.00
35 Joe Pisarcik 4.00 8.00
(no facsimile autograph)
36 Jerry Robinson 3.00 6.00
37 Max Runager 3.00 6.00
38 John Sciarra 3.00 6.00
39 Jerry Sisemore 3.00 6.00
40 Mark Slater 3.00 6.00
(no facsimile autograph)
41 Charles Smith 3.00 6.00
42 John Spagnola 3.00 6.00
43 Dick Vermeil 7.50 15.00
44 Steve Wagner 3.00 6.00
(no facsimile autograph)
45 Stan Walters 3.00 6.00
46 Reggie Wilkes 3.00 6.00
47 Brenard Wilson 3.00 6.00
48 Roynell Young 3.00 6.00
(no facsimile autograph)

1980 Eagles McDonald's Glasses

These standard-sized glasses were distributed by McDonald's in the Philadelphia area in 1980. Each glass contains 2 player drawings, with each player represented by a crude action drawing and a head shot superimposed over a fooball, with their name in script underneath the football. The glasses are unnumbered, and are catalogued below in alphabetical order by the first player name.

COMPLETE SET (5) 12.50 25.00
1 Bill Bergey 3.00 6.00
John Bunting
2 Billy Campfield 3.00 6.00
Wilbert Montgomery
3 Harold Carmichael 2.50 5.00
Randy Logan
4 Tony Franklin 2.50 5.00
Stan Walters
5 Ron Jaworski 3.00 8.00
Keith Krepfle

1983 Eagles Frito Lay

This set measures approximately 4 1/4" by 5 1/2" and features an action player shot and facsimile autograph enclosed in a white border. The team name and mascot appear in the top border while the player's name, position, and "Frito Lay" logo appear in the bottom border. Unless noted below, all cardbacks are blank. Frito Lay sponsored several Eagles sets throughout the 1970s and '80s. This release can be differentiated by the full "Frito Lay" logo in the lower right corner and the 1/8" left and right borders. Because this set is unnumbered, the cards are listed alphabetically.

COMPLETE SET (40) 100.00 200.00
1 Harvey Armstrong 3.00 6.00
2 Ron Baker 3.00 6.00
3 Bill Bergey 4.00 8.00
4 Greg Brown 3.00 6.00
5 Marion Campbell CO 3.00 6.00
(postcard style back)
6 Harold Carmichael 5.00 10.00
7 Ken Clarke 3.00 6.00
8 Dennis DeVaughn 3.00 6.00
9 Herman Edwards 3.00 6.00
10 Ray Ellis 3.00 6.00
11 Major Everett 3.00 6.00
12 Elbert Foules 3.00 6.00
13 Anthony Griggs 3.00 6.00
14 Michael Haddix 3.00 6.00
15 Perry Harrington 3.00 6.00
(with facsimile autograph)
16 Dennis Harrison 3.00 6.00
17 Melvin Hoover 3.00 6.00
18 Wes Hopkins 3.00 6.00
19 Ron Jaworski 5.00 10.00
20 Vyto Kab 3.00 6.00
21 Steve Kenney 3.00 6.00
22 Rich Kraynak 3.00 6.00
23 Dean Miraldi 3.00 6.00
24 Leonard Mitchell 3.00 6.00
25 Wilbert Montgomery 4.00 8.00
26 Hubie Oliver 3.00 6.00
27 Joe Pisarcik 4.00 8.00
(with facsimile autograph)
28 Mike Quick 4.00 8.00
(postcard style back)
29 Jerry Robinson 3.00 6.00
30 Max Runager 3.00 6.00
31 Lawrence Sampleton 3.00 6.00
(postcard style back)
32 Jody Schulz 3.00 6.00
33 Jerry Sisemore 3.00 6.00
34 John Spagnola 3.00 6.00
35 Reggie Wilkes 3.00 6.00
36 Joel Williams 3.00 6.00
37 Mike Williams 3.00 6.00
38 Tony Woodruff 3.00 6.00
39 Glen Young 3.00 6.00
40 Roynell Young 3.00 6.00
(with facsimile autograph)

1984 Eagles Police

This numbered eight-card set features the Philadelphia Eagles. Backs are printed in black ink with red accent. Cards measure approximately 2 5/8" by 4 1/8". The set was sponsored by Frito-Lay, the local police department, and the Philadelphia Eagles.

COMPLETE SET (8) 2.50 6.00
1 Mike Quick .50 1.25
2 Dennis Harrison .20 .50
3 Jerry Robinson .30 .75
4 Wilbert Montgomery .50 1.25
5 Herman Edwards .20 .50
6 Kenny Jackson .30 .75
7 Anthony Griggs .20 .50
8 Ron Jaworski .60 1.50

1985 Eagles Police

This 16-card set is numbered on the back. The card backs are printed in black and red ink on white card stock. Cards measure 2 5/8" by 4 1/8". The set was sponsored by Frito-Lay, local Police Departments, and the Eagles. Uniform numbers are printed on the card front before the player's name.

COMPLETE SET (16) 3.00 8.00
1 Ken Clarke .20 .50
2 Roynell Young .30 .75
3 Ray Ellis .20 .50
4 Ron Baker .20 .50
5 John Spagnola .25 .60
6 Reggie Wilkes .20 .50
7 Ron Jaworski .50 1.25
8 Steve Kenney .20 .50
9 Paul McFadden .20 .50
10 Mike Quick .40 1.00
11 Hubie Oliver .20 .50
12 Greg Brown .25 .60
13 Anthony Griggs .20 .50
14 Michael Haddix .25 .60
15 Kenny Jackson .30 .75
16 Vyto Kab .20 .50

1985 Eagles TastyKake

Cards from this set measure approximately 4 1/4" by 5 1/2" and feature a close-up player photo within a white border. The team name and team logo appear in the top border while the player's name, position, and TastyKake and Philadelphia Daily News sponsorship logos appear in the bottom border. All are blankbacked.

COMPLETE SET (16) 40.00 80.00
1 Ron Baker 3.00 6.00
2 Greg Brown 3.00 6.00
3 Randall Cunningham 6.00 12.00
4 Byron Darby 3.00 6.00
5 Michael Haddix 3.00 6.00
6 Wes Hopkins 3.00 6.00
7 Earnest Jackson ERR 3.00 6.00
8 Steve Kenney 3.00 6.00
9 Rich Kraynak 3.00 6.00
10 Dave Little 3.00 6.00
11 Paul McFadden 3.00 6.00
12 Leonard Mitchell 3.00 6.00
13 Mike Quick 4.00 8.00
14 Ken Reeves 3.00 6.00
15 Mike Reichenbach 3.00 6.00
16 John Spagnola 3.00 6.00

1985 Eagles Team Issue

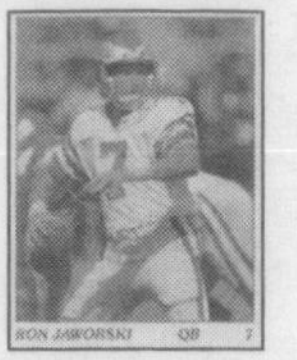

This 53-card team-issued set measures approximately 2 15/16" by 3 7/8". The fronts feature glossy color player photos bordered in white. The wider bottom border contains the player's name, position, and jersey number. Player information again appears on the top of the backs in green print; the career summary is printed in a black box that fills the rest of the backs. The cards are unnumbered and checklisted below alphabetically, with the miscellaneous cards listed at the end.

COMPLETE SET (53) 100.00 200.00
1 Harvey Armstrong 2.00 5.00
2 Ron Baker 2.00 5.00
3 Norman Braman PRES 2.00 5.00
4 Greg Brown 2.00 5.00
5 Marion Campbell CO 3.00 6.00
6 Jeff Christensen 2.00 5.00
7 Ken Clarke 2.00 5.00
8 Evan Cooper 2.00 5.00
9 Byron Darby 2.00 5.00
10 Mark Dennard 2.00 5.00
11 Herman Edwards 2.00 5.00
12 Ray Ellis 2.00 5.00
13 Major Everett 2.00 5.00
14 Gerry Feehery 2.00 5.00
15 Elbert Foules 2.00 5.00
16 Gregg Garrity 2.00 5.00
17 Anthony Griggs 2.00 5.00
18 Michael Haddix 2.00 5.00
19 Andre Hardy 2.00 5.00
20 Dennis Harrison 2.00 5.00
21 Joe Hayes 2.00 5.00
22 Melvin Hoover 2.00 5.00
23 Wes Hopkins 3.00 6.00
24 Mike Horan 2.00 5.00
25 Kenny Jackson 2.00 5.00
26 Ron Jaworski 4.00 8.00
27 Vyto Kab 2.00 5.00
28 Steve Kenney 2.00 5.00
29 Rich Kraynak 2.00 5.00
30 Dean May 2.00 5.00
31 Paul McFadden 2.00 5.00
32 Dean Miraldi 2.00 5.00
33 Leonard Mitchell 2.00 5.00
34 Wilbert Montgomery 3.00 6.00
35 Hubie Oliver 2.00 5.00
36 Mike Quick 3.00 6.00
37 Mike Reichenbach 2.00 5.00
38 Jerry Robinson 2.00 5.00
39 Rusty Russell 2.00 5.00
40 Lawrence Sampleton 2.00 5.00
41 Jody Schulz 2.00 5.00
42 John Spagnola 2.00 5.00
43 Tom Strauthers 2.00 5.00
44 Andre Waters 3.00 6.00
45 Reggie Wilkes 2.00 5.00
46 Joel Williams 2.00 5.00
47 Michael Williams 2.00 5.00
48 Brenard Wilson 2.00 5.00
49 Tony Woodruff 2.00 5.00
50 Roynell Young 2.00 5.00
51 Logo Card 2.00 5.00
(Eagle holding football on both sides)
52 1985 Schedule Card 2.00 5.00
(Both sides)
53 Title Card 1985-86 2.00 5.00
(Eagles' helmet)

1986 Eagles Frito Lay

Cards from this set measure approximately 4 1/4" by 5 1/2" and feature an action player shot and facsimile autograph enclosed within a white border. The team name and mascot appear in the top border while the player's name, position, and "Frito Lay" logo appear in the bottom border. All are blankbacked. Frito Lay sponsored several Eagles sets throughout the 1970s and '80s. This release can be differentiated by the full Frito Lay logo in the lower right corner and the 3/8" left and right borders. Because this set is unnumbered, the cards are listed alphabetically. Any additions to this checklist would be greatly appreciated.

COMPLETE SET 40.00 80.00
1 Ray Ellis 2.50 6.00
2 Wes Hopkins 2.50 6.00
3 Mike Horan 2.50 6.00
4 Earnest Jackson 3.00 8.00
5 Ron Jaworski 4.00 10.00
6 Ron Johnson WR 2.50 6.00
7 Mike Quick 3.00 8.00
8 Buddy Ryan CO 5.00 12.00
9 Tom Strauthers 2.50 6.00
10 Andre Waters 3.00 8.00
11 Reggie White 10.00 20.00

1986 Eagles Police

This 16-card set is numbered on the card backs, which are printed in black and red ink on white card stock. Cards measure approximately 2 5/8" by 4 1/8". The set was sponsored by Frito-Lay, local Police Departments, and the Eagles. Uniform numbers are printed on the card front before the player's name. Randall Cunningham's card predates his 1987 Topps Rookie Card by one year.

COMPLETE SET (16) 5.00 12.00
1 Greg Brown .15 .40
2 Reggie White 2.00 5.00
3 John Spagnola .15 .40
4 Mike Quick .30 .75
5 Ken Clarke .15 .40
6 Ken Reeves .15 .40
7 Mike Reichenbach .15 .40
8 Wes Hopkins .20 .50
9 Roynell Young .15 .40
10 Randall Cunningham 2.00 5.00
11 Paul McFadden .15 .40
12 Matt Cavanaugh .15 .40
13 Ron Jaworski .30 .75
14 Byron Darby .15 .40
15 Andre Waters .20 .50
16 Buddy Ryan CO .30 .75

1987 Eagles Police

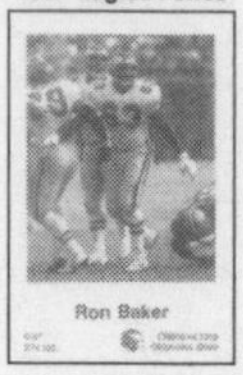

This set of 12 cards featuring Philadelphia Eagles was issued very late in the year and was not widely distributed. Reportedly 10,000 sets were distributed by officers of the New Jersey police force. The cards measure approximately 2 3/4" by 4 1/8" and feature a crime prevention tip on the back. The set was sponsored by the New Jersey State Police Crime Prevention Resource Center. The cards are unnumbered and are listed alphabetically below for reference.

COMPLETE SET (12) 40.00 100.00
1 Ron Baker 2.50 6.00
2 Keith Byars 3.00 8.00
3 Ken Clarke 2.50 6.00
4 Randall Cunningham 8.00 20.00
5 Paul McFadden 2.50 6.00
6 Mike Quick 3.00 8.00
7 Mike Reidenbach 2.50 6.00
8 Buddy Ryan CO 3.00 8.00
9 John Spagnola 2.50 6.00
10 Anthony Toney 2.50 6.00
11 Andre Waters 3.00 8.00
12 Reggie White 8.00 20.00

1988 Eagles Police

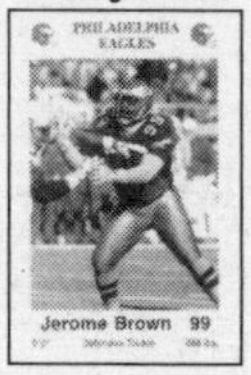

The 1988 Police Philadelphia Eagles set contains 12 unnumbered cards measuring approximately 2 3/4" by 4 1/8". There are 11 player cards and one coach card. The format is very similar to the 1990 set, however for 1988 the player's name and his jersey number is immediately below the image with his height, position, and weight below that. The backs have safety tips. The cards are listed below in alphabetical order by subject's name.

COMPLETE SET (12) 30.00 80.00
1 Jerome Brown 2.50 6.00
2 Keith Byars 2.50 6.00
3 Randall Cunningham 6.00 15.00
4 Matt Darwin 2.00 5.00
5 Keith Jackson 3.00 8.00
6 Seth Joyner 2.50 6.00
7 Mike Quick 2.50 6.00
8 Buddy Ryan CO 4.00 10.00
9 Clyde Simmons 2.50 6.00
(weight listed as 276)
10 John Teltschik 2.00 5.00
11 Anthony Toney 2.00 5.00
12 Reggie White 6.00 15.00

1989 Eagles Daily News

This 24-card set which measures approximately 5 9/16" by 4 1/4" features black and white portrait photos of the players. Above the player's photo is the Eagle logo and the Philadelphia Eagles team name while underneath are advertisments for McDonald's, radio station KYW, and the Philadelphia Daily News. The backs are blank. This was the third season that the Eagles had participated in this project. We have checklisted this set in alphabetical order.

COMPLETE SET (24) 75.00 150.00
1 Eric Allen 3.00 8.00
2 Jerome Brown 3.00 8.00
3 Keith Byars 3.00 8.00
4 Cris Carter UER 6.00 15.00
(Name misspelled Chris on front)
5 Randall Cunningham 4.00 10.00
6 Matt Darwin 2.50 6.00
7 Gerry Feehery 2.50 6.00
8 Ron Heller 2.50 6.00
9A Terry Hoage 2.50 6.00
(Solid color jersey)
9B Terry Hoage 2.50 6.00
(With white collar or undershirt)
10 Wes Hopkins 2.50 6.00
11 Keith Jackson 3.00 8.00
12 Seth Joyner 3.00 8.00
13 Mike Pitts 2.50 6.00
14 Mike Quick 3.00 8.00
15 Mike Reichenbach 2.50 6.00
16 Clyde Simmons 3.00 8.00
17 John Spagnola 2.50 6.00
18 Junior Tautalatasi 2.50 6.00
19 John Teltschik 2.50 6.00
20 Anthony Toney 2.50 6.00
21 Andre Waters 3.00 8.00
22 Reggie White 6.00 15.00
23 Luis Zendejas 2.50 6.00

1989 Eagles Police Jumbo

Cards from this set were distributed by the New Jersey State Police in Trenton, New Jersey over a period of years. These large unnumbered cards measure approximately 8 1/2" by 11" and feature action player photos of members of the Philadelphia Eagles inside white borders. Player bio information is centered beneath the picture between the New Jersey State Police Crime Prevention Resource Center emblem and Security Savings Bank logo. The 1989 issue is nearly identical to the 1990 issue, but can be differentiated by the bank logo missing the FDIC notation. The back carries the title "Alcohol and Other Drugs: Facts and Myths" and features five questions and answers on this topic. Sponsor and team logos at the bottom round out the back. The cards are unnumbered and checklisted below alphabetically.

COMPLETE SET (8) 50.00 100.00
1 Cris Carter 20.00 40.00
2 Mike Golic 5.00 10.00
3 Keith Jackson 6.00 12.00
4 Clyde Simmons 6.00 12.00
5 John Teltschik 10.00
6 Anthony Toney 5.00 10.00
7 Andre Waters 6.00 12.00
8 Luis Zendejas 5.00 10.00

1989 Eagles Smokey

This 50-card set features members of the Philadelphia Eagles. The cards measure approximately 3" by 5". The full-color photo on the front covers the complete card, although the player's name, number, and position are overprinted in the lower right corner. Each card back shows a different fire safety cartoon. Backs are printed in green ink in deference to the Eagles colors. Cards are unnumbered, except for uniform number which appears on the card front and back; cards are ordered below by uniform number. In a few cases, there were two cards produced of the same player; typically the two can be distinguished by home and away colors. The complete set price below includes all the variations listed.

COMPLETE SET (50) 100.00 200.00
6 Matt Cavanaugh 1.50 4.00
8 Luis Zendejas 1.50 4.00
9 Don McPherson 1.50 4.00
10 John Teltschik 1.50 4.00
12A Randall Cunningham 6.00 15.00
(White jersey)
12B Randall Cunningham 6.00 15.00
(Green jersey)
20 Andre Waters 2.00 5.00
21 Eric Allen 2.00 5.00
25 Anthony Toney 1.50 4.00
26 Michael Haddix 2.00 5.00
33 William Frizzell 1.50 4.00
34 Terry Hoage 1.50 4.00
35 Mark Konecny 1.50 4.00
41 Keith Byars 2.00 5.00
42 Eric Everett 1.50 4.00
43 Roynell Young 1.50 4.00
46 Izel Jenkins 1.50 4.00
48 Wes Hopkins 1.50 4.00
50 Dave Rimington 1.50 4.00
52 Todd Bell 1.50 4.00
53 Dwayne Jiles 1.50 4.00
55 Mike Reichenbach 1.50 4.00
56 Byron Evans 1.50 4.00
58 Ty Allert 1.50 4.00
59 Seth Joyner 2.00 5.00
61 Ben Tamburello 1.50 4.00
63 Ron Baker 1.50 4.00
66 Ken Reeves 1.50 4.00
68 Reggie Singletary 1.50 4.00
72 David Alexander 1.50 4.00
73 Ron Heller 1.50 4.00
74 Mike Pitts 1.50 4.00
78 Matt Darwin 1.50 4.00
80 Cris Carter 10.00 25.00
81 Kenny Jackson 1.50 4.00
82A Mike Quick 2.00 5.00
(White jersey)
82B Mike Quick 2.00 5.00
(Green jersey)
83 Jimmie Giles 2.00 5.00
85 Ron Johnson 1.50 4.00
86 Gregg Garrity 1.50 4.00
88 Keith Jackson 2.00 5.00
89 David Little 1.50 4.00
90 Mike Golic 1.50 4.00
91 Scott Curtis 1.50 4.00
92 Reggie White 6.00 15.00
96 Clyde Simmons 2.00 5.00
97 John Klingel 1.50 4.00
99 Jerome Brown 2.00 5.00
NNO Buddy Ryan CO 3.00 8.00
(Wearing white cap)
NNO Buddy Ryan CO 3.00 8.00
(Wearing green cap)

1990 Eagles Police

Sponsored by the N.J. Crime Prevention Officer's Association and the New Jersey State Police Crime Prevention Resource Center, this 12-card set measures approximately 2 5/8" by 4 1/8" and features action player photos on a white card face. The team name appears above the photo between two helmet icons so this year is often confused with the 1988 Eagles Police set. Except for 1990, just the player's name is immediately below the image, then his height and weight are listed below his name and oriented to the left and his position and college name are oriented to the right. The backs contains sponsor logos, safety tips, and the slogan "Take a bite out of crime" by McGruff the crime dog. The cards are unnumbered and checklisted below in alphabetical order.

COMPLETE SET (12) 24.00 60.00
1 David Alexander 1.60 4.00
2 Eric Allen 2.00 5.00
3 Randall Cunningham 4.80 12.00
4 Keith Byars 2.00 5.00
5 Jeff Feagles 1.60 4.00
6 Mike Golic 1.60 4.00
7 Keith Jackson 2.00 5.00
8 Rich Kotite CO 1.60 4.00
9 Roger Ruzek 1.60 4.00
10 Mickey Shuler 1.60 4.00
11 Clyde Simmons 2.00 5.00
(weight listed as 280)
12 Reggie White 4.80 12.00

1990 Eagles Police Jumbo

Cards from this set were distributed by the New Jersey State Police in Trenton, New Jersey over a period of years. These large unnumbered cards measure approximately 8 1/2" by 11" and feature action player photos of members of the Philadelphia Eagles inside white borders. Player bio information is centered beneath the picture between the New Jersey State Police Crime Prevention Resource Center emblem and Security Savings Bank logo. The 1990 issue is nearly identical to the 1989 issue, but can be differentiated by the bank logo including the FDIC notation. The back carries the title "Alcohol and Other Drugs: Facts and Myths" and features five questions and answers on this topic. Sponsor and team logos at the bottom round out the back. The cards are unnumbered and checklisted below alphabetically.

COMPLETE SET (15) 75.00 150.00
1 David Alexander 5.00 10.00
2 Eric Allen 6.00 12.00
3 Fred Barnett 6.00 12.00
4 Keith Byars 7.50 15.00
5 Randall Cunningham 12.50 25.00
6 Gregg Garrity 5.00 10.00
7 Mike Golic 5.00 10.00
8 Britt Hager 5.00 10.00
9 Ron Heller 5.00 10.00
10 Seth Joyner 7.50 15.00
11 Mike Pitts 5.00 10.00
12 Mike Schad 5.00 10.00
13 Jessie Small 6.00 12.00
14 Reggie White 15.00 30.00
15 Calvin Williams 6.00 12.00

1990 Eagles Sealtest Bookmarks

This six-card set (of bookmarks) which measures approximately 2" by 8" was produced by Sealtest to promote reading among children in Philadelphia. Apparently they were given out at The Free Library of Philadelphia on a weekly basis. The basic design of these bookmarks is identical to the 1990 Knudsen Chargers and 49ers bookmark sets. The color action player cut-out overlays a football stadium design. A box at the bottom whose color varies per bookmark gives biographical information and player profile. The backs have sponsor logos and describe two books that are available at the public library. The bookmarks are unnumbered and checklisted below in alphabetical order.

COMPLETE SET (6) 12.50 25.00
1 David Alexander 1.50 4.00
2 Eric Allen 2.00 5.00
3 Keith Byars 2.00 5.00
4 Randall Cunningham 4.00 8.00
5 Mike Pitts 1.50 4.00
6 Mike Quick 2.00 5.00

1992 Eagles Team Issue

These team issued photos measure approximately 4 1/4" by 5 1/2" and were produced for distribution by the Philadelphia Eagles. Each photo is blankbacked and unnumbered. Several photos were likely issued over a period of years. Any additions to this list would be appreciated.

COMPLETE SET (34) 60.00 120.00
1 David Alexander 1.50 4.00
2 Eric Allen 2.00 5.00
3 Fred Barnett 2.00 5.00
4 Pat Beach 1.50 4.00
5 Keith Byars 2.00 5.00
6 Antone Davis 1.50 4.00
7 Jeff Feagles 1.50 4.00
8 Mike Golic 1.50 4.00
9 Roy Green 2.00 5.00
10 Britt Hager 1.50 4.00

11 Andy Harmon	1.50	4.00
12 Wes Hopkins	1.50	4.00
13 Izel Jenkins	1.50	4.00
14 Tommy Jeter	1.50	4.00
15 Maurice Johnson	1.50	4.00
16 James Joseph	1.50	4.00
17 Seth Joyner	2.00	5.00
18 Rich Kotite	1.50	4.00
19 Scott Kowalkowski	1.50	4.00
20 Jim McMahon	3.00	8.00
21 Mark McMillian	1.50	4.00
22 Ken Rose	1.50	4.00
23 Roger Ruzek	1.50	4.00
24 Mike Schad	1.50	4.00
25 Rob Selby	1.50	4.00
26 Heath Sherman	1.50	4.00
27 Vai Sikahema	1.50	4.00
28 Clyde Simmons	2.00	5.00
29 William Thomas	2.00	5.00
30 Herschel Walker	3.00	8.00
31 Andre Waters	2.00	5.00
32 Casey Weldon	1.50	4.00
33 Reggie White	5.00	12.00
34 Calvin Williams	2.00	5.00

1997 Eagles Score

This 15-card set of the Philadelphia Eagles was distributed in five-card packs with a suggested retail price of $1.99. The fronts feature color action player photos with white borders and the player's name and team logo printed in team color foil at the bottom. The backs carry player information and career statistics. Platinum Team parallel cards were randomly seeded in packs featuring all foil cardfronts.

COMPLETE SET (15)	2.00	5.00
*PLATINUM TEAMS: 1X TO 2X		
1 Irving Fryar	.15	.40
2 Rodney Peete	.15	.40
3 Ricky Watters	.30	.75
4 Ty Detmer	.30	.75
5 Troy Vincent	.08	.25
6 Charlie Garner	.15	.40
7 Jason Dunn	.08	.25
8 Chris T. Jones	.15	.40
9 William Thomas	.08	.25
10 Brian Dawkins	.30	.75
11 Bobby Taylor	.08	.25
12 William Fuller	.08	.25
13 Mike Mamula	.08	.25
14 Ray Farmer	.08	.25
15 Mark Seay	.15	.40

2005 Eagles Activa Medallions

COMPLETE SET (25)	30.00	60.00
1 Keith Adams	1.25	3.00
2 David Akers	1.25	3.00
3 Shawn Andrews	1.25	3.00
4 Reggie Brown	1.25	3.00
5 Sheldon Brown	1.25	3.00
6 Brian Dawkins	1.25	3.00
7 Hank Fraley	1.25	3.00
8 Artis Hicks	1.25	3.00
9 Dirk Johnson	1.25	3.00
10 Dhani Jones	1.25	3.00
11 Jevon Kearse	1.25	3.00
12 Greg Lewis	1.25	3.00
13 Michael Lewis	1.25	3.00
14 Jerome McDougle	1.25	3.00
15 Donovan McNabb	1.50	4.00
16 Mike Patterson	1.25	3.00
17 Todd Pinkston	1.25	3.00
18 Jon Runyan	1.25	3.00
19 Lito Shepard	1.25	3.00
20 L.J. Smith	1.25	3.00
21 Tra Thomas	1.25	3.00
22 Jeremiah Trotter	1.25	3.00
23 Darwin Walker	1.25	3.00
24 Brian Westbrook	1.25	3.00
25 Eagles Logo	1.00	2.50

2005 Eagles Topps XXL

COMPLETE SET (4)	2.00	4.00
1 Donovan McNabb	.60	1.50
2 Terrell Owens	.50	1.25
3 Brian Westbrook	.40	1.00
4 Brian Dawkins	.40	1.00

2006 Eagles Topps

COMPLETE SET (12)	3.00	6.00
PHI1 Ryan Moats	.20	.50
PHI2 L.J. Smith	.20	.50
PHI3 Brian Dawkins	.25	.60
PHI4 Greg Lewis	.20	.50
PHI5 Brian Westbrook	.25	.60
PHI6 Donovan McNabb	.30	.75
PHI7 Reggie Brown	.20	.50
PHI8 Todd Pinkston	.20	.50
PHI9 Jeremiah Trotter	.20	.50
PHI10 Jevon Kearse	.25	.60
PHI11 Brodrick Bunkley	.25	.60
PHI12 Jason Avant	.20	.50

2007 Eagles Topps

COMPLETE SET (12)	2.50	5.00
1 Brian Westbrook	.25	.60
2 L.J. Smith	.20	.50
3 Brian Dawkins	.25	.60
4 Donovan McNabb	.30	.75
5 Reggie Brown	.20	.50
6 Tony Hunt	.20	.50
7 Lito Sheppard	.20	.50
8 Kevin Curtis	.20	.50
9 Takeo Spikes	.20	.50
10 Jeremiah Trotter	.20	.50
11 David Akers	.20	.50
12 Kevin Kolb	.50	1.25

2008 Eagles Donruss Thanksgiving Classic

Many fans who attended the 2008 Thanksgiving game in Philadelphia were treated to this complete set. Donruss reported that more than 120,000 cards were given away to fans at both the Dallas and Philadelphia games. Each team set also included one card from the NFL Network broadcasters set.

COMPLETE SET (5)	3.00	6.00
1 Donovan McNabb	.75	2.00
2 Brian Westbrook	.60	1.50
3 Brian Dawkins Youth Partnership	.60	1.50
4 Swoop - Mascot	.50	1.25
5 Pop Warner team of the year	.50	1.25

2008 Eagles Topps

COMPLETE SET (12)	2.50	5.00
1 Brian Westbrook	.25	.60
2 Donovan McNabb	.30	.75
3 Kevin Curtis	.20	.50
4 Correll Buckhalter	.25	.60
5 Asante Samuel	.20	.50
6 Reggie Brown	.20	.50
7 Trent Cole	.20	.50
8 A.J. Feeley	.20	.50
9 L.J. Smith	.20	.50
10 Brian Dawkins	.25	.60
11 DeSean Jackson	.75	2.00
12 Lito Sheppard	.20	.50

2012 Elite

COMP.SET w/o RC's (100)	8.00	20.00
101-200 ROOKIE PRINT RUN 699-999		
1 Larry Fitzgerald	.25	.60
2 Beanie Wells	.25	.60
3 Kevin Kolb	.25	.60
4 Michael Turner	.25	.60
5 Julio Jones	.25	.60
6 Roddy White	.25	.60
7 Matt Ryan	.25	.60
8 Ray Lewis	.30	.75
9 Ray Rice	.25	.60
10 Anquan Boldin	.25	.60
11 Joe Flacco	.25	.60
12 Ryan Fitzpatrick	.25	.60
13 Fred Jackson	.25	.60
14 Steve Johnson	.25	.60
15 Cam Newton	.50	1.25
16 DeAngelo Williams	.25	.60
17 Steve Smith WR	.25	.60
18 Brian Urlacher	.30	.75
19 Jay Cutler	.25	.60
20 Devin Hester	.30	.75
21 Matt Forte	.25	.60
22 Andy Dalton	.30	.75
23 Greg Little	.20	.50
24 A.J. Green	.25	.60
25 Colt McCoy	.25	.60
26 Peyton Hillis	.20	.50
27 DeMarcus Ware	.25	.60
28 Tony Romo	.30	.75
29 DeMarco Murray	.25	.60
30 Jason Witten	.30	.75
31 Von Miller	.25	.60
32 Tim Tebow	.50	1.25
33 Willis McGahee	.20	.50
34 Ndamukong Suh	.30	.75
35 Matthew Stafford	.30	.75
36 Calvin Johnson	.30	.75
37 Charles Woodson	.30	.75
38 Clay Matthews	.30	.75
39 Aaron Rodgers	.50	1.25
40 Greg Jennings	.25	.60
41 Andre Johnson	.25	.60
42 Arian Foster	.25	.60
43 Matt Schaub	.25	.60
44 Reggie Wayne	.25	.60
45 Peyton Manning	1.00	2.50
46 Maurice Jones-Drew	.25	.60
47 Blaine Gabbert	.25	.60
48 Jamaal Charles	.25	.60
49 Eric Berry	.25	.60
50 Dwayne Bowe	.25	.60
51 Matt Cassel	.25	.60
52 Reggie Bush	.25	.60
53 Brandon Marshall	.20	.50
54 Jared Allen	.25	.60
55 Adrian Peterson	.30	.75
56 Christian Ponder	.25	.60
57 Tom Brady	.50	1.25
58 BenJarvus Green-Ellis	.25	.60
59 Rob Gronkowski	.25	.60
60 Wes Welker	.30	.75
61 Drew Brees	.30	.75
62 Darren Sproles	.25	.60
63 Jimmy Graham	.25	.60
64 Marques Colston	.25	.60
65 Eli Manning	.30	.75
66 Brandon Jacobs	.25	.60
67 Victor Cruz	.30	.75
68 Darrelle Revis	.25	.60
69 Mark Sanchez	.25	.60
70 Plaxico Burress	.25	.60
71 Darren McFadden	.25	.60
72 Richard Seymour	.20	.50
73 Carson Palmer	.25	.60
74 Michael Vick	.30	.75
75 LeSean McCoy	.25	.60
76 DeSean Jackson	.25	.60
77 Ben Roethlisberger	.30	.75
78 Rashard Mendenhall	.25	.60
79 Troy Polamalu	.30	.75
80 Heath Miller	.25	.60
81 Philip Rivers	.25	.60
82 Ryan Mathews	.25	.60
83 Antonio Gates	.25	.60
84 Vincent Jackson	.25	.60
85 Patrick Willis	.25	.60
86 Alex Smith QB	.25	.60
87 Frank Gore	.25	.60
88 Vernon Davis	.25	.60
89 Tarvaris Jackson	.20	.50
90 Marshawn Lynch	.25	.60
91 Steven Jackson	.25	.60
92 James Laurinaitis	.20	.50
93 Sam Bradford	.30	.75
94 LeGarrette Blount	.20	.50
95 Josh Freeman	.25	.60
96 Matt Hasselbeck	.25	.60
97 Chris Johnson	.25	.60
98 Nate Washington	.20	.50
99 Brian Orakpo	.20	.50
100 Roy Helu Jr.	.25	.60
101 Andrew Luck/699 RC	20.00	40.00
102 Robert Griffin III/699 RC	20.00	40.00
103 Matt Kalil/799 RC	2.50	6.00
104 Morris Claiborne/799 RC	4.00	10.00
105 Justin Blackmon/699 RC	4.00	10.00
106 Trent Richardson/699 RC	8.00	20.00
107 Riley Reiff/999 RC	2.00	5.00
108 Quinton Coples/999 RC	2.00	5.00
109 Melvin Ingram/999 RC	2.50	6.00
110 Michael Brockers/999 RC	2.00	5.00
111 Ryan Tannehill/699 RC	5.00	12.00
112 David DeCastro/999 RC	2.50	6.00
113 Michael Floyd/699 RC	4.00	10.00
114 Luke Kuechly/999 RC	2.50	6.00
115 Janoris Jenkins/999 RC	2.00	5.00
116 Jonathan Martin/999 RC	1.50	4.00
117 Devon Still/999 RC	2.00	5.00
118 Dre Kirkpatrick/999 RC	3.00	8.00
119 Kendall Wright/799 RC	2.50	6.00
120 Fletcher Cox/999 RC	2.00	5.00
121 Courtney Upshaw/999 RC	2.50	6.00
122 Dontari Poe/999 RC	2.00	5.00
123 Rueben Randle/799 RC	2.00	5.00
124 Nick Perry/999 RC	2.00	5.00
125 Whitney Mercilus/999 RC	2.00	5.00
126 Dont'a Hightower/999 RC	3.00	8.00
127 Mark Barron/999 RC	3.00	8.00
128 Stephen Hill/799 RC	2.00	5.00
129 Zach Brown/999 RC	1.50	4.00
130 Andre Branch/999 RC	1.50	4.00
131 Dwayne Allen/799 RC	2.00	5.00
132 David Wilson/799 RC	4.00	10.00
133 Lamar Miller/799 RC	2.50	6.00
134 Brock Osweiler/799 RC	2.50	6.00
135 Lavonte David/999 RC	2.50	6.00
136 Alshon Jeffery/799 RC	3.00	8.00
137 Bobby Wagner/999 RC	2.00	5.00
138 Doug Martin/799 RC	3.00	8.00
139 Chris Givens/799 RC	1.50	4.00
140 Coby Fleener/799 RC	2.50	6.00
141 Brandon Weeden/699 RC	4.00	10.00
142 Jared Crick/999 RC	2.00	5.00
143 Shea McClellin/999 RC	2.50	6.00
144 Ronnell Lewis/999 RC	2.00	5.00
145 Orson Charles/999 RC	2.00	5.00
146 Vinny Curry/999 RC	2.00	5.00
147 Chandler Jones/999 RC	2.00	5.00
148 Isaiah Pead/799 RC	2.00	5.00
149 George Iloka/999 RC	1.50	4.00
150 Mohamed Sanu/799 RC	2.00	5.00
151 Nick Toon/799 RC	2.50	6.00
152 LaMichael James/799 RC	4.00	10.00
153 Kirk Cousins/999 RC	3.00	8.00
154 T.J. Graham/799 RC	2.00	5.00
155 Mychal Kendricks/999 RC	2.00	5.00
156 Juron Criner/999 RC	1.50	4.00
157 Stephon Gilmore/999 RC	2.00	5.00
158 Bernard Pierce/799 RC	2.00	5.00
159 Ladarius Green/999 RC	2.00	5.00
160 Cyrus Gray/999 RC	2.00	5.00
161 Brian Quick/799 RC	2.50	6.00
162 Nick Foles/799 RC	3.00	8.00
163 Ronnie Hillman/799 RC	2.50	6.00
164 Michael Egnew/799 RC	1.50	4.00
165 Keshawn Martin/999 RC	2.00	5.00
166 Chris Rainey/999 RC	2.00	5.00
167 Joe Adams/799 RC	2.00	5.00
168 Marvin Jones/999 RC	1.50	4.00
169 Ryan Lindley/999 RC	2.00	5.00
170 Greg Childs/999 RC	2.00	5.00
171 Jarius Wright/799 RC	2.00	5.00
172 Michael Smith/999 RC	1.50	4.00
173 Tommy Streeter/999 RC	2.00	5.00
174 Robert Turbin/799 RC	2.00	5.00
175 A.J. Jenkins/799 RC	2.50	6.00
176 DeVier Posey/799 RC	2.00	5.00
177 Bryce Brown/999 RC	2.00	5.00
178 Dan Herron/999 RC	2.00	5.00
179 Vick Ballard/999 RC	1.50	4.00
180 T.Y. Hilton/999 RC	2.00	5.00
181 Bruce Irvin/999 RC	2.50	6.00
182 Marvin McNutt/999 RC	2.00	5.00
183 Terrance Ganaway/999 RC	1.50	4.00
184 B.J. Coleman/999 RC	2.50	6.00
185 Alfred Morris/999 RC	1.50	4.00
186 Jeff Fuller/999 RC	2.50	6.00
187 Rishard Matthews/999 RC	2.00	5.00
188 B.J. Cunningham/799 RC	1.50	4.00
189 Ryan Broyles/799 RC	2.00	5.00
190 Russell Wilson/799 RC	3.00	8.00
191 Devon Wylie/999 RC	2.00	5.00
192 LaVon Brazill/999 RC	1.50	4.00
193 Travis Benjamin/999 RC	2.00	5.00
194 Kevin Zeitler/999 RC	1.50	4.00
195 Chandler Harnish/999 RC	2.00	5.00
196 Marc Tyler/999 RC	2.00	5.00
197 Harrison Smith/999 RC	2.00	5.00
198 Danny Coale/999 RC	3.00	8.00
199 Kellen Moore/999 RC	3.00	8.00
200 Case Keenum/999 RC	2.50	6.00

2012 Elite Aspirations

*VETS/70-99: 5X TO 12X BASIC CARDS
*ROOKIES/70-99: .8X TO 2X BASIC CARDS
*VETS/42-69: 6X TO 15X BASIC CARDS
*ROOKIES/42-69: 1X TO 2.5X BASIC CARDS
*VETS/31: 8X TO 20X BASIC CARDS
*ROOKIES/30: 1.2X TO 3X BASIC CARDS
*VETS/20: 10X TO 25X BASIC CARDS
*ROOKIES/23-29: 1.5X TO 4X BASIC CARDS
*VETS/10-19: 12X TO 30X BASIC CARDS
*ROOKIES/10-19: 2X TO 5X BASIC CARDS
STATED PRINT RUN 1-99

2012 Elite Status

*VETS/70-99: 5X TO 12X BASIC CARDS
*ROOKIES/70-99: .8X TO 2X BASIC CARDS
*VETS/40-69: 6X TO 15X BASIC CARDS
*ROOKIES/40-56: 1X TO 2.5X BASIC CARDS
*VETS/32-39: 8X TO 20X BASIC CARDS
*ROOKIES/30-32: 1.2X TO 3X BASIC CARDS
*VETS/20-29: 10X TO 25X BASIC CARDS
*ROOKIES/20-28: 1.5X TO 4X BASIC CARDS
*VETS/10-19: 12X TO 30X BASIC CARDS
*ROOKIES/10-19: 2X TO 5X BASIC CARDS
STATED PRINT RUN 1-99

2012 Elite Aspirations Autographs

1-100 VETERAN PRINT RUN 1-20		
101 200 ROOKIE PRINT RUN 49		
4 Michael Turner/20	10.00	25.00
15 Cam Newton/15	75.00	125.00
17 Steve Smith WR/20	10.00	25.00
20 Devin Hester/15	12.00	30.00
23 Greg Little/20	10.00	25.00
47 Blaine Gabbert/20	12.00	30.00
52 Reggie Bush/20	30.00	60.00
63 Jimmy Graham/20	12.00	30.00
64 Marques Colston/15	10.00	25.00
79 Troy Polamalu/20	60.00	100.00
87 Frank Gore/20	10.00	25.00
100 Roy Helu Jr./20	10.00	25.00
101 Andrew Luck/49	175.00	300.00
102 Robert Griffin III/49	175.00	300.00
103 Matt Kalil/49	12.00	30.00
104 Morris Claiborne/49	40.00	80.00
105 Justin Blackmon/49	30.00	80.00
106 Trent Richardson/49	60.00	120.00
107 Riley Reiff/49	10.00	25.00
108 Quinton Coples/49	10.00	25.00
109 Melvin Ingram/49	12.00	30.00
110 Michael Brockers/49	10.00	25.00
111 Ryan Tannehill/49	40.00	80.00
112 David DeCastro/49	12.00	30.00
113 Michael Floyd/49	20.00	50.00
114 Luke Kuechly/49	12.00	30.00
115 Janoris Jenkins/49 EXCH	10.00	25.00
116 Jonathan Martin/49	8.00	20.00
117 Devon Still/49	10.00	25.00
118 Dre Kirkpatrick/49 EXCH	15.00	40.00
119 Kendall Wright/49	12.00	30.00
120 Fletcher Cox/49	10.00	25.00
121 Courtney Upshaw/49	12.00	30.00
122 Dontari Poe/49	10.00	25.00
123 Rueben Randle/49	10.00	25.00
124 Nick Perry/49	10.00	25.00
125 Whitney Mercilus/49	10.00	25.00
126 Dont'a Hightower/49	15.00	40.00
127 Mark Barron/49	15.00	40.00
128 Stephen Hill/49 EXCH	10.00	25.00
129 Zach Brown/49	8.00	20.00
130 Andre Branch/49	8.00	20.00
131 Dwayne Allen/49	10.00	25.00
132 David Wilson/49	20.00	50.00
133 Lamar Miller/49	12.00	30.00
134 Brock Osweiler/49	15.00	40.00
135 Lavonte David/49 EXCH	12.00	30.00
136 Alshon Jeffery/49 EXCH	20.00	50.00
137 Bobby Wagner/49	10.00	25.00
138 Doug Martin/49	25.00	60.00
139 Chris Givens/49	8.00	20.00
140 Coby Fleener/49		
141 Brandon Weeden/49	40.00	80.00
142 Jared Crick/49	10.00	25.00
143 Shea McClellin/49	12.00	30.00
144 Ronnell Lewis/49	10.00	25.00
145 Orson Charles/49	10.00	25.00
146 Vinny Curry/49	10.00	25.00
147 Chandler Jones/49	10.00	25.00
148 Isaiah Pead/49	10.00	25.00
149 George Iloka/49	8.00	20.00
150 Mohamed Sanu/49	10.00	25.00
151 Nick Toon/49	12.00	30.00
152 LaMichael James/49	40.00	80.00
153 Kirk Cousins/49	15.00	40.00
154 T.J. Graham/49 EXCH	10.00	25.00
155 Mychal Kendricks/49	10.00	25.00
156 Juron Criner/49	8.00	20.00
157 Stephon Gilmore/49	10.00	25.00
158 Bernard Pierce/49 EXCH	10.00	25.00
159 Ladarius Green/49	10.00	25.00
160 Cyrus Gray/49	10.00	25.00
161 Brian Quick/49	12.00	30.00
162 Nick Foles/49	15.00	40.00
163 Ronnie Hillman/49 EXCH	12.00	30.00
164 Michael Egnew/49	8.00	20.00
165 Keshawn Martin/49	10.00	25.00
166 Chris Rainey/49 EXCH	10.00	25.00
167 Joe Adams/49	10.00	25.00
168 Marvin Jones/49	8.00	20.00
169 Ryan Lindley/49	10.00	25.00
170 Greg Childs/49	10.00	25.00
171 Jarius Wright/49	10.00	25.00
172 Michael Smith/49 EXCH	8.00	20.00
173 Tommy Streeter/49 EXCH	10.00	25.00
174 Robert Turbin/49 EXCH	10.00	25.00
175 A.J. Jenkins/49	12.00	30.00
176 DeVier Posey/49	10.00	25.00
177 Bryce Brown/49 EXCH	10.00	25.00
178 Dan Herron/49	10.00	25.00
179 Vick Ballard/49	8.00	20.00
180 T.Y. Hilton/49	10.00	25.00
181 Bruce Irvin/49 EXCH	12.00	30.00
182 Marvin McNutt/49	10.00	25.00
183 Terrance Ganaway/49	8.00	20.00
184 B.J. Coleman/49 EXCH	12.00	30.00
185 Alfred Morris/49	8.00	20.00
186 Jeff Fuller/49	12.00	30.00
187 Rishard Matthews/49	10.00	25.00
188 B.J. Cunningham/49	8.00	20.00
189 Ryan Broyles/49	15.00	40.00
190 Russell Wilson/49	15.00	40.00
191 Devon Wylie/49	10.00	25.00
192 LaVon Brazill/49	8.00	20.00
193 Travis Benjamin/49	10.00	25.00
194 Kevin Zeitler/49	8.00	20.00
195 Chandler Harnish/49	10.00	25.00
196 Marc Tyler/49	10.00	25.00
197 Harrison Smith/49	10.00	25.00
198 Danny Coale/49	15.00	40.00
199 Kellen Moore/49	15.00	40.00
200 Case Keenum/49	12.00	30.00

2012 Elite Back to the Future Jerseys

STATED PRINT RUN 180-199		
*PRIME/60-99: .5X TO 1.2X BASIC JSY		
*PRIME/31-49: .6X TO 1.5X BASIC JSY		
*PRIME/13: 1X TO 2.5X BASIC JSY		
1 Dan Fouts/199	5.00	12.00
2 Bob Hayes/180	8.00	20.00
3 Knute Rockne/199	15.00	30.00
4 Buck Buchanan/199	3.00	8.00
5 Bob Griese/199	5.00	12.00
6 Rocket Ismail/199	4.00	10.00
7 Todd Christensen/199	3.00	8.00
8 Doug Williams/199	4.00	10.00
9 Sterling Sharpe/199	4.00	10.00
10 Mark Carrier/195	4.00	10.00
11 Ted Hendricks/199	3.00	8.00
12 Doak Walker/199	5.00	12.00
13 John Fuqua/199	4.00	10.00
14 Steve Young/199	5.00	12.00
15 Don Meredith/199	8.00	20.00
16 John Hadl/199	4.00	10.00
17 Deion Sanders/199	5.00	12.00
18 George Blanda/199	5.00	12.00
19 Otto Graham/199	5.00	12.00
20 Junior Seau/199	4.00	10.00

2012 Elite Craftsmen

STATED PRINT RUN 999 SER.#'d SETS		
*GOLD/149: .6X TO 1.5X BASIC INSERTS		
*BLACK/49: 1X TO 2.5X BASIC INSERTS		
1 Andre Johnson	1.00	2.50
2 Ben Roethlisberger	1.25	3.00
3 Wes Welker	1.25	3.00
4 Reggie Wayne	1.00	2.50
5 Julio Jones	1.00	2.50
6 Darren McFadden	1.00	2.50
7 Peyton Manning	3.00	8.00
8 Hakeem Nicks	1.00	2.50
9 Miles Austin	1.00	2.50
10 Jason Witten	1.25	3.00
11 Michael Turner	1.00	2.50
12 Tony Romo	1.25	3.00
13 A.J. Green	1.00	2.50
14 Frank Gore	1.00	2.50
15 Darren Sproles	1.00	2.50

2012 Elite Craftsmen Jerseys Prime

STATED PRINT RUN 5-49		
3 Wes Welker/25	8.00	20.00
6 Darren McFadden/25	6.00	15.00
8 Hakeem Nicks/49	5.00	12.00
9 Miles Austin/49	5.00	12.00
11 Michael Turner/49	5.00	12.00
12 Tony Romo/49	6.00	15.00
13 A.J. Green/49	5.00	12.00

2012 Elite Down and Distance Jerseys

STATED PRINT RUN 8-299		
1 Matt Schaub/299	2.50	6.00
2 Aaron Ross/283	2.00	5.00
3 Anquan Boldin/299	2.50	6.00
4 Anthony Fasano/299	2.00	5.00
9 Brent Celek/299	2.50	6.00
10 Brian Hartline/47	4.00	10.00
11 Brian Urlacher/299	3.00	8.00
13 Cedric Benson/65	4.00	10.00
14 Devin Hester/36	6.00	15.00
15 Dez Bryant/299	3.00	8.00
16 Ed Reed/299	2.50	6.00
17 Haloti Ngata/299	2.00	5.00
18 Jacoby Ford/264	2.00	5.00
19 Jon Beason/19	5.00	12.00
20 Josh Cribbs/157	2.50	6.00
21 Knowshon Moreno/299	2.50	6.00
22 Mario Manningham/299	2.50	6.00
23 Mark Sanchez/299	2.50	6.00
24 Marques Colston/299	2.50	6.00
25 Miles Austin/299	2.50	6.00
26 Philip Rivers/63	4.00	10.00
27 Pierre Thomas/299	2.50	6.00
28 Shonn Greene/299	2.50	6.00
29 Tony Gonzalez/299	2.50	6.00
31 Devery Henderson/299	2.00	5.00
32 Joe Flacco/299	2.50	6.00
35 Eli Manning/299	4.00	10.00
36 Tony Romo/299	3.00	8.00
37 Steven Jackson/299	2.50	6.00
38 Hakeem Nicks/299	2.50	6.00
39 Sam Bradford/299	3.00	8.00
40 Reggie Wayne/299	2.50	6.00
41 Plaxico Burress/299	2.50	6.00
42 Patrick Willis/91	4.00	10.00
43 Wes Welker/19	8.00	20.00

2012 Elite Down and Distance Jerseys Prime

STATED PRINT RUN 2-49		
2 Aaron Ross/49	4.00	10.00
3 Anquan Boldin/25	6.00	15.00
4 Anthony Fasano/49	4.00	10.00
5 Antonio Gates/49	5.00	12.00
9 Brent Celek/38	5.00	12.00
10 Brian Hartline/49	4.00	10.00
13 Cedric Benson/49	5.00	12.00
14 Devin Hester/49	6.00	15.00
15 Dez Bryant/49	6.00	15.00
16 Ed Reed/49	5.00	12.00
17 Haloti Ngata/49	4.00	10.00
19 Jon Beason/49	4.00	10.00
20 Josh Cribbs/16	5.00	12.00
22 Mario Manningham/49	5.00	12.00
24 Marques Colston/49	5.00	12.00
25 Miles Austin/49	5.00	12.00
27 Pierre Thomas/49	5.00	12.00
30 Chad Greenway/40	5.00	12.00
31 Devery Henderson/49	4.00	10.00
33 Vincent Jackson/49	5.00	12.00
35 Eli Manning/35	8.00	20.00
36 Tony Romo/49	6.00	15.00
38 Hakeem Nicks/49	5.00	12.00
43 Wes Welker/49	6.00	15.00

2012 Elite Down and Distance Jerseys Autographs

STATED PRINT RUN 5-15		
7 Beanie Wells/15		
26 Philip Rivers/15		
27 Pierre Thomas/25	8.00	20.00
38 Hakeem Nicks/25 EXCH	10.00	25.00
40 Reggie Wayne/15 EXCH		

2012 Elite Down and Distance Jerseys Autographs Prime

PRIME STATED PRINT RUN 5-15		
6 Asante Samuel/15	12.00	30.00

2012 Elite Hit List

STATED PRINT RUN 999 SER.#'d SETS		
*BLACK/49: 1X TO 2.5X BASIC INSERTS		
*GOLD/149: .6X TO 1.5X BASIC INSERTS		
1 London Fletcher	.75	2.00
2 D'Qwell Jackson	.75	2.00
3 Chad Greenway	1.00	2.50
4 James Laurinaitis	.75	2.00
5 Clay Matthews	1.25	3.00
6 Sean Lee	.75	2.00
7 Curtis Lofton	.75	2.00
8 Jason Babin	.75	2.00
9 Jared Allen	1.00	2.50
10 Pat Angerer	.75	2.00
11 James Anderson	.75	2.00
12 Chris Long	.75	2.00
13 NaVorro Bowman	.75	2.00
14 Aldon Smith	1.00	2.50
15 Charles Woodson	1.25	3.00
16 Daryl Washington	.75	2.00
17 Derrick Johnson	.75	2.00
18 Desmond Bishop	.75	2.00
19 Karlos Dansby	.75	2.00
20 Lance Briggs	.75	2.00

2012 Elite New Breed Jerseys

STATED PRINT RUN 199-399		
*PRIME/50: .6X TO 1.5X BASIC JSY		
*PRIME/25: .8X TO 2X BASIC JSY		
1 Andrew Luck/199	20.00	50.00
2 Robert Griffin III/199	15.00	40.00
3 Trent Richardson/199	8.00	20.00
4 Justin Blackmon/199	5.00	12.00
5 Ryan Tannehill/199	5.00	12.00
6 Michael Floyd/299	5.00	12.00
7 Kendall Wright/299	4.00	10.00
8 Brandon Weeden/299	5.00	12.00
9 A.J. Jenkins/342	4.00	10.00
10 Doug Martin/399	5.00	12.00
11 David Wilson/399	5.00	12.00
12 Brian Quick/399	4.00	10.00
13 Coby Fleener/399	4.00	10.00
14 Stephen Hill/399	3.00	8.00
15 Alshon Jeffery/399	5.00	12.00
16 Isaiah Pead/399	3.00	8.00
17 Ryan Broyles/399	3.00	8.00
18 Brock Osweiler/399	4.00	10.00
19 LaMichael James/399	6.00	15.00
20 Rueben Randle/399	3.00	8.00
21 Dwayne Allen/399	3.00	8.00
22 Ronnie Hillman/399	4.00	10.00
23 DeVier Posey/399	3.00	8.00
24 T.J. Graham/399	3.00	8.00
25 Russell Wilson/399	5.00	12.00
26 Michael Egnew/399	2.50	6.00
27 Mohamed Sanu/399	3.00	8.00
28 Bernard Pierce/399	3.00	8.00
29 Nick Foles/399	5.00	12.00
30 Jarius Wright/399	3.00	8.00
31 Lamar Miller/399	4.00	10.00
32 Joe Adams/399	3.00	8.00
33 Robert Turbin/399	3.00	8.00
34 Chris Givens/399	2.50	6.00
35 Nick Toon/399	4.00	10.00

2012 Elite New Breed Jerseys Autographs

1-11 STATED PRINT RUN 25		
12-35 STATED PRINT RUN 50		
*PRIME/25: .5X TO 1.2X JSY AU/25		
*PRIME/25: .6X TO 1.5X JSY AU/50		
1 Andrew Luck/25	300.00	450.00
2 Robert Griffin III/25	200.00	350.00
3 Trent Richardson/25	75.00	150.00
4 Justin Blackmon/25	25.00	60.00
5 Ryan Tannehill/25	30.00	60.00
6 Michael Floyd/25	25.00	60.00
7 Kendall Wright/25	15.00	40.00
8 Brandon Weeden/25	30.00	60.00
9 A.J. Jenkins/25	15.00	40.00
10 Doug Martin/25	20.00	50.00
11 David Wilson/25 EXCH	25.00	60.00
12 Brian Quick/50	12.00	30.00
13 Coby Fleener/50	12.00	30.00
14 Stephen Hill/50 EXCH	10.00	25.00
15 Alshon Jeffery/50 EXCH	15.00	40.00
16 Isaiah Pead/50	10.00	25.00
17 Ryan Broyles/50	10.00	25.00
18 Brock Osweiler/50	12.00	30.00
19 LaMichael James/50	20.00	50.00
20 Rueben Randle/50	10.00	25.00
21 Dwayne Allen/50	10.00	25.00
22 Ronnie Hillman/50 EXCH	12.00	30.00
23 DeVier Posey/50	10.00	25.00
24 T.J. Graham/50 EXCH	10.00	25.00
25 Russell Wilson/50	15.00	40.00
26 Michael Egnew/50	8.00	20.00
27 Mohamed Sanu/50	10.00	25.00
28 Bernard Pierce/50 EXCH	10.00	25.00
29 Nick Foles/50	15.00	40.00
30 Jarius Wright/50	10.00	25.00
31 Lamar Miller/50	12.00	30.00
32 Joe Adams/50	10.00	25.00
33 Robert Turbin/50 EXCH	10.00	25.00
34 Chris Givens/50	8.00	20.00
35 Nick Toon/50	12.00	30.00

2012 Elite Passing the Torch Autograph

STATED PRINT RUN 5-25		
EXCH EXPIRATION: 1/25/2014		
1 Dan Marino/20 EXCH Drew Brees	250.00	350.00
2 Kellen Winslow Sr./20 Rob Gronkowski	60.00	120.00
4 Doug Williams/25 EXCH Robert Griffin III/25	150.00	250.00
8 Boomer Esiason/20 Andy Dalton	60.00	120.00
9 Fred Taylor/20 Maurice Jones-Drew	40.00	80.00
10 James Lofton/20 Donald Driver	40.00	80.00
11 Peyton Manning/20 Andrew Luck		
12 Emmitt Smith/20 EXCH DeMarco Murray	100.00	200.00
13 Bill Romanowski/20 EXCH Von Miller	50.00	100.00
15 Chad Ochocinco/20 A.J. Green	50.00	100.00
16 Jim Plunkett/20 EXCH Carson Palmer		
19 Fran Tarkenton/20 Christian Ponder		
20 John Elway/20 Peyton Manning	350.00	500.00

2012 Elite Prime Numbers

STATED PRINT RUN 999 SER.#'d SETS		
*BLACK/49: 1X TO 2.5X BASIC INSERTS		
*GOLD/149: .6X TO 1.5X BASIC INSERTS		
1 Aaron Rodgers	2.00	5.00
2 Mike Wallace	1.00	2.50
3 Steve Smith WR	1.00	2.50
4 LeSean McCoy	1.00	2.50
5 Adrian Peterson	1.25	3.00
6 BenJarvus Green-Ellis	1.00	2.50
7 Calvin Johnson	1.25	3.00
8 Jermichael Finley	1.00	2.50
9 Matthew Stafford	1.25	3.00
10 Jordy Nelson	1.00	2.50
11 Jimmy Graham	1.00	2.50
12 Roddy White	1.00	2.50
13 Eli Manning	1.25	3.00
14 Steven Jackson	1.00	2.50
15 Andy Dalton	1.25	3.00
16 Marshawn Lynch	1.00	2.50
17 Victor Cruz	1.25	3.00
18 Brandon Marshall	.75	2.00
19 Maurice Jones-Drew	1.00	2.50
20 Ahmad Bradshaw	1.00	2.50

2012 Elite Prime Numbers Jerseys Prime

STATED PRINT RUN 1-49		
4 LeSean McCoy/48	5.00	12.00
9 Matthew Stafford/24	8.00	20.00
12 Roddy White/47	5.00	12.00
13 Eli Manning/43	6.00	15.00
15 Andy Dalton/49	6.00	15.00
18 Brandon Marshall/17	5.00	12.00
19 Maurice Jones-Drew/49	5.00	12.00

2012 Elite Rookie Hard Hats

STATED PRINT RUN 399 SER.#'d SETS		
1 Andrew Luck	20.00	50.00
2 Robert Griffin III	15.00	40.00
3 Trent Richardson	8.00	20.00
4 Justin Blackmon	5.00	12.00
5 Ryan Tannehill	5.00	12.00
6 Michael Floyd	5.00	12.00
7 Kendall Wright	4.00	10.00
8 Brandon Weeden	5.00	12.00
9 A.J. Jenkins	4.00	10.00
10 Doug Martin	5.00	12.00
11 David Wilson	5.00	12.00
12 Alshon Jeffery	5.00	12.00
13 Bernard Pierce	3.00	8.00
14 Brian Quick	4.00	10.00
15 Brock Osweiler	4.00	10.00
16 Coby Fleener	4.00	10.00
17 DeVier Posey	3.00	8.00
18 Dwayne Allen	3.00	8.00
19 Isaiah Pead	3.00	8.00
20 Jarius Wright	3.00	8.00
21 Joe Adams	3.00	8.00
22 Lamar Miller	4.00	10.00
23 LaMichael James	5.00	12.00
24 Michael Egnew	2.50	6.00
25 Mohamed Sanu	3.00	8.00
26 Nick Foles	5.00	12.00
27 Nick Toon	4.00	10.00
28 Robert Turbin	3.00	8.00
29 Ronnie Hillman	4.00	10.00
30 Rueben Randle	3.00	8.00
31 Russell Wilson	5.00	12.00
32 Ryan Broyles	3.00	8.00
33 Stephen Hill	3.00	8.00
34 T.J. Graham	3.00	8.00
35 T.Y. Hilton	3.00	8.00
36 B.J. Coleman	4.00	10.00
37 Chandler Harnish	3.00	8.00
38 Chris Givens	2.50	6.00
39 Chris Rainey	3.00	8.00
40 Cyrus Gray	3.00	8.00
41 Dan Herron	3.00	8.00
42 Danny Coale	5.00	12.00
43 Devon Wylie	3.00	8.00
44 Juron Criner	2.50	6.00
45 Keshawn Martin	3.00	8.00
46 Kirk Cousins	5.00	12.00
47 Ladarius Green	3.00	8.00
48 Marvin Jones	2.50	6.00
49 Marvin McNutt	3.00	8.00
50 Orson Charles	3.00	8.00
51 Rishard Matthews	3.00	8.00
52 Ryan Lindley	3.00	8.00
53 Terrance Ganaway	2.50	6.00
54 Tommy Streeter	3.00	8.00
55 Travis Benjamin	3.00	8.00
56 Vick Ballard	2.50	6.00
57 Alfred Morris	2.50	6.00
58 Mark Barron	5.00	12.00
59 Dre Kirkpatrick	5.00	12.00
60 Morris Claiborne	5.00	12.00
61 Luke Kuechly	4.00	10.00
62 Melvin Ingram	4.00	10.00
63 Case Keenum	4.00	10.00
64 Jeff Fuller	4.00	10.00
65 Kellen Moore	5.00	12.00

2012 Elite Rookie Hard Hats Autographs

STATED PRINT RUN 49-199		
1 Andrew Luck/49	175.00	300.00
2 Robert Griffin III/49	175.00	300.00
3 Trent Richardson/49	60.00	120.00
4 Justin Blackmon/49	25.00	60.00
5 Ryan Tannehill/49	40.00	80.00
6 Michael Floyd/49	20.00	50.00
7 Kendall Wright/49	12.00	30.00
8 Brandon Weeden/49	30.00	60.00
9 A.J. Jenkins/49	12.00	30.00
10 Doug Martin/49	25.00	50.00
11 David Wilson/49	20.00	50.00
12 Alshon Jeffery/99 EXCH	12.00	30.00
13 Bernard Pierce/99 EXCH	8.00	20.00
14 Brian Quick/99	10.00	25.00
15 Brock Osweiler/99	12.00	30.00
16 Coby Fleener/99	10.00	25.00
17 DeVier Posey/99	8.00	20.00
18 Dwayne Allen/99	8.00	20.00
19 Isaiah Pead/99	8.00	20.00
20 Jarius Wright/99	8.00	20.00
21 Joe Adams/99	10.00	25.00
22 Lamar Miller/99	12.00	30.00
23 LaMichael James/99	15.00	40.00
24 Michael Egnew/99	6.00	15.00
25 Mohamed Sanu/99	8.00	20.00
26 Nick Foles/99	12.00	30.00
27 Nick Toon/99	8.00	20.00
28 Robert Turbin/99 EXCH	8.00	20.00
29 Ronnie Hillman/99 EXCH	8.00	20.00
30 Rueben Randle/99	10.00	25.00
31 Russell Wilson/99	12.00	30.00
32 Ryan Broyles/99	12.00	30.00
33 Stephen Hill/99 EXCH	8.00	20.00
34 T.J. Graham/99 EXCH	8.00	20.00
35 T.Y. Hilton/99	8.00	20.00
36 B.J. Coleman/199 EXCH	8.00	20.00
37 Chandler Harnish/199	6.00	15.00
38 Chris Givens/199	5.00	12.00
39 Chris Rainey/199 EXCH	8.00	20.00
40 Cyrus Gray/199	6.00	15.00
41 Dan Herron/199	6.00	15.00
42 Danny Coale/199	12.00	30.00
43 Devon Wylie/199	6.00	15.00
44 Juron Criner/199	8.00	20.00
45 Keshawn Martin/199	8.00	20.00
46 Kirk Cousins/199	10.00	25.00
47 Ladarius Green/199	6.00	15.00
48 Marvin Jones/199	5.00	12.00
49 Marvin McNutt/199	8.00	20.00
50 Orson Charles/199	6.00	15.00
51 Rishard Matthews/199	5.00	12.00
52 Ryan Lindley/199	6.00	15.00
53 Terrance Ganaway/199	6.00	15.00
54 Tommy Streeter/199 EXCH	5.00	12.00
55 Travis Benjamin/199	6.00	15.00
56 Vick Ballard/199	5.00	12.00
57 Alfred Morris/199	5.00	12.00
58 Mark Barron/199	10.00	25.00
59 Dre Kirkpatrick/199 EXCH	10.00	25.00
60 Morris Claiborne/49*	40.00	80.00
61 Luke Kuechly/199	8.00	20.00
62 Melvin Ingram/199	8.00	20.00
63 Case Keenum/199	8.00	20.00
64 Jeff Fuller/199	8.00	20.00
65 Kellen Moore/199	10.00	25.00

2012 Elite Rookie Inscriptions Black Ink

ANNOUNCED PRINT RUN 8-75		
3 Trent Richardson/25*	60.00	120.00
5 Ryan Tannehill/40*	30.00	60.00
6 Michael Floyd/40*	15.00	40.00
7 Kendall Wright/45*	15.00	40.00
9 A.J. Jenkins/75*	12.00	30.00
10 Doug Martin/45*	25.00	50.00
11 David Wilson/45*	25.00	60.00
12 Alshon Jeffery/50*	20.00	50.00
13 Bernard Pierce/45*	12.00	30.00
14 Brian Quick/25*	20.00	50.00
15 Brock Osweiler/35*	15.00	40.00
16 Coby Fleener/35*	15.00	40.00
17 DeVier Posey/45*	12.00	30.00
18 Dwayne Allen/45*	12.00	30.00
19 Isaiah Pead/75*	10.00	25.00
20 Chris Givens/30*	10.00	25.00
21 Joe Adams/50*	12.00	30.00
22 Lamar Miller/40*	15.00	40.00
23 LaMichael James/40*	15.00	40.00
25 Mohamed Sanu/55*	12.00	30.00
26 Nick Foles/50*	20.00	50.00
27 Nick Toon/21*	20.00	50.00
28 Robert Turbin/62*	10.00	25.00
29 Ronnie Hillman/35*	15.00	40.00

30 Rueben Randle/50*	12.00	30.00
31 Russell Wilson/35*	20.00	50.00
33 Stephen Hill/45*	12.00	30.00
34 T.J. Graham/40*	12.00	30.00

2012 Elite Rookie Inscriptions Blue Ink

ANNOUNCED PRINT RUN 15-196

1 Andrew Luck/40*	175.00	300.00
2 Robert Griffin III/40*	175.00	300.00
3 Trent Richardson/30*	60.00	120.00
4 Justin Blackmon/35*	60.00	120.00
5 Ryan Tannehill/15*	50.00	100.00
6 Michael Floyd/15*	30.00	80.00
7 Kendall Wright/15*	20.00	50.00
8 Brandon Weeden/55*	40.00	80.00
9 A.J. Jenkins/20*	20.00	50.00
10 Doug Martin/40*	25.00	50.00
11 David Wilson/40*	25.00	60.00
12 Alshon Jeffery/75*	15.00	40.00
13 Bernard Pierce/70*	10.00	25.00
14 Brian Quick/50*	15.00	40.00
15 Brock Osweiler/75*	12.00	30.00
16 Coby Fleener/15*	20.00	50.00
17 DeVier Posey/25*	15.00	40.00
18 Dwayne Allen/20*	15.00	40.00
19 Isaiah Pead/30*	12.00	30.00
20 Chris Givens/54*	10.00	25.00
21 Joe Adams/64*	10.00	25.00
22 Lamar Miller/25*	20.00	50.00
23 LaMichael James/75*	12.00	30.00
24 Michael Egnew/196*	6.00	15.00
25 Mohamed Sanu/64*	10.00	25.00
26 Nick Foles/38*	20.00	50.00
27 Nick Toon/79*	12.00	30.00
28 Robert Turbin/58*	12.00	30.00
29 Ronnie Hillman/75*	12.00	30.00
30 Rueben Randle/40*	12.00	30.00
31 Russell Wilson/50*	20.00	50.00
32 Ryan Broyles/150*	8.00	20.00
33 Stephen Hill/75*	10.00	25.00
34 T.J. Graham/40*	12.00	30.00

2012 Elite Rookie Inscriptions Green Ink

ANNOUNCED PRINT RUN 2-75

3 Trent Richardson/20*	75.00	150.00
5 Ryan Tannehill/30*	40.00	80.00
6 Michael Floyd/30*	20.00	50.00
7 Kendall Wright/15*	20.00	50.00
9 A.J. Jenkins/40*	15.00	40.00
10 Doug Martin/40*	25.00	50.00
11 David Wilson/55*	25.00	60.00
12 Alshon Jeffery/15*	25.00	60.00
13 Bernard Pierce	12.00	30.00
14 Brian Quick/30*	15.00	40.00
16 Coby Fleener/45*	15.00	40.00
17 DeVier Posey/55*	12.00	30.00
18 Dwayne Allen/75*	10.00	25.00
19 Isaiah Pead/50*	12.00	30.00
20 Chris Givens/25*	12.00	30.00
21 Joe Adams/56*	12.00	30.00
22 Lamar Miller/50*	15.00	40.00
23 LaMichael James/25*	30.00	80.00
25 Mohamed Sanu/45*	12.00	30.00
27 Nick Toon/32*	15.00	40.00
28 Robert Turbin/29*	15.00	40.00
30 Rueben Randle/25*	15.00	40.00
31 Russell Wilson/15*	25.00	60.00
34 T.J. Graham/35*	12.00	30.00

2012 Elite Rookie Inscriptions Red Ink

ANNOUNCED PRINT RUN 10-75

1 Andrew Luck/30*	175.00	300.00
2 Robert Griffin III/30*	175.00	300.00
3 Trent Richardson/15*	75.00	150.00
4 Justin Blackmon/30*	60.00	120.00
5 Ryan Tannehill/15*	50.00	100.00
7 Kendall Wright/30*	15.00	40.00
8 Brandon Weeden/30*	60.00	120.00
9 A.J. Jenkins/15*	20.00	50.00
10 Doug Martin/20*	25.00	60.00
11 David Wilson/40*	25.00	60.00
12 Alshon Jeffery/25*	25.00	60.00
14 Brian Quick/40*	15.00	40.00
15 Brock Osweiler/15*	20.00	50.00
16 Coby Fleener/50*	15.00	40.00
17 DeVier Posey/35*	12.00	30.00
18 Dwayne Allen/35*	12.00	30.00
19 Isaiah Pead/20*	15.00	40.00
20 Chris Givens/45*	10.00	25.00
21 Joe Adams/23*	15.00	40.00
22 Lamar Miller/30*	15.00	40.00
23 LaMichael James/15*	30.00	80.00
25 Mohamed Sanu/15*	15.00	40.00
26 Nick Foles/75*	15.00	40.00
27 Nick Toon/60*	12.00	30.00
28 Robert Turbin/37*	12.00	30.00
29 Ronnie Hillman/20*	20.00	50.00
30 Rueben Randle/30*	12.00	30.00
31 Russell Wilson/40*	20.00	50.00
33 Stephen Hill/20*	15.00	40.00
34 T.J. Graham/15*	15.00	40.00

2012 Elite Series

STATED PRINT RUN 999 SER.#'d SETS
*BLACK/49: 1X TO 2.5X BASIC INSERTS
*GOLD/149: .6X TO 1.5X BASIC INSERTS

1 Calvin Johnson	1.25	3.00
2 Greg Jennings	1.00	2.50
3 Rob Gronkowski	1.00	2.50
4 Chris Johnson	1.00	2.50
5 Arian Foster	1.00	2.50
6 DeAngelo Williams	1.00	2.50
7 Drew Brees	1.25	3.00
8 Aaron Rodgers	2.00	5.00
9 Ray Rice	1.00	2.50
10 Antonio Gates	1.00	2.50
11 Matt Ryan	1.00	2.50
12 Wes Welker	1.25	3.00
13 Larry Fitzgerald	1.00	2.50
14 Eli Manning	1.25	3.00
15 DeSean Jackson	1.00	2.50
16 Tom Brady	2.00	5.00
17 Dwayne Bowe	1.00	2.50
18 Michael Vick	1.25	3.00
19 Cam Newton	2.00	5.00
20 Maurice Jones-Drew	1.00	2.50

2012 Elite Series Jerseys Prime

STATED PRINT RUN 1-49

4 Chris Johnson/49	5.00	12.00
12 Wes Welker/49	6.00	15.00
20 Maurice Jones-Drew/49	5.00	12.00

2012 Elite Series Rookies

STATED PRINT RUN 999 SER.#'d SETS
*BLACK/49: 1X TO 2.5X BASIC INSERTS
*GOLD/149: .6X TO 1.5X BASIC INSERTS

1 Andrew Luck	8.00	20.00
2 Robert Griffin III	6.00	15.00
3 Trent Richardson	4.00	10.00
4 Justin Blackmon	2.50	6.00
5 Ryan Tannehill	3.00	8.00
6 Michael Floyd	2.50	6.00
7 Kendall Wright	1.50	4.00
8 Brandon Weeden	2.50	6.00
9 A.J. Jenkins	1.50	4.00
10 Doug Martin	2.00	5.00
11 David Wilson	2.50	6.00
12 Brian Quick	1.50	4.00
13 Coby Fleener	1.50	4.00
14 Stephen Hill	1.25	3.00
15 Alshon Jeffery	2.00	5.00
16 Isaiah Pead	1.25	3.00
17 Ryan Broyles	1.25	3.00
18 Brock Osweiler	1.50	4.00
19 LaMichael James	2.50	6.00
20 Rueben Randle	1.25	3.00
21 Dwayne Allen	1.25	3.00
22 Ronnie Hillman	1.50	4.00
23 DeVier Posey	1.25	3.00
24 T.J. Graham	1.25	3.00
25 Russell Wilson	2.00	5.00

2012 Elite Series Rookies Autographs

STATED PRINT RUN 99 SER.#'d SETS

1 Andrew Luck	150.00	250.00
2 Robert Griffin III	150.00	250.00
3 Trent Richardson	40.00	80.00
4 Justin Blackmon	20.00	50.00
5 Ryan Tannehill	25.00	50.00
6 Michael Floyd	12.00	30.00
7 Kendall Wright	8.00	20.00
8 Brandon Weeden	25.00	50.00
9 A.J. Jenkins	8.00	20.00
10 Doug Martin	12.00	30.00
11 David Wilson	15.00	40.00
12 Brian Quick	8.00	20.00
13 Coby Fleener	8.00	20.00
14 Stephen Hill EXCH	6.00	15.00
15 Alshon Jeffery EXCH	10.00	25.00
16 Isaiah Pead	6.00	15.00
17 Ryan Broyles	6.00	15.00
18 Brock Osweiler	10.00	25.00
19 LaMichael James	12.00	30.00
20 Rueben Randle	6.00	15.00
21 Dwayne Allen	6.00	15.00
22 Ronnie Hillman EXCH	8.00	20.00
23 DeVier Posey	6.00	15.00
24 T.J. Graham EXCH	6.00	15.00
25 Russell Wilson	12.00	30.00

2012 Elite Status Autographs

*1-100 VETS/15: .4X TO 1X ASPIRATION AU
1-100 VETERAN PRINT RUN 1-15
*ROOKIES/24: .6X TO 1.5X ASPRTION/49
101-200 ROOKIE PRINT RUN 24

101 Andrew Luck/24	350.00	500.00
102 Robert Griffin III/24		
106 Trent Richardson/24	100.00	175.00
141 Brandon Weeden/24	75.00	150.00

2012 Elite Throwback Threads

STATED PRINT RUN 15-199

1 Marshall Faulk/199	5.00	12.00
2 Steven Jackson/110	4.00	10.00
3 Ozzie Newsome/199	4.00	10.00
4 Tony Gonzalez/199	4.00	10.00
5 Sterling Sharpe/199	4.00	10.00
6 Jay Novacek/199	4.00	10.00
7 Rocket Ismail/199	4.00	10.00
8 Jerry Rice/199	6.00	15.00
9 Darrell Green/126	5.00	12.00
12 Julius Peppers/199	4.00	10.00
13 Doug Flutie/199	4.00	10.00
14 Eddie George/199	4.00	10.00
15 Chris Johnson/199	4.00	10.00
16 Eddie George/199	4.00	10.00
Chris Johnson		
17 Doug Flutie/15	6.00	15.00
Ryan Fitzpatrick		
18 Jay Novacek/111	5.00	12.00
Jason Witten		
19 Marshall Faulk/108	5.00	12.00
Steven Jackson		
20 Ozzie Newsome/199	4.00	10.00
Tony Gonzalez		

2012 Elite Throwback Threads Prime

*PRIME/30-49: X TO X BASIC JSY
*PRIME/25: X TO X BASIC JSY
PRIME STATED PRINT RUN 11-49

10 DeAngelo Hall/31	5.00	12.00

2012 Elite Throwback Threads Autographs

STATED PRINT RUN 15 SER.#'d SETS

5 Sterling Sharpe	30.00	60.00
8 Jerry Rice	60.00	120.00
11 Richard Dent	25.00	50.00
13 Doug Flutie	12.00	30.00

2012 Elite Turn of the Century Autographs

STATED PRINT RUN 99-699
EXCH EXPIRATION: 1/25/2014

101 Andrew Luck/99	150.00	250.00
102 Robert Griffin III/99	150.00	250.00
103 Matt Kalil/399	6.00	15.00
104 Morris Claiborne/199	30.00	60.00
105 Justin Blackmon/99	15.00	40.00
106 Trent Richardson/99	50.00	100.00
107 Riley Reiff/399	5.00	12.00
108 Quinton Coples/399	5.00	12.00
109 Melvin Ingram/242	6.00	15.00
110 Michael Brockers/399	5.00	12.00
111 Ryan Tannehill/99	30.00	60.00
112 David DeCastro/399	6.00	15.00
113 Michael Floyd/99	15.00	40.00
114 Luke Kuechly/299	6.00	15.00
115 Janoris Jenkins/399 EXCH	5.00	12.00
116 Jonathan Martin/399	4.00	10.00
117 Devon Still/399	5.00	12.00
118 Dre Kirkpatrick/299 EXCH	8.00	20.00
119 Kendall Wright/99	10.00	25.00
120 Fletcher Cox/399	5.00	12.00
121 Courtney Upshaw/299	6.00	15.00
122 Dontari Poe/599	5.00	12.00
123 Rueben Randle/99	8.00	20.00
124 Nick Perry/399	8.00	20.00
125 Whitney Mercilus/599	5.00	12.00
126 Dont'a Hightower/299	8.00	20.00
127 Mark Barron/299	8.00	20.00
128 Stephen Hill/99 EXCH	8.00	20.00
129 Zach Brown/299	4.00	10.00
130 Andre Branch/599	4.00	10.00
131 Dwayne Allen/99	8.00	20.00
132 David Wilson/99 EXCH	15.00	40.00
133 Lamar Miller/99	10.00	25.00
134 Brock Osweiler/99	12.00	30.00
135 Lavonte David/299 EXCH	6.00	15.00
136 Alshon Jeffery/99 EXCH	12.00	30.00
137 Bobby Wagner/299	5.00	12.00
138 Doug Martin/99	15.00	40.00
139 Chris Givens/199	5.00	12.00
140 Coby Fleener/99	10.00	25.00
141 Brandon Weeden/99	30.00	60.00
142 Jared Crick/599	5.00	12.00
143 Shea McClellin/299	6.00	15.00
144 Ronnell Lewis/599	5.00	12.00
145 Orson Charles/399	5.00	12.00
146 Vinny Curry/399	6.00	15.00
147 Chandler Jones/399	5.00	12.00
148 Isaiah Pead/99	8.00	20.00
149 George Iloka/699	4.00	10.00
150 Mohamed Sanu/99	8.00	20.00
151 Nick Toon/99	10.00	25.00
152 LaMichael James/99	20.00	40.00
153 Kirk Cousins/199	10.00	25.00
154 T.J. Graham/99 EXCH	8.00	20.00
155 Mychal Kendricks/599	5.00	12.00
156 Juron Criner/399	4.00	10.00
157 Stephon Gilmore/599	5.00	12.00
158 Bernard Pierce/99 EXCH	8.00	20.00
159 Ladarius Green/399	5.00	12.00
160 Cyrus Gray/199	6.00	15.00
161 Brian Quick/99	10.00	25.00
162 Nick Foles/99	12.00	30.00
163 Ronnie Hillman/99 EXCH	10.00	25.00
164 Michael Egnew/99	6.00	15.00
165 Keshawn Martin/399	5.00	12.00
166 Chris Rainey/199 EXCH	6.00	15.00
167 Joe Adams/99	8.00	20.00
168 Marvin Jones/599	4.00	10.00
169 Ryan Lindley/199	6.00	15.00
170 Greg Childs/399	5.00	12.00
171 Jarius Wright/99	8.00	20.00
172 Michael Smith/399 EXCH	4.00	10.00
173 Tommy Streeter/399 EXCH	5.00	12.00
174 Robert Turbin/99 EXCH	8.00	20.00
175 A.J. Jenkins/99	10.00	25.00
176 DeVier Posey/99	8.00	20.00
177 Bryce Brown/399 EXCH	5.00	12.00
178 Dan Herron/399	5.00	12.00
179 Vick Ballard/399	4.00	10.00
180 T.Y. Hilton/99	8.00	20.00
181 Bruce Irvin/399 EXCH	5.00	12.00
182 Marvin McNutt/399	5.00	12.00
183 Terrance Ganaway/599	4.00	10.00
184 B.J. Coleman/599 EXCH	5.00	12.00
185 Alfred Morris/399	4.00	10.00
186 Jeff Fuller/699	6.00	15.00
187 Rishard Matthews/599	5.00	12.00
188 B.J. Cunningham/599	4.00	10.00
189 Ryan Broyles/99	8.00	20.00
190 Russell Wilson/99	12.00	30.00
191 Devon Wylie/399	5.00	12.00
192 LaVon Brazill/399	4.00	10.00
193 Travis Benjamin/399	5.00	12.00
194 Kevin Zeitler/399	4.00	10.00
195 Chandler Harnish/399	5.00	12.00
196 Marc Tyler/699	5.00	12.00
197 Harrison Smith/399	5.00	12.00
198 Danny Coale/599	8.00	20.00
199 Kellen Moore/699	8.00	20.00
200 Case Keenum/699	6.00	15.00

1991 ENOR Pro Football HOF Promos

This six-card standard-size promo set was issued to preview the 160-card 1991 ENOR Pro Football Hall of Fame set. Apart from a slightly different shade of colors and card numbering differences, these promo cards differ from their counterparts in that the Team NFL logo on their card backs is black and white, while on the regular series cards, it is red, white, and blue.

COMPLETE SET (6)	2.80	7.00
1 Pro Football Hall of Fame (Building) (Regular issue card number is also 1)	.40	1.00
2 Earl Campbell	1.20	3.00
3 John Hannah	.40	1.00
4 Stan Jones	.40	1.00
5 Jan Stenerud	.40	1.00
6 Tex Schramm ADM	.40	1.00

1991 ENOR Pro Football HOF

The 1991 Pro Football Hall of Fame set contains 160 standard-size cards. The set, which includes this year's inductees, was issued in factory sets and wax packs. The fronts feature a mix of color or black and white player photos, with black and gold borders (the photos were obtained from the NFL's extensive archives). The player's position and name are given in a black stripe below the picture. A purple box with the words "Pro Football Hall of Fame" in white appears at the lower right corner of the card face. The backs have biography, career summary, and the year the individual was inducted. The backs are predominantly orange in color and have a picture of the Hall of Fame building at the bottom. The numbering is essentially in alphabetical order by subject. Randomly inserted throughout the packs were coupon cards that entitled the collector to receive a free Hall of Fame Album and free admission to the Pro Football Hall of Fame (offer expired December 31, 1993). The front design of the Free Admission card shows four different scenes of the Hall of Fame.

COMPLETE SET (160)	7.50	20.00
1 Pro Football Hall of Fame (Canton& OH)	.08	.25
1A Free Admission Pro Football Hall of Fame (Canton& OH)	.08	.25
2 Herb Adderley	.08	.25
3 Lance Alworth	.15	.40
4 Doug Atkins	.08	.25
5 Red Badgro	.07	.20
6 Cliff Battles	.07	.20
7 Sammy Baugh	.25	.60
8 Chuck Bednarik	.15	.40
9A Bert Bell FOUND OWN (Factory set version in coat and tie on phone)	.10	.30
9B Bert Bell FOUND OWN (Wax pack version in Steelers tee shirt)	.10	.30
10 Bobby Bell	.08	.25
11 Raymond Berry	.15	.40
12 Charles W. Bidwill OWN	.07	.20
13 Fred Biletnikoff	.15	.40
14 George Blanda	.15	.40
15 Mel Blount	.15	.40
16 Terry Bradshaw	.40	1.00
17 Jim Brown	.40	1.00
18 Paul Brown CO OWN/ FOUND	.10	.30
19 Roosevelt Brown	.08	.25
20 Willie Brown	.08	.25
21 Buck Buchanan	.08	.25
22 Dick Butkus	.30	.75
23 Earl Campbell	.30	.75
24 Tony Canadeo	.08	.25
25 Joe Carr PRES	.07	.20
26 Guy Chamberlin	.07	.20
27 Jack Christiansen	.07	.20
28 Dutch Clark	.08	.25
29 George Connor	.08	.25
30 Jimmy Conzelman	.07	.20
31 Larry Csonka	.15	.40
32 Willie Davis	.08	.25
33 Len Dawson	.15	.40
34 Mike Ditka	.30	.75
35 Art Donovan	.10	.30
36 Paddy Driscoll	.07	.20
37 Bill Dudley	.08	.25
38 Turk Edwards	.07	.20
39 Weeb Ewbank CO	.07	.20
40 Tom Fears	.08	.25
41 Ray Flaherty CO	.07	.20
42 Len Ford	.08	.25
43 Dan Fortmann	.07	.20
44 Frank Gatski	.07	.20
45 Bill George	.08	.25
46 Frank Gifford	.25	.60
47 Sid Gillman CO	.07	.20
48 Otto Graham	.30	.75
49 Red Grange	.30	.75
50 Joe Greene	.15	.40
51 Forrest Gregg	.08	.25
52 Bob Griese	.20	.50
53 Lou Groza	.10	.30
54 Joe Guyon	.07	.20
55 George Halas CO OWN FOUND	.30	.75
56 Jack Ham	.15	.40
57 John Hannah	.08	.25
58 Franco Harris	.25	.60
59 Ed Healey	.07	.20
60 Mel Hein	.07	.20
61 Ted Hendricks	.08	.25
62 Fats Henry	.07	.20
63 Arnie Herber	.08	.25
64 Bill Hewitt	.07	.20
65 Clarke Hinkle	.07	.20
66 Elroy Hirsch	.10	.30
67 Ken Houston	.08	.25
68 Cal Hubbard	.07	.20
69 Sam Huff	.10	.30
70 Lamar Hunt OWN FOUND	.08	.25
71 Don Hutson	.15	.40
72 John Henry Johnson	.08	.25
73 Deacon Jones	.10	.30
74 Stan Jones	.07	.20
75 Sonny Jurgensen	.10	.30
76 Walt Kiesling	.07	.20
77 Frank(Bruiser) Kinard	.07	.20
78 Earl(Curly) Lambeau CO FOUND OWN	.20	.50
79 Jack Lambert	.25	.60
80 Tom Landry CO	.30	.75
81 Dick Lane	.08	.25
82 Jim Langer	.08	.25
83 Willie Lanier	.08	.25
84 Yale Lary	.08	.25
85 Dante Lavelli	.08	.25
86 Bobby Layne	.25	.60
87 Tuffy Leemans	.07	.20
88 Bob Lilly	.15	.40
89 Sid Luckman	.15	.40
90 Link Lyman	.07	.20
91 Tim Mara FOUND OWN	.07	.20
92 Gino Marchetti	.08	.25
93 Geo.Preston Marshall FOUND OWN	.07	.20
94 Don Maynard	.10	.30
95 George McAfee	.07	.20
96 Mike McCormack	.08	.25
97 Johnny Blood McNally	.07	.20
98 Mike Michalske	.07	.20
99 Wayne Millner	.07	.20
100 Bobby Mitchell	.10	.30
101 Ron Mix	.08	.25
102 Lenny Moore	.10	.30
103 Marion Motley (See also 130)	.10	.30
104 George Musso	.08	.25
105 Bronko Nagurski	.30	.75
106 Greasy Neale CO	.07	.20
107 Ernie Nevers	.08	.25
108 Ray Nitschke	.20	.50
109 Leo Nomellini	.08	.25
110 Merlin Olsen	.10	.30
111 Jim Otto	.10	.30
112 Steve Owen CO	.07	.20
113 Alan Page	.08	.25
114 Clarence(Ace) Parker	.07	.20
115 Jim Parker	.08	.25
116 1958 NFL Championship	.07	.20
117 Pete Pihos	.08	.25
118 Hugh(Shorty) Ray OFF	.07	.20
119 Dan Reeves OWN	.07	.20
120 Jim Ringo	.08	.25
121 Andy Robustelli	.08	.25
122 Art Rooney FOUND ADMIN	.10	.30
123 Pete Rozelle COMM	.08	.25
124 Bob St.Clair	.08	.25
125 Gale Sayers	.30	.75
126 Joe Schmidt	.08	.25
127 Tex Schramm ADM	.07	.20
128 Art Shell	.10	.30
129 Roger Staubach	.40	1.00
130 Ernie Stautner UER (Numbered as 103)	.10	.30
131 Jan Stenerud	.08	.25
132 Ken Strong	.08	.25
133 Joe Stydahar	.07	.20
134 Fran Tarkenton	.25	.60
135 Charley Taylor	.08	.25
136 Jim Taylor	.10	.30
137 Jim Thorpe	.30	.75
138 Y.A. Tittle	.25	.60
139 George Trafton	.07	.20
140 Charley Trippi	.08	.25
141 Emlen Tunnell	.08	.25
142 Bulldog Turner	.10	.30
143 Johnny Unitas	.60	1.50
144 Gene Upshaw	.08	.25
145 Norm Van Brocklin	.10	.30
146 Steve Van Buren	.10	.30
147 Doak Walker	.20	.50
148 Paul Warfield	.10	.30
149 Bob Waterfield	.10	.30
150 Arnie Weinmeister	.07	.20
151 Bill Willis	.08	.25
152 Larry Wilson	.07	.20
153 Alex Wojciechowicz	.07	.20
154 Willie Wood	.08	.25
155 Enshrinement Day Hall of Fame Induction Ceremony	.07	.20
156 Mementoes Exhibit Enshrinee Mementoes Room	.07	.20
157 Checklist 1 The Beginning	.07	.20
158 Checklist 2 The Early Years	.07	.20
159 Checklist 3 The Modern Era	.07	.20
160A Checklist 4 Evolution of Uniform includes #133-160	.07	.20

1992 ENOR Pro Football HOF

1 Lem Barney	.75	2.00
2 Al Davis	.75	2.00
3 John Mackey black and white photo	.75	2.00
4 John Riggins	1.00	2.50

1994 ENOR Pro Football HOF

Packaged with 25 ProGard protective sheets, this six-card standard-size set was issued to commemorate five players and one coach who were inducted into the Football Hall of Fame in 1994. The cards have the same design as those in the 1991 ENOR set, except that they are unnumbered. The cards are listed below in alphabetical order.

COMPLETE SET (6)	20.00	40.00
1 Tony Dorsett	5.00	10.00
2 Bud Grant CO	3.00	6.00
3 Jim Johnson	3.00	6.00
4 Leroy Kelly	3.00	6.00
5 Jackie Smith	3.00	6.00
6 Randy White	4.00	8.00

1995 ENOR Pro Football HOF 5

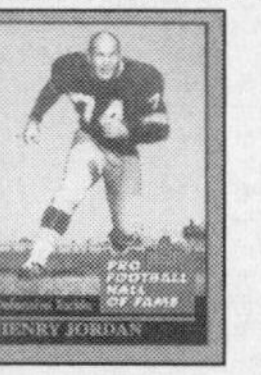

This 5-card standard-size set was issued to commemorate the new inductees into the Pro Football Hall of Fame in 1995. The cards have the same design as those in the 1991 and 1995 ENOR sets, except that they are unnumbered. The cards are listed below in alphabetical order.

COMPLETE SET (5)	20.00	40.00
1 Jim Finks	4.00	8.00
2 Hank Jordan	5.00	10.00
3 Steve Largent	6.00	12.00
4 Lee Roy Selmon	4.00	8.00
5 Kellen Winslow	4.00	8.00

1995 ENOR Pro Football HOF 180

ENOR re-issued its 1991 Pro Football Hall of Fame set in factory set form in 1995. The 1995 release contains the first 159-cards from the 1991 set in original form plus 21 new cards including a re-worked checklist 4. The new cards carry a 1995 copyright date, while the first 159-cards are dated 1991. We've included single card prices for just the 21 new cards. The original 159-cards are priced previously under 1991 ENOR.

160B Checklist 4 Evolution of Uniform includes 133-180	1.25	3.00
161 Lem Barney	1.25	3.00
162 Al Davis	2.00	5.00
163 John Mackey	1.25	3.00
164 John Riggins	2.00	5.00
165 Dan Fouts	2.00	5.00
166 Larry Little	1.25	3.00
167 Chuck Noll	1.50	4.00
168 Bill Walsh	2.00	5.00
169 Tony Dorsett	4.00	8.00
170 Bud Grant	1.50	4.00
171 Jim Johnson	1.25	3.00
172 Leroy Kelly	1.50	4.00
173 Jackie Smith	1.25	3.00
174 Randy White	2.00	5.00
175 O.J. Simpson	2.00	5.00
176 Jim Finks	1.25	3.00
177 Hank Jordan	1.50	4.00
178 Steve Largent	3.00	6.00
179 Lee Roy Selmon	1.25	3.00
180 Kellen Winslow	1.50	4.00

1996 ENOR Pro Football HOF

This five-card standard-size set was issued to commemorate the new inductees into the Pro Football Hall of Fame in 1996. The cards have the same design as those in the 1991 and 1995 ENOR sets, except that they are unnumbered. The cards are listed below in alphabetical order.

COMPLETE SET (5)	20.00	40.00
1 Lou Creekmur	4.00	8.00
2 Dan Dierdorf	4.00	8.00
3 Joe Gibbs	5.00	10.00
4 Charlie Joiner	4.00	8.00
5 Mel Renfro	4.00	8.00

2010 Epix

COMP.SET w/o RC's (100)	6.00	15.00
201-235 ROOKIE AU PRINT RUN 209-300		
1 Chris Wells	.15	.40
2 Larry Fitzgerald	.20	.50
3 Matt Leinart	.15	.40
4 Matt Ryan	.20	.50
5 Michael Turner	.12	.30
6 Roddy White	.15	.40
7 Anquan Boldin	.15	.40
8 Joe Flacco	.20	.50
9 Ray Rice	.15	.40
10 Lee Evans	.15	.40
11 Marshawn Lynch	.15	.40
12 Ryan Fitzpatrick	.20	.50
13 DeAngelo Williams	.15	.40
14 Matt Moore	.15	.40
15 Steve Smith	.15	.40
16 Devin Hester	.20	.50
17 Jay Cutler	.20	.50
18 Matt Forte	.15	.40
19 Carson Palmer	.15	.40
20 Cedric Benson	.15	.40
21 Chad Ochocinco	.15	.40
22 Jake Delhomme	.15	.40
23 Josh Cribbs	.20	.50
24 Mohamed Massaquoi	.15	.40
25 Felix Jones	.15	.40
26 Jason Witten	.20	.50
27 Miles Austin	.20	.50
28 Tony Romo	.25	.60
29 Eddie Royal	.12	.30
30 Knowshon Moreno	.15	.40
31 Kyle Orton	.15	.40
32 Calvin Johnson	.20	.50
33 Matthew Stafford	.20	.50
34 Nate Burleson	.12	.30
35 Aaron Rodgers	.40	1.00
36 Donald Driver	.15	.40
37 Ryan Grant	.15	.40
38 Andre Johnson	.15	.40
39 Matt Schaub	.15	.40
40 Steve Slaton	.12	.30
41 Dallas Clark	.15	.40
42 Joseph Addai	.15	.40
43 Peyton Manning	.30	.75
44 Reggie Wayne	.15	.40
45 David Garrard	.15	.40
46 Maurice Jones-Drew	.15	.40
47 Mike Sims-Walker	.15	.40
48 Dwayne Bowe	.15	.40
49 Jamaal Charles	.15	.40
50 Matt Cassel	.15	.40
51 Brandon Marshall	.15	.40
52 Chad Henne	.15	.40
53 Ronnie Brown	.15	.40
54 Adrian Peterson	.30	.75
55 Brett Favre	.75	2.00
56 Sidney Rice	.15	.40
57 Randy Moss	.20	.50
58 Tom Brady	.30	.75
59 Wes Welker	.20	.50
60 Drew Brees	.20	.50
61 Marques Colston	.15	.40
62 Pierre Thomas	.15	.40
63 Brandon Jacobs	.15	.40
64 Eli Manning	.20	.50
65 Steve Smith USC	.15	.40
66 Braylon Edwards	.15	.40
67 LaDainian Tomlinson	.20	.50
68 Mark Sanchez	.20	.50
69 Shonn Greene	.15	.40
70 Darren McFadden	.15	.40
71 Jason Campbell	.15	.40
72 Louis Murphy	.15	.40
73 DeSean Jackson	.15	.40
74 Kevin Kolb	.15	.40
75 LeSean McCoy	.15	.40
76 Ben Roethlisberger	.20	.50
77 Hines Ward	.15	.40
78 Rashard Mendenhall	.15	.40
79 Antonio Gates	.15	.40
80 Darren Sproles	.15	.40
81 Philip Rivers	.20	.50
82 Vincent Jackson	.12	.30
83 Frank Gore	.15	.40
84 Michael Crabtree	.20	.50
85 Vernon Davis	.15	.40
86 Julius Jones	.12	.30
87 Matt Hasselbeck	.12	.30
88 T.J. Houshmandzadeh	.15	.40
89 Donnie Avery	.15	.40
90 James Laurinaitis	.15	.40
91 Steven Jackson	.15	.40
92 Cadillac Williams	.15	.40
93 Josh Freeman	.20	.50
94 Kellen Winslow Jr.	.15	.40
95 Chris Johnson	.20	.50
96 Kenny Britt	.15	.40
97 Vince Young	.12	.30
98 Chris Cooley	.15	.40
99 Clinton Portis	.15	.40
100 Donovan McNabb	.20	.50
101 Aaron Hernandez RC	1.50	4.00
102 Amari Spievey RC	1.00	2.50
103 Andre Anderson RC	.75	2.00
104 Anthony Davis RC	.75	2.00
105 Anthony Dixon RC	1.00	2.50
106 Anthony McCoy RC	.75	2.00
107 Antonio Brown RC	1.50	4.00
108 Blair White RC	1.00	2.50
109 Brandon Graham RC	.75	2.00
110 Brandon Spikes RC	1.00	2.50
111 Brian Price RC	1.00	2.50
112 Bryan Bulaga RC	1.00	2.50
113 Carlos Dunlap RC	1.00	2.50
114 Carlton Mitchell RC	.75	2.00
115 Chad Jones RC	1.00	2.50
116 Charles Scott RC	.75	2.00
117 Chris Cook RC	1.00	2.50
118 Chris McGaha RC	.60	1.50
119 Corey Wootton RC	.75	2.00
120 Dan LeFevour RC	1.00	2.50
121 Dan Williams RC	.75	2.00
122 Daryl Washington RC	.75	2.00
123 David Gettis RC	1.00	2.50
124 David Reed RC	.75	2.00
125 Deji Karim RC	1.00	2.50
126 Dennis Pitta RC	1.00	2.50
127 Derrick Morgan RC	.75	2.00
128 Devin McCourty RC	1.00	2.50
129 Dezmon Briscoe RC	.75	2.00
130 Dominique Franks RC	.60	1.50
131 Donald Butler RC	.60	1.50
132 Earl Thomas RC	1.00	2.50
133 Ed Dickson RC	1.00	2.50
134 Everson Griffen RC	1.00	2.50
135 Freddie Barnes RC	.75	2.00
136 Garrett Graham RC	.75	2.00
137 Jacoby Ford RC	1.00	2.50
138 James Starks RC	1.50	4.00
139 Jared Odrick RC	1.00	2.50
140 Jarrett Brown RC	1.00	2.50
141 Jason Pierre-Paul RC	1.50	4.00
142 Jason Worilds RC	1.00	2.50
143 Javier Arenas RC	1.00	2.50
144 Jeremy Williams RC	.60	1.50
145 Jermaine Cunningham RC	1.00	2.50
146 Jerome Murphy RC	.75	2.00
147 Jerry Hughes RC	1.00	2.50
148 Jevan Snead RC	1.00	2.50
149 Jimmy Graham RC	2.00	5.00
150 Joe Haden RC	1.00	2.50
151 Joe Webb RC	1.00	2.50
152 John Conner RC	1.00	2.50
153 John Skelton RC	1.00	2.50
154 Joique Bell RC	.75	2.00
155 Jonathan Crompton RC	.75	2.00
156 Kareem Jackson RC	1.00	2.50
157 Kerry Meier RC	.75	2.00
158 Koa Misi RC	1.00	2.50
159 Kyle Williams RC	1.00	2.50
160 Kyle Wilson RC	1.00	2.50
161 Lamarr Houston RC	1.00	2.50
162 LeGarrette Blount RC	1.50	4.00
163 Levi Brown RC	.75	2.00
164 Linval Joseph RC	.75	2.00
165 Lonyae Miller RC	.75	2.00
166 Major Wright RC	1.00	2.50
167 Marc Mariani RC	1.00	2.50
168 Maurkice Pouncey RC	1.00	2.50
169 Mike Iupati RC	1.00	2.50
170 Mike Neal RC	1.00	2.50
171 Morgan Burnett RC	1.00	2.50
172 Myron Rolle RC	.60	1.50
173 Nate Allen RC	1.00	2.50
174 NaVorro Bowman RC	1.00	2.50
175 Pat Angerer RC	1.00	2.50
176 Pat Paschall RC	.75	2.00
177 Patrick Robinson RC	1.00	2.50
178 Perrish Cox RC	.75	2.00
179 Ricky Sapp RC	.75	2.00
180 Riley Cooper RC	1.00	2.50
181 Russell Okung RC	1.00	2.50
182 Rusty Smith RC	1.00	2.50
183 Sean Canfield RC	.75	2.00
184 Sean Lee RC	1.00	2.50
185 Sean Weatherspoon RC	1.00	2.50
186 Sergio Kindle RC	1.00	2.50
187 Seyi Ajirotutu RC	1.00	2.50
188 Shay Hodge RC	.75	2.00
189 T.J. Ward RC	1.00	2.50
190 Taylor Mays RC	1.00	2.50
191 Terrence Austin RC	.75	2.00
192 Terrence Cody RC	.75	2.00
193 Timothy Toone RC	.75	2.00
194 Tony Moeaki RC	1.00	2.50
195 Tony Pike RC	1.00	2.50
196 Torell Troup RC	.75	2.00
197 Trent Williams RC	1.00	2.50
198 Trindon Holliday RC	1.00	2.50
199 Tyson Alualu RC	.75	2.00
200 Zac Robinson RC	.75	2.00
201 C.J. Spiller AU/210 RC	15.00	40.00
202 Marcus Easley AU/210 RC	6.00	15.00
203 Demaryius Thomas AU/210 RC	10.00	25.00
204 Eric Decker AU/300 RC	10.00	25.00
205 Tim Tebow AU/270 RC	75.00	125.00
206 Jermaine Gresham AU/270 RC	10.00	25.00
207 Jordan Shipley AU/210 RC	10.00	25.00
208 Mike Kafka AU/210 RC	8.00	20.00
209 Eric Berry AU/210 RC	12.00	30.00
210 Dexter McCluster AU/300 RC	8.00	20.00
211 Armanti Edwards AU/210 RC	8.00	20.00
212 Brandon LaFell AU/210 RC	8.00	20.00
213 Jimmy Clausen AU/210 RC	8.00	20.00
214 Toby Gerhart AU/210 RC	8.00	20.00
215 Joe McKnight AU/210 RC	8.00	20.00
216 Rolando McClain AU/210 RC	8.00	20.00
217 Emmanuel Sanders AU/210 RC	8.00	20.00
218 Jonathan Dwyer AU/300 RC	8.00	20.00
219 Gerald McCoy AU/210 RC	8.00	20.00
220 Arrelious Benn AU/270 RC	8.00	20.00
221 Mike Williams AU/209 RC	12.00	30.00
222 Golden Tate AU/300 RC	8.00	20.00
223 Colt McCoy AU/270 RC	15.00	40.00
224 Montario Hardesty AU/300 RC	8.00	20.00
225 Ben Tate AU/210 RC	10.00	25.00
226 Damian Williams AU/210 RC	8.00	20.00
227 Mardy Gilyard AU/210 RC	8.00	20.00
228 Sam Bradford AU/270 RC	40.00	100.00
229 Jahvid Best AU/270 RC	20.00	50.00
230 Ndamukong Suh AU/210 RC	25.00	50.00
231 Dez Bryant AU/300 RC	25.00	60.00
232 Rob Gronkowski AU/300 RC	20.00	50.00
233 Taylor Price AU/300 RC	8.00	20.00
234 Andre Roberts AU/210 RC	8.00	20.00
235 Ryan Mathews AU/210 RC	20.00	50.00

2010 Epix Gold

*VETS 1-100: 5X TO 12X BASIC CARDS
*ROOKIES 101-200: 1.2X TO 3X BASIC CARDS
STATED PRINT RUN 100 SER.#'d SETS

2010 Epix Platinum
*VETS 1-100: 6X TO 15X BASIC CARDS
*ROOKIES 101-200: 1.5X TO 4X BASIC CARDS
STATED PRINT RUN 50 SER.#'d SETS

2010 Epix Silver
*VETS 1-100: 3X TO 8X BASIC CARDS
*ROOKIES 101-200: .8X TO 2X BASIC CARDS
STATED PRINT RUN 250 SER.#'d SETS

2010 Epix Ball Hawks
1 DeMarcus Ware 1.00 2.50
2 Troy Polamalu 1.25 3.00
3 Darrelle Revis 1.00 2.50
4 Ray Lewis 1.25 3.00
5 Charles Woodson 1.25 3.00
6 Patrick Willis 1.00 2.50
7 Will Smith .75 2.00
8 Brian Urlacher 1.25 3.00
9 Jared Allen 1.25 3.00
10 Dwight Freeney 1.00 2.50

2010 Epix Ball Hawks Materials
STATED PRINT RUN 140-299
*PRIME/40-50: .8X TO 2X BASIC JSY
1 DeMarcus Ware/200 3.00 8.00
2 Troy Polamalu/299 6.00 15.00
3 Darrelle Revis/299 2.50 6.00
4 Ray Lewis/299 4.00 10.00
5 Charles Woodson/299 3.00 8.00
6 Patrick Willis/299 2.50 6.00
7 Will Smith/299 2.00 5.00
8 Brian Urlacher/299 3.00 8.00
9 Jared Allen/299 4.00 10.00
10 Dwight Freeney/140 2.50 6.00

2010 Epix Canton Lettermen Autographs
STATED PRINT RUN 30-50
1 Emmitt Smith/50 100.00 175.00
2 Jerry Rice/50 90.00 150.00
3 Russ Grimm/50
4 Rickey Jackson/50 30.00 60.00
5 Floyd Little/50 20.00 40.00
6 John Randle/50 20.00 40.00
8 Bart Starr/50 90.00 150.00
9 Dan Marino/50 100.00 175.00
10 Don Maynard/50 20.00 40.00
11 Jim Taylor/50 30.00 60.00
12 Joe Montana/50 75.00 150.00
13 Joe Namath/50 60.00 120.00
14 John Elway/30 90.00 150.00
16 Troy Aikman/50 40.00 80.00
17 Roger Staubach/50 40.00 80.00
18 Steve Largent/50 25.00 50.00
19 Rod Woodson/50 25.00 50.00

2010 Epix Dallas Cowboys Lettermen Autographs
STATED PRINT RUN 35-70
1 Bob Lilly/70 25.00 50.00
2 Chuck Howley/70 25.00 50.00
3 Cliff Harris/70 20.00 40.00
4 Darren Woodson/70 25.00 60.00
5 Deion Sanders/35 50.00 100.00
6 Ed Too Tall Jones/70 25.00 50.00
7 Emmitt Smith/35 100.00 175.00
8 Erik Williams/70 20.00 40.00
9 Everson Walls/70 20.00 40.00
11 John Niland/70 20.00 40.00
12 Mark Stepnoski/70 20.00 40.00
14 Mel Renfro/70 20.00 40.00
15 Michael Irvin/35 40.00 80.00
18 Roger Staubach/35 60.00 100.00
19 Tony Dorsett/35 30.00 60.00
20 Troy Aikman/70 40.00 80.00
21 Jason Witten/35 40.00 80.00
23 D.D. Lewis/35 25.00 50.00
25 Randy White/35 40.00 80.00

2010 Epix Epix Game Orange
*GAME EMERALD: .5X TO 1.2X GAME ORG
*GAME PURPLE: .6X TO 1.5X GAME ORG
*MOMENT EMERALD: .4X TO 1X GAME ORG
*MOMENT ORANGE: .5X TO 1.2X GAME ORG
*MOMENT PURPLE: .8X TO 2X GAME ORG
*SEASON EMERALD: .6X TO 1.5X GAME ORG
*SEASON ORANGE: .4X TO 1X GAME ORG
*SEASON PURPLE: .5X TO 1.2X GAME ORG
1 Sidney Rice 1.00 2.50
2 Santana Moss 1.00 2.50
3 Ronnie Brown 1.00 2.50
4 Reggie Wayne 1.00 2.50
5 Ray Rice 1.00 2.50
6 Randy Moss 1.25 3.00
7 Pierre Garcon 1.00 2.50
8 Peyton Manning 2.00 5.00
9 Patrick Willis 1.00 2.50
10 Michael Turner .75 2.00
11 Matthew Stafford 1.25 3.00
12 Matt Ryan 1.25 3.00
13 Matt Forte 1.00 2.50
14 Mark Sanchez 1.25 3.00
15 LeSean McCoy 1.00 2.50
16 Larry Fitzgerald 1.25 3.00
17 Kyle Orton 1.00 2.50
18 Kevin Boss 1.00 2.50
19 Joseph Addai 1.00 2.50
20 Joe Flacco 1.25 3.00
21 Jason Witten 1.25 3.00
22 Hines Ward 1.00 2.50
23 Greg Jennings 1.00 2.50
24 Felix Jones 1.00 2.50
25 Eddie Royal .75 2.00
26 Dwayne Bowe 1.00 2.50
27 Drew Brees 1.25 3.00
28 Donald Driver 1.00 2.50
29 Devery Henderson .75 2.00
30 Aaron Rodgers 2.50 6.00
31 Antonio Gates 1.00 2.50
32 Bernard Berrian .75 2.00
33 Brett Favre 3.00 8.00
34 Derrick Mason 1.00 2.50
35 David Garrard 1.00 2.50
36 Darrelle Revis 1.00 2.50
37 Wes Welker 1.25 3.00
38 Vincent Jackson .75 2.00
39 Vernon Davis 1.00 2.50
40 Tony Romo 1.50 4.00
41 Tom Brady 2.00 5.00
42 Terrell Suggs .75 2.00
43 Steve Smith 1.00 2.50
44 Shonn Greene 1.00 2.50
45 Andre Johnson 1.00 2.50
46 Austin Collie 1.00 2.50
47 Brandon Jacobs 1.00 2.50
48 Brian Urlacher 1.25 3.00
49 Cadillac Williams 1.00 2.50
50 Chris Cooley 1.00 2.50
51 Ray Lewis 1.25 3.00
52 Percy Harvin 1.25 3.00
53 Maurice Jones-Drew 1.00 2.50
54 Matt Hasselbeck .75 2.00
55 Marion Barber 1.00 2.50
56 Ladell Betts .75 2.00
57 Adrian Peterson 2.00 5.00
58 DeSean Jackson 1.00 2.50
59 Dustin Keller 1.00 2.50
60 Eli Manning 1.25 3.00
61 Heath Miller 1.00 2.50
62 Jay Cutler 1.25 3.00
63 Darren Sproles 1.00 2.50
64 Calvin Johnson 1.25 3.00
65 Clinton Portis 1.00 2.50
66 Chad Ochocinco 1.00 2.50
67 Carson Palmer 1.00 2.50
68 Braylon Edwards 1.00 2.50
69 Chris Wells 1.00 2.50
70 Visanthe Shiancoe 1.00 2.50
71 Troy Polamalu 1.25 3.00
72 T.J. Houshmandzadeh 1.00 2.50
73 Ryan Grant 1.00 2.50
74 Devin Hester 1.25 3.00
75 Ed Reed 1.00 2.50
76 Jamaal Charles 1.00 2.50
77 Josh Cribbs 1.25 3.00
78 Lee Evans 1.00 2.50
79 Matt Schaub 1.00 2.50
80 Philip Rivers 1.25 3.00
81 Reggie Bush 1.25 3.00
82 Tony Gonzalez 1.00 2.50
83 Roddy White 1.00 2.50
84 Miles Austin 1.25 3.00
85 Knowshon Moreno 1.00 2.50
86 Frank Gore 1.00 2.50
87 Donovan McNabb 1.25 3.00
88 DeAngelo Williams 1.00 2.50
89 Dallas Clark 1.00 2.50
90 Cedric Benson 1.00 2.50
91 Darren McFadden 1.00 2.50
92 Brent Celek 1.00 2.50
93 Jonathan Stewart 1.00 2.50
94 Marques Colston 1.00 2.50
95 Vince Young .75 2.00
96 Anthony Gonzalez .75 2.00
97 Pierre Thomas 1.00 2.50
98 Steven Jackson 1.00 2.50
99 Chris Johnson 1.25 3.00
100 Ben Roethlisberger 1.25 3.00

2010 Epix Epix Jerseys Blue
*PRIME/35-50: .8X TO 2X BASIC JSY
*PRIME/19-25: 1X TO 2.5X BASIC JSY
1 Sidney Rice 2.50 6.00
2 Santana Moss 2.50 6.00
3 Ronnie Brown 2.50 6.00
4 Reggie Wayne 2.50 6.00
6 Randy Moss 3.00 8.00
8 Peyton Manning 5.00 12.00
9 Patrick Willis 2.50 6.00
11 Matthew Stafford 3.00 8.00
12 Matt Ryan 3.00 8.00
13 Matt Forte 2.50 6.00
14 Mark Sanchez 3.00 8.00
15 LeSean McCoy 2.50 6.00
16 Larry Fitzgerald 3.00 8.00
17 Kyle Orton 2.50 6.00
18 Kevin Boss 2.50 6.00
19 Joseph Addai 2.50 6.00
20 Joe Flacco 3.00 8.00
21 Jason Witten 3.00 8.00
22 Hines Ward 2.50 6.00
23 Greg Jennings 2.50 6.00
24 Felix Jones 2.50 6.00
25 Eddie Royal 2.00 5.00
26 Dwayne Bowe 2.50 6.00
28 Donald Driver 2.50 6.00
29 Devery Henderson 2.00 5.00
31 Antonio Gates 2.50 6.00
32 Bernard Berrian 2.00 5.00
33 Brett Favre 12.00 30.00
34 Derrick Mason 2.50 6.00
35 David Garrard 2.50 6.00
36 Darrelle Revis 2.50 6.00
37 Wes Welker 3.00 8.00
38 Vincent Jackson 2.00 5.00
39 Vernon Davis 2.50 6.00
40 Tony Romo 4.00 10.00
41 Tom Brady 5.00 12.00
42 Terrell Suggs 2.00 5.00
43 Steve Smith 2.50 6.00
44 Shonn Greene 2.50 6.00
45 Andre Johnson 2.50 6.00
47 Brandon Jacobs 2.50 6.00
48 Brian Urlacher 3.00 8.00
49 Cadillac Williams 2.50 6.00
50 Chris Cooley 2.50 6.00
51 Ray Lewis 4.00 10.00
52 Percy Harvin 3.00 8.00
53 Maurice Jones-Drew 2.50 6.00
54 Matt Hasselbeck 2.00 5.00
55 Marion Barber 2.50 6.00
56 Ladell Betts 2.00 5.00
57 Adrian Peterson 5.00 12.00
59 Dustin Keller 2.50 6.00
60 Eli Manning 3.00 8.00
61 Heath Miller 2.50 6.00
62 Jay Cutler 3.00 8.00
63 Darren Sproles 2.50 6.00
64 Calvin Johnson 3.00 8.00
65 Clinton Portis 2.50 6.00
66 Chad Ochocinco 2.50 6.00
67 Carson Palmer 2.50 6.00
68 Braylon Edwards 2.50 6.00
69 Chris Wells 2.50 6.00
70 Visanthe Shiancoe 2.50 6.00
71 Troy Polamalu 5.00 12.00
74 Devin Hester 3.00 8.00
75 Ed Reed 2.50 6.00
76 Jamaal Charles 2.50 6.00
77 Josh Cribbs 3.00 8.00
78 Lee Evans 2.50 6.00
79 Matt Schaub 2.50 6.00
80 Philip Rivers 3.00 8.00
81 Reggie Bush 3.00 8.00
82 Tony Gonzalez 2.50 6.00
83 Roddy White 2.50 6.00
84 Miles Austin 3.00 8.00
85 Knowshon Moreno 2.50 6.00
86 Frank Gore 2.50 6.00
87 Donovan McNabb 3.00 8.00
88 DeAngelo Williams 2.50 6.00
89 Dallas Clark 2.50 6.00
90 Cedric Benson 2.50 6.00
91 Darren McFadden 2.50 6.00
93 Jonathan Stewart 2.50 6.00
94 Marques Colston 2.50 6.00
95 Vince Young 2.00 5.00
96 Anthony Gonzalez 2.00 5.00
98 Steven Jackson 2.50 6.00
99 Chris Johnson 3.00 8.00
100 Ben Roethlisberger 3.00 8.00

2010 Epix Epix Signatures Red
STATED PRINT RUN 1-25
14 Mark Sanchez/25 25.00 50.00
18 Kevin Boss/25 8.00 20.00
26 Dwayne Bowe/25 8.00 20.00
32 Bernard Berrian/25 6.00 15.00
38 Vincent Jackson/25 6.00 15.00
46 Austin Collie/25 8.00 20.00
61 Heath Miller/20 8.00 20.00
78 Lee Evans/25 8.00 20.00

2010 Epix Highlight Zone
1 Miles Austin 1.25 3.00
2 Chris Johnson 1.25 3.00
3 Drew Brees 1.25 3.00
4 Josh Cribbs 1.25 3.00
5 Randy Moss 1.25 3.00
6 Adrian Peterson 2.00 5.00
7 Aaron Rodgers 2.50 6.00
8 Philip Rivers 1.25 3.00
9 Sidney Rice 1.00 2.50
10 Vince Young .75 2.00
11 DeAngelo Williams 1.00 2.50
12 Peyton Manning 2.00 5.00
13 Maurice Jones-Drew 1.00 2.50
14 Felix Jones 1.00 2.50
15 Brett Favre 3.00 8.00

2010 Epix Highlight Zone Materials
STATED PRINT RUN 125-200
*PRIME/50: .6X TO 1.5X BASIC JSY
*PRIME/25: .8X TO 2X BASIC JSY
2 Chris Johnson/200 4.00 10.00
4 Josh Cribbs/200 4.00 10.00
5 Randy Moss/200 4.00 10.00
6 Adrian Peterson/200 6.00 15.00
8 Philip Rivers/125 4.00 10.00
9 Sidney Rice/200 3.00 8.00
10 Vince Young/200 2.50 6.00
11 DeAngelo Williams/200 3.00 8.00
12 Peyton Manning/200 6.00 15.00
13 Maurice Jones-Drew/200 3.00 8.00
14 Felix Jones/200 3.00 8.00
15 Brett Favre/200 10.00 25.00

2010 Epix Materials
STATED PRINT RUN 75-299
1 Chris Wells/299 2.50 6.00
2 Larry Fitzgerald/299 3.00 8.00
3 Matt Leinart/299 2.50 6.00
4 Matt Ryan/250 3.00 8.00
6 Roddy White/299 2.50 6.00
8 Joe Flacco/299 3.00 8.00
10 Lee Evans/299 2.50 6.00
13 DeAngelo Williams/200 3.00 8.00
15 Steve Smith/75 4.00 10.00
16 Devin Hester/299 3.00 8.00
18 Matt Forte/299 2.50 6.00
19 Carson Palmer/299 2.50 6.00
20 Cedric Benson/299 2.50 6.00
21 Chad Ochocinco/200 3.00 8.00
23 Josh Cribbs/299 3.00 8.00
24 Mohamed Massaquoi/299 2.50 6.00
25 Felix Jones/100 3.00 8.00
26 Jason Witten/100 4.00 10.00
28 Tony Romo/200 5.00 12.00
29 Eddie Royal/299 2.00 5.00
30 Knowshon Moreno/299 2.50 6.00
31 Kyle Orton/299 2.50 6.00
32 Calvin Johnson/299 3.00 8.00
33 Matthew Stafford/299 3.00 8.00
36 Donald Driver/299 2.50 6.00
38 Andre Johnson/299 2.50 6.00
39 Matt Schaub/299 2.50 6.00
40 Steve Slaton/299 2.00 5.00
41 Dallas Clark/299 2.50 6.00
42 Joseph Addai/75 4.00 10.00
43 Peyton Manning/185 6.00 15.00
44 Reggie Wayne/160 3.00 8.00
45 David Garrard/299 2.50 6.00
46 Maurice Jones-Drew/299 2.50 6.00
48 Dwayne Bowe/299 2.50 6.00
49 Jamaal Charles/299 2.50 6.00
53 Ronnie Brown/100 3.00 8.00
54 Adrian Peterson/200 6.00 15.00
55 Brett Favre/299 12.00 30.00
56 Sidney Rice/250 2.50 6.00
57 Randy Moss/299 3.00 8.00
58 Tom Brady/299 5.00 12.00
59 Wes Welker/150 4.00 10.00
61 Marques Colston/299 2.50 6.00
63 Brandon Jacobs/299 2.50 6.00
64 Eli Manning/200 4.00 10.00
66 Braylon Edwards/75 4.00 10.00
68 Mark Sanchez/200 4.00 10.00
70 Darren McFadden/299 2.50 6.00
71 Jason Campbell/299 2.50 6.00
72 Louis Murphy/299 2.50 6.00
74 Kevin Kolb/299 2.50 6.00
76 Ben Roethlisberger/125 4.00 10.00
77 Hines Ward/110 3.00 8.00
78 Rashard Mendenhall/170 3.00 8.00
79 Antonio Gates/299 2.50 6.00
80 Darren Sproles/299 2.50 6.00
81 Philip Rivers/125 4.00 10.00
82 Vincent Jackson/299 2.00 5.00
83 Frank Gore/299 2.50 6.00
84 Michael Crabtree/130 4.00 10.00
85 Vernon Davis/299 2.50 6.00
87 Matt Hasselbeck/299 2.00 5.00
91 Steven Jackson/299 2.50 6.00
92 Cadillac Williams/299 2.50 6.00
93 Josh Freeman/299 3.00 8.00
95 Chris Johnson/299 3.00 8.00
96 Kenny Britt/299 2.50 6.00
97 Vince Young/299 2.00 5.00
98 Chris Cooley/299 2.50 6.00
99 Clinton Portis/250 2.50 6.00
100 Donovan McNabb/299 3.00 8.00

2010 Epix Materials Prime
COMMON CARD/30-50 4.00 10.00
SEMISTARS/30-50 5.00 12.00
UNL.STARS/30-50 6.00 15.00
COMMON CARD/20-25 6.00 15.00
UNL.STARS/20-25 8.00 20.00
PRIME PRINT RUN 4-50
28 Tony Romo/50 8.00 20.00
43 Peyton Manning/40 10.00 25.00
54 Adrian Peterson/50 10.00 25.00
58 Tom Brady/50 10.00 25.00
68 Mark Sanchez/50 6.00 15.00

2010 Epix Odyssey Combo Materials
STATED PRINT RUN 10-200
1 Cedric Benson/200 3.00 8.00
2 Donovan McNabb/100 4.00 10.00
4 Jason Campbell/200 3.00 8.00
6 Michael Turner/10
10 Santana Moss/200 3.00 8.00
11 T.J. Houshmandzadeh/90 4.00 10.00
12 Brett Favre/200 20.00 50.00
18 Tony Gonzalez/15 6.00 15.00
19 Jay Cutler/45 6.00 15.00
20 Laveranues Coles/200 2.50 6.00

2010 Epix Odyssey Combo Materials Prime
COMMON CARD/50 5.00 12.00
UNL.STARS/50 6.00 15.00
COMMON CARD/25 6.00 15.00
PRIME PRINT RUN 5-50

2010 Epix Odyssey Materials
STATED PRINT RUN 40-299
1 Cedric Benson/299 2.50 6.00
2 Donovan McNabb/299 3.00 8.00
4 Jason Campbell/299 2.50 6.00
5 Anquan Boldin/40 5.00 12.00
7 Jake Delhomme/299 2.50 6.00
10 Santana Moss/299 2.50 6.00
12 Brett Favre/299 12.00 30.00
14 Santonio Holmes/190 3.00 8.00
15 Ted Ginn/299 2.50 6.00
16 Chad Pennington/299 2.50 6.00
17 Chester Taylor/299 2.00 5.00
19 Jay Cutler/299 3.00 8.00
20 Laveranues Coles/299 2.00 5.00

2010 Epix Odyssey Materials Prime
COMMON CARD/75 3.00 8.00
SEMISTARS/75 4.00 10.00
UNL.STARS/75 5.00 12.00
COMMON CARD/35-50 5.00 12.00
UNL.STARS/35-50 6.00 15.00
COMMON CARD/15 6.00 15.00
PRIME PRINT RUN 15-75

2010 Epix Rookie Campaign Materials
STATED PRINT RUN 499 SER.#'d SETS
*PRIME/50: .6X TO 1.5X BASIC JSY/499
1 Ryan Mathews 6.00 15.00
2 Taylor Price 2.50 6.00
3 Dez Bryant 6.00 15.00
4 Jahvid Best 6.00 15.00
5 Mardy Gilyard 2.50 6.00
6 Ben Tate 3.00 8.00
7 Colt McCoy 5.00 12.00
8 Mike Williams 4.00 10.00
9 Gerald McCoy 2.50 6.00
10 Emmanuel Sanders 2.50 6.00
11 Joe McKnight 2.50 6.00
12 Jimmy Clausen 2.50 6.00
13 Armanti Edwards 2.50 6.00
14 Eric Berry 2.50 6.00
15 Jordan Shipley 2.50 6.00
16 Tim Tebow 10.00 25.00
17 Demaryius Thomas 3.00 8.00
18 C.J. Spiller 5.00 12.00
19 Jonathan Dwyer 2.50 6.00
20 Arrelious Benn 2.50 6.00
21 Golden Tate 2.50 6.00
22 Montario Hardesty 2.50 6.00
23 Damian Williams 2.50 6.00
24 Sam Bradford 8.00 20.00
25 Ndamukong Suh 5.00 12.00
26 Rob Gronkowski 6.00 15.00
27 Andre Roberts 2.50 6.00
28 Rolando McClain 2.50 6.00
29 Toby Gerhart 2.50 6.00
30 Brandon LaFell 2.50 6.00
31 Dexter McCluster 2.50 6.00
32 Mike Kafka 2.50 6.00
33 Jermaine Gresham 3.00 8.00
34 Eric Decker 3.00 8.00
35 Marcus Easley 2.00 5.00

2010 Epix Rookie Campaign Materials Signatures
STATED PRINT RUN 100 SER.#'d SETS
1 Ryan Mathews 15.00 40.00
2 Taylor Price 6.00 15.00
3 Dez Bryant 25.00 60.00
4 Jahvid Best 10.00 25.00
5 Mardy Gilyard 6.00 15.00
6 Ben Tate 8.00 20.00
7 Colt McCoy 12.00 30.00
8 Mike Williams 10.00 25.00
10 Emmanuel Sanders 6.00 15.00
12 Jimmy Clausen 6.00 15.00
13 Armanti Edwards 6.00 15.00
14 Eric Berry 6.00 15.00
15 Jordan Shipley 6.00 15.00
16 Tim Tebow 60.00 100.00
18 C.J. Spiller 10.00 25.00
19 Jonathan Dwyer 6.00 15.00
20 Arrelious Benn 6.00 15.00
21 Golden Tate 6.00 15.00
22 Montario Hardesty 6.00 15.00
23 Damian Williams 6.00 15.00
24 Sam Bradford 50.00 100.00
25 Ndamukong Suh 15.00 40.00
26 Rob Gronkowski 25.00 50.00
27 Andre Roberts 6.00 15.00
28 Rolando McClain 6.00 15.00
29 Toby Gerhart 6.00 15.00
30 Brandon LaFell 6.00 15.00
31 Dexter McCluster 6.00 15.00
32 Mike Kafka 6.00 15.00
34 Eric Decker 8.00 20.00
35 Marcus Easley 5.00 12.00

2010 Epix Rookie Campaign Materials Prime Signatures
*PRIME/25: .6X TO 1.5X BASIC JSY AU/100
PRIME PRINT RUN 25 SER.#'d SETS
16 Tim Tebow 100.00 175.00
24 Sam Bradford 75.00 150.00

2010 Epix Rush Hour
1 Ryan Grant 1.00 2.50
2 Clinton Portis 1.00 2.50
3 Cadillac Williams 1.00 2.50
4 Cedric Benson 1.00 2.50
5 Chris Wells 1.00 2.50
6 LeSean McCoy 1.00 2.50
7 Ray Rice 1.00 2.50
8 Jonathan Stewart 1.00 2.50
9 Shonn Greene 1.00 2.50
10 Steven Jackson 1.00 2.50
11 Joseph Addai 1.00 2.50
12 Matt Forte 1.00 2.50
13 Darren Sproles 1.00 2.50
14 Reggie Bush 1.25 3.00
15 Rashard Mendenhall 1.00 2.50
16 Ronnie Brown 1.00 2.50
17 Knowshon Moreno 1.00 2.50
18 Marion Barber 1.00 2.50
19 Brandon Jacobs 1.00 2.50
20 Jamaal Charles 1.00 2.50

2010 Epix Rush Hour Materials
STATED PRINT RUN 95-150
*PRIME/50: .6X TO 1.5X BASIC JSY
*PRIME/15: .8X TO 2X BASIC JSY
2 Clinton Portis/150 3.00 8.00
3 Cadillac Williams/150 3.00 8.00
4 Cedric Benson/150 3.00 8.00
5 Chris Wells/150 3.00 8.00
6 LeSean McCoy/150 3.00 8.00
8 Jonathan Stewart/150 3.00 8.00
10 Steven Jackson/150 3.00 8.00
11 Joseph Addai/150 3.00 8.00
12 Matt Forte/150 3.00 8.00
13 Darren Sproles/150 3.00 8.00
14 Reggie Bush/95 4.00 10.00
15 Rashard Mendenhall/150 3.00 8.00
16 Ronnie Brown/150 3.00 8.00
17 Knowshon Moreno/150 3.00 8.00
18 Marion Barber/150 3.00 8.00
19 Brandon Jacobs/150 3.00 8.00
20 Jamaal Charles/150 3.00 8.00

2010 Epix Saints Who Dat Lettermen Autographs
STATED PRINT RUN 240 SER.#'d SETS
1 Tracy Porter 15.00 40.00
2 Garrett Hartley 15.00 40.00
3 Pierre Thomas 15.00 40.00
4 Marques Colston 15.00 40.00
5 Drew Brees 50.00 100.00

2010 Epix Signatures
VETERAN PRINT RUN 1-30
ROOKIE PRINT RUN 299-499
10 Lee Evans/25 8.00 20.00
29 Eddie Royal/30 5.00 12.00
64 Eli Manning/15 50.00 100.00
68 Mark Sanchez/25 25.00 50.00
72 Louis Murphy/50 6.00 15.00
74 Kevin Kolb/25 8.00 20.00
84 Michael Crabtree/25 12.00 30.00
96 Kenny Britt/25 8.00 20.00
101 Aaron Hernandez/499 8.00 20.00
103 Andre Anderson/499 4.00 10.00
105 Anthony Dixon/399 5.00 12.00
106 Anthony McCoy/499 4.00 10.00
107 Antonio Brown/499 8.00 20.00
108 Blair White/499 5.00 12.00
109 Brandon Graham/499 4.00 10.00
110 Brandon Spikes/499 5.00 12.00
112 Bryan Bulaga/499 5.00 12.00
113 Carlos Dunlap/499 5.00 12.00
114 Carlton Mitchell/499 4.00 10.00
115 Chad Jones/499 5.00 12.00
116 Charles Scott/499 4.00 10.00
118 Chris McGaha/499 3.00 8.00
119 Corey Wootton/499 4.00 10.00
120 Dan LeFevour/499 5.00 12.00
123 David Gettis/499 5.00 12.00
127 Derrick Morgan/499 4.00 10.00
128 Devin McCourty/499 5.00 12.00
129 Dezmon Briscoe/499 4.00 10.00
130 Dominique Franks/499 3.00 8.00
132 Earl Thomas/499 5.00 12.00
133 Ed Dickson/499 5.00 12.00
134 Everson Griffen/499 5.00 12.00
135 Freddie Barnes/499 4.00 10.00
136 Garrett Graham/499 4.00 10.00
137 Jacoby Ford/499 8.00 20.00
138 James Starks/499 15.00 30.00
140 Jarrett Brown/499 5.00 12.00
141 Jason Pierre-Paul/499 8.00 20.00
142 Jason Worilds/499 5.00 12.00
144 Jeremy Williams/499 0.00 0.00
147 Jerry Hughes/499 5.00 12.00
148 Jevan Snead/499 5.00 12.00
149 Jimmy Graham/499 12.50 25.00
150 Joe Haden/499 5.00 12.00
153 John Skelton/499 5.00 12.00
154 Joique Bell/499 4.00 10.00
155 Jonathan Crompton/499 4.00 10.00
156 Kareem Jackson/299 5.00 12.00
162 LeGarrette Blount/499 10.00 25.00
166 Lonyae Miller/499 4.00 10.00
171 Morgan Burnett/499 5.00 12.00
177 Patrick Robinson/499 5.00 12.00
178 Perrish Cox/499 4.00 10.00
179 Ricky Sapp/499 4.00 10.00
180 Riley Cooper/499 5.00 12.00
183 Sean Canfield/499 4.00 10.00
184 Sean Lee/499 5.00 12.00
185 Sean Weatherspoon/499 5.00 12.00
187 Seyi Ajirotutu/499 5.00 12.00
188 Shay Hodge/499 4.00 10.00
190 Taylor Mays/499 5.00 12.00
195 Tony Pike/499 5.00 12.00
200 Zac Robinson/499 4.00 10.00

2010 Epix Spellbound
1 Aaron Rodgers 4.00 10.00
2 Adrian Peterson 3.00 8.00
3 Andre Johnson 1.50 4.00
4 Brett Favre 5.00 12.00
5 Brian Urlacher 2.00 5.00
6 Calvin Johnson 2.00 5.00
7 Carson Palmer 1.50 4.00
8 Chad Ochocinco 1.50 4.00
9 Chris Johnson 2.00 5.00
10 Darrelle Revis 1.50 4.00
11 Darren Sproles 1.50 4.00
12 DeAngelo Williams 1.50 4.00
13 DeSean Jackson 1.50 4.00
14 Donovan McNabb 2.00 5.00
15 Drew Brees 2.00 5.00
16 Eli Manning 2.00 5.00
17 Frank Gore 1.50 4.00
18 Jamaal Charles 1.50 4.00
19 Jason Witten 2.00 5.00
20 Knowshon Moreno 1.50 4.00
21 Larry Fitzgerald 2.00 5.00
22 Mark Sanchez 2.00 5.00
23 Matt Ryan 2.00 5.00
24 Matthew Stafford 2.00 5.00
25 Maurice Jones-Drew 1.50 4.00
26 Michael Crabtree 2.00 5.00
27 Michael Turner 1.25 3.00
28 Ray Lewis 2.00 5.00
29 Ray Rice 1.50 4.00
30 Reggie Wayne 1.50 4.00
31 Steve Smith 1.50 4.00
32 Steven Jackson 1.50 4.00
33 Tom Brady 3.00 8.00
34 Tony Romo 2.50 6.00
35 Troy Polamalu 2.00 5.00
36 Vernon Davis 1.50 4.00

2010 Epix Sunday Showdown Materials
STATED PRINT RUN 5-200
*PRIME/50: .6X TO 1.5X BASIC DUAL JSY
1 Drew Brees/5
DeMarcus Ware
2 Tony Romo/200 6.00 15.00
Eli Manning
3 Peyton Manning/200 8.00 20.00
Tom Brady
4 Chad Ochocinco/200 6.00 15.00
Troy Polamalu
7 Adrian Peterson/14
Ryan Grant
8 Philip Rivers/200 4.00 10.00
Vince Young
9 Chris Johnson/200 6.00 15.00
Ray Lewis
10 Larry Fitzgerald/200 4.00 10.00
Frank Gore
11 Carson Palmer/200 5.00 12.00
Joe Flacco
12 Shonn Greene/110 4.00 10.00
Ronnie Brown
13 Darren McFadden/200 4.00 10.00
Knowshon Moreno
14 Clinton Portis/200 4.00 10.00
LeSean McCoy
15 Calvin Johnson/200 5.00 12.00
Matt Forte

1967-73 Equitable Sports Hall of Fame
This set consists of copies of art work found over a number of years in many national magazines, especially "Sports Illustrated," honoring sports heroes that Equitable Life Assurance Society selected to be in its very own Sports Hall of Fame. The cards consists of charcoal-type drawings on white backgrounds by artists, George Loh and Robert Riger, and measure approximately 11" by 7 3/4". The unnumbered cards have been assigned numbers below using a sport prefix (BB- baseball, BK- basketball, FB- football, HK- hockey, OT-other).

COMPLETE SET (95) 250.00 500.00
FB1 Jim Brown 4.00 8.00
FB2 Charley Conerly 2.00 4.00
FB3 Bill Dudley 1.25 2.50
FB4 Roman Gabriel 1.25 2.50
FB5 Red Grange 4.00 8.00
FB6 Elroy Hirsch 2.00 4.00
FB7 Jerry Kramer 2.00 4.00
FB8 Vince Lombardi 4.00 8.00
FB9 Earl Morrall 1.25 2.50
FB10 Bronko Nagurski 3.00 6.00
FB11 Gale Sayers 4.00 8.00
FB12 Jim Thorpe 4.00 8.00
FB13 Johnny Unitas 4.00 8.00
FB14 Alex Webster 2.00 4.00

1969 Eskimo Pie

The 1969 Eskimo Pie football card set contains 15 panel pairs of American Football League players. Each pair of individual player cards is most commonly collected together and, thus, cataloged as pairs below. Each could be cut off of Eskimo Pie Ice Cream boxes at the time and most, if not all, can also be found in a thinner sticker version originally attached to a green colored backing paper two per panel for a total of four players. This thin sticker version apppears to be more difficult to find than the card/box version. The panels measure approximately 2 1/2" by 3" when neatly cut. It is thought that the "card/box" versions are actually stickers as well which could be removed from the cardboard to which they are attached. The unnumbered pairs are checklisted below alphabetically according to the last name of the player on the left. The names are mistakenly reversed on the card containing Jim Otto and Len Dawson (card number 14). Finally, a 16th sticker was uncovered in 2012 which included an offer for four different NFL team logo jewelry premiums: tie clasp, tie tac, pendant, and charm bracelet with the Jets team logo featured. This premium offer sticker was issued along with the Lamonica/Frazier sticker pair and it measures the same size as a standard sticker pair. The catalog designation for this set is F73.

COMPLETE SET (15) 2,500.00 3,500.00
*STICKER: .6X TO 1.2X CARD VERSION
1 Lance Alworth 100.00 200.00
John Charles
2 Al Atkinson 100.00 200.00
George Goeddeke
3 Marlin Briscoe SP 250.00 400.00
Billy Shaw
4 Gino Cappelletti SP 250.00 400.00
Dale Livingston
5 Eric Crabtree 100.00 200.00
Jim Dunaway
6 Ben Davidson 250.00 400.00
Bob Griese
7 Hewritt Dixon 100.00 175.00
Pete Beathard
8 Mike Garrett SP 125.00 250.00
Bobby Hunt
9 Daryle Lamonica 150.00 300.00
Willie Frazier
10 Jim Lynch 100.00 200.00
John Hadl
11 Kent McCloughan 100.00 200.00
Tom Regner
12 Jim Nance SP 250.00 400.00
Billy Neighbors
13 Rick Norton 100.00 200.00
Paul Costa
14 Jim Otto 250.00 400.00
Len Dawson UER
(Names reversed)
15 Matt Snell 100.00 175.00
Dick Post

1995 ESPN Magazine

This set of 6 cards was released in ESPN magazine. It features ESPN broadcasters on cards styled after the 1956 Topps set. The cards were printed on thin glossy stock and issued as a perforated sheet. They were skip numbered.

COMPLETE SET (6) 7.50 15.00
7 Joe Theismann 2.00 5.00
12 Chris Berman 1.25 3.00
32 Chris Mortensen 1.25 3.00
57 Tom Jackson 1.25 3.00
70 Art Donovan 1.50 4.00
84 Sterling Sharpe 1.25 3.00

2000 eTopps
Available only through a limited offering on the Topps website, these cards were initially meant to be sold in a stock market like atmosphere on eBay. Each card was issued with an IPO price that ranged from $3.50-$9.50 per card. Announced print runs are included below.

ANNOUNCED RPINT RUNS BELOW
1 Ricky Williams/1423* 6.00 12.00
4 Daunte Culpepper/1000* 7.50 15.00
5 Peter Warrick/1000* 6.00 12.00
6 Emmitt Smith/938* 20.00 40.00
9 Peyton Manning/1000* 20.00 40.00
11 Ron Dayne/1000* 6.00 12.00
12 Randy Moss/982* 12.50 25.00
13 Eddie George/496* 15.00 30.00
18 Kurt Warner/1070* 7.50 15.00
21 Marshall Faulk/850* 6.00 12.00
23 Jamal Lewis/500* 30.00 60.00
24 Edgerrin James/758* 10.00 20.00

2001 eTopps
The 2001 eTopps cards were issued via Topps' website and initially sold exclusively on eBay's eTopps Trade Floor. Owners of the cards could hold the cards on account with Topps and freely trade those cards similar to shares of stock. They also could pay a fee to take actual delivery of their cards, but most are still held on account with Topps. Since most do not trade hands as physical cards, we've simply listed the checklist here without pricing.

1 Ray Lewis/649 4.00 8.00
2 Peter Warrick/281 7.50 15.00
3 James Stewart/465 2.50 5.00
4 Junior Seau/389 35.00 60.00
6 Amani Toomer/538 3.00 6.00
7 Elvis Grbac/230 35.00 60.00
8 David Boston/560 3.00 6.00
9 Jimmy Smith/354 10.00 20.00
10 Warrick Dunn/571 3.00 6.00
11 James Thrash/431 7.50 15.00
12 Joe Horn/606 2.50 5.00
13 Stephen Davis/236 7.50 15.00
14 Tyrone Wheatley/237 7.50 15.00
15 Brian Urlacher/1146 4.00 8.00
16 Fred Taylor/283 10.00 20.00
17 Jerry Rice/933 10.00 20.00
18 Keyshawn Johnson/254 20.00 35.00
19 Jay Fiedler/478 2.50 5.00
20 Jamal Anderson/274 10.00 20.00
21 Emmitt Smith/1975 6.00 12.00
22 Tiki Barber/861 3.00 6.00
23 Daunte Culpepper/457 3.00 6.00
24 Torry Holt/553 4.00 8.00
25 Peyton Manning/1104 12.50 25.00
26 Eddie George/292 7.50 15.00
27 Jamal Lewis/237 12.50 25.00
28 Ricky Williams/683 3.00 6.00
29 Ahman Green/1105 2.00 4.00
30 Ed McCaffrey/330 4.00 8.00
31 Curtis Martin/404 7.50 15.00
32 Isaac Bruce/772 2.50 6.00
33 Doug Flutie/684 3.00 6.00
34 Steve McNair/341 7.50 15.00
35 Donovan McNabb/987 4.00 8.00
36 Keenan McCardell/243 10.00 20.00
37 Charlie Batch/322 4.00 8.00
38 Cade McNown/333 7.50 15.00
39 Terrell Owens/528 6.00 12.00
40 Brad Johnson/231 50.00 100.00
41 Tim Dwight/586 5.00 10.00
42 Muhsin Muhammad/270 7.50 15.00
43 Kurt Warner/785 4.00 8.00
44 Lamar Smith/371 3.00 6.00
45 Brian Griese/505 2.50 5.00
46 Matthew Hatchette/317 3.00 0.00
47 Jeff Garcia/585 2.50 5.00
48 Derrick Mason/207 15.00 30.00
49 Drew Bledsoe/372 25.00 50.00
50 Marshall Faulk/2742 2.50 5.00
51 Corey Dillon/726 2.00 4.00
52 Tony Gonzalez/950 2.50 5.00
53 Chad Lewis/313 7.50 15.00
54 Shaun Alexander/1442 2.50 5.00
55 Edgerrin James/473 4.00 8.00
56 Eric Moulds/217 15.00 30.00
57 Aaron Brooks/434 2.50 5.00
58 Zach Thomas/380 7.50 15.00
59 Jerome Bettis/826 4.00 8.00
60 Shannon Sharpe/302 7.50 15.00
61 Kerry Collins/355 7.50 15.00
62 Ricky Watters/384 4.00 8.00
63 Tim Couch/677 2.00 4.00
64 Marvin Harrison/391 10.00 20.00
65 Tim Brown/377 12.50 25.00
66 Mark Brunell/299 7.50 15.00
67 Wayne Chrebet/380 4.00 8.00
68 Terry Glenn/260 12.50 25.00
69 Mike Anderson/352 2.50 5.00
70 Randy Moss/881 5.00 10.00
71 Freddie Jones/339 3.00 6.00
72 Ike Hilliard/280 5.00 10.00
73 Derrick Alexander/349 4.00 8.00
74 Travis Prentice/443 2.50
75 Brett Favre/1066 10.00 25.00
76 Rod Smith/521 2.00 4.00
77 Todd Pinkston/1005 2.00 4.00
78 Cris Carter/540 4.00 8.00
79 Rich Gannon/327 5.00 10.00
80 Charlie Garner/518 4.00 8.00
81 Michael Pittman/338 4.00 8.00
82 Jeff Graham/425 3.00 6.00
83 Albert Connell/275 5.00 10.00
84 Bill Schroeder/673 2.00 4.00
85 Jeff Blake/361 3.00 6.00
86 Jon Kitna/537 3.00 6.00
87 Qadry Ismail/431 12.50 25.00
88 Joey Galloway/413 4.00 8.00
89 Duce Staley/688 2.00 4.00
90 Troy Brown/559 2.00 4.00
91 Johnnie Morton/231 7.50 15.00
92 Chris Chandler/307 4.00 8.00
93 Donald Hayes/291 4.00 8.00
94 Mike Alstott/999 2.00 4.00
95 Vinny Testaverde/459 7.50 15.00
96 James Allen/467 3.00 6.00
97 Jake Plummer/600 2.50 5.00
98 Antonio Freeman/348 7.50 15.00
99 Darrell Jackson/502 3.00 6.00
100 Ron Dayne/257 4.00 8.00
101 Rob Johnson/389 2.50 5.00
102 Kordell Stewart/346 3.00 6.00
103 Akili Smith/202 15.00 30.00
104 Shawn Jefferson/226 7.50 15.00
105 Germane Crowell/281 3.00 6.00
106 Kevin Johnson/478 10.00 20.00
108 Marcus Robinson/662 2.00 4.00
109 Priest Holmes/418 5.00 10.00
111 Kevin Lockett/319 3.00 6.00
112 Tony Banks/186 60.00 100.00
113 Terrell Davis/269 15.00 30.00
114 Trent Green/313 4.00 8.00
115 Sylvester Morris/299 4.00 8.00
116 J.R. Redmond/272 20.00 40.00
117 Willie Jackson/282 5.00 10.00
118 Chad Pennington/507 4.00 8.00
119 Tai Streets/462 2.00 4.00

120 Matt Hasselbeck/237	25.00	50.00
121 LaMont Jordan/678	2.50	5.00
122 Quincy Morgan/811	2.00	4.00
123 Chad Johnson/331	40.00	80.00
124 Anthony Thomas/2186	2.00	4.00
125 Drew Brees/1290	25.00	50.00
126 Kevan Barlow/1724	2.00	4.00
127 Chris Chambers/1715	2.00	4.00
128 Mike McMahon/1697	2.00	4.00
129 Todd Heap/755	3.00	6.00
130 Robert Ferguson/315	10.00	20.00
131 Dan Morgan/645	2.00	4.00
132 Jesse Palmer/521	2.00	4.00
133 Travis Minor/637	3.00	6.00
134 Rudi Johnson/532	5.00	10.00
135 Rod Gardner/510	2.50	5.00
136 Snoop Minnis/837	2.00	4.00
137 Koren Robinson/482	2.50	5.00
138 Chris Weinke/875	3.00	6.00
139 James Jackson/1053	2.00	4.00
140 Michael Vick/5721	12.50	30.00
141 Marques Tuiasosopo/616	2.50	5.00
142 Michael Bennett/658	2.00	4.00
143 LaDainian Tomlinson/1536	15.00	30.00
144 Freddie Mitchell/634	2.00	4.00
145 Deuce McAllister/597	3.00	8.00
146 Quincy Carter/923	2.00	4.00
147 Santana Moss/620	4.00	8.00
148 David Terrell/638	2.00	4.00
149 Reggie Wayne/595	10.00	20.00
150 Travis Henry/1117	2.00	4.00

2001 eTopps Super Bowl XXXV Promos

Topps issued these 7-cards to promote the upcoming eTopps card releases for 2001. Each card features a 2000 NFL season award winner or starting quarterback in Super Bowl XXXV. The cards were distributed free to attendees of the 2001 NFL Experience Super Bowl Card Show in Tampa, Florida at the Topps booth one card at a time. The Super Bowl XXXV logo can be found on the cardfronts and the cardbacks feature an advertisement for eTopps cards. A Refractor parallel set was also produced with each being serial numbered of 2000-cards made.

COMPLETE SET (7)	35.00	50.00
*REFRACTORS: 1X TO 2X BASIC CARDS		
1 Marshall Faulk NFL MVP	5.00	8.00
2 Marshall Faulk Off.POY	5.00	8.00
3 Brian Urlacher	6.00	12.00
4 Mike Anderson	10.00	20.00
5 Trent Dilfer	3.00	5.00
6 Kerry Collins	3.00	5.00
7 Ray Lewis	3.00	5.00

2002 eTopps

The 2002 eTopps cards were issued via Topps' website and initially sold exclusively on eBay's eTopps Trade Floor. Owner's of the cards could hold the cards on account with Topps and freely trade those cards similar to shares of stock. They also could pay a fee to take actual delivery of their cards, but most are still held on account with Topps. Since most of these cards do not trade hands as physical cards, we've simply listed the checklist here without pricing. We've also included the announced print runs when known. Card #76 was not issued. Collectors were given a chance in 2004 to have their Tom Brady and Brian Westbrook cards held in account signed by the athletes and certified by Topps. Each signed card was certified with a Topps hologram and accompanied by a matching card certificate of authenticity. We've listed those two variations below.

ANNOUNCED PRINT RUNS BELOW

1 Tom Brady/5000	10.00	20.00
2 Jeff Garcia/1724	1.25	3.00
3 Rod Smith/4000	1.00	2.50
4 Anthony Thomas/6000	1.25	3.00
5 Chris Chambers/4000	1.50	4.00
6 Kendrell Bell/5000	1.25	3.00
7 Curtis Martin/1311	1.50	4.00
8 Eddie George/3169	1.25	3.00
9 Stephen Davis/3961	1.25	3.00
10 Edgerrin James/3773	1.50	4.00
11 Michael Vick/6000	1.25	3.00
12 Peter Warrick/1533	1.25	3.00
13 Priest Holmes/5000	1.50	4.00
14 Jake Plummer/2000	1.25	3.00
15 Jimmy Smith/1692	1.25	3.00
16 Jerry Rice/2000	2.00	5.00
17 LaDainian Tomlinson/5000	1.50	4.00
18 Keyshawn Johnson/1492	1.25	3.00
19 Shaun Alexander/2986	1.50	4.00
20 Terrell Owens/5000	1.50	4.00
21 Rod Gardner/1757	1.50	4.00
22 Donovan McNabb/5000	1.50	4.00
23 Randy Moss/3000	1.50	4.00
24 Brian Griese/2909	1.25	3.00
25 Marcus Robinson/2000	1.25	3.00
26 Jamal Lewis/3528	1.50	4.00
27 Peyton Manning/2336	6.00	15.00
28 Mike McMahon/2790	1.25	3.00
29 Rich Gannon/3166	1.25	3.00
30 Jerome Bettis/2017	1.50	4.00
31 Matt Hasselbeck/3000	1.25	3.00
32 Marshall Faulk/3554	1.50	4.00
33 Plaxico Burress/3000	1.50	4.00
34 Ricky Williams/4000	1.25	3.00
35 Jay Fiedler/4000	1.00	2.50
36 Ahman Green/3730	1.50	4.00
37 Chris Weinke/2168	1.25	3.00
38 David Boston/2000	1.00	2.50
39 Troy Brown/3410	1.25	3.00
40 Tim Brown/1739	1.50	4.00
41 Darrell Jackson/4000	1.25	3.00
42 Steve McNair/2000	1.50	4.00
43 Torry Holt/4000	1.25	3.00
44 Tiki Barber/2000	1.50	4.00
45 Brett Favre/3466	4.00	10.00
46 Corey Dillon/4000	1.50	4.00
47 Emmitt Smith/2000	3.00	8.00
48 Marvin Harrison/4000	1.50	4.00
49 Daunte Culpepper/1508	1.50	4.00
50 Kurt Warner/1114	1.50	4.00
51 Tim Couch/5735	1.25	3.00
52 Eric Moulds/2000	1.25	3.00
53 Vinny Testaverde/3000	1.25	3.00
54 Trent Green/2000	1.25	3.00
55 Kordell Stewart/1538	1.25	3.00
56 Drew Brees/5000	1.50	4.00
57 Aaron Brooks/5000	1.25	3.00
58 Mark Brunell/4000	1.00	2.50
59 Tony Gonzalez/3274	1.25	3.00
60 Doug Flutie/1000	1.50	4.00
61 David Carr/6000	1.25	3.00
62 Travis Stephens/4000	1.00	2.50
63 Patrick Ramsey/5000	1.25	3.00
64 T.J. Duckett/6000	1.25	3.00
65 Javon Walker/5000	1.25	3.00
66 DeShaun Foster/3000	1.50	4.00
67 William Green/3000	1.25	3.00
68 Ashley Lelie/5000	1.25	3.00
69 Jabar Gaffney/5000	1.25	3.00
70 Ron Johnson/3000	1.00	2.50
71 Reche Caldwell/5000	1.00	2.50
72 Daniel Graham/4000	1.25	3.00
73 Josh Reed/3765	1.25	3.00
74 Andre Davis/2000	1.25	3.00
75 Joey Harrington/8000	1.25	3.00
77 Donte Stallworth/5000	1.25	3.00
78 Rohan Davey/3000	1.25	3.00
79 Maurice Morris/4000	1.25	3.00
80 Antwaan Randle El/4000	1.50	4.00
81 Cliff Russell/3000	1.00	2.50
82 Jeremy Shockey/7000	1.25	3.00
83 Julius Peppers/6000	1.50	4.00
84 Antonio Bryant/5000	1.25	3.00
85 Clinton Portis/6000	1.50	4.00
86 Ladell Betts/2302	1.25	3.00
87 Josh McCown/2127	1.50	4.00
88 Roy Williams/5000	1.50	4.00
89 Tim Carter/3000	1.25	3.00
90 Marquise Walker/2000	1.25	3.00
91 Chad Hutchinson/5000	1.00	2.50
92 Deion Branch/5000	1.50	4.00
93 Brian Westbrook/5000	3.00	6.00
94 Jonathan Wells/5000	1.00	2.50
95 Tommy Maddox/3397	1.25	3.00
96 Deuce McAllister/2822	1.50	4.00
97 Drew Bledsoe/2000	1.50	4.00
98 Brian Urlacher/2000	1.50	4.00
99 Donald Driver/2788	1.50	4.00
100 Peerless Price/2298	1.25	3.00
101 Chad Pennington/3000	1.50	4.00
102 Randy McMichael/2220	1.25	3.00
103 Marty Booker/1309	1.25	3.00
104 Hines Ward/2112	1.50	4.00
105 Warren Sapp/1621	1.25	3.00
106 Marc Bulger/3000	1.50	4.00
107 Lavernues Coles/2285	1.25	3.00

2002 eTopps Classic

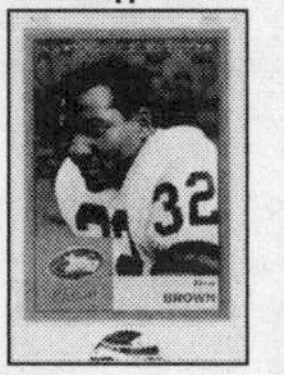

1 Barry Sanders/3000	4.00	8.00
2 Ray Nitschke/983	10.00	20.00
3 Dan Marino/3000	6.00	12.00
4 Chuck Bednarik/1291	4.00	8.00
5 Sammy Baugh/1259	5.00	10.00
6 Frank Gifford/1270	4.00	8.00
7 Terry Bradshaw/3000	4.00	8.00
7 Kellen Winslow/777	6.00	12.00
8 Jim Brown/3000	4.00	8.00
9 Jim Kelly/985	7.50	15.00
10 Y.A. Tittle/1064	5.00	10.00
11 Deacon?áJones/865	6.00	12.00
11 Fran Tarkenton/1106	6.00	12.00
12 Joe Montana/3000	10.00	20.00
13 Joe Namath/3000	4.00	8.00
14 John Elway/2422	5.00	10.00
14 Elroy Hirsch/906	5.00	10.00
15 Norm Van Brocklin/975	6.00	12.00
19 Bubba Smith/805	5.00	10.00
20 Dan Fouts/843	7.50	15.00

2002 eTopps Event Series

ES8 Marvin Harrison/952	3.00	8.00
ES6A Emmitt Smith/7184	3.00	8.00
ES6B Jerry Rice/3579	2.50	6.00

2003 eTopps

The 2003 eTopps cards were issued via Topps' website and initially sold exclusively on eBay's eTopps Trade Floor. Owner's of the cards could hold the cards on account with Topps and freely trade those cards similar to shares of stock. They also could pay a fee to take actual delivery of their cards, but most are still held on account with Topps. Since most of these cards do not trade hands as physical cards, we've simply listed the checklist here without pricing. We've also included the announced print runs when known. Collectors were given a chance in 2004 to have their Tom Brady card held in account signed and certified by Topps. Each signed card was certified with a Topps hologram and accompanied by a matching card certificate of authenticity.

ANNOUNCED PRINT RUNS BELOW

1 Aaron?áBrooks/638	2.50	5.00
2 Ahman Green/917	2.50	5.00
3 Amani Toomer/706	2.50	5.00
4 Brett Favre/1197	6.00	15.00
5 Brian Urlacher/1000	4.00	8.00
6 Brian Finneran/577	4.00	8.00
7 Chad Pennington/910	3.00	6.00
8 Clinton Portis/1495	2.50	5.00
9 Corey Dillon/1193	2.50	5.00
10 Curtis Martin/806	2.50	5.00
11 Darrell Jackson/1000	1.50	4.00
12 Jake Delhomme/1158	2.50	5.00
13 David Carr/1490	2.50	5.00
14 Derrick Mason/488	5.00	10.00
15 Deuce McAllister/772	3.00	6.00
16 Donald Driver/899	2.50	5.00
17 Donovan McNabb/812	4.00	8.00
18 Drew Bledsoe/918	2.50	5.00
19 Drew Brees/647	4.00	8.00
20 Kelly Holcomb/2565	1.25	3.00
21 Edgerrin James/920	2.50	5.00
22 Jamel White/1063	1.25	3.00
23 Hugh Douglas/578	4.00	8.00
24 Hines Ward/778	3.00	6.00
25 Jason Taylor/1012	1.50	4.00
26 Jeff Garcia/773	2.50	5.00
27 Jeremy Shockey/1763	4.00	8.00
28 Jerry Rice/1416	2.50	5.00
29 Jimmy Smith/785	1.50	4.00
30 Joe Horn/815	1.50	4.00
31 Joey Harrington/881	2.50	5.00
32 Kerry Collins/740	3.00	6.00
33 Keyshawn Johnson/1500	1.50	4.00
34 Kurt Warner/840	2.50	5.00
35 LaDainian Tomlinson/842	3.00	6.00
36 Marshall Faulk/634	5.00	10.00
37 Marty Booker/693	1.25	3.00
38 Marvin Harrison/1939	2.50	5.00
39 Michael Vick/1512	4.00	8.00
40 Peerless Price/724	1.50	4.00
41 Trent Green/1111	1.50	4.00
42 Troy Brown/1000	1.50	4.00
43 Priest Holmes/1033	2.50	5.00
44 Randy Moss/1050	3.00	6.00
45 Ray Lewis/1074	2.50	5.00
46 Rich Gannon/818	1.50	4.00
47 Ricky Williams/1052	2.50	5.00
48 Laveranues Coles/819	1.50	4.00
49 Rod Smith/951	1.25	3.00
50 Shaun Alexander/840	3.00	6.00
51 Steve McNair/1712	1.50	4.00
52 Terrell Owens/1003	2.50	5.00
53 Tiki Barber/1338	2.50	5.00
54 Champ Bailey/1072	2.50	5.00
55 Tom Brady/665	35.00	60.00
56 Tommy Maddox/772	1.50	4.00
57 Torry Holt/1069	2.50	5.00
58 Travis Henry/600	4.00	8.00
59 DeWayne Robertson/1197	1.25	3.00
60 Jerome McDougle/838	1.25	3.00
61 Andre Johnson/2551	1.50	4.00
62 Anquan Boldin/3500	1.50	4.00
63 Artose Pinner/1166	1.50	4.00
64 Bethel Johnson/1949	1.50	4.00
65 Brian St.Pierre/1511	1.25	3.00
66 Bryant Johnson/822	2.50	5.00
67 Byron Leftwich/5000	2.50	5.00
68 Carson Palmer/6000	5.00	12.00
69 Charles Rogers/2500	1.50	4.00
70 Chris Brown/1568	1.50	4.00
71 Chris Simms/1852	2.50	5.00
72 Dallas Clark/2829	4.00	10.00
73 Dave Ragone/842	1.50	4.00
74 Justin Fargas/2000	1.25	3.00
75 Kelley Washington/704	4.00	8.00
76 Kevin Curtis/785	4.00	8.00
77 Kliff Kingsbury/1000	1.50	4.00
78 Kyle Boller/3189	1.50	4.00
79 Larry Johnson/1858	3.00	8.00
80 Musa Smith/757	2.50	5.00
81 Nate Burleson/1491	1.25	3.00
82 Onterrio Smith/2000	1.50	4.00
83 Rex Grossman/3287	3.00	6.00
84 Seneca Wallace/1159	1.50	4.00
85 Taylor Jacobs/845	1.50	4.00
86 Terence Newman/1369	1.50	4.00
87 Terrell Suggs/1855	1.50	4.00
88 Teyo Johnson/1076	1.25	3.00
89 Tyrone Calico/1690	1.25	3.00
90 Willis McGahee/2000	2.50	5.00
91 Jerry Porter/1148	1.50	4.00
92 Dante Hall/2000	1.50	4.00
93 Trung Canidate/614	2.50	5.00
94 Curtis Conway/586	5.00	10.00
95 Kevin Faulk/689	4.00	8.00
96 Troy Hambrick/992	1.25	3.00
97 Domanick Davis/2000	1.50	4.00
98 Nick Barnett/955	1.50	4.00
99 Tim Rattay/880	2.50	5.00
100 Moe Williams/924	1.25	3.00
101 Correll Buckhalter/953	1.50	4.00
102 Steve Smith/765	3.00	6.00

2003 eTopps Classic

21 Lawrence Taylor/702	7.50	15.00
22 Gale Sayers/947	7.50	15.00
23 Johnny Unitas/661	12.50	25.00
24 Bo Jackson/1000	7.50	15.00
25 Walter Payton/1500	10.00	20.00
26 Phil Simms/781	10.00	20.00
27 Tony Dorsett/788	10.00	25.00
28 Steve Largent/639	7.50	15.00
29 Steve Young/592	75.00	125.00
30 Marcus Allen/722	10.00	20.00
31 Mike Singletary/953	6.00	12.00
32 Eric Dickerson/774	7.50	15.00
33 Otto Graham/547	10.00	20.00
34 Troy Aikman/587	12.50	25.00
35 Fred Biletnikoff/450	25.00	50.00
36 Jim Thorpe/785	6.00	15.00
37 Ronnie Lott/711	10.00	20.00
38 Jack Lambert/754	6.00	12.00
39 Raymond Berry/477	12.50	25.00
40 Earl Campbell/523	10.00	20.00

2003 eTopps Event Series

ES12 Jamal Lewis/938	2.00	5.00

2004 eTopps

ANNOUNCED PRINT RUNS BELOW

1 Green Bay Packers/2500	2.50	6.00
2 Chicago Bears/1495	2.00	5.00
3 New England Patriots/2500	2.50	6.00
4 Cleveland Browns/1239	1.50	4.00
5 Carolina Panthers/1668	1.50	4.00
6 New York Jets/1510	1.50	4.00
7 Baltimore Ravens/1404	1.50	4.00
8 Detroit Lions/1192	1.50	4.00
9 Buffalo Bills/952	2.00	5.00
10 Washington Redskins/1283	2.00	5.00
11 Philadelphia Eagles/1750	1.50	4.00
12 Pittsburgh Steelers/1320	5.00	12.00
13 Seattle Seahawks/1632	1.50	4.00
14 New York Giants/981	2.50	6.00
15 Houston Texans/839	2.00	5.00
16 Minnesota Vikings/1123	2.50	6.00
17 Denver Broncos/777	2.50	6.00
18 Cincinnati Bengals/751	2.00	5.00
19 Jacksonville Jaguars/908	1.50	4.00
20 Tennessee Titans/685	2.00	5.00
21 Atlanta Falcons/1750	2.50	6.00
22 Tampa Bay Buccaneers/595	2.50	6.00
23 St. Louis Rams/758	2.50	6.00
24 Arizona Cardinals/584	2.50	6.00
25 Kansas City Chiefs/826	2.00	5.00
26 Indianapolis Colts/1750	2.00	5.00
27 Oakland Raiders/663	3.00	8.00
28 Dallas Cowboys/812	3.00	8.00
29 Miami Dolphins/672	2.50	6.00
30 New Orleans Saints/591	2.50	6.00
31 San Francisco 49ers/750	3.00	8.00
32 San Diego Chargers/900	2.50	6.00
33 Rashaun Woods/1250	1.50	4.00
34 Kellen Winslow/3750	2.50	6.00
35 Ben Roethlisberger/2500	12.50	25.00
36 Marvin Harrison/1250	2.00	5.00
37 Terrell Owens/1562	2.00	5.00
38 Stephen Davis/1250	1.50	4.00
39 Daunte Culpepper/1250	2.00	5.00
40 Roy Williams WR/2500	2.50	6.00
41 Brian Westbrook/1250	1.50	4.00
42 Julius Jones/1750	2.00	5.00
43 J.P. Losman/2500	2.00	5.00
44 Eli Manning/3750	12.50	25.00
45 Reggie Williams/2276	1.50	4.00
46 Tatum Bell/1750	2.00	5.00
47 Philip Rivers/2500	6.00	12.00
48 Matt Schaub/1750	5.00	10.00
49 LaDainian Tomlinson/1250	2.50	6.00
50 Rudi Johnson/1250	1.50	4.00
51 Robert Gallery/1750	2.50	6.00
52 Keary Colbert/1669	2.00	5.00
53 Greg Jones/1481	1.50	4.00
54 Priest Holmes/1738	2.00	5.00
55 Peyton Manning/1750	5.00	10.00
56 Deuce McAllister/1211	1.50	4.00
57 Larry Fitzgerald/2500	5.00	10.00
58 Steven Jackson/1750	6.00	12.00
59 Lee Evans/1540	2.50	6.00
60 Chad Pennington/1091	2.00	5.00
61 Chad Johnson/1573	2.00	5.00
62 Randy Moss/1250	2.00	5.00
63 Michael Clayton/1446	2.50	6.00
64 Kevin Jones/1750	2.50	6.00
65 Ben Watson/1113	1.50	4.00
66 Clinton Portis/1028	2.00	5.00
67 Hines Ward/871	2.50	6.00
68 Quentin Griffin/1750	1.50	4.00
69 Boo Williams/703	2.00	5.00
70 Tom Brady/1750	7.50	15.00
71 Adam Vinatieri/1250	2.00	5.00
72 Lee Suggs/1250	1.50	4.00
73 Chris Brown/1046	1.50	4.00
74 Drew Henson/1559	1.50	4.00
75 Michael Jenkins/995	2.50	6.00
76 Darius Watts/1042	1.50	4.00
77 Chris Perry/1133	2.50	6.00
78 Donovan McNabb/1418	2.50	6.00
79 Mike Vanderjagt/688	1.50	4.00
80 Tiki Barber/839	2.50	6.00
81 Takeo Spikes/710	2.50	6.00
82 Deion Sanders/1099	2.50	6.00
83 Mewelde Moore/1250	1.50	4.00
84 Brett Favre/900	7.50	15.00
85 Lavar Arrington/900	2.00	5.00
86 Jason Elam/900	1.50	4.00
87A Reuben Droughns/1282	1.50	4.00
87B Matt Hasselbeck/900	2.00	5.00
88 Antonio Gates/1000	2.50	6.00
89 Craig Krenzel/1000	2.00	5.00

2004 eTopps Autographs

1 Tom Brady 02eTop/155	125.00	225.00
2 Tom Brady 03eTop/50		
3 Chad Pennington 01eTop/19		
4 Chad Pennington 02eTop/54		
5 Chad Pennington 03eTop/27		
6 Ben Roethlisberger 04eTop/150	150.00	250.00
7 Brian Westbrook 02eTop/143	40.00	75.00

2004 eTopps ECON Cleveland

These cards were given away to VIP attendees to the 2004 edition of The National Sports Collectors Convention in Cleveland. Each card features a famous Cleveland area athlete with The National logo at the top of the card and the eTopps and player names at the bottom.

3 Bernie Kosar/984	2.00	5.00

2004 eTopps Event Series

ES14 Peyton Manning/2844	2.00	5.00

2004 eTopps Event Series Playoffs

ES1 Marc Bulger/727	2.00	5.00
ES2 Chad Pennington/843	2.00	5.00
ES3 Peyton Manning/1500 Reggie Wayne	2.50	6.00
ES4 Daunte Culpepper/830	2.00	5.00
ES5 Jerome Bettis/1029 Duce Staley	2.00	5.00
ES6 Michael Vick/990	2.00	5.00
ES7 Donovan McNabb/892	2.00	5.00
ES8 Tom Brady/1207 Tedy Bruschi	2.50	6.00
ES9 Brian Westbrook/923 Brian Dawkins	2.00	5.00
ES10 Corey Dillon/1083	2.00	5.00
ES11 Rodney Harrison/987	2.00	5.00
ES12 Deion Branch/963	2.00	5.00

2005 eTopps

1 Michael Vick/1200	3.00	8.00
3 Alge Crumpler/690	2.50	6.00
4 Willis McGahee/885	2.50	6.00
5 Ben Roethlisberger/1200	5.00	10.00
7 T.J. Houshmandzadeh/881	2.50	6.00
8 Antonio Gates/852	3.00	8.00
9 J.P. Losman/1045	2.50	6.00
10 Shaun Alexander/893	3.00	8.00
13 Peyton Manning/1200	3.00	8.00
14 Julius Peppers/661	2.50	6.00
15 Clinton Portis/650	2.50	6.00
16 Randy Moss/1200	2.50	6.00
17 LaDainian Tomlinson/1200	2.50	6.00
18 Brett Favre/1200	6.00	12.00
19 Dunta Robinson/572	2.50	6.00
20 LaMont Jordan/660	2.50	6.00
21 Corey Dillon/591	2.00	5.00
22 Donovan McNabb/1169	2.00	5.00
23 Jason Witten/1012	2.50	6.00
24 Eli Manning/1200	2.50	6.00
25 Tony Gonzalez/638	2.50	6.00
26 Brandon Stokley/842	2.50	6.00
27 Larry Fitzgerald/684	2.50	6.00
28 Julius Jones/1200	2.00	5.00
29 Carson Palmer/1200	2.00	5.00
30 Tom Brady/1200	7.50	15.00
31 Byron Leftwich/667	2.00	5.00
32 Plaxico Burress/762	2.50	6.00
33 Brian Westbrook/786	2.50	6.00
34 Dwight Freeney/1026	2.00	5.00
35 Drew Brees/951	2.00	5.00
36 J.J. Arrington/2000	2.00	5.00
37 Cedric Benson/2000	2.00	5.00
38 Mark Bradley/1200	2.00	5.00
39 Reggie Brown/1200	2.00	5.00
40 Ronnie Brown/2000	3.00	8.00
41 Jason Campbell/1200	2.50	6.00
42 Maurice Clarett/1200	2.00	5.00
43 Mark Clayton/1200	2.00	5.00
44 Braylon Edwards/2000	3.00	8.00
45 Charlie Frye/1200	1.50	4.00
46 Frank Gore/1200	5.00	10.00
47 Vincent Jackson/1018	3.00	8.00
48 Matt Jones/1200	1.50	4.00
49 Stefan LeFors/1200	1.50	4.00
50 Heath Miller/1200	2.00	5.00
51 Ryan Moats/1158	2.00	5.00
52 Vernand Morency/1121	1.50	4.00
53 Terrence Murphy/1139	1.50	4.00
54 Kyle Orton/1200	1.50	4.00
55 Roscoe Parrish/1200	1.50	4.00
56 Courtney Roby/1200	1.50	4.00
57 Aaron Rodgers/1200	50.00	80.00
58 Mike Williams/2000	1.50	4.00
59 Eric Shelton/1200	1.50	4.00
60 Alex Smith/2400	6.00	12.00
62 Roddy White/1200	2.00	5.00
63 Cadillac Williams/2000	2.50	6.00
64 Troy Williamson/2000	1.50	4.00
67 Demarcus Ware/1127	2.50	6.00
68 Willie Parker/1200	2.00	5.00
69 Brandon Jones/599	2.50	6.00
70 Zach Thomas/600	2.00	5.00
71 Michael Strahan/741	2.00	5.00
72 Samie Parker/637	2.00	5.00
85 Mike Nugent/1200	1.50	4.00
86 Chris Henry/1067	1.50	4.00
87 David Greene/863	2.00	5.00
88 Brandon Jacobs/1200	2.50	6.00
89 Adrian McPherson/1200	1.50	4.00
TC1 Seattle Seahawks/1000	3.00	8.00
TC2 Indianapolis Colts/1000	2.50	6.00
TC3 Cincinnati Bengals/935	2.00	5.00
TC4 Chicago Bears/1000	2.00	5.00
TC5 New England Patriots/1000	2.50	6.00
TC6 Denver Broncos/947	2.00	5.00
TC7 New York Giants/881	2.00	5.00
TC8 Jacksonville Jaguars/476	3.00	8.00
TC9 Washington Redskins/604	2.50	6.00
TC10 Tampa Bay Buccaneers/647	2.50	6.00
TC11 Carolina Panthers/571	2.00	5.00
TC12 Pittsburgh Steelers/1000	3.00	8.00

2005 eTopps Autographs

BR1 Ben Roethlisberger
2004 eTopps/150
BW1 Brian Westbrook
2002 eTopps/143
CW1 Cadillac Williams
2005 eTopps/103
PM1 Peyton Manning 2000 eTopps/24
PM2 Peyton Manning 2001 eTopps/25
PM3 Peyton Manning 2002 eTopps/25
PM4 Peyton Manning 2005 eTopps/25
TB1 Tom Brady 2002 eTopps/155
TB2 Tom Brady 2003 eTopps/50

2005 eTopps Event Series

1 Brett Favre/1000	6.00	12.00
2 Peyton Manning Eli Manning/1000	4.00	8.00

2005 eTopps Classic

41 Merlin Olsen/1000	4.00	8.00
42 Joe Greene/1000	4.00	8.00
43 Roger Staubach/2000	4.00	8.00
44 Reggie White/2000	4.00	8.00
45 Alan Page/1000	4.00	8.00
46 Ed Jones/1000	4.00	8.00
47 George Blanda/1000	4.00	8.00
48 Bob Lilly/1000	4.00	8.00
49 Brian Piccolo/1000	7.50	15.00
50 Herschel Walker/1000	4.00	8.00

2006 eTopps

1 Peyton Manning/849	4.00	10.00
2 Ben Roethlisberger/999	3.00	8.00
3 Steve Smith/999	1.50	4.00
4 Carson Palmer/849	3.00	8.00
5 Larry Johnson/899	2.50	6.00
6 Michael Huff/539	40.00	80.00
7 Chad Johnson/849	2.00	5.00
8 LaDainian Tomlinson/999	3.00	8.00
9 Michael Vick/999	1.50	4.00
10 Edgerrin James/547	2.00	5.00
11 Mario Williams/717	3.00	8.00
12 Tom Brady/749	12.50	25.00
13 Eli Manning/999	3.00	8.00
14 Marcedes Lewis/749	1.50	4.00
15 Terrell Owens/749	3.00	8.00
16 Donovan McNabb/460	3.00	8.00
17 Shaun Alexander/749	1.50	4.00
18 Brett Favre/749	7.50	15.00
20 Owen Daniels/599	2.00	5.00
21 Troy Polamalu/999	2.50	6.00
22 Anthony Fasano/499	2.50	6.00
23 Brian Urlacher/715	2.00	5.00
24 A.J. Hawk/183	100.00	175.00
25 Marques Colston/999	3.00	8.00
26 Kellen Clemens/499	7.50	15.00
27 Brodie Croyle/499	7.50	15.00
28 Jay Cutler/254	90.00	150.00
29 Bruce Gradkowski/999	2.00	5.00
30 Tarvaris Jackson/599	6.00	12.00
31 Demetrius Williams/499	2.50	6.00
32 Matt Leinart/2499	6.00	12.00
33 Vernon Davis/1454	3.00	8.00
34 D.J. Shockley/499	2.50	6.00
35 Dominique Byrd/499	1.50	4.00
36 Vince Young/2499	6.00	12.00
37 Joseph Addai/1499	7.50	15.00
38 Reggie Bush/2525	7.50	15.00
39 Brian Calhoun/762	1.50	4.00
40 Bernard Berrian/700	2.00	5.00
41 Maurice Jones-Drew/1499	4.00	10.00
42 Chester Taylor/749	2.00	5.00
43 Laurence Maroney/1499	4.00	10.00
44 Jerious Norwood/1113	3.00	8.00
45 Leon Washington/313	15.00	30.00
46 LenDale White/1499	2.50	6.00
47 DeAngelo Williams/1999	2.50	6.00
48 Tony Romo/999	10.00	20.00
50 Jerricho Cotchery/699	2.00	5.00
51 Mike Bell/249	12.50	25.00
52 Maurice Stovall/499	3.00	8.00
53 Derek Hagan/749	2.00	5.00
54 D'Brickashaw Ferguson/785	2.00	5.00
55 Devin Hester/599	12.50	25.00
56 Santonio Holmes/999	3.00	8.00
57 Chad Jackson/999	2.00	5.00
58 Greg Jennings/1759	2.50	6.00
60 Sinorice Moss/999	2.00	5.00
61 Drew Brees/700	3.00	8.00
62 Shawne Merriman/749	2.50	6.00
63 Michael Robinson/499	3.00	8.00
64 Wali Lundy/799	1.50	4.00

2006 eTopps Classic

51 Vince Papale/749	5.00	10.00
52 Bronko Nagurski/999	4.00	8.00
53 Paul Hornung/849	7.50	15.00
54 Jim Plunkett/749	5.00	10.00
55 Joe Theismann/749	5.00	10.00

2006 eTopps Event Series

3 Hines Ward Jerome Bettis/1000	4.00	8.00

2006 eTopps Event Series Playoffs

1 Chicago Bears/1000	2.00	5.00
2 San Deigo Chargers/1000	2.00	5.00
3 Indianapolis Colts/799	2.00	5.00
4 Baltimore Ravens/799	2.00	5.00
5 Dallas Cowboys/999	3.00	8.00
6 New Orleans Saints/999	2.00	5.00
7 New England Patriots/899	2.50	6.00
8 Philadelphia Eagles/670	2.00	5.00
9 Seattle Seahawks/579	2.50	6.00
10 New York Jets/639	2.00	5.00
11 New York Giants/649	2.00	5.00
12 Kansas City Chiefs/599	2.50	6.00

2006 eTopps Event Series National VIP Promos

LB Matt Leinart Reggie Bush	2.00	5.00

2007 eTopps

1 Ben Roethlisberger/849	3.00	8.00
2 Peyton Manning/849	6.00	12.00
3 Randy Moss/749	6.00	12.00
4 Adrian Peterson/1999	25.00	40.00
5 Brandon Jackson/749	3.00	8.00
6 Tom Brady/749	15.00	30.00
7 Willis McGahee/749	2.00	5.00
8 Calvin Johnson/1999	3.00	8.00
9 Marshawn Lynch/999	10.00	20.00
10 Eli Manning/849	3.00	8.00
11 Thomas Jones/749	2.00	5.00
12 Anthony Gonzalez/749	3.00	8.00
13 James Jones/749	3.00	8.00
14 Brett Favre/499	30.00	50.00
15 Trent Edwards/749	7.50	15.00
16 Brian Leonard/749	2.00	5.00
17 Dwayne Bowe/2257	2.00	5.00
18 Vince Young/999	2.00	5.00
19 Greg Olsen/749	2.50	6.00
20 LaDainian Tomlinson/999	3.00	8.00
21 Reggie Bush/999	2.50	6.00
22 Sidney Rice/749	3.00	8.00
23 John Beck/749	5.00	10.00
24 Chad Johnson/749	2.00	5.00
25 Frank Gore/749	2.00	5.00
26 Selvin Young/749	5.00	10.00
27 Chris Henry/749	2.00	5.00
28 Braylon Edwards/749	2.50	6.00
29 Ted Ginn/1499	2.50	6.00
30 Wes Welker/749	2.50	6.00
31 DeShawn Wynn/749	2.00	5.00
32 Terrell Owens/499	25.00	50.00
33 Derek Anderson/749	3.00	8.00
34 Lorenzo Booker/749	2.00	5.00
35 Troy Smith/749	7.50	15.00
36 Tony Romo/999	5.00	10.00
37 Kevin Kolb/749	6.00	12.00
38 Brady Quinn/1499	6.00	12.00
39 T.J. Houshmandzadeh/749	2.00	5.00
40 Kolby Smith/749	2.50	6.00
41 Andre Hall/749	2.00	5.00
42 Brian Westbrook/749	2.50	6.00
43 JaMarcus Russell/1499	6.00	12.00
44 Zach Miller/499	7.50	15.00
45 Marion Barber/499	20.00	35.00
46 Ryan Grant/749	7.50	15.00
47 Drew Stanton/749	3.00	8.00

2007 eTopps Autographs

AF1 Anthony Fasano/2006 eTopps/49
AG1 Antonio Gates/2005 eTopps/75
AP1 Adrian Peterson/2007 eTopps/195 125.00 200.00
CP4 Chad Pennington/2004 eTopps Event Series/44
DA1 DeAngelo Williams/2006 eTopps/100
ES1 Emmitt Smith/2002 eTopps/25
ES2 Emmitt Smith/2002 eTopps Event Series/25
FG1 Frank Gore/2005 eTopps/99
GJ1 Greg Jennings/2006 eTopps/100
GS1 Gale Sayers/2003 eTopps Classic/50
JA1 Joseph Addai/2006 eTopps/100
JN1 Jerious Norwood/2006 eTopps/100
JP1 Jim Plunkett/2006 eTopps Classic/146
JT1 Joe Theismann/2006 eTopps Classic/150
LJ1 Larry Johnson/2003 eTopps/50
LT1 LaDainian Tomlinson/2001 eTopps/25 125.00 200.00
LT2 LaDainian Tomlinson/2006 eTopps/25
MC1 Marques Colston/2006 eTopps/100
MD1 Maurice Jones-Drew/2006 eTopps/100
ML1 Matt Leinart/2006 eTopps/100
MM1 Muhsin Muhammad/2006 eTopps/47
MS1 Maurice Stovall/2006 eTopps/49
PH1 Paul Hornung/2006 eTopps Classic/199
PM5 Peyton Manning/2006 eTopps/50
RB1 Reggie Bush/2006 eTopps/100 75.00 150.00
TD1 Tony Dorsett /2003 eTopps Classic/48
TD1 Terrell Davis/2001 eTopps/31
VP1 Vince Papale/2006 eTopps Classic/199
VY1 Vince Young/2006 eTopps/100
WP1 Willie Parker/2005 eTopps/50

2007 eTopps Event Series Playoffs

1 Green Bay Packers/999	3.00	6.00
2 Indianapolis Colts/999	3.00	6.00
3 New England Patriots/999	3.00	8.00
4 Dallas Cowboys/999	3.00	8.00
5 Tampa Bay Buccaneers/477	3.00	6.00
6 San Diego Chargers/586	3.00	6.00
7 Jacksonville Jaguars/590	3.00	6.00
8 Seattle Seahawks/497	3.00	6.00
9 New York Giants/641	3.00	6.00
10 Tennessee Titans/499	3.00	6.00
11 Washington Redskins/649	3.00	6.00
12 Pittsburgh Steelers/499	4.00	8.00

2008 eTopps

1 James Hardy/749		
2 Matt Forte/999		
3 Joe Flacco/999		
4 Peyton Manning/849		
5 Michael Turner/799		
6 Eddie Royal/799		
7 Jonathan Stewart/999		
8 J.T. O'Sullivan/749		
9 Felix Jones/999		
10 Tim Hightower/799		
11 Brett Favre/799		
12 Steve Slaton/749		
13 Chris Johnson/999		
14 Matt Ryan/999		
15 Matt Cassel/749		
16 Rashard Mendenhall/1319		
17 Drew Brees/699		
18 DeSean Jackson/749		
19 Kevin Smith/749		
20 Adrian Peterson/799		
21 Donnie Avery/699		
22 Steve Breaston/699		
23 Chad Pennington/499		
24 Benjarvus Green-Ellis/749	7.50	15.00
25 Jamaal Charles/699		
26 Clinton Portis/649		
27 Dustin Keller/699		
28 Brian Brohm/499		
30 Ray Rice/699		
31 Tony Romo/999		
32 Andre Johnson/686		
33 Darren McFadden/999		
34 Kevin O'Connell/499		
35 Peyton Hillis/499		
36 Kurt Warner/599		
37 Chad Henne/649		
38 John Carlson/599		
39 Davone Bess/699		
40 Tashard Choice/499		
41 New York Giants/999		
42 Tennessee Titans/749		
43 Pittsburgh Steelers/999		
44 Arizona Cardinals/699		
45 Indianapolis Colts/964		
46 Carolina Panthers/749		
47 Atlanta Falcons/699		
48 San Diego Chargers/599		
49 Philadelphia Eagles/694		
50 Miami Dolphins/681		
51 Minnesota Vikings/599		
52 Baltimore Ravens/699		
53 Colt Brennan/699		
54 John David Booty/699		

2008 eTopps Allen and Ginter Super Bowl Champions

1 Terry Bradshaw/749
2 John Elway/999
3 Joe Montana/999
4 Tom Brady/999
5 Troy Aikman/999
6 Joe Namath/999

2008 eTopps Allen and Ginter Yankee Tribute

5 Johnny Unitas/1499 *	4.00	10.00

2009 eTopps

1 Drew Brees/999		
2 Chris Wells/749		
3 Matthew Stafford/999		
4 Brett Favre/999		
5 Percy Harvin/999		
6 Johnny Knox/749		
7 Randy Moss/749		
8 Peyton Manning/849		
9 Ben Roethlisberger/849		
10 Knowshon Moreno/749		
11 Glen Coffee/749		
12 Tom Brady/749		
13 Steve Smith/749		
14 Austin Collie/749		
15 Kenny Britt/749		
16 Josh Johnson/749		
17 Adrian Peterson/999		
18 Hakeem Nicks/749		
19 Mike Wallace/749		
20 Shonn Greene/749		
21 Miles Austin/749		
22 Kyle Orton/749		
23 Mark Sanchez/999		
24 Chris Johnson/749		
25 Jeremy Maclin/749		
26 LeSean McCoy/749		
27 Cedric Benson/749		
28 Mohamed Massaquoi/749		
29 Josh Freeman/799		
30 Reggie Wayne/749		
31 Maurice Jones-Drew/749		
32 Jason Snelling/669		
33 Bernard Scott/729		
34 Chris Jennings/609		
35 Aaron Rodgers/649	6.00	12.00
36 Terrell Owens/599		
37 Michael Crabtree/749		
38 Donald Brown/699		
39 Louis Murphy/699		
40 Chad Ochocinco/599		
41 Indianapolis Colts/749		
42 New Orleans Saints/749		
43 Minnesota Vikings/749		
44 Tony Romo/749		
45 San Diego Chargers/749		
46 Arizona Cardinals/599		
47 Philadelphia Eagles/659		
48 Jared Allen/649		
49 Cincinnati Bengals/539		
50 New England Patriots/749		
51 Dallas Cowboys/749		
52 Green Bay Packers/749		
53 New York Jets/499		
54 Baltimore Ravens/509		
55 Julian Edelman/649		

2009 eTopps Allen and Ginter Super Bowl Champions

7 Brett Favre/999
8 Tom Landry/749
9 Emmitt Smith/999
10 Walter Payton/999
11 Jerry Rice/999
12 Peyton Manning/999
13 Roger Staubach/999
14 Tony Dorsett/999
15 Lawrence Taylor/999

1997 E-X2000

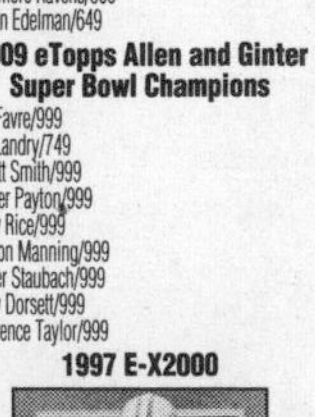

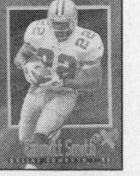

This 60-card, hobby-exclusive set features color action player images with a die-cut holofoil border and wet-look laminate. The player is silhouetted in front of a transparent window displaying a variety of sky patterns. The backs carry a modified mirror image of the front with 1996 season and career statistics.

COMPLETE SET (60)	12.50	30.00
1 Jake Plummer RC	4.00	10.00
2 Jamal Anderson	.60	1.50
3 Rae Carruth RC	.25	.60
4 Kerry Collins	.60	1.50
5 Darnell Autry RC	.60	1.50
6 Rashaan Salaam	.25	.60
7 Troy Aikman	1.25	3.00
8 Deion Sanders	.60	1.50
9 Emmitt Smith	2.00	5.00
10 Herman Moore	.40	1.00
11 Barry Sanders	2.00	5.00
12 Mark Chmura	.40	1.00
13 Brett Favre	2.50	6.00
14 Antonio Freeman	.60	1.50
15 Reggie White	.60	1.50
16 Cris Carter	.60	1.50
17 Brad Johnson	.60	1.50
18 Troy Davis RC	.40	1.00
19 Danny Wuerffel RC	.60	1.50
20 Dave Brown	.25	.60
21 Ike Hilliard RC	1.25	3.00
22 Ty Detmer	.40	1.00
23 Ricky Watters	.40	1.00
24 Tony Banks	.40	1.00
25 Eddie Kennison	.40	1.00
26 Jim Druckenmiller RC	.40	1.00
27 Jerry Rice	1.25	3.00
28 Steve Young	.75	2.00
29 Trent Dilfer	.60	1.50
30 Warrick Dunn RC	3.00	8.00
31 Terry Allen	.60	1.50
32 Gus Frerotte	.25	.60
33 Vinny Testaverde	.40	1.00
34 Antowain Smith RC	2.50	6.00
35 Thurman Thomas	.60	1.50
36 Jeff Blake	.40	1.00
37 Carl Pickens	.40	1.00
38 Terrell Davis	.75	2.00
39 John Elway	2.50	6.00
40 Eddie George	.60	1.50
41 Steve McNair	.75	2.00
42 Marshall Faulk	.75	2.00
43 Marvin Harrison	.60	1.50
44 Mark Brunell	.75	2.00
45 Marcus Allen	.60	1.50
46 Elvis Grbac	.40	1.00
47 Karim Abdul-Jabbar	.40	1.00
48 Dan Marino	2.50	6.00
49 Drew Bledsoe	.75	2.00
50 Terry Glenn	.60	1.50
51 Curtis Martin	.75	2.00
52 Keyshawn Johnson	.60	1.50
53 Tim Brown	.60	1.50
54 Jeff George	.40	1.00
55 Jerome Bettis	.60	1.50
56 Kordell Stewart	.60	1.50
57 Stan Humphries	.40	1.00
58 Junior Seau	.60	1.50
59 Joey Galloway	.40	1.00
60 Chris Warren	.40	1.00

1997 E-X2000 Essential Credentials

*STARS: 8X TO 20X BASIC CARDS
*RCs: 2.5X TO 6X BASIC CARDS
STATED PRINT RUN 100 SERIAL #'d SETS

1997 E-X2000 A Cut Above

STATED ODDS 1:288

1 Barry Sanders	20.00	50.00
2 Brett Favre	25.00	60.00
3 Dan Marino	25.00	60.00
4 Eddie George	6.00	15.00
5 Emmitt Smith	20.00	50.00
6 Jerry Rice	15.00	40.00
7 Joey Galloway	5.00	12.00
8 John Elway	20.00	50.00
9 Mark Brunell	6.00	15.00
10 Terrell Davis	10.00	25.00

1997 E-X2000 Fleet of Foot

COMPLETE SET (20)	40.00	100.00
STATED ODDS 1:20		
1 Antonio Freeman	2.50	6.00
2 Barry Sanders	8.00	20.00
3 Carl Pickens	1.50	4.00
4 Chris Warren	1.50	4.00
5 Curtis Martin	3.00	8.00
6 Deion Sanders	2.50	6.00
7 Emmitt Smith	8.00	20.00
8 Jerry Rice	5.00	12.00
9 Joey Galloway	1.50	4.00
10 Karim Abdul-Jabbar	1.50	4.00
11 Kordell Stewart	2.50	6.00
12 Lawrence Phillips	1.00	2.50
13 Mark Brunell	3.00	8.00
14 Marvin Harrison	2.50	6.00
15 Rae Carruth	1.00	2.50
16 Ricky Watters	1.50	4.00
17 Steve Young	3.00	8.00
18 Terrell Davis	3.00	8.00
19 Terry Glenn	2.50	6.00
20 Shawn Springs	1.50	4.00

1997 E-X2000 Star Date 2000

COMPLETE SET (15)	15.00	40.00
STATED ODDS 1:9		
1 Curtis Martin	1.25	3.00
2 Darnell Autry	.75	2.00
3 Darrell Russell	.50	1.25
4 Eddie Kennison	.75	2.00
5 Jim Druckenmiller	.75	2.00
6 Karim Abdul-Jabbar	1.25	3.00
7 Kerry Collins	.75	2.00
8 Keyshawn Johnson	1.25	3.00
9 Marvin Harrison	1.25	3.00
10 Orlando Pace	1.25	3.00
11 Pat Barnes	1.25	3.00
12 Reidel Anthony	.75	2.00
13 Tim Biakabutuka	.75	2.00
14 Warrick Dunn	2.00	5.00
15 Yatil Green	.75	2.00

1998 E-X2001

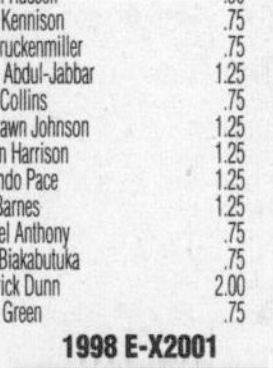

The 1998 SkyBox E-X2001 hobby only set was issued in one series totalling 60 cards and was distributed in two-card packs with a suggested retail price of $3.99. The set features color action player images printed with holographic and gold-foil stamping and player-specific die-cuts mounted on durable, see-thru plastic stock. Two parallel versions of this set were also produced: Essential Credentials Now with a holofoil gold background and each card sequentially numbered according to the player's card number in the basic set; Essential Credentials Future with a holofoil rose colored background and each card sequentially numbered to the opposite of the player's card number in the basic set.

COMPLETE SET (60)	20.00	50.00
1 Kordell Stewart	.20	.50
2 Steve Young	.60	1.50
3 Mark Brunell	.30	.75
4 Brett Favre	2.00	5.00
5 Barry Sanders	1.50	4.00
6 Warrick Dunn	.30	.75
7 Jerry Rice	1.00	2.50
8 Dan Marino	2.00	5.00
9 Emmitt Smith	1.50	4.00
10 John Elway	2.00	5.00
11 Eddie George	.30	.75
12 Jake Plummer	.30	.75
13 Terrell Davis	.30	.75
14 Curtis Martin	.30	.75
15 Troy Aikman	1.00	2.50
16 Terry Glenn	.20	.50
17 Mike Alstott	.30	.75
18 Drew Bledsoe	.30	.75
19 Keyshawn Johnson	.30	.75
20 Dorsey Levens	.20	.50
21 Elvis Grbac	.20	.50
22 Ricky Watters	.20	.50
23 Robert Smith	.20	.50
24 Trent Dilfer	.30	.75
25 Joey Galloway	.20	.50
26 Rob Moore	.20	.50
27 Steve McNair	.30	.75
28 Jim Harbaugh	.20	.50
29 Troy Davis	.10	.30
30 Rob Johnson	.20	.50
31 Shannon Sharpe	.30	.75
32 Jerome Bettis	.30	.75
33 Tim Brown	.30	.75
34 Kerry Collins	.20	.50
35 Garrison Hearst	.20	.50
36 Antonio Freeman	.30	.75
37 Charlie Garner	.20	.50
38 Glenn Foley	.10	.30
39 Yatil Green	.10	.30
40 Tiki Barber	.30	.75
41 Bobby Hoying	.20	.50
42 Corey Dillon	.20	.50
43 Antowain Smith	.20	.50
44 Robert Edwards RC	1.00	2.50
45 Jammi German RC	.60	1.50
46 Ahman Green RC	2.50	6.00
47 Hines Ward RC	5.00	10.00
48 Skip Hicks RC	1.00	2.50
49 Brian Griese RC	2.50	6.00
50 Charlie Batch RC	1.25	3.00
51 Jacquez Green RC	1.00	2.50
52 John Avery RC	1.00	2.50
53 Kevin Dyson RC	1.25	3.00
54 Peyton Manning RC	12.50	25.00
55 Randy Moss RC	6.00	15.00
56 Ryan Leaf RC	1.25	3.00
57 Curtis Enis RC	.60	1.50
58 Charles Woodson RC	1.50	4.00
59 Robert Holcombe RC	1.00	2.50
60 Fred Taylor RC	2.00	5.00
NNO Checklist Card 1	.10	.30
NNO Jake Plummer PROMO	.40	1.00
NNO Checklist Card 2	.10	.30

1998 E-X2001 Essential Credentials Future

*FUTURE/50-60: 25X TO 60X BASIC CARDS
*FUTURE/40-49: 40X TO 100X BASIC CARDS
*FUTURE/30-39: 50X TO 120X BASIC CARDS
*FUTURE/20-29: 60X TO 150X BASIC CARDS
*VETS FUT/10-19: 80X TO 200X BASIC CARDS
*ROOKIES FUT/10-19: 15X TO 40X BASIC RC
STATED PRINT RUN 1-60

1998 E-X2001 Essential Credentials Now

*ROOKIES NOW/50-60: 4X TO 10X BASIC RC
*ROOKIES NOW/44-49: 5X TO 12X BASIC RC
*VETS NOW/40-43: 40X TO 100X BASIC CARDS
*NOW/30-39: 50X TO 120X BASIC CARDS
*NOW/20-29: 60X TO 150X BASIC CARDS
*NOW/11-19: 80X TO 200X BASIC CARDS
STATED PRINT RUN 1-60

15 Troy Aikman/15	150.00	300.00
54 Peyton Manning/54	200.00	400.00

1998 E-X2001 Destination Honolulu

STATED ODDS 1:720 HOBBY

1 Peyton Manning	40.00	100.00
2 Terrell Davis	8.00	20.00
3 Corey Dillon	6.00	15.00
4 Eddie George	8.00	20.00
5 Emmitt Smith	30.00	80.00
6 Warrick Dunn	8.00	20.00
7 Brett Favre	40.00	100.00
8 Antowain Smith	6.00	15.00
9 Barry Sanders	30.00	80.00
10 Ryan Leaf	6.00	15.00

1998 E-X2001 Helmet Heroes

COMPLETE SET (20)	60.00	120.00
STATED ODDS 1:24 HOBBY		
1 Barry Sanders	5.00	12.00
2 Emmitt Smith	5.00	12.00
3 Brett Favre	6.00	15.00
4 Mark Brunell	1.00	2.50
5 Jerry Rice	3.00	8.00
6 Steve Young	2.00	5.00
7 Warrick Dunn	1.00	2.50
8 Kordell Stewart	1.00	2.50
9 John Elway	6.00	15.00
10 Troy Aikman	3.00	8.00
11 Dan Marino	6.00	15.00
12 Curtis Martin	1.00	2.50
13 Dorsey Levens	1.00	2.50
14 Jake Plummer	1.00	2.50
15 Corey Dillon	1.00	2.50
16 Yancey Thigpen	.60	1.50
17 Randy Moss	5.00	12.00
18 Curtis Enis	.50	1.25
19 Charles Woodson	1.25	3.00
20 Fred Taylor	1.50	4.00

1998 E-X2001 Star Date 2001

COMPLETE SET (15)	15.00	40.00
STATED ODDS 1:12 HOBBY		
1 Randy Moss	5.00	12.00
2 Fred Taylor	1.50	4.00
3 Corey Dillon	.60	1.50
4 Jake Plummer	.60	1.50
5 Antowain Smith	.60	1.50
6 Wilmont Perry	.25	.60
7 Donald Hayes	.25	.60
8 Tavian Banks	2.50	6.00
9 John Dutton	.25	.60
10 Kevin Dyson	1.00	2.50
11 Germane Crowell	.40	1.00
12 Bobby Hoying	.40	1.00
13 Jerome Pathon	1.00	2.50
14 Ryan Leaf	1.00	2.50
15 Peyton Manning	10.00	20.00

1999 E-X Century

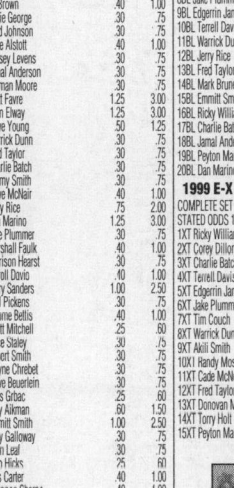

This 90 card set is done on a thick transparent card stock with a color action shot of each player. Key rookies include Tim Couch, Edgerrin James, and Ricky Williams. Also randomly inserted in packs at a rate of 1 in 68 packs is the cross brand autographics insert set which features hand signed autographed cards of stars and rookies.

COMPLETE SET (90)	50.00	120.00
COMP.SET w/o SP's (60)	20.00	40.00
1 Keyshawn Johnson	.30	.75
2 Natrone Means	.30	.75
3 Antonio Freeman	.30	.75
4 Muhsin Muhammad	.30	.75
5 Curtis Martin	.40	1.00
6 Chris Chandler	.30	.75
7 Priest Holmes	.40	1.00
8 Vinny Testaverde	.30	.75
9 Tim Brown	.40	1.00
10 Eddie George	.30	.75
11 Brad Johnson	.30	.75
12 Mike Alstott	.40	1.00
13 Dorsey Levens	.30	.75
14 Jamal Anderson	.30	.75
15 Herman Moore	.30	.75
16 Brett Favre	1.25	3.00
17 John Elway	1.25	3.00
18 Steve Young	.50	1.25
19 Warrick Dunn	.30	.75
20 Fred Taylor	.30	.75
21 Charlie Batch	.30	.75
22 Jimmy Smith	.30	.75
23 Steve McNair	.40	1.00
24 Jerry Rice	.75	2.00
25 Dan Marino	1.25	3.00
26 Jake Plummer	.30	.75
27 Marshall Faulk	.40	1.00
28 Garrison Hearst	.30	.75
29 Terrell Davis	.40	1.00
30 Barry Sanders	1.00	2.50
31 Carl Pickens	.30	.75
32 Jerome Bettis	.40	1.00
33 Scott Mitchell	.25	.60
34 Duce Staley	.30	.75
35 Robert Smith	.30	.75
36 Wayne Chrebet	.30	.75
37 Steve Beuerlein	.30	.75
38 Elvis Grbac	.25	.60
39 Troy Aikman	.60	1.50
40 Emmitt Smith	1.00	2.50
41 Joey Galloway	.30	.75
42 Ryan Leaf	.30	.75
43 Skip Hicks	.25	.60
44 Cris Carter	.40	1.00
45 Shannon Sharpe	.40	1.00
46 Mark Brunell	.30	.75
47 Kerry Collins	.30	.75
48 Corey Dillon	.30	.75
49 Kordell Stewart	.30	.75
50 Randy Moss	.40	1.00
51 Jon Kitna	.30	.75
52 Deion Sanders	.40	1.00
53 Rod Smith	.30	.75
54 Drew Bledsoe	.40	1.00
55 Terrell Owens	.40	1.00
56 Napoleon Kaufman	.25	.60
57 Trent Green	.30	.75
58 Ricky Watters	.30	.75
59 Randall Cunningham	.40	1.00
60 Peyton Manning	1.25	3.00
61 Tim Couch RC	1.50	4.00
62 Amos Zereoue RC	1.25	3.00
63 Cade McNown RC	1.25	3.00
64 Donovan McNabb RC	4.00	10.00
65 Ricky Williams RC	2.50	6.00
66 Daunte Culpepper RC	1.50	4.00
67 Troy Edwards RC	1.25	3.00
68 Peerless Price RC	1.25	3.00
69 Edgerrin James RC	2.00	5.00
70 Champ Bailey RC	3.00	8.00
71 Akili Smith RC	1.25	3.00
72 Kevin Johnson RC	1.25	3.00
73 Cecil Collins RC	1.00	2.50
74 David Boston RC	1.25	3.00
75 Torry Holt RC	2.50	6.00
76 James Johnson RC	1.00	2.50
77 Na Brown RC	1.00	2.50
78 Rob Konrad RC	1.00	2.50
79 Mike Cloud RC	1.00	2.50
80 Craig Yeast RC	1.00	2.50
81 Brock Huard RC	1.25	3.00
82 Chris McAlister RC	1.25	3.00
83 Shaun King RC	1.25	3.00
84 Wane McGarity RC	1.00	2.50
85 Joe Germaine RC	1.25	3.00
86 D'Wayne Bates RC	1.00	2.50
87 Kevin Faulk RC	1.50	4.00
88 Antoine Winfield RC	1.00	2.50
89 Reginald Kelly RC	1.00	2.50
90 Antuan Edwards RC	1.00	2.50
P1 Jake Plummer Promo	.40	1.00

1999 E-X Century Essential Credentials Future

*VETS/70-90: 8X TO 20X BASIC CARDS
*VETS/45-69: 12X TO 30X
*VETS/31-44: 20X TO 50X
*ROOKIES/20-30: 5X TO 10X
*ROOKIES/10-19: 6X TO 12X
STATED PRINT RUN 1-90

1999 E-X Century Essential Credentials Now

*ROOKIES/70-90: 2X TO 5X BASIC CARDS
*VETS/45-69: 12X TO 30X BASIC CARDS
*ROOKIES/45-69: 2.5X TO 6X
*VETS/30-44: 20X TO 50X
*VETS/20-29: 25X TO 60X
*VETS/10-19: 30X TO 80X
STATED PRINT RUN 1-90
CARDS #'d UNDER 10 NOT PRICED

1999 E-X Century Authen-Kicks

1AK Travis McGriff/235	6.00	15.00
2AK Trent Green/190	12.50	30.00
3AK Brock Huard/280	6.00	15.00
4AK Randall Cunningham/290	15.00	40.00
5AK Donovan McNabb/210	30.00	60.00
6AK Torry Holt/285	15.00	40.00
7AK Joe Germaine/280	6.00	15.00
8AK Cade McNown/260	6.00	15.00
9AK Doug Flutie/215	12.50	30.00
10AK O.J. McDuffie/285	6.00	15.00
11AK Ricky Williams/215	12.50	30.00
12AK Dan Marino/285	40.00	80.00

1999 E-X Century Bright Lights

COMPLETE SET (20)	50.00	120.00
STATED ODDS 1:24		
*ORANGE CARDS: 1.2X TO 3X GREENS		
1BL Randy Moss	5.00	12.00
2BL Tim Couch	2.00	5.00
3BL Eddie George	2.00	5.00
4BL Brett Favre	6.00	15.00
5BL Steve Young	2.50	6.00
6BL Barry Sanders	6.00	15.00
7BL Troy Aikman	4.00	10.00
8BL Jake Plummer	1.25	3.00
9BL Edgerrin James	5.00	12.00
10BL Terrell Davis	2.00	5.00
11BL Warrick Dunn	2.00	5.00
12BL Jerry Rice	4.00	10.00
13BL Fred Taylor	2.00	5.00
14BL Mark Brunell	2.00	5.00
15BL Emmitt Smith	4.00	10.00
16BL Ricky Williams	2.50	6.00
17BL Charlie Batch	2.00	5.00
18BL Jamal Anderson	2.00	5.00
19BL Peyton Manning	6.00	15.00
20BL Dan Marino	6.00	15.00

1999 E-X Century E-Xtraordinary

COMPLETE SET (15)	40.00	80.00
STATED ODDS 1:9		
1XT Ricky Williams	1.25	3.00
2XT Corey Dillon	1.00	2.50
3XT Charlie Batch	1.00	2.50
4XT Terrell Davis	1.00	2.50
5XT Edgerrin James	2.50	6.00
6XT Jake Plummer	.60	1.50
7XT Tim Couch	.75	2.00
8XT Warrick Dunn	1.00	2.50
9XT Akili Smith	.60	1.50
10XT Randy Moss	2.50	6.00
11XT Cade McNown	.60	1.50
12XT Fred Taylor	1.00	2.50
13XT Donovan McNabb	3.00	8.00
14XT Torry Holt	2.00	5.00
15XT Peyton Manning	3.00	8.00

2000 E-X

Released in early October 2000, E-X features a 150-card base set comprised of 100 veteran cards and 50 short-printed rookie cards, each sequentially numbered to 1500. Base cards are holographic foil board and showcase full-color action photography. E-X was packaged in 24-pack boxes with each pack containing five cards and carried a suggested retail price of $4.99.

COMPLETE SET (150)	100.00	200.00
COMP.SET w/o RC's (100)	6.00	15.00
1 Tim Couch	.20	.50
2 Daunte Culpepper	.20	.50
3 Jake Reed	.20	.50
4 Donovan McNabb	.25	.60
5 Terry Glenn	.20	.50
6 Vinny Testaverde	.20	.50
7 Michael Westbrook	.15	.40
8 Errict Rhett	.20	.50
9 Joey Galloway	.20	.50
10 O.J. McDuffie	.20	.50
11 Rob Johnson	.20	.50
12 Warren Sapp	.20	.50
13 Brian Griese	.20	.50
14 Derrick Mayes	.15	.40
15 Ike Hilliard	.20	.50
16 Kevin Dyson	.20	.50
17 Shannon Sharpe	.25	.60
18 Cade McNown	.15	.40
19 Damon Huard	.20	.50
20 James Stewart	.15	.40
21 Kevin Johnson	.15	.40
22 Muhsin Muhammad	.20	.50
23 Shaun King	.15	.40
24 Corey Dillon	.20	.50
25 Fred Taylor	.25	.60
26 Peyton Manning	.60	1.50
27 Steve McNair	.25	.60
28 Tim Brown	.25	.60
29 Brad Johnson	.20	.50
30 Edgerrin James	.25	.60
31 Germane Crowell	.15	.40
32 Kordell Stewart	.20	.50
33 Randy Moss	.25	.60
34 Tony Banks	.15	.40
35 Akili Smith	.15	.40
36 Charlie Batch	.20	.50
37 Duce Staley	.20	.50
38 Jerome Bettis	.25	.60
39 Rich Gannon	.20	.50
40 Steve Young	.30	.75
41 Tony Gonzalez	.25	.60
42 Curtis Martin	.25	.60
43 Eddie George	.20	.50
44 Marshall Faulk	.25	.60
45 Troy Edwards	.15	.40
46 Curtis Enis	.15	.40
47 Jake Plummer	.20	.50
48 Jon Kitna	.20	.50
49 Qadry Ismail	.20	.50
50 Terrell Davis	.25	.60
51 Troy Aikman	.40	1.00
52 Elvis Grbac	.15	.40
53 Jeff Blake	.20	.50
54 Kurt Warner	.40	1.00
55 Ricky Watters	.20	.50
56 Torry Holt	.25	.60
57 Brett Favre	.75	2.00
58 Chris Chandler	.20	.50
59 Eric Moulds	.20	.50
60 Jimmy Smith	.20	.50
61 Ricky Williams	.25	.60
62 Antonio Freeman	.20	.50
63 Curtis Conway	.20	.50
64 Emmitt Smith	.60	1.50
65 Kerry Collins	.20	.50
66 Marvin Harrison	.25	.60
67 Tyrone Wheatley	.15	.40
68 Charlie Garner	.20	.50
69 Derrick Alexander	.15	.40
70 Jamal Anderson	.20	.50
71 Mike Alstott	.25	.60
72 Ryan Leaf	.20	.50
73 Tim Biakabutuka	.20	.50
74 Amani Toomer	.20	.50
75 Dorsey Levens	.20	.50
76 Frank Sanders	.15	.40
77 Junior Seau	.25	.60
78 Steve Beuerlein	.20	.50
79 Wayne Chrebet	.20	.50
80 Carl Pickens	.20	.50
81 Drew Bledsoe	.25	.60
82 Isaac Bruce	.25	.60
83 Marcus Robinson	.20	.50
84 Stephen Davis	.20	.50
85 Cris Carter	.25	.60
86 Ed McCaffrey	.20	.50
87 Jerry Rice	.50	1.25
88 Mark Brunell	.20	.50
89 Peerless Price	.20	.50
90 Terance Mathis	.15	.40
91 Tony Martin	.20	.50
92 Jevon Kearse	.20	.50
93 Robert Smith	.20	.50
94 Rob Moore	.15	.40
95 Charles Johnson	.15	.40
96 Doug Flutie	.25	.60
97 Sean Dawkins	.15	.40
98 Keenan McCardell	.20	.50
99 Bill Schroeder	.20	.50
100 Rod Smith	.20	.50
101 Peter Warrick RC	2.50	6.00
102 Corey Simon RC	2.00	5.00
103 Danny Farmer RC	1.50	4.00
104 Jamal Lewis RC	2.50	6.00
105 Jerry Porter RC	2.50	6.00
106 Joe Hamilton RC	1.50	4.00
107 Marc Bulger RC	2.50	6.00
108 R.Jay Soward RC	1.50	4.00
109 Ron Dugans RC	1.50	4.00
110 Shaun Alexander RC	3.00	8.00
111 Travis Prentice RC	2.00	5.00
112 Anthony Becht RC	2.00	5.00
113 Bubba Franks RC	2.50	6.00
114 Chris Redman RC	2.00	5.00
115 Dennis Northcutt RC	2.00	5.00
116 Dez White RC	2.00	5.00
117 Gari Scott RC	1.50	4.00
118 Mareno Philyaw RC	1.50	4.00
119 Ron Dayne RC	2.50	6.00
120 Shyrone Stith RC	1.50	4.00
121 Tee Martin RC	2.50	6.00
122 Tom Brady RC	100.00	175.00
123 Trung Canidate RC	2.00	5.00
124 Chad Pennington RC	4.00	10.00
125 Chris Cole RC	2.00	5.00
126 Courtney Brown RC	2.00	5.00
127 Doug Chapman RC	1.50	4.00
128 Giovanni Carmazzi RC	1.50	4.00
129 J.R. Redmond RC	1.50	4.00
130 Michael Wiley RC	1.50	4.00
131 Reuben Droughns RC	2.50	6.00
132 Terrelle Smith RC	1.50	4.00
133 Thomas Jones RC	3.00	8.00
134 Travis Taylor RC	2.00	5.00
135 Anthony Lucas RC	1.50	4.00
136 Curtis Keaton RC	1.50	4.00
137 Frank Moreau RC	1.50	4.00
138 Darrell Jackson RC	2.00	5.00
139 Laveranues Coles RC	2.50	6.00
140 Brian Urlacher RC	10.00	25.00
141 Plaxico Burress RC	2.50	6.00
142 Sammy Morris RC	2.00	5.00
143 Sylvester Morris RC	1.50	4.00
144 Tim Rattay RC	2.00	5.00
145 Todd Pinkston RC	1.50	4.00
146 Troy Walters RC	1.50	4.00
147 Sebastian Janikowski RC	2.50	6.00
148 JaJuan Dawson RC	1.50	4.00
149 Trevor Gaylor RC	1.50	4.00
150 Rondell Mealey RC	1.50	4.00

2000 E-X Essential Credentials

*VETS 1-100: 10X TO 25X BASIC CARDS
1-100 VETERAN PRINT RUN 50
*ROOKIES 101-150: 1.5X TO 4X
101-150 ROOKIE PRINT RUN 25

122 Tom Brady	800.00	1,200.00

2000 E-X E-Xceptional Red

COMPLETE SET (15)	10.00	25.00
STATED ODDS 1:12		
*GREEN: 2X TO 5X BASIC INSERTS		
GREEN STATED ODDS 1:288		
*BLUE/100: 3X TO 8X BASIC INSERTS		
BLUE PRINT RUN 100 SER.#'d SETS		
1 Kurt Warner	1.00	2.50
2 Peyton Manning	1.50	4.00
3 Brett Favre	2.00	5.00
4 Tim Couch	.50	1.25
5 Keyshawn Johnson	.50	1.25
6 Mark Brunell	.50	1.25
7 Eddie George	.50	1.25
8 Edgerrin James	.60	1.50
9 Ricky Williams	.60	1.50
10 Randy Moss	.60	1.50
11 Jamal Lewis	.60	1.50
12 Emmitt Smith	1.50	4.00
13 Thomas Jones	.75	2.00
14 Fred Taylor	.60	1.50
15 Chad Pennington	1.00	2.50

2000 E-X E-Xciting

COMPLETE SET (10)	12.00	30.00
STATED ODDS 1:24		
1 Fred Taylor	1.00	2.50
2 Troy Aikman	1.50	4.00
3 Edgerrin James	1.00	2.50
4 Brett Favre	3.00	8.00
5 Peyton Manning	2.50	6.00
6 Emmitt Smith	2.50	6.00
7 Randy Moss	1.00	2.50
8 Kurt Warner	1.50	4.00
9 Marshall Faulk	1.00	2.50
10 Peter Warrick	1.00	2.50

2000 E-X E-Xplosive

COMPLETE SET (20)	12.00	30.00
STATED ODDS 1:8		
1 Kurt Warner	1.00	2.50
2 Marvin Harrison	.60	1.50
3 Ricky Williams	.60	1.50
4 Eddie George	.50	1.25
5 Emmitt Smith	1.50	4.00
6 Troy Aikman	1.00	2.50
7 Randy Moss	.60	1.50
8 Edgerrin James	.60	1.50
9 Keyshawn Johnson	.50	1.25
10 Tim Couch	.50	1.25
11 Fred Taylor	.60	1.50
12 Brett Favre	2.00	5.00
13 Peyton Manning	1.50	4.00
14 Donovan McNabb	.60	1.50
15 Ron Dayne	.60	1.50
16 Jake Plummer	.50	1.25
17 Marshall Faulk	.60	1.50
18 Travis Taylor	.50	1.25
19 Terrell Davis	.60	1.50
20 Shaun Alexander	.75	2.00

2000 E-X Generation E-X

COMPLETE SET (15)	5.00	12.00
STATED ODDS 1:4		
1 Peter Warrick	.30	.75
2 Plaxico Burress	.30	.75
3 R.Jay Soward	.20	.50
4 Shaun Alexander	.40	1.00
5 Chad Pennington	.50	1.25
6 Giovanni Carmazzi	.20	.50
7 Thomas Jones	.40	1.00
8 Todd Pinkston	.20	.50
9 Chris Redman	.25	.60
10 Jamal Lewis	.30	.75
11 Ron Dayne	.30	.75
12 Dez White	.25	.60
13 J.R. Redmond	.20	.50
14 Sylvester Morris	.20	.50
15 Travis Taylor	.25	.60

2000 E-X NFL Debut Postmarks

COMPLETE SET (15)	75.00	150.00
STATED ODDS 1:288		
1 Peter Warrick	4.00	10.00
2 Travis Taylor	3.00	8.00
3 Thomas Jones	5.00	12.00
4 Ron Dayne	4.00	10.00
5 Plaxico Burress	4.00	10.00
6 Sylvester Morris	2.50	6.00
7 Todd Pinkston	2.50	6.00
8 Jamal Lewis	4.00	10.00
9 Shaun Alexander	5.00	12.00
10 J.R. Redmond	2.50	6.00
11 Dennis Northcutt	3.00	8.00
12 Bubba Franks	4.00	10.00
13 R.Jay Soward	2.50	6.00
14 Jerry Porter	4.00	10.00
15 Chad Pennington	6.00	15.00

2001 E-X

This 140 card set was issued in four card packs which were packed 24 to a box. Cards numbered 91 through 140 featured rookies and were randomly inserted in packs. These cards were printed in quantities between 1000 and 1500 copies and most of the rookies featured signed some of the Rookie Cards.

COMP.SET w/o RC's (90)	10.00	25.00
91-140 ROOKIE PRINT RUN 1000-1500		
1 Jamal Anderson	.25	.60
2 Tim Couch	.20	.50
3 Jeff Garcia	.25	.60
4 Brett Favre	1.00	2.50
5 Donovan McNabb	.30	.75
6 Kerry Collins	.25	.60
7 Doug Flutie	.30	.75
8 Steve McNair	.30	.75
9 Kordell Stewart	.25	.60
10 Daunte Culpepper	.25	.60
11 Rich Gannon	.25	.60
12 Kurt Warner	.50	1.25
13 Brian Griese	.25	.60
14 Brad Johnson	.25	.60
15 Jake Plummer	.25	.60
16 Mark Brunell	.25	.60
17 Peyton Manning	.75	2.00
18 Keyshawn Johnson	.25	.60
19 Derrick Alexander	.20	.50
20 Emmitt Smith	.75	2.00
21 Rob Johnson	.25	.60
22 Aaron Brooks	.25	.60
23 Charlie Garner	.25	.60
24 Lamar Smith	.25	.60
25 Eddie George	.30	.75
26 Marshall Faulk	.30	.75
27 Tiki Barber	.30	.75
28 Terrell Davis	.30	.75
29 Jamal Lewis	.30	.75
30 Edgerrin James	.30	.75
31 Duce Staley	.25	.60
32 Ricky Williams	.30	.75
33 Dorsey Levens	.25	.60
34 Jerome Bettis	.30	.75
35 Ron Dayne	.25	.60
36 Mike Anderson	.25	.60
37 Peter Warrick	.25	.60
38 Mike Alstott	.25	.60
39 Fred Taylor	.30	.75
40 Curtis Martin	.30	.75
41 Warrick Dunn	.30	.75
42 Vinny Testaverde	.25	.60
43 Stephen Davis	.25	.60
44 Ahman Green	.30	.75
45 James Stewart	.20	.50
46 Ricky Watters	.25	.60
47 Ray Lewis	.30	.75
48 Thomas Jones	.25	.60
49 Zach Thomas	.30	.75
50 Junior Seau	.30	.75
51 Brian Urlacher	.40	1.00
52 Isaac Bruce	.30	.75
53 Corey Dillon	.25	.60
54 Cris Carter	.30	.75
55 Terrell Owens	.30	.75
56 Drew Bledsoe	.30	.75
57 Torry Holt	.25	.60
58 Charlie Batch	.25	.60
59 Germane Crowell	.20	.50
60 Jimmy Smith	.25	.60
61 Tim Biakabutuka	.20	.50
62 Jay Fiedler	.25	.60
63 Joey Galloway	.25	.60
64 Michael Westbrook	.20	.50
65 Shaun Alexander	.30	.75
66 Matt Hasselbeck	.30	.75
67 Elvis Grbac	.25	.60
68 Derrick Mason	.25	.60
69 Trent Green	.30	.75
70 Wayne Chrebet	.25	.60
71 Rod Smith	.25	.60
72 Jerry Rice	.60	1.50
73 Tim Brown	.30	.75
74 Shannon Sharpe	.30	.75
75 Joe Horn	.25	.60
76 Randy Moss	.30	.75
77 Amani Toomer	.25	.60
78 Antonio Freeman	.30	.75
79 Ed McCaffrey	.25	.60
80 Marvin Harrison	.30	.75
81 Muhsin Muhammad	.25	.60
82 Chad Pennington	.30	.75
83 Kevin Johnson	.20	.50
84 Tony Gonzalez	.30	.75
85 Terry Glenn	.25	.60
86 David Boston	.20	.50
87 Jevon Kearse	.25	.60
88 Marcus Robinson	.25	.60
89 Warren Sapp	.25	.60
90 Eric Moulds	.25	.60
91 Andre Carter/1250 RC	2.50	6.00
92 Kevan Barlow/1250 RC	2.50	6.00
93 Michael Bennett/1000 RC	2.50	6.00
94 Josh Booty/1500 RC	2.50	6.00
95 Drew Brees/1000 RC	20.00	50.00
96 Correll Buckhalter/1500 RC	3.00	8.00
97 Quincy Carter/1250 RC	2.50	6.00
98 Chris Chambers/1000 RC	3.00	8.00
99 Nick Goings/1500 RC	3.00	8.00
100 Kevin Kasper/1500 RC	2.00	5.00
101 Dave Dickenson/1500 RC	2.50	6.00
102 Robert Ferguson/1250 RC	3.00	8.00
103 Jamar Fletcher/1500 RC	2.00	5.00
104 Rod Gardner/1250 RC	2.50	6.00
105 Justin McCareins/1250 RC	2.50	6.00
106 Jason Brookins/1500 RC	3.00	8.00
107 Todd Heap/1500 RC	3.00	8.00
108 Travis Henry/1000 RC	2.50	6.00
109 Gerard Warren/1500 RC	2.50	6.00
110 James Jackson/1250 RC	2.00	5.00
111 Chad Johnson/1250 RC	5.00	12.00
112 Rudi Johnson/1500 RC	3.00	8.00
113 LaMont Jordan/1250 RC	3.00	8.00
114 Deuce McAllister/1250 RC	3.00	8.00
115 Mike McMahon/1250 RC	2.50	6.00
116 Snoop Minnis/1000 RC	2.00	5.00
117 Travis Minor/1500 RC	2.50	6.00
118 Freddie Mitchell/1000 RC	2.00	5.00
119 Quincy Morgan/1250 RC	2.50	6.00
120 Santana Moss/1250 RC	4.00	10.00
121 Cedrick Wilson/1500 RC	2.50	6.00
122 Jesse Palmer/1500 RC	2.50	6.00
123 Ken-Yon Rambo/1500 RC	2.00	5.00
124 Jamal Reynolds/1500 RC	2.00	5.00
125 Koren Robinson/1250 RC	2.50	6.00
126 Sage Rosenfels/1500 RC	3.00	8.00
127 Dan Morgan/1250 RC	2.50	6.00
128 Justin Smith/1500 RC	3.00	8.00
129 Fred Smoot/1500 RC	3.00	8.00
130 Vinny Sutherland/1500 RC	2.00	5.00
131 David Terrell/1000 RC	2.50	6.00
132 Anthony Thomas/1250 RC	3.00	8.00
133 LaDainian Tomlinson/1000 RC	12.00	30.00
134 Dan Alexander/1500 RC	2.50	6.00
135 Marques Tuiasosopo/1250 RC	2.50	6.00
136 Michael Vick/1000 RC	12.00	30.00
137 Steve Smith/1250 RC	6.00	15.00
138 Reggie Wayne/1250 RC	6.00	15.00
139 Chris Weinke/1000 RC	2.50	6.00
140 Alex Bannister/1250 RC	2.00	5.00

2001 E-X Essential Credentials

*VETS 1-90: 4X TO 10X BASIC CARDS
1-90 VETERAN PRINT RUN 299
*ROOKIES 91-140: 1.5X TO 4X
91-140 ROOKIE PRINT RUN 29

95 Drew Brees	125.00	200.00

2001 E-X Rookie Autographs

OVERALL AUTO/MEMORABILIA ODDS 1:10
ANNOUNCED PRINT RUNS BELOW

92 Kevan Barlow/275*	5.00	12.00
93 Michael Bennett/125*	6.00	15.00
95 Drew Brees/125*	150.00	225.00
96 Correll Buckhalter/375*	6.00	15.00
98 Chris Chambers/125*	12.00	30.00
101 Dave Dickenson/375*	5.00	12.00
105 Justin McCareins/375*	5.00	12.00
107 Todd Heap/125*	8.00	20.00
110 James Jackson/375*	4.00	10.00
111 Chad Johnson/125*	40.00	100.00
112 Rudi Johnson/275*	6.00	15.00

114 Deuce McAllister/125* 12.00 30.00
115 Mike McMahon/375 5.00 12.00
117 Travis Minor/375* 5.00 12.00
119 Quincy Morgan/125* 6.00 15.00
120 Santana Moss/125* 10.00 25.00
122 Jesse Palmer/275* 5.00 12.00
124 Jamal Reynolds/125* 5.00 12.00
125 Koren Robinson/125* 6.00 15.00
126 Sage Rosenfels/275* 6.00 15.00
127 Dan Morgan/375* 5.00 12.00
128 Justin Smith/275* 6.00 15.00
130 Vinny Sutherland/375* 4.00 10.00
131 David Terrell/125* 6.00 15.00
132 Anthony Thomas/275* 6.00 15.00
134 Dan Alexander/125* 6.00 15.00
135 Marques Tuiasosopo/125* 6.00 15.00
136 Michael Vick/125* 100.00 200.00
137 Steve Smith/375* 50.00 100.00
139 Chris Weinke/125* 6.00 15.00
140 Alex Bannister/375* 4.00 10.00

2001 E-X Behind the Numbers Jerseys

JERSEY/712-796 ODDS 1:24
OVERALL AUTO/MEMORABILIA ODDS 1:10
1 Mike Alstott/760 5.00 12.00
2 Jamal Anderson/768 5.00 12.00
3 Tim Brown/719 6.00 15.00
4 Isaac Bruce/720 6.00 15.00
5 Mark Brunell/792 5.00 12.00
6 Daunte Culpepper/789 5.00 12.00
7 Stephen Davis/752 5.00 12.00
8 Terrell Davis/770 6.00 15.00
9 Ron Dayne/773 5.00 12.00
10 Corey Dillon/772 5.00 12.00
11 Marshall Faulk/772 6.00 15.00
12 Brett Favre/796 20.00 50.00
13 Antonio Freeman/714 6.00 15.00
14 Jeff Garcia/795 5.00 12.00
15 Eddie George/773 6.00 15.00
16 Brian Griese/786 5.00 12.00
17 Marvin Harrison/712 6.00 15.00
18 Edgerrin James/768 6.00 15.00
19 Curtis Martin/772 6.00 15.00
20 Donovan McNabb/795 6.00 15.00
21 Randy Moss/716 6.00 15.00
22 Emmitt Smith/778 15.00 40.00
23 Fred Taylor/772 6.00 15.00
24 Ricky Williams/766 6.00 15.00

2001 E-X Behind the Numbers Jerseys Autographs

OVERALL AUTO/MEMORABILIA ODDS 1:10
1 Tim Brown/81 35.00 60.00
2 Isaac Bruce/80 20.00 50.00
3 Ron Dayne/27 15.00 40.00
4 Corey Dillon/28 15.00 40.00
5 Eddie George/27 30.00 60.00
6 Randy Moss/84 50.00 120.00
7 Emmitt Smith/22 175.00 300.00
8 Mike Alstott/40 15.00 40.00
9 Marvin Harrison/88 20.00 50.00
11 Stephen Davis/48 15.00 40.00
13 Marshall Faulk/28 40.00 100.00
18 Edgerrin James/32 20.00 50.00

2001 E-X Constant Threads

STATED ODDS 1:40
OVERALL AUTO/MEMORABILIA ODDS 1:10
1 Tim Brown 5.00 12.00
2 Mark Brunell JSY 4.00 10.00
3 Mark Brunell Pants 4.00 10.00
4 Germane Crowell JSY 3.00 8.00
5 Germane Crowell Pants 3.00 8.00
6 Tim Dwight SP 5.00 12.00
7 Brett Favre 15.00 40.00
8 Doug Flutie 6.00 15.00
9 Eddie George SP 6.00 15.00
10 Torry Holt 4.00 10.00
11 Edgerrin James 5.00 12.00
12 Brad Johnson 4.00 10.00
13 Kevin Johnson SP 4.00 10.00
14 Dan Marino 12.00 30.00
15 Steve McNair 5.00 12.00
16 Herman Moore JSY 4.00 10.00
17 Herman Moore Pants 4.00 10.00
18 Jake Plummer Pants UER 4.00 10.00
(swatches are actually jersey pieces)
19 Jerry Rice DP 10.00 25.00
20 Fred Taylor SP 6.00 15.00

2001 E-X E-Xtra Yards

COMPLETE SET (10) 10.00 25.00
STATED ODDS 1:20 RETAIL
1 Randy Moss .75 2.00
2 Donovan McNabb .75 2.00
3 Eddie George .75 2.00
4 Kurt Warner 1.25 3.00
5 Marshall Faulk .75 2.00
6 Peyton Manning 2.00 5.00
7 Ricky Williams .75 2.00
8 Emmitt Smith 2.00 5.00
9 Jamal Lewis .75 2.00
10 Edgerrin James .75 2.00

2001 E-X Turf Team

STATED ODDS 1:240
OVERALL AUTO/MEMORABILIA ODDS 1:10
1 Troy Aikman 12.00 30.00
2 Jamal Anderson 6.00 15.00
3 Drew Bledsoe 8.00 20.00
4 Stephen Davis 6.00 15.00
5 Ron Dayne 6.00 15.00
6 Corey Dillon 6.00 15.00
7 Marshall Faulk 8.00 20.00
8 Eddie George 8.00 20.00
9 Marvin Harrison 8.00 20.00
10 Torry Holt 6.00 15.00
11 Edgerrin James 8.00 20.00
12 Keyshawn Johnson 6.00 15.00
13 Peyton Manning 20.00 50.00
14 Donovan McNabb 8.00 20.00
15 Steve McNair 8.00 20.00
16 Jake Plummer 6.00 15.00
17 Emmitt Smith 20.00 50.00
18 Duce Staley 6.00 15.00
19 Kurt Warner 12.00 30.00
20 Peter Warrick 6.00 15.00

2004 E-X

E-X initially released in mid-February 2005. The base set consists of 65-cards including 16-rookies serial numberd to 500 and 9-rookie jersey serial numbered autographs. Hobby boxes contained 1-pack of 7-cards and carried an S.R.P. of $150 per pack. Two parallel sets and a variety of inserts can be found seeded in hobby and retail packs highlighted by the multi-tiered Clearly Authentics and Signings of the Times inserts. Some signed cards were issued via mail-in exchange or redemption cards with a number of those EXCH cards not yet appearing live on the secondary market as of the printing of this book.

UNSIGNED RC PRINT RUN 500 SER.#'d SETS
1 Travis Henry 1.00 2.50
2 Deion Sanders 1.50 4.00
3 Donovan McNabb 1.50 4.00
4 LaDainian Tomlinson 1.50 4.00
5 Shaun Alexander 1.25 3.00
6 Daunte Culpepper 1.25 3.00
7 Peyton Manning 3.00 8.00
8 Deuce McAllister 1.25 3.00
9 Marshall Faulk 1.50 4.00
10 Jamal Lewis 1.25 3.00
11 Chad Pennington 1.50 4.00
12 Clinton Portis 1.50 4.00
13 Brett Favre 4.00 10.00
14 Anquan Boldin 1.50 4.00
15 Priest Holmes 1.50 4.00
16 Brian Urlacher 1.50 4.00
17 David Carr 1.00 2.50
18 Joey Harrington 1.25 3.00
19 Tom Brady 3.00 8.00
20 Michael Vick 2.00 5.00
21 Jerry Rice 3.00 8.00
22 Mike Alstott 1.25 3.00
23 Keyshawn Johnson 1.25 3.00
24 Jeremy Shockey 1.25 3.00
25 Stephen Davis 1.25 3.00
26 Kevan Barlow 1.00 2.50
27 Carson Palmer 1.50 4.00
28 Steve McNair 1.50 4.00
29 Jake Plummer 1.25 3.00
30 Jeff Garcia 1.25 3.00
31 Byron Leftwich 1.25 3.00
32 Hines Ward 1.50 4.00
33 Randy Moss 1.50 4.00
34 Marvin Harrison 1.50 4.00
35 Terrell Owens 1.50 4.00
36 Ahman Green 1.25 3.00
37 Edgerrin James 1.25 3.00
38 Emmitt Smith 4.00 10.00
39 Torry Holt 1.25 3.00
40 Drew Bledsoe 1.50 4.00
42 Philip Rivers JSY AU/90 RC 40.00 100.00
43 Larry Fitzgerald RC 8.00 20.00
44 Roy Williams JSY AU/100 RC 20.00 50.00
45 Drew Henson JSY AU/95 RC 12.50 30.00
46 Ben Roethlisberger JSY AU/100 RC 100.00 200.00
48 Kellen Winslow RC 3.00 8.00
49 Chris Perry RC 2.50 6.00
50 Reggie Williams JSY AU/100 RC 12.50 30.00
51 Steven Jackson RC 5.00 12.00
52 Rashaun Woods RC 2.00 5.00
53 Tatum Bell RC 2.50 6.00
54 J.P. Losman RC 2.50 6.00
55 Sean Taylor RC 6.00 15.00
56 Michael Clayton JSY AU/80 RC 15.00 40.00
57 Lee Evans RC 3.00 8.00
58 Julius Jones RC 2.50 6.00
59 Jonathan Vilma RC 3.00 8.00
60 Michael Jenkins JSY AU/96 RC 12.50 30.00
61 Greg Jones RC 2.00 5.00
62 Will Smith RC 2.50 6.00
63 Ernest Wilford RC 2.50 6.00
64 Quincy Wilson RC 2.50 6.00
65 Cody Pickett RC 2.50 6.00

2004 E-X Essential Credentials Future

*VET/40-65: 2X TO 5X BASIC CARDS
*VETS/26-39: 2.5X TO 6X BASIC CARDS
COMMON ROOKIE/20-25 5.00 12.00
COMMON ROOKIE/10-19 6.00 15.00
ROOK.SEMISTARS/10-19 8.00 20.00
ROOK.UNL.STARS/10-19 10.00 25.00
STATED PRINT RUN 1-65
41 Eli Manning/25 50.00 125.00
42 Philip Rivers/24 30.00 80.00
43 Larry Fitzgerald/23 20.00 50.00
44 Roy Williams WR/22 8.00 20.00
46 Ben Roethlisberger/20 50.00 125.00
51 Steven Jackson/15 15.00 40.00

2004 E-X Essential Credentials Now

*VETS/20-40: 2.5X TO 6X BASIC CARDS
*VETS/10-19: 3X TO 8X BASIC CARDS
COMMON ROOKIE/45-65 3.00 8.00
ROOK.SEMISTARS/45-65 4.00 10.00
ROOK.UNL.STARS/45-65 5.00 12.00
STATED PRINT RUN 1-65
41 Eli Manning/41 40.00 100.00
42 Philip Rivers/42 25.00 60.00
43 Larry Fitzgerald/43 15.00 40.00
44 Roy Williams WR/44 6.00 15.00
46 Ben Roethlisberger/46 30.00 80.00
51 Steven Jackson/51 8.00 20.00

2004 E-X Rookie Die Cuts

*SINGLES: .4X TO 1X BASIC RCs
DIE CUT PRINT RUN 500 SER.#'d SETS
CARDS #41, 46 RELEASED IN LATE 2005
41 Eli Manning No Ser.# 12.00 30.00
46 Ben Roethlisberger No Ser.# 20.00 50.00

2004 E-X Rookie Jersey Autographs Gold

UNPRICED BURGUNDY PRINT RUN 5
UNPRICED EMERALD PRINT RUN 1
42 Philip Rivers/27 60.00 100.00
44 Roy Williams WR/54 15.00 40.00
45 Drew Henson/32 15.00 40.00
46 Ben Roethlisberger/77 100.00 200.00
50 Reggie Williams/73 10.00 25.00
56 Michael Clayton/24 15.00 40.00
60 Michael Jenkins/81 10.00 25.00

2004 E-X Rookie Dual Jersey Autographs Pewter

STATED PRINT RUN 9-63
41 Eli Manning/47 125.00 200.00
42 Philip Rivers/60 60.00 100.00
44 Roy Williams WR/26 25.00 60.00
45 Drew Henson/63 20.00 50.00
46 Ben Roethlisberger/55 100.00 200.00
49 Chris Perry/55 12.00 30.00
50 Reggie Williams/63 15.00 40.00
60 Michael Jenkins/54 15.00 40.00

2004 E-X Rookie Patch Autographs Tan

56 Michael Clayton/80 12.00 30.00

2004 E-X Check Mates Dual Autographs

STATED PRINT RUN 25 SER.#'d SETS
6 John Elway 250.00 450.00
Dan Marino
8 Jim Kelly 60.00 120.00
Steve Largent
11 Eli Manning 175.00 300.00
Peyton Manning
13 Joe Montana 200.00 350.00
Steve Young

2004 E-X Classic ConnEXions Dual Jerseys

STATED PRINT RUN 22 SER.#'d SETS
DMJE Dan Marino 30.00 60.00
John Elway
DSMI Deion Sanders 15.00 40.00
Michael Irvin
FHTD Franco Harris
Tony Dorsett
FTDC Fran Tarkenton
Daunte Culpepper
JKTA Jim Kelly
Troy Aikman
JLMS Jack Lambert 15.00 40.00
Mike Singletary
JMJN Joe Montana 40.00 80.00
Joe Namath
JMSY Joe Montana 20.00 50.00
Steve Young
JNMI Jay Novacek
Michael Irvin
JPRG Jim Plunkett 10.00 25.00
Rich Gannon
MSWP Mike Singletary 40.00 80.00
Walter Payton
PHBS Paul Hornung 20.00 50.00
Bart Starr
SLSA Steve Largent
Shaun Alexander
SSJE Shannon Sharpe
John Elway
SSSS Sterling Sharpe
Shannon Sharpe
TAES Troy Aikman 20.00 50.00
Emmitt Smith
TASY Troy Aikman
Steve Young
TTBS Thurman Thomas
Barry Sanders
TTJK Thurman Thomas 20.00 50.00
Jim Kelly
WPBS Walter Payton
Barry Sanders

2004 E-X Classic ConnEXions Triple Jerseys

UNPRICED PRINT RUN 13 SETS
UNPRICED EMERALD PRINT RUN 1 SET

2004 E-X Clearly Authentics Patch Silver

UNPRICED BLUE PRINT RUN 8 SETS
UNPRICED BRONZE PRINT RUN 11 SETS
UNPRICED BURGUNDY PRINT RUN 13 SETS
UNPRICED EMERALD PRINT RUN 1 SET
*GOLD/50: .5X TO 1.2X PATCH SILVER
GOLD PRINT RUN 50 SER.#'d SETS
*PEWTER/44: .6X TO 1.5X SILVER
PEWTER PRINT RUN 44 SER.#'d SETS
*DUAL TAN/22: .8X TO 2X SILVER
UNPRICED TURQUOISE SER.#'d 4-14
CAAB Anquan Boldin/81 7.50 20.00
CAAG Ahman Green/75 10.00 25.00
CABF Brett Favre/90 20.00 50.00
CABL Byron Leftwich/90 10.00 25.00
CABR Ben Roethlisberger/90 25.00 60.00
CABU Brian Urlacher/90 12.50 30.00
CACJ Chad Johnson/85 10.00 25.00
CACP Carson Palmer/90 10.00 25.00
CACP2 Clinton Portis/75 10.00 25.00
CACP3 Chad Pennington/90 10.00 25.00
CADC David Carr/65 10.00 25.00
CADC2 Daunte Culpepper/90 10.00 25.00
CADH Drew Henson/90 10.00 25.00
CADM Deuce McAllister/80 7.50 20.00
CADM2 Donovan McNabb/90 12.50 30.00
CADS Deion Sanders/65 15.00 40.00
CAEJ Edgerrin James/75 10.00 25.00
CAEM Eli Manning/90 25.00 60.00
CAES Emmitt Smith/90 12.50 30.00
CAJD Jake Delhomme/90 7.50 20.00
CAJH Joey Harrington/90 7.50 20.00
CAJL Jamal Lewis/90 7.50 20.00
CAJR Jerry Rice/80 15.00 40.00
CAJS Jeremy Shockey/80 10.00 25.00
CALF Larry Fitzgerald/90 12.50 30.00
CALT LaDainian Tomlinson/90 10.00 25.00
CAMF Marshall Faulk/90 7.50 20.00
CAMH Marvin Harrison/88 7.50 20.00
CAMV Michael Vick/90 15.00 40.00
CAPH Priest Holmes/90 12.50 30.00
CAPM Peyton Manning/90 15.00 40.00
CAPR Philip Rivers/50 15.00 40.00
CARL Ray Lewis/90 10.00 25.00
CARM Randy Moss/84 12.50 30.00
CASA Shaun Alexander/90 10.00 25.00
CASM Steve McNair/50
CATB Tom Brady/90 20.00 50.00
CATH Torry Holt/81 7.50 20.00
CATO Terrell Owens/81 10.00 25.00

2004 E-X Clearly Authentics Dual Emerald

UNPRICED EMERALD PRINT RUN 1 SET

2004 E-X Clearly Authentics Jersey Autographs

STATED PRINT RUN 2-100
SER.#'d UNDER 25 NOT PRICED
AB1 Anquan Boldin/100 12.00 30.00
AB2 Anquan Boldin/23 15.00 40.00
AG Ahman Green/85 20.00 40.00
BF1 Brett Favre/90 150.00 250.00
BL1 Byron Leftwich/100 15.00 40.00
BL2 Byron Leftwich/77 20.00 50.00
CJ1 Chad Johnson/65 12.00 30.00
CP2A Chad Pennington/80 15.00 40.00
DM1 Deuce McAllister/100 12.00 30.00
DM2 Deuce McAllister/88 15.00 40.00
EJ1 Edgerrin James/100 15.00 40.00
EJ2 Edgerrin James/52 20.00 50.00
JH1 Joey Harrington/36 20.00 50.00
JH2 Joey Harrington/95 15.00 40.00
KW Kellen Winslow Jr./90 20.00 50.00
MV1 Michael Vick/50 30.00 60.00
SJ1 Steven Jackson/100 15.00 40.00
SJ2 Steven Jackson/45 20.00 50.00
SM1 Santana Moss/90 12.00 30.00
SM2 Santana Moss/21
MV2 Michael Vick/22

2004 E-X Clearly Authentics Dual Jersey Autographs Pewter

UNPRICED BURGUNDY PRINT RUN 5 SETS
UNPRICED EMERALD PRINT RUN 1 SET
CAAB Anquan Boldin/41 15.00 40.00
CAAG Ahman Green/60 15.00 40.00
CAAJ Andre Johnson/39 20.00 50.00
CABL Byron Leftwich/68 15.00 40.00
CACJ Chad Johnson/39 15.00 40.00
CAEJ Edgerrin James/59 15.00 40.00
CAJD Jake Delhomme/46 15.00 40.00
CAJH Joey Harrington/74 12.00 30.00
CAJL Jamal Lewis/26 20.00 50.00
CAKW Kellen Winslow Jr./65 20.00 50.00
CAMV Michael Vick/104 30.00 60.00
CASA Shaun Alexander/30 15.00 40.00
CASJ Steven Jackson/56 50.00 100.00
CASM Santana Moss/54 15.00 40.00

2004 E-X Clearly Authentics Patch Autographs Tan

CARDS SER.#'d UNDER 25 NOT PRICED
CAAB Anquan Boldin/81 15.00 40.00
CAAG Ahman Green/30 20.00 50.00
CACJ Chad Johnson/85 15.00 40.00
CADM Deuce McAllister/26 20.00 50.00
CAEJ Edgerrin James/32 25.00 60.00
CAKW Kellen Winslow Jr./80 20.00 50.00
CASA Shaun Alexander/37 15.00 40.00
CASJ Steven Jackson/39 60.00 120.00
CASM Santana Moss/83 12.00 30.00

2004 E-X ConnEXions Dual Autographs

BBCB Boss Bailey/50 20.00 50.00
Champ Bailey
CJRJ Chad Johnson/50 20.00 50.00
Rudi Johnson
DFGP Doug Flutie/150 20.00 50.00
Gerard Phelan
FFFH Frenchy Fuqua/50 40.00 80.00
Franco Harris
JMLM Josh McCown/50 20.00 50.00
Luke McCown
RBTB Ronde Barber/150 20.00 50.00
Tiki Barber

2004 E-X Signings of the Times Jersey Bronze

BRONZE PRINT RUN 50 UNLESS NOTED
UNPRICED EMERALD PRINT RUN 1 SET
*GOLD: .6X TO 1.5X BRONZE
GOLD PRINT RUN 25 SER.#'d SETS
JK Jim Kelly 50.00 100.00
JM Joe Montana 75.00 150.00
RS Roger Staubach 50.00 100.00
SL Steve Largent/48 30.00 80.00
SY Steve Young 50.00 100.00
TA Troy Aikman 50.00 100.00
EC Earl Campbell No Auto 4.00 10.00
(released via Fleer inventory liquidation)

2004 E-X Signings of the Times Red

STATED PRINT RUN 50-350
AO Adewale Ogunleye/56 20.00 50.00
BB Boss Bailey/300 6.00 15.00
BS Billy Sims/255 15.00 40.00
BW Brian Westbrook/50 15.00 40.00
CB Champ Bailey/300 15.00 40.00
CC Chris Chambers/52 15.00 40.00
JB Jim Brown/100 40.00 80.00
JD Jake Delhomme/250 15.00 40.00
JM Luke McCown/250 6.00 15.00
RG Rex Grossman/52 20.00 50.00
TA Troy Aikman/100 40.00 80.00
TB Troy Brown/350 15.00 40.00
TB Tiki Barber/200 20.00 50.00

1994 Excalibur Elway Promos

COMPLETE SET (3) 4.80 12.00
COMMON CARD (SL1-SL3) 1.60 4.00

1994 Excalibur

The 1994 Collector's Edge Excalibur set consists of 75 standard-size cards based on the medieval theme of "Excalibur", the silver sword pulled from the stone in the legend of King Arthur. The cards are checklisted alphabetically according to teams. There are no key Rookie Cards in this set.

COMPLETE SET (75) 7.50 20.00
1 Bobby Hebert .08 .25
2 Deion Sanders .40 1.00
3 Andre Rison .20 .50
4 Cornelius Bennett .20 .50
5 Jim Kelly .30 .75
6 Andre Reed .20 .50
7 Bruce Smith .30 .75
8 Thurman Thomas .30 .75
9 Curtis Conway .30 .75
10 Richard Dent .20 .50
11 Jim Harbaugh .30 .75
12 Troy Aikman .75 2.00
13 Michael Irvin .30 .75
14 Russell Maryland .08 .25
15 Emmitt Smith 1.25 3.00
16 Steve Atwater .08 .25
17 Rod Bernstine .08 .25
18 John Elway 1.50 4.00
19 Glyn Milburn .20 .50
20 Shannon Sharpe .20 .50
21 Barry Sanders 1.25 3.00
22 Edgar Bennett .30 .75
23 Brett Favre 1.50 4.00
24 Sterling Sharpe .20 .50
25 Reggie White .30 .75
26 Warren Moon .30 .75
27 Wilber Marshall .08 .25
28 Haywood Jeffires .20 .50
29 Lorenzo White .08 .25
30 Quentin Coryatt .08 .25
31 Roosevelt Potts .08 .25
32 Jeff George .30 .75
33 Joe Montana 1.50 4.00
34 Neil Smith .20 .50
35 Marcus Allen .30 .75
36 Derrick Thomas .30 .75
37 Jeff Hostetler .20 .50
38 Tim Brown .30 .75
39 Rocket Ismail .20 .50
40 Randall Cunningham .30 .75
41 Jerome Bettis .40 1.00
42 Dan Marino 1.50 4.00
43 Keith Jackson .08 .25
44 O.J. McDuffie .30 .75
45 Drew Bledsoe .60 1.50
46 Leonard Russell .08 .25
47 Wade Wilson .08 .25
48 Eric Martin .08 .25
49 Phil Simms .20 .50
50 Gary Brown RB .30 .75
51 Rodney Hampton .20 .50
52 Boomer Esiason .20 .50
53 Johnny Johnson .08 .25
54 Ronnie Lott .20 .50
55 Fred Barnett .20 .50
56 Leroy Thompson .08 .25
57 Barry Foster .08 .25
58 Neil O'Donnell .30 .75
59 Stan Humphries .20 .50
60 Marion Butts .08 .25
61 Anthony Miller .20 .50
62 Natrone Means .30 .75
63 Dana Stubblefield .20 .50
64 John Taylor .20 .50
65 Ricky Watters .20 .50
66 Steve Young .60 1.50
67 Jerry Rice .75 2.00
68 Tom Rathman .08 .25
69 Rick Mirer .30 .75
70 Chris Warren .20 .50
71 Cortez Kennedy .20 .50
72 Mark Rypien .08 .25
73 Desmond Howard .20 .50
74 Art Monk .20 .50
75 Reggie Brooks .20 .50

1994 Excalibur FX

COMPLETE SET (7) 7.50 20.00
STATED ODDS 1:7
*FX GOLD SHIELDS: 1.2X to 3X BASIC INSERTS
*EQ GOLD SHIELDS: SAME VALUE
STATED ODDS 1:170
ONE SET PER EDGEQUEST REDEMPTI
*EQ SILVER SHIELDS: SAME VALUE
ONE SET PER EDGEQUEST REDEMPTI
1 Emmitt Smith 4.00 8.00
2 Rodney Hampton .60 1.25
3 Jerome Bettis 1.25 2.50
4 Steve Young 2.00 4.00
5 Rick Mirer 1.00 2.00
6 John Elway 5.00 10.00
7 Troy Aikman UER 2.50 5.00
(RB on front)

1994 Excalibur 22K

COMPLETE SET (25) 12.50 30.00
STATED ODDS 1:2
1 Troy Aikman 1.50 3.00
2 Michael Irvin .60 1.25
3 Emmitt Smith 2.50 5.00
4 Edgar Bennett .60 1.25
5 Brett Favre 3.00 6.00
6 Sterling Sharpe .30 .75
7 Rodney Hampton .30 .75
8 Jerome Bettis .75 1.50
9 Jerry Rice 1.50 3.00
10 Steve Young 1.25 2.50
11 Ricky Watters .30 .75
12 Thurman Thomas .60 1.25
13 John Elway 3.00 6.00
14 Shannon Sharpe .30 .75
15 Joe Montana 3.00 6.00
16 Marcus Allen .60 1.25
17 Tim Brown .60 1.25
18 Rocket Ismail .30 .75
19 Barry Foster .15 .40
20 Natrone Means .60 1.25
21 Rick Mirer .60 1.25
22 Dan Marino 3.00 6.00
23 AFC Card .15 .40
24 NFC Card .15 .40
25 Excalibur Card .15 .40
NNO Uncut Sheet 10.00 25.00

1995 Excalibur

For the second consecutive year, Collector's Edge issued an Excalibur brand. This 150-card medieval-themed card set was released in two series: the Sword (1-75) and the Stone (76-150). Fifteen-hundred, 12-box cases of each series were produced. The suggested retail price for each seven-card pack was $3.49. The cards are grouped alphabetically within teams. Jeff Blake is the only Rookie Card of note in this set. Collector's Edge issued a large number of Sword and Stone parallel cards for the base set as well as nearly every insert set. These Sword and Stone cards with printed with a bronze, silver, gold, or diamond "S/S" logo on the fronts and printed in quantities too low to establish secondary market values for.

COMPLETE SET (150) 15.00 30.00
COMP.SERIES 1 (75) 7.50 15.00
COMP.SERIES 2 (75) 7.50 15.00
1 Gary Clark .05 .15
2 Randal Hill .05 .15
3 Anthony Edwards .05 .15
4 Terance Mathis .10 .30
5 Erric Pegram .10 .30
6 Jeff George .10 .30
7 Pete Metzelaars .05 .15
8 Jim Kelly .20 .50
9 Andre Reed .10 .30
10 Lewis Tillman .05 .15
11 Curtis Conway .20 .50
12 Steve Walsh .05 .15
13 Derrick Fenner .05 .15
14 Harold Green .05 .15
15 Michael Jackson .10 .30
16 Eric Metcalf .10 .30
17 Antonio Langham .05 .15
18 Troy Aikman .75 2.00
19 Alvin Harper .05 .15
20 Jay Novacek .10 .30
21 John Elway 1.50 4.00
22 Glyn Milburn .05 .15
23 Steve Atwater .05 .15
24 Mel Gray .05 .15
25 Herman Moore .20 .50
26 Scott Mitchell .10 .30
27 Guy McIntyre .05 .15
28 Edgar Bennett .10 .30
29 Sterling Sharpe .10 .30
30 Gary Brown .05 .15
31 Haywood Jeffires .05 .15
32 Marshall Faulk 1.00 2.50
33 Roosevelt Potts .05 .15
34 Marcus Allen .20 .50
35 Willie Davis .10 .30
36 Lake Dawson .10 .30
37 Jeff Hostetler .10 .30
38 Rocket Ismail .10 .30
39 Troy Drayton .05 .15
40 Jerome Bettis .20 .50
41 Dan Marino 1.50 4.00
42 Mark Ingram .05 .15
43 O.J. McDuffie .20 .50
44 Warren Moon .10 .30
45 Qadry Ismail .10 .30
46 Jake Reed .10 .30
47 Ben Coates .10 .30
48 Vincent Brisby .05 .15
49 Michael Timpson .05 .15
50 Brad Daluiso .05 .15
51 Rodney Hampton .10 .30
52 Chris Calloway .05 .15
53 Rob Moore .10 .30
54 Boomer Esiason .10 .30
55 Michael Haynes .10 .30
56 Vaughn Dunbar .05 .15
57 Calvin Williams .10 .30
58 Herschel Walker .10 .30
59 Charlie Garner .20 .50
60 Neil O'Donnell .10 .30
61 Deon Figures .05 .15
62 Byron Bam Morris .05 .15
63 Junior Seau .20 .50
64 Leslie O'Neal .10 .30
65 Natrone Means .10 .30
66 Jerry Rice .75 2.00
67 Deion Sanders .50 1.25
68 William Floyd .10 .30
69 Chris Warren .10 .30
70 Cortez Kennedy .10 .30
71 Hardy Nickerson .05 .15
72 Craig Erickson .05 .15
73 Heath Shuler .10 .30
74 Reggie Brooks .10 .30
75 Henry Ellard .10 .30
76 Garrison Hearst .10 .30
77 Steve Beuerlein .10 .30
78 Seth Joyner .05 .15
79 Andre Rison .10 .30
80 Norm Johnson .05 .15
81 Craig Heyward .10 .30
82 Darryl Talley .05 .15
83 Kenneth Davis .05 .15
84 Bruce Smith .20 .50
85 Tom Waddle .05 .15
86 Erik Kramer .05 .15
87 Carl Pickens .10 .30
88 Dan Wilkinson .10 .30
89 Jeff Blake RC .30 .75
90 Vinny Testaverde .10 .30
91 Tommy Vardell .05 .15
92 Leroy Hoard .05 .15
93 Emmitt Smith 1.25 3.00
94 Michael Irvin .20 .50
95 Daryl Johnston .10 .30
96 Shannon Sharpe .10 .30
97 Anthony Miller .10 .30
98 Leonard Russell .05 .15
99 Barry Sanders 1.25 3.00
100 Brett Perriman .10 .30
101 Johnnie Morton .10 .30
102 Brett Favre 1.50 4.00
103 Bryce Paup .10 .30
104 Ernest Givins .05 .15
105 Webster Slaughter .05 .15
106 Jim Harbaugh .10 .30
107 Joe Montana 1.50 4.00
108 J.J. Birden .05 .15
109 Steve Bono .10 .30
110 James Jett .10 .30
111 Tim Brown .20 .50
112 Rob Fredrickson .05 .15
113 Chris Miller .05 .15
114 Bernie Parmalee .10 .30
115 Terry Kirby .10 .30
116 Bryan Cox .05 .15
117 Irving Fryar .10 .30
118 Terry Allen .10 .30
119 Cris Carter .20 .50
120 Fuad Reveiz .05 .15
121 Drew Bledsoe .50 1.25
122 Greg McMurtry .05 .15
123 Dave Brown .10 .30
124 Dave Meggett .05 .15
125 Johnny Johnson .05 .15
126 Ronnie Lott .10 .30
127 Johnny Mitchell .05 .15
128 Eric Martin .05 .15
129 Jim Everett .05 .15
130 Randall Cunningham .20 .50
131 Eric Allen .05 .15
132 Fred Barnett .10 .30
133 Barry Foster .10 .30
134 Kevin Greene .10 .30
135 Eric Green .05 .15
136 Stan Humphries .10 .30
137 Mark Seay .10 .30
138 Alfred Pupunu RC .05 .15
139 Steve Young .60 1.50
140 John Taylor .05 .15
141 Ricky Watters .10 .30
142 Brian Blades .10 .30
143 Rick Mirer .10 .30
144 Cortez Kennedy .10 .30
145 Jackie Harris .05 .15
146 Errict Rhett .10 .30
147 Trent Dilfer .20 .50
148 Brian Mitchell .05 .15
149 Ricky Ervins .05 .15
150 Darrell Green .05 .15

1995 Excalibur Die Cuts

*DIE CUTS: 2.5X TO 6X BASIC CARDS
STATED ODDS 1:9

1995 Excalibur Gold

*DC STARS: 2.5X to 6X

1995 Excalibur Challengers Draft Day Rookie Redemption Prizes

COMPLETE SET (31) 12.00 30.00
ONE SILV.CARD PER TEAM LOGO REDEMP.
*GOLD CARDS: SAME VALUE
DD1 Derrick Alexander .40 1.00
DD2 Tony Boselli .75 2.00
DD3 Kyle Brady .60 1.50
DD4 Mark Bruener .60 1.50
DD5 Jamie Brown .40 1.00
DD6 Ruben Brown .75 2.00
DD7 Devin Bush .40 1.00
DD8 Kevin Carter .75 2.00
DD9 Ki-Jana Carter .75 2.00
DD10 Kerry Collins 1.25 3.00
DD11 Kordell Stewart 1.25 3.00
DD12 Mark Fields .75 2.00
DD13 Joey Galloway 1.25 3.00
DD14 Trezelle Jenkins .40 1.00
DD15 Ellis Johnson .40 1.00
DD16 Napoleon Kaufman 1.00 2.50
DD17 Ty Law 1.00 2.50
DD18 Mike Mamula .40 1.00
DD19 Steve McNair 2.50 6.00
DD20 Billy Milner .40 1.00
DD21 Craig Newsome .60 1.50
DD22 Craig Powell .40 1.00
DD23 Rashaan Salaam .75 2.00
DD24 Frank Sanders .75 2.00
DD25 Warren Sapp .60 1.50
DD26 Terrance Shaw .40 1.00
DD27 J.J.Stokes .75 2.00
DD28 Michael Westbrook .75 2.00
DD29 Tyrone Wheatley 1.00 2.50
DD30 Sherman Williams .60 1.50
DD31 Cover Card .40 1.00
Checklist back

1995 Excalibur Dragon Slayers

COMPLETE SET (14) 15.00 30.00
STATED ODDS 1:12 STONE
1 Troy Aikman 2.00 4.00
2 Jerome Bettis .40 1.00
3 Drew Bledsoe 1.25 2.50
4 Marshall Faulk 2.50 5.00
5 Natrone Means .25 .60
6 Joe Montana 4.00 8.00
7 Byron Bam Morris .10 .30
8 Errict Rhett .25 .60
9 Jerry Rice 2.00 4.00
10 Barry Sanders 3.00 6.00
11 Deion Sanders 1.25 2.50
12 Junior Seau .40 1.00
13 Emmitt Smith 3.00 6.00
14 Ricky Watters .25 .60

1995 Excalibur EdgeTech

COMPLETE SET (12) 20.00 50.00
STATED ODDS 1:75 SWORD
1 Emmitt Smith 8.00 20.00
2 Errict Rhett .75 2.00
3 Steve Young 4.00 10.00
4 Jerry Rice 5.00 12.00
5 Ben Coates .75 2.00
6 Marcus Allen 1.25 3.00
7 John Elway 10.00 25.00
8 Keith Jackson .40 1.00
9 Garrison Hearst 1.25 3.00
10 Natrone Means .75 2.00

11 Michael Haynes	.75	2.00
12 Byron Bam Morris	.40	1.00

1995 Excalibur Rookie Roundtable

COMPLETE SET (25)	6.00	15.00
COMP.SERIES 1 (13)	2.00	5.00
COMP.SERIES 2 (12)	4.00	10.00
1-13 INSERTS IN SER.1 SWORD PA		
14-25 INSERTS IN SER.2 STONE P		
1 Sam Adams	.20	.50
2 Joe Johnson	.20	.50
3 Tim Bowens	.20	.50
4 Bryant Young	.20	.50
5 Aubrey Beavers	.20	.50
6 Willie McGinest	.20	.50
7 Rob Fredrickson	.20	.50
8 Lee Woodall	.20	.50
9 Antonio Langham	.20	.50
10 Dewayne Washington	.20	.50
11 Darryl Morrison	.20	.50
12 Keith Lyle	.20	.50
13 Antonio Langham	.20	.50
14 Darnay Scott	.20	.50
15 Derrick Alexander WR	.40	1.00
16 Todd Steussie	.20	.50
17 Larry Allen	.20	.50
18 Anthony Redmon	.20	.50
19 Joe Panos	.20	.50
20 Kevin Mawae	.20	.50
21 Andrew Jordan	.40	1.00
22 Heath Shuler	.40	1.00
23 Marshall Faulk	3.00	8.00
24 Errict Rhett	.40	1.00
25 Marshall Faulk POY	3.00	8.00

1995 Excalibur TekTech

COMPLETE SET (12)	20.00	50.00
RANDOM INSERTS IN SER.2 STONE		
1 Troy Aikman	4.00	10.00
2 Jerome Bettis	1.00	2.50
3 Drew Bledsoe	2.50	6.00
4 Tim Brown	1.00	2.50
5 Marshall Faulk	5.00	12.00
6 Haywood Jeffires	.30	.75
7 Dan Marino	8.00	20.00
8 Barry Sanders	6.00	15.00
9 Deion Sanders	2.50	6.00
10 Junior Seau	1.00	2.50
11 Darryl Talley	.30	.75
12 Ricky Watters	.60	1.50

1995 Excalibur 22K

COMPLETE SET (50)	75.00	200.00
COMP.SWORD SER.1 (25)	40.00	100.00
COMP.STONE SER.2 (25)	40.00	100.00
1SW-25SW STATED ODDS 1:36 SWORD		
1ST-25ST STATED ODDS 1:36 STONE		
*PRISM: .6X TO 1.5X BASIC INSERTS		
RAINDROP PRISM ANNC'D PRINT RUN 200		
*GOLD SHIELD SILVER PRISM/750: .2X to .5X		
GOLD SHIELD SILVER PRINT RUN 750		
*GOLD SHIELD GOLD PRISM/250: .4X to 1X		
GOLD SHIELD GOLD PRINT RUN 250		
SWORD/STONE VERSIONS NOT PRICED		
1SW Steve Young	2.50	6.00
2SW Barry Sanders	4.00	10.00
3SW John Elway	6.00	15.00
4SW Warren Moon	1.50	4.00
5SW Chris Warren	1.00	2.50
6SW William Floyd	1.00	2.50
7SW Jim Kelly	1.50	4.00
8SW Troy Aikman	3.00	8.00
9SW Jerome Bettis	1.50	4.00
10SW Terance Mathis	1.00	2.50
11SW Marcus Allen	1.50	4.00
12SW Antonio Langham	.60	1.50
13SW Sterling Sharpe	1.50	4.00
14SW Leonard Russell	.60	1.50
15SW Drew Bledsoe	1.50	4.00
16SW Rodney Hampton	1.00	2.50
17SW Herschel Walker	1.00	2.50
18SW Jim Everett	1.00	2.50
19SW Terry Allen	1.00	2.50
20SW Junior Seau	1.50	4.00
21SW Natrone Means	1.00	2.50
22SW Deion Sanders	2.00	5.00
23SW Charlie Garner	1.00	2.50
24SW Marshall Faulk	1.50	4.00
25SW Ben Coates	1.00	2.50
1ST Emmitt Smith	5.00	12.00
2ST Jerry Rice	4.00	10.00
3ST Stan Humphries	.60	1.50
4ST Joe Montana	8.00	20.00
5ST Steve Atwater	.60	1.50
6ST Eric Metcalf	.60	1.50
7ST Andre Rison	1.00	2.50
8ST Brett Favre	10.00	25.00
9ST Dan Marino	8.00	20.00
10ST Byron Bam Morris	.60	1.50
11ST Heath Shuler	1.00	2.50
12ST Trent Dilfer	1.50	4.00
13ST Errict Rhett	1.00	2.50
14ST Herman Moore	1.00	2.50
15ST Eric Allen	.60	1.50
16ST Cris Carter	1.50	4.00
17ST Ronnie Lott	1.50	4.00
18ST Randall Cunningham	1.50	4.00
19ST Barry Foster	.60	1.50
20ST John Taylor	1.00	2.50
21ST Rick Mirer	1.00	2.50
22ST Tim Brown	1.50	4.00
23ST Michael Irvin	1.50	4.00
24ST Ricky Watters	1.00	2.50
25ST Jay Novacek	1.00	2.50

1997 Excalibur

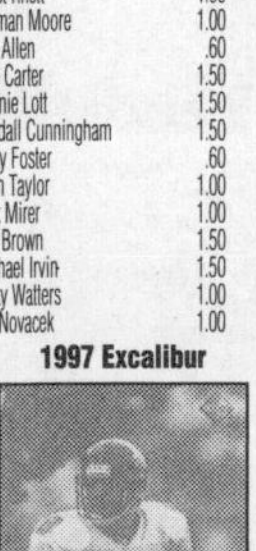

The 1997 Excalibur set was issued in one series totaling 150 cards and was distributed in six-card packs with a suggested retail price of $2.49. The cardfronts feature a foil stamped textured dragon detailed with black ink. The backs carry another player photo and player information and statistics. A second non-foil version of the set was released later. These cards were originally intended to be part of a retail parallel version set, but the idea was scrapped.

COMPLETE SET (150)	30.00	60.00
1 Larry Centers	.30	.75
2 Leeland McElroy	.20	.50
3 Simeon Rice	.30	.75
4 Eric Swann	.20	.50
5 Jamal Anderson	.50	1.25
6 Bert Emanuel	.30	.75
7 Eric Metcalf	.30	.75
8 Ray Lewis	.75	2.00
9 Derrick Alexander WR	.30	.75
10 Michael Jackson	.30	.75
11 Vinny Testaverde	.30	.75
12 Todd Collins	.20	.50
13 Jim Kelly	.50	1.25
14 Eric Moulds	.50	1.25
15 Andre Reed	.30	.75
16 Bruce Smith	.30	.75
17 Thurman Thomas	.50	1.25
18 Tim Biakabutuka	.30	.75
19 Kerry Collins	.50	1.25
20 Kevin Greene	.30	.75
21 Anthony Johnson	.20	.50
22 Lamar Lathon	.20	.50
23 Muhsin Muhammad	.30	.75
24 Curtis Conway	.30	.75
25 Bryan Cox	.20	.50
26 Walt Harris	.20	.50
27 Erik Kramer	.20	.50
28 Rick Mirer	.20	.50
29 Rashaan Salaam	.20	.50
30 Jeff Blake	.30	.75
31 Ki-Jana Carter	.20	.50
32 Carl Pickens	.30	.75
33 Troy Aikman	1.50	3.00
34 Michael Irvin	.50	1.25
35 Daryl Johnston	.30	.75
36 Emmitt Smith	2.50	5.00
37 Broderick Thomas	.20	.50
38 Terrell Davis	.60	1.50
39 John Elway	2.50	6.00
40 Anthony Miller	.20	.50
41 John Mobley	.20	.50
42 Shannon Sharpe	.30	.75
43 Neil Smith	.30	.75
44 Scott Mitchell	.30	.75
45 Herman Moore	.30	.75
46 Brett Perriman	.20	.50
47 Barry Sanders	2.00	5.00
48 Edgar Bennett	.30	.75
49 Robert Brooks	.30	.75
50 Brett Favre	3.00	6.00
51 Antonio Freeman	.50	1.25
52 Dorsey Levens	.50	1.25
53 Reggie White	.50	1.25
54 Eddie George	.50	1.25
55 Darryll Lewis	.20	.50
56 Steve McNair	.60	1.50
57 Chris Sanders	.20	.50
58 Marshall Faulk	.60	1.50
59 Jim Harbaugh	.30	.75
60 Marvin Harrison	.50	1.25
61 Jimmy Smith	.30	.75
62 Tony Brackens	.20	.50
63 Mark Brunell	.60	1.50
64 Kevin Hardy	.20	.50
65 Keenan McCardell	.30	.75
66 Natrone Means	.30	.75
67 Marcus Allen	.50	1.25
68 Elvis Grbac	.30	.75
69 Derrick Thomas	.50	1.25
70 Tamarick Vanover	.30	.75
71 Karim Abdul-Jabbar	.30	.75
72 Terrell Buckley	.20	.50
73 Irving Fryar	.30	.75
74 Dan Marino	2.50	6.00
75 O.J. McDuffie	.30	.75
76 Zach Thomas	.50	1.25
77 Terry Kirby	.30	.75
78 Cris Carter	.50	1.25
79 Brad Johnson	.50	1.25
80 John Randle	.30	.75
81 Jake Reed	.30	.75
82 Robert Smith	.30	.75
83 Drew Bledsoe	.60	1.50
84 Ben Coates	.30	.75
85 Terry Glenn	.50	1.25
86 Ty Law	.30	.75
87 Curtis Martin	.60	1.50
88 Willie McGinest	.20	.50
89 Mario Bates	.20	.50
90 Jim Everett	.20	.50
91 Wayne Martin	.20	.50
92 Heath Shuler	.20	.50
93 Torrance Small	.20	.50
94 Ray Zellars	.20	.50
95 Dave Brown	.20	.50
96 Jason Sehorn	.30	.75
97 Amani Toomer	.30	.75
98 Tyrone Wheatley	.30	.75
99 Hugh Douglas	.20	.50
100 Aaron Glenn	.20	.50
101 Jeff Graham	.20	.50
102 Keyshawn Johnson	.50	1.25
103 Adrian Murrell	.30	.75
104 Neil O'Donnell	.30	.75
105 Tim Brown	.50	1.25
106 Jeff George	.30	.75
107 Jeff Hostetler	.20	.50
108 Napoleon Kaufman	.50	1.25
109 Chester McGlockton	.20	.50
110 Fred Barnett	.20	.50
111 Ty Detmer	.30	.75
112 Chris T. Jones	.20	.50
113 Ricky Watters	.30	.75
114 Bobby Engram	.30	.75
115 Jerome Bettis	.50	1.25
116 Charles Johnson	.30	.75
117 Greg Lloyd	.20	.50
118 Kordell Stewart	.50	1.25
119 Yancey Thigpen	.30	.75
120 Rod Woodson	.30	.75
121 Stan Humphries	.30	.75
122 Tony Martin	.30	.75
123 Leonard Russell	.20	.50
124 Junior Seau	.50	1.25
125 Chad Brown	.20	.50
126 John Friesz	.20	.50
127 Joey Galloway	.30	.75
128 Cortez Kennedy	.20	.50
129 Warren Moon	.50	1.25
130 Chris Warren	.30	.75
131 Garrison Hearst	.30	.75
132 Terrell Owens	.60	1.50
133 Jerry Rice	1.50	3.00
134 Dana Stubblefield	.20	.50
135 Bryant Young	.20	.50
136 Steve Young	.75	2.00
137 Tony Banks	.30	.75
138 Isaac Bruce	.50	1.25
139 Eddie Kennison	.30	.75
140 Keith Lyle	.20	.50
141 Lawrence Phillips	.20	.50
142 Mike Alstott	.50	1.25
143 Hardy Nickerson	.20	.50
144 Errict Rhett	.20	.50
145 Warren Sapp	.30	.75
146 Gus Frerotte	.20	.50
147 Sean Gilbert	.20	.50
148 Ken Harvey	.20	.50
149 Terry Allen	.50	1.25
150 Michael Westbrook	.30	.75

1997 Excalibur Non-Foil Parallel

COMP.NO-FOIL SET (150)	7.50	15.00
*NO-FOIL CARDS: .1X TO .25X FOILS		

1997 Excalibur Castles

COMPLETE SET (25)	125.00	250.00
CASTLES: SAME PRICE AS OVERLORDS		

1997 Excalibur Crusaders

COMPLETE SET (25)	75.00	150.00
STATED ODDS 1:30		
STATED PRINT RUN 750 SERIAL #'d SETS		
1 Brett Favre	15.00	40.00
2 Mark Brunell	4.00	10.00
3 Jim Kelly	3.00	8.00
4 Michael Westbrook	2.00	5.00
5 Emmitt Smith	12.50	30.00
6 Marshall Faulk	4.00	10.00
7 Kerry Collins	3.00	8.00
8 Jeff Hostetler	1.25	3.00
9 Rashaan Salaam	1.25	3.00
10 Garrison Hearst	2.00	5.00
11 Tamarick Vanover	2.00	5.00
12 Rodney Hampton	3.00	8.00
13 Leeland McElroy	1.25	3.00
14 Tony Banks	2.00	5.00
15 Deion Sanders	3.00	8.00
16 Errict Rhett	1.25	3.00
17 Thurman Thomas	3.00	8.00
18 Chris Warren	2.00	5.00
19 Andre Reed	2.00	5.00
20 Napoleon Kaufman	3.00	8.00
21 Terry Allen	3.00	8.00
22 Carl Pickens	2.00	5.00
23 Marvin Harrison	3.00	8.00
24 Lawrence Phillips	1.25	3.00
25 Troy Aikman	8.00	20.00

1997 Excalibur Dragon Slayers Redemption

COMPLETE SET (12)	15.00	40.00
STATED PRINT RUN 1000 SERIAL #'d SETS		
1 Mark Brunell	2.00	5.00
2 Terrell Davis	2.50	6.00
3 Jim Druckenmiller	1.00	2.50
4 Warrick Dunn	2.00	5.00
5 Brett Favre	6.00	15.00
6 Terry Glenn	1.50	4.00
7 Keyshawn Johnson	1.50	4.00
8 Dan Marino	6.00	15.00
9 Curtis Martin	1.50	4.00
10 Emmitt Smith	4.00	10.00
11 Shawn Springs	.60	1.50
12 Eddie George	2.00	5.00

1997 Excalibur Game Helmets

COMP.UNSIGNED SET (25)	300.00	600.00
STATED PRINT RUN 249 UNSIGNED SETS		
SIGNED CARDS STATED ODDS 1:350		
1 Brett Favre	30.00	80.00
2 Mark Brunell SP	12.50	30.00
2AU Mark Brunell	20.00	40.00
AUTO/700		
3 Barry Sanders	25.00	60.00
4 John Elway	30.00	80.00
5 Emmitt Smith	25.00	60.00
6 Drew Bledsoe	12.50	30.00
7 Troy Aikman	20.00	50.00
8 Dan Marino	30.00	80.00
9 Eddie George	12.50	30.00
10 Terry Glenn	7.50	20.00
11 Keyshawn Johnson	12.50	30.00
12AU Terrell Davis	20.00	50.00
AUTO/500		
13 Curtis Martin	12.50	30.00
14 Steve McNair	12.50	30.00
15 Muhsin Muhammad	7.50	20.00
16 Antonio Freeman	8.00	20.00
17 Ricky Watters	7.50	20.00
18 Jerome Bettis SP	40.00	80.00
18AU Jerome Bettis	60.00	120.00
AUTO/100		
(released as dealer premium only)		
19 Herman Moore	6.00	15.00
20 Isaac Bruce	12.50	30.00
21 Deion Sanders	15.00	40.00
22 Cris Carter	15.00	40.00
23 Tim Biakabutuka	6.00	15.00
24 Karim Abdul-Jabbar	6.00	15.00
25 Mike Alstott	12.50	30.00
26 Jamal Anderson SP	12.50	30.00
26AU Jamal Anderson	40.00	100.00
AUTO/100		
27AU Kevin Greene	30.00	60.00
AUTO/100		
28 Tim Brown SP	30.00	60.00
28AU Tim Brown AU/100	50.00	120.00

1997 Excalibur Gridiron Wizards Draft

COMPLETE SET (25)	60.00	120.00
STATED ODDS 1:20		
STATED PRINT RUN 1000 SER.#'d SETS		
1 Reidel Anthony	2.00	5.00
2 Darnell Autry	2.00	5.00
3 Tiki Barber	7.50	20.00
4 Pat Barnes	2.00	5.00
5 Peter Boulware	2.00	5.00
6 Chris Canty	1.25	3.00
7 Rae Carruth	1.25	3.00
8 Troy Davis	2.00	5.00
9 Corey Dillon	5.00	12.00
10 Jim Druckenmiller	2.00	5.00
11 Warrick Dunn	4.00	10.00
12 James Farrior	2.00	5.00
13 Tony Gonzalez	5.00	10.00
14 Yatil Green	2.00	5.00
15 Marcus Harris	1.25	3.00
16 Ike Hilliard	2.00	5.00
17 David LaFleur	1.25	3.00
18 Orlando Pace	2.00	5.00
19 Jake Plummer	5.00	12.00
20 Dwayne Rudd	1.25	3.00
21 Darrell Russell	1.25	3.00
22 Antowain Smith	3.00	8.00
23 Shawn Springs	2.00	5.00
24 Bryant Westbrook	1.25	3.00
25 Danny Wuerffel	2.00	5.00

1997 Excalibur Marauders

COMPLETE SET (25)	75.00	200.00
STATED ODDS 1:20		
*SUPREME EDGE: 2X TO 5X BASIC INS.		
SUPREME EDGE PRINT RUN 50 SETS		
1 Tony Banks	2.50	6.00
Antonio Freeman		
2 Tim Biakabutuka	1.00	2.50
Heath Shuler		
3 Eddie Kennison	15.00	30.00
Brett Favre		
4 Todd Collins	2.50	6.00
Marcus Allen		
5 Shannon Sharpe	12.50	30.00
Dan Marino		
6 Napoleon Kaufman	2.50	6.00
Desmond Howard		
7 Mushin Muhammad	1.50	4.00
Dorsey Levens		
8 Mike Alstott	3.00	8.00
Drew Bledsoe		
9 Michael Westbrook	12.50	25.00
Emmitt Smith		
10 Marvin Harrison	2.50	6.00
Heath Shuler		
11 Marshall Faulk	3.00	8.00
Jeff Blake		
12 Lawrence Phillips	1.00	2.50
Jeff George		
13 Edgar Bennett	1.00	2.50
Tony Martin		
14 Karim Abdul-Jabbar	7.50	15.00
Jerry Rice		
15 Terrell Owens	4.00	10.00
Jim Harbaugh		
16 Isaac Bruce	12.50	30.00
John Elway		
17 Eric Metcalf	1.00	2.50
Dave Brown		
18 Eddie Kennison	2.50	6.00
Junior Seau		
19 Eddie George	2.50	6.00
Mark Brunell		
20 Deion Sanders	4.00	8.00
Cris Carter		
21 Eric Moulds	5.00	12.00
Steve Young		
22 Chris Warren	1.50	4.00
Ben Coates		
23 Carl Pickens	1.50	4.00
Robert Brooks		
24 Bobby Engram	2.50	6.00
Tim Brown		
25 Ben Coates	7.50	15.00
Troy Aikman		

1997 Excalibur Overlords

COMPLETE SET (25)	75.00	200.00
STATED ODDS 1:30		
STATED PRINT RUN 750 SERIAL #'d SETS		
CASTLE PRINT RUN 750 SERIAL #'d SETS		
1 Jeff Blake	2.50	6.00
2 Mark Brunell	5.00	12.00
3 Bobby Engram	2.50	6.00
4 Joey Galloway	2.50	6.00
5 Eddie Kennison	2.50	6.00
6 Terrell Davis	5.00	12.00
7 Chris Calloway	2.50	6.00
8 Hardy Nickerson	1.50	4.00
9 Errict Rhett	1.50	4.00
10 Emmitt Smith	15.00	40.00
11 Kordell Stewart	4.00	10.00
12 Steve Young	6.00	15.00
13 Marcus Allen	4.00	10.00
14 Edgar Bennett	2.50	6.00
15 Robert Brooks	2.50	6.00
16 Kerry Collins	4.00	10.00
17 Todd Collins	1.50	4.00
18 Brett Favre	20.00	50.00
19 Gus Frerotte	1.50	4.00
20 Elvis Grbac	2.50	6.00
21 Jeff Hostetler	1.50	4.00
22 Tony Martin	2.50	6.00
23 Terrell Owens	5.00	12.00
24 Dorsey Levens	4.00	10.00
25 Thurman Thomas	4.00	10.00

1997 Excalibur Quest Redemption

COMPLETE SET (12)	25.00	50.00
1 Jim Druckenmiller	.75	2.00
2 Brett Favre	6.00	15.00
3 Joey Galloway	1.25	3.00
4 Eddie George	2.50	6.00
5 Terry Glenn	.75	2.00
6 Marvin Harrison	1.25	3.00
7 Karim Abdul-Jabbar	.75	2.00
8 Keyshawn Johnson	1.25	3.00
9 Eddie Kennison	.75	2.00
10 Dan Marino	6.00	15.00
11 Curtis Martin	2.00	5.00
12 Emmitt Smith	4.00	10.00

1997 Excalibur 22K Knights

COMPLETE SET (25)	100.00	200.00
STATED ODDS 1:20		
STATED PRINT RUN 2000 SERIAL #'d SETS		
*BLACK MAGNUMS: 1X TO 2.5X BASIC INSERTS		
BL STATED ODDS 1:75 SUPER PREM.HOBBY		
BL STATED PRINT RUN 250 SERIAL #'d SETS		
*SUPREME EDGE: 1.2X TO 3X BASIC INSERTS		
SUPREME EDGE STATED PRINT RUN 50 SETS		
1 Troy Aikman	5.00	12.00
2 John Elway	10.00	25.00
3 Brett Favre	10.00	25.00
4 Dan Marino	10.00	25.00
5 Barry Sanders	8.00	20.00
6 Emmitt Smith	8.00	20.00
7 Mark Brunell	2.50	6.00
8 Jerry Rice	5.00	12.00
9 Terrell Davis	2.50	6.00
10 Natrone Means	1.25	3.00
11 Joey Galloway	1.25	3.00
12 Keyshawn Johnson	2.00	5.00
13 Curtis Martin	2.50	6.00
14 Herman Moore	1.25	3.00
15 Eddie George	2.00	5.00
16 Terry Glenn	2.00	5.00
17 Steve McNair	2.50	6.00
18 Marshall Faulk	2.50	6.00
19 Ricky Watters	1.25	3.00
20 Karim Abdul-Jabbar	1.25	3.00
21 Gus Frerotte	.75	2.00
22 Terry Allen	2.00	5.00
23 Andre Reed	1.25	3.00
24 Jerome Bettis	2.00	5.00
25 Tim Brown	2.00	5.00

1997 Excalibur National

The 1997 Excalibur National set was released in single card form over the course of The National Sports Collector's Convention in Cleveland. Each card was printed on gold foil textured stock with a player photo and Excalibur logo on the cardfront. The cardbacks are essentially parallel to the base Excalibur release including the card number. A second card number was added, with each numbered "XX of 24."

COMPLETE SET (25)	50.00	125.00
1 Leeland McElroy	.40	1.00
2 Mark Brunell	2.00	5.00
3 Emmitt Smith	4.00	10.00
4 Troy Aikman	2.40	6.00
5 Carl Pickens	.80	2.00
6 Terrell Davis	3.00	8.00
7 John Elway	4.80	12.00
8 Eddie George	2.40	6.00
9 Brett Favre	4.80	12.00
10 Barry Sanders	4.00	10.00
11 Steve McNair	2.00	5.00
12 Eddie Kennison	.80	2.00
13 Dan Marino	4.80	12.00
14 Cris Carter	1.20	3.00
15 Curtis Martin	2.00	5.00
16 Terry Glenn	1.20	3.00
17 Drew Bledsoe	2.00	5.00
18 Jerome Bettis	1.20	3.00
19 Kordell Stewart	1.50	4.00
20 Napoleon Kaufman	1.60	4.00
21 Joey Galloway	1.50	4.00
22 Kerry Collins	.80	2.00
23 Jerry Rice	2.40	6.00
24 Isaac Bruce	1.20	3.00
NNO Checklist Card	.40	1.00

1948-52 Exhibit W468 Black and White

Produced by the Exhibit Supply Company of Chicago, the 1948-52 Football Exhibit cards are unnumbered, blank-backed, and produced on thick card stock. Although we list the more common black and white cards below, some of the cards were issued in other colors as well including sepia, tan, green, red, pink, blue, and yellow. The primary method of distribution for the cards was through mechanical vending machines. Advertising panels on the front of these machines displayed from one to nine cards as well as the price for a card which was originally one cent but later raised to two cents. Each card measures approximately 3 1/4" by 5 3/8" and features a pro or college player. Several cards in the checklist below (Sammy Baugh, Glenn Dobbs, Otto Graham, Pat Harder, Jack Jacobs, Sid Luckman, Johnny Lujack, Marion Motley, Emil Sitko, Steve Van Buren, Bob Waterfield, and Tank Younger) have the same photo as in the Exhibit Sports Champions set of 1948; however, cards in this series do not have the single agate line of type describing the player at the bottom of the card. The cards were issued in three groups of 32 primarily during 1948, 1950, and 1951. We've included what is thought to be the year/years of issue for each card. The 16-cards in the 1951/1952 group are the most plentiful as they were reissued intact in sepia tone in 1952 (and perhaps 1953 as well). Some veteran collectors believe the second group may have been issued in 1949 rather than 1950. Cards issued during and after 1951 are marked as DP's as they are quite common compared to the other cards in the set. Several players, such as Creekmur, Houck, and Martin, are rumored to exist, but they have not been verified and are assumed not to exist in the checklist below. The American Card Catalog designation is W468. A football exhibit checklist card has also been found but was apparently produced in very limited quantity in 1950 only. This checklist card is known to exist in green and black-and-white and is identical to the Bednarik card but has the 32 players from the 1950 set listed on its front. The Bednarik checklist is usually found on the 9-card advertising display piece

COMPLETE SET (59)	2,500.00	5,000.00
1 Frankie Albert DP/48/50/51/52	3.00	8.00
2 Dick Barwegan DP/51/52	2.50	6.00
3 Sammy Baugh DP/48/50/51/52	12.50	25.00
4 Chuck Bednarik SP50	90.00	150.00
5 Tony Canadeo DP 51/52	6.00	15.00
6 Paul Christman 48/50	25.00	40.00
7 Bob Cifers SP48	175.00	300.00
8 Irv Comp SP48	175.00	300.00
9A Charley Conerly DP/48/50/51/52	6.00	15.00
(with extraneous line near/ football in photo)		
9B Charley Conerly DP/48/50/51/52	6.00	15.00
(without extraneous line)		
10 George Connor DP 51/52	4.00	10.00
11 Tex Coulter SP48	175.00	300.00
12 Glenn Davis SP50	175.00	300.00
13 Glenn Dobbs 48/50	25.00	40.00
14 John Dottley DP 51/52	2.50	6.00
15 Bill Dudley 48/50	35.00	60.00
16 Tom Fears DP 51/52	5.00	12.00
17 Joe Geri DP 51/52	2.50	6.00
18 Otto Graham DP/48/50/51/52	15.00	30.00
19 Pat Harder 48/50	25.00	40.00
20 Elroy Hirsch DP 51/52	6.00	15.00
21 Dick Hoerner SP50	60.00	100.00
22 Bob Hoernschemeyer DP/51/52	2.50	6.00
23 Les Horvath SP48	175.00	300.00
24 Jack Jacobs SP48	175.00	300.00
25 Nate Johnson SP48	175.00	300.00
26 Charlie Justice SP50	90.00	150.00
27 Bobby Layne DP/48/50/51/52	10.00	25.00
28 Clyde LeForce SP48	175.00	300.00
29 Sid Luckman 48/50	45.00	80.00
30 Johnny Lujack 48/50	35.00	60.00
31 John Mastrangelo SP48	175.00	300.00
32 Ollie Matson DP 51/52	6.00	15.00
33 Bill McColl DP 51/52	2.50	6.00
34 Fred Morrison DP/50/51/52	2.50	6.00
35 Marion Motley DP/48/50/51/52	10.00	20.00
36 Chuck Ortmann DP/51/52	2.50	6.00
37 Joe Perry SP50	75.00	135.00
38 Pete Pihos 48/50	30.00	50.00
39 Steve Pritko SP48	175.00	300.00
40 George Ratterman DP/48/50/51/52	2.50	6.00
41 Jay Rhodemyre DP/51/52	2.50	6.00
42 Martin Ruby SP50	75.00	125.00
43 Julie Rykovich DP/51/52	2.50	6.00
44 Walt Schlinkman SP48	175.00	300.00
45 Emil Sitko DP 51/52	2.50	6.00
46 Vitamin Smith DP/50/51/52	2.50	6.00
47 Norm Standlee/48/50	25.00	40.00
48 George Taliaferro DP/50/51/52	2.50	6.00
49 Y.A. Tittle 48/50	60.00	100.00
50 Charley Trippi DP/48/50/51/52	4.00	10.00
51 Frank Tripucka DP/50/51/52	3.00	8.00
52 Emlen Tunnell DP/51/52	5.00	12.00
53 Bulldog Turner DP/48/50/51/52	5.00	12.00
54 Steve Van Buren 48/50	35.00	60.00
55 Bob Waterfield DP/48/50/51/52	7.50	20.00
56 Herm Wedemeyer SP48	500.00	800.00
57 Bob Williams DP 51/52	2.50	6.00
58 Buddy Young DP	3.00	8.00
(passing)48/50/51/52		
59 Tank Younger DP/50/51/52	3.00	8.00
NNO Checklist Card SP50	500.00	800.00
Chuck Bednarik pictured		

1948-52 Exhibit W468 Variations

1A Frankie Albert B&W	12.50	25.00
(postcard back)		
1B Frankie Albert Sepia	7.50	15.00
2B Dick Barwegan Sepia	6.00	12.00
3A Sammy Baugh B&W	25.00	50.00
(postcard back)		
3B Sammy Baugh Yellow	75.00	125.00
5B Tony Canadeo Sepia	15.00	30.00
6A Paul Christman Lt.Blue	60.00	100.00
7A Bob Cifers Dark Green	200.00	350.00
7B Bob Cifers Yellow	200.00	350.00
8A Irv Comp Yellow	200.00	350.00
9A Charley Conerly B&W	20.00	40.00
(postcard back)		
10B George Connor Sepia	10.00	20.00
11A Tex Coulter Green	200.00	350.00
11B Tex Coulter Pink	200.00	350.00
14B John Dottley Sepia	6.00	12.00
15A Bill Dudley Red	60.00	100.00
16A Tom Fears B&W	12.50	25.00
(postcard back)		
16B Tom Fears Sepia	12.50	25.00
17A Joe Geri Sepia	6.00	12.00
18A Otto Graham B&W	30.00	60.00
(postcard back)		
18B Otto Graham Sepia	30.00	60.00
19A Pat Harder Blue	50.00	80.00
20A Elroy Hirsch B&W	20.00	40.00
(postcard back)		
20B Elroy Hirsch Sepia	15.00	30.00
22B Bob Hoernschemeyer Sepia	6.00	12.00
23A Les Horvath Dark Red	200.00	350.00
23B Les Horvath Yellow	200.00	350.00
24A Jack Jacobs	200.00	350.00
Dark Green		
25A Nate Johnson Green	200.00	350.00
25B Nate Johnson Dark Red	200.00	350.00
27A Bobby Layne B&W	25.00	50.00
(postcard back)		
27B Bobby Layne Sepia	25.00	50.00
28A Clyde LeForce Green	200.00	350.00
29A Sid Luckman Lt.Green	90.00	150.00
30A Johnny Lujack Yellow	75.00	125.00
30B Johnny Lujack Pink	75.00	125.00
31A John Mastrangelo Lt.Blue	175.00	300.00
32A Ollie Matson B&W	20.00	40.00
(postcard back)		
32D Ollie Matson Sepia	15.00	30.00
33B Bill McColl Sepia	6.00	15.00
34A Fred Morrison B&W	25.00	50.00
(postcard back)		
34B Fred Morrison Sepia	6.00	12.00
34C Fred Morrison Tan	7.50	15.00
35A Marion Motley B&W	25.00	50.00
(postcard back)		
35B Marion Motley Sepia	20.00	40.00
36B Chuck Ortmann Sepia	6.00	12.00
38A Pete Pihos Yellow	60.00	100.00
39A Steve Pritko Yellow	200.00	350.00
40A George Ratterman B&W	12.50	25.00
(postcard back)		
40B George Ratterman Sepia	6.00	12.00
41B Jay Rhodemyre Sepia	6.00	12.00
41C Jay Rhodemyre Tan	7.50	15.00
43A Julie Rykovich B&W	12.50	25.00
(postcard back)		
43B Julie Rykovich Sepia	6.00	12.00
44A Walt Schlinkman Pink	200.00	350.00
45B Emil Sitko Sepia	6.00	12.00
48B George Taliaferro Sepia	6.00	12.00
48C George Taliaferro Tan	7.50	15.00
49A Y.A. Tittle Green	90.00	150.00
49B Y.A. Tittle Yellow	90.00	150.00
50A Charley Trippi B&W	15.00	30.00
(postcard back)		
50B Charley Trippi Sepia	10.00	20.00
51B Frank Tripucka Sepia	7.50	15.00
52B Emlen Tunnell Sepia	12.50	25.00
53A Bulldog Turner B&W	25.00	50.00
(postcard back)		
53B Bulldog Turner Green	60.00	100.00
53C Bulldog Turner Sepia	12.50	25.00
54A Steve Van Buren Lt.Blue	75.00	125.00
55A Bob Waterfield B&W	25.00	50.00
(postcard back)		
55B Bob Waterfield Sepia	15.00	40.00
56A Herm Wedemeyer	600.00	1,000.00
Light Green		
57A Bob Williams B&W	25.00	50.00
(postcard back)		
57B Bob Williams Sepia	6.00	12.00
58A Buddy Young B&W	12.50	25.00
(postcard back)		
58B Buddy Young Sepia	7.50	15.00
58C Buddy Young Yellow	60.00	100.00
59B Tank Younger Sepia	6.00	12.00
NNO Chuck Bednarik CL Green	500.00	800.00

1926 Exhibit Red Grange One Minute to Play

These Exhibit cards were issued for the movie "One Minute to play' starring Red Grange. Each was produced in the standard oversized Exhibit style with a single color cardfront picturing Grange in a scene from the movie. The backs are blank.

1 Red Grange Punting
(Green)
2 Red Grange in sweater
(Purple)

2005 Exquisite Collection

This 127-card set was released in January, 2006. The set was issued in a six-card pack with an $500 SRP. Cards numbered 1-42 feature veterans in team alphabetical order while cards numbered 43-127 were all signed by the rookie. Within the rookie subset, cards numbered 85-118 also have a player-worn jersey swatch. With the exception of the game-worn autographed cards, which had a stated print run of 199 serial numbered sets, all the cards in this set were issued to a stated print run of 150 serial numbered sets.

1-42 VETERAN PRINT RUN 150		
ROOKIE AU PRINT RUN 150		
ROOKIE JSY AU PRINT RUN 99-199		
1 Larry Fitzgerald	15.00	40.00
2 Michael Vick	15.00	40.00
3 Jamal Lewis	12.00	30.00
4 Ray Lewis	15.00	40.00
5 Willis McGahee	15.00	40.00
6 Jake Delhomme	12.00	30.00
7 Brian Urlacher	15.00	40.00
8 Carson Palmer	15.00	40.00
9 Julius Jones	10.00	25.00
10 Drew Bledsoe	15.00	40.00
11 Jake Plummer	12.00	30.00
12 Kevin Jones	10.00	25.00
13 Roy Williams WR	12.00	30.00
14 Ahman Green	12.00	30.00
15 Brett Favre	75.00	150.00
16 David Carr	10.00	25.00
17 Edgerrin James	12.00	30.00
18 Marvin Harrison	15.00	40.00
19 Peyton Manning	40.00	80.00
20 Byron Leftwich	12.00	30.00
21 Priest Holmes	12.00	30.00
22 Daunte Culpepper	12.00	30.00
23 Tom Brady	40.00	80.00
24 Deuce McAllister	12.00	30.00
25 Eli Manning	25.00	60.00
26 Jeremy Shockey	15.00	40.00
27 Chad Pennington	15.00	40.00
28 Curtis Martin	15.00	40.00
29 Randy Moss	15.00	40.00
30 Donovan McNabb	15.00	40.00
31 Terrell Owens	15.00	40.00
32 Jerome Bettis	15.00	40.00
33 Ben Roethlisberger	25.00	60.00
34 Drew Brees	15.00	40.00
35 LaDainian Tomlinson	15.00	40.00
36 Antonio Gates	15.00	40.00
37 Shaun Alexander	12.00	30.00
38 Marc Bulger	12.00	30.00
39 Torry Holt	12.00	30.00
40 Steven Jackson	15.00	40.00
41 Steve McNair	15.00	40.00
42 Clinton Portis	12.00	30.00
43 Dan Orlovsky AU RC	15.00	40.00
44 Darren Sproles AU RC	75.00	125.00
45 Marion Barber AU RC	25.00	60.00
46 Chris Henry AU RC	15.00	40.00
47 Derek Anderson AU RC	12.00	30.00
48 Erasmus James AU RC	12.00	30.00
49 Thomas Davis AU RC	10.00	25.00
50 David Pollack AU RC	12.00	30.00
51 Fred Gibson AU RC	12.00	30.00
52 Craphonso Thorpe AU RC	10.00	25.00
53 Derrick Johnson AU RC	12.00	30.00
54 Brandon Jacobs AU RC	40.00	100.00
55 Adrian McPherson AU RC	10.00	25.00
56 Matt Cassel AU RC	75.00	150.00
57 Anthony Davis AU RC	10.00	25.00
58 Alvin Pearman AU RC	10.00	25.00
59 Brandon Jones AU RC	12.00	30.00
60 Jerome Mathis AU RC	15.00	40.00
61 Chase Lyman AU RC	10.00	25.00
62 Roydell Williams AU RC	12.00	30.00
63 DeMarcus Ware AU RC	150.00	250.00
64 Mike Patterson AU RC	10.00	25.00
65 Mike Nugent AU RC	12.00	30.00
66 Ryan Fitzpatrick AU RC	100.00	200.00
67 Barrett Ruud AU RC	15.00	40.00
68 Kevin Burnett AU RC	12.00	30.00
69 J.R. Russell AU RC	10.00	25.00
71 Marlin Jackson AU RC	10.00	25.00
72 Shawne Merriman AU RC	15.00	40.00
73 Alex Smith TE AU RC	10.00	25.00
74 Fabian Washington AU RC	12.00	30.00
75 Corey Webster AU RC	12.00	30.00
76 Larry Brackins AU RC	10.00	25.00
77 Kay-Jay Harris AU RC	10.00	25.00
78 Airese Currie AU RC	10.00	25.00
79 Taylor Stubblefield AU RC	10.00	25.00
80 James Kilian AU RC	10.00	25.00
81 Travis Johnson AU RC	10.00	25.00
82 Walter Reyes AU RC	10.00	25.00
83 Anttaj Hawthorne AU RC	10.00	25.00
84 Chad Owens AU RC	12.00	30.00
85 J.J. Arrington JSY AU RC	12.00	30.00
86 Mark Bradley JSY AU RC	10.00	25.00
87 Reggie Brown JSY AU RC	10.00	25.00
88 Jason Campbell JSY AU RC	40.00	100.00
89 Maurice Clarett JSY AU	10.00	25.00
90 Mark Clayton JSY AU RC	12.00	30.00
91 Ciatrick Fason JSY AU RC	10.00	25.00
92 Charlie Frye JSY AU RC	15.00	40.00
93 Frank Gore JSY AU RC	125.00	200.00
94 David Greene JSY AU RC	10.00	25.00
95 Vincent Jackson JSY AU RC	60.00	120.00
96 Adam Jones JSY AU RC	10.00	25.00
97 Matt Jones JSY AU RC	12.00	30.00
98 Stefan LeFors JSY AU RC	10.00	25.00
99 Heath Miller JSY AU RC	40.00	80.00
100 Ryan Moats JSY AU RC	10.00	25.00
101 Vernand Morency JSY AU RC	10.00	25.00
102 Terrence Murphy JSY AU RC	10.00	25.00
103 Kyle Orton JSY AU RC	50.00	100.00
104 Roscoe Parrish JSY AU RC	10.00	25.00
105 Courtney Roby JSY AU RC	12.00	30.00
106 Aaron Rodgers JSY AU RC	1,500.00	2,500.00
107 Carlos Rogers JSY AU RC	15.00	40.00
108 Antrel Rolle JSY AU RC	30.00	60.00
109 Eric Shelton JSY AU RC	10.00	25.00
110 Andrew Walter JSY AU RC	12.00	30.00
111 Roddy White JSY AU RC	75.00	150.00
112 Troy Williamson	20.00	50.00
JSY AU/99 RC		

113 Mike Williams JSY AU	20.00	50.00
114 Ronnie Brown JSY AU/99 RC	50.00	120.00
115 Braylon Edwards	40.00	100.00
JSY AU/99 RC		
116 Cedric Benson	50.00	120.00
JSY AU/99 RC		
117 Cadillac Williams	40.00	100.00
JSY AU/99 RC		
118 Alex Smith QB	300.00	500.00
JSY AU/99 RC		
120 Tyson Thompson AU RC	10.00	25.00
121 Chris Carr AU RC	10.00	25.00
122 Fred Amey AU RC	10.00	25.00
123 Brodney Pool AU RC	10.00	25.00
124 Stanford Routt AU RC	10.00	25.00
125 Justin Tuck AU RC	50.00	100.00
126 Luis Castillo AU RC	10.00	25.00
127 Kirk Morrison AU RC	15.00	40.00
128 DeAndra Cobb AU RC	10.00	25.00

2005 Exquisite Collection Rookie Autographed Materials Holofoil

STATED PRINT RUN 5 SER.#'d SETS
NOT PRICED DUE TO SCARCITY

2005 Exquisite Collection Cuts

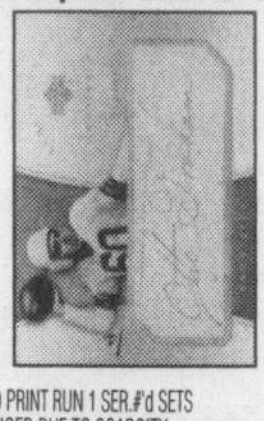

STATED PRINT RUN 1 SER.#'d SETS
NOT PRICED DUE TO SCARCITY

2005 Exquisite Collection Debut Signatures

STATED PRINT RUN 25 SER.#'d SETS

EDAJ Adam Jones	12.00	30.00
EDAN Antrel Rolle	20.00	50.00
EDAR Aaron Rodgers	350.00	600.00
EDAS Alex Smith QB	125.00	250.00
EDAW Andrew Walter	15.00	40.00
EDBE Braylon Edwards	25.00	60.00
EDCB Cedric Benson	20.00	50.00
EDCF Charlie Frye	20.00	50.00
EDCR Courtney Roby	15.00	40.00
EDCW Cadillac Williams	20.00	50.00
EDJC Jason Campbell	25.00	60.00
EDKO Kyle Orton	30.00	80.00
EDMA Mark Clayton	15.00	40.00
EDMC Maurice Clarett	12.00	30.00
EDMJ Matt Jones	15.00	40.00
EDMW Mike Williams	20.00	50.00
EDRB Reggie Brown	12.00	30.00
EDRM Ryan Moats	12.00	30.00
EDRO Ronnie Brown	40.00	100.00
EDRP Roscoe Parrish	12.00	30.00
EDRW Roddy White	25.00	60.00
EDTM Terrence Murphy	12.00	30.00
EDTW Troy Williamson	15.00	40.00
EDVJ Vincent Jackson	25.00	60.00
EDVM Vernand Morency	12.00	30.00

2005 Exquisite Collection Debut Signatures Dual

STATED PRINT RUN 15 SER.#'d SETS
NOT PRICED DUE TO SCARCITY

2005 Exquisite Collection Endorsement Autographs

STATED PRINT RUN 15 SER.#'d SETS

EEAB Anquan Boldin	15.00	40.00
EECB Chris Brown	12.00	30.00
EECJ Chad Johnson	15.00	40.00
EEDD Domanick Davis	12.00	30.00
EEJH Joe Horn	15.00	40.00
EEJI Jim Plunkett	20.00	50.00
EEJL James Lofton	20.00	50.00
EEJP J.P. Losman	12.00	30.00
EEJT Joe Theismann	40.00	80.00
EEKC Keary Colbert	12.00	30.00
EELJ Larry Johnson	15.00	40.00
EEMC Michael Clayton	12.00	30.00
EENB Nate Burleson	12.00	30.00
EERW Reggie Wayne	30.00	60.00
EETB Tiki Barber	30.00	60.00

2005 Exquisite Collection Equipment Helmet Autographs

STATED PRINT RUN 5 SER.#'d SETS
NOT PRICED DUE TO SCARCITY

2005 Exquisite Collection Equipment Pads Autographs

STATED PRINT RUN 5 SER.#'d SETS
NOT PRICED DUE TO SCARCITY

2005 Exquisite Collection NFL Logo Dual Autographs

STATED PRINT RUN 1 SER.#'d SETS
NOT PRICED DUE TO SCARCITY

2005 Exquisite Collection NFL Logo Quad Autographs

STATED PRINT RUN 1 SER.#'d SETS
NOT PRICED DUE TO SCARCITY

2005 Exquisite Collection Patch Gold

GOLD PRINT RUN 35 SER.#'d SETS
*SILVER HOLO/15: .6X TO 1.5X GOLD/35
SILVER HOLO SER.#'d TO 15

EPAA Aaron Brooks	6.00	15.00
EPAB Anquan Boldin	8.00	20.00
EPAG Ahman Green	8.00	20.00
EPAJ Adam Jones	6.00	15.00
EPAL Marcus Allen	12.00	30.00
EPAN Antonio Gates	10.00	25.00
EPAR Aaron Rodgers	75.00	135.00
EPAS Alex Smith QB	12.00	30.00
EPAW Andrew Walter	8.00	20.00
EPBE Braylon Edwards	10.00	25.00
EPBF Brett Favre	25.00	60.00
EPBJ Bo Jackson	15.00	40.00
EPBK Bernie Kosar	8.00	20.00
EPBL Byron Leftwich	8.00	20.00
EPBN Reggie Brown	5.00	12.00
EPBR Ben Roethlisberger	15.00	40.00
EPBS Barry Sanders	20.00	50.00
EPCA Carlos Rogers	8.00	20.00
EPCB Cedric Benson	8.00	20.00
EPCF Charlie Frye	8.00	20.00
EPCJ Chad Johnson	8.00	20.00
EPCP Carson Palmer	10.00	25.00
EPCR Courtney Roby	6.00	15.00
EPCW Cadillac Williams	8.00	20.00
EPDB Drew Bledsoe	10.00	25.00
EPDD Domanick Davis	6.00	15.00
EPDE Deuce McAllister	8.00	20.00
EPDM1 Dan Marino Home	30.00	80.00
EPDM2 Dan Marino Away	30.00	80.00
EPDO Donovan McNabb	10.00	25.00
EPDR Drew Bennett	8.00	20.00
EPDS Deion Sanders	15.00	40.00
EPEC Earl Campbell	12.00	30.00
EPEJ Edgerrin James	8.00	20.00
EPEM Eli Manning	15.00	40.00
EPES Eric Shelton	5.00	12.00
EPFG Frank Gore	12.00	30.00
EPFR Fred Taylor	8.00	20.00
EPGO Tony Gonzalez	8.00	20.00
EPJA J.J. Arrington	6.00	15.00
EPJC Jason Campbell	10.00	25.00
EPJE John Elway	25.00	60.00
EPJH Joe Horn	8.00	20.00
EPJJ Julius Jones	6.00	15.00
EPJK Jim Kelly	15.00	40.00
EPJM Joe Montana	30.00	80.00
EPJP J.P. Losman	6.00	15.00
EPJT Joe Theismann	12.00	30.00
EPKC Keary Colbert	6.00	15.00
EPKO Kyle Orton	8.00	20.00
EPLE Lee Evans	8.00	20.00
EPLJ LaMont Jordan	8.00	20.00
EPLT LaDainian Tomlinson	10.00	25.00
EPMA Maurice Clarett	6.00	15.00
EPMB Marc Bulger	8.00	20.00
EPMC Mark Clayton	8.00	20.00
EPMI Michael Clayton	6.00	15.00
EPMJ Matt Jones	8.00	20.00
EPMK Mark Bradley	5.00	12.00
EPMM Muhsin Muhammad	8.00	20.00
EPMO Randy Moss	10.00	25.00
EPMV Michael Vick	10.00	25.00
EPMW Mike Williams	8.00	20.00
EPNB Nate Burleson	6.00	15.00
EPPM Peyton Manning	20.00	50.00
EPRB Ronnie Brown	10.00	25.00
EPRE Reggie Wayne	10.00	25.00
EPRM Ryan Moats	6.00	15.00
EPRO Roddy White	10.00	25.00
EPRP Roscoe Parrish	5.00	12.00
EPRW Roy Williams WR	8.00	20.00
EPSF Stefan LeFors	5.00	12.00
EPSJ Steven Jackson	10.00	25.00
EPTA Troy Aikman	15.00	40.00
EPTB Tiki Barber	10.00	25.00
EPTG Trent Green	8.00	20.00
EPTM Terrence Murphy	5.00	12.00
EPTW Troy Williamson	6.00	15.00
EPVJ Vincent Jackson	10.00	25.00

2005 Exquisite Collection Patch Autographs

STATED PRINT RUN 10 SER.#'d SETS
NOT PRICED DUE TO SCARCITY

2005 Exquisite Collection Patch Duals

STATED PRINT RUN 25 SER.#'d SETS

AD Aaron Brooks	12.00	30.00
Deuce McAllister		
AJ Marcus Allen	25.00	60.00
Bo Jackson		
BD Tom Brady	30.00	80.00
Corey Dillon		
BJ Marc Bulger	15.00	40.00
Steven Jackson		
BK Barry Sanders	30.00	80.00
Kevin Jones		
BL Jerome Bettis	20.00	50.00
Jamal Lewis		
BM Tom Brady	30.00	80.00
Donovan McNabb		
CB Curtis Martin	20.00	50.00
Jerome Bettis		
DJ Tony Dorsett	20.00	50.00
Julius Jones		
EB John Elway	40.00	100.00
Tom Brady		
EK John Elway	30.00	80.00
Bernie Kosar		
FM Brett Favre	50.00	120.00
Dan Marino		
HG Priest Holmes	12.00	30.00
Trent Green		
JC Bo Jackson	20.00	50.00
Earl Campbell		
JD Joe Montana	50.00	120.00
Dan Marino		
JJ Joe Theismann	30.00	80.00
Joe Montana		
JM Julius Jones	15.00	40.00
Willis McGahee		
JS Bo Jackson	25.00	60.00
Deion Sanders		
JT Edgerrin James	15.00	40.00
LaDainian Tomlinson		
JW J.P. Losman	15.00	40.00
Willis McGahee		
KK Jim Kelly	20.00	50.00
Bernie Kosar		
KL Jim Kelly	20.00	50.00
J.P. Losman		
KW Kevin Jones	12.00	30.00
Roy Williams WR		
LM Byron Leftwich	15.00	40.00
Steve McNair		
LS Ray Lewis	25.00	60.00
Deion Sanders		
MB Eli Manning	25.00	60.00
Tiki Barber		
MF Joe Montana	50.00	120.00
Brett Favre		
MH Peyton Manning	30.00	80.00
Marvin Harrison		
MJ Peyton Manning	30.00	80.00
Edgerrin James		
MM Dan Marino	40.00	100.00
Peyton Manning		
MO Donovan McNabb	15.00	40.00
Terrell Owens		
MW Peyton Manning	30.00	80.00
Reggie Wayne		
OM Terrell Owens	15.00	40.00
Randy Moss		
PJ Carson Palmer	15.00	40.00
Chad Johnson		
RC Randy Moss	15.00	40.00
Chad Johnson		
RP Ben Roethlisberger	30.00	80.00
Carson Palmer		
SJ Barry Sanders	25.00	60.00
Julius Jones		
SR Roger Staubach	25.00	60.00
Ben Roethlisberger		
TM LaDainian Tomlinson	15.00	40.00
Deuce McAllister		
UL Brian Urlacher	15.00	40.00
Ray Lewis		
VB Michael Vick	15.00	40.00
Marc Bulger		
VC Michael Vick	15.00	40.00
Daunte Culpepper		

2005 Exquisite Collection Patch Quads

STATED PRINT RUN 10 SER.#'d SETS
NOT PRICED DUE TO SCARCITY

2005 Exquisite Collection Patch Triples

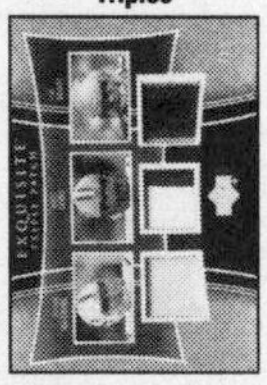

STATED PRINT RUN 15 SER.#'d SETS

BAS Drew Bledsoe	30.00	80.00
Troy Aikman		
Roger Staubach		
DHP Corey Dillon	15.00	40.00
Priest Holmes		
Clinton Portis		
FAM Brett Favre	50.00	120.00
Troy Aikman		
Joe Montana		
JJJ Julius Jones	20.00	50.00
Kevin Jones		
Steven Jackson		
MEM Joe Montana	50.00	120.00
John Elway		
Dan Marino		
MFB Peyton Manning	50.00	120.00
Brett Favre		
Tom Brady		
MJH Peyton Manning	40.00	100.00
Edgerrin James		
Marvin Harrison		
MMM Peyton Manning	50.00	120.00
Joe Montana		
Dan Marino		
MMT Willis McGahee	20.00	50.00
Deuce McAllister		
LaDainian Tomlinson		
MOH Randy Moss	20.00	50.00
Terrell Owens		
Marvin Harrison		
PAS Walter Payton	50.00	120.00
Marcus Allen		
Barry Sanders		
RCL Ben Roethlisberger	30.00	80.00
Daunte Culpepper		
Byron Leftwich		
VBF Michael Vick	50.00	120.00
Tom Brady		
Brett Favre		

2005 Exquisite Collection Signatures

STATED PRINT RUN 10-35

ESAB Anquan Boldin	20.00	50.00
ESAG Ahman Green	20.00	50.00
ESAL Marcus Allen	40.00	80.00
ESAN Antonio Gates	25.00	60.00
ESAR Aaron Rodgers	400.00	600.00
ESAS Alex Smith QB	90.00	150.00
ESBF Brett Favre	150.00	300.00
ESBJ Bo Jackson	75.00	150.00
ESBK Bernie Kosar	20.00	50.00
ESBL Byron Leftwich	20.00	50.00
ESBR Ben Roethlisberger	75.00	150.00
ESBS Barry Sanders	100.00	200.00
ESCB Cedric Benson	30.00	80.00
ESCF Charlie Frye	20.00	50.00
ESCJ Chad Johnson	20.00	50.00
ESCP Carson Palmer	25.00	60.00
ESCW Cadillac Williams	20.00	50.00
ESDB Drew Bledsoe	25.00	60.00
ESDE Deuce McAllister	20.00	50.00
ESDM1 Dan Marino Home	100.00	200.00
ESDM2 Dan Marino Away	100.00	200.00
ESDS Deion Sanders	40.00	80.00
ESEC Earl Campbell	40.00	80.00
ESEJ Edgerrin James	20.00	50.00
ESEM Eli Manning	90.00	150.00
ESFT Fran Tarkenton	25.00	60.00
ESGS Gale Sayers	40.00	80.00
ESJA J.J. Arrington	15.00	40.00
ESJC Jason Campbell	25.00	60.00
ESJE John Elway	100.00	200.00
ESJJ Julius Jones	15.00	40.00
ESJK Jim Kelly	60.00	100.00
ESJL James Lofton	15.00	40.00
ESJM Joe Montana	125.00	250.00
ESJP J.P. Losman	15.00	40.00
ESJT Joe Theismann	25.00	60.00
ESKO-Kyle Orton	25.00	60.00
ESLE Lee Evans	20.00	50.00
ESLJ LaMont Jordan	20.00	50.00
ESLT LaDainian Tomlinson	40.00	100.00
ESMA Maurice Clarett	12.00	30.00
ESMB Marc Bulger	20.00	50.00
ESMC Mark Clayton	15.00	40.00
ESMI Michael Clayton	15.00	40.00
ESMS Mike Singletary	40.00	80.00
ESMV Michael Vick	40.00	80.00
ESMW Mike Williams	20.00	50.00
ESNB Nate Burleson	15.00	40.00
ESPM Peyton Manning	100.00	200.00
ESRB Ronnie Brown	25.00	60.00
ESRE Reggie Wayne	25.00	60.00
ESRO Roddy White	25.00	60.00
ESRP Roscoe Parrish	12.00	30.00
ESRW Roy Williams WR/20	20.00	50.00
ESSJ Steven Jackson	25.00	60.00
ESTA Troy Aikman	75.00	150.00
ESTB Tiki Barber	25.00	60.00
ESTG Trent Green	20.00	50.00
ESTW Troy Williamson	15.00	40.00

2005 Exquisite Collection Signature Champions

STATED PRINT RUN 5 SER.#'d SETS
NOT PRICED DUE TO SCARCITY

2005 Exquisite Collection Signature Numbers

#'d UNDER 20 NOT PRICED DUE TO SCARCITY

SNBJ Bo Jackson/34	75.00	150.00
SNBS Barry Sanders/20	125.00	250.00
SNDS Deion Sanders/21	50.00	100.00
SNJJ Julius Jones/21		
SNMA Marcus Allen/32	40.00	80.00
SNTD Tony Dorsett/33	60.00	100.00

2005 Exquisite Collection Signature Duals

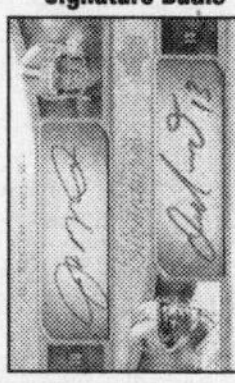

STATED PRINT RUN 25 SER.#'d SETS

AC Maurice Clarett	20.00	50.00
J.J. Arrington		
AH Herb Adderley	75.00	150.00
Paul Hornung		
BJ Marc Bulger	25.00	60.00
Steven Jackson		
BW Ronnie Brown	60.00	150.00
Cadillac Williams		
DJ Tony Dorsett	60.00	120.00
Julius Jones		
EA John Elway	125.00	250.00
Troy Aikman		
EK John Elway	125.00	250.00
Bernie Kosar		
FM Brett Favre	300.00	450.00
Peyton Manning		
JS Bo Jackson	125.00	200.00
Deion Sanders		
MM Joe Montana	200.00	400.00
Dan Marino		
MS Joe Montana	150.00	300.00
Alex Smith QB		
PJ Carson Palmer	30.00	80.00
Chad Johnson		
RL Ben Roethlisberger	75.00	150.00
J.P. Losman		
SB Gale Sayers	60.00	120.00
Cedric Benson		
SR Barry Sanders	125.00	250.00
Ronnie Brown		
TC Joe Theismann	40.00	100.00
Jason Campbell		
TJ LaDainian Tomlinson	40.00	100.00
Edgerrin James		
WC Roddy White	25.00	60.00
Mark Clayton		
WE Troy Williamson	30.00	80.00
Braylon Edwards		
WW Mike Williams	25.00	60.00
Roy Williams WR		

2005 Exquisite Collection Signature Quads

STATED PRINT RUN 10 SER.#'d SETS
NOT PRICED DUE TO SCARCITY

2005 Exquisite Collection Signature Triples

STATED PRINT RUN 15 SER.#'d SETS
NOT PRICED DUE TO SCARCITY

2005 Exquisite Collection Super Jersey Silver

STATED PRINT RUN 50 SER.#'d SETS
*GOLD/25: .5X TO 1.2X SILVER/50

SJAB Anquan Boldin	10.00	25.00
SJAG Ahman Green	10.00	25.00
SJAJ Adam Jones	6.00	15.00
SJAL Marcus Allen	12.00	30.00
SJAN Antonio Gates	12.00	30.00
SJAR Aaron Rodgers	50.00	100.00
SJAS Alex Smith QB	15.00	40.00
SJAW Andrew Walter	8.00	20.00
SJBD Brian Dawkins	10.00	25.00
SJBE Braylon Edwards	12.00	30.00
SJBF Brett Favre	30.00	80.00
SJBJ Bo Jackson	15.00	40.00
SJBK Bernie Kosar	10.00	25.00
SJBL Byron Leftwich	10.00	25.00
SJBN Reggie Brown	8.00	20.00
SJBR Ben Roethlisberger	20.00	50.00
SJBS Barry Sanders	20.00	50.00
SJCA Carlos Rogers	10.00	25.00
SJCB Cedric Benson	10.00	25.00
SJCF Charlie Frye	10.00	25.00
SJCJ Chad Johnson	10.00	25.00
SJCP Carson Palmer	12.00	30.00
SJCR Courtney Roby	8.00	20.00
SJCW Cadillac Williams	10.00	25.00
SJDB Drew Bledsoe	12.00	30.00
SJDD Domanick Davis	8.00	20.00
SJDE Deuce McAllister	10.00	25.00
SJDM1 Dan Marino Home	30.00	80.00
SJDM2 Dan Marino Away	30.00	80.00
SJDO Donovan McNabb	12.00	30.00
SJDR Drew Bennett	10.00	25.00
SJDS Deion Sanders	15.00	40.00
SJEC Earl Campbell	12.00	30.00
SJEJ Edgerrin James	10.00	25.00
SJEM Eli Manning	20.00	50.00
SJES Eric Shelton	6.00	15.00
SJFG Frank Gore	15.00	40.00
SJFT Fran Tarkenton	12.00	30.00
SJJA J.J. Arrington	8.00	20.00
SJJC Jason Campbell	12.00	30.00
SJJE John Elway	25.00	60.00
SJJH Joe Horn	10.00	25.00
SJJJ Julius Jones	8.00	20.00
SJJK Jim Kelly	15.00	40.00
SJJM Joe Montana	30.00	80.00
SJJP J.P. Losman	8.00	20.00
SJJT Joe Theismann	12.00	30.00
SJKC Keary Colbert	8.00	20.00
SJKO Kyle Orton	10.00	25.00
SJLE Lee Evans	10.00	25.00
SJLJ LaMont Jordan	10.00	25.00
SJLT LaDainian Tomlinson	12.00	30.00
SJMA Maurice Clarett	8.00	20.00
SJMB Marc Bulger	10.00	25.00
SJMC Mark Clayton	10.00	25.00
SJMJ Matt Jones	10.00	25.00
SJMK Mark Bradley	8.00	20.00
SJMM Muhsin Muhammad	10.00	25.00
SJMV Michael Vick	12.00	30.00
SJMW Mike Williams	10.00	25.00
SJNB Nate Burleson	8.00	20.00
SJPM Peyton Manning	25.00	60.00
SJRB Ronnie Brown	12.00	30.00
SJRE Reggie Wayne	12.00	30.00
SJRM Ryan Moats	8.00	20.00
SJRO Roddy White	12.00	30.00
SJRP Roscoe Parrish	6.00	15.00
SJRW Roy Williams WR	10.00	25.00
SJSA Shaun Alexander	10.00	25.00
SJSF Stefan LeFors	8.00	20.00
SJSJ Steven Jackson	12.00	30.00
SJTA Troy Aikman	15.00	40.00
SJTB Tiki Barber	12.00	30.00
SJTG Trent Green	10.00	25.00
SJTM Terrence Murphy	8.00	20.00
SJTW Troy Williamson	8.00	20.00
SJVJ Vincent Jackson	12.00	30.00
SJWM Willis McGahee	12.00	30.00

2005 Exquisite Collection Super Jersey Autographs

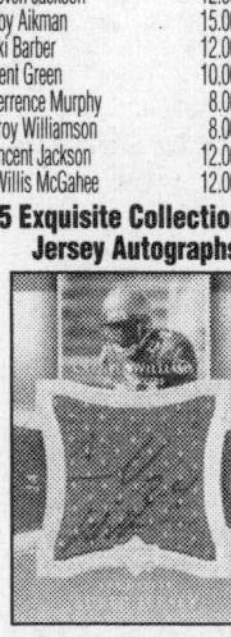

STATED PRINT RUN 15 SER.#'d SETS
NOT PRICED DUE TO SCARCITY

2005 Exquisite Collection Super Patch

STATED PRINT RUN 15 SER.#'d SETS

SUAB Anquan Boldin	25.00	60.00
SUAG Antonio Gates	30.00	80.00
SUBF Brett Favre	80.00	200.00
SUBK Bernie Kosar	25.00	60.00
SUBL Byron Leftwich	25.00	60.00
SUBO Bo Jackson	40.00	100.00
SUBR Ben Roethlisberger	50.00	125.00
SUBS Barry Sanders	50.00	120.00
SUCJ Chad Johnson	25.00	60.00
SUCP Carson Palmer	30.00	80.00
SUDB Drew Bledsoe	30.00	80.00
SUDD Domanick Davis	20.00	50.00
SUDE Deuce McAllister	25.00	60.00
SUDM Dan Marino	80.00	200.00
SUDO Donovan McNabb	30.00	80.00
SUDS Deion Sanders	40.00	100.00
SUEJ Edgerrin James	25.00	60.00
SUEM Eli Manning	50.00	125.00
SUJE John Elway	60.00	150.00
SUJJ Julius Jones	20.00	50.00
SUJM Joe Montana	80.00	200.00
SUJT Joe Theismann	30.00	80.00
SULE Lee Evans	25.00	60.00
SULT LaDainian Tomlinson	30.00	80.00
SUMA Marcus Allen	30.00	80.00
SUMB Marc Bulger	25.00	60.00
SUMC Michael Clayton	20.00	50.00
SUMS Mike Singletary	30.00	80.00
SUMV Michael Vick	30.00	80.00
SUNB Nate Burleson	20.00	50.00
SUPM Peyton Manning	60.00	150.00
SURO Roy Williams WR	25.00	60.00
SURS Roger Staubach	50.00	125.00
SURW Reggie Wayne	30.00	80.00
SUSJ Steven Jackson	30.00	80.00
SUTA Troy Aikman	40.00	100.00
SUTB Tiki Barber	30.00	80.00
SUTD Tony Dorsett	25.00	60.00
SUTG Trent Green	25.00	60.00
SUWP Walter Payton	80.00	200.00

2005 Exquisite Collection Super Patch Autographs

STATED PRINT RUN 5 SER.#'d SETS
NOT PRICED DUE TO SCARCITY

2006 Exquisite Collection

This 135-card set was released in January, 2007. The set was issued into the hobby in six-card packs (actually a box) which had a $600 SRP. Cards numbered 1-60 are veterans in team alphabetical order while cards numbered 61-135 are 2006 rookies. The veteran players were all issued to a stated print run of 150 serial numbered sets while the rookies are all signed by the featured players and cards numbered 103-135 also feature player-worn swatches. Cards numbered 61-102 were also issued to a stated print run of 150 serial numbered sets while cards numbered 103-108 and 135 were issued to a stated print run of 99 serial numbered sets. Cards numbered 109-133 were issued to a stated print run of 225 serial numbered sets. Cards number 134, Jay Cutler, was issued to a stated print run of 20 serial numbered sets and is the key card to completing this set. A few players did not return their signatures in time for pack out and those signatures could be redeemed until January 9, 2010.

1-102 PRINT RUN 150
103-108/135 JSY AU PRINT RUN 99
109-133 JSY AU PRINT RUN 225

1 Larry Fitzgerald	10.00	25.00
2 Edgerrin James	8.00	20.00
3 Michael Vick	10.00	25.00
4 Warrick Dunn	8.00	20.00
5 Steve McNair	8.00	20.00
6 Jamal Lewis	8.00	20.00
7 J.P. Losman	8.00	20.00
8 Willis McGahee	8.00	20.00
9 Jake Delhomme	8.00	20.00
10 Steve Smith	10.00	25.00
11 Rex Grossman	8.00	20.00
12 Thomas Jones	8.00	20.00
13 Carson Palmer	10.00	25.00
14 Chad Johnson	8.00	20.00
15 Charlie Frye	8.00	20.00
16 Julius Jones	6.00	15.00
17 Terrell Owens	10.00	25.00
18 Jake Plummer	8.00	20.00
19 Tatum Bell	6.00	15.00
20 Kevin Jones	6.00	15.00
21 Roy Williams WR	8.00	20.00
22 Brett Favre	40.00	80.00
23 Ahman Green	8.00	20.00
24 David Carr	6.00	15.00
25 Andre Johnson	10.00	25.00
26 Peyton Manning	25.00	50.00
27 Marvin Harrison	10.00	25.00
28 Byron Leftwich	8.00	20.00
29 Fred Taylor	8.00	20.00
30 Trent Green	8.00	20.00
31 Larry Johnson	8.00	20.00
32 Daunte Culpepper	8.00	20.00
33 Ronnie Brown	10.00	25.00
34 Chester Taylor	8.00	20.00
35 Tom Brady	15.00	40.00
36 Corey Dillon	8.00	20.00
37 Drew Brees	12.00	30.00
38 Deuce McAllister	8.00	20.00
39 Eli Manning	12.00	30.00
40 Tiki Barber	10.00	25.00
41 Chad Pennington	8.00	20.00
42 Laveranues Coles	6.00	15.00
43 Randy Moss	10.00	25.00
44 LaMont Jordan	8.00	20.00
45 Donovan McNabb	10.00	25.00
46 Brian Westbrook	8.00	20.00
47 Ben Roethlisberger	12.00	30.00
48 Willie Parker	8.00	20.00
49 Philip Rivers	10.00	25.00
50 LaDainian Tomlinson	10.00	25.00
51 Alex Smith QB	10.00	25.00
52 Frank Gore	10.00	25.00
53 Matt Hasselbeck	8.00	20.00
54 Shaun Alexander	8.00	20.00
55 Marc Bulger	8.00	20.00
56 Steven Jackson	10.00	25.00
57 Cadillac Williams	8.00	20.00
58 Drew Bennett	8.00	20.00
59 Clinton Portis	10.00	25.00
60 Santana Moss	8.00	20.00
61 Andre Hall AU RC	12.00	30.00
62 Anthony Fasano AU RC	15.00	40.00
63 Antonio Cromartie AU RC	25.00	60.00
64 Ashton Youboty AU RC	10.00	25.00
65 Brad Smith AU RC	15.00	40.00
66 Brodrick Bunkley AU RC	12.00	30.00
67 Bruce Gradkowski AU RC	15.00	40.00
68 Chad Greenway AU RC	15.00	40.00
69 Cory Rodgers AU RC	12.00	30.00
70 D.J. Shockley AU RC	12.00	30.00
71 Darnell Bing AU RC	12.00	30.00
72 Darrell Hackney AU RC	12.00	30.00
73 D'Brickashaw Ferguson AU RC	15.00	40.00
74 Dominique Byrd AU RC	12.00	30.00
75 Drew Olson AU RC	10.00	25.00
76 Ernie Sims AU RC	12.00	30.00
77 Garrett Mills AU RC	15.00	40.00
78 Gerald Riggs AU RC	12.00	30.00
79 Greg Jennings AU RC	75.00	125.00
80 Greg Lee AU RC	10.00	25.00
81 Ingle Martin AU RC	12.00	30.00
82 Jason Allen AU RC	12.00	30.00
83 Jerome Harrison AU RC	25.00	60.00
84 Jimmy Williams AU RC	15.00	40.00
85 Joseph Addai AU RC	25.00	60.00
86 Josh Betts AU RC	12.00	30.00
87 Kelly Jennings AU RC	12.00	30.00
88 Leonard Pope AU RC	15.00	40.00
89 Marcus McNeill AU RC	12.00	30.00
90 Martin Nance AU RC	12.00	30.00
91 Mathias Kiwanuka AU RC	15.00	40.00
92 Mike Bell AU RC	15.00	40.00
93 Mike Hass AU RC	12.00	30.00
94 Owen Daniels AU RC	15.00	40.00
95 P.J. Daniels AU RC	10.00	25.00
96 Reggie McNeal AU RC	12.00	30.00
97 Skyler Green AU RC	10.00	25.00
98 Terrence Whitehead AU RC	12.00	30.00
99 Thomas Howard AU RC	12.00	30.00
100 Tye Hill AU RC	10.00	25.00
101 Will Blackmon AU RC	12.00	30.00
102 Winston Justice AU RC	12.00	30.00
103 DeAngelo Williams JSY AU/99 RC	100.00	200.00
104 Matt Leinart JSY AU/99 RC	60.00	120.00
105 Reggie Bush JSY AU/99 RC	150.00	300.00
106 Santonio Holmes JSY AU/99 RC	60.00	120.00
107 Sinorice Moss JSY AU/99 RC	30.00	80.00
108 Vince Young JSY AU/99 RC	100.00	200.00
109 A.J. Hawk JSY AU RC	20.00	50.00
110 Brandon Marshall JSY AU RC	60.00	120.00
111 Brandon Williams JSY AU RC	12.00	30.00
112 Brian Calhoun JSY AU RC	12.00	30.00
113 Chad Jackson JSY AU RC	12.00	30.00
114 Charlie Whitehurst JSY AU RC	25.00	60.00
115 Demetrius Williams JSY AU RC	15.00	40.00
116 Derek Hagan JSY AU RC	15.00	40.00
117 Jason Avant JSY AU RC	12.00	30.00
118 Jerious Norwood JSY AU RC	15.00	40.00
119 Joe Klopfenstein JSY AU RC	12.00	30.00
120 Kellen Clemens JSY AU RC	15.00	40.00
121 Laurence Maroney JSY AU RC	15.00	40.00
122 LenDale White JSY AU RC	15.00	40.00
123 Leon Washington JSY AU RC	15.00	40.00
124 Marcedes Lewis JSY AU RC	20.00	50.00
125 Mario Williams JSY AU RC	30.00	80.00
126 Maurice Drew JSY AU RC	100.00	200.00
127 Maurice Stovall JSY AU RC	12.00	30.00
128 Michael Huff JSY AU RC	15.00	40.00
129 Michael Robinson JSY AU RC	15.00	40.00
130 Omar Jacobs JSY AU RC	12.00	30.00
131 Tarvaris Jackson JSY AU RC	25.00	60.00
132 Travis Wilson JSY AU RC	12.00	30.00
133 Vernon Davis JSY AU RC	75.00	150.00
134 Jay Cutler JSY AU/20 RC	2,000.00	3,000.00
135 Marques Colston JSY AU/99 RC	200.00	350.00
(EXCH card in packs; released in 2010 wearing college jersey)		

2006 Exquisite Collection Gold

UNPRICED VETERAN 1-60 PRINT RUN 1
*ROOKIES 61-102: .5X TO 1.2X BASIC CARDS
*ROOK.JSY AU/99 109-133: .5X TO 1.2X
ROOKIE PRINT RUN 60 SER.#'d SETS

103 DeAngelo Williams JSY AU/25	125.00	250.00
104 Matt Leinart JSY AU/25	100.00	250.00
105 Reggie Bush JSY AU/25	250.00	500.00
106 Santonio Holmes JSY AU/25	125.00	250.00
108 Vince Young JSY AU/25	150.00	300.00
126 Maurice Drew JSY AU/99	125.00	250.00
133 Vernon Davis JSY AU/99	125.00	200.00

2006 Exquisite Collection Debut Signatures

STATED PRINT RUN 35 SER.#'d SETS

EDSAH A.J. Hawk	12.00	30.00
EDSCJ Chad Jackson	8.00	20.00
EDSDH Derek Hagan	10.00	25.00
EDSDW DeAngelo Williams	15.00	40.00
EDSJC Jay Cutler	25.00	60.00
EDSKC Kellen Clemens	10.00	25.00
EDSLE Marcedes Lewis	12.00	30.00
EDSLM Laurence Maroney	10.00	25.00
EDSLW LenDale White	10.00	25.00
EDSMD Maurice Drew	20.00	50.00
EDSMH Michael Huff	10.00	25.00
EDSML Matt Leinart	12.00	30.00
EDSMS Maurice Stovall	8.00	20.00
EDSMW Mario Williams	12.00	30.00
EDSRB Reggie Bush	25.00	60.00
EDSSH Santonio Holmes	15.00	40.00
EDSSM Sinorice Moss	12.00	30.00
EDSTJ Tarvaris Jackson	12.00	30.00
EDSVD Vernon Davis	25.00	50.00
EDSVY Vince Young	15.00	40.00

2006 Exquisite Collection Dual Legendary Cuts

UNPRICED DUAL CUT PRINT RUN 1

2006 Exquisite Collection Dual Logo Signatures

UNPRICED DUAL SIG PRINT RUN 1

2006 Exquisite Collection Endorsements

STATED PRINT RUN 35 SER.#'d SETS
UNPRICED HOLOFOIL PRINT RUN 1
EEAC Alge Crumpler

EEAD Joseph Addai 15.00 40.00
EEAG Antonio Gates 15.00 40.00
EEAH A.J. Hawk 15.00 40.00
EEBA Ronde Barber 12.00 30.00
EEBC Brian Calhoun 10.00 25.00
EEBE Braylon Edwards 12.00 30.00
EEBF Brett Favre 125.00 250.00
EEBG Bob Griese 30.00 60.00
EEBM Brandon Marshall 15.00 40.00
EEBR Ben Roethlisberger 75.00 135.00
EECB Cedric Benson 12.00 30.00
EECF Charlie Frye 12.00 30.00
EECJ Chad Jackson 10.00 25.00
EECS Chris Simms 12.00 30.00
EEDB Drew Bledsoe 15.00 40.00
EEDO Dwight Clark 12.00 30.00
EEDF D'Brickashaw Ferguson 15.00 40.00
EEDH Derek Hagan 12.00 30.00
EEDM Dan Marino 100.00 200.00
EEDW DeAngelo Williams
EEEM Eli Manning 60.00 100.00
EEFO DeShaun Foster 12.00 30.00
EEFT Fran Tarkenton 50.00 100.00
EEGS Gale Sayers 50.00 100.00
EEJA Jason Avant 10.00 25.00
EEJC Jay Cutler 75.00 150.00
EEJJ Julius Jones 10.00 25.00
EEJK Jim Kelly/30 50.00 100.00
EEJO LaMont Jordan 12.00 30.00
EEJT Joe Theismann 30.00 60.00
EEJW Jason Witten 25.00 60.00
EEKC Kellen Clemens 12.00 30.00
EEKJ Keyshawn Johnson 12.00 30.00
EELD Len Dawson 15.00 40.00
EELE Matt Leinart 30.00 80.00
EELG L.C. Greenwood 25.00 50.00
EELJ Larry Johnson 12.00 30.00
EELM Laurence Maroney 12.00 30.00
EELT Lofa Tatupu 12.00 30.00
EELW LenDale White 12.00 30.00
EEMB Marc Bulger 12.00 30.00
EEMC Michael Clayton 10.00 25.00
EEMD Maurice Drew 60.00 120.00
EEMH Michael Huff 12.00 30.00
EEML Marcedes Lewis 15.00 40.00
EEMM Muhsin Muhammad 12.00 30.00
EEMR Michael Robinson 12.00 30.00
EEMS Maurice Stovall 10.00 25.00
EEMW Mario Williams 15.00 40.00
EEOJ Omar Jacobs 10.00 25.00
EEPH Paul Hornung 40.00 80.00
EEPM Peyton Manning 100.00 200.00
EEPR Philip Rivers 30.00 60.00
EERB Reggie Bush 60.00 150.00
EERO Ronnie Brown 15.00 40.00
EERW Reggie Wayne 12.00 30.00
EETA Troy Aikman 60.00 120.00
EETB Tiki Barber 15.00 40.00
EETG Trent Green 12.00 30.00
EETH T.J. Houshmandzadeh 12.00 30.00
EETJ Tarvaris Jackson 15.00 40.00
EETW Travis Wilson 10.00 25.00
EEVD Vernon Davis 20.00 50.00
EEVY Vince Young 60.00 120.00
EEWH Charlie Whitehurst 25.00 40.00
EEWP Willie Parker 12.00 30.00

2006 Exquisite Collection Foursome Signature Patch

UNPRICED FOUR SIG PRINT RUN 5

2006 Exquisite Collection Inscriptions

STATED PRINT RUN 25 SER.#'d SETS
UNPRICED HOLOFOIL PRINT RUN 1
EIBF Brett Favre 125.00 250.00
EIBR Ben Roethlisberger 60.00 120.00
EIBS Barry Sanders 100.00 200.00
EICW Cadillac Williams 20.00 50.00
EIDC Dwight Clark 25.00 60.00
EIJK Jim Kelly 50.00 100.00
EIKS Ken Stabler 50.00 100.00
EILC L.C. Greenwood 25.00 60.00
EIPM Peyton Manning 125.00 250.00
EISS Steve Smith 25.00 60.00
EITA Troy Aikman 60.00 120.00
EITD Tony Dorsett 30.00 80.00
EIWP Willie Parker 20.00 50.00

2006 Exquisite Collection Legendary Signatures

STATED PRINT RUN 10-25
UNPRICED HOLOFOIL PRINT RUN 1
SERIAL #'d UNDER 25 NOT PRICED
ELSBG Bob Griese 30.00 80.00
ELSDC Dwight Clark 25.00 60.00
ELSDF Dan Fouts 30.00 80.00
ELSDM Dan Marino 175.00 300.00
ELSFH Franco Harris 100.00 175.00
ELSGS Gale Sayers 30.00 80.00
ELSJE John Elway 125.00 200.00
ELSJK Jim Kelly 40.00 100.00
ELSJT Joe Theismann 25.00 60.00
ELSKS Ken Stabler 75.00 150.00
ELSLC L.C. Greenwood 25.00 60.00
ELSLD Len Dawson 25.00 60.00
ELSPH Paul Hornung 30.00 80.00
ELSTA Troy Aikman 75.00 150.00

2006 Exquisite Collection Maximum Jersey Silver

SILVER PRINT RUN 75 SER.#'d SETS
*GOLD/35: .6X TO 1.5X SILVER/75
GOLD PRINT RUN 35 SER.#'d SETS
UNPRICED SPECTRUM PRINT RUN 1
UNPRICED SIGNATURE PRINT RUN 5
XXLAG Antonio Gates 8.00 20.00
XXLAH A.J. Hawk 6.00 15.00
XXLBA Ronde Barber 6.00 15.00
XXLBC Brian Calhoun 4.00 10.00
XXLBE Braylon Edwards 6.00 15.00
XXLBF Brett Favre 15.00 40.00
XXLBM Brandon Marshall 6.00 15.00
XXLBR Ben Roethlisberger 10.00 25.00
XXLBU Reggie Bush 12.00 30.00
XXLBW Brandon Williams 4.00 10.00
XXLCB Cedric Benson 6.00 15.00
XXLCF Charlie Frye 6.00 15.00
XXLCJ Chad Jackson 4.00 10.00
XXLCL Mark Clayton 6.00 15.00
XXLCP Carson Palmer 8.00 20.00
XXLCS Chris Simms 6.00 15.00
XXLCU Kevin Curtis 6.00 15.00
XXLCW Cadillac Williams 6.00 15.00
XXLDB Drew Bledsoe 8.00 20.00
XXLDE Demetrius Williams 5.00 12.00
XXLDF DeShaun Foster 6.00 15.00
XXLDG David Givens 6.00 15.00
XXLDH Derek Hagan 5.00 12.00
XXLDM Derrick Mason 6.00 15.00
XXLDO Donovan McNabb 8.00 20.00
XXLDW DeAngelo Williams 8.00 20.00
XXLEM Eli Manning 10.00 25.00
XXLGJ Greg Jones 5.00 12.00
XXLHA Matt Hasselbeck 6.00 15.00
XXLHO T.J. Houshmandzadeh 6.00 15.00
XXLJA Jason Avant 4.00 10.00
XXLJC Jay Cutler 12.00 30.00
XXLJJ Julius Jones 5.00 12.00
XXLJK Joe Klopfenstein 4.00 10.00
XXLJN Jerious Norwood 5.00 12.00
XXLJO LaMont Jordan 6.00 15.00
XXLJW Jason Witten 8.00 20.00
XXLKC Kellen Clemens 5.00 12.00
XXLKJ Keyshawn Johnson 6.00 15.00
XXLKO Kyle Orton 8.00 20.00
XXLLC Dyron Loftwich 6.00 15.00
XXLLJ Larry Johnson 6.00 15.00
XXLLM Laurence Maroney 5.00 12.00
XXLLT LaDainian Tomlinson 8.00 20.00
XXLLW LenDale White 5.00 12.00
XXLMA Matt Leinart 6.00 15.00
XXLMB Marc Bulger 6.00 15.00
XXLMC Deuce McAllister 6.00 15.00
XXLMD Maurice Drew 10.00 25.00
XXLMH Michael Huff 5.00 12.00
XXLMI Michael Clayton 5.00 12.00
XXLML Marcedes Lewis 6.00 15.00
XXLMM Muhsin Muhammad 6.00 15.00
XXLMR Michael Robinson 5.00 12.00
XXLMS Maurice Stovall 4.00 10.00
XXLMV Michael Vick 8.00 20.00
XXLMW Mario Williams 6.00 15.00
XXLNB Nate Burleson 5.00 12.00
XXLOJ Omar Jacobs 4.00 10.00
XXLPM Peyton Manning 12.00 30.00
XXLPR Philip Rivers 8.00 20.00
XXLRB Reggie Brown 5.00 12.00
XXLRJ Rudi Johnson 6.00 15.00
XXLRM Randy Moss 8.00 20.00
XXLRO Ronnie Brown 8.00 20.00
XXLRW Reggie Wayne 6.00 15.00
XXLSA Shaun Alexander 6.00 15.00
XXLSH Santonio Holmes 8.00 20.00
XXLSM Sinorice Moss 6.00 15.00
XXLSS Steve Smith 8.00 20.00
XXLTB Tedy Bruschi 8.00 20.00
XXLTG Trent Green 6.00 15.00
XXLTH Thomas Jones 6.00 15.00
XXLTI Tiki Barber 8.00 20.00
XXLTJ Tarvaris Jackson 6.00 15.00
XXLTO Tom Brady 12.00 30.00
XXLTW Travis Wilson 4.00 10.00
XXLVD Vernon Davis 8.00 20.00
XXLVY Vince Young 8.00 20.00
XXLWA Leon Washington 5.00 12.00
XXLWH Charlie Whitehurst 6.00 15.00
XXLWI Mike Williams 5.00 12.00
XXLWP Willie Parker 6.00 15.00

2006 Exquisite Collection Maximum Jersey Signature

UNPRICED AUTO PRINT RUN 5 SETS

2006 Exquisite Collection Maximum Patch

STATED PRINT RUN 30 SER.#'d SETS
EMPBA Tiki Barber 15.00 40.00
EMPBF Brett Favre 30.00 80.00
EMPBL Byron Leftwich 12.00 30.00
EMPBR Ben Roethlisberger 20.00 50.00
EMPCJ Chad Jackson 10.00 25.00
EMPCP Carson Palmer 15.00 40.00
EMPCW Cadillac Williams 12.00 30.00
EMPDB Drew Bledsoe 16.00 40.00
EMPDC Daunte Culpepper 12.00 30.00
EMPDM Deuce McAllister 12.00 30.00
EMPDR Drew Brees 15.00 40.00
EMPDW DeAngelo Williams 15.00 40.00
EMPEJ Edgerrin James 12.00 30.00
EMPEM Eli Manning 20.00 50.00
EMPHW Hines Ward 15.00 40.00
EMPJJ Julius Jones 10.00 25.00
EMPJO Chad Johnson 12.00 30.00
EMPJP Jake Plummer 12.00 30.00
EMPLJ Larry Johnson 12.00 30.00
EMPLM Laurence Maroney 10.00 25.00
EMPLT LaDainian Tomlinson 15.00 40.00
EMPLW LenDale White 10.00 25.00
EMPMB Marc Bulger 12.00 30.00
EMPMC Donovan McNabb 15.00 40.00
EMPMH Marvin Harrison 15.00 40.00
EMPML Matt Leinart 12.00 30.00
EMPMV Michael Vick 15.00 40.00
EMPMW Mario Williams 12.00 30.00
EMPPM Peyton Manning 25.00 60.00
EMPPO Clinton Portis 15.00 40.00
EMPPR Philip Rivers 15.00 40.00
EMPRB Reggie Bush 25.00 60.00
EMPRJ Rudi Johnson 12.00 30.00
EMPRM Randy Moss 15.00 40.00
EMPRO Ronnie Brown 15.00 40.00
EMPSA Shaun Alexander 12.00 30.00
EMPSH Santonio Holmes 15.00 40.00
EMPTB Tom Brady 25.00 60.00
EMPTG Trent Green 12.00 30.00
EMPTO Terrell Owens 15.00 40.00
EMPVD Vernon Davis 15.00 40.00
EMPVY Vince Young 15.00 40.00

2006 Exquisite Collection Patch Silver

SILVER PRINT RUN 50 SER.#'d SETS
*GOLD/30: .5X TO 1.2X SILVER/50
GOLD PRINT RUN 30 SER.#'d SETS
UNPRICED SPECTRUM PRINT RUN 1
UNPRICED PATCH TRIO PRINT RUN 20
UNPRICED PATCH QUAD PRINT RUN 15
EPAB Anquan Boldin 8.00 20.00
EPAC Alge Crumpler 8.00 20.00
EPAG Ahman Green 8.00 20.00
EPAH A.J. Hawk 8.00 20.00
EPAR Antwaan Randle El 8.00 20.00
EPAS Alex Smith QB 10.00 25.00
EPBD Brian Dawkins 8.00 20.00
EPBE Braylon Edwards 8.00 20.00
EPBF Brett Favre 20.00 50.00
EPBL Byron Leftwich 8.00 20.00
EPBR Ben Roethlisberger 12.00 30.00
EPBS Barry Sanders 25.00 60.00
EPBU Brian Urlacher 10.00 25.00
EPBW Brian Westbrook 8.00 20.00
EPCC Chris Chambers 8.00 20.00
EPCF Charlie Frye 8.00 20.00
EPCJ Chad Johnson 8.00 20.00
EPCM Curtis Martin 10.00 25.00
EPCP Clinton Portis 10.00 25.00
EPCW Cadillac Williams 8.00 20.00
EPDB Drew Bledsoe 10.00 25.00
EPDC Daunte Culpepper 8.00 20.00
EPDF DeShaun Foster 8.00 20.00
EPDM Deuce McAllister 8.00 20.00
EPDR Drew Brees 10.00 25.00
EPDW DeAngelo Williams 10.00 25.00
EPEJ Edgerrin James 8.00 20.00
EPEM Eli Manning 12.00 30.00
EPER Ed Reed 8.00 20.00
EPFL Doug Flutie 15.00 40.00
EPFT Fred Taylor 8.00 20.00
EPGA Antonio Gates 10.00 25.00
EPGO Tony Gonzalez 8.00 20.00
EPHA Matt Hasselbeck 8.00 20.00
EPHO Torry Holt 8.00 20.00
EPIB Isaac Bruce 8.00 20.00
EPJA Chad Jackson 6.00 15.00
EPJE John Elway 25.00 60.00
EPJI Jim Plunkett 12.00 30.00
EPJJ Julius Jones 6.00 15.00
EPJK Jim Kelly 20.00 50.00
EPJL Jamal Lewis 8.00 20.00
EPJM Joe Montana 30.00 80.00
EPJO LaMont Jordan 8.00 20.00
EPJP Julius Peppers 8.00 20.00
EPJS Jeremy Shockey 10.00 25.00
EPJW Javon Walker 8.00 20.00
EPKJ Kevin Jones 6.00 15.00
EPKW Kurt Warner 10.00 25.00
EPLA LaVar Arrington 8.00 20.00
EPLJ Larry Johnson 8.00 20.00
EPLM Laurence Maroney 6.00 15.00
EPLT LaDainian Tomlinson 10.00 25.00
EPLW LenDale White 6.00 15.00
EPMA Dan Marino 30.00 80.00
EPMB Marc Bulger 8.00 20.00
EPMC Donovan McNabb 10.00 25.00
EPMF Marshall Faulk 8.00 20.00
EPMH Marvin Harrison 10.00 25.00
EPML Matt Leinart 8.00 20.00
EPMM Muhsin Muhammad 8.00 20.00
EPMO Sinorice Moss 10.00 25.00
EPMS Michael Strahan 8.00 20.00
EPMV Michael Vick 10.00 25.00
EPMW Mario Williams 8.00 20.00
EPOW Terrell Owens 10.00 25.00
EPPA Carson Palmer 10.00 25.00
EPPB Plaxico Burress 8.00 20.00
EPPL Jake Plummer 8.00 20.00
EPPM Peyton Manning 15.00 40.00
EPPR Philip Rivers 10.00 25.00
EPRB Reggie Bush 15.00 40.00
EPRJ Rudi Johnson 8.00 20.00
EPRL Ray Lewis 10.00 25.00
EPRM Randy Moss 10.00 25.00
EPRO Ronnie Brown 10.00 25.00
EPRW Roy Williams WR 8.00 20.00
EPSA Shaun Alexander 8.00 20.00
EPSH Santonio Holmes 10.00 25.00
EPSJ Steven Jackson 10.00 25.00
EPSM Steve McNair 8.00 20.00
EPSS Steve Smith 10.00 25.00
EPTA Tatum Bell 6.00 15.00
EPTB Tiki Barber 10.00 25.00
EPTD Tony Dorsett 15.00 40.00
EPTG Trent Green 8.00 20.00
EPTH T.J. Houshmandzadeh 8.00 20.00
EPTJ Thomas Jones 8.00 20.00
EPTO Tom Brady 15.00 40.00
EPTP Troy Polamalu 12.00 30.00
EPVD Vernon Davis 12.00 30.00
EPVY Vince Young 10.00 25.00
EPWA Reggie Wayne 8.00 20.00
EPWM Willis McGahee 8.00 20.00
EPWP Willie Parker 8.00 20.00

2006 Exquisite Collection Patch Combos

STATED PRINT RUN 25 SER.#'d SETS
AW Jason Avant 12.00 30.00
  Brian Westbrook
BM Reggie Bush 20.00 50.00
  Deuce McAllister
CS Michael Clayton 6.00 15.00
  Maurice Stovall
CW Brian Calhoun 10.00 25.00
  Mike Williams
DH Brian Dawkins 12.00 30.00
  Michael Huff
DW Vernon Davis 12.00 30.00
  Brandon Williams
FJ Marshall Faulk 15.00 40.00
  Steven Jackson
HC Derek Hagan 12.00 30.00
  Chris Chambers
JH Omar Jacobs 12.00 30.00
  Santonio Holmes
JL Edgerrin James 10.00 25.00
  Matt Leinart
JM Chad Jackson 8.00 20.00
  Laurence Maroney
JT Larry Johnson 15.00 40.00
  LaDainian Tomlinson
JW Tarvaris Jackson 10.00 25.00
  Charlie Whitehurst
LD Marcedes Lewis 15.00 40.00
  Maurice Drew
MB Eli Manning 20.00 50.00
  Tiki Barber
MF Peyton Manning 60.00 120.00
  Brett Favre
MW Donovan McNabb 15.00 40.00
  Brian Westbrook
NW Jerious Norwood 8.00 20.00
  Leon Washington
PJ Carson Palmer 15.00 40.00
  Chad Johnson
PM Chad Pennington 15.00 40.00
  Curtis Martin
PW Julius Peppers 10.00 25.00
  Mario Williams
RH Ben Roethlisberger 20.00 50.00
  Santonio Holmes
RW Philip Rivers 15.00 40.00
  Charlie Whitehurst
SR Alex Smith 15.00 40.00
  Michael Robinson
TB Tatum Bell 15.00 40.00
  Brandon Marshall
VY Michael Vick 12.00 30.00
  Vince Young
WH Mario Williams 10.00 25.00
  A.J. Hawk
WW Travis Wilson 8.00 20.00
  Demetrius Williams

2006 Exquisite Collection Patch Quads

UNPRICED PATCH QUAD PRINT RUN 15

2006 Exquisite Collection Patch Trios

STATED PRINT RUN 20 SER.#'d SETS
BLW Reggie Bush 20.00 50.00
  Matt Leinart
  LenDale White
BMJ Tom Brady 15.00 40.00
  Laurence Maroney
  Chad Jackson
DWR Vernon Davis 12.00 30.00
  Brandon Williams
  Michael Robinson
FBM Brett Favre 30.00 80.00
  Tom Brady
  Peyton Manning
FEW Charlie Frye 12.00 30.00
  Braylon Edwards
  Travis Williams
FPW DeShaun Foster 12.00 30.00
  Julius Peppers
  DeAngelo Williams
GJG Trent Green 12.00 30.00
  Larry Johnson
  Tony Gonzalez
JHK Steven Jackson 15.00 40.00
  Torry Holt
  Joe Klopfenstein
MKS Dan Marino 40.00 100.00
  Jim Kelly
  Roger Staubach
MLW Steve McNair 12.00 30.00
  Jamal Lewis
  Demetrius Williams
MMS Eli Manning 20.00 50.00
  Sinorice Moss
  Jeremy Shockey
MWB Donovan McNabb 15.00 40.00
  Brian Westbrook
  Reggie Brown
RHW Ben Roethlisberger 20.00 50.00
  Santonio Holmes
  Hines Ward
STB Barry Sanders 20.00 50.00
  LaDainian Tomlinson
  Reggie Bush
WHH Mario Williams 10.00 25.00
  A.J. Hawk
  Michael Huff

2006 Exquisite Collection Rare Materials Signatures

UNPRICED RARE SIG PRIINT RUN 1

2006 Exquisite Collection Rookie Signature Patch Spectrum

UNPRICED SPECTRUM PRINT RUN 1

2006 Exquisite Collection Signature Duals

DUAL SIGNATURE PRINT RUN 20
BB Tiki Barber 15.00 40.00
  Ronde Barber
BJ Drew Bledsoe
  Julius Jones
BW Reggie Bush 40.00 80.00
  LenDale White
CC Mark Clayton 12.00 30.00
  Michael Clayton
CD Dwight Clark 20.00 50.00
  Vernon Davis
CW Kellen Clemens 12.00 30.00
  Leon Washington
EC John Elway 100.00 200.00
  Jay Cutler
FE Charlie Frye 12.00 30.00
  Braylon Edwards
HW Derek Hagan 12.00 30.00
  Demetrius Williams
JR Omar Jacobs 12.00 30.00
  Willie Reid
LD Marcedes Lewis 25.00 60.00
  Maurice Drew
MA Laurence Maroney 15.00 40.00
  Joseph Addai
RW Philip Rivers
  Mario Williams
SB Gale Sayers
  Cedric Benson
SL Ken Stabler 40.00 80.00
  Matt Leinart
TH Lofa Tatupu 15.00 40.00
  A.J. Hawk
TW LaDainian Tomlinson 40.00 80.00
  DeAngelo Williams
WM Reggie Wayne 15.00 40.00
  Sinorice Moss
WR Brandon Williams 12.00 30.00
  Michael Robinson
YH Vince Young 25.00 60.00
  Michael Huff

2006 Exquisite Collection Signature Numbers

STATED PRINT RUN 10-90 SER.#'d SETS
UNPRICED DUAL SIG PRINT RUN 20
UNPRICED QUAD SIG PRINT RUN 10
UNPRICED QUAD SIG LOGO PRINT RUN 10
UNPRICED TRIO SIG PRINT RUN 15
SERIAL #'d UNDER 25 NOT PRICED
ESNAG Antonio Gates/85 15.00 40.00
ESNAH A.J. Hawk/50 25.00 60.00
ESNBA Tiki Barber/21 30.00 60.00
ESNBC Brian Calhoun/29 15.00 40.00
ESNBR Ronnie Brown/23 20.00 50.00
ESNBS Barry Sanders/20 125.00 250.00
ESNCW Cadillac Williams/24 15.00 40.00
ESNDH Derek Hagan/82 12.00 30.00
ESNDW DeAngelo Williams/34 30.00 80.00
ESNGS Gale Sayers/40 60.00 100.00
ESNJA Jason Avant/81 10.00 25.00
ESNJJ Julius Jones/21 15.00 40.00
ESNJN Jerious Norwood/32 15.00 40.00
ESNJO LaMont Jordan/34 15.00 40.00
ESNLJ Larry Johnson/27 15.00 40.00
ESNLM Laurence Maroney/39 12.00 30.00
ESNLW LenDale White/25 15.00 40.00
ESNMD Maurice Drew/32 40.00 100.00
ESNMH Michael Huff/24 15.00 40.00
ESNML Marcedes Lewis/89 15.00 40.00
ESNMR Michael Robinson/35 15.00 40.00
ESNMS Maurice Stovall/85 10.00 25.00
ESNMW Mario Williams/90 15.00 40.00
ESNRB Reggie Bush/25 40.00 100.00
ESNSM Sinorice Moss/83 15.00 40.00
ESNTW Travis Wilson/81 10.00 25.00
ESNVD Vernon Davis/05 30.00 60.00
ESNWA Leon Washington/29 15.00 40.00
ESNWI Demetrius Williams/87 12.00 30.00
ESNWP Willie Parker/39 15.00 40.00

2006 Exquisite Collection Signature Patch

UNPRICED PATCH PRINT RUN 10

2006 Exquisite Collection Signature Quads

UNPRICED QUAD SIG PRINT RUN 10

2006 Exquisite Collection Signature Swatches

STATED PRINT RUN 25 SER.#'d SETS
UNPRICED SIG PATCH PRINT RUN 10
ESSAG Antonio Gates 20.00 50.00
ESSAH A.J. Hawk 20.00 50.00
ESSBA Tiki Barber 20.00 50.00
ESSBC Brian Calhoun 12.00 30.00
ESSBE Braylon Edwards 15.00 40.00
ESSBF Brett Favre 125.00 250.00
ESSBL Byron Leftwich 15.00 40.00
ESSBR Ben Roethlisberger 40.00 100.00
ESSBU Reggie Bush 60.00 120.00
ESSCB Cedric Benson 15.00 40.00
ESSCF Charlie Frye 15.00 40.00
ESSCJ Chad Jackson 12.00 30.00
ESSCS Chris Simms 15.00 40.00
ESSCW Cadillac Williams 15.00 40.00
ESSDB Drew Bledsoe 20.00 50.00
ESSDF DeShaun Foster 15.00 40.00
ESSDG David Givens 15.00 40.00
ESSDH Derek Hagan 15.00 40.00
ESSDM Deuce McAllister 15.00 40.00
ESSDW DeAngelo Williams 30.00 80.00
ESSEM Eli Manning 60.00 120.00
ESSHO T.J. Houshmandzadeh 15.00 40.00
ESSJJ Julius Jones 12.00 30.00
ESSJM Joe Montana 100.00 200.00
ESSJO LaMont Jordan 15.00 40.00
ESSKC Kellen Clemens 15.00 40.00
ESSKJ Keyshawn Johnson 15.00 40.00
ESSKO Kyle Orton 20.00 50.00
ESSLE Matt Leinart 20.00 50.00
ESSLJ Larry Johnson 15.00 40.00
ESSLM Laurence Maroney 15.00 40.00
ESSLT LaDainian Tomlinson 40.00 100.00
ESSLW LenDale White 15.00 40.00
ESSMB Marc Bulger 15.00 40.00
ESSMC Michael Clayton 12.00 30.00
ESSMD Maurice Drew 30.00 80.00
ESSMH Michael Huff 15.00 40.00
ESSML Marcedes Lewis 20.00 50.00
ESSMM Muhsin Muhammad 15.00 40.00
ESSMS Maurice Stovall 12.00 30.00
ESSMV Michael Vick 50.00 100.00
ESSMW Mario Williams 20.00 50.00
ESSPM Peyton Manning 100.00 200.00
ESSPR Philip Rivers 30.00 80.00
ESSRB Reggie Brown 12.00 30.00
ESSRJ Rudi Johnson 15.00 40.00
ESSRO Ronnie Brown 20.00 50.00
ESSRW Reggie Wayne 15.00 40.00
ESSSH Santonio Holmes 25.00 60.00
ESSSM Sinorice Moss 20.00 50.00
ESSSS Steve Smith 20.00 50.00
ESSTA Lofa Tatupu 15.00 40.00
ESSTD Tony Dorsett 30.00 80.00
ESSTG Trent Green 15.00 40.00
ESSTH Thomas Jones 15.00 40.00
ESSTJ Tarvaris Jackson 20.00 50.00
ESSVD Vernon Davis 25.00 60.00
ESSVY Vince Young 50.00 120.00
ESSWH Charlie Whitehurst 20.00 50.00
ESSWP Willie Parker

2006 Exquisite Collection Signature Trios

UNPRICED TRIO SIG PRINT RUN 15

2006 Exquisite Collection Ticket Matchup Signatures

STATED PRINT RUN 25 SER.#'d SETS
BJ Drew Bledsoe 25.00 60.00
  Keyshawn Johnson
BM Drew Bledsoe 50.00 100.00
  Eli Manning
BW Reggie Bush 40.00 100.00
  DeAngelo Williams
CJ Kellen Clemens 25.00 60.00
  Tarvaris Jackson
DK Vernon Davis 40.00 80.00
  Joe Klopfenstein
HG A.J. Hawk 40.00 100.00
  Chad Greenway
HJ Derek Hagan 25.00 60.00
  Tarvaris Jackson
JB Larry Johnson 25.00 60.00
  Ronnie Brown
JH Keyshawn Johnson 25.00 60.00
  Santonio Holmes
JJ Chad Jackson 30.00 80.00
  Greg Jennings
LH Matt Leinart 25.00 60.00
  Michael Huff
MA Laurence Maroney 25.00 60.00
  Joseph Addai
MS Sinorice Moss 25.00 60.00
  Maurice Stovall
MY Peyton Manning 100.00 200.00
  Vince Young
RL Ben Roethlisberger 60.00 120.00
  Byron Leftwich
TJ LaDainian Tomlinson 40.00 80.00
  LaMont Jordan
WB Cadillac Williams 50.00 120.00
  Reggie Bush
WD LenDale White 25.00 60.00
  Maurice Drew

2007 Exquisite Collection

1-60 STATED PRINT RUN 150
61-102 AU ROOKIE PRINT RUN 150
104-125 JSY AU RC PRINT RUN 225
126-135 JSY AU RC PRINT RUN 99
1 Matt Leinart 6.00 15.00
2 Larry Fitzgerald 8.00 20.00
3 Julius Jones 5.00 12.00
4 Warrick Dunn 6.00 15.00
5 Steve McNair 6.00 15.00
6 Willis McGahee 6.00 15.00
7 J.P. Losman 5.00 12.00
8 Lee Evans 6.00 15.00
9 Jake Delhomme 6.00 15.00
10 Steve Smith 6.00 15.00
11 Rex Grossman 6.00 15.00
12 Cedric Benson 6.00 15.00
13 Carson Palmer 6.00 15.00
14 Chad Johnson 6.00 15.00
15 Jamal Lewis 6.00 15.00
16 Braylon Edwards 6.00 15.00
17 Tony Romo 20.00 50.00
18 Terrell Owens 8.00 20.00
19 Jay Cutler 8.00 20.00
20 Travis Henry 6.00 15.00
21 Jon Kitna 5.00 12.00
22 Roy Williams WR 6.00 15.00
23 Brett Favre 25.00 60.00
24 Donald Driver 8.00 20.00
25 Matt Schaub 6.00 15.00
26 Andre Johnson 6.00 15.00
27 Peyton Manning 12.00 30.00
28 Joseph Addai 6.00 15.00
29 David Garrard 6.00 15.00
30 Maurice Jones-Drew 8.00 20.00
31 Larry Johnson 5.00 12.00
32 Tony Gonzalez 6.00 15.00
33 Trent Green 6.00 15.00
34 Ronnie Brown 6.00 15.00
35 Tarvaris Jackson 5.00 12.00
36 Chester Taylor 5.00 12.00
37 Tom Brady 12.00 30.00
38 Randy Moss 8.00 20.00
39 Drew Brees 10.00 25.00
40 Reggie Bush 8.00 20.00
41 Eli Manning 8.00 20.00
42 Brandon Jacobs 6.00 15.00
43 Chad Pennington 6.00 15.00
44 Thomas Jones 6.00 15.00
45 Ronald Curry 6.00 15.00
46 Donovan McNabb 8.00 20.00
47 Brian Westbrook 6.00 15.00
48 Ben Roethlisberger 8.00 20.00
49 Willie Parker 6.00 15.00
50 Philip Rivers 8.00 20.00
51 LaDainian Tomlinson 8.00 20.00
52 Alex Smith QB 8.00 20.00
53 Frank Gore 8.00 20.00
54 Matt Hasselbeck 6.00 15.00
55 Shaun Alexander 6.00 15.00
56 Marc Bulger 6.00 15.00
57 Steven Jackson 8.00 20.00
58 Cadillac Williams 6.00 15.00
59 Vince Young 6.00 15.00
60 Jason Campbell 6.00 15.00
61 Aaron Ross AU RC 12.00 30.00
62 Adam Carriker AU RC 10.00 25.00
63 Ahmad Bradshaw AU RC 50.00 80.00
64 Amobi Okoye AU RC 12.00 30.00
65 Anthony Spencer AU RC 12.00 30.00
66 Aundrae Allison AU RC 8.00 20.00
67 Chris Davis AU RC 8.00 20.00
68 Chris Leak AU RC 10.00 25.00
69 Courtney Taylor AU RC 10.00 25.00
70 Korey Hall AU RC 10.00 25.00
71 Darrelle Revis AU RC 75.00 135.00
72 David Clowney AU RC 10.00 25.00
73 DeShawn Wynn AU RC 10.00 25.00
74 Dwayne Wright AU RC 10.00 25.00
75 Isaiah Stanback AU RC 8.00 20.00
76 Jacoby Jones AU RC 12.00 30.00
77 Jamaal Anderson AU RC 10.00 25.00
78 James Jones AU RC 12.00 30.00
79 Danny Ware AU RC 12.00 30.00
80 Jeff Rowe AU RC 8.00 20.00
81 Joel Filani AU RC 10.00 25.00
82 John Broussard AU RC 10.00 25.00
83 Jon Beason AU RC 10.00 25.00
84 Jordan Kent AU RC 10.00 25.00
85 Jordan Palmer AU RC 10.00 25.00
86 Justise Hairston AU RC 10.00 25.00
87 Kenneth Darby AU RC 10.00 25.00
88 Kolby Smith AU RC 10.00 25.00
89 LaRon Landry AU RC 12.00 30.00
90 Laurent Robinson AU RC 25.00 50.00
91 Lawrence Timmons AU RC 20.00 50.00
92 Legedu Naanee AU RC 12.00 30.00
93 Leon Hall AU RC 10.00 25.00
94 Michael Griffin AU RC 12.00 30.00
95 Mike Walker AU RC 20.00 50.00
96 Paul Posluszny AU RC 12.00 30.00
97 Reggie Nelson AU RC 10.00 25.00
98 Roy Hall AU RC 12.00 30.00
99 Ryne Robinson AU RC 10.00 25.00
100 Steve Breaston AU RC 25.00 50.00
101 Tyler Thigpen AU RC 12.00 30.00
102 Zach Miller AU RC 12.00 30.00
103 Craig Buster Davis JSY AU/30 RC 150.00 300.00
104 John Beck JSY AU RC 40.00 80.00
105 Lorenzo Booker JSY AU RC 15.00 40.00
106 Michael Bush JSY AU RC 30.00 80.00
107 Trent Edwards JSY AU RC 20.00 50.00
108 Yamon Figurs JSY AU RC 12.00 30.00
109 Chris Henry JSY AU RC 12.00 30.00
110 Johnnie Lee Higgins JSY AU RC 15.00 40.00
111 Jason Hill JSY AU RC 20.00 50.00
112 Tony Hunt JSY AU RC 12.00 30.00
113 Kenny Irons JSY AU RC 12.00 30.00
114 Brandon Jackson JSY AU RC 15.00 40.00
115 Kevin Kolb JSY AU RC 100.00 200.00
116 Brian Leonard JSY AU RC 15.00 40.00
117 Greg Olsen JSY AU RC 15.00 40.00
118 Antonio Pittman JSY AU RC 12.00 30.00
119 Sidney Rice JSY AU RC 30.00 80.00
120 Joe Thomas JSY AU RC 20.00 50.00
121 Steve Smith JSY AU RC 30.00 80.00
122 Drew Stanton JSY AU RC 12.00 30.00
123 Paul Williams JSY AU RC 12.00 30.00
124 Patrick Willis JSY AU RC 60.00 120.00
125 Garrett Wolfe JSY AU RC 12.00 30.00
126 Dwayne Bowe JSY AU RC 60.00 120.00
128 Anthony Gonzalez JSY AU RC 30.00 80.00
129 Dwayne Jarrett JSY AU RC 25.00 60.00
130 Calvin Johnson JSY AU RC 500.00 800.00
131 Marshawn Lynch JSY AU RC 50.00 100.00
132 Robert Meachem JSY AU RC 40.00 100.00
133 Adrian Peterson JSY AU RC 750.00 1,250.00
134 Brady Quinn JSY AU RC 60.00 120.00
135 JaMarcus Russell JSY AU RC 30.00 80.00

2007 Exquisite Collection Gold

1-60 VET UNPRICED PRINT RUN 1
*61-102 ROOKIE/60: .5X TO 1.2X BASE AU
*104-125 ROOKIE/99: .5X TO 1.2X BASE JSY AU
*126-135 ROOKIE/25: .5X TO 1.2X BASE JSY AU
61-102 ROOKIE AU PRINT RUN 60
104-125 ROOKIE JSY AU PRINT RUN 99
126-135 ROOKIE JSY AU PRINT RUN 25
71 Darrelle Revis AU 100.00 200.00
115 Kevin Kolb JSY AU 150.00 300.00
127 Ted Ginn JSY AU 100.00 200.00
130 Calvin Johnson JSY AU 600.00 1,000.00
131 Marshawn Lynch JSY AU 60.00 120.00
133 Adrian Peterson JSY AU 1,250.00 2,000.00
134 Brady Quinn JSY AU 100.00 250.00

2007 Exquisite Collection Debut Signatures

STATED PRINT RUN 20 SER.#'d SETS
UNPRICED GOLD SPECTRUM PRINT RUN 1
AG Anthony Gonzalez 15.00 40.00
AP Adrian Peterson 200.00 400.00
AP2 Adrian Peterson 200.00 400.00
BJ Brandon Jackson 12.00 30.00
BQ Brady Quinn 15.00 40.00
BQ2 Brady Quinn 15.00 40.00
CD Craig Buster Davis 12.00 30.00
CH Chris Henry RB 10.00 25.00
CJ Calvin Johnson 90.00 150.00
DB Dwayne Bowe 20.00 50.00
DB2 Dwayne Bowe 20.00 50.00
DJ Dwayne Jarrett 12.00 30.00
DS Drew Stanton 10.00 25.00
GO Greg Olsen 12.00 30.00
JB John Beck 15.00 40.00
JR JaMarcus Russell 10.00 25.00
JR2 JaMarcus Russell 10.00 25.00
KI Kenny Irons 10.00 25.00
KK Kevin Kolb 50.00 100.00
ML Marshawn Lynch 25.00 50.00
ML2 Marshawn Lynch 25.00 50.00
PI Antonio Pittman 10.00 25.00
PW Patrick Willis 40.00 80.00
RM Robert Meachem 20.00 50.00
RM2 Robert Meachem 15.00 40.00
SS Steve Smith USC 15.00 40.00
TE Trent Edwards 15.00 40.00
TG Ted Ginn Jr. 12.00 30.00
TG2 Ted Ginn Jr. 12.00 30.00
TH Tony Hunt 10.00 25.00

2007 Exquisite Collection Dual Legendary Cuts

DUAL CUT PRINT RUN 1

2007 Exquisite Collection Dual Logo Signatures

UNPRICED DUAL LOGO AU PRINT RUN 1

2007 Exquisite Collection Endorsements

STATED PRINT RUN 20 SER.#'d SETS
UNPRICED GOLD SPECTRUM PRINT RUN 1
AB Anquan Boldin 20.00 50.00
AS Alex Smith QB 25.00 60.00
BF Brett Favre 125.00 250.00
BJ Brandon Jacobs 20.00 50.00
BO Bo Jackson 30.00 80.00
BQ Brady Quinn 25.00 60.00
BU Reggie Bush 25.00 60.00
BU2 Reggie Bush 25.00 60.00
CJ Chad Johnson 20.00 50.00
CT Chester Taylor 15.00 40.00
DB Drew Brees 50.00 100.00
EM Eli Manning 75.00 150.00
FG Frank Gore 25.00 60.00
GS Gale Sayers 30.00 80.00
JA Joseph Addai 20.00 50.00
JC Jason Campbell 20.00 50.00
JO Calvin Johnson 50.00 125.00
JT Joe Theismann 25.00 60.00
LE Lee Evans 20.00 50.00
LF Larry Fitzgerald 25.00 60.00
LJ Larry Johnson 15.00 40.00
LT LaDainian Tomlinson 50.00 100.00
LY Marshawn Lynch 25.00 50.00
MA Marc Bulger 20.00 50.00
MB Marion Barber 25.00 60.00
ML Matt Leinart 20.00 50.00
PH Paul Hornung 25.00 50.00
PR Philip Rivers 25.00 60.00
RB Ronnie Brown 20.00 50.00
RW Reggie Wayne 20.00 50.00
SI Mike Singletary 25.00 60.00
SY Steve Young 50.00 120.00
TG Ted Ginn Jr. 12.00 30.00
TJ T.J. Houshmandzadeh 20.00 50.00
VY Vince Young 20.00 50.00
WP Willie Parker 20.00 50.00

2007 Exquisite Collection Inscriptions

STATED PRINT RUN 25 SER.#'d SETS
UNPRICED GOLD SPECTRUM PRINT RUN 1
AB Anquan Boldin 20.00 50.00
AS Alex Smith QB 25.00 60.00
BO Bo Jackson 60.00 120.00
CJ Chad Johnson 20.00 50.00
CW Cadillac Williams 20.00 50.00
DM Dan Marino 100.00 200.00
GS Gale Sayers 30.00 80.00
JA Joseph Addai 20.00 50.00
JN Joe Namath 50.00 100.00
JR JaMarcus Russell 10.00 25.00
LC L.C. Greenwood 20.00 50.00
LJ Larry Johnson 15.00 40.00
LT LaDainian Tomlinson 40.00 100.00
ML Matt Leinart 20.00 50.00
MS Mike Singletary 25.00 60.00
PH Paul Hornung 25.00 50.00
RB Reggie Bush 40.00 100.00
RW Reggie Wayne 20.00 50.00
VY Vince Young 30.00 80.00
WP Willie Parker 20.00 50.00

2007 Exquisite Collection Legendary Signatures

STATED PRINT RUN 20 SER.#'d SETS
UNPRICED GOLD SPECTRUM PRINT RUN 1
BO Bo Jackson 60.00 120.00
BS Barry Sanders
DM Dan Marino 100.00 200.00
DP Drew Pearson 20.00 50.00
ES Emmitt Smith 125.00 250.00
GS Gale Sayers 30.00 80.00

JM Joe Montana	100.00	200.00
JN Joe Namath	50.00	100.00
JT Joe Theismann	25.00	50.00
LC L.C. Greenwood	20.00	50.00
MS Mike Singletary	25.00	60.00
PH Paul Hornung	20.00	50.00
RC Roger Craig	20.00	50.00
SY Steve Young	60.00	120.00

2007 Exquisite Collection Maximum Jersey Silver

SILVER PRINT RUN 75 SER.#'d SETS
*SILVER SPECTRUM/15: .8X TO 2X BASIC JSY/75
SILVER SPECTRUM PRINT RUN 15 SER.#'d SETS
UNPRICED GOLD SPECTRUM PRINT RUN 1

AD Joseph Addai	6.00	15.00
AG Anthony Gonzalez	4.00	10.00
AJ Andre Johnson	6.00	15.00
AP Adrian Peterson	15.00	40.00
AP2 Adrian Peterson	15.00	40.00
AS Alex Smith QB	8.00	20.00
AV Adam Vinatieri	15.00	30.00
BA Champ Bailey	8.00	20.00
BF Brett Favre	20.00	50.00
BF2 Brett Favre	20.00	50.00
BJ Brandon Jackson	3.00	8.00
BL Byron Leftwich	6.00	15.00
BM Marion Barber	10.00	25.00
BO Dwayne Bowe	5.00	12.00
BO2 Dwayne Bowe	5.00	12.00
BQ Brady Quinn	4.00	10.00
BQ2 Brady Quinn	4.00	10.00
BR Ben Roethlisberger	12.00	30.00
BU Brian Urlacher	10.00	25.00
CB Cedric Benson	6.00	15.00
CH Chris Henry RB	2.50	6.00
CJ Calvin Johnson	12.00	30.00
CJ2 Calvin Johnson	12.00	30.00
CO Marques Colston	8.00	20.00
CP Carson Palmer	6.00	15.00
CT Chester Taylor	5.00	12.00
CU Jay Cutler	8.00	20.00
DB Drew Brees	8.00	20.00
DJ Dwayne Jarrett	3.00	8.00
DJ2 Dwayne Jarrett	3.00	8.00
DM Dan Marino	20.00	50.00
DM2 Dan Marino	20.00	50.00
DS Drew Stanton	2.50	6.00
DW DeAngelo Williams	8.00	20.00
EM Eli Manning	10.00	25.00
ER Ed Reed	8.00	20.00
FG Frank Gore	8.00	20.00
GA Gaines Adams	4.00	10.00
GL Terry Glenn	6.00	15.00
GS Gale Sayers	12.00	30.00
GW Garrett Wolfe	2.50	6.00
HI Johnnie Lee Higgins	3.00	8.00
HO Torry Holt	6.00	15.00
HU Tony Hunt	2.50	6.00
JA Jason Taylor	6.00	15.00
JB John Beck	4.00	10.00
JC Jason Campbell	6.00	15.00
JH Jason Hill	4.00	10.00
JJ Julius Jones	5.00	12.00
JM Joe Montana	20.00	50.00
JM2 Joe Montana	20.00	50.00
JN Joe Namath	12.00	30.00
JO Chad Johnson	6.00	15.00
JR JaMarcus Russell	2.50	6.00
JR2 JaMarcus Russell	2.50	6.00
JS Jeremy Shockey	6.00	15.00
JT Joe Thomas	4.00	10.00
JW Javon Walker	6.00	15.00
KI Kenny Irons	2.50	6.00
KK Kevin Kolb	6.00	15.00
KW Kellen Winslow	6.00	15.00
LB Lorenzo Booker	3.00	8.00
LJ Larry Johnson	5.00	12.00
LM Laurence Maroney	6.00	15.00
LT LaDainian Tomlinson	8.00	20.00
MB Marc Bulger	6.00	15.00
MC Donovan McNabb	8.00	20.00
ME Shawne Merriman	6.00	15.00
MH Matt Hasselbeck	6.00	15.00
MI Michael Bush	4.00	10.00
ML Marshawn Lynch	4.00	10.00
ML2 Marshawn Lynch	4.00	10.00
PI Antonio Pittman	2.50	6.00
PM Peyton Manning	15.00	40.00
PM2 Peyton Manning	15.00	40.00
PO Clinton Portis	6.00	15.00
PW Patrick Willis	8.00	20.00
RM Robert Meachem	4.00	10.00
RM2 Robert Meachem	4.00	10.00
RW Roy Williams WR	6.00	15.00
SA Shaun Alexander	6.00	15.00
SJ Steven Jackson	8.00	20.00
SM Steve Smith	6.00	15.00
SR Sidney Rice	5.00	12.00
SS Steve Smith USC	4.00	10.00
TB Tom Brady	12.00	30.00
TB2 Tom Brady	12.00	30.00
TE Trent Edwards	4.00	10.00
TG Ted Ginn Jr.	3.00	8.00
TG2 Ted Ginn Jr.	3.00	8.00
TH Joe Theismann	10.00	25.00
TH2 Joe Theismann	10.00	25.00
TS Troy Smith	4.00	10.00
VY Vince Young	6.00	15.00
VY2 Vince Young	6.00	15.00
WI Paul Williams	2.50	6.00
WM Willis McGahee	6.00	15.00
WM2 Willis McGahee	6.00	15.00
WP Walter Payton	20.00	50.00
WP2 Walter Payton	20.00	50.00

2007 Exquisite Collection Maximum Patch

PATCH PRINT RUN 25 SER.#'d SETS
UNPRICED PATCH GOLD SPECTRUM PRINT RUN 1

AG Antonio Gates	15.00	40.00
AP Adrian Peterson	30.00	80.00
BE Braylon Edwards	12.00	30.00
BQ Brady Quinn	8.00	20.00
BR Ben Roethlisberger	25.00	60.00
BU Brian Urlacher	20.00	50.00
CB Cedric Benson	12.00	30.00
CJ Chad Johnson	12.00	30.00
CP Clinton Portis	12.00	30.00
CW Cadillac Williams	12.00	30.00
DB Dwayne Bowe	10.00	25.00
DM Dan Marino	50.00	120.00
EJ Edgerrin James	12.00	30.00
ES Emmitt Smith	40.00	100.00
FG Frank Gore	15.00	40.00
FT Fred Taylor	12.00	30.00
GL Terry Glenn	12.00	30.00
JJ Julius Jones	10.00	25.00
JP Julius Peppers	12.00	30.00
JR JaMarcus Russell	5.00	12.00
JW Javon Walker	12.00	30.00
LE Lee Evans	12.00	30.00
LF Larry Fitzgerald	15.00	40.00
LJ Larry Johnson	10.00	25.00
LT LaDainian Tomlinson	15.00	40.00
MB Marion Barber	20.00	50.00
MC Donovan McNabb	15.00	40.00
MH Matt Hasselbeck	12.00	30.00
MJ Maurice Jones-Drew	15.00	40.00
ML Marshawn Lynch	8.00	20.00
PM Peyton Manning	30.00	80.00
PR Philip Rivers	15.00	40.00
RB Ronnie Brown	12.00	30.00
RM Randy Moss	15.00	40.00
RW Roy Williams WR	12.00	30.00
SA Shaun Alexander	12.00	30.00
TB Tom Brady	25.00	60.00
TG Ted Ginn Jr.	6.00	15.00
TH Torry Holt	12.00	30.00
TO Terrell Owens	15.00	40.00
TS Troy Smith	8.00	20.00
VY Vince Young	12.00	30.00

2007 Exquisite Collection Patch Combos

STATED PRINT RUN 25 SER.#'d SETS
UNPRICED PATCH QUAD PRINT RUN 10
UNPRICED PATCH TRIO PRINT RUN 15

AJ Shaun Alexander	12.00	30.00
Steven Jackson		
BF Larry Fitzgerald	12.00	30.00
Anquan Boldin		
BG Dwayne Bowe	15.00	40.00
Ted Ginn Jr.		
BM Eli Manning	15.00	40.00
Plaxico Burress		
CM Troy Smith	12.00	30.00
Mark Clayton		
FM Dan Marino	60.00	120.00
Brett Favre		
GG Tony Gonzalez	12.00	30.00
Antonio Gates		
GS Alex Smith QB	12.00	30.00
Frank Gore		
HB Marc Bulger	10.00	25.00
Torry Holt		
HW Marvin Harrison	12.00	30.00
Reggie Wayne		
JB Julius Jones	12.00	30.00
Marion Barber		
JH Chad Johnson	12.00	30.00
T.J. Houshmandzadeh		
JL Larry Johnson	12.00	30.00
Marshawn Lynch		
LB Ray Lewis	15.00	40.00
Champ Bailey		
MB Peyton Manning	40.00	100.00
Tom Brady		
MP Deuce McAllister	10.00	25.00
Antonio Pittman		
MY Donovan McNabb	15.00	40.00
Vince Young		
PC Jason Campbell	12.00	30.00
Clinton Portis		
PR Carson Palmer	20.00	50.00
Ben Roethlisberger		
QR JaMarcus Russell	15.00	40.00
Brady Quinn		
SJ Steve Smith	12.00	30.00
Dwayne Jarrett		
SP Walter Payton	60.00	120.00
Emmitt Smith		
ST Jason Taylor	12.00	30.00
Michael Strahan		
TJ Fred Taylor	15.00	40.00
Maurice Jones-Drew		
TP Adrian Peterson	30.00	80.00
Chester Taylor		
TR LaDainian Tomlinson	20.00	50.00
Philip Rivers		
WH Hines Ward	15.00	40.00
Santonio Holmes		
WJ Roy Williams WR	15.00	40.00
Calvin Johnson		

2007 Exquisite Collection Patch Gold

GOLD PRINT RUN 50 SER.#'d SETS
*SPECTRUM/15: .6X TO 1.5X GOLD/50
SPECTRUM PRINT RUN 15

AC Alge Crumpler	8.00	20.00
AD Joseph Addai	8.00	20.00
AG Anthony Gonzalez	5.00	12.00
AJ Andre Johnson	8.00	20.00
AN Antonio Gates	10.00	25.00
AP Adrian Peterson	20.00	50.00
AV Adam Vinatieri	15.00	40.00
BA Ronde Barber	8.00	20.00
BE Braylon Edwards	8.00	20.00
BF Brett Favre	25.00	60.00
BL Byron Leftwich	8.00	20.00
BO Dwayne Bowe	6.00	15.00
BQ Brady Quinn	5.00	12.00
BR Isaac Bruce	8.00	20.00
BS Barry Sanders	20.00	50.00
BU Brian Urlacher	10.00	25.00
BW Brian Westbrook	8.00	20.00
CB Champ Bailey	10.00	25.00
CJ Calvin Johnson	15.00	40.00
CL Mark Clayton	8.00	20.00
CO Marques Colston	10.00	25.00
CP Carson Palmer	8.00	20.00
CW Cadillac Williams	8.00	20.00
DB Drew Brees	10.00	25.00
DC Marion Barber	12.00	30.00
DE Deuce McAllister	8.00	20.00
DJ Dwayne Jarrett	8.00	20.00
DM Dan Marino	25.00	60.00
DO Donovan McNabb	10.00	25.00
ED Trent Edwards	5.00	12.00
EJ Edgerrin James	8.00	20.00
EM Eli Manning	12.00	30.00
ER Ed Reed	10.00	25.00
ES Emmitt Smith	25.00	60.00
FA Brett Favre	20.00	50.00
FG Frank Gore	10.00	25.00
FT Fred Taylor	8.00	20.00
GA Antonio Gates	10.00	25.00
GO Greg Olsen	8.00	20.00
GT Tony Gonzalez	8.00	20.00
GZ Tony Gonzalez	8.00	20.00
HM Heath Miller	6.00	15.00
HU Tony Hunt	6.00	15.00
HW Hines Ward	10.00	25.00
IB Isaac Bruce	8.00	20.00
JA Steven Jackson	10.00	25.00
JC Jay Cutler	10.00	25.00
JH Jason Witten	10.00	25.00
JJ Julius Jones	6.00	15.00
JK Jevon Kearse	8.00	20.00
JM Joe Montana	25.00	60.00
JO Chad Johnson	8.00	20.00
JP Julius Peppers	8.00	20.00
JR JaMarcus Russell	3.00	8.00
JS Jeremy Shockey	8.00	20.00
JT Jason Taylor	8.00	20.00
JU Julius Jones	6.00	15.00
JW Javon Walker	8.00	20.00
KJ Kevin Jones	6.00	15.00
LD Brian Leonard	6.00	15.00
LE Lee Evans	8.00	20.00
LF Larry Fitzgerald	10.00	25.00
LJ Larry Johnson	6.00	15.00
LT LaDainian Tomlinson	10.00	25.00
MA Matt Leinart	8.00	20.00
MB Marc Bulger	8.00	20.00
MC Deuce McAllister	8.00	20.00
ME Robert Meachem	6.00	15.00
MH Marvin Harrison	10.00	25.00
ML Marshawn Lynch	5.00	12.00
MS Michael Strahan	8.00	20.00
PB Plaxico Burress	8.00	20.00
PE Peyton Manning	20.00	50.00
PM Peyton Manning	20.00	50.00
PO Clinton Portis	8.00	20.00
PR Philip Rivers	10.00	25.00
RB Reggie Brown	6.00	15.00
RE Reggie Bush	10.00	25.00
RG Rex Grossman	8.00	20.00
RL Ray Lewis	10.00	25.00
RM Randy Moss	10.00	25.00
RO Ronnie Brown	8.00	20.00
RW Reggie Wayne	8.00	20.00
SA Shaun Alexander	8.00	20.00
SJ Steven Jackson	10.00	25.00
SM Shawne Merriman	8.00	20.00
SS Steve Smith	8.00	20.00
TA Fred Taylor	8.00	20.00
TE Tedy Bruschi	10.00	25.00
TG Ted Ginn Jr.	4.00	10.00
TH Torry Holt	8.00	20.00
TO Tom Brady	15.00	40.00
TR Tony Romo	12.00	30.00
TS Terrell Suggs	8.00	20.00
VY Vince Young	8.00	20.00
WD Warrick Dunn	8.00	20.00
WI Cadillac Williams	8.00	20.00
WP Willie Parker	8.00	20.00
WR Roy Williams S	8.00	20.00
ZT Zach Thomas	8.00	20.00

2007 Exquisite Collection Patch Quads

UNPRICED PATCH QUAD PRINT RUN 10

2007 Exquisite Collection Patch Trios

UNPRICED PATCH TRIO PRINT RUN 15

2007 Exquisite Collection Quad Legendary Cuts

UNPRICED QUAD CUT PRINT RUN 1

2007 Exquisite Collection Quad Logo Signatures

UNPRICED QUAD SIG PRINT RUN 1

2007 Exquisite Collection Rare Materials Signatures

UNPRICED RARE MAT SIG PRINT RUN 1

2007 Exquisite Collection Rookie Signature Spectrum

UNPRICED PRINT RUN 1

2007 Exquisite Collection Signature Combos

STATED PRINT RUN 25 SER.#'d SETS
UNPRICED SIG DUAL PATCH #'d TO 10

BL Champ Bailey	30.00	80.00
John Lynch		
BS Marc Bulger	20.00	50.00
Matt Schaub		
CT Chad Johnson	25.00	60.00
T.J. Houshmandzadeh		
EB Emmitt Smith	300.00	500.00
Barry Sanders		
EL Lee Evans	25.00	60.00
Marshawn Lynch		
FJ Larry Fitzgerald	75.00	150.00
Calvin Johnson		
GC Frank Gore	30.00	80.00
Roger Craig		
GS L.C. Greenwood	30.00	80.00
Mike Singletary		
HG Santonio Holmes	25.00	60.00
Ted Ginn Jr.		
HJ Santonio Holmes	25.00	60.00
Greg Jennings		
HQ Paul Hornung	75.00	150.00
Brady Quinn		
JB Larry Johnson	25.00	60.00
Dwayne Bowe		
JT Bo Jackson	75.00	150.00
LaDainian Tomlinson		
LF Matt Leinart	25.00	60.00
Larry Fitzgerald		
MJ Eli Manning	60.00	120.00
Brandon Jacobs		
MY Joe Montana	175.00	300.00
Steve Young		
NM Joe Namath	150.00	300.00
Dan Marino		
PB Drew Pearson	25.00	60.00
Marion Barber		
PL Willie Parker	25.00	60.00
Marshawn Lynch		
RD Philip Rivers	25.00	60.00
Craig Buster Davis		
SB Alex Smith QB	30.00	80.00
Reggie Bush		
SG Alex Smith QB	30.00	80.00
Frank Gore		
SJ Alex Smith QB	20.00	50.00
Darrell Jackson		
SS Gale Sayers	60.00	120.00
Mike Singletary		
ST Barry Sanders	150.00	300.00
LaDainian Tomlinson		
WA Reggie Wayne		
Joseph Addai		
WB Cadillac Williams	20.00	50.00
Ronnie Brown		
WJ DeAngelo Williams	25.00	60.00
Dwayne Jarrett		
WN DeAngelo Williams	20.00	50.00
Jerious Norwood		

2007 Exquisite Collection Signature Jersey Numbers

STATED PRINT RUN 4-89
SERIAL #'d UNDER 18 NOT PRICED

AP Adrian Peterson/28	300.00	600.00
BJ Brandon Jacobs/27	20.00	50.00
BO Bo Jackson/34	60.00	120.00
BU Michael Bush/43	20.00	50.00
CB Champ Bailey/24	25.00	60.00
CD Craig Buster Davis/84	15.00	40.00
CH Chris Henry RB/29	15.00	40.00
CO Jerricho Cotchery/89	15.00	40.00
CT Chester Taylor/29	15.00	40.00
DB Dwayne Bowe/82	25.00	60.00
DJ Darrell Jackson/82	12.00	30.00
DW Dwayne Jarrett/80	15.00	40.00
GJ Greg Jennings/85	20.00	50.00
GS Gale Sayers/40	50.00	100.00
JA Brandon Jackson/32	20.00	50.00
LJ Larry Johnson/27	15.00	40.00
LT LaDainian Tomlinson/21	90.00	150.00
ML Marshawn Lynch/23	30.00	80.00
PM Peyton Manning/18	90.00	150.00
PW Patrick Willis/52	30.00	80.00
RC Roger Craig/33	20.00	50.00
SI Mike Singletary/50	30.00	60.00
TG Ted Ginn/19	25.00	60.00
VJ Vincent Jackson/83	15.00	40.00
WI DeAngelo Williams/34	25.00	60.00

2007 Exquisite Collection Signature Swatches Patch

STATED PRINT RUN 25 SER.#'d SETS
UNPRICED SIG SWATCH PRINT RUN 10
UNPRICED SIG SWATCH DUAL #'d TO 15
UNPRICED SIG SWATCH QUAD #'d TO 10
UNPRICED SIG QUAD PATCH #'d TO 5

AB Anquan Boldin	15.00	40.00
AD Joseph Addai	15.00	40.00
AG Anthony Gonzalez	15.00	40.00
AP Adrian Peterson	200.00	400.00
AS Alex Smith QB	20.00	50.00
BJ Brandon Jacobs	15.00	40.00
BQ Brady Quinn	50.00	120.00
BR Drew Brees	75.00	150.00
CB Champ Bailey	25.00	60.00
CJ Chad Johnson	15.00	40.00
CO Jerricho Cotchery	15.00	40.00
CT Chester Taylor	20.00	50.00
CW Cadillac Williams	15.00	40.00
DB Dwayne Bowe	20.00	50.00
DD Donald Driver	20.00	50.00
DJ Dwayne Jarrett	12.00	30.00
DJ2 Dwayne Jarrett	12.00	30.00
DW DeAngelo Williams	20.00	50.00
JA Darrell Jackson	12.00	30.00
JC Jason Campbell	15.00	40.00
JL John Lynch	15.00	40.00
JO Calvin Johnson	75.00	150.00
JR JaMarcus Russell	10.00	25.00
JR2 JaMarcus Russell	10.00	25.00
LE Lee Evans	15.00	40.00
LF Larry Fitzgerald	20.00	50.00
MA Marques Colston	20.00	50.00
MB Marc Bulger	15.00	40.00
MC Mark Clayton	15.00	40.00
ML Marshawn Lynch	30.00	60.00
ML2 Marshawn Lynch	30.00	60.00
PM Peyton Manning	125.00	250.00
PR Philip Rivers	20.00	50.00
RB Ronnie Brown	15.00	40.00
RM Robert Meachem	15.00	40.00
RW Reggie Wayne	15.00	40.00
SH Santonio Holmes	15.00	40.00
SR Sidney Rice	40.00	80.00
SS Steve Smith USC	15.00	40.00
TG Ted Ginn Jr.	12.00	30.00
TG2 Ted Ginn Jr.	12.00	30.00
VY Vince Young	15.00	40.00

2007 Exquisite Collection Signature Quads

UNPRICED SIG QUAD PRINT RUN 10
UNPRICED SIG QUAD SWATCH #'d TO 10

2007 Exquisite Collection Signature Swatches

UNPRICED SIG SWATCH PRINT RUN 10
UNPRICED DUAL PRINT RUN 15
UNPRICED QUAD PRINT RUN 10

2007 Exquisite Collection Signature Swatches Dual

UNPRICED DUAL PRINT RUN 15

2007 Exquisite Collection Signature Swatches Quads

UNPRICED QUAD PRINT RUN 10

2007 Exquisite Collection Signature Trios

STATED PRINT RUN 20 SER.#'d SETS

ABD Joseph Addai	40.00	100.00
Dwayne Bowe		
Craig Buster Davis		
AWN Joseph Addai	40.00	100.00
DeAngelo Williams		
Jerious Norwood		
BBB Anquan Boldin	25.00	60.00
Reggie Brown		
Bernard Berrian		
BBC Drew Brees	125.00	250.00
Reggie Bush		
Marques Colston		
CCE Jerricho Cotchery	25.00	60.00
Mark Clayton		
Lee Evans		
GGP Ted Ginn Jr.		
Anthony Gonzalez		
Antonio Pittman		
GPH L.C. Greenwood	50.00	100.00
Willie Parker		
Santonio Holmes		
JGW Larry Johnson	40.00	100.00
Frank Gore		
DeAngelo Williams		
JHI Chad Johnson	25.00	60.00
T.J. Houshmandzadeh		
Kenny Irons		
JTJ Bo Jackson	75.00	150.00
LaDainian Tomlinson		
Larry Johnson		
LBD LaRon Landry	25.00	60.00
Dwayne Bowe		
Craig Buster Davis		
LFB Matt Leinart	40.00	100.00
Larry Fitzgerald		
Anquan Boldin		
LHJ Marshawn Lynch	30.00	80.00
Chris Henry RB		
Brandon Jackson		
MAW Peyton Manning	125.00	250.00
Joseph Addai		
Reggie Wayne		
MDG Robert Meachem	30.00	80.00
Craig Buster Davis		
Anthony Gonzalez		
MJS Eli Manning	75.00	150.00
Brandon Jacobs		
Steve Smith USC		
MRC Eli Manning	60.00	120.00
Philip Rivers		
Jason Campbell		
MTQ Joe Montana	150.00	300.00
Joe Theismann		
Brady Quinn		
NFR Joe Namath	200.00	400.00
Brett Favre		
JaMarcus Russell		
PTR Adrian Peterson	150.00	300.00
Chester Taylor		
Sidney Rice		
RJP JaMarcus Russell	150.00	300.00
Calvin Johnson		
Adrian Peterson		
SGJ Alex Smith QB	40.00	100.00
Frank Gore		
Darrell Jackson		
SSB Gale Sayers	60.00	120.00
Mike Singletary		
Bernard Berrian		
SST Emmitt Smith	250.00	500.00
Barry Sanders		
LaDainian Tomlinson		
TCL Joe Theismann	30.00	80.00
Jason Campbell		
LaRon Landry		
WEH Reggie Wayne	25.00	60.00
Lee Evans		
T.J. Houshmandzadeh		
YLY Steve Young	60.00	120.00
Matt Leinart		
Vince Young		

2007 Exquisite Collection Ticket Matchup Signatures

STATED PRINT RUN 30 SER.#'d SETS

AW Joseph Addai	40.00	80.00
DeAngelo Williams		
CA Calvin Johnson	75.00	150.00
Anquan Boldin		
FB Brett Favre	125.00	250.00
Marc Bulger		
GJ Frank Gore	30.00	60.00
Brandon Jacobs		
GW Frank Gore	30.00	60.00
DeAngelo Williams		
JA Larry Johnson	40.00	80.00
Joseph Addai		
JB Chad Johnson	40.00	80.00
Dwayne Bowe		
JE Chad Johnson	30.00	60.00
Lee Evans		
LB Marshawn Lynch	25.00	60.00
Marion Barber		
LJ Marshawn Lynch	40.00	80.00
Brandon Jacobs		
LQ Matt Leinart	40.00	100.00
Brady Quinn		
MB Peyton Manning	125.00	250.00
Drew Brees		
MM Joe Montana	200.00	400.00
Dan Marino		
PB Willie Parker	30.00	60.00
Ronnie Brown		
PN Adrian Peterson	125.00	250.00
Jerious Norwood		
SB Alex Smith QB	30.00	60.00
Marc Bulger		
TJ LaDainian Tomlinson	40.00	100.00
Larry Johnson		
WW Cadillac Williams	30.00	60.00
DeAngelo Williams		
YR Vince Young	50.00	100.00
Philip Rivers		

2007 Exquisite Collection Trophy Signature Patch

SIGNATURE PATCH PRINT RUN 25
UNPRICED SIG SWATCH PRINT RUN 10

ES Emmitt Smith	125.00	250.00
JA Joseph Addai	25.00	60.00
JL John Lynch	20.00	50.00
JN Joe Namath	60.00	120.00
JT Joe Theismann	25.00	60.00
PM Peyton Manning	100.00	200.00
RW Reggie Wayne	20.00	50.00
WP Willie Parker	20.00	50.00

2008 Exquisite Collection

This set was released on March 4, 2009. The base set consists of 177 cards. Cards 1-100 feature veterans serial numbered of 75. Cards 101-142 are autographed rookies serial numbered of 150, and cards 143-166 are autographed jersey rookies serial numbered of 199. Cards 167-176 are autographed jersey rookies serial numbered of 99. Card 177 is an autographed jersey card of Tiger Woods serial numbered of 10. This product was released with 7 cards per pack and 1 pack per hobby box.

1-100 VETERAN PRINT RUN 75
101-142 AU ROOKIE PRINT RUN 150
143-166 JSY AU RC PRINT RUN 191-199
167-176 JSY AU RC PRINT RUN 99
UNPRICED #177 PRINT RUN 10

1 Kurt Warner	10.00	25.00
2 Larry Fitzgerald	10.00	25.00
3 Anquan Boldin	8.00	20.00
4 Edgerrin James	8.00	20.00
5 Michael Turner	10.00	25.00
6 Roddy White	8.00	20.00
7 Willis McGahee	8.00	20.00
8 Ed Reed	8.00	20.00
9 Ray Lewis	10.00	25.00
10 Todd Heap	6.00	15.00
11 Trent Edwards	6.00	15.00
12 Marshawn Lynch	8.00	20.00
13 Lee Evans	8.00	20.00
14 Jake Delhomme	8.00	20.00
15 DeAngelo Williams	8.00	20.00
16 Steve Smith	8.00	20.00
17 Brian Urlacher	10.00	25.00
18 Kyle Orton	8.00	20.00
19 Devin Hester	10.00	25.00
20 Carson Palmer	10.00	25.00
21 Chad Johnson	8.00	20.00
22 T.J. Houshmandzadeh	8.00	20.00
23 Derek Anderson	6.00	15.00
24 Jamal Lewis	8.00	20.00
25 Kellen Winslow	8.00	20.00
26 Braylon Edwards	8.00	20.00
27 Tony Romo	12.00	30.00
28 Terrell Owens	10.00	25.00
29 Marion Barber	8.00	20.00
30 DeMarcus Ware	8.00	20.00
31 Jay Cutler	10.00	25.00
32 Brandon Marshall	8.00	20.00
33 Champ Bailey	8.00	20.00
34 Jon Kitna	8.00	20.00
35 Calvin Johnson	10.00	25.00
36 Roy Williams WR	8.00	20.00
37 Aaron Rodgers	40.00	80.00
38 Ryan Grant	10.00	25.00
39 Greg Jennings	10.00	25.00
40 Andre Johnson	8.00	20.00
41 Peyton Manning	25.00	50.00
42 Dallas Clark	8.00	20.00
43 Joseph Addai	8.00	20.00
44 Reggie Wayne	8.00	20.00
45 Fred Taylor	8.00	20.00
46 David Garrard	8.00	20.00
47 Maurice Jones-Drew	8.00	20.00
48 Selvin Young	6.00	15.00
49 Larry Johnson	8.00	20.00
50 Dwayne Bowe	8.00	20.00
51 Ronnie Brown	8.00	20.00
52 Joey Porter	6.00	15.00
53 Chad Pennington	8.00	20.00
54 Adrian Peterson	75.00	150.00
55 Jared Allen	10.00	25.00
56 Matt Jones	8.00	20.00
57 Tom Brady	30.00	60.00
58 Randy Moss	10.00	25.00
59 Rodney Harrison	6.00	15.00
60 Wes Welker	10.00	25.00
61 Drew Brees	12.00	30.00
62 Reggie Bush	10.00	25.00
63 Marques Colston	8.00	20.00
64 Eli Manning	12.00	30.00
65 Brandon Jacobs	8.00	20.00
66 Plaxico Burress	8.00	20.00
67 Brett Favre	40.00	80.00
68 Jerricho Cotchery	8.00	20.00
69 Laveranues Coles	6.00	15.00
70 JaMarcus Russell	8.00	20.00
71 Donovan McNabb	10.00	25.00
72 Brian Westbrook	8.00	20.00
73 Brian Dawkins	8.00	20.00
74 Willie Parker	8.00	20.00
75 Ben Roethlisberger	10.00	25.00
76 Troy Polamalu	12.00	30.00
77 Hines Ward	8.00	20.00
78 James Harrison RC	35.00	60.00
79 Philip Rivers	10.00	25.00
80 LaDainian Tomlinson	10.00	25.00
81 Antonio Gates	10.00	25.00
82 Antonio Cromartie	6.00	15.00
83 J.T. O'Sullivan	6.00	15.00
84 Patrick Willis	8.00	20.00
85 Frank Gore	8.00	20.00
86 Matt Hasselbeck	8.00	20.00
87 Jonathan Vilma	8.00	20.00
88 Lofa Tatupu	8.00	20.00
89 Marc Bulger	8.00	20.00
90 Torry Holt	8.00	20.00
91 Steven Jackson	10.00	25.00
92 Jeff Garcia	8.00	20.00
93 Earnest Graham	6.00	15.00
94 Joey Galloway	8.00	20.00
95 Vince Young	8.00	20.00
96 LenDale White	8.00	20.00
97 Santana Moss	6.00	15.00
98 Jason Campbell	8.00	20.00
99 Clinton Portis	8.00	20.00
100 Chris Cooley	8.00	20.00
101 Bruce Davis AU RC	8.00	20.00
102 Calais Campbell AU RC	8.00	20.00
103 Josh Johnson AU RC	20.00	50.00
104 Alex Brink AU RC	10.00	25.00
105 Andre Woodson AU RC	10.00	25.00
106 Antoine Cason AU RC	10.00	25.00
107 Aqib Talib AU RC	10.00	25.00
108 Chevis Jackson AU RC	6.00	15.00
109 Colt Brennan AU RC	20.00	50.00
110 DJ Hall AU RC	8.00	20.00
111 Dan Connor AU RC	10.00	25.00
112 Owen Schmitt AU RC	10.00	25.00
113 DeMario Pressley AU RC	8.00	20.00
114 Dennis Dixon AU RC	20.00	50.00
115 Dennis Keyes AU RC	6.00	15.00
116 Derrick Harvey AU RC	6.00	15.00
117 Dominique Rodgers-Cromartie AU RC	15.00	30.00
118 Mike Jenkins AU RC	10.00	25.00
119 Dwight Lowery AU RC	10.00	25.00
120 Erik Ainge AU RC	10.00	25.00
121 Erin Henderson AU RC	10.00	25.00
122 Chris Long AU RC	10.00	25.00
123 Frank Okam AU RC	6.00	15.00
124 Fred Davis AU RC	12.00	30.00
125 Tashard Choice AU RC	15.00	40.00
126 Jack Ikegwuonu AU RC	6.00	15.00
127 Jacob Hester AU RC	10.00	25.00
128 Jacob Tamme AU RC	15.00	30.00
129 Matt Flynn AU RC	200.00	350.00
130 Jermichael Finley AU RC	75.00	125.00
131 John Carlson AU RC	20.00	40.00
132 Justin Forsett AU RC	25.00	40.00
133 Justin King AU RC	8.00	20.00
134 Keenan Burton AU RC	6.00	15.00
135 Keith Rivers AU RC	10.00	25.00
136 Kenny Phillips AU RC	10.00	25.00
137 Lavelle Hawkins AU RC	6.00	15.00
138 Leodis McKelvin AU RC	8.00	20.00
139 Mike Hart AU RC	10.00	25.00
140 Ryan Clady AU RC	10.00	25.00
141 Sedrick Ellis AU RC	10.00	25.00
142 Vernon Gholston AU RC	8.00	20.00
143 Donnie Avery JSY AU RC	20.00	50.00
144 Earl Bennett JSY AU RC	15.00	40.00
145 John David Booty JSY AU RC	12.00	30.00
146 Brian Brohm JSY AU RC	25.00	60.00
147 Andre Caldwell JSY AU RC	12.00	30.00
148 Jamaal Charles JSY AU RC	125.00	250.00
150 Early Doucet JSY AU RC	12.00	30.00
151 Harry Douglas JSY AU RC	12.00	30.00
152 Matt Forte JSY AU RC	125.00	200.00
153 James Hardy JSY AU RC	12.00	30.00
154 DeSean Jackson JSY AU RC	100.00	200.00
155 Dexter Jackson JSY AU RC	12.00	30.00
156 Chris Johnson JSY AU RC	200.00	400.00
157 Dustin Keller JSY AU/191 RC	25.00	60.00
158 Malcolm Kelly JSY AU RC	12.00	30.00
159 Mario Manningham JSY AU RC	50.00	80.00
160 Jordy Nelson JSY AU RC	90.00	150.00
161 Kevin O'Connell JSY AU RC	12.00	30.00
162 Ray Rice JSY AU RC	125.00	250.00
163 Eddie Royal JSY AU RC	25.00	60.00
164 Jerome Simpson JSY AU RC	15.00	40.00
165 Steve Slaton JSY AU RC	15.00	40.00
166 Jake Long JSY AU RC	15.00	40.00
167 Darren McFadden JSY AU RC	300.00	450.00
168 Matt Ryan JSY AU RC	500.00	800.00
169 Felix Jones JSY AU RC	150.00	300.00
170 Joe Flacco JSY AU RC	350.00	600.00
171 Rashard Mendenhall JSY AU RC	125.00	250.00
172 Kevin Smith JSY AU RC	25.00	60.00
173 Jonathan Stewart JSY AU RC	100.00	200.00
175 Chad Henne JSY AU RC	75.00	200.00
176 Devin Thomas JSY AU RC	20.00	50.00

2008 Exquisite Collection Rookie Signature Spectrum

UNPRICED SIG.SPECTRUM PRINT RUN 1

2008 Exquisite Collection Silver Holofoil

UNPRICED VET 1-100 PRINT RUN 1
*ROOKIE AU 101-142: .5X TO 1.2X BASE AU RC
ROOKIE AU 101-142 PRINT RUN 30
*JSY AU 143-166: .4X TO 1X JSY AU/191-199
ROOKIE JSY AU 143-166 PRINT RUN 75
*JSY AU 167-176: .5X TO 1.2X JSY AU/99
ROOKIE JSY AU 167-176 PRINT RUN 25
UNPRICED #177 PRINT RUN 3

103 Josh Johnson AU	30.00	80.00
129 Matt Flynn AU	250.00	500.00
148 Jamaal Charles JSY AU	150.00	300.00
152 Matt Forte JSY AU	150.00	250.00
154 DeSean Jackson JSY AU	150.00	250.00
156 Chris Johnson JSY AU	300.00	600.00
160 Jordy Nelson JSY AU	125.00	200.00
162 Ray Rice JSY AU	200.00	400.00
167 Darren McFadden JSY AU/25	250.00	500.00
168 Matt Ryan JSY AU/25	600.00	1,200.00
169 Felix Jones JSY AU/25	200.00	400.00
170 Joe Flacco JSY AU/25	600.00	1,000.00
171 Rashard Mendenhall JSY AU/25	200.00	350.00
173 Jonathan Stewart JSY AU/25	100.00	200.00
175 Chad Henne JSY AU/25	200.00	400.00

2008 Exquisite Collection Black and Gold Steelers Champion Redemptions

ANNOUNCED PRINT RUN 25-150

BGBR Ben Roethlisberger/25*	125.00	250.00
BGDS Donnie Shell/150*	20.00	40.00
BGFH Franco Harris/100*	30.00	60.00
BGJH Jack Ham/150*	25.00	50.00
BGLG L.C. Greenwood/150*	20.00	40.00
BGRB Rocky Bleier/150*	25.00	50.00

2008 Exquisite Collection Champions Signatures

AUTO STATED PRINT RUN 15

ECSBF Brett Favre EXCH	100.00	200.00
ECSEM Eli Manning	50.00	100.00
ECSFH Franco Harris	50.00	100.00
ECSJE John Elway	75.00	150.00
ECSPM Peyton Manning	75.00	150.00
ECSRC Roger Craig	20.00	50.00
ECSTB Terry Bradshaw	75.00	150.00

2008 Exquisite Collection Cut Signatures

UNPRICED CUT SIG PRINT RUN 1-7

2008 Exquisite Collection Debut Signatures

GOLD PRINT RUN 15-60
UNPRICED PLATINUM PRINT RUN 1

EGDSCH Chad Henne/50	25.00	50.00
EGDSCL Chris Long/25	12.00	30.00
EGDSDM Darren McFadden/15	30.00	80.00
EGDSDT Devin Thomas/60	12.00	30.00
EGDSFJ Felix Jones/60	25.00	60.00
EGDSHD Harry Douglas/60	12.00	30.00
EGDSJF Joe Flacco/35	50.00	100.00
EGDSJH James Hardy/60	12.00	30.00
EGDSJS Jonathan Stewart/60	25.00	50.00
EGDSKS Kevin Smith/60	12.00	30.00
EGDSMF Matt Forte/60	25.00	60.00
EGDSMR Matt Ryan/15	100.00	200.00
EGDSRM Rashard Mendenhall/35	35.00	60.00
EGDSSS Steve Slaton/40	15.00	40.00

2008 Exquisite Collection Endorsements

STATED PRINT RUN 15-30
UNPRICED PLATINUM #'d TO 1

EEAP Adrian Peterson/15	100.00	200.00
EEAR Aaron Rodgers/30	175.00	300.00
EEBB Brian Bosworth/30	40.00	80.00
EEBF Brett Favre/30	100.00	200.00
EEBR Ben Roethlisberger/30	60.00	120.00
EEBS Barry Sanders/30	60.00	120.00
EECH Chad Henne/30	20.00	40.00
EECL Chris Long/30	12.00	30.00
EECP Clinton Portis/30	15.00	40.00
EEDA Donnie Avery/30	12.00	30.00
EEDG David Garrard/30	12.00	30.00
EEDJ Daryl Johnston/30	30.00	60.00
EEDT Devin Thomas/30	12.00	30.00
EEEM Eli Manning/30	50.00	100.00
EEES Emmitt Smith/30	75.00	150.00
EEFT Fran Tarkenton/30	25.00	60.00

EEJC Jason Campbell/30 12.00 30.00
EEJF Joe Flacco/30 40.00 100.00
EEJS Jonathan Stewart/30 25.00 50.00
EEJT Joe Theismann/30 20.00 50.00
EEKS Kevin Smith/30 12.00 30.00
EEKW Kurt Warner/30 40.00 80.00
EELE Jamal Lewis/30 10.00 25.00
EELT LaDainian Tomlinson/30 30.00 60.00
EEMA Peyton Manning/30 60.00 120.00
(blue jersey)
EEMF Matt Forte/30 25.00 60.00
EEML Marshawn Lynch/30 15.00 40.00
EEMR Matt Ryan/30 60.00 120.00
EEPH Paul Hornung/30 15.00 40.00
EEPM Peyton Manning/30 60.00 120.00
(white jersey)
EERG Roman Gabriel/30 25.00 50.00
EERM Rashard Mendenhall/30 35.00 60.00
EEWI Kellen Winslow Sr./30 12.00 30.00
EEYT Y.A. Tittle/30 15.00 40.00

2008 Exquisite Collection Ensemble 3 Signatures

ENSEMBLE 3 PRINT RUN 10-20
UNPRICED ENSEMBLE 4 PRINT RUN 10
UNPRICED ENSEMBLE 6 PRINT RUN 6
UNPRICED ENSEMBLE 8 PRINT RUN 5
BJC Marion Barber 30.00 80.00
Felix Jones
Tashard Choice
BRO Matt Ryan 100.00 200.00
Kevin O'Connell
John David Booty
CGR Frank Gore 50.00 100.00
Tom Rathman
Roger Craig
CMB Dwayne Bowe 15.00 40.00
Brandon Marshall
Jerricho Cotchery
FMR Brett Favre 150.00 300.00
Peyton Manning
Tony Romo
GGC David Garrard 15.00 40.00
Jason Campbell
Jeff Garcia
JTL LaDainian Tomlinson 50.00 100.00
Larry Johnson
Jamal Lewis
LPA Clinton Portis 25.00 50.00
Joseph Addai
Jamal Lewis
MFS Darren McFadden 60.00 120.00
Matt Forte
Kevin Smith
RBF Aaron Rodgers 175.00 300.00
Brian Brohm
Matt Flynn
SCW Ben Watson 15.00 40.00
Dallas Clark
Jeremy Shockey
SWH A.J. Hawk 25.00 50.00
DeMarcus Ware
Aaron Schobel
TMT Eli Manning 60.00 120.00
Y.A. Tittle
Fran Tarkenton
WGB Kurt Warner EXCH 30.00 60.00
Jeff Garcia
Marc Bulger
WMR Peyton Manning 125.00 200.00
Kurt Warner
Tony Romo
WWH Patrick Willis 25.00 50.00
DeMarcus Ware
A.J. Hawk

2008 Exquisite Collection Ensemble 4 Signatures

UNPRICED ENSEMBLE 4 PRINT RUN 10

2008 Exquisite Collection Ensemble 6 Signatures

UNPRICED ENSEMBLE 6 PRINT RUN 6

2008 Exquisite Collection Ensemble 8 Signatures

UNPRICED ENSEMBLE 8 PRINT RUN 5

2008 Exquisite CollectionGenerations Signatures

STATED PRINT RUN 15-35
UNPRICED PLATINUM PRINT RUN 1
AHM Franco Harris 40.00 80.00
Ottis Anderson
Rashard Mendenhall/35
CGR Roger Craig 40.00 80.00
Tom Rathman
Frank Gore/35
FRB Brett Favre 300.00 500.00
Aaron Rodgers
Brian Brohm/15
HHB Jack Ham 25.00 50.00
Brian Bosworth
A.J. Hawk/35
HSL Gale Sayers 50.00 100.00
Franco Harris
Marshawn Lynch/25
MMM Archie Manning 300.00 450.00
Peyton Manning
Eli Manning/15
SBJ Emmitt Smith 125.00 250.00
Marion Barber
Felix Jones/15
TCJ Colt Brennan 50.00 100.00
Joe Theismann
Jason Campbell/25
TMT Y.A. Tittle 60.00 120.00
Fran Tarkenton
Eli Manning/15
WBG Roman Gabriel 30.00 80.00
Kurt Warner
Marc Bulger/25

2008 Exquisite Collection Immortals Signatures

STATED PRINT RUN 10-55
SERIAL #'d UNDER 15 NOT PRICED
UNPRICED PLATINUM PRINT RUN 1
EGIIBS Barry Sanders/15 75.00 150.00
EGIIDB Dick Butkus/25 50.00 100.00
EGIIFT Fran Tarkenton/45 25.00 50.00
EGIIGS Gale Sayers/25 40.00 80.00
EGIIJH Jack Ham/35 30.00 60.00
EGIIKW Kellen Winslow Sr./25 12.00 30.00
EGIIPH Paul Hornung/55 15.00 40.00
EGIITB Terry Bradshaw/15 75.00 150.00
EGIIYT Y.A. Tittle/55 15.00 40.00

2008 Exquisite Collection Inscriptions

STATED PRINT RUN 30 SER.#'d SETS
UNPRICED PLATINUM PRINT RUN 1
UNPRICED QUAD AUTO PRINT RUN 4
EIBR Ben Roethlisberger 60.00 120.00
EICJ Chad Johnson 15.00 40.00
EIDJ Daryl Johnston 30.00 60.00
EIFH Franco Harris 40.00 80.00
EIJG Joe Greene 25.00 60.00
EIJK Jerry Kramer 20.00 40.00
EIML Marshawn Lynch 15.00 40.00
EIPH Paul Hornung 15.00 40.00

2008 Exquisite Collection Legendary Signatures

STATED PRINT RUN 35 SER.#'d SETS
UNPRICED PLATINUM PRINT RUN 1
ELBG Bob Griese 20.00 50.00
ELBS Barry Sanders 60.00 120.00
ELFH Franco Harris 30.00 80.00
ELFT Fran Tarkenton 25.00 60.00
ELJK Jerry Kramer 15.00 40.00
ELJR Jerry Rice 125.00 225.00
ELJT Joe Theismann 20.00 50.00
ELKA Ken Anderson 12.00 30.00
ELKW Kellen Winslow Sr. 12.00 30.00
ELPH Paul Hornung 15.00 40.00
ELTA Troy Aikman 50.00 100.00
ELTB Terry Bradshaw 60.00 120.00
ELYT Y.A. Tittle 15.00 40.00

2008 Exquisite Collection Legendary Signatures Gold Ink

BASIC GOLD INK PRINT RUN 10-60
*GOLD HOLO/15-30: .5X TO 1.2X GOLD INK
GOLD HOLOFOIL PRINT RUN 5-30
UNPRICED PLATINUM PRINT RUN 1
SERIAL #'d UNDER 15 NOT PRICED
EGSAM Archie Manning/40 15.00 40.00
EGSAR Aaron Rodgers/30 125.00 200.00
EGSBB Brian Brohm/40 10.00 25.00
EGSBG Bob Griese/40 15.00 40.00
EGSBG2 Bob Griese/40 15.00 40.00
EGSBJ Bo Jackson/35 60.00 120.00
EGSBR Ben Roethlisberger/15 60.00 120.00
EGSCH Chad Henne/60 25.00 50.00
EGSCL Chris Long/50 12.00 30.00
EGSCL2 Chris Long/50 12.00 30.00
EGSCP Clinton Portis/40 15.00 40.00
EGSDA Derek Anderson/40 15.00 40.00
EGSDB Dick Butkus/20 30.00 80.00
EGSDB2 Dick Butkus/20 30.00 80.00
EGSDM Darren McFadden/30 30.00 60.00
EGSDM2 Darren McFadden/30 30.00 60.00
EGSDT Devin Thomas/60 12.00 30.00
EGSDT2 Devin Thomas/60 12.00 30.00
EGSEB Earl Bennett/50 12.00 30.00
EGSEM Eli Manning/50 40.00 100.00
EGSEM2 Eli Manning/50 40.00 100.00
EGSFH Franco Harris/20 40.00 80.00
EGSFJ Felix Jones/60 20.00 50.00
EGSGS Gale Sayers/25 40.00 80.00
EGSHA James Hardy/50 12.00 30.00
EGSHD Harry Douglas/50 12.00 30.00
EGSJA Joseph Addai/15 15.00 40.00
EGSJC Jamaal Charles/50 15.00 40.00
EGSJF Joe Flacco/50 40.00 100.00
EGSJH Jack Ham/30 30.00 60.00
EGSJK Jerry Kramer/50 20.00 50.00
EGSJL Jake Long/50 12.00 30.00
EGSJN Jordy Nelson/50 30.00 60.00
EGSJS Jonathan Stewart/20 25.00 60.00
EGSJS2 Jonathan Stewart/20 25.00 60.00
EGSJT Joe Theismann/50 15.00 40.00
EGSJT2 Joe Theismann/50 15.00 40.00
EGSKS Kevin Smith/60 10.00 25.00
EGSKW Kellen Winslow Sr./45 12.00 30.00
EGSLE Jamal Lewis/40 10.00 25.00
EGSLT LaDainian Tomlinson/15 40.00 80.00
EGSMB Marion Barber/40 15.00 40.00
EGSPH Paul Hornung/50 15.00 40.00
EGSPH2 Paul Hornung/50 15.00 40.00
EGSPM Peyton Manning/25 60.00 120.00
EGSPM2 Peyton Manning/25 60.00 120.00
EGSRM Rashard Mendenhall/60 25.00 50.00
EGSRM2 Rashard Mendenhall/60 25.00 50.00
EGSSS Steve Slaton/40 15.00 40.00
EGSSS2 Steve Slaton/40 15.00 40.00
EGSTR Tony Romo/60 40.00 80.00
EGSYT Y.A. Tittle/50 15.00 40.00
EGSYT2 Y.A. Tittle/50 15.00 40.00

2008 Exquisite Collection Legendary Signatures Dual

STATED PRINT RUN 15
UNPRICED PLATINUM PRINT RUN 1
ELCAS Ottis Anderson 30.00 60.00
Billy Sims
ELCBH Terry Bradshaw 75.00 150.00
Franco Harris
ELCGG Roman Gabriel 30.00 60.00
Bob Griese
ELCHK Paul Hornung 30.00 60.00
Jerry Kramer
ELCHT Y.A. Tittle 30.00 60.00
Paul Hornung
ELCJP Joe Theismann 30.00 60.00
Paul Hornung
ELCJR Daryl Johnston 40.00 80.00
Tom Rathman
ELCTT Fran Tarkenton 30.00 60.00
Y.A. Tittle

2008 Exquisite Collection Legendary Signatures Dual Gold Ink

STATED PRINT RUN 15-35
UNPRICED PLATINUM PRINT RUN 1
BJ Marion Barber 40.00 80.00
Daryl Johnston/15
BR Ben Roethlisberger 175.00 300.00
Terry Bradshaw/15
CS Jerome Simpson 15.00 40.00
Andre Caldwell/35
DS Jonathan Stewart 40.00 80.00
Dennis Dixon/15
DT Harry Douglas 15.00 40.00
Devin Thomas/35
FN Jordy Nelson 75.00 125.00
Matt Flynn/35
FS Matt Forte 40.00 80.00
Kevin Smith/35
JM Darren McFadden 75.00 150.00
Bo Jackson/15
LL Chris Long 15.00 40.00
Jake Long/35
RB Aaron Rodgers 150.00 250.00
Brian Brohm/15
TB Fran Tarkenton 30.00 60.00
John David Booty/35
WG Kurt Warner EXCH 50.00 100.00
Roman Gabriel/15
WH A.J. Hawk 25.00 50.00
Patrick Willis/25

2008 Exquisite Collection Legendary Signatures Trios

UNPRICED TRIOS PRINT RUN 10-15
UNPRICED PLATINUM PRINT RUN 1

2008 Exquisite Collection Legendary Signatures Trios Gold Ink

STATED PRINT RUN 10-99
UNPRICED PLATINUM PRINT RUN 1
SERIAL #'d UNDER 20 NOT PRICED
ARJ Troy Aikman 125.00 250.00
Felix Jones
Tony Romo/25
FJS Matt Forte 60.00 120.00
Kevin Smith
Chris Johnson/99
HAS Ottis Anderson 25.00 50.00
Billy Sims
Paul Hornung/99
HFR Chad Henne 40.00 100.00
Joe Flacco
John David Booty/99
MCA Peyton Manning 100.00 200.00
Dallas Clark
Joseph Addai/20
SSS Billy Sims 75.00 150.00
Barry Sanders
Kevin Smith/25
TGT Y.A. Tittle 40.00 80.00
Bob Griese
Joe Theismann/75
WGC Jeff Garcia 30.00 60.00
Kurt Warner
Brodie Croyle/75

2008 Exquisite Collection Legendary Signatures Jersey Gold Ink

STATED PRINT RUN 35 SER.#'d SETS
*GOLD HOLO/20: .5X TO 1.2X JSY SIG/35
GOLD HOLOFOIL PRINT RUN 20
UNPRICED PLATINUM PRINT RUN 1
SERIAL #'d UNDER 20 NOT PRICED
EGSJBB Brian Brohm 15.00 40.00
EGSJBF Brett Favre 125.00 200.00
EGSJBR Ben Roethlisberger 75.00 150.00
EGSJCH Chad Henne 40.00 80.00
EGSJCJ Chris Johnson 75.00 125.00
EGSJDM Darren McFadden 40.00 100.00
EGSJDT Devin Thomas 15.00 40.00
EGSJEM Eli Manning 50.00 100.00
EGSJFH Franco Harris 40.00 80.00
EGSJFJ Felix Jones 40.00 100.00
EGSJFT Fran Tarkenton 30.00 60.00
EGSJGS Gale Sayers 40.00 80.00
EGSJJF Joe Flacco 75.00 150.00
EGSJJS Jonathan Stewart 30.00 80.00
EGSJJT Joe Theismann 30.00 60.00
EGSJLT LaDainian Tomlinson 50.00 100.00
EGSJMK Malcolm Kelly 15.00 40.00
EGSJML Marshawn Lynch 15.00 40.00
EGSJMR Matt Ryan 75.00 150.00
EGSJPM Peyton Manning 75.00 150.00
EGSJPW Patrick Willis 15.00 40.00
EGSJRM Rashard Mendenhall 30.00 60.00

2008 Exquisite Collection Logo Signatures

UNPRICED LOGO SIG PRINT RUN 1

2008 Exquisite Collection Logo Signatures Dual

UNPRICED LOGO SIG DUAL PRINT RUN 1

2008 Exquisite Collection Notations

UNPRICED NOTATIONS PRINT RUN 5

2008 Exquisite Collection Patch Combos

STATED PRINT RUN 35 SER.#'d SETS
*GOLD HOLO/15: .5X TO 1.2X COMBO/35
GOLD HOLOFOIL PRINT RUN 15
UNPRICED PLATINUM PRINT RUN 1
ECP1 Darren McFadden 15.00 40.00
Jonathan Stewart
ECP2 Matt Ryan 25.00 60.00
Joe Flacco
ECP3 Rashard Mendenhall 12.00 30.00
Felix Jones
ECP4 Devin Thomas 6.00 15.00
Limas Sweed
ECP5 Tom Brady 20.00 50.00
Peyton Manning
ECP6 Eli Manning 15.00 40.00
Peyton Manning
ECP7 LaDainian Tomlinson 15.00 40.00
Adrian Peterson
ECP8 Walter Payton 30.00 80.00
Matt Forte
ECP10 Matt Ryan 25.00 60.00
Chad Henne
ECP11 Malcolm Kelly 12.00 30.00
DeSean Jackson
ECP12 Brian Brohm 5.00 12.00
John David Booty
ECP13 Randy Moss 10.00 25.00
Terrell Owens
ECP14 Tony Romo 12.00 30.00
Donovan McNabb
ECP15 Brian Urlacher 10.00 25.00
Patrick Willis
ECP17 Kevin Smith 15.00 40.00
Barry Sanders
ECP19 Matt Forte 10.00 25.00
Earl Bennett
ECP20 Marion Barber 8.00 20.00
Jamal Lewis
ECP21 Clinton Portis 25.00 60.00
Chris Johnson
ECP22 Joe Theismann 10.00 25.00
Ken Stabler
ECP23 Aaron Rodgers 20.00 50.00
Brian Brohm
ECP24 Rashard Mendenhall 12.00 30.00
Limas Sweed
ECP25 Brett Favre 30.00 80.00
John Elway

2008 Exquisite Collection Patch Trios

STATED PRINT RUN 25 SER.#'d SETS
UNPRICED GOLD HOLOFOIL PRINT RUN 10
UNPRICED PLATINUM PRINT RUN 1
ETP1 Darren McFadden 20.00 50.00
Jonathan Stewart
Chris Johnson
ETP2 Matt Ryan 30.00 80.00
Brian Brohm
Joe Flacco
ETP3 Devin Thomas 10.00 25.00
Jordy Nelson
Donnie Avery
ETP4 Tom Brady 25.00 60.00
Peyton Manning
Tony Romo
ETP5 Walter Payton 40.00 100.00
Emmitt Smith
Franco Harris
ETP6 Adrian Peterson 20.00 50.00
LaDainian Tomlinson
Marshawn Lynch
ETP7 Franco Harris 30.00 80.00
Terry Bradshaw
Lynn Swann
ETP8 Darren McFadden 20.00 50.00
Matt Forte
Kevin Smith
ETP9 Felix Jones 15.00 40.00
Rashard Mendenhall
Ray Rice
ETP10 Randy Moss 12.00 30.00
Terrell Owens
Chad Johnson
ETP11 Patrick Willis 10.00 25.00
DeMarcus Ware
Aaron Schobel
ETP12 Derek Anderson 10.00 25.00
Braylon Edwards
Jamal Lewis
ETP13 Brett Favre 30.00 80.00
Aaron Rodgers
Brian Brohm

2008 Exquisite Collection Patch Quads

QUAD PATCH PRINT RUN 15
UNPRICED GOLD HOLOFOIL PRINT RUN 4
UNPRICED PLATINUM PRINT RUN 1
EQP1 Darren McFadden 25.00 60.00
Rashard Mendenhall
Felix Jones
Jonathan Stewart
EQP2 Matt Ryan 30.00 80.00
Brian Brohm
Chad Henne
Joe Flacco
EQP3 Malcolm Kelly 20.00 50.00
Devin Thomas
Limas Sweed
Rashard Mendenhall
EQP4 DeSean Jackson 20.00 50.00
Dexter Jackson
Earl Bennett
Donnie Avery
EQP5 Tom Brady 40.00 100.00
Tony Romo
Peyton Manning
Eli Manning
EQP7 Adrian Peterson 25.00 60.00
Clinton Portis
LaDainian Tomlinson
Larry Johnson
EQP8 Randy Moss 15.00 40.00
Terrell Owens
Chad Johnson
Reggie Wayne
EQP9 Joe Montana 50.00 120.00
Jerry Rice
Terry Bradshaw
Lynn Swann
EQP10 Adrian Peterson 75.00 150.00
Walter Payton
Franco Harris
Barry Sanders

2008 Exquisite Collection Patch Duals

STATED PRINT RUN 50 SER.#'d SETS
*GOLD HOLO/15: .5X TO 1.2X PATCH/50
GOLD HOLOFOIL PRINT RUN 15
UNPRICED PLATINUM PRINT RUN 1
EP1 Darren McFadden 15.00 40.00
EP2 Matt Ryan 20.00 50.00
EP3 Rashard Mendenhall 10.00 25.00
EP4 Joe Flacco 15.00 40.00
EP5 Felix Jones 10.00 25.00
EP6 Jonathan Stewart 12.00 30.00
EP7 Brian Brohm 6.00 15.00
EP8 Steve Slaton 6.00 15.00
EP9 Limas Sweed 6.00 15.00
EP10 Peyton Manning 15.00 40.00
EP11 Tom Brady 15.00 40.00
EP16 Walter Payton 25.00 60.00
EP17 Tony Romo 12.00 30.00
EP18 Fran Tarkenton 12.00 30.00
EP19 Joe Theismann 12.00 30.00
EP20 Barry Sanders 20.00 50.00
EP21 Emmitt Smith 25.00 60.00
EP22 Jack Lambert 12.00 30.00
EP23 James Hardy 5.00 12.00
EP24 Chad Henne 6.00 15.00
EP25 Randy Moss 10.00 25.00
EP26 LaDainian Tomlinson 10.00 25.00
EP27 Donovan McNabb 10.00 25.00
EP28 Terrell Owens 10.00 25.00
EP29 Bo Jackson 15.00 40.00
EP30 Brett Favre 25.00 60.00
EP31 Marshawn Lynch 8.00 20.00
EP32 Chad Johnson 8.00 20.00
EP33 Kurt Warner 10.00 25.00
EP34 Chris Johnson 15.00 40.00
EP35 Darren McFadden 15.00 40.00
EP36 Matt Ryan 20.00 50.00
EP37 Jonathan Stewart 12.00 30.00
EP38 Felix Jones 10.00 25.00
EP39 Devin Thomas 5.00 12.00
EP40 Eli Manning 10.00 25.00
EP41 Joseph Addai 8.00 20.00
EP42 Kellen Winslow Sr. 10.00 25.00
EP43 Adrian Peterson 15.00 40.00
EP44 Rashard Mendenhall 10.00 25.00
EP45 Matt Forte 12.00 30.00
EP47 Malcolm Kelly 5.00 12.00
EP48 Jerry Rice 25.00 60.00
EP49 Mel Blount 10.00 25.00
EP50 Aaron Rodgers 25.00 50.00

2008 Exquisite Collection Rare Materials

STATED PRINT RUN 35 SER.#'d SETS
UNPRICED PLATINUM PRINT RUN 10
ERMAC Andre Caldwell 6.00 15.00
ERMBB Brian Brohm 8.00 20.00
ERMBE Braylon Edwards 10.00 25.00
ERMBJ Brandon Jacobs 10.00 25.00
ERMBS Barry Sanders 25.00 60.00
ERMCH Chad Henne 8.00 20.00
ERMCJ Chris Johnson 20.00 50.00
ERMDA Donnie Avery 6.00 15.00
ERMDJ DeSean Jackson 15.00 40.00
ERMDK Dustin Keller 8.00 20.00
ERMDM Darren McFadden 20.00 50.00
ERMDT Devin Thomas 6.00 15.00
ERMDW DeMarcus Ware 10.00 25.00
ERMEM Eli Manning 12.00 30.00
ERMER Eddie Royal 8.00 20.00
ERMFH Franco Harris 15.00 40.00
ERMFJ Felix Jones 12.00 30.00
ERMJB John David Booty 6.00 15.00
ERMJC Jamaal Charles 12.00 30.00
ERMJE John Elway 25.00 60.00
ERMJF Joe Flacco 25.00 60.00
ERMJO Chad Johnson 10.00 25.00
ERMJS Jonathan Stewart 12.00 30.00
ERMKO Kevin O'Connell 6.00 15.00
ERMKS Kevin Smith 8.00 20.00
ERMLS Limas Sweed 8.00 20.00
ERMLT LaDainian Tomlinson 12.00 30.00
ERMMF Matt Forte 12.00 30.00
ERMMK Malcolm Kelly 6.00 15.00
ERMMR Matt Ryan 30.00 80.00
ERMNE Jordy Nelson 10.00 25.00
ERMPM Peyton Manning 20.00 50.00
ERMRM Rashard Mendenhall 15.00 40.00
ERMRR Ray Rice 15.00 40.00
ERMSS Steve Slaton 8.00 20.00
ERMST Ken Stabler 15.00 40.00
ERMTB Tom Brady 20.00 50.00

2008 Exquisite Collection Signature Combos

STATED PRINT RUN 35 SER.#'d SETS
ECSAJ Ken Anderson 15.00 40.00
Bert Jones
ECSBR Matt Ryan 100.00 200.00
Brian Brohm
ECSHF Joe Flacco 50.00 120.00
Chad Henne
ECSHK Paul Hornung 30.00 60.00
Jerry Kramer
ECSHT Paul Hornung 30.00 60.00
Y.A. Tittle
ECSJB Brian Bosworth 50.00 100.00
Bo Jackson
ECSJR Tom Rathman 40.00 80.00
Daryl Johnston
ECSJS Felix Jones 30.00 80.00
Kevin Smith
ECSJT Devin Thomas 20.00 50.00
DeSean Jackson
ECSLL Chris Long 15.00 40.00
Jake Long
ECSMA Joseph Addai 60.00 120.00
Peyton Manning
ECSMC Peyton Manning 60.00 120.00
Dallas Clark
ECSMM Peyton Manning 100.00 200.00
Eli Manning
ECSSM Jonathan Stewart 30.00 60.00
Rashard Mendenhall
ECSWH A.J. Hawk 20.00 50.00
DeMarcus Ware

2008 Exquisite Collection Signature Jersey

STATED PRINT RUN 25 SER.#'d SETS
UNPRICED PATCH AU PRINT RUN 10
ESSAP Adrian Peterson 100.00 200.00
ESSAR Aaron Rodgers 200.00 400.00
ESSBB Brian Brohm 12.00 30.00
ESSBR Ben Roethlisberger 75.00 150.00
ESSCH Chad Henne 12.00 30.00
ESSCJ Chris Johnson 75.00 150.00
ESSCP Clinton Portis 12.00 30.00
ESSDA Derek Anderson 10.00 25.00
ESSDB Dwayne Bowe 12.00 30.00
ESSDJ DeSean Jackson 40.00 80.00
ESSDM Darren McFadden 40.00 100.00
ESSDT Devin Thomas 12.00 30.00
ESSEM Eli Manning 50.00 100.00
ESSFH Franco Harris 40.00 80.00
ESSFJ Felix Jones 30.00 80.00
ESSJA Joseph Addai 12.00 30.00
ESSJB John David Booty 10.00 25.00
ESSJC Jamaal Charles 20.00 50.00
ESSJF Joe Flacco 75.00 150.00
ESSJL Jamal Lewis 12.00 30.00
ESSJN Jordy Nelson 30.00 60.00
ESSJR Jerry Rice 100.00 200.00
ESSJS Jonathan Stewart 30.00 60.00
ESSKO Kevin O'Connell 10.00 25.00
ESSKS Kevin Smith 12.00 30.00
ESSMF Matt Forte 30.00 80.00
ESSPM Peyton Manning 75.00 150.00
ESSPW Patrick Willis 20.00 50.00
ESSRC Roger Craig 12.00 30.00
ESSRM Rashard Mendenhall 30.00 80.00
ESSRR Ray Rice 20.00 50.00
ESSSS Steve Slaton 12.00 30.00
ESSTA Troy Aikman 50.00 100.00
ESSTB Terry Bradshaw 75.00 150.00
ESSTE Trent Edwards 10.00 25.00
ESSTR Tony Romo 50.00 100.00

2008 Exquisite Collection Signature Jersey Dual

DUAL JSY AU PRINT RUN 25
UNPRICED DUAL PATCH AU PRINT RUN 5
AR Troy Aikman 75.00 150.00
Tony Romo
BN Brian Brohm 30.00 60.00
Jordy Nelson
BR Matt Ryan 75.00 150.00
Brian Brohm
CG Roger Craig 30.00 60.00
Frank Gore
CW Ben Watson 20.00 50.00
Dallas Clark
EL Trent Edwards 20.00 50.00
Marshawn Lynch
EM John Elway 75.00 150.00
Brandon Marshall
FO Kevin O'Connell 60.00 120.00
Joe Flacco
FR Joe Flacco 100.00 175.00
Ray Rice
JE Chad Johnson
Braylon Edwards
JS Kevin Smith 60.00 120.00
Chris Johnson
LP Clinton Portis 20.00 50.00
Jamal Lewis
MJ Darren McFadden 40.00 80.00
Felix Jones
RM Jerry Rice 100.00 200.00
Don Maynard
SB Emmitt Smith 100.00 200.00
Marion Barber
SM Rashard Mendenhall 40.00 80.00
Jonathan Stewart
TM LaDainian Tomlinson 40.00 80.00
Darren McFadden
WW DeMarcus Ware
A.J. Hawk

2008 Exquisite Collection Signature Jersey Numbers

STATED PRINT RUN 2-80
SERIAL #'d UNDER 21 NOT PRICED
UNPRICED PATCH PRINT RUN 10
ESNCP Clinton Portis/26 20.00 50.00
ESNES Emmitt Smith/22 125.00 250.00
ESNFJ Felix Jones/25 40.00 100.00
ESNJA Joseph Addai/29 20.00 50.00
ESNJR Jerry Rice/80 100.00 175.00
ESNJS Jonathan Stewart/28 25.00 60.00
ESNLT LaDainian Tomlinson/21 40.00 80.00
ESNPM Peyton Manning/18 75.00 150.00

2008 Exquisite Collection Signature Jersey Numbers Dual

STATED PRINT RUN RUN 15
UNPRICED DUAL PATCH AU PRINT RUN 5
FB Brett Favre 125.00 200.00
Brian Brohm
FR Matt Ryan 125.00 250.00
Joe Flacco
JF Chris Johnson 75.00 150.00
Matt Forte
JM Bo Jackson 60.00 120.00
Darren McFadden
JS Jerome Simpson 20.00 50.00
Chad Johnson
MC Peyton Manning 75.00 150.00
Dallas Clark
PD John David Booty 75.00 150.00
Adrian Peterson
SJ Emmitt Smith 125.00 200.00
Felix Jones
WH DeMarcus Ware 30.00 60.00
A.J. Hawk

2008 Exquisite Collection Super Swatch

STATED PRINT RUN 50 SER.#'d SETS
*BLUE/20: .5X TO 1.2X SUPER SWATCH/50
BLUE PRINT RUN 20 SER.#'d SETS
UNPRICED BLUE PATCH PRINT RUN 5
UNPRICED GOLD HOLOFOIL PRINT RUN 5
UNPRICED PLATINUM PRINT RUN 1
UNPRICED SIGNATURE PRINT RUN 4
SSAN Derek Anderson 5.00 12.00
SSAP Adrian Peterson 12.00 30.00
SSAR Aaron Rodgers 15.00 40.00
SSAV Donnie Avery 4.00 10.00
SSBA Marion Barber 6.00 15.00
SSBB Brian Brohm 5.00 12.00
SSBC Brodie Croyle 6.00 15.00
SSBE Braylon Edwards 6.00 15.00
SSBF Brett Favre 20.00 50.00
SSBJ Bo Jackson 12.00 30.00
SSBO Brian Bosworth 10.00 25.00
SSBR Brian Brohm 5.00 12.00
SSBS Barry Sanders 15.00 40.00
SSBU Marc Bulger 6.00 15.00
SSCA Carson Palmer 8.00 20.00
SSCH Chad Henne 5.00 12.00
SSCJ Chad Johnson 6.00 15.00
SSCO Chris Johnson 12.00 30.00
SSCP Clinton Portis 6.00 15.00
SSCR Chris Johnson 12.00 30.00
SSDB Dwayne Bowe 6.00 15.00
SSDC Dallas Clark 6.00 15.00
SSDE Dexter Jackson 4.00 10.00
SSDG David Garrard 6.00 15.00
SSDJ DeSean Jackson 8.00 20.00
SSDM Darren McFadden 12.00 30.00
SSDO Donovan McNabb 8.00 20.00
SSDT Devin Thomas 4.00 10.00
SSEB Earl Bennett 5.00 12.00
SSEM Eli Manning 8.00 20.00
SSES Emmitt Smith 20.00 50.00
SSFA Brett Favre 20.00 50.00
SSFH Franco Harris 10.00 25.00
SSFJ Felix Jones 8.00 20.00
SSFL Joe Flacco 12.00 30.00
SSFT Fran Tarkenton 10.00 25.00
SSGS Gale Sayers 12.00 30.00
SSHE Chad Henne 5.00 12.00
SSJA Joseph Addai 6.00 15.00
SSJD Daryl Johnston 12.00 30.00
SSJDB John David Booty 4.00 10.00
SSJE John Elway 15.00 40.00
SSJF Joe Flacco 12.00 30.00
SSJH James Hardy 4.00 10.00
SSJL Jack Lambert 10.00 25.00
SSJO Felix Jones 8.00 20.00
SSJR Jerry Rice 15.00 40.00
SSJS Jonathan Stewart 10.00 25.00
SSJT Joe Theismann 10.00 25.00
SSKA Ken Anderson 8.00 20.00
SSKO Kevin O'Connell 4.00 10.00
SSKS Kevin Smith 5.00 12.00
SSKW Kurt Warner 8.00 20.00
SSLE Jamal Lewis 6.00 15.00
SSLJ Larry Johnson 6.00 15.00
SSLO Jake Long 5.00 12.00
SSLS Lynn Swann 15.00 40.00
SSLT LaDainian Tomlinson 8.00 20.00
SSMB Mel Blount 10.00 25.00
SSMC Darren McFadden 20.00 50.00
SSME Rashard Mendenhall 8.00 20.00
SSMF Matt Forte 10.00 25.00
SSMJ Joe Montana 20.00 50.00
SSMK Malcolm Kelly 4.00 10.00
SSML Marshawn Lynch 6.00 15.00
SSMO Randy Moss 8.00 20.00
SSMR Matt Ryan 15.00 40.00
SSNE Jordy Nelson 6.00 15.00
SSOA Ottis Anderson 6.00 15.00
SSPA Walter Payton 25.00 60.00
SSPE Peyton Manning 12.00 30.00
SSPH Paul Hornung 10.00 25.00
SSPM Peyton Manning 12.00 30.00
SSPW Patrick Willis 6.00 15.00
SSRC Roger Craig 8.00 20.00
SSRM Rashard Mendenhall 8.00 20.00
SSRO Ben Roethlisberger 8.00 20.00
SSRY Matt Ryan 15.00 40.00
SSSA Barry Sanders 15.00 40.00
SSSI Billy Sims 8.00 20.00
SSSM Kevin Smith 5.00 12.00
SSSS Steve Slaton 5.00 12.00
SSST Jonathan Stewart 10.00 25.00
SSSW Limas Sweed 5.00 12.00
SSTA Troy Aikman 12.00 30.00
SSTB Terry Bradshaw 15.00 40.00
SSTO Tom Brady 12.00 30.00
SSTR Tony Romo 10.00 25.00
SSVY Vince Young 6.00 15.00
SSWI Kellen Winslow Sr. 8.00 20.00
SSWP Walter Payton 25.00 60.00
SSWW Wes Welker 8.00 20.00

2009 Exquisite Collection

101-160 ROOKIE AU PRINT RUN 99
161-182 ROOKJSY AU PRINT RUN 225
183-188 ROOKIE JSY AU PRINT RUN 99
EXCH EXPIRATION: 3/5/2012
1 Peyton Manning 25.00 50.00
2 Eli Manning 15.00 40.00
3 Adrian Peterson 40.00 80.00
4 Tony Romo 15.00 40.00
5 Drew Brees 10.00 25.00
6 LaDainian Tomlinson 8.00 20.00
7 Donovan McNabb 8.00 20.00
8 Tom Brady 20.00 50.00
9 Randy Moss 8.00 20.00
10 Steve Smith 6.00 15.00
11 Ben Roethlisberger 12.00 30.00
12 Matt Ryan 10.00 25.00
13 Joe Flacco 8.00 20.00
14 Matt Forte 8.00 20.00
15 Brian Westbrook 6.00 15.00
16 Philip Rivers 8.00 20.00
17 Jay Cutler 8.00 20.00
18 Kurt Warner 8.00 20.00
19 Larry Fitzgerald 8.00 20.00
20 Anquan Boldin 6.00 15.00
21 Chad Henne 6.00 15.00
22 Ray Lewis 8.00 20.00
23 Brady Quinn 6.00 15.00
24 Steven Jackson 6.00 15.00
25 Matt Cassel 6.00 15.00
26 Andre Johnson 6.00 15.00
27 Jake Delhomme 6.00 15.00
28 Matt Schaub 6.00 15.00
29 Frank Gore 6.00 15.00
30 Brian Urlacher 8.00 20.00
31 Matt Hasselbeck 6.00 15.00
32 Reggie Wayne 6.00 15.00
33 Steve Smith USC 6.00 15.00
34 Steve Slaton 6.00 15.00
35 Calvin Johnson 8.00 20.00
36 Kevin Smith 6.00 15.00
37 Devin Hester 8.00 20.00
38 Hines Ward 6.00 15.00
39 James Harrison 8.00 20.00
40 Trent Edwards 5.00 12.00
41 Marshawn Lynch 6.00 15.00
42 JaMarcus Russell 5.00 12.00
43 Chris Cooley 6.00 15.00
44 Carson Palmer 8.00 20.00
45 Chad Johnson 6.00 15.00
46 T.J. Houshmandzadeh 6.00 15.00
47 Aaron Rodgers 40.00 80.00
48 Greg Jennings 8.00 20.00
49 Ryan Grant 8.00 20.00
50 Bernard Berrian 6.00 15.00
51 Jason Campbell 5.00 12.00
52 David Garrard 6.00 15.00
53 Maurice Jones-Drew 6.00 15.00
54 Ed Reed 6.00 15.00
55 Jerricho Cotchery 6.00 15.00
56 Marques Colston 6.00 15.00
57 Reggie Bush 8.00 20.00
58 Mario Williams 6.00 15.00
59 DeMarcus Ware 6.00 15.00
60 Ronnie Brown 6.00 15.00
61 Ted Ginn 6.00 15.00
62 Asante Samuel 5.00 12.00
63 Troy Polamalu 8.00 20.00
64 Rashard Mendenhall 6.00 15.00
65 Marion Barber 6.00 15.00
66 Brandon Jacobs 6.00 15.00
67 Marc Bulger 6.00 15.00
68 Torry Holt 6.00 15.00
69 Jason Witten 8.00 20.00
70 Tony Gonzalez 6.00 15.00
71 DeSean Jackson 6.00 15.00
72 Kyle Orton 6.00 15.00
73 Shawne Merriman 6.00 15.00
74 Dwayne Bowe 6.00 15.00
75 Dwight Freeney 6.00 15.00
76 DeAngelo Williams 8.00 20.00
77 Roddy White 6.00 15.00
78 Braylon Edwards 6.00 15.00
79 Santonio Holmes 6.00 15.00
80 Champ Bailey 6.00 15.00
81 Cedric Benson 6.00 15.00
82 Nnamdi Asomugha 6.00 15.00
83 Lance Briggs 6.00 15.00
84 Adrian Wilson 5.00 12.00
85 Thomas Jones 6.00 15.00
86 Vince Young 6.00 15.00
87 Patrick Willis 6.00 15.00
88 Justin Tuck 6.00 15.00
89 Jared Allen 8.00 20.00
90 Julius Peppers 6.00 15.00
91 Antonio Bryant 5.00 12.00
92 Vernon Davis 6.00 15.00
93 Vincent Jackson 6.00 15.00
94 Darren McFadden 8.00 20.00
95 Roy Williams WR 6.00 15.00
96 Felix Jones 8.00 20.00
97 Michael Turner 6.00 15.00
98 Donald Driver 6.00 15.00
99 Dallas Clark 6.00 15.00
100 Brett Favre 50.00 100.00
101 Curtis Painter AU RC 20.00 50.00
102 Bernard Scott AU RC 12.00 30.00
103 James Laurinaitis AU RC 15.00 40.00
104 Malcolm Jenkins AU RC 12.00 30.00
105 Brian Orakpo AU RC 25.00 50.00
106 Graham Harrell AU RC 50.00 100.00
107 Brian Cushing AU RC 20.00 50.00
108 Rey Maualuga AU RC 12.00 30.00
109 Clay Matthews AU RC 125.00 200.00
110 Phil Loadholt AU RC 10.00 25.00
111 Duke Robinson AU RC 8.00 20.00
112 Terrance Taylor AU RC 10.00 25.00
113 Tyson Jackson AU RC 10.00 25.00
114 Brandon Tate AU RC 20.00 50.00
115 Darius Butler AU RC 12.00 30.00
116 Larry English AU RC 12.00 30.00
117 B.J. Raji AU RC 20.00 40.00
118 Eugene Monroe AU RC 8.00 20.00
119 Vontae Davis AU RC 12.00 30.00
120 Mike Thomas AU RC 20.00 40.00
121 Deon Butler AU RC 10.00 25.00
122 Chase Coffman AU RC 10.00 25.00
123 Richard Quinn AU RC 10.00 25.00
124 Travis Beckum AU RC 10.00 25.00
125 Brian Hartline AU RC 12.00 30.00
126 Mike Goodson AU RC 12.00 30.00
127 Austin Collie AU RC 30.00 60.00
128 Gartrell Johnson AU RC 8.00 20.00
129 Brooks Foster AU RC 8.00 20.00
130 Johnny Knox AU RC 25.00 50.00
131 Tom Brandstater AU RC 12.00 30.00
132 Mike Teel AU RC 15.00 40.00
133 Cedric Peerman AU RC 10.00 25.00
134 Andre Smith AU RC 10.00 25.00
135 Alex Mack AU RC 10.00 25.00
137 Michael Oher AU RC 40.00 80.00
138 Evander Hood AU RC 30.00 60.00
139 Patrick Chung AU RC 12.00 30.00
140 Mike Mitchell AU RC 10.00 25.00
141 Louis Delmas AU RC 12.00 30.00
142 Alphonso Smith AU RC 10.00 25.00
143 Clint Sintim AU RC 12.00 30.00
144 Sen'Derrick Marks AU RC 8.00 20.00
145 Cody Brown AU RC 8.00 20.00
146 Michael Johnson AU RC 8.00 20.00
148 Dominique Edison AU RC 8.00 20.00
149 Kenny McKinley AU RC 15.00 40.00
150 Cornelius Ingram AU RC 8.00 20.00
151 Aaron Brown AU RC 12.00 30.00
152 Bear Pascoe AU RC 10.00 25.00
153 Keith Null AU RC 10.00 25.00
154 Rashad Jennings AU RC 25.00 50.00
155 Quinten Lawrence AU RC 8.00 20.00
156 Javarris Williams AU RC 10.00 25.00
157 Mike Mickens AU RC 10.00 25.00
158 Julian Edelman AU RC 12.00 30.00
159 Chris Ogbonnaya AU RC 10.00 25.00
160 Quinn Johnson AU RC 10.00 25.00

161 Jeremy Maclin JSY AU RC 40.00 80.00
162 Percy Harvin JSY AU RC 50.00 100.00
163 Brian Robiskie JSY AU RC 12.00 30.00
164 Hakeem Nicks JSY AU RC 50.00 100.00
165 Ramses Barden JSY AU RC 8.00 20.00
166 Rhett Bomar JSY AU RC 10.00 25.00
167 Pat White JSY AU RC 12.00 30.00
168 Brandon Pettigrew JSY AU RC 25.00 50.00
169 Derrick Williams JSY AU RC 10.00 25.00
170 Aaron Curry JSY AU RC 40.00 80.00
171 Kenny Britt JSY AU RC 40.00 80.00
172 Stephen McGee JSY AU RC 30.00 60.00
173 Juaquin Iglesias JSY AU RC 10.00 25.00
174 Nate Davis JSY AU RC 20.00 40.00
175 Glen Coffee JSY AU RC 10.00 25.00
176 Jason Smith JSY AU RC 10.00 25.00
177 Mike Wallace JSY AU RC 75.00 125.00
178 Javon Ringer JSY AU RC 40.00 80.00
179 Shonn Greene JSY AU RC 40.00 100.00
180 Andre Brown JSY AU RC 8.00 20.00
181 LeSean McCoy JSY AU RC 125.00 250.00
182 Patrick Turner JSY AU RC 10.00 25.00
183 Matthew Stafford JSY AU RC 500.00 800.00
184 Knowshon Moreno JSY AU RC 40.00 100.00
185 Michael Crabtree JSY AU RC 100.00 200.00
186 Darrius Heyward-Bey JSY AU RC 40.00 100.00
187 Mark Sanchez JSY AU RC 200.00 400.00
188 Donald Brown JSY AU RC 30.00 80.00
189 Chris Wells JSY AU RC 60.00 150.00
190 Josh Freeman JSY AU RC 200.00 400.00

2009 Exquisite Collection Rookie Silver Holofoil
*ROOKIE AU 101-160: .5X TO 1.2X BASIC CARD
101-160 ROOKIE AU PRINT RUN 25
*ROOK.JSY AU 161-182: .5X TO 1.2X
161-182 ROOKIE AU PRINT RUN 99
*ROOK.JSY AU 183-188: .6X TO 1.5X
183-188 ROOKIE AU PRINT RUN 25
109 Clay Matthews AU 250.00 400.00
162 Percy Harvin JSY AU 75.00 150.00
181 LeSean McCoy JSY AU 150.00 300.00
183 Matthew Stafford JSY AU 800.00 1,500.00
184 Knowshon Moreno JSY AU 100.00 200.00
185 Michael Crabtree JSY AU 200.00 400.00
187 Mark Sanchez JSY AU 500.00 1,000.00
189 Chris Wells JSY AU 125.00 250.00
190 Josh Freeman JSY AU 400.00 800.00

2009 Exquisite Collection Autobiography Jersey Signatures
STATED PRINT RUN 25-99
*GOLD/35: .5X TO 1.2X BASIC JSY AU
GOLD PRINT RUN 10-35
EXCH EXPIRATION: 3/6/2012
AB Anquan Boldin/99 12.00 30.00
AP Adrian Peterson/25 100.00 200.00
BM Brandon Marshall/99 20.00 50.00
BR Lance Briggs/99 15.00 40.00
BS Billy Sims/99 15.00 40.00
BW Brian Westbrook/75 15.00 40.00
CJ Chris Johnson/50 EXCH 50.00 100.00
DB Drew Brees/75 50.00 100.00
DM Donovan McNabb/25 30.00 60.00
DW DeMarcus Ware/99 25.00 50.00
EC Earl Campbell/75 30.00 60.00
EM Eli Manning/25 60.00 120.00
ES Emmitt Smith/25 100.00 200.00
FB Fred Biletnikoff/99 25.00 60.00
KW Kurt Warner/75 40.00 80.00
LE Lee Evans/99 12.00 30.00
LT Lawrence Taylor/99 30.00 60.00
MF Matt Forte/99 20.00 50.00
MT Michael Turner/75 15.00 40.00
MW Mario Williams/99 15.00 40.00
PH Paul Hornung/75 20.00 50.00
PM Peyton Manning/75 75.00 150.00
PS Phil Simms/75 20.00 50.00
RC Randall Cunningham/75 25.00 60.00
RO Ben Roethlisberger/25 60.00 120.00
RS Roger Staubach/75 50.00 100.00
RW Reggie Wayne/99 15.00 40.00
SL Steve Largent/75 20.00 50.00
SS Steve Slaton/99 12.00 30.00
TR Tony Romo/75 40.00 80.00

2009 Exquisite Collection Eight Patch
STATED PRINT RUN 20 SER.#'d SETS
1 Adrian Peterson 40.00 100.00
Brian Westbrook
Frank Gore
LaDainian Tomlinson
Larry Johnson
Marshawn Lynch
Maurice Jones-Drew
Ronnie Brown
2 Andre Johnson 30.00 60.00
Anquan Boldin
Braylon Edwards
Chad Johnson
Lee Evans
Randy Moss
Steve Smith
Terrell Owens
3 Aaron Rodgers 100.00 200.00
Brett Favre
Donovan McNabb
Eli Manning
Marc Bulger
Peyton Manning
Philip Rivers
Tom Brady
4 Dan Marino 100.00 200.00
Donovan McNabb
Jim Kelly
John Elway
Peyton Manning
Philip Rivers
Steve Young
Tom Brady
5 Chris Johnson 40.00 80.00
Darren McFadden
Felix Jones
Jonathan Stewart
Matt Forte
Rashard Mendenhall
Ray Rice
Steve Slaton
6 Andre Johnson 50.00 100.00
Isaac Bruce
Jerry Rice
Larry Fitzgerald
Randy Moss
Steve Largent
Steve Smith
Torry Holt
7 Chris Wells 50.00 100.00
Donald Brown
Josh Freeman
Knowshon Moreno
LeSean McCoy
Mark Sanchez
Matthew Stafford
Rhett Bomar
8 Brian Robiskie 40.00 80.00
Darrius Heyward-Bey
Hakeem Nicks
Jeremy Maclin
Kenny Britt
Michael Crabtree
Patrick Turner
Percy Harvin
9 Jeremy Maclin 40.00 80.00
Juaquin Iglesias
Michael Crabtree
Mike Thomas
Mike Wallace
Mohamed Massaquoi
Percy Harvin
Ramses Barden
10 Donovan McNabb 50.00 100.00
Josh Freeman
Mark Sanchez
Matthew Stafford
Nate Davis
Peyton Manning
Philip Rivers
Tom Brady
11 Adrian Peterson 40.00 100.00
Brian Westbrook
Chris Wells
Clinton Portis
Donald Brown
Knowshon Moreno
LaDainian Tomlinson
LeSean McCoy
12 Andre Johnson 40.00 100.00
Darrius Heyward-Bey
Jeremy Maclin
Michael Crabtree
Percy Harvin
Randy Moss
Steve Smith
Terrell Owens
13 Aaron Rodgers 60.00 150.00
Dan Marino
Donovan McNabb
Eli Manning
John Elway
Peyton Manning
Randall Cunningham
Tom Brady
14 Darrius Heyward-Bey 50.00 100.00
Jeremy Maclin
Josh Freeman
Mark Sanchez
Matthew Stafford
Michael Crabtree
Percy Harvin
Stephen McGee
15 Aaron Curry 40.00 80.00
Brian Urlacher
DeMarcus Ware
Julius Peppers
Patrick Willis
Ray Lewis
Shawne Merriman
Tyson Jackson
16 Bernard Berrian 75.00 150.00
Brett Favre
DeSean Jackson
Donovan McNabb
Peyton Manning
Randy Moss
Reggie Wayne
Tom Brady
17 Brady Quinn 30.00 60.00
Brian Robiskie
Deon Butler
Donovan McNabb
Eli Manning
Hakeem Nicks
Jeremy Maclin
Matt Hasselbeck
18 Brandon Jacobs 40.00 80.00
Dallas Clark
Donald Brown
Eli Manning
Hakeem Nicks
Peyton Manning
Ramses Barden
Reggie Wayne
19 Brian Westbrook 30.00 60.00
DeMarcus Ware
DeSean Jackson
Donovan McNabb
Felix Jones
Jason Witten
Jeremy Maclin
Marion Barber
20 Brian Urlacher 75.00 150.00
Devin Hester
Gale Sayers
Juaquin Iglesias
Lance Briggs
Matt Forte
Mike Singletary
Walter Payton
21 Bo Jackson 60.00 120.00
Darren McFadden
Daryl Johnston
Emmitt Smith
Jason Witten
Jerry Rice
Marion Barber
Tim Brown
22 Brett Favre 60.00 150.00
Donovan McNabb
Fran Tarkenton
Jason Campbell
Jim Kelly
Joe Theismann
Randall Cunningham
Trent Edwards
23 Brady Quinn 30.00 60.00
Carson Palmer
Donovan McNabb
Jason Campbell
Marc Bulger
Matt Leinart
Philip Rivers
Trent Edwards
24 Aaron Curry 40.00 80.00
Brian Urlacher
Joey Porter
Kirk Morrison
Mike Singletary
Patrick Willis
Ray Lewis
Tedy Bruschi
25 Aaron Rodgers 75.00 150.00
Dan Marino
Donovan McNabb
Eli Manning
Fran Tarkenton
Joe Theismann
John Elway
Peyton Manning
26 A.J. Hawk 40.00 80.00
Aaron Curry
Brian Urlacher
DeMarcus Ware
Lance Briggs
Patrick Willis
Ray Lewis
Shawne Merriman
27 Aaron Rodgers 100.00 200.00
Brett Favre
Carson Palmer
Donovan McNabb
Eli Manning
Matt Hasselbeck
Peyton Manning
Tom Brady
28 Asante Samuel 50.00 100.00
Bob Sanders
Brian Dawkins
Charles Woodson
Darrell Green
Ed Reed
Ronde Barber
Troy Polamalu
29 Jake Delhomme 40.00 80.00
Kurt Warner
Larry Fitzgerald
Peyton Manning
Philip Rivers
Reggie Wayne
Steve Smith
Vincent Jackson
30 Heath Miller 90.00 150.00
Hines Ward
Jack Ham
Limas Sweed
Mike Wallace
Rod Woodson
Troy Polamalu
Willie Parker
31 Aaron Curry 50.00 100.00
Brandon Pettigrew
Chris Wells
Darrius Heyward-Bey
Knowshon Moreno
Mark Sanchez
Matthew Stafford
Michael Crabtree
32 Andre Johnson 30.00 60.00
Chad Johnson
Donald Driver
Hines Ward
Larry Fitzgerald
Randy Moss
Steve Smith
Terrell Owens
33 Barry Sanders 75.00 150.00
Bo Jackson
Emmitt Smith
Gale Sayers
LaDainian Tomlinson
Mike Alstott
Roger Craig
Walter Payton
34 Brian Robiskie 50.00 100.00
Donald Brown
Jeremy Maclin
Josh Freeman
LeSean McCoy
Percy Harvin
Rhett Bomar
Shonn Greene
35 Adrian Peterson 40.00 100.00
Brandon Jacobs
Clinton Portis
LaDainian Tomlinson
Larry Johnson
LenDale White
Maurice Jones-Drew
Willie Parker
36 Chris Johnson 40.00 100.00
Clinton Portis
Darren McFadden
LaDainian Tomlinson
Marion Barber
Matt Forte
Steve Slaton
Steven Jackson
37 Aaron Schobel 30.00 60.00
Alan Page
Bob Lilly
Bruce Smith
Dwight Freeney
Julius Peppers
Merlin Olsen
Tyson Jackson
38 Aaron Rodgers 50.00 100.00
Eli Manning
Greg Jennings
Peyton Manning
Plaxico Burress
Randy Moss
Reggie Wayne
Tom Brady
39 Emmitt Smith 75.00 150.00
Gale Sayers
Jason Witten
Matt Forte
Mike Singletary
Roy Williams WR
Stephen McGee
Walter Payton
40 Dan Marino 75.00 150.00
Joe Flacco
Mark Sanchez
Matt Ryan
Matthew Stafford
Peyton Manning
Phil Simms
Philip Rivers

2009 Exquisite Collection Endorsements
STATED PRINT RUN 25-99
*GOLD/15: .6X TO 1.5X AU/50-99
*GOLD/15: .5X TO 1.2X AU/25-35
GOLD PRINT RUN 15
EAB Anquan Boldin/65 8.00 20.00
EAC Aaron Curry/99 8.00 20.00
EAH Albert Haynesworth/75 8.00 20.00
EAP Adrian Peterson/25 75.00 150.00
EBP Brandon Pettigrew/99 8.00 20.00
EBR Brian Robiskie/99 8.00 20.00
EBW Brian Westbrook/35 10.00 25.00
ECJ Chris Johnson/75 10.00 25.00
ECP Clinton Portis/65 8.00 20.00
ECR Michael Crabtree/35 30.00 60.00
EDB Drew Brees/30 50.00 100.00
EDH Darrius Heyward-Bey/50 8.00 20.00
EDM Donovan McNabb/25 40.00 80.00
EEM Eli Manning/25 30.00 60.00
EHN Hakeem Nicks/99 20.00 40.00
EJA Jared Allen/75 25.00 50.00
EJM Jeremy Maclin/75 12.00 30.00
EJP Joey Porter/75 8.00 20.00
EKB Kenny Britt/99 10.00 25.00
ELB Lance Briggs/75 10.00 25.00
ELM LeSean McCoy/99 15.00 40.00
EMC Matt Cassel/50 10.00 25.00
EMF Matt Forte/50 10.00 30.00
EMJ Maurice Jones-Drew/75 8.00 20.00
EMR Matt Ryan/25 40.00 80.00
EMS Matthew Stafford/25 75.00 150.00
EMT Michael Turner/50 10.00 25.00
EMW Mario Williams/75 8.00 20.00
EPM Peyton Manning/50 60.00 100.00
EPW Patrick Willis/99 12.00 30.00
ERL Ray Lewis/60 50.00 100.00
ERO Ben Roethlisberger/25 50.00 100.00
ESA Mark Sanchez/35 40.00 100.00
ESG Shonn Greene/99 15.00 40.00
EWH Pat White/75 8.00 20.00

2009 Exquisite Collection Ensemble 2 Signatures
DUAL AUTO PRINT RUN 25-50
EXCH EXPIRATION: 3/8/2012
BN Hakeem Nicks/50 15.00 40.00
Ramses Barden
BW Lance Briggs/35 30.00 60.00
Patrick Willis
CH Darrius Heyward-Bey/35 25.00 60.00
Michael Crabtree
CM Donovan McNabb/25 50.00 100.00
Randall Cunningham
HW Albert Haynesworth/50 15.00 40.00
Mario Williams
KT Jim Kelly/35 40.00 80.00
Thurman Thomas
MC Brian Cushing/50 40.00 80.00
Clay Matthews
ML Don Maynard/35 25.00 60.00
Steve Largent
MM Jeremy Maclin/50 25.00 60.00
LeSean McCoy
MS Peyton Manning/25 90.00 150.00
Roger Staubach
RB Javon Ringer/50 15.00 40.00
Kenny Britt
RH Brian Robiskie/50 40.00 80.00
Percy Harvin
SF Gale Sayers/35 40.00 80.00
Matt Forte
SP Adrian Peterson/25 75.00 150.00
Billy Sims
SS Mark Sanchez/25 100.00 175.00
Matthew Stafford
TR Matt Ryan/25 40.00 80.00
Michael Turner
WB Anquan Boldin/35 15.00 40.00
Reggie Wayne
WJ Brian Westbrook/35
DeSean Jackson
WM Chris Wells/35 30.00 80.00
Knowshon Moreno

2009 Exquisite Collection Ensemble 3 Signatures
STATED PRINT RUN 10-30
EXCH EXPIRATION: 3/8/2012
BRH Darrius Heyward-Bey/20 125.00 200.00
(Jerry Rice
Tim Brown
CHM Jeremy Maclin/20 100.00 175.00
Michael Crabtree
Percy Harvin
FSJ Chris Johnson/20
Matt Forte
Steve Slaton
KLP Alex Karras/20 40.00 80.00
Bob Lilly
William Perry
MCM Brian Cushing/30 50.00 100.00
Clay Matthews
Rey Maualuga
MMB Donald Brown/20 50.00 100.00
Knowshon Moreno
LeSean McCoy
MWB Donald Brown/20 100.00 175.00
Peyton Manning
Reggie Wayne
PJF Clinton Portis/20 30.00 60.00
Matt Forte
Maurice Jones-Drew
RMG Javon Ringer/20 40.00 80.00
LeSean McCoy
Shonn Greene
RWN Brian Robiskie/30 20.00 50.00
Derrick Williams
Hakeem Nicks
SKM Jim Kelly/20 50.00 100.00
Phil Simms
Warren Moon
WAH Albert Haynesworth/20 40.00 80.00
DeMarcus Ware
Jared Allen
WMB Chris Wells/20 40.00 80.00
Donald Brown
Knowshon Moreno
WTC Aaron Curry/30
DeMarcus Ware
Lawrence Taylor

2009 Exquisite Collection Ensemble 4 Signatures
CBJR Daryl Johnston 60.00 120.00
Earl Campbell
Rocky Bleier
Tom Rathman
ECLB Dwayne Bowe 25.00 60.00
Lee Evans
Marshawn Lynch
Matt Cassel
IBNW Hakeem Nicks 25.00 60.00
Juaquin Iglesias
Mike Wallace
Ramses Barden
JJDC Aaron Curry 20.00 50.00
Malcolm Jenkins
Tyson Jackson
Vontae Davis
STPS Adrian Peterson 250.00 400.00
Barry Sanders
Gale Sayers
LaDainian Tomlinson
WBBC Anquan Boldin 100.00 200.00
Drew Brees
Kurt Warner
Marques Colston
WBBP Derrick Brooks 60.00 120.00
Joey Porter
Lance Briggs
Patrick Willis
WMBM Drew Brees 250.00 400.00
Eli Manning
Kurt Warner
Peyton Manning

2009 Exquisite Collection Inscriptions
IAK Alex Karras 40.00 80.00
IAP Alan Page 50.00 100.00
IBJ Bo Jackson 75.00 150.00
ICP Clinton Portis 40.00 80.00
IDB Drew Brees 100.00 200.00
IDJ Deacon Jones 50.00 100.00
IEC Earl Campbell 40.00 80.00
IKW Kurt Warner 75.00 150.00
ILM LeSean McCoy 50.00 100.00
ILT Lawrence Taylor
IMA Matthew Stafford 100.00 175.00
IMS Mark Sanchez 60.00 120.00
IPH Percy Harvin 75.00 150.00
IPM Peyton Manning 100.00 200.00
IPS Phil Simms 40.00 80.00
IRB Rocky Bleier 50.00 100.00
ISL Steve Largent 40.00 80.00
ITR Tony Romo 50.00 100.00
ITT Thurman Thomas 40.00 80.00

2009 Exquisite Collection Legendary Signatures
STATED PRINT RUN 15-45
EXCH EXPIRATION: 3/8/2012
LAP Alan Page/45 15.00 40.00
LBL Bob Lilly/45 12.00 30.00
LDJ Deacon Jones/45 12.00 30.00
LEC Earl Campbell/25 25.00 50.00
LES Emmitt Smith/15 125.00 250.00
LJE John Elway/15 125.00 250.00
LJH Jack Ham/35 25.00 50.00
LJR Jerry Rice/15 125.00 200.00
LLB Lem Barney/45 10.00 25.00
LRC Randall Cunningham/35 30.00 60.00
LRS Roger Staubach/25 EXCH 75.00 125.00
LSL Steve Largent/45 15.00 40.00
LSY Steve Young/15 40.00 80.00
LWM Warren Moon/25 30.00 60.00

2009 Exquisite Collection Legendary Signatures Dual
STATED PRINT RUN 20 SER.#'d SETS
BH Terry Bradshaw EXCH
Franco Harris
CM Earl Campbell 30.00 60.00
Warren Moon
JO Deacon Jones 30.00 60.00
Merlin Olsen
KT Jim Kelly 50.00 100.00
Thurman Thomas
LJ Bob Lilly EXCH
Ed Too Tall Jones
LM Herman Moore 30.00 60.00
Steve Largent
MM Archie Manning 150.00 250.00
Dan Marino
PS Alan Page 30.00 60.00
Bubba Smith
TC Harry Carson EXCH
Lawrence Taylor
WB Lem Barney 50.00 100.00
Rod Woodson

2009 Exquisite Collection Notable Nameplates
STATED PRINT RUN 15 SER.#'d SETS
NAB Andre Brown 6.00 15.00
NAC Aaron Curry 10.00 25.00
NAP Adrian Peterson 25.00 60.00
NBA Ramses Barden 6.00 15.00
NBP Brandon Pettigrew 10.00 25.00
NBR Brian Robiskie 10.00 25.00
NBS Barry Sanders 30.00 80.00
NBU Deon Butler 8.00 20.00
NCW Chris Wells 20.00 50.00
NDB Donald Brown 10.00 25.00
NDH Darrius Heyward-Bey 10.00 25.00
NDM Dan Marino 40.00 100.00
NDW Derrick Williams 8.00 20.00
NEM Eli Manning 20.00 50.00
NGC Glen Coffee 8.00 20.00
NHN Hakeem Nicks 15.00 40.00
NJF Josh Freeman 15.00 40.00
NJI Juaquin Iglesias 8.00 20.00
NJM Jeremy Maclin 15.00 40.00
NJR Javon Ringer 10.00 25.00
NKB Kenny Britt 12.00 30.00
NKM Knowshon Moreno 10.00 25.00
NLM LeSean McCoy 20.00 50.00
NLT LaDainian Tomlinson 15.00 40.00
NMC Michael Crabtree 20.00 50.00
NMM Mohamed Massaquoi 8.00 20.00
NMS Mark Sanchez 30.00 80.00
NMT Mike Thomas 10.00 25.00
NMW Mike Wallace 25.00 60.00
NND Nate Davis 8.00 20.00
NPH Percy Harvin 40.00 100.00
NPM Peyton Manning 40.00 80.00
NPT Patrick Turner 8.00 20.00
NPW Pat White 10.00 25.00
NRB Rhett Bomar 8.00 20.00
NSG Shonn Greene 15.00 40.00
NST Matthew Stafford 50.00 120.00
NTB Tom Brady 40.00 80.00
NTH Mike Thomas 10.00 25.00
NTO Terrell Owens 15.00 40.00

2009 Exquisite Collection Patch
STATED PRINT RUN 75 SER.#'d SETS
*GOLD/40: .4X TO 1X BASIC PATCH/75
GOLD PRINT RUN 40 SER.#'d SETS
PAB Anquan Boldin 6.00 15.00
PAH A.J. Hawk 6.00 15.00
PAP Adrian Peterson 12.00 30.00
PAR Aaron Rodgers 30.00 60.00
PAS Aaron Schobel 6.00 15.00
PBD Brian Dawkins 8.00 20.00
PBJ Bo Jackson 15.00 40.00
PBO Dwayne Bowe 6.00 15.00
PBS Barry Sanders 15.00 40.00
PBU Brian Urlacher 10.00 25.00
PBW Brian Westbrook 6.00 15.00
PCJ Calvin Johnson 8.00 20.00
PCO Chad Johnson 6.00 15.00
PCP Clinton Portis 6.00 15.00
PCW Cadillac Williams 6.00 15.00
PDC Dallas Clark 6.00 15.00
PDH Devin Hester 12.00 30.00
PDJ Daryl Johnston 10.00 25.00
PDM Dan Marino 20.00 50.00
PDW DeAngelo Williams 8.00 20.00
PEM Eli Manning 8.00 20.00
PES Emmitt Smith 15.00 40.00
PFG Frank Gore 6.00 15.00
PGJ Greg Jennings 10.00 25.00
PJC Jason Campbell 5.00 12.00
PJK Jim Kelly 10.00 25.00
PJP Julius Peppers 6.00 15.00
PJR Jerry Rice 15.00 40.00
PJT Joe Theismann 10.00 25.00
PJW Jason Witten 8.00 20.00
PKW Kellen Winslow Sr. 8.00 20.00
PLJ Larry Johnson 6.00 15.00
PLT LaDainian Tomlinson 8.00 20.00
PMB Marion Barber 6.00 15.00
PMC Donovan McNabb 8.00 20.00
PML Marshawn Lynch 6.00 15.00
POW Terrell Owens 8.00 20.00
PPL Philip Rivers 8.00 20.00
PPM Peyton Manning 15.00 40.00
PPW Patrick Willis 6.00 15.00
PRB Ronnie Brown 6.00 15.00
PRL Ray Lewis 10.00 25.00
PRW Reggie Wayne 6.00 15.00
PSA Bob Sanders 6.00 15.00
PSJ Steven Jackson 6.00 15.00
PSM Shawne Merriman 6.00 15.00
PTO Tom Brady 12.00 30.00
PWI Willie Parker 5.00 12.00
PWP Walter Payton 25.00 60.00
PWW Wes Welker 10.00 25.00

2009 Exquisite Collection Patch Combos
STATED PRINT RUN 50 SER.#'d SETS
*GOLD/20: .6X TO 1.5X DUAL/50
GOLD STATED PRINT RUN 20
BM Peyton Manning 20.00 40.00
Tom Brady
CC Calvin Johnson 8.00 20.00
Chad Johnson
EB Barry Sanders 25.00 50.00
Emmitt Smith
EW Lee Evans 10.00 25.00
Wes Welker
GJ Antonio Gates 6.00 15.00
Vincent Jackson
GW Antonio Gates 8.00 20.00
Jason Witten
JB Marc Bulger 6.00 15.00
Steven Jackson
JJ Andre Johnson 8.00 20.00
Greg Jennings
JP Carson Palmer 8.00 20.00
Chad Johnson
JW Chad Johnson 10.00 25.00
Wes Welker
KM Dan Marino 30.00 60.00
Jim Kelly
LU Brian Urlacher 10.00 25.00
Ray Lewis
MB Donovan McNabb 12.00 30.00
Tom Brady
MM Dan Marino 25.00 50.00
Peyton Manning
MR Eli Manning 8.00 20.00
Philip Rivers
OJ Chad Johnson 8.00 20.00
Terrell Owens
PC Carson Palmer 8.00 20.00
Jason Campbell
PJ Brandon Jacobs 6.00 15.00
Clinton Portis
PS Adrian Peterson 15.00 40.00
Barry Sanders
PW DeMarcus Ware 8.00 20.00
Julius Peppers
RR Aaron Rodgers 20.00 50.00
Philip Rivers
TP Adrian Peterson 12.00 30.00
LaDainian Tomlinson
WG Brian Westbrook 8.00 20.00
Frank Gore
WM Brian Westbrook 12.00 30.00
Donovan McNabb
WP Hines Ward 12.00 30.00
Willie Parker

2009 Exquisite Collection Patch Quads
QUAD PATCH PRINT RUN 20
QB Carson Palmer 25.00 50.00
Donovan McNabb
Peyton Manning
Tom Brady
RB Clinton Portis 20.00 40.00
DeAngelo Williams
Frank Gore
Maurice Jones-Drew
WR Andre Johnson 20.00 40.00
Calvin Johnson
Reggie Wayne
Steve Smith
49OR Darrius Heyward-Bey 25.00 50.00
Jerry Rice
Jerry Rice
Michael Crabtree
BEAR Devin Hester 30.00 60.00
Gale Sayers
Matt Forte
Walter Payton
FKTM Brett Favre 50.00 120.00
Dan Marino
Fran Tarkenton
Jim Kelly
LUMW Brian Urlacher 25.00 50.00
DeMarcus Ware
Ray Lewis
Shawne Merriman
MRMR Aaron Rodgers 40.00 80.00
Eli Manning
Peyton Manning
Philip Rivers
OJJS Andre Johnson 20.00 40.00
Chad Johnson
Steve Smith
Terrell Owens
TPBL Adrian Peterson 30.00 60.00
LaDainian Tomlinson
Marshawn Lynch
Ronnie Brown

2009 Exquisite Collection Patch Trios
STATED PRINT RUN 25 SER.#'d SETS
BRL Isaac Bruce 30.00 60.00
Jerry Rice
Steve Largent
BRM Aaron Rodgers 50.00 100.00
Eli Manning
Tom Brady
DRF Aaron Rodgers 40.00 80.00
Brett Favre
Donald Driver
DSS Asante Samuel 10.00 25.00
Bob Sanders
Brian Dawkins
FBM Brett Favre 50.00 100.00
Dan Marino
Tom Brady
JBL Larry Johnson 10.00 25.00
Marshawn Lynch
Ronnie Brown
JES Braylon Edwards 10.00 25.00
Chad Johnson
Steve Smith
JJJ Andre Johnson 10.00 25.00
Calvin Johnson
Chad Johnson
JTP Adrian Peterson 20.00 50.00
LaDainian Tomlinson
Larry Johnson
LUW Brian Urlacher 15.00 40.00
DeMarcus Ware
Ray Lewis
MBM Eli Manning 25.00 50.00
Peyton Manning
Tom Brady
MMM Dan Marino 30.00 60.00
Eli Manning
Peyton Manning
SSP Barry Sanders 40.00 80.00
Emmitt Smith
Walter Payton
TKM Dan Marino 30.00 60.00
Fran Tarkenton
Jim Kelly
WWS Hines Ward 15.00 40.00
Steve Smith
Wes Welker

2009 Exquisite Collection Rare Materials
STATED PRINT RUN 35 SER.#'d SETS
4AB Andre Brown 6.00 15.00
4AC Aaron Curry 10.00 25.00
4AJ Andre Johnson 10.00 25.00
4AP Adrian Peterson
4BA Ramses Barden 6.00 15.00
4BF Brett Favre 60.00 120.00
4BJ Bo Jackson 20.00 50.00
4BO Anquan Boldin 10.00 25.00
4BP Brandon Pettigrew 10.00 25.00
4BR Brian Robiskie 10.00 25.00
4BU Deon Butler 8.00 20.00
4CJ Calvin Johnson 12.00 30.00
4CO Chad Johnson 10.00 25.00
4CP Carson Palmer 12.00 30.00
4CW Chris Wells 15.00 40.00
4DB Donald Brown 10.00 25.00
4DE DeAngelo Williams 12.00 30.00
4DH Darrius Heyward-Bey 10.00 25.00
4DM Dan Marino 30.00 80.00
4DO Donovan McNabb 15.00 40.00
4DW Derrick Williams 8.00 20.00
4FG Frank Gore 12.00 30.00
4GC Glen Coffee 8.00 20.00
4GS Gale Sayers
4HN Hakeem Nicks 15.00 40.00
4HO Paul Hornung
4JF Josh Freeman 12.00 30.00
4JK Jim Kelly 15.00 40.00
4JM Jeremy Maclin 15.00 40.00
4JR Javon Ringer 10.00 25.00
4JS Jason Smith 8.00 20.00
4KB Kenny Britt 12.00 30.00
4KM Knowshon Moreno 10.00 25.00
4LJ Larry Johnson 10.00 25.00
4LM LeSean McCoy 20.00 50.00
4LT LaDainian Tomlinson 12.00 30.00
4MA Marques Colston 10.00 25.00
4MC Michael Crabtree 20.00 50.00
4ML Marshawn Lynch 10.00 25.00
4MM Mohamed Massaquoi 8.00 20.00
4MS Mark Sanchez 30.00 60.00
4MT Mike Thomas 10.00 25.00
4MW Mike Wallace 20.00 50.00
4ND Nate Davis 8.00 20.00
4PH Percy Harvin 30.00 60.00
4PM Peyton Manning 40.00 80.00
4PT Patrick Turner 8.00 20.00
4PW Pat White 10.00 25.00
4RB Ronnie Brown 10.00 25.00
4RH Rhett Bomar 8.00 20.00
4RI Jerry Rice 40.00 80.00
4SG Shonn Greene 15.00 40.00
4SM Stephen McGee 10.00 25.00
4SS Steve Smith 10.00 25.00
4ST Matthew Stafford 25.00 60.00
4TJ Tyson Jackson 8.00 20.00
4TR Tony Romo 20.00 50.00
4UR Brian Urlacher 25.00 50.00
4VJ Vincent Jackson 10.00 25.00
4WP Walter Payton

2009 Exquisite Collection Rookie Big Patch Match-Up
STATED PRINT RUN 50 SER.#'d SETS
BC Andre Brown 6.00 15.00
Glen Coffee
BM Rhett Bomar 8.00 20.00
Stephen McGee
BN Hakeem Nicks 12.00 30.00
Ramses Barden
CH Darrius Heyward-Bey 15.00 40.00
Michael Crabtree
CM Jeremy Maclin 20.00 50.00
Michael Crabtree
FD Josh Freeman 15.00 40.00
Nate Davis
HM Jeremy Maclin 12.00 30.00
Percy Harvin
IM Juaquin Iglesias 6.00 15.00
Mohamed Massaquoi
MG LeSean McCoy 15.00 40.00
Shonn Greene
MN Hakeem Nicks 12.00 30.00
Jeremy Maclin
RB Javon Ringer 10.00 25.00
Kenny Britt
RW Brian Robiskie 15.00 40.00
Mike Wallace
SG Mark Sanchez 30.00 80.00
Shonn Greene
SP Brandon Pettigrew 50.00 100.00
Matthew Stafford
SS Mark Sanchez 50.00 100.00
Matthew Stafford
SW Derrick Williams 40.00 100.00
Matthew Stafford
WC Aaron Curry 12.00 30.00
Chris Wells
WM Chris Wells 12.00 30.00
Knowshon Moreno
WP Brandon Pettigrew 8.00 20.00
Derrick Williams
WT Pat White 8.00 20.00
Patrick Turner

2009 Exquisite Collection Rookie Bookmark Patch Autographs

STATED PRINT RUN 35-99
*PLATINUM/50: .5X TO 1.2X DUAL AU/99
PLATINUM PRINT RUN 10-50
EXCH EXPIRATION: 3/5/2012
BC Aaron Curry/99 15.00 40.00
Deon Butler
BG Donald Brown/99 15.00 40.00
Shonn Greene
BM Donald Brown/35 20.00 50.00
Knowshon Moreno
BN Hakeem Nicks/99 20.00 50.00
Rhett Bomar
BS Mark Sanchez/35 60.00 120.00
Rhett Bomar
CC Glen Coffee/35 25.00 60.00
Michael Crabtree
CD Michael Crabtree/35 40.00 80.00
Nate Davis
CH Darrius Heyward-Bey/35 25.00 60.00
Michael Crabtree
CM Jeremy Maclin/35 40.00 80.00
Michael Crabtree
FD Josh Freeman/99 30.00 80.00
Nate Davis
GB Andre Brown/99 20.00 50.00
Shonn Greene
HB Darrius Heyward-Bey/99 15.00 40.00
Deon Butler
HT Mike Thomas/99 25.00 60.00
Percy Harvin
IH Juaquin Iglesias/99 25.00 60.00
Percy Harvin
IP Brandon Pettigrew/99 15.00 40.00
Juaquin Iglesias
JS Jason Smith/99 12.00 30.00
Tyson Jackson
MB Deon Butler/99 12.00 30.00
Mohamed Massaquoi
MF Josh Freeman/99 40.00 80.00
Stephen McGee
MM Knowshon Moreno/99 30.00 80.00
LeSean McCoy
NB Hakeem Nicks/99 20.00 50.00
Kenny Britt
RB Brian Robiskie/99 20.00 50.00
Kenny Britt
RM Brian Robiskie/99 15.00 40.00
Mohamed Massaquoi
RW Brian Robiskie/99 25.00 60.00
Mike Wallace
SG Mark Sanchez/35 60.00 120.00
Shonn Greene
SM Knowshon Moreno/35 75.00 135.00
Matthew Stafford
SS Mark Sanchez/35 150.00 300.00
Matthew Stafford
SW Matthew Stafford/35 75.00 135.00
Pat White
TS Mark Sanchez/35 60.00 120.00
Patrick Turner
TT Mike Thomas/99 15.00 40.00
Patrick Turner
WB Deon Butler/99 12.00 30.00
Derrick Williams
WD Nate Davis/99 12.00 30.00
Pat White
WG Chris Wells/99 25.00 60.00
Shonn Greene
WH Chris Wells/35 20.00 50.00
Darrius Heyward-Bey
WI Derrick Williams/99 12.00 30.00
Juaquin Iglesias
WM Chris Wells/99 25.00 60.00
LeSean McCoy
WR Brian Robiskie/99 20.00 50.00
Chris Wells

2009 Exquisite Collection Signature Jersey

STATED PRINT RUN 20-50
EXCH EXPIRATION: 3/5/2012
SJAB Anquan Boldin/30 12.00 30.00
SJAC Aaron Curry/35 12.00 30.00
SJBG Bob Griese/30 20.00 50.00
SJBP Brandon Pettigrew/35 12.00 30.00
SJBR Brian Robiskie/35 12.00 30.00
SJBS Barry Sanders/20 100.00 175.00
SJCW Chris Wells/35 20.00 50.00
SJDB Drew Brees/25 75.00 135.00
SJDM Dan Marino/20 100.00 200.00
SJDW DeMarcus Ware/30 12.00 30.00
SJEM Eli Manning/20 40.00 80.00
SJFH Franco Harris/25 40.00 80.00
SJGS Gale Sayers/30 40.00 80.00
SJHN Hakeem Nicks/50 20.00 50.00
SJJE John Elway/30 75.00 150.00
SJJH Jack Ham/30 30.00 60.00
SJJI Juaquin Iglesias/50 10.00 25.00
SJJM Jeremy Maclin/35 20.00 50.00
SJKB Kenny Britt/50 15.00 40.00
SJKM Knowshon Moreno/35 25.00 60.00
SJKW Kurt Warner/30 50.00 100.00
SJLB Lance Briggs/30 12.00 30.00
SJLM LeSean McCoy/35 40.00 80.00
SJMA Peyton Manning/30 75.00 150.00
SJMC Michael Crabtree/30 40.00 100.00
SJMR Matt Ryan/20 40.00 80.00
SJMS Matthew Stafford/20 90.00 150.00
SJMT Michael Turner/30 12.00 30.00
SJMW Mario Williams/30 12.00 30.00
SJNI Hakeem Nicks/50 20.00 50.00
SJPM Peyton Manning/30 75.00 150.00
SJPS Phil Simms/30 12.00 30.00
SJPW Pat White/35 12.00 30.00
SJRC Randall Cunningham/30 30.00 60.00
SJSA Mark Sanchez/30 60.00 120.00
SJSG Shonn Greene/50 20.00 50.00
SJSL Steve Largent/30 30.00 60.00
SJTR Tony Romo/20 40.00 80.00
SJWM Warren Moon/30 40.00 80.00

2009 Exquisite Collection Signature Jersey Dual

STATED PRINT RUN 10-35
BN Hakeem Nicks/35 12.00 30.00
Ramses Barden
HJ Albert Haynesworth/25 15.00 40.00
Tyson Jackson
LB Lance Briggs/15 60.00 120.00
Ray Lewis
WP Brandon Pettigrew/35 15.00 40.00
Derrick Williams

2009 Exquisite Collection Single Player Triple Patch

STATED PRINT RUN 30 SER.#'d SETS
3PAG Antonio Gates 10.00 25.00
3PAJ Andre Johnson 8.00 20.00
3PAP Adrian Peterson 40.00 80.00
3PBE Braylon Edwards 8.00 20.00
3PBF Brett Favre 75.00 150.00
3PBJ Brandon Jacobs 8.00 20.00
3PBP Brandon Pettigrew 8.00 20.00
3PBR Tedy Bruschi 10.00 25.00
3PBS Barry Sanders 20.00 50.00
3PBU Brian Urlacher 12.00 30.00
3PCJ Chad Johnson 8.00 20.00
3PCP Clinton Portis 8.00 20.00
3PCR Michael Crabtree 15.00 40.00
3PCW Chris Wells 15.00 40.00
3PDA Darren McFadden 10.00 25.00
3PDE DeAngelo Williams 10.00 25.00
3PDG David Garrard 8.00 20.00
3PDH Darrius Heyward-Bey 8.00 20.00
3PDM Donovan McNabb 12.00 30.00
3PDO Donald Brown 8.00 20.00
3PDW DeMarcus Ware 8.00 20.00
3PES Emmitt Smith 25.00 60.00
3PFG Frank Gore 8.00 20.00
3PFR Josh Freeman 12.00 30.00
3PFT Fred Taylor 8.00 20.00
3PJC Jason Campbell 6.00 15.00
3PJF Joe Flacco 12.00 30.00
3PJK Jim Kelly 12.00 30.00
3PJM Jeremy Maclin 12.00 30.00
3PJO Chris Johnson 12.00 30.00
3PJP Julius Peppers 8.00 20.00
3PJR Jerry Rice 25.00 60.00
3PJW Jason Witten 10.00 25.00
3PKM Knowshon Moreno 15.00 40.00
3PKW Kurt Warner 10.00 25.00
3PLE Lee Evans 8.00 20.00
3PLM LeSean McCoy 12.00 30.00
3PLT LaDainian Tomlinson 10.00 25.00
3PMB Marion Barber 8.00 20.00
3PMC Marques Colston 8.00 20.00
3PMF Matt Forte 10.00 25.00
3PML Marshawn Lynch 8.00 20.00
3PMR Matt Ryan 12.00 30.00
3PMS Matthew Stafford 25.00 60.00
3PPA Carson Palmer 10.00 25.00
3PPH Percy Harvin 15.00 40.00
3PPM Peyton Manning 25.00 60.00
3PRB Ronnie Brown 8.00 20.00
3PRE Reggie Bush 12.00 30.00
3PRI Jerry Rice 25.00 60.00
3PRW Reggie Wayne 8.00 20.00
3PSA Mark Sanchez 25.00 60.00
3PSJ Steven Jackson 8.00 20.00
3PSM Shawne Merriman 8.00 20.00
3PSS Steve Smith 8.00 20.00
3PTO LaDainian Tomlinson 10.00 25.00
3PTR Tony Romo 15.00 40.00
3PVJ Vincent Jackson 8.00 20.00
3PVY Vince Young 8.00 20.00
3PWW Wes Welker 12.00 30.00

2009-10 Exquisite Collection Rookie Patch Flashback

STATED PRINT RUN 25 SER.#'d SETS
78J Peyton Manning/25 400.00 700.00
78K John Elway/25 300.00 600.00
78L Jerry Rice/25 300.00 600.00
78M Barry Sanders/25 400.00 800.00
78O Adrian Peterson/25 400.00 800.00

2010 Exquisite Collection

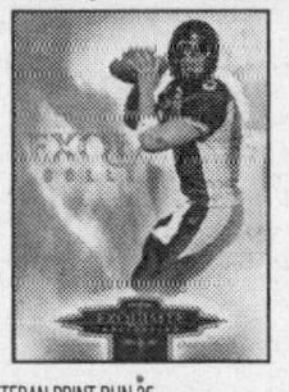

1-99 VETERAN PRINT RUN 35
100 132 JSY AU RC PRINT RUN 75-120
133-190 AU ROOKIE PRINT RUN 65
EXCH EXPIRATION: 3/17/2013
1 Aaron Rodgers 40.00 80.00
2 Adrian Peterson 30.00 60.00
3 Ahmad Bradshaw 6.00 15.00
4 Alex Smith QB 8.00 20.00
5 Andre Johnson 8.00 20.00
6 Anquan Boldin 8.00 20.00
7 Arian Foster 10.00 25.00
8 Austin Collie 8.00 20.00
9 Ben Roethlisberger 12.00 30.00
10 Brandon Marshall 8.00 20.00
11 Brett Favre 60.00 120.00
12 Calvin Johnson 10.00 25.00
13 Zach Miller 8.00 20.00
14 Carson Palmer 8.00 20.00
15 Cedric Benson 8.00 20.00
16 Chad Henne 8.00 20.00
17 Chad Johnson 6.00 15.00
18 Charles Woodson 20.00 40.00
19 Peyton Hillis 30.00 60.00
20 Chris Johnson 12.00 30.00
21 Brandon Jacobs 8.00 20.00
22 Clay Matthews 20.00 40.00
23 Ryan Fitzpatrick 10.00 25.00
24 Dallas Clark 8.00 20.00
25 Darren McFadden 8.00 20.00
26 David Garrard 8.00 20.00
27 DeAngelo Williams 8.00 20.00
28 DeSean Jackson 8.00 20.00
29 Donovan McNabb 20.00 40.00
30 Drew Brees 25.00 50.00
31 Eli Manning 25.00 50.00
32 Felix Jones 8.00 20.00
33 Frank Gore 8.00 20.00
34 Greg Jennings 10.00 25.00
35 Hakeem Nicks 8.00 20.00
36 Hines Ward 8.00 20.00
37 Jamaal Charles 8.00 20.00
38 Jason Campbell 8.00 20.00
39 Jason Witten 10.00 25.00
40 Jay Cutler 10.00 25.00
41 Brandon Lloyd 8.00 20.00
42 Jeremy Maclin 8.00 20.00
43 Joe Flacco 10.00 25.00
44 Jonathan Stewart 8.00 20.00
45 Joseph Addai 8.00 20.00
46 Josh Freeman 10.00 25.00
47 Josh Cribbs 10.00 25.00
48 Kevin Kolb 8.00 20.00
49 Knowshon Moreno 8.00 20.00
50 Kyle Orton 8.00 20.00
51 LaDainian Tomlinson 10.00 25.00
52 Larry Fitzgerald 8.00 20.00
53 LeSean McCoy 8.00 20.00
54 Braylon Edwards 8.00 20.00
55 Marion Barber 8.00 20.00
56 Mark Sanchez 10.00 25.00
57 Marques Colston 8.00 20.00
58 Matt Cassel 6.00 15.00
59 Matt Forte 8.00 20.00
60 Matt Hasselbeck 6.00 15.00
61 Matt Ryan 10.00 25.00
62 Matt Schaub 8.00 20.00
63 Matthew Stafford 15.00 40.00
64 Maurice Jones-Drew 8.00 20.00
65 Michael Turner 6.00 15.00
66 Michael Vick 15.00 40.00
67 Mike Wallace 8.00 20.00
68 Miles Austin 10.00 25.00
69 Patrick Willis 8.00 20.00
70 Percy Harvin 10.00 25.00
71 Peyton Manning 50.00 100.00
72 Philip Rivers 10.00 25.00
73 Kenny Britt 8.00 20.00
74 Randy Moss 8.00 20.00
75 Rashard Mendenhall 8.00 20.00
76 Ray Lewis 10.00 25.00
77 Ray Rice 8.00 20.00
78 Reggie Wayne 8.00 20.00
79 Ricky Williams 8.00 20.00
80 Roddy White 6.00 15.00
81 Ronnie Brown 8.00 20.00
82 Santana Moss 6.00 15.00
83 Santonio Holmes 8.00 20.00
84 Shonn Greene 8.00 20.00
85 Sidney Rice 10.00 25.00
86 Steve Breaston 6.00 15.00
87 Steve Smith USC 8.00 20.00
88 Steve Smith 8.00 20.00
89 Steven Jackson 8.00 20.00
90 Terrell Owens 10.00 25.00
91 Thomas Jones 8.00 20.00
92 Tim Hightower 6.00 15.00
93 Tom Brady 40.00 80.00
94 Tony Romo 12.00 30.00
95 Troy Polamalu 10.00 25.00
96 Vernon Davis 8.00 20.00
97 Vince Young 6.00 15.00
98 Vincent Jackson 6.00 15.00
99 Wes Welker 10.00 25.00
100 Dez Bryant JSY AU/75 RC 175.00 350.00
101 Arrelious Benn JSY AU/75 RC 20.00 50.00
102 C.J. Spiller JSY AU/75 RC 75.00 150.00
103 Colt McCoy JSY AU/75 RC 125.00 250.00
104 Demaryius Thomas JSY AU/75 RC 100.00 175.00
105 Dexter McCluster JSY AU/75 RC 40.00 80.00
106 Jimmy Clausen JSY AU/75 RC 25.00 60.00
107 Ndamukong Suh JSY AU/75 RC 125.00 250.00
108 Ryan Mathews JSY AU/75 RC 150.00 300.00
109 Sam Bradford JSY AU/75 RC 500.00 800.00
110 Tim Tebow JSY AU/75 RC 400.00 700.00
111 Toby Gerhart JSY AU/75 RC 25.00 60.00
112 Andre Roberts JSY AU/120 RC 20.00 50.00
113 Armanti Edwards JSY AU/120 RC 20.00 50.00
114 Ben Tate JSY AU/120 RC 40.00 80.00
115 Damian Williams JSY AU/120 RC 20.00 50.00
116 Emmanuel Sanders JSY AU/75 RC 25.00 60.00
117 Eric Berry JSY AU/75 75.00 135.00
118 Eric Decker JSY AU/120 RC 75.00 125.00
119 Gerald McCoy JSY AU/120 RC 20.00 50.00
120 Golden Tate JSY AU/120 RC 25.00 60.00
121 Jahvid Best JSY AU/120 RC 40.00 100.00
122 Jermaine Gresham JSY AU/120 RC 25.00 60.00
123 Joe McKnight JSY AU/120 RC 20.00 50.00
124 Jonathan Dwyer JSY AU/120 RC 20.00 50.00
125 Jordan Shipley JSY AU/120 RC 25.00 60.00
126 Marcus Easley JSY AU/120 RC 15.00 40.00
127 Mardy Gilyard JSY AU/120 RC 20.00 50.00
128 Mike Kafka JSY AU/75 RC 40.00 80.00
129 Mike Williams JSY AU/120 RC 40.00 100.00
130 Montario Hardesty JSY AU/120 RC 20.00 50.00
131 Rob Gronkowski JSY AU/120 RC 150.00 250.00
132 Rolando McClain JSY AU/120 RC 20.00 50.00
133 Anthony Dixon AU RC 30.00 60.00
134 Antonio Brown AU RC 60.00 120.00
135 Daryl Washington AU RC 25.00 50.00
136 Koa Misi AU RC 12.00 30.00
137 Brandon Graham AU RC 10.00 25.00
138 David Nelson AU RC 30.00 60.00
139 Carlton Mitchell AU RC 8.00 20.00
140 Charles Scott AU RC 8.00 20.00
141 Trent Williams AU RC 12.00 30.00
142 Dan LeFevour AU RC 15.00 40.00
143 Dan Williams AU RC 10.00 25.00
144 NaVorro Bowman AU RC 12.00 30.00
145 David Reed AU RC 10.00 25.00
146 Derrick Morgan AU EXCH
147 Tyson Alualu AU RC 10.00 25.00
148 Dezmon Briscoe AU RC 10.00 25.00
149 Earl Thomas AU RC 25.00 50.00
150 Ed Dickson AU RC 12.00 30.00
151 Jacoby Ford AU RC 40.00 80.00
152 James Starks AU RC 50.00 100.00
153 Jared Odrick AU RC EXCH
154 Taylor Mays AU RC 12.00 30.00
155 Jason Pierre-Paul AU RC EXCH
156 Jerry Hughes AU RC EXCH
157 Jermaine Cunningham AU RC 15.00 40.00
158 Jimmy Graham AU RC EXCH
159 Joe Haden AU RC EXCH
160 Joe Webb AU RC 30.00 60.00
161 John Skelton AU RC 60.00 100.00
162 Anthony McCoy AU RC 8.00 20.00
163 Kareem Jackson AU RC 12.00 30.00
164 Kerry Meier AU RC 10.00 25.00
165 Sean Lee AU RC 40.00 80.00
166 LeGarrette Blount AU RC 60.00 120.00
167 Levi Brown AU RC 12.00 30.00
168 Taylor Price AU RC 12.00 30.00
169 Zac Robinson AU RC 10.00 25.00
170 Bryan Bulaga AU RC 20.00 40.00
171 Javier Arenas AU RC 15.00 40.00
172 Patrick Robinson AU RC 12.00 30.00
173 Riley Cooper AU RC 20.00 40.00
174 Russell Okung AU RC EXCH
175 Rusty Smith AU RC 12.00 30.00
176 Garrett Graham AU RC 10.00 25.00
177 Rennie Curran AU RC 10.00 25.00
178 Sean Weatherspoon AU RC 12.00 30.00
179 Sergio Kindle AU RC 12.00 30.00
180 Stafon Johnson AU RC 10.00 25.00
181 Aaron Hernandez AU RC 75.00 125.00
182 Tony Pike AU RC 12.00 30.00
183 Carlos Dunlap AU RC EXCH
184 Brian Price AU RC 12.00 30.00
185 Lamarr Houston AU RC 12.00 30.00
186 T.J. Ward AU RC EXCH
187 Dennis Pitta AU RC 15.00 40.00
188 Jarrett Brown AU RC 10.00 25.00
189 Jonathan Crompton AU RC 10.00 25.00
190 Sean Canfield AU RC 10.00 25.00

2010 Exquisite Collection Autobiography Jersey Signatures

STATED PRINT RUN 20-99
EABAP Adrian Peterson/20 100.00 200.00
EABBB Brian Bosworth/20 40.00 80.00
EABBJ Bo Jackson/20 75.00 150.00
EABBR Drew Brees/20 50.00 100.00
EABBS Barry Sanders/20 100.00 175.00
EABCM Colt McCoy/20 75.00 150.00
EABCS C.J. Spiller/20 50.00 100.00
EABDJ DeSean Jackson/20 25.00 50.00
EABDM Dexter McCluster/99 12.00 30.00
EABDT Demaryius Thomas/99 15.00 40.00
EABEC Earl Campbell/20 40.00 80.00
EABEM Eli Manning/20 50.00 100.00
EABGT Golden Tate/99 12.00 30.00
EABJB Jahvid Best/99 25.00 60.00
EABJR Jerry Rice/20 125.00 200.00
EABJT Joe Theismann/20 40.00 80.00
EABNS Ndamukong Suh/20 100.00 200.00
EABPH Paul Hornung/99 30.00 60.00
EABPM Peyton Manning/20 125.00 200.00
EABRB Ronnie Brown/99 12.00 30.00
EABRM Ryan Mathews/99 25.00 60.00
EABSB Sam Bradford/20 125.00 250.00
EABSH Jordan Shipley/99 12.00 30.00
EABSI Billy Sims/20 30.00 60.00
EABSY Steve Young/20 75.00 125.00
EABTA Troy Aikman/20 75.00 125.00
EABTG Toby Gerhart/99 12.00 30.00
EABTT Tim Tebow/20 150.00 250.00

2010 Exquisite Collection Bio Script Signatures

STATED PRINT RUN 5-20
BSAH A.J. Hawk/20 15.00 40.00
BSCS C.J. Spiller/20 30.00 80.00
BSFG Frank Gore/20 12.00 30.00
BSMC Rolando McClain/20 12.00 30.00
BSRM Ryan Mathews/20 40.00 80.00
BSTH Thurman Thomas/20 20.00 50.00

2010 Exquisite Collection Draft Picks

STATED PRINT RUN 99 SER.#'d SETS
ERAD Andy Dalton 60.00 120.00
ERAG A.J. Green 40.00 80.00
ERBG Blaine Gabbert 30.00 80.00
ERCK Colin Kaepernick 20.00 50.00
ERCN Cam Newton 250.00 450.00
ERCP Christian Ponder 40.00 80.00
ERDC Delone Carter 12.00 30.00
ERDM DeMarco Murray 50.00 100.00
ERDT Daniel Thomas 20.00 50.00
ERER Evan Royster 12.00 30.00
ERGL Greg Little 15.00 40.00
ERGS Greg Salas 12.00 30.00
ERJJ Jerrel Jernigan 10.00 25.00
ERJL Jake Locker 50.00 100.00
ERJO Julio Jones 40.00 80.00
ERKH Kendall Hunter 15.00 40.00
ERLH Leonard Hankerson 12.00 30.00
ERMI Mark Ingram 40.00 80.00
ERND Noel Devine 10.00 25.00
ERNP Niles Paul 12.00 30.00
ERPA Prince Amukamara 12.00 30.00
ERPD Pat Devlin 12.00 30.00
ERRJ Ronald Johnson 10.00 25.00
ERRM Ryan Mallett 30.00 80.00
ERSV Shane Vereen 12.00 30.00
ERTS Torrey Smith 15.00 40.00
ERTT Tyrod Taylor 12.00 30.00
ERTY Titus Young 15.00 40.00
ERVB Vincent Brown 10.00 25.00
ERVM Von Miller 15.00 40.00

2010 Exquisite Collection Draft Picks Bronze

*BRONZE/25: .6X TO 1.5X BASIC INSERT/99
ERAD Andy Dalton 125.00 250.00
ERCN Cam Newton 400.00 800.00

2010 Exquisite Collection Endorsements

STATED PRINT RUN 10-50
EAB Arrelious Benn/50 10.00 25.00
EBT Ben Tate/50 20.00 40.00
EDC Dallas Clark/20 20.00 50.00
EDM Dexter McCluster/50 10.00 25.00
EDT Demaryius Thomas/50 12.00 30.00
EGJ Greg Jennings/20 20.00 50.00
EGT Golden Tate/50 10.00 25.00
EJA Jamaal Charles/20 15.00 40.00
EJB Jahvid Best/20 25.00 60.00
EJC Jason Campbell/20
EJM Joe McKnight/50 10.00 25.00
EPA Alan Page/20 15.00 40.00
EPW Patrick Willis/20 15.00 40.00
ERM Ryan Mathews/20 25.00 60.00
ERO Rolando McClain/50 10.00 25.00
ESH Jordan Shipley/50 10.00 25.00
ETG Toby Gerhart/50 10.00 25.00

2010 Exquisite Collection Ensemble 2 Signatures

ENSEMBLE TWO AU PRINT RUN 10-25
GH Rob Gronkowski/25 125.00 200.00
Aaron Hernandez
HW Patrick Willis/25 30.00 60.00
A.J. Hawk
TB Arrelious Benn/25 15.00 40.00
Golden Tate
TI Golden Tate/25 30.00 60.00
Rocket Ismail
TT Golden Tate/25 20.00 50.00
Demaryius Thomas
TW Demaryius Thomas/25 25.00 60.00
Mike Williams

2010 Exquisite Collection Inscriptions

STATED PRINT RUN 5-25
IBS Billy Sims/25 15.00 40.00
IJB Jahvid Best/25 20.00 50.00
IPH Paul Hornung/25 20.00 50.00
IPW Patrick Willis/25 15.00 40.00

2010 Exquisite Collection Legacy Signatures

STATED PRINT RUN 5-20
LBK Bernie Kosar/20 15.00 40.00
LGR George Rogers/20 15.00 40.00
LJT Joe Theismann/20 15.00 40.00
LPH Paul Hornung/20 20.00 50.00
LRI Rocket Ismail/20 30.00 60.00
LSI Billy Sims/20 15.00 40.00
LSL Steve Largent/20 20.00 50.00

2010 Exquisite Collection NCAA All-Time Defense Autographs

STATED PRINT RUN 10-20
ATDAH A.J. Hawk/20 20.00 50.00
ATDAP Alan Page/20 15.00 40.00
ATDEB Eric Berry/20 75.00 125.00
ATDHC Harry Carson/20 12.00 30.00
ATDJY Jack Youngblood/20 15.00 40.00
ATDMW Mario Williams/20 12.00 30.00
ATDNS Ndamukong Suh/20 60.00 120.00
ATDPW Patrick Willis/20 15.00 40.00
ATDSM Bubba Smith/20 15.00 40.00

2010 Exquisite Collection NCAA All-Time Offense Autographs

STATED PRINT RUN 5-20
EXCH EXPIRATION: 3/18/2013
ATOKW Kellen Winslow Sr./20 15.00 40.00
ATOPH Paul Hornung/20 20.00 50.00
ATORG Roman Gabriel/20 EXCH 20.00 50.00
ATORI Rocket Ismail/20 30.00 60.00
ATOSI Billy Sims/20 15.00 40.00

2010 Exquisite Collection Patch Combos

STATED PRINT RUN 50 SER.#'d SETS
AB Billy Sims 20.00 50.00
Adrian Peterson
AM Troy Aikman 30.00 60.00
Dan Marino
BH Chad Henne 15.00 40.00
Tom Brady
FR Doug Flutie 12.00 30.00
Matt Ryan
MB Peyton Manning 20.00 50.00
Drew Brees
MC Colt McCoy 15.00 40.00
Jimmy Clausen
MM Eli Manning 20.00 50.00
Peyton Manning
PB Adrian Peterson 30.00 80.00
Sam Bradford
PJ Adrian Peterson 15.00 40.00
Chris Johnson
PS Mark Sanchez 12.00 30.00
Carson Palmer
RB Tim Brown 15.00 40.00
Jerry Rice
SC Earl Campbell 15.00 40.00
Barry Sanders
SP Adrian Peterson 20.00 50.00
Barry Sanders
ST Barry Sanders 15.00 40.00
Thurman Thomas
TB Sam Bradford 30.00 80.00
Tim Tebow
WC Ricky Williams 12.00 30.00
Earl Campbell

2010 Exquisite Collection Patch Quads

STATED PRINT RUN 15 SER.#'d SETS
AEYM Troy Aikman 60.00 120.00
Dan Marino
John Elway
Steve Young
BRSR Matt Schaub 25.00 60.00
Tony Romo
Tom Brady
Philip Rivers
BTWS Dez Bryant 25.00 60.00
Jordan Shipley
Mike Williams
Demaryius Thomas
CPTB Jimmy Clausen 25.00 60.00
Golden Tate
Tim Brown
Alan Page
ESRW Kellen Winslow 90.00 175.00
Barry Sanders
John Elway
Jerry Rice
FPTB Tim Tebow 50.00 100.00
Carson Palmer
Sam Bradford
Doug Flutie
MBBM Drew Brees 40.00 80.00
Peyton Manning
Eli Manning
Tom Brady
MBMR Eli Manning 30.00 60.00
Peyton Manning
Drew Brees
Tony Romo
PGJB Chris Johnson 25.00 60.00
Ronnie Brown
Adrian Peterson
Frank Gore
SSFP Carson Palmer 30.00 80.00
Doug Flutie
Barry Sanders
Billy Sims
SWCS Billy Sims 40.00 80.00
Barry Sanders
Ricky Williams
Earl Campbell
TMBC Jimmy Clausen 30.00 80.00
Tim Tebow
Sam Bradford
Colt McCoy
YKKG Jim Kelly 40.00 80.00
Bernie Kosar
Bob Griese
Steve Young

2010 Exquisite Collection Patch Trios

STATED PRINT RUN 25 SER.#'d SETS
BCM Jimmy Clausen 30.00 80.00
Colt McCoy
Sam Bradford
BPR Philip Rivers 20.00 50.00
Tom Brady
Carson Palmer
BRL Tim Brown 25.00 60.00
Steve Largent
Jerry Rice
EAY Steve Young 25.00 60.00
John Elway
Troy Aikman
EMA Troy Aikman 30.00 80.00
John Elway
Dan Marino
MBB Tom Brady 25.00 60.00
Peyton Manning
Drew Brees
MMB Drew Brees 25.00 60.00
Peyton Manning
Eli Manning
MWC Dallas Clark 20.00 50.00
Peyton Manning
Reggie Wayne
RRR Philip Rivers 20.00 50.00
Tony Romo
Aaron Rodgers
SPB Sam Bradford 40.00 100.00
Adrian Peterson
Billy Sims
SRF Doug Flutie 25.00 60.00
Barry Sanders
Jerry Rice
SRM Jerry Rice 30.00 80.00
Dan Marino
Barry Sanders
TBC Sam Bradford 40.00 100.00
Tim Tebow
Jimmy Clausen
TMB Colt McCoy 40.00 100.00
Sam Bradford
Tim Tebow

2010 Exquisite Collection Premium Patch

STATED PRINT RUN 35-75
EPPAP Adrian Peterson/75 10.00 25.00
EPPAR Aaron Rodgers/50 40.00 80.00
EPPBB Brian Bosworth/75 12.00 30.00
EPPBJ Bo Jackson/50 15.00 40.00
EPPBK Bernie Kosar/50 6.00 15.00
EPPBR Tom Brady/75 15.00 40.00
EPPBS Barry Sanders/75 12.00 30.00
EPPCJ Calvin Johnson/35 10.00 25.00
EPPCM Colt McCoy/50 15.00 40.00
EPPCP Carson Palmer/75 6.00 15.00
EPPDD Drew Brees/35 10.00 25.00
EPPDF Doug Flutie/75 8.00 20.00
EPPDJ DeSean Jackson/50 6.00 15.00
EPPEC Earl Campbell/35 10.00 25.00
EPPEM Eli Manning/75 8.00 20.00
EPPFG Frank Gore/75 6.00 15.00
EPPGJ Greg Jennings/75 8.00 20.00
EPPJK Jim Kelly/75 8.00 20.00
EPPJN Chris Johnson/50 8.00 20.00
EPPJR Jerry Rice/75 12.00 30.00
EPPMA Miles Austin/75 15.00 40.00
EPPMS Mark Sanchez/75 8.00 20.00
EPPPM Peyton Manning/75 40.00 80.00
EPPPR Philip Rivers/50 8.00 20.00
EPPRW Reggie Wayne/35 8.00 20.00
EPPSB Sam Bradford/50 25.00 60.00
EPPSL Steve Largent/75 8.00 20.00
EPPSY Steve Young/75 12.00 30.00
EPPTA Troy Aikman/75 12.00 30.00
EPPTB Tim Brown/75 12.00 30.00
EPPTH Thurman Thomas/75 8.00 20.00
EPPTR Tony Romo/35 10.00 25.00
EPPTT Tim Tebow/50 25.00 60.00

2010 Exquisite Collection Rare Materials

STATED PRINT RUN 30-60
ERMAB Arrelious Benn/60 10.00 25.00
ERMAE Armanti Edwards/60 8.00 20.00
ERMAP Adrian Peterson/60 20.00 50.00
ERMAR Andre Roberts/60 8.00 20.00
ERMBL Brandon LaFell/60 8.00 20.00
ERMBR Dez Bryant/60 20.00 50.00
ERMBS Barry Sanders/60 20.00 50.00
ERMBT Ben Tate/60 10.00 25.00
ERMBU Brian Urlacher/60 15.00 40.00
ERMCH Chad Henne/30 10.00 25.00
ERMCJ Calvin Johnson/30 12.00 30.00
ERMCM Colt McCoy/60 15.00 40.00
ERMCS C.J. Spiller/60 12.00 30.00
ERMDB Drew Brees/30 12.00 30.00
ERMDJ DeSean Jackson/30 10.00 25.00
ERMDM Dan Marino/30 50.00 100.00
ERMDT Demaryius Thomas/60 10.00 25.00
ERMDW Damian Williams/60 8.00 20.00
ERMDX Dexter McCluster/60 8.00 20.00
ERMEB Eric Berry/60 15.00 40.00
ERMEC Earl Campbell/30 15.00 40.00
ERMED Eric Decker/60 10.00 25.00
ERMES Emmanuel Sanders/60 8.00 20.00
ERMGJ Greg Jennings/30 15.00 40.00
ERMGM Gerald McCoy/60 8.00 20.00
ERMGT Golden Tate/60 8.00 20.00
ERMJB Jahvid Best/60 12.00 30.00
ERMJC Jimmy Clausen/60 12.00 30.00
ERMJD Jonathan Dwyer/60 8.00 20.00
ERMJE John Elway/30 25.00 60.00
ERMJG Jermaine Gresham/60 10.00 25.00
ERMJK Jim Kelly/60 12.00 30.00
ERMJM Joe McKnight/60 8.00 20.00
ERMJN Chris Johnson/30 12.00 30.00
ERMJO Chad Johnson/60 8.00 20.00
ERMJR Jerry Rice/60 20.00 50.00
ERMJS Jordan Shipley/60 8.00 20.00
ERMLF Larry Fitzgerald/30 12.00 30.00
ERMMA Ryan Mathews/60 15.00 40.00
ERMMB Marion Barber/60 8.00 20.00
ERMME Marcus Easley/60 6.00 15.00
ERMMG Mardy Gilyard/60 8.00 20.00
ERMMH Montario Hardesty/60 10.00 25.00
ERMMK Mike Kafka/60 8.00 20.00
ERMMS Mark Sanchez/60 10.00 25.00
ERMMW Mike Williams/60 10.00 25.00
ERMNS Ndamukong Suh/60 30.00 60.00
ERMPM Peyton Manning/60 20.00 50.00
ERMPW Patrick Willis/60 12.00 30.00
ERMRB Ronnie Brown/60 10.00 25.00
ERMRG Rob Gronkowski/60 12.00 30.00
ERMRM Rolando McClain/60 8.00 20.00
ERMRW Ricky Williams/60 8.00 20.00
ERMSB Sam Bradford/60 25.00 60.00
ERMSY Steve Young/60 15.00 40.00
ERMTA Troy Aikman/60 15.00 40.00
ERMTB Tom Brady/60 25.00 60.00
ERMTG Toby Gerhart/60 8.00 20.00
ERMTR Tony Romo/60 12.00 30.00
ERMTT Tim Tebow/60 30.00 80.00

2010 Exquisite Collection Rookie Bookmark Patch Autographs

STATED PRINT RUN 50-99
EXCH EXPIRATION: 3/18/2013
BG Toby Gerhart/50 25.00 60.00
Jahvid Best
BH Eric Berry/99 30.00 60.00
Montario Hardesty
BM Ryan Mathews/50 40.00 80.00
Jahvid Best
BM2 Eric Berry/50 20.00 50.00
Dexter McCluster
BW Arrelious Benn/99 30.00 60.00
Mike Williams
DA Arrelious Benn/99 20.00 50.00
Demaryius Thomas
DG Demaryius Thomas/50 40.00 80.00
Golden Tate
DJ Dexter McCluster/50 25.00 60.00
Jahvid Best
DT Jonathan Dwyer/99 20.00 50.00
Demaryius Thomas
GG Jermaine Gresham/50 50.00 100.00
Rob Gronkowski
MB Sam Bradford/50 150.00 300.00
Colt McCoy
MC Colt McCoy/50 50.00 100.00
Jimmy Clausen
MS Colt McCoy/50 50.00 120.00
Jordan Shipley
NJ Ndamukong Suh/50 60.00 120.00
Jahvid Best
SG Jermaine Gresham/50 25.00 60.00
Jordan Shipley
SM Ryan Mathews/50 50.00 100.00
C.J. Spiller
TB Sam Bradford/50 175.00 350.00
Tim Tebow
TD Demaryius Thomas/99 40.00 80.00
Eric Decker
TT Tim Tebow/50 100.00 175.00
Demaryius Thomas
WT Damian Williams/50 15.00 40.00
Golden Tate
WW Damian Williams/99 15.00 40.00
Mike Williams

2010 Exquisite Collection Signature Jersey

STATED PRINT RUN 10-99
ESJAB Arrelious Benn/99 12.00 30.00
ESJDM Dexter McCluster/99 12.00 30.00
ESJDT Demaryius Thomas/99 15.00 40.00
ESJGT Golden Tate/99 12.00 30.00
ESJJB Jahvid Best/99 25.00 60.00
ESJMK Mike Kafka/99 12.00 30.00
ESJRM Rolando McClain/99 12.00 30.00
ESJJS Jordan Shipley/99 12.00 30.00
ESJTG Toby Gerhart/99 12.00 30.00

2010 Exquisite Collection Signature Jersey Dual

STATED PRINT RUN 5-25
BT Golden Tate/25 15.00 40.00
Arrelious Benn
TT Golden Tate/25 20.00 50.00
Demaryius Thomas

2010 Exquisite Collection Single Player Dual Patch

STATED PRINT RUN 25 SER.#'d SETS
EDPBB Brian Bosworth 10.00 25.00
EDPBK Bernie Kosar 10.00 25.00
EDPBS Barry Sanders 20.00 50.00
EDPDF Doug Flutie 10.00 25.00
EDPEC Earl Campbell 12.00 30.00
EDPJE John Elway 20.00 50.00
EDPJK Jim Kelly 12.00 30.00
EDPJR Jerry Rice 20.00 50.00
EDPSY Steve Young 15.00 40.00
EDPTA Troy Aikman 15.00 40.00
EDPTB Tim Brown 12.00 30.00
EDPTT Thurman Thomas 12.00 30.00

2010 Exquisite Collection Single Player Triple Patch

STATED PRINT RUN 50-75
ETPAJ Andre Johnson/75 8.00 20.00
ETPAP Adrian Peterson/75 15.00 40.00
ETPBS Barry Sanders/75 15.00 40.00
ETPCJ Calvin Johnson/50 10.00 25.00
ETPCP Carson Palmer/50 8.00 20.00
ETPDB Drew Brees/75 12.00 30.00
ETPDJ DeSean Jackson/75 8.00 20.00
ETPFG Frank Gore/50 8.00 20.00
ETPJC Jamaal Charles/75 8.00 20.00
ETPJR Jerry Rice/75 12.00 30.00
ETPMS Mark Sanchez/75 10.00 25.00
ETPPM Peyton Manning/50 15.00 40.00
ETPPR Philip Rivers/50 10.00 25.00
ETPRW Reggie Wayne/75 8.00 20.00
ETPSI Billy Sims/75 10.00 25.00
ETPTA Troy Aikman/50 15.00 40.00
ETPTB Tom Brady/75 20.00 50.00
ETPTR Tony Romo/75 12.00 30.00
ETPWW Wes Welker/75 10.00 25.00

1990 FACT Pro Set Cincinnati

The 1990 Pro Set FACT (Football and Academics: A Cincinnati Team) set was aimed at fourth graders in 29 schools in the Cincinnati school system. The special cards were used as motivational learning tools to promote public health and education. Twenty-five cards per week were issued in 25-card cello packs for fifteen consecutive weeks beginning October 1990. Moreover, a Teacher Instructional Game Plan, measuring approximately 8 1/2" by 11" and containing answers to all of the questions, was also issued. The standard-size cards are identical to first series cards, with the exception that the backs have interactive educational (Math, grammar, and science) questions instead of player information. Each 1990 Pro Set first series card was reprinted. The cards are numbered on the back. Each cello-wrapped pack led off with a header card which indicated the "week" number at the bottom. Initially, the missing numbers from the first series were 338, 376, and 377 but the Eric Dickerson PB card surfaced in limited quantities nearly twenty years later.

COMPLETE SET (375) 720.00 1,800.00
1 Barry Sanders W1 40.00 100.00
2 Joe Montana W1 50.00 120.00
3 Lindy Infante W1 UER 1.25 3.00
Coach of the Year
(missing Coach next
to Packers)
4 Warren Moon W1 UER 1.50 4.00
Man of the Year
(missing R symbol)
5 Keith Millard W1 1.25 3.00
Defensive Player
of the Year
6 Derrick Thomas W1 UER 1.50 4.00
Defensive Rookie
of the Year
(no 1989 on front
banner of card)
7 Ottis Anderson W1 1.25 3.00
Comeback Player
of the Year
8 Joe Montana W2 50.00 120.00
Passing Leader
9 Christian Okoye W2 1.25 3.00
Rushing Leader
10 Thurman Thomas W2 2.50 6.00
Total Yardage Leader
11 Mike Cofer W2 1.25 3.00
Kick Scoring Leader
12 Dalton Hilliard W2 UER 1.25 3.00
TD Scoring Leader
(O.J. Simpson not
listed in stats, but
is mentioned in text)
13 Sterling Sharpe W2 2.50 6.00
Receiving Leader
14 Rich Camarillo W3 1.25 3.00
Punting Leader
15 Walter Stanley W3 1.25 3.00
Punt Return Leader
16 Rod Woodson W3 1.50 4.00
Kickoff Return Leader

17 Felix Wright W3	1.25	3.00
Interception Leader		
18 Chris Doleman W3	1.25	3.00
Sack Leader		
19 Andre Ware W3	1.50	4.00
Heisman Trophy		
20 Mo Elewonibi W4	1.25	3.00
Outland Trophy		
21 Percy Snow W4	1.25	3.00
Lombardi Award		
22 Anthony Thompson W4	1.25	3.00
Maxwell Award		
23 Buck Buchanan W4	1.25	3.00
(Sacking Bart Starr)/1990 HOF Selection		
24 Bob Griese W4/1990 HOF Selection	1.50	4.00
25 Franco Harris W5/1990 HOF Selection	1.50	4.00
26 Ted Hendricks W4/1990 HOF Selection	1.50	4.00
27 Jack Lambert W5/1990 HOF Selection	1.50	4.00
28 Tom Landry W5/1990 HOF Selection	1.50	4.00
29 Bob St.Clair W5/1990 HOF Selection	1.25	3.00
30 Aundray Bruce W5 UER	1.25	3.00
(Stats say Falcons)		
31 Tony Casillas W5 UER	1.25	3.00
(Stats say Falcons)		
32 Shawn Collins W5	1.25	3.00
33 Marcus Cotton W6	1.25	3.00
34 Bill Fralic W6	1.25	3.00
35 Chris Miller W6	1.50	4.00
36 Deion Sanders W6 UER	15.00	40.00
(Stats say Falcons)		
37 John Settle W6	1.25	3.00
38 Jerry Glanville CO W6	1.25	3.00
39 Cornelius Bennett W7	1.50	4.00
40 Jim Kelly W7	6.00	15.00
41 Mark Kelso W7 UER	1.25	3.00
(No fumble rec. in '88;		
mentioned in '89)		
42 Scott Norwood W7	1.25	3.00
43 Nate Odomes W7	1.25	3.00
44 Scott Radecic W7	1.25	3.00
45 Jim Ritcher W8	1.25	3.00
46 Leonard Smith W8	1.25	3.00
47 Darryl Talley W8	1.25	3.00
48 Marv Levy CO W8	1.25	3.00
49 Neal Anderson W8	1.50	4.00
50 Kevin Butler W8	1.25	3.00
51 Jim Covert W9	1.25	3.00
52 Richard Dent W9	1.50	4.00
53 Jay Hilgenberg W9	1.25	3.00
54 Steve McMichael W9	1.25	3.00
55 Ron Morris W9	1.25	3.00
56 John Roper W9	1.25	3.00
57 Mike Singletary W9	1.50	4.00
58 Keith Van Horne W10	1.25	3.00
59 Mike Ditka CO W10	1.50	4.00
60 Lewis Billups W10	1.25	3.00
61 Eddie Brown W10	1.25	3.00
62 Jason Buck W10	1.25	3.00
63 Rickey Dixon W10	1.25	3.00
64 Tim McGee W11	1.25	3.00
65 Eric Thomas W11	1.25	3.00
66 Ickey Woods W11	1.25	3.00
67 Carl Zander W11	1.25	3.00
68 Sam Wyche CO W11	1.25	3.00
69 Paul Farren W11	1.25	3.00
70 Thane Gash W12	1.25	3.00
71 David Grayson W12	1.25	3.00
72 Bernie Kosar W12	1.50	4.00
73 Reggie Langhorne W12	1.25	3.00
74 Eric Metcalf W12	1.50	4.00
75 Ozzie Newsome W12	1.50	4.00
76 Felix Wright W13	1.25	3.00
77 Bud Carson CO W13	1.25	3.00
78 Troy Aikman W13	30.00	80.00
79 Michael Irvin W13	5.00	12.00
80 Jim Jeffcoat W13	1.25	3.00
81 Crawford Ker W13	1.25	3.00
82 Eugene Lockhart W13	1.25	3.00
83 Kelvin Martin W14	1.25	3.00
84 Ken Norton Jr. W14	1.50	4.00
85 Jimmy Johnson CO W14	1.50	4.00
86 Steve Atwater W14	1.25	3.00
87 Tyrone Braxton W14	1.25	3.00
88 John Elway W14	60.00	150.00
89 Simon Fletcher W15	1.25	3.00
90 Ron Holmes W15	1.25	3.00
91 Bobby Humphrey W15	1.25	3.00
92 Vance Johnson W15	1.25	3.00
93 Ricky Nattiel W15	1.25	3.00
94 Dan Reeves CO W15	1.50	4.00
95 Jim Arnold W1	1.25	3.00
96 Jerry Ball W1	1.25	3.00
97 Bennie Blades W1	1.25	3.00
98 Lomas Brown W1	1.25	3.00
99 Michael Cofer W1	1.25	3.00
100 Richard Johnson W4	1.25	3.00
101 Eddie Murray W4	1.25	3.00
102 Barry Sanders W2	60.00	150.00
103 Chris Spielman W2	1.25	3.00
104 William White W2	1.25	3.00
105 Eric Williams W2	1.25	3.00
106 Wayne Fontes CO W3 UER	1.25	3.00
(Says born in MO		
actually born in MA)		
107 Brent Fullwood W3	1.25	3.00
108 Ron Hallstrom W3	1.25	3.00
109 Tim Harris W8	1.25	3.00
110 Johnny Holland W8	1.25	3.00
111 Perry Kemp W8	1.25	3.00
112 Don Majkowski W9	1.25	3.00
113 Mark Murphy W9	1.25	3.00
114 Sterling Sharpe W9	2.50	6.00
115 Ed West W9	1.25	3.00
116 Lindy Infante CO W9	1.25	3.00
117 Steve Brown W9	1.25	3.00
118 Ray Childress W10	1.25	3.00
119 Ernest Givins W10	1.25	3.00
120 John Grimsley W10	1.25	3.00
121 Alonzo Highsmith W10	1.25	3.00
122 Drew Hill W10	1.50	4.00
123 Bubba McDowell W10	1.25	3.00
124 Dean Steinkuhler W10	1.25	3.00
125 Lorenzo White W11	1.25	3.00
126 Tony Zendejas W11	1.25	3.00
127 Jack Pardee CO W11	1.25	3.00
128 Albert Bentley W11	1.25	3.00
129 Dean Biasucci W11	1.25	3.00
130 Duane Bickett W11	1.25	3.00
131 Bill Brooks W12	1.25	3.00
132 Jon Hand W12	1.25	3.00
133 Mike Prior W12	1.25	3.00
134 Andre Rison W12	1.60	4.00
135 Rohn Stark W12	1.25	3.00
136 Donnell Thompson W12	1.25	3.00
137 Clarence Verdin W13	1.25	3.00
138 Fredd Young W13	1.25	3.00
139 Ron Meyer CO W14	1.25	3.00
140 John Alt W14	1.25	3.00
141 Steve DeBerg W14	1.25	3.00
142 Irv Eatman W1	1.25	3.00
143 Dino Hackett W2	1.25	3.00
144 Nick Lowery W2	1.25	3.00
145 Bill Maas W2	1.25	3.00
146 Stephone Paige W5	1.25	3.00
147 Neil Smith W3	1.50	4.00
148 Marty Schottenheimer	1.25	3.00
CO W3		
149 Steve Beuerlein W3	1.50	4.00
150 Tim Brown W4	6.00	15.00
151 Mike Dyal W4	1.25	3.00
152 Mervyn Fernandez W4	1.25	3.00
153 Willie Gault W4	1.25	3.00
154 Bob Golic W5	1.25	3.00
155 Bo Jackson W5	2.50	6.00
156 Don Mosebar W5	1.25	3.00
157 Steve Smith W5	1.25	3.00
158 Greg Townsend W5	1.25	3.00
159 Bruce Wilkerson W6	1.25	3.00
160 Steve Wisniewski W6	1.25	3.00
(Blocking for Bo Jackson)		
161 Art Shell CO W6	1.50	4.00
162 Flipper Anderson W6	1.25	3.00
163 Greg Bell W6 UER	1.25	3.00
(Stats have 5 catches		
should be 9)		
164 Henry Ellard W6	1.50	4.00
165 Jim Everett W6	1.25	3.00
166 Jerry Gray W7	1.25	3.00
167 Kevin Greene W7	1.50	4.00
168 Pete Holohan W13	1.25	3.00
169 Larry Kelm W13	1.25	3.00
170 Tom Newberry W13	1.25	3.00
171 Vince Newsome W13	1.25	3.00
172 Irv Pankey W14	1.25	3.00
173 Jackie Slater W14	1.25	3.00
174 Fred Strickland W14	1.25	3.00
175 Mike Wilcher W14 UER	1.25	3.00
(Fumble rec. number		
different from/1989 Pro Set card)		
176 John Robinson CO W7	1.25	3.00
UER (Stats say Rams		
should say L.A. Rams)		
177 Mark Clayton W7	1.50	4.00
178 Roy Foster W7	1.25	3.00
179 Harry Galbreath W7	1.25	3.00
180 Jim C. Jensen W8	1.25	3.00
181 Dan Marino W15	60.00	150.00
182 Louis Oliver W15	1.25	3.00
183 Sammie Smith W15	1.25	3.00
184 Brian Sochia W15	1.25	3.00
185 Don Shula CO W15	2.50	6.00
186 Joey Browner W8	1.25	3.00
187 Anthony Carter W15	1.50	4.00
188 Chris Doleman W8	1.25	3.00
189 Steve Jordan W4	1.25	3.00
190 Carl Lee W4	1.25	3.00
191 Randall McDaniel W5	1.50	4.00
192 Mike Merriweather W5	1.25	3.00
193 Keith Millard W14	1.25	3.00
194 Al Noga W12	1.25	3.00
195 Scott Studwell W5	1.25	3.00
196 Henry Thomas W12	1.25	3.00
197 Herschel Walker W5	1.50	4.00
198 Wade Wilson W5	1.50	4.00
199 Gary Zimmerman W5	1.25	3.00
200 Jerry Burns CO W6	1.25	3.00
201 Vincent Brown W6	1.25	3.00
202 Hart Lee Dykes W14	1.25	3.00
203 Sean Farrell W6	1.25	3.00
204 Fred Marion W6	1.25	3.00
205 Stanley Morgan W15 UER	1.50	4.00
(Text says he reached/10,000 yards fastest;/3 players did it		
in.10 seasons)		
206 Eric Sievers W6	1.25	3.00
207 John Stephens W15	1.25	3.00
208 Andre Tippett W15	1.25	3.00
209 Rod Rust CO W15	1.25	3.00
210 Morten Andersen W6	1.25	3.00
211 Brad Edelman W12	1.25	3.00
212 John Fourcade W12	1.25	3.00
213 Dalton Hilliard W13	1.25	3.00
214 Rickey Jackson W13	1.25	3.00
(Forcing Jim Kelly fumble)		
215 Vaughan Johnson W13	1.25	3.00
216 Eric Martin W13	1.25	3.00
217 Sam Mills W7	1.25	3.00
218 Pat Swilling W7 UER	1.50	4.00
(Total fumble		
recoveries listed		
as 4; should be 5)		
219 Frank Warren W7	1.25	3.00
220 Jim Wilks W7	1.25	3.00
221 Jim Mora CO W7	1.25	3.00
222 Raul Allegre W2	1.25	3.00
223 Carl Banks W1	1.25	3.00
224 Jumbo Elliott W1	1.25	3.00
225 Erik Howard W7	1.25	3.00
226 Pepper Johnson W2	1.25	3.00
227 Leonard Marshall W7	1.25	3.00
UER (In Super Bowl XXI		
George Martin had		
the safety)		
228 Dave Meggett W2	1.50	4.00
229 Bart Oates W3	1.25	3.00
230 Phil Simms W8	1.50	4.00
231 Lawrence Taylor W8	1.50	4.00
232 Bill Parcells CO W8	1.50	4.00
233 Troy Benson W8	1.25	3.00
234 Kyle Clifton W8 UER	1.25	3.00
(Born: Onley		
should be Olney)		
235 Johnny Hector W8	1.25	3.00
236 Jeff Lageman W9	1.25	3.00
237 Pat Leahy W9	1.25	3.00
238 Freeman McNeil W9	1.50	4.00
239 Ken O'Brien W9	1.25	3.00
240 Al Toon W9	1.50	4.00
241 Jo Jo Townsell W9	1.25	3.00
242 Bruce Coslet CO W10	1.25	3.00
243 Eric Allen W10	1.25	3.00
244 Jerome Brown W10	1.50	4.00
245 Keith Byars W10	1.50	4.00
246 Cris Carter W13	15.00	40.00
247 Randall Cunningham W13	2.50	6.00
248 Keith Jackson W14	1.50	4.00
249 Mike Quick W14	1.50	4.00
250 Clyde Simmons W14	1.50	4.00
251 Andre Waters W14	1.25	3.00
252 Reggie White W15	2.50	6.00
253 Buddy Ryan CO W15	1.25	3.00
254 Rich Camarillo W15	1.25	3.00
255 Earl Ferrell W10	1.25	3.00
(No mention of retire-		
ment on card front)		
256 Roy Green W10	1.50	4.00
257 Ken Harvey W3	1.25	3.00
258 Ernie Jones W1	1.25	3.00
259 Tim McDonald W11	1.25	3.00
260 Timm Rosenbach W11 UER	1.25	3.00
(Born '67; should be '66)		
261 Luis Sharpe W3	1.25	3.00
262 Vai Sikahema W3	1.25	3.00
263 J.T. Smith W1	1.25	3.00
264 Ron Wolfley W1 UER	1.25	3.00
(Born Blaisdel		
should be Blasdel)		
265 Joe Bugel CO W11	1.25	3.00
266 Gary Anderson W11	1.25	3.00
267 Bubby Brister W1	1.50	4.00
268 Merril Hoge W11	1.25	3.00
269 Carnell Lake W2	1.25	3.00
270 Louis Lipps W11	1.25	3.00
271 David Little W3	1.25	3.00
272 Greg Lloyd W3	1.50	4.00
273 Keith Willis W11	1.25	3.00
274 Tim Worley W3	1.25	3.00
275 Chuck Noll CO W4	1.50	4.00
276 Marion Butts W4	1.25	3.00
277 Gill Byrd W2	1.25	3.00
278 Vencie Glenn W2 UER	1.25	3.00
(Sack total should		
be 2, not 2.5)		
279 Burt Grossman W4	1.25	3.00
280 Gary Plummer W4	1.25	3.00
281 Billy Ray Smith W12	1.25	3.00
282 Billy Joe Tolliver W12	1.25	3.00
283 Dan Henning CO W1	1.25	3.00
284 Harris Barton W1	1.25	3.00
285 Michael Carter W1	1.25	3.00
286 Mike Cofer W1	1.25	3.00
287 Roger Craig W1	1.50	4.00
288 Don Griffin W1	1.25	3.00
289 Charles Haley W2	1.25	3.00
290 Pierce Holt W2	1.25	3.00
291 Ronnie Lott W2	2.50	6.00
292 Guy McIntyre W2	1.25	3.00
293 Joe Montana W2	60.00	150.00
294 Tom Rathman W2	1.25	3.00
295 Jerry Rice W3	30.00	75.00
296 Jesse Sapolu W3	1.25	3.00
297 John Taylor W3	1.50	4.00
298 Michael Walter W3	1.25	3.00
299 George Seifert CO W3	1.50	4.00
300 Jeff Bryant W3	1.25	3.00
301 Jacob Green W4	1.25	3.00
302 Norm Johnson W4 UER	1.25	3.00
(Card shop not in		
Garden Grove, should		
say Fullerton)		
303 Bryan Millard W4	1.25	3.00
304 Joe Nash W4	1.25	3.00
305 Eugene Robinson W4	1.25	3.00
306 John L. Williams W14	1.25	3.00
307 David Wyman W14	1.25	3.00
(NFL EXP is in caps		
inconsistent with rest		
of the set)		
308 Chuck Knox CO W14	1.25	3.00
309 Mark Carrier W14	1.50	4.00
310 Paul Gruber W14	1.25	3.00
311 Harry Hamilton W15	1.25	3.00
312 Bruce Hill W15	1.25	3.00
313 Donald Igwebuike W15	1.25	3.00
314 Kevin Murphy W15	1.25	3.00
315 Ervin Randle W12	1.25	3.00
316 Mark Robinson W12	1.25	3.00
317 Lars Tate W12	1.25	3.00
318 Vinny Testaverde W12	1.50	4.00
319 Ray Perkins CO W12	1.25	3.00
320 Earnest Byner W12	1.25	3.00
321 Gary Clark W12	1.50	4.00
322 Darryl Grant W13	1.25	3.00
323 Darrell Green W13	1.25	3.00
324 Jim Lachey W13	1.25	3.00
325 Charles Mann W13	1.25	3.00
326 Wilber Marshall W13	1.25	3.00
327 Ralf Mojsiejenko W13	1.25	3.00
328 Art Monk W15	2.50	6.00
329 Gerald Riggs W15	1.25	3.00
330 Mark Rypien W14	1.50	4.00
331 Ricky Sanders W4	1.25	3.00
332 Alvin Walton W4	1.25	3.00
333 Joe Gibbs CO W5	1.50	4.00
334 Aloha Stadium W5	1.25	3.00
335 Brian Blades PB W5	1.50	4.00
336 James Brooks PB W5	1.25	3.00
337 Shane Conlan PB W5	1.25	3.00
338 Eric Dickerson PB		
339 Ray Donaldson PB W5	1.25	3.00
340 Ferrell Edmunds PB W6	1.25	3.00
341 Boomer Esiason PB W6	1.50	4.00
342 David Fulcher PB W6	1.25	3.00
343 Chris Hinton PB W6	1.25	3.00
344 Rodney Holman PB W6	1.25	3.00
345 Kent Hull PB W6	1.25	3.00
346 Tunch Ilkin PB W7	1.25	3.00
347 Mike Johnson PB W7	1.25	3.00
348 Greg Kragen PB W7	1.25	3.00
349 Dave Krieg PB W7	1.25	3.00
350 Albert Lewis PB W7	1.25	3.00
351 Howie Long PB W7	1.50	4.00
352 Bruce Matthews PB W8	1.50	4.00
353 Clay Matthews PB W8	1.25	3.00
354 Erik McMillan PB W8	1.25	3.00
355 Karl Mecklenburg PB W8	1.25	3.00
356 Anthony Miller PB W8	1.50	4.00
357 Frank Minnifield PB W8	1.25	3.00
358 Max Montoya PB W8	1.25	3.00
359 Warren Moon PB W10	2.50	6.00
360 Mike Munchak PB W9	1.50	4.00
361 Anthony Munoz PB W9	1.50	4.00
362 John Offerdahl PB W9	1.25	3.00
363 Christian Okoye PB W9	1.25	3.00
364 Leslie O'Neal PB W9	1.50	4.00
365 Rufus Porter PB W9 UER	1.25	3.00
(TM logo missing)		
366 Andre Reed PB W10	1.50	4.00
367 Johnny Rembert PB W10	1.25	3.00
368 Reggie Roby PB W10	1.25	3.00
369 Kevin Ross PB W10	1.25	3.00
370 Webster Slaughter PB W10	1.25	3.00
371 Bruce Smith PB W11	1.50	4.00
372 Dennis Smith PB W11	1.25	3.00
373 Derrick Thomas PB W11	1.50	4.00
374 Thurman Thomas PB W11	1.50	4.00
375 David Treadwell PB W11	1.25	3.00
376 Lee Williams PB W11	1.25	3.00

1991 FACT Pro Set Mobil

Sponsored by Pro Set and Mobil Oil, the 1991 Pro Set FACT (Football and Academics: A Championship Team) set marks the second year that Pro Set produced cards to serve as motivational learning tools to promote public health and education. This year's program was expanded to include all 26 NFL cities and to target 200,000 fourth grade students in low socio-economic areas. Six monthly lessons were featured in the set, and each lesson had an educational theme. Teachers utilized in-classroom educational materials and distributed a set of 17 Pro Set cards (along with one title/header card) each month, with the reverse sides carrying specific educational lessons corresponding to the educational theme. The standard-size cards are identical to first series cards, with the exception that the backs have interactive educational questions instead of player information. The particular set in which the card was issued is indicated below by S for set number.

COMPLETE SET (108)	100.00	250.00
3 Joe Montana S1	30.00	50.00
5 Mike Singletary S2	.80	2.00
12 Jay Novacek S3	.80	2.00
20 Ottis Anderson S2	.80	2.00
40 Tim Brown S1	3.20	8.00
44 Herschel Walker S1	.80	2.00
59 Eric Dorsey S3	.60	1.50
60 Jumbo Elliott S1	.60	1.50
63 Jeff Hostetler S2	.80	2.00
69 Eric Moore S4	.60	1.50
70 Bart Oates S3	.60	1.50
71 Gary Reasons S4	.60	1.50
75 Shane Conlan S3	.60	1.50
78 Jim Kelly S4	1.60	4.00
84 Darryl Talley S6	.60	1.50
90 Marv Levy CO S1	.60	1.50
94 Tim Green S2	.60	1.50
99 Jerry Glanville CO S3	.60	1.50
101 Mark Carrier S3	.60	1.50
104 Jim Harbaugh S6	.80	2.00
105 Brad Muster S4	.60	1.50
107 Keith Van Horne S6	.60	1.50
111 Boomer Esiason S1	.80	2.00
114 Rodney Holman S5	.60	1.50
116 Anthony Munoz S2	.80	2.00
117 Sam Wyche CO S4	.60	1.50
118 Paul Farren S6	.60	1.50
119 Thane Gash S3	.60	1.50
122 Clay Matthews S2	.60	1.50
123 Eric Metcalf S6	.80	2.00
127 Tommie Agee S4	.60	1.50
128 Troy Aikman S6	10.00	25.00
132 Michael Irvin S6	1.60	4.00
134 Daniel Stubbs S6	.60	1.50
136 Steve Atwater S1	.60	1.50
138 John Elway S2	16.00	40.00
141 Mark Jackson S6	.60	1.50
142 Karl Mecklenburg S3	.60	1.50
143 Doug Widell S2	.60	1.50
153 Wayne Fontes CO S2	.60	1.50
156 Don Majkowski S1	.60	1.50
157 Tony Mandarich S6	.60	1.50
158 Mark Murphy S6	.60	1.50
161 Sterling Sharpe S4	1.60	4.00
162 Lindy Infante CO S3	.60	1.50
163 Ray Childress S6	.60	1.50
166 Bruce Matthews S3	.80	2.00
167 Warren Moon S6	1.60	4.00
168 Mike Munchak S4	.80	2.00
169 Al Smith S6	.60	1.50
174 Bill Brooks S1	.80	2.00
179 Clarence Verdin S3	.60	1.50
182 Steve DeBerg S1	.60	1.50
185 Christian Okoye S3	.60	1.50
189 M.Schottenheimer CO S1	.60	1.50
191 Howie Long S2	.80	2.00
194 Steve Smith S4	.60	1.50
196 Lionel Washington S6	.60	1.50
198 Art Shell CO S3	.80	2.00
203 Buford McGee S2	.60	1.50
204 Tom Newberry S6	.60	1.50
205 Frank Stams S1	.60	1.50
210 Dan Marino S4	16.00	40.00
212 John Offerdahl S1	.60	1.50
216 Don Shula CO S4	.80	2.00
217 Darrell Fullington S6	.60	1.50
218 Tim Irwin S2	.60	1.50
219 Mike Merriweather S3	.60	1.50
231 Ed Reynolds S3	.60	1.50
238 Robert Massey S4	.60	1.50
246 James Hasty S1	.60	1.50
247 Erik McMillan S2	.60	1.50
249 Ken O'Brien S4	.60	1.50
260 Andre Waters S2	.60	1.50
270 Joe Bugel CO S2	.60	1.50
271 Gary Anderson S1	.60	1.50
272 Dermontti Dawson S4	.60	1.50
275 Tunch Ilkin S2	.60	1.50
282 Gill Byrd S4	.60	1.50
290 Michael Carter S2	.60	1.50
292 Pierce Holt S3	.60	1.50
297 George Seifert CO S1	.80	2.00
306 Chuck Knox CO S3	.60	1.50
310 Harry Hamilton S4	.60	1.50
321 Martin Mayhew S4	.60	1.50
322 Mark Rypien S1	.80	2.00
NNO S1 Title Card	.60	1.50
Stay Fit		
NNO S2 Title Card	.60	1.50
Eat Smart		
NNO S3 Title Card	.60	1.50
Stay Off Drugs		
NNO S4 Title Card	.60	1.50
Stay In Tune		
NNO S5 Title Card	.60	1.50
Stay True to Yourself		
NNO S6 Title Card	.60	1.50
Stay In School		

1992 FACT NFL Properties

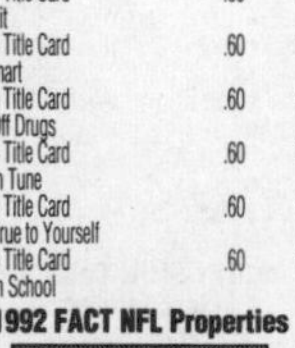

Sponsored by NFL Properties, Inc., this 18-card FACT (Football and Academics: A Championship Team) set measures the standard size and features NFL star players. The color photos on the fronts are full-bleed on the sides but bordered by black above and below. In white block lettering, the top of each card reads "It's A Fact," while the bottom slogan varies from card to card. On a white background with "It's A Fact" printed in pale blue, the horizontal backs have an extended player quote on the theme of the card.

COMPLETE SET (18)	16.00	40.00
1 Warren Moon	1.60	4.00
Crack Kills		
2 Boomer Esiason	1.00	2.50
Think Before You Drink		
3 Troy Aikman	3.20	8.00
Play It Straight		
4 Anthony Munoz	1.00	2.50
Quedate en la Escuela		
5 Charles Mann	.60	1.50
Steroids Destroy		
6 Earnest Byner	.60	1.50
Never Give Up		
7 Joe Jacoby	.60	1.50
Don't Pollute		
8 Howie Long	1.00	2.50
Aids Kills		
9 Dan Marino	6.00	15.00
School's The Ticket		
10 Mike Singletary	1.00	2.50
11 Cornelius Bennett	1.00	2.50
Chill		
12 Chris Doleman	1.00	2.50
Turn It Off		
13 Jim Harbaugh	1.00	2.50
Eat To Win		
14 Chris Hinton	.60	1.50
Say It Don't Spray It		
15 Nick Lowery	.60	1.50
Heal The Planet		
16 Rodney Peete	1.00	2.50
Respect The Law		
17 Pat Swilling	1.00	2.50
Vote		
18 Jim Everett	1.00	2.50
Study		

1992 FACT Pro Set Mobil

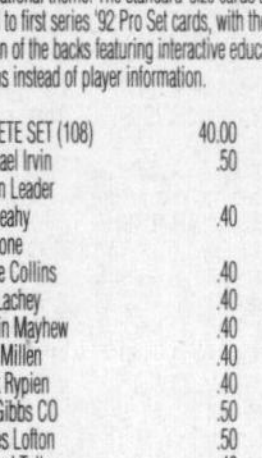

Sponsored by Pro Set and Mobil Oil, the 1992 Pro Set FACT (Football and Academics: A Championship Team) set marks the third year that Pro Set produced cards to serve as motivational learning tools to promote public health and education. Six monthly lessons were featured in the set, and each lesson had an educational theme. Teachers utilized in-classroom educational materials and distributed a set of 18-Pro Set cards (including one title/header card) each month, with the reverse sides carrying specific educational lessons corresponding to the educational theme. The standard-size cards are identical to first series '92 Pro Set cards, with the exception of the backs featuring interactive educational questions instead of player information.

COMPLETE SET (108)	40.00	100.00
10 Michael Irvin	.50	1.25
Season Leader		
20 Pat Leahy	.40	1.00
Milestone		
76 Andre Collins	.40	1.00
79 Jim Lachey	.40	1.00
82 Martin Mayhew	.40	1.00
83 Matt Millen	.40	1.00
87 Mark Rypien	.40	1.00
90 Joe Gibbs CO	.50	1.25
98 James Lofton	.50	1.25
104 Darryl Talley	.40	1.00
108 Marv Levy CO	.50	1.25
111 Moe Gardner	.40	1.00
117 Jerry Glanville CO	.40	1.00
118 Neal Anderson	.40	1.00
119 Trace Armstrong	.40	1.00
125 Tom Waddle	.40	1.00
132 Anthony Munoz	.50	1.25
135 David Shula CO	.40	1.00
136 Mike Babb	.40	1.00
137 Brian Brennan	.40	1.00
141 Clay Matthews	.40	1.00
142 Eric Metcalf	.50	1.25
144 Bill Belichick CO	.80	2.00
145 Steve Beuerlein	.50	1.25
147 Ray Horton	.40	1.00
152 Alexander Wright	.40	1.00
153 Jimmy Johnson CO	.50	1.25
155 John Elway	4.80	12.00
158 Karl Mecklenburg	.40	1.00
161 Doug Widell	.40	1.00
170 Chris Spielman	.40	1.00
171 Wayne Fontes	.40	1.00
173 Tony Mandarich	.40	1.00
175 Bryce Paup	.50	1.25
176 Sterling Sharpe	.50	1.25
177 Darrell Thompson	.40	1.00
180 Mike Holmgren CO	.80	2.00
181 Ray Childress	.40	1.00
183 Curtis Duncan	.40	1.00
186 Warren Moon	.80	2.00
189 Jack Pardee CO	.40	1.00
192 Bill Brooks	.40	1.00
195 Mike Prior	.40	1.00
197 Clarence Verdin	.40	1.00
199 John Alt	.40	1.00
200 Deron Cherry	.40	1.00
202 Nick Lowery	.40	1.00
205 Joe Valerio	.40	1.00
207 Marty Schottenheimer	.40	1.00
210 Tim Brown	.80	2.00
211 Howie Long	.80	2.00
212 Ronnie Lott	.80	2.00
216 Art Shell	.50	1.25
222 Tom Newberry	.40	1.00
225 Chuck Knox CO	.40	1.00
230 Jim Jensen	.40	1.00
231 Louis Oliver	.40	1.00
234 Don Shula CO	.80	2.00
238 Steve Jordan	.40	1.00
241 Herschel Walker	.50	1.25
242 Felix Wright	.40	1.00
243 Dennis Green CO	.40	1.00
248 Hugh Millen	.40	1.00
250 Andre Tippett	.40	1.00
252 Dick MacPherson CO	.40	1.00
254 Bobby Hebert	.40	1.00
259 Floyd Turner	.40	1.00
261 Jim Mora CO	.40	1.00
265 Jeff Hostetler	.50	1.25
268 Gary Reasons	.40	1.00
269 Everson Walls	.40	1.00
270 Ray Handley CO	.40	1.00
275 Jeff Lageman	.40	1.00
277 Rob Moore	.50	1.25
278 Lonnie Young	.40	1.00
279 Bruce Coslet CO	.40	1.00
283 Keith Jackson	.50	1.25
286 Andre Waters	.40	1.00
288 Rich Kotite CO	.40	1.00
290 Garth Jax	.40	1.00
291 Ernie Jones	.40	1.00
297 Joe Bugel CO	.40	1.00
298 Gary Anderson K	.40	1.00
300 Eric Green	.40	1.00
301 Bryan Hinkle	.40	1.00
302 Tunch Ilkin	.40	1.00
303 Louis Lipps	.40	1.00
304 Neil O'Donnell	.50	1.25
306 Bill Cowher CO	.50	1.25
312 Henry Rolling	.40	1.00
315 Bobby Ross CO	.40	1.00
317 Michael Carter	.40	1.00
320 Brent Jones	.50	1.25
324 George Seifert CO	.50	1.25
328 Tommy Kane	.40	1.00
330 Dave Krieg	.40	1.00
333 Tom Flores CO	.40	1.00
336 Reuben Davis	.40	1.00
342 Sam Wyche CO	.40	1.00
375 Steve Atwater	.40	1.00
386 Haywood Jeffires	.40	1.00
Pro Bowl		
398 Richmond Webb	.40	1.00
Pro Bowl		
NNO S1 Title Card	.40	1.00
Stay in School		
NNO S2 Title Card	.40	1.00
Stay Fit		
NNO S3 Title Card	.40	1.00
Eat Smart		
NNO S4 Title Card	.40	1.00
Stay in Tune		
NNO S5 Title Card	.40	1.00
Stay off Drugs		
NNO S6 Title Card	.40	1.00
Stay True to Yourself		

1993 FACT Fleer Shell

This 108-card set was issued by Fleer and co-sponsored by Shell and Russell Athletic. The FACT (Football and Academics: A Championship Team) sets were originally produced by Pro Set to serve as motivational learning tools to promote public health and education. Teachers utilized in-classroom educational materials and distributed a set of 18 Fleer cards each month, with the reverse sides carrying specific educational lessohs corresponding to the educational theme. The standard-size cards are identical to the regular 1993 Fleer set, with the exception that the backs include interactive educational questions along with player information. The cards are numbered on the back with 1-18 being in set 1, 19-36 in set 2, 37-54 in set 3, etc.

COMPLETE SET (108)	15.00	40.00
1 Stay in School	.10	.30
Scorecard		
2 Andre Rison	.20	.50
3 Jim Kelly	.30	.75
4 Mark Carrier DB	.10	.30
5 David Fulcher	.10	.30
6 Eric Metcalf	.20	.50
7 Emmitt Smith	2.00	5.00
8 John Elway	2.40	6.00
9 Rodney Peete	.20	.50
10 Brett Favre	2.40	6.00
11 Warren Moon	.30	.75
Houson Oilers		
12 Reggie Langhorne	.10	.30
13 Christian Okoye	.20	.50
14 Nick Bell	.10	.30
15 Jim Everett	.20	.50
16 Dan Marino	2.40	6.00
17 Chris Doleman	.20	.50
18 Leonard Russell	.20	.50
19 Stay Fit	.10	.30
Scorecard		
20 Sam Mills	.10	.30
21 Rodney Hampton	.20	.50
22 Rob Moore	.20	.50
23 Seth Joyner	.20	.50
24 Chris Chandler	.20	.50
25 Barry Foster	.20	.50
26 Stan Humphries	.20	.50
27 Steve Young	1.00	2.50
28 Cortez Kennedy	.20	.50
29 Reggie Cobb	.10	.30
30 Mark Rypien	.10	.30
31 Michael Haynes	.20	.50
32 Thurman Thomas	.30	.75
33 Tom Waddle	.10	.30
34 Harold Green	.10	.30
35 Tommy Vardell	.10	.30
36 Michael Irvin	.30	.75
37 Eat Smart	.10	.30
Scorecard		
38 Mike Croel	.10	.30
39 Barry Sanders	2.00	5.00
40 Sterling Sharpe	.30	.75
41 Haywood Jeffires	.20	.50
42 Duane Bickett	.10	.30
43 Nick Lowery	.10	.30
44 Greg Townsend	.10	.30
45 Todd Lyght	.10	.30
46 Ritchmond Webb	.10	.30
47 Cris Carter	.60	1.50
48 Marv Cook	.10	.30
49 Vaughan Johnson	.10	.30
50 Pepper Johnson	.10	.30
51 Kyle Clifton	.10	.30
52 Fred Barnett	.20	.50
53 Ken Harvey	.10	.30
54 Rod Woodson	.20	.50
55 Stay in Tune	.10	.30
Scorecard		
56 Marion Butts	.10	.30
57 Ricky Watters	.20	.50
58 Brian Blades	.20	.50
59 Broderick Thomas	.10	.30
60 Charles Mann	.10	.30
61 Chris Hinton	.10	.30
62 Cornelius Bennett	.20	.50
63 Jim Harbaugh	.20	.50
64 Tim Krumrie	.10	.30
65 Bernie Kosar	.20	.50
66 Troy Aikman	1.20	3.00
67 Shannon Sharpe	.30	.75
68 Chris Spielman	.20	.50
69 Brian Noble	.10	.30
70 Curtis Duncan	.10	.30
71 Quentin Coryatt	.10	.30
72 Derrick Thomas	.30	.75
73 Stay off Drugs	.10	.30
Scorecard		
74 Tim Brown	.30	.75
75 Jackie Slater	.10	.30
76 Keith Jackson	.20	.50
77 Terry Allen	.30	.75
78 Andre Tippett	.10	.30
79 Morten Andersen	.10	.30
80 Phil Simms	.20	.50
81 Jeff Lageman	.10	.30
82 Randall Cunningham	.30	.75
83 Randal Hill	.10	.30
84 Neil O'Donnell	.20	.50
85 Gill Byrd	.10	.30
86 John Taylor	.20	.50
87 Eugene Robinson	.10	.30
88 Paul Gruber	.10	.30
89 Andre Collins	.10	.30
90 Chris Miller	.20	.50
91 Stay True to Yourself	.10	.30
Scorecard		
92 Andre Reed	.20	.50
93 Richard Dent	.20	.50
94 David Klingler	.10	.30
95 Jay Novacek	.20	.50
96 Steve Atwater	.10	.30
97 Bennie Blades	.10	.30
98 Terrell Buckley	.10	.30
99 Ray Childress	.10	.30
100 Harvey Williams	.20	.50
101 Howie Long	.30	.75
102 Lawrence Taylor	.20	.50
103 Johnny Mitchell	.10	.30
104 Carnell Lake	.10	.30
105 Junior Seau	.30	.75
106 Kevin Fagan	.10	.30
107 Lawrence Dawsey	.10	.30
108 Art Monk	.20	.50

1994 FACT Fleer Shell

For the second consecutive year, Fleer and Shell Oil teamed up to produce a 108-card FACT (Football and Academics: A Championship Team) set. Consisting of six 18-card subsets, each subset features one title card, 17 player cards, and a different theme. The fronts feature white-bordered color action photos with a gold-foil stamped player signature, name and position, and team logo. The horizontal backs carry a ghosted action shot, and a close-up color photo. The set is arranged according to themes as follows: Stay in School (1-18), Stay Fit (19-36), Eat Smart (37-54), Stay in Tune (55-72), Stay off Drugs (73-90), and Stay True to Yourself (91-108).

COMPLETE SET (108)	15.00	40.00
1 Cover Card	.08	.25
Stay in School		
2 Steve Beuerlein	.15	.40
3 Erric Pegram	.08	.25
4 Darryl Talley	.08	.25
5 Tom Waddle	.08	.25
6 Darryl Williams	.08	.25
7 Tony Jones	.08	.25
8 Jay Novacek	.08	.25
9 Simon Fletcher	.08	.25
10 Jason Hanson	.08	.25
11 Reggie White	.25	.60
12 Ernest Givins	.08	.25
13 Kerry Cash	.08	.25
14 Joe Montana	2.40	6.00
15 Anthony Smith	.08	.25
16 Jackie Slater	.08	.25
17 Terry Kirby	.15	.40
18 John Randle	.15	.40
19 Cover Card	.08	.25
Stay Fit		
20 Drew Bledsoe	.80	2.00
21 Vaughan Johnson	.08	.25
22 Greg Jackson	.08	.25
23 Rob Moore	.15	.40
24 Byron Evans	.08	.25
25 Rod Woodson	.15	.40
26 Junior Seau	.25	.60
27 Steve Young	.80	2.00
28 Cortez Kennedy	.15	.40
29 Paul Gruber	.08	.25
30 Darrell Green	.08	.25
31 Tyronne Stowe	.08	.25
32 Pierce Holt	.08	.25
33 Steve Tasker	.15	.40
34 Chris Zorich	.15	.40
35 Ricardo McDonald	.08	.25
36 Mark Carrier WR	.15	.40
37 Cover Card	.08	.25
Eat Smart		
38 Emmitt Smith	2.00	5.00
39 Shannon Sharpe	.25	.60
40 Chris Spielman	.15	.40
41 Ken Ruettgers	.08	.25
42 Bubba McDowell	.08	.25
43 Rohn Stark	.08	.25
44 Derrick Thomas	.15	.40
45 Tim Brown	.25	.60
46 Shane Conlan	.08	.25
47 Marco Coleman	.08	.25
48 Steve Jordan	.08	.25
49 Ben Coates	.15	.40
50 Willie Roaf	.08	.25
51 Carlton Bailey	.08	.25
52 Ronnie Lott	.15	.40
53 Eric Allen	.08	.25
54 Dermontti Dawson	.08	.25
55 Cover Card	.08	.25
Stay in Tune		
56 Ronnie Harmon	.08	.25
57 Dana Stubblefield	.15	.40

58 Rick Mirer	.15	.40
59 Santana Dotson	.08	.25
60 Jim Lachey	.08	.25
61 Ricky Proehl	.08	.25
62 Jessie Tuggle	.08	.25
63 Jim Kelly	.25	.60
64 Mark Carrier DB	.08	.25
65 David Klingler	.08	.25
66 Eric Turner	.08	.25
67 Darrin Smith	.08	.25
68 Glyn Milburn	.15	.40
69 Herman Moore	.25	.60
70 Sterling Sharpe	.15	.40
71 Ray Childress	.08	.25
72 Quentin Coryatt	.08	.25
73 Cover Card	.08	.25
Stay off Drugs		
74 Marcus Allen	.25	.60
75 Jeff Hostetler	.15	.40
76 Jerome Bettis	.50	1.25
77 Richmond Webb	.08	.25
78 Randall McDaniel	.08	.25
79 Maurice Hurst	.08	.25
80 Morten Andersen	.08	.25
81 Dave Meggett	.15	.40
82 Brian Washington	.08	.25
83 Randall Cunningham	.25	.60
84 Kevin Greene	.15	.40
85 Leslie O'Neal	.08	.25
86 Tim McDonald	.08	.25
87 Eugene Robinson	.08	.25
88 Hardy Nickerson	.08	.25
89 Chip Lohmiller	.08	.25
90 Jeff George	.15	.40
91 Cover Card	.08	.25
Stay True to Yourself		
92 Cornelius Bennett	.15	.40
93 Erik Kramer	.08	.25
94 Tommy Vardell	.08	.25
95 Troy Aikman	1.20	3.00
96 John Elway	2.00	5.00
97 Barry Sanders	1.60	4.00
98 Dan Saleaumua	.08	.25
99 Dan Marino	2.00	5.00
100 Jack Del Rio	.08	.25
101 Bruce Armstrong	.08	.25
102 Renaldo Turnbull	.08	.25
103 Phil Simms	.15	.40
104 Boomer Esiason	.15	.40
105 Fred Barnett	.15	.40
106 Greg Lloyd	.08	.25
107 John Carney	.08	.25
108 Jerry Rice	1.20	3.00

1994 FACT NFL Properties

Sponsored by NFL Properties, Inc., this 18-card FACT (Football and Academics: A Championship Team) measures the standard-size and features NFL star players as well as Lesley Visser, a sports journalist. Inside a black picture frame, the fronts feature color posed photos. The words "It's A Fact" appears in white block lettering across the top, while the specific slogan, which varies from card to card, is printed across the bottom. On a white panel edged above and below in black, the backs present an extended player quote on the theme of the card.

COMPLETE SET (18)	12.00	30.00
1 Troy Aikman	1.60	4.00
Play It Straight		
2 Cornelius Bennett	.30	.75
Chill		
3 Lesley Visser ANN	.30	.75
Aim High		
4 Junior Seau	.40	1.00
Eat Smart		
5 Chris Hinton	.25	.60
Clean Up Your Act		
6 Howie Long	.40	1.00
Plan Ahead		
7 Nick Lowery	.25	.60
Heal The Planet		
8 Tony Casillas	.25	.60
Guns Are For Fools		
9 Dan Marino	3.20	8.00
School's The Ticket		
10 Warren Moon	.40	1.00
Make A Difference		
11 Rod Bernstine	.25	.60
Jim Kelly		
We're The Same Inside		
12 Rohn Stark	.25	.60
Smoking Is Stupid		
13 Michael Irvin	.50	1.25
Respect the Law		
14 Steve Young	1.20	3.00
Education Works		
15 Bart Oates	.25	.60
Kids Deserve Love		
16 Erik Kramer	.30	.75
Be Fit!		
17 Emmitt Smith	2.40	6.00
Don't Quit		
18 Steve Beuerlein	.30	.75
Think		

1994 FACT NFL Properties Artex

Issued in a cello pack, these three standard-size FACT cards are identical to their counterparts in the 18-card FACT set except for the numbering of cards 2-3 (Marino is #9 and Smith is #17 in the 18-card set) and the Artex Sportswear logo on their back. These sets were also distributed through various K-Mart outlets.

COMPLETE SET (3)	4.00	10.00
1 Troy Aikman	.80	2.00
Play It Straight		
2 Dan Marino	1.60	4.00
School's The Ticket		
3 Emmitt Smith	1.60	4.00
Don't Quit		

1995 FACT Fleer Shell

This FACT (Football and Academics: A Championship Team) set was produced by Fleer and Shell Oil and consists of six subsets of 18 cards each. The set features color action player photos with questions relating to the subset theme. The set is arranged according to themes as follows: Stay in School (1-18), Stay Fit (19-36), Eat Smart (37-54), Stay in Tune (55-72), Stay off Drugs (73-90), and Stay True to Yourself (91-108).

COMPLETE SET (108)	15.00	40.00
1 Cover Card	.07	.20
Stay in School		
2 Seth Joyner	.07	.20
3 J.J. Birden	.10	.30
4 Jim Kelly	.25	.60
5 Pete Metzelaars	.07	.20
6 Joe Cain	.07	.20
7 Carl Pickens	.10	.30
8 Leroy Hoard	.10	.30
9 Troy Aikman	1.00	2.50
10 Steve Atwater	.07	.20
11 Bennie Blades	.07	.20
12 Brett Favre	2.00	5.00
13 Mel Gray	.07	.20
14 Tony Bennett	.07	.20
15 Steve Beuerlein	.10	.30
16 Marcus Allen	.25	.60
17 Tim Brown	.25	.60
18 Tim Bowens	.07	.20
19 Cover Card	.07	.20
Stay Fit		
20 Jack Del Rio	.07	.20
21 Drew Bledsoe	1.00	2.50
22 Jim Everett	.07	.20
23 Michael Brooks	.07	.20
24 Tony Casillas	.07	.20
25 Fred Barnett	.10	.30
26 Kevin Greene	.10	.30
27 Jerome Bettis	.25	.60
28 John Carney	.07	.20
29 Ken Norton	.10	.30
30 Cortez Kennedy	.10	.30
31 Alvin Harper	.07	.20
32 Henry Ellard	.10	.30
33 Aeneas Williams	.07	.20
34 Jeff George	.10	.30
35 Bryce Paup	.07	.20
36 Sam Mills	.10	.30
37 Cover Card	.07	.20
Eat Smart		
38 Mark Carrier	.07	.20
39 Darnay Scott	.10	.30
40 Pepper Johnson	.07	.20
41 Michael Irvin	.25	.60
42 John Elway	2.00	5.00
43 Herman Moore	.25	.60
44 John Jurkovic	.07	.20
45 Al Smith	.07	.20
46 Steve Emtman	.07	.20
47 Darren Carrington	.07	.20
48 Kimble Anders	.07	.20
49 Jeff Hostetler	.10	.30
50 Eric Green	.10	.30
51 Cris Carter	.25	.60
52 Ben Coates	.10	.30
53 Michael Haynes	.07	.20
54 Dave Brown	.10	.30
55 Cover Card	.07	.20
Stay in Tune		
56 Boomer Esiason	.10	.30
57 Randall Cunningham	.25	.60
58 Byron Bam Morris	.07	.20
59 Sean Gilbert	.10	.30
60 Stan Humphries	.10	.30
61 Jerry Rice	1.00	2.50
62 Rick Mirer	.10	.30
63 Hardy Nickerson	.10	.30
64 Ricky Ervins	.07	.20
65 Eric Swann	.10	.30
66 Craig Heyward	.10	.30
67 Andre Reed	.10	.30
68 Frank Reich	.10	.30
69 Steve Walsh	.07	.20
70 Dan Wilkinson	.07	.20
71 Vinny Testaverde	.10	.30
72 Russell Maryland	.07	.20
73 Cover Card	.07	.20
Stay Off Drugs		
74 Shannon Sharpe	.10	.30
75 Brett Perriman	.10	.30
76 Reggie White	.25	.60
77 Mark Stepnoski	.07	.20
78 Marshall Faulk	1.00	2.50
79 Reggie Cobb	.07	.20
80 Lake Dawson	.07	.20
81 Rocket Ismail	.10	.30
82 Dan Marino	2.00	5.00
83 Warren Moon	.25	.60
84 Willie McGinest	.10	.30
85 William Roaf	.07	.20
86 Rodney Hampton	.10	.30
87 Marvin Washington	.07	.20
88 Charlie Garner	.25	.60
89 Neil O'Donnell	.10	.30
90 Todd Lyght	.07	.20
91 Cover Card	.07	.20
Stay True to Yourself		
92 Natrone Means	.10	.30
93 Deion Sanders	.40	1.00
94 Chris Warren	.10	.30
95 Errict Rhett	.10	.30
96 Ken Harvey	.07	.20
97 Bruce Smith	.25	.60
98 Chris Zorich	.10	.30
99 Eric Turner	.10	.30
100 Emmitt Smith	1.60	4.00
101 Barry Sanders	1.60	4.00
102 Neil Smith	.10	.30
103 Chester McGlockton	.07	.20
104 Fuad Reveiz	.07	.20
105 Thomas Lewis	.07	.20
106 Rod Woodson	.10	.30
107 Junior Seau	.10	.30
108 Steve Young	.60	1.50

1995 FACT NFL Properties

This 18-card set was produced by the NFL to promote it's FACT (Football and Academics: a Championship Team) program. The cards feature black-bordered color player photos with the NFL logo and words, "IT'S A FACT," at the top. The subject and a related message are printed at the bottom. The backs carry a paragraph of the player's thoughts on the card subject.

COMPLETE SET (18)	14.00	35.00
1 Troy Aikman	1.60	4.00
2 Rocket Ismail	.30	.75
Qadry Ismail		
3 Robin Roberts	.30	.75
4 Junior Seau	.50	1.25
5 Chris Hinton	.25	.60
6 Sean Jones	.30	.75
7 Thurman Thomas	.50	1.25
8 Neil Smith	.30	.75
9 Dan Marino	3.20	8.00
10 Reggie Williams	.25	.60
11 Rob Bernstine	.50	1.25
Jim Kelly		
12 Drew Bledsoe	1.60	4.00
13 Michael Irvin	.50	1.25
14 Steve Young	1.20	3.00
15 Jerry Rice	1.60	4.00
16 Herschel Walker	.30	.75
17 Emmitt Smith	2.40	6.00
18 Barry Sanders	3.20	8.00

1996 FACT Fleer Shell

This FACT set was produced by Fleer and sponsored by Shell Oil and consists of six subsets of 18-cards each. The set features color action player photos with questions relating to the subset theme. The set is essentially a parallel to the base 1996 Fleer set on the cardfronts with a community service message on the cardbacks.

COMPLETE SET (108)	15.00	25.00
1 Cover Card	.05	.15
Stay in School		
2 Garrison Hearst	.08	.25
3 Jeff George	.08	.25
4 Michael Jackson	.05	.15
5 Jim Kelly	.20	.50
6 Kerry Collins	.20	.50
7 Curtis Conway	.08	.25
8 Jeff Blake	.20	.50
9 Troy Aikman	.40	1.00
10 Steve Atwater	.05	.15
11 Scott Mitchell	.08	.25
12 Edgar Bennett	.05	.15
13 Mel Gray	.05	.15
14 Quentin Coryatt	.05	.15
15 Tony Boselli	.05	.15
16 Marcus Allen	.20	.50
17 Dan Marino	.60	1.50
18 Cris Carter	.20	.50
19 Cover Card	.05	.15
Stay Fit		
20 Drew Bledsoe	.30	.75
21 Mario Bates	.05	.15
22 Dave Brown	.05	.15
23 Kyle Brady	.08	.25
24 Tim Brown	.20	.50
25 William Fuller	.05	.15
26 Greg Lloyd	.05	.15
27 Isaac Bruce	.20	.50
28 Marco Coleman	.05	.15
29 Brent Jones	.05	.15
30 Joey Galloway	.20	.50
31 Trent Dilfer	.08	.25
32 Terry Allen	.08	.25
33 Rob Moore	.08	.25
34 Craig Heyward	.05	.15
35 Vinny Testaverde	.08	.25
36 Bryce Paup	.05	.15
37 Cover Card	.05	.15
Eat Smart		
38 Lamar Lathon	.05	.15
39 Erik Kramer	.05	.15
40 Ki-Jana Carter	.08	.25
41 Daryl Johnston	.05	.15
42 Terrell Davis	.60	1.50
43 Herman Moore	.08	.25
44 Mark Chmura	.08	.25
45 Steve McNair	.25	.60
46 Ken Dilger	.05	.15
47 Mark Brunell	.30	.75
48 Neil Smith	.08	.25
49 O.J. McDuffie	.08	.25
50 Qadry Ismail	.08	.25
51 Ben Coates	.08	.25
52 Jim Everett	.05	.15
53 Rodney Hampton	.05	.15
54 Hugh Douglas	.08	.25
55 Cover Card	.05	.15
Stay in Tune		
56 Chester McGlockton	.05	.15
57 Ricky Watters	.08	.25
58 Kordell Stewart	.20	.50
59 Troy Drayton	.05	.15
60 Aaron Hayden	.05	.15
61 Ken Norton	.05	.15
62 Rick Mirer	.08	.25
63 Hardy Nickerson	.05	.15
64 Henry Ellard	.05	.15
65 Aeneas Williams	.05	.15
66 Terance Mathis	.08	.25
67 Eric Turner	.05	.15
68 Bruce Smith	.08	.25
69 Tyrone Poole	.05	.15
70 Rashaan Salaam	.08	.25
71 Carl Pickens	.08	.25
72 Deion Sanders	.25	.60
73 Cover Card	.05	.15
Stay off Drugs		
74 John Elway	.60	1.50
75 Barry Sanders	.60	1.50
76 Robert Brooks	.08	.25
77 Chris Sanders	.05	.15
78 Marshall Faulk	.20	.50
79 James O. Stewart	.08	.25
80 Derrick Thomas	.08	.25
81 Bernie Parmalee	.05	.15
82 Robert Smith	.20	.50
83 Curtis Martin	.20	.50
84 Renaldo Turnbull	.05	.15
85 Thomas Lewis	.05	.15
86 Aaron Glenn	.05	.15
87 Harvey Williams	.05	.15
88 Calvin Williams	.05	.15
89 Yancey Thigpen	.05	.15
90 Leslie O'Neal	.05	.15
91 Cover Card	.05	.15
Stay True to Yourself		
92 Stan Humphries	.05	.15
93 Jerry Rice	.40	1.00
94 Chris Warren	.05	.15
95 Errict Rhett	.08	.25
96 Heath Shuler	.08	.25
97 Eric Metcalf	.05	.15
98 Thurman Thomas	.08	.25
99 Emmitt Smith	.50	1.25
100 Shannon Sharpe	.08	.25
101 Reggie White	.20	.50
102 Rodney Thomas	.05	.15
103 Jim Harbaugh	.05	.15
104 Tamarick Vanover	.08	.25
105 Neil O'Donnell	.05	.15
106 Rod Woodson	.08	.25
107 Junior Seau	.08	.25
108 Steve Young	.25	.60

1968-69 Falcons Team Issue

Printed on glossy thick paper stock, each of these black-and-white photos measure approximately 7 1/2" by 9 1/2" and have white borders. With the exception of the Berry photo (a portrait), all the photos are posed action shots. The cardbacks are blank. The photos are unnumbered and checklisted below in alphabetical order. Each includes the player's name and team name below the photo in the card border. This series can be differentiated from the 1970 and 1971 issues by the much larger type used in printing the player name and team name below the photo.

COMPLETE SET (23)	100.00	200.00
1 Bob Berry	5.00	10.00
2 Greg Brezina	5.00	10.00
3 Junior Coffey	5.00	10.00
4 Carlton Dabney	5.00	10.00
5 Bob Etter	5.00	10.00
6 Paul Gipson	5.00	10.00
7 Don Hansen	5.00	10.00
8 Bill Harris	5.00	10.00
9 Ralph Heck	5.00	10.00
10 Claude Humphrey	6.00	12.00
11 Randy Johnson	5.00	10.00
12 George Kunz	5.00	10.00
(Notre Dame photo)		
13 Errol Linden	5.00	10.00
14 Billy Lothridge	5.00	10.00
15 Tommy McDonald	7.50	15.00
16 Jim Mitchell	5.00	10.00
17 Tommy Nobis	7.50	15.00
18 Ken Reaves	5.00	10.00
19 Jerry Shay	5.00	10.00
20 John Small	5.00	10.00
21 Norm Van Brocklin CO	7.50	15.00
22 Harmon Wages	5.00	10.00
23 John Zook	5.00	10.00

1970 Falcons Stadium Issue

This 10-card set of the Atlanta Falcons features black and white player portraits in a white border and measures approximately 5 1/2" by 7 1/2". The backs are blank. The cards are unnumbered and checklisted below in alphabetical order.

COMPLETE SET (10)	40.00	80.00
1 Mike Brunson	5.00	10.00
2 Charlie Bryant	5.00	10.00
3 Sonny Campbell	5.00	10.00
4 Dean Halverson	5.00	10.00
5 Greg Lens	5.00	10.00
6 Randy Marshall	5.00	10.00
7 John Matlock	5.00	10.00
8 Gary Roberts	5.00	10.00
9 Jim Sullivan	5.00	10.00
10 Kenny Vinyard	5.00	10.00

1970 Falcons Team Issue

This set of the Atlanta Falcons features 8" by 10" black-and-white player photos with white borders. The photos are very similar to the 1971 set except that most players are wearing their black Falcons jersey and the pictures were taken inside the stadium. Unless noted below, all players also include their position (initials) below the photo along with their name and team name. The backs are blank. The cards are unnumbered and checklisted below in alphabetical order.

COMPLETE SET (41)	150.00	300.00
1 Ron Acks	5.00	10.00
2 Grady Allen	5.00	10.00
3A Bob Berry ERR	5.00	10.00
(team misspelled Flacons)		
3B Bob Berry COR	5.00	10.00
(Falcons spelled correctly)		
4 Bob Breitenstein	5.00	10.00
5 Greg Brezina	5.00	10.00
6 Jim Butler	5.00	10.00
7 Gail Cogdill	5.00	10.00
8 Glen Condren	5.00	10.00
9 Ted Cottrell	5.00	10.00
10 Carlton Dabney	5.00	10.00
11 Mike Donohoe	5.00	10.00
12 Dick Enderle	5.00	10.00
13 Paul Flatley	5.00	10.00
(no position abbreviation)		
14 Mike Freeman	5.00	10.00
15 Paul Gipson	5.00	10.00
16 Don Hansen	5.00	10.00
17 Tom Hayes	5.00	10.00
18 Dave Hettema	5.00	10.00
19 Claude Humphrey	6.00	12.00
20 Randy Johnson	6.00	12.00
21 George Kunz	5.00	10.00
22 Al Lavan	5.00	10.00
23 Bruce Lemmerman	5.00	10.00
24 Billy Lothridge	5.00	10.00
25 John Mallory	5.00	10.00
26 Art Malone	5.00	10.00
27 Andy Maurer	5.00	10.00
28 Tom McCauley	5.00	10.00
29 Jim Mitchell	5.00	10.00
30A Tommy Nobis	6.00	12.00
(with position abbreviation)		
30B Tommy Nobis	6.00	12.00
(without position abbreviation)		
31 Rudy Redmond	5.00	10.00
(no position abbreviation)		
32 Bill Sandeman	5.00	10.00
33 Dick Shiner	5.00	10.00
34 John Small	5.00	10.00
35 Malcolm Snider	5.00	10.00
36 Todd Snyder	5.00	10.00
37 Norm Van Brocklin CO	6.00	12.00
(not wearing a cap)		
38 Jeff Van Note	5.00	10.00
39 Harmon Wages	5.00	10.00
40 John Zook	5.00	10.00
41 Team Photo	5.00	10.00

1971 Falcons Team Issue

The 1971 Falcons Team Issue set consists of black-and-white photos measuring 8" by 10" with a white border on all four sides. The photos are similar to the 1970 set, but each player is wearing his red Falcons jersey and the pictures were taken outdoors. Only the player's name and team name appear below the photo. They are unnumbered and checklisted in alphabetical order.

COMPLETE SET (15)	75.00	150.00
1 Bob Berry	5.00	10.00
2 Mike Brunson	5.00	10.00
3 Ken Burrow	5.00	10.00
4 Sonny Campbell	5.00	10.00
5 Don Hansen	5.00	10.00
6 Leo Hart	5.00	10.00
7 Claude Humphrey	5.00	10.00
8 Ray Jarvis	5.00	10.00
9 Greg Lens	5.00	10.00
10 John Matlock	5.00	10.00
11 Tommy Nobis	6.00	12.00
12 Malcolm Snider	5.00	10.00
13 Pat Sullivan	6.00	12.00
14 Norm Van Brocklin CO	6.00	12.00
(wearing a cap)		
15 Harmon Wages	5.00	10.00

1973 Falcons Team Issue

The 1973 Falcons Team Issue features black-and-white photos measuring 8" by 10" with a white border. The photos are similar to the 1970 and 1972 sets, but the player's name and position initials (on the left) and the team name (on the right) are oriented very close to the outside borders. They are blankbacked, unnumbered and checklisted below in alphabetical order.

COMPLETE SET (11)	40.00	80.00
1 Greg Brezina	4.00	8.00
2 Ray Brown	4.00	8.00
3 Ken Burrow	4.00	8.00
4 Dave Hampton	4.00	8.00
5 Don Hansen	4.00	8.00
6A Claude Humphrey	5.00	10.00
(vertical)		
6B Claude Humphrey	5.00	10.00
(horizontal)		
7 Art Malone	4.00	8.00
8 Tommy Nobis	5.00	10.00
9 Ken Reaves	4.00	8.00
10 Bill Sandeman	4.00	8.00
11 Pat Sullivan	5.00	10.00

1975 Falcons Team Sheets

This three-card set was printed on sheets each measuring approximately 8 1/2" by 11" and features black-and-white player portraits. They were produced to be used by media and as public relations photos. Sheet 3 contains 15-players and the set title, while sheets 1 and 2 contain 16 players. The backs are blank.

COMPLETE SET (3)	10.00	20.00
1 Greg Brezina	2.50	5.00
Ray Brown		
Ken Burrow		
Rick Byas		
Larron Jackson		
John James		
Alfred Jenkins		
Bob Jones		
Greg McCrary		
Kim McQuilken		
Tommy Nobis		
Ralph Ortega		
Gerald Tinker		
Jeff Van Note		
Chuck Walker		
John Zook		
2 Marion Campbell	5.00	10.00
Brent Adams		
Steve Bartkowski		
Nick Bebout		
Dave Hampton		
Don Hansen		
Dennis Havig		
Tom Hayes		
Rosie Manning		
Jeff Merrow		
Nick Mike-Mayer		
Jim Mitchell		
Haskel Stanback		
Pat Sullivan		
Woody Thompson		
Mike Tilleman		
3 Team Name	2.50	5.00
Rankin Smith		
Frank Wall		
Pat Peppler		
Brad Davis		
Ray Easterling		
Wallace Francis		
Len Gotshalk		
Fulton Kuykendall		
Rolland Lawrence		
Mike Lewis		
Ron Mabra		
Oscar Reed		
Carl Russ		
Paul Ryczek		
Royce Smith		

1978 Falcons Kinnett Dairies

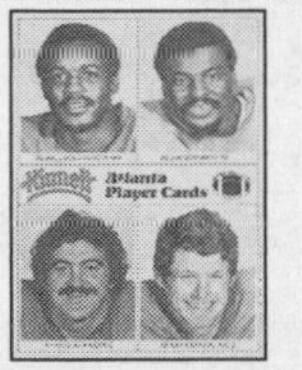

These six blank-backed white panels measure approximately 4 1/4" by 6" and feature four black-and-white player headshots per panel, all framed by a thin red line. A narrow strip running across the center of the panel contains the sponsor name, the words "Atlanta Player Cards," and the NFLPA logo. The cards are unnumbered and checklisted below in the alphabetical order of the players shown in the upper left corners.

COMPLETE SET (6)	20.00	40.00
1 William Andrews	3.75	7.50
Jeff Yeates		
Wilson Faumuina		
Phil McKinnely		
2 Warren Bryant	5.00	10.00
R.C. Thieleman		
Steve Bartkowski		
Frank Reed		
3 Wallace Francis	3.75	7.50
Jim Mitchell		
Jeff Van Note		
Ray Easterling		
4 Dewey McClain	2.50	5.00
Billy Ryckman		
Paul Ryczek		
Bubba Bean		
5 Robert Pennywell	2.50	5.00
Dave Scott		
Jim Bailey		
John James		
6 Haskel Stanback	3.75	7.50
Rick Byas		
Mike Esposito		
Tom Moriarty		

1980 Falcons Police

The 1980 Atlanta Falcons set contains 30 unnumbered cards each measuring approximately 2 5/8" by 4 1/8". Although uniform numbers can be found on the front of the cards, the cards have been listed alphabetically on the checklist below for convenience. Logos of the three sponsors, the Atlanta Police Athletic League, the Northside Atlanta Jaycees, and Coca-Cola, can be found on the back of the cards with short "Tips from the Falcons". Card backs have black printing with red accent. The Falcon helmet and stylized logo appear on the front of the cards with the player's name, uniform number, position, height, weight and college.

COMPLETE SET (30)	25.00	50.00
1 William Andrews	2.50	5.00
2 Steve Bartkowski	4.00	8.00
3 Bubba Bean	.75	2.00
4 Warren Bryant	.60	1.50
5 Rick Byas	.60	1.50
6 Lynn Cain	1.50	3.00
7 Buddy Curry	.60	1.50
8 Edgar Fields	.60	1.50
9 Wallace Francis	2.00	4.00
10 Alfred Jackson	1.50	3.00
11 John James	.60	1.50
12 Alfred Jenkins	2.00	4.00
13 Kenny Johnson	.60	1.50
14 Mike Kenn	1.50	3.00
15 Fulton Kuykendall	.75	2.00
16 Rolland Lawrence	.75	2.00
17 Tim Mazzetti	.60	1.50
18 Dewey McLean	.60	1.50
19 Jeff Merrow	.75	2.00
20 Junior Miller	.75	2.00
21 Tom Pridemore	.60	1.50
22 Frank Reed	.60	1.50
23 Al Richardson	.60	1.50
24 Dave Scott	.60	1.50
25 Don Smith	.60	1.50
26 Reggie Smith	.60	1.50
27 R.C. Thielemann	.75	2.00
28 Jeff Van Note	1.50	3.00
29 Joel Williams	.60	1.50
30 Jeff Yeates	.60	1.50

1981 Falcons Police

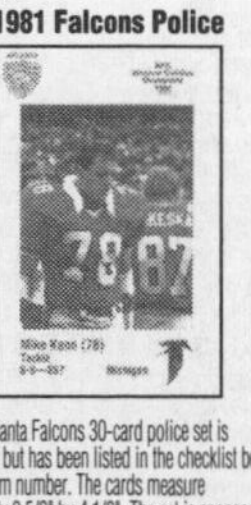

The 1981 Atlanta Falcons 30-card police set is unnumbered but has been listed in the checklist below by player uniform number. The cards measure approximately 2 5/8" by 4 1/8". The set is sponsored by the Atlanta Police Athletic League, whose logo appears on the front, and Coca-Cola and Chevron, whose logos appear on the back. The player's name and brief biographical data, in addition to "Tips from the Falcons," are contained on the backs of the cards. Card backs have black printing with red and blue accent on thin white card stock. The fronts inform the public that the Atlanta Falcons were the NFC Western Division Champions of 1980.

COMPLETE SET (30)	7.50	15.00
6 John James	.15	.40
10 Steve Bartkowski	1.25	3.00
16 Reggie Smith	.15	.40
18 Mick Luckhurst	.15	.40
21 Lynn Cain	.25	.60
23 Bobby Butler	.15	.40
27 Tom Pridemore	.15	.40
30 Scott Woerner	.15	.40
31 William Andrews	.60	1.50
36 Bob Glazebrook	.15	.40
37 Kenny Johnson	.15	.40
50 Buddy Curry	.15	.40
51 Jim Laughlin	.15	.40
54 Fulton Kuykendall	.15	.40
56 Al Richardson	.15	.40
57 Jeff Van Note	.25	.60
58 Joel Williams	.15	.40
65 Don Smith	.15	.40
66 Warren Bryant	.15	.40
68 R.C. Thielemann	.15	.40
70 Dave Scott	.15	.40
74 Wilson Faumuina	.15	.40
75 Jeff Merrow	.15	.40
78 Mike Kenn	.25	.60
79 Jeff Yeates	.15	.40
80 Junior Miller	.25	.60
84 Alfred Jenkins	.40	1.00
85 Alfred Jackson	.30	.75
89 Wallace Francis	.40	1.00
NNO Leeman Bennett CO	.15	.40

1981 Falcons Team Issue

The 1981 Falcons Team Issue set was issued with a total of 22-cards. The black-and-white photos measure 8" by 10" and have a white border. The player's name and team name appear below the photo with some pictures also including the player's position (initials) between his name and team name. The cards are unnumbered and checklisted below in alphabetical order.

COMPLETE SET (22)	14.00	35.00
1 William Andrews	1.25	3.00
2 Lynn Cain	1.00	2.50
3 Buddy Curry	.75	2.00
4 Tony Daykin	.75	2.00
5 Wilson Faumuina	.75	2.00
6 Wallace Francis	.75	2.00
7 Bob Glazebrook	.75	2.00
8 John James	.75	2.00
9 Kenny Johnson	.75	2.00
10 Mike Kenn	.75	2.00
11 Jim Laughlin	.75	2.00
12 Rolland Lawrence	1.00	2.50
13 James Mayberry	.75	2.00
14 Tim Mazzetti	.75	2.00
15 Junior Miller	.75	2.00
16 Al Richardson	.75	2.00
17 Eric Sanders	.75	2.00
18 John Scully	.75	2.00
19 Don Smith	.75	2.00
20 Reggie Smith	.75	2.00
21 Jeff Van Note	1.00	2.50
22 Joel Williams	.75	2.00

1982 Falcons Frito Lay

This set was sponsored by Frito Lay and contains 28-photo cards. The cards measure approximately 4 1/4" by 5 1/2" and are printed on thin paper stock. The white-bordered fronts display black-and-white player photos with a facsimile autograph over the player image. The "Compliments of..." note and Frito Lay logo in the lower right corner rounds out the front. The backs are blank. The cards are unnumbered and checklisted below alphabetically.

COMPLETE SET (28)	48.00	120.00
1 William Andrews	3.00	8.00
2 Steve Bartkowski	3.00	8.00
3 Warren Bryant	1.50	4.00
4 Bobby Butler	1.50	4.00
5 Lynn Cain	1.50	4.00
6 Buddy Curry	1.50	4.00
7 Pat Howell	1.50	4.00
8 Alfred Jackson	2.00	5.00
9 Alfred Jenkins	2.00	5.00
10 Kenny Johnson	1.50	4.00
11 Earl Jones	1.50	4.00
12 Mike Kenn	1.50	4.00
13 Fulton Kuykendall	1.50	4.00
14 Jim Laughlin	1.50	4.00
15 Mick Luckhurst	1.50	4.00
16 Jeff Merrow	1.50	4.00
17 Russ Mikeska	1.50	4.00
18 Junior Miller	2.00	5.00
19 Tom Pridemore	1.50	4.00
20 Al Richardson	1.50	4.00
21 Gerald Riggs	2.00	5.00
22 Eric Sanders	1.50	4.00
23 Dave Scott	1.50	4.00
24 John Scully	1.50	4.00
25 Don Smith	1.50	4.00
26 Ray Strong	1.50	4.00
27 Lyman White	1.50	4.00
28 Joel Williams	1.50	4.00

1995 Falcons A and P Food Market

These 8 X 10 glossy black and white action photos were issued by A and P Food Stores for promotional autograph signings within their stores. These unnumbered photos are checklisted alphabetically below. The checklist below may be incomplete, any additional submissions would be welcomed.

COMPLETE SET (9)	10.00	25.00
1 Terance Mathis	2.40	6.00
2 Eric Metcalf	1.60	4.00
3 Ross Schulte	1.20	3.00
4 Ken Tippins	1.20	3.00
5 Jessie Tuggle	1.60	4.00
6 Scott Tyner	1.20	3.00
7 Darnell Walker	1.20	3.00
8 Thomas Williams	1.20	3.00
9 Mike Zandofsky	1.20	3.00

2006 Falcons Topps

COMPLETE SET (12)	3.00	6.00
ATL1 Keith Brooking	.20	.50
ATL2 Roddy White	.25	.60
ATL3 Michael Vick	.30	.75
ATL4 Alge Crumpler	.25	.60
ATL5 DeAngelo Hall	.25	.60
ATL6 Patrick Kerney	.15	.40
ATL7 Warrick Dunn	.25	.60
ATL8 Matt Schaub	.25	.60
ATL9 Brian Finneran	.20	.50
ATL10 Michael Jenkins	.25	.60
ATL11 T.J. Duckett	.20	.50
ATL12 John Abraham	.20	.50

2007 Falcons Donruss Thanksgiving Classic

COMPLETE SET (4)	2.00	5.00
1 Alge Crumpler	.50	1.25
2 Jerious Norwood	.50	1.25
3 Warrick Dunn	.50	1.25
4 Joe Horn	.50	1.25

2007 Falcons Topps

COMPLETE SET (12)	2.50	5.00
1 Alge Crumpler	.25	.60
2 Warrick Dunn	.25	.60
3 Michael Vick	.30	.75
4 Michael Jenkins	.25	.60
5 Roddy White	.25	.60
6 Jerious Norwood	.25	.60
7 Joe Horn	.25	.60
8 DeAngelo Hall	.25	.60
9 Keith Brooking	.20	.50
10 Rod Coleman	.20	.50
11 John Abraham	.20	.50
12 Jamaal Anderson	.25	.60

2008 Falcons Topps

COMPLETE SET (12)	3.00	6.00
1 Joey Harrington	.20	.50
2 Roddy White	.25	.60
3 Jerious Norwood	.25	.60
4 Laurent Robinson	.20	.50
5 Chris Redman	.20	.50
6 Michael Turner	.30	.75
7 John Abraham	.20	.50
8 Michael Jenkins	.20	.50
9 Keith Brooking	.20	.50
10 Michael Boley	.20	.50
11 Matt Ryan	1.50	4.00
12 Harry Douglas	.25	.60

2008 Fathead Tradeables Game Time

Fatheads are 5x7 vinyls sticker featuring NFL players and team helmets. Each pack included one Team Helmet, 2-3 Game Time stickers and 1-2 Authentic insert stickers.

G1 Eli Manning	1.00	2.50
G2 Adrian Peterson	1.50	4.00
G3 Terrell Owens	1.00	2.50
G4 Tom Brady	1.50	4.00
G5 Peyton Manning	1.50	4.00
G6 LaDainian Tomlinson	1.00	2.50
G7 Larry Fitzgerald	1.00	2.50
G8 David Garrard	.75	2.00
G9 Hines Ward	.75	2.00
G10 Andre Johnson	.75	2.00
G11 Willis McGahee	.75	2.00
G12 Antonio Cromartie	.60	1.50
G13 Reggie Wayne	.75	2.00
G14 DeMarcus Ware	.75	2.00
G15 Frank Gore	.75	2.00
G16 LenDale White	.75	2.00
G17 Chad Johnson	.75	2.00
G18 Dwayne Bowe	.75	2.00
G19 Michael Huff	.60	1.50
G20 Keith Brooking	.60	1.50
G21 Kellen Winslow	.75	2.00
G22 Donovan McNabb	1.00	2.50
G23 Vince Young	.75	2.00
G24 John Lynch	.75	2.00
G25 Marvin Harrison	1.00	2.50
G26 Kyle Vanden Bosch	.60	1.50
G27 TJ Houshmandzadeh	.75	2.00
G28 Reggie Bush	1.00	2.50
G29 Steve Smith	.75	2.00
G30 Joseph Addai	.75	2.00
G31 Tedy Bruschi	1.00	2.50
G32 Matt Hasselbeck	.75	2.00
G33 Brian Westbrook	.75	2.00
G34 A.J. Hawk	.75	2.00
G35 Brandon Marshall	.75	2.00
G36 Jason Campbell	.75	2.00
G37 JaMarcus Russell	.75	2.00
G38 Michael Strahan	.75	2.00
G39 Shawne Merriman	.75	2.00
G40 Aaron Kampman	.75	2.00
G41 Terence Newman	.60	1.50
G42 Dallas Clark	.75	2.00
G43 Jason Witten	1.00	2.50
G44 Anquan Boldin	.75	2.00
G45 Brady Quinn	.75	2.00
G46 Charles Woodson	1.00	2.50
G47 Marshawn Lynch	.75	2.00
G48 James Harrison	1.00	2.50
G49 Steven Jackson	1.00	2.50
G50 Roddy White	.75	2.00
G51 Derek Anderson	.60	1.50
G52 Fred Taylor	.75	2.00
G53 Marion Barber	.75	2.00
G54 Larry Johnson	.75	2.00
G55 Ed Reed	.75	2.00
G56 Julian Peterson	.60	1.50
G57 Ray Lewis	1.00	2.50
G58 Randy Moss	1.00	2.50
G59 Ronnie Brown	.75	2.00
G60 Tony Romo	1.25	3.00
G61 Todd Heap	.60	1.50
G62 Ronde Barber	.60	1.50
G63 Calvin Johnson	1.00	2.50
G64 Derrick Mason	.75	2.00
G65 Marc Bulger	.75	2.00
G66 Ben Roethlisberger	1.00	2.50
G67 Brian Urlacher	1.00	2.50
G68 Wes Welker	1.00	2.50
G69 Willie Parker	.75	2.00
G70 Jay Cutler	1.00	2.50
G71 Carson Palmer	1.00	2.50
G72 Darren Sharper	.75	2.00
G73 Devin Hester	1.00	2.50
G74 Deuce McAllister	.75	2.00
G75 Donald Driver	.75	2.00
G76 Rudi Johnson	.75	2.00
G77 Jason Taylor	.75	2.00
G78 Richard Seymour	.60	1.50
G79 Derrick Brooks	.75	2.00
G80 Braylon Edwards	.75	2.00
G81 Plaxico Burress	.75	2.00
G82 Drew Brees	1.00	2.50
G83 Laveranues Coles	.60	1.50
G84 Edgerrin James	.75	2.00
G85 Santonio Holmes	.75	2.00
G86 Antonio Gates	1.00	2.50
G87 Lance Briggs	.60	1.50
G88 Greg Jennings	1.00	2.50
G89 Patrick Willis	.75	2.00
G90 Tommie Harris	.60	1.50
G91 Clinton Portis	.75	2.00
G92 Jamal Lewis	.75	2.00
G93 Jeff Garcia	.75	2.00
G94 Marques Colston	.75	2.00
G95 Mario Williams	.75	2.00
G96 Brandon Jacobs	.75	2.00
G97 Ernie Sims	.60	1.50
G98 Lee Evans	.75	2.00
G99 DeMeco Ryans	.75	2.00
G100 Kellen Clemens	.75	2.00
G101 Osi Umenyiora	.75	2.00
G102 Brian Dawkins	.75	2.00
G103 Chris Chambers	.75	2.00
G104 Bob Sanders	.75	2.00
G105 Julius Peppers	.75	2.00
G106 Philip Rivers	1.00	2.50
G107 Trent Edwards	.60	1.50
G108 Santana Moss	.60	1.50
G109 Roy Williams WR	.75	2.00
G110 Torry Holt	.75	2.00
G111 Marcus Trufant	.60	1.50
G112 Ryan Grant	1.00	2.50
G113 Troy Polamalu	1.00	2.50
G114 Lofa Tatupu	.75	2.00
G115 Maurice Jones-Drew	.75	2.00
G116 Joey Galloway	.75	2.00
G117 Matt Schaub	.75	2.00
G118 Jeremy Shockey	.75	2.00
G119 Kamerion Wimbley	.60	1.50
G120 Champ Bailey	.75	2.00
G121 Chris Cooley	.75	2.00
G122 Dwight Freeney	.75	2.00
G123 Laurence Maroney	.75	2.00
G124 Jerricho Cotchery	.75	2.00
G125 Tony Gonzalez	.75	2.00

2008 Fathead Tradeables Authentic

A1 Tom Brady	1.50	4.00
A2 LaDainian Tomlinson	1.00	2.50
A3 Peyton Manning	1.50	4.00
A4 Tony Romo	1.25	3.00
A5 Eli Manning	1.00	2.50
A6 Drew Brees	1.00	2.50
A7 Terrell Owens	1.00	2.50
A8 Adrian Peterson	1.50	4.00
A9 Brian Urlacher	1.00	2.50
A10 Champ Bailey	.75	2.00
A11 Ben Roethlisberger	1.00	2.50
A12 Vince Young	.75	2.00
A13 Maurice Jones-Drew	.75	2.00
A14 Clinton Portis	.75	2.00
A15 Brian Westbrook	.75	2.00
A16 Carson Palmer	1.00	2.50
A17 Shawne Merriman	.75	2.00
A18 Steve Smith	.75	2.00
A19 Larry Johnson	.75	2.00
A20 Devin Hester	1.00	2.50
A21 Marvin Harrison	1.00	2.50
A22 Reggie Bush	1.00	2.50
A23 Troy Polamalu	1.00	2.50
A24 Ray Lewis	1.00	2.50
A25 Andre Johnson	.75	2.00

2008 Fathead Tradeables Helmets

H1 Arizona Cardinals	.60	1.50
H2 Atlanta Falcons	.60	1.50
H3 Baltimore Ravens	.60	1.50
H4 Buffalo Bills	.60	1.50
H5 Carolina Panthers	.60	1.50
H6 Chicago Bears	.60	1.50
H7 Cincinnati Bengals	.60	1.50
H8 Cleveland Browns	.60	1.50
H9 Dallas Cowboys	.60	1.50
H10 Denver Broncos	.60	1.50
H11 Detroit Lions	.60	1.50
H12 Green Bay Packers	.60	1.50
H13 Houston Texans	.60	1.50
H14 Indianapolis Colts	.60	1.50
H15 Jacksonville Jaguars	.60	1.50
H16 Kansas City Chiefs	.60	1.50
H17 Miami Dolphins	.60	1.50
H18 Minnesota Vikings	.60	1.50
H19 New England Patriots	.60	1.50
H20 New Orleans Saints	.60	1.50
H21 New York Giants	.60	1.50
H22 New York Jets	.60	1.50
H23 Oakland Raiders	.60	1.50
H24 Philadelphia Eagles	.60	1.50
H25 Pittsburgh Steelers	.60	1.50
H26 San Diego Chargers	.60	1.50
H27 San Francisco 49ers	.60	1.50
H28 Seattle Seahawks	.60	1.50
H29 St. Louis Rams	.60	1.50
H30 Tampa Bay Buccaneers	.60	1.50
H31 Tennessee Titans	.60	1.50
H32 Washington Redskins	.60	1.50

2009 Fathead Tradeables Gameday

G1 Peyton Manning	1.50	4.00
G2 James Harrison	1.00	2.50
G3 Matt Ryan	1.00	2.50
G4 Tony Romo	1.50	4.00
G5 Lance Briggs	.75	2.00
G6 Marion Barber	.75	2.00
G7 Drew Brees	1.00	2.50
G8 Jared Allen	1.00	2.50
G9 Kyle Vanden Bosch	.60	1.50
G10 Lee Evans	.75	2.00
G11 Thomas Jones	.75	2.00
G12 Reggie Bush	1.00	2.50
G13 DeSean Jackson	.75	2.00
G14 Joe Flacco	1.00	2.50
G15 Chris Cooley	.75	2.00
G16 Maurice Jones-Drew	.75	2.00
G17 David Garrard	.75	2.00
G18 Darrelle Revis	.75	2.00
G19 Larry Johnson	.75	2.00
G20 Ray Lewis	1.00	2.50
G21 Bernard Berrian	.75	2.00
G22 Felix Jones	1.00	2.50
G23 Jamal Lewis	.75	2.00
G24 Anquan Boldin	.75	2.00
G25 Steven Jackson	.75	2.00
G26 Antonio Bryant	.60	1.50
G27 Julius Jones	.60	1.50
G28 Dwayne Bowe	.75	2.00
G29 Steve Smith	.75	2.00
G30 Jason Campbell	.60	1.50
G31 Ryan Grant	.75	2.00
G32 Lamarr Woodley	.60	1.50
G33 Philip Rivers	1.00	2.50
G34 Chad Pennington	.75	2.00
G35 Jerod Mayo	.75	2.00
G36 Greg Jennings	1.00	2.50
G37 Cortland Finnegan	.60	1.50
G38 Matt Schaub	.75	2.00
G39 Vincent Jackson	.75	2.00
G40 Clinton Portis	.75	2.00
G41 Derrick Mason	.75	2.00
G42 Demeco Ryans	.75	2.00
G43 Darren McFadden	1.00	2.50
G44 Antonio Gates	.75	2.00
G45 Roy Williams WR	.75	2.00
G46 Joe Thomas	.75	2.00
G47 Trent Edwards	.60	1.50
G48 Patrick Willis	.75	2.00
G49 Nnamdi Asomugha	.75	2.00
G50 Brady Quinn	.75	2.00
G51 Heath Miller	.75	2.00
G52 Ronnie Brown	.75	2.00
G53 Champ Bailey	.75	2.00
G54 Joey Porter	.75	2.00
G55 Troy Polamalu	1.00	2.50
G56 Matt Hasselbeck	.75	2.00
G57 Ed Reed	.75	2.00
G58 Kerry Collins	.75	2.00
G59 Reggie Wayne	.75	2.00
G60 Adrian Peterson	1.50	4.00
G61 Adrian Wilson	.60	1.50
G62 Jake Delhomme	.75	2.00
G63 Jason Witten	1.00	2.50
G64 Kurt Warner	1.00	2.50
G65 Ben Roethlisberger	1.00	2.50
G66 Calvin Johnson	1.00	2.50
G67 Marshawn Lynch	.75	2.00
G68 A.J. Hawk	.75	2.00
G69 Aaron Rodgers	2.00	5.00
G70 Carson Palmer	1.00	2.50
G71 Jerricho Cotchery	.75	2.00
G72 Jonathan Stewart	.75	2.00
G73 Derrick Johnson	.60	1.50
G74 Marques Colston	.75	2.00
G75 Bob Sanders	.75	2.00
G76 JaMarcus Russell	.60	1.50
G77 Barrett Ruud	.60	1.50
G78 Tom Brady	1.50	4.00
G79 Roddy White	.75	2.00
G80 Eli Manning	1.00	2.50
G81 Chad Ochocinco	.75	2.00
G82 LenDale White	.75	2.00
G83 Donovan McNabb	1.00	2.50
G84 Aaron Kampman	.75	2.00
G85 Larry Fitzgerald	1.00	2.50
G86 Donnie Avery	.75	2.00
G87 Steve Slaton	.75	2.00
G88 Dwight Freeney	.75	2.00
G89 Randy Moss	1.00	2.50
G90 Antonio Pierce	.60	1.50
G91 Julius Peppers	.75	2.00
G92 LaDainian Tomlinson	1.00	2.50
G93 D'Qwell Jackson	.60	1.50
G94 Willie Parker	.60	1.50
G95 Charles Woodson	1.00	2.50
G96 Brian Urlacher	1.00	2.50
G97 Michael Turner	.75	2.00
G98 Chris Johnson	1.00	2.50
G99 Shawne Merriman	.75	2.00
G100 Matt Forte	1.00	2.50
G101 Brandon Marshall	.75	2.00
G102 Jon Beason	.60	1.50
G103 Asante Samuel	.60	1.50
G104 Santana Moss	.75	2.00
G105 Justin Tuck	.75	2.00
G106 Terrell Suggs	.60	1.50
G107 Jeremy Shockey	.60	1.50
G108 Laron Landry	.60	1.50
G109 Hines Ward	.75	2.00
G110 Andre Johnson	.75	2.00
G111 Braylon Edwards	.75	2.00
G112 James Farrior	.60	1.50
G113 Robert Mathis	.60	1.50
G114 DeAngelo Williams	1.00	2.50
G115 Santonio Holmes	.75	2.00
G116 Devin Hester	1.00	2.50
G117 Frank Gore	.75	2.00
G118 Mario Williams	.75	2.00
G119 Kevin Smith	.75	2.00
G120 Brian Westbrook	.75	2.00
G121 Brandon Jacobs	.75	2.00
G122 Dallas Clark	.75	2.00
G123 Eddie Royal	.75	2.00
G124 Wes Welker	1.00	2.50
G125 Ronde Barber	.60	1.50
G126 DeMarcus Ware	.75	2.00
G127 Joseph Addai	1.00	2.50
G128 John Abraham	.60	1.50

2009 Fathead Tradeables Authentic

A1 Troy Polamalu	1.00	2.50
A2 Larry Fitzgerald	1.00	2.50
A3 Donovan McNabb	1.00	2.50
A4 Randy Moss	1.00	2.50
A5 Peyton Manning	1.50	4.00
A6 Brian Urlacher	1.00	2.50
A7 Clinton Portis	.75	2.00
A8 Marion Barber	.75	2.00
A9 Aaron Rodgers	2.00	5.00
A10 Chris Johnson	1.00	2.50
A11 Marshawn Lynch	.75	2.00
A12 Matt Ryan	1.00	2.50
A13 Eli Manning	1.00	2.50
A14 Steven Jackson	.75	2.00
A15 Braylon Edwards	.75	2.00

2009 Fathead Tradeables Helmets

COMPLETE SET (32)	12.00	30.00
H1 Arizona Cardinals	.60	1.50
H2 Atlanta Falcons	.60	1.50
H3 Baltimore Ravens	.60	1.50
H4 Buffalo Bills	.60	1.50
H5 Carolina Panthers	.60	1.50
H6 Chicago Bears	.60	1.50
H7 Cincinnati Bengals	.60	1.50
H8 Cleveland Browns	.60	1.50
H9 Dallas Cowboys	.60	1.50
H10 Denver Broncos	.60	1.50
H11 Detroit Lions	.60	1.50
H12 Green Bay Packers	.60	1.50
H13 Houston Texans	.60	1.50
H14 Indianapolis Colts	.60	1.50
H15 Jacksonville Jaguars	.60	1.50
H16 Kansas City Chiefs	.60	1.50
H17 Miami Dolphins	.60	1.50
H18 Minnesota Vikings	.60	1.50
H19 New England Patriots	.60	1.50
H20 New Orleans Saints	.60	1.50
H21 New York Giants	.60	1.50
H22 New York Jets	.60	1.50
H23 Oakland Raiders	.60	1.50
H24 Philadelphia Eagles	.60	1.50
H25 Pittsburgh Steelers	.60	1.50
H26 San Diego Chargers	.60	1.50
H27 San Francisco 49ers	.60	1.50
H28 Seattle Seahawks	.60	1.50
H29 St. Louis Rams	.60	1.50
H30 Tampa Bay Buccaneers	.60	1.50
H31 Tennessee Titans	.60	1.50
H32 Washington Redskins	.60	1.50

2010 Fathead Tradeables

1 Drew Brees	1.00	2.50
2 Peyton Manning	1.50	4.00
3 Chris Johnson	1.00	2.50
4 Charles Woodson	1.00	2.50
5 Larry Fitzgerald	1.00	2.50
6 Brett Favre	2.50	6.00
7 Darrelle Revis	.75	2.00
8 Tom Brady	1.50	4.00
9 DeSean Jackson	.75	2.00
10 Philip Rivers	1.00	2.50
11 Maurice Jones-Drew	.75	2.00
12 Hines Ward	.75	2.00
13 Patrick Willis	.75	2.00
14 Roddy White	.75	2.00
15 Ray Rice	.75	2.00
16 Cedric Benson	.75	2.00
17 Tony Romo	1.25	3.00
18 Matthew Stafford	1.00	2.50
19 Ricky Williams	.75	2.00
20 Josh Cribbs	1.00	2.50
21 Knowshon Moreno	.75	2.00
22 Eli Manning	1.00	2.50
23 James Harrison	1.00	2.50
24 Shawne Merriman	.75	2.00
25 Kellen Winslow	.75	2.00
26 Matt Schaub	.75	2.00
27 Clinton Portis	.75	2.00
28 Shonn Greene	.75	2.00
29 Dwight Freeney	.75	2.00
30 Percy Harvin	1.00	2.50
31 Donnie Avery	.75	2.00
32 LeSean McCoy	.75	2.00
33 Ryan Grant	.75	2.00
34 Joe Flacco	1.00	2.50
35 Paul Posluszny	.75	2.00
36 Jonathan Stewart	.75	2.00
37 Carson Palmer	.75	2.00
38 DeMarcus Ware	.75	2.00
39 Marques Colston	.75	2.00
40 Vincent Jackson	.60	1.50
41 Vince Young	.60	1.50
42 Nnamdi Asomugha	.75	2.00
43 Matt Cassel	.75	2.00
44 Andre Johnson	.75	2.00
45 Matt Hasselbeck	.60	1.50
46 Cadillac Williams	.75	2.00
47 Steve Smith USC	.75	2.00
48 Reggie Bush	1.00	2.50
49 Marion Barber	.75	2.00
50 Donald Driver	.75	2.00
51 Dallas Clark	.75	2.00
52 Wes Welker	1.00	2.50
53 Heath Miller	.75	2.00
54 Frank Gore	.75	2.00
55 Darren McFadden	.75	2.00
56 Vernon Davis	.75	2.00
57 T.J. Houshmandzadeh	.75	2.00
58 Steven Jackson	.75	2.00
59 Jerod Mayo	.75	2.00
60 Chad Henne	.75	2.00
61 Adrian Peterson	1.50	4.00
62 Mark Sanchez	1.00	2.50
63 Rashard Mendenhall	.75	2.00
64 DeAngelo Williams	.75	2.00
65 Matt Forte	.75	2.00
66 Ed Reed	.75	2.00
67 Miles Austin	1.00	2.50
68 Champ Bailey	.75	2.00
69 Kevin Kolb	.75	2.00
70 Aaron Rodgers	2.00	5.00
71 Chad Ochocinco	.75	2.00
72 Laurence Maroney	.75	2.00
73 Darren Sharper	.75	2.00
74 Brandon Meriweather	.60	1.50
75 Darren Sproles	.75	2.00
76 LaMarr Woodley	.60	1.50
77 Chris Cooley	.75	2.00
78 Matt Ryan	1.00	2.50
79 Beanie Wells	.75	2.00
80 Jay Cutler	1.00	2.50
81 Felix Jones	.75	2.00
82 Calvin Johnson	1.00	2.50
83 Joseph Addai	.75	2.00
84 David Garrard	.75	2.00
85 Sidney Rice	.75	2.00
86 Antonio Gates	.75	2.00
87 Troy Polamalu	1.00	2.50
88 Jared Allen	1.00	2.50
89 Ronnie Brown	.75	2.00
90 Brian Urlacher	1.00	2.50
91 Michael Turner	.60	1.50
92 Lee Evans	.75	2.00
93 Jason Witten	1.00	2.50
94 Steve Smith	.75	2.00
95 Joe Thomas	.60	1.50
96 Pierre Garcon	.75	2.00
97 Dwayne Bowe	.75	2.00
98 Randy Moss	1.00	2.50
99 Ray Lewis	1.00	2.50
100 Reggie Wayne	.75	2.00

1993 Fax Pax World of Sport

COMPLETE SET (40)	10.00	20.00
15 Dan Marino FB	1.50	4.00
16 Joe Montana FB	1.50	4.00
17 Emmitt Smith FB	1.25	3.00

1993 FCA 50

This 50-card standard-size set was sponsored by Fellowship of Christian Athletes. The color player photos on the fronts are accented on three sides by a thin pink stripe; the card face itself shades from blue to white as one moves toward the bottom. The FCA logo, featuring a cross with two olive branches, is superimposed in the upper left corner, while the player's name is printed beneath the picture and his sport in the pink stripe on the left. On a blue background, the backs carry a close-up photo, biography, and the player's testimony.

COMPLETE SET (50)	10.00	20.00
2 Zenon Andrusyshyn FB	.20	.50
3 Bobby Bowden CO FB	.20	.50
5 John Brandes FB	.20	.50
7 Brian Cabral FB	.20	.50
9 Paul Coffman FB	.20	.50
12 Doug Dawson FB	.20	.50
13 Donnie Dee FB	.20	.50
15 Mitch Donahue FB	.20	.50
16 Curtis Duncan FB	.20	.50
21 Bobby Hebert FB	.30	.75
23 David Dean FB	.20	.50
25 Brian Kinchen FB	.20	.50
26 Todd Kinchen FB	.20	.50
30 Neil Lomax FB	.30	.75
32 Dan Meers FB Mascot	.20	.50
33 Mike Merriweather FB	.20	.50
34 Ken Norton Jr. FB	.30	.75
38 Steve Pelluer FB	.30	.75
44 R.C. Slocum CO FB	.20	.50
45 Grant Teaff CO FB	.20	.50
46 Pat Tilley FB	.20	.50

1993 FCA Super Bowl

This six-card standard-size set features color player photos on a gradated blue background. The pictures are bordered on three sides by a thin hot pink line. The left side is bordered by a gradated blue border that also runs across the the bottom creating a double hot pink and blue bottom border. At the upper left of the picture is the FCA (Fellowship of Christian Athletes) emblem. The player's name appears in the bottom border, while his position is printed in the bottom margin. A hot pink stripe on the left edge contains the words "Professional Football." The backs are blue and display a color close-up photo, biographical information (including favorite scripture), and the player's testimony in yellow print.

COMPLETE SET (6)	6.00	15.00
1 Alfred Anderson	.75	2.00
2 Bob Lilly	1.25	3.00
3 Tom Landry CO	1.50	4.00
4 Brent Jones	.75	2.00
5 Bruce Matthews	1.00	2.50
6 Title Card	.75	2.00

1992 Finest

Manufactured with Topps Poly-tech process, this 44-card standard-size set features 33 established NFL stars and 11 top rookies. Three thousand cases were produced, with 20 sets per case. The cards are checklisted alphabetically according to veterans (1-33) and rookies (34-44).

COMPLETE SET (45)	7.50	20.00
1 Neal Anderson	.20	.50
2 Cornelius Bennett	.20	.50
3 Marion Butts	.10	.30
4 Anthony Carter	.20	.50
5 Mike Croel	.10	.30
6 John Elway	2.00	5.00
7 Jim Everett	.20	.50
8 Ernest Givins	.10	.30
9 Rodney Hampton	.20	.50
10 Alvin Harper	.10	.30
11 Michael Irvin	.40	1.00
12 Rickey Jackson	.10	.30
13 Seth Joyner	.10	.30
14 James Lofton	.20	.50
15 Ronnie Lott	.20	.50
16 Eric Metcalf	.20	.50
17 Chris Miller	.20	.50
18 Art Monk	.20	.50
19 Warren Moon	.40	1.00
20 Rob Moore	.20	.50
21 Anthony Munoz	.20	.50
22 Christian Okoye	.10	.30
23 Andre Rison	.20	.50
24 Leonard Russell	.10	.30
25 Mark Rypien	.20	.50
26 Barry Sanders	2.00	5.00
27 Emmitt Smith	2.50	6.00
28 Pat Swilling	.10	.30
29 John Taylor	.20	.50
30 Derrick Thomas	.40	1.00
31 Thurman Thomas	.40	1.00
32 Reggie White	.40	1.00
33 Rod Woodson	.40	1.00
34 Edgar Bennett	.20	.50
35 Terrell Buckley	.10	.30
36 Keith Hamilton	.20	.50
37 Amp Lee	.10	.30
38 Ricardo McDonald	.10	.30
39 Chris Mims	.10	.30
40 Robert Porcher	.40	1.00
41 Leon Searcy	.10	.30
42 Siran Stacy	.10	.30
43 Tommy Vardell	.10	.30
44 Bob Whitfield	.10	.30
NNO Checklist	.10	.30

1994 Finest

The 1994 Finest football set consists of 220 standard-size cards. Specially designed refracting foil cards were produced for each of the 220 cards. One of these foil cards was inserted in approximately every nine packs. Thirty-seven cards displayed a special rookie design, and one of these rookie cards was included in each five-card pack. Moreover, oversized 4" by 6" versions of these 37 rookie cards were produced and inserted at a rate of one in each 24-count box. There are no key Rookie Cards in this set.

COMPLETE SET (220)	15.00	40.00
1 Emmitt Smith	2.50	6.00
2 Calvin Williams	.30	.75
3 Mark Collins	.20	.50
4 Steve McMichael	.30	.75
5 Jim Kelly	.60	1.50
6 Michael Dean Perry	.30	.75
7 Wayne Simmons	.20	.50
8 Rocket Ismail	.30	.75
9 Mark Rypien	.20	.50
10 Brian Blades	.20	.50
11 Barry Word	.20	.50
12 Jerry Rice	1.50	4.00
13 Derrick Fenner	.20	.50
14 Karl Mecklenburg	.20	.50
15 Reggie Cobb	.20	.50
16 Eric Swann	.20	.50
17 Neil Smith	.30	.75
18 Barry Foster	.20	.50
19 Willie Roaf	.20	.50
20 Troy Drayton	.20	.50
21 Warren Moon	.50	1.25
22 Richmond Webb	.20	.50
23 Anthony Miller	.30	.75
24 Chris Slade	.20	.50
25 Mel Gray	.20	.50
26 Ronnie Lott	.50	1.25
27 Andre Rison	.30	.75
28 Jeff George	.30	.75
29 John Copeland	.20	.50
30 Derrick Thomas	.50	1.25
31 Sterling Sharpe	.30	.75
32 Chris Doleman	.20	.50
33 Monte Coleman	.20	.50
34 Mark Bavaro	3.00	.75
35 Kevin Williams	.20	.50
36 Eric Metcalf	.30	.75
37 Brent Jones	.30	.75
38 Steve Tasker	.30	.75
39 Dave Meggett	.20	.50
40 Howie Long	.50	1.25
41 Rick Mirer	.30	.75
42 Jerome Bettis	1.50	4.00
43 Marion Butts	.20	.50
44 Barry Sanders	2.50	6.00
45 Jason Elam	.30	.75
46 Broderick Thomas	.20	.50
47 Derek Brown RBK	.20	.50
48 Lorenzo White	.20	.50
49 Neil O'Donnell	.30	.75
50 Chris Burkett	.20	.50
51 John Offerdahl	.20	.50
52 Rohn Stark	.20	.50
53 Neal Anderson	.30	.75
54 Steve Beuerlein	.30	.75
55 Bruce Armstrong	.20	.50
56 Lincoln Kennedy	.20	.50
57 Darrell Green	.30	.75
58 Ricardo McDonald	.20	.50
59 Chris Warren	.30	.75
60 Mark Jackson	.20	.50
61 Pepper Johnson	.20	.50
62 Chris Spielman	.30	.75
63 Marcus Allen	.50	1.25
64 Jim Everett	.30	.75
65 Greg Townsend	.20	.50
66 Cris Carter	.50	1.25
67 Don Beebe	.30	.75
68 Reggie Langhorne	.20	.50
69 Randall Cunningham	.50	1.25
70 Johnny Holland	.20	.50
71 Morten Andersen	.20	.50
72 Leonard Marshall	.20	.50
73 Keith Jackson	.30	.75
74 Leslie O'Neal	.20	.50
75 Hardy Nickerson	.30	.75
76 Dan Williams	.20	.50
77 Steve Young	1.25	3.00
78 Deon Figures	.20	.50
79 Michael Irvin	.60	1.50
80 Luis Sharpe	.20	.50
81 Andre Tippett	.30	.75
82 Ricky Sanders	.20	.50
83 Erric Pegram	.20	.50
84 Albert Lewis	.20	.50
85 Anthony Blaylock	.20	.50
86 Pat Swilling	.20	.50
87 Duane Bickett	.20	.50
88 Myron Guyton	.20	.50
89 Clay Matthews	.20	.50
90 Jim McMahon	.30	.75
91 Bruce Smith	.50	1.25
92 Reggie White	.50	1.25
93 Shannon Sharpe	.50	1.25
94 Rickey Jackson	.20	.50
95 Ronnie Harmon	.20	.50
96 Terry McDaniel	.20	.50
97 Bryan Cox	.20	.50
98 Webster Slaughter	.20	.50
99 Boomer Esiason	.30	.75
100 Tim Krumrie	.20	.50
101 Cortez Kennedy	.30	.75
102 Henry Ellard	.30	.75
103 Clyde Simmons	.20	.50
104 Craig Erickson	.20	.50
105 Eric Green	.20	.50
106 Gary Clark	.30	.75
107 Jay Novacek	.30	.75
108 Dana Stubblefield	.30	.75
109 Mike Johnson	.20	.50
110 Ray Crockett	.20	.50
111 Leonard Russell	.20	.50
112 Robert Smith	.50	1.25
113 Art Monk	.30	.75
114 Ray Childress	.20	.50
115 O.J. McDuffie	.30	.75
116 Tim Brown	.50	1.25
117 Kevin Ross	.20	.50
118 Richard Dent	.30	.75
119 John Elway	2.50	6.00
120 James Hasty	.20	.50
121 Gary Plummer	.20	.50
122 Pierce Holt	.20	.50
123 Eric Martin	.20	.50
124 Brett Favre	3.00	8.00
125 Cornelius Bennett	.30	.75
126 Jessie Hester	.20	.50
127 Lewis Tillman	.20	.50
128 Qadry Ismail	.30	.75
129 Jay Schroeder	.20	.50
130 Curtis Conway	.50	1.25
131 Santana Dotson	.30	.75
132 Nick Lowery	.20	.50
133 Lomas Brown	.20	.50
134 Reggie Roby	.20	.50
135 John L. Williams	.20	.50
136 Vinny Testaverde	.30	.75
137 Seth Joyner	.20	.50
138 Ethan Horton	.20	.50
139 Jackie Slater	.20	.50
140 Rod Bernstine	.20	.50
141 Rob Moore	.30	.75
142 Dan Marino	2.50	6.00
143 Ken Harvey	.20	.50
144 Ernest Givins	.30	.75
145 Russell Maryland	.20	.50
146 Drew Bledsoe	1.00	2.50
147 Kevin Greene	.30	.75
148 Bobby Hebert	.20	.50
149 Junior Seau	.50	1.25
150 Tim McDonald	.20	.50
151 Thurman Thomas	.50	1.25
152 Phil Simms	.30	.75
153 Terrell Buckley	.20	.50
154 Sam Mills	.20	.50
155 Anthony Carter	.30	.75
156 Kelvin Martin	.20	.50
157 Shane Conlan	.20	.50
158 Irving Fryar	.30	.75
159 Demetrius DuBose	.20	.50
160 David Klingler	.20	.50
161 Herman Moore	.30	.75
162 Jeff Hostetler	.30	.75
163 Tommy Vardell	.20	.50
164 Craig Heyward	.30	.75
165 Wilber Marshall	.20	.50
166 Quentin Coryatt	.20	.50
167 Glyn Milburn	.20	.50
168 Fred Barnett	.30	.75
169 Charles Haley	.30	.75
170 Carl Banks	.30	.75
171 Ricky Proehl	.20	.50
172 Joe Montana	2.50	6.00
173 Johnny Mitchell	.20	.50
174 Andre Reed	.30	.75
175 Marco Coleman	.20	.50
176 Vaughan Johnson	.20	.50
177 Carl Pickens	.30	.75
178 Dwight Stone	.20	.50
179 Ricky Watters	.30	.75
180 Michael Haynes	.30	.75
181 Roger Craig	.30	.75
182 Cleveland Gary	.20	.50
183 Steve Emtman	.20	.50
184 Patrick Bates	.20	.50
185 Mark Carrier WR	.30	.75
186 Brad Hopkins	.20	.50
187 Dennis Smith	.20	.50
188 Natrone Means	.50	1.25
189 Michael Jackson	.30	.75
190 Ken Norton Jr.	.20	.50
191 Carlton Gray	.20	.50
192 Edgar Bennett	.50	1.25
193 Lawrence Taylor	.50	1.25
194 Marv Cook	.20	.50
195 Eric Curry	.20	.50
196 Victor Bailey	.20	.50
197 Ryan McNeil	.20	.50
198 Rod Woodson	.30	.75
199 Earnest Byner	.20	.50
200 Marvin Jones	.20	.50
201 Thomas Smith	.20	.50
202 Troy Aikman	1.50	4.00
203 Audray McMillian	.20	.50
204 Wade Wilson	.20	.50
205 George Teague	.20	.50
206 Deion Sanders	.75	2.00
207 Will Shields	.30	.75
208 John Taylor	.30	.75
209 Jim Harbaugh	.50	1.25
210 Micheal Barrow	.20	.50
211 Harold Green	.20	.50
212 Steve Everitt	.20	.50
213 Flipper Anderson	.20	.50
214 Rodney Hampton	.30	.75
215 Steve Atwater	.20	.50
216 James Trapp	.20	.50
217 Terry Kirby	.30	.75
218 Garrison Hearst	.50	1.25
219 Jeff Bryant	.20	.50
220 Roosevelt Potts	.20	.50

1994 Finest Refractors

COMPLETE SET (220)	250.00	500.00

*REFRACTORS: 2.5X TO 6X BASIC CARDS

1994 Finest Rookie Jumbos

COMPLETE SET (37)	40.00	100.00

ONE JUMBO CARD PER SEALED BOX

7 Wayne Simmons	.50	1.25

19 Willie Roaf	.50	1.25
20 Troy Drayton	.50	1.25
24 Chris Slade	.50	1.25
29 John Copeland	.50	1.25
35 Kevin Williams	1.00	2.50
41 Rick Mirer	2.00	5.00
42 Jerome Bettis	6.00	15.00
45 Jason Elam	1.00	2.50
47 Derek Brown RBK	.50	1.25
56 Lincoln Kennedy	.50	1.25
78 Deon Figures	.50	1.25
108 Dana Stubblefield	1.00	2.50
112 Robert Smith	2.00	5.00
115 O.J. McDuffie	2.00	5.00
128 Qadry Ismail	2.00	5.00
130 Curtis Conway	2.00	5.00
146 Drew Bledsoe	5.00	12.00
159 Demetrius DuBose	.50	1.25
167 Glyn Milburn	1.00	2.50
184 Patrick Bates	.50	1.25
186 Brad Hopkins	.50	1.25
188 Natrone Means	2.00	5.00
191 Carlton Gray	.50	1.25
195 Eric Curry	.50	1.25
196 Victor Bailey	.50	1.25
197 Ryan McNeil	.50	1.25
200 Marvin Jones	.50	1.25
201 Thomas Smith	.50	1.25
205 George Teague	.50	1.25
207 Will Shields	1.00	2.50
210 Micheal Barrow	.50	1.25
212 Steve Everitt	.50	1.25
216 James Trapp	.50	1.25
217 Terry Kirby	2.00	5.00
218 Garrison Hearst	2.00	5.00
220 Roosevelt Potts	.50	1.25

1995 Finest

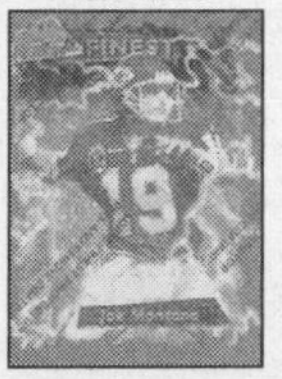

This 275 standard-size set was issued in seven card packs. These packs were in 24 count boxes and had a suggested retail price of $5.00 per pack. These high-tech cards each came with a protective peel-off laminate that prevented the cards from being scratched. Rookie Cards in this set include Jeff Blake, Ki-Jana Carter, Kerry Collins, Joey Galloway, Curtis Martin, Rashaan Salaam and Michael Westbrook.

COMPLETE SET (275)	30.00	80.00
COMP.SERIES 1 (165)	10.00	20.00
COMP.SERIES 2 (110)	25.00	60.00
1 Natrone Means	.25	.60
2 Dave Meggett	.08	.25
3 Tim Bowens	.08	.25
4 Jay Novacek	.25	.60
5 Michael Jackson	.25	.60
6 Calvin Williams	.25	.60
7 Neil Smith	.25	.60
8 Chris Gardocki	.08	.25
9 Jeff Burris	.08	.25
10 Warren Moon	.25	.60
11 Gary Anderson K	.08	.25
12 Bert Emanuel	.50	1.25
13 Rick Tuten	.08	.25
14 Steve Wallace	.08	.25
15 Marion Butts	.08	.25
16 Johnnie Morton	.25	.60
17 Rob Moore	.25	.60
18 Wayne Gandy	.08	.25
19 Quentin Coryatt	.25	.60
20 Richmond Webb	.08	.25
21 Errict Rhett	.25	.60
22 Joe Johnson	.08	.25
23 Gary Brown	.08	.25
24 Jeff Hostetler	.25	.60
25 Larry Centers	.25	.60
26 Tom Carter	.08	.25
27 Steve Atwater	.08	.25
28 Doug Pelfrey	.08	.25
29 Bryce Paup	.25	.60
30 Erik Williams	.08	.25
31 Henry Jones	.08	.25
32 Stanley Richard	.08	.25
33 Marcus Allen	.50	1.25
34 Antonio Langham	.08	.25
35 Lewis Tillman	.08	.25
36 Thomas Randolph	.08	.25
37 Byron Bam Morris	.08	.25
38 David Palmer	.25	.60
39 Ricky Watters	.25	.60
40 Brett Perriman	.25	.60
41 Will Wolford	.08	.25
42 Burt Grossman	.08	.25
43 Vincent Brisby	.25	.60
44 Ronnie Lott	.25	.60
45 Brian Blades	.25	.60
46 Brent Jones	.08	.25
47 Anthony Newman	.08	.25
48 Willie Roaf	.08	.25
49 Paul Gruber	.08	.25
50 Jeff George	.25	.60
51 Jamir Miller	.08	.25
52 Anthony Miller	.25	.60
53 Darrell Green	.08	.25
54 Steve Wisniewski	.08	.25
55 Dan Wilkinson	.25	.60
56 Brett Favre	2.00	5.00
57 Leslie O'Neal	.25	.60
58 Keith Byars	.08	.25
59 James Washington	.08	.25
60 Andre Reed	.25	.60
61 Ken Norton Jr.	.25	.60
62 John Randle	.25	.60
63 Lake Dawson	.25	.60
64 Greg Montgomery	.08	.25
65 Erric Pegram	.25	.60
66 Steve Everitt	.08	.25
67 Chris Brantley	.08	.25
68 Rod Woodson	.25	.60
69 Eugene Robinson	.08	.25
70 Dave Brown	.25	.60
71 Ricky Reynolds	.08	.25
72 Rohn Stark	.08	.25
73 Randal Hill	.08	.25
74 Brian Washington	.08	.25
75 Heath Shuler	.25	.60
76 Darion Conner	.08	.25
77 Terry McDaniel	.08	.25
78 Al Del Greco	.08	.25
79 Allen Aldridge	.08	.25
80 Trace Armstrong	.08	.25
81 Darnay Scott	.25	.60
82 Charlie Garner	.50	1.25
83 Harold Bishop	.08	.25
84 Reggie White	.50	1.25
85 Shawn Jefferson	.08	.25
86 Irving Spikes	.25	.60
87 Mel Gray	.08	.25
88 D.J. Johnson	.08	.25
89 Daryl Johnston	.25	.60
90 Joe Montana	2.00	5.00
91 Michael Strahan	.50	1.25
92 Robert Blackmon	.08	.25
93 Ryan Yarborough	.25	.60
94 Terry Allen	.25	.60
95 Michael Haynes	.25	.60
96 Jim Harbaugh	.25	.60
97 Micheal Barrow	.08	.25
98 John Thierry	.08	.25
99 Seth Joyner	.08	.25
100 Deion Sanders	.75	2.00
101 Eric Turner	.08	.25
102 LeShon Johnson	.25	.60
103 John Copeland	.08	.25
104 Cornelius Bennett	.25	.60
105 Sean Gilbert	.25	.60
106 Herschel Walker	.25	.60
107 Henry Ellard	.25	.60
108 Neil O'Donnell	.25	.60
109 Charles Wilson	.08	.25
110 Willie McGinest	.25	.60
111 Tim Brown	.50	1.25
112 Simon Fletcher	.08	.25
113 Broderick Thomas	.08	.25
114 Tom Waddle	.08	.25
115 Jessie Tuggle	.08	.25
116 Maurice Hurst	.08	.25
117 Aubrey Beavers	.08	.25
118 Donnell Bennett	.25	.60
119 Shante Carver	.08	.25
120 Eric Metcalf	.25	.60
121 John Carney	.08	.25
122 Thomas Lewis	.25	.60
123 Johnny Mitchell	.08	.25
124 Trent Dilfer	.50	1.25
125 Marshall Faulk	1.25	3.00
126 Ernest Givins	.08	.25
127 Aeneas Williams	.08	.25
128 Bucky Brooks	.08	.25
129 Todd Steussie	.08	.25
130 Randall Cunningham	.50	1.25
131 Reggie Brooks	.25	.60
132 Morten Andersen	.08	.25
133 James Jett	.25	.60
134 George Teague	.08	.25
135 John Taylor	.08	.25
136 Charles Johnson	.25	.60
137 Isaac Bruce	1.00	2.50
138 Jason Elam	.25	.60
139 Carl Pickens	.25	.60
140 Chris Warren	.25	.60
141 Bruce Armstrong	.08	.25
142 Mark Carrier DB	.08	.25
143 Irving Fryar	.25	.60
144 Van Malone	.08	.25
145 Charles Haley	.25	.60
146 Chris Calloway	.08	.25
147 J.J. Birden	.08	.25
148 Tony Bennett	.08	.25
149 Lincoln Kennedy	.08	.25
150 Stan Humphries	.25	.60
151 Hardy Nickerson	.08	.25
152 Randall McDaniel	.08	.25
153 Marcus Robertson	.08	.25
154 Ronald Moore	.08	.25
155 Thurman Thomas	.50	1.25
156 Tommy Vardell	.08	.25
157 Ken Ruettgers	.08	.25
158 Rob Fredrickson	.08	.25
159 Johnny Bailey	.08	.25
160 Greg Lloyd	.25	.60
161 David Alexander	.08	.25
162 Kevin Mawae	.08	.25
163 Derek Brown RBK	.08	.25
164 William Floyd	.25	.60
165 Aaron Glenn	.08	.25
166 Joey Galloway RC	3.00	8.00
167 Troy Drayton	.08	.25
168 Dormontti Dawson	.25	.60
169 Ronald Moore	.08	.25
170 Dan Marino	2.00	5.00
171 Dennis Gibson	.08	.25
172 Raymont Harris	.08	.25
173 Shannon Sharpe	.25	.60
174 Kevin Williams	.25	.60
175 Jim Everett	.08	.25
176 Rocket Ismail	.25	.60
177 Mark Fields RC	.50	1.25
178 George Koonce	.08	.25
179 Chris Hudson	.08	.25
180 Jerry Rice	1.00	2.50
181 Dewayne Washington	.25	.60
182 Dale Carter	.25	.60
183 Pete Stoyanovich	.08	.25
184 Blake Brockermeyer	.08	.25
185 Troy Aikman	1.00	2.50
186 Jeff Blake RC	1.00	2.50
187 Troy Vincent	.08	.25
188 Lamar Lathon	.08	.25
189 Tony Boselli	.50	1.25
190 Emmitt Smith	1.50	4.00
191 Bobby Houston	.08	.25
192 Edgar Bennett	.25	.60
193 Derrick Brooks RC	3.00	8.00
194 Ricky Proehl	.08	.25
195 Rodney Hampton	.25	.60
196 Dave Krieg	.08	.25
197 Vinny Testaverde	.25	.60
198 Erik Kramer	.08	.25
199 Ben Coates	.25	.60
200 Steve Young	.75	2.00
201 Glyn Milburn	.08	.25
202 Bryan Cox	.08	.25
203 Luther Elliss	.08	.25
204 Mark McMillian	.08	.25
205 Jerome Bettis	.50	1.25
206 Craig Heyward	.25	.60
207 Ray Buchanan	.08	.25
208 Kimble Anders	.25	.60
209 Kevin Greene	.25	.60
210 Eric Allen	.08	.25
211 Ricardo McDonald	.08	.25
212 Ruben Brown RC	.60	1.50
213 Harvey Williams	.08	.25
214 Broderick Thomas	.08	.25
215 Frank Reich	.08	.25
216 Frank Sanders RC UER Plays Wide Receiver Defensive Record on Back	.60	1.50
217 Craig Newsome	.08	.25
218 Merton Hanks	.08	.25
219 Chris Miller	.08	.25
220 John Elway	2.00	5.00
221 Ernest Givins	.08	.25
222 Boomer Esiason	.25	.60
223 Reggie Roby	.08	.25
224 Qadry Ismail	.25	.60
225 Ki-Jana Carter RC	.60	1.50
226 Leon Lett	.08	.25
227 Eric Hill	.08	.25
228 Scott Mitchell	.25	.60
229 Craig Erickson	.08	.25
230 Drew Bledsoe	.75	2.00
231 Sean Landeta	.08	.25
232 Barrett Brooks	.08	.25
233 Brian Mitchell	.08	.25
234 Tyrone Poole	.50	1.25
235 Desmond Howard	.25	.60
236 Wayne Simmons	.08	.25
237 Michael Westbrook RC	.60	1.50
238 Quinn Early	.25	.60
239 Willie Davis	.25	.60
240 Rashaan Salaam RC	.30	.75
241 Devin Bush	.08	.25
242 Dana Stubblefield	.25	.60
243 Dexter Carter	.08	.25
244 Shane Conlan	.08	.25
245 Keith Elias RC	.08	.25
246 Robert Brooks	.50	1.25
247 Garrison Hearst	.50	1.25
248 Eric Zeier RC	.60	1.50
249 Nate Newton	.25	.60
250 Barry Sanders	1.50	4.00
251 Dave Meggett	.08	.25
252 Courtney Hawkins	.08	.25
253 Cortez Kennedy	.25	.60
254 Mario Bates	.25	.60
255 Junior Seau	.50	1.25
256 Brian Washington	.08	.25
257 Darius Holland	.08	.25
258 Jeff Graham	.08	.25
259 Rob Moore	.25	.60
260 Andre Rison	.25	.60
261 Kerry Collins RC	4.00	8.00
262 Roosevelt Potts	.08	.25
263 Cris Carter	.50	1.25
264 Curtis Martin RC	6.00	15.00
265 Rick Mirer	.25	.60
266 Mo Lewis	.08	.25
267 Mike Sherrard	.08	.25
268 Herman Moore	.50	1.25
269 Eric Metcalf	.25	.60
270 Ray Childress	.08	.25
271 Chris Slade	.08	.25
272 Michael Irvin	.50	1.25
273 Jim Kelly	.50	1.25
274 Terance Mathis	.25	.60
275 LeRoy Butler	.08	.25

1995 Finest Refractors

COMPLETE SET (275)	300.00	600.00
COMP.SERIES 1 (165)	100.00	200.00
COMP.SERIES 2 (110)	200.00	400.00

*REFRACT.STARS: 2.5X to 6 BASIC CARDS
*REFRACTOR RCs: 1.5X to 4X BASIC CARDS
STATED ODDS 1:12

1995 Finest Fan Favorites

COMPLETE SET (25)	25.00	60.00
STATED ODDS 1:12 SER.1		
FF1 Drew Bledsoe	1.50	4.00
FF2 Jerome Bettis	1.00	2.50
FF3 Rick Mirer	.50	1.25
FF4 Andre Rison	.50	1.25
FF5 Troy Aikman	2.00	5.00
FF6 Cortez Kennedy	.50	1.25
FF7 Emmitt Smith	3.00	8.00
FF8 Sterling Sharpe	.50	1.25
FF9 Junior Seau	1.00	2.50
FF10 Michael Irvin	1.00	2.50
FF11 Jim Kelly	1.00	2.50
FF12 Steve Young	1.50	4.00
FF13 John Elway	4.00	10.00
FF14 Jerry Rice	2.00	5.00
FF15 Barry Sanders	3.00	8.00
FF16 Dan Marino	4.00	10.00
FF17 Dan Wilkinson	.50	1.25
FF18 Reggie White	1.00	2.50
FF19 Deion Sanders	1.50	4.00
FF20 Willie McGinest	.50	1.25
FF21 Stan Humphries	.50	1.25
FF22 Heath Shuler	.50	1.25
FF23 Natrone Means	.50	1.25
FF24 Warren Moon	.50	1.25
FF25 Marshall Faulk	2.50	6.00

1995 Finest Landmark

These standard-size "cards" are actually metal cards that were overlaid on a 4-ounce ingot of solid bronze. Using Topps' finest technology, the cards also feature the players personal achievements on the back. The first four cards were originally available only as a set through Topps direct mailers at a cost of $99 plus shipping. Two additional series were released later seperately and re-released together as "series two." These 12-card series two sets were available directly from Topps. We've assigned numbers to the cards alphabetically by series.

COMPLETE SET (16)	150.00	400.00
1 Troy Aikman	12.00	30.00
2 Jerry Rice	12.00	30.00
3 Emmitt Smith	16.00	40.00
4 Steve Young	8.00	20.00
5 Drew Bledsoe	10.00	25.00
6 Randall Cunningham	8.00	20.00
7 John Elway	20.00	50.00
8 Brett Favre	20.00	50.00
9 Michael Irvin	8.00	20.00
10 Jim Kelly	8.00	20.00
11 Dan Marino	20.00	50.00
12 Rick Mirer	4.80	12.00
13 Warren Moon	8.00	20.00
14 Barry Sanders	20.00	50.00
15 Junior Seau	8.00	20.00
16 Heath Shuler	4.80	12.00

1995-96 Finest Pro Bowl Jumbos

This 22-card set measures approximately 4" by 5 5/8". The fronts feature a color player cut-out on a metallic, lightning-effect background with the player's name printed in silver foil on a violet and black marblized band at the bottom. The cards are essentially enlarged versions of regular issue 1995 Finest cards and were distributed at the 1996 NFL Experience Pro Bowl show in Hawaii. The original card number is included on the backs as well as the new numbering of 22-cards. Refractor parallel versions of each card were produced in much shorter quantities. A poster sized Steve Young Finest promo card was produced as well and distributed at the Pro Bowl Card Show. It is priced separately below.

COMPLETE SET (22)	15.00	40.00
*REFRACTOR STARS: 5X TO 12X		
1 Troy Aikman	2.00	5.00
2 Tim Brown	.75	2.00
3 Cris Carter	.75	2.00
4 Marshall Faulk	1.25	3.00
5 Brett Favre	5.00	10.00
6 Merton Hanks	.40	1.00
7 Michael Irvin	.75	2.00
8 Greg Lloyd	.40	1.00
9 Dan Marino	5.00	10.00
10 Curtis Martin	2.00	5.00
11 Herman Moore	.75	2.00
12 Terry McDaniel	.40	1.00
13 Ken Norton	.40	1.00
14 Bryce Paup	.40	1.00
15 John Randle	.75	2.00
16 Jerry Rice	2.00	5.00
17 Barry Sanders	4.00	8.00
18 Junior Seau	.75	2.00
19 Steve Young	1.50	4.00
20 Reggie White	.75	2.00
21 Chris Warren	.40	1.00
22 Emmitt Smith	4.00	8.00
P1 Steve Young Promo/20 X 14 poster	7.50	15.00

1996 Finest

This 359 card standard-size set was issued in two series by Topps. The set was issued in six-card packs and had a suggested retail price of $5 per pack. The set is broken down into a total of 220 bronze cards, 91 silver cards (1:4 packs), and 48 gold cards (1:24 packs). All of the cards feature chromium technology and the "Topps Finest" protector. Cards are numbered on the back both by set order and by card theme.

COMPLETE SET (359)	150.00	300.00
COMP.SERIES 1 (191)	100.00	200.00
COMP.SERIES 2 (168)	50.00	100.00
COMP.BRONZE SER.1 (110)	15.00	40.00
COMP.BRONZE SER.2 (110)	15.00	40.00
B2 Jay Novacek B	.25	.60
B3 Ray Buchanan B	.10	.30
B5 Phil Hansen B	.10	.30
B6 Mike Mamula B	.10	.30
B9 Bernie Parmalee B	.10	.30
B10 Herman Moore B	.25	.60
B11 Shawn Jefferson B	.10	.30
B12 Chris Doleman B	.10	.30
B13 Erik Kramer B	.25	.60
B15 Orlando Thomas B	.10	.30
B16 Terrell Davis B	1.50	4.00
B18 Roman Phifer B	.10	.30
B19 Trent Dilfer B	.25	.60
B21 Darnay Scott B	.25	.60
B22 Steve McNair B	1.50	4.00
B23 Lamar Lathon B	.10	.30
B26 Thomas Randolph B	.10	.30
B27 Michael Jackson B	.25	.60
B28 Seth Joyner B	.10	.30
B29 Jeff Lageman B	.10	.30
B30 Darryl Williams B	.10	.30
B32 Erric Pegram B	.25	.60
B34 Sean Dawkins B	.25	.60
B38 Dan Saleaumua B UER card misnumbered 20	.10	.30
B39 Henry Thomas B	.10	.30
B43 Pat Swilling B	.10	.30
B44 Marty Carter B	.10	.30
B45 Anthony Miller B	.25	.60
B48 Chris Warren B	.25	.60
B49 Derek Brown RBK B	.10	.30
B51 Blaine Bishop B	.10	.30
B52 Jake Reed B	.25	.60
B55 Vencie Glenn B	.10	.30
B58 Derrick Alexander WR B	.25	.60
B64 Jessie Tuggle B	.10	.30
B65 Terrance Shaw B	.10	.30
B66 David Sloan B	.25	.60
B68 Brent Jones B	.10	.30
B70 William Thomas B	.10	.30
B71 Robert Smith B	.25	.60
B72 Wayne Simmons B	.10	.30
B73 Jim Harbaugh B	.25	.60
B76 Wayne Chrebet B	.40	1.00
B77 Chris Hudson B	.10	.30
B79 Stevon Moore B	.10	.30
B80 Chris Calloway B	.10	.30
B81 Tom Carter B	.10	.30
B82 Dave Meggett B	.10	.30
B83 Sam Mills B	.25	.60
B86 Renaldo Turnbull B	.10	.30
B87 Derrick Brooks B	.40	1.00
B89 Eugene Robinson B	.10	.30
B91 Rodney Thomas B	.10	.30
B92 Dan Wilkinson B	.10	.30
B93 Mark Fields B	.10	.30
B94 Warren Sapp B	.10	.30
B95 Curtis Martin B	1.50	4.00
B97 Ray Crockett B	.10	.30
B98 Ed McDaniel B	.10	.30
B101 Craig Heyward B	.10	.30
B102 Ellis Johnson B	.10	.30
B104 O.J. McDuffie B	.25	.60
B105 J.J. Stokes B	.40	1.00
B106 Mo Lewis B	.10	.30
B108 Rob Moore B	.25	.60
B110 Tyrone Wheatley B	.25	.60
B111 Ken Harvey B	.10	.30
B113 Willie Green B	.10	.30
B114 Willie Davis B	.25	.60
B115 Andy Harmon B	.10	.30
B117 Bryan Cox B	.10	.30
B119 Bert Emanuel B	.25	.60
B120 Greg Lloyd B	.25	.60
B122 Willie Jackson B	.25	.60
B123 Lorenzo Lynch B	.10	.30
B124 Pepper Johnson B	.10	.30
B128 Tyrone Poole B	.10	.30
B129 Neil Smith B	.25	.60
B130 Eddie Robinson B	.10	.30
B131 Bryce Paup B	.25	.60
B134 Troy Aikman B	2.00	5.00
B136 Chris Sanders B	.25	.60
B138 Jim Everett B	.10	.30
B139 Frank Sanders B	.25	.60
B141 Cortez Kennedy B	.25	.60
B143 Derrick Alexander DE B	.10	.30
B144 Rob Fredrickson B	.10	.30
B145 Chris Zorich B	.10	.30
B146 Devin Bush B	.10	.30
B149 Troy Vincent B	.10	.30
B151 Deion Sanders B	1.00	2.50
B152 James O. Stewart B	.25	.60
B156 Lawrence Dawsey B	.10	.30
B157 Robert Brooks B	.40	1.00
B158 Rashaan Salaam B	.25	.60
B161 Tim Brown B	.25	.60
B162 Brendan Stai B	.10	.30
B163 Sean Gilbert B	.10	.30
B169 Calvin Williams B	.25	.60
B171 Ruben Brown B	.10	.30
B172 Eric Green B	.10	.30
B175 Jerry Rice B	2.00	5.00
B176 Bruce Smith B	.40	1.00
B177 Mark Bruener B	.10	.30
B179 Lamont Warren B	.10	.30
B180 Tamarick Vanover B	.40	1.00
B182 Scott Mitchell B	.25	.60
B186 Terry Wooden B	.10	.30
B187 Ken Norton B	.25	.60
B188 Jeff Herrod B	.10	.30
B192 Gus Frerotte B	.25	.60
B194 Brett Maxie B	.10	.30
B198 Eddie Kennison B RC	.40	1.00
B201 Marcus Jones B RC	.10	.30
B202 Terry Allen B	.25	.60
B203 Leroy Hoard B	.10	.30
B205 Reggie White B	.40	1.00
B206 Larry Centers B	.25	.60
B208 Vincent Brisby B	.10	.30
B209 Michael Timpson B	.10	.30
B211 John Mobley B RC	.10	.30
B212 Clay Matthews B	.25	.60
B213 Shannon Sharpe B	.25	.60
B214 Tony Bennett B	.10	.30
B216 Mickey Washington B	.10	.30
B217 Fred Barnett B	.25	.60
B218 Michael Haynes B	.25	.60
B219 Stan Humphries B	.25	.60
B221 Winston Moss B	.10	.30
B222 Tim Biakabutuka B RC	.40	1.00
B223 Leeland McElroy B RC	.25	.60
B224 Vinnie Clark B	.10	.30
B225 Keyshawn Johnson B RC	2.00	5.00
B228 Tony Woods B	.10	.30
B231 Anthony Pleasant B	.10	.30
B232 Jeff George B	.25	.60
B233 Curtis Conway B	.40	1.00
B235 Jeff Lewis B RC	.25	.60
B236 Edgar Bennett B	.25	.60
B237 Regan Upshaw B RC	.10	.30
B240 William Fuller B	.10	.30
B241 Willie Anderson B RC	.10	.30
B242 Derrick Thomas B	.40	1.00
B243 Marvin Harrison B RC	6.00	15.00
B244 Darion Conner B	.10	.30
B245 Antonio Langham B	.10	.30
B246 Rodney Peete B	.10	.30
B247 Tim McDonald B	.10	.30
B248 Robert Jones B	.10	.30
B251 Mark Carrier DB B	.10	.30
B252 Stephon Grant B	.10	.30
B254 Jeff Hostetler B	.25	.60
B255 Darrell Green B	.10	.30
B261 Eric Swann B	.25	.60
B263 Irv Smith B	.10	.30
B264 Tim McKyer B	.10	.30
B266 Sean Jones B	.10	.30
B271 Yancey Thigpen B	.25	.60
B273 Quentin Coryatt B	.10	.30
B274 Hardy Nickerson B	.10	.30
B275 Ricardo McDonald B	.10	.30
B277 Robert Blackmon B	.10	.30
B279 Alonzo Spellman B	.10	.30
B281 Rickey Dudley B RC	.40	1.00
B282 Joe Cain B	.10	.30
B284 John Randle B	.25	.60
B286 Vinny Testaverde B	.25	.60
B289 Henry Jones B	.10	.30
B290 Simeon Rice B RC	1.00	2.50
B295 Leslie O'Neal B	.10	.30
B297 Greg Hill B	.25	.60
B301 Eric Metcalf B	.25	.60
B303 Jerome Woods B RC	.10	.30
B306 Anthony Smith B	.10	.30
B307 Darren Perry B	.10	.30
B311 James Hasty B	.10	.30
B312 Cris Carter B	.40	1.00
B314 Lawrence Phillips B RC	.25	.60
B317 Aeneas Williams B	.10	.30
B318 Eric Hill B	.10	.30
B319 Kevin Hardy B RC	.40	1.00
B321 Chris Chandler B	.25	.60
B322 Rocket Ismail B	.25	.60
B323 Anthony Parker B	.10	.30
B324 John Thierry B	.10	.30
B325 Micheal Barrow B	.10	.30
B326 Henry Ford B	.10	.30
B327 Aaron Hayden B RC	.10	.30
B328 Terance Mathis B	.10	.30
B329 Kirk Pointer B RC	.10	.30
B330 Ray Mickens B RC	.10	.30
B331 Jermane Mayberry B RC	.10	.30
B332 Mario Bates B	.25	.60
B333 Carlton Gray B	.10	.30
B334 Derek Loville B	.10	.30
B335 Mike Alstott B RC	2.00	5.00
B336 Eric Guliford B	.10	.30
B337 Marvcus Patton B	.10	.30
B338 Terrell Owens B RC	6.00	15.00
B339 Lance Johnstone B RC	.25	.60
B340 Lake Dawson B	.25	.60
B341 Winslow Oliver B RC	.10	.30
B342 Adrian Murrell B	.25	.60
B343 Jason Belser B	.10	.30
B344 Brian Dawkins B RC	3.00	8.00
B345 Reggie Brown B RC	.10	.30
B346 Shaun Gayle B	.10	.30
B347 Tony Brackens B RC	.40	1.00
B348 Thomas Lewis B	.10	.30
B349 Kelvin Pritchett B	.10	.30
B350 Bobby Engram B RC	.40	1.00
B351 Moe Williams B RC	1.00	2.50
B352 Thomas Smith B	.10	.30
B353 Dexter Carter B	.10	.30
B354 Qadry Ismail B	.25	.60
B355 Marco Battaglia B RC	.10	.30
B356 Levon Kirkland B	.10	.30
B357 Eric Allen B	.10	.30
B358 Bobby Hoying B RC	.40	1.00
B359 Checklist B	.10	.30
G1 Kordell Stewart G	2.00	5.00
G7 Kimble Anders G	.60	1.50
G8 Merton Hanks G	.60	1.50
G17 Rick Mirer G	1.25	3.00
G33 Craig Newsome G	.60	1.50
G36 Bryce Paup G	1.25	3.00
G40 Dan Marino G	10.00	25.00
G42 Andre Coleman G	.60	1.50
G47 Kevin Carter G	.60	1.50
G60 Mark Brunell G	2.00	5.00
G61 David Palmer G	1.25	3.00
G75 Carnell Lake G	.60	1.50
G96 Joey Galloway G	2.00	5.00
G112 Melvin Tuten G	.60	1.50
G121 Aaron Glenn G	.60	1.50
G132 Brett Favre G	10.00	25.00
G133 Ken Dilger G	1.25	3.00
G140 Barry Sanders G	7.50	20.00
G142 Glyn Milburn G	.60	1.50
G148 Brett Perriman G	1.25	3.00
G160 Kerry Collins G	2.00	5.00
G164 Lee Woodall G	.60	1.50
G173 Marshall Faulk G	2.50	6.00
G178 Troy Aikman G	5.00	12.00
G190 Drew Bledsoe G	2.00	5.00
G191 Checklist G	.60	1.50
G193 Michael Irvin G	2.00	5.00
G196 Warren Moon G	1.25	3.00
G200 Steve Young G	5.00	12.00
G207 Alex Van Dyke G RC	1.25	3.00
G220 Cris Carter G	2.00	5.00
G230 John Elway G	10.00	25.00
G234 Charles Haley G	1.25	3.00
G240 Jim Kelly G	2.00	5.00
G250 Rodney Hampton G	1.25	3.00
G256 Errict Rhett G	1.25	3.00
G257 Alex Molden G	.60	1.50
G260 Kevin Hardy G	1.25	3.00
G267 Bryant Young G	1.25	3.00
G268 Jeff Blake G	2.00	5.00
G270 Keyshawn Johnson G	2.00	5.00
G278 Junior Seau G	2.00	5.00
G285 Terry Kirby G	1.25	3.00
G293 Hugh Douglas G	1.25	3.00
G296 Reggie White G	2.00	5.00
G298 Elvis Grbac G	2.00	5.00
G300 Emmitt Smith G	7.50	20.00
G309 Ricky Watters G	1.25	3.00
S4 Brett Favre S	6.00	15.00
S14 Chester McGlockton S	.30	.75
S20 Tyrone Hughes S	.30	.75
S24 Ty Law S	1.25	3.00
S25 Brian Mitchell S	.30	.75
S31 Darren Woodson S	.60	1.50
S35 Brian Mitchell S	.30	.75
S37 Dana Stubblefield S	.60	1.50
S41 Kerry Collins S	1.25	3.00
S46 Orlando Thomas S	.30	.75
S50 Jerry Rice S	3.00	8.00
S53 Willie McGinest S	.30	.75
S54 Blake Brockermeyer S	.30	.75
S56 Michael Westbrook S	1.25	3.00
S57 Garrison Hearst S	1.25	3.00
S59 Kyle Brady S	.60	1.50
S62 Tim Brown S	.60	1.50
S63 Jeff Graham S	.30	.75
S67 Dan Marino S	6.00	15.00
S69 Tamarick Vanover S	1.25	3.00
S74 Daryl Johnston S	.60	1.50
S78 Frank Sanders S	.60	1.50
S84 Darryll Lewis S	.30	.75
S85 Carl Pickens S	.60	1.50
S88 Jerome Bettis S	1.25	3.00
S90 Terrell Davis S	2.50	6.00
S99 Napoleon Kaufman S	1.25	3.00
S100 Rashaan Salaam S	.60	1.50
S103 Barry Sanders S	6.00	15.00
S107 Tony Boselli S	.60	1.50
S109 Eric Zeier S	.60	1.50
S116 Bruce Smith S	1.25	3.00
S118 Zack Crockett S	.30	.75
S125 Joey Galloway S	1.25	3.00
S126 Heath Shuler S	.60	1.50
S127 Curtis Martin S	2.50	6.00
S135 Greg Lloyd S	.60	1.50
S137 Marshall Faulk S	1.50	4.00
S147 Tyrone Poole S	.30	.75
S150 J.J. Stokes S	1.25	3.00
S153 Drew Bledsoe S	1.25	3.00
S154 Terry McDaniel S	.30	.75
S155 Terrell Fletcher S	.30	.75
S159 Dave Brown S	.30	.75
S165 Jim Harbaugh S	.60	1.50
S166 Larry Brown S	.30	.75
S167 Neil Smith S	.60	1.50
S168 Herman Moore S	.60	1.50
S170 Deion Sanders S	2.00	5.00
S174 Mark Chmura S	.60	1.50
S181 Chris Warren S	.60	1.50
S183 Robert Brooks S	1.25	3.00
S184 Steve McNair S	2.50	6.00
S185 Kordell Stewart S	1.25	3.00
S189 Charlie Garner S	.60	1.50
S195 Harvey Williams S	.30	.75
S197 Jeff George S	.60	1.50
S199 Ricky Watters S	.60	1.50
S204 Steve Bono S	.60	1.50
S210 Jeff Blake S	1.25	3.00
S215 Phillippi Sparks S	.30	.75
S226 William Floyd S	.60	1.50
S227 Troy Drayton S	.30	.75
S229 Rodney Hampton S	.60	1.50
S239 Duane Clemons S RC	.30	.75
S249 Curtis Conway S	1.25	3.00
S253 John Mobley S	.30	.75
S258 Chris Slade S	.30	.75
S259 Derrick Thomas S	1.25	3.00
S262 Eric Metcalf S	.60	1.50
S265 Emmitt Smith S	5.00	12.00
S269 Jeff Hostetler S	.60	1.50
S272 Thurman Thomas S	1.25	3.00
S276 Steve Atwater S	.30	.75
S280 Isaac Bruce S	1.25	3.00
S283 Neil O'Donnell S	.60	1.50
S287 Jim Kelly S	1.25	3.00
S288 Lawrence Phillips S	1.25	3.00
S291 Terance Mathis S	.30	.75
S292 Errict Rhett S	.60	1.50
S294 Santo Stephens S	.30	.75
S299 Walt Harris S RC	.30	.75
S302 Jamir Miller S	.30	.75
S304 Ben Coates S	.60	1.50
S305 Marcus Allen S	1.25	3.00
S308 Jonathan Ogden S RC	1.25	3.00
S310 John Elway S	6.00	15.00
S313 Irving Fryar S	.60	1.50
S315 Junior Seau S	1.25	3.00
S316 Alex Molden S RC	.30	.75
S320 Steve Young S	2.50	6.00

1996 Finest Refractors

COMP.BRONZE SET (220)	500.00	1,000.00
COMP.BRONZE SER.1 (110)	250.00	500.00
COMP.BRONZE SER.2 (110)	250.00	500.00

*BRONZE VETS: 3X TO 8X BASIC CARDS
*BRONZE ROOKIE STARS: 1.5X TO 4X
*BRNZ ROOK.COMM/SEMI: 3X TO 8X
BRONZE REFRACTOR ODDS 1:12
*GOLD VETS: 2X TO 5X BASIC CARDS
GOLD REFRACTOR ODDS 1:288
*SILVER VETS: 2.5X TO 6X BASIC CARDS
SILVER REFRACTOR ODDS 1:48

1996-97 Finest Pro Bowl Jumbos

This 22-card set measures approximately 4" by 5-5/8". The fronts feature a color player photo on a metallic background. The cards are essentially enlarged versions of regular issue 1996 Finest gold cards but were distributed at the 1997 NFL Experience Pro Bowl show in Hawaii. Each is numbered "XX of 22" cards. Refractor parallel versions of each card were produced in much shorter quantities.

COMPLETE SET (22)	24.00	60.00
*REFRACTOR STARS: 6X TO 15X		
1 Brett Favre	3.20	8.00
2 Herman Moore	.60	1.50
3 Terrell Davis	2.00	5.00
4 Jerry Rice	2.00	5.00
5 Tim Brown	.60	1.50
6 Dan Marino	3.20	8.00
7 Curtis Martin	1.60	4.00
8 Barry Sanders	3.20	8.00
9 Bruce Smith	.80	2.00
10 Troy Aikman	2.00	5.00
11 Deion Sanders	1.20	3.00
12 Drew Bledsoe	1.60	4.00
13 Steve Young	1.60	4.00
14 Terry Allen	.60	1.50
15 Reggie White	.80	2.00
16 Shannon Sharpe	.60	1.50
17 John Elway	3.20	8.00
18 Emmitt Smith	2.40	6.00
19 Keyshawn Johnson	1.20	3.00
20 Ben Coates	.40	1.00
21 Ricky Watters	.40	1.00
22 Junior Seau	.80	2.00

1996-97 Finest Pro Bowl Promos 5X7

In addition to the 22-card Finest Pro Bowl set, six promo cards were released at the 1997 NFL Experience Pro Bowl Card Show in Hawaii. Each is simply an enlarged (5" by 7") copy of a 1996 Finest card. The backs carry a 1996 copyright date along with a player bio and card number. A Refractor parallel was also produced for each card.

COMPLETE SET (6)	14.00	35.00
*REFRACTORS: 4X TO 10X BASIC CARDS		
1 Curtis Martin	2.00	5.00
2 Brett Favre	4.00	10.00
3 Barry Sanders	4.00	10.00
4 Jerry Rice	2.40	6.00
5 Troy Aikman	2.40	6.00
6 John Elway	4.00	10.00

1997 Finest

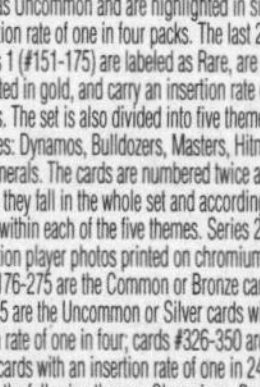

The 1997 Finest set was issued in two series totalling 350 cards and was distributed in six-card packs with a suggested retail price of $5. The set features borderless metallic design with the first 100 cards labeled as Common and highlighted in bronze. Cards #101-150 are labeled as Uncommon and are highlighted in silver with an insertion rate of one in four packs. The last 25 cards of Series 1 (#151-175) are labeled as Rare, are highlighted in gold, and carry an insertion rate of one in 24 packs. The set is also divided into five theme categories: Dynamos, Bulldozers, Masters, Hitmen, and Field Generals. The cards are numbered twice according to where they fall in the whole set and according to where they fall within each of the five themes. Series 2 features color action player photos printed on chromium cards. Cards #176-275 are the Common or Bronze cards; cards #276-325 are the Uncommon or Silver cards with an insertion rate of one in four; cards #326-350 are the Rare or Gold cards with an insertion rate of one in 24. Series 2 contains the following themes: Champions, Dominators, Impact, Stalwarts, and Masters. Series 2 cards are also numbered twice according to where they fall in the whole set and according to where they fall within each of the five themes.

COMPLETE SET (350)	250.00	500.00
COMP.SERIES 1 SET (175)	125.00	250.00
COMP.SERIES 2 SET (175)	125.00	250.00
COMP.BRONZE SET (200)	25.00	60.00
COMP.BRONZE SER.1 (100)	10.00	25.00
COMP.BRONZE SER.2 (100)	15.00	40.00
1 Mark Brunell B	.60	1.50
2 Chris Slade B	.25	.60
3 Chris Doleman B	.25	.60
4 Chris Hudson B	.25	.60
5 Karim Abdul-Jabbar B	.40	1.00
6 Darren Perry B	.25	.60
7 Daryl Johnston B	.40	1.00
8 Rob Moore B UER listed as uncommon	.40	1.00
9 Robert Smith B	.40	1.00
10 Terry Allen B	.40	1.00
11 Jason Dunn B	.25	.60
12 Henry Thomas B	.25	.60
13 Rod Stephens B	.25	.60
14 Ray Mickens B	.25	.60
15 Ty Detmer B	.40	1.00
16 Fred Barnett B	.25	.60

17 Derrick Alexander WR B	.40	1.00
18 Marcus Robertson B	.25	.60
19 Robert Blackmon B	.25	.60
20 Isaac Bruce B	.60	1.50
21 Chester McGlockton B	.25	.60
22 Stan Humphries B	.40	1.00
23 Lonnie Marts B	.25	.60
24 Jason Sehorn B	.40	1.00
25 Bobby Engram B UER listed as uncommon	.40	1.00
26 Brett Perriman B UER listed as uncommon	.25	.60
27 Stevon Moore B	.25	.60
28 Jamal Anderson B	.40	1.00
29 Wayne Martin B	.25	.60
30 Michael Irvin B UER listed as uncommon	.60	1.50
31 Thomas Smith B	.25	.60
32 Tony Brackens B	.25	.60
33 Eric Davis B	.25	.60
34 James O.Stewart B	.40	1.00
35 Ki-Jana Carter B	.25	.60
36 Ken Norton B	.25	.60
37 William Thomas B	.25	.60
38 Tim Brown B	.60	1.50
39 Lawrence Phillips B	.25	.60
40 Ricky Watters B	.40	1.00
41 Tony Bennett B	.25	.60
42 Jessie Armstead B	.25	.60
43 Trent Dilfer B	.60	1.50
44 Rodney Hampton B	.40	1.00
45 Sam Mills B	.25	.60
46 Rodney Harrison B RC	1.25	3.00
47 Rob Fredrickson B	.25	.60
48 Eric Hill B	.25	.60
49 Bennie Blades B	.25	.60
50 Eddie George B	.60	1.50
51 Dave Brown B	.25	.60
52 Raymont Harris B	.25	.60
53 Steve Tovar B	.25	.60
54 Thurman Thomas B	.60	1.50
55 Leeland McElroy B	.25	.60
56 Brian Mitchell B UER listed as uncommon	.25	.60
57 Eric Allen B	.25	.60
58 Vinny Testaverde B	.40	1.00
59 Marvin Washington B	.25	.60
60 Junior Seau B	.60	1.50
61 Bert Emanuel B	.40	1.00
62 Kevin Carter B	.25	.60
63 Mark Carrier DB B	.25	.60
64 Andre Coleman B	.25	.60
65 Chris Warren B	.40	1.00
66 Aeneas Williams B	.25	.60
67 Eugene Robinson B	.25	.60
68 Darren Woodson B	.25	.60
69 Anthony Johnson B	.25	.60
70 Terry Glenn B	.40	1.00
71 Troy Vincent B	.25	.60
72 John Copeland B	.25	.60
73 Warren Sapp B	.40	1.00
74 Bobby Hebert B	.25	.60
75 Jeff Hostetler B	.25	.60
76 Willie Davis B	.25	.60
77 Mickey Washington B	.25	.60
78 Cortez Kennedy B	.25	.60
79 Michael Strahan B	.40	1.00
80 Jerome Bettis B	.60	1.50
81 Andre Hastings B UER listed as uncommon	.25	.60
82 Simeon Rice B	.40	1.00
83 Cornelius Bennett B	.25	.60
84 Napoleon Kaufman B	.40	1.00
85 Jim Harbaugh B	.40	1.00
86 Aaron Hayden B	.25	.60
87 Gus Frerotte B	.25	.60
88 Jeff Blake B	.40	1.00
89 Anthony Miller B UER listed as uncommon	.25	.60
90 Deion Sanders B	.60	1.50
91 Curtis Conway B	.40	1.00
92 William Floyd B	.40	1.00
93 Eric Moulds B UER listed as uncommon	.40	1.00
94 Mel Gray B	.25	.60
95 Andre Rison B UER listed as uncommon	.40	1.00
96 Eugene Daniel B	.25	.60
97 Jason Belser B	.25	.60
98 Mike Mamula B	.25	.60
99 Jim Everett B	.25	.60
100 Checklist B	.25	.60
101 Drew Bledsoe S	1.25	3.00
102 Shannon Sharpe S	.75	2.00
103 Ken Harvey S	.50	1.25
104 Isaac Bruce S	1.25	3.00
105 Terry Allen S	.75	2.00
106 Lawyer Milloy S	.75	2.00
107 Ashley Ambrose S	.50	1.25
108 Alfred Williams S	.50	1.25
109 Hugh Douglas S	.50	1.25
110 Junior Seau S	1.25	3.00
111 Kordell Stewart S	.75	2.00
112 Adrian Murrell S	.75	2.00
113 Byron Bam Morris S	.50	1.25
114 Terrell Buckley S	.50	1.25
115 Dan Marino S	5.00	12.00
116 Willie Clay S	.50	1.25
117 Neil Smith S	.75	2.00
118 Blaine Bishop S	.50	1.25
119 John Mobley S	.50	1.25
120 Herman Moore S	.75	2.00
121 Keyshawn Johnson S	1.25	3.00
122 Boomer Esiason S	.75	2.00
123 Marshall Faulk S	1.25	3.00
124 Keith Jackson S	.50	1.25
125 Ricky Watters S	.75	2.00
126 Carl Pickens S	.75	2.00
127 Cris Carter S	1.25	3.00
128 Mike Alstott S	1.25	3.00
129 Simeon Rice S	.75	2.00
130 Troy Aikman S	2.50	6.00
131 Tamarick Vanover S	.75	2.00
132 Marquez Pope S	.50	1.25
133 Winslow Oliver S	.50	1.25
134 Edgar Bennett S	.75	2.00
135 Dave Meggett S	.50	1.25
136 Marcus Allen S	1.25	3.00
137 Jerry Rice S	2.50	6.00
138 Steve Atwater S	.50	1.25
139 Tim McDonald S	.50	1.25
140 Barry Sanders S	4.00	10.00
141 Eddie George S	1.25	3.00
142 Wesley Walls S	.50	1.25
143 Jerome Bettis S	1.25	3.00
144 Kevin Greene S	.75	2.00
145 Terrell Davis S	1.25	3.00
146 Gus Frerotte S	.75	2.00
147 Joey Galloway S	.75	2.00
148 Vinny Testaverde S	.75	2.00
149 Hardy Nickerson S	.50	1.25
150 Brett Favre S	5.00	12.00
151 Desmond Howard G	1.25	3.00
152 Keyshawn Johnson G	2.00	5.00
153 Tony Banks G	2.00	5.00
154 Chris Spielman G	.60	1.50
155 Reggie White G	2.00	5.00
156 Zach Thomas G	2.00	5.00
157 Carl Pickens G	1.25	3.00
158 Karim Abdul-Jabbar G	2.00	5.00
159 Chad Brown G	.60	1.50
160 Kerry Collins G	2.00	5.00
161 Marvin Harrison G	2.00	5.00
162 Steve Young G	3.00	8.00
163 Deion Sanders G	2.00	5.00
164 Trent Dilfer G	2.00	5.00
165 Barry Sanders G	6.00	15.00
166 Cris Carter G	2.00	5.00
167 Keenan McCardell G	1.25	3.00
168 Terry Glenn G	2.00	5.00
169 Emmitt Smith G	6.00	15.00
170 John Elway G	7.50	20.00
171 Jerry Rice G	4.00	10.00
172 Troy Aikman G	4.00	10.00
173 Curtis Martin G	2.00	5.00
174 Darrell Green G	1.25	3.00
175 Mark Brunell G	2.00	5.00
176 Corey Dillon B RC	3.00	8.00
177 Tyrone Poole B	.25	.60
178 Anthony Pleasant B	.25	.60
179 Frank Sanders B	.40	1.00
180 Troy Aikman B	1.50	3.00
181 Bill Romanowski B	.25	.60
182 Ty Law B	.40	1.00
183 Orlando Thomas B	.25	.60
184 Quentin Coryatt B	.25	.60
185 Kenny Holmes B RC	.40	1.00
186 Bryant Young B	.25	.60
187 Michael Sinclair B	.25	.60
188 Mike Tomczak B	.25	.60
189 Bobby Taylor B	.25	.60
190 Brett Favre B	3.00	6.00
191 Kent Graham B	.25	.60
192 Jessie Tuggle B	.25	.60
193 Jimmy Smith B	.40	1.00
194 Greg Hill B	.25	.60
195 Yatil Green B RC	.25	.60
196 Mark Fields B	.25	.60
197 Phillippi Sparks B	.25	.60
198 Aaron Glenn B	.25	.60
199 Pat Swilling B	.25	.60
200 Barry Sanders B	2.00	5.00
201 Mark Chmura B	.40	1.00
202 Marco Coleman B	.25	.60
203 Merton Hanks B	.25	.60
204 Brian Blades B	.25	.60
205 Errict Rhett B	.25	.60
206 Henry Ellard B	.25	.60
207 Andre Reed B	.40	1.00
208 Bryan Cox B	.25	.60
209 Darnay Scott B	.40	1.00
210 John Elway B	3.00	6.00
211 Glyn Milburn B	.25	.60
212 Don Beebe B	.25	.60
213 Kevin Lockett B RC	.25	.60
214 Dorsey Levens B	.60	1.50
215 Kordell Stewart B	.60	1.50
216 Larry Centers B	.40	1.00
217 Cris Carter B	.60	1.50
218 Willie McGinest B	.25	.60
219 Renaldo Wynn B RC	.25	.60
220 Jerry Rice B	1.50	3.00
221 Reidel Anthony B RC	.25	.60
222 Mark Carrier WR B	.25	.60
223 Quinn Early B	.25	.60
224 Chris Sanders B	.25	.60
225 Shawn Springs B RC	.25	.60
226 Kevin Smith B	.25	.60
227 Ben Coates B	.40	1.00
228 Tyrone Wheatley B	.40	1.00
229 Antonio Freeman B	.60	1.50
230 Dan Marino B	3.00	6.00
231 Dwayne Rudd B RC	.40	1.00
232 Leslie O'Neal B	.25	.60
233 Brent Jones B	.25	.60
234 Jake Plummer B RC	3.00	8.00
235 Kerry Collins B	.60	1.50
236 Rashaan Salaam B	.25	.60
237 Tyrone Braxton B	.25	.60
238 Herman Moore B	.40	1.00
239 Keyshawn Johnson B	.60	1.50
240 Drew Bledsoe B	.60	1.50
241 Rickey Dudley B	.40	1.00
242 Antowain Smith B RC	2.00	5.00
243 Jeff Lageman B	.25	.60
244 Chris T. Jones B	.25	.60
245 Steve Young B	1.00	2.50
246 Eddie Robinson B	.25	.60
247 Chad Cota B	.25	.60
248 Michael Jackson B	.40	1.00
249 Robert Porcher B	.25	.60
250 Reggie White B	.60	1.50
251 Carnell Lake B	.25	.60
252 Chris Calloway B	.25	.60
253 Terance Mathis B	.40	1.00
254 Carl Pickens B	.40	1.00
255 Curtis Martin B	.60	1.50
256 Jeff Graham B	.25	.60
257 Regan Upshaw B RC	.25	.60
258 Sean Gilbert B	.25	.60
259 Will Blackwell B RC	.25	.60
260 Emmitt Smith B	2.50	5.00
261 Reinard Wilson B RC	.25	.60
262 Darrell Russell B RC	.25	.60
263 Wayne Chrebet B	.40	1.00
264 Kevin Hardy B	.25	.60
265 Shannon Sharpe B	.60	1.50
266 Harvey Williams B	.25	.60
267 John Randle B	.40	1.00
268 Tim Bowens B	.25	.60
269 Tony Gonzalez B RC	3.00	8.00
270 Warrick Dunn B RC	2.50	6.00
271 Sean Dawkins B	.25	.60
272 Darryll Lewis B	.25	.60
273 Alonzo Spellman B	.25	.60
274 Mark Collins B	.25	.60
275 Checklist Card B	.25	.60
276 Pat Barnes S RC	.50	1.25
277 Dana Stubblefield S	.75	2.00
278 Dan Wilkinson S	.50	1.25
279 Bryce Paup S	.50	1.25
280 Kerry Collins S	1.25	3.00
281 Derrick Brooks S	1.25	3.00
282 Walter Jones S RC	1.25	3.00
283 Terry McDaniel S	.50	1.25
284 James Farrior S RC	1.25	3.00
285 Curtis Martin S	1.25	3.00
286 O.J. McDuffie S	.75	2.00
287 Natrone Means S	.75	2.00
288 Bryant Westbrook S RC	.75	2.00
289 Peter Boulware S RC	1.25	3.00
290 Emmitt Smith S	4.00	10.00
291 Joey Kent S RC	.75	2.00
292 Eddie Kennison S	.75	2.00
293 LeRoy Butler S	.50	1.25
294 Dale Carter S	.50	1.25
295 Jim Druckenmiller S RC	.75	2.00
296 Byron Hanspard S RC	.75	2.00
297 Jeff Blake S	.75	2.00
298 Levon Kirkland S	.50	1.25
299 Michael Westbrook S	.50	1.25
300 John Elway S	5.00	12.00
301 Lamar Lathon S	.50	1.25
302 Ray Lewis S	2.00	5.00
303 Steve McNair S	1.25	3.00
304 Shawn Springs S	.50	1.25
305 Karim Abdul-Jabbar S	.75	2.00
306 Orlando Pace S RC	1.25	3.00
307 Scott Mitchell S	.50	1.25
308 Walt Harris S	.50	1.25
309 Bruce Smith S	.75	2.00
310 Reggie White S	1.25	3.00
311 Eric Swann S	.50	1.25
312 Derrick Thomas S	1.25	3.00
313 Tony Martin S	.75	2.00
314 Darrell Russell S RC	.75	2.00
315 Mark Brunell S	1.25	3.00
316 Trent Dilfer S	1.25	3.00
317 Irving Fryar S	.50	1.25
318 Amani Toomer S	.75	2.00
319 Jake Reed S	.75	2.00
320 Steve Young S	2.00	5.00
321 Troy Davis S RC	.75	2.00
322 Jim Harbaugh S	.75	2.00
323 Neil O'Donnell S	.50	1.25
324 Terry Glenn S	.75	2.00
325 Deion Sanders S	1.25	3.00
326 Gus Frerotte G	1.25	3.00
327 Tom Knight G RC	1.25	3.00
328 Peter Boulware G	1.25	3.00
329 Jerome Bettis G	2.00	5.00
330 Orlando Pace G	2.00	5.00
331 Darnell Autry G RC	1.25	3.00
332 Ike Hilliard G RC	3.00	8.00
333 David LaFleur G RC	.60	1.50
334 Jim Harbaugh G	1.25	3.00
335 Eddie George G	2.00	5.00
336 Vinny Testaverde G	1.25	3.00
337 Terry Allen G	1.25	3.00
338 Jim Druckenmiller G	1.25	3.00
339 Ricky Watters G	1.25	3.00
340 Brett Favre G	7.50	20.00
341 Simeon Rice G	1.25	3.00
342 Shannon Sharpe G	2.00	5.00
343 Kordell Stewart G	2.00	5.00
344 Isaac Bruce G	2.00	5.00
345 Drew Bledsoe G	2.00	5.00
346 Jeff Blake G	1.25	3.00
347 Herman Moore G	1.25	3.00
348 Junior Seau G	2.00	5.00
349 Rae Carruth G RC	.60	1.50
350 Dan Marino G	7.50	20.00
P5 K.Abdul-Jabbar Promo	.60	1.50
P20 Isaac Bruce Promo	.75	2.00
P32 Tony Brackens Promo	.60	1.50
P45 Sam Mills Promo	.60	1.50
P70 Terry Glenn Promo	.60	1.50
P87 Gus Frerotte Promo	.60	1.50

1997 Finest Atomic Refractors

*GOLD: 2.5X TO 6X BASIC CARDS

1997 Finest Embossed

*SILVER: .8X TO 2X BASIC CARDS
SILVER STATED ODDS 1:16
*GOLD: 1X TO 2.5X BASIC CARDS
GOLD STATED ODDS 1:96

1997 Finest Embossed Refractors

*SILVER: 2X TO 5X BASIC CARDS
SILVER STATED ODDS 1:192
*GOLD: 2.5X TO 6X BASIC CARDS
GOLD STATED ODDS 1:1152

1997 Finest Refractors

*BRONZE VETS: 1.2X TO 3X BASIC CARDS
*BRONZE ROOKIES: 1X TO 2.5X
BRONZE REFRACTOR ODDS 1:12
*SILVER: 1X TO 2.5X BASIC CARDS
SILVER REFRACTOR ODDS 1:48
*GOLD: 1.2X TO 3X BASIC CARDS
GOLD REFRACTOR ODDS 1:288

1998 Finest Promos

This set of cards was distributed to hobbyists to promote the upcoming 1998 Finest football card release. Each card is nearly identical to the matching base issue card except for the card number on back.

COMPLETE SET (6)	4.00	10.00
PP1 Jerome Bettis	.60	1.50
PP2 Cris Carter	.60	1.50
PP3 Tony Gonzalez	.80	2.00
PP4 Tim Brown	.60	1.50
PP5 Mark Brunell	1.20	3.00
PP6 Antonio Freeman	.60	1.50

1998 Finest

The 1998 Finest set was issued in two series totalling 270 cards and was distributed in six-card packs with a suggested price of $5. The fronts feature color action player photos printed on 29 pt. card stock, while the backs display player information. Series 1 contains the subset Rookies (121-150). The 120 cards in Series 2 are organized by player position, each of which is identified by a different graphic.

COMPLETE SET (270)	30.00	80.00
COMP.SERIES 1 (150)	20.00	50.00
COMP.SERIES 2 (120)	12.50	30.00
1 John Elway	1.50	4.00
2 Terance Mathis	.25	.60
3 Jermaine Lewis	.25	.60
4 Fred Lane	.15	.40
5 Simeon Rice	.25	.60
6 David Dunn	.15	.40
7 Dexter Coakley	.15	.40
8 Carl Pickens	.25	.60
9 Antonio Freeman	.40	1.00
10 Herman Moore	.25	.60
11 Kevin Hardy	.15	.40
12 Tony Gonzalez	.40	1.00
13 O.J. McDuffie	.25	.60
14 David Palmer	.15	.40
15 Lawyer Milloy	.25	.60
16 Danny Kanell	.25	.60
17 Randal Hill	.15	.40
18 Chris Slade	.15	.40
19 Charlie Garner	.25	.60
20 Mark Brunell	.40	1.00
21 Donnell Woolford	.15	.40
22 Freddie Jones	.15	.40
23 Ken Norton	.15	.40
24 Tony Banks	.25	.60
25 Isaac Bruce	.40	1.00
26 Willie Davis	.15	.40
27 Cris Dishman	.15	.40
28 Aeneas Williams	.15	.40
29 Michael Booker	.15	.40
30 Cris Carter	.40	1.00
31 Michael McCrary	.15	.40
32 Eric Moulds	.40	1.00
33 Rae Carruth	.15	.40
34 Bobby Engram	.25	.60
35 Jeff Blake	.25	.60
36 Deion Sanders	.40	1.00
37 Rod Smith	.25	.60
38 Bryant Westbrook	.15	.40
39 Mark Chmura	.25	.60
40 Tim Brown	.40	1.00
41 Bobby Taylor	.15	.40
42 James Stewart	.25	.60
43 Kimble Anders	.25	.60
44 Karim Abdul-Jabbar	.40	1.00
45 Willie McGinest	.15	.40
46 Jessie Armstead	.15	.40
47 Brad Johnson	.40	1.00
48 Greg Lloyd	.15	.40
49 Stephen Davis	.15	.40
50 Jerome Bettis	.40	1.00
51 Warren Sapp	.25	.60
52 Horace Copeland	.15	.40
53 Chad Brown	.15	.40
54 Chris Canty	.15	.40
55 Robert Smith	.40	1.00
56 Pete Mitchell	.15	.40
57 Aaron Bailey	.15	.40
58 Robert Porcher	.15	.40
59 John Mobley	.15	.40
60 Tony Martin	.25	.60
61 Michael Irvin	.40	1.00
62 Charles Way	.15	.40
63 Raymont Harris	.15	.40
64 Chuck Smith	.15	.40
65 Larry Centers	.15	.40
66 Greg Hill	.15	.40
67 Kenny Holmes	.15	.40
68 John Lynch	.25	.60
69 Michael Sinclair	.15	.40
70 Steve Young	.50	1.25
71 Michael Strahan	.25	.60
72 Levon Kirkland	.15	.40
73 Rickey Dudley	.15	.40
74 Marcus Allen	.40	1.00
75 John Randle	.25	.60
76 Erik Kramer	.15	.40
77 Neil Smith	.25	.60
78 Byron Hanspard	.15	.40
79 Quinn Early	.15	.40
80 Warren Moon	.40	1.00
81 William Thomas	.15	.40
82 Ben Coates	.25	.60
83 Lake Dawson	.15	.40
84 Steve McNair	.40	1.00
85 Gus Frerotte	.15	.40
86 Rodney Harrison	.25	.60
87 Reggie White	.40	1.00
88 Derrick Thomas	.40	1.00
89 Dale Carter	.15	.40
90 Warrick Dunn	.40	1.00
91 Will Blackwell	.15	.40
92 Troy Vincent	.15	.40
93 Johnnie Morton	.25	.60
94 David LaFleur	.15	.40
95 Tony McGee	.15	.40
96 Lonnie Johnson	.15	.40
97 Thurman Thomas	.40	1.00
98 Chris Chandler	.25	.60
99 Jamal Anderson	.40	1.00
100 Checklist	.15	.40
101 Marshall Faulk	.60	1.50
102 Chris Calloway	.15	.40
103 Chris Spielman	.15	.40
104 Zach Thomas	.40	1.00
105 Jeff George	.25	.60
106 Darrell Russell	.15	.40
107 Darryll Lewis	.15	.40
108 Reidel Anthony	.25	.60
109 Terrell Owens	.40	1.00
110 Rob Moore	.25	.60
111 Darrell Green	.25	.60
112 Merton Hanks	.15	.40
113 Shawn Jefferson	.15	.40
114 Chris Sanders	.15	.40
115 Scott Mitchell	.25	.60
116 Vaughn Hebron	.15	.40
117 Ed McCaffrey	.25	.60
118 Bruce Smith	.25	.60
119 Peter Boulware	.15	.40
120 Brett Favre	1.50	4.00
121 Peyton Manning RC	15.00	40.00
122 Brian Griese RC	2.00	5.00
123 Tavian Banks RC	.60	1.50
124 Duane Starks RC	.40	1.00
125 Robert Holcombe RC	.60	1.50
126 Brian Simmons RC	.60	1.50
127 Skip Hicks RC	.60	1.50
128 Keith Brooking RC	1.00	2.50
129 Ahman Green RC	2.50	6.00
130 Jerome Pathon RC	1.00	2.50
131 Curtis Enis RC	.40	1.00
132 Grant Wistrom RC	.60	1.50
133 Germane Crowell RC	.60	1.50
134 Jacquez Green RC	.60	1.50
135 Randy Moss RC	6.00	15.00
136 Jason Peter RC	.40	1.00
137 John Avery RC	.60	1.50
138 Takeo Spikes RC	1.00	2.50
139 Pat Johnson RC	.60	1.50
140 Andre Wadsworth RC	.60	1.50
141 Fred Taylor RC	1.50	4.00
142 Charles Woodson RC	1.25	3.00
143 Marcus Nash RC	.40	1.00
144 Robert Edwards RC	.60	1.50
145 Kevin Dyson RC	1.00	2.50
146 Joe Jurevicius RC	1.00	2.50
147 Anthony Simmons RC	.60	1.50
148 Hines Ward RC	5.00	10.00
149 Greg Ellis RC	.40	1.00
150 Ryan Leaf RC	1.00	2.50
151 Jerry Rice	.75	2.00
152 Tony Martin	.25	.60
153 Checklist	.15	.40
154 Rob Johnson	.25	.60
155 Shannon Sharpe	.25	.60
156 Bert Emanuel	.25	.60
157 Eric Metcalf	.15	.40
158 Natrone Means	.25	.60
159 Derrick Alexander	.25	.60
160 Emmitt Smith	1.25	3.00
161 Jeff Burris	.15	.40
162 Chris Warren	.25	.60
163 Corey Fuller	.15	.40
164 Courtney Hawkins	.15	.40
165 James McKnight	.40	1.00
166 Shawn Springs	.15	.40
167 Wayne Martin	.15	.40
168 Michael Westbrook	.25	.60
169 Michael Jackson	.15	.40
170 Dan Marino	1.50	4.00
171 Amp Lee	.15	.40
172 James Jett	.25	.60
173 Ty Law	.25	.60
174 Kerry Collins	.25	.60
175 Robert Brooks	.25	.60
176 Blaine Bishop	.15	.40
177 Stephen Boyd	.15	.40
178 Keyshawn Johnson	.40	1.00
179 Deon Figures	.15	.40
180 Allen Aldridge	.15	.40
181 Corey Miller	.15	.40
182 Chad Lewis	.25	.60
183 Derrick Rodgers	.15	.40
184 Troy Drayton	.15	.40
185 Darren Woodson	.15	.40
186 Ken Dilger	.15	.40
187 Elvis Grbac	.25	.60
188 Terrell Fletcher	.15	.40
189 Frank Sanders	.25	.60
190 Curtis Martin	.40	1.00
191 Derrick Brooks	.40	1.00
192 Darrien Gordon	.15	.40
193 Andre Reed	.25	.60
194 Darnay Scott	.25	.60
195 Curtis Conway	.25	.60
196 Tim McDonald	.15	.40
197 Sean Dawkins	.15	.40
198 Napoleon Kaufman	.40	1.00
199 Willie Clay	.15	.40
200 Terrell Davis	.40	1.00
201 Wesley Walls	.25	.60
202 Santana Dotson	.15	.40
203 Frank Wycheck	.15	.40
204 Wayne Chrebet	.40	1.00
205 Andre Rison	.25	.60
206 Jason Sehorn	.25	.60
207 Jessie Tuggle	.15	.40
208 Kevin Turner	.15	.40
209 Jason Taylor	.25	.60
210 Yancey Thigpen	.15	.40
211 Jake Reed	.25	.60
212 Carnell Lake	.15	.40
213 Joey Galloway	.25	.60
214 Andre Hastings	.15	.40
215 Terry Allen	.40	1.00
216 Jim Harbaugh	.25	.60
217 Tony Banks	.25	.60
218 Greg Clark	.15	.40
219 Corey Dillon	.40	1.00
220 Troy Aikman	.75	2.00
221 Antowain Smith	.40	1.00
222 Steve Atwater	.15	.40
223 Trent Dilfer	.40	1.00
224 Junior Seau	.40	1.00
225 Garrison Hearst	.40	1.00
226 Eric Allen	.15	.40
227 Chad Cota	.15	.40
228 Vinny Testaverde	.25	.60
229 Duce Staley	.50	1.25
230 Drew Bledsoe	.60	1.50
231 Charles Johnson	.15	.40
232 Jake Plummer	.40	1.00
233 Errict Rhett	.25	.60
234 Doug Evans	.15	.40
235 Phillippi Sparks	.15	.40
236 Ashley Ambrose	.15	.40
237 Bryan Cox	.15	.40
238 Kevin Smith	.15	.40
239 Hardy Nickerson	.15	.40
240 Terry Glenn	.40	1.00
241 Lee Woodall	.15	.40
242 Andre Coleman	.15	.40
243 Michael Bates	.15	.40
244 Mark Fields	.15	.40
245 Eddie Kennison	.25	.60
246 Dana Stubblefield	.15	.40
247 Bobby Hoying	.25	.60
248 Mo Lewis	.15	.40
249 Derrick Mayes	.25	.60
250 Eddie George	.40	1.00
251 Mike Alstott	.40	1.00
252 J.J. Stokes	.25	.60
253 Adrian Murrell	.25	.60
254 Kevin Greene	.25	.60
255 LeRoy Butler	.15	.40
256 Glenn Foley	.25	.60
257 Jimmy Smith	.25	.60
258 Tiki Barber	.40	1.00
259 Irving Fryar	.25	.60
260 Ricky Watters	.25	.60
261 Jeff Graham	.15	.40
262 Kordell Stewart	.40	1.00
263 Rod Woodson	.25	.60
264 Leslie Shepherd	.15	.40
265 Ryan McNeil	.15	.40
266 Ike Hilliard	.25	.60
267 Keenan McCardell	.25	.60
268 Marvin Harrison	.40	1.00
269 Dorsey Levens	.40	1.00
270 Barry Sanders	1.25	3.00

1998 Finest No-Protectors

COMPLETE SET (270) 150.00 300.00
*NO-PROTECTOR STARS: 1.25X TO 3X BASIC CARDS
*NO-PROTECTOR RCs: .5X TO 1.2X BASIC CARDS
STATED ODDS 1:2 HOB/RET, 1 PER JUMBO

1998 Finest No-Protectors Refractors

COMPLETE SET (270) 1,000.00 1,800.00
*NP REF STARS: 6X TO 15X BASIC CARDS
*NP REF RC'S: 1.5X TO 4X BASIC CARDS
NP.REFRACT.ODDS 1:24 H/R, 1:10 JUM

1998 Finest Refractors

COMP.REFRACT.SET (270) 500.00 1,000.00
*REFRACT.STARS: 3X TO 8X
*REFRACTOR RCs: 1X TO 2.5X
REFRACTOR ODDS 1:12H/R, 1:5J
1-120 REFRACTORS IN SERIES 1 PACKS
121-270 REFRACTORS SERIES 2 PACKS

1998 Finest Centurions

COMPLETE SET (20) 125.00 250.00
CENTURIAN/500 ODDS 1:125H/R, 1:58J
*REFRACT/75: .75X TO 2X BASIC INSERT
REFRACTOR/75 ODDS 1:831H/R, 1:383J

C1 Brett Favre	25.00	60.00
C2 Eddie George	6.00	15.00
C3 Antonio Freeman	6.00	15.00
C4 Napoleon Kaufman	6.00	15.00
C5 Terrell Davis	6.00	15.00
C6 Keyshawn Johnson	6.00	15.00
C7 Peter Boulware	2.50	6.00
C8 Mike Alstott	6.00	15.00
C9 Jake Plummer	6.00	15.00
C10 Mark Brunell	6.00	15.00
C11 Marvin Harrison	6.00	15.00
C12 Antowain Smith	6.00	15.00
C13 Dorsey Levens	4.00	10.00
C14 Terry Glenn	4.00	10.00
C15 Warrick Dunn	6.00	15.00
C16 Joey Galloway	4.00	10.00
C17 Steve McNair	6.00	15.00
C18 Corey Dillon	6.00	15.00
C19 Drew Bledsoe	10.00	25.00
C20 Kordell Stewart	6.00	15.00

1998 Finest Future's Finest

COMPLETE SET (20) 125.00 250.00
STATED PRINT RUN 500 SERIAL #'d SETS
*REFRACT/75: 1X TO 2.5X BASIC INSERTS
REFRACTOR/75 ODDS 1:557
REF.STATED PRINT RUN 75 SERIAL #'d SETS

F1 Peyton Manning	30.00	60.00
F2 Napoleon Kaufman	5.00	12.00
F3 Jake Plummer	5.00	12.00
F4 Terry Glenn	5.00	12.00
F5 Ryan Leaf	5.00	12.00
F6 Drew Bledsoe	7.50	20.00
F7 Dorsey Levens	4.00	10.00
F8 Andre Wadsworth	4.00	10.00
F9 Joey Galloway	4.00	10.00
F10 Curtis Enis	4.00	10.00
F11 Warrick Dunn	5.00	12.00
F12 Kordell Stewart	4.00	10.00
F13 Randy Moss	15.00	40.00
F14 Robert Edwards	4.00	10.00
F15 Eddie George	5.00	12.00
F16 Fred Taylor	5.00	12.00
F17 Corey Dillon	5.00	12.00
F18 Brett Favre	20.00	50.00
F19 Kevin Dyson	5.00	12.00
F20 Terrell Davis	5.00	12.00

1998 Finest Jumbos 1

COMPLETE SET (8) 50.00 100.00
STATED ODDS 1:3 BOXES
*REFRACTORS: .8X TO 2X BASIC INSERTS
REFRACTOR ODDS 1:12 BOXES

1 John Elway	8.00	20.00
2 Peyton Manning	20.00	40.00
3 Mark Brunell	2.00	5.00
4 Curtis Enis	.60	1.50
5 Jerome Bettis	2.00	5.00
6 Ryan Leaf	.60	1.50
7 Warrick Dunn	2.00	5.00
8 Brett Favre	8.00	20.00

1998 Finest Jumbos 2

COMPLETE SET (7) 40.00 80.00
STATED ODDS 1:3 BOXES
*REFRACTORS: .8X TO 2X BASIC INSERTS
REFRACTOR STATED ODDS 1:12 BOXES

151 Jerry Rice	4.00	10.00
160 Emmitt Smith	6.00	15.00
170 Dan Marino	8.00	20.00
213 Joey Galloway	1.25	3.00
230 Drew Bledsoe	3.00	8.00
250 Eddie George	2.00	5.00
270 Barry Sanders	6.00	15.00

1998 Finest Mystery Finest 1

COMPLETE SET (50) 300.00 600.00
STATED ODDS 1:36H/R, 1:15J
*REFRACTORS: .6X TO 1.5X
REFRACT.STATED ODDS 1:144H/R, 1:64J

M1 Brett Favre Mark Brunell	10.00	25.00
M2 Brett Favre Jake Plummer	10.00	25.00
M3 Brett Favre Steve Young	10.00	25.00
M4 Brett Favre Brett Favre	12.50	30.00
M5 Mark Brunell Steve Young	4.00	10.00
M6 Mark Brunell Mark Brunell	4.00	10.00
M7 Jake Plummer Mark Brunell	4.00	10.00
M8 Jake Plummer Jake Plummer	4.00	10.00
M9 Steve Young Jake Plummer	4.00	10.00
M10 Steve Young Steve Young	4.00	10.00
M11 John Elway Drew Bledsoe	10.00	25.00
M12 John Elway Troy Aikman	10.00	25.00
M13 John Elway Dan Marino	12.50	30.00
M14 John Elway John Elway	12.50	30.00
M15 Drew Bledsoe Troy Aikman	6.00	15.00
M16 Drew Bledsoe Drew Bledsoe	5.00	12.00
M17 Troy Aikman Dan Marino	10.00	25.00
M18 Troy Aikman Troy Aikman	6.00	15.00
M19 Dan Marino Drew Bledsoe	10.00	25.00
M20 Dan Marino Dan Marino	12.50	30.00
M21 Kordell Stewart Corey Dillon	2.50	6.00
M22 Kordell Stewart Tim Brown	2.50	6.00
M23 Kordell Stewart Barry Sanders	7.50	20.00
M24 Kordell Stewart Kordell Stewart	2.50	6.00
M25 Corey Dillon Tim Brown	4.00	10.00
M26 Corey Dillon Corey Dillon	4.00	10.00
M27 Tim Brown Barry Sanders	7.50	20.00
M28 Tim Brown Tim Brown	2.50	6.00
M29 Barry Sanders Corey Dillon	7.50	20.00
M30 Barry Sanders Barry Sanders	10.00	25.00
M31 Terrell Davis Emmitt Smith	7.50	20.00
M32 Terrell Davis Jerome Bettis	4.00	10.00
M33 Terrell Davis Eddie George	4.00	10.00
M34 Terrell Davis Terrell Davis	4.00	10.00
M35 Emmitt Smith Eddie George	7.50	20.00
M36 Emmitt Smith Emmitt Smith	10.00	25.00
M37 Jerome Bettis Emmitt Smith	7.50	20.00
M38 Jerome Bettis Jerome Bettis	4.00	10.00
M39 Eddie George Jerome Bettis	4.00	10.00
M40 Eddie George Eddie George	4.00	10.00
M41 Herman Moore Jerry Rice	6.00	15.00
M42 Herman Moore Herman Moore	1.50	4.00
M43 Warrick Dunn Herman Moore	2.50	6.00
M44 Warrick Dunn Jerry Rice	6.00	15.00
M45 Warrick Dunn Dorsey Levens	2.50	6.00
M46 Warrick Dunn Warrick Dunn	4.00	10.00
M47 Jerry Rice Dorsey Levens	6.00	15.00
M48 Jerry Rice Jerry Rice	7.50	20.00
M49 D.Levens Herman Moore	1.50	4.00
M50 Dorsey Levens Dorsey Levens	1.50	4.00

1998 Finest Mystery Finest 2

COMPLETE SET (40) 200.00 400.00
STATED ODDS 1:36
*REFRACTORS: .6X TO 1.5X
REFRACTOR STATED ODDS 1:144

M1 Brett Favre Dan Marino	10.00	25.00
M2 Brett Favre Peyton Manning	15.00	30.00
M3 Brett Favre Ryan Leaf	6.00	15.00
M4 Dan Marino Peyton Manning	15.00	30.00
M5 Dan Marino Ryan Leaf	6.00	15.00
M6 Peyton Manning Ryan Leaf	12.50	25.00
M7 Barry Sanders Emmitt Smith	10.00	25.00
M8 Barry Sanders Curtis Enis	6.00	15.00
M9 Barry Sanders Fred Taylor	5.00	12.00
M10 Emmitt Smith Curtis Enis	5.00	12.00
M11 Emmitt Smith Fred Taylor	5.00	12.00
M12 Curtis Enis Fred Taylor	2.50	6.00
M13 John Elway Jerry Rice	7.50	20.00
M14 John Elway Randy Moss	20.00	40.00
M15 John Elway Charles Woodson	6.00	15.00
M16 Jerry Rice Randy Moss	15.00	30.00
M17 Jerry Rice Charles Woodson	4.00	10.00
M18 Randy Moss Charles Woodson	15.00	30.00
M19 Terrell Davis Kordell Stewart	4.00	10.00
M20 Terrell Davis Ricky Watters	4.00	10.00
M21 Terrell Davis Kevin Dyson	4.00	10.00
M22 Kordell Stewart Ricky Watters	4.00	10.00
M23 Kordell Stewart Kevin Dyson	4.00	10.00
M24 Ricky Watters Kevin Dyson	1.50	4.00
M25 Warrick Dunn Eddie George	4.00	10.00
M26 Warrick Dunn Curtis Martin	1.50	4.00
M27 Warrick Dunn Robert Edwards	2.50	6.00
M28 Eddie George Curtis Martin	4.00	10.00
M29 Eddie George Robert Edwards	4.00	10.00
M30 Curtis Martin Robert Edwards	4.00	10.00
M31 Peyton Manning Peyton Manning	15.00	30.00
M32 Ryan Leaf Ryan Leaf	4.00	10.00
M33 Curtis Enis Curtis Enis	1.50	4.00
M34 Fred Taylor Fred Taylor	2.50	6.00
M35 Randy Moss Randy Moss	15.00	30.00
M36 Charles Woodson Charles Woodson	4.00	10.00
M37 Ricky Watters Ricky Watters	1.50	4.00
M38 Kevin Dyson Kevin Dyson	2.50	6.00
M39 Curtis Martin Curtis Martin	2.50	6.00
M40 Robert Edwards Robert Edwards	2.50	6.00

1998 Finest Mystery Finest Jumbos 2

COMPLETE SET (3) 12.50 30.00
STATED ODDS 1:4 BOXES
*REFRACTORS: .75X TO 2X
REFRACTOR STATED ODDS 1:17 BOXES

M3 Brett Favre Ryan Leaf	6.00	15.00
M8 Barry Sanders Curtis Enis	6.00	15.00
M16 Jerry Rice Randy Moss	12.50	25.00

1998 Finest Stadium Stars

COMPLETE SET (20) 40.00 100.00
STATED ODDS 1:45

S1 Barry Sanders	4.00	10.00
S2 Steve Young	1.50	4.00
S3 Emmitt Smith	4.00	10.00
S4 Mark Brunell	1.25	3.00
S5 Curtis Martin	1.25	3.00
S6 Kordell Stewart	1.25	3.00
S7 Jerry Rice	2.50	6.00
S8 Warrick Dunn	1.25	3.00
S9 Peyton Manning	10.00	20.00
S10 Brett Favre	5.00	12.00
S11 Terrell Davis	1.25	3.00
S12 Cris Carter	1.25	3.00
S13 Herman Moore	.75	2.00

S14 Troy Aikman	2.50	6.00
S15 Tim Brown	1.25	3.00
S16 Dan Marino	5.00	12.00
S17 Drew Bledsoe	2.00	5.00
S18 Jerome Bettis	1.25	3.00
S19 Ryan Leaf	.60	1.50
S20 John Elway	5.00	12.00

1998 Finest Undergrads

COMPLETE SET (20)	50.00	120.00
STATED ODDS 1:72H/R, 1:32J		
*REFRACTORS: .6X TO 1.5X BASIC INSERTS		
REFRACT.STATED ODDS 1:216H/R, 1:96J		
U1 Warrick Dunn	1.00	2.50
U2 Tony Gonzalez	1.00	2.50
U3 Antowain Smith	.60	1.50
U4 Jake Plummer	1.00	2.50
U5 Peter Boulware	.30	.75
U6 Derrick Rodgers	.30	.75
U7 Freddie Jones	.30	.75
U8 Reidel Anthony	.30	.75
U9 Bryant Westbrook	.30	.75
U10 Corey Dillon	1.00	2.50
U11 Curtis Enis	.30	.75
U12 Andre Wadsworth	.60	1.50
U13 Fred Taylor	1.50	4.00
U14 Greg Ellis	.30	.75
U15 Ryan Leaf	.60	1.50
U16 Robert Edwards	.60	1.50
U17 Germane Crowell	.30	.75
U18 Brian Griese	2.00	5.00
U19 Kevin Dyson	1.00	2.50
U20 Peyton Manning	15.00	30.00

1998-99 Finest Pro Bowl Jumbos

This set of cards was distributed by Topps for the 1999 Pro Bowl Card Show in Hawaii. Each card measures roughly 4" by 5 5/8" and is essentially an enlarged version of the base Finest card with a Pro Bowl logo on the cardfronts. A Refractor version of each card was also issued.

COMPLETE SET (12)	20.00	50.00
*REFRACTORS: 3X TO 8X		
1 John Elway	3.00	8.00
2 Steve Young	1.50	4.00
3 Brett Favre	3.00	8.00
4 Fred Taylor	2.00	5.00
5 Robert Edwards	1.25	3.00
6 Peyton Manning	4.00	10.00
7 Randy Moss	2.00	5.00
8 Jerry Rice	1.50	4.00
9 Dan Marino	3.00	8.00
10 Terrell Davis	1.50	4.00
11 Drew Bledsoe	1.25	3.00
12 Barry Sanders	2.50	6.00

1998-99 Finest Pro Bowl Promos 5X7

1 John Elway	3.00	8.00
2 Brett Favre	3.00	8.00
3 Terrell Davis	1.50	4.00
4 Randy Moss	2.00	5.00
5 Barry Sanders	2.50	6.00
6 Steve Young	1.25	3.00

1998-99 Finest Super Bowl Jumbos

This set of cards was distributed by Topps for the Super Bowl XXXIII Card Show in Miami. Each card measures roughly 4" by 5 5/8" and is essentially an enlarged version of the base Finest card. Each card was distributed in exchange for 5-Topps wrappers at the show.

COMPLETE SET (12)	24.00	60.00
1 John Elway	3.20	8.00
2 Steve Young	1.20	3.00
3 Brett Favre	3.20	8.00
4 Fred Taylor	2.40	6.00
5 Robert Edwards	1.20	3.00
6 Peyton Manning	4.00	10.00
7 Randy Moss	5.00	10.00
8 Jerry Rice	1.60	4.00
9 Dan Marino	3.20	8.00
10 Terrell Davis	2.40	6.00
11 Drew Bledsoe	1.20	3.00
12 Barry Sanders	3.20	8.00

1998-99 Finest Super Bowl Promos

This six card set and accompaning Refractors set was released at the 1999 Super Bowl Card Show in Miami and the Hawaii Trade Conference in February 1999. Each is numbered "X of 6" and features the Super Bowl XXXIII logo on the cardfront.

COMPLETE SET (6)	10.00	25.00
*REFRACTORS: 2X TO 4X BASE CARD		
1 Terrell Davis	2.00	5.00
2 Steve Young	1.20	3.00
3 Brett Favre	2.40	6.00
4 Fred Taylor	1.60	4.00
5 Robert Edwards	1.20	3.00
6 Randy Moss	5.00	10.00

1999 Finest Promos

This set of cards was distributed to hobbyists to promote the upcoming 1999 Finest football card release. Each card is nearly identical to the matching base issue card except for the card number on the back.

COMPLETE SET (6)	3.00	8.00
PP1 Charlie Batch	.40	1.00
PP2 Jimmy Smith	.50	1.25
PP3 Jake Plummer	.60	1.50
PP4 O.J. McDuffie	.40	1.00
PP5 Curtis Martin	.75	2.00
PP6 Corey Dillon	.60	1.50

1999 Finest

The 1999 Finest set was released in mid September 1999 as a 175-card single series set consisting of 124 veterans and 51 bonus base cards, divided into three subsets, Rookies, Gems, and Sensations. The short printed Rookies subset contains the games best young players such as Edgerrin James and Ricky Williams each being designated with the Finest Rookie Card logo stamp. Gems showcases 11 of todays biggest stars with each cards background featuring an etched "gem" pattern. Sensations features 11 emerging talents such as Peyton Manning and Randy Moss. Each cards background is highlighted with a multi-etched design. Each base card is printed on a 27 pt. thickness stock. The S.R.P. is $5.00 per pack with five cards in a pack. Thirteen card collector packs, available exclusively through Home Team Advantage stores, contain eleven base cards plus two bonus cards with an S.R.P. of $10.00 per pack.

COMPLETE SET (175)	30.00	80.00
COMP.SET w/o SPs (124)	15.00	30.00
1 Peyton Manning	1.25	3.00
2 Priest Holmes	.40	1.00
3 Kordell Stewart	.30	.75
4 Shannon Sharpe	.40	1.00
5 Andre Rison	.30	.75
6 Rickey Dudley	.25	.60
7 Duce Staley	.30	.75
8 Randall Cunningham	.40	1.00
9 Warrick Dunn	.30	.75
10 Dan Marino	1.25	3.00
11 Kevin Greene	.30	.75
12 Garrison Hearst	.30	.75
13 Eric Moulds	.30	.75
14 Marvin Harrison	.40	1.00
15 Eddie George	.30	.75
16 Vinny Testaverde	.30	.75
17 Brad Johnson	.30	.75
18 Derrick Thomas	.40	1.00
19 Chris Chandler	.30	.75
20 Troy Aikman	.60	1.50
21 Terance Mathis	.25	.60
22 Terrell Owens	.40	1.00
23 Junior Seau	.40	1.00
24 Cris Carter	.40	1.00
25 Fred Taylor	.30	.75
26 Adrian Murrell	.30	.75
27 Terry Glenn	.30	.75
28 Rod Smith	.30	.75
29 Darnay Scott	.25	.60
30 Brett Favre	1.25	3.00
31 Cam Cleeland	.25	.60
32 Ricky Watters	.30	.75
33 Derrick Alexander	.25	.60
34 Bruce Smith	.40	1.00
35 Steve McNair	.40	1.00
36 Wayne Chrebet	.30	.75
37 Herman Moore	.30	.75
38 Bert Emanuel	.30	.75
39 Michael Irvin	.40	1.00
40 Steve Young	.50	1.25
41 Napoleon Kaufman	.25	.60
42 Tim Biakabutuka	.30	.75
43 Isaac Bruce	.40	1.00
44 J.J. Stokes	.25	.60
45 Antonio Freeman	.30	.75
46 John Randle	.30	.75
47 Frank Sanders	.25	.60
48 O.J. McDuffie	.30	.75
49 Keenan McCardell	.30	.75
50 Randy Moss	.40	1.00
51 Ed McCaffrey	.30	.75
52 Yancey Thigpen	.25	.60
53 Curtis Conway	.30	.75
54 Mike Alstott	.40	1.00
55 Deion Sanders	.40	1.00
56 Dorsey Levens	.30	.75
57 Joey Galloway	.30	.75
58 Natrone Means	.30	.75
59 Tim Brown	.40	1.00
60 Jerry Rice	.75	2.00
61 Robert Smith	.30	.75
62 Carl Pickens	.30	.75
63 Ben Coates	.30	.75
64 Jerome Bettis	.40	1.00
65 Corey Dillon	.30	.75
66 Curtis Martin	.40	1.00
67 Jimmy Smith	.30	.75
68 Keyshawn Johnson	.30	.75
69 Charlie Batch	.30	.75
70 Jamal Anderson	.30	.75
71 Mark Brunell	.30	.75
72 Antowain Smith	.25	.60
73 Aeneas Williams	.25	.60
74 Wesley Walls	.30	.75
75 Jake Plummer	.30	.75
76 Oronde Gadsden	.25	.60
77 Gary Brown	.25	.60
78 Peter Boulware	.25	.60
79 Stephen Alexander	.25	.60
80 Barry Sanders	1.00	2.50
81 Warren Sapp	.30	.75
82 Michael Sinclair	.25	.60
83 Freddie Jones	.25	.60
84 Ike Hilliard	.30	.75
85 Jake Reed	.30	.75
86 Tim Dwight	.30	.75
87 Johnnie Morton	.30	.75
88 Robert Brooks	.30	.75
89 Rocket Ismail	.30	.75
90 Emmitt Smith	1.00	2.50
91 Ricky Proehl	.25	.60
92 James Jett	.25	.60
93 Karim Abdul-Jabbar	.30	.75
94 Mark Chmura	.25	.60
95 Andre Reed	.40	1.00
96 Michael Westbrook	.25	.60
97 Michael Strahan	.30	.75
98 Chad Brown	.25	.60
99 Trent Dilfer	.30	.75
100 Terrell Davis	.40	1.00
101 Aaron Glenn	.25	.60
102 Skip Hicks	.25	.60
103 Tony Gonzalez	.40	1.00
104 Ty Law	.30	.75
105 Jermaine Lewis	.25	.60
106 Ray Lewis	.40	1.00
107 Zach Thomas	.40	1.00
108 Reidel Anthony	.25	.60
109 Levon Kirkland	.25	.60
110 Drew Bledsoe	.40	1.00
111 Bobby Engram	.30	.75
112 Jerome Pathon	.25	.60
113 Muhsin Muhammad	.30	.75
114 Vonnie Holliday	.25	.60
115 Bill Romanowski	.30	.75
116 Marshall Faulk	.40	1.00
117 Ty Detmer	.30	.75
118 Mo Lewis	.25	.60
119 Charles Woodson	.40	1.00
120 Doug Flutie	.40	1.00
121 Jon Kitna	.30	.75
122 Courtney Hawkins	.25	.60
123 Trent Green	.30	.75
124 John Elway	1.25	3.00
125 Barry Sanders GM	2.00	5.00
126 Brett Favre GM	2.50	6.00
127 Curtis Martin GM	.75	2.00
128 Dan Marino GM	2.50	6.00
129 Eddie George GM	.60	1.50
130 Emmitt Smith GM	2.00	5.00
131 Jamal Anderson GM	.60	1.50
132 Jerry Rice GM	1.50	4.00
133 John Elway GM	2.50	6.00
134 Terrell Davis GM	.75	2.00
135 Troy Aikman GM	1.25	3.00
136 Skip Hicks SN	.50	1.25
137 Charles Woodson SN	.75	2.00
138 Charlie Batch SN	.60	1.50
139 Curtis Enis SN	.50	1.25
140 Fred Taylor SN	.60	1.50
141 Jake Plummer SN	.60	1.50
142 Peyton Manning SN	2.50	6.00
143 Randy Moss SN	.75	2.00
144 Corey Dillon SN	.60	1.50
145 Priest Holmes SN	.75	2.00
146 Warrick Dunn SN	.60	1.50
147 Jevon Kearse RC	1.00	2.50
148 Chris Claiborne RC	.60	1.50
149 Akili Smith RC	.75	2.00
150 Brock Huard RC	.75	2.00
151 Daunte Culpepper RC	1.00	2.50
152 Edgerrin James RC	1.25	3.00
153 Cecil Collins RC	.60	1.50
154 Kevin Faulk RC	1.00	2.50
155 Amos Zereoue RC	.75	2.00
156 James Johnson RC	.60	1.50
157 Sedrick Irvin RC	.60	1.50
158 Ricky Williams RC	1.50	4.00
159 Mike Cloud RC	.60	1.50
160 Chris McAlister RC	.75	2.00
161 Rob Konrad RC	.60	1.50
162 Champ Bailey RC	2.00	5.00
163 Ebenezer Ekuban RC	.60	1.50
164 Tim Couch RC	1.00	2.50
165 Cade McNown RC	.75	2.00
166 Donovan McNabb RC	2.50	6.00
167 Joe Germaine RC	.75	2.00
168 Shaun King RC	.75	2.00
169 Peerless Price RC	.75	2.00
170 Kevin Johnson RC	.75	2.00
171 Troy Edwards RC	.75	2.00
172 Karsten Bailey RC	.60	1.50
173 David Boston RC	.75	2.00
174 D'Wayne Bates RC	.60	1.50
175 Torry Holt RC	1.50	4.00

1999 Finest Gold Refractors

*1-124 VETS: 12X TO 30X BASIC CARDS
*125-135 GEMS: 6X TO 15X BASIC CARDS
*136-146 SENSATION: 6X TO 15X BASIC SN
*147-175 ROOKIES: 5X TO 12X BASIC RC
STATED ODDS 1:72 H/R, 1:33 HTA
STATED PRINT RUN 100 SERIAL #'d SETS

1999 Finest Refractors

*1-124 VETS: 3X TO 8X BASIC CARDS
*125-135 GEMS: 1.5X TO 4X BASIC GEM
*136-146 SENSATION: 1.5X TO 4X BASIC SN
*147-175 ROOKIES: 1.5X TO 3X BASIC RC
STATED ODDS 1:12 H/R, 1:5 HTA

1999 Finest Double Team Left Side Refractors

COMPLETE SET (7)	6.00	15.00
*RIGHT/LEFT REF.VARIATIONS EQUAL VALUE		
STATED ODDS 1:50 H/R, 1:24 HTA		
*DUAL REFRACTORS: .8X TO 2X		
DUAL REFRACTOR ODDS 1:150H/R, 1:72HTA		
DT1 Akili Smith	.60	1.50
Carl Pickens		
DT2 Cade McNown	.60	1.50
Curtis Enis		
DT3 Doug Flutie	1.25	3.00
Eric Moulds		
DT4 Mark Brunell	1.25	3.00
Fred Taylor		
DT5 Kordell Stewart	1.25	3.00
Jerome Bettis		
DT6 Jon Kitna	1.00	2.50
Joey Galloway		
DT7 Warrick Dunn	1.25	3.00
Mike Alstott		

1999 Finest Future's Finest

COMPLETE SET (10)	60.00	120.00
STATED ODDS 1:253 H/R, 1:117 HTA		
STATED PRINT RUN 500 SER.#'d SETS		
*REFRACTORS: 1X TO 2.5X BASIC INSERT		
REFRACTOR ODDS 1:1262 H/R, 1:583 HTA		
REFRACTOR PRINT RUN 100 SER.#'d SETS		
F1 Akili Smith	2.50	6.00
F2 Cade McNown	3.00	8.00
F3 Champ Bailey	3.00	8.00
F4 Daunte Culpepper	6.00	15.00
F5 David Boston	3.00	8.00
F6 Donovan McNabb	7.50	20.00
F7 Edgerrin James	6.00	15.00
F8 Ricky Williams	3.00	8.00
F9 Tim Couch	3.00	8.00
F10 Torry Holt	5.00	12.00

1999 Finest Leading Indicators

COMPLETE SET (10)	12.00	30.00
STATED ODDS 1:30 H/R, 1:14 HTA		
L1 Jamal Anderson	1.50	4.00
L2 Doug Flutie	1.50	4.00
L3 Drew Bledsoe	2.00	5.00
L4 Eddie George	1.50	4.00
L5 Emmitt Smith	3.00	8.00
L6 John Elway	5.00	12.00
L7 Keyshawn Johnson	1.50	4.00
L8 Steve Young	2.00	5.00
L9 Terrell Owens	1.50	4.00
L10 Vinny Testaverde	1.00	2.50

1999 Finest Main Attractions

COMPLETE SET (7)	15.00	40.00
*RIGHT/LEFT REF.VARIATIONS SAME VALUE		
STATED ODDS 1:50 H/R, 1:24 HTA		
*DUAL REFRACTORS: .75X TO 2X		
DUAL REFRACTOR ODDS 1:150H/R, 1:72HTA		
MA1 Champ Bailey	1.50	4.00
Deion Sanders		
MA2 Daunte Culpepper	4.00	10.00
Steve McNair		
MA3 Donovan McNabb	5.00	12.00
Kordell Stewart		
MA4 Edgerrin James	4.00	10.00
Marshall Faulk		
MA5 Kevin Faulk	1.50	4.00
Warrick Dunn		
MA6 Joe Germaine	3.00	8.00
Troy Aikman		
MA7 Rob Konrad	1.25	3.00
Mike Alstott		

1999 Finest Prominent Figures

QB-YARDAGE PRINT RUN 5084 SER.#'d SETS		
QB-YARDAGE ODDS 1:25H/R,1:11HTA		
QB-TDs PRINT RUN 48 SER.#'d SETS		
QB-TDs STATED ODDS 1:2634H/R,1:1220HTA		
RB-TDs PRINT RUN 25 SER.#'d SETS		
RB-TDs STATED ODDS 1:5099H/R,1:2333HTA		
RB-YARDAGE PRINT RUN 2105 SER.#'d SETS		
RB-YARD.STATED ODDS 1:60H/R,1:28HTA		
WR-TDs PRINT RUN 22 SER.#'d SETS		
WR-TDs STATED ODDS 1:5779H/R,1:2660HTA		
WR-YARDAGE PRINT RUN 1848 SER.#'d SETS		
WR-YARDAGE ODDS 1:68H/R, 1:32HTA		
PF1 Brett Favre	4.00	10.00
PF2 Dan Marino	4.00	10.00
PF3 Drew Bledsoe	1.50	4.00
PF4 Jake Plummer	.60	1.50
PF5 Mark Brunell	.60	1.50
PF6 Peyton Manning	3.00	8.00
PF7 Randall Cunningham	1.00	2.50
PF8 Steve Young	1.50	4.00
PF9 Tim Couch	1.00	2.50
PF10 Vinny Testaverde	.60	1.50
PF11 Brett Favre	60.00	150.00
PF12 Dan Marino	60.00	150.00
PF13 Drew Bledsoe	25.00	60.00
PF14 Jake Plummer	10.00	25.00
PF15 Mark Brunell	10.00	25.00
PF16 Peyton Manning	50.00	120.00
PF17 Randall Cunningham	15.00	40.00
PF18 Steve Young	25.00	60.00
PF19 Tim Couch	15.00	40.00
PF20 Vinny Testaverde	.60	1.50
PF21 Barry Sanders	100.00	250.00
PF22 Curtis Martin	35.00	80.00
PF23 Eddie George	35.00	80.00
PF24 Emmitt Smith	60.00	150.00
PF25 Fred Taylor	35.00	80.00
PF26 Garrison Hearst	25.00	60.00
PF27 Jamal Anderson	25.00	60.00
PF28 Marshall Faulk	40.00	100.00
PF29 Ricky Williams	40.00	100.00
PF30 Terrell Davis	35.00	80.00
PF31 Barry Sanders	7.50	20.00
PF32 Curtis Martin	2.50	6.00
PF33 Eddie George	2.50	6.00
PF34 Emmitt Smith	5.00	12.00
PF35 Fred Taylor	2.50	6.00
PF36 Garrison Hearst	2.00	5.00
PF37 Jamal Anderson	2.00	5.00
PF38 Marshall Faulk	4.00	10.00
PF39 Ricky Williams	4.00	10.00
PF40 Terrell Davis	2.50	6.00
PF41 Antonio Freeman	25.00	60.00
PF42 David Boston	15.00	40.00
PF43 Cris Carter	25.00	60.00
PF44 Jerry Rice	60.00	150.00
PF45 Joey Galloway	15.00	40.00
PF46 Keyshawn Johnson	25.00	60.00
PF47 Randy Moss	75.00	150.00
PF48 Terrell Owens	25.00	60.00
PF49 Tim Brown	25.00	60.00
PF50 Torry Holt	30.00	80.00
PF51 Antonio Freeman	2.00	5.00
PF52 David Boston	2.00	5.00
PF53 Eric Moulds	2.00	5.00
PF54 Jerry Rice	5.00	12.00
PF55 Joey Galloway	1.25	3.00
PF56 Keyshawn Johnson	2.00	5.00
PF57 Randy Moss	5.00	12.00
PF58 Terrell Owens	2.00	5.00
PF59 Jimmy Smith	1.25	3.00
PF60 Torry Holt	4.00	10.00

1999 Finest Salute

COMPLETE SET (3)	125.00	250.00
STATED ODDS 1:53 HOB, 1:25 HTA		
REFRACTOR ODDS 1:1900 HOB,1:790 HTA		
GOLD REF.ODDS 1:12,384 HOB,1:5782 HTA		
GOLD REFRACTOR PRINT RUN 100 CARDS		
FS Terrell Davis	4.00	10.00
John Elway		
Randy Moss		
FSR Terrell Davis	15.00	40.00
John Elway		
Randy Moss		
(Refractor version)		
FSGR Terrell Davis	75.00	150.00
John Elway		
Randy Moss		
(Gold Refractor version)		

1999 Finest Team Finest

COMPLETE SET (10)	50.00	100.00
BLUE PRINT RUN 1500 SER.#'d SETS		
BLUE STATED ODDS 1:84HOB, 1:39 HTA		
*BLUE REFRACTORS: 1.5X TO 4X BLUES		
BLUE REF.PRINT RUN 150 SER.#'d SETS		
BLUE REF.STATED ODDS 1:843HOB,1:389HTA		
*GOLDS: 1.2X TO 3X BLUES		
GOLD PRINT RUN 250 SER.#'d SETS		
GOLD STATED ODDS 1:57 HTA		
*GOLD REFRACTORS: 6X TO 15X BLUES		
GOLD REF.PRINT RUN 25 SER. #'d SETS		
GOLD REF.STATED ODDS 1:573 HTA		
*REDS: .75X TO 2X BLUES		
RED PRINT RUN 500 SER.#'d SETS		
RED STATED ODDS 1:29 HTA		
*RED REFRACTORS: 3X TO 8X BLUES		
RED REF.PRINT RUN 50 SER.#'d SETS		
RED REF.STATED ODDS 1:285 HTA		
T1 Barry Sanders	6.00	15.00
T2 Brett Favre	6.00	15.00
T3 Dan Marino	6.00	15.00
T4 Drew Bledsoe	2.50	6.00
T5 Jamal Anderson	2.00	5.00
T6 John Elway	6.00	15.00
T7 Peyton Manning	6.00	15.00
T8 Randy Moss	5.00	12.00
T9 Terrell Davis	2.00	5.00
T10 Troy Aikman	4.00	10.00

1999-00 Finest Pro Bowl Jumbos

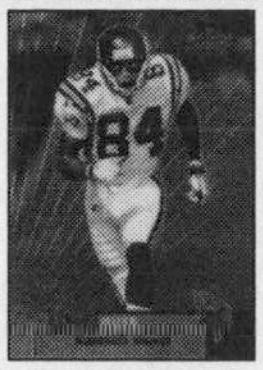

This set of cards was distributed by Topps directly to dealers at the 2000 Pro Bowl Card Show in Hawaii. Each card measures roughly 3 1/2" by 4 7/8" and is essentially an enlarged version of the Finest Pro Bowl and Super Bowl promos printed in the bi-fold format. A Refractor version was produced as well.

COMPLETE SET (12)	24.00	60.00
*REFRACTORS: 4X TO 10X BASIC CARDS		
1 Brett Favre	3.20	8.00
2 Marvin Harrison	.80	2.00
3 Marshall Faulk		
4 Randy Moss	3.20	8.00
5 Kurt Warner	6.00	15.00
6 Stephen Davis	.80	2.00
7 Peyton Manning	3.20	8.00
8 Edgerrin James	4.80	12.00
9 Drew Bledsoe	1.00	2.50
10 Emmitt Smith	2.00	5.00
11 Terrell Davis	2.00	5.00
12 Brad Johnson	.80	2.00

1999-00 Finest Pro Bowl Promos

This 12-card standard sized set was released at the 2000 Pro Bowl Card Show in Hawaii. Each player's card is essentially a parallel to the Finest Super Bowl set released a week earlier in Atlanta except that the Super Bowl logo has been replaced by the Pro Bowl logo.

COMPLETE SET (12)	24.00	60.00
*REFRACTORS: 4X TO 10X BASIC CARDS		
1 Brett Favre	3.20	8.00
2 Marvin Harrison	.60	1.50
3 Marshall Faulk	.60	1.50
4 Randy Moss	3.20	8.00
5 Kurt Warner	6.00	15.00
6 Stephen Davis	.60	1.50
7 Peyton Manning	3.20	8.00
8 Edgerrin James	4.80	12.00
9 Drew Bledsoe	1.00	2.50
10 Emmitt Smith	.60	1.50
11 Terrell Davis	2.00	5.00
12 Brad Johnson	.60	1.50

1999-00 Finest Super Bowl Promos

This 12-card set and accompaning Refractors parallel set was released at the 2000 Super Bowl Card Show in Atlanta as a wrapper redemption. Eight player's cards were similar to their base 1999 Finest card with 4-additional player's added to the set. Each features the Super Bowl XXXIV logo on the cardfront and was produced in a bi-fold format.

COMPLETE SET (12)	24.00	60.00
*REFRACTORS: 4X TO 10X BASIC CARDS		
1 Brett Favre	3.20	8.00
2 Marvin Harrison	.60	1.50
3 Marshall Faulk	.60	1.50
4 Randy Moss	3.20	8.00
5 Kurt Warner	6.00	15.00
6 Stephen Davis	.60	1.50
7 Peyton Manning	3.20	8.00
8 Edgerrin James	4.80	12.00
9 Drew Bledsoe	1.00	2.50
10 Emmitt Smith	2.00	5.00
11 Terrell Davis	2.00	5.00
12 Brad Johnson	.60	1.50

2000 Finest

Released as a 190-card base set, Finest football features 125 veteran cards, 40 rookie cards inserted in packs at one in 11 and one in five HTA sequentially numbered to 2400, 30 dual player Inherent Fire cards (card numbers 166-195) inserted at one in eight packs and one in three HTA, and 10 Gems cards (card numbers 195-205) inserted at one in 24 and one in nine HTA. Finest was packaged in 24-pack boxes with each pack containing five cards and carried a suggested retail price of $3.25; and Finest HTA was packaged in 12-pack boxes with packs containing 11 cards and carried a suggested retail price of $9.99. A special PSA redemption card limited to 10 total was inserted in packs at the rate of one in 12278 HTA which is redeemable for a complete set of the graded rookie subset.

COMPLETE SET (205)	150.00	300.00
COMP.SET w/o SP's (125)	12.50	30.00
126-165 ROOKIE/2400 ODDS 1:11, 1:5 HTA		
1 Tim Dwight	.25	.60
2 Cade McNown	.20	.50
3 Drew Bledsoe	.30	.75
4 Torry Holt	.30	.75
5 Derrick Mayes	.20	.50
6 Vinny Testaverde	.25	.60
7 Patrick Jeffers	.25	.60
8 Dorsey Levens	.25	.60
9 James Johnson	.20	.50
10 Champ Bailey	.25	.60
11 Jeff George	.25	.60
12 Shawn Jefferson	.20	.50
13 Terrence Wilkins	.20	.50
14 J.J. Stokes	.25	.60
15 Doug Flutie	.30	.75
16 Corey Dillon	.25	.60
17 Rod Smith	.25	.60
18 Jimmy Smith	.25	.60
19 Amani Toomer	.25	.60
20 Curtis Conway	.25	.60
21 Brad Johnson	.25	.60
22 Edgerrin James	.30	.75
23 Derrick Alexander	.20	.50
24 Terrell Owens	.30	.75
25 Kurt Warner	.50	1.25
26 Frank Sanders	.20	.50
27 Tony Banks	.20	.50
28 Troy Aikman	.50	1.25
29 Curtis Enis	.20	.50
30 Eddie George	.25	.60
31 Bill Schroeder	.25	.60
32 Kent Graham	.20	.50
33 Mike Alstott	.30	.75
34 Steve Young	.40	1.00
35 Jacquez Green	.20	.50
36 Frank Wycheck	.25	.60
37 Kerry Collins	.25	.60
38 Stephen Davis	.25	.60
39 Tony Gonzalez	.30	.75
40 Tyrone Wheatley	.20	.50
41 Brett Favre	1.00	2.50
42 Joey Galloway	.25	.60
43 Terrell Davis	.30	.75
44 Marvin Harrison	.30	.75
45 Zach Thomas	.30	.75
46 Jerry Rice	.60	1.50
47 Keyshawn Johnson	.25	.60
48 Rob Johnson	.25	.60
49 Rocket Ismail	.25	.60
50 Elvis Grbac	.20	.50
51 Warrick Dunn	.25	.60
52 Jevon Kearse	.25	.60
53 Albert Connell	.20	.50
54 Muhsin Muhammad	.25	.60
55 Carl Pickens	.25	.60
56 Peyton Manning	.75	2.00
57 Daunte Culpepper	.25	.60
58 Ike Hilliard	.25	.60
59 Steve McNair	.30	.75
60 Sean Dawkins	.20	.50
61 Steve Beuerlein	.25	.60
62 Priest Holmes	.30	.75
63 Jim Harbaugh	.25	.60
64 Germane Crowell	.20	.50
65 Cris Carter	.30	.75
66 Jamal Anderson	.25	.60
67 Kevin Johnson	.20	.50
68 Herman Moore	.25	.60
69 Ricky Williams	.30	.75
70 Rich Gannon	.25	.60
71 Isaac Bruce	.30	.75
72 Peerless Price	.25	.60
73 Az-Zahir Hakim	.20	.50
74 Mark Brunell	.30	.75
75 Rob Moore	.20	.50
76 Antowain Smith	.25	.60
77 Tim Biakabutuka	.25	.60
78 Ed McCaffrey	.25	.60
79 Tony Martin	.20	.50
80 Marcus Robinson	.25	.60
81 Kevin Dyson	.20	.50
82 Wesley Walls	.20	.50
83 Chris Chandler	.20	.50
84 Keenan McCardell	.25	.60
85 Napoleon Kaufman	.25	.60
86 Emmitt Smith	.75	2.00
87 James Stewart	.20	.50
88 Tim Brown	.30	.75
89 Ricky Watters	.25	.60
90 Johnnie Morton	.25	.60
91 Jake Plummer	.25	.60
92 Olandis Gary	.25	.60
93 Jerome Bettis	.30	.75
94 Terry Glenn	.25	.60
95 Kordell Stewart	.25	.60
96 Charlie Garner	.25	.60
97 Yancey Thigpen	.20	.50
98 Michael Westbrook	.20	.50
99 Bobby Engram	.25	.60
100 Eric Moulds	.25	.60
101 Darnay Scott	.25	.60
102 Antonio Freeman	.25	.60
103 Wayne Chrebet	.25	.60
104 Akili Smith	.20	.50
105 Jeff Blake	.25	.60
106 Curtis Martin	.30	.75
107 Errict Rhett	.25	.60
108 Damon Huard	.25	.60
109 Jeff Graham	.20	.50
110 Terance Mathis	.20	.50
111 Jon Kitna	.25	.60
112 Tim Couch	.25	.60
113 Fred Taylor	.30	.75
114 Qadry Ismail	.25	.60
115 Donovan McNabb	.30	.75
116 Charles Johnson	.20	.50
117 Troy Edwards	.20	.50
118 Shaun King	.20	.50
119 Charlie Batch	.25	.60
120 Robert Smith	.25	.60
121 Marshall Faulk	.30	.75
122 Brian Griese	.25	.60
123 O.J. McDuffie	.25	.60
124 Randy Moss	.30	.75
125 Duce Staley	.25	.60
126 Peter Warrick RC	2.50	6.00
127 Dez White RC	2.00	5.00
128 Ron Dayne RC	2.50	6.00
129 J.R. Redmond RC	1.50	4.00
130 Thomas Jones RC	3.00	8.00
131 Plaxico Burress RC	2.50	6.00
132 Reuben Droughns RC	2.50	6.00
133 Shaun Alexander RC	3.00	8.00
134 Ron Dugans RC	1.50	4.00
135 Travis Prentice RC	2.00	5.00
136 Joe Hamilton RC	1.50	4.00
137 Curtis Keaton RC	1.50	4.00
138 Chris Redman RC	1.50	4.00
139 Chad Pennington RC	4.00	10.00
140 Travis Taylor RC	2.00	5.00
141 Bubba Franks RC	2.50	6.00
142 Dennis Northcutt RC	2.00	5.00
143 Jerry Porter RC	2.50	6.00
144 Sylvester Morris RC	1.50	4.00
145 Anthony Becht RC	2.00	5.00
146 Trung Canidate RC	2.00	5.00
147 Jamal Lewis RC	2.50	6.00
148 R.Jay Soward RC	1.50	4.00
149 Tee Martin RC	2.50	6.00
150 Courtney Brown RC	2.00	5.00
151 Brian Urlacher RC	10.00	25.00
152 Danny Farmer RC	1.50	4.00
153 Laveranues Coles RC	2.50	6.00
154 Todd Pinkston RC	1.50	4.00
155 Corey Simon RC	2.00	5.00
156 Spergon Wynn RC	2.00	5.00
157 Tim Rattay RC	2.00	5.00
158 Todd Husak RC	1.50	4.00
159 Aaron Shea RC	1.50	4.00
160 Giovanni Carmazzi RC	1.50	4.00
161 Trevor Gaylor RC	1.50	4.00
162 JaJuan Dawson RC	1.50	4.00
163 Jarious Jackson RC	2.00	5.00
164 Chris Samuels RC	2.00	5.00
165 Rob Morris RC	2.00	5.00
166 Peter Warrick	.75	2.00
Randy Moss		
167 Randy Moss	.75	2.00
Peter Warrick		
168 Travis Prentice	.60	1.50
Stephen Davis		
169 Stephen Davis	.60	1.50
Travis Prentice		
170 Chris Redman	.60	1.50
Kurt Warner		
171 Kurt Warner	.60	1.50
Chris Redman		
172 Sylvester Morris	.50	1.25
Jimmy Smith		
173 Jimmy Smith	.50	1.25
Sylvester Morris		
174 Chad Pennington	1.25	3.00
Peyton Manning		
175 Peyton Manning	1.25	3.00
Chad Pennington		
176 R.Jay Soward	.50	1.25
Marvin Harrison		
177 Marvin Harrison	.50	1.25
R.Jay Soward		
178 Ron Dayne	.75	2.00
Jamal Anderson		
179 Jamal Anderson	.75	2.00
Ron Dayne		
180 Shaun Alexander	.60	1.50
Eddie George		
181 Eddie George	.60	1.50
Shaun Alexander		
182 Courtney Brown	.75	2.00
Bruce Smith		
183 Bruce Smith	.75	2.00
Courtney Brown		
184 Jamal Lewis	.50	1.25
Edgerrin James		
185 Edgerrin James	.50	1.25
Jamal Lewis		
186 Trung Canidate	2.00	5.00
Emmitt Smith		
187 Emmitt Smith	2.00	5.00
Trung Canidate		
188 Travis Taylor	.75	2.00
Cris Carter		
189 Cris Carter	.75	2.00
Travis Taylor		
190 Curtis Keaton	.50	1.25
Marshall Faulk		
191 Marshall Faulk	.50	1.25
Curtis Keaton		
192 Plaxico Burress	1.50	4.00
Jerry Rice		
193 Jerry Rice	1.50	4.00
Plaxico Burress		
194 Thomas Jones	.60	1.50
Terrell Davis		
195 Terrell Davis	.60	1.50
Thomas Jones		
196 Peyton Manning GM	1.50	4.00
197 Randy Moss GM	.60	1.50
198 Terrell Davis GM	.60	1.50
199 Marshall Faulk GM	.60	1.50
200 Edgerrin James GM	.60	1.50
201 Emmitt Smith GM	1.50	4.00
202 Ricky Williams GM	.60	1.50
203 Kurt Warner GM	1.00	2.50
204 Eddie George GM	.50	1.25
205 Brett Favre GM	2.00	5.00

2000 Finest Gold/Refractors

*VETS 1-125: 5X TO 12X BASIC CARDS
1-125 VET/300 ODDS 1:26, 1:14 HTA
1-125 VETERAN PRINT RUN 300
*ROOKIES 126-165: 1X TO 2.5X
126-165 ROOKIE/200 ODDS 1:132, 1:54 HTA
126-165 ROOKIE PRINT RUN 200
*IF 166-195: 3X TO 8X BASIC CARDS
166-195 IF/100 ODDS 1:365, 1:134 HTA
166-195 IF PRINT RUN 100
*GM 196-205: 5X TO 12X BASIC CARDS
196-205 GM/50 ODDS 1:2372, 1:703 HTA
196-205 GM PRINT RUN 50

2000 Finest Moments

COMPLETE SET (25)	10.00	25.00
STATED ODDS 1:8, 1:4 HTA		
*REFRACTOR: .8X TO 2X BASIC INSERTS		
REFRACTOR ODDS 1:18, 1:8 HTA		
FM1 Bart Starr	1.50	4.00
FM2 Phil Simms	.60	1.50
FM3 John Elway	1.50	4.00
FM4 Dan Marino	2.00	5.00
FM5 Kellen Winslow	.50	1.25
FM6 Franco Harris	.75	2.00
FM7 Stephen Davis	.50	1.25
FM8 Isaac Bruce	.60	1.50
FM9 Edgerrin James	.60	1.50
FM10 Marshall Faulk	.60	1.50
FM11 Patrick Jeffers	.50	1.25
FM12 Kurt Warner	1.00	2.50
FM13 Joe Montana	2.00	5.00
FM14 Kevin Carter	.40	1.00
FM15 Andre Reed	.60	1.50
FM16 Torry Holt	.60	1.50
FM17 Frank Wycheck	.50	1.25
Kevin Dyson		
FM18 Jason Elam	.40	1.00
FM19 Mike Jones LB	.40	1.00
FM20 Cade McNown	.40	1.00
FM21 Germane Crowell	.40	1.00
FM22 Bruce Matthews	.50	1.25
FM23 Champ Bailey	.50	1.25
FM24 Qadry Ismail	.50	1.25
FM25 Tony Brackens	.40	1.00

2000 Finest Moments Refractors Autographs

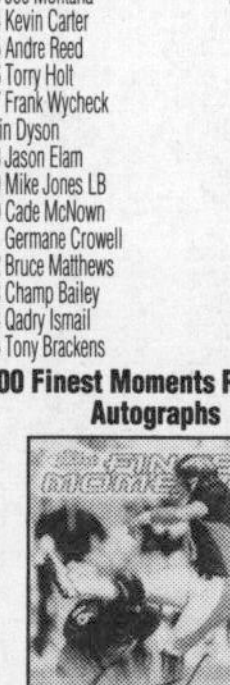

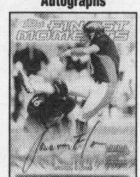

OVERALL STATED ODDS 1:48, 1:22 HTA		
FM1 Bart Starr	90.00	150.00
FM2 Phil Simms	15.00	40.00
FM3 John Elway	90.00	150.00
FM4 Dan Marino	100.00	200.00
FM5 Kellen Winslow	20.00	50.00
FM6 Franco Harris	50.00	100.00
FM7 Stephen Davis	8.00	20.00
FM8 Isaac Bruce	15.00	40.00
FM9 Edgerrin James	10.00	25.00
FM10 Marshall Faulk	30.00	60.00
FM11 Patrick Jeffers	8.00	20.00
FM12 Kurt Warner	50.00	100.00

FM13 Joe Montana 75.00 150.00
FM14 Kevin Carter 6.00 15.00
FM15 Andre Reed 10.00 25.00
FM16 Torry Holt 10.00 25.00
FM17A Frank Wycheck 8.00 20.00
Kevin Dyson
FM17B Frank Wycheck 8.00 20.00
Kevin Dyson AU
FM18 Jason Elam 12.00 30.00
FM19 Mike Jones LB 6.00 15.00
FM20 Cade McNown 6.00 15.00
FM21 Germane Crowell 6.00 15.00
FM22 Bruce Matthews 15.00 40.00
FM23 Champ Bailey 8.00 20.00
FM24 Qadry Ismail 8.00 20.00
FM25 Tony Brackens 6.00 15.00

2000 Finest Moments Jumbos

COMPLETE SET (7) 12.50 30.00
ONE PER BOX
1 Bart Starr 2.50 6.00
2 Phil Simms 1.00 2.50
3 John Elway 2.50 6.00
4 Dan Marino 3.00 8.00
5 Edgerrin James 1.00 2.50
6 Marshall Faulk 1.00 2.50
7 Joe Montana 3.00 8.00

2000 Finest NFL Europe's Finest

COMPLETE SET (10) 4.00 10.00
STATED ODDS 1:24, 1:12 HTA
E1 Kurt Warner 1.25 3.00
E2 Bill Schroeder .60 1.50
E3 Andy McCullough .50 1.25
E4 Dameyune Craig .50 1.25
E5 Marcus Robinson .60 1.50
E6 La'Roi Glover .50 1.25
E7 Damon Huard .60 1.50
E8 Brad Johnson .60 1.50
E9 Jake Delhomme 2.00 5.00
E10 Jon Kitna .60 1.50

2000 Finest Out of the Blue

COMPLETE SET (15) 7.50 20.00
STATED ODDS 1:24, 1:12 HTA
B1 Kurt Warner 1.00 2.50
B2 Patrick Jeffers .50 1.25
B3 Stephen Davis .50 1.25
B4 Amani Toomer .50 1.25
B5 Marcus Robinson .50 1.25
B6 Tyrone Wheatley .40 1.00
B7 Kevin Johnson .40 1.00
B8 Tony Gonzalez .60 1.50
B9 Olandis Gary .50 1.25
B10 Brad Johnson .50 1.25
B11 Germane Crowell .40 1.00
B12 Ricky Williams .60 1.50
B13 Edgerrin James .60 1.50
B14 Tim Couch .50 1.25
B15 Steve Beuerlein .50 1.25

2000 Finest Moments Pro Bowl Jerseys

COMPLETE SET (33) 250.00 500.00
STATED ODDS 1:77, 1:35 HTA
KMC Kevin Mawae 6.00 15.00
MBP Mitch Berger 8.00 20.00
TTP Tom Tupa 6.00 15.00
BDFS Brian Dawkins 12.00 25.00
BJQB Brad Johnson 8.00 20.00
CDRB Corey Dillon 8.00 20.00
DCOLB Dexter Coakley 6.00 15.00
DSST Detron Smith 6.00 15.00
DSTE David Sloan 6.00 15.00
EJRB Edgerrin James 10.00 25.00
JKDE Jevon Kearse 8.00 20.00
KCDE Kevin Carter 6.00 15.00
KHOLB Kevin Hardy 6.00 15.00
KWQB Kurt Warner 15.00 40.00
LEILM Luther Elliss 6.00 15.00
LSFS Lance Schulters 6.00 15.00
LSOT Leon Searcy 6.00 15.00
MHWR Marvin Harrison 10.00 25.00
MMWR Muhsin Muhammad 8.00 20.00
OMPK Olindo Mare 6.00 15.00
OPOT Orlando Pace 8.00 20.00
RGQB Rich Gannon 8.00 20.00
SBILB Stephen Boyd 6.00 15.00
SBQB Steve Beuerlein 8.00 20.00
SDRB Stephen Davis 8.00 20.00
SMCB Sam Madison 6.00 15.00
TBDE Tony Brackens 6.00 15.00
TGTE Tony Gonzalez 10.00 25.00
TJOG Tre Johnson 6.00 15.00
TLCB Todd Lyght 6.00 15.00
TMKR Tremain Mack 6.00 15.00
TPILM Trevor Pryce 6.00 15.00
ZTILB Zach Thomas 10.00 25.00

2000 Finest Superstars

COMPLETE SET (15) 7.50 20.00
STATED ODDS 1:16, 1:8 HTA
S1 Dan Marino 1.50 4.00
S2 Eddie George .40 1.00
S3 Marshall Faulk .50 1.25
S4 Stephen Davis .40 1.00
S5 Jerry Rice 1.00 2.50
S6 Emmitt Smith 1.25 3.00
S7 Terrell Davis .50 1.25
S8 Jimmy Smith .40 1.00
S9 Cris Carter .50 1.25
S10 Troy Aikman .75 2.00
S11 Curtis Martin .50 1.25
S12 Brett Favre 1.50 4.00
S13 Kurt Warner .75 2.00
S14 Marvin Harrison .50 1.25
S15 Steve Young .60 1.50

2000-01 Finest Pro Bowl Jumbos

This set was distributed to attendees (one card at a time) of the NFL Experience Pro Bowl Show in Hawaii in February 2001. The cards are essentially a Jumbo (roughly 4" by 5 5/8") version of the player's base 2000 Finest card with each featuring the Pro Bowl 2001 logo. A Jumbo Refractor parallel set was also produced.

COMPLETE SET (12) 15.00 30.00
*REFRACTORS: 3X TO 8X BASIC CARDS
1 Jeff Garcia 1.00 2.50
2 Randy Moss 2.50 6.00
3 Warren Sapp .60 1.50
4 Peyton Manning 2.50 6.00
5 Eddie George 1.25 3.00
6 Edgerrin James 2.50 6.00
7 Stephen Davis 1.00 2.50
8 Jamal Lewis 3.00 8.00
9 Marvin Harrison 1.00 2.50
10 Marshall Faulk 1.25 3.00
11 Rich Gannon 1.00 2.50
12 Daunte Culpepper 2.00 5.00

2000-01 Finest Pro Bowl Promos

These 6-cards were distributed to attendees (one card at a time) of the NFL Experience Pro Bowl Show in Hawaii in February 2001. The cards are essentially a parallel version of the player's base 2000 Finest card with each featuring the Pro Bowl 2001 logo.

COMPLETE SET (6) 12.50 25.00
1 Daunte Culpepper 2.00 5.00
2 Jamal Lewis 3.00 8.00
3 Peyton Manning 2.50 6.00
4 Edgerrin James 2.50 6.00
5 Randy Moss 2.50 6.00
6 Jeff Garcia 1.25 3.00

2000-01 Finest Super Bowl Jumbos

This set was distributed to hobby dealers primarily at the NFL Experience Super Bowl Card Show in Tampa, Florida. The cards are essentially a Jumbo (roughly 4" by 5 5/8") version of the player's base issue card with each featuring the Super Bowl XXXV logo. A Jumbo Refractor parallel set was also produced.

COMPLETE SET (12) 18.00 30.00
*REFRACTORS: 2.5X TO 5X BASIC CARDS
1 Jeff Garcia .75 2.00
2 Randy Moss 2.00 5.00
3 Warren Sapp .50 1.25
4 Peyton Manning 2.50 6.00
5 Eddie George 1.25 3.00
6 Edgerrin James 2.50 6.00
7 Stephen Davis .75 2.00
8 Jamal Lewis 2.50 6.00
9 Marvin Harrison .75 2.00
10 Marshall Faulk 1.25 3.00
11 Rich Gannon 1.25 3.00
12 Daunte Culpepper 1.50 4.00

2001 Finest

This 140 card set was released in October, 2001. The set is broken down into two parts: The first 100 cards are veterans while the final 40 cards are 2001 NFL rookies serial numbered to 1000. The first 500 of those rookies were graded by PSA. Both the ungraded and graded rookies were inserted at a one per box level. Each box contained 10 packs and each box was supposed to contain the following elements: Graded Rookie Card, Sequentially numbered Rookie Card, three Relic Cards and 2 Autographed cards.

COMP.SET w/o SP's (100) 20.00 40.00
1 Eddie George .40 1.00
2 Jay Fiedler .30 .75
3 Peter Warrick .30 .75
4 Vinny Testaverde .30 .75
5 Charles Johnson .25 .60
6 Ahman Green .40 1.00
7 Isaac Bruce .40 1.00
8 Junior Seau .40 1.00
9 Daunte Culpepper .30 .75
10 Ike Hilliard .30 .75
11 Tony Banks .25 .60
12 Steve Beuerlein .30 .75
13 Jamal Anderson .30 .75
14 Tyrone Wheatley .30 .75
15 Sylvester Morris .25 .60
16 Edgerrin James .40 1.00
17 Shaun King .25 .60
18 Terrell Owens .40 1.00
19 Donovan Mcnabb .40 1.00
20 Cade Mcnown .30 .75
21 Elvis Grbac .30 .75
22 James Stewart .25 .60
23 Joe Horn .30 .75
24 Randy Moss .40 1.00
25 Matt Hasselbeck .40 1.00
26 Jerome Bettis .40 1.00
27 Bill Schroeder .30 .75
28 Jake Plummer .30 .75
29 Rod Smith .30 .75
30 Akili Smith .25 .60
31 Jimmy Smith .30 .75
32 Oronde Gadsden .25 .60
33 Kerry Collins .30 .75
34 Warrick Dunn .40 1.00
35 Jeff Graham .25 .60
36 Ray Lewis .40 1.00
37 Joey Galloway .30 .75
38 Tim Brown .40 1.00
39 Derrick Alexander .25 .60
40 Jerry Rice .75 2.00
41 Muhsin Muhammad .30 .75
42 Shawn Jefferson .25 .60
43 Curtis Martin .40 1.00
44 Terry Glenn .30 .75
45 Marvin Harrison .40 1.00
46 Mike Anderson .30 .75
47 Stephen Davis .30 .75
48 Chad Lewis .25 .60
49 Fred Taylor .40 1.00
50 Corey Dillon .30 .75
51 Charlie Batch .30 .75
52 Kevin Johnson .25 .60
53 Brett Favre 1.25 3.00
54 Marshall Faulk .40 1.00
55 Kordell Stewart .30 .75
56 Steve McNair .40 1.00
57 Jeff Blake .30 .75
58 Eric Moulds .30 .75
59 Emmitt Smith 1.00 2.50
60 David Boston .25 .60
61 Cris Carter .40 1.00
62 Peyton Manning 1.00 2.50
63 Keyshawn Johnson .30 .75
64 Doug Flutie .40 1.00
65 Drew Bledsoe .40 1.00
66 Ricky Williams .40 1.00
67 Keenan Mccardell .30 .75
68 Brian Urlacher .50 1.25
69 Jamal Lewis .40 1.00
70 Ed McCaffrey .30 .75
71 Antonio Freeman .40 1.00
72 Darrell Jackson .30 .75
73 Jeff George .30 .75
74 Chris Chandler .30 .75
75 Germane Crowell .25 .60
76 Tim Biakabutuka .25 .60
77 Jon Kitna .30 .75
78 Troy Brown .30 .75
79 Lamar Smith .30 .75
80 Derrick Mason .30 .75
81 Hines Ward .40 1.00
82 Mark Brunell .30 .75
83 Trent Dilfer .30 .75
84 Tim Couch .25 .60
85 Donald Hayes .25 .60
86 Amani Toomer .30 .75
87 Tony Gonzalez .40 1.00
88 Rich Gannon .30 .75
89 Rob Johnson .30 .75
90 Torry Holt .30 .75
91 Jeff Garcia .30 .75
92 Kurt Warner .60 1.50
93 Aaron Brooks .30 .75
94 Brian Griese .30 .75
95 James Allen .25 .60
96 Wayne Chrebet .30 .75
97 Tiki Barber .40 1.00
98 Brad Johnson .30 .75
99 Ricky Watters .30 .75
100 Charlie Garner .30 .75
101 Andre Carter RC 2.50 6.00
102 Dan Morgan RC 2.50 6.00
103 Gerard Warren RC 2.50 6.00
104 Jesse Palmer RC 2.50 6.00
105 Josh Heupel RC 3.00 8.00
106 Justin Smith RC 3.00 8.00
107 LaMont Jordan RC 3.00 8.00
108 Leonard Davis RC 3.00 8.00
109 Marques Tuiasosopo RC 2.50 6.00
110 Snoop Minnis RC 2.00 5.00
111 Quincy Carter RC 2.50 6.00
112 Quincy Morgan RC 2.50 6.00
113 Richard Seymour RC 3.00 8.00
114 Rudi Johnson RC 3.00 8.00
115 Sage Rosenfels RC 3.00 8.00
116 Todd Heap RC 3.00 8.00
117 Travis Minor RC 2.50 6.00
118 Will Allen RC 3.00 8.00
119 Jamal Reynolds RC 2.00 5.00
120 Scotty Anderson RC 2.00 5.00
121 Anthony Thomas RC 3.00 8.00
122 Chad Johnson RC 5.00 12.00
123 Chris Chambers RC 3.00 8.00
124 Chris Weinke RC 2.50 6.00
125 David Terrell RC 2.50 6.00
126 Deuce McAllister RC 3.00 8.00
127 Drew Brees RC 50.00 80.00
128 Freddie Mitchell RC 2.00 5.00
129 James Jackson RC 2.00 5.00
130 Kevan Barlow RC 2.50 6.00
131 Koren Robinson RC 2.50 6.00
132 LaDainian Tomlinson RC 15.00 40.00
133 Michael Bennett RC 2.50 6.00
134 Michael Vick RC 20.00 50.00
135 Mike McMahon RC 2.50 6.00
136 Reggie Wayne RC 6.00 15.00
137 Robert Ferguson RC 3.00 8.00
138 Rod Gardner RC 2.50 6.00
139 Santana Moss RC 4.00 10.00
140 Travis Henry RC 2.50 6.00

2001 Finest Autographs

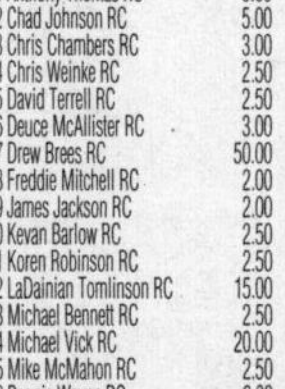

GROUP A STATED ODDS 1:1174
GROUP B, D, E STATED ODDS 1:220
GROUP C STATED ODDS 1:587
GROUP F STATED ODDS 1:176
GROUP G STATED ODDS 1:135
GROUP H STATED ODDS 1:98
GROUP I STATED ODDS 1:10
GROUP J STATED ODDS 1:84
GROUP K STATED ODDS 1:80
GROUP L STATED ODDS 1:59
GROUP M STATED ODDS 1:44
OVERALL STATED ODDS 1:5
FAAB Aaron Brooks K 6.00 15.00
FABN Bobby Newcombe M 6.00 15.00
FABS Bill Schroeder I 6.00 15.00
FACW Chris Weinke C SP 6.00 15.00
FADA Dan Alexander J 6.00 15.00
FADC Daunte Culpepper B SP 10.00 25.00
FADH Donald Hayes I 5.00 12.00
FAEG Eddie George B SP 8.00 20.00
FAEJ Edgerrin James A SP 25.00 50.00
FAEM Eric Moulds H 6.00 15.00
FAES Emmitt Smith D SP 100.00 200.00
FAJG Jeff Garcia E 10.00 25.00
FAJH Joe Horn I 6.00 15.00
FAJJ James Jackson I 5.00 12.00
FAJL Jamal Lewis G 8.00 20.00
FAJS Jimmy Smith I 6.00 15.00
FALS Lamar Smith I 6.00 15.00
FAMB Michael Bennett B SP 6.00 15.00
FAMR Marcus Robinson L 6.00 15.00
FARG Reggie Germany F 5.00 12.00
FASCM Sammy Morris D SP 6.00 15.00
FASM Sylvester Morris I 5.00 12.00
FASMO Santana Moss B SP 20.00 40.00
FATH Travis Henry I 6.00 15.00
FATM Travis Minor I 6.00 15.00

2001 Finest Moments Autographs

STATED ODDS 1:160
FMACW Chris Weinke 6.00 15.00
FMADC Daunte Culpepper 12.00 30.00
FMAEJ Edgerrin James 12.00 30.00
FMAEM Eric Moulds 6.00 15.00
FMAJG Jeff Garcia 12.00 30.00
FMAMV Michael Vick 60.00 120.00

2001 Finest Moments Relics

STATED ODDS 1:176
FMRCJ Chad Johnson 8.00 20.00
FMRDA Dan Alexander 6.00 15.00
FMRDC Daunte Culpepper 6.00 15.00
FMREJ Edgerrin James 8.00 20.00
FMRKB Kevan Barlow 6.00 15.00
FMRLJ LaMont Jordan 8.00 20.00
FMRLT LaDainian Tomlinson FB 15.00 40.00
FMRRG Rich Gannon 6.00 15.00
FMRRG Rod Gardner JSY 6.00 15.00
FMRRW Reggie Wayne 10.00 25.00

2001 Finest Rookie Premiere Jerseys

GROUP A STATED ODDS 1:88
GROUP B STATED ODDS 1:35
GROUP C STATED ODDS 1:11
GROUP D STATED ODDS 1:70
GROUP E STATED ODDS 1:15
OVERALL STATED ODDS 1:5
RPJAC Andre Carter A 3.00 8.00
RPJAT Anthony Thomas C 4.00 10.00
RPJCJ Chad Johnson B 6.00 15.00
RPJCW Chris Weinke E 3.00 8.00
RPJGW Gerard Warren A 3.00 8.00
RPJJH Josh Heupel B 4.00 10.00
RPJJP Jesse Palmer B 3.00 8.00
RPJJS Justin Smith A 4.00 10.00
RPJKB Kevan Barlow B 3.00 8.00
RPJKR Koren Robinson E 3.00 8.00
RPJLD Leonard Davis A 4.00 10.00
RPJMM Mike McMahon B 3.00 8.00
RPJMT Marques Tuiasosopo C 3.00 8.00
RPJMMI Snoop Minnis C 2.50 6.00
RPJRF Robert Ferguson 4.00 10.00
RPJRG Rod Gardner E 3.00 8.00
RPJRJ Rudi Johnson C 4.00 10.00
RPJRW Reggie Wayne E 8.00 20.00
RPJSM Santana Moss D 5.00 12.00
RPJSR Sage Rosenfels C 4.00 10.00
RPJTH Todd Heap C 4.00 10.00
RPJTM Travis Minor C 3.00 8.00

2001 Finest Stadium Throwback Relics

STATED ODDS 1:10
FSBF Brett Favre 15.00 40.00
FSCC Cris Carter 5.00 12.00
FSCD Corey Dillon 4.00 10.00
FSDB Drew Brees 15.00 40.00
FSDC Daunte Culpepper 4.00 10.00
FSDM Donovan McNabb 5.00 12.00
FSEJ Edgerrin James 5.00 12.00
FSEM Eric Moulds 4.00 10.00
FSJB Jerome Bettis 5.00 12.00
FSKR Koren Robinson 4.00 10.00
FSKW Kurt Warner 8.00 20.00
FSLT LaDainian Tomlinson 8.00 20.00
FSMF Marshall Faulk 5.00 12.00
FSMH Marvin Harrison 5.00 12.00
FSMM Snoop Minnis 3.00 8.00
FSPM Peyton Manning 12.00 30.00
FSRG Rod Gardner 4.00 10.00
FSRM Randy Moss 5.00 12.00
FSTC Tim Couch 3.00 8.00
FSTG Tony Gonzalez 5.00 12.00

2002 Finest

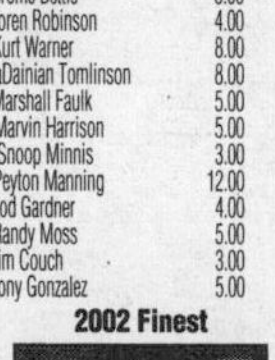

Released in late September, 2002, this set contains 62 veteran base cards, 14 veteran jersey cards, 40 rookies and 22 autographed rookies. The jersey cards #'d/999 were inserted 1:30, and the jersey cards #'d/499 were inserted 1:102 packs. The rookie autographs were inserted 1:18 packs. Please note some autographed rookies were issued via exchange card. The EXCH expiration date was September 30, 2004. The Hobby S.R.P. is $40.00/per mini-box. Each pack contains 5 cards. There are 6 packs per mini-box. Three mini-boxes per full box. Twelve boxes per case.

COMP.SET w/o SP's (62) 15.00 40.00
1 Peyton Manning 1.00 2.50
2 Troy Brown .40 1.00
3 Curtis Martin .50 1.25
4 Kordell Stewart .40 1.00
5 Michael Pittman .40 1.00
6 Rod Gardner .30 .75
7 Germane Crowell .30 .75
8 Terrell Davis .50 1.25
9 Eric Moulds .40 1.00
10 Jake Plummer .40 1.00
11 Tony Gonzalez .50 1.25
12 Ricky Williams .40 1.00
13 Deuce McAllister .40 1.00
14 Jerry Rice 1.00 2.50
15 Torry Holt .50 1.25
16 Michael Vick .75 2.00
17 David Terrell .30 .75
18 Terry Glenn .40 1.00
19 Mark Brunell .40 1.00
20 Vinny Testaverde .40 1.00
21 Jerome Bettis .50 1.25
22 Randy Moss .50 1.25
23 Marvin Harrison .50 1.25
24 Chris Weinke .30 .75
25 Tiki Barber .50 1.25
26 Corey Bradford .30 .75
27 David Boston .30 .75
28 Emmitt Smith 1.25 3.00
29 Santana Moss .40 1.00
30 Brian Griese .40 1.00
31 Priest Holmes .50 1.25
32 Rich Gannon .40 1.00
33 Antowain Smith .40 1.00
34 Marcus Robinson .40 1.00
35 Warrick Dunn .40 1.00
36 Daunte Culpepper .40 1.00
37 Shaun Alexander .40 1.00
38 Kurt Warner .50 1.25
39 Quincy Carter .30 .75
40 Ray Lewis .50 1.25
41 Aaron Brooks .40 1.00
42 Plaxico Burress .40 1.00
43 Jamal Lewis .40 1.00
44 Ahman Green .40 1.00
45 Rod Smith .40 1.00
46 Tim Couch .30 .75
47 Muhsin Muhammad .40 1.00
48 Drew Bledsoe .50 1.25
49 Anthony Thomas .40 1.00
50 Tom Brady 1.25 3.00
51 Trent Green .40 1.00
52 Charlie Garner .40 1.00
53 Darrell Jackson .40 1.00
54 Mike McMahon .30 .75
55 Donovan McNabb .50 1.25
56 Fred Taylor .40 1.00
57 Corey Dillon .40 1.00
58 Keyshawn Johnson .40 1.00
59 Drew Brees .75 2.00
60 Steve McNair .50 1.25
61 Jimmy Smith .40 1.00
62 Terrell Owens .50 1.25
63 Eddie George JSY/499 6.00 15.00
64 Jeff Garcia JSY/999 5.00 12.00
65 LaDain Tomlinson JSY/999 8.00 20.00
66 Cris Carter JSY/499 8.00 20.00
67 Chris Chambers JSY/499 6.00 15.00
68 Brian Urlacher JSY/999 6.00 15.00
69 Tim Brown JSY/999 6.00 15.00
70 Marshall Faulk JSY/999 6.00 15.00
71 Stephen Davis JSY/999 5.00 12.00
72 Jevon Kearse JSY/999 5.00 12.00
73 Edgerrin James JSY/999 5.00 12.00
74 Mike Anderson JSY/999 5.00 12.00
75 Warren Sapp JSY/499 6.00 15.00
76 Brett Favre JSY/499 20.00 50.00
77 Julius Peppers RC 2.50 6.00
78 Tim Carter RC 1.00 2.50
79 Travis Stephens RC .75 2.00
80 Jabar Gaffney RC 1.25 3.00
81 Cliff Russell RC .75 2.00
82 Reche Caldwell RC 1.25 3.00
83 Maurice Morris RC 1.00 2.50
84 Antwaan Randle El RC 1.25 3.00
85 Ladell Betts RC 1.25 3.00
86 Daniel Graham RC 1.00 2.50
87 Jeremy Shockey RC 2.00 5.00
88 Mike Williams RC .75 2.00
89 Josh McCown RC 1.25 3.00
90 Rohan Davey RC 1.25 3.00
91 David Garrard RC 1.50 4.00
92 Dwight Freeney RC 1.50 4.00
93 Leonard Henry RC .75 2.00
94 Albert Haynesworth RC 1.25 3.00
95 Herb Haygood RC .75 2.00
96 Kurt Kittner RC .75 2.00
97 Jason McAddley RC 1.00 2.50
98 Bryan Thomas RC .75 2.00
99 Wendell Bryant RC .75 2.00
100 Mike Rumph RC .75 2.00
101 Chad Hutchinson RC .75 2.00
102 Brian Westbrook RC 2.00 5.00
103 Deion Branch RC 1.25 3.00
104 John Henderson RC 1.00 2.50
105 Jerramy Stevens RC 1.25 3.00
106 Tracey Wistrom RC 1.00 2.50
107 Phillip Buchanon RC 1.25 3.00
108 Matt Schobel RC 1.25 3.00
109 Ed Reed RC 5.00 12.00
110 Randy Fasani RC 1.00 2.50
111 Josh Scobey RC 1.00 2.50
112 Luke Staley RC .75 2.00
113 Anthony Weaver RC .75 2.00
114 Kyle Johnson RC .75 2.00
115 David Carr AU RC 8.00 20.00
116 Joey Harrington AU RC 8.00 20.00
117 Donte Stallworth AU RC 8.00 20.00
118 Ashley Lelie AU RC 6.00 15.00
119 Patrick Ramsey AU RC 8.00 20.00
120 William Green AU RC 6.00 15.00
121 Josh Reed AU RC 6.00 15.00
122 Clinton Portis AU RC 25.00 50.00
123 Antonio Bryant AU RC 8.00 20.00
124 Javon Walker AU RC 8.00 20.00
125 Roy Williams AU RC 8.00 20.00
126 Marquise Walker AU RC 5.00 12.00
127 Quentin Jammer AU RC 8.00 20.00
128 DeShaun Foster AU RC 8.00 20.00
129 Andre Davis AU RC 6.00 15.00
130 Ron Johnson AU RC 6.00 15.00
131 Lamar Gordon AU RC 6.00 15.00
132 T.J. Duckett AU/300 RC 8.00 20.00
133 Freddie Milons AU RC 5.00 12.00
134 Eric Crouch AU RC 8.00 20.00
135 Adrian Peterson AU RC 8.00 20.00
136 Damien Anderson AU RC 5.00 12.00

2002 Finest Refractors

*VETS 1-62: 3X TO 8X BASIC CARDS
1-62 VETERAN ODDS 1:12 PACKS
*JSY/250: .5X TO 1.2X BASE JSY/999
*JSY/250: .4X TO 1X BASE JSY/499
63-76 JERSEY ODDS 1:72 PACKS
*ROOKIES 77-114: 1.2X TO 3X
77-114 ROOKIE PRINT RUN 250
*ROOKIE AU 115-136: .6X TO 1.5X
115-136 ROOKIE AU/175 ODDS 1:66
115-136 PRINT RUN 175 SER.#'d SETS
122 Clinton Portis AU 60.00 150.00

2002 Finest Gold Refractors

*VETS 1-62: 12X TO 30X BASIC CARDS
*JSY/25: 1X TO 2.5X BASIC JSY/999
JSY/999 ODDS 1:1746 PACKS
*JSY/25: .8X TO 2X BASIC JSY/499
JSY/499 ODDS 1:1470 PACKS
*ROOKIES 77-114: 5X TO 12X
*ROOKIE AU 115-136: 1.2X TO 3X
GOLD REF/25 OVERALL ODDS 1:102
STATED PRINT RUN 25 SER.#'d SETS
122 Clinton Portis AU 100.00 200.00

2002 Finest Xfractors

*JSY/20: 1X TO 2.5X BASE JSY/999
*JSY/20: .8X TO 2X BASE JSY/499
*ROOKIES 77-114: 5X TO 12X
*ROOKIE AU 115-136: 1.2X TO 3X
XFRACTOR/20 ODDS 1:3810
STATED PRINT RUN 20 SER.#'d SETS

2003 Finest

Released in October of 2003, this set consists of 149 cards including 60 veterans, 40 rookies, 18 jerseys, and 31 rookie autographs. The boxes contained three mini-boxes of 6 packs, with each pack featuring five cards. The SRP for the mini-boxes was $40. Card #149 was initially issued in packs as an exchange card, but the card was never fulfilled.

COMP.SET w/o SP's (100) 20.00 50.00
101-118 GROUP A ODDS 1:171 MINI-BOXES
101-118 GROUP B ODDS 1:38 MINI-BOXES
101-118 GROUP C ODDS 1:4 MINI-BOXES
ROOKIE AU/999 ODDS 1:3 MINI-BOXES
ROOKIE AU/399 ODDS 1:30 MINI-BOXES
1 Chad Pennington .40 1.00
2 Tommy Maddox .30 .75
3 Brett Favre 1.00 2.50
4 Eric Moulds .30 .75
5 Randy Moss .40 1.00
6 Duce Staley .30 .75
7 Derrick Mason .30 .75
8 Shaun Alexander .30 .75
9 Peyton Manning .75 2.00
10 Kerry Collins .30 .75
11 Joe Horn .30 .75
12 Laveranues Coles .25 .60
13 Marty Booker .30 .75
14 Emmitt Smith 1.00 2.50
15 Edgerrin James .40 1.00
16 Aaron Brooks .30 .75
17 Curtis Martin .40 1.00
18 Hines Ward .40 1.00
19 Rod Smith .30 .75
20 Priest Holmes .40 1.00
21 Jerry Rice .75 2.00
22 Peerless Price .25 .60
23 Mark Brunell .30 .75
24 Trent Green .30 .75
25 David Boston .25 .60
26 Chris Chambers .30 .75
27 Marshall Faulk .40 1.00
28 Fred Taylor .30 .75
29 Tim Couch .25 .60
30 Amani Toomer .30 .75
31 Travis Henry .25 .60
32 Jeff Blake .30 .75
33 Troy Brown .30 .75
34 Charlie Garner .30 .75
35 Tom Brady 1.00 2.50
36 Warrick Dunn .30 .75
37 Plaxico Burress .30 .75
38 Marvin Harrison .40 1.00
39 Clinton Portis .30 .75
40 Deuce McAllister .30 .75
41 Matt Hasselbeck .30 .75
42 Jeff Garcia .30 .75
43 David Carr .30 .75
44 Ahman Green .30 .75
45 Eddie George .30 .75
46 Drew Brees .40 1.00
47 Tiki Barber .40 1.00
48 Jay Fiedler .25 .60
49 Curtis Conway .25 .60
50 Steve McNair .40 1.00
51 Donald Driver .40 1.00
52 Jake Plummer .30 .75
53 Jamal Lewis .30 .75
54 Corey Dillon .30 .75
55 Stephen Davis .30 .75
56 Terrell Owens .40 1.00
57 Torry Holt .40 1.00
58 Chad Johnson .40 1.00
59 Chad Hutchinson .25 .60
60 Kurt Warner .40 1.00
61 Troy Polamalu RC 12.00 30.00
62 Eugene Wilson RC 1.25 3.00
63 Juston Wood RC .75 2.00
64 Anquan Boldin RC 2.00 5.00
65 Doug Gabriel RC 1.00 2.50
66 Domanick Davis RC 1.00 2.50
67 J.R. Tolver RC 1.00 2.50
68 Jerome McDougle RC .75 2.00
69 Keenan Howry RC .75 2.00
70 Teyo Johnson RC 1.00 2.50
71 Bethel Johnson RC .75 2.00
72 Ken Hamlin RC 1.25 3.00
73 L.J. Smith RC 1.25 3.00
74 Rashean Mathis RC 1.00 2.50
75 Arnaz Battle RC 1.25 3.00
76 B.J. Askew RC 1.00 2.50
77 Mike Doss RC 1.25 3.00
78 Kevin Curtis RC 1.25 3.00
79 Terence Newman RC 1.00 2.50
80 Shaun McDonald RC 1.00 2.50
81 Kevin Williams RC 1.25 3.00
82 Nate Burleson RC 1.00 2.50
83 Tyrone Calico RC 1.00 2.50
84 DeWayne White RC .75 2.00
85 Marcus Trufant RC 1.00 2.50
86 Nick Barnett RC 1.25 3.00
87 Bennie Joppru RC .75 2.00
88 Andre Woolfolk RC 1.00 2.50
89 Billy McMullen RC .75 2.00
90 Boss Bailey RC 1.00 2.50
91 William Joseph RC .75 2.00
92 Michael Haynes RC .75 2.00
93 DeWayne Robertson RC 1.00 2.50
94 LaTarence Dunbar RC .75 2.00
95 David Tyree RC 1.25 3.00
96 Walter Young RC .75 2.00
97 E.J. Henderson RC 1.00 2.50
98 Ty Warren RC 1.00 2.50
99 Zuriel Smith RC .75 2.00
100 Brock Forsey RC 1.00 2.50
101 Ricky Williams JSY C 4.00 10.00
102 Drew Bledsoe JSY C 5.00 12.00
103 Joey Harrington JSY C 3.00 8.00
104 Tim Brown JSY C 5.00 12.00
105 Brian Urlacher JSY C 5.00 12.00
106 Zach Thomas JSY C 5.00 12.00
107 Jeremy Shockey JSY C 5.00 12.00
108 Michael Strahan JSY A 6.00 15.00
109 Jason Taylor JSY C 4.00 10.00
110 Donovan McNabb JSY C 5.00 12.00
111 LaDainian Tomlinson JSY B 6.00 15.00
112 Rich Gannon JSY C 4.00 10.00
113 Brad Johnson JSY C 4.00 10.00
114 Daunte Culpepper JSY C 4.00 10.00
115 Michael Vick JSY C 6.00 15.00
116 Jimmy Smith JSY B 5.00 12.00
117 Keyshawn Johnson JSY C 5.00 12.00
118 Keith Brooking JSY C 4.00 10.00
119 Carson Palmer AU/399 RC 25.00 50.00
120 Byron Leftwich AU/399 RC 10.00 25.00
121 Chris Simms AU/399 RC 10.00 25.00
122 Kyle Boller AU/399 RC 10.00 25.00
123 Justin Fargas AU RC 6.00 15.00
124 Seneca Wallace AU RC 6.00 15.00
125 Larry Johnson AU RC 6.00 15.00
126 Kareem Kelly AU RC 4.00 10.00
127 Willis McGahee AU/399 RC 12.00 30.00
128 Kelley Washington AU RC 4.00 10.00
129 Brian St.Pierre AU RC 5.00 12.00
130 Kliff Kingsbury AU RC 5.00 12.00
131 Ken Dorsey AU RC 5.00 12.00
132 Bryant Johnson AU RC 6.00 15.00
133 Dallas Clark AU RC 15.00 40.00
134 Chris Brown AU RC 4.00 10.00
135 Taylor Jacobs AU RC 4.00 10.00
136 Artose Pinner AU RC 4.00 10.00
137 Lee Suggs AU RC 5.00 12.00
138 LaBrandon Toefield AU RC 5.00 12.00
139 Jason Witten AU RC 20.00 40.00
140 Brad Banks AU RC 5.00 12.00
141 Earnest Graham AU RC 8.00 20.00
142 Bobby Wade AU RC 5.00 12.00
143 Talman Gardner AU RC 4.00 10.00
144 Justin Gage AU RC 5.00 12.00
145 Sam Aiken AU RC 5.00 12.00
146 Musa Smith AU RC 4.00 10.00
147 Terrell Suggs AU RC 12.50 25.00
148 Brandon Lloyd AU RC 8.00 20.00
150 Rex Grossman AU RC 8.00 15.00

2003 Finest Refractors

*STARS: 2.5X TO 6X BASIC CARDS
*ROOKIES 61-100: 1.5X TO 4X
1-100 ODDS 1:3 MINI-BOX
*VET JSY 101-118: .4X TO 1X GRP A-B
*VET JSY 101-118: .5X TO 1.2X GRP C
101-118 VET JSY ODDS 1:17 MINI-BOX
*ROOK.AU: .5X TO 1.2X BASE AU/399
*ROOK.AU: .8X TO 2X BASE AU/999
ROOKIE AU ODDS 1:10 MINI-BOXES
PRINT RUN 199 SERIAL #'d SETS
119 Carson Palmer AU 60.00 120.00
139 Jason Witten AU 40.00 100.00

2003 Finest Gold Refractors

*VETS 1-60: 6X TO 15X BASIC CARDS
*ROOKIES 61-100: 3X TO 8X
1-100 ODDS 1:12 MINI-BOX
*VET JSY 101-118: .5X TO 1.2X GRP A-B
*VET JSY 101-118: .6X TO 1.5X GRP C
101-118 VET JSY ODDS 1:68 MINI-BOX
*ROOKIE AU/399: .6X TO 1.5X
*ROOK.AU/50: 1.2X TO 3X BASE AU/999
ROOKIE AU ODDS 1:38 MINI-BOXES
PRINT RUN 50 SERIAL #'d SETS
119 Carson Palmer AU 75.00 150.00
139 Jason Witten AU 60.00 120.00
150 Rex Grossman AU 20.00 50.00

2003 Finest Xfractors

*VETS 1-60: 3X TO 8X BASIC CARDS
*ROOKIES 61-100: 2X TO 5X
1-100 PRINT RUN 175
*VET JSY 101-118: .5X TO 1.2X GRP A-B
*VET JSY 101-118: .6X TO 1.5X GRP C
*ROOKIE AU/399: .6X TO 1.5X
*ROOKIE AU/999: 1.2X TO 3X
101-150 PRINT RUN 50
119 Carson Palmer AU 50.00 120.00
139 Jason Witten AU 50.00 120.00

2004 Finest

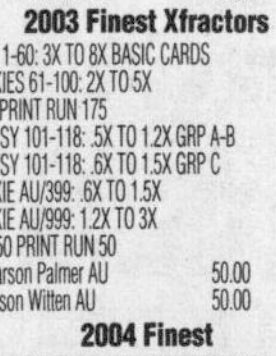

Finest initially released in early November 2004. The base set consists of 134-cards including 40-rookies (#61-100), 7-veteran jersey cards, and 27-signed and serial numbered rookies. Hobby boxes contained 18-packs of 5-cards and carried an S.R.P. of $6 per pack. Four basic parallel sets can be found seeded in hobby packs with four additional 1/1 Printing Plate parallels produced as well.

COMP.SET w/o SP's (100) 15.00 40.00
COMP.SET w/o RC's (60) 5.00 12.00

108-134 AU/399 RC STATED ODDS 1:120
108-134 AU/999 RC STATED ODDS 1:12
1 Steve McNair .30 .75
2 Corey Dillon .25 .60
3 Joey Harrington .25 .60
4 Travis Henry .20 .50
5 Donovan McNabb .30 .75
6 Jamal Lewis .25 .60
7 Jeff Garcia .25 .60
8 Fred Taylor .25 .60
9 Aaron Brooks .25 .60
10 Marc Bulger .25 .60
11 Keenan McCardell .20 .50
12 David Carr .20 .50
13 Charles Rogers .20 .50
14 Ray Lewis .30 .75
15 Priest Holmes .30 .75
16 Curtis Martin .30 .75
17 Plaxico Burress .25 .60
18 Shaun Alexander .25 .60
19 Brad Johnson .25 .60
20 Marvin Harrison .30 .75
21 Rod Smith .25 .60
22 Jake Delhomme .25 .60
23 Santana Moss .25 .60
24 Trent Green .25 .60
25 Michael Vick .40 1.00
26 Tim Rattay .20 .50
27 Chris Chambers .25 .60
28 Robert Ferguson .20 .50
29 Tiki Barber .30 .75
30 Terrell Owens .30 .75
31 Marshall Faulk .30 .75
32 Quincy Carter .20 .50
33 Stephen Davis .25 .60
34 Josh McCown .25 .60
35 Jeremy Shockey .25 .60
36 Tommy Maddox .25 .60
37 Derrick Mason .25 .60
38 Kerry Collins .25 .60
39 Jimmy Smith .25 .60
40 Chad Pennington .30 .75
41 Domanick Davis .20 .50
42 Darrell Jackson .25 .60
43 Steve Smith .30 .75
44 Drew Bledsoe .30 .75
45 Deuce McAllister .25 .60
46 Jerry Porter .20 .50
47 Peerless Price .20 .50
48 Eric Moulds .25 .60
49 Garrison Hearst .25 .60
50 Brett Favre .75 2.00
51 Amani Toomer .25 .60
52 Andre Johnson .30 .75
53 Edgerrin James .25 .60
54 Rex Grossman .25 .60
55 Daunte Culpepper .25 .60
56 Tony Gonzalez .30 .75
57 Byron Leftwich .25 .60
58 Mark Brunell .25 .60
59 Laveranues Coles .20 .50
60 Matt Hasselbeck .25 .60
61 Chris Gamble RC .60 1.50
62 Michael Turner RC 1.00 2.50
63 Julius Jones RC .60 1.50
64 Dunta Robinson RC .50 1.25
65 Sean Taylor RC 1.50 4.00
66 Ahmad Carroll RC .50 1.25
67 Derrick Strait RC .50 1.25
68 Dontarrious Thomas RC .60 1.50
69 Jason Babin RC .75 2.00
70 Reggie Williams RC .60 1.50
71 Dwan Edwards RC .50 1.25
72 Rashaun Woods RC .50 1.25
73 Ricardo Colclough RC .60 1.50
74 Will Smith RC .60 1.50
75 Kellen Winslow RC .75 2.00
76 Roy Williams RC .75 2.00
77 B.J. Symons RC .50 1.25
78 Carlos Francis RC .50 1.25
79 Triandos Luke RC .50 1.25
80 Drew Henson RC .50 1.25
81 Keiwan Ratliff RC .50 1.25
82 Will Poole RC .75 2.00
83 Tommie Harris RC .75 2.00
84 Steven Jackson RC 1.25 3.00
85 Greg Jones RC .50 1.25
86 Vince Wilfork RC .75 2.00
87 DeAngelo Hall RC .75 2.00
88 Daryl Smith RC .50 1.25
89 Teddy Lehman RC .50 1.25
90 Casey Bramlet RC .50 1.25
91 Marcus Tubbs RC .50 1.25
92 Andy Hall RC .50 1.25
93 Jim Sorgi RC .60 1.50
94 Kenechi Udeze RC .60 1.50
95 Darius Watts RC .50 1.25
96 Tank Johnson RC .50 1.25
97 Matt Mauck RC .50 1.25
98 Bradlee Van Pelt RC .60 1.50
99 D.J. Williams RC .75 2.00
100 Larry Fitzgerald RC 2.00 5.00
101 Peyton Manning JSY 6.00 15.00
102 Clinton Portis JSY 3.00 8.00
103 Chad Johnson JSY 3.00 8.00
104 Randy Moss JSY 3.00 8.00
105 Tom Brady JSY 6.00 15.00
106 LaDainian Tomlinson JSY 3.00 8.00
107 Ahman Green JSY 2.50 6.00
108 Ben Roethlisberger AU/399 RC 125.00 200.00
109 Philip Rivers AU/399 RC 40.00 80.00
110 Eli Manning AU/399 RC 100.00 200.00
111 Kevin Jones AU/399 RC 6.00 15.00
112 Bernard Berrian AU RC 6.00 15.00
113 Jeff Smoker AU RC 5.00 12.00
114 Mewelde Moore AU RC 5.00 12.00
115 Michael Clayton AU RC 5.00 12.00
116 Jonathan Vilma AU RC 6.00 15.00
117 Johnnie Morant AU RC 4.00 10.00
118 Devard Darling AU RC 4.00 10.00
119 Cedric Cobbs AU RC 4.00 10.00
120 Chris Perry AU/399 RC 6.00 15.00
121 Ernest Wilford AU RC 5.00 12.00
122 Michael Jenkins AU RC 6.00 15.00
123 Jerricho Cotchery AU RC 5.00 12.00
124 P.K. Sam AU RC 4.00 10.00
125 Tatum Bell AU RC 5.00 12.00
126 Derrick Hamilton AU RC 4.00 10.00
127 Luke McCown AU RC 5.00 12.00
128 Devery Henderson AU RC 6.00 15.00
129 Craig Krenzel AU RC 5.00 12.00
130 J.P. Losman AU RC 5.00 12.00
131 Lee Evans AU RC 6.00 15.00
132 Matt Schaub AU RC 20.00 50.00
133 Robert Gallery AU RC 6.00 15.00
134 Keary Colbert AU RC 4.00 10.00

2004 Finest Refractors

*STARS: 2.5X TO 6X BASE CARD HI
*ROOKIES 61-100: 1.5X TO 4X
1-100 SER.#'d TO 199, STATED ODDS 1:12
*VETERAN JSY: .5X TO 1.2X BASE JSYs
VETERAN JERSEY STATED ODDS 1:168
*ROOKIE AUs: .6X TO 1.5X BASE AU/999
ROOKIE AUTO SER.#'d TO 199, ODDS 1:48
108 Ben Roethlisberger AU 175.00 300.00
109 Philip Rivers AU 40.00 100.00
110 Eli Manning AU 150.00 300.00
132 Matt Schaub AU 40.00 100.00

2004 Finest Gold Refractors

*STARS: 6X TO 15X BASE CARD HI
*ROOKIES 61-100: 3X TO 8X BASE CARD HI
1-100 SER.#'d TO 50, STATED ODDS 1:48
*VETERAN JSY: 1.2X TO 3X BASE CARD HI
VETERAN JERSEY STATED ODDS 1:684
*ROOKIE AUs: 1.2X TO 3X BASE AU/999
ROOKIE AUTO SER.#'d TO 50, ODDS 1:180
108 Ben Roethlisberger AU 250.00 400.00
109 Philip Rivers AU 75.00 150.00
110 Eli Manning AU 250.00 400.00
132 Matt Schaub AU 75.00 150.00

2004 Finest Refractors Xfractors

1-100 STATED ODDS 1:468
VETERAN JERSEY STATED ODDS 1:8856
ROOKIE AUTO STATED ODDS 1:2166
UNPRICED XFRACTORS SER.#'d TO 5

2004 Finest Uncirculated Gold Xfractors

*STARS: 5X TO 12X BASE CARD HI
*ROOKIES: 2.5X TO 6X BASE CARD HI
STATED PRINT RUN 150 SER.#'d SETS

2005 Finest

This 183-card set was released in October, 2005. The set was issued through the hobby in five-card packs with an $8 SRP which came 18 packs to a box. Cards numbered 1-120 feature veterans while cards 121-183 were NFL rookies. In the rookie grouping, cards numbered 151-183 were all signed. Cards numbered 151-160 were signed to a stated print run of 299 serial numbered cards while there was no serial numbering for cards 151-183.

COMP.SET w/o AUs (150) 25.00 60.00
UNPRICED FRAMED REF. PRINT RUN 1 SET
UNPRICED FRAM.XFRAC. PRINT RUN 1 SET
UNPRICED GOLD XFRAC.PRINT RUN 10 SETS
UNPRICED PRINT.PLATE PRINT RUN 1 SET
UNPRICED SUPERFRACTORS #'d TO 1
1 Muhsin Muhammad .25 .60
2 Kevin Jones .20 .50
3 Eli Manning .50 1.25
4 Kevan Barlow .20 .50
5 Randy Moss .30 .75
6 Brian Griese .25 .60
7 Dante Hall .20 .50
8 Chris Brown .20 .50
9 Antonio Gates .30 .75
10 Champ Bailey .25 .60
11 Eric Moulds .20 .50
12 Ray Lewis .30 .75
13 Larry Fitzgerald .30 .75
14 Byron Leftwich .25 .60
15 Marvin Harrison .30 .75
16 Stephen Davis .25 .60
17 Laveranues Coles .20 .50
18 Shaun Alexander .25 .60
19 Drew Bledsoe .30 .75
20 Sean Taylor .30 .75
21 Deuce McAllister .25 .60
22 Nate Burleson .20 .50
23 A.J. Feeley .20 .50
24 Jerome Bettis .30 .75
25 Torry Holt .25 .60
26 LaDainian Tomlinson .30 .75
27 Travis Henry .20 .50
28 T.J. Houshmandzadeh .25 .60
29 Fred Taylor .25 .60
30 Michael Jenkins .25 .60
31 Edgerrin James .25 .60
32 Terrell Owens .30 .75
33 Jason Witten .30 .75
34 Clinton Portis .25 .60
35 Deion Branch .20 .50
36 Priest Holmes .25 .60
37 Javon Walker .20 .50
38 Rex Grossman .25 .60
39 Domanick Davis .20 .50
40 Allen Rossum .20 .50
41 Dwight Freeney .25 .60
42 Jimmy Smith .25 .60
43 Tiki Barber .30 .75
44 Steve McNair .30 .75
45 Steven Jackson .30 .75
46 Joe Horn .25 .60
47 Randy McMichael .20 .50
48 J.P. Losman .20 .50
49 Warrick Dunn .25 .60
50 Tatum Bell .20 .50
51 Roy Williams WR .25 .60
52 Curtis Martin .30 .75
53 Donovan McNabb .30 .75
54 LaMont Jordan .25 .60
55 Marc Bulger .25 .60
56 Drew Bennett .25 .60
57 Julius Jones .20 .50
58 Santana Moss .25 .60
59 Michael Bennett .25 .60
60 Tony Gonzalez .25 .60
61 Jamal Lewis .25 .60
62 Keary Colbert .20 .50
63 Carson Palmer .30 .75
64 Dunta Robinson .20 .50
65 Brandon Stokley .20 .50
66 Brett Favre .75 2.00
67 Jonathan Vilma .25 .60
68 Darrell Jackson .20 .50
69 Michael Pittman .20 .50
70 Drew Brees .30 .75
71 Amani Toomer .25 .60
72 Corey Dillon .25 .60
73 Willis McGahee .30 .75
74 Michael Vick .30 .75
75 Chad Johnson .25 .60
76 Anquan Boldin .25 .60
77 Kerry Collins .25 .60
78 Marshall Faulk .30 .75
79 Roy Williams S .20 .50
80 Trent Green .25 .60
81 Chris Gamble .20 .50
82 Ahman Green .25 .60
83 Todd Heap .25 .60
84 Brandon Lloyd .20 .50
85 Andre Johnson .30 .75
86 Lee Suggs .20 .50
87 Plaxico Burress .25 .60
88 Hines Ward .30 .75
89 Rod Smith .25 .60
90 Joey Harrington .25 .60
91 Derrick Mason .25 .60
92 Rudi Johnson .25 .60
93 Isaac Bruce .25 .60
94 Chris Chambers .25 .60
95 Matt Hasselbeck .25 .60
96 Donte Stallworth .20 .50
97 Philip Rivers .30 .75
98 Michael Clayton .20 .50
99 Alge Crumpler .25 .60
100 Chad Pennington .30 .75
101 Brian Westbrook .25 .60
102 Daunte Culpepper .25 .60
103 Jeremy Shockey .30 .75
104 Jerry Porter .20 .50
105 Tom Brady .60 1.50
106 Lee Evans .25 .60
107 Jake Delhomme .25 .60
108 Ben Roethlisberger .50 1.25
109 Jake Plummer .25 .60
110 Charles Rogers .20 .50
111 Patrick Ramsey .25 .60
112 Reggie Wayne .30 .75
113 Reuben Droughns .20 .50
114 Aaron Brooks .20 .50
115 David Carr .20 .50
116 Thomas Jones .30 .75
117 Ashley Lelie .20 .50
118 Donald Driver .30 .75
119 Billy Volek .20 .50
120 Peyton Manning .60 1.50
121 Frank Gore RC 1.50 4.00
122 Adam Jones RC .60 1.50
123 Antrel Rolle RC 1.00 2.50
124 Roddy White RC 1.25 3.00
125 Derrick Johnson RC .75 2.00
126 Troy Williamson RC .75 2.00
127 Maurice Clarett .60 1.50
128 Dan Orlovsky RC 1.00 2.50
129 Andrew Walter RC .75 2.00
130 Reggie Brown RC .60 1.50
131 Matt Jones RC .75 2.00
132 David Greene RC .60 1.50
133 Jerome Mathis RC 1.00 2.50
134 Thomas Davis RC .60 1.50
135 Roscoe Parrish RC .60 1.50
136 Ciatrick Fason RC .60 1.50
137 David Pollack RC .75 2.00
138 Kyle Orton RC 1.00 2.50
139 Heath Miller RC 1.25 3.00
140 Courtney Roby RC .75 2.00
141 Terrence Murphy RC .60 1.50
142 DeMarcus Ware RC 2.00 5.00
143 Fabian Washington RC .75 2.00
144 J.J. Arrington RC .75 2.00
145 Fred Gibson RC .75 2.00
146 Carlos Rogers RC 1.00 2.50
147 Eric Shelton RC .60 1.50
148 Craphonso Thorpe RC .60 1.50
149 Anthony Davis RC .60 1.50
150 Marion Barber RC 1.00 2.50
151 Aaron Rodgers AU/299 RC 350.00 500.00
152 Alex Smith QB AU/299 RC 30.00 60.00
153 Braylon Edwards AU/299 RC 20.00 50.00
154 Cadillac Williams AU/299 RC 15.00 40.00
155 Cedric Benson AU/299 RC 15.00 40.00
156 Charlie Frye AU/299 RC 12.00 30.00
157 Jason Campbell AU/299 RC 15.00 40.00
158 Mark Clayton AU/299 RC 12.00 30.00
159 Mike Williams AU/299 12.00 30.00
160 Ronnie Brown AU/299 RC 15.00 40.00
161 Alex Smith TE AU RC 3.00 8.00
162 Alvin Pearman AU RC 3.00 8.00
163 Brandon Jacobs AU RC 10.00 25.00
164 Channing Crowder AU RC 4.00 10.00
165 Chris Henry AU RC 5.00 12.00
166 Courtney Roby AU RC 4.00 10.00
167 Derek Anderson AU RC 4.00 10.00
168 Mark Bradley AU RC 3.00 8.00
169 Ryan Fitzpatrick AU RC 12.50 25.00
170 Ryan Moats AU RC 3.00 8.00
171 Stefan LeFors AU RC 3.00 8.00
172 Steve Savoy AU RC 3.00 8.00
173 Tab Perry AU RC 3.00 8.00
174 Timmy Chang AU RC 4.00 10.00
175 Vincent Jackson AU RC 8.00 20.00
176 Charles Frederick AU RC 3.00 8.00
177 Kay-Jay Harris AU RC 3.00 8.00
178 Darren Sproles AU RC 8.00 20.00
179 Adrian McPherson AU RC 3.00 8.00
180 Craig Bragg AU RC 3.00 8.00
181 J.R. Russell AU RC 3.00 8.00
182 Gino Guidugli AU RC 3.00 8.00
183 Vernand Morency AU RC 3.00 8.00

2005 Finest Refractors

*VETERANS: 2X TO 5X BASIC CARDS
*ROOKIE 121-150: .6X TO 1.5X BASIC CARD
*ROOKIE AU 161-183: .4X TO 1X BASIC AU
STATED PRINT RUN 399 SER.#'d SETS

2005 Finest Xfractors

*VETERANS 1-120: 2.5X TO 6X BASIC CARDS
*ROOKIES 121-150: .8X TO 2X BASIC CARDS
*ROOKIE AU 161-183: .5X TO 1.2X
STATED PRINT RUN 250 SER.#'d SETS

2005 Finest Black Refractors

*VETERANS: 5X TO 12X BASIC CARDS
*ROOKIES 121-150: 1.5X TO 4X BASIC CARDS
*ROOKIE AU 161-183: 1X TO 2.5X
STATED PRINT RUN 99 SER.#'d SETS

2005 Finest Black Xfractors

*VETERANS: 10X TO 25X BASIC CARDS
*ROOKIES 121-150: 4X TO 10X BASIC CARDS
*ROOKIE AU 161-183: 2X TO 5X BASIC AUTOS
STATED PRINT RUN 25 SER.#'d SETS

2005 Finest Gold Refractors

*VETERANS: 6X TO 15X BASIC CARDS
*ROOKIES 121-150: 2.5X TO 6X BASIC CARDS
*ROOKIE AU 161-183: 1.2X TO 3X
STATED PRINT RUN 49 SER.#'d SETS

2005 Finest Green Refractors

*VETERANS: 3X TO 8X BASIC CARDS
*ROOKIES 121-150: 1X TO 2.5X BASIC CARDS
*ROOKIE AU 161-183: .6X TO 1.5X
STATED PRINT RUN 199 SER.#'d SETS

2005 Finest Green Xfractors

*VETERANS: 6X TO 15X BASIC CARDS
*ROOKIES 121-150: 2.5X TO 6X BASIC CARDS
*ROOKIE AU 161-183: 1.2X TO 3X
STATED PRINT RUN 50 SER.#'d SETS

2005 Finest Blue Refractors

*VETERANS: 2.5X TO 6X BASIC CARDS
*ROOKIES 121-150: .8X TO 2X BASIC CARDS
*ROOKIE AU 161-183: .5X TO 1.2X
STATED PRINT RUN 299 SER.#'d SETS

2005 Finest Blue Xfractors

*VETERANS: 4X TO 10X BASIC CARDS
*ROOKIES 121-150: 1.2X TO 3X BASIC CARDS
*ROOKIE AU 161-183: .8X TO 2X
STATED PRINT RUN 150 SER.#'d SETS

2005 Finest Autographs Refractor

UNPRICED SUPERFRACTORS #'d TO 1
*XFRACTOR/199: .6X TO 1.5X BASIC AU
FAAM Adrian McPherson 4.00 10.00
FAAR Antrel Rolle 6.00 15.00
FABJ Brandon Jones 5.00 12.00
FACF Ciatrick Fason 4.00 10.00
FACT Craphonso Thorpe 4.00 10.00
FADJ Derrick Johnson 5.00 12.00
FADO Dan Orlovsky 6.00 15.00
FADS Darren Sproles 6.00 15.00
FAFW Fabian Washington 5.00 12.00
FAKC Kevin Curtis 5.00 12.00
FAMB Marion Barber 6.00 15.00
FANB Nate Burleson 4.00 10.00
FAOS Onterrio Smith 4.00 10.00
FARP Roscoe Parrish 4.00 10.00
FARW Roddy White 8.00 20.00
FASM Shawne Merriman 6.00 15.00
FATB Tatum Bell 4.00 10.00
FATW Troy Williamson 5.00 12.00

2005 Finest Peyton Manning Finest Moments

COMMON CARD (FM1-FM49) 2.50 6.00
STATED PRINT RUN 599 SER.#'d SETS
UNPRICED AUTOS PRINT RUN 1 SET

2006 Finest

This 186-card set was released In October, 2006. The set was issued in five-card packs; with an $8.50 SRP, which came six packs to a mini-box and three mini-boxes to a full box. Cards numbered 1-105 feature veterans while cards numbered 106-186 feature rookies. Within the rookie subset, cards numbered 151-186 were signed by the featured players. A few of those players who signed cards autographed fewer cards then the other players and those signed cards were serial numbered. The serial numbering of those signed cards are notated in our checklist.

COMP.SET w/o AU's (150) 12.50 30.00
1 Muhsin Muhammad .25 .60
2 Kevin Jones .20 .50
3 Eli Manning .40 1.00
4 Marion Barber .25 .60
5 Randy Moss .30 .75
6 Odell Thurman .20 .50
7 Dante Hall .25 .60
8 Chris Brown .20 .50
9 Antonio Gates .30 .75
10 Champ Bailey .25 .60
11 Eric Moulds .20 .50
12 Ray Lewis .30 .75
13 Larry Fitzgerald .30 .75
14 Byron Leftwich .25 .60
15 Marvin Harrison .30 .75
16 Larry Johnson .25 .60
17 Steve Smith .30 .75
18 Shaun Alexander .25 .60
19 Drew Bledsoe .30 .75
20 Joey Galloway .25 .60
21 Deuce McAllister .25 .60
22 Ben Obomanu RC 1.50 4.00
23 Chester Taylor .25 .60
24 Delanie Walker RC 1.50 4.00
25 Torry Holt .25 .60
26 LaDainian Tomlinson .30 .75
27 Derrick Mason .25 .60
28 T.J. Houshmandzadeh .25 .60
29 Fred Taylor .25 .60
30 Michael Jenkins .25 .60
31 Edgerrin James .25 .60
32 Terrell Owens .30 .75
33 Jason Witten .30 .75
34 Clinton Portis .30 .75
35 Deion Branch .25 .60
36 Priest Holmes .25 .60
37 Quinton Ganther RC 1.00 2.50
38 Kurt Warner .30 .75
39 Domanick Davis .20 .50
40 Chris Simms .25 .60
41 Dwight Freeney .25 .60
42 Daniel Bullocks RC 1.50 4.00
43 Tiki Barber .30 .75
44 Steve McNair .25 .60
45 Steven Jackson .30 .75
46 Joe Horn .25 .60
47 Randy McMichael .20 .50
48 Cedric Humes RC 1.00 2.50
49 Warrick Dunn .25 .60
50 Tatum Bell .20 .50
51 P.J. Pope RC 1.50 4.00
52 Curtis Martin .30 .75
53 Donovan McNabb .30 .75
54 LaMont Jordan .25 .60
55 Marc Bulger .25 .60
56 Drew Bennett .25 .60
57 Julius Jones .20 .50
58 Santana Moss .25 .60
59 Ronnie Brown .30 .75
60 Tony Gonzalez .25 .60
61 Jamal Lewis .25 .60
62 D.J. Shockley RC 1.25 3.00
63 Carson Palmer .30 .75
64 Jonathan Orr RC 1.25 3.00
65 Brandon Stokley .25 .60
66 Brett Favre .60 1.50
67 Jonathan Vilma .25 .60
68 Darrell Jackson .25 .60
69 Brian Urlacher .30 .75
70 Drew Brees .30 .75
71 Mike Williams .20 .50
72 Corey Dillon .25 .60
73 Willis McGahee .25 .60
74 Michael Vick .30 .75
75 Chad Johnson .25 .60
76 Anquan Boldin .25 .60
77 Shawne Merriman .25 .60
78 Willie Parker .25 .60
79 Roy Williams S .25 .60
80 Trent Green .25 .60
81 Chris Gamble .20 .50
82 Ahman Green .25 .60
83 Todd Heap .25 .60
84 Brett Basanez RC 1.50 4.00
85 Andre Johnson .30 .75
86 Abdul Hodge RC 1.00 2.50
87 Plaxico Burress .25 .60
88 Hines Ward .30 .75
89 Rod Smith .25 .60
90 Cadillac Williams .25 .60
91 Braylon Edwards .25 .60
92 Rudi Johnson .25 .60
93 Isaac Bruce .25 .60
94 Chris Chambers .25 .60
95 Matt Hasselbeck .25 .60
96 Donte Stallworth .20 .50
97 Philip Rivers .30 .75
98 Will Blackmon RC 1.25 3.00
99 Alge Crumpler .25 .60
100 Chad Pennington .25 .60
101 Darnell Bing RC 1.25 3.00
102 Daunte Culpepper .25 .60
103 Jeremy Shockey .30 .75
104 Jerry Porter .20 .50
105 Tom Brady .50 1.25
106 Jeff Webb RC 1.25 3.00
107 Jake Delhomme .25 .60
108 Ben Roethlisberger .40 1.00
109 Jake Plummer .25 .60
110 Paul Pinegar RC 1.00 2.50
111 Kevin McMahan RC 1.25 3.00
112 Reggie Wayne .25 .60
113 Bennie Brazell RC 1.25 3.00
114 Todd Watkins RC 1.25 3.00
115 David Carr .20 .50
116 Cory Rodgers RC 1.25 3.00
117 Leon Washington RC 1.25 3.00
118 Michael Strahan .25 .60
119 P.J. Daniels RC 1.00 2.50
120 Peyton Manning .50 1.25
121 Brandon Marshall RC 1.50 4.00
122 Jerome Harrison RC 1.50 4.00
123 Mario Williams RC 1.50 4.00
124 Ernie Sims RC 1.25 3.00
125 Devin Hester RC 2.50 6.00
126 Jimmy Williams RC 1.50 4.00
127 Charlie Whitehurst RC 1.50 4.00
128 Jason Avant RC 1.00 2.50
129 Marcus Vick RC 1.00 2.50
130 Mathias Kiwanuka RC 1.50 4.00
131 Brodrick Bunkley RC 1.25 3.00
132 Reggie McNeal RC 1.25 3.00
133 Dominique Byrd RC 1.25 3.00
134 Jason Allen RC 1.25 3.00
135 D'Qwell Jackson RC 1.25 3.00
136 Donte Whitner RC 1.50 4.00
137 Willie Reid RC 1.25 3.00
138 Kamerion Wimbley RC 1.50 4.00
139 Martin Nance RC 1.25 3.00
140 Haloti Ngata RC 1.50 4.00
141 Devin Aromashodu RC 1.50 4.00
142 Jeremy Bloom RC 1.25 3.00
143 Manny Lawson RC 1.25 3.00
144 Johnathan Joseph RC 1.25 3.00
145 Brad Smith RC 1.50 4.00
146 Thomas Howard RC 1.25 3.00
147 Demetrius Williams RC 1.25 3.00
148 Antonio Cromartie RC 1.50 4.00
149 Bobby Carpenter RC 1.00 2.50
150 Tamba Hali RC 1.50 4.00
151 Reggie Bush AU/199 RC 30.00 80.00
152 Matt Leinart AU/199 RC 10.00 25.00
153 Vince Young AU/199 RC 12.00 30.00
154 Jay Cutler AU/199 RC 30.00 80.00
155 Santonio Holmes AU/199 RC 12.00 30.00
156 LenDale White AU/199 RC 8.00 20.00
157 DeAngelo Williams AU/199 RC 12.00 30.00
158 Sinorice Moss AU/199 RC 10.00 25.00
159 Vernon Davis AU/199 RC 15.00 30.00
160 Joseph Addai AU/199 RC 10.00 25.00
161 Omar Jacobs AU/199 RC 6.00 15.00
162 Chad Jackson AU/199 RC 6.00 15.00
163 Chad Greenway AU RC 5.00 12.00
164 Maurice Drew AU RC 8.00 20.00
165 D'Brickashaw Ferguson AU RC 5.00 12.00
166 Anthony Fasano AU RC 5.00 12.00
167 Derek Hagan AU/199 RC 8.00 20.00
168 A.J. Hawk AU/199 RC 10.00 25.00
169 David Thomas AU RC 4.00 10.00
170 Brian Calhoun AU RC 3.00 8.00
171 Kellen Clemens AU RC 4.00 10.00
172 Tarvaris Jackson AU RC 5.00 12.00
173 Maurice Stovall AU RC 4.00 10.00
174 Michael Huff AU/199 RC 8.00 20.00
175 Greg Jennings AU RC 12.50 25.00
176 Joe Klopfenstein AU RC 3.00 8.00
177 Leonard Pope AU RC 5.00 12.00
178 Michael Robinson AU RC 4.00 10.00
179 Ingle Martin AU RC 4.00 10.00
180 Wali Lundy AU RC 4.00 10.00
181 Drew Olson AU RC 3.00 8.00
182 Jerious Norwood AU RC 4.00 10.00
183 Travis Wilson AU RC 3.00 8.00
184 Tye Hill AU RC 3.00 8.00
185 Brandon Williams AU RC 3.00 8.00
186 Marques Hagans AU RC 3.00 8.00

2006 Finest Black Refractors

*VETS: 5X TO 12X BASIC CARDS
*ROOKIES: 1.2X TO 3X BASIC CARDS
*ROOKIE AU: .8X TO 2X BASIC AU
STATED PRINT RUN 99 SER.#'d SETS

2006 Finest Black Xfractors

*VETERANS: 10X TO 25X BASIC CARDS
*ROOKIES: 2.5X TO 6X BASIC CARDS
*ROOKIE AU: 1.2X TO 3X BASIC CARDS
STATED PRINT RUN 25 SER.#'d SETS

2006 Finest Blue Refractors

*VETERANS: 2.5X TO 6X BASIC CARDS
*ROOKIES: .6X TO 1.5X BASIC CARDS
*ROOKIE AU: .5X TO 1.2X BASIC CARDS
STATED PRINT RUN 299 SER.#'d SETS

2006 Finest Blue Xfractors

*VETERANS: 4X TO 10X BASIC CARDS
*ROOKIES: 1X TO 2.5X BASIC CARDS
*ROOKIE AU: .6X TO 1.5X BASIC CARDS
STATED PRINT RUN 150 SER.#'d SETS

2006 Finest Gold Refractors

*VETERANS: 6X TO 15X BASIC CARDS
*ROOKIES: 1.5X TO 4X BASIC CARDS
*ROOKIE AU: 1X TO 2.5X BASIC CARDS
STATED PRINT RUN 49 SER.#'d SETS

2006 Finest Gold Xfractors

UNPRICED GOLD XFRACT #'d TO 10

2006 Finest Green Refractors

*VETERANS: 3X TO 8X BASIC CARDS
*ROOKIES: .8X TO 2X BASIC CARDS
*ROOKIE AU: .5X TO 1.2X BASIC CARDS
STATED PRINT RUN 199 SER.#'d SETS

2006 Finest Green Xfractors

*VETERANS: 6X TO 15X BASIC CARDS
*ROOKIES: 1.5X TO 4X BASIC CARDS
*ROOKIE AU: 1X TO 2.5X BASIC CARDS
STATED PRINT RUN 50 SER.#'d SETS

2006 Finest Refractors

*VETERANS: 2X TO 5X BASIC CARDS
*ROOKIES: .5X TO 1.2X BASIC CARDS
*ROOKIE AU: .4X TO 1X BASIC CARDS
*ROOKIE AU/50: .6X TO 1.5X BASIC CARDS
STATED PRINT RUN 50-399

2006 Finest SuperFractors

UNPRICED SUPERFRACTOR #'d TO 1

2006 Finest White Framed Refractors

UNPRICED WHITE REF #'d TO 1

2006 Finest White Framed Xfractors

UNPRICED WHT XFRACT #'d TO 1

2006 Finest Xfractors

*VETERANS: 2.5X TO 6X BASIC CARDS
*ROOKIES: .6X TO 1.5X BASIC CARDS
*ROOKIE AU: .4X TO 1X BASIC CARDS
*ROOKIE AU/25: 1X TO 2.5X AUTO/199
STATED PRINT RUN 25-250

2006 Finest Autographs Refractor

GROUP A ODDS 1:1896 HOB
GROUP B ODDS 1:126 HOB
GROUP C ODDS 1:36 HOB
*XFRCT/25: .6X TO 1.5X BASE GRP A
*XFRCT/25: .8X TO 2X BASE GRP B-C
XFRACTOR PRINT RUN 25
UNPRICED PRINT PLATES #'d TO 1
UNPRICED SUPERFRACTOR #'d TO 1
FABM Brandon Marshall C 10.00 25.00
FACH Cedric Humes C 3.00 8.00
FACR Cory Rodgers C 4.00 10.00
FADA Devin Aromashodu C 5.00 12.00
FAEM Eli Manning A 60.00 100.00
FAES Emmitt Smith A 150.00 250.00
FAJA Jason Avant B 3.00 8.00
FAJC Jay Cutler A 60.00 135.00
FAJH Jerome Harrison B 5.00 12.00
FALT LaDainian Tomlinson A 50.00 100.00
FAMK Mathias Kiwanuka C 5.00 12.00
FAML Matt Leinart A 20.00 50.00
FAPM Peyton Manning A 60.00 120.00
FAQG Quinton Ganther C 3.00 8.00
FARB Reggie Bush A 50.00 120.00
FASM Shawne Merriman A 10.00 25.00
FASS Steve Smith A 15.00 30.00
FAVY Vince Young A 25.00 60.00
FAWB Will Blackmon B 4.00 10.00
FAWJ Winston Justice C 4.00 10.00

2006 Finest Brett Favre Finest Moments

COMMON CARD (1-20) 2.50 6.00
*BLACK REFRACTOR/99: 1.2X TO 3X
*BLACK XFRACTOR/25: 3X TO 8X
*BLUE REFRACTOR/299: .6X TO 1.5X
*BLUE XFRACTOR/150: 1X TO 2.5X
*GOLD REFRACTOR/49: 2X TO 5X
*GOLD XFRACTOR/10: 6X TO 12X
*GREEN REFRACTOR/199: .8X TO 2X
*GREEN XFRACTOR/50: 2X TO 5X
UNPRICED PRINT PLATES #'d TO 1
*REFRACTOR/399: .5X TO 1.2X
UNPRICED SUPERFRACTOR #'d TO 1
UNPRICED WHT REFRACT #'d TO 1
UNPRICED WHT XFRACT #'d TO 1
*XFRACTOR/250: .8X TO 2X
UNPRICED AUTOS #'d TO 4
UNPRICED AU PRINT PLATES #'d TO 1

2006 Finest Johnny Unitas Finest Moments

COMMON CARD (1-10) 2.50 6.00
*BLACK REFRACTOR/99: 1X TO 2.5X
*BLUE REFRACTOR/299: .6X TO 1.5X
UNPRICED CUT AUTOS #'d TO 5
*GREEN REFRACTOR/199: .8X TO 2X
UNPRICED PRINT PLATES #'d TO 1
*REFRACTOR/399: .5X TO 1.2X
ONE UNITAS MOMENT PER HOBBY BOX

2007 Finest

This 150-card set was relased in October, 2007. The set was issued into the hobby in five-card packs, with a $10 SRP, which came 18 packs to a box. The set is divided between veterans which are cards 1-100 and 2007 NFL rookies which are cards 101-150.

COMPLETE SET (150) 30.00 60.00
UNPRICED PRINT.PLATE PRINT RUN 1
UNPRICED SUPERFRACTOR PRINT RUN 1
UNPRICED WHT XFRACTOR PRINT RUN 1
1 Peyton Manning .50 1.25
2 Drew Brees .30 .75
3 Donovan McNabb .30 .75
4 Tony Romo .40 1.00
5 Carson Palmer .25 .60
6 Marc Bulger .25 .60
7 Philip Rivers .30 .75
8 Tom Brady .50 1.25
9 J.P. Losman .20 .50
10 Steve McNair .25 .60
11 Eli Manning .30 .75
12 Matt Hasselbeck .25 .60
13 Alex Smith QB .30 .75
14 Ben Roethlisberger .30 .75
15 Matt Leinart .25 .60
16 Rex Grossman .25 .60
17 Brett Favre .60 1.50
18 Vince Young .25 .60
19 Jay Cutler .30 .75
20 Chad Pennington .25 .60
21 LaDainian Tomlinson .30 .75
22 Larry Johnson .20 .50
23 Frank Gore .30 .75
24 Steven Jackson .30 .75
25 Willie Parker .25 .60
26 Rudi Johnson .25 .60
27 Brian Westbrook .25 .60
28 Chester Taylor .20 .50
29 Travis Henry .25 .60
30 Thomas Jones .25 .60
31 Edgerrin James .25 .60
32 Fred Taylor .25 .60
33 Warrick Dunn .25 .60
34 Jamal Lewis .25 .60
35 Julius Jones .20 .50
36 Joseph Addai .25 .60
37 Ahman Green .25 .60
38 Deuce McAllister .25 .60
39 Ronnie Brown .25 .60
40 Maurice Jones-Drew .30 .75
41 DeShaun Foster .25 .60
42 Shaun Alexander .25 .60
43 Cadillac Williams .25 .60
44 Laurence Maroney .25 .60
45 Cedric Benson .25 .60
46 Dominic Rhodes .25 .60
47 Jerious Norwood .25 .60
48 Brandon Jacobs .25 .60
49 DeAngelo Williams .30 .75
50 Willis McGahee .25 .60
51 Clinton Portis .25 .60
52 Chad Johnson .25 .60
53 Marvin Harrison .30 .75
54 Roy Williams WR .25 .60
55 Reggie Wayne .25 .60
56 Donald Driver .30 .75
57 Lee Evans .25 .60
58 Anquan Boldin .25 .60
59 Torry Holt .25 .60
60 Terrell Owens .30 .75
61 Steve Smith .25 .60
62 Andre Johnson .25 .60
63 Laveranues Coles .20 .50
64 Javon Walker .25 .60
65 T.J. Houshmandzadeh .25 .60
66 Marques Colston .30 .75
67 Terry Glenn .25 .60
68 Plaxico Burress .25 .60
69 Hines Ward .30 .75
70 Jerricho Cotchery .25 .60
71 Larry Fitzgerald .30 .75
72 Braylon Edwards .25 .60
73 Santana Moss .25 .60
74 Santonio Holmes .25 .60
75 Mike Furrey .25 .60
76 Isaac Bruce .25 .60
77 Derrick Mason .25 .60
78 Randy Moss .30 .75
79 Greg Jennings .30 .75
80 Devin Hester .30 .75
81 Muhsin Muhammad .25 .60
82 Kellen Winslow .25 .60
83 Todd Heap .20 .50
84 Tony Gonzalez .25 .60
85 Antonio Gates .30 .75
86 Jeremy Shockey .25 .60
87 Jason Witten .30 .75
88 Randy McMichael .20 .50
89 Alge Crumpler .25 .60
90 L.J. Smith .20 .50
91 Champ Bailey .25 .60
92 DeAngelo Hall .25 .60
93 Asante Samuel .20 .50
94 Julius Peppers .25 .60
95 Jason Taylor .25 .60
96 Michael Strahan .25 .60
97 Shawne Merriman .25 .60
98 Brian Urlacher .30 .75
99 Troy Polamalu .30 .75
100 Ed Reed .25 .60
101 JaMarcus Russell RC 1.00 2.50
102 Brady Quinn RC 1.50 4.00
103 John Beck RC 1.50 4.00
104 Kevin Kolb RC 2.50 6.00
105 Trent Edwards RC 1.50 4.00
106 Troy Smith RC 1.50 4.00
107 Drew Stanton RC 1.00 2.50
108 Chris Leak RC 1.25 3.00
109 Jordan Palmer RC 1.25 3.00
110 Drew Tate RC 1.25 3.00
111 Isaiah Stanback RC 1.00 2.50
112 Adrian Peterson RC 6.00 15.00
113 Marshawn Lynch RC 1.50 4.00
114 Brandon Jackson RC 1.25 3.00
115 Kenny Irons RC 1.00 2.50
116 Michael Bush RC 1.25 3.00
117 Lorenzo Booker RC 1.25 3.00
118 Brian Leonard RC 1.25 3.00
119 Garrett Wolfe RC 1.00 2.50
120 Antonio Pittman RC 1.00 2.50
121 Selvin Young RC 1.25 3.00
122 Chris Henry RB RC 1.00 2.50
123 Tony Hunt RC 1.00 2.50
124 Kenneth Darby RC 1.25 3.00
125 Kolby Smith RC 1.25 3.00
126 Darius Walker RC 1.00 2.50
127 Greg Olsen RC 1.25 3.00
128 Dwayne Bowe RC 2.00 5.00
129 Craig Buster Davis RC 1.25 3.00
130 Ted Ginn Jr. RC 1.25 3.00
131 Anthony Gonzalez RC 1.50 4.00

132 Yamon Figurs RC 1.00 2.50
133 Jason Hill RC 1.50 4.00
134 Dwayne Jarrett RC 1.25 3.00
135 Calvin Johnson RC 5.00 12.00
136 Robert Meachem RC 1.50 4.00
137 Sidney Rice RC 2.00 5.00
138 Steve Smith USC RC 1.50 4.00
139 Paul Williams RC 1.00 2.50
140 Steve Breaston RC 1.50 4.00
141 David Clowney RC 1.25 3.00
142 Aundrae Allison RC 1.00 2.50
143 Ryne Robinson RC 1.25 3.00
144 Joe Thomas RC 1.50 4.00
145 Leon Hall RC 1.25 3.00
146 Gaines Adams RC 1.50 4.00
147 LaRon Landry RC 1.50 4.00
148 Amobi Okoye RC 1.50 4.00
149 Patrick Willis RC 3.00 8.00
150 Lawrence Timmons RC 1.50 4.00

2007 Finest Black Refractors

*VETS 1-100: 5X TO 12X BASIC CARDS
*ROOKIES 101-150: 1X TO 2.5X BASIC CARDS
BLK REF/99 ODDS 1:4 6-PACK MINI BOX

2007 Finest Blue Refractors

*VETS 1-100: 2.5X TO 6X BASIC CARDS
*ROOKIES 101-150: .5X TO 1.2X BASIC CARDS
BLUE REF/299 ODDS 1:2 6-PACK MINI BOX

2007 Finest Gold Refractors

*VETS 1-100: 6X TO 15X BASIC CARDS
*ROOKIES 101-150: 1.5X TO 4X BASIC CARDS
GOLD REF/50 ODDS 1:7 6-PACK MINI BOX

2007 Finest Green Refractors

*VETS 1-100: 3X TO 8X BASIC CARDS
*ROOKIES 101-150: .6X TO 1.5X BASIC CARDS
GRN REF/199 ODDS 1:2 6-PACK MINI BOX

2007 Finest Refractors

*VETS 1-100: 2.5X TO 6X BASIC CARDS
*ROOKIES 101-150: .5X TO 1.2X BASIC CARDS
ODDS 1:1 6-PACK MINI BOX
112 Adrian Peterson 15.00 40.00

2007 Finest Xfractors

*VETS 1-100: 8X TO 20X BASIC CARDS
*ROOKIES 101-150: 2X TO 5X BASIC CARDS
XFRACTOR/25 ODDS 1:14 6-PACK MINI BOX
102 Brady Quinn 8.00 20.00
112 Adrian Peterson 60.00 120.00
135 Calvin Johnson 25.00 60.00

2007 Finest Moments

STATED ODDS 1:1 6-PACK MINI BOX
*REFRACTORS: .5X TO 1.2X
REFRACT.ODDS 1:1 6-PACK MINI BOX
*BLUE REFRACTORS/299: .6X TO 1.5X
BLUE REF/299 ODDS 1:4 6-PACK MINI BOX
*GREEN REFRACTORS/199: .8X TO 2X
GREEN REF/199 ODDS 1:5 6-PACK MINI BOX
*BLACK REFRACTORS/99: 1X TO 2.5X
BLK REF/99 ODDS 1:10 6-PACK MINI BOX
*GOLD REFRACTORS/50: 1.2X TO 3X
GOLD REF/50 ODDS 1:20 6-PACK MINI BOX
*XFRACTORS/25: 2X TO 5X
XFRACT/25 ODDS 1:40 6-PACK MINI BOX
UNPRICED PRINT.PLATES PRINT RUN 1
UNPRICED SUPERFRACT.PRINT RUN 1
UNPRICED WHT XFRACT.PRINT RUN 1
AG Anthony Gonzalez 1.25 3.00
AP Adrian Peterson 5.00 12.00
BJ Brandon Jackson 1.00 2.50
BL Brian Leonard 1.00 2.50
BQ Brady Quinn 1.25 3.00
CJ Chad Johnson 1.00 2.50
CJA Chad Jackson .75 2.00
CJO Calvin Johnson 4.00 10.00
CW Cadillac Williams 1.00 2.50
DB Dwayne Bowe 1.50 4.00
DBR Drew Brees 1.25 3.00
DH Devin Hester 1.25 3.00
DJ Dwayne Jarrett 1.00 2.50
DS Drew Stanton .75 2.00
DW DeAngelo Williams 1.25 3.00
EM Eli Manning 1.25 3.00
FG Frank Gore 1.25 3.00
GJ Greg Jennings 1.25 3.00
GO Greg Olsen 1.00 2.50
JA Joseph Addai 1.00 2.50
JB John Beck 1.25 3.00
JC Jay Cutler 1.25 3.00
JN Jerious Norwood 1.00 2.50
JR JaMarcus Russell .75 2.00
KK Kevin Kolb 2.00 5.00
LB Lorenzo Booker 1.00 2.50
LJ Larry Johnson .75 2.00
LM Laurence Maroney 1.00 2.50
LT LaDainian Tomlinson 1.25 3.00
MB Michael Bush 1.25 3.00
MC Marques Colston 1.25 3.00
MD Maurice Jones-Drew 1.25 3.00
ML Matt Leinart 1.00 2.50
MLY Marshawn Lynch 1.25 3.00
MW Mario Williams 1.00 2.50
PM Peyton Manning 2.00 5.00
RB Reggie Bush 1.25 3.00
RM Robert Meachem 1.25 3.00
RW Roy Williams WR 1.00 2.50
SA Shaun Alexander 1.00 2.50
SH Santonio Holmes 1.00 2.50
SJ Steven Jackson 1.25 3.00
SR Sidney Rice 1.50 4.00
SS Steve Smith USC 1.25 3.00
SSM Steve Smith 1.00 2.50
TB Tom Brady 2.00 5.00
TG Ted Ginn Jr. 1.00 2.50
TJ Thomas Jones 1.00 2.50
VY Vince Young 1.00 2.50
WM Willis McGahee 1.00 2.50

2007 Finest Moments Autographs

GROUP A ODDS 1:328 6-PACK BOX
GROUP B ODDS 1:143 6-PACK BOX
GROUP C ODDS 1:125 6-PACK BOX
GROUP D ODDS 1:34 6-PACK BOX
*REFRACT/25: .4X TO 1X GROUP A-B AUs
*REFRACT/25: .6X TO 1.5X GROUP C-D AUs
REFRACT/25 ODDS 1:83 6-PACK BOX
UNPRICED SUPERFR.PRINT RUN 1
UNPRICED PRINT.PLATE PRINT RUN 1
AP Adrian Peterson A 150.00 300.00
BJ Brandon Jackson D 8.00 20.00
BL Brian Leonard D 8.00 20.00
BQ Brady Quinn A 40.00 100.00
CJ Chad Johnson B 12.00 30.00
DB Dwayne Bowe B 20.00 50.00
DW DeAngelo Williams B 10.00 25.00
FG Frank Gore B 12.00 30.00
GJ Greg Jennings C 10.00 25.00
JB John Beck D 12.00 30.00
JR JaMarcus Russell A 20.00 50.00
KK Kevin Kolb C 12.00 30.00
LJ Larry Johnson B 12.00 30.00
LT LaDainian Tomlinson A 50.00 100.00
MC Marques Colston B 10.00 25.00
ML Matt Leinart B 20.00 50.00
RB Reggie Bush A 25.00 60.00
RM Robert Meachem B 12.00 30.00
SA Shaun Alexander A 12.00 30.00
SJ Steven Jackson B 12.00 30.00
SS Steve Smith B 12.00 30.00
TB Tom Brady A 125.00 200.00
TG Ted Ginn Jr. B 12.00 30.00
TJ Thomas Jones B 10.00 25.00
VY Vince Young A 20.00 50.00

2007 Finest Moments Autographs Dual

STATED PRINT RUN 20 SER.#'d SETS
UNPRICED REFRACTOR PRINT RUN 10
BG John Beck / Ted Ginn 25.00 60.00
BM Drew Brees / Robert Meachem 40.00 80.00
BQ Tom Brady / Brady Quinn 200.00 400.00
JL Steven Jackson / Brian Leonard 20.00 50.00
JS Dwayne Jarrett / Steve Smith 20.00 50.00
JT Larry Johnson / LaDainian Tomlinson 40.00 100.00
PL Adrian Peterson / Marshawn Lynch 125.00 250.00
RJ JaMarcus Russell / Calvin Johnson 60.00 120.00
RP JaMarcus Russell / Adrian Peterson 125.00 250.00
RQ JaMarcus Russell / Brady Quinn 40.00 100.00

2007 Finest Reggie Bush Finest Moments

COMMON CARD 2.00 5.00
REG.BUSH MOMENT/899 ODDS 1:36 HOB
*REFRACTORS/149: .6X TO 1.5X
REFRACTOR/149 ODDS 1:144 HOB
*XFRACTORS/50: 1X TO 2.5X
XFRACTOR/50 ODDS 1:414 HOB
UNPRICED GOLD REF. PRINT RUN 1

2007 Finest Rookie Autographs

GROUP A ODDS 1:415 6-PACK BOX
GROUP B ODDS 1:51 6-PACK BOX
GROUP C/D ODDS 1:33 6-PACK BOX
GROUP E ODDS 1:14 6-PACK BOX
GROUP F/G ODDS 1:17 6-PACK BOX
GROUP H ODDS 1:2 6-PACK BOX
*BLUE XFRACT/50: .4X TO 1X GRP A AU
*BLUE XFRACT/50: .6X TO 1.5X GRP B-H AU
BLUE XFRACT/50 1:21 6-PACK MINI BOX
UNPRICED BLK XFRACT/10 1:104 MINI BOX
UNPRICED GOLD XFRACT.PRINT RUN 1
UNPRICED PRINT.PLATE PRINT RUN 1
101 JaMarcus Russell A 8.00 20.00
102 Brady Quinn A 12.00 30.00
103 John Beck D 6.00 15.00
104 Kevin Kolb B 10.00 25.00
105 Trent Edwards D 6.00 15.00
106 Troy Smith B 6.00 15.00
107 Drew Stanton B 4.00 10.00
109 Jordan Palmer F 5.00 12.00
110 Drew Tate H 5.00 12.00
111 Isaiah Stanback H 4.00 10.00
112 Adrian Peterson A 150.00 300.00
113 Marshawn Lynch A 12.00 30.00
114 Brandon Jackson D 5.00 12.00
116 Michael Bush C 6.00 15.00
117 Lorenzo Booker E 5.00 12.00
118 Brian Leonard E 5.00 12.00
119 Garrett Wolfe E 4.00 10.00
120 Antonio Pittman E 4.00 10.00
121 Selvin Young H 5.00 12.00
122 Chris Henry RB H 4.00 10.00
123 Tony Hunt G 4.00 10.00
124 Kenneth Darby H 5.00 12.00
125 Kolby Smith H 5.00 12.00
126 Darius Walker H 4.00 10.00
127 Greg Olsen C 5.00 12.00
128 Dwayne Bowe B 8.00 20.00
129 Craig Buster Davis H 5.00 12.00
130 Ted Ginn Jr. B 5.00 12.00
131 Anthony Gonzalez C 6.00 15.00
132 Yamon Figurs H 4.00 10.00
133 Jason Hill F 6.00 15.00
134 Dwayne Jarrett B 5.00 12.00
135 Calvin Johnson A 50.00 100.00
136 Robert Meachem B 6.00 15.00
137 Sidney Rice B 8.00 20.00
138 Steve Smith USC F 6.00 15.00
139 Paul Williams H 4.00 10.00
140 Steve Breaston H 6.00 15.00
141 David Clowney H 5.00 12.00
142 Aundrae Allison G 4.00 10.00
143 Ryne Robinson H 5.00 12.00
144 Joe Thomas C 6.00 15.00
145 Leon Hall C 5.00 12.00
146 Gaines Adams B 6.00 15.00
147 LaRon Landry E 6.00 15.00
148 Amobi Okoye B 6.00 15.00
149 Patrick Willis C 15.00 40.00
150 Lawrence Timmons H 6.00 15.00

2007 Finest Rookie Autographs Green Xfractors

*GREEN XFRACT/25: .6X TO 1.5X GRP A AUs
*GREEN XFRACT/25: .8X TO 2X GRP B-H AUs
GREEN XFRACTORS PRINT RUN 25 SER.#'d SETS
104 Kevin Kolb 20.00 50.00
112 Adrian Peterson 250.00 400.00
135 Calvin Johnson 100.00 200.00

2007 Finest Vince Young Finest Moments

COMMON CARD 2.00 5.00
VIN.YOUNG MOMENT/899 ODDS 1:36 HOB
*REFRACTORS/149: .6X TO 1.5X
REFRACTOR/149 ODDS 1:144 HOB
*XFRACTORS/50: 1X TO 2.5X
XFRACTOR/50 ODDS 1:414 HOB
UNPRICED GOLD REF. PRINT RUN 1

2008 Finest

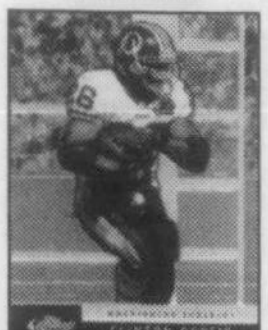

This set was released on September 17, 2008. The base set consists of 151 cards. Cards 1-100 and 151 feature veterans, and cards 101-150 are rookies serial numbered of 699.

COMP.SET w/o RC's (100) 10.00 25.00
ROOKIE REFRACTOR/699 ODDS 1:12
UNPRICED PRINT PLATE/1 ODDS 1:396
1 Drew Brees .30 .75
2 Tom Brady .50 1.25
3 Peyton Manning .50 1.25
4 Carson Palmer .30 .75
5 Ben Roethlisberger .30 .75
6 Tony Romo .40 1.00
7 Vince Young .25 .60
8 David Garrard .25 .60
9 Jeff Garcia .25 .60
10 Derek Anderson .20 .50
11 Matt Hasselbeck .25 .60
12 Donovan McNabb .30 .75
13 Philip Rivers .30 .75
14 Jay Cutler .30 .75
15 Matt Leinart .30 .75
16 Jason Campbell .25 .60
17 Matt Schaub .25 .60
18 Jon Kitna .25 .60
19 Marc Bulger .25 .60
20 Eli Manning .30 .75
21 Willie Parker .25 .60
22 Clinton Portis .25 .60
23 Adrian Peterson .50 1.25
24 LaDainian Tomlinson .30 .75
25 Marion Barber .25 .60
26 Brian Westbrook .25 .60
27 Fred Taylor .25 .60
28 Marshawn Lynch .25 .60
29 Joseph Addai .25 .60
30 Willis McGahee .25 .60
31 Frank Gore .25 .60
32 Larry Johnson .25 .60
33 Jamal Lewis .25 .60
34 Edgerrin James .25 .60
35 Thomas Jones .25 .60
36 Brandon Jacobs .25 .60
37 LenDale White .25 .60
38 Justin Fargas .20 .50
39 Ryan Grant .30 .75
40 Earnest Graham .20 .50
41 Laurence Maroney .25 .60
42 Steven Jackson .30 .75
43 DeAngelo Williams .25 .60
44 Shaun Alexander .25 .60
45 Maurice Jones-Drew .25 .60
46 Reggie Bush .30 .75
47 Chester Taylor .20 .50
48 Rudi Johnson .25 .60
49 Ronnie Brown .25 .60
50 Travis Henry .20 .50
51 Cedric Benson .25 .60
52 Chad Johnson .25 .60
53 Reggie Wayne .25 .60
54 Anquan Boldin .25 .60
55 Randy Moss .30 .75
56 Plaxico Burress .25 .60
57 Terrell Owens .30 .75
58 Andre Johnson .25 .60
59 Larry Fitzgerald .30 .75
60 Braylon Edwards .25 .60
61 Steve Smith .25 .60
62 Wes Welker .30 .75
63 T.J. Houshmandzadeh .25 .60
64 Derrick Mason .25 .60
65 Brandon Marshall .25 .60
66 Marques Colston .25 .60
67 Bobby Engram .20 .50
68 Torry Holt .25 .60
69 Roddy White .25 .60
70 Jerricho Cotchery .25 .60
71 Donald Driver .25 .60
72 Roy Williams WR .25 .60
73 Hines Ward .25 .60
74 Santonio Holmes .25 .60
75 Joey Galloway .25 .60
76 Greg Jennings .30 .75
77 Dwayne Bowe .25 .60
78 Calvin Johnson .30 .75
79 Santana Moss .20 .50
80 Kevin Curtis .20 .50
81 Chris Chambers .25 .60
82 Kellen Winslow .25 .60
83 Tony Gonzalez .25 .60
84 Antonio Gates .30 .75
85 Jeremy Shockey .25 .60
86 Jason Witten .30 .75
87 Chris Cooley .25 .60
88 Owen Daniels .20 .50
89 Dallas Clark .25 .60
90 Vernon Davis .25 .60
91 Antonio Cromartie .20 .50
92 Marcus Trufant .20 .50
93 Terence Newman .20 .50
94 Osi Umenyiora .25 .60
95 Mario Williams .25 .60
96 Patrick Willis .25 .60
97 Shawne Merriman .25 .60
98 DeMarcus Ware .25 .60
99 Ed Reed .25 .60
100 Bob Sanders .25 .60
101 Erik Ainge RC 2.00 5.00
102 John David Booty RC 1.50 4.00
103 Colt Brennan RC 2.00 5.00
104 Brian Brohm RC 2.00 5.00
105 Joe Flacco RC 6.00 15.00
106 Chad Henne RC 2.00 5.00
107 Josh Johnson RC 2.00 5.00
108 Anthony Morelli RC 1.50 4.00
109 Matt Ryan RC 8.00 20.00
110 Andre Woodson RC 2.00 5.00
111 Kyle Wright RC 1.50 4.00
112 Jamaal Charles RC 3.00 8.00
113 Tashard Choice RC 1.50 4.00
114 Matt Forte RC 3.00 8.00
115 Mike Hart RC 2.00 5.00
116 Chris Johnson RC 5.00 12.00
117 Felix Jones RC 3.00 8.00
118 Darren McFadden RC 5.00 12.00
119 Rashard Mendenhall RC 4.00 10.00
120 Allen Patrick RC 1.50 4.00
121 Ray Rice RC 4.00 10.00
122 Dustin Keller RC 2.00 5.00
123 Steve Slaton RC 2.00 5.00
124 Kevin Smith RC 2.00 5.00
125 Jonathan Stewart RC 3.00 8.00
126 Kevin O'Connell RC 1.50 4.00
127 Adrian Arrington RC 1.50 4.00
128 Donnie Avery RC 1.50 4.00
129 Earl Bennett RC 2.00 5.00
130 Dexter Jackson RC 1.50 4.00
131 Jerome Simpson RC 2.00 5.00
132 Keenan Burton RC 1.25 3.00
133 Andre Caldwell RC 1.50 4.00
134 Early Doucet RC 1.50 4.00
135 Harry Douglas RC 1.50 4.00
136 James Hardy RC 1.50 4.00
137 Jordy Nelson RC 2.50 6.00
138 DeSean Jackson RC 4.00 10.00
139 Malcolm Kelly RC 1.50 4.00
140 Mario Manningham RC 2.00 5.00
141 Limas Sweed RC 2.00 5.00
142 Eddie Royal RC 2.00 5.00
143 Devin Thomas RC 1.50 4.00
144 John Carlson RC 2.00 5.00
145 Chris Long RC 2.00 5.00
146 Vernon Gholston RC 1.50 4.00
147 Dominique Rodgers-Cromartie RC 2.00 5.00
148 Keith Rivers RC 2.00 5.00
149 Jake Long RC 2.00 5.00
150 Glenn Dorsey RC 2.00 5.00
151 Brett Favre SP 20.00 40.00

2008 Finest Black Refractors/Xfractors

*VETS 1-100: 4X TO 10X BASIC CARDS
*ROOKIES 101-150: 1.5X TO 4X BASIC CARDS
1-100 REFRACTOR/99 ODDS 1:24
101-150 XFRACTOR/10 ODDS 1:474

2008 Finest Blue Refractors/Xfractors

*VETS 1-100: 2.5X TO 6X BASIC CARDS
*ROOKIES 101-150: .8X TO 2X BASIC CARDS
101-150 ROOKIE XFRACTOR/50 ODDS 1:96

2008 Finest Gold Refractors/Xfractors

*VETS 1-100: 5X TO 12X BASIC CARDS
1-100 VET REFRACTOR/50 ODDS 1:48
UNPRICED 101-150 XFRACT/1 ODDS 1:4812

2008 Finest Green Refractors/Xfractors

*VETS 1-100: 2.5X TO 6X BASIC CARDS
*ROOKIES 101-150: 1X TO 2.5X BASIC CARDS
1-100 VET REFRACTOR/299 ODDS 1:12
101-150 XFRACTOR/25 ODDS 1:192

2008 Finest Red Refractors

*VETS 1-100: 8X TO 20X BASIC CARDS
RED REFRACTOR/25 ODDS 1:96

2008 Finest White Xfractors

UNPRICED WHITE XFRACT/1 ODDS 1:2370

2008 Finest Adrian Peterson Finest Moments

COMMON CARD (AP1-AP16) 3.00 8.00
*REFRACTOR/149: .5X TO 1.2X BASIC INSERTS
REFRACTORS PRINT RUN 149 SER.#'d SETS
*XFRACTOR/50: .6X TO 1.5X BASIC INSERTS
XFRACTORS PRINT RUN 50 SER.#'d SETS
UNPRICED GOLD REF. PRINT RUN 1
ONE PETERSON PER MINI-BOX

2008 Finest Autograph Patches

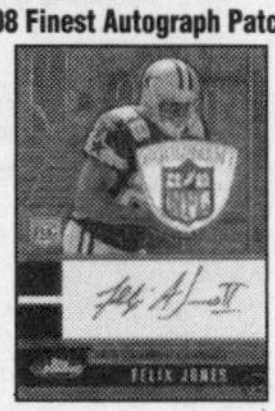

AUTO PATCH/15 ODDS 1:498
102 John David Booty 12.00 30.00
104 Brian Brohm 15.00 40.00
105 Joe Flacco 100.00 200.00
106 Chad Henne 15.00 40.00
109 Matt Ryan 150.00 300.00
112 Jamaal Charles 25.00 60.00
114 Matt Forte 25.00 60.00
116 Chris Johnson 75.00 150.00
117 Felix Jones 25.00 60.00
118 Darren McFadden 40.00 100.00
119 Rashard Mendenhall 30.00 80.00
121 Ray Rice 30.00 80.00
122 Dustin Keller 15.00 40.00
123 Steve Slaton 15.00 40.00
124 Kevin Smith 15.00 40.00
125 Jonathan Stewart 25.00 60.00
126 Kevin O'Connell 12.00 30.00
128 Donnie Avery 12.00 30.00
129 Earl Bennett 15.00 40.00
130 Dexter Jackson 12.00 30.00
131 Jerome Simpson 15.00 40.00
133 Andre Caldwell 12.00 30.00
134 Early Doucet 12.00 30.00
135 Harry Douglas 12.00 30.00
136 James Hardy 12.00 30.00
137 Jordy Nelson 40.00 80.00
138 DeSean Jackson 30.00 80.00
139 Malcolm Kelly 12.00 30.00
140 Mario Manningham 25.00 50.00
141 Limas Sweed 15.00 40.00
142 Eddie Royal 15.00 40.00
143 Devin Thomas 12.00 30.00
149 Jake Long 15.00 40.00
150 Glenn Dorsey 15.00 40.00

2008 Finest Autographs

GROUP A/40* ODDS 1:606
GROUP B/150* ODDS 1:126
GROUP C/400* ODDS 1:66
GROUP D/750* ODDS 1:84
GROUP E/1200* ODDS 1:102
GROUP F/1499* ODDS 1:54
GROUP G/1999* ODDS 1:18
ANNOUNCED PRINT RUNS BELOW
CARDS COULD BE SER.#'d VIA MAIL OFFER
UNPRICED BLACK XFRACT/5 ODDS 1:948
UNPRICED GOLD XFRACT/1 ODDS 1:4812
UNPRICED PRINT.PLATE/1 ODDS 1:1584
101 Erik Ainge/400* 5.00 12.00
102 John David Booty/40* 8.00 20.00
103 Colt Brennan/40* 10.00 25.00
104 Brian Brohm/40* 10.00 25.00
105 Joe Flacco/40* 60.00 120.00
106 Chad Henne/150* 20.00 40.00
107 Josh Johnson/1999* 4.00 10.00
108 Anthony Morelli/1499* 3.00 8.00
109 Matt Ryan/40* 75.00 150.00
110 Andre Woodson/40* 10.00 25.00
111 Kyle Wright/1200* 3.00 8.00
112 Jamaal Charles/400* 10.00 25.00
113 Tashard Choice/400* 4.00 10.00
114 Matt Forte/1999* 12.00 30.00
115 Mike Hart/1499* 4.00 10.00
116 Chris Johnson/1200* 20.00 50.00
117 Felix Jones/40* 30.00 80.00
118 Darren McFadden/40* 25.00 60.00
119 Rashard Mendenhall/40* 20.00 50.00
120 Allen Patrick/1999* 3.00 8.00
121 Ray Rice/150* 20.00 40.00
122 Dustin Keller/400* 5.00 12.00
123 Steve Slaton/150* 6.00 15.00
124 Kevin Smith/1999* 4.00 10.00
125 Jonathan Stewart/40* 40.00 80.00
126 Kevin O'Connell/150* 5.00 12.00
127 Adrian Arrington/1999* 3.00 8.00
128 Donnie Avery/1499* 3.00 8.00
129 Earl Bennett/750* 4.00 10.00
130 Dexter Jackson/150* 5.00 12.00
131 Jerome Simpson/150* 6.00 15.00
132 Keenan Burton/1999* 2.50 6.00
133 Andre Caldwell/1999* 3.00 8.00
134 Early Doucet/400* 4.00 10.00
135 Harry Douglas/1999* 3.00 8.00
136 James Hardy/150* 5.00 12.00
137 Jordy Nelson/150* 15.00 30.00
138 DeSean Jackson/400* 15.00 40.00
139 Malcolm Kelly/400* 4.00 10.00
140 Mario Manningham/750* 7.50 15.00
141 Limas Sweed/150* 6.00 15.00
142 Eddie Royal/1999* 4.00 10.00
143 Devin Thomas/150* 5.00 12.00
144 John Carlson/750* 4.00 10.00
145 Chris Long/150* 6.00 15.00
146 Vernon Gholston/150* 5.00 12.00
147 Dominique Rodgers-Cromartie/750* 4.00 10.00
148 Keith Rivers/400* 5.00 12.00
149 Jake Long/400* 5.00 12.00
150 Glenn Dorsey/150* EXCH 6.00 15.00
151 Brett Favre/25 175.00 300.00

2008 Finest Autographs Blue Xfractors

*BLUE XFRACT/30: .4X TO 1X BASIC AU/40
*BLUE XFRACT/30: .6X TO 1.5X BASIC AU/150
*BLUE XFRACT/30: .8X TO 2X BASIC AU/400
*BLUE XFRACT/30: 1X TO 2.5X BASIC AU/750-1999
BLUE XFRACTOR/30 ODDS 1:168
105 Joe Flacco 60.00 120.00
106 Chad Henne 30.00 80.00
109 Matt Ryan 75.00 150.00
116 Chris Johnson 60.00 120.00
117 Felix Jones 25.00 60.00
118 Darren McFadden 30.00 80.00
121 Ray Rice 40.00 100.00

2008 Finest Autographs Green Xfractors

*GRN XFRACT/30: .5X TO 1.2X BASIC AU/40
*GRN XFRACT/30: .8X TO 2X BASIC AU/150
*GRN XFRACT/30: 1X TO 2.5X BASIC AU/400
*GRN XFRACT/30: 1.2X TO 3X AUTO/750-1999
GREEN XFRACTOR/20 ODDS 1:252
105 Joe Flacco 100.00 175.00
106 Chad Henne 40.00 100.00
109 Matt Ryan 125.00 250.00
116 Chris Johnson 100.00 200.00
117 Felix Jones 40.00 100.00
118 Darren McFadden 40.00 100.00
121 Ray Rice 60.00 120.00

2008 Finest Moments

OVERALL MOMENTS ODDS 1:2
*REFRACTORS: .5X TO 1.2X BASIC INSERTS
*BLUE REF/299: .5X TO 1.2X BASIC INSERT
BLUE REFRACTOR/299 ODDS 1:18
*GREEN REF/199: .6X TO 1.5X BASIC INSERT
GREEN REFRACTOR/199 ODDS 1:24
*BLACK REFRACT/99: .8X TO 2X BASIC INSERTS
BLACK REFRACTOR/99 ODDS 1:48
*GOLD REFRACT/50: 1X TO 2.5X BASIC INSERTS
GOLD REFRACTOR/50 ODDS 1:96
*XFRACTOR/25: 1.5X TO 4X BASIC INSERTS
XFRACTOR/25 ODDS 1:192
UNPRICED WHITE XFRACT/1 ODDS 1:4812
UNPRICED SUPERFRACT/1 ODDS 1:4812
UNPRICED PRINT PLATE/1 ODDS 1:1203
FMAP Adrian Peterson 2.00 5.00
FMAW Andre Woodson .75 2.00
FMBB Bernard Berrian 1.00 2.50
FMBB Brian Brohm .75 2.00
FMBE Braylon Edwards 1.00 2.50
FMBS Barry Sanders 2.50 6.00
FMCB Colt Brennan .75 2.00
FMCH Chad Henne .75 2.00
FMCJ Chris Johnson 2.00 5.00
FMCL Chris Long .75 2.00
FMDB Drew Brees 1.25 3.00
FMDE Derek Anderson .75 2.00
FMDJ DeSean Jackson 1.50 4.00
FMDM Darren McFadden 2.00 5.00
FMDT Devin Thomas .60 1.50
FMED Early Doucet .60 1.50
FMEM Eli Manning 1.25 3.00
FMFJ Felix Jones 1.25 3.00
FMGD Glenn Dorsey .75 2.00
FMJB John David Booty .60 1.50
FMJC Jamaal Charles 1.25 3.00
FMJE John Elway 2.50 6.00
FMJF Joe Flacco 2.50 6.00
FMJH James Hardy .60 1.50
FMJL Jake Long .75 2.00
FMJM Joe Montana 3.00 8.00
FMJS Jonathan Stewart 1.25 3.00
FMLS Limas Sweed .75 2.00
FMLT LaDainian Tomlinson 1.25 3.00
FMLTA Lawrence Taylor 1.50 4.00
FMMF Matt Forte 1.25 3.00
FMMH Mike Hart .75 2.00
FMMK Malcolm Kelly .60 1.50
FMML Marshawn Lynch 1.00 2.50
FMMM Mario Manningham .75 2.00
FMMR Matt Ryan 3.00 8.00
FMPM Peyton Manning 2.00 5.00
FMRC Randall Cunningham 1.50 4.00
FMRG Ryan Grant 1.25 3.00
FMRM Randy Moss 1.25 3.00
FMRME Rashard Mendenhall 1.50 4.00
FMRR Ray Rice 1.50 4.00
FMRW Reggie Wayne 1.00 2.50
FMSJ Steven Jackson 1.25 3.00
FMSS Steve Slaton .75 2.00
FMTB Tom Brady 2.00 5.00
FMTO Terrell Owens 1.25 3.00
FMTR Tony Romo 1.50 4.00
FMVY Vince Young 1.00 2.50
FMWW Wes Welker 1.25 3.00

2008 Finest Moments Autographs

GROUP A ODDS 1:804
GROUP B ODDS 1:948
GROUP C ODDS 1:198
UNPRICED REFRACTOR/10 ODDS 1:948
UNPRICED SUPERFRACT/1 ODDS 1:10,152
UNPRICED PRINT PLATE/1 ODDS 1:3174
UNPRICED CUT AUTO/1 ODDS 1:23,712
FMAAP Adrian Peterson A 100.00 175.00
FMAAW Andre Woodson A 10.00 25.00
FMABB Brian Brohm A 10.00 25.00
FMABE Braylon Edwards A 10.00 25.00
FMABS Barry Sanders A 60.00 120.00
FMACH Chad Henne C 10.00 25.00
FMADM Darren McFadden A 30.00 80.00
FMADT Devin Thomas C 5.00 12.00
FMAEM Eli Manning A 60.00 120.00
FMAFJ Felix Jones A 30.00 80.00
FMAJE John Elway A 75.00 150.00
FMAJF Joe Flacco A 50.00 100.00
FMAJM Joe Montana A 75.00 150.00
FMAJS Jonathan Stewart A 30.00 60.00
FMALS Limas Sweed C 8.00 20.00
FMALT LaDainian Tomlinson A 50.00 100.00
FMALTA Lawrence Taylor A 40.00 80.00
FMAMK Malcolm Kelly B 5.00 12.00
FMAMR Matt Ryan A 60.00 120.00
FMAPM Peyton Manning A 75.00 150.00
FMARC Randall Cunningham A 20.00 40.00
FMARM Randy Moss A 150.00 225.00
FMARME Rashard Mendenhall A 20.00 50.00
FMASJ Steven Jackson A 20.00 40.00
FMATB Tom Brady A 150.00 250.00

2008 Finest Moments Autographs Dual

DUAL AU/15 ODDS 1:1692
UNPRICED REFRACT/10 ODDS 1:2370
UNPRICED GOLD REF/1 ODDS 1:29,196
BH Tom Brady / Chad Henne 150.00 250.00
BM Tom Brady / Randy Moss 150.00 300.00
EK Braylon Edwards / Malcolm Kelly 60.00 120.00
ML Rashard Mendenhall / Marshawn Lynch
MM Eli Manning / Peyton Manning 125.00 200.00
RM Matt Ryan / Darren McFadden 125.00 200.00
SM Barry Sanders / Darren McFadden 125.00 200.00
TC Lawrence Taylor / Randall Cunningham 50.00 100.00
TP LaDainian Tomlinson / Adrian Peterson 75.00 150.00
WF Andre Woodson / Joe Flacco

2008 Finest Moments Cut Signatures

UNPRICED CUT AUTO/1 ODDS 1:23,712
FCS1 Bronko Nagurski
FCS2 Bronko Nagurski
FCS3 Bronko Nagurski
FCS4 Bronko Nagurski
FCS5 Bronko Nagurski
FCS6 Vince Lombardi
FCS7 Vince Lombardi
FCS8 Vince Lombardi
FCS9 Vince Lombardi
FCS10 Vince Lombardi

2008 Finest Tom Brady Finest Moments

COMMON CARD (TB1-TB16) 2.50 6.00
STATED PRINT RUN 629 SER.#'d SETS
*REFRACTOR/149: .5X TO 1.2X BASIC INSERTS
REFRACTORS PRINT RUN 149 SER.#'d SETS
*XFRACTOR/50: .6X TO 1.5X BASIC INSERTS
XFRACTORS PRINT RUN 50 SER.#'d SETS
UNPRICED GOLD REF.PRINT RUN 1
ONE BRADY PER MINI BOX

2008 Finest Tom Brady/Randy Moss Autographs

UNPRICED AU/1 ODDS 1:10,728

2009 Finest

COMP.SET w/o AU's (100) 30.00 80.00
101-130 AUTO OVERALL ODDS 1:3 HOB
101-130 AU ANNOUNCED PRINT RUN 187-495
101-130 AU PER LETTER SER.#'s 17-102
1 Larry Fitzgerald .30 .75
2 Willis McGahee .25 .60
3 Darren McFadden .30 .75
4 Brett Favre 3.00 8.00
5 Brian Westbrook .25 .60
6 Anquan Boldin .25 .60
7 Hines Ward .25 .60
8 Drew Brees .30 .75
9 Terrell Owens .30 .75
10 Matt Ryan .30 .75
11 Steve Slaton .25 .60
12 Matt Cassel .25 .60
13 Clinton Portis .25 .60
14 Kurt Warner .30 .75
15 Santana Moss .25 .60
16 Steven Jackson .25 .60
17 Brandon Jacobs .25 .60
18 LaDainian Tomlinson .30 .75
19 DeAngelo Williams .30 .75
20 Marion Barber .25 .60
21 Randy Moss .30 .75
22 Aaron Rodgers .60 1.50
23 Jay Cutler .30 .75
24 Chad Ochocinco .25 .60
25 Adrian Peterson .50 1.25
26 Joe Flacco .30 .75
27 Chris Johnson .30 .75
28 Reggie Wayne .25 .60
29 Tom Brady .50 1.25
30 Steve Smith .25 .60
31 Braylon Edwards .25 .60
32 Donovan McNabb .30 .75
33 Michael Turner .25 .60
34 Michael Vick .40 1.00
35 Eli Manning .30 .75
36 Brandon Marshall .25 .60
37 Roy Williams WR .25 .60
38 Reggie Bush .30 .75
39 Philip Rivers .30 .75
40 Marshawn Lynch .25 .60
41 Tony Romo .50 1.25
42 Jonathan Stewart .25 .60
43 Matt Forte .30 .75
44 Ryan Grant .25 .60
45 Ben Roethlisberger .30 .75
46 Dwayne Bowe .25 .60
47 Antonio Gates .25 .60
48 Maurice Jones-Drew .25 .60
49 DeSean Jackson .25 .60
50 Calvin Johnson .30 .75
51 Joseph Addai .30 .75
52 Eddie Royal .25 .60
53 Andre Johnson .25 .60
54 Jason Witten .30 .75
55 Ronnie Brown .25 .60
56 T.J. Houshmandzadeh .25 .60
57 Frank Gore .25 .60
58 LenDale White .25 .60
59 Greg Jennings .30 .75
60 Peyton Manning .50 1.25
61 Josh Freeman RC 2.00 5.00
62 Shonn Greene RC 1.50 4.00
63 Mike Wallace RC 2.00 5.00
64 Javon Ringer RC 1.00 2.50
65 Hakeem Nicks RC 1.50 4.00
66 Brandon Pettigrew RC 1.00 2.50
67 Brian Robiskie RC 1.00 2.50
68 Chris Wells RC 1.50 4.00
69 Pat White RC 1.00 2.50
70 Michael Crabtree RC 2.00 5.00
71 Mike Thomas RC 1.00 2.50
72 Nate Davis RC .75 2.00
73 Percy Harvin RC 1.50 4.00
74 Tyson Jackson RC .75 2.00
75 Darrius Heyward-Bey RC 1.00 2.50
76 Aaron Curry RC 1.00 2.50
77 Juaquin Iglesias RC .75 2.00
78 Mohamed Massaquoi RC .75 2.00
79 Andre Brown RC .60 1.50
80 Mark Sanchez RC 3.00 8.00
81 Jason Smith RC .75 2.00
82 Patrick Turner RC .75 2.00
83 Donald Brown RC 1.00 2.50
84 Derrick Williams RC .75 2.00
85 Jeremy Maclin RC 1.50 4.00
86 Rhett Bomar RC .75 2.00
87 Glen Coffee RC .75 2.00
88 James Davis RC 1.00 2.50
89 Jarett Dillard RC 1.00 2.50
90 Knowshon Moreno RC 1.00 2.50
91 Kenny Britt RC 1.25 3.00
92 Stephen McGee RC 1.00 2.50
93 Austin Collie RC 1.00 2.50
94 Gartrell Johnson RC .60 1.50
95 LeSean McCoy RC 2.00 5.00
96 Deon Butler RC .75 2.00
97 Brandon Tate RC 1.00 2.50
98 Tom Brandstater RC 1.00 2.50
99 Ramses Barden RC .60 1.50
100 Matthew Stafford RC 6.00 15.00
101 James Laurinaitis AU/330* (serial numbered to 30) 8.00 20.00
102 James Casey AU/495* (serial numbered to 99) 6.00 15.00
103 Brian Cushing AU/476* (serial numbered to 68) 8.00 20.00
105 Austin Collie AU/486* (serial numbered to 81) 10.00 25.00
106 Johnny Knox AU/408* (serial numbered to 102) 12.00 30.00
107 Chris Wells AU/245* (serial numbered to 49) 12.00 30.00
108 Quan Cosby AU/495* (serial numbered to 99) 6.00 15.00
109 Cedric Peerman AU/476* (serial numbered to 68) 6.00 15.00
110 Chase Coffman AU/378* (serial numbered to 54) 6.00 15.00
112 Glen Coffee AU/384* (serial numbered to 64) 6.00 15.00
113 Gartrell Johnson AU/476* (serial numbered to 68) 5.00 12.00
114 Rashad Jennings AU/464* (serial numbered to 58) 8.00 20.00
115 James Davis AU/495* (serial numbered to 99) 8.00 20.00
116 Jarett Dillard AU/476* (serial numbered to 68) 8.00 20.00
117 Jeremy Maclin AU/234* (serial numbered to 39) 15.00 40.00
119 Rey Maualuga AU/368* (serial numbered to 46) 8.00 20.00
120 Kenny Britt AU/245* (serial numbered to 49) 10.00 25.00
121 LeSean McCoy AU/245* (serial numbered to 49) 15.00 40.00
122 Nate Davis AU/495* (serial numbered to 99) 6.00 15.00
123 Percy Harvin AU/288* (serial numbered to 48) 40.00 80.00
124 Patrick Turner AU/384* (serial numbered to 64) 6.00 15.00
128 Shonn Greene AU/486* (serial numbered to 81) 12.00 30.00
129 Stephen McGee AU/395* (serial numbered to 79) 8.00 20.00
130 Tom Brandstater AU/187* (serial numbered to 17) 8.00 20.00

2009 Finest Blue Refractors 429

*VETS 1-60: 2.5X TO 6X BASIC CARDS
*ROOKIES 61-100: .6X TO 1.5X BASIC CARDS
1-100 BLUE REF PRINT RUN 429
4 Brett Favre 10.00 25.00
34 Michael Vick 2.50 6.00

2009 Finest Gold Refractors 75

*VETS 1-60: 4X TO 10X BASIC CARDS
*ROOKIES 61-100: 1X TO 2.5X BASIC CARDS
1-100 GOLD REF PRINT RUN 75
4 Brett Favre 20.00 40.00
34 Michael Vick 4.00 10.00

2009 Finest Green Refractors 199
*VETS 1-60: 3X TO 8X BASIC CARDS
*ROOKIES 61-100: .8X TO 2X BASIC CARDS
1-100 GREEN REF PRINT RUN 199
4 Brett Favre 12.50 30.00
34 Michael Vick 3.00 8.00

2009 Finest Pigskin Gold Refractors
*VETS 1-60: 6X TO 15X BASIC CARDS
*ROOKIES 61-100: 1.5X TO 4X BASIC CARDS
1-100 PIGSKIN GOLD REF PRINT RUN 25
4 Brett Favre 30.00 60.00
34 Michael Vick 6.00 15.00
80 Mark Sanchez 25.00 60.00
100 Matthew Stafford 30.00 60.00

2009 Finest Pigskin Refractors
*VETS 1-60: 3X TO 8X BASIC CARDS
*ROOKIES 61-100: .8X TO 2X BASIC CARDS
1-100 PIGSKIN REF ODDS 1:9 HOB
4 Brett Favre 12.50 30.00
34 Michael Vick 3.00 8.00

2009 Finest Red Refractors 25
*VETS 1-60: 6X TO 15X BASIC CARDS
*ROOKIES 61-100: 1.5X TO 4X BASIC CARDS
1-100 RED REF PRINT RUN 25
4 Brett Favre 30.00 60.00
34 Michael Vick 6.00 15.00
80 Mark Sanchez 25.00 60.00
100 Matthew Stafford 40.00 80.00

2009 Finest Refractors
*VETS 1-60: 2.5X TO 6X BASIC CARDS
*ROOKIES 61-100: .6X TO 1.5X BASIC CARDS
1-100 REFRACTOR ODDS 1:3 HOB
AUTO/40-80*: .6X TO 1.5X BASIC AU
AUTO/110: .5X TO 1.2X BASIC AU
101-130 AU ANNOUNCED PRINT RUN 40-110
101-130 AU PER LETTER SER.#'d TO 10
4 Brett Favre 6.00 15.00
34 Michael Vick 2.50 6.00

2009 Finest Moments Autographs
GROUP A/15 ODDS 1:138 HOB
GROUP B/25 ODDS 1:74 HOB
FMAAP Adrian Peterson/15 75.00 150.00
FMABE Braylon Edwards/25 12.00 30.00
FMACW Chris Wells/25 30.00 60.00
FMADB Drew Brees/15 50.00 100.00
FMADM Darren McFadden/15 15.00 40.00
FMAEM Eli Manning/15 50.00 100.00
FMAFG Frank Gore/25 12.00 30.00
FMAHN Hakeem Nicks/25 12.00 30.00
FMAJC Jay Cutler/15 15.00 40.00
FMAJF Joe Flacco/15 30.00 60.00
FMAJM Jeremy Maclin/25 15.00 40.00
FMAKM Knowshon Moreno/25 40.00 80.00
FMALT LaDainian Tomlinson/15 25.00 50.00
FMAMC Michael Crabtree/25 40.00 80.00
FMAMS Matthew Stafford/25 60.00 120.00
FMAPM Peyton Manning/15 90.00 150.00
FMARM Randy Moss/15 60.00 120.00
FMARW Reggie Wayne/15 15.00 40.00
FMATB Tom Brady/15 100.00 200.00
FMADEB Donald Brown/25 12.00 30.00
FMADHB Darrius Heyward-Bey/25 12.00 30.00
FMAJFR Josh Freeman/25 20.00 50.00
FMAMJS Mark Sanchez/25 60.00 120.00

2009 Finest Rookie Jersey Autographs
GROUP A/109 ODDS 1:17 HOB
GROUP B/209 ODDS 1:13 HOB
GROUP C/309 ODDS 1:8 HOB
GROUP D/409 ODDS 1:11 HOB
*REFRACT/50: .5X TO 1.2X BASIC AU/209-409
*REFRACT/50: .4X TO 1X BASIC AU/109
61 Josh Freeman/109 40.00 80.00
62 Shonn Greene/309 12.00 30.00
63 Mike Wallace/309 25.00 50.00
64 Javon Ringer/309 8.00 20.00
65 Hakeem Nicks/209 12.00 30.00
66 Brandon Pettigrew/209 8.00 20.00
67 Brian Robiskie/209 8.00 20.00
68 Chris Wells/109 15.00 40.00
69 Pat White/109 10.00 25.00
70 Michael Crabtree/109 20.00 50.00
71 Mike Thomas/409 8.00 20.00
72 Nate Davis/409 6.00 15.00
73 Percy Harvin/209 20.00 50.00
74 Tyson Jackson/209 6.00 15.00
75 Darrius Heyward-Bey/109 10.00 25.00
76 Aaron Curry/209 8.00 20.00
77 Juaquin Iglesias/309 6.00 15.00
78 Mohamed Massaquoi/309 6.00 15.00
79 Andre Brown/409 5.00 12.00
80 Mark Sanchez/109 60.00 120.00
81 Jason Smith/209 6.00 15.00
82 Patrick Turner/309 6.00 15.00
83 Donald Brown/109 10.00 25.00
84 Derrick Williams/309 6.00 15.00
85 Jeremy Maclin/109 15.00 40.00
86 Rhett Bomar/309 6.00 15.00
87 Glen Coffee/309 6.00 15.00
90 Knowshon Moreno/109 10.00 25.00
91 Kenny Britt/109 12.00 30.00
92 Stephen McGee/209 10.00 25.00
95 LeSean McCoy/109 20.00 50.00
96 Deon Butler/409 6.00 15.00
99 Ramses Barden/409 5.00 12.00
100 Matthew Stafford/109 75.00 135.00

2009 Finest Rookie Jersey Autographs Gold Refractors
*GOLD REF/25: .8X TO 2X BASIC AU/209-409
*GOLD REF/25: .6X TO 1.5X BASIC AU/109
GOLD REFRACTOR PRINT RUN 25
61 Josh Freeman 60.00 120.00
80 Mark Sanchez 100.00 200.00
100 Matthew Stafford 150.00 300.00

2009 Finest Rookie Jersey Autographs Red Refractors
*RED REF/15: .8X TO 2X BASIC AU/209-409
*RED REF/15: .6X TO 1.5X BASIC AU/109
RED REFRACTOR PRINT RUN 15
80 Mark Sanchez 125.00 250.00
100 Matthew Stafford 200.00 350.00

2010 Finest

COMPLETE SET (125) 30.00 60.00
1 Adrian Peterson .50 1.25
2 Marcus Easley RC .60 1.50
3 Miles Austin .30 .75
4 Calvin Johnson .30 .75
5 Hines Ward .25 .60
6 Brandon Jacobs .25 .60
7 C.J. Spiller RC 1.25 3.00
8 Mark Sanchez .30 .75
9 Brent Celek .25 .60
10 Peyton Manning .50 1.25
11 Charles Woodson .30 .75
12 Steven Jackson .25 .60
13 Greg Jennings .25 .60
14 Matt Forte .25 .60
15 Jay Cutler .30 .75
16 Jason Witten .30 .75
17 Toby Gerhart RC .75 2.00
18 Reggie Bush .30 .75
19 Ray Rice .25 .60
20 Chris Johnson .30 .75
21 Matt Schaub .25 .60
22 Steve Smith .25 .60
23 Eric Decker RC 1.00 2.50
24 Emmanuel Sanders RC .75 2.00
25 Jerome Harrison .20 .50
26 DeMarcus Ware .25 .60
27 Jermaine Gresham RC 1.00 2.50
28 Hakeem Nicks .25 .60
29 Sidney Rice .25 .60
30 Andre Johnson .25 .60
31 Demaryius Thomas RC 1.00 2.50
32 Mardy Gilyard RC .75 2.00
33 Adrian Wilson .20 .50
34 Joseph Addai .25 .60
35 Darren McFadden .25 .60
36 Donovan McNabb .30 .75
37 Jonathan Dwyer RC .75 2.00
38 Mike Kafka RC .75 2.00
39 Fred Jackson .30 .75
40 Tom Brady .50 1.25
41 Damian Williams RC .75 2.00
42 Rob Gronkowski RC 2.00 5.00
43 Jimmy Clausen RC .75 2.00
44 Michael Crabtree .30 .75
45 Ray Lewis .30 .75
46 Jared Allen .30 .75
47 Lee Evans .25 .60
48 Ryan Grant .25 .60
49 Santonio Holmes .25 .60
50 Drew Brees .30 .75
51 Knowshon Moreno .25 .60
52 Ndamukong Suh RC 1.50 4.00
53 Ryan Mathews RC 1.50 4.00
54 Brandon Marshall .25 .60
55 DeAngelo Williams .25 .60
56 Aaron Rodgers .60 1.50
57 Steve Smith USC .25 .60
58 Mike Sims-Walker .25 .60
59 Jahvid Best RC 1.25 3.00
60 Maurice Jones-Drew .25 .60
61 Dwight Freeney .25 .60
62 Brett Favre .75 2.00
63 Ricky Williams .25 .60
64 LaDainian Tomlinson .30 .75
65 Golden Tate RC .75 2.00
66 Armanti Edwards RC .75 2.00
67 Reggie Wayne .25 .60
68 Rashard Mendenhall .25 .60
69 Tony Gonzalez .25 .60
70 Troy Polamalu .30 .75
71 Kellen Winslow .25 .60
72 Vincent Jackson .20 .50
73 Frank Gore .25 .60
74 Thomas Jones .25 .60
75 Matt Ryan .30 .75
76 Percy Harvin .30 .75
77 Colt McCoy RC 1.50 4.00
78 Michael Turner .20 .50
79 Wes Welker .30 .75
80 Chad Ochocinco .25 .60
81 Dexter McCluster RC .75 2.00
82 Mike Williams RC 1.25 3.00
83 Montario Hardesty RC .75 2.00
84 Kevin Kolb .25 .60
85 Darrelle Revis .25 .60
86 Jonathan Stewart .25 .60
87 Marques Colston .25 .60
88 Anquan Boldin .25 .60
89 Vince Young .20 .50
90 Larry Fitzgerald .30 .75
91 Taylor Price RC .75 2.00
92 Matthew Stafford .30 .75
93 Andre Roberts RC .75 2.00
94 Patrick Willis .25 .60
95 Elvis Dumervil .20 .50
96 Randy Moss .30 .75
97 Cedric Benson .25 .60
98 Eli Manning .30 .75
99 Shonn Greene .25 .60
100 Tim Tebow RC 5.00 10.00
101 Ben Tate RC 1.00 2.50
102 Eric Berry RC .75 2.00
103 Jamaal Charles .25 .60
104 Brandon LaFell RC .75 2.00
105 Joe Flacco .30 .75
106 T.J. Houshmandzadeh .25 .60
107 Ronnie Brown .25 .60
108 Antonio Gates .25 .60
109 DeSean Jackson .25 .60
110 Dez Bryant RC 2.50 6.00
111 Joe McKnight RC .75 2.00
112 Philip Rivers .30 .75
113 Chris Wells .25 .60
114 Roddy White .25 .60
115 LeSean McCoy .25 .60
116 Arrelious Benn RC .75 2.00
117 Pierre Thomas .25 .60
118 Gerald McCoy RC .75 2.00
119 Rolando McClain RC .75 2.00
120 Tony Romo .40 1.00
121 Dallas Clark .25 .60
122 Jordan Shipley RC .75 2.00
123 Clinton Portis .25 .60
124 Marion Barber .25 .60
125 Sam Bradford RC 3.00 8.00

2010 Finest Black Refractors
*VETS: 5X TO 12X BASIC CARDS
*ROOKIES: 2X TO 5X BASIC CARDS
BLACK REFRACTOR PRINT RUN 99

2010 Finest Gold Refractors
*VETS: 6X TO 15X BASIC CARDS
*ROOKIES: 2.5X TO 6X BASIC CARDS
GOLD REFRACTOR PRINT RUN 50

2010 Finest Mosaic Refractors
*VETS: 12X TO 30X BASIC CARDS
*ROOKIES: 5X TO 12X BASIC CARDS
MOSAIC REFRACTOR PRINT RUN 10
100 Tim Tebow 200.00 350.00
125 Sam Bradford 150.00 300.00

2010 Finest Red Refractors
*VETS: 8X TO 20X BASIC CARDS
*ROOKIES: 3X TO 8X BASIC CARDS
RED REFRACTOR PRINT RUN 25

2010 Finest Refractors
*VETS: 2X TO 5X BASIC CARDS
*ROOKIES: .8X TO 2X BASIC CARDS
STATED ODDS 1:3 HOBBY

2010 Finest Xfractors
*VETS: 2.5X TO 6X BASIC CARDS
*ROOKIES: 1X TO 2.5X BASIC CARDS
XFRACTOR/399 ODDS 1:4 HOBBY

2010 Finest Atomic Refractor Rookies
COMPLETE SET (25) 40.00 80.00
ONE PER 6-PACK MINI HOBBY BOX
*GOLD/50: 1.2X TO 3X BASIC INSERTS
FAR1 Sam Bradford 5.00 12.00
FAR2 Eric Berry 1.25 3.00
FAR3 Ben Tate 1.50 4.00
FAR4 Dexter McCluster 1.25 3.00
FAR5 Ryan Mathews 2.50 6.00
FAR6 Jahvid Best 2.00 5.00
FAR7 Montario Hardesty 1.25 3.00
FAR8 Jermaine Gresham 1.50 4.00
FAR9 Mike Williams 2.00 5.00
FAR10 Dez Bryant 4.00 10.00
FAR11 Joe McKnight 1.25 3.00
FAR12 Colt McCoy 2.50 6.00
FAR13 Brandon LaFell 1.25 3.00
FAR14 Ndamukong Suh 2.50 6.00
FAR15 Jimmy Clausen 1.25 3.00
FAR16 Demaryius Thomas 1.50 4.00
FAR17 Jonathan Dwyer 1.25 3.00
FAR18 Golden Tate 1.25 3.00
FAR19 Rolando McClain 1.25 3.00
FAR20 C.J. Spiller 2.00 5.00
FAR21 Arrelious Benn 1.25 3.00
FAR22 Toby Gerhart 1.25 3.00
FAR23 Jordan Shipley 1.25 3.00
FAR24 Emmanuel Sanders 1.25 3.00
FAR25 Tim Tebow 8.00 20.00

2010 Finest Dual Jersey Autographs
STATED PRINT RUN 100-350
*REF/75: .6X TO 1.5X JSY AU/300-350
*REF/75: .5X TO 1.2X JSY AU/200-250
*REF/75: .4X TO 1X JSY AU/100-160
EXCH EXPIRATION: 9/30/2013
AB Arrelious Benn/250 6.00 15.00
AD Anthony Dixon/350 5.00 12.00
AE Armanti Edwards/350 5.00 12.00
AG Anthony Gonzalez/110 6.00 15.00
AH Aaron Hernandez/350 10.00 25.00
AR Andre Roberts/350 5.00 12.00
BL Brandon LaFell/250 6.00 15.00
BT Ben Tate/110 12.00 30.00
CH Chad Henne/110 12.00 30.00
CM Colt McCoy/100 40.00 80.00
CS C.J. Spiller/110 15.00 40.00
DB Dez Bryant/100 50.00 100.00
DK Dustin Keller/110 8.00 20.00
DM Dexter McCluster/160 8.00 20.00
DT Demaryius Thomas/100 12.00 30.00
DTH Devin Thomas/300 3.00 8.00
DW Damian Williams/250 6.00 15.00
EB Eric Berry/160 15.00 40.00
ED Eric Decker/350 6.00 15.00
EDO Early Doucet/300 3.00 8.00
ES Emmanuel Sanders/250 6.00 15.00
GM Gerald McCoy/110 8.00 20.00
GT Golden Tate/100 10.00 25.00
JA Joseph Addai/110 8.00 20.00
JB Jahvid Best/100 40.00 100.00
JC Jimmy Clausen/100 10.00 25.00
JD Jonathan Dwyer/350 5.00 12.00
JF Jacoby Ford/350 10.00 25.00
JFL Joe Flacco/110 15.00 30.00
JG Jermaine Gresham/200 8.00 20.00
JGR Jimmy Graham/300 12.00 30.00
JH James Hardy/300 3.00 8.00
JM Joe McKnight/200 6.00 15.00
JMA Jerod Mayo/110 8.00 20.00
JS Jordan Shipley/350 5.00 12.00
ME Marcus Easley/350 4.00 10.00
MG Mardy Gilyard/350 5.00 12.00
MH Montario Hardesty/200 6.00 15.00
MK Mike Kafka/250 6.00 15.00
MW Mike Williams 8.00 20.00
NS Ndamukong Suh/110 30.00 60.00
PM Peyton Manning/100 60.00 120.00
RG Rob Gronkowski/200 25.00 50.00
RM Rolando McClain/100 10.00 25.00
RMA Ryan Mathews/100 30.00 80.00
SB Sam Bradford/100 75.00 150.00
SS Steve Slaton/110 6.00 15.00
TG Toby Gerhart/200 10.00 25.00
TP Taylor Price/350 6.00 15.00
TT Tim Tebow/100 75.00 150.00

2010 Finest Dual Jersey Autographs Black Refractors
*BLACK REF: .8X TO 2X DUAL/300-350
*BLACK REF: .6X TO 1.5X DUAL/200-250
*BLACK REF: .5X TO 1.2X DUAL/160
*BLACK REF: .4X TO 1X DUAL/100-110
STATED PRINT RUN 50 SER.#'d SETS
EXCH EXPIRATION: 9/30/2013

2010 Finest Dual Jersey Autographs Gold Refractors
*GOLD REF: 1.2X TO 3X DUAL/300-350
*GOLD REF: 1X TO 2.5X DUAL/200-250
*GOLD REF: .8X TO 2X DUAL/160
*GOLD REF: .6X TO 1.5X DUAL/100-110
GOLD REFRACTOR PRINT RUN 25
EXCH EXPIRATION: 9/30/2013
PM Peyton Manning 75.00 150.00
SB Sam Bradford
TT Tim Tebow 150.00 250.00

2010 Finest Moments
COMPLETE SET (25) 25.00 50.00
ONE PER 6-PACK MINI HOBBY BOX
FM1 Dez Bryant 2.50 6.00
FM2 Jonathan Dwyer .75 2.00
FM3 Jermaine Gresham 1.00 2.50
FM4 Toby Gerhart .75 2.00
FM5 Montario Hardesty .75 2.00
FM6 LeSean McCoy 1.00 2.50
FM7 Rob Gronkowski 2.00 5.00
FM8 Ben Tate 1.00 2.50
FM9 Ryan Mathews 1.50 4.00
FM10 Adrian Peterson 2.00 5.00
FM11 Darren McFadden 1.00 2.50
FM12 Arrelious Benn .75 2.00
FM13 Brandon LaFell .75 2.00
FM14 Jimmy Clausen .75 2.00
FM15 Ray Rice 1.00 2.50
FM16 Earl Thomas .75 2.00
FM17 Marques Colston 1.00 2.50
FM18 Joe Flacco 1.25 3.00
FM19 DeSean Jackson 1.00 2.50
FM20 Sam Bradford 3.00 8.00
FM21 Mike Sims-Walker 1.00 2.50
FM22 Jonathan Stewart 1.00 2.50
FM23 Jamaal Charles 1.00 2.50
FM24 Brandon Marshall 1.00 2.50
FM25 Tim Tebow 3.00 8.00

2010 Finest Moments Autographs
GROUP A ODDS 1:402 HOB
GROUP B ODDS 1:186 HOB
GROUP C ODDS 1:42 HOB
AB Arrelious Benn C 5.00 12.00
AP Adrian Peterson B 50.00 100.00
BL Brandon LaFell C 5.00 12.00
BM Brandon Marshall B 8.00 20.00
BT Ben Tate C 6.00 15.00
DB Dez Bryant A 30.00 60.00
DJ DeSean Jackson C 10.00 25.00
DM Darren McFadden C 8.00 20.00
ET Earl Thomas C 5.00 12.00
JC Jimmy Clausen A 8.00 20.00
JCH Jamaal Charles B 6.00 15.00
JD Jonathan Dwyer C 5.00 12.00
JF Joe Flacco C 12.00 30.00
JG Jermaine Gresham C 6.00 15.00
JS Jonathan Stewart C 6.00 15.00
LM LeSean McCoy C 10.00 25.00
MC Marques Colston B 6.00 15.00
MH Montario Hardesty C 5.00 12.00
MSW Mike Sims-Walker C 6.00 15.00
RG Rob Gronkowski C 15.00 40.00
RMA Ryan Mathews B 20.00 50.00
RR Ray Rice A 10.00 25.00
SB Sam Bradford A 50.00 100.00
TG Toby Gerhart C 5.00 12.00
TT Tim Tebow A 75.00 125.00

2010 Finest Rookie Patch Autographs
STATED PRINT RUN 100-450
EXCH EXPIRATION: 9/30/2013
2 Marcus Easley/450 5.00 12.00
7 C.J. Spiller/150 25.00 60.00
17 Toby Gerhart/300 10.00 25.00
23 Eric Decker/400 8.00 20.00
24 Emmanuel Sanders/350 6.00 15.00
27 Jermaine Gresham/300 8.00 20.00
31 Demaryius Thomas/100 15.00 40.00
32 Mardy Gilyard/400 6.00 15.00
37 Jonathan Dwyer/400 6.00 15.00
38 Mike Kafka/250 8.00 20.00
41 Damian Williams/350 6.00 15.00
42 Rob Gronkowski/350 30.00 60.00
43 Jimmy Clausen/100 12.00 30.00
52 Ndamukong Suh/210 30.00 60.00
53 Ryan Mathews/150 40.00 100.00
59 Jahvid Best/150 15.00 40.00
65 Golden Tate/100 12.00 30.00
66 Armanti Edwards/400 6.00 15.00
77 Colt McCoy/100 50.00 100.00
81 Dexter McCluster/150 10.00 25.00
82 Mike Williams 10.00 25.00
83 Montario Hardesty/400 6.00 15.00
91 Taylor Price/400 6.00 15.00
93 Andre Roberts/450 6.00 15.00
100 Tim Tebow/100 75.00 150.00
101 Ben Tate/150 20.00 40.00
102 Eric Berry/150 10.00 25.00
104 Brandon LaFell/350 6.00 15.00
110 Dez Bryant/100 50.00 120.00
111 Joe McKnight 6.00 15.00
116 Arrelious Benn/300 6.00 15.00
118 Gerald McCoy/150 10.00 25.00
119 Rolando McClain/250 8.00 20.00
122 Jordan Shipley/350 6.00 15.00
125 Sam Bradford/100 75.00 150.00

2010 Finest Rookie Patch Autographs Black Refractors
*BLK REF: .6X TO 1.5X BASE JSY AU/300-450
*BLK REF: .5X TO 1.2X BASE JSY AU/210-250
*BLACK REF: .4X TO 1X BASE JSY AU/150
BLACK REFRACTOR PRINT RUN 75
EXCH EXPIRATION: 9/30/2013

2010 Finest Rookie Patch Autographs Gold Refractors
*GOLD REF: 1X TO 2.5X BASIC JSY AU/300-450
*GOLD REF: .8X TO 2X BASIC JSY AU/210-250
*GOLD REF: .6X TO 1.5X BASIC JSY AU/150
*GOLD REF: .6X TO 1.5X BASIC JSY AU/100
GOLD REFRACTOR PRINT RUN 25
EXCH EXPIRATION: 9/30/2013
43 Jimmy Clausen 15.00 40.00
100 Tim Tebow 150.00 300.00
110 Dez Bryant 100.00 200.00
125 Sam Bradford 125.00 250.00

2010 Finest Rookie Patch Autographs Red Refractors
*RED REF: .8X TO 2X BASIC JSY AU/300-450
*RED REF: .6X TO 1.5X BASIC JSY AU/210-250
*RED REF: .5X TO 1.2X BASIC JSY AU/150
*RED REF: .4X TO 1X BASIC JSY AU/100
RED REFRACTOR PRINT RUN 50
EXCH EXPIRATION: 9/30/2013
100 Tim Tebow 100.00 200.00
110 Dez Bryant 60.00 120.00
125 Sam Bradford 100.00 200.00

2010 Finest Rookie Patch Autographs Refractors
*REFRACT: .6X TO 1.5X BASIC JSY AU/300-450
*REFRACT: .5X TO 1.2X BASIC JSY AU/210-250
*REFRACT: .4X TO 1X BASIC JSY AU/150
REFRACTOR STATED PRINT RUN 99
EXCH EXPIRATION: 9/30/2013

2011 Finest

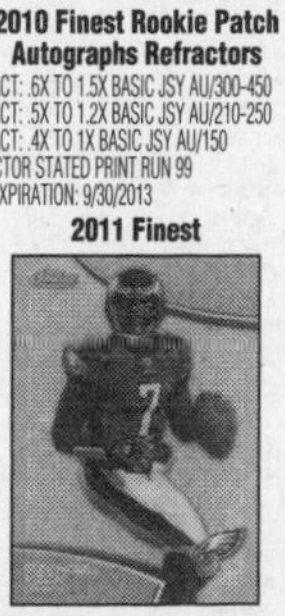

COMPLETE SET (125) 20.00 50.00
1 Michael Vick .30 .75
2 Pierre Garcon .25 .60
3 Jeremy Maclin .25 .60
4 Mike Wallace .30 .75
5 Jahvid Best .25 .60
6 Vernon Davis .25 .60
7 Greg Little RC .75 2.00
8 Greg Jennings .25 .60
9 Santana Moss .25 .60
10 Adrian Peterson .40 1.00
11 Matt Schaub .25 .60
12 Julio Jones RC 1.50 4.00
13 Matt Ryan .30 .75
14 Ray Rice .25 .60
15 Ryan Torain .20 .50
16 Dallas Clark .25 .60
17 Ahmad Bradshaw .25 .60
18 Randall Cobb RC 1.00 2.50
19 Frank Gore .25 .60
20 Chris Johnson .25 .60
21 A.J. Green RC 1.50 4.00
22 Shane Vereen RC .75 2.00
23 Jon Baldwin RC .75 2.00
24 Edmond Gates RC .60 1.50
25 Tim Tebow .60 1.50
26 Miles Austin .25 .60
27 Sidney Rice .25 .60
28 Von Miller RC 1.00 2.50
29 Jason Witten .30 .75
30 Arian Foster .25 .60
31 Cedric Benson .25 .60
32 Mike Williams .25 .60
33 Bilal Powell RC .50 1.25
34 Reggie Wayne .25 .60
35 Jamie Harper RC .75 2.00
36 Andre Johnson .25 .60
37 Brandon Marshall .25 .60
38 Jermichael Finley .25 .60
39 Austin Pettis RC .60 1.50
40 Roddy White .25 .60
41 Steven Jackson .25 .60
42 Vincent Jackson .25 .60
43 Jonathan Stewart .25 .60
44 Vincent Brown RC .75 2.00
45 Daniel Thomas RC .75 2.00
46 Michael Turner .25 .60
47 Christian Ponder RC 1.50 4.00
48 Ben Roethlisberger .30 .75
49 Jay Cutler .25 .60
50 Aaron Rodgers .50 1.25
51 Jerrel Jernigan RC .60 1.50
52 Colin Kaepernick RC 1.00 2.50
53 Thomas Jones .25 .60
54 Alex Green RC .75 2.00
55 Dwayne Bowe .25 .60
56 Kenny Britt .25 .60
57 Austin Collie .25 .60
58 Dez Bryant .30 .75
59 Santonio Holmes .25 .60
60 Drew Brees .30 .75
61 Maurice Jones-Drew .25 .60
62 Mike Tolbert .25 .60
63 Marcell Dareus RC .75 2.00
64 Brandon Lloyd .25 .60
65 Philip Rivers .30 .75
66 Eli Manning .30 .75
67 LeSean McCoy .25 .60
68 Johnny Knox .25 .60
69 Taiwan Jones RC .75 2.00
70 Tom Brady .50 1.25
71 Terrell Owens .30 .75
72 Anquan Boldin .25 .60
73 Ryan Mathews .25 .60
74 DeAngelo Williams .25 .60
75 Peyton Hillis .25 .60
76 Derrick Mason .20 .50
77 Jordan Todman RC .50 1.25
78 Darren McFadden .25 .60
79 BenJarvus Green-Ellis .25 .60
80 Peyton Manning .50 1.25
81 Torrey Smith RC 1.00 2.50
82 Delone Carter RC .60 1.50
83 Antonio Gates .25 .60
84 Shonn Greene .25 .60
85 Marshawn Lynch .25 .60
86 Mikel Leshoure RC .75 2.00
87 DeSean Jackson .25 .60
88 Josh Freeman .30 .75
89 Matthew Stafford .30 .75
90 Larry Fitzgerald .25 .60
91 Michael Crabtree .25 .60
92 Kyle Rudolph RC .75 2.00
93 Ryan Williams RC 1.00 2.50
94 Owen Daniels .20 .50
95 Stevan Ridley RC .75 2.00
96 Fred Jackson .30 .75
97 Beanie Wells .25 .60
98 Percy Harvin .25 .60
99 Jamaal Charles .25 .60
100 Blaine Gabbert RC 1.25 3.00
101 DeMarco Murray RC 1.50 4.00
102 Titus Young RC 1.00 2.50
103 Ryan Mallett RC 1.50 4.00
104 LaDainian Tomlinson .30 .75
105 Joseph Addai .25 .60
106 Mario Manningham .25 .60
107 Hakeem Nicks .25 .60
108 Steve Johnson .25 .60
109 Braylon Edwards .25 .60
110 Felix Jones .25 .60
111 Jake Locker RC 2.00 5.00
112 Matt Forte .25 .60
113 Knowshon Moreno .25 .60
114 Joe Flacco .30 .75
115 Marques Colston .25 .60
116 Andy Dalton RC 2.00 5.00
117 Calvin Johnson .30 .75
118 Tony Romo .30 .75
119 Wes Welker .30 .75
120 Mark Ingram RC 1.50 4.00
121 Leonard Hankerson RC .75 2.00
122 Kendall Hunter RC .75 2.00
123 LeGarrette Blount .25 .60
124 Rashard Mendenhall .25 .60
125 Cam Newton RC 5.00 12.00

2011 Finest Blue Refractors
*VETS: 6X TO 15X BASIC CARDS
*ROOKIES: 2.5X TO 6X BASIC CARDS
BLUE REFRACTOR/99 ODDS 1:24 HOB
125 Cam Newton 40.00 80.00

2011 Finest Gold Refractors
*VETS: 8X TO 20X BASIC CARDS
*ROOKIES: 3X TO 8X BASIC CARDS
GOLD REFRACTOR/50 ODDS 1:42 HOB
125 Cam Newton 75.00 150.00

2011 Finest Mosaic Refractors
*VETS: 20X TO 50X BASIC CARDS
*ROOKIES: 8X TO 20X BASIC CARDS
MOSAIC REFRACTOR/10 ODDS 1:210 HOB
125 Cam Newton 350.00 600.00

2011 Finest Red Refractors
*VETS: 10X TO 25X BASIC CARDS
*ROOKIES: 4X TO 10X BASIC CARDS
RED REFRACTOR/25 ODDS 1:84 HOB
125 Cam Newton 125.00 200.00

2011 Finest Refractors
*VETS: 2.5X TO 6X BASIC CARDS
*ROOKIES: 1X TO 2.5X BASIC CARDS

2011 Finest Xfractors
*VETS: 3X TO 8X BASIC CARDS
*ROOKIES: 1.2X TO 3X BASIC CARDS
STATED PRINT RUN 399 SER.#'d SETS

2011 Finest Atomic Refractor Rookies
*GOLD REF/50: 1.5X TO 4X BASIC INSERTS
*MOSAIC REF/10: 4X TO 10X BASIC INSERTS
*RED REF/25: 2.5X TO 6X BASIC INSERTS
FARAD Andy Dalton 4.00 10.00
FARAG A.J. Green 3.00 8.00
FARBG Blaine Gabbert 2.50 6.00
FARCK Colin Kaepernick 2.00 5.00
FARCN Cam Newton 12.00 30.00
FARCP Christian Ponder 3.00 8.00
FARDB Da'Quan Bowers 1.50 4.00
FARDM DeMarco Murray 3.00 8.00
FARGL Greg Little 1.50 4.00
FARJB Jon Baldwin 1.50 4.00
FARJH Jamie Harper 1.50 4.00
FARJJ Julio Jones 3.00 8.00
FARJJE Jerrel Jernigan 1.25 3.00
FARJL Jake Locker 4.00 10.00
FARKR Kyle Rudolph 1.50 4.00
FARLH Leonard Hankerson 1.50 4.00
FARMI Mark Ingram 3.00 8.00
FARML Mikel Leshoure 1.50 4.00
FARNF Nick Fairley 2.00 5.00
FARPA Prince Amukamara 1.50 4.00
FARRC Randall Cobb 2.00 5.00
FARRM Ryan Mallett 3.00 8.00
FARRW Ryan Williams 2.00 5.00
FARTS Torrey Smith 2.00 5.00
FARVM Von Miller 2.00 5.00

2011 Finest Jumbo Jersey Autographs
*BASE JSY AU/589: .25X TO .6X REF/75
*BASE JSY AU/339: .3X TO .8X REF/75
*BASE JSY AU/89-189: .4X TO 1X REF/75
EXCH EXPIRATION: 8/31/2014
AJRRM Ryan Mallett/189 25.00 50.00

2011 Finest Jumbo Jersey Autographs Gold Refractors
*GOLD REF/25: .6X TO 1.5X BASIC REF/75
AJRCN Cam Newton 200.00 350.00
AJRDB2 Drew Brees 60.00 120.00
AJRMV Michael Vick 100.00 175.00

2011 Finest Jumbo Jersey Autographs Red Refractors
*RED REF/10: .8X TO 2X BASIC REF/75
AJRAD Andy Dalton 125.00 200.00
AJRAJG A.J. Green 75.00 150.00
AJRCK Colin Kaepernick 30.00 80.00
AJRCN Cam Newton 350.00 600.00
AJRCP Christian Ponder 125.00 200.00
AJRJL Jake Locker 100.00 200.00
AJRMI Mark Ingram 100.00 200.00
AJRJJ2 Julio Jones 100.00 200.00

2011 Finest Jumbo Jersey Autographs Refractors
REFRACTOR STATED PRINT RUN 75
EXCH EXPIRATION: 8/31/2014
AJRAB Ahmad Bradshaw 8.00 20.00
AJRAG Alex Green 12.00 30.00
AJRAP Austin Pettis 6.00 15.00
AJRBP Bilal Powell 5.00 12.00
AJRCC Chris Cooley 10.00 25.00
AJRCS Cecil Shorts 6.00 15.00
AJRDB Dwayne Bowe 8.00 20.00
AJRDC Delone Carter 6.00 15.00
AJRDH David Harris 6.00 15.00
AJRDHA DeAngelo Hall 8.00 20.00
AJRDK Dustin Keller 6.00 15.00
AJRDM DeMarco Murray 50.00 100.00
AJRDMA Derrick Mason 6.00 15.00
AJRDT Daniel Thomas 12.00 30.00
AJREG Edmond Gates 6.00 15.00
AJRGL Greg Little 10.00 25.00
AJRJB Jon Baldwin 8.00 20.00
AJRJH Jamie Harper 8.00 20.00
AJRJJ Jerrel Jernigan 6.00 15.00
AJRJT Jordan Todman 5.00 12.00
AJRKH Kendall Hunter 10.00 25.00
AJRKM Knowshon Moreno 8.00 20.00
AJRKR Kyle Rudolph 8.00 20.00
AJRLH Leonard Hankerson 8.00 20.00
AJRLM LeSean McCoy 10.00 25.00
AJRMD Marcell Dareus 8.00 20.00
AJRML Mikel Leshoure 8.00 20.00
AJRNP Niles Paul 8.00 20.00
AJRPA Prince Amukamara 8.00 20.00
AJRPP Paul Posluszny 8.00 20.00
AJRPW Patrick Willis 10.00 25.00
AJRRC Randall Cobb 10.00 25.00
AJRRW Ryan Williams 10.00 25.00
AJRSH Santonio Holmes 10.00 25.00
AJRSR Sidney Rice 8.00 20.00
AJRSR2 Stevan Ridley 12.00 30.00
AJRSV Shane Vereen 8.00 20.00
AJRTD Tandon Doss 6.00 15.00
AJRTJ Taiwan Jones 10.00 25.00
AJRTS Torrey Smith 12.00 30.00
AJRTY Titus Young 10.00 25.00
AJRVB Vincent Brown 8.00 20.00
AJRVM Von Miller 12.00 30.00

2011 Finest Moments
*REFRACTORS: .6X TO 1.5X BASIC INSERTS
FMAB Antonio Brown 1.25 3.00
FMAJG A.J. Green 1.50 4.00
FMAP Adrian Peterson 1.50 4.00
FMAR Antrel Rolle .75 2.00
FMBG Blaine Gabbert 1.25 3.00
FMCN Cam Newton 5.00 12.00
FMDK Dustin Keller 1.00 2.50
FMDM DeMarco Murray 1.50 4.00
FMJB Jon Baldwin .75 2.00
FMJG Jabar Gaffney .75 2.00
FMJM Jerod Mayo .75 2.00
FMKR Kyle Rudolph .75 2.00
FMLH Leonard Hankerson .75 2.00
FMMI Mark Ingram 1.50 4.00
FMML Mikel Leshoure .75 2.00
FMMS Mark Sanchez 1.25 3.00
FMMT Mike Thomas 1.00 2.50
FMPH Peyton Hillis 1.00 2.50
FMRC Randall Cobb 1.00 2.50
FMRM Ryan Mallett 1.50 4.00
FMRW Ryan Williams 1.00 2.50
FMSV Shane Vereen .75 2.00
FMTJ Thomas Jones 1.00 2.50
FMTS Torrey Smith 1.00 2.50
FMTY Titus Young 1.00 2.50

2011 Finest Moments Autographs
STATED PRINT RUN 25 SER.#'d SETS
FMAAB Antonio Brown 10.00 25.00
FMAAJG A.J. Green 30.00 60.00
FMAAP Adrian Peterson 50.00 100.00
FMAAR Antrel Rolle 10.00 25.00
FMABG Blaine Gabbert 30.00 60.00
FMACN Cam Newton 100.00 200.00
FMADK Dustin Keller 6.00 15.00
FMADM DeMarco Murray 40.00 80.00
FMAJB Jon Baldwin 8.00 20.00
FMAJG Jabar Gaffney 6.00 15.00
FMAJM Jerod Mayo 6.00 15.00
FMAKR Kyle Rudolph 8.00 20.00
FMALH Leonard Hankerson 8.00 20.00
FMAMI Mark Ingram 40.00 80.00
FMAML Mikel Leshoure 8.00 20.00
FMAMS Mark Sanchez 40.00 80.00
FMAMT Mike Thomas 6.00 15.00
FMAPH Peyton Hillis 25.00 50.00
FMARC Randall Cobb 30.00 60.00
FMARM Ryan Mallett 25.00 50.00
FMARW Ryan Williams 10.00 25.00
FMASV Shane Vereen 8.00 20.00
FMATJ Thomas Jones 10.00 25.00
FMATS Torrey Smith 10.00 25.00
FMATY Titus Young 10.00 25.00

2011 Finest Rookie Autograph Refractors
REFRACTOR AU/30-150 ODDS 1:26 HOB
EXCH EXPIRATION: 8/31/2014
7 Greg Little/30 15.00 40.00
18 Randall Cobb/30 30.00 80.00
22 Shane Vereen/30 12.00 30.00
23 Jon Baldwin/30 12.00 30.00
24 Edmond Gates/150 8.00 20.00
28 Von Miller/30 20.00 50.00
33 Bilal Powell/30 8.00 20.00
35 Jamie Harper/90 15.00 40.00
39 Austin Pettis/150 8.00 20.00
44 Vincent Brown/150 10.00 25.00
45 Daniel Thomas/30 25.00 50.00
51 Jerrel Jernigan/30 10.00 25.00
54 Alex Green/150 10.00 25.00
63 Marcell Dareus/30 12.00 30.00
69 Taiwan Jones/90 10.00 25.00
77 Jordan Todman/90 6.00 15.00
81 Torrey Smith/30 15.00 40.00
82 Delone Carter/90 12.00 30.00
86 Mikel Leshoure/30 12.00 30.00
92 Kyle Rudolph/90 12.00 30.00
93 Ryan Williams
95 Stevan Ridley/90 10.00 25.00
101 DeMarco Murray/30 60.00 120.00
102 Titus Young/30 15.00 40.00
121 Leonard Hankerson/30 12.00 30.00
122 Kendall Hunter/150 10.00 25.00

2011 Finest Rookie Autograph Red Refractors
*RED REF/25: .5X TO 1.2X REF/90-150
*RED REF/25: .4X TO 1X REF/30
12 Julio Jones 125.00 200.00
93 Ryan Williams 20.00 50.00
101 DeMarco Murray 125.00 200.00

2011 Finest Rookie Patch Autographs
STATED PRINT RUN 100-599
EXCH EXPIRATION: 8/13/2014
*BLUE REF/75: .6X TO 1.5X PATCH AU/599
*BLUE REF/75: .5X TO 1.2X PATCH AU/310
*BLUE REF/75: .4X TO 1X PATCH AU/100
*RED REF/50: .8X TO 2X PATCH AU/599
*RED REF/50: .6X TO 1.5X PATCH AU/310
*RED REF/50: .5X TO 1.2X PATCH AU/100
RAPAD Andy Dalton/100 50.00 100.00
RAPAG Alex Green/599 6.00 15.00
RAPAJG A.J. Green/100 50.00 100.00
RAPAP Austin Pettis/599 5.00 12.00
RAPBP Bilal Powell/599 4.00 10.00
RAPCK Colin Kaepernick/100 15.00 40.00
RAPCN Cam Newton/100 150.00 250.00
RAPCP Christian Ponder/100 50.00 100.00
RAPCS Cecil Shorts/599 5.00 12.00
RAPDC Delone Carter/599 5.00 12.00
RAPDM DeMarco Murray/310 25.00 60.00
RAPDT Daniel Thomas/310 8.00 20.00
RAPEG Edmond Gates/599 5.00 12.00
RAPGL Greg Little/310 10.00 25.00
RAPJB Jon Baldwin/100 10.00 25.00
RAPJH Jamie Harper/599 6.00 15.00
RAPJJ Julio Jones/100 50.00 100.00
RAPJJE Jerrel Jernigan/310 6.00 15.00
RAPJR Jacquizz Rodgers/599 6.00 15.00
RAPJT Jordan Todman/599 4.00 10.00
RAPKH Kendall Hunter/599 8.00 20.00
RAPKR Kyle Rudolph/310 8.00 20.00
RAPLH Leonard Hankerson/310 8.00 20.00
RAPMD Marcell Dareus/100 12.00 30.00
RAPML Mikel Leshoure/100 10.00 25.00
RAPNP Niles Paul/599 6.00 15.00
RAPRC Randall Cobb/310 15.00 40.00
RAPRM Ryan Mallett/100 25.00 60.00
RAPRW Ryan Williams/100 12.00 30.00
RAPSR Stevan Ridley/599 6.00 15.00
RAPSV Shane Vereen/310 8.00 20.00
RAPTD Tandon Doss/599 5.00 12.00
RAPTJ Taiwan Jones/599 8.00 20.00
RAPTS Torrey Smith/310 10.00 25.00
RAPTY Titus Young/100 12.00 30.00
RAPVB Vincent Brown/599 6.00 15.00
RAPVM Von Miller/100 15.00 40.00

2011 Finest Rookie Patch Autographs Gold Refractors
*GOLD REF/25: 1X TO 2.5X PATCH AU/599
*GOLD REF/25: .8X TO 2X PATCH AU/310
*GOLD REF/25: .6X TO 1.5X PATCH AU/100
RAPAD Andy Dalton 100.00 200.00
RAPCN Cam Newton 200.00 350.00
RAPJL Jake Locker 100.00 200.00
RAPMI Mark Ingram 100.00 200.00

2011 Finest Rookie Patch Autographs Refractors
*REFRACT/99: .6X TO 1.5X PATCH AU/599
*REFRACT/99: .5X TO 1.2X PATCH AU/310
*REFRACT/99: .4X TO 1X PATCH AU/100
RAPBG Blaine Gabbert 30.00 80.00
RAPCN Cam Newton 150.00 250.00

1995 Flair

The debut issue for Flair contains 220 standard-size cards. Rookie Cards include Ki-Jana Carter, Kerry

Collins, Curtis Martin, Steve McNair, Rashaan Salaam, J.J. Stokes, Kordell Stewart and Michael Westbrook.

COMPLETE SET (220) 12.50 30.00
1 Larry Centers .15 .40
2 Garrison Hearst .30 .75
3 Seth Joyner .07 .20
4 Dave Krieg .07 .20
5 Rob Moore .15 .40
6 Frank Sanders RC .30 .75
Wearing 18 on front
Wearing 81 on back
7 Eric Swann .15 .40
8 Devin Bush .07 .20
9 Chris Doleman .07 .20
10 Bert Emanuel .30 .75
11 Jeff George .15 .40
12 Craig Heyward .15 .40
13 Terance Mathis .15 .40
14 Eric Metcalf .15 .40
15 Cornelius Bennett .15 .40
16 Jeff Burris .07 .20
17 Todd Collins RC 1.00 2.50
18 Russell Copeland .07 .20
19 Jim Kelly .30 .75
20 Andre Reed .15 .40
21 Bruce Smith .30 .75
22 Don Beebe .07 .20
23 Mark Carrier .15 .40
24 Kerry Collins RC 1.00 2.50
25 Barry Foster .15 .40
26 Pete Metzelaars .07 .20
27 Tyrone Poole .30 .75
28 Frank Reich .07 .20
29 Curtis Conway .30 .75
30 Chris Gedney .07 .20
31 Jeff Graham .07 .20
32 Raymont Harris .07 .20
33 Erik Kramer .07 .20
34 Rashaan Saleam RC .15 .40
35 Lewis Tillman .07 .20
36 Michael Timpson .07 .20
37 Jeff Blake RC .40 1.00
38 Ki-Jana Carter RC .30 .75
39 Tony McGee .07 .20
40 Carl Pickens .15 .40
41 Corey Sawyer .07 .20
42 Darnay Scott .15 .40
43 Dan Wilkinson .15 .40
44 Derrick Alexander .30 .75
45 Leroy Hoard .07 .20
46 Michael Jackson .15 .40
47 Antonio Langham .07 .20
48 Andre Rison .15 .40
49 Vinny Testaverde .15 .40
50 Eric Turner .07 .20
51 Troy Aikman .75 2.00
52 Charles Haley .15 .40
53 Michael Irvin .30 .75
54 Daryl Johnston .15 .40
55 Leon Lett .07 .20
56 Jay Novacek .15 .40
57 Emmitt Smith 1.25 3.00
58 Kevin Williams WR .15 .40
59 Steve Atwater .07 .20
60 Rod Bernstine .07 .20
61 John Elway 1.50 4.00
62 Glyn Milburn .07 .20
63 Anthony Miller .15 .40
64 Mike Pritchard .07 .20
65 Shannon Sharpe .15 .40
66 Scott Mitchell .15 .40
67 Herman Moore .30 .75
68 Johnnie Morton .15 .40
69 Brett Perriman .15 .40
70 Barry Sanders 1.25 3.00
71 Chris Spielman .15 .40
72 Edgar Bennett .15 .40
73 Robert Brooks .30 .75
74 Brett Favre 1.50 4.00
75 LeShon Johnson .15 .40
76 Sean Jones .07 .20
77 George Teague .07 .20
78 Reggie White .30 .75
79 Micheal Barrow .07 .20
80 Gary Brown .07 .20
81 Mel Gray .07 .20
82 Haywood Jeffires .07 .20
83 Steve McNair RC 1.50 4.00
84 Rodney Thomas RC .15 .40
85 Trev Alberts .07 .20
86 Flipper Anderson .07 .20
87 Tony Bennett .07 .20
88 Quentin Coryatt .15 .40
89 Sean Dawkins .15 .40
90 Craig Erickson .07 .20
91 Marshall Faulk 1.00 2.50
92 Steve Beuerlein .15 .40
93 Tony Boselli RC .30 .75
94 Reggie Cobb .07 .20
95 Ernest Givins .07 .20
96 Desmond Howard .15 .40
97 Jeff Lageman .07 .20
98 James O. Stewart RC .60 1.50
99 Marcus Allen .30 .75
100 Steve Bono .15 .40
101 Dale Carter .15 .40
102 Willie Davis .15 .40
103 Lake Dawson .15 .40
104 Greg Hill .15 .40
105 Neil Smith .15 .40
106 Tim Bowens .07 .20
107 Bryan Cox .07 .20
108 Irving Fryar .15 .40
109 Eric Green .07 .20
110 Terry Kirby .15 .40
111 Dan Marino 1.50 4.00
112 O.J. McDuffie .30 .75
113 Bernie Parmalee .15 .40
114 Derrick Alexander RC .07 .20
115 Cris Carter .30 .75
116 Qadry Ismail .15 .40
117 Warren Moon .15 .40
118 Jake Reed .15 .40
119 Robert Smith .30 .75
120 Dewayne Washington .15 .40
121 Drew Bledsoe .50 1.25
122 Vincent Brisby .07 .20
123 Ben Coates .15 .40
124 Curtis Martin RC 1.50 4.00
125 Willie McGinest .15 .40
126 Dave Meggett .07 .20
127 Chris Slade UER 126 .07 .20
128 Eric Allen .07 .20
129 Mario Bates .15 .40
130 Jim Everett .07 .20
131 Michael Haynes .15 .40
132 Tyrone Hughes .15 .40
133 Renaldo Turnbull .07 .20
134 Ray Zellars RC .15 .40
135 Michael Brooks .07 .20
136 Dave Brown .15 .40
137 Rodney Hampton .15 .40
138 Thomas Lewis .15 .40
139 Mike Sherrard .07 .20
140 Herschel Walker .15 .40
141 Tyrone Wheatley RC .60 1.50
142 Kyle Brady RC .30 .75
143 Boomer Esiason .15 .40
144 Aaron Glenn .07 .20
145 Mo Lewis .07 .20
146 Johnny Mitchell .07 .20
147 Ronald Moore .07 .20
148 Joe Aska .15 .40
149 Tim Brown .30 .75
150 Jeff Hostetler .15 .40
151 Rocket Ismail .15 .40
152 Napoleon Kaufman RC .60 1.50
153 Chester McGlockton .15 .40
154 Harvey Williams .07 .20
155 Fred Barnett .15 .40
156 Randall Cunningham .30 .75
157 Charlie Garner .30 .75
158 Mike Mamula RC .07 .20
159 Kevin Turner .07 .20
160 Ricky Watters .15 .40
161 Calvin Williams .15 .40
162 Mark Bruener RC .15 .40
163 Kevin Greene .15 .40
164 Charles Johnson .15 .40
165 Greg Lloyd .15 .40
166 Byron Bam Morris .07 .20
167 Neil O'Donnell .15 .40
168 Kordell Stewart RC .75 2.00
169 John L. Williams .07 .20
170 Rod Woodson .15 .40
171 Jerome Bettis .30 .75
172 Isaac Bruce .50 1.25
173 Kevin Carter RC .30 .75
174 Troy Drayton .07 .20
175 Sean Gilbert .15 .40
176 Carlos Jenkins .07 .20
177 Todd Lyght .07 .20
178 Chris Miller .07 .20
179 Andre Coleman .07 .20
180 Stan Humphries .15 .40
181 Shawn Jefferson .07 .20
182 Natrone Means .15 .40
183 Leslie O'Neal .15 .40
184 Junior Seau .30 .75
185 Mark Seay .15 .40
186 William Floyd .15 .40
187 Merton Hanks .07 .20
188 Brent Jones .07 .20
189 Ken Norton .15 .40
190 Jerry Rice .75 2.00
191 Deion Sanders .40 1.00
192 J.J. Stokes RC .30 .75
193 Dana Stubblefield .15 .40
194 Steve Young .60 1.50
195 Sam Adams .07 .20
196 Brian Blades .15 .40
197 Joey Galloway RC .75 2.00
198 Cortez Kennedy .15 .40
199 Rick Mirer .15 .40
200 Chris Warren .15 .40
201 Derrick Brooks RC .75 2.00
202 Lawrence Dawsey .07 .20
203 Trent Dilfer .30 .75
204 Alvin Harper .07 .20
205 Jackie Harris .07 .20
206 Courtney Hawkins .07 .20
207 Hardy Nickerson .07 .20
208 Errict Rhett .15 .40
209 Warren Sapp RC .75 2.00
210 Terry Allen .15 .40
211 Tom Carter .07 .20
212 Henry Ellard .15 .40
213 Darrell Green .07 .20
214 Brian Mitchell .07 .20
215 Heath Shuler .15 .40
216 Michael Westbrook RC .30 .75
217 Tydus Winans .07 .20
218 Checklist .07 .20
219 Checklist .07 .20
220 Checklist .15 .40
S1 Michael Irvin Sample .50 1.25

1995 Flair Hot Numbers

COMPLETE SET (10) 12.50 30.00
STATED ODDS 1:6
1 Jeff Blake .50 1.25
2 Tim Brown .50 1.25
3 Drew Bledsoe 1.50 4.00
4 Ben Coates .50 1.25
5 Trent Dilfer .50 1.25
6 Brett Favre 5.00 12.00
7 Dan Marino 5.00 12.00
8 Byron Bam Morris .50 1.25
9 Ricky Watters .50 1.25
10 Steve Young 2.00 5.00

1995 Flair TD Power

COMPLETE SET (10) 7.50 20.00
STATED ODDS 1:12
1 Marshall Faulk 2.00 5.00
2 Natrone Means .30 .75
3 William Floyd .30 .75
4 Byron Bam Morris .15 .40
5 Errict Rhett .30 .75
6 Andre Rison .30 .75
7 Jerry Rice 1.50 4.00
8 Barry Sanders 2.50 6.00
9 Emmitt Smith 2.50 6.00
10 Chris Warren .30 .75

1995 Flair Wave of the Future

COMPLETE SET (9) 20.00 50.00
STATED ODDS 1:37
1 Kyle Brady 1.00 2.50
2 Ki-Jana Carter 2.50 6.00
3 Kerry Collins 4.00 10.00
4 Joey Galloway 4.00 10.00
5 Steve McNair 7.50 20.00
6 Rashaan Salaam 2.50 6.00
7 James O. Stewart 3.00 8.00
8 Michael Westbrook 2.50 6.00
9 Tyrone Wheatley 3.00 8.00

2002 Flair

Released in September, 2002, this set contains 100 veterans and 35 rookies. The rookies are serial #'d to 1250. Each box contained 10 packs of 5 cards. Cases were available in either 12, 6 or 4 box configurations.

COMP.SET w/o SP's (90) 10.00 25.00
1 Jeff Garcia .40 1.00
2 Jevon Kearse .40 1.00
3 Chris Weinke .30 .75
4 Ray Lewis .50 1.25
5 Donovan McNabb .50 1.25
6 Tiki Barber .50 1.25
7 Rich Gannon .40 1.00
8 Jamal Anderson .40 1.00
9 Curtis Martin .50 1.25
10 Darrell Jackson .40 1.00
11 Ricky Williams .40 1.00
12 Drew Brees .75 2.00
13 Mark Brunell .40 1.00
14 Johnnie Morton .40 1.00
15 Quincy Carter .30 .75
16 Brian Urlacher .50 1.25
17 Peerless Price .30 .75
18 Drew Bledsoe .50 1.25
19 Aaron Brooks .40 1.00
20 Derrick Mason .40 1.00
21 Charlie Garner .40 1.00
22 Mike Alstott .40 1.00
23 Freddie Mitchell .30 .75
24 Isaac Bruce .50 1.25
25 Hines Ward .50 1.25
26 Doug Flutie .50 1.25
27 Terrell Owens .50 1.25
28 Peyton Manning 1.00 2.50
29 Ron Dayne .40 1.00
30 Peter Warrick .40 1.00
31 Randy Moss .50 1.25
32 Priest Holmes .50 1.25
33 Joey Galloway .40 1.00
34 Jimmy Smith .40 1.00
35 Marvin Harrison .50 1.25
36 Junior Seau .50 1.25
37 Zach Thomas .50 1.25
38 Antowain Smith .40 1.00
39 Marty Booker .40 1.00
40 Deuce McAllister .40 1.00
41 Rod Smith .40 1.00
42 Michael Westbrook .30 .75
43 Antonio Freeman .50 1.25
44 Kerry Collins .40 1.00
45 Koren Robinson .30 .75
46 Jamal Lewis .40 1.00
47 Duce Staley .40 1.00
48 Jerome Bettis .50 1.25
49 David Terrell .30 .75
50 Daunte Culpepper .40 1.00
51 Tim Couch .30 .75
52 Brian Griese .40 1.00
53 Marshall Faulk .50 1.25
54 Brad Johnson .40 1.00
55 Eddie George .40 1.00
56 Kurt Warner .50 1.25
57 Steve McNair .50 1.25
58 Stephen Davis .40 1.00
59 Corey Dillon .40 1.00
60 Troy Brown .40 1.00
61 Warrick Dunn .40 1.00
62 Ed McCaffrey .40 1.00
63 Amani Toomer .40 1.00
64 Rod Gardner .30 .75
65 Mike McMahon .30 .75
66 Wayne Chrebet .40 1.00
67 Jake Plummer .40 1.00
68 Edgerrin James .40 1.00
69 Eric Moulds .40 1.00
70 Tony Gonzalez .50 1.25
71 Marcus Robinson .40 1.00
72 Muhsin Muhammad .40 1.00
73 Trent Dilfer .40 1.00
74 Kevin Johnson .30 .75
75 Fred Taylor .40 1.00
76 Terrell Davis .50 1.25
77 Emmitt Smith 1.25 3.00
78 Az-Zahir Hakim .30 .75
79 Tim Brown .50 1.25
80 Jerry Rice 1.00 2.50
81 Warren Sapp .40 1.00
82 Michael Strahan .50 1.25
83 Garrison Hearst .40 1.00
84 David Boston .30 .75
85 Michael Vick .75 2.00
86 Anthony Thomas .40 1.00
87 Ahman Green .40 1.00
88 Chris Chambers .40 1.00
89 Tom Brady 1.25 3.00
90 Plaxico Burress .40 1.00
91 LaDainian Tomlinson .60 1.50
92 Shaun Alexander .40 1.00
93 Torry Holt .50 1.25
94 Kordell Stewart .40 1.00
95 Chad Pennington .50 1.25
96 Chris Redman .30 .75
97 Kendrell Bell .30 .75
98 Michael Bennett .40 1.00
99 Joe Horn .40 1.00
100 Brett Favre 1.25 3.00
101 David Carr RC 2.00 5.00
102 Joey Harrington RC 2.00 5.00
103 Ashley Lelie RC 1.50 4.00
104 Javon Walker RC 2.00 5.00
105 Reche Caldwell RC 2.00 5.00
106 Andre Davis RC 1.50 4.00
107 William Green RC 1.50 4.00
108 Antonio Bryant RC 2.00 5.00
109 Clinton Portis RC 2.50 6.00
110 Luke Staley RC 1.25 3.00
111 Josh Reed RC 1.50 4.00
112 Ron Johnson RC 1.50 4.00
113 Lamar Gordon RC 1.25 3.00
114 Cliff Russell RC 1.25 3.00
115 Eric Crouch RC 2.00 5.00
116 Ladell Betts RC 2.00 5.00
117 Patrick Ramsey RC 2.00 5.00
118 Adrian Peterson RC 2.00 5.00
119 DeShaun Foster RC 2.00 5.00
120 Tim Carter RC 1.50 4.00
121 Jabar Gaffney RC 2.00 5.00
122 T.J. Duckett RC 2.00 5.00
123 Julius Peppers RC 4.00 10.00
124 Rohan Davey RC 2.00 5.00
125 Antwaan Randle El RC 2.00 5.00
126 Jeremy Shockey RC 3.00 8.00
127 Donte Stallworth RC 2.00 5.00
128 Marquise Walker RC 1.25 3.00
129 Brian Westbrook RC 3.00 8.00
130 Randy Fasani RC 1.50 4.00
131 Jonathan Wells RC 2.00 5.00
132 Travis Stephens RC 1.25 3.00
133 Daniel Graham RC 1.50 4.00
134 Maurice Morris RC 1.50 4.00
135 David Garrard RC 2.50 6.00

2002 Flair Collection

*VETS/200: 2.5X TO 6X BASIC CARDS
1-100 VETERAN PRINT RUN 200
*ROOKIES/50: 1.2X TO 3X
101-135 ROOKIE PRINT RUN 50

2002 Flair Franchise Favorites

COMPLETE SET (18) 15.00 40.00
STATED ODDS 1:4
1 Donovan McNabb .75 2.00
2 Tim Brown .75 2.00
3 Michael Vick 1.25 3.00
4 Peerless Price .50 1.25
5 Anthony Thomas .60 1.50
6 Corey Dillon .60 1.50
7 Emmitt Smith 2.00 5.00
8 Brett Favre 2.00 5.00
9 Edgerrin James .60 1.50
10 Fred Taylor .60 1.50
11 Tony Gonzalez .75 2.00
12 Daunte Culpepper .60 1.50
13 Tom Brady 2.00 5.00
14 Deuce McAllister .60 1.50
15 Jerome Bettis .75 2.00
16 LaDainian Tomlinson 1.00 2.50
17 Kurt Warner .75 2.00
18 Eddie George .60 1.50

2002 Flair Franchise Favorites Jerseys

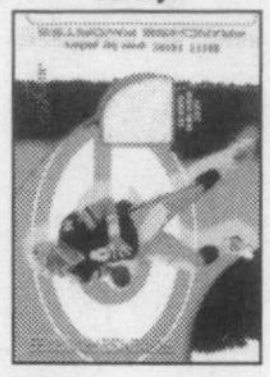

STATED ODDS 1:10
1 Jerome Bettis 5.00 12.00
2 Daunte Culpepper 4.00 10.00
3 Corey Dillon 4.00 10.00
4 Brett Favre 12.00 30.00
5 Eddie George 4.00 10.00
6 Edgerrin James 4.00 10.00
7 Donovan McNabb 5.00 12.00
8 Fred Taylor SP/300* 4.00 10.00
9 Anthony Thomas 4.00 10.00
10 LaDainian Tomlinson 6.00 15.00
11 Michael Vick 8.00 20.00
12 Kurt Warner 5.00 12.00

2002 Flair Franchise Tools Memorabilia

STATED ODDS 1:40
*GOLD/50: .8X TO 2X BASIC JSY-FB
GOLD/50: .6X TO 1.5X JSY-FB/50-100
GOLD PRINT RUN 50 SER.#'d SETS
1 Ladell Betts 5.00 12.00
2 Tim Carter 4.00 10.00
3 Rohan Davey 5.00 12.00
4 Andre Davis 4.00 10.00
5 T.J. Duckett SP/100* 6.00 15.00
6 DeShaun Foster SP/250* 5.00 12.00
7 Jabar Gaffney 5.00 12.00
8 David Garrard 6.00 15.00
9 Joey Harrington SP/200* 5.00 12.00
10 Ron Johnson 4.00 10.00
11 Ashley Lelie SP/75* 5.00 12.00
12 Maurice Morris 4.00 10.00
13 Clinton Portis SP/50* 12.00 30.00
14 Patrick Ramsey SP/200* 5.00 12.00
15 Antwaan Randle El SP/200* 5.00 12.00
16 Cliff Russell 3.00 8.00
17 Jeremy Shockey 6.00 15.00
18 Donte Stallworth SP/100* 6.00 15.00
19 Travis Stephens 3.00 8.00
20 Javon Walker 5.00 12.00

2002 Flair Jersey Heights

STATED ODDS 1:10
1 Ricky Williams 1.25 3.00
2 Marvin Harrison 1.50 4.00
3 Brian Urlacher 1.50 4.00
4 Terrell Davis 1.50 4.00
5 Randy Moss 1.50 4.00
6 Fred Taylor 1.25 3.00
7 Aaron Brooks 1.25 3.00
8 Jerry Rice 3.00 8.00
9 Curtis Martin 1.50 4.00
10 Kordell Stewart 1.25 3.00
11 Doug Flutie 1.50 4.00
12 Steve McNair 1.50 4.00
13 Marshall Faulk 1.50 4.00
14 Jeff Garcia 1.25 3.00
15 Brian Griese 1.25 3.00
16 Isaac Bruce 1.50 4.00
17 Drew Bledsoe 1.50 4.00
18 Rich Gannon 1.25 3.00

2002 Flair Jersey Heights Jerseys

STATED ODDS 1:18
*HOT NUMBER/100: .8X TO 2X BASIC JSY
HOT NUMBER JSY PRINT RUN 100
1 Drew Bledsoe 4.00 10.00
2 Aaron Brooks 3.00 8.00
3 Isaac Bruce 4.00 10.00
4 Doug Flutie 4.00 10.00
5 Rich Gannon 3.00 8.00
6 Jeff Garcia 3.00 8.00
7 Brian Griese 3.00 8.00
8 Steve McNair 4.00 10.00
9 Randy Moss 4.00 10.00
10 Kordell Stewart 3.00 8.00
11 Brian Urlacher 4.00 10.00

2002 Flair Sweet Swatch Memorabilia

STATED ODDS ONE PER BOX
ANNC'D PRINT RUN 375-750
*PATCH/150-300: .8X TO 2X BASIC JSY
PATCH PRINT RUN 150-300
AGSS Ahman Green/750* 5.00 12.00
BFSS Brett Favre/400* 15.00 40.00
CMSS Curtis Martin/400* 6.00 15.00
DCSS Daunte Culpepper/400* 5.00 12.00
EGSS Eddie George/400* 5.00 12.00
EJSS Edgerrin James/400* 5.00 12.00
JPSS Jake Plummer/400* 5.00 12.00
KWSS Kurt Warner/400* 6.00 15.00
MHSS Marvin Harrison/450* 6.00 15.00
MVSS Michael Vick/400* 10.00 25.00
TCSS Tim Couch/400* 4.00 10.00
THSS Torry Holt/375* 6.00 15.00
TOSS Terrell Owens/400* 6.00 15.00

2002 Flair Sweet Swatch Memorabilia Autographs

RANDOM INSERTS IN BOXES
ANNC'D PRINT RUN 50-800
*GOLD/50: .6X TO 1.5X BASIC AUTO
GOLD PRINT RUN 50 SER.#'d SETS
1 Kurt Warner/500* 20.00 50.00
2 Jeff Garcia/500* 15.00 40.00
3 Donovan McNabb/500* 20.00 50.00
4 Joe Montana SP/50* 75.00 150.00
5 Chad Pennington/800* 20.00 50.00

2003 Flair

Released in June of 2003, this set consists of 90 veterans and 40 rookies which were serial numbered to 500. Boxes contained 20 packs of five cards. Each hobby box also contained one oversized pack containing a Sweet Swatch Jumbo autograph or memorabilia card. The pack SRP was $5.99.

COMP.SET w/o SP's (90) 10.00 25.00
91-130 ROOKIE PRINT RUN 500
1 Jamal Lewis .30 .75
2 Aaron Brooks .30 .75
3 Joey Harrington .25 .60
4 Brett Favre 1.00 2.50
5 Donovan McNabb .40 1.00
6 Marcel Shipp .25 .60
7 Michael Vick .50 1.25
8 David Carr .30 .75
9 Tommy Maddox .30 .75
10 Drew Brees .40 1.00
11 Chad Pennington .40 1.00
12 Drew Bledsoe .40 1.00
13 Rich Gannon .30 .75
14 Kurt Warner .40 1.00
15 Brian Griese .30 .75
16 William Green .25 .60
17 Jake Plummer .30 .75
18 Eric Moulds .30 .75
19 Peyton Manning .75 2.00
20 Keyshawn Johnson .40 1.00
21 Travis Henry .25 .60
22 Tiki Barber .40 1.00
23 Emmitt Smith 1.00 2.50
24 Michael Bennett .30 .75
25 Curtis Martin .40 1.00
26 Donald Driver .40 1.00
27 Clinton Portis .30 .75
28 Eddie George .30 .75
29 Marshall Faulk .40 1.00
30 Jeremy Shockey .40 1.00
31 Ahman Green .30 .75
32 Priest Holmes .40 1.00
33 Edgerrin James .40 1.00
34 Plaxico Burress .30 .75
35 Ricky Williams .30 .75
36 Anthony Thomas .30 .75
37 Jerome Bettis .40 1.00
38 Shaun Alexander .30 .75
39 Fred Taylor .30 .75
40 Isaac Bruce .40 1.00
41 Mike Alstott .40 1.00
42 Peerless Price .25 .60
43 Corey Dillon .30 .75
44 Amani Toomer .30 .75
45 Warrick Dunn .30 .75
46 Tim Brown .40 1.00
47 Deuce McAllister .30 .75
48 Terrell Owens .40 1.00
49 Stephen Davis .30 .75
50 Torry Holt .40 1.00
51 Duce Staley .30 .75
52 Jimmy Smith .30 .75
53 Ray Lewis .40 1.00
54 Brian Urlacher .40 1.00
55 Zach Thomas .40 1.00
56 Joey Galloway .30 .75
57 LaDainian Tomlinson .40 1.00
58 Chris Chambers .30 .75
59 Ronde Barber .30 .75
60 Randy Moss .40 1.00
61 Tom Brady 1.00 2.50
62 Jerry Porter .25 .60
63 Patrick Ramsey .30 .75
64 Derrick Mason .30 .75
65 Daunte Culpepper .30 .75
66 Marty Booker .30 .75
67 Steve McNair .40 1.00
68 Hines Ward .40 1.00
69 Matt Hasselbeck .30 .75
70 Joe Horn .30 .75
71 Mark Brunell .30 .75
72 Laveranues Coles .25 .60
73 Chad Hutchinson .25 .60
74 Tony Gonzalez .40 1.00
75 Jeff Garcia .30 .75
76 Kendrell Bell .25 .60
77 Kerry Collins .30 .75
78 Warren Sapp .30 .75
79 Tim Couch .25 .60
80 Jerry Rice .75 2.00
81 Koren Robinson .30 .75
82 Antwaan Randle El .30 .75
83 Donte Stallworth .25 .60
84 Shannon Sharpe .40 1.00
85 Chad Johnson .40 1.00
86 Todd Heap .30 .75
87 Rod Gardner .25 .60
88 Marvin Harrison .40 1.00
89 David Boston .25 .60
90 Julius Peppers .40 1.00
91 Byron Leftwich RC 4.00 10.00
92 Terrell Suggs RC 4.00 10.00
93 Kelley Washington RC 2.50 6.00
94 Brandon Lloyd RC 6.00 15.00
95 Kliff Kingsbury RC 3.00 8.00
96 Willis McGahee RC 5.00 12.00
97 Terence Newman RC 3.00 8.00
98 Bryant Johnson RC 4.00 10.00
99 Musa Smith RC 2.50 6.00
100 Ken Dorsey RC 3.00 8.00
101 Larry Johnson RC 4.00 10.00
102 DeWayne Robertson RC 3.00 8.00
103 Onterrio Smith RC 2.50 6.00
104 Tyrone Calico RC 3.00 8.00
105 Kareem Kelly RC 2.50 6.00
106 Chris Brown RC 2.50 6.00
107 Andrew Pinnock RC 3.00 8.00
108 Taylor Jacobs RC 2.50 6.00
109 Dallas Clark RC 6.00 15.00
110 Marcus Trufant RC 3.00 8.00
111 Charles Rogers RC 3.00 8.00
112 Lee Suggs RC 3.00 8.00
113 Rex Grossman RC 4.00 10.00
114 Doug Gabriel RC 3.00 8.00
115 Arnaz Battle RC 4.00 10.00
116 William Joseph RC 2.50 6.00
117 Justin Fargas RC 4.00 10.00
118 Anquan Boldin RC 6.00 15.00
119 Teyo Johnson RC 3.00 8.00
120 Bobby Wade RC 3.00 8.00
121 Brian St.Pierre RC 3.00 8.00
122 Carson Palmer RC 8.00 20.00
123 Kyle Boller RC 4.00 10.00
124 Andre Johnson RC 10.00 25.00
125 Dave Ragone RC 2.50 6.00
126 Chris Simms RC 4.00 10.00
127 Seneca Wallace RC 4.00 10.00
128 Justin Gage RC 3.00 8.00
129 LaBrandon Toefield RC 3.00 8.00
130 Talman Gardner RC 2.50 6.00

2003 Flair Collection

*VETS 1-90: 4X TO 10X BASIC CARDS
*91-130 ROOKIES: .5X TO 1.2X
STATED PRINT RUN 125 SER.#'d SETS

2003 Flair A Cut Above

STATED PRINT RUN 500 SER.#'d SETS
*FINAL CUT/50: .8X TO 2X BASE JSY/500
FINAL CUT PRINT RUN 50 SER.#'d SETS
ACADB Drew Bledsoe 5.00 12.00
ACADC Daunte Culpepper 4.00 10.00
ACAEJ Edgerrin James 5.00 12.00
ACAIB Isaac Bruce 5.00 12.00
ACAJH Joe Horn 4.00 10.00
ACAKJ Keyshawn Johnson 5.00 12.00
ACAMA Mike Alstott 5.00 12.00
ACAMF Marshall Faulk 5.00 12.00
ACAPP Peerless Price 3.00 8.00
ACATB Tim Brown 5.00 12.00

2003 Flair Canton Calling

STATED ODDS 1:20
*PATCH/150: .6X TO 1.5X BASIC JSY
PATCHES PRINT RUN 150 SER.#'d SETS
CCBF Brett Favre 12.00 30.00
CCCC Cris Carter 5.00 12.00
CCCD Corey Dillon 4.00 10.00
CCCM Curtis Martin 5.00 12.00
CCEM Ed McCaffrey 4.00 10.00
CCES Emmitt Smith 12.00 30.00
CCJR Jerry Rice 10.00 25.00
CCJS Junior Seau 5.00 12.00
CCKW Kurt Warner 5.00 12.00
CCMF Marshall Faulk 5.00 12.00
CCRM Randy Moss 5.00 12.00
CCRW Ray Lewis 5.00 12.00
CCTG Tony Gonzalez 5.00 12.00
CCTO Terrell Owens 5.00 12.00

2003 Flair Sunday Showdown

STATED PRINT RUN 500 SER.#'d SETS
*PATCH/100: .6X TO 1.5X BASE JSY/500
PATCHES PRINT RUN 100 SER.#'d SETS
SSAG Ahman Green 4.00 10.00
SSBU Brian Urlacher 5.00 12.00
SSCC Chris Chambers 4.00 10.00
SSCP Clinton Portis 4.00 10.00
SSDB Drew Bledsoe 5.00 12.00
SSDM Donovan McNabb 5.00 12.00
SSDM Deuce McAllister 4.00 10.00
SSEG Eddie George 4.00 10.00
SSFT Fred Taylor 4.00 10.00
SSJL Jamal Lewis 4.00 10.00
SSJP Julius Peppers 5.00 12.00
SSJS Jeremy Shockey 5.00 12.00
SSMH Marvin Harrison Pants 5.00 12.00
SSRG Rich Gannon 4.00 10.00
SSSM Steve McNair 5.00 12.00
SSWG William Green 3.00 8.00

2003 Flair Sunday Showdown Dual Patches

STATED PRINT RUN 50 SER.#'d SETS
AGBU Ahman Green 12.00 30.00
Brian Urlacher
DMJS Donovan McNabb 12.00 30.00
Jeremy Shockey
FTEG Fred Taylor 10.00 25.00
Eddie George
JHDC Joey Harrington 10.00 25.00
Daunte Culpepper
JLWG Jamal Lewis 10.00 25.00
William Green
MADM Mike Alstott 12.00 30.00
Deuce McAllister
MHCC Marvin Harrison 12.00 30.00
Chris Chambers
SMPM Steve McNair 25.00 60.00
Peyton Manning

2003 Flair Sweet Swatch Autographs

STATED PRINT RUN 175 SER.#'d SETS
*GOLD/25: .8X TO 2X BASIC AU/175
GOLD PRINT RUN 25 SER.#'d SETS
UNPRICED MASTERPIECE PRINT RUN 1
LT LaDainian Tomlinson 40.00 80.00
TB Tom Brady 100.00 200.00
WM Willis McGahee 15.00 40.00

2003 Flair Sweet Swatch Jerseys

STATED PRINT RUN 200 SER.#'d SETS
PATCHES/25 NOT PRICED DUE TO SCARCITY
*JUMBO/180-520: .4X TO 1X BASE JSY/200
*JUMBO PATCH/61-165: .6X TO 1.5X BASE JSY/200
UNPRICED MASTERPIECE JUMBO #'d TO 1
AB Aaron Brooks 5.00 12.00
CM Curtis Martin 6.00 15.00
CP Chad Pennington 6.00 15.00
DB Drew Brees 6.00 15.00
DC David Carr 5.00 12.00
DM Deuce McAllister 5.00 12.00
ES Emmitt Smith 15.00 40.00
HW Hines Ward 6.00 15.00
JH Joey Harrington 4.00 10.00
KB Kendrell Bell 4.00 10.00
LT LaDainian Tomlinson 6.00 15.00
MB Michael Bennett 5.00 12.00
MH Marvin Harrison 6.00 15.00
MV Michael Vick 8.00 20.00
PH Priest Holmes 6.00 15.00
PM Peyton Manning 12.00 30.00
PP Peerless Price 4.00 10.00
RM Randy Moss 6.00 15.00
RW Ricky Williams 5.00 12.00
TG Tony Gonzalez 6.00 15.00

2003 Flair Sweet Swatch Jerseys Patches Jumbo

STATED PRINT RUN 61-165

2003 Flair Sweet Swatch Jerseys Duals Jumbo

STATED PRINT RUN 25 SER.#'d SETS
CPCM Chad Pennington 15.00 30.00
Curtis Martin
DBLT Drew Brees 20.00 50.00
LaDainian Tomlinson
DCJH David Carr
Joey Harrington
DMAB Deuce McAllister
Aaron Brooks
ESRW Emmitt Smith 20.00 50.00
Ricky Williams
MVPP Michael Vick 20.00 40.00
Peerless Price
PHTG Priest Holmes 15.00 30.00
Tony Gonzalez
PMMH Peyton Manning
Marvin Harrison
RMMB Randy Moss
Michael Bennett

2004 Flair

Flair initially released in mid-July 2004. The base set consists of -cards including 5-Power Pick short prints at the end of the set. Hobby boxes contained 1-pack of 12-cards and retail contained 24-packs of 4-cards with an S.R.P. of $2.99 per pack. Two parallel sets and a variety of inserts can be found seeded in hobby and retail packs highlighted by the multi-tiered Autograph Collection and Significant Cuts inserts. Some signed cards were issued via mail-in exchange or redemption cards with a number of those EXCH cards not yet appearing live on the secondary market as of the printing of this book.

COMP.SET w/o SP's (60) 20.00 40.00
ROOKIE STATED ODDS 1:100 RETAIL
ROOKIE PRINT RUN 799 SER.#'d SETS
1 Clinton Portis .60 1.50
2 Deuce McAllister .50 1.25
3 Marshall Faulk .60 1.50
4 Tom Brady 1.25 3.00
5 Ahman Green .50 1.25
6 LaDainian Tomlinson .60 1.50
7 Lee Suggs .50 1.25
8 Amani Toomer .50 1.25
9 Priest Holmes .60 1.50
10 Peerless Price .40 1.00
11 Warren Sapp .50 1.25
12 Andre Davis .40 1.00
13 Chad Pennington .60 1.50
14 Quincy Carter .40 1.00
15 Santana Moss .50 1.25
16 Antonio Bryant .50 1.25
17 Jerry Porter .40 1.00
18 Laveranues Coles .40 1.00
19 Daunte Culpepper .50 1.25
20 Stephen Davis .50 1.25
21 Rich Gannon .50 1.25
22 Chad Johnson .60 1.50
23 Ashley Lelie .40 1.00

24 Ray Lewis .60 1.50
25 Joey Harrington .50 1.25
26 Brian Westbrook .60 1.50
27 Marvin Harrison .60 1.50
28 Torry Holt .50 1.25
29 Kevan Barlow .40 1.00
30 Peyton Manning 1.25 3.00
31 Andre Johnson .60 1.50
32 Steve Smith .60 1.50
33 Troy Brown .50 1.25
34 Brian Urlacher .60 1.50
35 Anquan Boldin .60 1.50
36 Matt Hasselbeck .50 1.25
37 Edgerrin James .50 1.25
38 Dante Hall .50 1.25
39 Brad Johnson .50 1.25
40 Jamal Lewis .50 1.25
41 Rudi Johnson .50 1.25
42 Michael Strahan .60 1.50
43 Donovan McNabb .60 1.50
44 Steve McNair .60 1.50
45 Ricky Williams .50 1.25
46 Jake Delhomme .50 1.25
47 Patrick Ramsey .50 1.25
48 Randy Moss .60 1.50
49 David Carr .40 1.00
50 Jeff Garcia .50 1.25
51 Shaun Alexander .50 1.25
52 Byron Leftwich .50 1.25
53 Michael Vick .75 2.00
54 Brett Favre 1.50 4.00
55 Hines Ward .60 1.50
56 Chris Chambers .50 1.25
57 Eddie George .50 1.25
58 Eric Moulds .50 1.25
59 Plaxico Burress .50 1.25
60 Charles Rogers .40 1.00
61 Eli Manning RC 12.00 30.00
62 Larry Fitzgerald RC 4.00 10.00
63 Chris Perry RC 1.25 3.00
64 Ben Roethlisberger RC 12.00 30.00
65 Roy Williams RC 1.50 4.00
66 Kellen Winslow RC 1.50 4.00
67 Steven Jackson RC 2.50 6.00
68 Kevin Jones RC 1.25 3.00
69 Reggie Williams RC 1.25 3.00
70 Michael Clayton RC 1.25 3.00
71 Rashaun Woods RC 1.00 2.50
72 Ben Troupe RC 1.25 3.00
73 Greg Jones RC 1.00 2.50
74 J.P. Losman RC 1.25 3.00
75 Philip Rivers RC 6.00 15.00
76 Michael Jenkins RC 1.50 4.00
77 Darius Watts RC 1.00 2.50
78 Michael Turner RC 2.00 5.00
79 Lee Evans RC 1.50 4.00
80 Drew Henson RC 1.00 2.50
81 Luke McCown RC 1.25 3.00
82 Julius Jones RC 1.25 3.00
83 Bernard Berrian RC 1.60 4.00
84 Keary Colbert RC 1.00 2.50
85 Tatum Bell RC 1.25 3.00

2004 Flair Collection Row 1

*STARS: 2X TO 5X BASIC CARDS
*ROOKIES: .8X TO 2X BASIC CARDS
ROW 1/2 OVERALL ODDS 1:7H, 1:55R
ROW 1 PRINT RUN 100 SER.#'d SETS
UNPRICED ROW 2 PRINT RUN 1 SET

2004 Flair Autograph Collection Bronze

OVERALL AUTO ODDS 1:1 HOB
UNPRICED MASTERPIECE #'d OF 1
ACAL Ashley Lelie/150 5.00 12.00
ACBR Ben Roethlisberger/250 50.00 100.00
ACDC David Carr/100 5.00 12.00
ACDHA Dante Hall/150 6.00 15.00
ACEM Eli Manning/200 60.00 120.00
ACJD Jake Delhomme/150 6.00 15.00
ACJJ Julius Jones/150 6.00 15.00
ACJL J.P. Losman/150 6.00 15.00
ACKJ Kevin Jones/150 6.00 15.00
ACLE Lee Evans/220 6.00 15.00
ACLF Larry Fitzgerald/82 30.00 80.00
ACMC Michael Clayton/150 6.00 15.00
ACMJ Michael Jenkins/150 8.00 20.00
ACPRA Patrick Ramsey/158 6.00 15.00
ACPRI Philip Rivers/350 25.00 60.00
ACRAW Rashaun Woods/350 4.00 10.00
ACREW Reggie Williams/350 5.00 12.00
ACRG Rex Grossman/150 6.00 15.00
ACROW Roy Williams WR/150 8.00 20.00
ACSJ Steven Jackson/150 12.00 30.00
ACTB Tatum Bell/150 6.00 15.00
ACWM Willis McGahee/175 8.00 20.00

2004 Flair Autograph Collection Silver

SILVER PRINT RUN 100 SER.#'d SETS
ACKW Kellen Winslow 20.00 50.00
ACLF Larry Fitzgerald 30.00 80.00

2004 Flair Autograph Collection Gold Parchment

*GOLD/25: .8X TO 2X BRNZ/82-175
*GOLD/25: 1X TO 2.5X BRNZ/200-350
GOLD PRINT RUN 25 SER.#'d SETS
ACBR Ben Roethlisberger 100.00 200.00
ACEM Eli Manning 125.00 200.00
ACLF Larry Fitzgerald 40.00 100.00
ACPRI Philip Rivers 60.00 120.00

2004 Flair Cuts and Glory Bronze

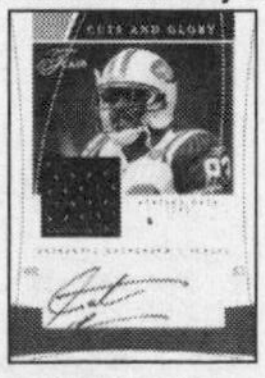

BRONZE PRINT RUN 100 SER.#'d SETS
*SILVER/50: .6X TO 1.5X BRONZE AU/100
SILVER PRINT RUN 50 SER.#'d SETS
GOLD STATED PRINT RUN 10-15
UNPRICED MASTERPIECE PRINT RUN 1 SET
CAGAB Anquan Boldin 12.00 30.00
CAGAG Ahman Green 12.00 30.00
CAGBL Byron Leftwich 10.00 25.00
CAGBW Brian Westbrook 12.00 30.00
CAGDC David Carr 8.00 20.00
CAGDF DeShaun Foster 10.00 25.00
CAGDM Donovan McNabb 30.00 60.00
CAGJD Jake Delhomme 10.00 25.00
CAGKB Kyle Boller 10.00 25.00
CAGMF Marshall Faulk 12.00 30.00
CAGMH Matt Hasselbeck 10.00 25.00
CAGSM Santana Moss 10.00 25.00
CHAD Chad Pennington 12.00 30.00

2004 Flair Gridiron Cuts Green

GREEN STATED ODDS 1:48 RETAIL
*BLUE/200: .5X TO 1.2X GREEN JSY
BLUE PRINT RUN 200 SER.#'d SETS
*DIE CUT PATCH/25: 1.5X TO 4X GREEN JSY
DIE CUT PATCH PRINT RUN 25 SER.#'d SETS
UNPRICED PURPLE PRINT RUN 1 SET
*RED/150: .5X TO 1.2X GREEN JSY
RED PRINT RUN 150 SER.#'d SETS
*SILVER/75: .8X TO 2X GREEN JSY
SILVER PRINT RUN 75 SER.#'d SETS
UNPRICED GOLD PRINT RUN 10 SETS
GCAG Ahman Green 2.50 6.00
GCAJ Andre Johnson 3.00 8.00
GCBF Brett Favre 8.00 20.00
GCCR Charles Rogers 2.00 5.00
GCDC David Carr 2.00 5.00
GCDC2 Daunte Culpepper 2.50 6.00
GCDM Deuce McAllister 2.50 6.00
GCDM2 Donovan McNabb 3.00 8.00
GCES Emmitt Smith 8.00 20.00
GCJH Joey Harrington 2.50 6.00
GCJL Jamal Lewis 2.50 6.00
GCLT LaDainian Tomlinson 3.00 8.00
GCMF Marshall Faulk 3.00 8.00
GCMH Matt Hasselbeck 2.50 6.00
GCPM Peyton Manning 6.00 15.00
GCRM Randy Moss 3.00 8.00
GCSA Shaun Alexander 2.50 6.00
GCSM Steve McNair 3.00 8.00
GCTB Tom Brady 6.00 15.00
GCTH Torry Holt 2.50 6.00

2004 Flair Hot Numbers

STATED PRINT RUN 500 SER.#'d SETS
*GOLD/52-99: 1.2X TO 3X BASIC INSERTS
*GOLD/21-37: 1.5X TO 4X BASIC INSERTS
*GOLD/10-19: 2X TO 5X BASIC INSERTS
GOLDS/3-8 NOT PRICED DUE TO SCARCITY
GOLD STATED PRINT RUN 3-99
1HN Peyton Manning 5.00 12.00
2HN Brett Favre 6.00 15.00
3HN Shaun Alexander 2.00 5.00
4HN Charles Rogers 1.50 4.00
5HN Jamal Lewis 2.00 5.00
6HN Clinton Portis 2.50 6.00
7HN Jeremy Shockey 2.00 5.00
8HN Daunte Culpepper 2.00 5.00
9HN Jake Delhomme 2.00 5.00
10HN Tom Brady 5.00 12.00
11HN Quincy Carter 1.50 4.00
12HN Donovan McNabb 2.50 6.00
13HN Byron Leftwich 2.00 5.00
14HN Santana Moss 2.00 5.00
15HN Marvin Harrison 2.50 6.00
16HN Randy Moss 2.50 6.00
17HN Laveranues Coles 1.50 4.00
18HN Andre Johnson 2.50 6.00
19HN Marshall Faulk 2.50 6.00
20HN Edgerrin James 2.00 5.00
21HN Ray Lewis 2.50 6.00
22HN Joey Harrington 2.00 5.00
23HN David Carr 1.50 4.00
24HN Ahman Green 2.00 5.00
25HN Torry Holt 2.00 5.00
26HN Chad Pennington 2.50 6.00
27HN LaDainian Tomlinson 2.50 6.00
28HN Chad Johnson 2.50 6.00
29HN Priest Holmes 2.50 6.00
30HN Marc Bulger 2.00 5.00
31HN Roy Williams S 2.00 5.00
32HN Plaxico Burress 2.00 5.00
33HN Jerry Porter 1.50 4.00
34HN Warren Sapp 2.00 5.00
35HN Brian Urlacher 2.50 6.00

2004 Flair Hot Numbers Game Used Green

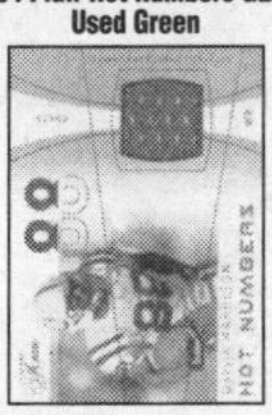

STATED ODDS 1:48 RETAIL
*BLUE/200: .5X TO 1.2X GREEN JSY
BLUE PRINT RUN 200 SER.#'d SETS
*DIE CUT PATCH/25: 1.5X TO 4X GREEN JSY
DC PATCH PRINT RUN 25 SER.#'d SETS
GOLD/21-54: 1.5X TO 4X GREEN JSY
*GOLD/80-99: .8X TO 2X GREEN JSY
GOLDS/3-18 NOT PRICED DUE TO SCARCITY
GOLDS #'d TO PLAYER'S JERSEY NUMBER
UNPRICED PURPLE PRINT RUN 1 SET
*RED/150: .5X TO 1.2X GREEN JSY
RED PRINT RUN 150 SER.#'d SETS
*SILVER/75: .8X TO 2X GREEN JSY
SILVER PRINT RUN 75 SER.#'d SETS
HNAG Ahman Green 2.50 6.00
HNAJ Andre Johnson 3.00 8.00
HNBF Brett Favre 8.00 20.00
HNBL Byron Leftwich 2.50 6.00
HNBU Brian Urlacher 3.00 8.00
HNCJ Chad Johnson 3.00 8.00
HNCP Chad Pennington 3.00 8.00
HNCR Charles Rogers 2.00 5.00
HNDC Daunte Culpepper 2.50 6.00
HNDC David Carr 2.00 5.00
HNDM Donovan McNabb 3.00 8.00
HNEJ Edgerrin James 2.50 6.00
HNJD Jake Delhomme 2.50 6.00
HNJH Joey Harrington 2.50 6.00
HNJL Jamal Lewis 2.50 6.00
HNJP Jerry Porter 2.00 5.00
HNJS Jeremy Shockey 2.50 6.00
HNLT LaDainian Tomlinson 3.00 8.00
HNMF Marshall Faulk 3.00 8.00
HNMH Marvin Harrison 3.00 8.00
HNPB Plaxico Burress 2.50 6.00
HNPH Priest Holmes 3.00 8.00
HNPM Peyton Manning 6.00 15.00
HNQC Quincy Carter 2.00 5.00
HNRL Ray Lewis 3.00 8.00
HNRW Roy Williams S 2.50 6.00
HNSA Shaun Alexander 2.50 6.00
HNTB Tom Brady 6.00 15.00
HNTH Torry Holt 2.50 6.00
HNWS Warren Sapp 2.50 6.00

2004 Flair Lettermen

STATED PRINT RUN 4-10 SETS
NOT PRICED DUE TO SCARCITY

2004 Flair Power Swatch Blue

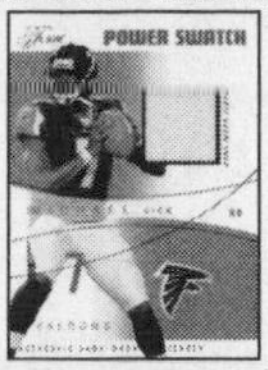

BLUE PRINT RUN 200 SER.#'d SETS
*DIE CUT PATCH/25: 1.2X TO 3X BLUE JSY
DIE CUT PATCH PRINT RUN 25 SER.#'d SETS
*GOLDS/28-48: 1X TO 2.5X BLUE JSY
*GOLDS/80-88: .6X TO 1.5X BLUE JSY
GOLDS/5-8 NOT PRICED DUE TO SCARCITY
GOLDS #'d TO PLAYER'S JERSEY NUMBER
UNPRICED PURPLE PRINT RUN 1 SET
*RED/150: .4X TO 1X BLUE JSY
RED PRINT RUN 150 SER.#'d SETS
*SILVER/75: .6X TO 1.5X BLUE JSY
SILVER PRINT RUN 75 SER.#'d SETS
PSAB Anquan Boldin 4.00 10.00
PSAJ Andre Johnson 4.00 10.00
PSBL Byron Leftwich 3.00 8.00
PSCJ Chad Johnson 4.00 10.00
PSDM Donovan McNabb 4.00 10.00
PSEJ Edgerrin James 3.00 8.00
PSJS Jeremy Shockey 3.00 8.00
PSMF Marshall Faulk 4.00 10.00
PSMH Marvin Harrison 4.00 10.00
PSMV Michael Vick 5.00 12.00
PSPH Priest Holmes 4.00 10.00
PSRG Rex Grossman 3.00 8.00
PSRM Randy Moss 4.00 10.00
PSRW Ricky Williams 3.00 8.00
PSST Stephen Davis 3.00 8.00

2004 Flair SIGnificant Cuts

STATED PRINT RUN 25-100
AV Adam Vinatieri/58 50.00 100.00
BL Byron Leftwich/25 20.00 40.00
BS Barry Sanders/50 75.00 150.00
BW Brian Westbrook/25 20.00 40.00
DM2 Donovan McNabb/100 25.00 50.00
DM3 Deuce McAllister/100 10.00 25.00
JH Joey Harrington/50 10.00 25.00
PM Peyton Manning/75 50.00 100.00
SA Shaun Alexander/100 12.00 30.00
CP2 Chad Pennington/25 20.00 40.00

1997 Flair Showcase Row 2

The 1997 Flair Showcase set was issued in one series totalling 360 cards and was distributed in five-card packs with a suggested retail price of $4.99. This hobby exclusive set is divided into three 120-card sets (Row 2/Style, Row1/Grace, and Row0/Showcase) and features holographic foil fronts with an action photo of the player silhouetted over a larger black-and-white head-shot image in the background. The backs carry a third photo, bio information and year-by-year and career statistics. The 24 pt. card stock is laminated with a shiny glossy coating for a super-premium style.

COMPLETE SET (120) 15.00 40.00
1 Jerry Rice .75 2.00
2 Mark Brunell .50 1.25
3 Eddie Kennison .25 .60
4 Brett Favre 1.50 4.00
5 Karim Abdul-Jabbar .25 .60
6 David LaFleur RC .15 .40
7 John Elway 1.50 4.00
8 Troy Aikman .75 2.00
9 Steve McNair .50 1.25
10 Kordell Stewart .40 1.00
11 Drew Bledsoe .50 1.25
12 Kerry Collins .40 1.00
13 Dan Marino 1.50 4.00
14 Steve Young .50 1.25
15 Marvin Harrison .40 1.00
16 Lawrence Phillips .15 .40
17 Jeff Blake .25 .60
18 Yatil Green RC .25 .60
19 Jake Plummer RC 2.50 6.00
20 Barry Sanders 1.25 3.00
21 Deion Sanders .40 1.00
22 Emmitt Smith 1.25 3.00
23 Rae Carruth RC .15 .40
24 Chris Warren .25 .60
25 Terry Glenn .40 1.00
26 Jim Druckenmiller RC .25 .60
27 Eddie George .40 1.00
28 Curtis Martin .50 1.25
29 Warrick Dunn RC 2.00 5.00
30 Terrell Davis .50 1.25
31 Rashaan Salaam .15 .40
32 Marcus Allen .40 1.00
33 Jeff George .25 .60
34 Thurman Thomas .40 1.00
35 Keyshawn Johnson .40 1.00
36 Jerome Bettis .40 1.00
37 Larry Centers .25 .60
38 Tony Banks .25 .60
39 Marshall Faulk .50 1.25
40 Mike Alstott .40 1.00
41 Elvis Grbac .25 .60
42 Errict Rhett .15 .40
43 Edgar Bennett .25 .60
44 Jim Harbaugh .25 .60
45 Antonio Freeman .50 1.25
46 Tiki Barber RC 4.00 10.00
47 Tim Biakabutuka .25 .60
48 Joey Galloway .30 .75
49 Tony Gonzalez RC 2.50 6.00
50 Keenan McCardell .25 .60
51 Darnay Scott .25 .60
52 Brad Johnson .50 1.25
53 Herman Moore .25 .60
54 Reidel Anthony RC .50 1.25
55 Junior Seau .40 1.00
56 Ricky Watters .25 .60
57 Amani Toomer .25 .60
58 Andre Reed .25 .60
59 Antowain Smith RC 2.00 4.00
60 Ike Hilliard RC 1.00 2.50
61 Byron Hanspard RC .30 .75
62 Robert Smith .25 .60
63 Gus Frerotte .15 .40
64 Charles Way .15 .40
65 Trent Dilfer .40 1.00
66 Adrian Murrell .25 .60
67 Stan Humphries .25 .60
68 Robert Brooks .25 .60
69 Jamal Anderson .40 1.00
70 Natrone Means .25 .60
71 John Friesz .15 .40
72 Ki-Jana Carter .15 .40
73 Marc Edwards RC .15 .40
74 Michael Westbrook .25 .60
75 Neil O'Donnell .25 .60
76 Scott Mitchell .25 .60
77 Wesley Walls .25 .60
78 Bruce Smith .25 .60
79 Corey Dillon RC 2.50 6.00
80 Wayne Chrebet .40 1.00
81 Tony Martin .25 .60
82 Jimmy Smith .25 .60
83 Terry Allen .40 1.00
84 Shannon Sharpe .25 .60
85 Derrick Alexander WR .25 .60
86 Garrison Hearst .25 .60
87 Tamarick Vanover .25 .60
88 Michael Irvin .40 1.00
89 Mark Chmura .25 .60
90 Bert Emanuel .25 .60
91 Eric Metcalf .25 .60
92 Reggie White .40 1.00
93 Carl Pickens .25 .60
94 Chris Sanders .15 .40
95 Frank Sanders .25 .60
96 Desmond Howard .25 .60
97 Michael Jackson .25 .60
98 Tim Brown .40 1.00
99 O.J. McDuffie .25 .60
100 Mario Bates .15 .40
101 Warren Moon .40 1.00
102 Curtis Conway .25 .60
103 Irving Fryar .25 .60
104 Isaac Bruce .40 1.00
105 Cris Carter .40 1.00
106 Chris Chandler .25 .60
107 Charles Johnson .25 .60
108 Kevin Lockett RC .25 .60
109 Rob Moore .25 .60
110 Napoleon Kaufman .40 1.00
111 Henry Ellard .15 .40
112 Vinny Testaverde .25 .60
113 Rick Mirer .15 .40
114 Ty Detmer .25 .60
115 Todd Collins .15 .40
116 Jake Reed .25 .60
117 Dave Brown .15 .40
118 Dedric Ward RC .25 .60
119 Heath Shuler .15 .40
120 Ben Coates .25 .60
S1 Rae Carruth Sample .08 .25
(three card strip)

1997 Flair Showcase Row 1

COMPLETE SET (120) 50.00 120.00
*STARS 1-40: 1X TO 2X ROW 2
*RCs 1-40: .5X TO 1.2X ROW 2
ROW 1 1-40 ODDS 1:2.5
*STARS 41-80: .5X TO 1.2X ROW 2
*RCs 41-80: .5X TO 1.2X ROW 2
ROW 1 41-80 ODDS 1:2
*STARS 81-120: 1.2X TO 3X ROW 2
*RCs 81-120: .8X TO 2X ROW 2
ROW 1 81-120 ODDS 1:3

1997 Flair Showcase Row 0

COMPLETE SET (120) 400.00 800.00
*STARS 1-40: 5X TO 12X ROW 2
*RCs 1-40: 3X TO 8X ROW 2
ROW 0 1-40 ODDS 1:24
*STARS 41-80: 3X TO 8X ROW 2
*RCs 41-80: 2X TO 5X ROW 2
ROW 0 41-80 ODDS 1:12
*STARS 81-120: 2X TO 5X ROW 2
*RCs 81-120: 1.2X TO 3X ROW 2
ROW 0 81-120 ODDS 1:5

1997 Flair Showcase Legacy Collection

*VETS 1-40: 10X TO 25X ROW 2
*ROOKIE STARS 1-40: 6X TO 15X ROW 2
*VETS 41-80: 6X TO 15X ROW 2
*ROOKIE STARS 41-80: 4X TO 10X ROW 2
*LEGACY 81-120: 8X TO 20X ROW 2
STATED PRINT RUN 100 SER.#'d SETS
THREE CARDS PER PLAYER: SAME PRICE

1997 Flair Showcase Hot Hands

COMPLETE SET (12) 40.00 100.00
STATED ODDS 1:90
HH1 Kerry Collins 3.00 8.00
HH2 Emmitt Smith 10.00 25.00
HH3 Terrell Davis 4.00 10.00
HH4 Brett Favre 12.50 30.00
HH5 Eddie George 3.00 8.00
HH6 Marvin Harrison 3.00 8.00
HH7 Mark Brunell 4.00 10.00
HH8 Dan Marino 12.50 30.00
HH9 Curtis Martin 4.00 10.00
HH10 Terry Glenn 3.00 8.00
HH11 Keyshawn Johnson 3.00 8.00
HH12 Jerry Rice 6.00 15.00

1997 Flair Showcase Midas Touch

COMPLETE SET (12) 30.00 80.00
STATED ODDS 1:20
MT1 Troy Aikman 5.00 12.00
MT2 John Elway 10.00 25.00
MT3 Barry Sanders 8.00 20.00
MT4 Marshall Faulk 3.00 8.00
MT5 Karim Abdul-Jabbar 1.50 4.00
MT6 Drew Bledsoe 3.00 8.00
MT7 Ricky Watters 1.50 4.00
MT8 Kordell Stewart 2.50 6.00
MT9 Tony Martin 1.50 4.00
MT10 Steve Young 3.00 8.00
MT11 Joey Galloway 2.00 5.00
MT12 Isaac Bruce 2.50 6.00

1997 Flair Showcase Now and Then

COMPLETE SET (4) 60.00 120.00
STATED ODDS 1:400
NT1 Dan Marino 20.00 50.00
John Elway
Darrell Green
NT2 Troy Aikman 20.00 50.00
Barry Sanders
Deion Sanders
NT3 Emmitt Smith 12.50 30.00
Chris Warren
Junior Seau
NT4 Brett Favre 12.50 30.00
Herman Moore
Ricky Watters

1997 Flair Showcase Wave of the Future

COMPLETE SET (25) 15.00 30.00
STATED ODDS 1:4
WF1 Mike Adams .30 .75
WF2 John Allred .30 .75
WF3 Pat Barnes .75 2.00
WF4 Kenny Bynum .30 .75
WF5 Will Blackwell .50 1.25
WF6 Peter Boulware .75 2.00
WF7 Greg Clark .30 .75
WF8 Troy Davis .50 1.25
WF9 Albert Connell .75 2.00
WF10 Jay Graham .50 1.25
WF11 Leon Johnson .50 1.25
WF12 Damon Jones .30 .75
WF13 Freddie Jones .50 1.25
WF14 George Jones .50 1.25
WF15 Chad Levitt .30 .75
WF16 Joey Kent .75 2.00
WF17 Danny Wuerffel .75 2.00
WF18 Orlando Pace .75 2.00
WF19 Darnell Autry .50 1.25
WF20 Sedrick Shaw .50 1.25
WF21 Shawn Springs .50 1.25
WF22 Duce Staley 2.50 6.00
WF23 Darrell Russell .30 .75
WF24 Bryant Westbrook .30 .75
WF25 Antwuan Wyatt .30 .75

1998 Flair Showcase Row 3

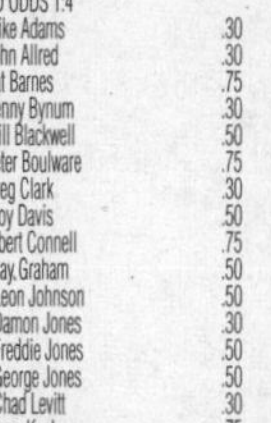

The 1998 Flair Showcase set was issued in one series totalling 80 cards and was distributed in five-card packs with a suggested retail price of $4.99. This hobby exclusive set is divided into four 80-card versions (Row 3/Flair/Showtime, Row 2/Style/Showstopper, Row 1/Grace/Showdown, and Row 0/Showcase/Showpiece) and features holographic foil fronts with an action photo of the player silhouetted over a larger black-and-white head-shot image in the background coated with a protective laminate finish. The backs display another player photo with player information and career statistics

COMPLETE SET (80) 40.00 80.00
ROW 3 FLAIR 1-20 STATED ODDS 1:0.9
ROW 3 FLAIR 21-40 STATED ODDS 1:1.1
ROW 3 FLAIR 41-60 STATED ODDS 1:1.4
ROW 3 FLAIR 61-80 STATED ODDS 1:1.8
1 Brett Favre 1.25 3.00
2 Emmitt Smith 1.00 2.50
3 Peyton Manning RC 7.50 15.00
4 Mark Brunell .40 1.00
5 Randy Moss RC 4.00 10.00
6 Jerry Rice .60 1.50
7 John Elway 1.25 3.00
8 Troy Aikman .60 1.50
9 Warrick Dunn .40 1.00
10 Kordell Stewart .40 1.00
11 Drew Bledsoe .50 1.25
12 Eddie George .40 1.00
13 Dan Marino 1.25 3.00
14 Antowain Smith .40 1.00
15 Curtis Enis RC .30 .75
16 Jake Plummer .40 1.00
17 Steve Young .40 1.00
18 Ryan Leaf RC .60 1.50
19 Terrell Davis .40 1.00
20 Barry Sanders 1.00 2.50
21 Corey Dillon .40 1.00
22 Fred Taylor RC 1.00 2.50
23 Herman Moore .25 .60
24 Marshall Faulk .50 1.25
25 John Avery RC .25 .60
26 Terry Glenn .40 1.00
27 Keyshawn Johnson .40 1.00
28 Charles Woodson RC 1.25 3.00
29 Garrison Hearst .40 1.00
30 Steve McNair .40 1.00
31 Deion Sanders .40 1.00
32 Robert Holcombe RC .25 .60
33 Jerome Bettis .40 1.00
34 Robert Edwards RC .50 1.25
35 Skip Hicks RC .50 1.25
36 Marcus Nash RC .30 .75
37 Fred Lane .15 .40
38 Kevin Dyson RC .60 1.50
39 Dorsey Levens .40 1.00
40 Jacquez Green RC .50 1.25
41 Shannon Sharpe .30 .75
42 Michael Irvin .50 1.25
43 Jim Harbaugh .30 .75
44 Curtis Martin .50 1.25
45 Bobby Hoying .30 .75
46 Trent Dilfer .50 1.25
47 Yancey Thigpen .20 .50
48 Warren Moon .50 1.25
49 Danny Kanell .30 .75
50 Rob Johnson .30 .75
51 Carl Pickens .30 .75
52 Scott Mitchell .30 .75
53 Tim Brown .50 1.25
54 Tony Banks .50 1.25
55 Jamal Anderson .50 1.25
56 Kerry Collins .30 .75
57 Elvis Grbac .30 .75
58 Mike Alstott .50 1.25
59 Glenn Foley .30 .75
60 Brad Johnson .50 1.25
61 Robert Brooks .50 1.25
62 Irving Fryar .50 1.25
63 Natrone Means .50 1.25
64 Rae Carruth .30 .75
65 Isaac Bruce .75 2.00
66 Andre Rison .50 1.25
67 Jeff George .50 1.25
68 Charles Way .30 .75
69 Derrick Alexander .50 1.25
70 Michael Jackson .30 .75
71 Rob Moore .50 1.25
72 Ricky Watters .50 1.25
73 Curtis Conway .50 1.25
74 Antonio Freeman .75 2.00
75 Jimmy Smith .50 1.25
76 Troy Davis .30 .75
77 Robert Smith .75 2.00
78 Terry Allen .75 2.00
79 Joey Galloway .50 1.25
80 Charles Johnson .30 .75
NNO Checklist Card .15 .40

1998 Flair Showcase Row 2

COMPLETE SET (80) 60.00 120.00
*STARS 1-20: 1X TO 2.5X ROW 3
*ROOKIES 1-20: .5X TO 1.2X ROW 3
ROW 2 STYLE 1-20 STATED ODDS 1:3
*STARS 21-40: .75X TO 2X ROW 3
*ROOKIES 21-40: .6X TO 1.5X ROW 3
ROW 2 STYLE 21-40 STATED ODDS 1:2.5
*STARS 41-60: 1X TO 2.5X ROW 3
ROW 2 STYLE 41-60 STATED ODDS 1:4
*STARS 61-80: .6X TO 1.5X ROW 3
ROW 2 STYLE 61-80 STATED ODDS 1:3.4

1998 Flair Showcase Row 1

*STARS 1-20: 3X TO 8X ROW 3
*ROOKIES 1-20: 1.5X TO 4X ROW 3
ROW 1 GRACE 1-20 STATED ODDS 1:16
*STARS 21-40: 4X TO 10X ROW 3
*ROOKIES 21-40: 2X TO 5X ROW 3
ROW 1 GRACE 21-40 STATED ODDS 1:24
*STARS 41-60: 1.2X TO 3X ROW 3
ROW 1 GRACE 41-60 STATED ODDS 1:6
*STARS 61-80: 1.2X TO 3X ROW 3
ROW 1 GRACE 61-80 STATED ODDS 1:9.6

1998 Flair Showcase Row 0

*STARS 1-20: 10X TO 25X ROW 3
*ROOKIES 1-20: 3X TO 8X ROW 3
ROW 0 SHOWCASE 1-20 PRINT RUN 250
*STARS 21-40: 6X TO 15X ROW 3
*ROOKIES 21-40: 2.5X TO 6X ROW 3
ROW 0 SHOWCASE 21-40 PRINT RUN 500
*STARS 41-60: 5X TO 12X ROW 3
ROW 0 SHOWCASE 41-60 PRINT RUN 1000
*STARS 61-80: 2.5X TO 6X ROW 3
ROW 0 SHOWCASE 61-80 PRINT RUN 2000

1998 Flair Showcase Legacy Collection Row 3

*VETS 1-40: 8X TO 20X BASIC ROW 3
*ROOKIES 1-40: 4X TO 10X BASIC ROW 3
*VETS 41-60: 6X TO 15X BASIC ROW 3
*VETS 61-80: 6X TO 15X BASIC ROW 3
STATED PRINT RUN 100 SER.#'d SETS
*ROW 0/1/2 CARDS: .4X TO 1X ROW 3
UNPRICED MASTERPIECES #'d TO 1
3 Peyton Manning 100.00 200.00
28 Charles Woodson 50.00 100.00

1998 Flair Showcase Feature Film

COMPLETE SET (10) 75.00 150.00
STATED ODDS 1:60
UNPRICED MASTERS SERIAL #'d TO 1
1 Terrell Davis 4.00 10.00
2 Brett Favre 12.50 30.00
3 Antowain Smith 4.00 10.00
4 Emmitt Smith 10.00 25.00
5 Dan Marino 12.50 30.00
6 Kordell Stewart 4.00 10.00
7 Warrick Dunn 4.00 10.00
8 Barry Sanders 10.00 25.00
9 Peyton Manning 15.00 30.00
10 Ryan Leaf 1.25 3.00

1999 Flair Showcase

Released as a 192-card set, the 1999 Flair Showcase set is divided into three subsets. The power version contains 32 cards featuring a full color action photo set against a silver silhouette background, the passion version is comprised of 64 cards that feature two full color action photos set against the player's jersey number, and the Showcase version features 96 players and rookies on a split-front card with two silhouette photos segmented by an action shot. The last 32 cards in this set are numbered out of 1999. 1999 Flair Showcase was packaged in 24-pack boxes with packs of five cards each and carried a suggested retail price of $4.99.

COMPLETE SET (192) 300.00 600.00
COMP.SET w/o SPs (160) 20.00 50.00
1 Troy Aikman PW .50 1.25
2 Jamal Anderson PW .25 .60
3 Charlie Batch PW .25 .60
4 Jerome Bettis PW .30 .75
5 Drew Bledsoe PW .30 .75
6 Mark Brunell PW .25 .60
7 Randall Cunningham PW .30 .75
8 Terrell Davis PW .30 .75
9 Corey Dillon PW .25 .60
10 Warrick Dunn PW .25 .60
11 Curtis Enis PW .20 .50
12 Marshall Faulk PW .30 .75
13 Brett Favre PW 1.00 2.50
14 Doug Flutie PW .30 .75
15 Eddie George PW .25 .60
16 Brian Griese PW .25 .60
17 Keyshawn Johnson PW .25 .60
18 Peyton Manning PW 1.00 2.50
19 Dan Marino PW 1.00 2.50
20 Curtis Martin PW .30 .75
21 Steve McNair PW .30 .75
22 Randy Moss PW .30 .75
23 Terrell Owens PW .30 .75
24 Jake Plummer PW .25 .60
25 Jerry Rice PW .60 1.50
26 Barry Sanders PW .75 2.00
27 Antowain Smith PW .20 .50
28 Emmitt Smith PW .75 2.00
29 Kordell Stewart PW .25 .60
30 J.J. Stokes PW .20 .50
31 Fred Taylor PW .25 .60
32 Steve Young PW .40 1.00
33 Troy Aikman PN .50 1.25
34 Mike Alstott PN .30 .75
35 Jamal Anderson PN .25 .60
36 Charlie Batch PN .25 .60
37 Jerome Bettis PN .30 .75
38 Drew Bledsoe PN .30 .75
39 Mark Brunell PN .25 .60
40 Cris Carter PN .30 .75
41 Mark Chmura PN .20 .50
42 Wayne Chrebet PN .25 .60
43 Kerry Collins PN .25 .60
44 Randall Cunningham PN .30 .75
45 Terrell Davis PN .30 .75
46 Trent Dilfer PN .25 .60
47 Corey Dillon PN .25 .60
48 Warrick Dunn PN .25 .60
49 Kevin Dyson PN .20 .50
50 Curtis Enis PN .20 .50
51 Marshall Faulk PN .30 .75
52 Brett Favre PN 1.00 2.50
53 Doug Flutie PN .30 .75
54 Antonio Freeman PN .25 .60
55 Eddie George PN .25 .60
56 Terry Glenn PN .25 .60
57 Tony Gonzalez PN .30 .75
58 Elvis Grbac PN .20 .50
59 Jacquez Green PN .20 .50
60 Brian Griese PN .25 .60
61 Marvin Harrison PN .30 .75
62 Garrison Hearst PN .25 .60
63 Skip Hicks PN .20 .50
64 Priest Holmes PN .30 .75
65 Michael Irvin PN .30 .75
66 Brad Johnson PN .25 .60
67 Keyshawn Johnson PN .25 .60
68 Napoleon Kaufman PN .20 .50
69 Dorsey Levens PN .25 .60
70 Peyton Manning PN 1.00 2.50
71 Dan Marino PN 1.00 2.50
72 Curtis Martin PN .30 .75
73 Ed McCaffrey PN .25 .60
74 Keenan McCardell PN .25 .60
75 O.J. McDuffie PN .25 .60
76 Steve McNair PN .30 .75
77 Scott Mitchell PN .20 .50
78 Randy Moss PN .30 .75
79 Eric Moulds PN .25 .60
80 Terrell Owens PN .30 .75
81 Lawrence Phillips PN .25 .60
82 Jake Plummer PN .25 .60
83 Jerry Rice PN .60 1.50
84 Andre Rison PN .25 .60
85 Barry Sanders PN .75 2.00
86 Shannon Sharpe PN .30 .75
87 Antowain Smith PN .20 .50
88 Emmitt Smith PN .75 2.00
89 Rod Smith PN .25 .60
90 Duce Staley PN .25 .60
91 Kordell Stewart PN .25 .60
92 J.J. Stokes PN .20 .50
93 Fred Taylor PN .25 .60
94 Vinny Testaverde PN .25 .60
95 Ricky Watters PN .25 .60
96 Steve Young PN .40 1.00
97 Mike Alstott .30 .75
98 Jamal Anderson .25 .60
99 Charlie Batch .25 .60
100 Jerome Bettis .30 .75
101 Tim Biakabutuka .25 .60
102 Drew Bledsoe .30 .75
103 Tim Brown .30 .75
104 Mark Brunell .25 .60
105 Cris Carter .30 .75
106 Chris Chandler .25 .60
107 Mark Chmura .20 .50
108 Wayne Chrebet .25 .60
109 Ben Coates .25 .60
110 Kerry Collins .25 .60
111 Randall Cunningham .30 .75
112 Trent Dilfer .25 .60
113 Corey Dillon .25 .60
114 Warrick Dunn .25 .60
115 Kevin Dyson .20 .50
116 Curtis Enis .20 .50
117 Marshall Faulk .30 .75
118 Doug Flutie .30 .75
119 Antonio Freeman .25 .60
120 Joey Galloway .25 .60
121 Rich Gannon .25 .60
122 Eddie George .25 .60
123 Terry Glenn .25 .60
124 Tony Gonzalez .30 .75
125 Elvis Grbac .20 .50
126 Jacquez Green .20 .50
127 Brian Griese .25 .60
128 Marvin Harrison .30 .75
129 Garrison Hearst .25 .60
130 Skip Hicks .20 .50
131 Priest Holmes .30 .75
132 Michael Irvin .30 .75
133 Brad Johnson .25 .60
134 Napoleon Kaufman .20 .50
135 Terry Kirby .20 .50
136 Dorsey Levens .25 .60
137 Curtis Martin .30 .75
138 Ed McCaffrey .25 .60
139 Keenan McCardell .25 .60
140 O.J. McDuffie .25 .60
141 Steve McNair .30 .75
142 Natrone Means .25 .60
143 Scott Mitchell .20 .50
144 Herman Moore .25 .60
145 Eric Moulds .25 .60
146 Terrell Owens .30 .75
147 Lawrence Phillips .25 .60
148 Jerry Rice .60 1.50
149 Andre Rison .25 .60
150 Deion Sanders .30 .75
151 Shannon Sharpe .30 .75
152 Antowain Smith .20 .50
153 Rod Smith .25 .60
154 Duce Staley .25 .60
155 Kordell Stewart .25 .60
156 J.J. Stokes .20 .50
157 Vinny Testaverde .25 .60
158 Yancey Thigpen .20 .50
159 Ricky Watters .25 .60
160 Steve Young .40 1.00
161 Troy Aikman SP 4.00 10.00
162 Champ Bailey RC 6.00 15.00
163 Karsten Bailey RC 2.00 5.00
164 D'Wayne Bates RC 2.00 5.00
165 David Boston RC 2.50 6.00
166 Mike Cloud RC 2.00 5.00
167 Cecil Collins RC 2.00 5.00
168 Tim Couch RC 3.00 8.00
169 Daunte Culpepper RC 3.00 8.00
170 Terrell Davis SP 2.50 6.00
171 Troy Edwards RC 2.50 6.00

172 Kevin Faulk RC	3.00	8.00
173 Brett Favre SP	8.00	20.00
174 Torry Holt RC	5.00	12.00
175 Sedrick Irvin RC	2.00	5.00
176 Edgerrin James RC	4.00	10.00
177 James Johnson RC	2.00	5.00
178 Kevin Johnson RC	2.50	6.00
179 Keyshawn Johnson SP	2.00	5.00
180 Peyton Manning SP	8.00	20.00
181 Dan Marino SP	8.00	20.00
182 Donovan McNabb RC	8.00	20.00
183 Cade McNown RC	2.50	6.00
184 Joe Montgomery RC	2.00	5.00
185 Randy Moss SP	2.50	6.00
186 Jake Plummer SP	2.00	5.00
187 Peerless Price RC	2.50	6.00
188 Barry Sanders SP	6.00	15.00
189 Akili Smith RC	2.50	6.00
190 Emmitt Smith SP	6.00	15.00
191 Fred Taylor SP	2.00	5.00
192 Ricky Williams RC	5.00	12.00
P24 Jake Plummer PW Promo	.40	1.00
P82 Jake Plummer PN Promo	.40	1.00
P147 Jake Plummer Promo	.40	1.00

1999 Flair Showcase Legacy Collection

*STARS: 8X TO 20X BASIC CARDS
*SP STARS: 2.5X TO 6X BASIC CARDS
*ROOKIES: .8X TO 2X BASIC CARDS
STATED PRINT RUN 99 SERIAL #'d SETS
UNPRICED MASTERPIECES SER.#'d TO 1

1999 Flair Showcase Class of '99

COMPLETE SET (15)	125.00	250.00
STATED PRINT RUN 500 SER.#'d SETS		
1 Tim Couch	4.00	10.00
2 Donovan McNabb	12.50	30.00
3 Akili Smith	4.00	10.00
4 Cade McNown	4.00	10.00
5 Daunte Culpepper	10.00	25.00
6 Ricky Williams	5.00	12.00
7 Edgerrin James	10.00	25.00
8 Kevin Faulk	4.00	10.00
9 Torry Holt	7.50	20.00
10 David Boston	4.00	10.00
11 Sedrick Irvin	3.00	8.00
12 Peerless Price	4.00	10.00
13 Joe Germaine	4.00	10.00
14 Brock Huard	4.00	10.00
15 Shaun King	4.00	10.00

1999 Flair Showcase Feel The Game

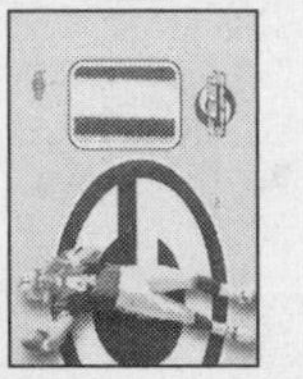

STATED ODDS 1:168		
1FG Edgerrin James Glove	40.00	100.00
2FG Antowain Smith Shorts	6.00	15.00
3FG Peyton Manning JSY	20.00	50.00
4FG Cecil Collins Shoes	6.00	15.00
5FG Brett Favre JSY	25.00	60.00
6FG Jake Plummer Shoes	7.50	20.00
7FG Dan Marino JSY	25.00	60.00
8FG Sean Dawkins Shoes	6.00	15.00
9FG Torry Holt Shoes	10.00	25.00
10FG Marshall Faulk JSY	12.50	30.00

1999 Flair Showcase First Rounders

COMPLETE SET (10)	15.00	40.00
STATED ODDS 1:10		
1FR Tim Couch	1.00	2.50
2FR Donovan McNabb	3.00	8.00
3FR Akili Smith	1.00	2.50
4FR Cade McNown	1.00	2.50
5FR Daunte Culpepper	2.50	6.00
6FR David Boston	1.00	2.50
7FR Torry Holt	1.50	4.00
8FR Ricky Williams	1.25	3.00
9FR Edgerrin James	2.50	6.00
10FR Troy Edwards	1.00	2.50

1999 Flair Showcase Shrine Time

COMPLETE SET (15)	50.00	100.00
STATED PRINT RUN 1500 SER.#'d SETS		
1 Peyton Manning	6.00	15.00
2 Fred Taylor	2.00	5.00
3 Terrell Owens	2.00	5.00
4 Charlie Batch	2.00	5.00
5 Jerry Rice	4.00	10.00
6 Randy Moss	5.00	12.00
7 Warrick Dunn	2.00	5.00
8 Mark Brunell	2.00	5.00
9 Emmitt Smith	4.00	10.00
10 Eddie George	2.00	5.00
11 Barry Sanders	6.00	15.00
12 Terrell Davis	2.00	5.00
13 Dan Marino	6.00	15.00
14 Troy Aikman	4.00	10.00
15 Brett Favre	6.00	15.00

2006 Flair Showcase

This 268-card set was released in November, 2006. The set was issued in five-card packs, with a $4.99 SRP, which came 18 packs to a box. The set is broken down into veterans (1-100, 237-268) both groupings of which are in team alphabetical order and rookies (101-236) also broken down several times into team alphabetical order. The following groups of cards have these stated print runs: Cards numbered 101-142 were issued to a stated print run of 699 serial numbered copies, Cards numbered 143-184 were issued to a stated print run of 499 serial numbered sets, cards numbered 185-226 were issued to a stated print run of 299 serial numbered sets and the veterans from 237-268 were issued to a stated print run of 999 serial numbered sets.

COMP.SET w/o SP's (100)	8.00	20.00
101-142 PRINT RUN 699 SER.#'d SETS		
143-184 PRINT RUN 499 SER.#'d SETS		
185-226 PRINT RUN 299 SER.#'d SETS		
227-236 PRINT RUN 199 SER.#'d SETS		
237-268 PRINT RUN 999 SER.#'d SETS		
1 Edgerrin James	.25	.60
2 Larry Fitzgerald	.30	.75
3 Anquan Boldin	.25	.60
4 Michael Vick	.30	.75
5 Warrick Dunn	.25	.60
6 Roddy White	.25	.60
7 Steve McNair	.25	.60
8 Jamal Lewis	.25	.60
9 Derrick Mason	.25	.60
10 Willis McGahee	.25	.60
11 Lee Evans	.25	.60
12 J.P. Losman	.25	.60
13 Jake Delhomme	.25	.60
14 DeShaun Foster	.25	.60
15 Steve Smith	.30	.75
16 Rex Grossman	.25	.60
17 Thomas Jones	.25	.60
18 Muhsin Muhammad	.25	.60
19 Brian Urlacher	.30	.75
20 Carson Palmer	.30	.75
21 Rudi Johnson	.25	.60
22 Chad Johnson	.25	.60
23 Charlie Frye	.25	.60
24 Reuben Droughns	.25	.60
25 Braylon Edwards	.25	.60
26 Drew Bledsoe	.30	.75
27 Julius Jones	.20	.50
28 Terrell Owens	.30	.75
29 Jake Plummer	.25	.60
30 Tatum Bell	.20	.50
31 Javon Walker	.25	.60
32 Kevin Jones	.20	.50
33 Roy Williams WR	.25	.60
34 Mike Williams	.20	.50
35 Brett Favre	.60	1.50
36 Ahman Green	.25	.60
37 Donald Driver	.30	.75
38 David Carr	.20	.50
39 Eric Moulds	.20	.50
40 Andre Johnson	.30	.75
41 Peyton Manning	.50	1.25
42 Marvin Harrison	.30	.75
43 Reggie Wayne	.25	.60
44 Byron Leftwich	.25	.60
45 Fred Taylor	.25	.60
46 Ernest Wilford	.20	.50
47 Trent Green	.25	.60
48 Larry Johnson	.25	.60
49 Tony Gonzalez	.25	.60
50 Eddie Kennison	.20	.50
51 Daunte Culpepper	.25	.60
52 Ronnie Brown	.30	.75
53 Chris Chambers	.25	.60
54 Brad Johnson	.25	.60
55 Chester Taylor	.25	.60
56 Troy Williamson	.20	.50
57 Tom Brady	.50	1.25
58 Corey Dillon	.25	.60
59 Troy Brown	.20	.50
60 Drew Brees	.30	.75
61 Deuce McAllister	.25	.60
62 Joe Horn	.25	.60
63 Eli Manning	.40	1.00
64 Tiki Barber	.30	.75
65 Plaxico Burress	.25	.60
66 Jeremy Shockey	.30	.75
67 Chad Pennington	.25	.60
68 Curtis Martin	.30	.75
69 Laveranues Coles	.20	.50
70 Aaron Brooks	.25	.60
71 LaMont Jordan	.25	.60
72 Randy Moss	.30	.75
73 Jerry Porter	.20	.50
74 Donovan McNabb	.30	.75
75 Brian Westbrook	.25	.60
76 Reggie Brown	.20	.50
77 Ben Roethlisberger	.40	1.00
78 Willie Parker	.25	.60
79 Hines Ward	.30	.75
80 Philip Rivers	.30	.75
81 LaDainian Tomlinson	.30	.75
82 Antonio Gates	.30	.75
83 Alex Smith QB	.30	.75
84 Frank Gore	.30	.75
85 Antonio Bryant	.20	.50
86 Matt Hasselbeck	.25	.60
87 Shaun Alexander	.25	.60
88 Nate Burleson	.20	.50
89 Marc Bulger	.25	.60
90 Steven Jackson	.30	.75
91 Torry Holt	.25	.60
92 Chris Simms	.25	.60
93 Cadillac Williams	.25	.60
94 Joey Galloway	.25	.60
95 Kerry Collins	.25	.60
96 David Givens	.25	.60
97 Drew Bennett	.25	.60
98 Mark Brunell	.25	.60
99 Clinton Portis	.30	.75
100 Santana Moss	.25	.60
101 Todd Watkins RC	1.50	4.00
102 Adam Jennings RC	2.00	5.00
103 David Pittman RC	2.00	5.00
104 Dawan Landry RC	2.50	6.00
105 Ko Simpson RC	2.00	5.00
106 James Anderson RC	1.50	4.00
107 Dusty Dvoracek RC	2.50	6.00
108 Jamar Williams RC	2.00	5.00
109 Bennie Brazell RC	2.00	5.00
110 Leon Williams RC	2.00	5.00
111 Lawrence Vickers RC	2.00	5.00
112 Elvis Dumervil RC	2.50	6.00
113 Domenik Hixon RC	2.50	6.00
114 Antoine Bethea RC	3.00	8.00
115 David Anderson RC	2.00	5.00
116 Freddie Keiaho RC	2.00	5.00
117 Clint Ingram RC	2.50	6.00
118 Jeff Webb RC	2.00	5.00
119 Devin Aromashodu RC	2.50	6.00
120 Mike Hass RC	2.00	5.00
121 Josh Lay RC	1.50	4.00
122 Marques Colston RC	5.00	12.00
123 Gerris Wilkinson RC	1.50	4.00
124 Barry Cofield RC	2.50	6.00
125 Guy Whimper RC	1.50	4.00
126 Nick Mangold RC	1.25	3.00
127 Anthony Schlegel RC	2.00	5.00
128 Eric Smith RC	2.00	5.00
129 Darnell Bing RC	2.00	5.00
130 Anthony Smith RC	2.50	6.00
131 Charlie Whitehurst RC	2.50	6.00
132 Delanie Walker RC	2.50	6.00
133 Marcus Hudson RC	2.00	5.00
134 David Kirtman RC	2.00	5.00
135 Victor Adeyanju RC	2.00	5.00
136 Davin Joseph RC	2.00	5.00
137 Marcus McNeill RC	2.00	5.00
138 Calvin Lowry RC	2.50	6.00
139 Stephen Tulloch RC	2.00	5.00
140 Terna Nande RC	2.00	5.00
141 Jonathan Orr RC	2.00	5.00
142 Jon Alston RC	1.50	4.00
143 Jimmy Williams RC	3.00	8.00
144 D.J. Shockley RC	2.50	6.00
145 Demetrius Williams RC	2.50	6.00
146 P.J. Daniels RC	2.00	5.00
147 Quinn Sypniewski RC	2.50	6.00
148 Ashton Youboty RC	2.00	5.00
149 Richard Marshall RC	2.50	6.00
150 Jeff King RC	2.50	6.00
151 Danieal Manning RC	3.00	8.00
152 Reggie McNeal RC	2.50	6.00
153 D'Qwell Jackson RC	2.50	6.00
154 Jerome Harrison RC	3.00	8.00
155 Skyler Green RC	2.00	5.00
156 Brandon Marshall RC	3.00	8.00
157 Daniel Bullocks RC	3.00	8.00
158 Abdul Hodge RC	2.00	5.00
159 Cory Rodgers RC	2.50	6.00
160 Ingle Martin RC	2.50	6.00
161 Stephen Gostkowski RC	5.00	12.00
162 Wali Lundy RC	2.50	6.00
163 Bernard Pollard RC	2.50	6.00
164 Marcus Vick RC	2.00	5.00
165 Cedric Griffin RC	2.50	6.00
166 Garrett Mills RC	3.00	8.00
167 Roman Harper RC	2.50	6.00
168 Brad Smith RC	3.00	8.00
169 Leon Washington RC	2.50	6.00
170 Ahmad Brooks RC	3.00	8.00
171 Thomas Howard RC	2.50	6.00
172 Jason Avant RC	2.00	5.00
173 Jeremy Bloom RC	2.50	6.00
174 Omar Jacobs RC	2.00	5.00
175 Mike Bell RC	3.00	8.00
176 Cedric Humes RC	2.00	5.00
177 Michael Robinson RC	2.50	6.00
178 Ben Obomanu RC	3.00	8.00
179 Darryl Tapp RC	2.50	6.00
180 Claude Wroten RC	2.00	5.00
181 Dominique Byrd RC	2.50	6.00
182 Marques Hagans RC	2.00	5.00
183 Bruce Gradkowski RC	3.00	8.00
184 Rocky McIntosh RC	2.50	6.00
185 Leonard Pope RC	3.00	8.00
186 Jerious Norwood RC	2.50	6.00
187 Haloti Ngata RC	3.00	8.00
188 Donte Whitner RC	3.00	8.00
189 John McCargo RC	2.00	5.00
190 Devin Hester RC	5.00	12.00
191 Johnathan Joseph RC	2.50	6.00
192 Kamerion Wimbley RC	3.00	8.00
193 Travis Wilson RC	2.00	5.00
194 Bobby Carpenter RC	2.00	5.00
195 Anthony Fasano RC	3.00	8.00
196 Tony Scheffler RC	3.00	8.00
197 Ernie Sims RC	2.50	6.00
198 Brian Calhoun RC	2.00	5.00
199 A.J. Hawk RC	3.00	8.00
200 Greg Jennings RC	6.00	15.00
201 Mario Williams RC	3.00	8.00
202 DeMeco Ryans RC	3.00	8.00
203 Marcedes Lewis RC	3.00	8.00
204 Maurice Drew RC	5.00	12.00
205 Tamba Hali RC	3.00	8.00
206 Brodie Croyle RC	3.00	8.00
207 Jason Allen RC	2.50	6.00
208 Derek Hagan RC	2.50	6.00
209 Chad Greenway RC	3.00	8.00
210 Tarvaris Jackson RC	3.00	8.00
211 Chad Jackson RC	2.00	5.00
212 David Thomas RC	2.50	6.00
213 Mathias Kiwanuka RC	3.00	8.00
214 Sinorice Moss RC	3.00	8.00
215 D'Brickashaw Ferguson RC	3.00	8.00
216 Kellen Clemens RC	2.50	6.00
217 Michael Huff RC	2.50	6.00
218 Brodrick Bunkley RC	2.50	6.00
219 Willie Reid RC	2.50	6.00
220 Antonio Cromartie RC	3.00	8.00
221 Manny Lawson RC	2.50	6.00
222 Brandon Williams RC	2.00	5.00
223 Kelly Jennings RC	2.50	6.00
224 Tye Hill RC	2.00	5.00
225 Joe Klopfenstein RC	2.00	5.00
226 Maurice Stovall RC	2.00	5.00
227 Matt Leinart RC	4.00	10.00
228 DeAngelo Williams RC	5.00	12.00
229 Jay Cutler RC	8.00	20.00
230 Joseph Addai RC	4.00	10.00
231 Laurence Maroney RC	3.00	8.00
232 Reggie Bush RC	8.00	20.00
233 Santonio Holmes RC	5.00	12.00
234 Vernon Davis RC	5.00	12.00
235 Vince Young RC	5.00	12.00
236 LenDale White RC	3.00	8.00
237 Edgerrin James	1.25	3.00
238 Michael Vick	1.50	4.00
239 Jamal Lewis	1.25	3.00
240 Willis McGahee	1.25	3.00
241 Steve Smith	1.50	4.00
242 Brian Urlacher	1.50	4.00
243 Carson Palmer	1.50	4.00
244 Charlie Frye	1.25	3.00
245 Terrell Owens	1.50	4.00
246 Jake Plummer	1.25	3.00
247 Kevin Jones	1.00	2.50
248 Brett Favre	3.00	8.00
249 David Carr	1.00	2.50
250 Peyton Manning	2.50	6.00
251 Byron Leftwich	1.25	3.00
252 Larry Johnson	1.25	3.00
253 Daunte Culpepper	1.25	3.00
254 Brad Johnson	1.25	3.00
255 Tom Brady	2.50	6.00
256 Drew Brees	1.50	4.00
257 Eli Manning	2.00	5.00
258 Curtis Martin	1.50	4.00
259 Randy Moss	1.50	4.00
260 Donovan McNabb	1.50	4.00
261 Ben Roethlisberger	2.00	5.00
262 LaDainian Tomlinson	1.50	4.00
263 Alex Smith QB	1.50	4.00
264 Shaun Alexander	1.25	3.00
265 Marc Bulger	1.25	3.00
266 Cadillac Williams	1.25	3.00
267 Drew Bennett	1.25	3.00
268 Clinton Portis	1.50	4.00

2006 Flair Showcase Emerald

*VETS 1-100: 5X TO 12X BASIC CARDS
1-100 PRINT RUN 50 SER.#'d SETS
*ROOKIES 101-142: 1X TO 2.5X
*ROOKIES 143-184: .8X TO 2X
*ROOKIES 185-226: .8X TO 2X
*ROOKIES 227-236: .6X TO 1.5X
*VETS 237-268: 1.5X TO 4X BASIC CARDS
101-236 PRINT RUN 25 SER.#'d SETS

2006 Flair Showcase Gold

*VETS 1-100: 3X TO 8X BASIC CARDS
*ROOKIES 101-142: .6X TO 1.5X
*ROOKIES 143-184: .5X TO 1.2X
*ROOKIES 185-226: .5X TO 1.2X
1-226 PRINT RUN 99 SER.#'d SETS
*ROOKIES 227-236: .5X TO 1.2X
*VETS 237-268: .8X TO 2X BASIC CARDS
227-268 PRINT RUN 75 SER.#'d SETS

2006 Flair Showcase Autographics

AUAF Anthony Fasano	6.00	15.00
AUAH Andre Hall	5.00	12.00
AUBA Ronde Barber SP	10.00	25.00
AUBB Brodrick Bunkley	4.00	10.00
AUBC Brian Calhoun	8.00	20.00
AUBD Brian Dawkins	10.00	25.00
AUBG Bruce Gradkowski	6.00	15.00
AUBM Brandon Marshall	8.00	20.00
AUBR Reggie Brown SP	6.00	15.00
AUCJ Chad Jackson	8.00	20.00
AUCS Chris Simms SP	6.00	15.00
AUCU Kevin Curtis	4.00	10.00
AUCW Charlie Whitehurst	8.00	20.00
AUDF D'Brickashaw Ferguson	6.00	15.00
AUDM DonTrell Moore	4.00	10.00
AUDW DeAngelo Williams SP	25.00	60.00
AUES Ernie Sims	6.00	15.00
AUJA Joseph Addai	10.00	25.00
AUJC Jay Cutler SP	30.00	80.00
AUJJ Julius Jones SP	15.00	30.00
AUJK Joe Klopfenstein	4.00	10.00
AUJW Jimmy Williams	4.00	10.00
AUKC Kellen Clemens	6.00	15.00
AUKJ Kelly Jennings	4.00	10.00
AULJ Larry Johnson	8.00	20.00
AULP Leonard Pope SP	6.00	15.00
AULT Lofa Tatupu	10.00	25.00
AULW LenDale White SP	10.00	25.00
AUMB Mike Bell	8.00	20.00
AUMC Deuce McAllister SP	8.00	20.00
AUMI Mike Williams	4.00	10.00
AUMM Marcus McNeill	4.00	10.00
AUMN Martin Nance	4.00	10.00
AUMS Maurice Stovall	6.00	15.00
AUMU Muhsin Muhammad SP	8.00	20.00
AUMW Mario Williams	8.00	20.00
AUPR Philip Rivers	15.00	40.00
AURB Reggie Bush SP	30.00	80.00
AURM Reggie McNeal	6.00	15.00
AUSM Sinorice Moss	8.00	20.00
AUSS Steve Smith SP	15.00	30.00
AUTB Tedy Bruschi	20.00	40.00
AUTH Tye Hill	6.00	15.00
AUTJ Thomas Jones	8.00	20.00
AUTR Travis Wilson	4.00	10.00
AUTW Terrence Whitehead	4.00	10.00
AUVD Vernon Davis SP	10.00	25.00

2006 Flair Showcase Clear Path to Greatness

CPTG1 A.J. Hawk	5.00	12.00
CPTG2 Anthony Fasano	5.00	12.00
CPTG3 Brandon Marshall	5.00	12.00
CPTG4 Brandon Williams	3.00	8.00
CPTG5 Brian Calhoun	3.00	8.00
CPTG6 Brodie Croyle	5.00	12.00
CPTG7 Chad Jackson	3.00	8.00
CPTG8 Charlie Whitehurst	5.00	12.00
CPTG9 D'Brickashaw Ferguson	5.00	12.00
CPTG10 DeAngelo Williams	6.00	15.00
CPTG11 Demetrius Williams	4.00	10.00
CPTG12 Derek Hagan	4.00	10.00
CPTG13 Donte Whitner	5.00	12.00
CPTG14 Ernie Sims	4.00	10.00
CPTG15 Greg Jennings	10.00	25.00
CPTG16 Jason Allen	4.00	10.00
CPTG17 Jason Avant	3.00	8.00
CPTG18 Jay Cutler	10.00	25.00
CPTG19 Jerious Norwood	4.00	10.00
CPTG20 Joe Klopfenstein	3.00	8.00
CPTG21 Joseph Addai	5.00	12.00
CPTG22 Kamerion Wimbley	5.00	12.00
CPTG23 Kellen Clemens	4.00	10.00
CPTG24 Laurence Maroney	4.00	10.00
CPTG25 LenDale White	4.00	10.00
CPTG26 Leon Washington	4.00	10.00
CPTG27 Marcedes Lewis	5.00	12.00
CPTG28 Mario Williams	5.00	12.00
CPTG29 Matt Leinart	5.00	12.00
CPTG30 Maurice Drew	8.00	20.00
CPTG31 Maurice Stovall	3.00	8.00
CPTG32 Michael Huff	4.00	10.00
CPTG33 Michael Robinson	4.00	10.00
CPTG34 Omar Jacobs	3.00	8.00
CPTG35 Reggie Bush	10.00	25.00
CPTG36 Santonio Holmes	6.00	15.00
CPTG37 Sinorice Moss	5.00	12.00
CPTG38 Tarvaris Jackson	5.00	12.00
CPTG39 Travis Wilson	3.00	8.00
CPTG40 Tye Hill	3.00	8.00
CPTG41 Vernon Davis	6.00	15.00
CPTG42 Vince Young	6.00	15.00

2006 Flair Showcase Fresh Ink

FIAG Antonio Gates	8.00	20.00
FIAH A.J. Hawk	15.00	40.00
FIAY Ashton Youboty SP	5.00	12.00
FIBE Braylon Edwards SP	6.00	15.00
FIBI Darnell Bing	6.00	15.00
FIBW Brandon Williams	5.00	12.00
FIBY Dominique Byrd	6.00	15.00
FICG Chad Greenway	8.00	20.00
FICI Clint Ingram	8.00	20.00
FICR Cory Rodgers	6.00	15.00
FIDB Drew Bennett	6.00	15.00
FIDF DeShaun Foster	6.00	15.00
FIDG David Givens	6.00	15.00
FIDH Darrell Hackney	6.00	15.00
FIDM Derrick Mason	6.00	15.00
FIDO Drew Olson	5.00	12.00
FIDR DeMeco Ryans	8.00	20.00
FIEM Eli Manning SP	25.00	60.00
FIGJ Greg Jennings	15.00	40.00
FIGL Greg Lee	5.00	12.00
FIGR Gerald Riggs	6.00	15.00
FIHA Derek Hagan	6.00	15.00
FIHB Hank Baskett	8.00	20.00
FIHO T.J. Houshmandzadeh	6.00	15.00
FIHU Michael Huff	6.00	15.00
FIJB Josh Betts	6.00	15.00
FIJH Jerome Harrison	8.00	20.00
FIJN Jerious Norwood	6.00	15.00
FIJW Jason Witten SP	20.00	40.00
FIKO Kyle Orton SP	8.00	20.00
FILE Matt Leinart SP	20.00	50.00
FILJ LaMont Jordan SP	6.00	15.00
FILM Laurence Maroney	8.00	20.00
FILW Leon Washington	6.00	15.00
FIMD Maurice Drew	12.00	30.00
FIMH Mike Hass	6.00	15.00
FIMK Mathias Kiwanuka	8.00	20.00
FIMR Michael Robinson	6.00	15.00
FINB Nate Burleson	5.00	12.00
FIOD Owen Daniels	8.00	20.00
FIOJ Omar Jacobs	5.00	12.00
FIPM Peyton Manning	40.00	80.00
FIRJ Rudi Johnson SP	6.00	15.00
FIRW Reggie Wayne	6.00	15.00
FISH Santonio Holmes SP	10.00	25.00
FITH Thomas Howard	6.00	15.00
FITJ Tarvaris Jackson	8.00	20.00
FIVY Vince Young SP	25.00	50.00
FIWJ Winston Justice SP	6.00	15.00
FIWP Willie Parker SP	10.00	25.00

2006 Flair Showcase Hot Hands

HH1 Anquan Boldin	1.00	2.50
HH2 Bob Sanders	1.00	2.50
HH3 Brian Dawkins	1.00	2.50
HH4 Chad Johnson	1.00	2.50
HH5 Champ Bailey	1.00	2.50
HH6 Chris Chambers	1.00	2.50
HH7 Darren Sharper	1.00	2.50
HH8 DeAngelo Hall	1.00	2.50
HH9 Donald Driver	1.25	3.00
HH10 Ed Reed	1.00	2.50
HH11 Hines Ward	1.25	3.00
HH12 Javon Walker	1.00	2.50
HH13 Joey Galloway	1.00	2.50
HH14 Ken Lucas	.75	2.00
HH15 Larry Fitzgerald	1.25	3.00
HH16 Marvin Harrison	1.25	3.00
HH17 Nathan Vasher	.75	2.00
HH18 Plaxico Burress	1.00	2.50
HH19 Randy Moss	1.25	3.00
HH20 Ronde Barber	1.00	2.50
HH21 Santana Moss	1.00	2.50
HH22 Steve Smith	1.25	3.00
HH23 Terrell Owens	1.25	3.00
HH24 Torry Holt	1.00	2.50
HH25 Troy Polamalu	1.50	4.00

2006 Flair Showcase Hot Numbers

HN1 Anquan Boldin	1.00	2.50
HN2 Antonio Gates	1.25	3.00
HN3 Ben Roethlisberger	1.50	4.00
HN4 Brett Favre	2.50	6.00
HN5 Brian Urlacher	1.25	3.00
HN6 Carson Palmer	1.25	3.00
HN7 Chad Johnson	1.00	2.50
HN8 Champ Bailey	1.00	2.50
HN9 Donovan McNabb	1.25	3.00
HN10 Dwight Freeney	1.00	2.50
HN11 Edgerrin James	1.00	2.50
HN12 Eli Manning	1.50	4.00
HN13 Julius Peppers	1.00	2.50
HN14 LaDainian Tomlinson	1.25	3.00
HN15 Larry Johnson	1.00	2.50
HN16 Michael Vick	1.25	3.00
HN17 Peyton Manning	2.00	5.00
HN18 Randy Moss	1.25	3.00
HN19 Santana Moss	1.00	2.50
HN20 Shaun Alexander	1.00	2.50
HN21 Steve Smith	1.25	3.00
HN22 Terrell Owens	1.25	3.00
HN23 Tiki Barber	1.25	3.00
HN24 Tom Brady	2.00	5.00
HN25 Tony Gonzalez	1.00	2.50

2006 Flair Showcase Lettermen

UNPRICED LETTERMEN PRINT RUN 4-10

2006 Flair Showcase Showcase Stars

SS1 Antonio Gates	1.25	3.00
SS2 Brett Favre	2.50	6.00
SS3 Brian Urlacher	1.25	3.00
SS4 Carson Palmer	1.25	3.00
SS5 Chad Johnson	1.00	2.50
SS6 Clinton Portis	1.25	3.00
SS7 Dwight Freeney	1.00	2.50
SS8 Edgerrin James	1.00	2.50
SS9 LaDainian Tomlinson	1.25	3.00
SS10 Larry Johnson	1.00	2.50
SS11 Michael Vick	1.25	3.00
SS12 Peyton Manning	2.00	5.00
SS13 Randy Moss	1.25	3.00
SS14 Santana Moss	1.00	2.50
SS15 Shaun Alexander	1.00	2.50
SS16 Steve Smith	1.25	3.00
SS17 Terrell Owens	1.25	3.00
SS18 Tiki Barber	1.25	3.00
SS19 Tom Brady	2.00	5.00
SS20 Troy Polamalu	1.50	4.00

2006 Flair Showcase Showcase Stitches Jersey

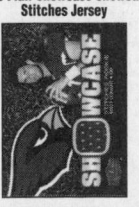

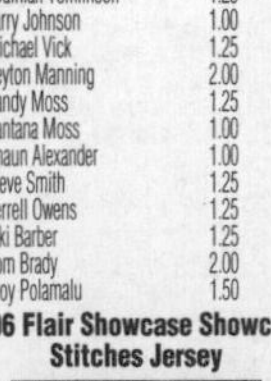

*PATCHES: .8X TO 2X BASIC INSERTS		
PATCH PRINT RUN 50 SER.#'d SETS		
SHSAC Alge Crumpler	3.00	8.00
SHSAH A.J. Hawk	2.50	6.00
SHSAS Alex Smith QB	4.00	10.00
SHSBC Brian Calhoun	2.50	6.00
SHSBL Byron Leftwich	3.00	8.00
SHSBU Reggie Bush	5.00	12.00
SHSBW Brandon Williams	1.50	4.00
SHSCJ Chad Jackson	2.50	6.00
SHSCW Cadillac Williams	3.00	8.00
SHSDB Drew Bledsoe	4.00	10.00
SHSDH Derek Hagan	2.00	5.00
SHSDM Deuce McAllister	3.00	8.00
SHSDW DeAngelo Williams	3.00	8.00
SHSEJ Edgerrin James	3.00	8.00
SHSJC Jay Cutler	5.00	12.00
SHSJP Jake Plummer	3.00	8.00
SHSJS Jeremy Shockey	4.00	10.00
SHSKJ Kevin Jones	2.50	6.00
SHSKO Kyle Orton	4.00	10.00
SHSLJ Larry Johnson	3.00	8.00
SHSLM Laurence Maroney	2.00	5.00
SHSLW LenDale White	2.00	5.00
SHSMD Maurice Drew	4.00	10.00
SHSMH Michael Huff	2.00	5.00
SHSML Matt Leinart	2.50	6.00
SHSMS Maurice Stovall	1.50	4.00
SHSMW Mario Williams	2.50	6.00
SHSOJ Omar Jacobs	2.50	6.00
SHSPB Plaxico Burress	3.00	8.00
SHSPH Priest Holmes	3.00	8.00
SHSRB Ronnie Brown	4.00	10.00
SHSRM Randy Moss	4.00	10.00
SHSRW Reggie Wayne	3.00	8.00
SHSSH Santonio Holmes	3.00	8.00
SHSSJ Steven Jackson	4.00	10.00
SHSSM Sinorice Moss	2.50	6.00
SHSTB Tatum Bell	2.50	6.00
SHSTJ Tarvaris Jackson	2.50	6.00
SHSTO Terrell Owens	4.00	10.00
SHSTW Troy Williamson	2.50	6.00
SHSVD Vernon Davis	3.00	8.00
SHSVY Vince Young	3.00	8.00

2006 Flair Showcase Wave of the Future

WOTF1 Alex Smith QB	1.50	4.00
WOTF2 Antonio Gates	1.50	4.00
WOTF3 Ben Roethlisberger	2.00	5.00
WOTF4 Braylon Edwards	1.25	3.00
WOTF5 Cadillac Williams	1.25	3.00
WOTF6 Chad Jackson	1.00	2.50
WOTF7 Chris Simms	1.25	3.00
WOTF8 Eli Manning	2.00	5.00
WOTF9 Jay Cutler	1.50	4.00
WOTF10 Joseph Addai	.75	2.00
WOTF11 Julius Jones	1.00	2.50
WOTF12 Kellen Clemens	1.00	2.00
WOTF13 Kevin Jones	1.00	2.50
WOTF14 Larry Fitzgerald	1.50	4.00
WOTF15 Larry Johnson	1.25	3.00
WOTF16 Laurence Maroney	.60	1.50
WOTF17 LenDale White	.60	1.50
WOTF18 Lofa Tatupu	1.25	3.00
WOTF19 Mario Williams	.75	2.00
WOTF20 Matt Leinart	.75	2.00
WOTF21 Philip Rivers	1.50	4.00
WOTF22 Reggie Bush	1.50	4.00
WOTF23 Ronnie Brown	1.50	4.00
WOTF24 Santonio Holmes	1.00	2.50
WOTF25 Shawne Merriman	1.25	3.00
WOTF26 Steven Jackson	1.50	4.00
WOTF27 Tatum Bell	1.00	2.50
WOTF28 Vernon Davis	1.25	3.00
WOTF29 Vince Young	1.00	2.50
WOTF30 Willie Parker	1.25	3.00

1960 Fleer

The 1960 Fleer set of 132 standard-size cards was Fleer's first venture into football card production. This set features players of the American Football League's debut season. Several well-known coaches are featured in the set; the set is the last regular issue set to feature coaches (on their own specific card) until the 1989 Pro Set release. The card backs are printed in red and black. The key card in the set is Jack Kemp's Rookie Card. Other Rookie Cards include Sid Gillman, Ron Mix and Hank Stram. The cards are frequently found off-centered as Fleer's first effort into the football card market left much to be desired in the area of quality control. A large quantity of color separations and "proofs" are widely available.

COMPLETE SET (132)	500.00	750.00
WRAPPER (5-CENT)	20.00	25.00
1 Harvey White RC	12.00	20.00
2 Tom Corky Tharp RC	2.00	3.50
3 Dan McGrew RC	2.00	3.50
4 Bob White RC	2.00	3.50
5 Dick Jamieson RC	2.00	3.50
6 Sam Salerno RC	2.00	3.50
7 Sid Gillman CO RC	12.00	20.00
8 Ben Preston RC	2.00	3.50
9 George Blanch RC	2.00	3.50
10 Bob Stransky RC	2.00	3.50
11 Fran Curci RC	2.00	3.50
12 George Shirkey RC	2.00	3.50
13 Paul Larson	2.00	3.50
14 John Stolte RC	2.00	3.50
15 Serafino Fazio RC	2.50	5.00
16 Tom Dimitroff RC	2.00	3.50
17 Elbert Dubenion RC	6.00	12.00
18 Hogan Wharton RC	2.00	3.50
19 Tom O'Connell	2.00	3.50
20 Sammy Baugh CO	25.00	40.00
21 Tony Sardisco RC	2.00	3.50
22 Alan Cann RC	2.00	3.50
23 Mike Hudock RC	2.00	3.50
24 Bill Atkins RC	2.00	3.50
25 Charlie Jackson RC	2.00	3.50
26 Frank Tripucka	3.00	6.00
27 Tony Teresa RC	2.00	3.50
28 Joe Amstutz RC	2.00	3.50
29 Bob Fee RC	2.00	3.50
30 Jim Baldwin RC	2.00	3.50
31 Jim Yates RC	2.00	3.50
32 Don Flynn RC	2.00	3.50
33 Ken Adamson RC	2.00	3.50
34 Ron Drzewiecki	2.00	3.50
35 J.W. Slack RC	2.00	3.50
36 Bob Yates RC	2.00	3.50
37 Gary Cobb RC	2.00	3.50
38 Jacky Lee RC	2.50	5.00
39 Jack Spikes RC	2.50	5.00
40 Jim Padgett RC	2.00	3.50
41 Jack Larscheid UER RC (name misspelled Larsheid)	2.00	3.50
42 Bob Reifsnyder RC	2.00	3.50
43 Fran Rogel	2.00	3.50
44 Ray Moss RC	2.00	3.50
45 Tony Banfield RC	2.50	5.00
46 George Herring RC	2.00	3.50
47 Willie Smith RC	2.00	3.50
48 Buddy Allen RC	2.00	3.50
49 Bill Brown LB RC	2.00	3.50
50 Ken Ford RC	2.00	3.50
51 Billy Kinard RC	2.00	3.50
52 Buddy Mayfield RC	2.00	3.50
53 Bill Krisher RC	2.00	3.50
54 Frank Bernardi RC	2.00	3.50
55 Lou Saban CO RC	2.50	5.00
56 Gene Cockrell RC	2.00	3.50
57 Sam Sanders RC	2.00	3.50
58 George Blanda	30.00	50.00
59 Sherrill Headrick RC	2.50	5.00
60 Carl Larpenter RC	2.00	3.50
61 Gene Prebola RC	2.00	3.50
62 Dick Chorovich RC	2.00	3.50
63 Bob McNamara RC	2.00	3.50
64 Tom Saidock RC	2.00	3.50
65 Willie Evans RC	2.00	3.50
66 Billy Cannon RC UER (Hometown: Istruma, should be Istrouma)	10.00	20.00
67 Sam McCord RC	2.00	3.50
68 Mike Simmons RC	2.00	3.50
69 Jim Swink RC	2.50	5.00
70 Don Hitt RC	2.00	3.50
71 Gerhard Schwedes RC	2.00	3.50
72 Thurlow Cooper RC	2.00	3.50
73 Abner Haynes RC	10.00	20.00
74 Billy Shoemake RC	2.00	3.50
75 Marv Lasater RC	2.00	3.50
76 Paul Lowe RC	7.50	15.00
77 Bruce Hartman RC	2.00	3.50
78 Blanche Martin RC	2.00	3.50
79 Gene Grabosky RC	2.00	3.50
80 Lou Rymkus CO	2.50	5.00
81 Chris Burford RC	4.00	8.00
82 Don Allen RC	2.00	3.50
83 Bob Nelson C RC	2.00	3.50
84 Jim Woodard RC	2.00	3.50
85 Tom Rychlec RC	2.00	3.50
86 Bob Cox RC	2.00	3.50
87 Jerry Cornelison RC	2.00	3.50
88 Jack Work	2.00	3.50
89 Sam DeLuca RC	2.00	3.50
90 Rommie Loudd RC	2.00	3.50
91 Teddy Edmondson RC	2.00	3.50
92 Buster Ramsey CO	2.00	3.50
93 Doug Asad RC	2.00	3.50
94 Jimmy Harris	2.00	3.50
95 Larry Cundiff RC	2.00	3.50
96 Richie Lucas RC	3.00	6.00
97 Don Norwood RC	2.00	3.50
98 Larry Grantham RC	2.50	5.00
99 Bill Mathis RC	3.00	6.00
100 Mel Branch RC	2.50	5.00
101 Marvin Terrell RC	2.00	3.50
102 Charlie Flowers RC	2.00	3.50
103 John McMullan RC	2.00	3.50
104 Charlie Kaaihue RC	2.00	3.50
105 Joe Schaffer RC	2.00	3.50
106 Al Day RC	2.00	3.50
107 Johnny Carson	2.00	3.50
108 Alan Goldstein RC	2.00	3.50
109 Doug Cline RC	2.00	3.50
110 Al Carmichael	2.00	3.50
111 Bob Dee RC	2.00	3.50
112 John Bredice RC	2.00	3.50
113 Don Floyd RC	2.00	3.50
114 Ronnie Cain RC	2.00	3.50
115 Stan Flowers RC	2.00	3.50
116 Hank Stram CO RC	25.00	40.00
117 Bob Dougherty RC	2.00	3.50
118 Ron Mix RC	25.00	40.00
119 Roger Ellis RC	2.00	3.50
120 Elvin Caldwell RC	2.00	3.50
121 Bill Kimber RC	2.00	3.50
122 Jim Matheny RC	2.00	3.50
123 Curley Johnson RC	2.00	3.50
124 Jack Kemp RC	60.00	120.00
125 Ed Denk RC	2.00	3.50
126 Jerry McFarland RC	2.00	3.50
127 Dan Lanphear RC	2.00	3.50
128 Paul Maguire RC	10.00	18.00
129 Ray Collins	2.00	3.50
130 Ron Burton RC	3.00	6.00
131 Eddie Erdelatz CO RC	2.00	3.50
132 Ron Beagle RC	7.50	15.00

1960 Fleer AFL Team Decals

This set of nine logo decals was inserted with the 1960 Fleer regular issue inaugural AFL football set. These inserts measure approximately 2 1/4" by 3" and one decal was to be inserted in each wax pack. The decals are unnumbered and are ordered below alphabetically by team name for convenience. There is one decal for each of the eight AFL teams as well as a decal with the league logo. The backs of the decal backing contained instructions on the proper application of the decal.

COMPLETE SET (9)	100.00	200.00
1 AFL Logo	12.50	25.00
2 Boston Patriots	10.00	20.00
3 Buffalo Bills	12.50	25.00
4 Dallas Texans	15.00	30.00
5 Denver Broncos	12.50	25.00
6 Houston Oilers	12.50	25.00
7 Los Angeles Chargers	12.50	25.00
8 New York Titans	10.00	20.00
9 Oakland Raiders	15.00	30.00

1960 Fleer College Pennant Decals

This set of 19 pennant decal pairs was distributed as an insert with the 1960 Fleer regular issue inaugural AFL football set along with and at the same time as the AFL Team Decals described immediately above. Some dealers feel that these college decals are tougher to find than the AFL team decals. These inserts were approximately 2 1/4" by 3" and one decal was to be inserted in each wax pack. The decals are unnumbered and are ordered below alphabetically according to the lower alphabetically of each college pair. The backs of the decal backing contained instructions on the proper application of the decal printed in very light blue.

COMPLETE SET (19)	87.50	175.00
1 Alabama Yale	6.00	12.00
2 Army Mississippi	3.75	7.50
3 California Indiana	3.75	7.50
4 Duke Notre Dame	10.00	20.00
5 Florida St. Kentucky	6.00	12.00
6 Georgia Oklahoma	6.00	12.00
7 Houston Iowa	3.75	7.50
8 Idaho St Penn.	3.75	7.50
9 Iowa St. Penn State	6.00	12.00
10 Kansas UCLA	5.00	10.00
11 Marquette New Mexico	3.75	7.50
12 Maryland Missouri	3.75	7.50
13 Miss.South. N.Carolina	3.75	7.50
14 Navy Stanford	5.00	10.00
15 Nebraska Purdue	6.00	12.00
16 Pittsburgh Utah	3.75	7.50
17 SMU West Virginia	3.75	7.50
18 So.Carolina USC	5.00	10.00
19 Wake Forest Wisconsin	3.75	7.50

1961 Fleer

The 1961 Fleer football set contains 220 standard-size cards. The set contains NFL (1-132) and AFL (133-220) players. The cards are grouped alphabetically by team nicknames within league. The backs are printed in black and lime green on a white card stock. The AFL cards are often found in uncut sheet form. The key Rookie Cards in this set are John Brodie, Tom Flores, Don Maynard, Don Meredith, and Jim Otto.

COMPLETE SET (220)	1,000.00	1,600.00
WRAPPER (5-CENT, SER.1)	20.00	25.00
WRAPPER (5-CENT, SER.2)	25.00	30.00
1 Ed Brown	7.50	15.00
2 Rick Casares	3.00	6.00
3 Willie Galimore	3.00	6.00
4 Jim Dooley	2.50	4.00
5 Harlon Hill	2.50	4.00
6 Stan Jones	4.00	8.00
7 J.C. Caroline	2.50	4.00
8 Joe Fortunato	2.50	4.00
9 Doug Atkins	4.00	8.00
10 Milt Plum	3.00	6.00
11 Jim Brown	90.00	150.00
12 Bobby Mitchell	5.00	10.00
13 Ray Renfro	3.00	6.00
14 Gern Nagler	2.50	4.00
15 Jim Shofner	2.50	4.00
16 Vince Costello	2.50	4.00
17 Galen Fiss RC	2.50	4.00
18 Walt Michaels	3.00	6.00
19 Bob Gain	2.50	4.00
20 Mal Hammack	2.50	4.00
21 Frank Mestnik RC	2.50	4.00
22 Bobby Joe Conrad	3.00	6.00
23 John David Crow	3.00	6.00
24 Sonny Randle RC	3.00	6.00
25 Don Gillis	2.50	4.00
26 Jerry Norton	2.50	4.00
27 Bill Stacy RC	2.50	4.00
28 Leo Sugar	2.50	4.00
29 Frank Fuller	2.50	4.00
30 John Unitas	35.00	60.00
31 Alan Ameche	4.00	8.00
32 Lenny Moore	7.50	15.00
33 Raymond Berry	7.50	15.00
34 Jim Mutscheller	2.50	4.00
35 Jim Parker	4.00	8.00
36 Bill Pellington	2.50	4.00
37 Gino Marchetti	5.00	10.00
38 Gene Lipscomb	4.00	8.00
39 Art Donovan	7.50	15.00
40 Eddie LeBaron	3.00	6.00
41 Don Meredith RC	90.00	150.00
42 Don McIlhenny	2.50	4.00
43 L.G. Dupre	2.50	4.00
44 Fred Dugan RC	2.50	4.00
45 Billy Howton	3.00	6.00
46 Duane Putnam	2.50	4.00
47 Gene Cronin	2.50	4.00
48 Jerry Tubbs	2.50	4.00
49 Clarence Peaks	2.50	4.00
50 Ted Dean RC	2.50	4.00
51 Tommy McDonald	4.00	8.00
52 Bill Barnes	2.50	4.00
53 Pete Retzlaff	3.00	6.00
54 Bobby Walston	2.50	4.00
55 Chuck Bednarik	6.00	12.00
56 Maxie Baughan RC	3.00	6.00
57 Bob Pellegrini	2.50	4.00
58 Jesse Richardson	2.50	4.00
59 John Brodie RC	30.00	50.00
60 J.D. Smith RB	3.00	6.00
61 Ray Norton RC	2.50	4.00
62 Monty Stickles RC	2.50	4.00
63 Bob St. Clair	4.00	8.00
64 Dave Baker RC	2.50	4.00
65 Abe Woodson	2.50	4.00
66 Matt Hazeltine	2.50	4.00
67 Leo Nomellini	5.00	10.00
68 Charley Conerly	5.00	10.00
69 Kyle Rote	4.00	8.00
70 Jack Stroud RC	2.50	4.00
71 Roosevelt Brown	4.00	8.00
72 Jim Patton	2.50	4.00
73 Erich Barnes	2.50	4.00
74 Sam Huff	7.50	15.00
75 Andy Robustelli	5.00	10.00
76 Dick Modzelewski RC	2.50	4.00
77 Roosevelt Grier	4.00	8.00
78 Earl Morrall	4.00	8.00
79 Jim Ninowski	2.50	4.00
80 Nick Pietrosante RC	3.00	6.00
81 Howard Cassady	3.00	6.00
82 Jim Gibbons	2.50	4.00
83 Gail Cogdill RC	3.00	6.00
84 Dick Lane	4.00	8.00
85 Yale Lary	4.00	8.00
86 Joe Schmidt	4.00	8.00
87 Darris McCord	2.50	4.00
88 Bart Starr	35.00	60.00
89 Jim Taylor	30.00	50.00
90 Paul Hornung	30.00	55.00
91 Tom Moore RC	4.00	8.00
92 Boyd Dowler RC	7.50	15.00
93 Max McGee	4.00	8.00
94 Forrest Gregg	5.00	10.00
95 Jerry Kramer	5.00	10.00
96 Jim Ringo	4.00	8.00
97 Bill Forester	3.00	6.00
98 Frank Ryan	3.00	6.00
99 Ollie Matson	6.00	12.00
100 Jon Arnett	3.00	6.00
101 Dick Bass RC	3.00	6.00
102 Jim Phillips	2.50	4.00
103 Del Shofner	3.00	6.00
104 Art Hunter	2.50	4.00
105 Lindon Crow	2.50	4.00
106 Les Richter	3.00	6.00
107 Lou Michaels	2.50	4.00
108 Ralph Guglielmi	2.50	4.00
109 Don Bosseler	2.50	4.00
110 John Olszewski	2.50	4.00
111 Bill Anderson	2.50	4.00
112 Joe Walton	2.50	4.00
113 Jim Schrader	2.50	4.00
114 Gary Glick	2.50	4.00
115 Ralph Felton	2.50	4.00
116 Bob Toneff	2.50	4.00
117 Bobby Layne	25.00	40.00
118 John Henry Johnson	4.00	8.00
119 Tom Tracy	3.00	6.00
120 Jimmy Orr RC	4.00	8.00
121 John Nisby	2.50	4.00
122 Dean Derby	2.50	4.00
123 John Reger	2.50	4.00
124 George Tarasovic	2.50	4.00
125 Ernie Stautner	5.00	10.00
126 George Shaw	2.50	4.00
127 Hugh McElhenny	6.00	12.00
128 Dick Haley RC	2.50	4.00
129 Dave Middleton	2.50	4.00
130 Perry Richards RC	2.50	4.00
131 Gene Johnson DB RC	2.50	4.00
132 Don Joyce RC	2.50	4.00
133 Johnny Green RC	4.00	8.00
134 Wray Carlton RC	4.00	8.00
135 Richie Lucas	4.00	8.00
136 Elbert Dubenion	4.00	8.00
137 Tom Rychlec	3.50	6.00
138 Mack Yoho RC	3.50	6.00
139 Phil Blazer RC	3.50	6.00
140 Dan McGrew	3.50	6.00
141 Bill Atkins	3.50	6.00
142 Archie Matsos RC	3.50	6.00
143 Gene Grabosky	3.50	8.00
144 Frank Tripucka	5.00	10.00
145 Al Carmichael	3.50	6.00
146 Bob McNamara	3.50	6.00
147 Lionel Taylor RC	7.50	15.00
148 Eldon Danenhauer RC	3.50	6.00
149 Willie Smith	3.50	6.00
150 Carl Larpenter	3.50	6.00
151 Ken Adamson	3.50	6.00
152 Goose Gonsoulin UER RC (Photo actually Darryl Rodgers)	5.00	10.00
153 Joe Young RC	3.50	6.00
154 Gordy Holz RC	3.50	6.00
155 Jack Kemp	50.00	80.00
156 Charlie Flowers	3.50	6.00
157 Paul Lowe	5.00	10.00
158 Don Norton RC	3.50	6.00
159 Howard Clark RC	3.50	6.00
160 Paul Maguire	7.50	15.00
161 Ernie Wright RC	4.00	8.00
162 Ron Mix	7.50	15.00
163 Fred Cole RC	3.50	6.00
164 Jim Sears RC	3.50	6.00
165 Volney Peters	3.50	6.00
166 George Blanda	25.00	40.00
167 Jacky Lee	4.00	8.00
168 Bob White	3.50	6.00
169 Doug Cline	3.50	6.00
170 Dave Smith RB RC	3.50	6.00
171 Billy Cannon	7.50	15.00
172 Bill Groman RC	3.50	6.00
173 Al Jamison RC	3.50	6.00
174 Jim Norton RC	3.50	6.00
175 Dennit Morris RC	3.50	6.00
176 Don Floyd	3.50	6.00
177 Butch Songin	3.50	6.00
178 Billy Lott RC	3.50	6.00
179 Ron Burton	5.00	10.00
180 Jim Colclough RC	3.50	6.00
181 Charley Leo RC	3.50	6.00
182 Walt Cudzik RC	3.50	6.00
183 Fred Bruney	3.50	6.00
184 Ross O'Hanley RC	3.50	6.00
185 Tony Sardisco	3.50	6.00
186 Harry Jacobs RC	3.50	6.00
187 Bob Dee	3.50	6.00
188 Tom Flores RC	15.00	30.00
189 Jack Larscheid	3.50	6.00
190 Dick Christy RC	3.50	6.00
191 Alan Miller RC	3.50	6.00
192 James Smith	3.50	6.00
193 Gerald Burch RC	3.50	6.00
194 Gene Prebola	3.50	6.00
195 Alan Goldstein	3.50	6.00
196 Don Manoukian RC	3.50	6.00
197 Jim Otto RC	40.00	75.00
198 Wayne Crow	3.50	6.00
199 Cotton Davidson RC	4.00	8.00
200 Randy Duncan RC	4.00	8.00
201 Jack Spikes	4.00	8.00
202 Johnny Robinson RC	7.50	15.00
203 Abner Haynes	7.50	15.00
204 Chris Burford	4.00	8.00
205 Bill Krisher	3.50	6.00
206 Marvin Terrell	3.50	6.00
207 Jimmy Harris	3.50	6.00
208 Mel Branch	4.00	8.00
209 Paul Miller	3.50	6.00
210 Al Dorow	3.50	6.00
211 Dick Jamieson	3.50	6.00
212 Pete Hart RC	3.50	6.00
213 Bill Shockley RC	3.50	6.00
214 Dewey Bohling RC	3.50	6.00
215 Don Maynard RC	40.00	80.00
216 Bob Mischak RC	3.50	6.00
217 Mike Hudock	3.50	6.00
218 Bob Reifsnyder	3.50	6.00
219 Tom Saidock	3.50	6.00
220 Sid Youngelman	12.00	20.00

1961 Fleer Magic Message Blue Inserts

Q.
What player was selected in 1950 by the Associated Press as "Greatest Player in the half-century"?

This unattractive set contains 40 cards that were inserted in 1961 Fleer football wax packs. The cards are light blue in color and measure approximately 3" by 2 1/8". The fronts feature a question and a crude line drawing. For the answer, the collector is instructed to "Turn card and wet; when dry, wet again." A tag line at the bottom of the front indicates that the cards were printed by Business Service of Long Island, New York. The backs are blank, and the cards are numbered on the front in the lower right corner.

COMPLETE SET (40)	75.00	150.00
1 When was the first Sugar Bowl game played	2.00	4.00
2 Which school was famous for its Point-A-Minute team	2.00	4.00
3 What famous coach was known as Gloomy Gil	2.00	4.00
4 Which college coach holds the longest record for years coached	2.00	4.00
5 What is meant by two Platoon System	2.00	4.00
6 When was the only Sudden Death playoff in NFL history	2.00	4.00
7 What is a Sudden Death playoff in professional football	2.00	4.00
8 What is the longest field goal kicked in pro football (place kick)	2.00	4.00
9 What famous Colorado All-American now holds a key position in President Kennedy's administration (Whizzer White)	2.00	4.00
10 What Michigan All-American has gained added fame as a radio and television sportscaster (Tom Harmon)	3.00	6.00
11 The North-South game has become an annual classic. Do you know where it was first played	2.00	4.00
12 The Army-Navy game has become an annual classic. Do you know when it was first played	2.00	4.00
13 What slugging major league outfielder was an All-American back during his college days	2.00	4.00
14 What All-Americans were known as Mr. Inside and Mr. Outside (Glenn Davis and Doc Blanchard)	2.00	4.00
15 Which team was called the Thundering Hord	2.00	4.00
16 When was the first championship playoff in the National Football League	2.00	4.00
17 What is the record for field goals dropkicked in a single game	2.00	4.00
18 What is the longest winning streak in college football	2.00	4.00
19 Who was the first collegian gained by draft in the National Football League	2.00	4.00
20 Which team was the first to use the huddle	2.00	4.00
21 Who was the first Intercollegiate Champion	2.00	4.00
22 When was the first broadcast of a football game	2.00	4.00
23 What is the longest field goal (placement kick) on record	2.00	4.00
24 What is the origin of the tackling dummy	2.00	4.00
25 What player was selected in 1950 as Greatest Player in the half-century (Jim Thorpe)	3.00	6.00
26 What is the record for the most touchdowns in a game	2.00	4.00
27 What player ran the wrong way in a bowl game	2.00	4.00
28 When was the first field goal attempted in college football	2.00	4.00
29 When and by whom was the first All-American team selected	2.00	4.00
30 When was the forward pass first used	2.00	4.00
31 What was the first college to put numbers on player's jerseys	2.00	4.00
32 When was the first professional football game played	2.00	4.00
33 Where is the Football Hall of Fame to be erected (Canton& Ohio)	2.00	4.00
34 Who were the Four Horsemen	2.00	4.00
35 When was the first Rose Bowl game played	2.00	4.00
36 Who holds the record for the most forward passes attempted in a professional game	2.00	4.00
37 Who was known as the Galloping Ghost (Red Grange)	3.00	6.00
38 Has the Rose Bowl always been played in California	2.00	4.00
39 Which team featured the Seven Blocks of Granite (Fordham)	2.00	4.00
40 Where and when was the first football game played in the United States	3.00	6.00

1961 Fleer Wallet Pictures

These "cards" were issued as part of the 1961-62 issue of Complete Sports Pro-Football Illustrated magazine. The magazine section was entitled "Wallet Picture Album, photos courtesy of Frank H. Fleer Corp." The AFL and NFL sections were issued seperately and each photo inside the magazine was printed in black and white on newsprint stock. The pictures were to be cut from the pages and, once neatly cut, the photos measure roughly 2 1/2" by 3 3/8" with the backs including only the player's name and team name. The interior pages included 52-NFL players and 90-AFL players. Twelve additional photos were included as the back cover to the magazine and they measure roughly 2 3/8" by 2 3/8" when neatly cut out. Those twleve were printed on white stock with a light single color tone. Most of the photos were the same as used for the 1961 Fleer card set. We've arranged the unnumbered photos below alphabetically by team and then by player starting with the AFL (1-90) then the NFL (91-145).

COMPLETE SET (145)	125.00	300.00
1 Tommy Addison	.75	2.00
2 Jim Colclough	.75	2.00
3 Walt Cudzik	.75	2.00
4 Bob Dee	.75	2.00
5 Harry Jacobs	.75	2.00
6 Charley Leo	.75	2.00
7 Billy Lott	.75	2.00
8 Ross O'Hanley	.75	2.00
9 Tony Sardisco UER (name spelled Sandisco)	.75	2.00
10 Butch Songin	.75	2.00
11 Bill Atkins	.75	2.00
12 Phil Blazer	.75	2.00
13 Wray Carlton	.75	2.00
14 Monte Crockett	.75	2.00
15 Elbert Dubenion	1.00	2.50
16 Willmer Fowler	.75	2.00
17 Gene Grabosky	.75	2.00
18 Richie Lucas	1.00	2.50
19 Archie Matsos	.75	2.00
20 Richard McCabe	.75	2.00
21 Dan McGrew UER (reverse negative)	.75	2.00
22 Tom Rychlec	.75	2.00
23 Laverne Torczon	.75	2.00
24 Mack Yoho	.75	2.00
25 Mel Branch	.75	2.00
26 Chris Burford	.75	2.00
27 Cotton Davidson	.75	2.00
28 Randy Duncan	.75	2.00
29 Jimmy Harris	.75	2.00
30 E.J. Holub	.75	2.00
31 Bill Krisher	.75	2.00
32 Paul Miller	.75	2.00
33 Johnny Robinson	1.00	2.50
34 Jack Spikes	.75	2.00
35 Marvin Terrell	.75	2.00
36 Ken Adamson	.75	2.00
37 Al Carmichael	.75	2.00
38 Eldon Danenhauer	.75	2.00
39 Goose Gonsoulin UER (name spelled Consoulin)	.75	2.00
40 Gordy Holz	.75	2.00
41 Carl Larpenter	.75	2.00
42 Bud McFadin	.75	2.00
43 Bob McNamara	.75	2.00
44 Dave Rolle	.75	2.00
45 Willie Smith	.75	2.00
46 Lionel Taylor	1.50	4.00
47 Frank Tripucka UER (name spelled Tripuka)	1.50	4.00
48 Joe Young	.75	2.00
49 George Blanda	4.00	10.00
50 Doug Cline	.75	2.00
51 Don Floyd	.75	2.00
52 Bobby Gordon	.75	2.00
53 Bill Groman	.75	2.00
54 Al Jamison	.75	2.00
55 Jacky Lee	.75	2.00
56 Richard Michael	.75	2.00
57 Dennit Morris	.75	2.00
58 Jim Norton	.75	2.00
59 Dave Smith	.75	2.00
60 Bob White	.75	2.00
61 Dewey Bohling	.75	2.00
62 Pete Hart	.75	2.00
63 Mike Hudock	.75	2.00
64 Bob Mischak	.75	2.00
65 Sid Youngelman UER (name spelled Youngleman)	.75	2.00
66 Gerald Burch	.75	2.00
67 Dick Christy	.75	2.00
68 Bob Coolbaugh	.75	2.00
69 Wayne Crow	.75	2.00
70 Don Deskins	.75	2.00
71 Tom Flores	1.50	4.00
72 Alan Goldstein	.75	2.00
73 Jack Larscheid	.75	2.00
74 Dan Manoukian UER (name spelled Manoukin)	.75	2.00
75 Alan Miller UER name misspelled Millis)	.75	2.00
76 Jim Otto	3.00	8.00
77 Charley Powell	.75	2.00
78 Gene Prebola	.75	2.00
79 Jim Smith RB	.75	2.00
80 Howard Clark	.75	2.00
81 Fred Cole	.75	2.00
82 Charlie Flowers	.75	2.00
83 Dick Harris	.75	2.00
84 Jack Kemp	6.00	15.00
85 Paul Lowe	1.00	2.50
86 Ron Mix	1.50	4.00
87 Don Norton	.75	2.00
88 Volney Peters	.75	2.00
89 Jim Sears	.75	2.00
90 Ernie Wright	1.00	2.50
91 Alan Ameche	1.00	2.50
92 Raymond Berry	3.00	8.00
93 Lenny Moore	2.50	6.00
94 Jim Mutscheller	.75	2.00
95 Ed Brown (yellow color)	1.00	2.50
96 Rick Casares	1.00	2.50
97 J.C. Caroline	.75	2.00
98 Willie Galimore	.75	2.00
99 Harlon Hill UER (name misspelled Horton Hill)	.75	2.00
100 Bobby Mitchell	2.00	5.00
101 Gern Nagler	.75	2.00
102 Milt Plum (magenta color)	1.00	2.50
103 Ray Renfro	1.00	2.50
104 Billy Howton UER (team identified as Texans)	1.00	2.50
105 Don Meredith (yellow color)	6.00	15.00
106 Howard Cassady (yellow color)	1.00	2.50
107 Gail Cogdill	.75	2.00
108 Dick Lane	1.50	4.00
109 Nick Pietrosante	.75	2.00
110 Paul Hornung	6.00	15.00
111 Tom Moore	1.00	2.50
112 Bart Starr	10.00	25.00
113 Jim Taylor (cyan color)	5.00	12.00
114 Les Richter (cyan color)	.75	2.00
115 Frank Ryan	1.00	2.50
116 Del Shofner	.75	2.00
117 Dick Haley UER (name spelled Pick)	.75	2.00
118 Perry Richards	.75	2.00
119 Charley Conerly UER (name spelled Charlie)/(cyan color)	2.00	5.00
120 Kyle Rote	1.00	2.50
121 Bill Barnes (cyan color)	.75	2.00
122 Chuck Bednarik	2.00	5.00
123 Clarence Peaks	.75	2.00
124 Pete Retzlaff	1.00	2.50
125 Bobby Walston	.75	2.00
126 Dean Derby	.75	2.00
127 John Henry Johnson	1.50	4.00
128 Bobby Layne (cyan color)	4.00	10.00
129 Jimmy Orr	1.00	2.50
130 Tom Tracy	1.00	2.50
131 Bobby Joe Conrad	.75	2.00
132 John David Crow (magenta color)	1.00	2.50
133 Mal Hammack UER (name spelled Harmack)	.75	2.00
134 Sonny Randle	.75	2.00
135 Bill Stacy UER (name misspelled Stacey)	.75	2.00
136 Dave Baker	.75	2.00
137 John Brodie (cyan color)	3.00	8.00
138 Matt Hazeltine	.75	2.00
139 Ray Norton	.75	2.00
140 J.D Smith RB	.75	2.00
141 Bill Anderson	.75	2.00
142 Don Bosseler (magenta color)	.75	2.00
143 Ralph Guglielmi	.75	2.00
144 John Olszewski	.75	2.00
145 Joe Walton	.75	2.00

1962 Fleer

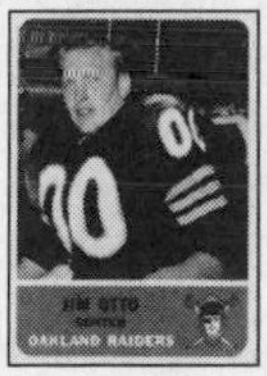

The 1962 Fleer football set contains 88 standard-size cards featuring AFL players only. The set was issued in six-card nickel packs which came 24 packs to a box with a slab of bubble gum. Card numbering is alphabetical by team city. The card backs are printed in black and blue on a white card stock. Key Rookie Cards in this set are Gino Cappelletti, Charlie Hennigan, Ernie Ladd and Fred Williamson.

COMPLETE SET (88)	500.00	900.00
WRAPPER (5-CENT)	100.00	200.00
1 Billy Lott	8.00	16.00
2 Ron Burton	5.00	10.00
3 Gino Cappelletti RC	10.00	20.00
4 Babe Parilli	5.00	10.00
5 Jim Colclough	3.50	7.00
6 Tony Sardisco	3.50	7.00
7 Walt Cudzik	3.50	7.00
8 Bob Dee	3.50	7.00
9 Tommy Addison RC	4.00	8.00
10 Harry Jacobs	3.50	7.00
11 Ross O'Hanley	3.50	7.00
12 Art Baker	3.50	7.00
13 Johnny Green	3.50	7.00
14 Elbert Dubenion	5.00	10.00
15 Tom Rychlec	3.50	7.00
16 Billy Shaw RC	20.00	40.00
17 Ken Rice	3.50	7.00
18 Bill Atkins	3.50	7.00
19 Richie Lucas	4.00	8.00
20 Archie Matsos	3.50	7.00
21 Laverne Torczon	3.50	7.00
22 Warren Rabb RC UER (name misspelled Raab)	3.50	7.00
23 Jack Spikes	4.00	8.00
24 Cotton Davidson	4.00	8.00
25 Abner Haynes	7.50	15.00
26 Jimmy Saxton RC	3.50	7.00
27 Chris Burford	4.00	8.00
28 Bill Miller RC	3.50	7.00
29 Sherrill Headrick	4.00	8.00
30 E.J. Holub RC	4.00	8.00
31 Jerry Mays RC	5.00	10.00
32 Mel Branch	4.00	8.00
33 Paul Rochester RC	3.50	7.00
34 Frank Tripucka	5.00	10.00
35 Gene Mingo	3.50	7.00
36 Lionel Taylor	6.00	12.00
37 Ken Adamson	3.50	7.00
38 Eldon Danenhauer	3.50	7.00
39 Goose Gonsoulin	5.00	10.00
40 Gordy Holz	3.50	7.00
41 Bud McFadin	4.00	8.00
42 Jim Stinnette RC	3.50	7.00
43 Bob Hudson RC	3.50	7.00
44 George Herring	3.50	7.00
45 Charley Tolar RC	3.50	7.00
46 George Blanda	30.00	50.00
47 Billy Cannon	7.50	15.00
48 Charlie Hennigan RC	7.50	15.00
49 Bill Groman	3.50	7.00
50 Al Jamison	3.50	7.00
51 Tony Banfield	3.50	7.00
52 Jim Norton	3.50	7.00
53 Dennit Morris	3.50	7.00
54 Don Floyd	3.50	7.00
55 Ed Husmann UER RCMisspelled Hussman on both sides)	3.50	7.00
56 Robert Brooks RC	3.50	7.00
57 Al Dorow	3.50	7.00
58 Dick Christy	3.50	7.00
59 Don Maynard	30.00	50.00
60 Art Powell	5.00	10.00
61 Mike Hudock	3.50	7.00
62 Bill Mathis	4.00	8.00
63 Butch Songin	3.50	7.00
64 Larry Grantham	3.50	7.00
65 Nick Mumley RC	3.50	7.00
66 Tom Saidock	3.50	7.00
67 Alan Miller	3.50	7.00
68 Tom Flores	7.50	15.00
69 Bob Coolbaugh	3.50	7.00
70 George Fleming RC	3.50	7.00
71 Wayne Hawkins RC	4.00	8.00
72 Jim Otto	25.00	40.00
73 Wayne Crow	3.50	7.00
74 Fred Williamson RC	18.00	30.00
75 Tom Louderback RC	3.50	7.00
76 Volney Peters	3.50	7.00
77 Charley Powell RC	3.50	7.00
78 Don Norton	3.50	7.00
79 Jack Kemp	50.00	100.00
80 Paul Lowe	5.00	10.00
81 Dave Kocourek	3.50	7.00
82 Ron Mix	7.50	15.00
83 Ernie Wright	5.00	10.00
84 Dick Harris RC	3.50	7.00
85 Bill Hudson RC	3.50	7.00
86 Ernie Ladd RC	15.00	25.00
87 Earl Faison RC	4.00	8.00
88 Ron Nery	9.00	18.00

1963 Fleer

The 1963 Fleer football set of 88 standard-size cards features AFL players only. Card numbers is in team order. Card numbers 6 and 64 are more difficult to obtain than the other cards in the set; their shortage is believed to be attributable to their possible replacement on the printing sheet by the unnumbered checklist. The card backs are printed in red and black on a white card stock. The set price below does not include the checklist card. Cards with numbers divisible by four can be found with or without a red stripe on the bottom of the card back; it is thought that those without the red stripe are in lesser supply. Currently, there is no difference in value. The key Rookie Cards in this set are Lance Alworth, Nick Buoniconti, and Len Dawson.

COMPLETE SET (88)	1,200.00	1,800.00
WRAPPER (5-CENT)	60.00	120.00
1 Larry Garron RC	10.00	20.00
2 Babe Parilli	5.00	10.00
3 Ron Burton	6.00	12.00
4 Jim Colclough	4.00	8.00
4B Jim Colclough NS	4.00	8.00
5 Gino Cappelletti	6.00	12.00
6 Charles Long SP RC	50.00	100.00
7 Bill Neighbors RC	4.00	8.00
8 Dick Felt RC	4.00	8.00
8B Dick Felt NS RC	4.00	8.00
9 Tommy Addison	4.00	8.00
10 Nick Buoniconti RC	45.00	80.00
11 Larry Eisenhauer RC	4.00	8.00
12 Bill Mathis	4.00	8.00
12B Bill Mathis NS	4.00	8.00
13 Lee Grosscup RC	5.00	10.00
14 Dick Christy	4.00	8.00
15 Don Maynard	30.00	50.00
16 Alex Kroll RC	4.00	8.00
16B Alex Kroll NS RC	4.00	8.00
17 Bob Mischak	4.00	8.00
18 Dainard Paulson RC	4.00	8.00
19 Lee Riley	4.00	8.00
20 Larry Grantham	5.00	10.00
20B Larry Grantham NS	5.00	10.00
21 Hubert Bobo RC	4.00	8.00
22 Nick Mumley	4.00	8.00
23 Cookie Gilchrist RC	30.00	50.00
24 Jack Kemp	75.00	150.00
24B Jack Kemp NS	75.00	150.00
25 Wray Carlton	4.00	8.00
26 Elbert Dubenion	5.00	10.00
27 Ernie Warlick RC	5.00	10.00
28 Billy Shaw	7.50	15.00
28B Billy Shaw NS	7.50	15.00
29 Ken Rice	4.00	8.00
30 Booker Edgerson RC	4.00	8.00
31 Ray Abruzzese RC	4.00	8.00
32 Mike Stratton RC	7.50	15.00
32B Mike Stratton NS RC	7.50	15.00
33 Tom Sestak RC	6.00	12.00
34 Charley Tolar	4.00	8.00
35 Dave Smith	4.00	8.00
36 George Blanda	30.00	50.00
36B George Blanda NS	30.00	50.00
37 Billy Cannon	7.50	15.00
38 Charlie Hennigan	5.00	10.00
39 Bob Talamini RC	4.00	8.00
40 Jim Norton	4.00	8.00
40B Jim Norton NS	4.00	8.00
41 Tony Banfield	4.00	8.00
42 Doug Cline	4.00	8.00
43 Don Floyd	4.00	8.00
44 Ed Husmann	4.00	8.00
44B Ed Husmann NS	4.00	8.00
45 Curtis McClinton RC	7.50	15.00
46 Jack Spikes	5.00	10.00
47 Len Dawson RC	150.00	250.00
48 Abner Haynes	7.50	15.00
48B Abner Haynes NS	7.50	15.00
49 Chris Burford	5.00	10.00
50 Fred Arbanas RC	6.00	12.00
51 Johnny Robinson	5.00	10.00
52 E.J. Holub	5.00	10.00
52B E.J. Holub NS	5.00	10.00
53 Sherrill Headrick	5.00	10.00
54 Mel Branch	5.00	10.00
55 Jerry Mays	5.00	10.00
56 Cotton Davidson	5.00	10.00
56B Cotton Davidson NS	5.00	10.00
57 Clem Daniels RC	10.00	20.00
58 Bo Roberson RC	5.00	10.00
59 Art Powell	6.00	12.00
60 Bob Coolbaugh	4.00	8.00
60B Bob Coolbaugh NS	4.00	8.00
61 Wayne Hawkins	4.00	8.00
62 Jim Otto	18.00	30.00
63 Fred Williamson	10.00	20.00
64 Bob Dougherty SP	60.00	120.00
64B Bob Dougherty SP NS	60.00	120.00
65 Dalva Allen RC	4.00	8.00
66 Chuck McMurtry RC	4.00	8.00
67 Gerry McDougall RC	4.00	8.00
68 Tobin Rote	5.00	10.00
68B Tobin Rote NS	5.00	10.00
69 Paul Lowe	6.00	12.00
70 Keith Lincoln RC	25.00	40.00
71 Dave Kocourek	4.00	8.00
72 Lance Alworth RC	125.00	250.00
72B Lance Alworth NS RC	125.00	250.00
73 Ron Mix	15.00	25.00
74 Charlie McNeil RC	4.00	8.00
75 Emil Karas RC	4.00	8.00
76 Ernie Ladd	10.00	20.00
76B Ernie Ladd NS	10.00	20.00
77 Earl Faison	4.00	8.00
78 Jim Stinnette	4.00	8.00
79 Frank Tripucka	6.00	12.00
80 Don Stone RC	4.00	8.00
80B Don Stone NS RC	4.00	8.00
81 Bob Scarpitto RC	4.00	8.00
82 Lionel Taylor	6.00	12.00
83 Jerry Tarr RC	4.00	8.00
84 Eldon Danenhauer	4.00	8.00
84B Eldon Danenhauer NS	4.00	8.00
85 Goose Gonsoulin	5.00	10.00
86 Jim Fraser RC	4.00	8.00
87 Chuck Gavin RC	4.00	8.00
88 Bud McFadin	10.00	20.00
88B Bud McFadin NS	10.00	20.00
NNO Checklist Card SP	250.00	350.00

1968 Fleer Big Signs

This set of 26 "Big Signs" was produced by Fleer. They are blank backed and measure approximately 7 3/4" by 11 1/2" with rounded corners. They are unnumbered so they are listed below alphabetically by team city name. They are credited at the bottom as 1968 in roman numerals, but in fact were probably issued several years later, perhaps as late as 1974. As another point of reference in dating the set, the New England Patriots changed their name from Boston in 1970. There were two distinct versions of this set, with each version including all 26 teams. The 1970 version was issued in a green box, while the 1974 version was issued in a brown box. Both boxes carry a 1968 copyright date; however, 1974 is generally considered to be the issue date of the second series. Though they are considerably different in design, the size of the collectibles is similar. The generic drawings (of a faceless player from each team) are in color with a white border. The set was licensed by NFL Properties so there are no players shown.

COMPLETE SET (26)	150.00	250.00
1 Atlanta Falcons	5.00	10.00
2 Baltimore Colts	5.00	10.00
3 Buffalo Bills	5.00	10.00
4 Chicago Bears	6.00	12.00
5 Cincinnati Bengals	5.00	10.00
6 Cleveland Browns	5.00	10.00
7 Dallas Cowboys	10.00	20.00
8 Denver Broncos	5.00	10.00
9 Detroit Lions	5.00	10.00
10 Green Bay Packers	10.00	20.00
11 Houston Oilers	5.00	10.00
12 Kansas City Chiefs	5.00	10.00
13 Los Angeles Rams	5.00	10.00
14 Miami Dolphins	7.50	15.00
15 Minnesota Vikings	5.00	10.00
16 New England Patriots	5.00	10.00
17 New Orleans Saints	5.00	10.00
18 New York Giants	5.00	10.00
19 New York Jets	5.00	10.00
20 Oakland Raiders	10.00	20.00
21 Philadelphia Eagles	5.00	10.00
22 Pittsburgh Steelers	7.50	15.00
23 St. Louis Cardinals	5.00	10.00
24 San Diego Chargers	5.00	10.00
25 San Francisco 49ers	7.50	15.00
26 Washington Redskins	7.50	15.00

1972 Fleer Quiz

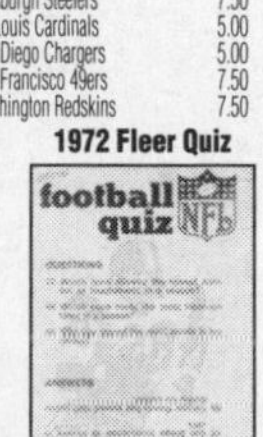

The 28 cards in this set measure approximately 2 1/2" by 4" and feature three questions and (upside down) answers about football players and events. The cards were issued one per pack with Fleer cloth team patches. The words "Official Football Quiz" are printed at the top and are accented by the NFL logo. The backs are blank. The cards are numbered in the lower right hand corner.

COMPLETE SET (28)	25.00	50.00
COMMON CARD (1-28)	1.00	2.00

1972-73 Fleer Cloth Patches

These cloth stickers were issued 3-per pack as a stand alone product, inserted one per pack in 1972 Fleer Quiz, and one per pack in 1973 Fleer Pro Scouting Report. Each blankbacked sticker includes one small team name sticker at the top and a larger team helmet or team logo at the bottom. We've catalogued and priced the stickers as pairs according to the smaller team name sticker first and the larger sticker second. Many of the stickers were identical for both years (and all contain a 1972 copyright date) except for the conference champions stickers as noted below. Variations on some sticker combinations do exist and we have cataloged all known versions below. The 1972-73 helmet stickers can be differentiated from the 1974-75 listings (those also feature a 1972 copyright year) by a single-bar face mask design instread of dual-bar.

COMPLETE SET (64) 125.00 250.00
1 Bears Name 4.00 8.00
Cowboys Small Helmet
2 Bears Name 3.00 6.00
Jets helmet
3 Bengals Name 2.00 4.00
Cardinals Helmet
4 Bengals Name 3.00 6.00
Giants Logo Blue
5A Bills Name 4.00 10.00
Chiefs Logo ERR
(Redskins logo instead of Chiefs logo
issued in 1972 packs)
5B Bills Name 2.00 4.00
Chiefs Logo Gold
(Gold background on Chiefs logo
issued in 1973 pack)
6 Bills Name 4.00 8.00
Cowboys Large Helmet
7 Broncos Name 2.00 4.00
Colts Helmet
8 Broncos Name 2.00 4.00
Patriots Logo
9 Broncos Name 4.00 8.00
Redskins Helmet
10 Browns Name 2.00 4.00
Chargers Helmet
11 Browns Name 2.00 4.00
Saints Helmet
12 Cardinals Name (Gold St. Louis) 2.00 4.00
Bengals Logo
13 Cardinals Name 4.00 8.00
Raiders Helmet
14A Chargers Name Lt Blue 1972 3.00 6.00
Bears Helmet White C
14B Chargers Name Lt Blue 1973 3.00 6.00
Bears Helmet Orange C
15 Chiefs Name 2.00 4.00
Browns Helmet
16 Chiefs Name 2.00 4.00
NFL Logo
17 Chiefs Name 2.00 4.00
Rams Helmet
18 Colts Name 2.00 4.00
Saints Logo
19 Colts Name 4.00 8.00
Steelers Logo
20 Cowboys Name 4.00 8.00
Broncos Helmet
21A Cowboys Name 4.00 8.00
Dolphins Helmet
(Dolphins written in print style)
21B Cowboys Name 4.00 8.00
Dolphins Helmet
(Dolphins written in script style)
22 Dolphins Name 3.00 6.00
Vikings Helmet
23 Eagles Name 2.00 4.00
Chiefs Helmet
24 Eagles Name 4.00 8.00
Steelers Helmet
25 Falcons Name 3.00 6.00
Browns Logo
26 Falcons Name 3.00 6.00
Giants Logo Red
27 Falcons Name 2.00 4.00
Oilers Helmet
28 49ers Name 3.00 6.00
Colts Logo
29 49ers Name 4.00 8.00
Packers Logo
30 Giants Name Red 3.00 6.00
Bills Logo
31 Giants Name Blue 2.00 4.00
Lions Logo
32 Jets Name 4.00 8.00
Broncos Logo
33 Jets Name 2.00 4.00
Falcons Logo
34 Lions Name 2.00 4.00
Oilers Logo
35 Lions Name 2.00 4.00
Rams Logo Yellow
36 Lions Name 2.00 4.00
Rams Logo White
37 Oilers Name 2.00 4.00
Cardinals Logo
38 Oilers Name 2.00 4.00
Eagles Helmet
39 Packers Name 3.00 6.00
Chargers Logo light blue
40 Packers Name 3.00 6.00
Eagles Logo
41 Patriots Name 2.00 4.00
Falcons Helmet
42 Patriots Name 3.00 6.00
Jets Logo
43 Raiders Name 4.00 8.00
Redskins Logo Gold
44 Raiders Name 3.00 6.00
Giants Helmet
45A Rams Name 4.00 8.00
Dolphins Logo
(Dolphins written in print style)
45B Rams Name 4.00 8.00
Dolphins Logo
(Dolphins written in script style)
46 Rams Name/49ers Logo 4.00 8.00
47 Redskins Name 2.00 4.00
Bengals Helmet
48 Redskins Name/49ers Helmet 4.00 8.00
49 Saints Name 2.00 4.00
Lions Helmet
50 Saints Name 4.00 8.00
Raiders Logo
51 Steelers Name 4.00 8.00
Packers Helmet
52 Steelers Name 3.00 6.00
Rams Helmet
53 Steelers Name 3.00 6.00
Vikings Logo
54 Vikings Name 3.00 6.00
Bears Logo
55 Vikings Name 3.00 6.00
Bills Helmet
56 Vikings Name 2.00 4.00
Patriots Helmet
57 AFC Conference 4.00 8.00
NFL Logo
Dolphins 1971-72 Champs
58 AFC Conference 4.00 8.00
NFL Logo
Dolphins 1972-73 Champs
59 NFC Conference 4.00 8.00
NFL Logo
Cowboys 1971-72 Champs
60 NFC Conference 4.00 8.00
NFL Logo
Redskins 1972-73 Champs

1973 Fleer Pro Bowl Scouting Report

The 14 cards in this set measure approximately 2 1/2" by 4" and feature an explanation of the ideal size, responsibilities, and assignments of each player on the team. Each card shows a different position. Color artwork illustrates examples of how a player might appear. A diagram shows the position on the field. The words "AFC-NFC Pro Bowl Scouting Cards" are printed at the top and are accented by the NFL logo and underscored by a blue stripe. The backs are blank. The cards are unnumbered and checklisted below in alphabetical order. The cards came one per pack with two cloth football logo patches that are dated 1972. It appears that the same cloth patches were sold each year from 1972 to 1975. In the first year, they were sold alone in packs, while in the following years, they were sold again through packs with the Scouting Report and Hall of Fame issues, respectively.

COMPLETE SET (14) 20.00 40.00
1 Center 1.50 3.00
2 Cornerback 1.50 3.00
3 Defensive End 1.50 3.00
4 Defensive Tackle 1.50 3.00
5 Guard 1.50 3.00
6 Kicker 1.50 3.00
7 Linebacker 1.50 3.00
8 Offensive Tackle 1.50 3.00
9 Punter 1.50 3.00
10 Quarterback 1.50 3.00
11 Running Back 1.50 3.00
12 Safety 1.50 3.00
13 Tight End 1.50 3.00
14 Wide Receiver 1.50 3.00

1974 Fleer Big Signs

This set of 26 "Big Signs" was produced by Fleer in 1974. They are blank backed and measure approximately 7 3/4" by 11 1/2" with rounded corners. They are unnumbered so they are listed below alphabetically by team city name. They are credited at the bottom as 1968 in roman numerals, but in fact were probably issued several years later, perhaps as late as 1974. As another point of reference in dating the set, the New England Patriots changed their name from Boston in 1970. There were two distinct versions of this set, with each version including all 26 teams. The 1968 version was issued in a green box, while the 1974 version was issued in a brown box. Both boxes carry a 1968 copyright date; however, 1974 is generally considered to be the issue date of this second series. Though they are considerably different in design, the size of the collectibles is similar. The generic drawings (of a faceless player from each team) are in color with a white border. The set was licensed by NFL Properties so there are no players identifiably shown.

COMPLETE SET (26) 60.00 100.00
1 Atlanta Falcons 2.00 4.00
2 Baltimore Colts 2.00 4.00
3 Buffalo Bills 2.00 4.00
4 Chicago Bears 2.00 4.00
5 Cincinnati Bengals 2.00 4.00
6 Cleveland Browns 2.00 4.00
7 Dallas Cowboys 4.00 8.00
8 Denver Broncos 2.00 4.00
9 Detroit Lions 2.00 4.00
10 Green Bay Packers 4.00 8.00
11 Houston Oilers 2.00 4.00
12 Kansas City Chiefs 2.00 4.00
13 Los Angeles Rams 2.00 4.00
14 Miami Dolphins 3.00 6.00
15 Minnesota Vikings 2.00 4.00
16 New England Patriots 2.00 4.00
17 New Orleans Saints 2.00 4.00
18 New York Giants 2.00 4.00
19 New York Jets 2.00 4.00
20 Oakland Raiders 4.00 8.00
21 Philadelphia Eagles 2.00 4.00
22 Pittsburgh Steelers 3.00 6.00
23 St. Louis Cardinals 2.00 4.00
24 San Diego Chargers 2.00 4.00
25 San Francisco 49ers 3.00 6.00
26 Washington Redskins 3.00 6.00

1974 Fleer Hall of Fame

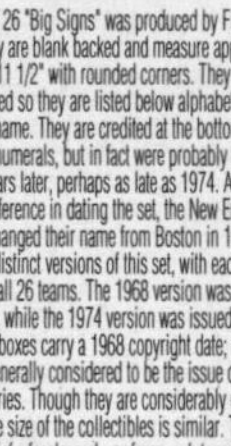

The 1974 Fleer Hall of Fame football card set contains 50 players inducted into the Pro Football Hall of Fame in Canton, Ohio. The cards measure approximately 2 1/2" by 4". The fronts feature black and white photos, white borders, and a cartoon head of a football player flanked by the words "The Immortal Roll." The backs contain biographical data and a stylized Pro Football Hall of Fame logo. The cards are unnumbered and can be distinguished from cards of the 1975 Fleer Hall of Fame set by this lack of numbering as well as the white border on the fronts. The cards are arranged and numbered below alphabetically by player's name for convenience. The cards were originally issued in wax packs with one Hall of Fame card and two cloth team logo stickers.

COMPLETE SET (50) 35.00 70.00
1 Cliff Battles .50 1.25
2 Sammy Baugh 1.50 3.00
3 Chuck Bednarik .75 1.50
4 Bert Bell COMM .40 1.00
OWN
5 Paul Brown CO 1.00 2.00
OWN
FOUNDER
6 Joe Carr PRES .40 1.00
7 Guy Chamberlin .40 1.00
8 Dutch Clark .50 1.25
9 Jimmy Conzelman .40 1.00
10 Art Donovan .75 1.50
11 Paddy Driscoll .40 1.00
12 Bill Dudley .50 1.25
13 Dan Fortmann .40 1.00
14 Otto Graham 1.50 3.00
15 Red Grange 2.00 4.00
16 George Halas CO 1.00 2.00
OWN
FOUNDER
17 Mel Hein .40 1.00
18 Fats Henry .40 1.00
19 Bill Hewitt .40 1.00
20 Clarke Hinkle .40 1.00
21 Elroy Hirsch .75 1.50
22 Robert(Cal) Hubbard .40 1.00
23 Lamar Hunt OWN .40 1.00
FOUNDER
24 Don Hutson .50 1.25
25 Earl Lambeau CO .40 1.00
OWN
FOUNDER
26 Bobby Layne 1.25 2.50
27 Vince Lombardi CO 2.00 4.00
28 Sid Luckman 1.00 2.00
29 Gino Marchetti .50 1.25
30 Ollie Matson .75 1.50
31 George McAfee .50 1.25
32 Hugh McElhenny .75 1.50
33 Johnny Blood McNally .40 1.00
34 Marion Motley .75 1.50
35 Bronko Nagurski 1.25 2.50
36 Ernie Nevers .50 1.25
37 Leo Nomellini .50 1.25
38 Steve Owen CO .40 1.00
39 Joe Perry .75 1.50
40 Pete Pihos .50 1.25
41 Andy Robustelli .75 1.50
42 Ken Strong .50 1.25
43 Jim Thorpe 2.00 4.00
44 Y.A. Tittle 1.25 2.50
45 Charley Trippi .50 1.25
46 Emlen Tunnell .50 1.25
47 Bulldog Turner .75 1.50
48 Norm Van Brocklin 1.00 2.00
49 Steve Van Buren .75 1.50
50 Bob Waterfield 1.00 2.00

1974-75 Fleer Cloth Patches

These cloth stickers were inserted one per pack in 1974 and 1975 Fleer Hall of Fame packs although each includes a 1972 copyright year on the fronts. The blankbacked stickers include one small team name sticker at the top and a larger team helmet or team logo at the bottom. We've catalogued and priced the stickers as pairs according to the smaller team name sticker first and the larger sticker second. Most of the stickers were nearly identical for both years except that the 1974 issue features no trademark (TM) notation on the fronts while the 1975 stickers include two trademark (TM) symbols. They are also very similar to the 1972-73 stickers and are often confused with them due to the 1972 copyright year printed on the fronts. However, the helmet stickers can be differentiated from the 1972-73 listings by the double-bar face mask design instead of single-bar. Most of the 1974 team logo stickers cannot be differentiated from the 1972-73 logo stickers and therefore are not listed below. However, the 1975 team logo stickers are priced below (marked with an *) since they do feature the trademark (TM) symbol distinction on the logo sticker portion.

COMPLETE SET (62) 125.00 250.00
1 Bears Name 4.00 8.00
Cowboys Small Helmet
2 Bears Name 3.00 6.00
Jets helmet
3 Bengals Name 2.00 4.00
Cardinals Helmet
4 Bengals Name 3.00 6.00
Giants Logo TM *
5A Bills Name 2.00 4.00
Chiefs Logo Yellow *
5B Bills Name 2.00 4.00
Chiefs Logo Yellow TM
6 Bills Name 4.00 8.00
Cowboys Large Helmet
7 Broncos Name 2.00 4.00
Colts Helmet
8 Broncos Name 2.00 4.00
Patriots Logo *
9 Broncos Name 4.00 8.00
Redskins Helmet
10 Browns Name 2.00 4.00
Chargers Helmet
11 Browns Name 2.00 4.00
Saints Helmet
12A Cardinals Name No TM 2.00 4.00
(yellow St. Louis)
Bengals Logo
12B Cardinals Name TM 2.00 4.00
(yellow St. Louis)
Bengals Logo
13 Cardinals Name 4.00 8.00
Raiders Helmet
14 Chargers Name Dark Blue 3.00 6.00
Bears Helmet Orange C
15 Chiefs Name 2.00 4.00
Browns Helmet
16 Chiefs Name 2.00 4.00
NFL Logo *
17 Colts Name 2.00 4.00
Saints Logo *
18 Colts Name 4.00 8.00
Steelers Logo *
19 Cowboys Name 4.00 8.00
Broncos Helmet
20 Cowboys Name 4.00 8.00
Dolphins Helmet
21 Dolphins Name 3.00 6.00
Vikings Helmet
22 Eagles Name 2.00 4.00
Chiefs Helmet
23 Eagles Name 4.00 8.00
Steelers Helmet
24 Falcons Name 3.00 6.00
Browns Logo *
25 Falcons Name 3.00 6.00
Giants Logo *
26 Falcons Name 2.00 4.00
Oilers Helmet
27 49ers Name 3.00 6.00
Colts Logo *
28 49ers Name 4.00 8.00
Packers Logo *
29 Giants Name 3.00 6.00
Bills Logo *
30 Giants Name 2.00 4.00
Lions Logo *
31 Jets Name 4.00 8.00
Broncos Logo *
32 Jets Name 2.00 4.00
Falcons Logo *
33 Lions Name 2.00 4.00
Oilers Logo *
34 Lions Name 2.00 4.00
Rams Logo Yellow *
35 Oilers Name 2.00 4.00
Cardinals Logo *
36 Oilers Name 2.00 4.00
Eagles Helmet
37A Packers Name 3.00 6.00
Chargers Logo No TM
(dark blue)
37B Packers Name 3.00 6.00
Chargers Logo TM
(dark blue)
38 Packers Name 3.00 6.00
Eagles Logo *
39 Patriots Name 2.00 4.00
Falcons Helmet
40 Patriots Name 3.00 6.00
Jets Logo *
41A Raiders Name 4.00 8.00
Redskins Logo TM
(yellow Redskins name)
41B Raiders Name 4.00 8.00
Redskins Logo No TM
(yellow Redskins name)
42 Raiders Name 3.00 6.00
Giants Helmet
43 Rams Name 4.00 8.00
Dolphins Logo *
44 Rams Name/49ers Logo * 4.00 8.00
45 Redskins Name 2.00 4.00
Bengals Helmet
46 Redskins Name/49ers Helmet 4.00 8.00
47 Saints Name 2.00 4.00
Lions Helmet
48 Saints Name 4.00 8.00
Raiders Logo *
49 Steelers Name 4.00 8.00
Packers Helmet
50 Steelers Name 3.00 6.00
Rams Helmet
51 Steelers Name 3.00 6.00
Vikings Logo *
52 Vikings Name 3.00 6.00
Bears Logo *
53 Vikings Name 3.00 6.00
Bills Helmet
54 Vikings Name 2.00 4.00
Patriots Helmet
55 AFC Conference 4.00 8.00
AFC Logo
Dolphins 1973-74 Champs
56 AFC Conference 4.00 8.00
AFC Logo
Steelers 1974-75 Champs
57 NFC Conference 4.00 8.00
NFC Logo
Vikings 1973-74 Champs
58 NFC Conference 4.00 8.00
NFC Logo
Vikings 1974-75 Champs

1975 Fleer Hall of Fame

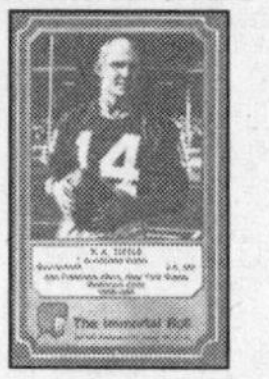

The 1975 Fleer Hall of Fame football card set contains 84 cards. The cards measure 2 1/2" by 4". Except for the change in border color from white to brown and the different set numbering contained on the backs of the cards, fifty of the cards in this set are very similar to the cards in the 1974 Fleer set. Thirty-four additional cards have been added to this set in comparison to the 1974 set. These cards are numbered and were issued in wax packs with cloth team logo stickers.

COMPLETE SET (84) 40.00 80.00
1 Jim Thorpe 1.50 3.00
2 Cliff Battles .40 1.00
3 Bronko Nagurski 1.00 2.00
4 Red Grange 1.50 3.00
5 Guy Chamberlin .30 .75
6 Joe Carr PRES .30 .75
7 George Halas CO .75 1.50
OWN/
FOUNDER
8 Jimmy Conzelman .30 .75
9 George McAfee .40 1.00
10 Clarke Hinkle .30 .75
11 Paddy Driscoll .30 .75
12 Mel Hein .30 .75
13 Johnny Blood McNally .30 .75
14 Dutch Clark .40 1.00
15 Steve Owen CO .30 .75
16 Bill Hewitt .30 .75
17 Robert(Cal) Hubbard .30 .75
18 Don Hutson .63 1.25
19 Ernie Nevers .40 1.00
20 Dan Fortmann .30 .75
21 Ken Strong .40 1.00
22 Chuck Bednarik .63 1.25
23 Bert Bell COMM .30 .75
OWN
24 Paul Brown CO .75 1.50
OWN
FOUND
25 Art Donovan .63 1.25
26 Bill Dudley .40 1.00
27 Otto Graham 1.00 2.00
28 Fats Henry .40 1.00
29 Elroy Hirsch .63 1.25
30 Lamar Hunt OWN .30 .75
FOUND
31 Curly Lambeau CO .30 .75
OWN
FOUNDER
32 Vince Lombardi CO 1.50 3.00
33 Sid Luckman .75 1.50
34 Gino Marchetti .40 1.00
35 Ollie Matson .63 1.25
36 Hugh McElhenny .63 1.25
37 Marion Motley .40 1.00
38 Leo Nomellini .40 1.00
39 Joe Perry .63 1.25
40 Andy Robustelli .40 1.00
41 Pete Pihos .40 1.00
42 Y.A. Tittle 1.00 2.00
43 Charley Trippi .40 1.00
44 Emlen Tunnell .40 1.00
45 Bulldog Turner .63 1.25
46 Norm Van Brocklin .75 1.50
47 Steve Van Buren .63 1.25
48 Bob Waterfield .75 1.50
49 Bobby Layne 1.00 2.00
50 Sammy Baugh 1.25 2.50
51 Joe Guyon .30 .75
52 Roy(Link) Lyman .30 .75
53 George Trafton .30 .75
54 Turk Edwards .30 .75
55 Ed Healey .30 .75
56 Mike Michalske .30 .75
57 Alex Wojciechowicz .30 .75
58 Dante Lavelli .63 1.25
59 George Connor .40 1.00
60 Wayne Millner .30 .75
61 Jack Christiansen .30 .75
62 Roosevelt Brown .30 .75
63 Joe Stydahar .30 .75
64 Ernie Stautner .40 1.00
65 Jim Parker .40 1.00
66 Raymond Berry .63 1.25
67 Geo.Preston Marshall .30 .75
OWN
FOUND
68 Clarence(Ace) Parker .30 .75
69 Greasy Neale CO .30 .75
70 Tim Mara OWN .30 .75
FOUND
71 Hugh(Shorty) Ray OFF .30 .75
72 Tom Fears .40 1.00
73 Arnie Herber .30 .75
74 Walt Kiesling .30 .75
75 Frank(Bruiser) Kinard .30 .75
76 Tony Canadeo .30 .75
77 Bill George .30 .75
78 Art Rooney FOUND .30 .75
OWN
ADMIN
79 Joe Schmidt .40 1.00
80 Dan Reeves OWN .30 .75
81 Lou Groza .63 1.25
82 Charles W. Bidwill OWN .30 .75
83 Lenny Moore .63 1.25
84 Dick(Night Train) Lane .40 1.00

1976 Fleer Cloth Patches

These cloth stickers were sold as a stand alone product and do not feature any copyright year on them. The blankbacked stickers include one small team name sticker at the top and a larger team helmet or team logo at the bottom. We've catalogued and priced the stickers as pairs according to the smaller team name sticker first and the larger sticker second. Many of the stickers can be confused with the 1972-73 and 1974-75 sets, but this year has no date designation.

1 Bears Name 3.00 6.00
Cowboys Small Helmet
2 Bears Name 2.50 5.00
Jets helmet
3 Bengals Name 2.00 4.00
Cardinals Helmet
4 Bengals Name 2.50 5.00
Giants Logo
6 Bills Name 2.00 4.00
Chiefs Logo
7 Bills Name 3.00 6.00
Cowboys Large Helmet
8 Broncos Name 2.00 4.00
Colts Helmet
9 Broncos Name 2.00 4.00
Patriots Logo
10 Broncos Name 3.00 6.00
Redskins Helmet.
11 Browns Name 2.00 4.00
- Chargers Helmet
12 Browns Name 2.00 4.00
Saints Helmet
13 Buccaneers Name 2.00 4.00
Seahawks Helmet
14 Buccaneers Name 2.00 4.00
Seahawks Logo
15 Cardinals Name 2.00 4.00
Bengals Logo
16 Cardinals Name 3.00 6.00
Raiders Helmet
17 Chargers Name 2.50 5.00
Bears Helmet
18 Chiefs Name 2.50 5.00
Browns Helmet
19 Colts Name 2.00 4.00
Saints Logo
20 Colts Name 3.00 6.00
Steelers Logo
21 Cowboys Name 3.00 6.00
Broncos Helmet
22 Cowboys Name 3.00 6.00
Dolphins Helmet
23 Dolphins Name 2.50 5.00
Vikings Logo
24 Eagles Name 2.00 4.00
Chiefs Helmet
25 Eagles Name 3.00 6.00
Steelers Helmet
26 Falcons Name 2.50 5.00
Browns Logo
27 Falcons Name 2.00 4.00
Oilers Helmet
28 49ers Name 2.50 5.00
Colts Logo
29 49ers Name 3.00 6.00
Packers Logo
30 Giants Name 2.50 5.00
Bills Logo
31 Giants Name 2.00 4.00
Lions Logo
32 Jets Name 3.00 6.00
Broncos Logo
33 Jets Name 2.00 4.00
Falcons Logo
34 Lions Name 2.00 4.00
Oilers Helmet
35 Lions Name 2.00 4.00
Rams Logo
36 Oilers Name 2.00 4.00
Cardinals Logo
37 Oilers Name 2.00 4.00
Eagles Helmet
38 Packers Name 2.50 5.00
Chargers Logo
39 Packers Name 2.50 5.00
Eagles Logo
40 Patriots Name 2.00 4.00
Falcons Helmet
41 Patriots Name 2.50 5.00
Jets Logo
42 Raiders Name 3.00 6.00
Redskins Logo
43 Raiders Name 2.50 5.00
Giants Helmet
44 Rams Name 3.00 6.00
Dolphins Logo
45 Rams Name/49ers Logo 3.00 6.00
46 Redskins Name 2.00 4.00
Bengals Helmet
47 Redskins Name/49ers Helmet 3.00 6.00
48 Saints Name 2.00 4.00
Lions Helmet
49 Saints Name 3.00 6.00
Raiders Logo
49 Seahawks Name 2.00 4.00
Buccaneers Helmet
50 Seahawks Name 2.00 4.00
Buccaneers Logo
51 Steelers Name 3.00 6.00
Packers Helmet
52 Steelers Name 2.50 5.00
Rams Helmet
53 Steelers Name 2.50 5.00
Vikings Logo
54 Vikings Name 2.50 5.00
Bears Logo
55 Vikings Name 2.50 5.00
Bills Helmet
56 Vikings Name 2.00 4.00
Patriots Helmet

1976 Fleer Hi Gloss Patches

Fleer issued these helmet and logo stickers in 1976 as a separate product packaged in its own wrapper with two Hi Gloss paper stickers and one Cloth Patch in each pack. Each card is blankbacked and features a small team name sticker at the top and a larger logo or helmet sticker at the bottom. We've cataloged the set in order by the team name on top. Note that no year of issue was printed on the stickers.

COMPLETE SET (56) 125.00 225.00
*CLOTH VERSION: .5X TO 1.2X
1 Bears Name 3.00 6.00
Cowboys Small Helmet
2 Bears Name 2.50 5.00
Jets helmet
3 Bengals Name 2.00 4.00
Cardinals Helmet
4 Bengals Name 2.50 5.00
Giants Logo
6 Bills Name 2.00 4.00
Chiefs Logo
7 Bills Name 3.00 6.00
Cowboys Large Helmet
8 Broncos Name 2.00 4.00
Colts Helmet
9 Broncos Name 2.00 4.00
Patriots Logo
10 Broncos Name 3.00 6.00
Redskins Helmet
11 Browns Name 2.00 4.00
Chargers Helmet
12 Browns Name 2.00 4.00
Saints Helmet
13 Buccaneers Name 2.00 4.00
Seahawks Helmet
14 Buccaneers Name 2.00 4.00
Seahawks Logo
15 Cardinals Name 2.00 4.00
Bengals Logo
16 Cardinals Name 3.00 6.00
Raiders Helmet
17 Chargers Name 2.50 5.00
Bears Helmet
18 Chiefs Name 2.50 5.00
Browns Helmet
19 Colts Name 2.00 4.00
Saints Logo
20 Colts Name 3.00 6.00
Steelers Logo
21 Cowboys Name 3.00 6.00
Broncos Helmet
22 Cowboys Name 3.00 6.00
Dolphins Helmet
23 Dolphins Name 2.50 5.00
Vikings Logo
24 Eagles Name 2.00 4.00
Chiefs Helmet
25 Eagles Name 3.00 6.00
Steelers Helmet
26 Falcons Name 2.50 5.00
Browns Logo
27 Falcons Name 2.00 4.00
Oilers Helmet
28 49ers Name 2.50 5.00
Colts Logo
29 49ers Name 3.00 6.00
Packers Logo
30 Giants Name 2.50 5.00
Bills Logo
31 Giants Name 2.00 4.00
Lions Logo
32 Jets Name 3.00 6.00
Broncos Logo
33 Jets Name 2.00 4.00
Falcons Logo
34 Lions Name 2.00 4.00
Oilers Helmet
35 Lions Name 2.00 4.00
Rams Logo
36 Oilers Name 2.00 4.00
Cardinals Logo
37 Oilers Name 2.00 4.00
Eagles Helmet
38 Packers Name 2.50 5.00
Chargers Logo
39 Packers Name 2.50 5.00
Eagles Logo
40 Patriots Name 2.00 4.00
Falcons Helmet
41 Patriots Name 2.50 5.00
Jets Logo
42 Raiders Name 3.00 6.00
Redskins Logo
43 Raiders Name 2.50 5.00
Giants Helmet
44 Rams Name 3.00 6.00
Dolphins Logo
45 Rams Name/49ers Logo 3.00 6.00
46 Redskins Name 2.00 4.00
Bengals Helmet
47 Redskins Name/49ers Helmet 3.00 6.00
48 Saints Name 2.00 4.00
Lions Helmet
49 Seahawks Name 2.00 4.00
Buccaneers Helmet
49 Saints Name 3.00 6.00
Raiders Logo
50 Seahawks Name 2.00 4.00
Buccaneers Logo
51 Steelers Name 3.00 6.00
Packers Helmet
52 Steelers Name 2.50 5.00
Rams Helmet
53 Steelers Name 2.50 5.00
Vikings Logo
54 Vikings Name 2.50 5.00
Bears Logo
55 Vikings Name 2.50 5.00
Bills Helmet
56 Vikings Name 2.00 4.00
Patriots Helmet

1976 Fleer Team Action

This 66-card standard-size set contains cards picturing action scenes with two cards for every NFL team and then a card for each previous Super Bowl. The first card in each team pair, i.e., the odd-numbered card, is an offensive card; the even-numbered cards are defensive scenes. Cards have a white border with a red outline on the front; the backs are printed with black ink on white cardboard stock with a light blue NFL emblem superimposed in the middle of the write-up on the back of the card. These cards are actually stickers as they may be peeled and stuck. The instructions on the back of the sticker say, "For use as sticker, bend corner and peel." The cards were issued in four-card packs with no inserts, unlike earlier Fleer football issues.

COMPLETE SET (66) 300.00 600.00
1 Baltimore Colts 4.50 9.00
High Scorers
2 Baltimore Colts 4.00 8.00
Effective Tackle
3 Buffalo Bills 4.00 8.00
Perfect Blocking
4 Buffalo Bills 4.00 8.00
The Sack
5 Cincinnati Bengals 4.00 8.00
Being Hit Behind
The Runner
6 Cincinnati Bengals 6.00 12.00
A Little Help
(Tackling Franco Harris)
7 Cleveland Browns 4.00 8.00
Blocking Tight End
8 Cleveland Browns 4.00 8.00
Stopping the
Double Threat
9 Denver Broncos 4.00 8.00
The Swing Pass
10 Denver Broncos 4.00 8.00
The Gang Tackle
11 Houston Oilers 5.00 10.00
Short Zone Flood
(Dan Pastorini passing)
12 Houston Oilers 6.00 12.00
Run Stoppers
(Franco Harris running)
13 Kansas City Chiefs 4.00 8.00
Off On the Ball
14 Kansas City Chiefs 4.00 8.00
Forcing the Scramble
15 Miami Dolphins 6.00 12.00
Pass Protection
(Bob Griese)
16 Miami Dolphins 5.00 10.00
Natural Turf
17 New England Patriots 4.00 8.00
Quicker Than the Eye
18 New England Patriots 4.00 8.00
The Rugby Touch
19 New York Jets 7.50 15.00
They Run& Too
(John Riggins and
Joe Namath)
20 New York Jets 6.00 12.00
The Buck Stops Here
(O.J.Simpson tackled)
21 Oakland Raiders 5.00 10.00
A Strong Offense
22 Oakland Raiders 5.00 10.00
High and Low
23 Pittsburgh Steelers 7.50 15.00
The Pitch-Out
(Terry Bradshaw&
Franco Harris& and
Rocky Bleier)
24 Pittsburgh Steelers 6.00 12.00
The Takeaway
(Jack Ham)
25 San Diego Chargers 4.00 8.00
Run to Daylight
26 San Diego Chargers 4.00 8.00
The Swarm
27 Tampa Bay Buccaneers 4.00 8.00
Stadium
28 Tampa Bay Buccaneers 4.00 8.00
Buccaneers Uniform
29 Atlanta Falcons 4.00 8.00
A Key Block
30 Atlanta Falcons 4.00 8.00
Breakthrough
(Robert Newhouse)
31 Chicago Bears 4.00 8.00
An Inside Look
32 Chicago Bears 4.00 8.00
Defensive Emphasis

33 Dallas Cowboys 5.00 10.00
Eight-Yard Burst
(Robert Newhouse)
34 Dallas Cowboys 5.00 10.00
The Big Return
(Cliff Harris)
35 Detroit Lions 4.00 8.00
Power Sweep
36 Detroit Lions 4.00 8.00
A Tough Defense
37 Green Bay Packers 4.00 8.00
Tearaway Gain
38 Green Bay Packers 4.00 8.00
Good Support
39 Los Angeles Rams 4.00 8.00
(Cullen Bryant)
40 Los Angeles Rams 4.00 8.00
Low-Point Defense
(Lydell Mitchell)
41 Minnesota Vikings 6.00 12.00
The Running Guards
(Fran Tarkenton and
Chuck Foreman)
42 Minnesota Vikings 4.00 8.00
A Stingy Defense
43 New York Giants 4.00 8.00
The Quick Opener
44 New York Giants 4.00 8.00
Defending a Tradition
45 New Orleans Saints 5.00 10.00
Head for the Hole
(Archie Manning)
46 New Orleans Saints 4.00 8.00
The Contain Man
47 Philadelphia Eagles 4.00 8.00
Line Signals
48 Philadelphia Eagles 4.00 8.00
Don't Take Sides
49 San Francisco 49ers 4.00 8.00
The Clues
50 San Francisco 49ers 4.00 8.00
Goal-Line Stand
51 St. Louis Cardinals 5.00 10.00
Nonskid Handoff
(Jim Hart)
52 St. Louis Cardinals 4.00 8.00
Strong Pursuit
53 Seattle Seahawks 4.00 8.00
Stadium
54 Seattle Seahawks 4.00 8.00
Uniform
55 Washington Redskins 5.00 10.00
A Fancy Passing
(Billy Kilmer)
56 Washington Redskins 4.00 8.00
Let's Go Defense
(Chris Hanburger)
57 Super Bowl I 6.00 12.00
Green Bay NFL 35
Kansas City AFL 10
(Jim Taylor)
58 Super Bowl II 6.00 12.00
Green Bay NFL 33
Oakland AFL 14
(Ben Davidson)
59 Super Bowl III 6.00 12.00
New York AFL 16
Baltimore NFL 7
60 Super Bowl IV 6.00 12.00
Kansas City AFL 23
Minnesota NFL 7
61 Super Bowl V 6.00 12.00
Baltimore AFC 16
Dallas NFC 13
62 Super Bowl VI 10.00 20.00
Dallas NFC 24
Miami AFC 3
(Walt Garrison and
Roger Staubach)
63 Super Bowl VII 7.50 15.00
Miami AFC 14
Washington NFC 7
(Larry Csonka)
64 Super Bowl VIII 7.50 15.00
Miami AFC 24
Minnesota NFC 7
(Larry Csonka diving)
65 Super Bowl IX 6.00 12.00
Pittsburgh AFC 16
Minnesota NFC 6
66 Super Bowl X 25.00 40.00
Pittsburgh AFC 21
Dallas NFC 17
(Terry Bradshaw and
Franco Harris)

1977 Fleer Team Action

The 1977 Fleer Teams in Action football set contains 67 standard-size cards depicting action scenes. There are two cards for each NFL team and one card for each Super Bowl. The first card in each team pair, i.e., the odd-numbered card, is an offensive card; the even-numbered cards are defensive scenes. The cards have white borders and the backs are printed in dark blue ink on gray stock. The cards are numbered and contain a 1977 copyright date. The cards were issued in four-card wax packs along with four team logo stickers.

COMPLETE SET (67) 40.00 80.00
1 Baltimore Colts 1.25 2.50
The Easy Chair
(Bert Jones)
2 Baltimore Colts .63 1.25
A Handy Solution
3 Buffalo Bills .63 1.25
Blocking Tight End
4 Buffalo Bills .63 1.25
Search And Destroy
5 Cincinnati Bengals 1.00 2.00
Cutting on a Rug
(Ken Anderson hand off)
6 Cincinnati Bengals .63 1.25
Strength in
the Middle
7 Cleveland Browns .75 1.50
Snap& Drop& Set
(Brian Sipe)
8 Cleveland Browns .63 1.25
High and Low
9 Denver Broncos .63 1.25
Green Light
10 Denver Broncos .63 1.25
Help From Behind
11 Houston Oilers .63 1.25
Room to Move
12 Houston Oilers .63 1.25
For The Defense
13 Kansas City Chiefs .63 1.25
Chance to Motor
14 Kansas City Chiefs .63 1.25
From the Ground Up
15 Miami Dolphins .75 1.50
Eye of the Storm
16 Miami Dolphins .75 1.50
When Man Takes
Flight
17 New England Patriots .63 1.25
Turning the Corner
18 New England Patriots .63 1.25
A Matter of Inches
19 New York Jets 4.00 8.00
Keeping Him Clean
(Joe Namath)
20 New York Jets .63 1.25
Plugging the Leaks
21 Oakland Raiders .75 1.50
On Solid Ground
22 Oakland Raiders/3-4& Shut The Door .75 1.50
23 Pittsburgh Steelers 1.00 2.00
Daylight Saving
Time (Rocky Bleier)
24 Pittsburgh Steelers .75 1.50
A Controlled Swarm
25 San Diego Chargers 2.00 4.00
Youth on the Move
(Dan Fouts)
26 San Diego Chargers .63 1.25
A Rude Housewarming
27 Seattle Seahawks 1.00 2.00
Play Action Pass
(Jim Zorn faking)
28 Seattle Seahawks .75 1.50
Birds of Prey
29 Atlanta Falcons .63 1.25
Ad-Libbing
on Offense
30 Atlanta Falcons .63 1.25
A Futile Chase
31 Chicago Bears 3.00 6.00
Follow Me
(Walter Payton blocking)
32 Chicago Bears .63 1.25
A Nose for
the Ball
33 Dallas Cowboys .75 1.50
The Plunge
34 Dallas Cowboys 1.25 2.50
Unassisted Sack
(Ed Too Tall Jones)
35 Detroit Lions .63 1.25
Motor City Might
36 Detroit Lions .63 1.25
Block Party
37 Green Bay Packers .63 1.25
Another Era
38 Green Bay Packers 3.00 6.00
Face-to-Face
(Walter Payton tackled)
39 Los Angeles Rams .63 1.25
Personal Escort
40 Los Angeles Rams .63 1.25
A Closed Case
41 Minnesota Vikings .63 1.25
Nothing Fancy
42 Minnesota Vikings .63 1.25
Lending A Hand
43 New Orleans Saints .63 1.25
Ample Protection
44 New Orleans Saints .63 1.25
Well-Timed Contact
45 New York Giants .63 1.25
Quick Pitch
46 New York Giants .63 1.25
In A Pinch
47 Philadelphia Eagles .63 1.25
When to Fly
48 Philadelphia Eagles .63 1.25
Swooping Defense
49 St. Louis Cardinals .75 1.50
Speed Outside
(Jim Hart)
50 St. Louis Cardinals .63 1.25
The Circle Tightens
51 San Francisco 49ers .75 1.50
Sideline Route
(Gene Washington)
52 San Francisco 49ers .75 1.50
The Gold Rush
53 Tampa Bay Buccaneers .63 1.25
A Rare Occasion
54 Tampa Bay Buccaneers .63 1.25
Expansion Blues
55 Washington Redskins 1.25 2.50
Splitting the Seam
(Joe Theismann passing)
56 Washington Redskins .75 1.50
The Hands of Time
57 Super Bowl I .75 1.50
Green Bay NFL 35
Kansas City AFL 10
58 Super Bowl II .75 1.50
Green Bay NFL 33
Oakland AFL 14
59 Super Bowl III .75 1.50
New York AFL 16
Baltimore NFL 7
(Tom Matte running)
60 Super Bowl IV .75 1.50
Kansas City AFL 23
Minnesota NFL 7
61 Super Bowl V .75 1.50
Baltimore AFC 16
Dallas NFC 13
62 Super Bowl VI 2.00 4.00
Dallas NFC 24
Miami AFC 3
(Walt Garrison
running; Roger Staubach
also shown)
63 Super Bowl VII 1.25 2.50
Miami AFC 14
Washington NFC 7
(Larry Csonka
running)
64 Super Bowl VIII 1.25 2.50
Miami AFC 24
Minnesota NFC 7
(Larry Csonka
running)
65 Super Bowl IX .75 1.50
Pittsburgh AFC 16
Minnesota NFC 6
66 Super Bowl X 2.00 4.00
Pittsburgh AFC 21
Dallas NFC 17
(Terry Bradshaw
and Franco Harris)
67 Super Bowl XI 2.00 4.00
Oakland AFC 32
Minnesota NFC 14
(Ken Stabler)

1977 Fleer Team Action Stickers

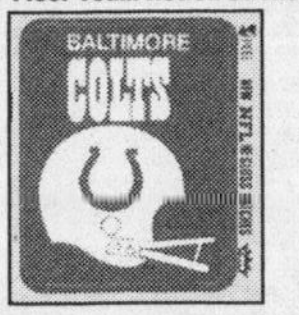

This set of stickers was issued one per pack in the 1977 Fleer Team Action card release. Each NFL team is represented with two stickers, with all but the Cowboys and Seahawks having both a helmet sticker and logo/insignia sticker. Several were produced with slight color variations in the border as noted below. Although these and other similar stickers were released over a number of years, the exact year of issue can be identified by the unique sticker back -- an artist's drawing of fingers peeling away a Jets helmet sticker. Two separate posters were also released to house the stickers; one for each conference. Each sticker measures roughly 2 3/8" by 2 3/4."

COMPLETE SET (65) 100.00 200.00
1A Atlanta Falcons 1.25 3.00
Helmet
(blue border)
1B Atlanta Falcons 1.25 3.00
Helmet
(red border)
2 Atlanta Falcons 1.25 3.00
Logo
3A Baltimore Colts 1.25 3.00
Helmet
(blue border)
3B Baltimore Colts 1.25 3.00
Helmet
(yellow border)
4 Baltimore Colts 1.25 3.00
Logo
5 Buffalo Bills 1.50 4.00
Helmet
6 Buffalo Bills 1.50 4.00
Logo
7A Chicago Bears 1.50 4.00
Helmet
(blue border)
7B Chicago Bears 1.50 4.00
Helmet
(red border)
8 Chicago Bears 1.50 4.00
Logo
9 Cincinnati Bengals 1.25 3.00
Helmet
10 Cincinnati Bengals 1.25 3.00
Logo
11 Cleveland Browns 1.50 4.00
Helmet
12 Cleveland Browns 1.50 4.00
Logo
13 Dallas Cowboys 2.00 5.00
Helmet
(large helmet)
14 Dallas Cowboys 2.00 5.00
Helmet
(small helmet)
15 Denver Broncos 2.00 5.00
Helmet
16 Denver Broncos 2.00 5.00
Logo
17 Detroit Lions 1.25 3.00
Helmet
18 Detroit Lions 1.25 3.00
Logo
19 Green Bay Packers 2.00 5.00
Helmet
20 Green Bay Packers 2.00 5.00
Logo
21 Houston Oilers 1.25 3.00
Helmet
22 Houston Oilers 1.25 3.00
Logo
23 Kansas City Chiefs 1.25 3.00
Helmet
24 Kansas City Chiefs 1.25 3.00
Logo
25 Los Angeles Rams 1.25 3.00
Helmet
26A Los Angeles Rams 1.25 3.00
Logo
(blue border)
26B Los Angeles Rams 1.25 3.00
Logo
(red border)
27 Miami Dolphins 2.00 5.00
Helmet
28 Miami Dolphins 2.00 5.00
Logo
29 Minnesota Vikings 1.50 4.00
Helmet
30 Minnesota Vikings 1.50 4.00
Logo
31A New England Patriots 1.25 3.00
Helmet
(blue border)
31B New England Patriots 1.25 3.00
Helmet
(red border)
32 New England Patriots 1.25 3.00
Logo
33 New Orleans Saints 1.25 3.00
Helmet
34 New Orleans Saints 1.25 3.00
Logo
35 New York Giants 1.50 4.00
Helmet
36 New York Giants 1.50 4.00
Logo
37 New York Jets 1.50 4.00
Helmet
38A New York Jets 1.50 4.00
Logo
(blue border)
38B New York Jets 1.50 4.00
Logo
(green border)
39 Oakland Raiders 2.00 5.00
Helmet
40A Oakland Raiders 2.00 5.00
Logo
(blue border)
40B Oakland Raiders 2.00 5.00
Logo
(yellow border)
41A Philadelphia Eagles 1.25 3.00
Helmet
(blue border)
41B Philadelphia Eagles 1.25 3.00
Helmet
(green border)
42 Philadelphia Eagles 1.25 3.00
Logo
43 Pittsburgh Steelers 2.00 5.00
Helmet
44A Pittsburgh Steelers 2.00 5.00
Logo
(blue border)
44B Pittsburgh Steelers 2.00 5.00
Logo
(yellow border)
45 St. Louis Cardinals 1.25 3.00
Helmet
46 St. Louis Cardinals 1.25 3.00
Logo
47 San Diego Chargers 1.25 3.00
Helmet
48 San Diego Chargers 1.25 3.00
Logo
49 San Francisco 49ers 2.00 5.00
Helmet
50 San Francisco 49ers 2.00 5.00
Logo
51 Seattle Seahawks 1.25 3.00
Helmet
(red border)
52 Seattle Seahawks 1.25 3.00
Helmet
(yellow border)
53 Tampa Bay Bucs 1.25 3.00
Helmet
54 Tampa Bay Bucs 1.25 3.00
Logo
55 Washington Redskins 2.00 5.00
Helmet
56 Washington Redskins 2.00 5.00
Logo
NNO AFC Poster 5.00 10.00
NNO NFC Poster 5.00 10.00

1978 Fleer Team Action

The 1978 Fleer Teams in Action football set contains 68 action scenes. The cards measure the standard size. As in the previous year, each team is depicted on two cards and each Super Bowl is depicted on one card. The additional card in comparison to last year's set comes from the additional Super Bowl which was played during the year. The fronts have yellow borders. The card backs are printed with black ink on gray stock. The cards are numbered and feature a 1978 copyright date. Cards were issued in wax packs of seven team cards plus four team logo stickers.

COMPLETE SET (68) 20.00 40.00
1 Atlanta Falcons .63 1.25
Sticking to Basics
2 Atlanta Falcons .25 .50
In Pursuit
3 Baltimore Colts .25 .50
Forward Plunge
4 Baltimore Colts .25 .50
Stacking It Up
5 Buffalo Bills .25 .50
Daylight Breakers
6 Buffalo Bills .25 .50
Swarming Defense
7 Chicago Bears 3.00 6.00
Up The Middle
(Walter Payton
running)
8 Chicago Bears .25 .50
Rejuvenated Defense
9 Cincinnati Bengals .75 1.50
Poise and Execution
(Ken Anderson)
10 Cincinnati Bengals .25 .50
Down-to-Earth
11 Cleveland Browns .38 .75
Breakaway
(Greg Pruitt)
12 Cleveland Browns .50 1.00
Red Dogs
(Ken Anderson tackled)
13 Dallas Cowboys 3.00 6.00
Up and Over
(Tony Dorsett)
14 Dallas Cowboys .50 1.00
Doomsday II
15 Denver Broncos .25 .50
Mile-High Offense
16 Denver Broncos 2.00 4.00
Orange Crush
(Walter Payton tackled)
17 Detroit Lions .25 .50
End-Around
18 Detroit Lions .25 .50
Special Teams
19 Green Bay Packers .25 .50
Running Strong
20 Green Bay Packers .25 .50
Tearin' em Down
21 Houston Oilers .25 .50
Goal-Line Drive
22 Houston Oilers .25 .50
Interception
23 Kansas City Chiefs .25 .50
Running Wide
(Ed Podolak)
24 Kansas City Chiefs .25 .50
Armed Defense
25 Los Angeles Rams .25 .50
Rushing Power
26 Los Angeles Rams .25 .50
Backing the Line
27 Miami Dolphins 1.50 3.00
Protective Pocket
(Bob Griese passing)
28 Miami Dolphins .38 .75
Life in the Pit
29 Minnesota Vikings .50 1.00
Storm Breakers
(Foreman in snow)
30 Minnesota Vikings .25 .50
Blocking the Kick
31 New England Patriots .25 .50
Clearing The Way
32 New England Patriots .25 .50
One-on-One
33 New Orleans Saints .25 .50
Extra Yardage
34 New Orleans Saints .25 .50
Drag-Down Defense
35 New York Giants .25 .50
Ready& Aim& Fire
36 New York Giants .25 .50
Meeting of Minds
37 New York Jets .25 .50
Take-Off
38 New York Jets .25 .50
Ambush
39 Oakland Raiders .50 1.00
Power 31 Left
40 Oakland Raiders .50 1.00
Welcoming Committee
41 Philadelphia Eagles .40 1.00
Taking Flight
(Vince Papale)
42 Philadelphia Eagles .25 .50
Soaring High
43 Pittsburgh Steelers .38 .75
Ironclad Offense
44 Pittsburgh Steelers .75 1.50
Curtain Closes
(Jack Lambert)
45 St. Louis Cardinals .25 .50
A Good Bet
46 St. Louis Cardinals .25 .50
Gang Tackle
47 San Diego Chargers .25 .50
Circus Catch
48 San Diego Chargers .25 .50
Charge
49 San Francisco 49ers .50 1.00
Follow the Block
50 San Francisco 49ers .50 1.00
Goal-Line Stand
51 Seattle Seahawks .25 .50
Finding Daylight
52 Seattle Seahawks .25 .50
Rushing The Pass
53 Tampa Bay Buccaneers .25 .50
Play Action
54 Tampa Bay Buccaneers .25 .50
Youth on the Move
55 Washington Redskins .38 .75
Renegade Runners
56 Washington Redskins .38 .75
Dual Action
57 Super Bowl I 1.00 2.00
Green Bay NFL 35
Kansas City AFL 10
(Bart Starr)
58 Super Bowl II .38 .75
Green Bay NFL 33
Oakland AFL 14
59 Super Bowl III .38 .75
New York AFL 16
Baltimore NFL 7
60 Super Bowl IV .38 .75
Kansas City AFL 23
Minnesota NFL 7
61 Super Bowl V .38 .75
Baltimore AFC 16
Dallas NFC 13
62 Super Bowl VI .38 .75
Dallas NFC 24
Miami AFC 3
63 Super Bowl VII .38 .75
Miami AFC 14
Washington NFC 7
64 Super Bowl VIII 1.00 2.00
Miami AFC 24
Minnesota NFC 7
(Larry Csonka
running)
65 Super Bowl IX 1.50 3.00
Pittsburgh AFC 16
Minnesota NFC 6
(Terry Bradshaw
and Franco Harris)
66 Super Bowl X .38 .75
Pittsburgh AFC 21
Dallas NFC 17
67 Super Bowl XI .75 1.50
Oakland AFC 32
Minnesota NFC 14
(Ken Stabler hand off)
68 Super Bowl XII 2.00 4.00
Dallas NFC 27
Denver AFC 10
(Roger Staubach and
Tony Dorsett)

1978 Fleer Team Action Stickers

This set of stickers was issued one per pack in the 1978 Fleer Team Action card release and is virtually identical to the 1979 set. Each NFL team is represented with two stickers, with all but the Cowboys and Seahawks having both a helmet sticker and logo/insignia sticker. Several were produced with slight color variations in the border as noted below. Although these and other similar stickers were released over a number of years, the exact year of issue can be identified by the unique sticker back -- a puzzle piece that forms a photo from Super Bowl XII when fully assembled. Note that there are a number of puzzle back variations for each team. Very few collectors attempt to assemble a full set with all back variations. Reportedly, there are 170-total different sticker combinations of fronts and backs. We've noted the number of known back variations for each sticker below. Each sticker measures roughly 2 3/8" by 2 3/4."

COMPLETE SET (65) 70.00 120.00
1A Atlanta Falcons .75 1.50
Helmet 1
(blue border)
1B Atlanta Falcons .75 1.50
Helmet 3
(red border)
2 Atlanta Falcons .75 1.50
Logo 3
3A Baltimore Colts 1.25 2.50
Helmet 1
(blue border)
3B Baltimore Colts 1.25 2.50
Helmet 2
(yellow border)
4 Baltimore Colts 1.25 2.50
Logo 3
5 Buffalo Bills 1.25 2.50
Helmet 3
6 Buffalo Bills 1.25 2.50
Logo 3
7A Chicago Bears 1.25 2.50
Helmet 1
(blue border)
7B Chicago Bears .75 1.50
Helmet 2
(red border)
8 Chicago Bears 1.25 2.50
Logo 3
9 Cincinnati Bengals .75 1.50
Helmet 3
10 Cincinnati Bengals .75 1.50
Logo 3
11 Cleveland Browns 1.25 2.50
Helmet 3
12 Cleveland Browns 1.25 2.50
Logo 3
13 Dallas Cowboys 2.00 4.00
Helmet 3
14 Dallas Cowboys 2.00 4.00
Logo 3
15 Denver Broncos 2.00 4.00
Helmet 2
16 Denver Broncos .75 1.50
Logo 3
17 Detroit Lions .75 1.50
Helmet 2
18 Detroit Lions .75 1.50
Logo 3
19 Green Bay Packers 2.00 4.00
Helmet 3
20 Green Bay Packers 2.00 4.00
Logo 3
21 Houston Oilers .75 1.50
Helmet 4
22 Houston Oilers .75 1.50
Logo 3
23 Kansas City Chiefs .75 1.50
Helmet 3
24 Kansas City Chiefs .75 1.50
Logo 3
25 Los Angeles Rams .75 1.50
Helmet 3
26A Los Angeles Rams .75 1.50
Logo 1
(blue border)
26B Los Angeles Rams .75 1.50
Logo 3
(red border)
27 Miami Dolphins 2.00 4.00
Helmet 3
28 Miami Dolphins 1.50 3.00
Logo 3
29 Minnesota Vikings 1.25 2.50
Helmet 3
30 Minnesota Vikings 1.25 2.50
Logo 3
31A New England Pats .75 1.50
Helmet 1
(blue border)
31B New England Pats .75 1.50
Helmet 2
(red border)
32 New England Pats .75 1.50
Logo 3
33 New Orleans Saints .75 1.50
Helmet 3
34 New Orleans Saints .75 1.50
Logo 3
35 New York Giants 1.25 2.50
Helmet 3
36 New York Giants 1.25 2.50
Logo 3
37 New York Jets 1.25 2.50
Helmet 3
38A New York Jets .75 1.50
Logo 1
(blue border)
38B New York Jets 1.25 2.50
Logo 3
(green border)
39 Oakland Raiders 2.00 4.00
Helmet 3
40A Oakland Raiders .75 1.50
Logo 1
(blue border)
40B Oakland Raiders 2.00 4.00
Logo 3
(yellow border)
41A Philadelphia Eagles .75 1.50
Helmet 1
(blue border)
41B Philadelphia Eagles .75 1.50
Helmet 2
(green border)
42 Philadelphia Eagles .75 1.50
Logo 3
43 Pittsburgh Steelers 2.00 4.00
Helmet 3
44A Pittsburgh Steelers .75 1.50
Logo 1
(blue border)
44B Pittsburgh Steelers 2.00 4.00
Logo 3
(yellow border)
45 St. Louis Cardinals .75 1.50
Helmet 3
46 St. Louis Cardinals .75 1.50
Logo 3
47 San Diego Chargers .75 1.50
Helmet 2
48 San Diego Chargers .75 1.50
Logo 3
49 San Francisco 49ers 2.00 4.00
Helmet 3
50 San Francisco 49ers 2.00 4.00
Logo 3
51 Seattle Seahawks .75 1.50
Helmet 3
(red border)
52 Seattle Seahawks .75 1.50
Helmet 3
(yellow border)
53 Tampa Bay Bucs .75 1.50
Helmet 3
54 Tampa Bay Bucs .75 1.50
Logo 3
55 Washington Redskins 2.00 4.00
Helmet 3
56 Washington Redskins 2.00 4.00
Logo 3

1979 Fleer Team Action

The 1979 Fleer Teams in Action football set mirrors the previous two sets in design (colorful action scenes with specific players not identified) and contains an additional card for the most recent Super Bowl making a total of 69 standard-size cards in the set. The fronts have white borders, and the backs are printed in black ink on gray stock. The backs have a 1979 copyright date. The card numbering follows team name alphabetical order followed by Super Bowl cards in chronological order. Cards were issued in wax packs of seven team cards plus three team logo stickers.

COMPLETE SET (69) 15.00 30.00
1 Atlanta Falcons .50 1.00
What's Up
Front Counts
2 Atlanta Falcons .20 .40
Following The
Bouncing Ball
3 Baltimore Colts .20 .40
Big Enough To Drive
A Truck Through
4 Baltimore Colts .20 .40
When The Defense
Becomes The Offense
5 Buffalo Bills .20 .40
Full Steam Ahead
6 Buffalo Bills .20 .40
Three's A Crowd
7 Chicago Bears .20 .40
Moving Out As One
8 Chicago Bears .20 .40
Stack 'Em Up
9 Cincinnati Bengals .20 .40
Out In The
Open Field
10 Cincinnati Bengals .20 .40
Sandwiched
11 Cleveland Browns .20 .40
Protective Pocket
12 Cleveland Browns .20 .40
Shake Rattle
And Roll
13 Dallas Cowboys 1.50 3.00
Paving The Way
(Tony Dorsett running)
14 Dallas Cowboys .30 .60
The Right Place
At The Right Time
15 Denver Broncos .20 .40
A Stable Of Runners
16 Denver Broncos .20 .40
Orange Crush
17 Detroit Lions .20 .40
Through The Line
18 Detroit Lions .20 .40
Tracked Down
19 Green Bay Packers .20 .40
Power Play
20 Green Bay Packers .20 .40
Four-To-One Odds
21 Houston Oilers 3.00 6.00
Offensive Gusher
(Earl Campbell running)
22 Houston Oilers .20 .40
Gotcha
23 Kansas City Chiefs .20 .40
Get Wings
24 Kansas City Chiefs .20 .40
Ambushed
25 Los Angeles Rams .20 .40
Men In The Middle
26 Los Angeles Rams .20 .40
Nowhere To Go
But Down
27 Miami Dolphins .30 .60
Escort Service
28 Miami Dolphins .30 .60
All For One
29 Minnesota Vikings .20 .40
Up And Over
30 Minnesota Vikings .20 .40
The Purple Gang
31 New England Patriots .20 .40
Prepare For Takeoff
32 New England Patriots .20 .40
Dept. Of Defense
33 New Orleans Saints .50 1.00
Bombs Away
(Archie Manning)
34 New Orleans Saints .20 .40
Duel In The Dome
35 New York Giants .20 .40
Battle Of The Line
Of Scrimmage
36 New York Giants .20 .40
Piled Up
37 New York Jets .20 .40
Hitting The Hole
38 New York Jets .20 .40
Making Sure
39 Oakland Raiders 1.00 2.00
Left-Handed
Strength
Ken Stabler
40 Oakland Raiders .30 .60
Black Sunday
41 Philadelphia Eagles .20 .40
Ready Aim Fire
42 Philadelphia Eagles .20 .40
Closing In
43 Pittsburgh Steelers .30 .60
Anchor Man
44 Pittsburgh Steelers .50 1.00
The Steel Curtain
45 St. Louis Cardinals .30 .60
High Altitude Bomber
(Jim Hart)
46 St. Louis Cardinals .20 .40
Three On One
47 San Diego Chargers .20 .40
Charge
48 San Diego Chargers .20 .40
Special Teams Shot
49 San Francisco 49ers .30 .60
In For The Score

50 San Francisco 49ers .30 .60
Nothing But
Red Shirts
51 Seattle Seahawks .20 .40
North-South Runner
52 Seattle Seahawks .20 .40
The Sting
53 Tampa Bay Buccaneers .20 .40
Hitting Paydirt
54 Tampa Bay Buccaneers .20 .40
Making 'Em Pay
The Price
55 Washington Redskins .30 .60
On The Warpath
56 Washington Redskins .30 .60
Drawing A Crowd
57 Super Bowl I .50 1.00
Green Bay NFL 35
Kansas City AFL 10
(Jim Taylor running)
58 Super Bowl II .75 1.50
Green Bay NFL 33
Oakland AFL 14
(Bart Starr passing)
59 Super Bowl III .30 .60
New York AFL 16
Baltimore NFL 7
60 Super Bowl IV .30 .60
Kansas City AFL 23
Minnesota NFL 7
61 Super Bowl V .30 .60
Baltimore AFC 16
Dallas NFC 13
62 Super Bowl VI 1.00 2.00
Dallas NFC 24
Miami AFC 3
(Bob Griese
and Bob Lilly)
63 Super Bowl VII .30 .60
Miami AFC 14
Washington NFC 7
64 Super Bowl VIII 1.00 2.00
Miami AFC 24
Minnesota NFC 7
(Bob Griese and
Larry Csonka)
65 Super Bowl IX 1.50 3.00
Pittsburgh AFC 16
Minnesota NFC 6
(Terry Bradshaw and
Franco Harris)
66 Super Bowl X .30 .60
Pittsburgh AFC 21
Dallas NFC 17
67 Super Bowl XI .30 .60
Oakland AFC 32
Minnesota NFC 14
Ken Stabler pictured
68 Super Bowl XII .30 .60
Dallas NFC 27
Denver AFC 10
69 Super Bowl XIII .75 1.50
Pittsburgh AFC 35
Dallas NFC 31

1979 Fleer Team Action Stickers

This set of stickers was issued one per pack in the 1979 Fleer Team Action card release and is virtually identical to the 1978 set. Each NFL team is represented with two stickers, with all but the Cowboys and Seahawks having both a helmet sticker and logo/insignia sticker. Several were produced with slight color variations in the border as noted below. Although these and other similar stickers were released over a number of years, the exact year of issue can be identified by the unique sticker back -- a puzzle piece that forms a photo from Super Bowl XIII when fully assembled. Note that there are a number of puzzle back variations for each team. Very few collectors attempt to assemble a full set with all back variations. Reportedly, there are 170-total different sticker combinations of fronts and backs. We've noted the number of known back variations for each sticker below. Each sticker measures roughly 2 3/8" by 2 3/4."

COMPLETE SET (65) 30.00 60.00
1A Atlanta Falcons .50 1.00
Helmet 1
(blue border)
1B Atlanta Falcons .50 1.00
Helmet 3
(red border)
2 Atlanta Falcons .50 1.00
Logo 3
3A Baltimore Colts .75 1.50
Helmet 1
(blue border)
3B Baltimore Colts .75 1.50
Helmet 2
(yellow border)
4 Baltimore Colts .75 1.50
Logo 3
5 Buffalo Bills .75 1.50
Helmet 3
6 Buffalo Bills .75 1.50
Logo 3
7A Chicago Bears .75 1.50
Helmet 1
(blue border)
7B Chicago Bears .75 1.50
Helmet 2
(red border)
8 Chicago Bears .75 1.50
Logo 3
9 Cincinnati Bengals .50 1.00
Helmet 3
10 Cincinnati Bengals .50 1.00
Logo 3
11 Cleveland Browns .75 1.50
Helmet 3
12 Cleveland Browns .75 1.50
Logo 3
13 Dallas Cowboys 1.25 2.50
Helmet 3
14 Dallas Cowboys 1.25 2.50
Helmet 3
15 Denver Broncos .75 1.50
Helmet 2
16 Denver Broncos .75 1.50
Logo 3
17 Detroit Lions .50 1.00
Helmet 2
18 Detroit Lions .50 1.00
Logo 3
19 Green Bay Packers 1.25 2.50
Helmet 3
20 Green Bay Packers 1.25 2.50
Logo 3
21 Houston Oilers .50 1.00
Helmet 4
22 Houston Oilers .50 1.00
Logo 3
23 Kansas City Chiefs .50 1.00
Helmet 3
24 Kansas City Chiefs .50 1.00
Logo 3
25 Los Angeles Rams .50 1.00
Helmet 3
26A Los Angeles Rams .50 1.00
Logo 1#(blue border)
26B Los Angeles Rams .50 1.00
Logo 3#(red border)
27 Miami Dolphins 1.25 2.50
Helmet 3
28 Miami Dolphins 1.25 2.50
Logo 3
29 Minnesota Vikings .75 1.50
Helmet 3
30 Minnesota Vikings .75 1.50
Logo 3
31A New England Pats .50 1.00
Helmet 1
(blue border)
31B New England Pats .50 1.00
Helmet 2
(red border)
32 New England Pats .50 1.00
Logo 3
33 New Orleans Saints .50 1.00
Helmet 3
34 New Orleans Saints .50 1.00
Logo 3
35 New York Giants .75 1.50
Helmet 3
36 New York Giants .75 1.50
Logo 3
37 New York Jets .75 1.50
Helmet 3
38A New York Jets .75 1.50
Logo 1
(blue border)
38B New York Jets .75 1.50
Logo 3
(green border)
39 Oakland Raiders 1.25 2.50
Helmet 3
40A Oakland Raiders 1.25 2.50
Logo 1
(blue border)
40B Oakland Raiders 1.25 2.50
Logo 3
(yellow border)
41A Philadelphia Eagles .50 1.00
Helmet 1
(blue border)
41B Philadelphia Eagles .50 1.00
Helmet 2
(green border)
42 Philadelphia Eagles .50 1.00
Logo 3
43 Pittsburgh Steelers 1.25 2.50
Helmet 3
44A Pittsburgh Steelers 1.25 2.50
Logo 1
(blue border)
44B Pittsburgh Steelers 1.25 2.50
Logo 3
(yellow border)
45 St. Louis Cardinals .50 1.00
Helmet 3
46 St. Louis Cardinals .50 1.00
Logo 3
47 San Diego Chargers .50 1.00
Helmet 2
48 San Diego Chargers .50 1.00
Logo 3
49 San Francisco 49ers 1.25 2.50
Helmet 3
50 San Francisco 49ers 1.25 2.50
Logo 3
51 Seattle Seahawks .50 1.00
Helmet 3
(red border)
52 Seattle Seahawks .50 1.00
Helmet 3
(yellow border)
53 Tampa Bay Bucs .50 1.00
Helmet 3
54 Tampa Bay Bucs .50 1.00
Logo 3
55 Washington Redskins .75 1.50
Helmet 3
56 Washington Redskins .75 1.50
Logo 3

1980 Fleer Team Action

The 1980 Fleer Teams in Action football set continues the tradition of earlier sets but has one additional card for the most recent Super Bowl, i.e., now 70 full color standard-size cards in the set. The fronts have white borders and the backs are printed in black on gray stock. The cards are numbered on back and feature a 1980 copyright date. The card numbering follows team name alphabetical order followed by Super Bowl cards in chronological order. Cards were issued in seven-card wax packs along with three team logo stickers.

COMPLETE SET (70) 10.00 20.00
1 Atlanta Falcons .30 .75
Getting The
Extra Yards
2 Atlanta Falcons .10 .30
Falcons Get
Their Prey
3 Baltimore Colts .10 .30
Looking For Daylight
(Joe Washington)
4 Baltimore Colts .10 .30
Ready If Needed
5 Buffalo Bills .10 .30
You Block For Me and
I'll Block For You
6 Buffalo Bills .10 .30
Stand Em Up And
Push 'Em Back
7 Chicago Bears 2.00 4.00
Coming Through
(Walter Payton)
8 Chicago Bears .10 .30
Four On One
9 Cincinnati Bengals .10 .30
Power Running
10 Cincinnati Bengals .10 .30
Out Of Running Room
11 Cleveland Browns .40 1.00
End Around
(Ozzie Newsome)
12 Cleveland Browns .10 .30
Rubber Band Defense
13 Dallas Cowboys .75 2.00
Point Of Attack
(Tony Dorsett)
14 Dallas Cowboys .25 .60
Man In The Middle
(Bob Breunig)
15 Denver Broncos .10 .30
Strong And Steady
16 Denver Broncos .10 .30
Orange Power
17 Detroit Lions .10 .30
On The March
18 Detroit Lions .10 .30
The Silver Rush
19 Green Bay Packers .10 .30
Getting Underway
20 Green Bay Packers .10 .30
The Best Offense
Is A Good Defense
21 Houston Oilers .10 .30
Airborne
22 Houston Oilers .10 .30
Search And Destroy
23 Kansas City Chiefs .10 .30
Blazing The Trail
24 Kansas City Chiefs .10 .30
Making Sure
25 Los Angeles Rams .10 .30
One Good Turn
Deserves Another
26 Los Angeles Rams .10 .30
Shedding The Block
27 Miami Dolphins .10 .30
Sweeping The Flanks
28 Miami Dolphins .10 .30
Keep 'Em Busy
29 Minnesota Vikings .10 .30
One Man To Beat
30 Minnesota Vikings .10 .30
Purple People
Eaters II
31 New England Patriots .10 .30
Hitting The Hole
32 New England Patriots .10 .30
Getting To The Ball
33 New Orleans Saints .10 .30
Splitting The
Defenders
34 New Orleans Saints .40 1.00
Don't Let Him
Get Outside
(Joe Theismann)
35 New York Giants 1.25 2.50
Audible
(Phil Simms)
36 New York Giants .10 .30
Wrong Side Up
37 New York Jets .10 .30
Make Him Miss
38 New York Jets .10 .30
The Only Way To
Play (Mark Gastineau)
39 Oakland Raiders .10 .30
Pulling Out All
The Stops
40 Oakland Raiders .10 .30
Right On
41 Philadelphia Eagles .10 .30
Not Pretty& But
Still Points
42 Philadelphia Eagles .10 .30
Applying The Clamps
43 Pittsburgh Steelers .75 2.00
All Systems Go
(Franco Harris sweep)
44 Pittsburgh Steelers .10 .30
Still The Steel
Curtain
45 St. Louis Cardinals .40 1.00
On The Move
(Ottis Anderson)
46 St. Louis Cardinals .10 .30
Long Gone
47 San Diego Chargers .10 .30
Short-Range Success
48 San Diego Chargers .10 .30
Pursuit
49 San Francisco 49ers .10 .30
Getting Field Position
50 San Francisco 49ers .10 .30
Finding A Nugget
51 Seattle Seahawks .10 .30
They'll Try
Anything Once
52 Seattle Seahawks .10 .30
Paying The Price
53 Tampa Bay Buccaneers .10 .30
Coming Of Age
54 Tampa Bay Buccaneers/3-4 Shut The Door 1.50
3.00
(Walter Payton
tackled)
55 Washington Redskins .10 .30
Wide Open
56 Washington Redskins .10 .30
Rude Reception
57 Super Bowl I .20 .50
Green Bay NFL 35
Kansas City AFL 10
58 Super Bowl II .40 1.00
Green Bay NFL 33
Oakland AFL 14
(Bart Starr)
59 Super Bowl III 1.25 2.50
New York AFL 16
Baltimore NFL 7
(Joe Namath)
60 Super Bowl IV .20 .50
Kansas City AFL 23
Minnesota NFL 7
61 Super Bowl V .20 .50
Baltimore AFC 16
Dallas NFC 13
62 Super Bowl VI 1.25 2.50
Dallas NFC 24
Miami AFC 3
(Roger Staubach)
63 Super Bowl VII .20 .50
Miami AFC 14
Washington NFC 7
64 Super Bowl VIII .20 .50
Miami AFC 24
Minnesota NFC 7
65 Super Bowl IX .60 1.50
Pittsburgh AFC 16
Minnesota NFC 6
(Terry Bradshaw
Rocky Bleier)
66 Super Bowl X .40 1.00
Pittsburgh AFC 21
Dallas NFC 17
(Jack Lambert)
67 Super Bowl XI .20 .50
Oakland AFC 44
Minnesota NFC 14
(Chuck Foreman)
68 Super Bowl XII .20 .50
Dallas NFC 27
Denver AFC 10
69 Super Bowl XIII .75 2.00
Pittsburgh AFC 35
Dallas NFC 31
(Terry Bradshaw)
70 Super Bowl XIV .60 1.50
Pittsburgh AFC 31
Los Angeles NFC 19
(Franco Harris)

1980 Fleer Team Action Stickers

This set of stickers was issued one per pack in the 1980 Fleer Team Action card release and is virtually identical to the 1977 set. Each NFL team is represented with two stickers, with all but the Cowboys and Seahawks having both a helmet sticker and logo/insignia sticker. Several were produced with slight color variations in the border as noted below. Although these and other similar stickers were released over a number of years, the exact year of issue can be identified by the unique blank white sticker back. Each sticker measures roughly 2 3/8" by 2 3/4."

COMPLETE SET (65) 25.00 50.00
1A Atlanta Falcons .30 .75
Helmet
(blue border)
1B Atlanta Falcons .30 .75
Helmet
(red border)
2 Atlanta Falcons .30 .75
Logo
3A Baltimore Colts .50 1.25
Helmet
(blue border)
3B Baltimore Colts .50 1.25
Helmet
(yellow border)
4 Baltimore Colts .50 1.25
Logo
5 Buffalo Bills .50 1.25
Helmet
6 Buffalo Bills .50 1.25
Logo
7A Chicago Bears .50 1.25
Helmet
(blue border)
7B Chicago Bears .50 1.25
Helmet
(red border)
8 Chicago Bears .50 1.25
Logo
9 Cincinnati Bengals .30 .75
Helmet
10 Cincinnati Bengals .30 .75
Logo
11 Cleveland Browns .50 1.25
Helmet
12 Cleveland Browns .50 1.25
Logo
13 Dallas Cowboys .75 2.00
Helmet
(large helmet)
14 Dallas Cowboys .75 2.00
Helmet
(small helmet)
15 Denver Broncos .50 1.25
Helmet
16 Denver Broncos .50 1.25
Logo
17 Detroit Lions .30 .75
Helmet
18 Detroit Lions .30 .75
Logo
19 Green Bay Packers .75 2.00
Helmet
20 Green Bay Packers .75 2.00
Logo
21 Houston Oilers .30 .75
Helmet
22 Houston Oilers .30 .75
Logo
23 Kansas City Chiefs .30 .75
Helmet
24 Kansas City Chiefs .30 .75
Logo
25 Los Angeles Rams .30 .75
Helmet
26A Los Angeles Rams .30 .75
Logo
(blue border)
26B Los Angeles Rams .30 .75
Logo
(red border)
27 Miami Dolphins .75 2.00
Helmet
28 Miami Dolphins .75 2.00
Logo
29 Minnesota Vikings .50 1.25
Helmet
30 Minnesota Vikings .50 1.25
Logo
31A New England Patriots .30 .75
Helmet
(blue border)
31B New England Patriots .30 .75
Helmet
(red border)
32 New England Patriots .30 .75
Logo
33 New Orleans Saints .30 .75
Helmet
34 New Orleans Saints .30 .75
Logo
35 New York Giants .50 1.25
Helmet
36 New York Giants .50 1.25
Logo
37 New York Jets .50 1.25
Helmet
38A New York Jets .50 1.25
Logo
(blue border)
38B New York Jets .50 1.25
Logo
(green border)
39 Oakland Raiders .75 2.00
Helmet
40A Oakland Raiders .75 2.00
Logo
(blue border)
40B Oakland Raiders .75 2.00
Logo
(yellow border)
41A Philadelphia Eagles .30 .75
Helmet
(blue border)
41B Philadelphia Eagles .30 .75
Helmet
(green border)
42 Philadelphia Eagles .30 .75
Logo
43 Pittsburgh Steelers .75 2.00
Helmet
44A Pittsburgh Steelers .75 2.00
Logo
(blue border)
44B Pittsburgh Steelers .75 2.00
Logo
(yellow border)
45 St. Louis Cardinals .30 .75
Helmet
46 St. Louis Cardinals .30 .75
Logo
47 San Diego Chargers .30 .75
Helmet
48 San Diego Chargers .30 .75
Logo
49 San Francisco 49ers .75 2.00
Helmet
50 San Francisco 49ers .75 2.00
Logo
51 Seattle Seahawks .30 .75
Helmet
(red border)
52 Seattle Seahawks .30 .75
Helmet
(yellow border)
53 Tampa Bay Bucs .30 .75
Helmet
54 Tampa Bay Bucs .30 .75
Logo
55 Washington Redskins .50 1.25
Helmet
56 Washington Redskins .50 1.25
Logo

1981 Fleer Team Action

The 1981 Fleer Teams in Action football set deviates from previous years in that, while each team is depicted on two cards and each Super Bowl is depicted on one card, an additional group of cards (72-88) have been added to make the set number 88 standard-size cards, no doubt to accomodate the press sheet size. The card numbering follows team name alphabetical order followed by Super Bowl cards in chronological order and the last group of miscellaneous cards. The card fronts are in full color with white borders, and the card backs are printed in blue and red on white stock. The backs feature a 1981 copyright. Cards were issued in eight-card wax packs along with three team logo stickers.

COMPLETE SET (88) 8.00 20.00
1 Atlanta Falcons .20 .50
Out In The Open
(William Andrews)
2 Atlanta Falcons .08 .25
Grits Blitz
3 Baltimore Colts .08 .25
Sprung Through
The Line
4 Baltimore Colts .08 .25
Human Pyramid
5 Buffalo Bills .08 .25
Buffalo Bills'
Wild West Show
6 Buffalo Bills .08 .25
Buffaloed
7 Chicago Bears 1.00 2.50
About To Hit Paydirt
(Walter Payton)
8 Chicago Bears .08 .25
Bear Trap
9 Cincinnati Bengals .08 .25
Behind The Wall
(Pete Johnson)
10 Cincinnati Bengals .08 .25
Black Cloud
11 Cleveland Browns .15 .40
Point Of Attack
(Mike Pruitt)
12 Cleveland Browns .20 .50
The Only Way To
Go Is Down
(Rocky Bleier tackled)
13 Dallas Cowboys .20 .50
Big O In Big D
(Ron Springs fumble)
14 Dallas Cowboys .20 .50
Headed Off At The Pass
15 Denver Broncos .08 .25
Man Versus Elements
(Craig Morton in snow)
16 Denver Broncos .08 .25
The Old High-Low
Treatment
17 Detroit Lions .20 .50
Play Acfion
(Billy Sims)
18 Detroit Lions .08 .25
Into The Lions' Den
19 Green Bay Packers .08 .25
A Packer Packs
The Pigskin
20 Green Bay Packers .08 .25
Sandwiched
21 Houston Oilers .08 .25
Wait A Minute
22 Houston Oilers/3-4 Shut The Door .08 .25
23 Kansas City Chiefs .08 .25
On The Ball
24 Kansas City Chiefs .08 .25
Seeing Red
25 Los Angeles Rams .08 .25
The Point Of Attack
26 Los Angeles Rams .08 .25
Get Your Hands Up
27 Miami Dolphins .15 .40
Plenty Of Time
(David Woodley)
28 Miami Dolphins .15 .40
Pursuit
29 Minnesota Vikings .08 .25
Tough Yardage
30 Minnesota Vikings .08 .25
Purple Avalanche
(Pete Johnson)
31 New England Patriots .08 .25
In High Gear
32 New England Patriots .40 1.00
Keep 'Em Covered
(Ken Stabler)
33 New Orleans Saints .20 .50
Setting Up
(Archie Manning)
34 New Orleans Saints .08 .25
Air Ball
35 New York Giants .08 .25
Off Tackle
36 New York Giants .08 .25
In The Land Of
The Giants
37 New York Jets .15 .40
Cleared For Lauching
(Richard Todd)
38 New York Jets .08 .25
Airborne
39 Oakland Raiders .15 .40
Off And Running
40 Oakland Raiders .15 .40
Block That Kick
41 Philadelphia Eagles .08 .25
About To Take Flight
42 Philadelphia Eagles .08 .25
Birds Of Prey
(Robert Newhouse)
43 Pittsburgh Steelers .40 1.00
Here Come The
Infantry
(Franco Harris)
44 Pittsburgh Steelers .15 .40
Like A Steel Trap
45 St. Louis Cardinals .08 .25
Run To Daylight
46 St. Louis Cardinals .08 .25
Stacked Up And Up
47 San Diego Chargers .08 .25
Straight-Ahead Power
48 San Diego Chargers .08 .25
Stonewalled
49 San Francisco 49ers .15 .40
Follow The Leader
50 San Francisco 49ers .15 .40
Search And Destroy
51 Seattle Seahawks .08 .25
Short-Range Success
52 Seattle Seahawks .08 .25
Take Down
53 Tampa Bay Buccaneers .08 .25
Orange Blossom Special
(Jerry Eckwood)
54 Tampa Bay Buccaneers .08 .25
Tropical Storm Buc
55 Washington Redskins .15 .40
Alone For A Moment
56 Washington Redskins .15 .40
Ambushed
57 Super Bowl I .20 .50
Green Bay NFL 35
Kansas City AFL 10
(Jim Taylor)
58 Super Bowl II .08 .25
Green Bay NFL 35
Oakland AFL 14
59 Super Bowl III .08 .25
New York AFL 16
Baltimore NFL 7
60 Super Bowl IV .08 .25
Kansas City AFL 23
Minnesota NFL 7
61 Super Bowl V .08 .25
Baltimore AFC 16
Dallas NFC 13
62 Super Bowl VI .15 .40
Dallas NFC 24
Miami AFC 3
63 Super Bowl VII .08 .25
Miami AFC 14
Washington NFC 7
64 Super Bowl VIII .40 1.00
Miami AFC 24
Minnesota NFC 7
(Larry Csonka running)
65 Super Bowl IX .40 1.00
Pittsburgh AFC 16
Minnesota NFC 6
(Franco Harris)
66 Super Bowl X .15 .40
Pittsburgh AFC 21
Dallas NFC 17
67 Super Bowl XI .40 1.00
Oakland AFC 32
Minnesota NFC 14
(Ken Stabler)
68 Super Bowl XII .75 2.00
Dallas NFC 27
Denver AFC 10
(Roger Staubach
and Tony Dorsett)
69 Super Bowl XIII 1.00 2.50
Pittsburgh AFC 35
Dallas NFC 31
(Roger Staubach
and Tony Dorsett)
70 Super Bowl XIV .40 1.00
Pittsburgh AFC 31
Los Angeles NFC 19
(Franco Harris)
71 Super Bowl XV .15 .40
Oakland AFC 27
Philadelphia NFC 10
(Jim Plunkett)
72 Training Camp .20 .50
(Steelers)/(Chuck Noll)
73 Practice Makes .08 .25
Perfect
74 Airborn Carrier .08 .25
75 The National Anthem .08 .25
Chargers
76 Filling Up .08 .25
(Stadium)
77 Away In Time .75 2.00
(Terry Bradshaw)
78 Flat Out .08 .25
79 Halftime .08 .25
(Band playing)
80 Warm Ups Patriots .08 .25
81 Getting To The .08 .25
Bottom Of It
82 Souvenir (Crowd) .08 .25
83 A Game Of Inches .08 .25
(Officials measuring)
84 The Overview .08 .25
85 The Dropback .08 .25
86 Pregame Huddle .08 .25
(Redskins)
87 Every Way But Loose UER .08 .25
(Giants helmet on back&
should be Rams)
88 Mudders UER .15 .40
(Redskins helmet on
back& should be 49ers)

1981 Fleer Team Action Stickers

Fleer re-designed the Team Action Sticker sets in 1981 to feature the team's helmet or logo against a green football field pattern. This set was issued one sticker per pack and features each NFL team in two different stickers. The cardbacks contain the team's 1981 NFL schedule and each sticker measures roughly 2 1/4" by 2 3/4." Over the years a large number of variations have been discovered, but we've listed only the more significant variations below. Minor variations in colors and tones exist on virtually every sticker and some collectors attempt to assemble complete sets of all minor variations.

COMPLETE SET (56) 20.00 50.00
1 Atlanta Falcons .30 .75
Helmet
2 Atlanta Falcons .30 .75
Logo
3A Baltimore Colts .50 1.25
Helmet COR
(both front and back
helmet logo correct)
3B Baltimore Colts .50 1.25
Helmet ERR
(front helmet logo correct
back helmet logo upside down)
3C Baltimore Colts .50 1.25
Helmet ERR
(both front and back
helmet logos upside down)
4A Baltimore Colts .50 1.25
Logo COR
(helmet logo on back right side up)
4B Baltimore Colts .50 1.25
Logo ERR
(helmet logo on back upside down)
5A Buffalo Bills .50 1.25
Helmet
(blue face mask)
5B Buffalo Bills .50 1.25
Helmet
(white face mask)
6 Buffalo Bills .50 1.25
Logo
7A Chicago Bears .50 1.25
Helmet
(gray face mask)
7B Chicago Bears .50 1.25
Helmet
(white face mask)
8 Chicago Bears .50 1.25
Logo
9A Cincinnati Bengals .30 .75
Large Helmet
(black face mask)
9B Cincinnati Bengals .30 .75
Large Helmet
(white face mask)
10A Cincinnati Bengals .30 .75
Small Helmet
(black face mask)
10B Cincinnati Bengals .30 .75
Small Helmet
(white face mask)
11 Cleveland Browns .50 1.25
Large Helmet
12 Cleveland Browns .50 1.25
Small Helmet
13 Dallas Cowboys .75 2.00
Large Helmet
14 Dallas Cowboys .75 2.00
Small Helmet
15 Denver Broncos .50 1.25
Helmet
16 Denver Broncos .50 1.25
Logo
17A Detroit Lions .30 .75
Helmet
(gray face mask)
17B Detroit Lions .30 .75
Helmet
(white face mask)
18A Detroit Lions .30 .75
Logo
(blue bars on logo)
18B Detroit Lions .30 .75
Logo
(gray bars on logo)
19A Green Bay Packers .75 2.00
Helmet
(green face mask)
19B Green Bay Packers .75 2.00
Helmet
(white face mask)
20A Green Bay Packers .75 2.00
Logo
(green uniform in logo)
20B Green Bay Packers .75 2.00
Logo
(copper uniform in logo)
21A Houston Oilers .30 .75
Helmet
(orange face mask)
21B Houston Oilers .30 .75
Helmet
(white face mask)

22 Houston Oilers Logo .30 .75
23 Kansas City Chiefs Helmet .30 .75
24 Kansas City Chiefs Logo .30 .75
25A Los Angeles Rams Helmet (gray face mask) .30 .75
25B Los Angeles Rams Helmet (white face mask) .30 .75
26A L.A. Rams Logo White (Ram head is white on front) .30 .75
26B L.A. Rams Logo Orange (Ram head is orange on front) .30 .75
27A Miami Dolphins Helmet (gray face mask) .75 2.00
27B Miami Dolphins Helmet (white face mask) .75 2.00
28 Miami Dolphins Logo .75 2.00
29 Minnesota Vikings Helmet .50 1.25
30 Minnesota Vikings Logo .50 1.25
31 New England Patriots Helmet .30 .75
32 New England Patriots Logo .30 .75
33A New Orleans Saints Helmet (black face mask) .30 .75
33B New Orleans Saints Helmet (white face mask) .30 .75
34 New Orleans Saints Logo .30 .75
35 New York Giants Large Helmet .50 1.25
36 New York Giants Small Helmet .50 1.25
37 New York Jets Large Helmet .50 1.25
38 New York Jets Small Helmet .50 1.25
39A Oakland Raiders Helmet (gray face mask) .75 2.00
39B Oakland Raiders Helmet (white face mask) .75 2.00
40 Oakland Raiders Logo .75 2.00
41 Philadelphia Eagles Helmet .30 .75
42 Philadelphia Eagles Logo .30 .75
43A Pittsburgh Steelers Helmet (yellow trim) .75 2.00
43b Pittsburgh Steelers Helmet (white trim) .75 2.00
44 Pittsburgh Steelers Logo .75 2.00
45A St. Louis Cardinals Helmet (gray face mask) .30 .75
45B St. Louis Cardinals Helmet (white face mask) .30 .75
46 St. Louis Cardinals Logo .30 .75
47 San Diego Chargers Helmet .30 .75
48 San Diego Chargers Logo .30 .75
49A San Francisco 49ers Helmet (gray face mask) .75 2.00
49B San Francisco 49ers Helmet (white face mask) .75 2.00
50 San Francisco 49ers Logo .75 2.00
51A Seattle Seahawks Large Helmet (gray face mask) .30 .75
51B Seattle Seahawks Large Helmet (white face mask) .30 .75
52 Seattle Seahawks Small Helmet .30 .75
53A Tampa Bay Bucs Helmet (dark orange face mask) .30 .75
53B Tampa Bay Bucs Helmet (white face mask) .30 .75
54 Tampa Bay Bucs Logo .30 .75
55A Washington Redskins Helmet (orange face mask) .50 1.25
55B Washington Redskins Helmet (white face mask) .50 1.25
56 Washington Redskins Logo .50 1.25

1982 Fleer Team Action

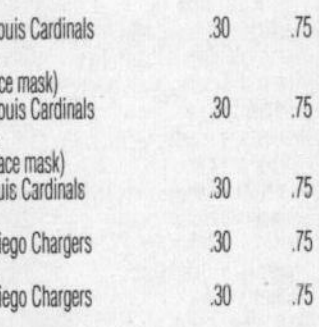

The 1982 Fleer Teams in Action football set is very similar to the 1981 set (with again 88 standard-size cards) and other Fleer Teams in Action sets of previous years. The backs are printed in yellow and gray on a white stock. These cards feature a 1982 copyright date. The card numbering follows team name alphabetical order followed by Super Bowl cards in chronological order and NFL Team Highlights cards. Cards were issued in wax packs of seven team cards along with three team logo stickers.

COMPLETE SET (88) 14.00 35.00
1 Atlanta Falcons Running to Daylight (William Andrews) .25 .60
2 Atlanta Falcons Airborne Falcons .08 .25
3 Baltimore Colts Plenty of Time To Throw (Bert Jones and Mark Gastineau) .15 .40
4 Baltimore Colts Lassoing the Opponent .08 .25
5 Buffalo Bills Point of Attack (Joe Ferguson) .15 .40
6 Buffalo Bills Capturing the Enemy .08 .25
7 Chicago Bears Three on One (Walter Payton) 1.00 2.50
8 Chicago Bears Stretched Out .08 .25
9 Cincinnati Bengals About to Hit Paydirt (Pete Johnson) .08 .25
10 Cincinnati Bengals Tiger-Striped Attack .08 .25
11 Cleveland Browns Reading the Field (Brian Sipe) .15 .40
12 Cleveland Browns Covered From All Angles .08 .25
13 Dallas Cowboys Blocking Convoy (Tony Dorsett) .40 1.00
14 Dallas Cowboys Encircled .15 .40
15 Denver Broncos Springing Into Action (Craig Morton) .15 .40
16 Denver Broncos High and Low .08 .25
17 Detroit Lions Setting Up The Screen Pass .08 .25
18 Detroit Lions Poised and Ready To Attack (Doug Williams) .15 .40
19 Green Bay Packers Flying Through The Air .08 .25
20 Green Bay Packers Hitting The Pack .08 .25
21 Houston Oilers Waiting For The Hole To Open (Gifford Nielsen and Earl Campbell) 1.50 4.00
22 Houston Oilers Biting The Dust .08 .25
23 Kansas City Chiefs Going In Untouched .08 .25
24 Kansas City Chiefs No Place To Go .08 .25
25 Los Angeles Rams Getting To The Outside (Wendell Tyler) .08 .25
26 Los Angeles Rams Double Team& Double Trouble (John Riggins tackled) .30 .75
27 Miami Dolphins Cutting Back Against The Grain (Tony Nathan) .15 .40
28 Miami Dolphins Taking Two Down .15 .40
29 Minnesota Vikings Running Inside For Tough Yardage .08 .25
30 Minnesota Vikings Bowling Over The Opponent .08 .25
31 New England Patriots Leaping For The First Down .08 .25
32 New England Patriots Gang Tackling .08 .25
33 New Orleans Saints Breaking Into The Clear (George Rogers) .15 .40
34 New Orleans Saints Double Jeopardy .08 .25
35 New York Giants Getting Ready To Hit The Opening .08 .25
36 New York Giants Negative Yardage (Tony Dorsett, Lawrence Taylor) .50 1.25
37 New York Jets Off To The Races (Freeman McNeil) .15 .40
38 New York Jets Sandwiched .08 .25
39 Oakland Raiders Throwing The Down and Out (Marc Wilson) .15 .40
40 Oakland Raiders The Second Wave Is On The Way .15 .40
41 Philadelphia Eagles Blasting Up The Middle (Ron Jaworski) .15 .40
42 Philadelphia Eagles Triple-Teaming (Carl Hairston and John Riggins) .30 .75
43 Pittsburgh Steelers Stretching For A Score .15 .40
44 Pittsburgh Steelers Rising Above The Crowd .15 .40
45 St. Louis Cardinals Sweeping To The Right (Jim Hart) .15 .40
46 St. Louis Cardinals No Place To Go But Down .08 .25
47 San Diego Chargers Looking For Someone To Block .08 .25
48 San Diego Chargers Being In The Right Place .08 .25
49 San Francisco 49ers Giving Second Effort (Joe Montana) 6.00 15.00
50 San Francisco 49ers In Your Face (Steve Bartkowski) .20 .50
51 Seattle Seahawks Nothing But Open Space (Jack Lambert) .30 .75
52 Seattle Seahawks Attacking From The Blind Side (Brian Sipe) .15 .40
53 Tampa Bay Buccaneers Everyone In Motion (Doug Williams) .15 .40
54 Tampa Bay Buccaneers Ring Around The Running Back .08 .25
55 Washington Redskins Knocking Them Down One-By-One (Joe Theismann) .30 .75
56 Washington Redskins Coming From All Directions .15 .40
57 Super Bowl I Green Bay NFL 35 Kansas City AFL 10 (Jim Taylor) .20 .50
58 Super Bowl II Green Bay NFL 33 Oakland AFL 14 .08 .25
59 Super Bowl III New York AFL 16 Baltimore NFL 7 .08 .25
60 Super Bowl IV Kansas City AFL 23 Minnesota NFL 7 .08 .25
61 Super Bowl V Baltimore AFC 16 Dallas NFC 13 .08 .25
62 Super Bowl VI Dallas NFC 24 Miami AFC 3 (Bob Griese and Bob Lilly) .40 1.00
63 Super Bowl VII Miami AFC 14 Washington NFC 7 (Larry Csonka running) .30 .75
64 Super Bowl VIII Miami AFC 24 Minnesota NFC 7 (Larry Csonka and Paul Warfield) .40 1.00
65 Super Bowl IX Pittsburgh AFC 16 Minnesota NFC 6 .08 .25
66 Super Bowl X Pittsburgh AFC 21 Dallas NFC 17 (Roger Staubach) .60 1.50
67 Super Bowl XI Oakland AFC 32 Minnesota NFC 14 (Mark Van Eeghen) .15 .40
68 Super Bowl XII Dallas NFC 27 Denver AFC 10 (Roger Staubach) .60 1.50
69 Super Bowl XIII Pittsburgh AFC 35 Dallas NFC 31 (Lynn Swann) .50 1.25
70 Super Bowl XIV Pittsburgh AFC 31 Los Angeles NFC 19 .08 .25
71 Super Bowl XV Oakland AFC 27 Philadelphia NFC 10 (Jim Plunkett) .15 .40
72 Super Bowl XVI San Francisco NFC 26 Cincinnati AFC 21 (Dwight Clark) .40 1.00
73 NFL Team Highlights/1982 AFC-NFC Pro Bowl Action (Montana rolling out) 5.00 12.00
74 NFL Team Highlights/1982 AFC-NFC Pro Bowl Action (Ken Anderson and Anthony Munoz) .40 1.00
75 NFL Team Highlights Aloha Stadium .08 .25
76 NFL Team Highlights On The Field Meeting .08 .25
77 NFL Team Highlights First Down (Joe Theismann) .25 .60
78 NFL Team Highlights The Man In Charge (Jerry Markbright) .08 .25
79 NFL Team Highlights Coming Onto The Field .08 .25
80 NFL Team Highlights In The Huddle (Bill Kenney and Carlos Carson) .08 .25
81 NFL Team Highlights Lying In Wait (Atlanta defense) .08 .25
82 NFL Team Highlights Celebration .08 .25
83 NFL Team Highlights Men In Motion (Lawrence Taylor) .08 .25
84 NFL Team Highlights Shotgun Formation .08 .25
85 NFL Team Highlights Training Camp .08 .25
86 NFL Team Highlights Halftime Instructions (Bill Walsh in locker room) .40 1.00
87 NFL Team Highlights Field Goal Attempt (Rolf Benirschke) .08 .25
88 NFL Team Highlights Free Kick .15 .40

1982 Fleer Team Action Stickers

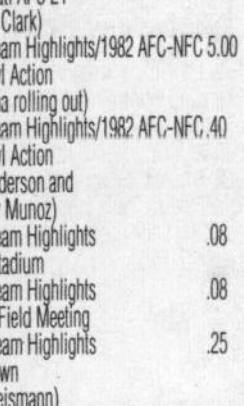

Fleer again re-designed the Team Action Sticker sets in 1982 to feature the team's helmet or logo against a gold colored background along with a team name sticker. This set was issued one sticker per pack and features all NFL teams with most in two different stickers. Cardbacks contain the team's 1982 NFL schedule printed in red ink. Each sticker measures roughly 2" by 3".

COMPLETE SET (50) 20.00 50.00
1 Atlanta Falcons Helmet .30 .75
2 Atlanta Falcons Logo .30 .75
3 Baltimore Colts Helmet (COLTS printed in smaller letters on front) .50 1.25
4 Baltimore Colts Helmet (COLTC printed in larger letters on front) .50 1.25
5 Buffalo Bills Helmet .50 1.25
6 Buffalo Bills Logo .50 1.25
7 Chicago Bears Helmet .50 1.25
8 Chicago Bears Logo .50 1.25
9 Cincinnati Bengals Helmet .50 1.25
10 Cleveland Browns Helmet .50 1.25
11 Dallas Cowboys Large Helmet .75 2.00
12 Dallas Cowboys Small Helmet .75 2.00
13 Denver Broncos Helmet .50 1.25
14 Denver Broncos Logo .50 1.25
15 Detroit Lions Helmet .30 .75
16 Detroit Lions Logo .30 .75
17 Green Bay Packers Helmet .75 2.00
18 Green Bay Packers Helmet (green outline missing from ear hole) .75 2.00
19 Houston Oilers Helmet .30 .75
20 Houston Oilers Logo .30 .75
21 Kansas City Chiefs Helmet .30 .75
22 Kansas City Chiefs Logo .30 .75
23 Los Angeles Rams Helmet .30 .75
24 Los Angeles Rams Logo .30 .75
25 Miami Dolphins Helmet .75 2.00
26 Miami Dolphins Logo .75 2.00
27 Minnesota Vikings Helmet .50 1.25
28 Minnesota Vikings Logo .50 1.25
29 New England Patriots Helmet .30 .75
30 New England Patriots Logo .30 .75
31 New Orleans Saints Helmet .30 .75
32 New Orleans Saints Logo .30 .75
33 New York Giants Helmet (with TM) .50 1.25
34 New York Giants Helmet (without TM) .50 1.25
35 New York Jets Helmet .50 1.25
36 Oakland Raiders Helmet .75 2.00
37 Oakland Raiders Logo .75 2.00
38 Philadelphia Eagles Helmet .30 .75
39 Philadelphia Eagles Logo .30 .75
40 Pittsburgh Steelers Helmet .75 2.00
41 Pittsburgh Steelers Logo .75 2.00
42 St. Louis Cardinals Helmet .30 .75
43 St. Louis Cardinals Logo .30 .75
44 San Diego Chargers Helmet .30 .75
45 San Francisco 49ers Helmet .75 2.00
46 San Francisco 49ers Logo .75 2.00
47 Seattle Seahawks Helmet .30 .75
48 Tampa Bay Bucs Helmet .30 .75
49 Tampa Bay Bucs Logo .30 .75
50 Washington Redskins Helmet .50 1.25
51 Washington Redskins Logo .50 1.25

1983 Fleer Team Action

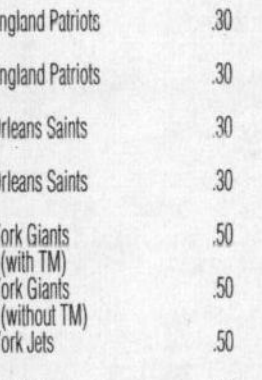

The 1983 Fleer Teams in Action football set contains 88 standard-size cards. There are two cards numbered 67, one of which was obviously intended to be card number 66. The backs are printed in blue on white card stock. These cards feature a 1983 copyright date. The card numbering follows team name alphabetical order followed by Super Bowl cards in chronological order and NFL Team Highlights cards. Cards were issued in seven-card packs along with three team logo stickers.

COMPLETE SET (88) 8.00 20.00
1 Atlanta Falcons Breaking Away to Daylight (Ronnie Lott) .40 1.00
2 Atlanta Falcons Piled Up .08 .25
3 Baltimore Colts Cutting Back to Daylight .08 .25
4 Baltimore Colts Pressuring the QB (Joe Ferguson) .08 .25
5 Buffalo Bills Moving to the Outside (Roosevelt Leaks running) .08 .25
6 Buffalo Bills Buffalo Stampede .08 .25
7 Chicago Bears Ready to Let It Fly (Jim McMahon and Walter Payton) 1.00 2.50
8 Chicago Bears Jump Ball .08 .25
9 Cincinnati Bengals Hurdling Into Open .08 .25
10 Cincinnati Bengals Hands Up .08 .25
11 Cleveland Browns An Open Field Ahead (Mike Pruitt) .08 .25
12 Cleveland Browns Reacting to the Ball Carrier .08 .25
13 Dallas Cowboys Mid-Air Ballet (Tony Dorsett) .50 1.25
14 Dallas Cowboys/3& 2& 1 Takeoff .15 .40
15 Denver Broncos Clear Sailing .08 .25
16 Denver Broncos Stacking Up Offense .08 .25
17 Detroit Lions Hitting the Wall .08 .25
18 Detroit Lions Snapping into Action .08 .25
19 Green Bay Packers Fingertip Control (Ed Too Tall Jones) .30 .75
20 Green Bay Packers QB Sack .08 .25
21 Houston Oilers Sweeping to Outside .08 .25
22 Houston Oilers Halting Forward Progress (Freeman McNeil) .08 .25
23 Kansas City Chiefs Waiting for the Key Block .08 .25
24 Kansas City Chiefs Going Head to Head (John Hannah) .15 .40
25 Los Angeles Raiders Bombs Away (Jim Plunkett passing) .20 .50
26 Los Angeles Raiders Caged Bengal .15 .40
27 Los Angeles Rams Clearing Out Mildle .08 .25
28 Los Angeles Rams One on One Tackle .08 .25
29 Miami Dolphins Skating through Hole .15 .40
30 Miami Dolphins Follow the Bouncing Ball .15 .40
31 Minnesota Vikings Dropping into Pocket (Tommy Kramer) .15 .40
32 Minnesota Vikings Attacking from All Angles .08 .25
33 New England Patriots Touchdown .08 .25
34 New England Patriots Pouncing Patriots (Walter Payton tackled) 1.00 2.50
35 New Orleans Saints Only One Man to Beat .08 .25
36 New Orleans Saints Closing In (Tony Dorsett) .50 1.25
37 New York Giants Setting Up to Pass .08 .25
38 New York Giants In Pursuit .08 .25
39 New York Jets Just Enough Room .08 .25
40 New York Jets Wrapping Up Runner .08 .25
41 Philadelphia Eagles Play Action Fakers (Ron Jaworski and Harry Carson) .15 .40
42 Philadelphia Eagles Step Away from Sack (Archie Manning) .15 .40
43 Pittsburgh Steelers Exploding Through a Hole (Franco Harris and Terry Bradshaw) .40 1.00
44 Pittsburgh Steelers Outnumbered (Jack Lambert) .30 .75
45 St. Louis Cardinals Keeping His Balance .08 .25
46 St. Louis Cardinals Waiting for the Reinforcements .08 .25
47 San Diego Chargers Supercharged Charger .08 .25
48 San Diego Chargers Triple Team Tackle .08 .25
49 San Francisco 49ers There's No Stopping Him Now .15 .40
50 San Francisco 49ers Heading 'Em Off at the Pass .15 .40
51 Seattle Seahawks Calling the Signals (Jim Zorn) .15 .40
52 Seattle Seahawks The Hands Have It .08 .25
53 Tampa Bay Buccaneers Off to the Races .08 .25
54 Tampa Bay Buccaneers Buccaneer Sandwich .08 .25
55 Washington Redskins Looking for Daylight .15 .40
56 Washington Redskins Smothering the Ball Carrier .15 .40
57 Super Bowl I Green Bay NFL 35 Kansas City AFL 10 (Jim Taylor) .30 .75
58 Super Bowl II Green Bay NFL 33 Oakland AFL 14 .08 .25
59 Super Bowl III New York AFL 16 Baltimore NFL 7 .08 .25
60 Super Bowl IV Kansas City AFL 23 Minnesota NFL 7 .08 .25
61 Super Bowl V Baltimore AFC 16 Dallas NFC 13 (Johnny Unitas) .60 1.50
62 Super Bowl VI Dallas NFC 24 Miami AFC 3 (Bob Griese and Bob Lilly) .40 1.00
63 Super Bowl VII Miami AFC 14 Washington NFC 7 (Manny Fernandez) .15 .40
64 Super Bowl VIII Miami AFC 24 Minnesota NFC 7 (Larry Csonka diving) .30 .75
65 Super Bowl IX Pittsburgh AFC 16 Minnesota NFC 6 (Franco Harris) .40 1.00
66 Super Bowl X UER Pittsburgh AFC 21 Dallas NFC 17 (Terry Bradshaw; number on back 67) .60 1.50
67 Super Bowl XI Oakland AFC 32 Minnesota NFC 14 (see also card 66) .15 .40
68 Super Bowl XII Dallas NFC 27 Denver AFC 10 .08 .25
69 Super Bowl XIII Pittsburgh AFC 35 Dallas NFC 31 (Terry Bradshaw passing) .60 1.50
70 Super Bowl XIV Pittsburgh AFC 31 Los Angeles NFC 19 (Vince Ferragamo passing) .08 .25
71 Super Bowl XV Oakland AFC 27 Philadelphia NFC 10 .08 .25
72 Super Bowl XVI San Francisco NFC 26 Cincinnati AFC 21 .08 .25
73 Super Bowl XVII Washington NFC 27 Miami AFC 17 (John Riggins running) .30 .75
74 NFL Team Highlights/1983 AFC-NFC Pro Bowl (Dan Fouts) .40 1.00
75 NFL Team Highlights Super Bowl XVII Spectacular .08 .25
76 NFL Team Highlights Tampa Stadium: Super Bowl XVIII .08 .25
77 NFL Team Highlights Up& Up& and Away .08 .25
78 NFL Team Highlights Sideline Conference (Steve Bartkowski) .15 .40
79 NFL Team Highlights Barefoot Follow-Through (Mike Lansford) .08 .25
80 NFL Team Highlights Fourth and Long (Max Runager punting) .08 .25
81 NFL Team Highlights Blocked Punt .08 .25
82 NFL Team Highlights Fumble .08 .25
83 NFL Team Highlights National Anthem .08 .25
84 NFL Team Highlights Concentrating on the Ball (Tony Franklin) .08 .25
85 NFL Team Highlights Splashing Around .08 .25
86 NFL Team Highlights Loading in Shotgun .08 .25
87 NFL Team Highlights Taking the Snap .08 .25
88 NFL Team Highlights Line of Scrimmage .15 .40

1983 Fleer Team Action Stickers

The 1983 Fleer Team Action Sticker set is virtually identical to the 1982 release. Each features the team's helmet or logo against a gold colored background along with a team name sticker. This set was issued one sticker per pack and features all NFL teams with most in two different stickers. The cardbacks contain the team's 1983 NFL schedule printed in red ink. Each sticker measures roughly 2" by 3".

COMPLETE SET (51) 14.00 35.00
1 Atlanta Falcons Helmet .25 .60
2 Atlanta Falcons Logo .25 .60
3 Baltimore Colts Helmet (COLTS printed in smaller letters on front) .40 1.00
4 Baltimore Colts Helmet (COLTS printed in larger letters on front) .40 1.00
5 Buffalo Bills Helmet .40 1.00
6 Buffalo Bills Logo .40 1.00
7 Chicago Bears Helmet .40 1.00
8 Chicago Bears Logo .40 1.00
9 Cincinnati Bengals Helmet .40 1.00
10 Cleveland Browns Helmet .40 1.00
11 Dallas Cowboys Large Helmet .60 1.50
12 Dallas Cowboys Small Helmet .60 1.50
13 Denver Broncos Helmet .40 1.00
14 Denver Broncos Logo .40 1.00
15 Detroit Lions Helmet .25 .60
16 Detroit Lions Logo .25 .60
17 Green Bay Packers Helmet .60 1.50
18 Green Bay Packers Helmet (green outline missing from ear hole) .60 1.50
19 Houston Oilers Helmet .25 .60
20 Houston Oilers Logo .25 .60
21 Kansas City Chiefs Helmet .25 .60
22 Kansas City Chiefs Logo .25 .60
23 Los Angeles Raiders Helmet .60 1.50
24 Los Angeles Raiders Logo .60 1.50
25 Los Angeles Rams Helmet .25 .60
26 Los Angeles Rams Logo .25 .60
27 Miami Dolphins Helmet .60 1.50
28 Miami Dolphins Logo .60 1.50
29 Minnesota Vikings Helmet .40 1.00
30 Minnesota Vikings Logo .40 1.00
31 New England Patriots Helmet .25 .60
32 New England Patriots Logo .25 .60
33 New Orleans Saints Helmet .25 .60
34 New Orleans Saints Logo .25 .60
35 New York Giants Helmet (with TM) .40 1.00
36 New York Giants Helmet (without TM) .40 1.00
37 New York Jets Helmet .40 1.00
38 Philadelphia Eagles Helmet .25 .60
39 Philadelphia Eagles Logo .25 .60
40 Pittsburgh Steelers Helmet .60 1.50
41 Pittsburgh Steelers Logo .60 1.50
42 St. Louis Cardinals Helmet .25 .60
43 St. Louis Cardinals Logo .25 .60
44 San Diego Chargers Helmet .25 .60
45 San Francisco 49ers Helmet .60 1.50
46 San Francisco 49ers Logo .60 1.50
47 Seattle Seahawks Helmet .25 .60
48 Tampa Bay Bucs Helmet .25 .60
49 Tampa Bay Bucs Logo .25 .60
50 Washington Redskins Helmet .40 1.00
51 Washington Redskins Logo .40 1.00

1984 Fleer Team Action

The 1984 Fleer Teams in Action football card set contains 88 standard-size cards. The cards feature a 1984 copyright date. The cards show action scenes with specific players not identified. There is a green border on the fronts of the cards with the title of the card inside a yellow strip; the backs are red and white. The card fronts are in full color. The card numbering follows team name alphabetical order (with the exception of the Indianapolis Colts whose last-minute move from Baltimore apparently put them out of order) followed by Super Bowl cards in chronological order and NFL Team Highlights cards. Cards were issued in seven-card wax packs along with three team logo stickers.

COMPLETE SET (88) 8.00 20.00
1 Atlanta Falcons .15 .40
2 Atlanta Falcons Gang Tackle .08 .25
3 Indianapolis Colts About to Break Free .08 .25
4 Indianapolis Colts Cutting Off All the Angles .08 .25
5 Buffalo Bills Cracking the First Line of Defense .08 .25
6 Buffalo Bills Getting Help From A Friend .08 .25
7 Chicago Bears Over the Top (Jim McMahon and Walter Payton) 1.00 2.50
8 Chicago Bears You Grab Him High I'll Grab Him Low .08 .25
9 Cincinnati Bengals Skipping Through an Opening .08 .25
10 Cincinnati Bengals Saying Hello to a QB (Joe Ferguson) .08 .25
11 Cleveland Browns Free Sailing into .08 .25

1984 Fleer Team Action

the End Zone
(Greg Pruitt)
12 Cleveland Browns .08 .25
Making Sure of
the Tackle
13 Dallas Cowboys .20 .50
(Danny White)
14 Dallas Cowboys .25 .60
Cowboy's Corral
(Ed Too Tall Jones)
15 Denver Broncos .08 .25
Sprinting into the Open
16 Denver Broncos .08 .25
Ready to Pounce
(Curt Warner)
17 Detroit Lions .15 .40
Lion on the Prowl
(Billy Sims)
18 Detroit Lions .25 .60
Stacking Up
the Ball Carrier
(John Riggins)
19 Green Bay Packers .08 .25
Waiting For the
Hole to Open
20 Green Bay Packers .08 .25
Packing Up
Your Opponent
21 Houston Oilers 1.50 4.00
Nothing But Open
Spaces Ahead
(Earl Campbell)
22 Houston Oilers .08 .25
Meeting Him Head On
23 Kansas City Chiefs .08 .25
Going Outside for
Extra Yardage
24 Kansas City Chiefs .08 .25
A Running Back
in Trouble
25 Los Angeles Raiders .75 2.00
No Defenders in Sight
(Marcus Allen)
26 Los Angeles Raiders .40 1.00
Rampaging Raiders
(Howie Long and
John Riggins)
27 Los Angeles Rams .08 .25
Making the Cut
28 Los Angeles Rams .08 .25
Caught From Behind
29 Miami Dolphins .15 .40
Sliding Down the Line
30 Miami Dolphins .15 .40
Making Sure
31 Minnesota Vikings .08 .25
Stretching For
Touchdown
32 Minnesota Vikings .08 .25
Hitting the Wall
33 New England Patriots .15 .40
Straight Up the Middle
(Steve Grogan)
34 New England Patriots 1.25 3.00
Come here and
Give Me a Hug
(Earl Campbell tackled)
35 New Orleans Saints .08 .25
One Defender to Beat
36 New Orleans Saints .08 .25
Saints Sandwich
37 New York Giants .08 .25
A Six Point Landing
38 New York Giants .08 .25
Leaping to the Aid
of a Teammate
39 New York Jets .08 .25
Galloping through
Untouched
40 New York Jets .08 .25
Capturing the Enemy
41 Philadelphia Eagles .08 .25
One More Block and
He's Gone
42 Philadelphia Eagles .08 .25
Meeting an Opponent
With Open Arms
43 Pittsburgh Steelers .15 .40
The Play Begins
to Develop
44 Pittsburgh Steelers .15 .40
Rally Around the
Ball Carrier
45 St. Louis Cardinals .08 .25
Sprinting Around
the Corner
46 St. Louis Cardinals .08 .25
Overmatched
47 San Diego Chargers .08 .25
Up& Up& and Away
48 San Diego Chargers .08 .25
Engulfing the Opponent
49 San Francisco 49ers .15 .40
Tunneling Up
the Middle
(Wendell Tyler)
50 San Francisco 49ers .25 .60
Nowhere to Go but
Down (John Riggins)
51 Seattle Seahawks .08 .25
Letting the Ball Fly
(Jim Zorn)
52 Seattle Seahawks .08 .25
Handing Out
Some Punishment
53 Tampa Bay Buccaneers .08 .25
When he Hits the
Ground He's Gone
54 Tampa Bay Buccaneers .08 .25
One Leg Takedown
55 Washington Redskins .25 .60
Plenty of Room to Run
(John Riggins)
56 Washington Redskins .15 .40
Squashing the Opponent
57 Super Bowl I .20 .50
Green Bay NFL 35
Kansas City AFL 10
(Jim Taylor)
58 Super Bowl II .30 .75
Green Bay NFL 33
Oakland AFL 14
(Bart Starr)
59 Super Bowl III .08 .25
New York AFL 16
Baltimore NFL 7
60 Super Bowl IV .08 .25
Kansas City AFL 23
Minnesota NFL 7
61 Super Bowl V .20 .50
Baltimore AFC 16
Dallas NFC 13
(Earl Morrall)
62 Super Bowl VI .50 1.25
Dallas NFC 24
Miami AFC 3
(Roger Staubach)
63 Super Bowl VII .25 .60
Miami AFC 14
Washington NFC 7
(Jim Kiick and
Bob Griese)
64 Super Bowl VIII .30 .75
Miami AFC 24
Minnesota NFC 7
(Larry Csonka diving)
65 Super Bowl IX .50 1.25
Pittsburgh AFC 16
Minnesota NFC 6
(Terry Bradshaw)
66 Super Bowl X .30 .75
Pittsburgh AFC 21
Dallas NFC 17
(Franco Harris)
67 Super Bowl XI .08 .25
Oakland AFC 32
Minnesota NFC 14
68 Super Bowl XII .40 1.00
Dallas NFC 27
Denver AFC 10
(Tony Dorsett)
69 Super Bowl XIII .30 .75
Pittsburgh AFC 35
Dallas NFC 31
(Franco Harris)
70 Super Bowl XIV .30 .75
Pittsburgh AFC 31
Los Angeles NFC 19
(Franco Harris)
71 Super Bowl XV .08 .25
Oakland AFC 27
Philadelphia NFC 10
(Jim Plunkett)
72 Super Bowl XVI .08 .25
San Francisco NFC 26
Cincinnati AFC 21
73 Super Bowl XVII .08 .25
Washington NFC 27
Miami AFC 17
74 Super Bowl XVIII .30 .75
Los Angeles AFC 38
Washington NFC 9
(Howie Long)
75 NFL Team Highlights .08 .25
Official's Conference
76 NFL Team Highlights .08 .25
Leaping for the
Ball Carrier
77 NFL Team Highlights .08 .25
Setting Up in the
Passing Pocket
(Jim Plunkett)
78 NFL Team Highlights .08 .25
Field Goal Block
79 NFL Team Highlights .15 .40
Stopped For No Gain
(Steve Grogan)
80 NFL Team Highlights .08 .25
Double Team Block
81 NFL Team Highlights .08 .25
Kickoff
82 NFL Team Highlights .08 .25
Punt Block
83 NFL Team Highlights .08 .25
Coaches Signals
84 NFL Team Highlights .08 .25
Training Camp
85 NFL Team Highlights .08 .25
Fumble
(Dwight Stephenson)
86 NFL Team Highlights/1984 AFC-NFC Pro Bowl .08
.25
87 NFL Team Highlights .08 .25
Cheerleaders
88 NFL Team Highlights .25 .60
In the Huddle
(Joe Theismann)

1984 Fleer Team Action Stickers

The 1984 Fleer Team Action Sticker set is virtually identical to the 1983 release with only a small change in the border color. Each features the team's helmet or logo against a yellow colored background along with a team name sticker. This set was issued one sticker per pack and features all NFL teams with most in two different stickers. The cardbacks contain the team's 1984 NFL schedule printed in blue ink. Each sticker measures roughly 2" by 3."

COMPLETE SET (51) 14.00 35.00
1 Atlanta Falcons .25 .60
Helmet
2 Atlanta Falcons .25 .60
Logo
3 Buffalo Bills .40 1.00
Helmet
4 Buffalo Bills .40 1.00
Logo
5 Chicago Bears .40 1.00
Helmet
6 Chicago Bears .40 1.00
Logo
7 Cincinnati Bengals .25 .60
Helmet
8 Cleveland Browns .40 1.00
Helmet
9 Dallas Cowboys .60 1.50
Large Helmet
10 Dallas Cowboys .60 1.50
Small Helmet
11 Denver Broncos .40 1.00
Helmet
12 Denver Broncos .40 1.00
Logo
13 Detroit Lions .25 .60
Helmet
14 Detroit Lions .25 .60
Logo
15 Green Bay Packers .60 1.50
Helmet
16 Green Bay Packers .60 1.50
Helmet
(green outline missing from ear hole)
17 Houston Oilers .25 .60
Helmet
18 Houston Oilers .25 .60
Logo
19 Indianapolis Colts Helmet .40 1.00
(COLTS printed in
smaller letters on front)
20 Indianapolis Colts Helmet .40 1.00
(COLTS printed in
larger letters on front)
21 Kansas City Chiefs .25 .60
Helmet
22 Kansas City Chiefs .25 .60
Logo
23 Los Angeles Raiders .60 1.50
Helmet
24 Los Angeles Raiders .60 1.50
Logo
25 Los Angeles Rams .25 .60
Helmet
26 Los Angeles Rams .25 .60
Logo
27 Miami Dolphins .60 1.50
Helmet
28 Miami Dolphins .60 1.50
Logo
29 Minnesota Vikings .40 1.00
Helmet
30 Minnesota Vikings .40 1.00
Logo
31 New England Patriots .25 .60
Helmet
32 New England Patriots .25 .60
Logo
33 New Orleans Saints .25 .60
Helmet
34 New Orleans Saints .25 .60
Logo
35 New York Giants .40 1.00
Helmet (with TM)
36 New York Giants .40 1.00
Helmet (without TM)
37 New York Jets .40 1.00
Helmet
38 Philadelphia Eagles .25 .60
Helmet
39 Philadelphia Eagles .25 .60
Logo
40 Pittsburgh Steelers .60 1.50
Helmet
41 Pittsburgh Steelers .60 1.50
Logo
42 St. Louis Cardinals .25 .60
Helmet
43 St. Louis Cardinals .25 .60
Logo
44 San Diego Chargers .25 .60
Helmet
45 San Francisco 49ers .60 1.50
Helmet
46 San Francisco 49ers .60 1.50
Logo
47 Seattle Seahawks .25 .60
Helmet
48 Tampa Bay Bucs .25 .60
Helmet
49 Tampa Bay Bucs .25 .60
Logo
50 Washington Redskins .40 1.00
Helmet
51 Washington Redskins .40 1.00
Logo

1985 Fleer Team Action

This 88-card standard-size set, entitled Fleer Teams in Action, is essentially organized alphabetically by the name of the team. There are three cards for each team, the first subtitled "On Offense" with offensive team statistics on the back, the second "On Defense" with defensive team statistics on the back, and the third "In Action" with a team schedule for the upcoming 1985 season. The last four cards feature highlights of the previous three Super Bowls and Pro Bowl. The cards are typically oriented horizontally. The cards feature a 1985 copyright date. The cards show full-color action scenes with specific players not identified. The card backs are printed in orange and black on white card stock. Cards were issued in wax packs of 15 cards and one sticker.

COMPLETE SET (88) 10.00 25.00
1 Atlanta Falcons .15 .40
Nothing But Open
Spaces Ahead
2 Atlanta Falcons .08 .25
Leveling Ball Carrier
3 Atlanta Falcons .25 .60
Flying Falcon
(John Riggins)
4 Buffalo Bills .08 .25
Ducking Under
the Pressure
5 Buffalo Bills .08 .25
Swallowing Up
the Opponent
6 Buffalo Bills .08 .25
Avoiding Late Hit
7 Chicago Bears .75 2.00
Picking His Spot
(Walter Payton)
8 Chicago Bears .08 .25
C'Mon Guys& Give Me
Some Room to Breathe
9 Chicago Bears .30 .75
Just Hanging Around
in Case They're Needed
(Richard Dent)
10 Cincinnati Bengals .08 .25
Struggling for
Every Extra Yard
11 Cincinnati Bengals .08 .25
Making Opponent Pay
12 Cincinnati Bengals .08 .25
Just Out of the
Reach of the Defender
13 Cleveland Browns .08 .25
Plenty of Time to
Fire the Ball
14 Cleveland Browns .08 .25
Hitting the Wall
15 Cleveland Browns .08 .25
Look What We Found
16 Dallas Cowboys .40 1.00
Waiting for the Right
Moment to Burst Upfield
(Tony Dorsett and
Wilber Marshall)
17 Dallas Cowboys .50 1.25
Sorry Buddy& This is
the End of the Line
(Ed Too Tall Jones
tackling Walter Payton)
18 Dallas Cowboys .25 .60
Following Through
for Three Points
(Ed Too Tall Jones)
19 Denver Broncos .08 .25
Blasting Up the Middle
20 Denver Broncos .08 .25
Finishing Off
the Tackle
21 Denver Broncos .08 .25
About to Hit Paydirt
22 Detroit Lions .08 .25
Waiting to Throw
Until the Last Second
(Dexter Manley)
23 Detroit Lions .08 .25
Double Trouble on
the Tackle
24 Detroit Lions .08 .25
Quick Pitch
25 Green Bay Packers .15 .40
Unleashing the
Long Bomb
(Steve McMichael)
26 Green Bay Packers .40 1.00
Encircling the
Ball Carrier
(Marcus Allen)
27 Green Bay Packers .08 .25
Piggy-Back Ride
28 Houston Oilers 1.50 4.00
Retreating into
the Pocket
(Warren Moon and
Earl Campbell)
29 Houston Oilers .08 .25
Punishing the Enemy
30 Houston Oilers .08 .25
No Chance to
Block This One
31 Indianapolis Colts .08 .25
Getting Ready to
Let It Fly
32 Indianapolis Colts .08 .25
Pushing the Ball
Carrier Backward
33 Indianapolis Colts .08 .25
Nowhere to Go
34 Kansas City Chiefs .08 .25
Cutting Back for
Extra Yardage
35 Kansas City Chiefs .08 .25
Reaching for
the Deflection
36 Kansas City Chiefs .08 .25
Rising to the Occasion
37 Los Angeles Raiders .15 .40
Hurdling Into
the Open Field
38 Los Angeles Raiders .15 .40
No Place To Go
39 Los Angeles Raiders .15 .40
Standing Tall
In the Pocket
40 Los Angeles Rams .40 1.00
One More Barrier and
He's Off to the Races
(Eric Dickerson)
41 Los Angeles Rams .08 .25
Driving A Shoulder
Into the Opponent
42 Los Angeles Rams .08 .25
The Kickoff
43 Miami Dolphins .15 .40
Sidestepping Trouble
(Tony Nathan)
44 Miami Dolphins .15 .40
Hold On& We're Coming
45 Miami Dolphins 4.00 10.00
The Release Point
(Dan Marino)
46 Minnesota Vikings .08 .25
Putting As Much As
He Has Into the Pass
(Tommy Kramer)
47 Minnesota Vikings .08 .25
Gang Tackling
48 Minnesota Vikings .08 .25
You're Not Getting Away
From Me This Time
49 New England Patriots .08 .25
Throwing On the Run
(Tony Eason)
50 New England Patriots .08 .25
The Only Place to Go
Is Down
51 New England Patriots .08 .25
Standing the Ball
Carrier Up
52 New Orleans Saints .08 .25
Going Up the Middle
Under A Full Head
of Steam
53 New Orleans Saints .08 .25
Putting Everything
They've Got Into
the Tackle
54 New Orleans Saints .08 .25
Getting Off the Ground
to Block the Kick
55 New York Giants .08 .25
Over the Top
56 New York Giants .08 .25
Rallying Around
the Opposition
57 New York Giants .20 .50
The Huddle
(Phil Simms)
58 New York Jets .08 .25
Following His Blockers
59 New York Jets .08 .25
This Is As Far
As You Go
60 New York Jets .08 .25
Looking Over
the Defense
61 Philadelphia Eagles .08 .25
Going Through the
Opening Untouched
62 Philadelphia Eagles .08 .25
Squashing the Enemy
63 Philadelphia Eagles .08 .25
There's No Room
Here& So Let's
Go Outside
64 Pittsburgh Steelers .15 .40
Sprinting Around
the End
65 Pittsburgh Steelers .15 .40
Mismatch
66 Pittsburgh Steelers .15 .40
About to Be Thrown
Back
67 St.Louis Cardinals .08 .25
In for Six
68 St.Louis Cardinals .08 .25
Piling Up the
Ball Carrier
69 St.Louis Cardinals .20 .50
Causing the Fumble
(Joe Theismann tackled)
70 San Diego Chargers .08 .25
Plenty of Open
Space Ahead
71 San Diego Chargers .08 .25
Ready to Be
Swallowed Up
72 San Diego Chargers .08 .25
A Quarterback in
Serious Trouble
73 San Francisco 49ers .15 .40
Reading the Hole and
Exploding Through It
74 San Francisco 49ers .15 .40
Burying the Opponent
75 San Francisco 49ers 3.00 8.00
Waiting to Throw
Until His Receiver
Breaks Free
(Joe Montana and
Russ Francis)
76 Seattle Seahawks .15 .40
Getting Just Enough
Time to Pass
(Dave Krieg)
77 Seattle Seahawks .15 .40
Capturing the Enemy
(Craig James tackled)
78 Seattle Seahawks .08 .25
It's Going to Be
A Footrace Now
79 Tampa Bay Buccaneers .08 .25
Heading Outside Away
From Trouble
80 Tampa Bay Buccaneers .08 .25
One-On-One Tackle
81 Tampa Bay Buccaneers .25 .60
A Buccaneers Sandwich
(Dickerson tackled)
82 Washington Redskins .25 .60
Just Enough Room
To Get Through
(John Riggins)
83 Washington Redskins .15 .40
Wrapping Up
the Opponent
84 Washington Redskins .15 .40
Field-Goal Attempt
(Mark Moseley)
85 Super Bowl XIX .25 .60
San Francisco NFC 38
Miami AFC 16
(Roger Craig running)
86 Super Bowl XIX 2.00 5.00
San Francisco NFC 38
Miami AFC 16
(Joe Montana passing)
87 Super Bowl XIX .15 .40
San Francisco NFC 38
Miami AFC 16
(Tony Nathan tackled)
88 1985 Pro Bowl .15 .40
AFC 22& NFC 14
(Runner stopped)

1985 Fleer Team Action Stickers

The 1985 Fleer Team Action Sticker set is very similar to previous releases. Each features the team's helmet or logo against a blue colored background along with a team name sticker. This set was issued one sticker per pack and features all NFL teams with most in two different stickers. The cardbacks contain an offer to participate in a Fleer Cheer Contest. Each sticker measures roughly 2" by 3."

COMPLETE SET (50) 15.00 30.00
1 Atlanta Falcons .30 .75
Helmet
2 Atlanta Falcons .30 .75
Logo
3 Buffalo Bills .40 1.00
Helmet
4 Buffalo Bills .40 1.00
Logo
5 Chicago Bears .40 1.00
Helmet
6 Chicago Bears .40 1.00
Logo
7 Cincinnati Bengals .30 .75
Helmet
8 Cleveland Browns .40 1.00
Helmet
9 Dallas Cowboys .60 1.50
Large Helmet
10 Dallas Cowboys .60 1.50
Small Helmet
11 Denver Broncos .40 1.00
Helmet
12 Denver Broncos .40 1.00
Logo
13 Detroit Lions .30 .75
Helmet
14 Detroit Lions .30 .75
Logo
15 Green Bay Packers .60 1.50
Helmet
16 Green Bay Packers .60 1.50
Helmet
(green outline missing from ear hole)
17 Houston Oilers .30 .75
Helmet
18 Houston Oilers .30 .75
Logo
19 Indianapolis Colts .40 1.00
Small Helmet
20 Indianapolis Colts .40 1.00
Large Helmet
21 Kansas City Chiefs .30 .75
Helmet
22 Kansas City Chiefs .30 .75
Logo
23 Los Angeles Raiders .60 1.50
Helmet
24 Los Angeles Raiders .60 1.50
Logo
25 Los Angeles Rams .30 .75
Helmet
26 Los Angeles Rams .30 .75
Logo
27 Miami Dolphins .60 1.50
Helmet
28 Miami Dolphins .60 1.50
Logo
29 Minnesota Vikings .40 1.00
Helmet
30 Minnesota Vikings .40 1.00
Logo
31 New England Patriots .30 .75
Helmet
32 New England Patriots .30 .75
Logo
33 New Orleans Saints .30 .75
Helmet
34 New Orleans Saints .30 .75
Logo
35 New York Giants .40 1.00
Helmet
36 New York Jets .40 1.00
Helmet
37 Philadelphia Eagles .30 .75
Helmet
38 Philadelphia Eagles .30 .75
Logo
39 Pittsburgh Steelers .60 1.50
Helmet
40 Pittsburgh Steelers .60 1.50
Logo
41 St. Louis Cardinals .30 .75
Helmet
42 St. Louis Cardinals .30 .75
Logo
43 San Diego Chargers .30 .75
Helmet
44 San Francisco 49ers .60 1.50
Helmet
45 San Francisco 49ers .60 1.50
Logo
46 Seattle Seahawks .30 .75
Helmet
47 Tampa Bay Bucs .30 .75
Helmet
48 Tampa Bay Bucs .30 .75
Logo
49 Washington Redskins .40 1.00
Helmet
50 Washington Redskins .40 1.00
Logo

1986 Fleer Team Action

This 88-card standard-size set, entitled "Live Action Football," is essentially organized alphabetically by the name of the team. There are three cards for each team; the first subtitled "On Offense" with offensive team statistics on the back, the second "On Defense" with defensive team statistics on the back, and the third "In Action" with a team schedule for the upcoming 1986 season. The last four cards feature highlights of the previous three Super Bowls and Pro Bowl. The cards are typically oriented horizontally. The cards feature a 1986 copyright date. The cards show full-color action scenes (with a light blue border around the photo) with specific players not identified. The card backs are printed in blue and black on white card stock. Cards were issued in wax packs of seven team action cards and three team logo stickers.

COMPLETE SET (88) 10.00 25.00
1 Atlanta Falcons .15 .40
Preparing to Make Cut
2 Atlanta Falcons .08 .25
Everybody Gets
Into the Act
3 Atlanta Falcons .08 .25
Where Do You Think
You're Going
4 Buffalo Bills .08 .25
Turning On the
After-Burners
5 Buffalo Bills .08 .25
Running Into a
Wall of Blue
6 Buffalo Bills .08 .25
Up and Over
7 Chicago Bears .60 1.50
Pocket Forms Around
Passer (Jim McMahon
and Walter Payton)
8 Chicago Bears .30 .75
Monsters of the
Midway II (Richard
Dent and Dan Hampton)
9 Chicago Bears .30 .75
Blitz in a Blizzard
(Mike Singletary)
10 Cincinnati Bengals .15 .40
Plowing through
Defense
(Dave Rimington
and Anthony Munoz)
11 Cincinnati Bengals .08 .25
Zeroing In for the Hit
12 Cincinnati Bengals .30 .75
Oh& No You Don't
(Marcus Allen)
13 Cleveland Browns .40 1.00
Looking for a Hole
to Develop
(Bernie Kosar
and Kevin Mack)
14 Cleveland Browns .08 .25
Buried by the Browns
15 Cleveland Browns .08 .25
Another Runner
Pounded Into the Turf
16 Dallas Cowboys .40 1.00
Hole You Could Drive
Truck Through
(Tony Dorsett)
17 Dallas Cowboys .20 .50
We've Got You
Surrounded
(Jim Jeffcoat)
18 Dallas Cowboys .20 .50
Giving the Referee
Some Help
(Randy White)
19 Denver Broncos 3.00 8.00
The Blockers Spring
Into Action (John Elway)
20 Denver Broncos .08 .25
The Orange Crush
Shows Its Stuff
21 Denver Broncos .08 .25
A Stampede to Block
the Kick
22 Detroit Lions .08 .25
A Runner's Eye View
of the Situation
23 Detroit Lions .08 .25
Levelling the
Ball Carrier
24 Detroit Lions .08 .25
Going All Out to Get
the Quarterback
25 Green Bay Packers .08 .25
Sweeping Around
the Corner
26 Green Bay Packers .08 .25
Not Afraid to Go
Head to Head
27 Green Bay Packers .08 .25
Taking the Snap
28 Houston Oilers .08 .25
Plunging for that
Extra Yard
29 Houston Oilers .08 .25
Tightening the Vise
30 Houston Oilers .08 .25
Launching a Field Goal
31 Indianapolis Colts .08 .25
Galloping Out of
an Arm-Tackle
32 Indianapolis Colts .08 .25
Ball Is Knocked Loose
33 Indianapolis Colts .08 .25
Busting Out of the
Backfield
34 Kansas City Chiefs .08 .25
About to Head Upfield
35 Kansas City Chiefs .08 .25
On the Warpath
36 Kansas City Chiefs .08 .25
Getting the Point
Across
37 Los Angeles Raiders .08 .25
Looks Like Clear
Sailing Ahead
38 Los Angeles Raiders .08 .25
Surrounded by
Unfriendly Faces
39 Los Angeles Raiders .08 .25
Vaulting for Six Points
40 Los Angeles Rams .25 .60
Breaking into an Open
Field (Eric Dickerson)
41 Los Angeles Rams .08 .25
Swept Away By a
Wave of Rams
42 Los Angeles Rams .08 .25
Alertly Scooping
Up a Fumble
43 Miami Dolphins .08 .25
Clearing a Path for
the Running Back
44 Miami Dolphins .08 .25
Teaching a Painful
Lesson
45 Miami Dolphins .08 .25
Trying for a Piece
of the Ball
46 Minnesota Vikings .08 .25
All Day to Throw
(Tommy Kramer)
47 Minnesota Vikings .60 1.50
The Moment before
Impact (Walter Payton
tackled)
48 Minnesota Vikings .08 .25
Leaving the
Competition Behind
49 New England Patriots .08 .25
Solid Line of Blockers
50 New England Patriots .08 .25
Surprise Attack from
the Rear
51 New England Patriots .08 .25
Getting a Grip on
the Opponent
52 New Orleans Saints .08 .25
Look Out& I'm Coming
Through
53 New Orleans Saints .08 .25
A Furious Assault
54 New Orleans Saints .08 .25
Line of Scrimmage
55 New York Giants .20 .50
Pass Play Develops
(Phil Simms
and Joe Morris)
56 New York Giants .08 .25
Putting Squeeze on
Offense
57 New York Giants .08 .25
Using a Great Block
to Turn Corner
58 New York Jets .08 .25
The Runner Spots Lane
59 New York Jets .08 .25
About to Deliver
a Headache
60 New York Jets .08 .25
Flying Formation
61 Philadelphia Eagles .20 .50
Slipping a Tackle
(Keith Byars)
62 Philadelphia Eagles .08 .25
Airborne Eagles
Break Up Pass
63 Philadelphia Eagles .08 .25
Connecting on Toss
Over Middle
(Ron Jaworski passing)
64 Pittsburgh Steelers .08 .25
Letting Big Guy
Lead The Way
65 Pittsburgh Steelers .15 .40
Converging From
Every Direction
66 Pittsburgh Steelers .15 .40
All Eyes Are on
the Football
(Gary Anderson K)
67 St.Louis Cardinals .08 .25
Calmly Dropping Back
to Pass (Neil Lomax
and Jim Burt)
68 St.Louis Cardinals .08 .25
Applying Some Bruises
69 St.Louis Cardinals .08 .25
Looking for Yardage
on Interception Return
70 San Diego Chargers UER .08 .25

Human Cannonball
(reverse negative)
71 San Diego Chargers .15 .40
Another One Bites
the Dust
(Dave Krieg)
72 San Diego Chargers .08 .25
A Clean Steal by
the Defense
73 San Francisco 49ers 2.50 6.00
Looking for Safe
Passage
(Joe Montana
handing off)
74 San Francisco 49ers .15 .40
An Uplifting Experience
75 San Francisco 49ers .20 .50
In Hot Pursuit
(Danny White)
76 Seattle Seahawks .08 .25
Preparing for Collision
77 Seattle Seahawks .08 .25
A Group Effort
78 Seattle Seahawks .25 .60
Forcing a Hurried Throw
(Dan Fouts)
79 Tampa Bay Buccaneers .08 .25
Protecting Quarterback
at All Costs
80 Tampa Bay Buccaneers .08 .25
Dishing Out Some
Punishment
81 Tampa Bay Buccaneers .08 .25
No Trespassing
82 Washington Redskins .15 .40
Squaring Off in the
Trenches
83 Washington Redskins .20 .50
Pouncing on the
Passer (Danny White)
84 Washington Redskins .15 .40
Two Hits Are Better
Than One
85 Super Bowl XX .60 1.50
86 Super Bowl XX .20 .50
Chicago NFC 46
New England AFC 10
(Jim McMahon passing)
87 Super Bowl XX .08 .25
Chicago NFC 46
New England AFC 10
(Bears defense)
88 Pro Bowl 1986 .30 .75
NFC 28& AFC 24
(Marcus Allen running)

1986 Fleer Team Action Stickers

The 1986 Fleer Team Action Sticker set is very similar to previous releases. Each features the team's helmet or logo against a blue colored background along with a team name sticker. The helmets were re-designed with a new facemask. This set was issued one sticker per pack and features all NFL teams with most in two different stickers. There are no known variations and cardbacks contain advertisements for various Fleer Candy products printed with red ink. Each sticker measures roughly 2" by 3."

COMPLETE SET (49) 10.00 25.00
1 Atlanta Falcons .20 .50
Helmet
2 Atlanta Falcons .20 .50
Logo
3 Buffalo Bills .30 .75
Helmet
4 Buffalo Bills .30 .75
Logo
5 Chicago Bears .30 .75
Helmet
6 Chicago Bears .30 .75
Logo
7 Cincinnati Bengals .20 .50
Helmet
8 Cleveland Browns .30 .75
Helmet
9 Dallas Cowboys .50 1.25
Large Helmet
10 Dallas Cowboys .50 1.25
Small Helmet
11 Denver Broncos .30 .75
Helmet
12 Denver Broncos .30 .75
Logo
13 Detroit Lions .20 .50
Helmet
14 Detroit Lions .20 .50
Logo
15 Green Bay Packers .50 1.25
Helmet
16 Houston Oilers .20 .50
Helmet
17 Houston Oilers .20 .50
Logo
18 Indianapolis Colts Helmet .30 .75
(COLTS printed in
smaller letters on front)
19 Indianapolis Colts Helmet .30 .75
(COLTS printed in
larger letters on front)
20 Kansas City Chiefs .20 .50
Helmet
21 Kansas City Chiefs .20 .50
Logo
22 Los Angeles Raiders .50 1.25
Helmet
23 Los Angeles Raiders .50 1.25
Logo
24 Los Angeles Rams .20 .50
Helmet
25 Los Angeles Rams .20 .50
Logo
26 Miami Dolphins .50 1.25
Helmet
27 Miami Dolphins .50 1.25
Logo
28 Minnesota Vikings .30 .75
Helmet
29 Minnesota Vikings .30 .75
Logo
30 New England Patriots .20 .50
Helmet
31 New England Patriots .20 .50
Logo
32 New Orleans Saints .20 .50
Helmet
33 New Orleans Saints .20 .50
Logo
34 New York Giants .30 .75
Helmet
35 New York Jets .30 .75
Helmet
36 Philadelphia Eagles .20 .50
Helmet
37 Philadelphia Eagles .20 .50
Logo
38 Pittsburgh Steelers .50 1.25
Helmet
39 Pittsburgh Steelers .50 1.25
Logo
40 St. Louis Cardinals .20 .50
Helmet
41 St. Louis Cardinals .20 .50
Logo
42 San Diego Chargers .20 .50
Helmet
43 San Francisco 49ers .50 1.25
Helmet
44 San Francisco 49ers .50 1.25
Logo
45 Seattle Seahawks .20 .50
Helmet
46 Tampa Bay Bucs .20 .50
Helmet
47 Tampa Bay Bucs .20 .50
Logo
48 Washington Redskins .30 .75
Helmet
49 Washington Redskins .30 .75
Logo

1987 Fleer Team Action

This 88-card standard-size set, entitled "Live Action Football," is essentially organized alphabetically by the name of the team. There are two cards for each team; basically odd-numbered cards feature the team's offense and even-numbered cards feature the team's defense. The cards are typically oriented horizontally. The cards feature a 1987 copyright date. The cards show full-color action scenes (with a yellow and black border around the photo) with specific players not identified. The card backs are printed in gold and black on white card stock. Cards were issued in wax packs of seven team action cards and three team logo stickers.

COMPLETE SET (88) 20.00 35.00
1 Atlanta Falcons .10 .30
A Clear View Downfield
2 Atlanta Falcons .07 .20
Pouncing on a Runner
(Roger Craig tackled)
3 Buffalo Bills .07 .20
Buffalo Stampede
4 Buffalo Bills UER .07 .20
Double Bill
(Bengals and Oilers
pictured)
5 Chicago Bears .50 1.25
Stay Out of Our Way
(Walter Payton)
6 Chicago Bears .10 .30
Quarterback's Night-
mare (Dan Hampton)
7 Cincinnati Bengals .07 .20
Irresistible Force
(Eddie Brown)
8 Cincinnati Bengals UER .07 .20
Bengals on the Prowl
(Bills defense
tackling Bengal)
9 Cleveland Browns .07 .20
Following the
Lead Blocker
10 Cleveland Browns .07 .20
Block That Kick
11 Dallas Cowboys .10 .30
Next Stop...End Zone
12 Dallas Cowboys .10 .30
Ride 'em Cowboys
13 Denver Broncos 1.50 4.00
Pitchout in Progress
(John Elway)
14 Denver Broncos .07 .20
Broncos' Busters
15 Detroit Lions .07 .20
Off to the Races
16 Detroit Lions .07 .20
Entering the Lions' Den
17 Green Bay Packers .07 .20
Setting the Wheels
in Motion
18 Green Bay Packers .07 .20
Stack of Packers
19 Houston Oilers .07 .20
Making a Cut at the
Line of Scrimmage
20 Houston Oilers .07 .20
Hit Parade
21 Indianapolis Colts .07 .20
The Horses Up Front
22 Indianapolis Colts .07 .20
Stopping the Runner
in His Tracks
23 Kansas City Chiefs .07 .20
It's a Snap
24 Kansas City Chiefs .30 .75
Nowhere to Hide
(Bo Jackson getting
tackled)
25 Los Angeles Raiders .40 1.00
Looking for Daylight
(Bo Jackson running)
26 Los Angeles Raiders .10 .30
Wrapped Up by Raiders
27 Los Angeles Rams .10 .30
Movers and Shakers
(Jim Everett)
28 Los Angeles Rams .07 .20
In the Quarter-
back's Face
29 Miami Dolphins .10 .30
Full Speed Ahead
30 Miami Dolphins .10 .30
Acrobatic Interception
31 Minnesota Vikings .07 .20
Solid Line
of Protection
(Tommy Kramer)
32 Minnesota Vikings .07 .20
Bearing a Heavy Load
33 New England Patriots .10 .30
The Blockers Fan Out
(Craig James)
34 New England Patriots .07 .20
Converging Linebackers
35 New Orleans Saints .07 .20
Saints Go Diving In
(Dalton Hilliard
and Jim Burt)
36 New Orleans Saints .07 .20
Crash Course
37 New York Giants .07 .20
Armed and Dangerous
(Phil Simms)
38 New York Giants .30 .75
A Giant-sized Hit
(Lawrence Taylor)
39 New York Jets .07 .20
Jets Prepare
for Takeoff
(Ken O'Brien)
40 New York Jets .07 .20
Showing No Mercy
41 Philadelphia Eagles .07 .20
Taking It Straight
Up the Middle
42 Philadelphia Eagles .50 1.25
The Strong Arm
of the Defense
(Reggie White)
43 Pittsburgh Steelers .10 .30
Double-team Trouble
44 Pittsburgh Steelers .10 .30
Caught in a Steel Trap
45 St. Louis Cardinals .07 .20
The kick is up
and...it's good
46 St. Louis Cardinals .07 .20
Seeing Red
47 San Diego Chargers .07 .20
Blast Off
48 San Diego Chargers .07 .20
Lightning Strikes
(Todd Christensen
tackled)
49 San Francisco 49ers UER .10 .30
The Rush Is On
(reverse negative
photo on front)
50 San Francisco 49ers .10 .30
Shoulder to Shoulder
51 Seattle Seahawks .07 .20
Not a Defender in Sight
(Curt Warner)
52 Seattle Seahawks .07 .20
Hard Knocks
53 Tampa Bay Buccaneers 1.25 3.00
Rolling Out Against
the Grain
(Steve Young)
54 Tampa Bay Buccaneers .07 .20
Crunch Time
55 Washington Redskins .10 .30
Getting the Drop
on the Defense
(Jay Schroeder)
56 Washington Redskins .10 .30
The Blitz Claims
Another Victim
57 AFC Championship Game .07 .20
Denver 23&
Cleveland 20 (OT)
58 AFC Divisional Playoff .07 .20
Cleveland 23&
New York Jets 20 (OT)
59 AFC Divisional Playoff .07 .20
Denver 22&
New England 17
(Andre Tippett)
60 AFC Wild Card Game .07 .20
New York Jets 35&
Kansas City 15
61 NFC Championship .20 .50
New York Giants 17&
Washington 0
(Lawrence Taylor)
62 NFC Divisional Playoff .10 .30
63 NFC Divisional Playoff .10 .30
New York Giants 49&
San Francisco 3
(Joe Morris)
64 NFC Wild Card Game .20 .50
Washington 19&
Los Angeles Rams 7
(Eric Dickerson)
65 Super Bowl I .07 .20
Green Bay NFL 35
Kansas City AFL 10
66 Super Bowl II .20 .50
Green Bay NFL 33
Oakland AFL 14
(Bart Starr)
67 Super Bowl III .07 .20
New York AFL 16
Baltimore NFL 7
(Matt Snell running)
68 Super Bowl IV .07 .20
Kansas City AFL 23
Minnesota NFL 7
69 Super Bowl V .10 .30
Baltimore AFC 16
Dallas NFC 13
(Duane Thomas tackled)
70 Super Bowl VI .50 1.25
Dallas NFC 24
Miami AFC 3
(Roger Staubach)
71 Super Bowl VII .20 .50
Miami AFC 14
Washington NFC 7
(Bob Griese
and Jim Kiick)
72 Super Bowl VIII .20 .50
Miami AFC 24
Minnesota NFC 7
(Larry Csonka running)
73 Super Bowl IX .20 .50
Pittsburgh AFC 16
Minnesota NFC 6
(Fran Tarkenton
loose ball)
74 Super Bowl X .20 .50
Pittsburgh AFC 21
Dallas NFC 17
(Franco Harris)
75 Super Bowl XI .07 .20
Oakland AFC 32
Minnesota NFC 14
(Chuck Foreman
tackled)
76 Super Bowl XII .30 .75
Dallas NFC 27
Denver AFC 10
(Tony Dorsett running)
77 Super Bowl XIII .40 1.00
Pittsburgh AFC 35
Dallas NFC 31
(Terry Bradshaw
passing)
78 Super Bowl XIV .10 .30
Pittsburgh AFC 31
Los Angeles NFC 19
(Cullen Bryant tackled)
79 Super Bowl XV .10 .30
Oakland AFC 27&
Philadelphia NFC 10
(Jim Plunkett passing)
80 Super Bowl XVI .10 .30
San Francisco NFC 26&
Cincinnati AFC 21
81 Super Bowl XVII .07 .20
Washington NFC 27&
Miami AFC 17
82 Super Bowl XVIII .07 .20
Los Angeles AFC 38&
Washington NFC 9
(Punt blocked)
83 Super Bowl XIX 2.00 5.00
San Francisco NFC 38&
Miami AFC 16
(Roger Craig and
Joe Montana)
84 Super Bowl XX .10 .30
Chicago NFC 46&
New England AFC 10
(Wilber Marshall
and Richard Dent)
85 Super Bowl XXI .20 .50
New York NFC 39&
Denver AFC 20
(Lawrence Taylor)
86 Super Bowl XXI .07 .20
New York NFC 39&
Denver AFC 20
(Phil Simms)
87 Super Bowl XXI .20 .50
Giants erupt in 3rd&
Score 17 points
(Lawrence Taylor
and Carl Banks)/(Checklist 1-44 on back)
88 Super Bowl XXI .10 .30
Giants Outrun Broncos
by only 27 yards
(Checklist 45-88
on card back)

1987 Fleer Team Action Stickers

The 1987 Fleer Team Action Sticker set is very similar to previous releases. Each features the team's helmet or logo against a blue colored background along with a team name sticker. This set was issued one sticker per pack and features all NFL teams with most in two different stickers. There are no known variations and cardbacks contain advertisements for various Fleer Candy products printed with blue ink. Each sticker measures roughly 2" by 3."

COMPLETE SET (49) 8.00 20.00
1 Atlanta Falcons .15 .40
Helmet
2 Atlanta Falcons .15 .40
Logo
3 Buffalo Bills .25 .60
Helmet
4 Buffalo Bills .25 .60
Logo
5 Chicago Bears .25 .60
Helmet
6 Chicago Bears .25 .60
Logo
7 Cincinnati Bengals .15 .40
Helmet
8 Cleveland Browns .25 .60
Helmet
9 Dallas Cowboys .40 1.00
Large Helmet
10 Dallas Cowboys .40 1.00
Small Helmet
11 Denver Broncos .25 .60
Helmet
12 Denver Broncos .25 .60
Logo
13 Detroit Lions .15 .40
Helmet
14 Detroit Lions .15 .40
Logo
15 Green Bay Packers .40 1.00
Helmet
16 Houston Oilers .15 .40
Helmet
17 Houston Oilers .15 .40
Logo
18 Indianapolis Colts Helmet .25 .60
(COLTS printed in
smaller letters on front)
19 Indianapolis Colts Helmet .25 .60
(COLTS printed in
larger letters on front)
20 Kansas City Chiefs .15 .40
Helmet
21 Kansas City Chiefs .15 .40
Logo
22 Los Angeles Raiders .40 1.00
Helmet
23 Los Angeles Raiders .40 1.00
Logo
24 Los Angeles Rams .15 .40
Helmet
25 Los Angeles Rams .15 .40
Logo
26 Miami Dolphins .40 1.00
Helmet
27 Miami Dolphins .40 1.00
Logo
28 Minnesota Vikings .25 .60
Helmet
29 Minnesota Vikings .25 .60
Logo
30 New England Patriots .15 .40
Helmet
31 New England Patriots .15 .40
Logo
32 New Orleans Saints .15 .40
Helmet
33 New Orleans Saints .15 .40
Logo
34 New York Giants .25 .60
Helmet
35 New York Jets .25 .60
Helmet
36 Philadelphia Eagles .15 .40
Helmet
37 Philadelphia Eagles .15 .40
Logo
38 Pittsburgh Steelers .40 1.00
Helmet
39 Pittsburgh Steelers .40 1.00
Logo
40 St. Louis Cardinals .15 .40
Helmet
41 St. Louis Cardinals .15 .40
Logo
42 San Diego Chargers .15 .40
Helmet
43 San Francisco 49ers .40 1.00
Helmet
44 San Francisco 49ers .40 1.00
Logo
45 Seattle Seahawks .15 .40
Helmet
46 Tampa Bay Bucs .15 .40
Helmet
47 Tampa Bay Bucs .15 .40
Logo
48 Washington Redskins .25 .60
Helmet
49 Washington Redskins .25 .60
Logo

1988 Fleer Team Action

This 88-card standard-size set, entitled "Live Action Football," is essentially organized alphabetically by the nickname of the team within each conference. There are two cards for each team. Basically odd-numbered cards feature the team's offense and even-numbered cards feature the team's defense. The Super Bowl cards included in this set are subtitled "Super Bowls of the Decade." The cards are typically oriented horizontally. The cards feature a 1988 copyright date. The cards show full-color action scenes with specific players not identified. The card backs are printed in blue and green on white card stock. Cards were issued in wax packs of seven team action cards and three team logo stickers.

COMPLETE SET (88) 20.00 35.00
1 Bengals Offense .20 .50
A Great Wall
(Boomer Esiason)
2 Bengals Defense .07 .20
Stacking the Odds
3 Bills Offense .40 1.00
Play-Action
(Jim Kelly)
4 Bills Defense .07 .20
Buffalo Soldiers
5 Broncos Offense 1.25 3.00
Sneak Attack
(John Elway)
6 Broncos Defense .07 .20
Crushing the Opposition
7 Browns Offense .10 .30
On the Run
(Bernie Kosar
and Kevin Mack)
8 Browns Defense .10 .30
Dogs' Day
(Eric Dickerson)
9 Chargers Offense .07 .20
A Bolt of Blue
(Gary Anderson RB)
10 Chargers Defense .07 .20
That's a Wrap
11 Chiefs Offense .07 .20
Last Line of Offense
12 Chiefs Defense .07 .20
Hard-Hitting in the
Heartland
13 Colts Offense .07 .20
An Eye To the End Zone
14 Colts Defense .07 .20
Free Ball
15 Dolphins Offense 2.00 5.00
Miami Scoring Machine
(Dan Marino takes snap)
16 Dolphins Defense .10 .30
No Mercy
17 Jets Offense .07 .20
On a Roll
(Ken O'Brien)
18 Jets Defense .07 .20
Jets Win a Dogfight
19 Oilers Offense .30 .75
Well-Oiled Machine
(Warren Moon
hands off)
20 Oilers Defense .07 .20
Hard Shoulder
21 Patriots Offense .10 .30
A Clean Sweep
(Craig James)
22 Patriots Defense .10 .30
A Fall in New England
(Bo Jackson tackled)
23 Raiders Offense .20 .50
Rush Hour in Los
Angeles (Bo Jackson)
24 Raiders Defense .10 .30
Cut Me Some Slack
(Howie Long)
25 Seahawks Offense .07 .20
Follow the Leader
(Curt Warner)
26 Seahawks Defense .07 .20
Pain& But No Gain
(Brian Bosworth)
27 Steelers Offense .10 .30
Life in the Fast Lane
28 Steelers Defense .10 .30
No Exit
29 Bears Offense .07 .20
Bearly Audible
30 Bears Defense .07 .20
Here& Kitty& Kitty
31 Buccaneers Offense .20 .50
Letting Loose
(Vinny Testaverde)
32 Buccaneers Defense .07 .20
In The Grasp
33 Cardinals Offense .07 .20
You've Gotta Hand It
to Him (Neil Lomax)
34 Cardinals Defense .10 .30
Stack of Cards
(Roger Craig)
35 Cowboys Offense .10 .30
Take It Away
(Herschel Walker)
36 Cowboys Defense .10 .30
Howdy& Pardner
(Randy White)
37 Eagles Offense .20 .50
Eagle in Flight
(Randall Cunningham)
38 Eagles Defense .30 .75
Buffalo Sandwich
(Reggie White)
39 Falcons Offense .07 .20
Rumbling Runner
40 Falcons Defense .07 .20
The Brink of Disaster
41 49ers Offense .10 .30
Move aside
(Roger Craig)
42 49ers Defense .20 .50
Bullies by the Bay
(Ronnie Lott)
43 Giants Offense .10 .30
Firing a Fastball
(Phil Simms passing)
44 Giants Defense .07 .20
A Giant Headache
45 Lions Offense .07 .20
Charge Up the Middle
46 Lions Defense .07 .20
Rocking and Rolling
in Motown
47 Packers Offense .07 .20
Gaining Altitude
(Carl Lee)
48 Packers Defense .07 .20
This Play is a Hit
49 Rams Offense .07 .20
Rams Lock Horns
(Jim Everett)
50 Rams Defense .07 .20
Greetings from L.A.
51 Redskins Offense .10 .30
Capital Gains
52 Redskins Defense .10 .30
No More Mr. Nice Guy
53 Saints Offense .07 .20
Roamin' in the Dome
54 Saints Defense .07 .20
He'll Feel This One
Tomorrow
55 Vikings Offense .07 .20
Passing Fancy
(Wade Wilson)
56 Vikings Defense .07 .20
A Vikings' Siege
57 Super Bowl XXII .07 .20
Washington 42
Denver 10
(Timmy Smith)
58 Super Bowl Checklist .07 .20
(Timmy Smith running;
Checklist 1-50
on back)
59 Super Bowl Checklist .40 1.00
(John Elway sacked;
Checklist 51-88
on back)
60 Super Bowl XXI .20 .50
New York Giants 39
Denver 20
(Lawrence Taylor
and Carl Banks)
61 Super Bowl XX .40 1.00
62 Super Bowl XIX .10 .30
San Francisco 38
Miami 16
(Roger Craig running)
63 Super Bowl XVIII .20 .50
L.A. Raiders 38
Washington 9
(Marcus Allen running)
64 Super Bowl XVII .07 .20
Washington 27
Miami 17
65 Super Bowl XVI 1.00 2.50
San Francisco 26
Cincinnati 21
(Joe Montana pitching)
66 Super Bowl XV .10 .30
Oakland 27
Philadelphia 10
(Jim Plunkett)
67 Super Bowl XIV .07 .20
Pittsburgh 31
Los Angeles Rams 19
68 NFC Championship .07 .20
Washington 17
Minnesota 10
69 AFC Championship .40 1.00
Denver 38
Cleveland 33
(John Elway)
70 NFC Playoff Game 1.00 2.50
Minnesota 36
San Francisco 24
(Joe Montana chased)
71 NFC Playoff Game .07 .20
Washington 21
Chicago 17
72 AFC Playoff Game .10 .30
Cleveland 38
Indianapolis 21
(Ozzie Newsome
and Kevin Mack)
73 AFC Playoff Game .07 .20
Denver 34
Houston 10
74 NFC Wild Card Game .07 .20
Minnesota 44
New Orleans 10
75 AFC Wild Card Game .07 .20
Houston 23
Seattle 20 (OT)
76 League Leading Team .10 .30
Rushing: 49ers
(Roger Craig running)
77 League Leading Team 1.50 4.00
Passing: Dolphins
(Dan Marino drops back)
78 League Leading Team .07 .20
Interceptions: Saints
79 League Leading Team .07 .20
Fumble Recovery:
Eagles
80 League Leading Team .10 .30
Sacks: Bears
(Richard Dent)
81 League Leading Team .07 .20
Defense Against
Kickoff Returns: Bills
82 League Leading Team .07 .20
Defense Against
Punt Returns: Jets
83 League Leading Team .07 .20
Punt Returns:
Cardinals
84 League Leading Team .07 .20
Kickoff Returns:
Falcons
85 League Leading Team .07 .20
Fewest Fumbles:
Steelers
86 League Leading Team .10 .30
Fewest Interceptions:
Browns (Bernie Kosar)
87 League Leading Team .07 .20
Fewest Points Allowed:
Colts
88 League Leading Team .20 .50
TD's on Returns: Rams
(Henry Ellard)

1988 Fleer Team Action Stickers

The 1988 Fleer Team Action Sticker set is very similar to previous releases. Each features the team's helmet or logo against a red colored background along with a team name sticker. This set was issued one sticker per pack and features all NFL teams with most in two different stickers. There are no known variations and cardbacks contain the team's 1988 NFL Schedule printed in blue ink. Each sticker measures roughly 2" by 3."

COMPLETE SET (49) 8.00 20.00
1 Atlanta Falcons .15 .40
Helmet
2 Atlanta Falcons .15 .40
Logo
3 Buffalo Bills .25 .60
Helmet
4 Buffalo Bills .25 .60
Logo
5 Chicago Bears .25 .60
Helmet
6 Chicago Bears .25 .60
Logo
7 Cincinnati Bengals .15 .40
Helmet
8 Cleveland Browns .25 .60
Helmet
9 Dallas Cowboys .40 1.00
Large Helmet
10 Dallas Cowboys .40 1.00
Small Helmet
11 Denver Broncos .25 .60
Helmet
12 Denver Broncos .25 .60
Logo
13 Detroit Lions .15 .40
Helmet
14 Detroit Lions .15 .40
Logo
15 Green Bay Packers .40 1.00
Helmet
16 Houston Oilers .15 .40
Helmet
17 Houston Oilers .15 .40
Logo
18 Indianapolis Colts Helmet .25 .60
(COLTS printed in
smaller letters on front)
19 Indianapolis Colts Helmet .25 .60
(COLTS printed in
larger letters on front)
20 Kansas City Chiefs .15 .40
Helmet
21 Kansas City Chiefs .15 .40
Logo
22 Los Angeles Raiders .40 1.00
Helmet
23 Los Angeles Raiders .40 1.00
Logo
24 Los Angeles Rams .15 .40
Helmet
25 Los Angeles Rams .15 .40
Logo
26 Miami Dolphins .40 1.00
Helmet
27 Miami Dolphins .40 1.00
Logo
28 Minnesota Vikings .25 .60
Helmet
29 Minnesota Vikings .25 .60
Logo
30 New England Patriots .15 .40
Helmet
31 New England Patriots .15 .40
Logo
32 New Orleans Saints .15 .40
Helmet
33 New Orleans Saints .15 .40
Logo
34 New York Giants .25 .60
Helmet
35 New York Jets .25 .60
Helmet
36 Philadelphia Eagles .15 .40
Helmet
37 Philadelphia Eagles .15 .40
Logo
38 Phoenix Cardinals .15 .40
Helmet
39 Phoenix Cardinals .15 .40
Logo
40 Pittsburgh Steelers .40 1.00
Helmet
41 Pittsburgh Steelers .40 1.00
Logo
42 San Diego Chargers .15 .40
Helmet
43 San Francisco 49ers .40 1.00
Helmet
44 San Francisco 49ers .40 1.00
Logo
45 Seattle Seahawks .15 .40
Helmet
46 Tampa Bay Bucs .15 .40
Helmet

47 Tampa Bay Bucs Logo	.15	.40
48 Washington Redskins Helmet	.25	.60
49 Washington Redskins Logo	.25	.60

1990 Fleer

The 1990 Fleer set contains 400 standard-size cards. This set was issued in fifteen-card baggy packs as well as 43 card pre-priced ($1.49) jumbo packs. The card numbering is alphabetical within team which are are essentially ordered by their respective order of finish during the 1989 season. The following cards have AFC logo location variations: 18, 20-22, 24, 27-30, 32, 49-56, 58, 60, 110-111, 113-117, 119, 122, 124, 198, 200-211, 213-217, and 221-223. Jim Covert (290) and Mark May (162) can be found with or without a thin line just above the text on the back. Rookie Cards include Jeff George and Jeff Hostetler.

COMPLETE SET (400)	5.00	12.00
1 Harris Barton	.01	.05
2 Chet Brooks	.01	.05
3 Michael Carter	.01	.05
4 Mike Cofer UER (FGA and FGM columns switched)	.01	.05
5 Roger Craig	.02	.10
6 Kevin Fagan RC	.01	.05
7 Charles Haley UER (Fumble recoveries should be 2 in 1986 and 5 career, card says 1 and 4)	.02	.10
8 Pierce Holt RC	.01	.05
9 Ronnie Lott	.02	.10
10A Joe Montana ERR (31,054 TD's)	.50	1.25
10B Joe Montana COR (216 TD's)	.50	1.25
11 Bubba Paris	.01	.05
12 Tom Rathman	.01	.05
13 Jerry Rice	.30	.75
14 John Taylor	.08	.25
15 Keena Turner	.01	.05
16 Michael Walter	.01	.05
17 Steve Young	.20	.50
18 Steve Atwater	.01	.05
19 Tyrone Braxton	.01	.05
20 Michael Brooks RC	.01	.05
21 John Elway	.50	1.25
22 Simon Fletcher	.01	.05
23 Bobby Humphrey	.01	.05
24 Mark Jackson	.01	.05
25 Vance Johnson	.01	.05
26 Greg Kragen	.01	.05
27 Ken Lanier RC	.01	.05
28 Karl Mecklenburg	.01	.05
29 Orson Mobley RC	.01	.05
30 Steve Sewell	.01	.05
31 Dennis Smith	.01	.05
32 David Treadwell	.01	.05
33 Flipper Anderson	.01	.05
34 Greg Bell	.01	.05
35 Henry Ellard	.02	.10
36 Jim Everett	.02	.10
37 Jerry Gray	.01	.05
38 Kevin Greene	.02	.10
39 Pete Holohan	.01	.05
40 LeRoy Irvin	.01	.05
41 Mike Lansford	.01	.05
42 Buford McGee RC	.01	.05
43 Tom Newberry	.01	.05
44 Vince Newsome RC	.01	.05
45 Jackie Slater	.01	.05
46 Mike Wilcher	.01	.05
47 Matt Bahr	.01	.05
48 Brian Brennan	.01	.05
49 Thane Gash RC	.01	.05
50 Mike Johnson	.01	.05
51 Bernie Kosar	.02	.10
52 Reggie Langhorne	.01	.05
53 Tim Manoa	.01	.05
54 Clay Matthews	.02	.10
55 Eric Metcalf	.08	.25
56 Frank Minnifield	.01	.05
57 Gregg Rakoczy RC UER (First line of text calls him Greg)	.01	.05
58 Webster Slaughter	.02	.10
59 Bryan Wagner	.01	.05
60 Felix Wright	.01	.05
61 Raul Allegre	.01	.05
62 Ottis Anderson UER (Stats say 9.317 yards, should be 9,317)	.02	.10
63 Carl Banks	.01	.05
64 Mark Bavaro	.01	.05
65 Maurice Carthon	.01	.05
66 Mark Collins UER (Total fumble recoveries should be 5, not 3)	.01	.05
67 Jeff Hostetler RC	.08	.25
68 Erik Howard	.01	.05
69 Pepper Johnson	.01	.05
70 Sean Landeta	.01	.05
71 Lionel Manuel	.01	.05
72 Leonard Marshall	.01	.05
73 Dave Meggett	.02	.10
74 Bart Oates	.01	.05
75 Doug Riesenberg RC	.01	.05
76 Phil Simms	.02	.10
77 Lawrence Taylor	.08	.25
78 Eric Allen	.01	.05
79 Jerome Brown	.01	.05
80 Keith Byars	.01	.05
81 Cris Carter	.20	.50
82A Byron Evans ERR RC	.05	.15
82B Randall Cunningham	.05	.15
83A Ron Heller RC ERR (should be 84 according to checklist)	.05	.15
83B Byron Evans COR RC	.05	.15
84 Ron Heller COR RC	.01	.05
85 Terry Hoage RC	.01	.05
86 Keith Jackson	.02	.10
87 Seth Joyner	.02	.10
88 Mike Quick	.01	.05
89 Mike Schad	.01	.05
90 Clyde Simmons	.01	.05
91 John Teltschik	.01	.05
92 Anthony Toney	.01	.05
93 Reggie White	.08	.25
94 Ray Berry	.01	.05
95 Joey Browner	.01	.05
96 Anthony Carter	.02	.10
97 Chris Doleman	.01	.05
98 Rick Fenney	.01	.05
99 Rich Gannon RC	.60	1.50
100 Hassan Jones	.01	.05
101 Steve Jordan	.01	.05
102 Rich Karlis	.01	.05
103 Andre Ware RC	.08	.25
104 Kirk Lowdermilk	.01	.05
105 Keith Millard	.01	.05
106 Scott Studwell	.01	.05
107 Herschel Walker	.02	.10
108 Wade Wilson	.02	.10
109 Gary Zimmerman	.02	.10
110 Don Beebe	.02	.10
111 Cornelius Bennett	.02	.10
112 Shane Conlan	.01	.05
113 Jim Kelly	.08	.25
114 Scott Norwood UER (FGA and FGM columns switched)	.01	.05
115 Mark Kelso UER (Some stats added wrong on back)	.01	.05
116 Larry Kinnebrew	.01	.05
117 Pete Metzelaars	.01	.05
118 Scott Radecic	.01	.05
119 Andre Reed	.08	.25
120 Jim Ritcher RC	.01	.05
121 Bruce Smith	.08	.25
122 Leonard Smith	.01	.05
123 Art Still	.01	.05
124 Thurman Thomas	.08	.25
125 Steve Brown	.01	.05
126 Ray Childress	.01	.05
127 Ernest Givins	.02	.10
128 John Grimsley	.01	.05
129 Alonzo Highsmith	.01	.05
130 Drew Hill	.01	.05
131 Bruce Matthews	.02	.10
132 Johnny Meads	.01	.05
133 Warren Moon UER (186 completions in 1987 and 1341 career, should be 184 and 1339)	.08	.25
134 Mike Munchak	.02	.10
135 Mike Rozier	.01	.05
136 Dean Steinkuhler	.01	.05
137 Lorenzo White	.01	.05
138 Tony Zendejas	.01	.05
139 Gary Anderson K	.01	.05
140 Bubby Brister	.01	.05
141 Thomas Everett	.01	.05
142 Derek Hill	.01	.05
143 Merril Hoge	.01	.05
144 Tim Johnson	.01	.05
145 Louis Lipps	.02	.10
146 David Little	.01	.05
147 Greg Lloyd	.08	.25
148 Mike Mularkey	.01	.05
149 John Rienstra RC	.01	.05
150 Gerald Williams RC UER (Tackles and fumble recovery headers are switched)	.01	.05
151 Keith Willis UER (Tackles and fumble recovery headers are switched)	.01	.05
152 Rod Woodson	.08	.25
153 Tim Worley	.01	.05
154 Gary Clark	.08	.25
155 Darryl Grant	.01	.05
156 Darrell Green	.02	.10
157 Joe Jacoby	.01	.05
158 Jim Lachey	.01	.05
159 Chip Lohmiller	.01	.05
160 Charles Mann	.01	.05
161 Wilber Marshall	.01	.05
162 Mark May	.01	.05
163 Ralf Mojsiejenko	.01	.05
164 Art Monk UER (No explanation of How Acquired)	.02	.10
165 Gerald Riggs	.02	.10
166 Mark Rypien	.02	.10
167 Ricky Sanders	.01	.05
168 Don Warren	.01	.05
169 Robert Brown RC	.01	.05
170 Blair Bush	.01	.05
171 Brent Fullwood	.01	.05
172 Tim Harris	.01	.05
173 Chris Jacke	.01	.05
174 Perry Kemp	.01	.05
175 Don Majkowski	.01	.05
176 Tony Mandarich	.01	.05
177 Mark Murphy	.01	.05
178 Brian Noble	.01	.05
179 Ken Ruettgers	.01	.05
180 Sterling Sharpe	.08	.25
181 Ed West RC	.01	.05
182 Keith Woodside	.01	.05
183 Morten Andersen	.01	.05
184 Stan Brock	.01	.05
185 Jim Dombrowski RC	.01	.05
186 John Fourcade	.01	.05
187 Bobby Hebert	.01	.05
188 Craig Heyward	.02	.10
189 Dalton Hilliard	.01	.05
190 Rickey Jackson	.02	.10
191 Buford Jordan	.01	.05
192 Eric Martin	.01	.05
193 Robert Massey	.01	.05
194 Sam Mills	.02	.10
195 Pat Swilling	.02	.10
196 Jim Wilks	.01	.05
197 John Alt RC	.01	.05
198 Walker Lee Ashley RC	.01	.05
199 Steve DeBerg	.01	.05
200 Leonard Griffin RC	.01	.05
201 Albert Lewis	.01	.05
202 Nick Lowery	.01	.05
203 Bill Maas	.01	.05
204 Pete Mandley	.01	.05
205 Chris Martin RC	.01	.05
206 Christian Okoye	.01	.05
207 Stephone Paige	.01	.05
208 Kevin Porter RC	.01	.05
209 Derrick Thomas	.08	.25
210 Lewis Billups	.01	.05
211 James Brooks	.02	.10
212 Jason Buck	.01	.05
213 Rickey Dixon RC	.01	.05
214 Boomer Esiason	.02	.10
215 David Fulcher	.01	.05
216 Rodney Holman	.01	.05
217 Lee Johnson	.01	.05
218 Tim Krumrie	.01	.05
219 Tim McGee	.01	.05
220 Anthony Munoz	.02	.10
221 Bruce Reimers RC	.01	.05
222 Leon White	.01	.05
223 Ickey Woods	.01	.05
224 Harvey Armstrong RC	.01	.05
225 Michael Ball RC	.01	.05
226 Chip Banks	.01	.05
227 Pat Beach	.01	.05
228 Duane Bickett	.01	.05
229 Bill Brooks	.01	.05
230 Jon Hand	.01	.05
231 Andre Rison	.08	.25
232 Rohn Stark	.01	.05
233 Donnell Thompson	.01	.05
234 Jack Trudeau	.01	.05
235 Clarence Verdin	.01	.05
236 Mark Clayton	.02	.10
237 Jeff Cross	.01	.05
238 Jeff Dellenbach RC	.01	.05
239 Mark Duper	.02	.10
240 Ferrell Edmunds	.01	.05
241 Hugh Green UER (Back says Traded 1986, should be 1985)	.01	.05
242 E.J. Junior	.01	.05
243 Marc Logan	.01	.05
244 Dan Marino	.50	1.25
245 John Offerdahl	.01	.05
246 Reggie Roby	.01	.05
247 Sammie Smith	.01	.05
248 Pete Stoyanovich	.01	.05
249 Marcus Allen	.08	.25
250 Eddie Anderson RC	.01	.05
251 Steve Beuerlein	.02	.10
252 Mike Dyal RC	.01	.05
253 Mervyn Fernandez	.01	.05
254 Bob Golic	.01	.05
255 Mike Harden	.01	.05
256 Bo Jackson	.10	.30
257 Howie Long UER (Born Sommerville, should be Somerville)	.08	.25
258 Don Mosebar	.01	.05
259 Jay Schroeder	.01	.05
260 Steve Smith	.01	.05
261 Greg Townsend	.01	.05
262 Lionel Washington	.01	.05
263 Brian Blades	.02	.10
264 Jeff Bryant	.01	.05
265 Grant Feasel RC	.01	.05
266 Jacob Green	.01	.05
267 James Jefferson	.01	.05
268 Norm Johnson	.01	.05
269 Dave Krieg UER (Misspelled Kreig on card front)	.02	.10
270 Travis McNeal	.01	.05
271 Joe Nash	.01	.05
272 Rufus Porter	.01	.05
273 Kelly Stouffer	.01	.05
274 John L. Williams	.01	.05
275 Jim Arnold	.01	.05
276 Jerry Ball	.01	.05
277 Bennie Blades	.01	.05
278 Lomas Brown	.01	.05
279 Michael Cofer	.01	.05
280 Bob Gagliano	.01	.05
281 Richard Johnson	.01	.05
282 Eddie Murray	.01	.05
283 Rodney Peete	.02	.10
284 Barry Sanders	.50	1.25
285 Eric Sanders	.01	.05
286 Chris Spielman	.08	.25
287 Eric Williams RC	.01	.05
288 Neal Anderson	.02	.10
289A Kevin Butler ERR ERR (Listed as Punter on front and back)	.08	.25
289B Kevin Butler COR ERR (Listed as Placekicker on front and Punter on back)	.08	.25
289C Kevin Butler ERR COR (Listed as Punter on front and Placekicker on back)	.08	.25
289D Kevin Butler COR COR (Listed as Placekicker on front and back)	.01	.05
290 Jim Covert	.01	.05
291 Richard Dent	.02	.10
292 Dennis Gentry	.01	.05
293 Jim Harbaugh	.08	.25
294 Jay Hilgenberg	.01	.05
295 Vestee Jackson	.01	.05
296 Steve McMichael	.02	.10
297 Ron Morris	.01	.05
298 Brad Muster	.01	.05
299 Mike Singletary	.02	.10
300 James Thornton UER (Missing birthdate)	.01	.05
301 Mike Tomczak	.02	.10
302 Keith Van Horne	.01	.05
303 Chris Bahr UER ('86 FGA and FGM stats are reversed)	.01	.05
304 Martin Bayless RC	.01	.05
305 Marion Butts	.02	.10
306 Gill Byrd	.01	.05
307 Arthur Cox	.01	.05
308 Burt Grossman	.01	.05
309 Jamie Holland	.01	.05
310 Jim McMahon	.02	.10
311 Anthony Miller	.08	.25
312 Leslie O'Neal	.02	.10
313 Billy Ray Smith	.01	.05
314 Tim Spencer	.01	.05
315 Broderick Thompson RC	.01	.05
316 Lee Williams	.01	.05
317 Bruce Armstrong	.01	.05
318 Tim Goad RC	.01	.05
319 Steve Grogan	.02	.10
320 Roland James	.01	.05
321 Cedric Jones	.01	.05
322 Fred Marion	.01	.05
323 Stanley Morgan	.01	.05
324 Robert Perryman (Back says Robert, front says Bob)	.01	.05
325 Johnny Rembert	.01	.05
326 Ed Reynolds	.01	.05
327 Kenneth Sims	.01	.05
328 John Stephens	.01	.05
329 Danny Villa RC	.01	.05
330 Robert Awalt	.01	.05
331 Anthony Bell	.01	.05
332 Rich Camarillo	.01	.05
333 Earl Ferrell	.01	.05
334 Roy Green	.02	.10
335 Gary Hogeboom	.01	.05
336 Cedric Mack	.01	.05
337 Freddie Joe Nunn	.01	.05
338 Luis Sharpe	.01	.05
339 Vai Sikahema	.01	.05
340 J.T. Smith	.01	.05
341 Tom Tupa RC	.01	.05
342 Percy Snow RC	.01	.05
343 Mark Carrier WR	.08	.25
344 Randy Grimes	.01	.05
345 Paul Gruber	.01	.05
346 Ron Hall	.01	.05
347 Jeff George RC	.20	.50
348 Bruce Hill UER (Photo on back is actually Jerry Bell)	.01	.05
349 William Howard UER (Yards rec. says 284, should be 285)	.01	.05
350 Donald Igwebuike	.01	.05
351 Chris Mohr RC	.01	.05
352 Winston Moss RC	.01	.05
353 Ricky Reynolds	.01	.05
354 Mark Robinson	.01	.05
355 Lars Tate	.01	.05
356 Vinny Testaverde	.02	.10
357 Broderick Thomas	.01	.05
358 Troy Benson	.01	.05
359 Jeff Criswell RC	.01	.05
360 Tony Eason	.01	.05
361 James Hasty	.01	.05
362 Johnny Hector	.01	.05
363 Bobby Humphery UER (Photo on back is actually Bobby Humphrey)	.01	.05
364 Pat Leahy	.01	.05
365 Erik McMillan	.01	.05
366 Freeman McNeil	.01	.05
367 Ken O'Brien	.01	.05
368 Ron Stallworth	.01	.05
369 Al Toon	.02	.10
370 Blair Thomas RC	.01	.05
371 Aundray Bruce	.01	.05
372 Tony Casillas	.01	.05
373 Shawn Collins	.01	.05
374 Evan Cooper	.01	.05
375 Bill Fralic	.01	.05
376 Scott Funhage	.01	.05
377 Mike Gann	.01	.05
378 Ron Heller	.01	.05
379 Keith Jones	.01	.05
380 Mike Kenn	.01	.05
381 Chris Miller	.08	.25
382 Deion Sanders UER (Stats say no 1989 fumble recoveries, should be 1)	.20	.50
383 John Settle	.01	.05
384 Troy Aikman	.30	.75
385 Bill Bates	.02	.10
386 Willie Broughton	.01	.05
387 Steve Folsom	.01	.05
388 Ray Horton UER (Extra line after career totals)	.01	.05
389 Michael Irvin	.08	.25
390 Jim Jeffcoat	.01	.05
391 Eugene Lockhart	.01	.05
392 Kelvin Martin RC	.01	.05
393 Nate Newton	.02	.10
394 Mike Saxon UER (6 career blocked kicks, stats add up to 4)	.01	.05
395 Derrick Shepard RC	.01	.05
396 Steve Walsh UER (Yards Passing 50.2; Percentage and yards data are switched)	.02	.10
397 Super Bowl MVP's (Jerry Rice and Joe Montana) HOR	.30	.75
398 Checklist Card UER (Card 103 not listed)	.01	.05
399 Checklist Card UER (Bengals misspelled)	.01	.05
400 Checklist Card	.01	.05

1990 Fleer All-Pros

COMPLETE SET (25)	2.50	6.00
1 Joe Montana	.60	1.50
2 Jerry Rice UER (photo on front is actually John Taylor)	.40	1.00
3 Keith Jackson	.02	.10
4 Barry Sanders	.60	1.50
5 Christian Okoye	.01	.05
6 Tom Newberry	.01	.05
7 Jim Covert	.01	.05
8 Anthony Munoz	.02	.10
9 Mike Munchak	.02	.10
10 Jay Hilgenberg	.01	.05
11 Chris Doleman	.01	.05
12 Keith Millard	.01	.05
13 Derrick Thomas	.10	.30
14 Lawrence Taylor	.10	.30
15 Karl Mecklenburg	.01	.05
16 Reggie White	.10	.30
17 Tim Harris	.01	.05
18 David Fulcher	.01	.05
19 Ronnie Lott	.02	.10
20 Eric Allen	.01	.05
21 Steve Atwater	.01	.05
22 Rich Camarillo	.01	.05
23 Morten Andersen	.01	.05
24 Andre Reed	.10	.30
25 Rod Woodson	.10	.30

1990 Fleer Stars and Stripes

This 90-card standard size set was issued by Fleer in conjunction with their subsidiary, the Asher Candy Company, in a packaging which included two red, white, and blue striped candy sticks as well as eight cards. This set features members of the 1990 Pro Bowl teams as well as ten of the leading rookies in the 1990 season. Cards were arranged as follows, AFC Pro Bowlers (1-39), NFC Pro Bowlers (40-80), and leading draftees (81-90). Some of the same mistakes made in the regular Fleer set were carried over into the Stars'n'Stripes set including the misspelling of Dave Krieg's name as Kreig. Since this set did not sell that well at the retail level, much of the production was remaindered. However some of these leftover sealed cases are susceptible to damaged cards from the candy "leaking" into or onto the cards.

COMPLETE SET (90)	4.80	12.00
1 Warren Moon	.20	.50
2 Reggie Roby	.05	.15
3 David Treadwell	.05	.15
4 Dave Krieg UER (Misspelled Kreig)	.10	.30
5 James Brooks	.05	.15
6 Erik McMillan	.05	.15
7 Rod Woodson	.10	.30
8 Albert Lewis	.05	.15
9 Kevin Ross	.05	.15
10 Frank Minnifield	.05	.15
11 David Fulcher	.05	.15
12 Thurman Thomas	.20	.50
13 Christian Okoye	.05	.15
14 Dennis Smith	.05	.15
15 Johnny Rembert	.05	.15
16 Ray Donaldson	.05	.15
17 John Offerdahl	.05	.15
18 Clay Matthews	.05	.15
19 Shane Conlan	.05	.15
20 Derrick Thomas	.10	.30
21 Tunch Ilkin	.05	.15
22 Mike Munchak	.10	.30
23 Max Montoya	.05	.15
24 Kent Hull	.05	.15
25 Greg Kragen	.05	.15
26 Bruce Matthews	.10	.30
27 Howie Long	.20	.50
28 Chris Hinton	.05	.15
29 Anthony Munoz	.05	.15
30 Bruce Smith	.10	.30
31 Ferrell Edmunds	.05	.15
32 Rodney Holman	.05	.15
33 Andre Reed	.10	.30
34 Webster Slaughter	.05	.15
35 Anthony Miller	.10	.30
36 Brian Blades	.05	.15
37 Leslie O'Neal	.05	.15
38 Rufus Porter	.05	.15
39 Lee Williams	.05	.15
40 Eddie Murray	.05	.15
41 Mark Rypien	.05	.15
42 Randall Cunningham	.20	.50
43 Rich Camarillo	.05	.15
44 Barry Sanders	1.60	4.00
45 Dalton Hilliard	.05	.15
46 Eric Allen	.05	.15
47 Brent Fullwood	.05	.15
48 Ron Wolfley	.05	.15
49 Jerry Gray	.05	.15
50 Dave Meggett	.05	.15
51 Roger Craig	.10	.30
52 Carl Lee	.05	.15
53 Ronnie Lott	.20	.50
54 Tim McDonald	.05	.15
55 Joey Browner	.05	.15
56 Mike Singletary	.10	.30
57 Vaughan Johnson	.05	.15
58 Chris Spielman	.05	.15
59 Doug Smith	.05	.15
60 Lawrence Taylor	.20	.50
61 Chris Doleman	.05	.15
62 Guy McIntyre	.05	.15
63 Jay Hilgenberg	.05	.15
64 Randall McDaniel	.10	.30
65 Gary Zimmerman	.05	.15
66 Luis Sharpe	.05	.15
67 Charles Mann	.05	.15
68 Keith Millard	.05	.15
69 Jackie Slater	.05	.15
70 Bill Fralic	.05	.15
71 Henry Ellard	.10	.30
72 Jerry Rice	.80	2.00
73 Steve Jordan	.05	.15
74 Sterling Sharpe	.10	.30
75 Keith Jackson	.05	.15
76 Mark Carrier WR	.10	.30
77 Kevin Greene	.10	.30
78 Reggie White	.20	.50
79 Jerry Ball	.05	.15
80 Tim Harris	.05	.15
81 Jeff George	.20	.50
82 Blair Thomas	.05	.15
83 Cortez Kennedy	.10	.30
84 Junior Seau	.20	.50
85 Mark Carrier DB	.05	.15
86 Andre Ware	.10	.30
87 Chris Singleton	.05	.15
88 Percy Snow	.05	.15
89 Steve Broussard	.05	.15
90 Rodney Hampton	.10	.30

1990 Fleer Update

This 120-card standard size set features some of the leading rookies and traded players in their new uniforms. The set is the same design as the regular issue with color photos bordered by a team color. The set is arranged in team order. The cards are numbered on the back with a "U" prefix. Rookie Cards include Brad Baxter, Mark Carrier (DB), Reggie Cobb, Andre Collins, Barry Foster, Eric Green, Harold Green, Rodney Hampton, Leroy Hoard, Stan Humphries, Haywood Jeffires, Johnny Johnson, Brent Jones, Cortez Kennedy, Rob Moore, Ken Norton Jr., Junior Seau, Emmitt Smith and Calvin Williams.

COMP.FACT.SET (120)	12.50	25.00
U1 Albert Bentley	.01	.05
U2 Dean Biasucci	.01	.05
U3 Ray Donaldson	.01	.05
U4 Jeff George	.50	1.25
U5 Ray Agnew RC	.01	.05
U6 Greg McMurtry RC	.01	.05
U7 Chris Singleton RC	.01	.05
U8 James Francis RC	.01	.05
U9 Harold Green RC	.02	.10
U10 John Elliott	.01	.05
U11 Rodney Hampton RC	.08	.25
U12 Gary Reasons	.01	.05
U13 Lewis Tillman	.01	.05
U14 Everson Walls	.01	.05
U15 David Alexander RC	.01	.05
U16 Jim McMahon	.02	.10
U17 Ben Smith RC	.01	.05
U18 Andre Waters	.02	.10
U19 Calvin Williams RC	.02	.10
U20 Earnest Byner	.02	.10
U21 Andre Collins RC	.01	.05
U22 Russ Grimm	.02	.10
U23 Stan Humphries RC	.08	.25
U24 Martin Mayhew RC	.01	.05
U25 Barry Foster RC	.08	.25
U26 Eric Green RC	.02	.10
U27 Tunch Ilkin	.01	.05
U28 Hardy Nickerson	.02	.10
U29 Jerrol Williams	.01	.05
U30 Mike Baab	.01	.05
U31 Leroy Hoard RC	.20	.50
U32 Eddie Johnson RC	.01	.05
U33 William Fuller	.02	.10
U34 Haywood Jeffires RC	.08	.25
U35 Don Maggs RC	.01	.05
U36 Allen Pinkett	.01	.05
U37 Robert Awalt	.01	.05
U38 Dennis McKinnon	.01	.05
U39 Ken Norton RC	.08	.25
U40 Emmitt Smith RC	7.50	20.00
U41 Alexander Wright RC	.01	.05
U42 Eric Hill	.01	.05
U43 Johnny Johnson RC	.02	.10
U44 Timm Rosenbach	.01	.05
U45 Anthony Thompson RC	.01	.05
U46 Dexter Carter RC	.01	.05
U47 Eric Davis RC UER (Listed as WR on front, DB on back)	.02	.10
U48 Keith DeLong	.01	.05
U49 Brent Jones RC	.08	.25
U50 Darryl Pollard RC	.01	.05
U51 Steve Wallace RC	.08	.25
U52 Bern Brostek RC	.01	.05
U53 Aaron Cox	.01	.05
U54 Cleveland Gary	.01	.05
U55 Fred Strickland RC	.01	.05
U56 Pat Terrell RC	.01	.05
U57 Steve Broussard RC	.01	.05
U58 Scott Case	.01	.05
U59 Brian Jordan RC	.02	.10
U60 Andre Rison	.08	.25
U61 Kevin Haverdink	.01	.05
U62 Rueben Mayes	.01	.05
U63 Steve Walsh	.02	.10
U64 Greg Bell	.01	.05
U65 Tim Brown	.08	.25
U66 Willie Gault	.02	.10
U67 Vance Mueller RC	.01	.05
U68 Bill Pickel	.01	.05
U69 Aaron Wallace RC	.02	.10
U70 Glenn Parker RC	.01	.05
U71 Frank Reich	.08	.25
U72 Leon Seals RC	.01	.05
U73 Darryl Talley	.01	.05
U74 Brad Baxter RC	.01	.05
U75 Jeff Criswell	.01	.05
U76 Jeff Lageman	.01	.05
U77 Rob Moore RC	.60	1.50
U78 Blair Thomas	.02	.10
U79 Louis Oliver	.01	.05
U80 Tony Paige	.01	.05
U81 Richmond Webb RC	.01	.05
U82 Robert Blackmon RC	.01	.05
U83 Derrick Fenner RC	.01	.05
U84 Andy Heck	.01	.05
U85 Cortez Kennedy RC	.08	.25
U86 Terry Wooden RC	.01	.05
U87 Jeff Donaldson	.01	.05
U88 Tim Grunhard RC	.01	.05
U89 Emile Harry RC	.01	.05
U90 Dan Saleaumua	.01	.05
U91 Percy Snow	.01	.05
U92 Andre Ware	.08	.25
U93 Darrell Fullington RC	.01	.05
U94 Mike Merriweather	.01	.05
U95 Henry Thomas	.01	.05
U96 Robert Brown	.01	.05
U97 LeRoy Butler RC	.08	.25
U98 Anthony Dilweg	.01	.05
U99 Darrell Thompson RC	.01	.05
U100 Keith Woodside	.01	.05
U101 Gary Plummer	.01	.05
U102 Junior Seau RC	2.00	5.00
U103 Billy Joe Tolliver	.01	.05
U104 Mark Vlasic	.01	.05
U105 Gary Anderson RB	.01	.05
U106 Ian Beckles RC	.01	.05
U107 Reggie Cobb RC	.01	.05
U108 Keith McCants RC	.01	.05
U109 Mark Bortz RC	.01	.05
U110 Maury Buford	.01	.05
U111 Mark Carrier DB RC	.08	.25
U112 Dan Hampton	.02	.10
U113 William Perry	.02	.10
U114 Ron Rivera	.01	.05
U115 Lemuel Stinson	.01	.05
U116 Melvin Bratton RC	.01	.05
U117 Gary Kubiak RC	.08	.25
U118 Alton Montgomery RC	.01	.05
U119 Ricky Nattiel	.01	.05
U120 Checklist 1-132	.01	.05

1991 Fleer

This 432-card standard-size set features color action photos with the player removed from the action. The card numbering is alphabetical by player within team by conference. Subsets include Hot Hitters (396-407), League Leaders (408-419) and Rookie Prospects (420-428). Rookie Cards in this set include Russell Maryland.

COMPLETE SET (432)	4.00	8.00
1 Shane Conlan	.01	.05
2 John Davis RC	.01	.05
3 Kent Hull	.01	.05
4 James Lofton	.02	.10
5 Keith McKeller	.01	.05
6 Scott Norwood	.01	.05
7 Nate Odomes	.01	.05
8 Andre Reed	.02	.10
9 Jim Ritcher	.01	.05
10 Leon Seals	.01	.05
11 Bruce Smith	.08	.25
12 Leonard Smith	.01	.05
13 Steve Tasker	.02	.10
14 Thurman Thomas	.08	.25
15 Lewis Billups	.01	.05
16 James Brooks	.02	.10
17 Eddie Brown	.01	.05
18 Carl Carter	.01	.05
19 Boomer Esiason	.02	.10
20 James Francis	.01	.05
21 David Fulcher	.01	.05
22 Harold Green	.02	.10
23 Rodney Holman	.01	.05
24 Bruce Kozerski	.01	.05
25 Tim McGee	.01	.05
26 Anthony Munoz	.02	.10
27 Bruce Reimers	.01	.05
28 Ickey Woods	.01	.05
29 Carl Zander	.01	.05
30 Mike Baab	.01	.05
31 Brian Brennan	.01	.05
32 Rob Burnett RC	.02	.10
33 Paul Farren	.01	.05
34 Thane Gash	.01	.05
35 David Grayson	.01	.05
36 Mike Johnson	.01	.05
37 Reggie Langhorne	.01	.05
38 Kevin Mack	.01	.05
39 Eric Metcalf	.02	.10
40 Frank Minnifield	.01	.05
41 Gregg Rakoczy	.01	.05
42 Felix Wright	.01	.05
43 Steve Atwater	.01	.05
44 Michael Brooks	.01	.05
45 John Elway	.50	1.25
46 Simon Fletcher	.01	.05
47 Bobby Humphrey	.01	.05
48 Mark Jackson	.01	.05
49 Keith Kartz	.01	.05
50 Clarence Kay	.01	.05
51 Greg Kragen	.01	.05
52 Karl Mecklenburg	.01	.05
53 Warren Powers	.01	.05
54 Dennis Smith	.01	.05
55 Jim Szymanski	.01	.05
56 David Treadwell	.01	.05
57 Michael Young	.01	.05
58 Ray Childress	.01	.05
59 Curtis Duncan	.01	.05
60 William Fuller	.02	.10
61 Ernest Givins	.02	.10
62 Drew Hill	.01	.05
63 Haywood Jeffires	.02	.10
64 Richard Johnson DB	.01	.05
65 Sean Jones	.02	.10
66 Don Maggs	.01	.05
67 Bruce Matthews	.02	.10
68 Johnny Meads	.01	.05
69 Greg Montgomery	.01	.05
70 Warren Moon	.08	.25
71 Mike Munchak	.02	.10
72 Allen Pinkett	.01	.05
73 Lorenzo White	.01	.05
74 Pat Beach	.01	.05
75 Albert Bentley	.01	.05
76 Dean Biasucci	.01	.05
77 Duane Bickett	.01	.05
78 Bill Brooks	.01	.05
79 Sam Clancy	.01	.05
80 Ray Donaldson	.01	.05
81 Jeff George	.08	.25
82 Alan Grant	.01	.05
83 Jessie Hester	.01	.05
84 Jeff Herrod	.01	.05
85 Rohn Stark	.01	.05
86 Jack Trudeau	.01	.05
87 Clarence Verdin	.01	.05
88 John Alt	.01	.05
89 Steve DeBerg	.01	.05
90 Tim Grunhard	.01	.05
91 Dino Hackett	.01	.05
92 Jonathan Hayes	.01	.05
93 Albert Lewis	.01	.05
94 Nick Lowery	.01	.05
95 Bill Maas UER (Back photo actually David Szott)	.01	.05
96 Christian Okoye	.01	.05
97 Stephone Paige	.01	.05
98 Kevin Porter	.01	.05
99 David Szott RC	.01	.05
100 Derrick Thomas	.08	.25
101 Barry Word FFC	.01	.05
102 Marcus Allen	.08	.25
103 Thomas Benson	.01	.05
104 Tim Brown	.08	.25
105 Riki Ellison	.01	.05
106 Mervyn Fernandez	.01	.05
107 Willie Gault	.02	.10
108 Bob Golic	.01	.05
109 Ethan Horton FFC	.01	.05
110 Bo Jackson	.10	.30
111 Howie Long	.08	.25
112 Don Mosebar	.01	.05
113 Jerry Robinson	.01	.05
114 Jay Schroeder	.01	.05
115 Steve Smith	.01	.05
116 Greg Townsend	.01	.05
117 Steve Wisniewski	.01	.05
118 Mark Clayton	.02	.10
119 Mark Duper	.02	.10
120 Ferrell Edmunds	.01	.05
121 Hugh Green	.01	.05
122 David Griggs	.01	.05
123 Jim C. Jensen	.01	.05
124 Dan Marino	.50	1.25
125 Tim McKyer	.01	.05
126 John Offerdahl	.01	.05
127 Louis Oliver	.01	.05
128 Tony Paige	.01	.05
129 Reggie Roby	.01	.05
130 Keith Sims	.01	.05
131 Sammie Smith	.01	.05
132 Pete Stoyanovich	.01	.05
133 Richmond Webb	.01	.05
134 Bruce Armstrong	.01	.05
135 Vincent Brown	.01	.05
136 Hart Lee Dykes	.01	.05
137 Irving Fryar	.02	.10
138 Tim Goad	.01	.05
139 Tommy Hodson	.01	.05
140 Maurice Hurst	.01	.05
141 Ronnie Lippett	.01	.05
142 Greg McMurtry	.01	.05
143 Ed Reynolds	.01	.05
144 John Stephens	.01	.05
145 Andre Tippett	.01	.05
146 Danny Villa	.01	.05
147 Brad Baxter	.01	.05
148 Kyle Clifton	.01	.05
149 Jeff Criswell	.01	.05
150 James Hasty	.01	.05
151 Jeff Lageman	.01	.05
152 Pat Leahy	.01	.05
153 Rob Moore	.08	.25
154 Al Toon	.02	.10

155 Gary Anderson K .01 .05
156 Bubby Brister .01 .05
157 Chris Calloway .01 .05
158 Donald Evans .01 .05
159 Eric Green .01 .05
160 Bryan Hinkle .01 .05
161 Merril Hoge .01 .05
162 Tunch Ilkin .01 .05
163 Louis Lipps .01 .05
164 David Little .01 .05
165 Mike Mularkey .01 .05
166 Gerald Williams .01 .05
167 Warren Williams .01 .05
168 Rod Woodson .08 .25
169 Tim Worley .01 .05
170 Martin Bayless .01 .05
171 Marion Butts .02 .10
172 Gill Byrd .01 .05
173 Frank Cornish .01 .05
174 Arthur Cox .01 .05
175 Burt Grossman .01 .05
176 Anthony Miller .02 .10
177 Leslie O'Neal .02 .10
178 Gary Plummer .01 .05
179 Junior Seau .08 .25
180 Billy Joe Tolliver .01 .05
181 Derrick Walker RC .01 .05
182 Lee Williams .01 .05
183 Robert Blackmon .01 .05
184 Brian Blades .02 .10
185 Grant Feasel .01 .05
186 Derrick Fenner .01 .05
187 Andy Heck .01 .05
188 Norm Johnson .01 .05
189 Tommy Kane .01 .05
190 Cortez Kennedy .08 .25
191 Dave Krieg .02 .10
192 Travis McNeal .01 .05
193 Eugene Robinson .01 .05
194 Chris Warren .08 .25
195 John L. Williams .01 .05
196 Steve Broussard .01 .05
197 Scott Case .01 .05
198 Shawn Collins .01 .05
199 Darion Conner UER .01 .05
200 Tory Epps .01 .05
201 Bill Fralic .01 .05
202 Michael Haynes .08 .25
203 Chris Hinton .01 .05
204 Keith Jones .01 .05
205 Brian Jordan .02 .10
206 Mike Kenn .01 .05
207 Chris Miller .02 .10
208 Andre Rison .02 .10
209 Mike Rozier .01 .05
210 Deion Sanders .15 .40
211 Gary Wilkins .01 .05
212 Neal Anderson .02 .10
213 Trace Armstrong .01 .05
214 Mark Bortz .01 .05
215 Kevin Butler .01 .05
216 Mark Carrier DB .02 .10
217 Wendell Davis FFC .01 .05
218 Richard Dent .02 .10
219 Dennis Gentry .01 .05
220 Jim Harbaugh .08 .25
221 Jay Hilgenberg .01 .05
222 Steve McMichael .02 .10
223 Ron Morris .01 .05
224 Brad Muster .01 .05
225 Mike Singletary .02 .10
226 James Thornton .01 .05
227 Tommie Agee .01 .05
228 Troy Aikman .30 .75
229 Jack Del Rio .02 .10
230 Issiac Holt .01 .05
231 Ray Horton .01 .05
232 Jim Jeffcoat .01 .05
233 Eugene Lockhart .01 .05
234 Kelvin Martin .01 .05
235 Nate Newton .02 .10
236 Mike Saxon .01 .05
237 Emmitt Smith 1.00 2.50
238A Daniel Stubbs .02 .10
238B Daniel Stubbs .02 .10
239 Jim Arnold .01 .05
240 Jerry Ball .01 .05
241 Bennie Blades .01 .05
242 Lomas Brown .01 .05
243 Robert Clark .01 .05
244 Mike Cofer .01 .05
245 Mel Gray .02 .10
246 Rodney Peete .02 .10
247 Barry Sanders .50 1.25
248 Andre Ware .02 .10
249 Matt Brock RC .01 .05
250 Robert Brown .01 .05
251 Anthony Dilweg .01 .05
252 Johnny Holland .01 .05
253 Tim Harris .01 .05
254 Chris Jacke .01 .05
255 Perry Kemp .01 .05
256 Don Majkowski UER .01 .05
257 Tony Mandarich .01 .05
258 Mark Murphy .01 .05
259 Brian Noble .01 .05
260 Jeff Query .01 .05
261 Sterling Sharpe .08 .25
262 Ed West .01 .05
263 Keith Woodside .01 .05
264 Flipper Anderson .01 .05
265 Aaron Cox .01 .05
266 Henry Ellard .02 .10
267 Jim Everett .02 .10
268 Cleveland Gary .01 .05
269 Kevin Greene .02 .10
270 Pete Holohan .01 .05
271 Mike Lansford .01 .05
272 Duval Love RC .01 .05
273 Buford McGee .01 .05
274 Tom Newberry .01 .05
275 Jackie Slater .01 .05
276 Frank Stams .01 .05
277 Alfred Anderson .01 .05
278 Joey Browner .01 .05
279 Anthony Carter .02 .10
280 Chris Doleman .01 .05
281 Rick Fenney .01 .05
282 Rich Gannon .08 .25
283 Hassan Jones .01 .05
284 Steve Jordan .01 .05
285 Carl Lee .01 .05
286 Randall McDaniel .02 .10
287 Keith Millard .01 .05
288 Herschel Walker .02 .10
289 Wade Wilson .02 .10
290 Gary Zimmerman .02 .10
291 Morten Andersen .01 .05
292 Jim Dombrowski .01 .05
293 Gill Fenerty .01 .05
294 Craig Heyward .02 .10
295 Dalton Hilliard .01 .05
296 Rickey Jackson .01 .05
297 Vaughan Johnson .01 .05
298 Eric Martin .01 .05
299 Robert Massey .01 .05
300 Rueben Mayes .01 .05
301 Sam Mills .01 .05
302 Brett Perriman .08 .25
303 Pat Swilling .02 .10
304 Steve Walsh .01 .05
305 Ottis Anderson .02 .10
306 Matt Bahr .01 .05
307 Mark Bavaro .01 .05
308 Maurice Carthon .01 .05
309 Mark Collins .01 .05
310 John Elliott .01 .05
311 Rodney Hampton .08 .25
312 Jeff Hostetler .02 .10
313 Erik Howard .01 .05
314 Pepper Johnson .01 .05
315 Sean Landeta .01 .05
316 Dave Meggett .02 .10
317 Bart Oates .01 .05
318 Phil Simms .02 .10
319 Lawrence Taylor .08 .25
320 Reyna Thompson .01 .05
321 Everson Walls .01 .05
322 Eric Allen .01 .05
323 Fred Barnett .08 .25
324 Jerome Brown .01 .05
325 Keith Byars .01 .05
326 Randall Cunningham .08 .25
327 Byron Evans .01 .05
328 Ron Heller .01 .05
329 Keith Jackson .02 .10
330 Seth Joyner .02 .10
331 Heath Sherman .01 .05
332 Clyde Simmons .01 .05
333 Ben Smith .01 .05
334 Anthony Toney .01 .05
335 Andre Waters .01 .05
336 Reggie White .08 .25
337 Calvin Williams .02 .10
338 Anthony Bell .01 .05
339 Rich Camarillo .01 .05
340 Roy Green .01 .05
341 Tim Jorden RC .01 .05
342 Cedric Mack .01 .05
343 Dexter Manley .01 .05
344 Freddie Joe Nunn .01 .05
345 Ricky Proehl .01 .05
346 Tootie Robbins .01 .05
347 Timm Rosenbach .01 .05
348 Luis Sharpe .01 .05
349 Vai Sikahema .01 .05
350 Anthony Thompson .01 .05
351 Lonnie Young .01 .05
352 Dexter Carter .01 .05
353 Mike Cofer .01 .05
354 Kevin Fagan .01 .05
355 Don Griffin .01 .05
356 Charles Haley UER .02 .10
(Total fumbles should be 6, not 5)
357 Pierce Holt .01 .05
358 Brent Jones .08 .25
359 Guy McIntyre .01 .05
360 Joe Montana .50 1.25
361 Darryl Pollard .01 .05
362 Tom Rathman .01 .05
363 Jerry Rice .30 .75
364 Bill Romanowski .01 .05
365 John Taylor .02 .10
366 Steve Wallace UER .02 .10
Listed as a DL on front of card
367 Steve Young .30 .75
368 Gary Anderson RB .01 .05
369 Ian Beckles .01 .05
370 Mark Carrier WR .08 .25
371 Reggie Cobb .01 .05
372 Reuben Davis .01 .05
373 Randy Grimes .01 .05
374 Wayne Haddix .01 .05
375 Ron Hall .01 .05
376 Harry Hamilton .01 .05
377 Bruce Hill .01 .05
378 Keith McCants .01 .05
379 Bruce Perkins .01 .05
380 Vinny Testaverde UER .02 .10
(Misspelled Vinnie on card front)
381 Broderick Thomas .01 .05
382 Jeff Bostic .01 .05
383 Earnest Byner .01 .05
384 Gary Clark .08 .25
385 Darryl Grant .01 .05
386 Darrell Green .01 .05
387 Stan Humphries .08 .25
388 Jim Lachey .01 .05
389 Charles Mann .01 .05
390 Wilber Marshall .01 .05
391 Art Monk .02 .10
392 Gerald Riggs .01 .05
393 Mark Rypien .02 .10
394 Ricky Sanders .01 .05
395 Don Warren .01 .05
396 Bruce Smith HIT .02 .10
397 Reggie White HIT .02 .10
398 Lawrence Taylor HIT .02 .10
399 David Fulcher HIT .01 .05
400 Derrick Thomas HIT .02 .10
401 Mark Carrier DB HIT .01 .05
402 Mike Singletary HIT .02 .10
403 Charles Haley HIT .01 .05
404 Jeff Cross HIT .01 .05
405 Leslie O'Neal HIT .02 .10
406 Tim Harris HIT .01 .05
407 Steve Atwater HIT .01 .05
408 Joe Montana LL UER .20 .50
(4th on yardage list, not 3rd)
409 Randall Cunningham LL .02 .10
410 Warren Moon LL .02 .10
411 Andre Rison LL UER .02 .10
(Card incorrectly numbered as 412 and Michigan State misspelled as Stage)
412 Haywood Jeffires LL .02 .10
(See number 411)
413 Stephone Paige LL .01 .05
414 Phil Simms LL .02 .10
415 Barry Sanders LL .20 .50
416 Bo Jackson LL .02 .10
417 Thurman Thomas LL .02 .10
418 Emmitt Smith LL .50 1.25
419 John L. Williams LL .01 .05
420 Nick Bell RC .01 .05
421 Eric Bieniemy RC .01 .05
422 Mike Dumas RP RC UER .01 .05
(Returned interception vs. Purdue, not Michigan State)
423 Russell Maryland RC .08 .25
424 Derek Russell RC .01 .05
425 Chris Smith RC .01 .05
426 Mike Stonebreaker RP .01 .05
427 Pat Tyrance RP .01 .05
428 Kenny Walker RC .01 .05
429 Checklist 1-108 UER .01 .05
430 Checklist 109-216 .01 .05
431 Checklist 217-324 .01 .05
432 Checklist 325-432 .01 .05

1991 Fleer All-Pros

COMPLETE SET (26) 2.00 5.00
1 Andre Reed UER .02 .10
(Caught 81 passes in 1989, should say 88 passes)
2 Bobby Humphrey .01 .05
3 Kent Hull .01 .05
4 Mark Bortz .01 .05
5 Bruce Smith .08 .25
6 Greg Townsend .01 .05
7 Ray Childress .01 .05
8 Andre Rison .02 .10
9 Barry Sanders .50 1.25
10 Bo Jackson .10 .30
11 Neal Anderson .02 .10
12 Keith Jackson .02 .10
13 Derrick Thomas .08 .25
14 John Offerdahl .01 .05
15 Lawrence Taylor .08 .25
16 Darrell Green .01 .05
17 Mark Carrier DB UER .02 .10
(No period in last sentence of bio)
18 David Fulcher UER .01 .05
(Bill Wyche, should be Sam)
19 Joe Montana .50 1.25
20 Jerry Rice .30 .75
21 Charles Haley .02 .10
22 Mike Singletary .02 .10
23 Nick Lowery .01 .05
24 Jim Lachey UER .01 .05
(Acquired by trade in 1987, not 1988)
25 Anthony Munoz .02 .10
26 Thurman Thomas .08 .25

1991 Fleer Pro-Vision

COMPLETE SET (10) 2.00 5.00
1 Joe Montana .60 1.50
2 Barry Sanders .60 1.50
3 Lawrence Taylor .10 .30
4 Mike Singletary .02 .10
5 Dan Marino .60 1.50
6 Bo Jackson .15 .40
7 Randall Cunningham .10 .30
8 Bruce Smith .10 .30
9 Derrick Thomas .10 .30
10 Howie Long .10 .30

1991 Fleer Stars and Stripes

This 140-card standard-size set marked the second year that Fleer, in conjunction with Asher Candy, marketed a set sold with candy sticks. The set features full-color game action shots on the front and a large color portrait, as well as complete statistical information on the back. The cards are arranged by alphabetical team order within each conference.

COMPLETE SET (140) 4.80 12.00
1 Shane Conlan .02 .10
2 Kent Hull .02 .10
3 Andre Reed .07 .20
4 Bruce Smith .07 .20
5 Thurman Thomas .10 .30
6 James Brooks .02 .10
7 Boomer Esiason .07 .20
8 David Fulcher .02 .10
9 Rodney Holman .02 .10
10 Anthony Munoz .07 .20
11 Reggie Langhorne .02 .10
12 Clay Matthews .02 .10
13 Eric Metcalf .07 .20
14 Gregg Rakoczy .02 .10
15 Steve Atwater .02 .10
16 John Elway 1.00 2.50
17 Bobby Humphrey .02 .10
18 Karl Mecklenburg .02 .10
19 Dennis Smith .02 .10
20 Ray Childress .02 .10
21 Ernest Givins .02 .10
22 Haywood Jeffires .07 .20
23 Warren Moon .10 .30
24 Mike Munchak .07 .20
25 Albert Bentley .02 .10
26 Jeff George .07 .20
27 Rohn Stark .02 .10
28 Clarence Verdin .02 .10
29 Albert Lewis .02 .10
30 Nick Lowery .02 .10
31 Christian Okoye .02 .10
32 Stephone Paige .02 .10
33 Derrick Thomas .07 .20
34 Barry Word .02 .10
35 Bo Jackson .10 .30
36 Howie Long .10 .30
37 Greg Townsend .02 .10
38 Steve Wisniewski UER .02 .10
(Acquired by trade in/1989, not draft)
39 Mark Clayton .02 .10
40 Dan Marino 1.00 2.50
41 John Offerdahl .02 .10
42 Richmond Webb .02 .10
43 Irving Fryar .07 .20
44 Ed Reynolds .02 .10
45 John Stephens .02 .10
46 Rob Moore .10 .30
47 Ken O'Brien .02 .10
48 Al Toon .02 .10
49 Bubby Brister .02 .10
50 Eric Green .02 .10
51 Merril Hoge .02 .10
52 David Little .02 .10
53 Rod Woodson .07 .20
54 Marion Butts .02 .10
55 Leslie O'Neal .02 .10
56 Junior Seau .10 .30
57 Billy Joe Tolliver .02 .10
58 Cortez Kennedy .07 .20
59 Dave Krieg .02 .10
60 John L. Williams .02 .10
61 Steve Broussard .02 .10
62 Bill Fralic .02 .10
63 Andre Rison .07 .20
64 Neal Anderson .02 .10
65 Mark Carrier DB .02 .10
66 Richard Dent .02 .10
67 Jim Harbaugh .07 .20
68 Mike Singletary .07 .20
69 Troy Aikman .50 1.25
70 Emmitt Smith 1.25 3.00
71 Mel Gray .02 .10
72 Rodney Peete .02 .10
73 Barry Sanders 1.00 2.50
74 Tim Harris .02 .10
75 Perry Kemp .02 .10
76 Sterling Sharpe .07 .20
77 Henry Ellard .07 .20
78 Jim Everett .02 .10
79 Kevin Greene .07 .20
80 Jackie Slater .02 .10
81 Joey Browner .02 .10
82 Chris Doleman .02 .10
83 Steve Jordan .02 .10
84 Carl Lee .02 .10
85 Herschel Walker .07 .20
86 Morten Andersen .02 .10
87 Dalton Hilliard .02 .10
88 Vaughan Johnson .02 .10
89 Steve Walsh .02 .10
90 Ottis Anderson .02 .10
91 John Elliott .02 .10
92 Rodney Hampton .07 .20
93 Sean Landeta .02 .10
94 Dave Meggett .02 .10
95 Phil Simms .07 .20
96 Lawrence Taylor .07 .20
97 Randall Cunningham .10 .30
98 Keith Jackson .02 .10
99 Seth Joyner .02 .10
100 Reggie White .10 .30
101 Roy Green .02 .10
102 Johnny Johnson .02 .10
103 Ricky Proehl .02 .10
104 Tootie Robbins .02 .10
105 Kevin Fagan UER .02 .10
(4th round pick in/1987, not 1986)
106 Charles Haley .07 .20
107 Guy McIntyre .02 .10
108 Joe Montana 1.00 2.50
109 Tom Rathman .02 .10
110 Jerry Rice .50 1.25
111 John Taylor .07 .20
112 Wayne Haddix .02 .10
113 Vinny Testaverde .02 .10
114 Earnest Byner .02 .10
115 Gary Clark .07 .20
116 Darrell Green .02 .10
117 Jim Lachey .02 .10
118 Art Monk .07 .20
119 Mark Rypien .02 .10
120 Nick Bell .02 .10
121 Eric Bieniemy .02 .10
122 Jarrod Bunch .02 .10
123 Aaron Craver .02 .10
124 Lawrence Dawsey .02 .10
125 Mike Dumas .02 .10
126 Jeff Graham .10 .30
127 Paul Justin .02 .10
128 Darryll Lewis UER .02 .10
(Darryll misspelled as Darryl)
120 Todd Marinovich .02 .10
130 Russell Maryland .07 .20
131 Kanavis McGhee .02 .10
132 Ernie Mills .02 .10
133 Herman Moore .30 .75
134 Godfrey Myles .02 .10
135 Browning Nagle .02 .10
136 Esera Tuaolo .02 .10
137 Mark Vander Poel .02 .10
138 Harvey Williams .07 .20
139 Chris Zorich .02 .10
140 Checklist Card UER .02 .10
(Darryll Lewis mispelled Darryl)

1992 Fleer Prototypes

The 1992 Fleer Prototype football set contains six standard-size cards. The cards were distributed as two-card and three-card panels or strips in an attempt to show off the new design features of the 1992 Fleer football cards. The cards prominently pronounce "1992 Pre-Production Sample" in the middle of the reverse.

93 Mike Croel .30 .75
191 Tim Brown .50 1.25
428 Mark Rypien .30 .75
435 Terrell Buckley .30 .75
457 Barry Sanders LL 2.00 5.00
475 Emmitt Smith PV 2.00 5.00

1992 Fleer

The 1992 Fleer football set contains 480 standard-size cards. The cards were available in 17-card wax packs, 42-card rack packs, and 32-card cello packs. The cards are checklisted alphabetically according to teams. Subsets included are Prospects (432-451), League Leaders (452-470), Pro-Visions (471-476), and Checklists (477-480). Rookie Cards include Edgar Bennett, Steve Bono, Amp Lee and Tommy Vardell.

COMPLETE SET (480) 5.00 10.00
1 Steve Broussard .01 .05
2 Rick Bryan .01 .05
3 Scott Case .01 .05
4 Tory Epps .01 .05
5 Bill Fralic .01 .05
6 Moe Gardner .01 .05
7 Michael Haynes .02 .10
8 Chris Hinton .01 .05
9 Brian Jordan .02 .10
10 Mike Kenn .01 .05
11 Tim McKyer .01 .05
12 Chris Miller .02 .10
13 Erric Pegram .02 .10
14 Mike Pritchard .02 .10
15 Andre Rison .02 .10
16 Jessie Tuggle .01 .05
17 Carlton Bailey RC .02 .10
18 Howard Ballard .01 .05
19 Don Beebe .01 .05
20 Cornelius Bennett .02 .10
21 Shane Conlan .01 .05
22 Kent Hull .01 .05
23 Mark Kelso .01 .05
24 James Lofton .02 .10
25 Keith McKeller .01 .05
26 Scott Norwood .01 .05
27 Nate Odomes .01 .05
28 Frank Reich .02 .10
29 Jim Ritcher .01 .05
30 Leon Seals .01 .05
31 Darryl Talley .01 .05
32 Steve Tasker .02 .10
33 Thurman Thomas .08 .25
34 Will Wolford .01 .05
35 Neal Anderson .01 .05
36 Trace Armstrong .01 .05
37 Mark Carrier DB .01 .05
38 Richard Dent .02 .10
39 Shaun Gayle .01 .05
40 Jim Harbaugh .08 .25
41 Jay Hilgenberg .01 .05
42 Darren Lewis .01 .05
43 Steve McMichael .02 .10
44 Brad Muster .01 .05
45 William Perry .02 .10
46 John Roper .01 .05
47 Lemuel Stinson .01 .05
48 Stan Thomas .01 .05
49 Keith Van Horne .01 .05
50 Tom Waddle .01 .05
51 Donnell Woolford .01 .05
52 Chris Zorich .02 .10
53 Eddie Brown .01 .05
54 James Francis .01 .05
55 David Fulcher .01 .05
56 David Grant .01 .05
57 Harold Green .01 .05
58 Rodney Holman .01 .05
59 Lee Johnson .01 .05
60 Tim Krumrie .01 .05
61 Anthony Munoz .02 .10
62 Joe Walter RC .01 .05
63 Mike Baab .01 .05
64 Stephen Braggs .01 .05
65 Richard Brown RC .01 .05
66 Dan Fike .01 .05
67 Scott Galbraith RC .01 .05
68 Randy Hilliard RC .01 .05
69 Michael Jackson .02 .10
70 Tony Jones T .01 .05
71 Ed King .01 .05
72 Kevin Mack .01 .05
73 Clay Matthews .02 .10
74 Eric Metcalf .02 .10
75 Vince Newsome .01 .05
76 John Rienstra .01 .05
77 Steve Beuerlein .02 .10
78 Larry Brown DB .01 .05
79 Tony Casillas .01 .05
80 Alvin Harper .02 .10
81 Issiac Holt .01 .05
82 Ray Horton .01 .05
83 Michael Irvin .08 .25
84 Daryl Johnston .08 .25
85 Kelvin Martin .01 .05
86 Nate Newton .02 .10
87 Ken Norton .02 .10
88 Jay Novacek .02 .10
89 Emmitt Smith .60 1.50
90 Vinson Smith RC .01 .05
91 Mark Stepnoski .02 .10
92 Steve Atwater .01 .05
93 Mike Croel .01 .05
94 John Elway .50 1.25
95 Simon Fletcher .01 .05
96 Gaston Green .01 .05
97 Mark Jackson .01 .05
98 Keith Kartz .01 .05
99 Greg Kragen .01 .05
100 Greg Lewis .01 .05
101 Karl Mecklenburg .01 .05
102 Derek Russell .01 .05
103 Steve Sewell .01 .05
104 Dennis Smith .01 .05
105 David Treadwell .01 .05
106 Kenny Walker .01 .05
107 Doug Widell .01 .05
108 Michael Young .01 .05
109 Jerry Ball .01 .05
110 Bennie Blades .01 .05
111 Lomas Brown .01 .05
112 Scott Conover RC .01 .05
113 Ray Crockett .01 .05
114 Mike Farr .01 .05
115 Mel Gray .02 .10
116 Willie Green .01 .05
117 Tracy Hayworth RC .01 .05
118 Erik Kramer .02 .10
119 Herman Moore .08 .25
120 Dan Owens .01 .05
121 Rodney Peete .02 .10
122 Brett Perriman .08 .25
123 Barry Sanders .50 1.25
124 Chris Spielman .02 .10
125 Marc Spindler .01 .05
126 Tony Bennett .01 .05
127 Matt Brock .01 .05
128 LeRoy Butler .01 .05
129 Johnny Holland .01 .05
130 Perry Kemp .01 .05
131 Don Majkowski .01 .05
132 Mark Murphy .01 .05
133 Brian Noble .01 .05
134 Bryce Paup .08 .25
135 Sterling Sharpe .08 .25
136 Scott Stephen .01 .05
137 Darrell Thompson .01 .05
138 Mike Tomczak .01 .05
139 Esera Tuaolo .01 .05
140 Keith Woodside .01 .05
141 Ray Childress .01 .05
142 Cris Dishman .01 .05
143 Curtis Duncan .01 .05
144 John Flannery .01 .05
145 William Fuller .02 .10
146 Ernest Givins .02 .10
147 Haywood Jeffires .02 .10
148 Sean Jones .02 .10
149 Lamar Lathon .01 .05
150 Bruce Matthews .01 .05
151 Bubba McDowell .01 .05
152 Johnny Meads .01 .05
153 Warren Moon .08 .25
154 Mike Munchak .02 .10
155 Al Smith .01 .05
156 Doug Smith .01 .05
157 Lorenzo White .01 .05
158 Michael Ball .01 .05
159 Chip Banks .01 .05
160 Duane Bickett .01 .05
161 Bill Brooks .01 .05
162 Ken Clark .01 .05
163 Jon Hand .01 .05
164 Jeff Herrod .01 .05
165 Jessie Hester .01 .05
166 Scott Radecic .01 .05
167 Rohn Stark .01 .05
168 Clarence Verdin .01 .05
169 John Alt .01 .05
170 Tim Barnett .01 .05
171 Tim Grunhard .01 .05
172 Dino Hackett .01 .05
173 Jonathan Hayes .01 .05
174 Bill Maas .01 .05
175 Chris Martin .01 .05
176 Christian Okoye .01 .05
177 Stephone Paige .01 .05
178 Jayice Pearson RC .01 .05
179 Kevin Porter .01 .05
180 Kevin Ross .01 .05
181 Dan Saleaumua .01 .05
182 Tracy Simien RC .01 .05
183 Neil Smith .08 .25
184 Derrick Thomas .08 .25
185 Robb Thomas .01 .05
186 Mark Vlasic .01 .05
187 Barry Word .01 .05
188 Marcus Allen .08 .25
189 Eddie Anderson .01 .05
190 Nick Bell .01 .05
191 Tim Brown .08 .25
192 Scott Davis .01 .05
193 Riki Ellison .01 .05
194 Mervyn Fernandez .01 .05
195 Willie Gault .02 .10
196 Jeff Gossett .01 .05
197 Ethan Horton .01 .05
198 Jeff Jaeger .01 .05
199 Howie Long .08 .25
200 Ronnie Lott .02 .10
201 Todd Marinovich .01 .05
202 Don Mosebar .01 .05
203 Jay Schroeder .01 .05
204 Greg Townsend .01 .05
205 Lionel Washington .01 .05
206 Steve Wisniewski .01 .05
207 Flipper Anderson .01 .05
208 Bern Brostek .01 .05
209 Robert Delpino .01 .05
210 Henry Ellard .02 .10
211 Jim Everett .02 .10
212 Cleveland Gary .01 .05
213 Kevin Greene .02 .10
214 Darryl Henley .01 .05
215 Damone Johnson .01 .05
216 Larry Kelm .01 .05
217 Todd Lyght .01 .05
218 Jackie Slater .01 .05
219 Michael Stewart .01 .05
220 Pat Terrell UER .01 .05
221 Robert Young .01 .05
222 Mark Clayton .02 .10
223 Bryan Cox .02 .10
224 Aaron Craver .01 .05
225 Jeff Cross .01 .05
226 Mark Duper .01 .05
227 Harry Galbreath .01 .05
228 David Griggs .01 .05
229 Mark Higgs .01 .05
230 Vestee Jackson .01 .05
231 John Offerdahl .01 .05
232 Louis Oliver .01 .05
233 Tony Paige .01 .05
234 Reggie Roby .01 .05
235 Sammie Smith .01 .05
236 Pete Stoyanovich .01 .05
237 Richmond Webb .01 .05
238 Terry Allen .08 .25
239 Ray Berry .01 .05
240 Joey Browner .01 .05
241 Anthony Carter .02 .10
242 Cris Carter .20 .50
243 Chris Doleman .01 .05
244 Rich Gannon .08 .25
245 Tim Irwin .01 .05
246 Steve Jordan .01 .05
247 Carl Lee .01 .05
248 Randall McDaniel .02 .10
249 Mike Merriweather .01 .05
250 Harry Newsome .01 .05
251 John Randle .02 .10
252 Henry Thomas .01 .05
253 Herschel Walker .02 .10
254 Ray Agnew .01 .05
255 Bruce Armstrong .01 .05
256 Vincent Brown .01 .05
257 Marv Cook .01 .05
258 Irving Fryar .02 .10
259 Pat Harlow .01 .05
260 Tommy Hodson .01 .05
261 Maurice Hurst .01 .05
262 Ronnie Lippett .01 .05
263 Eugene Lockhart .01 .05
264 Greg McMurtry .01 .05
265 Hugh Millen .01 .05
266 Leonard Russell .02 .10
267 Andre Tippett .01 .05
268 Brent Williams .01 .05
269 Morten Andersen .01 .05
270 Gene Atkins .01 .05
271 Wesley Carroll .01 .05
272 Jim Dombrowski .01 .05
273 Quinn Early .02 .10
274 Gill Fenerty .01 .05
275 Bobby Hebert .01 .05
276 Joel Hilgenberg .01 .05
277 Rickey Jackson .01 .05
278 Vaughan Johnson .01 .05
279 Eric Martin .01 .05
280 Brett Maxie .01 .05
281 Fred McAfee RC .01 .05
282 Sam Mills .01 .05
283 Pat Swilling .02 .10
284 Floyd Turner .01 .05
285 Steve Walsh .01 .05
286 Frank Warren .01 .05
287 Stephen Baker .01 .05
288 Maurice Carthon .01 .05
289 Mark Collins .01 .05
290 John Elliott .01 .05
291 Myron Guyton .01 .05
292 Rodney Hampton .02 .10
293 Jeff Hostetler .02 .10
294 Mark Ingram .01 .05
295 Pepper Johnson .01 .05
296 Sean Landeta .01 .05
297 Leonard Marshall .01 .05
298 Dave Meggett .02 .10
299 Bart Oates .01 .05
300 Phil Simms .02 .10
301 Reyna Thompson .01 .05
302 Lewis Tillman .01 .05
303 Brad Baxter .01 .05
304 Kyle Clifton .01 .05
305 James Hasty .01 .05
306 Joe Kelly .01 .05
307 Jeff Lageman .01 .05
308 Mo Lewis .01 .05
309 Erik McMillan .01 .05
310 Rob Moore .02 .10
311 Tony Stargell .01 .05
312 Jim Sweeney .01 .05
313 Marvin Washington .01 .05
314 Lonnie Young .01 .05
315 Eric Allen .01 .05
316 Fred Barnett .08 .25
317 Jerome Brown .01 .05
318 Keith Byars .01 .05
319 Wes Hopkins .01 .05
320 Keith Jackson .02 .10
321 James Joseph .01 .05
322 Seth Joyner .02 .10
323 Jeff Kemp .01 .05
324 Roger Ruzek .01 .05
325 Clyde Simmons .01 .05
326 William Thomas .01 .05
327 Reggie White .08 .25
328 Calvin Williams .02 .10
329 Rich Camarillo .01 .05
330 Ken Harvey .01 .05
331 Eric Hill .01 .05
332 Johnny Johnson .01 .05
333 Ernie Jones .01 .05
334 Tim Jorden .01 .05
335 Tim McDonald .01 .05
336 Freddie Joe Nunn .01 .05
337 Luis Sharpe .01 .05
338 Eric Swann .02 .10
339 Aeneas Williams .02 .10
340 Gary Anderson K .01 .05
341 Bubby Brister .01 .05
342 Adrian Cooper .01 .05
343 Barry Foster .02 .10
344 Eric Green .01 .05
345 Bryan Hinkle .01 .05
346 Tunch Ilkin .01 .05
347 Carnell Lake .01 .05
348 Louis Lipps .01 .05
349 David Little .01 .05
350 Greg Lloyd .02 .10
351 Neil O'Donnell .08 .25
352 Dwight Stone .01 .05
353 Rod Woodson .08 .25
354 Rod Bernstine .01 .05
355 Eric Bieniemy .01 .05
356 Marion Butts .01 .05
357 Gill Byrd .01 .05
358 John Friesz .02 .10
359 Burt Grossman .01 .05
360 Courtney Hall .01 .05
361 Ronnie Harmon .01 .05
362 Shawn Jefferson .01 .05
363 Nate Lewis .01 .05
364 Craig McEwen RC .01 .05
365 Eric Moten .01 .05
366 Joe Phillips .01 .05
367 Gary Plummer .01 .05
368 Henry Rolling .01 .05
369 Broderick Thompson .01 .05
370 Harris Barton .01 .05
371 Steve Bono RC .08 .25
372 Todd Bowles .01 .05
373 Dexter Carter .01 .05
374 Michael Carter .01 .05
375 Mike Cofer .01 .05
376 Keith DeLong .01 .05
377 Charles Haley .02 .10
378 Merton Hanks .02 .10
379 Tim Harris .01 .05
380 Brent Jones .02 .10
381 Guy McIntyre .01 .05
382 Tom Rathman .01 .05
383 Bill Romanowski .01 .05
384 Jesse Sapolu .01 .05
385 John Taylor .02 .10
386 Steve Young .25 .60
387 Robert Blackmon .01 .05
388 Brian Blades .02 .10
389 Jacob Green .01 .05
390 Dwayne Harper .01 .05
391 Andy Heck .01 .05
392 Tommy Kane .01 .05
393 John Kasay .01 .05
394 Cortez Kennedy .02 .10
395 Bryan Millard .01 .05
396 Rufus Porter .01 .05
397 Eugene Robinson .01 .05
398 John L. Williams .01 .05
399 Terry Wooden .01 .05
400 Gary Anderson RB .01 .05
401 Ian Beckles .01 .05
402 Mark Carrier WR .02 .10
403 Reggie Cobb .01 .05
404 Lawrence Dawsey .02 .10
405 Ron Hall .01 .05
406 Keith McCants .01 .05
407 Charles McRae .01 .05
408 Tim Newton .01 .05
409 Jesse Solomon .01 .05
410 Vinny Testaverde .02 .10
411 Broderick Thomas .01 .05
412 Robert Wilson .01 .05
413 Jeff Bostic .01 .05
414 Earnest Byner .01 .05
415 Gary Clark .08 .25
416 Andre Collins .01 .05
417 Brad Edwards .01 .05
418 Kurt Gouveia .01 .05
419 Darrell Green .01 .05
420 Joe Jacoby .01 .05
421 Jim Lachey .01 .05
422 Chip Lohmiller .01 .05
423 Charles Mann .01 .05
424 Wilber Marshall .01 .05
425 Ron Middleton RC .01 .05
426 Brian Mitchell .02 .10
427 Art Monk UER .02 .10
(Born in 1967 should say 1957)
428 Mark Rypien .01 .05
429 Ricky Sanders .01 .05
430 Mark Schlereth RC .01 .05
431 Fred Stokes .01 .05
432 Edgar Bennett RC .08 .25
433 Brian Bollinger RC .01 .05
434 Joe Bowden RC .01 .05
435 Terrell Buckley RC .01 .05
436 Willie Clay RC .01 .05
437 Steve Gordon RC .01 .05

438 Keith Hamilton RC .02 .10
439 Carlos Huerta .01 .05
440 Matt LaBounty RC .01 .05
441 Amp Lee RC .01 .05
442 Ricardo McDonald RC .01 .05
443 Chris Mims RC .02 .10
444 Michael Moody RC .01 .05
445 Patrick Rowe RC .01 .05
446 Leon Searcy RC .02 .10
447 Siran Stacy RC .01 .05
448 Kevin Turner RC .01 .05
449 Tommy Vardell RC .02 .10
450 Bob Whitfield RC .01 .05
451 Darryl Williams RC .01 .05
452 Thurman Thomas LL .02 .10
453 Emmitt Smith LL UER .30 .75
(Thr at start of second paragraph should be the)
454 Haywood Jeffires LL .01 .05
455 Michael Irvin LL .02 .10
456 Mark Clayton LL .01 .05
457 Barry Sanders LL .25 .60
458 Pete Stoyanovich LL .01 .05
459 Chip Lohmiller LL .01 .05
460 William Fuller LL .01 .05
461 Pat Swilling LL .01 .05
462 Ronnie Lott LL .01 .05
463 Ray Crockett LL .01 .05
464 Tim McKyer LL .01 .05
465 Aeneas Williams LL .01 .05
466 Rod Woodson LL .02 .10
467 Mel Gray LL .01 .05
468 Nate Lewis LL .01 .05
469 Steve Young LL .10 .30
470 Reggie Roby LL .01 .05
471 John Elway PV .25 .60
472 Ronnie Lott PV .01 .05
473 Art Monk PV UER .01 .05
474 Warren Moon PV .02 .10
475 Emmitt Smith PV .30 .75
476 Thurman Thomas PV .02 .10
477 Checklist 1-120 .01 .05
478 Checklist 121-240 .01 .05
479 Checklist 241-360 .01 .05
480 Checklist 361-480 .01 .05

1992 Fleer All-Pros

COMPLETE SET (24) 2.00 5.00
1 Marv Cook .02 .10
2 Mike Kenn .02 .10
3 Steve Wisniewski .02 .10
4 Jim Ritcher .02 .10
5 Jim Lachey .02 .10
6 Michael Irvin .30 .75
7 Andre Rison .10 .30
8 Thurman Thomas .30 .75
9 Barry Sanders 2.00 4.00
10 Bruce Matthews .02 .10
11 Mark Rypien .02 .10
12 Jeff Jaeger .02 .10
13 Reggie White .30 .75
14 Clyde Simmons .02 .10
15 Pat Swilling .10 .30
16 Sam Mills .02 .10
17 Ray Childress .02 .10
18 Jerry Ball .02 .10
19 Derrick Thomas .30 .75
20 Darrell Green .02 .10
21 Ronnie Lott .10 .30
22 Steve Atwater .02 .10
23 Mark Carrier DB .02 .10
24 Jeff Gossett .02 .10

1992 Fleer Rookie Sensations

COMPLETE SET (20) 4.00 10.00
RANDOM INSERTS IN JUMBO PACKS
1 Moe Gardner .15 .40
2 Mike Pritchard .40 1.00
3 Stan Thomas .15 .40
4 Larry Brown DB .15 .40
5 Todd Lyght .15 .40
6 James Joseph .15 .40
7 Aeneas Williams .40 1.00
8 Michael Jackson .40 1.00
9 Ed King .15 .40
10 Mike Croel .15 .40
11 Kenny Walker .15 .40
12 Tim Barnett .15 .40
13 Nick Bell .15 .40
14 Todd Marinovich .15 .40
15 Leonard Russell .40 1.00
16 Pat Harlow .15 .40
17 Mo Lewis .15 .40
18 John Kasay .15 .40
19 Lawrence Dawsey .40 1.00
20 Charles McRae .15 .40

1992 Fleer Mark Rypien

COMPLETE SET (12) 1.50 3.00
COMMON RYPIEN (1-12) .10 .30
COMMON SEND-OFF (13-15) .20 .50
AU Mark Rypien AUTO 12.50 30.00
(Certified Autograph)

1992 Fleer Team Leaders

COMPLETE SET (24) 15.00 40.00
ONE TL OR RYPIEN PER RACK PACK
1 Chris Miller .25 .60
2 Neal Anderson .08 .25
3 Emmitt Smith 4.00 10.00
4 Chris Spielman .25 .60
5 Brian Noble .08 .25
6 Jim Everett .25 .60
7 Joey Browner .08 .25
8 Sam Mills .08 .25
9 Rodney Hampton .25 .60
10 Reggie White .60 1.50
11 Tim McDonald .08 .25
12 Charles Haley .25 .60
13 Mark Rypien .08 .25
14 Cornelius Bennett .25 .60
15 Clay Matthews .25 .60
16 John Elway 3.00 8.00
17 Warren Moon .60 1.50
18 Derrick Thomas .60 1.50
19 Greg Townsend .08 .25
20 Bruce Armstrong .08 .25
21 Brad Baxter .08 .25
22 Rod Woodson .60 1.50
23 Marion Butts .08 .25
24 Rufus Porter .08 .25

1993 Fleer

The 1993 Fleer football set consists of 500 standard-size cards. Cards were available in 15 and 29-card packs as well as 27-card rack packs. Topical subsets featured are Award Winners (236-240, 253-257), League Leaders (241-243, 258-262), and Pro Visions (246-248, 263-264). Rookie Cards include Dave Brown. A Promo Panel with eight cards was produced and is priced as uncut at the end of our checklist.

COMPLETE SET (500) 10.00 20.00
1 Dan Saleaumua .01 .05
2 Bryan Cox .01 .05
3 Dermontti Dawson .01 .05
4 Michael Jackson .02 .10
5 Calvin Williams .02 .10
6 Terry McDaniel .01 .05
7 Jack Del Rio .01 .05
8 Steve Atwater .01 .05
9 Ernie Jones .01 .05
10 Brad Muster .01 .05
(Signed with New Orleans Saints)
11 Harold Green .01 .05
12 Eric Bieniemy .01 .05
13 Eric Dorsey .01 .05
14 Fred Barnett .02 .10
15 Cleveland Gary .01 .05
16 Darion Conner .01 .05
17 Jerry Ball .01 .05
(Traded to Cleveland Browns)
18 Tony Casillas .01 .05
19 Brian Blades .02 .10
20 Tony Bennett .01 .05
21 Reggie Cobb .01 .05
22 Kurt Gouveia .01 .05
23 Greg McMurtry .01 .05
24 Kyle Clifton .01 .05
25 Trace Armstrong .01 .05
26 Terry Allen .08 .25
27 Steve Bono .02 .10
28 Barry Word .01 .05
29 Mark Duper .01 .05
30 Nate Newton .02 .10
31 Will Wolford .01 .05
(Signed with Indianapolis Colts)
32 Curtis Duncan .01 .05
33 Nick Bell .01 .05
34 Don Beebe .01 .05
35 Mike Croel .01 .05
36 Rich Camarillo .01 .05
37 Wade Wilson .01 .05
(Signed with New Orleans Saints)
38 John Taylor .02 .10
39 Marion Butts .01 .05
40 Rodney Hampton .02 .10
41 Seth Joyner .01 .05
42 Wilber Marshall .01 .05
43 Bobby Hebert .01 .05
(Signed with Atlanta Falcons)
44 Bennie Blades .01 .05
45 Thomas Everett .01 .05
46 Ricky Sanders .01 .05
47 Matt Brock .01 .05
48 Lawrence Dawsey .01 .05
49 Brad Edwards .01 .05
50 Vincent Brown .01 .05
51 Jeff Lageman .01 .05
52 Mark Carrier DB .01 .05
53 Cris Carter .08 .25
54 Brent Jones .02 .10
55 Barry Foster .02 .10
56 Derrick Thomas .08 .25
57 Scott Zolak .01 .05
58 Mark Stepnoski .01 .05
59 Eric Metcalf .02 .10
60 Al Smith .01 .05
61 Ronnie Harmon .01 .05
62 Cornelius Bennett .02 .10
63 Karl Mecklenburg .01 .05
64 Chris Chandler .02 .10
65 Toi Cook .01 .05
66 Tim Krumrie .01 .05
67 Gill Byrd .01 .05
68 Mark Jackson .01 .05
(Signed with New York Giants)
69 Tim Harris .01 .05
(Signed with Philadelphia Eagles)
70 Shane Conlan .01 .05
(Signed with Los Angeles Rams)
71 Moe Gardner .01 .05
72 Lomas Brown .01 .05
73 Charles Haley .02 .10
74 Mark Rypien .01 .05
75 LeRoy Butler .01 .05
76 Steve DeBerg .01 .05
77 Darrell Green .01 .05
78 Marv Cook .01 .05
79 Chris Burkett .01 .05
80 Richard Dent .02 .10
81 Roger Craig .02 .10
82 Amp Lee .01 .05
83 Eric Green .01 .05
84 Willie Davis .08 .25
85 Mark Higgs .01 .05
86 Carlton Haselrig .01 .05
87 Tommy Vardell .01 .05
88 Haywood Jeffires .02 .10
89 Tim Brown .08 .25
90 Randall McDaniel .02 .10
91 John Elway .60 1.50
92 Ken Harvey .01 .05
93 Joel Hilgenberg .01 .05
94 Steve Wallace .01 .05
95 Stan Humphries .02 .10
96 Greg Jackson .01 .05
97 Clyde Simmons .01 .05
98 Jim Everett .02 .10
99 Michael Haynes .02 .10
100 Mel Gray .02 .10
101 Alvin Harper .02 .10
102 Art Monk .02 .10
103 Brett Favre .75 2.00
104 Keith McCants .01 .05
105 Charles Mann .01 .05
106 Leonard Russell .02 .10
107 Mo Lewis .01 .05
108 Shaun Gayle .01 .05
109 Chris Doleman .01 .05
110 Tim McDonald .01 .05
(Signed with San Francisco 49ers)
111 Louis Oliver .01 .05
112 Greg Lloyd .02 .10
113 Chip Banks .01 .05
114 Sean Jones .01 .05
115 Ethan Horton .01 .05
116 Kenneth Davis .01 .05
117 Simon Fletcher .01 .05
118 Johnny Johnson .01 .05
(Traded to New York Jets)
119 Vaughan Johnson .01 .05
120 Derrick Fenner .01 .05
121 Nate Lewis .01 .05
122 Pepper Johnson .01 .05
123 Heath Sherman .01 .05
124 Darryl Henley .01 .05
125 Pierce Holt .01 .05
(Signed with Atlanta Falcons)
126 Herman Moore .08 .25
127 Michael Irvin .08 .25
128 Tommy Kane .01 .05
129 Jackie Harris .01 .05
130 Hardy Nickerson .02 .10
(Signed with Tampa Bay Buccaneers)
131 Chip Lohmiller .01 .05
132 Andre Tippett .01 .05
133 Leonard Marshall .01 .05
(Signed with New York Jets)
134 Craig Heyward .02 .10
(Signed with Chicago Bears)
135 Anthony Carter .02 .10
136 Tom Rathman .01 .05
137 Lorenzo White .01 .05
138 Nick Lowery .01 .05
139 John Offerdahl .01 .05
140 Neil O'Donnell .08 .25
141 Clarence Verdin .01 .05
142 Ernest Givins .02 .10
143 Todd Marinovich .01 .05
144 Jeff Wright .01 .05
145 Michael Brooks .01 .05
146 Freddie Joe Nunn .01 .05
147 William Perry .02 .10
148 Daniel Stubbs .01 .05
149 Morten Andersen .01 .05
150 Dave Meggett .01 .05
151 Andre Waters .01 .05
152 Todd Lyght .01 .05
153 Chris Miller .02 .10
154 Rodney Peete .01 .05
155 Jim Jeffcoat .01 .05
156 Cortez Kennedy .02 .10
157 Johnny Holland .01 .05
158 Ricky Reynolds .01 .05
159 Kevin Greene .02 .10
(Signed with Pittsburgh Steelers)
160 Jeff Herrod .01 .05
161 Bruce Matthews .01 .05
162 Anthony Smith .01 .05
163 Henry Jones .01 .05
164 Rob Burnett .01 .05
165 Eric Swann .02 .10
166 Tom Waddle .01 .05
167 Alfred Williams .01 .05
168 Darren Carrington RC .01 .05
169 Mike Sherrard .01 .05
(Signed with New York Giants)
170 Frank Reich .02 .10
171 Anthony Newman RC .01 .05
172 Mike Pritchard .02 .10
173 Andre Ware .01 .05
174 Daryl Johnston .08 .25
175 Rufus Porter .01 .05
176 Reggie White .08 .25
(Signed with Green Bay Packers)
177 Charles Mincy RC .01 .05
178 Pete Stoyanovich .01 .05
179 Rod Woodson .08 .25
180 Anthony Johnson .02 .10
181 Cody Carlson .01 .05
182 Gaston Green .01 .05
(Traded to Los Angeles Raiders)
183 Audray McMillian .01 .05
184 Mike Johnson .01 .05
185 Aeneas Williams .01 .05
186 Jarrod Bunch .01 .05
187 Dennis Smith .01 .05
188 Quinn Early .02 .10
189 James Hasty .01 .05
190 Darryl Talley .01 .05
191 Jon Vaughn .01 .05
192 Andre Rison .02 .10
193 Kelvin Pritchett .01 .05
194 Ken Norton Jr. .02 .10
195 Chris Warren .02 .10
196 Sterling Sharpe .08 .25
197 Christian Okoye .01 .05
198 Richmond Webb .01 .05
199 James Francis .01 .05
200 Reggie Langhorne .01 .05
201 J.J. Birden .01 .05
202 Aaron Wallace .01 .05
203 Henry Thomas .01 .05
204 Clay Matthews .02 .10
205 Robert Massey .01 .05
206 Donnell Woolford .01 .05
207 Ricky Watters .08 .25
208 Wayne Martin .01 .05
209 Rob Moore .02 .10
210 Steve Tasker .02 .10
211 Jackie Slater .01 .05
212 Steve Young .30 .75
213 Barry Sanders .50 1.25
214 Jay Novacek .02 .10
215 Eugene Robinson .01 .05
216 Duane Bickett .01 .05
217 Broderick Thomas .01 .05
218 David Fulcher .01 .05
219 Rohn Stark .01 .05
220 Warren Moon .08 .25
221 Steve Wisniewski .01 .05
222 Nate Odomes .01 .05
223 Shannon Sharpe .08 .25
224 Byron Evans .01 .05
225 Mark Collins .01 .05
226 Rod Bernstine .01 .05
(Signed with Denver Broncos)
227 Sam Mills .01 .05
228 Marvin Washington .01 .05
229 Thurman Thomas .08 .25
230 Brent Williams .01 .05
231 Jessie Tuggle .01 .05
232 Chris Spielman .02 .10
233 Emmitt Smith .60 1.50
234 John L. Williams .01 .05
235 Jeff Cross .01 .05
236 Chris Doleman AW .01 .05
237 John Elway AW .30 .75
238 Barry Foster AW .01 .05
239 Cortez Kennedy AW .01 .05
240 Steve Young AW .15 .40
241 Barry Foster LL .01 .05
242 Warren Moon LL .01 .05
243 Sterling Sharpe LL .01 .05
244 Emmitt Smith LL .30 .75
245 Thurman Thomas LL .02 .10
246 Michael Irvin PV .02 .10
247 Steve Young PV .15 .40
248 Barry Foster PV .01 .05
249 Checklist .01 .05
Teams Atlanta through Detroit
250 Checklist .01 .05
Teams Detroit through Miami
251 Checklist .01 .05
Teams Minnesota through Pittsburgh
252 Checklist .01 .05
Teams Pittsburgh through Washington and Specials
253 Troy Aikman AW .15 .40
254 Jason Hanson AW .01 .05
255 Carl Pickens AW .02 .10
256 Santana Dotson AW .01 .05
257 Dale Carter AW .01 .05
258 Clyde Simmons LL .01 .05
259 Audray McMillian LL .01 .05
260 Henry Jones LL .01 .05
261 Deion Sanders LL .08 .25
262 Haywood Jeffires LL .01 .05
263 Deion Sanders PV .08 .25
264 Andre Reed PV .02 .10
265 Vince Workman .01 .05
(Signed with Tampa Bay Buccaneers)
266 Robert Brown .01 .05
267 Ray Agnew .01 .05
268 Ronnie Lott .02 .10
(Signed with New York Jets)
269 Wesley Carroll .01 .05
270 John Randle .02 .10
271 Rodney Culver .01 .05
272 David Alexander .01 .05
273 Troy Aikman .30 .75
274 Bernie Kosar .02 .10
275 Scott Case .01 .05
276 Dan McGwire .01 .05
277 John Alt .01 .05
278 Dan Marino .60 1.50
279 Santana Dotson .02 .10
280 Johnny Mitchell .01 .05
281 Alonzo Spellman .01 .05
282 Adrian Cooper .01 .05
283 Gary Clark .02 .10
(Signed with Phoenix Cardinals)
284 Vance Johnson .01 .05
285 Eric Martin .01 .05
286 Jesse Solomon .01 .05
287 Carl Banks .01 .05
288 Harris Barton .01 .05
289 Jim Harbaugh .08 .25
290 Bubba McDowell .01 .05
291 Anthony McDowell RC .01 .05
292 Terrell Buckley .01 .05
293 Bruce Armstrong .01 .05
294 Kurt Barber .01 .05
295 Reginald Jones .01 .05
296 Steve Jordan .01 .05
297 Kerry Cash .01 .05
298 Ray Crockett .01 .05
299 Keith Byars .01 .05
300 Russell Maryland .01 .05
301 Johnny Bailey .01 .05
302 Vinnie Clark .01 .05
(Traded to Atlanta Falcons)
303 Terry Wooden .01 .05
304 Harvey Williams .02 .10
305 Marco Coleman .01 .05
306 Mark Wheeler .01 .05
307 Greg Townsend .01 .05
308 Tim McGee .01 .05
(Signed with Washington Redskins)
309 Donald Evans .01 .05
310 Randal Hill .01 .05
311 Kenny Walker .01 .05
312 Dalton Hilliard .01 .05
313 Howard Ballard .01 .05
314 Phil Simms .02 .10
315 Jerry Rice .40 1.00
316 Courtney Hall .01 .05
317 Darren Lewis .01 .05
318 Greg Montgomery .01 .05
319 Paul Gruber .01 .05
320 George Koonce RC .01 .05
321 Eugene Chung .01 .05
322 Mike Brim .01 .05
323 Patrick Hunter .01 .05
324 Todd Scott .01 .05
325 Steve Emtman .01 .05
326 Andy Harmon RC .02 .10
327 Larry Brown DB .01 .05
328 Chuck Cecil .01 .05
(Signed with Phoenix Cardinals)
329 Tim McKyer .01 .05
330 Jeff Bryant .01 .05
331 Tim Barnett .01 .05
332 Irving Fryar .02 .10
(Traded to Miami Dolphins)
333 Tyji Armstrong .01 .05
334 Brad Baxter .01 .05
335 Shane Collins .01 .05
336 Jeff Graham .02 .10
337 Ricky Proehl .01 .05
338 Tommy Maddox .08 .25
339 Jim Dombrowski .01 .05
340 Bill Brooks .01 .05
(Signed with Buffalo Bills)
341 Dave Brown RC .08 .25
342 Eric Davis .01 .05
343 Leslie O'Neal .02 .10
344 Jim Morrissey .01 .05
345 Mike Munchak .02 .10
346 Ron Hall .01 .05
347 Brian Noble .01 .05
348 Chris Singleton .01 .05
349 Boomer Esiason UER .02 .10
(Signed with New York Jets)/(Card front notes he was signed instead of traded)
350 Ray Roberts .01 .05
351 Gary Zimmerman .01 .05
352 Quentin Coryatt .02 .10
353 Willie Green .01 .05
354 Randall Cunningham .08 .25
355 Kevin Smith .02 .10
356 Michael Dean Perry .02 .10
357 Tim Green .01 .05
358 Dwayne Harper .01 .05
359 Dale Carter .01 .05
360 Keith Jackson .02 .10
361 Martin Mayhew .01 .05
(Signed with Tampa Bay Buccaneers)
362 Brian Washington .01 .05
363 Earnest Byner .01 .05
364 D.J. Johnson .01 .05
365 Timm Rosenbach .01 .05
366 Doug Widell .01 .05
367 Vaughn Dunbar .01 .05
368 Phil Hansen .01 .05
369 Mike Fox .01 .05
370 Dana Hall .01 .05
371 Junior Seau .08 .25
372 Steve McMichael .02 .10
373 Eddie Robinson .01 .05
374 Milton Mack RC .01 .05
375 Mike Prior .01 .05
(Signed with Green Bay Packers)
376 Jerome Henderson .01 .05
377 Scott Mersereau .01 .05
378 Neal Anderson .01 .05
379 Harry Newsome .01 .05
380 John Baylor .01 .05
381 Bill Fralic .01 .05
(Signed with Detroit Lions)
382 Mark Bavaro .01 .05
(Signed with Philadelphia Eagles)
383 Robert Jones .01 .05
384 Tyronne Stowe .01 .05
385 Deion Sanders .20 .50
386 Robert Blackmon .01 .05
387 Neil Smith .08 .25
388 Mark Ingram .01 .05
(Signed with Miami Dolphins)
389 Mark Carrier WR .02 .10
(Signed with Cleveland Browns)
390 Browning Nagle .01 .05
391 Ricky Ervins .01 .05
392 Carnell Lake .01 .05
393 Luis Sharpe .01 .05
394 Greg Kragen .01 .05
395 Tommy Barnhardt .01 .05
396 Mark Kelso .01 .05
397 Kent Graham RC .08 .25
398 Bill Romanowski .01 .05
399 Anthony Miller .02 .10
400 John Roper .01 .05
401 Lamar Rogers .01 .05
402 Troy Auzenne .01 .05
403 Webster Slaughter .01 .05
404 David Brandon .01 .05
405 Chris Hinton .01 .05
406 Andy Heck .01 .05
407 Tracy Simien .01 .05
408 Troy Vincent .01 .05
409 Jason Hanson .01 .05
410 Rod Jones RC .01 .05
411 Al Noga .01 .05
(Signed with Washington Redskins)
412 Ernie Mills .01 .05
413 Willie Gault .01 .05
414 Henry Ellard .02 .10
415 Rickey Jackson .01 .05
416 Bruce Smith .08 .25
417 Derek Brown TE .01 .05
418 Kevin Fagan .01 .05
419 Gary Plummer .01 .05
420 Wendell Davis .01 .05
421 Craig Thompson .01 .05
422 Wes Hopkins .01 .05
423 Ray Childress .01 .05
424 Pat Harlow .01 .05
425 Howie Long .08 .25
426 Shane Dronett .01 .05
427 Sean Salisbury .01 .05
428 Dwight Hollier RC .01 .05
429 Brett Perriman .08 .25
430 Donald Hollas RC .01 .05
431 Jim Lachey .01 .05
432 Darren Perry .01 .05
433 Lionel Washington .01 .05
434 Sean Gilbert .02 .10
435 Gene Atkins .01 .05
436 Jim Kelly .08 .25
437 Ed McCaffrey .08 .25
438 Don Griffin .01 .05
439 Jerrol Williams .01 .05
(Signed with San Diego Chargers)
440 Bryce Paup .02 .10
441 Darryl Williams .01 .05
442 Vai Sikahema .01 .05
443 Cris Dishman .01 .05
444 Kevin Mack .01 .05
445 Winston Moss .01 .05
446 Tyrone Braxton .01 .05
447 Mike Merriweather .01 .05
448 Tony Paige .01 .05
449 Robert Porcher .01 .05
450 Ricardo McDonald .01 .05
451 Danny Copeland .01 .05
452 Tony Tolbert .01 .05
453 Eric Dickerson .02 .10
454 Flipper Anderson .01 .05
455 Dave Krieg .02 .10
456 Brad Lamb RC .01 .05
457 Bart Oates .01 .05
458 Guy McIntyre .01 .05
459 Stanley Richard .01 .05
460 Edgar Bennett .08 .25
461 Pat Carter .01 .05
462 Eric Allen .01 .05
463 William Fuller .01 .05
464 James Jones .01 .05
465 Chester McGlockton .02 .10
466 Charles Dimry .01 .05
467 Tim Grunhard .01 .05
468 Jarvis Williams .01 .05
469 Tracy Scroggins .01 .05
470 David Klingler .01 .05
471 Andre Collins .01 .05
472 Erik Williams .01 .05
473 Eddie Anderson .01 .05
474 Marc Boutte .01 .05
475 Joe Montana .60 1.50
476 Andre Reed .02 .10
477 Lawrence Taylor .08 .25
478 Jeff George .08 .25
479 Chris Mims .01 .05
480 Ken Ruettgers .01 .05
481 Roman Phifer .01 .05
482 William Thomas .01 .05
483 Lamar Lathon .01 .05
484 Vinny Testaverde .02 .10
(Signed with Cleveland Browns)
485 Mike Kenn .01 .05
486 Greg Lewis .01 .05
487 Chris Martin .01 .05
(Traded to Los Angeles Rams)
488 Maurice Hurst .01 .05
489 Pat Swilling .01 .05
(Traded to Detroit Lions)
490 Carl Pickens .02 .10
491 Tony Smith .01 .05
492 James Washington .01 .05
493 Jeff Hostetler .02 .10
(Signed with Los Angeles Raiders)
494 Jeff Chadwick .01 .05
495 Kevin Ross .01 .05
496 Jim Ritcher .01 .05
497 Jessie Hester .01 .05
498 Burt Grossman .01 .05
499 Keith Van Horne .01 .05
500 Gerald Robinson .01 .05
P1 Promo Panel 2.00 5.00

1993 Fleer All-Pros

COMPLETE SET (25) 10.00 25.00
1 Steve Atwater .15 .40
2 Rich Camarillo .15 .40
3 Ray Childress .15 .40
4 Chris Doleman .15 .40
5 Barry Foster .30 .75
6 Henry Jones .15 .40
7 Cortez Kennedy .30 .75
8 Nick Lowery .15 .40
9 Wilber Marshall .15 .40
10 Bruce Matthews .15 .40
11 Randall McDaniel .15 .40
12 Audray McMillian .15 .40
13 Sam Mills .15 .40
14 Jay Novacek .30 .75
15 Jerry Rice 3.00 8.00
16 Junior Seau .75 2.00
17 Sterling Sharpe .75 2.00
18 Clyde Simmons .15 .40
19 Emmitt Smith 5.00 12.00
20 Derrick Thomas .75 2.00
21 Steve Wallace .15 .40
22 Richmond Webb .15 .40
23 Steve Wisniewski .15 .40
24 Rod Woodson .75 2.00
25 Steve Young 2.50 6.00

1993 Fleer Prospects

COMPLETE SET (30) 15.00 40.00
1 Drew Bledsoe 5.00 12.00
2 Garrison Hearst 1.50 4.00
3 John Copeland .30 .75
4 Eric Curry .30 .75
5 Curtis Conway 1.25 3.00
6 Lincoln Kennedy .30 .75
7 Jerome Bettis 6.00 15.00
8 Patrick Bates .30 .75
9 Brad Hopkins .30 .75
10 Tom Carter .30 .75
11 Irv Smith .30 .75
12 Robert Smith 2.50 6.00
13 Deon Figures .30 .75
14 Leonard Renfro .30 .75
15 O.J. McDuffie 1.25 3.00
16 Dana Stubblefield .60 1.50
17 Todd Kelly .30 .75
18 George Teague .30 .75
19 Demetrius DuBose .30 .75
20 Coleman Rudolph .30 .75
21 Carlton Gray .30 .75
22 Troy Drayton .30 .75
23 Natrone Means UER 1.25 3.00
(San Diego Chargers Receiver spelled Reveiver)
24 Qadry Ismail 1.25 3.00
25 Gino Torretta .60 1.50
26 Carl Simpson .30 .75
27 Glyn Milburn .30 .75
28 Chad Brown .30 .75
29 Reggie Brooks .30 .75
30 Billy Joe Hobert .60 1.50

1993 Fleer Rookie Sensations

COMPLETE SET (20) 30.00 80.00
RANDOM INSERTS IN JUMBO PACKS
1 Dale Carter 2.50 6.00
2 Eugene Chung 2.00 5.00
3 Marco Coleman 2.50 6.00
4 Quentin Coryatt 2.00 5.00
5 Santana Dotson 2.00 5.00
6 Vaughn Dunbar 2.00 5.00
7 Steve Emtman 2.50 6.00
8 Sean Gilbert 2.50 6.00
9 Dana Hall 2.00 5.00
10 Jason Hanson 2.00 5.00
11 Robert Jones 2.00 5.00
12 David Klingler 2.50 6.00
13 Amp Lee 2.00 5.00
14 Troy Auzenne 2.00 5.00
15 Ricardo McDonald 2.00 5.00
16 Chris Mims 2.00 5.00
17 Johnny Mitchell 2.50 6.00
18 Carl Pickens 2.50 6.00
19 Darren Perry 2.00 5.00
20 Troy Vincent 2.50 6.00

1993 Fleer Team Leaders

COMPLETE SET (5) 15.00 30.00
1 Brett Favre 8.00 15.00
2 Derrick Thomas 1.00 2.00
3 Steve Young 3.00 6.00
4 John Elway 6.00 12.00
5 Cortez Kennedy .30 .75

1993 Fleer Steve Young

COMPLETE SET (10) 3.00 8.00
COMMON YOUNG (1-10) .40 1.00
COMMON SEND-OFF (11-13) .75 2.00

1993 Fleer Steve Young Autographs

COMMON AUTO (1-10) 20.00 50.00

1993 Fleer Fruit of the Loom

This 50-card standard-size set issued by Fleer was sponsored by Fruit of the Loom. Each specially marked underwear package contained six cards. The color action player photos on the fronts are framed with silver metallic borders. At the bottom of the photo, the player's last name is printed in transparent lettering that has an embossed look. The team affiliation and position appear at the lower right corner. Fruit of the Loom's logo is in the upper left corner. On a team color-coded panel, the horizontal backs carry a close-up color shot, biography, player profile, team logo, and statistics.

COMPLETE SET (50) 70.00 175.00
1 Andre Rison 1.20 3.00
2 Deion Sanders 4.00 8.00
3 Neal Anderson .50 1.25
4 Jim Harbaugh 1.20 3.00
5 Bernie Kosar .80 2.00
6 Eric Metcalf .80 2.00
7 John Elway 10.00 20.00
8 Karl Mecklenburg .50 1.25
9 Sterling Sharpe .80 2.00
10 Reggie White 1.20 3.00
(Traded to Green Bay Packers)
11 Steve Emtman .50 1.25
12 Jeff George 1.20 3.00
13 Willie Gault .50 1.25
14 Jim Kelly 1.20 3.00
15 Thurman Thomas 1.20 3.00
16 Harold Green .50 1.25
17 Carl Pickens .80 2.00
18 Troy Aikman 6.00 12.00
19 Emmitt Smith 6.00 15.00
20 Barry Sanders 6.00 15.00
21 Pat Swilling .50 1.25
(Traded to Detroit Lions)
22 Haywood Jeffires .50 1.25
23 Warren Moon 1.20 3.00
24 Derrick Thomas 1.20 3.00
25 Christian Okoye .50 1.25
26 Flipper Anderson .50 1.25
27 Jim Everett .50 1.25
28 Keith Jackson .50 1.25
29 Dan Marino 10.00 20.00
30 Andre Tippett .50 1.25
31 Lawrence Taylor 1.20 3.00
32 Randall Cunningham 1.20 3.00
33 Barry Foster .50 1.25
34 Rod Woodson .80 2.00
35 Jerry Rice 6.00 12.00
36 Steve Young 5.00 10.00
37 Reggie Cobb .50 1.25
38 Roger Craig .80 2.00
39 Chris Doleman .50 1.25
40 Morten Andersen .50 1.25
41 Dalton Hilliard .50 1.25
42 Ronnie Lott .80 2.00
(Traded to New York Jets)
43 Chris Chandler .80 2.00
44 Stan Humphries .80 2.00
45 Junior Seau 1.20 3.00
46 Brian Blades .50 1.25
47 Cortez Kennedy .80 2.00
48 Wilber Marshall .50 1.25
49 Art Monk .80 2.00
50 Checklist Card .50 1.25

1994 Fleer

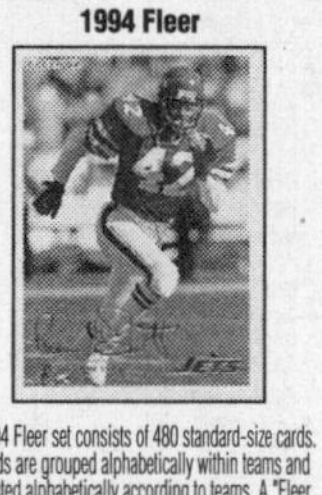

The 1994 Fleer set consists of 480 standard-size cards. The cards are grouped alphabetically within teams and checklisted alphabetically according to teams. A "Fleer Hot Pack" was inserted in about every other box. It looks like a regular pack but it is filled with 15 insert cards. Otherwise, one insert card was included per pack. Cards were available in 15 and 21-card packs.There are no key Rookie Cards in this set. A Jerome Bettis prototype/promo card was produced and priced below.

COMPLETE SET (480) 10.00 20.00
1 Michael Bankston .01 .05
2 Steve Beuerlein .02 .10
3 John Booty .01 .05
4 Rich Camarillo .01 .05
5 Chuck Cecil .01 .05
6 Larry Centers .08 .25
7 Gary Clark .02 .10
8 Garrison Hearst .08 .25
9 Eric Hill .01 .05
10 Randal Hill .01 .05
11 Ronald Moore .01 .05
12 Ricky Proehl .01 .05
13 Luis Sharpe .01 .05
14 Clyde Simmons .01 .05
15 Tyronne Stowe .01 .05
16 Eric Swann .02 .10
17 Aeneas Williams .01 .05
18 Darion Conner .01 .05
19 Moe Gardner .01 .05
20 Jumpy Geathers .01 .05
21 Jeff George .08 .25
22 Roger Harper .01 .05
23 Bobby Hebert .01 .05
24 Pierce Holt .01 .05
25 D.J. Johnson .01 .05
26 Mike Kenn .01 .05
27 Lincoln Kennedy .01 .05
28 Erric Pegram .01 .05
29 Mike Pritchard .01 .05
30 Andre Rison .02 .10
31 Deion Sanders .20 .50
32 Tony Smith .01 .05
33 Jesse Solomon .01 .05
34 Jessie Tuggle .01 .05

35 Don Beebe	.01	.05
36 Cornelius Bennett	.02	.10
37 Bill Brooks	.01	.05
38 Kenneth Davis	.01	.05
39 John Fina	.01	.05
40 Phil Hansen	.01	.05
41 Kent Hull	.01	.05
42 Henry Jones	.01	.05
43 Jim Kelly	.08	.25
44 Pete Metzelaars	.01	.05
45 Marvcus Patton	.01	.05
46 Andre Reed	.02	.10
47 Frank Reich	.02	.10
48 Bruce Smith	.08	.25
49 Thomas Smith	.01	.05
50 Darryl Talley	.01	.05
51 Steve Tasker	.02	.10
52 Thurman Thomas	.08	.25
53 Jeff Wright	.01	.05
54 Neal Anderson	.01	.05
55 Trace Armstrong	.01	.05
56 Troy Auzenne	.01	.05
57 Joe Cain RC	.01	.05
58 Mark Carrier DB	.01	.05
59 Curtis Conway	.08	.25
60 Richard Dent	.02	.10
61 Shaun Gayle	.01	.05
62 Andy Heck	.01	.05
63 Dante Jones	.01	.05
64 Erik Kramer	.02	.10
65 Steve McMichael	.02	.10
66 Terry Obee	.01	.05
67 Vinson Smith	.01	.05
68 Alonzo Spellman	.01	.05
69 Tom Waddle	.01	.05
70 Donnell Woolford	.01	.05
71 Tim Worley	.01	.05
72 Chris Zorich	.01	.05
73 Mike Brim	.01	.05
74 John Copeland	.01	.05
75 Derrick Fenner	.01	.05
76 James Francis	.01	.05
77 Harold Green	.01	.05
78 Rod Jones	.01	.05
79 David Klingler	.01	.05
80 Bruce Kozerski	.01	.05
81 Tim Krumrie	.01	.05
82 Ricardo McDonald	.01	.05
83 Tim McGee	.01	.05
84 Tony McGee	.01	.05
85 Louis Oliver	.01	.05
86 Carl Pickens	.02	.10
87 Jeff Query	.01	.05
88 Daniel Stubbs	.01	.05
89 Steve Tovar	.01	.05
90 Alfred Williams	.01	.05
91 Darryl Williams	.01	.05
92 Rob Burnett	.01	.05
93 Mark Carrier WR	.02	.10
94 Leroy Hoard	.01	.05
95 Michael Jackson	.02	.10
96 Mike Johnson	.01	.05
97 Pepper Johnson	.01	.05
98 Tony Jones	.01	.05
99 Clay Matthews	.01	.05
100 Eric Metcalf	.02	.10
101 Stevon Moore	.01	.05
102 Michael Dean Perry	.02	.10
103 Anthony Pleasant	.01	.05
104 Vinny Testaverde	.02	.10
105 Eric Turner	.01	.05
106 Tommy Vardell	.01	.05
107 Troy Aikman	.40	1.00
108 Larry Brown DB	.01	.05
109 Dixon Edwards	.01	.05
110 Charles Haley	.02	.10
111 Alvin Harper	.02	.10
112 Michael Irvin	.08	.25
113 Jim Jeffcoat	.01	.05
114 Daryl Johnston	.02	.10
115 Leon Lett	.01	.05
116 Russell Maryland	.01	.05
117 Nate Newton	.01	.05
118 Ken Norton Jr.	.02	.10
119 Jay Novacek	.02	.10
120 Darrin Smith	.01	.05
121 Emmitt Smith	.60	1.50
122 Kevin Smith	.01	.05
123 Mark Stepnoski	.01	.05
124 Tony Tolbert	.01	.05
125 Erik Williams	.01	.05
126 Kevin Williams	.02	.10
127 Darren Woodson	.02	.10
128 Steve Atwater	.01	.05
129 Rod Bernstine	.01	.05
130 Ray Crockett	.01	.05
131 Mike Croel	.01	.05
132 Robert Delpino	.01	.05
133 Shane Dronett	.01	.05
134 Jason Elam	.02	.10
135 John Elway	.75	2.00
136 Simon Fletcher	.01	.05
137 Greg Kragen	.01	.05
138 Karl Mecklenburg	.01	.05
139 Glyn Milburn	.02	.10
140 Anthony Miller	.02	.10
141 Derek Russell	.01	.05
142 Shannon Sharpe	.02	.10
143 Dennis Smith	.01	.05
144 Dan Williams	.01	.05
145 Gary Zimmerman	.01	.05
146 Bennie Blades	.01	.05
147 Lomas Brown	.01	.05
148 Bill Fralic	.01	.05
149 Mel Gray	.01	.05
150 Willie Green	.01	.05
151 Jason Hanson	.01	.05
152 Robert Massey	.01	.05
153 Ryan McNeil	.01	.05
154 Scott Mitchell	.02	.10
155 Derrick Moore	.01	.05
156 Herman Moore	.08	.25
157 Brett Perriman	.02	.10
158 Robert Porcher	.01	.05
159 Kelvin Pritchett	.01	.05
160 Barry Sanders	.60	1.50
161 Tracy Scroggins	.01	.05
162 Chris Spielman	.02	.10
163 Pat Swilling	.01	.05
164 Edgar Bennett	.08	.25
165 Robert Brooks	.08	.25
166 Terrell Buckley	.01	.05
167 LeRoy Butler	.01	.05
168 Brett Favre	.75	2.00
169 Harry Galbreath	.01	.05
170 Jackie Harris	.01	.05
171 Johnny Holland	.01	.05
172 Chris Jacke	.01	.05
173 George Koonce	.01	.05
174 Bryce Paup	.02	.10
175 Ken Ruettgers	.01	.05
176 Sterling Sharpe	.02	.10
177 Wayne Simmons	.01	.05
178 George Teague	.01	.05
179 Darrell Thompson	.01	.05
180 Reggie White	.08	.25
181 Gary Brown	.01	.05
182 Cody Carlson	.01	.05
183 Ray Childress	.01	.05
184 Cris Dishman	.01	.05
185 Ernest Givins	.02	.10
186 Haywood Jeffires	.02	.10
187 Sean Jones	.01	.05
188 Lamar Lathon	.01	.05
189 Bruce Matthews	.01	.05
190 Bubba McDowell	.01	.05
191 Glenn Montgomery	.01	.05
192 Greg Montgomery	.01	.05
193 Warren Moon	.08	.25
194 Do Orlando	.01	.05
195 Marcus Robertson	.01	.05
196 Eddie Robinson	.01	.05
197 Webster Slaughter	.01	.05
198 Lorenzo White	.01	.05
199 John Baylor	.01	.05
200 Jason Belser	.01	.05
201 Tony Bennett	.01	.05
202 Dean Biasucci	.01	.05
203 Ray Buchanan	.01	.05
204 Kerry Cash	.01	.05
205 Quentin Coryatt	.01	.05
206 Eugene Daniel	.01	.05
207 Steve Emtman	.01	.05
208 Jon Hand	.01	.05
209 Jim Harbaugh	.08	.25
210 Jeff Herrod	.01	.05
211 Anthony Johnson	.02	.10
212 Roosevelt Potts	.01	.05
213 Rohn Stark	.01	.05
214 Will Wolford	.01	.05
215 Marcus Allen	.08	.25
216 John Alt	.01	.05
217 Kimble Anders	.02	.10
218 J.J. Birden	.01	.05
219 Dale Carter	.01	.05
220 Keith Cash	.01	.05
221 Tony Casillas	.01	.05
222 Willie Davis	.02	.10
223 Tim Grunhard	.01	.05
224 Nick Lowery	.01	.05
225 Charles Mincy	.01	.05
226 Joe Montana	.75	2.00
227 Dan Saleaumua	.01	.05
228 Tracy Simien	.01	.05
229 Neil Smith	.02	.10
230 Derrick Thomas	.08	.25
231 Eddie Anderson	.01	.05
232 Tim Brown	.08	.25
233 Nolan Harrison	.01	.05
234 Jeff Hostetler	.02	.10
235 Rocket Ismail	.02	.10
236 Jeff Jaeger	.01	.05
237 James Jett	.01	.05
238 Joe Kelly	.01	.05
239 Albert Lewis	.01	.05
240 Terry McDaniel	.01	.05
241 Chester McGlockton	.01	.05
242 Winston Moss	.01	.05
243 Gerald Perry	.01	.05
244 Greg Robinson	.01	.05
245 Anthony Smith	.01	.05
246 Steve Smith	.01	.05
247 Greg Townsend	.01	.05
248 Lionel Washington	.01	.05
249 Steve Wisniewski	.01	.05
250 Alexander Wright	.01	.05
251 Flipper Anderson	.01	.05
252 Jerome Bettis	.20	.50
253 Marc Boutte	.01	.05
254 Shane Conlan	.01	.05
255 Troy Drayton	.01	.05
256 Henry Ellard	.02	.10
257 Sean Gilbert	.01	.05
258 Nate Lewis	.01	.05
259 Todd Lyght	.01	.05
260 Chris Miller	.01	.05
261 Anthony Newman	.01	.05
262 Roman Phifer	.01	.05
263 Henry Rolling	.01	.05
264 I.J. Rubley RC	.01	.05
265 Jackie Slater	.01	.05
266 Fred Stokes	.01	.05
267 Robert Young	.01	.05
268 Gene Atkins	.01	.05
269 J.B. Brown	.01	.05
270 Keith Byars	.01	.05
271 Marco Coleman	.01	.05
272 Bryan Cox	.01	.05
273 Jeff Cross	.01	.05
274 Irving Fryar	.02	.10
275 Mark Higgs	.01	.05
276 Dwight Hollier	.01	.05
277 Mark Ingram	.01	.05
278 Keith Jackson	.01	.05
279 Terry Kirby	.08	.25
280 Bernie Kosar	.02	.10
281 Dan Marino	.75	2.00
282 O.J. McDuffie	.08	.25
283 Keith Sims	.01	.05
284 Pete Stoyanovich	.01	.05
285 Troy Vincent	.01	.05
286 Richmond Webb	.01	.05
287 Terry Allen	.02	.10
288 Anthony Carter	.02	.10
289 Cris Carter	.20	.50
290 Jack Del Rio	.01	.05
291 Chris Doleman	.01	.05
292 Vencie Glenn	.01	.05
293 Scottie Graham RC	.02	.10
294 Chris Hinton	.01	.05
295 Qadry Ismail	.08	.25
296 Carlos Jenkins	.01	.05
297 Steve Jordan	.01	.05
298 Carl Lee	.01	.05
299 Randall McDaniel	.02	.10
300 John Randle	.02	.10
301 Todd Scott	.01	.05
302 Robert Smith	.08	.25
303 Fred Strickland	.01	.05
304 Henry Thomas	.01	.05
305 Bruce Armstrong	.01	.05
306 Harlon Barnett	.01	.05
307 Drew Bledsoe	.30	.75
308 Vincent Brown	.01	.05
309 Ben Coates	.02	.10
310 Todd Collins	.01	.05
311 Myron Guyton	.01	.05
312 Pat Harlow	.01	.05
313 Maurice Hurst	.01	.05
314 Leonard Russell	.01	.05
315 Chris Slade	.01	.05
316 Michael Timpson	.01	.05
317 Andre Tippett	.01	.05
318 Morten Andersen	.01	.05
319 Derek Brown RBK	.01	.05
320 Vince Buck	.01	.05
321 Toi Cook	.01	.05
322 Quinn Early	.02	.10
323 Jim Everett	.02	.10
324 Michael Haynes	.02	.10
325 Tyrone Hughes	.02	.10
326 Rickey Jackson	.01	.05
327 Vaughan Johnson	.01	.05
328 Eric Martin	.01	.05
329 Wayne Martin	.01	.05
330 Sam Mills	.01	.05
331 Willie Roaf	.01	.05
332 Irv Smith	.01	.05
333 Keith Taylor	.01	.05
334 Renaldo Turnbull	.01	.05
335 Carlton Bailey	.01	.05
336 Michael Brooks	.01	.05
337 Jarrod Bunch	.01	.05
338 Chris Calloway	.01	.05
339 Mark Collins	.01	.05
340 Howard Cross	.01	.05
341 Stacey Dillard RC	.01	.05
342 John Elliott	.01	.05
343 Rodney Hampton	.02	.10
344 Greg Jackson	.01	.05
345 Mark Jackson	.01	.05
346 Dave Meggett	.01	.05
347 Corey Miller	.01	.05
348 Mike Sherrard	.01	.05
349 Phil Simms	.02	.10
350 Lewis Tillman	.01	.05
351 Brad Baxter	.01	.05
352 Kyle Clifton	.01	.05
353 Boomer Esiason	.02	.10
354 James Hasty	.01	.05
355 Bobby Houston	.01	.05
356 Johnny Johnson	.01	.05
357 Jeff Lageman	.01	.05
358 Mo Lewis	.01	.05
359 Ronnie Lott	.02	.10
360 Leonard Marshall	.01	.05
361 Johnny Mitchell	.01	.05
362 Rob Moore	.02	.10
363 Eric Thomas	.01	.05
364 Brian Washington	.01	.05
365 Marvin Washington	.01	.05
366 Eric Allen	.01	.05
367 Fred Barnett	.02	.10
368 Bubby Brister	.01	.05
369 Randall Cunningham	.08	.25
370 Byron Evans	.01	.05
371 William Fuller	.01	.05
372 Andy Harmon	.01	.05
373 Seth Joyner	.01	.05
374 William Perry	.02	.10
375 Leonard Renfro	.01	.05
376 Heath Sherman	.01	.05
377 Ben Smith	.01	.05
378 William Thomas	.01	.05
379 Herschel Walker	.02	.10
380 Calvin Williams	.02	.10
381 Chad Brown	.01	.05
382 Dermontti Dawson	.01	.05
383 Deon Figures	.01	.05
384 Barry Foster	.01	.05
385 Jeff Graham	.01	.05
386 Eric Green	.01	.05
387 Kevin Greene	.02	.10
388 Carlton Haselrig	.01	.05
389 Levon Kirkland	.01	.05
390 Carnell Lake	.01	.05
391 Greg Lloyd	.02	.10
392 Neil O'Donnell	.08	.25
393 Darren Perry	.01	.05
394 Dwight Stone	.01	.05
395 Leroy Thompson	.01	.05
396 Rod Woodson	.02	.10
397 Marion Butts	.01	.05
398 John Carney	.01	.05
399 Darren Carrington	.01	.05
400 Burt Grossman	.01	.05
401 Courtney Hall	.01	.05
402 Ronnie Harmon	.01	.05
403 Stan Humphries	.02	.10
404 Shawn Jefferson	.01	.05
405 Vance Johnson	.01	.05
406 Chris Mims	.01	.05
407 Leslie O'Neal	.01	.05
408 Stanley Richard	.01	.05
409 Junior Seau	.08	.25
410 Harris Barton	.01	.05
411 Dennis Brown	.01	.05
412 Eric Davis	.01	.05
413 Merton Hanks	.02	.10
414 John Johnson	.01	.05
415 Brent Jones	.02	.10
416 Marc Logan	.01	.05
417 Tim McDonald	.01	.05
418 Gary Plummer	.01	.05
419 Tom Rathman	.01	.05
420 Jerry Rice	.40	1.00
421 Bill Romanowski	.01	.05
422 Jesse Sapolu	.01	.05
423 Dana Stubblefield	.02	.10
424 John Taylor	.02	.10
425 Steve Wallace	.01	.05
426 Ted Washington	.01	.05
427 Ricky Watters	.02	.10
428 Troy Wilson RC	.01	.05
429 Steve Young	.30	.75
430 Howard Ballard	.01	.05
431 Michael Bates	.01	.05
432 Robert Blackmon	.01	.05
433 Brian Blades	.02	.10
434 Ferrell Edmunds	.01	.05
435 Carlton Gray	.01	.05
436 Patrick Hunter	.01	.05
437 Cortez Kennedy	.02	.10
438 Kelvin Martin	.01	.05
439 Rick Mirer	.08	.25
440 Nate Odomes	.01	.05
441 Ray Roberts	.01	.05
442 Eugene Robinson	.01	.05
443 Rod Stephens	.01	.05
444 Chris Warren	.02	.10
445 John L. Williams	.01	.05
446 Terry Wooden	.01	.05
447 Marty Carter	.01	.05
448 Reggie Cobb	.01	.05
449 Lawrence Dawsey	.01	.05
450 Santana Dotson	.02	.10
451 Craig Erickson	.01	.05
452 Thomas Everett	.01	.05
453 Paul Gruber	.01	.05
454 Courtney Hawkins	.01	.05
455 Martin Mayhew	.01	.05
456 Hardy Nickerson	.02	.10
457 Ricky Reynolds	.01	.05
458 Vince Workman	.01	.05
459 Reggie Brooks	.02	.10
460 Earnest Byner	.01	.05
461 Andre Collins	.01	.05
462 Brad Edwards	.01	.05
463 Kurt Gouveia	.01	.05
464 Darrell Green	.01	.05
465 Ken Harvey	.01	.05
466 Ethan Horton	.01	.05
467 A.J. Johnson	.01	.05
468 Tim Johnson	.01	.05
469 Jim Lachey	.01	.05
470 Chip Lohmiller	.01	.05
471 Art Monk	.02	.10
472 Sterling Palmer RC	.01	.05
473 Mark Rypien	.01	.05
474 Ricky Sanders	.01	.05
475 Checklist 1-106	.01	.05
476 Checklist 107-214	.01	.05
477 Checklist 215-317	.01	.05
478 Checklist 318-409	.01	.05
479 Checklist 410-480 Inserts	.01	.05
480 Inserts Checklist	.01	.05
P244 Jerome Bettis Promo Numbered 244	.40	1.00

1994 Fleer All-Pros

COMPLETE SET (24)	7.50	20.00
1 Troy Aikman	1.25	3.00
2 Eric Allen	.07	.20
3 Jerome Bettis	.60	1.50
4 Barry Foster	.07	.20
5 Michael Irvin	.30	.75
6 Cortez Kennedy	.10	.30
7 Joe Montana	2.50	6.00
8 Hardy Nickerson	.10	.30
9 Jerry Rice	1.25	3.00
10 Andre Rison	.10	.30
11 Barry Sanders	2.00	5.00
12 Deion Sanders	.60	1.50
13 Junior Seau	.30	.75
14 Shannon Sharpe	.10	.30
15 Sterling Sharpe	.10	.30
16 Bruce Smith	.30	.75
17 Emmitt Smith	2.00	5.00
18 Neil Smith	.10	.30
19 Derrick Thomas	.30	.75
20 Thurman Thomas	.30	.75
21A Renaldo Turnbull ERR (Photo of Reggie White on front)	.40	1.00
21B Renaldo Turnbull COR	.07	.20
22 Reggie White	.30	.75
23 Rod Woodson	.10	.30
24 Steve Young	1.00	2.50

1994 Fleer Award Winners

COMPLETE SET (5)	1.50	4.00
1 Jerome Bettis	.30	.75
2 Rick Mirer	.10	.30
3 Deion Sanders	.40	1.00
4 Emmitt Smith	1.25	2.50
5 Dana Stubblefield	.10	.30

1994 Fleer Jerome Bettis

COMPLETE SET (15)	3.00	8.00
COMPLETE SET (12)	2.50	6.00
COMMON BETTIS (1-12)	.25	.60
COMMON SEND-OFF (13-15)	.40	1.00

1994 Fleer League Leaders

COMPLETE SET (10)	4.00	10.00
1 Marcus Allen	.20	.50
2 Tim Brown	.20	.50
3 John Elway	1.50	4.00
4 Tyrone Hughes	.07	.20
5 Jerry Rice	.75	2.00
6 Sterling Sharpe	.07	.20
7 Emmitt Smith	1.25	3.00
8 Neil Smith	.07	.20
9 Thurman Thomas	.20	.50
10 Steve Young	.60	1.50

1994 Fleer Living Legends

COMPLETE SET (6)	12.50	30.00
STATED ODDS 1:60 HOB/JUM		
1 Marcus Allen	.60	1.50
2 John Elway	5.00	12.00
3 Joe Montana	5.00	12.00
4 Jerry Rice	2.50	6.00
5 Emmitt Smith	4.00	10.00
6 Reggie White	.60	1.50

1994 Fleer Prospects

COMPLETE SET (25)	6.00	15.00
1 Sam Adams	.25	.60
2 Trev Alberts	.25	.60
3 Derrick Alexander WR	.40	1.00
4 Mario Bates	.40	1.00
5 Jeff Burris	.25	.60
6 Shante Carver	.15	.40
7 Marshall Faulk	2.50	6.00
8 William Floyd	.40	1.00
9 Rob Fredrickson	.25	.60
10 Wayne Gandy	.15	.40
11 Charlie Garner	1.00	2.50
12 Aaron Glenn	.40	1.00
13 Charles Johnson	.40	1.00
14 Joe Johnson	.15	.40
15 Tre Johnson	.15	.40
16 Antonio Langham	.25	.60
17 Chuck Levy	.15	.40
18 Willie McGinest	.40	1.00
19 David Palmer	.40	1.00
20 Errict Rhett UER (Florida played in '94 Sugar Bowl, not Copper Bowl)	.40	1.00
21 Jason Sehorn	.40	1.00
22 Heath Shuler	.40	1.00
23 Charlie Ward Not Drafted	.40	1.00
24 Dewayne Washington	.25	.60
25 Bryant Young	.40	1.00

1994 Fleer Pro-Vision

COMPLETE SET (9)	2.50	6.00
*JUMBO CARDS: 1.2X to 3X BASIC CARDS		
ONE JUMBO SET PER HOBBY CASE		
1 Rodney Hampton	.05	.15
2 Ricky Watters	.05	.15
3 Rick Mirer	.15	.40
4 Brett Favre	1.50	3.00
5 Troy Aikman	.75	1.50
6 Jerome Bettis	.30	.75
7 Joe Montana	1.50	3.00
8 Cornelius Bennett	.05	.15
9 Rod Woodson	.05	.15

1994 Fleer Rookie Exchange

COMPLETE SET (12)	12.50	30.00
ONE SET PER TRADE CARD BY MAIL		
1 Derrick Alexander WR	1.25	3.00
2 Trent Dilfer	2.50	6.00
3 Marshall Faulk	7.50	20.00
4 Charlie Garner	3.00	8.00
5 Greg Hill	1.25	3.00
6 Charles Johnson	1.25	3.00
7 Antonio Langham	.40	1.00
8 Willie McGinest	1.25	3.00
9 Heath Shuler	1.25	3.00
10 Dewayne Washington	.60	1.50
11 Dan Wilkinson	.60	1.50
12 Bryant Young	1.25	3.00
NNO Rookie Exch. Expired	.20	.50

1994 Fleer Rookie Sensations

COMPLETE SET (20)	50.00	100.00
RANDOM INSERTS IN JUMBO PACKS		
1 Jerome Bettis	5.00	12.00
2 Drew Bledsoe	7.50	20.00
3 Reggie Brooks	2.50	6.00
4 Tom Carter	1.50	4.00
5 John Copeland	1.50	4.00
6 Jason Elam	1.50	4.00
7 Garrison Hearst	3.00	8.00
8 Tyrone Hughes	1.50	4.00
9 James Jett	3.00	8.00
10 Lincoln Kennedy	1.50	4.00
11 Terry Kirby	3.00	8.00
12 Glyn Milburn	2.50	6.00
13 Rick Mirer	3.00	8.00
14 Ronald Moore	1.50	4.00
15 Willie Roaf	1.50	4.00
16 Wayne Simmons	1.50	4.00
17 Chris Slade	1.50	4.00
18 Darrin Smith	1.50	4.00
19 Dana Stubblefield	2.50	6.00
20 George Teague	1.50	4.00

1994 Fleer Scoring Machines

COMPLETE SET (20)	15.00	40.00
1 Marcus Allen	.50	1.25
2 Natrone Means	1.00	2.50
3 Jerome Bettis	1.00	2.50
4 Tim Brown	.50	1.25
5 Barry Foster	.08	.25
6 Rodney Hampton	.20	.50
7 Michael Irvin	.50	1.25
8 Nick Lowery	.08	.25
9 Dan Marino	4.00	10.00
10 Joe Montana	4.00	10.00
11 Warren Moon	.50	1.25
12 Andre Reed	.20	.50
13 Jerry Rice	2.00	5.00
14 Andre Rison	.20	.50
15 Barry Sanders	3.00	8.00
16 Shannon Sharpe	.20	.50
17 Sterling Sharpe	.20	.50
18 Emmitt Smith	3.00	8.00
19 Thurman Thomas	.50	1.25
20 Ricky Watters	.20	.50

1995 Fleer

The 1995 Fleer set consists of 400 standard-size cards issued as one series. The cards were issued in 11-card packs with a suggested retail price of $1.49. These packs included nine basic cards, one insert and one Flair preview card. Hot packs containing only insert cards were included one out of 72 packs. Seventeen-card jumbo ($2.29) included 15 basic cards, one insert as well as one Flair preview. The cards are grouped alphabetically within teams, and checklisted alphabetically according to teams. Jeff Blake is the key Rookie Card in this set. A Promo Panel of three cards was produced and is priced at the end of our checklist as an uncut panel.

COMPLETE SET (400)	10.00	25.00
1 Michael Bankston	.02	.10
2 Larry Centers	.07	.20
3 Gary Clark	.02	.10
4 Eric Hill	.02	.10
5 Seth Joyner	.02	.10
6 Dave Krieg	.02	.10
7 Lorenzo Lynch	.02	.10
8 Jamir Miller	.02	.10
9 Ronald Moore	.02	.10
10 Ricky Proehl	.02	.10
11 Clyde Simmons	.02	.10
12 Eric Swann	.07	.20
13 Aeneas Williams	.02	.10
14 J.J. Birden	.02	.10
15 Chris Doleman	.02	.10
16 Bert Emanuel	.10	.30
17 Jumpy Geathers	.02	.10
18 Jeff George	.07	.20
19 Roger Harper	.02	.10
20 Craig Heyward	.07	.20
21 Pierce Holt	.02	.10
22 D.J. Johnson	.02	.10
23 Terance Mathis	.07	.20
24 Clay Matthews	.07	.20
25 Andre Rison	.07	.20
26 Chuck Smith	.02	.10
27 Jessie Tuggle	.02	.10
28 Cornelius Bennett	.07	.20
29 Bucky Brooks	.02	.10
30 Jeff Burris	.02	.10
31 Russell Copeland	.02	.10
32 Matt Darby	.02	.10
33 Phil Hansen	.02	.10
34 Henry Jones	.02	.10
35 Jim Kelly	.10	.30
36 Mark Maddox RC	.02	.10
37 Bryce Paup	.07	.20
38 Andre Reed	.07	.20
39 Bruce Smith	.10	.30
40 Darryl Talley	.02	.10
41 Dewell Brewer RC	.02	.10
42 Mike Fox	.02	.10
43 Eric Guliford	.02	.10
44 Lamar Lathon	.02	.10
45 Pete Metzelaars	.02	.10
46 Sam Mills	.07	.20
47 Frank Reich	.02	.10
48 Rod Smith DB	.07	.20
49 Jack Trudeau	.02	.10
50 Tracy Armstrong	.02	.10
51 Joe Cain	.02	.10
52 Mark Carrier DB	.02	.10
53 Curtis Conway	.10	.30
54 Shaun Gayle	.02	.10
55 Jeff Graham	.02	.10
56 Raymont Harris	.02	.10
57 Erik Kramer	.02	.10
58 Lewis Tillman	.02	.10
59 Tom Waddle	.02	.10
60 Steve Walsh	.02	.10
61 Donnell Woolford	.02	.10
62 Chris Zorich	.02	.10
63 Jeff Blake RC	.25	.60
64 Mike Brim	.02	.10
65 Steve Broussard	.02	.10
66 James Francis	.02	.10
67 Ricardo McDonald	.02	.10
68 Tony McGee	.02	.10
70 Darnay Scott	.07	.20
71 Steve Tovar	.02	.10
72 Dan Wilkinson	.07	.20
73 Alfred Williams	.02	.10
74 Darryl Williams	.02	.10
75 Derrick Alexander WR	.10	.30
76 Randy Baldwin	.02	.10
77 Carl Banks	.02	.10
78 Rob Burnett	.02	.10
79 Steve Everitt	.02	.10
80 Leroy Hoard	.02	.10
81 Michael Jackson	.07	.20
82 Pepper Johnson	.02	.10
83 Tony Jones	.02	.10
84 Antonio Langham	.02	.10
85 Eric Metcalf	.07	.20
86 Stevon Moore	.02	.10
87 Anthony Pleasant	.02	.10
88 Vinny Testaverde	.07	.20
89 Eric Turner	.02	.10
90 Troy Aikman	.40	1.00
91 Charles Haley	.07	.20
92 Michael Irvin	.10	.30
93 Daryl Johnston	.07	.20
94 Robert Jones	.02	.10
95 Leon Lett	.02	.10
96 Russell Maryland	.02	.10
97 Nate Newton	.07	.20
98 Jay Novacek	.07	.20
99 Darrin Smith	.02	.10
100 Emmitt Smith	.60	1.50
101 Kevin Smith	.02	.10
102 Erik Williams	.02	.10
103 Kevin Williams WR	.07	.20
104 Darren Woodson	.07	.20
105 Elijah Alexander	.02	.10
106 Steve Atwater	.02	.10
107 Ray Crockett	.02	.10
108 Shane Dronett	.02	.10
109 Jason Elam	.07	.20
110 John Elway	.75	2.00
111 Simon Fletcher	.02	.10
112 Glyn Milburn	.02	.10
113 Anthony Miller	.07	.20
114 Michael Dean Perry	.02	.10
115 Mike Pritchard	.02	.10
116 Derek Russell	.02	.10
117 Leonard Russell	.02	.10
118 Shannon Sharpe	.07	.20
119 Gary Zimmerman	.02	.10
120 Bennie Blades	.02	.10
121 Lomas Brown	.02	.10
122 Willie Clay	.02	.10
123 Mike Johnson	.02	.10
124 Robert Massey	.02	.10
125 Scott Mitchell	.07	.20
126 Herman Moore	.10	.30
127 Brett Perriman	.07	.20
128 Robert Porcher	.02	.10
129 Barry Sanders	.60	1.50
130 Chris Spielman	.07	.20
131 Henry Thomas	.02	.10
132 Edgar Bennett	.07	.20
134 LeRoy Butler	.02	.10
135 Brett Favre	.75	2.00
136 Sean Jones	.02	.10
137 John Jurkovic	.02	.10
138 George Koonce	.02	.10
139 Wayne Simmons	.02	.10
140 George Teague	.02	.10
141 Reggie White	.10	.30
142 Micheal Barrow	.02	.10
143 Gary Brown	.02	.10
144 Cody Carlson	.02	.10
145 Ray Childress	.02	.10
146 Cris Dishman	.02	.10
147 Ernest Givins	.02	.10
148 Mel Gray	.02	.10
149 Darryll Lewis	.02	.10
150 Bruce Matthews	.02	.10
151 Marcus Robertson	.02	.10
152 Webster Slaughter	.02	.10
153 Al Smith	.02	.10
154 Mark Stepnoski	.02	.10
155 Trev Alberts	.02	.10
156 Flipper Anderson	.02	.10
157 Jason Belser	.02	.10
158 Tony Bennett	.02	.10
159 Ray Buchanan	.02	.10
160 Quentin Coryatt	.07	.20
161 Sean Dawkins	.07	.20
162 Steve Emtman	.02	.10
163 Marshall Faulk	.50	1.25
164 Stephen Grant RC	.02	.10
165 Jim Harbaugh	.07	.20
166 Jeff Herrod	.02	.10
167 Tony Siragusa	.02	.10
168 Steve Beuerlein	.07	.20
169 Darren Carrington	.02	.10
170 Reggie Cobb	.02	.10
171 Kelvin Martin	.02	.10
172 Kelvin Pritchett	.02	.10
173 Joel Smeenge	.02	.10
174 James Williams	.02	.10
175 Marcus Allen	.10	.30
176 Kimble Anders	.07	.20
177 Dale Carter	.07	.20
178 Mark Collins	.02	.10
179 Willie Davis	.07	.20
180 Lake Dawson	.07	.20
181 Greg Hill	.07	.20
182 Darren Mickell RC	.02	.10
183 Joe Montana	.75	2.00
184 Tracy Simien	.02	.10
185 Neil Smith	.07	.20
186 William White	.02	.10
187 Greg Biekert	.02	.10
188 Tim Brown	.10	.30
189 Rob Fredrickson	.02	.10
190 Andrew Glover RC	.02	.10
191 Nolan Harrison	.02	.10
192 Jeff Hostetler	.07	.20
193 Rocket Ismail	.07	.20
194 Terry McDaniel	.02	.10
195 Chester McGlockton	.07	.20
196 Winston Moss	.02	.10
197 Anthony Smith	.02	.10
198 Harvey Williams	.02	.10
199 Steve Wisniewski	.02	.10
200 Johnny Bailey	.02	.10
201 Jerome Bettis	.10	.30
202 Isaac Bruce	.20	.50
203 Shane Conlan	.02	.10
204 Troy Drayton	.02	.10
205 Sean Gilbert	.07	.20
206 Jessie Hester	.02	.10
207 Jimmie Jones	.02	.10
208 Todd Lyght	.02	.10
209 Chris Miller	.02	.10
210 Roman Phifer	.02	.10
211 Marquez Pope	.02	.10
212 Robert Young	.02	.10
213 Gene Atkins	.02	.10
214 Aubrey Beavers	.02	.10
215 Tim Bowens	.02	.10
216 Bryan Cox	.02	.10
217 Jeff Cross	.02	.10
218 Irving Fryar	.07	.20
219 Eric Green	.02	.10
220 Mark Ingram	.02	.10
221 Terry Kirby	.07	.20
222 Dan Marino	.75	2.00
223 O.J. McDuffie	.10	.30
224 Bernie Parmalee	.07	.20
225 Keith Sims	.02	.10
226 Irving Spikes	.07	.20
227 Michael Stewart	.02	.10
228 Troy Vincent	.02	.10
229 Richmond Webb	.02	.10
230 Terry Allen	.07	.20
231 Cris Carter	.10	.30
232 Jack Del Rio	.02	.10
233 Vencie Glenn	.02	.10
234 Qadry Ismail	.07	.20
235 Carlos Jenkins	.02	.10
236 Ed McDaniel	.02	.10
237 Randall McDaniel	.05	.15
238 Warren Moon	.07	.20
239 Anthony Parker	.02	.10
240 John Randle	.07	.20
241 Jake Reed	.07	.20
242 Fuad Reveiz	.02	.10
243 Broderick Thomas	.02	.10
244 Dewayne Washington	.07	.20
245 Bruce Armstrong	.02	.10
246 Drew Bledsoe	.25	.60
247 Vincent Brisby	.02	.10
248 Vincent Brown	.02	.10
249 Marion Butts	.02	.10
250 Ben Coates	.07	.20
251 Tim Goad	.02	.10
252 Myron Guyton	.02	.10
253 Maurice Hurst	.02	.10
254 Mike Jones	.02	.10
255 Willie McGinest	.07	.20
256 Dave Meggett	.02	.10
257 Ricky Reynolds	.02	.10
258 Chris Slade	.07	.20
259 Michael Timpson	.02	.10
260 Mario Bates	.07	.20
261 Derek Brown RBK	.02	.10
262 Darion Conner	.02	.10
263 Quinn Early	.07	.20
264 Jim Everett	.02	.10
265 Michael Haynes	.07	.20
266 Tyrone Hughes	.07	.20
267 Joe Johnson	.02	.10
268 Wayne Martin	.02	.10
269 Willie Roaf	.02	.10
270 Irv Smith	.02	.10
271 Jimmy Spencer	.02	.10
272 Winfred Tubbs	.02	.10
273 Renaldo Turnbull	.02	.10
274 Michael Brooks	.02	.10
275 Dave Brown	.07	.20
276 Chris Calloway	.02	.10
277 Jesse Campbell	.02	.10
278 Howard Cross	.02	.10
279 John Elliott	.02	.10
280 Keith Hamilton	.02	.10
281 Rodney Hampton	.07	.20
282 Thomas Lewis	.07	.20
283 Thomas Randolph	.02	.10
284 Mike Sherrard	.02	.10
285 Michael Strahan	.10	.30
286 Brad Baxter	.02	.10
287 Tony Casillas	.02	.10
288 Kyle Clifton	.02	.10
289 Boomer Esiason	.07	.20
290 Aaron Glenn	.02	.10
291 Bobby Houston	.02	.10
292 Johnny Johnson	.02	.10
293 Jeff Lageman	.02	.10
294 Mo Lewis	.02	.10
295 Johnny Mitchell	.02	.10
296 Rob Moore	.07	.20
297 Marcus Turner	.02	.10
298 Marvin Washington	.02	.10
299 Eric Allen	.02	.10
300 Fred Barnett	.07	.20
301 Randall Cunningham	.10	.30
302 Byron Evans	.02	.10
303 William Fuller	.02	.10
304 Charlie Garner	.10	.30
305 Andy Harmon	.02	.10
306 Greg Jackson	.02	.10
307 Bill Romanowski	.02	.10
308 William Thomas	.02	.10
309 Herschel Walker	.07	.20
310 Calvin Williams	.07	.20
311 Michael Zordich	.02	.10
312 Chad Brown	.07	.20
313 Dermontti Dawson	.07	.20
314 Barry Foster	.07	.20
315 Kevin Greene	.07	.20
316 Charles Johnson	.07	.20
317 Levon Kirkland	.02	.10
318 Carnell Lake	.02	.10
319 Greg Lloyd	.07	.20
320 Byron Bam Morris	.02	.10
321 Neil O'Donnell	.07	.20
322 Darren Perry	.02	.10
323 Ray Seals	.02	.10
324 John L. Williams	.02	.10
325 Rod Woodson	.07	.20
326 John Carney	.02	.10
327 Andre Coleman	.02	.10
328 Courtney Hall	.02	.10
329 Ronnie Harmon	.02	.10
330 Dwayne Harper	.02	.10
331 Stan Humphries	.07	.20
332 Shawn Jefferson	.02	.10
333 Tony Martin	.07	.20
334 Natrone Means	.07	.20
335 Chris Mims	.02	.10
336 Leslie O'Neal	.07	.20
337 Alfred Pupunu RC	.02	.10
338 Junior Seau	.10	.30
339 Mark Seay	.07	.20
340 Eric Davis	.02	.10
341 William Floyd	.07	.20
342 Merton Hanks	.02	.10
343 Rickey Jackson	.02	.10

344 Brent Jones .02 .10
345 Tim McDonald .02 .10
346 Ken Norton Jr. .07 .20
347 Gary Plummer .02 .10
348 Jerry Rice .40 1.00
349 Deion Sanders .15 .40
350 Jesse Sapolu .02 .10
351 Dana Stubblefield .07 .20
352 John Taylor .02 .10
353 Steve Wallace .02 .10
354 Ricky Watters .07 .20
355 Lee Woodall .02 .10
356 Bryant Young .07 .20
357 Steve Young .30 .75
358 Sam Adams .02 .10
359 Howard Ballard .02 .10
360 Robert Blackmon .02 .10
361 Brian Blades .07 .20
362 Carlton Gray .02 .10
363 Cortez Kennedy .07 .20
364 Rick Mirer .07 .20
365 Eugene Robinson .02 .10
366 Chris Warren .07 .20
367 Terry Wooden .02 .10
368 Brad Culpepper .02 .10
369 Lawrence Dawsey .02 .10
370 Trent Dilfer .10 .30
371 Santana Dotson .02 .10
372 Craig Erickson .02 .10
373 Thomas Everett .02 .10
374 Paul Gruber .02 .10
375 Alvin Harper .02 .10
376 Jackie Harris .02 .10
377 Courtney Hawkins .02 .10
378 Martin Mayhew .02 .10
379 Hardy Nickerson .02 .10
380 Errict Rhett .07 .20
381 Charles Wilson .02 .10
382 Reggie Brooks .07 .20
383 Tom Carter .02 .10
384 Andre Collins .02 .10
385 Henry Ellard .07 .20
386 Ricky Ervins .02 .10
387 Darrell Green .02 .10
388 Ken Harvey .02 .10
389 Brian Mitchell .02 .10
390 Stanley Richard .02 .10
391 Heath Shuler .07 .20
392 Rod Stephens .02 .10
393 Tyronne Stowe .02 .10
394 Tydus Winans .02 .10
395 Tony Woods .02 .10
396 Checklist (1-104) .02 .10
397 Checklist (105-212) .02 .10
398 Checklist (213-298) .02 .10
399 Checklist (299-400) .02 .10
400 Checklist (Inserts) .02 .10
P1 Promo Panel 1.00 2.50
Reggie Brooks
Jerome Bettis
Rick Mirer

1995 Fleer Aerial Attack

COMPLETE SET (6) 15.00 30.00
STATED ODDS 1:37
1 Tim Brown 1.25 2.50
2 Dan Marino 8.00 15.00
3 Joe Montana 8.00 15.00
4 Jerry Rice 4.00 8.00
5 Andre Rison .75 1.50
6 Sterling Sharpe .75 1.50

1995 Fleer Flair Preview

COMPLETE SET (30) 7.50 20.00
ONE PER PACK
1 Aeneas Williams .07 .20
2 Jeff George .15 .40
3 Andre Reed .15 .40
4 Kerry Collins .40 1.00
5 Mark Carrier DB .07 .20
6 Jeff Blake .50 1.25
7 Leroy Hoard .07 .20
8 Emmitt Smith 1.25 3.00
9 Shannon Sharpe .15 .40
10 Barry Sanders 1.25 3.00
11 Reggie White .25 .60
12 Bruce Matthews .07 .20
13 Marshall Faulk 1.00 2.50
14 Tony Boselli .07 .20
15 Joe Montana 1.50 4.00
16 Tim Brown .25 .60
17 Jerome Bettis .25 .60
18 Dan Marino 1.50 4.00
19 Cris Carter .25 .60
20 Drew Bledsoe .50 1.25
21 Willie Roaf .07 .20
22 Rodney Hampton .15 .40
23 Rob Moore .15 .40
24 Fred Barnett .15 .40
25 Rod Woodson .15 .40
26 Natrone Means .15 .40
27 Jerry Rice .75 2.00
28 Chris Warren .15 .40
29 Errict Rhett .15 .40
30 Henry Ellard .15 .40

1995 Fleer Gridiron Leaders

COMPLETE SET (10) 2.50 6.00
STATED ODDS 1:4
1 Cris Carter .15 .40
2 Ben Coates .08 .25
3 Marshall Faulk .75 1.50
4 Jerry Rice .60 1.25
5 Barry Sanders 1.00 2.00
6 Deion Sanders .20 .50
7 Emmitt Smith 1.00 2.00
8 Eric Turner .02 .10
9 Chris Warren .08 .25
10 Steve Young .40 1.00

1995 Fleer Prospects

COMPLETE SET (20) 10.00 20.00
STATED ODDS 1:6
1 Tony Boselli .60 1.50
2 Kyle Brady .30 .75
3 Ruben Brown .60 1.50
4 Kevin Carter .60 1.50
5 Ki-Jana Carter .60 1.50
6 Kerry Collins 1.25 3.00
7 Luther Elliss .20 .50
8 Jimmy Hitchcock .20 .50
9 Jack Jackson .20 .50
10 Ellis Johnson .20 .50
11 Rob Johnson .60 1.50
12 Steve McNair 2.00 5.00
13 Rashaan Salaam .60 1.50
14 Warren Sapp .20 .50
15 J.J. Stokes .60 1.50
16 Bobby Taylor .60 1.50
17 John Walsh .20 .50
18 Michael Westbrook .60 1.50
19 Tyrone Wheatley .75 2.00
20 Sherman Williams .30 .75

1995 Fleer Pro-Vision

COMPLETE SET (6) 1.00 2.50
STATED ODDS 1:6
1 Natrone Means .07 .20
2 Sterling Sharpe .07 .20
3 Ken Norton .07 .20
4 Drew Bledsoe .25 .60
5 Marshall Faulk .50 1.25
6 Tim Brown .10 .30

1995 Fleer Rookie Sensations

COMPLETE SET (20) 20.00 40.00
STATED ODDS 1:3 JUMBO
1 Derrick Alexander WR 2.00 4.00
2 Mario Bates .50 1.25
3 Tim Bowens .50 1.25
4 Lake Dawson 1.00 2.50
5 Bert Emanuel 2.00 4.00
6 Marshall Faulk 4.00 10.00
7 William Floyd 1.00 2.50
8 Rob Fredrickson .50 1.25
9 Greg Hill 1.00 2.50
10 Charles Johnson 1.00 2.50
11 Antonio Langham .50 1.25
12 Willie McGinest 1.00 2.50
13 Byron Bam Morris .50 1.25
14 Errict Rhett 1.00 2.50
15 Darnay Scott 3.00 6.00
16 Heath Shuler 1.00 2.50
17 Dewayne Washington .50 1.25
18 Dan Wilkinson .50 1.25
19 Lee Woodall .50 1.25
20 Bryant Young 1.00 2.50

1995 Fleer TD Sensations

COMPLETE SET (10) 4.00 8.00
STATED ODDS 1:3 FOIL
1 Marshall Faulk .75 1.50
2 Dan Marino 1.25 2.50
3 Natrone Means .08 .25
4 Herman Moore .15 .40
5 Jerry Rice .60 1.25
6 Sterling Sharpe .08 .25
7 Emmitt Smith 1.00 2.00
8 Chris Warren .08 .25
9 Ricky Watters .08 .25
10 Steve Young .40 1.00

1995 Fleer Bettis/Mirer Sheet

At the Super Bowl card show in Miami, commemorative sheets of Bettis and Mirer insert cards could be purchased for five wrappers and 1.00. Just 2,500 were produced; 400 of these were signed by one of the two players and sold for 25.00. The sheets measure 8 1/2" by 11". One side features ten insert cards of Jerome Bettis, while the other side shows ten Rick Mirer insert cards. Sheets containing autograph's of Bettis and Mirer were embossed with the Fleer mark of Authenticity stamp.

1 Jerome Bettis .80 2.00
Rick Mirer
2 Jerome Bettis 12.50 25.00
AU

1995 Fleer Shell

Produced by Fleer, this 10-card set was issued by Shell in the "Drive to the Super Bowl XXX" sweepstakes. The standard-size cards are perforated at one end and were originally attached to a tab card of equal size. The tab features three rub-offs on its front and abbreviated rules on its back. The three rub-offs were titled "your score," "their score," and "prize." If the first rub-off had a higher score than the second one, then the holder could scratch the prize box to determine the prize. The contest expired 9/17/95. The cards themselves feature horizontal fronts with either color or black-and-white action photos that fade along the edges into white borders. The card title and final game score are presented in a yellow rectangle at the bottom. The circumstances surrounding the particular game are summarized on the back. Reportedly, 65 million game pieces (cards) were created.

COMPLETE SET (10) 3.20 8.00
1 Super Bowl XXIII .80 2.00
Joe Montana's drive
2 1967 NFL Championship .50 1.25
Bart Starr's TD
3 1986 AFC Championship .30 .75
The Drive
Mark Jackson
4 Super Bowl XIII .50 1.25
Steeler's drive
Terry Bradshaw
Franco Harris
5 1975 NFC Divisional Playoffs .30 .75
Cowboy's drive
Doug Dennison featured
6 1968 AFL Championship .30 .75
Jet's drive
7 1981 NFC Championship/49ers team shot .40
1.00
8 1983 NFC Championship .40 1.00
Redskins' drive
John Riggins' TD
9 1969 AFL Divisional Playoffs .40 1.00
Len Dawson in huddle
10 Super Bowl V .40 1.00
Colts' field goal
Bob Lilly and
Mel Renfro pictured

1996 Fleer

The 1996 Fleer set was issued in one series totalling 200 cards. The 11-card packs retail for $1.49 each. The cards are grouped alphabetically within teams and checklisted below alphabetically according to teams. The set contains the topical subsets: Rookies (141-180) and PFW Weekly Previews (181-197). A three-card promo sheet (cards numbered S1-S3) was produced and is priced below in complete sheet form.

COMPLETE SET (200) 7.50 20.00
1 Garrison Hearst .07 .20
2 Rob Moore .07 .20
3 Frank Sanders .07 .20
4 Eric Swann .02 .10
5 Aeneas Williams .02 .10
6 Jeff George .07 .20
7 Craig Heyward .02 .10
8 Terance Mathis .02 .10
9 Eric Metcalf .02 .10
10 Michael Jackson .07 .20
11 Andre Rison .07 .20
12 Vinny Testaverde .07 .20
13 Eric Turner .02 .10
14 Darick Holmes .02 .10
15 Jim Kelly .10 .30
16 Bryce Paup .02 .10
17 Bruce Smith .07 .20
18 Thurman Thomas .10 .30
19 Kerry Collins .10 .30
20 Lamar Lathon .02 .10
21 Derrick Moore .02 .10
22 Tyrone Poole .02 .10
23 Curtis Conway .10 .30
24 Bryan Cox .02 .10
25 Erik Kramer .02 .10
26 Rashaan Salaam .07 .20
27 Jeff Blake .10 .30
28 Ki-Jana Carter .07 .20
29 Carl Pickens .07 .20
30 Darnay Scott .07 .20
31 Troy Aikman .30 .75
32 Charles Haley .07 .20
33 Michael Irvin .10 .30
34 Daryl Johnston .07 .20
35 Jay Novacek .02 .10
36 Deion Sanders .15 .40
37 Emmitt Smith .50 1.25
38 Steve Atwater .02 .10
39 Terrell Davis .25 .60
40 John Elway .60 1.50
41 Anthony Miller .07 .20
42 Shannon Sharpe .07 .20
43 Scott Mitchell .07 .20
44 Herman Moore .07 .20
45 Johnnie Morton .07 .20
46 Brett Perriman .02 .10
47 Barry Sanders .50 1.25
48 Edgar Bennett .07 .20
49 Robert Brooks .10 .30
50 Mark Chmura .07 .20
51 Brett Favre .60 1.50
52 Reggie White .10 .30
53 Mel Gray .02 .10
54 Steve McNair .25 .60
55 Chris Sanders .07 .20
56 Rodney Thomas .02 .10
57 Quentin Coryatt .02 .10
58 Sean Dawkins .02 .10
59 Ken Dilger .07 .20
60 Marshall Faulk .15 .40
61 Jim Harbaugh .07 .20
62 Tony Boselli .02 .10
63 Mark Brunell .20 .50
64 Natrone Means .07 .20
65 James O.Stewart .07 .20
66 Marcus Allen .10 .30
67 Steve Bono .02 .10
68 Neil Smith .07 .20
69 Derrick Thomas .10 .30
70 Tamarick Vanover .07 .20
71 Fred Barnett .02 .10
72 Eric Green .02 .10
73 Dan Marino .60 1.50
74 O.J. McDuffie .07 .20
75 Bernie Parmalee .02 .10
76 Cris Carter .10 .30
77 Qadry Ismail .07 .20
78 Warren Moon .07 .20
79 Jake Reed .07 .20
80 Robert Smith .07 .20
81 Drew Bledsoe .20 .50
82 Vincent Brisby .02 .10
83 Ben Coates .07 .20
84 Curtis Martin .25 .60
85 Dave Meggett .02 .10
86 Mario Bates .07 .20
87 Jim Everett .02 .10
88 Michael Haynes .02 .10
89 Renaldo Turnbull .02 .10
90 Dave Brown .02 .10
91 Rodney Hampton .07 .20
92 Thomas Lewis .02 .10
93 Tyrone Wheatley .07 .20
94 Kyle Brady .02 .10
95 Hugh Douglas .07 .20
96 Aaron Glenn .02 .10
97 Jeff Graham .02 .10
98 Adrian Murrell .07 .20
99 Neil O'Donnell .07 .20
100 Tim Brown .10 .30
101 Jeff Hostetler .02 .10
102 Napoleon Kaufman .10 .30
103 Chester McGlockton .02 .10
104 Harvey Williams .02 .10
105 William Fuller .02 .10
106 Charlie Garner .07 .20
107 Ricky Watters .07 .20
108 Calvin Williams .02 .10
109 Jerome Bettis .10 .30
110 Greg Lloyd .07 .20
111 Byron Bam Morris .02 .10
112 Kordell Stewart .10 .30
113 Yancey Thigpen .07 .20
114 Rod Woodson .07 .20
115 Isaac Bruce .10 .30
116 Troy Drayton .02 .10
117 Leslie O'Neal .02 .10
118 Steve Walsh .02 .10
119 Marco Coleman .02 .10
120 Aaron Hayden .02 .10
121 Stan Humphries .07 .20
122 Junior Seau .10 .30
123 William Floyd .07 .20
124 Brent Jones .02 .10
125 Ken Norton .02 .10
126 Jerry Rice .30 .75
127 J.J. Stokes .10 .30
128 Steve Young .25 .60
129 Brian Blades .02 .10
130 Joey Galloway .10 .30
131 Rick Mirer .07 .20
132 Chris Warren .07 .20
133 Trent Dilfer .10 .30
134 Alvin Harper .02 .10
135 Hardy Nickerson .02 .10
136 Errict Rhett .07 .20
137 Terry Allen .07 .20
138 Henry Ellard .02 .10
139 Heath Shuler .07 .20
140 Michael Westbrook .10 .30
141 Karim Abdul-Jabbar RC .10 .30
142 Mike Alstott RC .40 1.00
143 Marco Battaglia RC .02 .10
144 Tim Biakabutuka RC .10 .30
145 Tony Brackens RC .10 .30
146 Duane Clemons RC .02 .10
147 Ernie Conwell RC .02 .10
148 Chris Darkins RC .02 .10
149 Stephen Davis RC .60 1.50
150 Brian Dawkins RC .50 1.25
151 Rickey Dudley RC .10 .30
152 Jason Dunn RC .07 .20
153 Bobby Engram RC .10 .30
154 Daryl Gardener RC .02 .10
155 Eddie George RC .50 1.25
156 Terry Glenn RC .40 1.00
157 Kevin Hardy RC .10 .30
158 Walt Harris RC .02 .10
159 Marvin Harrison RC 1.00 2.50
160 Bobby Hoying RC .10 .30
161 Keyshawn Johnson RC .40 1.00
162 Cedric Jones RC .02 .10
163 Marcus Jones RC .02 .10
164 Eddie Kennison RC .10 .30
165 Ray Lewis RC 1.00 2.50
166 Derrick Mayes RC .10 .30
167 Leeland McElroy RC .07 .20
168 Johnny McWilliams RC .07 .20
169 John Mobley RC .02 .10
170 Alex Molden RC .02 .10
171 Eric Moulds RC .50 1.25
172 Muhsin Muhammad RC UER .40 1.00
(name misspelled on front)
173 Jonathan Ogden RC .10 .30
174 Lawrence Phillips RC .10 .30
175 Stanley Pritchett RC .07 .20
176 Simeon Rice RC .30 .75
177 Bryan Still RC .07 .20
178 Amani Toomer RC .40 1.00
179 Regan Upshaw RC .02 .10
180 Alex Van Dyke RC .07 .20
181 Barry Sanders PFW .25 .60
182 Marcus Allen PFW .10 .30
183 Bryce Paup PFW .02 .10
184 Jerry Rice PFW .15 .40
185 Desmond Howard PFW .07 .20
Bob Christian
186 Leon Lett PFW .02 .10
187 Brett Favre PFW .30 .75
188 Greg Lloyd PFW .02 .10
Derrick Thomas
189 Jeff Blake PFW .07 .20
190 Emmitt Smith PFW .25 .60
191 John Elway PFW .15 .40
Jeff Hostetler
192 Chiefs PFW .02 .10
193 Marshall Faulk PFW .10 .30
194 Troy Aikman PFW .15 .40
Steve Young
195 Dan Marino PFW .30 .75
196 Donta Jones PFW .02 .10
197 Jim Kelly PFW .10 .30
198 Checklist .02 .10
199 Checklist .02 .10
200 Checklist .02 .10
P1 Promo Sheet 1.50 4.00
William Floyd
Trent Dilfer
Brett Favre

1996 Fleer Breakthroughs

COMPLETE SET (24) 6.00 15.00
STATED ODDS 1:3
1 Tim Bowens .15 .40
2 Kyle Brady .15 .40
3 Devin Bush .15 .40
4 Kevin Carter .15 .40
5 Ki-Jana Carter .30 .75
6 Kerry Collins .50 1.25
7 Trent Dilfer .50 1.25
8 Ken Dilger .30 .75
9 Joey Galloway .50 1.25
10 Aaron Hayden .15 .40
11 Napoleon Kaufman .50 1.25
12 Craig Newsome .15 .40
13 Tyrone Poole .15 .40
14 Jake Reed .30 .75
15 Rashaan Salaam .30 .75
16 Chris Sanders .30 .75
17 Frank Sanders .30 .75
18 Kordell Stewart .50 1.25
19 J.J. Stokes .50 1.25
20 Bobby Taylor .15 .40
21 Orlando Thomas .15 .40
22 Michael Timpson .15 .40
23 Tamarick Vanover .30 .75
24 Michael Westbrook .50 1.25

1996 Fleer RAC Pack

COMPLETE SET (10) 6.00 15.00
STATED ODDS 1:18
1 Robert Brooks 1.50 4.00
2 Tim Brown 1.50 4.00
3 Isaac Bruce 1.50 4.00
4 Cris Carter 1.50 4.00
5 Curtis Conway 1.50 4.00
6 Michael Irvin 1.50 4.00
7 Eric Metcalf .50 1.25
8 Herman Moore 1.00 2.50
9 Carl Pickens 1.00 2.50
10 Jerry Rice 4.00 10.00

1996 Fleer Rookie Autographs

COMPLETE SET (3) 30.00 60.00
STATED ODDS 1:288 HOBBY
*BLUE SIGS: .6X TO 1.5X BASIC AUTOS
A1 Tim Biakabutuka 5.00 12.00
A2 Eddie George 10.00 25.00
A3 Leeland McElroy 5.00 12.00

1996 Fleer Rookie Sensations

COMPLETE SET (11) 25.00 60.00
STATED ODDS 1:72
*HOT PACK: .3X TO .8X BASIC INSERTS
HOT PACK SET STATED ODDS 1:960
1 Karim Abdul-Jabbar 2.00 5.00
2 Tim Biakabutuka UER 2.00 5.00
(photo actually Muhsin Muhammad)
3 Rickey Dudley 1.25 3.00
4 Eddie George 4.00 10.00
5 Terry Glenn 3.00 8.00
6 Kevin Hardy 1.25 3.00
7 Marvin Harrison 7.50 20.00
8 Keyshawn Johnson 3.00 8.00
9 Jonathan Ogden 2.50 6.00
10 Lawrence Phillips 2.00 5.00
11 Simeon Rice 5.00 12.00

1996 Fleer Rookie Write-Ups

COMPLETE SET (10) 6.00 15.00
STATED ODDS 1:12 HOBBY
1 Tim Biakabutuka .30 .75
2 Rickey Dudley .30 .75
3 Eddie George 1.25 3.00
4 Terry Glenn 1.00 2.50
5 Kevin Hardy .30 .75
6 Marvin Harrison 2.50 6.00
7 Keyshawn Johnson 1.00 2.50
8 Leeland McElroy .20 .50
9 Lawrence Phillips .30 .75
10 Simeon Rice .75 2.00

1996 Fleer Statistically Speaking

COMPLETE SET (20) 25.00 60.00
STATED ODDS 1:37
1 Troy Aikman 2.50 6.00
2 Larry Centers .60 1.50
3 Ben Coates .60 1.50
4 Brett Favre 5.00 12.00
5 Joey Galloway 1.00 2.50
6 Rodney Hampton .60 1.50
7 Dan Marino 5.00 12.00
8 Curtis Martin 2.00 5.00
9 Anthony Miller .40 1.00
10 Brian Mitchell .60 1.50
11 Herman Moore .60 1.50
12 Errict Rhett .60 1.50
13 Rashaan Salaam .40 1.00
14 Barry Sanders 4.00 10.00
15 Deion Sanders 1.25 3.00
16 Emmitt Smith 4.00 10.00
17 Kordell Stewart .60 1.50
18 Chris Warren .40 1.00
19 Ricky Watters .60 1.50
20 Steve Young 2.00 5.00

1997 Fleer

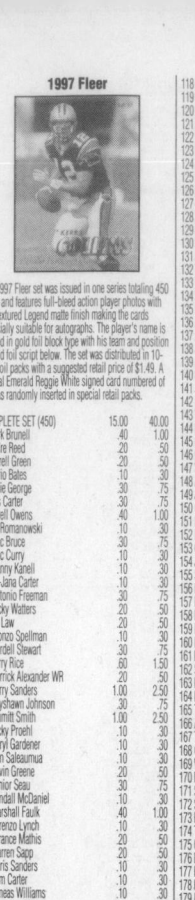

The 1997 Fleer set was issued in one series totaling 450 cards and features full-bleed action player photos with the Textured Legend matte finish making the cards especially suitable for autographs. The player's name is printed in gold foil block type with his team and position in gold foil script below. The set was distributed in 10-card foil packs with a suggested retail price of $1.49. A special Emerald Reggie White signed card numbered of 80 was randomly inserted in special retail packs.

COMPLETE SET (450) 15.00 40.00
1 Mark Brunell .40 1.00
2 Andre Reed .20 .50
3 Darrell Green .20 .50
4 Mario Bates .10 .30
5 Eddie George .30 .75
6 Cris Carter .30 .75
7 Terrell Owens .40 1.00
8 Bill Romanowski .10 .30
9 Isaac Bruce .30 .75
10 Eric Curry .10 .30
11 Danny Kanell .10 .30
12 Ki-Jana Carter .10 .30
13 Antonio Freeman .30 .75
14 Ricky Watters .20 .50
15 Ty Law .20 .50
16 Alonzo Spellman .10 .30
17 Kordell Stewart .30 .75
18 Jerry Rice .60 1.50
19 Derrick Alexander WR .20 .50
20 Barry Sanders 1.00 2.50
21 Keyshawn Johnson .30 .75
22 Emmitt Smith 1.00 2.50
23 Ricky Proehl .10 .30
24 Daryl Gardener .10 .30
25 Dan Saleaumua .10 .30
26 Kevin Greene .20 .50
27 Junior Seau .30 .75
28 Randall McDaniel .10 .30
29 Marshall Faulk .40 1.00
30 Lorenzo Lynch .10 .30
31 Terance Mathis .20 .50
32 Warren Sapp .20 .50
33 Chris Sanders .10 .30
34 Tom Carter .10 .30
35 Aeneas Williams .10 .30
36 Lawrence Phillips .10 .30
37 John Elway 1.25 3.00
38 Stanley Richard .10 .30
39 Darryl Williams .10 .30
40 Phillippi Sparks .10 .30
41 Tedy Bruschi .60 1.50
42 Merton Hanks .10 .30
43 Ray Lewis .50 1.25
44 Erik Williams .10 .30
45 Jason Gildon .10 .30
46 George Koonce .10 .30
47 Louis Oliver .10 .30
48 Muhsin Muhammad .20 .50
49 Daryl Hobbs .10 .30
50 Terry Glenn .30 .75
51 Marvin Harrison .30 .75
52 Brian Dawkins .30 .75
53 Dale Carter .10 .30
54 Alex Molden .10 .30
55 Raymont Harris .10 .30
56 Jeff Burris .10 .30
57 Don Beebe .10 .30
58 Jamir Miller .10 .30
59 Carl Pickens .20 .50
60 Antonio London .10 .30
61 Courtney Hall .10 .30
62 Derrick Brooks .30 .75
63 Chris Boniol .10 .30
64 Jeff Lageman .10 .30
65 Roy Barker .10 .30
66 Devin Bush .10 .30
67 Aaron Glenn .10 .30
68 Wayne Simmons .10 .30
69 Steve Atwater .10 .30
70 Jimmie Jones .10 .30
71 Mark Carrier WR .10 .30
72 Chris Chandler .20 .50
73 Andy Harmon .10 .30
74 John Friesz .10 .30
75 Karim Abdul-Jabbar .20 .50
76 Levon Kirkland .10 .30
77 Torrance Small .10 .30
78 Harvey Williams .10 .30
79 Chris Calloway .10 .30
80 Vinny Testaverde .20 .50
81 Bryant Young .10 .30
82 Ray Buchanan .10 .30
83 Robert Smith .20 .50
84 Robert Brooks .20 .50
85 Ray Crockett .10 .30
86 Bennie Blades .10 .30
87 Mark Carrier DB .10 .30
88 Mike Tomczak .10 .30
89 Darick Holmes .10 .30
90 Drew Bledsoe .40 1.00
91 Darren Woodson .10 .30
92 Dan Wilkinson .10 .30
93 Charles Way .10 .30
94 Ray Farmer .10 .30
95 Marcus Allen .30 .75
96 Marco Coleman .10 .30
97 Zach Thomas .30 .75
98 Wesley Walls .20 .50
99 Frank Wycheck .10 .30
100 Troy Aikman .60 1.50
101 Clyde Simmons .10 .30
102 Courtney Hawkins .10 .30
103 Chuck Smith .10 .30
104 Neil O'Donnell .20 .50
105 Kevin Carter .10 .30
106 Chris Slade .10 .30
107 Jessie Armstead .10 .30
108 Sean Dawkins .10 .30
109 Robert Blackmon .10 .30
110 Kevin Smith .10 .30
111 Lonnie Johnson .10 .30
112 Craig Newsome .10 .30
113 Jonathan Ogden .10 .30
114 Chris Zorich .10 .30
115 Tim Brown .30 .75
116 Fred Barnett .10 .30
117 Michael Haynes .10 .30
118 Eric Hill .10 .30
119 Ronnie Harmon .10 .30
120 Sean Gilbert .10 .30
121 Derrick Alexander DE .10 .30
122 Derrick Thomas .30 .75
123 Tyrone Wheatley .20 .50
124 Cortez Kennedy .10 .30
125 Jeff George .20 .50
126 Chad Cota .10 .30
127 Gary Zimmerman .10 .30
128 Johnnie Morton .20 .50
129 Chad Brown .10 .30
130 Marvcus Patton .10 .30
131 James O.Stewart .20 .50
132 Terry Kirby .20 .50
133 Chris Mims .10 .30
134 William Thomas .10 .30
135 Steve Tasker .10 .30
136 Jason Belser .10 .30
137 Bryan Cox .10 .30
138 Jessie Tuggle .10 .30
139 Ashley Ambrose .10 .30
140 Mark Chmura .20 .50
141 Jeff Hostetler .10 .30
142 Rich Owens .10 .30
143 Willie Davis .10 .30
144 Hardy Nickerson .10 .30
145 Curtis Martin .40 1.00
146 Ken Norton .10 .30
147 Victor Green .10 .30
148 Anthony Miller .10 .30
149 John Kasay .10 .30
150 O.J. McDuffie .20 .50
151 Darren Perry .10 .30
152 Luther Elliss .10 .30
153 Greg Hill .10 .30
154 John Randle .20 .50
155 Stephen Grant .10 .30
156 Leon Lett .10 .30
157 Darrien Gordon .10 .30
158 Ray Zellars .10 .30
159 Michael Jackson .20 .50
160 Leslie O'Neal .10 .30
161 Bruce Smith .20 .50
162 Santana Dotson .10 .30
163 Bobby Hebert .10 .30
164 Keith Hamilton .10 .30
165 Tony Boselli .10 .30
166 Alfred Williams .10 .30
167 Ty Detmer .20 .50
168 Chester McGlockton .10 .30
169 William Floyd .20 .50
170 Bruce Matthews .10 .30
171 Simeon Rice .20 .50
172 Scott Mitchell .20 .50
173 Ricardo McDonald .10 .30
174 Tyrone Poole .10 .30
175 Greg Lloyd .10 .30
176 Bruce Armstrong .10 .30
177 Erik Kramer .10 .30
178 Kimble Anders .20 .50
179 Lamar Smith .30 .75
180 Tony Tolbert .10 .30
181 Joe Aska .10 .30
182 Eric Allen .10 .30
183 Eric Turner .10 .30
184 Brad Johnson .30 .75
185 Tony Martin .20 .50
186 Mike Mamula .10 .30
187 Irving Spikes .10 .30
188 Keith Jackson .10 .30
189 Carlton Bailey .10 .30
190 Tyrone Braxton .10 .30
191 Chad Bratzke .10 .30
192 Adrian Murrell .20 .50
193 Roman Phifer .10 .30
194 Todd Collins .10 .30
195 Chris Warren .20 .50
196 Kevin Hardy .10 .30
197 Rick Mirer .10 .30
198 Cornelius Bennett .10 .30
199 Jimmy Hitchcock .10 .30
200 Michael Irvin .30 .75
201 Quentin Coryatt .10 .30
202 Reggie White .30 .75
203 Larry Centers .20 .50
204 Rodney Thomas .10 .30
205 Dana Stubblefield .10 .30
206 Rod Woodson .20 .50
207 Rhett Hall .10 .30
208 Steve Tovar .10 .30
209 Michael Westbrook .20 .50
210 Steve Wisniewski .10 .30
211 Carlester Crumpler .10 .30
212 Elvis Grbac .20 .50
213 Tim Bowens .10 .30
214 Robert Porcher .10 .30
215 John Carney .10 .30
216 Anthony Newman .10 .30
217 Earnest Byner .10 .30
218 Dewayne Washington .10 .30
219 Willie Green .10 .30
220 Terry Allen .30 .75
221 William Fuller .10 .30
222 Al Del Greco .10 .30
223 Trent Dilfer .30 .75
224 Michael Dean Perry .10 .30
225 Larry Allen .10 .30
226 Mark Bruener .10 .30
227 Clay Matthews .10 .30
228 Reuben Brown UER .10 .30
229 Edgar Bennett .20 .50
230 Neil Smith .20 .50
231 Ken Harvey .10 .30
232 Kyle Brady .10 .30
233 Corey Miller .10 .30
234 Tony Siragusa .10 .30
235 Todd Sauerbrun .10 .30
236 Daniel Stubbs .10 .30
237 Robb Thomas .10 .30
238 Jimmy Smith .20 .50
239 Marquez Pope .10 .30
240 Tim Biakabutuka .20 .50
241 Jamie Asher .10 .30
242 Steve McNair .40 1.00
243 Harold Green .10 .30
244 Frank Sanders .20 .50
245 Joe Johnson .10 .30
246 Eric Bieniemy .10 .30
247 Kevin Turner .10 .30
248 Rickey Dudley .20 .50
249 Orlando Thomas .10 .30
250 Dan Marino 1.25 3.00
251 Deion Sanders .30 .75
252 Dan Williams .10 .30
253 Sam Gash .10 .30
254 Lonnie Marts .10 .30
255 Mo Lewis .10 .30
256 Charles Johnson .20 .50
257 Chris Jacke .10 .30
258 Keenan McCardell .20 .50
259 Donnell Woolford .10 .30
260 Terrance Shaw .10 .30
261 Jason Dunn .10 .30

262 Willie McGinest	.10	.30
263 Ken Dilger	.10	.30
264 Keith Lyle	.10	.30
265 Antonio Langham	.10	.30
266 Carlton Gray	.10	.30
267 LeShon Johnson	.10	.30
268 Thurman Thomas	.30	.75
269 Jesse Campbell	.10	.30
270 Carnell Lake	.10	.30
271 Cris Dishman	.10	.30
272 Kevin Williams	.10	.30
273 Troy Brown	.20	.50
274 William Roaf	.10	.30
275 Terrell Davis	.40	1.00
276 Herman Moore	.20	.50
277 Walt Harris	.10	.30
278 Mark Collins	.10	.30
279 Bert Emanuel	.20	.50
280 Qadry Ismail	.20	.50
281 Phil Hansen	.10	.30
282 Steve Young	.40	1.00
283 Michael Sinclair	.10	.30
284 Jeff Graham	.10	.30
285 Sam Mills	.10	.30
286 Terry McDaniel	.10	.30
287 Eugene Robinson	.10	.30
288 Tony Bennett	.10	.30
289 Daryl Johnston	.20	.50
290 Eric Swann	.10	.30
291 Byron Bam Morris	.10	.30
292 Thomas Lewis	.10	.30
293 Terrell Fletcher	.10	.30
294 Gus Frerotte	.10	.30
295 Stanley Pritchett	.10	.30
296 Mike Alstott	.30	.75
297 Will Shields	.10	.30
298 Errict Rhett	.10	.30
299 Garrison Hearst	.20	.50
300 Kerry Collins	.30	.75
301 Darryll Lewis	.10	.30
302 Chris T. Jones	.10	.30
303 Yancey Thigpen	.20	.50
304 Jackie Harris	.10	.30
305 Steve Christie	.10	.30
306 Gilbert Brown	.20	.50
307 Terry Wooden	.10	.30
308 Pete Mitchell	.10	.30
309 Tim McDonald	.10	.30
310 Jake Reed	.20	.50
311 Ed McCaffrey	.20	.50
312 Chris Doleman	.10	.30
313 Eric Metcalf	.20	.50
314 Ricky Reynolds	.10	.30
315 David Sloan	.10	.30
316 Marvin Washington	.10	.30
317 Herschel Walker	.20	.50
318 Michael Timpson	.10	.30
319 Blaine Bishop	.10	.30
320 Irv Smith	.10	.30
321 Seth Joyner	.10	.30
322 Terrell Buckley	.10	.30
323 Michael Strahan	.20	.50
324 Sam Adams	.10	.30
325 Leslie Shepherd	.10	.30
326 James Jett	.20	.50
327 Anthony Pleasant	.10	.30
328 Lee Woodall	.10	.30
329 Shannon Sharpe	.20	.50
330 Jamal Anderson	.30	.75
331 Andre Hastings	.10	.30
332 Troy Vincent	.10	.30
333 Sean LaChapelle	.10	.30
334 Winslow Oliver	.10	.30
335 Sean Jones	.10	.30
336 Darnay Scott	.20	.50
337 Todd Lyght	.10	.30
338 Leonard Russell	.10	.30
339 Nate Newton	.10	.30
340 Zack Crockett	.10	.30
341 Amp Lee	.10	.30
342 Bobby Engram	.20	.50
343 Mike Hollis	.10	.30
344 Rodney Hampton	.20	.50
345 Mel Gray	.10	.30
346 Van Malone	.10	.30
347 Aaron Craver	.10	.30
348 Jim Everett	.10	.30
349 Trace Armstrong	.10	.30
350 Pat Swilling	.10	.30
351 Brent Jones	.10	.30
352 Chris Spielman	.10	.30
353 Brett Perriman	.10	.30
354 Brian Kinchen	.10	.30
355 Joey Galloway	.20	.50
356 Henry Ellard	.10	.30
357 Ben Coates	.20	.50
358 Dorsey Levens	.30	.75
359 Charlie Garner	.20	.50
360 Eric Pegram	.10	.30
361 Anthony Johnson	.10	.30
362 Rashaan Salaam	.10	.30
363 Jeff Blake	.20	.50
364 Kent Graham	.10	.30
365 Broderick Thomas	.10	.30
366 Richmond Webb	.10	.30
367 Alfred Pupunu	.10	.30
368 Mark Stepnoski	.10	.30
369 David Dunn	.10	.30
370 Bobby Houston	.10	.30
371 Anthony Parker	.10	.30
372 Quinn Early	.10	.30
373 LeRoy Butler	.10	.30
374 Kurt Gouveia	.10	.30
375 Greg Biekert	.10	.30
376 Jim Harbaugh	.20	.50
377 Eric Bjornson	.10	.30
378 Craig Heyward	.10	.30
379 Steve Bono	.20	.50
380 Tony Banks	.20	.50
381 John Mobley	.10	.30
382 Irving Fryar	.20	.50
383 Dermontti Dawson	.10	.30
384 Eric Davis	.10	.30
385 Natrone Means	.20	.50
386 Jason Sehorn	.20	.50
387 Michael McCrary	.10	.30
388 Corwin Brown	.10	.30
389 Kevin Glover	.10	.30
390 Jerris McPhail	.10	.30
391 Bobby Taylor	.10	.30
392 Tony McGee	.10	.30
393 Curtis Conway	.20	.50
394 Napoleon Kaufman	.30	.75
395 Brian Blades	.10	.30
396 Richard Dent	.10	.30
397 Dave Brown	.10	.30
398 Stan Humphries	.20	.50
399 Stevon Moore	.10	.30
400 Brett Favre	1.50	3.00
401 Jerome Bettis	.30	.75
402 Darrin Smith	.10	.30
403 Chris Penn	.10	.30
404 Rob Moore	.20	.50
405 Micheal Barrow	.10	.30
406 Tony Brackens	.10	.30
407 Wayne Martin	.10	.30
408 Warren Moon	.30	.75
409 Jason Elam	.20	.50
410 J.J. Birden	.10	.30
411 Hugh Douglas	.10	.30
412 Lamar Lathon	.10	.30
413 John Kidd	.10	.30
414 Bryce Paup	.10	.30
415 Shawn Jefferson	.10	.30
416 Leeland McElroy SS	.10	.30
417 Flbert Shelley SS	.10	.30
418 Jermaine Lewis SS	.20	.50
419 Eric Moulds SS	.30	.75
420 Michael Bates SS	.10	.30
421 John Mangum SS	.10	.30
422 Corey Sawyer SS	.10	.30
423 Jim Schwantz SS RC	.10	.30
424 Rod Smith WR SS	.30	.75
425 Glyn Milburn SS	.10	.30
426 Desmond Howard SS	.20	.50
427 John Henry Mills SS RC	.10	.30
428 Cary Blanchard SS RC	.10	.30
429 Chris Hudson SS	.10	.30
430 Tamarick Vanover SS	.20	.50
431 Kirby Dar Dar SS RC	.20	.50
432 David Palmer SS	.10	.30
433 Dave Meggett SS	.10	.30
434 Tyrone Hughes SS	.10	.30
435 Amani Toomer SS	.20	.50
436 Wayne Chrebet SS	.20	.50
437 Carl Kidd SS RC	.10	.30
438 Derrick Witherspoon SS	.10	.30
439 Jahine Arnold SS	.10	.30
440 Andre Coleman SS	.10	.30
441 Jeff Wilkins SS	.10	.30
442 Jay Bellamy SS RC	.10	.30
443 Eddie Kennison SS	.20	.50
444 Nilo Silvan SS	.10	.30
445 Brian Mitchell SS	.10	.30
446 Garrison Hearst Checklist back	.20	.50
447 Napoleon Kaufman Checklist back	.30	.75
448 Brian Mitchell Checklist back	.10	.30
449 Rodney Hampton Checklist back	.10	.30
450 Edgar Bennett Checklist back	.10	.30
S1 Mark Chmura Sample	.40	1.00
AU1 Reggie White AUTO (numbered of 80)	75.00	125.00

1997 Fleer Crystal Silver

COMPLETE SET (445)	60.00	120.00
*CRYSTAL SILVER STARS: 1.5X TO 3X BASIC CARDS		
STATED ODDS 1:2		

1997 Fleer Tiffany Blue

COMPLETE SET (445)	500.00	1,000.00
*TIFFANY BLUE STARS: 10X TO 25X BASIC CARDS		
STATED ODDS 1:20 HOBBY		

1997 Fleer All-Pros

COMPLETE SET (24)	60.00	120.00
STATED ODDS 1:36 RETAIL		
1 Troy Aikman	5.00	12.00
2 Larry Allen	1.00	2.50
3 Drew Bledsoe	3.00	8.00
4 Terrell Davis	3.00	8.00
5 Dermontti Dawson	1.00	2.50
6 John Elway	10.00	25.00
7 Brett Favre	10.00	25.00
8 Herman Moore	1.50	4.00
9 Jerry Rice	5.00	12.00
10 Barry Sanders	8.00	20.00
11 Shannon Sharpe	1.50	4.00
12 Erik Williams	1.00	2.50
13 Ashley Ambrose	1.00	2.50
14 Chad Brown	1.00	2.50
15 LeRoy Butler	1.00	2.50
16 Kevin Greene	1.50	4.00
17 Sam Mills	1.00	2.50
18 John Randle	1.50	4.00
19 Deion Sanders	2.50	6.00
20 Junior Seau	2.50	6.00
21 Bruce Smith	1.50	4.00
22 Alfred Williams	1.00	2.50
23 Darren Woodson	1.00	2.50
24 Bryant Young	1.00	2.50

1997 Fleer Decade of Excellence

COMPLETE SET (12)	20.00	50.00
STATED ODDS 1:36 HOBBY		
*RARE TRAD.: 1X TO 2.5X BASIC INSERTS		
1 Marcus Allen	1.50	4.00
2 Cris Carter	1.50	4.00
3 John Elway	6.00	15.00
4 Irving Fryar	1.00	2.50
5 Darrell Green	1.00	2.50
6 Dan Marino	6.00	15.00
7 Jerry Rice	3.00	8.00
8 Bruce Smith	1.00	2.50
9 Herschel Walker	1.00	2.50
10 Reggie White	1.50	4.00
11 Rod Woodson	1.00	2.50
12 Steve Young	2.00	5.00

1997 Fleer Game Breakers

COMPLETE SET (20)	7.50	15.00
STATED ODDS 1:2 RETAIL		
*SUPREMES: 2X TO 5X BASIC INSERTS		
SUPREME ODDS 1:18 HOB/RET		
1 Troy Aikman	.75	2.00
2 Jerome Bettis	.40	1.00
3 Drew Bledsoe	.50	1.25
4 Isaac Bruce	.40	1.00
5 Mark Brunell	.50	1.25
6 Kerry Collins	.40	1.00
7 Terrell Davis	.50	1.25
8 Marshall Faulk	.50	1.25
9 Antonio Freeman	.40	1.00
10 Joey Galloway	.25	.60
11 Terry Glenn	.40	1.00
12 Desmond Howard	.25	.60
13 Keyshawn Johnson	.40	1.00
14 Eddie Kennison	.25	.60
15 Curtis Martin	.50	1.25
16 Herman Moore	.25	.60
17 Lawrence Phillips	.15	.40
18 Barry Sanders	1.25	3.00
19 Shannon Sharpe	.25	.60
20 Emmitt Smith	1.25	3.00

1997 Fleer Million Dollar Moments

COMPLETE SET (45)	2.00	4.00
COMP.PRIZE SET (50)	6.00	10.00
*PRIZE CARDS: SAME PRICE AS INSERTS		
46A-50A: PRICED ONLY AS PRIZE VERSIONS		
ONE PER PACK IN FLEER PRODUCTS		
1 Checklist Card	.01	.05
2 Troy Aikman	.20	.50
3 Sid Luckman	.05	.15
4 Barry Sanders	.20	.50
5 Tom Fears	.05	.15
6 Reggie White	.08	.25
7 Lou Groza not shown in photo	.05	.15
8 John Elway	.20	.50
9 Raymond Berry	.05	.15
10 Marcus Allen	.08	.25
11 Paul Hornung	.08	.25
12 Herschel Walker	.05	.15
13 Norm Van Brocklin	.05	.15
14 Bruce Smith	.05	.15
15 Bill Wade	.01	.05
16 Andre Reed	.05	.15
17 Gale Sayers	.08	.25
18 Terrell Davis	.15	.40
19 Jim Bakken	.01	.05
20 Marshall Faulk	.10	.30
21 Tom Dempsey	.01	.05
22 Dan Marino	.40	1.00
23 Garo Yepremian	.01	.05
24 Jerry Rice	.20	.50
25 Herman Edwards	.01	.05
26 Derrick Thomas	.05	.15
27 Kellen Winslow	.01	.05
28 Steve Young	.08	.25
29 Tony Dorsett	.08	.25
30 Desmond Howard	.05	.15
31 Roger Craig	.01	.05
32 Drew Bledsoe	.10	.30
33 Doug Williams	.01	.05
34 Jerome Bettis	.08	.25
35 Bobby Layne	.05	.15
36 Junior Seau	.08	.25
37 Roman Gabriel	.01	.05
38 Cris Carter	.08	.25
39 Drew Pearson	.05	.15
40 Warren Moon	.08	.25
41 Wesley Walker	.01	.05
42 Ricky Watters	.05	.15
43 Carl Eller	.01	.05
44 Kordell Stewart	.15	.40
45 John Mackey	.01	.05
46A Thurman Thomas Prize	.08	.25
47A Ken Stabler Prize	.20	.50
48A Emmitt Smith Prize	.75	2.00
49A Jim Brown Prize	.20	.50
50A Eddie George Prize	.30	.75

1997 Fleer Prospects

COMPLETE SET (10)	6.00	12.00
STATED ODDS 1:6		
1 Peter Boulware	.75	2.00
2 Rae Carruth	.40	1.00
3 Jim Druckenmiller	.60	1.50
4 Warrick Dunn	1.25	3.00
5 Tony Gonzalez	1.50	4.00
6 Yatil Green	.40	1.00
7 Ike Hilliard	.75	2.00
8 Orlando Pace	.75	2.00
9 Darrell Russell	.40	1.00
10 Shawn Springs	.60	1.50

1997 Fleer Rookie Sensations

COMPLETE SET (20)	10.00	25.00
STATED ODDS 1:4		
1 Karim Abdul-Jabbar	.75	2.00
2 Mike Alstott	1.25	3.00
3 Tony Banks	.75	2.00
4 Tony Brackens	.50	1.25
5 Rickey Dudley	.75	2.00
6 Bobby Engram	.75	2.00
7 Eddie George	1.25	3.00
8 Terry Glenn	1.25	3.00
9 Kevin Hardy	.50	1.25
10 Marvin Harrison	1.25	3.00
11 Keyshawn Johnson	1.25	3.00
12 Eddie Kennison	.75	2.00
13 Jermaine Lewis	.75	2.00
14 Ray Lewis	2.00	5.00
15 John Mobley	.50	1.25
16 Eric Moulds	1.25	3.00
17 Jonathan Ogden	.50	1.25
18 Lawrence Phillips	.50	1.25
19 Simeon Rice	.75	2.00
20 Zach Thomas	1.25	3.00

1997 Fleer Thrill Seekers

COMPLETE SET (12)	100.00	200.00
STATED ODDS 1:288		
1 Karim Abdul-Jabbar	2.50	6.00
2 Jerome Bettis	4.00	10.00
3 Terrell Davis	5.00	12.00
4 John Elway	15.00	40.00
5 Brett Favre	15.00	40.00
6 Eddie George	4.00	10.00
7 Terry Glenn	4.00	10.00
8 Keyshawn Johnson	4.00	10.00
9 Dan Marino	15.00	40.00
10 Curtis Martin	5.00	12.00
11 Deion Sanders	4.00	10.00
12 Emmitt Smith	12.50	30.00

1997 Fleer SkyBox Brett Favre Promo

1 Brett Favre/2500	2.00	5.00

2006 Fleer

This 200-card set was released in June, 2006. The set was issued into the hobby in 10-card packs, with a $1.59 SRP, which came 36 packs to a box. Cards 1-100 feature veterans sequenced in alphabetical team order while cards 101-200 feature 2006 rookies sequenced in first name alphabetical order. Those rookie cards were inserted into packs at a stated rate of two per.

COMPLETE SET (200)	20.00	50.00
COMP.SET w/o RC's (100)	6.00	15.00
TWO ROOKIES PER PACK		
ONE INSERT CARD PER PACK		
1 Anquan Boldin	.15	.40
2 Larry Fitzgerald	.20	.50
3 J.J. Arrington	.12	.30
4 Michael Vick	.20	.50
5 Warrick Dunn	.15	.40
6 Roddy White	.15	.40
7 Jamal Lewis	.15	.40
8 Kyle Boller	.15	.40
9 Derrick Mason	.15	.40
10 Willis McGahee	.15	.40
11 J.P. Losman	.15	.40
12 Lee Evans	.15	.40
13 Steve Smith	.20	.50
14 Jake Delhomme	.15	.40
15 DeShaun Foster	.15	.40
16 Rex Grossman	.15	.40
17 Brian Urlacher	.20	.50
18 Thomas Jones	.15	.40
19 Carson Palmer	.20	.50
20 Chad Johnson	.15	.40
21 Rudi Johnson	.15	.40
22 Charlie Frye	.15	.40
23 Braylon Edwards	.15	.40
24 Reuben Droughns	.15	.40
25 Julius Jones	.12	.30
26 Drew Bledsoe	.20	.50
27 Terry Glenn	.15	.40
28 Jake Plummer	.15	.40
29 Tatum Bell	.12	.30
30 Champ Bailey	.15	.40
31 Rod Smith	.15	.40
32 Roy Williams WR	.15	.40
33 Kevin Jones	.12	.30
34 Mike Williams	.12	.30
35 Brett Favre	.40	1.00
36 Ahman Green	.15	.40
37 Javon Walker	.15	.40
38 David Carr	.12	.30
39 Andre Johnson	.20	.50
40 Domanick Davis	.12	.30
41 Peyton Manning	.30	.75
42 Edgerrin James	.15	.40
43 Marvin Harrison	.20	.50
44 Reggie Wayne	.15	.40
45 Byron Leftwich	.15	.40
46 Fred Taylor	.15	.40
47 Ernest Wilford	.12	.30
48 Larry Johnson	.15	.40
49 Trent Green	.15	.40
50 Tony Gonzalez	.15	.40
51 Ronnie Brown	.20	.50
52 Ricky Williams	.12	.30
53 Chris Chambers	.15	.40
54 Daunte Culpepper	.15	.40
55 Troy Williamson	.12	.30
56 Brad Johnson	.15	.40
57 Tom Brady	.30	.75
58 Deion Branch	.15	.40
59 Corey Dillon	.15	.40
60 Deuce McAllister	.15	.40
61 Donte Stallworth	.12	.30
62 Joe Horn	.15	.40
63 Eli Manning	.25	.60
64 Tiki Barber	.20	.50
65 Plaxico Burress	.15	.40
66 Jeremy Shockey	.20	.50
67 Chad Pennington	.15	.40
68 Curtis Martin	.20	.50
69 Laveranues Coles	.12	.30
70 Randy Moss	.20	.50
71 Aaron Brooks	.15	.40
72 LaMont Jordan	.15	.40
73 Donovan McNabb	.20	.50
74 Brian Westbrook	.15	.40
75 Terrell Owens	.20	.50
76 Ben Roethlisberger	.25	.60
77 Hines Ward	.20	.50
78 Willie Parker	.15	.40
79 Heath Miller	.15	.40
80 LaDainian Tomlinson	.20	.50
81 Drew Brees	.20	.50
82 Antonio Gates	.20	.50
83 Alex Smith QB	.20	.50
84 Antonio Bryant	.12	.30
85 Frank Gore	.20	.50
86 Shaun Alexander	.15	.40
87 Matt Hasselbeck	.15	.40
88 Darrell Jackson	.15	.40
89 Marc Bulger	.15	.40
90 Steven Jackson	.20	.50
91 Torry Holt	.15	.40
92 Cadillac Williams	.15	.40
93 Chris Simms	.15	.40
94 Joey Galloway	.15	.40
95 Steve McNair	.15	.40
96 Chris Brown	.12	.30
97 Drew Bennett	.15	.40
98 Clinton Portis	.20	.50
99 Santana Moss	.15	.40
100 Mark Brunell	.15	.40
101 A.J. Hawk RC	.75	2.00
102 A.J. Nicholson RC	.50	1.25
103 Abdul Hodge RC	.50	1.25
104 Andre Hall RC	.60	1.50
105 Anthony Fasano RC	.75	2.00
106 Antonio Cromartie RC	.75	2.00
107 Ashton Youboty RC	.50	1.25
108 Bobby Carpenter RC	.50	1.25
109 Brad Smith RC	.75	2.00
110 Greg Jennings RC	1.50	4.00
111 Brandon Williams RC	.50	1.25
112 Brian Calhoun RC	.50	1.25
113 Brodie Croyle RC	.75	2.00
114 Brodrick Bunkley RC	.60	1.50
115 Bruce Gradkowski RC	.75	2.00
116 Chad Greenway RC	.75	2.00
117 Chad Jackson RC	.50	1.25
118 Charles Davis RC	.60	1.50
119 Charles Gordon RC	.60	1.50
120 Charlie Whitehurst RC	.75	2.00
121 Claude Wroten RC	.50	1.25
122 Cory Rodgers RC	.60	1.50
123 D.J. Shockley RC	.60	1.50
124 Darnell Bing RC	.60	1.50
125 Darrell Hackney RC	.60	1.50
126 David Thomas RC	.60	1.50
127 D'Brickashaw Ferguson RC	.75	2.00
128 DeAngelo Williams RC	1.00	2.50
129 DeMeco Ryans RC	.75	2.00
130 Demetrius Williams RC	.60	1.50
131 Derek Hagan RC	.60	1.50
132 Devin Hester RC	1.25	3.00
133 Dominique Byrd RC	.60	1.50
134 DonTrell Moore RC	.60	1.50
135 D'Qwell Jackson RC	.60	1.50
136 Drew Olson RC	.50	1.25
137 Elvis Dumervil RC	.75	2.00
138 Ernie Sims RC	.60	1.50
139 Garrett Mills RC	.75	2.00
140 Gerald Riggs RC	.60	1.50
141 Greg Lee RC	.50	1.25
142 Haloti Ngata RC	.75	2.00
143 Hank Baskett RC	.75	2.00
144 Jason Allen RC	.60	1.50
145 Jason Avant RC	.50	1.25
146 Jay Cutler RC	1.50	4.00
147 Jeff Webb RC	.60	1.50
148 Jeremy Bloom RC	.60	1.50
149 Jerome Harrison RC	.75	2.00
150 Jimmy Williams RC	.75	2.00
151 Joe Klopfenstein RC	.50	1.25
152 Johnathan Joseph RC	.60	1.50
153 Joseph Addai RC	.75	2.00
154 Jovon Bouknight RC	.60	1.50
155 Kai Parham RC	.75	2.00
156 Kamerion Wimbley RC	.75	2.00
157 Kellen Clemens RC	.60	1.50
158 Kelly Jennings RC	.60	1.50
159 Ko Simpson RC	.60	1.50
160 Laurence Maroney RC	.60	1.50
161 Lawrence Vickers RC	.60	1.50
162 LenDale White RC	.60	1.50
163 Leon Washington RC	.60	1.50
164 Leonard Pope RC	.75	2.00
165 Manny Lawson RC	.60	1.50
166 Marcedes Lewis RC	.75	2.00
167 Marcus McNeill RC	.60	1.50
168 Donte Whitner RC	.75	2.00
169 Mario Williams RC	.75	2.00
170 Martin Nance RC	.60	1.50
171 Mathias Kiwanuka RC	.75	2.00
172 Matt Bernstein RC	.50	1.25
173 Matt Leinart RC	.75	2.00
174 Maurice Drew RC	1.25	3.00
175 Maurice Stovall RC	.50	1.25
176 Michael Huff RC	.60	1.50
177 Michael Robinson RC	.60	1.50
178 Mike Hass RC	.60	1.50
179 Omar Jacobs RC	.50	1.25
180 Orien Harris RC	.60	1.50
181 Owen Daniels RC	.75	2.00
182 Miles Austin RC	2.00	5.00
183 Reggie Bush RC	1.50	4.00
184 Reggie McNeal RC	.60	1.50
185 Santonio Holmes RC	1.00	2.50
186 Sinorice Moss RC	.75	2.00
187 Skyler Green RC	.50	1.25
188 Tony Scheffler RC	.75	2.00
189 Tamba Hali RC	.75	2.00
190 Tarvaris Jackson RC	.75	2.00
191 Thomas Howard RC	.60	1.50
192 Tim Day RC	.60	1.50
193 Todd Watkins RC	.50	1.25
194 Travis Wilson RC	.50	1.25
195 Tye Hill RC	.50	1.25
196 Vernon Davis RC	1.00	2.50
197 Vince Young RC	1.00	2.50
198 Wali Lundy RC	.60	1.50
199 Will Blackmon RC	.60	1.50
200 Winston Justice RC	.60	1.50

2006 Fleer Gold

*VETERANS 1-100: 5X TO 12X BASIC CARDS
*ROOKIES 101-200: 1X TO 2.5X BASIC CARDS

2006 Fleer Silver

*VETERANS 1-100: 3X TO 8X BASIC CARDS
*ROOKIES 101-200: .6X TO 1.5X BASIC CARDS

2006 Fleer Autographics

AUAG Antonio Gates		
AUAV Jason Avant	5.00	12.00
AUBA Ronde Barber		
AUBE Braylon Edwards		
AUBL Byron Leftwich		
AUBY Dominique Byrd	6.00	15.00
AUCG Chad Greenway	8.00	20.00
AUCJ Chad Jackson	5.00	12.00
AUCW Cadillac Williams		
AUDB Drew Bledsoe		
AUDF D'Brickashaw Ferguson	8.00	20.00
AUDO Drew Olson		
AUDR DeMeco Ryans	10.00	25.00
AUDW DeAngelo Williams SP	25.00	60.00
AUGR Gerald Riggs	6.00	15.00
AUHB Hank Baskett		
AUJC Jay Cutler SP		
AUJH Jerome Harrison	8.00	20.00
AUKJ Keyshawn Johnson		
AUKO Kyle Orton	8.00	20.00
AULE Matt Leinart SP		
AULJ Larry Johnson SP	12.00	30.00
AULM Laurence Maroney		
AULP Leonard Pope	8.00	20.00
AULT LaDainian Tomlinson SP		
AULW Leon Washington	15.00	30.00
AUMD Maurice Drew	30.00	60.00
AUMK Mathias Kiwanuka	8.00	20.00
AUML Marcedes Lewis	8.00	20.00
AUMO Sinorice Moss SP	8.00	20.00
AURB Reggie Bush SP	40.00	100.00
AURJ Rudi Johnson	6.00	15.00
AURM Reggie McNeal	6.00	15.00
AURY Ryan Moats	5.00	12.00
AUTH T.J. Houshmandzadeh		
AUTJ Thomas Jones	6.00	15.00
AUTW Travis Wilson	5.00	12.00
AUWH LenDale White SP		
AUWI Jason Witten	20.00	40.00

2006 Fleer Fabrics

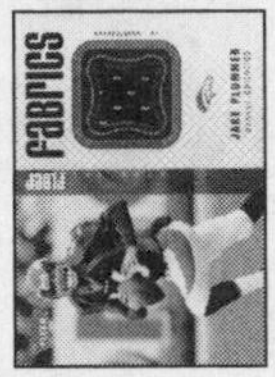

FFAB Aaron Brooks	2.50	6.00
FFAC Alge Crumpler	2.50	6.00
FFAG Ahman Green	2.50	6.00
FFAL Ashley Lelie	2.50	6.00
FFAR Antwaan Randle El	3.00	8.00
FFBL Byron Leftwich	2.50	6.00
FFBR Troy Brown	2.50	6.00
FFBU Marc Bulger	2.50	6.00
FFBW Brian Westbrook	2.50	6.00
FFCF Charlie Frye	4.00	10.00
FFCM Curtis Martin	4.00	10.00
FFCP Chad Pennington	2.50	6.00
FFCW Cadillac Williams	4.00	10.00
FFDB Drew Brees	2.50	6.00
FFDC David Carr	2.50	6.00
FFDD Domanick Davis SP	2.50	6.00
FFDM Deuce McAllister	2.50	6.00
FFEJ Edgerrin James	4.00	10.00
FFGR Trent Green	2.50	6.00
FFHO Torry Holt SP	2.50	6.00
FFIB Isaac Bruce	2.50	6.00
FFJD Jake Delhomme SP	3.00	8.00
FFJG Jeff Garcia	2.50	6.00
FFJJ Julius Jones	4.00	10.00
FFJL Jamal Lewis	2.50	6.00
FFJM Josh McCown	2.50	6.00
FFJO Larry Johnson	4.00	10.00
FFJP Jake Plummer	2.50	6.00
FFJS Jeremy Shockey	4.00	10.00
FFJW Javon Walker	2.50	6.00
FFKJ Kevin Jones	4.00	10.00
FFKM Keenan McCardell	2.50	6.00
FFKO Kyle Orton	2.50	6.00
FFLA LaVar Arrington	4.00	10.00
FFMB Mark Brunell	3.00	8.00
FFMF Marshall Faulk	2.50	6.00
FFMH Matt Hasselbeck	2.50	6.00
FFPB Plaxico Burress	2.50	6.00
FFPM Peyton Manning SP	8.00	20.00
FFPO Jerry Porter	2.50	6.00
FFPR Philip Rivers	4.00	10.00
FFRB Ronnie Brown	4.00	10.00
FFRG Rex Grossman	2.50	6.00
FFRM Randy Moss	4.00	10.00
FFRW Ricky Williams	2.50	6.00
FFSD Stephen Davis	2.50	6.00
FFSJ Steven Jackson	4.00	10.00
FFSM Steve McNair	4.00	10.00
FFTA Tatum Bell	2.50	6.00
FFTB Tom Brady SP	8.00	20.00
FFTG Tony Gonzalez SP	2.50	6.00
FFTH Todd Heap	2.50	6.00
FFTO Terrell Owens	4.00	10.00
FFTW Troy Williamson	2.50	6.00
FFWA Reggie Wayne	2.50	6.00
FFWO Charles Woodson	2.50	6.00
FFZT Zach Thomas	4.00	10.00
FFEJ2 Edgerrin James	4.00	10.00

2006 Fleer Faces of the Game

COMPLETE SET (10)	8.00	20.00
FGBA Tiki Barber	1.00	2.50
FGBF Brett Favre	2.00	5.00
FGCJ Chad Johnson	.75	2.00
FGDM Donovan McNabb	1.00	2.50
FGHW Hines Ward	1.00	2.50
FGLT LaDainian Tomlinson	1.00	2.50
FGMV Michael Vick	1.00	2.50
FGPM Peyton Manning	1.50	4.00
FGSA Shaun Alexander	.75	2.00
FGTB Tom Brady	1.50	4.00

2006 Fleer Fantastic 40

RANDOM INSERTS IN WAL-MART PACKS		
F40AB Anquan Boldin	.50	1.25
F40AG Antonio Gates	.60	1.50
F40BA Tiki Barber	.60	1.50
F40BF Brett Favre	1.25	3.00
F40BR Ben Roethlisberger	.75	2.00
F40CC Chris Chambers	.50	1.25
F40CD Corey Dillon	.50	1.25
F40CJ Chad Johnson	.50	1.25
F40CM Curtis Martin	.60	1.50
F40CP Carson Palmer	.60	1.50
F40CW Cadillac Williams	.50	1.25
F40DC Daunte Culpepper	.50	1.25
F40DM Donovan McNabb	.60	1.50
F40EJ Edgerrin James	.50	1.25
F40EM Eli Manning	.75	2.00
F40HA Matt Hasselbeck	.50	1.25
F40HW Hines Ward	.60	1.50
F40JG Joey Galloway	.50	1.25
F40JJ Julius Jones	.40	1.00
F40JL Jamal Lewis	.50	1.25
F40JP Jake Plummer	.50	1.25
F40LF Larry Fitzgerald	.60	1.50
F40LJ Larry Johnson	.50	1.25
F40LT LaDainian Tomlinson	.60	1.50
F40MH Marvin Harrison	.60	1.50
F40MV Michael Vick	.60	1.50
F40PM Peyton Manning	1.00	2.50
F40PO Clinton Portis	.60	1.50
F40RB Ronnie Brown	.60	1.50
F40RJ Rudi Johnson	.50	1.25
F40RM Randy Moss	.60	1.50
F40RW Reggie Wayne	.50	1.25
F40SA Shaun Alexander	.50	1.25
F40SM Santana Moss	.50	1.25
F40SS Steve Smith	.60	1.50
F40TB Tom Brady	1.00	2.50
F40TG Tony Gonzalez	.50	1.25
F40TH Torry Holt	.50	1.25
F40TO Terrell Owens	.60	1.50
F40WD Warrick Dunn	.50	1.25

2006 Fleer Fantasy Standouts

COMPLETE SET (20)	10.00	25.00
FSBR Tom Brady	1.50	4.00
FSCJ Chad Johnson	.75	2.00
FSCP Clinton Portis	1.00	2.50
FSDM Donovan McNabb	1.00	2.50
FSEJ Edgerrin James	.75	2.00
FSEM Eli Manning	1.25	3.00
FSHA Marvin Harrison	1.00	2.50
FSJO LaMont Jordan	.75	2.00
FSLF Larry Fitzgerald	1.00	2.50
FSLJ Larry Johnson	.75	2.00
FSLT LaDainian Tomlinson	1.00	2.50
FSMH Matt Hasselbeck	.75	2.00
FSPA Carson Palmer	1.00	2.50
FSPM Peyton Manning	1.50	4.00
FSRJ Rudi Johnson	.75	2.00
FSRM Randy Moss	1.00	2.50
FSSA Shaun Alexander	.75	2.00
FSSS Steve Smith	1.00	2.50
FSTB Tiki Barber	1.00	2.50
FSTH Torry Holt	.75	2.00

2006 Fleer Fresh Faces

COMPLETE SET (18)	15.00	40.00
FRAH A.J. Hawk	.75	2.00
FRCJ Chad Jackson	.50	1.25
FRCR Brodie Croyle	.75	2.00
FRDF D'Brickashaw Ferguson	.75	2.00
FRDW DeAngelo Williams	1.00	2.50
FRJA Joseph Addai	.75	2.00
FRJC Jay Cutler	1.50	4.00
FRLM Laurence Maroney	.60	1.50
FRLW LenDale White	.60	1.50
FRMH Michael Huff	.60	1.50
FRML Matt Leinart	.75	2.00
FRMS Maurice Stovall	.50	1.25
FRMW Mario Williams	.75	2.00
FRRB Reggie Bush	1.50	4.00
FRSH Santonio Holmes	1.00	2.50
FRSM Sinorice Moss	.75	2.00
FRVD Vernon Davis	1.00	2.50
FRVY Vince Young	1.00	2.50

2006 Fleer Seek and Destroy

COMPLETE SET (10)	6.00	15.00
SDBU Brian Urlacher	1.25	3.00
SDCB Champ Bailey	1.00	2.50
SDDF Dwight Freeney	1.00	2.50
SDJP Julius Peppers	1.00	2.50
SDJV Jonathan Vilma	1.00	2.50
SDMS Michael Strahan	1.00	2.50
SDRL Ray Lewis	1.25	3.00
SDSM Shawne Merriman	1.00	2.50
SDTB Tedy Bruschi	1.25	3.00
SDTP Troy Polamalu	1.50	4.00

2006 Fleer Stretching the Field

COMPLETE SET (10)	6.00	15.00
SFAB Anquan Boldin	.75	2.00
SFCJ Chad Johnson	.75	2.00
SFJG Joey Galloway	.75	2.00
SFLF Larry Fitzgerald	1.00	2.50
SFMH Marvin Harrison	1.00	2.50
SFPB Plaxico Burress	.75	2.00
SFRM Randy Moss	1.00	2.50
SFSM Santana Moss	.75	2.00
SFSS Steve Smith	1.00	2.50
SFTH Torry Holt	.75	2.00

2006 Fleer The Franchise

COMPLETE SET (32)	12.00	30.00
TFAS Alex Smith QB	1.00	2.50
TFBF Brett Favre	2.00	5.00
TFBJ Brad Johnson	.75	2.00
TFBL Byron Leftwich	.75	2.00
TFBR Ben Roethlisberger	1.25	3.00
TFBU Brian Urlacher	1.00	2.50
TFCF Charlie Frye	.75	2.00
TFCP Carson Palmer	1.00	2.50
TFCW Cadillac Williams	.75	2.00
TFDC David Carr	.60	1.50
TFDM Deuce McAllister	.75	2.00
TFEM Eli Manning	1.25	3.00
TFJJ Julius Jones	.60	1.50
TFJP Jake Plummer	.75	2.00
TFKJ Kevin Jones	.60	1.50
TFLF Larry Fitzgerald	1.00	2.50
TFLJ Larry Johnson	.75	2.00
TFLT LaDainian Tomlinson	1.00	2.50
TFMB Marc Bulger	.75	2.00
TFMC Donovan McNabb	1.00	2.50
TFMV Michael Vick	1.00	2.50
TFPE Chad Pennington	.75	2.00
TFPM Peyton Manning	1.50	4.00
TFPO Clinton Portis	1.00	2.50
TFRB Ronnie Brown	1.00	2.50
TFRL Ray Lewis	1.00	2.50
TFRM Randy Moss	1.00	2.50
TFSA Shaun Alexander	.75	2.00
TFSM Steve McNair	.75	2.00
TFSS Steve Smith	1.00	2.50
TFTB Tom Brady	1.50	4.00
TFWM Willis McGahee	.75	2.00

2002 Fleer Collectibles

This set of cards was issued one card at a time packaged with a 1:55 scale Howler die-cast car. Each card and die-cast combo was issued together in a blister style package. The cards feature foil highlights and a "Fleer Collectibles" logo on the front. The cardbacks include a brief player bio and a large card number at the top. One card and die-cast was produced for each NFL team.

COMPLETE SET (32)	25.00	60.00
1 Michael Vick	1.50	4.00
2 Brian Urlacher	1.00	2.50
3 Emmitt Smith	2.50	6.00
4 Mike McMahon	.60	1.50
5 Brett Favre	2.50	6.00
6 Kurt Warner	1.00	2.50
7 Daunte Culpepper	.75	2.00
8 Aaron Brooks	.75	2.00
9 Tiki Barber	1.00	2.50
10 Donovan McNabb	1.00	2.50
11 Jake Plummer	.75	2.00
12 Jeff Garcia	.75	2.00
13 Keyshawn Johnson	.75	2.00
14 Stephen Davis	.75	2.00
15 Eric Moulds	.75	2.00
16 Corey Dillon	.75	2.00
17 Ray Lewis	1.00	2.50
18 Brian Griese	.75	2.00
19 Peyton Manning	2.00	5.00
20 Eddie George	.75	2.00
21 Tony Gonzalez	1.00	2.50
22 Tim Brown	1.00	2.50
23 Chris Chambers	.75	2.00
24 Tom Brady	2.50	6.00
25 Curtis Martin	1.00	2.50
26 Jerome Bettis	1.00	2.50
27 LaDainian Tomlinson	1.25	3.00
28 Trent Dilfer	.75	2.00
29 Mark Brunell	.75	2.00
30 Muhsin Muhammad	.75	2.00
31 Tim Couch	.60	1.50
32 Tony Boselli	.75	2.00

2004 Fleer Authentic Player Autographs

Cards from this set were issued as replacements for a variety of older autograph exchange cards from different Fleer football products. Each card includes a cut signature of the featured player with his name above the player image and the notation "Player Autograph Card." The Fleer logo appears at the top of the card but no specific Fleer brand is mentioned. Some players have more than one serial numbered version as noted below while others feature a swatch of jersey as well as the signature. However, on some cards, little or no difference can be found between the serial numbered versions except for the serial numbering while others were printed with a variation in the foil color used.

BL1 Byron Leftwich JSY/50	10.00	25.00
BL2 Byron Leftwich JSY/75	10.00	25.00
DC1 David Carr/25	12.00	30.00
DC2 David Carr/75	10.00	25.00
DC3 David Carr/100	10.00	25.00
DC4 David Carr/250	8.00	20.00
JL1 Jamal Lewis/25	8.00	20.00
JL2 Jamal Lewis/100	8.00	20.00
MH1 Matt Hasselbeck/50	10.00	25.00
MH2 Matt Hasselbeck/75	10.00	25.00
MH3 Matt Hasselbeck/100	10.00	25.00
MV1 Michael Vick JSY/25	25.00	50.00
MV2 Michael Vick JSY/50	25.00	50.00
MV3 Michael Vick JSY/100	25.00	50.00

2005 Fleer Authentic Player Autographs

Cards from this set first hit the secondary market in Spring 2005. They were issued as replacements for a variety of older autograph exchange cards from different Fleer football products. Each card includes a cut signature of the featured player with his first inital and last name above the player image and the simple set name "Authentic Player Autograph." The Fleer logo appears at the bottom of the card but no specific Fleer brand is mentioned. Most players have more than serial numbered version as noted below. However little or no difference can be found between the versions except for the serial numbering.

AM2 Archie Manning/150	7.50	20.00
BR1 Ben Roethlisberger/50	90.00	150.00
CC1 Chris Chambers/50	5.00	12.00
CC2 Chris Chambers/150	5.00	12.00
CC4 Chris Chambers/300	5.00	12.00
DH1 Drew Henson/50	7.50	20.00
DH2 Drew Henson/150	7.50	20.00
DS2 Donte Stallworth/150	5.00	12.00
JM1 Josh McCown/50	6.00	15.00
JM2 Josh McCown/150	6.00	15.00
JM3 Josh McCown/300	6.00	15.00
KW1 Kellen Winslow Jr./50	7.50	20.00
KW2 Kellen Winslow Jr./150	7.50	20.00
WM1 Willis McGahee/50	7.50	20.00
AM1 Archie Manning/50	7.50	20.00
CC3 Chris Chambers JSY/100	6.00	15.00
DS1 Donte Stallworth/50	6.00	15.00
SJ1 Steven Jackson/50	10.00	25.00
JMJ2 Josh McCown JSY/100	7.50	20.00
JMJ1 Josh McCown JSY/25	7.50	20.00

2002 Fleer Authentix

Released in June 2002, this 140-card base set includes 100 veterans and 40 rookies. The rookies are numbered to 1,250. Some Hot Boxes exist which contain a bonus pack with a memorabilia card of the team noted on the box. The card fronts feature a color action shot surrounded by a white border. The background resembles that of a game ticket. Special "Home Team Edition" foil boxes were produced for these teams: Dallas Cowboys, Green Bay Packers, San Francisco 49ers, Pittsburgh Steelers, Miami Dolphins, and Philadelphia Eagles. Each of the Home Team boxes included additional cards from the second series (cards #141-230) of players from the team featured in that box as well as randomly seeded parallel inserts for that team. Due to market scarcity, the basic issue Hometown Heroes subset cards (#141-230) are not priced below.

COMP.SET w/o SP's (100)	7.50	20.00
1 Jake Plummer	.25	.60
2 Chad Pennington	.30	.75
3 Corey Bradford	.20	.50
4 Mike Anderson	.25	.60
5 Donovan McNabb	.30	.75
6 Brian Griese	.25	.60
7 Keyshawn Johnson	.25	.60
8 Michael Strahan	.30	.75
9 Rod Smith	.25	.60
10 Warren Sapp	.25	.60
11 Joe Horn	.25	.60
12 Anthony Thomas	.25	.60
13 Jeff Garcia	.25	.60
14 Michael Bennett	.25	.60
15 Richard Huntley	.20	.50
16 Doug Flutie	.30	.75
17 Tony Gonzalez	.30	.75
18 David Boston	.20	.50
19 Freddie Mitchell	.20	.50
20 Terrell Davis	.30	.75
21 Torry Holt	.30	.75
22 Drew Bledsoe	.30	.75
23 Peter Warrick	.25	.60
24 Darrell Jackson	.25	.60
25 Chris Chambers	.25	.60
26 Marvin Harrison	.30	.75
27 Warrick Dunn	.25	.60
28 Tim Brown	.30	.75
29 Terry Glenn	.25	.60
30 Rod Gardner	.20	.50
31 Aaron Brooks	.25	.60
32 Johnnie Morton	.25	.60
33 Steve McNair	.30	.75
34 Deuce McAllister	.25	.60
35 Emmitt Smith	.75	2.00
36 Isaac Bruce	.30	.75
37 Cris Carter	.30	.75
38 Marty Booker	.25	.60
39 Garrison Hearst	.25	.60
40 Jay Fiedler	.25	.60
41 Eric Moulds	.25	.60
42 Hines Ward	.30	.75
43 Peyton Manning	.60	1.50
44 Trent Dilfer	.25	.60
45 Ricky Williams	.25	.60
46 Quincy Carter	.20	.50
47 Kurt Warner	.30	.75
48 Tom Brady	.75	2.00
49 Chris Weinke	.20	.50
50 LaDainian Tomlinson	.40	1.00
51 Antowain Smith	.25	.60
52 Corey Dillon	.25	.60
53 Shaun Alexander	.25	.60
54 Daunte Culpepper	.25	.60
55 Ray Lewis	.30	.75
56 Kordell Stewart	.25	.60
57 Trent Green	.25	.60
58 Chris Redman	.20	.50
59 Plaxico Burress	.25	.60
60 Fred Taylor	.25	.60
61 Snoop Minnis	.20	.50
62 Jerry Rice	.60	1.50
63 James Allen	.20	.50
64 Peerless Price	.20	.50
65 Curtis Martin	.30	.75
66 Mike McMahon	.20	.50
67 Brad Johnson	.25	.60
68 Troy Brown	.25	.60
69 Jamal Lewis	.25	.60
70 Jerome Bettis	.30	.75
71 Dominic Rhodes	.25	.60
72 Az-Zahir Hakim	.20	.50
73 Rich Gannon	.25	.60
74 Ahman Green	.25	.60
75 Eddie George	.25	.60
76 Tim Couch	.20	.50
77 Ricky Watters	.25	.60
78 Randy Moss	.30	.75
79 Brian Urlacher	.30	.75
80 Terrell Owens	.30	.75
81 Jimmy Smith	.25	.60
82 Travis Henry	.20	.50
83 Drew Brees	.50	1.25
84 Priest Holmes	.30	.75
85 Michael Vick	.50	1.25
86 James Thrash	.25	.60
87 Jamie Sharper	.25	.60
88 Marcus Robinson	.25	.60
89 Laveranues Coles	.25	.60
90 Brett Favre	.75	2.00
91 Stephen Davis	.25	.60
92 Tiki Barber	.30	.75
93 Kevin Johnson	.20	.50
94 Marshall Faulk	.30	.75
95 Mark Brunell	.25	.60
96 Jamal Anderson	.25	.60
97 Duce Staley	.25	.60
98 Edgerrin James	.25	.60
99 Kevan Barlow	.20	.50
100 Kerry Collins	.25	.60
101 David Carr RC	2.50	6.00
102 Joey Harrington RC	2.50	6.00
103 William Green RC	2.00	5.00
104 Donte Stallworth RC	2.50	6.00
105 Ashley Lelie RC	2.00	5.00
106 Jabar Gaffney RC	2.50	6.00
107 Antonio Bryant RC	2.50	6.00
108 Josh Reed RC	2.00	5.00
109 Daniel Graham RC	2.00	5.00
110 Reche Caldwell RC	2.50	6.00
111 Jeremy Shockey RC	4.00	10.00
112 T.J. Duckett RC	2.50	6.00
113 Marquise Walker RC	1.50	4.00
114 Lamar Gordon RC	2.00	5.00
115 DeShaun Foster RC	2.50	6.00
116 Patrick Ramsey RC	2.50	6.00
117 Andre Davis RC	2.00	5.00
118 Ron Johnson RC	2.00	5.00
119 Luke Staley RC	1.50	4.00
120 Clinton Portis RC	3.00	8.00
121 Freddie Milons RC	1.50	4.00
122 Javon Walker RC	2.50	6.00
123 David Garrard RC	3.00	8.00
124 Kurt Kittner RC	1.50	4.00
125 Adrian Peterson RC	2.50	6.00
126 Roy Williams RC	2.50	6.00
127 Maurice Morris RC	2.00	5.00
128 Cliff Russell RC	1.50	4.00
129 Antwaan Randle El RC	2.50	6.00
130 Verron Haynes RC	1.50	4.00
131 Eric Crouch RC	2.50	6.00
132 Kahlil Hill RC	1.50	4.00
133 Brian Westbrook RC	4.00	10.00
134 Travis Stephens RC	1.50	4.00
135 Julius Peppers RC	5.00	12.00
136 Quentin Jammer RC	2.50	6.00
137 Rohan Davey RC	2.50	6.00
138 Ladell Betts RC	2.50	6.00
139 Tim Carter RC	2.00	5.00
140 Josh McCown RC	2.50	6.00
141 Emmitt Smith HH	2.50	6.00
142 Quincy Carter HH	.60	1.50
143 Joey Galloway HH	.75	2.00
144 Anthony Wright HH	.60	1.50
145 La'Roi Glover HH	.60	1.50
146 Greg Ellis HH	.60	1.50
147 Dexter Coakley HH	.60	1.50
148 Dat Nguyen HH	.60	1.50
149 Darren Woodson HH	.75	2.00
150 Troy Hambrick HH	.60	1.50
151 Larry Allen HH	.60	1.50
152 Ebenezer Ekuban HH	.60	1.50
153 Reggie Swinton HH	.60	1.50
154 Michael Wiley HH	.60	1.50
155 Duane Hawthorne HH	.60	1.50
156 Brett Favre HH	2.50	6.00
157 Ahman Green HH	.75	2.00
158 Terry Glenn HH	.75	2.00
159 Donald Driver HH	1.00	2.50
160 Ryan Longwell HH	.60	1.50
161 Nate Wayne HH	.60	1.50
162 Darren Sharper HH	.75	2.00
163 Kabeer Gbaja-Biamila HH	.75	2.00
164 Vonnie Holliday HH	.60	1.50
165 Bubba Franks HH	.75	2.00
166 LeRoy Butler HH	.75	2.00
167 Dorsey Levens HH	.75	2.00
168 William Henderson HH	.75	2.00
169 Tyrone Williams HH	.60	1.50
170 Robert Ferguson HH	.75	2.00
171 Jeff Garcia HH	.75	2.00
172 Garrison Hearst HH	.75	2.00
173 Terrell Owens HH	1.00	2.50
174 Kevan Barlow HH	.60	1.50
175 J.J. Stokes HH	.60	1.50
176 Tai Streets HH	.60	1.50
177 Eric Johnson HH	.60	1.50
178 Fred Beasley HH	.60	1.50
179 Tim Rattay HH	.75	2.00
180 Derek Smith HH RC	1.00	2.50
181 Zack Bronson HH	.60	1.50
182 Ahmed Plummer HH	.60	1.50
183 Bryant Young HH	.60	1.50
184 Vinny Sutherland HH	.60	1.50
185 Andre Carter HH	.60	1.50
186 Kordell Stewart HH	.75	2.00
187 Jerome Bettis HH	1.00	2.50
188 Hines Ward HH	1.00	2.50
189 Plaxico Burress HH	.75	2.00
190 Kendrell Bell HH	.60	1.50
191 Amos Zereoue HH	.60	1.50
192 Jason Gildon HH	.75	2.00
193 Chad Scott HH	.60	1.50
194 Joey Porter HH	.75	2.00
195 Hank Poteat HH	.60	1.50
196 Troy Edwards HH	.60	1.50
197 Lee Flowers HH	.60	1.50
198 Aaron Smith HH RC	6.00	15.00
199 Dan Kreider HH RC	6.00	15.00
200 Tommy Maddox HH	.75	2.00
201 Jay Fiedler HH	.75	2.00
202 Ricky Williams HH	.75	2.00
203 Chris Chambers HH	.75	2.00
204 Oronde Gadsden HH	.60	1.50
205 Travis Minor HH	.60	1.50
206 Zach Thomas HH	1.00	2.50
207 Jason Taylor HH	.75	2.00
208 Olindo Mare HH	.60	1.50
209 Sam Madison HH	.60	1.50
210 Patrick Surtain HH	.60	1.50
211 Tim Bowens HH	.60	1.50
212 Daryl Gardener HH	.60	1.50
213 Dedric Ward HH	.60	1.50
214 James McKnight HH	.60	1.50
215 Deon Dyer HH	.60	1.50
216 Donovan McNabb HH	1.00	2.50
217 Duce Staley HH	.75	2.00
218 James Thrash HH	.75	2.00
219 Correll Buckhalter HH	.75	2.00
220 Freddie Mitchell HH	.60	1.50
221 Chad Lewis HH	.60	1.50
222 Hugh Douglas HH	.60	1.50
223 Brian Dawkins HH	.75	2.00
224 David Akers HH	.60	1.50
225 Troy Vincent HH	.75	2.00
226 Bobby Taylor HH	.75	2.00
227 Rod Smart HH RC	1.00	2.50
228 Todd Pinkston HH	.60	1.50
229 Corey Simon HH	.60	1.50
230 A.J. Feeley HH	.60	1.50

2002 Fleer Authentix Front Row

*VETS 1-100: 4X TO 10X BASIC CARDS
*ROOKIES 101-140: .8X TO 2X
STATED PRINT RUN 150 SER.#'d SETS

2002 Fleer Authentix Second Row

*VETS 1-100: 3X TO 8X BASIC CARDS
*ROOKIES 101-140: .6X TO 1.5X
STATED PRINT RUN 250 SER.#'d SETS

2002 Fleer Authentix Buy Backs

1 Kevan Barlow 01Leg/42
4 Quincy Carter 01Leg/41
6 Chris Chambers 01Leg/40
8 Robert Ferguson 01Leg/58
9 Bubba Franks 01E-X/20
10 Freddie Mitchell 01Leg/42
12 Todd Pinkston 01E-X/20

2002 Fleer Authentix Hometown Heroes

COMPLETE SET (15)	10.00	25.00
STATED ODDS 1:6		
1 Michael Vick	1.25	3.00
2 William Green	.60	1.50
3 Donte Stallworth	.75	2.00
4 Ashley Lelie	.60	1.50
5 Anthony Thomas	.60	1.50
6 Eddie George	.60	1.50
7 Peyton Manning	1.50	4.00
8 Ricky Williams	.60	1.50
9 Tom Brady	2.00	5.00
10 Kurt Warner	.75	2.00
11 Daunte Culpepper	.60	1.50
12 David Carr	.75	2.00
13 Joey Harrington	.75	2.00
14 Edgerrin James	.60	1.50
15 Randy Moss	.75	2.00

2002 Fleer Authentix Hometown Heroes Memorabilia

ONE PER HOME TEAM EDITION BOX
*CHINATOWN/50: .8X TO 2X BASIC JSY
49ERS CHINATOWN PRINT RUN 50
UNPRICED 49ERS FISHER.WHARF #'d TO 5
UNPRICED 49ERS LOMBARD ST. #'d TO 1
*LOWER.GRNVL/25: 1X TO 2.5X BASIC JSY
COWBOY LOWER GRNVILLE #'d TO 25
UNPRICED COWBOY HIGH.PARK #'d TO 5
UNPRICED COWBOY WEST END #'d TO 1
*FT.LAUDER/50: .8X TO 2X BASIC JSY
DOLPHIN FT.LAUDERDALE #'d TO 50
UNPRICED DOLPHIN S.BEACH #'d TO 5
UNPRICED DOLPHIN OCEAN DR.#'d TO 1
*SOUTH ST/25: 1X TO 2.5X BASIC JSY
EAGLE SOUTH ST.PRINT RUN 25
UNPRICED EAGLE MANAYUNK #'d TO 5
UNPRICED EAGLE PENN'S LAND. #'d TO 1
*KEWAUNEE/25: 1X TO 2.5X BASIC JSY
PACKERS KEWAUNEE #'d TO 25
UNPRICED PACKER IOLA #'d TO 5
UNPRICED PACKER BAY BEACH #'d TO 1
*OHIO RIVER/25: 1X TO 2.5X BASIC JSY
STEELER OHIO RIVER #'d TO 25
UNPRICED STEELER ALLEGHENY #'d TO 5
UNPRICED STEELER MONGHLA #'d TO 1

HHM49 Jeff Garcia	10.00	25.00
Terrell Owens		
HHMBD Brian Dawkins	6.00	15.00
HHMBF Brett Favre	20.00	50.00
HHMBS Bart Starr Pants	20.00	50.00
HHMCO Troy Aikman	25.00	60.00
Emmitt Smith		
HHMDL Dorsey Levens SP	6.00	15.00
HHMDM2 Donovan McNabb	8.00	20.00
HHMDM1 Dan Marino	20.00	50.00
HHMDO Jason Taylor	8.00	20.00
Sam Madison		
HHMDS Duce Staley	6.00	15.00
HHMEA Brian Dawkins	8.00	20.00
Troy Vincent		
HHMES Emmitt Smith	20.00	50.00
HHMJB Jerome Bettis	8.00	20.00
HHMJG Jeff Garcia	6.00	15.00
HHMJR Jerry Rice	15.00	40.00
HHMJT Jason Taylor	6.00	15.00
HHMKS Kordell Stewart	6.00	15.00
HHMPA Brett Favre	25.00	60.00
Dorsey Levens		
HHMPB Plaxico Burress	6.00	15.00
HHMPH Paul Hornung Pants	12.00	30.00
HHMRN Ray Nitschke Pants	15.00	40.00
HHMRS Roger Staubach	15.00	40.00
HHMSM Sam Madison		
HHMST Kordell Stewart	10.00	25.00
Jerome Bettis		
HHMTA Troy Aikman	12.00	30.00
HHMTD Tony Dorsett Pants	10.00	25.00
HHMTO Terrell Owens	8.00	20.00
HHMTP Todd Pinkston SP	5.00	12.00
HHMTV Troy Vincent	6.00	15.00
HHMZT Zach Thomas	8.00	20.00

2002 Fleer Authentix Jersey Authentix Ripped

STATED ODDS 1:11
*UNRIPPED/50: .8X TO 2X BASIC JSY
UNRIPPED PRINT RUN 50 SER.#'d SETS
*RIPPED PRO BOWL: .6X TO 1.5X BASIC JSY
RIPPED PB RANDOM INSERTS IN PACKS
UNPRICED UNRIPPED PRO BOWL #'d TO 1

JAAF Antonio Freeman	5.00	12.00
JABF Brett Favre	12.00	30.00
JABU Brian Urlacher	5.00	12.00
JACD Corey Dillon	4.00	10.00
JACP Chad Pennington	5.00	12.00
JACW Charles Woodson	5.00	12.00
JADB1 David Boston	3.00	8.00
JADB2 Drew Bledsoe	5.00	12.00
JADM Donovan McNabb	5.00	12.00
JADW Dez White	3.00	8.00
JAEJ Edgerrin James	4.00	10.00
JAEM1 Ed McCaffrey	4.00	10.00
JAEM2 Eric Moulds	4.00	10.00
JAGC Germane Crowell	3.00	8.00
JAIB Isaac Bruce	5.00	12.00
JAJA Jamal Anderson	4.00	10.00
JAJG Jeff Garcia	4.00	10.00
JAJS Jimmy Smith	4.00	10.00
JAKJ Kevin Johnson	3.00	8.00
JAKM Keenan McCardell	4.00	10.00
JAKW Kurt Warner	5.00	12.00
JAMF Marshall Faulk	5.00	12.00
JAPW Peter Warrick	4.00	10.00
JARD Ron Dayne	4.00	10.00
JASD Stephen Davis	4.00	10.00
JATB Tim Brown	5.00	12.00
JATH Torry Holt	5.00	12.00
JATP Todd Pinkston	3.00	8.00
JATS Thomas Jones	5.00	12.00
JAWS Warren Sapp	4.00	10.00

2002 Fleer Authentix Stadium Classics

COMPLETE SET (15)	20.00	50.00
STATED ODDS 1:12		
1 Donovan McNabb	1.25	3.00
2 Marshall Faulk	1.25	3.00
3 Mark Brunell	1.00	2.50
4 Brett Favre	3.00	8.00
5 Emmitt Smith	3.00	8.00
6 Kurt Warner	1.25	3.00
7 Daunte Culpepper	1.00	2.50
8 Jerry Rice	2.50	6.00
9 Tim Couch	.75	2.00
10 Edgerrin James	1.00	2.50
11 Randy Moss	1.25	3.00
12 Fred Taylor	1.00	2.50
13 Brian Urlacher	1.25	3.00
14 Jeff Garcia	1.00	2.50
15 Shaun Alexander	1.00	2.50

2002 Fleer Authentix Stadium Classics Memorabilia

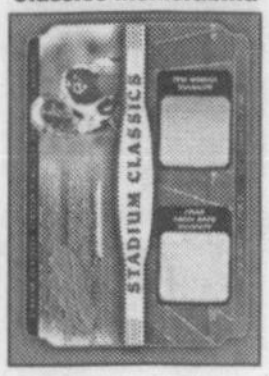

STATED ODDS 1:58
*GOLD/100: .6X TO 1.5X BASIC JSY
GOLD STATED PRINT RUN 100

SCBA Brian Urlacher	5.00	12.00
SCBF Brett Favre	12.00	30.00
SCDC Daunte Culpepper	4.00	10.00
SCDM Donovan McNabb	5.00	12.00
SCEJ Edgerrin James	4.00	10.00
SCES Emmitt Smith	12.00	30.00
SCFT Fred Taylor	4.00	10.00
SCJG Jeff Garcia	4.00	10.00
SCJR Jerry Rice	10.00	25.00
SCKW Kurt Warner	5.00	12.00
SCMB Mark Brunell	4.00	10.00
SCMF Marshall Faulk	5.00	12.00
SCRM Randy Moss	5.00	12.00
SCTC Tim Couch	3.00	8.00

2002 Fleer Authentix Ticket for Four

STATED PRINT 200 SER.#'d SETS		
1 Brett Favre	20.00	50.00
Daunte Culpepper		
Donovan McNabb		
Tim Couch		
2 Bo Jackson	10.00	25.00
Ricky Williams		
Marshall Faulk		
Stephen Davis		
3 Terrell Owens	8.00	20.00
David Boston		
Rod Smith		
Tim Brown		
4 Junior Seau	8.00	20.00
Bruce Smith		
Brian Urlacher		
Warren Sapp		
5 Kurt Warner	8.00	20.00
Marshall Faulk		
Torry Holt		
Isaac Bruce		

2003 Fleer Authentix

Released in July of 2003, this set consists of 165 cards, including 100 veterans, 30 rookies, and 35 Hometown Heroes subset cards. The rookies are serial numbered to 1250. The Hometown Heroes cards are only available in Home Team Edition boxes. Boxes featured 24 packs of 5 cards, with an SRP of $3.99. In addition to hobby boxes, Fleer also produced Home Team Edition boxes for the Dallas Cowboys, Green Bay Packers, New York Giants, Oakland Raiders, and Pittsburgh Steelers. Each Home Team Editon box contained one special pack with a Hometown Heroes memorabilia card, along with three Hometown Heroes subset cards.

COMP.SET w/o SP's (100)	7.50	20.00
1 Donovan McNabb	.30	.75
2 Tim Brown	.30	.75
3 Donald Driver	.30	.75
4 Eddie George	.25	.60
5 Curtis Martin	.30	.75
6 Chad Hutchinson	.20	.50
7 Shaun Alexander	.25	.60
8 Kerry Collins	.25	.60
9 Trent Green	.25	.60
10 Marc Bulger	.30	.75
11 Donte Stallworth	.20	.50
12 Julius Peppers	.30	.75
13 Ronde Barber	.25	.60
14 Jason Taylor	.25	.60
15 Eric Moulds	.25	.60
16 Amos Zereoue	.20	.50
17 Fred Taylor	.25	.60
18 Jake Plummer	.25	.60
19 Jerry Rice	.60	1.50
20 Quincy Morgan	.20	.50
21 Koren Robinson	.25	.60
22 Tom Brady	.75	2.00
23 Brian Urlacher	.30	.75
24 Terrell Owens	.30	.75
25 Priest Holmes	.30	.75
26 Brett Favre	.75	2.00
27 Derrick Mason	.25	.60
28 Charlie Garner	.25	.60
29 Clinton Portis	.25	.60
30 Warren Sapp	.25	.60
31 Joe Horn	.25	.60
32 Michael Lewis	.20	.50
33 Torry Holt	.30	.75
34 Aaron Brooks	.25	.60
35 William Green	.20	.50
36 Matt Hasselbeck	.25	.60
37 Ricky Williams	.25	.60
38 Travis Henry	.20	.50
39 Junior Seau	.30	.75
40 Duce Staley	.25	.60
41 Todd Heap	.25	.60
42 Hines Ward	.30	.75
43 David Carr	.25	.60
44 Rod Gardner	.20	.50
45 Deuce McAllister	.25	.60
46 Chad Johnson	.30	.75
47 Garrison Hearst	.25	.60
48 Daunte Culpepper	.25	.60
49 Ray Lewis	.30	.75
50 Plaxico Burress	.25	.60
51 Randy Moss	.30	.75
52 Drew Bledsoe	.30	.75
53 LaDainian Tomlinson	.30	.75
54 Chris Chambers	.25	.60
55 Chris Redman	.20	.50
56 Jerome Bettis	.30	.75
57 Tony Gonzalez	.30	.75
58 Michael Vick	.40	1.00
59 Tommy Maddox	.25	.60
60 Marvin Harrison	.30	.75
61 Stephen Davis	.25	.60
62 Chad Pennington	.30	.75
63 James Stewart	.20	.50
64 Simeon Rice	.20	.50
65 Jeremy Shockey	.30	.75
66 Emmitt Smith	.75	2.00
67 Marshall Faulk	.30	.75
68 Troy Brown	.25	.60
69 Warrick Dunn	.25	.60
70 David Boston	.20	.50
71 Edgerrin James	.30	.75
72 Patrick Ramsey	.25	.60
73 Rich Gannon	.25	.60
74 Ed McCaffrey	.25	.60
75 Kurt Warner	.30	.75
76 Marty Booker	.25	.60
77 Tai Streets	.20	.50
78 Michael Bennett	.25	.60
79 Peerless Price	.20	.50
80 Drew Brees	.30	.75
81 Mark Brunell	.25	.60
82 Jamal Lewis	.25	.60
83 Brad Johnson	.25	.60
84 Jimmy Smith	.25	.60
85 T.J. Duckett	.25	.60
86 Todd Pinkston	.20	.50
87 Joey Harrington	.20	.50
88 Derrick Brooks	.25	.60
89 Laveranues Coles	.20	.50
90 Shannon Sharpe	.30	.75
91 Keyshawn Johnson	.30	.75
92 Tiki Barber	.30	.75
93 Corey Dillon	.25	.60
94 Jeff Garcia	.25	.60
95 Peyton Manning	.60	1.50
96 Marcel Shipp	.20	.50
97 Brian Dawkins	.25	.60
98 Ahman Green	.25	.60
99 Steve McNair	.30	.75
100 Amani Toomer	.25	.60
101 Carson Palmer RC	4.00	10.00
102 Taylor Jacobs RC	1.25	3.00
103 Kyle Boller RC	2.00	5.00
104 Anquan Boldin RC	3.00	8.00
105 Willis McGahee RC	2.50	6.00
106 Kevin Curtis RC	2.00	5.00
107 Musa Smith RC	1.25	3.00
108 Dallas Clark RC	3.00	8.00
109 Larry Johnson RC	2.00	5.00
110 Billy McMullen RC	1.25	3.00
111 B.J. Askew RC	1.50	4.00
112 Bennie Joppru RC	1.25	3.00
113 Bryant Johnson RC	2.00	5.00
114 Byron Leftwich RC	2.00	5.00
115 Onterrio Smith RC	1.25	3.00
116 Justin Fargas RC	2.00	5.00
117 Terence Newman RC	1.50	4.00
118 Andre Johnson RC	5.00	12.00
119 Rex Grossman RC	2.00	5.00
120 Tyrone Calico RC	1.50	4.00
121 Chris Simms RC	2.00	5.00
122 Kelley Washington RC	1.25	3.00
123 Dave Ragone RC	1.25	3.00
124 Teyo Johnson RC	1.50	4.00
125 Seneca Wallace RC	2.00	5.00
126 Lee Suggs RC	1.50	4.00
127 Chris Brown RC	1.25	3.00
128 L.J. Smith RC	2.00	5.00
129 Charles Rogers RC	1.50	4.00
130 Terrell Suggs RC	2.00	5.00
131 Antonio Bryant HH	1.25	3.00
132 Roy Williams HH	1.50	4.00
133 Joey Galloway HH	1.50	4.00
134 Dexter Coakley HH	1.50	4.00
135 Greg Ellis HH	2.00	5.00
136 Troy Hambrick HH	1.25	3.00
137 La'Roi Glover HH	1.25	3.00
138 Tony Fisher HH	1.25	3.00
139 Javon Walker HH	1.50	4.00
140 Robert Ferguson HH	1.25	3.00
141 Bubba Franks HH	1.50	4.00
142 Kabeer Gbaja-Biamila HH	1.50	4.00
143 Na'il Diggs HH	1.25	3.00
144 Darren Sharper HH	1.50	4.00
145 Jerry Porter HH	1.25	3.00
146 Doug Jolley HH	1.25	3.00
147 Sebastian Janikowski HH	1.50	4.00
148 Rod Woodson HH	2.00	5.00
149 Phillip Buchanon HH	1.25	3.00
150 Charles Woodson HH	2.00	5.00
151 Zack Crockett HH	1.50	4.00
152 Michael Strahan HH	2.00	5.00
153 Dhani Jones HH RC	2.00	5.00
154 Will Allen HH	1.50	4.00
155 Will Peterson HH	1.50	4.00
156 Ron Dixon HH	1.25	3.00
157 Mike Barrow HH	1.25	3.00
158 Ike Hilliard HH	1.25	3.00
159 Antwaan Randle El HH	1.50	4.00
160 Joey Porter HH	2.00	5.00
161 Jason Gildon HH	1.50	4.00
162 Chris Fuamatu-Ma'afala HH	1.50	4.00
163 Kendrell Bell HH	1.25	3.00
164 Chad Scott HH	1.25	3.00
165 Dan Kreider HH	2.00	5.00

2003 Fleer Authentix Balcony

*VETS 1-100: 2X TO 5X BASE CARDS
*ROOKIES 101-130: .5X TO 1.2X
STATED PRINT RUN 250 SER.#'d SETS

2003 Fleer Authentix Booster Tickets Lower Level

LUXURY BOX NOT PRICED DUE TO SCARCITY
*UPPER LEVEL: .8X TO 2X LOWER LEVEL
OVERALL ANNC'D BOOSTER PRINT RUN 250

101 Carson Palmer	4.00	10.00
102 Taylor Jacobs	1.25	3.00
103 Kyle Boller	2.00	5.00
104 Anquan Boldin	3.00	8.00
105 Willis McGahee	2.50	6.00
106 Kevin Curtis	2.00	5.00
107 Musa Smith	1.25	3.00
108 Dallas Clark	3.00	8.00
109 Larry Johnson	2.00	5.00
110 Billy McMullen	1.25	3.00
111 B.J. Askew	1.50	4.00
112 Bennie Joppru	1.25	3.00
113 Bryant Johnson	2.00	5.00
114 Byron Leftwich	2.00	5.00
115 Onterrio Smith	1.25	3.00
116 Justin Fargas	2.00	5.00
117 Terence Newman	1.50	4.00
118 Andre Johnson	5.00	12.00
119 Rex Grossman	2.00	5.00
120 Tyrone Calico	1.50	4.00
121 Chris Simms	2.00	5.00
122 Kelley Washington	1.25	3.00
123 Dave Ragone	1.25	3.00
124 Teyo Johnson	1.50	4.00
125 Seneca Wallace	2.00	5.00
126 Lee Suggs	1.50	4.00
127 Chris Brown	1.25	3.00
128 L.J. Smith	2.00	5.00
129 Charles Rogers	1.50	4.00
130 Terrell Suggs	2.00	5.00

2003 Fleer Authentix Club Box

*VETS 1-100: 3X TO 8X BASIC CARDS
*ROOKIES 101-130: .8X TO 2X
STATED PRINT RUN 100 SER.#'d SETS

2003 Fleer Authentix Standing Room Only

*VETS 1-100: 10X TO 25X BASIC CARDS
*ROOKIES 101-30: 1.5X TO 4X
PRINT RUN 25 SER.#'d SETS

2003 Fleer Authentix Autographs

1 Michael Bennett	7.50	20.00
3 Plaxico Burress	7.50	20.00
4 Joey Harrington	15.00	40.00
7 Donovan McNabb	25.00	50.00
8 Chad Pennington	15.00	30.00
11 Michael Vick	30.00	60.00

2003 Fleer Authentix Hometown Heroes Memorabilia

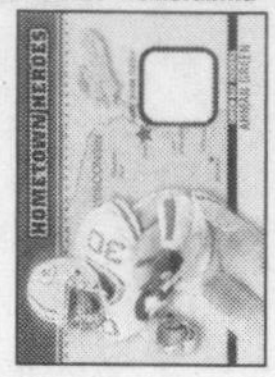

ONE PER HOME TEAM BOX		
AB Antonio Bryant	4.00	10.00
AG Ahman Green	5.00	12.00
BF Brett Favre	15.00	40.00
DD Donald Driver	6.00	15.00
HW Hines Ward	6.00	15.00
JB Jerome Bettis	6.00	15.00
JG Joey Galloway	5.00	12.00
JR Jerry Rice	12.00	30.00
JS Jeremy Shockey	6.00	15.00
MS Michael Strahan	6.00	15.00
PB Plaxico Burress	5.00	12.00
RG Rich Gannon	5.00	12.00
RW Roy Williams	5.00	12.00
TB1 Tiki Barber	6.00	15.00
TB2 Tim Brown	6.00	15.00
WPB Hines Ward	8.00	20.00
Plaxico Burress		
BFAG Brett Favre	20.00	50.00
Ahman Green		
JGAB Joey Galloway	6.00	15.00
Antonio Bryant		
JRRG Jerry Rice	15.00	40.00
Rich Gannon		
JSTB Jeremy Shockey	8.00	20.00
Tiki Barber		

2003 Fleer Authentix Jersey Authentix Ripped

STATED ODDS 1:18
*UNRIPPED/50: .8X TO 2X RIPPED JSY
UNRIPPED PRINT RUN 50 SER.#'d SETS

JAAB Antonio Bryant	2.50	6.00
JACP Clinton Portis	3.00	8.00
JACP2 Chad Pennington	4.00	10.00
JADM Deuce McAllister	3.00	8.00
JADM2 Donovan McNabb	4.00	10.00
JAJG Jeff Garcia	3.00	8.00
JAJH Joey Harrington	2.50	6.00
JAJR Brian Urlacher	4.00	10.00
JALT LaDainian Tomlinson	4.00	10.00
JAMB Michael Bennett	3.00	8.00
JAMF Marshall Faulk	4.00	10.00
JAPB Plaxico Burress	3.00	8.00
JARM Randy Moss	4.00	10.00
JARW Ricky Williams	3.00	8.00
JATH Travis Henry	2.50	6.00

2003 Fleer Authentix Jersey Authentix Ripped Pro Bowl

RANDOM INSERTS IN PACKS
UNPRICED UNRIPPED PRINT RUN 1

JADM Deuce McAllister/91	8.00	20.00
JADM Donovan McNabb/39	12.00	30.00
JAJG Jeff Garcia/87	8.00	20.00
JAJR Brian Urlacher/50	10.00	25.00
JALT LaDainian Tomlinson/103	10.00	25.00
JAMB Michael Bennett/19	10.00	25.00
JAMF Marshall Faulk/80	10.00	25.00
JARM Randy Moss/66	10.00	25.00
JARW Ricky Williams/74	8.00	20.00
JATH Travis Henry/42	8.00	20.00

2003 Fleer Authentix Jersey Authentix Autographs Pro Bowl

PRO BOWL PRINT RUN 75 SER.#'d SETS
*REG.SEASON/270: .3X TO .8X PRO BOWL/75
*REG.SEASON/100-135: .4X TO 1X PB/75
*REG.SEASON/25: .6X TO 1.5X PRO BOWL/75

AJACP Chad Pennington	15.00	40.00
AJAMV Michael Vick	50.00	100.00
AJAWM Willis McGahee	15.00	40.00

2003 Fleer Authentix Jersey Authentix Game of the Week Ripped

RIPPED STATED ODDS 1:240
*UNRIPPED/50: .8X TO 2X BASE DUAL JSY
UNRIPPED PRINT RUN 50 SER.#'d SETS

ABDM Antonio Bryant	6.00	15.00
Deuce McAllister		
CPDM Chad Pennington	8.00	20.00
Donovan McNabb		
CPLT Clinton Portis	8.00	20.00
LaDainian Tomlinson		
CPTH Chad Pennington	8.00	20.00
Travis Henry		
DMRW Donovan McNabb	8.00	20.00
Ricky Williams		
JHMB Joey Harrington	6.00	15.00
Michael Bennett		

MFJG Marshall Faulk	8.00	20.00
Jeff Garcia		
MFPB Marshall Faulk	8.00	20.00
Plaxico Burress		
RMBU Randy Moss	8.00	20.00
Brian Urlacher		
THAB Travis Henry	5.00	12.00
Antonio Bryant		

2003 Fleer Authentix Stadium Classics

COMPLETE SET (10)	12.50	30.00
STATED ODDS 1:12		
1SC Brian Urlacher	1.25	3.00
2SC Donovan McNabb	1.25	3.00
3SC Peyton Manning	2.50	6.00
4SC Deuce McAllister	1.00	2.50
5SC Brett Favre	3.00	8.00
6SC Chad Pennington	1.25	3.00
7SC Randy Moss	1.25	3.00
8SC Michael Vick	1.50	4.00
9SC Ricky Williams	1.00	2.50
10SC LaDainian Tomlinson	1.25	3.00

2003 Fleer Authentix Ticket Studs

STATED ODDS 1:26		
1TS Michael Vick	2.00	5.00
2TS Tom Brady	4.00	10.00
3TS Brett Favre	4.00	10.00
4TS Emmitt Smith	4.00	10.00
5TS Randy Moss	1.50	4.00
6TS Jerry Rice	3.00	8.00
7TS Peyton Manning	3.00	8.00
8TS Chad Pennington	1.50	4.00
9TS Donovan McNabb	1.50	4.00
10TS LaDainian Tomlinson	1.50	4.00
11TS Jeremy Shockey	1.50	4.00
12TS Drew Brees	1.50	4.00
13TS Brian Urlacher	1.50	4.00
14TS Clinton Portis	1.25	3.00
15TS David Carr	1.25	3.00

2003 Fleer Authentix Ticket Studs Jerseys

STATED ODDS 1:24		
TSBF Brett Favre	10.00	25.00
TSBU Brian Urlacher	4.00	10.00
TSCP1 Chad Pennington	4.00	10.00
TSCP2 Clinton Portis	3.00	8.00
TSDB Drew Brees	4.00	10.00
TSDC David Carr	3.00	8.00
TSDM Donovan McNabb	4.00	10.00
TSES Emmitt Smith	10.00	25.00
TSJR Jerry Rice	8.00	20.00
TSJS Jeremy Shockey	4.00	10.00
TSLT LaDainian Tomlinson	4.00	10.00
TSMV Michael Vick	5.00	12.00
TSPM Peyton Manning	8.00	20.00
TSRM Randy Moss	4.00	10.00
TSTB Tom Brady	10.00	25.00

2004 Fleer Authentix

Fleer Authentix initially released in late July 2004. The base set consists of 150-cards including 30-rookies, 10-rookies issued with an autograph of that player?ÇOs team?ÇOs coach, and 10-additional veteran Home Team cards. Hobby boxes contained 24-packs of 5-cards and carried an S.R.P. of $4.99 per pack. Five parallel sets and a variety of inserts can be found seeded in hobby and retail packs highlighted by the multi-tiered Autograph inserts. Some signed cards were issued via mail-in exchange or redemption cards with a number of those EXCH cards not yet appearing live on the secondary market as of the printing of this book.

COMP.SET w/o SP's (100)	10.00	25.00
OVERALL ROOKIE 101-140 ODDS 1:12H, 1:60R		
131-140 PRINT RUN 250 SER.#'d SETS		
1 Tom Brady	.60	1.50
2 Amani Toomer	.25	.60
3 Terry Glenn	.25	.60
4 Eddie George	.25	.60
5 Bryant Johnson	.20	.50
6 Carson Palmer	.30	.75
7 Matt Hasselbeck	.25	.60
8 Randy Moss	.30	.75
9 Chad Johnson	.30	.75
10 Darrell Jackson	.25	.60
11 Chris Chambers	.25	.60
12 Jake Delhomme	.25	.60
13 Plaxico Burress	.25	.60
14 Marvin Harrison	.30	.75
15 Drew Bledsoe	.30	.75
16 Terrell Owens	.30	.75
17 Andre Johnson	.30	.75
18 Anquan Boldin	.30	.75
19 Jeremy Shockey	.25	.60
20 Champ Bailey	.25	.60
21 Shaun Alexander	.25	.60
22 Dant?? Hall	.25	.60
23 Julius Peppers	.25	.60
24 Duce Staley	.25	.60
25 Domanick Davis	.20	.50
26 Quentin Griffin	.20	.50
27 Clinton Portis	.30	.75
28 Aaron Brooks	.25	.60
29 Justin McCareins	.20	.50
30 Joey Galloway	.25	.60
31 David Boston	.20	.50
32 Lee Suggs	.25	.60
33 Torry Holt	.25	.60
34 Daunte Culpepper	.25	.60
35 Brian Urlacher	.30	.75
36 Kevan Barlow	.20	.50
37 Fred Taylor	.25	.60
38 Eric Moulds	.25	.60
39 Donovan McNabb	.30	.75
40 Edgerrin James	.25	.60
41 Ray Lewis	.30	.75
42 Rich Gannon	.25	.60
43 Joey Harrington	.25	.60
44 Laveranues Coles	.20	.50
45 Ricky Williams	.25	.60
46 Rex Grossman	.25	.60
47 Drew Brees	.30	.75
48 Priest Holmes	.30	.75
49 Travis Henry	.20	.50
50 Tim Rattay	.20	.50
51 Tony Gonzalez	.30	.75
52 Stephen Davis	.25	.60
53 Hines Ward	.30	.75
54 Peyton Manning	.60	1.50
55 Peerless Price	.20	.50
56 Jerry Rice	.00	1.50
57 David Carr	.20	.50
58 Jamal Lewis	.25	.60
59 Tim Brown	.30	.75
60 Warren Sapp	.25	.60
61 Tommy Maddox	.25	.60
62 Joe Horn	.25	.60
63 Roy Williams S	.25	.60
64 Charlie Garner	.25	.60
65 Deion Branch	.25	.60
66 Corey Dillon	.25	.60
67 Marc Bulger	.25	.60
68 Trent Green	.25	.60
69 Michael Vick	.40	1.00
70 Chad Pennington	.30	.75
71 Charles Rogers	.20	.50
72 Mark Brunell	.25	.60
73 Tiki Barber	.30	.75
74 Jeff Garcia	.25	.60
75 Marshall Faulk	.30	.75
76 DeShaun Foster	.25	.60
77 LaVar Arrington	.25	.60
78 Byron Leftwich	.25	.60
79 Willis McGahee	.30	.75
80 Brian Westbrook	.30	.75
81 Ahman Green	.25	.60
82 Kyle Boller	.25	.60
83 Jevon Kearse	.25	.60
84 Donald Driver	.30	.75
85 Warrick Dunn	.25	.60
86 Santana Moss	.25	.60
87 Keyshawn Johnson	.25	.60
88 Steve McNair	.30	.75
89 Deuce McAllister	.25	.60
90 A.J. Feeley	.20	.50
91 Keenan McCardell	.20	.50
92 Michael Bennett	.25	.60
93 Terrell Suggs	.25	.60
94 LaDainian Tomlinson	.30	.75
95 Brett Favre	.75	2.00
96 Emmitt Smith	.75	2.00
97 Curtis Martin	.30	.75
98 Jake Plummer	.25	.60
99 Derrick Mason	.25	.60
100 Ty Law	.25	.60
101 Don Troupe RC	1.60	4.00
102 DeAngelo Hall RC	2.00	5.00
103 Eli Manning RC	12.00	30.00
104 Cody Pickett RC	1.50	4.00
105 Matt Schaub RC	4.00	10.00
106 J.P. Losman RC	1.50	4.00
107 Chris Perry RC	1.50	4.00
108 Steven Jackson RC	3.00	8.00
109 Kevin Jones RC	1.50	4.00
110 Michael Turner RC	2.50	6.00
111 Philip Rivers RC	8.00	20.00
112 Quincy Wilson RC	1.50	4.00
113 Luke McCown RC	1.50	4.00
114 Greg Jones RC	1.25	3.00
115 Julius Jones RC	1.50	4.00
116 Sean Taylor RC	4.00	10.00
117 Kellen Winslow RC	2.00	5.00
118 Rashaun Woods RC	1.25	3.00
119 Ben Watson RC	2.00	5.00
120 Devery Henderson RC	2.00	5.00
121 Ernest Wilford RC	1.50	4.00
122 Michael Jenkins RC	2.00	5.00
123 Roy Williams RC	2.00	5.00
124 Lee Evans RC	2.00	5.00
125 Bernard Berrian RC	2.00	5.00
126 Mewelde Moore RC	1.50	4.00
127 Jammal Lord RC	1.25	3.00
128 Darius Watts RC	1.25	3.00
129 Derrick Hamilton RC	1.25	3.00
130 Devard Darling RC	1.25	3.00
131 Andy Hall RC	7.50	20.00
Andy Reid AU RC		
132 Tatum Bell RC	12.50	30.00
Mike Shanahan AU		
133 Drew Henson RC	25.00	50.00
Bill parcells AU		
134 Ben Roethlisberger RC	50.00	100.00
Bill Cowher AU		
135 Robert Gallery RC	10.00	25.00
Norv Turner AU RC		
136 Cedric Cobbs RC	40.00	80.00
Bill Belichick AU		
137 Reggie Williams RC	7.50	20.00
Jack Del Rio AU		
138 Larry Fitzgerald RC	12.50	30.00
Dennis Green AU		
139 Michael Clayton RC	10.00	25.00
Jon Gruden AU RC		
140 Keary Colbert RC	10.00	25.00
John Fox AU RC		
141 Najeh Davenport HT	.60	1.50
142 Javon Walker HT	.50	1.25
143 Robert Ferguson HT	.50	1.25
144 Nick Barnett HT	.60	1.50
145 Kabeer Gbaja-Biamila HT	.60	1.50
146 Terence Newman HT	.60	1.50
147 Dexter Coakley HT	.50	1.25
148 Darren Woodson HT	.60	1.50
149 Jason Witten HT	.75	2.00
150 Antonio Bryant HT	.60	1.50

2004 Fleer Authentix Balcony Blue

*VETS 1-100: 5X TO 12X BASIC CARDS
*ROOKIES 101-130: .8X TO 2X
*ROOKIES 131-140: .5X TO 1.2X
*VETS 141-150: 2X TO 5X
STATED PRINT RUN 75 SER.#'d SETS

2004 Fleer Authentix Club Box Gold

*VETS 1-100: 10X TO 25X
*ROOKIES 101-130: 1.5X TO 4X
*ROOKIES 131-140: 1.2X TO 3X
*VETS 141-150: 4X TO 10X
STATED PRINT RUN 25 SER.#'d SETS

134 Ben Roethlisberger	75.00	200.00
Bill Cowher AU		

2004 Fleer Authentix General Admission Green

*VETS 1-100: 4X TO 10X BASIC CARDS
*ROOKIES 101-130: .6X TO 1.5X
*ROOKIES 131-140: .5X TO 1.2X
*VETS 141-150: 1.5X TO 4X
OVERALL PARALLEL ODDS 1:8 HOB, 1:48 RET
STATED PRINT RUN 100 SER.#'d SETS

2004 Fleer Authentix Mezzanine Bronze

*VETS 1-100: 6X TO 15X
*ROOKIES 101-130: 1X TO 2.5X
*ROOKIES 131-140: .6X TO 1.5X
*VETS 141-150: 2.5X TO 6X
STATED PRINT RUN 50 SER.#'d SETS

2004 Fleer Authentix Standing Room Only Purple

*VETS 1-100: 15X TO 40X BASIC CARDS
*ROOKIES 101-130: 2.5X TO 6X
*ROOKIES 131-140: 2X TO 5X
*VETS 141-150: 6X TO 15X
STATED PRINT RUN 10 SER.#'d SETS

134 Ben Roethlisberger	150.00	300.00
Bill Cowher AU		

2004 Fleer Authentix Autographs General Admission

GENERAL ADMISSION PRINT RUN 100
*BALCONY/75: .4X TO 1X GEN.ADM/100
BALCONY PRINT RUN 75 SER.#'d SETS
*CLUB BOX/25: .8X TO 2X GEN.ADM/100
CLUB BOX PRINT RUN 25 SER.#'d SETS
*MEZZANINE/50: .5X TO 1.2X GEN.ADM/100
MEZZANINE PRINT RUN 50 SER.#'d SETS
UNPRICED STANDING ROOM #'d TO 5

AABW Brian Westbrook	10.00	25.00
AADH Dante Hall	8.00	20.00
AAJW2 Jason Witten	12.00	30.00
AAMJ Michael Jenkins	10.00	25.00
AATC Tyrone Calico	8.00	20.00
AAWM Willis McGahee	10.00	25.00

2004 Fleer Authentix Autographed Jersey Balcony

*BALCONY: .5X TO 1.2X GEN.ADMISS.
BALCONY PRINT RUN 50 SER.#'d SETS

2004 Fleer Authentix Autographed Jersey General Admission

GENERAL ADMISSION PRINT RUN 75		
UNPRICED STANDING ROOM #'d TO 1		
AJABW Brian Westbrook	12.00	30.00
AJADH Dante Hall	10.00	25.00
AJAJD Jake Delhomme	10.00	25.00
AJAJW2 Jason Witten	15.00	40.00
AJAMH Matt Hasselbeck	12.00	30.00
AJATC Tyrone Calico	10.00	25.00
AJAWM Willis McGahee	12.00	30.00

2004 Fleer Authentix Autographed Jersey Mezzanine

*MEZZANINE/25: .8X TO 2X GEN.ADMISS.
MEZZANINE PRINT RUN 25 SER.#'d SETS

2004 Fleer Authentix Draft Day Tickets

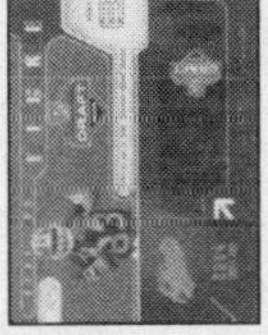

STATED ODDS 1:240 H, 1:480 R		
DDTBR Ben Roethlisberger	20.00	50.00
DDTEM Eli Manning	20.00	50.00
DDTKW Kellen Winslow Jr.	4.00	10.00
DDTLE Lee Evans	4.00	10.00
DDTLF Larry Fitzgerald	10.00	25.00
DDTPR Philip Rivers	12.00	30.00
DDTRW Roy Williams WR	4.00	10.00
DDTRW2 Reggie Williams	3.00	8.00
DDTRW3 Rashaun Woods	2.50	6.00
DDTSJ Steven Jackson	6.00	15.00

2004 Fleer Authentix Hot Ticket

STATED ODDS 1:12 H, 1:18 R		
1HT Donovan McNabb	1.25	3.00
2HT Tom Brady	2.50	6.00
3HT Brett Favre	3.00	8.00
4HT Clinton Portis	1.25	3.00
5HT Michael Vick	1.50	4.00
6HT Jeremy Shockey	1.00	2.50
7HT Peyton Manning	2.50	6.00
8HT Emmitt Smith	3.00	8.00
9HT Chad Pennington	1.25	3.00
10HT Randy Moss	1.25	3.00
11HT Ricky Williams	1.00	2.50
12HT Byron Leftwich	1.00	2.50
13HT Brian Urlacher	1.25	3.00
14HT Terrell Owens	1.25	3.00
15HT Jerry Rice	2.50	6.00

2004 Fleer Authentix Hot Ticket Jersey

STATED PRINT RUN 200-500		
*PATCH/54-81: .8X TO 2X JSY/410-500		
*PATCH/84: .5X TO 1.2X JSY/200		
*PATCH/34: 1X TO 2.5X JSY/500		
*PATCH/18-26: 1.2X TO 3X JSY/410-500		
PATCH STATED PRINT RUN 4-84		
UNPRICED NFL SHIELD SER.#'d TO 1		
HTBF Brett Favre/500	8.00	20.00
HTBL Byron Leftwich/500	2.50	6.00
HTBU Brian Urlacher/450	3.00	8.00
HTCP Chad Pennington/500	3.00	8.00
HTCP2 Clinton Portis/500	3.00	8.00
HTDM Donovan McNabb/500	3.00	8.00
HTES Emmitt Smith/485	8.00	20.00
HTJR Jerry Rice/410	6.00	15.00
HTJS Jeremy Shockey/500	2.50	6.00
HTMV Michael Vick/200	6.00	15.00
HTPM Peyton Manning/500	6.00	15.00
HTRM Randy Moss/500	3.00	8.00
HTRW Ricky Williams/500	2.50	6.00
HTTB Tom Brady/500	6.00	15.00
HTTO Terrell Owens/460	3.00	8.00

2004 Fleer Authentix Jersey Authentix Balcony

BALCONY PRINT RUN 150 SER.#'d SETS		
*GEN.ADM/205-350: .3X TO .8X BALCONY		
*GEN.ADM/145-170: .4X TO 1X BALCONY		
*CLUB BOX/25: 1X TO 2.5X BALCONY		
CLUB BOX PRINT RUN 25 SER.#'d SETS		
*MEZZANINE/75: .6X TO 1.5X BALCONY		
MEZZANINE PRINT RUN 75 SER.#'d SETS		
*STAND.ROOM/10: 1.5X TO 4X BALCONY		
STANDING ROOM ONLY PRINT RUN 10		
JAAB Anquan Boldin	4.00	10.00
JAAG Ahman Green HT	3.00	8.00
JAAJ Andre Johnson	4.00	10.00
JABF Brett Favre HT	10.00	25.00
JABL Byron Leftwich	3.00	8.00
JABW Brian Westbrook	4.00	10.00
JACJ Chad Johnson	4.00	10.00
JACP Clinton Portis	4.00	10.00
JACP2 Chad Pennington	4.00	10.00
JADC Daunte Culpepper	3.00	8.00
JADM Donovan McNabb	4.00	10.00
JADM2 Deuce McAllister	3.00	8.00
JAEJ Edgerrin James	3.00	8.00
JAES Emmitt Smith	10.00	25.00
JAJH Joey Harrington	3.00	8.00
JAJL Jamal Lewis	3.00	8.00
JAJR Jerry Rice	8.00	20.00
JAJS Jeremy Shockey	3.00	8.00
JAKG Donald Driver HT	4.00	10.00
JALA LaVar Arrington	8.00	20.00
JALT LaDainian Tomlinson	4.00	10.00
JAMF Marshall Faulk	4.00	10.00
JAMH Marvin Harrison	4.00	10.00
JAMV Michael Vick	5.00	12.00
JAPM Peyton Manning	8.00	20.00
JAQC Quincy Carter HT	2.50	6.00
JARM Randy Moss	4.00	10.00
JARW Ricky Williams	3.00	8.00
JARW2 Roy Williams S HT	3.00	8.00
JASA Shaun Alexander	3.00	8.00
JASM Santana Moss	3.00	8.00
JASM2 Steve McNair	4.00	10.00
JATB Tom Brady	8.00	20.00
JATN Terence Newman HT	3.00	8.00
JATO Terrell Owens	4.00	10.00

2004 Fleer Authentix Monday Night Matchup Jersey

STATED PRINT RUN 10-160		
*PATCH/10: 1X TO 2.5X JSY/80-160		
*PATCH/10: .8X TO 2X JSY/40-70		
*PATCH/10: .6X TO 1.5X JSY/30		
*PATCH/10: .5X TO 1.2X JSY/20		
*PATCH/10: .4X TO 1X JSY/10		
PATCH STATED PRINT RUN 10		
AGEG Ahman Green/50	5.00	12.00
Eddie George		
BFMF Brett Favre/120	12.00	30.00
Marshall Faulk		
CPJP Carson Palmer/70	6.00	15.00
Jake Plummer		
CPRW Clinton Portis/30	8.00	20.00
Roy Williams S		
CPRW Chad Pennington/80	5.00	12.00
Ricky Williams		
DBMF Derrick Brooks/60	6.00	15.00
Marshall Faulk		
DCPM Peyton Manning/90	10.00	25.00
Daunte Culpepper		
DMKJ Keyshawn Johnson/100	5.00	12.00
Donovan McNabb		
JDBF Jake Delhomme/10	40.00	100.00
Brett Favre		
RLPH Jamal Lewis/40	6.00	15.00
Priest Holmes		
RWTB Ricky Williams/150	10.00	25.00
Tom Brady		
SARW Shaun Alexander/130	4.00	10.00
Roy Williams S		
SMTG Steve McNair/140	5.00	12.00
Tony Gonzalez		
TGTB Trent Green/110	10.00	25.00
Tom Brady		
THTO Torry Holt/160	5.00	12.00
Terrell Owens		
TORM Terrell Owens/20	10.00	25.00
Randy Moss		

2004 Fleer Authentix Stadium Standouts

COMPLETE SET (10)	10.00	25.00
STATED ODDS 1:8 HOB, 1:12 RET		
1SS Ricky Williams	.75	2.00
2SS Anquan Boldin	1.00	2.50
3SS Tom Brady	2.00	5.00
4SS Brett Favre	2.50	6.00
5SS Peyton Manning	2.00	5.00
6SS Marshall Faulk	1.00	2.50
7SS Michael Vick	1.25	3.00
8SS David Carr	.60	1.50
9SS Carson Palmer	1.00	2.50
10SS Randy Moss	1.00	2.50

2004 Fleer Authentix Tailgate Trios Jerseys

STATED PRINT RUN 75 SER.#'d SETS		
*HOMETOWN/25: .6X TO 1.5X BASIC INSERTS		
HOMETOWN 25 PRINT RUN 25 SETS		
UNPRICED HOMETOWN 5 PRINT RUN 5		
BHM Aaron Brooks	8.00	20.00
Joe Horn		
Deuce McAllister		
BJG Antonio Bryant	8.00	20.00
Keyshawn Johnson		
Terry Glenn		
BMH Drew Bledsoe	10.00	25.00
Eric Moulds		
Travis Henry		
BWM Plaxico Burress	10.00	25.00
Hines Ward		
Tommy Maddox		
DGF Donald Driver	25.00	60.00
Ahman Green		
Brett Favre		
GRB Rich Gannon	20.00	50.00
Jerry Rice		
Tim Brown		
HBF Torry Holt	10.00	25.00
Isaac Bruce		
Marshall Faulk		
HJA Matt Hasselbeck	8.00	20.00
Darrell Jackson		
Shaun Alexander		
HJM Marvin Harrison	20.00	50.00
Edgerrin James		
Peyton Manning		
MCB Randy Moss	10.00	25.00
Daunte Culpepper		
Michael Bennett		
MMG Steve McNair	10.00	25.00
Derrick Mason		
Eddie George		
OMW Donovan McNabb	10.00	25.00
Terrell Owens		
Brian Westbrook		
PCB Clinton Portis	10.00	25.00
Laveranues Coles		
Mark Brunell		
PMM Chad Pennington	10.00	25.00
Santana Moss		
Curtis Martin		
TSB Amani Toomer	10.00	25.00
Jeremy Shockey		
Tiki Barber		

2001 Fleer Authority

This 155 card set was issued by Fleer in Novermber, 2001. The first 100 cards in the set ware veterans while cards 101-155 are rookie cards which are serial numbered to 1350.

COMP.SET w/o SP's (100)	10.00	25.00
1 Brian Urlacher	.40	1.00
2 James Stewart	.20	.50
3 Lamar Smith	.25	.60
4 Curtis Martin	.30	.75
5 Shannon Sharpe	.30	.75
6 Germane Crowell	.20	.50
7 Daunte Culpepper	.25	.60
8 Charlie Garner	.25	.60
9 Jake Plummer	.25	.60
10 Eric Moulds	.25	.00
11 Brett Favre	1.00	2.50
12 Robert Smith	.25	.60
13 Tim Brown	.30	.75
14 David Boston	.20	.50
15 Cade McNown	.25	.60
16 Ahman Green	.30	.75
17 Terry Glenn	.25	.60
18 Wayne Chrebet	.25	.60
19 Jamal Lewis	.30	.75
20 Peter Warrick	.25	.60
21 Peyton Manning	.75	2.00
22 Ricky Williams	.30	.75
23 Donovan McNabb	.30	.75
24 Isaac Bruce	.30	.75
25 Tim Couch	.20	.50
26 Marvin Harrison	.30	.75
27 Kerry Collins	.25	.60
28 Kordell Stewart	.25	.60
29 Keyshawn Johnson	.25	.60
30 Kevin Johnson	.20	.50
31 Mark Brunell	.25	.60
32 Ron Dayne	.25	.60
33 Doug Flutie	.30	.75
34 Warrick Dunn	.30	.75
35 Emmitt Smith	.75	2.00
36 Jimmy Smith	.25	.60
37 Amani Toomer	.25	.60
38 Chad Pennington	.30	.75
39 Steve McNair	.30	.75
40 Brian Griese	.25	.60
41 Derrick Alexander	.20	.50
42 Vinny Testaverde	.25	.60
43 Terrell Owens	.30	.75
44 Derrick Mason	.25	.60
45 Mike Anderson	.25	.60
46 Michael Westbrook	.20	.50
47 Rich Gannon	.25	.60
48 Shaun Alexander	.30	.75
49 Jevon Kearse	.25	.60
50 Ed McCaffrey	.25	.60
51 Tony Gonzalez	.30	.75
52 Tyrone Wheatley	.25	.60
53 Kurt Warner	.50	1.25
54 Stephen Davis	.25	.60
55 Rod Smith	.25	.60
56 Deion Sanders	.30	.75
57 Brad Johnson	.25	.60
58 Ike Hilliard	.25	.60
59 Trent Green	.30	.75
60 Terrell Davis	.30	.75
61 Warren Sapp	.25	.60
62 Marshall Faulk	.30	.75
63 Tiki Barber	.30	.75
64 Keenan McCardell	.25	.60
65 Joey Galloway	.25	.60
66 Frank Wycheck	.20	.50
67 Ricky Watters	.25	.60
68 Joe Horn	.25	.60
69 Fred Taylor	.30	.75
70 Troy Aikman	.50	1.25
71 Mike Alstott	.25	.60
72 Matt Hasselbeck	.30	.75
73 Aaron Brooks	.25	.60
74 Terrence Wilkins	.20	.50
75 Travis Prentice	.20	.50
76 Eddie George	.30	.75
77 Jeff Garcia	.25	.60
78 Randy Moss	.30	.75
79 Edgerrin James	.30	.75
80 Corey Dillon	.25	.60
81 Torry Holt	.25	.60
82 Todd Pinkston	.20	.50
83 Drew Bledsoe	.30	.75
84 Antonio Freeman	.30	.75
85 Marcus Robinson	.25	.60
86 Muhsin Muhammad	.25	.60
87 Junior Seau	.30	.75
88 Zach Thomas	.30	.75
89 Dorsey Levens	.25	.60
90 Tim Biakabutuka	.20	.50
91 Elvis Grbac	.25	.60
92 Jerome Bettis	.30	.75
93 Cris Carter	.30	.75
94 Jerry Rice	.60	1.50
95 Rob Johnson	.25	.60
96 Thomas Jones	.25	.60
97 Duce Staley	.25	.60
98 Ray Lucas	.20	.50
99 Charlie Batch	.25	.60
100 Jamal Anderson	.25	.60
101 Michael Vick RC	6.00	15.00
102 Drew Brees RC	10.00	25.00
103 Andre Carter RC	1.25	3.00
104 David Terrell RC	1.25	3.00
105 Koren Robinson RC	1.25	3.00
106 Rod Gardner RC	1.25	3.00
107 Santana Moss RC	2.00	5.00
108 Deuce McAllister RC	1.50	4.00
109 Freddie Mitchell RC	1.00	2.50
110 Michael Bennett RC	1.25	3.00
111 Reggie Wayne RC	3.00	8.00
112 Todd Heap RC	1.50	4.00
113 LaDainian Tomlinson RC	5.00	12.00
114 Chad Johnson RC	2.50	6.00
115 Anthony Thomas RC	1.50	4.00
116 Robert Ferguson RC	1.50	4.00
117 LaMont Jordan RC	1.50	4.00
118 Chris Chambers RC	1.50	4.00
119 Travis Henry RC	1.25	3.00
120 Marques Tuiasosopo RC	1.25	3.00
121 James Jackson RC	1.00	2.50
122 Heath Evans RC	1.25	3.00
123 Travis Minor RC	1.25	3.00
124 Rudi Johnson RC	1.50	4.00
125 Chris Weinke RC	1.25	3.00
126 Sage Rosenfels RC	1.50	4.00
127 Fred Smoot RC	1.50	4.00
128 Correll Buckhalter RC	1.50	4.00
129 Justin McCareins RC	1.25	3.00
130 Jesse Palmer RC	1.25	3.00
131 Scotty Anderson RC	1.00	2.50
132 Kevan Barlow RC	1.25	3.00
133 John Capel RC	1.00	2.50
134 Mike McMahon RC	1.25	3.00
135 Snoop Minnis RC	1.00	2.50
136 Quincy Morgan RC	1.25	3.00
137 Vinny Sutherland RC	1.00	2.50
138 Dan Alexander RC	1.25	3.00
139 Cedrick Wilson RC	1.25	3.00
140 Josh Booty RC	1.25	3.00
141 Bobby Newcombe RC	1.25	3.00
142 Josh Heupel RC	1.50	4.00
143 Ken-Yon Rambo RC	1.00	2.50
144 Eddie Berlin RC	1.00	2.50
145 Reggie Germany RC	1.00	2.50
146 Quincy Carter RC	1.25	3.00
147 Steve Smith RC	3.00	8.00
148 Dan Morgan RC	1.25	3.00
149 Chris Barnes RC	1.00	2.50
150 Alex Bannister RC	1.00	2.50
151 A.J. Feeley RC	1.25	3.00
152 Jason Brookins RC	1.50	4.00
153 Kevin Kasper RC	1.00	2.50
154 Nick Goings RC	1.50	4.00
155 Gerard Warren RC	1.25	3.00

2001 Fleer Authority Prominence 25

*ROOKIES 101-155: 2X TO 5X BASIC CARD
STATED PRINT RUN 25 SER.#'d SETS

2001 Fleer Authority Prominence 75

*VETS 1-100: 6X TO 15X BASIC CARDS
*ROOKIES 101-155: 1X TO 2.5X
STATED PRINT RUN 75 SER.#'d SETS

2001 Fleer Authority Prominence 125

*VETS 1-100: 5X TO 12X BASIC CARDS
STATED PRINT RUN 125 SER.#'d SETS

2001 Fleer Authority Autographs

STATED ODDS 1:59 HOB, 1:206 RET		
ANNOUNCED PRIINT RUNS 25-500		
1 Shaun Alexander/500*	6.00	15.00
2 Drew Brees/150*	75.00	135.00
3 Isaac Bruce/95*	8.00	20.00
4 Chris Chambers/450*	5.00	12.00
5 Wayne Chrebet/500*	4.00	10.00
6 Daunte Culpepper/25*	12.00	30.00
7 Stephen Davis/500*	4.00	10.00
8 Corey Dillon/500*	4.00	10.00
9 Marshall Faulk/25*	15.00	40.00
10 Travis Henry/400*	4.00	10.00
11 Josh Heupel/500*	5.00	12.00
12 Torry Holt/500*	5.00	12.00
13 Edgerrin James/25*	15.00	40.00
14 Jamal Lewis/450*	5.00	12.00
15 Deuce McAllister	8.00	20.00
16 Donovan McNabb/100*	15.00	40.00
17 Travis Minor/500*	4.00	10.00
18 Quincy Morgan/500*	4.00	10.00
19 Randy Moss	25.00	50.00
20 Santana Moss/250*	6.00	15.00
21 Ken-Yon Rambo/500*	3.00	8.00
22 Sage Rosenfels/500*	5.00	12.00
23 Jimmy Smith/225*	4.00	10.00
24 Duce Staley/250*	4.00	10.00
25 David Terrell/225*	4.00	10.00
26 Anthony Thomas/500*	5.00	12.00
27 LaDainian Tomlinson/250*	40.00	100.00
28 Marques Tuiasosopo/500*	4.00	10.00
29 Chris Weinke/100*	6.00	15.00

2001 Fleer Authority Figure

COMPLETE SET (20)	12.50	30.00
STATED PRINT RUN 1750 SER.#'d SETS		
1 Michael Vick/Jamal Anderson	1.50	4.00
2 Drew Brees	2.50	6.00
Doug Flutie		
3 David Terrell	.30	.75
Marcus Robinson		
4 Koren Robinson	.40	1.00
Matt Hasselbeck		
5 Rod Gardner	.30	.75
Stephen Davis		
6 Santana Moss	.50	1.25
Wayne Chrebet		
7 Deuce McAllister	.40	1.00
Ricky Williams		
8 Dan Morgan	.50	1.25
Brian Urlacher		
9 Reggie Wayne	.75	2.00
Marvin Harrison		
10 Marques Tuiasosopo	.40	1.00
Tim Brown		
11 Freddie Mitchell	.40	1.00
Donovan McNabb		
12 Quincy Morgan	.30	.75
Tim Couch		
13 Chad Johnson	.60	1.50
Peter Warrick		
14 Robert Ferguson	1.25	3.00
Brett Favre		
15 Josh Heupel	.40	1.00
Chris Weinke		
16 Anthony Thomas	.40	1.00
Cade McNown		
17 Quincy Carter	1.00	2.50
Emmitt Smith		
18 Kevan Barlow	.30	.75
Jeff Garcia		
19 James Jackson	.40	1.00
Edgerrin James		
20 Michael Bennett	.40	1.00
Randy Moss		

2001 Fleer Authority Goal Line Gear

STATED ODDS 1:14 HOB, 1:44 RET		
1 David Boston Hat/100	4.00	10.00
2 David Boston JSY/450	2.50	6.00
3 Mark Brunell Hat/100	5.00	12.00
4 Mark Brunell JSY/650	3.00	8.00
5 Tim Couch Hat/200	3.00	8.00
6 Tim Couch Pants/800	2.50	6.00
7 Ron Dayne JSY/800	3.00	8.00
8 Warrick Dunn JSY/800	4.00	10.00
9 Marshall Faulk FB/200	5.00	12.00
10 Marshall Faulk Hat/200	5.00	12.00
11 Marshall Faulk JSY/500	4.00	10.00
12 Marshall Faulk Pants/175	5.00	12.00
13 Brett Favre JSY/200	15.00	40.00
14 Rich Gannon JSY/800	3.00	8.00
15 Eddie George Hat/200	5.00	12.00
16 Eddie George JSY/800	4.00	10.00
17 Marvin Harrison JSY/550	4.00	10.00
18 Marvin Harrison Pants/325	5.00	12.00
19 Torry Holt Hat/200	4.00	10.00
20 Torry Holt JSY/800	3.00	8.00
21 Torry Holt Pants/300	4.00	10.00
22 Torry Holt Shoes/400	3.00	8.00
23 Edgerrin James FB/200	5.00	12.00
24 Edgerrin James Pants/800	4.00	10.00
25 Kevin Johnson Hat/100	4.00	10.00
26 Kevin Johnson Pants/400	2.50	6.00
27 Thomas Jones Hat/100	5.00	12.00
28 Thomas Jones JSY/100	5.00	12.00
29 Jevon Kearse Hat/100	5.00	12.00
30 Jevon Kearse JSY/650	3.00	8.00
31 Jevon Kearse Pants/200	4.00	10.00
32 Donovan McNabb FB/200	5.00	12.00
33 Donovan McNabb Hat/300	5.00	12.00
34 Donovan McNabb JSY/625	4.00	10.00
35 Donovan McNabb Pants/800	4.00	10.00
36 Steve McNair Hat/100	6.00	15.00
37 Cade McNown Jsy	3.00	8.00
38 Cade McNown Hat	3.00	8.00
39 Chad Pennington JSY/800	4.00	10.00
40 Jake Plummer Hat/100	5.00	12.00
41 Jake Plummer JSY/250	4.00	10.00
42 Jake Plummer Pants/900	3.00	8.00
43 Warren Sapp JSY/800	3.00	8.00
44 Junior Seau JSY/800	4.00	10.00
45 Emmitt Smith FB/200	12.00	30.00
46 Emmitt Smith JSY/600	10.00	25.00
47 Duce Staley Hat/100	5.00	12.00
48 R.Jay Soward JSY	2.50	6.00
49 Duce Staley JSY/150	5.00	12.00
50 Fred Taylor FB/100	6.00	15.00
51 Fred Taylor Hat/750	4.00	10.00
52 Fred Taylor JSY/360	5.00	12.00
53 Brian Urlacher Hat/200	6.00	15.00
54 Brian Urlacher JSY/200	6.00	15.00
55 Kurt Warner FB/100	10.00	25.00
56 Kurt Warner Hat/100	10.00	25.00
57 Kurt Warner JSY/250	8.00	20.00
58 Kurt Warner Pants/150	10.00	25.00
59 Dez White Hat	3.00	8.00
60 Dez White JSY	3.00	8.00

2001 Fleer Authority Seal of Approval

COMPLETE SET (15)	30.00	60.00
STATED ODDS 1:80 HOB, 1:120 RET		
1 Donovan McNabb	1.50	4.00
2 Emmitt Smith	4.00	10.00
3 Edgerrin James	1.50	4.00
4 Brett Favre	5.00	12.00
5 Michael Vick	6.00	15.00
6 Daunte Culpepper	1.25	3.00
7 Eddie George	1.50	4.00
8 LaDainian Tomlinson	2.50	6.00
9 Jamal Lewis	1.50	4.00
10 Marshall Faulk	1.50	4.00
11 Peyton Manning	4.00	10.00
12 Randy Moss	1.50	4.00
13 Ricky Williams	1.50	4.00
14 Fred Taylor	1.50	4.00
15 Kurt Warner	2.50	6.00

2001 Fleer Authority We're Number One

COMPLETE SET (10)	12.50	25.00
STATED ODDS 1:20 HOB, 1:40 RET		
1 Tim Couch	.60	1.50
2 Drew Bledsoe	1.00	2.50
3 Troy Aikman	2.00	5.00
4 Bo Jackson	1.50	4.00
5 George Rogers	1.00	2.50
6 Earl Campbell	1.25	3.00
7 Jim Plunkett	1.00	2.50
8 Terry Bradshaw	2.00	5.00
9 Paul Hornung	1.25	3.00
10 Michael Vick	2.50	6.00

2001 Fleer Authority We're Number One Autographs

STATED ODDS 1:100
1 Troy Aikman 30.00 80.00
2 Drew Bledsoe 15.00 30.00
3 Terry Bradshaw 50.00 100.00
4 Earl Campbell 15.00 30.00
5 Irving Fryar 15.00 30.00
6 Paul Hornung 15.00 30.00
7 Bo Jackson 50.00 120.00
8 Jim Plunkett 10.00 20.00
9 George Rogers 15.00 30.00
10 Michael Vick 75.00 150.00

2001 Fleer Authority We're Number One Jerseys

STATED ODDS 1:100
1 Drew Bledsoe 7.50 20.00
2 Terry Bradshaw 15.00 40.00
3 Tim Couch 6.00 15.00
4 John Elway 20.00 50.00
5 Bo Jackson 15.00 40.00
6 Jim Plunkett 6.00 15.00

2003 Fleer Avant

Released in November of 2003, this set consists of 90 cards, including 60 veterans and 30 rookies. Rookies 61-90 are serial numbered to 699. Boxes contained 18 packs of 4 cards. SRP was $7.99.

COMP.SET w/o SP's (60) 12.50 30.00
ROOKIE PRINT RUN 699 SER.#'d SETS
1 Priest Holmes .50 1.25
2 Hines Ward .50 1.25
3 Patrick Ramsey .40 1.00
4 Deuce McAllister .40 1.00
5 Tony Gonzalez .50 1.25
6 Daunte Culpepper .40 1.00
7 Edgerrin James .50 1.25
8 Jeremy Shockey .50 1.25
9 Donovan McNabb .50 1.25
10 Eddie George .40 1.00
11 Ray Lewis .50 1.25
12 LaDainian Tomlinson .50 1.25
13 Peyton Manning 1.00 2.50
14 Charlie Garner .40 1.00
15 Brad Johnson .40 1.00
16 David Carr .40 1.00
17 Jerry Rice 1.00 2.50
18 Keyshawn Johnson .50 1.25
19 Ahman Green .40 1.00
20 Rich Gannon .40 1.00
21 William Green .30 .75
22 Torry Holt .50 1.25
23 Brett Favre 1.25 3.00
24 Curtis Martin .50 1.25
25 Derrick Brooks .40 1.00
26 Joey Harrington .30 .75
27 Chad Pennington .50 1.25
28 Koren Robinson .40 1.00
29 Clinton Portis .40 1.00
30 Michael Strahan .50 1.25
31 Marvin Harrison .50 1.25
32 Travis Henry .30 .75
33 Aaron Brooks .40 1.00
34 Antwaan Randle El .40 1.00
35 Antonio Bryant .30 .75
36 Shaun Alexander .40 1.00
37 Jake Plummer .40 1.00
38 Emmitt Smith 1.25 3.00
39 Plaxico Burress .40 1.00
40 Peerless Price .30 .75
41 Drew Bledsoe .50 1.25
42 Jeff Garcia .40 1.00
43 Fred Taylor .40 1.00
44 Correll Buckhalter .40 1.00
45 Steve McNair .50 1.25
46 Stephen Davis .40 1.00
47 Terrell Owens .50 1.25
48 Corey Dillon .40 1.00
49 Marshall Faulk .50 1.25
50 Tom Brady 1.25 3.00
51 Tiki Barber .50 1.25
52 Michael Vick .60 1.50
53 Drew Brees .50 1.25
54 Chad Johnson .50 1.25
55 Randy Moss .50 1.25
56 Eric Moulds .40 1.00
57 Brian Urlacher .50 1.25
58 Kurt Warner .50 1.25
59 Ricky Williams .40 1.00
60 Laveranues Coles .30 .75
61 Carson Palmer RC 4.00 10.00
62 Charles Rogers RC 1.50 4.00
63 Andre Johnson RC 5.00 12.00
64 DeWayne Robertson RC 1.50 4.00
65 Terence Newman RC 1.50 4.00
66 Byron Leftwich RC 2.00 5.00
67 Terrell Suggs RC 2.00 5.00
68 Bryant Johnson RC 2.00 5.00
69 Kyle Boller RC 2.00 5.00
70 Rex Grossman RC 2.00 5.00
71 Willis McGahee RC 2.50 6.00
72 Dallas Clark RC 3.00 8.00
73 Larry Johnson RC 2.00 5.00
74 Bennie Joppru RC 1.25 3.00
75 Taylor Jacobs RC 1.25 3.00
76 Anquan Boldin RC 3.00 8.00
77 Tyrone Calico RC 1.50 4.00
78 L.J. Smith RC 2.00 5.00
79 Teyo Johnson RC 1.50 4.00
80 Kelley Washington RC 1.25 3.00
81 Jason Witten RC 5.00 12.00
82 Nate Burleson RC 1.50 4.00
83 Musa Smith RC 1.25 3.00
84 Tony Hollings RC 1.50 4.00
85 Chris Brown RC 1.25 3.00
86 Billy McMullen RC 1.25 3.00
87 Chris Simms RC 2.00 5.00
88 Artose Pinner RC 1.25 3.00
89 Quentin Griffin RC 1.50 4.00
90 Onterrio Smith RC 1.25 3.00

2003 Fleer Avant Black

*VETS 1-60: 2X TO 5X BASIC CARDS
*ROOKIES 61-90: .8X TO 2X
BLACK/199 STATED ODDS 1:3
STATED PRINT RUN 199 SER.#'d SETS

2003 Fleer Avant Candid Collection

OVERALL #'d INSERT ODDS 1:199
STATED PRINT RUN 99 SER.#'d SETS
1 Donovan McNabb 3.00 8.00
2 Brett Favre 8.00 20.00
3 Terrell Owens 3.00 8.00
4 Michael Vick 4.00 10.00
5 Kurt Warner 3.00 8.00
6 Emmitt Smith 8.00 20.00
7 Clinton Portis 2.50 6.00
8 Rich Gannon 2.50 6.00
9 Ricky Williams 2.50 6.00
10 Daunte Culpepper 2.50 6.00
11 Peyton Manning 6.00 15.00
12 Chad Pennington 3.00 8.00
13 Warren Sapp 2.50 6.00
14 Shaun Alexander 2.50 6.00
15 Priest Holmes 3.00 8.00
16 LaDainian Tomlinson 3.00 8.00
17 Jeremy Shockey 3.00 8.00
18 Randy Moss 3.00 8.00
19 Joey Harrington 2.00 5.00
20 David Carr 2.50 6.00

2003 Fleer Avant Candid Collection Jerseys

OVERALL MEMORABILIA ODDS 1:3
STATED PRINT RUN 100 SER.#'d SETS
1 Daunte Culpepper 4.00 10.00
2 Brett Favre 12.00 30.00
3 Joey Harrington 3.00 8.00
4 Priest Holmes 5.00 12.00
5 Peyton Manning 10.00 25.00
6 Donovan McNabb 5.00 12.00
7 Terrell Owens 5.00 12.00
8 Clinton Portis 4.00 10.00
9 Warren Sapp 4.00 10.00
10 Jeremy Shockey 5.00 12.00

2003 Fleer Avant Draw Play

COMPLETE SET (15) 15.00 40.00
OVERALL #'d INSERT ODDS 1:199
STATED PRINT RUN 535 SER.#'d SETS
1 Ricky Williams 1.00 2.50
2 Michael Vick 1.50 4.00
3 Travis Henry .75 2.00
4 Deuce McAllister 1.00 2.50
5 Clinton Portis 1.00 2.50
6 Ahman Green 1.00 2.50
7 Priest Holmes 1.25 3.00
8 Marshall Faulk 1.25 3.00
9 Emmitt Smith 3.00 8.00
10 LaDainian Tomlinson 1.25 3.00
11 Steve McNair 1.25 3.00
12 Daunte Culpepper 1.00 2.50
13 Tiki Barber 1.25 3.00
14 Donovan McNabb 1.25 3.00
15 Edgerrin James 1.25 3.00

2003 Fleer Avant Draw Play Jerseys

OVERALL MEMORABILIA ODDS 1:3
SER.#'d UNDER 20 NOT PRICED
1 Marshall Faulk/28 15.00 40.00
2 Edgerrin James/32 15.00 40.00
3 Deuce McAllister/26 12.00 30.00
5 LaDainian Tomlinson/21 15.00 40.00

2003 Fleer Avant Materials Blue

PRINT RUN 250 SER.#'d SETS
*PATCH/25: 1.5X TO 4X BLUE JSY
PATCHES PRINT RUN 25 SER.#'d SETS
*RED/75: .6X TO 1.5X BLUE JSY
RED PRINT RUN 75 SER.#'d SETS
OVERALL MEMORABILIA ODDS 1:3
1 Drew Bledsoe 4.00 10.00
2 Tom Brady 10.00 25.00
3 Drew Brees 4.00 10.00
4 David Carr 3.00 8.00
5 Daunte Culpepper 3.00 8.00
6 Corey Dillon 3.00 8.00
7 Marshall Faulk 4.00 10.00
8 Brett Favre 10.00 25.00
9 Rich Gannon 3.00 8.00
10 Eddie George 3.00 8.00
11 Ahman Green 3.00 8.00
12 Rex Grossman 3.00 8.00
13 Joey Harrington 2.00 5.00
14 Torry Holt 4.00 10.00
15 Taylor Jacobs 2.50 6.00
16 Edgerrin James 4.00 10.00
17 Andre Johnson 8.00 20.00
18 Larry Johnson 3.00 8.00
19 Byron Leftwich 3.00 8.00
20 Peyton Manning 8.00 20.00
21 Deuce McAllister 3.00 8.00
22 Donovan McNabb 4.00 10.00
23 Steve McNair 4.00 10.00
24 Peerless Price 2.50 6.00
25 Antwaan Randle El 3.00 8.00
26 Jeremy Shockey 4.00 10.00
27 Chris Simms 3.00 8.00
28 LaDainian Tomlinson 4.00 10.00
29 Brian Urlacher 4.00 10.00
30 Hines Ward 4.00 10.00

2003 Fleer Avant Work of Heart

COMPLETE SET (10) 15.00 40.00
PRINT RUN 300 SER.#'d SETS
OVERALL #'d INSERT ODDS 1:199
1 Brett Favre 4.00 10.00
2 Marshall Faulk 1.50 4.00
3 Jerry Rice 3.00 8.00
4 Michael Vick 2.00 5.00
5 Jeff Garcia 1.25 3.00
6 Joey Harrington 1.00 2.50
7 Edgerrin James 1.50 4.00
8 Donovan McNabb 1.50 4.00
9 Jeremy Shockey 1.50 4.00
10 Randy Moss 1.50 4.00

2003 Fleer Avant Work of Heart Jerseys

OVERALL MEMORABILIA ODDS 1:3
PRINT RUN 300 SER.#'d SETS
1 Brett Favre 10.00 25.00
2 Marshall Faulk 4.00 10.00
3 Jerry Rice 8.00 20.00
4 Michael Vick 5.00 12.00
5 Jeff Garcia 3.00 8.00
6 Joey Harrington 2.50 6.00
7 Edgerrin James 4.00 10.00
8 Donovan McNabb 4.00 10.00
9 Jeremy Shockey 4.00 10.00
10 Randy Moss 4.00 10.00

2002 Fleer Box Score

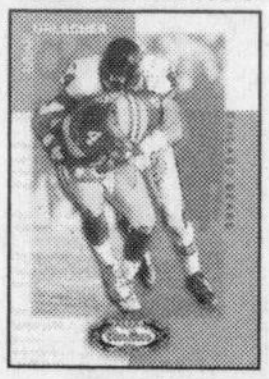

Released in late November 2002, this set consists of 240-cards including 115-veterans, 35-rookies, 30-rising stars, 30-quarterbacks, and 30-all-pros. The rookies were serial numbered to 1500. Cards 151-180 were only available in rising stars mini boxes, cards 181-210 were only found in QBC mini boxes, and cards 211-240 were only found in All Pro mini boxes.

COMP.SET w/o SP's (115) 10.00 25.00
1 Brian Urlacher .40 1.00
2 Edgerrin James .30 .75
3 Ricky Williams .30 .75
4 Tim Brown .40 1.00
5 Tim Couch .25 .60
6 Kurt Warner .40 1.00
7 Kendrell Bell .25 .60
8 Daunte Culpepper .30 .75
9 Anthony Thomas .30 .75
10 Marvin Harrison .40 1.00
11 Jerry Rice .75 2.00
12 Eddie George .30 .75
13 Donovan McNabb .40 1.00
14 Chris Chambers .30 .75
15 Emmitt Smith 1.00 2.50
16 David Boston .25 .60
17 Plaxico Burress .30 .75
18 Randy Moss .40 1.00
19 Peyton Manning .75 2.00
20 Michael Vick .60 1.50
21 Marshall Faulk .40 1.00
22 Tom Brady 1.00 2.50
23 LaDainian Tomlinson .50 1.25
24 Shaun Alexander .30 .75
25 Curtis Martin .40 1.00
26 Brett Favre 1.00 2.50
27 Drew Bledsoe .40 1.00
28 Jeff Garcia .30 .75
29 Terrell Davis .40 1.00
30 Corey Dillon .30 .75
31 Troy Brown .30 .75
32 Drew Brees .60 1.50
33 Jamal Lewis .30 .75
34 Derrick Alexander .25 .60
35 Az-Zahir Hakim .25 .60
36 Antowain Smith .30 .75
37 Muhsin Muhammad .30 .75
38 Warrick Dunn .30 .75
39 Curtis Conway .30 .75
40 Antonio Freeman .40 1.00
41 Bill Schroeder .25 .60
42 Joe Horn .30 .75
43 Peerless Price .25 .60
44 Ahman Green .30 .75
45 Marcus Robinson .30 .75
46 Aaron Brooks .30 .75
47 Cris Carter .40 1.00
48 Tiki Barber .40 1.00
49 Terry Glenn .30 .75
50 Ed McCaffrey .30 .75
51 Darrell Jackson .30 .75
52 Garrison Hearst .30 .75
53 Hines Ward .40 1.00
54 Deuce McAllister .30 .75
55 Rod Gardner .25 .60
56 Amani Toomer .30 .75
57 Thomas Jones .40 1.00
58 Travis Henry .25 .60
59 Koren Robinson .25 .60
60 Travis Taylor .25 .60
61 Ron Dayne .30 .75
62 Robert Ferguson .30 .75
63 Chad Pennington .40 1.00
64 James Allen .25 .60
65 Chris Weinke .25 .60
66 Torry Holt .40 1.00
67 Chris Chandler .30 .75
68 Shane Matthews .25 .60
69 Ike Hilliard .30 .75
70 Charlie Garner .30 .75
71 Laveranues Coles .30 .75
72 Lamar Smith .30 .75
73 Rob Johnson .30 .75
74 Qadry Ismail .30 .75
75 James Jackson .25 .60
76 Wayne Chrebet .30 .75
77 Priest Holmes .40 1.00
78 Michael Westbrook .25 .60
79 Michael Pittman .30 .75
80 Derrick Mason .30 .75
81 Dominic Rhodes .30 .75
82 Eric Moulds .30 .75
83 Fred Taylor .30 .75
84 Corey Bradford .25 .60
85 Steve McNair .40 1.00
86 Tyrone Wheatley .30 .75
87 Peter Warrick .30 .75
88 Freddie Mitchell .25 .60
89 Peter Boulware .25 .60
90 Kevin Johnson .25 .60
91 Jermaine Lewis .25 .60
92 Joey Galloway .30 .75
93 Stephen Davis .30 .75
94 James Thrash .30 .75
95 James Stewart .25 .60
96 Quincy Morgan .25 .60
97 Dorsey Levens .30 .75
98 Johnnie Morton .30 .75
99 Rocket Ismail .30 .75
100 Rod Smith .30 .75
101 David Terrell .25 .60
102 Kordell Stewart .30 .75
103 Marty Booker .30 .75
104 Brian Griese .30 .75
105 Snoop Minnis .25 .60
106 Jake Plummer .30 .75
107 Keenan McCardell .30 .75
108 Duce Staley .30 .75
109 Isaac Bruce .40 1.00
110 Bubba Franks .30 .75
111 Keyshawn Johnson .30 .75
112 Kevan Barlow .25 .60
113 Reggie Wayne .40 1.00
114 Michael Bennett .30 .75
115 Santana Moss .30 .75
116 David Carr RC 1.00 2.50
117 Joey Harrington RC 1.00 2.50
118 Antwaan Randle El RC 1.00 2.50
119 Eric Crouch RC 1.00 2.50
120 Javon Walker RC 1.00 2.50
121 William Green RC .75 2.00
122 Patrick Ramsey RC 1.00 2.50
123 Clinton Portis RC 1.25 3.00
124 Andre Davis RC .75 2.00
125 T.J. Duckett RC 1.00 2.50
126 Ladell Betts RC 1.00 2.50
127 Marquise Walker RC .60 1.50
128 Maurice Morris RC .75 2.00
129 Brian Westbrook RC 1.50 4.00
130 Phillip Buchanon RC 1.00 2.50
131 Tim Carter RC .75 2.00
132 Zak Kustok RC .60 1.50
133 Chester Taylor RC 1.00 2.50
134 Josh Reed RC .75 2.00
135 Kurt Kittner RC .60 1.50
136 Cliff Russell RC .60 1.50
137 Travis Fisher RC .75 2.00
138 Jerramy Stevens RC 1.00 2.50
139 Verron Haynes RC .60 1.50
140 Ricky Williams RC .75 2.00
141 Randy McMichael RC 1.00 2.50
142 Dwight Freeney RC 1.25 3.00
143 Lito Sheppard RC 1.00 2.50
144 Mike Williams RC .60 1.50
145 Jason McAddley RC .75 2.00
146 Deion Branch RC 1.00 2.50
147 Daniel Graham RC .75 2.00
148 J.T. O'Sullivan RC .75 2.00
149 Freddie Milons RC .60 1.50
150 Ron Johnson RC .75 2.00
151 Ashley Lelie RC .50 1.25
152 Roy Williams RC .60 1.50
153 Donte Stallworth RC .60 1.50
154 Randy Fasani RC .50 1.25
155 Antonio Bryant RC .60 1.50
156 Julius Peppers RC 1.25 3.00
157 Jabar Gaffney RC .60 1.50
158 Chad Hutchinson RC .40 1.00
159 DeShaun Foster RC .60 1.50
160 Micah Ross RC .40 1.00
161 Rocky Calmus RC .50 1.25
162 Travis Stephens RC .40 1.00
163 Quentin Jammer RC .60 1.50
164 Napoleon Harris RC .50 1.25
165 Jeremy Shockey RC 1.00 2.50
166 Rohan Davey RC .60 1.50
167 Najeh Davenport RC .60 1.50
168 Adrian Peterson RC .60 1.50
169 Ed Reed RC 2.50 6.00
170 Ben Leber RC .40 1.00
171 Robert Thomas RC .40 1.00
172 Lamar Gordon RC .50 1.25
173 Reche Caldwell RC .60 1.50
174 Michael Lewis RC .60 1.50
175 Ryan Sims RC .60 1.50
176 David Garrard RC .75 2.00
177 Jonathan Wells RC .60 1.50
178 Albert Haynesworth RC .60 1.50
179 Josh McCown RC .60 1.50
180 John Henderson RC .50 1.25
181 Jake Plummer QBC .40 1.00
182 Michael Vick QBC .75 2.00
183 Chris Redman QBC .30 .75
184 Drew Bledsoe QBC .50 1.25
185 Jim Miller QBC .30 .75
186 Jon Kitna QBC .40 1.00
187 Tim Couch QBC .30 .75
188 Quincy Carter QBC .30 .75
189 Brian Griese QBC .40 1.00
190 Mike McMahon QBC .30 .75
191 Brett Favre QBC 1.25 3.00
192 David Carr QBC .50 1.25
193 Peyton Manning QBC 1.00 2.50
194 Mark Brunell QBC .40 1.00
195 Trent Green QBC .40 1.00
196 Jay Fiedler QBC .40 1.00
197 Daunte Culpepper QBC .40 1.00
198 Tom Brady QBC 1.25 3.00
199 Aaron Brooks QBC .40 1.00
200 Kerry Collins QBC .40 1.00
201 Vinny Testaverde QBC .40 1.00
202 Rich Gannon QBC .40 1.00
203 Donovan McNabb QBC .50 1.25
204 Kordell Stewart QBC .40 1.00
205 Doug Flutie QBC .50 1.25
206 Jeff Garcia QBC .40 1.00
207 Trent Dilfer QBC .40 1.00
208 Kurt Warner QBC .50 1.25
209 Brad Johnson QBC .40 1.00
210 Steve McNair QBC .50 1.25
211 Sam Madison AP .30 .75
212 Bruce Matthews AP .40 1.00
213 Brett Favre AP 1.25 3.00
214 Cris Carter AP .50 1.25
215 Michael Strahan AP .50 1.25
216 Ray Lewis AP .50 1.25
217 Randy Moss AP .50 1.25
218 Jerome Bettis AP .50 1.25
219 Warren Sapp AP .40 1.00
220 Junior Seau AP .50 1.25
221 Emmitt Smith AP 1.25 3.00
222 Jimmy Smith AP .40 1.00
223 Mike Alstott AP .40 1.00
224 Zach Thomas AP .50 1.25
225 Marshall Faulk AP .50 1.25
226 John Lynch AP .40 1.00
227 Larry Allen AP .30 .75
228 Kurt Warner AP .50 1.25
229 Eddie George AP .40 1.00
230 Tony Gonzalez AP .50 1.25
231 Marvin Harrison AP .50 1.25
232 Terrell Davis AP .50 1.25
233 Peyton Manning AP 1.00 2.50
234 Terrell Owens AP .50 1.25
235 Jevon Kearse AP .40 1.00
236 Jerry Rice AP 1.00 2.50
237 Shannon Sharpe AP .50 1.25
238 Rod Woodson AP .50 1.25
239 Mark Brunell AP .40 1.00
240 Tim Brown AP .50 1.25

2002 Fleer Box Score Classic Miniatures

COMPLETE SET (30) 12.50 30.00
*MINIS: .8X TO 2X BASIC CARDS
CLASSIC MINIATURE SET IN MINI BOXES

2002 Fleer Box Score Classic Miniatures First Edition

*MIN FIRST EDIT/100: 3X TO 8X BASIC CARDS
FIRST EDITION PRINT RUN 100

2002 Fleer Box Score First Edition

*VETS 1-115: 3X TO 8X BASIC CARDS
*ROOKIES 116-150: .8X TO 2X
*ROOKIES 151-180: 1.2X TO 3X
*QBC 181-210: 2.5X TO 6X
*AP 211-240: 2.5X TO 6X
STATED PRINT RUN 100 SER.#'d SETS

2002 Fleer Box Score All Pro Roster Jerseys

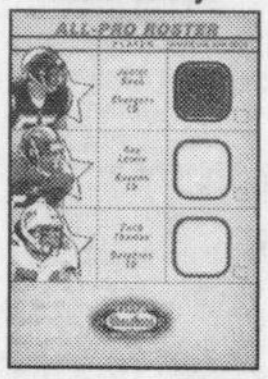

ONE PER ALL PRO MINI BOX
1 Cris Carter 12.00 30.00
Randy Moss
Jerry Rice
Tim Brown
2 Brett Favre 15.00 40.00
Emmitt Smith
Jerry Rice
Randy Moss
3 Brett Favre 15.00 40.00
Kurt Warner
Peyton Manning
Mark Brunell
4 Tony Gonzalez 6.00 15.00
Shannon Sharpe
Mike Alstott
5 Sam Madison 6.00 15.00
John Lynch
Rod Woodson
6 Junior Seau 6.00 15.00
Ray Lewis
Zach Thomas
7 Emmitt Smith 15.00 40.00
Marshall Faulk
Eddie George
Terrell Davis
8 Jimmy Smith 6.00 15.00
Marvin Harrison
Terrell Owens
9 Michael Strahan 6.00 15.00
Jevon Kearse
Warren Sapp
10 Kurt Warner 12.00 30.00
Marshall Faulk
Peyton Manning
Eddie George

2002 Fleer Box Score Classic Miniatures Jerseys

ONE PER CLASSIC MINIATURES MINI BOX
1 Brian Urlacher 4.00 10.00
2 Ricky Williams 3.00 8.00
3 Tom Brady 10.00 25.00
4 Shaun Alexander 3.00 8.00
5 Anthony Thomas 3.00 8.00
6 Chris Chambers 3.00 8.00
7 David Boston 2.50 6.00
8 LaDainian Tomlinson 5.00 12.00
9 Plaxico Burress 3.00 8.00
10 Corey Dillon 3.00 8.00

2002 Fleer Box Score Debuts

COMPLETE SET (15) 15.00 40.00
STATED PRINT RUN 2002 SER.#'d SETS
1 Antwaan Randle El 1.00 2.50
2 T.J. Duckett 1.00 2.50
3 Donte Stallworth 1.00 2.50
4 Deion Branch 1.00 2.50
5 William Green .75 2.00
6 Brian Westbrook 1.50 4.00
7 Jabar Gaffney 1.00 2.50
8 Clinton Portis 1.25 3.00
9 Joey Harrington 1.00 2.50
10 Andre Davis .75 2.00
11 Javon Walker 1.00 2.50
12 Antonio Bryant 1.00 2.50
13 Jeremy Shockey 1.50 4.00
14 Josh Reed .75 2.00
15 David Carr 1.00 2.50

2002 Fleer Box Score Jersey Rack Quads

STATED PRINT RUN 100 SER.#'d SETS
1 Eddie George 10.00 25.00
Steve McNair
Donovan McNabb
Antonio Freeman
2 Jeff Garcia 10.00 25.00
Terrell Owens
Marshall Faulk
Kurt Warner
3 Randy Moss 25.00 60.00
Daunte Culpepper
Ahman Green
Brett Favre
4 Jamal Lewis 25.00 60.00
Peyton Manning
Emmitt Smith
Fred Taylor
5 David Boston 12.00 30.00
Marvin Harrison
LaDainian Tomlinson
Curtis Martin
6 Ricky Williams 10.00 25.00
Chris Chambers
Edgerrin James
Marvin Harrison
7 Tom Brady 25.00 60.00
Antowain Smith
Marshall Faulk
Kurt Warner

2002 Fleer Box Score Jersey Rack Triples

STATED PRINT RUN 300 SER.#'d SETS
1 Tom Brady 25.00 60.00
Brett Favre
Kurt Warner
2 Randy Moss 15.00 40.00
Jerry Rice
Torry Holt
3 Kordell Stewart 8.00 20.00
Plaxico Burress
Jerome Bettis
4 Anthony Thomas 6.00 15.00
Ahman Green
Shaun Alexander
5 Michael Vick 12.00 30.00
Daunte Culpepper
Donovan McNabb

2002 Fleer Box Score Press Clippings

STATED ODDS 1:18
1 David Carr 1.25 3.00
2 Joey Harrington 1.25 3.00
3 Drew Bledsoe 1.25 3.00
4 Michael Vick 2.00 5.00
5 Kordell Stewart 1.00 2.50
6 Aaron Brooks 1.00 2.50
7 Donovan McNabb 1.25 3.00
8 Rich Gannon 1.00 2.50
9 Drew Brees 2.00 5.00
10 Peyton Manning 2.50 6.00
11 Tom Brady 3.00 8.00
12 Brett Favre 3.00 8.00
13 Jeff Garcia 1.00 2.50
14 Kurt Warner 1.25 3.00
15 Daunte Culpepper 1.00 2.50

2002 Fleer Box Score Press Clippings Jerseys

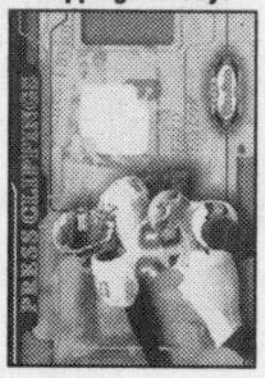

STATED ODDS 1:14
*PATCH/50: 1X TO 2.5X BASIC JSY
PATCHES PRINT RUN 50 SER.#'d SETS
1 Shaun Alexander 3.00 8.00
2 Jerome Bettis 4.00 10.00
3 David Boston 2.50 6.00
4 Tim Couch 2.50 6.00
5 Marvin Harrison 4.00 10.00
6 Torry Holt 4.00 10.00
7 Jamal Lewis 3.00 8.00
8 Curtis Martin 4.00 10.00
9 Jerry Rice 8.00 20.00
10 Emmitt Smith 10.00 25.00
11 Fred Taylor 3.00 8.00
12 Anthony Thomas 3.00 8.00
13 LaDainian Tomlinson 5.00 12.00
14 Brian Urlacher 4.00 10.00
15 Michael Vick 6.00 15.00

2002 Fleer Box Score QBXtra Jerseys

ONE PER QBC MINI BOX
1 Tom Brady SP 10.00 25.00
2 Tim Couch 2.50 6.00
3 Daunte Culpepper 3.00 8.00
4 Brett Favre 10.00 25.00
5 Jeff Garcia 3.00 8.00
6 Brian Griese 3.00 8.00
7 Peyton Manning SP 8.00 20.00
8 Donovan McNabb 4.00 10.00
9 Michael Vick SP 6.00 15.00
10 Kurt Warner 4.00 10.00

2002 Fleer Box Score Red Shirt Freshman

ONE PER RISING STARS MINI BOX
1 Deion Branch 4.00 10.00
2 Antonio Bryant 4.00 10.00
3 David Carr 4.00 10.00
4 DeShaun Foster 4.00 10.00
5 William Green 3.00 8.00
6 Joey Harrington 4.00 10.00
7 Clinton Portis SP 5.00 12.00
8 Josh Reed 3.00 8.00
9 Jeremy Shockey 6.00 15.00
10 Javon Walker 4.00 10.00

2002 Fleer Box Score Yard Markers

COMPLETE SET (20) 15.00 40.00
STATED ODDS 1:9
1 Tom Brady 2.50 6.00
2 Antowain Smith .75 2.00
3 Randy Moss 1.00 2.50
4 Daunte Culpepper .75 2.00
5 Edgerrin James .75 2.00
6 Peyton Manning 2.00 5.00
7 Eddie George .75 2.00
8 Steve McNair 1.00 2.50
9 Ricky Williams .75 2.00
10 Chris Chambers .75 2.00
11 Jeff Garcia .75 2.00
12 Terrell Owens 1.00 2.50
13 Marshall Faulk 1.00 2.50
14 Kurt Warner 1.00 2.50
15 Donovan McNabb 1.00 2.50
16 Freddie Mitchell .60 1.50
17 Ahman Green .75 2.00
18 Brett Favre 2.50 6.00
19 Plaxico Burress .75 2.00
20 Kordell Stewart .75 2.00

2002 Fleer Box Score Yard Markers Jerseys

STATED ODDS 1:14
1 Tom Brady 12.00 30.00
2 Plaxico Burress 4.00 10.00
3 Chris Chambers 4.00 10.00
4 Daunte Culpepper 4.00 10.00
5 Marshall Faulk 5.00 12.00
6 Brett Favre 12.00 30.00
7 Antonio Freeman 5.00 12.00
8 Jeff Garcia 4.00 10.00
9 Eddie George 4.00 10.00
10 Ahman Green 4.00 10.00
11 Edgerrin James 4.00 10.00
12 Peyton Manning 10.00 25.00
13 Donovan McNabb 5.00 12.00
14 Steve McNair 5.00 12.00
15 Randy Moss 5.00 12.00
16 Terrell Owens 5.00 12.00
17 Antowain Smith 4.00 10.00
18 Kordell Stewart 4.00 10.00
19 Kurt Warner 5.00 12.00
20 Ricky Williams 4.00 10.00

2002 Fleer Box Score Yard Markers Duals

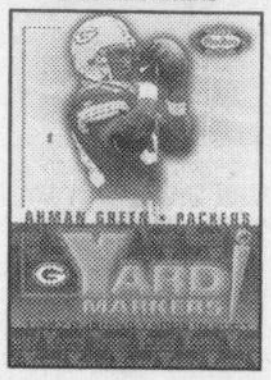

COMPLETE SET (10) 25.00 60.00
STATED ODDS 1:108
1 Tom Brady 5.00 12.00
Antowain Smith
2 Randy Moss 2.00 5.00
Daunte Culpepper
3 Edgerrin James 4.00 10.00
Peyton Manning
4 Eddie George 2.00 5.00
Steve McNair
5 Ricky Williams 1.50 4.00
Chris Chambers
6 Jeff Garcia 2.00 5.00
Terrell Owens
7 Marshall Faulk 2.00 5.00
Kurt Warner
8 Donovan McNabb 2.00 5.00
Freddie Mitchell
9 Ahman Green 5.00 12.00
Brett Favre
10 Plaxico Burress 1.50 4.00
Kordell Stewart

2002 Fleer Box Score Yard Markers Duals Jerseys

STATED PRINT RUN 100 SER.#'d SETS
1 Tom Brady 15.00 40.00
Antowain Smith
2 Plaxico Burress 5.00 12.00
Kordell Stewart
3 Marshall Faulk 6.00 15.00
Kurt Warner
4 Jeff Garcia 6.00 15.00
Terrell Owens
5 Eddie George 6.00 15.00
Steve McNair
6 Ahman Green 15.00 40.00
Brett Favre
7 Edgerrin James 12.00 30.00
Peyton Manning
8 Donovan McNabb 6.00 15.00
Antonio Freeman
9 Randy Moss 6.00 15.00
Daunte Culpepper
10 Ricky Williams 5.00 12.00
Chris Chambers

1998 Fleer Brilliants

The 1998 Fleer Brilliants set was issued in one series totalling 150 cards and was distriubted in five-card packs with a suggested price of $4.99. The set featues color action player photos printed using super-bright mirror foil laminate on 24 pt. plastic styrene card stock with an etched radial pattern background. The set contains a 50-card Rookie subset seeded into packs at the rate of 1:2.

COMPLETE SET (150) 40.00 100.00
1 John Elway 1.50 4.00
2 Curtis Conway .40 1.00
3 Danny Wuerffel .40 1.00
4 Emmitt Smith 1.25 3.00
5 Marvin Harrison .40 1.00
6 Antowain Smith .40 1.00
7 James Stewart .30 .75
8 Junior Seau .40 1.00
9 Herman Moore .40 1.00
10 Drew Bledsoe .50 1.25
11 Rae Carruth .30 .75
12 Trent Dilfer .40 1.00
13 Derrick Alexander .40 1.00
14 Ike Hilliard .40 1.00
15 Bruce Smith .50 1.25
16 Warren Moon .40 1.00
17 Jermaine Lewis .30 .75
18 Mike Alstott .40 1.00
19 Robert Brooks .40 1.00
20 Jerome Bettis .50 1.25
21 Brett Favre 1.50 4.00
22 Garrison Hearst .40 1.00
23 Neil O'Donnell .40 1.00
24 Joey Galloway .40 1.00
25 Barry Sanders 1.25 3.00

26 Donnell Bennett .30 .75
27 Jamal Anderson .40 1.00
28 Isaac Bruce .40 1.00
29 Chris Chandler .40 1.00
30 Kordell Stewart .40 1.00
31 Corey Dillon .40 1.00
32 Troy Aikman .75 2.00
33 Frank Sanders .30 .75
34 Cris Carter .50 1.25
35 Greg Hill .30 .75
36 Tony Martin .40 1.00
37 Shannon Sharpe .50 1.25
38 Wayne Chrebet .40 1.00
39 Trent Green .40 1.00
40 Warrick Dunn .40 1.00
41 Michael Irvin .60 1.25
42 Eddie George .40 1.00
43 Carl Pickens .40 1.00
44 Wesley Walls .40 1.00
45 Steve McNair .50 1.25
46 Bert Emanuel .40 1.00
47 Terry Glenn .40 1.00
48 Elvis Grbac .40 1.00
49 Charles Way .30 .75
50 Steve Young .60 1.50
51 Deion Sanders .60 1.50
52 Keyshawn Johnson .40 1.00
53 Kerry Collins .40 1.00
54 O.J. McDuffie .40 1.00
55 Ricky Watters .40 1.00
56 Derrick Thomas .50 1.25
57 Antonio Freeman .40 1.00
58 Jake Plummer .40 1.00
59 Andre Reed .50 1.25
60 Jerry Rice 1.00 2.50
61 Dorsey Levens .40 1.00
62 Eddie Kennison .30 .75
63 Marshall Faulk .50 1.25
64 Michael Jackson .30 .75
65 Karim Abdul-Jabbar .30 .75
66 Andre Rison .40 1.00
67 Glenn Foley .30 .75
68 Jake Reed .40 1.00
69 Tony Banks .40 1.00
70 Dan Marino 1.50 4.00
71 Bryan Still .30 .75
72 Tim Brown .50 1.25
73 Charles Johnson .30 .75
74 Jeff George .40 1.00
75 Jimmy Smith .40 1.00
76 Ben Coates .40 1.00
77 Rob Moore .30 .75
78 Johnnie Morton .40 1.00
79 Peter Boulware .30 .75
80 Curtis Martin .50 1.25
81 James McKnight .30 .75
82 Danny Kanell .30 .75
83 Brad Johnson .40 1.00
84 Amani Toomer .40 1.00
85 Terry Allen .40 1.00
86 Rod Smith .40 1.00
87 Keenan McCardell .40 1.00
88 Leslie Shepherd .30 .75
89 Irving Fryar .40 1.00
90 Terrell Davis .50 1.25
91 Robert Smith .40 1.00
92 Duce Staley .40 1.00
93 Rickey Dudley .30 .75
94 Bobby Hoying .40 1.00
95 Terrell Owens .50 1.25
96 Fred Lane .30 .75
97 Natrone Means .40 1.00
98 Yancey Thigpen .30 .75
99 Reggie White .50 1.25
100 Mark Brunell .40 1.00
101 Ahman Green RC 2.00 5.00
102 Skip Hicks RC .75 2.00
103 Hines Ward RC 4.00 10.00
104 Marcus Nash RC .60 1.50
105 Terry Hardy RC .60 1.50
106 Pat Johnson RC .75 2.00
107 Tremayne Stephens RC .60 1.50
108 Joe Jurevicius RC 1.00 2.50
109 Moses Moreno RC .60 1.50
110 Charles Woodson RC 2.50 6.00
111 Kevin Dyson RC 1.00 2.50
112 Alvis Whitted RC .75 2.00
113 Michael Pittman RC 1.00 2.50
114 Stephen Alexander RC .75 2.00
115 Tavian Banks RC .75 2.00
116 John Avery RC .75 2.00
117 Keith Brooking RC 1.00 2.50
118 Jerome Pathon RC 1.00 2.50
119 Terry Fair RC .75 2.00
120 Peyton Manning RC 15.00 30.00
121 R.W. McQuarters RC 1.00 2.50
122 Charlie Batch RC 1.00 2.50
123 Jonathan Quinn RC .75 2.00
124 C.Fuamatu-Ma'afala RC .75 2.00
125 Jacquez Green RC .75 2.00
126 Germane Crowell RC .75 2.00
127 Oronde Gadsden RC .75 2.00
128 Koy Detmer .75 2.00
129 Robert Holcombe RC .75 2.00
130 Curtis Enis RC .75 2.00
131 Brian Griese RC 2.00 5.00
132 Tony Simmons RC .75 2.00
133 Vonnie Holliday RC .75 2.00
134 Alonzo Mayes RC .60 1.50
135 Jon Ritchie RC .75 2.00
136 Robert Edwards RC .75 2.00
137 Mike Vanderjagt RC .75 2.00
138 Jonathan Linton RC .75 2.00
139 Fred Taylor RC 2.00 5.00
140 Randy Moss RC 6.00 15.00
141 Rod Rutledge RC .60 1.50
142 Andre Wadsworth RC 1.00 2.50
143 Rashaan Shehee RC .60 1.50
144 Shaun Williams RC .75 2.00
145 Mikhael Ricks RC .75 2.00
146 Wade Richey RC .60 1.50
147 Carlos King RC .60 1.50
148 Tim Dwight RC 1.00 2.50
149 Scott Frost RC .60 1.50
150 Ryan Leaf RC 1.00 2.50
P74 Jeff George Promo .40 1.00

1998 Fleer Brilliants 24-Karat Gold

*1-100 VETS24: 15X TO 40X BASIC CARDS
*101-150 ROOKIES/24: 6X TO 15X
STATED PRINT RUN 24 SETS
120 Peyton Manning 300.00 450.00

1998 Fleer Brilliants Blue

COMPLETE SET (150) 150.00 300.00
*1-100 VETS: 1.5X TO 4X BASIC CARDS
*101-150 ROOKIES: .6X TO 1.5X BASIC CARDS
1-100 VETERAN STATED ODDS 1:3
101-150 ROOKIE STATED ODDS 1:6

1998 Fleer Brilliants Gold

*1-100 VETS/99: 8X TO 20X BASIC CARDS
*101-150 ROOKIES/99: 2X TO 5X
STATED PRINT RUN 99 SER.#'d SETS

1998 Fleer Brilliants Illuminators

COMPLETE SET (15) 30.00 60.00
STATED ODDS 1:10
1 Robert Edwards .75 2.00
2 Fred Taylor 1.50 4.00
3 Kordell Stewart 1.50 4.00
4 Troy Aikman 3.00 8.00
5 Curtis Enis .50 1.25
6 Drew Bledsoe 2.50 6.00
7 Curtis Martin 1.50 4.00
8 Joey Galloway 1.00 2.50
9 Jerome Bettis 1.50 4.00
10 Glenn Foley 1.00 2.50
11 Karim Abdul-Jabbar 1.50 4.00
12 Jake Plummer 1.50 4.00
13 Jerry Rice 0.00 0.00
14 Charlie Batch 1.00 2.50
15 Jacquez Green .75 2.00

1998 Fleer Brilliants Shining Stars

COMPLETE SET (15) 30.00 80.00
STATED ODDS 1:20
*PULSAR STARS: 2X TO 5X BASIC INSERTS
*PULSAR ROOKIES: 1.2X TO 3X BAS.INS.
PULSARS STATED ODDS 1:400
1 Terrell Davis 1.50 4.00
2 Emmitt Smith 4.00 10.00
3 Barry Sanders 4.00 10.00
4 Mark Brunell 1.25 3.00
5 Brett Favre 5.00 12.00
6 Ryan Leaf 1.00 2.50
7 Randy Moss 3.00 8.00
8 Warrick Dunn 1.25 3.00
9 Peyton Manning 8.00 20.00
10 Corey Dillon 1.25 3.00
11 Dan Marino 5.00 12.00
12 Keyshawn Johnson 1.25 3.00
13 John Elway 4.00 10.00
14 Eddie George 1.25 3.00
15 Antowain Smith 1.00 2.50

1999 Fleer Focus

Released as a 175-card set, 1999 Fleer Focus football is comprised of 100 veteran cards and 75 rookie subset cards seeded at one in two packs. Base cards are white-bordered and highlighted with gold foil. Rookie cards are divided up into four tiers, Quarterbacks are serial numbered out of 2250, Running Backs are numbered out of 2500, Receivers are numbered out 3850, and Defense/others are not serial numbered. Fleer Focus was packaged in 24-pack boxes with five cards per pack and carried a suggested retail price of $2.99.

COMPLETE SET (175) 100.00 200.00
COMP.SET w/o SP's (100) 20.00 40.00
1 Randy Moss .30 .75
2 Andre Rison .25 .60
3 Ed McCaffrey .25 .60
4 Jerry Rice .60 1.50
5 Tim Biakabutuka .25 .60
6 Wayne Chrebet .25 .60
7 Deion Sanders .30 .75
8 Ricky Watters .25 .60
9 Skip Hicks .20 .50
10 Charlie Batch .25 .60
11 Joey Galloway .25 .60
12 Stephen Alexander .20 .50
13 Curtis Conway .25 .60
14 Garrison Hearst .25 .60
15 Kerry Collins .25 .60
16 Cris Carter .30 .75
17 Eddie George .25 .60
18 Eric Moulds .25 .60
19 Vinny Testaverde .25 .60
20 Curtis Enis .20 .50
21 Gary Brown .20 .50
22 Junior Seau .30 .75
23 Kevin Dyson .20 .50
24 Jeff Blake .25 .60
25 Herman Moore .25 .60
26 Natrone Means .25 .60
27 Terry Glenn .25 .60
28 Fred Taylor .25 .60
29 Ben Coates .25 .60
30 Corey Dillon .25 .60
31 Eddie Kennison .25 .60
32 Byron Bam Morris .20 .50
33 Doug Pederson .20 .50
34 Jamal Anderson .25 .60
35 Michael Westbrook .20 .50
36 Peyton Manning 1.00 2.50
37 Carl Pickens .25 .60
38 Drew Bledsoe .30 .75
39 Jim Harbaugh .25 .60
40 Kurt Warner RC 2.00 5.00
41 Mark Chmura .20 .50
42 Hines Ward .30 .75
43 Terry Kirby .20 .50
44 Brett Favre 1.00 2.50
45 Kordell Stewart .25 .60
46 Leslie Shepherd .20 .50
47 Marshall Faulk .30 .75
48 Troy Aikman .50 1.25
49 Isaac Bruce .30 .75
50 Michael Irvin .30 .75
51 Robert Smith .25 .60
52 Dorsey Levens .25 .60
53 Duce Staley .25 .60
54 Jake Plummer .25 .60
55 Adrian Murrell .25 .60
56 Antonio Freeman .25 .60
57 Jerome Bettis .30 .75
58 Elvis Grbac .20 .50
59 Keyshawn Johnson .25 .60
60 Steve Beuerlein .25 .60
61 Yancey Thigpen .20 .50
62 Doug Flutie .30 .75
63 Jacquez Green .20 .50
64 Jimmy Smith .25 .60
65 Tim Brown .30 .75
66 Jason Sehorn .25 .60
67 Muhsin Muhammad .25 .60
68 Shannon Sharpe .30 .75
69 Terrell Owens .30 .75
70 Keenan McCardell .25 .60
71 Rich Gannon .25 .60
72 Scott Mitchell .20 .50
73 Warrick Dunn .25 .60
74 Brad Johnson .25 .60
75 Charles Johnson .20 .50
76 Chris Chandler .25 .60
77 Marcus Pollard .20 .50
78 Mike Alstott .30 .75
79 Bubby Brister .20 .50
80 Jon Kitna .25 .60
81 Randall Cunningham .30 .75
82 Antowain Smith .20 .50
83 Curtis Martin .30 .75
84 Steve McNair .30 .75
85 Tony Gonzalez .30 .75
86 O.J. McDuffie .25 .60
87 Steve Young .40 1.00
88 Terrell Davis .30 .75
89 Mark Brunell .25 .60
90 Napoleon Kaufman .20 .50
91 Priest Holmes .30 .75
92 Trent Dilfer .25 .60
93 Brian Griese .25 .60
94 J.J. Stokes .20 .50
95 Karim Abdul-Jabbar .25 .60
96 Barry Sanders .75 2.00
97 Dan Marino 1.00 2.50
98 Emmitt Smith .75 2.00
99 Marvin Harrison .30 .75
100 Rod Smith .25 .60
101 Champ Bailey RC 1.25 3.00
102 Fernando Bryant RC .40 1.00
103 Chris Claiborne RC .40 1.00
104 Antuan Edwards RC .40 1.00
105 Martin Gramatica RC .40 1.00
106 Andy Katzenmoyer RC .50 1.25
107 Jevon Kearse RC .60 1.50
108 Chris McAlister RC .50 1.25
109 Al Wilson RC .60 1.50
110 Antoine Winfield RC .40 1.00
111 Karsten Bailey RC 1.00 2.50
112 D'Wayne Bates RC 1.00 2.50
113 Marty Booker RC 1.25 3.00
114 David Boston RC 1.25 3.00
115 Na Brown RC 1.00 2.50
116 Desmond Clark RC 1.25 3.00
117 Dameane Douglas RC 1.00 2.50
118 Donald Driver RC 20.00 40.00
119 Troy Edwards RC 1.25 3.00
120 Torry Holt RC 2.50 6.00
121 Kevin Johnson RC 1.25 3.00
122 Reginald Kelly RC 1.00 2.50
123 Jimmy Kleinsasser RC 1.50 4.00
124 Jeremy McDaniel RC 1.00 2.50
125 Darnell McDonald RC 1.00 2.50
126 Travis McGriff RC 1.00 2.50
127 Billy Miller RC 1.00 2.50
128 Dee Miller RC 1.00 2.50
129 Peerless Price RC 1.25 3.00
130 Troy Smith RC 1.25 3.00
131 Brandon Stokley RC 1.50 4.00
132 Wane McGarity RC 1.00 2.50
133 Mark Campbell RC 1.00 2.50
134 Jerame Tuman RC 1.00 2.50
135 Craig Yeast RC 1.00 2.50
136 Jerry Azumah RC 1.50 4.00
137 Marlon Barnes RC 1.50 4.00
138 Michael Basnight RC 1.50 4.00
139 Shawn Bryson RC 1.50 4.00
140 Mike Cloud RC 1.50 4.00
141 Cecil Collins RC 1.50 4.00
142 Autry Denson RC 1.50 4.00
143 Kevin Faulk RC 2.50 6.00
144 Jermaine Fazande RC 1.50 4.00
145 Jim Finn RC 1.50 4.00
146 Madre Hill RC 1.50 4.00
147 Sedrick Irvin RC 1.50 4.00
148 Terry Jackson RC 1.50 4.00
149 Edgerrin James RC 3.00 8.00
150 James Johnson RC 1.50 4.00
151 Rob Konrad RC 1.50 4.00
152 Joel Makovicka RC 1.50 4.00
153 Cecil Martin RC 1.50 4.00
154 Joe Montgomery RC 1.50 4.00
155 De'Mond Parker RC 1.50 4.00
156 Sirr Parker RC 1.50 4.00
157 Jeff Paulk RC 1.50 4.00
158 Nick Williams RC 1.50 4.00
159 Ricky Williams RC 4.00 10.00
160 Amos Zereoue RC 2.00 5.00
161 Michael Bishop RC 2.00 5.00
162 Aaron Brooks RC 2.50 6.00
163 Tim Couch RC 2.50 6.00
164 Scott Covington RC 1.50 4.00
165 Daunte Culpepper RC 2.50 6.00
166 Kevin Daft RC 1.50 4.00
167 Joe Germaine RC 2.00 5.00
168 Chris Greisen RC 1.50 4.00
169 Brock Huard RC 2.00 5.00
170 Shaun King RC 2.00 5.00
171 Cory Sauter RC 1.50 4.00
172 Donovan McNabb RC 6.00 15.00
173 Cade McNown RC 2.00 5.00
174 Chad Plummer RC 1.50 4.00
175 Akili Smith RC 2.00 5.00
P1 Promo Sheet 1.50 4.00
(SBXXXIV NFL Experience)
NFLX1 Kurt Warner
NFLX2 Jamal Anderson
NFLX3 Edgerrin James
NFLX4 Peyton Manning
NFLX5 Randy Moss
NFLX6 Dan Marino
P54 Jake Plummer PROMO .40 1.00

1999 Fleer Focus Masterpieces

STATED PRINT RUN 1 SET

1999 Fleer Focus Stealth

*STARS 1-100: 3X TO 8X BASIC CARDS
*101-110 RCs: .8X TO 2X
*111-135 RCs: .6X TO 1.5X
*136-175 RCs: .5X TO 1.2X
STATED PRINT RUN 300 SER.#'d SETS

1999 Fleer Focus Feel the Game

COMPLETE SET (10) 125.00 300.00
STATED ODDS 1:192
1FG Vinny Testaverde 6.00 15.00
2FG Mark Brunell 12.50 30.00
3FG Brett Favre Shoe 30.00 80.00
4FG Fred Taylor 12.50 30.00
5FG Jeff Blake 6.00 15.00
6FG Emmitt Smith 20.00 50.00
7FG Joe Germaine 6.00 15.00
8FG Cecil Collins 6.00 15.00
9FG Charles Woodson 10.00 25.00
10FG Kurt Warner 15.00 40.00

1999 Fleer Focus Fresh Ink

STATED ODDS 1:48
1 Reidel Anthony 5.00 12.00
2 Charlie Batch 5.00 12.00
3 Jeff Blake 8.00 20.00
4 Darrin Chiaverini 5.00 12.00
5 Wayne Chrebet 8.00 20.00
6 Daunte Culpepper 10.00 25.00
7 Terrell Davis 12.50 30.00
8 Koy Detmer 5.00 12.00
9 Corey Dillon 10.00 25.00
10 Troy Edwards 5.00 12.00
11 Doug Flutie 10.00 25.00
12 Eddie George 10.00 25.00
13 Trent Green 8.00 20.00
14 Marvin Harrison 12.50 30.00
15 Torry Holt 10.00 25.00
16 Sedrick Irvin 5.00 12.00
17 Edgerrin James 12.50 30.00
18 Brad Johnson 8.00 20.00
19 Charles Johnson 5.00 12.00
20 Jon Kitna 10.00 25.00
21 Jim Kleinsasser 8.00 20.00
22 Peyton Manning 60.00 100.00
23 O.J. McDuffie 5.00 12.00
24 Travis McGriff 5.00 12.00
25 Donovan McNabb 25.00 60.00
26 Cade McNown 5.00 12.00
27 Joe Montgomery 5.00 12.00
28 Randy Moss 30.00 60.00
29 Jake Plummer 8.00 20.00
30 Akili Smith 5.00 12.00
31 Antowain Smith 8.00 20.00
32 Duce Staley 10.00 25.00
33 Brandon Stokley 8.00 20.00
34 Fred Taylor 10.00 25.00
35 Vinny Testaverde 8.00 20.00
36 Ricky Williams 10.00 25.00
37 Steve Young 20.00 50.00

1999 Fleer Focus Glimmer Men

COMPLETE SET (10) 20.00 40.00
STATED ODDS 1:20
1R Tim Couch 1.25 3.00
2R Barry Sanders 4.00 10.00
3R Terrell Davis 1.25 3.00
4R Dan Marino 4.00 10.00
5R Troy Aikman 2.50 6.00
6R Brett Favre 4.00 10.00
7R Randy Moss 3.00 8.00
8R Emmitt Smith 2.50 6.00
9R Edgerrin James 2.50 6.00
10R Fred Taylor 1.25 3.00

1999 Fleer Focus Reflexions

COMPLETE SET (10) 150.00 300.00
STATED PRINT RUN 100 SER.#'d SETS
1R Tim Couch 7.50 20.00
2R Barry Sanders 15.00 40.00
3R Terrell Davis 5.00 12.00
4R Dan Marino 15.00 40.00
5R Troy Aikman 10.00 25.00
6R Brett Favre 15.00 40.00
7R Randy Moss 12.50 30.00
8R Emmitt Smith 10.00 25.00
9R Edgerrin James 20.00 40.00
10R Fred Taylor 5.00 12.00

1999 Fleer Focus Sparklers

COMPLETE SET (10) 12.50 30.00
STATED ODDS 1:10
1S Tim Couch .60 1.50
2S Donovan McNabb 2.50 6.00
3S Akili Smith .60 1.50
4S Cade McNown .60 1.50
5S Daunte Culpepper 2.00 5.00
6S Ricky Williams 1.00 2.50
7S Edgerrin James 2.00 5.00
8S Kevin Faulk .60 1.50
9S Torry Holt 1.25 3.00
10S David Boston .60 1.50
11S Sedrick Irvin .60 1.50
12S Peerless Price .60 1.50
13S Troy Edwards .60 1.50
14S Brock Huard .60 1.50
15S Shaun King .60 1.50

1999 Fleer Focus Wondrous

COMPLETE SET 30.00 60.00
STATED ODDS 1:20
1W Peyton Manning 4.00 10.00
2W Fred Taylor 1.25 3.00
3W Tim Couch .60 1.50
4W Charlie Batch 1.25 3.00
5W Jerry Rice 2.50 6.00
6W Randy Moss 3.00 8.00
7W Warrick Dunn 1.25 3.00
8W Mark Brunell 1.25 3.00
9W Emmitt Smith 2.50 6.00
10W Eddie George .75 2.00
11W Brian Griese 1.25 3.00
12W Terrell Davis 1.25 3.00
13W Dan Marino 4.00 10.00
14W Ricky Williams 1.25 3.00
15W Brett Favre 4.00 10.00
16W Jake Plummer .75 2.00
17W Troy Aikman 2.50 6.00
18W Drew Bledsoe 2.00 5.00
19W Edgerrin James 2.50 6.00
20W Cade McNown .60 1.50

2000 Fleer Focus

Released as a 260-card set, Fleer Focus features 200 base issue cards and 60 sequentially numbered rookie cards. Card numbers 201-211 are numbered to 3999, card numbers 212-233 are numbered to 1999, card numbers 234-250 are numbered to 2499, and card numbers 251-260 are numbered to 2999. Focus was packaged in 24-pack boxes with packs containing 10 cards and carried a suggested retail price of $2.99.

COMPLETE SET (260) 200.00 400.00
COMP.SET w/o SPs (200) 10.00 25.00
201-211 ROOKIE PRINT RUN 3999
212-233 ROOKIE PRINT RUN 1999
234-250 ROOKIE PRINT RUN 2499
251-260 ROOKIE PRINT RUN 2999
1 Tim Couch .20 .50
2 Germane Crowell .15 .40
3 Curtis Martin .25 .60
4 Samari Rolle .15 .40
5 Brian Griese .20 .50
6 Kerry Collins .20 .50
7 Jevon Kearse .20 .50
8 Rocket Ismail .20 .50
9 Cam Cleeland .15 .40
10 Warrick Dunn .20 .50
11 Carl Pickens .20 .50
12 Cris Carter .25 .60
13 Mike Pritchard .15 .40
14 Corey Dillon .20 .50
15 Randy Moss .25 .60
16 Derrick Mayes .15 .40
17 Marcus Robinson .20 .50
18 Thurman Thomas .25 .60
19 J.J. Stokes .20 .50
20 Muhsin Muhammad .20 .50
21 Derrick Alexander .15 .40
22 Curtis Conway .20 .50
23 Qadry Ismail .20 .50
24 Ken Dilger .15 .40
25 Troy Edwards .15 .40
26 Shawn Jefferson .15 .40
27 Terrence Wilkins .15 .40
28 Duce Staley .20 .50
29 Aeneas Williams .15 .40
30 Antonio Freeman .20 .50
31 Tim Brown .25 .60
32 Darrell Green .20 .50
33 Herman Moore .20 .50
34 Vinny Testaverde .20 .50
35 Yancey Thigpen .15 .40
36 Emmitt Smith .60 1.50
37 Ricky Williams .25 .60
38 Keyshawn Johnson .20 .50
39 Eddie Kennison .15 .40
40 Zach Thomas .25 .60
41 Shawn Springs .15 .40
42 Wesley Walls .15 .40
43 Andre Rison .20 .50
44 Jerry Rice .50 1.25
45 Rob Johnson .20 .50
46 Keenan McCardell .20 .50
47 Ryan Leaf .20 .50
48 Michael McCrary .15 .40
49 Marvin Harrison .25 .60
50 Donovan McNabb .25 .60
51 Curtis Enis .15 .40
52 Tony Martin .20 .50
53 Jeff Garcia .20 .50
54 Tim Biakabutuka .20 .50
55 Tony Gonzalez .25 .60
56 Jim Harbaugh .20 .50
57 Peerless Price .20 .50
58 Fred Taylor .25 .60
59 Kordell Stewart .20 .50
60 Chris Chandler .20 .50
61 Bill Schroeder .20 .50
62 Charles Woodson .25 .60
63 Terance Mathis .15 .40
64 Brett Favre .75 2.00
65 Rickey Dudley .15 .40
66 Rob Moore .15 .40
67 Charlie Batch .20 .50
68 Wayne Chrebet .20 .50
69 Jeff George .20 .50
70 Olandis Gary .20 .50
71 Amani Toomer .20 .50
72 Kevin Dyson .20 .50
73 Darrin Chiaverini .15 .40
74 Willie McGinest .20 .50
75 Ricky Proehl .15 .40
76 Craig Yeast .15 .40
77 Dwayne Rudd .15 .40
78 Marshall Faulk .25 .60
79 Bobby Engram .20 .50
80 Jay Fiedler .20 .50
81 Jon Kitna .20 .50
82 Patrick Jeffers .20 .50
83 James Johnson .15 .40
84 Charlie Garner .20 .50
85 Eric Moulds .20 .50
86 Mark Brunell .20 .50
87 Richard Huntley .15 .40
88 Frank Sanders .15 .40
89 Robert Porcher .15 .40
90 Aaron Glenn .15 .40
91 Stephen Davis .20 .50
92 Ed McCaffrey .20 .50
93 Pete Mitchell .15 .40
94 Frank Wycheck .20 .50
95 David LaFleur .15 .40
96 Jake Delhomme RC .60 1.50
97 John Lynch .20 .50
98 Michael Pittman .15 .40
99 Andy Katzenmoyer .15 .40
100 Isaac Bruce .25 .60
101 Terry Kirby .15 .40
102 Kevin Faulk .20 .50
103 Kevin Carter .15 .40
104 Darnay Scott .20 .50
105 Robert Smith .20 .50
106 Brian Mitchell .15 .40
107 Shane Matthews .15 .40
108 O.J. McDuffie .20 .50
109 Bryant Young .15 .40
110 Jay Riemersma .15 .40
111 Elvis Grbac .15 .40
112 Jermaine Fazande .15 .40
113 Jonathan Linton .15 .40
114 Kyle Brady .15 .40
115 Junior Seau .25 .60
116 Shannon Sharpe .25 .60
117 Jerome Pathon .15 .40
118 Jerome Bettis .25 .60
119 O.J. Santiago .15 .40
120 Ahman Green .20 .50
121 Troy Vincent .15 .40
122 David Boston .15 .40
123 James Stewart .15 .40
124 Ray Lucas .15 .40
125 Brad Johnson .20 .50
126 Rod Smith .20 .50
127 Joe Jurevicius .15 .40
128 Eddie George .20 .50
129 Darren Woodson .15 .40
130 Jake Reed .20 .50
131 Mike Alstott .25 .60
132 Leslie Shepherd .15 .40
133 Terry Glenn .20 .50
134 Az-Zahir Hakim .15 .40
135 Alonzo Mayes .15 .40
136 Sam Madison .15 .40
137 Ricky Watters .20 .50
138 Antowain Smith .20 .50
139 Jimmy Smith .20 .50
140 Hines Ward .25 .60
141 Priest Holmes .25 .60
142 Edgerrin James .25 .60
143 Charles Johnson .15 .40
144 Jamal Anderson .20 .50
145 Dorsey Levens .20 .50
146 Rich Gannon .20 .50
147 Champ Bailey .20 .50
148 Bill Romanowski .15 .40
149 Jason Sehorn .15 .40
160 Steve McNair .25 .60
151 Jermaine Lewis .15 .40
152 Cornelius Bennett .15 .40
153 Torrance Small .15 .40
154 Tim Dwight .20 .50
155 Corey Bradford .15 .40
156 Napoleon Kaufman .20 .50
157 Jake Plummer .20 .50
158 David Sloan .15 .40
159 Dedric Ward .15 .40
160 Michael Westbrook .15 .40
161 Terrell Davis .25 .60
162 Ike Hilliard .20 .50
163 Derrick Brooks .25 .60
164 Greg Ellis .15 .40
165 Keith Poole .15 .40
166 Jacquez Green .15 .40
167 Joey Galloway .20 .50
168 Lawyer Milloy .15 .40
169 Warren Sapp .20 .50
170 Takeo Spikes .15 .40
171 John Randle .20 .50
172 Torry Holt .25 .60
173 Cade McNown .15 .40
174 Damon Huard .20 .50
175 Terrell Owens .25 .60
176 Steve Beuerlein .20 .50
177 Tony Richardson RC .20 .50
178 Jeff Graham .15 .40
179 Doug Flutie .25 .60
180 Kevin Hardy .15 .40
181 Mark Bruener .20 .50
182 Tony Banks .15 .40
183 Peyton Manning .60 1.50
184 Hugh Douglas .15 .40
185 Simeon Rice .20 .50
186 Terry Fair .15 .40
187 James Jett .20 .50
188 Albert Connell .15 .40
189 Troy Aikman .40 1.00
190 Jeff Blake .20 .50
191 Shaun King .15 .40
192 Kevin Johnson .15 .40
193 Drew Bledsoe .25 .60
194 Kurt Warner .40 1.00
195 Akili Smith .15 .40
196 Daunte Culpepper .20 .50
197 Sean Dawkins .15 .40
198 Natrone Means .20 .50
199 Kimble Anders .15 .40
200 Steve Young .30 .75
201 Courtney Brown RC 1.00 2.50
202 Chris Samuels RC 1.00 2.50
203 Corey Simon RC 1.00 2.50
204 Deon Grant RC .75 2.00
205 Darren Howard RC .75 2.00
206 Rob Morris RC 1.00 2.50
207 Ahmed Plummer RC .75 2.00
208 Anthony Becht RC 1.00 2.50
209 Brian Urlacher RC 5.00 12.00
210 Shaun Ellis RC 1.25 3.00
211 Bubba Franks RC 1.25 3.00
212 Plaxico Burress RC 2.00 5.00
213 R.Jay Soward RC 1.25 3.00
214 Dez White RC 1.50 4.00
215 Peter Warrick RC 2.00 5.00
216 Jerry Porter RC 2.00 5.00
217 Ron Dugans RC 1.25 3.00
218 Laveranues Coles RC 2.00 5.00
219 Travis Taylor RC 1.50 4.00
220 Anthony Lucas RC 1.25 3.00
221 Sylvester Morris RC 1.25 3.00
222 Dennis Northcutt RC 1.50 4.00
223 Chafie Fields RC 1.25 3.00
224 Danny Farmer RC 1.25 3.00
225 Chris Cole RC 1.50 4.00
226 Sherrod Gideon RC 1.25 3.00
227 Todd Pinkston RC 1.25 3.00
228 Gari Scott RC 1.25 3.00
229 Darrell Jackson RC 1.50 4.00
230 JaJuan Dawson RC 1.25 3.00
231 Trevor Gaylor RC 1.25 3.00
232 Bashir Yamini RC 1.25 3.00
233 Quinton Spotwood RC 1.25 3.00
234 Michael Wiley RC 1.00 2.50
235 Ron Dayne RC 1.50 4.00
236 Thomas Jones RC 2.00 5.00
237 Jamal Lewis RC 1.50 4.00
238 Travis Prentice RC 1.25 3.00
239 J.R. Redmond RC 1.00 2.50
240 Trung Canidate RC 1.25 3.00
241 Shaun Alexander RC 2.00 5.00
242 Frank Murphy RC 1.00 2.50
243 Shyrone Stith RC 1.00 2.50
244 Rondell Mealey RC 1.00 2.50
245 Terrelle Smith RC 1.00 2.50
246 Reuben Droughns RC 1.50 4.00
247 Chad Morton RC 1.50 4.00
248 Mike Anderson RC 1.50 4.00
249 Paul Smith RC 1.00 2.50
250 Curtis Keaton RC 1.00 2.50
251 Jarious Jackson RC 1.25 3.00
252 Marc Bulger RC 1.50 4.00
253 Tee Martin RC 1.50 4.00
254 Todd Husak RC 1.00 2.50
255 Joe Hamilton RC 1.00 2.50
256 Doug Johnson RC 1.25 3.00
257 Giovanni Carmazzi RC 1.00 2.50
258 Chris Redman RC 1.25 3.00
259 Tim Rattay RC 1.25 3.00
260 Chad Pennington RC 2.50 6.00
P16 Tim Couch Promo .40 1.00

2000 Fleer Focus Draft Position

*VETS/823-1220: 2.5X TO 6X BASIC CARD
*VETS/401-735: 3X TO 8X BASIC CARD
*VETS/300-331: 4X TO 10X BASIC CARD
*VETS/201-230: 5X TO 12X BASIC CARD
*VETS/90-131: 6X TO 15X BASIC CARD
1-200 VETERAN PRINT RUN 90-1220
*201-211 ROOK/202-226: 1X TO 2.5X
*201-211 ROOK/101-128: 1.2X TO 3X
*212-233 ROOK/405-634: .4X TO 1X
*212-233 ROOK/304-318: .5X TO 1.2X
*212-233 ROOK/201-216 .6X TO 1.5X
*212-233 ROOK/100-129: .8X TO 2X
*234-250 ROOK/402-746: .5X TO 1.2X
*234-250 ROOK/301-319: .6X TO 1.5X
*234-250 ROOK/105-131: 1X TO 2.5X
*251-260 ROOK/403-728: .5X TO 1.2X
*251-260 ROOK/303-313: .6X TO 1.5X
*251-260 ROOK/100-118: 1X TO 2.5X
201-260 ROOKIE PRINT RUN 100-746

2000 Fleer Focus Good Hands

COMPLETE SET (15) 12.50 30.00
STATED ODDS 1:18
*TD/12-17: 6X TO 15X BASIC INSERTS
TD EDITION PRINT RUN 1-17
1 Keyshawn Johnson .60 1.50
2 Joey Galloway .60 1.50
3 Jerry Rice 1.50 4.00
4 Cris Carter .75 2.00
5 Randy Moss .75 2.00
6 Marvin Harrison .75 2.00
7 Marcus Robinson .60 1.50
8 Edgerrin James .75 2.00
9 Tim Brown .75 2.00
10 Jimmy Smith .60 1.50
11 Isaac Bruce .75 2.00
12 Peter Warrick .75 2.00
13 Marshall Faulk .75 2.00
14 Germane Crowell .50 1.25
15 Plaxico Burress .75 2.00

2000 Fleer Focus Last Man Standing

COMPLETE SET (25) 25.00 60.00
STATED ODDS 1:12
*TD/42: 5X TO 12X BASIC INSERTS
*TD/20-28: 6X TO 15X BASIC INSERTS
*TD/11-18: 8X TO 20X BASIC INSERTS
TD EDITION PRINT RUN 2-42
1 Tim Couch .50 1.25
2 Randy Moss .60 1.50
3 Akili Smith .40 1.00
4 Peyton Manning 1.50 4.00
5 Kurt Warner 1.00 2.50
6 Ricky Williams .60 1.50
7 Edgerrin James .60 1.50
8 Eddie George .50 1.25
9 Emmitt Smith 1.50 4.00
10 Terrell Davis .60 1.50
11 Brett Favre 2.00 5.00
12 Brian Griese .50 1.25
13 Donovan McNabb .60 1.50
14 Charlie Batch .50 1.25
15 Shaun King .40 1.00
16 Marshall Faulk .60 1.50
17 Jake Plummer .50 1.25
18 Cade McNown .40 1.00
19 Jerry Rice 1.25 3.00
20 Troy Aikman 1.00 2.50
21 Keyshawn Johnson .50 1.25
22 Peter Warrick .60 1.50
23 Ron Dayne .60 1.50
24 Mark Brunell .50 1.25
25 Fred Taylor .60 1.50

2000 Fleer Focus Sparklers

COMPLETE SET (15) 12.50 30.00
STATED ODDS 1:6
*TD/32-40. 8X TO 20X BASIC INSERTS
*TD/20-26: 10X TO 25X BASIC INSERTS
*TD/11-18: 12X TO 30X BASIC INSERTS
TD EDITION PRINT RUN 5-40
1 Chad Pennington .60 1.50
2 Ron Dayne .40 1.00
3 Shaun Alexander .50 1.25
4 Plaxico Burress .40 1.00
5 Peter Warrick .40 1.00
6 Thomas Jones .50 1.25
7 Chris Redman .30 .75
8 Sylvester Morris .25 .60
9 J.R. Redmond .25 .60
10 Dez White .30 .75
11 Jamal Lewis .40 1.00
12 Travis Taylor .30 .75
13 R.Jay Soward .25 .60
14 Todd Pinkston .25 .60
15 Dennis Northcutt .30 .75

2000 Fleer Focus Star Studded

COMPLETE SET (25) 60.00 120.00
STATED ODDS 1:24
*TD/40-42: 2X TO 5X BASIC INSERTS
*TD/20-28: 2.5X TO 6X BASIC INSERTS
*TD/11 19: 3X TO 8X BASIC INSERTS
TD EDITION PRINT RUN 2-42
1 Peyton Manning 4.00 10.00
2 Fred Taylor 1.50 4.00
3 Tim Couch 1.25 3.00
4 Charlie Batch 1.25 3.00
5 Jerry Rice 3.00 8.00
6 Randy Moss 1.50 4.00
7 Ron Dayne 1.50 4.00
8 Mark Brunell 1.25 3.00
9 Emmitt Smith 4.00 10.00
10 Thomas Jones 2.00 5.00
11 Brian Griese 1.25 3.00
12 Terrell Davis 1.50 4.00
13 Brad Johnson 1.25 3.00
14 Ricky Williams 1.50 4.00
15 Brett Favre 5.00 12.00
16 Jake Plummer 1.25 3.00
17 Troy Aikman 2.50 6.00
18 Drew Bledsoe 1.50 4.00
19 Edgerrin James 1.50 4.00
20 Steve McNair 1.50 4.00
21 Doug Flutie 1.50 4.00
22 Chad Pennington 2.50 6.00
23 Jamal Lewis 1.50 4.00
24 Plaxico Burress 1.50 4.00
25 Kurt Warner 2.50 6.00

2001 Fleer Focus

This 230 card set was issued in fall, 2001. The set consists of 180 veterans and fifty 2001 NFL rookies. The Rookie Cards, numbered from 181 through 230 had a stated print run of 1850 sets.

COMP.SET w/o SP's (180) 10.00 25.00
181-230 ROOKIE PRINT RUN 1850
1 Marshall Faulk .25 .60
2 Randy Moss .25 .60
3 Cade McNown .20 .50
4 Jeff Graham .15 .40
5 Donovan McNabb .25 .60
6 Shannon Sharpe .25 .60
7 Todd Pinkston .15 .40
8 Terrence Wilkins .15 .40
9 Michael Strahan .25 .60
10 Rich Gannon .20 .50

11 Germane Crowell .15 .40
12 Warren Sapp .20 .50
13 La'Roi Glover .15 .40
14 Peter Warrick .20 .50
15 Shaun Alexander .25 .60
16 Ray Lucas .15 .40
17 Muhsin Muhammad .20 .50
18 Curtis Conway .20 .50
19 R.Jay Soward .15 .40
20 Jamal Lewis .25 .60
21 Tony Gonzalez .25 .60
22 Bill Schroeder .20 .50
23 Frank Sanders .15 .40
24 Charles Woodson .25 .60
25 Johnnie Morton .20 .50
26 Frank Wycheck .15 .40
27 Ron Dayne .20 .50
28 Travis Prentice .15 .40
29 Isaac Bruce .25 .60
30 Drew Bledsoe .25 .60
31 James Allen .15 .40
32 Matt Hasselbeck .25 .60
33 Zach Thomas .25 .60
34 Shawn Bryson .15 .40
35 Jerry Rice .50 1.25
36 Mike Cloud .15 .40
37 Sammy Morris .20 .50
38 Corey Simon .15 .40
39 Peyton Manning .60 1.50
40 Thomas Jones .20 .50
41 Tyrone Wheatley .20 .50
42 Herman Moore .20 .50
43 Jeff George .20 .50
44 Kerry Collins .20 .50
45 Rocket Ismail .20 .50
46 Andre Rison .20 .50
47 David Sloan .15 .40
48 Michael Westbrook .15 .40
49 Ron Dixon .15 .40
50 Randall Cunningham .25 .60
51 Keyshawn Johnson .20 .50
52 Aaron Brooks .20 .50
53 Corey Dillon .20 .50
54 John Randle .20 .50
55 Cris Carter .25 .60
56 Donald Hayes .15 .40
57 Hines Ward .25 .60
58 Edgerrin James .25 .60
59 Terance Mathis .15 .40
60 Doug Johnson .15 .40
61 Rod Smith .20 .50
62 Kevin Dyson .15 .40
63 Amani Toomer .20 .50
64 Courtney Brown .15 .40
65 Mike Alstott .20 .50
66 Kevin Faulk .20 .50
67 Shane Matthews .15 .40
68 Ricky Watters .20 .50
69 Peter Boulware .15 .40
70 Tim Biakabutuka .15 .40
71 Troy Aikman .40 1.00
72 Keenan McCardell .20 .50
73 Priest Holmes .25 .60
74 Duce Staley .20 .50
75 Antonio Freeman .25 .60
76 David Boston .15 .40
77 Chad Pennington .25 .60
78 Brian Griese .20 .50
79 Stephen Davis .20 .50
80 Curtis Martin .25 .60
81 Tony Banks .15 .40
82 Warrick Dunn .25 .60
83 Willie McGinest .15 .40
84 Marty Booker .20 .50
85 James Williams .15 .40
86 Oronde Gadsden .15 .40
87 Patrick Jeffers .15 .40
88 Junior Seau .25 .60
89 Frank Moreau .15 .40
90 Ray Lewis .25 .60
91 Doug Flutie .25 .60
92 Jimmy Smith .20 .50
93 Qadry Ismail .20 .50
94 Jeremiah Trotter .15 .40
95 Dorsey Levens .20 .50
96 Michael Pittman .20 .50
97 Wayne Chrebet .20 .50
98 Mike Anderson .20 .50
99 Derrick Mason .20 .50
100 Jason Sehorn .20 .50
101 Kevin Johnson .15 .40
102 Terrell Owens .25 .60
103 Lamar Smith .20 .50
104 Eric Moulds .20 .50
105 Jerome Bettis .25 .60
106 Marvin Harrison .25 .60
107 Shawn Jefferson .15 .40
108 Rickey Dudley .15 .40
109 James Stewart .15 .40
110 Bruce Smith .25 .60
111 Matthew Hatchette .15 .40
112 Emmitt Smith .60 1.50
113 Steve McNair .25 .60
114 Ricky Williams .25 .60
115 Tim Couch .15 .40
116 Darrell Jackson .20 .50
117 Doug Chapman .15 .40
118 Jeff Lewis .15 .40
119 Freddie Jones .15 .40
120 Sylvester Morris .15 .40
121 Elvis Grbac .20 .50
122 Plaxico Burress .20 .50
123 Marcus Pollard .15 .40
124 Chris Chandler .20 .50
125 James Thrash .20 .50
126 Brett Favre .75 2.00
127 Jake Plummer .20 .50
128 Vinny Testaverde .20 .50
129 Terrell Davis .25 .60
130 Jevon Kearse .20 .50
131 Albert Connell .15 .40
132 Dennis Northcutt .15 .40
133 Az-Zahir Hakim .15 .40
134 J.R. Redmond .15 .40
135 Marcus Robinson .20 .50
136 Eddie George .25 .60
137 Ike Hilliard .20 .50
138 Hugh Douglas .15 .40
139 Kurt Warner .40 1.00
140 Terry Glenn .20 .50
141 Brian Urlacher .30 .75
142 Charlie Garner .20 .50
143 Jay Fiedler .20 .50
144 Rob Johnson .20 .50
145 Kordell Stewart .20 .50
146 Mark Brunell .20 .50
147 Travis Taylor .15 .40
148 Laveranues Coles .20 .50
149 Ed McCaffrey .20 .50
150 Jacquez Green .15 .40
151 Joe Horn .20 .50
152 Darnay Scott .20 .50
153 Torry Holt .20 .50
154 Daunte Culpepper .20 .50
155 Wesley Walls .15 .40
156 Jeff Garcia .20 .50
157 Derrick Alexander .15 .40
158 Peerless Price .15 .40
159 Bobby Shaw .15 .40
160 Fred Taylor .25 .60
161 Chris Redman .25 .60
162 Tim Brown .25 .60
163 Charlie Batch .20 .50
164 Champ Bailey .25 .60
165 Tiki Barber .25 .60
166 Joey Galloway .20 .50
167 Brad Johnson .20 .50
168 Jeff Blake .20 .50
169 Jon Kitna .20 .50
170 Trent Green .25 .60
171 Troy Brown .20 .50
172 Eddie Kennison .20 .50
173 J.J. Stokes .15 .40
174 James McKnight .15 .40
175 Jeremy McDaniel .15 .40
176 Richard Huntley .15 .40
177 Kyle Brady .15 .40
178 Jamal Anderson .20 .50
179 Chad Lewis .15 .40
180 Ahman Green .25 .60
181 Michael Vick RC 6.00 15.00
182 Deuce McAllister RC 1.50 4.00
183 David Terrell RC 1.25 3.00
184 Koren Robinson RC 1.25 3.00
185 LaDainian Tomlinson RC 5.00 12.00
186 Michael Bennett RC 1.25 3.00
187 Chris Chambers RC 1.50 4.00
188 Chad Johnson RC 2.50 6.00
189 Santana Moss RC 2.00 5.00
190 Todd Heap RC 1.50 4.00
191 Freddie Mitchell RC 1.00 2.50
192 Quincy Morgan RC 1.25 3.00
193 Rod Gardner RC 1.25 3.00
194 Kevan Barlow RC 1.25 3.00
195 Drew Brees RC 10.00 25.00
196 Robert Ferguson RC 1.50 4.00
197 Ken-Yon Rambo RC 1.00 2.50
198 Travis Henry RC 1.25 3.00
199 LaMont Jordan RC 1.50 4.00
200 Chris Weinke RC 1.25 3.00
201 Sage Rosenfels RC 1.50 4.00
202 Josh Heupel RC 1.50 4.00
203 Quincy Carter RC 1.25 3.00
204 Jesse Palmer RC 1.25 3.00
205 Mike McMahon RC 1.25 3.00
206 Rudi Johnson RC 1.50 4.00
207 Anthony Thomas RC 1.50 4.00
208 James Jackson RC 1.00 2.50
209 Snoop Minnis RC 1.00 2.50
210 Derek Combs RC 1.00 2.50
211 Ronney Daniels RC 1.00 2.50
212 Alex Bannister RC 1.00 2.50
213 Cedrick Wilson RC 1.25 3.00
214 Travis Minor RC 1.25 3.00
215 Marques Tuiasosopo RC 1.25 3.00
216 Reggie Wayne RC 3.00 8.00
217 Josh Booty RC 1.25 3.00
218 Jamal Reynolds RC 1.00 2.50
219 Gerard Warren RC 1.25 3.00
220 Justin Smith RC 1.50 4.00
221 Andre Carter RC 1.25 3.00
222 Milton Wynn RC 1.00 2.50
223 Fred Smoot RC 1.50 4.00
224 Jamar Fletcher RC 1.00 2.50
225 Dan Morgan RC 1.25 3.00
226 Jonathan Carter RC 1.00 2.50
227 Correll Buckhalter RC 1.50 4.00
228 Kevin Kasper RC 1.00 2.50
229 Derrick Blaylock RC 1.25 3.00
230 Justin McCareins RC 1.25 3.00

2001 Fleer Focus Numbers

*VETS/200-403: 3X TO 8X BASIC CARDS
*ROOKIES/200-403: .5X TO 1.2X
*VETS/100-199: 5X TO 12X BASIC CARDS
*ROOKIES/100-199: .8X TO 2X
*VETS/70-99: 6X TO 15X BASIC CARDS
*ROOKIES/70-99: 1X TO 2.5X
*VETS/45-69: 8X TO 20X BASIC CARDS
*ROOKIES/45-69: 1.2X TO 3X
*VETS/30-44: 12X TO 30X BASIC CARDS
*ROOKIES/30-44: 2X TO 5X
*VETS/20-29: 15X TO 40X BASIC CARDS
*VETS/10-19: 20X TO 50X BASIC CARDS

2001 Fleer Focus Certified Cuts

STATED ODDS 1:72
CCCC Chris Chambers 8.00 20.00
CCCW Chris Weinke SP 6.00 15.00
CCDB Drew Brees SP 75.00 125.00
CCDM Deuce McAllister 8.00 20.00
CCDM2 Donovan McNabb SP 25.00 50.00
CCDT David Terrell 6.00 15.00
CCJH Josh Heupel 8.00 20.00
CCJJ James Jackson 5.00 12.00
CCJP Jesse Palmer 6.00 15.00
CCKB Kevan Barlow 6.00 15.00
CCKR Koren Robinson 6.00 15.00
CCLJ LaMont Jordan EXCH 1.25 3.00
CCLT LaDainian Tomlinson 50.00 120.00
CCMB Michael Bennett 6.00 15.00
CCMV Michael Vick SP EXCH 1.50 4.00
CCRJ Rudi Johnson 8.00 20.00
CCRW Reggie Wayne EXCH 1.50 4.00
CCSM Santana Moss 10.00 25.00

2001 Fleer Focus Property Of

STATED ODDS 1:192
*SHIRTS/SKINS/50: .6X TO 1.5X JSY
SHIRTS/SKINS PRINT RUN 50
POBF Brett Favre 15.00 40.00
POCD Corey Dillon 4.00 10.00
PODM Dan Marino 12.00 30.00
POJR Jerry Rice 10.00 25.00
POKS Kordell Stewart 4.00 10.00
POKW Kurt Warner 8.00 20.00
POMF Marshall Faulk 5.00 12.00
PORL Ray Lewis 5.00 12.00
PORS Rod Smith 4.00 10.00
POWC Wayne Chrebet 4.00 10.00

2001 Fleer Focus Rookie Premiere Jersey

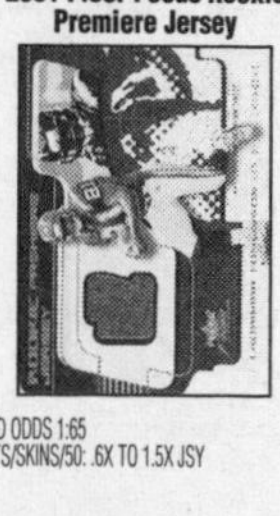

STATED ODDS 1:65
*SHIRTS/SKINS/50: .6X TO 1.5X JSY
SHIRTS/SKINS PRINT RUN 50
RPAC Andre Carter 3.00 8.00
RPAT Anthony Thomas 4.00 10.00
RPCC Chris Chambers 4.00 10.00
RPCJ Chad Johnson 6.00 15.00
RPCW Chris Weinke 3.00 8.00
RPDB Drew Brees 25.00 60.00
RPDM1 Dan Morgan 3.00 8.00
RPDM2 Deuce McAllister 4.00 10.00
RPDT David Terrell 3.00 8.00
RPFM Freddie Mitchell 2.50 6.00
RPGW Gerard Warren 3.00 8.00
RPJH Josh Heupel 4.00 10.00
RPJJ James Jackson 2.50 6.00
RPJP Jesse Palmer 3.00 8.00
RPJS Justin Smith 4.00 10.00
RPKB Kevan Barlow 3.00 8.00
RPKR Koren Robinson 3.00 8.00
RPLD Leonard Davis 4.00 10.00
RPLT LaDainian Tomlinson 12.00 30.00
RPMB Michael Bennett 3.00 8.00
RPMM1 Mike McMahon 3.00 8.00
RPMM2 Snoop Minnis 2.50 6.00
RPMT Marques Tuiasosopo 3.00 8.00
RPMV Michael Vick 15.00 40.00
RPQC Quincy Carter 3.00 8.00
RPQM Quincy Morgan 3.00 8.00
RPRF Robert Ferguson 4.00 10.00
RPRG Rod Gardner 3.00 8.00
RPRJ Rudi Johnson 4.00 10.00
RPRS Richard Seymour 4.00 10.00
RPRW Reggie Wayne 8.00 20.00
RPSM Santana Moss 5.00 12.00
RPSR Sage Rosenfels 4.00 10.00
RPTH1 Todd Heap 4.00 10.00
RPTH2 Travis Henry 3.00 8.00
RPTM Travis Minor 3.00 8.00

2001 Fleer Focus Tag Team

STATED ODDS 1:140
TTBF Brett Favre 20.00 50.00
TTBJ Bo Jackson 12.00 30.00
TTBU Brian Urlacher 10.00 25.00
TTDC Daunte Culpepper 6.00 15.00
TTDM1 Dan Marino 25.00 60.00
TTDM2 Deuce McAllister 6.00 15.00
TTDM3 Donovan McNabb 8.00 20.00
TTED Eric Dickerson 8.00 20.00
TTEG Eddie George 8.00 20.00
TTEJ Edgerrin James 8.00 20.00
TTES Emmitt Smith 20.00 40.00
TTJE John Elway 25.00 60.00
TTJM Joe Montana 30.00 60.00
TTJR Jerry Rice 15.00 40.00
TTJU Johnny Unitas 25.00 60.00
TTMA Marcus Allen 10.00 25.00
TTMF Marshall Faulk 8.00 20.00
TTPH Paul Hornung Pants 10.00 25.00
TTRC Randall Cunningham 10.00 25.00
TTRM Randy Moss 8.00 20.00
TTRS Roger Staubach 20.00 50.00
TTSM Steve McNair 8.00 20.00
TTSY Steve Young 12.00 30.00
TTTA Troy Aikman 15.00 40.00
TTTD1 Terrell Davis 8.00 20.00
TTTD2 Tony Dorsett 10.00 25.00
TTWM Warren Moon 10.00 25.00
TTWP1 Walter Payton 40.00 100.00
TTWP2 William Perry 8.00 20.00

2001 Fleer Focus Tag Team Tandems

STATED PRINT RUN 50 SER.#'d SETS
BJMA Bo Jackson 30.00 80.00
Marcus Allen
DCWM Daunte Culpepper 20.00 50.00
Warren Moon
DMRC Donovan McNabb 20.00 50.00
Randall Cunningham
DMRW Deuce McAllister 15.00 40.00
Ricky Williams
ESTD Emmitt Smith 50.00 120.00
Tony Dorsett
JETD John Elway 40.00 100.00
Terrell Davis
JMSY Joe Montana 40.00 100.00
Steve Young
JRSY Jerry Rice 40.00 100.00
Steve Young
JUEJ Johnny Unitas 40.00 100.00
Edgerrin James
MFED Marshall Faulk 20.00 50.00
Eric Dickerson
PHBF Paul Hornung 50.00 120.00
Brett Favre
RMDC Randy Moss 20.00 50.00
Daunte Culpepper
SMEG Steve McNair 20.00 50.00
Eddie George
TARS Troy Aikman 30.00 80.00
Roger Staubach
WPBU William Perry 25.00 60.00
Brian Urlacher

2001 Fleer Focus Toast of the Town

COMPLETE SET (20) 15.00 40.00
STATED ODDS 1:6
1 Donovan McNabb .75 2.00
2 Brett Favre 2.50 6.00
3 Jerome Bettis .75 2.00
4 Stephen Davis .60 1.50
5 Emmitt Smith 2.00 5.00
6 Cris Carter .75 2.00
7 Peyton Manning 2.00 5.00
8 Eddie George .75 2.00
9 Edgerrin James .75 2.00
10 Daunte Culpepper .60 1.50
11 Kurt Warner 1.25 3.00
12 Mark Brunell .60 1.50
13 Randy Moss .75 2.00
14 Marvin Harrison .75 2.00
15 Jamal Lewis .75 2.00
16 Warren Sapp .60 1.50
17 Jerry Rice 1.50 4.00
18 Ricky Williams .75 2.00
19 Ron Dayne .60 1.50
20 Brian Griese .60 1.50

2001 Fleer Focus Tunnel Vision

COMPLETE SET (15) 15.00 40.00
STATED ODDS 1:12
1 Peyton Manning 2.00 5.00
2 Jamal Lewis .75 2.00
3 Emmitt Smith 2.00 5.00
4 Eddie George .75 2.00
5 Michael Vick 2.00 5.00
6 Brett Favre 2.50 6.00
7 Ricky Williams .75 2.00
8 Edgerrin James .75 2.00
9 Ron Dayne .60 1.50
10 Eric Moulds .60 1.50
11 Tim Brown .75 2.00
12 Terrell Davis .75 2.00
13 Jevon Kearse .60 1.50
14 Peter Warrick .60 1.50
15 Ray Lewis .75 2.00

2002 Fleer Focus JE

Released in October 2002, this 160 card set was made up of 100 veterans and 60 rookies. Boxes contained 24 packs with 7 cards per pack. The rookies were serial numbered to 1850. Boxes contained 1 oversized materialistic jumbo card as a box topper.

COMP.SET w/o SP's (100) 7.50 20.00
ROOKIE PRINT RUN 1850 SER.#'d SETS
1 Tom Brady .75 2.00
2 Curtis Martin .30 .75
3 Brett Favre .75 2.00
4 Michael Pittman .25 .60
5 Donovan McNabb .30 .75
6 Quincy Carter .20 .50
7 Trent Dilfer .25 .60
8 Troy Brown .25 .60
9 Ed McCaffrey .25 .60
10 Shaun Alexander .25 .60
11 Daunte Culpepper .25 .60
12 Marty Booker .25 .60
13 Junior Seau .30 .75
14 Zach Thomas .30 .75
15 Muhsin Muhammad .25 .60
16 Kordell Stewart .25 .60
17 Jimmy Smith .25 .60
18 David Boston .20 .50
19 Laveranues Coles .25 .60
20 Emmitt Smith .75 2.00
21 Darrell Jackson .25 .60
22 Charlie Garner .25 .60
23 Marcus Robinson .25 .60
24 Drew Brees .50 1.25
25 Tony Gonzalez .30 .75
26 James Allen .20 .50
27 Steve McNair .30 .75
28 Kerry Collins .25 .60
29 Az-Zahir Hakim .20 .50
30 Marshall Faulk .30 .75
31 Derrick Mason .25 .60
32 Rod Smith .25 .60
33 Torry Holt .30 .75
34 Jake Plummer .25 .60
35 Kevin Johnson .20 .50
36 Kevan Barlow .20 .50
37 Priest Holmes .30 .75
38 Anthony Thomas .25 .60
39 Jerome Bettis .30 .75
40 Johnnie Morton .25 .60
41 Eric Moulds .25 .60
42 James Thrash .25 .60
43 Jamie Sharper .25 .60
44 Eddie George .25 .60
45 Randy Moss .30 .75
46 Tim Couch .20 .50
47 Terrell Owens .30 .75
48 Jay Fiedler .25 .60
49 Travis Henry .20 .50
50 Hines Ward .30 .75
51 Ricky Williams .25 .60
52 Brian Urlacher .30 .75
53 LaDainian Tomlinson .40 1.00
54 Trent Green .25 .60
55 Chris Redman .20 .50
56 Deuce McAllister .25 .60
57 Mark Brunell .25 .60
58 Jamal Lewis .25 .60
59 Freddie Mitchell .20 .50
60 Peyton Manning .60 1.50
61 Stephen Davis .25 .60
62 Tiki Barber .30 .75
63 Terry Glenn .25 .60
64 Keyshawn Johnson .25 .60
65 Aaron Brooks .25 .60
66 Brian Griese .25 .60
67 Koren Robinson .20 .50
68 Michael Bennett .25 .60
69 Ray Lewis .30 .75
70 Rich Gannon .25 .60
71 Marvin Harrison .30 .75
72 Rod Gardner .20 .50
73 Chad Pennington .30 .75
74 Terrell Davis .30 .75
75 Isaac Bruce .30 .75
76 Peter Warrick .25 .60
77 Jeff Garcia .25 .60
78 Chris Chambers .25 .60
79 Chris Weinke .20 .50
80 Plaxico Burress .25 .60
81 Edgerrin James .25 .60
82 Drew Bledsoe .30 .75
83 Duce Staley .25 .60
84 Fred Taylor .25 .60
85 Warrick Dunn .25 .60
86 Jerry Rice .60 1.50
87 Ahman Green .25 .60
88 Warren Sapp .25 .60
89 Michael Strahan .30 .75
90 Bill Schroeder .20 .50
91 Kurt Warner .30 .75
92 Antowain Smith .25 .60
93 Corey Dillon .25 .60
94 Garrison Hearst .25 .60
95 Joey Galloway .25 .60
96 Michael Vick .50 1.25
97 Tim Brown .30 .75
98 Corey Bradford .20 .50
99 Brad Johnson .25 .60
100 Joe Horn .25 .60
101 Quentin Jammer RC 1.25 3.00
102 Rohan Davey RC 1.25 3.00
103 David Garrard RC 1.50 4.00
104 Ron Johnson RC 1.00 2.50
105 Jeremy Shockey RC 2.00 5.00
106 Marquise Walker RC .75 2.00
107 Luke Staley RC .75 2.00
108 Josh Scobey RC 1.00 2.50
109 Adrian Peterson RC 1.25 3.00
110 Lito Sheppard RC 1.25 3.00
111 Daniel Graham RC 1.00 2.50
112 Ryan Sims RC 1.25 3.00
113 William Green RC 1.00 2.50
114 Ashley Lelie RC 1.00 2.50
115 Deion Branch RC 1.25 3.00
116 Omar Easy RC 1.00 2.50
117 Jake Schifino RC .75 2.00
118 Donte Stallworth RC 1.25 3.00
119 Craig Nall RC 1.00 2.50
120 Clinton Portis RC 1.50 4.00
121 Brandon Doman RC .75 2.00
122 Eric Crouch RC 1.25 3.00
123 Josh McCown RC 1.25 3.00
124 Cliff Russell RC .75 2.00
125 T.J. Duckett RC 1.25 3.00
126 Jason McAddley RC 1.00 2.50
127 Chad Hutchinson RC .75 2.00
128 Jonathan Wells RC 1.25 3.00
129 Antwaan Randle El RC 1.25 3.00
130 Terry Charles RC .75 2.00
131 Lamar Gordon RC 1.00 2.50
132 Antonio Bryant RC 1.25 3.00
133 Brian Westbrook RC 2.00 5.00
134 Javon Walker RC 1.25 3.00
135 J.T. O'Sullivan RC 1.00 2.50
136 Maurice Morris RC 1.00 2.50
137 Tim Carter RC 1.00 2.50
138 Antwoine Womack RC .75 2.00
139 Ladell Betts RC 1.25 3.00
140 Joey Harrington RC 1.25 3.00
141 Chester Taylor RC 1.25 3.00
142 David Carr RC 1.25 3.00
143 Roy Williams RC 1.25 3.00
144 Reche Caldwell RC 1.25 3.00
145 Lamont Brightful RC .75 2.00
146 Patrick Ramsey RC 1.25 3.00
147 Travis Stephens RC .75 2.00
148 Andre Davis RC 1.00 2.50
149 Herb Haygood RC .75 2.00
150 Randy Fasani RC 1.00 2.50
151 Jabar Gaffney RC 1.25 3.00
152 Kahlil Hill RC .75 2.00
153 Julius Peppers RC 2.50 6.00
154 Kurt Kittner RC .75 2.00
155 DeShaun Foster RC 1.25 3.00
156 Verron Haynes RC .75 2.00
157 Josh Reed RC 1.00 2.50
158 Freddie Milons RC .75 2.00
159 Robert Thomas RC .75 2.00
160 Sam Simmons RC .75 2.00

2002 Fleer Focus JE Jersey Numbers

*VETS/80-99: 4X TO 10X BASIC CARDS
*ROOKIES/80-99: .8X TO 2X
*VETS/45-55: 5X TO 12X BASIC CARDS
*ROOKIES/45-55: 1X TO 2.5X
*VETS/30-43: 8X TO 20X BASIC CARDS
*ROOKIES/30-43: 1.5X TO 4X
*VETS/20-29: 12X TO 30X BASIC CARDS
*ROOKIES/20-29: 2.5X TO 6X
*VETS/10-19: 20X TO 50X BASIC CARDS
*ROOKIES/10-19: 4X TO 10X
SERIAL #'d UNDER 10 NOT PRICED

2002 Fleer Focus JE Jersey Numbers Century

*VETS: 2.5X TO 6X BASIC CARDS
*ROOKIES: .6X TO 1.5X BASIC CARDS
STATED PRINT RUN 101-199

2002 Fleer Focus JE Franchise Focus

STATED ODDS 1:12
1 David Boston .75 2.00
2 Michael Vick 2.00 5.00
3 Ray Lewis 1.25 3.00
4 Drew Bledsoe 1.25 3.00
5 Julius Peppers 2.50 6.00
6 Brian Urlacher 1.25 3.00
7 Corey Dillon 1.00 2.50
8 Tim Couch .75 2.00
9 Emmitt Smith 3.00 8.00
10 Rod Smith 1.00 2.50
11 Joey Harrington 1.25 3.00
12 Brett Favre 3.00 8.00
13 David Carr 1.25 3.00
14 Peyton Manning 2.50 6.00
15 Jimmy Smith 1.00 2.50
16 Tony Gonzalez 1.25 3.00
17 Ricky Williams 1.00 2.50
18 Randy Moss 1.25 3.00
19 Tom Brady 3.00 8.00
20 Aaron Brooks 1.00 2.50
21 Michael Strahan 1.25 3.00
22 Curtis Martin 1.25 3.00
23 Jerry Rice 2.50 6.00
24 Donovan McNabb 1.25 3.00
25 Jerome Bettis 1.25 3.00
26 Junior Seau 1.25 3.00
27 Jeff Garcia 1.00 2.50
28 Shaun Alexander 1.00 2.50
29 Kurt Warner 1.25 3.00
30 Keyshawn Johnson 1.00 2.50
31 Eddie George 1.00 2.50
32 Stephen Davis 1.00 2.50

2002 Fleer Focus JE Franchise Focus Jerseys

STATED ODDS 1:82
1 Tim Couch 3.00 8.00
2 Stephen Davis 4.00 10.00
3 Keyshawn Johnson 4.00 10.00
4 Ray Lewis 5.00 12.00
5 Donovan McNabb 5.00 12.00
6 Randy Moss 5.00 12.00
7 Junior Seau 5.00 12.00
8 Brian Urlacher 5.00 12.00
9 Kurt Warner 5.00 12.00
10 Ricky Williams 4.00 10.00

2002 Fleer Focus JE Franchise Focus Rivals

STATED PRINT RUN 100 SER.#'d SETS
ABMV Aaron Brooks 10.00 25.00
Michael Vick
CMRB Curtis Martin 15.00 40.00
Tom Brady
DBSA David Boston 5.00 12.00
Shaun Alexander
DMMS Donovan McNabb 6.00 15.00
Michael Strahan
ESSD Emmitt Smith 15.00 40.00
Stephen Davis
JGKW Jeff Garcia 6.00 15.00
Kurt Warner
JRJS Jerry Rice 12.00 30.00
Junior Seau
JSEG Jimmy Smith 5.00 12.00
Eddie George
RMBF Randy Moss 15.00 40.00
Brett Favre
TCJB Tim Couch 6.00 15.00
Jerome Bettis

2002 Fleer Focus JE Freeze Frame

STATED ODDS 1:24
1 Kurt Warner 1.50 4.00
2 Eddie George 1.25 3.00
3 Marshall Faulk 1.50 4.00
4 Emmitt Smith 4.00 10.00
5 Randy Moss 1.50 4.00
6 Brett Favre 4.00 10.00
7 Drew Bledsoe 1.50 4.00
8 LaDainian Tomlinson 2.00 5.00
9 Tom Brady 4.00 10.00
10 Donovan McNabb 1.50 4.00
11 Ricky Williams 1.25 3.00
12 Jerry Rice 3.00 8.00
13 Daunte Culpepper 1.25 3.00
14 Peyton Manning 3.00 8.00
15 Brian Urlacher 1.50 4.00

2002 Fleer Focus JE Freeze Frame Jerseys

STATED ODDS 1:187
*PATCH/50: .6X TO 1.5X BASIC JSY
PATCHES PRINT RUN 50 SER.#'d SETS
1 Marshall Faulk 6.00 15.00
2 Brett Favre 15.00 40.00
3 Eddie George 5.00 12.00
4 Peyton Manning 12.00 30.00
5 Donovan McNabb 6.00 15.00
6 Randy Moss 6.00 15.00
7 Emmitt Smith 15.00 40.00
8 Brian Urlacher 6.00 15.00
9 Kurt Warner 6.00 15.00
10 Ricky Williams 5.00 12.00

2002 Fleer Focus JE Lettermen

UNPRICED LETTERMEN #'d TO 1

2002 Fleer Focus JE Materialistic Home

STATED ODDS 1:24
*AWAY/50: .8X TO 2X HOME JSY
AWAY PRINT RUN 50 SER.#'d SETS
1 Kurt Warner 3.00 8.00
2 Tom Brady 8.00 20.00
3 Daunte Culpepper 2.50 6.00
4 Drew Bledsoe 3.00 8.00
5 Emmitt Smith 8.00 20.00
6 Jerry Rice 6.00 15.00
7 Eddie George 2.50 6.00
8 Donovan McNabb 3.00 8.00
9 Brett Favre 8.00 20.00
10 Peyton Manning 6.00 15.00
11 Randy Moss 3.00 8.00
12 Marshall Faulk 3.00 8.00
13 Ricky Williams 2.50 6.00
14 Brian Urlacher 3.00 8.00
15 Edgerrin James 2.50 6.00

2002 Fleer Focus JE Materialistic Jumbos

STATED ODDS ONE PER BOX
*GOLD/50: 1X TO 2.5X BASIC INSERT
GOLD PRINT RUN 50 SER.#'d SETS
1 Joey Harrington 2.00 5.00
2 William Green 1.50 4.00
3 Donte Stallworth 2.00 5.00
4 Ashley Lelie 1.50 4.00
5 Jabar Gaffney 2.00 5.00
6 Antonio Bryant 2.00 5.00
7 Josh Reed 1.50 4.00
8 Antwaan Randle El 2.00 5.00
9 Reche Caldwell 2.00 5.00
10 Javon Walker 2.00 5.00
11 T.J. Duckett 2.00 5.00
12 Marquise Walker 1.25 3.00
13 Clinton Portis 2.50 6.00
14 DeShaun Foster 2.00 5.00
15 Patrick Ramsey 2.00 5.00

2002 Fleer Focus JE Materialistic Plus

STATED PRINT RUN 250 SER.#'d SETS
1 Brett Favre 12.00 30.00
2 Eddie George 4.00 10.00
3 Peyton Manning 10.00 25.00
4 Donovan McNabb 5.00 12.00
5 Randy Moss 5.00 12.00
6 Emmitt Smith 12.00 30.00
7 Brian Urlacher 5.00 12.00
8 Kurt Warner 5.00 12.00
9 Ricky Williams 4.00 10.00
10 Marshall Faulk 5.00 12.00

2002 Fleer Focus JE ROY Collection

STATED ODDS 1:144
1 Emmitt Smith 8.00 20.00
2 Curtis Martin 3.00 8.00
3 Anthony Thomas 2.50 6.00
4 Brian Urlacher 3.00 8.00
5 Jerome Bettis 3.00 8.00
6 Edgerrin James 2.50 6.00
7 Jevon Kearse 2.50 6.00
8 Marshall Faulk 3.00 8.00
9 Eric Dickerson 2.50 6.00
10 Randy Moss 3.00 8.00
11 Tony Dorsett 3.00 8.00
12 Kendrell Bell 2.00 5.00
13 Eddie George 2.50 6.00
14 Charles Woodson 3.00 8.00
15 Warrick Dunn 2.50 6.00

2002 Fleer Focus JE ROY Collection Jerseys

STATED ODDS 1:187
*PATCH/97-101: .6X TO 1.5X BASIC JSY
PATCH PRINT RUN 97-101
1 Kendrell Bell SP 4.00 10.00
2 Tony Dorsett SP 10.00 25.00
3 Warrick Dunn 5.00 12.00
4 Marshall Faulk 6.00 15.00
5 Eddie George 5.00 12.00
6 Jevon Kearse 5.00 12.00
7 Randy Moss 6.00 15.00
8 Anthony Thomas SP 5.00 12.00
9 Brian Urlacher SP 6.00 15.00

2003 Fleer Focus

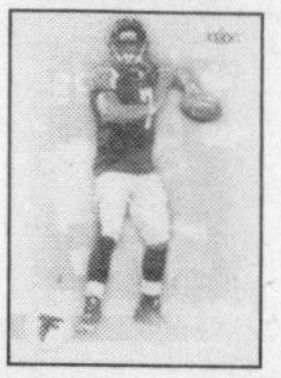

Released in November of 2003, this set features 160 cards consisting of 120 veterans and 40 rookies. Rookies 121-160 are serial numbered to 699. Boxes contained 24 packs of 5 cards. SRP was $2.99.

COMP.SET w/o SP's (120) 10.00 25.00
121-160 ROOKIE PRINT RUN 699
1 Tony Gonzalez .30 .75
2 Aaron Brooks .25 .60
3 Joey Harrington .20 .50
4 Brett Favre .75 2.00
5 Donovan McNabb .30 .75
6 Jerome Bettis .30 .75
7 Michael Vick .40 1.00
8 Travis Taylor .20 .50
9 Jay Fiedler .20 .50
10 David Boston .20 .50
11 Peerless Price .20 .50
12 Kevan Barlow .20 .50
13 LaDainian Tomlinson .30 .75
14 Jevon Kearse .25 .60
15 Peyton Manning .60 1.50
16 T.J. Duckett .25 .60
17 Drew Brees .30 .75
18 Brian Dawkins .25 .60
19 Charles Woodson .30 .75
20 Emmitt Smith .75 2.00
21 Joe Jurevicius .25 .60
22 Duce Staley .25 .60
23 Rod Gardner .20 .50
24 Jamal Lewis .25 .60
25 Jeff Garcia .25 .60
26 Clinton Portis .25 .60
27 Priest Holmes .30 .75
28 Mike Alstott .30 .75
29 Shaun Alexander .25 .60
30 Randy Moss .30 .75
31 Eric Moulds .25 .60
32 Troy Brown .25 .60
33 Michael Bennett .25 .60
34 Ricky Williams .25 .60
35 Champ Bailey .30 .75
36 Hugh Douglas .20 .50
37 Travis Henry .20 .50
38 Daunte Culpepper .25 .60
39 Koren Robinson .25 .60
40 Todd Heap .25 .60
41 John Abraham .25 .60
42 Drew Bledsoe .30 .75
43 Tom Brady .75 2.00
44 Torry Holt .30 .75
45 Jake Delhomme .30 .75
46 Joe Horn .25 .60
47 Julius Peppers .30 .75
48 Ray Lewis .30 .75
49 Deuce McAllister .25 .60
50 Marshall Faulk .30 .75
51 Takeo Spikes .20 .50
52 Kordell Stewart .25 .60
53 Brian Urlacher .30 .75
54 Zach Thomas .30 .75
55 Kurt Warner .30 .75
56 Peter Warrick .25 .60
57 Marty Booker .25 .60
58 Warren Sapp .25 .60
59 Jon Kitna .25 .60
60 Chad Johnson .30 .75
61 Jeremy Shockey .30 .75
62 Keyshawn Johnson .30 .75
63 Kelly Holcomb .20 .50
64 Corey Dillon .25 .60
65 Tiki Barber .30 .75
66 Eddie George .25 .60
67 Joey Galloway .25 .60
68 Tim Couch .20 .50
69 Amani Toomer .25 .60
70 Steve McNair .30 .75
71 Troy Hambrick .20 .50
72 William Green .20 .50
73 Chad Pennington .30 .75
74 Laveranues Coles .20 .50
75 Quincy Carter .20 .50
76 Antonio Bryant .20 .50
77 Curtis Martin .30 .75
78 Terrell Owens .30 .75
79 Patrick Ramsey .25 .60
80 Ashley Lelie .20 .50
81 Donte Stallworth .20 .50
82 Roy Williams .25 .60
83 Charlie Garner .25 .60
84 Chris Chambers .25 .60
85 Warrick Dunn .25 .60

86 Shannon Sharpe	.30	.75
87 Rod Smith	.25	.60
88 Marvin Harrison	.30	.75
89 Rich Gannon	.25	.60
90 Stephen Davis	.25	.60
91 James Stewart	.20	.50
92 Tim Brown	.30	.75
93 Anthony Thomas	.25	.60
94 Stacey Mack	.20	.50
95 Jake Plummer	.25	.60
96 Jerry Rice	.60	1.50
97 Quincy Morgan	.20	.50
98 Dwight Freeney	.25	.60
99 Jason Taylor	.25	.60
100 Ahman Green	.25	.60
101 Hines Ward	.30	.75
102 Kerry Collins	.25	.60
103 Plaxico Burress	.25	.60
104 Santana Moss	.25	.60
105 Michael Strahan	.30	.75
106 Donald Driver	.30	.75
107 Tommy Maddox	.25	.60
108 Jerry Porter	.20	.50
109 David Carr	.25	.60
110 Garrison Hearst	.25	.60
111 Edgerrin James	.30	.75
112 Isaac Bruce	.30	.75
113 Marc Bulger	.30	.75
114 Brad Johnson	.25	.60
115 Fred Taylor	.25	.60
116 Derrick Brooks	.25	.60
117 Jimmy Smith	.25	.60
118 Derrick Mason	.25	.60
119 Mark Brunell	.25	.60
120 Trent Green	.25	.60
121 Mike Doss RC	2.00	5.00
122 Carson Palmer RC	4.00	10.00
123 Charles Rogers RC	1.50	4.00
124 Andre Johnson RC	5.00	12.00
125 Tony Hollings RC	1.50	4.00
126 Terence Newman RC	1.50	4.00
127 Byron Leftwich RC	2.00	5.00
128 Terrell Suggs RC	2.00	5.00
129 Bryant Johnson RC	2.00	5.00
130 Kyle Boller RC	2.00	5.00
131 Rex Grossman RC	2.00	5.00
132 Willis McGahee RC	2.50	6.00
133 Dallas Clark RC	3.00	8.00
134 Bobby Wade RC	1.50	4.00
135 Tony Romo RC	20.00	50.00
136 Michael Haynes RC	1.25	3.00
137 Bethel Johnson RC	1.25	3.00
138 Anquan Boldin RC	3.00	8.00
139 Seneca Wallace RC	2.00	5.00
140 Nick Barnett RC	2.00	5.00
141 Teyo Johnson RC	1.50	4.00
142 Kelley Washington RC	1.25	3.00
143 Nate Burleson RC	1.50	4.00
144 Ken Dorsey RC	1.50	4.00
145 Dewayne White RC	1.25	3.00
146 Chris Kelsay RC	1.50	4.00
147 Dave Ragone RC	1.25	3.00
148 David Tyree RC	2.00	5.00
149 Billy McMullen RC	1.25	3.00
150 Chris Simms RC	2.00	5.00
151 Onterrio Smith RC	1.25	3.00
152 Marcus Trufant RC	1.50	4.00
153 Jason Witten RC	5.00	12.00
154 Johnathan Sullivan RC*	1.25	3.00
155 Kevin Williams RC	2.00	5.00
156 Justin Fargas RC	2.00	5.00
157 Domanick Davis RC	1.50	4.00
158 LaBrandon Toefield RC	1.50	4.00
159 Shaun McDonald RC	1.50	4.00
160 Brandon Lloyd RC	3.00	8.00

2003 Fleer Focus Anniversary Gold

*VETS 1-120: 5X TO 12X BASIC CARDS
*ROOKIES 121-160: .8X TO 2X
STATED PRINT RUN 50 SER.#'d SETS

135 Tony Romo	50.00	120.00

2003 Fleer Focus Anniversary Silver

*VETS 1-120: 8X TO 20X BASIC CARDS
*ROOKIES 121-160: 1.2X TO 3X
STATED PRINT RUN 25 SER.#'d SETS

135 Tony Romo	75.00	200.00

2003 Fleer Focus Numbers Century

*VETS 1-120: 3X TO 8X BASIC CARDS
*ROOKIES 121-160: .5X TO 1.2X
STATED PRINT RUN 100 SER.#'d SETS
UNPRICED DECADE SER.#'d TO 10

135 Tony Romo	25.00	60.00

2003 Fleer Focus Numbers Decade

UNPRICED DECADE SER.#'d TO 10
NOT PRICED DUE TO SCARCITY

2003 Fleer Focus Diamond Focus

STATED PRINT RUN 350 SER.#'d SETS

1 Ricky Williams	1.50	4.00
2 Chad Pennington	2.00	5.00
3 Michael Vick	2.50	6.00
4 Brett Favre	5.00	12.00
5 Peyton Manning	4.00	10.00
6 Marshall Faulk	2.00	5.00
7 Carson Palmer	2.50	6.00
8 Charles Rogers	1.50	4.00
9 Willis McGahee	1.50	4.00
10 Andre Johnson	3.00	8.00
11 Byron Leftwich	1.25	3.00
12 Kyle Boller	2.00	5.00
13 LaDainian Tomlinson	2.00	5.00
14 Drew Bledsoe	2.00	5.00
15 Jerry Rice	4.00	10.00

2003 Fleer Focus Diamond Focus Jerseys 200

STATED PRINT RUN 200 SER.#'d SETS
*JERSEYS/100: .5X TO 1.2X JSY/200
*JERSEYS/50: .8X TO 2X JSY/200
JERSEYS/5 TOO SCARCE TO PRICE

1 Drew Bledsoe	4.00	10.00
2 Marshall Faulk	4.00	10.00
3 Brett Favre	10.00	25.00
4 Peyton Manning	8.00	20.00
5 Chad Pennington	4.00	10.00
6 Jerry Rice	8.00	20.00
7 Charles Rogers	3.00	8.00
8 LaDainian Tomlinson	4.00	10.00
9 Michael Vick	5.00	12.00
10 Ricky Williams	3.00	8.00

2003 Fleer Focus Emerald Focus

COMPLETE SET (10)	20.00	50.00
STATED PRINT RUN 500 SER.#'d SETS		
1 Donovan McNabb	1.50	4.00
2 Kurt Warner	1.50	4.00
3 David Carr	1.25	3.00
4 Tom Brady	4.00	10.00
5 Brian Urlacher	1.50	4.00
6 Randy Moss	1.50	4.00
7 Joey Harrington	1.00	2.50
8 Edgerrin James	1.50	4.00
9 Emmitt Smith	4.00	10.00
10 Jeremy Shockey	1.50	4.00

2003 Fleer Focus Emerald Focus Jerseys 250

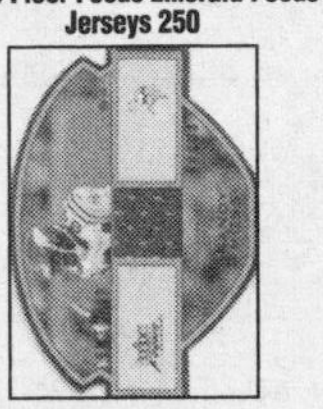

STATED PRINT RUN 250 SER.#'d SETS
*JERSEYS/150: .5X TO 1.2X JSY/250
*JERSEYS/75: .6X TO 1.5X JSY/250
JERSEYS/10 TOO SCARCE TO PRICE

1 Tom Brady	10.00	25.00
2 David Carr	3.00	8.00
3 Joey Harrington	2.50	6.00
4 Edgerrin James	4.00	10.00
5 Jeremy Shockey	4.00	10.00
6 Donovan McNabb	4.00	10.00
7 Randy Moss	4.00	10.00
8 Emmitt Smith	10.00	25.00
9 Brian Urlacher	4.00	10.00
10 Kurt Warner	4.00	10.00

2003 Fleer Focus Extra Effort

COMPLETE SET (10)	15.00	40.00
STATED PRINT RUN 500 SER.#'d SETS		
1 Emmitt Smith	4.00	10.00
2 Brett Favre	4.00	10.00
3 Hines Ward	1.50	4.00
4 Jerry Rice	3.00	8.00
5 Jeff Garcia	1.25	3.00
6 Chad Pennington	1.50	4.00
7 Eric Moulds	1.25	3.00
8 Daunte Culpepper	1.25	3.00
9 Fred Taylor	1.25	3.00
10 Drew Brees	1.50	4.00

2003 Fleer Focus Shirtified

COMPLETE SET (15)	12.00	30.00
STATED PRINT RUN 750 SER.#'d SETS		
1 Torry Holt	1.25	3.00
2 Michael Vick	1.50	4.00
3 Jeremy Shockey	1.25	3.00
4 Terrell Owens	1.25	3.00
5 Plaxico Burress	1.00	2.50
6 Steve McNair	1.25	3.00
7 Ricky Williams	1.00	2.50
8 Tim Brown	1.25	3.00
9 Brian Urlacher	1.25	3.00
10 Priest Holmes	1.25	3.00
11 Tommy Maddox	1.00	2.50
12 Deuce McAllister	1.00	2.50
13 Marvin Harrison	1.25	3.00
14 Clinton Portis	1.00	2.50
15 Tiki Barber	1.25	3.00

2003 Fleer Focus Shirtified Jerseys 175

STATED PRINT RUN 175 SER.#'d SETS
*JERSEYS/75: .6X TO 1.5X JSY/175
*NAMEPLATE/25: 1.5X TO 3X JSY/175
UNPRICED NFL LOGO PRINT RUN 1
*NUMBERS/80-90: .6X TO 1.5X JSY/175
*NUMBERS/52-54: .8X TO 2X JSY/175
*NUMBERS/31-37: 1X TO 2.5X JSY/175
*NUMBERS/20-27: 1.2X TO 3X JSY/175
NUMBERS STATED PRINT RUN 4-90

1 Shaun Alexander	3.00	8.00
2 Tiki Barber	4.00	10.00
3 Tim Brown	4.00	10.00
4 Plaxico Burress	3.00	8.00
5 Daunte Culpepper	3.00	8.00
6 Brett Favre	10.00	25.00
7 Eddie George	3.00	8.00
8 William Green	2.50	6.00
9 Marvin Harrison	4.00	10.00
10 Travis Henry	2.50	6.00
11 Priest Holmes	4.00	10.00
12 Torry Holt	4.00	10.00
13 Andre Johnson	6.00	15.00
14 Ray Lewis	4.00	10.00
15 Tommy Maddox	3.00	8.00
16 Deuce McAllister	3.00	8.00
17 Steve McNair	4.00	10.00
18 Terrell Owens	4.00	10.00
19 Julius Peppers	4.00	10.00
20 Clinton Portis	3.00	8.00
21 Jeremy Shockey	4.00	10.00
22 Emmitt Smith	10.00	25.00
23 Brian Urlacher	4.00	10.00
24 Michael Vick	5.00	12.00
25 Ricky Williams	3.00	8.00

2001 Fleer Game Time

Fleer Game Time released in July of 2001. The 150-card set featured 110 veterans and 40 rookies called Next Game. The cardfronts had 3 pictures of the featured player, a full color photo is the main focus, a two-color image of the the main photo is used in the background, and the headshot was taken from the main photo and placed on the left side of the card. The cardbacks were horizontal and contained statistics up through 2000. The rookie cards were serial numbered to 2001.

COMP.SET w/o SP's (110)	6.00	15.00
1 Donovan McNabb	.20	.50
2 Travis Prentice	.12	.30
3 Keenan McCardell	.15	.40
4 Kurt Warner	.30	.75
5 Ray Lewis	.20	.50
6 Terrell Davis	.20	.50
7 Kevin Faulk	.15	.40
8 Terrell Owens	.20	.50
9 Jeff George	.15	.40
10 Dennis Northcutt	.12	.30
11 Fred Taylor	.20	.50
12 Cris Carter	.20	.50
13 Aaron Brooks	.15	.40
14 Marshall Faulk	.20	.50
15 David Boston	.12	.30
16 Rocket Ismail	.15	.40
17 Jerome Bettis	.20	.50
18 Warrick Dunn	.20	.50
19 Corey Dillon	.15	.40
20 Mark Brunell	.15	.40
21 Torry Holt	.15	.40
22 Michael McCrary	.12	.30
23 Rod Smith	.15	.40
24 Charlie Garner	.15	.40
25 Bruce Smith	.20	.50
26 Doug Johnson	.12	.30
27 Brian Griese	.15	.40
28 Jeff Garcia	.15	.40
29 Eddie George	.20	.50
30 Shawn Bryson	.12	.30
31 Marvin Harrison	.20	.50
32 Hugh Douglas	.12	.30
33 Terance Mathis	.12	.30
34 Emmitt Smith	.50	1.25
35 Lamar Smith	.15	.40
36 Junior Seau	.20	.50
37 Steve McNair	.20	.50
38 Jake Plummer	.15	.40
39 Tim Couch	.12	.30
40 Jay Fiedler	.15	.40
41 Plaxico Burress	.15	.40
42 Keyshawn Johnson	.15	.40
43 Jason Taylor	.20	.50
44 Charlie Batch	.15	.40
45 Terry Glenn	.15	.40
46 Laveranues Coles	.15	.40
47 Darrell Jackson	.15	.40
48 Jamal Lewis	.20	.50
49 Ed McCaffrey	.15	.40
50 Vinny Testaverde	.15	.40
51 Ricky Watters	.15	.40
52 Champ Bailey	.20	.50
53 Peter Warrick	.15	.40
54 Eric Moulds	.15	.40
55 Michael Strahan	.20	.50
56 Warren Sapp	.15	.40
57 Tony Gonzalez	.20	.50
58 Kerry Collins	.15	.40
59 Shaun King	.12	.30
60 Jason Sehorn	.15	.40
61 Marcus Robinson	.15	.40
62 James Stewart	.12	.30
63 Curtis Martin	.20	.50
64 Brian Urlacher	.25	.60
65 Germane Crowell	.12	.30
66 Wesley Walls	.12	.30
67 Antonio Freeman	.20	.50
68 Ron Dayne	.15	.40
69 Tyrone Wheatley	.15	.40
70 Zach Thomas	.20	.50
71 Shannon Sharpe	.20	.50
72 Mike Anderson	.15	.40
73 Wayne Chrebet	.15	.40
74 Shaun Alexander	.20	.50
75 Stephen Davis	.15	.40
76 Derrick Mason	.15	.40
77 Dorsey Levens	.15	.40
78 Jessie Armstead	.12	.30
79 Rich Gannon	.15	.40
80 Muhsin Muhammad	.15	.40
81 Brett Favre	.60	1.50
82 Randy Moss	.20	.50
83 Joe Horn	.15	.40
84 Charles Woodson	.20	.50
85 Brad Hoover	.15	.40
86 Terrence Wilkins	.12	.30
87 Sylvester Morris	.12	.30
88 Tim Brown	.20	.50
89 Jamal Anderson	.15	.40
90 Joey Galloway	.15	.40
91 Drew Bledsoe	.20	.50
92 Rodney Harrison	.15	.40
93 Jevon Kearse	.15	.40
94 Rob Johnson	.15	.40
95 Edgerrin James	.20	.50
96 Thomas Jones	.15	.40
97 Courtney Brown	.12	.30
98 Jimmy Smith	.15	.40
99 Ricky Williams	.20	.50
100 Isaac Bruce	.20	.50
101 Akili Smith	.12	.30
102 Derrick Alexander	.12	.30
103 Daunte Culpepper	.15	.40
104 Amani Toomer	.15	.40
105 Mike Alstott	.15	.40
106 Sam Cowart	.12	.30
107 Peyton Manning	.50	1.25
108 Robert Smith	.15	.40
109 Duce Staley	.15	.40
110 Cade McNown	.15	.40
111 Michael Vick RC	6.00	15.00
112 David Terrell RC	1.25	3.00
113 Deuce McAllister RC	1.50	4.00
114 Koren Robinson RC	1.25	3.00
115 Rod Gardner RC	1.25	3.00
116 Chris Chambers RC	1.50	4.00
117 Santana Moss RC	2.00	5.00
118 Reggie Wayne RC	3.00	8.00
119 Quincy Morgan RC	1.25	3.00
120 Rudi Johnson RC	1.50	4.00
121 Robert Ferguson RC	1.50	4.00
122 Ja'Mar Toombs RC	1.00	2.50
123 Michael Bennett RC	1.25	3.00
124 Ronney Daniels RC	1.00	2.50
125 Drew Brees RC	10.00	25.00
126 Josh Heupel RC	1.50	4.00
127 Chris Weinke RC	1.25	3.00
128 LaDainian Tomlinson RC	5.00	12.00
129 Chad Johnson RC	2.50	6.00
130 LaMont Jordan RC	1.50	4.00
131 Freddie Mitchell RC	1.00	2.50
132 Anthony Thomas RC	1.50	4.00
133 Ben Leard RC	1.00	2.50
134 Sage Rosenfels RC	1.50	4.00
135 Marques Tuiasosopo RC	1.25	3.00
136 Gerard Warren RC	1.25	3.00
137 Jamar Fletcher RC	1.00	2.50
138 Justin Smith RC	1.50	4.00
139 Dan Morgan RC	1.25	3.00
140 Jamal Reynolds RC	1.00	2.50
141 Shaun Rogers RC	1.50	4.00
142 Todd Heap RC	1.50	4.00
143 Travis Minor RC	1.25	3.00
144 Mike McMahon RC	1.25	3.00
145 Travis Henry RC	1.25	3.00
146 Kevan Barlow RC	1.25	3.00
147 Javon Green RC	1.00	2.50
148 Ken-Yon Rambo RC	1.00	2.50
149 Tim Hasselbeck RC	1.25	3.00
150 Snoop Minnis RC	1.00	2.50
CL1 Checklist	.05	.15
CL2 Checklist	.05	.15

2001 Fleer Game Time Extra

*VETS 1-110: 2.5X TO 6X BASIC CARDS
*ROOKIES 111-150: .8X TO 2X
OVERALL STATED ODDS 1:8
111-150 ROOKIE PRINT RUN 201

2001 Fleer Game Time Crunch Time

COMPLETE SET (20)	7.50	20.00
STATED ODDS 1:4 HOB, 1:5 RET		
1 Emmitt Smith	2.00	5.00
2 Isaac Bruce	.75	2.00
3 James Stewart	.50	1.25
4 Warrick Dunn	.75	2.00
5 Jake Plummer	.60	1.50
6 Shannon Sharpe	.75	2.00
7 Robert Smith	.60	1.50
8 Jamal Anderson	.60	1.50
9 Terrell Owens	.75	2.00
10 Marcus Robinson	.60	1.50
11 Ed McCaffrey	.60	1.50
12 Jamal Lewis	.75	2.00
13 Amani Toomer	.60	1.50
14 Jerome Bettis	.75	2.00
15 Cris Carter	.75	2.00
16 Stephen Davis	.60	1.50
17 Marvin Harrison	.75	2.00
18 Joe Horn	.60	1.50
19 Tim Couch	.50	1.25
20 Drew Bledsoe	.75	2.00

2001 Fleer Game Time Double Trouble

COMPLETE SET (15)	12.50	30.00
STATED ODDS 1:24 HOB. 1:30 RET.		
1 Daunte Culpepper / Randy Moss	1.00	2.50
2 Kurt Warner / Marshall Faulk	1.50	4.00
3 Peyotn Manning / Edgerrin James	2.50	6.00
4 Warrick Dunn / Keyshawn Johnson	1.00	2.50
5 Brett Favre / Antonio Freeman	3.00	8.00
6 Tiki Barber / Ron Dayne	1.00	2.50
7 Corey Dillon / Peter Warrick	.75	2.00
8 Donovan McNabb / Duce Staley	1.00	2.50
9 Fred Taylor / Jimmy Smith	1.00	2.50
10 Rich Gannon / Tim Brown	1.00	2.50
11 Steve McNair / Eddie George	1.00	2.50
12 Curtis Martin / Wayne Chrebet	1.00	2.50
13 Ricky Williams / Aaron Brooks	1.00	2.50
14 Derrick Alexander / Tony Gonzalez	1.00	2.50
15 Brian Griese / Terrell Davis	1.00	2.50

2001 Fleer Game Time Eleven-Up

COMPLETE SET (15)	12.50	30.00
STATED ODDS 1:12 HOB. 1:15 RET.		
1 Jamal Lewis	1.00	2.50
2 Randy Moss	1.00	2.50
3 Ricky Williams	1.00	2.50
4 Terrell Davis	1.00	2.50
5 Donovan McNabb	1.00	2.50
6 Curtis Martin	1.00	2.50
7 Brett Favre	3.00	8.00
8 Aaron Brooks	.75	2.00
9 Kurt Warner	1.50	4.00
10 Eddie George	1.00	2.50
11 Daunte Culpepper	.75	2.00
12 Jamal Anderson	.75	2.00
13 Marshall Faulk	1.00	2.50
14 Ray Lewis	1.00	2.50
15 Ron Dayne	.75	2.00

2001 Fleer Game Time Fame Time Jerseys

STATED PRINT RUN 100 SER.#'d SETS
*RED: .3X TO .8X BASIC JSY

1 Terry Bradshaw	25.00	60.00
2 Eric Dickerson	15.00	40.00
3 Tony Dorsett	25.00	50.00
4 Paul Hornung	30.00	60.00
5 Howie Long	35.00	60.00
6 Joe Montana	40.00	100.00
7 Walter Payton	50.00	120.00
8 Roger Staubach	30.00	80.00
9 Fran Tarkenton	15.00	40.00
10 Lawrence Taylor	25.00	50.00
11 Johnny Unitas	30.00	80.00

2001 Fleer Game Time Fame Time Jerseys Autographs

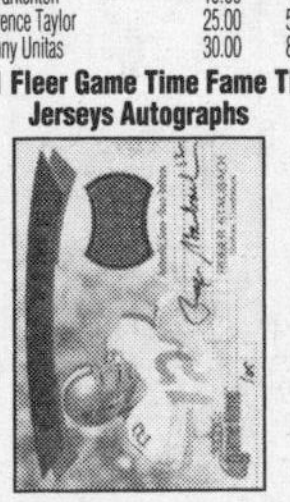

STATED PRINT RUN 25 SER.#'d SETS

1 Terry Bradshaw	100.00	200.00
2 Eric Dickerson	30.00	80.00
3 Tony Dorsett	60.00	120.00
4 Paul Hornung	30.00	80.00
5 Howie Long	60.00	120.00
6 Joe Montana	150.00	300.00
7 Roger Staubach	75.00	150.00
8 Fran Tarkenton	30.00	80.00
10 Johnny Unitas	175.00	300.00

2001 Fleer Game Time In the Zone

STATED ODDS 1:73		
CM Curtis Martin	6.00	15.00
DB Drew Bledsoe	6.00	15.00
DC Daunte Culpepper	5.00	12.00
EJ Edgerrin James	6.00	15.00
JR J.R. Redmond	4.00	10.00
JS James Stewart	4.00	10.00
JS Jimmy Smith	5.00	12.00
MH Marvin Harrison	6.00	15.00
OG Oronde Gadsden	4.00	10.00
PM Peyton Manning	15.00	40.00
PP Peerless Price	4.00	10.00
RG Rich Gannon	5.00	12.00
RM Randy Moss	6.00	15.00
TW Tyrone Wheatley	5.00	12.00

2001 Fleer Game Time Uniformity

STATED ODDS 1:19 HOBBY		
1 Jessie Armstead	4.00	10.00
2 Champ Bailey	6.00	15.00
3 David Boston	4.00	10.00
4 Kyle Brady Pants	4.00	10.00
5 Courtney Brown	4.00	10.00
6 Isaac Bruce	6.00	15.00
7 Mark Brunell	5.00	12.00
8 Plaxico Burress	5.00	12.00
9 Trung Canidate Pants	4.00	10.00
10 Wayne Chrebet	5.00	12.00
11 Tim Couch Pants	4.00	10.00
12 Marshall Faulk Pants	6.00	15.00
13 Marvin Harrison	6.00	15.00
14 Torry Holt	5.00	12.00
15 Kevin Johnson Pants	4.00	10.00
16 Jevon Kearse	5.00	12.00
17 Shaun King	4.00	10.00
18 Dorsey Levens	5.00	12.00
19 Dan Marino	15.00	40.00
20 Keenan McCardell	5.00	12.00
21 Donovan McNabb	6.00	15.00
22 Cade McNown	5.00	12.00
23 Jake Plummer	5.00	12.00
24 Travis Prentice	4.00	10.00
25 Peerless Price	4.00	10.00
26 Chris Redman	6.00	15.00
27 Jerry Rice	12.00	30.00
28 Marcus Robinson	5.00	12.00
29 Corey Simon	4.00	10.00
30 Jimmy Smith	5.00	12.00
31 Duce Staley	5.00	12.00
32 Kordell Stewart	5.00	12.00
33 Michael Strahan Pants	6.00	15.00
34 Fred Taylor	6.00	15.00
35 Kurt Warner	10.00	25.00

2000 Fleer Gamers

Released as a 145-card set, Fleer Gamers features 100 veteran cards and 45 rookie cards. Base card is half foil and features full color action player shots, and the Next Gamers rookie cards feature an all-foil card stock. Fleer Gamers was packaged in 24-pack boxes with packs containing five cards and carried a suggested retail price of $3.99.

COMPLETE SET (145)	50.00	100.00
COMP.SET w/o SPs (100)	7.50	20.00
1 Edgerrin James	.25	.60
2 Tim Couch	.20	.50
3 Cris Carter	.25	.60
4 Rich Gannon	.20	.50
5 Akili Smith	.15	.40
6 Muhsin Muhammad	.20	.50
7 Dorsey Levens	.20	.50
8 Dedric Ward	.15	.40
9 Jevon Kearse	.20	.50
10 Peerless Price	.20	.50
11 Mike Alstott	.25	.60
12 Michael Strahan	.20	.50
13 Stephen Davis	.20	.50
14 Rob Moore	.15	.40
15 James Stewart	.15	.40
16 Robert Smith	.20	.50
17 Napoleon Kaufman	.20	.50
18 Peyton Manning	.60	1.50
19 Keyshawn Johnson	.20	.50
20 Tony Martin	.20	.50
21 Jermaine Fazande	.15	.40
22 Jamal Anderson	.20	.50
23 Ed McCaffrey	.20	.50
24 Drew Bledsoe	.25	.60
25 Duce Staley	.20	.50
26 Warrick Dunn	.20	.50
27 Chris Chandler	.20	.50
28 Olandis Gary	.20	.50
29 Terry Glenn	.20	.50
30 Donovan McNabb	.25	.60
31 Torry Holt	.25	.60
32 Tim Dwight	.20	.50
33 Terrell Davis	.25	.60
34 Tony Simmons	.15	.40
35 Jerome Bettis	.25	.60
36 Az-Zahir Hakim	.15	.40
37 Darrin Chiaverini	.15	.40
38 Fred Taylor	.25	.60
39 Jon Kitna	.20	.50
40 Tony Banks	.15	.40
41 Brian Griese	.20	.50
42 Jeff Blake	.20	.50
43 Kordell Stewart	.20	.50
44 Isaac Bruce	.25	.60
45 Shannon Sharpe	.25	.60
46 Rocket Ismail	.20	.50
47 Ricky Williams	.25	.60
48 Marshall Faulk	.25	.60
49 Qadry Ismail	.20	.50
50 Joey Galloway	.20	.50
51 Jake Reed	.20	.50
52 Kurt Warner	.40	1.00
53 Cade McNown	.15	.40
54 Herman Moore	.20	.50
55 Curtis Martin	.25	.60
56 Steve McNair	.25	.60
57 Tim Biakabutuka	.20	.50
58 Brett Favre	.75	2.00
59 Wayne Chrebet	.20	.50
60 Eddie George	.20	.50
61 Troy Aikman	.40	1.00
62 Jimmy Smith	.20	.50
63 Derrick Mayes	.15	.40
64 Emmitt Smith	.60	1.50
65 Mark Brunell	.20	.50
66 Ricky Watters	.20	.50
67 Marcus Robinson	.20	.50
68 Randy Moss	.25	.60
69 Troy Edwards	.15	.40
70 Carl Pickens	.20	.50
71 Damon Huard	.20	.50
72 Mikhael Ricks	.15	.40
73 David Boston	.15	.40
74 Charlie Batch	.20	.50
75 Randall Cunningham	.25	.60
76 Tim Brown	.25	.60
77 Shaun King	.15	.40
78 Darnay Scott	.20	.50
79 Derrick Alexander	.15	.40
80 Steve Young	.30	.75
81 Kevin Johnson	.15	.40
82 Elvis Grbac	.15	.40
83 Tai Streets	.15	.40
84 Steve Beuerlein	.20	.50
85 Antonio Freeman	.20	.50
86 Vinny Testaverde	.20	.50
87 Brad Johnson	.20	.50
88 Curtis Enis	.15	.40
89 Jay Fiedler	.20	.50
90 Junior Seau	.25	.60
91 Eric Moulds	.20	.50
92 Jake Plummer	.20	.50
93 Amani Toomer	.20	.50
94 Champ Bailey	.20	.50
95 Germane Crowell	.15	.40
96 Tony Gonzalez	.25	.60
97 Jerry Rice	.50	1.25
98 Rob Johnson	.20	.50
99 Marvin Harrison	.25	.60
100 Kerry Collins	.20	.50
101 Thomas Jones RC	1.25	3.00
102 Jarious Jackson RC	.75	2.00
103 R.Jay Soward RC	.60	1.50
104 Trung Canidate RC	.75	2.00
105 Travis Taylor RC	.75	2.00
106 Giovanni Carmazzi RC	.60	1.50
107 Jerry Porter RC	1.00	2.50
108 Chris Redman RC	.75	2.00
109 Tee Martin RC	1.00	2.50
110 Dez White RC	.75	2.00
111 Danny Farmer RC	.60	1.50
112 Brian Urlacher RC	4.00	10.00
113 Reuben Droughns RC	1.00	2.50
114 Marc Bulger RC	1.00	2.50
115 Peter Warrick RC	1.00	2.50
116 Plaxico Burress RC	1.00	2.50
117 Ron Dugans RC	.60	1.50
118 Gari Scott RC	.60	1.50
119 Curtis Keaton RC	.60	1.50
120 Corey Simon RC	.75	2.00
121 Rob Morris RC	.75	2.00
122 Chad Morton RC	1.00	2.50
123 Hank Poteat RC	.60	1.50
124 Ahmed Plummer RC	.60	1.50
125 Bashir Yamini RC	.60	1.50
126 J.R. Redmond RC	.60	1.50
127 Travis Prentice RC	.75	2.00
128 Todd Pinkston RC	.60	1.50
129 Courtney Brown RC	.75	2.00
130 Laveranues Coles RC	1.00	2.50
131 Jamal Lewis RC	1.00	2.50
132 Tim Rattay RC	.75	2.00
133 Anthony Becht RC	.75	2.00
134 Chris Cole RC	.75	2.00
135 Ron Dayne RC	1.00	2.50
136 Sylvester Morris RC	.60	1.50
137 Joe Hamilton RC	.60	1.50
138 Dennis Northcutt RC	.75	2.00
139 Doug Johnson RC	.75	2.00
140 Shyrone Stith RC	.60	1.50
141 Darrell Jackson RC	.75	2.00
142 Michael Wiley RC	.60	1.50
143 Chad Pennington RC	1.50	4.00
144 Bubba Franks RC	1.00	2.50
145 Shaun Alexander RC	1.25	3.00

2000 Fleer Gamers Extra

COMPLETE SET (145)	100.00	200.00
*VETS 1-100: 1.5X TO 4X BASIC CARDS		
1-100 VETERAN ODDS 1:8		
*ROOKIES 101-145: .6X TO 1.5X		
101-145 ROOKIE ODDS 1:24		

2000 Fleer Gamers Change the Game

COMPLETE SET (15)	25.00	60.00
STATED ODDS 1:24		
1 Kurt Warner	1.50	4.00
2 Brett Favre	3.00	8.00
3 Eddie George	.75	2.00
4 Keyshawn Johnson	.75	2.00
5 Randy Moss	1.00	2.50
6 Tim Couch	.75	2.00
7 Ricky Williams	1.00	2.50
8 Peyton Manning	2.50	6.00
9 Terrell Davis	1.00	2.50
10 Troy Aikman	1.50	4.00
11 Fred Taylor	1.00	2.50
12 Cade McNown	.60	1.50
13 Edgerrin James	1.00	2.50
14 Peter Warrick	1.00	2.50
15 Jamal Lewis	1.00	2.50

2000 Fleer Gamers Contact Sport

COMPLETE SET (20)	10.00	25.00
STATED ODDS 1:4		
1 Peter Warrick	.30	.75
2 Jamal Lewis	.30	.75
3 Thomas Jones	.40	1.00
4 Plaxico Burress	.30	.75
5 Travis Taylor	.25	.60
6 Ron Dayne	.30	.75
7 Bubba Franks	.30	.75
8 Chad Pennington	.50	1.25
9 Shaun Alexander	.40	1.00
10 Sylvester Morris	.20	.50
11 R.Jay Soward	.20	.50
12 Trung Canidate	.25	.60
13 Dennis Northcutt	.25	.60
14 Todd Pinkston	.20	.50
15 Jerry Porter	.30	.75
16 Travis Prentice	.25	.60
17 Courtney Brown	.25	.60
18 Ron Dugans	.20	.50
19 Dez White	.25	.60
20 Chris Redman	.25	.60

2000 Fleer Gamers Uniformity

STATED ODDS 1:44		
1 Troy Aikman	12.50	30.00
2 Jamal Anderson Pants	8.00	20.00
3 Charlie Batch Uniform	8.00	20.00
4 David Boston Pants	6.00	15.00
5 Tim Brown	10.00	25.00
6 Isaac Bruce Pants	10.00	25.00
7 Mark Brunell	8.00	20.00
8 Chris Chandler Pants	8.00	20.00
9 Tim Couch Pants	8.00	20.00
10 Germane Crowell Pants	6.00	15.00
11 Randall Cunningham	10.00	25.00
12 Stephen Davis	8.00	20.00
13 Tim Dwight Pants	8.00	20.00
14 Curtis Enis	6.00	15.00
15 Marshall Faulk	10.00	25.00
16 Az-Zahir Hakim	6.00	15.00
17 Marvin Harrison Pants	10.00	25.00
18 Torry Holt Pants	10.00	25.00
19 Edgerrin James Pants	10.00	25.00
20 Kevin Johnson Pants	6.00	15.00
21 Terry Kirby Pants	6.00	15.00
22 John Lynch	8.00	20.00
23 Peyton Manning Pants	20.00	50.00
24 Ed McCaffrey	8.00	20.00
25 Herman Moore Pants	8.00	20.00
26 Rob Moore Pants	6.00	15.00
27 Johnnie Morton Pants	8.00	20.00
28 Jake Plummer Pants	8.00	20.00
29 Jerry Rice	15.00	40.00
30 Frank Sanders Pants	6.00	15.00
31 Bruce Smith	10.00	25.00
32 Emmitt Smith	15.00	40.00
33 Kurt Warner	15.00	40.00
34 Steve Young	12.50	30.00

2000 Fleer Gamers Yard Chargers

COMPLETE SET (15)	25.00	60.00
1-5 STATED ODDS 1:9		
6-10 STATED ODDS 1:24		
11-15 STATED ODDS 1:144		
1 Marvin Harrison	.50	1.25
2 Randy Moss	.50	1.25
3 Keyshawn Johnson	.40	1.00
4 Tim Brown	.50	1.25
5 Jerry Rice	1.00	2.50
6 Terrell Davis	.75	2.00
7 Emmitt Smith	2.00	5.00
8 Eddie George	.60	1.50
9 Edgerrin James	.75	2.00
10 Marshall Faulk	.75	2.00
11 Tim Couch	2.00	5.00
12 Kurt Warner	4.00	10.00
13 Peyton Manning	6.00	15.00
14 Brett Favre	8.00	20.00
15 Troy Aikman	4.00	10.00

2001 Fleer Genuine

Fleer Genuine was released in July of 2001. The base set consisted of 155 cards, with the last 30 from the set being short-printed rookies. The rookies were serial numbered to 1000, and each had a swatch of a jersey. The cardfronts were highlighted by silver foil lettering and the border is split vertically with the left side white and the right side a team color.

COMP.SET w/o RC's (125)	10.00	25.00
1 Donovan McNabb	.30	.75
2 Daunte Culpepper	.25	.60
3 Derrick Alexander	.20	.50
4 Jessie Armstead	.20	.50
5 Hines Ward	.30	.75
6 Peter Warrick	.25	.60
7 Jay Fiedler	.25	.60
8 Cris Carter	.30	.75
9 Az-Zahir Hakim	.20	.50
10 Michael Westbrook	.20	.50
11 Akili Smith	.20	.50
12 Lamar Smith	.25	.60
13 Eric Moulds	.25	.60
14 Shaun Alexander	.30	.75
15 Jeff George	.25	.60
16 Brad Hoover	.25	.60
17 Brian Griese	.25	.60
18 Keenan McCardell	.25	.60
19 Freddie Jones	.20	.50
20 Brian Urlacher	.40	1.00
21 Thomas Jones	.25	.60
22 Charlie Batch	.25	.60
23 Aaron Brooks	.25	.60
24 Hugh Douglas	.20	.50
25 Mike Alstott	.25	.60
26 Darrell Russell	.20	.50
27 Muhsin Muhammad	.25	.60
28 Rocket Ismail	.25	.60
29 Fred Taylor	.30	.75
30 Tyrone Wheatley	.25	.60
31 Rodney Harrison	.25	.60
32 Curtis Martin	.30	.75
33 Jason Sehorn	.25	.60
34 James McKnight	.20	.50
35 Jimmy Smith	.25	.60
36 Laveranues Coles	.25	.60
37 Jeff Garcia	.25	.60
38 Sam Cowart	.20	.50
39 Joey Galloway	.25	.60
40 Mark Brunell	.25	.60
41 Vinny Testaverde	.25	.60
42 Terrell Owens	.30	.75
43 Ray Lewis	.30	.75
44 Ahman Green	.30	.75
45 Ron Dayne	.25	.60
46 Samari Rolle	.20	.50
47 Shawn Bryson	.20	.50
48 Emmitt Smith	.75	2.00
49 Terrence Wilkins	.20	.50
50 Charlie Garner	.25	.60
51 Rob Johnson	.25	.60
52 Courtney Brown	.20	.50
53 Edgerrin James	.30	.75
54 Kurt Warner	.50	1.25
55 Michael McCrary	.20	.50
56 Dennis Northcutt	.20	.50
57 Marvin Harrison	.30	.75
58 Rich Gannon	.25	.60
59 Marshall Faulk	.30	.75
60 Travis Prentice	.20	.50
61 Terrell Davis	.30	.75
62 Charles Woodson	.30	.75
63 Isaac Bruce	.30	.75
64 Tim Couch	.20	.50

65 Oronde Gadsden	.20	.50
66 Randy Moss	.30	.75
67 Torry Holt	.25	.60
68 Shannon Sharpe	.30	.75
69 Antonio Freeman	.30	.75
70 Michael Strahan	.30	.75
71 Jevon Kearse	.25	.60
72 Jamal Lewis	.30	.75
73 Peyton Manning	.75	2.00
74 Amani Toomer	.25	.60
75 Derrick Mason	.25	.60
76 Jake Plummer	.25	.60
77 Rod Smith	.25	.60
78 Terry Glenn	.25	.60
79 Plaxico Burress	.25	.60
80 Warren Sapp	.25	.60
81 Jamal Anderson	.25	.60
82 James Stewart	.20	.50
83 Ricky Williams	.30	.75
84 Chad Lewis	.20	.50
85 Shaun King	.20	.50
86 Wesley Walls	.20	.50
87 Mike Anderson	.25	.60
88 Corey Simon	.20	.50
89 Wayne Chrebet	.25	.60
90 Junior Seau	.30	.75
91 Terance Mathis	.20	.50
92 Germane Crowell	.20	.50
93 Joe Horn	.25	.60
94 Duce Staley	.25	.60
95 Keyshawn Johnson	.25	.60
96 Qadry Ismail	.25	.60
97 Dorsey Levens	.25	.60
98 Kerry Collins	.25	.60
99 Corey Dillon	.25	.60
100 Zach Thomas	.30	.75
101 Chad Pennington	.30	.75
102 Ricky Watters	.25	.60
103 Bruce Smith	.30	.75
104 David Boston	.20	.50
105 Ed McCaffrey	.25	.60
106 Kevin Faulk	.25	.60
107 Jerome Bettis	.30	.75
108 Warrick Dunn	.30	.75
109 Tim Brown	.30	.75
110 Marcus Robinson	.25	.60
111 Tony Gonzalez	.30	.75
112 Drew Bledsoe	.30	.75
113 Darrell Jackson	.25	.60
114 Stephen Davis	.25	.60
115 Doug Johnson	.20	.50
116 Brett Favre	1.00	2.50
117 Darren Howard	.20	.50
118 Cade McNown	.25	.60
119 Steve McNair	.30	.75
120 James Allen	.20	.50
121 Sylvester Morris	.20	.50
122 J.R. Redmond	.20	.50
123 Jacquez Green	.20	.50
124 Champ Bailey	.30	.75
125 Eddie George	.30	.75
126 Michael Vick JSY RC	15.00	40.00
127 David Terrell JSY RC	3.00	8.00
128 Deuce McAllister JSY RC	4.00	10.00
129 Koren Robinson JSY RC	3.00	8.00
130 Rod Gardner JSY RC	3.00	8.00
131 Chris Chambers JSY RC	4.00	10.00
132 Santana Moss JSY RC	5.00	12.00
133 Reggie Wayne JSY RC	8.00	20.00
134 Quincy Morgan JSY RC	3.00	8.00
135 Rudi Johnson JSY RC	4.00	10.00
136 Robert Ferguson JSY RC	4.00	10.00
137 Todd Heap JSY RC	4.00	10.00
138 Michael Bennett JSY RC	3.00	8.00
139 Jesse Palmer JSY RC	3.00	8.00
140 Drew Brees JSY RC	20.00	50.00
141 James Jackson JSY RC	2.50	6.00
142 Chris Weinke JSY RC	3.00	8.00
143 LaDainian Tomlinson JSY RC	12.00	30.00
144 Chad Johnson JSY RC	6.00	15.00
145 Quincy Carter JSY RC	3.00	8.00
146 Freddie Mitchell JSY RC	2.50	6.00
147 Anthony Thomas JSY RC	4.00	10.00
148 Travis Henry JSY RC	3.00	8.00
149 Snoop Minnis JSY RC	2.50	6.00
150 Marques Tuiasosopo JSY RC	3.00	8.00
151 Travis Minor JSY RC	3.00	8.00
152 Mike McMahon JSY RC	3.00	8.00
153 Josh Heupel JSY RC	4.00	10.00
154 Sage Rosenfels JSY RC	4.00	10.00
155 Kevan Barlow JSY RC	3.00	8.00

2001 Fleer Genuine Coverage Plus Jerseys

STATED ODDS 1:24		
1 Courtney Brown	4.00	10.00
2 Isaac Bruce	6.00	15.00
3 Mark Brunell	5.00	12.00
4 Az-Zahir Hakim	4.00	10.00
5 Marvin Harrison	6.00	15.00
6 Torry Holt	5.00	12.00
7 Edgerrin James	6.00	15.00
8 Brad Johnson	5.00	12.00
9 Kevin Johnson	4.00	10.00
10 Rob Johnson	5.00	12.00
11 Thomas Jones	5.00	12.00
12 Ed McCaffrey	5.00	12.00
13 Keenan McCardell	5.00	12.00
14 Cade McNown	5.00	12.00
15 Eric Moulds	5.00	12.00
16 Jake Plummer	5.00	12.00
17 Travis Prentice	4.00	10.00
18 Marcus Robinson	5.00	12.00
19 Warren Sapp	5.00	12.00
20 Corey Simon	4.00	10.00
21 Jimmy Smith	5.00	12.00
22 Duce Staley	5.00	12.00
23 Fred Taylor	6.00	15.00
24 Brian Urlacher	8.00	20.00
25 Kurt Warner	10.00	25.00
26 Dez White	5.00	12.00

2001 Fleer Genuine Final Cut Jerseys

STATED ODDS 1:24		
1 Troy Aikman	12.00	30.00
2 Jamal Anderson	5.00	12.00
3 Charlie Batch	5.00	12.00
4 David Boston	4.00	10.00
5 Isaac Bruce	6.00	15.00
6 Tim Couch	4.00	10.00
7 Terrell Davis	6.00	15.00
8 Kevin Dyson	4.00	10.00
9 L.C. Greenwood	6.00	15.00
10 Marvin Harrison	6.00	15.00
11 Edgerrin James	6.00	15.00
12 Rob Johnson	5.00	12.00
13 Jevon Kearse	5.00	12.00
14 Jim Kelly	10.00	25.00
15 James Lofton	5.00	12.00
16 Ed McCaffrey	5.00	12.00
17 Rob Moore	4.00	10.00
18 Johnnie Morton	5.00	12.00
19 Jake Plummer	5.00	12.00
20 Jerry Rice	12.00	30.00
21 Mike Singletary	8.00	20.00
22 Emmitt Smith	15.00	40.00
23 Charles Woodson	6.00	15.00
24 Steve Young	10.00	25.00

2001 Fleer Genuine Future Swatch Tandems

STATED PRINT RUN 50 SER.#'d SETS		
1 Michael Vick	50.00	120.00
Drew Brees		
2 David Terrell	8.00	20.00
Anthony Thomas		
3 Santana Moss	15.00	40.00
Reggie Wayne		
4 Deuce McAllister	40.00	100.00
LaDainian Tomlinson		
5 Koren Robinson	6.00	15.00
Rod Gardner		

2001 Fleer Genuine Hawaii Live O

COMPLETE SET (15)	10.00	25.00
STATED ODDS 1:23		
1 Daunte Culpepper	.75	2.00
2 Donovan McNabb	1.00	2.50
3 Torry Holt	.75	2.00
4 Terrell Owens	1.00	2.50
5 Jimmy Smith	.75	2.00
6 Jeff Garcia	.75	2.00
7 Rich Gannon	.75	2.00
8 Peyton Manning	2.50	6.00
9 Joe Horn	.75	2.00
10 Tony Gonzalez	1.00	2.50
11 Edgerrin James	1.00	2.50
12 Eddie George	1.00	2.50
13 Corey Dillon	.75	2.00
14 Warrick Dunn	1.00	2.50
15 Marvin Harrison	1.00	2.50

2001 Fleer Genuine Names of the Game Jerseys

STATED PRINT RUN 100 SER.#'d SETS		
1 Daunte Culpepper	6.00	15.00
2 Terrell Davis	8.00	20.00
3 Ron Dayne	6.00	15.00
4 Eric Dickerson	8.00	20.00
5 Tony Dorsett	10.00	25.00
6 Edgerrin James	8.00	20.00
7 Jevon Kearse	6.00	15.00
8 Curtis Martin	8.00	20.00
9 Steve McNair	8.00	20.00
10 Joe Montana	50.00	120.00
11 Randy Moss	8.00	20.00
12 Walter Payton	40.00	100.00
13 William Perry	6.00	15.00
14 Deion Sanders	8.00	20.00
15 Roger Staubach	30.00	80.00
16 Lawrence Taylor	10.00	25.00
17 Johnny Unitas	30.00	80.00

2001 Fleer Genuine Names of the Game Jerseys Autographs

STATED PRINT RUN 50 SER.#'d SETS		
3 Ron Dayne	12.50	30.00
4 Eric Dickerson	30.00	60.00
5 Tony Dorsett	40.00	80.00
6 Edgerrin James	30.00	60.00
7 Joe Montana	125.00	200.00
8 Randy Moss	40.00	100.00
9 William Perry	30.00	60.00
10 Roger Staubach	75.00	150.00
11 Lawrence Taylor	50.00	80.00
12 Johnny Unitas	200.00	350.00

2001 Fleer Genuine Pennant Aggression

COMPLETE SET (10)	7.50	20.00
STATED ODDS 1:23		
1 Kurt Warner	1.25	3.00
2 Brett Favre	2.50	6.00
3 Emmitt Smith	2.00	5.00
4 Daunte Culpepper	.60	1.50
5 Terrell Davis	.75	2.00
6 Peyton Manning	2.00	5.00
7 Eddie George	.75	2.00
8 Donovan McNabb	.75	2.00
9 Ricky Williams	.75	2.00
10 Tim Couch	.50	1.25

2001 Fleer Genuine Seek and Deploy

COMPLETE SET (15)	12.50	30.00
STATED ODDS 1:23		
1 Jamal Lewis	1.00	2.50
2 Randy Moss	1.00	2.50
3 Ricky Williams	1.00	2.50
4 Terrell Davis	1.00	2.50
5 Donovan McNabb	1.00	2.50
6 Curtis Martin	1.00	2.50
7 Brett Favre	3.00	8.00
8 Aaron Brooks	.75	2.00
9 Kurt Warner	1.50	4.00
10 Eddie George	1.00	2.50
11 Daunte Culpepper	.75	2.00
12 Jamal Anderson	.75	2.00
13 Marshall Faulk	1.00	2.50
14 Ray Lewis	1.00	2.50
15 Ron Dayne	.75	2.00

2002 Fleer Genuine

Released in December, 2002, this set features 125 veterans and 50 rookies. The rookies were serial #'d to 599. Each box contained 24 packs of 5 cards.

COMP.SET w/o SP's (125)	7.50	20.00
126-175 ROOKIE PRINT RUN 599		
1 Brian Urlacher	.30	.75
2 Keyshawn Johnson	.25	.60
3 Donovan McNabb	.30	.75
4 Tim Couch	.20	.50
5 Junior Seau	.30	.75
6 Eric Moulds	.25	.60
7 Randy Moss	.30	.75
8 Rod Smith	.25	.60
9 Torry Holt	.30	.75
10 Plaxico Burress	.25	.60
11 Kordell Stewart	.25	.60
12 Brett Favre	.75	2.00
13 Stephen Davis	.25	.60
14 Santana Moss	.25	.60
15 Kurt Warner	.30	.75
16 Jake Plummer	.25	.60
17 Jimmy Smith	.25	.60
18 Quincy Carter	.20	.50
19 Marvin Harrison	.30	.75
20 Fred Taylor	.25	.60
21 Warren Sapp	.25	.60
22 Curtis Martin	.30	.75
23 Isaac Bruce	.30	.75
24 Drew Brees	.50	1.25
25 Ray Lewis	.30	.75
26 Hines Ward	.30	.75
27 Koren Robinson	.20	.50
28 Jevon Kearse	.25	.60
29 Jerry Rice	.60	1.50
30 Jeff Garcia	.25	.60
31 Edgerrin James	.25	.60
32 Warrick Dunn	.25	.60
33 Ricky Williams	.25	.60
34 Doug Flutie	.30	.75
35 Brian Griese	.25	.60
36 Chad Pennington	.30	.75
37 Duce Staley	.25	.60
38 Eddie George	.25	.60
39 Daunte Culpepper	.25	.60
40 Jerome Bettis	.30	.75
41 Michael Vick	.50	1.25
42 Tim Brown	.30	.75
43 Tom Brady	.75	2.00
44 Steve McNair	.30	.75
45 Terrell Owens	.30	.75
46 Corey Dillon	.25	.60
47 Peyton Manning	.60	1.50
48 Rich Gannon	.25	.60
49 Emmitt Smith	.75	2.00
50 David Boston	.20	.50
51 Mark Brunell	.25	.60
52 Ron Dayne	.25	.60
53 Wayne Chrebet	.25	.60
54 Terrell Davis	.30	.75
55 Zach Thomas	.30	.75
56 Kevin Johnson	.20	.50
57 Marshall Faulk	.30	.75
58 Anthony Thomas	.25	.60
59 Deuce McAllister	.25	.60
60 LaDainian Tomlinson	.40	1.00
61 Thomas Jones	.30	.75
62 Ahman Green	.25	.60
63 Aaron Brooks	.25	.60
64 Courtney Brown	.20	.50
65 Chris Chambers	.25	.60
66 Jamal Lewis	.25	.60
67 David Terrell	.20	.50
68 Tony Gonzalez	.30	.75
69 Laveranues Coles	.25	.60
70 Shaun Alexander	.25	.60
71 Chris Weinke	.20	.50
72 Antowain Smith	.25	.60
73 Rod Gardner	.20	.50
74 Mike Anderson	.25	.60
75 Antonio Freeman	.30	.75
76 Kevan Barlow	.20	.50
77 Jim Miller	.20	.50
78 Bill Schroeder	.20	.50
79 Joe Horn	.25	.60
80 Travis Henry	.20	.50
81 Michael Bennett	.25	.60
82 Michael Pittman	.25	.60
83 Keenan McCardell	.25	.60
84 Amani Toomer	.25	.60
85 Peerless Price	.20	.50
86 Az-Zahir Hakim	.20	.50
87 James Thrash	.25	.60
88 Drew Bledsoe	.30	.75
89 Mike McMahon	.20	.50
90 Derrick Mason	.25	.60
91 Joey Galloway	.25	.60
92 Snoop Minnis	.20	.50
93 Ed McCaffrey	.25	.60
94 Johnnie Morton	.25	.60
95 Richard Huntley	.20	.50
96 Troy Brown	.25	.60
97 Shane Matthews	.20	.50
98 Muhsin Muhammad	.25	.60
99 David Patten	.20	.50
100 Jon Kitna	.25	.60
101 Terrence Wilkins	.20	.50
102 Kerry Collins	.25	.60
103 Tiki Barber	.30	.75
104 Fred Beasley	.20	.50
105 Trent Dilfer	.25	.60
106 Chris Redman	.20	.50
107 Jay Fiedler	.25	.60
108 Charlie Garner	.25	.60
109 Mike Alstott	.25	.60
110 Darnay Scott	.25	.60
111 Garrison Hearst	.25	.60
112 James Jackson	.20	.50
113 Darrell Jackson	.25	.60
114 Freddie Mitchell	.20	.50
115 Brad Johnson	.25	.60
116 Olandis Gary	.25	.60
117 Priest Holmes	.30	.75
118 Vinny Testaverde	.25	.60
119 Takeo Spikes	.20	.50
120 Marty Booker	.25	.60
121 Curtis Conway	.25	.60
122 Jacquez Green	.20	.50
123 Champ Bailey	.30	.75
124 Trent Green	.25	.60
125 Terry Glenn	.25	.60
126 Ladell Betts RC	2.00	5.00
127 DeShaun Foster RC	2.00	5.00
128 Maurice Morris RC	1.50	4.00
129 Chester Taylor RC	2.00	5.00
130 Randy McMichael RC	2.00	5.00
131 Verron Haynes RC	1.25	3.00
132 Cliff Russell RC	1.25	3.00
133 Brandon Doman RC	1.25	3.00
134 Ashley Lelie RC	1.50	4.00
135 Roy Williams RC	2.00	5.00
136 Antonio Bryant RC	2.00	5.00
137 William Green RC	1.50	4.00
138 Clinton Portis RC	2.50	6.00
139 J.T. O'Sullivan RC	1.50	4.00
140 Javon Walker RC	2.00	5.00
141 Randy Fasani RC	1.50	4.00
142 Chad Hutchinson RC	1.25	3.00
143 Ben Leber RC	1.25	3.00
144 Tim Carter RC	1.50	4.00
145 Jason McAddley RC	1.50	4.00
146 Donte Stallworth RC	2.00	5.00
147 Andre Davis RC	1.50	4.00
148 Julius Peppers RC	4.00	10.00
149 Patrick Ramsey RC	2.00	5.00
150 Deion Branch RC	2.00	5.00
151 Jonathan Wells RC	2.00	5.00
152 Jabar Gaffney RC	2.00	5.00
153 Josh McCown RC	2.00	5.00
154 Jeremy Shockey RC	3.00	8.00
155 Eric Crouch RC	2.00	5.00
156 Joey Harrington RC	2.00	5.00
157 Jerramy Stevens RC	2.00	5.00
158 T.J. Duckett RC	2.00	5.00
159 Ron Johnson RC	1.50	4.00
160 Josh Reed RC	1.50	4.00
161 Reche Caldwell RC	2.00	5.00
162 Lamar Gordon RC	1.50	4.00
163 David Garrard RC	2.50	6.00
164 Freddie Milons RC	1.25	3.00
165 Marquise Walker RC	1.25	3.00
166 Rohan Davey RC	2.00	5.00
167 Coy Wire RC	1.50	4.00
168 Quentin Jammer RC	2.00	5.00
169 Omar Easy RC	1.50	4.00
170 Kurt Kittner RC	1.25	3.00
171 Travis Stephens RC	1.25	3.00
172 David Carr RC	2.00	5.00
173 Daniel Graham RC	1.50	4.00
174 Antwaan Randle El RC	2.00	5.00
175 Brian Westbrook RC	3.00	8.00

2002 Fleer Genuine Reflection Ascending

*VETS/100-125: 3X TO 8X
*VETS/70-99: 4X TO 10X
*VETS/45-69: 5X TO 12X
*VETS/30-44: 6X TO 15X
*VETS/20-29: 10X TO 25X
*VETS/10-19: 15X TO 40X
STATED PRINT RUN 1-125
SER.#'d UNDER 10 NOT PRICED

2002 Fleer Genuine Reflection Descending

*VETS/100-125: 3X TO 8X
*VETS/70-99: 4X TO 10X
*VETS/45-69: 5X TO 12X
*VETS/30-44: 6X TO 15X
*VETS/20-29: 10X TO 25X
*VETS/10-19: 15X TO 40X
STATED PRINT RUN 1-125
SER.#'d UNDER 10 NOT PRICED

2002 Fleer Genuine Article

STATED ODDS 1:24		
*INSIDER/500: .5X TO 1.2X BASIC JSY		
INSIDER PRINT RUN 500 SER.#'d SETS		
UNPRICED TAG PRINT RUN 5-19		
GABF Brett Favre	10.00	25.00
GABU Brian Urlacher	4.00	10.00
GADB Drew Brees	6.00	15.00
GADC Daunte Culpepper	3.00	8.00
GAES Emmitt Smith	10.00	25.00
GAIB Isaac Bruce	4.00	10.00
GAJB Jerome Bettis	5.00	12.00
GAJG Jeff Garcia	3.00	8.00
GAJR Jerry Rice	8.00	20.00
GAJS Junior Seau	4.00	10.00
GAKJ Keyshawn Johnson	3.00	8.00
GAKR Koren Robinson	2.50	6.00
GALT LaDainian Tomlinson	5.00	12.00
GAPM Peyton Manning	8.00	20.00
GAQC Quincy Carter	2.50	6.00
GARL Ray Lewis	4.00	10.00
GARM Randy Moss	4.00	10.00
GARS Rod Smith	3.00	8.00
GASD Stephen Davis	3.00	8.00
GASM Santana Moss	3.00	8.00
GATB Tom Brady	10.00	25.00
GATH Torry Holt	4.00	10.00
GAWS Warren Sapp	3.00	8.00
GAZT Zach Thomas	4.00	10.00

2002 Fleer Genuine Authen-Kicks

STATED ODDS 1:240		
*COMBO/25: .8X TO 2X BASIC INSERTS		
COMBO STATED PRINT RUN 25		
ADM Donovan McNabb	6.00	15.00
AEJ Edgerrin James	5.00	12.00
AMH Marvin Harrison	6.00	15.00
APM Peyton Manning	12.00	30.00
ARGO Rich Gannon	5.00	12.00
ATH Torry Holt	6.00	15.00

2002 Fleer Genuine Names of the Game

COMPLETE SET (20)	15.00	40.00
STATED ODDS 1:20		
1 Kurt Warner	1.00	2.50
2 Brett Favre	2.50	6.00
3 Brian Urlacher	1.00	2.50
4 Jeff Garcia	.75	2.00
5 Donovan McNabb	1.00	2.50
6 Tom Brady	2.50	6.00
7 Tim Couch	.60	1.50
8 Daunte Culpepper	.75	2.00
9 Michael Vick	1.50	4.00
10 Edgerrin James	.75	2.00
11 Marshall Faulk	1.00	2.50
12 Emmitt Smith	2.50	6.00
13 Eddie George	.75	2.00
14 Jerome Bettis	1.00	2.50
15 Drew Brees	1.50	4.00
16 Quincy Carter	.60	1.50
17 Randy Moss	1.00	2.50
18 Isaac Bruce	1.00	2.50
19 Jerry Rice	2.00	5.00
20 Junior Seau	1.00	2.50

2002 Fleer Genuine Names of the Game Jerseys

STATED PRINT RUN 500 SER.#'d SETS		
1 Jerome Bettis	4.00	10.00
2 Tom Brady	10.00	25.00
3 Drew Brees	6.00	15.00
4 Isaac Bruce	4.00	10.00
5 Quincy Carter	2.50	6.00
6 Tim Couch	2.50	6.00
7 Daunte Culpepper	3.00	8.00
8 Marshall Faulk	4.00	10.00
9 Brett Favre	10.00	25.00
10 Jeff Garcia	3.00	8.00
11 Eddie George	3.00	8.00
12 Edgerrin James	3.00	8.00
13 Donovan McNabb	4.00	10.00
14 Randy Moss	4.00	10.00
15 Jerry Rice	8.00	20.00
16 Junior Seau	4.00	10.00
17 Emmitt Smith	10.00	25.00
18 Brian Urlacher	4.00	10.00
19 Michael Vick	6.00	15.00
20 Kurt Warner	4.00	10.00

2002 Fleer Genuine Names of the Game Jerseys Duals

STATED PRINT RUN 50 SER.#'d SETS		
BFDC Brett Favre	25.00	60.00
Daunte Culpepper		
BUJS Brian Urlacher	10.00	25.00
Junior Seau		
DBQC Drew Brees	15.00	40.00
Quincy Carter		
EGJB Eddie George	10.00	25.00
Jerome Bettis		
EJMF Edgerrin James	10.00	25.00
Marshall Faulk		
ESJR Emmitt Smith	25.00	60.00
Jerry Rice		
KWDM Kurt Warner	10.00	25.00
Donovan McNabb		
MVJG Michael Vick	15.00	40.00
Jeff Garcia		
RMIB Randy Moss	10.00	25.00
Isaac Bruce		
TBTC Tom Brady	25.00	60.00
Tim Couch		

2002 Fleer Genuine TD Threats

STATED ODDS 1:8		
1 Edgerrin James	.60	1.50
Eddie George		
2 Terrell Owens	.75	2.00
Tim Brown		
3 Emmitt Smith	2.00	5.00
Marshall Faulk		
4 David Boston	.60	1.50
Jimmy Smith		
5 Santana Moss	.75	2.00
Randy Moss		
6 Daunte Culpepper	.60	1.50
Tim Couch		
7 Donovan McNabb	1.50	4.00
Peyton Manning		
8 Jerry Rice	1.50	4.00
Chris Chambers		
9 Eric Moulds	.60	1.50
Rod Smith		
10 Fred Taylor	1.00	2.50
LaDainian Tomlinson		
11 Duce Staley	.75	2.00
Jerome Bettis		
12 Michael Vick	2.00	5.00
Brett Favre		
13 Tom Brady	2.00	5.00
Drew Brees		
14 Ahman Green	.75	2.00
Curtis Martin		
15 Kurt Warner	.75	2.00
Jeff Garcia		
16 Quincy Carter	.60	1.50
Jake Plummer		
17 Terrell Davis	.75	2.00
Corey Dillon		
18 Mark Brunell	.60	1.50
Kordell Stewart		
19 Hines Ward	.75	2.00
Plaxico Burres		
20 Joe Horn	.75	2.00
Torry Holt		
21 Brian Griese	.75	2.00
Drew Bledsoe		
22 Donte Stallworth	.75	2.00
Darrell Jackson		
23 Rod Gardner	.50	1.25
David Terrell		
24 Deuce McAllister	.60	1.50
Anthony Thomas		
25 Aaron Brooks	.75	2.00
David Carr		

2002 Fleer Genuine TD Threats Jerseys

STATED ODDS 1:22
*PATCH/56-73: .6X TO 1.5X BASIC DUAL
*PATCH/36-38: 1X TO 2.5X BASIC DUAL
*PATCH/21-26: 1.2X TO 3X BASIC DUAL
*PATCH/10-19: 1.5X TO 4X BASIC DUAL
PATCH STATED PRINT RUN 8-73
PATCH SER.#'d UNDER 10 NOT PRICED

1 Edgerrin James	4.00	10.00
Eddie George		
2 Terrell Owens	5.00	12.00
Tim Brown		
3 Emmitt Smith	12.00	30.00
Marshall Faulk		
4 David Boston	4.00	10.00
Jimmy Smith		
5 Santana Moss	5.00	12.00
Randy Moss		
6 Daunte Culpepper	4.00	10.00
Tim Couch		
7 Donovan McNabb	10.00	25.00
Peyton Manning		
8 Jerry Rice	10.00	25.00
Chris Chambers		
9 Eric Moulds	4.00	10.00
Rod Smith		
10 Fred Taylor	6.00	15.00
LaDainian Tomlinson		
11 Michael Vick	12.00	30.00
Brett Favre		
12 Tom Brady	12.00	30.00
Drew Brees		
13 Ahman Green	5.00	12.00
Curtis Martin		
14 Kurt Warner	5.00	12.00
Jeff Garcia		
15 Quincy Carter	4.00	10.00
Jake Plummer		
16 Terrell Davis	5.00	12.00
Corey Dillon		
17 Mark Brunell	4.00	10.00
Kordell Stewart		
18 Hines Ward	5.00	12.00
Plaxico Burress		
19 Joe Horn	5.00	12.00
Torry Holt		

2003 Fleer Genuine Insider

Released in August of 2003, this set consists of 140 cards, including 100 veterans and 40 rookies. Rookies 101-110 are serial numbered to 499. Rookies 111-130 are serial numbered to 799. Rookies 131-140 are serial numbered to 350. Boxes contained 24 packs of 5 cards.

COMP.SET w/o SP's (100)	7.50	20.00
101-110 ROOKIE PRINT RUN 499		
111-130 ROOKIE PRINT RUN 799		
131-140 ROOKIE PRINT RUN 350		
1 Donovan McNabb	.40	1.00
2 Rich Gannon	.30	.75
3 Joey Harrington	.25	.60
4 Eddie George	.30	.75
5 Jeremy Shockey	.40	1.00
6 Tim Couch	.25	.60
7 Shaun Alexander	.30	.75
8 Tiki Barber	.40	1.00
9 Antonio Bryant	.25	.60
10 Marc Bulger	.40	1.00
11 Tom Brady	1.00	2.50
12 Julius Peppers	.40	1.00
13 Junior Seau	.40	1.00
14 Trent Green	.30	.75
15 Eric Moulds	.30	.75
16 Santana Moss	.30	.75
17 Hugh Douglas	.25	.60
18 Emmitt Smith	1.00	2.50
19 Tim Brown	.40	1.00
20 William Green	.25	.60
21 Koren Robinson	.30	.75
22 Randy Moss	.40	1.00
23 Anthony Thomas	.30	.75
24 Terrell Owens	.40	1.00
25 Fred Taylor	.30	.75
26 Ahman Green	.30	.75
27 Derrick Mason	.30	.75
28 Chad Pennington	.40	1.00
29 Shannon Sharpe	.40	1.00
30 Warren Sapp	.30	.75
31 Deuce McAllister	.30	.75
32 Rod Smith	.30	.75
33 Torry Holt	.40	1.00
34 Joe Horn	.30	.75
35 Chad Johnson	.40	1.00
36 Matt Hasselbeck	.30	.75
37 Chris Chambers	.30	.75
38 Travis Henry	.25	.60
39 David Boston	.25	.60
40 Tony Gonzalez	.40	1.00
41 Todd Heap	.30	.75
42 Hines Ward	.40	1.00
43 Brett Favre	1.00	2.50
44 Rod Gardner	.25	.60
45 Donte Stallworth	.25	.60
46 Corey Dillon	.30	.75
47 Garrison Hearst	.30	.75
48 Ricky Williams	.30	.75
49 Ray Lewis	.40	1.00
50 Plaxico Burress	.30	.75
51 Michael Bennett	.30	.75
52 Stephen Davis	.30	.75
53 LaDainian Tomlinson	.40	1.00
54 Priest Holmes	.40	1.00
55 Jonathan Wells	.25	.60
56 Jerome Bettis	.40	1.00
57 Jimmy Smith	.30	.75
58 Michael Vick	.50	1.25
59 Tommy Maddox	.30	.75
60 Edgerrin James	.40	1.00
61 Laveranues Coles	.25	.60
62 Curtis Conway	.25	.60
63 Clinton Portis	.30	.75
64 Derrick Brooks	.30	.75
65 Amani Toomer	.30	.75
66 Roy Williams	.30	.75
67 Marshall Faulk	.40	1.00
68 Daunte Culpepper	.30	.75
69 Peerless Price	.25	.60
70 Marcel Shipp	.25	.60
71 David Carr	.30	.75
72 Patrick Ramsey	.30	.75
73 Charlie Garner	.30	.75
74 Jake Plummer	.30	.75
75 Kurt Warner	.40	1.00
76 Brian Urlacher	.40	1.00
77 Tai Streets	.25	.60
78 Jason Taylor	.30	.75
79 Drew Bledsoe	.40	1.00
80 Drew Brees	.40	1.00
81 Peyton Manning	.75	2.00
82 Jamal Lewis	.30	.75
83 Antwaan Randle El	.30	.75
84 Mark Brunell	.30	.75
85 Warrick Dunn	.30	.75
86 Brian Dawkins	.30	.75
87 James Stewart	.25	.60
88 Ronde Barber	.30	.75
89 Curtis Martin	.40	1.00
90 Jon Kitna	.30	.75
91 Keyshawn Johnson	.40	1.00
92 Aaron Brooks	.30	.75
93 Marty Booker	.30	.75
94 Jeff Garcia	.30	.75
95 Marvin Harrison	.40	1.00
96 T.J. Duckett	.30	.75
97 Jerry Rice	.75	2.00
98 Donald Driver	.40	1.00
99 Steve McNair	.40	1.00
100 Kerry Collins	.30	.75
101 Carson Palmer RC	5.00	12.00
102 Kyle Boller RC	2.50	6.00
103 Willis McGahee RC	3.00	8.00
104 Larry Johnson RC	2.50	6.00
105 Bryant Johnson RC	2.50	6.00
106 Byron Leftwich RC	2.50	6.00
107 Andre Johnson RC	6.00	15.00
108 Rex Grossman RC	2.50	6.00
109 Kelley Washington RC	1.50	4.00
110 Charles Rogers RC	2.00	5.00
111 Taylor Jacobs RC	1.25	3.00
112 Sam Aiken RC	1.50	4.00
113 Dallas Clark RC	3.00	8.00
114 B.J. Askew RC	1.50	4.00
115 Quentin Griffin RC	1.50	4.00
116 Terence Newman RC	1.50	4.00
117 Chris Simms RC	2.00	5.00
118 Brandon Lloyd RC	3.00	8.00
119 Lee Suggs RC	1.50	4.00
120 L.J. Smith RC	2.00	5.00
121 Anquan Boldin RC	3.00	8.00
122 Musa Smith RC	1.25	3.00
123 Billy McMullen RC	1.25	3.00
124 Bennie Joppru RC	1.25	3.00
125 Justin Fargas RC	2.00	5.00
126 Tyrone Calico RC	1.50	4.00
127 Dave Ragone RC	1.25	3.00
128 Seneca Wallace RC	2.00	5.00
129 Chris Brown RC	1.25	3.00
130 Terrell Suggs RC	2.00	5.00
131 Bethel Johnson RC	2.00	5.00
132 Nate Burleson RC	2.50	6.00
133 Teyo Johnson RC	2.50	6.00
134 Kevin Curtis RC	3.00	8.00
135 Jason Witten RC	8.00	20.00
136 Artose Pinner RC	2.00	5.00
137 Boss Bailey RC	2.50	6.00
138 Jerome McDougle RC	2.00	5.00
139 LaBrandon Toefield RC	2.50	6.00
140 Domanick Davis RC	2.50	6.00

2003 Fleer Genuine Insider Mini 149

*SINGLES: .3X TO .8X BASIC CARDS
STATED PRINT RUN 149 SER.#'d SETS

2003 Fleer Genuine Insider Reflection

*VETS 1-100: 3X TO 8X BASIC CARDS
*ROOKIES 111-130: 1X TO 2.5X
STATED PRINT RUN 99 SER.#'d SETS

2003 Fleer Genuine Insider Genuine Article

STATED ODDS 1:24		
*PATCH/50: 1.5X TO 4X BASIC JSY		
PATCH PRINT RUN 50 SER.#'d SETS		
GAAB Aaron Brooks	3.00	8.00
GABF Brett Favre	10.00	25.00
GABU Brian Urlacher	4.00	10.00
GACP Clinton Portis	3.00	8.00
GACP2 Chad Pennington	4.00	10.00
GADB Drew Brees	4.00	10.00
GADC Daunte Culpepper	3.00	8.00
GADC2 David Carr	3.00	8.00
GADM Donovan McNabb	4.00	10.00
GADM2 Deuce McAllister	3.00	8.00
GAES Emmitt Smith	10.00	25.00
GAJH Joey Harrington	2.50	6.00
GAJR Jerry Rice	8.00	20.00
GAJS Jeremy Shockey	4.00	10.00
GAKW Kurt Warner	4.00	10.00
GALT LaDainian Tomlinson	4.00	10.00
GAMF Marshall Faulk	4.00	10.00
GAMH Marvin Harrison	4.00	10.00
GAMV Michael Vick	5.00	12.00
GAPM Peyton Manning	8.00	20.00
GARM Randy Moss	4.00	10.00
GARW Ricky Williams	3.00	8.00
GATB Tom Brady	10.00	25.00
GATO Terrell Owens	4.00	10.00

2003 Fleer Genuine Insider Autographs

STATED ODDS 1:24		
AICS Chris Simms	8.00	20.00
AIDB Drew Brees	30.00	60.00
AIKB Kyle Boller	6.00	15.00
AIKW Kelley Washington	6.00	15.00
AILJ Larry Johnson	10.00	25.00
AIMB Michael Bennett	6.00	15.00
AITM Tommy Maddox	10.00	25.00

2003 Fleer Genuine Insider Tools of the Game

COMPLETE SET (15)	15.00	40.00
STATED ODDS 1:8		
1 Brett Favre	2.50	6.00
2 Clinton Portis	.75	2.00
3 Donovan McNabb	1.00	2.50

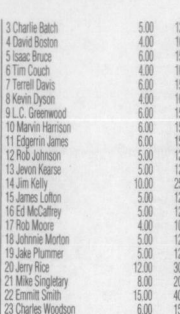

4 Daunte Culpepper	.75	2.00
5 LaDainian Tomlinson	1.00	2.50
6 Tom Brady	2.50	6.00
7 Peyton Manning	2.00	5.00
8 Emmitt Smith	2.50	6.00
9 Brian Urlacher	1.00	2.50
10 Michael Vick	1.25	3.00
11 Randy Moss	1.00	2.50
12 Marshall Faulk	1.00	2.50
13 Kurt Warner	1.00	2.50
14 Marvin Harrison	1.00	2.50
15 Joey Harrington	.60	1.50

2003 Fleer Genuine Insider Tools of the Game Memorabilia

STATED PRINT RUN 199 SER.#'d SETS

TGBF Brett Favre	12.00	30.00
TGBU Brian Urlacher	5.00	12.00
TGCP Clinton Portis	4.00	10.00
TGDC Daunte Culpepper	4.00	10.00
TGDM Donovan McNabb	5.00	12.00
TGJH Joey Harrington	3.00	8.00
TGJR Jerry Rice	10.00	25.00
TGKW Kurt Warner	5.00	12.00
TGLT LaDainian Tomlinson	5.00	12.00
TGMF Marshall Faulk	5.00	12.00
TGMH Marvin Harrison	5.00	12.00
TGMV Michael Vick	6.00	15.00
TGPM Peyton Manning	10.00	25.00
TGRM Randy Moss	5.00	12.00
TGTB Tom Brady	12.00	30.00

2003 Fleer Genuine Insider Tools of the Game Memorabilia Duals

STATED PRINT RUN 99 SER.#'d SETS

TGBF Brett Favre	20.00	50.00
TGBU Brian Urlacher	8.00	20.00
TGDC Daunte Culpepper	6.00	15.00
TGDM Donovan McNabb	8.00	20.00
TGKW Kurt Warner	8.00	20.00
TGMF Marshall Faulk	8.00	20.00
TGMH Marvin Harrison	8.00	20.00
TGMV Michael Vick	10.00	25.00
TGPM Peyton Manning	15.00	40.00
TGRM Randy Moss	8.00	20.00

2003 Fleer Genuine Insider Touchdown Threats

COMPLETE SET (10)	15.00	40.00
STATED ODDS 1:20		
1 Donovan McNabb	1.25	3.00
Michael Vick		
2 Brett Favre	2.00	5.00
Peyton Manning		
3 Jeremy Shockey	1.00	2.50
Todd Heap		
4 Randy Moss	1.00	2.50
Terrell Owens		
5 LaDainian Tomlinson	1.00	2.50
Clinton Portis		
6 Emmitt Smith	2.00	5.00
Jerry Rice		
7 Deuce McAllister	.75	2.00
Travis Henry		
8 Ricky Williams	.75	2.00
Fred Taylor		
9 Marshall Faulk	1.00	2.50
Edgerrin James		
10 David Carr	1.00	2.50
Chad Pennington		

2003 Fleer Genuine Insider Touchdown Threats Jerseys

STATED ODDS 1:48

BFPM Brett Favre JSY	12.50	30.00
Peyton Manning		
BFPM1 Brett Favre	6.00	15.00
Peyton Manning JSY		
DCCP David Carr JSY	5.00	12.00
Chad Pennington		
DCCP1 David Carr	5.00	12.00
Chad Pennington JSY		
DMMV Donovan McNabb JSY	6.00	15.00
Michael Vick		
DMMV1 Donovan McNabb	10.00	25.00
Michael Vick JSY		
ESJR Emmitt Smith JSY	12.50	30.00
Jerry Rice		
JSTH Jeremy Shockey JSY	5.00	12.00
Todd Heap		
LTCP LaDainian Tomlinson JSY	6.00	15.00
Clinton Portis		
LTCP1 LaDainian Tomlinson	3.00	8.00
Clinton Portis JSY		
MFEJ Marshall Faulk JSY	5.00	12.00
Edgerrin James		
MFEJ1 Marshall Faulk	5.00	12.00
Edgerrin James JSY		
RMTO Randy Moss JSY	6.00	15.00
Terrell Owens		
RMTO1 Randy Moss	5.00	12.00
Terrell Owens JSY		
RWFT Ricky Williams JSY	4.00	10.00
Fred Taylor		

2003 Fleer Genuine Insider Touchdown Threats Jersey Duals

STATED PRINT RUN 200 SER.#'d SETS

BFPM Brett Favre	15.00	40.00
Peyton Manning		
DCCP David Carr	8.00	20.00
Chad Pennington		
DMMV Donovan McNabb	10.00	25.00
Michael Vick		
ESJR Emmitt Smith	15.00	40.00
Jerry Rice		
LTCP LaDainian Tomlinson	8.00	20.00
Clinton Portis		
MFEJ Marshall Faulk	8.00	20.00
Edgerrin James		
RMTO Randy Moss	8.00	20.00
Terrell Owens		

2004 Fleer Genuine

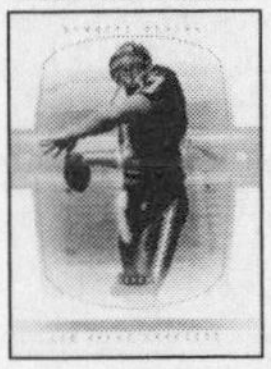

Fleer Genuine initially released in late October 2004. The base set consists of 100-cards including 25-rookies serial numbered to 500. Hobby boxes contained 12-packs of 5-cards. One parallel set and a variety of inserts can be found seeded in hobby and retail packs highlighted by the multi-tiered Big Time Autograph inserts. Some signed cards were issued via mail-in exchange or redemption cards with a number of those EXCH cards not yet appearing live on the secondary market as of the printing of this book.

76-100 ROOKIE PRINT RUN 500 SER.#'d SETS

1 Anquan Boldin	.40	1.00
2 Rod Smith	.30	.75
3 Randy Moss	.40	1.00
4 Drew Brees	.40	1.00
5 Jamal Lewis	.30	.75
6 Ahman Green	.30	.75
7 Aaron Brooks	.30	.75
8 Torry Holt	.30	.75
9 Steve Smith	.40	1.00
10 Marvin Harrison	.40	1.00
11 Santana Moss	.30	.75
12 Eddie George	.30	.75
13 Lee Suggs	.30	.75
14 Randy McMichael	.25	.60
15 Hines Ward	.40	1.00
16 Drew Bledsoe	.40	1.00
17 Andre Johnson	.40	1.00
18 Jeremy Shockey	.30	.75
19 Mike Alstott	.30	.75
20 Chad Johnson	.40	1.00
21 Priest Holmes	.40	1.00
22 Brian Westbrook	.40	1.00
23 Rudi Johnson	.30	.75
24 Keyshawn Johnson	.30	.75
25 Chris Chambers	.30	.75
26 LaDainian Tomlinson	.40	1.00
27 Ray Lewis	.40	1.00
28 Brett Favre	1.00	2.50
29 Deuce McAllister	.30	.75
30 Marshall Faulk	.40	1.00
31 Brian Urlacher	.40	1.00
32 Byron Leftwich	.30	.75
33 Jerry Rice	.75	2.00
34 Clinton Portis	.40	1.00
35 Derrick Mason	.30	.75
36 Emmitt Smith	1.00	2.50
37 Plaxico Burress	.30	.75
38 Peerless Price	.25	.60
39 Joey Harrington	.30	.75
40 Corey Dillon	.30	.75
41 Matt Hasselbeck	.30	.75
42 Stephen Davis	.30	.75
43 Peyton Manning	.75	2.00
44 Tiki Barber	.40	1.00
45 Derrick Brooks	.30	.75
46 Jeff Garcia	.30	.75
47 Trent Green	.30	.75
48 Donovan McNabb	.40	1.00
49 Michael Vick	.50	1.25
50 Jake Plummer	.30	.75
51 Tom Brady	.75	2.00
52 Brandon Lloyd	.30	.75
53 Eric Moulds	.30	.75
54 David Carr	.25	.60
55 Joe Horn	.30	.75
56 Isaac Bruce	.30	.75
57 Rex Grossman	.30	.75
58 Fred Taylor	.30	.75
59 Rich Gannon	.30	.75
60 Laveranues Coles	.25	.60
61 T.J. Duckett	.30	.75
62 Charles Rogers	.25	.60
63 Deion Branch	.30	.75
64 Shaun Alexander	.30	.75
65 Jake Delhomme	.30	.75
66 Edgerrin James	.30	.75
67 Chad Pennington	.40	1.00
68 Steve McNair	.40	1.00
69 Carson Palmer	.40	1.00
70 Tony Gonzalez	.40	1.00
71 Terrell Owens	.40	1.00
72 Josh McCown	.30	.75
73 Ashley Lelie	.25	.60
74 Daunte Culpepper	.30	.75
75 Kevan Barlow	.25	.60
76 Eli Manning RC	10.00	25.00
77 Larry Fitzgerald RC	4.00	10.00
78 Philip Rivers RC	6.00	15.00
79 Kellen Winslow RC	1.50	4.00
80 Roy Williams RC	1.50	4.00
81 Reggie Williams RC	1.25	3.00
82 Ben Roethlisberger RC	10.00	25.00
83 Lee Evans RC	1.50	4.00
84 Michael Clayton RC	1.25	3.00
85 J.P. Losman RC	1.25	3.00
86 Steven Jackson RC	2.50	6.00
87 Chris Perry RC	1.25	3.00
88 Michael Jenkins RC	1.50	4.00
89 Kevin Jones RC	1.25	3.00
90 Rashaun Woods RC	1.00	2.50
91 Ben Watson RC	1.50	4.00
92 Ben Troupe RC	1.25	3.00
93 Tatum Bell RC	1.25	3.00
94 Julius Jones RC	1.25	3.00
95 Devery Henderson RC	1.50	4.00
96 Darius Watts RC	1.00	2.50
97 Greg Jones RC	1.00	2.50
98 Keary Colbert RC	1.00	2.50
99 Derrick Hamilton RC	1.00	2.50
100 Drew Henson RC	1.00	2.50

2004 Fleer Genuine Reflections

*STARS: 3X TO 8X BASE CARD HI
1-75 PRINT RUN 99 SER.#'d SETS
76-100 SER.#'d TO DRAFT PICK POSITION
ROOKIES SER.#'d UNDER 20 NOT PRICED

85 J.P. Losman/22	5.00	12.00
86 Steven Jackson/24	10.00	25.00
87 Chris Perry/26	5.00	12.00
88 Michael Jenkins/29	6.00	15.00
89 Kevin Jones/30	4.00	10.00
90 Rashaun Woods/31	3.00	8.00
91 Ben Watson/32	5.00	12.00
92 Ben Troupe/40	4.00	10.00
93 Tatum Bell/41	4.00	10.00
94 Julius Jones/43	4.00	10.00
95 Devery Henderson/50	3.00	8.00
96 Darius Watts/54	2.00	5.00
97 Greg Jones/55	2.00	5.00
98 Keary Colbert/62	2.00	5.00
99 Derrick Hamilton/77	2.00	5.00
100 Drew Henson/192	1.25	3.00

2004 Fleer Genuine At Large

STATED ODDS 1:45

1AL Anquan Boldin	1.50	4.00
2AL LaDainian Tomlinson	1.50	4.00
3AL Michael Vick	2.00	5.00
4AL Daunte Culpepper	1.25	3.00
5AL Brian Urlacher	1.50	4.00
6AL Ahman Green	1.25	3.00
7AL Peyton Manning	3.00	8.00
8AL Byron Leftwich	1.25	3.00
9AL Priest Holmes	1.50	4.00
10AL Chad Pennington	1.50	4.00
11AL Jeremy Shockey	1.25	3.00
12AL Joe Horn	1.25	3.00
13AL Santana Moss	1.25	3.00
14AL Donovan McNabb	1.50	4.00
15AL Randy Moss	1.50	4.00

2004 Fleer Genuine At Large Patch Autographs

STATED PRINT RUN 25-44

AB Anquan Boldin/25	15.00	40.00
BL Byron Leftwich/25	30.00	60.00
CP Chad Pennington/44	75.00	150.00

2004 Fleer Genuine At Large Patch White

WHITE PRINT RUN 75 SER.#'d SETS
*BLACK BORDER/35: .5X TO 1.2X WHT/75
BLACK PRINT RUN 35 SER.#'d SETS
*ORANGE/10: 1X TO 2.5X WHITE/75
ORANGE PRINT RUN 10 SETS

AB Anquan Boldin	6.00	15.00
AB2 Aaron Brooks	5.00	12.00
AG Ahman Green	5.00	12.00
BL Byron Leftwich	5.00	12.00
BU Brian Urlacher	6.00	15.00
CC Chris Chambers	5.00	12.00
CP Chad Pennington	6.00	15.00
DB Derrick Brooks	5.00	12.00
DC Daunte Culpepper	5.00	12.00
DM Donovan McNabb	6.00	15.00
HW Hines Ward	6.00	15.00
JD Jake Delhomme	5.00	12.00
JF Justin Fargas	5.00	12.00
JH Joey Harrington	5.00	12.00
JH2 Joe Horn	5.00	12.00
JL Jamal Lewis	5.00	12.00
JS Jeremy Shockey	5.00	12.00
LT LaDainian Tomlinson	6.00	15.00
MA Mike Alstott	5.00	12.00
MF Marshall Faulk	6.00	15.00
MH Matt Hasselbeck	5.00	12.00
MV Michael Vick	8.00	20.00
PH Priest Holmes	6.00	15.00
PM Peyton Manning	12.00	30.00
RG Rich Gannon	5.00	12.00
RG2 Rex Grossman	5.00	12.00
RM Randy Moss	6.00	15.00
RW Roy Williams S	5.00	12.00
SM Santana Moss	5.00	12.00
TH Travis Henry	4.00	10.00

2004 Fleer Genuine Big Time

STATED ODDS 1:500

1BT Clinton Portis	5.00	12.00
2BT Donovan McNabb	5.00	12.00
3BT Jeff Garcia	4.00	10.00
4BT Chad Johnson	5.00	12.00
5BT Michael Vick	6.00	15.00
6BT Tony Gonzalez	5.00	12.00
7BT Deuce McAllister	4.00	10.00
8BT Carson Palmer	5.00	12.00
9BT Peyton Manning	10.00	25.00
10BT LaDainian Tomlinson	5.00	12.00
11BT Brett Favre	12.00	30.00
12BT Marvin Harrison	5.00	12.00
13BT Terrell Owens	5.00	12.00
14BT Priest Holmes	5.00	12.00
15BT Jamal Lewis	4.00	10.00

2004 Fleer Genuine Big Time Autographs Blue

BLUE BORDER PRINT RUN 150
*ORANGE/25: .8X TO 2X BLUE/150
ORANGE BORDER PRINT RUN 25
*RED/50: .5X TO 1.2X BLUE/150
RED BORDER PRINT RUN 50

CJ Chad Johnson	8.00	20.00
CP2 Chris Perry	6.00	15.00
DM Deuce McAllister	6.00	15.00
DS Donte Stallworth	5.00	12.00
JJ Joe Jurevicius	5.00	12.00
JL Jamal Lewis	6.00	15.00
RW Reggie Williams	6.00	15.00

2004 Fleer Genuine Big Time Jersey Autographs White

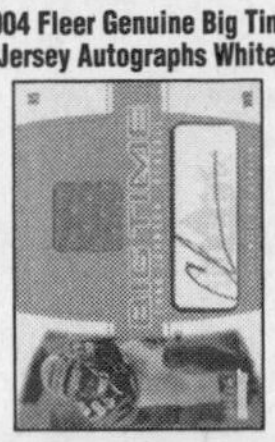

WHITE BORDER PRINT RUN 75 SER.#'d SETS
*BLACK BORDER: .6X TO 1.5X WHITE
BLACK BORDER PRINT RUN 25 SER.#'d SETS

CJ Chad Johnson	10.00	25.00

2004 Fleer Genuine Big Time Patch Autographs

STATED PRINT RUN 25 SER.#'d SETS

DM Deuce McAllister	25.00	60.00

2004 Fleer Genuine Big Time Patch Black

BLACK BORDER PRINT RUN 25
UNPRICED ORANGE PRINT RUN 5 SETS
*WHITE BORDER/54-97: .25X TO .6X BLACK
*WHITE BORDER/31-44: .3X TO .8X BLACK
*WHITE BORDER/21-28: .4X TO 1X BLACK
WHITE BORDER SER.#'d TO JSY NUMBER

BB Boss Bailey	6.00	15.00
BF Brett Favre	25.00	60.00
BU Brian Urlacher	10.00	25.00
CJ Chad Johnson	10.00	25.00
CM Curtis Martin	10.00	25.00
CP Carson Palmer	10.00	25.00
CP2 Clinton Portis	10.00	25.00
DC David Carr	6.00	15.00
DM Deuce McAllister	8.00	20.00
DM2 Donovan McNabb	10.00	25.00
DS Donte Stallworth	6.00	15.00
FM Freddie Mitchell	6.00	15.00
FT Fred Taylor	8.00	20.00
IB Isaac Bruce	8.00	20.00
JG Jeff Garcia	8.00	20.00
JL Jamal Lewis	8.00	20.00
JP Julius Peppers	8.00	20.00
LS Lee Suggs	8.00	20.00
LT LaDainian Tomlinson	10.00	25.00
MH Marvin Harrison	10.00	25.00
MV Michael Vick	12.00	30.00
PB Plaxico Burress	8.00	20.00
PH Priest Holmes	10.00	25.00
PM Peyton Manning	20.00	50.00
PP Peerless Price	6.00	15.00
PW Peter Warrick	8.00	20.00
TB Tiki Barber	10.00	25.00
TG Tony Gonzalez	10.00	25.00
TO Terrell Owens	10.00	25.00
ZT Zach Thomas	10.00	25.00

2004 Fleer Genuine Genuine Article

COMPLETE SET (15)	12.50	30.00
STATED ODDS 1:7		
1GA Brett Favre	2.50	6.00
2GA Marvin Harrison	1.00	2.50
3GA Clinton Portis	1.00	2.50
4GA Peyton Manning	2.00	5.00
5GA Randy Moss	1.00	2.50
6GA Donovan McNabb	1.00	2.50
7GA Tom Brady	2.00	5.00
8GA Terrell Owens	1.00	2.50
9GA Torry Holt	.75	2.00
10GA Steve McNair	1.00	2.50
11GA Ray Lewis	1.00	2.50
12GA Michael Vick	1.25	3.00
13GA Deuce McAllister	.75	2.00
14GA Shaun Alexander	.75	2.00
15GA Priest Holmes	1.00	2.50

2004 Fleer Genuine Genuine Article Jerseys Red

*ORANGE BORDER/25: 1.2X TO 3X RED
ORANGE BORDER PRINT RUN 25
*WHITE BORDER/150: .6X TO 1.5X RED
WHITE BORDER PRINT RUN 150

BF Brett Favre	8.00	20.00
CP Clinton Portis	3.00	8.00
DM Deuce McAllister	2.50	6.00
DM2 Donovan McNabb	3.00	8.00
MH Marvin Harrison	3.00	8.00
MV Michael Vick	4.00	10.00
PH Priest Holmes	3.00	8.00
PM Peyton Manning	6.00	15.00
RL Ray Lewis	3.00	8.00
RM Randy Moss	3.00	8.00
SA Shaun Alexander	2.50	6.00
SM Steve McNair	3.00	8.00
TB Tom Brady	6.00	15.00
TH Torry Holt	2.50	6.00
TO Terrell Owens	3.00	8.00

2004 Fleer Genuine Genuine Article Jersey Autographs Silver

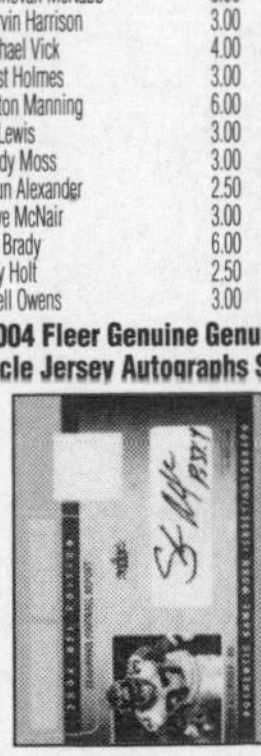

SILVER BORDER PRINT RUN 100
UNPRICED ORANGE PRINT RUN 1 SET

SA Shaun Alexander	15.00	40.00

1997 Fleer Goudey

The 1997 Fleer Goudey set was issued in two series, each totaling 150 cards. The small almost square shaped (2 3/8" x 2 7/8") cards measured the same as the 1930's Goudey sets. Inspired by the classic look of the 1930's cards these cards have the same "Art Deco-style" graphics and same matte finish. The cards in Series 1 were issued in 10 card packs in 36 count hobby boxes. An unnumbered base card of Brett Favre was released to promote the set.

COMPLETE SET (150)	6.00	15.00
1 Michael Jackson	.10	.30
2 Ray Lewis	.30	.75
3 Vinny Testaverde	.10	.30
4 Eric Turner	.07	.20
5 Jim Kelly	.20	.50
6 Bryce Paup	.07	.20
7 Andre Reed	.10	.30
8 Bruce Smith	.10	.30
9 Thurman Thomas	.20	.50
10 Jeff Blake	.10	.30
11 Ki-Jana Carter	.07	.20
12 Carl Pickens	.10	.30
13 Darnay Scott	.10	.30
14 Terrell Davis	.25	.60
15 John Elway	.75	2.00
16 Anthony Miller	.07	.20
17 John Mobley	.07	.20
18 Shannon Sharpe	.10	.30
19 Chris Chandler	.10	.30
20 Eddie George	.20	.50
21 Steve McNair	.25	.60
22 Chris Sanders	.07	.20
23 Quentin Coryatt	.07	.20
24 Sean Dawkins	.07	.20
25 Ken Dilger	.07	.20
26 Marshall Faulk	.25	.60
27 Jim Harbaugh	.10	.30
28 Marvin Harrison	.20	.50
29 Tony Brackens	.07	.20
30 Mark Brunell	.25	.60
31 Kevin Hardy	.07	.20
32 Keenan McCardell	.10	.30
33 James O.Stewart	.10	.30
34 Marcus Allen	.20	.50
35 Steve Bono	.10	.30
36 Dale Carter	.07	.20
37 Neil Smith	.10	.30
38 Derrick Thomas	.20	.50
39 Tamarick Vanover	.10	.30
40 Karim Abdul-Jabbar	.10	.30
41 Dan Marino	.75	2.00
42 O.J. McDuffie	.10	.30
43 Stanley Pritchett	.07	.20
44 Zach Thomas	.20	.50
45 Drew Bledsoe	.25	.60
46 Ben Coates	.10	.30
47 Terry Glenn	.20	.50
48 Shawn Jefferson	.07	.20
49 Curtis Martin	.25	.60
50 Dave Meggett	.07	.20
51 Hugh Douglas	.07	.20
52 Keyshawn Johnson	.20	.50
53 Adrian Murrell	.10	.30
54 Tim Brown	.20	.50
55 Rickey Dudley	.10	.30
56 Jeff Hostetler	.07	.20
57 Napoleon Kaufman	.20	.50
58 Chester McGlockton	.07	.20
59 Jerome Bettis	.20	.50
60 Andre Hastings	.07	.20
61 Greg Lloyd	.07	.20
62 Kordell Stewart	.20	.50
63 Yancey Thigpen	.10	.30
64 Rod Woodson	.10	.30
65 Andre Coleman	.07	.20
66 Stan Humphries	.10	.30
67 Tony Martin	.10	.30
68 Leonard Russell	.07	.20
69 Junior Seau	.20	.50
70 Brian Blades	.07	.20
71 Joey Galloway	.10	.30
72 Chris Warren	.10	.30
73 Larry Centers	.10	.30
74 Leeland McElroy	.07	.20
75 Simeon Rice	.10	.30
76 Frank Sanders	.10	.30
77 Eric Swann	.07	.20
78 Jamal Anderson	.20	.50
79 Bert Emanuel	.10	.30
80 Terance Mathis	.10	.30
81 Eric Metcalf	.10	.30
82 Tim Biakabutuka	.10	.30
83 Kerry Collins	.20	.50
84 Kevin Greene	.10	.30
85 Muhsin Muhammad	.10	.30
86 Wesley Walls	.10	.30
87 Curtis Conway	.10	.30
88 Bryan Cox	.07	.20
89 Walt Harris	.07	.20
90 Erik Kramer	.07	.20
91 Rashaan Salaam	.07	.20
92 Troy Aikman	.40	1.00
93 Michael Irvin	.20	.50
94 Daryl Johnston	.10	.30
95 Leon Lett	.07	.20
96 Deion Sanders	.20	.50
97 Emmitt Smith	.60	1.50
98 Scott Mitchell	.10	.30
99 Herman Moore	.10	.30
100 Johnnie Morton	.10	.30
101 Brett Perriman	.07	.20
102 Barry Sanders	.60	1.50
103 Edgar Bennett	.10	.30
104 Robert Brooks	.10	.30
105 Brett Favre	.75	2.00
106 Antonio Freeman	.20	.50
107 Keith Jackson	.07	.20
108 Reggie White	.20	.50
109 Cris Carter	.20	.50
110 Warren Moon	.20	.50
111 John Randle	.10	.30
112 Jake Reed	.10	.30
113 Robert Smith	.10	.30
114 Jim Everett	.07	.20
115 Michael Haynes	.07	.20
116 Alex Molden	.07	.20
117 Ray Zellars	.07	.20
118 Chris Calloway	.07	.20
119 Rodney Hampton	.10	.30
120 Phillippi Sparks	.07	.20
121 Amani Toomer	.10	.30
122 Ty Detmer	.10	.30
123 Jason Dunn	.07	.20
124 Irving Fryar	.10	.30
125 Chris T. Jones	.07	.20
126 Ricky Watters	.10	.30
127 Tony Banks	.10	.30
128 Isaac Bruce	.20	.50
129 Eddie Kennison	.10	.30
130 Lawrence Phillips	.07	.20
131 Merton Hanks	.07	.20
132 Terry Kirby	.10	.30
133 Ken Norton	.07	.20
134 Jerry Rice	.40	1.00
135 J.J. Stokes	.10	.30
136 Steve Young	.25	.60
137 Alvin Harper	.07	.20
138 Jackie Harris	.07	.20
139 Hardy Nickerson	.07	.20
140 Errict Rhett	.07	.20
141 Terry Allen	.20	.50
142 Henry Ellard	.07	.20
143 Gus Frerotte	.07	.20
144 Brian Mitchell	.07	.20
145 Michael Westbrook	.10	.30
146 Chuck Bednarik	.10	.30
146AU Chuck Bednarik	20.00	50.00
(Signed Card)		
147 Y.A. Tittle	.10	.30
147AU Y.A. Tittle	20.00	50.00
(Signed Card)		
148 Checklist	.07	.20
149 Checklist	.07	.20
150 Checklist	.07	.20
P1 Brett Favre Promo	.75	2.00

1997 Fleer Goudey Gridiron Greats

COMPLETE SET (147)	40.00	80.00
*GG STARS: 2.5X TO 5X BASIC CARDS		
STATED ODDS 1:3		

1997 Fleer Goudey Bednarik Says

COMPLETE SET (15)	40.00	80.00
STATED ODDS 1:60		
1 Kevin Greene	2.00	4.00
2 Ray Lewis	3.00	8.00
3 Greg Lloyd	1.25	2.50
4 Chester McGlockton	1.25	2.50
5 Hardy Nickerson	1.25	2.50
6 Bryce Paup	1.25	2.50
7 Simeon Rice	2.00	4.00
8 Deion Sanders	3.00	6.00
9 Junior Seau	3.00	6.00
10 Bruce Smith	2.00	4.00
11 Derrick Thomas	3.00	6.00
12 Zach Thomas	3.00	6.00
13 Eric Turner	1.25	2.50
14 Reggie White	4.00	8.00
15 Rod Woodson	2.00	4.00

1997 Fleer Goudey Heads Up

COMPLETE SET (20)	50.00	100.00
STATED ODDS 1:30		
1 Troy Aikman	4.00	10.00
2 Marcus Allen	2.00	5.00
3 Tim Biakabutuka	1.25	3.00
4 Robert Brooks	1.25	3.00
5 Isaac Bruce	2.00	5.00
6 Kerry Collins	2.00	5.00
7 Terrell Davis	2.50	6.00
8 Brett Favre	8.00	20.00
9 Terry Glenn	2.00	5.00
10 Rodney Hampton	1.25	3.00
11 Michael Irvin	2.00	5.00
12 Chris T. Jones	.75	2.00
13 Carl Pickens	1.25	3.00
14 Barry Sanders	6.00	15.00
15 Kordell Stewart	2.00	5.00
16 Thurman Thomas	2.00	5.00
17 Tamarick Vanover	1.25	3.00
18 Chris Warren	1.25	3.00
19 Ricky Watters	1.25	3.00
20 Steve Young	2.50	6.00

1997 Fleer Goudey Pigskin 2000

COMPLETE SET (15)	100.00	200.00
STATED ODDS 1:360		
1 Karim Abdul-Jabbar	4.00	10.00
2 Jeff Blake	4.00	10.00
3 Drew Bledsoe	8.00	20.00
4 Robert Brooks	4.00	10.00
5 Terrell Davis	8.00	20.00
6 Marshall Faulk	8.00	20.00
7 Joey Galloway	4.00	10.00
8 Eddie George	6.00	15.00
9 Terry Glenn	6.00	15.00
10 Keyshawn Johnson	6.00	15.00
11 Chris T. Jones	2.50	6.00
12 Curtis Martin	8.00	20.00
13 Steve McNair	8.00	20.00
14 Lawrence Phillips	2.50	6.00
15 Kordell Stewart	6.00	15.00

1997 Fleer Goudey Tittle Says

COMPLETE SET (20)	75.00	150.00
STATED ODDS 1:72		
1 Karim Abdul-Jabbar	1.25	3.00
2 Jerome Bettis	2.00	5.00
3 Tim Brown	2.00	5.00
4 Isaac Bruce	2.00	5.00
5 Cris Carter	2.00	5.00
6 Curtis Conway	1.25	3.00
7 John Elway	8.00	20.00
8 Marshall Faulk	2.50	6.00
9 Brett Favre	8.00	20.00
10 Joey Galloway	1.25	3.00
11 Eddie George	2.00	5.00
12 Keyshawn Johnson	2.00	5.00
13 Dan Marino	8.00	20.00
14 Curtis Martin	2.50	6.00
15 Herman Moore	1.25	3.00
16 Jerry Rice	4.00	10.00
17 Barry Sanders	6.00	15.00
18 Emmitt Smith	6.00	15.00
19 Thurman Thomas	2.00	5.00
20 Ricky Watters	1.25	3.00

1997 Fleer Goudey II

The 1997 Fleer Goudey set was issued in two series, each totaling 150 cards. Series II cards were issued in eight-card packs with a suggested retail price of $1.49. These cards were designed to match the card stock, color (off-white), size and graphics of the 1934 Goudey set. The back of each card displayed what Gale Sayers reported on the pictured player. Series II contained three Gale Sayers commemorative cards that were seeded at 1:9 packs with one percent foil stamped as "Rare Traditions" versions. A Reggie White promo card was released to promote the set that is identical to the base #92 Reggie White card except that it was printed on white card stock instead of off-white. Additionally there was a Reggie White display card measuring standard size that was to be used in the retailer's box display.

COMPLETE SET (150)	7.50	20.00
1 Gale Sayers SP	.20	.50
1AU Gale Sayers AUTO	40.00	100.00
1RT Gale Sayers	4.00	8.00
Rare Traditions Foil		
2 Vinny Testaverde	.10	.30
3 Jeff George	.10	.30
4 Brett Favre	.75	2.00
5 Eddie Kennison	.10	.30
6 Ken Norton	.07	.20
7 John Elway	.75	2.00
8 Troy Aikman	.40	1.00
9 Steve McNair	.25	.60
10 Kordell Stewart	.20	.50
11 Drew Bledsoe	.25	.60
12 Kerry Collins	.20	.50
13 Dan Marino	.75	2.00
14 Brad Johnson	.20	.50
15 Todd Collins	.07	.20
16 Ki-Jana Carter	.07	.20
17 Pat Barnes RC	.20	.50
18 Aeneas Williams	.07	.20
19 Keyshawn Johnson	.20	.50
20 Barry Sanders	.60	1.50
21 Tiki Barber RC	1.25	3.00
22 Emmitt Smith	.60	1.50
23 Kevin Hardy	.07	.20
24 Mario Bates	.07	.20
25 Ricky Watters	.10	.30
26 Chris Canty RC	.07	.20
27 Eddie George	.20	.50
28 Curtis Martin	.25	.60
29 Adrian Murrell	.10	.30
30 Terrell Davis	.25	.60
31 Rashaan Salaam	.07	.20
32 Marcus Allen	.20	.50
33 Karim Abdul-Jabbar	.20	.50
34 Thurman Thomas	.20	.50
35 Marvin Harrison	.20	.50
36 Jerome Bettis	.20	.50
37 Larry Centers	.10	.30
38 Stan Humphries	.10	.30
39 Lawrence Phillips	.07	.20
40 Gale Sayers SP	.20	.50
40AU Gale Sayers AUTO	40.00	100.00
40RT Gale Sayers	4.00	8.00
Rare Traditions Foil		
41 Henry Ellard	.07	.20
42 Chris Warren	.10	.30
43 Robert Brooks	.10	.30
44 Sedrick Shaw RC	.10	.30
45 Muhsin Muhammad	.10	.30
46 Napoleon Kaufman	.20	.50
47 Reidel Anthony RC	.20	.50
48 Jamal Anderson	.20	.50
49 Scott Mitchell	.10	.30
50 Mark Brunell	.25	.60
51 William Thomas	.07	.20
52 Bryan Cox	.07	.20
53 Carl Pickens	.10	.30
54 Chris Spielman	.07	.20
55 Junior Seau	.20	.50
56 Hardy Nickerson	.07	.20
57 Dwayne Rudd RC	.20	.50
58 Peter Boulware RC	.20	.50
59 Jim Druckenmiller RC	.10	.30
60 Michael Westbrook	.10	.30
61 Shawn Springs RC	.10	.30
62 Zach Thomas	.20	.50
63 David LaFleur RC	.07	.20
64 Darrell Russell RC	.07	.20
65 Jake Plummer RC	.75	2.00
66 Tim Biakabutuka	.10	.30
67 Tyrone Wheatley	.10	.30
68 Elvis Grbac	.10	.30
69 Antonio Freeman	.20	.50
70 Wayne Chrebet	.20	.50
71 Walter Jones RC	.20	.50
72 Marshall Faulk	.25	.60
73 Jason Dunn	.07	.20
74 Darnay Scott	.10	.30
75 Errict Rhett	.07	.20
76 Orlando Pace RC	.20	.50
77 Natrone Means	.10	.30
78 Bruce Smith	.10	.30
79 Jamie Sharper RC	.10	.30
80 Jerry Rice	.40	1.00
81 Tim Brown	.20	.50
82 Brian Mitchell	.07	.20
83 Andre Reed	.10	.30
84 Herman Moore	.10	.30
85 Rob Moore	.10	.30
86 Rae Carruth RC	.07	.20
87 Bert Emanuel	.10	.30
88 Michael Irvin	.20	.50
89 Mark Chmura	.10	.30
90 Tony Brackens	.07	.20
91 Kevin Greene	.10	.30
92 Reggie White	.20	.50
93 Derrick Thomas	.20	.50
94 Troy Davis RC	.10	.30
95 Greg Lloyd	.07	.20
96 Cortez Kennedy	.07	.20
97 Simeon Rice	.10	.30
98 Terrell Owens	.25	.60
99 Hugh Douglas	.07	.20
100 Terry Glenn	.20	.50
101 Jim Harbaugh	.10	.30
102 Shannon Sharpe	.10	.30
103 Joey Kent RC	.20	.50
104 Jeff Blake	.10	.30
105 Terry Allen	.20	.50
106 Cris Carter	.20	.50
107 Amani Toomer	.10	.30
108 Derrick Alexander WR	.10	.30
109 Darnell Autry RC	.10	.30
110 Irving Fryar	.10	.30
111 Bryant Westbrook RC	.07	.20
112 Tony Banks	.10	.30
113 Michael Booker RC	.07	.20
114 Yatil Green RC	.10	.30
115 James Farrior RC	.20	.50
116 Warrick Dunn RC	.60	1.50
117 Greg Hill	.07	.20
118 Tony Martin	.10	.30
119 Chris Sanders	.07	.20
120 Charles Johnson	.10	.30
121 John Mobley	.07	.20
122 Keenan McCardell	.10	.30
123 Willie McGinest	.07	.20
124 O.J. McDuffie	.10	.30
125 Deion Sanders	.20	.50
126 Curtis Conway	.10	.30
127 Desmond Howard	.10	.30
128 Johnnie Morton	.10	.30
129 Ike Hilliard RC	.30	.75

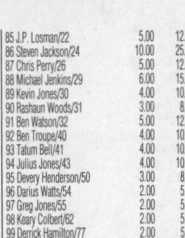

130 Gus Frerotte	.07	.20
131 Tom Knight	.07	.20
132 Sean Dawkins	.07	.20
133 Isaac Bruce	.20	.50
134 Wesley Walls	.10	.30
135 Danny Wuerffel RC	.20	.50
136 Tony Gonzalez RC	.75	2.00
137 Ben Coates	.10	.30
138 Joey Galloway	.10	.30
139 Michael Jackson	.10	.30
140 Steve Young	.25	.60
141 Corey Dillon RC	.75	2.00
142 Jake Reed	.10	.30
143 Edgar Bennett	.10	.30
144 Ty Detmer	.10	.30
145 Darrell Green	.10	.30
146 Antowain Smith RC	.50	1.25
147 Mike Alstott	.20	.50
148 Checklist	.07	.20
149 Checklist	.07	.20
150 Gale Sayers SP	.20	.50
150AU Gale Sayers AUTO	40.00	100.00
150RT Gale Sayers Rare Traditions Foil	4.00	8.00
D92 Reggie White Display card (ad back, measures 2 1/2" x 3 1/2")	.40	1.00
P92 Reggie White Promo (printed on white stock)	.40	1.00

1997 Fleer Goudey II Greats

COMPLETE SET (148) 750.00 1,500.00
*GREATS STARS: 15X TO 40X BASIC CARDS
*GREATS RCs: 15X TO 30X BASIC CARDS
STATED PRINT RUN 150 SERIAL #'d SETS

1997 Fleer Goudey II Gridiron Greats

COMPLETE SET (148) 60.00 120.00
*STARS: 2.5X TO 5X BASIC CARDS
*RC'S: 1.25X TO 2.5X BASIC CARDS
STATED ODDS 1:3

1997 Fleer Goudey II Big Time Backs

COMPLETE SET (10) 125.00 250.00
STATED ODDS 1:72
UNPRICED WOODEN CARDS #'d OF 10

1 Karim Abdul-Jabbar	4.00	10.00
2 Marcus Allen	4.00	10.00
3 Jerome Bettis	4.00	10.00
4 Terrell Davis	5.00	12.00
5 Brett Favre	15.00	40.00
6 Eddie George	4.00	10.00
7 Dan Marino	15.00	40.00
8 Curtis Martin	5.00	12.00
9 Barry Sanders	12.50	30.00
10 Emmitt Smith	12.50	30.00

1997 Fleer Goudey II Glory Days

COMPLETE SET (15) 35.00 70.00
STATED ODDS 1:18 RETAIL

1 Troy Aikman	5.00	12.00
2 Isaac Bruce	2.50	6.00
3 Mark Brunell	3.00	8.00
4 Cris Carter	2.50	6.00
5 Joey Galloway	1.50	4.00
6 Terry Glenn	2.50	6.00
7 Marvin Harrison	2.50	6.00
8 Dan Marino	10.00	25.00
9 Deion Sanders	2.50	6.00
10 Shannon Sharpe	1.50	4.00
11 Bruce Smith	1.50	4.00
12 Emmitt Smith	8.00	20.00
13 Kordell Stewart	2.50	6.00
14 Ricky Watters	1.50	4.00
15 Reggie White	2.50	6.00

1997 Fleer Goudey II Rookie Classics

COMPLETE SET (20) 7.50 15.00
STATED ODDS 1:3

1 Reidel Anthony	.30	.75
2 Pat Barnes	.30	.75
3 Peter Boulware	.30	.75
4 Rae Carruth	.10	.30
5 Troy Davis	.20	.50
6 Corey Dillon	1.25	3.00
7 Jim Druckenmiller	.20	.50
8 Warrick Dunn	1.00	2.50
9 Tony Gonzalez	1.25	3.00
10 Yatil Green	.20	.50
11 Ike Hilliard	.50	1.25
12 Walter Jones	.30	.75
13 David LaFleur	.10	.30
14 Orlando Pace	.30	.75
15 Jake Plummer	1.25	3.00
16 Darrell Russell	.10	.30
17 Antowain Smith	.75	2.00
18 Shawn Springs	.20	.50
19 Bryant Westbrook	.10	.30
20 Danny Wuerffel	.30	.75

1997 Fleer Goudey II Vintage Goudey

COMPLETE SET (15) 75.00 150.00
STATED ODDS 1:36 HOBBY

1 Karim Abdul-Jabbar	3.00	8.00
2 Kerry Collins	3.00	8.00
3 Terrell Davis	4.00	10.00
4 John Elway	12.50	30.00
5 Brett Favre	12.50	30.00
6 Eddie George	3.00	8.00
7 Terry Glenn	3.00	8.00
8 Keyshawn Johnson	3.00	8.00
9 Curtis Martin	4.00	10.00
10 Herman Moore	2.00	5.00
11 Jerry Rice	6.00	15.00
12 Barry Sanders	10.00	25.00
13 Deion Sanders	3.00	8.00
14 Zach Thomas	3.00	8.00
15 Steve Young	4.00	10.00

2004 Fleer Inscribed

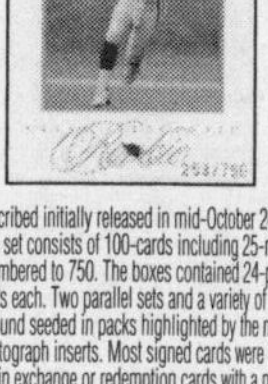

Fleer Inscribed initially released in mid-October 2004. The base set consists of 100-cards including 25-rookies serial numbered to 750. The boxes contained 24-packs of 5-cards each. Two parallel sets and a variety of inserts can be found seeded in packs highlighted by the multi-tiered Autograph inserts. Most signed cards were issued via mail-in exchange or redemption cards with a number of those EXCH cards not yet appearing live on the secondary market as of the printing of this book.

COMP.SET w/o SP's (75) 10.00 25.00
76-100 RC ODDS: 1:12 HOB, 1:100 RET
76-100 RC PRINT RUN 750 SER.#'d SETS
UNPRICED RED PRINT RUN 5 SETS

1 Terrell Owens	.40	1.00
2 David Carr	.25	.60
3 Jerry Porter	.25	.60
4 Charles Rogers	.25	.60
5 Torry Holt	.30	.75
6 Byron Leftwich	.30	.75
7 Laveranues Coles	.25	.60
8 Edgerrin James	.30	.75
9 Brian Urlacher	.40	1.00
10 Hines Ward	.40	1.00
11 LaDainian Tomlinson	.40	1.00
12 Ahman Green	.30	.75
13 Kevan Barlow	.25	.60
14 Trent Green	.30	.75
15 Deuce McAllister	.30	.75
16 Lee Suggs	.30	.75
17 Drew Brees	.40	1.00
18 Randy Moss	.40	1.00
19 Brandon Lloyd	.30	.75
20 Jeff Garcia	.30	.75
21 Roy Williams S	.30	.75
22 Daunte Culpepper	.30	.75
23 Matt Hasselbeck	.30	.75
24 Keyshawn Johnson	.30	.75
25 Michael Vick	.50	1.25
26 Shaun Alexander	.30	.75
27 Chad Pennington	.40	1.00
28 Ashley Lelie	.25	.60
29 Anquan Boldin	.40	1.00
30 Carson Palmer	.40	1.00
31 Jeremy Shockey	.30	.75
32 Peerless Price	.25	.60
33 Chad Johnson	.40	1.00
34 Tiki Barber	.40	1.00
35 Warrick Dunn	.30	.75
36 Jamal Lewis	.30	.75
37 Brian Westbrook	.40	1.00
38 Stephen Davis	.30	.75
39 Steve McNair	.40	1.00
40 Donovan McNabb	.40	1.00
41 Fred Taylor	.30	.75
42 Clinton Portis	.40	1.00
43 Santana Moss	.30	.75
44 Rod Smith	.30	.75
45 Josh McCown	.30	.75
46 Ray Lewis	.40	1.00
47 Marshall Faulk	.40	1.00
48 Eric Moulds	.30	.75
49 Jerry Rice	.75	2.00
50 Jake Delhomme	.30	.75
51 Tony Gonzalez	.40	1.00
52 Aaron Brooks	.30	.75
53 Randy McMichael	.25	.60
54 David Boston	.25	.60
55 Plaxico Burress	.30	.75
56 Rich Gannon	.30	.75
57 Brett Favre	1.00	2.50
58 Isaac Bruce	.30	.75
59 Tom Brady	.75	2.00
60 Priest Holmes	.40	1.00
61 Joe Horn	.30	.75
62 Troy Brown	.30	.75
63 Jake Plummer	.30	.75
64 Derrick Brooks	.30	.75
65 Marvin Harrison	.40	1.00
66 LaVar Arrington	.30	.75
67 Drew Bledsoe	.40	1.00
68 Steve Smith	.40	1.00
69 Peyton Manning	.75	2.00
70 Rex Grossman	.30	.75
71 Corey Dillon	.30	.75
72 Mike Alstott	.30	.75
73 Andre Johnson	.40	1.00
74 Joey Harrington	.30	.75
75 Tyrone Calico	.30	.75
76 Eli Manning RC	12.00	30.00
77 Larry Fitzgerald RC	5.00	12.00
78 Philip Rivers RC	8.00	20.00
79 Kellen Winslow RC	2.00	5.00
80 Roy Williams RC	2.00	5.00
81 Reggie Williams RC	1.50	4.00
82 Ben Roethlisberger RC	12.00	30.00
83 Lee Evans RC	2.00	5.00
84 Michael Clayton RC	1.50	4.00
85 J.P. Losman RC	1.50	4.00
86 Steven Jackson RC	3.00	8.00
87 Chris Perry RC	1.50	4.00
88 Michael Jenkins RC	2.00	5.00
89 Kevin Jones RC	1.50	4.00
90 Rashaun Woods RC	1.25	3.00
91 Ben Watson RC	2.00	5.00
92 Ben Troupe RC	1.50	4.00
93 Tatum Bell RC	1.50	4.00
94 Julius Jones RC	1.50	4.00
95 Devery Henderson RC	2.00	5.00
96 Darius Watts RC	1.25	3.00
97 Greg Jones RC	1.25	3.00
98 Keary Colbert RC	1.25	3.00
99 Derrick Hamilton RC	1.25	3.00
100 Bernard Berrian RC	2.00	5.00

2004 Fleer Inscribed Black Border Gold

*1-75 VETS: 2X TO 5X BASIC CARDS
*76-100 ROOKIES: .6X TO 1.5X BASIC CARDS
STATED PRINT RUN 199 SER.#'d SETS

2004 Fleer Inscribed Autographs Bronze

*BRONZE: .4X TO 1X SILVER AUTO
BRONZE STATED PRINT RUN 50-350

LF Larry Fitzgerald/50	40.00	80.00

2004 Fleer Inscribed Autographs Purple

STATED PRINT RUN 21-88

AB Antonio Bryant/88	8.00	20.00
DH Dante Hall/82	10.00	25.00
DS Donte Stallworth/83	10.00	25.00
KW Kelley Washington/87	8.00	20.00
WM Willis McGahee/21	12.00	30.00
CJ Chad Johnson/85	10.00	25.00

2004 Fleer Inscribed Autographs Silver

SILVER STATED PRINT RUN 100-450
*RED/25: 1X TO 2.5X SILVER/300-450
RED STATED PRINT RUN 25
*GOLD/300-450: .4X TO 1X SLVR/300-450

AB Antonio Bryant/300	8.00	20.00
DH Dante Hall/350	8.00	20.00
DS Donte Stallworth/450	6.00	15.00
JL J.P. Losman/100	10.00	25.00
LM Luke McCown/300	8.00	20.00
WM Willis McGahee/350	10.00	25.00

2004 Fleer Inscribed Award Winners

STATED PRINT RUN 150 SER.#'d SETS

1AW Randy Moss	2.00	5.00
2AW Ray Lewis	2.00	5.00
3AW Warrick Dunn	1.50	4.00
4AW Edgerrin James	1.50	4.00
5AW Brian Urlacher	2.00	5.00
6AW Derrick Brooks	1.50	4.00
7AW Tommy Maddox	1.50	4.00
8AW Marshall Faulk	2.00	5.00
9AW Priest Holmes	2.00	5.00
10AW Jevon Kearse	1.50	4.00
11AW Warren Sapp	1.50	4.00
12AW Michael Strahan	2.00	5.00
13AW Eddie George	1.50	4.00
14AW Clinton Portis	2.00	5.00
15AW Anquan Boldin	2.00	5.00

2004 Fleer Inscribed Award Winners Autographs

STATED PRINT RUN 100 SER.#'d SETS

AWAAB Anquan Boldin/100	10.00	25.00

2004 Fleer Inscribed Award Winners Autographs Notated

NOTATED STATED PRINT RUN 3-97

AWAWD Warrick Dunn/97	10.00	25.00

2004 Fleer Inscribed Award Winners Jersey Silver

SILVER PRINT RUN 175 SER.#'d SETS
*COPPER/75: .6X TO 1.5X SILVER/175
COPPER PRINT RUN 75 SER.#'d SETS
*PURPLE PATCH/49: .8X TO 2X SILVER/175
PURPLE PRINT RUN 49 SER.#'d SETS

AWJAB Anquan Boldin	4.00	10.00
AWJBU Brian Urlacher	4.00	10.00
AWJCP Clinton Portis	4.00	10.00
AWJDB Derrick Brooks	3.00	8.00
AWJEG Eddie George	3.00	8.00
AWJEJ Edgerrin James	3.00	8.00
AWJJK Jevon Kearse	3.00	8.00
AWJMF Marshall Faulk	4.00	10.00
AWJMS Michael Strahan	4.00	10.00
AWJPH Priest Holmes	4.00	10.00
AWJRL Ray Lewis	4.00	10.00
AWJRM Randy Moss	4.00	10.00
AWJTM Tommy Maddox	3.00	8.00
AWJWD Warrick Dunn	3.00	8.00
AWJWS Warren Sapp	3.00	8.00

2004 Fleer Inscribed Names of the Game

STATED PRINT RUN 299 SER.#'d SETS

1NG Priest Holmes	1.00	2.50
2NG LaDainian Tomlinson	1.00	2.50
3NG Donovan McNabb	1.00	2.50
4NG Deuce McAllister	.75	2.00
5NG Edgerrin James	.75	2.00
6NG Plaxico Burress	.75	2.00
7NG Jake Plummer	.75	2.00
8NG Steve McNair	1.00	2.50
9NG Boo Williams	.60	1.50
10NG Jevon Kearse	.75	2.00
11NG Tiki Barber	1.00	2.50
12NG Peyton Manning	2.00	5.00
13NG Peerless Price	.60	1.50
14NG Jerome Bettis	1.00	2.50
15NG Tom Brady	2.00	5.00
16NG Dante Hall	.75	2.00
17NG Randy Moss	1.00	2.50
18NG Emmitt Smith	2.50	6.00
19NG Ahman Green	.75	2.00
20NG Daunte Culpepper	.75	2.00
21NG Kellen Winslow Jr.	.75	2.00
22NG Terrell Owens	.75	2.00
23NG Larry Fitzgerald	2.00	5.00
24NG Eli Manning	5.00	12.00
25NG Dick Butkus	2.00	5.00
26NG Ken Stabler	2.00	5.00
27NG Paul Hornung	1.25	3.00
28NG Earl Campbell	1.00	2.50
29NG John Elway	4.00	10.00
30NG Dan Marino	5.00	12.00

2004 Fleer Inscribed Names of the Game Autographs

STATED PRINT RUN 99 SER.#'d SETS
*NOTATED/25: .5X TO 1.2X BASIC AU/99
NOTATED STATED PRINT RUN 25

NGADH Dante Hall	8.00	20.00
NGADM2 Deuce McAllister	8.00	20.00
NGADM3 Dan Marino	100.00	175.00
NGAEM Eli Manning	100.00	175.00
NGAJE John Elway	75.00	125.00

2004 Fleer Inscribed Names of the Game Jersey Copper

COPPER PRINT RUN 225 SER.#'d SETS
*GOLD/150: .5X TO 1.2X COPPER JSY
GOLD PRINT RUN 150 SER.#'d SETS
*PURPLE PATCH/33: 1X TO 2.5X COPPER
PURPLE PRINT RUN 33 SER.#'d SETS
*RED/79: .6X TO 1.5X COPPER JSY
RED PRINT RUN 79 SER.#'d SETS
*SILVER: .3X TO .8X COPPER JSY

NGJAG Ahman Green	3.00	8.00
NGJBW Boo Williams	2.50	6.00
NGJDC Daunte Culpepper	3.00	8.00
NGJDH Dante Hall	3.00	8.00
NGJDM Dan Marino	10.00	25.00
NGJDM2 Deuce McAllister	3.00	8.00
NGJDM3 Donovan McNabb	4.00	10.00
NGJEC Earl Campbell	5.00	12.00
NGJEJ Edgerrin James	3.00	8.00
NGJEM Eli Manning	12.00	30.00
NGJES Emmitt Smith	10.00	25.00
NGJJB Jerome Bettis	6.00	15.00
NGJJE John Elway	10.00	25.00
NGJJK Jevon Kearse	3.00	8.00
NGJJP Jake Plummer	3.00	8.00
NGJKS Ken Stabler	6.00	15.00
NGJKW Kellen Winslow Jr.	2.00	5.00
NGJLF Larry Fitzgerald	5.00	12.00
NGJLT LaDainian Tomlinson	4.00	10.00
NGJPB Plaxico Burress	3.00	8.00
NGJPH Paul Hornung	5.00	12.00
NGJPM Peyton Manning	8.00	20.00
NGJPP Peerless Price	2.50	6.00
NGJPH2 Priest Holmes	4.00	10.00
NGJRM Randy Moss	4.00	10.00
NGJSM Steve McNair	4.00	10.00
NGJTB Tiki Barber	4.00	10.00
NGJTO Terrell Owens	4.00	10.00
NGJTB2 Tom Brady	8.00	20.00

2004 Fleer Inscribed Valuable Players

STATED PRINT RUN 74-104

1VP Dan Marino/84	7.50	20.00
2VP John Elway/87	6.00	15.00
3VP Earl Campbell/79	2.00	5.00
4VP Emmitt Smith/93	4.00	10.00
5VP Ken Stabler/74	3.00	8.00
6VP Brett Favre/95	5.00	12.00
7VP Marshall Faulk/100	2.00	5.00
8VP Rich Gannon/103	1.25	3.00
9VP Steve McNair/104	2.00	5.00
10VP Peyton Manning/104	2.50	6.00

2004 Fleer Inscribed Valuable Players Autographs

STATED PRINT RUN 199 SER.#'d SETS
UNPRICED NOTATED PRINT RUN 9 SETS

VPADM Dan Marino	100.00	200.00
VPAJE John Elway	75.00	150.00

2004 Fleer Inscribed Valuable Players Jersey Blue

STATED PRINT RUN 74-104
UNPRICED MASTERPIECE PRINT RUN 1 SET

BF Brett Favre/95	15.00	40.00
DM Dan Marino/84	20.00	50.00
EC Earl Campbell/79	8.00	20.00
ES Emmitt Smith/93	15.00	40.00
JE John Elway/87	20.00	50.00
KS Ken Stabler/74	10.00	25.00
MF Marshall Faulk/100	6.00	15.00
PM Peyton Manning/104	12.00	30.00
RG Rich Gannon/103	5.00	12.00
SM Steve McNair/104	6.00	15.00

2001 Fleer Legacy

This 120 card set was released in December, 2001. It was issued in five card packs with an SRP of $4.99 per pack which came 24 to a box. Cards numbered 91-120 featured rookies and were serial numbered to 999. The first 300 of those rookie cards featured a "postmark" on them as part of an insert set.

COMP.SET w/o SP's (90) 10.00 25.00
91-120 ROOKIE PRINT RUN 999

1 Donovan McNabb	.30	.75
2 Doug Flutie	.30	.75
3 Amani Toomer	.25	.60
4 Jay Fiedler	.25	.60
5 Antonio Freeman	.30	.75
6 Jon Kitna	.25	.60
7 Jake Plummer	.25	.60
8 Ricky Watters	.25	.60
9 Jerry Rice	.60	1.50
10 Troy Brown	.25	.60
11 Jimmy Smith	.25	.60
12 Edgerrin James	.30	.75
13 Todd Pinkston	.20	.50
14 Eric Moulds	.25	.60
15 Stephen Davis	.25	.60
16 Matt Hasselbeck	.30	.75
17 Vinny Testaverde	.25	.60
18 Priest Holmes	.30	.75
19 Mike Anderson	.25	.60
20 Shane Matthews	.20	.50
21 Qadry Ismail	.25	.60
22 Torry Holt	.25	.60
23 Duce Staley	.25	.60
24 Ahman Green	.30	.75
25 Corey Dillon	.25	.60
26 Peerless Price	.20	.50
27 Steve McNair	.30	.75
28 Junior Seau	.30	.75
29 Doug Chapman	.20	.50
30 Mark Brunell	.25	.60
31 Joey Galloway	.25	.60
32 James Allen	.20	.50
33 David Boston	.20	.50
34 Marshall Faulk	.30	.75
35 Shaun Alexander	.30	.75
36 Wayne Chrebet	.25	.60
37 Randy Moss	.30	.75
38 Marvin Harrison	.30	.75
39 Tim Couch	.20	.50
40 Jamal Anderson	.25	.60
41 Warren Sapp	.25	.60
42 Brad Johnson	.25	.60
43 Kerry Collins	.25	.60
44 Derrick Alexander	.20	.50
45 Terrell Davis	.30	.75
46 Tiki Barber	.30	.75
47 Trent Green	.30	.75
48 James Stewart	.20	.50
49 Kevin Johnson	.20	.50
50 Ray Lewis	.30	.75
51 Warrick Dunn	.30	.75
52 Tim Brown	.30	.75
53 Daunte Culpepper	.25	.60
54 Fred Taylor	.30	.75
55 Brian Griese	.25	.60
56 Wesley Walls	.20	.50
57 Rob Johnson	.25	.60
58 Travis Taylor	.20	.50
59 Jeff Garcia	.25	.60
60 Rich Gannon	.25	.60
61 Cris Carter	.30	.75
62 Peyton Manning	.75	2.00
63 Peter Warrick	.25	.60
64 Terance Mathis	.20	.50
65 Kurt Warner	.50	1.25
66 Kordell Stewart	.25	.60
67 Aaron Brooks	.25	.60
68 JaJuan Dawson	.20	.50
69 Elvis Grbac	.25	.60
70 Keyshawn Johnson	.25	.60
71 Terrell Owens	.30	.75
72 Curtis Martin	.30	.75
73 Lamar Smith	.25	.60
74 Rod Smith	.25	.60
75 Tim Biakabutuka	.20	.50
76 Thomas Jones	.25	.60
77 Isaac Bruce	.30	.75
78 Joe Horn	.25	.60
79 Drew Bledsoe	.30	.75
80 Oronde Gadsden	.20	.50
81 Brett Favre	1.00	2.50
82 Emmitt Smith	.75	2.00
83 Muhsin Muhammad	.25	.60
84 Eddie George	.30	.75
85 Jerome Bettis	.30	.75
86 Ricky Williams	.30	.75
87 Tony Gonzalez	.30	.75
88 Germane Crowell	.20	.50
89 Brian Urlacher	.40	1.00
90 Shawn Jefferson	.20	.50
91 Michael Vick RC	10.00	25.00
92 David Terrell RC	2.00	5.00
93 Chris Chambers RC	2.50	6.00
94 Freddie Mitchell RC	1.50	4.00
95 Drew Brees RC	15.00	40.00
96 LaMont Jordan RC	2.50	6.00
97 Quincy Carter RC	2.00	5.00
98 Anthony Thomas RC	2.50	6.00
99 LaDainian Tomlinson RC	8.00	20.00
100 Santana Moss RC	3.00	8.00
101 Rod Gardner RC	2.00	5.00
102 Nick Goings RC	2.50	6.00
103 Sage Rosenfels RC	2.50	6.00
104 Mike McMahon RC	2.00	5.00
105 Snoop Minnis RC	1.50	4.00
106 Michael Bennett RC	2.00	5.00
107 Todd Heap RC	2.50	6.00
108 Kevan Barlow RC	2.00	5.00
109 Travis Henry RC	2.00	5.00
110 Jason Brookins RC	2.50	6.00
111 Rudi Johnson RC	2.50	6.00
112 Reggie Wayne RC	5.00	12.00
113 Koren Robinson RC	2.00	5.00
114 Chad Johnson RC	4.00	10.00
115 Quincy Morgan RC	2.00	5.00
116 Robert Ferguson RC	2.50	6.00
117 Chris Weinke RC	2.00	5.00
118 Jesse Palmer RC	2.00	5.00
119 James Jackson RC	1.50	4.00
120 Deuce McAllister RC	2.50	6.00

2001 Fleer Legacy Ultimate Legacy

*VETS 1-90: 3X TO 8X BASIC CARDS
*ROOKIES 91-120: .5X TO 1.2X
STATED PRINT RUN 250

2001 Fleer Legacy Rookie Postmarks

FIRST 300 SER.#'d RCs POSTMARKED
FIRST 100 #'d POSTMARKS WERE SIGNED

91 Michael Vick	12.00	30.00
92 David Terrell	2.50	6.00
93 Chris Chambers	3.00	8.00
94 Freddie Mitchell	2.00	5.00
95 Drew Brees	20.00	50.00
96 LaMont Jordan	3.00	8.00
97 Quincy Carter	2.50	6.00
98 Anthony Thomas	3.00	8.00
99 LaDainian Tomlinson	10.00	25.00
100 Santana Moss	4.00	10.00
101 Rod Gardner	2.50	6.00
102 Nick Goings	3.00	8.00
103 Sage Rosenfels	3.00	8.00
104 Mike McMahon	2.50	6.00
105 Snoop Minnis	2.00	5.00
106 Michael Bennett	2.50	6.00
107 Todd Heap	3.00	8.00
108 Kevan Barlow	2.50	6.00
109 Travis Henry	2.50	6.00
110 Jason Brookins	3.00	8.00
111 Rudi Johnson	3.00	8.00
112 Reggie Wayne	6.00	15.00
113 Koren Robinson	2.50	6.00
114 Chad Johnson	5.00	12.00
115 Quincy Morgan	2.50	6.00
116 Robert Ferguson	3.00	8.00
117 Chris Weinke	2.50	6.00
118 Jesse Palmer	2.50	6.00
119 James Jackson	2.00	5.00
120 Deuce McAllister	3.00	8.00

2001 Fleer Legacy Rookie Postmarks Autographs

FIRST 100 #'d POSTMARKS SIGNED

91 Michael Vick	125.00	200.00
92 David Terrell	8.00	20.00
93 Chris Chambers	10.00	25.00
95 Drew Brees	100.00	175.00
100 Santana Moss	12.00	30.00
103 Sage Rosenfels	10.00	25.00
104 Mike McMahon	8.00	20.00
106 Michael Bennett	8.00	20.00
108 Kevan Barlow	8.00	20.00
114 Chad Johnson	50.00	100.00
118 Jesse Palmer	8.00	20.00

2001 Fleer Legacy 1000 Yard Club Jerseys

STATED ODDS 1:115
OVERALL MEMORABILIA ODDS 1:12

BS Barry Sanders	15.00	40.00
CD Corey Dillon	5.00	12.00
CM Curtis Martin	6.00	15.00
DS Duce Staley	5.00	12.00
EJ Edgerrin James	6.00	15.00
FS Frank Sanders	4.00	10.00
FT Fred Taylor	6.00	15.00
IB Isaac Bruce	6.00	15.00
JA Jamal Anderson	5.00	12.00
JB Jerome Bettis	6.00	15.00
JL Jamal Lewis	6.00	15.00
MH Marvin Harrison	6.00	15.00
MR Marcus Robinson	5.00	12.00
RM Randy Moss	6.00	15.00
RS Rod Smith	5.00	12.00
SD Stephen Davis	5.00	12.00
TB Tiki Barber	6.00	15.00
TH Torry Holt	5.00	12.00
TO Terrell Owens	6.00	15.00
WC Wayne Chrebet	5.00	12.00
WD Warrick Dunn	6.00	15.00
EMC Ed McCaffrey	5.00	12.00
EMO Eric Moulds	5.00	12.00

2001 Fleer Legacy 1000 Yard Club Dual Jerseys

STATED PRINT RUN 400 SER.#'d SETS
OVERALL MEMORABILIA ODDS 1:12

BSRM Barry Sanders	15.00	40.00
Randy Moss		
CDTD Corey Dillon	6.00	15.00
Terrell Davis		
EGWD Eddie George	6.00	15.00
Warrick Dunn		
EMJS Ed McCaffrey	5.00	12.00
Jimmy Smith		
IBMR Isaac Bruce	6.00	15.00
Marcus Robinson		
IBTO Isaac Bruce	6.00	15.00
Terrell Owens		
JABS Jamal Anderson	15.00	40.00
Barry Sanders		
JBEJ Jerome Bettis	6.00	15.00
Edgerrin James		
JBFT Jerome Bettis	6.00	15.00
Fred Taylor		
MHIB Marvin Harrison	6.00	15.00
Isaac Bruce		
MHRS Marvin Harrison	6.00	15.00
Rod Smith		
MRMH Marcus Robinson	6.00	15.00
Marvin Harrison		
RSEM Rod Smith	5.00	12.00
Ed McCaffrey		
SDDS Stephen Davis	5.00	12.00
Duce Staley		
SDTD Stephen Davis	6.00	15.00
Terrell Davis		
SDWD Stephen Davis	6.00	15.00
Warrick Dunn		
TBEG Tiki Barber	6.00	15.00
Eddie George		
TBWD Tiki Barber	6.00	15.00
Warrick Dunn		
WCCM Wayne Chrebet	6.00	15.00
Curtis Martin		
WCJM Wayne Chrebet	5.00	12.00
Jimmy Smith		

2001 Fleer Legacy Game Issue 2nd Quarter

2ND QUARTER PRINT RUN 100
*1ST QUARTER: .4X TO 1X 2ND QUARTER
*3RD QUARTER/50: .5X TO 1.2X 2ND QRTR
3RD QUARTER PRINT RUN 50
*4TH QUARTER/25: 1X TO 2.5X 2ND QRTR
4TH QUARTER PRINT RUN 25
OVERALL MEMORABILIA ODDS 1:12

BF Brett Favre	20.00	50.00
BG Brian Griese	5.00	12.00
BJ Bo Jackson	10.00	25.00
CC Cris Carter	6.00	15.00
DB David Boston	4.00	10.00
DC Daunte Culpepper	5.00	12.00
DM Donovan McNabb	6.00	15.00
EJ Edgerrin James	6.00	15.00
GC Germane Crowell	4.00	10.00
JG Jeff Garcia	5.00	12.00
JP Jake Plummer	5.00	12.00
KJ Kevin Johnson	4.00	10.00
KS Kordell Stewart	5.00	12.00
KW Kurt Warner	10.00	25.00
MB Mark Brunell	5.00	12.00
RD Ron Dayne	5.00	12.00
RG Rich Gannon	5.00	12.00
RJ Rob Johnson	5.00	12.00
RL Ray Lewis	6.00	15.00
VT Vinny Testaverde	5.00	12.00

2001 Fleer Legacy Hall of Fame Material

STATED ODDS 1:288
OVERALL MEMORABILIA ODDS 1:12

BF Brett Favre	25.00	60.00
BJ Bo Jackson	12.00	30.00
DM Dan Marino	30.00	80.00
ES Emmitt Smith	25.00	60.00
JE John Elway	25.00	60.00
JR Jerry Rice	20.00	50.00
JS Junior Seau	8.00	20.00
MA Marcus Allen	10.00	25.00
MF Marshall Faulk	8.00	20.00
TA Troy Aikman	15.00	40.00

2001 Fleer Legacy Triple Threads

STATED ODDS 1:48
OVERALL MEMORABILIA ODDS 1:12

BBJ Kevan Barlow	6.00	15.00
Michael Bennett		
Rudi Johnson		
CGR Chris Chambers	6.00	15.00
Rod Gardner		
Koren Robinson		
CMF Chris Chambers	6.00	15.00
Snoop Minnis		
Robert Ferguson		
FWM Robert Ferguson	12.00	30.00
Reggie Wayne		
Marvin Minnis		
HCV Josh Heupel	25.00	60.00
Quincy Carter		
Michael Vick		
HMC Todd Heap	6.00	15.00
Quincy Morgan		
Chris Chambers		
HPT Josh Heupel	6.00	15.00
Jesse Palmer		
Marques Tuiasosopo		
HRH Josh Heupel	6.00	15.00
Sage Rosenfels		
Todd Heap		
HTJ Travis Henry	6.00	15.00
Anthony Thomas		
James Jackson		
JHM Chad Johnson	12.00	30.00
Todd Heap		
Santana Moss		
JJM Rudi Johnson	6.00	15.00
James Jackson		
Travis Minor		
MFM Quincy Morgan	6.00	15.00
Robert Ferguson		
Snoop Minnis		
MHB Travis Minor	5.00	12.00
Travis Henry		
Michael Bennett		
MJJ Deuce McAllister	12.00	30.00
Rudi Johnson		
Chad Johnson		
MMJ Santana Moss	12.00	30.00
Freddie Mitchell		
Chad Johnson		
MMT Deuce McAllister	6.00	15.00
Travis Minor		
Anthony Thomas		
MPW Mike McMahon	5.00	12.00
Jesse Palmer		
Chris Weinke		
MTR Mike McMahon	6.00	15.00
Marques Tuiasosopo		
Sage Rosenfels		
MWT Mike McMahon	5.00	12.00
Chris Weinke		
Marques Tuiasosopo		
PBR Jesse Palmer	25.00	60.00
Drew Brees		
Sage Rosenfels		
RMM Koren Robinson	5.00	12.00
Freddie Mitchell		
Quincy Morgan		
TBH LaDainian Tomlinson	25.00	60.00
Kevan Barlow		
Travis Henry		
TGW David Terrell	12.00	30.00
Rod Gardner		
Reggie Wayne		
TJB Anthony Thomas	6.00	15.00
James Jackson		
Kevan Barlow		
TMB LaDainian Tomlinson	25.00	60.00
Deuce McAllister		
Michael Bennett		
TMG David Terrell	5.00	12.00
Freddie Mitchell		
Rod Gardner		
VBC Michael Vick	25.00	60.00
Drew Brees		
Quincy Carter		
VTT Michael Vick	20.00	50.00
LaDainian Tomlinson		
David Terrell		
WBC Chris Weinke	25.00	60.00
Drew Brees		
Quincy Carter		
WMR Reggie Wayne	8.00	20.00
Santana Moss		
Koren Robinson		

2002 Fleer Maximum

This 290-card base set contains 250 veterans and 40 rookies. The rookies are divided into subsets: Maximum Rookie Home Whites sequentially numbered to 3500 and Maximum Rookie True Colors sequentially numbered to 3500.

COMP.SET w/o RC's (250) 10.00 25.00
251-290 ROOKIE PRINT RUN 3500

1 Tom Brady	.75	2.00
2 Kurt Warner	.30	.75
3 Mike McMahon	.20	.50
4 Ronney Jenkins	.20	.50
5 Tyrone Wheatley	.25	.60
6 Germane Crowell	.20	.50
7 James Jackson	.20	.50
8 Eric Metcalf	.20	.50
9 Muhsin Muhammad	.25	.60
10 Tony Richardson	.20	.50
11 Wayne Chrebet	.25	.60
12 Daunte Culpepper	.25	.60
13 Trent Dilfer	.25	.60
14 Kevin Dyson	.25	.60
15 Chris Fuamatu-Ma'afala	.20	.50
16 Dominic Rhodes	.25	.60
17 David Terrell	.20	.50
18 Rod Woodson	.30	.75
19 Anthony Wright	.20	.50
20 Jerome Bettis	.30	.75
21 Kendrell Bell	.20	.50
22 Edgerrin James	.25	.60
23 Jamal Lewis	.25	.60
24 Jim Miller	.20	.50

25 Warren Sapp	.25	.60
26 Clint Stoerner	.20	.50
27 Michael Strahan	.30	.75
28 Vinny Sutherland	.20	.50
29 Mike Alstott	.25	.60
30 Jay Fiedler	.25	.60
31 Willie Jackson	.20	.50
32 Earl Little RC	.25	.60
33 Robert Porcher	.20	.50
34 Junior Seau	.30	.75
35 Darrick Vaughn	.20	.50
36 Wesley Walls	.25	.60
37 Michael Westbrook	.20	.50
38 Freddie Mitchell	.20	.50
39 Drew Bledsoe	.30	.75
40 Gus Frerotte	.25	.60
41 Travis Henry	.20	.50
42 MarTay Jenkins	.20	.50
43 Curtis Keaton	.20	.50
44 Keenan McCardell	.25	.60
45 Neil O'Donnell	.25	.60
46 Chad Pennington	.30	.75
47 Charlie Rogers	.20	.50
48 Hines Ward	.30	.75
49 Jason Gildon	.25	.60
50 Travis Taylor	.20	.50
51 Dre Bly	.20	.50
52 Oronde Gadsden	.20	.50
53 Danny Wuerffel	.25	.60
54 Jamir Miller	.20	.50
55 Cory Schlesinger	.20	.50
56 LaDainian Tomlinson	.40	1.00
57 Michael Vick	.50	1.25
58 Chris Weinke	.20	.50
59 Brandon Stokley	.25	.60
60 James Allen	.20	.50
61 Correll Buckhalter	.25	.60
62 Jameel Cook	.20	.50
63 Deuce McAllister	.25	.60
64 Travis Minor	.20	.50
65 James Stewart	.20	.50
66 Kwamie Lassiter	.20	.50
67 Jamel White	.20	.50
68 Ronde Barber	.25	.60
69 Kevan Barlow	.20	.50
70 Marty Booker	.25	.60
71 Peter Boulware	.20	.50
72 Quincy Carter	.20	.50
73 Warrick Dunn	.25	.60
74 Brett Favre	.75	2.00
75 Chad Lewis	.20	.50
76 Jeff Ogden	.25	.60
77 Todd Sauerbrun	.20	.50
78 Ricky Williams	.25	.60
79 Charlie Batch	.20	.50
80 Courtney Brown	.20	.50
81 Stephen Davis	.25	.60
82 Fred Smoot	.25	.60
83 Marshall Faulk	.30	.75
84 Doug Flutie	.30	.75
85 Rich Gannon	.25	.60
86 Dante Hall	.25	.60
87 Frank Sanders	.20	.50
88 Antowain Smith	.25	.60
89 Tiki Barber	.30	.75
90 Fred Beasley	.20	.50
91 Jason Brookins	.20	.50
92 Rocket Ismail	.25	.60
93 Bubba Franks	.25	.60
94 Joey Galloway	.25	.60
95 Keyshawn Johnson	.25	.60
96 Donovan McNabb	.30	.75
97 Lamar Smith	.25	.60
98 Corey Bradford	.20	.50
99 Kerry Collins	.25	.60
100 Autry Denson	.20	.50
101 Antonio Freeman	.30	.75
102 Fred Taylor	.25	.60
103 Troy Hambrick	.20	.50
104 Brad Johnson	.25	.60
105 Brian Mitchell	.25	.60
106 Zach Thomas	.30	.75
107 Michael Bennett	.25	.60
108 Ron Dayne	.25	.60
109 Jeff Garcia	.25	.60
110 Ahman Green	.25	.60
111 Scotty Anderson	.20	.50
112 Qadry Ismail	.25	.60
113 Ed McCaffrey	.25	.60
114 Shaun King	.20	.50
115 Duce Staley	.25	.60
116 Travis Brown	.20	.50
117 Mark Brunell	.25	.60
118 Chris Cole	.20	.50
119 Aaron Glenn	.20	.50
120 Darrell Jackson	.25	.60
121 Jevon Kearse	.25	.60
122 Randy Moss	.30	.75
123 Hank Poteat	.20	.50
124 Brian Urlacher	.30	.75
125 Mike Anderson	.25	.60
126 David Akers	.20	.50
127 Laveranues Coles	.25	.60
128 Eddie George	.25	.60
129 J.J. Stokes	.20	.50
130 Matt Hasselbeck	.30	.75
131 Nate Jacquet	.20	.50
132 Anthony Thomas	.25	.60
133 Terrence Wilkins	.20	.50
134 Tim Couch	.20	.50
135 Ty Detmer	.25	.60
136 Rod Gardner	.20	.50
137 Charlie Garner	.25	.60
138 Terry Glenn	.25	.60
139 Az-Zahir Hakim	.20	.50
140 Donald Hayes	.20	.50
141 Priest Holmes	.30	.75
142 Jermaine Wiggins	.20	.50
143 Aaron Brooks	.25	.60
144 Alge Crumpler	.25	.60
145 Benjamin Gay	.20	.50
146 Marcellus Wiley	.20	.50
147 Torry Holt	.30	.75
148 Desmond Howard	.25	.60
149 Richard Huntley	.20	.50
150 Bryan Johnson RC	.25	.60
151 Terry Kirby	.20	.50
152 Snoop Minnis	.20	.50
153 David Boston	.20	.50
154 Shawn Bryson	.20	.50
155 Scott Covington	.20	.50
156 Terrell Davis	.30	.75
157 Damon Gibson	.20	.50
158 Curtis Martin	.30	.75
159 Derrick Mason	.25	.60
160 Jacquez Green	.20	.50
161 Chad Scott	.20	.50
162 Tony Boselli	.25	.60
163 Derrick Alexander	.20	.50
164 Ian Gold	.20	.50
165 Rob Johnson	.25	.60
166 Thomas Jones	.30	.75
167 Steve Smith	.30	.75
168 Jonathan Quinn	.20	.50
169 Mack Strong	.20	.50
170 Vinny Testaverde	.25	.60
171 Frank Wycheck	.20	.50
172 Amos Zereoue	.20	.50
173 Chris Chambers	.25	.60
174 Joe Horn	.25	.60
175 Kevin Johnson	.20	.50
176 Ryan McNeil	.20	.50
177 Marcus Pollard	.20	.50
178 Jerry Rice	.60	1.50
179 Jon Kitna	.25	.60
180 Maurice Smith	.20	.50
181 Jerome Pathon	.20	.50
182 Darrien Gordon	.20	.50
183 Champ Bailey	.30	.75
184 Drew Brees	.50	1.25
185 Troy Brown	.25	.60
186 Brian Griese	.25	.60
187 Jamal Anderson	.25	.60
188 Eric Moulds	.25	.60
189 Darnay Scott	.25	.60
190 Jimmy Smith	.25	.60
191 Ricky Watters	.25	.60
192 Craig Yeast	.20	.50
193 Michael Bates	.20	.50
194 Trung Canidate	.20	.50
195 David Dunn	.20	.50
196 Tim Dwight	.20	.50
197 Trent Green	.25	.60
198 David Patten	.20	.50
199 Jake Plummer	.25	.60
200 Rod Smith	.25	.60
201 Alex Van Pelt	.20	.50
202 Peter Warrick	.25	.60
203 Shaun Alexander	.25	.60
204 Plaxico Burress	.25	.60
205 Byron Chamberlain	.20	.50
206 Peyton Manning	.60	1.50
207 Marcus Robinson	.25	.60
208 Desmond Clark	.25	.60
209 Reggie Swinton	.20	.50
210 Amani Toomer	.25	.60
211 Karl Williams	.20	.50
212 Larry Centers	.25	.60
213 Corey Dillon	.25	.60
214 Jason Elam	.25	.60
215 Arnold Jackson	.20	.50
216 Stacey Mack	.20	.50
217 Steve McNair	.30	.75
218 Santana Moss	.25	.60
219 Koren Robinson	.20	.50
220 Kordell Stewart	.25	.60
221 Spergon Wynn	.20	.50
222 Todd Bouman	.20	.50
223 Marvin Harrison	.30	.75
224 Joe Jurevicius	.20	.50
225 Terry Allen	.25	.60
226 Jermaine Lewis	.20	.50
227 Terrell Owens	.30	.75
228 Shane Matthews	.20	.50
229 Emmitt Smith	.75	2.00
230 Jeremiah Trotter	.20	.50
231 Tony Banks	.20	.50
232 Tim Brown	.30	.75
233 Isaac Bruce	.30	.75
234 Curtis Conway	.25	.60
235 Marc Edwards	.20	.50
236 Tony Gonzalez	.30	.75
237 Deltha O'Neal	.20	.50
238 Michael Pittman	.25	.60
239 Peerless Price	.20	.50
240 Takeo Spikes	.20	.50
241 Charlie Clemons RC	.20	.50
242 Garrison Hearst	.25	.60
243 Ike Hilliard	.25	.60
244 Leonard Johnson	.20	.50
245 Chris Redman	.20	.50
246 Ray Lewis	.30	.75
247 John Lynch	.25	.60
248 Bill Schroeder	.20	.50
249 James Thrash	.25	.60
250 Chad Johnson	.30	.75
251 David Carr RC	1.00	2.50
252 Joey Harrington RC	1.00	2.50
253 DeShaun Foster RC	1.00	2.50
254 William Green RC	.75	2.00
255 Julius Peppers RC	2.00	5.00
256 Javon Walker RC	1.00	2.50
257 Ashley Lelie RC	.75	2.00
258 Adrian Peterson RC	1.00	2.50
259 Patrick Ramsey RC	1.00	2.50
260 Kurt Kittner RC	.60	1.50
261 Josh Reed RC	.75	2.00
262 David Garrard RC	1.25	3.00
263 Reche Caldwell RC	1.00	2.50
264 Quentin Jammer RC	1.00	2.50
265 Rohan Davey RC	1.00	2.50
266 Eric Crouch RC	1.00	2.50
267 Kahlil Hill RC	.60	1.50
268 Antwaan Randle El RC	1.00	2.50
269 Josh McCown RC	1.00	2.50
270 Maurice Morris RC	.75	2.00
271 Jeremy Shockey RC	1.50	4.00
272 Travis Stephens RC	.60	1.50
273 Jonathan Wells RC	1.00	2.50
274 Roy Williams RC	1.00	2.50
275 Brian Westbrook RC	1.50	4.00
276 Daniel Graham RC	.75	2.00
277 Marquise Walker RC	.60	1.50
278 Lamar Gordon RC	.75	2.00
279 Jason McAddley RC	.75	2.00
280 Jabar Gaffney RC	1.00	2.50
281 Luke Staley RC	.60	1.50
282 Clinton Portis RC	1.25	3.00
283 Cliff Russell RC	.60	1.50
284 Andre Davis RC	.75	2.00
285 Ron Johnson RC	.75	2.00
286 Ladell Betts RC	1.00	2.50
287 T.J. Duckett RC	1.00	2.50
288 Donte Stallworth RC	1.00	2.50
289 Antonio Bryant RC	1.00	2.50
290 Chad Hutchinson RC	.60	1.50

2002 Fleer Maximum To The Max

*VETS 1-250: 2.5X TO 6X BASIC CARDS
1-250 VETERAN PRINT RUN 250
*ROOKIES 251-290: 2X TO 5X
251-290 ROOKIE PRINT RUN 100

2002 Fleer Maximum Dressed to Thrill

STATED ODDS 1:16 HOB, 1:72 RET

1 Courtney Brown	2.50	6.00
2 Tim Brown	4.00	10.00
3 Mark Brunell	3.00	8.00
4 Plaxico Burress	3.00	8.00
5 Trung Canidate	2.50	6.00
6 Stephen Davis	3.00	8.00
7 Corey Dillon	3.00	8.00
8 Brett Favre	10.00	25.00
9 Rich Gannon	3.00	8.00
10 Tony Gonzalez	4.00	10.00
11 Marvin Harrison	4.00	10.00
12 Jevon Kearse	3.00	8.00
13 Donovan McNabb	4.00	10.00
14 Eric Moulds	3.00	8.00
15 Terrell Owens	4.00	10.00
16 Jerry Rice	8.00	20.00
17 Marcus Robinson	3.00	8.00
18 Warren Sapp	3.00	8.00
19 Ricky Williams	3.00	8.00
20 Vinny Testaverde	3.00	8.00
21 Zach Thomas	4.00	10.00
22 LaDainian Tomlinson	5.00	12.00
23 Peter Warrick	3.00	8.00

2002 Fleer Maximum Dressed to Thrill Nameplates

STATED PRINT RUN 100 SER.#'d SETS

1 Courtney Brown	5.00	12.00
2 Tim Brown	8.00	20.00
3 Trung Canidate	5.00	12.00
4 Corey Dillon	6.00	15.00
5 Brett Favre	20.00	50.00
6 Rich Gannon	6.00	15.00
7 Tony Gonzalez	8.00	20.00
8 Donovan McNabb	8.00	20.00
9 Terrell Owens	8.00	20.00
10 Warren Sapp	6.00	15.00
11 Vinny Testaverde	6.00	15.00
12 Zach Thomas	8.00	20.00
13 LaDainian Tomlinson	10.00	25.00
14 Peter Warrick	6.00	15.00
15 Ricky Williams	6.00	15.00

2002 Fleer Maximum Dressed to Thrill Numbers

STATED PRINT RUN 250 SER.#'d SETS

1 Jamal Anderson	5.00	12.00
2 Courtney Brown	4.00	10.00
3 Tim Brown	6.00	15.00
4 Mark Brunell	5.00	12.00
5 Trung Canidate	4.00	10.00
6 Corey Dillon	5.00	12.00
7 Brett Favre	15.00	40.00
8 Rich Gannon	5.00	12.00
9 Tony Gonzalez	6.00	15.00
10 Marvin Harrison	6.00	15.00
11 Jevon Kearse	5.00	12.00
12 Donovan McNabb	6.00	15.00
13 Terrell Owens	6.00	15.00
14 Jerry Rice	12.00	30.00
15 Marcus Robinson	5.00	12.00
16 Warren Sapp	5.00	12.00
17 Vinny Testaverde	5.00	12.00
18 Zach Thomas	6.00	15.00
19 LaDainian Tomlinson	8.00	20.00
20 Peter Warrick	5.00	12.00
21 Ricky Williams	5.00	12.00

2002 Fleer Maximum First and Ten

STATED PRINT RUN 25 SER.#'d SETS

1 AFC	125.00	250.00
Terrell Davis		
Ricky Williams		
Jerry Rice		
Edgerrin James		
Jamal Lewis		
Kordell Stewart		
Tim Couch		
Brian Griese		
Mark Brunell		
Rich Gannon		
2 NFC	150.00	300.00
Marshall Faulk		
Brett Favre		
Emmitt Smith		
Jeff Garcia		
Jake Plummer		
Randy Moss		
Brian Urlacher		
Daunte Culpepper		
Donovan McNabb		
Kurt Warner		

2002 Fleer Maximum K Corps

1-18 PRINT RUN 3040-4830
19-58 PRINT RUN 1003-1598

1 Kurt Warner/4830	1.00	2.50
2 Peyton Manning/4131	2.00	5.00
3 Brett Favre/3921	2.50	6.00
4 Aaron Brooks/3832	.75	2.00
5 Rich Gannon/3828	.75	2.00
6 Trent Green/3783	.75	2.00
7 Kerry Collins/3764	.75	2.00
8 Jake Plummer/3653	.75	2.00
9 Jeff Garcia/3538	.75	2.00
10 Doug Flutie/3464	1.00	2.50
11 Brad Johnson/3406	.75	2.00
12 Steve McNair/3350	1.00	2.50
13 Mark Brunell/3309	.75	2.00
14 Jay Fiedler/3290	.75	2.00
15 Donovan McNabb/3233	1.00	2.50
16 Jon Kitna/3216	.75	2.00
17 Kordell Stewart/3109	.75	2.00
18 Tim Couch/3040	.60	1.50
19 David Boston/1598	1.00	2.50
20 Priest Holmes/1555	1.50	4.00
21 Marvin Harrison/1524	1.50	4.00
22 Curtis Martin/1513	1.50	4.00
23 Stephen Davis/1432	1.25	3.00
24 Terrell Owens/1412	1.50	4.00
25 Ahman Green/1387	1.25	3.00
26 Marshall Faulk/1382	1.50	4.00
27 Jimmy Smith/1373	1.25	3.00
28 Torry Holt/1363	1.50	4.00
29 Rod Smith/1343	1.25	3.00
30 Shaun Alexander/1318	1.25	3.00
31 Corey Dillon/1315	1.25	3.00
32 Keyshawn Johnson/1266	1.25	3.00
33 Joe Horn/1265	1.25	3.00
34 Ricky Williams/1245	1.25	3.00
35 LaDainian Tomlinson/1236	2.00	5.00
36 Randy Moss/1233	1.50	4.00
37 Garrison Hearst/1206	1.25	3.00
38 Troy Brown/1199	1.25	3.00
39 Anthony Thomas/1183	1.25	3.00
40 Tim Brown/1199	1.50	4.00
41 Antowain Smith/1157	1.25	3.00
42 Johnnie Morton/1154	1.25	3.00
43 Jerry Rice/1139	3.00	8.00
44 Derrick Mason/1128	1.25	3.00
45 Curtis Conway/1125*	1.25	3.00
46 Keenan McCardell/1110	1.25	3.00
47 Isaac Bruce/1106	1.50	4.00
48 Dominic Rhodes/1104	1.25	3.00
49 Kevin Johnson/1097	1.00	2.50
50 Darrell Jackson/1081	1.25	3.00
51 Jerome Bettis/1072	1.50	4.00
52 Marty Booker/1071	1.25	3.00
53 Qadry Ismail/1059	1.25	3.00
54 Amani Toomer/1054	1.25	3.00
55 Willie Jackson/1046	1.00	2.50
56 Emmitt Smith/1021	4.00	10.00
57 Plaxico Burress/1008	1.25	3.00
58 Hines Ward/1003	1.50	4.00

2002 Fleer Maximum Playbook X's and O's

COMPLETE SET (20)	12.00	30.00
STATED ODDS 1:6 HOB, 1:8 RET		
1 Tom Brady	2.00	5.00
2 Tiki Barber	.75	2.00
3 Brian Griese	.60	1.50
4 Jake Plummer	.60	1.50
5 Chris Chambers	.60	1.50
6 Terrell Davis	.75	2.00
7 Daunte Culpepper	.60	1.50
8 Ron Dayne	.60	1.50
9 Cris Carter	.75	2.00
10 Jamal Lewis	.60	1.50
11 Duce Staley	.60	1.50
12 Brian Urlacher	.75	2.00
13 Edgerrin James	.60	1.50
14 Michael Vick	1.25	3.00
15 Drew Brees	1.25	3.00
16 Jerry Rice	1.50	4.00
17 Marshall Faulk	.75	2.00
18 Brett Favre	2.00	5.00
19 Jerome Bettis	.75	2.00
20 Kurt Warner	.75	2.00

2002 Fleer Maximum Playbook Xs Jerseys

X's JERSEY ODDS 1:24 HOB, 1:144 RET
*O's JSY/50: .8X TO 2X X's JSY
O's STATED PRINT RUN 50

1 Jerome Bettis	5.00	12.00
2 Drew Brees	8.00	20.00
3 Cris Carter	5.00	12.00
4 Daunte Culpepper	4.00	10.00
5 Ron Dayne	4.00	10.00
6 Marshall Faulk	5.00	12.00
7 Brett Favre	12.00	30.00
8 Brian Griese	4.00	10.00
9 Edgerrin James	4.00	10.00
10 Jamal Lewis	4.00	10.00
11 Jake Plummer	4.00	10.00
12 Jerry Rice	10.00	25.00
13 Duce Staley	4.00	10.00
14 Brian Urlacher	5.00	12.00
15 Kurt Warner	5.00	12.00

2002 Fleer Maximum Post Pattern

STATED ODDS 1:40 HOB, 1:72 RET

1 Edgerrin James	4.00	10.00
2 Marvin Harrison	5.00	12.00
3 Curtis Martin	5.00	12.00
4 Mark Brunell	4.00	10.00
5 Fred Taylor	4.00	10.00
6 Tim Brown	5.00	12.00
7 Randy Moss	5.00	12.00
8 Daunte Culpepper	4.00	10.00
9 Emmitt Smith	12.00	30.00
10 Steve McNair	5.00	12.00

1999 Fleer Mystique

Released as a 160-card set, 1999 Fleer Mystique is comprised of 100 veterans, 50 rookies which are sequentially numbered to 2999, and 10 star player cards which are sequentially numbered to 2500. Each pack contained one "covered" card which had to be peeled to reveal either a numbered insert/basic card or one of the few non-numbered base cards. Mystique was packaged in 24-pack boxes with each pack containing four cards and carried a suggested retail price of $4.99.

COMPLETE SET (160)	100.00	200.00
COMP.SHORT SET (100)	25.00	50.00
1 Terrell Davis SP	.60	1.50
2 Jerome Bettis SP	.60	1.50
3 J.J. Stokes	.25	.60
4 Frank Wycheck	.30	.75
5 O.J. McDuffie	.30	.75
6 Johnnie Morton	.30	.75
7 Marshall Faulk SP	.60	1.50
8 Ryan Leaf	.30	.75
9 Sean Dawkins	.25	.60
10 Brett Favre SP	2.00	5.00
11 Steve Young SP	.75	2.00
12 Jimmy Smith	.30	.75
13 Isaac Bruce	.40	1.00
14 Trent Dilfer	.30	.75
15 Brian Mitchell	.30	.75
16 Kordell Stewart SP	.50	1.25
17 Herman Moore	.30	.75
18 Troy Aikman SP	1.00	2.50
19 Cris Carter	.40	1.00
20 Barry Sanders SP	1.50	4.00
21 Tony Gonzalez	.40	1.00
22 Skip Hicks	.25	.60
23 Steve McNair SP	.60	1.50
24 Brad Johnson	.30	.75
25 Mark Chmura	.25	.60
26 Randall Cunningham SP	.60	1.50
27 Jerry Rice SP	1.25	3.00
28 Jamie Asher	.25	.60
29 Brian Griese SP	.50	1.25
30 Peyton Manning SP	2.00	5.00
31 Keith Poole	.25	.60
32 Wayne Chrebet	.30	.75
33 Rich Gannon	.30	.75
34 Michael Irvin	.40	1.00
35 Yancey Thigpen	.25	.60
36 Corey Dillon	.30	.75
37 Steve Beuerlein	.30	.75
38 Terry Kirby	.25	.60
39 Jacquez Green	.25	.60
40 Mark Brunell SP	.50	1.25
41 Rickey Dudley	.25	.60
42 Shannon Sharpe	.40	1.00
43 Andre Rison	.30	.75
44 Chris Chandler	.30	.75
45 Fred Taylor SP	.50	1.25
46 Kerry Collins	.30	.75
47 Antowain Smith SP	.40	1.00
48 Wesley Walls	.30	.75
49 Rob Moore	.25	.60
50 Dan Marino SP	2.00	5.00
51 Robert Smith	.30	.75
52 Keenan McCardell	.30	.75
53 Joey Galloway	.30	.75
54 Fred Lane	.25	.60
55 Napoleon Kaufman	.25	.60
56 Curtis Martin	.40	1.00
57 Rod Smith	.30	.75
58 Curtis Conway	.30	.75
59 Kevin Dyson	.25	.60
60 Warrick Dunn SP	.50	1.25
61 Ahman Green	.30	.75
62 Duce Staley	.30	.75
63 Emmitt Smith SP	1.50	4.00
64 Adrian Murrell	.30	.75
65 Dorsey Levens	.30	.75
66 Drew Bledsoe SP	.60	1.50
67 Ed McCaffrey	.30	.75
68 Natrone Means	.30	.75
69 Deion Sanders	.40	1.00
70 Keyshawn Johnson SP	.50	1.25
71 Antonio Freeman	.30	.75
72 James Stewart	.25	.60
73 Ben Coates	.30	.75
74 Priest Holmes	.40	1.00
75 Jake Reed	.30	.75
76 Mike Alstott	.40	1.00
77 Vinny Testaverde	.30	.75
78 Ricky Watters	.30	.75
79 Garrison Hearst	.30	.75
80 Junior Seau	.40	1.00
81 Tim Brown	.40	1.00
82 Jamal Anderson	.30	.75
83 Robert Brooks	.30	.75
84 Marc Edwards	.30	.75
85 Curtis Enis	.25	.60
86 Doug Flutie	.40	1.00
87 Terry Glenn	.30	.75
88 Charlie Batch SP	.50	1.25
89 Marvin Harrison	.40	1.00
90 Jake Plummer SP	.50	1.25
91 Terrell Owens	.40	1.00
92 Scott Mitchell	.25	.60
93 Tim Dwight	.30	.75
94 Eddie George SP	.50	1.25
95 Ike Hilliard	.30	.75
96 Robert Holcombe	.25	.60
97 Charles Johnson	.25	.60
98 Eric Moulds	.30	.75
99 Michael Westbrook	.25	.60
100 Randy Moss SP	.60	1.50
101 Tim Couch RC	2.00	5.00
102 Donovan McNabb RC	8.00	20.00
103 Akili Smith RC	1.50	4.00
104 Cade McNown RC	1.50	4.00
105 Daunte Culpepper RC	2.00	5.00
106 Ricky Williams RC	3.00	8.00
107 Edgerrin James RC	2.50	6.00
108 Kevin Faulk RC	2.00	5.00
109 Torry Holt RC	3.00	8.00
110 David Boston RC	1.50	4.00
111 Chris Claiborne RC	1.25	3.00
112 Mike Cloud RC	1.25	3.00
113 Joe Germaine RC	1.50	4.00
114 Cecil Collins RC	1.25	3.00
115 Tim Alexander RC	1.25	3.00
116 Brandon Stokley RC	2.00	5.00
117 Lamarr Glenn RC	1.25	3.00
118 Shawn Bryson RC	1.25	3.00
119 Jeff Paulk RC	1.25	3.00
120 Kevin Johnson RC	1.50	4.00
121 Charlie Rogers RC	1.25	3.00
122 Joe Montgomery RC	1.25	3.00
123 Travis McGriff RC	1.25	3.00
124 Dee Miller RC	1.25	3.00
125 Rob Konrad RC	1.25	3.00
126 Peerless Price RC	1.50	4.00
127 D'Wayne Bates RC	1.25	3.00
128 Craig Yeast RC	1.25	3.00
129 Malcolm Johnson RC	1.25	3.00
130 Brock Huard RC	1.50	4.00
131 Sedrick Irvin RC	1.25	3.00
132 Troy Smith RC	1.50	4.00
133 Troy Edwards RC	1.50	4.00
134 Al Wilson RC	2.00	5.00
135 Terry Jackson RC	1.25	3.00
136 Dameane Douglas RC	1.25	3.00
137 Amos Zereoue RC	1.50	4.00
138 Shaun King RC	1.50	4.00
139 James Johnson RC	1.25	3.00
140 Jermaine Fazande RC	1.25	3.00
141 Autry Denson RC	1.25	3.00
142 Darran Hall RC	1.25	3.00
143 Na Brown RC	1.25	3.00
144 Mike Lucky RC	1.25	3.00
145 Karsten Bailey RC	1.25	3.00
146 Kevin Daft RC	1.25	3.00
147 Sean Bennett RC	1.25	3.00
148 Madre Hill RC	1.25	3.00
149 Michael Bishop RC	1.50	4.00
150 Scott Covington RC	1.25	3.00
151 Randy Moss STAR	1.50	4.00
152 Fred Taylor STAR	1.25	3.00
153 Brett Favre STAR	5.00	12.00
154 Dan Marino STAR	5.00	12.00
155 Terrell Davis STAR	1.50	4.00
156 Barry Sanders STAR	4.00	10.00
157 Emmitt Smith STAR	4.00	10.00
158 Jake Plummer STAR	1.25	3.00
159 Warrick Dunn STAR	1.25	3.00
160 Troy Aikman STAR	2.50	6.00
P86 Doug Flutie Promo	.50	1.25

1999 Fleer Mystique Gold

COMPLETE SET (100)	150.00	300.00

*GOLD STARS: 2X TO 5X BASE CARDS
*GOLD SPs: 2.5X TO 6X BASIC CARDS
GOLDS RANDOM INSERTS IN PACKS

1999 Fleer Mystique Feel the Game

COMPLETE SET (10)	150.00	300.00
1 Terrell Davis/545	10.00	25.00
2 Charles Johnson/325	8.00	20.00
3 Jon Kitna/640	6.00	15.00
4 Dorsey Levens/515	6.00	15.00
5 Dan Marino Sock/220	30.00	80.00
6 Curtis Martin/690	10.00	25.00
7 Johnnie Morton/580	6.00	15.00
8 Randy Moss/510	15.00	40.00
9 Brandon Stokley Glove/85	15.00	40.00
10 Steve Young/580	20.00	40.00

1999 Fleer Mystique Fresh Ink

STATED PRINT RUN 45-750

1 Charlie Batch/250	7.50	20.00
2 Mark Brunell/45	30.00	60.00
3 Shawn Bryson/650	5.00	12.00
4 Cecil Collins/725	5.00	12.00
5 Daunte Culpepper/300	12.00	30.00
6 Randall Cunningham/200	15.00	40.00
7 Terrell Davis/50	40.00	80.00
8 Sean Dawkins/700	5.00	12.00
9 Corey Dillon/250	10.00	25.00
10 Dameane Douglas/750	5.00	12.00
11 Tim Dwight/725	7.50	20.00
12 Troy Edwards/200	7.50	20.00
13 Doug Flutie/250	15.00	40.00
14 Eddie George/250	10.00	25.00
15 Joe Germaine/575	5.00	12.00
16 Trent Green/350	10.00	25.00
17 Torry Holt/350	12.00	30.00
18 Brock Huard/700	7.50	20.00
19 Edgerrin James/150	15.00	40.00
20 Brad Johnson/300	10.00	25.00
21 Jon Kitna/350	10.00	25.00
22 Peyton Manning/250	60.00	120.00
23 Randy Moss/150	30.00	80.00
24 Doug Pederson/750	5.00	12.00
25 Jake Plummer/300	7.50	20.00
26 Peerless Price/675	7.50	20.00
27 Akili Smith/100	5.00	12.00
28 Emmitt Smith/125	100.00	175.00
29 Antowain Smith/150	10.00	25.00
30 Ricky Williams/150	12.00	30.00

1999 Fleer Mystique NFL 2000

COMPLETE SET (10)	20.00	40.00
STATED PRINT RUN 999 SER.#'d SETS		
1N Peyton Manning	6.00	15.00
2N Ryan Leaf	.75	2.00
3N Charlie Batch	2.00	5.00
4N Fred Taylor	2.00	5.00
5N Keyshawn Johnson	1.25	3.00
6N J.J. Stokes	1.25	3.00
7N Jake Plummer	1.25	3.00
8N Brian Griese	2.00	5.00
9N Antowain Smith	1.25	3.00
10N Jamal Anderson	1.25	3.00

1999 Fleer Mystique Protential

COMPLETE SET (10)	30.00	60.00
STATED PRINT RUN 1999 SER.#'d SETS		
1PT Tim Couch	2.00	5.00
2PT Donovan McNabb	6.00	15.00
3PT Akili Smith	2.00	5.00
4PT Cade McNown	2.00	5.00
5PT Daunte Culpepper	5.00	12.00
6PT Ricky Williams	2.50	6.00
7PT Edgerrin James	5.00	12.00
8PT Kevin Faulk	2.00	5.00
9PT Torry Holt	3.00	8.00
10PT David Boston	2.00	5.00

1999 Fleer Mystique Star Power

COMPLETE SET (10)	150.00	300.00
STATED PRINT RUN 100 SER.#'d SETS		
1SP Randy Moss	20.00	50.00
2SP Warrick Dunn	8.00	20.00
3SP Mark Brunell	6.00	15.00
4SP Emmitt Smith	15.00	40.00
5SP Eddie George	8.00	20.00
6SP Barry Sanders	25.00	60.00
7SP Terrell Davis	8.00	20.00
8SP Dan Marino	25.00	60.00
9SP Troy Aikman	15.00	40.00
10SP Brett Favre	25.00	60.00

2000 Fleer Mystique

Released as a 145-card set, Fleer Mystique is comprised of 100 veteran cards and 45 rookie cards sequentially numbered to 2000. Base cards are all foil and feature full color action photography with the word mystique appearing behind the player in silver foil. All inserts and rookie cards were produced with an opaque covering that needed to be peeled to reveal the card. Mystique was packaged in 20-pack boxes with packs containing five cards and carried a suggested retail price of $4.99.

COMPLETE SET (145)	125.00	250.00
COMP.SET w/o SP's (100)	6.00	15.00
1 Tim Couch	.25	.60
2 Edgerrin James	.30	.75
3 Terrell Davis	.30	.75
4 Eddie George	.25	.60
5 Jevon Kearse	.25	.60
6 Mike Alstott	.30	.75
7 Tony Martin	.25	.60
8 Jermaine Fazande	.20	.50
9 Akili Smith	.20	.50
10 Damon Huard	.25	.60
11 Kordell Stewart	.25	.60
12 Peyton Manning	.75	2.00
13 Michael Westbrook	.20	.50
14 Tim Biakabutuka	.25	.60
15 Curtis Martin	.30	.75
16 Shaun King	.20	.50
17 Jamal Anderson	.25	.60
18 Terry Allen	.25	.60
19 Sean Dawkins	.20	.50
20 Muhsin Muhammad	.25	.60
21 Vinny Testaverde	.25	.60
22 Warren Sapp	.25	.60
23 Wesley Walls	.20	.50
24 Mark Brunell	.25	.60
25 Tim Brown	.30	.75
26 Kevin Dyson	.25	.60
27 Curtis Enis	.20	.50
28 Keenan McCardell	.25	.60
29 Rich Gannon	.25	.60
30 Jermaine Lewis	.20	.50
31 Johnnie Morton	.25	.60
32 Kerry Collins	.25	.60
33 Az-Zahir Hakim	.20	.50
34 Cade McNown	.20	.50
35 Jimmy Smith	.25	.60
36 Tyrone Wheatley	.20	.50
37 Marcus Robinson	.25	.60
38 Fred Taylor	.30	.75
39 Donovan McNabb	.30	.75
40 Steve McNair	.30	.75
41 Corey Dillon	.25	.60
42 Tony Gonzalez	.30	.75
43 Duce Staley	.25	.60
44 Albert Connell	.20	.50
45 Isaac Bruce	.30	.75
46 Troy Aikman	.50	1.25
47 Charlie Garner	.25	.60
48 Kevin Johnson	.20	.50
49 Cris Carter	.30	.75
50 Ryan Leaf	.25	.60
51 Doug Flutie	.30	.75
52 Brett Favre	1.00	2.50
53 Joe Montgomery	.20	.50
54 Torry Holt	.30	.75
55 Jonathan Linton	.20	.50
56 Antonio Freeman	.25	.60
57 Amani Toomer	.25	.60
58 Kurt Warner	.50	1.25
59 Jake Plummer	.25	.60
60 Rob Johnson	.25	.60
61 Randy Moss	.30	.75
62 Jerry Rice	.60	1.50
63 Chris Chandler	.25	.60
64 Joey Galloway	.25	.60
65 Olandis Gary	.25	.60
66 Drew Bledsoe	.30	.75
67 Steve Beuerlein	.25	.60
68 Marvin Harrison	.30	.75
69 Keyshawn Johnson	.25	.60
70 Warrick Dunn	.25	.60
71 Tim Dwight	.25	.60
72 Brian Griese	.25	.60
73 Terry Glenn	.25	.60
74 Jon Kitna	.25	.60
75 Qadry Ismail	.25	.60
76 Germane Crowell	.20	.50
77 Ricky Williams	.30	.75
78 Marshall Faulk	.30	.75
79 Karim Abdul-Jabbar	.20	.50
80 James Johnson	.20	.50
81 Hines Ward	.30	.75
82 Frank Sanders	.20	.50
83 Emmitt Smith	.75	2.00
84 Robert Smith	.25	.60
85 Steve Young	.40	1.00
86 Darnay Scott	.25	.60
87 Tamarick Vanover	.20	.50
88 Troy Edwards	.20	.50
89 Brad Johnson	.25	.60
90 Tony Banks	.20	.50
91 Charlie Batch	.25	.60
92 Jeff Blake	.25	.60
93 Ricky Watters	.25	.60
94 Carl Pickens	.25	.60
95 Elvis Grbac	.20	.50
96 Jerome Bettis	.30	.75
97 Eric Moulds	.25	.60
98 Dorsey Levens	.25	.60
99 Wayne Chrebet	.25	.60
100 Stephen Davis	.25	.60
101 Shaun Alexander RC	2.00	5.00
102 Sebastian Janikowski RC	1.50	4.00
103 Tom Brady RC	60.00	120.00
104 Courtney Brown RC	1.25	3.00
105 Marc Bulger RC	1.50	4.00
106 Plaxico Burress RC	1.50	4.00
107 Trung Canidate RC	1.25	3.00
108 Giovanni Carmazzi RC	1.00	2.50
109 Trevor Gaylor RC	1.00	2.50
110 Laveranues Coles RC	1.50	4.00
111 Ron Dayne RC	1.50	4.00
112 Reuben Droughns RC	1.50	4.00
113 Danny Farmer RC	1.00	2.50
114 Chafie Fields RC	1.00	2.50
115 Bubba Franks RC	1.50	4.00
116 Sherrod Gideon RC	1.00	2.50
117 Joe Hamilton RC	1.00	2.50
118 Chris Cole RC	1.25	3.00
119 Darrell Jackson RC	1.25	3.00
120 Thomas Jones RC	2.00	5.00
121 Jamal Lewis RC	1.50	4.00
122 Anthony Lucas RC	1.00	2.50
123 Tee Martin RC	1.50	4.00
124 Frank Murphy RC	1.00	2.50
125 Rondell Mealey RC	1.00	2.50
126 Sylvester Morris RC	1.00	2.50
127 Dennis Northcutt RC	1.25	3.00
128 Chad Pennington RC	2.50	6.00
129 Travis Prentice RC	1.25	3.00
130 Tim Rattay RC	1.25	3.00
131 Chris Redman RC	1.25	3.00
132 J.R. Redmond RC	1.00	2.50
133 R.Jay Soward RC	1.00	2.50
134 Quinton Spotwood RC	1.00	2.50
135 Shyrone Stith RC	1.00	2.50
136 Travis Taylor RC	1.25	3.00
137 Troy Walters RC	1.00	2.50
138 Peter Warrick RC	1.50	4.00
139 Dez White RC	1.25	3.00
140 Michael Wiley RC	1.00	2.50
141 Jerry Porter RC	1.50	4.00
142 Mareno Philyaw RC	1.00	2.50
143 Anthony Becht RC	1.25	3.00
144 JaJuan Dawson RC	1.00	2.50
145 Ron Dugans RC	1.00	2.50

2000 Fleer Mystique Gold

*VETS 1-100: 1.5X TO 4X BASIC CARDS
*ROOKIES 101-145: .4X TO 1X
GOLD STATED ODDS 1:20

103 Tom Brady	75.00	135.00

2000 Fleer Mystique Big Buzz

COMPLETE SET (10)	6.00	15.00
STATED ODDS 1:10		
1 Peter Warrick	.50	1.25
2 Shaun Alexander	.60	1.50
3 Ron Dayne	.50	1.25
4 Joe Hamilton	.30	.75
5 Thomas Jones	.60	1.50
6 Jamal Lewis	.50	1.25
7 Chad Pennington	.75	2.00
8 Tim Rattay	.40	1.00
9 Chris Redman	.40	1.00
10 Plaxico Burress	.50	1.25

2000 Fleer Mystique Canton Calling

COMPLETE SET (10) 10.00 25.00
STATED ODDS 1:20
1 Jerry Rice 1.50 4.00
2 Troy Aikman 1.25 3.00
3 Dan Marino 2.50 6.00
4 Brett Favre 2.50 6.00
5 Peyton Manning 2.00 5.00
6 Emmitt Smith 2.00 5.00
7 Randy Moss .75 2.00
8 Marvin Harrison .75 2.00
9 Marshall Faulk .75 2.00
10 Thurman Thomas .75 2.00

2000 Fleer Mystique Destination Tampa

COMPLETE SET (10) 6.00 15.00
STATED ODDS 1:10
1 Kurt Warner .75 2.00
2 Peyton Manning 1.25 3.00
3 Brett Favre 1.50 4.00
4 Tim Couch .40 1.00
5 Keyshawn Johnson .40 1.00
6 Mark Brunell .40 1.00
7 Eddie George .40 1.00
8 Edgerrin James .50 1.25
9 Ricky Williams .50 1.25
10 Randy Moss .50 1.25

2000 Fleer Mystique Numbers Game

COMPLETE SET (10) 15.00 40.00
STATED ODDS 1:40
*RED ZONE/100: 1.5X TO 4X BASIC INSERTS
RED ZONE PRINT RUN 100
1 Kurt Warner 2.00 5.00
2 Peyton Manning 3.00 8.00
3 Keyshawn Johnson 1.00 2.50
4 Terrell Davis 1.25 3.00
5 Brett Favre 4.00 10.00
6 Jevon Kearse 1.00 2.50
7 Troy Aikman 2.00 5.00
8 Edgerrin James 1.25 3.00
9 Eddie George 1.00 2.50
10 Marshall Faulk 1.25 3.00

2000 Fleer Mystique Running Men

COMPLETE SET (20) 5.00 12.00
STATED ODDS 1:5
1 Antowain Smith .40 1.00
2 Corey Dillon .40 1.00
3 Terrell Davis .50 1.25
4 Edgerrin James .50 1.25
5 Fred Taylor .50 1.25
6 Kevin Faulk .40 1.00
7 Jerome Bettis .50 1.25
8 Ricky Watters .40 1.00
9 Eddie George .40 1.00
10 Jamal Anderson .40 1.00
11 Tim Biakabutuka .40 1.00
12 Curtis Enis .30 .75
13 Emmitt Smith 1.25 3.00
14 James Stewart .30 .75
15 Dorsey Levens .40 1.00
16 Robert Smith .40 1.00
17 Duce Staley .40 1.00
18 Marshall Faulk .50 1.25
19 Stephen Davis .40 1.00
20 Mike Alstott .50 1.25

2003 Fleer Mystique

Released in September of 2003, this set consists of 130 cards including 80 veterans and 50 rookies. The rookies were serial numbered to 699, and were inserted into packs at a rate of 1:15. Boxes contained 20 packs of 4 cards, with one pack containing a sealed mystery pack. Pack SRP was $5.99.

COMP. SET w/o SP's (80) 12.00 30.00
81-130 ROOKIE/699 ODDS 1:15
1 Emmitt Smith 1.00 2.50
2 Marcel Shipp .25 .60
3 Michael Vick .50 1.25
4 Warrick Dunn .30 .75
5 T.J. Duckett .30 .75
6 Peerless Price .25 .60
7 Ray Lewis .40 1.00
8 Todd Heap .30 .75
9 Jamal Lewis .30 .75
10 Eric Moulds .30 .75
11 Drew Bledsoe .40 1.00
12 Travis Henry .25 .60
13 Stephen Davis .30 .75
14 Julius Peppers .40 1.00
15 Marty Booker .30 .75
16 Brian Urlacher .40 1.00
17 Chad Johnson .40 1.00
18 Corey Dillon .30 .75
19 William Green .25 .60
20 Tim Couch .25 .60
21 Joey Galloway .30 .75
22 Chad Hutchinson .25 .60
23 Jake Plummer .30 .75
24 Ed McCaffrey .30 .75
25 Clinton Portis .30 .75
26 Joey Harrington .25 .60
27 Ahman Green .30 .75
28 Brett Favre 1.00 2.50
29 Jabar Gaffney .25 .60
30 David Carr .30 .75
31 Peyton Manning .75 2.00
32 Marvin Harrison .40 1.00
33 Edgerrin James .40 1.00
34 Mark Brunell .30 .75
35 Fred Taylor .30 .75
36 Trent Green .30 .75
37 Priest Holmes .40 1.00
38 Tony Gonzalez .40 1.00
39 Chris Chambers .30 .75
40 Zach Thomas .40 1.00
41 Ricky Williams .30 .75
42 Michael Bennett .30 .75
43 Daunte Culpepper .30 .75
44 Randy Moss .40 1.00
45 Deion Branch .30 .75
46 Tom Brady 1.00 2.50
47 Aaron Brooks .30 .75
48 Deuce McAllister .30 .75
49 Joe Horn .30 .75
50 Jeremy Shockey .40 1.00
51 Amani Toomer .30 .75
52 Tiki Barber .40 1.00
53 Chad Pennington .40 1.00
54 Curtis Martin .40 1.00
55 Rich Gannon .30 .75
56 Tim Brown .40 1.00
57 Jerry Rice .75 2.00
58 Donovan McNabb .40 1.00
59 Duce Staley .30 .75
60 Hines Ward .40 1.00
61 Tommy Maddox .30 .75
62 Plaxico Burress .30 .75
63 Jerome Bettis .40 1.00
64 David Boston .25 .60
65 Drew Brees .40 1.00
66 LaDainian Tomlinson .40 1.00
67 Jeff Garcia .30 .75
68 Terrell Owens .40 1.00
69 Koren Robinson .30 .75
70 Shaun Alexander .30 .75
71 Kurt Warner .40 1.00
72 Torry Holt .40 1.00
73 Marshall Faulk .40 1.00
74 Keyshawn Johnson .40 1.00
75 Mike Alstott .40 1.00
76 Warren Sapp .30 .75
77 Steve McNair .40 1.00
78 Eddie George .30 .75
79 Patrick Ramsey .30 .75
80 Rod Gardner .25 .60
81 Bennie Joppru RC 1.25 3.00
82 Musa Smith RC 1.25 3.00
83 Ken Dorsey RC 1.50 4.00
84 Billy McMullen RC 1.25 3.00
85 Bethel Johnson RC 1.25 3.00
86 Terence Newman RC 1.50 4.00
87 Jason Witten RC 5.00 12.00
88 Jimmy Kennedy RC 1.50 4.00
89 Johnathan Sullivan RC 1.25 3.00
90 Chris Simms RC 2.00 5.00
91 Brian St.Pierre RC 1.50 4.00
92 Quentin Griffin RC 1.50 4.00
93 Tyrone Calico RC 1.50 4.00
94 DeWayne Robertson RC 1.50 4.00
95 Bryant Johnson RC 2.00 5.00
96 Charles Rogers RC 1.50 4.00
97 William Joseph RC 1.25 3.00
98 Dallas Clark RC 3.00 8.00
99 Michael Haynes RC 1.25 3.00
100 Larry Johnson RC 2.00 5.00
101 Terrell Suggs RC 2.00 5.00
102 Marcus Trufant RC 1.50 4.00
103 Dave Ragone RC 1.25 3.00
104 Seneca Wallace RC 2.00 5.00
105 Willis McGahee RC 2.50 6.00
106 Andre Woolfolk RC 1.50 4.00
107 LaBrandon Toefield RC 1.50 4.00
108 Andre Johnson RC 5.00 12.00
109 Lee Suggs RC 1.50 4.00
110 Brandon Lloyd RC 3.00 8.00
111 Kyle Boller RC 2.00 5.00
112 B.J. Askew RC 1.50 4.00
113 Anquan Boldin RC 3.00 8.00
114 Kelley Washington RC 1.25 3.00
115 Kevin Williams RC 2.00 5.00
116 Kliff Kingsbury RC 1.50 4.00
117 Jerome McDougle RC 1.25 3.00
118 L.J. Smith RC 2.00 5.00
119 J.R. Tolver RC 1.50 4.00
120 Carson Palmer RC 4.00 10.00
121 Kevin Curtis RC 2.00 5.00
122 Shaun McDonald RC 1.50 4.00
123 Byron Leftwich RC 2.00 5.00
124 Bobby Wade RC 1.50 4.00
125 Nate Burleson RC 1.50 4.00
126 Justin Fargas RC 2.00 5.00
127 DeWayne White RC 1.25 3.00
128 Taylor Jacobs RC 1.25 3.00
129 Rex Grossman RC 2.00 5.00
130 Boss Bailey RC 1.50 4.00
P28 Brett Favre PROMO 1.00 2.50
P41 Ricky Williams PROMO .50 1.25
P123 Byron Leftwich PROMO .75 2.00

2003 Fleer Mystique Gold

*1-80 VETS/150: 4X TO 10X BASIC CARDS
1-80 VET STATED PRINT RUN 150
*81-130 ROOKIES: .8X TO 2X
81-130 ROOKIE PRINT RUN 75
OVERALL STATED ODDS 1:15

2003 Fleer Mystique Rookie Blue

*ROOKIES: .5X TO 1.2X BASIC CARDS
STATED PRINT RUN 350 SER.#'d SETS

2003 Fleer Mystique Awe Pairs

COMPLETE SET (20) 25.00 60.00
STATED PRINT RUN 250 SER.#'d SETS
UNPRICED GOLD PRINT RUN 6-12
1 Drew Bledsoe 1.50 4.00
Travis Henry
2 Peyton Manning 3.00 8.00
Marvin Harrison
3 Tommy Maddox 1.25 3.00
Plaxico Burress
4 Marshall Faulk 1.50 4.00
Torry Holt
5 Ricky Williams 1.25 3.00
Chris Chambers
6 Trent Green 1.50 4.00
Priest Holmes
7 Steve McNair 1.50 4.00
Eddie George
8 Donovan McNabb 1.50 4.00
Duce Staley
9 Rich Gannon 1.50 4.00
Tim Brown
10 Chad Pennington 1.50 4.00
Curtis Martin
11 Drew Brees 1.50 4.00
LaDainian Tomlinson
12 Kerry Collins 1.50 4.00
Jeremy Shockey
13 Keyshawn Johnson 1.50 4.00
Mike Alstott
14 Michael Bennett 1.50 4.00
Randy Moss
15 Jeff Garcia 1.50 4.00
Terrell Owens
16 Brett Favre 4.00 10.00
Donald Driver
17 Jamal Lewis 1.25 3.00
Todd Heap
18 Koren Robinson 1.25 3.00
Shaun Alexander
19 Aaron Brooks 1.25 3.00
Deuce McAllister
20 Michael Vick 2.00 5.00
Warrick Dunn

2003 Fleer Mystique Awe Pairs Jerseys

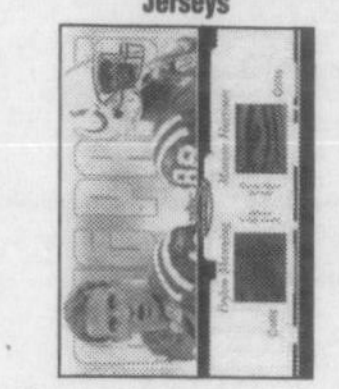

STATED PRINT RUN 199 SER.#'d SETS
ABDM Aaron Brooks 5.00 12.00
Deuce McAllister
DBLT Drew Brees 6.00 15.00
LaDainian Tomlinson
DBTH Drew Bledsoe 6.00 15.00
Travis Henry
DMDS Donovan McNabb 6.00 15.00
Duce Staley
JGTO Jeff Garcia 6.00 15.00
Terrell Owens
JLTH Jamal Lewis 5.00 12.00
Todd Heap
KCJS Kerry Collins 6.00 15.00
Jeremy Shockey
KJMA Keyshawn Johnson 6.00 15.00
Mike Alstott
KRSA Koren Robinson 5.00 12.00
Shaun Alexander
MBRM Michael Bennett 6.00 15.00
Randy Moss
MFTH Marshall Faulk 6.00 15.00
Torry Holt
PMMH Peyton Manning 12.00 30.00
Marvin Harrison
RGTB Rich Gannon 6.00 15.00
Tim Brown
RWCC Ricky Williams 5.00 12.00
Chris Chambers
SMEG Steve McNair 6.00 15.00
Eddie George
TMPB Tommy Maddox 5.00 12.00
Plaxico Burress

2003 Fleer Mystique End Zone Eminence

COMPLETE SET (10) 15.00 40.00
STATED PRINT RUN 100 SER.#'d SETS
*GOLD/77-88: .5X TO 1.2X BASIC INSERT
*GOLD/54-67: .6X TO 1.5X BASIC INSERT
*GOLD/26: .8X TO 2X BASIC INSERT
GOLD PRINT RUN 26-88
1 Priest Holmes 2.50 6.00
2 Shaun Alexander 2.00 5.00
3 Ricky Williams 2.00 5.00
4 Clinton Portis 2.00 5.00
5 Deuce McAllister 2.00 5.00
6 LaDainian Tomlinson 2.50 6.00
7 Travis Henry 1.50 4.00
8 Eddie George 2.00 5.00
9 Terrell Owens 2.50 6.00
10 Hines Ward 2.50 6.00

2003 Fleer Mystique End Zone Eminence Jerseys

STATED PRINT RUN 100 SER.#'d SETS
CP Clinton Portis 5.00 12.00
DM Deuce McAllister 5.00 12.00
EG Eddie George 5.00 12.00
HW Hines Ward 6.00 15.00
LT LaDainian Tomlinson 6.00 15.00
PH Priest Holmes 6.00 15.00
RW Ricky Williams 5.00 12.00
SA Shaun Alexander 5.00 12.00
TH Travis Henry 4.00 10.00
TO Terrell Owens 6.00 15.00

2003 Fleer Mystique Ink Appeal

INK APPEAL PRINT RUN 20-75
AJ Andre Johnson/75 30.00 60.00
DM Donovan McNabb/20 50.00 100.00
LT LaDainian Tomlinson/75 50.00 100.00
MB Michael Bennett/20 15.00 40.00
PB Plaxico Burress/20 20.00 50.00
TB Tom Brady/75 100.00 200.00
WM Willis McGahee/55 25.00 60.00

2003 Fleer Mystique Ink Appeal Gold

GOLD PRINT RUN 3-80
SERIAL #'d UNDER 20 NOT PRICED
AJ Andre Johnson/80 40.00 80.00
LT LaDainian Tomlinson/21 60.00 120.00
MB Michael Bennett/23 15.00 40.00
PB Plaxico Burress/80 15.00 40.00
WM Willis McGahee/21 30.00 80.00

2003 Fleer Mystique Rare Finds

COMPLETE SET (10) 12.00 30.00
STATED PRINT RUN 350 SER.#'d SETS
1 Ricky Williams 1.25 3.00
Priest Holmes
LaDainian Tomlinson
2 Marshal Faulk 1.25 3.00
Deuce McAllister
Shaun Alexander
3 Rich Gannon 2.50 6.00
Drew Bledsoe
Peyton Manning
4 Brett Favre 3.00 8.00
Aaron Brooks
Michael Vick
5 Marvin Harrison 1.25 3.00
Hines Ward
Eric Moulds
6 Randy Moss 1.25 3.00
Terrell Owens
Keyshawn Johnson
7 Julius Peppers 1.25 3.00
Brian Urlacher
Ray Lewis
8 David Carr 1.00 2.50
Joey Harrington
Patrick Ramsey
9 Clinton Portis 1.00 2.50
Travis Henry
William Green
10 Jerry Rice 2.50 6.00
Tim Brown
Jerry Porter

2003 Fleer Mystique Rare Finds Autographs

STATED PRINT RUN 100 SER.#'d SETS
CP Chad Pennington 12.00 30.00
DM Donovan McNabb 20.00 50.00
JH Joey Harrington 8.00 20.00
MB Michael Bennett 10.00 25.00
PB Plaxico Burress 10.00 25.00

2003 Fleer Mystique Rare Finds Jersey Autographs

STATED PRINT RUN 50 SER.#'d SETS
CP Chad Pennington 20.00 50.00
DM Donovan McNabb 30.00 80.00
JH Joey Harrington 12.00 30.00
MB Michael Bennett 15.00 40.00
PB Plaxico Burress 15.00 40.00

2003 Fleer Mystique Rare Finds Jersey Singles

STATED PRINT RUN 299 SER.#'d SETS
BF Brett Favre JSY 10.00 25.00
Aaron Brooks
Michael Vick
BU Brian Urlacher JSY 4.00 10.00
Julius Peppers
Ray Lewis
CP Clinton Portis JSY 3.00 8.00
Travis Henry
William Green
DB Drew Bledsoe JSY 4.00 10.00
Rich Gannon
Peyton Manning
DC David Carr JSY 3.00 8.00
Joey Harrington
Patrick Ramsey
DM Deuce McAllister JSY 4.00 10.00
Marshall Faulk
Shaun Alexander
HW Hines Ward JSY 4.00 10.00
Marvin Harrison
Eric Moulds
JH Joey Harrington JSY 3.00 8.00
David Carr
Patrick Ramsey
JP Julius Peppers JSY 4.00 10.00
Brian Urlacher
Ray Lewis
MF Marshall Faulk JSY 4.00 10.00
Deuce McAllister
Shaun Alexander
MH Marvin Harrison JSY 4.00 10.00
Hines Ward
Eric Moulds
RW Ricky Williams JSY 4.00 10.00
Priest Holmes
LaDainian Tomlinson
TO Terrell Owens JSY 4.00 10.00
Randy Moss
Keyshawn Johnson
WG William Green JSY 4.00 10.00
Travis Henry
Clinton Portis

2003 Fleer Mystique Rare Finds Jersey Doubles

STATED PRINT RUN 250 SER.#'d SETS
CPTH Clinton Portis JSY 5.00 12.00
Travis Henry JSY
William Green
DBPM Rich Gannon 12.00 30.00
Drew Bledsoe JSY
Peyton Manning JSY
DCJH David Carr JSY 5.00 12.00
Joey Harrington JSY
Patrick Ramsey
DMSA Marshall Faulk 6.00 15.00
Deuce McAllister JSY
Shaun Alexander JSY
JPBU Julius Peppers JSY 6.00 15.00
Brian Urlacher JSY
Jamal Lewis
MFDM Marshall Faulk JSY 6.00 15.00
Deuce McAllister JSY
Shaun Alexander
MHHW Marvin Harrison JSY 6.00 15.00
Hines Ward JSY
Eric Moulds
RWLT Ricky Williams JSY 6.00 15.00
Priest Holmes
LaDainian Tomlinson JSY
RWPH Ricky Williams JSY 6.00 15.00
Priest Holmes JSY
LaDainian Tomlinson
TOKJ Randy Moss 6.00 15.00
Terrell Owens JSY
Keyhawn Johnson JSY

2003 Fleer Mystique Rare Finds Jersey Triples

STATED PRINT RUN 150 SER.#'d SETS
CPTHWG Clinton Portis 6.00 15.00
Travis Henry
William Green
DCJHPR David Carr 6.00 15.00
Joey Harrington
Patrick Ramsey
JPBURL Julius Peppers 8.00 20.00
Brian Urlacher
Jamal Lewis
MFDMSA Marshall Faulk 8.00 20.00
Deuce McAllister
Shaun Alexander
MHHWEM Marvin Harrison 8.00 20.00
Hines Ward
Eric Moulds
RGDBPM Rich Gannon 15.00 40.00
Drew Bledsoe
Peyton Manning
RWPHLT Ricky Williams 8.00 20.00
Priest Holmes
LaDainian Tomlinson

2003 Fleer Mystique Secret Weapons

COMPLETE SET (15) 15.00 40.00
STATED PRINT RUN 500 SER.#'d SETS
*GOLD/80-83: .8X TO 2X BASIC INSERT
*GOLD/55: 1X TO 2.5X BASIC INSERT
*GOLD/34-41: 1.2X TO 3X BASIC INSERT
*GOLD/21-22: 1.5X TO 4X BASIC INSERT
GOLD PRINT RUN 2-80
1 Willis McGahee 1.25 3.00
2 Carson Palmer 2.00 5.00
3 Charles Rogers .75 2.00
4 Byron Leftwich 1.00 2.50
5 Andre Johnson 2.50 6.00
6 Larry Johnson 1.00 2.50
7 Quentin Griffin .75 2.00
8 Dave Ragone .60 1.50
9 Kyle Boller 1.00 2.50
10 Chris Simms 1.00 2.50
11 Terrell Suggs 1.00 2.50
12 Rex Grossman 1.00 2.50
13 Bryant Johnson 1.00 2.50
14 Seneca Wallace 1.00 2.50
15 Terence Newman .75 2.00

2003 Fleer Mystique Shining Stars

COMPLETE SET (15) 15.00 40.00
STATED PRINT RUN 500 SER.#'d SETS
*GOLD/192-326: .6X TO 1.5X BASIC INSERTS
*GOLD/85-164: .8X TO 2X BASIC INSERTS
*GOLD/47-60: 1X TO 2.5X BASIC INSERTS
*GOLD/27: 1.5X TO 4X BASIC INSERTS
GOLD PRINT RUN 2-326
1 Emmitt Smith 2.50 6.00
2 Michael Vick 1.25 3.00
3 Brian Urlacher 1.00 2.50
4 Joey Harrington .60 1.50
5 Brett Favre 2.50 6.00
6 Peyton Manning 2.00 5.00
7 Tom Brady 2.50 6.00
8 Kurt Warner 1.00 2.50
9 Jeremy Shockey 1.00 2.50
10 Jerry Rice 2.00 5.00
11 Marshall Faulk 1.00 2.50
12 Randy Moss 1.00 2.50
13 Donovan McNabb 1.00 2.50
14 Corey Dillon .75 2.00
15 David Carr .75 2.00

2003 Fleer Mystique Shining Stars Jerseys

STATED PRINT RUN 250 SER.#'d SETS
*PATCH/25: 1X TO 2.5X BASIC JSY
PATCH STATED PRINT RUN 25
BF Brett Favre 10.00 25.00
BU Brian Urlacher 4.00 10.00
CD Corey Dillon 3.00 8.00
DC David Carr 3.00 8.00
DM Donovan McNabb 4.00 10.00
ES Emmitt Smith 10.00 25.00
JH Joey Harrington 2.50 6.00
JR Jerry Rice 8.00 20.00
JS Jeremy Shockey 4.00 10.00
KW Kurt Warner 4.00 10.00
MF Marshall Faulk 4.00 10.00
PM Peyton Manning 8.00 20.00
TB Tom Brady 10.00 25.00

2002 Fleer Platinum

Released in late December 2002, this set features 320 cards including 230 veterans, and 90 rookies. Rookies 231-290 were found in all packs. Rookies 291-300 were only available in wax packs, and rookies 301-310 were only available in jumbo packs. Each box contained 10 wax packs of 10 cards, 4 jumbo packs of 25 cards, and one rack pack of 45 cards.

COMP.SET w/o RC's (230) 12.00 30.00
1 Donovan McNabb .30 .75
2 Tom Brady .75 2.00
3 Kurt Warner .30 .75
4 Jerry Porter .20 .50
5 LaDainian Tomlinson .40 1.00
6 Rod Gardner .20 .50
7 Dorsey Levens .25 .60
8 Drew Bledsoe .30 .75
9 David Terrell .20 .50
10 Ahman Green .25 .60
11 D'Wayne Bates .20 .50
12 Wayne Chrebet .25 .60
13 Doug Flutie .30 .75
14 Steve McNair .30 .75
15 Nate Clements .20 .50
16 Gerard Warren .20 .50
17 James Allen .20 .50
18 David Patten .20 .50
19 Jerry Rice .60 1.50
20 Garrison Hearst .25 .60
21 Samari Rolle .20 .50
22 Jay Riemersma .20 .50
23 Quincy Carter .20 .50
24 Lamar Smith .25 .60
25 Jacquez Green .20 .50
26 John Abraham .25 .60
27 Kevin Dyson .25 .60
28 James Thrash .25 .60
29 Todd Heap .25 .60
30 Gus Frerotte .25 .60
31 Terry Glenn .25 .60
32 Mark Brunell .25 .60
33 Randy Moss .30 .75
34 John Lynch .25 .60
35 Curtis Conway .25 .60
36 Bill Romanowski .25 .60
37 Thomas Jones .30 .75
38 Dez White .20 .50
39 Greg Ellis .20 .50
40 Trent Green .25 .60
41 Deuce McAllister .25 .60
42 Hines Ward .30 .75
43 Isaac Bruce .30 .75
44 Edgerrin James .25 .60
45 Chad Lewis .20 .50
46 Ray Lewis .30 .75
47 Corey Dillon .25 .60
48 Brett Favre .75 2.00
49 Daunte Culpepper .25 .60
50 Vinny Testaverde .25 .60
51 Warren Sapp .25 .60
52 Corey Simon .20 .50
53 Chris McAlister .20 .50
54 Peter Warrick .25 .60
55 Luther Elliss .20 .50
56 Sam Madison .20 .50
57 Will Allen .20 .50
58 Michael Pittman .25 .60
59 Jamal Lewis .25 .60
60 Takeo Spikes .20 .50
61 Robert Porcher .20 .50
62 Peyton Manning .60 1.50
63 Robert Edwards .20 .50
64 Rob Johnson .25 .60
65 Willie Jackson .20 .50
66 Dan Morgan .20 .50
67 Ian Gold .20 .50
68 Donald Driver .30 .75
69 Fred Taylor .25 .60
70 Dante Hall .25 .60
71 Jerome Pathon .20 .50
72 Amos Zereoue .20 .50
73 Darrell Jackson .25 .60
74 Chris Redman .20 .50
75 Chad Johnson .30 .75
76 Az-Zahir Hakim .20 .50
77 Jermaine Lewis .20 .50
78 Zach Thomas .30 .75
79 Michael Strahan .30 .75
80 Junior Seau .30 .75
81 Brad Johnson .25 .60
82 Keith Brooking .20 .50
83 Shawn Springs .20 .50
84 Tim Couch .20 .50
85 Bill Schroeder .20 .50
86 Jamie Sharper .25 .60
87 Ricky Williams .25 .60
88 Ron Dayne .25 .60
89 Brian Finneran .20 .50
90 Kevin Johnson .20 .50
91 Scotty Anderson .20 .50
92 Chris Chambers .25 .60
93 Amani Toomer .25 .60
94 Jeff Garcia .25 .60
95 Chad Brown .20 .50
96 Rodney Peete .25 .60
97 Dennis Northcutt .20 .50
98 Jamel White .20 .50
99 Patrick Johnson .20 .50
100 Ty Law .25 .60
101 Charles Woodson .30 .75
102 Stephen Davis .25 .60
103 Charlie Garner .25 .60
104 Courtney Brown .20 .50
105 Aaron Glenn .20 .50
106 Antowain Smith .25 .60
107 Tim Brown .30 .75
108 Shane Matthews .20 .50
109 Warrick Dunn .25 .60
110 Wesley Walls .25 .60
111 Jason Elam .25 .60
112 Jay Fiedler .25 .60
113 Kerry Collins .25 .60
114 Jerome Bettis .30 .75
115 Koren Robinson .20 .50
116 Patrick Kerney .20 .50
117 Muhsin Muhammad .25 .60
118 Mike McMahon .20 .50
119 Qadry Ismail .25 .60
120 Oronde Gadsden .20 .50
121 Tiki Barber .30 .75
122 Kordell Stewart .25 .60
123 Shaun Alexander .25 .60
124 Jake Plummer .25 .60
125 Marty Booker .25 .60
126 La'Roi Glover .20 .50
127 Marvin Harrison .30 .75
128 Bobby Shaw .20 .50
129 Kevin Faulk .25 .60
130 Drew Brees .50 1.25
131 Marshall Faulk .30 .75
132 MarTay Jenkins .20 .50
133 Anthony Thomas .25 .60
134 Brian Griese .25 .60
135 Johnnie Morton .25 .60
136 Aaron Brooks .25 .60
137 Ernie Conwell .20 .50
138 Rod Smith .25 .60
139 Antonio Freeman .30 .75
140 Travis Taylor .20 .50
141 Jon Kitna .25 .60
142 Robert Ferguson .25 .60
143 Derrick Alexander .20 .50
144 Laveranues Coles .25 .60
145 Keyshawn Johnson .25 .60
146 Freddie Jones .20 .50
147 Jim Miller .20 .50
148 Mike Anderson .25 .60
149 Marcus Pollard .20 .50
150 Priest Holmes .30 .75
151 Joe Horn .25 .60
152 Plaxico Burress .25 .60
153 Shannon Sharpe .30 .75
154 Michael Vick .50 1.25
155 Steve Smith .30 .75
156 Ed McCaffrey .25 .60
157 Eddie Kennison .25 .60
158 Darren Howard .20 .50
159 Trent Dilfer .25 .60
160 Peerless Price .20 .50
161 Quincy Morgan .20 .50
162 Corey Bradford .20 .50
163 Jimmy Smith .25 .60
164 Troy Brown .25 .60
165 Rich Gannon .25 .60
166 Kevan Barlow .20 .50
167 Jevon Kearse .25 .60
168 David Boston .20 .50
169 Marcel Shipp .20 .50
170 Joey Galloway .25 .60
171 Kyle Brady .20 .50
172 Donald Hayes .20 .50
173 Chad Scott .20 .50
174 Torry Holt .30 .75
175 Champ Bailey .30 .75
176 Travis Henry .20 .50
177 Troy Hambrick .20 .50
178 Hardy Nickerson .20 .50
179 Michael Bennett .25 .60
180 Chad Pennington .30 .75
181 Eric Johnson .20 .50
182 Derrick Mason .25 .60
183 Kwamie Lassiter .20 .50
184 Brian Urlacher .30 .75
185 Olandis Gary .25 .60
186 Tony Gonzalez .30 .75
187 David Sloan .20 .50
188 Kendrell Bell .20 .50
189 Jamie Martin .25 .60
190 Eric Moulds .25 .60
191 Emmitt Smith .75 2.00
192 Bubba Franks .25 .60
193 Byron Chamberlain .20 .50
194 Santana Moss .25 .60
195 Dana Stubblefield .20 .50
196 Eddie George .25 .60
197 Brian Dawkins .25 .60
198 Stephen Alexander .20 .50
199 Terrell Owens .30 .75
200 Curtis Martin .30 .75
201 Larry Izzo UH .20 .50
202 Brian Simmons UH .20 .50
203 Jason Fisk UH RC .20 .50
204 Carlos Emmons UH .20 .50
205 Justin McCareins UH .25 .60
206 Adam Vinatieri UH .30 .75
207 Cornelius Griffin UH .20 .50
208 Trevor Pryce UH .20 .50
209 Sam Shade UH .20 .50
210 Rod Smart UH RC .25 .60
211 Tony Richardson UH .20 .50
212 Kevin Kasper UH .20 .50
213 Rodney Harrison UH .25 .60
214 Patrick Surtain UH .20 .50
215 Fred Beasley UH .20 .50
216 James Farrior UH .25 .60
217 Rosevelt Colvin UH RC .40 1.00
218 Anthony McFarland UH .20 .50
219 Dat Nguyen UH .20 .50
220 Greg Comella UH .20 .50
221 Rob Konrad UH .20 .50
222 London Fletcher UH .20 .50
223 Omar Stoutmire UH .20 .50
224 Warrick Holdman UH .20 .50
225 Bob Christian UH .20 .50
226 David Akers UH .20 .50
227 Tony Brackens UH .20 .50
228 Deon Grant UH .20 .50
229 Olin Kreutz UH RC .40 1.00
230 Gary Walker UH .20 .50
231 Lito Sheppard RC 1.00 2.50
232 Kalimba Edwards RC .75 2.00
233 Hayden Epstein RC .60 1.50
234 Napoleon Harris RC .75 2.00
235 Josh McCown RC 1.00 2.50
236 J.T. O'Sullivan RC .75 2.00
237 Omar Easy RC .75 2.00
238 Adrian Peterson RC 1.00 2.50
239 Jarrod Baxter RC .60 1.50
240 John Henderson RC .75 2.00
241 Jon McGraw RC .60 1.50
242 Terry Jones RC .60 1.50
243 Ron Johnson RC .75 2.00
244 Josh Reed RC .75 2.00
245 Jason McAddley RC .75 2.00
246 Sheldon Brown RC 1.00 2.50
247 Rocky Bernard RC .75 2.00
248 Nick Davis RC .60 1.50
249 Robert Thomas RC .60 1.50
250 Rohan Davey RC 1.00 2.50
251 Seth Burford RC .60 1.50
252 Najeh Davenport RC 1.00 2.50
253 Verron Haynes RC .60 1.50
254 Tellis Redmon RC .60 1.50
255 Vernon Fox RC .60 1.50
256 Willie Offord RC .60 1.50
257 Marquise Walker RC .60 1.50
258 Antonio Bryant RC 1.00 2.50
259 Andre Davis RC .75 2.00
260 Eddie Drummond RC .60 1.50
261 Marques Anderson RC .75 2.00
262 Charles Stackhouse RC .60 1.50
263 Rocky Calmus RC .75 2.00
264 Mike Williams RC .60 1.50
265 Brandon Doman RC .60 1.50
266 Maurice Morris RC .75 2.00
267 Ladell Betts RC 1.00 2.50
268 Ricky Williams RC .75 2.00
269 Tony Fisher RC .75 2.00
270 Michael Lewis RC 1.00 2.50
271 Jerramy Stevens RC 1.00 2.50
272 Reche Caldwell RC 1.00 2.50
273 Antwaan Randle El RC 1.00 2.50
274 Charles Grant RC 1.00 2.50
275 Lee Mays RC .60 1.50
276 Phillip Buchanon RC 1.00 2.50
277 Carlos Hall RC .60 1.50
278 Billy Cundiff RC .75 2.00
279 Saleem Rasheed RC .60 1.50
280 David Garrard RC 1.25 3.00
281 Preston Parsons RC .60 1.50
282 Travis Stephens RC .60 1.50
283 Clinton Portis RC 1.25 3.00
284 James Mungro RC 1.00 2.50
285 Tank Williams RC .75 2.00
286 Ed Reed RC 4.00 10.00
287 Javon Walker RC 1.00 2.50
288 Cliff Russell RC .60 1.50
289 Daryl Jones RC .60 1.50
290 Freddie Milons RC .60 1.50
291 Dwight Freeney RC 2.50 6.00
292 Lamar Gordon RC 1.50 4.00
293 Donte Stallworth RC 2.00 5.00
294 Craig Nall RC 1.50 4.00
295 Coy Wire RC 1.50 4.00
296 T.J. Duckett RC 2.00 5.00
297 Jeremy Shockey RC 3.00 8.00
298 Patrick Ramsey RC 2.00 5.00
299 Chester Taylor RC 2.00 5.00
300 Tim Carter RC 1.50 4.00
301 Joey Harrington RC 2.50 6.00
302 Roy Williams RC 2.50 6.00
303 Julius Peppers RC 5.00 12.00
304 William Green RC 2.00 5.00
305 Ashley Lelie RC 2.00 5.00
306 Rock Cartwright RC 2.50 6.00
307 DeShaun Foster RC 2.50 6.00
308 Marc Boerigter RC 2.50 6.00
309 Chad Hutchinson RC 1.50 4.00
310 Daniel Graham RC 2.00 5.00
311 Ryan Sims RC 3.00 8.00
312 Kurt Kittner RC 2.00 5.00
313 Jabar Gaffney RC 3.00 8.00
314 David Carr RC 3.00 8.00
315 Brian Westbrook RC 5.00 12.00
316 Randy Fasani RC 2.50 6.00
317 Randy McMichael RC 3.00 8.00

318 Ben Leber RC	2.00	5.00
319 Jonathan Wells RC	3.00	8.00
320 Deion Branch RC	3.00	8.00

2002 Fleer Platinum Finish

*VETS 1-230: 4X TO 10X BASIC CARDS
*ROOKIES 231-290: 1.5X TO 4X
*ROOKIES 291-300: .8X TO 2X
*ROOKIES 301-310: .6X TO 1.5X
*ROOKIES 311-320: .5X TO 1.2X
STATED PRINT RUN 100 SER.#'d SETS

2002 Fleer Platinum Bad to the Bone

COMPLETE SET (20)	20.00	50.00
STATED ODDS 1:12, 1:6 JUM, 1:3 RACK		
BB1 Julius Peppers	2.00	5.00
BB2 Josh Reed	.75	2.00
BB3 Antonio Bryant	1.00	2.50
BB4 DeShaun Foster	1.00	2.50
BB5 Joey Harrington	1.00	2.50
BB6 Patrick Ramsey	1.00	2.50
BB7 Jeremy Shockey	1.50	4.00
BB8 Marquise Walker	.60	1.50
BB9 Reche Caldwell	1.00	2.50
BB10 Jabar Gaffney	1.00	2.50
BB11 Antwaan Randle El	1.00	2.50
BB12 Donte Stallworth	1.00	2.50
BB13 Roy Williams	1.00	2.50
BB14 Tim Carter	.75	2.00
BB15 T.J. Duckett	1.00	2.50
BB16 William Green	.75	2.00
BB17 Ashley Lelie	.75	2.00
BB18 Clinton Portis	1.25	3.00
BB19 Javon Walker	1.00	2.50
BB20 Andre Davis	.75	2.00

2002 Fleer Platinum Guts and Glory

COMPLETE SET (20)	12.00	30.00
STATED ODDS 1:4, 1:2 JUM, 1:1 RACK		
1 Zach Thomas	1.00	2.50
2 Junior Seau	1.00	2.50
3 Michael Strahan	1.00	2.50
4 Mike Alstott	.75	2.00
5 Darren Woodson	.75	2.00
6 Garrison Hearst	.75	2.00
7 Jake Plummer	.75	2.00
8 Grant Wistrom	.60	1.50
9 Wayne Chrebet	.75	2.00
10 Rich Gannon	.75	2.00
11 Brian Griese	.75	2.00
12 Ed McCaffrey	.75	2.00
13 Jerome Bettis	1.00	2.50
14 Tedy Bruschi	1.00	2.50
15 Keith Brooking	.60	1.50
16 Peter Boulware	.60	1.50
17 Brian Dawkins	.75	2.00
18 Vinny Testaverde	.75	2.00
19 Warren Sapp	.75	2.00
20 Antowain Smith	.75	2.00

2002 Fleer Platinum Inside the Playbook

STATED PRINT RUN 400 SER.#'d SETS		
1 Jake Plummer	1.50	4.00
2 Michael Vick	3.00	8.00
3 Ray Lewis	2.00	5.00
4 Drew Bledsoe	2.00	5.00
5 Julius Peppers	4.00	10.00
6 Brian Urlacher	2.00	5.00
7 Corey Dillon	1.50	4.00
8 Tim Couch	1.25	3.00
9 Emmitt Smith	5.00	12.00
10 Rod Smith	1.50	4.00
11 Joey Harrington	2.00	5.00
12 Brett Favre	5.00	12.00
13 David Carr	2.00	5.00
14 Peyton Manning	4.00	10.00
15 Jimmy Smith	1.50	4.00
16 Tony Gonzalez	2.00	5.00
17 Ricky Williams	1.50	4.00
18 Randy Moss	2.00	5.00
19 Tom Brady	5.00	12.00
20 Deuce McAllister	1.50	4.00
21 Jeremy Shockey	3.00	8.00
22 Curtis Martin	2.00	5.00
23 Jerry Rice	4.00	10.00
24 Donovan McNabb	2.00	5.00
25 Hines Ward	2.00	5.00
26 LaDainian Tomlinson	2.50	6.00
27 Terrell Owens	2.00	5.00
28 Shaun Alexander	1.50	4.00
29 Marshall Faulk	2.00	5.00
30 Keyshawn Johnson	1.50	4.00
31 Steve McNair	2.00	5.00
32 Stephen Davis	1.50	4.00

2002 Fleer Platinum Inside the Playbook Jerseys

STATED PRINT RUN 250 SER.#'d SETS		
1 Tim Couch	3.00	8.00
2 Stephen Davis	4.00	10.00
3 Corey Dillon	4.00	10.00
4 Marshall Faulk	5.00	12.00
5 Brett Favre	12.00	30.00
6 Joey Harrington	5.00	12.00
7 Keyshawn Johnson	4.00	10.00
8 Ray Lewis	5.00	12.00
9 Peyton Manning	10.00	25.00
10 Curtis Martin	5.00	12.00
11 Donovan McNabb	5.00	12.00
12 Steve McNair	5.00	12.00
13 Randy Moss	5.00	12.00
14 Terrell Owens	5.00	12.00
15 Julius Peppers	6.00	15.00
16 Jake Plummer	4.00	10.00
17 Jerry Rice	10.00	25.00
18 Emmitt Smith	12.00	30.00
19 Jimmy Smith	4.00	10.00
20 Rod Smith	4.00	10.00
21 LaDainian Tomlinson	6.00	15.00
22 Brian Urlacher	5.00	12.00
23 Michael Vick	8.00	20.00
24 Hines Ward	5.00	12.00
25 Ricky Williams	4.00	10.00

2002 Fleer Platinum Nameplates

NAMEPLATE/20-240 ODDS 1:8 JUMBO		
STATED PRINT RUN 20-240		
NAG Ahman Green/33	10.00	25.00
NAH Az-Zahir Hakim/45	6.00	15.00
NAS Antowain Smith/60	6.00	15.00
NBF Brett Favre/33	30.00	80.00
NBG Brian Griese/20	12.00	30.00
NBS Bruce Smith/40	10.00	25.00
NBU Brian Urlacher/65	8.00	20.00
NCC Chris Chambers/80	6.00	15.00
NCD Corey Dillon/90	6.00	15.00
NCP Clinton Portis/50	8.00	20.00
NDB1 David Boston/48	6.00	15.00
NDB2 Drew Brees/135	10.00	25.00
NDC Daunte Culpepper/200	4.00	10.00
NDF Doug Flutie/44	10.00	25.00
NEM1 Ed McCaffrey/240	4.00	10.00
NEM2 Eric Moulds/100	5.00	12.00
NES Emmitt Smith/150	15.00	40.00
NHW Hines Ward/52	10.00	25.00
NIB Isaac Bruce/95	8.00	20.00
NJB Jerome Bettis/52	10.00	25.00
NJG Jeff Garcia/70	6.00	15.00
NJK Jevon Kearse/45	8.00	20.00
NJM Johnnie Morton/90	6.00	15.00
NJP1 Jake Plummer/125	5.00	12.00
NJP2 Julius Peppers/54	12.00	30.00
NJR Jerry Rice/35	25.00	60.00
NJS Jimmy Smith/45	8.00	20.00
NKD Kevin Dyson/80	6.00	15.00
NKJ Kevin Johnson/75	5.00	12.00
NKR Koren Robinson/60	5.00	12.00
NKS Kordell Stewart/60	6.00	15.00
NKW Kurt Warner/75	8.00	20.00
NLT LaDainian Tomlinson/150	8.00	20.00
NMA Mike Alstott/65	6.00	15.00
NMB Mark Brunell/150	5.00	12.00
NMF Marshall Faulk/40	10.00	25.00
NMH Marvin Harrison/55	10.00	25.00
NPB Plaxico Burress/130	5.00	12.00
NPM Peyton Manning/55	20.00	50.00
NPW Peter Warrick/65	6.00	15.00
NQC Quincy Carter/95	5.00	12.00
NRL Ray Lewis/35	12.00	30.00
NRM Randy Moss/40	10.00	25.00
NRS Rod Smith/110	5.00	12.00
NSD Stephen Davis/75	6.00	15.00
NSM1 Steve McNair/50	10.00	25.00
NSM2 Santana Moss/20	12.00	30.00
NTB1 Tim Brown/105	6.00	15.00
NTB2 Tom Brady/61	20.00	50.00
NTC Tim Couch/35	8.00	20.00
NTD Terrell Davis/40	10.00	25.00
NTH Torry Holt/60	8.00	20.00
NTO Terrell Owens/45	10.00	25.00
NVT Vinny Testaverde/75	6.00	15.00
NWS Warren Sapp/110	5.00	12.00
NZT Zach Thomas/60	8.00	20.00

2002 Fleer Platinum Portraits

COMPLETE SET (20)	20.00	50.00
STATED ODDS 1:20, 1:10 JUM, 1:5 RACK		
1 Brett Favre	2.50	6.00
2 Jerry Rice	2.00	5.00
3 Emmitt Smith	2.50	6.00
4 Michael Vick	1.50	4.00
5 Marshall Faulk	1.00	2.50
6 Peyton Manning	2.00	5.00
7 Kurt Warner	1.00	2.50
8 Donovan McNabb	1.00	2.50
9 Tom Brady	2.50	6.00
10 Ricky Williams	.75	2.00
11 LaDainian Tomlinson	1.25	3.00
12 Drew Brees	1.50	4.00
13 Daunte Culpepper	.75	2.00
14 Randy Moss	1.00	2.50
15 Brian Urlacher	1.00	2.50
16 Jeff Garcia	.75	2.00
17 Jerome Bettis	1.00	2.50
18 Clinton Portis	.60	1.50
19 Fred Taylor	.75	2.00
20 Julius Peppers	1.00	2.50

2002 Fleer Platinum Portraits Memorabilia

STATED ODDS 1:66 WAX PACK		
SOME PRINT RUNS FLEER ANNOUNCED		
*PATCH/100: .6X TO 1.5X BASIC JSY		
*PATCH/100: .5X TO 1.2X JSY SP		
PATCHES PRINT RUN 100 SER.#'d SETS		
PATCH/100 ISSUED IN WAX PACKS		
PPBU Brian Urlacher	4.00	10.00
PPCP Clinton Portis	3.00	8.00
PPDB Drew Brees	6.00	15.00
PPDC Daunte Culpepper	3.00	8.00
PPDM Donovan McNabb	4.00	10.00
PPES Emmitt Smith SP/326*	12.00	30.00
PPFT Fred Taylor	3.00	8.00
PPJG Jeff Garcia	3.00	8.00
PPJP Julius Peppers	5.00	12.00
PPJR Jerry Rice	8.00	20.00
PPKW Kurt Warner	4.00	10.00
PPLT LaDainian Tomlinson	5.00	12.00
PPMF Marshall Faulk Pants	4.00	10.00
PPMV Michael Vick	6.00	15.00
PPPM Peyton Manning SP/380*	10.00	25.00
PPRM Randy Moss SP/393*	5.00	12.00
PPRW Ricky Williams	3.00	8.00

2002 Fleer Platinum Run with History Jerseys

STATED PRINT RUN 222 SER.#'d SETS		
ESBS Emmitt Smith Barry Sanders	35.00	60.00
ESES Emmitt Smith	20.00	50.00
ESTA Emmitt Smith Troy Aikman AUTO	50.00	120.00
ESTD Emmitt Smith Tony Dorssett	35.00	60.00
ESWP Emmitt Smith Walter Payton	40.00	100.00
NNO Emmitt Smith Barry Sanders Troy Aikman Tony Dorsett Walter Payton/22	175.00	300.00

2002 Fleer Platinum Run with History Jersey Autographs

FIRST 20 CARDS OF PRINT RUN SIGNED		
FSBS Emmitt Smith AU Barry Sanders	150.00	300.00
ESES Emmitt Smith AU	150.00	300.00
ESTA Emmitt Smith AU Troy Aikman AU	200.00	400.00
ESTD Emmitt Smith AU Tony Dorssett	150.00	300.00
ESWP Emmitt Smith AU Walter Payton	150.00	300.00

2003 Fleer Platinum

Released in July of 2003, this set consists of 270 cards, including 210 veterans, and 60 rookies. Cards 211-240 were inserted at a rate of 1:2 jumbo packs, one per rack pack, and 1:14 wax packs. Cards 241-250 were serial numbered to 1500, and were only available in wax packs. Cards 251-260 were serial numbered to 750, and were only available in jumbo packs. Cards 261-270 were serial numbered to 500, and were only available in rack packs. Boxes contained 14 wax packs of 7 cards, 4 jumbo packs of 20 cards, and 1 rack pack with 30 cards.

COMP.SET w/o SP's (210)	12.00	30.00
1 Donovan McNabb	.30	.75
2 Jonathan Wells	.20	.50
3 Amos Zereoue	.20	.50
4 Ray Lewis	.30	.75
5 Trent Green	.25	.60
6 Jeff Garcia	.25	.60
7 Marty Booker	.25	.60
8 Antowain Smith	.25	.60
9 Brad Johnson	.25	.60
10 Joey Galloway	.25	.60
11 Chad Pennington	.30	.75
12 Patrick Ramsey	.25	.60
13 James Stewart	.20	.50
14 Charles Woodson	.30	.75
15 Warrick Dunn	.25	.60
16 Marvin Harrison	.30	.75
17 Jerome Bettis	.30	.75
18 Muhsin Muhammad	.25	.60
19 Zach Thomas	.30	.75
20 Darrell Jackson	.25	.60
21 Kelly Holcomb	.20	.50
22 Deuce McAllister	.25	.60
23 Mike Alstott	.30	.75
24 Kabeer Gbaja-Biamila	.25	.60
25 Todd Pinkston	.20	.50
26 Chris Redman	.20	.50
27 Jimmy Smith	.25	.60
28 Tim Dwight	.20	.50
29 Kordell Stewart	.25	.60
30 Daunte Culpepper	.25	.60
31 Isaac Bruce	.30	.75
32 William Green	.20	.50
33 Tiki Barber	.30	.75
34 Jevon Kearse	.25	.60
35 Ashley Lelie	.20	.50
36 Charlie Garner	.25	.60
37 Marcel Shipp	.20	.50
38 Corey Bradford	.20	.50
39 Hines Ward	.30	.75
40 Josh Reed	.20	.50
41 Jay Fiedler	.20	.50
42 Matt Hasselbeck	.25	.60
43 Corey Dillon	.25	.60
44 David Patten	.20	.50
45 Warren Sapp	.25	.60
46 Chad Johnson	.30	.75
47 Troy Brown	.25	.60
48 Keyshawn Johnson	.30	.75
49 Roy Williams	.25	.60
50 Curtis Martin	.30	.75
51 Rod Gardner	.20	.50
52 David Carr	.25	.60
53 Tommy Maddox	.25	.60
54 Todd Heap	.25	.60
55 Hugh Douglas	.20	.50
56 Julian Peterson	.20	.50
57 Julius Peppers	.30	.75
58 Sam Madison	.25	.60
59 Jerramy Stevens	.25	.60
60 Andre Davis	.20	.50
61 Joe Horn	.25	.60
62 Ronde Barber	.25	.60
63 Joey Harrington	.20	.50
64 Jerry Porter	.20	.50
65 T.J. Duckett	.25	.60
66 Edgerrin James	.30	.75
67 Joey Porter	.30	.75
68 Brian Urlacher	.30	.75
69 Randy Moss	.30	.75
70 Torry Holt	.30	.75
71 Quincy Morgan	.20	.50
72 Amani Toomer	.25	.60
73 Derrick Mason	.25	.60
74 Donald Driver	.30	.75
75 Duce Staley	.25	.60
76 Peerless Price	.20	.50
77 Mark Brunell	.25	.60
78 David Boston	.20	.50
79 Takeo Spikes	.20	.50
80 Ricky Williams	.25	.60
81 Shaun Alexander	.25	.60
82 Jon Kitna	.25	.60
83 Deion Branch	.25	.60
84 Derrick Brooks	.25	.60
85 Rod Smith	.25	.60
86 Rich Gannon	.25	.60
87 Jason McAddley	.20	.50
88 Jabar Gaffney	.20	.50
89 Plaxico Burress	.25	.60
90 Troy Hambrick	.20	.50
91 Santana Moss	.25	.60
92 Champ Bailey	.30	.75
93 Bubba Franks	.25	.60
94 Brian Westbrook	.30	.75
95 Ed Reed	.30	.75
96 Priest Holmes	.30	.75
97 Terrell Owens	.30	.75
98 Anthony Thomas	.25	.60
99 Michael Bennett	.25	.60
100 Marshall Faulk	.30	.75
101 Kevin Johnson	.20	.50
102 Kerry Collins	.25	.60
103 Eddie George	.25	.60
104 Shannon Sharpe	.30	.75
105 Tim Brown	.30	.75
106 Brian Finneran	.20	.50
107 Reggie Wayne	.30	.75
108 Drew Brees	.30	.75
109 Jake Delhomme	.30	.75
110 Chris Chambers	.25	.60
111 Maurice Morris	.20	.50
112 Antonio Bryant	.20	.50
113 Michael Strahan	.30	.75
114 Laveranues Coles	.20	.50
115 Ahman Green	.25	.60
116 Jeff Blake	.25	.60
117 Jamal Lewis	.25	.60
118 Fred Taylor	.25	.60
119 Marcellus Wiley	.20	.50
120 Stephen Davis	.25	.60
121 Randy McMichael	.20	.50
122 Kurt Warner	.30	.75
123 Tim Couch	.20	.50
124 Aaron Brooks	.25	.60
125 John Lynch	.25	.60
126 Clinton Portis	.25	.60
127 Wayne Chrebet	.25	.60
128 Emmitt Smith	.75	2.00
129 Aaron Glenn	.20	.50
130 Antwaan Randle El	.25	.60
131 Travis Henry	.20	.50
132 Tony Gonzalez	.30	.75
133 Garrison Hearst	.25	.60
134 Drew Bledsoe	.30	.75
135 Eddie Kennison	.20	.50
136 Kevan Barlow	.20	.50
137 David Terrell	.20	.50
138 Tom Brady	.75	2.00
139 Joe Jurevicius	.25	.60
140 Terry Glenn	.25	.60
141 Curtis Conway	.20	.50
142 Trung Canidate	.20	.50
143 Javon Walker	.25	.60
144 Brian Dawkins	.25	.60
145 Keith Brooking	.25	.60
146 Dwight Freeney	.25	.60
147 LaDainian Tomlinson	.30	.75
148 Kevin Dyson	.20	.50
149 Jason Taylor	.25	.60
150 Koren Robinson	.25	.60
151 Dennis Northcutt	.20	.50
152 Donte Stallworth	.20	.50
153 Steve McNair	.30	.75
154 Ed McCaffrey	.25	.60
155 Jerry Rice	.60	1.50
156 Travis Taylor	.20	.50
157 Kyle Brady	.20	.50
158 Quentin Jammer	.20	.50
159 DeShaun Foster	.25	.60
160 Derrius Thompson	.20	.50
161 Marc Bulger	.30	.75
162 Chad Hutchinson	.20	.50
163 Jeremy Shockey	.30	.75
164 Frank Wycheck	.20	.50
165 Brett Favre	.75	2.00
166 Phillip Buchanon	.20	.50
167 Michael Vick	.40	1.00
168 Peyton Manning	.60	1.50
169 Kendrell Bell	.20	.50
170 Eric Moulds	.25	.60
171 Johnnie Morton	.25	.60
172 Tai Streets	.20	.50
173 Ron Dugans	.20	.50
174 Ty Law	.25	.60
175 Simeon Rice	.20	.50
176 Jake Plummer	.25	.60
177 John Abraham	.25	.60
178 Fred Smoot	.20	.50
179 Arizona TC Shipp	.15	.40
180 Atlanta TC Michael Vick	.30	.75
181 Baltimore TC Ray Lewis	.25	.60
182 Buffalo TC Drew Bledsoe	.25	.60
183 Carolina TC Chris Weinke	.20	.50
184 Chicago TC Anthony Thomas	.20	.50
185 Cincinnati TC Corey Dillon	.20	.50
186 Cleveland TC Jamel White	.15	.40
187 Dallas TC Troy Hambrick	.15	.40
188 Denver TC Al Wilson	.15	.40
189 Detroit TC Cory Schlesinger	.15	.40
190 Green Bay TC Tony Fisher	.15	.40
191 Houston TC David Carr	.20	.50
192 Indianapolis TC Peyton Manning	.50	1.25
193 Jacksonville TC Fred Taylor	.20	.50
194 Kansas City TC Trent Green	.20	.50
195 Miami TC Jay Fiedler	.15	.40
196 Minnesota TC Moe Williams	.15	.40
197 New England TC Ted Johnson	.15	.40
198 New Orleans TC Deuce McAllister	.20	.50
199 NY Giants TC Micheal Barrow	.15	.40
200 NY Jets TC LaMont Jordan	.20	.50
201 Oakland TC Tyrone Wheatley	.20	.50
202 Philadelphia TC Duce Staley	.20	.50
203 Pittsburgh TC Tommy Maddox	.20	.50
204 San Diego TC LaDainian Tomlinson	.25	.60
205 San Francisco TC Garrison Hearst	.20	.50
206 Seattle TC Matt Hasselbeck	.20	.50
207 St. Louis TC Kurt Warner	.25	.60
208 Tampa Bay TC Aaron Stecker	.15	.40
209 Tennessee TC Robaire Smith	.15	.40
210 Washington TC Patrick Ramsey	.20	.50
211 L.J. Smith RC	1.00	2.50
212 Taylor Jacobs RC	.60	1.50
213 J.R. Tolver RC	.75	2.00
214 Musa Smith RC	.60	1.50
215 Bennie Joppru RC	.60	1.50
216 Ken Dorsey RC	.75	2.00
217 Kareem Kelly RC	.60	1.50
218 Andre Woolfolk RC	.75	2.00
219 Brian St.Pierre RC	.75	2.00
220 Jerome McDougle RC	.60	1.50
221 Avon Cobourne RC	.60	1.50
222 William Joseph RC	.60	1.50
223 Dallas Clark RC	1.50	4.00
224 Anquan Boldin RC	1.50	4.00
225 Mike Doss RC	1.00	2.50
226 Cecil Sapp RC	.60	1.50
227 Domanick Davis RC	.75	2.00
228 Brad Banks RC	.75	2.00
229 Justin Gage RC	.75	2.00
230 Nate Burleson RC	.75	2.00
231 Earnest Graham RC	1.00	2.50
232 DeWayne White RC	.60	1.50
233 Kevin Williams RC	1.00	2.50
234 Billy McMullen RC	.60	1.50
235 Talman Gardner RC	.60	1.50
236 Marcus Trufant RC	.75	2.00
237 Quentin Griffin RC	.75	2.00
238 LaBrandon Toefield RC	.75	2.00
239 Kliff Kingsbury RC	.75	2.00
240 Doug Gabriel RC	.75	2.00
241 Kyle Boller RC	1.50	4.00
242 Dave Ragone RC	1.00	2.50
243 Larry Johnson RC	1.50	4.00
244 Lee Suggs RC	1.25	3.00
245 Charles Rogers RC	1.25	3.00
246 Jimmy Kennedy RC	1.25	3.00
247 Onterrio Smith RC	1.00	2.50
248 Artose Pinner RC	1.00	2.50
249 Tyrone Calico RC	1.25	3.00
250 Terence Newman RC	1.25	3.00
251 Byron Leftwich RC	2.00	5.00
252 Kelley Washington RC	1.25	3.00
253 Justin Fargas RC	2.00	5.00
254 DeWayne Robertson RC	1.50	4.00
255 Boss Bailey RC	1.50	4.00
256 Sam Aiken RC	1.50	4.00
257 Bryant Johnson RC	2.00	5.00
258 Rex Grossman RC	2.00	5.00
259 Teyo Johnson RC	1.50	4.00
260 Willis McGahee RC	2.50	6.00
261 Carson Palmer RC	5.00	12.00
262 Chris Simms RC	2.50	6.00
263 Andre Johnson RC	6.00	15.00
264 Seneca Wallace RC	2.50	6.00
265 Terrell Suggs RC	2.50	6.00
266 Chris Brown RC	1.50	4.00
267 Kevin Curtis RC	2.50	6.00
268 Brandon Lloyd RC	4.00	10.00
269 Jason Witten RC	6.00	15.00
270 Dobby Wade RC	2.00	5.00

2003 Fleer Platinum Finish

*VETS/1-210: 5X TO 12X BASIC CARDS
*ROOKIES 211-240: 1.5X TO 4X
*ROOKIES 241-250: 1X TO 2.5X
*ROOKIES 251-260: .8X TO 2X
*ROOKIES 261-270: .6X TO 1.5X
STATED PRINT RUN 100 SER.#'d SETS

2003 Fleer Platinum Alma Materials

ONE PER RACK PACK		
1 Ken Dorsey	3.00	8.00
2 Justin Fargas	4.00	10.00
3 Quentin Griffin	3.00	8.00
4 Edgerrin James	4.00	10.00
5 Peyton Manning	8.00	20.00
6 Carson Palmer	5.00	12.00
7 Julius Peppers	4.00	10.00
8 Michael Vick	5.00	12.00
9 Seneca Wallace	4.00	10.00

2003 Fleer Platinum Alma Materials Prep to Pro

STATED PRINT RUN 200 SER.#'d SETS		
1 Edgerrin James	6.00	15.00
2 Peyton Manning	12.00	30.00
3 Julius Peppers	6.00	15.00
4 Michael Vick	8.00	20.00

2003 Fleer Platinum Big Signs

COMPLETE SET (10)	6.00	15.00
ODDS 1:2 JUM, 1:RACK, 1:7 WAX		
*PLATINUM/100: 1.5X TO 4X BASIC INSERTS		
PLATINUM PRINT RUN 100 SER.#'d SETS		
1 Donovan McNabb	.75	2.00
2 Brett Favre	2.00	5.00
3 Ricky Williams	.60	1.50
4 Brian Urlacher	.75	2.00
5 Clinton Portis	.60	1.50
6 Jeremy Shockey	.75	2.00
7 Jerry Rice	1.50	4.00
8 Randy Moss	.75	2.00
9 Chad Pennington	.75	2.00
10 Michael Vick	1.00	2.50

2003 Fleer Platinum Big Signs Autographs

STATED PRINT RUN 200 SER.#'d SETS		
BSACP Clinton Portis	20.00	40.00
BSADM Donovan McNabb	20.00	40.00

2003 Fleer Platinum Patch of Honor

PATCH/142-220 ODDS 1:8 JUMBO		
STATED PRINT RUN 142-220		
PHBF Brett Favre/220	15.00	40.00
PHBU Brian Urlacher/220	6.00	15.00
PHCM Curtis Martin/220	6.00	15.00
PHCP Clinton Portis/220	5.00	12.00
PHCP2 Chad Pennington/219	6.00	15.00
PHDC Daunte Culpepper/220	5.00	12.00
PHDM Donovan McNabb/220	6.00	15.00
PHDM2 Deuce McAllister/220	5.00	12.00
PHEG Eddie George/220	5.00	12.00
PHES Emmitt Smith/220	15.00	40.00
PHFT Fred Taylor/220	5.00	12.00
PHHT Travis Henry/215	4.00	10.00
PHHW Hines Ward/219	6.00	15.00
PHJG Jeff Garcia/220	5.00	12.00
PHJR Jerry Rice/205	12.00	30.00
PHJS Jeremy Shockey/220	6.00	15.00
PHLT LaDainian Tomlinson/220	6.00	15.00
PHMF Marshall Faulk/220	6.00	15.00
PHMH Marvin Harrison/219	6.00	15.00
PHMV Michael Vick/219	8.00	20.00
PHPH Priest Holmes/220	6.00	15.00
PHPMO Peyton Manning/220	12.00	30.00
PHRL Ray Lewis/220	6.00	15.00
PHRM Randy Moss/220	6.00	15.00
PHRWO Ricky Williams/220	5.00	12.00
PHSA Shaun Alexander/220	5.00	12.00
PHTB Tom Brady/220	15.00	40.00
PHTB2 Tim Brown/142	6.00	15.00
PHTO Terrell Owens/220	6.00	15.00
PHWS Warren Sapp/220	5.00	12.00

2003 Fleer Platinum Portrayals

COMPLETE SET (15)	15.00	40.00
ODDS 1:4 JUM, 1:2 RACK, 1:14 WAX		
*PLATINUM/100: 1X TO 2.5X BASIC INSERT		
PLATINUM PRINT RUN 100 SER.#'d SETS		
1 LaDainian Tomlinson	1.00	2.50
2 Shaun Alexander	.75	2.00
3 Ray Lewis	1.00	2.50
4 Brett Favre	2.50	6.00
5 Jerry Rice	2.00	5.00
6 Joey Harrington	.60	1.50
7 Donovan McNabb	1.00	2.50
8 Brian Urlacher	1.00	2.50
9 Jeremy Shockey	1.00	2.50
10 Emmitt Smith	2.50	6.00
11 Chad Pennington	1.00	2.50
12 Randy Moss	1.00	2.50
13 Michael Vick	1.25	3.00
14 Clinton Portis	.75	2.00
15 Ricky Williams	.75	2.00

2003 Fleer Platinum Portrayals Jerseys

STATED ODDS 1:50 WAX		
*PATCH/100: 1X TO 2.5X BASIC JSY		
PATCHES PRINT RUN 100 SER.#'d SETS		
PPBF Brett Favre	12.00	30.00
PPBU Brian Urlacher	5.00	12.00
PPDM Donovan McNabb	5.00	12.00
PPJH Joey Harrington	3.00	8.00
PPJRO Jerry Rice	10.00	25.00
PPJS Jeremy Shockey	5.00	12.00
PPMV Michael Vick	6.00	15.00
PPRL Ray Lewis	5.00	12.00
PPRM Randy Moss	5.00	12.00
PPSA Shaun Alexander	4.00	10.00

2003 Fleer Platinum Pro Bowl Scouting Report

COMPLETE SET (15)	20.00	50.00
STATED PRINT RUN 400 SER.#'d SETS		
*PLATINUM/100: .6X TO 1.5X BASIC INSERTS		
PLATINUM PRINT RUN 100 SER.#'d SETS		
1 Ricky Williams	1.25	3.00
2 Rich Gannon	1.25	3.00
3 Drew Bledsoe	1.50	4.00
4 Brad Johnson	1.25	3.00
5 Jeff Garcia	1.25	3.00
6 Donovan McNabb	1.50	4.00
7 Peyton Manning	3.00	8.00
8 Todd Heap	1.25	3.00
9 Terrell Owens	1.50	4.00
10 Marshall Faulk	1.50	4.00
11 Marvin Harrison	1.50	4.00
12 Deuce McAllister	1.25	3.00
13 LaDainian Tomlinson	1.50	4.00
14 Eric Moulds	1.25	3.00
15 Jerry Rice	3.00	8.00

2003 Fleer Platinum Pro Bowl Scouting Report Jerseys

STATED PRINT RUN 250 SER.#'d SETS		
PBSRDM Deuce McAllister	4.00	10.00
PBSRJG Jeff Garcia	4.00	10.00
PBSRJR Jerry Rice	10.00	25.00
PBSRLT LaDainian Tomlinson	5.00	12.00
PBSRMH Marvin Harrison	5.00	12.00
PBSRPM Peyton Manning	10.00	25.00
PBSRRG Rich Gannon	4.00	10.00
PBSRRW Ricky Williams	4.00	10.00
PBSRTH Todd Heap	4.00	10.00
PBSRTO Terrell Owens	5.00	12.00

2004 Fleer Platinum

Fleer Platinum initially released in early September 2004. The base set consists of 185-cards including 50-rookies featuring prints runs between 299 and 999. Hobby boxes contained sixteen 7-card packs and four 20-card jumbo packs and carried an S.R.P. of $6 per pack. One parallel set and a variety of inserts can be found seeded in hobby and retail packs highlighted by the Pro Material Jersey Autograph inserts. Some signed cards were issued via mail-in exchange or redemption cards with a number of those EXCH cards not yet appearing live on the secondary market as of the printing of this book.

COMP.SET w/o SP's (135)	7.50	20.00
136-145 RC PRINT RUN 299 SER.#'d SETS		
146-155 RC PRINT RUN 499 SER.#'d SETS		
156-165 RC PRINT RUN 799 SER.#'d SETS		
166-185 RC PRINT RUN 999 SER.#'d SETS		
1 Joey Harrington	.25	.60
2 Kyle Boller	.25	.60
3 Randy McMichael	.20	.50
4 David Tyree	.25	.60
5 Darrell Jackson	.25	.60
6 Brian Urlacher	.30	.75
7 Ahman Green	.25	.60
8 Onterrio Smith	.20	.50
9 Jevon Kearse	.25	.60
10 Eddie George	.25	.60
11 Julius Peppers	.25	.60
12 Donald Driver	.30	.75
13 Randy Moss	.30	.75
14 Brian Westbrook	.30	.75
15 Derrick Brooks	.25	.60
16 Jamal Lewis	.25	.60
17 Artose Pinner	.20	.50
18 Ricky Williams	.25	.60
19 Chad Pennington	.30	.75
20 Matt Hasselbeck	.25	.60
21 Josh McCown	.25	.60
22 Carson Palmer	.30	.75
23 Byron Leftwich	.25	.60
24 Tedy Bruschi	.30	.75
25 Duce Staley	.25	.60
26 Laveranues Coles	.20	.50
27 Drew Bledsoe	.30	.75
28 Shannon Sharpe	.30	.75
29 A.J. Feeley	.20	.50
30 Santana Moss	.25	.60
31 Adam Archuleta	.20	.50
32 Travis Henry	.20	.50
33 Ashley Lelie	.20	.50
34 Dante Hall	.25	.60
35 Curtis Martin	.30	.75
36 Isaac Bruce	.25	.60
37 Eric Moulds	.25	.60
38 Jake Plummer	.25	.60
39 Trent Green	.25	.60
40 Shaun Ellis	.20	.50
41 Torry Holt	.25	.60
42 T.J. Duckett	.25	.60
43 Quincy Morgan	.20	.50
44 Jabar Gaffney	.20	.50
45 Tiki Barber	.30	.75
46 Tim Rattay	.20	.50
47 Champ Bailey	.25	.60
48 Tony Gonzalez	.30	.75
49 Rich Gannon	.25	.60
50 Marshall Faulk	.30	.75
51 Jake Delhomme	.25	.60
52 Antonio Bryant	.25	.60
53 Priest Holmes	.30	.75
54 Jerry Rice	.60	1.50
55 Marc Bulger	.25	.60
56 Stephen Davis	.25	.60
57 Roy Williams S	.25	.60
58 Willis McGahee	.30	.75
59 Julian Peterson	.25	.60
60 Thomas Jones	.30	.75
61 Dre Bly	.20	.50
62 Corey Dillon	.25	.60
63 Tommy Maddox	.25	.60
64 Derrick Mason	.25	.60
65 Marty Booker	.25	.60
66 Brett Favre	.75	2.00
67 Tom Brady	.60	1.50
68 Correll Buckhalter	.25	.60
69 Steve McNair	.30	.75
70 Alge Crumpler	.25	.60
71 Quincy Carter	.20	.50
72 Andre Johnson	.30	.75
73 Jeremy Shockey	.25	.60
74 Kevan Barlow	.20	.50
75 Jerry Porter	.20	.50
76 Ray Lewis	.30	.75
77 Keyshawn Johnson	.25	.60
78 Domanick Davis	.20	.50
79 Michael Strahan	.30	.75
80 Brandon Lloyd	.25	.60
81 Anquan Boldin	.30	.75
82 Chad Johnson	.30	.75
83 Jimmy Smith	.25	.60
84 Troy Brown	.25	.60
85 Hines Ward	.30	.75
86 Tyrone Calico	.25	.60
87 Marcel Shipp	.20	.50
88 Peter Warrick	.25	.60
89 Reggie Wayne	.30	.75
90 Aaron Brooks	.25	.60
91 Antwaan Randle El	.25	.60
92 Mark Brunell	.25	.60
93 Todd Heap	.25	.60
94 Charles Rogers	.20	.50
95 Chris Chambers	.25	.60
96 Amani Toomer	.25	.60
97 Shaun Alexander	.25	.60
98 Michael Vick	.40	1.00
99 Jeff Garcia	.25	.60
100 Edgerrin James	.25	.60
101 Deuce McAllister	.25	.60
102 LaDainian Tomlinson	.30	.75
103 Warrick Dunn	.25	.60
104 Andre Davis	.20	.50
105 Peyton Manning	.60	1.50
106 Boo Williams	.20	.50
107 Drew Brees	.30	.75
108 Rex Grossman	.25	.60

109 Javon Walker .20 .50
110 Michael Bennett .25 .60
111 Terrell Owens .30 .75
112 Michael Pittman .25 .60
113 Emmitt Smith .75 2.00
114 Rudi Johnson .25 .60
115 Fred Taylor .25 .60
116 Deion Branch .25 .60
117 Plaxico Burress .25 .60
118 Clinton Portis .30 .75
119 DeShaun Foster .25 .60
120 Najeh Davenport .25 .60
121 Daunte Culpepper .25 .60
122 Donovan McNabb .30 .75
123 Charles Lee .20 .50
124 Peerless Price .20 .50
125 Lee Suggs .25 .60
126 Marvin Harrison .30 .75
127 Joe Horn .25 .60
128 Antonio Gates .30 .75
129 Steve Smith .30 .75
130 David Carr .20 .50
131 Jason Taylor .25 .60
132 Phillip Buchanon .25 .60
133 Brad Johnson .25 .60
134 Takeo Spikes .20 .50
135 Koren Robinson .20 .50
136 Eli Manning RC 20.00 50.00
137 Ben Roethlisberger RC 20.00 50.00
138 Drew Henson RC 2.00 5.00
139 Kellen Winslow RC 3.00 8.00
140 Kevin Jones RC 2.50 6.00
141 Larry Fitzgerald RC 8.00 20.00
142 Roy Williams RC 3.00 8.00
143 Philip Rivers RC 12.00 30.00
144 Lee Evans RC 3.00 8.00
145 Julius Jones RC 2.50 6.00
146 Chris Perry RC 1.50 4.00
147 Michael Clayton RC 1.50 4.00
148 Sean Taylor RC 4.00 10.00
149 Reggie Williams RC 1.50 4.00
150 Steven Jackson RC 3.00 8.00
151 Tatum Bell RC 1.50 4.00
152 Keary Colbert RC 1.25 3.00
153 J.P. Losman RC 1.50 4.00
154 Devery Henderson RC 2.00 5.00
155 Ben Troupe RC 1.50 4.00
156 Luke McCown RC 1.25 3.00
157 Greg Jones RC 1.00 2.50
158 Ben Watson RC 1.50 4.00
159 Bernard Berrian RC 1.50 4.00
160 Devard Darling RC 1.00 2.50
161 Cedric Cobbs RC 1.00 2.50
162 Darius Watts RC 1.00 2.50
163 Derrick Hamilton RC 1.00 2.50
164 Matt Schaub RC 3.00 8.00
165 Mewelde Moore RC 1.25 3.00
166 Michael Jenkins RC 1.25 3.00
167 Rashaun Woods RC .75 2.00
168 Quincy Wilson RC 1.00 2.50
169 Jonathan Vilma RC 1.25 3.00
170 Jerricho Cotchery RC 1.00 2.50
171 John Navarre RC .75 2.00
172 Josh Harris RC .75 2.00
173 Teddy Lehman RC .75 2.00
174 Ernest Wilford RC 1.00 2.50
175 P.K. Sam RC .75 2.00
176 Jeff Smoker RC 1.00 2.50
177 Chris Gamble RC 1.00 2.50
178 Johnnie Morant RC .75 2.00
179 DeAngelo Hall RC 1.25 3.00
180 Vince Wilfork RC 1.25 3.00
181 Michael Turner RC 1.50 4.00
182 Robert Gallery RC 1.25 3.00
183 Ricardo Colclough RC 1.00 2.50
184 Kenechi Udeze RC 1.00 2.50
185 Dunta Robinson RC .75 2.00

2004 Fleer Platinum Finish

*VETS: 4X TO 10X BASIC CARDS
*ROOKIES 136-145: .5X TO 1.2X BASE RCs
*ROOKIES 146-155: .8X TO 2X BASE RCs
*ROOKIES 156-165: 1X TO 2.5X BASE RCs
*ROOKIES 166-185: 1.2X TO 3X BASE RCs
STATED PRINT RUN 100 SER.#'d SETS

2004 Fleer Platinum Autographs Blue

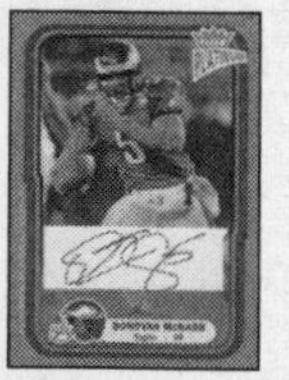

BLUE AU/15-99 ODDS 1:256 HOBBY
BLUE #'d UNDER 20 NOT PRICED
UNPRICED RED PRINT RUN 5 SETS
14 Brian Westbrook/43 12.50 30.00
16 Jamal Lewis/23 15.00 40.00
19 Chad Pennington/71 15.00 40.00
50 Marshall Faulk/15 30.00 60.00
51 Jake Delhomme/35 15.00 40.00
81 Anquan Boldin/19 15.00 40.00
101 Deuce McAllister/47 15.00 40.00
122 Donovan McNabb/19 30.00 60.00
138 Drew Henson/99 12.50 30.00

2004 Fleer Platinum Deep Six

STATED ODDS 1:108 HOB/JUM, 1:270 RET
1DS Joey Harrington 2.00 5.00
Roy Williams WR
2DS Eli Manning 8.00 20.00
Jeremy Shockey
3DS Donovan McNabb 3.00 8.00
Terrell Owens
4DS Daunte Culpepper 3.00 8.00
Randy Moss
5DS David Carr 3.00 8.00
Andre Johnson
6DS Chad Pennington 3.00 8.00
Santana Moss
7DS Michael Vick 4.00 10.00
Michael Jenkins
8DS Peyton Manning 6.00 15.00
Marvin Harrison
9DS Drew Bledsoe 3.00 8.00
Eric Moulds
10DS Rich Gannon 6.00 15.00
Jerry Rice

2004 Fleer Platinum Jerseys

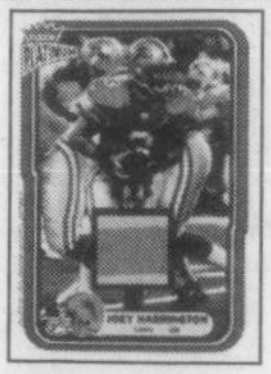

OVERALL JERSEY ODDS 1:4 JUMBO
STATED PRINT RUN 40-765
*NAMEPLATE/105-120: .8X TO 2X JSY/765
*NAMEPLATE/40-60: 1.2X TO 3X JSY/765
*NAMEPLATE/25-35: 1.5X TO 4X JSY/765
NAMEPLATE/25-120 INSERTS IN JUMBO
UNPRICED PATCH PRINT RUN 5 SETS
1 Joey Harrington/765 2.50 6.00
6 Brian Urlacher/80 5.00 12.00
22 Carson Palmer/120 5.00 12.00
41 Torry Holt/765 2.50 6.00
66 Brett Favre/765 8.00 20.00
67 Tom Brady/765 6.00 15.00
69 Steve McNair/765 3.00 8.00
73 Jeremy Shockey/100 4.00 10.00
76 Ray Lewis/765 3.00 8.00
90 Aaron Brooks/765 2.50 6.00
98 Michael Vick/40 7.50 20.00
101 Deuce McAllister/765 2.50 6.00
102 LaDainian Tomlinson/765 3.00 8.00
105 Peyton Manning/765 6.00 15.00
121 Daunte Culpepper/220 4.00 10.00
126 Marvin Harrison/765 3.00 8.00
130 David Carr/765 2.00 5.00

2004 Fleer Platinum Platinum Memorabilia

STATED ODDS 1:24 HOB, 1:96 RET
*DUAL/50: .8X TO 2X SINGLE JSY
*DUAL/50: .6X TO 1.5X SINGLE JSY SP
DUAL PRINT RUN 50 SER.#'d SETS
PMAG Ahman Green SP 4.00 10.00
PMBF Brett Favre 10.00 25.00
PMBL Byron Leftwich 3.00 8.00
PMCJ Chad Johnson SP 5.00 12.00
PMCP Chad Pennington SP 5.00 12.00
PMCP2 Clinton Portis 4.00 10.00
PMDC David Carr 2.50 6.00
PMDM Donovan McNabb SP 5.00 12.00
PMDM2 Deuce McAllister 3.00 8.00
PMJH Joey Harrington 3.00 8.00
PMJL Jamal Lewis 3.00 8.00
PMJR Jerry Rice SP 10.00 25.00
PMJS Jeremy Shockey SP 4.00 10.00
PMLT LaDainian Tomlinson 4.00 10.00
PMMF Marshall Faulk 4.00 10.00
PMMH Marvin Harrison 4.00 10.00
PMMV Michael Vick SP 6.00 15.00
PMPH Priest Holmes 4.00 10.00
PMPM Peyton Manning 8.00 20.00
PMRI Ricky Williams SP 4.00 10.00
PMRM Randy Moss 4.00 10.00
PMRW Roy Williams S SP 4.00 10.00
PMSA Shaun Alexander SP 4.00 10.00
PMSM Steve McNair 4.00 10.00
PMTB Tom Brady 8.00 20.00

2004 Fleer Platinum Platinum Portraits

COMPLETE SET (10) 10.00 25.00
STATED ODDS 1:18 HOB,1:4 JUM, 1:24 RET
1PP Deuce McAllister 1.00 2.50
2PP Marshall Faulk 1.25 3.00
3PP Brian Westbrook 1.25 3.00
4PP Shaun Alexander 1.00 2.50
5PP Andre Johnson 1.25 3.00
6PP Charles Rogers .75 2.00
7PP Brett Favre 3.00 8.00
8PP Edgerrin James 1.00 2.50
9PP Byron Leftwich 1.00 2.50
10PP Hines Ward 1.25 3.00

2004 Fleer Platinum Platinum Portraits Jersey

STATED ODDS 1:48 HOB, 1:120 RET
*PATCH/80-100: .6X TO 1.5X BASIC JSY
PATCH PRINT RUN 80-100 SER.#'d SETS
PPAJ Andre Johnson SP 4.00 10.00
PPBF Brett Favre 10.00 25.00
PPBL Byron Leftwich 3.00 8.00
PPBW Brian Westbrook 4.00 10.00
PPCR Charles Rogers SP 2.50 6.00
PPDM Deuce McAllister 3.00 8.00
PPEJ Edgerrin James 3.00 8.00
PPHW Hines Ward 4.00 10.00
PPMF Marshall Faulk 4.00 10.00
PPSA Shaun Alexander SP 3.00 8.00

2004 Fleer Platinum Pro Material Jerseys

ONE PER RACK PACK
STATED PRINT RUN 250 SER.#'d SETS
*DIE CUT/99: .6X TO 1.5X BASIC JSY
DIE CUT PRINT RUN 99 SER.#'d SETS
UNPRICED DC PATCH PRINT RUN 5 SETS
PMBB Bernard Berrian 3.00 8.00
PMBR Ben Roethlisberger 12.00 30.00
PMBT Ben Troupe 2.50 6.00
PMBW Ben Watson 3.00 8.00
PMOC Cedric Cobbs 2.00 5.00
PMCP Chris Perry 2.50 6.00
PMDD Devard Darling 2.00 5.00
PMDH DeAngelo Hall 3.00 8.00
PMDH2 Derrick Hamilton 2.00 5.00
PMDH3 Devery Henderson 3.00 8.00
PMDW Darius Watts 2.00 5.00
PMEM Eli Manning 12.00 30.00
PMGJ Greg Jones 2.00 5.00
PMJJ Julius Jones 2.50 6.00
PMJL J.P. Losman 2.50 6.00
PMKC Keary Colbert 2.00 5.00
PMKJ Kevin Jones 3.00 8.00
PMKW Kellen Winslow Jr. 3.00 8.00
PMLE Lee Evans 3.00 8.00
PMLF Larry Fitzgerald 8.00 20.00
PMLM Luke McCown 2.50 6.00
PMMC Michael Clayton 2.50 6.00
PMMJ Michael Jenkins 3.00 8.00
PMMM Mewelde Moore 2.50 6.00
PMMS Matt Schaub 6.00 15.00
PMPR Philip Rivers 12.00 30.00
PMRW Reggie Williams 2.50 6.00
PMRW2 Roy Williams WR 3.00 8.00
PMRW3 Rashaun Woods 2.00 5.00
PMSJ Steven Jackson 5.00 12.00
PMTB Tatum Bell 2.50 6.00

2004 Fleer Platinum Pro Material Jerseys Autographs

JSY AU/10-394 ODDS 1:4 RACK PACK
UNPRICED DC PATCH PRINT RUN 5
PMCP Chris Perry/394 6.00 15.00
PMEM Eli Manning/224 90.00 150.00
PMKC Keary Colbert/78 6.00 15.00
PMMC Michael Clayton/166 8.00 20.00
PMPR Philip Rivers/294 25.00 60.00
PMRW Rashaun Woods/274 5.00 12.00
PMSJ Steven Jackson/22 40.00 100.00

2004 Fleer Platinum Pro Material Jerseys Autographs Die Cut

DIE CUT PRINT RUN 25 SER.#'d SETS
PMBR Ben Roethlisberger 125.00 250.00
PMCP Chris Perry 12.00 30.00
PMEM Eli Manning 125.00 250.00
PMKC Keary Colbert 10.00 25.00
PMLF Larry Fitzgerald 60.00 120.00
PMMC Michael Clayton 12.00 30.00
PMMS Matt Schaub 30.00 80.00
PMPR Philip Rivers 75.00 150.00
PMRW Rashaun Woods 10.00 25.00
PMSJ Steven Jackson 50.00 100.00

2004 Fleer Platinum Scouting Report

STATED ODDS 1:60 H,1:160 JUM,1:432 R
STATED PRINT RUN 250 SER.#'d SETS
1SR Tom Brady 4.00 10.00
2SR Peyton Manning 4.00 10.00
3SR Priest Holmes 2.00 5.00
4SR Donovan McNabb 2.00 5.00
5SR Torry Holt 1.50 4.00
6SR Clinton Portis 2.00 5.00
7SR LaDainian Tomlinson 2.00 5.00
8SR Jeremy Shockey 1.50 4.00
9SR Steve McNair 2.00 5.00
10SR Chad Pennington 2.00 5.00
11SR Michael Vick 2.50 6.00
12SR Brett Favre 5.00 12.00
13SR Randy Moss 2.00 5.00
14SR Byron Leftwich 1.50 4.00
15SR David Carr 1.25 3.00
16SR Ricky Williams 1.50 4.00
17SR Stephen Davis 1.50 4.00
18SR Terrell Owens 2.00 5.00
19SR Marvin Harrison 2.00 5.00
20SR Jerry Rice 4.00 10.00

2004 Fleer Platinum Scouting Report Jersey

STATED PRINT RUN 35-250
SRBF Brett Favre 10.00 25.00
SRBL Byron Leftwich 3.00 8.00
SRCP2 Clinton Portis 4.00 10.00
SRDC David Carr 2.50 6.00
SRDM Donovan McNabb/35 6.00 15.00
SRJR Jerry Rice 8.00 20.00
SRJS Jeremy Shockey 3.00 8.00
SRLT LaDainian Tomlinson 4.00 10.00
SRMH Marvin Harrison 4.00 10.00
SRMV Michael Vick 5.00 12.00
SRPH Priest Holmes 4.00 10.00
SRPM Peyton Manning 8.00 20.00
SRRM Randy Moss 4.00 10.00
SRSD Stephen Davis 3.00 8.00
SRSM Steve McNair 4.00 10.00
SRTB Tom Brady 8.00 20.00
SRTH Torry Holt 3.00 8.00
SRTO Terrell Owens 4.00 10.00

2004 Fleer Platinum Youth Movement

COMPLETE SET (15) 12.50 30.00
STATED ODDS 1:9 HOB, 1:2 JUM, 1:8 RET
1YM Eli Manning 3.00 8.00
2YM Kevin Jones .40 1.00
3YM Philip Rivers 2.00 5.00
4YM Kellen Winslow Jr. .50 1.25
5YM Ben Roethlisberger 3.00 8.00
6YM Roy Williams WR .50 1.25
7YM Drew Henson .30 .75
8YM Larry Fitzgerald 1.25 3.00
9YM J.P. Losman .40 1.00
10YM Steven Jackson .75 2.00
11YM Chris Perry .40 1.00
12YM Reggie Williams .40 1.00
13YM Michael Clayton .40 1.00
14YM Lee Evans .50 1.25
15YM Tatum Bell .40 1.00

2001 Fleer Premium

Fleer released Premium in August of 2001. This 250-card set featured 200 base cards and 50 rookies which were short printed. The rookies were serial numbered to 2001. The base set design used foilboard and gold-foil highlights fro the lettering and logo. The cards were issued in eight card packs with an SRP of $3.99 per pack and 24 packs in the box.

COMP.SET w/o SP's (200) 10.00 25.00
201-250 ROOKIE PRINT RUN 2001
1 Ricky Williams .25 .60
2 Dez White .20 .50
3 Jay Riemersma .15 .40
4 Derrick Mason .20 .50
5 Chad Lewis .15 .40
6 Shaun King .15 .40
7 Jevon Kearse .20 .50
8 Bobby Engram .20 .50
9 Warrick Dunn .25 .60
10 Randall Cunningham .25 .60
11 Stephen Alexander .15 .40
12 Jimmy Smith .20 .50
13 Az-Zahir Hakim .15 .40
14 Antonio Freeman .25 .60
15 Curtis Conway .20 .50
16 Tim Biakabutuka .15 .40
17 Peter Warrick .20 .50
18 Kurt Warner .40 1.00
19 Brian Urlacher .30 .75
20 Rod Smith .20 .50
21 Frank Sanders .15 .40
22 Trevor Pryce .15 .40
23 Sammy Morris .20 .50
24 Cade McNown .20 .50
25 Keyshawn Johnson .20 .50
26 Tim Couch .15 .40
27 Dedric Ward .15 .40
28 Bill Schroeder .20 .50
29 John Randle .20 .50
30 Donovan McNabb .25 .60
31 Marvin Harrison .25 .60
32 Trent Dilfer .20 .50
33 David Boston .15 .40
34 Donnell Bennett .15 .40
35 Trace Armstrong .15 .40
36 Sam Adams .15 .40
37 Jeremiah Trotter .15 .40
38 Zach Thomas .25 .60
39 Shawn Jefferson .15 .40
40 J.J. Stokes .15 .40
41 Akili Smith .15 .40
42 Tony Siragusa .20 .50
43 William Roaf .20 .50
44 Muhsin Muhammad .20 .50
45 Terance Mathis .15 .40
46 Tee Martin .20 .50
47 Ray Lewis .25 .60
48 Matt Hasselbeck .25 .60
49 Todd Pinkston .15 .40
50 Rob Johnson .20 .50
51 Edgerrin James .25 .60
52 Rocket Ismail .20 .50
53 Trent Green .25 .60
54 Tim Dwight .20 .50
55 Anthony Becht .15 .40
56 Jessie Armstead .15 .40
57 Mike Anderson .20 .50
58 Jamal Anderson .20 .50
59 Anthony Wright .15 .40
60 Regan Upshaw .15 .40
61 John Holecek .15 .40
62 Shaun Alexander .25 .60
63 Troy Aikman .40 1.00
64 Peter Boulware .15 .40
65 Hines Ward .25 .60
66 Michael Strahan .25 .60
67 Herman Moore .20 .50
68 Rich Gannon .20 .50
69 Ken Dilger .15 .40
70 Terrell Davis .25 .60
71 Terrence Wilkins .15 .40
72 Fred Taylor .25 .60
73 Napoleon Kaufman .15 .40
74 Tony Horne .15 .40
75 Ahman Green .25 .60
76 Jay Fiedler .20 .50
77 Albert Connell .15 .40
78 Charlie Batch .20 .50
79 James Allen .15 .40
80 Sylvester Morris .15 .40
81 Isaac Bruce .25 .60
82 Charles Woodson .25 .60
83 Lamar Smith .20 .50
84 Peyton Manning .60 1.50
85 Sam Madison .15 .40
86 Olandis Gary .15 .40
87 Kevin Faulk .20 .50
88 Jeff Garcia .20 .50
89 JaJuan Dawson .15 .40
90 Sam Cowart .15 .40
91 David Sloan .15 .40
92 Bobby Shaw .15 .40
93 Travis Prentice .15 .40
94 Terrell Owens .25 .60
95 John Lynch .20 .50
96 Jim Harbaugh .20 .50
97 Brian Griese .20 .50
98 Jeff Graham .15 .40
99 La'Roi Glover .15 .40
100 Joey Galloway .20 .50
101 Wesley Walls .15 .40
102 Vinny Testaverde .20 .50
103 Jason Taylor .25 .60
104 Darnay Scott .20 .50
105 Samari Rolle .15 .40
106 Adrian Murrell .20 .50
107 Eric Moulds .20 .50
108 Keenan McCardell .20 .50
109 Donald Hayes .15 .40
110 Brett Favre .75 2.00
111 Troy Edwards .15 .40
112 Ron Dayne .20 .50
113 Daunte Culpepper .20 .50
114 Chris Chandler .20 .50
115 Mark Brunell .20 .50
116 Courtney Brown .15 .40
117 Aaron Brooks .20 .50
118 Fred Beasley .15 .40
119 Mike Alstott .20 .50
120 Tyrone Wheatley .20 .50
121 R.Jay Soward .15 .40
122 Deion Sanders .25 .60
123 Jake Reed .20 .50
124 Jamal Lewis .25 .60
125 Tony Gonzalez .25 .60
126 Terrell Fletcher .15 .40
127 Wayne Chrebet .20 .50
128 Cris Carter .25 .60
129 Drew Bledsoe .25 .60
130 Tiki Barber .25 .60
131 Derrick Alexander .15 .40
132 Frank Wycheck .15 .40
133 Jerome Pathon .15 .40
134 Warren Sapp .20 .50
135 Joe Horn .20 .50
136 Ricky Watters .20 .50
137 Amani Toomer .20 .50
138 Bruce Smith .25 .60
139 Andre Rison .20 .50
140 J.R. Redmond .15 .40
141 Steve McNair .25 .60
142 Michael McCrary .15 .40
143 Ike Hilliard .20 .50
144 Charlie Garner .20 .50
145 Mark Bruener .20 .50
146 Emmitt Smith .60 1.50
147 Darren Sharper .20 .50
148 Peerless Price .15 .40
149 Johnnie Morton .20 .50
150 Curtis Martin .25 .60
151 Joe Johnson .15 .40
152 MarTay Jenkins .15 .40
153 Priest Holmes .25 .60
154 Terry Glenn .20 .50
155 Oronde Gadsden .15 .40
156 Germane Crowell .15 .40
157 Steve Beuerlein .20 .50
158 Champ Bailey .25 .60
159 Troy Vincent .20 .50
160 James Stewart .15 .40
161 Jerry Rice .50 1.25
162 Randy Moss .25 .60
163 Dave Moore .15 .40
164 Ed McCaffrey .20 .50
165 Thomas Jones .20 .50
166 Rickey Dudley .15 .40
167 Hugh Douglas .15 .40
168 Stephen Davis .20 .50
169 Kerry Collins .20 .50
170 Cam Cleeland .15 .40
171 Stephen Boyd .15 .40
172 Jerome Bettis .25 .60
173 Aeneas Williams .20 .50
174 Chad Pennington .25 .60
175 Dorsey Levens .20 .50
176 Desmond Howard .20 .50
177 Torry Holt .20 .50
178 Plaxico Burress .20 .50
179 Kevin Johnson .15 .40
180 Kyle Brady .15 .40
181 Jake Plummer .20 .50
182 Brad Johnson .20 .50
183 Eddie George .25 .60
184 Corey Dillon .20 .50
185 Curtis Enis .15 .40
186 Tim Brown .25 .60
187 Tony Boselli .20 .50
188 Duce Staley .20 .50
189 Junior Seau .25 .60
190 Marshall Faulk .25 .60
191 Kordell Stewart .20 .50
192 Corey Simon .15 .40
193 Shannon Sharpe .25 .60
194 Marcus Robinson .20 .50
195 Carl Pickens .20 .50
196 Doug Flutie .25 .60
197 Freddie Jones .15 .40
198 Patrick Jeffers .15 .40
199 Shawn Bryson .15 .40
200 Kevin Dyson .15 .40
201 David Terrell RC 1.25 3.00
202 Dan Morgan RC 1.25 3.00
203 Chris Weinke RC 1.25 3.00
204 Correll Buckhalter RC 1.50 4.00
205 Chad Johnson RC 2.50 6.00
206 LaDainian Tomlinson RC 5.00 12.00
207 Reggie Wayne RC 3.00 8.00
208 Tim Hasselbeck RC 1.25 3.00
209 Michael Vick RC 6.00 15.00
210 Heath Evans RC 1.25 3.00
211 Damione Lewis RC 1.25 3.00
212 Richard Seymour RC 1.50 4.00
213 Quincy Morgan RC 1.25 3.00
214 Drew Brees RC 10.00 25.00
215 Freddie Mitchell RC 1.00 2.50
216 Justin McCareins RC 1.25 3.00
217 Mike McMahon RC 1.25 3.00
218 Derrick Gibson RC 1.00 2.50
219 Rudi Johnson RC 1.50 4.00
220 Todd Heap RC 1.50 4.00
221 Josh Booty RC 1.25 3.00
222 Justin Smith RC 1.50 4.00
223 Marcus Stroud RC 1.25 3.00
224 Rod Gardner RC 1.25 3.00
225 Vinny Sutherland RC 1.00 2.50
226 Marques Tuiasosopo RC 1.25 3.00
227 Anthony Thomas RC 1.50 4.00
228 Bobby Newcombe RC 1.25 3.00
229 Michael Bennett RC 1.25 3.00
230 Snoop Minnis RC 1.00 2.50
231 Travis Minor RC 1.25 3.00
232 Travis Henry RC 1.25 3.00
233 Kevan Barlow RC 1.25 3.00
234 Gerard Warren RC 1.25 3.00
235 Sage Rosenfels RC 1.50 4.00
236 Chris Chambers RC 1.50 4.00
237 James Jackson RC 1.00 2.50
238 Deuce McAllister RC 1.50 4.00
239 Koren Robinson RC 1.25 3.00
240 Andre Carter RC 1.25 3.00
241 Santana Moss RC 2.00 5.00
242 LaMont Jordan RC 1.50 4.00
243 Ken-Yon Rambo RC 1.00 2.50
244 Jamal Reynolds RC 1.00 2.50
245 Fred Smoot RC 1.50 4.00
246 Robert Ferguson RC 1.50 4.00
247 Alex Bannister RC 1.00 2.50
248 Dan Alexander RC 1.25 3.00
249 Nate Clements RC 1.25 3.00
250 Quincy Carter RC 1.25 3.00
CL1 Checklist .05 .15
CL2 Checklist .05 .15

2001 Fleer Premium Star Ruby

*VETS 1-200: 6X TO 15X BASIC CARDS
*ROOKIES 201-250: 1X TO 2.5X
STATED PRINT RUN 125 SER.#'d SETS

2001 Fleer Premium Clothes to the Game

STATED ODDS 1:59
1 Jessie Armstead 3.00 8.00
2 Champ Bailey 5.00 12.00
3 David Boston 3.00 8.00
4 Courtney Brown 3.00 8.00
5 Isaac Bruce 5.00 12.00
6 Ken Dilger 3.00 8.00
7 Curtis Enis 3.00 8.00
8 E.G. Green 3.00 8.00
9 Marvin Harrison 5.00 12.00
10 Torry Holt 4.00 10.00
11 Edgerrin James 5.00 12.00
12 Cade McNown 4.00 10.00
13 Johnnie Morton 4.00 10.00
14 Todd Pinkston 3.00 8.00
15 Michael Pittman 4.00 10.00
16 Jake Plummer 4.00 10.00
17 Travis Prentice 3.00 8.00
18 Jerry Rice 10.00 25.00
19 R.Jay Soward 3.00 8.00
20 Kordell Stewart 4.00 10.00
21 Kurt Warner 8.00 20.00

2001 Fleer Premium Commanding Respect

COMPLETE SET (15) 7.50 20.00
STATED ODDS 1:20
1 Brian Griese .60 1.50
2 Jamal Lewis .75 2.00
3 Fred Taylor .75 2.00
4 Stephen Davis .60 1.50
5 Marcus Robinson .60 1.50
6 Marvin Harrison .75 2.00
7 Marshall Faulk .75 2.00
8 Doug Flutie .75 2.00
9 Jamal Anderson .60 1.50
10 Donovan McNabb .75 2.00
11 Steve McNair .75 2.00
12 Jeff Garcia .60 1.50
13 Daunte Culpepper .60 1.50
14 Isaac Bruce .75 2.00
15 Jimmy Smith .60 1.50

2001 Fleer Premium Greatest Plays

COMP.SET w/o SP's (19) 12.50 30.00
STATED ODDS 1:10
1 Dave Casper SP 10.00 20.00
2 Emmitt Smith 1.50 4.00
3 Roger Staubach 1.25 3.00
4 Jerry Rice 1.25 3.00
5 Doug Flutie .75 2.00
6 Earl Campbell .75 2.00
7 Bart Starr SP 15.00 30.00
8 John Elway 2.00 5.00
9 Joe Montana 2.00 5.00
10 Dan Marino 2.00 5.00
11 Dwight Clark .60 1.50
12 Franco Harris .75 2.00
13 Gale Sayers 1.00 2.50
14 Ken Stabler 1.00 2.50
15 Steve Young 1.00 2.50
16 William Perry .60 1.50
17 Michael Westbrook .50 1.25
18 Kordell Stewart .50 1.25
19 Terry Bradshaw 1.25 3.00
20 Tony Dorsett .75 2.00
21 Eric Dickerson .60 1.50

2001 Fleer Premium Greatest Plays Jerseys

STATED ODDS 1:91
1 Tony Dorsett 10.00 25.00
2 John Elway 15.00 40.00
3 Doug Flutie 10.00 25.00
4 Dan Marino 20.00 40.00
5 Joe Montana 20.00 50.00
6 Jerry Rice 12.50 30.00
7 Bart Starr 12.50 30.00
8 Steve Young 10.00 25.00

2001 Fleer Premium Home Field Advantage

COMPLETE SET (12) 20.00 50.00
STATED ODDS 1:72
1 Eddie George 1.50 4.00
2 Edgerrin James 1.50 4.00
3 Ricky Williams 1.50 4.00
4 Jeff Garcia 1.25 3.00
5 Brett Favre 5.00 12.00
6 Warrick Dunn 1.50 4.00
7 Donovan McNabb 1.50 4.00
8 Brian Urlacher 2.00 5.00
9 Kurt Warner 2.50 6.00
10 Emmitt Smith 4.00 10.00
11 Rich Gannon 1.25 3.00
12 Cris Carter 1.50 4.00

2001 Fleer Premium Home Field Advantage Turf

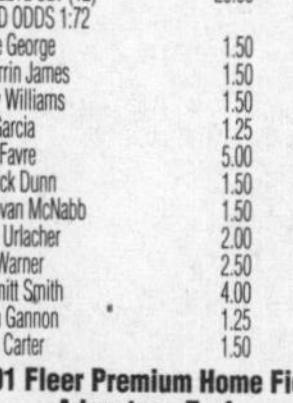

STATED PRINT RUN 314 SER.#'d SETS
1 Cris Carter 6.00 15.00
2 Warrick Dunn 6.00 15.00
3 Brett Favre 20.00 50.00
4 Rich Gannon 5.00 12.00
5 Jeff Garcia 5.00 12.00
6 Eddie George 6.00 15.00
7 Edgerrin James 6.00 15.00
8 Donovan McNabb 6.00 15.00
9 Emmitt Smith 15.00 40.00
10 Brian Urlacher 8.00 20.00
11 Kurt Warner 10.00 25.00
12 Ricky Williams 6.00 15.00

2001 Fleer Premium Performers Jerseys

STATED PRINT RUN 900 SER.#'d SETS
1 Jerome Bettis 5.00 12.00
2 David Boston 3.00 8.00
3 Az-Zahir Hakim 3.00 8.00
4 Torry Holt 4.00 10.00
5 Edgerrin James 5.00 12.00
6 Kevin Johnson 3.00 8.00
7 Rob Johnson 4.00 10.00
8 Thomas Jones 4.00 10.00
9 Jim Kelly 6.00 15.00
10 Jamal Lewis 5.00 12.00
11 Keenan McCardell 4.00 10.00
12 Donovan McNabb 5.00 12.00
13 Cade McNown 4.00 10.00
14 Jake Plummer 4.00 10.00
15 Travis Prentice 3.00 8.00
16 Jerry Rice 10.00 25.00
17 Marcus Robinson 4.00 10.00
18 Duce Staley 4.00 10.00
19 Kordell Stewart 4.00 10.00
20 Kurt Warner 8.00 20.00

2001 Fleer Premium Respect Patches

STATED PRINT RUN 80 SER.#'d SETS
1 Jamal Anderson 8.00 20.00
2 Isaac Bruce 10.00 25.00
3 Daunte Culpepper 8.00 20.00
4 Stephen Davis 8.00 20.00
5 Marshall Faulk 10.00 25.00
6 Doug Flutie 10.00 25.00
7 Jeff Garcia 8.00 20.00
8 Brian Griese 8.00 20.00
9 Marvin Harrison 10.00 25.00
10 Jamal Lewis 10.00 25.00
11 Donovan McNabb 10.00 25.00
12 Steve McNair 10.00 25.00
13 Marcus Robinson 8.00 20.00
14 Jimmy Smith 8.00 20.00
15 Fred Taylor 10.00 25.00

2001 Fleer Premium Rookie Game Ball

STATED PRINT RUN 250 SER.#'d SETS
201 David Terrell 4.00 10.00
202 Dan Morgan 4.00 10.00
203 Chris Weinke 4.00 10.00
205 Chad Johnson 8.00 20.00
206 LaDainian Tomlinson 25.00 60.00
207 Reggie Wayne 10.00 25.00
209 Michael Vick 20.00 50.00
213 Quincy Morgan 4.00 10.00
214 Drew Brees 25.00 50.00
215 Freddie Mitchell 3.00 8.00
219 Rudi Johnson 5.00 12.00
224 Rod Gardner 4.00 10.00
226 Marques Tuiasosopo 4.00 10.00
227 Anthony Thomas 5.00 12.00
229 Michael Bennett 4.00 10.00
230 Snoop Minnis 3.00 8.00
231 Travis Minor 4.00 10.00
232 Travis Henry 4.00 10.00
233 Kevan Barlow 4.00 10.00
236 Chris Chambers 5.00 12.00
237 James Jackson 3.00 8.00
238 Deuce McAllister 5.00 12.00
239 Koren Robinson 4.00 10.00
241 Santana Moss 6.00 15.00
250 Quincy Carter 4.00 10.00

2001 Fleer Premium Rookie Revolution

COMPLETE SET (10) 10.00 25.00
STATED ODDS 1:10
1 Deuce McAllister .60 1.50
2 David Terrell .50 1.25
3 Drew Brees 4.00 10.00
4 Chad Johnson 1.00 2.50
5 LaDainian Tomlinson 2.00 5.00
6 Marques Tuiasosopo .50 1.25
7 Michael Vick 2.50 6.00
8 Michael Bennett .50 1.25
9 Anthony Thomas .60 1.50
10 Santana Moss .75 2.00

2001 Fleer Premium Rookie Revolution Autographs

STATED PRINT RUN 50 SER.#'d SETS
1 Michael Bennett 8.00 20.00
2 Drew Brees 100.00 175.00
3 Chad Johnson 15.00 40.00
5 Santana Moss 12.00 30.00
6 David Terrell 8.00 20.00
7 Anthony Thomas 10.00 25.00
8 LaDainian Tomlinson 75.00 150.00
9 Marques Tuiasosopo 8.00 20.00
10 Michael Vick 100.00 175.00

2001 Fleer Premium Solid Performers

COMPLETE SET (20) 12.00 30.00
STATED ODDS 1:20
1 Jerome Bettis .75 2.00
2 David Boston .50 1.25
3 Cade McNown .60 1.50
4 Keenan McCardell .60 1.50
5 Thomas Jones .60 1.50
6 Edgerrin James .75 2.00
7 Torry Holt .60 1.50
8 Az-Zahir Hakim .50 1.25
9 Jake Plummer .60 1.50
10 Travis Prentice .50 1.25
11 Marcus Robinson .60 1.50
12 Duce Staley .60 1.50

13 Kurt Warner 1.25 3.00
14 Kordell Stewart .60 1.50
15 Rob Johnson .60 1.50
16 Jamal Lewis .75 2.00
17 Donovan McNabb .75 2.00
18 Kevin Johnson .50 1.25
19 Jim Kelly 1.00 2.50
20 Jerry Rice 1.50 4.00

2001 Fleer Premium Suiting Up Jerseys

STATED ODDS 1:109 RETAIL
1 Jessie Armstead 4.00 10.00
2 Champ Bailey 6.00 15.00
3 David Boston 4.00 10.00
4 Courtney Brown 4.00 10.00
5 Isaac Bruce 6.00 15.00
6 Ken Dilger 4.00 10.00
7 Curtis Enis 4.00 10.00
8 E.G. Green 4.00 10.00
9 Marvin Harrison 6.00 15.00
10 Torry Holt 5.00 12.00
11 Edgerrin James 6.00 15.00
12 Cade McNown 5.00 12.00
13 Johnnie Morton 5.00 12.00
14 Todd Pinkston 4.00 10.00
15 Michael Pittman 5.00 12.00
16 Jake Plummer 5.00 12.00
17 Travis Prentice 4.00 10.00
18 Jerry Rice 12.00 30.00
19 R.Jay Soward 4.00 10.00

2002 Fleer Premium

Released in September 2002, this 200-card set contains 130 veterans and 39 rookies. S.R.P. was $2.99 per pack. Both hobby and retail boxes contained 24 packs each with 5 cards per pack. Rookies were serial numbered to 1250.

COMP.SET w/o SP's (160) 15.00 40.00
131-170 ROOKIE PRINT RUN 1250
1 Kevin Dyson .30 .75
2 Kerry Collins .30 .75
3 Marty Booker .30 .75
4 Curtis Conway .30 .75
5 Drew Bledsoe .40 1.00
6 Kurt Warner .40 1.00
7 Hines Ward .40 1.00
8 Terrell Owens .40 1.00
9 Todd Pinkston .25 .60
10 Eric Moulds .30 .75
11 Quincy Morgan .25 .60
12 Fred Taylor .30 .75
13 Santana Moss .30 .75
14 Peyton Manning .75 2.00
15 Qadry Ismail .30 .75
16 Mike McMahon .25 .60
17 David Patten .25 .60
18 Wayne Chrebet .30 .75
19 David Terrell .25 .60
20 Corey Bradford .25 .60
21 Derrick Mason .30 .75
22 Anthony Thomas .30 .75
23 James Allen .25 .60
24 Vinny Testaverde .30 .75
25 Trent Green .30 .75
26 Thomas Jones .40 1.00
27 Rocket Ismail .30 .75
28 Duce Staley .30 .75
29 Drew Brees .60 1.50
30 Chris Chandler .30 .75
31 Kordell Stewart .30 .75
32 Koren Robinson .25 .60
33 Jon Kitna .30 .75
34 Jamie Sharper .30 .75
35 Germane Crowell .25 .60
36 Lamar Smith .30 .75
37 LaDainian Tomlinson .50 1.25
38 Freddie Mitchell .25 .60
39 Corey Dillon .30 .75
40 Isaac Bruce .40 1.00
41 James Thrash .30 .75
42 Brian Griese .30 .75
43 Marvin Harrison .40 1.00
44 Aaron Brooks .30 .75
45 Rich Gannon .30 .75
46 Mike Alstott .30 .75
47 Shannon Sharpe .40 1.00
48 Travis Henry .25 .60
49 Keyshawn Johnson .30 .75
50 Daunte Culpepper .30 .75
51 James Jackson .25 .60
52 Justin McCareins .30 .75
53 Quincy Carter .25 .60
54 Stephen Davis .30 .75
55 Joey Galloway .30 .75
56 Joe Horn .30 .75
57 Plaxico Burress .30 .75
58 Brett Favre 1.00 2.50
59 Brian Urlacher .40 1.00
60 David Boston .25 .60
61 Darrell Jackson .30 .75
62 Trung Canidate .25 .60
63 Shaun Alexander .30 .75
64 Steve McNair .40 1.00
65 Doug Flutie .40 1.00
66 LaMont Jordan .30 .75
67 Rod Smith .30 .75
68 Marshall Faulk .40 1.00
69 Tiki Barber .40 1.00
70 James Stewart .25 .60
71 Frank Wycheck .25 .60
72 Peerless Price .25 .60
73 Derrick Alexander .25 .60
74 Charlie Garner .30 .75
75 Peter Warrick .30 .75
76 Warren Sapp .30 .75
77 Kevan Barlow .25 .60
78 Edgerrin James .30 .75
79 Willie Jackson .25 .60
80 Keenan McCardell .30 .75
81 Bill Schroeder .25 .60
82 Curtis Martin .40 1.00
83 Torry Holt .40 1.00
84 Tony Gonzalez .40 1.00
85 Jeff Garcia .30 .75
86 Travis Taylor .25 .60
87 Johnnie Morton .30 .75
88 Tim Couch .25 .60
89 Troy Brown .30 .75
90 Emmitt Smith 1.00 2.50
91 Aeneas Williams .30 .75
92 Rod Gardner .25 .60
93 Brandon Stokley .30 .75
94 Warrick Dunn .30 .75
95 Jay Riemersma .25 .60
96 Kevin Johnson .25 .60
97 Antowain Smith .30 .75
98 James McKnight .25 .60
99 Amani Toomer .30 .75
100 Ricky Williams .30 .75
101 Priest Holmes .40 1.00
102 Muhsin Muhammad .30 .75
103 Jake Plummer .30 .75
104 Marcus Robinson .30 .75
105 Donovan McNabb .40 1.00
106 Tom Brady 1.00 2.50
107 Jimmy Smith .30 .75
108 Jamal Lewis .30 .75
109 Antonio Freeman .40 1.00
110 Ron Dayne .30 .75
111 Tim Brown .40 1.00
112 Chris Chambers .30 .75
113 Garrison Hearst .30 .75
114 Michael Vick .60 1.50
115 Snoop Minnis .25 .60
116 Terrell Davis .40 1.00
117 Ahman Green .30 .75
118 Donald Hayes .25 .60
119 Jermaine Lewis .25 .60
120 Chad Johnson .40 1.00
121 Jay Fiedler .30 .75
122 Randy Moss .40 1.00
123 Wesley Walls .30 .75
124 Eddie George .30 .75
125 Jerry Rice .75 2.00
126 Michael Bennett .30 .75
127 Jerome Bettis .40 1.00
128 Mark Brunell .30 .75
129 Adam Vinatieri .40 1.00
130 Ed McCaffrey .30 .75
131 Maurice Morris RC 1.25 3.00
132 Ron Johnson RC 1.25 3.00
133 Antwaan Randle El RC 1.50 4.00
134 Brian Westbrook RC 2.50 6.00
135 Julius Peppers RC 3.00 8.00
136 Travis Stephens RC 1.00 2.50
137 David Carr RC 1.50 4.00
138 Clinton Portis RC 2.00 5.00
139 Reche Caldwell RC 1.50 4.00
140 Tim Carter RC 1.25 3.00
141 Daniel Graham RC 1.25 3.00
142 Rohan Davey RC 1.50 4.00
143 T.J. Duckett RC 1.50 4.00
144 Luke Staley RC 1.00 2.50
145 Ashley Lelie RC 1.25 3.00
146 Josh Reed RC 1.25 3.00
147 Randy Fasani RC 1.25 3.00
148 Andre Davis RC 1.25 3.00
149 Joey Harrington RC 1.50 4.00
150 David Garrard RC 2.00 5.00
151 Ladell Betts RC 1.50 4.00
152 Donte Stallworth RC 1.50 4.00
153 Adrian Peterson RC 1.50 4.00
154 Lamar Gordon RC 1.25 3.00
155 Jonathan Wells RC 1.50 4.00
156 Jabar Gaffney RC 1.50 4.00
157 Patrick Ramsey RC 1.50 4.00
158 Roy Williams RC 1.50 4.00
159 Jeremy Shockey RC 2.50 6.00
160 Javon Walker RC 1.50 4.00
161 Marquise Walker RC 1.00 2.50
162 Antonio Bryant RC 1.50 4.00
163 Josh McCown RC 1.50 4.00
164 Najeh Davenport RC 1.50 4.00
165 William Green RC 1.25 3.00
166 Jerramy Stevens RC 1.50 4.00
167 DeShaun Foster RC 1.50 4.00
168 Cliff Russell RC 1.00 2.50
169 Kurt Kittner RC 1.00 2.50
170 Eric Crouch RC 1.50 4.00
171 Michael Pittman PP .30 .75
172 Darnay Scott PP .30 .75
173 Charles Woodson PP .40 1.00
174 Ty Law PP .30 .75
175 Tony Boselli PP .30 .75
176 Zach Thomas PP .40 1.00
177 Trent Dilfer PP .30 .75
178 Bubba Franks PP .30 .75
179 Laveranues Coles PP .30 .75
180 John Lynch PP .30 .75
181 Kendrell Bell PP .25 .60
182 Mike Anderson PP .30 .75
183 Amos Zereoue PP .25 .60
184 Michael Strahan PP .40 1.00
185 Chad Lewis PP .25 .60
186 Travis Minor PP .25 .60
187 Jevon Kearse PP .30 .75
188 Darren Sharper PP .30 .75
189 Az-Zahir Hakim PP .25 .60
190 Ray Lewis PP .40 1.00
191 Deuce McAllister PP .30 .75
192 Chris Weinke PP .25 .60
193 Desmond Howard PP .30 .75
194 Dominic Rhodes PP .30 .75
195 Joe Jurevicius PP .25 .60
196 Tim Dwight PP .25 .60
197 Jeff Zgonina PP .25 .60
198 Junior Seau PP .40 1.00
199 Rosevelt Colvin PP RC .50 1.25
200 Chad Pennington PP .40 1.00

2002 Fleer Premium Star Ruby

*VETS 1-130: 2.5X TO 6X BASIC CARDS
*ROOKIES 131-170: 1X TO 2.5X
STATED PRINT RUN 100 SER.#'d SETS

2002 Fleer Premium All-Pro Team

COMPLETE SET (25) 25.00 60.00
STATED PRINT RUN 1000 SER.#'d SETS
1 David Boston .75 2.00
2 Jerome Bettis 1.25 3.00
3 Brett Favre 3.00 8.00
4 Brian Urlacher 1.25 3.00
5 Marshall Faulk 1.25 3.00
6 Rich Gannon 1.00 2.50
7 Emmitt Smith 3.00 8.00
8 Corey Dillon 1.00 2.50
9 Jerry Rice 2.50 6.00
10 Donovan McNabb 1.25 3.00
11 Curtis Martin 1.25 3.00
12 Isaac Bruce 1.25 3.00
13 Junior Seau 1.25 3.00
14 Jeff Garcia 1.00 2.50
15 Mike Alstott 1.00 2.50
16 Ray Lewis 1.25 3.00
17 Daunte Culpepper 1.00 2.50
18 Tony Gonzalez 1.25 3.00
19 Terrell Owens 1.25 3.00
20 Peyton Manning 2.50 6.00
21 Randy Moss 1.25 3.00
22 Kurt Warner 1.25 3.00
23 Jimmy Smith 1.00 2.50
24 Edgerrin James 1.00 2.50
25 Tom Brady 3.00 8.00

2002 Fleer Premium All-Pro Team Jerseys

STATED ODDS 1:36 HOB, 1:150 RET
1 David Boston 2.50 6.00
2 Tom Brady 10.00 25.00
3 Daunte Culpepper 3.00 8.00
4 Corey Dillon 3.00 8.00
5 Brett Favre 10.00 25.00
6 Jeff Garcia 3.00 8.00
7 Ray Lewis 4.00 10.00
8 Curtis Martin 4.00 10.00
9 Randy Moss 4.00 10.00
10 Terrell Owens 4.00 10.00
11 Jerry Rice 8.00 20.00
12 Junior Seau 4.00 10.00
13 Emmitt Smith 10.00 25.00
14 Jimmy Smith 3.00 8.00
15 Brian Urlacher 4.00 10.00
16 Kurt Warner 4.00 10.00

2002 Fleer Premium All-Pro Team Jersey Patches

STATED PRINT RUN 100 SER.#'d SETS
1 Mike Alstott 6.00 15.00
2 Jerome Bettis 8.00 20.00
3 David Boston 5.00 12.00
4 Tom Brady 20.00 50.00
5 Isaac Bruce 8.00 20.00
6 Daunte Culpepper 6.00 15.00
7 Corey Dillon 6.00 15.00
8 Marshall Faulk 8.00 20.00
9 Brett Favre 20.00 50.00
10 Rich Gannon 6.00 15.00
11 Jeff Garcia 6.00 15.00
12 Edgerrin James 6.00 15.00
13 Ray Lewis 8.00 20.00
14 Donovan McNabb 8.00 20.00
15 Randy Moss 8.00 20.00
16 Terrell Owens 8.00 20.00
17 Jerry Rice 15.00 40.00
18 Brian Urlacher 8.00 20.00
19 Kurt Warner 8.00 20.00

2002 Fleer Premium All-Rookie Team

STATED ODDS 1:6 HOB/RET
1 David Carr .50 1.25
2 William Green .40 1.00
3 Ashley Lelie .40 1.00
4 Clinton Portis .60 1.50
5 Reche Caldwell .50 1.25
6 Donte Stallworth .50 1.25
7 DeShaun Foster .50 1.25
8 T.J. Duckett .50 1.25
9 Antwaan Randle El .50 1.25
10 Julius Peppers 1.00 2.50
11 Joey Harrington .50 1.25
12 Jabar Gaffney .50 1.25
13 Antonio Bryant .50 1.25
14 Ladell Betts .50 1.25
15 Ron Johnson .40 1.00

2002 Fleer Premium All-Rookie Team Memorabilia

STATED PRINT RUN 50 SER.#'d SETS
1 T.J. Duckett 6.00 15.00
2 DeShaun Foster 6.00 15.00
3 Jabar Gaffney 6.00 15.00
4 William Green 5.00 12.00
5 Joey Harrington 6.00 15.00
6 Ashley Lelie 5.00 12.00
7 Julius Peppers 12.00 30.00
8 Donte Stallworth 6.00 15.00

2002 Fleer Premium Fantasy Team

COMPLETE SET (20) 25.00 60.00
STATED PRINT RUN 1200 SER.#'d SETS
1 Kurt Warner 1.00 2.50
2 Peyton Manning 2.00 5.00
3 Brett Favre 2.50 6.00
4 Michael Vick 1.50 4.00
5 Tom Brady 2.50 6.00
6 Edgerrin James .75 2.00
7 Marshall Faulk 1.00 2.50
8 Ricky Williams .75 2.00
9 Emmitt Smith 2.50 6.00
10 Anthony Thomas .75 2.00
11 Randy Moss 1.00 2.50
12 Jerry Rice 2.00 5.00
13 Marvin Harrison 1.00 2.50
14 Chris Chambers .75 2.00
15 Torry Holt 1.00 2.50
16 David Carr 1.00 2.50
17 Joey Harrington 1.00 2.50
18 William Green .75 2.00
19 Donte Stallworth 1.00 2.50
20 Ashley Lelie .75 2.00

2002 Fleer Premium Fantasy Team Memorabilia

STATED ODDS 1:60 HOB, 1:240 RET
1 Tom Brady 10.00 25.00
2 Brett Favre 10.00 25.00
3 William Green 3.00 8.00
4 Joey Harrington 4.00 10.00
5 Marvin Harrison Pants 4.00 10.00
6 Torry Holt 4.00 10.00
7 Edgerrin James 3.00 8.00
8 Randy Moss 4.00 10.00
9 Jerry Rice 8.00 20.00
10 Emmitt Smith 10.00 25.00
11 Anthony Thomas 3.00 8.00
12 Kurt Warner 4.00 10.00
13 Ricky Williams 3.00 8.00

2002 Fleer Premium Fantasy Team Memorabilia Duals

STATED PRINT RUN 75 SER.#'d SETS
1 William Green 8.00 20.00
2 Joey Harrington 10.00 25.00
3 Donte Stallworth 10.00 25.00
4 Anthony Thomas 8.00 20.00
5 Michael Vick 15.00 40.00

2002 Fleer Premium Prem Team

COMPLETE SET (27) 50.00 100.00
STATED ODDS 1:12 HOB/RET
*RUBY/500: .5X TO 1.2X BASIC INSERTS
RUBY PRINT RUN 500 SER.#'d SETS
1 Jeff Garcia 1.25 3.00
2 Garrison Hearst 1.25 3.00
3 Emmitt Smith 4.00 10.00
4 Brett Favre 4.00 10.00
5 Ahman Green 1.25 3.00
6 Plaxico Burress 1.25 3.00
7 Jerome Bettis 1.50 4.00
8 Kordell Stewart 1.25 3.00
9 Kendrell Bell 1.00 2.50
10 Randall Cunningham 1.50 4.00
11 Donovan McNabb 1.50 4.00
12 Duce Staley 1.25 3.00
13 Chad Lewis 1.00 2.50
14 Ricky Williams 1.25 3.00
15 Zach Thomas 1.50 4.00
16 Rich Gannon 1.25 3.00
17 Jerry Rice 3.00 8.00
18 Tim Brown 1.50 4.00
19 Brian Urlacher 1.50 4.00
20 Marcus Robinson 1.25 3.00
21 Anthony Thomas 1.25 3.00
22 Kurt Warner 1.50 4.00
23 Marshall Faulk 1.50 4.00
24 Isaac Bruce 1.50 4.00
25 Brian Griese 1.25 3.00
26 Terrell Davis 1.50 4.00
27 Ed McCaffrey 1.25 3.00

2002 Fleer Premium Prem Team Jerseys

STATED ODDS 1:10 HOB, 1:65 RET
1 Jerome Bettis 5.00 12.00
2 Tim Brown 4.00 10.00
3 Terrell Davis 4.00 10.00
4 Brett Favre 10.00 26.00
5 Rich Gannon 3.00 8.00
6 Jeff Garcia 3.00 8.00
7 Brian Griese 3.00 8.00
8 Jerry Rice 8.00 20.00
9 Emmitt Smith 10.00 25.00
10 Duce Staley 3.00 8.00
11 Anthony Thomas 3.00 8.00
12 Brian Urlacher 4.00 10.00
13 Kurt Warner 4.00 10.00
14 Ricky Williams 3.00 8.00
15 Donovan McNabb 4.00 10.00

2002 Fleer Premium Prem Team Jersey Patches

STATED PRINT RUN 100 SER.#'d SETS
1 Jerome Bettis 12.00 30.00
2 Tim Brown 10.00 25.00
3 Brett Favre 25.00 60.00
4 Rich Gannon 8.00 20.00
5 Jeff Garcia 8.00 20.00
6 Brian Griese 8.00 20.00
7 Donovan McNabb 10.00 25.00
8 Jerry Rice 20.00 50.00
9 Emmitt Smith 25.00 60.00
10 Duce Staley 8.00 20.00
11 Kordell Stewart 8.00 20.00
12 Anthony Thomas 8.00 20.00
13 Brian Urlacher 10.00 25.00
14 Kurt Warner 10.00 25.00
15 Ricky Williams 8.00 20.00

2000 Fleer Showcase

Released in late November 2000, Showcase features a 160-card base set comprised of 100 Veteran cards, 20 Rookie cards, numbers 101-120, sequentially numbered to 1000, and 40 Rookie cards, numbers 121-160, sequentially numbered to 2000. Base cards are all holographic foil and are enhanced with gold foil highlights. Showcase was packaged in 24-pack boxes with packs containing five cards and carried a suggested retail price of $4.99.

COMP.SET w/o SP's (100) 10.00 25.00
1 Tim Couch .25 .60
2 Deion Sanders .30 .75
3 Darnay Scott .25 .60
4 Brett Favre 1.00 2.50
5 Mark Brunell .25 .60
6 Randy Moss .30 .75
7 Tyrone Wheatley .20 .50
8 Isaac Bruce .30 .75
9 Eddie George .25 .60
10 Troy Aikman .50 1.25
11 Charlie Batch .25 .60
12 Marvin Harrison .30 .75
13 Terry Glenn .25 .60
14 Charles Johnson .20 .50
15 Jerry Rice .60 1.50
16 Kurt Warner .50 1.25
17 Kevin Johnson .20 .50
18 Jay Fiedler .25 .60
19 Vinny Testaverde .25 .60
20 Curtis Enis .20 .50
21 Elvis Grbac .20 .50
22 Kordell Stewart .25 .60
23 Jamal Anderson .25 .60
24 Dorsey Levens .25 .60
25 Derrick Mayes .20 .50
26 Marcus Robinson .25 .60
27 Cam Cleeland .20 .50
28 Charlie Garner .25 .60
29 Germane Crowell .20 .50
30 Cade McNown .20 .50
31 Tony Gonzalez .30 .75
32 Shaun King .20 .50
33 Wayne Chrebet .25 .60
34 Muhsin Muhammad .25 .60
35 Olandis Gary .25 .60
36 Ray Lewis .30 .75
37 Terrell Davis .30 .75
38 Steve Beuerlein .25 .60
39 James Stewart .20 .50
40 Jon Kitna .25 .60
41 Tim Biakabutuka .25 .60
42 Ryan Leaf .25 .60
43 Mike Alstott .30 .75
44 Yancey Thigpen .20 .50
45 Champ Bailey .25 .60
46 Peerless Price .25 .60
47 Ken Dilger .20 .50
48 Derrick Alexander .20 .50
49 Drew Bledsoe .30 .75
50 Jerome Bettis .30 .75
51 Jermaine Fazande .20 .50
52 Joey Galloway .25 .60
53 Jeff Blake .25 .60
54 Emmitt Smith .75 2.00
55 Ricky Williams .30 .75
56 Marshall Faulk .30 .75
57 Stephen Davis .25 .60
58 Rob Johnson .25 .60
59 Brian Griese .25 .60
60 Damon Huard .25 .60
61 Jevon Kearse .25 .60
62 Doug Flutie .30 .75
63 Curtis Martin .30 .75
64 Torry Holt .30 .75
65 David Boston .20 .50
66 Cris Carter .30 .75
67 Jason Sehorn .20 .50
68 Keyshawn Johnson .25 .60
69 Chris Chandler .25 .60
70 Antonio Freeman .25 .60
71 Kerry Collins .25 .60
72 Akili Smith .20 .50
73 Troy Edwards .20 .50
74 Tim Dwight .25 .60
75 Donovan McNabb .30 .75
76 Tony Banks .20 .50
77 Ed McCaffrey .25 .60
78 Errict Rhett .25 .60
79 Fred Taylor .30 .75
80 Terrell Owens .30 .75
81 Steve McNair .30 .75
82 Rob Moore .20 .50
83 Jimmy Smith .25 .60
84 Daunte Culpepper .25 .60
85 Carl Pickens .25 .60
86 Moses Moreno .20 .50
87 Brad Johnson .25 .60
88 Jake Plummer .25 .60
89 Edgerrin James .30 .75
90 Zach Thomas .30 .75
91 Rich Gannon .25 .60
92 Warrick Dunn .25 .60
93 Shannon Sharpe .30 .75
94 Peyton Manning .75 2.00
95 Keenan McCardell .25 .60
96 Tony Simmons .20 .50
97 Duce Staley .25 .60
98 Corey Dillon .25 .60
99 Tim Brown .30 .75
100 Ricky Watters .25 .60
101 Peter Warrick RC 3.00 8.00
102 Shaun Alexander RC 4.00 10.00
103 Anthony Becht RC 2.50 6.00
104 Courtney Brown RC 2.50 6.00
105 Plaxico Burress RC 3.00 8.00
106 Trung Canidate RC 2.50 6.00
107 Giovanni Carmazzi RC 2.00 5.00
108 Laveranues Coles RC 3.00 8.00
109 Ron Dayne RC 3.00 8.00
110 Reuben Droughns RC 3.00 8.00
111 Danny Farmer RC 2.00 5.00
112 Bubba Franks RC 3.00 8.00
113 Thomas Jones RC 4.00 10.00
114 Jamal Lewis RC 3.00 8.00
115 Sylvester Morris RC 2.00 5.00
116 Chad Pennington RC 5.00 12.00
117 Travis Prentice RC 2.50 6.00
118 J.R. Redmond RC 2.00 5.00
119 R.Jay Soward RC 2.00 5.00
120 Dez White RC 2.50 6.00
121 Sebastian Janikowski RC 2.00 5.00
122 Todd Pinkston RC 1.25 3.00
123 Marc Bulger RC 2.00 5.00
124 Ron Dugans RC 1.25 3.00
125 Joe Hamilton RC 1.25 3.00
126 Curtis Keaton RC 1.25 3.00
127 Tee Martin RC 2.00 5.00
128 Dennis Northcutt RC 1.50 4.00
129 Corey Simon RC 1.50 4.00
130 Chris Redman RC 1.50 4.00
131 Brian Urlacher RC 8.00 20.00
132 Travis Taylor RC 1.50 4.00
133 Michael Wiley RC 1.25 3.00
134 Tim Rattay RC 1.50 4.00
135 Jerry Porter RC 2.00 5.00
136 Tom Brady RC 60.00 120.00
137 Deon Dyer RC 1.25 3.00
138 Mareno Philyaw RC 1.25 3.00
139 Spergon Wynn RC 1.50 4.00
140 John Abraham RC 2.00 5.00
141 Ahmed Plummer RC 1.25 3.00
142 Chris Hovan RC 1.50 4.00
143 Rob Morris RC 1.50 4.00
144 Keith Bulluck RC 1.50 4.00
145 JaJuan Dawson RC 1.25 3.00
146 Chris Cole RC 1.50 4.00
147 Chafie Fields RC 1.25 3.00
148 Darrell Jackson RC 1.50 4.00
149 Marcus Knight RC 1.25 3.00
150 Gari Scott RC 1.25 3.00
151 Kwame Cavil RC 1.25 3.00
152 Frank Moreau RC 1.25 3.00
153 Doug Chapman RC 1.25 3.00
154 Erron Kinney RC 1.25 3.00
155 Ron Dixon RC 1.25 3.00
156 Ben Kelly RC 1.25 3.00
157 Bashir Yamini RC 1.25 3.00
158 Anthony Lucas RC 1.25 3.00
159 Avion Black RC 1.25 3.00
160 Ian Gold RC 1.25 3.00

2000 Fleer Showcase Rookie Showcase Firsts

*1-20: .5X TO 1.2X BASIC RC/1000
*21-60: .8X TO 2X BASIC RC/2000
SHOWCASE FIRST PRINT RUN 250
36 Tom Brady 150.00 300.00

2000 Fleer Showcase Legacy

*VETS 1-100: 15X TO 40X BASIC CARDS
*ROOKIES 101-120: 1.5X TO 4X
*ROOKIES 121-160: 2.5X TO 6X
LEGACY PRINT RUN 20 SER.#'d SETS
136 Tom Brady 600.00 1,000.00

2000 Fleer Showcase Air to the Throne

COMPLETE SET (10) 5.00 12.00
STATED ODDS 1:10
1 Peyton Manning 1.50 4.00
2 Charlie Batch .50 1.25
3 Giovanni Carmazzi .40 1.00
4 Brian Griese .50 1.25
5 Daunte Culpepper .50 1.25
6 Steve McNair .60 1.50
7 Brad Johnson .50 1.25
8 Rob Johnson .50 1.25
9 Cade McNown .40 1.00
10 Chad Pennington 1.00 2.50

2000 Fleer Showcase License to Skill

COMPLETE SET (10) 10.00 25.00
STATED ODDS 1:20
1 Tim Couch .75 2.00
2 Keyshawn Johnson .75 2.00
3 Peyton Manning 2.50 6.00
4 Brett Favre 3.00 8.00
5 Terrell Davis 1.00 2.50
6 Cade McNown .60 1.50
7 Marvin Harrison 1.00 2.50
8 Eddie George .75 2.00
9 Randy Moss 1.00 2.50
10 Emmitt Smith 2.50 6.00

2000 Fleer Showcase Mission Possible

COMPLETE SET (10) 3.00 8.00
STATED ODDS 1:5
1 Tim Couch .30 .75
2 Brett Favre 1.25 3.00
3 Ricky Williams .40 1.00
4 Akili Smith .25 .60
5 Shaun King .25 .60
6 Marvin Harrison .40 1.00
7 Vinny Testaverde .30 .75
8 Terrell Davis .40 1.00
9 Edgerrin James .40 1.00
10 Eddie George .30 .75

2000 Fleer Showcase Next

COMPLETE SET (20) 7.50 20.00
STATED ODDS 1:2.5
1 Peter Warrick .30 .75
2 Bubba Franks .30 .75
3 Jamal Lewis .30 .75
4 Anthony Becht .25 .60
5 R.Jay Soward .20 .50
6 Courtney Brown .25 .60
7 Plaxico Burress .30 .75
8 Trung Canidate .25 .60
9 Chris Redman .25 .60
10 Laveranues Coles .30 .75
11 Ron Dayne .30 .75
12 Reuben Droughns .30 .75
13 Danny Farmer .20 .50
14 Travis Prentice .25 .60
15 Dez White .25 .60
16 Shaun Alexander .40 1.00
17 Thomas Jones .40 1.00
18 J.R. Redmond .20 .50
19 Sylvester Morris .20 .50
20 Chad Pennington .50 1.25

2000 Fleer Showcase Super Natural

COMPLETE SET (10) 10.00 25.00
STATED ODDS 1:20
1 Randy Moss 1.00 2.50
2 Marshall Faulk 1.00 2.50
3 Edgerrin James 1.00 2.50
4 Terrell Davis 1.00 2.50
5 Kurt Warner 1.50 4.00
6 Fred Taylor 1.00 2.50
7 Peyton Manning 2.50 6.00
8 Brett Favre 3.00 8.00
9 Brad Johnson .75 2.00
10 Warrick Dunn .75 2.00

2000 Fleer Showcase Touch Football

STATED ODDS 1:150
1 Shaun Alexander 10.00 25.00
2 Anthony Becht 6.00 15.00
3 Courtney Brown 6.00 15.00
4 Plaxico Burress 8.00 20.00
5 Trung Canidate 6.00 15.00
6 Laveranues Coles 8.00 20.00
7 Ron Dayne 8.00 20.00
8 Reuben Droughns 8.00 20.00
9 Ron Dugans 5.00 12.00
10 Danny Farmer 5.00 12.00
11 Bubba Franks 8.00 20.00
12 Joe Hamilton 5.00 12.00
13 Thomas Jones 10.00 25.00
14 Curtis Keaton 5.00 12.00
15 Jamal Lewis 8.00 20.00
16 Tee Martin 8.00 20.00
17 Sylvester Morris 5.00 12.00
18 Dennis Northcutt 6.00 15.00
19 Chad Pennington 12.00 30.00
20 Todd Pinkston 5.00 12.00
21 Jerry Porter 8.00 20.00
22 Travis Prentice 6.00 15.00
23 Chris Redman 6.00 15.00
24 J.R. Redmond 5.00 12.00
25 Corey Simon 6.00 15.00
26 R.Jay Soward 5.00 12.00
27 Travis Taylor 6.00 15.00
28 Brian Urlacher 20.00 50.00
29 Peter Warrick 8.00 20.00
30 Dez White 6.00 15.00

2001 Fleer Showcase

This 160 card set was issued in September, 2001. The cards were issued in five card packs with a suggested retail price of $4.99 per pack. Twenty four packs were included in each box. The last 60 cards in the set were short printed as cards numbered 101 through 115 were inserted at a rate of two per box. The final 45 cards of the set featured Rookie Cards and they were all printed in different amounts. Cards numbered 116 to 125 had a print run of 500, cards numbered from 126 through 145 had a print run of 1500 and cards numbered 146 through 160 had a print run of 2500 cards. In addition, an signed Avant Card of Donovan McNabb (numbered to 300) was randomly inserted in packs.

COMP.SET w/o SP's (100) 10.00 25.00
146-160 ROOKIE PRINT RUN 2000
1 Cris Carter .30 .75
2 Sylvester Morris .20 .50
3 Vinny Testaverde .25 .60
4 Jevon Kearse .25 .60
5 Terance Mathis .20 .50
6 Mike Anderson .25 .60
7 Aaron Brooks .25 .60
8 Jerry Rice .60 1.50
9 Mike Alstott .25 .60
10 Jon Kitna .25 .60
11 Derrick Alexander .20 .50
12 Shaun Alexander .30 .75
13 Thomas Jones .25 .60
14 James Stewart .20 .50
15 Ron Dayne .25 .60
16 Az-Zahir Hakim .20 .50
17 Terrell Owens .30 .75
18 Travis Prentice .20 .50
19 Lamar Smith .25 .60
20 James Thrash .25 .60
21 Doug Flutie .30 .75
22 Derrick Mason .25 .60
23 Ray Lewis .30 .75
24 Ed McCaffrey .25 .60
25 Ricky Williams .30 .75
26 Tyrone Wheatley .25 .60
27 Chris Chandler .25 .60
28 Rod Smith .25 .60
29 Joe Horn .25 .60
30 Jerome Bettis .30 .75
31 Brian Urlacher .40 1.00
32 Dorsey Levens .25 .60
33 Kordell Stewart .25 .60
34 Michael Westbrook .20 .50
35 Jamal Anderson .25 .60
36 Charlie Batch .25 .60
37 Kerry Collins .25 .60
38 Jake Plummer .25 .60
39 Robert Porcher .20 .50
40 Jason Sehorn .25 .60
41 Junior Seau .30 .75
42 Warren Sapp .25 .60
43 Champ Bailey .30 .75
44 Jamal Lewis .30 .75
45 Tony Banks .20 .50
46 Doug Chapman .20 .50
47 Stephen Davis .25 .60
48 Elvis Grbac .25 .60
49 Joey Galloway .25 .60
50 Terry Glenn .25 .60
51 Todd Pinkston .20 .50
52 JaJuan Dawson .20 .50
53 Zach Thomas .30 .75
54 Tim Couch .20 .50
55 Cade McNown .25 .60
56 Charlie Garner .25 .60
57 Jeff George .25 .60
58 Peerless Price .20 .50
59 Tony Gonzalez .30 .75
60 Rob Johnson .25 .60
61 Keenan McCardell .25 .60
62 Eric Moulds .25 .60
63 Jimmy Smith .25 .60
64 Jeff Garcia .25 .60
65 Rod Woodson .30 .75
66 Brian Griese .25 .60
67 Kevin Faulk .25 .60
68 Plaxico Burress .25 .60
69 Isaac Bruce .30 .75
70 Keyshawn Johnson .25 .60
71 Tim Biakabutuka .20 .50
72 Mark Brunell .25 .60
73 Wesley Walls .20 .50
74 Jerome Pathon .20 .50
75 Wayne Chrebet .25 .60
76 Muhsin Muhammad .25 .60
77 Marvin Harrison .30 .75
78 David Boston .20 .50
79 Germane Crowell .20 .50
80 Tiki Barber .30 .75
81 Laveranues Coles .25 .60
82 Tim Brown .30 .75
83 Matt Hasselbeck .30 .75
84 Brad Johnson .25 .60
85 Marcus Robinson .25 .60
86 Ahman Green .30 .75
87 Curtis Martin .30 .75
88 Peter Warrick .25 .60
89 Ray Lucas .20 .50
90 Duce Staley .25 .60
91 Darrell Jackson .25 .60
92 Steve McNair .30 .75
93 Rickey Dudley .20 .50
94 Jason Taylor .30 .75
95 Rich Gannon .25 .60
96 Torry Holt .25 .60
97 James Allen .20 .50
98 Antonio Freeman .30 .75
99 Trent Green .30 .75
100 Ricky Watters .25 .60
101 Corey Dillon AC 1.25 3.00
102 Emmitt Smith AC 4.00 10.00
103 Terrell Davis AC 1.50 4.00
104 Brett Favre AC 5.00 12.00
105 Peyton Manning AC 4.00 10.00
106 Edgerrin James AC 1.50 4.00
107 Fred Taylor AC 1.50 4.00
108 Daunte Culpepper AC 1.25 3.00
109 Randy Moss AC 1.50 4.00
110 Drew Bledsoe AC 1.50 4.00
111 Donovan McNabb AC 1.50 4.00
112 Kurt Warner AC 2.50 6.00
113 Marshall Faulk AC 1.50 4.00
114 Warrick Dunn AC 1.50 4.00
115 Eddie George AC 1.50 4.00
116 Michael Vick AC RC 15.00 40.00
117 David Terrell AC RC 3.00 8.00
118 Deuce McAllister AC RC 4.00 10.00
119 Koren Robinson AC RC 3.00 8.00
120 Rod Gardner AC RC 3.00 8.00
121 Santana Moss AC RC 5.00 12.00
122 Drew Brees AC RC 25.00 60.00
123 Chris Weinke AC RC 3.00 8.00
124 LaDainian Tomlinson AC RC 12.00 30.00
125 Freddie Mitchell AC RC 2.50 6.00
126 Chris Chambers RC 2.00 5.00
127 Reggie Wayne RC 4.00 10.00
128 Quincy Morgan RC 1.50 4.00
129 Rudi Johnson RC 2.00 5.00
130 Robert Ferguson RC 2.00 5.00
131 Todd Heap RC 2.00 5.00
132 Michael Bennett RC 1.50 4.00
133 Jesse Palmer RC 1.50 4.00
134 James Jackson RC 1.25 3.00

135 Chad Johnson RC	3.00	8.00
136 LaMont Jordan RC	2.00	5.00
137 Anthony Thomas RC	2.00	5.00
138 Travis Henry RC	1.50	4.00
139 Snoop Minnis RC	1.25	3.00
140 Marques Tuiasosopo RC	1.50	4.00
141 Travis Minor RC	1.50	4.00
142 Mike McMahon RC	1.50	4.00
143 Josh Heupel RC	2.00	5.00
144 Sage Rosenfels RC	2.00	5.00
145 Quincy Carter RC	1.50	4.00
146 Alge Crumpler RC	2.00	5.00
147 Kevan Barlow RC	1.50	4.00
148 Heath Evans RC	1.50	4.00
149 Correll Buckhalter RC	2.00	5.00
150 Justin McCareins RC	1.50	4.00
151 Reggie Germany RC	1.25	3.00
152 Vinny Sutherland RC	1.25	3.00
153 Scotty Anderson RC	1.25	3.00
154 Tim Hasselbeck RC	1.50	4.00
155 Alex Bannister RC	1.25	3.00
156 Andre Carter RC	1.50	4.00
157 Adam Archuleta RC	1.50	4.00
158 Ken-Yon Rambo RC	1.25	3.00
159 Gerard Warren RC	1.50	4.00
160 Justin Smith RC	2.00	5.00
CL1 Checklist	.05	.15
CL2 Checklist	.05	.15
NNO Donovan McNabb AU/300	20.00	50.00

2001 Fleer Showcase Legacy

*VETS 1-100: 6X TO 15X BASIC CARDS
*VETS AC 101-115: 1.5X TO 4X
*ROOKIES 116-125: .8X TO 2X
*ROOKIES 126-145: 1.2X TO 3X
*ROOKIES 146-160: 1.2X TO 3X
STATED PRINT RUN 50 SER.#'d SETS

2001 Fleer Showcase Awards Showcase

STATED ODDS 1:20 RETAIL

1 Randy Moss	1.25	3.00
2 Marvin Harrison	1.25	3.00
3 Tony Gonzalez	1.25	3.00
4 Rich Gannon	1.00	2.50
5 Marshall Faulk	1.25	3.00
6 Edgerrin James	1.25	3.00
7 Warren Sapp	1.00	2.50
8 Ray Lewis	1.25	3.00
9 Brian Urlacher	1.50	4.00
10 Chris Weinke	1.00	2.50
11 Eric Moulds	1.00	2.50
12 Isaac Bruce	1.25	3.00
13 Daunte Culpepper	1.00	2.50
14 Curtis Martin	1.25	3.00
15 Kurt Warner	2.00	5.00
16 Mike Anderson	1.00	2.50
17 Robert Smith	1.00	2.50
18 Jamal Lewis	1.25	3.00
19 Rod Smith	1.00	2.50
20 Junior Seau	1.25	3.00

2001 Fleer Showcase Awards Showcase Memorabilia

STATED PRINT RUN 100 SER.#'d SETS

1 Marcus Allen	12.00	30.00
2 Terry Bradshaw	20.00	50.00
3 Terrell Davis	10.00	25.00
4 Eric Dickerson	10.00	25.00
5 Tony Dorsett	12.00	30.00
6 Marshall Faulk	10.00	25.00
7 Brett Favre	30.00	80.00
8 Eddie George	10.00	25.00
9 Edgerrin James	10.00	25.00
10 Joe Montana	30.00	80.00
11 Randy Moss	10.00	25.00
12 Walter Payton	30.00	80.00
13 Jerry Rice	20.00	50.00
14 Emmitt Smith	25.00	60.00
15 Fran Tarkenton	15.00	40.00
16 Lawrence Taylor	12.00	30.00
17 Johnny Unitas	25.00	60.00
18 Steve Young	15.00	40.00

2001 Fleer Showcase Awards Showcase Memorabilia Autographs

STATED PRINT RUN 25 SER.#'d SETS

2 Terry Bradshaw	100.00	200.00
4 Eric Dickerson	40.00	100.00
5 Tony Dorsett	40.00	100.00
6 Marshall Faulk	40.00	100.00
7 Edgerrin James	30.00	80.00
8 Joe Montana	125.00	250.00
9 Randy Moss	60.00	120.00
11 Emmitt Smith	150.00	300.00
13 Lawrence Taylor	40.00	100.00
14 Johnny Unitas	250.00	400.00

2001 Fleer Showcase Patchwork

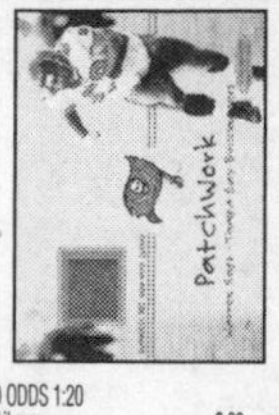

STATED ODDS 1:20

1 Troy Aikman	8.00	20.00
2 Jamal Anderson	4.00	10.00
3 Charlie Batch	4.00	10.00
4 Drew Bledsoe	5.00	12.00
5 Mark Brunell	4.00	10.00
6 Chris Chandler	4.00	10.00
7 Terrell Davis	5.00	12.00
8 Marshall Faulk	5.00	12.00
9 Brian Griese	4.00	10.00
10 Marvin Harrison	5.00	12.00
11 Torry Holt	4.00	10.00
12 Edgerrin James	5.00	12.00
13 Dorsey Levens	4.00	10.00
14 Ronnie Lott	6.00	12.00
15 Dan Marino	12.00	30.00
16 Steve McNair	5.00	12.00
17 Johnnie Morton	4.00	10.00
18 Todd Pinkston	3.00	8.00
19 Travis Prentice	3.00	8.00
20 Peerless Price	3.00	8.00
21 Chris Redman	5.00	12.00
22 Jerry Rice	10.00	25.00
23 Warren Sapp	4.00	10.00
24 Deion Sanders	5.00	12.00
25 Junior Seau	5.00	12.00
26 Bruce Smith	5.00	12.00
27 Rod Smith	4.00	10.00
28 Fred Taylor	5.00	12.00
29 Lawrence Taylor	5.00	12.00
30 Brian Urlacher	6.00	15.00
31 Kurt Warner	8.00	20.00
32 Charles Woodson	8.00	20.00
33 Steve Young	6.00	15.00

2001 Fleer Showcase Stitches

STATED ODDS 1:20

1 Cris Carter	5.00	12.00
2 Daunte Culpepper	4.00	10.00
3 Corey Dillon	4.00	10.00
4 John Elway	12.00	30.00
5 Marshall Faulk	5.00	12.00
6 Brett Favre	15.00	40.00
7 Marvin Harrison	5.00	12.00
8 Dan Marino	12.00	30.00
9 Steve McNair	5.00	12.00
10 Joe Montana	12.00	30.00
11 Todd Pinkston	3.00	8.00
12 Robert Smith	4.00	10.00
13 Fred Taylor	5.00	12.00
14 Kurt Warner	8.00	20.00
15 Peter Warrick	4.00	10.00
16 Ricky Williams	5.00	12.00
17 Steve Young	6.00	15.00

2002 Fleer Showcase

Released in May 2002, this 166 card set is composed of 125 basic cards, 10 Avant veteran cards and 6 rookie Avant cards serial numbered to 500 and 25 Rookie Showcase serial numbered to 1500. The veteran Avant cards were issued at a stated rate of one in 12. Boxes contained 24 packs per box with 5 cards per pack. SRP per pack was $4.99.

COMP.SET w/o SP's (125)	10.00	25.00
136-141 ROOKIE AC PRINT RUN 500		
142-166 ROOKIE PRINT RUN 1500		
1 Kevin Johnson	.25	.60
2 Chris Walsh	.25	.60
3 Vinny Testaverde	.30	.75
4 Kordell Stewart	.30	.75
5 Chris Redman	.25	.60
6 Johnnie Morton	.30	.75
7 Tony Gonzalez	.40	1.00
8 Torry Holt	.40	1.00
9 Champ Bailey	.40	1.00
10 Eric Moulds	.30	.75
11 Az-Zahir Hakim	.25	.60
12 Mark Brunell	.30	.75
13 Laveranues Coles	.30	.75
14 Kevan Barlow	.25	.60
15 Stephen Davis	.30	.75
16 Benjamin Gay	.25	.60
17 Randy Moss	.40	1.00
18 Hines Ward	.40	1.00
19 Brian Urlacher	.40	1.00
20 Dominic Rhodes	.30	.75
21 David Patten	.25	.60
22 Tim Brown	.40	1.00
23 Trent Dilfer	.30	.75
24 David Boston	.25	.60
25 Quincy Carter	.25	.60
26 Daunte Culpepper	.30	.75
27 Plaxico Burress	.30	.75
28 Michael Pittman	.30	.75
29 Joey Galloway	.30	.75
30 Jason Taylor	.30	.75
31 Drew Brees	.60	1.50
32 Jamal Anderson	.30	.75
33 Dat Nguyen	.25	.60
34 Chris Chambers	.30	.75
35 Tiki Barber	.40	1.00
36 LaDainian Tomlinson	.50	1.25
37 Peter Warrick	.30	.75
38 Bubba Franks	.30	.75
39 Joe Horn	.30	.75
40 Correll Buckhalter	.30	.75
41 Mike Alstott	.30	.75
42 Brian Finneran	.25	.60
43 Troy Hambrick	.25	.60
44 Zach Thomas	.40	1.00
45 Kerry Collins	.30	.75
46 Junior Seau	.40	1.00
47 Alvis Whitted	.25	.60
48 Terrell Davis	.40	1.00
49 Ricky Williams	.30	.75
50 Curtis Conway	.30	.75
51 Travis Taylor	.25	.60
52 Brian Griese	.30	.75
53 Sylvester Morris	.25	.60
54 Amani Toomer	.30	.75
55 Jeff Garcia	.30	.75
56 Michael McCrary	.25	.60
57 Ahman Green	.30	.75
58 Trent Green	.30	.75
59 Trung Canidate	.25	.60
60 Jamal Lewis	.30	.75
61 Larry Foster	.25	.60
62 Priest Holmes	.40	1.00
63 Isaac Bruce	.40	1.00
64 Bruce Smith	.40	1.00
65 Darnay Scott	.30	.75
66 Terry Glenn	.30	.75
67 Darren Howard	.25	.60
68 Hugh Douglas	.25	.60
69 Milton Wynn	.25	.60
70 Tim Couch	.25	.60
71 Bill Schroeder	.25	.60
72 Michael Strahan	.40	1.00
73 James Thrash	.30	.75
74 Steve McNair	.40	1.00
75 Patrick Jeffers	.30	.75
76 Marcus Pollard	.25	.60
77 Willie McGinest	.30	.75
78 Santana Moss	.30	.75
79 Grant Wistrom	.25	.60
80 Jim Miller	.25	.60
81 Marvin Harrison	.40	1.00
82 Troy Brown	.30	.75
83 Rich Gannon	.30	.75
84 Shaun Alexander	.30	.75
85 Jake Plummer	.30	.75
86 Quincy Morgan	.25	.60
87 Michael Bennett	.30	.75
88 Jerome Bettis	.40	1.00
89 Marty Booker	.30	.75
90 Trevor Insley	.25	.60
91 Adam Vinatieri	.40	1.00
92 Charles Woodson	.40	1.00
93 Darrell Jackson	.30	.75
94 Corey Dillon	.30	.75
95 Corey Bradford	.25	.60
96 Deuce McAllister	.30	.75
97 Todd Pinkston	.25	.60
98 Warren Sapp	.30	.75
99 Alex Van Pelt	.25	.60
100 Mike McMahon	.25	.60
101 Fred Taylor	.30	.75
102 Ron Dayne	.30	.75
103 Ernie Conwell	.25	.60
104 Rod Gardner	.25	.60
105 Muhsin Muhammad	.30	.75
106 Reggie Wayne	.40	1.00
107 Antowain Smith	.30	.75
108 Chad Pennington	.40	1.00
109 Koren Robinson	.25	.60
110 Travis Henry	.25	.60
111 Ed McCaffrey	.30	.75
112 Keenan McCardell	.30	.75
113 Curtis Martin	.40	1.00
114 Bryant Young	.25	.60
115 Derrick Mason	.30	.75
116 Anthony Thomas	.30	.75
117 Jermaine Lewis	.25	.60
118 Aaron Brooks	.30	.75
119 Charlie Garner	.30	.75
120 Keyshawn Johnson	.30	.75
121 Chris Weinke	.25	.60
122 Rod Smith	.30	.75
123 Jimmy Smith	.30	.75
124 Terrell Owens	.40	1.00
125 Eddie George	.30	.75
126 Tom Brady AC	3.00	8.00
127 Donovan McNabb AC	1.25	3.00
128 Kurt Warner AC	1.25	3.00
129 Peyton Manning AC	2.50	6.00
130 Marshall Faulk AC	1.25	3.00
131 Michael Vick AC	2.00	5.00
132 Emmitt Smith AC	3.00	8.00
133 Jerry Rice AC	2.50	6.00
134 Edgerrin James AC	1.00	2.50
135 Brett Favre AC	3.00	8.00
136 David Carr AC RC	3.00	8.00
137 Joey Harrington AC RC	3.00	8.00
138 Ashley Lelie AC RC	2.50	6.00
139 William Green AC RC	2.50	6.00
140 T.J. Duckett AC RC	3.00	8.00
141 Donte Stallworth AC RC	3.00	8.00
142 Ron Johnson RC	1.50	4.00
143 Jeremy Shockey RC	3.00	8.00
144 Daniel Graham RC	1.50	4.00
145 Reche Caldwell RC	2.00	5.00
146 Antonio Bryant RC	2.00	5.00
147 DeShaun Foster RC	2.00	5.00
148 Clinton Portis RC	2.50	6.00
149 Patrick Ramsey RC	2.00	5.00
150 Lamar Gordon RC	1.50	4.00
151 Josh Reed RC	1.50	4.00
152 Ladell Betts RC	2.00	5.00
153 Kurt Kittner RC	1.25	3.00
154 Jabar Gaffney RC	2.00	5.00
155 Josh McCown RC	2.00	5.00
156 Marquise Walker RC	1.25	3.00
157 Brian Westbrook RC	3.00	8.00
158 Andre Davis RC	1.50	4.00
159 David Garrard RC	2.50	6.00
160 Cliff Russell RC	1.25	3.00
161 Julius Peppers RC	4.00	10.00
162 Adrian Peterson RC	2.00	5.00
163 Antwaan Randle El RC	2.00	5.00
164 Javon Walker RC	2.00	5.00
165 Rohan Davey RC	2.00	5.00
166 Luke Staley RC	1.25	3.00

2002 Fleer Showcase Legacy

*VETS 1-125: 5X TO 12X BASIC CARDS
*AC VETS 126-135: 1.5X TO 4X
*ROOKIE AC 136-141: .6X TO 1.5X
*ROOKIES 142-166: 1X TO 2.5X
STATED PRINT RUN 100 SER.#'d SETS
UNPRICED MASTERPIECES #d TO 1

2002 Fleer Showcase Masterpiece

STATED PRINT RUN 1 SER.#'d SET
UNPRICED MASTERPIECE PRINT RUN 1

2002 Fleer Showcase Air to the Throne

COMPLETE SET (17)	20.00	50.00
STATED ODDS 1:8		
AT16, AT17, AT19 NOT RELEASED		
AT1 Mark Brunell	1.00	2.50
AT2 Tim Couch	.75	2.00
AT3 Daunte Culpepper	1.00	2.50
AT4 Brett Favre	3.00	8.00
AT5 Rich Gannon	1.00	2.50
AT6 Jeff Garcia	1.00	2.50
AT7 Brian Griese	1.00	2.50
AT8 Kurt Warner	1.25	3.00
AT9 Donovan McNabb	1.25	3.00
AT10 Steve McNair	1.25	3.00
AT11 Jake Plummer	1.00	2.50
AT12 Kordell Stewart	1.00	2.50
AT13 Troy Aikman	2.00	5.00
AT14 Jim Kelly	1.50	4.00
AT15 John Elway	2.50	6.00
AT18 Dan Marino	3.00	8.00
AT20 Roger Staubach	2.00	5.00

2002 Fleer Showcase Air to the Throne Jerseys

STATED ODDS 1:24
*GOLD/50: .8X TO 2X BASIC JSY
GOLD STATED PRINT RUN 50 SER.#'d SETS

1 Troy Aikman	8.00	20.00
2 Mark Brunell	4.00	10.00
3 Tim Couch	3.00	8.00
4 Daunte Culpepper	4.00	10.00
5 John Elway	10.00	25.00
6 Brett Favre	12.00	30.00
7 Rich Gannon	4.00	10.00
8 Jeff Garcia	4.00	10.00
9 Brian Griese	4.00	10.00
10 Jim Kelly	6.00	15.00
11 Dan Marino	12.00	30.00
12 Donovan McNabb	5.00	12.00
13 Steve McNair	5.00	12.00
14 Joe Montana	25.00	60.00
15 Jake Plummer	4.00	10.00
16 Roger Staubach	8.00	20.00
17 Kordell Stewart	4.00	10.00
18 Kurt Warner	5.00	12.00

2002 Fleer Showcase Football's Best

COMPLETE SET (32)	50.00	120.00
STATED PRINT RUN 799 SER.#'d SETS		
FB1 Edgerrin James	1.50	4.00
FB2 Shaun Alexander	1.50	4.00
FB3 Mike Alstott	1.50	4.00
FB4 Tiki Barber	2.00	5.00
FB5 Jerome Bettis	2.00	5.00
FB6 David Boston	1.25	3.00
FB7 Tim Brown	2.00	5.00
FB8 Isaac Bruce	2.00	5.00
FB9 Plaxico Burress	1.50	4.00
FB10 Tim Couch	1.25	3.00
FB11 Wayne Chrebet	1.50	4.00
FB12 Daunte Culpepper	1.50	4.00
FB13 Stephen Davis	1.50	4.00
FB14 Terrell Davis	2.00	5.00
FB15 Ron Dayne	1.50	4.00
FB16 Corey Dillon	1.50	4.00
FB17 Marshall Faulk	2.00	5.00
FB18 Brett Favre	5.00	12.00
FB19 Rich Gannon	1.50	4.00
FB20 Eddie George	1.50	4.00
FB21 Randy Moss	2.00	5.00
FB22 Junior Seau	2.00	5.00
FB23 Jerry Rice	4.00	10.00
FB24 Torry Holt	2.00	5.00
FB25 Jamal Anderson	1.50	4.00
FB26 Ray Lewis	2.00	5.00
FB27 Antowain Smith	1.50	4.00
FB28 Peter Warrick	1.50	4.00
FB29 Ed McCaffrey	1.50	4.00
FB30 Marvin Harrison	2.00	5.00
FB31 Jimmy Smith	1.50	4.00
FB32 Fred Taylor	1.50	4.00

2002 Fleer Showcase Football's Best Memorabilia

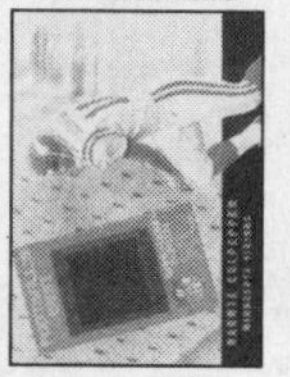

STATED ODDS 1:15
*SILVER PATCH/100: .6X TO 1.5X BASIC JSY
SILVER PATCH PRINT RUN 100 SER.#'d SETS
*GOLD PATCH/25: 1.5X TO 4X BASIC JSY
GOLD PATCH PRINT RUN 25 SER.#'d SETS

FB1 Mike Alstott	4.00	10.00
FB2 Jamal Anderson	4.00	10.00
FB3 Tiki Barber	5.00	12.00
FB4 Jerome Bettis	12.00	30.00
FB5 David Boston	3.00	8.00
FB6 Tim Brown	5.00	12.00
FB7 Isaac Bruce	5.00	12.00
FB8 Plaxico Burress	4.00	10.00
FB9 Wayne Chrebet	4.00	10.00
FB10 Tim Couch	3.00	8.00
FB11 Daunte Culpepper	4.00	10.00
FB12 Stephen Davis	4.00	10.00
FB13 Terrell Davis	5.00	12.00
FB14 Ron Dayne	4.00	10.00
FB15 Corey Dillon	4.00	10.00
FB16 Marshall Faulk	5.00	12.00
FB17 Brett Favre	12.00	30.00
FB18 Rich Gannon	4.00	10.00
FB19 Eddie George	4.00	10.00
FB20 Marvin Harrison	5.00	12.00
FB21 Torry Holt	5.00	12.00
FB22 Edgerrin James	4.00	10.00
FB23 Ray Lewis	5.00	12.00
FB24 Ed McCaffrey	4.00	10.00
FB25 Randy Moss	5.00	12.00
FB26 Jerry Rice	10.00	25.00
FB27 Junior Seau	5.00	12.00
FB28 Antowain Smith	4.00	10.00
FB29 Jimmy Smith	4.00	10.00
FB30 Fred Taylor	4.00	10.00
FB31 Peter Warrick	4.00	10.00

2002 Fleer Showcase Top to Bottom

STATED PRINT RUN 250 SER.#'d SETS

1 David Boston	4.00	10.00
2 Eddie George	5.00	12.00
3 Marvin Harrison	6.00	15.00
4 Edgerrin James	5.00	12.00
5 Jake Plummer	5.00	12.00
6 Marcus Robinson	5.00	12.00
7 Duce Staley	5.00	12.00
8 Brian Urlacher	6.00	15.00

2003 Fleer Showcase

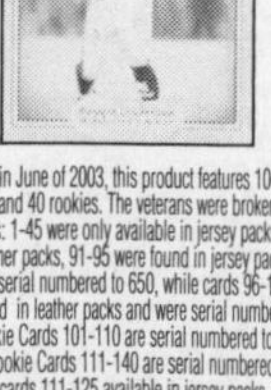

Released in June of 2003, this product features 100 veterans, and 40 rookies. The veterans were broken down as follows: 1-45 were only available in jersey packs, 46-90 in leather packs, 91-95 were found in jersey packs and were serial numbered to 650, while cards 96-100 were found in leather packs and were serial numbered to 350. Rookie Cards 101-110 are serial numbered to 350 or 650. Rookie Cards 111-140 are serial numbered to 750, with cards 111-125 available in jersey packs, and cards 126-140 available in leather packs. Each box contained two 12-pack mini-boxes, one Leather Edition and one Jersey Edition. Each pack featured five cards for an SRP of $4.99.

COMP.SET w/o SP's (90)	10.00	25.00
1 Edgerrin James	.40	1.00
2 Donald Driver	.40	1.00
3 Drew Brees	.40	1.00
4 Corey Dillon	.30	.75
5 Jerome Bettis	.40	1.00
6 Charlie Garner	.30	.75
7 Eddie George	.30	.75
8 Mark Brunell	.30	.75
9 David Boston	.25	.60
10 Todd Heap	.30	.75
11 Terrell Owens	.40	1.00
12 Tommy Maddox	.30	.75
13 Keyshawn Johnson	.40	1.00
14 Jamal Lewis	.30	.75
15 Zach Thomas	.40	1.00
16 Isaac Bruce	.40	1.00
17 Michael Bennett	.30	.75
18 Rod Smith	.30	.75
19 Eric Moulds	.30	.75
20 T.J Duckett	.30	.75
21 Hines Ward	.40	1.00
22 Tiki Barber	.40	1.00
23 Julius Peppers	.40	1.00
24 Rich Gannon	.30	.75
25 Rod Gardner	.25	.60
26 Curtis Martin	.40	1.00
27 Donte Stallworth	.25	.60
28 Anthony Thomas	.30	.75
29 Warren Sapp	.30	.75
30 Jake Plummer	.30	.75
31 Patrick Ramsey	.30	.75
32 Tai Streets	.25	.60
33 Matt Hasselbeck	.30	.75
34 James Stewart	.25	.60
35 Chad Hutchinson	.25	.60
36 Hugh Douglas	.25	.60
37 Jimmy Smith	.30	.75
38 Kerry Collins	.30	.75
39 Junior Seau	.40	1.00
40 Ed McCaffrey	.30	.75
41 Marshall Faulk	.40	1.00
42 Deuce McAllister	.30	.75
43 Drew Bledsoe	.40	1.00
44 Brian Urlacher	.40	1.00
45 William Green	.25	.60
46 Chris Chambers	.30	.75
47 Daunte Culpepper	.30	.75
48 Warrick Dunn	.30	.75
49 Antwaan Randle El	.30	.75
50 Joey Harrington	.25	.60
51 Tim Brown	.40	1.00
52 Duce Staley	.30	.75
53 Laveranues Coles	.25	.60
54 Ray Lewis	.40	1.00
55 Marvin Harrison	.40	1.00
56 Tony Gonzalez	.40	1.00
57 Torry Holt	.40	1.00
58 Jeff Garcia	.30	.75
59 Peerless Price	.25	.60
60 Marcel Shipp	.25	.60
61 Brian Finneran	.25	.60
62 Fred Taylor	.30	.75
63 Koren Robinson	.30	.75
64 Shaun Alexander	.30	.75
65 Plaxico Burress	.30	.75
66 Ahman Green	.30	.75
67 Simeon Rice	.25	.60
68 Joe Horn	.30	.75
69 Steve McNair	.40	1.00
70 Amani Toomer	.30	.75
71 Kendrell Bell	.25	.60
72 Marty Booker	.30	.75
73 Stephen Davis	.30	.75
74 David Carr	.30	.75
75 Garrison Hearst	.30	.75
76 Joey Galloway	.30	.75
77 Aaron Brooks	.30	.75
78 Mike Alstott	.40	1.00
79 Shannon Sharpe	.40	1.00
80 Derrick Mason	.30	.75
81 Tim Couch	.25	.60
82 Chad Johnson	.40	1.00
83 Jason Taylor	.30	.75
84 Travis Henry	.25	.60
85 Curtis Conway	.25	.60
86 Peyton Manning	.75	2.00
87 Kurt Warner	.40	1.00
88 LaDainian Tomlinson	.40	1.00
89 Emmitt Smith	1.00	2.50
90 Priest Holmes	.40	1.00
91 Ricky Williams AC	1.50	4.00
92 Brett Favre AC	5.00	12.00
93 Clinton Portis AC	1.50	4.00
94 Randy Moss AC	2.00	5.00
95 Tom Brady AC	5.00	12.00
96 Chad Pennington AC	2.50	6.00
97 Michael Vick AC	3.00	8.00
98 Jeremy Shockey AC	2.50	6.00
99 Donovan McNabb AC	2.50	6.00
100 Jerry Rice AC	5.00	12.00
101 Carson Palmer AC/350 RC	8.00	20.00
102 Lee Suggs AC/350 RC	3.00	8.00
103 Larry Johnson AC/350 RC	4.00	10.00
104 Taylor Jacobs AC/650 RC	2.00	5.00
105 Andre Johnson AC/350 RC	10.00	25.00
106 Justin Fargas AC/650 RC	3.00	8.00
107 Charles Rogers AC/350 RC	3.00	8.00
108 Willis McGahee AC/650 RC	4.00	10.00
109 Byron Leftwich AC/350 RC	4.00	10.00
110 Kyle Boller AC/650 RC	3.00	8.00
111 Bobby Wade RC	2.50	6.00
112 Brian St.Pierre RC	2.50	6.00
113 Doug Gabriel RC	2.50	6.00
114 Chris Brown RC	2.00	5.00
115 DeWayne Robertson RC	2.50	6.00
116 Anquan Boldin RC	5.00	12.00
117 Brandon Lloyd RC	5.00	12.00
118 Brad Banks RC	2.50	6.00
119 Dallas Clark RC	5.00	12.00
120 Artose Pinner RC	2.00	5.00
121 Dave Ragone RC	2.00	5.00
122 Arnaz Battle RC	3.00	8.00
123 Andrew Pinnock RC	2.50	6.00
124 Billy McMullen RC	2.00	5.00
125 Avon Cobourne RC	2.00	5.00
126 Terence Newman RC	2.50	6.00
127 Jimmy Kennedy RC	2.50	6.00
128 Terrell Suggs RC	3.00	8.00
129 Rex Grossman RC	3.00	8.00
130 Musa Smith RC	2.00	5.00
131 William Joseph RC	2.00	5.00
132 Tyrone Calico RC	2.50	6.00
133 Teyo Johnson RC	2.50	6.00
134 Onterrio Smith RC	2.00	5.00
135 Mike Doss RC	3.00	8.00
136 Kliff Kingsbury RC	2.50	6.00
137 Kelley Washington RC	2.00	5.00
138 Kareem Kelly RC	2.00	5.00
139 Jason Gesser RC	2.50	6.00
140 Chris Simms RC	3.00	8.00

2003 Fleer Showcase Legacy

*VETS 1-90: 3X TO 8X BASIC CARDS
*AC STARS 91-95: .8X TO 2X
*AC STARS 96-100: ..6X TO 1.5X
*AC ROOKIES: .4X TO 1X AC RC/350
*AC ROOKIES: .5X TO 1.2X AC RC/650
*ROOKIES 111-140: .8X TO 2X
STATED PRINT RUN 125 SER.#'d SETS
UNPRICED MASTERPIECES #'d TO 1

2003 Fleer Showcase Avant Card Jerseys

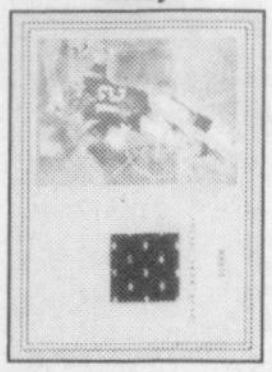

STATED PRINT RUN 999 SER.#'d SETS

AVBF Brett Favre JE	10.00	25.00
AVCP Chad Pennington LE	4.00	10.00
AVCP2 Clinton Portis JE	3.00	8.00
AVDM Donovan McNabb LE	4.00	10.00
AVJR Jerry Rice LE	8.00	20.00
AVJS Jeremy Shockey LE	4.00	10.00
AVMV Michael Vick LE	5.00	12.00
AVRM Randy Moss JE	4.00	10.00
AVRW Ricky Williams JE	3.00	8.00
AVTB Tom Brady JE	10.00	25.00

2003 Fleer Showcase Football's Best

COMPLETE SET (8)	8.00	20.00
STATED ODDS 1:12 LEATHER		
1 Michael Vick	1.50	4.00
2 Ricky Williams	1.00	2.50
3 Brian Urlacher	1.25	3.00
4 Jeff Garcia	1.00	2.50
5 Chad Pennington	1.25	3.00
6 William Green	.75	2.00
7 Kurt Warner	1.25	3.00
8 Drew Bledsoe	1.25	3.00

2003 Fleer Showcase Football's Best Jerseys

STATED ODDS 1:28 LEA, 1:38 JER
*GOLD/150: .6X TO 1.5X BASIC JSY
GOLD PRINT RUN 150 SER.#'d SETS

FBAG Ahman Green LE	3.00	8.00
FBBU Brian Urlacher JE	4.00	10.00
FBCP Chad Pennington JE	4.00	10.00
FBDC David Carr LE	3.00	8.00
FBEG Eddie George JE	3.00	8.00
FBEM Eric Moulds JE	3.00	8.00
FBES Emmitt Smith JE	10.00	25.00
FBJG Jeff Garcia LE	3.00	8.00
FBJK Jevon Kearse LE	3.00	8.00
FBJS Jeremy Shockey JE	4.00	10.00
FBKJ Keyshawn Johnson LE	4.00	10.00
FBKR Koren Robinson JE	3.00	8.00
FBKW Kurt Warner LE	4.00	10.00
FBMB Michael Bennett LE	3.00	8.00
FBMF Marshall Faulk JE	4.00	10.00
FBMV Michael Vick LE	5.00	12.00
FBPB Plaxico Burress JE	3.00	8.00
FBRW Ricky Williams LE	3.00	8.00
FBWG William Green LE	2.50	6.00
FBWS Warren Sapp JE	3.00	8.00

2003 Fleer Showcase Hot Hands

STATED ODDS 1:144 LEATHER

1 Jerry Rice	6.00	15.00
2 Randy Moss	3.00	8.00
3 Terrell Owens	3.00	8.00
4 Marvin Harrison	3.00	8.00
5 Jeremy Shockey	3.00	8.00
6 Marshall Faulk	3.00	8.00
7 Priest Holmes	3.00	8.00
8 Deuce McAllister	2.50	6.00

2003 Fleer Showcase Hot Hands Jerseys

STATED PRINT RUN 599 SER.#'d SETS
FOUND ONLY IN LEATHER PACKS

HHAB Antonio Bryant	2.50	6.00
HHAR Antwaan Randle El	3.00	8.00
HHDB David Boston	2.50	6.00
HHDB2 Drew Brees	4.00	10.00
HHDC Daunte Culpepper	3.00	8.00
HHDM Deuce McAllister	3.00	8.00
HHEM Eric Moulds	3.00	8.00
HHJR Jerry Rice	8.00	20.00
HHJS Jeremy Shockey	4.00	10.00
HHKR Koren Robinson	3.00	8.00
HHKW Kurt Warner	4.00	10.00
HHLT LaDainian Tomlinson	4.00	10.00
HHMF Marshall Faulk	4.00	10.00
HHMH Marvin Harrison	4.00	10.00
HHPH Priest Holmes	4.00	10.00
HHPM Peyton Manning	8.00	20.00
HHPP Peerless Price	2.50	6.00
HHRM Randy Moss	4.00	10.00
HHTH Todd Heap	3.00	8.00
HHTO Terrell Owens	4.00	10.00

2003 Fleer Showcase Sweet Stitches

COMPLETE SET (8)	10.00	25.00
STATED ODDS 1:12 JERSEY		
1 Brett Favre	3.00	8.00
2 Clinton Portis	1.00	2.50
3 Donovan McNabb	1.25	3.00
4 Daunte Culpepper	1.00	2.50
5 LaDainian Tomlinson	1.25	3.00
6 Tom Brady	3.00	8.00
7 Peyton Manning	2.50	6.00
8 Emmitt Smith	3.00	8.00

2003 Fleer Showcase Sweet Stitches Jerseys

STATED PRINT RUN 899 SER.#'d SETS
ISSUED IN JERSEY PACKS
*PATCH/201: .6X TO 1.5X BASIC JSY
PATCHES PRINT RUN 201 SER.#'d SETS
*PURPLE PATCH/46-56: 1X TO 2.5X BASIC JSY
*PURPLE PATCH/27: 1.2X TO 3X BASIC JSY
PURPLE PATCH PRINT RUN 27-56

1 Drew Brees	4.00	10.00
2 Antonio Bryant	2.50	6.00
3 David Carr	3.00	8.00
4 Daunte Culpepper	3.00	8.00
5 Brett Favre	10.00	25.00
6 Eddie George	3.00	8.00
7 Ahman Green	3.00	8.00
8 Edgerrin James	4.00	10.00
9 Peyton Manning	8.00	20.00
10 Donovan McNabb	4.00	10.00
11 Clinton Portis	3.00	8.00
12 Peerless Price	2.50	6.00
13 Antwaan Randle El	3.00	8.00
14 Emmitt Smith	10.00	25.00
15 LaDainian Tomlinson	4.00	10.00

2004 Fleer Showcase

Showcase released in early June of 2004 and was Fleer's second football product of the year. The base set consists of 149-cards including 100-veterans and 48-rookies each serial numbered to 599. Hobby box included 20-packs with 5-cards per pack at an SRP of $6.50 and retail boxes contained 24-packs of 4-cards with an SRP of $2.99. Card #150, Mike Williams, was initially pulled from the pack-out after he was declared ineligible for the NFL Draft. Copies of the card hit the secondary in late 2005, however, after the Fleer inventory liquidation sale took place. Due to the unigue distribution of the card, it is not considered a Rookie Card. Two parallel sets and a large section of inserts with a variety of game-used versions can be found seeded in packs. Insert highlights include Sweet Sigs autographs produced in three foil colors and Feature Film with each card produced with an original photographic slide.

COMP.SET w/o SP's (100)	10.00	25.00
UNPRICED MASTERPIECE PRINT RUN 1		
1 Jamal Lewis	.30	.75
2 Kevan Barlow	.25	.60
3 Travis Henry	.25	.60
4 Jon Kitna	.30	.75
5 David Boston	.25	.60
6 Andre Davis	.25	.60
7 Steve McNair	.40	1.00
8 Freddie Mitchell	.25	.60
9 Plaxico Burress	.30	.75
10 Jake Delhomme	.30	.75
11 Andre Johnson	.40	1.00
12 T.J. Duckett	.30	.75
13 Ray Lewis	.40	1.00
14 Shaun Alexander	.30	.75
15 Stephen Davis	.30	.75
16 Priest Holmes	.40	1.00
17 Edgerrin James	.30	.75
18 Josh McCown	.30	.75
19 Jerry Rice	.75	2.00
20 Fred Taylor	.30	.75
21 Marty Booker	.30	.75
22 Eddie George	.30	.75
23 Jake Plummer	.30	.75
24 LaDainian Tomlinson	.40	1.00
25 David Carr	.25	.60
26 Keenan McCardell	.25	.60
27 Jerry Porter	.25	.60
28 Drew Bledsoe	.40	1.00
29 Brian Dawkins	.30	.75
30 Curtis Martin	.40	1.00
31 Troy Brown	.30	.75
32 Peyton Manning	.75	2.00
33 Clinton Portis	.40	1.00
34 Brett Favre	1.00	2.50
35 Joey Harrington	.30	.75
36 Tiki Barber	.40	1.00
37 Hines Ward	.40	1.00
38 Laveranues Coles	.25	.60
39 Deuce McAllister	.30	.75
40 Kyle Boller	.30	.75
41 Jeff Garcia	.30	.75
42 Julius Peppers	.30	.75
43 Chris Chambers	.30	.75
44 Willis McGahee	.40	1.00
45 Michael Vick	.50	1.25
46 Carson Palmer	.40	1.00
47 Ricky Williams	.30	.75
48 Matt Hasselbeck	.30	.75
49 Anquan Boldin	.40	1.00
50 Tony Gonzalez	.40	1.00
51 Marvin Harrison	.40	1.00
52 Santana Moss	.30	.75
53 Ahman Green	.30	.75
54 Eric Moulds	.30	.75
55 Byron Leftwich	.30	.75
56 Daunte Culpepper	.30	.75
57 Terrell Owens	.40	1.00
58 Kerry Collins	.30	.75
59 Tommy Maddox	.30	.75
60 Chad Johnson	.40	1.00
61 Rich Gannon	.30	.75
62 Patrick Ramsey	.30	.75
63 Quincy Morgan	.25	.60
64 Koren Robinson	.25	.60
65 Deion Branch	.30	.75
66 Rex Grossman	.30	.75
67 Darnerien McCants	.25	.60
68 Ashley Lelie	.25	.60
69 Roy Williams S	.30	.75

70 Michael Bennett	.30	.75
71 Domanick Davis	.25	.60
72 Warren Sapp	.30	.75
73 Randy Moss	.40	1.00
74 Drew Brees	.40	1.00
75 Brian Westbrook	.40	1.00
76 Kelly Holcomb	.25	.60
77 Jason Taylor	.30	.75
78 Charles Rogers	.25	.60
79 Marc Bulger	.30	.75
80 Donald Driver	.40	1.00
81 Trent Green	.30	.75
82 Peerless Price	.25	.60
83 Quincy Carter	.25	.60
84 Torry Holt	.30	.75
85 Derrick Mason	.30	.75
86 Donte Stallworth	.25	.60
87 Derrick Brooks	.30	.75
88 Dre Bly	.25	.60
89 Antonio Bryant	.30	.75
90 DeShaun Foster	.30	.75
91 Emmitt Smith	1.00	2.50
92 Chad Pennington	.40	1.00
93 Jeremy Shockey	.30	.75
94 Aaron Brooks	.30	.75
95 Marshall Faulk	.40	1.00
96 Dante Hall	.30	.75
97 Brian Urlacher	.40	1.00
98 Corey Dillon	.30	.75
99 Donovan McNabb	.40	1.00
100 Tom Brady	.75	2.00
101 Derrick Strait RC	1.25	3.00
102 Michael Clayton RC	1.50	4.00
103 Larry Fitzgerald RC	5.00	12.00
104 Chris Gamble RC	1.50	4.00
105 Devery Henderson RC	2.00	5.00
106 Steven Jackson RC	3.00	8.00
107 Michael Jenkins RC	2.00	5.00
108 Greg Jones RC	1.25	3.00
109 Kevin Jones RC	1.50	4.00
110 Eli Manning RC	12.00	30.00
111 Chris Perry RC	1.50	4.00
112 Philip Rivers RC	8.00	20.00
113 Ben Roethlisberger RC	12.00	30.00
114 Bernard Berrian RC	2.00	5.00
115 Sean Taylor RC	4.00	10.00
116 Reggie Williams RC	1.50	4.00
117 Roy Williams RC	2.00	5.00
118 Kellen Winslow RC	2.00	5.00
119 Rashaun Woods RC	1.25	3.00
120 J.P. Losman RC	1.50	4.00
121 Will Poole RC	2.00	5.00
122 Will Smith RC	1.50	4.00
123 Devard Darling RC	1.25	3.00
124 Jonathan Vilma RC	2.00	5.00
125 Drew Henson RC	1.25	3.00
126 Michael Turner RC	2.50	6.00
127 Lee Evans RC	2.00	5.00
128 Ernest Wilford RC	1.50	4.00
129 Cedric Cobbs RC	1.25	3.00
130 Ricardo Colclough RC	1.50	4.00
131 Ryan Dinwiddie RC	1.25	3.00
132 DeAngelo Hall RC	2.00	5.00
133 Cody Pickett RC	1.50	4.00
134 Quincy Wilson RC	1.50	4.00
135 Ahmad Carroll RC	1.25	3.00
136 Robert Gallery RC	2.00	5.00
137 John Navarre RC	1.25	3.00
138 P.K. Sam RC	1.25	3.00
139 Jeff Smoker RC	1.50	4.00
140 Ben Troupe RC	1.50	4.00
141 Marquise Hill RC	1.25	3.00
142 D.J. Williams RC	2.00	5.00
143 Tommie Harris RC	2.00	5.00
144 Ben Watson RC	2.00	5.00
145 Tatum Bell RC	1.50	4.00
146 B.J. Symons RC	1.25	3.00
147 Matt Schaub RC	4.00	10.00
148 Casey Clausen RC	1.50	4.00
149 Jason Fife RC	1.25	3.00
150 Mike Williams No Ser.#	3.00	8.00

2004 Fleer Showcase Legacy

*VETS 1-100: 3X TO 8X BASIC CARDS
*ROOKIES 101-149: .8X TO 2X BASIC CARD
STATED PRINT RUN 125 SER.#'d SETS

2004 Fleer Showcase Feature Film

STATED ODDS 1:480 HOB,1:2000 RET
STATED PRINT RUN 50 SER.#'d SETS

1FF Brian Urlacher	8.00	20.00
2FF Jerry Rice	15.00	40.00
3FF Michael Vick	10.00	25.00
4FF Jeremy Shockey	6.00	15.00
5FF Emmitt Smith	20.00	50.00
6FF Brett Favre	20.00	50.00
7FF David Carr	5.00	12.00
8FF Joey Harrington	6.00	15.00
9FF Randy Moss	8.00	20.00
10FF Peyton Manning	15.00	40.00

2004 Fleer Showcase Feature Film Game Used

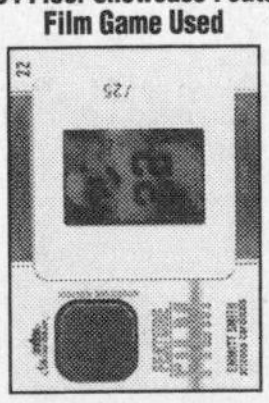

OVERALL GAME USED ODDS 1:10H,1:24R
STATED PRINT RUN 25 SER.#'d SETS

FFBF Brett Favre	30.00	80.00
FFBU Brian Urlacher	12.00	30.00
FFDC David Carr	8.00	20.00
FFES Emmitt Smith	30.00	80.00
FFJH Joey Harrington	10.00	25.00
FFJR Jerry Rice	25.00	60.00
FFJS Jeremy Shockey	10.00	25.00
FFMV Michael Vick	15.00	40.00
FFPM Peyton Manning	25.00	60.00
FFRM Randy Moss	12.00	30.00

2004 Fleer Showcase Grace

COMPLETE SET (20)	15.00	40.00
STATED ODDS 1:8 HOB/RET		
1SG Brian Urlacher	1.25	3.00
2SG Plaxico Burress	1.00	2.50
3SG Andre Johnson	1.25	3.00
4SG Shaun Alexander	1.00	2.50
5SG Stephen Davis	1.00	2.50
6SG Edgerrin James	1.00	2.50
7SG LaDainian Tomlinson	1.25	3.00
8SG Peyton Manning	2.50	6.00
9SG Clinton Portis	1.25	3.00
10SG Brett Favre	3.00	8.00
11SG Deuce McAllister	1.00	2.50
12SG Julius Peppers	1.00	2.50
13SG Jerry Rice	2.50	6.00
14SG Ricky Williams	1.00	2.50
15SG Daunte Culpepper	1.00	2.50
16SG Santana Moss	1.00	2.50
17SG Roy Williams S	1.00	2.50
18SG Chad Pennington	1.25	3.00
19SG Donovan McNabb	1.25	3.00
20SG Tom Brady	2.50	6.00

2004 Fleer Showcase Grace Game Used

OVERALL GAME USED ODDS 1:10H,1:24R
SERIAL #'d UNDER 16 NOT PRICED
UNPRICED MASTERPIECE PRINT RUN 1

AJ1 Andre Johnson	4.00	10.00
AJ2 Andre Johnson/300	4.00	10.00
AJ3 Andre Johnson/100	5.00	12.00
AJ5 Andre Johnson/80	5.00	12.00
BF1 Brett Favre	10.00	25.00
BF2 Brett Favre/300	10.00	25.00
BF3 Brett Favre/100	12.00	30.00
BF4 Brett Favre/358	10.00	25.00
BU1 Brian Urlacher	4.00	10.00
BU2 Brian Urlacher/300	4.00	10.00
BU3 Brian Urlacher/100	5.00	12.00
BU5 Brian Urlacher/54	12.00	30.00
CP1 Clinton Portis	4.00	10.00
CP2 Clinton Portis/300	4.00	10.00
CP3 Clinton Portis/100	5.00	12.00
CP4 Clinton Portis/31	10.00	25.00
CP5 Clinton Portis/26	12.00	30.00
DC1 Daunte Culpepper	3.00	8.00
DC2 Daunte Culpepper/300	3.00	8.00
DC3 Daunte Culpepper/100	4.00	10.00
DC4 Daunte Culpepper/116	4.00	10.00
EJ1 Edgerrin James	3.00	8.00
EJ2 Edgerrin James/300	3.00	8.00
EJ3 Edgerrin James/100	4.00	10.00
EJ4 Edgerrin James/52	6.00	15.00
EJ5 Edgerrin James/32	8.00	20.00
JP1 Julius Peppers	3.00	8.00
JP2 Julius Peppers/300	3.00	8.00
JP3 Julius Peppers/100	4.00	10.00
JP5 Julius Peppers/90	4.00	10.00
JR1 Jerry Rice	8.00	20.00
JR2 Jerry Rice/300	8.00	20.00
JR3 Jerry Rice/100	10.00	25.00
JR4 Jerry Rice/205	8.00	20.00
JR5 Jerry Rice/80	10.00	25.00
LT1 LaDainian Tomlinson	4.00	10.00
LT2 LaDainian Tomlinson/300	4.00	10.00
LT3 LaDainian Tomlinson/100	5.00	12.00
LT4 LaDainian Tomlinson/42	8.00	20.00
LT5 LaDainian Tomlinson/21	12.00	30.00
PB1 Plaxico Burress	3.00	8.00
PB2 Plaxico Burress/300	3.00	8.00
PB3 Plaxico Burress/100	4.00	10.00
PB4 Plaxico Burress/17	10.00	25.00
PB5 Plaxico Burress/80	4.00	10.00
PM1 Peyton Manning	8.00	20.00
PM2 Peyton Manning/300	8.00	20.00
PM3 Peyton Manning/100	10.00	25.00
PM4 Peyton Manning/176	8.00	20.00
PM5 Peyton Manning/18	25.00	60.00
RW1 Ricky Williams	3.00	8.00
RW2 Ricky Williams/300	3.00	8.00
RW3 Ricky Williams/100	4.00	10.00
RW4 Ricky Williams/45	6.00	15.00
RW5 Ricky Williams/34	8.00	20.00
SA1 Shaun Alexander	3.00	8.00
SA2 Shaun Alexander/300	3.00	8.00
SA3 Shaun Alexander/100	4.00	10.00
SA4 Shaun Alexander/52	6.00	15.00
SA5 Shaun Alexander/37	8.00	20.00
SD1 Stephen Davis	3.00	8.00
SD2 Stephen Davis/300	3.00	8.00
SD3 Stephen Davis/100	4.00	10.00
SD4 Stephen Davis/56	6.00	15.00
SD5 Stephen Davis/48	6.00	15.00
SM1 Santana Moss	3.00	8.00
SM2 Santana Moss/300	3.00	8.00
SM3 Santana Moss/100	4.00	10.00
SM4 Santana Moss/16	10.00	25.00
SM5 Santana Moss/83	4.00	10.00
TB1 Tom Brady	10.00	25.00
TB2 Tom Brady/300	10.00	25.00
TB3 Tom Brady/100	12.00	30.00
TB4 Tom Brady/71	12.00	30.00
DEM1 Deuce McAllister	3.00	8.00
DEM2 Deuce McAllister/300	3.00	8.00
DEM3 Deuce McAllister/100	4.00	10.00
DEM4 Deuce McAllister GLD/26	10.00	25.00
DEM5 Deuce McAllister GRN/26	10.00	25.00
DOM1 Donovan McNabb	4.00	10.00
DOM2 Donovan McNabb/300	4.00	10.00
DOM3 Donovan McNabb/100	5.00	12.00
DOM4 Donovan McNabb/104	5.00	12.00
ROY1 Roy Williams S	3.00	8.00
ROY2 Roy Williams S/300	3.00	8.00
ROY3 Roy Williams S/100	4.00	10.00
ROY5 Roy Williams S/31	8.00	20.00
CHAD1 Chad Pennington	4.00	10.00
CHAD2 Chad Pennington/300	4.00	10.00
CHAD3 Chad Pennington/100	5.00	12.00
CHAD4 Chad Pennington/41	8.00	20.00

2004 Fleer Showcase Hot Hands

STATED ODDS 1:240 HOB,1:480 RET

1HH Anquan Boldin	5.00	12.00
2HH Ahman Green	4.00	10.00
3HH Chad Johnson	5.00	12.00
4HH Jeremy Shockey	4.00	10.00
5HH Priest Holmes	5.00	12.00
6HH Torry Holt	4.00	10.00
7HH Marvin Harrison	5.00	12.00
8HH LaDainian Tomlinson	5.00	12.00
9HH Deuce McAllister	4.00	10.00
10HH Randy Moss	5.00	12.00

2004 Fleer Showcase Hot Hands Game Used

STATED PRINT RUN 50 SER.#'d SETS

HHAB Anquan Boldin	8.00	20.00
HHAG Ahman Green	6.00	15.00
HHCJ Chad Johnson	8.00	20.00
HHDM Deuce McAllister	6.00	15.00
HHJS Jeremy Shockey	6.00	15.00
HHLT LaDainian Tomlinson	8.00	20.00
HHMH Marvin Harrison	8.00	20.00
HHPH Priest Holmes	8.00	20.00
HHRM Randy Moss	8.00	20.00
HHTH Torry Holt	6.00	15.00

2004 Fleer Showcase Playmakers

COMPLETE SET (15)	15.00	40.00
STATED ODDS 1:24 HOB/RET		
1PM Jamal Lewis	1.25	3.00
2PM Michael Vick	2.00	5.00
3PM Marvin Harrison	1.50	4.00
4PM Ahman Green	1.25	3.00
5PM Terrell Owens	1.50	4.00
6PM Chad Johnson	1.50	4.00
7PM Marshall Faulk	1.50	4.00
8PM Priest Holmes	1.50	4.00
9PM Hines Ward	1.50	4.00
10PM Ricky Williams	1.25	3.00
11PM Randy Moss	1.50	4.00
12PM Charles Rogers	1.00	2.50
13PM Donovan McNabb	1.50	4.00
14PM Anquan Boldin	1.50	4.00
15PM Chad Pennington	1.50	4.00

2004 Fleer Showcase Playmakers Game Used

JERSEYS SER.#'d UNDER 20 NOT PRICED
OVERALL GAME USED ODDS 1:10H,1:24R
UNPRICED MASTERPIECE PRINT RUN 1

AB1 Anquan Boldin/300	4.00	10.00
AB2 Anquan Boldin/100	5.00	12.00
AB5 Anquan Boldin/81	5.00	12.00
AB6 Anquan Boldin/16	12.00	30.00
AG1 Ahman Green/300	3.00	8.00
AG2 Ahman Green/100	4.00	10.00
AG3 Ahman Green/42	6.00	15.00
AG4 Ahman Green/15	10.00	25.00
AG5 Ahman Green/30	8.00	20.00
AG6 Ahman Green/57	6.00	15.00
CJ1 Chad Johnson/300	4.00	10.00
CJ2 Chad Johnson/100	5.00	12.00
CJ3 Chad Johnson/16	12.00	30.00
CJ5 Chad Johnson/85	5.00	12.00
CJ6 Chad Johnson/21	12.00	30.00
CP1 Chad Pennington/300	4.00	10.00
CP2 Chad Pennington/100	5.00	12.00
CP3 Chad Pennington/41	8.00	20.00
CP4 Chad Pennington/15	12.00	30.00
CP6 Chad Pennington/21	12.00	30.00
CR1 Charles Rogers/300	2.50	6.00
CR2 Charles Rogers/100	3.00	8.00
CR5 Charles Rogers/80	3.00	8.00
DM1 Donovan McNabb/300	4.00	10.00
DM2 Donovan McNabb/100	5.00	12.00
DM3 Donovan McNabb/104	5.00	12.00
DM4 Donovan McNabb/19	12.00	30.00
DM6 Donovan McNabb/64	8.00	20.00
HW1 Hines Ward/300	4.00	10.00
HW2 Hines Ward/100	5.00	12.00
HW3 Hines Ward/37	10.00	25.00
HW5 Hines Ward/86	5.00	12.00
HW6 Hines Ward/77	5.00	12.00
JL1 Jamal Lewis/300	3.00	8.00
JL2 Jamal Lewis/100	4.00	10.00
JL3 Jamal Lewis/27	10.00	25.00
JL5 Jamal Lewis/31	8.00	20.00
JL6 Jamal Lewis/44	6.00	15.00
MF1 Marshall Faulk/300	4.00	10.00
MF2 Marshall Faulk/100	5.00	12.00
MF3 Marshall Faulk/131	5.00	12.00
MF5 Marshall Faulk/28	12.00	30.00
MF6 Marshall Faulk/141	5.00	12.00
MH1 Marvin Harrison/300	4.00	10.00
MH2 Marvin Harrison/100	5.00	12.00
MH3 Marvin Harrison/83	5.00	12.00
MH5 Marvin Harrison/88	5.00	12.00
MH6 Marvin Harrison/121	5.00	12.00
MV1 Michael Vick/300	5.00	12.00
MV2 Michael Vick/100	6.00	15.00
MV3 Michael Vick/32	12.00	30.00
MV6 Michael Vick/21	15.00	40.00
PH1 Priest Holmes/300	4.00	10.00
PH2 Priest Holmes/100	5.00	12.00
PH3 Priest Holmes/72	5.00	12.00
PH4 Priest Holmes/27	12.00	30.00
PH5 Priest Holmes/31	10.00	25.00
PH6 Priest Holmes/65	8.00	20.00
RM1 Randy Moss/300	4.00	10.00
RM2 Randy Moss/100	5.00	12.00
RM3 Randy Moss/77	5.00	12.00
RM4 Randy Moss/17	12.00	30.00
RM5 Randy Moss/84	5.00	12.00
RM6 Randy Moss/91	5.00	12.00
RW1 Ricky Williams/300	3.00	8.00
RW2 Ricky Williams/100	4.00	10.00
RW3 Ricky Williams/45	6.00	15.00
RW5 Ricky Williams/34	8.00	20.00
RW6 Ricky Williams/70	4.00	10.00
TO1 Terrell Owens/300	4.00	10.00
TO2 Terrell Owens/100	5.00	12.00
TO3 Terrell Owens/83	5.00	12.00
TO5 Terrell Owens/81	5.00	12.00
TO6 Terrell Owens/107	5.00	12.00

2004 Fleer Showcase Sweet Sigs Gold

OVERALL AUTO STATED ODDS 1:20H, 1:24R
CARDS #'d UNDER 20 NOT PRICED

AL Ashley Lelie JSY/85	8.00	20.00
DF DeShaun Foster JSY/20	20.00	50.00
DS Donte Stallworth JSY/83	8.00	20.00
JD Jake Delhomme JSY/17	20.00	50.00
KJ Kevin Jones/34	15.00	40.00
LE Lee Evans/88	12.00	30.00
MC Michael Clayton/88	10.00	25.00
MW Mike Williams No AU	4.00	10.00
SA Shaun Alexander JSY/37	15.00	40.00
WP Will Poole/29	25.00	60.00
AM1 Archie Manning/50	10.00	25.00
CJ1 Chad Johnson/148	12.00	30.00
CJ2 Chad Johnson JSY/85	12.00	30.00
RG1 Rex Grossman/76	10.00	25.00
ROW Roy Williams WR/88	12.00	30.00

2004 Fleer Showcase Sweet Sigs Red

RED FOIL AU/12-68 ODDS 1:20H, 1:24R
CARDS #'d UNDER 20 NOT PRICED

AL Ashley Lelie/15	15.00	40.00
AM Archie Manning/42	30.00	60.00
AV Adam Vinatieri/46	50.00	100.00
BL Byron Leftwich/43	12.00	30.00
BR Ben Roethlisberger/68	60.00	120.00
CJ Chad Johnson/15	25.00	60.00
DC David Carr/67	10.00	25.00
DF DeShaun Foster/30	15.00	40.00
DH Drew Henson/26	15.00	40.00
DM Donovan McNabb/45	40.00	80.00
DS Donte Stallworth/67	10.00	25.00
EM Eli Manning/41	60.00	120.00
JD Jake Delhomme/33	15.00	40.00
KJ Kevin Jones/16	20.00	50.00
LE Lee Evans/12	25.00	60.00
MC Michael Clayton/12	20.00	50.00
ROW Roy Williams WR/12	25.00	60.00
SA Shaun Alexander/38	15.00	40.00
WP Will Poole/22	25.00	60.00
RG Rex Grossman/38	15.00	40.00

2004 Fleer Showcase Sweet Sigs Silver

OVERALL AUTO ODDS 1:20H, 1:24R
STATED PRINT RUN 25-300

AL1 Ashley Lelie/300	6.00	15.00
AL2 Ashley Lelie/100	8.00	20.00
AV1 Adam Vinatieri/200	35.00	60.00
AV2 Adam Vinatieri/100	40.00	80.00
BL1 Byron Leftwich/250	8.00	20.00
BL2 Byron Leftwich/100	10.00	25.00
BR1 Ben Roethlisberger/270	40.00	100.00
BR2 Ben Roethlisberger/100	50.00	120.00
CJ1 Chad Johnson/148	12.00	30.00
CJ2 Chad Johnson/100	12.00	30.00
DC1 David Carr/25	15.00	40.00
DC2 David Carr/100	8.00	20.00
DF1 DeShaun Foster/300	8.00	20.00
DF2 DeShaun Foster/100	10.00	25.00
DH1 Drew Henson/50	10.00	25.00
DH2 Drew Henson/100	8.00	20.00
DS1 Donte Stallworth/60	10.00	25.00
DS2 Donte Stallworth/100	8.00	20.00
EM1 Eli Manning/200	50.00	100.00
EM2 Eli Manning/100	60.00	120.00
JD1 Jake Delhomme/275	10.00	25.00
JD2 Jake Delhomme/100	10.00	25.00
KJ1 Kevin Jones/300	8.00	20.00
KJ2 Kevin Jones/100	10.00	25.00
LE1 Lee Evans/300	10.00	25.00
LE2 Lee Evans/100	12.00	30.00
MC1 Michael Clayton/300	8.00	20.00
MC2 Michael Clayton/100	10.00	25.00
RG2 Rex Grossman/100	25.00	50.00
SA1 Shaun Alexander/125	10.00	25.00
SA2 Shaun Alexander/100	10.00	25.00
WP1 Will Poole/149	12.00	30.00
WP2 Will Poole/100	12.00	30.00
ROW1 Roy Williams WR/300	10.00	25.00
ROW2 Roy Williams WR/100	12.00	30.00
EC1 Earl Campbell No Auto	3.00	8.00
MW1 Mike Williams No Auto	3.00	8.00

2003 Fleer Snapshot

Released in January of 2004, this set consists of 135 cards including 90 veterans and 45 rookies. Rookies 91-135 are serial numbered to 500 and were inserted at a rate of 1:8 packs. Boxes contained 24 packs of 5 cards.

COMP.SET w/o SP's (90)	10.00	25.00
91-135 ROOKIE/500 ODDS 1:8		
1 Trent Green	.30	.75
2 Chad Johnson	.40	1.00
3 Randy Moss	.40	1.00
4 Brett Favre	1.00	2.50
5 Terrell Owens	.40	1.00
6 LaDainian Tomlinson	.40	1.00
7 Michael Vick	.50	1.25
8 Jerry Rice	.75	2.00
9 David Carr	.30	.75
10 Chad Pennington	.40	1.00
11 Torry Holt	.40	1.00
12 Edgerrin James	.40	1.00
13 Travis Henry	.25	.60
14 Warrick Dunn	.30	.75
15 Laveranues Coles	.25	.60
16 Fred Taylor	.30	.75
17 Todd Heap	.30	.75
18 Tim Brown	.40	1.00
19 Donovan McNabb	.40	1.00
20 Marvin Harrison	.40	1.00
21 Patrick Ramsey	.30	.75
22 Troy Brown	.30	.75
23 Antonio Bryant	.25	.60
24 Donte Stallworth	.25	.60
25 Joe Horn	.30	.75
26 Clinton Portis	.30	.75
27 Kurt Warner	.40	1.00
28 Quincy Morgan	.25	.60
29 James Stewart	.25	.60
30 Ashley Lelie	.25	.60
31 Kerry Collins	.30	.75
32 Julius Peppers	.40	1.00
33 Brad Johnson	.30	.75
34 Ricky Williams	.30	.75
35 Ahman Green	.30	.75
36 Plaxico Burress	.30	.75
37 Amani Toomer	.30	.75
38 Brian Urlacher	.40	1.00
39 Eddie George	.30	.75
40 Tony Gonzalez	.40	1.00
41 Chris Chambers	.30	.75
42 Tommy Maddox	.30	.75
43 Drew Brees	.40	1.00
44 Anthony Thomas	.30	.75
45 Brian Griese	.30	.75
46 Ray Lewis	.40	1.00
47 Peerless Price	.25	.60
48 Charlie Garner	.30	.75
49 Stacey Mack	.25	.60
50 Rod Gardner	.25	.60
51 Jevon Kearse	.30	.75
52 Tim Couch	.25	.60
53 Koren Robinson	.30	.75
54 Daunte Culpepper	.30	.75
55 Tom Brady	1.00	2.50
56 Jeff Blake	.30	.75
57 Jeff Garcia	.30	.75
58 Mike Alstott	.40	1.00
59 Corey Dillon	.30	.75
60 Antwaan Randle El	.30	.75
61 Deuce McAllister	.30	.75
62 William Green	.25	.60
63 Shaun Alexander	.30	.75
64 Eric Moulds	.30	.75
65 Jamal Lewis	.30	.75
66 Rich Gannon	.30	.75
67 Tiki Barber	.40	1.00
68 Peyton Manning	.75	2.00
69 Marshall Faulk	.40	1.00
70 Hines Ward	.40	1.00
71 Drew Bledsoe	.40	1.00
72 Stephen Davis	.30	.75
73 Mark Brunell	.30	.75
74 Priest Holmes	.40	1.00
75 Duce Staley	.30	.75
76 Jerome Bettis	.40	1.00
77 Rod Smith	.30	.75
78 Marty Booker	.30	.75
79 Aaron Brooks	.30	.75
80 Jake Plummer	.30	.75
81 Warren Sapp	.30	.75
82 David Boston	.25	.60
83 Joey Harrington	.25	.60
84 Emmitt Smith	1.00	2.50
85 Jimmy Smith	.30	.75
86 Curtis Martin	.40	1.00
87 Keyshawn Johnson	.40	1.00
88 Steve McNair	.40	1.00
89 Donald Driver	.40	1.00
90 Jeremy Shockey	.40	1.00
91 Tyrone Calico RC	2.00	5.00
92 Sam Aiken RC	2.00	5.00
93 Jason Witten RC	6.00	15.00
94 Dave Ragone RC	1.50	4.00
95 Billy McMullen RC	1.50	4.00
96 Musa Smith RC	1.50	4.00
97 Kelley Washington RC	1.50	4.00
98 Larry Johnson RC	2.50	6.00
99 Dallas Clark RC	4.00	10.00
100 Andre Johnson RC	6.00	15.00
101 Artose Pinner RC	1.50	4.00
102 B.J. Askew RC	2.00	5.00
103 Rex Grossman RC	2.50	6.00
104 Kevin Williams RC	2.50	6.00
105 Terence Newman RC	2.00	5.00
106 Teyo Johnson RC	2.00	5.00
107 Kevin Curtis RC	2.50	6.00
108 Brandon Lloyd RC	4.00	10.00
109 Kyle Boller RC	2.50	6.00
110 Bethel Johnson RC	1.50	4.00
111 E.J. Henderson RC	2.00	5.00
112 Quentin Griffin RC	2.00	5.00
113 Jerome McDougle RC	1.50	4.00
114 Justin Fargas RC	2.50	6.00
115 Michael Haynes RC	1.50	4.00
116 Tony Hollings RC	2.00	5.00
117 Bryant Johnson RC	2.50	6.00
118 L.J. Smith RC	2.50	6.00
119 Nate Burleson RC	2.00	5.00
120 Taylor Jacobs RC	1.50	4.00
121 Byron Leftwich RC	2.50	6.00
122 Charles Rogers RC	2.00	5.00
123 Chris Brown RC	1.50	4.00
124 DeWayne Robertson RC	2.00	5.00
125 Terrell Suggs RC	2.50	6.00
126 Johnathan Sullivan RC	1.50	4.00
127 Willis McGahee RC	3.00	8.00
128 Anquan Boldin RC	4.00	10.00
129 Chris Simms RC	2.50	6.00
130 Carson Palmer RC	5.00	12.00
131 Marcus Trufant RC	2.00	5.00
132 Jimmy Kennedy RC	2.00	5.00
133 Onterrio Smith RC	1.50	4.00
134 Boss Bailey RC	2.00	5.00
135 William Joseph RC	1.50	4.00

2003 Fleer Snapshot Projections

COMPLETE SET (15)	30.00	80.00
PRINT RUN 199 SER.#'d SETS		
1 Ricky Williams	2.00	5.00
2 Donovan McNabb	2.50	6.00
3 Brett Favre	6.00	15.00
4 Jerry Rice	5.00	12.00
5 Edgerrin James	2.50	6.00
6 Eddie George	2.00	5.00
7 Tom Brady	6.00	15.00
8 Marshall Faulk	2.50	6.00
9 Fred Taylor	2.00	5.00
10 Peyton Manning	5.00	12.00
11 Randy Moss	2.50	6.00
12 Chad Pennington	2.50	6.00
13 Kurt Warner	2.50	6.00
14 Tim Brown	2.50	6.00
15 Emmitt Smith	6.00	15.00

2003 Fleer Snapshot Projections Jerseys Silver

SILVER PRINT RUN 250 SER.#'d SETS
OVERALL MEM/AUTO ODDS 1:8
*GOLD/50: .8X TO 2X SILVER/250
GOLD PRINT RUN 50 SER.#'d SETS

NPBF Brett Favre	10.00	25.00
NPCP Chad Pennington	4.00	10.00
NPDM Donovan McNabb	4.00	10.00
NPEG Eddie George	3.00	8.00
NPEJ Edgerrin James	4.00	10.00
NPFT Fred Taylor	3.00	8.00
NPJR Jerry Rice	8.00	20.00
NPKW Kurt Warner	4.00	10.00
NPMF Marshall Faulk	4.00	10.00
NPPM Peyton Manning	8.00	20.00
NPRM Randy Moss	4.00	10.00
NPRWO Ricky Williams	3.00	8.00
NPTB Tim Brown	4.00	10.00
NPTB Tom Brady	10.00	25.00

2003 Fleer Snapshot Rookie Slides

STATED PRINT RUN 50 SER.#'d SETS

1 Tyrone Calico	4.00	10.00
2 Sam Aiken	4.00	10.00
3 Jason Witten	12.00	30.00
4 Dave Ragone	3.00	8.00
5 Billy McMullen	3.00	8.00
6 Musa Smith	3.00	8.00
7 Kelley Washington	3.00	8.00
8 Larry Johnson	5.00	12.00
9 Dallas Clark	8.00	20.00
10 Andre Johnson	12.00	30.00
11 Artose Pinner	3.00	8.00
12 B.J. Askew	4.00	10.00
13 Rex Grossman	5.00	12.00
14 Kevin Williams	5.00	12.00
15 Terence Newman	4.00	10.00
16 Teyo Johnson	4.00	10.00
17 Kevin Curtis	5.00	12.00
18 Brandon Lloyd	8.00	20.00
19 Kyle Boller	5.00	12.00
20 Bethel Johnson	3.00	8.00
21 E.J. Henderson	4.00	10.00
22 Quentin Griffin	4.00	10.00
23 Jerome McDougle	3.00	8.00
24 Justin Fargas	5.00	12.00
25 Michael Haynes	3.00	8.00
26 Tony Hollings	4.00	10.00
27 Bryant Johnson	5.00	12.00
28 L.J. Smith	5.00	12.00
29 Nate Burleson	4.00	10.00
30 Taylor Jacobs	3.00	8.00
31 Byron Leftwich	5.00	12.00
32 Charles Rogers	4.00	10.00
33 Chris Brown	3.00	8.00
34 DeWayne Robertson	4.00	10.00
35 Terrell Suggs	5.00	12.00
36 Johnathan Sullivan	3.00	8.00
37 Willis McGahee	6.00	15.00
38 Anquan Boldin	8.00	20.00
39 Chris Simms	5.00	12.00
40 Carson Palmer	10.00	25.00
41 Marcus Trufant	4.00	10.00
42 Jimmy Kennedy	4.00	10.00
43 Onterrio Smith	3.00	8.00
44 Boss Bailey	4.00	10.00
45 William Joseph	3.00	8.00

2003 Fleer Snapshot Seal of Approval

STATED ODDS 1:12
*GOLD/99: .8X TO 2X BASIC INSERTS
GOLD PRINT RUN 99 SER.#'d SETS

1 Clinton Portis	1.25	3.00
2 David Carr	1.25	3.00
3 Joey Harrington	1.00	2.50
4 Antwaan Randle El	1.25	3.00
5 Jeremy Shockey	1.50	4.00
6 Michael Vick	2.00	5.00
7 Drew Brees	1.50	4.00
8 Tommy Maddox	1.25	3.00
9 LaDainian Tomlinson	1.50	4.00
10 Deuce McAllister	1.25	3.00
11 Brett Favre	4.00	10.00
12 Jerry Rice	3.00	8.00
13 Eric Moulds	1.25	3.00
14 Ricky Williams	1.25	3.00
15 Terrell Owens	1.50	4.00
16 Taylor Jacobs	.60	1.50
17 Larry Johnson	1.00	2.50
18 Rex Grossman	1.00	2.50
19 Bryant Johnson	1.00	2.50
20 Kyle Boller	1.00	2.50
21 Andre Johnson	2.50	6.00
22 Charles Rogers	.75	2.00
23 Byron Leftwich	1.00	2.50
24 Willis McGahee	1.25	3.00
25 Carson Palmer	2.00	5.00

2003 Fleer Snapshot Seal of Approval Jerseys Bronze

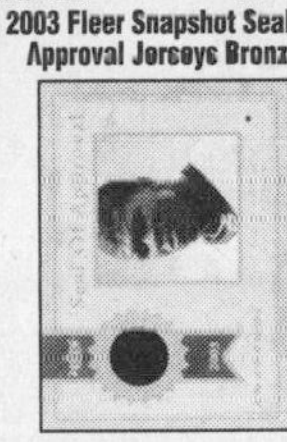

STATED PRINT RUN 375 SER.#'d SETS
OVERALL MEM/AUTO ODDS 1:8
*GOLD/99: .6X TO 1.5X BRONZE JSY
GOLD PRINT RUN 99 SER.#'d SETS

SAAJ Andre Johnson	6.00	15.00
SAAR Antwaan Randle El	3.00	8.00
SABF Brett Favre	10.00	25.00
SABL Byron Leftwich	2.50	6.00
SACP Carson Palmer	5.00	12.00
SACP Clinton Portis	2.00	5.00
SACR Charles Rogers	2.50	6.00
SADB Drew Brees	4.00	10.00
SADC David Carr	3.00	8.00
SADM Deuce McAllister	3.00	8.00
SAEM Eric Moulds	3.00	8.00
SAJH Joey Harrington	2.50	6.00
SAJR Jerry Rice	8.00	20.00
SAKB Kyle Boller	3.00	8.00
SALJ Larry Johnson	2.50	6.00
SALT LaDainian Tomlinson	4.00	10.00
SAMV Michael Vick	5.00	12.00
SARG Rex Grossman	2.50	6.00
SARW Ricky Williams	3.00	8.00
SATJ Taylor Jacobs	2.00	5.00
SATM Tommy Maddox	3.00	8.00
SATO Terrell Owens	4.00	10.00

2003 Fleer Snapshot Slides

PRINT RUN 100 SERIAL #'d SETS

1 Randy Moss	4.00	10.00
2 Brett Favre	10.00	25.00
3 LaDainian Tomlinson	4.00	10.00
4 Michael Vick	5.00	12.00
5 Jerry Rice	8.00	20.00
6 Chad Pennington	4.00	10.00
7 Donovan McNabb	4.00	10.00
8 Marvin Harrison	4.00	10.00
9 Clinton Portis	3.00	8.00
10 Ricky Williams	3.00	8.00
11 Daunte Culpepper	3.00	8.00
12 Tom Brady	10.00	25.00
13 Deuce McAllister	3.00	8.00
14 Shaun Alexander	3.00	8.00
15 Jamal Lewis	3.00	8.00
16 Peyton Manning	8.00	20.00
17 Marshall Faulk	4.00	10.00
18 Stephen Davis	3.00	8.00
19 Priest Holmes	4.00	10.00
20 Jeremy Shockey	4.00	10.00

2003 Fleer Snapshot Slides Autographs

PRINT RUN 50 SERIAL #'d SETS
OVERALL MEM/AUTO ODDS 1:8
UNPRICED GOLD PRINT RUN 10

1 T.J. Duckett	10.00	25.00
2 Joey Harrington	8.00	20.00
3 Josh Reed	8.00	20.00
4 Donte Stallworth	8.00	20.00
5 DeShaun Foster	10.00	25.00
6 Julius Peppers	50.00	80.00
7 Javon Walker	10.00	25.00
8 Daniel Graham	8.00	20.00
9 Ashley Lelie	8.00	20.00
10 Clinton Portis	10.00	25.00
11 Jabar Gaffney	8.00	20.00
12 Andre Davis	8.00	20.00
13 Antwaan Randle El	10.00	25.00
14 William Green	8.00	20.00
15 Patrick Ramsey	10.00	25.00
16 Roy Williams	10.00	25.00
17 Antonio Bryant	8.00	20.00
18 Ladell Betts	8.00	20.00
19 Tim Carter	8.00	20.00
20 Josh McCown	10.00	25.00

2003 Fleer Snapshot We're Number One

STATED PRINT RUN 1-2003

1A Carson Palmer/2003	1.50	4.00
2A David Carr/2002	1.25	3.00
3A Michael Vick/2001	2.00	5.00
4A Tim Couch/1999	1.00	2.50
4B Tim Couch/99	2.00	5.00
5A Peyton Manning/1998	3.00	8.00
5B Peyton Manning/98	6.00	15.00
6A Keyshawn Johnson/1996	1.50	4.00
6B Keyshawn Johnson/96	3.00	8.00
7A Drew Bledsoe/1993	1.50	4.00
7B Drew Bledsoe/93	3.00	8.00

2003 Fleer Snapshot We're Number One Jerseys

STATED PRINT RUN 111 SER.#'d SETS
*GOLD/25: .8X TO 2X BASIC JSY
GOLD STATED PRINT RUN 25

1 Carson Palmer	6.00	15.00
2 David Carr	5.00	12.00
3 Michael Vick	8.00	20.00
4 Tim Couch	4.00	10.00
5 Peyton Manning	12.00	30.00
6 Keyshawn Johnson	6.00	15.00
7 Drew Bledsoe	6.00	15.00

2004 Fleer Sweet Sigs

Fleer Sweet Sigs initially released in late November 2004. The base set consists of 100-cards including 25-rookies serial numbered to 999 at the end of the set. Hobby boxes contained 12-packs of 6-cards each. Two parallel sets and a variety of inserts can be found seeded in hobby and retail packs highlighted by the multi-tiered Autograph inserts. Some signed cards were issued via mail-in exchange or redemption cards with a number of those EXCH cards not yet appearing live on the secondary market as of the printing of this book.

COMP.SET w/o RC's (75)	6.00	15.00
1 Brett Favre	.75	2.00
2 Daunte Culpepper	.25	.60
3 Marshall Faulk	.30	.75
4 Ashley Lelie	.20	.50
5 Rex Grossman	.25	.60
6 Jeff Garcia	.25	.60
7 Jake Plummer	.25	.60
8 Tony Gonzalez	.30	.75
9 Terrell Owens	.30	.75
10 Plaxico Burress	.25	.60
11 Michael Vick	.40	1.00
12 Carson Palmer	.30	.75
13 Charles Rogers	.20	.50
14 Corey Dillon	.25	.60
15 Aaron Brooks	.25	.60
16 Torry Holt	.25	.60
17 Joey Galloway	.25	.60
18 Mark Brunell	.25	.60
19 Anquan Boldin	.30	.75
20 Domanick Davis	.20	.50
21 Edgerrin James	.25	.60
22 Hines Ward	.30	.75
23 Kyle Boller	.25	.60
24 Kurt Warner	.30	.75
25 Matt Hasselbeck	.25	.60
26 Chris Chambers	.25	.60
27 Deuce McAllister	.25	.60
28 Chad Pennington	.30	.75
29 Eddie George	.25	.60
30 Ray Lewis	.30	.75
31 Ahman Green	.25	.60
32 Marvin Harrison	.30	.75
33 Tiki Barber	.30	.75
34 Jerry Rice	.60	1.50
35 Emmitt Smith	.75	2.00
36 Chad Johnson	.30	.75
37 Roy Williams S	.25	.60
38 Peyton Manning	.60	1.50
39 Stephen Davis	.25	.60
40 Jamal Lewis	.25	.60
41 David Carr	.20	.50
42 A.J. Feeley	.20	.50
43 Jerry Porter	.20	.50
44 Willis McGahee	.30	.75
45 Quincy Morgan	.20	.50
46 Fred Taylor	.25	.60
47 Trent Green	.25	.60
48 Donovan McNabb	.30	.75
49 Marc Bulger	.25	.60
50 LaVar Arrington	.25	.60
51 Joey Harrington	.25	.60
52 Jake Delhomme	.25	.60
53 Jeremy Shockey	.25	.60

54 LaDainian Tomlinson	.30	.75
55 Brian Urlacher	.30	.75
56 Rudi Johnson	.25	.60
57 Shaun Alexander	.25	.60
58 Charlie Garner	.25	.60
59 Eric Moulds	.25	.60
60 Tom Brady	.60	1.50
61 Curtis Martin	.30	.75
62 Koren Robinson	.20	.50
63 Steve McNair	.30	.75
64 Travis Henry	.20	.50
65 Julius Peppers	.25	.60
66 Keyshawn Johnson	.25	.60
67 Andre Johnson	.30	.75
68 Priest Holmes	.30	.75
69 Drew Brees	.30	.75
70 Rich Gannon	.25	.60
71 Randy Moss	.30	.75
72 Peerless Price	.20	.50
73 Drew Bledsoe	.30	.75
74 Byron Leftwich	.25	.60
75 Clinton Portis	.30	.75
76 Roy Williams RC	1.50	4.00
77 Eli Manning RC	10.00	25.00
78 Kevin Jones RC	1.25	3.00
79 Tatum Bell RC	1.25	3.00
80 DeAngelo Hall RC	1.50	4.00
81 Michael Clayton RC	1.25	3.00
82 Rashaun Woods RC	1.00	2.50
83 Darius Watts RC	1.00	2.50
84 J.P. Losman RC	1.25	3.00
85 Drew Henson RC	1.00	2.50
86 Philip Rivers RC	6.00	15.00
87 Ben Roethlisberger RC	10.00	25.00
88 Larry Fitzgerald RC	4.00	10.00
89 Chris Perry RC	1.25	3.00
90 Devery Henderson RC	1.50	4.00
91 Sean Taylor RC	3.00	8.00
92 Reggie Williams RC	1.25	3.00
93 Lee Evans RC	1.50	4.00
94 Julius Jones RC	1.25	3.00
95 Dunta Robinson RC	1.00	2.50
96 Michael Jenkins RC	1.50	4.00
97 Greg Jones RC	1.00	2.50
98 Kellen Winslow RC	1.50	4.00
99 Steven Jackson RC	2.50	6.00
100 Matt Schaub RC	3.00	8.00

2004 Fleer Sweet Sigs Black

*VETS/80-90: 4X TO 10X BASIC CARDS
*ROOKIES/80-83: .8X TO 2X
*VETS/48-56: 5X TO 12X
*VETS/30-37: 6X TO 15X
*ROOKIES/33-39: 1.2X TO 3X
*VETS/20-28: 8X TO 20X
*ROOKIES/21-26: 1.5X TO 4X
*VETS/10-19: 12X TO 30X
*ROOKIES/10-19: 2.5X TO 6X
CARDS SER.#'d TO JERSEY NUMBER
CARDS #'d UNDER 25 NOT PRICED

2004 Fleer Sweet Sigs Gold

*VETS: 4X TO 10X BASIC CARDS
*ROOKIES: .9X TO 2X BASIC CARDS
STATED PRINT RUN 99 SER.#'d SETS

2004 Fleer Sweet Sigs Autographs Copper

UNPRICED MASTERPIECE PRINT RUN 1

BR Ben Roethlisberger/200	40.00	100.00
BW Brian Westbrook/150	8.00	20.00
CC Chris Chambers	6.00	15.00
CJ Chad Johnson/100	8.00	20.00
DC David Carr/40	8.00	20.00
EG Eddie George/27	12.00	30.00
GJ Greg Jones/175	4.00	10.00
JD Jake Delhomme/32	10.00	25.00
JJ Joe Jurevicius/75	6.00	15.00
KB Kyle Boller/75	8.00	20.00
MC Michael Clayton/205	5.00	12.00
MV Michael Vick/45	30.00	60.00
PR Philip Rivers/175	25.00	60.00
RG Rex Grossman/125	6.00	15.00
RJ Rudi Johnson/143	6.00	15.00
RW5 Rashaun Woods/150	4.00	10.00
TC Tyrone Calico/175	5.00	12.00
CRP Chris Perry	5.00	12.00
DEH Devery Henderson/150	6.00	15.00
DRH Drew Henson/50	6.00	15.00

2004 Fleer Sweet Sigs Autographs Gold

GOLD PRINT RUN 3-29

CB Chris Brown/29	8.00	20.00
GJ Greg Jones/29	8.00	20.00
JJ Joe Jurevicius/30	8.00	20.00
KC Keary Colbert/29	8.00	20.00
MC Michael Clayton/29	10.00	25.00

2004 Fleer Sweet Sigs Autographs Silver

SILVER PRINT RUN 11-153 CARDS
SILVERS SER.#'d UNDER 25 NOT PRICED

AB Anquan Boldin/54	8.00	20.00
AG Ahman Green/76	6.00	15.00
BF Brett Favre/33	150.00	250.00
BW Brian Westbrook/91	8.00	20.00
DH Dante Hall/153	5.00	12.00
GJ Greg Jones/55	5.00	12.00
KC Keary Colbert/62	5.00	12.00
RG Rex Grossman/22	12.00	30.00
RJ Rudi Johnson/150	5.00	12.00
RW5 Rashaun Woods/31	8.00	20.00
TC Tyrone Calico/60	6.00	15.00
CRP Chris Perry/26	12.00	30.00
DAM Dan Marino/27	150.00	300.00
DEH Devery Henderson/50	8.00	20.00

2004 Fleer Sweet Sigs End Zone Kings

STATED ODDS 1:12 HOB/RET

1 Ahman Green	.75	2.00
2 Priest Holmes	1.00	2.50
3 LaDainian Tomlinson	1.00	2.50
4 Jamal Lewis	.75	2.00
5 Clinton Portis	1.00	2.50
6 Marshall Faulk	1.00	2.50
7 Marvin Harrison	1.00	2.50
8 Tony Gonzalez	1.00	2.50
9 Hines Ward	1.00	2.50
10 Peyton Manning	2.00	5.00
11 Steve McNair	1.00	2.50
12 Daunte Culpepper	.75	2.00
13 Terrell Owens	1.00	2.50
14 Chad Pennington	1.00	2.50
15 Randy Moss	1.00	2.50

2004 Fleer Sweet Sigs End Zone Kings Jersey Silver

SILVER PRINT RUN 99-225
*GOLD/50: .8X TO 2X SILVER
GOLD PRINT RUN 50 SER.#'d SETS
*RED: .3X TO .8X SILVER
RED STATED ODDS 1:108 RETAIL
*BLACK DUAL: .8X TO 2X SILVER

AG Ahman Green/209	3.00	8.00
CP Chad Pennington/127	4.00	10.00
CP2 Clinton Portis/215	4.00	10.00
DC Daunte Culpepper/122	3.00	8.00
HW Hines Ward/223	4.00	10.00
JL Jamal Lewis/220	3.00	8.00
LT LaDainian Tomlinson/186	4.00	10.00
MF Marshall Faulk/208	4.00	10.00
MH Marvin Harrison/221	4.00	10.00
PH Priest Holmes/175	4.00	10.00
PM Peyton Manning/99	8.00	20.00
RM Randy Moss/212	4.00	10.00
SM Steve McNair/136	4.00	10.00
TG Tony Gonzalez/225	4.00	10.00
TO Terrell Owens/220	4.00	10.00

2004 Fleer Sweet Sigs End Zone Kings Jersey Quads

STATED PRINT RUN 12-35

GFMO Ahman Green/33	25.00	60.00
Marshall Faulk		
Randy Moss		
Terrell Owens		
PCMM Chad Pennington/35	30.00	80.00
Daunte Culpepper		
Peyton Manning		
Steve McNair		
PTFH Clinton Portis/26	20.00	50.00
LaDainian Tomlinson		
Marshall Faulk		
Priest Holmes		
WHMO Hines Ward/27	20.00	50.00
Marvin Harrison		
Randy Moss		
Terrell Owens		

2004 Fleer Sweet Sigs Gridiron Heroes

STATED ODDS 1:6 HOB/RET

1GH Brett Favre	2.50	6.00
2GH Michael Vick	1.25	3.00
3GH Jerry Rice	2.00	5.00
4GH Emmitt Smith	2.50	6.00
5GH Byron Leftwich	.75	2.00
6GH Donovan McNabb	1.00	2.50
7GH Clinton Portis	1.00	2.50
8GH Shaun Alexander	.75	2.00
9GH Tom Brady	2.00	5.00
10GH Eli Manning	3.00	8.00
11GH David Carr	.60	1.50
12GH Chad Johnson	1.00	2.50
13GH Brian Urlacher	1.00	2.50
14GH Joey Harrington	.75	2.00
15GH Andre Johnson	1.00	2.50
16GH Corey Dillon	.75	2.00
17GH Drew Bledsoe	1.00	2.50
18GH Plaxico Burress	.75	2.00
19GH Edgerrin James	.75	2.00
20GH Larry Fitzgerald	1.25	3.00
21GH Carson Palmer	1.00	2.50
22GH Philip Rivers	2.00	5.00
23GH Kellen Winslow Jr.	1.00	2.50
24GH Charles Rogers	.60	1.50
25GH Jeremy Shockey	.75	2.00

2004 Fleer Sweet Sigs Gridiron Heroes Jersey Silver

SILVER PRINT RUN 35-230
*BLACK/80-85: .6X TO 1.5X SILVER
*BLACK/54: .8X TO 2X SILVER
*BLACK/26-32: 1X TO 2.5X SILVER
*BLACK/26-32: .6X TO 1.5X SILVER/35
BLACK SER.#'d TO JERSEY NUMBER
BLACK SER.#'d UNDER 25 NOT PRICED
*GOLD/50: .8X TO 2X SILVER/155-230
*GOLD/50: .5X TO 1.2X SILVER/35
*RED: .3X TO .8X SILVER/155-230
*RED: .2X TO .5X SILVER/35
RED STATED ODDS 1:108 RETAIL
UNPRICED NFL LOGO PRINT RUN 1

AJ Andre Johnson/198	4.00	10.00
BF Brett Favre/230	10.00	25.00
BL Byron Leftwich/199	3.00	8.00
BU Brian Urlacher/155	4.00	10.00
CD Corey Dillon/210	3.00	8.00
CJ Chad Johnson/229	4.00	10.00
CP2 Clinton Portis/189	4.00	10.00
CR Charles Rogers/228	2.50	6.00
DB Drew Bledsoe/203	4.00	10.00
DC David Carr/227	2.50	6.00
DM Donovan McNabb/215	4.00	10.00
EJ Edgerrin James/216	3.00	8.00
ES Emmitt Smith/35	15.00	40.00
JH Joey Harrington/230	3.00	8.00
JR Jerry Rice/200	8.00	20.00
JS Jeremy Shockey/224	3.00	8.00
MV Michael Vick/213	5.00	12.00
PB Plaxico Burress/209	3.00	8.00
TB Tom Brady/226	8.00	20.00
CAP Carson Palmer/223	4.00	10.00

2004 Fleer Sweet Sigs Gridiron Heroes Jersey Duals

STATED PRINT RUN 2-36
CARDS SER.#'d UNDER 20 NOT PRICED

BD Tom Brady/36	20.00	50.00
Corey Dillon		
CJ David Carr/34	12.50	30.00
Andre Johnson		
HR Joey Harrington/25	12.50	30.00
Charles Rogers		
JP Edgerrin James/21	12.50	30.00
Clinton Portis		
JP2 Chad Johnson/29	10.00	25.00
Carson Palmer		
SF Emmitt Smith/31	15.00	40.00
Larry Fitzgerald		
VL Michael Vick/28	20.00	50.00
Byron Leftwich		

2004 Fleer Sweet Sigs Gridiron Heroes Jersey Quads

STATED PRINT RUN 29-42

BFSR Tom Brady	40.00	100.00
Brett Favre		
Emmitt Smith		
Jerry Rice/32		
BJJF Plaxico Burress	15.00	40.00
Chad Johnson		
Andre Johnson		
Larry Fitzgerald/29		
JPDA Edgerrin James	15.00	40.00
Clinton Portis		
Corey Dillon		
Shaun Alexander/37		
VHLM Michael Vick	25.00	60.00
Joey Harrington		
Byron Leftwich		
Donovan McNabb/42		

2004 Fleer Sweet Sigs Sweet Stitches Jersey Silver

SILVER PRINT RUN 99-250
*BLACK/15-48: 1X TO 2.5X SILVER
BLACK PRINT RUN 15-48
*GOLD/50: .8X TO 2X SILVER
GOLD PRINT RUN 50 SER.#'d SETS
*RED: .3X TO .8X SILVER
RED STATED ODDS 1:108 RETAIL

AB Anquan Boldin/244	4.00	10.00
AB2 Aaron Brooks/250	3.00	8.00
AL Ashley Lelie/230	2.50	6.00
AT Amani Toomer/244	3.00	8.00
BU Brian Urlacher/189	4.00	10.00
CC Chris Chambers/236	3.00	8.00
CM Curtis Martin/248	4.00	10.00
DB Drew Bledsoe/239	4.00	10.00
DB2 Drew Brees/125	4.00	10.00
DD Domanick Davis/198	2.50	6.00
DH Dante Hall/239	3.00	8.00
DH2 Drew Henson/99	2.50	6.00
DS Donte Stallworth/223	2.50	6.00
EGO Eddie George/236	3.00	8.00
HW Hines Ward/232	4.00	10.00
JD Jake Delhomme/247	3.00	8.00
JP Julius Peppers/221	3.00	8.00
JS Jeremy Shockey/230	3.00	8.00
KB Kyle Boller/226	3.00	8.00
LS Lee Suggs/231	3.00	8.00
MH Matt Hasselbeck/190	3.00	8.00
MP Marcus Pollard/210	2.50	6.00
PP Peerless Price/240	2.50	6.00
RG Rex Grossman/246	3.00	8.00
RJ Rudi Johnson/246	3.00	8.00
RL Ray Lewis/247	4.00	10.00
SD Stephen Davis/238	3.00	8.00
SM Santana Moss/239	3.00	8.00
TG Tony Gonzalez/201	4.00	10.00
ZT Zach Thomas/217	4.00	10.00

2004 Fleer Sweet Sigs Sweet Stitches Jersey Quads

STATED PRINT RUN 2-33

BBGS Klye Boller/26	15.00	40.00
Anquan Boldin		
Rex Grossman		
Lee Suggs		
BLSM Anquan Boldin/33	15.00	40.00
Ashley Lelie		
Donte Stallworth		
Santana Moss		
CTMM Chris Chambers/33	15.00	40.00
Zach Thomas		
Curtis Martin		
Santana Moss		
GSPF Tony Gonzalez/25	20.00	50.00
Jeremy Shockey		
Marcus Pollard		
Bubba Franks		
JSDG Rudi Johnson/27	12.00	30.00
Lee Suggs		
Domanick Davis		
Quentin Griffin		
MGDG Curtis Martin/28	20.00	50.00
Eddie George		
Stephen Davis		
Charlie Garner		

2002 Fleer Throwbacks

Released in September 2002, this 125 card set features 54 retired legends, 46 active veterans and 25 rookies. The rookies were inserted at a rate of 1:4 packs. Pack SRP was $5.99. Boxes contained 24 packs of 5 cards.

COMP.SET w/o SP's (100)	12.50	30.00
1 Terry Bradshaw	1.00	2.50
2 Franco Harris	.60	1.50
3 Y.A. Tittle	.50	1.25
4 Tony Dorsett	.60	1.50
5 Paul Hornung	.60	1.50
6 Rocky Bleier	.50	1.25
7 Archie Griffin	.40	1.00
8 Dwight Clark	.50	1.25
9 Bo Jackson	.75	2.00
10 Fran Tarkenton	.60	1.50
11 Howie Long	.60	1.50
12 Bob Griese	.60	1.50
13 George Rogers	.40	1.00
14 Roger Craig	.50	1.25
15 Jim Plunkett	.50	1.25
16 Eric Dickerson	.50	1.25
17 Marcus Allen	.60	1.50
18 Roger Staubach	1.00	2.50
19 Lawrence Taylor	.60	1.50
20 Joe Greene	.60	1.50
21 Earl Campbell	.60	1.50
22 Dave Casper	.40	1.00
23 Charles White	.40	1.00
24 Fred Biletnikoff	.60	1.50
25 Dan Pastorini	.40	1.00
26 John Cappelletti	.40	1.00
27 Paul Warfield	.50	1.25
28 Ozzie Newsome	.50	1.25
29 Johnny Rodgers	.50	1.25
30 William Perry	.50	1.25
31 Charley Taylor	.50	1.25
32 Deacon Jones	.50	1.25
33 Bubba Smith	.50	1.25
34 James Lofton	.40	1.00
35 Mike Rozier	.50	1.25
36 Ray Nitschke	.60	1.50
37 Dan Fouts	.60	1.50
38 Bob Lilly	.50	1.25
39 Ronnie Lott	.60	1.50
40 Barry Sanders	1.00	2.50
41 Troy Aikman	1.00	2.50
42 John Elway	1.25	3.00
43 Irving Fryar	.40	1.00
44 Jim Kelly	.75	2.00
45 Jim McMahon	.60	1.50
46 Joe Montana	1.50	4.00
47 Warren Moon	.60	1.50
48 Jay Novacek	.50	1.25
49 Mel Renfro	.40	1.00
50 Mike Singletary	.60	1.50
51 Johnny Unitas	1.00	2.50
52 Steve Young	.75	2.00
53 Walter Payton	2.50	6.00
54 Dan Marino	1.50	4.00
55 Torry Holt	.40	1.00
56 Rod Smith	.30	.75
57 Priest Holmes	.40	1.00
58 Anthony Thomas	.30	.75
59 Curtis Martin	.40	1.00
60 LaDainian Tomlinson	.50	1.25
61 Antowain Smith	.30	.75
62 Terrell Owens	.40	1.00
63 Tony Gonzalez	.40	1.00
64 Steve McNair	.40	1.00
65 Jerome Bettis	.40	1.00
66 Rich Gannon	.30	.75
67 Jake Plummer	.30	.75
68 Jamal Lewis	.30	.75
69 Drew Brees	.60	1.50
70 Jevon Kearse	.30	.75
71 Keyshawn Johnson	.30	.75
72 Kordell Stewart	.30	.75
73 Tim Brown	.40	1.00
74 Vinny Testaverde	.30	.75
75 Tom Brady	1.00	2.50
76 Drew Bledsoe	.40	1.00
77 Stephen Davis	.30	.75
78 Marvin Harrison	.40	1.00
79 Brian Griese	.30	.75
80 Michael Vick	.60	1.50
81 Emmitt Smith	1.00	2.50
82 Edgerrin James	.30	.75
83 Mark Brunell	.30	.75
84 Tim Couch	.25	.60
85 Randy Moss	.40	1.00
86 Brian Urlacher	.40	1.00
87 Marshall Faulk	.40	1.00
88 Corey Dillon	.30	.75
89 Eddie George	.30	.75
90 Terrell Davis	.40	1.00
91 Brett Favre	1.00	2.50
92 Peyton Manning	.75	2.00
93 Fred Taylor	.30	.75
94 Daunte Culpepper	.30	.75
95 Ricky Williams	.30	.75
96 Jerry Rice	.75	2.00
97 Donovan McNabb	.40	1.00
98 Doug Flutie	.40	1.00
99 Jeff Garcia	.30	.75
100 Kurt Warner	.40	1.00
101 Antonio Bryant RC	.75	2.00
102 Reche Caldwell RC	.75	2.00
103 David Carr RC	.75	2.00
104 Tim Carter RC	.60	1.50
105 Rohan Davey RC	.75	2.00
106 Andre Davis RC	.60	1.50
107 T.J. Duckett RC	.75	2.00
108 DeShaun Foster RC	.75	2.00
109 Jabar Gaffney RC	.75	2.00
110 William Green RC	.60	1.50
111 Joey Harrington RC	.75	2.00
112 Ron Johnson RC	.60	1.50
113 Ashley Lelie RC	.60	1.50
114 Josh McCown RC	.75	2.00
115 Julius Peppers RC	1.50	4.00
116 Clinton Portis RC	1.00	2.50
117 Patrick Ramsey RC	.75	2.00
118 Antwaan Randle El RC	.75	2.00
119 Josh Reed RC	.60	1.50
120 Cliff Russell RC	.50	1.25
121 Jeremy Shockey RC	1.25	3.00
122 Donte Stallworth RC	.75	2.00
123 Travis Stephens RC	.50	1.25
124 Javon Walker RC	.75	2.00
125 Marquise Walker RC	.50	1.25

2002 Fleer Throwbacks Classic Clippings

STATED ODDS 1:24 HOB, 1:240 RET

1 Fred Biletnikoff	6.00	15.00
2 Earl Campbell	6.00	15.00
3 Dave Casper	4.00	10.00
4 John Elway	12.00	30.00
5 Irving Fryar	4.00	10.00
6 Bob Lilly	5.00	12.00
7 Ronnie Lott	6.00	15.00
8 Joe Montana DP	12.00	30.00
9 Dan Marino DP	12.00	30.00
10 Jay Novacek	5.00	12.00
11 Walter Payton	20.00	50.00
12 Barry Sanders	10.00	25.00
13 Steve Young	8.00	20.00

2002 Fleer Throwbacks Classic Numbers

STATED PRINT RUN 100 SER.#'d SETS

1 Barry Sanders	20.00	50.00
2 Marcus Allen	12.00	30.00
3 Brett Favre	30.00	80.00
4 Irving Fryar	8.00	20.00
5 Steve Young	25.00	50.00
6 Jim Plunkett	10.00	25.00

2002 Fleer Throwbacks Greats of the Game Autographs

STATED ODDS 1:48 HOB, 1:240 RET

1 Marcus Allen	20.00	40.00
2 Fred Biletnikoff	20.00	40.00
3 Rocky Bleier SP	40.00	80.00
4 Terry Bradshaw SP	100.00	175.00
5 Earl Campbell	20.00	40.00
6 John Cappelletti	10.00	25.00
7 Dave Casper	10.00	25.00
8 Dwight Clark	10.00	25.00
9 Roger Craig	10.00	25.00
10 Daunte Culpepper	10.00	25.00
11 Eric Dickerson	15.00	30.00
12 Tony Dorsett	30.00	60.00
13 Joe Greene	25.00	60.00
14 Bob Griese	15.00	40.00
15 Archie Griffin	10.00	25.00
16 Franco Harris	35.00	60.00
17 Paul Hornung	25.00	50.00
18 Bo Jackson	50.00	80.00
19 Deacon Jones	10.00	25.00
20 Howie Long	25.00	50.00
21 Joe Montana	60.00	120.00
22 Randy Moss SP	50.00	100.00
23 Ozzie Newsome	10.00	25.00
24 Dan Pastorini	8.00	20.00
25 William Perry	10.00	25.00
26 Jim Plunkett	10.00	25.00
27 George Rogers	6.00	15.00
28 Johnny Rodgers	8.00	20.00
29 Mike Rozier	8.00	20.00
30 Bubba Smith	15.00	30.00
31 Emmitt Smith SP	175.00	300.00
32 Roger Staubach SP	50.00	80.00
33 Fran Tarkenton	15.00	40.00
34 Charley Taylor	8.00	20.00
35 Lawrence Taylor	25.00	50.00
36 Y.A. Tittle	15.00	40.00
37 Johnny Unitas SP	300.00	450.00
38 Paul Warfield	8.00	20.00
39 Charles White	8.00	20.00

2002 Fleer Throwbacks Lambeau Legends

STATED ODDS 1:48 HOB, 1:240 RET

1 Paul Hornung	8.00	20.00
2 Brett Favre	12.00	30.00
3 Dorsey Levens	4.00	10.00
4 Ray Nitschke	12.00	30.00
5 Antonio Freeman	5.00	12.00
6 Ahman Green	4.00	10.00

2002 Fleer Throwbacks On 2 Canton

STATED ODDS 1:12 HOB/RET

1 Walter Payton	4.00	10.00
Emmitt Smith		
2 Brian Griese	1.00	2.50
Bob Griese		
3 Fran Tarkenton	1.00	2.50
Daunte Culpepper		
4 Randy Moss	2.00	5.00
Jerry Rice		
5 Earl Campbell	1.00	2.50
Ricky Williams		

2002 Fleer Throwbacks On 2 Canton Memorabilia

STATED PRINT RUN 50 SER.#'d SETS

1 Earl Campbell	20.00	50.00
Ricky Williams		
2 Dan Marino	50.00	120.00
Joe Montana		
3 Randy Moss	40.00	100.00
Jerry Rice		
4 Walter Payton	60.00	150.00
Emmitt Smith		
5 Fran Tarkenton	20.00	50.00
Daunte Culpepper		

2002 Fleer Throwbacks QB Collection

COMPLETE SET (17)	20.00	50.00
STATED PRINT RUN 1500 SER.#'d SETS		
1 Donovan McNabb	1.00	2.50
2 Warren Moon	1.25	3.00
3 Jim Plunkett	1.00	2.50
4 Kurt Warner	1.00	2.50
5 Steve Young	1.50	4.00
6 Daunte Culpepper	.75	2.00
7 Brett Favre	2.50	6.00
8 Peyton Manning	2.00	5.00
9 Jeff Garcia	.75	2.00
10 Dan Fouts	1.25	3.00
11 John Elway	2.50	6.00
12 Jim McMahon	1.25	3.00
13 Jim Kelly	1.50	4.00
14 Troy Aikman	2.00	5.00
15 Y.A. Tittle	1.00	2.50
16 Fran Tarkenton	1.25	3.00
17 Bob Griese	1.25	3.00

2002 Fleer Throwbacks QB Collection Memorabilia

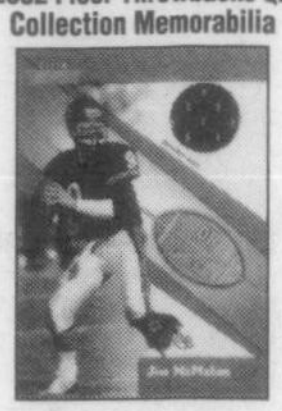

STATED ODDS 1:48 HOB, 1:240 RET

1 Troy Aikman	10.00	25.00
2 Daunte Culpepper	5.00	12.00
3 John Elway	12.00	30.00
4 Brett Favre	15.00	40.00
5 Dan Fouts	6.00	15.00
6 Jeff Garcia	5.00	12.00
8 Jim Kelly	8.00	20.00
10 Jim McMahon	6.00	15.00
11 Donovan McNabb	6.00	15.00
13 Jim Plunkett	5.00	12.00
16 Kurt Warner	6.00	15.00
17 Steve Young	8.00	20.00

2002 Fleer Throwbacks QB Collection Dream Backfield

STATED ODDS 1:24 HOB/RET

1 Brett Favre	3.00	8.00
Paul Hornung		
2 Warren Moon	1.25	3.00
Earl Campbell		
3 Kurt Warner	1.25	3.00
Eric Dickerson		
4 Dan Fouts	1.50	4.00
LaDainian Tomlinson		

2002 Fleer Throwbacks QB Collection Dream Backfield Memorabilia

STATED ODDS 1:30 HOB, 1:240 RET

1 Paul Hornung JSY	7.50	20.00
Brett Favre		
2 Earl Campbell JSY	6.00	15.00
Warren Moon		
3 Eric Dickerson JSY	6.00	15.00
Kurt Warner		
4 LaDainian Tomlinson JSY	6.00	15.00
Dan Fouts		

2002 Fleer Throwbacks QB Collection Dream Backfield Memorabilia Duals

STATED ODDS 1:120 HOB, 1:480 RET

1 Brett Favre	30.00	60.00
Paul Hornung		
2 Warren Moon	12.50	25.00
Earl Campbell		
3 Kurt Warner	12.50	30.00
Eric Dickerson		
4 Dan Fouts	12.50	25.00
LaDainian Tomlinson		

2002 Fleer Throwbacks Super Stars

COMPLETE SET (7)	7.50	20.00
STATED 1:6 HOB, 1:8 RET		
1 Jerry Rice	2.00	5.00
2 Terrell Davis	1.00	2.50
3 Marcus Allen	1.00	2.50
4 Jim Plunkett	.75	2.00
5 Fred Biletnikoff	1.00	2.50
6 Emmitt Smith	2.50	6.00
7 John Elway	2.00	5.00

2002 Fleer Throwbacks Super Stars Memorabilia

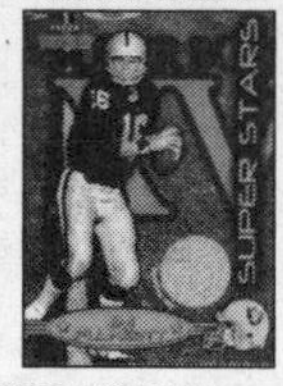

STATED ODDS 1:48 HOB, 1:240 RET

1 Marcus Allen	6.00	15.00
2 Fred Biletnikoff	6.00	15.00
3 Terrell Davis	6.00	15.00
4 John Elway	12.00	30.00
5 Jim Plunkett	5.00	12.00
6 Jerry Rice	12.00	30.00
7 Emmitt Smith	15.00	40.00

1998 Fleer Tradition

The 1998 Fleer Tradition set was issued in one series totalling 250 cards. The 10-card packs retail for $1.59 each. The fronts feature full-bleed color action photos with a clean background. The Fleer Tradition logo is found is the upper right corner. The backs offer complete stats on the featured player.

COMPLETE SET (250)	20.00	40.00
1 Brett Favre	.75	2.00
2 Barry Sanders	.60	1.50
3 John Elway	.75	2.00
4 Emmitt Smith	.60	1.50
5 Dan Marino	.75	2.00
6 Eddie George	.20	.50
7 Jerry Rice	.40	1.00
8 Jake Plummer	.20	.50
9 Joey Galloway	.10	.30
10 Mike Alstott	.20	.50
11 Brian Mitchell	.07	.20
12 Keyshawn Johnson	.20	.50
13 Jerald Moore	.07	.20
14 Randal Hill	.07	.20
15 Byron Hanspard	.07	.20
16 Jeff George	.10	.30
17 Terry Glenn	.20	.50
18 Jerome Bettis	.20	.50
19 Curtis Conway	.10	.30
20 Fred Lane	.07	.20
21 Isaac Bruce	.20	.50
22 Tiki Barber	.20	.50
23 Bobby Hoying	.10	.30
24 Marcus Allen	.20	.50
25 Dana Stubblefield	.07	.20
26 Peter Boulware	.07	.20
27 John Randle	.10	.30
28 Jason Sehorn	.10	.30
29 Rod Smith	.10	.30
30 Michael Sinclair	.07	.20
31 Marshall Faulk	.25	.60
32 Karl Williams	.07	.20
33 Kordell Stewart	.20	.50
34 Corey Dillon	.20	.50
35 Bryant Young	.07	.20
36 Charlie Garner	.10	.30
37 Andre Reed	.10	.30
38 Ray Buchanan	.07	.20
39 Brett Perriman	.07	.20
40 Leon Lett	.07	.20
41 Keenan McCardell	.10	.30
42 Eric Swann	.07	.20
43 Leslie Shepherd	.07	.20
44 Curtis Martin	.20	.50
45 Andre Rison	.10	.30
46 Keith Lyle	.07	.20
47 Rae Carruth	.07	.20
48 William Henderson	.10	.30
49 Sean Dawkins	.07	.20
50 Terrell Davis	.20	.50
51 Tim Brown	.20	.50
52 Willie McGinest	.07	.20
53 Jermaine Lewis	.10	.30
54 Ricky Watters	.10	.30
55 Freddie Jones	.07	.20
56 Robert Smith	.20	.50
57 Reidel Anthony	.10	.30
58 James Stewart	.10	.30
59 Earl Holmes RC	.20	.50
60 Dale Carter	.07	.20
61 Michael Irvin	.20	.50
62 Jason Taylor	.10	.30
63 Eric Metcalf	.07	.20
64 LeRoy Butler	.07	.20
65 Jamal Anderson	.20	.50
66 Jamie Asher	.07	.20
67 Chris Sanders	.07	.20
68 Warren Sapp	.10	.30
69 Ray Zellars	.07	.20
70 Carl Pickens	.10	.30
71 Garrison Hearst	.20	.50
72 Eddie Kennison	.10	.30
73 John Mobley	.07	.20
74 Rob Johnson	.10	.30
75 William Thomas	.07	.20
76 Drew Bledsoe	.30	.75
77 Micheal Barrow	.07	.20
78 Jim Harbaugh	.10	.30
79 Terry McDaniel	.07	.20
80 Johnnie Morton	.10	.30
81 Danny Kanell	.10	.30
82 Larry Centers	.07	.20
83 Courtney Hawkins	.07	.20
84 Tony Brackens	.07	.20
85 Tony Gonzalez	.20	.50
86 Aaron Glenn	.07	.20
87 Cris Carter	.20	.50
88 Chuck Smith	.07	.20
89 Tamarick Vanover	.07	.20
90 Karim Abdul-Jabbar	.20	.50
91 Bryant Westbrook	.07	.20
92 Mike Pritchard	.07	.20
93 Darren Woodson	.07	.20
94 Wesley Walls	.10	.30
95 Tony Banks	.10	.30
96 Michael Westbrook	.10	.30
97 Shannon Sharpe	.10	.30
98 Jeff Blake	.10	.30
99 Terrell Owens	.20	.50
100 Warrick Dunn	.20	.50
101 Levon Kirkland	.07	.20
102 Frank Wycheck	.07	.20
103 Gus Frerotte	.07	.20
104 Simeon Rice	.10	.30
105 Shawn Jefferson	.07	.20
106 Irving Fryar	.10	.30
107 Michael McCrary	.07	.20
108 Robert Brooks	.10	.30
109 Chris Chandler	.10	.30
110 Junior Seau	.20	.50
111 O.J. McDuffie	.10	.30
112 Glenn Foley	.10	.30
113 Darryl Williams	.07	.20
114 Elvis Grbac	.10	.30
115 Napoleon Kaufman	.20	.50
116 Anthony Miller	.07	.20
117 Troy Davis	.07	.20
118 Charles Way	.07	.20
119 Scott Mitchell	.10	.30
120 Ken Harvey	.07	.20
121 Tyrone Hughes	.07	.20
122 Mark Brunell	.20	.50
123 David Palmer	.07	.20
124 Rob Moore	.10	.30
125 Kerry Collins	.10	.30
126 Will Blackwell	.07	.20
127 Ray Crockett	.07	.20
128 Leslie O'Neal	.07	.20
129 Antowain Smith	.20	.50
130 Carlester Crumpler	.07	.20
131 Michael Jackson	.07	.20
132 Trent Dilfer	.20	.50
133 Dan Williams	.07	.20
134 Dorsey Levens	.20	.50
135 Ty Law	.10	.30
136 Rickey Dudley	.07	.20
137 Jessie Tuggle	.07	.20
138 Darrien Gordon	.07	.20
139 Kevin Turner	.07	.20
140 Willie Davis	.07	.20
141 Zach Thomas	.20	.50
142 Tony McGee	.07	.20
143 Dexter Coakley	.07	.20
144 Troy Brown	.10	.30
145 Leeland McElroy	.07	.20
146 Michael Strahan	.10	.30
147 Ken Dilger	.07	.20
148 Bryce Paup	.07	.20
149 Herman Moore	.10	.30
150 Reggie White	.20	.50
151 Dewayne Washington	.07	.20
152 Natrone Means	.10	.30
153 Ben Coates	.10	.30
154 Bert Emanuel	.10	.30
155 Steve Young	.25	.60
156 Jimmy Smith	.10	.30

157 Darrell Green .10 .30
158 Troy Aikman .40 1.00
159 Greg Hill .07 .20
160 Raymont Harris .07 .20
161 Troy Drayton .07 .20
162 Stevon Moore .07 .20
163 Warren Moon .20 .50
164 Wayne Martin .07 .20
165 Jason Gildon .07 .20
166 Chris Calloway .07 .20
167 Aeneas Williams .07 .20
168 Michael Bates .07 .20
169 Hugh Douglas .07 .20
170 Brad Johnson .20 .50
171 Bruce Smith .10 .30
172 Neil Smith .10 .30
173 James McKnight .20 .50
174 Robert Porcher .07 .20
175 Merton Hanks .07 .20
176 Ki-Jana Carter .07 .20
177 Mo Lewis .07 .20
178 Chester McGlockton .07 .20
179 Zack Crockett .07 .20
180 Derrick Thomas .20 .50
181 J.J. Stokes .10 .30
182 Derrick Rodgers .07 .20
183 Daryl Johnston .10 .30
184 Chris Penn .07 .20
185 Steve Atwater .07 .20
186 Amp Lee .07 .20
187 Frank Sanders .10 .30
188 Chris Slade .07 .20
189 Mark Chmura .10 .30
190 Kimble Anders .10 .30
191 Charles Johnson .07 .20
192 William Floyd .07 .20
193 Jay Graham .07 .20
194 Hardy Nickerson .07 .20
195 Terry Allen .20 .50
196 James Jett .10 .30
197 Jessie Armstead .07 .20
198 Yancey Thigpen .10 .30
199 Terance Mathis .10 .30
200 Steve McNair .20 .50
201 Wayne Chrebet .20 .50
202 Jamir Miller .07 .20
203 Duce Staley .25 .60
204 Deion Sanders .20 .50
205 Carnell Lake .07 .20
206 Ed McCaffrey .10 .30
207 Shawn Springs .07 .20
208 Tony Martin .10 .30
209 Jerris McPhail .07 .20
210 Darnay Scott .10 .30
211 Jake Reed .10 .30
212 Adrian Murrell .10 .30
213 Quinn Early .07 .20
214 Marvin Harrison .20 .50
215 Ryan McNeil .07 .20
216 Derrick Alexander .10 .30
217 Ray Lewis .20 .50
218 Antonio Freeman .20 .50
219 Dwayne Rudd .07 .20
220 Muhsin Muhammad .10 .30
221 Kevin Hardy .07 .20
222 Andre Hastings .07 .20
223 John Avery RC .30 .75
224 Keith Brooking RC .50 1.25
225 Kevin Dyson RC .50 1.25
226 Robert Edwards RC .30 .75
227 Greg Ellis RC .20 .50
228 Curtis Enis RC .20 .50
229 Terry Fair RC .30 .75
230 Ahman Green RC 1.50 4.00
231 Jacquez Green RC .30 .75
232 Brian Griese RC 1.25 3.00
233 Skip Hicks RC .30 .75
234 Ryan Leaf RC .50 1.25
235 Peyton Manning RC 7.50 15.00
236 R.W. McQuarters RC .30 .75
237 Randy Moss RC 4.00 10.00
238 Marcus Nash RC .20 .50
239 Anthony Simmons RC .30 .75
240 Brian Simmons RC .30 .75
241 Takeo Spikes RC .50 1.25
242 Duane Starks RC .20 .50
243 Fred Taylor RC .75 2.00
244 Andre Wadsworth RC .30 .75
245 Shaun Williams RC .30 .75
246 Grant Wistrom RC .30 .75
247 Charles Woodson RC .75 2.00
248 Checklist .07 .20
249 Checklist .07 .20
250 Checklist .07 .20
P16 Jeff George Promo .40 1.00

1998 Fleer Tradition Heritage

*1-250 VETS: 15X TO 40X BASIC CARDS
*221-247 ROOKIES: 5X TO 12X
HERITAGE PRINT RUN 125 SERIAL #'d SETS

1998 Fleer Tradition Big Numbers

COMPLETE SET (99) 40.00 100.00
STATED ODDS 1:4
EACH HAS 11-CARDS OF EQUAL VALUE
BN1A Tim Brown 0 .30 .75
BN2A Cris Carter 0 .30 .75
BN3A Terrell Davis 0 .30 .75
BN4A John Elway 0 1.25 3.00
BN5A Brett Favre 0 1.25 3.00
BN6A Eddie George 0 .30 .75
BN7A Dorsey Levens 0 .30 .75
BN8A Herman Moore 0 .20 .50
BN9A Steve Young 0 .40 1.00

1998 Fleer Tradition Big Numbers Prizes

COMPLETE SET (9) 6.00 15.00
SET ISSUED VIA MAIL REDEMPTION
1BN Tim Brown .50 1.25
2BN Cris Carter .50 1.25
3BN Terrell Davis .50 1.25
4BN John Elway 2.00 5.00
5BN Brett Favre 2.00 5.00
6BN Eddie George .50 1.25
7BN Dorsey Levens .50 1.25
8BN Herman Moore .30 .75
9BN Steve Young .60 1.50

1998 Fleer Tradition Playmakers Theatre

STATED PRINT RUN 100 SER.#'d SETS
PT1 Terrell Davis 12.00 30.00
PT2 Corey Dillon 10.00 25.00
PT3 Warrick Dunn 10.00 25.00
PT4 John Elway 50.00 100.00
PT5 Brett Favre 100.00 200.00
PT6 Antonio Freeman 12.00 30.00
PT7 Joey Galloway 10.00 25.00
PT8 Eddie George 10.00 25.00
PT9 Terry Glenn 10.00 25.00
PT10 Dan Marino 50.00 100.00
PT11 Curtis Martin 12.00 30.00
PT12 Jake Plummer 10.00 25.00
PT13 Barry Sanders 40.00 80.00
PT14 Deion Sanders 15.00 40.00
PT15 Kordell Stewart 8.00 20.00

1998 Fleer Tradition Red Zone Rockers

COMPLETE SET (10) 30.00 60.00
STATED ODDS 1:32
RZ1 Jerome Bettis 2.00 5.00
RZ2 Drew Bledsoe 3.00 8.00
RZ3 Mark Brunell 2.00 5.00
RZ4 Corey Dillon 2.00 5.00
RZ5 Joey Galloway 1.25 3.00
RZ6 Keyshawn Johnson 2.00 5.00
RZ7 Dorsey Levens 2.00 5.00
RZ8 Dan Marino 8.00 20.00
RZ9 Barry Sanders 6.00 15.00
RZ10 Emmitt Smith 6.00 15.00

1998 Fleer Tradition Rookie Sensations

COMPLETE SET (15) 30.00 60.00
STATED ODDS 1:16
1RS John Avery .50 1.25
2RS Keith Brooking .75 2.00
3RS Kevin Dyson .75 2.00
4RS Robert Edwards .50 1.25
5RS Greg Ellis .30 .75
6RS Curtis Enis .30 .75
7RS Terry Fair .50 1.25
8RS Ryan Leaf .75 2.00
9RS Peyton Manning 10.00 25.00
10RS Randy Moss 6.00 15.00
11RS Marcus Nash .30 .75
12RS Fred Taylor 1.25 3.00
13RS Andre Wadsworth .50 1.25
14RS Grant Wistrom .50 1.25
15RS Charles Woodson 1.00 2.50

1999 Fleer Tradition

This 300 card set was issued in August, 1999. The cards were in 10 card packs. Cards numbered from 251 through 300 feature the leading rookies entering the 1999 season. Notable Rookie Cards include Tim Couch, Edgerrin James and Ricky Williams. Four unnumbered checklist cards were issued at a rate of one every six packs.

COMPLETE SET (300) 20.00 40.00
1 Randy Moss .20 .50
2 Peyton Manning .60 1.50
3 Barry Sanders .50 1.25
4 Terrell Davis .20 .50
5 Brett Favre .60 1.50
6 Fred Taylor .15 .40
7 Jake Plummer .15 .40
8 John Elway .60 1.50
9 Emmitt Smith .50 1.25
10 Kerry Collins .15 .40
11 Peter Boulware .12 .30
12 Jamal Anderson .15 .40
13 Doug Flutie .20 .50
14 Michael Bates .12 .30
15 Corey Dillon .15 .40
16 Curtis Conway .15 .40
17 Ty Detmer .15 .40
18 Robert Brooks .15 .40
19 Dale Carter .12 .30
20 Charlie Batch .15 .40
21 Ken Dilger .12 .30
22 Troy Aikman .30 .75
23 Tavian Banks .12 .30
24 Cris Carter .20 .50
25 Derrick Alexander WR .12 .30
26 Chris Bordano RC .12 .30
27 Karim Abdul-Jabbar .15 .40
28 Jessie Armstead .15 .40
29 Drew Bledsoe .20 .50
30 Brian Dawkins .15 .40
31 Wayne Chrebet .15 .40
32 Garrison Hearst .15 .40
33 Eric Allen .15 .40
34 Tony Banks .15 .40
35 Jerome Bettis .20 .50
36 Stephen Alexander .12 .30
37 Rodney Harrison .15 .40
38 Mike Alstott .20 .50
39 Chad Brown .12 .30
40 Johnny McWilliams .12 .30
41 Kevin Dyson .12 .30
42 Keith Brooking .15 .40
43 Jim Harbaugh .15 .40
44 Bobby Engram .15 .40
45 John Holecek .12 .30
46 Steve Beuerlein .15 .40
47 Tony McGee .12 .30
48 Greg Ellis .12 .30
49 Corey Fuller .12 .30
50 Stephen Boyd .12 .30
51 Marshall Faulk .20 .50
52 LeRoy Butler .15 .40
53 Reggie Barlow .12 .30
54 Randall Cunningham .20 .50
55 Aeneas Williams .12 .30
56 Kimble Anders .12 .30
57 Cam Cleeland .12 .30
58 John Avery .12 .30
59 Gary Brown .12 .30
60 Ben Coates .15 .40
61 Koy Detmer .12 .30
62 Bryan Cox .15 .40
63 Edgar Bennett .15 .40
64 Tim Brown .20 .50
65 Isaac Bruce .20 .50
66 Eddie George .15 .40
67 Reidel Anthony .12 .30
68 Charlie Jones .12 .30
69 Terry Allen .15 .40
70 Joey Galloway .15 .40
71 Jamir Miller .12 .30
72 Will Blackwell .12 .30
73 Ray Buchanan .12 .30
74 Priest Holmes .20 .50
75 Michael Irvin .20 .50
76 Jonathan Linton .12 .30
77 Curtis Enis .12 .30
78 Neil O'Donnell .15 .40
79 Tim Biakabutuka .15 .40
80 Terry Kirby .12 .30
81 Germane Crowell .12 .30
82 Jason Elam .12 .30
83 Mark Chmura .12 .30
84 Marvin Harrison .20 .50
85 Jimmy Hitchcock .12 .30
86 Tony Brackens .12 .30
87 Sean Dawkins .12 .30
88 Tony Gonzalez .20 .50
89 Kent Graham .12 .30
90 Oronde Gadsden .12 .30
91 Hugh Douglas .15 .40
92 Robert Edwards .12 .30
93 R.W. McQuarters .12 .30
94 Aaron Glenn .12 .30
95 Kevin Carter .12 .30
96 Rickey Dudley .12 .30
97 Derrick Brooks .20 .50
98 Mark Bruener .12 .30
99 Darrell Green .20 .50
100 Jessie Tuggle .12 .30
101 Freddie Jones .12 .30
102 Rob Moore .12 .30
103 Ahman Green .15 .40
104 Chris Chandler .15 .40
105 Steve McNair .20 .50
106 Kevin Greene .15 .40
107 Jermaine Lewis .12 .30
108 Erik Kramer .15 .40
109 Eric Moulds .15 .40
110 Terry Fair .12 .30
111 Carl Pickens .15 .40
112 La'Roi Glover RC .20 .50
113 Chris Spielman .15 .40
114 Leroy Hoard .12 .30
115 Mark Brunell .15 .40
116 Patrick Jeffers RC .25 .60
117 Elvis Grbac .12 .30
118 Ike Hilliard .15 .40
119 Sam Madison .12 .30
120 Terrell Owens .20 .50
121 Rich Gannon .15 .40
122 Skip Hicks .12 .30
123 Eric Green .12 .30
124 Trent Dilfer .15 .40
125 Terry Glenn .15 .40
126 Trent Green .15 .40
127 Charles Johnson .12 .30
128 Adrian Murrell .15 .40
129 Jason Gildon .15 .40
130 Tim Dwight .15 .40
131 Ryan Leaf .15 .40
132 Rocket Ismail .15 .40
133 Jon Kitna .15 .40
134 Alonzo Mayes .12 .30
135 Yancey Thigpen .12 .30
136 David LaFleur .12 .30
137 Ray Lewis .20 .50
138 Herman Moore .15 .40
139 Brian Griese .15 .40
140 Antonio Freeman .15 .40
141 Darnay Scott .12 .30
142 Ed McDaniel .12 .30
143 Andre Reed .20 .50
144 Andre Hastings .12 .30
145 Chris Warren .15 .40
146 Kevin Hardy .12 .30
147 Joe Jurevicius .12 .30
148 Jerome Pathon .12 .30
149 Duce Staley .15 .40
150 Dan Marino .60 1.50
151 Jerry Rice .40 1.00
152 Byron Bam Morris .12 .30
153 Az-Zahir Hakim .12 .30
154 Ty Law .15 .40
155 Warrick Dunn .15 .40
156 Keyshawn Johnson .15 .40
157 Brian Mitchell .15 .40
158 James Jett .12 .30
159 Fred Lane .12 .30
160 Courtney Hawkins .12 .30
161 Andre Wadsworth .12 .30
162 Natrone Means .15 .40
163 Andrew Glover .12 .30
164 Anthony Simmons .12 .30
165 Leon Lett .12 .30
166 Frank Wycheck .15 .40
167 Barry Minter .12 .30
168 Michael McCrary .12 .30
169 Johnnie Morton .15 .40
170 Jay Riemersma .12 .30
171 Vonnie Holliday .12 .30
172 Brian Simmons .12 .30
173 Joe Johnson .12 .30
174 Ed McCaffrey .15 .40
175 Jason Sehorn .15 .40
176 Keenan McCardell .15 .40
177 Bobby Taylor .15 .40
178 Andre Rison .15 .40
179 Greg Hill .12 .30
180 O.J. McDuffie .15 .40
181 Darren Woodson .15 .40
182 Willie McGinest .15 .40
183 J.J. Stokes .12 .30
184 Leon Johnson .12 .30
185 Bert Emanuel .15 .40
186 Napoleon Kaufman .12 .30
187 Leslie Shepherd .12 .30
188 Levon Kirkland .12 .30
189 Simeon Rice .12 .30
190 Mikhael Ricks .12 .30
191 Robert Smith .15 .40
192 Michael Sinclair .12 .30
193 Muhsin Muhammad .15 .40
194 Duane Starks .12 .30
195 Terance Mathis .12 .30
196 Antowain Smith .12 .30
197 Tony Parrish .12 .30
198 Takeo Spikes .12 .30
199 Ernie Mills .12 .30
200 John Mobley .12 .30
201 Robert Porcher .12 .30
202 Pete Mitchell .12 .30
203 Darick Holmes .12 .30
204 Derrick Thomas .20 .50
205 David Palmer .12 .30
206 Jason Taylor .15 .40
207 Sammy Knight .12 .30
208 Dwayne Rudd .12 .30
209 Lawyer Milloy .15 .40
210 Michael Strahan .15 .40
211 Mo Lewis .12 .30
212 William Thomas .12 .30
213 Darrell Russell .12 .30
214 Brad Johnson .15 .40
215 Kordell Stewart .15 .40
216 Robert Holcombe .12 .30
217 Junior Seau .20 .50
218 Jacquez Green .12 .30
219 Shawn Springs .12 .30
220 Michael Westbrook .12 .30
221 Rod Woodson .20 .50
222 Frank Sanders .12 .30
223 Bruce Smith .20 .50
224 Eugene Robinson .15 .40
225 Bill Romanowski .15 .40
226 Wesley Walls .15 .40
227 Jimmy Smith .15 .40
228 Deion Sanders .20 .50
229 Lamar Thomas .12 .30
230 Dorsey Levens .15 .40
231 Tony Simmons .12 .30
232 John Randle .15 .40
233 Curtis Martin .20 .50
234 Bryant Young .15 .40
235 Charles Woodson .20 .50
236 Charles Way .12 .30
237 Zach Thomas .20 .50
238 Ricky Proehl .12 .30
239 Ricky Watters .15 .40
240 Hardy Nickerson .12 .30
241 Shannon Sharpe .20 .50
242 O.J. Santiago .12 .30
243 Vinny Testaverde .15 .40
244 Roell Preston .12 .30
245 James Stewart .12 .30
246 Jake Reed .15 .40
247 Steve Young .25 .60
248 Shaun Williams .12 .30
249 Rod Smith .15 .40
250 Warren Sapp .15 .40
251 Champ Bailey RC .60 1.50
252 Karsten Bailey RC .20 .50
253 D'Wayne Bates RC .20 .50
254 Michael Bishop RC .25 .60
255 David Boston RC .25 .60
256 Na Brown RC .20 .50
257 Fernando Bryant RC .20 .50
258 Shawn Bryson RC .20 .50
259 Darrin Chiaverini RC .20 .50
260 Chris Claiborne RC .20 .50
261 Mike Cloud RC .20 .50
262 Cecil Collins RC .20 .50
263 Tim Couch RC .30 .75
264 Scott Covington RC .20 .50
265 Daunte Culpepper RC .30 .75
266 Antuan Edwards RC .20 .50
267 Troy Edwards RC .25 .60
268 Ebenezer Ekuban RC .20 .50
269 Kevin Faulk RC .30 .75
270 Jermaine Fazande RC .20 .50
271 Joe Germaine RC .25 .60
272 Martin Gramatica RC .20 .50
273 Torry Holt RC .50 1.25
274 Brock Huard RC .25 .60
275 Sedrick Irvin RC .20 .50
276 Sheldon Jackson RC .20 .50
277 Edgerrin James RC .40 1.00
278 James Johnson RC .20 .50
279 Kevin Johnson RC .25 .60
280 Malcolm Johnson RC .20 .50
281 Andy Katzenmoyer RC .25 .60
282 Jevon Kearse RC .30 .75
283 Patrick Kerney RC .25 .60
284 Shaun King RC .25 .60
285 Jim Kleinsasser RC .30 .75
286 Rob Konrad RC .20 .50
287 Chris McAlister RC .25 .60
288 Donovan McNabb RC 2.00 5.00
289 Cade McNown RC .25 .60
290 Dee Miller RC .20 .50
291 Joe Montgomery RC .20 .50
292 De'Mond Parker RC .20 .50
293 Peerless Price RC .25 .60
294 Akili Smith RC .25 .60
295 Justin Swift RC .20 .50
296 Jerame Tuman RC .20 .50
297 Ricky Williams RC .50 1.25
298 Antoine Winfield .20 .50
299 Craig Yeast RC .20 .50
300 Amos Zereoue RC .25 .60
P6 Fred Taylor Promo .40 1.00

1999 Fleer Tradition Blitz Collection

COMPLETE SET (300) 50.00 120.00
*BC STARS: 1.2X TO 3X BASIC CARDS
*BLITZ COLL.RCs: .5X TO 1.2X BASIC CARDS
ONE BLITZ COLLECTION PER RETAIL PACK

1999 Fleer Tradition Trophy Collection

*TC STARS: 50X TO 120X BASIC CARDS
*TC ROOKIES: 8X TO 20X
STATED PRINT RUN 20 SERIAL #'d SETS

1999 Fleer Tradition Aerial Assault

COMPLETE SET (15) 25.00 50.00
STATED ODDS 1:24
1 Troy Aikman 2.00 5.00
2 Jamal Anderson 1.00 2.50
3 Charlie Batch 1.00 2.50
4 Mark Brunell 1.00 2.50
5 Terrell Davis 1.00 2.50
6 John Elway 3.00 8.00
7 Brett Favre 3.00 8.00
8 Keyshawn Johnson 1.00 2.50
9 Jon Kitna 1.00 2.50
10 Peyton Manning 3.00 8.00
11 Dan Marino 3.00 8.00
12 Randy Moss 2.50 6.00
13 Eric Moulds 1.00 2.50
14 Jake Plummer .60 1.50
15 Jerry Rice 2.00 5.00

1999 Fleer Tradition Fresh Ink

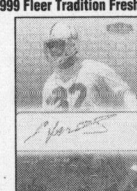

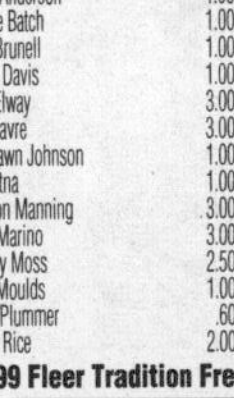

STATED PRINT RUN 200 SER.#'d SETS
1 Champ Bailey 15.00 30.00
2 David Boston 7.50 20.00
3 Chris Claiborne 6.00 15.00
4 Torry Holt 12.00 30.00
5 Edgerrin James 15.00 40.00
6 James Johnson 6.00 15.00
7 Kevin Johnson 7.50 20.00
8 Jevon Kearse 10.00 25.00
9 Shaun King 7.50 20.00
10 Rob Konrad 7.50 20.00
11 Donovan McNabb 30.00 80.00
12 Cade McNown 7.50 20.00
13 Akili Smith 7.50 20.00
14 Ricky Williams 12.00 30.00

1999 Fleer Tradition Rookie Sensations

COMPLETE SET (20) 15.00 40.00
STATED ODDS 1:6
1 Champ Bailey .75 2.00
2 Michael Bishop .60 1.50
3 David Boston .60 1.50
4 Chris Claiborne .20 .50
5 Tim Couch .60 1.50
6 Daunte Culpepper 2.50 6.00
7 Troy Edwards .40 1.00
8 Kevin Faulk .60 1.50
9 Torry Holt 1.50 4.00
10 Brock Huard .60 1.50
11 Edgerrin James 2.50 6.00
12 Kevin Johnson .60 1.50
13 Shaun King .40 1.00
14 Rob Konrad .60 1.50
15 Chris McAlister .40 1.00
16 Donovan McNabb 3.00 8.00
17 Cade McNown .40 1.00
18 Peerless Price .60 1.50
19 Akili Smith .40 1.00
20 Ricky Williams 1.25 3.00

1999 Fleer Tradition Under Pressure

COMPLETE SET (15) 50.00 120.00
STATED ODDS 1:96
1 Charlie Batch 3.00 8.00
2 Terrell Davis 3.00 8.00
3 Warrick Dunn 3.00 8.00
4 John Elway 10.00 25.00
5 Brett Favre 10.00 25.00
6 Keyshawn Johnson 3.00 8.00
7 Peyton Manning 10.00 25.00
8 Dan Marino 10.00 25.00
9 Curtis Martin 3.00 8.00
10 Randy Moss 8.00 20.00
11 Jake Plummer 2.00 5.00
12 Barry Sanders 10.00 25.00
13 Emmitt Smith 6.00 15.00
14 Fred Taylor 3.00 8.00
15 Charles Woodson 3.00 8.00

1999 Fleer Tradition Unsung Heroes

COMPLETE SET (30) 5.00 10.00
STATED ODDS 1:3
1UH Tommy Bennett .25 .60
2UH Lester Archambeau .25 .60
3UH James Jones DT .25 .60
4UH Phil Hansen .25 .60
5UH Anthony Johnson .25 .60
6UH Bobby Engram .25 .60
7UH Eric Bieniemy .25 .60
8UH Daryl Johnston .25 .60
9UH Maa Tanuvasa .25 .60
10UH Stephen Boyd .25 .60
11UH Adam Timmerman .25 .60
12UH Ken Dilger .25 .60
13UH Bryan Barker .25 .60
14UH Rich Gannon .40 1.00
15UH O.J. Brigance .25 .60
16UH Jeff Christy .25 .60
17UH Shawn Jefferson .25 .60
18UH Aaron Craver .25 .60
19UH Chris Calloway .25 .60
20UH Pepper Johnson .25 .60
21UH Greg Biekert .25 .60
22UH Duce Staley .25 .60
23UH Courtney Hawkins .25 .60
24UH D'Marco Farr .25 .60
25UH Rodney Harrison .25 .60
26UH Ray Brown .25 .60
27UH Jon Kitna .40 1.00
28UH Brad Culpepper .25 .60
29UH Steve Jackson .25 .60
30UH Brian Mitchell .25 .60

1999 Fleer Tradition Unsung Heroes Banquet

This set was distributed to attendees of the NFL Player's Inc. Unsung Heroes Awards Banquet on April 16, 1999. Each card features a full color photo of the player on front with a player profile on back. The cards were also issued in Fleer packs as an insert with a different suffix on the card numbers.

COMPLETE SET (31) 16.00 40.00
1AB Tommy Bennett .50 1.25
2AB Lester Archambeau .50 1.25
3AB James Jones DT .50 1.25
4AB Phil Hansen .50 1.25
5AB Anthony Johnson .50 1.25
6AB Bobby Engram .80 2.00
7AB Eric Bieniemy .50 1.25
8AB Daryl Johnston .80 2.00
9AB Maa Tanuvasa .50 1.25
10AB Stephen Boyd .50 1.25
11AB Adam Timmerman .50 1.25
12AB Ken Dilger .80 2.00
13AB Bryan Barker .50 1.25
14AB Rich Gannon 1.20 3.00
15AB O.J. Brigance .50 1.25
16AB Jeff Christy .50 1.25
17AB Shawn Jefferson .50 1.25
18AB Aaron Craver .50 1.25
19AB Chris Calloway .80 2.00
20AB Pepper Johnson .50 1.25
21AB Greg Biekert .50 1.25
22AB Duce Staley 1.20 3.00
23AB Courtney Hawkins .50 1.25
24AB D'Marco Farr .50 1.25
25AB Rodney Harrison .50 1.25
26AB Ray Brown OL .50 1.25
27AB Jon Kitna 1.20 3.00
28AB Brad Culpepper .50 1.25
29AB Steve Jackson .50 1.25
30AB Brian Mitchell .50 1.25
NNO Checklist Card UER .50 1.25
(several incorrect card #'s)

2000 Fleer Tradition

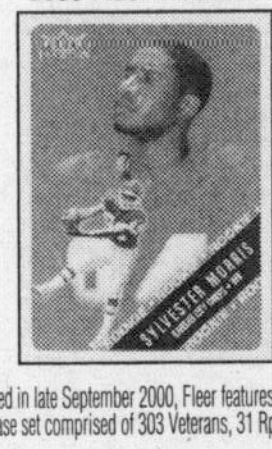

Released in late September 2000, Fleer features a 400-card base set comprised of 303 Veterans, 31 Rpploe Singles, 31 Rookies to Watch, 31 Team Action cards, and 4 Checklists. Base cards are white bordered and feature both action and portrait photos coupled with a facsimile player autograph on a single color background resembling sets from the 1950's. Fleer was packaged in 36-pack boxes with packs containing 10 cards.

COMPLETE SET (400) 25.00 60.00
1 Kevin Johnson .12 .30
2 Chris Chandler .15 .40
3 Peerless Price .15 .40
4 Andre Rison .15 .40
5 Curtis Enis .12 .30
6 Tim Couch .15 .40
7 Brian Dawkins .20 .50
8 Akili Smith .12 .30
9 Kevin Faulk .15 .40
10 Joey Galloway .15 .40
11 Bill Romanowski .12 .30
12 Charlie Batch .15 .40
13 Terrence Wilkins .12 .30
14 Kevin Hardy .12 .30
15 Cade McNown .12 .30
16 Elvis Grbac .12 .30
17 Cris Carter .20 .50
18 Willie McGinest .15 .40
19 Michael Bishop .12 .30
20 Lee Woodall .12 .30
21 Jake Reed .15 .40
22 Bryan Cox .12 .30
23 Chris Sanders .12 .30
24 Tavian Banks .12 .30
25 Levon Kirkland .12 .30
26 James Hundon .12 .30
27 Junior Seau .20 .50
28 Darren Woodson .12 .30
29 Kevin Carter .12 .30
30 Joe Jurevicius .12 .30
31 John Lynch .15 .40
32 Steve McNair .20 .50
33 Jake Plummer .15 .40
34 Antonio Freeman .15 .40
35 Peter Boulware .12 .30
36 Brad Johnson .15 .40
37 Bobby Engram .15 .40
38 David Boston .12 .30
39 Jason Tucker .12 .30
40 Troy Brown .15 .40
41 Brian Griese .15 .40
42 Dorsey Levens .15 .40
43 Cornelius Bennett .12 .30
44 Donovan McNabb .20 .50
45 Rob Johnson .15 .40
46 Robert Smith .15 .40
47 Stanley Pritchett .12 .30
48 Tedy Bruschi .30 .75
49 Dan Marino .60 1.50
50 Amani Toomer .15 .40
51 Aaron Glenn .12 .30
52 Rickey Dudley .12 .30
53 Tim Brown .20 .50
54 Jim Harbaugh .15 .40
55 Terrell Owens .20 .50
56 Jason Sehorn .12 .30
57 Cortez Kennedy .12 .30
58 London Fletcher RC .20 .50
59 Simeon Rice .15 .40
60 Shaun King .12 .30
61 Stephen Davis .15 .40
62 Andre Wadsworth .12 .30
63 Kyle Brady .12 .30
64 Priest Holmes .20 .50
65 Patrick Jeffers .15 .40
66 Barry Minter .12 .30
67 Curtis Martin .20 .50
68 Darrin Chiaverini .12 .30
69 Robert Thomas .12 .30
70 Samari Rolle .12 .30
71 Robert Porcher .12 .30
72 Jerry Rice .40 1.00
73 Bill Schroeder .15 .40
74 Chad Bratzke .12 .30
75 Tony Brackens .12 .30
76 O.J. McDuffie .15 .40
77 John Randle .15 .40
78 Michael Pittman .12 .30
79 Drew Bledsoe .20 .50
80 Ike Hilliard .15 .40
81 Victor Green .12 .30
82 Duce Staley .15 .40
83 Bruce Smith .20 .50
84 Amos Zereoue .12 .30
85 Charlie Garner .15 .40
86 Shawn Springs .12 .30
87 Kurt Warner .30 .75
88 Eddie George .15 .40
89 Michael Westbrook .12 .30
90 Dexter Coakley .12 .30
91 Rob Moore .12 .30
92 Duane Starks .12 .30
93 Steve Beuerlein .15 .40
94 Marty Booker .15 .40
95 Karim Abdul-Jabbar .12 .30
96 Troy Aikman .30 .75
97 Germane Crowell .12 .30
98 Matt Hasselbeck .20 .50
99 E.G. Green .12 .30
100 Mark Brunell .15 .40
101 Tony Martin .15 .40
102 Darrell Green .15 .40
103 Ricky Williams .20 .50
104 Michael Strahan .15 .40
105 Vinny Testaverde .15 .40
106 Charles Johnson .12 .30
107 Hines Ward .20 .50
108 Bryant Young .12 .30
109 Mo Lewis .12 .30
110 Greg Clark .12 .30
111 Jon Kitna .15 .40
112 Jacquez Green .12 .30
113 Kevin Dyson .15 .40
114 Stephen Alexander .12 .30
115 Cam Cleeland .12 .30
116 Keith Poole .12 .30
117 Az-Zahir Hakim .12 .30
118 Tim Dwight .15 .40
119 Corey Bradford .12 .30
120 Carlos Emmons .12 .30
121 Trent Dilfer .15 .40
122 Lance Schulters .12 .30
123 Byron Hanspard .12 .30
124 Tim Biakabutuka .15 .40
125 Eddie Kennison .12 .30
126 Terry Kirby .12 .30
127 Mike McKenzie .12 .30
128 Fred Beasley .12 .30
129 Chad Brown .12 .30
130 Terrell Davis .20 .50
131 Herman Moore .15 .40
132 Vonnie Holliday .12 .30
133 Jim Miller .12 .30
134 Peyton Manning .50 1.25
135 Derrick Alexander .12 .30
136 Oronde Gadsden .15 .40
137 Robert Griffith .12 .30
138 Troy Edwards .12 .30
139 Damon Huard .15 .40
140 Jessie Armstead .12 .30
141 Charles Woodson .20 .50
142 Troy Vincent .12 .30
143 Natrone Means .15 .40
144 Jeff Garcia .15 .40
145 Terry Glenn .15 .40
146 Marshall Faulk .20 .50
147 Pat Johnson .12 .30
148 Frank Wycheck .15 .40
149 Champ Bailey .15 .40
150 Jamal Anderson .15 .40
151 Doug Flutie .20 .50
152 Michael Bates .12 .30
153 Corey Dillon .15 .40
154 Keith McKenzie .12 .30
155 Orpheus Roye .12 .30
156 Olandis Gary .15 .40
157 Johnnie Morton .15 .40
158 Brett Favre .60 1.50
159 Adrian Murrell .12 .30
160 Fred Taylor .20 .50
161 Tony Gonzalez .20 .50
162 Zach Thomas .20 .50
163 Randy Moss .20 .50
164 Marcus Robinson .15 .40
165 Tiki Barber .20 .50
166 Rich Gannon .15 .40
167 Jeremiah Trotter RC .40 1.00
168 Jermaine Fazande .12 .30
169 Steve Young .25 .60
170 Isaac Bruce .20 .50
171 Warrick Dunn .15 .40
172 Yancey Thigpen .12 .30
173 Rod Smith .15 .40
174 Albert Connell .12 .30
175 Freddie Jones .12 .30
176 Terance Mathis .12 .30
177 Eric Moulds .15 .40
178 Brian Mitchell .12 .30
179 Wesley Walls .12 .30
180 Carl Pickens .15 .40
181 Errict Rhett .15 .40
182 Madre Hill .12 .30
183 Jason Elam .12 .30
184 Greg Ellis .12 .30
185 David Sloan .12 .30
186 Edgerrin James .20 .50
187 Jimmy Smith .15 .40
188 Tony Richardson RC .15 .40
189 James Hasty .12 .30
190 Sam Madison .12 .30
191 Tony Simmons .12 .30
192 Andre Hastings .12 .30
193 Keyshawn Johnson .15 .40
194 Na Brown .12 .30
195 Napoleon Kaufman .15 .40
196 Torrance Small .12 .30
197 Curtis Conway .15 .40
198 Jeff Graham .12 .30
199 Jason Hanson .12 .30
200 Derrick Mayes .12 .30
201 Torry Holt .20 .50
202 Warren Sapp .15 .40
203 Kimble Anders .12 .30
204 Blaine Bishop .12 .30
205 Leroy Hoard .12 .30
206 Larry Centers .12 .30
207 O.J. Santiago .12 .30
208 Antowain Smith .15 .40
209 Chuck Smith .12 .30
210 Takeo Spikes .12 .30
211 Rocket Ismail .15 .40
212 Ed McCaffrey .15 .40
213 Karsten Bailey .12 .30
214 Terry Fair .12 .30
215 Ken Dilger .12 .30
216 Jamie Martin .12 .30
217 Cris Dishman .12 .30
218 Jay Fiedler .15 .40
219 Lawyer Milloy .12 .30
220 Jake Delhomme RC .50 1.25
221 Wayne Chrebet .15 .40
222 Darrell Russell .12 .30
223 Christian Fauria .12 .30
224 Jerome Bettis .20 .50
225 Ryan Leaf .15 .40
226 Ricky Watters .15 .40
227 Keenan McCardell .15 .40
228 Grant Wistrom .12 .30
229 Jevon Kearse .15 .40
230 Frank Sanders .12 .30
231 Shannon Sharpe .20 .50
232 Jonathan Linton .12 .30
233 Alonzo Mayes .12 .30
234 Jason Garrett .20 .50
235 Kordell Stewart .15 .40
236 David LaFleur .12 .30
237 Kenny Bynum .12 .30
238 Byron Chamberlain .12 .30
239 Tyrone Davis .12 .30
240 Jerome Pathon .12 .30
241 Alvis Whitted .12 .30
242 Kevin Lockett .12 .30
243 Matthew Hatchette .12 .30
244 Rod Woodson .20 .50
245 Joe Horn .15 .40
246 Ronnie Powell .12 .30
247 Dedric Ward .12 .30
248 James Johnson .12 .30
249 James Jett .15 .40
250 Bobby Shaw RC .15 .40
251 J.J. Stokes .15 .40
252 Paul Shields RC .12 .30
253 Sean Dawkins .12 .30
254 Hardy Nickerson .12 .30
255 Stephen Boyd .12 .30
256 Chris Warren .12 .30
257 Kerry Collins .15 .40
258 Isaac Byrd .12 .30
259 Bobby Hoying .12 .30
260 Daunte Culpepper .15 .40
261 Moe Williams .12 .30
262 Kamil Loud .12 .30
263 Derrick Brooks .20 .50
264 Jay Riemersma .12 .30
265 Ray Lucas .12 .30
266 Jason Gildon .12 .30
267 James Stewart .12 .30
268 Marcellus Wiley .12 .30
269 Craig Yeast .12 .30
270 Michael Basnight .12 .30
271 Tyrone Wheatley .12 .30
272 Martin Gramatica .12 .30
273 Phillip Daniels RC .12 .30
274 Richard Huntley .12 .30
275 Muhsin Muhammad .15 .40
276 Todd Lyght .12 .30
277 Carlester Crumpler .12 .30
278 Jeff Lewis .12 .30
279 Jeff George .15 .40
280 Jeff Blake .15 .40

281 Michael McCrary .12 .30
282 Shawn Jefferson .12 .30
283 Mark Bruener .15 .40
284 Donnie Abraham .12 .30
285 Yatil Green .12 .30
286 Jermaine Lewis .12 .30
287 Rob Fredrickson .12 .30
288 Thurman Thomas .20 .50
289 Kent Graham .12 .30
290 Darnay Scott .15 .40
291 Tony Graziani .15 .40
292 Qadry Ismail .15 .40
293 Aeneas Williams .12 .30
294 Marvin Harrison .20 .50
295 Jimmy Hitchcock .12 .30
296 Bob Christian .12 .30
297 Pete Mitchell .12 .30
298 Mike Alstott .20 .50
299 Emmitt Smith .50 1.25
300 Trevor Pryce .12 .30
301 Tony Banks .12 .30
302 Mikhael Ricks .12 .30
303 Randall Cunningham .20 .50
304 Thomas Jones RC .40 1.00
305 Mark Simoneau RC .20 .50
306 Jamal Lewis RC .30 .75
307 Kwame Cavil RC .20 .50
308 Rashard Anderson RC .20 .50
309 Brian Urlacher RC 1.25 3.00
310 Peter Warrick RC .30 .75
311 Courtney Brown RC .25 .60
312 Michael Wiley RC .20 .50
313 Chris Cole RC .25 .60
314 Reuben Droughns RC .30 .75
315 Bubba Franks RC .30 .75
316 Rob Morris RC .25 .60
317 R.Jay Soward RC .20 .50
318 Sylvester Morris RC .20 .50
319 Ben Kelly RC .20 .50
320 Doug Chapman RC .20 .50
321 J.R. Redmond RC .20 .50
322 Darren Howard RC .20 .50
323 Ron Dayne RC .30 .75
324 Chad Pennington RC .50 1.25
325 Jerry Porter RC .30 .75
326 Corey Simon RC .25 .60
327 Plaxico Burress RC .30 .75
328 Trung Canidate RC .25 .60
329 Rogers Beckett RC .20 .50
330 Giovanni Carmazzi RC .20 .50
331 Shaun Alexander RC .40 1.00
332 Joe Hamilton RC .20 .50
333 Keith Bulluck RC .25 .60
334 Todd Husak RC .20 .50
335 Darwin Walker RC .20 .50
Raynoch Thompson RC
336 Mareno Philyaw RC .20 .50
Anthony Midget RC
337 Chris Redman RC .25 .60
Travis Taylor RC
338 Sammy Morris RC .25 .60
Avion Black RC
339 Deon Grant RC .20 .50
Alvin McKinley RC
340 Dez White RC .25 .60
Frank Murphy RC
341 Curtis Keaton RC .20 .50
Ron Dugans RC
342 Travis Prentice RC .25 .60
Dennis Northcutt RC
343 Orantes Grant RC .20 .50
Dwayne Goodrich RC
344 Deltha O'Neal RC .25 .60
Ian Gold RC
345 Stockar McDougle RC .20 .50
Barrett Green RC
346 Anthony Lucas RC .20 .50
Na'il Diggs RC
347 Marcus Washington RC .25 .60
Don Kendra RC
348 T.J. Slaughter RC .20 .50
Shyrone Stith RC
349 William Bartee RC .20 .50
Frank Moreau RC
350 Deon Dyer RC .20 .50
Todd Wade RC
351 Chris Hovan RC .20 .50
Troy Walters RC
352 David Stachelski RC 6.00 15.00
Tom Brady RC
353 Marc Bulger RC .30 .75
Terrelle Smith RC
354 Cornelius Griffin RC .20 .50
Ron Dixon RC
355 Laveranues Coles RC .30 .75
Anthony Becht RC
356 Sebastian Janikowski RC .30 .75
Shane Lechler RC
357 Todd Pinkston RC .20 .50
Gari Scott RC
358 Danny Farmer RC .30 .75
Tee Martin RC
359 Brian Young RC .20 .50
Jacoby Shepherd RC
360 JaJuan Seider RC .20 .50
Trevor Gaylor RC
361 Tim Rattay RC .25 .60
Chafie Fields RC
362 Darrell Jackson RC .25 .60
James Williams RC
363 Nate Webster RC .20 .50
James Whalen RC
364 Erron Kinney RC .20 .50
Chris Coleman RC
365 Chris Samuels RC .25 .60
Leon Murray RC
366 Arizona Cardinals IA .12 .30
Jake Plummer
367 Atlanta Falcons IA .12 .30
Chris Chandler
Jamal Anderson
368 Baltimore Ravens IA .12 .30
Peter Boulware
369 Buffalo Bills IA .12 .30
Doug Flutie
370 Carolina Panthers IA .12 .30
Steve Beuerlein
371 Chicago Bears IA .12 .30
Cade McNown
372 Cincinnati Bengals IA .12 .30
Corey Dillon
373 Cleveland Browns IA .12 .30
Tim Couch
374 Dallas Cowboys IA .30 .75
Emmitt Smith
375 Denver Broncos IA .12 .30
Olandis Gary
376 Detroit Lions IA .12 .30
Charlie Batch
377 Green Bay Packers IA .12 .30
Dorsey Levens
378 Indianapolis Colts IA .12 .30
Edgerrin James
379 Jacksonville Jaguars IA .12 .30
Tony Brackens
380 Kansas City Chiefs IA .12 .30
Elvis Grbac
381 Miami Dolphins IA .40 1.00
Dan Marino
382 Minnesota Vikings IA .12 .30
Robert Smith
383 New England Patriots IA .12 .30
Drew Bledsoe
384 New Orleans Saints IA .12 .30
Ricky Williams
385 New York Giants IA .12 .30
Jessie Armstead
386 New York Jets IA .12 .30
Curtis Martin
387 Oakland Raiders IA .12 .30
Napoleon Kaufman
388 Philadelphia Eagles IA .12 .30
Donovan McNabb
389 Pittsburgh Steelers IA .12 .30
Jerome Bettis
390 St. Louis Rams IA .12 .30
Marshall Faulk
391 San Diego Chargers IA .12 .30
Jermaine Fazande
392 San Francisco 49ers IA .12 .30
Charlie Garner
393 Seattle Seahawks IA .12 .30
Cortez Kennedy
394 Tampa Bay Bucs IA .12 .30
Mike Alstott
395 Tennessee Titans IA .12 .30
Steve McNair
396 Washington Redskins IA .12 .30
Stephen Davis
397 Tim Couch CL .12 .30
398 Peyton Manning CL .30 .75
399 Kurt Warner CL .20 .50
400 Randy Moss CL .12 .30

2000 Fleer Tradition Autographics

DOMINION STATED ODDS 1:192
E-X STATED ODDS 1:24
FLEER STAT.ODDS 1:144 HOB, 1:192 RET
FLEER FOCUS ODDS 1:72 HOB, 1:144 RET
FLEER GAMERS STATED ODDS 1:287
FLEER MYSTIQUE STAT.ODDS 1:120
FLEER SHOWCASE STAT.ODDS 1:24
IMPACT STATED ODDS 1:216
METAL STATED ODDS 1:96
SKYBOX AND ULTRA STATED ODDS 1:72
1 Karim Abdul-Jabbar 4.00 10.00
2 Troy Aikman 40.00 80.00
3 Shaun Alexander 6.00 15.00
4 Terry Allen 5.00 12.00
5 Mike Alstott 8.00 20.00
6 Kimble Anders 4.00 10.00
7 Jamal Anderson 5.00 12.00
8 Mike Anderson 6.00 15.00
9 Champ Bailey 10.00 25.00
10 Charlie Batch 5.00 12.00
11 Donnell Bennett 4.00 10.00
12 Jerome Bettis 40.00 80.00
13 Tim Biakabatuka 5.00 12.00
14 Drew Bledsoe 12.00 30.00
15 David Boston 4.00 10.00
16 Peter Boulware 4.00 10.00
17 Tom Brady 175.00 300.00
18 Tim Brown 15.00 40.00
19 Isaac Bruce 6.00 15.00
20 Mark Brunell 5.00 12.00
21 Marc Bulger 6.00 15.00
22 Trung Canidate 5.00 12.00
23 Giovanni Carmazzi 4.00 10.00
24 Cris Carter 15.00 40.00
25 Kwame Cavil 4.00 10.00
26 Darrin Chiaverini 4.00 10.00
27 Wayne Chrebet 5.00 12.00
28 Laveranues Coles 6.00 15.00
29 Kerry Collins 5.00 12.00
30 Tim Couch 5.00 12.00
31 Germane Crowell 4.00 10.00
32 Daunte Culpepper 5.00 12.00
33 Stephen Davis 5.00 12.00
34 Terrell Davis 12.00 30.00
35 Ron Dayne 6.00 15.00
36 Jake Delhomme 6.00 15.00
37 Corey Dillon 5.00 12.00
38 Reuben Droughns 6.00 15.00
39 Ron Dugans 4.00 10.00
40 Tim Dwight 5.00 12.00
41 Deon Dyer 4.00 10.00
42 Kevin Dyson 5.00 12.00
43 Troy Edwards 4.00 10.00
44 Danny Farmer 4.00 10.00
45 Kevin Faulk 5.00 12.00
46 Marshall Faulk 15.00 40.00
47 Christian Fauria 4.00 10.00
48 Jermaine Fazande 4.00 10.00
49 Jay Fiedler 5.00 12.00
50 Chafie Fields 4.00 10.00
51 Bubba Franks 6.00 15.00
52 Rich Gannon 6.00 15.00
53 Jeff Garcia 5.00 12.00
54 Charlie Garner 5.00 12.00
55 Olandis Gary 5.00 12.00
56 Jason Garrett 6.00 15.00
57 Trevor Gaylor 4.00 10.00
58 Eddie George 5.00 12.00
59 Sherrod Gideon 4.00 10.00
60 Tony Gonzalez 12.00 30.00
61 Jeff Graham 4.00 10.00
62 Tony Graziani 5.00 12.00
63 Damon Griffin 4.00 10.00
64 Az-Zahir Hakim 4.00 10.00
65 Joe Hamilton 4.00 10.00
66 Marvin Harrison 10.00 25.00
67 Tony Hartley 4.00 10.00
68 Priest Holmes 6.00 15.00
69 Torry Holt 8.00 20.00
70 Tony Horne 4.00 10.00
71 Damon Huard 5.00 12.00
72 Trevor Insley 4.00 10.00
73 Rocket Ismail 8.00 20.00
74 Darrell Jackson 5.00 12.00
75 Edgerrin James 6.00 15.00
76 Sebastian Janikowski 6.00 15.00
77 Patrick Jeffers 5.00 12.00
78 Ronney Jenkins 4.00 10.00
79 Brad Johnson 5.00 12.00
80 Kevin Johnson 4.00 10.00
81 Keyshawn Johnson 5.00 12.00
82 Rob Johnson 5.00 12.00
83 Thomas Jones 6.00 15.00
84 Jevon Kearse 5.00 12.00
85 Curtis Keaton 4.00 10.00
86 Terry Kirby 4.00 10.00
87 Jon Kitna 5.00 12.00
88 Marcus Knight 4.00 10.00
89 Dorsey Levens 5.00 12.00
90 Jamal Lewis 6.00 15.00
91 Anthony Lucas 4.00 10.00
92 Ray Lucas 4.00 10.00
93 Curtis Martin 50.00 100.00
94 Tee Martin 6.00 15.00
95 Shane Matthews 4.00 10.00
96 Derrick Mayes 4.00 10.00
97 Ed McCaffrey 5.00 12.00
98 Keenan McCardell 5.00 12.00
99 O.J.McDuffie 5.00 12.00
100 Cade McNown 4.00 10.00
101 Rondell Mealey 4.00 10.00
102 Joe Montgomery 4.00 10.00
103 Herman Moore 5.00 12.00
104 Frank Moreau 4.00 10.00
105 Sylvester Morris 4.00 10.00
106 Johnnie Morton 5.00 12.00
107 Randy Moss 30.00 60.00
108 Eric Moulds 5.00 12.00
109 Muhsin Muhammad 5.00 12.00
110 Dennis Northcutt 5.00 12.00
111 Terrell Owens 15.00 40.00
112 Chad Pennington 6.00 15.00
113 Mareno Philyaw 4.00 10.00
114 Todd Pinkston 4.00 10.00
115 Jake Plummer 5.00 12.00
116 Jerry Porter 6.00 15.00
117 Travis Prentice 5.00 12.00
118 Peerless Price 5.00 12.00
119 John Randle 10.00 25.00
120 Tim Rattay 5.00 12.00
121 Chris Redman 5.00 12.00
122 J.R. Redmond 4.00 10.00
123 Jake Reed 5.00 12.00
124 Jerry Rice 75.00 135.00
125 Jay Riemersma 4.00 10.00
126 Jon Ritchie 4.00 10.00
127 Marcus Robinson 5.00 12.00
128 Warren Sapp 15.00 40.00
129 Bill Schroeder 5.00 12.00
130 Gari Scott 4.00 10.00
131 Jason Sehorn 4.00 10.00
132 Shannon Sharpe 10.00 25.00
133 David Sloan 4.00 10.00
134 Akili Smith 4.00 10.00
135 Antowain Smith 5.00 12.00
136 Emmitt Smith 100.00 200.00
137 Jimmy Smith 5.00 12.00
138 Rod Smith 5.00 12.00
139 R.Jay Soward 4.00 10.00
140 Quinton Spotwood 4.00 10.00
141 Shawn Springs 4.00 10.00
142 Duce Staley 5.00 12.00
143 Kordell Stewart 5.00 12.00
144 Shyrone Stith 4.00 10.00
145 Michael Strahan 12.00 30.00
146 Travis Taylor 5.00 12.00
147 Amani Toomer 5.00 12.00
148 Troy Walters 4.00 10.00
149 Dedric Ward 4.00 10.00
150 Kurt Warner 15.00 40.00
151 Peter Warrick 6.00 15.00
152 Chris Watson 4.00 10.00
153 Michael Westbrook 4.00 10.00
154 Tyrone Wheatley 4.00 10.00
155 Dez White 5.00 12.00
156 Michael Wiley 4.00 10.00
157 Terrence Wilkins 4.00 10.00
158 James Williams 4.00 10.00
159 Ricky Williams 12.00 30.00
160 Frank Wycheck 5.00 12.00

2000 Fleer Tradition Autographics Gold

*GOLD/50: .8X TO 2X BASIC AUTO
GOLD PRINT RUN 50 SER.#'d SETS
17 Tom Brady 500.00 1,000.00
93 Curtis Martin 75.00 150.00
124 Jerry Rice 125.00 250.00
136 Emmitt Smith 150.00 300.00

2000 Fleer Tradition Autographics Silver

*SILVER/250: .5X TO 1.2X BASIC AUTO
SILVER PRINT RUN 250 SER.#'d SETS
17 Tom Brady 250.00 500.00
124 Jerry Rice 75.00 150.00
136 Emmitt Smith 100.00 200.00

2000 Fleer Tradition Feel the Game

E-X STATED ODDS 1:72
FLEER FOCUS STAT.ODDS 1:144 H, 1:288 R
FLEER MYSTIQUE STAT.ODDS 1:120
FLEER SHOWCASE STAT.ODDS 1:72
ULTRA STATED ODDS 1:144
*GOLD/50: .8X TO 2X BASIC JSY
GOLD PRINT RUN 50 SER.#'d SETS
1 Karim Abdul-Jabbar 3.00 8.00
2 Troy Aikman Blue 8.00 20.00
3 Troy Aikman White 8.00 20.00
4 Jamal Anderson 4.00 10.00
5 Drew Bledsoe 5.00 12.00
6 David Boston 3.00 8.00
7 Tim Brown 5.00 12.00
8 Mark Brunell 4.00 10.00
9 Chris Chandler 4.00 10.00
10 Curtis Conway 4.00 10.00
11 Curtis Conway Pants 4.00 10.00
12 Tim Couch 4.00 10.00
13 Germane Crowell 3.00 8.00
14 Terrell Davis 5.00 12.00
15 Tim Dwight Pants 4.00 10.00
16 Kevin Dyson Blue 4.00 10.00
17 Kevin Dyson White 4.00 10.00
18 Kevin Dyson Pants 4.00 10.00
19 Curtis Enis 3.00 8.00
20 Curtis Enis Pants 3.00 8.00
21 Brett Favre 15.00 40.00
22 Doug Flutie 5.00 12.00
23 Antonio Freeman 4.00 10.00
24 Eddie George 4.00 10.00
25 Eddie George Pants 4.00 10.00
26 Terry Glenn 4.00 10.00
27 Trent Green Blue 4.00 10.00
29 Brian Griese 4.00 10.00
30 Az-Zahir Hakim Pants 3.00 8.00
31 Marvin Harrison 5.00 12.00
32 Torry Holt 5.00 12.00
33 Edgerrin James 5.00 12.00
34 Kevin Johnson 3.00 8.00
35 Rob Johnson 4.00 10.00
36 Jevon Kearse Blue 4.00 10.00
37 Jevon Kearse White 4.00 10.00
38 Terry Kirby 3.00 8.00
39 Dorsey Levens 4.00 10.00
40 Peyton Manning 12.00 30.00
41 Terrance Mathis 3.00 8.00
42 Shane Matthews Pants 3.00 8.00
43 Steve McNair Blue 5.00 12.00
44 Steve McNair White 5.00 12.00
45 Steve McNair Pants 5.00 12.00
46 Cade McNown Pants 3.00 8.00
47 Herman Moore 4.00 10.00
48 Rob Moore 3.00 8.00
49 Johnnie Morton Blue 4.00 10.00
50 Johnnie Morton White 4.00 10.00
51 Jake Plummer White 4.00 10.00
52 Jake Plummer Red 4.00 10.00
53 Jerry Rice 10.00 25.00
54 Marcus Robinson Pants 4.00 10.00
55 Deion Sanders Blue 5.00 12.00
56 Deion Sanders White 5.00 12.00
57 Frank Sanders 3.00 8.00
58 Junior Seau 5.00 12.00
59 Shannon Sharpe 5.00 12.00
60 Emmitt Smith Blue 12.00 30.00
61 Emmitt Smith White 12.00 30.00
62 Jimmy Smith 4.00 10.00
63 Rod Smith 4.00 10.00
64 J.J. Stokes 4.00 10.00
65 Kordell Stewart 4.00 10.00
66 Fred Taylor 5.00 12.00
67 Amani Toomer 4.00 10.00
68 Kurt Warner Pants 8.00 20.00
69 Charles Woodson 5.00 12.00

2000 Fleer Tradition Genuine Coverage

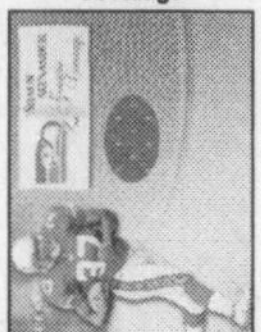

DOMINION STATED ODDS 1:720
METAL GEN.COVER.OR AUTO.ODDS 1:96
SKYBOX H STATED ODDS 1:144
SKYBOX HR STATED ODDS 1:288
1 Troy Aikman 15.00 40.00
2 Shaun Alexander 8.00 20.00
3 Jamal Anderson 8.00 20.00
4 Charlie Batch 8.00 20.00
5 David Boston 6.00 15.00
6 Courtney Brown 8.00 20.00
7 Isaac Bruce 10.00 25.00
8 Mark Brunell 8.00 20.00
9 Chris Chandler 8.00 20.00
10 Darrin Chiaverini 6.00 15.00
11 Tim Couch 8.00 20.00
12 Germane Crowell 6.00 15.00
13 Sean Dawkins 6.00 15.00
14 Ron Dayne 10.00 25.00
15 Corey Dillon 8.00 20.00
16 Reuben Droughns 10.00 25.00
17 Tim Dwight 8.00 20.00
18 Bubba Franks 10.00 25.00
19 Marvin Harrison 10.00 25.00
20 Torry Holt 10.00 25.00
21 Kevin Johnson 6.00 15.00
22 Terry Kirby 6.00 15.00
23 Shane Matthews 6.00 15.00
24 Ed McCaffrey 8.00 20.00
25 Cade McNown 6.00 15.00
26 Herman Moore 8.00 20.00
27 Rob Moore 6.00 15.00
28 Sylvester Morris 6.00 15.00
29 Johnnie Morton 8.00 20.00
30 Chad Pennington 10.00 25.00
31 Jake Plummer 8.00 20.00
32 Jerry Porter 10.00 25.00
33 Travis Prentice 8.00 20.00
34 J.R. Redmond 6.00 15.00
35 Marcus Robinson 8.00 20.00
36 Frank Sanders 6.00 15.00
37 Peter Warrick 10.00 25.00

2000 Fleer Tradition Genuine Coverage Nostalgic

STATED ODDS 1:360 HOB, 1:720 RET
1 Chad Pennington 10.00 25.00
2 Ron Dayne 6.00 15.00
3 Plaxico Burress 6.00 15.00
4 Brian Urlacher 25.00 60.00
5 Bubba Franks 6.00 15.00
6 Jerry Porter 6.00 15.00
7 Trung Canidate 5.00 12.00
8 Dez White 5.00 12.00
9 Courtney Brown 5.00 12.00

2000 Fleer Tradition Patchworks

RANDOM INSERTS IN SKYBOX HOBBY
1 Troy Aikman 12.00 30.00
2 Shaun Alexander 8.00 20.00
3 Jamal Anderson 6.00 15.00
4 Drew Bledsoe 8.00 20.00
5 Mark Brunell 6.00 15.00
6 Tim Couch 6.00 15.00
7 Ron Dayne 8.00 20.00
8 Brett Favre 25.00 60.00
9 Eddie George 6.00 15.00
10 Marvin Harrison 8.00 20.00
11 Peyton Manning 50.00
12 Edgerrin James 8.00 20.00
13 Cade McNown 5.00 12.00
14 Jake Plummer 6.00 15.00
15 Jerry Rice 15.00 40.00
16 Junior Seau 8.00 20.00
17 Emmitt Smith 20.00 50.00
18 Fred Taylor 8.00 20.00
19 Kurt Warner 12.00 30.00

2000 Fleer Tradition Rookie Retro

COMPLETE SET (10) 10.00 25.00
STATED ODDS 1:36
1 Chad Pennington 1.25 3.00
2 Ron Dayne .75 2.00
3 Plaxico Burress .75 2.00
4 Brian Urlacher 3.00 8.00
5 Bubba Franks .75 2.00
6 Jerry Porter .75 2.00
7 Trung Canidate .60 1.50
8 Dez White .60 1.50
9 Courtney Brown .60 1.50
10 Shaun Alexander 1.00 2.50

2000 Fleer Tradition Throwbacks

COMPLETE SET (20) 3.00 8.00
STATED ODDS 1:3
1 Troy Aikman .50 1.25
2 Junior Seau .30 .75
3 Ron Dayne .30 .75
4 Steve Young .40 1.00
5 Wesley Walls .20 .50
6 Duce Staley .25 .60
7 Brian Urlacher 1.25 3.00
8 Jerome Bettis .30 .75
9 Marshall Faulk .30 .75
10 Doug Flutie .30 .75
11 Brett Favre 1.00 2.50
12 Warren Sapp .25 .60
13 Charlie Batch .25 .60
14 Mike Alstott .30 .75
15 Cade McNown .20 .50
16 Jon Kitna .25 .60
17 Emmitt Smith .75 2.00
18 Tony Gonzalez .30 .75
19 Zach Thomas .30 .75
20 Cris Carter .30 .75

2000 Fleer Tradition Tradition of Excellence

COMPLETE SET (20) 15.00 40.00
STATED ODDS 1:9
1 Brett Favre 1.50 4.00
2 Randy Moss .50 1.25
3 Tim Couch .40 1.00
4 Peter Warrick .50 1.25
5 Ron Dayne .50 1.25
6 Kurt Warner .75 2.00
7 Jevon Kearse .40 1.00
8 Ricky Williams .50 1.25
9 Keyshawn Johnson .40 1.00
10 Emmitt Smith 1.25 3.00
11 Donovan McNabb .50 1.25
12 Jamal Lewis .50 1.25
13 Jerry Rice 1.00 2.50
14 Eddie George .40 1.00
15 Peyton Manning 1.25 3.00
16 Stephen Davis .40 1.00
17 Thomas Jones .60 1.50
18 Plaxico Burress .50 1.25
19 Troy Aikman .75 2.00
20 Edgerrin James .50 1.25

2000 Fleer Tradition Whole Ten Yards

COMPLETE SET (15) 12.50 30.00
STATED ODDS 1:18
1 Edgerrin James .60 1.50
2 Stephen Davis .50 1.25
3 Kurt Warner 1.00 2.50
4 Keyshawn Johnson .50 1.25
5 Mark Brunell .50 1.25
6 Peyton Manning 1.50 4.00
7 Emmitt Smith 1.50 4.00
8 Peter Warrick .60 1.50
9 Brett Favre 2.00 5.00
10 Marshall Faulk .60 1.50
11 Fred Taylor .60 1.50
12 Shaun Alexander .75 2.00
13 Terrell Davis .60 1.50
14 Eddie George .50 1.25
15 Randy Moss .60 1.50

2000 Fleer Tradition Glossy

COMP.FACT.SET (406) 30.00 60.00
COMP.SET w/o SP's (400) 15.00 30.00
*1-400 VETS: .5X TO 1.2X BASIC CARD
*304-365 ROOKIES: .5X TO 1.2X
401-450 PRINT RUN 750 SETS
7500 FACTORY SETS PRODUCED
401 JaJuan Dawson RC .75 2.00
402 Mike Anderson RC 1.25 3.00
403 Windrell Hayes RC .75 2.00
404 Shockmain Davis RC .75 2.00
405 Dante Hall RC 1.25 3.00
406 Charles Lee RC .75 2.00
407 Maurice Smith RC .75 2.00
408 Obafemi Ayanbadejo RC 1.00 2.50
409 Travis Taylor 1.00 2.50
410 Dez White 1.00 2.50
411 Sammy Morris 1.00 2.50
412 Darrell Jackson 1.00 2.50
413 Todd Pinkston .75 2.00
414 Ron Dixon .75 2.00
415 Frank Moreau .75 2.00
416 James Williams .75 2.00
417 Lenzie Jackson RC .75 2.00
418 Chad Morton RC 1.25 3.00
419 Matt Lytle RC .75 2.00
420 Travis Prentice 1.00 2.50
421 Laveranues Coles 1.25 3.00
422 Clint Stoerner RC 1.25 3.00
423 Karon Coleman RC .75 2.00
424 Ron Dugans .75 2.00
425 Dennis Northcutt 1.00 2.50
426 Herbert Goodman RC .75 2.00
427 Dane Looker RC 1.25 3.00
428 Mike Brown RC 1.25 3.00
429 Derrius Thompson RC .75 2.00
430 Danny Farmer .75 2.00
431 Bashir Yamini RC .75 2.00
432 Trevor Gaylor .75 2.00
433 Erron Kinney RC .75 2.00
434 James Hodgins RC .75 2.00
435 Aaron Shea RC 1.00 2.50
436 Patrick Pass RC 1.00 2.50
437 Terrelle Smith .75 2.00
438 Avion Black .75 2.00
439 Deltha O'Neal 1.00 2.50
440 Chris Coleman .75 2.00
441 Reggie Jones RC .75 2.00
442 Shyrone Stith .75 2.00
443 Aaron Stecker RC 1.00 2.50
444 Chris Redman 1.00 2.50
445 Curtis Keaton .75 2.00
446 Jamel White RC .75 2.00
447 Troy Walters .75 2.00
448 Spergon Wynn 1.00 2.50
449 Ronney Jenkins RC .75 2.00
450 Doug Johnson RC 1.00 2.50

2000 Fleer Tradition Glossy Traditional Threads

ONE PER FACTORY SET
1 Troy Aikman/140 10.00 25.00
2 Jamal Anderson/225 4.00 10.00
3 Charlie Batch/55 10.00 25.00
4 Drew Bledsoe/325 5.00 12.00
5 David Boston/55 8.00 20.00
6 Tim Brown/81 10.00 25.00
7 Mark Brunell/700 3.00 8.00
8 Tim Couch/430 3.00 8.00
9 Germane Crowell/82 6.00 15.00
10 Stephen Davis/155 5.00 12.00
11 Terrell Davis/100 10.00 25.00
12 Curtis Enis/44 8.00 20.00
13 Marshall Faulk/275 5.00 12.00
14 Brett Favre/585 12.00 30.00
15 Antonio Freeman/86 8.00 20.00
16 Brian Griese/165 5.00 12.00
17 Marvin Harrison/250 5.00 12.00
18 Torry Holt/55 12.00 30.00
19 Edgerrin James/285 5.00 12.00
20 Dorsey Levens/25 12.00 30.00
21 Peyton Manning/345 12.00 30.00
22 Dan Marino/140 20.00 50.00
23 Steve McNair/200 5.00 12.00
25 Johnnie Morton/25 12.00 30.00
26 Jake Plummer/250 4.00 10.00
27 Junior Seau/55 12.00 30.00
28 Antowain Smith/26 12.00 30.00
29 Emmitt Smith/750 10.00 25.00
30 Rod Smith/25 12.00 30.00
31 Fred Taylor/325 5.00 12.00
32 Vinny Testaverde/225 4.00 10.00
33 Amani Toomer/25 12.00 30.00
34 Kurt Warner/700 6.00 15.00
35 Steve Young/125 12.00 30.00

2001 Fleer Tradition

In July of 2001 Fleer released its base set of what is also referred to as Fleer Tradition. The version was available at retail stores nationwide.The cards had a vintage look to them. The cardfronts had a color photo of the the player close up and a color photo of the player in action and a faded stadium scene photo in the background. The cards were set horizontally. The cardbacks had the old greyback stock and no UV coating. The cardbacks also featured a small comic reminiscent of older cards. The cardfronts did not have a glossy coating.

COMPLETE SET (450) 20.00 40.00
1 Thomas Jones .20 .50
2 Bruce Smith .25 .60
3 Marvin Harrison .25 .60
4 Darrell Jackson .20 .50
5 Trent Green .25 .60
6 Wesley Walls .15 .40
7 Jimmy Smith .20 .50
8 Isaac Bruce .25 .60
9 Jamal Anderson .20 .50
10 Marty Booker .20 .50
11 Elvis Grbac .20 .50
12 Joe Jurevicius .15 .40
13 Reidel Anthony .15 .40
14 Darnay Scott .20 .50
15 Oronde Gadsden .15 .40
16 Shawn Bryson .15 .40
17 Jonathan Ogden .20 .50
18 Aaron Shea .15 .40
19 Randy Moss .25 .60
20 Eddie George .25 .60
21 Stephen Davis .20 .50
22 Emmitt Smith .60 1.50
23 Willie McGinest .15 .40
24 Trent Dilfer .20 .50
25 Peter Boulware .15 .40
26 Rod Smith .20 .50
27 Ricky Williams .25 .60
28 Albert Connell .15 .40
29 Robert Porcher .15 .40
30 Jessie Armstead .15 .40
31 Shane Matthews .15 .40
32 Eric Moulds .20 .50
33 Kurt Schulz .15 .40
34 Richie Anderson .15 .40
35 Ron Dugans .15 .40
36 Steve Beuerlein .20 .50
37 Darren Sharper .20 .50
38 Andre Rison .20 .50
39 Courtney Brown .15 .40
40 Eddie Kennison .20 .50
41 Ken Dilger .15 .40
42 Charles Johnson .15 .40
43 Dexter Coakley .15 .40
44 Akili Smith .15 .40
45 R.Jay Soward .15 .40
46 Danny Farmer .15 .40
47 Dez White .20 .50
48 Olandis Gary .15 .40
49 Wali Rainer .15 .40
50 Derrick Alexander .15 .40
51 Donnie Abraham .15 .40
52 David Sloan .15 .40
53 Larry Allen .20 .50
54 Sam Madison .15 .40
55 Troy Edwards .15 .40
56 Ryan Longwell .20 .50
57 Brian Griese .20 .50
58 John Randle .20 .50
59 Reggie Jones .15 .40
60 Mike Peterson .15 .40
61 Bill Romanowski .20 .50
62 Kevin Faulk .20 .50
63 Tai Streets .15 .40
64 Tony Brackens .15 .40
65 James Stewart .15 .40
66 Joe Horn .20 .50
67 Kurt Warner .40 1.00
68 Eric Hicks RC .25 .60
69 Bryan Westbrook .15 .40
70 Tiki Barber .25 .60
71 Frank Sanders .15 .40
72 Olindo Mare .15 .40
73 Bill Schroeder .20 .50
74 Anthony Becht .15 .40
75 Rob Johnson .20 .50
76 Troy Brown .20 .50
77 Chad Bratzke .15 .40
78 Rickey Dudley .15 .40
79 Doug Johnson .15 .40
80 Joe Johnson .15 .40
81 Keenan McCardell .20 .50
82 Tim Brown .25 .60
83 Blaine Bishop .15 .40
84 Ron Dixon .15 .40
85 Michael Cloud .15 .40
86 Todd Pinkston .15 .40
87 Shannon Sharpe .25 .60
88 Marvin Jones .15 .40
89 Zach Thomas .25 .60
90 Kordell Stewart .20 .50
91 Champ Bailey .25 .60
92 Jacquez Green .15 .40
93 Daunte Culpepper .20 .50
94 Freddie Jones .15 .40
95 Donald Hayes .15 .40
96 Rich Gannon .20 .50
97 Ty Law .20 .50
98 Grant Wistrom .15 .40
99 James Allen .15 .40
100 Corey Simon .15 .40
101 Jeff Blake .20 .50
102 Bryant Young .20 .50
103 Craig Yeast .15 .40
104 Bobby Shaw .15 .40
105 Kerry Collins .20 .50
106 Brock Huard .15 .40
107 JaJuan Dawson .15 .40
108 Jeff Graham .15 .40
109 Chad Pennington .25 .60
110 Jake Plummer .20 .50
111 James McKnight .15 .40
112 Terrell Owens .25 .60
113 Mo Lewis .15 .40
114 Jeremy McDaniel .15 .40
115 Ed McCaffrey .20 .50
116 Ricky Watters .20 .50
117 Jerry Porter .15 .40
118 Shawn Jefferson .15 .40
119 Charlie Batch .20 .50
120 Justin Watson .15 .40
121 Donovan McNabb .25 .60
122 Shaun King .15 .40
123 Brett Favre .75 2.00
124 Ronald McKinnon .15 .40
125 Richard Huntley .15 .40
126 Ray Lewis .25 .60
127 Jerome Pathon .15 .40
128 Sam Cowart .15 .40
129 Ryan Leaf .15 .40
130 Greg Clark .15 .40
131 Tony Boselli .20 .50
132 Frank Wycheck .15 .40
133 Charlie Garner .20 .50
134 Tony Siragusa .20 .50
135 Sylvester Morris .15 .40
136 Qadry Ismail .20 .50
137 Jon Kitna .20 .50
138 James Thrash .20 .50
139 Lamar Smith .20 .50
140 Brad Johnson .20 .50
141 London Fletcher .15 .40
142 Tim Biakabutuka .15 .40
143 Ed McDaniel .15 .40
144 Tony Parrish .15 .40
145 David Boston .15 .40
146 Brian Urlacher .30 .75
147 Drew Bledsoe .25 .60
148 David Patten .15 .40
149 Marcellus Wiley .15 .40
150 Peter Warrick .20 .50
151 La'Roi Glover .15 .40
152 Troy Aikman .40 1.00
153 Chris Chandler .20 .50
154 Travis Prentice .15 .40
155 Ike Hilliard .20 .50
156 John Mobley .15 .40
157 Warren Sapp .20 .50
158 Joey Galloway .20 .50
159 Laveranues Coles .20 .50
160 Germane Crowell .15 .40
161 Jamal Lewis .25 .60
162 Mike Anderson .20 .50
163 Charles Woodson .25 .60
164 Antonio Freeman .25 .60
165 Derrick Mason .20 .50
166 Chris Claiborne .15 .40
167 Brian Mitchell .20 .50
168 Mike Vanderjagt .15 .40
169 Rod Woodson .25 .60
170 Doug Chapman .15 .40
171 John Lynch .20 .50
172 Kevin Hardy .15 .40
173 Sam Shade .15 .40
174 Edgerrin James .25 .60
175 Brian Dawkins .20 .50
176 Donnie Edwards .15 .40
177 Patrick Jeffers .15 .40
178 Mark Brunell .20 .50
179 Junior Seau .25 .60
180 Trace Armstrong .15 .40
181 Marcus Robinson .20 .50
182 Tony Gonzalez .25 .60
183 J.J. Stokes .15 .40
184 Jake Reed .20 .50
185 Corey Dillon .20 .50
186 Jay Fiedler .20 .50
187 Christian Fauria .15 .40
188 Sammy Knight .15 .40
189 Kevin Johnson .15 .40
190 Matthew Hatchette .15 .40
191 Az-Zahir Hakim .15 .40
192 Keith Hamilton .15 .40
193 Darren Woodson .20 .50
194 Terry Glenn .20 .50
195 Simeon Rice .20 .50
196 Keyshawn Johnson .20 .50
197 Terrell Davis .25 .60
198 William Roaf .20 .50
199 Doug Flutie .25 .60
200 Kevin Carter .15 .40
201 Stephen Boyd .15 .40
202 Michael Strahan .25 .60
203 Ray Buchanan .15 .40
204 Tyrone Wheatley .20 .50
205 Jason Hanson .15 .40
206 Wayne Chrebet .20 .50
207 Samari Rolle .15 .40
208 Duce Staley .20 .50
209 Dorsey Levens .20 .50
210 Sebastian Janikowski .20 .50
211 Duane Starks .15 .40
212 Jason Gildon .15 .40
213 Terrence Wilkins .15 .40
214 Eric Allen .20 .50
215 Deion Sanders .25 .60
216 Curtis Conway .20 .50
217 Fred Taylor .25 .60

218 Troy Vincent .20 .50
219 Mike Minter RC .20 .50
220 Jeff Garcia .20 .50
221 Tony Richardson .15 .40
222 Jerome Bettis .25 .60
223 Chad Morton .15 .40
224 Tony Horne .15 .40
225 Dave Moore .15 .40
226 Victor Green .15 .40
227 Chris Sanders .15 .40
228 Marshall Faulk .25 .60
229 Cris Carter .25 .60
230 Rodney Harrison .20 .50
231 Tim Couch .15 .40
232 Antowain Smith .20 .50
233 Lawyer Milloy .20 .50
234 Lance Schulters .15 .40
235 Michael Wiley .15 .40
236 Steve McNair .25 .60
237 Aaron Brooks .20 .50
238 Anthony Simmons .15 .40
239 Dwayne Carswell .15 .40
240 Priest Holmes .25 .60
241 Amani Toomer .20 .50
242 Aeneas Williams .20 .50
243 MarTay Jenkins .15 .40
244 Jeff George .20 .50
245 Vinny Testaverde .20 .50
246 Peerless Price .15 .40
247 Bubba Franks .20 .50
248 Randall Cunningham .25 .60
249 Aaron Glenn .20 .50
250 Terance Mathis .15 .40
251 Peyton Manning .60 1.50
252 Terrell Buckley .20 .50
253 Greg Biekert .15 .40
254 Martin Gramatica .15 .40
255 Kyle Brady .15 .40
256 Johnnie Morton .20 .50
257 Jeremiah Trotter .15 .40
258 Travis Taylor .15 .40
259 Frank Moreau .15 .40
260 LeRoy Butler .20 .50
261 Plaxico Burress .20 .50
262 Randall Godfrey .15 .40
263 Jason Taylor .25 .60
264 Jeff Burris .15 .40
265 Jim Harbaugh .20 .50
266 Marco Coleman .15 .40
267 Robert Smith .20 .50
268 Mike Hollis .15 .40
269 Jerry Rice .50 1.25
270 Muhsin Muhammad .20 .50
271 J.R. Redmond .15 .40
272 Brian Walker .15 .40
273 Orlando Pace .20 .50
274 Cade McNown .20 .50
275 Darren Howard .15 .40
276 Ron Dayne .20 .50
277 Shaun Alexander .25 .60
278 Brandon Bennett .15 .40
279 Jason Sehorn .20 .50
280 Matt Hasselbeck .25 .60
281 Michael Pittman .20 .50
282 Dennis Northcutt .15 .40
283 Dedric Ward .15 .40
284 Curtis Martin .25 .60
285 Sammy Morris .20 .50
286 Rocket Ismail .20 .50
287 Jon Ritchie .15 .40
288 Shaun Ellis .15 .40
289 Tim Dwight .20 .50
290 Trevor Pryce .15 .40
291 Warrick Dunn .25 .60
292 Napoleon Kaufman .15 .40
293 Mike Alstott .20 .50
294 Herman Moore .20 .50
295 Chad Lewis .15 .40
296 Hugh Douglas .15 .40
297 Chris Redman .25 .60
298 Ahman Green .25 .60
299 Hines Ward .25 .60
300 Mark Bruener .20 .50
301 Jevon Kearse .20 .50
302 Jermaine Fazande .15 .40
303 Terrell Fletcher .15 .40
304 Torry Holt .20 .50
305 Chris McAlister .15 .40
306 Jason Elam .20 .50
307 Fred Beasley .15 .40
308 Frank Wycheck UH .15 .40
309 Michael McCrary UH .15 .40
310 Mark Brunell UH .20 .50
311 Tim Couch UH .15 .40
312 Takeo Spikes UH .15 .40
313 Jerome Bettis UH .25 .60
314 Zach Thomas UH .25 .60
315 Drew Bledsoe UH .25 .60
316 Wayne Chrebet UH .20 .50
317 Jay Riemersma UH .15 .40
318 Marvin Harrison UH .25 .60
319 Ed McCaffrey UH .20 .50
320 Tony Gonzalez UH .25 .60
321 Tim Brown UH .25 .60
322 Junior Seau UH .25 .60
323 Shawn Springs UH .15 .40
324 Troy Aikman UH .40 1.00
325 Pat Tillman UH RC 8.00 20.00
326 David Akers UH RC .15 .40
327 Michael Strahan UH .25 .60
328 Darrell Green UH .25 .60
329 Kurt Warner UH .40 1.00
330 Jeff Garcia UH .20 .50
331 Aaron Brooks UH .20 .50
332 Jamal Anderson UH .20 .50
333 Brad Hoover UH .20 .50
334 Cris Carter UH .25 .60
335 Derrick Brooks UH .25 .60
336 Antonio Freeman UH .25 .60
337 Luther Elliss UH .15 .40
338 James Allen UH .15 .40
339 Arizona Cardinals TC .20 .50
340 Atlanta Falcons TC .20 .50
341 Baltimore Ravens TC .15 .40
342 Buffalo Bills TC .15 .40
343 Carolina Panthers TC .15 .40
344 Chicago Bears TC .25 .60
345 Cincinnati Bengals TC .20 .50
346 Cleveland Browns TC .15 .40
347 Dallas Cowboys TC .30 .75
Emmitt Smith
348 Denver Broncos TC .20 .50
349 Detroit Lions TC .15 .40
350 Green Bay Packers TC .40 1.00
Brett Favre
351 Indianapolis Colts TC .20 .50
Edgerrin James
352 Jacksonville Jaguars TC .20 .50
353 Kansas City Chiefs TC .15 .40
354 Miami Dolphins TC .20 .50
355 Minnesota Vikings TC .25 .60
356 New England Patriots TC .25 .60
357 New Orleans Saints TC .15 .40
358 New York Giants TC .20 .50
359 New York Jets TC .20 .50
360 Oakland Raiders TC .20 .50
361 Philadelphia Eagles TC .25 .60
362 Pittsburgh Steelers TC .25 .60
363 San Diego Chargers TC .15 .40
364 San Francisco 49ers TC .15 .40
365 Seattle Seahawks TC .15 .40
366 St. Louis Rams TC .25 .60
Kurt Warner
367 Tampa Bay Buccaneers TC .20 .50
368 Tennessee Titans TC .20 .50
369 Washington Redskins TC .15 .60
370 Buffalo Bills TL .15 .40
371 Indianapolis Colts TL .25 .60
372 Miami Dolphins TL .15 .40
373 New England Patriots TL .20 .50
374 New York Jets TL .20 .50
375 Baltimore Ravens TL .20 .50
376 Cincinnati Bengals TL .15 .40
377 Cleveland Browns TL .15 .40
378 Jacksonville Jaguars TL .20 .50
379 Pittsburgh Steelers TL .25 .60
380 Tennessee Titans TL .20 .50
381 Denver Broncos TL .20 .50
382 Kansas City Chiefs TL .20 .50
383 Oakland Raiders TL .20 .50
384 San Diego Chargers TL .20 .50
385 Seattle Seahawks TL .15 .40
386 Arizona Cardinals TL .15 .40
387 Dallas Cowboys TL .25 .60
388 New York Giants TL .20 .50
389 Philadelphia Eagles TL .20 .50
390 Washington Redskins TL .20 .50
391 Chicago Bears TL .15 .40
392 Detroit Lions TL .15 .40
393 Green Bay Packers TL .25 .60
394 Minnesota Vikings TL .25 .60
395 Tampa Bay Buccaneers TL .20 .50
396 Atlanta Falcons TL .15 .40
397 Carolina Panthers TL .15 .40
398 New Orleans Saints TL .20 .50
399 San Francisco 49ersTL .20 .50
400 St. Louis Rams TL .25 .60
401 Michael Vick RC 3.00 8.00
402 Drew Brees RC 5.00 12.00
403 Michael Bennett RC .30 .75
404 David Terrell RC .30 .75
405 Deuce McAllister RC .40 1.00
406 Santana Moss RC .50 1.25
407 Koren Robinson RC .30 .75
408 Chris Weinke RC .30 .75
409 Reggie Wayne RC .75 2.00
410 Rod Gardner RC .30 .75
411 James Jackson RC .25 .60
412 Travis Henry RC .30 .75
413 Josh Heupel RC .40 1.00
414 LaDainian Tomlinson RC 3.00 8.00
415 Chad Johnson RC .60 1.50
416 Sage Rosenfels RC .40 1.00
417 Quincy Morgan RC .30 .75
418 Ken-Yon Rambo RC .25 .60
419 LaMont Jordan RC .40 1.00
420 Anthony Thomas RC .40 1.00
421 Dave Dickenson RC .30 .75
422 Travis Minor RC .30 .75
423 Kevan Barlow RC .30 .75
424 Chris Chambers RC .40 1.00
425 Richard Seymour RC .40 1.00
426 Gerard Warren RC .30 .75
427 Jamar Fletcher RC .25 .60
428 Freddie Mitchell RC .25 .60
429 Jamal Reynolds RC .25 .60
430 Marques Tuiasosopo RC .30 .75
431 Snoop Minnis RC .25 .60
432 Mike McMahon RC .30 .75
433 Robert Ferguson RC .40 1.00
434 Ronney Daniels RC .25 .60
435 Rudi Johnson RC .40 1.00
436 Vinny Sutherland RC .25 .60
437 Josh Booty RC .30 .75
438 Reggie White RC .25 .60
439 Todd Heap RC .40 1.00
440 Justin Smith RC .40 1.00
441 Andre Carter RC .30 .75
442 Bobby Newcombe RC .30 .75
443 Alex Bannister RC .25 .60
444 Correll Buckhalter RC .40 1.00
445 Quincy Carter RC .30 .75
446 Jesse Palmer RC .30 .75
447 Heath Evans RC .30 .75
448 Dan Morgan RC .30 .75
449 Justin McCareins RC .30 .75
450 Alge Crumpler RC .40 1.00

2001 Fleer Tradition Art of a Champion

STATED ODDS 1:120 GLOSSY, 1:240 RETAIL
1 Drew Brees 20.00 50.00
2 Daunte Culpepper 2.50 6.00
3 Ron Dayne 2.50 6.00
4 Marshall Faulk 3.00 8.00
5 Eddie George 3.00 8.00
6 Edgerrin James 3.00 8.00
7 Jamal Lewis 3.00 8.00
8 Randy Moss 3.00 8.00
9 Fred Taylor 3.00 8.00
10 Michael Vick 12.00 30.00

2001 Fleer Tradition Art of a Champion Autographs

RANDOM INSERTS IN GLOSSY AND RETAIL
1 Drew Brees 60.00 100.00
2 Daunte Culpepper 15.00 40.00
4 Marshall Faulk 25.00 50.00
5 Eddie George 15.00 40.00
6 Edgerrin James 15.00 40.00
7 Jamal Lewis 15.00 40.00
10 Michael Vick 60.00 120.00

2001 Fleer Tradition Autographics

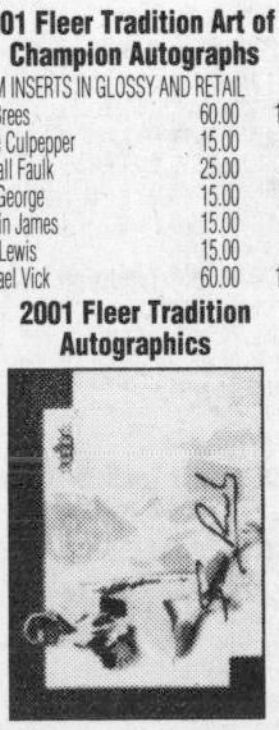

STATED ODDS 1:96 RETAIL GAME TIME
1 Shaun Alexander 8.00 20.00
2 Mike Anderson 6.00 15.00
3 Drew Brees 50.00 100.00
4 Isaac Bruce SP 10.00 25.00
5 Mark Brunell SP 8.00 20.00
6 Chris Chambers 8.00 20.00
8 Daunte Culpepper SP 8.00 20.00
9 Stephen Davis 6.00 15.00
10 Ron Dayne 6.00 15.00
11 Corey Dillon 6.00 15.00
12 Marshall Faulk SP 12.00 30.00
14 Brian Griese 6.00 15.00
15 Travis Henry 6.00 15.00
16 Josh Heupel 8.00 20.00
17 Torry Holt 6.00 15.00
18 Edgerrin James SP 10.00 25.00
21 Donovan McNabb SP 25.00 50.00
22 Travis Minor 6.00 15.00
23 Randy Moss SP 30.00 60.00
24 Santana Moss 10.00 25.00
25 Ken-Yon Rambo 5.00 12.00
26 Koren Robinson SP 8.00 20.00
27 Marcus Robinson 6.00 15.00
28 Sage Rosenfels 8.00 20.00
29 Jimmy Smith 6.00 15.00
30 Duce Staley SP 8.00 20.00
31 David Terrell 6.00 15.00
32 Anthony Thomas 8.00 20.00
33 LaDainian Tomlinson 30.00 80.00
34 Marques Tuiasosopo 6.00 15.00
36 Kurt Warner SP 25.00 50.00
37 Reggie Wayne EXCH 1.00 2.50
38 Chris Weinke SP 8.00 20.00

2001 Fleer Tradition Conference Clash

COMPLETE SET (15) 15.00 40.00
STATED ODDS 1:24 GLOSSY, 1:40 RETAIL
1 Peyton Manning 2.50 6.00
Drew Bledsoe
2 Randy Moss 1.00 2.50
Keyshawn Johnson
3 Stephen Davis 2.50 6.00
Emmitt Smith
4 Jeff Garcia 1.50 4.00
Kurt Warner
5 Jamal Lewis 1.00 2.50
Eddie George
6 Troy Aikman 1.50 4.00
Donovan McNabb
7 Edgerrin James 1.00 2.50
Curtis Martin
8 Terrell Owens 1.00 2.50
Isaac Bruce
9 Brett Favre 3.00 8.00
Daunte Culpepper
10 Corey Dillon 1.00 2.50
Fred Taylor
11 Ricky Williams 1.00 2.50
Marshall Faulk
12 Mark Brunell .75 2.00
Tim Couch
13 Torry Holt 2.00 5.00
Jerry Rice
14 Shaun Alexander 1.00 2.50
Terrell Davis
15 Eric Moulds 1.00 2.50
Marvin Harrison

2001 Fleer Tradition Grass Roots

COMPLETE SET (10) 7.50 20.00
STATED ODDS 1:24 GLOSSY, 1:40 RETAIL
1 Donovan McNabb 1.00 2.50
2 Edgerrin James 1.00 2.50
3 Ricky Williams 1.00 2.50
4 Fred Taylor 1.00 2.50
5 Terrell Davis 1.00 2.50
6 Eddie George 1.00 2.50
7 Jamal Lewis 1.00 2.50
8 Marshall Faulk 1.00 2.50
9 Daunte Culpepper .75 2.00
10 Emmitt Smith 2.50 6.00

2001 Fleer Tradition Grass Roots Turf

RANDOM INSERTS IN GLOSSY AND RETAIL
1 Donovan McNabb 8.00 20.00
2 Edgerrin James 8.00 20.00
3 Ricky Williams 8.00 20.00
4 Fred Taylor 8.00 20.00
5 Terrell Davis 8.00 20.00
6 Eddie George 8.00 20.00
7 Jamal Lewis 8.00 20.00
8 Marshall Faulk 8.00 20.00
9 Daunte Culpepper 6.00 15.00
10 Emmitt Smith 20.00 50.00

2001 Fleer Tradition Keeping Pace

COMPLETE SET (15) 12.50 30.00
STATED ODDS 1:12 GLOSSY, 1:20 RETAIL
1 Michael Vick 2.00 5.00
2 Drew Brees 3.00 8.00
3 Michael Bennett .40 1.00
4 David Terrell .40 1.00
5 Deuce McAllister .50 1.25
6 Santana Moss .60 1.50
7 Koren Robinson .40 1.00
8 Chris Weinke .40 1.00
9 Reggie Wayne 1.00 2.50
10 Rod Gardner .40 1.00
11 James Jackson .30 .75
12 Travis Henry .40 1.00
13 Josh Heupel .50 1.25
14 LaDainian Tomlinson 1.50 4.00
15 Chad Johnson .75 2.00

2001 Fleer Tradition Rookie Retro Threads

STATED ODDS 1:24 GLOSSY,1:240 RET
1 Kevan Barlow FB 3.00 8.00
2 Kevan Barlow JSY 3.00 8.00
3 Michael Bennett FB 3.00 8.00
4 Michael Bennett JSY 3.00 8.00
5 Drew Brees FB 25.00 60.00
6 Drew Brees JSY 25.00 60.00
7 Andre Carter JSY 3.00 8.00
8 Quincy Carter JSY 3.00 8.00
9 Chris Chambers FB 4.00 10.00
10 Chris Chambers JSY 4.00 10.00
11 Robert Ferguson FB 4.00 10.00
12 Robert Ferguson JSY 4.00 10.00
13 Rod Gardner FB 3.00 8.00
14 Rod Gardner JSY 3.00 8.00
15 Travis Henry FB 3.00 8.00
16 Travis Henry JSY 3.00 8.00
17 Josh Heupel FB 4.00 10.00
18 Josh Heupel JSY 4.00 10.00
19 James Jackson JSY 2.50 6.00
20 Deuce McAllister FB 4.00 10.00
21 Mike McMahon FB 3.00 8.00
22 Mike McMahon JSY 3.00 8.00
23 Travis Minor FB 3.00 8.00
24 Travis Minor JSY 3.00 8.00
25 Freddie Mitchell FB 2.50 6.00
26 Freddie Mitchell JSY 2.50 6.00
27 Quincy Morgan JSY 3.00 8.00
28 Santana Moss JSY 5.00 12.00
29 Jesse Palmer FB 3.00 8.00
30 Jesse Palmer JSY 3.00 8.00
31 Koren Robinson FB 3.00 8.00
32 Sage Rosenfels FB 4.00 10.00
33 Sage Rosenfels JSY 4.00 10.00
34 David Terrell JSY 3.00 8.00
35 Anthony Thomas FB 4.00 10.00
36 Anthony Thomas JSY 4.00 10.00
37 LaDainian Tomlinson FB 12.00 30.00
38 LaDainian Tomlinson JSY 12.00 30.00
39 Marques Tuiasosopo FB 3.00 8.00
40 Marques Tuiasosopo JSY 3.00 8.00
41 Michael Vick FB 12.00 30.00
42 Michael Vick JSY 12.00 30.00
43 Reggie Wayne JSY 8.00 20.00
44 Chris Weinke FB 3.00 8.00
45 LaDainian Tomlinson HEL 12.00 30.00
Michael Bennett HEL
46 Drew Brees 25.00 60.00
LaDainian Tomlinson FB
47 Drew Brees HEL 25.00 60.00
Michael Vick HEL
48 Freddie Mitchell HEL 3.00 8.00
Rod Gardner HEL
49 Todd Heap FB 4.00 10.00
Snoop Minnis FB
50 James Jackson FB 2.50 6.00
Quincy Morgan FB
51 Rudi Johnson FB 6.00 15.00
Chad Johnson FB
52 Deuce McAllister 15.00 40.00
Michael Vick FB
53 Dan Morgan FB 3.00 8.00
Chris Weinke FB
54 Santana Moss 8.00 20.00
Reggie Wayne FB
55 Santana Moss 8.00 20.00
Reggie Wayne HEL
56 David Terrell HEL 3.00 8.00
Koren Robinson HEL
57 Koren Robinson 3.00 8.00
Quincy Carter FB
58 Sage Rosenfels 4.00 10.00
Rod Gardner FB
59 David Terrell 4.00 10.00
Anthony Thomas FB

2001 Fleer Tradition Throwbacks

COMPLETE SET (20) 20.00 50.00
STATED ODDS 1:12 GLOSSY, 1:20 RETAIL
1 Jamal Lewis .75 2.00
2 Eddie George .75 2.00
3 Marvin Harrison .75 2.00
4 Brett Favre 2.50 6.00
5 Donovan McNabb .75 2.00
6 Troy Aikman 1.25 3.00
7 Edgerrin James .75 2.00
8 Brian Urlacher 1.00 2.50
9 Stephen Davis .60 1.50
10 Daunte Culpepper .60 1.50
11 Jerry Rice 1.50 4.00
12 Emmitt Smith 2.00 5.00
13 Kurt Warner 1.25 3.00
14 Ricky Williams .75 2.00
15 Cris Carter .75 2.00
16 Mark Brunell .60 1.50
17 Ron Dayne .60 1.50
18 Peyton Manning 2.00 5.00
19 Randy Moss .75 2.00
20 Brian Griese .60 1.50

2001 Fleer Tradition Glossy

In July of 2001 Fleer released the glossy version of what is also referred to as Fleer Tradition. The Glossy set was only available at hobby shops.The cards had a vintage look to them. The cardfronts had a color photo of the the player close up and a color photo of the player in action and a faded stadium scene photo in the background. The cards were set horizontally. The cardbacks had the old greyback stock and no UV coating. The cardbacks also featured a small comic reminiscent of older cards.

COMP.SET w/o SP's (400) 20.00 40.00
*1-400 GLOSSY: .5X TO 1.2X BASIC CARDS
401-500 ROOKIE PRINT RUN 2001
325 Pat Tillman UH RC 8.00 20.00
402 Drew Brees RC 10.00 25.00

2001 Fleer Tradition Glossy Rookie Minis

*MINI/350: .5X TO 1.2X GLOSSY RC
STATED PRINT RUN 350 SER.#'d SETS

2001 Fleer Tradition Glossy Rookie Stickers

*STICKER/699: .4X TO 1X GLOSSY RC
STATED PRINT RUN 699 SER.#'d SETS

2001 Fleer Tradition Glossy Nameplates

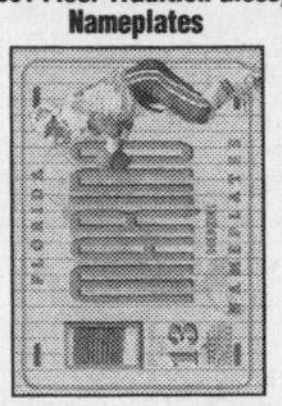

RANDOM INSERTS IN CELLO/JUMBO PACKS
1 Ron Dayne 8.00 20.00
2 Kurt Warner 15.00 40.00
3 Curtis Martin 10.00 25.00
4 Jake Plummer 8.00 20.00
5 Mark Brunell 8.00 20.00
6 Drew Bledsoe 10.00 25.00
7 Kevin Johnson 6.00 15.00
8 Brian Griese 8.00 20.00
9 Terrell Owens 10.00 25.00
10 Brian Urlacher 12.00 30.00
11 Jamal Anderson 8.00 20.00
12 Isaac Bruce 10.00 25.00
13 Jerome Bettis 10.00 25.00
14 Fred Taylor 10.00 25.00
15 Tim Couch 6.00 15.00
16 Stephen Davis 8.00 20.00
17 Warrick Dunn 10.00 25.00
18 Rod Smith 8.00 20.00
19 Marshall Faulk 10.00 25.00
20 Thomas Jones 8.00 20.00
21 Emmitt Smith 25.00 60.00
22 Marcus Robinson 8.00 20.00
23 Daunte Culpepper 8.00 20.00
24 Antonio Freeman 10.00 25.00
25 Marvin Harrison 10.00 25.00
26 Dan Marino 25.00 60.00
27 Steve Young 15.00 40.00
28 Deion Sanders 10.00 25.00
29 Edgerrin James 10.00 25.00
30 Jerry Rice 20.00 50.00

2001 Fleer Tradition Glossy Traditional Threads

ONE PER GLOSSY RACK PACK
1 Troy Aikman 8.00 20.00
2 Jamal Anderson 4.00 10.00
3 Jerome Bettis 5.00 12.00
4 Drew Bledsoe 5.00 12.00
5 Isaac Bruce 5.00 12.00
6 Mark Brunell 4.00 10.00
7 Tim Couch 3.00 8.00
8 Daunte Culpepper 4.00 10.00
9 Stephen Davis 4.00 10.00
10 Ron Dayne 4.00 10.00
11 Warrick Dunn 5.00 12.00
12 Marshall Faulk 5.00 12.00
13 Brett Favre 15.00 40.00
14 Antonio Freeman 5.00 12.00
15 Eddie George 5.00 12.00
16 Brian Griese 4.00 10.00
17 Marvin Harrison 5.00 12.00
18 Edgerrin James 5.00 12.00
19 Kevin Johnson 3.00 8.00
20 Thomas Jones 4.00 10.00
22 Ray Lewis 5.00 12.00
23 Dan Marino 12.00 30.00
24 Curtis Martin 5.00 12.00
25 Randy Moss 5.00 12.00
26 Terrell Owens 5.00 12.00
27 Jake Plummer 4.00 10.00
28 Jerry Rice 10.00 25.00
29 Rod Smith 4.00 10.00
30 Jimmy Smith 4.00 10.00
31 Kordell Stewart 4.00 10.00
32 Fred Taylor 6.00 15.00
33 Brian Urlacher 6.00 15.00
34 Kurt Warner 8.00 20.00
35 Steve Young 6.00 15.00

2002 Fleer Tradition

Released in August 2002, this 300-card set contains 260 veterans and 40 rookies. S.R.P. is $1.99 per pack. Both hobby and retail boxes contained 24 packs, each with 10 cards per pack.

COMPLETE SET (300) 30.00 80.00
1 Jeff Garcia .20 .50
2 Brian Simmons .15 .40
3 Kordell Stewart .20 .50
4 Chris Weinke .15 .40
5 Donovan McNabb .25 .60
6 Antoine Winfield .15 .40
7 Ray Lewis .25 .60
8 Drew Brees .40 1.00
9 Frank Sanders .15 .40
10 Rich Gannon .20 .50
11 Jamal Anderson .20 .50
12 Curtis Martin .25 .60
13 Darrell Jackson .20 .50
14 Micheal Barrow .15 .40
15 Jeff Wilkins .15 .40
16 Ricky Williams .20 .50
17 Brad Johnson .20 .50
18 Tedy Bruschi .25 .60
19 Frank Wycheck .15 .40
20 Byron Chamberlain .15 .40
21 Terry Glenn .20 .50
22 James McKnight .15 .40
23 Thomas Jones .25 .60
24 Jamie Sharper .20 .50
25 Trent Green .20 .50
26 Mike Rucker RC .25 .60
27 Mark Brunell .20 .50
28 Takeo Spikes .15 .40
29 Dominic Rhodes .20 .50
30 Jim Miller .15 .40
31 Corey Bradford .15 .40
32 Jamir Miller .15 .40
33 Johnnie Morton .20 .50
34 Rocket Ismail .20 .50
35 Mike Anderson .20 .50
36 James Allen .15 .40
37 Quincy Carter .15 .40
38 Germane Crowell .15 .40
39 Quincy Morgan .15 .40
40 Kabeer Gbaja-Biamila .20 .50
41 Reggie Wayne .25 .60
42 Brian Urlacher .25 .60
43 Stacey Mack .15 .40
44 Justin Smith .15 .40
45 Snoop Minnis .15 .40
46 Donald Hayes .15 .40
47 Jay Fiedler .20 .50
48 Nate Clements .15 .40
49 Drew Bledsoe .25 .60
50 Peter Boulware .15 .40
51 Lawyer Milloy .15 .40
52 Michael Pittman .20 .50
53 Aaron Brooks .20 .50
54 Maurice Smith .15 .40
55 Ike Hilliard .20 .50
56 Derrick Mason .20 .50
57 LaMont Jordan .20 .50
58 Charlie Garner .20 .50
59 Mike Alstott .20 .50
60 Freddie Mitchell .15 .40
61 Isaac Bruce .25 .60
62 Hines Ward .25 .60
63 John Randle .20 .50
64 Doug Flutie .25 .60
65 Terrell Owens .25 .60
66 Garrison Hearst .20 .50
67 Rodney Harrison .20 .50
68 Koren Robinson .15 .40
69 Amos Zereoue .15 .40
70 Aeneas Williams .20 .50
71 Hugh Douglas .15 .40
72 Jacquez Green .15 .40
73 Sebastian Janikowski .15 .40
74 Kevin Dyson .20 .50
75 Terance Mathis .15 .40
76 Vinny Testaverde .20 .50
77 Kwamie Lassiter .15 .40
78 Ron Dayne .20 .50
79 Jonathan Ogden .20 .50
80 Charlie Clemons RC .15 .40
81 Peter Warrick .20 .50
82 Adam Vinatieri .25 .60
83 Ted Washington .15 .40
84 Randy Moss .25 .60
85 Rosevelt Colvin RC .30 .75
86 Oronde Gadsden .15 .40
87 Anthony Henry .15 .40
88 Priest Holmes .25 .60
89 Joey Galloway .20 .50
90 Jimmy Smith .20 .50
91 Bill Romanowski .20 .50
92 Chris Claiborne .15 .40
93 Marvin Harrison .25 .60
94 Vonnie Holliday .15 .40
95 Darren Sharper .20 .50
96 Chad Bratzke .15 .40
97 James Stewart .15 .40
98 Fred Taylor .20 .50
99 Jason Elam .20 .50
100 Keyshawn Johnson .20 .50
101 Dexter Coakley .15 .40
102 Zach Thomas .25 .60
103 Jamel White .15 .40
104 Antowain Smith .20 .50
105 Marty Booker .20 .50
106 Deuce McAllister .20 .50
107 Adam Archuleta .15 .40
108 Rod Smith .20 .50
109 Tony Boselli .20 .50
110 Joe Johnson .15 .40
111 Simeon Rice .15 .40
112 Cory Schlesinger .15 .40
113 La'Roi Glover .15 .40
114 Tiki Barber .25 .60
115 Michael Westbrook .15 .40
116 Antonio Freeman .25 .60
117 Kerry Collins .20 .50
118 Laveranues Coles .20 .50
119 Jay Feely .15 .40
120 Champ Bailey .25 .60
121 Peyton Manning .50 1.25
122 Chad Pennington .25 .60
123 Anthony Dorsett .15 .40
124 Jamal Lewis .20 .50
125 Marcus Pollard .15 .40
126 Charles Woodson .25 .60
127 Duce Staley .20 .50
128 Travis Henry .15 .40
129 Tony Brackens .15 .40
130 Jeremiah Trotter .15 .40
131 Jerome Bettis .25 .60
132 Chad Johnson .25 .60
133 Lamar Smith .20 .50
134 Joey Porter .20 .50
135 Curtis Conway .20 .50
136 David Terrell .15 .40
137 Daunte Culpepper .20 .50
138 Chris Fuamatu-Ma'afala .15 .40
139 J.J. Stokes .15 .40
140 Tim Couch .15 .40
141 Ty Law .20 .50
142 Vinny Sutherland .15 .40
143 Trung Canidate .15 .40
144 Larry Allen .15 .40
145 Darren Howard .15 .40
146 Ricky Watters .20 .50
147 Grant Wistrom .15 .40
148 Brian Griese .20 .50
149 Jason Sehorn .20 .50
150 Marshall Faulk .25 .60
151 Martin Gramatica .15 .40
152 Robert Porcher .15 .40
153 Richie Anderson .15 .40
154 Derrick Brooks .25 .60
155 Jevon Kearse .20 .50
156 Bill Schroeder .15 .40
157 Marvin Jones .15 .40
158 Eddie George .20 .50
159 Keith Brooking .15 .40
160 Ryan Longwell .15 .40
161 Brian Dawkins .20 .50
162 Chris Redman .15 .40
163 Az-Zahir Hakim .15 .40
164 James Thrash .20 .50
165 Rob Johnson .20 .50
166 Hardy Nickerson .15 .40
167 Chad Scott .15 .40
168 Jon Kitna .20 .50
169 Donnie Edwards .15 .40
170 Andre Carter .15 .40
171 Warrick Holdman .15 .40
172 Jason Taylor .20 .50
173 Levon Kirkland .15 .40
174 Mike Brown .20 .50
175 David Patten .15 .40
176 Kurt Warner .25 .60
177 Fred Smoot .20 .50
178 Dat Nguyen .15 .40
179 Joe Horn .20 .50
180 John Lynch .20 .50
181 Troy Hambrick .15 .40
182 John Carney .15 .40
183 Wesley Walls .20 .50
184 Deltha O'Neal .15 .40
185 Joe Jurevicius .15 .40
186 Steve McNair .25 .60
187 Scotty Anderson .15 .40
188 John Abraham .20 .50
189 Stephen Davis .20 .50
190 Nate Wayne .15 .40
191 Corey Simon .15 .40
192 Joel Makovicka .15 .40
193 Rob Morris .15 .40
194 Correll Buckhalter .20 .50
195 Qadry Ismail .20 .50
196 Keenan McCardell .20 .50
197 Jason Gildon .20 .50
198 Peerless Price .15 .40
199 Tony Richardson .15 .40
200 Kevan Barlow .15 .40
201 Corey Dillon .20 .50
202 Sam Madison .15 .40
203 Chad Brown .15 .40
204 Dez White .15 .40
205 Troy Brown .20 .50
206 Orlando Pace .20 .50
207 Jermaine Lewis .15 .40
208 Willie Jackson .15 .40
209 Warrick Dunn .20 .50
210 James Jackson .15 .40
211 Sammy Knight .15 .40
212 Ronde Barber .20 .50
213 Ed McCaffrey .20 .50
214 Amani Toomer .20 .50
215 Rod Gardner .15 .40
216 Mike McMahon .15 .40
217 Wayne Chrebet .20 .50
218 Jake Plummer .20 .50
219 Bubba Franks .20 .50
220 Shane Lechler .15 .40
221 Travis Taylor .15 .40
222 Edgerrin James .20 .50
223 David Akers .15 .40
224 Eric Moulds .20 .50
225 Mike Vanderjagt .15 .40
226 Kendrell Bell .15 .40
227 Darnay Scott .20 .50
228 Tony Gonzalez .25 .60
229 Marcellus Wiley .15 .40
230 Marcus Robinson .20 .50
231 Muhsin Muhammad .20 .50
232 Trent Dilfer .20 .50
233 Kevin Johnson .15 .40
234 Travis Minor .15 .40
235 London Fletcher .15 .40
236 Reggie Swinton .15 .40
237 Michael Bennett .20 .50
238 Brett Favre DD .50 1.25
239 Terrell Davis DD .20 .50
240 Emmitt Smith DD .50 1.25
241 Shannon Sharpe DD .20 .50
242 Cris Carter DD .20 .50
243 Tim Brown DD .20 .50
244 Jerry Rice DD .40 1.00
245 Bruce Smith DD .20 .50
246 Warren Sapp DD .15 .40
247 Michael Strahan DD .20 .50
248 Junior Seau DD .20 .50
249 Darrell Green DD .20 .50
250 Rod Woodson DD .20 .50
251 David Boston BB .15 .40
252 Michael Vick BB .30 .75
253 Anthony Thomas BB .15 .40
254 Ahman Green BB .15 .40
255 Chris Chambers BB .15 .40
256 Tom Brady BB .50 1.25
257 Plaxico Burress BB .15 .40
258 LaDainian Tomlinson BB .25 .60
259 Shaun Alexander BB .15 .40
260 Torry Holt BB .20 .50
261 Julius Peppers RC 1.25 3.00
262 William Green RC .50 1.25
263 Joey Harrington RC .60 1.50
264 Jabar Gaffney RC .60 1.50
265 T.J. Duckett RC .60 1.50
266 Antwaan Randle El RC .60 1.50
267 Javon Walker RC .60 1.50
268 David Carr RC .60 1.50
269 DeShaun Foster RC .60 1.50
270 Donte Stallworth RC .60 1.50
271 Antonio Bryant RC .60 1.50
272 Clinton Portis RC .75 2.00
273 Josh Reed RC .50 1.25
274 Ashley Lelie RC .50 1.25
275 Patrick Ramsey RC .60 1.50
276 Jonathan Wells RC .60 1.50
Adrian Peterson RC
277 Quentin Jammer RC .60 1.50
Roy Williams RC
278 Jeremy Shockey RC 1.00 2.50
Daniel Graham RC
279 Eric Crouch RC .60 1.50
Major Applewhite RC
280 Phillip Buchanon RC .60 1.50
Lito Sheppard RC
281 Kahlil Hill RC .60 1.50
Deion Branch RC
282 Ryan Sims RC .60 1.50
Wendell Bryant RC
283 Josh Scobey RC 1.00 2.50
Brian Westbrook RC
284 Ladell Betts RC .60 1.50
Omar Easy RC
285 Andre Davis RC .50 1.25
Daryl Jones RC
286 Cliff Russell RC .60 1.50
Chester Taylor RC
287 Jason McAddley RC .60 1.50
Josh McCown RC
288 David Garrard RC .75 2.00
Rohan Davey RC
289 Marquise Walker RC .50 1.25
Ron Johnson RC
290 Luke Staley RC .50 1.25
Lamar Gordon RC
291 Reche Caldwell RC .60 1.50
Lee Mays RC
292 Robert Thomas RC .50 1.25
Napoleon Harris RC
293 Maurice Morris RC .50 1.25
Jerramy Stevens RC
294 Kurt Kittner RC .50 1.25
Randy Fasani RC
295 Rocky Calmus RC .50 1.25
Jake Schifino RC
296 Tim Carter RC .50 1.25
Freddie Milons RC
297 Tracey Wistrom RC .50 1.25
Travis Stephens RC
298 Mike Williams RC .75 2.00
Dwight Freeney RC
299 John Henderson RC .60 1.50
Albert Haynesworth RC
300 Najeh Davenport RC .60 1.50
Craig Nall RC

2002 Fleer Tradition Minis
*VETS 1-260: 6X TO 15X BASIC CARDS
*ROOKIES 261-300: 2.5X TO 6X
STATED PRINT RUN 125 SER.#'d SETS

2002 Fleer Tradition Tiffany
*VETS 1-260: 4X TO 10X BASIC CARDS
*ROOKIES 261-300: 1.5X TO 4X
STATED PRINT 225 SER.#'d SETS

2002 Fleer Tradition Career Highlights
COMPLETE SET (10) 15.00 40.00
STATED ODDS 1:24
1 Peyton Manning 2.50 6.00
2 Brett Favre 3.00 8.00
3 Kurt Warner 1.25 3.00
4 Emmitt Smith 3.00 8.00
5 Marshall Faulk 1.25 3.00
6 Jerome Bettis 1.25 3.00
7 Jerry Rice 2.50 6.00
8 Cris Carter 1.25 3.00
9 Randy Moss 1.25 3.00
10 Michael Strahan 1.25 3.00

2002 Fleer Tradition Classic Combinations Hobby
1-10 PRINT RUN 2000
11-20 PRINT RUN 1000
21-30 PRINT RUN 500
31-35 PRINT RUN 250
*RETAIL 1-10: .3X TO .8X HOBBY INSERTS
*RETAIL 11-20: .25X TO .6X HOBBY INSERTS
*RETAIL 21-30: .2X TO .5X HOBBY INSERTS
*RETAIL 31-35: .15X TO .4X HOBBY INSERTS
1 Kendrell Bell 1.00 2.50
Brian Urlacher
2 Daunte Culpepper 1.00 2.50
Randy Moss
3 Earl Campbell 1.00 2.50
Eddie George
4 Paul Hornung 2.50 6.00
Brett Favre
5 Peyton Manning 2.00 5.00
Edgerrin James
6 Donovan McNabb 1.00 2.50
Daunte Culpepper
7 Brian Griese 2.50 6.00
Tom Brady
8 Jerry Rice 2.00 5.00
Tim Brown
9 Anthony Thomas 4.00 10.00
Walter Payton
10 Torry Holt 1.00 2.50
Koren Robinson
11 Jerry Rice 2.50 6.00
Cris Carter
12 Chris Chambers 1.00 2.50
Plaxico Burress
13 Michael Vick 2.00 5.00
Donovan McNabb
14 Kurt Warner 1.25 3.00
Marshall Faulk
15 Brett Favre 3.00 8.00
Daunte Culpepper
16 Jeff Garcia 1.25 3.00
Kurt Warner
17 Peyton Manning 2.50 6.00
Jamal Lewis
18 Earl Campbell 1.25 3.00
Ricky Williams
19 David Carr 2.50 6.00
Peyton Manning
20 John Elway 2.50 6.00
Brian Griese
21 Jeff Garcia 1.50 4.00
Terrell Owens
22 Eric Dickerson 1.50 4.00
Marshall Faulk
23 Emmitt Smith 4.00 10.00
Marcus Allen
24 Roger Staubach 4.00 10.00
Emmitt Smith
25 Terrell Davis 1.50 4.00
Curtis Martin
26 Emmitt Smith 6.00 15.00
Walter Payton
27 Joe Montana 4.00 10.00
Kurt Warner
28 Kordell Stewart 1.50 4.00
Jerome Bettis
29 Eddie George 1.25 3.00
Archie Griffin
30 John Elway 3.00 8.00
Terrell Davis
31 Brian Griese 2.00 5.00
Bob Griese
32 Joey Harrington 2.00 5.00
David Carr
33 Bob Griese 3.00 8.00
Drew Brees
34 Randy Moss 4.00 10.00
Jerry Rice
35 Emmitt Smith 5.00 12.00
Fred Taylor

2002 Fleer Tradition Classic Combinations Memorabilia

STATED ODDS 1:24
1 Marcus Allen JSY 10.00 25.00
Emmitt Smith
2 Brian Griese 12.00 30.00
Tom Brady JSY
3 Bob Griese 8.00 20.00
Drew Brees JSY
4 Earl Campbell JSY 6.00 15.00
Eddie George
5 Earl Campbell JSY 6.00 15.00
Ricky Williams
6 Cris Carter JSY 6.00 15.00
Jerry Rice
7 Daunte Culpepper JSY 6.00 15.00
Donovan McNabb
8 Daunte Culpepper JSY 6.00 15.00
Randy Moss
9 Eric Dickerson JSY 6.00 15.00
Marshall Faulk
10 John Elway JSY 15.00 40.00
Terrell Davis
11 John Elway JSY 15.00 40.00
Brian Griese
12 Marshall Faulk JSY 6.00 15.00
Eric Dickerson
13 Marshall Faulk JSY 6.00 15.00
Kurt Warner
14 Brett Favre JSY 12.00 30.00
Daunte Culpepper
15 Brett Favre JSY 12.00 30.00
Paul Hornung
16 Jeff Garcia JSY 6.00 15.00
Terrell Owens
17 Jeff Garcia JSY 6.00 15.00
Kurt Warner
18 Eddie George JSY 5.00 12.00
Earl Campbell
19 Torry Holt JSY 6.00 15.00
Koren Robinson
20 Peyton Manning 5.00 12.00
Jamal Lewis JSY
21 Donovan McNabb JSY 6.00 15.00
Daunte Culpepper
22 Donovan McNabb JSY 8.00 20.00
Michael Vick
23 Joe Montana JSY 20.00 50.00
Kurt Warner
24 Randy Moss JSY 8.00 20.00
Daunte Culpepper
25 Randy Moss JSY 8.00 20.00
Jerry Rice
26 Terrell Owens JSY 6.00 15.00
Jeff Garcia
27 Walter Payton JSY 25.00 60.00
Emmitt Smith
28 Walter Payton JSY 25.00 60.00
Anthony Thomas
29 Jerry Rice JSY 10.00 25.00
Cris Carter
30 Jerry Rice JSY 10.00 25.00
Randy Moss
31 Emmitt Smith JSY 12.00 30.00
Marcus Allen
32 Emmitt Smith JSY 12.00 30.00
Walter Payton
33 Emmitt Smith JSY 12.00 30.00
Fred Taylor
34 Roger Staubach JSY 15.00 40.00
Emmitt Smith
35 Anthony Thomas JSY 6.00 15.00
Walter Payton
36 Kendrell Bell 8.00 20.00
Brian Urlacher JSY
37 Michael Vick JSY 8.00 20.00
Donovan McNabb
38 Kurt Warner JSY 6.00 15.00
Marshall Faulk
39 Kurt Warner JSY 6.00 15.00
Joe Montana
40 Ricky Williams JSY 6.00 15.00
Earl Campbell

2002 Fleer Tradition Classic Combinations Memorabilia Duals
STATED PRINT RUN 100 SER.#'d SETS
1 Emmitt Smith 30.00 80.00
Marcus Allen
2 Earl Campbell 12.00 30.00
Eddie George
3 Earl Campbell 12.00 30.00
Ricky Williams
4 Jerry Rice 25.00 60.00
Cris Carter
5 Daunte Culpepper 12.00 30.00
Randy Moss
6 Terrell Davis 12.00 30.00
Curtis Martin
7 Eric Dickerson 12.00 30.00
Marshall Faulk
8 John Elway 25.00 60.00
Terrell Davis
9 John Elway 25.00 60.00
Brian Griese
10 Brett Favre 30.00 80.00
Daunte Culpepper
11 Jeff Garcia 12.00 30.00
Terrell Owens
12 Brian Griese 30.00 80.00
Tom Brady
13 Paul Hornung 40.00 100.00
Brett Favre
14 Donovan McNabb 12.00 30.00
Daunte Culpepper
15 Donovan McNabb 20.00 50.00
Michael Vick
16 Joe Montana 30.00 80.00
Kurt Warner
17 Walter Payton 50.00 120.00
Emmitt Smith
18 Randy Moss 25.00 60.00
Jerry Rice
19 Roger Staubach 30.00 80.00
Emmitt Smith
20 Fred Taylor 30.00 80.00
Emmitt Smith
21 Anthony Thomas 50.00 120.00
Walter Payton
22 Kurt Warner 12.00 30.00
Marshall Faulk
23 Kurt Warner 12.00 30.00
Jeff Garcia

2002 Fleer Tradition Golden Memories
COMPLETE SET (15) 12.50 30.00
STATED ODDS 1:8
1 America Tribute .60 1.50
2 Kurt Warner .75 2.00
3 Tom Brady 2.00 5.00
4 David Carr .75 2.00
5 Shaun Alexander .60 1.50
6 Anthony Thomas .60 1.50
7 Kendrell Bell .50 1.25
8 Michael Vick 1.25 3.00
9 Donovan McNabb .75 2.00
10 LaDainian Tomlinson 1.00 2.50
11 Brian Urlacher .75 2.00
12 Marshall Faulk .75 2.00
13 Edgerrin James .60 1.50
14 Terrell Owens .75 2.00
15 Tim Brown .75 2.00

2002 Fleer Tradition Headliners
COMPLETE SET (20) 30.00 80.00
STATED ODDS 1:24
1 Donovan McNabb 1.50 4.00
2 Marshall Faulk 1.50 4.00
3 Randy Moss 1.50 4.00
4 Emmitt Smith 4.00 10.00
5 Jeff Garcia 1.25 3.00
6 Tim Brown 1.50 4.00
7 Brian Urlacher 1.50 4.00
8 Jerome Bettis 1.50 4.00
9 Edgerrin James 1.25 3.00
10 Kurt Warner 1.50 4.00
11 Terrell Davis 1.50 4.00
12 Tim Couch 1.00 2.50
13 Ricky Williams 1.25 3.00
14 Daunte Culpepper 1.25 3.00
15 Jerry Rice 3.00 8.00
16 Curtis Martin 1.50 4.00
17 Peyton Manning 3.00 8.00
18 Eddie George 1.25 3.00
19 Tom Brady 4.00 10.00
20 Brett Favre 4.00 10.00

2002 Fleer Tradition Rookie Sensations
COMPLETE SET (20) 30.00 80.00
STATED PRINT RUN 1250 SER.#'d SETS
1 David Carr 1.00 2.50
2 Joey Harrington 1.00 2.50
3 William Green .75 2.00
4 Ashley Lelie .75 2.00
5 Donte Stallworth 1.00 2.50
6 T.J. Duckett 1.00 2.50
7 DeShaun Foster 1.00 2.50
8 Josh Reed .75 2.00
9 Jabar Gaffney 1.00 2.50
10 Clinton Portis 1.25 3.00
11 Antonio Bryant 1.00 2.50
12 Reche Caldwell 1.00 2.50
13 Julius Peppers 2.00 5.00
14 Ron Johnson .75 2.00
15 Javon Walker 1.00 2.50
16 Josh McCown 1.00 2.50
17 Marquise Walker .60 1.50
18 Patrick Ramsey 1.00 2.50
19 Antwaan Randle El 1.00 2.50
20 Andre Davis .75 2.00

2002 Fleer Tradition School Colors
COMPLETE SET (15) 20.00 50.00
STATED PRINT RUN 750 SER.#'d SETS
1 Santana Moss 1.25 3.00
2 Edgerrin James 1.25 3.00
3 David Terrell 1.00 2.50
4 Anthony Thomas 1.25 3.00
5 Dan Morgan 1.00 2.50
6 Rod Gardner 1.00 2.50
7 Archie Griffin 1.00 2.50
8 Drew Brees 2.50 6.00
9 Chad Johnson 1.50 4.00
10 Chris Weinke 1.00 2.50
11 Reggie Wayne 1.50 4.00
12 DeShaun Foster 1.50 4.00
13 Robert Ferguson 1.25 3.00
14 Tom Brady 4.00 10.00
15 David Carr 1.50 4.00

2002 Fleer Tradition School Colors Memorabilia

STATED ODDS 1:30
1 Drew Brees 8.00 20.00
2 Robert Ferguson 4.00 10.00
3 DeShaun Foster 5.00 12.00
4 Rod Gardner 3.00 8.00
5 Archie Griffin 3.00 8.00
6 Edgerrin James 4.00 10.00
7 Chad Johnson 5.00 12.00
8 Dan Morgan 3.00 8.00
9 Santana Moss 4.00 10.00
10 David Terrell 3.00 8.00
11 Anthony Thomas 4.00 10.00
12 Chris Weinke 3.00 8.00

2002 Fleer Tradition School Colors Memorabilia Duals
STATED ODDS 1:211
1 Edgerrin James 8.00 20.00
2 Dan Morgan 6.00 15.00
3 Santana Moss 8.00 20.00
4 David Terrell 6.00 15.00
5 Anthony Thomas 8.00 20.00

2003 Fleer Tradition

Released in September of 2003, this set consists of 270 veterans, 10 single player rookie cards, and 20 triple player rookie cards.

COMPLETE SET (300) 15.00 40.00
1 Aaron Glenn .15 .40
2 Jerry Rice .50 1.25
3 Chad Hutchinson .15 .40
4 Kris Jenkins .15 .40
5 Ed Reed .25 .60
6 Ed McCaffrey .20 .50
7 Rod Gardner .15 .40
8 Aaron Brooks .20 .50
9 Chad Pennington .25 .60
10 Jevon Kearse .20 .50
11 Kurt Warner .25 .60
12 Eddie George .20 .50
13 Ron Dugans .15 .40
14 Adam Vinatieri .25 .60
15 Jimmy Smith .20 .50
16 Chad Johnson .25 .60
17 Kyle Brady .15 .40
18 Eddie Kennison .15 .40
19 Joe Jurevicius .20 .50
20 Ronde Barber .20 .50
21 Adam Archuleta .15 .40
22 Champ Bailey .25 .60
23 Joe Horn .20 .50
24 Ladell Betts .15 .40
25 Edgerrin James .25 .60
26 Rosevelt Colvin .20 .50
27 Ahman Green .20 .50
28 Joey Porter .25 .60
29 Charles Woodson .25 .60
30 Lance Schulters .15 .40
31 Edgerton Hartwell .15 .40
32 Joey Galloway .20 .50
33 Roy Williams .20 .50
34 Al Wilson .15 .40
35 Charlie Garner .20 .50
36 John Lynch .20 .50
37 La'Roi Glover .15 .40
38 Emmitt Smith .60 1.50
39 Ryan Longwell .20 .50
40 Alge Crumpler .20 .50
41 John Abraham .20 .50
42 Chris Hovan .20 .50
43 Laveranues Coles .15 .40
44 Eric Hicks .15 .40
45 Johnnie Morton .20 .50
46 Sam Madison .20 .50
47 Amani Toomer .20 .50
48 Chris Redman .15 .40
49 Jon Kitna .20 .50
50 Leonard Little .15 .40
51 Eric Moulds .20 .50
52 Santana Moss .20 .50
53 Amos Zereoue .15 .40
54 Jonathan Wells .15 .40
55 Chris Chambers .20 .50
56 London Fletcher .15 .40
57 Frank Wycheck .15 .40
58 Josh McCown .20 .50
59 Shannon Sharpe .25 .60
60 Andre Carter .15 .40
61 Corey Dillon .20 .50
62 Josh Reed .15 .40
63 Marc Boerigter .15 .40
64 Fred Smoot .15 .40
65 Shaun Alexander .20 .50
66 Andre Davis .15 .40
67 Julian Peterson .15 .40
68 Corey Bradford .15 .40
69 Marc Bulger .25 .60
70 Fred Taylor .20 .50
71 Junior Seau .25 .60
72 Simeon Rice .15 .40
73 Anthony Thomas .20 .50
74 Correll Buckhalter .20 .50
75 Justin Smith .20 .50
76 Marcel Shipp .15 .40
77 Garrison Hearst .20 .50
78 Stacey Mack .15 .40
79 Antowain Smith .20 .50
80 Kabeer Gbaja-Biamila .20 .50
81 Curtis Martin .25 .60
82 Marcellus Wiley .15 .40
83 Gary Walker .15 .40
84 Kalimba Edwards .15 .40
85 Stephen Davis .20 .50
86 Antwaan Randle El .20 .50
87 Curtis Conway .15 .40
88 Keith Brooking .20 .50
89 Mark Word RC .15 .40
90 Greg Ellis .25 .60
91 Steve McNair .25 .60
92 Ashley Lelie .15 .40
93 Kelly Holcomb .15 .40
94 Darrell Jackson .20 .50
95 Mark Brunell .20 .50
96 Hugh Douglas .15 .40
97 Kendrell Bell .15 .40
98 Steve Smith .25 .60
99 Bill Schroeder .15 .40
100 Darren Howard .20 .50
101 Kevan Barlow .15 .40
102 Marshall Faulk .25 .60
103 Ike Hilliard .15 .40
104 T.J. Duckett .20 .50
105 Bobby Taylor .20 .50
106 Kevin Carter .20 .50
107 Darren Sharper .20 .50
108 Marty Booker .20 .50
109 Isaac Bruce .25 .60
110 Kevin Hardy .15 .40
111 Tai Streets .15 .40
112 Brad Johnson .20 .50
113 Daunte Culpepper .20 .50
114 Kevin Johnson .15 .40
115 Matt Hasselbeck .20 .50
116 Jabar Gaffney .15 .40
117 Takeo Spikes .15 .40
118 Brett Favre .60 1.50
119 Keyshawn Johnson .25 .60
120 David Akers .20 .50
121 Maurice Morris .15 .40
122 Jake Delhomme .25 .60
123 Kordell Stewart .20 .50
124 Terrell Davis .25 .60
125 Brian Kelly .15 .40
126 David Terrell .15 .40
127 Koren Robinson .20 .50
128 Michael Strahan .25 .60
129 Jake Plummer .20 .50
130 Terrell Owens .25 .60
131 Brian Urlacher .25 .60
132 David Patten .15 .40
133 Michael Vick .30 .75
134 Jamal Lewis .20 .50
135 Terry Glenn .20 .50
136 Brian Simmons .15 .40
137 David Boston .15 .40
138 Michael Bennett .20 .50
139 James Stewart .15 .40
140 Tiki Barber .25 .60
141 Brian Griese .20 .50
142 Deion Branch .20 .50
143 Mike Peterson .15 .40
144 James Mungro .15 .40
145 Tim Couch .15 .40
146 Brian Dawkins .20 .50
147 Dennis Northcutt .15 .40
148 Mike Alstott .25 .60
149 James Thrash .15 .40
150 Tim Brown .25 .60
151 Brian Finneran .15 .40
152 Derrick Brooks .20 .50
153 Muhsin Muhammad .20 .50
154 Jason Elam .20 .50
155 Tim Dwight .15 .40
156 Bruce Smith .20 .50
157 Derrick Mason .20 .50
158 Napoleon Harris .15 .40
159 Jason Gildon .20 .50
160 Todd Heap .20 .50
161 Aaron Schobel .20 .50
162 Derrius Thompson .15 .40
163 Nate Clements .20 .50
164 Jason McAddley .15 .40
165 Todd Pinkston .15 .40
166 Bubba Franks .20 .50
167 Deuce McAllister .20 .50
168 Patrick Surtain .15 .40
169 Javon Walker .20 .50
170 Tom Brady .60 1.50
171 Dexter Coakley .20 .50
172 Patrick Kerney .20 .50
173 Jay Fiedler .15 .40
174 Tommy Maddox .20 .50
175 Donald Driver .25 .60
176 Patrick Ramsey .20 .50
177 Olandis Gary .15 .40
178 Tony Gonzalez .25 .60
179 Donnie Edwards .15 .40
180 Peter Boulware .20 .50
181 Jeff Blake .20 .50
182 Torry Holt .25 .60
183 Donovan McNabb .25 .60
184 Peter Warrick .20 .50
185 Jeff Garcia .20 .50
186 Travis Henry .15 .40
187 Doug Jolley .15 .40
188 Peyton Manning .50 1.25
189 Jerome Bettis .25 .60
190 Travis Taylor .15 .40
191 Drew Brees .25 .60
192 Phillip Buchanon .15 .40
193 Jerramy Stevens .20 .50
194 Trent Green .20 .50
195 Duce Staley .20 .50
196 Plaxico Burress .20 .50
197 Jerry Porter .15 .40
198 Trevor Pryce .20 .50
199 Dwight Freeney .20 .50
200 Quincy Morgan .15 .40
201 Troy Vincent .20 .50
202 Randy McMichael .15 .40
203 Troy Hambrick .15 .40
204 Randy Moss .25 .60
205 Troy Brown .20 .50
206 Ray Lewis .25 .60
207 Trung Canidate .15 .40
208 Raynoch Thompson .15 .40
209 Ty Law .20 .50
210 Reggie Wayne .25 .60
211 Warren Sapp .20 .50
212 Richard Seymour .20 .50
213 Warrick Dunn .20 .50
214 Robert Ferguson .15 .40
215 Wayne Chrebet .20 .50
216 Rod Coleman RC .15 .40
217 Will Allen .20 .50
218 Rod Woodson .25 .60
219 Zach Thomas .25 .60
220 Rod Smith .20 .50
221 Ricky Williams .20 .50
222 LaDainian Tomlinson .25 .60
223 Priest Holmes .25 .60
224 Rich Gannon .20 .50
225 Drew Bledsoe .25 .60
226 Kerry Collins .20 .50
227 Marvin Harrison .25 .60
228 Hines Ward .25 .60
229 Peerless Price .15 .40
230 Jason Taylor .20 .50
231 Jeremy Shockey .25 .60
232 Clinton Portis .20 .50
233 Antonio Bryant .15 .40
234 Donte Stallworth .15 .40
235 David Carr .20 .50
236 Joey Harrington .15 .40
237 William Green .15 .40
238 Julius Peppers .25 .60
239 Marcel Shipp .12 .30
Raynoch Thompson
Adrian Wilson
240 Michael Vick .25 .60
Warrick Dunn
Brian Finneran
Keith Brooking
241 Jamal Lewis .20 .50
Edgerton Hartwell
Travis Taylor
Ed Reed
242 Drew Bledsoe .20 .50
Travis Henry
Eric Moulds
London Fletcher
243 Julius Peppers .20 .50
Steve Smith
Muhsin Muhammad
244 Marty Booker .20 .50
Brian Urlacher
Anthony Thomas
245 Corey Dillon .20 .50
Justin Smith
Chad Johnson
Jon Kitna
246 Tim Couch .12 .30
William Green
Quincy Morgan
Mark Word
247 Chad Hutchinson .20 .50
Joey Galloway
Roy Williams
Greg Ellis
248 Clinton Portis .15 .40
Rod Smith
Al Wilson
249 Joey Harrington .12 .30
James Stewart
Bill Schroeder
Kalimba Edwards
250 Brett Favre .50 1.25
Ahman Green
Donald Driver
KGB
251 David Carr .15 .40
Jonathan Wells
Corey Bradford
Aaron Glenn
252 Peyton Manning .40 1.00
Edgerrin James
Marvin Harrison
Dwight Freeney
253 Mark Brunell .15 .40
Fred Taylor
Jimmy Smith
Marlon McCree
254 Treent Green .20 .50
Priest Holmes
Eddie Kennison
Eric Hicks
255 Ricky Williams .20 .50
Chris Chambers
Zach Thomas
Jason Taylor
256 Daunte Culpepper .20 .50
Michael Bennett
Randy Moss
Moe Williams
257 Tom Brady .50 1.25
Antowain Smith
Troy Brown
Adam Vinatieri
258 Aaron Brooks .15 .40
Deuce McAllister
Joe Horn
Darren Howard
259 Kerry Collins .20 .50
Tiki Barber
Amani Toomer
Michael Strahan
260 Chad Pennington .20 .50
Curtis Martin
Wayne Chrebet
John Abraham
261 Rich Gannon .40 1.00
Charlie Garner
Jerry Rice
Rod Woodson
262 Donovan McNabb .20 .50
Duce Staley
Todd Pinkston
Bobby Taylor
263 Tommy Maddox .20 .50
Amos Zereoue
Hines Ward
Jason Gildon
Jerry Porter
264 Drew Brees .20 .50
LaDainian Tomlinson
Donnie Edwards
265 Jeff Garcia .20 .50
Garrison Hearst
Terrell Owens
Andre Carter
266 Matt Hasselbeck .15 .40
Shaun Alexander
Koren Robinson
Reggie Tongue
267 Marc Bulger .20 .50
Marshall Faulk
Torry Holt
Leonard Little
268 Brad Johnson .40 1.00
Keyshawn Johnson
Simeon Rice
Brian Kelly
269 Steve McNair .20 .50
Eddie George
Derrick Mason
Lance Schulters
270 Patrick Ramsey .15 .40
Rod Gardner
Fred Smoot
271 Carson Palmer RC 1.00 2.50
272 Kyle Boller RC .50 1.25
273 Byron Leftwich RC .50 1.25
274 Willis McGahee RC .60 1.50
275 Larry Johnson RC .50 1.25
276 Charles Rogers RC .40 1.00
277 Andre Johnson RC 1.25 3.00
278 Bryant Johnson RC .50 1.25
279 Rex Grossman RC .50 1.25
280 Taylor Jacobs RC .30 .75
281 Dewayne Robertson RC .50 1.25
Johnathan Sullivan RC
Kevin Williams RC
282 Bennie Joppru RC .40 1.00
Domanick Davis RC
Dave Ragone RC
283 Jason Witten RC 1.25 3.00
Dallas Clark RC
L.J.Smith RC
284 Terrence Edwards RC .40 1.00
Musa Smith RC
Boss Bailey RC
285 Lee Suggs RC .40 1.00
Chris Brown RC
Onterrio Smith RC
286 Quentin Griffin RC .40 1.00
Artose Pinner RC
B.J. Askew RC
287 Justin Fargas RC .50 1.25
Doug Gabriel RC
Teyo Johnson RC
288 Jimmy Kennedy RC .40 1.00
William Joseph RC
Ty Warren RC
289 Terrell Suggs RC .50 1.25
Michael Haynes RC
Jerome McDougle RC
290 Kelley Washington RC .50 1.25
Kevin Curtis RC
Nate Burleson RC
291 Seneca Wallace RC .50 1.25
Ken Dorsey RC
Chris Simms RC
292 Bobby Wade RC .40 1.00
Sam Aiken RC
Justin Gage RC
293 Sultan McCullough RC .50 1.25
Cecil Sapp RC
Earnest Graham RC
294 Kareem Kelly RC .40 1.00
Talman Gardner RC
J.R. Tolver RC
295 Bethel Johnson RC .75 2.00
Anquan Boldin RC
Tyrone Calico RC
296 Brandon Lloyd RC .75 2.00
Billy McMullen RC
Shaun McDonald RC
297 Chris Kelsay RC .50 1.25
Dewayne White RC
Mike Doss RC
298 Terence Newman RC .40 1.00
Marcus Trufant RC
Andre Woolfolk RC
299 Kliff Kingsbury RC 5.00 12.00
Tony Romo RC
Brian St. Pierre RC
300 Andrew Pinnock RC .40 1.00
LaBrandon Toefield RC
Avon Cobourne RC

2003 Fleer Tradition Minis
*VETS 1-270: 5X TO 12X BASIC CARDS
*ROOKIES 271-300: 2.5X TO 6X
STATED PRINT RUN 125 SER.#'d SETS
RANDOM INSERTS IN RETAIL PACKS
299 Kliff Kingsbury RC 20.00 50.00
Tony Romo RC
Brian St. Pierre RC

2003 Fleer Tradition Tiffany
*VETS 1-270: 3X TO 8X BASIC CARDS
*ROOKIES 271-300: 1.5X TO 4X
STATED PRINT RUN 200 SER.#'d SETS
299 Kliff Kingsbury RC 12.00 30.00
Tony Romo RC
Brian St. Pierre RC

2003 Fleer Tradition Classic Combinations
1-10 STATED PRINT RUN 1500 SER.#'d SETS
11-20 STATED PRINT RUN 750 SER.#'d SETS
21-30 STATED PRINT RUN 375 SER.#'d SETS
1 Earl Campbell 1.00 2.50
Priest Holmes
2 Plaxico Burress .75 2.00
Charles Rogers
3 Ed Too Tall Jones .60 1.50
Terrell Suggs
4 Edgerrin James .75 2.00
Willis McGahee
5 Marcus Allen 1.25 3.00
Carson Palmer
6 Fran Tarkenton 1.00 2.50
Chad Pennington
7 Michael Vick 1.25 3.00
Byron Leftwich
8 Doug Flutie 1.00 2.50
Drew Bledsoe
9 Peyton Manning 2.00 5.00
Travis Henry
10 Ken Stabler 1.25 3.00
Rich Gannon
11 Randy Moss 1.25 3.00
Terrell Owens
12 Bob Griese 1.00 2.50
Ricky Williams
13 Ronnie Lott 1.00 2.50
Roy Williams
14 Jack Ham 1.00 2.50
Kendrell Bell
15 David Carr 2.00 5.00
Andre Johnson
16 Brett Favre 3.00 8.00
Kurt Warner
17 Fred Biletnikoff 2.50 6.00
Jerry Rice
18 Joey Harrington .60 1.50
Charles Rogers
19 Chad Pennington .75 2.00
Byron Leftwich
20 Ken Stabler 1.50 4.00
Michael Vick
21 Fran Tarkenton 1.50 4.00
Brett Favre
22 Donovan McNabb 1.50 4.00
Marvin Harrison
23 Clinton Portis 1.25 3.00
Willis McGahee
24 Emmitt Smith 4.00 10.00
Rex Grossman
25 Jack Ham 1.50 4.00
Brian Urlacher
26 Marcus Allen 1.50 4.00
Marshall Faulk
27 Jeremy Shockey 2.50 6.00
Andre Johnson
28 Fred Biletnikoff 1.50 4.00
Tim Brown
29 Carson Palmer 2.00 5.00
Byron Leftwich
30 Ed Too Tall Jones 1.50 4.00
Julius Peppers

2003 Fleer Tradition Classic Combinations Memorabilia

STATED ODDS 1:72
1 Earl Campbell JSY 5.00 12.00
Priest Holmes
2 Marcus Allen JSY 5.00 12.00
Carson Palmer
3 Bob Griese JSY 5.00 12.00
Ricky Williams
4 Michael Vick JSY 5.00 12.00
Ken Stabler
5 Kurt Warner JSY 6.00 15.00
Brett Favre
6 Fred Biletnikoff JSY 5.00 12.00
Tim Brown
7 Fred Biletnikoff JSY 5.00 12.00
Jerry Rice
8 Michael Vick JSY 5.00 12.00
Byron Leftwich
9 Edd Too Tall Jones JSY 4.00 10.00
Terrell Suggs
10 Ronnie Lott JSY 5.00 12.00
Roy Williams
11 Doug Flutie JSY 4.00 10.00
Drew Bledsoe
12 Chad Pennington JSY 4.00 10.00
Fran Tarkenton
13 Clinton Portis JSY 2.50 6.00
Willis McGahee
14 Marcus Allen JSY 5.00 12.00
Marshall Faulk
15 Jeremy Shockey JSY 4.00 10.00
Andre Johnson
16 Drew Bledsoe JSY 4.00 10.00
Doug Flutie
17 Brian Urlacher JSY 4.00 10.00
Jack Ham
18 Priest Holmes JSY 4.00 10.00
Earl Campbell
19 Plaxico Burress JSY 3.00 8.00
Charles Rogers
20 Peyton Manning JSY 8.00 20.00
Travis Henry
21 Edgerrin James JSY 5.00 12.00
Willis McGahee
22 Tim Brown JSY 4.00 10.00
Fred Biletnikoff
23 Marvin Harrison JSY 4.00 10.00
Donovan McNabb
24 Ricky Williams JSY 4.00 10.00
Bob Griese
25 Terrell Owens JSY 4.00 10.00
Randy Moss

2003 Fleer Tradition Classic Combinations Memorabilia Duals
1 Earl Campbell 6.00 15.00
Priest Holmes
2 Fred Biletnikoff 6.00 15.00
Tim Brown
3 Ed Too Tall Jones 6.00 15.00
Julius Peppers
4 Doug Flutie 6.00 15.00
Drew Bledsoe
5 Marcus Allen 6.00 15.00
Marshall Faulk
6 Fred Biletnikoff 12.00 30.00
Jerry Rice
7 Donovan McNabb 6.00 15.00
Marvin Harrison
8 Peyton Manning 12.00 30.00
Travis Henry
9 Brett Favre 15.00 40.00
Kurt Warner
10 Randy Moss 6.00 15.00
Terrell Owens
11 Ronnie Lott 5.00 12.00
Roy Williams
12 Fran Tarkenton 6.00 15.00
Brett Favre

13 Bob Griese 6.00 15.00
Ricky Williams
14 Ken Stabler 8.00 20.00
Michael Vick
15 Fran Tarkenton 6.00 15.00
Chad Pennington

2003 Fleer Tradition Rookie Sensations

STATED PRINT RUN 1250 SER.#'d SETS
1 Kyle Boller 1.00 2.50
2 Taylor Jacobs .60 1.50
3 Terence Newman .75 2.00
4 Kelley Washington .60 1.50
5 Carson Palmer 2.00 5.00
6 Byron Leftwich 1.00 2.50
7 Willis McGahee 1.25 3.00
8 Bethel Johnson .60 1.50
9 Kevin Curtis 1.00 2.50
10 Charles Rogers .75 2.00
11 Rex Grossman 1.00 2.50
12 Larry Johnson 1.00 2.50
13 Anquan Boldin 1.50 4.00
14 Andre Johnson 2.50 6.00
15 Bryant Johnson 1.00 2.50
16 Terrell Suggs 1.00 2.50
17 Tyrone Calico .75 2.00
18 Chris Simms 1.00 2.50
19 DeWayne Robertson .75 2.00
20 Nate Burleson .75 2.00

2003 Fleer Tradition Standouts

COMPLETE SET (10) 10.00 25.00
STATED ODDS 1:36
1 Ricky Williams .75 2.00
2 Michael Vick 1.25 3.00
3 Brett Favre 2.50 6.00
4 Randy Moss 1.00 2.50
5 Chad Pennington 1.00 2.50
6 Jerry Rice 2.00 5.00
7 Clinton Portis .75 2.00
8 Brian Urlacher 1.00 2.50
9 Donovan McNabb 1.00 2.50
10 Tom Brady 2.50 6.00

2003 Fleer Tradition Throwbacks

COMPLETE SET (10) 15.00 40.00
STATED ODDS 1:72
1 Marcus Allen 2.00 5.00
2 Bob Griese 2.00 5.00
3 Jack Ham 1.50 4.00
4 Ken Stabler 2.50 6.00
5 Fran Tarkenton 2.00 5.00
6 Earl Campbell 2.00 5.00
7 Fred Biletnikoff 2.00 5.00
8 Ed Too Tall Jones 1.50 4.00
9 Ronnie Lott 1.50 4.00
10 Doug Flutie 2.00 5.00

2003 Fleer Tradition Throwbacks Memorabilia

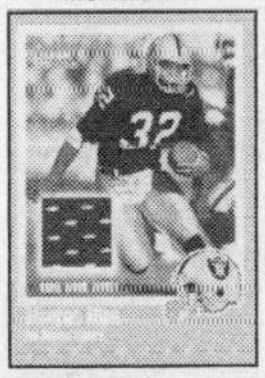

STATED ODDS 1:288
*PATCH/100: .6X TO 1.5X BASIC JSY
PATCHES PRINT RUN 100 SER.#'d SETS
1 Marcus Allen 5.00 12.00
2 Earl Campbell 5.00 12.00
3 Bob Griese 5.00 12.00
4 Ronnie Lott 4.00 10.00
5 Fran Tarkenton 5.00 12.00

2004 Fleer Tradition

Fleer Tradition initially released in early July 2004. The base set consists of 360-cards including 20-rookies and 10-multi player rookie cards. Hobby boxes contained 36-packs of 10-cards each and carried and S.R.P. of $1.49. Four parallel sets and a variety of inserts can be found seeded in hobby and retail packs highlighted by the multi-tiered Rookie Throwback Threads inserts.

COMPLETE SET (360) 50.00 100.00
COMP.SET w/o SP's (330) 15.00 30.00
331-ROOKIE STATED ODDS 1:4
351-360 ROOKIE STATED ODDS 1:18H, 1:24R
1 Ricky Williams TL .15 .40
Chris Chambers
Adewale Ogunleye
Patrick Surtain
2 Drew Bledsoe TL .15 .40
Travis Henry
Bobby Shaw
Aaron Schobel
3 Tom Brady TL .30 .75
Mike Cloud
David Givens
Mike Vrabel
4 Chad Pennington TL .15 .40
Curtis Martin
Santana Moss
Shaun Ellis
5 Peyton Manning TL .30 .75
Edgerrin James
Marvin Harrison
Dwight Freeney
6 Byron Leftwich TL .15 .40
Fred Taylor
Jimmy Smith
Mike Peterson
7 Steve McNair TL .08 .25
Eddie George
Derrick Mason
Samari Rolle
8 David Carr TL .15 .40
Domanick Davis
Andre Johnson
Marcus Coleman
9 Rich Gannon TL .25 .60
Zack Crockett
Jerry Rice
Phillip Buchanon
10 Jake Plummer TL .15 .40
Clinton Portis
Shannon Sharpe
Bertrand Berry
11 Trent Green TL .15 .40
Priest Holmes
Tony Gonzalez
Vonnie Holliday
12 Drew Brees TL .20 .50
LaDainian Tomlinson
David Boston
Quentin Jammer
13 Tommy Maddox TL .25 .60
Jerome Bettis
Hines Ward
Kimo von Oelhoffen
14 Kelly Holcomb TL .08 .25
William Green
Dennis Northcutt
Earl Little
15 Jon Kitna TL .15 .40
Rudi Johnson
Chad Johnson
Tory James
16 Kyle Boller TL .15 .40
Jamal Lewis
Terrell Suggs
Ray Lewis
17 Donovan McNabb TL .15 .40
Correll Buckhalter
Brian Westbrook
Corey Simon
18 Kerry Collins TL .15 .40
Tiki Barber
Amani Toomer
Michael Strahan
19 Patrick Ramsey TL .15 .40
Trung Canidate
Laveranues Coles
Fred Smoot
20 Quincy Carter TL .15 .40
Troy Hambrick
Terry Glenn
Terence Newman
21 Daunte Culpepper TL .25 .60
Moe Williams
Randy Moss
Kevin Williams
22 Brett Favre TL .30 .75
Ahman Green
Javon Walker
Kabeer Gbaja-Biamila
23 Kordell Stewart TL .25 .60
Anthony Thomas
Marty Booker
Brian Urlacher
24 Joey Harrington TL .15 .40
Shawn Bryson
Az-Zahir Hakim
Dre Bly
25 Jeff Garcia TL .15 .40
Kevan Barlow
Terrell Owens
Julian Peterson
26 Marc Bulger TL .15 .40
Marshall Faulk
Torry Holt
Leonard Little
27 Matt Hasselbeck TL .15 .40
Shaun Alexander
Darrell Jackson
Chike Okeafor
28 Jeff Blake TL .08 .25
Marcel Shipp
Anquan Boldin
Dexter Jackson
29 Jake Delhomme TL .15 .40
Stephen Davis
Steve Smith
Mike Rucker
30 Brad Johnson TL .08 .25
Michael Pittman
Keenan McCardell
Simeon Rice
31 Doug Johnson TL .08 .25
T.J. Duckett
Peerless Price
Keith Brooking
32 Aaron Brooks TL .15 .40
Deuce McAllister
Joe Horn
Charles Grant
33 Anquan Boldin .20 .50
34 Michael Vick .25 .60
35 Kyle Boller .15 .40
36 Aeneas Williams .12 .30
37 Jake Delhomme .15 .40
38 Rex Grossman .15 .40
39 Carson Palmer .20 .50
40 Quincy Morgan .12 .30
41 Terry Glenn .15 .40
42 Jake Plummer .15 .40
43 Joey Harrington .15 .40
44 Brett Favre .50 1.25
45 Jeff Garcia .15 .40
46 Peyton Manning .40 1.00
47 Byron Leftwich .15 .40
48 Trent Green .15 .40
49 A.J. Feeley .12 .30
50 Daunte Culpepper .15 .40
51 Tom Brady .40 1.00
52 Aaron Brooks .15 .40
53 Kerry Collins .15 .40
54 Chad Pennington .20 .50
55 Rich Gannon .15 .40
56 Donovan McNabb .20 .50
57 Tommy Maddox .15 .40
58 Drew Brees .20 .50
59 Terrell Owens .20 .50
60 Matt Hasselbeck .15 .40
61 Kurt Warner .20 .50
62 Brad Johnson .15 .40
63 Jerome Bettis .20 .50
64 Keith Bulluck .12 .30
65 Rod Gardner .12 .30
66 Eddie George .15 .40
67 Warren Sapp .15 .40
68 Marc Bulger .15 .40
69 Shaun Alexander .15 .40
70 Tai Streets .12 .30
71 LaDainian Tomlinson .20 .50
72 Steve McNair .20 .50
73 Brian Westbrook .20 .50
74 Jerry Rice .40 1.00
75 Santana Moss .15 .40
76 Moe Williams .12 .30
77 Deuce McAllister .15 .40
78 Adam Vinatieri .20 .50
79 Randy Moss .20 .50
80 Ricky Williams .15 .40
81 Priest Holmes .20 .50
82 Jimmy Smith .15 .40
83 Edgerrin James .15 .40
84 Andre Johnson .20 .50
85 Ahman Green .15 .40
86 Charles Rogers .12 .30
87 Champ Bailey .15 .40
88 Roy Williams S .15 .40
89 Tim Couch .15 .40
90 Corey Dillon .15 .40
91 Thomas Jones .20 .50
92 Stephen Davis .15 .40
93 Travis Henry .12 .30
94 Jamal Lewis .15 .40
95 Warrick Dunn .15 .40
96 Emmitt Smith .50 1.25
97 Mark Brunell .15 .40
98 Willis McGahee .20 .50
99 Duce Staley .15 .40
100 Lee Suggs .15 .40
101 Rod Smith .15 .40
102 Marvin Harrison .20 .50
103 Larry Johnson .15 .40
104 Michael Bennett .15 .40
105 Donte Stallworth .12 .30
106 DeShaun Foster .15 .40
107 Hines Ward .20 .50
108 T.J. Duckett .15 .40
109 Brian Urlacher .20 .50
110 Boss Bailey .12 .30
111 Tim Brown .20 .50
112 David Boston .12 .30
113 Marshall Faulk .20 .50
114 Jason Witten .20 .50
115 Richard Seymour .12 .30
116 Domanick Davis .12 .30
117 Jon Kitna .15 .40
118 Ray Lewis .20 .50
119 Tedy Bruschi .20 .50
120 Chris Chambers .15 .40
121 Freddie Mitchell .12 .30
122 Amani Toomer .15 .40
123 Curtis Martin .20 .50
124 Eric Moulds .15 .40
125 Darrell Jackson .15 .40
126 Clinton Portis .20 .50
127 Jay Fiedler .12 .30
128 Todd Heap .15 .40
129 Dexter Jackson .12 .30
130 James Jackson .12 .30
131 Shannon Sharpe .20 .50
132 Donald Driver .20 .50
133 Billy Miller .12 .30
134 Dante Hall .15 .40
135 Onterrio Smith .12 .30
136 Joe Horn .15 .40
137 Shaun Ellis .12 .30
138 L.J. Smith .15 .40
139 Jerry Porter .12 .30
140 Reggie Wayne .20 .50
141 Derrick Brooks .15 .40
142 Terrell Suggs .15 .40
143 Randy McMichael .12 .30
144 Mike Alstott .15 .40
145 Nate Poole RC .20 .50
146 Chris Brown .12 .30
147 Torry Holt .15 .40
148 Adewale Ogunleye .15 .40
149 Peter Warrick .15 .40
150 Alge Crumpler .15 .40
151 Charlie Garner .15 .40
152 Jeremy Shockey .15 .40
153 Simeon Rice .12 .30
154 Julian Peterson .15 .40
155 Patrick Ramsey .15 .40
156 Shawn Springs .12 .30
157 Marcus Stroud .12 .30
158 Keyshawn Johnson .15 .40
159 Steve Smith .20 .50
160 Ty Law .15 .40
161 Derrick Mason .15 .40
162 Josh Reed .12 .30
163 Fred Smoot .12 .30
164 Muhsin Muhammad .15 .40
165 Justin Gage .15 .40
166 Chad Johnson .20 .50
167 Dennis Northcutt .12 .30
168 Joey Galloway .15 .40
169 Ashley Lelie .12 .30
170 Casey Fitzsimmons .12 .30
171 Dwight Freeney .15 .40
172 Nick Barnett .15 .40
173 LaBrandon Toefield .12 .30
174 Jabar Gaffney .12 .30
175 Tony Gonzalez .20 .50
176 Zach Thomas .20 .50
177 Nate Burleson .15 .40
178 Deion Branch .15 .40
179 Boo Williams .12 .30
180 Michael Strahan .20 .50
181 Anthony Becht .12 .30
182 Charles Woodson .20 .50
183 Sheldon Brown .12 .30
184 Kendrell Bell .12 .30
185 Kassim Osgood .12 .30
186 Tony Parrish .12 .30
187 Marcel Shipp .12 .30
188 Bobby Engram .15 .40
189 Keith Brooking .12 .30
190 Isaac Bruce .15 .40
191 Travis Taylor .12 .30
192 Charles Lee .12 .30
193 Takeo Spikes .12 .30
194 Justin McCareins .12 .30
195 Julius Peppers .15 .40
196 LaVar Arrington .15 .40
197 Dez White .15 .40
198 Rudi Johnson .15 .40
199 Andre Davis .12 .30
200 Quincy Carter .12 .30
201 Quentin Griffin .12 .30
202 Dallas Clark .20 .50
203 Artose Pinner .12 .30
204 Kevin Johnson .12 .30
205 Kabeer Gbaja-Biamila .15 .40
206 Marcus Coleman .12 .30
207 Johnnie Morton .15 .40
208 Jason Taylor .15 .40
209 Kevin Williams .12 .30
210 David Givens .12 .30
211 Charles Grant .12 .30
212 Ike Hilliard .15 .40
213 Wayne Chrebet .15 .40
214 Teyo Johnson .12 .30
215 Brian Dawkins .15 .40
216 Antwaan Randle El .15 .40
217 Eric Parker .15 .40
218 Josh McCown .15 .40
219 Tim Rattay .12 .30
220 Brian Finneran .12 .30
221 Chad Brown .12 .30
222 Ed Reed .15 .40
223 Dane Looker .12 .30
224 Aaron Schobel .12 .30
225 Joe Jurevicius .12 .30
226 Ricky Manning .12 .30
227 Jevon Kearse .15 .40
228 Laveranues Coles .12 .30
229 Kelley Washington .12 .30
230 William Green .12 .30
231 Terence Newman .15 .40
232 Bryant Johnson .12 .30
233 Peerless Price .12 .30
234 Peter Boulware .15 .40
235 Drew Bledsoe .20 .50
236 Kris Jenkins .15 .40
237 Marty Booker .15 .40
238 Matt Schobel .12 .30
239 Earl Little .12 .30
240 Antonio Bryant .15 .40
241 Al Wilson .12 .30
242 Dre Bly .12 .30
243 Javon Walker .12 .30
244 David Carr .12 .30
245 Mike Vanderjagt .12 .30
246 Fred Taylor .15 .40
247 Eddie Kennison .15 .40
248 Patrick Surtain .12 .30
249 Jim Kleinsasser .12 .30
250 Daniel Graham .12 .30
251 Jerome Pathon .12 .30
252 Tiki Barber .20 .50
253 John Abraham .12 .30
254 Justin Fargas .15 .40
255 Correll Buckhalter .15 .40
256 Plaxico Burress .15 .40
257 Quentin Jammer .12 .30
258 Kevan Barlow .12 .30
259 Koren Robinson .12 .30
260 Leonard Little .12 .30
261 John Lynch .15 .40
262 Tyrone Calico .15 .40
263 Taylor Jacobs .12 .30
264 Joey Porter .15 .40
265 Freddie Jones .12 .30
266 Marcus Pollard .12 .30
267 Mike Peterson .12 .30
268 Justin Griffith .12 .30
269 Shawn Bryson .12 .30
270 Will Allen .12 .30
271 Antonio Gates .20 .50
272 Chris McAlister .12 .30
273 Tony Hollings .12 .30
274 Cedrick Wilson .12 .30
275 Adam Archuleta .12 .30
276 London Fletcher .12 .30
277 Drew Bennett .15 .40
278 Rod Smart .15 .40
279 LaMont Jordan .15 .40
280 Jerry Azumah .12 .30
281 Bubba Franks .12 .30
282 Troy Edwards .12 .30
283 Willie McGinest .15 .40
284 Morten Andersen .12 .30
285 Dat Nguyen .12 .30
286 Samari Rolle .12 .30
287 Brian Simmons .12 .30
288 Chike Okeafor .15 .40
289 Rodney Harrison .15 .40
290 Jason Elam .15 .40
291 Tim Dwight .12 .30
292 Corey Bradford .12 .30
293 Charles Tillman .15 .40
294 Tim Carter .12 .30
295 Ahmed Plummer .12 .30
296 Troy Walters .12 .30
297 Michael Lewis .15 .40
298 Tory James .12 .30
299 Doug Flutie .20 .50
300 Az-Zahir Hakim .12 .30
301 Itula Mili .12 .30
302 Jamie Sharper .12 .30
303 Vonnie Holliday .12 .30
304 Brian Russell RC .20 .50
305 Bryan Gilmore .12 .30
306 Darren Sharper .15 .40
307 Kyle Brady .15 .40
308 David Tyree .15 .40
309 Andre Carter .12 .30
310 Lawyer Milloy .12 .30
311 David Terrell .12 .30
312 Richie Anderson .12 .30
313 Darren Howard .12 .30
314 Sebastian Janikowski .12 .30
315 Kimo von Oelhoffen .12 .30
316 Donnie Edwards .15 .40
317 Brandon Lloyd .15 .40
318 Robert Ferguson .12 .30
319 Derek Smith .12 .30
320 Anthony Thomas .15 .40
321 Ken Hamlin .12 .30
322 Ronde Barber .15 .40
323 Erron Kinney .12 .30
324 Tom Brady AW .30 .75
325 Peyton Manning AW .30 .75
326 Steve McNair AW .15 .40
327 Jamal Lewis AW .12 .30
328 Ray Lewis AW .15 .40
329 Anquan Boldin AW .15 .40
330 Terrell Suggs AW .12 .30
331 Eli Manning RC 5.00 12.00
332 Larry Fitzgerald RC 2.00 5.00
333 Ben Roethlisberger RC 5.00 12.00
334 Tatum Bell RC .60 1.50
335 Roy Williams RC .75 2.00
336 Drew Henson RC .50 1.25
337 Philip Rivers RC 4.00 10.00
338 Rashaun Woods RC .50 1.25
339 Kevin Jones RC .60 1.50
340 Sean Taylor RC 1.50 4.00
341 Steven Jackson RC 1.25 3.00
342 Kellen Winslow RC .75 2.00
343 Chris Perry RC .60 1.50
344 J.P. Losman RC .60 1.50
345 Greg Jones RC .50 1.25
346 Reggie Williams RC .60 1.50
347 Michael Clayton RC .60 1.50
348 Jonathan Vilma RC .75 2.00
349 Julius Jones RC .60 1.50
350 Michael Jenkins RC .75 2.00
351 Eli Manning 15.00 30.00
Philip Rivers
Ben Roethlisberger
352 Larry Fitzgerald 3.00 8.00
Reggie Williams
Roy Williams WR
353 Lee Evans RC .75 2.00
Bernard Berrian RC
Derrick Hamilton RC
354 Kenechi Udeze RC .75 2.00
Will Poole RC
Keary Colbert RC
355 Chris Gamble RC .75 2.00
Dunta Robinson RC
DeAngelo Hall RC
356 Ben Troupe RC .75 2.00
Ben Watson RC
Ben Hartsock RC
357 Devard Darling RC .60 1.50
Johnnie Morant RC
Ernest Wilford RC
358 Luke McCown RC 1.50 4.00
Cody Pickett RC
Matt Schaub RC
359 Tatum Bell 1.00 2.50
Michael Turner RC
Cedric Cobbs RC
360 Mewelde Moore RC .60 1.50
Quincy Wilson RC
Derrick Knight RC

2004 Fleer Tradition Blue

*VETS: 1X TO 2.5X BASIC CARDS
*ROOKIES 331-350: .6X TO 1.5X
*ROOKIES 351-360: .6X TO 1.5X

2004 Fleer Tradition Crystal

*VETS: 5X TO 12X BASIC CARDS
*ROOKIES 331-350: 2.5X TO 6X
*ROOKIES 351-360: 2.5X TO 6X
1-330 PRINT RUN 150 SER.#'d SETS
331-350 PRINT RUN 75 SER.#'d SETS
351-360 PRINT RUN 25 SER.#'d SETS

2004 Fleer Tradition Draft Day

*ROOKIES 331-350: 1X TO 2.5X
*ROOKIES 351-360: 1X TO 2.5X
DRAFT DAY/375 ODDS ONE PER HOT PACK
STATED PRINT RUN 375 SER.#'d SETS

2004 Fleer Tradition Green

*VETS: 1.5X TO 4X BASIC CARDS
*ROOKIES 331-350: 1X TO 2.5X
*ROOKIES 351-360: 1X TO 2.5X

2004 Fleer Tradition Classic Combinations

COMBOS/250 ODDS 1:144 H, 1:360 R
STATED PRINT RUN 250 SER.#'d SETS
1CC Jerry Rice 5.00 12.00
Larry Fitzgerald
2CC Philip Rivers 10.00 25.00
Eli Manning
3CC Peyton Manning 12.50 25.00
Eli Manning
4CC Carson Palmer 2.00 5.00
Chris Perry
5CC Chad Pennington 10.00 25.00
Ben Roethlisberger
6CC Clinton Portis 2.00 5.00
Tatum Bell
7CC Tom Brady 4.00 10.00
Drew Henson
8CC Jeremy Shockey 2.00 5.00
Kellen Winslow Jr.
9CC Michael Vick 2.50 6.00
Kevin Jones
10CC Roy Williams S 4.00 10.00
Sean Taylor
11CC Ricky Williams 2.00 5.00
Roy Williams WR
12CC Anquan Boldin 2.00 5.00
Greg Jones
13CC Chad Johnson 3.00 8.00
Steven Jackson
14CC Byron Leftwich 1.50 4.00
Reggie Williams
15CC Charles Rogers 2.00 5.00
Roy Williams WR
16CC Brett Favre 8.00 20.00
Philip Rivers
17CC Randy Moss 2.00 5.00
Rashaun Woods
18CC Chris Chambers 2.00 5.00
Lee Evans
19CC Drew Henson 1.50 4.00
Julius Jones
20CC Patrick Ramsey 1.50 4.00
J.P. Losman

2004 Fleer Tradition Gridiron Tributes

COMPLETE SET (20) 15.00 40.00
STATED ODDS 1:6 HOB/RET
1GT Steve McNair .75 2.00
2GT Tom Brady 1.50 4.00
3GT Peyton Manning 1.50 4.00
4GT Chad Pennington .75 2.00
5GT Donovan McNabb .75 2.00
6GT Brett Favre 2.00 5.00
7GT Jerry Rice 1.50 4.00
8GT Emmitt Smith 2.00 5.00
9GT Ricky Williams .60 1.50
10GT Priest Holmes .75 2.00
11GT LaDainian Tomlinson .75 2.00
12GT Jeremy Shockey .60 1.50
13GT Byron Leftwich .60 1.50
14GT Marvin Harrison .75 2.00
15GT Jamal Lewis .60 1.50
16GT Ahman Green .60 1.50
17GT Brian Urlacher .75 2.00
18GT Michael Vick 1.00 2.50
19GT Clinton Portis .75 2.00
20GT Randy Moss .75 2.00

2004 Fleer Tradition Gridiron Tributes Game Used

STATED ODDS 1:51 HOB, 1:192 RET
*PATCH/50: 1X TO 2.5X BASIC JSY
PATCH STATED PRINT RUN 50
GTAG Ahman Green 2.50 6.00
GTBF Brett Favre 8.00 20.00
GTBL Byron Leftwich 2.50 6.00
GTBU Brian Urlacher 3.00 8.00
GTCP Chad Pennington 3.00 8.00
GTCP2 Clinton Portis 3.00 8.00
GTDM Donovan McNabb 3.00 8.00
GTES Emmitt Smith 8.00 20.00
GTJL Jamal Lewis 2.50 6.00
GTJR Jerry Rice 6.00 15.00
GTJS Jeremy Shockey 2.50 6.00
GTLT LaDainian Tomlinson 3.00 8.00
GTMH Marvin Harrison 3.00 8.00
GTMV Michael Vick 4.00 10.00
GTPH Priest Holmes 3.00 8.00
GTPM Peyton Manning 6.00 15.00
GTRM Randy Moss 3.00 8.00
GTRW Ricky Williams 2.50 6.00
GTSM Steve McNair 3.00 8.00
GTTB Tom Brady 6.00 15.00

2004 Fleer Tradition Rookie Hat's Off

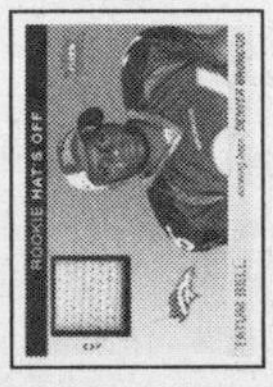

HAT'S OFF/100 ODDS 1:9 HOT PACKS
HOBR Ben Roethlisberger 20.00 50.00
HOCP Chris Perry 5.00 12.00
HOEM Eli Manning 20.00 50.00
HOGJ Greg Jones 4.00 10.00
HOJJ Julius Jones 5.00 12.00
HOJL J.P. Losman 5.00 12.00
HOKJ Kevin Jones 5.00 12.00
HOKW Kellen Winslow Jr. 6.00 15.00
HOLE Lee Evans 6.00 15.00
HOLF Larry Fitzgerald 15.00 40.00
HOMC Michael Clayton 5.00 12.00
HOMJ Michael Jenkins 6.00 15.00
HOPR Philip Rivers 15.00 40.00
HORW Roy Williams WR 6.00 15.00
HORW2 Rashaun Woods 4.00 10.00
HORW3 Reggie Williams 5.00 12.00
HOSJ Steven Jackson 10.00 25.00
HOTB Tatum Bell 5.00 12.00

2004 Fleer Tradition Rookie Throwback Threads Footballs

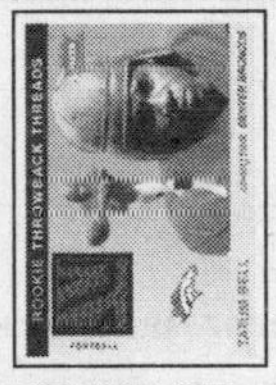

FOOTBALL ODDS 1:108 HOB, 1:480 RET
*HELMETS: .6X TO 1.5X FOOTBALLS
HELMET ODDS 1:360 HOB, 1:960 RET
*JERSEYS: .3X TO .8X FOOTBALLS
JERSEY ODDS 1:58 HOB, 1:240 RET
*JERSEY/BALL: 1X TO 2.5X FOOTBALLS
JSY/BALL PRINT RUN 50 SER.#'d SETS
*JERSEY/HELMET: 1.5X TO 4X FOOTBALLS
JSY/HELMET PRINT RUN 25 SER.#'d SETS
TTBR Ben Roethlisberger 20.00 50.00
TTCP Chris Perry 3.00 8.00
TTEM Eli Manning Blue 15.00 40.00
TTGJ Greg Jones 2.50 6.00
TTJJ Julius Jones 3.00 8.00
TTJL J.P. Losman 3.00 8.00
TTKJ Kevin Jones 3.00 8.00
TTKW Kellen Winslow Jr. Wht 4.00 10.00
TTLE Lee Evans 4.00 10.00
TTLF Larry Fitzgerald 10.00 25.00
TTLM Luke McCown 3.00 8.00
TTMC Michael Clayton 3.00 8.00
TTMJ Michael Jenkins 4.00 10.00
TTMS Matt Schaub 8.00 20.00
TTPR Philip Rivers 10.00 25.00
TTRW Roy Williams WR 4.00 10.00
TTSJ Steven Jackson 6.00 15.00
TTTB Tatum Bell 3.00 8.00
TTEM2 Eli Manning Wht 15.00 40.00
TTKW2 Kellen Winslow Jr. Blue 4.00 10.00
TTRW2 Rashaun Woods 2.50 6.00
TTRW3 Reggie Williams 3.00 8.00

2004 Fleer Tradition Rookie Throwback Threads Dual Jerseys

STATED PRINT RUN 100 SER.#'d SETS
*PATCH/75: .5X TO 1.2X BASIC DUAL
PATCH PRINT RUN 75 SER.#'d SETS
EMEM Eli Manning Dual 25.00 60.00
EMKW Eli Manning 25.00 60.00
Kellen Winslow Jr.
EMPR Eli Manning 25.00 60.00
Philip Rivers
JLLM J.P. Losman 6.00 15.00
Luke McCown
KJRW Kevin Jones 8.00 20.00
Roy Williams WR
KWKW Kellen Winslow Dual 8.00 20.00
KWLM Kellen Winslow Jr. 8.00 20.00
Luke McCown
MJCP Michael Jenkins 8.00 20.00
Chris Perry
PRBR Philip Rivers 25.00 60.00
Ben Roethlisberger
RWTB Rashaun Woods 6.00 15.00
Tatum Bell
SJKJ Steven Jackson 12.00 30.00
Kevin Jones
SJTB Steven Jackson 12.00 30.00
Tatum Bell

2004 Fleer Tradition Signing Day

COMPLETE SET (15) 20.00 50.00
STATED ODDS 1:12 HOB, 1:24 RET
*CHROME/50: 2.5X TO 6X BASIC INSERT
CHROME PRINT RUN 50 SER.#'d SETS
1SD Eli Manning 5.00 12.00
2SD Larry Fitzgerald 2.00 5.00
3SD Ben Roethlisberger 5.00 12.00
4SD J.P. Losman .60 1.50
5SD Roy Williams WR .75 2.00
6SD Steven Jackson 1.25 3.00
7SD Rashaun Woods .50 1.25
8SD Reggie Williams .60 1.50
9SD Michael Jenkins .75 2.00
10SD Philip Rivers 3.00 8.00
11SD Drew Henson .50 1.25
12SD Kevin Jones .60 1.50
13SD Lee Evans .75 2.00
14SD Michael Clayton .60 1.50
15SD Chris Perry .60 1.50

1995 FlickBall NFL Helmets

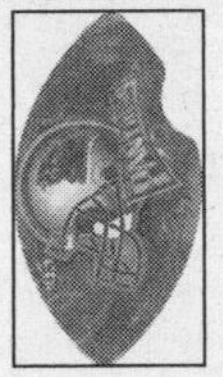

FlickBall produced its first full set of "paper footballs" in 1995 as NFL Team Helmets. Each flickball features an NFL helmet or Super Bowl logo and were packaged 6 per pack. There were two special inaugural season expansion team flickballs (#61-62) randomly inserted at the rate of 1:48 packs. They are not considered part of the complete set price.

COMPLETE SET (60) 8.00 20.00
1 Dallas Cowboys .20 .50
2 New York Giants .10 .30
3 Arizona Cardinals .10 .30
4 Philadelphia Eagles .10 .30
5 Washington Redskins .20 .50
6 Minnesota Vikings .10 .30
7 Chicago Bears .10 .30
8 Green Bay Packers .20 .50
9 Detroit Lions .10 .30
10 Tampa Bay Buccaneers .10 .30
11 San Francisco 49ers .20 .50
12 New Orleans Saints .10 .30
13 Atlanta Falcons .10 .30
14 Carolina Panthers .20 .50
15 St.Louis Rams .10 .30
16 New England Patriots .10 .30
17 Miami Dolphins .20 .50
18 Buffalo Bills .10 .30
19 Indianapolis Colts .10 .30
20 New York Jets .10 .30
21 Pittsburgh Steelers .20 .50
22 Cleveland Browns .10 .30
23 Cincinnati Bengals .10 .30
24 Jacksonville Jaguars .20 .50
25 Houston Oilers .10 .30
26 San Diego Chargers .10 .30
27 Oakland Raiders .20 .50
28 Kansas City Chiefs .10 .30
29 Denver Broncos .10 .30
30 Seattle Seahawks .10 .30
31 Super Bowl I .10 .30
32 Super Bowl II .10 .30
33 Super Bowl III .10 .30
34 Super Bowl IV .10 .30
35 Super Bowl V .10 .30
36 Super Bowl VI .10 .30
37 Super Bowl VII .10 .30
38 Super Bowl VIII .10 .30
39 Super Bowl IX .10 .30
40 Super Bowl X .10 .30
41 Super Bowl XI .10 .30
42 Super Bowl XII .10 .30
43 Super Bowl XIII .10 .30
44 Super Bowl XIV .10 .30
45 Super Bowl XV .10 .30
46 Super Bowl XVI .10 .30
47 Super Bowl XVII .10 .30
48 Super Bowl XVIII .10 .30
49 Super Bowl XIX .10 .30
50 Super Bowl XX .10 .30
51 Super Bowl XXI .10 .30
52 Super Bowl XXII .10 .30
53 Super Bowl XXIII .10 .30
54 Super Bowl XXIV .10 .30
55 Super Bowl XXV .10 .30
56 Super Bowl XXVI .10 .30
57 Super Bowl XXVII .10 .30
58 Super Bowl XXVIII .10 .30
59 Super Bowl XXIX .10 .30
60 Super Bowl XXX Logo .10 .30
61 Carolina Panthers 1.60 4.00
Inaugural Season
62 Jacksonville Jaguars 1.60 4.00
Inaugural Season

1995 FlickBall Prototypes

FlickBall produced this set as Prototypes for its 1996 premier FlickBall release. The 10-card, football-shaped set measures approximately 2 1/4" by 1 1/4" and features a finger-size cut-out space called the "flick zone" used to "flick" the card (ball) as part of a football game. The fronts feature color player photos while the backs include logos and the "Pre-Production" title. Card number seven is called a "Double Flick" and has a different player on each side. The cards are unnumbered and checklisted below in alphabetical order.

COMPLETE SET (10) 2.00 5.00
1 Bill Bates .07 .20
2 Jeff Blake .25 .60
3 Drew Bledsoe .30 .75
4 Brett Favre 1.00 2.50
5 Kevin Greene .07 .20
6 Daryl Johnston .07 .20
7 Steve McNair .50 1.25
Kerry Collins
8 Jerry Rice .40 1.00
9 Tamarick Vanover .15 .40
10 Chris Warren .07 .20

1996 FlickBall

FlickBall produced a complete 100-card set in 1996. The flickballs were packaged seven to a blister pack and included several random insert sets.

COMPLETE SET (100)	12.00	30.00
1 Troy Aikman	.60	1.50
2 Emmitt Smith	1.00	2.50
3 Michael Irvin	.15	.40
4 Deion Sanders	.30	.75
5 Bill Bates	.08	.25
6 Rodney Peete	.05	.15
7 Ricky Watters	.08	.25
8 Fred Barnett	.05	.15
9 Dave Krieg	.05	.15
10 Larry Centers	.08	.25
11 Garrison Hearst	.08	.25
12 Dave Brown	.05	.15
13 Rodney Hampton	.08	.25
14 Mike Sherrard	.05	.15
15 Gus Frerotte	.08	.25
16 Henry Ellard	.05	.15
17 Darrell Green	.05	.15
18 Scott Mitchell	.08	.25
19 Barry Sanders	1.20	3.00
20 Herman Moore	.08	.25
21 Erik Kramer	.05	.15
22 Curtis Conway	.08	.25
23 Jeff Graham	.05	.15
24 Brett Favre	1.20	3.00
25 Edgar Bennett	.08	.25
26 Robert Brooks	.08	.25
27 Reggie White	.15	.40
28 Warren Moon	.08	.25
29 Robert Smith	.15	.40
30 Cris Carter	.15	.40
31 Trent Dilfer	.15	.40
32 Errict Rhett	.08	.25
33 Santana Dotson	.05	.15
34 Steve Young	.50	1.25
35 Jerry Rice	.60	1.50
36 Merton Hanks	.05	.15
37 Ken Norton	.05	.15
38 Jesse Sapolu	.05	.15
39 Jim Everett	.05	.15
40 Willie Roaf	.05	.15
41 Tyrone Hughes	.05	.15
42 Chris Miller	.05	.15
43 Isaac Bruce	.15	.40
44 Shane Conlan	.05	.15
45 Jeff George	.08	.25
46 Eric Metcalf	.05	.15
47 Craig Heyward	.05	.15
48 Sam Mills	.05	.15
49 Mark Carrier WR	.05	.15
50 Brett Maxie	.05	.15
51 Jim Kelly	.15	.40
52 Andre Reed	.08	.25
53 Bruce Smith	.08	.25
54 Bryce Paup	.05	.15
55 Jim Harbaugh	.08	.25
56 Marshall Faulk	.30	.75
57 Sean Dawkins	.05	.15
58 Dan Marino	1.20	3.00
59 Terry Kirby	.08	.25
60 O.J. McDuffie	.08	.25
61 Bernie Parmalee	.05	.15
62 Wayne Chrebet	.08	.25
63 Adrian Murrell	.08	.25
64 Ronald Moore	.05	.15
65 Drew Bledsoe	.50	1.25
66 Vincent Brisby	.05	.15
67 Vincent Brown	.05	.15
68 Neil O'Donnell UER name spelled Niel	.08	.25
69 Eric Pegram	.05	.15
70 Rohn Stark	.05	.15
71 Kevin Greene	.08	.25
72 Greg Lloyd	.08	.25
73 Todd McNair	.05	.15
74 Mark Stepnoski	.05	.15
75 Bruce Matthews	.05	.15
76 Jeff Blake	.08	.25
77 Carl Pickens	.08	.25
78 John Copeland	.05	.15
79 Vinny Testaverde	.08	.25
80 Andre Rison	.08	.25
81 Leroy Hoard	.05	.15
82 Mark Brunell	.50	1.25
83 Cedric Tillman	.05	.15
84 Desmond Howard	.08	.25
85 Stan Humphries	.08	.25
86 Natrone Means	.08	.25
87 Junior Seau	.08	.25
88 Steve Bono	.05	.15
89 Marcus Allen	.15	.40
90 Derrick Thomas	.08	.25
91 Neil Smith	.05	.15
92 Rick Mirer	.08	.25
93 Chris Warren	.08	.25
94 Cortez Kennedy	.05	.15
95 Jeff Hostetler	.05	.15
96 Tim Brown	.15	.40
97 Terry McDaniel	.05	.15
98 John Elway	1.20	3.00
99 Shannon Sharpe	.08	.25
100 Steve Atwater	.05	.15

1996 FlickBall Commemoratives

These four inserts into 1996 FlickBall blister packs were hand numbered of 700. They feature four standout NFL players and were inserted at the rate of 1:357 packs.

COMPLETE SET (4)	28.00	70.00
C1 Emmitt Smith/25 Touchdowns	8.00	20.00
C2 Dan Marino Most passing yards	8.00	20.00
C3 Brett Favre	8.00	20.00
C4 Curtis Martin Rookie of the Year	6.00	15.00

1996 FlickBall DoubleFlicks

These 12-card were randomly inserted into 1996 FlickBall packs at the average rate of 1:3. They feature one player from the same position on each side of the card.

COMPLETE SET (12)	8.00	20.00
DF1 Dan Marino Drew Bledsoe	1.60	4.00
DF2 Troy Aikman Steve Young	1.00	2.50
DF3 Kerry Collins Steve McNair	.80	2.00
DF4 Eric Zeier Kordell Stewart	1.20	3.00
DF5 Emmitt Smith Marshall Faulk	1.20	3.00
DF6 Barry Sanders Errict Rhett	1.20	3.00
DF7 Curtis Martin Terrell Davis	2.00	5.00
DF8 Rashaan Salaam Napoleon Kaufman	.60	1.50
DF9 Michael Irvin Jerry Rice	.80	2.00
DF10 Tim Brown Cris Carter	.50	1.25
DF11 Joey Galloway J.J. Stokes	.60	1.50
DF12 Frank Sanders Michael Westbrook	.50	1.25

1996 FlickBall Hawaiian Flicks

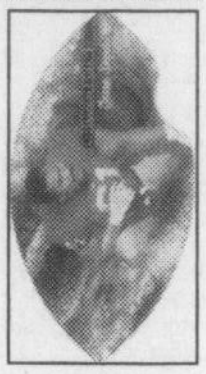

These 4-cards were randomly inserted into 1996 FlickBall blister packs at the rate of 1:8. They feature NFL players native to Hawaii.

COMPLETE SET (4)	2.00	5.00
H1 Mark Tuinei	.40	1.00
H2 Jesse Sapolu	.40	1.00
H3 Jason Elam	.40	1.00
H4 Junior Seau	.80	2.00

1996 FlickBall PreviewFlick Cowboys

Random 1996 FlickBall packs contained these 8-cards. They feature Dallas Cowboys players and carry a "P" card number prefix. The insertion ratio was 1:4 packs.

COMPLETE SET (8)	2.40	6.00
P1 Daryl Johnston	.40	1.00
P2 Jay Novacek	.40	1.00
P3 Kevin Williams WR	.30	.75
P4 Charles Haley	.40	1.00
P5 Darren Woodson	.30	.75
P6 Leon Lett	.30	.75
P7 Chad Hennings	.30	.75
P8 Mark Tuinei	.30	.75

1996 FlickBall Rookies

Randomly inserted into 1996 FlickBall packs at the rate of 1:2, these 20-cards feature top 1995 NFL rookies.

COMPLETE SET (20)	6.00	15.00
R1 Sherman Williams	.10	.30
R2 Mike Mamula	.10	.30
R3 Frank Sanders	.30	.75
R4 Steve Stenstrom	.10	.30
R5 Michael Westbrook	.40	1.00
R6 Warren Sapp	.15	.40
R7 Rashaan Salaam	.15	.40
R8 J.J. Stokes	.25	.60
R9 Kevin Carter	.10	.30
R10 Kerry Collins	.60	1.50
R11 Curtis Martin	.80	2.00
R12 Kordell Stewart	.80	2.00
R13 Steve McNair	1.00	2.50
R14 Rodney Thomas	.15	.40
R15 Eric Zeier	.15	.40
R16 Tony Boselli	.15	.40
R17 Tamarick Vanover	.15	.40
R18 Joey Galloway	.60	1.50
R19 Napoleon Kaufman	.50	1.25
R20 Terrell Davis	2.00	5.00

1996 FlickBall Team Sets

MGwhiz, Inc., the makers or FlickBall products, developed this set as a test. The three teams were primarily distributed in their respective areas. Each team was individually packaged with five players and one team helmet mounted on a display backer board. We've added the team name initials to the card numbers below to assist with cataloging. There are no prefixes on the actual card numbers.

COMPLETE SET (18)	6.00	15.00
COMP.COWBOYS SET (6)	2.80	7.00
COMP.VIKINGS SET (6)	1.40	3.50
COMP.PACKERS SET (6)	2.00	5.00
DC1 Troy Aikman	.80	2.00
DC2 Deion Sanders	.50	1.25
DC3 Emmitt Smith	1.20	3.00
DC4 Daryl Johnston	.30	.75
DC5 Cowboys Helmet	.20	.50
DC6 Darren Woodson	.20	.50
MV1 Warren Moon	.30	.75
MV2 Cris Carter	.30	.75
MV3 Robert Smith	.30	.75
MV4 Qadry Ismail	.20	.50
MV5 Vikings Helmet	.20	.50
MV6 David Palmer	.20	.50
GBP1 Brett Favre	1.60	4.00
GBP2 Edgar Bennett	.30	.75
GBP3 Reggie White	.40	1.00
GBP4 Robert Brooks	.60	1.50
GBP5 Packers Helmet	.20	.50
GBP6 George Teague	.20	.50

1997 FlickBall ProFlick

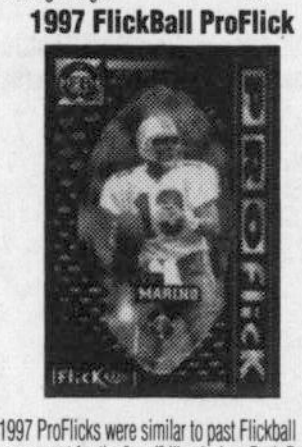

The 1997 ProFlicks were similar to past Flickball releases except for the "card" like design. Each ProFlick was produced and inserted in a 2" by 3" holder that roughly resembles a card. Packs contained 4-ProFlicks with one of the four being from the foil parallel set. A six-piece Rookies insert set was also produced.

COMPLETE SET (44)	12.00	30.00
1 Troy Aikman	.80	2.00
2 Terry Allen	.30	.75
3 Jerome Bettis	.30	.75
4 Drew Bledsoe	.60	1.50
5 Tim Brown	.30	.75
6 Isaac Bruce	.30	.75
7 Mark Brunell	.80	2.00
8 Larry Centers	.08	.25
9 Mark Chmura	.15	.40
10 Kerry Collins	.30	.75
11 Terrell Davis	1.20	3.00
12 Ty Detmer	.15	.40
13 John Elway	1.60	4.00
14 Marshall Faulk	.30	.75
15 Brett Favre	1.60	4.00
16 Joey Galloway	.40	1.00
17 Kevin Greene	.08	.25
18 Jim Harbaugh	.15	.40
19 Desmond Howard	.15	.40
20 Brad Johnson	.30	.75
21 Napoleon Kaufman	.30	.75
22 Erik Kramer	.08	.25
23 Dan Marino	1.60	4.00
24 Curtis Martin	.50	1.25
25 Tony Martin	.15	.40
26 Steve McNair	.60	1.50
27 Natrone Means	.15	.40
28 Herman Moore	.15	.40
29 Adrian Murrell	.15	.40
30 Carl Pickens	.15	.40
31 Jerry Rice	.80	2.00
32 Rashaan Salaam	.15	.40
33 Barry Sanders	1.60	4.00
34 Deion Sanders	.40	1.00
35 Junior Seau	.15	.40
36 Emmitt Smith	1.20	3.00
37 Jimmy Smith	.15	.40
38 Kordell Stewart	.40	1.00
39 Vinny Testaverde	.15	.40
40 Herschel Walker	.15	.40
41 Ricky Watters	.15	.40
42 Reggie White	.30	.75
43 Steve Young	.30	.75
44 Ray Zellars	.08	.25

1997 FlickBall ProFlick Foils

ProFlick packs contained four-ProFlicks with one of the four being from this foil parallel set. Each foil "card" is a parallel to the base cards with a prismatic foil design on the cardfronts.

COMPLETE SET (44)	25.00	60.00
*FOILS: .8X TO 2X BASIC CARDS		

1997 FlickBall ProFlick QB Greats

Six top NFL quarterbacks are featured in this ProFlick set. Each of the "cards" was printed in both standard card stock as well as prismatic silver foil stock and randomly inserted into special retail packs.

COMPLETE SET (6)	15.00	40.00
*FOIL: .6X TO 1.5X BASIC INSERTS		
QB1 Troy Aikman	1.50	4.00
QB2 Drew Bledsoe	1.25	3.00
QB3 Mark Brunell	1.00	2.50
QB4 John Elway	3.00	8.00
QB5 Brett Favre	3.00	8.00
QB6 Dan Marino	3.00	8.00

1997 FlickBall ProFlick Rookies

This 6-card set was randomly inserted into 1997 ProFlicks packs. Each features a top 1996 NFL rookie. Reportedly, they were inserted at the rate of 1:48 packs.

COMPLETE SET (6)	30.00	50.00
*FOIL: .6X TO 1.5X BASIC INSERTS		
R1 Karim Abdul-Jabbar	2.00	5.00
R2 Eddie George	4.00	10.00
R3 Terry Glenn	2.50	6.00
R4 Kevin Hardy	1.50	4.00
R5 Marvin Harrison	5.00	12.00
R6 Keyshawn Johnson	3.00	8.00

1997 FlickBall QB Club

MGwhiz, Inc., the makers or FlickBall products, developed this set featuring members of Quarterback Club. Two groups of six players each were packaged mounted on a display backer board, which was numbered of 2-different boards made. We've priced the flickballs separately, although they're most commonly sold in intact on sheets (display boards) of six.

COMPLETE SET (12)	4.00	10.00
1 Troy Aikman	.40	1.00
2 Jerry Rice	.40	1.00
3 Brett Favre	.80	2.00
4 John Elway	.80	2.00
5 Junior Seau	.20	.50
6 Jim Harbaugh	.20	.50
7 Dan Marino	.80	2.00
8 Emmitt Smith	.60	1.50
9 Steve Young	.30	.75
10 Drew Bledsoe	.30	.75
11 Barry Sanders	.80	2.00
12 Mark Brunell	.30	.75

2003 Flipp Sports Booklets

These booklets were issued to show, if fanned in quick order, two fast action photos of the featured player(s). Each player is mentioned on the outside covers and the inside covers feature biographical information as well as career statistics. Since these booklets are not numbered, we have sequenced them alphabetically.

1 Tiki Barber Jeremy Shockey	1.25	3.00
2 Jerry Rice	2.00	5.00

1974 Florida Blazers WFL Team Issue

These photos were issued by the team for promotional purposes and fan mail requests. Each includes a black and white image printed above the subject's name and team logo. Each measures 5 1/2" by 7."

COMPLETE SET (10)	25.00	60.00
1 Chuck Beatty	3.00	8.00
2 Bob Davis	3.00	8.00
3 Billy Hobbs	3.00	8.00
4 Billie Hayes	3.00	8.00
5 Rommie Loudd Mgr.	3.00	8.00
6 Jack Pardee CO	4.00	10.00
7 Tommy Reamon	3.00	8.00
8 John Ricca	3.00	8.00
9 Lou Ross	3.00	8.00
10 Paul Vellano	3.00	8.00

1988 Football Heroes Sticker Book

This sticker book contains 20 pages and measures approximately 9 1/4" by 12 1/2". It serves as an introduction to American football, with a discussion of how the game is played and a glossary of terms. The bulk of the book discusses various positions (e.g., quarterbacks, running backs, tight ends, wide receivers, kickers, offensive linemen, and defensive linemen), and outstanding NFL players who fill these positions. The stickers are approximately 3" in height and issued on two sheets, with 15 stickers per sheet. They are to be pasted on a glossy "Football Heroes" poster, which has an imitation-wood picture frame and slots for only 15 player stickers. The cards are unnumbered and checklisted below in alphabetical order.

COMPLETE SET (30)	125.00	250.00
1 Marcus Allen	4.00	10.00
2 Gary Anderson K	1.50	4.00
3 Brian Bosworth	2.00	5.00
4 Anthony Carter	2.00	5.00
5 Deron Cherry	1.50	4.00
6 Eric Dickerson	2.00	5.00
7 John Elway	12.50	25.00
8 Bo Jackson	5.00	12.00
9 Rich Karlis	1.50	4.00
10 Bernie Kosar	2.00	5.00
11 Steve Largent	4.00	10.00
12 Mick Luckhurst	1.50	4.00
13 Dexter Manley	1.50	4.00
14 Dan Marino	15.00	30.00
15 Jim McMahon	2.00	5.00
16 Joe Montana	20.00	40.00
17 Joe Morris	1.50	4.00
18 Anthony Munoz	2.00	5.00
19 Ozzie Newsome	2.00	5.00
20 Walter Payton	20.00	40.00
21 William Perry	2.00	5.00
22 Jerry Rice	10.00	20.00
23 Ricky Sanders	1.50	4.00
24 Phil Simms	2.00	5.00
25 Mike Singletary	2.50	6.00
26 Dwight Stephenson	2.00	5.00
27 Lawrence Taylor	2.50	6.00
28 Herschel Walker	2.50	6.00
29 Doug Williams	2.00	5.00
30 Kellen Winslow	2.00	5.00

1985-88 Football Immortals

This set was produced and released in factory set form in 1985, 1987 and 1988. With a few exceptions, the majority of the cards in the factory sets are exactly the same therefore they are combined below. The 1985 set had 135 cards and the 1987 and 1988 sets had 142 cards. In the checklist below the variation cards are listed using the following convention, that the A (or first) variety is from 1985 and the B variety is the version that was released with the 1987 and 1988 sets. Cards 6-128 are essentially in alphabetical order by subject's name. The cards are standard size. The horizontal card backs are light green and black on white card stock. The card photos are in black and white inside two color borders. The outer, thicker border is gold metallic. The inner border is color coded according to the number of the card, red border (1-45), blue border (46-90), green border (91-135), and yellow border (136-144). The set is titled "Football Immortals" at the top of every cardfront. Since all members of the set are Football Hall of Famers, their year of induction is given on the front and back of each card.

COMPLETE SET (150)	100.00	200.00
COMP.FACT.SET 1985 (135)	15.00	30.00
COMP.FACT.SET 1987 (142)	50.00	100.00
1 Pete Rozelle	.75	2.00
2 Joe Namath	1.50	4.00
3 Frank Gatski	.75	2.00
4 O.J. Simpson	1.00	2.50
5 Roger Staubach	1.50	4.00
6 Herb Adderley	1.00	2.50
7 Lance Alworth	1.00	2.50
8 Doug Atkins	1.00	2.50
9 Red Badgro	.75	2.00
10 Cliff Battles	.75	2.00
11 Sammy Baugh	1.25	3.00
12 Raymond Berry	1.00	2.50
13 Charles W. Bidwill	.75	2.00
14 Chuck Bednarik	1.00	2.50
15 Bert Bell	.75	2.00
16 Bobby Bell	1.00	2.50
17 George Blanda	1.00	2.50
18 Jim Brown	1.50	4.00
19 Paul Brown	1.00	2.50
20 Roosevelt Brown	.75	2.00
21 Ray Flaherty	.75	2.00
22 Len Ford	.75	2.00
23 Dan Fortmann	.75	2.00
24 Bill George	.75	2.00
25 Art Donovan	1.00	2.50
26 Paddy Driscoll	.75	2.00
27 Jimmy Conzelman	.75	2.00
28 Willie Davis	1.00	2.50
29 Dutch Clark	1.00	2.50
30 George Connor	.75	2.00
31 Guy Chamberlin	.75	2.00
32 Jack Christiansen	.75	2.00
33 Tony Canadeo	1.00	2.50
34 Joe Carr	.75	2.00
35 Willie Brown	1.00	2.50
36 Dick Butkus	1.25	3.00
37 Bill Dudley	.75	2.00
38 Turk Edwards	1.00	2.50
39 Weeb Ewbank	.75	2.00
40 Tom Fears	.75	2.00
41 Otto Graham	1.25	3.00
42 Red Grange	1.25	3.00
43 Frank Gifford	1.00	2.50
44 Sid Gillman	.75	2.00
45 Forrest Gregg	1.00	2.50
46 Lou Groza	1.00	2.50
47 Joe Guyon	.75	2.00
48 George Halas	1.25	3.00
49 Ed Healey	.75	2.00
50 Mel Hein	.75	2.00
51 Fats Henry	.75	2.00
52 Arnie Herber	1.00	2.50
53 Bill Hewitt	.75	2.00
54 Clarke Hinkle	1.00	2.50
55 Elroy Hirsch	1.00	2.50
56 Robert(Cal) Hubbard	.75	2.00
57 Sam Huff	1.00	2.50
58 Lamar Hunt	.75	2.00
59 Don Hutson	1.00	2.50
60 Dave(Deacon) Jones	1.00	2.50
61 Sonny Jurgensen	1.00	2.50
62 Walt Kiesling	.75	2.00
63 Frank(Bruiser) Kinard	.75	2.00
64 Earl(Curly) Lambeau	1.00	2.50
65 Dick(Night Train)Lane	1.00	2.50
66 Yale Lary	.75	2.00
67 Dante Lavelli	1.00	2.50
68 Bobby Layne	1.00	2.50
69 Tuffy Leemans	.75	2.00
70 Bob Lilly	1.00	2.50
71 Vince Lombardi	2.50	6.00
72 Sid Luckman	1.00	2.50
73 Link Lyman	.75	2.00
74 Tim Mara	.75	2.00
75 Gino Marchetti	1.00	2.50
76 Geo.Preston Marshall	.75	2.00
77 Ollie Matson	1.00	2.50
78 George McAfee	.75	2.00
79 Mike McCormack	.75	2.00
80 Hugh McElhenny	1.00	2.50
81 Johnny Blood McNally	1.00	2.50
82 Mike Michalske	.75	2.00
83 Wayne Millner	.75	2.00
84 Bobby Mitchell	1.00	2.50
85 Ron Mix	.75	2.00
86 Lenny Moore	1.00	2.50
87 Marion Motley	1.00	2.50
88 George Musso	.75	2.00
89 Bronko Nagurski	1.50	4.00
90 Greasy Neale	.75	2.00
91 Ernie Nevers	.75	2.00
92 Ray Nitschke	1.00	2.50
93 Leo Nomellini	.75	2.00
94 Merlin Olsen	1.00	2.50
95 Jim Otto	1.00	2.50
96 Steve Owen	.75	2.00
97 Clarence(Ace) Parker	.75	2.00
98 Jim Parker	.75	2.00
99 Joe Perry	1.00	2.50
100 Pete Pihos	.75	2.00
101 Hugh(Shorty) Ray	.75	2.00
102 Dan Reeves OWN	.75	2.00
103 Jim Ringo	1.00	2.50
104 Andy Robustelli	1.00	2.50
105 Art Rooney	.75	2.00
106 Gale Sayers	1.25	3.00
107 Joe Schmidt	1.00	2.50
108 Bart Starr	1.50	4.00
109 Ernie Stautner	1.00	2.50
110 Ken Strong	.75	2.00
111 Joe Stydahar	.75	2.00
112 Charley Taylor	.75	2.00
113 Jim Taylor	1.00	2.50
114 Jim Thorpe	1.50	4.00
115 Y.A. Tittle	1.00	2.50
116 George Trafton	.75	2.00
117 Charley Trippi	1.00	2.50
118 Emlen Tunnell	.75	2.00
119 Bulldog Turner	1.00	2.50
120 Johnny Unitas	1.50	4.00
121 Norm Van Brocklin	1.00	2.50
122 Steve Van Buren	1.00	2.50
123 Paul Warfield	1.00	2.50
124 Bob Waterfield	1.00	2.50
125 Arnie Weinmeister	.75	2.00
126 Bill Willis	.75	2.00
127 Larry Wilson	.75	2.00
128 Alex Wojciechowicz	.75	2.00
129 Pro Football Hall of Fame (Entrance pictured)	.75	2.00
130A Jim Thorpe Statue	1.25	3.00
130B Doak Walker	2.50	6.00
131A Enshrinement Galleries	1.00	2.50
131B Willie Lanier	1.50	4.00
132 Pro Football Hall of Fame on Enshrinement Day (Aerial shot of crowd)	.75	2.00
133A Eric Dickerson Display	1.25	3.00
133B Paul Hornung	3.00	8.00
134A Walter Payton	2.50	6.00
134B Ken Houston	1.50	4.00
135A Super Bowl Display	1.00	2.50
135B Fran Tarkenton	4.00	10.00
136 Don Maynard	2.00	5.00
137 Larry Csonka	3.00	8.00
138 Joe Greene	3.00	8.00
139 Len Dawson	2.50	6.00
140 Gene Upshaw	1.50	4.00
141A Jim Langer	1.50	4.00
141B Fred Biletnikoff	10.00	20.00
142A John Henry Johnson	1.50	4.00
142B Mike Ditka	12.50	25.00
143 Jack Ham	10.00	20.00
144 Alan Page	10.00	20.00

1988 Foot Locker Slam Fest

This nine-card set was produced by Foot Locker to commemorate the "Foot Locker Slam Fest" slam dunk contest, televised on ESPN on May 17, 1988. The cards were given out in May at participating Foot Locker stores to customers. Between May 18 and July 31, customers could turn in the winner's card (Mike Conley) and receive a free pair of Wilson athletic shoes and 50 percent off any purchase at Foot Locker. These standard size cards (2 1/2" by 3 1/2") feature color posed shots of the participants, who were professional athletes from sports other than basketball. The pictures have magenta and blue borders on a white card face. A colored banner with the words "Foot Locker" overlays the top of the picture. A line drawing of a referee overlays the lower left corner of the picture. The backs are printed in blue on white and promote the slam dunk contest and an in-store contest. The cards are unnumbered and checklisted below in alphabetical order.

COMPLETE SET (9)	12.00	30.00
1 Carl Banks FB	.75	2.00
4 Bo Jackson BB FB	2.50	6.00
5 Keith Jackson FB	.75	2.00
7 Ricky Sanders FB	.75	2.00

1989 Foot Locker Slam Fest

This ten-card standard-size set was produced by Foot Locker and Nike to commemorate the "Foot Locker Slam Fest" slam dunk contest, which was televised during halftimes of NBC college basketball games through March 12, 1989. The cards were wrapped in cellophane and issued with one stick of gum. They were given out at participating Foot Locker stores upon request with a purchase. The cards feature color posed shots of the participants, who were professional athletes from sports other than basketball. A banner with the words "Foot Locker" traverses the top of the card face. The cards are unnumbered and checklisted below in alphabetical order.

COMPLETE SET (10)	3.20	8.00
2 Keith Jackson FB	.20	.50
4 Eric Dickerson FB	.60	1.50
8 Mike Quick FB	.20	.50

1991 Foot Locker Slam Fest

This 30-card standard-size set was issued by Foot Locker in three ten-card series to commemorate the "Foot Locker Slam Fest" dunk contest televised during halftimes of NBC college basketball games through March 10, 1991. Each set contained two Domino's Pizza coupons and a 5.00 discount coupon on any purchase of 50.00 or more at Foot Locker. The set was released in substantial quantity after the promotional coupons expired. The fronts feature both posed and action photos enclosed in an arch like double red borders. The card top carries a blue border with "Foot Locker" in blue print on a white background. Beneath the photo appears "Limited Edition" and the player's name. The backs present career highlights, card series, and numbers placed within an arch of double red borders. The player's name and team name appear in black lettering at the bottom. The cards are numbered on the back; the card numbering below adds the number 10 to each card number in the second series and 20 to each card number in the third series.

COMPLETE SET (30)	2.00	5.00
6 Deion Sanders BB FB	.30	.75
8 Tim Brown FB	.10	.25
22 Bo Jackson BB FB	.10	.25
27 Eric Dickerson FB	.06	.15

2005 Ford Promos

3 Brett Favre	2.00	5.00

1966 Fortune Shoes

Fortune Shoe Company sponsored this set of 9" by 12" black-and-white pencil sketches. The unnumbered cards are blankbacked and were printed on thick paper stock. Any additions to this list would be appreciated.

COMPLETE SET (9)	125.00	250.00
1 Roman Gabriel	12.50	25.00
2 Charley Johnson	10.00	20.00
3 John Henry Johnson	15.00	25.00
4 Don Meredith	15.00	30.00
5 Lenny Moore	15.00	25.00
6 Frank Ryan	10.00	20.00
7 Gale Sayers	25.00	50.00
8 Jim Taylor	15.00	30.00
9 John Unitas	25.00	50.00

2003 Fort Wayne Freedom UIF

1 Vernard Alsberry	.20	.50
2 Jason Battershell	.20	.50
3 Carlton Bragg	.20	.50
4 Andrae Brooks	.20	.50
5 Ron Brown	.20	.50
6 Lewis Carter	.20	.50
7 Pat Cavanaugh	.20	.50
8 Vbrian Ceaser	.20	.50
9 Jamar Cottee	.20	.50
10 Rachman Crable	.20	.50
11 Charles Dempsey	.20	.50
12 John Diettrich	.20	.50
13 Jeremy Dutcher	.20	.50
14 Alf Fertil	.20	.50
15 Rocky Harvey	.20	.50
16 Rich Huff (HC)	.20	.50
17 Robin Johnson	.20	.50
18 Kevin Kemp	.20	.50
19 Dietrich Lapsley	.20	.50
20 Dayna Overton	.20	.50
21 Patrick Paulsen	.20	.50
22 Remele Penick	.20	.50
23 Bobby Petras	.20	.50
24 Adrian Reese	.20	.50
25 Juliamn Reese	.20	.50
26 Antoine Taylor	.20	.50
27 Evan Triggs	.20	.50
28 Lamont White	.20	.50
29 Team Card	.20	.50

2004 Fort Wayne Freedom UIF

1 Al Baysinger	.20	.50
2 Chris Bell	.20	.50
3 Andrae Brooks	.20	.50
4 Nick Brownfield	.20	.50
5 Lewis Carter	.20	.50
6 Jamar Cottee	.20	.50
7 Rachman Crable	.20	.50
8 John Diettrich	.20	.50
9 Alf Fertil	.20	.50
10 Alen Ganaway	.20	.50
11 Jamie Hanton	.20	.50
12 Rocky Harvey	.20	.50
13 Scott Heighland	.20	.50
14 Lamar Martin	.20	.50
15 Dayna Overton	.20	.50
16 Remele Penick	.20	.50
17 Bobby Petras	.20	.50
18 Adrian Reese	.20	.50
19 Ernie Smith	.20	.50
20 Luther Stroder	.20	.50
21 Jremy Swonger	.20	.50
22 Antoine Taylor	.20	.50
23 Adam Walter	.20	.50
24 Adam Wheatley	.20	.50
25 Bryan White	.20	.50
26 Team Card	.20	.50

2005 Fort Wayne Freedom UIF

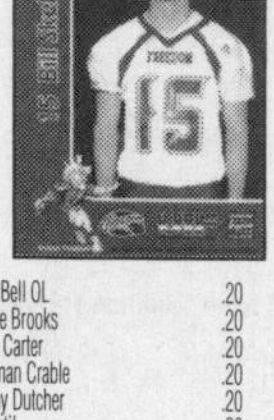

1 Chris Bell OL	.20	.50
2 Andrae Brooks	.20	.50
3 Lewis Carter	.20	.50
4 Rachman Crable	.20	.50
5 Jeremy Dutcher	.20	.50
6 Alf Fertil	.20	.50
7 Alan Ganaway	.20	.50
8 Jamarkus Gorman	.20	.50
9 Mike Hanley	.20	.50
10 Rocky Harvey	.20	.50
11 Scott Heighland	.20	.50
12 Lamar Martin	.20	.50
13 Terrance Miles	.20	.50
14 Dayna Overton	.20	.50
15 Remele Oenick	.20	.50
16 Bobby Petras	.20	.50
17 Adrian Reese	.20	.50
18 Scott Russell	.20	.50
19 Bill Skelton	.20	.50
20 Carlos Smith	.20	.50
21 Luther Stroder	.20	.50
22 Noah Swartz	.20	.50
23 Evan Triggs	.20	.50
24 Bryan White	.20	.50
25 Team Card	.20	.50

2006 Fort Wayne Freedom UIF

1 Andrae Brooks	.20	.50
2 Lewis Carter	.20	.50
3 Rachman Crable	.20	.50
4 Doug Daniel	.20	.50
5 Alf Fertil	.20	.50
6 Alan Ganaway	.20	.50
7 Jamarkus Gorman	.20	.50
8 Randall Guzman	.20	.50
9 Michael Hanley	.20	.50
10 Rocky Harvey	.20	.50
11 Scott Heighland	.20	.50
12 Jamie Holman	.20	.50
13 Mike Lane	.20	.50
14 Lamar Martin	.20	.50
15 Ronnie McCrae	.20	.50
16 Dan Musielewicz	.20	.50
17 Keith Recker	.20	.50
18 Adrian Reese	.20	.50
19 Scott Russell	.20	.50
20 Bill Skelton	.20	.50
21 Luther Stroder	.20	.50
22 Noah Swartz	.20	.50
23 Bryan White	.20	.50
24 Johnell Wyatte	.20	.50

2008 Fort Wayne Freedon CIFL

COMPLETE SET (24)	5.00	10.00
1 Shonn Bell	.30	.75
2 Lewis Carter	.20	.50
3 Brian Clawson	.20	.50
4 Kota-Carone Colors	.20	.50
5 Travis Colston	.20	.50

6 Thad Conley	.20	.50
7 Rachman Crable	.20	.50
8 Alfred Fertil	.20	.50
9 Rocky Harvey	.20	.50
10 Scott Heighland	.20	.50
11 Eric Hooks	.20	.50
12 Justin Hoover	.20	.50
13 Brandon Hurd	.20	.50
14 Glenn Johnson	.20	.50
15 Jeffrey Lewis	.20	.50
16 Ronnie McCrae	.20	.50
17 Remele Penick	.20	.50
18 Craig Plaster	.20	.50
19 Adrian Reese	.20	.50
20 JaRell Smith	.20	.50
21 Luther Stroder	.20	.50
22 Antoine Taylor	.20	.50
23 Bo Thompson	.20	.50
24 Team Card	.20	.50

1953-55 49ers Burgermeister Beer Team Photos

These oversized (roughly 6 1/4" by 9") color team photos were sponsored by Burgermeister Beer and distributed in the San Francisco area. Each were printed on thin card stock and featured a Burgermeister ad on the back along with the 49ers logo.

1953 San Francisco 49ers	25.00	50.00
1954 San Francisco 49ers	25.00	50.00
1955 San Francisco 49ers	25.00	50.00

1955 49ers Christopher Dairy

These cards were part of milk cartons released around 1955 by Christopher Dairy Farms. Two players were apparently included on each carton and printed in blue and white with the player's name and position next to the image. Three unfolded cartons were uncovered in 2001, but it is not yet known if these 6 constitute a full set. Any additions to this list are appreciated.

COMPLETE SET (6)	500.00	800.00
1 John Henry Johnson	125.00	200.00
2 Clay Matthews Sr.	75.00	125.00
3 Dick Moegle	75.00	125.00
4 Joe Perry	150.00	250.00
5 Dob Ct.Clair	00.00	150.00
6 Bob Toneff	75.00	125.00

1955 49ers Team Issue

This 38-card set measures approximately 4 1/4" by 6 1/4". The front features a black and white posed action photo enclosed by a white border, with the player's signature across the bottom portion of the picture. The back of the card lists the player's name, position, height, weight, and college, along with basic biographical information. Many of the cards in this and the other similar team issue sets are only distinguishable as to year by comparing text on the card back; the first few words of text are provided for many of the cards parenthetically below. The set was available direct from the team as part of a package for their fans. The cards are unnumbered and hence are listed alphabetically for convenience.

COMPLETE SET (38)	250.00	400.00
1 Frankie Albert CO	5.00	10.00
(One of Red ...)		
2 Joe Arenas	4.00	8.00
(The All-Time ...)		
3 Harry Babcock	4.00	8.00
4 Ed Beatty	4.00	8.00
(After searching ...)		
5 Phil Bengtson CO	4.00	8.00
(An All-America ...)		
6 Rex Berry	4.00	8.00
(One of the ...)		
7 Hardy Brown	4.00	10.00
8 Marion Campbell	4.00	10.00
9 Al Carapella	4.00	8.00
10 Paul Carr	4.00	8.00
(Drafted by ...)		
11 Maury Duncan	4.00	8.00
12 Bob Hantla	4.00	8.00
13 Carroll Hardy	4.00	8.00
14 Matt Hazeltine	4.00	8.00
(Won All-America ...)		
15 Howard(Red) Hickey CO	4.00	8.00
(After 14 years ...)		
16 Doug Hogland	4.00	8.00
17 Bill Johnson	4.00	8.00
(Here's one ... with ten lines of text)		
18 John Henry Johnson	15.00	30.00
(NFL rookies who ...)		
19 Eldred Kraemer	4.00	8.00
20 Bud Laughlin	4.00	8.00
21 Bobby Luna	4.00	8.00
22 George Maderos	4.00	8.00
(The greatest ...)		
23 Clay Matthews Sr.	4.00	10.00
24 Hugh McElhenny	15.00	30.00
(NFL Commissioner ...)		
25 Dick Moegle	5.00	10.00
(25 text lines)		
26 Leo Nomellini	12.50	25.00
(Leo was ...)		
27 Lou Palatella	4.00	8.00
(Like Eldred ...)		
28 Joe Perry	15.00	30.00
(First man ...)		
29 Charley Powell	4.00	8.00
(Charley, ...)		
30 Gordy Soltau	4.00	8.00
(One of the ...)		
31 Bob St. Clair	12.50	25.00
(In two years ...)		
32 Tom Stolhandske	4.00	8.00
33 Roy Storey ANN	4.00	8.00
Bob Fouts ANN		
Red Strader CO		
34 Red Strader CO	4.00	8.00
35 Y.A. Tittle	20.00	40.00
(Jinxed by ...)		
36 Bob Toneff	4.00	8.00
(Rated the ...)		
37 Billy Wilson	4.00	10.00
(Named the ...)		
38 Sid Youngelman	4.00	8.00

1956 49ers Team Issue

This set measures approximately 4 1/8" by 6 1/4". The front features a black and white posed action photo enclosed by a white border, with the player's signature across the bottom portion of the picture. The back of the card lists the player's name, position, height, weight, and college, along with basic biographical information. Many of the cards in this and the other similar team issue sets are only distinguishable as to year by comparing text on the card back; the first few words of text are provided for many of the cards parenthetically below. The set was available direct from the team as part of a package for their fans. The cards are unnumbered and hence are listed alphabetically for convenience. It is likely that this set contains more than the number of cards listed below. Any additions to this list are appreciated.

COMPLETE SET (35)	200.00	350.00
1 Frankie Albert CO	5.00	10.00
(Frank Culling Albert, who ...)		
2 Joe Arenas	4.00	8.00
(One of the NFL's ...)		
3 Ed Beatty	4.00	8.00
(Traded by ...)		
4 Phil Bengtson CO	4.00	8.00
(Phil is known ...)		
5 Rex Berry	4.00	8.00
(Unanimously ...)		
6 Bruce Bosley	4.00	8.00
(Bosley was ...)		
7 Fred Bruney	4.00	8.00
8 Paul Carr	4.00	8.00
(A redshirt draft ...)		
9 Clyde Conner	4.00	8.00
(One of the ...)		
10 Paul Goad	4.00	8.00
11 Matt Hazeltine	4.00	8.00
(Matt reported ...)		
12 Ed Henke	4.00	8.00
(After attending ...)		
13 Bill Herchman	4.00	8.00
(Bill was ...)		
14 Howard(Red) Hickey CO	4.00	8.00
(Red Hickey ...)		
15 Bill Jessup	4.00	8.00
(Bill is one ...)		
16 Bill Johnson	4.00	8.00
(Here's one ... with nine lines of text)		
17 John Henry Johnson	18.00	30.00
(According to coach ...)		
18 George Maderos	4.00	8.00
(A 21st ...)		
19 Hugh McElhenny	15.00	30.00
(The King has been ...)		
20 Dick Moegle	5.00	10.00
(San ... with/11 lines of text)		
21 Earl Morrall	12.00	20.00
(Unanimous All-America ...)		
22 George Morris	4.00	8.00
23 Leo Nomellini	12.50	25.00
(A 49er standby ...)		
24 Lou Palatella	4.00	8.00
(A tackle at Pitt ...)		
25 Joe Perry	15.00	30.00
(Joe is ...)		
26 Charley Powell	4.00	8.00
(Equipped ...)		
27 Leo Rucka	4.00	8.00
28 Ed Sharkey	4.00	8.00
29 Charles Smith	4.00	8.00
30 Gordy Soltau	4.00	8.00
(No all-time ...)		
31 Roy Storey ANN	4.00	8.00
Bob Fouts ANN		
(blankbacked)		
32 Bob St. Clair	10.00	20.00
(Tallest man ...)		
33 Y.A. Tittle	25.00	40.00
(Full handle is ...)		
34 Bob Toneff	4.00	8.00
(Another ...)		
35 Billy Wilson	4.00	8.00
(Billy is ...)		

1956-61 49ers Falstaff Beer Team Photos

These oversized (roughly 6 1/4" by 9") color team photos were sponsored by Falstaff Beer and distributed in the San Francisco area. Each was printed on card stock and features advertising and/or photos of the coaching staff on the back. Note that blankbacked reprints of the photos have circulated for a number of years.

1956 San Francisco 49ers	20.00	40.00
1957 San Francisco 49ers	20.00	40.00
1958 San Francisco 49ers	20.00	40.00
1959 San Francisco 49ers	20.00	40.00
1960 San Francisco 49ers	20.00	40.00
1961 San Francisco 49ers	20.00	40.00

1957 49ers Team Issue

This 43-card set measures approximatey 4 1/8" by 6 1/4". The front features a black and white posed action photo enclosed by a white border, with the player's signature across the bottom portion of the picture. For those players who were included in the 1956 set, the same photos were used in the 1957 set, with the exception of Bill Johnson, who appears as a coach in the 1957 set. The back lists the player's name, position, height, weight, and college, along with basic biographical information. Many of the cards in this and the other similar team issue sets are only distinguishable as to year by comparing text on the card back; the first few words of text are provided for many of the cards parenthetically below. The set was available direct from the team as part of a package for their fans. The John Brodie card in this set predates his Topps and Fleer Rookie Cards by four years. The cards are unnumbered and hence are listed alphabetically for convenience.

COMPLETE SET (43)	250.00	400.00
1 Frankie Albert CO	5.00	10.00
(Frank Culling Albert played ... same as 1958)		
2 Joe Arenas	4.00	8.00
(Again in 1956 ...)		
3 Gene Babb	4.00	8.00
(Drafted 19th ...)		
4 Larry Barnes	4.00	8.00
5 Phil Bengtson CO	4.00	8.00
(Beginning his eighth ...)		
6 Bruce Bosley	4.00	8.00
(After a ... same as 1958)		
7 John Brodie	20.00	40.00
(According to ...)		
8 Paul Carr	4.00	8.00
(Versatile on ...)		
9 Clyde Conner	4.00	8.00
(Football ...)		
10 Ted Connolly	4.00	8.00
(The 49er ...)		
11 Bobby Cross	4.00	8.00
12 Mark Duncan CO	4.00	8.00
(Mark ... same as 1958)		
13 Bob Fouts ANN	4.00	8.00
Lon Simmons ANN		
Frankie Albert CO		
(Same as 1958)		
14 John Gonzaga	4.00	8.00
(One of the ...)		
15 Tom Harmon ANN	5.00	10.00
(Kids' ages are/11, 8, and 5)		
16 Matt Hazeltine	4.00	8.00
(An All-American ...)		
17 Ed Henke	4.00	8.00
(Studious-looking ...)		
18 Bill Herchman	4.00	8.00
(The 49ers' ...)		
19 Howard(Red) Hickey CO	4.00	8.00
(After 14 campaigns ... same as 1958)		
20 Bob Holladay	4.00	8.00
21 Bill Jessup	4.00	8.00
(One of the ...)		
22 Bill Johnson CO	4.00	8.00
(No all-time ... same as 1958)		
23 Marv Matuszak	4.00	8.00
(Traded to ...)		
24 Hugh McElhenny	12.50	25.00
(Sidelined ...)		
25 Dick Moegle	5.00	10.00
(An ... with/11 lines of text)		
26 Frank Morze	4.00	8.00
(The 49ers, used ...)		
27 Leo Nomellini	10.00	20.00
(He was ...)		
28 R.C. Owens	5.00	10.00
(If the ...)		
29 Lou Palatella	4.00	8.00
(Most ... same as 1956)		
30 Joe Perry	12.50	25.00
(The greatest ...)		
31 Charley Powell	4.00	8.00
(Name almost ...)		
32 Jim Ridlon	4.00	8.00
(Teaming with ...)		
33 Karl Rubke	4.00	8.00
(The 16th ...)		
34 J.D. Smith	5.00	10.00
(J.D.'s football ...)		
35 Gordy Soltau	4.00	8.00
(Already listed ...)		
36 Bob St. Clair	7.50	15.00
(A born leader ...)		
37 Bill Stits	4.00	8.00
(An All-American ...)		
38 Y.A. Tittle	20.00	40.00
(For sheer ...)		
39 Bob Toneff	4.00	8.00
(After a ...)		
40A Lynn Waldorf	4.00	8.00
Director of Personnel		
(Vertical text, Ministry misspelled 'Minstry' on back)		
40B Lynn Waldorf	4.00	8.00
Director of Personnel		
(Vertical text, Ministry spelled correctly on back)		
41 Val Joe Walker	4.00	8.00
42 Billy Wilson	4.00	8.00
(Born on ...)		
43 49ers Coaches	5.00	10.00
Bill Johnson		
Phil Bengtson		
Frankie Albert		
Mark Duncan		
Howard(Red) Hickey		
(Blankback)		

1958 49ers Team Issue

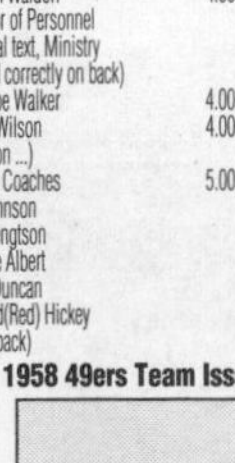

This 44-card set measures approximately 4 1/8" by 6 1/4". The front features a black and white posed action photo enclosed by a white border, with the player's signature across the bottom portion of the picture. The back lists the player's name, position, height, weight, and college, along with basic biographical information. Many of the cards in this and the other similar team issue sets are only distinguishable as to year by comparing text on the card back; the first few words of text are provided for many of the cards parenthetically below. The set was available direct from the team as part of a package for their fans. The John Brodie card in this set holds particular interest to some collectors in that it precedes Brodie's Topps and Fleer Rookie Cards by three years. The cards are unnumbered and hence are listed alphabetically for convenience.

COMPLETE SET (44)	250.00	400.00
1 Frankie Albert CO	5.00	10.00
(Frank Culling Albert played ... same as 1957)		
2 Bill Atkins	4.00	8.00
(Alabama ...)		
3 Gene Babb	4.00	8.00
(A great ...)		
4 Phil Bengtson CO	4.00	8.00
(Beginning his 9th ...)		
5 Bruce Bosley	4.00	8.00
(After a ... same as 1957)		
6 John Brodie	15.00	30.00
(With John ...)		
7 Clyde Conner	4.00	8.00
(In signing ... running pose)		
8 Ted Connolly	4.00	8.00
(When Santa Clara ...)		
9 Fred Dugan	4.00	8.00
(Butch Dugan ...)		
10 Mark Duncan CO	4.00	8.00
(Mark ... same as 1957)		
11 Bob Fouts ANN	4.00	8.00
Lon Simmons ANN		
Frankie Albert CO		
(Same as 1957)		
12 John Gonzaga	4.00	8.00
(Recommended ...)		
13 Tom Harmon ANN	5.00	10.00
(Kids' ages are/12, 9, and 6)		
14 Matt Hazeltine	4.00	8.00
(Improved ...)		
15 Ed Henke	4.00	8.00
(The Frank Buck ...)		
16 Bill Herchman	4.00	8.00
(A lineman's ...)		
17 Howard(Red) Hickey CO	4.00	8.00
(After 14 campaigns ... same as 1957)		
18 Bill Jessup	4.00	8.00
(Hard luck ...)		
19 Bill Johnson CO	4.00	8.00
(No all-time ... same as 1957)		
20 Marv Matuszak	4.00	8.00
(The best ...)		
21 Hugh McElhenny	12.50	25.00
(More people ...)		
22 Jerry Mertens	4.00	8.00
(A 20th draft selection& Jerry ...)		
23 Dick Moegle	5.00	10.00
(13 text lines)		
24 Dennit Morris	4.00	8.00
25 Frank Morze	4.00	8.00
(The 49ers drafted ...)		
26 Leo Nomellini	10.00	20.00
(Defensive ...)		
27 R.C. Owens	5.00	10.00
(There's always ...)		
28 Jim Pace	4.00	8.00
29 Lou Palatella	4.00	8.00
(When ...)		
30 Joe Perry	12.50	25.00
(The all-time ...)		
31 Jim Ridlon	4.00	8.00
(After a ...)		
32 Karl Rubke	4.00	8.00
(Desperately ...)		
33 J.D. Smith	5.00	10.00
(Used mainly ...)		
34 Gordy Soltau	4.00	8.00
(In his eight ...)		
35 Bob St. Clair	7.50	15.00
(The only ...)		
36 Bill Stits	4.00	8.00
(When the ...)		
37 John Thomas	4.00	8.00
(This is ...)		
38 Y.A. Tittle	17.50	35.00
(His real ...)		
39 Bob Toneff	4.00	8.00
(A chronic ...)		
40 Lynn Waldorf	4.00	8.00
Director of Personnel		
(Vertical text, Ministry spelled correctly on back)		
41 Billy Wilson	4.00	8.00
(Em Tunnell& great ...)		
42 John Wittenborn	4.00	8.00
(John ...)		
43 Abe Woodson	5.00	10.00
(The 49ers ...)		
44 49ers Coaches	5.00	10.00
Bill Johnson		
Mark Duncan		
Frankie Albert		
Joe Vetrano		
Red Hickey		
Phil Bengtson		
(blankbacked)		

1959 49ers Team Issue

This 45-card set measures approximately 4 1/8" by 6 1/4". The front features a black and white posed action photo enclosed by a white border, with the player's signature across the bottom portion of the picture. The back lists the player's name, position, height, weight, and college, along with basic biographical information. Many of the cards in this and the other similar team issue sets are only distinguishable as to year by comparing text on the card back; the first few words of text are provided for many of the cards parenthetically below. The set was available direct from the team as part of a package for their fans. The cards are unnumbered and hence are listed alphabetically for convenience.

COMPLETE SET (45)	250.00	400.00
1 Bill Atkins	4.00	8.00
(Played defensive ...)		
2 Dave Baker	4.00	8.00
(Rated the best ...)		
3 Bruce Bosley	4.00	8.00
(Starred as ...)		
4 John Brodie	12.50	25.00
(Led NFL ...)		
5 Jack Christiansen CO	7.50	15.00
6 Monte Clark	4.00	8.00
(One of the many ...)		
7 Clyde Conner	4.00	8.00
(Standing pose, jersey #88)/(In signing Clyde ...)		
8 Ted Connolly	4.00	8.00
(Realized his ...)		
9 Tommy Davis	4.00	8.00
(Red Hickey's prediction ...)		
10 Eddie Dove	4.00	8.00
11 Fred Dugan	4.00	8.00
(Made ...)		
12 Mark Duncan CO	4.00	8.00
(A versatile ...)		
13 Bob Fouts ANN	4.00	8.00
14 John Gonzaga	4.00	8.00
(One of few ...)		
15 Bob Harrison	4.00	8.00
(Bob topped off ...)		
16 Matt Hazeltine	4.00	8.00
(One of the ...)		
17 Ed Henke	4.00	8.00
(Suffered a ...)		
18 Bill Herchman	4.00	8.00
(Starting ...)		
19 Howard(Red) Hickey CO	4.00	8.00
(Baseball ...)		
20 Russ Hodges ANN	4.00	8.00
21 Bill Johnson CO	4.00	8.00
(Bill Johnson ...)		
22 Charlie Krueger	4.00	8.00
(A broken arm ...)		
23 Lenny Lyles	4.00	8.00
24 Hugh McElhenny	12.50	25.00
(One of the ...)		
25 Jerry Mertens	4.00	8.00
(A 20th draft selection last ...)		
26 Dick Moegle	5.00	10.00
(7 text lines)		
27 Frank Morze	4.00	8.00
(Transferred ...)		
28 Leo Nomellini	10.00	20.00
(Has never ...)		
29 Clancy Osborne	4.00	8.00
(Played through preseason ...)		
30 R.C. Owens	5.00	10.00
(Gave football its ...)		
31 Joe Perry	12.50	25.00
(Football's ...)		
32 Jim Ridlon	4.00	8.00
(Showed ...)		
33 Karl Rubke	4.00	8.00
(Started his ...)		
34 Bob St.Clair	7.50	15.00
(Tallest player ...)		
35 Henry Schmidt	4.00	8.00
(After two years ...)		
36 Bob Shaw CO	4.00	8.00
37 Lon Simmons ANN	4.00	8.00
38 J.D. Smith	5.00	10.00
(One of the ...)		
39 John Thomas	4.00	8.00
(Didn't make ...)		
40 Y.A. Tittle	15.00	30.00
(In 11 years ...)		
41 Jerry Tubbs	4.00	8.00
(Recently named as/ center-linebacker ...)		
42 Lynn Waldorf	4.00	8.00
Director of Personnel		
(Horizontal text)		
43 Billy Wilson	4.00	8.00
(Emlen Tunnell,/12-year ...)		
44 John Wittenborn	4.00	8.00
(Handy ...)		
45 Abe Woodson	5.00	10.00
(Received ...)		

1960 49ers Team Issue

This 44-card set measures approximately 4 1/8" by 6 1/4". The front features a black-and-white posed action photo with white borders. The player's facsimile autograph is inscribed across the picture. The back lists the player's name, position, height, weight, age, college, along with career summary and biographical notes. The set was available direct from the team as part of a package for their fans. The photos are unnumbered and checklisted below in alphabetical order.

COMPLETE SET (44)	200.00	350.00
1 Dave Baker	4.00	8.00
(David Lee Baker ...)		
2 Bruce Bosley	4.00	8.00
(Born in Fresno ...)		
3 John Brodie	12.50	25.00
(This could be ...)		
4 Jack Christiansen ACO	6.00	12.00
5 Monte Clark	4.00	8.00
(A special chapter ...)		
6 Dan Colchico	4.00	8.00
(Big Dan ...)		
7 Clyde Conner	4.00	8.00
(Clyde Raymond ...)		
8 Ted Connolly	4.00	8.00
(When Theodore ...)		
9 Tommy Davis	4.00	8.00
(San Francisco ...)		
10 Eddie Dove	4.00	8.00
(Edward Everett ...)		
11 Mark Duncan ACO	4.00	8.00
(A versatile ...)		
12 Bob Fouts ANN	4.00	8.00
13 Bob Harrison	4.00	8.00
(There is no more ...)		
14 Matt Hazeltine	4.00	8.00
(Matthew Hazeltine ...)		
15 Ed Henke	4.00	8.00
(Desire and ...)		
16 Howard(Red) Hickey CO	4.00	8.00
(Baseball ...)		
17 Russ Hodges ANN	4.00	8.00
18 Bill Johnson CO	4.00	8.00
(Bill Johnson ...)		
19 Gordon Kelley	4.00	8.00
(This Southern ...)		
20 Charlie Krueger	4.00	8.00
(The 49ers' ...)		
21 Lenny Lyles	4.00	8.00
(Leonard Lyles ...)		
22 Hugh McElhenny	12.50	25.00
(San Francisco's ...)		
23 Mike Magac	4.00	8.00
(Mike was ...)		
24 Jerry Mertens	4.00	8.00
(Jerome William ...)		
25 Frank Morze	4.00	8.00
(Anyone with ...)		
26 Leo Nomellini	10.00	20.00
(Leo Joseph ...)		
27 Clancy Osborne	4.00	8.00
('Desire' ...)		
28 R.C. Owens	5.00	10.00
(Few players ...)		
29 Jim Ridlon	4.00	8.00
(James Ridlon ...)		
30 C.R. Roberts	4.00	8.00
(After trials ...)		
31 Len Rohde	4.00	8.00
(Len, a three- ...)		
32 Karl Rubke	4.00	8.00
(Only 20 years ...)		
33 Bob St.Clair	6.00	12.00
(Robert Bruce ...)		
34 Henry Schmidt	4.00	8.00
(After two years ...)		
35 Lon Simmons ANN	4.00	8.00
36 J.D. Smith	4.00	8.00
(In J.D. Smith ...)		
37 Gordy Soltau ANN	4.00	8.00
38 Monty Stickles	4.00	8.00
(The football ...)		
39 John Thomas	4.00	8.00
(Noted more ...)		
40 Y.A. Tittle	15.00	30.00
(When Yelberton ...)		
41 Lynn Waldorf	4.00	8.00
(Director of Personnel)		
42 Bobby Waters	4.00	8.00
(A smart, ...)		
43 Billy Wilson	4.00	8.00
(Only Don Hutson ...)		
44 Abe Woodson	5.00	10.00
(A Big 10 ...)		

1961 49ers Team Issue

The 49ers issued this set of large (approximately 8" by 10") black and white player photos in 1961. The team logo (old style) and basic player information is contained beneath the player image. The photos are unnumbered and listed below alphabetically. Note that these photos are similar to other 49ers photos, but can be identified by the size (8" by 10") and by the text (position is in lower and upper case letters) and format used to identify the player's weight (example of style: 6-1).

COMPLETE SET (31)	125.00	250.00
1 Bruce Bosley	4.00	8.00
2 John Brodie	10.00	20.00
3 Bernie Casey	4.00	8.00
4 Monte Clark	4.00	8.00
5 Clyde Conner	4.00	8.00
6 Bill Cooper	4.00	8.00
7 Lou Cordileone	4.00	8.00
8 Tommy Davis	5.00	10.00
9 Bob Harrison	4.00	8.00
10 Matt Hazeltine	4.00	8.00
11 Ed Henke	4.00	8.00
12 Howard Red Hickey CO	4.00	8.00
13 Jim Johnson	5.00	10.00
14 Carl Kammerer	4.00	8.00
15 Billy Kilmer	7.50	15.00
16 Roland Lakes	4.00	8.00
17 Bill Lopasky	4.00	8.00
18 Hugh McElhenny	7.50	15.00
19 Dale Messer	4.00	8.00
20 Leo Nomellini	6.00	12.00
21 Ray Norton	4.00	8.00
22 R.C. Owens	5.00	10.00
23 Jim Ridlon	4.00	8.00
24 Karl Rubke	4.00	8.00
25 Bob St. Clair	5.00	10.00
26 Monty Stickles	4.00	8.00
27 Aaron Thomas	4.00	8.00
28 John Thomas	4.00	8.00
29 Y.A. Tittle	12.50	25.00
30 Abe Woodson	5.00	10.00
31 Coaching Staff	7.50	15.00
Bill Johnson		
Jack Christiansen		
Billy Wilson		
Mark Duncan		
Red Hickey CO		

1963 49ers Team Issue

The 49ers issued this set of large (approximately 8" by 10 7/8") black and white player photos around 1963. The team logo (old style) and basic player information is contained beneath the player image. The photos are unnumbered and listed below alphabetically. Note that these photos are similar to other 49ers photos, but can be identified by the larger size (8" by 10 7/8") and by the larger text used on the player's name (4/32" high) as well as the format used to identify the player's weight (example of style: 6' 1"). Note that the player's position was also printed in upper and lower case letters which helps to differentiate this year from later years.

COMPLETE SET (7)	25.00	50.00
1 Eddie Dove	4.00	8.00
2 Mike Magac	4.00	8.00
3 Ed Pine	4.00	8.00
4 Len Rohde	4.00	8.00
5 Monty Stickles	4.00	8.00
6 John Thomas	4.00	8.00
7 Bob Waters	4.00	8.00

1964 49ers Team Issue

The 49ers issued this set of large (approximately 8" by 10 7/8") black and white player photos around 1964. The team logo (old style) and basic player information is contained beneath the player image. The photos are unnumbered and listed below alphabetically. Note that these photos are similar to other 49ers photos, but can be identified by the larger size (8" by 10 7/8") and by the smaller text used on the player's name (3/32" high) and the format used to identify the player's height (example of style: 6' 1"). Note that the player's position was also printed in upper and lower case letters which helps to differentiate this year from later years.

COMPLETE SET (16)	60.00	120.00
1 Kermit Alexander	4.00	8.00
(Weight 186)		
2 John Brodie	7.50	15.00
(position: Quarter Back)		
3 Bernie Casey	5.00	10.00
(Weight 213)		
4 Jack Christiansen CO	6.00	12.00
5 Dan Colchico	4.00	8.00
6 Tommy Davis	5.00	10.00
7 Leon Donohue	4.00	8.00
8 Charlie Krueger	4.00	8.00
(Weight 250)		
9 Roland Lakes	4.00	8.00
10 Don Lisbon	4.00	8.00
11 Clark Miller	4.00	8.00
12 Walter Rock	4.00	8.00
13 Karl Rubke	4.00	8.00
14 Chuck Sieminski	4.00	8.00
15 J.D. Smith	5.00	10.00
16 Abe Woodson	4.00	8.00

1965 49ers Team Issue

The 49ers issued this set of large (approximately 8" by 10 7/8") black and white player photos around 1965. The team logo (old style) and basic player information is contained beneath the player image. The photos are unnumbered and listed below alphabetically. Note that these are virtually identical to the 1964 photos and likely were issued over a period of years. However, we've cataloged below photos which include distinct variations over the 1964 issue.

1 Kermit Alexander	4.00	8.00
(Weight 180)		
2 John Brodie	7.50	15.00
(position: Quarterback)		
3 Bernie Casey	4.00	8.00
(Weight 209)		
4 Dave Wilcox	5.00	10.00
(Weight 230)		

1966 49ers Team Issue

The 49ers issued this set of large (approximately 8" by 10 7/8") black and white player photos around 1966. The team logo (old style) and basic player information is contained beneath the player image. The photos are unnumbered and listed below alphabetically. Note that these photos are similar to other 49ers photos, but can be identified by the larger size (8" by 10 7/8") and by the text style used on the player's position which was printed in all capital letters.

COMPLETE SET (8)	40.00	80.00
1 Kermit Alexander	4.00	8.00
2 Tommy Davis	5.00	10.00
3 Billy Kilmer	7.50	15.00
4 Elbert Kimbrough	4.00	8.00
5 Dave Kopay	4.00	8.00
6 Charlie Krueger	4.00	8.00
7 Gary Lewis	4.00	8.00
8 George Mira	4.00	8.00
9 Ken Willard	5.00	10.00

1967 49ers Team Issue

This team issue set measures approximately 8" by 11" and features black and white posed action photos of the San Francisco 49ers on thin card stock. The backs are blank. The player's name, position, height, and weight are printed in the white lower border in all caps. The set is very similar to the 1968 and 1971-72 releases, but the size is slightly smaller. The team logo that appears in the white border below the player photo is also slightly different than the 1968 photos. Because this set is unnumbered, the photos are listed alphabetically.

COMPLETE SET	60.00	120.00
1 John David Crow	5.00	10.00
2 Tommy Davis	5.00	10.00
3 George Donnelly	4.00	8.00
4 Charlie Johnson DT	4.00	8.00
5 John Brodie	7.50	15.00
6 George Mira	4.00	8.00
7 Howard Mudd	4.00	8.00
8 Sonny Randle	4.00	8.00
9 Dave Wilcox	5.00	10.00
10 Dick Witcher	4.00	8.00
11 Ken Willard	5.00	10.00
12 Bob Windsor	4.00	8.00
13 Steve Spurrier	20.00	40.00

1968 49ers Team Issue

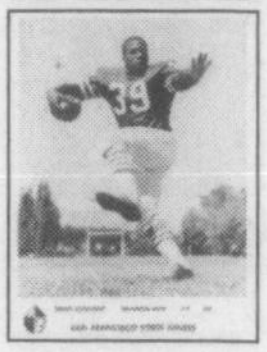

This team issue set measures approximately 8 1/2" by 11" and features black and white posed action photos of the San Francisco 49ers on thin card stock. The backs are blank. The player's name, position, height, and weight are printed in the white lower border in all caps. The set is very similar to the 1971-72 release, but the team logo is printed in black and silver. It also appears in the white border below the player information. Because this set is unnumbered, the players and coaches are listed alphabetically. Steve Spurrier's card predates his Rookie Card by four years.

COMPLETE SET (38)	125.00	250.00
1 Kermit Alexander	5.00	10.00
2 Cas Banaszek	4.00	8.00
3 Ed Beard	4.00	8.00
4 Forrest Blue	4.00	8.00
5 Bruce Bosley	4.00	8.00
6 John Brodie	7.50	15.00
posed action photo		
7 Elmer Collett	4.00	8.00
8 Doug Cunningham	4.00	8.00
9 Tommy Davis	5.00	10.00
10 Earl Edwards	4.00	8.00
11 Kevin Hardy	4.00	8.00
12 Matt Hazeltine	4.00	8.00
13 Stan Hindman	4.00	8.00
14 Tom Holzer	4.00	8.00
15 Jim Johnson	6.00	12.00
16 Charlie Krueger	4.00	8.00
17 Roland Lakes	4.00	8.00
18 Gary Lewis	4.00	8.00
19 Kay McFarland	4.00	8.00
20 Clifton McNeil	4.00	8.00
21 George Mira	5.00	10.00
22 Eugene Moore	4.00	8.00
23 Howard Mudd	4.00	8.00
24 Dick Nolan CO	4.00	8.00
25 Frank Nunley	4.00	8.00
26 Don Parker	4.00	8.00
27 Mel Phillips	4.00	8.00
28 Al Randolph	4.00	8.00
29 Len Rohde	4.00	8.00
30 Steve Spurrier	20.00	40.00
31 John Thomas	4.00	8.00
32 Bill Tucker	4.00	8.00
33 Gene Washington	5.00	10.00
34 Dave Wilcox	5.00	10.00
35 Ken Willard	5.00	10.00
36 Bob Windsor	4.00	8.00
37 Dick Witcher	4.00	8.00
38 Team Photo	7.50	15.00

1968 49ers Volpe Tumblers

These 49ers artist's renderings were part of a plastic cup tumbler product produced in 1968. The noted sports artist Volpe created the artwork which includes an action scene and a player portrait. The "cards" are unnumbered, each measures approximately 5" by 8 1/2" and is curved in the shape required to fit inside a plastic cup. There are likely 12 cups included in this set. Any additions to this list are appreciated.

COMPLETE SET (3)	62.50	125.00
1 John Brodie	30.00	60.00
2 John David Crow	20.00	40.00
3 Charlie Krueger	15.00	30.00

1969 49ers Team Issue 4X5

These small (roughly 4" by 5") black and white photos look very similar to the 1971 release. Each includes a player photo along with his team name, player name, and position. The cardbacks are blank. We've noted text or photo differences below on players that were included in both sets.

COMPLETE SET (20)	40.00	80.00
1 Elmer Collett	2.50	5.00
no comma after team		
2 Tommy Davis	3.00	6.00
3 Earl Edwards	2.50	5.00
listed as DE		
4 Johnny Fuller	2.50	5.00
comma after team		
5 Harold Hays	2.50	5.00
6 Stan Hindman	2.50	5.00
jersey number hidden		
7 Roland Lakes	2.50	5.00
8 Gary Lewis	2.50	5.00
9 Frank Nunley	2.50	5.00
listed as LB		
10 Clifton McNeil	2.50	5.00
11 Mel Phillips	2.50	5.00
listed as DB		
12 Al Randolph	2.50	5.00
13 Len Rohde	2.50	5.00
smiling in photo		
14 Jim Sniadecki	2.50	5.00
no comma after name		
15 Sam Silas	2.50	5.00
16 Jimmy Thomas	2.50	5.00
team name missing		
listed as RB		
17 Bill Tucker	2.50	5.00
18 Bob Windsor	2.50	5.00
(team name SF 49ers)		
19 Dick Witcher	3.00	6.00
listed as FL		
20 John Woitt	2.50	5.00

1971 49ers Team Issue 4X5

These small (roughly 4" by 5") black and white photos look very similar to the 1969 release. Each includes a player photo along with his team name, player name, and position. The cardbacks are blank. We've noted text or photo differences below on players that were included in both sets.

COMPLETE SET (20)	40.00	80.00
1 Elmer Collett	2.50	4.00
comma after team name		
2 Earl Edwards	2.50	4.00
listed as DT		
3 Johnny Fuller	2.50	4.00
no comma after team		
4 Tony Harris	2.50	4.00
5 Tommy Hart	3.00	6.00
6 Stan Hindman	2.50	4.00
jersey number showing		
7 Bob Hoskins	2.50	4.00
8 John Isenbarger	2.50	4.00
9 Jim McCann	2.50	4.00
10 Frank Nunley	2.50	4.00
listed as MLB		
11 Mel Phillips	2.50	4.00
listed as S		
12 Preston Riley	2.50	4.00
13 Len Rohde	2.50	5.00
not smiling in photo		
14 Larry Schreiber	2.50	4.00
15 Mike Simpson	2.50	4.00
16 Jim Sniadecki	2.50	4.00
comma after name		
17 Jimmy Thomas	2.50	4.00
listed as WR		
18 Vic Washington	2.50	5.00
19 Bob Windsor	2.50	5.00
(team name SF 49er)		
20 Dick Witcher	2.50	5.00
listed as WR		

1971 49ers Postcards

The San Francisco 49ers distributed this set of oversized postcards in 1971. Each measures approximately 5 3/4" by 8 7/8" and features a borderless black and white player photo on front with a postcard style back. The player's name, position, helmet logo, and some vital statistics are featured within a white border area below the photo. The unnumbered cardbacks also contain extensive player career information and stats.

COMPLETE SET (47)	200.00	400.00
1 Cas Banaszek	6.25	12.50
2 Ed Beard	5.00	10.00
3 Randy Beisler	5.00	10.00
4 Bill Belk	6.25	12.50
5 Forrest Blue	6.25	12.50
6 John Brodie	10.00	20.00
7 Elmer Collett	5.00	10.00
8 Doug Cunningham	5.00	10.00
9 Earl Edwards	5.00	10.00
10 Johnny Fuller	5.00	10.00
11 Bruce Gossett	6.25	12.50
12 Cedrick Hardman	6.25	12.50
13 Tony Harris	5.00	10.00
14 Tommy Hart	6.25	12.50
15 Stan Hindman	5.00	10.00
16 Bob Hoskins	5.00	10.00
17 Marty Huff	5.00	10.00
18 John Isenbarger	5.00	10.00
19 Ernie Janet	5.00	10.00
20 Jimmy Johnson	7.50	15.00
21 Charlie Krueger	6.25	12.50
22 Ted Kwalick	6.25	12.50
23 Jim McCann	5.00	10.00
24 Dick Nolan CO	6.25	12.50
25 Frank Nunley	5.00	10.00
26 Joe Orduna	5.00	10.00
27 Willie Parker	5.00	10.00
28 Woody Peoples	5.00	10.00
29 Mel Phillips	6.25	12.50
30 Joe Reed	6.25	12.50
31 Preston Riley	5.00	10.00
32 Len Rohde	6.25	12.50
33 Larry Schreiber	5.00	10.00
34 Sam Silas	5.00	10.00
35 Mike Simpson	5.00	10.00
36 Jim Sniadecki	5.00	10.00
37 Steve Spurrier	20.00	40.00
38 Bruce Taylor	6.25	12.50
39 Jimmy Thomas	5.00	10.00
40 Skip Vanderbundt	6.25	12.50
41 Gene Washington	6.25	12.50
42 Vic Washington	6.25	12.50
43 John Watson	5.00	10.00
44 Dave Wilcox	6.25	12.50
45 Ken Willard	6.25	12.50
46 Bob Windsor	5.00	10.00
47 Dick Witcher	5.00	10.00
48 Coaching Staff	6.25	12.50

1971-72 49ers Team Issue

This team issue set measures approximately 8 1/2" by 11" and features black and white posed action photos of the San Francisco 49ers on thin card stock. The backs are blank. The player's name, position, height, and weight are printed in the white lower border in all caps. The set is very similar to the 1967 and 1968 releases, but the team logo is printed in all black and appears in the white border below the player information. Because this set is unnumbered, the players are listed alphabetically.

COMPLETE SET (5)	15.00	30.00
1 Ed Beard	4.00	8.00
2 Bill Belk	4.00	8.00
3 John Brodie	7.50	15.00
head and shoulder shot		
4 Bruce Gossett	4.00	8.00
5 Ted Kwalick	4.00	8.00

1972 49ers Redwood City Tribune

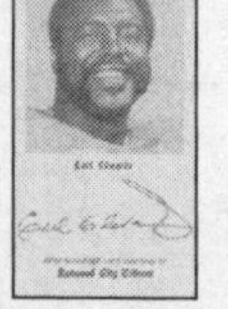

This set of six (approximately) 3" by 5 1/2" facsimile autograph cards features black-and-white head shots with white borders. The player's name is printed beneath the picture and in a large space immediately beneath, the card carries the player's signature. The bottom of the front reads "49er autograph card courtesy of Redwood City Tribune." The cards are unnumbered and checklisted below in alphabetical order. The set's date is bracketed by the fact that Frank Edwards last year with the San Francisco 49ers was 1972 and Larry Schreiber's first year with the 49ers was 1971.

COMPLETE SET (6)	37.50	75.00
1 Earl Edwards	3.75	7.50
2 Frank Nunley	3.75	7.50
3 Len Rohde	3.75	7.50
4 Larry Schreiber	3.75	7.50
5 Steve Spurrier	20.00	40.00
6 Gene Washington	6.25	12.50

1972-75 49ers Team Issue

The 49ers released similar player photos over a period of years in the 1970s. For ease in cataloging, we've included them together below. There are likely many missing from the checklist, any additions to the list would be appreciated. Each photo measures approximately 7" by 11" and was printed on very thin glossy stock. The fronts feature black-and-white action player photos on a white background. The player's picture measures roughly 6 1/4" by 7 1/2" and the cardbacks are blanks. The player's name, biographical information, career highlights, and a personal profile are printed in the white margin at the bottom. Most also include a 49ers helmet logo below the image. The player's statistics and years pro notation help in identifying the year of issue. The cards are unnumbered and checklisted below in alphabetical order.

1 Cas Banaszek	4.00	8.00
2 Forrest Blue	4.00	8.00
3 Bruce Gossett	4.00	8.00
4 Windlan Hall 1974	4.00	8.00
(NFL years 3)		
5 Cedrick Hardman	4.00	8.00
6 Mike Holmes	4.00	8.00
7 Tom Hull 1974	4.00	8.00
8 Wilbur Jackson 1974	5.00	10.00
(no helmet logo on front, mentions drafted No.1a - '74)		
9 Jim Johnson 1974	6.00	12.00
(NFL years 14)		
10 Manfred Moore 1974	4.00	8.00
(no helmet logo on front, mentions drafted No.9 - '74)		
11 Mel Phillips 1972	4.00	8.00
(years pro 7)		
12 Steve Spurrier 1974	12.50	25.00
(NFL years 8)		
13 Bruce Taylor	4.00	8.00
14 Skip Vanderbundt	4.00	8.00
15 Gene Washington 1973	5.00	10.00
(pro years 5)		
16 Gene Washington 1975	5.00	10.00
(NFL years 7)		
17 John Watson 1974	4.00	8.00
(NFL years 4)		

1977 49ers Team Issue

These team issued photos of the San Francisco 49ers measure approximately 5" by 8" and feature black-and-white player photos within a white border. The player's name is pirnted in all caps below the picture with his jersey number, position, height, weight, and college printed below that. The backs are blank so the cards are unnumbered and checklisted below in alphabetical order. It is thought that these photos may have been issued over a period of years since they closely resemble the 1980-82 release.

1 Cleveland Elam	2.00	5.00
2 Jim Plunkett	3.00	8.00
3 Dave Washington	2.00	5.00

1980-82 49ers Team Issue

This team issue set of the San Francisco 49ers measures approximately 5" by 8" and features a black-and-white player photo in a white border. The player's name, jersey number, height, weight, and college are printed in the wide bottom margin. The backs are blank. The cards are unnumbered and checklisted below in alphabetical order. It is thought that these photos may have been issued over a period of years since some feature the player's name in all caps while others use both upper and lower case letters. The set features an early Joe Montana card that is thought to have been issued in 1982.

COMPLETE SET (55)	125.00	250.00
1 Dan Audick	1.25	3.00
2 John Ayers	1.25	3.00
3 Jean Barrett	1.25	3.00
4 Guy Benjamin	1.25	3.00
5 Dwaine Board	1.25	3.00
6 Bob Bruer	1.25	3.00
7 Ken Bungarda	1.25	3.00
8 Dan Bunz	1.25	3.00
9 John Choma	1.25	3.00
10 Ricky Churchman	1.25	3.00
11 Dwight Clark	3.00	8.00
12 Earl Cooper	1.25	3.00
13 Randy Cross	1.50	4.00
14 Johnny Davis	1.25	3.00
15 Fred Dean	1.50	4.00
16 Walt Downing	1.25	3.00
17 Walt Easley	1.25	3.00
18 Lenvil Elliott	1.25	3.00
19 Keith Fahnhorst	1.25	3.00
20 Bob Ferrell	1.25	3.00
21 Phil Francis	1.25	3.00
22 Rick Gervais	1.25	3.00
23 Willie Harper	1.25	3.00
24 John Harty	1.25	3.00
25 Dwight Hicks	1.50	4.00
26 Scott Hilton	1.25	3.00
27 Paul Hofer	1.25	3.00
28 Pete Kugler	1.25	3.00
29 Amos Lawrence	1.25	3.00
30 Bobby Leopold	1.25	3.00
31 Ronnie Lott	6.00	15.00
32 Saladin Martin	1.25	3.00
33 Milt McColl	1.25	3.00
34 Jim Miller	1.25	3.00
35 Joe Montana	90.00	150.00
36 Ricky Patton	1.25	3.00
37 Lawrence Pillers	1.25	3.00
38 Craig Puki	1.25	3.00
39 Fred Quillan	1.25	3.00
40 Eason Ramson	1.25	3.00
41 Archie Reese	1.25	3.00
42 Jack Reynolds	1.50	4.00
43 Bill Ring	1.25	3.00
44 Mike Shumann	1.25	3.00
45 Freddie Solomon	2.00	5.00
46 Scott Stauch	1.25	3.00
47 Jim Stuckey	1.25	3.00
48 Lynn Thomas	1.25	3.00
49 Keena Turner	1.25	3.00
50 Jimmy Webb	1.25	3.00
51 Ray Wersching	1.25	3.00
52 Carlton Williamson	1.25	3.00
53 Mike Wilson	1.25	3.00
54 Eric Wright	1.50	4.00
55 Charlie Young	1.50	4.00

1982 49ers Prints

These large (roughly 11 1/2" by 18") prints were sponsored by Taco Bell and Dr. Pepper and issued in 1982. Each features several 49ers players in a color artist's rendering format on thick paper stock. The backs feature the art's title and a write-up on the featured players along with the Taco Bell and Dr. Pepper logos.

COMPLETE SET (4)	30.00	75.00
1 Deanfence	6.00	15.00
Fred Dean		
Jack Reynolds		
Dwight Hicks		
Ronnie Lott		
2 Joe, Freddie, and Dwight	25.00	40.00
Joe Montana		
Freddie Solomon		
Dwight Clark		
3 The Unsung Ones	4.00	10.00
Randy Cross		
John Ayers		
Fred Quillan		
Keith Fahnhorst		
4 Very Special Teams	4.00	10.00
Jim Miller		
Bill Ring		
Ray Wersching		

1984 49ers Police

This set of 12 cards was issued in three panels of four cards each. Individual cards measure approximately 2 1/2" by 4 1/16" and feature the San Francisco 49ers. Since the cards are unnumbered, they are ordered and numbered below alphabetically by the subject's name. The set is sponsored by 7-Eleven, Dr. Pepper, and KCBS.

COMPLETE SET (12)	12.00	30.00
1 Dwaine Board	.20	.50
2 Roger Craig	2.00	5.00
3 Riki Ellison	.20	.50
4 Keith Fahnhorst	.20	.50
5 Joe Montana	8.00	20.00
Dwight Clark		
6 Jack Reynolds	.30	.75
7 Freddie Solomon	.30	.75
8 Keena Turner	.30	.75
9 Wendell Tyler	.30	.75
10 Bill Walsh CO	1.50	4.00
11 Ray Wersching	.20	.50
12 Eric Wright	.20	.50

1985 49ers Police

This set of 16 cards was issued in four panels of four cards each. Individual cards measure approximately 2 1/2" by 4" and feature the San Francisco 49ers. Since the cards are unnumbered, they are ordered and numbered below alphabetically by the subject's name. The set is differentiated from the similar 1984 Police 49ers set since this 1985 set is only sponsored by 7-Eleven and Dr. Pepper.

COMPLETE SET (16)	10.00	25.00
1 John Ayers	.15	.40
2 Roger Craig	.75	2.00
3 Fred Dean	.30	.75
4 Riki Ellison	.20	.50
5 Keith Fahnhorst	.15	.40
6 Russ Francis	.30	.75
7 Dwight Hicks	.20	.50
8 Ronnie Lott	1.25	3.00
9 Dana McLemore	.15	.40
10 Joe Montana	6.00	15.00
11 Todd Shell	.20	.50
12 Freddie Solomon	.30	.75
13 Keena Turner	.30	.75
14 Bill Walsh CO	.50	1.25
15 Ray Wersching	.15	.40
16 Eric Wright	.20	.50

1985 49ers Smokey

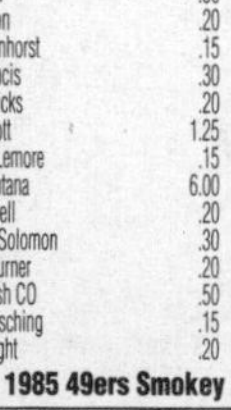

This set of seven large (approximately 2 15/16" by 4 3/8") cards was issued in the Summer of 1985 and features the San Francisco 49ers and Smokey Bear. The card backs are printed in black on a thin white card stock. Card backs have a cartoon fire safety message and a facsimile autograph of the player. Smokey Bear is pictured on each card along with the player (or players).

COMPLETE SET (7)	40.00	80.00
1 Group Picture with Smokey (Player list on back of card)	8.00	20.00
2 Joe Montana	35.00	60.00
3 Jack Reynolds	1.25	3.00
4 Eric Wright	1.25	3.00
5 Dwight Hicks	1.25	3.00
6 Dwight Clark	2.50	6.00
7 Keena Turner	1.25	3.00

1987 49ers Ace Fact Pack

This 33-card set measures approximately 2 1/4" by 3 5/8". This set was manufactured in West Germany (by Ace Fact Pack) for release in Great Britain and features rounded corners and a playing card type of design on the back. There are 22 player cards in this set and we have checklisted those cards in alphabetical order.

COMPLETE SET (33)	250.00	500.00
1 John Ayers	2.00	5.00
2 Dwaine Board	2.00	5.00
3 Michael Carter	2.50	6.00
4 Dwight Clark	4.00	10.00
5 Roger Craig	6.00	15.00
6 Joe Cribbs	2.50	6.00
7 Randy Cross	2.50	6.00
8 Riki Ellison	2.00	5.00
9 Jim Fahnhorst	2.00	5.00
10 Keith Fahnhorst	2.00	5.00
11 Russ Francis	2.50	6.00
12 Don Griffin	2.00	5.00
13 Ronnie Lott	10.00	25.00
14 Milt McColl	2.00	5.00
15 Tim McKyer	2.00	5.00
16 Joe Montana	125.00	300.00
17 Bubba Paris	2.00	5.00
18 Fred Quillan	2.00	5.00
19 Jerry Rice	75.00	150.00
20 Manu Tuiasosopo	2.00	5.00
21 Keena Turner	2.00	5.00
22 Carlton Williamson	2.00	5.00
23 49ers Helmet	2.00	5.00
24 49ers Information	2.00	5.00
25 49ers Uniform	2.00	5.00
26 Game Record Holders	2.00	5.00
27 Season Record Holders	2.00	5.00
28 Career Record Holders	2.00	5.00
29 Record 1967-86	2.00	5.00
30 1986 Team Statistics	2.00	5.00
31 All-Time Greats	2.00	5.00
32 Roll of Honour	2.00	5.00
33 Candlestick Park	2.00	5.00

1988 49ers Police

The 1988 Police San Francisco 49ers set contains 20 unnumbered cards measuring approximately 2 1/2" by 4". There are 19 player cards and one coach card. The fronts are basically "pure" with white borders. The backs have a football tip and a McGruff crime tip. The cards are listed below in alphabetical order by subject's name. The set is sponsored by 7-Eleven and Oscar Mayer, which differentiates this set from the similar-looking 1985 Police 49ers set.

COMPLETE SET (20)	25.00	60.00
1 Harris Barton	.30	.75
2 Dwaine Board	.20	.50
3 Michael Carter	.20	.50
4 Roger Craig	.40	1.00
5 Randy Cross	.30	.75
6 Riki Ellison	.20	.50
7 John Frank	.20	.50
8 Jeff Fuller	.20	.50
9 Pete Kugler	.20	.50
10 Ronnie Lott	1.00	2.50
11 Joe Montana	8.00	20.00
12 Tom Rathman	.30	.75
13 Jerry Rice	8.00	20.00
14 Jeff Stover	.20	.50
15 Keena Turner	.30	.75
16 Bill Walsh CO	.60	1.50
17 Michael Walter	.20	.50
18 Mike Wilson	.20	.50
19 Eric Wright	.30	.75
20 Steve Young	6.00	15.00

1988 49ers Smokey

This 35-card set features members of the San Francisco 49ers. The cards measure approximately 5" by 8". The printing on the card back is in black ink on white card stock. The cards are unnumbered except for uniform number; they are ordered below alphabetically for convenience. Each card back contains a fire safety cartoon (usually) featuring Smokey. Reportedly the Dwaine Board card is more difficult to find than the other cards in the set.

COMPLETE SET (35)	60.00	150.00
1 Harris Barton	.60	1.50
2 Dwaine Board SP	3.00	8.00
3 Michael Carter	.60	1.50
4 Bruce Collie	.40	1.00
5 Roger Craig	1.50	4.00
6 Randy Cross	.75	2.00
7 Eddie DeBartolo Jr.	.75	2.00
(Owner		
President)		
8 Riki Ellison	.40	1.00
9 Kevin Fagan	.40	1.00
10 Jim Fahnhorst	.40	1.00
11 John Frank	.60	1.50
12 Jeff Fuller	.40	1.00
13 Don Griffin	.60	1.50
14 Charles Haley	1.25	3.00
15 Ron Heller	.40	1.00
16 Tom Holmoe	.40	1.00
17 Pete Kugler	.40	1.00
18 Ronnie Lott	2.00	5.00
19 Tim McKyer	.50	1.50
20 Joe Montana	30.00	50.00
21 Tory Nixon	.40	1.00
22 Bubba Paris	.60	1.50
23 John Paye	.40	1.00
24 Tom Rathman	.75	2.00
25 Jerry Rice	30.00	50.00
26 Jeff Stover	.40	1.00
27 Harry Sydney	.40	1.00
28 John Taylor	1.50	4.00
29 Keena Turner	.60	1.50
30 Steve Wallace	.60	1.50
31 Bill Walsh CO	1.25	3.00
32 Michael Walter	.40	1.00
33 Mike Wilson	.40	1.00
34 Eric Wright	.50	1.50
35 Steve Young	10.00	25.00

1990 49ers Knudsen

This six-card set of bookmarks measures approximately 2" by 8" was produced by Knudsen's to help promote readership by people under 15 years old in the San Francisco area. They were given out in San Francisco libraries on a weekly basis. Between the Knudsen company name, the front features a color action photo of the player superimposed on a football stadium. The field is green, the bleachers are yellow with gray print, and the scoreboard above the player reads "The Reading Team". The box below the player gives brief biographical information and player highlights. The back has logos of the sponsors and describes two books that are available at the public library. We have checklisted this set in alphabetical order because they are otherwise unnumbered except for the player's uniform number displayed on the card front.

COMPLETE SET (6)	20.00	50.00
1 Roger Craig	1.60	4.00
2 Ronnie Lott	2.00	5.00
3 Joe Montana	8.00	20.00
4 Jerry Rice	8.00	20.00
5 George Seifert CO	1.60	4.00
6 Michael Walter	1.20	3.00

1990-91 49ers SF Examiner

This 16-card San Francisco Examiner 49ers set was issued on two unperforated sheets measuring approximately 14" by 11". Each sheet featured eight cards, with a newspaper headline at the top of the sheet reading "San Francisco Examiner Salutes the 49ers' Finest". If the cards were cut, they would measure approximately 3 1/4" by 4 1/8". The front design has color game shots, with a thin orange border on a red card face. A gold plaque at the card top reads "SF Examiner's Finest," while the gold plaque at the bottom has the player's position and name. The horizontally oriented backs have a black and white head shot, biographical information, statistics, and player profile. The cards are unnumbered and checklisted below in alphabetical order.

COMPLETE SET (16)	30.00	50.00
1 Harris Barton	.50	1.25
2 Michael Carter	.50	1.25
3 Mike Cofer	.50	1.25
4 Roger Craig	.75	2.00
5 Kevin Fagan	.50	1.25
6 Don Griffin	.50	1.25
7 Charles Haley	.75	2.00
8 Pierce Holt	.50	1.25
9 Brent Jones	.75	2.00
10 Ronnie Lott	1.50	4.00
11 Guy McIntyre	.50	1.25
12 Matt Millen	.50	1.25
13 Joe Montana	10.00	20.00
14 Tom Rathman	.75	2.00
15 Jerry Rice	7.50	15.00
16 John Taylor	.75	2.00

1992 49ers FBI

This 40-card standard-size set was sponsored by the San Francisco 49ers and the FBI (Federal Bureau of Investigation). According to the title card, a different pack of cards was available free with the 49ers' edition of GameDay Magazine at regular season home games each week at Candlestick Park. The fronts display color action player photos with white borders. In red and white lettering, the player's first and last names are overprinted on the picture at the upper left and lower right corners respectively. The team helmet at the lower left corner rounds out the front. Inside white borders on brick-red background, the backs feature a color close-up photo (inside a football helmet design), biographical information, and a public service message in the form of a player quote.

COMPLETE SET (40)	16.00	40.00
1 Michael Carter	.20	.50
2 Kevin Fagan	.20	.50
3 Charles Haley	.40	1.00
4 Guy McIntyre	.20	.50
5 George Seifert CO	.40	1.00
6 Harry Sydney	.20	.50
7 John Taylor	.50	1.25
8 Michael Walter	.20	.50
9 Steve Young	4.00	10.00
10 Mike Cofer	.20	.50
11 Keith DeLong	.20	.50
12 Don Griffin	.20	.50
13 Pierce Holt	.30	.75
14 Mike Sherrard	.40	1.00
15 Larry Roberts	.20	.50
16 Bill Romanowski	.20	.50
17 Tom Rathman	.40	1.00
18 Jesse Sapolu	.30	.75
19 Brent Jones	.40	1.00
20 Brian Bollinger	.20	.50
21 Eric Davis	.20	.50
22 Antonio Goss	.20	.50
23 Alan Grant	.20	.50
24 Harris Barton	.30	.75
25 Ricky Watters	1.60	4.00
26 Darin Jordan	.20	.50
27 Odessa Turner	.20	.50
28 David Wilkins	.20	.50
29 Merton Hanks	.40	1.00
30 David Whitmore	.20	.50
31 Joe Montana	6.00	15.00
32 Klaus Wilmsmeyer	.20	.50
33 Tim Harris	.30	.75
34 Roy Foster	.20	.50
35 Bill Musgrave	.30	.75
36 Dana Hall	.30	.75
37 Steve Wallace	.30	.75
38 Steve Bono	.80	2.00
39 Jerry Rice	4.80	12.00
NNO Title Card	.30	.75

1994 49ers Pro Mags/Pro Tags

Issued in a black cardboard box and featuring the San Francisco 49ers, this set consists of six Pro Mags and six Pro Tags, both with rounded corners and measuring 2 1/8" by 3 3/8". Each box was individually numbered out of 750. On a team color-coded background, the magnet fronts display borderless color action player photos. The player's name in big gold-foil letters appears along the left side, with the team name below. A gold-foil Super Bowl XXIX logo is printed in the lower right corner. On a computerized team color-coded background, the tag fronts feature a color action player cutout superimposed on the Roman numerals XXIX printed vertically in block lettering. The player's name is gold foil-stamped across the bottom, with a gold-foil Super Bowl XXIX logo beneath it. The backs carry a color closeup photo, an autograph strip, and player profile. The magnets and tags are unnumbered and checklisted below in alphabetical order, first the magnets (1-6) and then the tags (7-12).

COMPLETE SET (12)	8.00	20.00
1 Ken Norton Jr.	.50	1.25
2 Jerry Rice	1.20	3.00
3 Deion Sanders	.80	2.00
4 John Taylor	.50	1.25
5 Ricky Watters	.60	1.50
6 Steve Young	1.00	2.50
7 Ken Norton Jr.	.50	1.25
8 Jerry Rice	1.20	3.00
9 Deion Sanders	.80	2.00
10 John Taylor	.50	1.25
11 Ricky Watters	.60	1.50
12 Steve Young	1.00	2.50

1994-95 49ers Then and Now Coins

Each coin in this set measures 1 1/4" in diameter and features a member of the 49ers from the past or present. The reverse side of the coins features the year "1994-95" and set name and 49ers logo. The unnumbered coins were minted in a silver colored heavy alloy metal. A colorful album to house the collection was also produced.

COMPLETE SET (20)	125.00	200.00
1 John Brodie	4.00	10.00
2 Dwight Clark	4.00	10.00
3 Dwight Clark The Catch	5.00	12.00
4 Roger Craig	5.00	12.00
5 Randy Cross	4.00	10.00
6 Ronnie Lott	6.00	15.00
7 Leo Nomellini	4.00	10.00
8 R.C. Owens	4.00	10.00
9 Joe Perry	5.00	12.00
10 Jerry Rice	7.50	20.00
11 Jerry Rice 127 TDs	7.50	20.00
12 George Seifert CO	4.00	10.00
13 John Taylor	4.00	10.00
14 Y.A. Tittle	5.00	12.00
15 Keena Turner	4.00	10.00
16 Bill Walsh CO	5.00	12.00
17 Gene Washington	4.00	10.00
18 Eric Wright	4.00	10.00
19 Steve Young	6.00	15.00
20 Team of the Decade Copper	5.00	12.00
NNO Album	5.00	12.00

1995 49ers CommCard Phone Cards

Five 49ers players were featured on prepaid phone cards by CommCard. The various denominations included: 10, 29, 49, and 75-minutes.

COMPLETE SET (5)	2.00	5.00
1 Richard Dent	.60	1.50
2 Merton Hanks	.40	1.00
3 Tim McDonald	.40	1.00

4 Bart Oates	.40	1.00
5 Jesse Sapolu	.40	1.00

1996 49ers Save Mart Cards/Coins

The San Francisco 49ers, in conjunction with Save Mart Supermarkets, produced this nine card and coin set commemorating the team's Super Bowl teams past and present. The card fronts feature color action player photos with the player's name printed diagonally on one side of the cardfront. The backs display the complete nine-card checklist and individual card numbers. We've listed the cards below using a "CA" prefix. The coin fronts feature a player likeness with the player's name and jersey number. The backs display the 49ers team logo. The coins are unnumbered but have been listed below alphabetically using a "CO" prefix. A cardboard holder featuring Jerry Rice and Steve Young was produced to house the set.

COMP.CARD/COIN SET (18)	16.00	40.00
COMPLETE CARD SET (9)	10.00	25.00
COMPLETE COIN SET (9)	8.00	20.00
CA1 Steve Young	2.00	5.00
CA2 Roger Craig	1.00	2.50
CA3 Jerry Rice	2.40	6.00
CA4 Ronnie Lott	1.20	3.00
CA5 Ken Norton	.75	2.00
CA6 Dwight Clark	1.00	2.50
CA7 Brent Jones	.75	2.00
CA8 Joe Montana	3.20	8.00
CA9 Steve Young Jerry Rice Super Bowl XXIX	2.00	5.00
CO1 Dwight Clark	1.00	2.50
CO2 Roger Craig	1.00	2.50
CO3 Brent Jones	.75	2.00
CO4 Ronnie Lott	1.00	2.50
CO5 Joe Montana	2.40	6.00
CO6 Ken Norton	.75	2.00
CO7 Jerry Rice	2.00	5.00
CO8 Steve Young	1.60	4.00
CO9 Super Bowl XXIX Trophy Gold colored coin	1.20	3.00
NNO Set Display Holder Jerry Rice Steve Young	1.60	4.00

1997 49ers Collector's Choice

Upper Deck released several team sets in 1997 in a blister pack wrapper. Each of the 14-cards in this set are very similar to the base Collector's Choice cards except for the card numbering on the cardback A cover/checklist card was added featuring the team helmet.

COMPLETE SET (14)	1.20	3.00
SF1 Dana Stubblefield	.05	.15
SF2 Merton Hanks	.02	.10
SF3 Terrell Owens	.40	1.00
SF4 Bront Jonos	.02	.10
SF5 Ken Norton Jr.	.02	.10
SF6 Jerry Rice	.40	1.00
SF7 Terry Kirby	.05	.15
SF8 Bryant Young	.05	.15
SF9 Jim Druckenmiller	.05	.15
SF10 William Floyd	.05	.15
SF11 Steve Young	.25	.60
SF12 Lee Woodall	.02	.10
SF13 Garrison Hearst	.05	.15
SF14 49ers Logo Checklist (Jerry Rice on back)	.25	.60

1997 49ers Score

This 15-card set of the San Francisco 49ers was distributed in five-card packs with a suggested retail price of $1.99. The fronts feature color action player photos with white borders and the player's name and team logo printed in team color foil at the bottom. The backs carry player information and career statistics. A Platinum Team parallel set was randomly inserted in packs and featured red foil on the cardfronts.

COMPLETE SET (15)	3.20	8.00
*PLATINUM TEAMS: 1X TO 2X		
1 Jerry Rice	.80	2.00
2 Steve Young	.60	1.50
3 Garrison Hearst	.30	.75
4 Terry Kirby	.15	.40
5 Brent Jones	.08	.25
6 J.J. Stokes	.30	.75
7 Terrell Owens	.50	1.25
8 William Floyd	.15	.40
9 Ken Norton Jr.	.08	.25
10 Bryant Young	.15	.40
11 Dana Stubblefield	.15	.40
12 Ted Popson	.08	.25
13 Roy Barker	.08	.25
14 Tyronne Drakeford	.08	.25
15 Merton Hanks	.08	.25

1998 49ers UD Choice

COMPLETE SET (11)	3.00	8.00
SF1 Terrell Owens	.40	1.00
SF2 Merton Hanks	.20	.50
SF3 Chris Doleman	.20	.50
SF4 Steve Young	.60	1.50
SF5 Chuck Levy	.20	.50
SF6 J.J. Stokes	.20	.50
SF7 Ken Norton	.20	.50
SF8 R.W. McQuarters	.20	.50
SF9 Jerry Rice	1.00	2.50
SF10 Garrison Hearst	.30	.75
SF11 Ty Detmer	.30	.75

2002 49ers Topps Coke

This set was produced by Topps and sponsored by Coca-Cola. Each card features a red border with the Coke logo on the front and a standard cardback.

1 Jeff Garcia	.50	1.25
2 Terrell Owens	.75	2.00
3 Tai Streets	.40	1.00
4 Garrison Hearst	.50	1.25
5 Kevan Barlow	.50	1.25
6 Eric Johnson	.50	1.25
7 Bryant Young	.40	1.00
8 Dana Stubblefield	.40	1.00
9 Derek Smith LB	.40	1.00
10 Jeff Ulbrich	.40	1.00
11 Andre Carter	.40	1.00
12 Ahmed Plummer	.40	1.00

2006 49ers Topps

COMPLETE SET (12)	3.00	6.00
SF1 Alex Smith QB	.30	.75
SF2 Kevan Barlow	.20	.50
SF3 Arnaz Battle	.20	.50
SF4 Frank Gore	.30	.75
SF5 Derrick Johnson	.20	.50
SF6 Shawntae Spencer	.20	.50
SF7 Bryant Young	.20	.50
SF8 Antonio Bryant	.20	.50
SF9 Maurice Hicks	.20	.50
SF10 Trent Dilfer	.25	.60
SF11 Vernon Davis	.40	1.00
SF12 Manny Lawson	.25	.60

2007 49ers Topps

COMPLETE SET (12)	2.50	6.00
1 Frank Gore	.30	.75
2 Vernon Davis	.25	.60
3 Alex Smith QB	.30	.75
4 Arnaz Battle	.20	.50
5 Ashley Lelie	.25	.60
6 Nate Clements	.20	.50
7 Manny Lawson	.20	.50
8 Bryant Young	.20	.50
9 Walt Harris	.20	.50
10 Jason Hill	.30	.75
11 Darrell Jackson	.20	.50
12 Patrick Willis	.60	1.50

2008 49ers Topps

COMPLETE SET (12)	2.50	5.00
1 Vernon Davis	.25	.60
2 Patrick Willis	.25	.60
3 DeShaun Foster	.25	.60
4 Frank Gore	.25	.60
5 Trent Dilfer	.25	.60
6 Isaac Bruce	.25	.60
7 Alex Smith QB	.30	.75
8 Arnaz Battle	.20	.50
9 Nate Clements	.20	.50
10 Michael Lewis	.20	.50
11 Josh Morgan	.30	.75
12 Kentwan Balmer	.25	.60

2009 49ers Breast Cancer Awareness

This three card set was issued at a home game in 2009. Each unnumbered card was created by one of the three NFL licensed manufacturers and features the pink ribbon breast cancer awareness logo on the fronts.

COMPLETE SET (3)	2.00	5.00
1 Vernon Davis Panini	.75	2.00
2 Frank Gore Upper Deck	.75	2.00
3 Patrick Willis Topps	.75	2.00

1989 Franchise Game

The 1989 NFL Franchise Game was produced by Rohrwood Enterprises of Loveland, Colorado. The game is modeled after Monopoly, in that players begin with a sum of money (54.5 million dollars) and travel around the board, acquiring "property" (i.e., players) in exchange for money. The object of the game is to build a team of 23 players who fill all the different positions required by the team and who are under contract. The game cards measure approximately 3" by 3 1/2" and feature action player photos with rounded corners and white borders. Some collectors have observed a variation in photographic quality. The player's name and team appear above the picture, while the draft round, number of points player is worth to the franchise, and his salary are printed below the picture. The card backs display a teal panel printed with the home cities of NFL teams. A large numeral or acronym appears in the center of the panel. The player's position is printed across the top. The cards are unnumbered and checklisted below alphabetically according to and within teams. In addition to these player cards, the set includes 28 unnumbered team cards displaying the team helmet and 13 generic coaches' cards.

COMPLETE SET (332)	100.00	250.00
1 Neal Anderson	.60	1.50
2 Kevin Butler	.30	.75
3 Jim Covert	.30	.75
4 Dave Duerson	.30	.75
5 Dan Hampton	.60	1.50
6 Jay Hilgenberg	.30	.75
7 Mike Richardson	.30	.75
8 Ron Rivera	.30	.75
9 Mike Singletary	.60	1.50
10 Mike Tomczak	.30	.75
11 Keith Van Horne	.30	.75
12 Lewis Billups	.30	.75
13 Jim Breech	.30	.75
14 James Brooks	.30	.75
15 Eddie Brown	.60	1.50
16 Ross Browner	.30	.75
17 Jason Buck	.30	.75
18 Cris Collinsworth	.60	1.50
19 Eddie Edwards	.30	.75
20 Boomer Esiason	.60	1.50
21 David Fulcher	.30	.75
22 Ray Horton	.30	.75
23 Tim Krumrie	.30	.75
24 Max Montoya	.30	.75
25 Anthony Munoz	.60	1.50
26 Jim Skow	.30	.75
27 Reggie Williams	.30	.75
28 Ickey Woods	.30	.75
29 Cornelius Bennett	1.25	3.00
30 Shane Conlan	.30	.75
31 Joe Devlin	.30	.75
32 Nate Odomes	.30	.75
33 Scott Norwood	.30	.75
34 Andre Reed	.60	1.50
35 Jim Ritcher	.30	.75
36 Fred Smerlas	.30	.75
37 Bruce Smith	.60	1.50
38 Art Still	.30	.75
39 Keith Bishop	.30	.75
40 Bill Bryan	.30	.75
41 Tony Dorsett	1.25	3.00
42 Simon Fletcher	.30	.75
43 Mike Harden	.30	.75
44 Mark Haynes	.30	.75
45 Mike Horan	.30	.75
46 Vance Johnson	.30	.75
47 Rulon Jones	.30	.75
48 Rich Karlis	.30	.75
49 Karl Mecklenburg	.30	.75
50 Dennis Smith	.30	.75
51 Dave Studdard	.30	.75
52 Andre Townsend	.30	.75
53 Steve Watson	.30	.75
54 Sammy Winder	.30	.75
55 Matt Bahr	.30	.75
56 Rickey Bolden	.30	.75
57 Earnest Byner	.30	.75
58 Sam Clancy	.30	.75
59 Hanford Dixon	.30	.75
60 Bob Golic	.30	.75
61 Carl Hairston	.30	.75
62 Eddie Johnson	.30	.75
63 Kevin Mack	.30	.75
64 Clay Matthews	.30	.75
65 Frank Minnifield	.30	.75
66 Ozzie Newsome	.60	1.50
67 Cody Risien	.30	.75
68 John Cannon	.30	.75
69 Ron Holmes	.30	.75
70 Winston Moss	.30	.75
71 Rob Taylor	.30	.75
72 Joe Bostic	.30	.75
73 Roy Green	.30	.75
74 Ricky Hunley	.30	.75
75 E.J. Junior	.30	.75
76 Neil Lomax	.30	.75
77 Tim McDonald	.30	.75
78 Cedric Mack	.30	.75
79 Freddie Joe Nunn	.30	.75
80 Gary Anderson RBK	.60	1.50
81 Keith Baldwin	.30	.75
82 Gill Byrd	.30	.75
83 Elvis Patterson	.30	.75
84 Gary Plummer	.30	.75
85 Billy Ray Smith	.30	.75
86 Lee Williams	.30	.75
87 Mike Bell	.30	.75
88 Lloyd Burruss	.30	.75
89 Carlos Carson	.30	.75
90 Deron Cherry	.30	.75
91 Jack Del Rio	1.25	3.00
92 Irv Eatman	.30	.75
93 Dino Hackett	.30	.75
94 Bill Kenney	.30	.75
95 Albert Lewis	.30	.75
96 David Lutz	.30	.75
97 Bill Maas	.30	.75
98 Stephone Paige	.60	1.50
99 Neil Smith	1.25	3.00
100 Dean Biasucci	.30	.75
101 Duane Bickett	.30	.75
102 Chris Chandler	1.25	3.00
103 Eugene Daniel	.30	.75
104 Ray Donaldson	.30	.75
105 Jon Hand	.30	.75
106 Chris Hinton	.30	.75
107 Joe Klecko	.30	.75
108 Cliff Odom	.30	.75
109 Rohn Stark	.30	.75
110 Donnell Thompson	.30	.75
111 Willie Tullis	.30	.75
112 Freddie Young	.30	.75
113 Michael Downs	.30	.75
114 Michael Irvin	2.00	5.00
115 Jim Jeffcoat	.30	.75
116 Ed(Too Tall) Jones	.60	1.50
117 Tom Rafferty	.30	.75
118 Herschel Walker	.60	1.50
119 Everson Walls	.30	.75
120 Danny White	.60	1.50.
121 Randy White	.60	1.50
122 Bob Brudzinski	.30	.75
123 Mark Clayton	.60	1.50
124 Mark Duper	.60	1.50
125 Ron Jaworski	.60	1.50
126 Paul Lankford	.30	.75
127 Dan Marino	8.00	20.00
128 John Offerdahl	.30	.75
129 Reggie Roby	.30	.75
130 Dwight Stephenson	1.25	3.00
131 Randall Cunningham	1.25	3.00
132 Ron Heller	.30	.75
133 Mike Quick	.60	1.50
134 Ken Reeves	.30	.75
135 Dave Rimington	.30	.75
136 Reggie Singletary	.30	.75
137 Andre Waters	.30	.75
138 Reggie White	1.25	3.00
139 Roynell Young	.30	.75
140 Aundray Bruce	.30	.75
141 Bobby Butler	.30	.75
142 Bill Fralic	.30	.75
143 Mike Kenn	.30	.75
144 Chris Miller	.60	1.50
145 John Settle	.30	.75
146 George Yarno	.30	.75
147 Michael Carter	.30	.75
148 Wes Chandler	.60	1.50
149 Roger Craig	.60	1.50
150 Randy Cross	.30	.75
151 Riki Ellison	.30	.75
152 Jim Fahnhorst	.30	.75
153 Charles Haley	.60	1.50
154 Barry Helton	.30	.75
155 Guy McIntyre	.30	.75
156 Tim McKyer	.30	.75
157 Joe Montana	10.00	25.00
158 Jerry Rice	5.00	12.00
159 Keena Turner	.30	.75
160 Eric Wright	.30	.75
161 Steve Young	3.00	8.00
162 Raul Allegre	.30	.75
163 Ottis Anderson	.30	.75
164 Billy Ard	.30	.75
165 Carl Banks	.30	.75
166 Mark Bavaro	.30	.75
167 Jim Burt	.30	.75
168 Harry Carson	.30	.75
169 John Elliott	.30	.75
170 Terry Kinard	.30	.75
171 Coon Londota	.30	.75
172 Lionel Manuel	.30	.75
173 Joe Morris	.60	1.50
174 Bart Oates	.30	.75
175 Phil Simms	.60	1.50
176 Pat Leahy	.30	.75
177 Marty Lyons	.30	.75
178 Erik McMillan	.30	.75
179 Freeman McNeil	.60	1.50
180 Scott Mersereau	.30	.75
181 Ken O'Brien	.60	1.50
182 Jim Sweeney	.30	.75
183 Al Toon	.60	1.50
184 Wesley Walker	.60	1.50
185 Jim Arnold	.30	.75
186 Bennie Blades	.30	.75
187 Mike Cofer	.30	.75
188 Keith Ferguson	.30	.75
189 Steve Mott	.30	.75
190 Eddie Murray	.30	.75
191 Harvey Salem	.30	.75
192 Bobby Watkins	.30	.75
193 Keith Bostic	.30	.75
194 Richard Byrd	.30	.75
195 Ray Childress	.30	.75
196 Ernest Givins	.30	.75
197 Kenny Johnson	.30	.75
198 Sean Jones	.30	.75
199 Robert Lyles	.30	.75
200 Bruce Matthews	.30	.75
201 Johnny Meads	.30	.75
202 Warren Moon	1.25	3.00
203 Mike Munchak	.60	1.50
204 Mike Rozier	.30	.75
205 Dean Steinkuhler	.30	.75
206 Tony Zendejas	.30	.75
207 Mark Cannon	.30	.75
208 Alphonso Carreker	.30	.75
209 Phillip Epps	.30	.75
210 Tim Harris	.30	.75
211 Brian Noble	.30	.75
212 Raymond Clayborn	.30	.75
213 Steve Grogan	.60	1.50
214 Roland James	.30	.75
215 Fred Marion	.30	.75
216 Stanley Morgan	.60	1.50
217 Kenneth Sims	.30	.75
218 Andre Tippett	.60	1.50
219 Marcus Allen	1.25	3.00
220 Chris Bahr	.30	.75
221 Steve Beuerlein	1.25	3.00
222 Tim Brown	2.50	6.00
223 Todd Christensen	.30	.75
224 Ron Fellows	.30	.75
225 Willie Gault	.30	.75
226 Mike Haynes	.60	1.50
227 Bo Jackson	.60	1.50
228 James Lofton	.60	1.50
229 Howie Long	1.25	3.00
230 Vann McElroy	.30	.75
231 Hod Martin	.30	.75
232 Matt Millen	.30	.75
233 Bill Pickel	.30	.75
234 Jay Schroeder	.30	.75
235 Stacey Toran	.30	.75
236 Greg Townsend	.30	.75
237 Greg Bell	.30	.75
238 Henry Ellard	.60	1.50
239 Jerry Gray	.30	.75
240 LeRoy Irvin	.30	.75
241 Gary Jeter	.30	.75
242 Johnnie Johnson	.30	.75
243 Larry Kelm	.30	.75
244 Mike Lansford	.30	.75
245 Shawn Miller	.30	.75
246 Mel Owens	.30	.75
247 Jackie Slater	.30	.75
248 Charles White	.30	.75
249 Jeff Bostic	.30	.75
250 Kelvin Bryant	.30	.75
251 Dave Butz	.30	.75
252 Gary Clark	.60	1.50
253 Steve Cox	.30	.75
254 Darryl Grant	.30	.75
255 Darrell Green	.60	1.50
256 Joe Jacoby	.30	.75
257 Mel Kaufman	.30	.75
258 Jim Lachey	.30	.75
259 Dexter Manley	.30	.75
260 Charles Mann	.30	.75
261 Mark May	.30	.75
262 Art Monk	.60	1.50
263 Ricky Sanders	.30	.75
264 Alvin Walton	.30	.75
265 Doug Williams	.60	1.50
266 Morten Andersen	.60	1.50
267 Bruce Clark	.30	.75
268 Jim Dombrowski	.30	.75
269 Mel Gray	.30	.75
270 Bobby Hebert	.30	.75
271 Rickey Jackson	.30	.75
272 Van Jakes	.30	.75
273 Steve Korte	.30	.75
274 Rueben Mayes	.30	.75
275 Sam Mills	.60	1.50
276 Dave Waymer	.30	.75
277 Jeff Bryant	.30	.75
278 Blair Bush	.30	.75
279 Jacob Green	.30	.75
280 Melvin Jenkins	.30	.75
281 Norm Johnson	.30	.75
282 Dave Krieg	.60	1.50
283 Bryan Millard	.30	.75
284 Ruben Rodriguez	.30	.75
285 Terry Taylor	.30	.75
286 Curt Warner	.30	.75
287 Tony Woods	.30	.75
288 Gary Anderson	.30	.75
289 Tunch Ilkin	.30	.75
290 Earnest Jackson	.30	.75
291 Louis Lipps	.30	.75
292 Mike Webster	.60	1.50
293 Rod Woodson	1.25	3.00
294 Joey Browner	.30	.75
295 Anthony Carter	.60	1.50
296 Chris Doleman	.60	1.50
297 Tim Irwin	.30	.75
298 Tommy Kramer	.60	1.50
299 Carl Lee	.30	.75
300 Kirk Lowdermilk	.30	.75
301 Keith Millard	.30	.75
302 Scott Studwell	.30	.75
303 Wade Wilson	.60	1.50
304 Gary Zimmerman	.50	1.25
T1 Atlanta Falcons Team Helmet	.20	.50
T2 Buffalo Bills Team Helmet	.20	.50
T3 Chicago Bears Team Helmet	.20	.50
T4 Cincinnati Bengals Team Helmet	.20	.50
T5 Cleveland Browns Team Helmet	.20	.50
T6 Dallas Cowboys Team Helmet	.30	.75
T7 Denver Broncos Team Helmet	.30	.75
T8 Detroit Lions Team Helmet	.20	.50
T9 Green Bay Packers Team Helmet	.30	.75
T10 Houston Oilers Team Helmet	.20	.50
T11 Indianapolis Colts Team Helmet	.20	.50
T12 Kansas City Chiefs Team Helmet	.20	.50
T13 Los Angeles Raiders Team Helmet	.30	.75
T14 Los Angeles Rams Team Helmet	.20	.50
T15 Miami Dolphins Team Helmet	.30	.75
T16 Minnesota Vikings Team Helmet	.20	.50
T17 New England Patriots Team Helmet	.20	.50
T18 New Orleans Saints Team Helmet	.20	.50
T19 New York Giants Team Helmet	.20	.50
T20 New York Jets Team Helmet	.20	.50
T21 Philadelphia Eagles Team Helmet	.20	.50
T22 Phoenix Cardinals Team Helmet	.20	.50
T23 Pittsburgh Steelers Team Helmet	.30	.75
T24 San Diego Chargers Team Helmet	.20	.50
T25 San Francisco 49ers Team Helmet	.30	.75
T26 Seattle Seahawks Team Helmet	.20	.50
T27 Tampa Bay Buccaneers Team Helmet	.20	.50
T28 Washington Redskins Team Helmet	.30	.75

1972-74 Franklin Mint HOF Coins Bronze

Issued by the Pro Football Hall of Fame in Canton, Ohio and the Franklin Mint, this collection of 50-coins honors inducted players and coaches chosen by the Hall's Selection Committee. The larger coins were released by subsciption over the course of three years. The year of issue can be found on the serrated edge of the coin in very fine print. Reported mintage figures were 1,946 silver coins and 1,802 bronze coins with each coin containing 1-ounce of metal. The fronts feature a double image: a large portrait and an action scene. The unnumbered backs carry the Hall of Fame Logo, the player's name, position and a summary of his accomplishments. Each set came with a colorful album with a black-and-white action pencil drawing and a biography for each player. Another cardboard "mount" album was issued for use in housing the larger coin set. In 1976, the set was re-released in miniature form (roughly 1/2" diameter) as a complete set. These "minis" were issued sealed on a backer board and came with a jewelry style case to house the coins.

COMPLETE SET (50)	250.00	500.00
*SILVER MINI COINS: .3X TO .8X BRONZE		
1 Cliff Battles	4.00	10.00
2 Sammy Baugh	10.00	25.00
3 Chuck Bednarik	6.00	15.00
4 Bert Bell	4.00	10.00
5 Paul Brown 74	6.00	15.00
6 Joe Carr	4.00	10.00
7 Guy Chamberlin	4.00	10.00
8 Dutch Clark	5.00	12.00
9 Jimmy Conzelman	4.00	10.00
10 Art Donovan	6.00	15.00
11 Paddy Driscoll	4.00	10.00
12 Bill Dudley	5.00	12.00
13 Dan Fortmann	4.00	10.00
14 Otto Graham 73	10.00	25.00
15 Red Grange 72	12.00	30.00
16 George Halas 74	8.00	20.00
17 Mel Hein	4.00	10.00
18 Fats Henry	5.00	12.00
19 Bill Hewitt	4.00	10.00
20 Clarke Hinkle	4.00	10.00
21 Elroy Hirsch 73	6.00	15.00
22 Cal Hubbard	4.00	10.00
23 Lamar Hunt 74	4.00	10.00
24 Don Hutson	6.00	15.00
25 Curly Lambeau	5.00	12.00
26 Bobby Layne 73	8.00	20.00
27 Vince Lombardi 74	15.00	40.00
28 Sid Luckman	8.00	20.00
29 Gino Marchetti	5.00	12.00
30 Ollie Matson	6.00	15.00
31 George McAfee	5.00	12.00
32 Hugh McElhenny 73	6.00	15.00
33 Johnny Blood McNally	4.00	10.00
34 Marion Motley 73	6.00	15.00
35 Bronko Nagurski	12.00	30.00
36 Ernie Nevers 72	5.00	12.00
37 Leo Nomellini 74	5.00	12.00
38 Steve Owen	4.00	10.00
39 Joe Perry 73	5.00	12.00
40 Pete Pihos 73	5.00	12.00
41 Andy Robustelli	5.00	12.00
42 Ken Strong	5.00	12.00
43 Jim Thorpe	12.00	30.00
44 Y.A. Tittle 74	8.00	20.00
45 Charley Trippi 73	5.00	12.00
46 Emlen Tunnell 74	5.00	12.00
47 Bulldog Turner	5.00	12.00
48 Norm Van Brocklin 74	6.00	15.00
49 Steve Van Buren 73	6.00	15.00
50 Bob Waterfield 73	6.00	15.00

1972-74 Franklin Mint HOF Coins Silver

1 Cliff Battles	30.00	40.00
2 Sammy Baugh	30.00	40.00
3 Chuck Bednarik	30.00	40.00
4 Bert Bell	30.00	40.00
5 Paul Brown 74	30.00	40.00
6 Joe Carr	30.00	40.00
7 Guy Chamberlin	30.00	40.00
8 Dutch Clark	30.00	40.00
9 Jimmy Conzelman	30.00	40.00
10 Art Donovan	30.00	40.00
11 Paddy Driscoll	30.00	40.00
12 Bill Dudley	30.00	40.00
13 Dan Fortmann	30.00	40.00
14 Otto Graham 73	30.00	40.00
15 Red Grange 72	30.00	50.00
16 George Halas 74	30.00	40.00
17 Mel Hein	30.00	40.00
18 Fats Henry	30.00	40.00
19 Bill Hewitt	30.00	40.00
20 Clarke Hinkle	30.00	40.00
21 Elroy Hirsch 73	30.00	40.00
22 Cal Hubbard	30.00	40.00
23 Lamar Hunt 74	30.00	40.00
24 Don Hutson	30.00	40.00
25 Curly Lambeau	30.00	40.00
26 Bobby Layne 73	30.00	40.00
27 Vince Lombardi 74	30.00	60.00
28 Sid Luckman	30.00	40.00
29 Gino Marchetti	30.00	40.00
30 Ollie Matson	30.00	40.00
31 George McAfee	30.00	40.00
32 Hugh McElhenny 73	30.00	40.00
33 Johnny Blood McNally	30.00	40.00
34 Marion Motley 73	30.00	40.00
35 Bronko Nagurski	30.00	50.00
36 Ernie Nevers 72	30.00	40.00
37 Leo Nomellini 74	30.00	40.00
38 Steve Owen	30.00	40.00
39 Joe Perry 73	30.00	40.00
40 Pete Pihos 73	30.00	40.00
41 Andy Robustelli	30.00	40.00
42 Ken Strong	30.00	40.00
43 Jim Thorpe	30.00	50.00
44 Y.A. Tittle 74	30.00	40.00
45 Charley Trippi 73	30.00	40.00
46 Emlen Tunnell 74	30.00	40.00
47 Bulldog Turner	30.00	40.00
48 Norm Van Brocklin 74	30.00	40.00
49 Steve Van Buren 73	30.00	40.00
50 Bob Waterfield 73	30.00	40.00

1990 Fresno Bandits Smokey

This 25-card standard-size set features the Fresno Bandits, a semi-professional football team. The fronts display black-and-white posed player photos inside white borders. Red and black designs edge the picture. The Smokey the Bear logo appears in the upper left corner, while the team logo is printed in the lower right. The backs carry biography, a black-and-white photo picturing the player with Smokey, and a safety slogan. The cards are unnumbered and checklisted below in alphabetical order.

COMPLETE SET (25)	10.00	25.00
1 Allan Blades	.50	1.25
2 Corey Clark	.50	1.25
3 Darryl Duke	.50	1.25
4 Heikoti Fakava	.50	1.25
5 Charles Frazier	.50	1.25
6 Chris Geile	.50	1.25
7 Mike Henson	.50	1.25
8 James Hickey	.50	1.25
9 Anthony Howard	.50	1.25
10 Derrick Jinks	.50	1.25
11 Anthony Jones	.50	1.25
12 Marvin Jones	.50	1.25
13 Mike Jones	.50	1.25
14 Steve Loop	.50	1.25
15 Thomas Ireland	.50	1.25
16 Jay Lynch	.50	1.25
17 Sheldon Martin	.50	1.25
18 Chuckie McCutchen	.50	1.25
19 Lance Oberparleiter	.50	1.25
20 Darrell Rosette	.50	1.25
21 Fred Sims	.50	1.25
22 Bryan Turner	.50	1.25
23 Jim Woods CO	.50	1.25
24 Rick Zumwalt	.50	1.25
25 Coaching Staff	.50	1.25

1991 Fresno Bandits Smokey

This 27-card set of the Fresno Brandits was sponsored by Sierra National Forest and Fresno-Kings Ranger Unit. The fronts feature black-and-white player photos. The backs carry player information and a fire prevention cartoon starring Smokey the Bear. The cards are unnumbered and checklisted below in alphabetical order.

COMPLETE SET (27)	10.00	25.00
1 Kyle Cabott	.40	1.00
2 Derrick Chachere	.40	1.00
3 Eric Coleman WR	.40	1.00
4 Steve Domingos	.40	1.00
5 Carlos Hannon	.40	1.00
6 Tim Hardin	.40	1.00
7 Mike Henson	.40	1.00
8 Keith Hill	.40	1.00
9 Jeff Hulsey	.40	1.00
10 Keith Jenkins	.40	1.00
11 Derrick Jinks	.60	1.50
12 Niko Liulamaga	.40	1.00
13 Steve Loop	.40	1.00
14 Stacy Marshall	.40	1.00
15 Bob Martin CO	.40	1.00
16 Sheldon Martin	.40	1.00
17 Daren Miller	.40	1.00
18 Kevin Newton	.40	1.00
19 Shante' Rhodes	.40	1.00
20 James Sanders	.40	1.00
21 Sandy Sledge	.40	1.00
22 Anthony Stitt	.40	1.00
23 Bryan Tobey	.40	1.00
24 JJ Velasco	.40	1.00
25 Dave Walter	.40	1.00
26 Derrick Williams	.40	1.00
27 Smokey Bear CL	.40	1.00

1989 Frito Lay Stickers

These tiny (roughly 1-1/2" x 1-1/2") blankbacked color stickers feature one NFL player on the front along with his name, position, and team name. They were issued in bags of various Frito Lay chips and involve a redemption program around the winner of Super Bowl XXIV. The stickers were licensed through the NFLPA and MSA.

1 Bennie Blades	7.50	15.00
2 Bill Brooks	7.50	15.00
3 James Brooks	10.00	20.00
4 Joey Browner	7.50	15.00
5 Deron Cherry	7.50	15.00
6 Jim Everett	10.00	20.00
7 Willie Gault	10.00	20.00
8 Darrell Green	12.50	25.00
9 Roy Green	7.50	15.00
10 Dalton Hilliard	7.50	15.00
11 Vance Johnson	7.50	15.00
12 Louis Lipps	10.00	20.00
13 Dan Marino	50.00	100.00
14 Joe Montana	50.00	100.00
15 Warren Moon	12.50	25.00
16 Ozzie Newsome	10.00	20.00
17 Sterling Sharpe	10.00	20.00
18 Phil Simms	12.50	25.00
19 Mike Singletary	15.00	30.00
20 Tim Spencer	7.50	15.00
21 Andre Tippett	10.00	20.00
22 Al Toon	10.00	20.00
23 Everson Walls	7.50	15.00
24 James Wilder	7.50	15.00

1963 Gad Fun Cards

This set of 1963 Fun Cards were issued by a sports illustrator by the name of Gad from Minneapolis, Minnesota. The cards are printed on cardboard stock paper. The borderless fronts have black and white line drawings. A fun sport's fact or player career statistic is depicted in the drawing. The backs of the first six cards display numbers used to play the game explained on card number 6. The other backs carry a cartoon with a joke or riddle. Copyright information is listed on the lower portion of the card.

COMPLETE SET (84)	37.50	75.00
74 Minnesota Football Team/1949	.25	.50
81 Highest Football Game Score	.25	.50

1992 GameDay Draft Day Promos

This 13-card promo set was produced by NFL Properties. In the May 1, 1992 edition of USA Today, an ad ran offering to the public 2,500 sets for 50.00 each with the proceeds going to NFL Charities. Other unnumbered sets (originally reported as 10,000 sets but later discovered to be only a small percentage of the original reported amount with many of these other sets missing one player) were also available through various media and dealer channels. The cards were patterned after 1965 Topps football and thus measure approximately 2 1/2" by 4 11/16". Several cards of the same player were issued to reflect different draft day scenarios; 13 different combos existed. Card fronts feature a full-color action picture in a small colored border enclosed by a white border. The team name beneath the photo is in gray lettering, while the player's name appears in block lettering. The title "NFL GameDay" is below the name. Horizontal backs feature the player's team helmet in a box, biography, and the NFL Draft logo in the white border on the far left. A full-color photo is also on the back along with a summary of the player's collegiate career. Although all the cards are numbered "1" on the back, they are checklisted below in alphabetical order according to the player's last name.

COMPLETE SET (13)	6.00	15.00
1A Quentin Coryatt (Rams)	.60	1.50
1B Vaughn Dunbar (Falcons)	.60	1.50
1C Vaughn Dunbar (49ers)	.60	1.50
1D Vaughn Dunbar (Seahawks)	.60	1.50
1E Steve Emtman (Colts)	.60	1.50
1F Steve Emtman (Rams)	.60	1.50
1G Desmond Howard (Colts)	1.20	3.00
1H Desmond Howard (Redskins)	1.20	3.00
1I David Klingler (Chiefs)	.60	1.50
1J David Klingler (Giants)	.60	1.50
1K Troy Vincent (Bengals)	.60	1.50
1L Troy Vincent (Colts)	.60	1.50
1M Troy Vincent (Packers)	.60	1.50

1992 GameDay

This 500-card set measures 2 1/2" by 4 11/16" and was issued in 12-card packs. In terms of card size, it is the largest basic issue set since 1965 Topps. The set includes 14 multi-player special cards which feature 56 rookies chosen after the third round of the 1992 draft. Rookie Cards include Edgar Bennett, Steve Bono, Robert Brooks, Terrell Buckley, Mark Chmura, Marco Coleman, Quentin Coryatt, Steve Emtman, Chester McGlockton, Johnny Mitchell, Carl Pickens, and Tommy Vardell.

COMPLETE SET (500)	25.00	50.00
1 Jim Kelly	.15	.40

2 Mark Ingram	.02	.10
3 Travis McNeal	.02	.10
4 Ricky Ervins	.02	.10
5 Joe Montana	.75	2.00
6 Broderick Thompson	.02	.10
7 Darion Conner	.02	.10
8 Jim Harbaugh	.15	.40
9 Harvey Williams	.07	.20
10 Chip Banks	.02	.10
11 Henry Thomas	.02	.10
12 Derek Brown TE RC	.02	.10
13 James Joseph	.02	.10
14 Kevin Fagan	.02	.10
15 Chuck Klingbeil RC	.02	.10
16 Harlon Barnett	.02	.10
17 Jim Price	.02	.10
18 Terrell Buckley RC	.02	.10
19 Paul McJulien RC	.02	.10
20 James Hasty	.02	.10
21 James Francis	.02	.10
22 Andre Tippett	.02	.10
23 John Elway	.60	1.50
24 Eric Dickerson	.07	.20
25 James Jefferson	.02	.10
26 Danny Noonan	.02	.10
27 Warren Moon	.15	.40
28 Gene Atkins	.02	.10
29 Jessie Hester	.02	.10
30 Mike Mooney RC	.02	.10
Kevin Smith RBK RC		
Ron Humphrey RC		
Tracy Boyd RC		
31 Toby Caston RC	.02	.10
32 Howard Dinkins RC	.02	.10
33 James Patton RC	.02	.10
34 Walter Reeves	.02	.10
35 Johnny Mitchell RC	.02	.10
36 Mike Brim RC	.02	.10
37 Irving Fryar	.07	.20
38 Lewis Billups	.02	.10
39 Alonzo Spellman RC	.07	.20
40 John Friesz	.07	.20
41 Patrick Hunter	.02	.10
42 Reuben Davis	.02	.10
43 Tom Myslinski RC	.02	.10
Shawn Harper RC		
Mark Thomas RC		
Mike Frier RC		
44 Siran Stacy RC	.02	.10
45 Stephone Paige	.02	.10
46 Eddie Robinson RC	.02	.10
47 Tracy Scroggins RC	.02	.10
48 David Klingler RC	.02	.10
49A Deion Sanders ERR (Last line of card says outfielder)	.25	.60
49B Deion Sanders COR (Last line of card says plays outfield)	.25	.60
50 Tom Waddle	.02	.10
51 Gary Anderson RB	.02	.10
52 Kevin Butler	.02	.10
53 Bruce Smith	.15	.40
54 Steve Sewell	.02	.10
55 Wesley Walls	.02	.10
56 Lawrence Taylor	.15	.40
57 Mike Merriweather	.02	.10
58 Roman Phifer	.02	.10
59 Shaun Gayle	.02	.10
60 Marc Boutte RC	.02	.10
61 Tony Mayberry RC	.02	.10
62 Antone Davis UER (Card has 9th pick in/1991 draft, was 8th)	.02	.10
63 Rod Bernstine	.02	.10
64 Shane Collins RC	.02	.10
65 Martin Bayless	.02	.10
66 Corey Harris RC	.02	.10
67 Jason Hanson RC	.07	.20
68 John Fina RC	.02	.10
69 Cornelius Bennett	.07	.20
70 Mark Bortz	.02	.10
71 Gary Anderson K	.02	.10
72 Paul Siever RC	.02	.10
73 Flipper Anderson	.02	.10
74 Shane Dronett RC	.02	.10
75 Brian Noble	.02	.10
76 Tim Green	.02	.10
77 Percy Snow	.02	.10
78 Greg McMurtry	.02	.10
79 Dana Hall RC	.02	.10
80 Tyji Armstrong RC	.02	.10
81 Gary Clark	.07	.20
82 Steve Emtman RC	.02	.10
83 Eric Moore	.02	.10
84 Brent Jones	.07	.20
85 Ray Seals RC	.02	.10
86 James Jones	.02	.10
87 Jeff Hostetler	.07	.20
88 Keith Jackson	.07	.20
89 Gary Plummer	.02	.10
90 Robert Blackmon	.02	.10
91 Larry Tharpe RC	.02	.10
Michael Brandon RC		
Anthony Hamlet RC		
Mike Pawlawski RC		
92 Greg Skrepenak RC	.02	.10
93 Kevin Call	.02	.10
94 Clarence Kay	.02	.10
95 William Fuller	.02	.10
96 Troy Auzenne RC	.02	.10
97 Carl Pickens RC	.15	.40
98 Lorenzo White	.02	.10
99 Doug Smith	.02	.10
100 Dale Carter RC	.07	.20
101 Fred McAfee RC	.02	.10
102 Jack Del Rio	.02	.10
103 Vaughn Dunbar RC	.02	.10
104 J.J. Birden	.02	.10
105 Harris Barton	.02	.10
106 Ray Ethridge RC	.02	.10
107 John Gesek	.02	.10
108 Mike Singletary	.07	.20
109 Mark Rypien	.02	.10
110 Robb Thomas	.02	.10
111 Joe Kelly	.02	.10
112 Ben Smith	.02	.10
113 Neil O'Donnell	.07	.20
114 John L. Williams	.02	.10
115 Mike Sherrard	.02	.10
116 Chad Hennings RC	.07	.20
117 Henry Ellard	.07	.20
118 Jay Hilgenberg	.02	.10
119 Charles Dimry	.02	.10
120 Chuck Smith RC	.02	.10
121 Brian Mitchell	.07	.20
122 Eric Allen	.02	.10
123 Nate Lewis	.02	.10
124 Kevin Ross	.02	.10
125 Jimmy Smith RC	1.25	3.00
126 Kevin Smith RC	.02	.10
127 Larry Webster RC	.02	.10
128 Marv Cook	.02	.10
129 Calvin Williams	.07	.20
130 Harry Swayne RC	.02	.10
131 Jimmie Jones	.02	.10
132 Ethan Horton	.02	.10
133 Chris Mims RC	.02	.10
134 Derrick Thomas	.15	.40
135 Gerald Dixon RC	.02	.10
136 Gary Zimmerman	.02	.10
137 Robert Jones RC	.02	.10
138 Steve Broussard	.02	.10
139 David Wyman	.02	.10
140 Ian Beckles	.02	.10
141 Steve Bono RC	.15	.40
142 Cris Carter	.20	.50
143 Anthony Carter	.07	.20
144 Greg Townsend	.02	.10
145 Al Smith	.02	.10
146 Troy Vincent RC	.02	.10
147 Jessie Tuggle	.02	.10
148 David Fulcher	.02	.10
149 Johnny Rembert	.02	.10
150 Ernie Jones	.02	.10
151 Mark Royals	.02	.10
152 Jeff Bryant	.02	.10
153 Vai Sikahema	.02	.10
154 Tony Woods	.02	.10
155 Joe Bowden RC	.02	.10
Doug Rigby RC		
Marcus Dowdell RC		
Ostell Miles RC		
156 Mark Carrier WR	.07	.20
157 Joe Nash	.02	.10
158 Keith Van Horne	.02	.10
159 Kelvin Martin	.02	.10
160 Peter Tom Willis	.02	.10
161 Richard Johnson	.02	.10
162 Louis Oliver	.02	.10
163 Nick Lowery	.02	.10
164 Ricky Proehl	.02	.10
165 Terance Mathis	.07	.20
166 Keith Sims	.02	.10
167 E.J. Junior	.02	.10
168 Scott Mersereau	.02	.10
169 Tom Rathman	.02	.10
170 Robert Harris RC	.02	.10
171 Ashley Ambrose RC	.15	.40
172 David Treadwell	.02	.10
173 Mark Green	.02	.10
174 Clayton Holmes RC	.02	.10
175 Tony Sacca RC	.02	.10
176 Wes Hopkins	.02	.10
177 Mark Wheeler RC	.02	.10
178 Robert Clark	.02	.10
179 Eugene Daniel	.02	.10
180 Rob Burnett	.02	.10
181 Al Edwards	.02	.10
182 Clarence Verdin	.02	.10
183 Tom Newberry	.02	.10
184 Mike Jones	.02	.10
185 Roy Foster	.02	.10
186 Leslie O'Neal	.07	.20
187 Izel Jenkins	.02	.10
188 Willie Clay RC	.15	.40
Ty Detmer		
Mike Evans RC		
Ed McDaniel RC		
189 Mike Tomczak	.02	.10
190 Leonard Wheeler RC	.02	.10
191 Gaston Green	.02	.10
192 Maury Buford	.02	.10
193 Jeremy Lincoln RC	.02	.10
194 Todd Collins RC	.02	.10
195 Billy Ray Smith	.02	.10
196 Renaldo Turnbull	.02	.10
197 Michael Carter	.02	.10
198 Rod Milstead RC	.02	.10
Dion Lambert RC		
Hesham Ismail RC		
Reggie E. White RC		
199 Shawn Collins	.02	.10
200 Issiac Holt	.02	.10
201 Irv Eatman	.02	.10
202 Anthony Thompson	.02	.10
203 Chester McGlockton RC	.07	.20
204 Greg Briggs RC	.02	.10
Chris Crooms RC		
Ephesians Bartley RC		
Curtis Whitley RC		
205 James Brown RC	.02	.10
206 Marvin Washington	.02	.10
207 Richard Cooper RC	.02	.10
208 Jim C. Jensen	.02	.10
209 Sam Seale	.02	.10
210 Andre Reed	.07	.20
211 Thane Gash	.02	.10
212 Randal Hill	.02	.10
213 Brad Baxter	.02	.10
214 Michael Cofer	.02	.10
215 Ray Crockett	.02	.10
216 Tony Mandarich	.02	.10
217 Warren Williams	.02	.10
218 Erik Kramer	.07	.20
219 Bubby Brister	.07	.20
220 Steve Young	.30	.75
221 Jeff George	.15	.40
222 James Washington	.02	.10
223 Bruce Alexander RC	.02	.10
224 Broderick Thomas	.02	.10
225 Bern Brostek	.02	.10
226 Brian Blades	.07	.20
227 Troy Aikman	.40	1.00
228 Aaron Wallace	.02	.10
229 Tommy Jeter RC	.02	.10
230 Russell Maryland	.02	.10
231 Charles Haley	.07	.20
232 James Lofton	.07	.20
233 William White	.02	.10
234 Tim McGee	.02	.10
235 Haywood Jeffires	.07	.20
236 Charles Mann	.02	.10
237 Robert Lyles	.02	.10
238 Rohn Stark	.02	.10
239 Jim Morrissey	.02	.10
240 Mel Gray	.07	.20
241 Barry Word	.02	.10
242 Dave Widell RC	.02	.10
243 Sean Gilbert RC	.07	.20
244 Tommy Maddox RC	.75	2.00
245 Bernie Kosar	.07	.20
246 John Roper	.02	.10
247 Mark Higgs	.02	.10
248 Rob Moore	.07	.20
249 Dan Fike	.02	.10
250 Dan Saleaumua	.02	.10
251 Tim Krumrie	.02	.10
252 Tony Casillas	.02	.10
253 Jayice Pearson RC	.02	.10
254 Dan Marino	.60	1.50
255 Tony Martin	.07	.20
256 Mike Fox	.02	.10
257 Courtney Hawkins RC	.07	.20
258 Leonard Marshall	.02	.10
259 Willie Gault	.07	.20
260 Al Toon	.07	.20
261 Browning Nagle	.02	.10
262 Ronnie Lott	.07	.20
263 Sean Jones	.02	.10
264 Ernest Givins	.07	.20
265 Ray Donaldson	.02	.10
266 Vaughan Johnson	.02	.10
267 Tommy Hodson	.02	.10
268 Chris Doleman	.02	.10
269 Pat Swilling	.02	.10
270 Merril Hoge	.02	.10
271 Bill Maas	.02	.10
272 Sterling Sharpe	.15	.40
273 Mitchell Price	.02	.10
274 Richard Brown RC	.02	.10
275 Randall Cunningham	.15	.40
276 Chris Martin	.02	.10
277 Courtney Hall	.02	.10
278 Michael Walter	.02	.10
279 Ricardo McDonald RC	.02	.10
David Wilson RC		
Sean Lumpkin RC		
Tony Brooks RC		
280 Bill Brooks	.02	.10
281 Jay Schroeder	.02	.10
282 John Stephens	.02	.10
283 William Perry	.07	.20
284 Floyd Turner	.02	.10
285 Carnell Lake	.02	.10
286 Joel Steed RC	.02	.10
287 Vinnie Clark	.02	.10
288 Ken Norton	.07	.20
289 Eric Thomas	.02	.10
290 Derrick Fenner	.02	.10
291 Tony Smith RC	.02	.10
292 Eric Metcalf	.07	.20
293 Roger Craig	.07	.20
294 Leon Searcy RC	.02	.10
295 Tyrone Legette RC	.02	.10
296 Rob Taylor	.02	.10
297 Eric Williams	.02	.10
298 David Little	.02	.10
299 Wayne Martin	.02	.10
300 Eric Martin	.02	.10
301 Jim Everett	.07	.20
302 Michael Dean Perry	.07	.20
303 Dwayne White RC	.02	.10
304 Greg Lloyd	.07	.20
305 Ricky Reynolds	.02	.10
306 Anthony Smith	.02	.10
307 Robert Delpino	.02	.10
308 Ken Clark	.02	.10
309 Chris Jacke	.02	.10
310 Reggie Dwight RC	.02	.10
Anthony McCoy RC		
Craig Thompson RC		
Klaus Wilmsmeyer RC		
311 Doug Widell	.02	.10
312 Sammie Smith	.02	.10
313 Ken O'Brien	.02	.10
314 Timm Rosenbach	.02	.10
315 Jesse Sapolu	.02	.10
316 Ronnie Harmon	.02	.10
317 Bill Pickel	.02	.10
318 Lonnie Young	.02	.10
319 Chris Burkett	.02	.10
320 Ervin Randle	.02	.10
321 Ed West	.02	.10
322 Tom Thayer	.02	.10
323 Keith McKeller	.02	.10
324 Webster Slaughter	.02	.10
325 Duane Bickett	.02	.10
326 Howie Long	.15	.40
327 Sam Mills	.02	.10
328 Mike Golic	.02	.10
329 Bruce Armstrong	.02	.10
330 Pat Terrell	.02	.10
331 Mike Pritchard	.07	.20
332 Audray McMillian	.02	.10
333 Marquez Pope RC	.02	.10
334 Pierce Holt	.02	.10
335 Erik Howard	.02	.10
336 Jerry Rice	.40	1.00
337 Vinny Testaverde	.07	.20
338 Bart Oates	.02	.10
339 Nolan Harrison RC	.02	.10
340 Chris Goode	.02	.10
341 Ken Ruettgers	.02	.10
342 Brad Muster	.02	.10
343 Paul Farren	.02	.10
344 Corey Miller RC	.02	.10
345 Brian Washington	.02	.10
346 Jim Sweeney	.02	.10
347 Keith McCants	.02	.10
348 Louis Lipps	.02	.10
349 Keith Byars	.02	.10
350 Steve Walsh	.02	.10
351 Jeff Jaeger	.02	.10
352 Christian Okoye	.02	.10
353 Cris Dishman	.02	.10
354 Keith Kartz	.02	.10
355 Harold Green	.02	.10
356 Richard Shelton RC	.02	.10
357 Jacob Green	.02	.10
358 Al Noga	.02	.10
359 Dean Biasucci	.02	.10
360 Jeff Herrod	.02	.10
361 Bennie Blades	.02	.10
362 Mark Vlasic	.02	.10
363 Chris Miller	.07	.20
364 Bubba McDowell	.02	.10
365 Tyronne Stowe RC	.02	.10
366 Jon Vaughn	.02	.10
367 Winston Moss	.02	.10
368 Levon Kirkland RC	.02	.10
369 Ted Washington	.02	.10
370 Cortez Kennedy	.07	.20
371 Jeff Feagles	.02	.10
372 Aundray Bruce	.02	.10
373 Michael Irvin	.15	.40
374 Lemuel Stinson	.02	.10
375 Billy Joe Tolliver	.02	.10
376 Anthony Munoz	.07	.20
377 Nate Newton	.02	.10
378 Steve Smith	.02	.10
379 Eugene Chung RC	.02	.10
380 Bryan Hinkle	.02	.10
381 Dan McGwire	.02	.10
382 Jeff Cross	.02	.10
383 Ferrell Edmunds	.02	.10
384 Craig Heyward	.07	.20
385 Shannon Sharpe	.15	.40
386 Anthony Miller	.07	.20
387 Eugene Lockhart	.02	.10
388 Darryl Henley	.02	.10
389 LeRoy Butler	.02	.10
390 Scott Fulhage	.02	.10
391 Andre Ware	.02	.10
392 Lionel Washington	.02	.10
393 Rick Fenney	.02	.10
394 John Taylor	.07	.20
395 Chris Singleton	.02	.10
396 Monte Coleman	.02	.10
397 Brett Perriman	.07	.20
398 Hugh Millen	.02	.10
399 Dennis Gentry	.02	.10
400 Eddie Anderson	.02	.10
401 Lance Olberding RC	.02	.10
Eddie Miller RC		
Dwayne Sabb RC		
Corey Widmer RC		
402 Brent Williams	.02	.10
403 Tony Zendejas	.02	.10
404 Donnell Woolford	.02	.10
405 Boomer Esiason	.07	.20
406 Gill Fenerty	.02	.10
407 Kurt Barber RC	.02	.10
408 William Thomas	.02	.10
409 Keith Henderson	.02	.10
410 Paul Gruber	.02	.10
411 Alfred Oglesby	.02	.10
412 Wendell Davis	.02	.10
413 Robert Brooks RC	.30	.75
414 Ken Willis	.02	.10
415 Aaron Cox	.02	.10
416 Thurman Thomas	.15	.40
417 Alton Montgomery	.02	.10
418 Mike Prior	.02	.10
419 Albert Bentley	.02	.10
420 John Randle	.07	.20
421 Dermontti Dawson	.02	.10
422 Phillippi Sparks RC	.02	.10
423 Michael Jackson	.07	.20
424 Carl Banks	.02	.10
425 Chris Zorich	.07	.20
426 Dwight Stone	.02	.10
427 Bryan Millard	.02	.10
428 Neal Anderson	.02	.10
429 Michael Haynes	.07	.20
430 Michael Young	.02	.10
431 Dennis Byrd	.02	.10
432 Fred Barnett	.07	.20
433 Junior Seau	.15	.40
434 Mark Clayton	.07	.20
435 Marco Coleman RC	.02	.10
436 Lee Williams	.02	.10
437 Stan Thomas	.02	.10
438 Lawrence Dawsey	.07	.20
439 Tommy Vardell RC	.02	.10
440 Steve Israel RC	.02	.10
441 Ray Childress	.02	.10
442 Darren Woodson RC	.15	.40
443 Lamar Lathon	.02	.10
444 Reggie Roby	.02	.10
445 Eric Green	.02	.10
446 Mark Carrier DB	.02	.10
447 Kevin Walker	.02	.10
448 Vince Workman	.02	.10
449 Leonard Griffin	.02	.10
450 Robert Porcher RC	.15	.40
451 Hart Lee Dykes	.02	.10
452 Thomas McLemore RC	.02	.10
453 Jamie Dukes RC	.02	.10
454 Bill Romanowski	.02	.10
455 Deron Cherry	.02	.10
456 Burt Grossman	.02	.10
457 Lance Smith	.02	.10
458 Jay Novacek	.07	.20
459 Erric Pegram	.07	.20
460 Reggie Rutland	.02	.10
461 Rickey Jackson	.02	.10
462 Dennis Brown	.02	.10
463 Neil Smith	.15	.40
464 Rich Gannon	.15	.40
465 Herman Moore	.15	.40
466 Rodney Peete	.07	.20
467 Alvin Harper	.07	.20
468 Andre Rison	.07	.20
469 Rufus Porter	.02	.10
470 Robert Wilson	.02	.10
471 Phil Simms	.07	.20
472 Art Monk	.07	.20
473 Mike Tice	.02	.10
474 Quentin Coryatt RC	.02	.10
475 Chris Hinton	.02	.10
476 Vance Johnson	.02	.10
477 Kyle Clifton	.02	.10
478 Garth Jax	.02	.10
479 Ray Agnew	.02	.10
480 Patrick Rowe RC	.02	.10
481 Joe Jacoby	.02	.10
482 Bruce Pickens	.02	.10
483 Keith DeLong	.02	.10
484 Eric Swann	.07	.20
485 Steve McMichael	.07	.20
486 Leroy Hoard	.07	.20
487 Rickey Dixon	.02	.10
488 Robert Perryman	.02	.10
489 Darryl Williams RC	.02	.10
490 Emmitt Smith	.75	2.00
491 Dino Hackett	.02	.10
492 Earnest Byner	.02	.10
493 Bucky Richardson RC	.02	.10
Bernard Dafney RC		
Anthony Davis RC		
Tony Brown RC		
494 Bill Johnson RC	.02	.10
495 Darryl Ashmore RC	.02	.10
Joe Campbell RC		
Kelvin Harris RC		
Tim Lester RC		
496 Nick Bell	.02	.10
497 Jerry Ball	.02	.10
498 Edgar Bennett RC	.15	.40
Mark Chmura RC		
Chris Holder RC		
Mazio Royster RC		
499 Steve Christie	.02	.10
500 Kenneth Davis	.02	.10
P1 Promo Sheet	2.00	5.00
Joe Montana		
Lawrence Taylor		
Mark Rypien		
Bernie Kosar		
Chris Doleman		
Randall Cunningham		

1992 GameDay Promo Sheets

These 6-card perforated sheets were issued to preview the 1992 GameDay football card set. Each card appears to be exactly like the basic pack version single card but on close inspection differences on the cardbacks can be found as noted below.

5 Joe Montana	1.50	4.00
49 Deion Sanders	.75	2.00
56 Lawrence Taylor	.50	1.25
109 Mark Rypien	.40	1.00
227 Troy Aikman	1.00	2.50
245 Bernie Kosar	.40	1.00
268 Chris Doleman	.30	.75
269 Pat Swilling	.30	.75
275 Randall Cunningham	.40	1.00
326 Howie Long	.50	1.25
416 Thurman Thomas	.60	1.50
492 Earnest Byner	.30	.75
S1 Sheet 1/#5 Joe Montana/ reads 'only three time...' on back/ instead of 'lone three time...')/56 Lawrence Taylor/ sack total:131 instead of/ sack total: 131.0 for pack version/109 Mark Rypien/ reads 'and was named MVP...'/ instead of '	3.00	8.00
S2 49 Deion Sanders/ NFC logo missing on back/227 Troy Aikman/ NFC logo missing on back/416 Thurman Thomas/ AFC logo missing on back/326 Howie Long/ AFC logo missing on back/269 Pat Swilling/ NFC logo missing on back/492 Earnest Byner/	3.00	8.00

1992 GameDay National

The cards in this 46-card preview set were given away during the 13th National Sports Card Convention in Atlanta, Georgia. An attractive black vinyl notebook with a cardboard slip cover was available to hold the cards. Like the 1965 Topps football set, these cards measure approximately 2 1/2" by 4 11/16". The players featured on each card front are in color against a black and white background. The horizontally oriented backs have career statistics, biography, and a color head shot. The cards are numbered on the back. Reportedly the cards of Deron Cherry, Mark Rypien, and Deion Sanders were individually distributed in limited quantities at the National in Atlanta.

COMPLETE SET (46)	20.00	50.00
1 Deion Sanders SP	1.20	3.00
2 Jim Kelly	.40	1.00
3 Jim Harbaugh	.20	.50
4 Boomer Esiason	.20	.50
5 Bernie Kosar	.20	.50
6 Troy Aikman	1.60	4.00
7 John Elway	3.20	8.00
8 Rodney Peete	.08	.25
9 Sterling Sharpe	.20	.50
10 Warren Moon	.40	1.00
11 Jeff George	.20	.50
12 Derrick Thomas	.20	.50
13 Howie Long	.20	.50
14 Jim Everett	.08	.25
15 Dan Marino	3.20	8.00
16 Chris Doleman	.08	.25
17 Irving Fryar	.08	.25
18 Pat Swilling	.08	.25
19 Lawrence Taylor	.40	1.00
20 Ken O'Brien	.08	.25
21 Randall Cunningham	.40	1.00
22 Timm Rosenbach	.08	.25
23 Bubby Brister	.40	1.00
24 John Friesz	.08	.25
25 Joe Montana	3.20	8.00
26 Dan McGwire	.08	.25
27 Vinny Testaverde	.20	.50
28 Mark Rypien SP	.08	.25
29 Ronnie Lott	.40	1.00
30 Marco Coleman	.08	.25
31 Rob Moore	.20	.50
32 Bill Pickel	.08	.25
33 Brad Baxter	.08	.25
34 Steve Broussard	.08	.25
35 Darion Conner	.08	.25
36 Chris Hinton	.08	.25
37 Erric Pegram	.08	.25
38 Jessie Tuggle	.08	.25
39 Billy Joe Tolliver	.08	.25
40 David Klingler	.20	.50
41 Michael Irvin	.40	1.00
42 Emmitt Smith	3.20	8.00
43 Quentin Coryatt	.20	.50
44 Steve Emtman	.08	.25
45 Deron Cherry SP	.40	1.00
46 Ricky Ervins	.08	.25

1992-93 GameDay Gamebreakers

This 14-card set was first made available at the Super Bowl card show to preview the 1993 design. The cards, patterned after 1965 Topps football, measure approximately 2 1/2" by 4 11/16". The checklist card is printed with the individual number of the set and the total number produced (5,000).

COMPLETE SET (14)	3.20	8.00
1 Marco Coleman	.07	.20
2 Bill Cowher CO	.10	.30
3 John Elway	1.20	3.00
4 Barry Foster	.07	.20
5 Cortez Kennedy	.10	.30
6 James Lofton	.10	.30
7 Art Monk	.10	.30
8 Jerry Rice	.60	1.50
9 Sterling Sharpe	.10	.30
10 Emmitt Smith	1.20	3.00
11 Thurman Thomas	.20	.50
12 Gino Torretta	.07	.20
13 Steve Young	.50	1.25
14 Checklist Card	.07	.20

1992-93 GameDay Super Bowl Program Promos

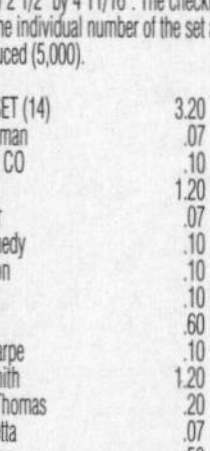

This six-card promo set was inserted one card per 1993 Super Bowl program. Each card measures approximately 2 1/2" by 4 3/4". The cards are numbered on the back and identified as promo cards.

COMPLETE SET (6)	4.80	12.00
1 Troy Aikman	2.00	5.00
2 Terry Allen	.80	2.00
3 Ray Childress	.50	1.25
4 Marco Coleman	.50	1.25
5 Barry Foster	.50	1.25
6 Sterling Sharpe	.80	2.00

1993 GameDay

Issued by Fleer in 12-card packs, this set consists of 480 cards measuring approximately 2 1/2" by 4 3/4". Rookie Cards include Jerome Bettis, Drew Bledsoe, Reggie Brooks, Curtis Conway, Andre Hastings, Garrison Hearst, Qadry Ismail, Terry Kirby, O.J. McDuffie, Natrone Means, Glyn Milburn, Rick Mirer, Roosevelt Potts, Robert Smith, Dana Stubblefield and Kevin Williams. A six-card promo sheet was produced and priced below.

COMPLETE SET (480)	12.50	30.00
1 Troy Aikman	.30	.75
2 Terry Allen	.08	.25
3 Ray Childress	.01	.05
4 Marco Coleman	.01	.05
5 Barry Foster	.02	.10
6 Sterling Sharpe	.08	.25
7 Steve McMichael	.02	.10
8 Steve Young	.30	.75
9 Derrick Thomas	.08	.25
10 John Elway	.60	1.50
11 Drew Bledsoe RC	1.00	2.50
12 Jim Kelly	.08	.25
13 Dan Marino	.60	1.50
14 Mo Lewis	.01	.05
15 David Klingler	.01	.05
16 Darrell Green	.01	.05
17 James Francis	.01	.05
18 John Copeland RC	.02	.10
19 Terry McDaniel	.01	.05
20 Barry Sanders	.50	1.25
21 Deion Sanders	.20	.50
22 Emmitt Smith	.60	1.50
23 Marion Butts	.01	.05
24 Darryl Talley	.01	.05
25 Randall Cunningham	.08	.25
26 Rod Woodson	.08	.25
27 Terrell Buckley	.01	.05
28 Michael Haynes	.02	.10
29 Tony Jones	.01	.05
30 Santana Dotson	.02	.10
31 Lomas Brown	.01	.05
32 Eric Metcalf	.02	.10
33 Morten Andersen	.01	.05
34 Reggie Cobb	.01	.05
35 Ferrell Edmunds	.01	.05
36 Joe Montana	.60	1.50
37 Ken Harvey	.01	.05
38 Rodney Hampton	.02	.10
39 Kurt Gouveia	.01	.05
40 Ken Norton Jr.	.02	.10
41 Frank Reich	.02	.10
42 Kevin Greene	.02	.10
43 Cleveland Gary	.01	.05
44 Maurice Hurst	.01	.05
45 Troy Vincent	.01	.05
46 Eric Curry RC	.01	.05
47 Curtis Conway RC	.15	.40
48 Christian Okoye	.01	.05
49 Tunch Ilkin	.01	.05
50 Michael Irvin	.08	.25
51 Bart Oates	.01	.05
52 Pepper Johnson	.01	.05
53 Vaughan Johnson	.01	.05
54 Lawrence Taylor	.08	.25
55 Junior Seau	.08	.25
56 Michael Brooks	.01	.05
57 Neal Anderson	.01	.05
58 D.J. Johnson	.01	.05
59 Seth Joyner	.01	.05
60 Marvin Washington	.01	.05
61 Ernest Givins	.02	.10
62 Jaime Fields RC	.01	.05
63 Vincent Brown	.01	.05
64 Randall McDaniel	.02	.10
65 Tommy Maddox	.08	.25
66 Steve Everitt RC	.01	.05
67 Brian Noble	.01	.05
68 Bryce Paup	.02	.10
69 Brad Baxter	.01	.05
70 Demetrius DuBose RC	.01	.05
71 Duane Bickett	.01	.05
72 Mark Rypien	.01	.05
73 Harris Barton	.01	.05
74 Bruce Matthews	.01	.05
75 Irving Fryar	.02	.10
76 Steve Wisniewski	.01	.05
77 Will Shields RC	.08	.25
78 Tom Carter RC	.02	.10
79 Steve Emtman	.01	.05
80 Jerry Rice	.40	1.00
81 Art Monk	.02	.10
82 Tony Tolbert	.01	.05
83 Johnny Mitchell	.01	.05
84 Deon Figures RC	.01	.05
85 Marv Cook	.01	.05
86 Darion Conner	.01	.05
87 Ricky Proehl	.01	.05
88 Tony Bennett	.01	.05
89 Jay Schroeder	.01	.05
90 Neil Smith	.08	.25
91 Jarvis Williams	.01	.05
92 James Hasty	.01	.05
93 Anthony Miller	.02	.10
94 Thomas Smith RC	.02	.10
95 Richard Dent	.02	.10
96 Henry Jones	.01	.05
97 Renaldo Turnbull	.01	.05
98 Jason Hanson	.01	.05
99 Cortez Kennedy	.02	.10
100 Brett Favre	.75	2.00
101 Anthony Carter	.02	.10
102 Cris Carter	.08	.25
103 Dana Stubblefield RC	.08	.25
104A Nick Bell	.01	.05
104B Don Griffin UER (No.104 on back, should have been #111)	.01	.05
105 Marcus Allen	.08	.25
106 Neil O'Donnell	.08	.25
107 Steve DeBerg	.01	.05
108 Leonard Russell	.02	.10
109 Ethan Horton	.01	.05
110 William Perry	.02	.10
112 Clarence Verdin	.01	.05
113 Amp Lee	.01	.05
114 Earnest Byner	.01	.05
115 Ricky Reynolds	.01	.05
116 Tom Waddle	.01	.05
117 Robert Jones	.01	.05
118 Willie Davis	.02	.10
119 Chris Miller	.02	.10
120 Drew Hill	.01	.05
121 Warren Moon	.08	.25
122 Flipper Anderson	.01	.05
123 George Teague RC	.02	.10
124 John L. Williams	.01	.05
125 Ed McCaffrey	.08	.25
126 Eric Green	.01	.05
127 Scott Mersereau	.01	.05
128 Charles Mann	.01	.05
129 Todd Lyght	.01	.05
130 Rodney Culver	.01	.05
131 Richmond Webb	.01	.05
132 John Parrella RC	.01	.05
133 Reggie Brooks RC	.02	.10
134 Lincoln Kennedy RC	.01	.05
135 Tim Johnson	.01	.05
136 Robert Massey	.01	.05
137 Keith Jackson	.02	.10
138 Alfred Williams	.01	.05
139 Leroy Hoard	.02	.10
140 Jessie Tuggle	.01	.05
141 Chris Mims	.01	.05
142 Herschel Walker	.02	.10
143 Clyde Simmons	.01	.05
144 Dana Hall	.01	.05
145 Nate Newton	.02	.10
146 Dennis Smith	.01	.05
147 Rich Camarillo	.01	.05
148 Chris Spielman	.02	.10
149 Jim Dombrowski	.01	.05
150 Steve Beuerlein	.02	.10
151 Mark Clayton	.01	.05
152 Lee Williams	.01	.05
153 Robert Smith RC	.50	1.25
154 Greg Jackson	.01	.05
155 Jay Hilgenberg	.01	.05
156 Howard Ballard	.01	.05
157 Mike Compton RC	.08	.25
158 Brent Williams	.01	.05
159 Tommy Kane	.01	.05
160 Barry Word	.01	.05
161 Darren Lewis	.01	.05
162 Steve Atwater	.01	.05
163 Gary Clark	.02	.10
164 Donnell Woolford	.01	.05
165 Henry Thomas	.01	.05
166 Tim Brown	.08	.25
167 Andre Ware	.01	.05
168 Jackie Harris	.01	.05
169 Browning Nagle	.01	.05
170 Chris Singleton	.01	.05
171 Ronnie Lott	.02	.10
172 Leonard Marshall	.01	.05
173 Dale Carter	.01	.05
174 Bruce Armstrong	.01	.05
175 Tommy Vardell	.01	.05
176 Bubba McDowell	.01	.05
177 Patrick Bates RC	.01	.05
178 Tyji Armstrong	.01	.05
179 Keith Byars	.01	.05
180 Boomer Esiason	.02	.10
181 Ricky Watters	.08	.25
182 Keith Sims	.01	.05
183 Burt Grossman	.01	.05
184 Richard Cooper	.01	.05
185 Marc Boutte	.01	.05
186 Shane Conlan	.01	.05
187 Luis Sharpe	.01	.05
188 O.J. McDuffie RC	.08	.25
189 Harvey Williams	.02	.10
190 Blair Thomas	.01	.05
191 Charles Haley	.02	.10
192 Chip Lohmiller	.01	.05
193 Vinny Testaverde	.02	.10
194 Desmond Howard	.02	.10
195 Johnny Johnson	.01	.05
196 Bennie Blades	.01	.05
197 Jeff Wright	.01	.05
198 Cody Carlson	.01	.05
199 Micheal Barrow RC	.08	.25
200 Pat Swilling	.01	.05
201 Willie Roaf RC	.02	.10
202 Michael Walter	.01	.05
203 Kevin Fagan	.01	.05
204 Nate Odomes	.01	.05
205 Michael Dean Perry	.02	.10
206 Bruce Pickens	.01	.05
207 Mel Gray	.02	.10
208 Jack Trudeau	.01	.05
209 Ricky Sanders	.01	.05
210 Bobby Hebert	.01	.05
211 Craig Heyward	.02	.10
212 Eric Bieniemy	.01	.05
213 Andre Rison	.02	.10
214 Bernie Kosar	.02	.10
215 Lester Holmes	.01	.05
216 Marcus Buckley RC	.01	.05
217 Tony Casillas	.01	.05
218 Cornelius Bennett	.02	.10
219 Kyle Clifton	.01	.05
220 Kirk Lowdermilk	.01	.05
221 Leon Searcy	.01	.05
222 Gary Anderson K	.01	.05
223 Tim Barnett	.01	.05
224 Gene Atkins	.01	.05
225 Jeff Cross	.01	.05
226 Darrin Smith RC	.02	.10
227 Rohn Stark	.01	.05
228 Chris Warren	.02	.10
229 Eric Allen	.01	.05
230 Wayne Simmons RC	.01	.05
231 Al Smith	.01	.05
232 Reggie Rivers RC	.01	.05
233 Kevin Smith	.02	.10
234 Vince Workman	.01	.05
235 Thurman Thomas	.08	.25
236 Kevin Williams RC	.08	.25
237 Dan McGwire	.01	.05
238 Greg Lloyd	.02	.10
239 Ray Buchanan RC	.08	.25
240 Shannon Sharpe	.08	.25
241 Ricardo McDonald	.01	.05
242 Aaron Wallace	.01	.05
243 Chris Hinton	.01	.05
244 Bill Romanowski	.01	.05
245 Randal Hill	.01	.05
246 Ray Agnew	.01	.05
247 Todd Kelly RC	.01	.05
248 John Stephens	.01	.05
249 Sean Salisbury	.01	.05
250 Roger Craig	.02	.10
251 Dave Krieg	.02	.10
252 Brian Blades	.02	.10
253 Jarrod Bunch	.01	.05
254 Phil Simms	.02	.10
255 Keith Van Horne	.01	.05
256 Jim Price	.01	.05
257 Garrison Hearst RC	.30	.75
258 Derrick Walker	.01	.05
259 Mike Pritchard	.02	.10
260 Leonard Renfro RC	.01	.05
261 Rodney Peete	.01	.05
262 Jeff Bryant	.01	.05
263 Dermontti Dawson	.01	.05
264 Greg McMurtry	.01	.05
265 Wendell Davis	.01	.05
266 Kerry Cash	.01	.05

267 Jackie Slater	.01	.05
268 Sam Mills	.01	.05
269 Carlton Bailey	.01	.05
270 Mark Wheeler	.01	.05
271 Darren Perry	.01	.05
272 Todd Scott	.01	.05
273 Johnny Holland	.01	.05
274 Mike Croel	.01	.05
275 Shane Dronett	.01	.05
276 Andre Collins	.01	.05
277 Eric Swann	.02	.10
278 Jessie Hester	.01	.05
279 Bryan Cox	.01	.05
280 Mark Jackson	.01	.05
281 Thomas Everett	.01	.05
282 James Lofton	.02	.10
283 Carl Pickens	.02	.10
284 Mark Carrier WR	.02	.10
285 Heath Sherman	.01	.05
286 Chris Burkett	.01	.05
287 Coleman Rudolph RC	.01	.05
288 Todd Marinovich	.01	.05
289 Nate Lewis	.01	.05
290 Fred Barnett	.02	.10
291 Jim Lachey	.01	.05
292 Jerry Ball	.01	.05
293 Jeff George	.08	.25
294 William Fuller	.01	.05
295 Courtney Hawkins	.01	.05
296 Kelvin Martin	.01	.05
297 Trace Armstrong	.01	.05
298 Carl Banks	.01	.05
299 Terry Kirby RC	.08	.25
300 John Offerdahl	.01	.05
301 Harry Swayne	.01	.05
302 Wilber Marshall	.01	.05
303 Guy McIntyre	.01	.05
304 Steve Wallace	.01	.05
305 Chris Slade RC	.02	.10
306 Anthony Newman	.01	.05
307 Chip Banks	.01	.05
308 Carlton Gray RC	.01	.05
309 Wayne Martin	.01	.05
310 Tom Rathman	.01	.05
311 Shaun Gayle	.01	.05
312 Billy Joe Hobert RC	.08	.25
313 Matt Brock	.01	.05
314 Arthur Marshall RC	.01	.05
315 Wade Wilson	.01	.05
316 Michael Jackson	.02	.10
317 Bruce Kozerski	.01	.05
318 Reggie Langhorne	.01	.05
319 Jerrol Williams	.01	.05
320 Aeneas Williams	.01	.05
321 Tony McGee RC	.02	.10
322 Carl Simpson RC	.01	.05
323 Russell Maryland	.01	.05
324 Nick Lowery	.01	.05
325 Steve Tasker	.02	.10
326 Alvin Harper	.02	.10
327 Haywood Jeffires	.02	.10
328 Hardy Nickerson	.02	.10
329 Alonzo Spellman	.01	.05
330 Eric Dickerson	.02	.10
331 Scott Zolak	.01	.05
332 Darryl Henley	.01	.05
333 Daniel Stubbs	.01	.05
334 Andy Heck	.01	.05
335 Mark May	.01	.05
336 Roosevelt Potts RC	.01	.05
337 Erik Howard	.01	.05
338 Sean Gilbert	.02	.10
339 Jerome Bettis RC	2.50	6.00
340 Darron Carrington RC	.01	.05
341 Gill Byrd	.01	.05
342 John Friesz	.02	.10
343 Roger Harper RC	.01	.05
344 Fred Stokes	.01	.05
345 Stanley Richard	.01	.05
346 Johnny Bailey	.01	.05
347 David Wyman	.01	.05
348 Merril Hoge	.01	.05
349 Brett Perriman	.00	.25
350 Kelvin Pritchett	.01	.05
351 Rod Bernstine	.01	.05
352 Jim Ritcher	.01	.05
353 Mark Stepnoski	.01	.05
354 Jeff Lageman	.01	.05
355 Darrien Gordon RC	.01	.05
356 Don Mosebar	.01	.05
357 Simon Fletcher	.01	.05
358 Charles Mincy RC	.01	.05
359 Ron Hall	.01	.05
360 Brent Jones	.02	.10
361 Byron Evans	.01	.05
362 Dan Footman RC	.01	.05
363 Mark Higgs	.01	.05
364 Brian Washington	.01	.05
365 Brad Hopkins RC	.01	.05
366 Tracy Simien	.01	.05
367 Derrick Fenner	.01	.05
368 Lorenzo White	.01	.05
369 Marvin Jones RC	.01	.05
370 Chris Doleman	.01	.05
371 Jeff Herrod	.01	.05
372 Jim Harbaugh	.08	.25
373 Jim Jeffcoat	.01	.05
374 Michael Strahan RC	1.00	2.50
375 Ricky Ervins	.01	.05
376 Joel Hilgenberg	.01	.05
377 Curtis Duncan	.01	.05
378 Glyn Milburn RC	.08	.25
379 Jack Del Rio	.01	.05
380 Eric Martin	.01	.05
381 Dave Meggett	.01	.05
382 Jeff Hostetler	.02	.10
383 Greg Townsend	.01	.05
384 Brad Muster	.01	.05
385 Irv Smith RC	.01	.05
386 Chris Jacke	.01	.05
387 Ernest Dye RC	.01	.05
388 Henry Ellard	.02	.10
389 John Taylor	.02	.10
390 Chris Chandler	.02	.10
391 Larry Centers RC	.08	.25
392 Henry Rolling	.01	.05
393 Dan Saleaumua	.01	.05
394 Moe Gardner	.01	.05
395 Darryl Williams	.01	.05
396 Paul Gruber	.01	.05
397 Dwayne Harper	.01	.05
398 Pat Harlow	.01	.05
399 Rickey Jackson	.01	.05
400 Quentin Coryatt	.02	.10
401 Steve Jordan	.01	.05
402 Rick Mirer RC	.08	.25
403 Howard Cross	.01	.05
404 Mike Johnson	.01	.05
405 Broderick Thomas	.01	.05
406 Stan Humphries	.02	.10
407 Ronnie Harmon	.01	.05
408 Andy Harmon RC	.02	.10
409 Troy Drayton RC	.02	.10
410 Dan Williams RC	.01	.05
411 Mark Bavaro	.01	.05
412 Bruce Smith	.08	.25
413 Elbert Shelley RC	.01	.05
414 Tim McGee	.01	.05
415 Tim Harris	.01	.05
416 Rob Moore	.02	.10
417 Rob Burnett	.01	.05
418 Howie Long	.08	.25
419 Chuck Cecil	.01	.05
420 Carl Lee	.01	.05
421 Anthony Smith	.01	.05
422 Jeff Graham	.02	.10
423 Clay Matthews	.02	.10
424 Jay Novacek	.02	.10
425 Phil Hansen	.01	.05
426 Andre Hastings RC	.02	.10
427 Toi Cook	.01	.05
428 Rufus Porter	.01	.05
429 Mike Pitts	.01	.05
430 Eddie Robinson	.01	.05
431 Herman Moore	.08	.25
432 Erik Kramer	.02	.10
433 Mark Carrier DB	.01	.05
434 Natrone Means RC	.08	.25
435 Carnell Lake	.01	.05
436 Carlton Haselrig	.01	.05
437 John Randle	.02	.10
438 Louis Oliver	.01	.05
439 Ray Roberts	.01	.05
440 Leslie O'Neal	.02	.10
441 Reggie White	.08	.25
442 Dalton Hilliard	.01	.05
443 Tim Krumrie	.01	.05
444 LeRoy Butler	.01	.05
445 Greg Kragen	.01	.05
446 Anthony Johnson	.02	.10
447 Audray McMillian	.01	.05
448 Lawrence Dawsey	.01	.05
449 Pierce Holt	.01	.05
450 Brad Edwards	.01	.05
451 J.J. Birden	.01	.05
452 Mike Munchak	.02	.10
453 Tracy Scroggins	.01	.05
454 Mike Tomczak	.01	.05
455 Harold Green	.01	.05
456 Vaughn Dunbar	.01	.05
457 Calvin Williams	.02	.10
458 Pete Stoyanovich	.01	.05
459 Willie Gault	.01	.05
460 Ken Ruettgers	.01	.05
461 Eugene Robinson	.01	.05
462 Larry Brown DB	.01	.05
463 Antonio London RC	.01	.05
464 Andre Reed	.02	.10
465 Daryl Johnston	.08	.25
466 Karl Mecklenburg	.01	.05
467 David Lang	.01	.05
468 Bill Brooks	.01	.05
469 Jim Everett	.02	.10
470 Qadry Ismail RC	.08	.25
471 Vai Sikahema	.01	.05
472 Andre Tippett	.01	.05
473 Eugene Chung	.01	.05
474 Cris Dishman	.01	.05
475 Tim McDonald	.01	.05
476 Freddie Joe Nunn	.01	.05
477 Checklist 1-134	.01	.05
478 Checklist 135-268	.01	.05
479 Checklist 269-402	.01	.05
480 CL 403-480	.01	.05
Inserts		
P1 Promo Sheet	1.20	3.00
Steve Young		
Thurman Thomas		
Junior Seau		
Jay Novacek		
Terrell Buckley		
Rick Mirer		

1993 GameDay Gamebreakers

COMPLETE SET (20)	10.00	25.00
STATED ODDS 1:3		
1 Troy Aikman	.75	2.00
2 Brett Favre	2.00	5.00
3 Steve Young	.75	2.00
4 Dan Marino	1.50	4.00
5 Joe Montana	1.50	4.00
6 Jim Kelly	.25	.60
7 Emmitt Smith	1.50	4.00
8 Ricky Watters	.25	.60
9 Barry Foster	.08	.25
10 Barry Sanders	1.25	3.00
11 Michael Irvin	.25	.60
12 Thurman Thomas	.25	.60
13 Sterling Sharpe	.25	.60
14 Jerry Rice	1.00	2.50
15 Andre Rison	.08	.25
16 Deion Sanders	.50	1.25
17 Harold Green	.05	.15
18 Lorenzo White	.05	.15
19 Terry Allen	.25	.60
20 Haywood Jeffires	.08	.25

1993 GameDay Rookie Standouts

COMPLETE SET (16)	10.00	25.00
STATED ODDS 1:4		
1 Drew Bledsoe	5.00	12.00
2 Rick Mirer	.50	1.25
3 Garrison Hearst	1.50	4.00
4 Jerome Bettis	12.50	30.00
5 Marvin Jones	.08	.25
6 Reggie Brooks	.20	.50
7 O.J. McDuffie	.50	1.25
8 Qadry Ismail	.50	1.25
9 Glyn Milburn	.50	1.25
10 Andre Hastings	.20	.50
11 Curtis Conway	.75	2.00
12 Eric Curry	.08	.25
13 John Copeland	.20	.50
14 Kevin Williams	.50	1.25
15 Patrick Bates	.08	.25
16 Lincoln Kennedy	.08	.25

1993 GameDay Second Year Stars

COMPLETE SET (16)	2.50	6.00
STATED ODDS 1:4		
1 Carl Pickens	.40	1.00
2 David Klingler	.20	.50
3 Santana Dotson	.40	1.00
4 Chris Mims	.20	.50
5 Steve Emtman	.20	.50
6 Marco Coleman	.20	.50
7 Robert Jones	.20	.50
8 Dale Carter	.20	.50
9 Troy Vincent	.20	.50
10 Tracy Scroggins	.20	.50
11 Vaughn Dunbar	.20	.50
12 Quentin Coryatt	.40	1.00
13 Dana Hall	.20	.50
14 Terrell Buckley	.20	.50
15 Tommy Vardell	.20	.50
16 Johnny Mitchell	.20	.50

1994 GameDay

Measuring 2 1/2" by 4 3/4", this 420-card set features full-bleed action photos on front with the player's name and team name at the bottom. The backs have a player photo with statistics and a write-up at the bottom. Biographical information runs along the right border. The players are grouped alphabetically within teams, and checklisted below alphabetically according to teams. Rookie Cards in this set include Mario Bates, Isaac Bruce, Bert Emanuel, Marshall Faulk, Errict Rhett, Darnay Scott and Heath Shuler. A Reggie Brooks promo card was produced and is priced below.

COMPLETE SET (420)	15.00	30.00
1 Michael Bankston	.01	.05
2 Steve Beuerlein	.02	.10
3 Gary Clark	.02	.10
4 Garrison Hearst	.08	.25
5 Eric Hill	.01	.05
6 Randal Hill	.01	.05
7 Seth Joyner	.01	.05
8 Jim McMahon	.02	.10
9 Jamir Miller RC	.02	.10
10 Ronald Moore	.01	.05
11 Ricky Proehl	.01	.05
12 Luis Sharpe	.01	.05
13 Clyde Simmons	.01	.05
14 Eric Swann	.02	.10
15 Aeneas Williams	.01	.05
16 Chris Doleman	.01	.05
17 Bert Emanuel RC	.08	.25
18 Moe Gardner	.01	.05
19 Jeff George	.08	.25
20 Roger Harper	.01	.05
21 Pierce Holt	.01	.05
22 Lincoln Kennedy	.01	.05
23 Erric Pegram	.01	.05
24 Andre Rison	.02	.10
25 Deion Sanders	.20	.50
26 Tony Smith	.01	.05
27 Jessie Tuggle	.01	.05
28 Don Beebe	.01	.05
29 Cornelius Bennett	.02	.10
30 Bill Brooks	.01	.05
31 Bucky Brooks RC	.01	.05
32 Jeff Burris RC	.02	.10
33 Kenneth Davis	.01	.05
34 Phil Hansen	.01	.05
35 Kent Hull	.01	.05
36 Henry Jones	.01	.05
37 Jim Kelly	.08	.25
38 Pete Metzelaars	.01	.05
39 Marvcus Patton	.01	.05
40 Andre Reed	.02	.10
41 Bruce Smith	.08	.25
42 Thomas Smith	.01	.05
43 Darryl Talley	.01	.05
44 Steve Tasker	.02	.10
45 Thurman Thomas	.08	.25
46 Jeff Wright	.01	.05
47 Trace Armstrong	.01	.05
48 Joe Cain	.01	.05
49 Mark Carrier DB	.01	.05
50 Curtis Conway	.08	.25
51 Shaun Gayle	.01	.05
52 Dante Jones	.01	.05
53 Erik Kramer	.02	.10
54 Terry Obee	.01	.05
55 Vinson Smith	.01	.05
56 Alonzo Spellman	.01	.05
57 John Thierry RC	.01	.05
58 Tom Waddle	.01	.05
59 Donnell Woolford	.01	.05
60 Tim Worley	.01	.05
61 Chris Zorich	.01	.05
62 Mike Brim	.01	.05
63 John Copeland	.01	.05
64 Derrick Fenner	.01	.05
65 James Francis	.01	.05
66 Harold Green	.01	.05
67 David Klingler	.01	.05
68 Ricardo McDonald	.01	.05
69 Tony McGee	.01	.05
70 Carl Pickens	.02	.10
71 Jeff Query	.01	.05
72 Darnay Scott RC	.20	.50
73 Steve Tovar	.01	.05
74 Dan Wilkinson RC	.02	.10
75 Alfred Williams	.01	.05
76 Darryl Williams	.01	.05
77 Derrick Alexander WR RC	.08	.25
78 Rob Burnett	.01	.05
79 Steve Everitt	.01	.05
80 Michael Jackson	.02	.10
81 Pepper Johnson	.01	.05
82 Tony Jones	.01	.05
83 Antonio Langham RC	.02	.10
84 Eric Metcalf	.02	.10
85 Stevon Moore	.01	.05
86 Michael Dean Perry	.02	.10
87 Anthony Pleasant	.01	.05
88 Vinny Testaverde	.02	.10
89 Eric Turner	.01	.05
90 Tommy Vardell	.01	.05
91 Troy Aikman	.40	1.00
92 Larry Brown DB	.01	.05
93 Shante Carver RC	.01	.05
94 Charles Haley	.02	.10
95 Alvin Harper	.02	.10
96 Michael Irvin	.08	.25
97 Daryl Johnston	.02	.10
98 Leon Lett	.01	.05
99 Russell Maryland	.01	.05
100 Nate Newton	.01	.05
101 Jay Novacek	.02	.10
102 Darrin Smith	.01	.05
103 Emmitt Smith	.60	1.50
104 Kevin Smith	.01	.05
105 Mark Stepnoski	.01	.05
106 Tony Tolbert	.01	.05
107 Erik Williams	.01	.05
108 Kevin Williams	.02	.10
109 Darren Woodson	.02	.10
110 Allen Aldridge RC	.01	.05
111 Steve Atwater	.01	.05
112 Rod Bernstine	.01	.05
113 Ray Crockett	.01	.05
114 Mike Croel	.01	.05
115 Robert Delpino	.01	.05
116 Shane Dronett	.01	.05
117 Jason Elam	.02	.10
118 John Elway	.75	2.00
119 Simon Fletcher	.01	.05
120 Glyn Milburn	.02	.10
121 Anthony Miller	.02	.10
122 Mike Pritchard	.01	.05
123 Shannon Sharpe	.02	.10
124 Dan Williams	.01	.05
125 Bennie Blades	.01	.05
126 Lomas Brown	.01	.05
127 Anthony Carter	.02	.10
128 Mel Gray	.01	.05
129 Jason Hanson	.01	.05
130 Robert Massey	.01	.05
131 Ryan McNeil	.01	.05
132 Scott Mitchell	.02	.10
133 Herman Moore	.08	.25
134 Johnnie Morton RC	.20	.50
135 Brett Perriman	.02	.10
136 Robert Porcher	.01	.05
137 Barry Sanders	.60	1.50
138 Tracy Scroggins	.01	.05
139 Chris Spielman	.02	.10
140 Pat Swilling	.01	.05
141 Edgar Bennett	.08	.25
142 Robert Brooks	.08	.25
143 Terrell Buckley	.01	.05
144 LeRoy Butler	.01	.05
145 Reggie Cobb	.01	.05
146 Curtis Duncan	.01	.05
147 Brett Favre	.75	2.00
148 Sean Jones	.01	.05
149 George Koonce	.01	.05
150 Ken Ruettgers	.01	.05
151 Sterling Sharpe	.02	.10
152 Wayne Simmons	.01	.05
153 Aaron Taylor RC	.01	.05
154 George Teague	.01	.05
155 Reggie White	.08	.25
156 Micheal Barrow	.01	.05
157 Gary Brown	.01	.05
158 Rich Camarillo	.01	.05
159 Cody Carlson	.01	.05
160 Ray Childress	.01	.05
161 Cris Dishman	.01	.05
162 Henry Ford RC	.01	.05
163 Ernest Givins	.02	.10
164 Steve Jackson	.01	.05
165 Haywood Jeffires	.02	.10
166 Bruce Matthews	.01	.05
167 Bubba McDowell	.01	.05
168 Marcus Robertson	.01	.05
169 Eddie Robinson	.01	.05
170 Webster Slaughter	.01	.05
171 Trev Alberts RC	.02	.10
172 Tony Bennett	.01	.05
173 Ray Buchanan	.01	.05
174 Kerry Cash	.01	.05
175 Quentin Coryatt	.01	.05
176 Eugene Daniel	.01	.05
177 Sean Dawkins RC	.08	.25
178 Steve Emtman	.01	.05
179 Marshall Faulk RC	2.00	5.00
180 Jon Hand	.01	.05
181 Jim Harbaugh	.08	.25
182 Jeff Herrod	.01	.05
183 Roosevelt Potts	.01	.05
184 Rohn Stark	.01	.05
185 Marcus Allen	.08	.25
186 Donnell Bennett RC	.08	.25
187 J.J. Birden	.01	.05
188 Dale Carter	.01	.05
189 Mark Collins	.01	.05
190 Willie Davis	.02	.10
191 Lake Dawson RC	.02	.10
192 Tim Grunhard	.01	.05
193 Greg Hill RC	.08	.25
194 Joe Montana	.75	2.00
195 Tracy Simien	.01	.05
196 Neil Smith	.02	.10
197 Derrick Thomas	.08	.25
198 Tim Brown	.08	.25
199 James Folston RC	.01	.05
200 Rob Fredrickson RC	.02	.10
201 Nolan Harrison	.01	.05
202 Jeff Hostetler	.02	.10
203 Rocket Ismail	.02	.10
204 Jeff Jaeger	.01	.05
205 James Jett	.01	.05
206 Terry McDaniel	.01	.05
207 Chester McGlockton	.01	.05
208 Winston Moss	.01	.05
209 Tom Rathman	.01	.05
210 Anthony Smith	.01	.05
211 Harvey Williams	.02	.10
212 Steve Wisniewski	.01	.05
213 Alexander Wright	.01	.05
214 Flipper Anderson	.01	.05
215 Jerome Bettis	.20	.50
216 Isaac Bruce RC	2.00	4.00
217 Troy Drayton	.01	.05
218 Wayne Gandy RC	.01	.05
219 Sean Gilbert	.01	.05
220 Nate Lewis	.01	.05
221 Todd Lyght	.01	.05
222 Chris Miller	.01	.05
223 Anthony Newman	.01	.05
224 Roman Phifer	.01	.05
225 Henry Rolling	.01	.05
226 Jackie Slater	.01	.05
227 Fred Stokes	.01	.05
228 Gene Atkins	.01	.05
229 Aubrey Beavers RC	.01	.05
230 Tim Bowens RC	.02	.10
231 J.B. Brown	.01	.05
232 Keith Byars	.01	.05
233 Marco Coleman	.01	.05
234 Bryan Cox	.01	.05
235 Jeff Cross	.01	.05
236 Irving Fryar	.02	.10
237 Mark Ingram	.01	.05
238 Keith Jackson	.01	.05
239 Terry Kirby	.08	.25
240 Dan Marino	.75	2.00
241 Michael Stewart	.01	.05
242 Troy Vincent	.01	.05
243 Richmond Webb	.01	.05
244 Terry Allen	.02	.10
245 Cris Carter	.20	.50
246 Jack Del Rio	.01	.05
247 Vencie Glenn	.01	.05
248 Chris Hinton	.01	.05
249 Qadry Ismail	.08	.25
250 Carlos Jenkins	.01	.05
251 Randall McDaniel	.02	.10
252 Warren Moon	.08	.25
253 David Palmer RC	.08	.25
254 John Randle	.02	.10
255 Jake Reed	.02	.10
256 Todd Scott	.01	.05
257 Todd Steussie RC	.02	.10
258 Henry Thomas	.01	.05
259 Dewayne Washington RC	.02	.10
260 Bruce Armstrong	.01	.05
261 Drew Bledsoe	.30	.75
262 Vincent Brisby	.02	.10
263 Vincent Brown	.01	.05
264 Marion Butts	.01	.05
265 Ben Coates	.02	.10
266 Pat Harlow	.01	.05
267 Maurice Hurst	.01	.05
268 Willie McGinest RC	.08	.25
269 Chris Slade	.01	.05
270 Michael Timpson	.01	.05
271 Morten Andersen	.01	.05
272 Mario Bates RC	.08	.25
273 Derek Brown RBK	.01	.05
274 Quinn Early	.02	.10
275 Jim Everett	.02	.10
276 Michael Haynes	.02	.10
277 Tyrone Hughes	.02	.10
278 Joe Johnson RC	.01	.05
279 Eric Martin	.01	.05
280 Wayne Martin	.01	.05
281 Sam Mills	.01	.05
282 Willie Roaf	.01	.05
283 Irv Smith	.01	.05
284 Renaldo Turnbull	.01	.05
285 Carlton Bailey	.01	.05
286 Michael Brooks	.01	.05
287 Dave Brown	.02	.10
288 Jarrod Bunch	.01	.05
289 Howard Cross	.01	.05
290 John Elliott	.01	.05
291 Keith Hamilton	.01	.05
292 Rodney Hampton	.02	.10
293 Mark Jackson	.01	.05
294 Thomas Lewis RC	.02	.10
295 Dave Meggett	.01	.05
296 Corey Miller	.01	.05
297 Mike Sherrard	.01	.05
298 Brad Baxter	.01	.05
299 Kyle Clifton	.01	.05
300 Boomer Esiason	.02	.10
301 Aaron Glenn RC	.08	.25
302 James Hasty	.01	.05
303 Johnny Johnson	.01	.05
304 Jeff Lageman	.01	.05
305 Mo Lewis	.01	.05
306 Ronnie Lott	.02	.10
307 Johnny Mitchell	.01	.05
308 Art Monk	.02	.10
309 Rob Moore	.02	.10
310 Brian Washington	.01	.05
311 Marvin Washington	.01	.05
312 Ryan Yarborough RC	.01	.05
313 Eric Allen	.01	.05
314 Victor Bailey	.01	.05
315 Fred Barnett	.02	.10
316 Mark Bavaro	.01	.05
317 Randall Cunningham	.08	.25
318 Byron Evans	.01	.05
319 William Fuller	.01	.05
320 Charlie Garner RC	.50	1.25
321 Andy Harmon	.01	.05
322 Vaughn Hebron	.01	.05
323 Mark McMillian	.01	.05
324 Bill Romanowski	.01	.05
325 William Thomas	.01	.05
326 Greg Townsend	.01	.05
327 Herschel Walker	.02	.10
328 Bernard Williams RC	.01	.05
329 Calvin Williams	.02	.10
330 Dermontti Dawson	.01	.05
331 Deon Figures	.01	.05
332 Barry Foster	.01	.05
333 Eric Green	.01	.05
334 Kevin Greene	.02	.10
335 Carlton Haselrig	.01	.05
336 Charles Johnson RC	.08	.25
337 Levon Kirkland	.01	.05
338 Carnell Lake	.01	.05
339 Greg Lloyd	.02	.10
340 Neil O'Donnell	.08	.25
341 Darren Perry	.01	.05
342 Dwight Stone	.01	.05
343 John L. Williams	.01	.05
344 Rod Woodson	.02	.10
345 John Carney	.01	.05
346 Darren Carrington	.01	.05
347 Isaac Davis RC	.01	.05
348 Courtney Hall	.01	.05
349 Ronnie Harmon	.01	.05
350 Dwayne Harper	.01	.05
351 Stan Humphries	.02	.10
352 Shawn Jefferson	.01	.05
353 Vance Johnson	.01	.05
354 Natrone Means	.08	.25
355 Chris Mims	.01	.05
356 Leslie O'Neal	.01	.05
357 Stanley Richard	.01	.05
358 Junior Seau	.08	.25
359 Harris Barton	.01	.05
360 Eric Davis	.01	.05
361 Richard Dent	.02	.10
362 William Floyd RC	.08	.25
363 Merton Hanks	.02	.10
364 Brent Jones	.02	.10
365 Marc Logan	.01	.05
366 Tim McDonald	.01	.05
367 Ken Norton	.02	.10
368 Jerry Rice	.40	1.00
369 Jesse Sapolu	.01	.05
370 Dana Stubblefield	.02	.10
371 John Taylor	.02	.10
372 Ricky Watters	.02	.10
373 Bryant Young RC	.15	.40
374 Steve Young	.30	.75
375 Sam Adams RC	.02	.10
376 Michael Bates	.01	.05
377 Robert Blackmon	.01	.05
378 Brian Blades	.02	.10
379 Ferrell Edmunds	.01	.05
380 John Kasay	.01	.05
381 Cortez Kennedy	.02	.10
382 Kelvin Martin	.01	.05
383 Rick Mirer	.08	.25
384 Rufus Porter	.01	.05
385 Eugene Robinson	.01	.05
386 Rod Stephens	.01	.05
387 Chris Warren	.02	.10
388 Marty Carter	.01	.05
389 Horace Copeland	.01	.05
390 Eric Curry	.01	.05
391 Lawrence Dawsey	.01	.05
392 Trent Dilfer RC	.50	1.25
393 Santana Dotson	.02	.10
394 Craig Erickson	.01	.05
395 Thomas Everett	.01	.05
396 Paul Gruber	.01	.05
397 Jackie Harris	.01	.05
398 Courtney Hawkins	.01	.05
399 Martin Mayhew	.01	.05
400 Hardy Nickerson	.02	.10
401 Errict Rhett RC	.08	.25
402 Vince Workman	.01	.05
403 Reggie Brooks	.02	.10
404 Tom Carter	.01	.05
405 Andre Collins	.01	.05
406 Henry Ellard	.02	.10
407 Kurt Gouveia	.01	.05
408 Darrell Green	.01	.05
409 Ken Harvey	.01	.05
410 Ethan Horton	.01	.05
411 Desmond Howard	.02	.10
412 Jim Lachey	.01	.05
413 Sterling Palmer RC	.01	.05
414 Heath Shuler RC	.08	.25
415 Tyronne Stowe	.01	.05
416 Tony Woods	.01	.05
417 Checklist 1-124	.01	.05
418 Checklist 125-243	.01	.05
419 Checklist 244-358	.01	.05
420 CL 359-420	.01	.05
Inserts		
P1 Reggie Brooks Promo	.20	.50
Numbered 000		

1994 GameDay Flashing Stars

COMPLETE SET (4)	7.50	20.00
1 Jerome Bettis	1.50	4.00
2 Rick Mirer	.75	2.00
3 Jerry Rice	3.00	8.00
4 Emmitt Smith	5.00	12.00

1994 GameDay Gamebreakers

COMPLETE SET (16)	6.00	15.00
1 Troy Aikman	.60	1.50
2 Marcus Allen	.15	.40
3 Tim Brown	.15	.40
4 John Elway	1.25	3.00
5 Michael Irvin	.15	.40
6 Dan Marino	1.25	3.00
7 Joe Montana	1.25	3.00
8 Jerry Rice	.60	1.50
9 Andre Rison	.05	.15
10 Barry Sanders	1.00	2.50
11 Deion Sanders	.30	.75
12 Sterling Sharpe	.05	.15
13 Emmitt Smith	1.00	2.50
14 Thurman Thomas	.15	.40
15 Rod Woodson	.05	.15
16 Steve Young	.50	1.25

1994 GameDay Rookie Standouts

COMPLETE SET (16)	4.00	10.00
1 Sam Adams	.05	.15
2 Trev Alberts	.05	.15
3 Lake Dawson	.05	.15
4 Trent Dilfer	.75	2.00
5 Marshall Faulk	3.00	8.00
6 Aaron Glenn	.15	.40
7 Charles Johnson	.15	.40
8 Willie McGinest	.15	.40
9 Jamir Miller	.05	.15
10 Johnnie Morton	.30	.75
11 David Palmer	.15	.40
12 Errict Rhett	.15	.40
13 Heath Shuler	.15	.40
14 John Thierry	.02	.10
15 Dan Wilkinson	.05	.15
16 Bryant Young	.15	.40

1994 GameDay Second Year Stars

COMPLETE SET (16)	2.50	6.00
1 Jerome Bettis	.75	2.00
2 Drew Bledsoe	1.25	3.00
3 Reggie Brooks	.15	.40
4 Tom Carter	.07	.20
5 Eric Curry	.07	.20
6 Steve Everitt	.07	.20
7 Tyrone Hughes	.15	.40
8 James Jett	.07	.20
9 Terry Kirby	.40	1.00
10 Natrone Means	.40	1.00
11 Rick Mirer	.40	1.00
12 Ronald Moore	.07	.20
13 Willie Roaf	.07	.20
14 Chris Slade	.07	.20
15 Darrin Smith	.07	.20
16 Dana Stubblefield	.15	.40

1971 Gatorade Team Lids

These lids were actually the tops off bottles of Gatorade sold during the 1971 and 1972 NFL seasons. Each white colored lid had a dark outline of an NFL helmet with the team name printed underneath.

COMPLETE SET (26)	75.00	150.00
1 Atlanta Falcons	2.50	5.00
2 Baltimore Colts	3.00	6.00
3 Buffalo Bills	2.50	5.00
4 Chicago Bears	3.00	6.00
5 Cincinnati Bengals	2.50	5.00
6 Cleveland Browns	3.00	6.00
7 Dallas Cowboys	4.00	8.00
8 Denver Broncos	3.00	6.00
9 Detroit Lions	2.50	5.00
10 Green Bay Packers	4.00	8.00
11A Houston Oilers Blue Helmet	4.00	10.00
11B Houston Oilers Gray Helmet	2.50	5.00
12 Kansas City Chiefs	2.50	5.00
13A Los Angeles Rams white Rams horns	4.00	10.00
13B Los Angeles Rams yellow Rams horns	2.50	5.00
14 Miami Dolphins	4.00	8.00
15 Minnesota Vikings	3.00	6.00
16 New England Patriots	2.50	5.00
17 New Orleans Saints	2.50	5.00
18 New York Giants	2.50	5.00
19 New York Jets	2.50	5.00
20 Oakland Raiders	4.00	8.00
21 Philadelphia Eagles	2.50	5.00
22 Pittsburgh Steelers	4.00	8.00
23 San Diego Chargers	2.50	5.00
24 San Francisco 49ers	4.00	8.00
25 St. Louis Cardinals	2.50	5.00
26A Washington Redskins ('R' logo old style)	4.00	8.00
26B Washington Redskins (Indian head logo new style)	4.00	8.00

1997 George Teague Softball

This card set was issued for the Geaorge Teague vs. Michael Bolton Celebrity Softball Challenge event. The two single Teague cards are similar in design to the 1997 Ultra football card set on the fronts with a newly designed cardback. The set was sponsored by the Rebecca Fund and Michael Bolton Foundation.

COMPLETE SET (32)	12.50	25.00
1 Mike Bolen	.40	1.00
2 Micheal Bolton	.60	1.50
3 Micheal Bolton	.60	1.50
4 Gilbert Brown	.75	2.00
5 Mugs Cain	.40	1.00
6 Johnny Dodd	.40	1.00
7 Bucky Ford	.40	1.00
8 Phil Higgins	.40	1.00
9 Bill Jartz	.40	1.00
10 Charles Jordan	.60	1.50
11 John Jurkovic	.75	2.00
12 Louis Levin	.40	1.00
13 Tom Mulhern	.40	1.00
14 Murphy in the morning	.40	1.00
15 Tim Nass	.40	1.00
16 Bobby Olah	.40	1.00
17 Bernie Parmalee	.75	2.00
18 Ron Peterson	.40	1.00
19 Lee Ann Rimes	.60	1.50
20 Jim Schwantz	.60	1.50
21 Donnie Slye	.40	1.00
22 Jimmy Slye	.40	1.00
23 Rebecca Slye	.40	1.00
24 George Teague	.60	1.50
25 George Teague	.60	1.50
26 J.T. Teague	.40	1.00
27 Quinn Teague	.40	1.00
28 Adam Timmerman	.60	1.50
29 Richie Vaughn	.40	1.00
30 Gary Whitefield	.40	1.00
31 Shawn Wooden	.60	1.50
32 Cover Card Team Photo	.40	1.00

1956 Giants Team Issue

The 1956 Giants Team Issue set contains 36 cards measuring approximately 4 7/8" by 6 7/8". The fronts have black and white posed player photos with white borders. A facsimile autograph appears below the picture. The backs have brief biographical information and career highlights. The cards are unnumbered and checklisted below in alphabetical order. Many of the cards in this set are similar to the 1957 release and are only distinguishable by the differences noted below in parenthesis. We've included the first line of text on the cardback of some to help differentiate the two sets.

COMPLETE SET (36)	125.00	250.00
1 Bill Austin (Austin was a Giant regular...)	4.00	8.00
2 Ray Beck (jersey #61)	4.00	8.00
3 Roosevelt Brown	6.00	12.00
4 Hank Burnine	4.00	8.00
5 Don Chandler kicking pose)	4.00	8.00
6 Bobby Clatterbuck (standing passing pose)	4.00	8.00
7 Charley Conerly (passing pose)	10.00	20.00
8 Frank Gifford	20.00	40.00
9 Roosevelt Grier	6.00	12.00
10 Don Heinrich (Heinrich was the Giants'...)	4.00	8.00
11 John Hermann	4.00	8.00
12 Jim Lee Howell CO	4.00	8.00
13 Sam Huff	10.00	20.00
14 Ed Hughes (handing off ball)	4.00	0.00
15 Gerald Huth (The Giants' No. 24...)	4.00	8.00
16 Jim Katcavage	4.00	8.00
17 Gene Kirby ANN	4.00	8.00
18 Ken MacAfee E (catching a pass)	4.00	8.00
19 Dick Modzelewski (Misspelled Modelewski on the cardback)	4.00	8.00
20 Henry Moore	4.00	8.00
21 Dick Nolan	4.00	8.00
22 Jim Patton (Jimmy Patton on front)	4.00	8.00
23 Andy Robustelli	7.50	15.00
24 Kyle Rote (catching a pass in mid-air)	5.00	10.00
25 Chris Schenkel ANN (Wearing a checkered suit)	4.00	8.00
26 Bob Schnelker	4.00	8.00
27 Jack Stroud (Stroud was a Pro Bowl...)	4.00	8.00
28 Harland Svare	4.00	8.00
29 Bill Svoboda (four-point stance)	4.00	8.00
30 Bob Topp	4.00	8.00
31 Mel Triplett (Triplett is a powerhouse...)	4.00	8.00
32 Emlen Tunnell	6.00	12.00
33 Alex Webster	5.00	10.00
34 Ray Wietecha (The Giants' Iron Man...)	4.00	8.00
35 Dick Yelvington (photo oriented horizontally)	4.00	8.00
36 Walt Yowarsky (four-point stance)	4.00	8.00

1957 Giants Team Issue

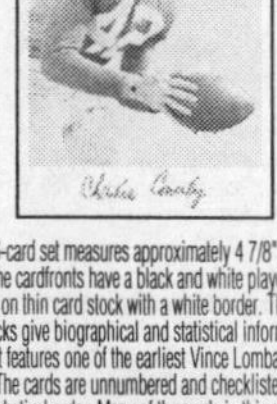

This 36-card set measures approximately 4 7/8" by 6 7/8". The cardfronts have a black and white player photo printed on thin card stock with a white border. The cardbacks give biographical and statistical information. This set features one of the earliest Vince Lombardi cards. The cards are unnumbered and checklisted below in alphabetical order. Many of the cards in this set are similar to the 1956 release and are only distinguishable by the differences noted below in parenthesis. We've included the first line of text on the cardback of some to help differentiate the two sets.

COMPLETE SET (36)	150.00	300.00
1 Ben Agajanian	4.00	8.00
2 Bill Austin (After five seasons...)	4.00	8.00
3 Ray Beck (jersey #65)	4.00	8.00
4 John Bookman	4.00	8.00
5 Roosevelt Brown	6.00	12.00

6 Don Chandler 4.00 8.00
(running pose)
7 Bobby Clatterbuck 4.00 8.00
(leaping passing pose)
8 Charley Conerly 10.00 20.00
(handing-off ball)
9 Gene Filipski 4.00 8.00
10 Frank Gifford 15.00 30.00
11 Don Heinrich 4.00 8.00
(For the second season...)
12 Sam Huff 6.00 12.00
13 Ed Hughes 4.00 8.00
(running pose)
14 Gerald Huth 4.00 8.00
(A pleasant surprise...)
15 Jim Katcavage 4.00 8.00
16 Les Keiter ANN 4.00 8.00
17 Cliff Livingston 4.00 8.00
18 Ken MacAfee E 4.00 8.00
(three-point stance)
19 Dennis Mendyk 4.00 8.00
20 Dick Modzelewski 4.00 8.00
(Spelled correctly on cardback)
21 Dick Nolan 4.00 8.00
22 Jim Patton 4.00 8.00
(Jim Patton on front)
23 Andy Robustelli 6.00 12.00
24 Kyle Rote 5.00 10.00
(running pose)
25 Chris Schenkel ANN 4.00 8.00
(Wearing a black suit)
26 Jack Spinks 4.00 8.00
27 Jack Stroud 4.00 8.00
(The best right guard...)
28 Harland Svare 4.00 8.00
29 Bill Svoboda 4.00 8.00
(portrait)
30 Mel Triplett 4.00 8.00
(Triplett in '56 was a...)
31 Emlen Tunnell 6.00 12.00
32 Alex Webster 5.00 10.00
33 Ray Wietecha 4.00 8.00
(Giant coaches rate...)
34 Dick Yelvington 4.00 8.00
(photo oriented vertically)
35 Walt Yowarsky 4.00 8.00
(blocking pose)
36 Giants Coaches 30.00 60.00
John Dell Isola
Jim Lee Howell
Ken Kavanaugh
Tom Landry
Vince Lombardi

1959 Giants Shell Glasses

These four drinking glasses were issued by Shell Gasoline Stations around 1959. Each features the same artwork and captions found on the 1959 Giants Shell Posters with the image etched on the glass with a frosted background.

COMPLETE SET (4) 100.00 200.00
1 Frank Gifford 40.00 80.00
2 Sam Huff 30.00 60.00
3 Dick Modzelewski 20.00 40.00
4 Kyle Rote 25.00 50.00

1959 Giants Shell Posters

This set of ten posters was distributed by Shell Oil in 1959. The pictures are black and white drawings by Robert Riger, and measure approximately 11 3/4" by 13 3/4". The unnumbered posters are arranged alphabetically by the player's last name and feature members of the New York Giants.

COMPLETE SET (10) 75.00 150.00
1 Charley Conerly 7.50 15.00
Gets it away under fire
2 Frank Gifford 18.00 30.00
Around the right side
3 Sam Huff 12.00 20.00
Shuts off the middle
4 Dick Modzelewski 6.00 12.00
Breaks through to nail his man
5 Jim Patton 6.00 12.00
Goes after the scatback
6 Andy Robustelli 7.50 15.00
Captain blitzes the quarterback
7 Kyle Rote 7.50 15.00
Catches one in the end zone
8 Bob Schnelker 6.00 12.00
Gets under a long one
9 Pat Summerall 7.50 15.00
Adds 3 points from the forty
10 Alex Webster and 7.50 15.00
Roosevelt Brown
Cuts back as Brown
clears the way

1960 Giants Jay Publishing

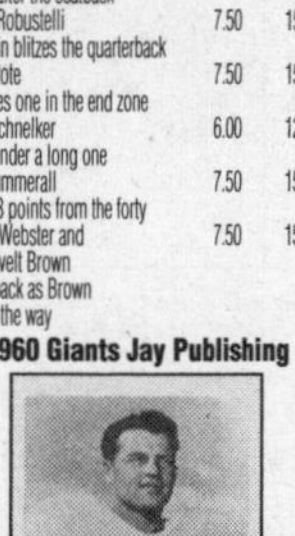

This 12-card set features (approximately) 5" by 7" black-and-white player photos. The photos show players in traditional poses with the quarterback preparing to throw, the runner heading downfield, and the defenseman ready for the tackle. These cards were packaged 12 to a packet and originally sold for 25 cents. The backs are blank. The cards are unnumbered and checklisted in alphabetical order.

COMPLETE SET (12) 75.00 135.00
1 Roosevelt Brown 6.00 12.00
2 Don Chandler 3.00 6.00
3 Charley Conerly 10.00 20.00
4 Frank Gifford 17.50 35.00
5 Roosevelt Grier 5.00 10.00
6 Sam Huff 10.00 20.00
7 Phil King 3.00 6.00
8 Andy Robustelli 7.50 15.00
9 Kyle Rote 4.00 8.00
10 Bob Schnelker 3.00 6.00
11 Pat Summerall 7.50 15.00
12 Alex Webster 4.00 8.00

1961 Giants Jay Publishing

This 12-card set features (approximately) 5" by 7" black-and-white player photos. The photos show players in traditional poses with the quarterback preparing to throw, the runner heading downfield, and the defenseman ready for the tackle. These cards were packaged 12 to a packet and originally sold for 25 cents. The backs are blank. The cards are unnumbered and checklisted below in alphabetical order.

COMPLETE SET (12) 50.00 100.00
1 Roosevelt Brown 4.00 8.00
2 Don Chandler 3.00 6.00
3 Charley Conerly 7.50 15.00
4 Roosevelt Grier 4.00 8.00
5 Sam Huff 6.00 12.00
6 Dick Modzelewski 3.00 6.00
7 Jimmy Patton 3.00 6.00
8 Jim Podoley 3.00 6.00
9 Andy Robustelli 5.00 10.00
10 Allie Sherman CO 3.00 6.00
11 Del Shofner 4.00 8.00
12 Y.A. Tittle 12.50 25.00

1962 Giants Team Issue

The New York Giants issued this set of player photos in 1962. The photos were distributed in set form complete with a paper checklist of the 10-players. Each measures approximately 8" by 10" and features a black and white photo with only the player's name directly below the picture within the border. The cards are blankbacked and unnumbered.

COMPLETE SET (10) 75.00 150.00
1 Roosevelt Brown 7.50 15.00
2 Don Chandler 6.00 12.00
3 Frank Gifford 17.50 35.00
4 Sam Huff 10.00 20.00
5 Dick Lynch 6.00 12.00
6 Jim Patton 6.00 12.00
7 Andy Robustelli 10.00 20.00
8 Del Shofner 7.50 15.00
9 Y.A. Tittle 12.50 25.00
10 Alex Webster 6.00 12.00

1965 Giants Team Issue Color

This set was originally released as a poster-sized sheet of color photos with facsimile player signatures. When cut, the photos measure roughly 5" by 7". The set is unnumbered and listed below alphabetically with prices for cut cards..

COMPLETE SET (15) 75.00 150.00
1 Roosevelt Brown 7.50 15.00
2 Tucker Frederickson 5.00 10.00
3 Jerry Hillebrand 5.00 10.00
4 Jim Katcavage 5.00 10.00
5 Spider Lockhart 6.00 12.00
6 Dick Lynch 5.00 10.00
7 Chuck Mercein 5.00 10.00
8 Earl Morrall 6.00 12.00
9 Joe Morrison 6.00 12.00
10 Del Shofner 6.00 12.00
11 Lou Slaby 5.00 10.00
12 Aaron Thomas 5.00 10.00
13 Steve Thurlow 5.00 10.00
14 Ernie Wheelwright 5.00 10.00
15 Giants Team Photo 6.00 12.00

1965-68 Giants Team Issue

The Giants issued a large number of roughly 8" x 10" black and white photos in the mid 1960s. Each photo includes only the player's name and position below the image in all capital letters and the backs are blank. Many player's were issued in various different poses as well as with variations in the text below the photo. We've included this detail below when known. Additions to this list are appreciated.

1A Erich Barnes 5.00 10.00
(Def. Halfback
running to his right)
1B Erich Barnes 5.00 10.00
(Def. Halfback
portrait)
1C Erich Barnes 5.00 10.00
(Defensive Back)
2 Roosevelt Brown 7.50 15.00
3 Henry Carr 5.00 10.00
4A Clarence Childs 5.00 10.00
Defensive Back, name
and position 1 1/4-in apart)
4B Clarence Childs 5.00 10.00
Defensive Back, name
and position 1 1/4-in apart)
5 Darrell Dess 5.00 10.00
6 Scott Eaton 5.00 10.00
7 Tucker Frederickson 6.00 12.00
8A Jerry Hillebrand 5.00 10.00
(Linebacker, name and
position 1 3/8-in apart)
8B Jerry Hillebrand 5.00 10.00
(Linebacker, name and
position 3/4-in apart)
9A Jim Katcavage 5.00 10.00
(Defensive End)
9B Jim Katcavage 5.00 10.00
(Def. End, name and
position 2 3/8-in apart)
9C Jim Katcavage 5.00 10.00
(Def. End, name and
position 1 1/4-in apart)
10A Ernie Koy 6.00 12.00
(Offensive Back)
10B Ernie Koy 6.00 12.00
(Running Back)
11 Greg Larson 5.00 10.00
12 Dick Lynch 5.00 10.00
13 Earl Morrall 6.00 12.00
14 Joe Morrison 6.00 12.00
15 Allie Sherman CO 6.00 12.00
(At chalkboard)
16 Del Shofner 6.00 12.00
17 Andy Stynchula 5.00 10.00
18 Fran Tarkenton 12.50 25.00
19 Aaron Thomas 5.00 10.00

1966 Giants Team Issue Color

This set was originally released as a poster-sized sheet of color photos with facsimile player signatures. When cut, the photos measure roughly 5" by 7". The set is unnumbered and listed below alphabetically with prices for cut photos.

1 Henry Carr 5.00 10.00
2 Tucker Frederickson 5.00 10.00
3 Pete Gogolak 5.00 10.00
4 Jerry Hillebrand 5.00 10.00
5 Homer Jones 5.00 10.00
6 Jim Katcavage 5.00 10.00
7 Ernie Koy 5.00 10.00
8 Spider Lockhart 6.00 12.00
9 Chuck Mercein 5.00 10.00
10 Earl Morrall 7.50 15.00
11 Joe Morrison 6.00 12.00
12 Jim Prestel 5.00 10.00
13 Aaron Thomas 5.00 10.00
14 Go-Go Giants '66 Title 5.00 10.00
15 Earl Morrall Action 7x10 6.00 12.00

1972 Giants Team Issue

These photos were issued by the Giants in 1972. Each measures roughly 4" by 5" with a white border on all 4-sides of the player image. The player's name and position is included below the photo and the cardbacks are blank and unnumbered.

COMPLETE SET (18) 50.00 100.00
1 Pete Athas 4.00 8.00
2 Bobby Duhon 4.00 8.00
3 Charlie Evans 4.00 8.00
4 Jim Files 4.00 8.00
5 Pete Gogolak 4.00 8.00
6 Jack Gregory 4.00 8.00
7 Bob Grim 4.00 8.00
8 Don Herrmann 4.00 8.00
9 Rich Houston 4.00 8.00
10 Pat Hughes 4.00 8.00
11 Randy Johnson 5.00 10.00
12 Ron Johnson 4.00 8.00
13 Carl Lockhart 4.00 8.00
14 Eldridge Small 4.00 8.00
15 Joe Taffoni 4.00 8.00
16 Rocky Thompson 4.00 8.00
17 Dave Tipton 4.00 8.00
18 Willie Williams 4.00 8.00

1973 Giants Color Litho

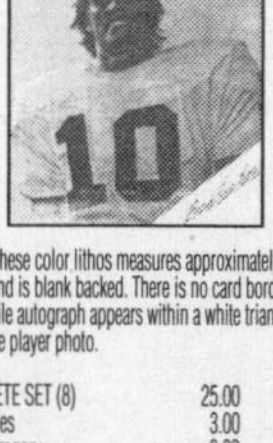

Each of these color lithos measures approximately 8 1/2" by 11" and is blank backed. There is no card border and a facsimile autograph appears within a white triangle below the player photo.

COMPLETE SET (8) 25.00 50.00
1 Jim Files 3.00 6.00
2 Jack Gregory 3.00 6.00
3 Ron Johnson 4.00 8.00
4 Greg Larson 3.00 6.00
5 Spider Lockhart 4.00 8.00
6 Norm Snead 5.00 10.00
7 Bob Tucker 4.00 8.00
8 Brad Van Pelt 4.00 8.00

1974 Giants Color Litho

Each of these color photos measures approximately 8 1/2" by 11" and is blankbacked. The photos are borderless and the player's name appears in white in the lower left or right of the player image.

COMPLETE SET (8) 25.00 50.00
1 Pete Athas 3.00 6.00
2 Pete Gogolak 3.00 6.00
3 Bob Grim 4.00 8.00
4 Don Herrmann 3.00 6.00
5 Pat Hughes 3.00 6.00
6 Bob Hyland 3.00 6.00
7 Ron Johnson 4.00 8.00
8 John Mendenhall 3.00 6.00

1974 Giants Team Issue

This photo pack set was issued by the Giants in 1974. Each photo measures roughly 8 1/2" by 10" with a white border on all 4-sides of the player image. The player's name and position is included below the photo and the cardbacks are blank and unnumbered.

COMPLETE SET (8) 25.00 50.00
1 Chuck Crist 3.00 6.00
2 Pete Gogolak 3.00 6.00
3 Bob Grim 3.00 6.00
4 Brian Kelley 3.00 6.00
5 Spider Lockhart 4.00 8.00
6 Norm Snead 5.00 10.00
7 Doug Van Horn 3.00 6.00
8 Willie Young 3.00 6.00

1975 Giants Team Issue

This photos were issued by the Giants around 1975. Each measures roughly 8" by 10" with a white border on all 4-sides of the player image. Just the player's name and position are included below the photo and the backs are blank and unnumbered.

1 Bobby Brooks 5.00 10.00
2 Pete Gogolak 5.00 10.00
3 Ron Johnson 6.00 12.00
4 Norm Snead 6.00 12.00
5 Willie Young 5.00 10.00

1979 Giants Team Sheets

This set consists of eight 8" by 10" sheets that display 5-8 black-and-white player/coach photos on each. Each individual photo measures approximately 2 1/4" by 3 1/4" and includes the player's name, jersey number, position, and brief vital stats below the photo. "1979 New York Football Giants" appears across the top of each sheet and the backs are blank. The sheets are unnumbered and checklisted below alphabetically according to the player featured in the upper left corner.

COMPLETE SET (8) 25.00 50.00
1 Bob Hammond 4.00 8.00
Billy Taylor
Bob Torrey
Doug Kotar
Alan Caldwell
Ken Johnson
Frank Marion
Harry Carson
2 Dan Lloyd 3.00 6.00
Brian Kelley
Jim Clack
John Skorupan
Keith Eck
Randy Coffield
Brad Benson
Ron Mikolajczyk
3 Coaches: 5.00 10.00
Ray Perkins
Ernie Adams
Bill Austin
Bill Belichick
Ralph Hawkins
Pat Hodgson
Bob Lord
Don Pollard
4 Ray Rhodes 3.00 6.00
Odis McKinney
Terry Jackson
Ray Oldham
Beasley Reece
Eddie Hicks
Emery Moorehead
Ernie Jones
5 Jimmy Robinson 3.00 6.00
Johnny Perkins
Gary Shirk
Dwight Scales
Loaird McCreary
6 Jim Stanley CO 5.00 10.00
Jim Williams CO
Joe Pisarcik
Brad Van Pelt
Phil Simms
Dave Jennings
Randy Dean
Joe Danelo
7 Doug Van Horn 3.00 6.00
John Mendenhall
Steve Spencer
J.T. Turner
Roy Simmons
Gary Jeter
Gordon Gravelle
Gordon King
8 Jeff Weston 3.00 6.00
Tom Neville
George Martin
Calvin Miller
Gus Coppens
Steve Young T
Phil Tabor
Earnest Gray

1981 Giants Team Sheets

This set consists of eight 8" by 10" sheets that display four to eight black-and-white player/coach photos on each. Each individual photo measures approximately 2 1/4" by 3 1/4" and includes the player's name, jersey number, position, and brief vital stats below the photo. "1981 New York Football Giants" appears across the top of each sheet and the backs are blank. The sheets are unnumbered and checklisted below alphabetically according to the player featured in the upper left corner.

COMPLETE SET (9) 40.00 75.00
1 Carl Barisich 3.00 6.00
Phil Tabor
Tom Mullady
Danny Pittman
Earnest Gray
Alvin Garrett
John Mistler
Johnny Perkins
2 Louis Jackson 3.00 6.00
Terry Jackson
Beasley Reece
Bill Currier
Leon Perry
Mark Haynes
Larry Flowers
Billy Taylor
3 Bob Lord CO 5.00 10.00
Bill Parcells CO
Jim Williams CO
Brad Van Pelt
Phil Simms
Scott Brunner
Dave Jennings
Joe Danelo
4 Bo Matthews 4.00 8.00
Doug Kotar
Leon Bright
Mike Dennis
Frank Marion
Joe McLaughlin
Harry Carson
Brian Kelley
5 Coaches: 5.00 10.00
Ray Perkins
Ernie Adams
Bill Austin
Bill Belichick
Romeo Crennel
Fred Glick
Pat Hodgson
Lamar Leachman
6 Mark Reed 3.00 6.00
Larry Heater
Mike Whittington
John Sinnott
Myron Lapka
Kevin Kurdyla
Mark Slawson
Clifford Chatman
7 Gary Shirk 3.00 6.00
Mike Friede
Dave Young
Rob Carpenter
8 Lawrence Taylor 7.50 15.00
Byron Hunt
Ed McGlasson
Brad Benson
Ernie Hughes
Jim Burt
Billy Ard
J.T. Turner
9 1981 Draft Picks: 7.50 15.00
Lawrence Taylor
Dave Young
John Mistler
Clifford Chatman
Bill Neill
Melvin Hoover
Edward O'Neal
Louis Jackson

1987 Giants Ace Fact Pack

This 33-card set, which measures approximately 2 1/4" by 3 5/8", was made in West Germany (by Ace Fact Pack) for distribution in England. This set features rounded corners and the back says "Ace" as if they were playing cards. We have checklisted the players in the set in alphabetical order.

COMPLETE SET (33) 50.00 120.00
1 Billy Ard 1.25 3.00
2 Carl Banks 2.50 6.00
3 Mark Bavaro 2.50 6.00
4 Brad Benson 1.25 3.00
5 Harry Carson 2.50 6.00
6 Maurice Carthon UER 2.00 5.00
(Misspelled Morris)
7 Mark Collins 2.00 5.00
8 Chris Godfrey 1.25 3.00
9 Kenny Hill 1.25 3.00
10 Erik Howard 2.00 5.00
11 Bobby Johnson 1.25 3.00
12 Leonard Marshall 2.50 6.00
13 George Martin 2.00 5.00
14 Joe Morris 2.00 5.00
15 Karl Nelson 1.25 3.00
16 Bart Oates UER 2.00 5.00
(Misspelled Oakes)
17 Gary Reasons 1.25 3.00
18 Stacy Robinson 1.25 3.00
19 Phil Simms 6.00 15.00
20 Lawrence Taylor 10.00 25.00
21 Herb Welch 1.25 3.00
22 Perry Williams 1.25 3.00
23 Giants Helmet 1.25 3.00
24 Giants Information 1.25 3.00
25 Giants Uniforms 1.25 3.00
26 Game Record Holders 1.25 3.00
27 Season Record Holders 1.25 3.00
28 Career Record Holders 1.25 3.00
29 Record 1967-86 1.25 3.00
30 1986 Team Statistics 1.25 3.00
31 All-Time Greats 1.25 3.00
32 Roll of Honour 1.25 3.00
33 Giants Stadium 1.25 3.00

1987 Giants Police

This set of 12 cards featuring New York Giants was issued very late in the year and was not widely distributed. Reportedly 10,000 sets were distributed by officers of the New Jersey police force. Cards measure approximately 2 3/4" by 4 1/8" and feature a crime prevention tip on the back. The set was sponsored by the New Jersey State Police Crime Prevention Resource Center. The Giants helmet appears below the player photo which differentiates this set from the very similar 1988 Police Giants set. These unnumbered cards are listed alphabetically in the checklist below.

COMPLETE SET (12) 50.00 125.00
1 Carl Banks 4.00 10.00
2 Mark Bavaro 3.00 8.00
3 Brad Benson 2.50 6.00
4 Jim Burt 2.50 6.00
5 Harry Carson 3.00 8.00
6 Maurice Carthon 2.50 6.00
7 Sean Landeta 2.50 6.00
8 Leonard Marshall 3.00 8.00
9 George Martin 2.50 6.00
10 Joe Morris 4.00 10.00
11 Bill Parcells CO 12.50 25.00
12 Phil Simms 15.00 30.00

1988 Giants Police

The 1988 Police New York Giants set contains 12 unnumbered cards measuring approximately 2 3/4" by 4 1/8". There are 11 player cards and one coach card. The backs have safety tips. The cards are listed below in alphabetical order by subject's name. The Giants team name and helmets appear above the player photo which differentiates this set from the very similar 1987 Police Giants set.

COMPLETE SET (12) 50.00 125.00
1 Billy Ard 2.50 6.00
2 Jim Burt 2.50 6.00
3 Harry Carson 4.00 10.00
4 Maurice Carthon 2.50 6.00
5 Leonard Marshall 4.00 10.00
6 George Martin 2.50 6.00
7 Phil McConkey 2.50 6.00
8 Joe Morris 3.00 8.00
9 Karl Nelson 2.50 6.00
10 Bart Oates 2.50 6.00
11 Bill Parcells CO 10.00 25.00
12 Phil Simms 15.00 30.00

1992 Giants Police

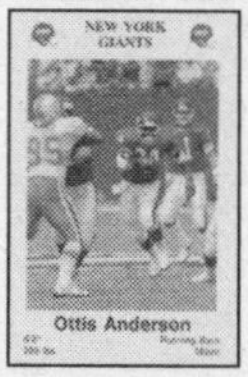

This 12-card set was printed and distributed by the New Jersey State Police Crime Prevention Resource Center. The cards measure approxiamtely 2 3/4" by 4 1/8". The fronts display color action player photos bordered in white. The team name appears at the top between two representations of the team helmet, while player information is printed beneath the picture. In dark blue print on white, the backs carry logos, "Tips from the Giants" in the form of public service announcements, and the McGruff the Crime Dog "Take a Bite out of Crime" slogan. The cards are unnumbered and checklisted below in alphabetical order.

COMPLETE SET (12) 32.00 80.00
1 Ottis Anderson 3.20 8.00
2 Matt Bahr 2.00 5.00
3 Eric Dorsey 2.00 5.00
4 John Elliott 2.00 5.00
5 Ray Handley CO 2.00 5.00
6 Jeff Hostetler 3.20 8.00
7 Erik Howard 2.00 5.00
8 Pepper Johnson 2.40 6.00
9 Leonard Marshall 2.40 6.00
10 Bart Oates 2.00 5.00
11 Gary Reasons 2.00 5.00
12 Phil Simms 8.00 20.00

1997 Giants Score

This 15-card set of the New York Giants was distributed in five-card packs with a suggested retail price of $1.99. The fronts feature color action player photos with white borders and the player's name and team logo printed in team color foil at the bottom. The backs carry player information and career statistics. Platinum Team parallel cards were randomly seeded in packs featuring all foil cardfronts.

COMPLETE SET (15) 2.40 6.00
*PLATINUM TEAMS: 1X TO 2X
1 Thomas Lewis .08 .25
2 Dave Brown .15 .40
3 Rodney Hampton .30 .75
4 Tyrone Wheatley .30 .75
5 Cedric Jones DE .08 .25
6 Amani Toomer .30 .75
7 Michael Strahan .15 .40
8 Chris Calloway .15 .40
9 Jessie Armstead .08 .25
10 Corey Miller .08 .25
11 Jason Sehorn .15 .40
12 Phillippi Sparks .08 .25
13 Charles Way .30 .75
14 Corey Widmer .08 .25
15 Danny Kanell .40 1.00

2004 Giants NY Post Stickers

This set of stickers was issued over a series of weeks within the NY Post newspaper. Each sheet features stickers of a number of Giants players intended to be pasted into an album.

COMPLETE SET (6) 5.00 12.00
1 Sheet 1 1.50 4.00
Luke Pettigout (2)
Kurt Warner
Will Allen
Eli Manning
Shaun Williams
Tiki Barber
Amani Toomer
Giants Logo
Giants Stadium
2 Sheet 2 1.00 2.50
3 Sheet 3 1.00 2.50
4 Sheet 4 1.00 2.50
5 Sheet 5 1.00 2.50
NNO Album .60 1.50

2005 Giants Topps XXL

COMPLETE SET (4) 2.00 5.00
1 Eli Manning 1.00 2.50
2 Jeremy Shockey .40 1.00
3 Plaxico Burress .30 .75
4 Tiki Barber .40 1.00

2006 Giants Topps

COMPLETE SET (12) 3.00 6.00
NYG1 Jeremy Shockey .30 .75
NYG2 Mathias Kiwanuka .30 .75
NYG3 Eli Manning .40 1.00
NYG4 Antonio Pierce .20 .50
NYG5 Tiki Barber .30 .75
NYG6 Amani Toomer .25 .60
NYG7 Osi Umenyiora .25 .60
NYG8 Plaxico Burress .25 .60
NYG9 Michael Strahan .25 .60
NYG10 LaVar Arrington .25 .60
NYG11 Sam Madison .20 .50
NYG12 Sinorice Moss .30 .75

2006 Giants Upper Deck Wachovia

Cards from this set were issued at the October 8, 2006 New York Giants home game. The cards were produced by Upper Deck and sponsored by Wachovia Bank.

COMPLETE SET (20) 6.00 15.00
1 LaVar Arrington .50 1.25
2 Tiki Barber .60 1.50
3 Plaxico Burress .50 1.25
4 Will Demps .60 1.50
5 Jeff Feagles .30 .75
6 Jay Feely .30 .75
7 Mathias Kiwanuka .60 1.50
8 Eli Manning .75 2.00
9 Kareem McKenzie .30 .75
10 Sinorice Moss .60 1.50
11 Shaun O'Hara .60 1.50
12 Luke Petitgout .30 .75
13 Antonio Pierce .40 1.00
14 Jeremy Shockey .60 1.50
15 Chris Snee .30 .75
16 Michael Strahan .50 1.25
17 Amani Toomer .50 1.25
18 David Tyree .50 1.25
19 Osi Umenyiora .50 1.25
20 Gibril Wilson .40 1.00

2007 Giants Merrick Mint Quarters

COMPLETE SET (11) 60.00 100.00
1 Plaxico Burress 5.00 10.00
2 Brandon Jacobs 5.00 10.00
3 Eli Manning 6.00 12.00
4 Eli Manning MVP 6.00 12.00
5 Antonio Pierce 5.00 10.00
6 Jeremy Shockey 5.00 10.00
7 Michael Strahan 5.00 10.00
8 Amani Toomer 5.00 10.00
9 Justin Tuck 5.00 10.00
10 David Tyree 5.00 10.00
11 Osi Umenyiora 5.00 10.00

2007 Giants Topps

COMPLETE SET (12) 3.00 6.00
1 Plaxico Burress .25 .60
2 Eli Manning .30 .75
3 Reuben Droughns .25 .60
4 Brandon Jacobs .25 .60
5 Sinorice Moss .25 .60
6 Jeremy Shockey .25 .60
7 Michael Strahan .25 .60
8 Steve Smith .30 .75
9 Antonio Pierce .20 .50
10 Amani Toomer .25 .60
11 Osi Umenyiora .25 .60
12 Aaron Ross .30 .75

2008 Giants Topps

COMPLETE SET (12) 2.50 5.00
1 Eli Manning .30 .75
2 Brandon Jacobs .25 .60
3 Jeremy Shockey .25 .60
4 Osi Umenyiora .25 .60
5 Michael Strahan .25 .60
6 Plaxico Burress .25 .60
7 Steve Smith USC .25 .60
8 Justin Tuck .25 .60
9 Ahmad Bradshaw .25 .60
10 Antonio Pierce .20 .50
11 Amani Toomer .25 .60
12 Mario Manningham .40 1.00

2008 Giants Topps Super Bowl XLII

COMP.FACT.SET (27)	10.00	20.00
1 Eli Manning	.50	1.25
2 Brandon Jacobs	.40	1.00
3 Ahmad Bradshaw	.40	1.00
4 Plaxico Burress	.40	1.00
5 Amani Toomer	.40	1.00
6 Steve Smith USC	.40	1.00
7 David Tyree	.40	1.00
8 Kevin Boss	.40	1.00
9 Shaun O'Hara	.30	.75
10 Chris Snee	.30	.75
11 Kareem McKenzie	.30	.75
12 Michael Strahan	.40	1.00
13 Osi Umenyiora	.40	1.00
14 Jeremy Shockey	.40	1.00
15 Fred Robbins	.30	.75
16 Antonio Pierce	.30	.75
17 Kawika Mitchell	.30	.75
18 Sam Madison	.30	.75
19 Corey Webster	.30	.75
20 Aaron Ross	.30	.75
21 Justin Tuck	.40	1.00
22 Gibril Wilson	.30	.75
23 New York Giants Win	.50	1.25
24 David Tyree TD Catch	.40	1.00
25 David Tyree Catch	.40	1.00
26 Plaxico Burress TD	.40	1.00
27 Jay Alford Sack	.30	.75

2008 Giants Upper Deck Super Bowl XLII

COMP.FACT SET (51)	10.00	20.00
1 Eli Manning	.50	1.25
2 R.W. McQuarters	.30	.75
3 Antonio Pierce	.30	.75
4 David Diehl	.30	.75
5 Corey Webster	.30	.75
6 Shaun O'Hara	.30	.75
7 Barry Cofield	.30	.75
8 Kevin Boss	.40	1.00
9 Reggie Torbor	.30	.75
10 Sam Madison	.30	.75
11 Jeff Feagles	.30	.75
12 Madison Hedgecock	.30	.75
13 David Tyree	.40	1.00
14 Grey Ruegamer	.30	.75
15 Gerris Wilkinson	.30	.75
16 Reuben Droughns	.40	1.00
17 Domenik Hixon	.40	1.00
18 Kawika Mitchell	.30	.75
19 Ahmad Bradshaw	.40	1.00
20 Jeremy Shockey	.40	1.00
21 Justin Tuck	.40	1.00
22 Amani Toomer	.40	1.00
23 Fred Robbins	.30	.75
24 James Butler	.30	.75
25 Brandon Jacobs	.40	1.00
26 Osi Umenyiora	.40	1.00
27 Aaron Ross	.30	.75
28 Derrick Ward	.30	.75
29 Chris Snee	.30	.75
30 Michael Strahan	.40	1.00
31 Gibril Wilson	.30	.75
32 Sinorice Moss	.40	1.00
33 Lawrence Tynes	.30	.75
34 Jay Alford	.30	.75
35 Kareem McKenzie	.30	.75
36 Zak DeOssie	.30	.75
37 Kevin Dockery	.30	.75
38 Rich Seubert	.30	.75
39 Michael Johnson	.30	.75
40 Plaxico Burress	.40	1.00
MM1 R.W. McQuarters MM	.30	.75
MM2 Lawrence Tynes MM	.30	.75
MM3 David Tyree MM	.40	1.00
MM4 Plaxico Burress MM	.40	1.00
SH1 Osi Umenyiora SH	.40	1.00
SH2 Michael Strahan SH	.40	1.00
SH3 Derrick Ward SH	.30	.75
SH4 Plaxico Burress SH	.40	1.00
SH5 Brandon Jacobs SH	.40	1.00
MVP1 Eli Manning MVP	.50	1.25
NYG1 Giants Team Jumbo	1.25	3.00

2009 Giants BP Mini Posters

These mini posters measuring roughly 9 1/2" by 12" feature great moments in Giants history. They were created for and distributed by BP Stores in the New York area.

COMPLETE SET (10)	10.00	20.00
1 Joe Morris	.75	2.00
2 Super Bowl Celebration	.75	2.00
3 Tiki Barber	1.00	2.50
4 Kerry Collins	1.00	2.50
5 Osi Umenyiora	.75	2.00
6 Joe Danelo	.75	2.00
7 Lawrence Taylor	1.25	3.00
8 Phil Simms	1.25	3.00
9 Phil McConkey	.75	2.00
10 Eli Manning	1.25	3.00

2009 Giants Breast Cancer Awareness

This three card set was issued at a home game in 2009. Each unnumbered card was created by one of the three NFL licensed manufacturers and features the pink ribbon breast cancer awareness logo on the fronts.

COMPLETE SET (3)	2.50	6.00
1 Eli Manning Panini	1.00	2.50
2 Justin Tuck Topps	.75	2.00
3 Brandon Jacobs Upper Deck	.75	2.00

2011 Giants Topps Super Bowl XLVI

This set was issued via a wrapper redemption program at the 2012 Super Bowl Card Show.

COMPLETE SET (5)	3.00	8.00
1 Eli Manning	.75	2.00
2 Victor Cruz	1.00	2.50
3 Ahmad Bradshaw	.60	1.50
4 Hakeem Nicks	.60	1.50
5 Jason Pierre-Paul	.75	2.00

2012 Giants Panini Super Bowl XLVI

COMPLETE SET (9)	4.00	10.00
1 Eli Manning	.75	2.00
2 Ahmad Bradshaw	.60	1.50
3 Brandon Jacobs	.60	1.50
4 Hakeem Nicks	.60	1.50
5 Victor Cruz	.75	2.00
6 Jason Pierre-Paul	.60	1.50
7 Justin Tuck	.50	1.25
8 Osi Umenyiora	.50	1.25
9 Antrel Rolle	.50	1.25

1969 Glendale Stamps

This set contains 312 stamps featuring NFL players each measuring approximately 1 13/16" by 2 15/16". The stamps were meant to be pasted in an accompanying album, which itself measures approximately 9" by 12". The stamps and the album positions are unnumbered so the stamps are ordered and numbered below according to the team order that they appear in the book. The team order is alphabetical as well, according to the city name. The stamp of O.J. Simpson predates his 1970 Topps Rookie Card by one year and the stamp of Gene Upshaw predates his Rookie Card by three years.

COMPLETE SET (312)	200.00	350.00
1 Bob Berry	.30	.75
2 Clark Miller	.30	.75
3 Jim Butler	.30	.75
4 Junior Coffey	.30	.75
5 Paul Flatley	.30	.75
6 Randy Johnson	.30	.75
7 Charlie Bryant	.30	.75
8 Billy Lothridge	.30	.75
9 Tommy Nobis	.75	1.50
10 Claude Humphrey	.30	.75
11 Ken Reaves	.30	.75
12 Jerry Simmons	.30	.75
13 Mike Curtis	.40	1.00
14 Dennis Gaubatz	.30	.75
15 Jerry Logan	.30	.75
16 Lenny Lyles	.30	.75
17 John Mackey	1.00	2.00
18 Tom Matte	.30	.75
19 Lou Michaels	.30	.75
20 Jimmy Orr	.30	.75
21 Willie Richardson	.30	.75
22 Don Shinnick	.30	.75
23 Dan Sullivan	.30	.75
24 Johnny Unitas	10.00	20.00
25 Houston Antwine	.30	.75
26 John Bramlett	.30	.75
27 Aaron Marsh	.30	.75
28 R.C. Gamble	.30	.75
29 Gino Cappelletti	.40	1.00
30 John Charles	.30	.75
31 Larry Eisenhauer	.30	.75
32 Jon Morris	.30	.75
33 Jim Nance	.30	.75
34 Len St. Jean	.30	.75
35 Mike Taliaferro	.30	.75
36 Jim Whalen	.30	.75
37 Stew Barber	.30	.75
38 Al Bemiller	.30	.75
39 George(Butch) Byrd	.30	.75
40 Booker Edgerson	.30	.75
41 Harry Jacobs	.30	.75
42 Jack Kemp	10.00	20.00
43 Ron McDole	.30	.75
44 Joe O'Donnell	.30	.75
45 John Pitts	.30	.75
46 George Saimes	.30	.75
47 Mike Stratton	.30	.75
48 O.J. Simpson	7.50	15.00
49 Ronnie Bull	.30	.75
50 Dick Butkus	7.50	15.00
51 Jim Cadile	.30	.75
52 Jack Concannon	.30	.75
53 Dick Evey	.30	.75
54 Bennie McRae	.30	.75
55 Ed O'Bradovich	.30	.75
56 Brian Piccolo	12.50	25.00
57 Mike Pyle	.30	.75
58 Gale Sayers	7.50	15.00
59 Dick Gordon	.30	.75
60 Roosevelt Taylor	.30	.75
61 Al Beauchamp	.30	.75
62 Dave Middendorf	.30	.75
63 Harry Gunner	.30	.75
64 Bobby Hunt	.30	.75
65 Bob Johnson	.30	.75
66 Charley King	.30	.75
67 Andy Rice	.30	.75
68 Paul Robinson	.30	.75
69 Bill Staley	.30	.75
70 Pat Matson	.30	.75
71 Bob Trumpy	.50	1.25
72 Sam Wyche	2.00	4.00
73 Erich Barnes	.30	.75
74 Gary Collins	.30	.75
75 Ben Davis	.30	.75
76 John Demarie	.30	.75
77 Gene Hickerson	.40	1.00
78 Jim Houston	.30	.75
79 Ernie Kellerman	.30	.75
80 Leroy Kelly	1.25	2.50
81 Dale Lindsey	.30	.75
82 Bill Nelsen	.30	.75
83 Jim Kanicki	.30	.75
84 Dick Schafrath	.30	.75
85 George Andrie	.30	.75
86 Mike Clark	.30	.75
87 Cornell Green	.30	.75
88 Bob Hayes	1.00	2.00
89 Chuck Howley	.40	1.00
90 Lee Roy Jordan	.75	1.50
91 Bob Lilly	2.50	5.00
92 Craig Morton	.40	1.00
93 John Niland	.30	.75
94 Dan Reeves	2.50	5.00
95 Mel Renfro	1.00	2.00
96 Lance Rentzel	.30	.75
97 Tom Beer	.30	.75
98 Billy Van Heusen	.30	.75
99 Mike Current	.30	.75
100 Al Denson	.30	.75
101 Pete Duranko	.30	.75
102 George Goeddeke	.30	.75
103 John Huard	.30	.75
104 Rich Jackson	.30	.75
105 Pete Jacques	.30	.75
106 Fran Lynch	.30	.75
107 Floyd Little	.75	1.50
108 Steve Tensi	.30	.75
109 Lem Barney	1.25	2.50
110 Nick Eddy	.30	.75
111 Mel Farr	.30	.75
112 Ed Flanagan	.30	.75
113 Larry Hand	.30	.75
114 Alex Karras	1.25	2.50
115 Dick LeBeau	.30	.75
116 Mike Lucci	.30	.75
117 Earl McCullouch	.30	.75
118 Bill Munson	.30	.75
119 Jerry Rush	.30	.75
120 Wayne Walker	.30	.75
121 Herb Adderley	1.00	2.00
122 Donny Anderson	.40	1.00
123 Lee Roy Caffey	.30	.75
124 Carroll Dale	.30	.75
125 Willie Davis	1.00	2.00
126 Boyd Dowler	.30	.75
127 Marv Fleming	.30	.75
128 Bob Jeter	.30	.75
129 Hank Jordan	1.00	2.00
130 Dave Robinson	.30	.75
131 Bart Starr	10.00	20.00
132 Willie Wood	1.00	2.00
133 Pete Beathard	.30	.75
134 Jim Beirne	.30	.75
135 Garland Boyette	.30	.75
136 Woody Campbell	.30	.75
137 Miller Farr	.30	.75
138 Hoyle Granger	.30	.75
139 Mac Haik	.30	.75
140 Ken Houston	1.25	2.50
141 Bobby Maples	.30	.75
142 Alvin Reed	.30	.75
143 Don Trull	.30	.75
144 George Webster	.30	.75
145 Bobby Bell	1.00	2.00
146 Aaron Brown	.30	.75
147 Buck Buchanan	1.00	2.00
148 Len Dawson	4.00	8.00
149 Mike Garrett	.40	1.00
150 Robert Holmes	.30	.75
151 Willie Lanier	1.25	2.50
152 Frank Pitts	.30	.75
153 Johnny Robinson	.40	1.00
154 Jan Stenerud	1.25	2.50
155 Otis Taylor	.40	1.00
156 Jim Tyrer	.30	.75
157 Dick Bass	.30	.75
158 Maxie Baughan	.30	.75
159 Richie Petitbon	.30	.75
160 Roger Brown	.30	.75
161 Roman Gabriel	.50	1.25
162 Bruce Gossett	.30	.75
163 Deacon Jones	1.00	2.00
164 Tom Mack	.50	1.25
165 Tommy Mason	.30	.75
166 Ed Meador	.30	.75
167 Merlin Olsen	1.25	2.50
168 Pat Studstill	.30	.75
169 Jack Clancy	.30	.75
170 Maxie Williams	.30	.75
171 Larry Csonka	7.50	15.00
172 Jim Warren	.30	.75
173 Norm Evans	.30	.75
174 Rick Norton	.30	.75
175 Bob Griese	6.00	12.00
176 Howard Twilley	.30	.75
177 Billy Neighbors	.30	.75
178 Nick Buoniconti	.75	1.50
179 Tom Goode	.30	.75
180 Dick Westmoreland	.30	.75
181 Grady Alderman	.30	.75
182 Bill Brown	.30	.75
183 Fred Cox	.30	.75
184 Clint Jones	.30	.75
185 Joe Kapp	.40	1.00
186 Paul Krause	.40	1.00
187 Gary Larsen	.30	.75
188 Jim Marshall	1.00	2.00
189 Dave Osborn	.30	.75
190 Alan Page	2.50	5.00
191 Mick Tingelhoff	.40	1.00
192 Roy Winston	.30	.75
193 Dan Abramowicz	.30	.75
194 Doug Atkins	1.00	2.00
195 Bo Burris	.30	.75
196 John Douglas	.30	.75
197 Don Shy	.30	.75
198 Billy Kilmer	.40	1.00
199 Tony Lorick	.30	.75
200 Dave Parks	.30	.75
201 Dave Rowe	.30	.75
202 Monty Stickles	.30	.75
203 Steve Stonebreaker	.30	.75
204 Del Williams	.30	.75
205 Pete Case	.30	.75
206 Tommy Crutcher	.30	.75
207 Scott Eaton	.30	.75
208 Tucker Frederickson	.30	.75
209 Pete Gogolak	.30	.75
210 Homer Jones	.30	.75
211 Ernie Koy	.30	.75
212 Spider Lockhart	.30	.75
213 Bruce Maher	.30	.75
214 Aaron Thomas	.30	.75
215 Fran Tarkenton	6.00	12.00
216 Jim Katcavage	.30	.75
217 Al Atkinson	.30	.75
218 Emerson Boozer	.30	.75
219 John Elliott	.30	.75
220 Dave Herman	.30	.75
221 Winston Hill	.30	.75
222 Jim Hudson	.30	.75
223 Pete Lammons	.30	.75
224 Gerry Philbin	.30	.75
225 George Sauer Jr.	.30	.75
226 Joe Namath	12.50	25.00
227 Matt Snell	.40	1.00
228 Jim Turner	.30	.75
229 Fred Biletnikoff	2.00	4.00
230 Willie Brown	1.00	2.00
231 Billy Cannon	.40	1.00
232 Dan Conners	.30	.75
233 Ben Davidson	.40	1.00
234 Hewritt Dixon	.30	.75
235 Daryle Lamonica	.50	1.25
236 Ike Lassiter	.30	.75
237 Kent McCloughan	.30	.75
238 Jim Otto	1.00	2.00
239 Harry Schuh	.30	.75
240 Gene Upshaw	1.25	2.50
241 Gary Ballman	.30	.75
242 Joe Carollo	.30	.75
243 Dave Lloyd	.30	.75
244 Fred Hill	.30	.75
245 Al Nelson	.30	.75
246 Joe Scarpati	.30	.75
247 Sam Baker	.30	.75
248 Fred Brown	.30	.75
249 Floyd Peters	.30	.75
250 Nate Ramsey	.30	.75
251 Norm Snead	.40	1.00
252 Tom Woodeshick	.30	.75
253 John Hilton	.30	.75
254 Kent Nix	.30	.75
255 Paul Martha	.30	.75
256 Ben McGee	.30	.75
257 Andy Russell	.40	1.00
258 Dick Shiner	.30	.75
259 J.R. Wilburn	.30	.75
260 Marv Woodson	.30	.75
261 Earl Gros	.30	.75
262 Dick Hoak	.30	.75
263 Roy Jefferson	.30	.75
264 Larry Gagner	.30	.75
265 Johnny Roland	.30	.75
266 Jackie Smith	1.00	2.00
267 Jim Bakken	.30	.75
268 Don Brumm	.30	.75
269 Bob DeMarco	.30	.75
270 Irv Goode	.30	.75
271 Ken Gray	.30	.75
272 Charley Johnson	.40	1.00
273 Ernie McMillan	.30	.75
274 Larry Stallings	.30	.75
275 Jerry Stovall	.30	.75
276 Larry Wilson	.75	1.50
277 Chuck Allen	.30	.75
278 Lance Alworth	2.50	5.00
279 Kenny Graham	.30	.75
280 Steve DeLong	.30	.75
281 Willie Frazier	.30	.75
282 Gary Garrison	.30	.75
283 Sam Gruneisen	.30	.75
284 John Hadl	.50	1.25
285 Brad Hubbert	.30	.75
286 Ron Mix	.75	1.50
287 Dick Post	.30	.75
288 Walt Sweeney	.30	.75
289 Kermit Alexander	.30	.75
290 Ed Beard	.30	.75
291 Bruce Bosley	.30	.75
292 John Brodie	1.25	2.50
293 Stan Hindman	.30	.75
294 Jim Johnson	1.00	2.00
295 Charlie Krueger	.30	.75
296 Clifton McNeil	.30	.75
297 Gary Lewis	.30	.75
298 Howard Mudd	.30	.75
299 Dave Wilcox	.40	1.00
300 Ken Willard	.30	.75
301 Charlie Gogolak	.30	.75
302 Len Hauss	.30	.75
303 Sonny Jurgensen	2.50	5.00
304 Carl Kammerer	.30	.75
305 Walter Rock	.30	.75
306 Ray Schoenke	.30	.75
307 Chris Hanburger	.40	1.00
308 Tom Brown	.30	.75
309 Sam Huff	1.25	2.50
310 Bob Long	.30	.75
311 Vince Promuto	.30	.75
312 Pat Richter	.30	.75
NNO Stamp Album	10.00	20.00

1989-97 Goal Line HOF

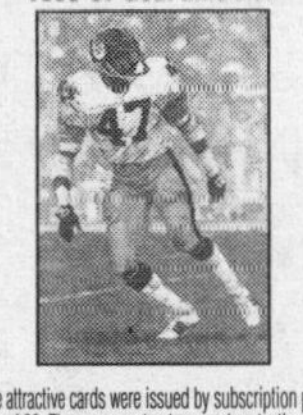

These attractive cards were issued by subscription per series of 30. They were sent out one series at a time in a custom box. The cards are postcard-size drawings (a full-color action painting) measuring approximately 4" by 6". The card backs contain brief biographical information and are printed in black on white card stock. Each card contains the specific set serial number out of 5,000 at the bottom of the cardbacks. The back also feature the player's name, college, position, NFL years, pro team, and the date he was enshrined in the Hall of Fame. The players featured are all members of the Pro Football Hall of Fame in Canton, Ohio. The second series was produced in 1990, the third series in 1991, and so forth. Collectors who ordered series five before August 31, 1993, received a free commemorative ticket signed by Pete Elliott (Commissioner of the Pro Football Hall of Fame) and were entered into a drawing for one of three uncut sheets of series five. In total, 50 fifth-series uncut sheets were produced, and they were signed and numbered by the artist. Within each series the cards have been numbered alphabetically. They are considered ideal for autographing and are often found signed. The artist for the set was Gary Thomas. Collectors who have been purchasing this set over the years have the continuation right to receive the same serial numbered card whenever the next series is issued.

COMPLETE SET (189)	300.00	600.00
1 Lance Alworth	12.50	25.00
2 Red Badgro	2.00	5.00
3 Cliff Battles	1.50	4.00
4 Mel Blount	12.50	25.00
5 Terry Bradshaw	20.00	40.00
6 Jim Brown	15.00	30.00
7 George Connor	10.00	20.00
8 Turk Edwards	1.50	4.00
9 Tom Fears	10.00	20.00
10 Frank Gifford	12.50	25.00
11 Otto Graham	7.50	15.00
12 Red Grange	3.00	8.00
13 George Halas	2.50	6.00
14 Clarke Hinkle	1.50	4.00
15 Robert(Cal) Hubbard	1.50	4.00
16 Sam Huff	12.50	25.00
17 Frank(Bruiser) Kinard	1.50	4.00
18 Dick(Night Train) Lane	2.00	5.00
19 Sid Luckman	2.50	6.00
20 Bobby Mitchell	10.00	20.00
21 Merlin Olsen	10.00	20.00
22 Jim Parker	10.00	20.00
23 Joe Perry	12.50	25.00
24 Pete Rozelle	2.00	5.00
25 Art Shell	10.00	20.00
26 Fran Tarkenton	10.00	20.00
27 Jim Thorpe	3.00	8.00
28 Paul Warfield	12.50	25.00
29 Larry Wilson	10.00	20.00
30 Willie Wood	10.00	20.00
31 Doug Atkins	1.00	2.50
32 Bobby Bell	1.00	2.50
33 Raymond Berry	1.25	3.00
34 Paul Brown	.60	1.50
35 Guy Chamberlin	.60	1.50
36 Dutch Clark	.60	1.50
37 Jimmy Conzelman	.60	1.50
38 Len Dawson	1.25	3.00
39 Mike Ditka	2.50	6.00
40 Dan Fortmann	.60	1.50
41 Frank Gatski	1.00	2.50
42 Bill George	.60	1.50
43 Elroy Hirsch	1.25	3.00
44 Paul Hornung	1.50	4.00
45 John Henry Johnson	1.00	2.50
46 Walt Kiesling	.60	1.50
47 Yale Lary	1.00	2.50
48 Bobby Layne	1.25	3.00
49 Tuffy Leemans	.60	1.50
50 Geo.Preston Marshall	.60	1.50
51 George McAfee	1.00	2.50
52 Wayne Millner	.60	1.50
53 Bronko Nagurski	1.50	4.00
54 Joe Namath	4.00	10.00
55 Ray Nitschke	1.25	3.00
56 Jim Ringo	1.00	2.50
57 Art Rooney	.60	1.50
58 Joe Stydahar	.60	1.50
59 Charley Taylor	1.25	3.00
60 Charley Trippi	1.00	2.50
61 Fred Biletnikoff	1.25	3.00
62 Buck Buchanan	.60	1.50
63 Dick Butkus	2.00	5.00
64 Earl Campbell	1.50	4.00
65 Tony Canadeo	1.00	2.50
66 Art Donovan	1.25	3.00
67 Ray Flaherty	.60	1.50
68 Forrest Gregg	1.00	2.50
69 Lou Groza	1.25	3.00
70 John Hannah	1.00	2.50
71 Don Hutson	1.00	2.50
72 Deacon Jones	1.25	3.00
73 Stan Jones	1.00	2.50
74 Sonny Jurgensen	1.25	3.00
75 Vince Lombardi	1.25	3.00
76 Tim Mara	.60	1.50
77 Ollie Matson	1.00	2.50
78 Mike McCormack	1.00	2.50
79 Johnny Blood McNally	.60	1.50
80 Marion Motley	1.25	3.00
81 George Musso	1.00	2.50
82 Greasy Neale	.60	1.50
83 Clarence(Ace) Parker	1.00	2.50
84 Pete Pihos	1.00	2.50
85 Tex Schramm	1.00	2.50
86 Roger Staubach	3.00	8.00
87 Jan Stenerud	1.00	2.50
88 Y.A. Tittle	1.50	4.00
89 Bulldog Turner	1.00	2.50
90 Steve Van Buren	1.00	2.50
91 Herb Adderley	1.00	2.50
92 Lem Barney	1.00	2.50
93 Sammy Baugh	2.00	5.00
94 Chuck Bednarik	1.25	3.00
95 Charles W. Bidwill	.60	1.50
96 Willie Brown	1.25	3.00
97 Al Davis	1.50	4.00
98 Bill Dudley	1.00	2.50
99 Weeb Ewbank	1.00	2.50
100 Len Ford	.60	1.50
101 Sid Gillman	1.00	2.50
102 Jack Ham	1.25	3.00
103 Mel Hein	.60	1.50
104 Bill Hewitt	.60	1.50
105 Dante Lavelli	1.00	2.50
106 Bob Lilly	1.25	3.00
107 John Mackey	1.00	2.50
108 Hugh McElhenny	1.25	3.00
109 Mike Michalske	.60	1.50
110 Ron Mix	1.00	2.50
111 Leo Nomellini	1.00	2.50
112 Steve Owen	.60	1.50
113 Alan Page	1.25	3.00
114 Dan Reeves OWN	.60	1.50
115 John Riggins	1.25	3.00
116 Gale Sayers	2.00	5.00
117 Ken Strong	.60	1.50
118 Gene Upshaw	1.00	2.50
119 Norm Van Brocklin	1.50	4.00
120 Alex Wojciechowicz	.60	1.50
121 Bert Bell COMM	.60	1.50
122 George Blanda	1.50	4.00
123 Joe Carr	.60	1.50
124 Larry Csonka	1.50	4.00
125 Paddy Driscoll	.60	1.50
126 Dan Fouts	1.25	3.00
127 Bob Griese	1.50	4.00
128 Ed Healey	.60	1.50
129 Fats Henry	.60	1.50
130 Ken Houston	1.00	2.50
131 Lamar Hunt OWN	1.00	2.50
132 Jack Lambert	1.25	3.00
133 Tom Landry	1.50	4.00
134 Willie Lanier	1.00	2.50
135 Larry Little	1.00	2.50
136 Don Maynard	1.00	2.50
137 Lenny Moore	1.25	3.00
138 Chuck Noll CO	1.25	3.00
139 Jim Otto	1.25	3.00
140 Walter Payton	4.00	10.00
141 Hugh(Shorty) Ray OFF	.60	1.50
142 Andy Robustelli	1.00	2.50
143 Bob St. Clair	1.00	2.50
144 Joe Schmidt	1.25	3.00
145 Jim Taylor	1.25	3.00
146 Doak Walker	1.25	3.00
147 Bill Walsh CO	1.25	3.00
148 Bob Waterfield	1.25	3.00
149 Arnie Weinmeister	1.00	2.50
150 Bill Willis	1.00	2.50
151 Roosevelt Brown	1.00	2.50
152 Jack Christiansen	.60	1.50
153 Willie Davis	1.00	2.50
154 Tony Dorsett	2.00	5.00
155 Bud Grant	1.00	2.50
156 Joe Greene	1.50	4.00
157 Joe Guyon	.60	1.50
158 Franco Harris	1.50	4.00
159 Ted Hendricks	1.25	3.00
160 Arnie Herber	.60	1.50
161 Jim Johnson	1.00	2.50
162 Leroy Kelly	1.25	3.00
163 Curly Lambeau	.60	1.50
164 Jim Langer	1.00	2.50
165 Link Lyman	.60	1.50
166 Gino Marchetti	1.00	2.50
167 Ernie Nevers	1.25	3.00
168 O.J. Simpson	1.50	4.00
169 Jackie Smith	1.00	2.50
170 Bart Starr	3.00	8.00
171 Ernie Stautner	1.25	3.00
172 George Trafton	.60	1.50
173 Emlen Tunnell	.60	1.50
174 Johnny Unitas	3.00	8.00
175 Randy White	1.25	3.00
176 Jim Finks	1.25	3.00
177 Hank Jordan	1.25	3.00
178 Steve Largent	2.00	5.00
179 Lee Roy Selmon	1.50	4.00
180 Kellen Winslow	2.00	5.00
181 Lou Creekmur	1.50	4.00
182 Dan Dierdorf	2.00	5.00
183 Joe Gibbs	1.50	4.00
184 Charlie Joiner	2.00	5.00
185 Mel Renfro	2.00	5.00
186 Mike Haynes	1.50	4.00
187 Wellington Mara	1.50	4.00
188 Don Shula	2.50	6.00
189 Mike Webster	1.50	4.00

1989-97 Goal Line HOF Autographs

COMPLETE SET (141)	3,000.00	5,000.00
1 Lance Alworth	20.00	40.00
2 Red Badgro	25.00	40.00
4 Mel Blount	20.00	40.00
5 Terry Bradshaw	40.00	75.00
6 Jim Brown	40.00	75.00
7 George Connor	15.00	30.00
9 Tom Fears	25.00	40.00
10 Frank Gifford	30.00	50.00
11 Otto Graham	20.00	40.00
12 Red Grange	150.00	250.00
16 Sam Huff	20.00	40.00
18 Dick(Night Train) Lane	15.00	30.00
19 Sid Luckman	40.00	75.00
20 Bobby Mitchell	15.00	30.00
21 Merlin Olsen	20.00	40.00
22 Jim Parker	15.00	30.00
23 Joe Perry	20.00	40.00
24 Pete Rozelle COMM	175.00	300.00
25 Art Shell	15.00	30.00
26 Fran Tarkenton	25.00	50.00
28 Paul Warfield	20.00	40.00
29 Larry Wilson	12.50	25.00
30 Willie Wood	15.00	30.00
31 Doug Atkins	7.50	15.00
32 Bobby Bell	10.00	20.00
33 Raymond Berry	12.50	25.00
34 Paul Brown CO	125.00	200.00
38 Len Dawson	15.00	30.00
39 Mike Ditka	20.00	40.00
40 Dan Fortmann (Proof card; thought to be signed by his wife)	90.00	150.00
41 Frank Gatski	12.50	25.00
43 Elroy Hirsch	15.00	30.00
44 Paul Hornung	15.00	30.00
45 John Henry Johnson	10.00	20.00
47 Yale Lary	10.00	20.00
51 George McAfee	7.50	15.00
54 Joe Namath	50.00	100.00
55 Ray Nitschke	35.00	60.00
56 Jim Ringo	15.00	30.00
59 Charley Taylor	12.50	25.00
60 Charley Trippi	10.00	20.00
61 Fred Biletnikoff	15.00	30.00
62 Buck Buchanan	60.00	100.00
63 Dick Butkus	25.00	40.00
64 Earl Campbell	20.00	40.00
65 Tony Canadeo	15.00	30.00
66 Art Donovan	12.50	25.00
67 Ray Flaherty	35.00	60.00
68 Forrest Gregg	12.50	25.00
69 Lou Groza	15.00	30.00
70 John Hannah	12.50	25.00
71 Don Hutson	100.00	175.00
72 Deacon Jones	12.50	25.00
73 Stan Jones	10.00	20.00
74 Sonny Jurgensen	30.00	45.00
77 Ollie Matson	15.00	30.00
78 Mike McCormack	10.00	20.00
80 Marion Motley	30.00	50.00
81 George Musso	15.00	30.00
83 Clarence(Ace) Parker	10.00	20.00
84 Pete Pihos	15.00	30.00
85 Tex Schramm GM	15.00	25.00
86 Roger Staubach	40.00	75.00
87 Jan Stenerud	10.00	20.00
88 Y.A. Tittle	15.00	30.00
89 Bulldog Turner	30.00	50.00
90 Steve Van Buren	10.00	20.00
91 Herb Adderley	10.00	20.00
92 Lem Barney	12.50	25.00
93 Sammy Baugh	40.00	80.00
94 Chuck Bednarik	10.00	20.00
96 Willie Brown	10.00	20.00
97 Al Davis OWN	250.00	450.00
98 Bill Dudley	12.50	25.00
99 Weeb Ewbank CO	25.00	40.00
101 Sid Gillman	12.50	25.00
102 Jack Ham	15.00	30.00
105 Dante Lavelli	12.50	25.00
106 Bob Lilly	12.50	25.00
107 John Mackey	10.00	20.00
108 Hugh McElhenny	10.00	20.00
110 Ron Mix	12.50	25.00
111 Leo Nomellini	15.00	30.00
113 Alan Page	15.00	30.00
115 John Riggins	90.00	150.00
116 Gale Sayers	30.00	50.00
118 Gene Upshaw	12.50	25.00
120 Alex Wojciechowicz	1,000.00	1,500.00
122 George Blanda	35.00	60.00
124 Larry Csonka	25.00	40.00
126 Dan Fouts	25.00	40.00
127 Bob Griese	20.00	40.00
130 Ken Houston	10.00	20.00
131 Lamar Hunt OWN	12.50	25.00
132 Jack Lambert	30.00	50.00
133 Tom Landry	50.00	80.00
134 Willie Lanier	10.00	20.00
135 Larry Little	10.00	20.00
136 Don Maynard	10.00	20.00
137 Lenny Moore	10.00	20.00
138 Chuck Noll CO	15.00	30.00
139 Jim Otto	10.00	20.00
140 Walter Payton	100.00	175.00
142 Andy Robustelli	10.00	20.00
143 Bob St. Clair	10.00	20.00
144 Joe Schmidt	10.00	20.00
145 Jim Taylor	12.50	25.00
146 Doak Walker	60.00	100.00
147 Bill Walsh CO	30.00	50.00
149 Arnie Weinmeister	25.00	40.00
150 Bill Willis	10.00	20.00
151 Roosevelt Brown	12.50	25.00
153 Willie Davis	10.00	20.00
154 Tony Dorsett	25.00	40.00
155 Bud Grant CO	30.00	50.00
156 Joe Greene	15.00	30.00
158 Franco Harris	30.00	50.00
159 Ted Hendricks	12.50	25.00
161 Jim Johnson	10.00	20.00
162 Leroy Kelly	12.50	25.00
164 Jim Langer	10.00	20.00
166 Gino Marchetti	12.50	25.00
168 O.J. Simpson	50.00	80.00
169 Jackie Smith	10.00	20.00
170 Bart Starr	50.00	80.00
171 Ernie Stautner	12.50	25.00
174 Johnny Unitas	90.00	150.00
175 Randy White	15.00	30.00
178 Steve Largent	15.00	30.00
179 Lee Roy Selmon	10.00	20.00
180 Kellen Winslow	25.00	40.00
181 Lou Creekmur	10.00	20.00
182 Dan Dierdorf	12.50	25.00
183 Joe Gibbs CO	30.00	45.00
184 Charlie Joiner	10.00	20.00
185 Mel Renfro	10.00	20.00
186 Mike Haynes	15.00	30.00
187 Wellington Mara OWN	12.50	25.00
188 Don Shula CO	30.00	50.00
189 Mike Webster	20.00	40.00

1989-97 Goal Line HOF Proofs

COMPLETE SET (189)	500.00	800.00

*PROOFS: .6X TO 1.5X BASIC CARDS

1998 Goal Line HOF

This update set was released by Goal Line Art primarily to collectors who held the rights to the original numbered sets. This set was issued in a blue and white factory set styled box. All five new inductees were included.

COMPLETE SET (5)	8.00	20.00
190 Paul Krause	1.60	4.00
191 Tommy McDonald	1.60	4.00
192 Anthony Munoz	1.60	4.00
193 Mike Singletary	2.40	6.00
194 Dwight Stephenson	2.40	6.00

1998 Goal Line HOF Autographs

This set was issued unsigned in 1998 to subscription holders. Although the cards were not released signed, the set is popular with autograph collectors and commonly traded signed.

190 Paul Krause	12.50	25.00
191 Tommy McDonald	7.50	15.00
192 Anthony Munoz	10.00	20.00
193 Mike Singletary	20.00	35.00
194 Dwight Stephenson	12.50	25.00

1999 Goal Line HOF

This update set was released by Goal Line Art primarily to collectors who held the rights to the original numbered sets. This set was issued in a red and white factory set styled box. All five new inductees were included. 5000 sets were produced.

COMPLETE SET (5)	10.00	20.00
195 Eric Dickerson	3.00	6.00
196 Tom Mack	2.00	4.00
197 Ozzie Newsome	3.00	6.00
198 Billy Shaw	2.00	4.00
199 Lawrence Taylor	3.00	6.00

1999 Goal Line HOF Autographs

This set was issued unsigned in 1998 to subscription holders. Although the cards were not released signed, the set is popular with autograph collectors and commonly traded signed.

195 Eric Dickerson	25.00	40.00
196 Tom Mack	12.50	25.00
197 Ozzie Newsome	20.00	35.00
198 Billy Shaw	12.50	25.00
199 Lawrence Taylor	12.50	25.00

2000 Goal Line HOF

This update set was released by Goal Line Art primarily to collectors who held the rights to the original numbered sets. This set was issued in a factory set box. Five new inductees were included. Reportedly, 5000 sets were produced.

COMPLETE SET (5)	15.00	25.00
200 Howie Long	3.00	6.00
201 Ronnie Lott	3.00	6.00
202 Joe Montana	5.00	10.00
203 Dan Rooney	2.00	4.00
204 Dave Wilcox	2.00	4.00

2000 Goal Line HOF Autographs

200 Howie Long	40.00	75.00
201 Ronnie Lott	25.00	40.00
202 Joe Montana	60.00	100.00
203 Dan Rooney	30.00	50.00
204 Dave Wilcox	12.50	25.00

2001 Goal Line HOF

This update set was released by Goal Line Art primarily to collectors who held the rights to the original numbered sets. This set was issued in a factory set box. Six new inductees were included. Reportedly, 5000 sets were produced.

COMPLETE SET (7)	15.00	30.00
205 Nick Buoniconti	4.00	8.00
206 Marv Levy	3.00	6.00
207 Mike Munchak	3.00	6.00
208 Jackie Slater	3.00	6.00
209 Lynn Swann	5.00	10.00
210 Ron Yary	3.00	6.00
211 Jack Youngblood	4.00	8.00

2001 Goal Line HOF Autographs

205 Nick Buoniconti	20.00	35.00
206 Marv Levy	30.00	50.00
207 Mike Munchak	25.00	40.00
208 Jackie Slater	20.00	35.00
209 Lynn Swann	50.00	100.00
210 Ron Yary	20.00	35.00
211 Jack Youngblood	20.00	35.00

2002 Goal Line HOF

This update set was released by Goal Line Art primarily to collectors who held the rights to the original numbered sets. This set was issued in a factory set box. Four new inductees were included. Reportedly, 5000 sets were produced.

COMPLETE SET (5)	12.50	25.00
212 George Allen	3.00	6.00

213 Dave Casper	4.00	8.00
214 Dan Hampton	3.00	6.00
215 Jim Kelly	5.00	10.00
216 John Stallworth	4.00	8.00

2002 Goal Line HOF Autographs

213 Dave Casper	15.00	30.00
214 Dan Hampton	15.00	30.00
215 Jim Kelly	30.00	50.00
216 John Stallworth	20.00	40.00

2003 Goal Line HOF

This update set was released by Goal Line Art primarily to collectors who held the rights to the original numbered sets. This set was issued in a factory set box. Five new inductees were included for 2003. Reportedly, 5000 sets were produced.

COMPLETE SET (5)	15.00	25.00
217 Marcus Allen	4.00	10.00
218 Elvin Bethea	2.50	6.00
219 Joe DeLamielleure	2.50	6.00
220 James Lofton	3.00	8.00
221 Hank Stram	2.50	6.00

2003 Goal Line HOF Autographs

217 Marcus Allen	25.00	40.00
218 Elvin Bethea	20.00	35.00
219 Joe DeLamielleure	20.00	35.00
220 James Lofton	20.00	35.00
221 Hank Stram	25.00	40.00

2004 Goal Line HOF

This update set was released by Goal Line Art primarily to collectors who held the rights to the original numbered sets. This set was issued in a factory set box. Four new inductees were included for 2004. Reportedly, 5000 sets were produced.

COMPLETE SET (4)	15.00	25.00
222 Bob Brown	3.00	6.00
223 Carl Eller	3.00	6.00
224 John Elway	5.00	10.00
225 Barry Sanders	5.00	10.00

2004 Goal Line HOF Autographs

222 Bob Brown	15.00	30.00
223 Carl Eller	15.00	30.00
224 John Elway	125.00	200.00
225 Barry Sanders	75.00	125.00

2005 Goal Line HOF

COMPLETE SET (4)	15.00	30.00
226 Benny Friedman	3.00	6.00
227 Dan Marino	5.00	10.00
228 Fritz Pollard	3.00	6.00
229 Steve Young	4.00	8.00

2005 Goal Line HOF Autographs

227 Dan Marino	125.00	200.00
229 Steve Young	40.00	80.00

2006 Goal Line HOF

COMPLETE SET (6)	15.00	30.00
230 Troy Aikman	4.00	8.00
231 Harry Carson	3.00	6.00
232 John Madden	3.00	6.00
233 Warren Moon	3.00	6.00
234 Reggie White	4.00	8.00
235 Rayfield Wright	3.00	6.00

2006 Goal Line HOF Autographs

230 Troy Aikman	90.00	150.00
231 Harry Carson	15.00	30.00
232 John Madden	20.00	40.00
233 Warren Moon	15.00	30.00
235 Rayfield Wright	15.00	30.00

2007 Goal Line HOF

COMPLETE SET (6)	15.00	30.00
236 Gene Hickerson	2.50	5.00
237 Michael Irvin	3.00	6.00
238 Bruce Matthews	2.50	5.00
239 Charlie Sanders	2.50	5.00
240 Thurman Thomas	3.00	6.00
241 Roger Wehrli	2.50	5.00

2007 Goal Line HOF Autographs

236 Gene Hickerson		
237 Michael Irvin	25.00	50.00
238 Bruce Matthews	12.50	25.00
239 Charlie Sanders	12.50	25.00
240 Thurman Thomas	25.00	50.00
241 Roger Wehrli	12.50	25.00

2008 Goal Line HOF

COMPLETE SET (6)	15.00	30.00
242 Fred Dean	2.50	5.00
243 Darrell Green	3.00	6.00
244 Art Monk	3.00	6.00
245 Emmitt Thomas	2.50	5.00
246 Andre Tippett	2.50	5.00
247 Gary Zimmerman	2.50	5.00

2008 Goal Line HOF Autographs

242 Fred Dean	12.50	25.00
243 Darrell Green	15.00	30.00
244 Art Monk	15.00	30.00
245 Emmitt Thomas	12.50	25.00
246 Andre Tippett	12.50	25.00
247 Gary Zimmerman	12.50	25.00

2009 Goal Line HOF

COMPLETE SET (6)	15.00	30.00
248 Bob Hayes	2.50	5.00
249 Randall McDaniel	2.50	5.00
250 Bruce Smith	3.00	6.00
251 Derrick Thomas	2.50	5.00
252 Ralph Wilson Jr.	2.50	5.00
253 Rod Woodson	2.50	5.00

2009 Goal Line HOF Autographs

249 Randall McDaniel	12.50	25.00
250 Bruce Smith	15.00	30.00
252 Ralph Wilson Jr.	12.50	25.00
253 Rod Woodson	15.00	30.00

2010 Goal Line HOF

COMPLETE SET (7)	25.00	40.00
254 Russ Grimm	2.50	6.00
255 Rickey Jackson	2.50	6.00
256 Dick LeBeau	2.50	6.00
257 Floyd Little	2.50	6.00
258 John Randle	2.50	6.00
259 Jerry Rice	3.00	8.00
260 Emmitt Smith	3.00	8.00

1888 Goodwin Champions N162

This 50-card set issued by Goodwin was one of the major competitors to the N28 and N29 sets marketed by Allen and Ginter. It contains individuals representing 18 sports, with eight baseball players pictured. Each color card is backlisted and bears advertising for "Old Judge" and "Gypsy Queen" cigarettes on the front. The set was released to the public in 1888 and an album (catalog: A36) is associated with it as a premium issue.

12 Harry Beecher (Football)	3,000.00	4,500.00

2003 Grand Rapids Rampage AFL

This set was sponsored by Choice Marketing, Inc. and features members of the Grand Papids Rampage of the Arena Football League. Each card includes the team name and player name below the color player photo on the front. The cardbacks are printed in black and white and feature another player photo and a player bio.

COMPLETE SET (10)	5.00	10.00
1 Chris Avery	.40	1.00
2 Clint Dolezel	.75	2.00
3 Cecil Doggette	.40	1.00
4 Brian Gowins	.40	1.00
5 Willis Marshall	.40	1.00
6 Corey Mayfield	.40	1.00
7 Ricky Ross	.40	1.00
8 Chris Ryan	.40	1.00
9 Terrill Shaw	.75	2.00
10 Steve Smith	.60	1.50

2000 Greats of the Game

Released in early January 2001, this 134-card set features base cards with maroon borders, a white out background and full color player action shots with silver foil highlights. Card numbers 131-134 were added late as redemptions and were limited in production to 500 of each card with #134, Mike Anderson, released as an autograph. Greats of the game was packaged in 24-pack boxes with each pack containing five cards and carried a suggested retail price of $4.99.

COMP.SET w/o SP's (100)	20.00	40.00
131-134 ROOKIE PRINT RUN 500		
1 Terry Bradshaw	.60	1.50
2 Paul Hornung	.25	.60
3 Tony Dorsett	.25	.60
4 L.C. Greenwood	.20	.50
5 Ozzie Newsome	.15	.40
6 Michael Irvin	.25	.60
7 Art Donovan	.20	.50
8 Don Maynard	.20	.50
9 Bobby Mitchell	.20	.50
10 Bob Lilly	.20	.50
11 Earl Morrall	.15	.40
12 Harvey Martin	.15	.40
13 Dan Fouts	.25	.60
14 Joe Theismann	.25	.60
15 Roger Staubach	.50	1.25
16 Otto Graham	.20	.50
17 Cliff Branch	.20	.50
18 Sonny Jurgensen	.25	.60
19 Eric Dickerson	.20	.50
20 Lee Roy Selmon	.20	.50
21 Roger Craig	.20	.50
22 Raymond Berry	.20	.50
23 Bob Hayes	.20	.50
24 Steve Largent	.25	.60
25 Lenny Moore	.20	.50
26 Chuck Bednarik	.20	.50
27 Ken Stabler	.30	.75
28 William Perry	.20	.50
29 Joe Greene	.25	.60
30 Joe Namath	.50	1.25
31 Jim Kelly	.30	.75
32 Steve Young	.30	.75
33 Randy White	.20	.50
34 Lawrence Taylor	.25	.60
35 Franco Harris	.30	.75
36 Marcus Allen	.25	.60
37 Mike Singletary	.25	.60
38 Fran Tarkenton	.30	.75
39 Mel Renfro	.15	.40
40 Len Dawson	.25	.60
41 Carl Eller	.15	.40
42 Chuck Foreman	.15	.40
43 Gino Marchetti	.15	.40
44 Jim Marshall	.15	.40
45 Jack Ham	.25	.60
46 Mercury Morris	.15	.40
47 Anthony Munoz	.20	.50
48 Herschel Walker	.20	.50
49 Drew Pearson	.20	.50
50 John Elway	.60	1.50
51 George Blanda	.25	.60
52 Earl Campbell	.25	.60
53 Bart Starr	.60	1.50
54 Dan Marino	.75	2.00
55 Johnny Unitas	.60	1.50
56 Sammy Baugh	.25	.60
57 Steve Van Buren	.15	.40
58 Mel Blount	.20	.50
59 Fred Biletnikoff	.25	.60
60 John Brodie	.20	.50
61 Daryle Lamonica	.15	.40
62 James Lofton	.15	.40
63 Ronnie Lott	.25	.60
64 Gale Sayers	.40	1.00
65 Art Monk	.20	.50
66 Jim Plunkett	.20	.50
67 Charlie Joiner	.15	.40
68 Deacon Jones	.20	.50
69 Paul Warfield	.25	.60
70 Jim Otto	.15	.40
71 Billy Kilmer	.20	.50
72 Archie Manning	.20	.50
73 Alex Karras	.20	.50
74 Tom Matte	.15	.40
75 Jay Novacek	.20	.50
76 Charley Taylor	.15	.40
77 Sam Huff	.20	.50
78 Jack Lambert	.25	.60
79 Mike Ditka	.25	.60
80 Frank Gifford	.25	.60
81 Jim Thorpe	.40	1.00
82 Walter Payton	1.00	2.50
83 Doak Walker	.25	.60
84 Sid Luckman	.20	.50
85 Bronko Nagurski	.25	.60
86 Alan Ameche	.15	.40
87 Merlin Olsen	.20	.50
88 Dick Butkus	.40	1.00
89 Elroy Hirsch	.15	.40
90 Max McGee	.20	.50
91 Ray Nitschke	.30	.75
92 Phil Simms	.25	.60
93 Vince Lombardi CC	.50	1.25
94 Tom Landry CC	.30	.75
95 Bill Walsh CC	.20	.50
96 Mike Ditka CC	.25	.60
97 Jimmy Johnson CC	.20	.50
98 Chuck Noll CC	.20	.50
99 Dan Reeves CC	.20	.50
100 Don Shula CC	.25	.60
101 Peter Warrick RC	2.00	5.00
102 Thomas Jones RC	2.50	6.00
103 Jamal Lewis RC	2.00	5.00
104 Chad Pennington RC	3.00	8.00
105 Chris Redman RC	1.50	4.00
106 Ron Dayne RC	2.00	5.00
107 Trung Canidate RC	1.50	4.00
108 Shaun Alexander RC	2.50	6.00
109 Plaxico Burress RC	2.00	5.00
110 J.R. Redmond RC	1.25	3.00
111 Travis Taylor RC	1.50	4.00
112 Dez White RC	1.50	4.00
113 Todd Pinkston RC	1.25	3.00
114 Laveranues Coles RC	2.00	5.00
115 Dennis Northcutt RC	1.50	4.00
116 Jerry Porter RC	2.00	5.00
117 R.Jay Soward RC	1.25	3.00
118 Sylvester Morris RC	1.25	3.00
119 Ron Dugans RC	1.25	3.00
120 Travis Prentice RC	1.50	4.00
121 Tee Martin RC	2.00	5.00
122 James Williams RC	1.25	3.00
123 Trevor Gaylor RC	1.25	3.00
124 Shyrone Stith RC	1.25	3.00
125 Frank Moreau RC	1.25	3.00
126 Kwame Cavil RC	1.25	3.00
127 Ron Dixon RC	1.25	3.00
128 Darrell Jackson RC	1.50	4.00
129 Sammy Morris RC	1.50	4.00
130 JaJuan Dawson RC	1.25	3.00
131 Doug Johnson RC	3.00	8.00
132 Brian Urlacher RC	15.00	40.00
133 Brad Hoover RC	3.00	8.00
134 Mike Anderson AUTO RC	15.00	30.00

2000 Greats of the Game Gold Border Autographs

STATED ODDS 1:24 HOB, 1:40 RET		
1 Marcus Allen	15.00	40.00
2 Sammy Baugh SP	100.00	200.00
3 Chuck Bednarik	12.50	30.00
4 Raymond Berry	12.50	30.00
5 Fred Biletnikoff	15.00	40.00
6 George Blanda	30.00	60.00
7 Mel Blount	15.00	40.00
8 Terry Bradshaw	60.00	120.00
9 Cliff Branch	12.50	30.00
11 Earl Campbell	25.00	50.00
12 Roger Craig	12.50	30.00
13 Len Dawson	15.00	40.00
14 Eric Dickerson	15.00	40.00
15 Mike Ditka	20.00	50.00
16 Mike Ditka CC	15.00	40.00
17 Art Donovan	12.50	30.00
18 Tony Dorsett	30.00	60.00
19 Carl Eller	15.00	40.00
20 John Elway SP	100.00	200.00
21 Chuck Foreman	12.50	30.00
22 Dan Fouts	15.00	40.00
23 Frank Gifford SP	40.00	80.00
24 Otto Graham	40.00	80.00
25 Joe Greene	30.00	60.00
26 L.C. Greenwood	15.00	40.00
27 Jack Ham	20.00	50.00
28 Franco Harris	30.00	60.00
29 Bob Hayes	75.00	150.00
30 Paul Hornung	25.00	50.00
31 Sam Huff	15.00	40.00
32 Michael Irvin	25.00	50.00
33 Jimmy Johnson SP	15.00	40.00
34 Charlie Joiner	10.00	25.00
35 Deacon Jones	12.50	30.00
36 Sonny Jurgensen	25.00	50.00
37 Alex Karras	15.00	40.00
38 Jim Kelly	35.00	60.00
39 Billy Kilmer	12.50	30.00
40 Jack Lambert	60.00	120.00
41 Daryle Lamonica	15.00	40.00
42 Steve Largent	15.00	40.00
43 Bob Lilly	15.00	40.00
44 James Lofton	15.00	40.00
45 Ronnie Lott	25.00	50.00
46 Archie Manning	15.00	40.00
47 Gino Marchetti	15.00	40.00
48 Dan Marino SP	100.00	200.00
49 Jim Marshall	15.00	40.00
50 Harvey Martin	30.00	80.00
51 Tom Matte	12.50	30.00
52 Don Maynard	12.50	30.00
53 Bobby Mitchell	15.00	40.00
54 Art Monk	25.00	50.00
55 Lenny Moore	15.00	40.00
56 Earl Morrall	10.00	25.00
57 Mercury Morris	12.50	30.00
58 Anthony Munoz	12.50	30.00
59 Joe Namath	40.00	100.00
60 Ozzie Newsome	12.50	30.00
61 Chuck Noll SP	40.00	80.00
62 Jay Novacek	12.50	30.00
63 Jim Otto	12.50	30.00
64 Drew Pearson	12.50	30.00
65 William Perry	12.50	30.00
66 Jim Plunkett	12.50	30.00
67 Dan Reeves SP	15.00	40.00
68 Mel Renfro	12.50	30.00
69 Gale Sayers	20.00	50.00
70 Lee Roy Selmon	12.50	30.00
71 Don Shula SP	40.00	80.00
72 Mike Singletary	15.00	40.00
73 Ken Stabler	20.00	50.00
74 Bart Starr SP	100.00	200.00
75 Roger Staubach SP	75.00	135.00
76 Fran Tarkenton	25.00	50.00
77 Charley Taylor	10.00	25.00
78 Lawrence Taylor SP	30.00	80.00
79 Joe Theismann	15.00	40.00
80 Johnny Unitas SP	200.00	350.00
81 Steve Van Buren SP	125.00	200.00
82 Herschel Walker	15.00	40.00
83 Bill Walsh	60.00	100.00
84 Paul Warfield	12.50	30.00
85 Randy White	10.00	25.00
86 Steve Young	40.00	80.00

2000 Greats of the Game Cowboy Clippings

STATED ODDS 1:72 HOB		
1CCL Troy Aikman	25.00	60.00
2CCL Tony Dorsett	20.00	50.00
4CCL Michael Irvin	12.50	30.00
5CCL Tom Landry SP	300.00	400.00
6CCL Bob Lilly	15.00	40.00
7CCL Harvey Martin Shoes SP	75.00	135.00
8CCL Jay Novacek	15.00	40.00
9CCL Mel Renfro	12.50	30.00
10CCL Roger Staubach	25.00	60.00

2000 Greats of the Game Feel The Game Classics

STATED ODDS 1:36 HOB		
1 Marcus Allen	10.00	25.00
2 Fred Biletnikoff	10.00	25.00
3 Terry Bradshaw	15.00	40.00
4 Eric Dickerson	8.00	20.00
5 John Elway	12.50	30.00
6 L.C. Greenwood Jersey	8.00	20.00
7 L.C. Greenwood Shoe	8.00	20.00
8 Paul Hornung Pants	10.00	25.00
9 Jim Kelly	12.00	30.00
10 James Lofton	6.00	15.00
11 Ronnie Lott	10.00	25.00
12 Dan Marino Wht	15.00	40.00
13 Dan Marino Teal	15.00	40.00
14 Joe Namath	15.00	40.00
15 Walter Payton	20.00	50.00
16 Jim Plunkett Blk	8.00	20.00
17 Jim Plunkett Wht	8.00	20.00
18 Mike Singletary	10.00	25.00
19 Bart Starr Pants	20.00	50.00
20 Fran Tarkenton	12.00	30.00
21 Lawrence Taylor	10.00	25.00
22 Johnny Unitas	20.00	50.00
23 Steve Young	12.00	30.00

2000 Greats of the Game Retrospection Collection

COMPLETE SET (10)	6.00	15.00
STATED ODDS 1:6		
1RC Terry Bradshaw	1.00	2.50
2RC John Elway	1.00	2.50
3RC Roger Staubach	.75	2.00
4RC Franco Harris	.40	1.00
5RC Paul Hornung	.40	1.00
6RC Dan Marino	1.25	3.00
7RC Fran Tarkenton	.50	1.25
8RC Joe Namath	.75	2.00
9RC Walter Payton	1.50	4.00
10RC Jim Thorpe	.60	1.50

2004 Greats of the Game

Greats of the Game was produced by Fleer and initially released in mid-December 2004. The base set consists of 86-cards including 20-rookies serial numbered to 999 at the end of the set. Note that cards #35, 39, and 41 reportedly were not produced but a few copies of each appeared on the market after Fleer ceased operations. Hobby boxes contained 15-packs of 5-cards each while retail boxes contained 20-packs of 4-cards each. One parallel set and a variety of inserts can be found seeded in hobby and retail packs highlighted by one of the most popular insert sets of the year -- Gold Border Autographs.

COMP.SET w/o RC's (67)	15.00	40.00
ROOKIE/999 ODDS: 1:15 HOB, 1:24 RET		
1 Jim Brown	1.25	3.00
2 Jim Thorpe	.75	2.00
3 Terry Bradshaw	1.25	3.00
4 Fran Tarkenton	.75	2.00
5 Joe Namath	1.25	3.00
6 Joe Montana	2.00	5.00
7 George Rogers	.50	1.25
8 Marcus Allen	.75	2.00
9 Walter Payton	3.00	8.00
10 Dick Butkus	1.25	3.00
11 Dan Fouts	.75	2.00
12 Kellen Winslow Sr.	.75	2.00
13 Sammy Baugh	.75	2.00
14 Bart Starr	2.00	5.00
15 Steve Young	1.00	2.50
16 Sid Luckman	.75	2.00
17 Y.A. Tittle	.75	2.00
18 Dan Marino	2.00	5.00
19 Paul Hornung	.75	2.00
20 John Elway	2.00	5.00
21 Earl Campbell	.75	2.00
22 Max McGee	.60	1.50
23 Alan Ameche	.50	1.25
24 Bronko Nagurski	.75	2.00
25 Elroy Hirsch	.60	1.50
26 Jack Lambert	1.00	2.50
27 Sam Huff	.60	1.50
28 Jay Novacek	.60	1.50
29 Roger Staubach	1.25	3.00
30 Bob Hayes	.60	1.50
31 Ken Stabler	1.00	2.50
32 Chuck Bednarik	.60	1.50
33 Ronnie Lott	.75	2.00
34 Steve Van Buren	.60	1.50
35 Art Monk SP	30.00	80.00
36 Gale Sayers	1.00	2.50
37 Jim Otto	.50	1.25
38 Jim Plunkett	.60	1.50
40 Don Maynard	.60	1.50
41 John Riggins	.75	2.00
42 Billy Sims	.60	1.50
43 Franco Harris	1.00	2.50
44 Tony Dorsett	.75	2.00
45 Wilbert Montgomery	.50	1.25
46 Eric Dickerson SP	5.00	12.00
47 Jim Taylor	.75	2.00
48 George Blanda	.75	2.00
49 Cris Carter	.75	2.00
50 Mike Quick	.50	1.25
51 James Lofton	.50	1.25
52 Lawrence Taylor	.75	2.00
53 Roger Craig	.75	2.00
54 Paul Warfield	.60	1.50
55 Dan Pastorini	.50	1.25
56 Ozzie Newsome	.60	1.50
57 Charley Taylor	.60	1.50
58 Deacon Jones	.60	1.50
59 Bob Lilly	.75	2.00
60 Mike Singletary	.75	2.00
61 Warren Moon	.60	1.50
62 Charles White	.50	1.25
63 Bob Griese	.75	2.00
64 Dwight Clark	.60	1.50
65 Joe Greene	.75	2.00
66 Dave Casper	.60	1.50
67 Harold Carmichael	.50	1.25
68 Drew Pearson	.60	1.50
69 Tony Hill	.50	1.25
70 Ray Nitschke	.75	2.00
71 Eli Manning RC	10.00	25.00
72 Philip Rivers RC	6.00	15.00
73 Ben Roethlisberger RC	10.00	25.00
74 Julius Jones RC	1.25	3.00
75 Larry Fitzgerald RC	4.00	10.00
76 Steven Jackson RC	2.50	6.00
77 Kevin Jones RC	1.25	3.00
78 Tatum Bell RC	1.25	3.00
79 Rashaun Woods RC	1.00	2.50
80 Roy Williams RC	1.50	4.00
81 Lee Evans RC	1.50	4.00
82 Michael Clayton RC	1.25	3.00
83 J.P. Losman RC	1.25	3.00
84 Drew Henson RC	1.00	2.50
85 Kellen Winslow RC	1.50	4.00
86 Chris Perry RC	1.25	3.00
87 Reggie Williams RC	1.25	3.00
88 Michael Jenkins RC	1.50	4.00
89 Darius Watts RC	1.00	2.50
90 Keary Colbert RC	1.00	2.50

2004 Greats of the Game Green/Red

*VETS 1-70: 1.2X TO 3X BASE CARD HI
VETERAN GREEN PRINT RUN 500 SETS
*ROOKIES 71-90: 1X TO 2.5X
ROOKIE RED PRINT RUN 99 SETS
STATED ODDS 1:7.5 HOB, 1:24 RET

2004 Greats of the Game Classic Combos

1CC Troy Aikman/1995 Michael Irvin	2.50	6.00
2CC Terry Bradshaw SP Lynn Swann	30.00	80.00
3CC Ken Stabler/1977 Fred Biletnikoff	2.00	5.00
4CC Roger Staubach/1974 Drew Pearson	2.00	5.00
5CC Joe Montana/1981 Dwight Clark	5.00	12.00
6CC Dan Marino/1984 Mark Clayton	4.00	10.00
7CC Steve Young/1995 Jerry Rice	3.00	8.00
8CC Joe Namath/1965 Don Maynard	2.50	6.00
9CC Bob Griese/1970 Paul Warfield	1.50	4.00
10CC Dan Fouts/1981 Kellen Winslow	1.50	4.00

2004 Greats of the Game Classic Combos Autographs

UNPRICED SINGLE AU PRINT RUN 10		
UNPRICED DUAL AU PRINT RUN 10		
4CC2 Roger Staubach No AU Drew Pearson No AU	15.00	40.00

2004 Greats of the Game Glory of Their Time

STATED PRINT RUN 1960-1997		
GOT1 Joe Namath/1967	2.50	6.00
GOT2 Troy Aikman/1992	2.50	6.00
GOT3 Walter Payton/1977	6.00	15.00
GOT4 Joe Montana/1987	4.00	10.00
GOT5 Bart Starr/1966	4.00	10.00
GOT6 Paul Hornung/1960	1.50	4.00
GOT7 Dan Marino/1984	4.00	10.00
GOT8 Roger Staubach/1979	2.50	6.00
GOT9 Warren Moon/1990	1.25	3.00
GOT10 Jack Lambert/1976	2.00	5.00
GOT11 Franco Harris/1979	2.00	5.00
GOT12 Steve Young/1994	2.00	5.00
GOT13 Eric Dickerson/1984	1.50	4.00
GOT14 Lawrence Taylor/1986	1.50	4.00
GOT15 Tony Dorsett/1981	1.50	4.00
GOT16 Ronnie Lott/1986	1.50	4.00
GOT17 Earl Campbell/1980	1.50	4.00
GOT18 Gale Sayers/1965	2.00	5.00
GOT19 Jim Kelly/1991	1.50	4.00
GOT20 Bob Griese/1977	1.50	4.00
GOT21 John Elway/1993	4.00	10.00
GOT22 Barry Sanders/1997	3.00	8.00
GOT23 Jim Plunkett/1985	1.25	3.00
GOT24 Bob Lilly/1963	1.50	4.00
GOT25 Fran Tarkenton/1975	1.50	4.00
GOT26 Mel Renfro/1969	1.25	3.00
GOT27 Fred Biletnikoff/1969	1.50	4.00
GOT28 Shannon Sharpe/1996	1.50	4.00
GOT29 Thurman Thomas/1992	1.25	3.00
GOT30 Michael Irvin/1995	1.50	4.00

2004 Greats of the Game Glory of Their Time Game Used Red

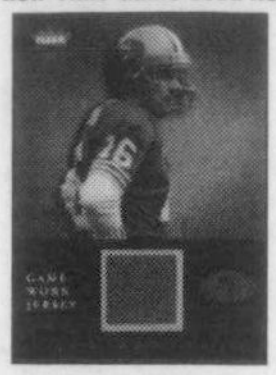

RED STATED ODDS 1:24 HOBBY		
*GOLD: .4X TO 1X RED		
GOLD STATED ODDS 1:24 RETAIL		
*SILVER/300: .5X TO 1.2X RED		
SILVER PRINT RUN 300 SER.#'d SETS		
*PATCH/25: 1X TO 2.5X RED		
PATCH PRINT RUN 25 SER.#'d SETS		
ALL ARE JERSEY SWATCH UNLESS NOTED		
BG Bob Griese	5.00	12.00
BS Bart Starr Pants	12.00	30.00
BS Barry Sanders	8.00	20.00
DM Dan Marino	10.00	25.00
EC Earl Campbell	5.00	12.00
FB Fred Biletnikoff	5.00	12.00
FH Franco Harris	6.00	15.00
FT Fran Tarkenton	8.00	20.00
GS Gale Sayers	6.00	15.00
JE John Elway	10.00	25.00
JK Jim Kelly	5.00	12.00
JL Jack Lambert	8.00	20.00
JM Joe Montana	10.00	25.00
JP Jim Plunkett	4.00	10.00
LT Lawrence Taylor	5.00	12.00
MF Mel Renfro	4.00	10.00
MI Michael Irvin	5.00	12.00
PH Paul Hornung Pants	6.00	15.00
RL Ronnie Lott	5.00	12.00
RS Roger Staubach	8.00	20.00
SS Shannon Sharpe SP	30.00	60.00
SY Steve Young	6.00	15.00
TA Troy Aikman	8.00	20.00
TD Tony Dorsett	5.00	12.00
TT Thurman Thomas	4.00	10.00
WM Warren Moon	4.00	10.00
WP Walter Payton	12.00	30.00

2004 Greats of the Game Gold Border Autographs

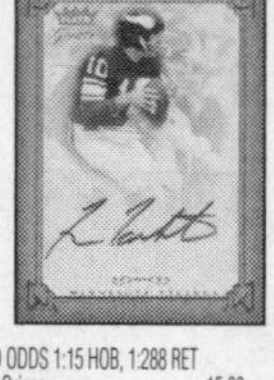

STATED ODDS 1:15 HOB, 1:288 RET		
BG Bob Griese	15.00	40.00
BL Bob Lilly	10.00	25.00
BR Ben Roethlisberger	100.00	200.00
BS1 Bart Starr SP	60.00	120.00
BS2 Billy Sims	10.00	25.00
CB Chuck Bednarik	10.00	25.00
CC Cris Carter	15.00	40.00
CT Charley Taylor	7.50	20.00
CW Charles White	7.50	20.00
DF Dan Fouts	15.00	40.00
DJ Deacon Jones	7.50	20.00
ED Eric Dickerson	15.00	40.00
FH Franco Harris	25.00	50.00
FT Fran Tarkenton	15.00	40.00
GB George Blanda	20.00	50.00
GS Gale Sayers	30.00	60.00
HC Harold Carmichael	7.50	20.00
JB Jim Brown SP	100.00	200.00
JE John Elway	90.00	150.00
JG Joe Greene	30.00	50.00
JM Joe Montana	60.00	120.00
JN Jay Novacek SP	15.00	40.00
JO Jim Otto	12.00	30.00
JP Jim Plunkett	10.00	25.00
JT Jim Taylor	30.00	80.00
KC Keary Colbert	7.50	20.00
KS Ken Stabler	25.00	50.00
LT Lawrence Taylor SP	25.00	60.00
MC Michael Clayton	10.00	25.00
MD Mike Ditka	25.00	50.00
MJ Michael Jenkins SP	10.00	25.00
MQ Mike Quick	10.00	25.00
MS Mike Singletary	15.00	40.00
ON Ozzie Newsome	7.50	20.00
PH Paul Hornung	15.00	40.00
PW Paul Warfield SP	15.00	40.00
RC Roger Craig	15.00	40.00
RL Ronnie Lott	15.00	40.00
RS Roger Staubach SP	50.00	100.00
RW2 Roy Williams WR SP	15.00	40.00
SH Sam Huff	20.00	50.00
SV Steve Van Buren SP	100.00	200.00
SY Steve Young SP	50.00	100.00
TH Tony Hill	15.00	40.00
YT Y.A. Tittle	20.00	50.00
DCA Dave Casper	10.00	25.00
DCL Dwight Clark	10.00	25.00
DMY Don Maynard	7.50	20.00
DPA Dan Pastorini	7.50	20.00
DPE Drew Pearson	10.00	25.00
DPE2 Drew Pearson ERR (Drew Henson autograph)	15.00	40.00
JLA Jack Lambert	40.00	80.00
JNA Joe Namath SP	60.00	120.00
KWS Kellen Winslow Sr.	10.00	25.00
KWS2 Kellen Winslow Sr. ERR (Winslow Jr. autograph)	15.00	40.00
WMN Warren Moon SP	20.00	50.00
WMY Wilbert Montgomery	7.50	20.00

2004 Greats of the Game Personality Cut Autographs

UNPRICED CUT AUTO PRINT RUN 1

1998 Green Bay Bombers PIFL

COMPLETE SET (30)	7.50	15.00
1 Coaches Dave Hochtritt#Dave Pisarik Bob Canney Bud Keyes	.30	.75
2 Mario Russo CO	.30	.75
3 Joel Banda	.30	.75
4 Dan Blohm	.30	.75
5 Darrick Bolton	.30	.75
6 Troy Bonk	.30	.75
7 Bruce Breecher	.30	.75
8 Tyrone Brown	.30	.75
9 Derric Coakley	.30	.75
10 Heath Garland	.30	.75
11 Mark Grapentine	.30	.75
12 Todd Hanley	.30	.75
13 Willie High	.30	.75
14 Jim Hobbins	.30	.75
15 Shane Konop	.30	.75
16 Dan Luedtke	.30	.75
17 Bryan Mader	.30	.75
18 Jay McDonagh	.30	.75
19 Chris Perry	.30	.75
20 Derf Reese	.30	.75
21 Eric Rice	.30	.75
22 Darrick Sanders	.30	.75
23 Kelly Schmitt	.30	.75
24 Sahl Shaheed	.30	.75
25 Matt Teske	.30	.75
26 Jeason Thomas	.30	.75
27 Jeff Timmerman	.30	.75
28 Mike Whitehouse	.30	.75
29 Bomber Explosion	.30	.75
30 Checklist	.30	.75

1991 Greenleaf Puzzles

Greenleaf Steel Rule Die Corp. produced these NFL player puzzles. Each measures roughly 4-1/2" by 6-3/8" and is sealed within a cardboard frame and thick plastic cover. The puzzle backs contain a postcard style format along with a short write-up on the featured player. The checklist below is presumed to be incomplete.

COMPLETE SET (6)	6.00	15.00
1001 Jim Kelly	1.00	2.50
1005 Dan Marino	3.20	8.00
1010 Lawrence Taylor	1.00	2.50
1013 Randall Cunningham	.80	2.00
1015 Troy Aikman	1.60	4.00
1016 Thurman Thomas	.80	2.00

1939 Gridiron Greats Blotters

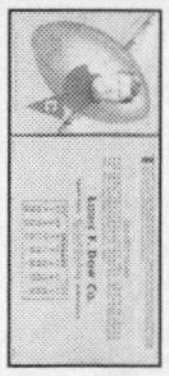

This set of 12 ink blotters was produced by the Louis F. Dow Company in honor of great college football players. These blotters were issued in two different sizes: legal sized blotter at approximately 9" by 3 7/8" and a smaller version at 3 3/8" by 6 1/4." They were issued in a brown paper sleeve as a complete set. The left portion of the blotter front has a head and shoulders sepia-toned drawing, with the player wearing either a red or a blue jersey. The right portion of the blotter has a brief player profile and one or more or even none of the following: a sponsor advertisement and/or monthly calendar (a different month on each of the 12 blotters). The backs are blank with just the felt-like blotter material and each is numbered in small print on the front. Many of these player blotters were issued over a period of years as some have been found with different calendar years, no calendar at all, and/or various advertisors such as Syracuse Letter Co., Famous Energy, or Pyott Foundry. Louis Dow also produced larger wall type calendars for some, or all, of these player works of art as well as bound notebooks using the player images on the covers.

COMPLETE SET (12)	7,000.00	10,000.00
B3941 Jim Thorpe	900.00	1,500.00
B3942 Walter Eckersall	300.00	500.00
B3943 Edward Mahan	300.00	500.00
B3944 Sammy Baugh	750.00	1,250.00
B3945 Thomas Shevlin	300.00	500.00
B3946 Red Grange	900.00	1,500.00
B3947 Ernie Nevers	400.00	750.00
B3948 George Gipp	600.00	1,000.00
B3949 Pudge Heffelfinger	300.00	500.00
B3950 Bronko Nagurski	900.00	1,500.00
B3951 Willie Heston	300.00	500.00
B3952 Jay Berwanger	300.00	500.00

1939 Gridiron Greats Notebooks

These notebook covers were produced by the Louis F. Dow Company in honor of great college football players. Each measures slightly smaller than 8" by 10" and was blank backed. They can be found bound with pages or with the pages carefully removed.

1 Jay Berwanger	300.00	500.00
2 George Gipp	600.00	1,000.00

3 Willie Heston	300.00	500.00
4 Bronko Nagurski	900.00	1,500.00

1941 Gridiron Greats Blotters

These oversized blotters are virtually identical to the 1939 Gridiron Greats Blotters and were produced by Louis F. Dow Company. The artwork featured for each player is the same but the calendar is for the year 1941. It is believed that there are likely a number of different advertising sponsors used on the calendars as well as the full complement of players.

1 Red Grange	900.00	1,500.00

1943 Gridiron Greats Calendars

These oversized calendars are very similar to the 1939 Gridiron Greats Blotters and were produced by Louis F. Dow Company. The artwork featured for each player is the same but these calendars are vertically oriented. The fronts contain a small attached calendar for the year 1943 along with sponsor advertising. It is believed that there are likely a number of different advertising sponsors used on the calendars as well as the full complement of players.

M3902 Walter Eckersall	250.00	400.00
M3910 Bronko Nagurski	600.00	1,000.00
M3952 Jay Berwanger	250.00	400.00

2002 Gridiron Kings Chicago Collection

NOT PRICED DUE TO SCARCITY

2002 Gridiron Kings National Promos

Distributed at the 2002 National Convention in Chicago, the first 6-cards of this set were distributed to promote the 2002 Donruss Gridiron Kings release. A seventh autographed card of Gale Sayers was made available to select members of the press who attended the Playoff press conference.

COMPLETE SET (7)	20.00	35.00
N1 Anthony Thomas	1.25	3.00
N2 Brian Urlacher	1.50	4.00
N3 Brett Favre	4.00	10.00
N4 Tom Brady	4.00	10.00
N5 Jeff Garcia	1.25	3.00
N6 Joey Harrington	1.50	4.00
N7 Gale Sayers AU/150	25.00	50.00

2002 Gridiron Kings Samples

*SAMPLES: .8X TO 2X BASE CARDS

2002 Gridiron Kings

Released in October 2002, this 175-card set includes 100 veterans, 50 rookies and 25 retired legends. Boxes contained 24 packs of 4 cards. The complete set was comprised of reprints from original oil paintings.

COMPLETE SET (175)	60.00	120.00
COMP.SET w/o SP's (100)	15.00	40.00
1 David Boston	.30	.75
2 Jake Plummer	.40	1.00
3 Michael Vick	.75	2.00
4 Warrick Dunn	.40	1.00
5 Jamal Lewis	.40	1.00
6 Ray Lewis	.50	1.25
7 Drew Bledsoe	.50	1.25
8 Travis Henry	.30	.75
9 Eric Moulds	.40	1.00
10 Chris Weinke	.30	.75
11 Lamar Smith	.40	1.00
12 Anthony Thomas	.40	1.00
13 Chris Chandler	.40	1.00
14 Brian Urlacher	.50	1.25
15 Corey Dillon	.40	1.00
16 Peter Warrick	.40	1.00
17 Tim Couch	.30	.75
18 James Jackson	.30	.75
19 Kevin Johnson	.30	.75
20 Quincy Carter	.30	.75
21 Emmitt Smith	1.25	3.00
22 Joey Galloway	.40	1.00
23 Brian Griese	.40	1.00
24 Terrell Davis	.50	1.25
25 Ed McCaffrey	.40	1.00
26 Rod Smith	.40	1.00
27 Mike McMahon	.30	.75
28 Az-Zahir Hakim	.30	.75
29 Germane Crowell	.30	.75
30 Brett Favre	1.25	3.00
31 Terry Glenn	.40	1.00
32 Ahman Green	.40	1.00
33 James Allen	.30	.75
34 Tony Simmons	.30	.75
35 Peyton Manning	1.00	2.50
36 Edgerrin James	.40	1.00
37 Marvin Harrison	.50	1.25
38 Dominic Rhodes	.40	1.00
39 Mark Brunell	.40	1.00
40 Jimmy Smith	.40	1.00
41 Keenan McCardell	.40	1.00
42 Fred Taylor	.40	1.00
43 Priest Holmes	.50	1.25
44 Snoop Minnis	.30	.75
45 Trent Green	.40	1.00
46 Tony Gonzalez	.50	1.25
47 Chris Chambers	.40	1.00
48 Ricky Williams	.40	1.00
49 Jay Fiedler	.40	1.00
50 Zach Thomas	.50	1.25
51 Randy Moss	.50	1.25
52 Cris Carter	.50	1.25
53 Daunte Culpepper	.40	1.00
54 Michael Bennett	.40	1.00
55 Tom Brady	1.25	3.00
56 Antowain Smith	.40	1.00
57 Troy Brown	.40	1.00
58 Aaron Brooks	.40	1.00
59 Deuce McAllister	.40	1.00
60 Joe Horn	.40	1.00
61 Kerry Collins	.40	1.00
62 Ron Dayne	.40	1.00
63 Michael Strahan	.50	1.25
64 Vinny Testaverde	.40	1.00
65 Curtis Martin	.50	1.25
66 Wayne Chrebet	.40	1.00
67 Rich Gannon	.40	1.00
68 Tim Brown	.50	1.25
69 Jerry Rice	1.00	2.50
70 Charlie Garner	.40	1.00
71 Donovan McNabb	.50	1.25
72 Duce Staley	.40	1.00
73 Freddie Mitchell	.30	.75
74 Kordell Stewart	.40	1.00
75 Jerome Bettis	.50	1.25
76 Plaxico Burress	.40	1.00
77 Kendrell Bell	.30	.75
78 LaDainian Tomlinson	.60	1.50
79 Drew Brees	.75	2.00
80 Doug Flutie	.50	1.25
81 Junior Seau	.50	1.25
82 Jeff Garcia	.40	1.00
83 Terrell Owens	.50	1.25
84 Garrison Hearst	.40	1.00
85 Trent Dilfer	.40	1.00
86 Shaun Alexander	.40	1.00
87 Koren Robinson	.30	.75
88 Marshall Faulk	.50	1.25
89 Kurt Warner	.50	1.25
90 Torry Holt	.50	1.25
91 Isaac Bruce	.50	1.25
92 Brad Johnson	.40	1.00
93 Keyshawn Johnson	.40	1.00
94 Mike Alstott	.40	1.00
95 Warren Sapp	.40	1.00
96 Steve McNair	.50	1.25
97 Eddie George	.40	1.00
98 Jevon Kearse	.40	1.00
99 Stephen Davis	.40	1.00
100 Rod Gardner	.30	.75
101 David Carr RC	1.50	4.00
102 Joey Harrington RC	1.50	4.00
103 Patrick Ramsey RC	1.50	4.00
104 Josh McCown RC	1.50	4.00
105 David Garrard RC	2.00	5.00
106 Rohan Davey RC	1.50	4.00
107 Randy Fasani RC	1.25	3.00
108 Kurt Kittner RC	1.00	2.50
109 William Green RC	1.25	3.00
110 T.J. Duckett RC	1.50	4.00
111 DeShaun Foster RC	1.50	4.00
112 Clinton Portis RC	2.00	5.00
113 Maurice Morris RC	1.25	3.00
114 Ladell Betts RC	1.50	4.00
115 Lamar Gordon RC	1.25	3.00
116 Brian Westbrook RC	2.50	6.00
117 Jonathan Wells RC	1.50	4.00
118 Travis Stephens RC	1.00	2.50
119 Josh Scobey RC	1.25	3.00
120 Donte Stallworth RC	1.50	4.00
121 Ashley Lelie RC	1.25	3.00
122 Javon Walker RC	1.50	4.00
123 Jabar Gaffney RC	1.50	4.00
124 Josh Reed RC	1.25	3.00
125 Tim Carter RC	1.25	3.00
126 Andre Davis RC	1.25	3.00
127 Reche Caldwell RC	1.50	4.00
128 Antwaan Randle El RC	1.50	4.00
129 Antonio Bryant RC	1.50	4.00
130 Deion Branch RC	1.50	4.00
131 Marquise Walker RC	1.00	2.50
132 Cliff Russell RC	1.00	2.50
133 Eric Crouch RC	1.50	4.00
134 Ron Johnson RC	1.25	3.00
135 Terry Charles RC	1.00	2.50
136 Jeremy Shockey RC	2.50	6.00
137 Daniel Graham RC	1.25	3.00
138 Julius Peppers RC	3.00	8.00
139 Dwight Freeney RC	2.00	5.00
140 Ryan Sims RC	1.50	4.00
141 John Henderson RC	1.25	3.00
142 Wendell Bryant RC	1.00	2.50
143 Albert Haynesworth RC	1.50	4.00
144 Quentin Jammer RC	1.50	4.00
145 Phillip Buchanon RC	1.50	4.00
146 Lito Sheppard RC	1.50	4.00
147 Roy Williams RC	1.50	4.00
148 Ed Reed RC	6.00	15.00
149 Napoleon Harris RC	1.25	3.00
150 Mike Williams RC	1.00	2.50
151 Art Monk	1.00	2.50
152 Barry Sanders	2.00	5.00
153 Bob Griese	1.25	3.00
154 Dan Marino	3.00	8.00
155 Dick Butkus	2.00	5.00
156 Earl Campbell	1.25	3.00
157 Eric Dickerson	1.00	2.50
158 Fran Tarkenton	1.25	3.00
159 Franco Harris	1.25	3.00
160 Herschel Walker	1.00	2.50
161 Joe Montana	3.00	8.00
162 Ronnie Lott	1.25	3.00
163 Joe Theismann	1.25	3.00
164 John Elway	2.50	6.00
165 John Riggins	1.25	3.00
166 Ken Stabler	1.50	4.00
167 Len Dawson	1.25	3.00
168 Marcus Allen	1.25	3.00
169 Mike Singletary	1.25	3.00
170 Roger Staubach	2.00	5.00
171 Walter Payton	5.00	12.00
172 Steve Largent	1.25	3.00
173 Terry Bradshaw	2.00	5.00
174 Thurman Thomas	1.25	3.00
175 Tony Dorsett	1.25	3.00

2002 Gridiron Kings Bronze

*VETS 1-100: 1.5X TO 4X BASIC CARDS
*ROOKIES 101-150: .5X TO 1.2X
*RETIRED 151-175: .6X TO 1.5X
OVERALL PARALLEL ODDS 1:6

2002 Gridiron Kings Gold

*VETS 1-100: 5X TO 12X BASIC CARDS
*ROOKIES 101-150: 1.5X TO 4X
*RETIRED 151-175: 2X TO 5X
GOLD PRINT RUN 100 SER.#'d SETS

2002 Gridiron Kings Silver

*VETS 1-100: 2.5X TO 6X BASIC CARDS
*ROOKIES 101-150: .8X TO 2X
*RETIRED 151-175: 1X TO 2.5X
SILVER PRINT RUN 400 SER.#'d SETS

2002 Gridiron Kings DK Originals

STATED PRINT RUN 1000 SER.#'d SETS

DK1 Emmitt Smith	5.00	12.00
DK2 Brett Favre	5.00	12.00
DK3 Shaun Alexander	1.50	4.00
DK4 Tom Brady	5.00	12.00
DK5 Chris Chambers	1.50	4.00
DK6 Mark Brunell	1.50	4.00
DK7 Jeff Garcia	1.50	4.00
DK8 Marvin Harrison	2.00	6.00
DK9 Ahman Green	1.50	4.00
DK10 LaDainian Tomlinson	2.50	6.00
DK11 Brian Griese	1.50	4.00
DK12 Jerome Bettis	2.00	5.00
DK13 Quincy Carter	1.25	3.00
DK14 Tim Couch	1.25	3.00
DK15 Donovan McNabb	2.00	5.00
DK16 Corey Dillon	1.50	4.00
DK17 Chris Weinke	1.25	3.00
DK18 Rich Gannon	1.50	4.00
DK19 Drew Bledsoe	2.00	5.00
DK20 Terrell Davis	2.00	5.00
DK21 Travis Henry	1.25	3.00
DK22 Curtis Martin	2.00	5.00
DK23 Aaron Brooks	1.50	4.00
DK24 Ray Lewis	2.00	5.00
DK25 Michael Vick	3.00	8.00

2002 Gridiron Kings Donruss 1894

STATED PRINT RUN 1000 SER.#'d SETS

MC1 Anthony Thomas	1.50	4.00
MC2 Randy Moss	2.00	5.00
MC3 Tom Brady	5.00	12.00
MC4 Jerry Rice	4.00	10.00
MC5 Jerome Bettis	2.00	5.00
MC6 Junior Seau	2.00	5.00
MC7 Emmitt Smith	5.00	12.00
MC8 Marshall Faulk	2.00	5.00
MC9 Eddie George	1.50	4.00
MC10 Barry Sanders	4.00	10.00
MC11 Kurt Warner	2.00	5.00
MC12 Peyton Manning	4.00	10.00
MC13 Dan Marino	6.00	15.00
MC14 Ricky Williams	1.50	4.00
MC15 Dick Butkus	4.00	10.00
MC16 Brett Favre	5.00	12.00
MC17 Earl Campbell	2.50	6.00
MC18 Zach Thomas	2.00	5.00
MC19 John Elway	5.00	12.00
MC20 Edgerrin James	1.50	4.00
MC21 Joey Harrington	2.00	5.00
MC22 William Green	1.50	4.00
MC23 Donte Stallworth	2.00	5.00
MC24 Roy Williams	2.00	5.00
MC25 Brian Urlacher	2.00	5.00

2002 Gridiron Kings Gridiron Cut Collection

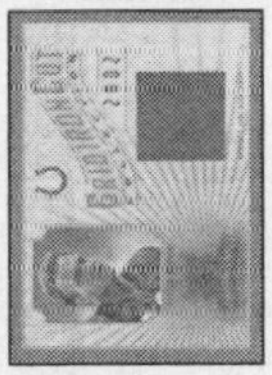

GC1-GC40 AUTO PRINT RUN 50-400
GC41-GC90/GC101-GC110 JSY PRINT RUN 400
GC91-GC100 FB PRINT RUN 550

GC1 Art Monk AU/219	12.00	30.00
GC2 Barry Sanders AU/83	75.00	150.00
GC3 Bob Griese AU/50	30.00	80.00
GC4 Dick Butkus AU/125	30.00	80.00
GC5 Earl Campbell AU/50	30.00	80.00
GC6 Eric Dickerson AU/50	25.00	60.00
GC7 Fran Tarkenton AU/50	30.00	80.00
GC8 Franco Harris AU/50	40.00	100.00
GC9 Herschel Walker AU/50	25.00	60.00
GC10 Joe Montana AU/50	125.00	250.00
GC11 Ronnie Lott AU/82	30.00	80.00
GC12 Joe Theismann AU/50	30.00	80.00
GC13 John Riggins AU/50	25.00	60.00
GC14 Ken Stabler AU/50	40.00	100.00
GC15 Len Dawson AU/50	25.00	60.00
GC16 Marcus Allen AU/50	30.00	80.00
GC17 Mike Singletary AU/50	30.00	80.00
GC18 Roger Staubach AU/83	60.00	120.00
GC19 Steve Largent AU/50	50.00	100.00
GC20 Terry Bradshaw AU/160	50.00	100.00
GC21 Thurman Thomas AU/400	12.00	30.00
GC22 Tony Dorsett AU/50	30.00	80.00
GC23 Brian Urlacher AU/197	30.00	60.00
GC24 Chris Weinke AU/300	8.00	20.00
GC25 David Boston AU/266	8.00	20.00
GC26 Deuce McAllister AU/310	10.00	25.00
GC27 Drew Brees AU/400	30.00	60.00
GC28A Zach Thomas AU/400	12.00	30.00
GC28B Zach Thomas Buddy Lee AU	30.00	60.00
GC29 Quincy Carter AU/400	8.00	20.00
GC30 Ray Lewis AU/245	25.00	50.00
GC31 Terrell Owens AU/200	12.00	30.00
GC32 Garrison Hearst AU/400	10.00	25.00
GC33 DeShaun Foster AU/400	12.00	30.00
GC34 Dwight Freeney AU/400	10.00	25.00
GC35 Lito Sheppard AU/400	12.00	30.00
GC36 Reche Caldwell AU/350	12.00	30.00
GC37 Rohan Davey AU/350	12.00	30.00
GC38 Maurice Morris AU/382	10.00	25.00
GC39 Phillip Buchanon No Auto	5.00	12.00
GC40 Travis Stephens AU/400	8.00	20.00
GC41 Dan Marino JSY/400	15.00	40.00
GC42 John Elway JSY/400	12.00	30.00
GC43 Daunte Culpepper JSY/400	5.00	12.00
GC44 Kordell Stewart JSY/400	5.00	12.00
GC45 Steve McNair JSY/400	6.00	15.00
GC46 Jeff Garcia JSY/400	5.00	12.00
GC47 Kurt Warner JSY/400	6.00	15.00
GC48 Jake Plummer JSY/400	5.00	12.00
GC49 Donovan McNabb JSY/400	6.00	15.00
GC50 Tim Couch JSY/400	4.00	10.00
GC51 Rich Gannon JSY/400	5.00	12.00
GC52 Quincy Carter JSY/400	4.00	10.00
GC53 Tom Brady JSY/400	15.00	40.00
GC54 Brian Griese JSY/400	5.00	12.00
GC55 Mark Brunell JSY/400	5.00	12.00
GC56 Brett Favre JSY/400	15.00	40.00
GC57 Peyton Manning JSY/400	12.00	30.00
GC58 Emmitt Smith JSY/400	15.00	40.00
GC59 Mike Alstott JSY/400	5.00	12.00
GC60 Jerome Bettis JSY/400	6.00	15.00
GC61 Marshall Faulk JSY/400	6.00	15.00
GC62 LaDainian Tomlinson JSY/400	8.00	20.00
GC63 Terrell Davis JSY/400	6.00	15.00
GC64 Antowain Smith JSY/400	5.00	12.00
GC65 Fred Taylor JSY/400	5.00	12.00
GC66 Edgerrin James JSY/400	5.00	12.00
GC67 Ron Dayne JSY/400	5.00	12.00
GC68 Curtis Martin JSY/400	6.00	15.00
GC69 Stephen Davis JSY/400	5.00	12.00
GC70 Walter Payton JSY/400	20.00	50.00
GC71 Freddie Mitchell JSY/400	4.00	10.00
GC72 Cris Carter JSY/400	6.00	15.00
GC73 David Boston JSY/400	4.00	10.00
GC74 Tony Gonzalez JSY/400	6.00	15.00
GC75 Marvin Harrison JSY/400	6.00	15.00
GC76 Torry Holt JSY/400	6.00	15.00
GC77 Jerry Rice JSY/400	12.00	30.00
GC78 Randy Moss JSY/400	6.00	15.00
GC79 Jimmy Smith JSY/400	5.00	12.00
GC80 Ed McCaffrey JSY/400	5.00	12.00
GC81 Eric Moulds JSY/400	5.00	12.00
GC82 Keyshawn Johnson JSY/400	5.00	12.00
GC83 Isaac Bruce JSY/400	6.00	15.00
GC84 Tim Brown JSY/400	6.00	15.00
GC85 Peter Warrick JSY/400	5.00	12.00
GC86 Zach Thomas JSY/400	6.00	15.00
GC87 Warren Sapp JSY/400	5.00	12.00
GC88 Junior Seau JSY/400	6.00	15.00
GC89 Jevon Kearse JSY/400	5.00	12.00
GC90 Ray Lewis JSY/400	6.00	15.00
GC91 Donovan McNabb FB/550	6.00	15.00
GC92 Eddie George FB/550	5.00	12.00
GC93 Curtis Martin FB/550	6.00	15.00
GC94 Anthony Thomas FB/550	5.00	12.00
GC95 Jeff Garcia FB/550	5.00	12.00
GC96 Shaun Alexander FB/550	5.00	12.00
GC97 Rod Smith FB/550	5.00	12.00
GC98 Aaron Brooks FB/550	5.00	12.00
GC99 Peyton Manning FB/550	12.00	30.00
GC100 Brett Favre FB/550	15.00	40.00
GC101 David Carr JSY/400	5.00	12.00
GC102 J.Harrington JSY/400	5.00	12.00
GC103 William Green JSY/400	5.00	12.00
GC104 T.J. Duckett JSY/400	5.00	12.00
GC105 Clinton Portis JSY/400	6.00	15.00
GC106 DeShaun Foster JSY/400	5.00	12.00
GC107 Donte Stallworth JSY/400	5.00	12.00
GC108 Ashley Lelie JSY/400	4.00	10.00
GC109 Antw Randle El JSY/400	5.00	12.00
GC110 Jeremy Shockey JSY/400	8.00	20.00

2002 Gridiron Kings Heritage Collection

COMPLETE SET (25)	50.00	120.00
STATED ODDS 1:23		
HC1 Art Monk	1.50	4.00
HC2 Barry Sanders	3.00	8.00
HC3 Bob Griese	2.00	5.00
HC4 Dan Marino	5.00	12.00
HC5 Dick Butkus	3.00	8.00
HC6 Earl Campbell	2.00	5.00
HC7 Eric Dickerson	1.50	4.00
HC8 Fran Tarkenton	2.00	5.00
HC9 Franco Harris	2.00	5.00
HC10 Herschel Walker	1.50	4.00
HC11 Joe Montana	5.00	12.00
HC12 Ronnie Lott	2.00	5.00
HC13 Joe Theismann	2.00	5.00
HC14 John Elway	4.00	10.00
HC15 John Riggins	2.00	5.00
HC16 Ken Stabler	2.50	6.00
HC17 Len Dawson	2.00	5.00
HC18 Marcus Allen	2.00	5.00
HC19 Mike Singletary	2.00	5.00
HC20 Roger Staubach	3.00	8.00
HC21 Walter Payton	8.00	20.00
HC22 Steve Largent	2.00	5.00
HC23 Terry Bradshaw	3.00	8.00
HC24 Thurman Thomas	2.00	5.00
HC25 Tony Dorsett	2.00	5.00

2002 Gridiron Kings Team Duos

COMPLETE SET (10)	30.00	80.00
STATED ODDS 1:72		
TD1 Anthony Thomas Brian Urlacher	2.50	6.00
TD2 Peyton Manning Edgerrin James	5.00	12.00
TD3 Ricky Williams Zach Thomas	2.50	6.00
TD4 Daunte Culpepper Randy Moss	2.50	6.00
TD5 David Carr Jabar Gaffney	2.50	6.00
TD6 Terry Bradshaw Franco Harris	5.00	12.00
TD7 Kurt Warner Marshall Faulk	2.50	6.00
TD8 Roger Staubach Tony Dorsett	5.00	12.00
TD9 Steve McNair Eddie George	2.50	6.00
TD10 Jerry Rice Tim Brown	5.00	12.00

2003 Gridiron Kings

Released in October of 2003, this set consists of 175 cards including 100 veterans, 50 rookies, and 25 retired players. Boxes contained 24 packs of 5 cards. Pack SRP was $4.

COMPLETE SET (175)	75.00	150.00
COMP.SET w/o SP's (100)	10.00	25.00
1 David Boston	.25	.60
2 Marcel Shipp	.25	.60
3 Jake Plummer	.30	.75
4 Michael Vick	.50	1.25
5 T.J. Duckett	.30	.75
6 Warrick Dunn	.30	.75
7 Ray Lewis	.40	1.00
8 Jamal Lewis	.30	.75
9 Todd Heap	.30	.75
10 Drew Bledsoe	.40	1.00
11 Eric Moulds	.30	.75
12 Travis Henry	.25	.60
13 Julius Peppers	.40	1.00
14 Steve Smith	.40	1.00
15 Muhsin Muhammad	.30	.75
16 Anthony Thomas	.30	.75
17 David Terrell	.25	.60
18 Brian Urlacher	.40	1.00
19 Corey Dillon	.30	.75
20 Chad Johnson	.40	1.00
21 William Green	.25	.60
22 Tim Couch	.25	.60
23 Quincy Morgan	.25	.60
24 Roy Williams	.30	.75
25 Emmitt Smith	1.00	2.50
26 Antonio Bryant	.25	.60
27 Clinton Portis	.30	.75
28 Ashley Lelie	.25	.60
29 Rod Smith	.30	.75
30 Brian Griese	.30	.75
31 Joey Harrington	.25	.60
32 James Stewart	.25	.60
33 Az-Zahir Hakim	.25	.60
34 Brett Favre	1.00	2.50
35 Ahman Green	.30	.75
36 Donald Driver	.40	1.00
37 Javon Walker	.30	.75
38 David Carr	.30	.75
39 Jabar Gaffney	.25	.60
40 Jonathan Wells	.25	.60
41 Edgerrin James	.40	1.00
42 Marvin Harrison	.40	1.00
43 Peyton Manning	.75	2.00
44 Mark Brunell	.30	.75
45 Jimmy Smith	.30	.75
46 Fred Taylor	.30	.75
47 Priest Holmes	.40	1.00
48 Tony Gonzalez	.40	1.00
49 Trent Green	.30	.75
50 Jay Fiedler	.25	.60
51 Chris Chambers	.30	.75
52 Zach Thomas	.40	1.00
53 Ricky Williams	.30	.75
54 Randy Moss	.40	1.00
55 Daunte Culpepper	.30	.75
56 Michael Bennett	.30	.75
57 Tom Brady	1.00	2.50
58 Deion Branch	.30	.75
59 Antowain Smith	.30	.75
60 Donte Stallworth	.25	.60
61 Deuce McAllister	.30	.75
62 Aaron Brooks	.30	.75
63 Kerry Collins	.30	.75
64 Jeremy Shockey	.40	1.00
65 Tiki Barber	.40	1.00
66 Curtis Martin	.40	1.00
67 Chad Pennington	.40	1.00
68 Santana Moss	.30	.75
69 Jerry Rice	.75	2.00
70 Rich Gannon	.30	.75
71 Tim Brown	.40	1.00
72 Charlie Garner	.30	.75
73 Donovan McNabb	.40	1.00
74 Duce Staley	.30	.75
75 Antonio Freeman	.30	.75
76 Tommy Maddox	.30	.75
77 Jerome Bettis	.40	1.00
78 Antwaan Randle El	.30	.75
79 Plaxico Burress	.30	.75
80 LaDainian Tomlinson	.40	1.00
81 Junior Seau	.40	1.00
82 Drew Brees	.40	1.00
83 Terrell Owens	.40	1.00
84 Jeff Garcia	.30	.75
85 Garrison Hearst	.30	.75
86 Koren Robinson	.30	.75
87 Shaun Alexander	.30	.75
88 Trent Dilfer	.30	.75
89 Marshall Faulk	.40	1.00
90 Kurt Warner	.40	1.00
91 Isaac Bruce	.40	1.00
92 Brad Johnson	.30	.75
93 Keyshawn Johnson	.40	1.00
94 Warren Sapp	.30	.75
95 Steve McNair	.40	1.00
96 Derrick Mason	.30	.75
97 Eddie George	.30	.75
98 Bruce Smith	.30	.75
99 Rod Gardner	.25	.60
100 Patrick Ramsey	.30	.75
101 Carson Palmer RC	2.00	5.00
102 Byron Leftwich RC	1.00	2.50
103 Kyle Boller RC	1.00	2.50
104 Chris Simms RC	1.00	2.50
105 Dave Ragone RC	.60	1.50
106 Rex Grossman RC	1.00	2.50
107 Brian St.Pierre RC	.75	2.00
108 Kliff Kingsbury RC	.75	2.00
109 Seneca Wallace RC	1.00	2.50
110 Larry Johnson RC	1.00	2.50
111 Lee Suggs RC	.75	2.00
112 Justin Fargas RC	1.00	2.50
113 Onterrio Smith RC	.60	1.50
114 Willis McGahee RC	1.25	3.00
115 Chris Brown RC	.60	1.50
116 Musa Smith RC	.60	1.50
117 Artose Pinner RC	.60	1.50
118 Domanick Davis RC	.75	2.00
119 Charles Rogers RC	.75	2.00
120 Andre Johnson RC	2.50	6.00
121 Taylor Jacobs RC	.60	1.50
122 Bryant Johnson RC	1.00	2.50
123 Kelley Washington RC	.60	1.50
124 Brandon Lloyd RC	1.50	4.00
125 Tyrone Calico RC	.75	2.00
126 Kevin Curtis RC	1.00	2.50
127 Bethel Johnson RC	.60	1.50
128 Anquan Boldin RC	1.50	4.00
129 Nate Burleson RC	.75	2.00
130 Jason Witten RC	2.50	6.00
131 Bennie Joppru RC	.60	1.50
132 Teyo Johnson RC	.75	2.00
133 Dallas Clark RC	1.50	4.00
134 Terrell Suggs RC	1.00	2.50
135 Chris Kelsay RC	.75	2.00
136 Jerome McDougle RC	.60	1.50
137 Michael Haynes RC	.60	1.50
138 Calvin Pace RC	.75	2.00
139 Jimmy Kennedy RC	.75	2.00
140 Kevin Williams RC	1.00	2.50
141 DeWayne Robertson RC	.75	2.00
142 William Joseph RC	.60	1.50
143 Johnathan Sullivan RC	.60	1.50
144 Boss Bailey RC	.75	2.00
145 E.J. Henderson RC	.75	2.00
146 Terence Newman RC	.75	2.00
147 Marcus Trufant RC	.75	2.00
148 Andre Woolfolk RC	.75	2.00
149 Troy Polamalu RC	12.50	25.00
150 Mike Doss RC	1.00	2.50
151 Andre Reed	.75	2.00
152 Bo Jackson	1.50	4.00
153 Dan Marino	2.50	6.00
154 Deacon Jones	.75	2.00
155 Deion Sanders	1.00	2.50
156 Doak Walker	1.00	2.50
157 Don Maynard	.75	2.00
158 Frank Gifford	1.00	2.50
159 Fred Biletnikoff	1.00	2.50
160 Gale Sayers	1.50	4.00
161 Jack Lambert	1.00	2.50
162 Jim Brown	1.50	4.00
163 Jim Kelly	1.25	3.00
164 Joe Greene	1.00	2.50
165 Joe Montana	2.50	6.00
166 John Elway	2.50	6.00
167 John Riggins	1.00	2.50
168 Johnny Unitas	2.00	5.00
169 Larry Csonka	1.00	2.50
170 Lawrence Taylor	1.00	2.50
171 Mike Ditka	1.00	2.50
172 Ozzie Newsome	.75	2.00
173 Red Grange	1.00	2.50
174 Troy Aikman	1.25	3.00
175 Warren Moon	.75	2.00

2003 Gridiron Kings Bronze

*VETS 1-100: 1.5X TO 4X BASIC CARDS
*ROOKIES 101-150: .6X TO 1.5X
*RETIRED 151-175: .8X TO 2X
STATED ODDS 1:6

2003 Gridiron Kings Gold

*VETS 1-100: 6X TO 15X BASIC CARDS
*ROOKIES 101-150: 2X TO 5X
*RETIRED 151-175: 3X TO 8X
STATED PRINT RUN 75 SER.#'d SETS

2003 Gridiron Kings Silver

*VETS 1-100: 2.5X TO 6X BASIC CARDS
*ROOKIES 101-150: .8X TO 2X
*RETIRED 151-175: 1.2X TO 3X
STATED PRINT RUN 150 SER.#'d SETS

2003 Gridiron Kings Donruss 1894

COMPLETE SET (25)	40.00	100.00
STATED PRINT RUN 600 SER.#'d SETS		
MC26 Michael Vick	2.50	6.00
MC27 Drew Bledsoe	2.00	5.00
MC28 Julius Peppers	2.00	5.00
MC29 Clinton Portis	1.50	4.00
MC30 Ahman Green	1.50	4.00
MC31 David Carr	1.50	4.00
MC32 Marvin Harrison	2.00	5.00
MC33 Priest Holmes	2.00	5.00
MC34 Michael Bennett	1.50	4.00
MC35 Deuce McAllister	1.50	4.00
MC36 Jeremy Shockey	2.00	5.00
MC37 Chad Pennington	2.00	5.00
MC38 Rich Gannon	1.50	4.00
MC39 Donovan McNabb	2.00	5.00
MC40 LaDainian Tomlinson	2.00	5.00
MC41 Jeff Garcia	1.50	4.00
MC42 Steve McNair	2.00	5.00
MC43 Doak Walker	2.00	5.00
MC44 Jim Brown	3.00	8.00
MC45 Jim Kelly	2.50	6.00
MC46 Joe Montana	5.00	12.00
MC47 Carson Palmer	2.00	5.00
MC48 Byron Leftwich	1.00	2.50
MC49 Charles Rogers	1.50	4.00
MC50 Andre Johnson	2.50	6.00

2003 Gridiron Kings GK Evolution

COMPLETE SET (25)	50.00	120.00
STATED ODDS 1:23		
GE1 Michael Vick	2.00	5.00
GE2 Travis Henry	1.00	2.50
GE3 Emmitt Smith	4.00	10.00
GE4 Clinton Portis	1.25	3.00
GE5 Joey Harrington	1.00	2.50
GE6 Brett Favre	4.00	10.00
GE7 David Carr	1.25	3.00
GE8 Peyton Manning	3.00	8.00
GE9 Priest Holmes	1.50	4.00
GE10 Ricky Williams	1.25	3.00
GE11 Randy Moss	1.50	4.00
GE12 Deuce McAllister	1.25	3.00
GE13 Jeremy Shockey	1.50	4.00
GE14 Chad Pennington	1.50	4.00
GE15 Jerry Rice	3.00	8.00
GE16 Donovan McNabb	1.50	4.00
GE17 Plaxico Burress	1.25	3.00
GE18 LaDainian Tomlinson	1.50	4.00
GE19 Terrell Owens	1.50	4.00
GE20 Shaun Alexander	1.25	3.00
GE21 Marshall Faulk	1.50	4.00
GE22 Warren Sapp	1.25	3.00
GE23 Eddie George	1.25	3.00
GE24 Dan Marino	4.00	10.00
GE25 John Elway	4.00	10.00

2003 Gridiron Kings Gridiron Cut Collection

GC1-GC23 RETIRED AU PRINT RUN 24-200
GC26-GC40 ROOKIE AU PRINT RUN 25-250
GC41-GC80 JSY PRINT RUN 225-475
GC81-GC90 FB PRINT RUN 275
GC91-GC100 JSY AU PRINT RUN 50

GC1 Andre Reed AU/200	10.00	25.00
GC2 Bo Jackson AU/100	40.00	80.00
GC3 Dan Marino AU/25	75.00	200.00
GC4 Deacon Jones AU/100	12.00	30.00
GC5 Deion Sanders AU/25	40.00	100.00
GC6 Don Maynard AU/100	12.00	30.00
GC7 Frank Gifford AU/100	20.00	50.00
GC8 Fred Biletnikoff AU/100	25.00	50.00
GC9 Gale Sayers AU/100	25.00	50.00
GC10 Jack Lambert AU/150	50.00	100.00
GC11 Jim Brown AU/50	40.00	80.00
GC12 Jim Kelly AU/25	60.00	120.00
GC13 Joe Greene AU/150	25.00	50.00
GC14 Joe Montana AU/50	75.00	150.00
GC15 John Elway AU/24	60.00	150.00
GC16 John Riggins AU/50	40.00	80.00
GC17 Johnny Unitas AU/40	200.00	350.00
GC18 Larry Csonka AU/100	25.00	60.00
GC19 Lawrence Taylor AU/100	30.00	50.00
GC20 Mike Ditka AU/100	20.00	40.00
GC21 Ozzie Newsome AU/100	10.00	25.00
GC22 Troy Aikman AU/25	60.00	120.00
GC23 Warren Moon AU/100	25.00	50.00
GC26 Boss Bailey AU/250	6.00	15.00
GC27 Brian St.Pierre AU/250	6.00	15.00
GC28 Bryant Johnson AU/150	8.00	20.00
GC29 Jimmy Kennedy AU/250	6.00	15.00
GC30 Chris Kelsay AU/250	6.00	15.00
GC31 Dallas Clark AU/250	12.50	25.00
GC34 Kelley Washington AU/107	5.00	12.00
GC35 Lee Suggs AU/250	6.00	15.00
GC36 Mike Doss AU/250	8.00	20.00
GC37 Onterrio Smith AU/150	5.00	12.00
GC38 Terrell Suggs AU/100	15.00	30.00
GC39 Tyrone Calico AU/150	6.00	15.00
GC40 Carson Palmer AU/25	60.00	120.00
GC41 David Boston JSY/475	2.50	6.00
GC42 T.J. Duckett JSY/275	3.00	8.00
GC43 Jamal Lewis JSY/375	3.00	8.00
GC44 Eric Moulds JSY/375	3.00	8.00
GC45 Travis Henry JSY/375	2.50	6.00
GC46 David Terrell JSY/375	2.50	6.00
GC47 Anthony Thomas JSY/375	3.00	8.00
GC48 Corey Dillon JSY/475	3.00	8.00
GC49 Tim Couch JSY/475	2.50	6.00
GC50 Emmitt Smith JSY/375	10.00	25.00
GC51 Antonio Bryant JSY/375	2.50	6.00
GC52 Clinton Portis JSY/275	3.00	8.00
GC53 Joey Harrington JSY/375	2.50	6.00
GC54 Brett Favre JSY/275	10.00	25.00
GC55 Javon Walker JSY/475	3.00	8.00
GC56 Edgerrin James JSY/375	4.00	10.00
GC57 Peyton Manning JSY/375	8.00	20.00
GC58 Fred Taylor JSY/475	3.00	8.00
GC59 Priest Holmes JSY/375	4.00	10.00
GC60 Trent Green JSY/475	3.00	8.00
GC61 Ricky Williams JSY/275	3.00	8.00
GC62 Randy Moss JSY/275	4.00	10.00
GC63 Jeremy Shockey JSY/375	4.00	10.00
GC64 Tiki Barber JSY/475	4.00	10.00
GC65 Santana Moss JSY/375	3.00	8.00
GC66 Curtis Martin JSY/375	4.00	10.00
GC67 Rich Gannon JSY/275	3.00	8.00
GC68 Donovan McNabb JSY/475	4.00	10.00
GC69 Duce Staley JSY/475	3.00	8.00
GC70 Jerome Bettis JSY/475	4.00	10.00
GC71 Antwaan Randle El JSY/375	3.00	8.00
GC72 LaDainain Tomlinson JSY/375	4.00	10.00
GC73 Junior Seau JSY/475	4.00	10.00
GC74 Terrell Owens JSY/375	4.00	10.00
GC75 Jeff Garcia JSY/275	3.00	8.00
GC76 Marshall Faulk JSY/275	4.00	10.00
GC77 Kurt Warner JSY/375	4.00	10.00
GC78 Warren Sapp JSY/375	3.00	8.00
GC79 Troy Aikman JSY/225	12.50	25.00
GC80 Joe Montana JSY/225	20.00	50.00
GC81 LaDainian Tomlinson FB/275	4.00	10.00
GC82 Jeremy Shockey FB/275	4.00	10.00
GC83 Antonio Bryant FB/275	2.50	6.00
GC84 Marshall Faulk FB/275	4.00	10.00
GC85 Jerry Rice FB/275	8.00	20.00
GC86 Joey Harrington FB/275	2.50	6.00
GC87 Jeff Garcia FB/275	3.00	8.00
GC88 Marvin Harrison FB/275	4.00	10.00
GC89 Rod Smith FB/275	3.00	8.00
GC90 Charlie Garner FB/275	3.00	8.00
GC91 Deacon Jones JSY AU/50	20.00	50.00
GC92 Don Maynard JSY AU/50	25.00	60.00
GC93 Fred Biletnikoff JSY AU/50	40.00	80.00
GC94 Jim Brown JSY AU/50	60.00	120.00
GC95 Jim Kelly JSY AU/50	50.00	100.00
GC96 Joe Montana JSY AU/50	75.00	150.00
GC97 John Riggins JSY AU/50	40.00	80.00
GC98 Ozzie Newsome JSY AU/50	20.00	50.00
GC99 Warren Moon JSY AU/50	20.00	50.00
GC100 Kurt Warner JSY AU/50	40.00	80.00

2003 Gridiron Kings Heritage Collection

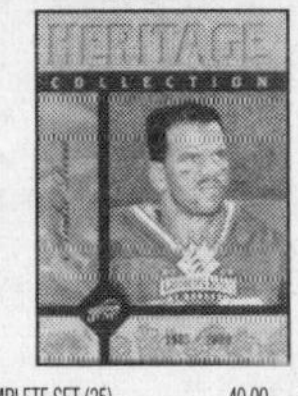

COMPLETE SET (25)	40.00	100.00
STATED ODDS 1:23		
HC1 Andre Reed	1.25	3.00
HC2 Bo Jackson	2.50	6.00
HC3 Dan Marino	4.00	10.00
HC4 Deacon Jones	1.25	3.00
HC5 Deion Sanders	1.50	4.00
HC6 Doak Walker	1.50	4.00
HC7 Don Maynard	1.25	3.00
HC8 Frank Gifford	1.50	4.00
HC9 Fred Biletnikoff	1.50	4.00
HC10 Gale Sayers	2.50	6.00
HC11 Jack Lambert	1.50	4.00
HC12 Jim Brown	2.50	6.00
HC13 Jim Kelly	2.00	5.00
HC14 Joe Greene	1.50	4.00
HC15 Joe Montana	4.00	10.00
HC16 John Elway	4.00	10.00
HC17 John Riggins	1.50	4.00
HC18 Johnny Unitas	3.00	8.00
HC19 Larry Csonka	1.50	4.00
HC20 Lawrence Taylor	1.50	4.00
HC21 Mike Ditka	1.50	4.00
HC22 Ozzie Newsome	1.25	3.00
HC23 Red Grange	1.50	4.00
HC24 Troy Aikman	2.00	5.00
HC25 Warren Moon	1.25	3.00

2003 Gridiron Kings Royal Expectations

COMPLETE SET (15)	20.00	50.00
STATED ODDS 1:23		
RE1 Andre Johnson	2.50	6.00
RE2 Byron Leftwich	1.00	2.50
RE3 Carson Palmer	2.00	5.00
RE4 Bryant Johnson	1.00	2.50
RE5 Chris Brown	.60	1.50
RE6 Dallas Clark	1.50	4.00
RE7 Justin Fargas	1.00	2.50
RE8 Kelley Washington	.60	1.50
RE9 Kyle Boller	1.00	2.50
RE10 Larry Johnson	1.00	2.50
RE11 Willis McGahee	1.25	3.00
RE12 Terence Newman	.75	2.00
RE13 Rex Grossman	1.00	2.50
RE14 Taylor Jacobs	.60	1.50
RE15 Terrell Suggs	1.00	2.50

2003 Gridiron Kings Royal Expectations Materials Gold

STATED ODDS 1:52
*SILVER: .4X TO 1X GOLD
SILVERS FEATURE SQUARE SWATCHES

RE1 Andre Johnson	8.00	20.00
RE2 Byron Leftwich	3.00	8.00
RE3 Carson Palmer	6.00	15.00
RE4 Bryant Johnson	3.00	8.00
RE5 Chris Brown	2.00	5.00
RE6 Dallas Clark	5.00	12.00
RE7 Justin Fargas	3.00	8.00
RE8 Kelley Washington	2.00	5.00
RE9 Kyle Boller	3.00	8.00
RE10 Larry Johnson	3.00	8.00
RE11 Willis McGahee	4.00	10.00
RE12 Terence Newman	2.50	6.00
RE13 Rex Grossman	3.00	8.00
RE14 Taylor Jacobs	2.00	5.00
RE15 Terrell Suggs	3.00	8.00

2003 Gridiron Kings Team Timeline

COMPLETE SET (10)	20.00	50.00
PRINT RUN 600 SERIAL #'d SETS		
TT1 Dan Marino	4.00	10.00
Jay Fiedler		
TT2 Deion Sanders	1.50	4.00
Roy Williams		
TT3 Doak Walker	1.50	4.00
Joey Harrington		
TT4 Fred Biletnikoff	1.50	4.00
Tim Brown		
TT5 Gale Sayers	2.50	6.00
Anthony Thomas		
TT6 Jim Brown	2.50	6.00
William Green		
TT7 Joe Montana	4.00	10.00
Jeff Garcia		
TT8 Johnny Unitas	3.00	8.00
Peyton Manning		
TT9 Larry Csonka	1.50	4.00
Ricky Williams		
TT10 Warren Moon	1.25	3.00
David Carr		

2003 Gridiron Kings Team Timeline Materials

PRINT RUN 100 SERIAL #'d SETS		
TT1 Dan Marino	15.00	40.00
Jay Fiedler		
TT2 Deion Sanders	10.00	25.00
Roy Williams		
TT3 Doak Walker	15.00	40.00
Joey Harrington		
TT4 Fred Biletnikoff	6.00	15.00
Tim Brown		
TT5 Gale Sayers	10.00	25.00
Anthony Thomas		
TT6 Jim Brown	10.00	25.00
William Green		
TT7 Joe Montana	15.00	40.00
Jeff Garcia		
TT8 Johnny Unitas	12.00	30.00
Peyton Manning		
TT9 Larry Csonka	6.00	15.00
Ricky Williams		
TT10 Warren Moon	5.00	12.00
David Carr		

1991 GTE Super Bowl Theme Art

This limited edition set of approximately 4 5/8" by 6" cards was issued on the occasion of Super Bowl XXV and sponsored by GTE, whose company logo appears at the bottom on the front of each card above a full color reproduction of the Super Bowl program cover enframed by black borders. The back includes information on the Super Bowl for that particular year, including location, teams, score, winning coach, MVP, and a GTE Super Bowl Telefact.

COMPLETE SET (25)	3.20	8.00
COMMON CARD (1-25)	.16	.40
1 Super Bowl I	.25	.60
25 Super Bowl XXV	.25	.60

1995 GTE Super Bowl XXIX Phone Cards

GTE produced and distributed these two cards for the 1995 NFL Experience Super Bowl Card Show in Miami. Each measures 3 3/8" by 2 1/8" and has rounded corners. Card #1 originally could be purchased for $8.85 and provided 15-units of long distance. Card #2 sold initially for $17.11 and provided 29-units. Each one was issued in a clear cellophane pack. The backs have instructions on how to use the calling card feature. Each is numbered of 3000 produced and expired on 12/31/95.

COMPLETE SET (2)	1.20	3.00
1 Super Bowl XXIX Teams	.60	1.50
Chargers Helmet/49ers Helmet		
2 Super Bowl XXIX Logo	.60	1.50

1995 GTE/Shell Super Bowl Phone Cards

GTE produced this phone card set sponsored and distributed by Shell Oil Co. Each card was valued at 5-units of GTE phone time that expired on January 31, 1996. Five previous Super Bowl game scores are included on each of the first five cards and four games on the last card.

COMPLETE SET (6)	3.20	8.00
COMMON CARD (1-6)	.60	1.50

1995-96 Hallmark Ornament Cards

HK1 Troy Aikman	1.00	2.50
(1995 Classic)		
HK3 Joe Namath#(1996 Score Board)	2.00	5.00

1963 Hall of Fame Postcards

1 Sammy Baugh	10.00	20.00
2 Dutch Clark	7.50	15.00
3 Fats Henry	7.50	15.00
4 Johnny Blood McNally	7.50	15.00
5 Ernie Nevers	7.50	15.00
6 Jim Thorpe	12.50	25.00

1982-08 Hall of Fame Metallics

This set features Pro Football Hall of Fame enshrinees and was distributed in separate series with each series containing the inductees for specific years. Only 2,000 of each series were produced and a purchase of a complete run of series' included a Letter of Authenticity. Each 10 mil 2 1/2" by 3 1/2" silver-toned metallic card carries an imprinted reproduction of the enshrinee's bust from the Hall of Fame along with appropriate statistical data of the enshrinee's football career along with a blank back. The first fifteen series' were produced together in 1982-83 and sold separately as 8-card series. Subsequent series' were sold as that year's enshrinees were announced, therefore they vary in number of cards. We've assigned numbers to the cards below according to alphabetical order within series. Note that Lynn Swann was not produced for the set.

COMPLETE SET (225)	600.00	1,200.00
1 Sammy Baugh	5.00	10.00
2 Joe Carr	2.00	4.00
3 George Halas	4.00	8.00
4 Mel Hein	2.00	4.00
5 Dick Lane	2.50	5.00
6 Bob Lilly	4.00	8.00
7 Marion Motley	3.00	6.00
8 Jim Thorpe	5.00	10.00
9 Herb Adderley	2.50	5.00
10 Dutch Clark	2.00	4.00
11 Red Grange	5.00	10.00
12 Vince Lombardi	7.50	15.00
13 Joe Perry	3.00	6.00
14 Art Rooney	2.50	5.00
15 Joe Schmidt	2.50	5.00
16 Bill Willis	2.50	5.00
17 Paul Brown	3.00	6.00
18 Fats Henry	2.00	4.00
19 Elroy Hirsch	3.00	6.00
20 Bronko Nagurski	6.00	12.00
21 Leo Nomellini	2.50	5.00
22 Jim Ringo	2.50	5.00
23 Joe Stydahar	2.00	4.00
24 Y.A. Tittle	4.00	8.00
25 Guy Chamberlin	2.00	4.00
26 George Connor	2.50	5.00
27 Willie Davis	2.50	5.00
28A Frank Gifford ERR	3.00	6.00
(bust is Raymond Berry)		
28B Frank Gifford COR	3.00	6.00
(bust is Gifford)		
29 Clarke Hinkle	2.00	4.00
30 Lamar Hunt	2.00	4.00
31 Bruiser Kinard	2.00	4.00
32 Curly Lambeau	2.50	5.00
33 Weeb Ewbank	2.00	4.00
34 Dan Fortmann	2.00	4.00
35 Yale Lary	2.50	5.00
36 Sid Luckman	4.00	8.00
37 Lenny Moore	4.00	8.00
38 Ernie Nevers	2.50	5.00
39 Jim Parker	2.50	5.00
40 Ernie Stautner	3.00	6.00
41 Lance Alworth	4.00	8.00
42 Red Badgro	2.00	4.00
43 Chuck Bednarik	3.00	6.00
44 Roosevelt Brown	2.50	5.00
45 Bill Dudley	2.00	4.00
46 Bobby Layne	4.00	8.00
47 Link Lyman	2.00	4.00
48 Steve Owen	2.00	4.00
49 Paddy Driscoll	2.00	4.00
50 Len Ford	2.50	5.00
51 Sam Huff	3.00	6.00
52 Deacon Jones	3.00	6.00
53 Dante Lavelli	2.50	5.00
54 Tuffy Leemans	2.00	4.00
55 Dan Reeves	2.00	4.00
56 Bulldog Turner	2.50	5.00
57 Doug Atkins	2.50	5.00
58 George Blanda	5.00	10.00
59 Dick Butkus	5.00	10.00
60 Joe Guyon	2.00	4.00
61 Arnie Herber	2.00	4.00
62 Don Hutson	3.00	6.00
63 Walt Kiesling	2.00	4.00
64 Ron Mix	2.00	4.00
65 Cliff Battles	2.00	4.00
66 Jim Brown	6.00	12.00
67 Lou Groza	3.00	6.00
68 Ed Healey	2.00	4.00
69 Jim Otto	2.50	5.00
70 Pete Pihos	2.50	5.00
71 Hugh Shorty Ray	2.00	4.00
72 Bob Waterfield	3.00	6.00
73 Raymond Berry	3.00	6.00
74 Turk Edwards	2.00	4.00
75 Johnny Blood McNally	2.00	4.00
76 Greasy Neale	2.00	4.00
77 Ace Parker	2.00	4.00
78 Andy Robustelli	2.50	5.00
79 Charley Trippi	2.00	4.00
80 Larry Wilson	2.00	4.00
81 Art Donovan	2.50	5.00
82 Forrest Gregg	2.50	5.00
83 Tim Mara	2.00	4.00
84 Mike Michalske	2.00	4.00
85 Wayne Millner	2.00	4.00
86 Gale Sayers	5.00	10.00
87 Ken Strong	2.50	5.00
88 Norm Van Brocklin	3.00	6.00
89 Charles Bidwill	2.00	4.00
90 Bill George	2.50	5.00
91 Bill Hewitt	2.00	4.00
92 Hugh McElhenny	3.00	6.00
93 Bart Starr	7.50	15.00
94 George Trafton	2.00	4.00
95 Steve Van Buren	3.00	6.00
96 Alex Wojciechowicz	2.00	4.00
97 Tony Canadeo	2.50	5.00
98 Jack Christiansen	2.00	4.00
99 Gino Marchetti	2.50	5.00
100 George Preston Marshall	2.00	4.00
101 Ollie Matson	2.50	5.00
102 George Musso	2.00	4.00
103 Ray Nitschke	4.00	8.00
104 Johnny Unitas	6.00	12.00
105 Bert Bell	2.00	4.00
106 Tom Fears	2.50	5.00
107 Ray Flaherty	2.00	4.00
108 Otto Graham	5.00	10.00
109 Cal Hubbard	2.00	4.00
110 George McAfee	2.00	4.00
111 Merlin Olsen	3.00	6.00
112 Jim Taylor	3.00	6.00
113 Bobby Bell	2.50	5.00
114 Jimmy Conzelman	2.00	4.00
115 Sid Gillman	2.00	4.00
116 Sonny Jurgensen	3.00	8.00
117 Bobby Mitchell	3.00	6.00
118 Emlen Tunnell	2.50	5.00
119 Paul Warfield	3.00	6.00
120 Hall of Fame logo	2.00	4.00
121 Willie Brown	2.00	4.00
122 Mike McCormack	2.00	4.00
123 Charley Taylor	2.50	5.00
124 Arnie Weinmeister	2.00	4.00
125 Frank Gatski	2.00	4.00
126 Joe Namath	10.00	20.00
127 Pete Rozelle	2.00	4.00
128 O.J. Simpson	5.00	10.00
129 Roger Staubach	7.50	15.00
130 Paul Hornung	5.00	10.00
131 Ken Houston	2.50	5.00
132 Willie Lanier	2.50	5.00
133 Fran Tarkenton	4.00	8.00
134 Doak Walker	3.00	6.00
135 Larry Csonka	4.00	8.00
136 Len Dawson	3.00	8.00
137 Joe Greene	3.00	6.00
138 John Henry Johnson	2.00	4.00
139 Jim Langer	2.00	4.00
140 Don Maynard	3.00	6.00
141 Gene Upshaw	2.50	5.00
142 Fred Biletnikoff	3.00	8.00
143 Mike Ditka	6.00	12.00
144 Jack Ham	3.00	6.00
145 Alan Page	2.50	5.00
146 Mel Blount	3.00	6.00
147 Terry Bradshaw	7.50	15.00
148 Art Shell	3.00	6.00
149 Willie Wood	2.50	5.00
150 Buck Buchanan	2.50	5.00
151 Bob Griese	4.00	8.00
152 Franco Harris	4.00	8.00
153 Ted Hendricks	2.50	5.00
154 Jack Lambert	3.00	6.00
155 Tom Landry	4.00	8.00
156 Bob St. Clair	2.50	5.00
157 Earl Campbell	3.00	6.00
158 John Hannah	2.50	5.00
159 Stan Jones	2.00	4.00
160 Tex Schramm	2.00	4.00
161 Jan Stenerud	2.50	5.00
162 Lem Barney	2.00	4.00
163 Al Davis	3.00	6.00
164 John Mackey	2.00	4.00
165 John Riggins	2.00	4.00
166 Dan Fouts	3.00	8.00
167 Larry Little	2.00	4.00
168 Chuck Noll	3.00	6.00
169 Walter Payton	15.00	30.00
170 Bill Walsh	3.00	6.00
171 Tony Dorsett	4.00	8.00
172 Bud Grant	3.00	6.00
173 Jim Johnson	2.00	4.00
174 Leroy Kelly	3.00	6.00
175 Jackie Smith	2.00	4.00
176 Randy White	3.00	6.00
177 Jim Finks	2.00	4.00
178 Hank Jordan	2.50	5.00
179 Steve Largent	3.00	6.00
180 Lee Roy Selmon	2.00	4.00
181 Kellen Winslow	2.00	4.00
182 Lou Creekmur	2.50	5.00
183 Dan Dierdorf	2.50	5.00
184 Joe Gibbs	2.50	5.00
185 Charlie Joiner	2.50	5.00
186 Mel Renfro	2.50	5.00
187 Mike Haynes	3.00	6.00
188 Wellington Mara	3.00	6.00
189 Don Shula	3.00	8.00
190 Mike Webster	3.00	6.00
191 Paul Krause	2.00	4.00
192 Tommy McDonald	2.00	4.00
193 Anthony Munoz	2.00	4.00
194 Mike Singletary	2.50	5.00
195 Dwight Stephenson	2.00	4.00
196 Eric Dickerson	2.50	5.00
197 Tom Mack	2.00	4.00
198 Ozzie Newsome	2.50	5.00
199 Billy Shaw	2.00	4.00
200 Lawrence Taylor	3.00	6.00
201 Howie Long	2.50	5.00
202 Ronnie Lott	2.50	5.00
203 Joe Montana	6.00	15.00
204 Dan Rooney	2.00	4.00
205 Dave Wilcox	2.00	4.00
206 Nick Buoniconti	2.50	5.00
207 Marv Levy	2.00	4.00
208 Mike Munchak	2.00	4.00
209 Jackie Slater	2.00	4.00
210 Ron Yary	2.00	4.00
211 Jack Youngblood	2.50	5.00
212 George Allen	2.50	5.00
213 Dave Casper	2.00	4.00
214 Dan Hampton	2.00	4.00
215 Jim Kelly	3.00	8.00
216 John Stallworth	2.50	5.00
217 Marcus Allen	3.00	6.00
218 Elvin Bethea	2.00	4.00
219 Joe DeLamielleure	2.00	4.00
220 James Lofton	2.50	5.00
221 Hank Stram	2.50	5.00
222 Bob Brown	2.00	4.00
223 Carl Eller	2.50	5.00
224 John Elway	3.00	8.00
225 Barry Sanders	3.00	8.00
226 Benny Friedman	1.50	4.00
227 Dan Marino	5.00	10.00
228 Fritz Pollard	1.50	4.00
229 Steve Young	2.50	6.00
230 Troy Aikman	2.50	6.00
231 Harry Carson	1.50	4.00
232 John Madden	1.50	4.00
233 Warren Moon	1.50	4.00
234 Reggie White	2.00	5.00
235 Rayfield Wright	1.50	4.00
236 Gene Hickerson	1.50	4.00
237 Michael Irvin	2.00	5.00
238 Bruce Matthews	1.50	4.00
239 Charlie Sanders	1.50	4.00
240 Thurman Thomas	2.00	5.00
241 Roger Wehrli	1.50	4.00
242 Fred Dean	1.50	4.00
243 Darrell Green	1.50	4.00
244 Art Monk	1.50	4.00
245 Emmitt Thomas	1.50	4.00
246 Andre Tippett	1.50	4.00
247 Gary Zimmerman	1.50	4.00

1990 Hall of Fame Stickers

This 80-sticker set is actually part of a book; the individual stickers in the book measure approximately 1 7/8" by 2 1/8". The book was entitled "The Official Pro Football Hall of Fame Fun and Fact Sticker Book." The original artwork from which the stickers were derived was performed by noted hobbyist Mark Rucker and featured 80 members of the Pro Football Hall of Fame.

COMPLETE SET (80)	20.00	35.00
1 Fats Henry	.25	.60
2 George Trafton	.25	.60
3 Mike Michalske	.25	.60
4 Turk Edwards	.25	.60
5 Bill Hewitt	.25	.60
6 Mel Hein	.25	.60
7 Joe Stydahar	.25	.60
8 Dan Fortmann	.25	.60
9 Alex Wojciechowicz	.25	.60
10 George Connor	.25	.60
11 Jim Thorpe	.50	1.25
12 Ernie Nevers	.25	.60
13 Johnny Blood McNally	.25	.60
14 Ken Strong	.25	.60
15 Bronko Nagurski	.50	1.25
16 Clarke Hinkle	.25	.60
17 Clarence(Ace) Parker	.25	.60
18 Bill Dudley	.25	.60
19 Don Hutson	.30	1.00
20 Dante Lavelli	.30	.75
21 Elroy Hirsch	.30	1.00
22 Raymond Berry	.30	1.00
23 Bobby Mitchell	.30	.75
24 Don Maynard	.30	1.00
25 Mike Ditka	.50	1.25
26 Lance Alworth	.30	1.00
27 Charley Taylor	.30	.75
28 Paul Warfield	.30	.75
29 Lou Groza	.30	.75
30 Art Donovan	.30	.75
31 Leo Nomellini	.25	.60
32 Andy Robustelli	.25	.60
33 Gino Marchetti	.30	.75
34 Forrest Gregg	.30	.75
35 Jim Otto	.30	.75
36 Ron Mix	.30	.75
37 Deacon Jones	.30	1.00
38 Bob Lilly	.30	1.00
39 Merlin Olsen	.30	1.00
40 Alan Page	.30	.75
41 Joe Greene	.30	1.00
42 Art Shell	.30	.75
43 Sammy Baugh	.50	1.25
44 Sid Luckman	.20	.75
45 Bob Waterfield	.30	.75
46 Bobby Layne	.40	1.00
47 Norm Van Brocklin	.30	.75
48 Y.A. Tittle	.50	1.25
49 Johnny Unitas	1.50	4.00
50 Bart Starr	1.50	4.00
51 Sonny Jurgensen	.30	1.00
52 Joe Namath	1.25	3.00
53 Roger Staubach	1.00	2.50
54 Terry Bradshaw	1.00	2.50
55 Steve Van Buren	.25	.60
56 Marion Motley	.30	.75
57 Joe Perry	.30	.75
58 Hugh McElhenny	.30	.75
59 Frank Gifford	.40	1.00
60 Jim Brown	.75	2.00
61 Jim Taylor	.30	1.00
62 Gale Sayers	.60	1.50
63 Larry Csonka	.30	1.00
64 Emlen Tunnell	.25	.60
65 Jack Christiansen	.25	.60
66 Dick(Night Train) Lane	.25	.60
67 Sam Huff	.30	.75
68 Ray Nitschke	.30	1.00
69 Larry Wilson	.25	.60
70 Willie Wood	.30	.75
71 Bobby Bell	.30	.75
72 Willie Brown	.30	.75
73 Dick Butkus	.60	1.50
74 Jack Ham	.30	1.00
75 George Halas	.40	1.00
76 Steve Owen	.25	.60
77 Art Rooney	.30	.75
78 Bert Bell	.25	.60
79 Paul Brown	.30	.75
80 Pete Rozelle	.25	.60

1974 Hawaii Hawaiians WFL Team Issue

These photos were issued by the team for promotional purposes and fan mail requests. Each includes a black and white image printed above the subject's name and team logo. Each measures 5 1/2" by 7".

COMPLETE SET (9)	25.00	60.00
1 Gary Baccus	3.00	8.00
2 Damone Bame CO	3.00	8.00
3 Lem Burnham	3.00	8.00
4 Ron East	3.00	8.00
5 John Kelsey	3.00	8.00
6 Al Oliver	3.00	8.00
7 Greg Slough	3.00	8.00
8 Levi Stanley	3.00	8.00
9 Norris Weese	3.00	8.00

1993 Heads and Tails SB XXVII

COMPLETE SET (25)	4.80	12.00
*GOLD CARDS: 1X TO 2X SILVERS		
1 Title Card CL	.08	.25
2 Lawrence Taylor	.15	.40
Mike Singletary		
3 Dennis Byrd	.08	.25
4 Junior Seau	.20	.50
5 Steve Young	.40	1.00
6 Sterling Sharpe	.15	.40
7 Cortez Kennedy	.15	.40
8 Terry Bradshaw	.40	1.00
9 Fred Biletnikoff	.15	.40
10 John Riggins	.15	.40
11 Phil Simms	.15	.40
12 Cornelius Bennett	.15	.40
13 Jim Kelly	.25	.60
14 Bruce Smith	.15	.40
15 Andre Reed	.15	.40
16 Keith McKeller	.08	.25
17 James Lofton	.15	.40
18 Thurman Thomas	.25	.60
19 Emmitt Smith	1.00	2.50
20 Kelvin Martin	.08	.25
21 Troy Aikman	.60	1.50
22 Charles Haley	.08	.25
23 Alvin Harper	.15	.40
24 Michael Irvin	.25	.60
25 Jay Novacek	.15	.40

1970 Hi-C Mini-Posters

This set of ten posters were the insides of the Hi-C drink can labels. They are numbered very subtly below the player's picture but they are listed below in alphabetical order. The players selected for the set were leaders at their positions during the 1969 season. The mini-posters measure approximately 6 5/8" by 13 3/4".

COMPLETE SET (10)	300.00	600.00
1 Greg Cook	30.00	60.00
2 Fred Cox	30.00	60.00
3 Sonny Jurgensen	50.00	100.00
4 David Lee	25.00	50.00
5 Dennis Partee	25.00	50.00
6 Dick Post	25.00	50.00
7 Mel Renfro	50.00	100.00
8 Gale Sayers	75.00	150.00
9 Emmitt Thomas	30.00	60.00
10 Jim Turner	25.00	50.00

1997 Highland Mint Football Shaped Medallions

These football-shaped medallions are 1 7/8 inches wide and 1 1/8 inches at their greatest width and manufactured with silver. Each medallion was numbered of either 5000 or 7500 and is housed with an astroturf-like holder in a pigskin textured box. The original suggested retail price for these medallions was $29.95. Many players were also produced with a real diamond piece included. The diamond version pieces were numbered of 500.

1 Dan Marino S/7500	20.00	30.00
2 Troy Aikman S/5000	20.00	30.00
3 Troy Aikman DIAM/500	65.00	125.00
4 Brett Favre S/5000	20.00	30.00
5 Brett Favre DIAM/500	65.00	125.00
6 Jerry Rice S/7500	20.00	30.00
7 Jerry Rice DIA/500	65.00	125.00
8 Emmitt Smith S/7500	20.00	30.00
9 Emmitt Smith DIA/500	65.00	125.00

1995 Highland Mint Legends Mint-Cards

The Highland Mint Legends Collection features NFL greats in a newly designed Mint-Card format. These standard-sized bronze metal cards are enclosed in a plastic display holder case with each being serial numbered of either 2500 or 5000. Silver versions of these cards (20% of total of bronzes) were produced as well.

1 Joe Namath S/1000	90.00	160.00
2 Joe Namath B/5000	20.00	35.00
3 Roger Staubach S/500	90.00	160.00
4 Roger Staubach B/2500	20.00	35.00
5 Johnny Unitas S/500	90.00	160.00
6 Johnny Unitas B/2500	20.00	35.00

1997 Highland Mint Mint-Cards Pinnacle/Score/UD

These cards are replicas of previously-issued Pinnacle, Score or Upper Deck cards. The silver and bronze cards contain 4.25 ounces of metal; the gold cards are 24-karat gold-plated on silver. Each card is individually numbered, packaged in a lucite display holder and accompanied by a certificate of authenticity. The production mintage according to Highland Mint is listed below.

1 Troy Aikman/89SCO	125.00	175.00
S/1000		
2 Troy Aikman/89SCO	12.50	25.00
B/5000		
3 Drew Bledsoe/94SCOSS	125.00	175.00
S/1000		
4 Drew Bledsoe/94SCOSS	12.50	25.00
B/5000		
5 Brett Favre 93	125.00	200.00
S/250		
6 Brett Favre 93	25.00	50.00
B/1500		
7 Dan Marino/94PIN	150.00	250.00
G/500		
8 Dan Marino/94PIN	125.00	175.00
S/1000		
9 Dan Marino/94PIN	17.50	35.00
B/5000		
10 Joe Montana/92UD	175.00	300.00
G/500		
11 Joe Montana/92UD	125.00	175.00
S/1000		
12 Joe Montana/92UD	20.00	40.00
B/5000		
13 Errict Rhett/94PIN	125.00	175.00
S/500		
14 Errict Rhett/94PIN	7.50	15.00
B/2500		
15 Jerry Rice/95ZEN	125.00	175.00
S/500		
16 Jerry Rice/95ZEN	15.00	30.00
B/2500		
17 Rashaan Salaam/95PIN	125.00	175.00
S/500		
18 Rashaan Salaam/95PIN	7.50	15.00
B/2500		
19 Barry Sanders 89	125.00	175.00
S/250		
20 Barry Sanders 89	20.00	40.00
B/1500		
21 Heath Shuler/94PIN	125.00	175.00
S/500		
22 Heath Shuler/94PIN	7.50	15.00
B/2500		
23 Emmitt Smith 90	150.00	250.00
G/500		
24 Emmitt Smith 90	125.00	175.00
S/1000		
25 Emmitt Smith 90	15.00	30.00
B/5000		
26 Kordell Stewart/95	125.00	175.00
S/500		
27 Kordell Stewart/95	10.00	20.00
B/2500		

1997 Highland Mint Mint-Cards Topps

Produced by Highland Mint, these cards measure the standard size and are metal reproductions of Topps football cards. The reported .999 fine silver content for both the silver and gold plated cards was 4.25 troy ounces. The reported final mintage figures for each card are listed below. Highland Mint also issued 40 bronze promos of the Smith card. Each card bears a serial number on its bottom edge. These cards were available only through direct distributors, and were packaged in a lucite display case within an album. Each card came with a sequentially numbered Certificate of Authenticity. The numbering on the card backs reflects the actual card numbers from the original Topps issues; however the listing below is ordered alphabetically for convenience.

1 Troy Aikman 89	125.00	250.00
G/375		
2 Troy Aikman 89	125.00	175.00
S/500		
3 Troy Aikman 89	20.00	50.00
B/2500		
4 Marcus Allen 83	125.00	175.00
S/88		
5 Marcus Allen 83	15.00	30.00
B/549		
6 Jerome Bettis 93	125.00	175.00
S/301		
7 Jerome Bettis 93	12.50	25.00
B/1566		
8 Drew Bledsoe 93	125.00	200.00
G/375		
9 Drew Bledsoe 93	125.00	175.00
S/500		
10 Drew Bledsoe 93	12.50	25.00
B/2500		
11 John Elway 84	125.00	175.00
S/500		
12 John Elway 84	20.00	40.00
B/2020		
13 Marshall Faulk 94	125.00	175.00
S/530		
14 Marshall Faulk 94	12.50	25.00
B/2500		
15 Brett Favre 92	125.00	200.00
S/110		
16 Brett Favre 92	30.00	60.00
B/714		
17 Michael Irvin 89	125.00	175.00
S/509		
18 Michael Irvin 89	12.50	25.00
B/1633		
19 Jim Kelly 87	125.00	175.00
S/419		
20 Jim Kelly 87	15.00	30.00
B/1165		
21 Dan Marino 84	150.00	300.00
G/375		
22 Dan Marino 84	125.00	200.00
S/500		
23 Dan Marino 84	20.00	40.00
B/2500		
24 Natrone Means 93	125.00	175.00
S/136		
25 Natrone Means/93	12.50	25.00
B/1026		
26 Rick Mirer 93	125.00	175.00
S/384		
27 Rick Mirer 93	12.50	25.00
B/1982		
28 Jerry Rice 86	150.00	300.00
G/375		
29 Jerry Rice 86	125.00	175.00
S/750		
30 Jerry Rice 86	15.00	30.00
B/2500		
31 Barry Sanders 89	150.00	300.00
G/375		
32 Barry Sanders 89	125.00	175.00
S/750		
33 Barry Sanders 89	15.00	30.00
B/2500		
34 Deion Sanders 89	125.00	175.00
S/191		
35 Deion Sanders 89	12.50	30.00
B/1033		
36 Sterling Sharpe 89	125.00	175.00
S/171		
37 Sterling Sharpe 89	12.50	25.00
B/901		
38 Emmitt Smith 90	150.00	300.00
G/375		
39 Emmitt Smith 90	125.00	175.00
S/750		
40 Emmitt Smith 90	17.50	35.00
B/2500		
41 Lawrence Taylor/84	125.00	175.00
S/585		
42 Lawrence Taylor/84	12.50	25.00
B/1630		
43 Steve Young 86	125.00	200.00
G/375		
44 Steve Young 86	125.00	175.00
S/500		
45 Steve Young 86	12.50	25.00
B/2500		

1997-00 Highland Mint Mint-Coins

Each medallion weighs one-troy ounce and is individually numbered. The fronts feature a player likeness as well as name, uniform number, and signature. The backs display the team logo and statistics. The medallions were packaged in a hard plastic capsule and a velvet jewelry box. Unless noted below, the unpriced solid gold coins were produced in quantities of 100, the bronze coins were printed in quantities of 25,000 and the silvers 7500. Highland Mint also produced two-tone "Signature Series" silver medallions with gold plate highlights and a production run of 1500 of each piece.

1 Troy Aikman B	5.00	12.00
2 Troy Aikman S	30.00	40.00
3 Troy Aikman SS	35.00	60.00
4 Jerome Bettis	30.00	40.00
Rams S/2100		
5 Jerome Bettis	30.00	40.00
Steelers S/5400		
6 Jerome Bettis S	30.00	40.00
Kordell Stewart S		
7 Drew Bledsoe B	5.00	12.00
8 Drew Bledsoe S	30.00	40.00
9 Drew Bledsoe SS	30.00	50.00
10 Mark Brunell B	5.00	12.00
11 Mark Brunell S	30.00	40.00
12 Ki-Jana Carter S	30.00	40.00
13 Kerry Collins S	30.00	40.00
14 Tim Couch S	30.00	40.00
15 Randall Cunningham B	5.00	12.00
16 Terrell Davis B	5.00	12.00
17 Terrell Davis S	30.00	40.00
18 Trent Dilfer S	30.00	40.00
19 Warrick Dunn S	30.00	40.00
20 John Elway B	6.00	15.00
21 John Elway S	30.00	40.00
22 John Elway RET S	30.00	40.00
23 John Elway SS	45.00	80.00
24 Marshall Faulk B	5.00	12.00
25 Marshall Faulk S	30.00	40.00
26 Brett Favre B	6.00	15.00
27 Brett Favre S	30.00	40.00
28 Favre	30.00	40.00
B.Sanders S		
29 Eddie George S/5000	30.00	40.00
30 Terry Glenn S	30.00	40.00
31 Michael Irvin S	30.00	40.00
32 Jim Kelly S	30.00	40.00
33 Ryan Leaf S	30.00	40.00
34 Peyton Manning B	6.00	15.00
35 Peyton Manning S	30.00	40.00
36 Dan Marino B	6.00	15.00
37 Dan Marino G/100		
38 Dan Marino S	30.00	40.00
39 Dan Marino SS	60.00	100.00
40 Curtis Martin S	30.00	40.00
41 Natrone Means S	30.00	40.00
42 Rick Mirer S	30.00	40.00
43 Joe Montana B	6.00	15.00
44 Joe Montana B	6.00	15.00
Jerry Rice B		
45 Joe Montana G/100		
46 Joe Montana S	30.00	40.00
47 Randy Moss B	6.00	15.00
48 Randy Moss S	30.00	40.00
49 Joe Namath S	30.00	40.00
50 Jake Plummer S	30.00	40.00
51 Jerry Rice B	5.00	12.00
52 Jerry Rice S	30.00	40.00
53 Jerry Rice SS	35.00	60.00
54 Rashaan Salaam S	30.00	40.00
55 Barry Sanders B	6.00	15.00
56 Barry Sanders S	30.00	40.00
57 Deion Sanders B	4.00	10.00
58 Deion Sanders	30.00	40.00
Cowboys S/4810		
59 Deion Sanders/49ers S/2690	30.00	40.00
60 Junior Seau S	30.00	40.00
61 Heath Shuler S	30.00	40.00
62 Emmitt Smith B	6.00	15.00
63 Emmitt Smith G/100		
64 Emmitt Smith S	30.00	40.00
65 Emmitt Smith SS	45.00	80.00
66 Kordell Stewart B	5.00	12.00
67 Kordell Stewart S	30.00	40.00
68 Reggie White S	30.00	40.00
69 Ricky Williams S	30.00	40.00
70 Steve Young B	4.00	10.00
71 Steve Young S	30.00	40.00
72 Cowboys Set B/2500	6.00	15.00
73 49ers B/2500	6.00	15.00

1991 Homers

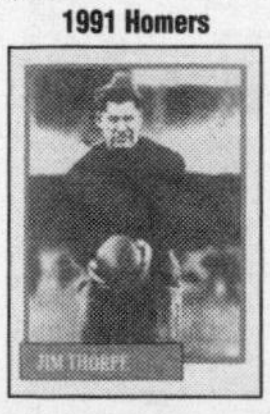

This six-card standard-size set was sponsored by Legend Food Products in honor of the listed Hall of Famers. One free card was randomly inserted in either 3 1/2 or 10 oz. boxes of QB's Cookies. The vanilla-flavored cookies came in six player shapes (wide receiver, kicker, linebacker, tackle, running back, and quarterback), with a trivia quiz and secret message featured on each box. The card fronts display sepia-toned photos enclosed by bronze borders on a white card face. The player's name appears in a bronze bar at the lower left corner. The backs present year of induction into the Pro Football Hall of Fame, biography, career highlights, and a checklist for the set.

COMPLETE SET (6)	75.00	135.00
1 Vince Lombardi CO	15.00	30.00
2 Hugh McElhenny	7.50	15.00
3 Elroy Hirsch	7.50	15.00

4 Jim Thorpe 12.50 25.00
5 Dick Lane 6.00 12.00
6 Bart Starr 20.00 40.00

2001 Hot Prospects

In August of 2001 Fleer released Hot Prospects as a 100-card base set in hobby packs. The cardfronts use a partial foilboard and glossy design highlighted with silver-foil lettering and team logos. The cardbacks use a 3-color design, brown, black, and one of the featured players' team colors. While the hobby version of this product contained no rookie cards, please note that cards 101-135 were available only in retail packs at the rate of 1:10.

COMP.SET w/o SP's (100) 10.00 25.00
1 Aaron Brooks .25 .60
2 Tim Couch .20 .50
3 Jeff George .25 .60
4 Brett Favre 1.00 2.50
5 Donovan McNabb .30 .75
6 Ray Lucas .20 .50
7 Doug Flutie .30 .75
8 Mark Brunell .25 .60
9 Steve McNair .30 .75
10 Trent Green .30 .75
11 Daunte Culpepper .25 .60
12 Rich Gannon .25 .60
13 Kurt Warner .50 1.25
14 Brian Griese .25 .60
15 Kerry Collins .25 .60
16 Vinny Testaverde .25 .60
17 David Boston .20 .50
18 Peyton Manning .75 2.00
19 Keyshawn Johnson .25 .60
20 Tim Biakabutuka .20 .50
21 J.R. Redmond .20 .50
22 Emmitt Smith .75 2.00
23 Terry Glenn .25 .60
24 Tony Gonzalez .30 .75
25 Charlie Garner .25 .60
26 Lamar Smith .25 .60
27 Eddie George .30 .75
28 Fred Taylor .30 .75
29 Marvin Harrison .30 .75
30 Terrell Davis .30 .75
31 Marcus Robinson .25 .60
32 Edgerrin James .30 .75
33 Ed McCaffrey .25 .60
34 Ricky Williams .30 .75
35 Todd Pinkston .20 .50
36 Jerome Bettis .30 .75
37 Shaun Alexander .30 .75
38 Mike Anderson .25 .60
39 Keenan McCardell .25 .60
40 Mike Alstott .25 .60
41 Terrell Fletcher .20 .50
42 Kevin Johnson .20 .50
43 Wesley Walls .20 .50
44 Derrick Mason .25 .60
45 Sammy Morris .25 .60
46 Joey Galloway .25 .60
47 Sylvester Morris .20 .50
48 Stephen Davis .25 .60
49 Terrell Owens .30 .75
50 Troy Edwards .20 .50
51 Amani Toomer .25 .60
52 Ray Lewis .30 .75
53 Terance Mathis .20 .50
54 Brian Urlacher .40 1.00
55 Junior Seau .30 .75
56 Rocket Ismail .25 .60
57 Wayne Chrebet .25 .60
58 Peter Warrick .25 .60
59 Andre Rison .25 .60
60 Desmond Howard .25 .60
61 Eric Moulds .25 .60
62 Jerry Rice .60 1.50
63 Stephen Alexander .20 .50
64 Isaac Bruce .30 .75
65 Travis Prentice .20 .50
66 James Stewart .20 .50
67 Jamal Anderson .25 .60
68 Ricky Watters .25 .60
69 Jamal Lewis .30 .75
70 Priest Holmes .30 .75
71 Ahman Green .30 .75
72 Marshall Faulk .30 .75
73 Warrick Dunn .30 .75
74 Curtis Martin .30 .75
75 Corey Dillon .25 .60
76 Ron Dayne .25 .60
77 Thomas Jones .25 .60
78 Duce Staley .25 .60
79 Tiki Barber .30 .75
80 Cris Carter .30 .75
81 Tim Brown .30 .75
82 Jimmy Smith .25 .60
83 Elvis Grbac .25 .60
84 Randy Moss .30 .75
85 Tim Dwight .25 .60
86 Antonio Freeman .30 .75
87 Muhsin Muhammad .25 .60
88 Torry Holt .25 .60
89 Frank Wycheck .20 .50
90 Jake Plummer .25 .60
91 Brad Johnson .25 .60
92 Chris Chandler .25 .60
93 Drew Bledsoe .30 .75
94 Rob Johnson .25 .60
95 Matt Hasselbeck .30 .75
96 Jon Kitna .25 .60
97 Kordell Stewart .25 .60
98 Charlie Batch .25 .60
99 Cade McNown .25 .60
100 Jeff Garcia .25 .60
101 Quincy Morgan RC .75 2.00
102 Jesse Palmer RC .75 2.00
103 Reggie Wayne RC 2.00 5.00
104 Deuce McAllister RC 1.00 2.50
105 Chad Johnson RC 1.50 4.00
106 Chris Weinke RC .75 2.00
107 Michael Bennett RC .75 2.00
108 Rod Gardner RC .75 2.00
109 Michael Vick RC 4.00 10.00
110 Anthony Thomas RC 1.00 2.50
111 Santana Moss RC 1.25 3.00
112 Kevan Barlow RC .75 2.00
113 Koren Robinson RC .75 2.00
114 Rudi Johnson RC 1.00 2.50
115 Josh Heupel RC 1.00 2.50
116 James Jackson RC .60 1.50
117 Freddie Mitchell RC .60 1.50
118 LaDainian Tomlinson RC 8.00 20.00
119 Marques Tuiasosopo RC .75 2.00
120 Drew Brees RC 6.00 15.00
121 David Terrell RC .75 2.00
122 Chris Chambers RC 1.00 2.50
123 Mike McMahon RC .75 2.00
124 Robert Ferguson RC 1.00 2.50
125 Justin Smith RC 1.00 2.50
126 Leonard Davis RC 1.00 2.50
127 Todd Heap RC 1.00 2.50
128 Dan Morgan RC .75 2.00
129 Gerard Warren RC .75 2.00
130 Travis Henry RC .75 2.00
131 Travis Minor RC .75 2.00
132 Richard Seymour RC 1.00 2.50
133 Quincy Carter RC .75 2.00
134 Snoop Minnis RC .60 1.50
135 Sage Rosenfels RC 1.00 2.50
CL1 Checklist .02 .10

2001 Hot Prospects Draft Day Postmarks

1 Kevan Barlow/1975 3.00 8.00
2 Michael Bennett/1825 3.00 8.00
3 Drew Brees/1775 12.00 30.00
4 Rod Gardner/1875 3.00 8.00
5 Josh Heupel/1825 4.00 10.00
6 James Jackson/1975 2.50 6.00
7 Chad Johnson/1875 6.00 15.00
8 Rudi Johnson/1975 4.00 10.00
9 Deuce McAllister/1825 4.00 10.00
10 Freddie Mitchell/1875 2.50 6.00
11 Quincy Morgan/1875 3.00 8.00
12 Santana Moss/1750 5.00 12.00
13 Jesse Palmer/1875 3.00 8.00
14 Koren Robinson/1825 3.00 8.00
15 David Terrell/1825 3.00 8.00
16 Anthony Thomas/1875 4.00 10.00
17 LaDainian Tomlinson/1775 12.00 30.00
18 Marques Tuiasosopo/1875 3.00 8.00
19 Michael Vick/1775 12.00 30.00
20 Reggie Wayne/1875 8.00 20.00
21 Chris Weinke/1775 3.00 8.00

2001 Hot Prospects Draft Day Postmarks Autographs

2 Michael Bennett 8.00 20.00
3 Drew Brees SP 100.00 175.00
5 Josh Heupel 10.00 25.00
7 Chad Johnson 30.00 60.00
8 Rudi Johnson 10.00 25.00
11 Quincy Morgan 8.00 20.00
12 Santana Moss SP 15.00 40.00
13 Jesse Palmer 8.00 20.00
14 Koren Robinson 8.00 20.00
15 David Terrell 8.00 20.00
16 Anthony Thomas 10.00 25.00
17 LaDainian Tomlinson SP 100.00 200.00
18 Marques Tuiasosopo 8.00 20.00
21 Chris Weinke SP 10.00 25.00

2001 Hot Prospects Honor Guard

COMPLETE SET (49) 40.00 80.00
STATED ODDS 1:5
1 Troy Aikman 1.25 3.00
2 Marcus Allen 1.00 2.50
3 Mike Alstott .60 1.50
4 Jerome Bettis .75 2.00
5 Drew Bledsoe .75 2.00
6 Isaac Bruce .75 2.00
7 Mark Brunell .60 1.50
8 Wayne Chrebet .60 1.50
9 Daunte Culpepper .60 1.50
10 Randall Cunningham 1.00 2.50
11 Terrell Davis .75 2.00
12 Stephen Davis .60 1.50
13 Corey Dillon .60 1.50
14 Warrick Dunn .75 2.00
15 Marshall Faulk .75 2.00
16 Brett Favre 2.50 6.00
17 Doug Flutie .75 2.00
18 Jeff Garcia .60 1.50
19 Eddie George .75 2.00
20 Brian Griese .60 1.50
21 Bo Jackson 1.25 3.00
22 Jamal Lewis .75 2.00
23 Dan Marino 2.50 6.00
24 Donovan McNabb .75 2.00
25 Steve McNair .75 2.00
26 Joe Montana 2.50 6.00
27 Randy Moss .75 2.00
28 Jerry Rice 1.50 4.00
29 Jerry Rice 1.50 4.00
30 Deion Sanders .75 2.00
31 Emmitt Smith 2.00 5.00
32 Fred Taylor .75 2.00
33 John Elway 2.50 6.00
34 Kurt Warner 1.25 3.00
35 Ricky Williams .75 2.00
36 Marvin Harrison .75 2.00
37 Edgerrin James .75 2.00
38 Curtis Martin .75 2.00
39 Vinny Testaverde .60 1.50
40 Rod Smith .60 1.50
41 Warren Moon 1.00 2.50
42 Steve Young 1.25 3.00
43 Jamal Anderson .60 1.50
44 Tim Brown .75 2.00
45 Plaxico Burress .60 1.50
46 Tim Couch .50 1.25
47 Az-Zahir Hakim .50 1.25
48 Ed McCaffrey .60 1.50
49 Ron Dayne .60 1.50

2001 Hot Prospects Pigskin Prospects

COMPLETE SET (15) 25.00 50.00
STATED ODDS 1:15
PP1 Drew Brees 5.00 12.00
PP2 Koren Robinson .60 1.50
PP3 Robert Ferguson .75 2.00
PP4 Rod Gardner .60 1.50
PP5 Chad Johnson 1.25 3.00
PP6 Reggie Wayne 1.50 4.00
PP7 Chris Weinke .60 1.50
PP8 Deuce McAllister .75 2.00
PP9 Chris Chambers .75 2.00
PP10 Freddie Mitchell .50 1.25
PP11 Quincy Carter .60 1.50
PP12 LaDainian Tomlinson 2.50 6.00
PP13 Santana Moss 1.00 2.50
PP14 David Terrell .60 1.50
PP15 Michael Vick 3.00 8.00

2001 Hot Prospects Pigskin Prospects Jerseys

STATED ODDS 1:51
1 Drew Brees 20.00 40.00
3 Robert Ferguson 4.00 10.00
4 Chad Johnson 6.00 15.00
5 Reggie Wayne 8.00 20.00
6 Chris Weinke 3.00 8.00

2001 Hot Prospects Rookie Premiere Postmarks Jerseys

STATED PRINT RUN 1500 SETS
1 Kevan Barlow 3.00 8.00
2 Michael Bennett 3.00 8.00
3 Drew Brees 20.00 40.00
4 Quincy Carter 3.00 8.00
5 Chris Chambers 4.00 10.00
6 Leonard Davis 4.00 10.00
7 Robert Ferguson 4.00 10.00
8 Rod Gardner 3.00 8.00
9 Todd Heap 4.00 10.00
10 Travis Henry 3.00 8.00
11 Josh Heupel 4.00 10.00
12 James Jackson 2.50 6.00
13 Chad Johnson 6.00 15.00
14 Rudi Johnson 4.00 10.00
15 Deuce McAllister 4.00 10.00
16 Mike McMahon 3.00 8.00
17 Snoop Minnis 2.50 6.00
18 Travis Minor 3.00 8.00
19 Freddie Mitchell 2.50 6.00
20 Dan Morgan 3.00 8.00
21 Quincy Morgan 3.00 8.00
22 Santana Moss 5.00 12.00
23 Jesse Palmer 3.00 8.00
24 Koren Robinson 3.00 8.00
25 Sage Rosenfels 4.00 10.00
26 Richard Seymour 4.00 10.00
27 Justin Smith 4.00 10.00
28 David Terrell 3.00 8.00
29 Anthony Thomas 4.00 10.00
30 LaDainian Tomlinson 12.00 30.00
31 Marques Tuiasosopo 3.00 8.00
32 Michael Vick 12.00 30.00
33 Gerard Warren 3.00 8.00
34 Reggie Wayne 8.00 20.00
35 Chris Weinke 3.00 8.00

2001 Hot Prospects Scoring King Jerseys

STATED ODDS 1:12
1 Troy Aikman SP 12.00 30.00
2 Marcus Allen 6.00 15.00
3 Mike Alstott 5.00 12.00
4 Jamal Anderson SP 6.00 15.00
5 Jerome Bettis 6.00 15.00
6 Drew Bledsoe SP 8.00 20.00
7 Tim Brown SP 8.00 20.00
8 Isaac Bruce SP 8.00 20.00
9 Mark Brunell SP 6.00 15.00
10 Plaxico Burress 5.00 12.00
11 Wayne Chrebet SP 6.00 15.00
12 Tim Couch SP 5.00 12.00
13 Daunte Culpepper SP 6.00 15.00
14 Randall Cunningham 6.00 15.00
15 Stephen Davis SP 6.00 15.00
16 Terrell Davis SP 8.00 20.00
17 Ron Dayne 5.00 12.00
18 Corey Dillon SP 6.00 15.00
19 Warrick Dunn 6.00 15.00
20 John Elway SP 20.00 50.00
21 Marshall Faulk 6.00 15.00
22 Brett Favre SP 25.00 60.00
23 Doug Flutie 6.00 15.00
24 Jeff Garcia SP 6.00 15.00
25 Eddie George 6.00 15.00
26 Brian Griese SP 6.00 15.00
27 Az-Zahir Hakim 4.00 10.00
28 Marvin Harrison SP 8.00 20.00
29 Bo Jackson 10.00 25.00
30 Edgerrin James SP 8.00 20.00
31 Jamal Lewis SP 8.00 20.00
32 Dan Marino SP 20.00 50.00
33 Curtis Martin SP 8.00 20.00
34 Ed McCaffrey 5.00 12.00
35 Donovan McNabb SP 8.00 20.00
36 Steve McNair 6.00 15.00
37 Joe Montana 15.00 40.00
38 Warren Moon SP 8.00 20.00
39 Randy Moss SP 8.00 20.00
40 Jerry Rice SP 15.00 40.00
41 Deion Sanders 6.00 15.00
42 Emmitt Smith SP 20.00 50.00
43 Rod Smith 5.00 12.00
44 Fred Taylor SP 8.00 20.00
45 Vinny Testaverde 5.00 12.00
46 Kurt Warner SP 12.00 30.00
47 Ricky Williams SP 8.00 20.00
48 Steve Young 8.00 20.00

2001 Hot Prospects TD Fever

STATED ODDS 1:21
1 Drew Bledsoe 5.00 12.00
2 Daunte Culpepper 4.00 10.00
3 Oronde Gadsden 3.00 8.00
4 Rich Gannon 4.00 10.00
5 Marvin Harrison 5.00 12.00
6 Edgerrin James 5.00 12.00
7 Peyton Manning 12.00 30.00
8 Curtis Martin 5.00 12.00
9 Randy Moss 5.00 12.00
10 Peerless Price 3.00 8.00
11 J.R. Redmond 3.00 8.00
12 Jimmy Smith 4.00 10.00
13 James Stewart 3.00 8.00
14 Tyrone Wheatley 4.00 10.00

2002 Hot Prospects

Released in July 2002, this 112-card base set includes 80 veterans and 32 rookies. The rookie cards offer swatches of game-worn jersey and are serial #'d to 1000. The product contains 15 packs per box, 5 cards per pack. The David Carr RC never made it into packs and was mailed out by Fleer to top dealers across the country. It does not feature a jersey swatch like the other Rookie Cards, and is serial numbered to 250.

COMP.SET w/o SP's (80) 10.00 25.00
ROOKIE JSY PRINT RUN 1000
1 Donovan McNabb .40 1.00
2 Drew Brees .60 1.50
3 Curtis Martin .40 1.00
4 Priest Holmes .40 1.00
5 Quincy Carter .25 .60
6 Chris Weinke .25 .60
7 Marshall Faulk .40 1.00
8 Jake Plummer .30 .75
9 Tom Brady 1.00 2.50
10 Ahman Green .30 .75
11 Brian Urlacher .40 1.00
12 Keyshawn Johnson .30 .75
13 Jerome Bettis .40 1.00
14 Tiki Barber .40 1.00
15 Edgerrin James .30 .75
16 Jamal Lewis .30 .75
17 Terrell Owens .40 1.00
18 Joe Horn .30 .75
19 Daunte Culpepper .30 .75
20 Terrell Davis .40 1.00
21 Fred Taylor .30 .75
22 Emmitt Smith 1.00 2.50
23 Jamal Anderson .30 .75
24 Garrison Hearst .30 .75
25 Chad Pennington .40 1.00
26 Michael Bennett .30 .75
27 James Allen .25 .60
28 Marty Booker .30 .75
29 Warren Sapp .30 .75
30 Jerry Rice .75 2.00
31 Antowain Smith .30 .75
32 Marvin Harrison .40 1.00
33 Tim Couch .25 .60
34 Stephen Davis .30 .75
35 Kordell Stewart .30 .75
36 Tony Gonzalez .40 1.00
37 Mike McMahon .25 .60
38 Eric Moulds .30 .75
39 Kurt Warner .40 1.00
40 Ricky Williams .30 .75
41 Michael Strahan .40 1.00
42 Trent Green .30 .75
43 Brian Griese .30 .75
44 David Boston .25 .60
45 LaDainian Tomlinson .50 1.25
46 Tim Brown .40 1.00
47 Deuce McAllister .30 .75
48 Jamie Sharper .30 .75
49 Rod Gardner .25 .60
50 Isaac Bruce .40 1.00
51 Freddie Mitchell .25 .60
52 Kerry Collins .30 .75
53 Mark Brunell .30 .75
54 Corey Dillon .30 .75
55 Steve McNair .40 1.00
56 Aaron Brooks .30 .75
57 Chris Chambers .30 .75
58 Bill Schroeder .25 .60
59 Ray Lewis .40 1.00
60 Shaun Alexander .30 .75
61 Kevin Johnson .25 .60
62 Michael Vick .60 1.50
63 Jeff Garcia .30 .75
64 Laveranues Coles .30 .75
65 Jimmy Smith .30 .75
66 Brett Favre 1.00 2.50
67 Anthony Thomas .30 .75
68 Torry Holt .40 1.00
69 Duce Staley .30 .75
70 Randy Moss .40 1.00
71 Peyton Manning .75 2.00
72 Peter Warrick .30 .75
73 Eddie George .30 .75
74 Plaxico Burress .30 .75
75 Troy Brown .30 .75
76 Rod Smith .30 .75
77 Drew Bledsoe .40 1.00
78 Darrell Jackson .30 .75
79 Rich Gannon .30 .75
80 Jay Fiedler .30 .75
81 David Carr/250 RC 8.00 20.00
82 Andre Davis JSY RC 2.50 6.00
83 Daniel Graham JSY RC 2.50 6.00
84 Ron Johnson JSY RC 2.50 6.00
85 Julius Peppers JSY RC 6.00 15.00
86 Josh Reed JSY RC 2.50 6.00
87 Travis Stephens JSY RC 2.00 5.00
88 Mike Williams JSY RC 2.00 5.00
89 Antonio Bryant JSY RC 3.00 8.00
90 Eric Crouch JSY RC 3.00 8.00
91 DeShaun Foster JSY RC 3.00 8.00
92 Joey Harrington JSY RC 3.00 8.00
93 Josh McCown JSY RC 3.00 8.00
94 Patrick Ramsey JSY RC 3.00 8.00
95 Jeremy Shockey JSY RC 5.00 12.00
96 Marquise Walker JSY RC
97 Reche Caldwell JSY RC 3.00 8.00
98 Rohan Davey JSY RC 3.00 8.00
99 Jabar Gaffney JSY RC 3.00 8.00
100 David Garrard JSY RC 4.00 10.00
101 Maurice Morris JSY RC 2.50 6.00
102 Antwaan Randle El JSY RC 3.00 8.00
103 Donte Stallworth JSY RC 3.00 8.00
104 Roy Williams JSY RC 3.00 8.00
105 Ladell Betts JSY RC 3.00 8.00
106 Tim Carter JSY RC 2.50 6.00
107 T.J. Duckett JSY RC 3.00 8.00
108 William Green JSY RC 2.50 6.00
109 Ashley Lelie JSY RC 2.50 6.00
110 Clinton Portis JSY RC 4.00 10.00
111 Cliff Russell JSY RC 2.00 5.00
112 Javon Walker JSY RC 3.00 8.00

2002 Hot Prospects Class Of

STATED PRINT RUN 750 SER.#'d SETS
1 Tim Couch 1.50 4.00
Donovan McNabb
2 Torry Holt 1.50 4.00
David Boston
3 Fred Taylor 1.25 3.00
Ahman Green
4 Jake Plummer 1.25 3.00
Corey Dillon
5 Keyshawn Johnson 1.50 4.00
Marvin Harrison
6 Warren Sapp 1.50 4.00
Curtis Martin
7 Aaron Brooks 1.25 3.00
Daunte Culpepper
8 Marshall Faulk 1.50 4.00
Isaac Bruce
9 Brian Griese 3.00 8.00
Peyton Manning
10 Stephen Davis 1.25 3.00
Eddie George
11 Edgerrin James 1.25 3.00
Ricky Williams
12 Randy Moss 1.50 4.00
Hines Ward
13 Michael Strahan 1.50 4.00
Jerome Bettis
14 Terrell Owens 1.50 4.00
Mike Alstott
15 Brett Favre 4.00 10.00
Ricky Watters
16 Ron Dayne 1.25 3.00
Shaun Alexander
17 Peter Warrick 1.50 4.00
Thomas Jones
18 Tom Brady 4.00 10.00
Chad Pennington
19 Michael Vick 2.50 6.00
Drew Brees
20 LaDainian Tomlinson 2.00 5.00
Anthony Thomas

2002 Hot Prospects Class Of Memorabilia

STATED PRINT RUN 375 SER.#'d SETS
ABDC Aaron Brooks 6.00 15.00
Daunte Culpepper
EJRW Edgerrin James 6.00 15.00
Ricky Williams
FTAG Fred Taylor 6.00 15.00
Ahman Green
JPCD Jake Plummer 6.00 15.60
Corey Dillon
KJMH Keyshawn Johnson 8.00 20.00
Marvin Harrison
LTAT LaDainian Tomlinson 10.00 25.00
Anthony Thomas
MFIB Marshall Faulk 8.00 20.00
Isaac Bruce
MSJB Michael Strahan 8.00 20.00
Jerome Bettis
MVDB Michael Vick 12.00 30.00
Drew Brees
PWTJ Peter Warrick 8.00 20.00
Thomas Jones
RDSA Ron Dayne 6.00 15.00
Shaun Alexander
RMHW Randy Moss 8.00 20.00
Hines Ward
SDEG Stephen Davis 6.00 15.00
Eddie George
TBCP Tom Brady 20.00 50.00
Chad Pennington
TCDM Tim Couch 8.00 20.00
Donovan McNabb
THDB Torry Holt 8.00 20.00
David Boston
TOMA Terrell Owens 8.00 20.00
Mike Alstott
WSCM Warren Sapp 8.00 20.00
Curtis Martin

2002 Hot Prospects Hat Trick

STATED ODDS 1:7
HTAMD Shaun Alexander 1.50 4.00
Deuce McAllister
T.J. Duckett
HTBMS Plaxico Burress 1.50 4.00
Freddie Mitchell
Donte Stallworth
HTDTF Ron Dayne 1.50 4.00
Anthony Thomas
DeShaun Foster
HTFHS Bubba Franks 2.50 6.00
Todd Heap
Jeremy Shockey
HTLTG Jaml Lewis 2.00 5.00
LaDainian Tomlinson
Ahman Green
HTRBH Chris Redman 2.50 6.00
Drew Brees
Joey Harrington
HTTRG Fred Taylor 1.50 4.00
Robinson
Jabar Gaffney
HTUMP Brian Urlacher 3.00 8.00
Julius Morgan
J.J. Peppers
HTWGL Peter Warrick 1.25 3.00
Rod Gardner
Ashley Lelie

2002 Hot Prospects Hat Trick Memorabilia

STATED PRINT RUN 150 SER.#'d SETS
HTAMD Shaun Alexander 10.00 25.00
Deuce McAllister
T.J. Duckett
HTBMS Plaxico Burress 10.00 25.00
Freddie Mitchell
Donte Stallworth
HTDTF Ron Dayne 10.00 25.00
Anthony Thomas
DeShaun Foster
HTFHS Bubba Franks 12.00 30.00
Todd Heap
Jeremy Shockey
HTLTG Jaml Lewis 12.00 30.00
LaDainian Tomlinson
Ahman Green
HTRBH Chris Redman 15.00 40.00
Drew Brees
Joey Harrington
HTTRG Fred Taylor 10.00 25.00
Robinson
Jabar Gaffney
HTUMP Brian Urlacher 15.00 40.00
Julius Morgan
J.J. Peppers
HTWGL Peter Warrick 8.00 20.00
Rod Gardner
Ashley Lelie

2002 Hot Prospects Hot Materials

STATED ODDS 1:6
*RED HOT/50: .8X TO 2X BASIC JSY
RED HOT PRINT RUN 50 SER.#'d SETS
HMAB Aaron Brooks 4.00 10.00
HMAB2 Antonio Bryant 5.00 12.00
HMAG Ahman Green 4.00 10.00
HMAL Ashley Lelie 4.00 10.00
HMAR Antwaan Randle El 5.00 12.00
HMAT Anthony Thomas 4.00 10.00
HMBF Brett Favre 12.00 30.00
HMBU Brian Urlacher 5.00 12.00
HMCD Corey Dillon SP/361 5.00 12.00
HMCM Curtis Martin 5.00 12.00
HMCP Clinton Portis 4.00 10.00
HMDB Drew Brees SP/124 10.00 25.00
HMDC Daunte Culpepper 4.00 10.00
HMDC2 Reche Caldwell 5.00 12.00
HMDF DeShaun Foster 5.00 12.00
HMDM Donovan McNabb 5.00 12.00
HMDS Donte Stallworth 5.00 12.00
HMEG Eddie George 4.00 10.00
HMES Emmitt Smith 12.00 30.00
HMIB Isaac Bruce 5.00 12.00
HMJG Jabar Gaffney 5.00 12.00
HMJG2 Jeff Garcia 4.00 10.00
HMJH Joey Harrington 5.00 12.00
HMJR Jerry Rice 10.00 25.00
HMJR2 Josh Reed 4.00 10.00
HMJW Javon Walker 5.00 12.00
HMKJ Keyshawn Johnson 4.00 10.00
HMKS Kordell Stewart SP/161 5.00 12.00
HMKW Kurt Warner 5.00 12.00
HMLC Laveranues Coles 4.00 10.00
HMLT LaDainian Tomlinson 6.00 15.00
HMMF Marshall Faulk 5.00 12.00
HMMW Marquise Walker 3.00 8.00
HMPR Patrick Ramsey SP/331 5.00 12.00
HMPW Peter Warrick 4.00 10.00
HMRM Randy Moss SP/62 10.00 25.00
HMRW Ricky Williams 4.00 10.00
HMSD Stephen Davis 4.00 10.00
HMTB Tom Brady 12.00 30.00
HMTC Tim Couch 3.00 8.00
HMTC2 Trung Canidate 3.00 8.00
HMTD T.J. Duckett 5.00 12.00
HMTH Torry Holt 5.00 12.00
HMTO Terrell Owens 5.00 12.00
HMWG William Green 4.00 10.00

2002 Hot Prospects Hot Tandems Memorabilia

STATED PRINT RUN 100 SER.#'d SETS
UNPRICED RED HOT PRINT RUN 10
ABJR Antonio Bryant 8.00 20.00
Josh Reed
ABRW Aaron Brooks 6.00 15.00
Ricky Williams
AGCD Ahman Green 6.00 15.00
Corey Dillon
ALJR Ashley Lelie 6.00 15.00
Josh Reed
ALTC Ashley Lelie 6.00 15.00
Trung Canidate
ARJW Antwaan Randle El 8.00 20.00
Javon Walker
ATBU Anthony Thomas 8.00 20.00
Brian Urlacher
BFCM Brett Favre 20.00 50.00
Curtis Martin
CPDF Clinton Portis 6.00 15.00
DeShaun Foster
DCRM Daunte Culpepper 8.00 20.00
Randy Moss
DFCM DeShaun Foster 8.00 20.00
Curtis Martin
DMAB Donovan McNabb 8.00 20.00
Aaron Brooks
DMDC Donovan McNabb 8.00 20.00
Daunte Culpepper
DMTC Donovan McNabb 8.00 20.00
Tim Couch
DSMW Donte Stallworth 8.00 20.00
Marquise Walker
EGTD Eddie George 8.00 20.00
T.J. Duckett
ESMF Emmitt Smith 20.00 50.00
Marshall Faulk
ESWG Emmitt Smith 20.00 50.00
William Green
JGAB Jabar Gaffney 8.00 20.00
Antonio Bryant
JGAG Jeff Garcia 6.00 15.00
Ahman Green
JGLT Jeff Garcia 10.00 25.00
LaDainian Tomlinson
JRBU Jerry Rice 15.00 40.00
Brian Urlacher
JRDS Jerry Rice 15.00 40.00
Donte Stallworth
KJMW Keyshawn Johnson 6.00 15.00
Marquise Walker
KSAR Kordell Stewart 8.00 20.00
Antwaan Randle El
KSTC Kordell Stewart 6.00 15.00
Tim Couch
LCJB Laveranues Coles 8.00 20.00
Jabar Gaffney
LTMM LaDainian Tomlinson 6.00 15.00
Maurice Morris
PWCD Peter Warrick 6.00 15.00
Corey Dillon
RCJW Reche Caldwell 8.00 20.00
Javon Walker
RCPR Reche Caldwell 8.00 20.00
Patrick Ramsey
RMTO Randy Moss 8.00 20.00
Terrell Owens
RWAT Ricky Williams 6.00 15.00
Anthony Thomas
SDEG Stephen Davis 6.00 15.00
Eddie George
SDLC Stephen Davis 6.00 15.00
Laveranues Coles
TBJH Tom Brady 20.00 50.00
Joey Harrington
TBKW Tom Brady 20.00 50.00
Kurt Warner
TCPR Tim Couch 8.00 20.00
Patrick Ramsey
THMF Torry Holt 8.00 20.00
Marshall Faulk
THTC Torry Holt 8.00 20.00
Trung Caniddate
TOBF Terrell Owens 20.00 50.00
Brett Favre
WGTD William Green 8.00 20.00
T.J.Duckett

2002 Hot Prospects Sweet Selections

STATED ODDS 1:15
1 David Carr 1.00 2.50
2 Julius Peppers 2.00 5.00
3 Joey Harrington 1.00 2.50
4 Donte Stallworth 1.00 2.50
5 William Green .75 2.00
6 T.J. Duckett 1.00 2.50
7 Ashley Lelie .75 2.00
8 Javon Walker 1.00 2.50
9 Patrick Ramsey 1.00 2.50
10 Jabar Gaffney 1.00 2.50

2003 Hot Prospects

Released in November of 2003, this set originally consisted of 120-cards, including 80-veterans and 40-rookies. The overall rookie odds were 1:4. Rookies 81-91 were issued as exchange cards in packs redeemable for a card featuring an authentic player autograph serial numbered to 400. Rookies 92-103 featured game worn jersey swatches and were serial numbered to 750. Rookies 104-109 were issued as exchange cards in packs redeemable for a card featuring an authentic player autograph serial numbered to 400. Rookies 110-120 were serial numbered to 1250. Boxes contained 15 packs of 4 cards and the SRP was $4.99. Ultimately Fleer never redeemed any of the signed rookies from the set so those have been removed from the checklist below leaving a complete skip-numbered set of 103-cards.

COMP.SET w/o SP's (80) 7.50 20.00
92-103 JSY ROOKIE PRINT RUN 750
110-120 ROOKIE PRINT RUN 1250
OVERALL ROOKIE STATED ODDS 1:4
1 Emmitt Smith 1.00 2.50
2 Terrell Owens .40 1.00
3 Tiki Barber .40 1.00
4 Trent Green .30 .75
5 Quincy Morgan .25 .60
6 Eric Moulds .30 .75
7 Simeon Rice .25 .60
8 Hines Ward .40 1.00
9 Michael Bennett .30 .75
10 Donald Driver .40 1.00
11 Stephen Davis .30 .75
12 Steve McNair .40 1.00
13 David Boston .25 .60
14 Deuce McAllister .30 .75
15 Marvin Harrison .40 1.00
16 Peerless Price .25 .60
17 Matt Hasselbeck .30 .75
18 Jerry Rice .75 2.00
19 Junior Seau .40 1.00
20 Clinton Portis .30 .75
21 Fred Taylor .30 .75
22 William Green .25 .60
23 Warrick Dunn .30 .75
24 Koren Robinson .30 .75
25 Jeremy Shockey .40 1.00
26 Chris Chambers .30 .75
27 Brett Favre 1.00 2.50
28 Julius Peppers .40 1.00
29 Eddie George .30 .75
30 Todd Pinkston .25 .60
31 Tom Brady 1.00 2.50
32 Edgerrin James .40 1.00
33 Chad Johnson .40 1.00
34 Laveranues Coles .25 .60
35 LaDainian Tomlinson .40 1.00
36 Priest Holmes .40 1.00
37 Shannon Sharpe .40 1.00
38 Jamal Lewis .30 .75
39 Warren Sapp .30 .75
40 Tim Brown .40 1.00
41 Kerry Collins .30 .75
42 Jimmy Smith .30 .75
43 Chad Hutchinson .25 .60
44 Marcel Shipp .25 .60
45 Jeff Garcia .30 .75
46 Donovan McNabb .40 1.00
47 Randy Moss .40 1.00
48 Ahman Green .30 .75
49 Travis Henry .25 .60
50 Brad Johnson .30 .75
51 Tommy Maddox .30 .75
52 Aaron Brooks .30 .75
53 Peyton Manning .75 2.00
54 Brian Urlacher .40 1.00
55 Rod Gardner .25 .60
56 Chad Pennington .40 1.00
57 Ricky Williams .30 .75
58 James Stewart .25 .60
59 Todd Heap .30 .75
60 Marshall Faulk .40 1.00
61 Corey Dillon .30 .75
62 Michael Vick .50 1.25
63 Shaun Alexander .30 .75
64 Curtis Martin .40 1.00
65 Mark Brunell .30 .75
66 Joey Harrington .25 .60
67 Drew Bledsoe .40 1.00
68 Keyshawn Johnson .40 1.00
69 Jerome Bettis .40 1.00
70 Daunte Culpepper .30 .75
71 David Carr .30 .75
72 Marty Booker .30 .75
73 Patrick Ramsey .30 .75
74 Drew Brees .40 1.00
75 Donte Stallworth .25 .60
76 Jake Plummer .30 .75
77 Ray Lewis .40 1.00
78 Kurt Warner .40 1.00
79 Rich Gannon .30 .75
80 Tony Gonzalez .40 1.00
92 Dallas Clark JSY RC 5.00 12.00
93 Terence Newman JSY RC 2.50 6.00
94 Rex Grossman JSY RC 3.00 8.00
95 Kelley Washington JSY RC 2.00 5.00
96 Kyle Boller JSY RC 3.00 8.00
97 Carson Palmer JSY RC 6.00 15.00
98 Charles Rogers JSY RC 2.50 6.00
99 Chris Simms JSY RC 3.00 8.00
100 Larry Johnson JSY RC 3.00 8.00
101 Andre Johnson JSY RC 8.00 20.00
102 Taylor Jacobs JSY RC 2.00 5.00
103 Byron Leftwich JSY RC 3.00 8.00
110 Tyrone Calico RC 1.25 3.00
111 Billy McMullen RC 1.00 2.50
112 Jerome McDougle RC 1.00 2.50
113 Willis McGahee RC 2.00 5.00
114 Anquan Boldin RC 2.50 6.00
115 Artose Pinner RC 1.00 2.50
116 Kevin Williams RC 1.50 4.00
117 Bethel Johnson RC 1.00 2.50
118 Quentin Griffin RC 1.25 3.00
119 Nate Burleson RC 1.25 3.00
120 DeWayne Robertson RC 1.25 3.00

2003 Hot Prospects Cream of the Crop

COMPLETE SET (15) 15.00 40.00
STATED ODDS 1:5

1 Byron Leftwich .75 2.00
2 Charles Rogers .60 1.50
3 Carson Palmer 1.50 4.00
4 Taylor Jacobs .50 1.25
5 Bryant Johnson .75 2.00
6 Kyle Boller .75 2.00
7 Rex Grossman .75 2.00
8 Andre Johnson 2.00 5.00
9 Kelley Washington .50 1.25
10 Larry Johnson .75 2.00
11 Willis McGahee 1.00 2.50
12 Chris Simms .75 2.00
13 Jason Witten 2.00 5.00
14 Anquan Boldin 1.25 3.00
15 Quentin Griffin .60 1.50

2003 Hot Prospects Hot Materials

STATED PRINT RUN 150 SER.#'d SETS
*RED HOT/50: .6X TO 1.5X JSY/150
RED HOT PRINT RUN 50 SER.#'d SETS
OVERALL MEMORABILIA ODDS 1:6
HMBF Brett Favre 10.00 25.00
HMBU Brian Urlacher 4.00 10.00
HMCP Clinton Portis 3.00 8.00
HMCP2 Chad Pennington 4.00 10.00
HMDB Drew Bledsoe 4.00 10.00
HMDB2 Drew Brees 4.00 10.00
HMDC Daunte Culpepper 3.00 8.00
HMDC2 David Carr 3.00 8.00
HMDM Deuce McAllister 3.00 8.00
HMDM2 Donovan McNabb 4.00 10.00
HMDS Donte Stallworth 2.50 6.00
HMEJ Edgerrin James 4.00 10.00
HMJG Jeff Garcia 3.00 8.00
HMJH Joey Harrington 2.50 6.00
HMJL Jamal Lewis 3.00 8.00
HMJR Jerry Rice 8.00 20.00
HMJS Jeremy Shockey 4.00 10.00
HMKW Kurt Warner 4.00 10.00
HMLT LaDainian Tomlinson 4.00 10.00
HMMF Marshall Faulk 4.00 10.00
HMMV Michael Vick 5.00 12.00
HMPM Peyton Manning 8.00 20.00
HMPR Patrick Ramsey 3.00 8.00
HMRG Rich Gannon 3.00 8.00
HMRG Rod Gardner 2.50 6.00
HMRM Randy Moss 4.00 10.00
HMRW Ricky Williams 3.00 8.00
HMSA Shaun Alexander 3.00 8.00
HMTB Tom Brady 10.00 25.00
HMTO Terrell Owens 4.00 10.00

2003 Hot Prospects Hot Tandems

STATED PRINT RUN 100 SER.#'d SETS
UNPRICED RED HOTS SER.#'d TO 10
OVERALL MEMORABILIA ODDS 1:6
BFTB Brett Favre 20.00 50.00
Tom Brady
BUJR Brian Urlacher 12.00 30.00
Jerry Rice
CPJL Clinton Portis 5.00 12.00
Jamal Lewis
CPMV Chad Pennington 8.00 20.00
Michael Vick
CPRW Chad Pennington 6.00 15.00
Ricky Williams
DBDB Drew Bledsoe 6.00 15.00
Drew Brees
DCDC Daunte Culpepper 5.00 12.00
David Carr
DCPR David Carr 5.00 12.00
Patrick Ramsey
DMRM Donovan McNabb 6.00 15.00
Randy Moss
DMSA Deuce McAllister 5.00 12.00
Shaun Alexander
EJLT Edgerrin James 6.00 15.00
LaDainian Tomlinson
JGDM Jeff Garcia 6.00 15.00
Donovan McNabb
JHDB Joey Harrington 6.00 15.00
Drew Bledsoe
JHDC Joey Harrington 5.00 12.00
Daunte Culpepper
JRRM Jerry Rice 12.00 30.00
Randy Moss
JSBF Jeremy Shockey 15.00 40.00
Brett Favre
JSRG Jeremy Shockey 6.00 15.00
Rod Gardner
KWRG Kurt Warner 6.00 15.00
Rich Gannon
LTJL LaDainian Tomlinson 6.00 15.00
Jamal Lewis
MFMV Marshall Faulk 8.00 20.00
Michael Vick
PMBU Peyton Manning 12.00 30.00
Brian Urlacher
PMKW Peyton Manning 12.00 30.00
Kurt Warner
RWMF Ricky Williams 6.00 15.00
Marshall Faulk
TODM Terrell Owens 6.00 15.00
Deuce McAllister
TODS Terrell Owens 6.00 15.00
Donte Stallworth

2003 Hot Prospects Hot Triple Patches

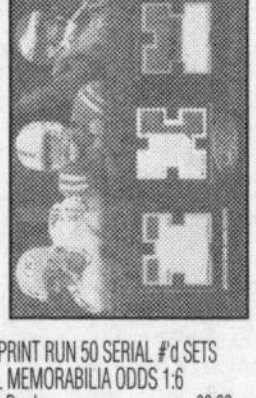

STATED PRINT RUN 50 SERIAL #'d SETS
OVERALL MEMORABILIA ODDS 1:6
BGP Tom Brady 30.00 80.00
Jeff Garcia
Chad Pennington
CRB David Carr 12.00 30.00
Patrick Ramsey
Drew Brees
FMM Brett Favre 30.00 80.00
Peyton Manning
Donovan McNabb
HBC Joey Harrington 12.00 30.00
Drew Bledsoe
Daunte Culpepper
JLA Edgerrin James 12.00 30.00
Jamal Lewis
Shaun Alexander
JTL Edgerrin James 12.00 30.00
LaDainian Tomlinson
Jamal Lewis
MMM Donovan McNabb 25.00 60.00
Randy Moss
Peyton Manning
MPT Deuce McAllister 12.00 30.00
Clinton Portis
LaDainian Tomlinson
ORM Terrell Owens 25.00 60.00
Jerry Rice
Randy Moss
SFB Jeremy Shockey 30.00 80.00
Brett Favre
Tom Brady
SSG Jeremy Shockey 12.00 30.00
Donte Stallworth
Rod Gardner
UWF Brian Urlacher 12.00 30.00
Ricky Williams
Marshall Faulk
VHC Michael Vick 15.00 40.00
Joey Harrington
Daunte Culpepper
WFV Ricky Williams 15.00 40.00
Marshall Faulk
Michael Vick
WGB Kurt Warner 12.00 30.00
Rich Gannon
Drew Bledsoe

2003 Hot Prospects Playergraphs Redemption

STATED PRINT RUN 200 SER.#'d SETS
*REDS: .6X TO 1.5X BASIC AUTOS
RED HOTS PRINT RUN 50 SER.#'d SETS
OVERALL AUTOGRAPH ODDS 1:60
PDM Donovan McNabb AU 20.00 50.00
PJH Joey Harrington AU 20.00 50.00
PMB Michael Bennett AU 10.00 25.00
PPB Plaxico Burress AU 10.00 25.00

2003 Hot Prospects Sweet Selections

COMPLETE SET (10) 12.00 30.00
STATED ODDS 1:15
1 Carson Palmer 1.50 4.00
David Carr
2 LaDainian Tomlinson 1.25 3.00
Jamal Lewis
3 Joey Harrington 1.25 3.00
Steve McNair
4 Brian Urlacher 1.25 3.00
Fred Taylor
5 Michael Vick 2.50 6.00
Peyton Manning
6 Torry Holt 1.25 3.00
Tim Brown
7 Ricky Williams 1.25 3.00
Junior Seau
8 Donovan McNabb 1.25 3.00
Marshall Faulk
9 Plaxico Burress 1.00 2.50
David Boston
10 Keyshawn Johnson 1.25 3.00
Drew Bledsoe

2003 Hot Prospects Sweet Selections Jerseys

STATED PRINT RUN 325 SER.#'d SETS
OVERALL MEMORABILIA ODDS 1:6
BUFT Brian Urlacher 4.00 10.00
Fred Taylor
DMMF Donovan McNabb 4.00 10.00
Marshall Faulk
JHSM Joey Harrington 4.00 10.00
Steve McNair
KJDB Keyshawn Johnson 4.00 10.00
Drew Bledsoe
LTJL LaDainian Tomlinson 4.00 10.00
Jamal Lewis
MVPM Michael Vick 8.00 20.00
Peyton Manning
PBDB Plaxico Burress 3.00 8.00
David Boston
PMDC Carson Palmer 5.00 12.00
David Carr
RWJS Ricky Williams 4.00 10.00
Junior Seau
THTB Torry Holt 4.00 10.00
Tim Brown

2004 Hot Prospects

Fleer Hot Prospects initially released in early August 2004. The base set consists of 112-cards including 24-jersey autographed rookie cards, 8-jersey rookie cards, and 10-rookies serial numbered of 1000. Hobby boxes contained 15-packs of 5-cards and carried an S.R.P. of $7.99 per pack while retail boxes contained 24-packs of 5-cards and carried an S.R.P. of $2.99. Two parallel sets and a variety of inserts can be found seeded in hobby and retail packs highlighted by the Notable Notations Autograph inserts. Some signed cards were issued via mail-in exchange or redemption cards. Card #92 Luke McCown was one of those exchange cards in packs, but the live card was never released.

COMP.SET w/o SP's (70) 7.50 20.00
71-94 AU JSY RC ODDS 1:20H, 1:840R
95-102 JSY RC ODDS 1:42H, 1:420R
95-102 JSY RC PRINT RUN 350 #'d SETS
103-112 ROOKIE ODDS 1:18H, 1:1440R
103-112 RC PRINT RUN 1000 SER. #'d SETS
UNPRICED WHITE HOT PRINT RUN 1
1 Donovan McNabb .30 .75
2 Charlie Garner .25 .60
3 Tim Rattay .20 .50
4 Drew Brees .30 .75
5 Jerry Rice .60 1.50
6 Aaron Brooks .25 .60
7 Chris Chambers .25 .60
8 Byron Leftwich .25 .60
9 Andre Johnson .30 .75
10 Edgerrin James .25 .60
11 Charles Rogers .20 .50
12 Quentin Griffin .20 .50
13 Carson Palmer .30 .75
14 Ray Lewis .30 .75
15 Clinton Portis .30 .75
16 Marc Bulger .25 .60
17 Matt Hasselbeck .25 .60
18 Plaxico Burress .25 .60
19 Priest Holmes .30 .75
20 David Carr .20 .50
21 Ahman Green .25 .60
22 Roy Williams S .25 .60
23 Travis Henry .20 .50
24 Michael Vick .40 1.00
25 Eddie George .25 .60
26 Marshall Faulk .30 .75
27 Kevan Barlow .20 .50
28 Shaun Alexander .25 .60
29 Hines Ward .30 .75
30 Anquan Boldin .30 .75
31 Chad Pennington .30 .75
32 Randy Moss .30 .75
33 Fred Taylor .25 .60
34 Marvin Harrison .30 .75
35 Joey Harrington .25 .60
36 Rich Gannon .25 .60
37 Deuce McAllister .25 .60
38 Deion Branch .25 .60
39 Tony Gonzalez .30 .75
40 Brett Favre .75 2.00
41 Keyshawn Johnson .25 .60
42 Lee Suggs .25 .60
43 Jake Delhomme .25 .60
44 Rex Grossman .25 .60
45 Drew Bledsoe .30 .75
46 Warrick Dunn .25 .60
47 Steve McNair .30 .75
48 Torry Holt .25 .60
49 Brian Westbrook .30 .75
50 Santana Moss .25 .60
51 Jeremy Shockey .25 .60
52 Daunte Culpepper .25 .60
53 Jeff Garcia .25 .60
54 Stephen Davis .25 .60
55 Eric Moulds .25 .60
56 Emmitt Smith .75 2.00
57 Keenan McCardell .20 .50
58 LaDainian Tomlinson .30 .75
59 Terrell Owens .30 .75
60 Curtis Martin .30 .75
61 Joe Horn .25 .60
62 Tiki Barber .30 .75
63 Tom Brady .60 1.50
64 Ricky Williams .25 .60
65 Peyton Manning .60 1.50
66 Jake Plummer .25 .60
67 Chad Johnson .30 .75
68 Brian Urlacher .30 .75
69 Jamal Lewis .25 .60
70 Laveranues Coles .20 .50
71 Tatum Bell JSY AU/350 RC 10.00 25.00
72 Bernard Berrian JSY AU/344 RC 20.00 40.00
73 Michael Clayton JSY AU/350 RC 8.00 20.00
74 Lee Evans JSY AU/350 RC 12.00 30.00
75 Larry Fitzgerald JSY AU/140 RC 60.00 120.00
76 Devery Henderson JSY AU/350 RC 12.00 30.00
77 Drew Henson JSY AU/331 RC 8.00 20.00
78 Steven Jackson JSY AU/300 RC 30.00 80.00
79 Michael Jenkins No AU
80 Greg Jones JSY AU/289 RC 8.00 20.00
81 Kevin Jones JSY AU/278 RC 8.00 20.00
82 J.P. Losman JSY AU/350 RC 10.00 25.00
83 Eli Manning JSY AU/350 RC 100.00 175.00
84 Chris Perry JSY AU/350 RC 10.00 25.00
85 Philip Rivers JSY AU/350 RC 50.00 100.00
86 Ben Roethlisberger JSY AU/150 RC 150.00 250.00
87 Reggie Williams JSY AU/350 RC 10.00 25.00
88 Roy Williams JSY AU/350 RC 12.00 30.00
89 Kellen Winslow Jr. JSY AU/50 RC 40.00 100.00
90 Rashaun Woods JSY AU/350 RC 8.00 20.00
91 Julius Jones JSY AU/350 RC 10.00 25.00
92 Luke McCown No AU
93 Keary Colbert JSY AU/349 RC 8.00 20.00
94 Matt Schaub JSY AU/120 RC 40.00 100.00
95 Cedric Cobbs JSY RC 3.00 8.00
96 Darius Watts JSY RC 3.00 8.00
97 DeAngelo Hall JSY RC 5.00 12.00
98 Derrick Hamilton JSY RC 3.00 8.00
99 Devard Darling JSY RC 3.00 8.00
100 Ben Troupe JSY RC 4.00 10.00
101 Mewelde Moore JSY RC 4.00 10.00
102 Ben Watson JSY RC 5.00 12.00
103 Sean Taylor RC 3.00 8.00
104 Ricky Ray RC 1.50 4.00
105 Carlos Francis RC 1.00 2.50
106 Samie Parker RC 1.00 2.50
107 Jerricho Cotchery RC 1.25 3.00
108 Ernest Wilford RC 1.25 3.00
109 Craig Krenzel RC 1.25 3.00
110 Robert Gallery RC 1.50 4.00
111 Dunta Robinson RC 1.00 2.50
112 Jonathan Vilma RC 1.50 4.00

2004 Hot Prospects Red Hot

*VETS 1-72: 6X TO 15X BASIC CARDS
*ROOK.71-94: .5X TO 1.2X AU RC/278-350
*ROOK.71-94: .4X TO 1X AU RC/50-150
*ROOKIES 95-102: .8X TO 2X
*ROOKIES 103-112: 1.2X TO 3X
OVERALL PARALLEL ODDS 1:26H, 1:420R
RED HOT PRINT RUN 50 SER.#'d SETS
89 Kellen Winslow JSY AU 40.00 100.00

2004 Hot Prospects Alumni Ink

STATED PRINT RUN 50 SER.#'d SETS
UNPRICED RED HOT PRINT RUN 10
UNPRICED WHITE HOT PRINT RUN 1
CPBL Chad Pennington 20.00 50.00
Byron Leftwich
DHMC Devery Henderson 12.00 30.00
Michael Clayton
DHTB Drew Henson 100.00 175.00
Tom Brady
DMEM Deuce McAllister 60.00 120.00
Eli Manning
LECC Lee Evans 10.00 25.00
Chris Chambers
TBRW Tatum Bell 8.00 20.00
Rashaun Woods

2004 Hot Prospects Double Team Autograph Patches

AUTO PRINT RUN 25 SER.#'d SETS
UNPRICED RED HOT PRINT RUN 5
UNPRICED WHITE HOT PRINT RUN 1
DTKJ Kevin Jones 15.00 40.00
DTMS Matt Schaub 40.00 100.00
DTRW Roy Williams WR 20.00 50.00
DTSJ Steven Jackson 30.00 80.00

2004 Hot Prospects Double Team Jersey

STATED PRINT RUN 100 SER.#'d SETS
*RED HOT/25: .8X TO 2X BASIC JSY/100
RED HOT PRINT RUN 25 SER.#'d SETS
UNPRICED WHITE HOT PRINT RUN 1
*PATCH/50: .6X TO 1.5X BASIC JSY/100
PATCH PRINT RUN 50 SER.#'d SETS
*RH PATCH/10: 1X TO 2.5X JSY/100
UNPRICED WHITE HOT PATCH PRINT RUN 1
DTDF DeShaun Foster 4.00 10.00
DTDH Drew Henson 3.00 8.00
DTEM Eli Manning 25.00 50.00
DTKJ Kevin Jones 4.00 10.00
DTKW Kellen Winslow Jr. 5.00 12.00
DTLE Lee Evans 5.00 12.00
DTMS Matt Schaub 10.00 25.00
DTQG Quentin Griffin 3.00 8.00
DTRW Roy Williams WR 5.00 12.00
DTSJ Steven Jackson 8.00 20.00

2004 Hot Prospects Draft Rewind

COMPLETE SET (30) 25.00 60.00
STATED ODDS 1:5
1DR Donovan McNabb 1.00 2.50
2DR Jerry Rice 2.00 5.00
3DR Andre Johnson 1.00 2.50
4DR Edgerrin James .75 2.00
5DR Charles Rogers .60 1.50
6DR Carson Palmer 1.00 2.50
7DR David Carr .60 1.50
8DR Roy Williams S .75 2.00
9DR Michael Vick 1.25 3.00
10DR Eddie George .75 2.00
11DR Marshall Faulk 1.00 2.50
12DR Anquan Boldin 1.00 2.50
13DR Chad Pennington 1.00 2.50
14DR Randy Moss 1.00 2.50
15DR Marvin Harrison 1.00 2.50
16DR Joey Harrington .75 2.00
17DR Deuce McAllister .75 2.00
18DR Brett Favre 2.50 6.00
19DR Steve McNair 1.00 2.50
20DR Jeremy Shockey .75 2.00
21DR Daunte Culpepper .75 2.00
22DR Emmitt Smith 2.50 6.00
23DR LaDainian Tomlinson 1.00 2.50
24DR Terrell Owens 1.00 2.50
25DR Eli Manning 4.00 10.00
26DR Ricky Williams .75 2.00
27DR Peyton Manning 2.00 5.00
28DR Chad Johnson 1.00 2.50
29DR Brian Urlacher 1.00 2.50
30DR Jamal Lewis .75 2.00

2004 Hot Prospects Draft Rewind Jersey

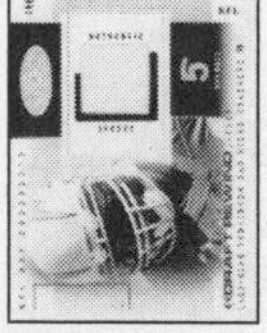

STATED PRINT RUN 101-189
*RED HOT/10: .8X TO 2X BASIC JSY
UNPRICED WHITE HOT PRINT RUN 1
*PATCH/43-99: .5X TO 1.2X BASIC JSY
*PATCH/31-33: .6X TO 1.5X BASIC JSY
*PATCH/21-29: .8X TO 2X BASIC JSY
*PATCH/11-19: 1X TO 2.5X BASIC JSY
UNPRICED RED HOT PATCH PRINT RUN 5
DRAB Anquan Boldin/154 5.00 12.00
DRAJ Andre Johnson/103 5.00 12.00
DRBF Brett Favre/133 12.00 30.00
DRBU Brian Urlacher/109 6.00 15.00
DRCJ Chad Johnson/136 5.00 12.00
DRCP Carson Palmer/101 5.00 12.00
DRCP2 Chad Pennington/118 5.00 12.00
DRCR Charles Rogers/102 3.00 8.00
DRDC David Carr/101 3.00 8.00
DRDC2 Daunte Culpepper/111 4.00 10.00
DRDM Deuce McAllister/123 4.00 10.00
DRDM2 Donovan McNabb/102 5.00 12.00
DREG Eddie George/114 4.00 10.00
DREJ Edgerrin James/104 4.00 10.00
DREM Eli Manning/101 20.00 50.00
DRES Emmitt Smith/117 10.00 25.00
DRJH Joey Harrington/103 4.00 10.00
DRJL Jamal Lewis/105 4.00 10.00
DRJR Jerry Rice/116 10.00 25.00
DRJS Jeremy Shockey/114 4.00 10.00
DRLT LaDainian Tomlinson/105 5.00 12.00
DRMF Marshall Faulk/102 5.00 12.00
DRMH Marvin Harrison/119 5.00 12.00
DRMV Michael Vick/101 6.00 15.00
DRPM Peyton Manning/101 10.00 25.00
DRRM Randy Moss/121 5.00 12.00
DRRW Ricky Williams/105 4.00 10.00
DRRW2 Roy Williams S/108 4.00 10.00
DRSM Steve McNair/103 5.00 12.00
DRTO Terrell Owens/189 5.00 12.00

2004 Hot Prospects Hot Materials

STATED PRINT RUN 500 SER.#'d SETS
*RED HOT/50: .8X TO 2X BASIC JSY/500
RED HOT PRINT RUN 50 SER.#'d SETS
UNPRICED WHITE HOT PRINT RUN 1
HMAB Anquan Boldin 3.00 8.00
HMBF Brett Favre 8.00 20.00
HMBR Ben Roethlisberger 15.00 40.00
HMBU Brian Urlacher 3.00 8.00
HMCP Carson Palmer 3.00 8.00
HMCP2 Chad Pennington 3.00 8.00
HMDC David Carr 2.00 5.00
HMDC2 Daunte Culpepper 2.50 6.00
HMDH Drew Henson 2.00 5.00
HMDM Donovan McNabb 3.00 8.00
HMDM2 Deuce McAllister 2.50 6.00
HMEJ Edgerrin James 2.50 6.00
HMEM Eli Manning 15.00 40.00
HMES Emmitt Smith 8.00 20.00
HMJH Joey Harrington 2.50 6.00
HMJL Jamal Lewis 2.50 6.00
HMJR Jerry Rice 6.00 15.00
HMJS Jeremy Shockey 2.50 6.00
HMKJ Kevin Jones 2.50 6.00
HMKW Kellen Winslow Jr. 3.00 8.00
HMLE Lee Evans 3.00 8.00
HMLF Larry Fitzgerald 6.00 15.00
HMLT LaDainian Tomlinson 3.00 8.00
HMMF Marshall Faulk 3.00 8.00
HMMH Marvin Harrison 3.00 8.00
HMMV Michael Vick 5.00 12.00
HMPM Peyton Manning 6.00 15.00
HMPR Philip Rivers 10.00 25.00
HMRM Randy Moss 3.00 8.00
HMRW Ricky Williams 2.50 6.00
HMRW2 Roy Williams WR 2.50 6.00
HMRW3 Reggie Williams 2.50 6.00
HMSM Steve McNair 3.00 8.00
HMTB Tom Brady 6.00 15.00
HMTO Terrell Owens 3.00 8.00

2004 Hot Prospects Notable Newcomers

COMPLETE SET (15) 20.00 50.00
STATED ODDS 1:15
1NN Eli Manning 6.00 15.00
2NN Larry Fitzgerald 2.50 6.00
3NN Ben Roethlisberger 6.00 15.00
4NN Roy Williams WR 1.00 2.50
5NN Kellen Winslow Jr. 1.00 2.50
6NN Kevin Jones .75 2.00
7NN Reggie Williams .75 2.00
8NN Michael Clayton .75 2.00
9NN Phillip Rivers 4.00 10.00
10NN Lee Evans 1.00 2.50
11NN Drew Henson .60 1.50
12NN Steven Jackson 1.50 4.00
13NN Chris Perry .75 2.00
14NN Greg Jones .60 1.50
15NN J.P. Losman .75 2.00

2004 Hot Prospects Notable Notations Autographs

STATED PRINT RUN 50 SER.#'d SETS
1NN Eli Manning 75.00 150.00
2NN Larry Fitzgerald 40.00 80.00
3NN Ben Roethlisberger 75.00 150.00
4NN Roy Williams WR 12.00 30.00
7NN Reggie Williams 10.00 25.00
8NN Michael Clayton
9NN Philip Rivers 40.00 80.00
10NN Lee Evans 12.00 30.00
11NN Drew Henson 8.00 20.00
12NN Steven Jackson 20.00 50.00
13NN Chris Perry 10.00 25.00
15NN J.P. Losman 10.00 25.00

2006 Hot Prospects

This 224-card set was released in October, 2006. The set was issued into the hobby five-card packs, with a $9.99 SRP which came 15 packs to a box. Cards numbered 1-100 feature veterans in team alphabetical order while cards numbered 101-224 feature 2006 rookies. Those Rookie Cards are broken into the follwing groupings: Cards numbered 101-160 were issued to a stated print run of 1150 serial numbered sets; cards numbered 161-190 which were signed by the player were issued to a stated print run of 299 serial numbered sets. Cards numbered 201-222 contained both player-worn swatches and an signature were issued to a stated print of 999 serial numbered sets and the set concludes with cards 223 and 224 which also had player-worn swatches and autographs and those two cards were issued to a stated print run of 399 serial numbered sets.

COMP.SET w/o RC's (100) 10.00 25.00
101-160 PRINT RUN 1150 SER.#'d SETS
161-190 AU PRINT RUN 299 SER.#'d SETS
191-200 JSY AU PRINT RUN 175 SETS
201-222 JSY AU PRINT RUN 999 SETS
223-224 JSY AU PRINT RUN 399 SETS
1 Edgerrin James .25 .60
2 Larry Fitzgerald .30 .75
3 Anquan Boldin .25 .60
4 Michael Vick .30 .75
5 Warrick Dunn .25 .60
6 Roddy White .25 .60
7 Jamal Lewis .25 .60
8 Steve McNair .25 .60
9 Mark Clayton .25 .60
10 Willis McGahee .25 .60
11 Lee Evans .25 .60
12 J.P. Losman .25 .60
13 Jake Delhomme .25 .60
14 Steve Smith .30 .75
15 DeShaun Foster .25 .60
16 Rex Grossman .25 .60
17 Thomas Jones .25 .60
18 Brian Urlacher .30 .75
19 Carson Palmer .30 .75
20 Chad Johnson .25 .60
21 Rudi Johnson .25 .60
22 T.J. Houshmandzadeh .25 .60
23 Braylon Edwards .25 .60
24 Charlie Frye .25 .60
25 Reuben Droughns .25 .60
26 Julius Jones .20 .50
27 Terrell Owens .30 .75
28 Drew Bledsoe .30 .75
29 Jake Plummer .25 .60
30 Tatum Bell .20 .50
31 Javon Walker .25 .60
32 Kevin Jones .20 .50
33 Roy Williams WR .25 .60
34 Mike Williams .20 .50
35 Brett Favre .60 1.50
36 Donald Driver .30 .75
37 Ahman Green .25 .60
38 David Carr .20 .50
39 Domanick Davis .20 .50
40 Andre Johnson .30 .75
41 Peyton Manning .50 1.25
42 Reggie Wayne .25 .60
43 Marvin Harrison .30 .75
44 Matt Jones .20 .50
45 Greg Jones .20 .50
46 Byron Leftwich .25 .60
47 Larry Johnson .25 .60
48 Trent Green .25 .60
49 Eddie Kennison .20 .50
50 Tony Gonzalez .25 .60
51 Daunte Culpepper .25 .60
52 Ronnie Brown .30 .75
53 Chris Chambers .25 .60
54 Troy Williamson .20 .50
55 Chester Taylor .25 .60
56 Koren Robinson .20 .50
57 Tom Brady .50 1.25
58 Corey Dillon .25 .60
59 Deion Branch .25 .60
60 Drew Brees .30 .75
61 Donte Stallworth .20 .50
62 Deuce McAllister .25 .60
63 Tiki Barber .30 .75
64 Eli Manning .40 1.00
65 Plaxico Burress .25 .60
66 Chad Pennington .25 .60
67 Curtis Martin .30 .75
68 Justin McCareins .20 .50
69 Randy Moss .30 .75
70 LaMont Jordan .25 .60
71 Aaron Brooks .25 .60
72 Jerry Porter .20 .50
73 Donovan McNabb .30 .75
74 Brian Westbrook .25 .60
75 Reggie Brown .20 .50
76 Ben Roethlisberger .40 1.00
77 Hines Ward .30 .75
78 Willie Parker .25 .60
79 LaDainian Tomlinson .30 .75
80 Philip Rivers .30 .75
81 Antonio Gates .30 .75
82 Alex Smith QB .30 .75
83 Frank Gore .30 .75
84 Antonio Bryant .20 .50
85 Shaun Alexander .25 .60
86 Matt Hasselbeck .25 .60
87 Nate Burleson .20 .50
88 Torry Holt .25 .60
89 Marc Bulger .25 .60
90 Steven Jackson .30 .75
91 Kevin Curtis .25 .60
92 Cadillac Williams .25 .60
93 Chris Simms .25 .60
94 Joey Galloway .25 .60
95 Drew Bennett .25 .60
96 David Givens .25 .60
97 Billy Volek .20 .50
98 Clinton Portis .30 .75
99 Santana Moss .25 .60
100 Antwaan Randle El .25 .60
101 Donte Whitner RC 3.00 8.00
102 Haloti Ngata RC 3.00 8.00
103 Kamerion Wimbley RC 3.00 8.00
104 Jason Allen RC 2.50 6.00
105 Bobby Carpenter RC 2.00 5.00
106 Antonio Cromartie RC 3.00 8.00
107 Tamba Hali RC 3.00 8.00
108 Manny Lawson RC 2.50 6.00
109 Davin Joseph RC 2.50 6.00
110 Johnathan Joseph RC 2.50 6.00
111 John McCargo RC 2.00 5.00
112 Nick Mangold RC 2.50 6.00
113 Marcus Vick RC 2.00 5.00
114 Rocky McIntosh RC 2.50 6.00
115 Tim Day RC 2.50 6.00
116 Danieal Manning RC 3.00 8.00
117 Roman Harper RC 2.50 6.00
118 Josh Lay RC 2.00 5.00
119 Chris Gocong RC 2.50 6.00
120 Greg Blue RC 2.50 6.00
121 Bernard Pollard RC 2.50 6.00
122 Richard Marshall RC 2.50 6.00
123 Tony Scheffler RC 3.00 8.00
124 Dawan Landry RC 3.00 8.00
125 Darryl Tapp RC 2.50 6.00
126 Anthony Schlegel RC 2.50 6.00
127 Jon Alston RC 2.00 5.00
128 Pat Watkins RC 2.50 6.00
129 Anthony Smith RC 3.00 8.00
130 David Thomas RC 2.50 6.00
131 David Pittman RC 2.50 6.00
132 Frostee Rucker RC 2.50 6.00
133 Troy Bergeron RC 2.50 6.00
134 Freddie Keiaho RC 2.50 6.00
135 Stephen Tulloch RC 2.50 6.00
136 Gerris Wilkinson RC 2.00 5.00
137 Eric Smith RC 2.50 6.00
138 Garrett Mills RC 3.00 8.00
139 Skyler Green RC 2.00 5.00
140 Brodie Croyle RC 3.00 8.00
141 P.J. Daniels RC 2.00 5.00
142 Marques Hagans RC 2.00 5.00
143 Jamar Williams RC 2.50 6.00
144 Ingle Martin RC 2.50 6.00
145 Charles Spencer RC 2.00 5.00
146 Andrew Whitworth RC 2.00 5.00
147 Jeff King RC 2.50 6.00
148 Taitusi Lutui RC 2.50 6.00
149 Quinn Sypniewski RC 2.50 6.00
150 P.J. Pope RC 3.00 8.00
151 Wali Lundy RC 2.50 6.00
152 Jonathan Orr RC 2.50 6.00
153 Jonathan Lewis RC 2.00 5.00
154 Adam Jennings RC 2.50 6.00
155 Jeff Webb RC 2.50 6.00
156 Cedric Humes RC 2.00 5.00
157 T.J. Williams RC 3.00 8.00
158 Todd Watkins RC 2.00 5.00
159 Bennie Brazell RC 2.50 6.00
160 Marques Colston RC 6.00 15.00
161 DonTrell Moore AU RC 5.00 12.00
162 Brad Smith AU RC 6.00 15.00
163 Gerald Riggs AU RC 5.00 12.00
164 Chad Greenway AU RC 6.00 15.00
165 Cory Rodgers AU RC 5.00 12.00
166 Darrell Hackney AU RC 5.00 12.00
167 D.J. Shockley AU RC 5.00 12.00
168 Dominique Byrd AU RC 5.00 12.00
169 Joseph Addai AU RC 10.00 25.00
170 Darnell Bing AU RC 5.00 12.00
171 Mike Bell AU RC 6.00 15.00
172 Ernie Sims AU RC 5.00 12.00
173 Brodrick Bunkley AU RC 5.00 12.00
174 Hank Baskett AU RC 6.00 15.00
175 Jerome Harrison AU RC 6.00 15.00
176 Jimmy Williams AU RC 6.00 15.00
177 D'Brickashaw Ferguson AU RC 6.00 15.00
178 Josh Betts AU RC 5.00 12.00
179 Leonard Pope AU RC 6.00 15.00
180 Terrence Whitehead AU RC 5.00 12.00
181 Mathias Kiwanuka AU RC 6.00 15.00
182 Ashton Youboty AU RC 4.00 10.00
183 DeMeco Ryans AU RC 6.00 15.00
184 Thomas Howard AU RC 5.00 12.00
185 Owen Daniels AU RC 6.00 15.00
186 Reggie McNeal AU RC 5.00 12.00
187 Tye Hill AU RC 4.00 10.00
188 Will Blackmon AU RC 5.00 12.00
189 Winston Justice AU RC 5.00 12.00
190 Greg Jennings AU RC 15.00 40.00
191 Matt Leinart AU/175 RC 12.00 30.00
192 Vince Young AU/175 RC 30.00 60.00
193 Jay Cutler AU/175 RC 40.00 80.00
194 Reggie Bush AU/175 RC 40.00 80.00
195 Laurence Maroney AU/175 RC 8.00 20.00
196 LenDale White AU/175 RC 8.00 20.00
197 DeAngelo Williams AU/175 RC 12.00 30.00
198 Vernon Davis AU/175 RC 15.00 30.00
199 Santonio Holmes AU/175 RC 12.00 30.00
200 Sinorice Moss AU/175 RC 10.00 25.00
201 Jason Avant JSY AU RC 4.00 10.00
202 Brian Calhoun JSY AU RC 4.00 10.00
203 Kellen Clemens JSY AU RC 5.00 12.00
204 Demetrius Williams JSY AU RC 5.00 12.00
205 Brandon Williams JSY AU RC 4.00 10.00
206 Maurice Drew JSY AU RC 10.00 25.00
207 Travis Wilson JSY AU RC 4.00 10.00
208 Joe Klopfenstein JSY AU RC 4.00 10.00
209 Derek Hagan JSY AU RC 5.00 12.00
210 A.J. Hawk JSY AU RC 6.00 15.00
211 Michael Huff JSY AU RC 5.00 12.00
212 Tarvaris Jackson JSY AU RC 6.00 15.00
213 Omar Jacobs JSY AU RC 4.00 10.00
214 Mario Williams JSY AU RC 6.00 15.00
215 Marcedes Lewis JSY AU RC 6.00 15.00
216 Brandon Marshall JSY AU RC 8.00 20.00
217 Chad Jackson JSY AU RC 4.00 10.00
218 Jerious Norwood JSY AU RC 5.00 12.00
219 Michael Robinson JSY AU RC 5.00 12.00
220 Maurice Stovall JSY AU RC 4.00 10.00
221 Leon Washington JSY AU RC 5.00 12.00
222 Charlie Whitehurst JSY AU RC 6.00 15.00
223 Kelly Jennings JSY AU/399 RC 6.00 15.00
224 Marcus McNeill JSY AU/399 RC 6.00 15.00

2006 Hot Prospects Red Hot

*VETERANS 1-100: 6X TO 15X BASIC CARDS
*ROOKIES 101-160: .8X TO 2X BASIC CARDS
*AU ROOK.161-190: .8X TO 2X
1-190 PRINT RUN 50
*FB AU ROOK.191-199: .4X TO 1X
*FB AU ROOK.201-222: .6X TO 1.5X
191-222 FB AUTO PRINT RUN 99

2006 Hot Prospects White Hot

UNPRICED PRINT RUN 1 SET

2006 Hot Prospects Red Hot Autographed Rookie Material Letters

STATED PRINT RUN 25 SER.#'d SETS
UNPRICED SET REDEMPTION #'d TO 5
191 Matt Leinart 20.00 50.00
192 Vince Young 25.00 60.00
193 Jay Cutler 50.00 120.00
194 Reggie Bush 50.00 120.00
195 Laurence Maroney 15.00 40.00
196 LenDale White 15.00 40.00
197 DeAngelo Williams 25.00 60.00
198 Vernon Davis
199 Santonio Holmes 25.00 60.00
200 Sinorice Moss

2006 Hot Prospects Endorsements

UNPRICED WHITE HOT PRINT RUN 1
HPAC Alge Crumpler 4.00 10.00
HPAG Antonio Gates 6.00 15.00
HPAH A.J. Hawk SP 25.00 50.00
HPBA Ronde Barber 6.00 15.00
HPBB Brodrick Bunkley SP 6.00 15.00
HPBC Brian Calhoun 6.00 15.00
HPBE Braylon Edwards 6.00 15.00
HPBF Brett Favre SP 75.00 150.00
HPBG Bruce Gradkowski 6.00 15.00
HPBL Byron Leftwich SP
HPBM Brandon Marshall SP 10.00 25.00
HPBR Ben Roethlisberger SP 40.00 80.00
HPBS Brad Smith 6.00 15.00
HPBU Reggie Bush SP 30.00 80.00
HPBW Brandon Williams SP 6.00 15.00
HPCF Charlie Frye 6.00 15.00
HPCG Chad Greenway 6.00 15.00
HPCI Clint Ingram 6.00 15.00
HPCJ Chad Jackson SP 8.00 20.00
HPCP Carson Palmer SP 40.00 80.00
HPCR Cory Rodgers 4.00 10.00
HPCS Chris Simms 6.00 15.00
HPCU Kevin Curtis 4.00 10.00
HPCW Cadillac Williams SP
HPDB Drew Bennett 4.00 10.00
HPDF D'Brickashaw Ferguson 6.00 15.00
HPDG David Givens 4.00 10.00
HPDH Darrell Hackney 3.00 8.00
HPDM Deuce McAllister 4.00 10.00
HPDO Drew Olson 3.00 8.00
HPDR Drew Bledsoe SP 15.00 30.00
HPDS D.J. Shockley 6.00 15.00
HPDW DeAngelo Williams SP 20.00 50.00
HPEM Eli Manning SP
HPFO DeShaun Foster 4.00 10.00
HPGJ Greg Jennings 10.00 25.00
HPGL Greg Lee 3.00 8.00
HPGR Gerald Riggs 4.00 10.00
HPHA Andre Hall 4.00 10.00
HPHB Hank Baskett 6.00 15.00
HPHI Tye Hill SP 6.00 15.00
HPJA Joseph Addai SP 12.00 30.00
HPJB Josh Betts 4.00 10.00
HPJC Jay Cutler SP 40.00 80.00

HPJH Jerome Harrison 6.00 15.00
HPJI Jimmy Williams 4.00 10.00
HPJJ Julius Jones SP
HPJN Jerious Norwood SP 12.00 30.00
HPJO Greg Jones 3.00 8.00
HPJW Jason Witten 15.00 30.00
HPKC Kellen Clemens SP
HPKJ Keyshawn Johnson 10.00 25.00
HPKO Kyle Orton 3.00 8.00
HPLA LaMont Jordan 4.00 10.00
HPLJ Larry Johnson SP 12.00 30.00
HPLM Laurence Maroney SP 8.00 20.00
HPLP Leonard Pope 4.00 10.00
HPLT LaDainian Tomlinson SP 40.00 80.00
HPLW LenDale White SP
HPMA Derrick Mason 4.00 10.00
HPMC Michael Clayton 4.00 10.00
HPMI Mike Williams 4.00 10.00
HPML Matt Leinart SP 20.00 50.00
HPMM Muhsin Muhammad 4.00 10.00
HPMN Martin Nance 3.00 8.00
HPMV Michael Vick SP 25.00 50.00
HPMW Mario Williams SP
HPOD Owen Daniels 6.00 15.00
HPPM Peyton Manning 50.00 100.00
HPPR Philip Rivers SP 20.00 40.00
HPRB Reggie Brown 4.00 10.00
HPRJ Rudi Johnson 6.00 15.00
HPRM Ryan Moats 4.00 10.00
HPRO Ronnie Brown SP
HPRW Reggie Wayne 6.00 15.00
HPSH Santonio Holmes SP 15.00 40.00
HPSM Sinorice Moss SP
HPTA Lofa Tatupu 10.00 25.00
HPTG Trent Green SP
HPTH T.J. Houshmandzadeh 6.00 15.00
HPTI Tiki Barber SP 15.00 30.00
HPTJ Thomas Jones 6.00 15.00
HPVD Vernon Davis SP 8.00 20.00
HPVY Vince Young SP 25.00 60.00
HPWI Demetrius Williams SP
HPWJ Winston Justice 4.00 10.00
HPWP Willie Parker SP 15.00 40.00

2006 Hot Prospects Endorsements Red Hot

*RED HOT: 1X TO 2.5X BASE AUTO
*RED HOT: .6X TO 1.5X BASE AUTO SP
RED HOT PRINT RUN 25 SER.#'d SETS
HPPM Peyton Manning 100.00 175.00

2006 Hot Prospects Dual Endorsements

STATED PRINT RUN 25 SER.#'d SETS
UNPRICED RED HOT PRINT RUN 10
UNPRICED WHITE HOT PRINT RUN 1
AC Brian Calhoun 20.00 50.00
Joseph Addai
BA Reggie Brown 15.00 40.00
Jason Avant
BH Ronnie Brown 20.00 50.00
Derek Hagan
CF D'Brickashaw Ferguson 20.00 50.00
Kellen Clemens
DG Antonio Gates 20.00 50.00
Vernon Davis
EF John Elway 175.00 300.00
Brett Favre
FW DeShaun Foster 20.00 50.00
DeAngelo Williams
GJ Chad Greenway 20.00 50.00
Tarvaris Jackson
HB Darnell Bing
Michael Huff
HS A.J. Hawk 30.00 60.00
Ernie Sims
HW Jimmy Williams
Tye Hill
JD Greg Jones 30.00 60.00
Maurice Drew
JH Omar Jacobs 25.00 60.00
Santonio Holmes
JJ Thomas Jones 15.00 40.00
Julius Jones
JS Keyshawn Johnson 15.00 40.00
Steve Smith
JT Larry Johnson 50.00 120.00
LaDainian Tomlinson
KB Dominique Byrd 12.00 30.00
Joe Klopfenstein
KM Mathias Kiwanuka 15.00 40.00
Sinorice Moss
LP Carson Palmer 20.00 50.00
Matt Leinart
MB Brandon Williams 15.00 40.00
Michael Robinson
MJ Chad Jackson 15.00 40.00
Laurence Maroney
MM Peyton Manning 150.00 250.00
Eli Manning
OM Muhsin Muhammad 15.00 40.00
Kyle Orton
RW Philip Rivers 25.00 60.00
Charlie Whitehurst
SC Michael Clayton
Maurice Stovall
SW Brad Smith 20.00 50.00
Leon Washington
WB Mario Williams 40.00 100.00
Reggie Bush
WF Jason Witten 30.00 60.00
Anthony Fasano
WR DeMeco Ryans 20.00 50.00
Mario Williams
YW LenDale White 25.00 60.00
Vince Young

2006 Hot Prospects Triple Endorsements

COMMON CARD 25.00 50.00
UNLISTED STARS 30.00 60.00
STATED PRINT RUN 25 SER.#'d SETS
UNPRICED RED HOT PRINT RUN 10
UNPRICED WHITE HOT PRINT RUN 1
CJW Charlie Whitehurst 30.00 60.00
Kellen Clemens
Tarvaris Jackson
CMJ Chad Jackson 75.00 150.00
Jay Cutler
Laurence Maroney
HTI Rocket Ismail 50.00 80.00
Paul Hornung
Joe Theismann
JWB Rudi Johnson 30.00 60.00
Ronnie Brown
Cadillac Williams
MBM Tiki Barber 75.00 125.00
Eli Manning
Sinorice Moss
RPH Ben Roethlisberger 60.00 120.00
Willie Parker
Santonio Holmes
SRO Chris Simms 30.00 60.00
Philip Rivers
Kyle Orton
WAW DeAngelo Williams 40.00 100.00
Joseph Addai
LenDale White
WHH A.J. Hawk 30.00 60.00
Mario Williams
Michael Huff
YLC Jay Cutler 75.00 150.00
Matt Leinart
Vince Young

2006 Hot Prospects Prospectus

STATED PRINT RUN 299 SER.#'d SETS
PRAH A.J. Hawk 1.00 2.50
PRBC Brian Calhoun .60 1.50
PRBM Brandon Marshall 1.00 2.50
PRBW Brandon Williams .60 1.50
PRCJ Chad Jackson .60 1.50
PRCW Charlie Whitehurst 1.00 2.50
PRDH Derek Hagan .75 2.00
PRDW DeAngelo Williams 1.25 3.00
PRJA Jason Avant .60 1.50
PRJK Joe Klopfenstein .60 1.50
PRKC Kellen Clemens .75 2.00
PRLE Matt Leinart 1.00 2.50
PRLM Laurence Maroney .75 2.00
PRLW Leon Washington .75 2.00
PRMD Maurice Drew 1.50 4.00
PRMH Michael Huff .75 2.00
PRML Marcedes Lewis 1.00 2.50
PRMR Michael Robinson .75 2.00
PRMS Maurice Stovall .60 1.50
PRMW Mario Williams 1.00 2.50
PROJ Omar Jacobs .60 1.50
PRRB Reggie Bush 2.00 5.00
PRSH Santonio Holmes 1.25 3.00
PRSM Sinorice Moss 1.00 2.50
PRTJ Tarvaris Jackson 1.00 2.50
PRTW Travis Wilson .60 1.50
PRVD Vernon Davis 1.25 3.00
PRVY Vince Young 1.25 3.00
PRWH LenDale White .75 2.00
PRWI Demetrius Williams .75 2.00

2006 Hot Prospects Prospectus Jerseys

PRAH A.J. Hawk/275 6.00 15.00
PRBC Brian Calhoun/250 2.50 6.00
PRBM Brandon Marshall/200 2.50 6.00
PRBW Brandon Williams/250 2.50 6.00
PRCJ Chad Jackson/250 2.50 6.00
PRCW Charlie Whitehurst/275 2.50 6.00
PRDH Derek Hagan/275 2.50 6.00
PRDW DeAngelo Williams/250 6.00 15.00
PRJA Jason Avant/250 2.50 6.00
PRJK Joe Klopfenstein/250 2.50 6.00
PRKC Kellen Clemens/200 2.50 6.00
PRLE Matt Leinart/199 6.00 15.00
PRLM Laurence Maroney/250 3.00 8.00
PRLW Leon Washington/250 3.00 8.00
PRMD Maurice Drew/250 5.00 12.00
PRMH Michael Huff/275 2.50 6.00
PRML Marcedes Lewis/250 2.50 6.00
PRMR Michael Robinson/250 2.50 6.00
PRMS Maurice Stovall/275 2.50 6.00
PRMW Mario Williams/250 3.00 8.00
PROJ Omar Jacobs/275 2.50 6.00
PRRB Reggie Bush/100 10.00 25.00
PRSH Santonio Holmes/250 4.00 10.00
PRSM Sinorice Moss/250 2.50 6.00
PRTJ Tarvaris Jackson/250 2.50 6.00
PRTW Travis Wilson/250 2.50 6.00
PRVD Vernon Davis/250 4.00 10.00
PRVY Vince Young/199 8.00 20.00
PRWH LenDale White/250 4.00 10.00
PRWI Demetrius Williams/400 2.50 6.00

2006 Hot Prospects Retrospective

STATED PRINT RUN 699 SER.#'d SETS
REAG Antonio Gates 1.50 4.00
REAR Aaron Rodgers 3.00 8.00
REAS Alex Smith QB 1.50 4.00
REBA Tiki Barber 1.50 4.00
REBE Braylon Edwards 1.25 3.00
REBF Brett Favre 3.00 8.00
REBJ Brad Johnson 1.25 3.00
REBL Byron Leftwich 1.25 3.00
REBR Ben Roethlisberger 2.00 5.00
REBU Brian Urlacher 1.50 4.00
RECB Cedric Benson 1.25 3.00
RECJ Chad Johnson 1.25 3.00
RECP Carson Palmer 1.50 4.00
RECR Charles Rogers 1.25 3.00
RECS Chris Simms 1.25 3.00
RECW Cadillac Williams 1.25 3.00
REDB Drew Bledsoe 1.50 4.00
REDC Daunte Culpepper 1.25 3.00
REDF DeShaun Foster 1.25 3.00
REDH Dante Hall 1.25 3.00
REDM Donovan McNabb 1.50 4.00
REDR Drew Brees 1.50 4.00
REEJ Edgerrin James 1.25 3.00
REEM Eli Manning 2.00 5.00
REGR Trent Green 1.25 3.00
REHM Heath Miller 1.25 3.00
REIB Isaac Bruce 1.25 3.00
REJD Jake Delhomme 1.25 3.00
REJH Joey Harrington 1.00 2.50
REJO LaMont Jordan 1.25 3.00
REJP Jerry Porter 1.00 2.50
REJS Junior Seau 1.50 4.00
REKJ Kevin Jones 1.00 2.50
REKM Keenan McCardell 1.25 3.00
REKO Kyle Orton 1.50 4.00
RELF Larry Fitzgerald 1.50 4.00
RELJ Larry Johnson 1.25 3.00
RELO Lofa Tatupu 1.25 3.00
RELT LaDainian Tomlinson 1.50 4.00
REMB Mark Brunell 1.25 3.00
REMC Deuce McAllister 1.25 3.00
REMO Ryan Moats 1.00 2.50
REMV Michael Vick 1.50 4.00
REMW Mike Williams 1.00 2.50
REPH Priest Holmes 1.25 3.00
REPM Peyton Manning 2.50 6.00
RERB Ronnie Brown 1.50 4.00
RERM Randy Moss 1.50 4.00
RERS Rod Smith 1.25 3.00
RESA Shaun Alexander 1.25 3.00
RESH Jeremy Shockey 1.50 4.00
RESJ Steven Jackson 1.50 4.00
RETA Tatum Bell 1.00 2.50
RETB Tom Brady 2.50 6.00
RETD T.J. Duckett 1.00 2.50
RETG Tony Gonzalez 1.25 3.00
RETO Terrell Owens 1.50 4.00
RETW Troy Williamson 1.00 2.50
REWM Willis McGahee 1.25 3.00

2006 Hot Prospects Retrospective Jerseys

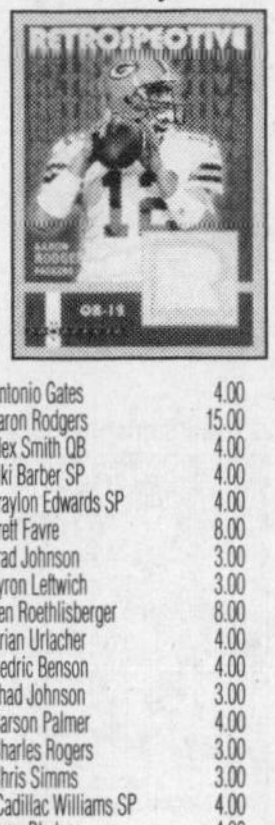

REAG Antonio Gates 4.00 10.00
REAR Aaron Rodgers 15.00 40.00
REAS Alex Smith QB 4.00 10.00
REBA Tiki Barber SP 4.00 10.00
REBE Braylon Edwards SP 4.00 10.00
REBF Brett Favre 8.00 20.00
REBJ Brad Johnson 3.00 8.00
REBL Byron Leftwich 3.00 8.00
REBR Ben Roethlisberger 8.00 20.00
REBU Brian Urlacher 4.00 10.00
RECB Cedric Benson 4.00 10.00
RECJ Chad Johnson 3.00 8.00
RECP Carson Palmer 4.00 10.00
RECR Charles Rogers 3.00 8.00
RECS Chris Simms 3.00 8.00
RECW Cadillac Williams SP 4.00 10.00
REDB Drew Bledsoe 4.00 10.00
REDC Daunte Culpepper 4.00 10.00
REDF DeShaun Foster SP 3.00 8.00
REDH Dante Hall 3.00 8.00
REDM Donovan McNabb 4.00 10.00
REDR Drew Brees 3.00 8.00
REEJ Edgerrin James 4.00 10.00
REEM Eli Manning 5.00 12.00
REGR Trent Green SP 3.00 8.00
REHM Heath Miller 4.00 10.00
REIB Isaac Bruce 3.00 8.00
REJD Jake Delhomme 3.00 8.00
REJH Joey Harrington 3.00 8.00
REJO LaMont Jordan SP 3.00 8.00
REJP Jerry Porter 3.00 8.00
REJS Junior Seau 4.00 10.00
REKJ Kevin Jones 4.00 10.00
REKM Keenan McCardell 2.50 6.00
REKO Kyle Orton SP 3.00 8.00
RELF Larry Fitzgerald 4.00 10.00
RELJ Larry Johnson SP 4.00 10.00
RELO Lofa Tatupu SP 3.00 8.00
RELT LaDainian Tomlinson SP 4.00 10.00
REMB Mark Brunell 3.00 8.00
REMC Deuce McAllister 3.00 8.00
REMO Ryan Moats 2.50 6.00
REMV Michael Vick SP 3.00 8.00
REMW Mike Williams SP 4.00 10.00
REPH Priest Holmes 3.00 8.00
REPM Peyton Manning SP 6.00 15.00
RERB Ronnie Brown SP 4.00 10.00
RERM Randy Moss 4.00 10.00
RERS Rod Smith 3.00 8.00
RESA Shaun Alexander 4.00 10.00
RESH Jeremy Shockey 4.00 10.00
RESJ Steven Jackson 4.00 10.00
RETA Tatum Bell 3.00 8.00
RETB Tom Brady 6.00 15.00
RETD T.J. Duckett 2.50 6.00
RETG Tony Gonzalez 3.00 8.00
RETO Terrell Owens 4.00 10.00
RETW Troy Williamson 3.00 8.00
REWM Willis McGahee 4.00 10.00

1974 Houston Texans WFL Team Issue 8X10

The photos measure roughly 8" x 10" and include black and white images with the player's name in the lower left below the photo, his position centered, and the team name on the right side below the photo. The backs are blank.

1 Garland Boyette 7.50 15.00
2 Joe Robb 7.50 15.00

1999 Houston ThunderBears AFL

COMPLETE SET (27) 7.50 15.00
1 Hunter Adams .30 .75
2 Rodney Blackshear .30 .75
3 Marcus Bradley .30 .75
4 Ben Bronson .30 .75
5 David Caldwell .30 .75
6 Joe Carollo .30 .75
7 Terence Davis .30 .75
8 Clint Dolezel .60 1.50
9 Murray Garrett .30 .75
10 Dietrich Griffin .30 .75
11 Robert Hall .30 .75
12 Michael Harrison .30 .75
13 Lucas Yarnell .30 .75
14 Bernard Holmes .30 .75
15 Ed Howard .30 .75
16 Conrad Lewis .30 .75
17 Steve Thonn CO .30 .75
18 Junior Soli .30 .75
19 Shawn Washington .30 .75
20 Jeff Mitchell .30 .75
21 Walter Shelton .30 .75
22 Justin Skinner .30 .75
23 Verone McKinley .30 .75
24 Clayton Baker .30 .75
25 Larry Jones .30 .75
26 Team Photo .30 .75
27 Cover Card .30 .75

1938 Huskies Cereal

These cards are actually entire backs of Huskies cereal boxes from the late 1930s. Each box back features an artist's rendering of the University of Washington Huskies coach Jimmy Phelan and one NFL player (or just a single player) at the top along with brief bios on each. A series of smaller drawings appears below the two that were intended to be cut out and used to form a moving picture simulating football action when flipped by the collector.

1 Jimmy Phelan 350.00 600.00
Sammy Baugh
2 Dutch Clark 300.00 500.00
3 Jimmy Phelan 350.00 600.00
Don Hutson

1994 Images

This premier edition of Classic Images features 125 standard-size cards. Production was limited to 1,994 cases. The full-bleed color action photos on the fronts have a metallic sheen to them. The player's name is printed toward the bottom, with the "Images" logo between the first and last name. A second black-and-white photo appears on the back, along with the player's name, position, team name and statistics, as well as a small color headshot on the left side. The cards were sold six cards to a pack, with no jumbo or periodical versions produced. Rookie Cards in this set include Derrick Alexander, Isaac Bruce, Trent Dilfer, Marshall Faulk, William Floyd, Greg Hill, Charles Johnson, Byron Bam Morris, Errict Rhett, Darnay Scott and Heath Shuler. The Emmitt Smith (one per box chiptopper) and Drew Bledsoe Throwbacks (random insert in packs) NFL Experience preview cards were included in the Images product. An Emmitt Smith Images promo card was produced as well and is priced below.

COMPLETE SET (125) 15.00 40.00
1 Emmitt Smith 1.25 3.00
2 Reggie White .30 .75
3 Michael Haynes .15 .40
4 Chris Warren .15 .40
5 Jeff George .30 .75
6 Sean Gilbert .07 .20
7 Ricky Watters .15 .40
8 Eric Metcalf .15 .40
9 Randall Cunningham .30 .75
10 Tim Brown .30 .75
11 Trent Dilfer RC .75 2.00
12 Marshall Faulk RC 3.00 8.00
13 David Klingler .07 .20
14 Barry Foster .07 .20
15 John Elway 1.50 4.00
16 Joe Montana 1.50 4.00
17 Rodney Hampton .15 .40
18 Todd Steussie RC .15 .40
19 Bruce Smith .30 .75
20 Wayne Gandy RC .07 .20
21 Anthony Miller .15 .40
22 Reggie Brooks .15 .40
23 Johnny Johnson .07 .20
24 Byron Bam Morris RC .15 .40
25 Drew Bledsoe .75 2.00
26 Jeff Hostetler .15 .40
27 Alvin Harper .15 .40
28 Cris Carter .40 1.00
29 Bert Emanuel RC .30 .75
30 Errict Rhett RC .30 .75
31 Scott Mitchell .15 .40
32 Deion Sanders .40 1.00
33 Lewis Tillman .07 .20
34 Tim Bowens RC .15 .40
35 Charles Haley .15 .40
36 Stan Humphries .15 .40
37 Haywood Jeffires .15 .40
38 Andre Reed .15 .40
39 Charles Johnson RC .30 .75
40 Ronald Moore .07 .20
41 Jim Everett .15 .40
42 Greg Hill RC .30 .75
43 Thurman Thomas .30 .75
44 Willie McGinest RC .30 .75
45 Aaron Glenn RC .30 .75
46 Erric Pegram .07 .20
47 Terry Kirby .30 .75
48 Warren Moon .30 .75
49 Clyde Simmons .07 .20
50 Eric Turner .07 .20
51 Heath Shuler RC .30 .75
52 Rickey Jackson .07 .20
53 Johnnie Morton RC .75 2.00
54 Charlie Garner RC .75 2.00
55 Mark Collins .07 .20
56 Mike Pritchard .07 .20
57 Bryant Young RC .50 1.25
58 Joe Johnson RC .07 .20
59 Erik Kramer .15 .40
60 Barry Sanders 1.25 3.00
61 Rod Woodson .15 .40
62 Dave Brown .15 .40
63 Gary Brown .07 .20
64 Brett Favre 1.50 4.00
65 Isaac Bruce RC 2.50 6.00
66 Boomer Esiason .15 .40
67 Jim Harbaugh .30 .75
68 Jackie Harris .07 .20
69 Art Monk .15 .40
70 Jamir Miller RC .15 .40
71 Neil O'Donnell .30 .75
72 Neil Smith .15 .40
73 Junior Seau .30 .75
74 Jerome Bettis .50 1.25
75 Bernard Williams RC .07 .20
76 Jeff Burris RC .15 .40
77 Henry Ellard .15 .40
78 Reggie Cobb .07 .20
79 Shante Carver RC .07 .20
80 Terry Allen .15 .40
81 Cortez Kennedy .15 .40
82 Trev Alberts RC .15 .40
83 Michael Irvin .30 .75
84 Herschel Walker .15 .40
85 Dan Marino 1.50 4.00
86 Dave Meggett .07 .20
87 Herman Moore .30 .75
88 Darnay Scott RC .40 1.00
89 Dewayne Washington RC .15 .40
90 Rob Fredrickson RC .15 .40
91 Rick Mirer .30 .75
92 Thomas Lewis RC .15 .40
93 Chris Miller .07 .20
94 Marion Butts .07 .20
95 Sam Adams RC .15 .40
96 Jerry Rice .75 2.00
97 Ben Coates .15 .40
98 David Palmer RC .30 .75
99 Antonio Langham RC .15 .40
100 Curtis Conway .30 .75
101 Derrick Thomas .30 .75
102 Ken Norton Jr. .15 .40
103 Ronnie Lott .15 .40
104 Sterling Sharpe .15 .40
105 Troy Aikman .75 2.00
106 Shannon Sharpe .15 .40
107 Natrone Means .30 .75
108 Derek Brown RBK .07 .20
109 Dan Wilkinson RC .15 .40
110 Andre Rison .15 .40
111 Quentin Coryatt .07 .20
112 Cody Carlson .07 .20
113 William Floyd RC .30 .75
114 Marcus Allen .30 .75
115 Steve Young .60 1.50
116 Jim Kelly .30 .75
117 LeShon Johnson RC .15 .40
118 Irving Fryar .15 .40
119 Carl Pickens .15 .40
120 Keith Jackson .07 .20
121 John Thierry RC .07 .20
122 Vinny Testaverde .15 .40
123 Der.Alexander WR RC .30 .75
124 Seth Joyner .07 .20
125 Checklist .07 .20
IF1 Emmitt Smith Promo 1.00 2.50
Numbered IF1
TP1 Drew Bledsoe 25.00 50.00
NFL Experience Throwbacks
preview card
NNO Emmitt Smith 4.00 10.00
NFL Experience
Sneak Preview card

1994 Images All-Pro

COMPLETE SET (25) 100.00 200.00
STATED ODDS 1:12
A1 Heath Shuler 1.00 2.50
A2 Steve Young 3.00 8.00
A3 Trent Dilfer 2.50 6.00
A4 Troy Aikman 4.00 10.00
A5 Emmitt Smith 6.00 15.00
A6 Barry Sanders 6.00 15.00
A7 Jerome Bettis 2.50 6.00
A8 Errict Rhett 1.00 2.50
A9 Jerry Rice 4.00 10.00
A10 Michael Irvin 1.50 4.00
A11 Andre Rison .75 2.00
A12 Sterling Sharpe .75 2.00
A13 Reggie White 1.50 4.00
A14 Rick Mirer 1.50 4.00
A15 Drew Bledsoe 4.00 10.00
A16 John Elway 8.00 20.00
A17 Joe Montana 8.00 20.00
A18 Dan Marino 8.00 20.00
A19 Thurman Thomas 1.50 4.00
A20 Marshall Faulk 10.00 25.00
A21 Marcus Allen 1.50 4.00
A22 Charles Johnson 1.00 2.50
A23 Tim Brown 1.50 4.00
A24 Anthony Miller .75 2.00
A25 Derrick Thomas 1.50 4.00

1994-95 Images Update

COMPLETE SET (10) 30.00 60.00
126 Emmitt Smith 8.00 15.00
127 Troy Aikman 5.00 10.00
128 Steve Young 4.00 8.00
129 Deion Sanders 2.50 5.00
130 Ben Coates 2.00 4.00
131 Natrone Means 2.00 4.00
132 Drew Bledsoe 6.00 12.00
133 Cris Carter 2.50 5.00
134 Marshall Faulk 6.00 12.00
135 Errict Rhett 1.50 3.00

1995 Images Limited

Classic issued Images NFL as a 125-card set in two separate releases: Live (retail) and Limited (hobby). Each set had different action photos of the same players on 24-point micro-lined foil-board cards. A few cards at the end of each set were changed. Card fronts have a silver background with the player's name along the bottom of the card. The Live version also contains the word "Live!" along the left side of the card. Limited card backs feature a full bleed shot with the player's name on the left of the card and statistical information at the bottom. Live card backs contain a player shot in a diagonal photo with the player's name and statistics at the bottom. Rookie Cards in this set include Jeff Blake, Ki-Jana Carter, Kerry Collins, Joey Galloway, Curtis Martin, Steve McNair, Rashaan Salaam, Kordell Stewart, J.J. Stokes and Michael Westbrook. Another bonus feature was Hot Boxes, where each pack contained approximately 50% inserts. Hot Boxes were specially marked and could be found in every five cases. Drew Bledsoe Promo cards were produced and priced below.

COMPLETE SET (125) 10.00 25.00
1 Emmitt Smith .75 2.00
2 Steve Young .40 1.00
3 Drew Bledsoe .30 .75
4 Dan Marino 1.00 2.50
5 John Elway 1.00 2.50
6 Barry Sanders .75 2.00
7 Brett Favre 1.00 2.50
8 Troy Aikman .50 1.25
9 Jim Kelly .15 .40
10 Marshall Faulk .60 1.50
11 Jerry Rice .50 1.25
12 Warren Moon .07 .20
13 Jim Everett .02 .10
14 Rodney Hampton .07 .20
15 Jeff Hostetler .07 .20
16 Errict Rhett .07 .20
17 Jerome Bettis .15 .40
18 Byron Bam Morris .02 .10
19 Randall Cunningham .15 .40
20 Rick Mirer .07 .20
21 Natrone Means .07 .20
22 Jeff George .07 .20
23 Garrison Hearst .15 .40
24 Michael Irvin .15 .40
25 Cris Carter .15 .40
26 Irving Fryar .07 .20
27 Jeff Blake RC .30 .75
28 Bruce Smith .15 .40
29 Shannon Sharpe .07 .20
30 Steve Beuerlein .07 .20
31 Stan Humphries .07 .20
32 Chris Warren .07 .20
33 Ben Coates .07 .20
34 Boomer Esiason .07 .20
35 Trent Dilfer .15 .40
36 Chris Miller .02 .10
37 Dave Brown .07 .20
38 Herman Moore .15 .40
39 Anthony Miller .07 .20
40 Andre Reed .07 .20
41 Reggie White .15 .40
42 Darnay Scott .07 .20
43 Erik Kramer .02 .10
44 Leroy Hoard .02 .10
45 Fred Barnett .07 .20
46 Junior Seau .15 .40
47 Vinny Testaverde .07 .20
48 Gus Frerotte .07 .20
49 William Floyd .07 .20
50 Mo Lewis .02 .10
51 Tim Brown .15 .40
52 Greg Lloyd .07 .20
53 Chester McGlockton .07 .20
54 Heath Shuler .07 .20
55 Rod Woodson .07 .20
56 Don Beebe .02 .10
57 Carl Pickens .07 .20
58 Charles Haley .07 .20
59 Steve Bono .07 .20
60 Harvey Williams .02 .10
61 Greg Hill .07 .20
62 Eric Metcalf .07 .20
63 Mario Bates .07 .20
64 Terry Allen .07 .20
65 Michael Timpson .02 .10
66 Mark Stepnoski .02 .10
67 Jeff Lageman .02 .10
68 Robert Smith .15 .40
69 Eric Allen .02 .10
70 Ricky Watters .07 .20
71 Derek Loville .02 .10
72 Bernie Parmalee .07 .20
73 Bryce Paup .07 .20
74 Frank Reich .02 .10
75 Henry Thomas .02 .10
76 Craig Erickson .02 .10
77 Eric Green .02 .10
78 Dave Meggett .02 .10
79 Deion Sanders .30 .75
80 Herschel Walker .07 .20
81 Andre Rison .07 .20
82 Ki-Jana Carter RC .15 .40
83 Tony Boselli RC .15 .40
84 Steve McNair RC 1.25 3.00
85 Michael Westbrook RC .15 .40
86 Kerry Collins RC .75 2.00
87 Kevin Carter RC .15 .40
88 Warren Sapp RC .60 1.50
89 Joey Galloway RC .60 1.50
90 J.J. Stokes RC .15 .40
92 Kyle Brady RC .15 .40
93 Napoleon Kaufman RC .40 1.00
94 Tyrone Wheatley RC .40 1.00
95 Mike Mamula RC .02 .10
96 Desmond Howard .07 .20
97 James O. Stewart RC .40 1.00
98 Craig Newsome RC .02 .10
99 Ty Law RC 1.00 2.50
100 Ellis Johnson RC .02 .10
101 Hugh Douglas RC .15 .40
102 Mark Bruener RC .07 .20
103 Tyrone Poole .15 .40
104 Luther Elliss .02 .10
105 Mark Fields RC .15 .40
106 Frank Sanders RC .15 .40
107 Rashaan Salaam RC .07 .20
108 Craig Powell RC .02 .10
109 Sherman Williams RC .02 .10
110 Chad May RC .02 .10
111 Rob Johnson RC .30 .75
112 Todd Collins RC .50 1.25
113 Terrell Davis RC 1.00 2.50
114 Eric Zeier RC .15 .40
115 Curtis Martin RC 1.25 3.00
116 Kordell Stewart RC .60 1.50
117 Troy Vincent .02 .10
118 Ray Zellars RC .07 .20
119 Dave Krieg .02 .10
120 Mike Sherrard .02 .10
121 Willie Davis .02 .10
122 Robert Brooks .07 .20
123 Chris Sanders RC .07 .20
124 Checklist #1 .15 .40
Drew Bledsoe
125 Emmitt Smith CL .25 .60
LT1 Drew Bledsoe Promo .60 1.50
numbered LT1, ad back

1995 Images Limited/Live Die Cuts

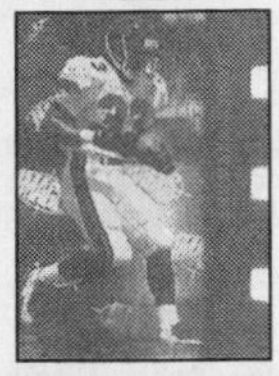

COMPLETE SET (30) 80.00 200.00
COMP.SERIES 1 (15) 30.00 80.00
COMP.SERIES 2 (15) 50.00 120.00
DC1-DC15 ODDS 1:99 LIMITED
DC16-DC30 ODDS 1:99 LIVE
DC1 Jim Kelly 2.50 6.00
DC2 Kerry Collins 3.00 8.00
DC3 Michael Irvin 2.00 5.00
DC4 Troy Aikman 6.00 15.00
DC5 John Elway 12.50 30.00
DC6 Barry Sanders 10.00 25.00
DC7 Marshall Faulk 2.50 6.00
DC8 James O. Stewart .75 2.00
DC9 Drew Bledsoe 2.00 5.00
DC10 Herman Moore 1.25 3.00
DC11 Byron Bam Morris .75 2.00
DC12 Jerry Rice 8.00 20.00
DC13 Joey Galloway 2.00 5.00
DC14 Rick Mirer 1.25 3.00
DC15 Errict Rhett 1.25 3.00
DC16 Rob Moore .75 2.00
DC17 Jeff George 1.25 3.00
DC18 Rashaan Salaam .75 2.00
DC19 Andre Rison 1.25 3.00
DC20 Emmitt Smith 12.50 30.00
DC21 Brett Favre 15.00 40.00
DC22 Dan Marino 15.00 40.00
DC23 Warren Moon 1.25 3.00
DC24 Dave Brown .75 2.00
DC25 Napoleon Kaufman .75 2.00
DC26 Natrone Means 1.25 3.00
DC27 Steve Young 5.00 12.00
DC28 Reggie White 2.00 5.00
DC29 Jerome Bettis 2.00 5.00
DC30 Michael Westbrook .75 2.00

1995 Images Limited Focused Gold

COMPLETE SET (30) 40.00 80.00
*LIVE BLUE: .4X TO 1X LIMITED GOLD
ONE PER BOX LIMITED/LIVE
F1 Rashaan Salaam .60 1.50
Erik Kramer
F2 Kerry Collins 1.00 2.50
Frank Reich
F3 Jim Kelly 1.25 3.00
Andre Reed
F4 Jeff George .60 1.50
Craig Heyward
F5 Garrison Hearst .75 2.00
Dave Krieg
F6 Barry Sanders 4.00 10.00
Herman Moore
F7 John Elway 5.00 12.00
Shannon Sharpe
F8 Emmitt Smith 4.00 10.00
Troy Aikman
F9 Andre Rison .60 1.50
Leroy Hoard
F10 Carl Pickens 1.25 3.00
Jeff Blake
F11 Willie Davis .60 1.50
Steve Bono
F12 James O.Stewart 1.25 3.00
Steve Beuerlein
F13 Marshall Faulk 3.00 8.00
Craig Erickson
F14 Steve McNair 2.50 6.00
Chris Chandler
F15 Brett Favre 6.00 12.00
Reggie White
F16 Rodney Hampton .60 1.50
Dave Brown
F17 Mario Bates .60 1.50
Jim Everett
F18 Drew Bledsoe 1.50 4.00
Ben Coates
F19 Warren Moon 1.25 3.00
Cris Carter
F20 Dan Marino 5.00 12.00
Irving Fryar
F21 Natrone Means .75 2.00
Stan Humphries
F22 Byron Bam Morris .60 1.50
Kevin Greene
F23 Ricky Watters .75 2.00
Randall Cunningham
F24 Tim Brown .60 1.50
Jeff Hostetler
F25 Boomer Esiason .60 1.50
Kyle Brady
F26 Michael Westbrook .75 2.00
Terry Allen
F27 Errict Rhett .75 2.00
Trent Dilfer
F28 Jerome Bettis 1.25 3.00
Kevin Carter
F29 Steve Young 4.00 8.00
Jerry Rice
F30 Joey Galloway 1.25 3.00
Rick Mirer

1995 Images Limited Icons

COMPLETE SET (20) 50.00 120.00
STATED ODDS 1:20 LIMITED
I1 Jim Kelly 1.25 2.50
I2 Rashaan Salaam .30 .75
I3 Andre Rison .60 1.25
I4 Troy Aikman 4.00 8.00
I5 Emmitt Smith 6.00 12.00
I6 John Elway 8.00 15.00
I7 Barry Sanders 6.00 12.00
I8 Brett Favre 8.00 15.00
I9 Marshall Faulk 5.00 10.00
I10 Irving Fryar .60 1.25
I11 Dan Marino 8.00 15.00
I12 Drew Bledsoe 2.50 5.00
I13 Rodney Hampton .60 1.25
I14 Ricky Watters .60 1.25
I15 Byron Bam Morris .25 .60
I16 Natrone Means .60 1.25
I17 Steve Young 3.00 6.00
I18 Jerry Rice 4.00 8.00
I19 Errict Rhett .60 1.25
I20 Michael Westbrook .75 1.50

1995 Images Limited Sculpted Previews

COMPLETE SET (5) 12.50 25.00
STATED ODDS 1:24 LIMITED
NX1 Emmitt Smith 5.00 10.00
NX2 Drew Bledsoe 2.00 4.00
NX3 Steve Young 2.50 5.00
NX4 Rashaan Salaam .40 1.00
NX5 Marshall Faulk 4.00 8.00

1995 Images Limited/Live Silks

COMPLETE SET (10) 40.00 100.00
COMP.SERIES 1 (5) 20.00 50.00
COMP.SERIES 2 (5) 20.00 50.00
S1-S5 ODDS 1:375 LIVE
S6-S10 ODDS 1:375 LIMITED
S1 Troy Aikman 10.00 25.00
S2 Marshall Faulk 5.00 12.00
S3 Drew Bledsoe 4.00 10.00
S4 Byron Bam Morris 2.00 5.00
S5 James O. Stewart 2.50 6.00
S6 Emmitt Smith 20.00 50.00
S7 Steve Young 8.00 20.00
S8 Rashaan Salaam 2.00 5.00
S9 Natrone Means 2.50 6.00
S10 Michael Westbrook 2.00 5.00

1995 Images Live

COMPLETE SET (125) 10.00 25.00
UNLESS LISTED LIMITED/LIVE SAME PRICE
119 Mark Brunell .30 .75
120 Keenan McCardell .07 .20
121 Terry Kirby .07 .20
122 Marcus Allen .15 .40
123 Charlie Garner .07 .20
LV1 Drew Bledsoe Promo .60 1.50
numbered LV1, ad back

1995 Images Live Untouchables

COMPLETE SET (25) 100.00 200.00
STATED ODDS 1:20 LIVE
U1 Jim Kelly 2.50 5.00
U2 Kerry Collins 3.00 6.00
U3 Rashaan Salaam .30 .75
U4 Troy Aikman 8.00 15.00
U5 Emmitt Smith 12.50 25.00
U6 John Elway 15.00 30.00
U7 Barry Sanders 12.50 25.00
U8 Reggie White 2.50 5.00
U9 Steve McNair 6.00 12.00
U10 Marshall Faulk 10.00 20.00
U11 Dan Marino 15.00 30.00
U12 Drew Bledsoe 5.00 10.00
U13 Ben Coates 1.25 2.50
U14 Tyrone Wheatley 2.00 4.00
U15 Chester McGlockton 1.25 2.50
U16 Ricky Watters 1.25 2.50
U17 Junior Seau 2.50 5.00
U18 Natrone Means 1.25 2.50
U19 Steve Young 6.00 12.00
U20 Jerry Rice 8.00 15.00
U21 Rick Mirer 1.25 2.50
U22 Jerome Bettis 2.50 5.00
U23 Warren Sapp 3.00 6.00
U24 Michael Westbrook .75 1.50
U25 Heath Shuler 1.25 2.50

2000 Impact

Released as a 199-card set, this set was numbered 1-200 due to the last minute pulling of card number 137. Base cards are white bordered and feature full color action photos. Impact was packaged in 36-pack boxes with packs containing 10 cards and carried a suggested retail price of $.99.

COMPLETE SET (199) 12.50 30.00
1 Kurt Warner .30 .75
2 Dan Marino .60 1.50
3 Sedrick Irvin .12 .30
4 Chris Redman RC .25 .60
5 Robert Smith .15 .40
6 Amani Toomer .15 .40
7 Richard Huntley .12 .30
8 Ahman Green .15 .40
9 Fred Lane .12 .30
10 Eddie George .15 .40
11 Rocket Ismail .15 .40
12 Shannon Sharpe .20 .50
13 Shawn Jefferson .12 .30
14 Michael Wiley RC .20 .50
15 Jeff Graham .12 .30
16 Steve Beuerlein .15 .40
17 Tim Biakabutuka .15 .40
18 Chris Watson .12 .30
19 Kevin Faulk .15 .40
20 Emmitt Smith .50 1.25
21 Plaxico Burress RC .30 .75
22 Hines Ward .20 .50
23 Jacquez Green .12 .30
24 Doug Flutie .20 .50
25 Leslie Shepherd .12 .30
26 Johnnie Morton .15 .40
27 Tom Brady RC 10.00 25.00
28 Jeff George .15 .40
29 Derrick Mason .15 .40
30 Marshall Faulk .20 .50
31 Derrick Mayes .12 .30
32 Jerome Bettis .20 .50
33 Adrian Murrell .12 .30
34 Curtis Enis .12 .30
35 Kimble Anders .12 .30
36 Travis Prentice RC .25 .60
37 Curtis Martin .20 .50
38 Ronnie Powell .12 .30
39 Steve Christie .12 .30
40 Brett Favre .60 1.50
41 Michael Bates .12 .30
42 Rondell Mealey RC .20 .50
43 Randall Cunningham .20 .50
44 Kerry Collins .15 .40
45 William Thomas .12 .30
46 Ricky Watters .15 .40
47 Marvin Harrison .20 .50
48 Corey Bradford .12 .30
49 Terry Kirby .12 .30
50 Troy Aikman .30 .75
51 Cris Carter .20 .50
52 Jamal Lewis RC .30 .75
53 Duce Staley .15 .40
54 Isaac Bruce .20 .50
55 Yancey Thigpen .12 .30
56 R.Jay Soward RC .20 .50
57 Jermaine Lewis .12 .30
58 Zach Thomas .20 .50
59 Sylvester Morris RC .20 .50
60 Steve McNair .20 .50
61 Tiki Barber .20 .50
62 Torrance Small .12 .30
63 Champ Bailey .15 .40
64 Tim Dwight .15 .40
65 Willie Jackson .12 .30
66 Edgerrin James .20 .50
67 Ron Dayne RC .30 .75
68 Rich Gannon .15 .40
69 Junior Seau .20 .50
70 Warren Sapp .15 .40
71 Rob Johnson .15 .40
72 Antonio Freeman .15 .40
73 O.J. McDuffie .15 .40
74 Tamarick Vanover .12 .30
75 Courtney Brown RC .25 .60
76 Donovan McNabb .20 .50
77 Az-Zahir Hakim .12 .30
78 Albert Connell .12 .30
79 Qadry Ismail .15 .40
80 Terrell Davis .20 .50
81 Dorsey Levens .15 .40
82 Tony Martin .15 .40
83 Laveranues Coles RC .30 .75
84 Karim Abdul-Jabbar .12 .30
85 Charles Johnson .12 .30
86 Torry Holt .20 .50
87 Stephen Davis .15 .40
88 Tony Banks .12 .30
89 Akili Smith .12 .30
90 Tim Couch .15 .40
91 Bill Schroeder .15 .40
92 Andre Hastings .12 .30
93 Eddie Kennison .12 .30
94 Randy Moss .20 .50
95 Tony Horne .12 .30
96 Sherrod Gideon RC .20 .50
97 Wesley Walls .12 .30
98 Brian Griese .15 .40
99 Jake Delhomme RC .75 2.00
100 Peyton Manning .50 1.25
101 Brad Johnson .15 .40
102 Trung Canidate RC .25 .60
103 Freddie Jones .12 .30
104 Muhsin Muhammad .15 .40
105 Eric Moulds .15 .40
106 Ed McCaffrey .15 .40
107 Joe Montgomery .12 .30
108 Olandis Gary .15 .40
109 J.J. Stokes .15 .40
110 Ricky Williams .20 .50
111 Jim Harbaugh .15 .40
112 Mike Alstott .20 .50
113 Errict Rhett .15 .40
114 Terance Mathis .12 .30
115 Kevin Johnson .12 .30
116 Tremain Mack .12 .30
117 Peter Warrick RC .30 .75
118 Lamont Warren .12 .30
119 Damon Huard .15 .40
120 Cade McNown .12 .30
121 Natrone Means .15 .40
122 Ken Oxendine .12 .30
123 J.R. Redmond RC .20 .50
124 Ken Dilger .12 .30
125 James Johnson .12 .30
126 Napoleon Kaufman .15 .40
127 Ryan Leaf .15 .40
128 Michael Westbrook .12 .30
129 Mario Bates .12 .30
130 Jake Plummer .15 .40
131 James Jett .15 .40
132 Darnay Scott .15 .40
133 Curtis Conway .15 .40
134 Fred Taylor .20 .50
135 Wayne Chrebet .15 .40
136 Sean Dawkins .12 .30
138 Keenan McCardell .15 .40
139 Donnell Bennett .12 .30
140 Jerry Rice .40 1.00
141 Vinny Testaverde .15 .40
142 Chad Pennington RC .50 1.25
143 Jonathan Linton .12 .30
144 Herman Moore .15 .40
145 David Patten .12 .30
146 Troy Edwards .12 .30
147 Jon Kitna .15 .40
148 Jimmy Smith .15 .40
149 Tee Martin RC .30 .75
150 Jevon Kearse .15 .40
151 Frank Sanders .12 .30
152 Marcus Robinson .15 .40
153 Mike Hollis .12 .30
154 Frank Wycheck .15 .40
155 Tim Rattay RC .25 .60
156 Dedric Ward .12 .30
157 Terrell Owens .20 .50
158 Chris Chandler .15 .40
159 Damon Griffin .12 .30
160 Mike Vanderjagt .12 .30
161 Elvis Grbac .12 .30
162 Rickey Dudley .12 .30
163 Jeff Garcia .15 .40
164 Thomas Jones RC .40 1.00
165 Tyrone Wheatley .12 .30
166 Rod Smith .15 .40
167 Bubba Franks RC .30 .75
168 Chris Warren .12 .30
169 Anthony Lucas RC .20 .50
170 Terry Glenn .15 .40
171 John Carney .12 .30
172 Warrick Dunn .15 .40
173 Shaun Alexander RC .40 1.00
174 David Boston .12 .30
175 Bobby Engram .15 .40
176 Travis Taylor RC .25 .60
177 Derrick Alexander .12 .30
178 Keyshawn Johnson .15 .40
179 Steve Young .25 .60
180 Deion Sanders .20 .50
181 Charlie Batch .15 .40
182 Drew Bledsoe .20 .50
183 Reuben Droughns RC .30 .75
184 Ray Lucas .12 .30
185 Shaun King .12 .30
186 Jamal Anderson .15 .40
187 Corey Dillon .15 .40
188 Joe Hamilton RC .20 .50
189 Terrence Wilkins .12 .30
190 Mark Brunell .15 .40
191 Tony Gonzalez .20 .50
192 Tim Brown .20 .50
193 Charlie Garner .15 .40
194 Antowain Smith .15 .40
195 David LaFleur .12 .30
196 Germane Crowell .12 .30
197 Terry Allen .15 .40
198 Marc Bulger RC .30 .75
199 Kevin Dyson .15 .40
200 Kordell Stewart .15 .40

2000 Impact Hats Off

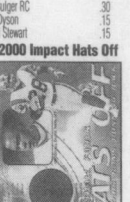

STATED ODDS 1:720H/1:1444R
1 Karim Abdul-Jabbar 8.00 20.00
2 Jamal Anderson 10.00 25.00
3 David Boston 8.00 20.00
4 Isaac Bruce 12.00 30.00
5 Chris Chandler 10.00 25.00
6 Curtis Conway 10.00 25.00
7 Tim Couch 10.00 25.00
8 Tim Dwight 10.00 25.00
9 Curtis Enis 8.00 20.00
10 Marshall Faulk 15.00 40.00
11 Az-Zahir Hakim 8.00 20.00
12 Torry Holt 12.00 30.00
13 Kevin Johnson 8.00 20.00
14 Terry Kirby 8.00 20.00
15 Terance Mathis 8.00 20.00
16 Shane Matthews 8.00 20.00
17 Cade McNown 8.00 20.00
18 Rob Moore 8.00 20.00
19 Jake Plummer 10.00 25.00
20 Marcus Robinson 10.00 25.00
21 Frank Sanders 8.00 20.00

2000 Impact Point of Impact

COMPLETE SET (10) 12.50 30.00
STATED ODDS 1:30
PI1 Peyton Manning 2.50 6.00
PI2 Edgerrin James 1.00 2.50
PI3 Brett Favre 3.00 8.00
PI4 Marshall Faulk 1.00 2.50
PI5 Fred Taylor 1.00 2.50
PI6 Tim Couch .75 2.00
PI7 Emmitt Smith 2.50 6.00
PI8 Eddie George .75 2.00
PI9 Randy Moss 1.00 2.50
PI10 Terrell Davis 1.00 2.50

2000 Impact Rewind '99

COMPLETE SET (40) 6.00 15.00
ONE PER PACK
1 Jake Plummer .20 .50
2 Tim Dwight .20 .50
3 Tony Banks .15 .40
4 Doug Flutie .25 .60
5 Tim Biakabutuka .20 .50
6 Marcus Robinson .20 .50
7 Corey Dillon .20 .50
8 Tim Couch .20 .50
9 Troy Aikman .40 1.00
10 Olandis Gary .20 .50
11 Germane Crowell .15 .40
12 Brett Favre .75 2.00
13 Peyton Manning .60 1.50
14 Mark Brunell .20 .50
15 Tony Gonzalez .25 .60
16 Dan Marino .75 2.00
17 Randy Moss .25 .60
18 Drew Bledsoe .25 .60
19 Ricky Williams .25 .60
20 Amani Toomer .20 .50
21 Keyshawn Johnson .20 .50
22 Rich Gannon .20 .50
23 Duce Staley .20 .50
24 Jerome Bettis .25 .60
25 Kenny Bynum .15 .40
26 Charlie Garner .20 .50
27 Jon Kitna .20 .50
28 Kurt Warner .40 1.00
29 Mike Alstott .25 .60
30 Eddie George .20 .50
31 Stephen Davis .20 .50
32 Kurt Warner .40 1.00
33 Edgerrin James .25 .60
34 Jevon Kearse .20 .50
35 Marshall Faulk .25 .60
36 Edgerrin James .25 .60
37 Marvin Harrison .25 .60
38 Jimmy Smith .20 .50
39 Steve Beuerlein .20 .50
40 Kurt Warner .40 1.00

2000 Impact Team Tattoos

COMPLETE SET (31) 10.00 25.00
COMMON TATTOO .40 1.00
STATED ODDS 1:4

2011 In The Game Canadiana Authentic Patch Gold

ANNOUNCED PRINT RUN 10
UNPRICED DUE TO SCARCITY

2011 In The Game Canadiana Authentic Patch Silver

ANNOUNCED PRINT RUN 30
AP2 Dave Cutler 25.00 50.00

2011 In The Game Canadiana Autographs

OVERALL AUTO/MEM ODDS THREE PER BOX
ADCU1 Dave Cutler 10.00 20.00
ADCU2 Dave Cutler 10.00 20.00

2011 In The Game Canadiana Autographs Blue

*BLUE: .75X TO 1.5X BLACK AUTOS
OVERALL AUTO ODDS ONE PER BOX

2011 In The Game Canadiana Mega Memorabilia Gold

ANNOUNCED PRINT RUN 10
UNPRICED DUE TO SCARCITY

2011 In The Game Canadiana Mega Memorabilia Silver

MM3 Dave Cutler L 10.00 20.00

2011 In The Game Canadiana Red

BLUE/50: .75X TO 2X BASIC RED
UNPRICED ONYX ANNOUNCED RUN 5
ANNOUNCED PRINT RUN 180 SETS
10 Bronko Nagurski .75 2.00
17 Dave Cutler .60 1.50

1992-93 Intimidator Bio Sheets

Produced by Intimidator, each of these bio sheets measures approximately 8 1/2" by 11" and is printed on card stock. The fronts display a large glossy color player photo framed by black and white inner borders. The right side of the photo is edged by a gold foil stripe that presents the player's name, team name, Intimidator logo, and uniform number. The surrounding card face, which constitutes the outer border, is team color-coded. The backs carry two black-and-white player photos, pro career summary, college career summary, and personal as well as biographical information. An autograph slot at the lower right corner and a date (1/93) rounds out the back. The bio sheets are unnumbered and checklisted below in alphabetical order. Two Derrick Thomas promos were also produced.

COMPLETE SET (36) 40.00 100.00
1 Troy Aikman 4.00 10.00
2 Jerry Ball .60 1.50
3 Cornelius Bennett .80 2.00
4 Earnest Byner .60 1.50
5 Randall Cunningham 1.20 3.00
6 Chris Doleman .80 2.00
7 John Elway 6.00 15.00
8 Jim Everett .80 2.00
9 Michael Irvin 1.20 3.00
10 Jim Kelly 1.20 3.00
11 James Lofton .80 2.00
12 Howie Long 1.20 3.00
13 Ronnie Lott .80 2.00
14 Nick Lowery .60 1.50
15 Charles Mann .60 1.50
16 Dan Marino 6.00 15.00
17 Art Monk .80 2.00
18 Joe Montana 10.00 20.00
19 Warren Moon 1.20 3.00
20 Christian Okoye .80 2.00
21 Leslie O'Neal .80 2.00
22 Andre Reed .80 2.00
23 Jerry Rice 4.00 10.00
24 Andre Rison .80 2.00
25 Deion Sanders 2.00 5.00
26 Junior Seau 1.20 3.00
27 Mike Singletary .80 2.00
28 Bruce Smith .80 2.00
29 Emmitt Smith 6.00 15.00
30 Neil Smith .80 2.00
31 Pat Swilling .80 2.00
32 Lawrence Taylor .80 2.00
33 Broderick Thomas .60 1.50
34 Derrick Thomas 1.20 3.00
35 Thurman Thomas 1.20 3.00
36 Lorenzo White .80 2.00
P1 Derrick Thomas Promo 1.60 4.00
(12/92 date at bottom on back)
P2 Derrick Thomas Promo 1.60 4.00
(no date nor Team
NFL logo on back)

1995 Iowa Barnstormers AFL

The Iowa Barnstormers Arena Football League team issued this set of cards in conjunction with Taco John's stores. Two cards were distributed each week of the season at participating stores and complete team sets reportedly were sold through the team. The cards are not numbered but have been arranged alphabetically below with players and coaches first and mascot and cheerleaders last. This was Kurt Warner's first football card.

COMPLETE SET (42) 75.00 150.00
1 Mike Black 1.25 3.00
2 Larry Blue 1.25 3.00
3 Lester Brinkley 1.25 3.00
4 Jim Burrow ACO 1.25 3.00
5 Toney Catchings 1.25 3.00
6 Andy Chilcote 1.25 3.00
7 Leonard Conley 1.25 3.00
8 Jim Foster OWN 1.25 3.00
9 John Gregory CO 1.25 3.00
10 Art Haege ACO 1.25 3.00
11 Weylan Harding 1.25 3.00
12 Todd Harrington 1.25 3.00
13 Willis Jacox 1.25 3.00
14 Carlos James 1.25 3.00
15 Brian Krulikowski 1.25 3.00
16 Jeff Loots 1.25 3.00
17 Ron Lopez 1.25 3.00
18 Adrian Lunsford 1.25 3.00
19 Ron Moran 1.25 3.00
20 Ryan Murray 1.25 3.00
21 Bob Rees 1.25 3.00
22 Jon Roehlk CO 1.25 3.00
23 Rick Schaaf 1.25 3.00
24 Mike Sunvold 1.25 3.00
25 Reggie Sutton 1.25 3.00
26 Kurt Warner 40.00 80.00
27 Ralph Young ACO 1.25 3.00
28 Tony Young 1.25 3.00
29 Jim Zabel ANN 1.25 3.00
30 Billy Barnstormer 1.25 3.00
(mascot)
31 Cheerleaders 1.25 3.00
Ginger Akason
Angela Thompson
32 Cheerleaders 1.25 3.00
Toni Barber
Denise Porter
33 Cheerleaders 1.25 3.00
Margaret Barrett
Carrie Leonard
34 Cheerleaders 1.25 3.00
Tama-Lea Bence
Amy Vacco
35 Cheerleaders 1.25 3.00
Jennifer Blomgren
Tracey Griffin
Krista Jagerson
36 Cheerleaders 1.25 3.00
Danielle Burns
Carmen Phelps
Wendy Wagner
37 Cheerleaders 1.25 3.00
Shelly Gascon
Jessi Kuhn
38 Cheerleaders 1.25 3.00
Merea Haugen
Tanya Ogden
39 Cheerleaders 1.25 3.00
Chloris Hock
Gina Moeckly
40 Cheerleaders 1.25 3.00
Lori Nicholas
Jiffy Puls
Jennifer Swanson
41 Cheerleaders 1.25 3.00
Staci Perkins
Allison Rowray
42 Cheerleaders 1.25 3.00
Molly Richardson
Maria Weaver

1996 Iowa Barnstormers AFL

For the second year, the Iowa Barnstormers Arena Football League team issued a set of cards. Complete team sets reportedly were sold through the team. The cards were numbered on the backs.

COMPLETE SET (42) 60.00 120.00
1 Mike Black 1.25 3.00
2 Matthew Sleeple 1.25 3.00
3 Ron Lopez 1.25 3.00
4 Ryan Murray 1.25 3.00
5 David Bush 1.25 3.00
6 Kurt Warner 30.00 60.00
7 Andy Chilcote 1.25 3.00
8 Mark Friday 1.25 3.00
9 Leonard Conley 1.25 3.00
10 Steve Houghton 1.25 3.00
11 Toney Catchings 1.25 3.00
12 Lamart Cooper 1.25 3.00
13 Chris Spencer 1.25 3.00
14 Todd Harrington 1.25 3.00
15 Carlos James 1.25 3.00
16 Larry Blue 1.25 3.00
17 Harold Jasper 1.25 3.00
18 Weylan Harding 1.25 3.00
19 Garry Howe 1.25 3.00
20 Matt Eller 1.25 3.00
21 Willis Jacox 1.25 3.00
22 Calvin Shakoor 1.25 3.00
23 Jim Burrow ACO 1.25 3.00
24 George Asleson ACO 1.25 3.00
25 Art Haege ACO 1.25 3.00
26 John Gregory CO 1.25 3.00
27 Jim Foster OWN 1.25 3.00
28 Cheerleaders 1.25 3.00
Amy Vacco
Merea Haugen
Lisa Thill
29 Cheerleaders 1.25 3.00
Ginger Akason
Margaret McCloud
30 Cheerleaders 1.25 3.00
Shelly Gascon
Jessi Kuhn
31 Cheerleaders 1.25 3.00
Tanya Ogden
Tama-Lea Bence
32 Cheerleaders 1.25 3.00
Kristy Bales
Angela Goddard
Shelene Riddle
33 Cheerleaders 1.25 3.00
Lauren Phommachakr
Christa Anderson
Nessa Wauters
34 Cheerleaders 1.25 3.00
Toni Barber
Carmen Phelps
35 Cheerleaders 1.25 3.00
Tracey Griffin
Wendy Wagner
36 Cheerleaders 1.25 3.00
Jennifer Swanson
April Samp
37 Cheerleaders 1.25 3.00
Renae Epp
Kara Lundin
Jennifer Day
38 Cheerleaders 1.25 3.00
Erin Gersdorf
Taylor Somers
Michelle Piercy
39 Cheerleaders 1.25 3.00
Stephanie Livingston
Jennifer Rawley
Stacie Carlson
40 Barnstormer Billy 1.25 3.00
Barnyard Bob
(mascots)
41 Harvie Herrington ANN 1.25 3.00
42 Ron Moran ANN 1.25 3.00

1997 Iowa Barnstormers AFL

For the third year, the Iowa Barnstormers Arena Football League team issued a set of cards that included Kurt Warner. Complete team sets were sold through the team with portions of the proceeds going to local charities. The cards were numbered on the backs.

COMPLETE SET (50) 60.00 120.00
1 John Gregory CO 1.25 3.00
2 Art Haege ACO 1.25 3.00
3 Jim Burrow ACO 1.25 3.00
4 George Asleson ACO 1.25 3.00
5 Jim Foster OWN 1.25 3.00
6 Mike Black 1.25 3.00
7 Carlos James 1.25 3.00
8 Larry Blue 1.25 3.00
9 Lamart Cooper 1.25 3.00
10 Andre Allen 1.25 3.00
11 Jarrod DeGeorgia 1.25 3.00
12 Kurt Warner 30.00 60.00
13 Mike Horacek 1.25 3.00
14 Charles Puleri 2.00 5.00
15 Todd Harrington 1.25 3.00
16 Hiawatha Philer 1.25 3.00
17 Greg Eaglin 1.25 3.00
18 John Anderson S 1.25 3.00
19 Leonard Conley 1.25 3.00
20 John Motton 1.25 3.00
21 Ron Moran 1.25 3.00
22 Steve Houghton 1.25 3.00
23 David Withun 1.25 3.00
24 David Bush 1.25 3.00
25 Garry Howe 1.25 3.00
26 Vernon Broughton 1.25 3.00
27 Matt Eller 1.25 3.00
28 Anthony Hutch 1.25 3.00
29 Chris Spencer 1.25 3.00
30 Willis Jacox 1.25 3.00
31 Toney Catchings 1.25 3.00
32 Evan Matautia 1.25 3.00
33 Barnyard Bob 1.25 3.00
Barnstormer Billy
34 Cheerleaders 1.25 3.00
Emily Reis
Cutina Johnson
35 Cheerleaders 1.25 3.00
Ginger Akason
Margaret McCloud
36 Cheerleaders 1.25 3.00
Stephani Livingston
Taylor Rounds
37 Cheerleaders 1.25 3.00
Tanya Ogden
Amy Vacco
38 Cheerleaders 1.25 3.00
Suzie Caldwell
Erin Gersdorf
39 Cheerleaders 1.25 3.00
Diane Yates
Tiffany Hagen
40 Cheerleaders 1.25 3.00
Jennifer Rawley
Tiffany Kilts
41 Cheerleaders 1.25 3.00
Tracy Schaffner
Angie Beenen
42 Cheerleaders 1.25 3.00
Karla Overton
Sabetha Clark
43 Cheerleaders 1.25 3.00
Lauren Phommachaker
Christa Anderson
44 Cheerleaders 1.25 3.00
Shelly Gascon
Jennifer Swanson
45 Cheerleaders 1.25 3.00
Stephanie Haworth
Jill Kemp
Amber Coppick
46 Cheerleaders 1.25 3.00
Julie Grove
Kristy Bales
47 Cheerleaders 1.25 3.00
Kara Lundin
Carla Erpelding
48 Team Support Staff 1.25 3.00
Shane Dunlevy
Michael Browne
Kevin McDonald
49 Front Office Team 1.25 3.00
50 Broadcast Team 1.25 3.00
Jim Zabel
Gary Fletcher

1999 Iowa Barnstormers AFL

The Iowa Barnstormers Arena Football League team issued this set of cards. Complete sets were sold through the team and at the arena with portions of the proceeds going to local charities.

COMPLETE SET (42) 20.00 40.00
1 George Asleson ACO .75 2.00
2 Larry Blue .75 2.00
3 Jim Burrow ACO .75 2.00
4 Toney Catchings .75 2.00
5 Scott Cloman .75 2.00
6 Leonard Conley .75 2.00
7 Rodney Filer .75 2.00
8 John Fisher .75 2.00
9 Jim Foster OWN .75 2.00
10 Aaron Garcia .75 2.00
11 Eric Gohlstin .75 2.00
12 Marvin Graves .75 2.00
13 John Gregory CO .75 2.00
14 Art Haege ACO .75 2.00
15 Todd Harrington .75 2.00
16 Mike Horacek .75 2.00
17 Garry Howe .75 2.00
18 Anthony Hutch .75 2.00
19 Carlos James .75 2.00
20 Kevin Kaesviharn .75 2.00
21 Skip McClendon .75 2.00
22 John Motton .75 2.00
23 Basil Proctor .75 2.00
24 Matt Sherman .75 2.00
25 Shea Showers .75 2.00
26 Chris Spencer .75 2.00
27 Kevin Swayne .75 2.00
28 Geoff Turner .75 2.00
29 Mathias Vavao .75 2.00
30 Jack Walker .75 2.00
31 Jim Zabel ANN .75 2.00
Gary Fletcher ANN
32 Chearleaders .75 2.00
Laura Belieu
Melissa Gale Da Costa
33 Chearleaders .75 2.00
Kim Bogenschutz
34 Chearleaders .75 2.00
Diane Claude
Karla Overton
35 Chearleaders .75 2.00
Amber Coppick
Jensie Grigsby
36 Chearleaders .75 2.00
Cristy Dauphin
Angie Beenen
37 Chearleaders .75 2.00
Brieanna Dodd
Chrissy Sitterle
38 Chearleaders .75 2.00
Carla Erpelding
Megan Linke
39 Chearleaders .75 2.00
Heather Johnson
Tiffany Koenig
40 Chearleaders .75 2.00
Tanya Ogden
41 Chearleaders .75 2.00
Stacy Peters
Traci Morris
42 Chearleaders .75 2.00
Amy Vacco
Jennifer Rawley

2007 Iowa Blackhawks APFL

COMPLETE SET (39) 6.00 12.00
1 Black Jack (Mascot) .20 .50
2 George Patterson III .20 .50
3 Paul Kosel .20 .50
4 Chris Moore .20 .50
5 Mike Wolff CO .20 .50
6 Justin Kammrad .20 .50
7 Ted Hennings .20 .50
8 Shawn Ronk .20 .50
9 Kurt Ferguson .20 .50
10 Mike Reynolds .20 .50
11 Tony Doremus Asst.CO .20 .50
12 Chuck Wright .20 .50
13 Mike Stuart .20 .50
14 Ray Rose .20 .50
15 Brett Ryan Asst.CO .20 .50
16 Elijah Simmons .20 .50
17 Dave Coberly Asst.CO .20 .50
18 Dedric Washington .20 .50
19 Burton Bosan .20 .50
20 Mike Paulson Asst.CO .20 .50
21 Eric Smith .20 .50
22 Ryan Dennhardt .20 .50
23 Dontae Allen .20 .50
24 Steve Rush .20 .50
25 Cameron Gales .20 .50
26 Yano Jones .20 .50
27 Matt Smoyer .20 .50
28 Scott Yates .20 .50
29 Djuan Johnson .20 .50
30 Jeremy Glynn .20 .50
31 Travis Kleinbeck .20 .50
32 Taylor Wallin .20 .50
33 Tyrice Ellebb .20 .50
34 Ryan Kauffman .20 .50
35 Ryan Hoden .20 .50
36 Dave Liebentritt .20 .50
37 Kaylon Price .20 .50
38 Jerry Lakin .20 .50
39 Team Picture .20 .50

2008 Iowa Blackhawks APFL

COMPLETE SET (32) 6.00 12.00
1 Mike Wolff and Staff .20 .50
2 Chuck Wright .20 .50
3 Dave Liebentritt .20 .50
4 Rich Rylee .20 .50
5 Jeremy Glynn .20 .50
6 Greg Ernster .20 .50
7 Djuan Johnson .20 .50
8 Jon Helget .20 .50
9 Elijah Simmons .20 .50
10 Eric Johnson .20 .50
11 Ryan Kauffman .20 .50
12 Brad Triplett .20 .50
13 Kurt Ferguson .20 .50
14 Mike Neville .20 .50
15 Mike Stuart .20 .50
16 Matt Smoyer .20 .50
17 Jerry Lakin .20 .50
18 Tyrice Ellebb .20 .50
19 Cameron Gales .20 .50
20 Marty Wolff .20 .50
21 Ryan Hoden .20 .50
22 Burton Bosan .20 .50
23 Ryan Dennhardt .20 .50
24 Josh Hayes .20 .50
25 Dontae Allen .20 .50
26 Jared Isenhart .20 .50
27 Chris Moore .20 .50
28 Travis Hines .20 .50
29 Scott Yates .20 .50
30 Brandon Carrera .20 .50
31 Eric Smith .20 .50
32 Iowa Hot Wings .20 .50

1997 Iron Kids Bread

These cards were issued in packages of Iron Kids Bread in 1997. Each includes a color photo of the featured player on the front along with the "Iron Kids Bread" sponsorship logo in the lower right corner. Any additions to the list below are appreciated.

1 Ken Norton .75 2.00

2007-08 ITG Ultimate Memorabilia Cityscapes

STATED PRINT RUN 24 SERIAL #'d SETS

3 Dominik Hasek	10.00	25.00
Doug Flutie		
4 Marty Turco	8.00	20.00
Deion Sanders		
9 Patrick Roy	30.00	80.00
John Elway		
10 Pavel Datsyuk	10.00	25.00
Barry Sanders		
15 Mike Modano	10.00	25.00
Michael Irvin		

1974 Jacksonville Sharks WFL Team Issue

These black and white photos were issued by the team and measure roughly 3 1/2" x 4 3/4." The backs are blank but the fronts include a large amount of information within the space below the player image: jersey number, player's name, team logo, position initials, height, and weight.

1 Tommy Durrance	6.00	12.00
2 Dennis Hughes	6.00	12.00
3 Grant Guthrie	6.00	12.00
4 Kay Stephenson	6.00	12.00

1975 Jacksonville Express Team Issue

The Jacksonville Express of the World Football League distributed this set of player photos. Each photo measures approxmately 4 1/2" by 5" and features a black and white player picture with a blank cardback. The photos contain no player names nor any other identifying text. We've listed the photos below according to the player's jersey number.

COMPLETE SET (38)	450.00	900.00
2 Johnny Osborne	12.50	25.00
3 Lee McGriff	12.50	25.00
6 Dan Callahan	12.50	25.00
7 Steve Barrios	12.50	25.00
8 Steve Foley	15.00	30.00
10 George Mira	15.00	30.00
12 David Fowler	12.50	25.00
16 Ron Coppenbarger	12.50	25.00
18 Bob Ansley	12.50	25.00
20 Jimmy Poulos	12.50	25.00
21 Tommy Reamon	12.50	25.00
23 Alfred Haywood	12.50	25.00
30 Jeff Davis	12.50	25.00
31 Fletcher Smith	12.50	25.00
32 Brian Duncan	12.50	25.00
42 Canary Simmons	12.50	25.00
44 Skip Johns	12.50	25.00
46 Willie Jackson	15.00	30.00
50 Rick Thomann	12.50	25.00
51 Jay Casey	12.50	25.00
52 Glen Gaspard	12.50	25.00
54 Howard Kindig	12.50	25.00
55 Fred Abbott	12.50	25.00
57 Ted Jarnov	12.50	25.00
58 Chip Myrtle	15.00	30.00
59 Sherman Miller	12.50	25.00
63 Tom Walker	12.50	25.00
68 Carleton Oats	12.50	25.00
70 Buck Baker	12.50	25.00
76 Carl Taibi	12.50	25.00
77 Joe Jackson	12.50	25.00
78 Kenny Moore	12.50	25.00
79 Larry Gagner	12.50	25.00
80 Dennis Hughes	12.50	25.00
81 Charles Hall	12.50	25.00
82 Don Brumm	15.00	30.00
87 Mike Creaney	12.50	25.00
88 Witt Beckman	12.50	25.00

1997 Jaguars Collector's Choice

Upper Deck released several team sets in 1997 in a blister pack wrapper. Each of the 14-cards in this set are very similar to the base Collector's Choice cards except for the card numbering on the cardback. A cover/checklist card was added featuring the team helmet.

COMPLETE SET (14)	1.20	3.00
JA1 Jimmy Smith	.08	.25
JA2 Pete Mitchell	.02	.10
JA3 Natrone Means	.05	.15
JA4 Mark Brunell	.50	1.25
JA5 Kevin Hardy	.05	.15
JA6 Tony Brackens	.05	.15
JA7 Aaron Beasley	.02	.10
JA8 Chris Hudson	.02	.10
JA9 Renaldo Wynn	.02	.10
JA10 John Jurkovic	.02	.10
JA11 Keenan McCardell	.08	.25
JA12 James O. Stewart	.05	.15
JA13 Deon Figures	.02	.10
JA14 Jaguars Logo	.20	.50
Checklist		
(Mark Brunell on back)		

1997 Jaguars Team Issue

This 37-card set features black-and-white player photos in blue borders measuring approximately 5" by 8". The set was sponsored by Champion Health Care and displays a "Jaguars Don't Smoke" logo in the bottom right. The backs are blank. The cards are unnumbered and checklisted below in alphabetical order.

COMPLETE SET (37)	32.00	80.00
1 Bryan Barker	.80	2.00
2 Aaron Beasley	.80	2.00
3 Tony Boselli	1.00	2.50
4 Brant Boyer	.80	2.00
5 Tony Brackens	1.00	2.50
6 Mark Brunell	4.80	12.00
7 Michael Cheever	.80	2.00
8 Ben Coleman	.80	2.00
9 Don Davey	.80	2.00
10 Travis Davis	.80	2.00
11 Brian DeMarco	.80	2.00
12 Deon Figures	.80	2.00
13 Dana Hall	.80	2.00
14 James Hamilton	.80	2.00
15 Kevin Hardy	1.00	2.50
16 Mike Hollis	.80	2.00
17 Willie Jackson	1.00	2.50
18 John Jurkovic	.80	2.00
19 Jeff Lageman	.80	2.00
20 Mike Logan	.80	2.00
21 Keenan McCardell	1.60	4.00
22 Tom McManus	.80	2.00
23 Pete Mitchell	1.00	2.50
24 Will Moore	.80	2.00
25 Jeff Novak	.80	2.00
26 Chris Parker	.80	2.00
27 Seth Payne	.80	2.00
28 Kelvin Pritchett	.80	2.00
29 Eddie Robinson	.80	2.00
30 Bryan Schwartz	.80	2.00
31 Leon Searcy	.80	2.00
32 Joel Smeenge	.80	2.00
33 Jimmy Smith	1.60	4.00
34 James Stewart	1.00	2.50
35 Dave Thomas	.80	2.00
36 Rich Tylski	.80	2.00
37 Renaldo Wynn	.80	2.00

2005 Jaguars Super Bowl XXXIX

Each card manufacturer produced 2-cards to be distributed at the Super Bowl Card Show XXXIX in Jacksonville via wrapper redemption programs. The design varies from manufacturer and from card-to-card but each is numbered on the back as part of the 8-card set.

COMPLETE SET (8)	10.00	20.00
1 Greg Jones	1.00	2.50
(Topps)		
2 Reggie Williams	1.25	3.00
(Upper Deck)		
3 Ernest Wilford	.75	2.00
(Fleer)		
4 Marcus Stroud	.75	2.00
(Donruss Playoff)		
5 Byron Leftwich	1.50	4.00
(Donruss Playoff)		
6 David Garrard	.75	2.00
(Upper Deck)		
7 Fred Taylor	1.25	3.00
(Fleer)		
8 Jimmy Smith	1.00	2.50
(Topps)		

2006 Jaguars Topps

COMPLETE SET (12)	3.00	6.00
JAC1 Greg Jones	.20	.50
JAC2 Fred Taylor	.25	.60
JAC3 Ernest Wilford	.20	.50
JAC4 David Garrard	.25	.60
JAC5 Byron Leftwich	.25	.60
JAC6 Matt Jones	.20	.50
JAC7 Alvin Pearman	.20	.50
JAC8 Jimmy Smith	.25	.60
JAC9 Mike Peterson	.20	.50
JAC10 Daryl Smith	.15	.40
JAC11 Maurice Drew	.50	1.25
JAC12 Marcedes Lewis	.30	.75

2007 Jaguars Topps

COMPLETE SET (12)	2.50	5.00
1 Fred Taylor	.25	.60
2 Matt Jones	.25	.60
3 Reggie Williams	.25	.60
4 Ernest Wilford	.20	.50
5 Jermaine Wiggins	.20	.50
6 Reggie Nelson	.25	.60
7 David Garrard	.25	.60
8 Maurice Jones-Drew	.30	.75
9 Rashean Mathis	.20	.50
10 Byron Leftwich	.25	.60
11 Dennis Northcutt	.20	.50
12 Mike Peterson	.20	.50

2008 Jaguars Topps

COMPLETE SET (12)	2.00	4.00
1 Maurice Jones-Drew	.25	.60
2 Fred Taylor	.25	.60
3 Cleo Lemon	.20	.50
4 David Garrard	.25	.60
5 Reggie Nelson	.20	.50
6 Jerry Porter	.20	.50
7 Reggie Williams	.25	.60
8 Dennis Northcutt	.20	.50
9 Marcedes Lewis	.20	.50
10 Rashean Mathis	.20	.50
11 Derrick Harvey	.20	.50
12 Mike Peterson	.25	.60

1985 Jeno's Pizza Logo Stickers

This set of stickers was originally issued in complete sheet form. Since the stickers are often found individually cut, we've cataloged them this way. Each is blankbacked and features either an NFL team helmet or Super Bowl logo on the fronts.

COMPLETE SET (48)	60.00	150.00
1 Atlanta Falcons	1.25	3.00
2 Buffalo Bills	1.25	3.00
3 Chicago Bears	1.25	3.00
4 Cincinnati Bengals	1.25	3.00
5 Cleveland Browns	1.25	3.00
6 Dallas Cowboys	2.00	5.00
7 Denver Broncos	1.25	3.00
8 Detroit Lions	1.25	3.00
9 Green Bay Packers	2.00	5.00
10 Houston Oilers	1.25	3.00
11 Indianapolis Colts	1.25	3.00
12 Kansas City Chiefs	1.25	3.00
13 Los Angeles Raiders	2.00	5.00
14 Los Angeles Rams	1.25	3.00
15 Miami Dolphins	2.00	5.00
16 Minnesota Vikings	1.25	3.00
17 New England Patriots	1.25	3.00
18 New Orleans Saints	1.25	3.00
19 New York Giants	1.25	3.00
20 New York Jets	1.25	3.00
21 Philadelphia Eagles	1.25	3.00
22 Pittsburgh Steelers	2.00	5.00
23 St. Louis Cardinals	1.25	3.00
24 San Diego Chargers	1.25	3.00
25 San Francisco 49ers	2.00	5.00
26 Seattle Seahawks	1.25	3.00
27 Tampa Bay Buccaneers	1.25	3.00
28 Washington Redskins	2.00	5.00
29 Super Bowl I	1.25	3.00
30 Super Bowl II	1.25	3.00
31 Super Bowl III	1.25	3.00
32 Super Bowl IV	1.25	3.00
33 Super Bowl V	1.25	3.00
34 Super Bowl VI	1.25	3.00
35 Super Bowl VII	1.25	3.00
36 Super Bowl VIII	1.25	3.00
37 Super Bowl IX	1.25	3.00
38 Super Bowl X	1.25	3.00
39 Super Bowl XI	1.25	3.00
40 Super Bowl XII	1.25	3.00
41 Super Bowl XIII	1.25	3.00
42 Super Bowl XIV	1.25	3.00
43 Super Bowl XV	1.25	3.00
44 Super Bowl XVI	1.25	3.00
45 Super Bowl XVII	1.25	3.00
46 Super Bowl XVIII	1.25	3.00
47 Super Bowl XIX	1.25	3.00
48 Super Bowl XX	1.25	3.00

1986 Jeno's Pizza

The 1986 Jeno's Pizza football set contains 56 cards (two for each of the 28 teams). The two cards for each team typically represent a retired star and a current player. The cards are standard sized (2 1/2" by 3 1/2") and were printed horizontally (most of them) on thin card stock. The cards were distributed as a promotion with one card, sealed in plastic, contained in each special Jeno's box. Reportedly 10,000 sets were produced. There was also a Terry Bradshaw Action Play Book to house the cards issued via a mail redemption coupon.

COMPLETE SET (56)	10.00	25.00
1 Duane Thomas	.15	.40
2 Butch Johnson	.15	.40
3 Lawrence Taylor	.40	1.00
Andy Headen		
Wendell Tyler		
4 Joe Morris	.10	.30
5 Wilbert Montgomery	.10	.30
6 Harold Carmichael	.15	.40
7 Ottis Anderson	.15	.40
8 Roy Green	.08	.25
9 Mark Murphy	.08	.25
10 Joe Theismann	.30	.75
John Riggins		
11 Jim McMahon	.30	.75
12 Walter Payton	2.00	5.00
13 Billy Sims	.15	.40
14 James Jones	.08	.25
15 Willie Davis	.15	.40
Hank Jordan		
Len Dawson		
16 Eddie Lee Ivery	.08	.25
17 Fran Tarkenton	.40	1.00
18 Alan Page	.15	.40
Lawrence McCutchen		
19 Ricky Bell	.10	.30
20 Cecil Johnson	.08	.25
21 Bubba Bean	.08	.25
22 Gerald Riggs	.08	.25
23 Eric Dickerson	.25	.60
Barry Redden		
Ed Too Tall Jones		
24 Jack Reynolds	.10	.30
25 Archie Manning	.15	.40
26 Wayne Wilson	.10	.30
27 Dan Bunz	.08	.25
Pete Johnson		
28 Roger Craig	1.25	3.00
Joe Montana		
29 O.J. Simpson	.40	1.00
30 Joe Cribbs	.10	.30
31 Rick Volk	.15	.40
Leroy Kelly		
32 Earl Morrall	.10	.30
33 Jim Kiick	.10	.30
34 Dan Marino	2.50	6.00
35 Craig James	.15	.40
36 Julius Adams	.08	.25
37 Joe Namath	1.25	3.00
38 Freeman McNeil	.10	.30
39 Pete Johnson	.08	.25
40 Larry Kinnebrew	.08	.25
41 Brian Sipe	.10	.30
42 Kevin Mack	.10	.30
Earnest Byner		
43 Dan Pastorini	.10	.30
44 Elvin Bethea	.15	.40
Carter Hartwig		
45 Fran Tarkenton	.40	1.00
Jack Lambert		
L.C. Greenwood		
46 Terry Bradshaw	1.00	2.50
Franco Harris		
47 Randy Gradishard	.10	.30
Steve Foley		
48 Sammy Winder	.08	.25
49 Robert Holmes	.08	.25
50 Buck Buchanan	.15	.40
Curley Culp		
51 Willie Jones	.08	.25
Cedrick Hardman		
52 Marcus Allen	.50	1.25
53 Dan Fouts	.25	.60
Don Macek		
54 Dan Fouts	.50	1.25
55 Blair Bush	.08	.25
56 Steve Largent	.50	1.25
NNO Play Book	1.25	3.00
(Terry Bradshaw)		

1963 Jets Team Issue

These 4" by 5" Black and White cards were issued by the New York Jets in their first season as the Jets. They had been the Titans for the previous three seasons. There are small facsimile autographs on the bottom of the cardfronts. As these cards are not numbered we have sequenced them in alphabetical order.

COMPLETE SET (8)	60.00	120.00
1 Weeb Ewbank CO	10.00	20.00
2 Larry Grantham	7.50	15.00
3 Gene Heeter	7.50	15.00
4 Bill Mathis	7.50	15.00
5 Don Maynard	12.50	25.00
6 Mark Smolinski	7.50	15.00
7 Bake Turner	7.50	15.00
8 Dick Wood	7.50	15.00

1963 Jets Team Issue 5x7

This set of the New York Jets measures approximately 5" by 7" and look very similar to the Jay Publishing issues of the early 1960s and the 1965-66 Jets set listings. The fronts feature black-and-white player photos with just the player's name and team name below the photo. It is very likely that the Jets issued these photos in groups over a number of years as they can be found in 6 or 8-card envelopes. The backs are blank. The cards are unnumbered and checklisted below in alphabetical order.

1 Bill Atkins	6.00	12.00
2 Dick Christy	6.00	12.00
3 Larry Grantham	6.00	12.00
4 Dick Guesman	6.00	12.00
5 Mike Hudock	6.00	12.00
6 Charlie Janerette	6.00	12.00
7 Don Maynard	10.00	20.00
8 Bill Mathis	6.00	12.00
9 LaVerne Torczon	6.00	12.00

1965 Jets Team Issue 8x10

This set of the New York Jets photos measures approximately 8 1/2" by 10 1/4" and are very similar in design to other Jets photos issued in the 1960s and 1970s. The fronts feature black and white player photos with just the player's name and position (spelled out on most) below the photo along with the team's logo. This year can be identified by the slightly slanted position of the Jets' logo below the player image. The blankbacked photos are unnumbered and checklisted below in alphabetical order.

COMPLETE SET (10)	125.00	200.00
1 Emerson Boozer	7.50	15.00
2 Larry Grantham	6.00	12.00
3 John Huarte	6.00	12.00
4 Bill Mathis	6.00	12.00
5 Don Maynard	12.50	25.00
6 Wahoo McDaniel	7.50	15.00
7 Joe Namath	50.00	100.00
8 George Sauer	6.00	12.00
9 Matt Snell	7.50	15.00
10 Bake Turner	6.00	12.00

1965-66 Jets Team Issue 5x7

This set of the New York Jets measures approximately 5" by 7" and look very similar to the Jay Publishing issues of the early 1960s. The fronts feature black-and-white player photos with just the player's name and team name below the photo. It is very likely that the Jets issued these photos in groups over a number of years as they can be found in 6 or 8-card envelopes. The backs are blank. The cards are unnumbered and checklisted below in alphabetical order.

COMPLETE SET (10)	100.00	175.00
1 Ralph Baker	6.00	12.00
2 Dan Ficca	6.00	12.00
3 Wahoo McDaniel UER	7.50	15.00
(name misspelled McDaniels)		
4 Joe Namath	45.00	80.00
5 Dainard Paulson	6.00	12.00
6 Gerry Philbin	6.00	12.00
7 Mark Smolinski	6.00	12.00
8 Matt Snell	7.50	15.00
9 Bake Turner	6.00	12.00
10 Dick Wood	6.00	12.00

1967 Jets Team Issue 8x10

This set of the New York Jets photos measures approximately 8" by 10" and are very similar in design to the 1965 issue except for the logo. The fronts feature black and white player photos with just the player's name and position (spelled out on most) below the photo along with the team's logo. This year can be identified by the horizontal position of the Jets' logo below the player image. The blankbacked photos are unnumbered and checklisted below in alphabetical order.

1 Al Atkinson	6.00	12.00
2 Emerson Boozer	7.50	15.00
3 Randy Rasmussen	6.00	12.00
4 Paul Rochester	6.00	12.00
5 George Sauer	6.00	12.00

1969 Jets Tasco Prints

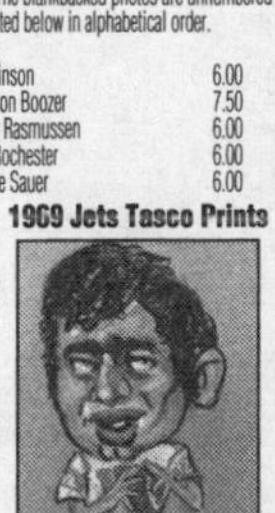

Tasco Associates produced this set of New York Jets prints. The fronts feature a large color artist's rendering of the player along with the player's name and position. The backs are blank. The prints measure approximately 11" by 16."

COMPLETE SET (6)	75.00	125.00
1 Winston Hill	7.50	15.00
2 Joe Namath	35.00	60.00
3 Gerry Philbin	7.50	15.00
4 Johnny Sample	7.50	15.00
5 Matt Snell	10.00	20.00
6 Jim Turner	7.50	15.00

1973-76 Jets Team Issue

The Jets issued these 8 " by 10" photos over the course of several years in the mid-1970s. Each includes a black and white photo of a Jets player with the older style (JETS within an oval) team logo, his name, and his position listed below the image. The type style and size varies slightly from photo to photo and several players were likely issued in differing styles. The backs are blank. Any additions to this list are appreciated.

1 Mike Adamle	5.00	10.00
4 Ralph Baker	5.00	10.00
6 Carl Barzilauskas	5.00	10.00
7 Mike Battle	5.00	10.00
9 Roger Bernhardt	5.00	10.00
10 Hank Bjorklund	5.00	10.00
11 Emerson Boozer	6.00	12.00
12 Willie Brister	5.00	10.00
13 Gordon Brown	5.00	10.00
14 Bob Burns	5.00	10.00
15 Greg Buttle	5.00	10.00
16 Duane Carrell	5.00	10.00
18 Bill Demory	5.00	10.00
19 John Dockery	5.00	10.00
21 Bill Ferguson	5.00	10.00
23 Richmond Flowers	5.00	10.00
25 Ed Galigher	5.00	10.00
26 Greg Gantt	5.00	10.00
27 Bruce Harper	5.00	10.00
28 Dave Herman	5.00	10.00
29 Winston Hill	5.00	10.00
2A Al Atkinson	5.00	10.00
(jersey number fully visible)		
2B Al Atkinson	5.00	10.00
(half of jersey number visible)		
30 Lou Holtz CO	7.50	15.00
(press conference holding ball)		
31 Delles Howell	5.00	10.00
32 Bobby Howfield	5.00	10.00
33 Clarence Jackson	5.00	10.00
34 J.J. Jones	5.00	10.00
35 Larry Keller	5.00	10.00
36 David Knight	5.00	10.00
37 Warren Koegel	5.00	10.00
38 Pete Lammons	5.00	10.00
39 Pat Leahy	5.00	10.00
3A Darrell Austin	5.00	10.00
(with neck pad)		
3B Darrell Austin	5.00	10.00
(without neck pad)		
40 John Little	5.00	10.00
41 Mark Lomas	5.00	10.00
42 Bob Martin	5.00	10.00
43 Don Maynard	10.00	20.00
44 Wayne Mulligan	5.00	10.00
45 Joe Namath Action	20.00	35.00
46 Jim Nance	6.00	12.00
47 Richard Neal	5.00	10.00
48 Burgess Owens	5.00	10.00
49 Gerry Philbin	5.00	10.00
(all-pro defensive end)		
50 Lou Piccone	5.00	10.00
51 Lawrence Pillers	5.00	10.00
52 Garry Puetz	5.00	10.00
53 Randy Rasmussen	5.00	10.00
54 Steve Reese	5.00	10.00
56 Jamie Rivers	5.00	10.00
57 Travis Roach	5.00	10.00
58 Joe Schmiesing	5.00	10.00
59 John Schmitt	5.00	10.00
5A Jerome Barkum	5.00	10.00
(photo from waist up)		
5B Jerome Barkum	5.00	10.00
(close-up of face)		
60 Richard Sowells	5.00	10.00
61 Shafer Suggs	5.00	10.00
62 Bob Svihus	5.00	10.00
63 Steve Tannen	5.00	10.00
64 Ed Taylor	5.00	10.00
65 Earlie Thomas	5.00	10.00
67 Godwin Turk	5.00	10.00
68 Phil Wise	5.00	10.00
70 Larry Woods	5.00	10.00
71 Robert Woods	5.00	10.00
72 Roscoe Word	5.00	10.00
8A Ed Bell	5.00	10.00
(facing straight forward)		
8B Ed Bell	5.00	10.00
(turned to his side)		
17A Richard Caster	6.00	12.00
(listed as Richard)		
17B Richard Caster	6.00	12.00
(listed as Rich)		
20A John Ebersole Portrait	5.00	10.00
(smiling, numbers hidden)		
20B John Ebersole Portrait	5.00	10.00
(numbers fully visible)		
20C John Ebersole	5.00	10.00
(warming up on field)		
22A Joe Fields mustache	5.00	10.00
22B Joe Fields smiling	5.00	10.00
24A Clark Gaines	5.00	10.00
(action pose)		
24B Clark Gaines	5.00	10.00
(standing wearing jacket)		
55A John Riggins	10.00	20.00
(close up portrait)		
55B John Riggins Action	10.00	20.00
66A Richard Todd	7.50	15.00
(action photo)		
66B Richard Todd	7.50	15.00
(portrait)		
69A Al Woodall	5.00	10.00
(green jersey)		
69B Al Woodall	5.00	10.00
(white jersey)		

1981 Jets Police

This unnumbered Police issue is complete at ten cards. Cards measure approximately 2 5/8" by 4 1/8" and have a green border around the photo on the front of the cards. The set was sponsored by New York City Crime Prevention Section, Frito-Lay, Kiwanis Club, and the New York Jets. The backs each contain a safety tip printed in red ink. The 1981 date is printed on the card backs. Apparently these Jets Police cards were printed on a sheet such that six of the cards were double printed and four of the cards were single printed. The single-printed cards, which are more difficult to find, are indicated below by SP.

COMPLETE SET (10)	14.00	35.00
14 Richard Todd SP	3.00	8.00
42 Bruce Harper	.60	1.50
51 Greg Buttle	.60	1.50
73 Joe Klecko	1.00	2.50
79 Marvin Powell	.60	1.50
80 Johnny Lam Jones SP	2.00	4.00
85 Wesley Walker SP	4.00	10.00
93 Marty Lyons	1.00	2.50
99 Mark Gastineau	1.00	2.50
NNO Team Effort SP	2.00	4.00

1987 Jets Ace Fact Pack

This 33-card set was made in West Germany (by Ace Fact Pack) for sale in England. This set measures approximately 2 1/4" by 3 5/8" and features members of the New York Jets. This set features cards with rounded corners; the card backs have a design for "Ace" like a playing card. We have checklisted the 22 players in the set in alphabetical order.

COMPLETE SET (33)	40.00	100.00
1 Dan Alexander	1.25	3.00
2 Tom Baldwin	1.25	3.00
3 Darry Bennett	1.25	3.00
4 Russell Carter	2.00	5.00
5 Kyle Clifton	2.00	5.00
6 Bob Crable	1.25	3.00
7 Joe Fields	2.00	5.00
8 Rusty Guilbeau	1.25	3.00
9 Harry Hamilton	1.25	3.00
10 Johnny Hector	2.00	5.00
11 Jerry Holmes	1.25	3.00
12 Gordon King	1.25	3.00
13 Lester Lyles	1.25	3.00
14 Marty Lyons	2.00	5.00
15 Kevin McArthur	1.25	3.00
16 Freeman McNeil	2.50	6.00
17 Ken O'Brien	2.50	6.00
18 Tony Paige	2.00	5.00
19 Mickey Shuler	2.00	5.00
20 Jim Sweeney	1.25	3.00
21 Al Toon	3.00	8.00
22 Wesley Walker	3.00	8.00
23 Jets Helmet	1.25	3.00
24 Jets Information	1.25	3.00
25 Jets Uniform	1.25	3.00
26 Game Record Holders	1.25	3.00
27 Season Record Holders	1.25	3.00
28 Career Record Holders	1.25	3.00
29 Record 1967-86	1.25	3.00
30 1986 Team Statistics	1.25	3.00
31 All-Time Greats	1.25	3.00
32 Roll of Honour	1.25	3.00
33 Giants Stadium	1.25	3.00

1988 Jets Ace Fact Pack

Cards from this 33-card set measure approximately 2 1/4" by 3 5/8". This set consists of 22-player cards and 11-additional informational cards about the Jets team. We've checklisted the cards alphabetically beginning with the 22-players. The cards have square corners (as opposed to rounded like the 1987 sets) and a playing card design on the back. These cards were manufactured in West Germany (by Ace Fact Pack) and released primarily in Great Britain.

COMPLETE SET (33)	60.00	120.00
1 Dan Alexander	1.50	4.00
2 Tom Baldwin	1.50	4.00
3 Kyle Clifton	1.50	4.00
4 Bob Crable	1.50	4.00
5 Mark Gastineau	3.00	8.00
6 Alex Gordon	1.50	4.00
7 Harry Hamilton	1.50	4.00
8 Johnny Hector	1.50	4.00
9 Jerry Holmes	1.50	4.00
10 Bobby Humphery	1.50	4.00
11 Lester Lyles	1.50	4.00
12 Marty Lyons	1.50	4.00
13 Kevin McArthur	1.50	4.00
14 Freeman McNeil	3.00	8.00
15 Matt Monger	1.50	4.00
16 Ken O'Brien	2.00	5.00
17 Mickey Shuler	1.50	4.00
18 Kurt Sohn	1.50	4.00
19 Jim Sweeney	1.50	4.00
20 Al Toon	2.00	5.00
21 Roger Vick	1.50	4.00
22 Wesley Walker	2.00	5.00
23 1987 Team Statistics	1.50	4.00
24 All-Time Greats	1.50	4.00
25 Career Record Holders	1.50	4.00
26 Game Record Holders	1.50	4.00
27 Giants Stadium	1.50	4.00
28 Jets Helmet	1.50	4.00
(Cover card)		
29 Jets Helmet	1.50	4.00
(Informational card)		
30 Jets Uniform	1.50	4.00
31 Record 1968-87	1.50	4.00
32 Roll Of Honour	1.50	4.00
33 Season Record Holders	1.50	4.00

2004 Jets NY Post Stickers

This set of stickers was issued over a series of weeks within the NY Post newspaper. Each sheet features stickers of a number of Jets players intended to be pasted into an album.

COMPLETE SET (6)	5.00	12.00
1 Sheet 1	1.25	3.00
Kevin Mawae		
Chad Pennington		
Sam Cowart		
Santana Moss		
Shaun Ellis (2)		
Curtis Martin		
Justin McCareins		
Giants Stadium		
Jets Logo		
2 Sheet 2	1.25	3.00
Kevin Mawae		
Wayne Chrebet		
Ray Mickens		
Curtis Martin		
Shaun Ellis		
Jason Fabini		
Santana Moss		
Jets Logo		
3 Sheet 3	1.25	3.00
Santana Moss		
Kevin Mawae		
Shaun Ellis		
Wayne Chrebet		
Curtis Martin		
Ray Mickens		
Jason Fabini		
Jets Logo		
4 Sheet 4	1.25	3.00
Jason Fabini		
Wayne Chrebet		
John Abraham		
Justin McCareins		
Sam Cowart (2)		
Santana Moss		
Ray Mickens		
Kevin Mawae		
5 Sheet 5	1.25	3.00
Wayne Chrebet		
Jason Fabini		
Justin McCareins		
John Abraham (2)		
Sam Cowart		
Ray Mickens		
Chad Pennington (2)		
Curtis Martin		
NNO Album	.60	1.50

2006 Jets Topps

COMPLETE SET (12)	3.00	6.00
NYJ1 Jonathan Vilma	.25	.60
NYJ2 Cedric Houston	.20	.50
NYJ3 Laveranues Coles	.20	.50
NYJ4 Chad Pennington	.25	.60
NYJ5 Patrick Ramsey	.25	.60
NYJ6 Curtis Martin	.30	.75
NYJ7 Tim Dwight	.15	.40
NYJ8 Justin Miller	.20	.50
NYJ9 B. J. Askew	.20	.50
NYJ10 Justin McCareins	.20	.50
NYJ11 D'Brickashaw Ferguson	.30	.75
NYJ12 Kellen Clemens	.25	.60

2007 Jets Delta

These cards were sponsored by Delta and Channel 2 and feature members of the Jets. Each was issued as part of a perforated 4-card sheet and measures roughly 4 14" by 5 1/4" when separated.

COMPLETE SET (16)	7.50	15.00
1 Laveranues Coles	.40	1.00
2 Jerricho Cotchery	.50	1.25
3 Shaun Ellis	.40	1.00
4 D'Brickashaw Ferguson	.40	1.00
5 David Harris	.50	1.25
6 Victor Hobson	.40	1.00
7 Thomas Jones	.50	1.25
8 Eric Mangini CO	.40	1.00
9 Nick Mangold	.40	1.00
10 Mike Nugent	.40	1.00
11 Chad Pennington	.50	1.25
12 Darrelle Revis	1.00	2.50
13 Kerry Rhodes	.40	1.00
14 Dewayne Robertson	.40	1.00
15 Jonathan Vilma	.50	1.25
16 Leon Washington	.50	1.25

2007 Jets Topps

COMPLETE SET (12)	2.50	6.00
1 Chad Pennington	.25	.60
2 Thomas Jones	.25	.60
3 Laveranues Coles	.20	.50
4 Leon Washington	.25	.60
5 Jerricho Cotchery	.25	.60
6 Kerry Rhodes	.20	.50
7 Justin Miller	.20	.50
8 Jonathan Vilma	.25	.60
9 Cedric Houston	.20	.50
10 Bryan Thomas	.20	.50
11 David Harris	.25	.60
12 Darrelle Revis	.50	1.25

2008 Jets Topps

COMPLETE SET (12)	2.50	5.00
1 Chad Pennington	.25	.60
2 Thomas Jones	.25	.60
3 Jerricho Cotchery	.25	.60
4 Kellen Clemens	.25	.60
5 David Harris	.20	.50
6 Jesse Chatman	.20	.50
7 Kerry Rhodes	.20	.50
8 Leon Washington	.25	.60
9 Laveranues Coles	.20	.50
10 Chris Baker	.20	.50
11 Dustin Keller	.40	1.00
12 Vernon Gholston	.30	.75

2009 Jets Breast Cancer Awareness

This three card set was issued at a Jets game in 2009. Each unnumbered card was created by one of the three NFL licensed manufacturers and features the pink ribbon breast cancer awareness logo on the fronts.

COMPLETE SET (3)	3.00	6.00
1 Jerricho Cotchery Topps	.75	2.00
2 Thomas Jones Upper Deck	.75	2.00
3 Mark Sanchez Panini	1.50	4.00

1963 Jewish Sports Champions

The 16 cards in this set, measuring roughly 2 2/3" x 3", are cut out of an "Activity Funbook" entitled Jewish Sports Champions. The set pays tribute to famous Jewish athletes from baseball, football, bull fighting to chess. The cards have a green border with a yellow background and a player close-up illustration. Cards that are still attached carry a premium over those that have been cut-out. The cards are unnumbered and listed below in alphabetical order with an assigned sport prefix (BB-baseball, BK- basketball, BX- boxing, FB- football, OT- other).

COMPLETE SET (16)	100.00	200.00
FB1 Benny Friedman FB	6.00	12.00
FB2 Sid Luckman FB	10.00	20.00

1996 Jimmy Dean All-Time Greats

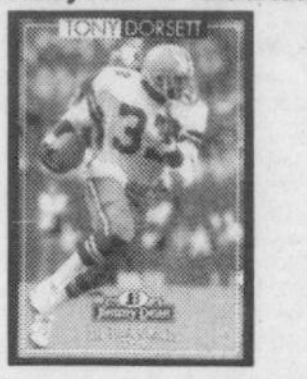

These cards were issued one per package of various Jimmy Dean products in 1996. The cards include a color photo of the player on the front and biographical information on the back. A mail order offer was included for obtaining a signed card from each player for $7.95 each.

COMPLETE SET (4)	1.60	4.00
1 Tony Dorsett	.40	1.00
2 Steve Largent	.40	1.00
3 Gale Sayers	.60	1.50
4 Bart Starr	.80	2.00

1996 Jimmy Dean All-Time Greats Autographs

These cards were distributed via a mail order offer included with 1996 Jimmy Dean cards. Each card could be originally obtained for $7.95 each and was issued along with a separate paper certificate of authenticity.

COMPLETE SET (4)	45.00	80.00
1 Tony Dorsett	10.00	20.00
2 Steve Largent	7.50	15.00
3 Gale Sayers	10.00	20.00
4 Bart Starr	25.00	40.00

1994-96 John Deere

Over a three year period, the John Deere tractor company used professional athletes to promote their products and included cards of these athletes in their set. These five cards were issued in 1994 (Ryan and Novacek), 1995 (Jackson and Petty) and 1996 (Larry Bird). For our cataloguing purposes we are sequencing these cards in alphabetical order. Larry Bird signed some cards for this promotion but these cards are so thinly traded that no pricing is available

COMPLETE SET (5)	15.00	40.00
3 Jay Novacek	1.00	2.50

1959 Kahn's

The 1959 Kahn's football set of 31 black and white cards features players from the Cleveland Browns and the Pittsburgh Steelers. The cards measure approximately 3 1/4" by 3 15/16". The backs contain height, weight and short football career data. The statistics on the back are single spaced. The cards are unnumbered and hence are listed below alphabetically for convenience.

COMPLETE SET (31)	3,000.00	5,000.00
1 Dick Alban	75.00	125.00
2 Jim Brown	800.00	1,200.00
3 Jack Butler	75.00	125.00
4 Lew Carpenter	75.00	125.00
5 Preston Carpenter	75.00	125.00
6 Vince Costello	75.00	125.00
7 Dale Dodrill	75.00	125.00
8 Bob Gain	75.00	125.00
9 Gary Glick	75.00	125.00
10 Lou Groza	125.00	200.00
11 Gene Hickerson	150.00	250.00
12 Bill Howton	90.00	150.00
13 Art Hunter	75.00	125.00
14 Joe Krupa	75.00	125.00
15 Bobby Layne	175.00	300.00
16 Joe Lewis	75.00	125.00
17 Jack McClairen	75.00	125.00
18 Mike McCormack	100.00	175.00
19 Walt Michaels	90.00	150.00
20 Bobby Mitchell	150.00	250.00
21 Jim Ninowski	75.00	125.00
22 Chuck Noll	500.00	800.00
23 Jimmy Orr	75.00	125.00
24 Milt Plum	90.00	150.00
25 Ray Renfro	90.00	150.00
26 Mike Sandusky	75.00	125.00
27 Billy Ray Smith	75.00	125.00
28 Jim Ray Smith	75.00	125.00
29 Ernie Stautner	150.00	250.00
30 Tom Tracy	90.00	150.00
31 Frank Varrichione	75.00	125.00

1960 Kahn's

The 1960 Kahn's football set of 38 cards features Cleveland Browns and Pittsburgh Steelers. The cards measure approximately 3 1/4" by 3 15/16". In addition to data similar to the backs of the 1959 Kahn's cards, the backs of the 1960 Kahn's cards contain an ad for a free professional album and instruction booklet, which could be obtained by sending two labels to Kahn's. The cards are unnumbered and hence are listed below alphabetically for convenience. Willie Davis' card predates his 1964 Philadelphia Rookie Card by four years.

COMPLETE SET (38)	2,500.00	4,000.00
1 Sam Baker	50.00	80.00
2 Jim Brown	300.00	500.00
3 Ray Campbell	50.00	80.00
4 Preston Carpenter	50.00	80.00
5 Vince Costello	50.00	80.00
6 Willie Davis	75.00	125.00
7 Galen Fiss	50.00	80.00
8 Bob Gain	50.00	80.00
9 Lou Groza	90.00	150.00
10 Gene Hickerson	100.00	175.00
11 John Henry Johnson	75.00	125.00
12 Rich Kreitling	50.00	80.00
13 Joe Krupa	50.00	80.00
14 Bobby Layne	150.00	250.00
15 Jack McClairen	50.00	80.00
16 Mike McCormack	75.00	125.00
17 Walt Michaels	50.00	100.00
18 Bobby Mitchell	90.00	150.00
19 Dick Moegle	50.00	100.00
20 John Morrow	50.00	80.00
21 Gern Nagler	50.00	80.00
22 John Nisby	50.00	80.00
23 Jimmy Orr	50.00	100.00
24 Bernie Parrish	50.00	80.00
25 Milt Plum	50.00	100.00
26 John Reger	50.00	80.00
27 Ray Renfro	50.00	100.00
28 Will Renfro	50.00	80.00
29 Mike Sandusky	50.00	80.00
30 Dick Schafrath	50.00	80.00
31 Jim Ray Smith	50.00	80.00
32 Billy Ray Smith	50.00	100.00
33 Ernie Stautner	90.00	150.00
34 George Tarasovic	50.00	80.00
35 Tom Tracy	50.00	100.00
36 Frank Varrichione	50.00	80.00
37 John Wooten	50.00	80.00
38 Lowe W. Wren	50.00	80.00

1961 Kahn's

The 1961 Kahn's football set of 36 cards features Cleveland and Pittsburgh players. The cards measure approximately 3 1/4" by 4 1/16". The backs are the same as the 1960 Kahn's cards; however, the free booklet ad requires but one label to be sent in rather than the two labels required for the 1960 offer. Pictures of Larry Krutko and Tom Tracy are reversed. The cards are unnumbered and hence are listed below alphabetically for convenience.

COMPLETE SET (36)	1,200.00	2,000.00
1 Sam Baker	25.00	40.00
2 Jim Brown	250.00	400.00
3 Preston Carpenter	25.00	40.00
4 Vince Costello	25.00	40.00
5 Dean Derby	25.00	40.00
6 Buddy Dial	25.00	40.00
7 Don Fleming	25.00	40.00
8 Bob Gain	25.00	40.00
9 Bobby Joe Green	25.00	40.00
10 Gene Hickerson	60.00	100.00
11 Jim Houston	25.00	40.00
12 Dan James	25.00	40.00
13 John Henry Johnson	60.00	100.00
14 Rich Kreitling	25.00	40.00
15 Joe Krupa	25.00	40.00
16 Larry Krutko UER (Photo actually Tom Tracy)	25.00	40.00
17 Bobby Layne	100.00	175.00
18 Joe Lewis	25.00	40.00
19 Gene Lipscomb	40.00	80.00
20 Mike McCormack	60.00	100.00
21 Bobby Mitchell	75.00	125.00
22 John Morrow	25.00	40.00
23 John Nisby	25.00	40.00
24 Jimmy Orr	25.00	40.00
25 Milt Plum	30.00	50.00
26 John Reger	25.00	40.00
27 Ray Renfro	30.00	50.00
28 Will Renfro	25.00	40.00
29 Mike Sandusky	25.00	40.00
30 Dick Schafrath	25.00	40.00
31 Jim Ray Smith	25.00	40.00
32 Ernie Stautner	60.00	100.00
33 George Tarasovic	25.00	40.00
34 Tom Tracy UER (Photo actually Larry Krutko)	30.00	50.00
35 Frank Varrichione	25.00	40.00
36 John Wooten	25.00	40.00

1962 Kahn's

The 1962 Kahn's football card set contains 38 players from eight different teams. New teams added in this year's set are the Chicago Bears, Detroit Lions, and Minnesota Vikings. The cards measure approximately 3 1/4" by 4 3/16". The backs contain information comparable to the backs of previous years; however, the statistics are double spaced, and the player's name on the back is in bold-faced type. The cards are unnumbered and hence are listed below alphabetically for conveniencee. An album was also issued to house the set.

COMPLETE SET (38)	1,200.00	2,000.00
1 Maxie Baughan	25.00	40.00
2 Charley Britt	25.00	40.00
3 Jim Brown	200.00	350.00
4 Preston Carpenter	25.00	40.00
5 Pete Case	25.00	40.00
6 Howard Cassady	25.00	50.00
7 Vince Costello	25.00	40.00
8 Buddy Dial	25.00	50.00
9 Gene Hickerson	40.00	80.00
10 Jim Houston	25.00	40.00
11 Dan James	25.00	40.00
12 Rich Kreitling	25.00	40.00
13 Joe Krupa	25.00	40.00
14 Bobby Layne	90.00	150.00
15 Ray Lemek	25.00	40.00
16 Gene Lipscomb	30.00	60.00
17 Dave Lloyd	25.00	40.00
18 Lou Michaels	25.00	40.00
19 Larry Morris	25.00	40.00
20 John Morrow	25.00	40.00
21 Jim Ninowski	25.00	40.00
22 Buzz Nutter	25.00	40.00
23 Jimmy Orr	25.00	40.00
24 Bernie Parrish	25.00	40.00
25 Milt Plum	25.00	50.00
26 Myron Pottios	25.00	40.00
27 John Reger	25.00	40.00
28 Ray Renfro	25.00	50.00
29 Frank Ryan	25.00	50.00
30 Johnny Sample	25.00	40.00
31 Mike Sandusky	25.00	40.00
32 Dick Schafrath	25.00	40.00
33 Jim Shofner	25.00	50.00
34 Jim Ray Smith	25.00	40.00
35 Ernie Stautner	40.00	80.00
36 Fran Tarkenton	150.00	250.00
37 Paul Wiggin	25.00	40.00
38 John Wooten	25.00	40.00

1963 Kahn's

The 1963 Kahn's football card set includes players from six new teams not appearing in previous Kahn sets. All 14 NFL teams are represented in this set. The new teams are Dallas Cowboys, Green Bay Packers, New York Giants, St. Louis Cardinals, San Francisco 49ers and Washington Redskins. The cards measure approximately 3 1/4" by 4 3/16". The backs contain player statistics comparable to previous years; however, this set may be distinguished from Kahn's sets of other years because it is the only Kahn's football card set that has a distinct white border surrounding the picture on the obverse. With a total of 92 different cards, this is the largest Kahn's football issue. The cards are unnumbered and hence are listed below alphabetically for convenience.

COMPLETE SET (92)	1,800.00	3,000.00
1 Bill Barnes	15.00	25.00
2 Erich Barnes	15.00	25.00
3 Dick Bass	18.00	30.00
4 Don Bosseler	15.00	25.00
5 Jim Brown	175.00	300.00
6 Roger Brown	15.00	25.00
7 Roosevelt Brown	25.00	40.00
8 Ronnie Bull	18.00	30.00
9 Preston Carpenter	15.00	25.00
10 Frank Clarke	25.00	40.00
11 Gail Cogdill	15.00	25.00
12 Bobby Joe Conrad	15.00	25.00
13 John David Crow	18.00	30.00
14 Dan Currie	18.00	30.00
15 Buddy Dial	18.00	30.00
16 Mike Ditka	90.00	150.00
17 Fred Dugan	15.00	25.00
18 Galen Fiss	15.00	25.00
19 Bill Forester	18.00	30.00
20 Bob Gain	15.00	25.00
21 Willie Galimore	18.00	30.00
22 Bill George	25.00	40.00
23 Frank Gifford	60.00	100.00
24 Bill Glass	18.00	30.00
25 Forrest Gregg	25.00	40.00
26 Fred Hageman	15.00	25.00
27 Jimmy Hill	15.00	25.00
28 Sam Huff	35.00	60.00
29 Dan James	15.00	25.00
30 John Henry Johnson	25.00	40.00
31 Sonny Jurgensen	35.00	60.00
32 Jim Katcavage	18.00	30.00
33 Ron Kostelnik	15.00	25.00
34 Jerry Kramer	25.00	40.00
35 Ron Kramer	18.00	30.00
36 Dick Lane	25.00	40.00
37 Yale Lary	25.00	40.00
38 Eddie LeBaron	25.00	40.00
39 Dick Lynch	15.00	25.00
40 Tommy Mason	18.00	30.00
41 Tommy McDonald	25.00	40.00
42 Lou Michaels	18.00	30.00
43 Bobby Mitchell	30.00	50.00
44 Dick Modzelewski	15.00	25.00
45 Lenny Moore	35.00	60.00
46 John Morrow	15.00	25.00
47 John Nisby	15.00	25.00
48 Ray Nitschke	50.00	80.00
49 Leo Nomellini	25.00	40.00
50 Jimmy Orr	15.00	25.00
51 John Paluck	15.00	25.00
52 Jim Parker	25.00	40.00
53 Bernie Parrish	15.00	25.00
54 Jim Patton	15.00	25.00
55 Don Perkins	25.00	40.00
56 Richie Petitbon	18.00	30.00
57 Jim Phillips	15.00	25.00
58 Nick Pietrosante	15.00	25.00
59 Milt Plum	18.00	30.00
60 Myron Pottios	15.00	25.00
61 Sonny Randle	18.00	30.00
62 John Reger	15.00	25.00
63 Ray Renfro	18.00	30.00
64 Pete Retzlaff	18.00	30.00
65 Pat Richter	15.00	25.00
66 Jim Ringo	25.00	40.00
67 Andy Robustelli	30.00	50.00
68 Joe Rutgens	15.00	25.00
69 Bob St. Clair	25.00	40.00
70 Johnny Sample	18.00	30.00
71 Lonnie Sanders	15.00	25.00
72 Dick Schafrath	15.00	25.00
73 Joe Schmidt	30.00	50.00
74 Del Shofner	18.00	30.00
75 J.D. Smith	15.00	25.00
76 Norm Snead	25.00	40.00
77 Bill Stacy	15.00	25.00
78 Bart Starr	125.00	225.00
79 Ernie Stautner	30.00	50.00
80 Jim Steffen	15.00	25.00
81 Andy Stynchula	15.00	25.00
82 Fran Tarkenton	60.00	100.00
83 Jim Taylor	50.00	80.00
84 Clendon Thomas	15.00	25.00
85 Fuzzy Thurston	25.00	40.00
86 Y.A. Tittle	60.00	100.00
87 Bob Toneff	15.00	25.00
88 Jerry Tubbs	25.00	40.00
89 Johnny Unitas	150.00	250.00
90 Bill Wade	18.00	30.00
91 Willie Wood	25.00	40.00
92 Abe Woodson	18.00	30.00

1964 Kahn's

The 1964 Kahn's football card set of 53 is the only Kahn's football card set in full color. It is also the only set which does not contain the statement "Compliments of Kahn's, the Wiener the World Awaited" on the cardfront. This slogan is contained on the back of the card which also contains player data similar to cards of other years. The cards measure approximately 3" by 3 5/8". The cards are unnumbered and hence are listed below alphabetically for convenience. Paul Warfield's card holds special interest in that it was issued very early in his career.

COMPLETE SET (53)	900.00	1,500.00
1 Doug Atkins	18.00	30.00
2 Terry Barr	10.00	20.00
3 Dick Bass	15.00	25.00
4 Ordell Braase	10.00	20.00
5 Ed Brown	15.00	25.00
6 Jimmy Brown	90.00	150.00
7 Gary Collins	15.00	25.00
8 Bobby Joe Conrad	10.00	20.00
9 Mike Ditka	60.00	100.00
10 Galen Fiss	10.00	20.00
11 Paul Flatley	15.00	25.00
12 Joe Fortunato	10.00	20.00
13 Bill George	18.00	30.00
14 Bill Glass	15.00	25.00
15 Ernie Green	15.00	25.00
16 Dick Hoak	10.00	20.00
17 Paul Hornung	30.00	50.00
18 Sam Huff	20.00	35.00
19 Charley Johnson	15.00	25.00
20 John Henry Johnson	18.00	30.00
21 Alex Karras	18.00	30.00
22 Jim Katcavage	15.00	25.00
23 Joe Krupa	10.00	20.00
24 Dick Lane	18.00	30.00
25 Tommy Mason	15.00	25.00
26 Don Meredith	50.00	80.00
27 Bobby Mitchell	20.00	35.00
28 Larry Morris	10.00	20.00
29 Jimmy Orr	15.00	25.00
30 Jim Parker	18.00	30.00
31 Bernie Parrish	10.00	20.00
32 Don Perkins	15.00	25.00
33 Jim Phillips	10.00	20.00
34 Sonny Randle	10.00	20.00
35 Pete Retzlaff	15.00	25.00
36 Jim Ringo	18.00	30.00
37 Frank Ryan	15.00	25.00
38 Dick Schafrath	10.00	20.00
39 Joe Schmidt	18.00	30.00
40 Del Shofner	15.00	25.00
41 J.D. Smith	10.00	20.00
42 Norm Snead	15.00	25.00
43 Bart Starr	60.00	100.00
44 Fran Tarkenton	50.00	80.00
45 Jim Taylor	25.00	40.00
46 Clendon Thomas	10.00	20.00
47 Y.A. Tittle	30.00	50.00
48 Jerry Tubbs	15.00	25.00
49 Johnny Unitas	60.00	100.00
50 Bill Wade	15.00	25.00
51 Paul Warfield	35.00	60.00
52 Alex Webster	15.00	25.00
53 Abe Woodson	10.00	20.00

1971 Keds KedKards

This set is composed of crude artistic renditions of popular subjects from various sports from 1971 who were apparently celebrity endorsers of Keds shoes. The cards actually form a complete panel on the Keds tennis shoes box. The three different panels are actually different sizes; the Bing panel contains smaller cards. The smaller Bubba Smith shows him without beard and standing straight; the large Bubba shows him leaning over, with beard, and jersey number partially visible. The individual player card portions of the card panels measure approximately 2 15/16" by 2 3/4" and 2 5/16" by 2 3/16" respectively, although it should noted that there are slight size differences among the individual cards even on the same panel. The panel background is colored in black and yellow. On the Bench/Reed card (number 3 below) each player measures approximately 5 1/4" by 3 1/2". A facsimile autograph appears in the upper left corner of each player's drawing. The Bench/Reed was issued with the Keds Champion boys basketball shoe box, printed on the box top with a black broken line around the card to follow when cutting the card out.

COMPLETE SET (3)	112.50	225.00
1FB Bubba Smith w beard	30.00	60.00
2FB Bubba Smith no beard	30.00	60.00

1937 Kellogg's Pep Stamps

Kellogg's distributed these multi-sport stamps inside specially marked Pep brand cereal boxes in 1937. They were originally issued in four-stamp blocks along with an instructional type tab at the top. The tab contained the sheet number. We've noted the sheet number after each athlete's name below. Note that six athletes appear on two sheets, thereby making those six double prints. There were 24-different sheets produced. We've catalogued the unnumbered stamps below in single loose form according to sport (AR- auto racing, AV- aviation, BB- baseball, BX- boxing, FB- football, GO- golf, HO- horses, SW- swimming, TN- tennis). Stamps can often be found intact in blocks of four along with the tab. Complete blocks of stamps are valued at roughly 50 percent more than the total value of the four individual stamps as priced below. An album was also produced to house the set.

COMPLETE SET (90)	1,000.00	2,000.00
FB1 Bill Alexander 2	12.00	20.00
FB2 Matty Bell 3	12.00	20.00
FB3 Fritz Crisler 14	25.00	40.00
FB4 Bill Cunningham 23	12.00	20.00
FB5 Red Grange 16/22	125.00	200.00
FB6 Howard Jones 18	15.00	25.00
FB7 Andy Kerr 4	15.00	25.00
FB8 Harry Kipke 19	12.00	20.00
FB9 Lou Little 8	25.00	40.00
FB10 Ed Madigan 12	12.00	20.00
FB11 Bronko Nagurski 15	125.00	200.00
FB12 Ernie Nevers 21	35.00	60.00
FB13 Jimmy Phelan 20	12.00	20.00
FB14 Bill Shakespeare 10	15.00	25.00
FB15 Frank Thomas 5	15.00	25.00
FB16 Tiny Thornhill 9	12.00	20.00
FB17 Jim Thorpe 17	125.00	200.00
FB18 Wallace Wade 11	12.00	20.00

1948 Kellogg's All Wheat Sport Tips Series 1

21 Football: Punting	3.00	8.00
22 Football: Passing	3.00	8.00
23 Football: Placement Kick	3.00	8.00
24 Football: Ball Carrying	3.00	8.00

1948 Kellogg's All Wheat Sport Tips Series 2

12 Football: Shoulder Block	3.00	8.00
26 Football: Cross Body Block	3.00	8.00
27 Football: Holding the Ball	3.00	8.00
28 Football: Punt	3.00	8.00

1948 Kellogg's Pep

These small cards measure approximately 1 7/16" by 1 5/8". The card front presents a black and white head-and-shoulders shot of the player, with a white border. The back has the player's name and a brief description of his accomplishments. The cards are unnumbered, but have been assigned numbers below using a sport (BB-baseball, FB- football, BK- basketball, OT- other) prefix. Other Movie Star Kellogg's Pep cards exist, but they are not listed below. The catalog designation for this set is F273-19. An album was also produced to house the set.

COMPLETE SET (20)	700.00	1,400.00
FB1 Lou Groza	80.00	120.00
FB2 George McAfee	25.00	40.00
FB3 Norm Standlee	18.00	30.00
FB4A Charley Trippi (Photo cropped closer; top of helmet fully visible)	50.00	80.00
FB4B Charley Trippi (Photo cropped further away top of helmet slightly cut off)	50.00	80.00
FB5 Bob Waterfield	80.00	120.00

1970 Kellogg's

The 1970 Kellogg's football set of 60 cards was Kellogg's first football issue. The cards have a 3D effect and are approximately 2 1/4" by 3 1/2". The cards could be obtained from boxes of cereal or as a set from a box top offer. The 1970 Kellogg's set can easily be distinguished from the 1971 Kellogg's set by recognizing the color of the helmet logo on the front of each card. In the 1970 set this helmet logo is blue, whereas with the 1971 set the helmet logo is red. The 1971 set also is distinguished by its thick blue (with white spots) border on each card front as well as by the small inset photo in the upper left corner of each reverse. The key card in the set is O.J. Simpson as 1970 was O.J.'s rookie year for cards.

COMPLETE SET (60)	50.00	100.00
1 Carl Eller	.60	1.50
2 Jim Otto	.60	1.50
3 Tom Matte	.40	1.00
4 Bill Nelsen	.30	.75
5 Travis Williams	.30	.75
6 Len Dawson	2.00	4.00
7 Gene Washington Vik	.30	.75
8 Jim Nance	.30	.75
9 Norm Snead	.40	1.00
10 Dick Butkus	4.00	8.00
11 George Sauer Jr.	.40	1.00
12 Billy Kilmer	.50	1.25
13 Alex Karras	1.25	2.50
14 Larry Wilson	.60	1.50
15 Dave Robinson	.30	.75
16 Bill Brown	.30	.75
17 Bob Griese	3.00	6.00
18 Al Denson	.30	.75
19 Dick Post	.30	.75
20 Jan Stenerud	.60	1.50
21 Paul Warfield	2.00	4.00
22 Mel Farr	.30	.75
23 Mel Renfro	.60	1.50
24 Roy Jefferson	.30	.75
25 Mike Garrett	.30	.75
26 Harry Jacobs	.30	.75
27 Carl Garrett	.30	.75
28 Dave Wilcox	.50	1.25
29 Matt Snell	.40	1.00
30 Tom Woodeshick	.30	.75
31 Leroy Kelly	.75	2.00
32 Floyd Little	.40	1.00
33 Ken Willard	.30	.75
34 John Mackey	.75	2.00
35 Merlin Olsen	1.50	3.00
36 Dave Grayson	.30	.75
37 Lem Barney	1.25	2.50
38 Deacon Jones	1.25	2.50
39 Bob Hayes	1.25	2.50
40 Lance Alworth	2.00	4.00
41 Larry Csonka	3.00	6.00
42 Bobby Bell	.75	2.00
43 George Webster	.30	.75
44 Johnny Roland	.30	.75
45 Dick Shiner	.30	.75
46 Bubba Smith	1.25	2.50
47 Daryle Lamonica	.50	1.25
48 O.J. Simpson	5.00	10.00
49 Calvin Hill	.50	1.25
50 Fred Biletnikoff	2.00	4.00
51 Gale Sayers	4.00	8.00
52 Homer Jones	.30	.75
53 Sonny Jurgensen	2.00	4.00
54 Bob Lilly	1.50	3.00
55 Johnny Unitas	6.00	12.00
56 Tommy Nobis	.50	1.25
57 Ed Meador	.30	.75
58 Spider Lockhart	.30	.75
59 Don Maynard	. 2.00	4.00
60 Greg Cook	.30	.75

1971 Kellogg's

The 1971 Kellogg's set of 60 cards could be obtained only from boxes of cereal. One card was inserted in each specially marked box of Kellogg's Corn Flakes and Kellogg's Raisin Bran cereals. The cards measure approximately 2 1/4" by 3 1/2". This set is much more difficult to obtain than the previous Kellogg's set since no box top offer was available. The 1971 Kellogg's set can easily be distinguished from the 1970 Kellogg's set by recognizing the color of the helmet logo on the front of each card. In the 1970 set this helmet logo is blue, whereas with the 1971 set the helmet logo is red. The 1971 set also is distinguished by its thick blue (with white spots) border on each card front as well as by the small inset photo in the uppper left corner of each reverse. Among the key cards in the set is Joe Greene as 1971 was "Mean" Joe's rookie year for cards.

COMPLETE SET (60)	200.00	400.00
1 Tom Barrington	2.50	5.00
2 Chris Hanburger	3.00	6.00
3 Frank Nunley	2.50	5.00
4 Houston Antwine	2.50	5.00
5 Ron Johnson	3.00	6.00
6 Craig Morton	4.00	8.00
7 Jack Snow	3.00	6.00
8 Mel Renfro	5.00	10.00
9 Les Josephson	2.50	5.00
10 Gary Garrison	2.50	5.00
11 Dave Herman	2.50	5.00
12 Fred Dryer	4.00	8.00
13 Larry Brown	3.00	6.00
14 Gene Washington 49er	3.00	6.00
15 Joe Greene	10.00	20.00
16 Marlin Briscoe	2.50	5.00
17 Bob Grant	2.50	5.00
18 Dan Conners	2.50	5.00
19 Mike Curtis	3.00	6.00
20 Harry Schuh	2.50	5.00
21 Rich Jackson	2.50	5.00
22 Clint Jones	2.50	5.00
23 Hewritt Dixon	2.50	5.00
24 Jess Phillips	2.50	5.00
25 Gary Cuozzo	2.50	5.00
26 Bo Scott	2.50	5.00
27 Glen Ray Hines	2.50	5.00
28 Johnny Unitas	17.50	35.00
29 John Gilliam	2.50	5.00
30 Harmon Wages	2.50	5.00
31 Walt Sweeney	2.50	5.00
32 Bruce Taylor	2.50	5.00
33 George Blanda	10.00	20.00
34 Ken Bowman	2.50	5.00
35 Johnny Robinson	3.00	6.00
36 Ed Podolak	2.50	5.00
37 Curley Culp	2.50	5.00
38 Jim Hart	3.00	6.00
39 Dick Butkus	12.50	25.00
40 Floyd Little	3.00	6.00
41 Nick Buoniconti	4.00	8.00
42 Larry Smith	2.50	5.00
43 Wayne Walker	3.00	6.00
44 MacArthur Lane	2.50	5.00
45 John Brodie	6.00	12.00
46 Dick LeBeau	2.50	5.00
47 Claude Humphrey	2.50	5.00
48 Jerry LeVias	2.50	5.00
49 Erich Barnes	2.50	5.00
50 Andy Russell	3.00	6.00
51 Donny Anderson	3.00	6.00
52 Mike Reid	4.00	8.00
53 Al Atkinson	2.50	5.00
54 Tom Dempsey	2.50	5.00
55 Bob Griese	10.00	20.00
56 Dick Gordon	2.50	5.00
57 Charlie Sanders	3.00	6.00
58 Doug Cunningham	2.50	5.00
59 Cyril Pinder	2.50	5.00
60 Dave Osborn	2.50	5.00

1978 Kellogg's Stickers

These stickers measure approximately 2 1/2" by 2 5/8". The fronts feature color team helmets with the team's name below. The backs carry a short team history and a quiz about referee's signals. The stickers are numbered on the back "X of 28."

COMPLETE SET (28)	60.00	100.00
1 Atlanta Falcons	3.00	6.00
2 Baltimore Colts	3.00	6.00
3 Buffalo Bills	3.00	6.00
4 Chicago Bears	4.00	8.00
5 Cincinnati Bengals	3.00	6.00
6 Cleveland Browns	4.00	8.00
7 Dallas Cowboys	4.00	8.00
8 Denver Broncos	3.00	6.00
9 Detroit Lions	3.00	6.00
10 Green Bay Packers	4.00	8.00
11 Houston Oilers	3.00	6.00
12 Kansas City Chiefs	3.00	6.00
13 Los Angeles Rams	3.00	6.00
14 Miami Dolphins	4.00	8.00
15 Minnesota Vikings	3.00	6.00
16 New England Patriots	3.00	6.00
17 New Orleans Saints	3.00	6.00
18 New York Giants	3.00	6.00
19 New York Jets	3.00	6.00
20 Oakland Raiders	4.00	8.00
21 Philadelphia Eagles	3.00	6.00
22 Pittsburgh Steelers	4.00	8.00
23 St. Louis Cardinals	3.00	6.00
24 San Diego Chargers	3.00	6.00
25 San Francisco 49ers	3.00	6.00
26 Seattle Seahawks	3.00	6.00
27 Tampa Bay Buccaneers	3.00	6.00
28 Washington Redskins	4.00	8.00

1982 Kellogg's Panels

The 1982 Kellogg's National Football League set of 24 cards was issued in eight panels of three cards each. The cards measure 2 1/2" by 3 1/2" and the panels are approximately 4 1/8" by 7 1/2". The cards came with Kellogg's Raisin Bran cereal and contain statistics on the back. Cards are in color and contain the Kellogg's logo in the lower right corner of the front of the card. While not numbered, the cards have been listed in the checklist below alphabetically according to the left hand side player, when the panel is viewed from the front. Prices below are for full panels of three. It is possible (but not recommended) to separate the cards at the perforation marks. Sharp-eyed Cowboy fans will notice that the photos for Harvey Martin and Billy Joe DuPree were erroneously switched.

COMPLETE SET (8)	4.00	10.00
1 Ken Anderson Frank Lewis Gifford Nielsen	.40	1.00
2 Ottis Anderson Cris Collinsworth Franco Harris	.75	2.00
3 William Andrews Brian Sipe Fred Smerlas	.40	1.00
4 Steve Bartkowski Robert Brazile Jack Rudnay	.40	1.00
5 Tony Dorsett Eric Hipple Pat McInally	.75	2.00
6 Billy Joe DuPree UER (Photo actually Harvey Martin) David Hill John Stallworth	.60	1.50
7 Harvey Martin UER (Photo actually Billy Joe DuPree) Mike Pruitt Joe Senser	.40	1.00
8 Art Still Mel Gray Tommy Kramer	.40	1.00

1982 Kellogg's Team Posters

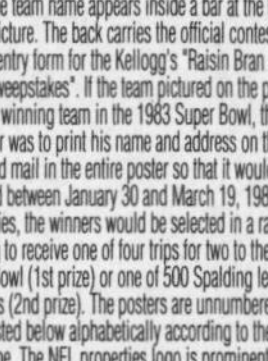

These 28 NFL team posters were inserted in specially marked boxes of Kellogg's Raisin Bran cereal. Each poster measures approximately 8" by 10 1/2" and is printed on thin paper stock. Inside a thin black border, the fronts feature a color painting of an action scene, with a smaller painting of another scene placed over to the side. The team name appears inside a bar at the bottom of the picture. The back carries the official contest rules and an entry form for the Kellogg's "Raisin Bran Super Bowl Sweepstakes". If the team pictured on the poster was the winning team in the 1983 Super Bowl, the collector was to print his name and address on the entry form and mail in the entire poster so that it would be received between January 30 and March 19, 1983. From the entries, the winners would be selected in a random drawing to receive one of four trips for two to the 1984 Super Bowl (1st prize) or one of 500 Spalding leather footballs (2nd prize). The posters are unnumbered and checklisted below alphabetically according to the team's city name. The NFL properties logo is prominently displayed on the card front. The posters are typically found with fold marks as they were folded into three parts both horizontally and vertically. The posters are copyrighted 1982 on the front. No players are explicitly identified on the cards. The poster backs are printed in light blue ink.

COMPLETE SET (28)	100.00	250.00
1 Atlanta Falcons	4.00	10.00
2 Buffalo Bills	4.00	10.00
3 Chicago Bears	4.00	10.00
4 Cincinnati Bengals	4.00	10.00
5 Cleveland Browns	4.00	10.00
6 Dallas Cowboys	6.00	15.00
7 Denver Broncos	6.00	15.00
8 Detroit Lions	4.00	10.00

9 Green Bay Packers	10.00	20.00
10 Houston Oilers	4.00	10.00
11 Indianapolis Colts	4.00	10.00
12 Kansas City Chiefs	4.00	10.00
13 Los Angeles Raiders	15.00	30.00
14 Los Angeles Rams	4.00	10.00
15 Miami Dolphins	6.00	15.00
16 Minnesota Vikings	4.00	10.00
17 New England Patriots	4.00	10.00
18 New Orleans Saints	4.00	10.00
19 New York Giants	4.00	10.00
20 New York Jets	4.00	10.00
21 Philadelphia Eagles	4.00	10.00
22 Pittsburgh Steelers	6.00	15.00
23 St. Louis Cardinals	4.00	10.00
24 San Diego Chargers	4.00	10.00
25 San Francisco 49ers	6.00	15.00
26 Seattle Seahawks	4.00	10.00
27 Tampa Bay Buccaneers	4.00	10.00
28 Washington Redskins WIN	15.00	30.00

1983 Kellogg's Stickers

Similar to the 1978 Kellogg's Stickers, these measure approximately 2 1/2" by 2 5/8" with the fronts featuring color team helmets with the team's name below. The backs carry a football game called "Touchdown" that could be played with the cards. A blankbacked version of the stickers was also released.

COMPLETE SET (28)	40.00	80.00
1 Atlanta Falcons	2.50	5.00
2 Baltimore Colts	2.50	5.00
3 Buffalo Bills	2.50	5.00
4 Chicago Bears	3.00	6.00
5 Cincinnati Bengals	2.50	5.00
6 Cleveland Browns	3.00	6.00
7 Dallas Cowboys	3.00	6.00
8 Denver Broncos	2.50	5.00
9 Detroit Lions	2.50	5.00
10 Green Bay Packers	3.00	6.00
11 Houston Oilers	2.50	5.00
12 Kansas City Chiefs	2.50	5.00
13 Los Angeles Raiders	3.00	6.00
14 Los Angeles Rams	2.50	5.00
15 Miami Dolphins	3.00	6.00
16 Minnesota Vikings	2.50	5.00
17 New England Patriots	2.50	5.00
18 New Orleans Saints	2.50	5.00
19 New York Giants	2.50	5.00
20 New York Jets	2.50	5.00
21 Philadelphia Eagles	2.50	5.00
22 Pittsburgh Steelers	3.00	6.00
23 St. Louis Cardinals	2.50	5.00
24 San Diego Chargers	2.50	5.00
25 San Francisco 49ers	2.50	5.00
26 Seattle Seahawks	2.50	5.00
27 Tampa Bay Buccaneers	2.50	5.00
28 Washington Redskins	3.00	6.00

1969 Kelly's Chips Zip Stickers

This set of small stickers was inserted one per package in Kelly's Brand Chips in 1969. Each includes a black and white head photo of the player against a red/orange (cards #1-6), green (#7-12), or blue (#13-20) colored background along with the word "ZIP" on the fronts. The backs contain the sticker number and instructions on obtaining a full color action signed photo of a player. Each sticker measures roughly 2" by 3."

1 Dave Williams UER (name misspelled William)	50.00	80.00
3 Willie Crenshaw	50.00	80.00
4 Jim Bakken	50.00	80.00
6 Larry Wilson	60.00	100.00
7 Bart Starr	300.00	500.00
8 John Mackey	60.00	100.00
9 Joe Namath	300.00	500.00
10 Ray Nitschke UER (name misspelled Nitchke)	100.00	175.00
11 Jim Grabowski	60.00	100.00
12 Bob Hayes	90.00	150.00
13 Gale Sayers	175.00	300.00
14 Dick Butkus	175.00	300.00
16 Brian Piccolo	175.00	300.00
17 Mike Pyle	50.00	80.00
19 Roman Gabriel	60.00	100.00
20 Bill Brown	60.00	100.00

1993 Kemper Walter Payton

Kemper Mutual Funds sponsored this card and pin set featuring Walter Payton. The card and pin together were given away at a 1993 Bears game honoring Walter Payton's induction into the Hall of Fame.

COMPLETE SET (2)	3.20	8.00
1 Walter Payton Card	2.00	5.00
2 Walter Payton Pin	1.20	3.00

1989 King B Discs

The 1989 King B Football Discs set has 24 red-bordered 2 3/8" diameter round discs. The fronts have helmetless color mug shots; the backs are white and have sparse bio and stats. One disc was included in each specially marked can of King B beef jerky. The discs are numbered on the back. The set is arranged alphabetically by teams, one player per team, with only 24 of the 28 NFL teams represented. The set, which was produced by Michael Schechter Associates, was apparently endorsed only by the NFLPA. There are many quarterbacks included in the set. The discs are referred to as "1st Annual Collectors Edition." It has been estimated that 500,000 total discs were produced for this issue.

COMPLETE SET (24)	40.00	80.00
1 Chris Miller	1.00	2.50
2 Shane Conlan	.60	1.50
3 Richard Dent	1.00	2.50
4 Boomer Esiason	1.00	2.50
5 Frank Minnifield	.60	1.50
6 Herschel Walker	1.00	2.50
7 Karl Mecklenburg	.60	1.50
8 Mike Cofer	.60	1.50
9 Warren Moon	1.50	4.00
10 Chris Chandler	1.50	4.00
11 Deron Cherry	.60	1.50
12 Bo Jackson	2.50	5.00
13 Jim Everett	1.00	2.50
14 Dan Marino	10.00	25.00
15 Anthony Carter	1.00	2.50
16 Andre Tippett	.60	1.50
17 Bobby Hebert	.60	1.50
18 Phil Simms	1.00	2.50
19 Al Toon	1.00	2.50
20 Gary Anderson RB	.60	1.50
21 Joe Montana	10.00	25.00
22 Dave Krieg	.60	1.50
23 Randall Cunningham	1.50	4.00
24 Bubby Brister	1.00	2.50

1990 King B Discs

The 1990 King B Discs set contains 24 discs each measuring approximately 2 3/8" in diameter. The fronts have color head shots of the players (without helmets), encircled by a red border on a yellow background. The year "1990" in green block lettering and a King B football icon overlay the bottom of the picture. On the backs, the biographical and statistical information is encircled by a ring of stars. The style of the set is very similar to the previous year.

COMPLETE SET (24)	30.00	75.00
1 Jim Everett	.50	1.25
2 Marcus Allen	1.20	3.00
3 Brian Blades	.50	1.25
4 Bubby Brister	.80	2.00
5 Mark Carrier WR	.80	2.00
6 Steve Jordan	.50	1.25
7 Barry Sanders	10.00	25.00
8 Ronnie Lott	.80	2.00
9 Howie Long	1.20	3.00
10 Steve Atwater	.50	1.25
11 Dan Marino	10.00	25.00
12 Boomer Esiason	.80	2.00
13 Dalton Hilliard	.50	1.25
14 Phil Simms	.80	2.00
15 Jim Kelly	1.20	3.00
16 Mike Singletary	.80	2.00
17 John Stephens	.50	1.25
18 Christian Okoye	.50	1.25
19 Art Monk	.80	2.00
20 Chris Miller	.80	2.00
21 Roger Craig	.80	2.00
22 Duane Bickett	.50	1.25
23 Don Majkowski	.50	1.25
24 Eric Metcalf	.80	2.00
NNO Uncut Sheet	35.00	60.00

1991 King B Discs

This set of 24 discs was produced by Michael Schechter Associates, and each one measures approximately 2 5/8" in diameter. One disc was included in each specially marked can of King B beef jerky. The front features a head shot of the player, his name, position, and team name printed in gold in the magenta border. The year and the King B logo are printed at the base of each picture. The circular backs are printed in scarlet and carry biographical and statistical information encircled by stars.

COMPLETE SET (24)	20.00	50.00
1 Mark Rypien	.60	1.50
2 Art Monk	.60	1.50
3 Sean Jones	.40	1.00
4 Bubby Brister	.60	1.50
5 Warren Moon	.80	2.00
6 Andre Rison	.60	1.50
7 Emmitt Smith	5.00	12.00
8 Mervyn Fernandez	.40	1.00
9 Rickey Jackson	.40	1.00
10 Bruce Armstrong	.40	1.00
11 Neal Anderson	.60	1.50
12 Christian Okoye	.40	1.00
13 Thurman Thomas	.80	2.00
14 Bruce Smith	.80	2.00
15 Jeff Hostetler	.60	1.50
16 Barry Sanders	6.00	15.00
17 Andre Reed	.60	1.50
18 Derrick Thomas	.80	2.00
19 Jim Everett	.60	1.50
20 Boomer Esiason	.60	1.50
21 Merril Hoge	.40	1.00
22 Steve Atwater	.40	1.00
23 Dan Marino	6.00	15.00
24 Mark Collins	.40	1.00
NNO Uncut Sheet	8.00	20.00

1992 King B Discs

For the fourth consecutive year, Mike Schechter Associates produced a 24-disc set for King B. One disc was included in each specially marked can of King B beef jerky. The discs measure approximately 2 3/8" in diameter. The fronts feature posed color player photos edged by a bright yellow border on a black face. The player's name appears in white at the top with his position and team name immediately below. The year in white block lettering and a bright yellow King B helmet icon are at the base of the picture. The backs are white with black print, and they carry biography, statistics, the player's name, and the King B helmet icon. The left and right edges are detailed with solid black and black outline stars.

COMPLETE SET (24)	12.00	30.00
1 Derrick Thomas	.40	1.00
2 Wilber Marshall	.30	.75
3 Andre Rison	.40	1.00
4 Thurman Thomas	.50	1.25
5 Emmitt Smith	3.20	8.00
6 Charles Mann	.30	.75
7 Michael Irvin	.50	1.25
8 Jim Everett	.40	1.00
9 Gary Anderson RB	.30	.75
10 Trace Armstrong	.30	.75
11 John Elway	3.20	8.00
12 Chip Lohmiller	.30	.75
13 Bobby Hebert	.30	.75
14 Cornelius Bennett	.40	1.00
15 Chris Miller	.30	.75
16 Warren Moon	.50	1.25
17 Charles Haley	.30	.75
18 Mark Rypien	.30	.75
19 Darrell Green	.30	.75
20 Barry Sanders	3.20	8.00
21 Rodney Hampton	.40	1.00
22 Shane Conlan	.30	.75
23 Jerry Ball	.30	.75
24 Morten Andersen	.30	.75
NNO Uncut Sheet	8.00	20.00

1993 King B Discs

This Fifth Annual Collectors Edition of the King B Discs set was produced by Michael Schechter Associates. One disc was included in each specially marked can of King B beef jerky. Each disc measures approximately 2 3/8" in diameter and features on its front a posed color player head shot bordered on the sides by a green gridiron design. The player's name, position, and team appear in orange and white lettering within the black margin above the photo. The year of the set, 1993, and a blue football helmet icon bearing the King B logo rest in the black margin at the bottom. The backs are white with black print, and they carry the player's name, team, position, biography, statistics (or highlights), and the King B helmet icon. The left and right edges are detailed with solid black and black outline stars. This set was also issued in an uncut sheet measuring 17 1/4" by 12 3/4".

COMPLETE SET (24)	12.50	25.00
1 Luis Sharpe	.40	1.00
2 Erik McMillan	.40	1.00
3 Chris Doleman	.40	1.00
4 Cortez Kennedy	.40	1.00
5 Howie Long	.50	1.25
6 Bill Romanowski	.40	1.00
7 Andre Tippett	.40	1.00
8 Simon Fletcher	.40	1.00
9 Derrick Thomas	.50	1.25
10 Rodney Peete	.40	1.00
11 Ronnie Lott	.50	1.25
12 Duane Bickett	.40	1.00
13 Steve Walsh	.40	1.00
14 Stan Humphries	.50	1.25
15 Jeff George	.50	1.25
16 Jay Novacek	.50	1.25
17 Andre Reed	.50	1.25
18 Andre Rison	.50	1.25
19 Emmitt Smith	4.00	8.00
20 Neal Anderson	.50	1.25
21 Ricky Sanders	.40	1.00
22 Thurman Thomas	1.00	2.50
23 Lorenzo White	.40	1.00
24 Barry Foster	.40	1.00

1994 King B Discs

Produced by Michael Schechter Associates, this was the Sixth Annual Collectors Edition of 1994 King B discs. One disc was included in each specially-marked can of King B beef jerky. The discs measure approximately 2 3/8" in diameter. On a green background, the fronts feature posed color closeups. The player's name, position and the team name appear inside a yellow ochre bar across the bottom part of the photo. The year 1994 and the King B logo are below. The backs are white with green print and carry player biography and statistics. The discs are basically arranged alphabetically and numbered on the back as "X of 24."

COMPLETE SET (24)	12.50	25.00
1 Marcus Allen	.60	1.50
2 Jerome Bettis	1.00	2.50
3 Terrell Buckley	.40	1.00
4 Craig Erickson	.40	1.00
5 Brett Favre	4.00	8.00
6 Barry Foster	.40	1.00
7 Irving Fryar	.40	1.00
8 Gary Brown	.40	1.00
9 Rodney Hampton	.40	1.00
10 Qadry Ismail	.50	1.25
11 Jim Jeffcoat	.40	1.00
12 Jim Lachey	.40	1.00
13 Natrone Means	.50	1.25
14 Tony Meola	.40	1.00
15 Pete Metzelaars	.40	1.00
16 Scott Mitchell	.40	1.00
17 Ronald Moore	.40	1.00
18 Andre Rison	.50	1.25
19 Jay Schroeder	.40	1.00
20 Junior Seau	.50	1.25
21 Shannon Sharpe	.50	1.25
22 Sterling Sharpe	.50	1.25
23 Tim Brown	.60	1.50
24 Chris Warren	.40	1.00

1995 King B Discs

Produced by Michael Schechter Associates, the "7th Annual Collectors Edition" was issued both as a 17 1/4" by 12 1/2" collector sheet and as individual discs in shredded beef jerky containers. The discs measure 2 5/8" in diameter and feature on their fronts color closeup photos on a white back picturing in gray a running back pursued by two defenders. The left side of the disc is dark brown with thin vertical gold stripes. Inside a circle formed by the player's name and alternating football and star icons, the backs present biography and statistics. The discs are numbered on the back "X of 24."

COMPLETE SET (24)	12.50	25.00
1 Errict Rhett	.40	1.00
2 Andre Reed	.50	1.25
3 Rodney Hampton	.40	1.00
4 Kevin Greene	.40	1.00
5 Merton Hanks	.40	1.00
6 Jerome Bettis	.75	2.00
7 Johnny Johnson	.40	1.00
8 Ricky Watters	.40	1.00
9 Harvey Williams	.40	1.00
10 Mel Gray	.40	1.00
11 Craig Erickson	.40	1.00
12 Stan Humphries	.40	1.00
13 Natrone Means	.40	1.00
14 Terance Mathis	.40	1.00
15 Ken Harvey	.40	1.00
16 Brian Mitchell	.40	1.00
17 Cris Carter	.60	1.50
18 Tim Brown	.60	1.50
19 Marshall Faulk	3.00	6.00
20 Eric Turner	.40	1.00
21 Terry Allen	.40	1.00
22 Chris Warren	.40	1.00
23 Randy Baldwin	.40	1.00
24 Ben Coates	.40	1.00

1996 King B Discs

Michael Schechter Associates again produced a King B Discs set in 1996. This "8th Annual Collectors Edition" was issued both as a 17 1/4" by 12 1/2" collector sheet and as individual discs in shredded beef jerky containers. The discs measure 2 5/8" in diameter and feature on their fronts color closeup photos on white paper stock. Only top NFL defensive players were included in the set. The backs present a player biography and statistics as well as the card's number "X of 24."

COMPLETE SET (24)	12.50	25.00
1 Reggie White	1.00	2.50
2 Rickey Jackson	.40	1.00
3 Kevin Greene	.50	1.25
4 Tony Bennett	.40	1.00
5 Bryce Paup	.40	1.00
6 John Copeland	.40	1.00
7 Pat Swilling	.40	1.00
8 Willie McGinest	.40	1.00
9 Charles Haley	.50	1.25
10 Chris Doleman	.40	1.00
11 Clyde Simmons	.40	1.00
12 Hugh Douglas	.40	1.00
13 Henry Thomas	.40	1.00
14 John Randle	.50	1.25
15 Phil Hansen	.40	1.00
16 Bruce Smith	.60	1.50
17 Jim Flanigan	.40	1.00
18 D'Marco Farr	.40	1.00
19 Ray Seals	.40	1.00
20 Neil Smith	.40	1.00
21 Andy Harmon	.40	1.00
22 William Fuller	.40	1.00
23 Tracy Scroggins	.40	1.00
24 Leslie O'Neal	.40	1.00

1997 King B Discs

Michael Schechter Associates produced a King B Discs set in 1997 for the 9th time. This set was issued both as a 17 1/4" by 12 1/2" collector sheet and as individual discs in shredded beef jerky containers. The discs measure 2 5/8" in diameter and feature on their fronts color closeup photos on white paper stock. Only top NFL rookies were included in the set. The backs present a player biography and college statistics as well as the card's number "X of 24."

COMPLETE SET (24)	40.00	75.00
1 Orlando Pace	1.00	2.50
2 Darrell Russell	1.00	2.50
3 Shawn Springs	.75	2.00
4 Peter Boulware	1.25	3.00
5 Bryant Westbrook	.75	2.00
6 Walter Jones	1.25	3.00
7 Ike Hilliard	1.25	3.00
8 James Farrior	1.00	2.50
9 Tom Knight	.75	2.00
10 Chris Naeole	.75	2.00
11 Warrick Dunn	3.00	8.00
12 Tony Gonzalez	3.00	8.00
13 Reinard Wilson	.75	2.00
14 Yatil Green	1.25	3.00
15 Reidel Anthony	1.25	3.00
16 Dwayne Rudd	.75	2.00
17 Renaldo Wynn	.75	2.00
18 David LaFleur	.75	2.00
19 Antowain Smith	2.50	6.00
20 Chad Scott	.75	2.00
21 Jim Druckenmiller	1.25	3.00
22 Rae Carruth	.75	2.00
23 Ronnie McAda	.75	2.00
24 Jake Plummer	3.00	8.00

1998 King B Discs

Produced by Michael Schechter Associates, the "10th Annual Collectors Edition" was issued both as a 17 1/4" by 12 1/2" collector sheet and as individual discs in shredded beef jerky containers. The discs measure 2 5/8" in diameter and feature on their fronts color closeup photos with an art drawing of a generic player in the background. Again, the set featured only NFL draft picks and was subtitled Hot Picks. The disc backs feature player vital statistics and career college stats. Each is numbered on the back "X of 24."

COMPLETE SET (24)	25.00	50.00
1 Grant Wistrom	.50	1.25
2 Jerome Pathon	.75	2.00
3 Skip Hicks	.50	1.25
4 Charles Woodson	1.50	4.00
5 Joe Jurevicius	.75	2.00
6 Tra Thomas	.40	1.00
7 Andre Wadsworth	.50	1.25
8 Fred Taylor	3.00	6.00
9 Duane Starks	.50	1.25
10 Takeo Spikes	.75	2.00
11 Anthony Simmons	.40	1.00
12 Brian Simmons	.40	1.00
13 Kevin Dyson	1.00	2.50
14 Curtis Enis	.75	2.00
15 Robert Edwards	1.00	2.50
16 Greg Ellis	.40	1.00
17 Marcus Nash	.40	1.00
18 Jason Peter	.50	1.25
19 Keith Brooking	.75	2.00
20 John Avery	.50	1.25
21 Ahman Green	2.00	5.00
22 Jacquez Green	.50	1.25
23 Brian Griese	3.00	6.00
24 Randy Moss	5.00	12.00

1999 King B Discs

Produced by Michael Schechter Associates (MSA), the "11th Annual Collectors Edition" was issued as individual discs in shredded beef jerky containers. The discs measure 2 5/8" in diameter and feature on their fronts color closeup photos of a top 1998 NFL Draft Pick. The disc backs feature player vital statistics and career college stats. Each is numbered on the back "X of 24."

COMPLETE SET (24)	25.00	50.00
1 Jevon Kearse	1.50	4.00
2 Kevin Johnson	1.50	4.00
3 Torry Holt	1.25	3.00
4 Jermaine Fazande	.50	1.25
5 Shaun King	.50	1.25
6 Edgerrin James	5.00	10.00
7 James Johnson	.50	1.25
8 Chris McAlister	.40	1.00
9 Antoine Winfield	.40	1.00
10 D'Wayne Bates	.40	1.00
11 Peerless Price	1.50	4.00
12 Troy Edwards	.50	1.25
13 Ebenezer Ekuban	.40	1.00
14 Andy Katzenmoyer	.50	1.25
15 Kevin Faulk	.75	2.00
16 David Boston	1.50	4.00
17 Brock Huard	.75	2.00
18 Daunte Culpepper	4.00	8.00
19 Akili Smith	.40	1.00
20 Mike Cloud	.50	1.25
21 Champ Bailey	.75	2.00
22 Rob Konrad	.50	1.25
23 Chris Claiborne	.40	1.00
24 Donovan McNabb	5.00	10.00

2000 King B Discs

This set is titled "Stars of the New Millennium" on the fronts and includes only 2000 NFL Draft picks. The discs were issued one per King B Jerky package. A color image of the player is included on the cardfronts with a simple blue and white cardback.

COMPLETE SET (24)	25.00	50.00
1 Ron Dayne	1.25	3.00
2 Trung Canidate	1.00	2.50
3 Plaxico Burress	1.50	4.00
4 Courtney Brown	.75	2.00
5 Anthony Becht	.60	1.50
6 Shaun Alexander	1.50	4.00
7 Sylvester Morris	.75	2.00
8 Jamal Lewis	2.50	6.00
9 Thomas Jones	.75	2.00
10 Bubba Franks	.75	2.00
11 Ron Dugans	.40	1.00
12 Reuben Droughns	.60	1.50
13 J.R. Redmond	.60	1.50
14 Travis Prentice	.60	1.50
15 Jerry Porter	1.00	2.50
16 Todd Pinkston	.60	1.50
17 Chad Pennington	2.50	6.00
18 Dennis Northcutt	.75	2.00
19 Peter Warrick	1.25	3.00
20 Brian Urlacher	2.50	6.00
21 Travis Taylor	1.00	2.50
22 R.Jay Soward	.60	1.50
23 Corey Simon	.75	2.00
24 Chris Samuels	.40	1.00
NNO Uncut Sheet	7.50	20.00

2001 King B Discs

For the 13th straight year, King B Jerky issued a set of NFL player discs. This set is titled "Prime Pros" as printed on the cardfronts and includes NFL stars licensed by Player's Inc. The discs were issued one per King B Jerky package. A color image of the player is included on the cardfronts with a standard black and white cardback.

COMPLETE SET (24)	25.00	50.00
1 Ray Lewis	.75	2.00
2 Emmitt Smith	2.00	5.00
3 Ed McCaffrey	.75	2.00
4 Dorsey Levens	.60	1.50
5 Edgerrin James	2.00	5.00
6 Mark Brunell	.75	2.00
7 Terrell Owens	.75	2.00
8 Randy Moss	1.50	4.00
9 Daunte Culpepper	.75	2.00
10 Ty Law	.60	1.50
11 Tony Gonzalez	.75	2.00
12 Jason Sehorn	.40	1.00
13 Tiki Barber	.60	1.50
14 Zach Thomas	.75	2.00
15 Kurt Warner	1.50	4.00
16 Marshall Faulk	1.00	2.50
17 Eddie George	.75	2.00
18 Stephen Davis	.60	1.50
19 Jamal Anderson	.60	1.50
20 Tony Siragusa	.40	1.00
21 Corey Dillon	.75	2.00
22 Wayne Chrebet	.60	1.50
23 Curtis Martin	.75	2.00
24 Marvin Harrison	.75	2.00
NNO Uncut Sheet	7.50	20.00

2002 King B Discs

For the 14th straight year, King B Jerky issued a set of NFL player discs. This set is titled "Team Stars" as printed on the cardfronts and includes NFL stars licensed by Player's Inc. The discs were issued one per King B Jerky package. A color image of the player is included on the cardfronts with a standard black and white cardback. A collectible uncut sheet of the entire set was also produced. Please note that two players were incorrectly numbered 21 and that no disc #23 was produced.

COMPLETE SET (24)	25.00	50.00
1 Corey Dillon	.60	1.50
2 Rod Smith	.60	1.50
3 Ahman Green	.75	2.00
4 Edgerrin James	1.25	3.00
5 Tony Gonzalez	.75	2.00
6 Tom Brady	2.50	6.00
7 Michael Strahan	.60	1.50
8 Curtis Martin	.75	2.00
9 Tim Brown	.75	2.00
10 Jerome Bettis	.75	2.00
11 Marshall Faulk	1.00	2.50
12 Kurt Warner	1.50	4.00
13 Terrell Owens	.75	2.00
14 Shaun Alexander	1.00	2.50
15 Warren Sapp	.60	1.50
16 Eddie George	.75	2.00
17 Brett Favre	2.50	6.00
18 Jeff Garcia	.75	2.00
19 Rich Gannon	.60	1.50
20 Jerry Rice	2.00	5.00
21A Kordell Stewart	.60	1.50
21B Adam Vinatieri	.75	2.00
22 Brian Griese	.75	2.00
23 Marvin Harrison	.75	2.00
NNO Uncut Sheet	7.50	20.00

1991 Knudsen

This 18-card set (of bookmarks) produced by Knudsen's Dairy in California measures approximately 2" by 8". They were presented to youngsters who checked out library books during the 1991 football season in order to promote reading. The fronts feature a player photo superimposed on the page of a book, with biography and career summary below. Card numbers appear in circles in the lower right corner of each card. The backs have logos of the sponsors and describe two books that are available at the public library. The bookmarks were distributed in the team's respective areas, San Diego Chargers (1-6), Los Angeles Rams (7-12), and San Francisco 49ers (13-18).

COMPLETE SET (18)	32.00	80.00
1 Gill Byrd	.80	2.00
2 Courtney Hall	.80	2.00
3 Ronnie Harmon	.80	2.00
4 Anthony Miller	.80	2.00
5 Joe Phillips	.80	2.00
6 Junior Seau	1.60	4.00
7 Jim Everett	1.20	3.00
8 Kevin Greene	1.20	3.00
9 Damone Johnson	.80	2.00
10 Tom Newberry	.80	2.00
11 John Robinson CO	.80	2.00
12 Michael Stewart	.80	2.00
13 Michael Carter	.80	2.00
14 Charles Haley	1.20	3.00
15 Joe Montana	14.00	35.00
16 Tom Rathman	.80	2.00
17 Jerry Rice	10.00	25.00
18 George Seifert CO	1.20	3.00

1971 Lake County Rifles Milk Cartons

These cards were cut from milk cartons and feature a small single color player image from the Lake County (Illinois) semi-pro football team. Each card also include a very short bio of the player as well as the team's season schedule. A coupon good for a discounted game ticket was also included at the bottom, but presumably would be removed from most cards. The cardbacks are blank.

1 Clifford Boyd	5.00	10.00
2 Bruce Hart	5.00	10.00
3 Terry Stanger	5.00	10.00

1993 Lakers Forum

COMPLETE SET (11)	4.00	10.00
7 Ken Norton	.20	.50

1976 Landsman Playing Cards

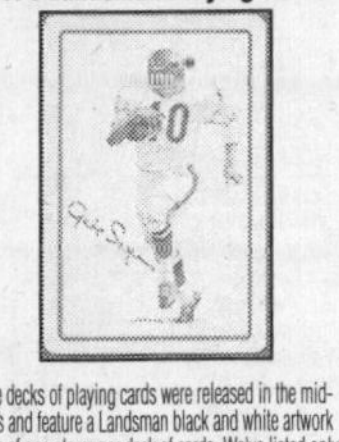

These decks of playing cards were released in the mid-1970s and feature a Landsman black and white artwork image of one player per deck of cards. We've listed only one player name below although each player can be found in all 54-card versions of a standard deck of playing cards. Any additions to this list are appreciated.

COMP.FOREMAN DECK (54)	15.00	30.00
COMP.NAMATH DECK (54)	20.00	50.00
COMP.SAYERS DECK (54)	15.00	40.00
COMP.STABLER DECK (54)	15.00	40.00
COMP.STARR DECK (54)	20.00	50.00
COMP.TARKENTON (54)	15.00	40.00
1 Chuck Foreman	.40	1.00
2 Joe Namath	1.00	2.50
3 Gale Sayers	.60	1.50
4 Ken Stabler	.75	2.00
5 Bart Starr	.75	2.00
6 Fran Tarkenton	.60	1.50

1976 Landsman Portraits

These 8 1/2" by 11" black-and-white portraits were issued around 1976 and feature art by Landsman. The checklist below is thought to be incomplete, however any additional information would be appreciated.

COMPLETE SET (3)	25.00	50.00
1 Chuck Foreman	5.00	10.00
2 Ken Stabler	12.50	25.00
3 Fran Tarkenton	7.50	15.00

1996 Laser View

The 1996 Laser View set was issued in one series totalling 40 cards and features 3.5 seconds of actual game footage printed on super premium 20pt. card stock with full-motion hologram technology. The one-card packs originally retailed for $4.99 each.

COMPLETE SET (40)	15.00	40.00
1 Jim Kelly	.50	1.25
2 Troy Aikman	1.25	3.00
3 Michael Irvin	.50	1.25
4 Emmitt Smith	2.00	5.00
5 John Elway	2.50	6.00
6 Barry Sanders	2.00	5.00
7 Brett Favre	2.50	6.00
8 Jim Harbaugh	.25	.60
9 Dan Marino	2.50	6.00
10 Warren Moon	.25	.60
11 Drew Bledsoe	.75	2.00
12 Jim Everett	.10	.30
13 Jeff Hostetler	.10	.30
14 Neil O'Donnell	.25	.60
15 Junior Seau	.50	1.25
16 Jerry Rice	1.25	3.00
17 Steve Young	1.00	2.50
18 Rick Mirer	.25	.60
19 Boomer Esiason	.25	.60
20 Bernie Kosar	.10	.30
21 Heath Shuler	.25	.60
22 Dave Brown	.10	.30
23 Jeff Blake	.50	1.25
24 Kerry Collins	.50	1.25
25 Kordell Stewart	.50	1.25
26 Scott Mitchell	.25	.60
27 Kerry Collins PE	.50	1.25
28 Troy Aikman PE	.75	2.00
29 Kordell Stewart PE	.50	1.25
30 Michael Irvin PE	.25	.60
31 Emmitt Smith PE	1.25	3.00
32 John Elway PE	1.50	4.00
33 Barry Sanders PE	1.25	3.00
34 Brett Favre PE	1.50	4.00
35 Dan Marino PE	1.50	4.00
36 Drew Bledsoe PE	.50	1.25
37 Neil O'Donnell PE	.25	.60
38 Jerry Rice PE	.75	2.00
39 Steve Young PE	.75	2.00
40 Jeff Blake PE	.25	.60
P5 John Elway Promo	1.25	3.00

1996 Laser View Gold

COMPLETE SET (40)	50.00	100.00
*GOLDS: 1X TO 2.5X BASIC CARDS		
STATED ODDS 1:12		

1996 Laser View Eye on the Prize

COMPLETE SET (12)	30.00	80.00
STATED ODDS 1:24		
1 Troy Aikman	4.00	10.00
2 Emmitt Smith	6.00	15.00
3 Michael Irvin	1.50	4.00
4 Steve Young	3.00	8.00
5 Jerry Rice	4.00	10.00
6 Dan Marino	8.00	20.00
7 John Elway	8.00	20.00
8 Junior Seau	1.50	4.00
9 Neil O'Donnell	.75	2.00
10 Jeff Hostetler	.40	1.00
11 Jim Kelly	1.50	4.00
12 Kordell Stewart	1.50	4.00

1996 Laser View Inscriptions

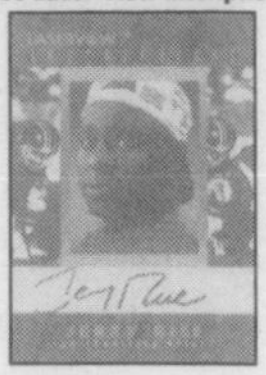

AUTO/900-4900 ODDS 1:24		
1 Jeff Blake/3125	8.00	20.00
2 Drew Bledsoe/2775	15.00	40.00
3 Dave Brown/3100	8.00	20.00
4 Mark Brunell/3200	10.00	25.00
5 Kerry Collins/3000	10.00	25.00
6 John Elway/3100	30.00	80.00
7 Boomer Esiason/1500	15.00	40.00
8 Jim Everett/3100	8.00	20.00
9 Brett Favre/4850	60.00	120.00
10 Jeff George/2900	8.00	20.00
11 Jim Harbaugh/3500	15.00	30.00
12 Jeff Hostetler/3750	8.00	20.00
13 Michael Irvin/3050	15.00	40.00
14 Jim Kelly/3100	15.00	40.00
15 Bernie Kosar/3200	12.00	30.00
16 Erik Kramer/3150	8.00	20.00
17 Rick Mirer/3150	10.00	25.00
18 Scott Mitchell/4900	8.00	20.00
19 Warren Moon/2800	12.00	30.00
20 Neil O'Donnell/1600	12.00	30.00
21 Jerry Rice/900	60.00	120.00
22 Barry Sanders/2900	40.00	80.00
23 Junior Seau/3000	20.00	40.00
24 Heath Shuler/3100	10.00	25.00
25 Steve Young/1950	25.00	50.00

1983 Latrobe Police

This 30-card standard-size set is subtitled "The Birth of Professional Football" in Latrobe, Pennsylvania. Cards were not printed in full color, rather either sepia or black and white. The set is not attractive and, hence, has never been very aggressively pursued by collectors. The set is available with two kinds of backs. There is no difference in value between the two sets of backs-although the set with safety tips on the back seems to be more in demand due to the many collectors of police issues.

COMPLETE SET (30)	6.00	12.00
1 John Kinport Brallier	.40	1.00
2 John K. Brallier	.20	.50
3 Latrobe YMCA Team 1895	.20	.50
4 Brallier and Team at W and J 1895	.20	.50
5 Latrobe A.A. Team 1896	.20	.50
6 Latrobe A.A. 1897	.20	.50
7 1st All Pro Team 1897	.20	.50
8 David J. Berry Mgr.	.20	.50
9 Harry Cap Ryan RT	.20	.50
10 Walter Okeson LE	.20	.50
11 Edward Wood RE	.20	.50
12 E.Big Bill Hammer C	.20	.50
13 Marcus Saxman LH	.20	.50
14 Charles Shumaker SUB	.20	.50
15 Charles McDyre LE	.20	.50
16 Edward Abbaticchio FB	.20	.50
17 George Flickinger C LT	.20	.50
18 Walter Howard RH	.20	.50
19 Thomas Trenchard	.20	.50
20 John Kinport Brallier QB	.40	1.00
21 Jack Gass LH	.20	.50
22 Dave Campbell LT	.20	.50
23 Edward Blair RH	.20	.50
24 John Johnston RG	.20	.50
25 Sam Johnston LG	.20	.50
26 Alex Laird SUB	.20	.50
27 Latrobe A.A. 1897 Team	.20	.50
28 Pro Football Memorial Plaque	.20	.50
29 Commemorative Medallion	.20	.50
30 Birth of Pro Football Checklist Card	.20	.50

1975 Laughlin Flaky Football

This 26-card set measures approximately 2 1/2" by 3 3/8". The title card indicates that the set was copyrighted in 1975 by noted artist, R.G. Laughlin. The typical orientation of the cards is that the city name is printed on the top of the card, with the mock team name running from top to bottom down the left side. The cartoon pictures are oriented horizontally inside the right angle formed by these two lines of text. The cards are numbered in the lower right hand corner (usually) and the backs of the cards are blank.

COMPLETE SET (27)	125.00	225.00
1 Pittsburgh Stealers	8.00	12.00
2 Minnesota Spikings	8.00	12.00
3 Cincinnati Bungles	6.00	10.00
4 Chicago Bares	8.00	12.00
5 Miami Dullfins	8.00	12.00
6 Philadelphia Eggles	6.00	10.00
7 Cleveland Brawns	8.00	12.00
8 New York Gianuts	8.00	12.00
9 Buffalo Bulls	6.00	10.00
10 Dallas Plowboys	8.00	12.00
11 New England Pastry Nuts	6.00	10.00
12 Green Bay Porkers	8.00	12.00
13 Denver Bonkos	6.00	10.00
14 St. Louis Cigardinals	6.00	10.00
15 New York Jests	8.00	12.00
16 Washington Redskins	8.00	12.00
17 Oakland Waders	8.00	12.00
18 Los Angeles Yams	6.00	10.00
19 Baltimore Kilts	6.00	10.00
20 New Orleans Scents	6.00	10.00
21 San Diego Charges	6.00	10.00
22 Detroit Loins	6.00	10.00
23 Kansas City Chefs	6.00	10.00
24 Atlanta Fakin's	6.00	10.00
25 Houston Owlers	6.00	10.00
26 San Francisco 40 Miners	8.00	12.00
NNO Title Card Flaky Football	8.00	12.00

1948 Leaf

The 1948 Leaf set of 98-cards features black and white player portraits against a solid colored background. The player's uniforms were also colored and quite a number of variations have been reported in the player's uniform and background colors. We've included the more collected variations in the listing below. Recently a Johnny Lujack variation surfaced with his name misspelled "Jonny" on the front. Any additions to the variations list are appreciated. The cards measure approximately 2 3/8" by 2 7/8" and can be found on gray or cream colored card stock or a lighter, nearly white, stock. These differences in paper stock may account for the large number of color variations discovered. The second series (50-98) cards are much more difficult to obtain than the first series (1-49). This set features the Rookie Cards of many football stars since it was, along with the 1948 Bowman set, the first major post-war set. The set included then current NFL players as well as current college players.

COMPLETE SET (98)	4,500.00	6,000.00
WRAPPER (5-CENT)	110.00	160.00
1A Sid Luckman YB RC (Yellow Background)	250.00	400.00
1B Sid Luckman WB RC (White Background)	300.00	500.00
2 Steve Suhey RC	20.00	30.00
3A Bulldog Turner RB RC (Red background)	75.00	135.00
3B Bulldog Turner WB RC (White background)	100.00	175.00
4 Doak Walker RC	125.00	200.00
5A Levi Jackson BJ RC (Blue jersey)	25.00	40.00
5B Levi Jackson WJ RC (White jersey)	30.00	50.00
6A Bobby Layne YP RC (Yellow pants on front, Name misspelled Bobbie)	250.00	400.00
6B Bobby Layne RP RC (Red pants on front, Name misspelled Bobbie)	300.00	500.00
7A Bill Fischer RB RC (Red background at knees)	20.00	30.00
7B Bill Fischer WB RC (White background at knees)	25.00	40.00
8A Vince Banonis BL RC (Black letter name on front)	20.00	30.00
8B Vince Banonis WL RC (White letter name on front)	30.00	50.00
8C Vince Banonis WB RC (White background)	30.00	50.00
9A Tommy Thompson YJN RC (Yellow jersey numbers)	25.00	40.00
9B Tommy Thompson BJN RC (Blue jersey numbers)	40.00	80.00
10 Perry Moss RC	20.00	30.00
11 Terry Brennan RC	25.00	40.00
12A Bill Swiacki BL RC (Black letter name on front)	20.00	30.00
12B Bill Swiacki WL RC (White letter name on front)	30.00	50.00
13A Johnny Lujack RC	125.00	200.00
13B Johnny Lujack RC ERR (misspelled Jonny on front)	175.00	300.00
14A Mal Kutner BL RC (Black letter name on front)	20.00	30.00
14B Mal Kutner WL RC (White letter name on front)	30.00	50.00
15 Charlie Justice RC	50.00	90.00
16A Pete Pihos YJN RC (Yellow jersey number)	90.00	150.00
16B Pete Pihos BJN RC (Blue jersey number)	125.00	200.00
17A Kenny Washington BL RC (Black letter name on front)	35.00	60.00
17B Kenny Washington WL RC (White letter name on front)	50.00	80.00
18 Harry Gilmer RC	30.00	50.00
19A George McAfee RC (no nickname on front)	90.00	150.00
19B George McAfee ERR RC (Gorgeous George on front)	125.00	200.00
20A George Taliaferro YB RC (Yellow background)	25.00	40.00
20B George Taliaferro WB RC (White background)	30.00	50.00
21 Paul Christman RC	30.00	50.00
22A Steve Van Buren GJ BL RC (Green jersey, Yellow Sock)	150.00	250.00
22B Steve Van Buren YJ RC (Yellow jersey, Yellow Sock)	175.00	300.00
22C Steve Van Buren GJ BS RC (Green Jersey, Blue Sock)	200.00	350.00
23A Ken Kavanaugh YS RC (Yellow stripes on sleeves)	25.00	40.00
23B Ken Kavanaugh RS RC (Red stripes on sleeves)		
24A Jim Martin RB RC (Red background)	25.00	40.00
24B Jim Martin WB RC (White background)	30.00	50.00
25A Bud Angsman RC (Black letter name on front)	25.00	40.00
25B Bud Angsman WL RC (White letter name on front)	35.00	60.00
25C Bud Angsman WB RC (White background)	35.00	60.00
26A Bob Waterfield BL RC (Black name on front)	150.00	250.00
26B Bob Waterfield WL RC (White name on front)	300.00	450.00
27A Fred Davis RC (Yellow background)	20.00	30.00
27B Fred Davis RC (White background)	30.00	50.00
28A Whitey Wistert YJ RC (Yellow jersey)	25.00	40.00
28B Whitey Wistert GJ RC (Green jersey)	30.00	50.00
29 Charley Trippi RC	65.00	110.00
30A Paul Governali BRH RC (darker brown helmet)	25.00	40.00
30B Paul Governali TH RC (light tan helmet)	25.00	40.00
30C Paul Governali BH RC (blue helmet)	30.00	50.00
31A Tom McWilliams MJ RC (Maroon jersey)	20.00	30.00
31B Tom McWilliams RJ RC (Red jersey)	25.00	40.00
32 Leroy Zimmerman RC	20.00	30.00
33 Pat Harder UER RC (Misspelled Harber on front)	30.00	50.00
34A Sammy Baugh MJ RC (Maroon jersey)	400.00	600.00
34B Sammy Baugh RJ RC (Red jersey)	400.00	600.00
35 Ted Fritsch Sr. RC	25.00	40.00
36 Bill Dudley RC	75.00	125.00
37 George Connor RC	50.00	100.00
38A Frank Dancewicz GN RC (greenish jersey numbers)	20.00	30.00
38B Frank Dancewicz BN RC (blue jersey numbers)	20.00	40.00
39 Billy Dewell RC	20.00	30.00
40A John Nolan GN RC (greenish jersey numbers)	20.00	30.00
40B John Nolan BN RC (blue jersey numbers)	20.00	40.00
40C John Nolan YN RC (bright yellow jersey numbers)	20.00	40.00
41A Harry Szulborski OP RC Orange Pants)	20.00	30.00
41B Harry Szulborski YP RC Yellow Pants)	30.00	50.00
42 Tex Coulter RC	25.00	40.00
43A Robert Nussbaumer MJ RC (Maroon Jersey)	20.00	30.00
43B Robert Nussbaumer RJ RC (Red Jersey)	30.00	50.00
44 Bob Mann RC	20.00	30.00
45 Jim White RC	25.00	40.00
46A Jack Jacobs JN RC (Jersey #27 in photo)	20.00	30.00
46B Jack Jacobs NJN RC (No jersey number in photo)	30.00	50.00
47A John Clement BFB RC (Brown football)	20.00	30.00
47B John Clement YFB RC (Yellow football)	20.00	35.00
48 Frank Reagan RC	20.00	30.00
49 Frank Tripucka RC	25.00	40.00
50 John Rauch RC	100.00	175.00
51 Mike DiMitro RC	100.00	175.00
52A Leo Nomellini BBMJ RC (Blue Background, Maroon jersey)	300.00	450.00
52B Leo Nomellini BBRJ RC (Blue background, Red Jersey)	350.00	500.00
52C Leo Nomellini WB RC (White background, red jersey)	350.00	500.00
53 Charley Conerly RC	300.00	450.00
54A Chuck Bednarik YB RC (Yellow background)	350.00	500.00
54B Chuck Bednarik WB RC (White background)	350.00	500.00
55 Chick Jagade RC	100.00	175.00
56 Bob Folsom RC	125.00	200.00
57 Gene Rossides RC	125.00	200.00
58 Art Weiner RC	100.00	175.00
59 Alex Sarkistian RC	100.00	175.00
60 Dick Harris RC	100.00	175.00
61 Len Younce RC	100.00	175.00
62 Gene Derricotte RC	100.00	175.00
63A Roy Rebel Steiner RJ RC (Red jersey)	100.00	175.00
63B Roy Rebel Steiner WJ RC (White jersey)	125.00	200.00
64 Frank Seno RC	100.00	175.00
65 Bob Hendren RC	100.00	175.00
66A Jack Cloud BB RC	100.00	175.00
66B Jack Cloud WB RC	125.00	200.00
67 Harrell Collins RC	100.00	175.00
68A Clyde LeForce ERR RC (Red Background) (name misspelled LaForce)	100.00	175.00
68B Clyde LeForce ERR RC (White Background) (name misspelled LaForce)	125.00	200.00
69 Larry Joe RC	100.00	175.00
70 Phil O'Reilly RC	100.00	175.00
71 Paul Campbell RC	100.00	175.00
72 Ray Evans RC	100.00	175.00
73A Jackie Jensen RB RC (Red Background Misspelled Jackey on card front)	250.00	400.00
73B Jackie Jensen WB RC (White background, name misspelled Jackey on front)	300.00	450.00
74 Russ Steger RC	100.00	175.00
75 Tony Minisi RC	100.00	175.00
76 Clayton Tonnemaker RC	100.00	175.00
77A George Savitsky GS RC (Green stripes on sleeve)	100.00	175.00
77B George Savitsky NGS RC (No green stripes on sleeve)	125.00	200.00
78 Clarence Self RC	100.00	175.00
79 Rod Franz RC	100.00	175.00
80A Jim Youle RB RC (Red background)	100.00	175.00
80B Jim Youle WB RC (White background)	125.00	200.00
81A Billy Bye YPMJ RC (Yellow pants, Maroon jersey)	100.00	175.00
81B Billy Bye YPRJ RC (Yellow pants, Red jersey)	125.00	200.00
81C Billy Bye WPMJ RC (White pants, Maroon jersey)	125.00	200.00
82 Fred Enke RC	100.00	175.00
83A Fred Folger GJ RC (Gray jersey)	100.00	175.00
83B Fred Folger WJ RC (White jersey)	125.00	200.00
84 Jug Girard RC	125.00	200.00
85 Joe Scott RC	100.00	175.00
86 Bob DeMoss RC	100.00	175.00
87 Dave Templeton RC	100.00	175.00
88 Herb Siegert RC	100.00	175.00
89A Bucky O'Conner BJ RC (Blue jersey)	100.00	175.00
89B Bucky O'Conner WJ RC (White jersey)	150.00	250.00
90 Joe Whisler RC	100.00	175.00
91 Leon Hart RC	150.00	250.00
92 Earl Banks RC	100.00	175.00
93 Frank Aschenbrenner RC	100.00	175.00
94 John Goldsberry RC	100.00	175.00
95 Porter Payne RC	100.00	175.00
96 Pete Perini RC	100.00	175.00
97 Jay Rhodemyre RC	100.00	175.00
98 Al DiMarco RC	125.00	250.00

1949 Leaf

Measuring approximately 2 3/8" by 2 7/8", the 1949 Leaf set contains 49 cards that are skip-numbered from 1 to 150. Designed much like the 1948 issue (use of many of the same portraits), the fronts feature player portraits against a solid background. The player's name is at the bottom. The backs carry career highlights and a bio. The cards can be found on either gray or cream colored card stock. The card backs detail an offer to send in five wrappers and a dime for a 12" by 6" felt pennant of one of the teams listed on the different card backs including college and pro teams. Unlike the 1948 set, all the players portrayed were in the NFL. There are no key Rookie Cards in this set as virtually all of the players in the 1949 set were also in the 1948 Leaf set.

COMPLETE SET (49)	1,500.00	2,200.00
WRAPPER (5-CENT)	250.00	300.00
1 Bob Hendren	40.00	80.00
2 Joe Scott	18.00	30.00
3 Frank Reagan	18.00	30.00
4 John Rauch	18.00	30.00
7 Bill Fischer	18.00	30.00
9 Elmer Bud Angsman	20.00	35.00
10 Billy Dewell	18.00	30.00
13 Tommy Thompson	25.00	35.00
15 Sid Luckman	75.00	125.00
16 Charley Trippi	35.00	60.00
17 Bob Mann	18.00	30.00
19 Paul Christman	25.00	35.00
22 Bill Dudley	35.00	60.00
23 Clyde LeForce	18.00	30.00
26 Sammy Baugh	200.00	350.00
28 Pete Pihos	50.00	70.00
31 Tex Coulter	25.00	35.00
32 Mal Kutner	25.00	35.00
35 Whitey Wistert	25.00	35.00
37 Ted Fritsch Sr.	25.00	35.00
38 Vince Banonis	18.00	30.00
39 Jim White	18.00	30.00
40 George Connor	35.00	60.00
41 George McAfee	35.00	60.00
43 Frank Tripucka	30.00	50.00
47 Fred Enke	18.00	30.00
49 Charley Conerly	60.00	100.00
51 Ken Kavanaugh	25.00	35.00
52 Bob Demoss	18.00	30.00
56 John Lujack	60.00	100.00
57 Jim Youle	18.00	30.00
62 Harry Gilmer	25.00	35.00
65 Robert Nussbaumer	18.00	30.00
67 Bobby Layne	125.00	200.00
70 Herb Siegert	18.00	30.00
74 Tony Minisi	18.00	30.00
79 Steve Van Buren	90.00	150.00
81 Perry Moss	18.00	30.00
89 Bob Waterfield	75.00	125.00
90 Jack Jacobs	18.00	30.00
95 Kenny Washington	30.00	50.00
101 Pat Harder UER (Misspelled Harber on front)	25.00	35.00
110 Bill Swiacki	25.00	35.00
118 Fred Davis	18.00	30.00
126 Jay Rhodemyre	18.00	30.00
127 Frank Seno	18.00	30.00
134 Chuck Bednarik	110.00	175.00
144 George Savitsky	18.00	30.00
150 Bulldog Turner	90.00	150.00

1983 Leaf Football Facts Booklets

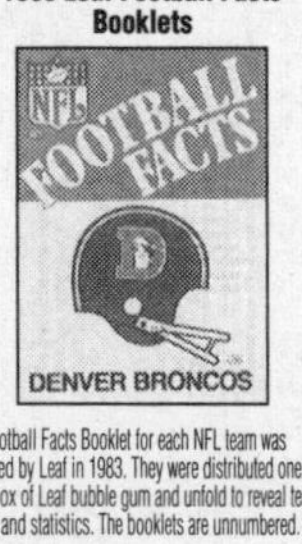

One Football Facts Booklet for each NFL team was produced by Leaf in 1983. They were distributed one per small box of Leaf bubble gum and unfold to reveal team history and statistics. The booklets are unnumbered.

COMPLETE SET (28)	30.00	75.00
1 Atlanta Falcons	1.25	3.00
2 Baltimore Colts	1.25	3.00
3 Buffalo Bills	1.25	3.00
4 Chicago Bears	2.00	5.00
5 Cincinnati Bengals	1.25	3.00
6 Cleveland Browns	1.25	3.00
7 Dallas Cowboys	2.50	6.00
8 Denver Broncos	1.25	3.00
9 Detroit Lions	1.25	3.00
10 Green Bay Packers	2.50	6.00
11 Houston Oilers	1.25	3.00
12 Kansas City Chiefs	1.25	3.00
13 Los Angeles Rams	1.25	3.00
14 Miami Dolphins	2.50	6.00
15 Minnesota Vikings	1.25	3.00
16 New England Patriots	1.25	3.00
17 New Orleans Saints	1.25	3.00
18 New York Giants	1.25	3.00
19 New York Jets	1.25	3.00
20 Oakland Raiders	2.50	6.00
21 Philadelphia Eagles	1.25	3.00
22 Pittsburgh Steelers	2.50	6.00
23 St. Louis Cardinals	1.25	3.00
24 San Diego Chargers	1.25	3.00
25 San Francisco 49ers	2.50	6.00
26 Seattle Seahawks	1.25	3.00
27 Tampa Bay Buccaneers	1.25	3.00
28 Washington Redskins	2.50	6.00

1996 Leaf

This 190-card set was distributed in 10-card packs with a suggested retail price of $2.99. The fronts feature borderless action color player photos with silver foil highlights. The backs carry another player photo with career statistics.

COMPLETE SET (190)	7.50	20.00
1 Troy Aikman	.40	1.00
2 Ricky Watters	.07	.20
3 Robert Brooks	.15	.40
4 Ki-Jana Carter	.07	.20
5 Drew Bledsoe	.25	.60
6 Eric Swann	.02	.10
7 Hardy Nickerson	.02	.10
8 Tony Martin	.07	.20
9 Garrison Hearst	.07	.20
10 Bernie Parmalee	.02	.10
11 Neil Smith	.07	.20
12 Aaron Craver	.02	.10
13 Rashaan Salaam	.07	.20
14 Greg Hill	.07	.20
15 Charlie Garner	.07	.20
16 Kimble Anders	.07	.20
17 Steve McNair	.30	.75
18 Neil O'Donnell	.07	.20
19 Greg Lloyd	.07	.20
20 Warren Moon	.07	.20
21 Bernie Kosar	.02	.10
22 Derrick Thomas	.15	.40
23 Andre Hastings	.02	.10
24 Wayne Chrebet	.25	.60
25 Mark Seay	.02	.10
26 Eric Metcalf	.02	.10
27 Shawn Jefferson	.02	.10
28 Napoleon Kaufman	.15	.40
29 Steve Walsh	.02	.10
30 Derrick Alexander DE	.02	.10
31 Rodney Peete	.02	.10
32 Terance Mathis	.02	.10
33 Michael Westbrook	.15	.40
34 Kevin Carter	.02	.10
35 Aaron Hayden RC	.02	.10
36 J.J. Stokes	.15	.40
37 Andre Reed	.07	.20
38 Chris Warren	.07	.20
39 Jerry Rice	.40	1.00
40 Ben Coates	.07	.20
41 Reggie White	.15	.40
42 Joey Galloway	.15	.40
43 Sean Dawkins	.02	.10
44 Brett Favre	.75	2.00
45 Jeff George	.07	.20
46 Robert Smith	.07	.20
47 Ken Dilger	.07	.20
48 Larry Centers	.07	.20
49 Jackie Harris	.02	.10
50 Hugh Douglas	.07	.20
51 Herschel Walker	.07	.20
52 Kerry Collins	.15	.40
53 Michael Irvin	.15	.40
54 Willie McGinest	.02	.10
55 Herman Moore	.07	.20
56 Leroy Hoard	.02	.10
57 Scott Mitchell	.07	.20
58 Terrell Davis	.30	.75
59 Kevin Greene	.07	.20
60 Yancey Thigpen	.07	.20
61 Kevin Smith	.02	.10
62 Trent Dilfer	.15	.40
63 Cortez Kennedy	.02	.10
64 Carnell Lake	.02	.10
65 Quinn Early	.02	.10
66 Kyle Brady	.02	.10
67 Marshall Faulk	.20	.50
68 Fred Barnett	.02	.10
69 Quentin Coryatt	.02	.10
70 Dan Marino	.75	2.00
71 Junior Seau	.15	.40
72 Andre Coleman	.02	.10
73 Terry Kirby	.07	.20
74 Curtis Martin	.30	.75
75 Isaac Bruce	.15	.40
76 Mark Chmura	.07	.20
77 Edgar Bennett	.07	.20
78 Mario Bates	.07	.20
79 Eric Zeier	.02	.10
80 Adrian Murrell	.07	.20
81 Mark Brunell	.25	.60
82 Mark Rypien	.02	.10
83 Eric Pegram	.02	.10
84 Bryan Cox	.02	.10
85 Heath Shuler	.07	.20
86 Lake Dawson	.07	.20
87 O.J. McDuffie	.07	.20
88 Emmitt Smith	.60	1.50
89 Jim Harbaugh	.07	.20
90 Aaron Bailey	.02	.10
91 Jim Kelly	.15	.40
92 Rodney Hampton	.07	.20
93 Cris Carter	.15	.40
94 Henry Ellard	.02	.10
95 Darnay Scott	.07	.20
96 Daryl Johnston	.07	.20
97 Tamarick Vanover	.07	.20
98 Jeff Blake	.15	.40
99 Anthony Miller	.07	.20
100 Darren Woodson	.07	.20
101 Irving Fryar	.07	.20
102 Craig Hayward	.02	.10
103 Derek Loville	.02	.10
104 Ernie Mills	.02	.10
105 Brian Blades	.02	.10
106 Gus Frerotte	.07	.20
107 Alvin Harper	.02	.10
108 Tyrone Wheatley	.07	.20
109 John Elway	.75	2.00
110 Charles Haley	.07	.20
111 Terrell Fletcher	.02	.10
112 Vincent Brisby	.02	.10
113 Jerome Bettis	.15	.40
114 Barry Sanders	.60	1.50
115 Ken Norton Jr.	.02	.10
116 Sherman Williams	.02	.10
117 Antonio Freeman	.15	.40
118 Bert Emanuel	.07	.20
119 Marcus Allen	.15	.40
120 Stan Humphries	.07	.20
121 Chris Sanders	.07	.20
122 Jeff Graham	.02	.10
123 Jay Novacek	.02	.10
124 Aeneas Williams	.02	.10
125 Kordell Stewart	.15	.40
126 Steve Young	.30	.75
127 Jake Reed	.07	.20
128 Rick Mirer	.07	.20
129 Jeff Hostetler	.02	.10
130 Tim Brown	.15	.40
131 Shannon Sharpe	.07	.20
132 Dave Brown	.02	.10
133 Harvey Williams	.02	.10
134 Rodney Thomas	.02	.10
135 Frank Sanders	.07	.20
136 Brett Perriman	.02	.10
137 Steve Bono	.02	.10
138 Steve Atwater	.02	.10
139 Andre Rison	.07	.20
140 Orlando Thomas	.02	.10
141 Terry Allen	.07	.20
142 Carl Pickens	.07	.20
143 William Floyd	.07	.20
144 Bryce Paup	.02	.10
145 James O. Stewart	.07	.20
146 Eric Bjornson	.02	.10
147 Errict Rhett	.07	.20
148 Darick Holmes	.02	.10
149 Brian Mitchell	.02	.10
150 Brent Jones	.02	.10
151 Natrone Means	.07	.20
152 Rod Woodson	.07	.20
153 Bruce Smith	.07	.20
154 Deion Sanders	.25	.60
155 Kevin Williams	.02	.10
156 Erik Kramer	.02	.10
157 Jim Everett	.02	.10
158 Vinny Testaverde	.07	.20
159 Boomer Esiason	.07	.20
160 Leslie O'Neal	.02	.10
161 Curtis Conway	.15	.40
162 Thurman Thomas	.15	.40
163 Tony Brackens RC	.15	.40
164 Stepfret Williams RC	.07	.20
165 Alex Van Dyke RC	.07	.20
166 Cedric Jones RC	.02	.10
167 Stanley Pritchett RC	.07	.20
168 Willie Anderson RC	.02	.10
169 Regan Upshaw RC	.02	.10
170 Daryl Gardener RC	.02	.10
171 Alex Molden RC	.02	.10
172 John Mobley RC	.02	.10
173 Danny Kanell RC	.15	.40
174 Marco Battaglia RC	.02	.10
175 Simeon Rice RC	.40	1.00
176 Tony Banks RC	.15	.40
177 Stephen Davis RC	.60	1.50
178 Walt Harris RC	.02	.10
179 Amani Toomer RC	.40	1.00
180 Derrick Mayes RC	.15	.40
181 Jeff Lewis RC	.07	.20
182 Chris Darkins RC	.02	.10
183 Rickey Dudley RC	.15	.40
184 Jonathan Ogden RC	.15	.40
185 Mike Alstott RC	.50	1.25
186 Eric Moulds RC	.60	1.50
187 Karim Abdul-Jabbar RC	.15	.40
188 Jerry Rice Checklist Card	.15	.40
189 Dan Marino Checklist Card	.15	.40
190 Emmitt Smith Checklist Card	.15	.40

1996 Leaf Collector's Edition

COMP.FACT.SET (191)	12.50	30.00
COMPLETE SET (190)	7.50	20.00
*COLLECTOR EDITION: 4X TO 1X BASIC CARDS		

1996 Leaf Press Proofs

COMPLETE SET (190)	100.00	200.00
*STARS: 4X TO 10X BASIC CARDS		
*RCs: 2.5X TO 6X BASIC CARDS		
ANNOUNCED PRINT RUN 2000 SETS		

1996 Leaf Red

*STARS: .6X TO 1.5X BASIC CARDS
*ROOKIES: .4X TO 1X BASIC CARDS

1996 Leaf American All-Stars

COMPLETE SET (20)	75.00	150.00
STATED PRINT RUN 5000 SERIAL #'d SETS		
*GOLDS: .8X TO 2X BASIC INSERTS		
GOLDS PRINT RUN 1000 SERIAL #'d SETS		
1 Emmitt Smith	5.00	12.00
2 Drew Bledsoe	2.00	5.00
3 Jerry Rice	3.00	8.00
4 Kerry Collins	1.25	3.00
5 Eddie George	.60	1.50
6 Keyshawn Johnson	2.50	6.00
7 Lawrence Phillips	1.00	2.50
8 Rashaan Salaam	.60	1.50
9 Deion Sanders	2.00	5.00
10 Marshall Faulk	1.50	4.00
11 Steve Young	2.50	6.00
12 Ki-Jana Carter	.60	1.50
13 Curtis Martin	2.50	6.00
14 Joey Galloway	1.25	3.00
15 Troy Aikman	3.00	8.00
16 Barry Sanders	5.00	12.00
17 Dan Marino	6.00	15.00
18 John Elway	6.00	15.00
19 Steve McNair	2.50	6.00
20 Tim Biakabutuka	1.00	2.50

1996 Leaf Collector's Edition Autographs

COMPLETE SET (9)	75.00	150.00
ONE PER COLLEDITION FACT.SET		
ANNOUNCED PRINT RUN 2000 SETS		
1 Karim Abdul-Jabbar	5.00	12.00
2 Isaac Bruce	6.00	15.00
3 Terrell Davis	15.00	40.00
4 Bobby Engram	4.00	10.00
5 Joey Galloway	6.00	15.00
6 Marvin Harrison	30.00	50.00
7 Eddie Kennison	5.00	12.00
8 Leeland McElroy	4.00	10.00
9 Tamarick Vanover	5.00	12.00

1996 Leaf Gold Leaf Rookies

COMPLETE SET (10)	7.50	20.00
1 Leeland McElroy	.60	1.50
2 Marvin Harrison	2.50	6.00
3 Lawrence Phillips	1.00	2.50
4 Bobby Engram	.60	1.50
5 Kevin Hardy	.60	1.50
6 Keyshawn Johnson	1.00	2.50
7 Eddie Kennison	.60	1.50
8 Tim Biakabutuka	1.00	2.50
9 Eddie George	2.00	5.00
10 Terry Glenn	1.00	2.50

1996 Leaf Gold Leaf Stars

COMPLETE SET (15)	100.00	200.00
RANDOM INSERTS IN RETAIL PACKS		
STATED PRINT RUN 2500 SERIAL #'d SETS		
1 Drew Bledsoe	4.00	10.00
2 Jerry Rice	6.00	15.00
3 Emmitt Smith	10.00	25.00
4 Dan Marino	12.50	30.00
5 Isaac Bruce	2.50	6.00
6 Kerry Collins	2.50	6.00
7 Barry Sanders	10.00	25.00
8 Keyshawn Johnson	3.00	8.00
9 Errict Rhett	1.25	3.00
10 Joey Galloway	2.50	6.00
11 Brett Favre	12.50	30.00
12 Curtis Martin	5.00	12.00
13 Steve Young	5.00	12.00
14 Troy Aikman	6.00	15.00
15 John Elway	12.50	30.00

1996 Leaf Grass Roots

COMPLETE SET (20)	25.00	50.00
STATED PRINT RUN 5000 SERIAL #'d SETS		
*PROMOS: .4X TO 1X BASIC INSERTS		
1 Thurman Thomas	1.00	2.50
2 Eddie George	3.00	8.00
3 Rodney Hampton	.50	1.25
4 Rashaan Salaam	.50	1.25
5 Natrone Means	.50	1.25
6 Errict Rhett	.50	1.25
7 Leeland McElroy	.25	.60
8 Emmitt Smith	4.00	10.00
9 Marshall Faulk	1.25	3.00
10 Ricky Watters	.50	1.25
11 Chris Warren	.50	1.25
12 Tim Biakabutuka	1.00	2.50
13 Barry Sanders	4.00	10.00
14 Karim Abdul-Jabbar	1.00	2.50
15 Darick Holmes	.25	.60
16 Terrell Davis	2.00	5.00
17 Lawrence Phillips	1.00	2.50
18 Ki-Jana Carter	.50	1.25
19 Curtis Martin	2.00	5.00
20 Kordell Stewart	1.00	2.50

1996 Leaf Grass Roots Promos

8 Emmitt Smith	4.00	10.00
13 Barry Sanders	3.00	8.00
20 Kordell Stewart	1.00	2.50

1996 Leaf Shirt Off My Back

COMPLETE SET (10)	50.00	125.00
RANDOM INS.IN MAGAZINE PACKS		
STATED PRINT RUN 2500 SETS		
1 Steve Young	5.00	12.00
2 Jeff Blake	2.50	6.00
3 Drew Bledsoe	3.00	8.00
4 Kordell Stewart	2.50	6.00
5 Troy Aikman	6.00	15.00
6 Steve McNair	5.00	12.00
7 John Elway	10.00	25.00
8 Dan Marino	10.00	25.00
9 Kerry Collins	2.50	6.00
10 Brett Favre	12.50	30.00

1996 Leaf Statistical Standouts

COMPLETE SET (15)	75.00	150.00
RANDOM INSERTS IN HOBBY PACKS		
STATED PRINT RUN 2500 SERIAL #'d SETS		
1 John Elway	10.00	25.00
2 Jerry Rice	5.00	12.00
3 Reggie White	2.00	5.00
4 Drew Bledsoe	3.00	8.00
5 Chris Warren	1.00	2.50
6 Bruce Smith	1.00	2.50
7 Barry Sanders	8.00	20.00
8 Greg Lloyd	1.00	2.50
9 Emmitt Smith	8.00	20.00
10 Dan Marino	10.00	25.00
11 Steve Young	4.00	10.00
12 Steve Atwater	.50	1.25
13 Isaac Bruce	2.00	5.00
14 Deion Sanders	3.00	8.00
15 Brett Favre	10.00	25.00

1997 Leaf

This 200-card set features color action player photos and was distributed in 10-card packs with a suggested retail price of $2.99. The set contains the following subsets: Gold Leaf Rookies (#153-182) and Legacy (#183-197).

COMPLETE SET (200)	10.00	25.00
1 Steve Young	.30	.75
2 Brett Favre	1.00	2.50
3 Barry Sanders	.75	2.00
4 Drew Bledsoe	.30	.75
5 Troy Aikman	.50	1.25
6 Kerry Collins	.25	.60
7 Dan Marino	1.00	2.50
8 Jerry Rice	.50	1.25
9 John Elway	1.00	2.50
10 Emmitt Smith	.75	2.00
11 Tony Banks	.15	.40
12 Gus Frerotte	.08	.25
13 Elvis Grbac	.15	.40
14 Neil O'Donnell	.15	.40
15 Michael Irvin	.25	.60
16 Marshall Faulk	.30	.75
17 Todd Collins	.08	.25
18 Scott Mitchell	.15	.40
19 Trent Dilfer	.25	.60
20 Rick Mirer	.08	.25
21 Frank Sanders	.15	.40
22 Larry Centers	.15	.40
23 Brad Johnson	.25	.60
24 Garrison Hearst	.15	.40
25 Steve McNair	.30	.75
26 Dorsey Levens	.25	.60
27 Eric Metcalf	.15	.40
28 Jeff George	.15	.40
29 Rodney Hampton	.15	.40
30 Michael Westbrook	.15	.40
31 Cris Carter	.25	.60
32 Heath Shuler	.08	.25
33 Warren Moon	.25	.60
34 Rod Woodson	.15	.40
35 Ken Dilger	.08	.25
36 Ben Coates	.15	.40
37 Andre Reed	.15	.40
38 Terrell Owens	.30	.75
39 Jeff Blake	.15	.40
40 Vinny Testaverde	.15	.40
41 Robert Brooks	.15	.40

42 Shannon Sharpe	.15	.40
43 Terry Allen	.25	.60
44 Terance Mathis	.15	.40
45 Bobby Engram	.15	.40
46 Rickey Dudley	.15	.40
47 Alex Molden	.08	.25
48 Lawrence Phillips	.08	.25
49 Curtis Martin	.30	.75
50 Jim Harbaugh	.15	.40
51 Wayne Chrebet	.25	.60
52 Quentin Coryatt	.08	.25
53 Eddie George	.25	.60
54 Michael Jackson	.15	.40
55 Greg Lloyd	.08	.25
56 Natrone Means	.15	.40
57 Marcus Allen	.25	.60
58 Desmond Howard	.15	.40
59 Stan Humphries	.15	.40
60 Reggie White	.25	.60
61 Brett Perriman	.08	.25
62 Warren Sapp	.15	.40
63 Adrian Murrell	.15	.40
64 Mark Brunell	.30	.75
65 Carl Pickens	.15	.40
66 Kordell Stewart	.25	.60
67 Ricky Watters	.15	.40
68 Tyrone Wheatley	.15	.40
69 Stanley Pritchett	.08	.25
70 Kevin Greene	.15	.40
71 Karim Abdul-Jabbar	.15	.40
72 Ki-Jana Carter	.08	.25
73 Rashaan Salaam	.08	.25
74 Simeon Rice	.15	.40
75 Napoleon Kaufman	.25	.60
76 Muhsin Muhammad	.15	.40
77 Bruce Smith	.15	.40
78 Eric Moulds	.25	.60
79 O.J. McDuffie	.15	.40
80 Danny Kanell	.08	.25
81 Harvey Williams	.08	.25
82 Greg Hill	.08	.25
83 Terrell Davis	.30	.75
84 Dan Wilkinson	.08	.25
85 Yancey Thigpen	.15	.40
86 Darrell Green	.15	.40
87 Tamarick Vanover	.15	.40
88 Mike Alstott	.25	.60
89 Johnnie Morton	.15	.40
90 Dale Carter	.08	.25
91 Jerome Bettis	.25	.60
92 James O.Stewart	.15	.40
93 Irving Fryar	.15	.40
94 Junior Seau	.25	.60
95 Sean Dawkins	.08	.25
96 J.J. Stokes	.15	.40
97 Tim Biakabutuka	.15	.40
98 Bert Emanuel	.15	.40
99 Eddie Kennison	.15	.40
100 Ray Zellars	.08	.25
101 Dave Brown	.08	.25
102 Leeland McElroy	.08	.25
103 Chris Warren	.15	.40
104 Byron Bam Morris	.08	.25
105 Thurman Thomas	.25	.60
106 Kyle Brady	.08	.25
107 Anthony Miller	.08	.25
108 Derrick Thomas	.25	.60
109 Mark Chmura	.15	.40
110 Deion Sanders	.25	.60
111 Eric Swann	.08	.25
112 Amani Toomer	.15	.40
113 Raymont Harris	.08	.25
114 Jake Reed	.15	.40
115 Bryant Young	.08	.25
116 Keenan McCardell	.15	.40
117 Herman Moore	.25	.60
118 Errict Rhett	.08	.25
119 Henry Ellard	.08	.25
120 Bobby Hoying	.15	.40
121 Robert Smith	.15	.40
122 Keyshawn Johnson	.25	.60
123 Zach Thomas	.25	.60
124 Charlie Garner	.15	.40
125 Terry Kirby	.15	.40
126 Darren Woodson	.08	.25
127 Darnay Scott	.15	.40
128 Chris Sanders	.08	.25
129 Charles Johnson	.15	.40
130 Joey Galloway	.15	.40
131 Curtis Conway	.15	.40
132 Isaac Bruce	.25	.60
133 Bobby Taylor	.08	.25
134 Jamal Anderson	.25	.60
135 Ken Norton	.08	.25
136 Darick Holmes	.08	.25
137 Tony Brackens	.08	.25
138 Tony Martin	.15	.40
139 Antonio Freeman	.25	.60
140 Neil Smith	.15	.40
141 Terry Glenn	.25	.60
142 Marvin Harrison	.25	.60
143 Daryl Johnston	.15	.40
144 Tim Brown	.25	.60
145 Kimble Anders	.15	.40
146 Derrick Alexander WR	.15	.40
147 LeShon Johnson	.08	.25
148 Anthony Johnson	.08	.25
149 Leslie Shepherd	.08	.25
150 Chris T. Jones	.08	.25
151 Edgar Bennett	.15	.40
152 Ty Detmer	.15	.40
153 Ike Hilliard RC	.40	1.00
154 Jim Druckenmiller RC	.15	.40
155 Warrick Dunn RC	.75	2.00
156 Yatil Green RC	.15	.40
157 Reidel Anthony RC	.25	.60
158 Antowain Smith RC	.60	1.50
159 Rae Carruth RC	.08	.25
160 Tiki Barber RC	1.50	4.00
161 Byron Hanspard RC	.15	.40
162 Jake Plummer RC	1.00	2.50
163 Joey Kent RC	.25	.60
164 Corey Dillon RC	1.00	2.50
165 Kevin Lockett RC	.15	.40
166 Will Blackwell RC	.15	.40
167 Troy Davis RC	.15	.40
168 James Farrior RC	.25	.60
169 Danny Wuerffel RC	.25	.60
170 Pat Barnes RC	.25	.60
171 Darnell Autry RC	.15	.40
172 Tom Knight RC	.08	.25
173 David LaFleur RC	.08	.25
174 Tony Gonzalez RC	1.00	2.50
175 Kenny Holmes RC	.25	.60
176 Reinard Wilson RC	.15	.40
177 Renaldo Wynn RC	.08	.25
178 Bryant Westbrook RC	.08	.25
179 Darrell Russell RC	.08	.25
180 Orlando Pace RC	.25	.60
181 Shawn Springs RC	.15	.40
182 Peter Boulware RC	.25	.60
183 Dan Marino L	.50	1.25
184 Brett Favre L	.50	1.25
185 Emmitt Smith L	.40	1.00
186 Eddie George L	.25	.60
187 Curtis Martin L	.15	.40
188 Tim Brown L	.15	.40
189 Mark Brunell L	.25	.60
190 Isaac Bruce L	.15	.40
191 Deion Sanders L	.15	.40
192 John Elway L	.50	1.25
193 Jerry Rice L	.25	.60
194 Barry Sanders L	.40	1.00
195 Herman Moore L	.15	.40
196 Carl Pickens L	.15	.40
197 Karim Abdul-Jabbar L	.15	.40
198 Drew Bledsoe CL	.25	.60
199 Troy Aikman CL	.25	.60
200 Terrell Davis CL	.25	.60

1997 Leaf Fractal Matrix

1 Steve Young GZ	6.00	15.00
2 Brett Favre GX	20.00	50.00
3 Barry Sanders GZ	12.50	30.00
4 Drew Bledsoe GZ	5.00	12.00
5 Troy Aikman GZ	7.50	20.00
6 Kerry Collins GZ	4.00	10.00
7 Dan Marino GX	20.00	50.00
8 Jerry Rice GZ	7.50	20.00
9 John Elway GZ	15.00	40.00
10 Emmitt Smith GX	15.00	40.00
11 Tony Banks GY	4.00	10.00
12 Gus Frerotte SX	1.25	3.00
13 Elvis Grbac SX	3.00	8.00
14 Neil O'Donnell BX	.40	1.00
15 Michael Irvin SY	2.00	5.00
16 Marshall Faulk SY	2.00	5.00
17 Todd Collins SX	1.25	3.00
18 Scott Mitchell BX	.40	1.00
19 Trent Dilfer SY	1.50	4.00
20 Rick Mirer SX	1.25	3.00
21 Frank Sanders SX	2.00	5.00
22 Larry Centers BX	.40	1.00
23 Brad Johnson BX	1.25	3.00
24 Garrison Hearst SY	1.50	4.00
25 Steve McNair GZ	5.00	12.00
26 Dorsey Levens BX	1.25	3.00
27 Eric Metcalf BX	.40	1.00
28 Jeff George SX	2.00	5.00
29 Rodney Hampton BX	.40	1.00
30 Michael Westbrook SY	1.50	4.00
31 Cris Carter SY	2.00	5.00
32 Heath Shuler SX	1.25	3.00
33 Warren Moon BX	1.25	3.00
34 Rod Woodson SX	1.25	3.00
35 Ken Dilger BX	.60	1.50
36 Ben Coates BX	.60	1.50
37 Andre Reed BX	.60	1.50
38 Terrell Owens SZ	2.00	5.00
39 Jeff Blake SY	1.50	4.00
40 Vinny Testaverde BX	.60	1.50
41 Robert Brooks SY	1.00	2.50
42 Shannon Sharpe SX	2.00	5.00
43 Terry Allen SY	1.50	4.00
44 Terance Mathis BX	.60	1.50
45 Bobby Engram BZ	.30	.75
46 Rickey Dudley BX	1.25	3.00
47 Alex Molden BX	.40	1.00
48 Lawrence Phillips SY	1.00	2.50
49 Curtis Martin GZ	5.00	12.00
50 Jim Harbaugh BX	.60	1.50
51 Wayne Chrebet BX	1.25	3.00
52 Quentin Coryatt BX	.40	1.00
53 Eddie George GX	5.00	12.00
54 Michael Jackson BX	.40	1.00
55 Greg Lloyd BX	.40	1.00
56 Natrone Means SZ	1.50	4.00
57 Marcus Allen GY	4.00	10.00
58 Desmond Howard BX	.60	1.50
59 Stan Humphries BX	.40	1.00
60 Reggie White GY	4.00	10.00
61 Brett Perriman SY	1.00	2.50
62 Warren Sapp BX	1.25	3.00
63 Adrian Murrell SZ	1.50	4.00
64 Mark Brunell GZ	4.00	10.00
65 Carl Pickens GY	2.50	6.00
66 Kordell Stewart GZ	4.00	10.00
67 Ricky Watters GY	2.50	6.00
68 Tyrone Wheatley BX	1.25	3.00
69 Stanley Pritchett BX	.40	1.00
70 Kevin Greene BX	.40	1.00
71 Karim Abdul-Jabbar GZ	2.50	6.00
72 Ki-Jana Carter SY	1.50	4.00
73 Rashaan Salaam SY	1.00	2.50
74 Simeon Rice BX	.60	1.50
75 Napoleon Kaufman SY	2.00	5.00
76 Muhsin Muhammad SZ	2.00	5.00
77 Bruce Smith GY	2.50	6.00
78 Eric Moulds SX	3.00	8.00
79 O.J. McDuffie BX	.60	1.50
80 Danny Kanell BZ	.30	.75
81 Harvey Williams BX	.40	1.00
82 Greg Hill SY	1.00	2.50
83 Terrell Davis GZ	5.00	12.00
84 Dan Wilkinson BX	.40	1.00
85 Yancey Thigpen BX	.60	1.50
86 Darrell Green SX	1.25	3.00
87 Tamarick Vanover SX	2.00	5.00
88 Mike Alstott BX	1.25	3.00
89 Johnnie Morton SX	2.00	5.00
90 Dale Carter BX	.40	1.00
91 Jerome Bettis GY	4.00	10.00
92 James O.Stewart BX	.60	1.50
93 Irving Fryar SX	2.00	5.00
94 Junior Seau SY	2.00	5.00
95 Sean Dawkins BX	.40	1.00
96 J.J. Stokes BZ	2.50	6.00
97 Tim Biakabutuka SY	1.50	4.00
98 Bert Emanuel BX	.60	1.50
99 Eddie Kennison GY	2.50	6.00
100 Ray Zellars BX	.40	1.00
101 Dave Brown BX	.60	1.50
102 Leeland McElroy SY	1.00	2.50
103 Chris Warren SY	1.00	2.50
104 Byron Bam Morris BX	.40	1.00
105 Thurman Thomas GY	2.50	6.00
106 Kyle Brady BX	1.25	3.00
107 Anthony Miller GY	2.50	6.00
108 Derrick Thomas SY	2.00	5.00
109 Mark Chmura BX	.60	1.50
110 Deion Sanders GZ	4.00	10.00
111 Eric Swann BX	.60	1.50
112 Amani Toomer SX	3.00	8.00
113 Raymont Harris BX	.40	1.00
114 Jake Reed BX	.60	1.50
115 Bryant Young BX	.60	1.50
116 Keenan McCardell SX	2.00	5.00
117 Herman Moore GZ	2.50	6.00
118 Errict Rhett SZ	1.50	4.00
119 Henry Ellard BX	.60	1.50
120 Bobby Hoying SX	3.00	8.00
121 Robert Smith BX	1.25	3.00
122 Keyshawn Johnson GZ	4.00	10.00
123 Zach Thomas BX	1.25	3.00
124 Charlie Garner BX	.60	1.50
125 Terry Kirby BX	.60	1.50
126 Darren Woodson BX	.40	1.00
127 Darnay Scott SX	2.00	5.00
128 Chris Sanders SY	1.00	2.50
129 Charles Johnson SX	1.25	3.00
130 Joey Galloway SZ	1.50	4.00
131 Curtis Conway SY	1.50	4.00
132 Isaac Bruce GZ	4.00	10.00
133 Bobby Taylor BX	.40	1.00
134 Jamal Anderson SY	2.00	6.00
135 Ken Norton BX	.40	1.00
136 Darick Holmes BX	.40	1.00
137 Tony Brackens BX	.60	1.50
138 Tony Martin BX	.60	1.50
139 Antonio Freeman SZ	2.00	5.00
140 Neil Smith BX	.40	1.00
141 Terry Glenn GZ	2.50	6.00
142 Marvin Harrison SY	2.00	5.00
143 Daryl Johnston BX	.60	1.50
144 Tim Brown GY	4.00	10.00
145 Kimble Anders BX	.60	1.50
146 Derrick Alexander SX	2.00	5.00
147 LeShon Johnson BX	.40	1.00
148 Anthony Johnson BX	.40	1.00
149 Leslie Shepherd BX	.60	1.50
150 Chris T. Jones BX	.40	1.00
151 Edgar Bennett BX	.40	1.00
152 Ty Detmer BX	.60	1.50
153 Ike Hilliard GX	4.00	10.00
154 Jim Druckenmiller SZ	1.00	2.50
155 Warrick Dunn GZ	4.00	10.00
156 Yatil Green GZ	1.50	4.00
157 Reidel Anthony GZ	2.50	6.00
158 Antowain Smith GZ	4.00	10.00
159 Rae Carruth SY	1.00	2.50
160 Tiki Barber GZ	6.00	15.00
161 Byron Hanspard SZ	1.50	4.00
162 Jake Plummer SY	4.00	10.00
163 Joey Kent SZ	1.00	2.50
164 Corey Dillon SY	4.00	10.00
165 Kevin Lockett BZ	1.50	4.00
166 Will Blackwell BY	.30	.75
167 Troy Davis GZ	1.50	4.00
168 James Farrior BX	.60	1.50
169 Danny Wuerffel SY	2.00	5.00
170 Pat Barnes SY	1.00	2.50
171 Darnell Autry SY	2.00	5.00
172 Tom Knight BX	.40	1.00
173 David LaFleur BY	.30	.75
174 Tony Gonzalez BY	2.50	6.00
175 Kenny Holmes BX	.40	1.00
176 Reinard Wilson BX	.40	1.00
177 Renaldo Wynn BX	.40	1.00
178 Bryant Westbrook BX	.60	1.50
179 Darrell Russell BX	.60	1.50
180 Orlando Pace BX	1.25	3.00
181 Shawn Springs BX	.60	1.50
182 Peter Boulware BX	1.25	3.00
183 Dan Marino L BY	7.50	20.00
184 Brett Favre L BY	7.50	20.00
185 Emmitt Smith L BY	6.00	15.00
186 Eddie George L BY	1.00	2.50
187 Curtis Martin L BY	1.50	4.00
188 Tim Brown L BZ	1.00	2.50
189 Mark Brunell L BY	2.50	6.00
190 Isaac Bruce L BY	1.00	2.50
191 Deion Sanders L BY	1.00	2.50
192 John Elway L BY	7.50	20.00
193 Jerry Rice L BY	4.00	10.00
194 Barry Sanders L BY	6.00	15.00
195 Herman Moore L BY	.50	1.25
196 Carl Pickens L BY	.50	1.25
197 Karim Abdul-Jabbar L BY	.50	1.25
198 Drew Bledsoe CL BY	1.50	4.00
199 Troy Aikman CL BY	2.50	6.00
200 Terrell Davis CL BY	1.50	4.00

1997 Leaf Fractal Matrix Die-Cuts

1 Steve Young GZ	20.00	50.00
2 Brett Favre GX	25.00	60.00
3 Barry Sanders GZ	40.00	100.00
4 Drew Bledsoe GZ	15.00	40.00
5 Troy Aikman GZ	25.00	60.00
6 Kerry Collins GZ	7.50	20.00
7 Dan Marino GX	30.00	80.00
8 Jerry Rice GZ	25.00	60.00
9 John Elway GZ	50.00	120.00
10 Emmitt Smith GX	25.00	60.00
11 Tony Banks GY	7.50	20.00
12 Gus Frerotte SX	2.50	6.00
13 Elvis Grbac SX	4.00	10.00
14 Neil O'Donnell BX	1.00	2.50
15 Michael Irvin SY	7.50	20.00
16 Marshall Faulk SY	7.50	20.00
17 Todd Collins SX	2.00	5.00
18 Scott Mitchell BX	1.00	2.50
19 Trent Dilfer SY	5.00	12.00
20 Rick Mirer SX	2.00	5.00
21 Frank Sanders SX	2.50	6.00
22 Larry Centers BX	1.00	2.50
23 Brad Johnson BX	2.00	5.00
24 Garrison Hearst SY	5.00	12.00
25 Steve McNair GZ	15.00	40.00
26 Dorsey Levens BX	2.00	5.00
27 Eric Metcalf BX	1.00	2.50
28 Jeff George SX	2.50	6.00
29 Rodney Hampton BX	1.00	2.50
30 Michael Westbrook SY	5.00	12.00
31 Cris Carter SY	7.50	20.00
32 Heath Shuler SX	2.50	6.00
33 Warren Moon BX	2.00	5.00
34 Rod Woodson SX	2.00	5.00
35 Ken Dilger BX	1.50	4.00
36 Ben Coates BX	1.50	4.00
37 Andre Reed BX	1.50	4.00
38 Terrell Owens SZ	12.50	30.00
39 Jeff Blake SY	7.50	20.00
40 Vinny Testaverde BX	1.50	4.00
41 Robert Brooks SY	5.00	12.00
42 Shannon Sharpe SX	4.00	10.00
43 Terry Allen SY	5.00	12.00
44 Terance Mathis BX	1.50	4.00
45 Bobby Engram BZ	3.00	8.00
46 Rickey Dudley BX	1.50	4.00
47 Alex Molden BX	1.00	2.50
48 Lawrence Phillips SY	3.00	8.00
49 Curtis Martin GZ	15.00	40.00
50 Jim Harbaugh BX	1.50	4.00
51 Wayne Chrebet BX	2.00	5.00
52 Quentin Coryatt BX	1.00	2.50
53 Eddie George GX	7.50	20.00
54 Michael Jackson BX	1.50	4.00
55 Greg Lloyd BX	1.00	2.50
56 Natrone Means SZ	7.50	20.00
57 Marcus Allen GY	7.50	20.00
58 Desmond Howard BX	1.50	4.00
59 Stan Humphries BX	1.50	4.00
60 Reggie White GY	5.00	12.00
61 Brett Perriman SY	3.00	8.00
62 Warren Sapp BX	2.00	5.00
63 Adrian Murrell SZ	7.50	20.00
64 Mark Brunell GZ	15.00	40.00
65 Carl Pickens GY	5.00	12.00
66 Kordell Stewart GZ	12.50	30.00
67 Ricky Watters GY	5.00	12.00
68 Tyrone Wheatley BX	2.00	5.00
69 Stanley Pritchett BX	1.00	2.50
70 Kevin Greene BX	1.00	2.50
71 Karim Abdul-Jabbar GZ	7.50	20.00
72 Ki-Jana Carter SY	5.00	12.00
73 Rashaan Salaam SY	3.00	8.00
74 Simeon Rice BX	1.50	4.00
75 Napoleon Kaufman SY	7.50	20.00
76 Muhsin Muhammad SZ	12.50	30.00
77 Bruce Smith GY	5.00	12.00
78 Eric Moulds SX	4.00	10.00
79 O.J. McDuffie BX	1.50	4.00
80 Danny Kanell BZ	5.00	12.00
81 Harvey Williams BX	1.00	2.50
82 Greg Hill SY	3.00	8.00
83 Terrell Davis GZ	15.00	40.00
84 Dan Wilkinson BX	1.00	2.50
85 Yancey Thigpen BX	1.50	4.00
86 Darrell Green SX	2.00	5.00
87 Tamarick Vanover SX	2.50	6.00
88 Mike Alstott BX	2.00	5.00
89 Johnnie Morton SX	2.50	6.00
90 Dale Carter BX	1.00	2.50
91 Jerome Bettis GY	7.50	20.00
92 James O.Stewart BX	1.50	4.00
93 Irving Fryar SX	2.50	6.00
94 Junior Seau SY	7.50	20.00
95 Sean Dawkins BX	1.50	4.00
96 J.J. Stokes BZ	5.00	12.00
97 Tim Biakabutuka SY	5.00	12.00
98 Bert Emanuel BX	1.50	4.00
99 Eddie Kennison GY	5.00	12.00
100 Ray Zellars BX	1.00	2.50
101 Dave Brown BX	1.50	4.00
102 Leeland McElroy SY	3.00	8.00
103 Chris Warren SY	3.00	8.00
104 Byron Bam Morris BX	1.00	2.50
105 Thurman Thomas GY	5.00	12.00
106 Kyle Brady BX	2.00	5.00
107 Anthony Miller GY	3.00	8.00
108 Derrick Thomas SY	7.50	20.00
109 Mark Chmura BX	1.50	4.00
110 Deion Sanders GZ	12.50	30.00
111 Eric Swann BX	1.00	2.50
112 Amani Toomer SX	4.00	10.00
113 Raymont Harris BX	1.00	2.50
114 Jake Reed BX	1.50	4.00
115 Bryant Young BX	1.50	4.00
116 Keenan McCardell SX	2.50	6.00
117 Herman Moore GZ	7.50	20.00
118 Errict Rhett SZ	5.00	12.00
119 Henry Ellard BX	1.50	4.00
120 Bobby Hoying SX	2.50	6.00
121 Robert Smith BX	2.00	5.00
122 Keyshawn Johnson GZ	12.50	30.00
123 Zach Thomas BX	2.00	5.00
124 Charlie Garner BX	1.50	4.00
125 Terry Kirby BX	1.50	4.00
126 Darren Woodson BX	1.00	2.50
127 Darnay Scott SX	2.50	6.00
128 Chris Sanders SY	3.00	8.00
129 Charles Johnson SX	2.00	5.00
130 Joey Galloway SZ	7.50	20.00
131 Curtis Conway SY	5.00	12.00
132 Isaac Bruce GZ	12.50	30.00
133 Bobby Taylor BX	1.00	2.50
134 Jamal Anderson SY	7.50	20.00
135 Ken Norton BX	1.00	2.50
136 Darick Holmes BX	1.00	2.50
137 Tony Brackens BX	1.50	4.00
138 Tony Martin BX	1.50	4.00
139 Antonio Freeman SZ	12.50	30.00
140 Neil Smith BX	1.00	2.50
141 Terry Glenn GZ	7.50	20.00
142 Marvin Harrison SY	7.50	20.00
143 Daryl Johnston BX	1.50	4.00
144 Tim Brown GY	7.50	20.00
145 Kimble Anders BX	1.50	4.00
146 Derrick Alexander SX	2.50	6.00
147 LeShon Johnson BX	1.00	2.50
148 Anthony Johnson BX	1.00	2.50
149 Leslie Shepherd BX	1.50	4.00
150 Chris T. Jones BX	1.00	2.50
151 Edgar Bennett BX	1.50	4.00
152 Ty Detmer BX	1.50	4.00
153 Ike Hilliard GX	4.00	10.00
154 Jim Druckenmiller SZ	5.00	12.00
155 Warrick Dunn GZ	12.50	30.00
156 Yatil Green GZ	5.00	12.00
157 Reidel Anthony GZ	7.50	20.00
158 Antowain Smith GZ	12.50	30.00
159 Rae Carruth SY	3.00	8.00
160 Tiki Barber GZ	15.00	40.00
161 Byron Hanspard SZ	7.50	20.00
162 Jake Plummer SY	8.00	20.00
163 Joey Kent SZ	5.00	12.00
164 Corey Dillon SY	8.00	20.00
165 Kevin Lockett BZ	3.00	8.00
166 Will Blackwell BY	2.00	5.00
167 Troy Davis GZ	5.00	12.00
168 James Farrior BX	1.50	4.00
169 Danny Wuerffel SY	7.50	20.00
170 Pat Barnes SY	3.00	8.00
171 Darnell Autry SY	7.50	20.00
172 Tom Knight BX	1.00	2.50
173 David LaFleur BY	2.00	5.00
174 Tony Gonzalez BY	8.00	20.00
175 Kenny Holmes BX	1.00	2.50
176 Reinard Wilson BX	1.00	2.50
177 Renaldo Wynn BX	1.00	2.50
178 Bryant Westbrook BX	1.00	2.50
179 Darrell Russell BX	1.00	2.50
180 Orlando Pace BX	2.00	5.00
181 Shawn Springs BX	1.50	4.00
182 Peter Boulware BX	2.00	5.00
183 Dan Marino L BY	20.00	50.00
184 Brett Favre L BY	20.00	50.00
185 Emmitt Smith L BY	15.00	40.00
186 Eddie George L BY	4.00	10.00
187 Curtis Martin L BY	6.00	15.00
188 Tim Brown L BZ	7.50	20.00
189 Mark Brunell L BY	6.00	15.00
190 Isaac Bruce L BY	4.00	10.00
191 Deion Sanders L BY	4.00	10.00
192 John Elway L BY	20.00	50.00
193 Jerry Rice L BY	10.00	25.00
194 Barry Sanders L BY	15.00	40.00
195 Herman Moore L BY	2.50	6.00
196 Carl Pickens L BY	2.50	6.00
197 Karim Abdul-Jabbar L BY	2.50	6.00
198 Drew Bledsoe CL BY	4.00	10.00
199 Troy Aikman CL BY	6.00	15.00
200 Terrell Davis CL BY	6.00	15.00

1997 Leaf Signature Proofs

COMPLETE SET (200)	300.00	600.00
*STARS: 8X TO 20X BASIC CARDS		
*RCs: 4X TO 10X BASIC CARDS		
STATED PRINT RUN 200 SER.#'d SETS		

1997 Leaf Hardwear

COMPLETE SET (20)	75.00	150.00
STATED PRINT RUN 3500 SERIAL #'d SETS		
1 Dan Marino	8.00	20.00
2 Brett Favre	8.00	20.00
3 Emmitt Smith	6.00	15.00
4 Jerry Rice	4.00	10.00
5 Barry Sanders	6.00	15.00
6 Deion Sanders	2.00	5.00
7 Reggie White	2.00	5.00
8 Tim Brown	2.00	5.00
9 Steve McNair	2.50	6.00
10 Steve Young	2.50	6.00
11 Mark Brunell	2.50	6.00
12 Ricky Watters	1.25	3.00
13 Eddie Kennison	1.25	3.00
14 Kordell Stewart	2.00	5.00
15 Kerry Collins	2.00	5.00
16 Joey Galloway	1.25	3.00
17 Terrell Owens	2.50	6.00
18 Terry Glenn	2.00	5.00
19 Keyshawn Johnson	2.00	5.00
20 Eddie George	2.00	5.00

1997 Leaf Letterman

COMPLETE SET (15)	125.00	250.00
STATED PRINT RUN 1000 SERIAL #'d SETS		
1 Brett Favre	12.50	30.00
2 Emmitt Smith	10.00	25.00
3 Dan Marino	12.50	30.00
4 Jerry Rice	6.00	15.00
5 Mark Brunell	4.00	10.00
6 Barry Sanders	10.00	25.00
7 John Elway	12.50	30.00
8 Eddie George	3.00	8.00
9 Troy Aikman	6.00	15.00
10 Curtis Martin	4.00	10.00
11 Karim Abdul-Jabbar	2.00	5.00
12 Terrell Davis	4.00	10.00
13 Ike Hilliard	5.00	12.00
14 Terry Glenn	3.00	8.00
15 Drew Bledsoe	4.00	10.00

1997 Leaf Reproductions

COMPLETE SET (24)	125.00	250.00
STATED PRINT RUN 1948 SERIAL #'d SETS		
*PROMO: .2X TO .5X BASIC INSERTS		
1 Emmitt Smith	12.50	30.00
2 Brett Favre	15.00	40.00
3 Dan Marino	15.00	40.00
4 Barry Sanders	12.50	30.00
5 Jerry Rice	8.00	20.00
6 Terrell Davis	5.00	12.00
7 Curtis Martin	5.00	12.00
8 Troy Aikman	8.00	20.00
9 Drew Bledsoe	5.00	12.00
10 Herman Moore	4.00	10.00
11 Isaac Bruce	4.00	10.00
12 Carl Pickens	2.50	6.00
13 Len Dawson	4.00	10.00
14 Dan Fouts	4.00	10.00
15 Jim Plunkett	4.00	10.00
16 Ken Stabler	4.00	10.00
17 Joe Theismann	4.00	10.00
18 Billy Kilmer	4.00	10.00
19 Danny White	4.00	10.00
20 Archie Manning	4.00	10.00
21 Ron Jaworski	2.50	6.00
22 Y.A. Tittle	4.00	10.00
23 Sid Luckman	4.00	10.00
24 Sammy Baugh	4.00	10.00

1997 Leaf Reproductions Autographs

STATED PRINT RUN 500 SETS		
13 Len Dawson	15.00	40.00
14 Dan Fouts	15.00	40.00
15 Jim Plunkett	12.00	30.00
16 Ken Stabler	15.00	40.00
17 Joe Theismann	15.00	40.00
18 Billy Kilmer	12.00	30.00
18P Billy Kilmer Gold Holofoil	12.00	30.00
19 Danny White	15.00	40.00
20 Archie Manning	12.00	30.00
21 Ron Jaworski	12.00	30.00
22 Y.A. Tittle	25.00	50.00
23 Sid Luckman	100.00	200.00
24 Sammy Baugh	100.00	175.00
24P Sammy Baugh Gold Holofoil	90.00	150.00

1997 Leaf Run and Gun

COMPLETE SET (18)	100.00	200.00
STATED PRINT RUN 3500 SERIAL #'d SETS		
1 Dan Marino Karim Abdul-Jabbar	10.00	25.00
2 Troy Aikman Emmitt Smith	10.00	25.00
3 John Elway Terrell Davis	12.50	30.00
4 Drew Bledsoe Curtis Martin	5.00	12.00
5 Kordell Stewart Jerome Bettis	6.00	15.00
6 Mark Brunell Natrone Means	6.00	15.00
7 Kerry Collins Tim Biakabutuka	3.00	8.00
8 Rick Mirer Rashaan Salaam	2.00	5.00
9 Scott Mitchell Barry Sanders	10.00	25.00
10 Steve McNair Eddie George	3.00	8.00
11 Trent Dilfer Warrick Dunn	4.00	10.00
12 Jeff Blake Ki-Jana Carter	3.00	8.00
13 Tony Banks Lawrence Phillips	3.00	8.00
14 Steve Young Garrison Hearst	5.00	12.00
15 Jim Harbaugh Marshall Faulk	4.00	10.00
16 Elvis Grbac Marcus Allen	3.00	8.00
17 Neil O'Donnell Adrian Murrell	2.00	5.00
18 Gus Frerotte Tery Allen	3.00	8.00

1999 Leaf Certified

The 1999 Leaf Certified set was released as a 225 card set. The set was broken down in four card groups as folows: the first 100 cards in the set were done with one blue star on card front and were available four cards in each pack. The two star level was a 50 card set inserted one in each pack. The three star level was done as a 25 card set and inserted one in three packs. The four star level was a 50 card short printed set of the 1999 rookies and was inserted at a rate of one in five packs. Only the rookie cards were available in the four star format.

COMPLETE SET (225)	100.00	200.00
COMP.SET w/o RCs 175)	15.00	40.00
1 Simeon Rice	.25	.60
2 Frank Sanders	.25	.60
3 Andre Wadsworth	.25	.60
4 Larry Centers	.30	.75
5 Byron Hanspard	.25	.60
6 Terance Mathis	.25	.60
7 O.J. Santiago	.25	.60
8 Chris Calloway	.25	.60
9 Michael Jackson	.25	.60
10 Rod Woodson	.40	1.00
11 Pat Johnson	.25	.60
12 Rob Johnson	.30	.75
13 Andre Reed	.40	1.00
14 Tim Biakabutuka	.30	.75
15 Rae Carruth	.25	.60
16 Fred Lane	.25	.60
17 Muhsin Muhammad	.30	.75
18 Wesley Walls	.30	.75
19 Edgar Bennett	.30	.75
20 Curtis Conway	.30	.75
21 Bobby Engram	.30	.75
22 Jeff Blake	.30	.75
23 Darnay Scott	.25	.60
24 Ty Detmer	.30	.75
25 Sedrick Shaw	.25	.60
26 Leslie Shepherd	.25	.60
27 Terry Kirby	.25	.60
28 Chris Warren	.30	.75
29 Rocket Ismail	.30	.75
30 Marcus Nash	.25	.60
31 Neil Smith	.25	.60
32 Bubby Brister	.25	.60
33 Brian Griese	.30	.75
34 Germane Crowell	.25	.60
35 Johnnie Morton	.30	.75
36 Gus Frerotte	.25	.60
37 Robert Brooks	.30	.75
38 Mark Chmura	.25	.60
39 Derrick Mayes	.25	.60
40 Jerome Pathon	.25	.60
41 Jimmy Smith	.30	.75
42 James Stewart	.25	.60
43 Tavian Banks	.25	.60
44 Derrick Alexander WR	.25	.60
45 Kimble Anders	.25	.60
46 Elvis Grbac	.25	.60
47 Derrick Thomas	.40	1.00
48 Byron Bam Morris	.25	.60
49 Tony Gonzalez	.40	1.00
50 John Avery	.25	.60
51 Tyrone Wheatley	.30	.75
52 Zach Thomas	.40	1.00
53 Lamar Thomas	.25	.60
54 Jeff George	.25	.60
55 John Randle	.30	.75
56 Jake Reed	.30	.75
57 Leroy Hoard	.25	.60
58 Robert Edwards	.25	.60
59 Ben Coates	.30	.75
60 Tony Simmons	.25	.60
61 Shawn Jefferson	.25	.60
62 Eddie Kennison	.30	.75
63 Lamar Smith	.25	.60
64 Tiki Barber	.40	1.00
65 Kerry Collins	.30	.75
66 Ike Hilliard	.30	.75
67 Gary Brown	.25	.60
68 Joe Jurevicius	.25	.60
69 Kent Graham	.25	.60
70 Dedric Ward	.25	.60
71 Terry Allen	.30	.75
72 Neil O'Donnell	.30	.75
73 Desmond Howard	.30	.75
74 James Jett	.25	.60
75 Jon Ritchie	.25	.60
76 Rickey Dudley	.25	.60
77 Charles Johnson	.25	.60
78 Chris Fuamatu-Ma'afala	.25	.60
79 Hines Ward	.40	1.00
80 Ryan Leaf	.30	.75
81 Jim Harbaugh	.30	.75
82 Junior Seau	.40	1.00
83 Mikhael Ricks	.25	.60
84 J.J. Stokes	.25	.60
85 Ahman Green	.30	.75
86 Tony Banks	.30	.75
87 Robert Holcombe	.25	.60
88 Az-Zahir Hakim	.25	.60
89 Greg Hill	.25	.60
90 Trent Green	.30	.75
91 Eric Zeier	.25	.60
92 Reidel Anthony	.25	.60
93 Bert Emanuel	.30	.75
94 Warren Sapp	.30	.75
95 Kevin Dyson	.25	.60
96 Yancey Thigpen	.25	.60
97 Frank Wycheck	.30	.75
98 Michael Westbrook	.25	.60
99 Albert Connell	.25	.60
100 Darrell Green	.40	1.00
101 Rob Moore	.30	.75
102 Adrian Murrell	.40	1.00
103 Jake Plummer	.40	1.00
104 Chris Chandler	.40	1.00
105 Jamal Anderson	.40	1.00
106 Tim Dwight	.40	1.00
107 Jermaine Lewis	.30	.75
108 Priest Holmes	.50	1.25
109 Bruce Smith	.50	1.25
110 Eric Moulds	.40	1.00
111 Antowain Smith	.30	.75
112 Curtis Enis	.30	.75
113 Corey Dillon	.40	1.00
114 Michael Irvin	.50	1.25
115 Ed McCaffrey	.40	1.00
116 Shannon Sharpe	.50	1.25
117 Terrell Davis	.50	1.25
118 Charlie Batch	.40	1.00
119 Antonio Freeman	.40	1.00
120 Dorsey Levens	.40	1.00
121 Marvin Harrison	.50	1.25
122 Peyton Manning	1.50	4.00
123 Keenan McCardell	.40	1.00
124 Fred Taylor	.40	1.00
125 Andre Rison	.40	1.00
126 O.J. McDuffie	.40	1.00
127 Karim Abdul-Jabbar	.40	1.00
128 Randy Moss	[illegible]	1.25
129 Terry Glenn	.40	1.00
130 Vinny Testaverde	.40	1.00
131 Keyshawn Johnson	.40	1.00
132 Curtis Martin	.50	1.25
133 Wayne Chrebet	.40	1.00
134 Napoleon Kaufman	.30	.75
135 Charles Woodson	.50	1.25
136 Duce Staley	.40	1.00
137 Kordell Stewart	.40	1.00
138 Terrell Owens	.50	1.25
139 Ricky Watters	.40	1.00
140 Joey Galloway	.40	1.00
141 Jon Kitna	.40	1.00
142 Isaac Bruce	.50	1.25
143 Jacquez Green	.30	.75
144 Warrick Dunn	.40	1.00
145 Mike Alstott	.50	1.25
146 Trent Dilfer	.40	1.00
147 Steve McNair	.50	1.25
148 Eddie George	.40	1.00
149 Skip Hicks	.30	.75
150 Brad Johnson	.40	1.00
151 Doug Flutie	.75	2.00
152 Thurman Thomas	.75	2.00
153 Carl Pickens	.60	1.50
154 Emmitt Smith	2.00	5.00
155 Troy Aikman	1.25	3.00
156 Deion Sanders	.75	2.00
157 John Elway	2.50	6.00
158 Rod Smith	.60	1.50
159 Barry Sanders	2.00	5.00
160 Herman Moore	.60	1.50
161 Brett Favre	2.50	6.00
162 Mark Brunell	.60	1.50
163 Warren Moon	.75	2.00
164 Dan Marino	2.50	6.00
165 Randall Cunningham	.75	2.00
166 Robert Smith	.60	1.50
167 Cris Carter	.75	2.00
168 Drew Bledsoe	.75	2.00
169 Tim Brown	.75	2.00
170 Jerome Bettis	.75	2.00
171 Natrone Means	.60	1.50
172 Jerry Rice	1.50	4.00
173 Steve Young	1.00	2.50
174 Garrison Hearst	.60	1.50
175 Marshall Faulk	.75	2.00
176 David Boston RC	1.25	3.00
177 Jeff Paulk RC	1.00	2.50
178 Reginald Kelly RC	1.00	2.50
179 Scott Covington RC	1.00	2.50
180 Chris McAlister RC	1.25	3.00
181 Shawn Bryson RC	1.00	2.50
182 Peerless Price RC	1.25	3.00
183 Cade McNown RC	1.25	3.00
184 Michael Bishop RC	1.25	3.00
185 D'Wayne Bates RC	1.00	2.50
186 Marty Booker RC	1.25	3.00
187 Akili Smith RC	1.25	3.00
188 Craig Yeast RC	1.00	2.50
189 Tim Couch RC	1.50	4.00
190 Kevin Johnson RC	1.25	3.00
191 Wane McGarity RC	1.00	2.50
192 Olandis Gary RC	1.50	4.00
193 Travis McGriff RC	1.00	2.50
194 Sedrick Irvin RC	1.00	2.50
195 Chris Claiborne RC	1.00	2.50
196 De'Mond Parker RC	1.00	2.50
197 Dee Miller RC	1.00	2.50
198 Edgerrin James RC	2.00	5.00
199 Mike Cloud RC	1.00	2.50
200 Larry Parker RC	1.25	3.00
201 Cecil Collins RC	1.00	2.50
202 James Johnson RC	1.00	2.50
203 Rob Konrad RC	1.00	2.50
204 Daunte Culpepper RC	1.50	4.00
205 Jim Kleinsasser RC	1.50	4.00
206 Kevin Faulk RC	1.50	4.00
207 Andy Katzenmoyer RC	1.25	3.00
208 Ricky Williams RC	2.50	6.00
209 Joe Montgomery RC	1.00	2.50
210 Sean Bennett RC	1.00	2.50
211 Dameane Douglas RC	1.00	2.50
212 Donovan McNabb RC	6.00	15.00
213 Na Brown RC	1.00	2.50
214 Amos Zereoue RC	1.25	3.00
215 Troy Edwards RC	1.25	3.00
216 Jermaine Fazande RC	1.00	2.50
217 Tai Streets RC	1.25	3.00
218 Brock Huard RC	1.25	3.00
219 Charlie Rogers RC	1.00	2.50
220 Karsten Bailey RC	1.00	2.50
221 Joe Germaine RC	1.25	3.00
222 Torry Holt RC	2.50	6.00
223 Shaun King RC	1.25	3.00
224 Jevon Kearse RC	1.50	4.00
225 Champ Bailey RC	3.00	8.00

1999 Leaf Certified Mirror Gold

*1-STAR 1-100: 15X TO 40X BASIC CARDS
1-STAR 1-100 PRINT RUN 45 SER.#'d SETS
*2-STAR 101-150: 10X TO 25X BASIC CARDS
2-STAR 101-150 PRINT RUN 35 SER.#'d SETS
3-STAR 151-175: 10X TO 25X BASIC CARDS
3-STAR 151-175 PRINT RUN 25 SER.#'d SETS
4-STAR 176-225: 1.2X TO 3X BASIC CARDS
4-STAR 176-225 PRINT RUN 30 SER.#'d SETS

1999 Leaf Certified Mirror Red

1-STAR 1-100: 6X TO 16X BASIC CARD
1-STAR 1-100 STATED ODDS 1:17
2-STAR 101-150: 3X TO 8X BASIC CARD
2-STAR 101-150 STATED ODDS 1:53
3-STAR 151-175: 3X TO 8X BASIC CARD
3-STAR 151-175 STATED ODDS 1:125
4-STAR 176-225: .6X TO 1.5X BASIC CARD
4-STAR 176-225 STATED ODDS 1:89

1999 Leaf Certified Skills

COMPLETE SET (20)	60.00	120.00
STATED ODDS 1:35		
*MIRROR BLACK: 3X TO 8X BASIC INSERT		
MIRROR BLACK PRINT RUN 25 SER.#'d SETS		
CS1 Deion Sanders Champ Bailey	2.50	6.00
CS2 John Elway Cade McNown	6.00	15.00

CS3 Cris Carter Daivd Boston	2.50	6.00
CS4 Marshall Faulk Edgerrin James	3.00	8.00
CS5 Jerry Rice Randy Moss	5.00	12.00
CS6 Antonio Freeman Terrell Owens	2.50	6.00
CS7 Terrell Davis Ricky Williams	2.50	6.00
CS8 Drew Bledsoe Doug Flutie	2.50	6.00
CS9 Eddie George Jamal Anderson	2.50	6.00
CS10 Troy Aikman Peyton Manning	5.00	12.00
CS11 Barry Sanders Warrick Dunn	6.00	15.00
CS12 Randall Cunningham Daunte Culpepper	3.00	8.00
CS13 Dan Marino Tim Couch	7.50	20.00
CS14 Emmitt Smith Fred Taylor	5.00	12.00
CS15 Keyshawn Johnson Eric Moulds	2.50	6.00
CS16 Steve Young Mark Brunell	2.50	6.00
CS17 Donovan McNabb Akili Smith	4.00	10.00
CS18 Brett Favre Jake Plummer	6.00	15.00
CS19 Kordell Stewart Steve McNair	2.50	6.00
CS20 Torry Holt Troy Edwards	2.50	6.00

1999 Leaf Certified Fabric of the Game

FG1 John Elway/100	30.00	80.00
FG2 Barry Sanders/100	30.00	80.00
FG3 Jerry Rice/100	20.00	50.00
FG4 Brett Favre/250	15.00	40.00
FG5 Steve Young/250	10.00	25.00
FG6 Troy Aikman/250	15.00	40.00
FG7 Deion Sanders/250	5.00	12.00
FG8 Terrell Davis/500	4.00	10.00
FG9 Mark Brunell/500	4.00	10.00
FG10 Drew Bledsoe/500	6.00	15.00
FG11 R.Cunningham/500	4.00	10.00
FG12 Eddie George/500	4.00	10.00
FG13 Jamal Anderson/750	3.00	8.00
FG14 Doug Flutie/750	3.00	8.00
FG15 Robert Smith/750	3.00	8.00
FG16 Garrison Hearst/750	3.00	8.00
FG17 Keyshawn Johnson/750	3.00	8.00
FG18 Randy Moss/750	10.00	25.00
FG19 Eric Moulds/1000	2.50	6.00
FG20 Curtis Enis/1000	2.50	6.00
FG21 Ricky Williams/1000	4.00	10.00
FG22 Peyton Manning/1000	10.00	25.00
FG23 Tim Couch/1000	3.00	8.00
FG24 Cade McNown/1000	3.00	8.00
FG25 Akili Smith/1000	2.50	6.00
FG26 Dan Marino/100	30.00	80.00
FG27 Jerry Rice/100	20.00	50.00
FG28 Emmitt Smith/100	20.00	50.00
FG29 Cris Carter/250	5.00	12.00
FG30 Steve Young/250	10.00	25.00
FG31 Herman Moore/250	5.00	12.00
FG32 Tim Brown/250	5.00	12.00
FG33 Jerome Bettis/500	4.00	10.00
FG34 Natrone Means/500	4.00	10.00
FG35 Antonio Freeman/500	4.00	10.00
FG36 Terrell Davis/500	4.00	10.00
FG37 Carl Pickens/500	2.00	5.00
FG38 K.Abdul-Jabbar/750	3.00	8.00
FG39 Mike Alstott/750	3.00	8.00
FG40 Jake Plummer/750	3.00	8.00
FG41 Steve McNair/750	3.00	8.00
FG42 Terrell Owens/750	3.00	8.00
FG43 Kordell Stewart/750	3.00	8.00
FG44 Randy Moss/1000	7.50	20.00
FG45 Fred Taylor/1000	3.00	8.00
FG46 Peyton Manning/1000	10.00	25.00
FG47 Tim Couch/1000	3.00	8.00
FG48 Akili Smith/1000	2.50	6.00
FG49 Torry Holt/1000	6.00	15.00
FG50 Donovan McNabb/1000	12.50	25.00
FG51 Barry Sanders/100	30.00	80.00
FG52 Dan Marino/100	30.00	80.00
FG53 Jerry Rice/100	20.00	50.00
FG54 John Elway/250	20.00	50.00
FG55 Brett Favre/250	15.00	40.00
FG56 Emmitt Smith/250	15.00	30.00
FG57 Mark Brunell/250	5.00	12.00
FG58 Jake Plummer/500	4.00	10.00
FG59 Ricky Watters/500	2.00	5.00
FG60 Dorsey Levens/500	4.00	10.00
FG61 Curtis Martin/500	4.00	10.00
FG62 Marshall Faulk/500	6.00	15.00
FG63 Eddie George/750	3.00	8.00
FG64 Corey Dillon/750	3.00	8.00
FG65 Warrick Dunn/750	3.00	8.00
FG66 Antowain Smith/750	3.00	8.00
FG67 Napoleon Kaufman/750	3.00	8.00
FG68 Joey Galloway/750	3.00	8.00
FG69 Fred Taylor/1000	3.00	8.00
FG70 Charlie Batch/1000	3.00	8.00
FG71 Ricky Williams/1000	4.00	10.00
FG72 Edgerrin James/1000	7.50	20.00
FG73 Jon Kitna/1000	3.00	8.00
FG74 Daunte Culpepper/1000	7.50	20.00
FG75 Skip Hicks/1000	2.50	6.00

1999 Leaf Certified Gold Future

COMPLETE SET (30)	60.00	120.00

STATED ODDS 1:17
*MIRROR BLACK: 4X TO 10X BASIC INSERT
MIRROR BLACK PRINT RUN 25 SER.#'d SETS

1 Travis McGriff	.60	1.50
2 Jermaine Fazande	1.00	2.50
3 Kevin Faulk	1.50	4.00
4 Edgerrin James	5.00	12.00
5 Ricky Williams	2.50	6.00
6 Tim Couch	1.50	4.00
7 Torry Holt	3.00	8.00
8 Kevin Johnson	1.50	4.00
9 Amos Zereoue	1.50	4.00
10 Joe Germaine	1.00	2.50
11 Shawn Bryson	1.50	4.00
12 D'Wayne Bates	1.00	2.50
13 Akili Smith	.60	1.50
14 Shaun King	1.00	2.50
15 Joe Montgomery	1.00	2.50
16 Troy Edwards	1.00	2.50
17 Rob Konrad	1.50	4.00
18 David Boston	1.50	4.00
19 Reginald Kelly	.60	1.50
20 Donovan McNabb	6.00	15.00
21 Champ Bailey	2.00	5.00
22 Craig Yeast	1.00	2.50
23 Daunte Culpepper	5.00	12.00
24 Peerless Price	1.50	4.00
25 Cecil Collins	.60	1.50
26 Cade McNown	1.00	2.50
27 Karsten Bailey	1.00	2.50
28 James Johnson	1.00	2.50
29 Brock Huard	1.50	4.00
30 Mike Cloud	1.00	2.50

1999 Leaf Certified Gold Team

COMPLETE SET (30)	100.00	200.00

STATED ODDS 1:17
*MIRROR BLACK: 4X TO 10X BASIC INSERT
MIRROR BLACK PRINT RUN 25 SER.#'d SETS

CGT1 Randy Moss	5.00	12.00
CGT2 Terrell Davis	2.00	5.00
CGT3 Peyton Manning	6.00	15.00
CGT4 Fred Taylor	2.50	6.00
CGT5 Jake Plummer	2.00	5.00
CGT6 Drew Bledsoe	3.00	8.00
CGT7 John Elway	7.50	20.00
CGT8 Mark Brunell	2.00	5.00
CGT9 Joey Galloway	2.00	5.00
CGT10 Troy Aikman	5.00	12.00
CGT11 Jerome Bettis	2.50	6.00
CGT12 Tim Brown	2.50	6.00
CGT13 Dan Marino	7.50	20.00
CGT14 Antonio Freeman	2.50	6.00
CGT15 Steve Young	3.00	8.00
CGT16 Jamal Anderson	2.50	6.00
CGT17 Brett Favre	7.50	20.00
CGT18 Jerry Rice	5.00	12.00
CGT19 Corey Dillon	2.50	6.00
CGT20 Barry Sanders	7.50	20.00
CGT21 Doug Flutie	2.50	6.00
CGT22 Emmitt Smith	5.00	12.00
CGT23 Curtis Martin	2.50	6.00
CGT24 Dorsey Levens	2.50	6.00
CGT25 Kordell Stewart	2.00	5.00
CGT26 Eddie George	2.50	6.00
CGT27 Terrell Owens	2.50	6.00
CGT28 Keyshawn Johnson	2.50	6.00
CGT29 Steve McNair	2.50	6.00
CGT30 Cris Carter	2.50	6.00

1999 Leaf Certified Gridiron Gear

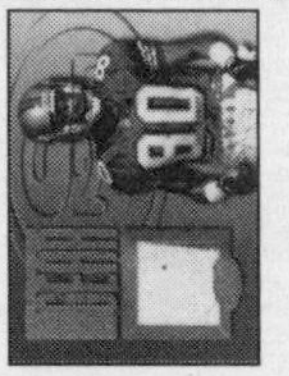

STATED PRINT RUN 300 SER.#'d SETS

AF86 Antonio Freeman	6.00	15.00
BC87 Ben Coates	6.00	15.00
BF4A Brett Favre White	25.00	60.00
BF4H Brett Favre Green	25.00	60.00
BS20 Barry Sanders	20.00	50.00
CC80 Curtis Conway	6.00	15.00
CM28 Curtis Martin	8.00	20.00
CS81 Chris Sanders	5.00	12.00
CW24 Charles Woodson	8.00	20.00
DB11 Drew Bledsoe	8.00	20.00
DF7A Doug Flutie White	8.00	20.00
DF7H Doug Flutie Blue	8.00	20.00
DG28 Darrell Green	8.00	20.00
DH80 Desmond Howard	6.00	15.00
DL25A Dorsey Levens White	6.00	15.00
DL25H Dorsey Levens Green	6.00	15.00
DM13A Dan Marino White	25.00	60.00
DM13H Dan Marino Teal	25.00	60.00
DS21 Deion Sanders	8.00	20.00
DT58 Derrick Thomas	40.00	80.00
EG27 Eddie George	6.00	15.00
ES22 Emmitt Smith	20.00	50.00
HM84 Herman Moore	6.00	15.00
IB80 Isaac Bruce	8.00	20.00
JA32 Jamal Anderson	6.00	15.00
JB36 Jerome Bettis	8.00	20.00
JE7H John Elway Blue	25.00	60.00
JE7HC John Elway Orange	25.00	60.00
JJ82 James Jett	5.00	12.00
JK12 Jim Kelly	10.00	25.00
JM19 Joe Montana	25.00	60.00
JP16 Jake Plummer	6.00	15.00
JR80A Jerry Rice White	15.00	40.00
JR80H Jerry Rice Red	15.00	40.00
JS33 James Stewart	5.00	12.00
JS55 Junior Seau	8.00	20.00
JS82 Jimmy Smith	6.00	15.00
KA33 Karim Abdul-Jabbar	6.00	15.00
KJ19 Keyshawn Johnson	6.00	15.00
KM87 Keenan McCardell	6.00	15.00
KS10 Kordell Stewart	6.00	15.00
MB8A Mark Brunell White	6.00	15.00
MB8H Mark Brunell Teal	6.00	15.00
MC89 Mark Chmura	5.00	12.00
MH88 Marvin Harrison	8.00	20.00
MI88 Michael Irvin	8.00	20.00
NK26A Nap.Kaufman White	5.00	12.00
NK26H Nap.Kaufman Black	5.00	12.00
NM20 Natrone Means	6.00	15.00
NS90 Neil Smith	5.00	12.00
OM81 O.J. McDuffie	6.00	15.00
PM18 Peyton Manning	25.00	60.00
PS12 Phil Simms	8.00	20.00
RB87 Robert Brooks	6.00	15.00
RC7 Randall Cunningham	8.00	20.00
RL16 Ryan Leaf	6.00	15.00
RM84A Randy Moss White	8.00	20.00
RM84H Randy Moss Purple	8.00	20.00
SM9 Steve McNair	8.00	20.00
SY8 Steve Young	10.00	25.00
TA8 Troy Aikman	12.00	30.00
TB71 Tony Boselli	6.00	15.00
TB81 Tim Brown	8.00	20.00
TD12 Trent Dilfer	6.00	15.00
TD30A Terrell Davis White	8.00	20.00
TD30H Terrell Davis Blue	8.00	20.00
TT34 Thurman Thomas	8.00	20.00
VT12 Vinny Testaverde	6.00	15.00
WD28 Warrick Dunn	6.00	15.00
WM1 Warren Moon	8.00	20.00
WS99 Warren Sapp	6.00	15.00
ZT54 Zach Thomas	8.00	20.00

2000 Leaf Certified

Released as a 250-card original set, Leaf Certified contained 150-veteran player cards and 100 Rookie cards. Base cards have blue borders with a holographic fractal foil stock. Leaf Certified was packaged in 18-pack boxes with packs containing five cards each.

COMP.SET w/o RC's (150)	15.00	40.00

151-190 RC 3-STAR PRINT RUN 2000
221-250 RC 5-STAR PRINT RUN 1000

1 Frank Sanders	.25	.60
2 Rob Moore .	.25	.60
3 Simeon Rice	.30	.75
4 David Boston	.25	.60
5 Tim Dwight	.30	.75
6 Jamal Anderson	.30	.75
7 Chris Chandler	.30	.75
8 Terance Mathis	.25	.60
9 Priest Holmes	.40	1.00
10 Rod Woodson	.40	1.00
11 Tony Banks	.25	.60
12 Jermaine Lewis	.25	.60
13 Shannon Sharpe	.40	1.00
14 Qadry Ismail	.30	.75
15 Doug Flutie	.40	1.00
16 Antowain Smith	.30	.75
17 Peerless Price	.30	.75
18 Rob Johnson	.30	.75
19 Muhsin Muhammad	.30	.75
20 Wesley Walls	.25	.60
21 Tim Biakabutuka	.30	.75
22 Steve Beuerlein	.30	.75
23 Patrick Jeffers	.30	.75
24 Natrone Means	.30	.75
25 Curtis Enis	.25	.60
26 Bobby Engram	.30	.75
27 Marcus Robinson	.30	.75
28 Eddie Kennison	.25	.60
29 Marty Booker	.30	.75
30 Darnay Scott	.30	.75
31 Carl Pickens	.30	.75
32 Karim Abdul-Jabbar	.25	.60
33 Errict Rhett	.30	.75
34 Darrin Chiaverini	.25	.60
35 Randall Cunningham	.40	1.00
36 Michael Irvin	.40	1.00
37 Rocket Ismail	.30	.75
38 Ed McCaffrey	.30	.75
39 Rod Smith	.30	.75
40 Herman Moore	.30	.75
41 Johnnie Morton	.30	.75
42 James Stewart	.25	.60
43 Bill Schroeder	.30	.75
44 Ahman Green	.30	.75
45 Terrence Wilkins	.25	.60
46 Keenan McCardell	.30	.75
47 Derrick Alexander	.25	.60
48 Elvis Grbac	.25	.60
49 Tony Gonzalez	.40	1.00
50 O.J. McDuffie	.30	.75
51 Tony Martin	.30	.75
52 James Johnson	.25	.60
53 Thurman Thomas	.40	1.00
54 Jay Fiedler	.30	.75
55 Damon Huard	.30	.75
56 Leroy Hoard	.25	.60
57 Terry Glenn	.30	.75
58 Kevin Faulk	.30	.75
59 Jeff Blake	.30	.75
60 Jake Reed	.30	.75
61 Amani Toomer	.30	.75
62 Kerry Collins	.30	.75
63 Ike Hilliard	.30	.75
64 Joe Montgomery	.25	.60
65 Vinny Testaverde	.30	.75
66 Wayne Chrebet	.30	.75
67 Ray Lucas	.25	.60
68 Napoleon Kaufman	.30	.75
69 Charles Woodson	.40	1.00
70 Tyrone Wheatley	.25	.60
71 Rich Gannon	.30	.75
72 Duce Staley	.30	.75
73 Kordell Stewart	.30	.75
74 Jerome Bettis	.40	1.00
75 Troy Edwards	.25	.60
76 Junior Seau	.40	1.00
77 Jim Harbaugh	.30	.75
78 Curtis Conway	.30	.75
79 Jermaine Fazande	.25	.60
80 Terrell Owens	.40	1.00
81 Charlie Garner	.30	.75
82 Garrison Hearst	.25	.60
83 Jeff Garcia	.30	.75
84 Derrick Mayes	.25	.60
85 Az-Zahir Hakim	.25	.60
86 Mike Alstott	.40	1.00
87 Warrick Dunn	.30	.75
88 Jacquez Green	.25	.60
89 Warren Sapp	.30	.75
90 Yancey Thigpen	.25	.60
91 Kevin Dyson	.30	.75
92 Frank Wycheck	.30	.75
93 Jevon Kearse	.30	.75
94 Adrian Murrell	.25	.60
95 Bruce Smith	.40	1.00
96 Michael Westbrook	.25	.60
97 Albert Connell	.25	.60
98 Champ Bailey	.30	.75
99 Jeff George	.30	.75
100 Deion Sanders	.40	1.00
101 Jake Plummer	.40	1.00
102 Eric Moulds	.40	1.00
103 Cade McNown	.30	.75
104 Corey Dillon	.40	1.00
105 Akili Smith	.30	.75
106 Tim Couch	.40	1.00
107 Kevin Johnson	.30	.75
108 Emmitt Smith	1.25	3.00
109 Troy Aikman	.75	2.00
110 Joey Galloway	.40	1.00
111 John Elway	1.25	3.00
112 Terrell Davis	.50	1.25
113 Olandis Gary	.40	1.00
114 Brian Griese	.40	1.00
115 Charlie Batch	.40	1.00
116 Barry Sanders	1.00	2.50
117 Germane Crowell	.30	.75
118 Brett Favre	1.50	4.00
119 Dorsey Levens	.40	1.00
120 Antonio Freeman	.40	1.00
121 Peyton Manning	1.25	3.00
122 Edgerrin James	.50	1.25
123 Marvin Harrison	.50	1.25
124 Mark Brunell	.40	1.00
125 Fred Taylor	.50	1.25
126 Jimmy Smith	.40	1.00
127 Dan Marino	1.50	4.00
128 Randy Moss	.50	1.25
129 Daunte Culpepper	.40	1.00
130 Cris Carter	.50	1.25
131 Robert Smith	.40	1.00
132 Drew Bledsoe	.50	1.25
133 Ricky Williams	.50	1.25
134 Curtis Martin	.50	1.25
135 Tim Brown	.50	1.25
136 Donovan McNabb	.50	1.25
137 Jerry Rice	1.00	2.50
138 Steve Young	.60	1.50
139 Jon Kitna	.40	1.00
140 Ricky Watters	.40	1.00
141 Kurt Warner	.75	2.00
142 Marshall Faulk	.50	1.25
143 Torry Holt	.50	1.25
144 Isaac Bruce	.50	1.25
145 Shaun King	.30	.75
146 Keyshawn Johnson	.40	1.00
147 Eddie George	.40	1.00
148 Steve McNair	.50	1.25
149 Stephen Davis	.40	1.00
150 Brad Johnson	.40	1.00
151 Rogers Beckett RC	1.25	3.00
152 Erik Flowers RC	1.25	3.00
153 Demario Brown RC	1.25	3.00
154 Doug Johnson RC	1.50	4.00
155 Deon Grant RC	1.25	3.00
156 Ian Gold RC	1.25	3.00
157 Brian Urlacher RC	8.00	20.00
158 Frank Murphy RC	1.25	3.00
159 James Whalen RC	1.25	3.00
160 JaJuan Dawson RC	1.25	3.00
161 William Bartee RC	1.25	3.00
162 Aaron Shea RC	1.50	4.00
163 Deltha O'Neal RC	1.50	4.00
164 Jarious Jackson RC	1.50	4.00
165 Muneer Moore RC	1.25	3.00
166 Hank Poteat RC	1.25	3.00
167 Jacoby Shepherd RC	1.25	3.00
168 Ben Kelly RC	1.25	3.00
169 Orantes Grant RC	1.25	3.00
170 Chris Hovan RC	1.50	4.00
171 Leon Murray RC	1.25	3.00
172 Marc Bulger RC	2.00	5.00
173 Chad Morton RC	2.00	5.00
174 Na'il Diggs RC	1.25	3.00
175 Shaun Ellis RC	2.00	5.00
176 John Abraham RC	2.00	5.00
177 Fred Robbins RC	1.25	3.00
178 Marcus Knight RC	1.25	3.00
179 Thomas Hamner RC	1.25	3.00
180 Cornelius Griffin RC	1.25	3.00
181 Raynoch Thompson RC	1.25	3.00
182 Paul Smith RC	1.25	3.00
183 Ahmed Plummer RC	1.25	3.00
184 John Engelberger RC	1.25	3.00
185 Darren Howard RC	1.25	3.00
186 Corey Moore RC	1.25	3.00
187 Joe Hamilton RC	1.25	3.00
188 Rob Morris RC	1.50	4.00
189 Keith Bulluck RC	1.50	4.00
190 Todd Husak RC	1.25	3.00
191 Mareno Philyaw RC	1.50	4.00
192 Kwame Cavil RC	1.50	4.00
193 Sammy Morris RC	2.00	5.00
194 Avion Black RC	1.50	4.00
195 Bashir Yamini RC	1.50	4.00
196 Curtis Keaton RC	1.50	4.00
197 Mike Anderson RC	2.50	6.00
198 Bubba Franks RC	2.50	6.00
199 Anthony Lucas RC	1.50	4.00
200 Rondell Mealey RC	1.50	4.00
201 Terrelle Smith RC	1.50	4.00
202 Frank Moreau RC	1.50	4.00
203 Deon Dyer RC	1.50	4.00
204 Quinton Spotwood RC	1.50	4.00
205 Troy Walters RC	1.50	4.00
206 Doug Chapman RC	1.50	4.00
207 Tom Brady RC	100.00	175.00
208 Sherrod Gideon RC	1.50	4.00
209 Ron Dixon RC	1.50	4.00
210 Anthony Becht RC	2.00	5.00
211 James Williams RC	1.50	4.00
212 Sebastian Janikowski RC	2.50	6.00
213 Corey Simon RC	2.00	5.00
214 Gari Scott RC	1.50	4.00
215 Dante Hall RC	2.50	6.00
216 Tim Rattay RC	2.00	5.00
217 Chafie Fields RC	1.50	4.00
218 Trung Canidate RC	2.00	5.00
219 Chris Coleman RC	1.50	4.00
220 Erron Kinney RC	1.50	4.00
221 Thomas Jones RC	4.00	10.00
222 Travis Taylor RC	2.50	6.00
223 Chris Redman RC	2.50	6.00
224 Jamal Lewis RC	3.00	8.00
225 Dez White RC	2.50	6.00
226 Peter Warrick RC	3.00	8.00
227 Ron Dugans RC	2.00	5.00
228 Courtney Brown RC	2.50	6.00
229 Travis Prentice RC	2.50	6.00
230 Dennis Northcutt RC	2.50	6.00
231 Michael Wiley RC	2.00	5.00
232 Chris Cole RC	2.50	6.00
233 Reuben Droughns RC	3.00	8.00
234 R.Jay Soward RC	2.00	5.00
235 Shyrone Stith RC	2.00	5.00
236 Sylvester Morris RC	2.00	5.00
237 J.R. Redmond RC	2.00	5.00
238 Ron Dayne RC	3.00	8.00
239 Chad Pennington RC	5.00	12.00
240 Laveranues Coles RC	3.00	8.00
241 Jerry Porter RC	3.00	8.00
242 Todd Pinkston RC	2.00	5.00
243 Plaxico Burress RC	3.00	8.00
244 Danny Farmer RC	2.00	5.00
245 Tee Martin RC	3.00	8.00
246 Trevor Gaylor RC	2.00	5.00
247 Giovanni Carmazzi RC	2.00	5.00
248 Darrell Jackson RC	2.50	6.00
249 Shaun Alexander RC	4.00	10.00
250 Chris Samuels RC	2.50	6.00

2000 Leaf Certified Mirror Gold

*VETS 1-100: 12X TO 30X BASIC CARDS
1-100 1-STAR PRINT RUN 20
*VETS 101-150: 10X TO 25X BASIC CARD
101-150 2-STAR PRINT RUN 25
*ROOKIES 151-190: 1.2X TO 5X
151-190 3-STAR ROOKIE PRINT RUN 30
*ROOKIES 191-220: 1.5X TO 4X
191-220 4-STAR ROOKIE PRINT RUN 35
*ROOKIES 221-250: 1X TO 2.5X
221-250 5-STAR ROOKIE PRINT RUN 40

207 Tom Brady	600.00	1,000.00

2000 Leaf Certified Mirror Red

*VETS 1-100: 2X TO 5X BASIC CARD
1-100 1-STAR VETERAN ODDS 1:17
*VETS 101-150: 1.5X TO 4X BASIC CARD
101-150 2-STAR VETERAN ODDS 1:53
*ROOKIES 151-190: .6X TO 1.5X
151-190 3-STAR ROOKIE ODDS 1:89
*ROOKIES 191-220: .5X TO 1.2X
191-220 4-STAR ROOKIE ODDS 1:125
*ROOKIES 221-250: .4X TO 1X
221-250 5-STAR ROOKIE ODDS 1:161

207 Tom Brady	250.00	400.00

2000 Leaf Certified Rookie Die Cuts

*3-STAR 151-190: 1X TO 2.5X BASIC CARDS
*4-STAR 191-220: .75X TO 2X BASIC CARDS
*5-STAR 221-250: .4X TO 1X BASIC CARDS
FIRST 250 CARDS OF PRINT RUN DIE CUT

207 Tom Brady	175.00	300.00

2000 Leaf Certified Fabric of the Game

STATED PRINT RUN 100-1000

FG1 Barry Sanders/100	12.00	30.00
FG2 John Elway/100	15.00	40.00
FG3 Jerry Rice/100	12.00	30.00
FG4 Cris Carter/250	4.00	10.00
FG5 Emmitt Smith/250	10.00	25.00
FG6 Troy Aikman/250	6.00	15.00
FG7 Deion Sanders/250	4.00	10.00
FG8 Terrell Davis/500	3.00	8.00
FG9 Marshall Faulk/500	3.00	8.00
FG10 Mark Brunell/500	2.50	6.00
FG11 Randy Moss/500	3.00	8.00
FG12 Peyton Manning/500	8.00	20.00
FG13 Kurt Warner/750	4.00	10.00
FG14 Jamal Anderson/750	2.00	5.00
FG15 Edgerrin James/750	2.50	6.00
FG16 Isaac Bruce/750	2.50	6.00
FG17 Jimmy Smith/750	2.00	5.00
FG18 Keyshawn Johnson/750	2.00	5.00
FG19 Brian Griese/1000	2.00	5.00
FG20 Cade McNown/1000	1.50	4.00
FG21 Shaun King/1000	1.50	4.00
FG22 Chad Pennington/1000	4.00	10.00
FG23 Plaxico Burress/1000	2.50	6.00
FG24 Thomas Jones/1000	3.00	8.00
FG25 Peter Warrick/1000	2.50	6.00
FG26 Dan Marino/100	20.00	50.00
FG27 John Elway/100	15.00	40.00
FG28 Emmitt Smith/100	15.00	40.00
FG29 Brett Favre/250	12.00	30.00
FG30 Steve Young/250	5.00	12.00
FG31 Cris Carter/250	4.00	10.00
FG32 Michael Irvin/250	4.00	10.00
FG33 Eddie George/500	2.50	6.00
FG34 Drew Bledsoe/500	3.00	8.00
FG35 Antonio Freeman/500	2.50	6.00
FG36 Steve McNair/500	3.00	8.00
FG37 Randy Moss/500	3.00	8.00
FG38 Kurt Warner/750	4.00	10.00
FG39 Eric Moulds/750	2.00	5.00
FG40 Fred Taylor/750	2.50	6.00
FG41 Charlie Batch/750	2.00	5.00
FG42 Marvin Harrison/750	2.50	6.00
FG43 Joey Galloway/750	2.00	5.00
FG44 Tim Couch/1000	2.00	5.00
FG45 Ricky Williams/1000	2.50	6.00
FG46 Donovan McNabb/1000	2.50	6.00
FG47 Akili Smith/1000	1.50	4.00
FG48 Kevin Johnson/1000	1.50	4.00
FG49 Thomas Jones/1000	3.00	8.00
FG50 Ron Dayne/1000	2.50	6.00
FG51 Dan Marino/100	20.00	50.00
FG52 Barry Sanders/100	12.00	30.00
FG53 Jerry Rice/100	12.00	30.00
FG54 Brett Favre/250	12.00	30.00
FG55 Tim Brown/250	4.00	10.00
FG56 Steve Young/250	5.00	12.00
FG57 Thurman Thomas/250	4.00	10.00
FG58 Jeff George/500	2.50	6.00
FG59 Curtis Martin/500	3.00	8.00
FG60 Terrell Davis/500	3.00	8.00
FG61 Peyton Manning/500	8.00	20.00
FG62 Ricky Watters/500	2.50	6.00
FG63 Edgerrin James/750	2.50	6.00
FG64 Fred Taylor/750	2.50	6.00
FG65 Stephen Davis/750	2.00	5.00
FG66 Jake Plummer/750	2.00	5.00
FG67 Brad Johnson/750	2.00	5.00
FG68 Jon Kitna/750	2.00	5.00
FG69 Tim Couch/1000	2.00	5.00
FG70 Daunte Culpepper/1000	2.00	5.00
FG71 Olandis Gary/1000	2.00	5.00
FG72 Jamal Lewis/1000	2.50	6.00
FG73 Peter Warrick/1000	2.50	6.00
FG74 Stephen Alexander/1000	1.50	4.00
FG75 Travis Taylor/1000	2.00	5.00

2000 Leaf Certified Gold Future

COMPLETE SET (30)	20.00	50.00

STATED ODDS 1:17
*MIRROR BLACK/25: 5X TO 12X BASIC INSERTS
MIRROR BLACK PRINT RUN 25 SER #'D SETS

CGF1 Peter Warrick	.75	2.00
CGF2 Chad Pennington	1.25	3.00
CGF3 Thomas Jones	1.00	2.50
CGF4 Plaxico Burress	.75	2.00
CGF5 Jamal Lewis	.75	2.00
CGF6 Travis Taylor	.60	1.50
CGF7 Chris Redman	.60	1.50
CGF8 Dez White	.60	1.50
CGF9 Shaun Alexander	1.00	2.50
CGF10 Sylvester Morris	.50	1.25
CGF11 Ron Dayne	.75	2.00
CGF12 R.Jay Soward	.50	1.25
CGF13 Travis Prentice	.60	1.50
CGF14 Giovanni Carmazzi	.50	1.25
CGF15 Todd Pinkston	.50	1.25
CGF16 J.R. Redmond	.50	1.25
CGF17 Trevor Gaylor	.50	1.25
CGF18 Trung Canidate	.60	1.50
CGF19 Danny Farmer	.50	1.25
CGF20 Tee Martin	.75	2.00
CGF21 Darrell Jackson	.60	1.50
CGF22 Gari Scott	.50	1.25
CGF23 Dennis Northcutt	.60	1.50
CGF24 Jerry Porter	.75	2.00
CGF25 Reuben Droughns	.75	2.00
CGF26 Laveranues Coles	.75	2.00
CGF27 Bubba Franks	.75	2.00
CGF28 Doug Chapman	.50	1.25
CGF29 Chris Cole	.60	1.50
CGF30 Ron Dugans	.50	1.25

2000 Leaf Certified Gold Team

COMPLETE SET (40)	40.00	100.00

STATED ODDS 1:17
*MIRROR BLACKS: 5X TO 12X BASIC INSERTS
MIRROR BLACKS PRINT RUN 25 SER.#'d SETS

CGT1 Randy Moss	1.25	3.00
CGT2 Brett Favre	4.00	10.00
CGT3 Dan Marino	4.00	10.00
CGT4 Barry Sanders	2.50	6.00
CGT5 John Elway	3.00	8.00
CGT6 Peyton Manning	3.00	8.00
CGT7 Terrell Davis	1.25	3.00
CGT8 Emmitt Smith	3.00	8.00
CGT9 Troy Aikman	2.00	5.00
CGT10 Jerry Rice	2.50	6.00
CGT11 Fred Taylor	1.25	3.00
CGT12 Jake Plummer	1.00	2.50
CGT13 Charlie Batch	1.00	2.50
CGT14 Drew Bledsoe	1.25	3.00
CGT15 Mark Brunell	1.00	2.50
CGT16 Steve Young	1.50	4.00
CGT17 Eddie George	1.00	2.50
CGT18 Tim Brown	1.25	3.00
CGT19 Cris Carter	1.25	3.00
CGT20 Stephen Davis	1.00	2.50
CGT21 Marshall Faulk	1.25	3.00
CGT22 Antonio Freeman	1.00	2.50
CGT23 Marvin Harrison	1.25	3.00
CGT24 Brad Johnson	1.00	2.50
CGT25 Keyshawn Johnson	1.00	2.50
CGT26 Jon Kitna	1.00	2.50
CGT27 Curtis Martin	1.25	3.00
CGT28 Steve McNair	1.25	3.00
CGT29 Isaac Bruce	1.25	3.00
CGT30 Kurt Warner	2.00	5.00
CGT31 Edgerrin James	1.25	3.00
CGT32 Tim Couch	1.00	2.50
CGT33 Ricky Williams	1.25	3.00
CGT34 Donovan McNabb	1.25	3.00
CGT35 Cade McNown	.75	2.00
CGT36 Daunte Culpepper	1.00	2.50
CGT37 Torry Holt	1.25	3.00
CGT38 Robert Smith	1.00	2.50
CGT39 Mike Alstott	1.25	3.00
CGT40 Dorsey Levens	1.00	2.50

2000 Leaf Certified Gridiron Gear

AF86H Antonio Freeman/300	5.00	12.00
BF4A Brett Favre W/300	20.00	50.00
BF4H Brett Favre G/100	25.00	60.00
BG14H Brian Griese/100	6.00	15.00
BS20H Barry Sanders/100	15.00	40.00
CB12H Charlie Batch/300	5.00	12.00
CB24H Champ Bailey/300	5.00	12.00
CC80H Cris Carter/100	8.00	20.00
CD28H Corey Dillon/300	5.00	12.00
CE44A Curtis Enis W/300	4.00	10.00
CE44H Curtis Enis Blu/300	4.00	10.00
CM8A Cade McNown/300	4.00	10.00
CM28H Curtis Martin/100	8.00	20.00
CW24H Charles Woodson/300	6.00	15.00
DB11H Drew Bledsoe/100	8.00	20.00
DF7H Doug Flutie/300	6.00	15.00
DH11H Damon Huard/300	5.00	12.00
DL25A Dorsey Levens W/300	5.00	12.00
DL25H Dorsey Levens G/300	5.00	12.00
DM5A Donovan McNabb/300	6.00	15.00
DM13A Dan Marino White/300	20.00	50.00
DM13H Dan Marino Teal/100	25.00	60.00
DS21H Deion Sanders/300	6.00	15.00
EG27A Eddie George/100	6.00	15.00
EJ32H Edg.James Blu/100	8.00	20.00
EJ32PB Edg.James PB/300	6.00	15.00
EM80A Eric Moulds/300	5.00	12.00
EM87H Ed McCaffrey/300	5.00	12.00
ES22H Emmitt Smith/100	20.00	50.00
FT28A Fred Taylor W/300	6.00	15.00
FT28H Fred Taylor Teal/100	8.00	20.00
IB80A Isaac Bruce W/100	8.00	20.00
IB80H Isaac Bruce Blu/300	6.00	15.00
JB36H Jerome Bettis/100	8.00	20.00
JE7A John Elway/100	20.00	50.00
JH4A Jim Harbaugh/300	5.00	12.00
JK90A Jevon Kearse/300	5.00	12.00
JM87A Johnnie Morton/300	5.00	12.00
JP16A Jake Plummer/300	5.00	12.00
JR80A Jerry Rice W/100	15.00	40.00
JR80H Jerry Rice R/300	12.00	30.00
JS82A Jimmy Smith W/100	6.00	15.00
JS82H Jimmy Smith Teal/300	5.00	12.00
KM87H Keenan McCardell/300	5.00	12.00
KS10A Kordell Stewart/300	5.00	12.00
KW13A Kurt Warner W/300	10.00	25.00
KW13H Kurt Warner Blu/100	12.00	30.00
MA40H Mike Alstott/300	6.00	15.00
MB8A Mark Brunell W/100	6.00	15.00
MB8H Mark Brunell Teal/300	5.00	12.00
MF28A Marshall Faulk White/100	8.00	20.00
MF28H Marshall Faulk Blue/300	6.00	15.00
MH88H Marvin Harrison/300	6.00	15.00
NK26A Napoleon Kaufman/100	6.00	15.00
OG22H Olandis Gary/100	6.00	15.00
PM18A Peyton Manning/100	20.00	50.00
RC7H Randall Cunningham/300	6.00	15.00
RL6A Ray Lucas/100	5.00	12.00
RM84H Randy Moss/100	8.00	20.00
RS80H Rod Smith/300	5.00	12.00
RW32A Ricky Watters/300	5.00	12.00
RW34A Ricky Williams White/100	8.00	20.00
RW34H Ricky Williams Black/100	8.00	20.00
SK10H Shaun King/100	5.00	12.00
SM9H Steve McNair/100	8.00	20.00
SY8H Steve Young/100	10.00	25.00
TA8H Troy Aikman/100	12.00	30.00
TB81A Tim Brown W/300	6.00	15.00
TB81H Tim Brown Blk/300	6.00	15.00
TC2H Tim Couch/100	6.00	15.00
TD30A Terrell Davis/100	8.00	20.00
TO81H Terrell Owens/300	6.00	15.00
TW47H Tyrone Wheatley/300	4.00	10.00
WC80H Wayne Chrebet/300	5.00	12.00
WD28A Warrick Dunn/300	5.00	12.00

2000 Leaf Certified Gridiron Gear Century

BF4A Brett Favre W AU	200.00	350.00
DM13A Dan Marino White AUTO	175.00	300.00
EJ32H Edgerrin James Blue AUTO	40.00	100.00
JE7A John Elway AU	175.00	300.00
JP16A Jake Plummer AU	30.00	80.00
KW13A Kurt Warner White AUTO	60.00	120.00
KW13H Kurt Warner Blue AUTO	60.00	120.00
RW34A Ricky Williams White AUTO	30.00	80.00
RW34H Ricky Williams Black AUTO	30.00	80.00
SY8H Steve Young AU	75.00	150.00
TA8H Troy Aikman AU	100.00	200.00

2000 Leaf Certified Heritage Collection

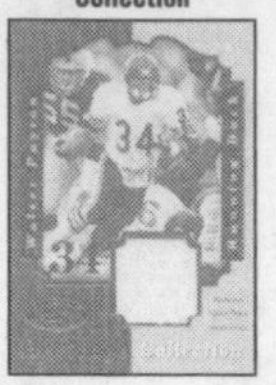

STATED PRINT RUN 100 SER.#'d SETS

BE7H Boomer Esiason	10.00	25.00
BG12A Bob Griese	10.00	25.00
BJ7H Bert Jones	6.00	15.00
BK19H Bernie Kosar	8.00	20.00
BS15H Bart Starr	30.00	80.00
CJ32A Craig James	6.00	15.00
DF14A Dan Fouts W	10.00	25.00
DF14H Dan Fouts Blu	10.00	25.00
DM13H Don Maynard	8.00	20.00
DT58H Derrick Thomas	40.00	80.00
EC34A Earl Campbell	10.00	25.00
ED29A Eric Dickerson W	8.00	20.00
ED29H Eric Dickerson Blu	8.00	20.00
FG16H Frank Gifford	10.00	25.00
FT10H Fran Tarkenton	12.00	30.00
GS40H Gale Sayers	15.00	40.00
HL75A Howie Long	15.00	40.00
HW34 Herschel Walker	8.00	20.00
JB12H John Brodie	8.00	20.00
JB32H Jim Brown	15.00	40.00
JK12A Jim Kelly	12.00	30.00
JM16A Joe Montana 49ers	25.00	60.00
JM19A Joe Montana Chiefs	25.00	60.00
JN12A Joe Namath	20.00	50.00
JP16H Jim Plunkett	8.00	20.00
JT7H Joe Theismann	10.00	25.00
JU19H Johnny Unitas	40.00	100.00
KJ88H Keith Jackson	6.00	15.00
KS12A Ken Stabler	12.00	30.00
LS39A Larry Csonka	10.00	25.00
LT56A Lawrence Taylor	10.00	25.00
MA32A Marcus Allen W	12.00	30.00
MA32H Marcus Allen R	12.00	30.00
MO74H Merlin Olsen	8.00	20.00
ON82A Ozzie Newsome	6.00	15.00
PS11H Phil Simms	10.00	25.00
RB82A Raymond Berry	8.00	20.00
RL42H Ronnie Lott	10.00	25.00
RN66H Ray Nitschke	30.00	80.00
RW92H Reggie White	30.00	60.00
SJ9H Sonny Jurgensen	10.00	25.00
SL80A Steve Largent	10.00	25.00
TB12A Terry Bradshaw W	25.00	60.00
TB12P Terry Bradshaw PB	25.00	60.00
TD33H Tony Dorsett	15.00	40.00
TH83A Ted Hendricks	8.00	20.00
WM1A Warren Moon	10.00	25.00
WP34A Walter Payton W	40.00	100.00
WP34H Walter Payton Blu	40.00	100.00

2000 Leaf Certified Heritage Collection Century

BE7H Boomer Esiason	15.00	40.00
BG12A Bob Griese AU	60.00	120.00
BJ7H Bert Jones	10.00	25.00
BK19H Bernie Kosar	12.00	30.00
BS15H Bart Starr AU	150.00	250.00
CJ32A Craig James	10.00	25.00
DF14A Dan Fouts W AU	50.00	100.00
DF14H Dan Fouts Blue AU	50.00	100.00
DM13H Don Maynard	12.00	30.00
DT58H Derrick Thomas	50.00	120.00
EC0034 Earl Campbell AU	60.00	120.00
ED29A Eric Dickerson White AUTO	50.00	100.00
ED29H E.Dickerson Blue AUTO	50.00	100.00
FG16H Frank Gifford	15.00	40.00
FT10H Fran Tarkenton AU	60.00	120.00
GS40H Gale Sayers	25.00	60.00
HL75A Howie Long AU	75.00	150.00
HW34 Herschel Walker	12.00	30.00
JB12H John Brodie	12.00	30.00
JB32A Jim Brown	25.00	60.00
JK12A Jim Kelly	20.00	50.00
JM16A Joe Montana/49ers AUTO	125.00	250.00
JM19A Joe Montana Chiefs AUTO	100.00	200.00
JN12A Joe Namath AUTO	100.00	200.00
JP16H Jim Plunkett	12.00	30.00
JT7H Joe Theismann	15.00	40.00
JU19H Johnny Unitas AU	300.00	550.00
KJ88H Keith Jackson	10.00	25.00
KS12A Ken Stabler AU		
LT56A Lawrence Taylor AUTO	75.00	150.00
MA32A Marcus Allen White AUTO	60.00	120.00
MA32H Marcus Allen Red AUTO	60.00	120.00
MO74H Merlin Olsen	12.00	30.00
ON82A Ozzie Newsome	10.00	25.00
PS11H Phil Simms	15.00	40.00
RB82A Raymond Berry	12.00	30.00
RL42H Ronnie Lott AUTO	50.00	100.00
RN66H Ray Nitschke	50.00	120.00
RW92H Reggie White	40.00	100.00

SJ9H Sonny Jurgensen AUTO	50.00	100.00
SL80A Steve Largent	15.00	40.00
TB12A Terry Bradshaw White AUTO	100.00	200.00
TB12P Terry Bradshaw Pro Bowl AUTO	100.00	200.00
TD33H Tony Dorsett	25.00	60.00
TH83A Ted Hendricks	12.00	30.00
WM1A Warren Moon	15.00	40.00
WP34A Walter Payton W	60.00	150.00
WP34H Walter Payton Blue	60.00	150.00

2000 Leaf Certified Skills

COMPLETE SET (30) 40.00 100.00
STATED ODDS 1:35
*MIRROR BLACK/25: 3X TO 8X BASIC INSERTS
MIRROR BLACK PRINT RUN 25 SER.#'d SETS

CS1 Jamal Anderson Thomas Jones	1.50	4.00
CS2 Randy Moss Germane Crowell	1.25	3.00
CS3 Brett Favre Donovan McNabb	4.00	10.00
CS4 Dan Marino Tim Couch	1.00	2.50
CS5 Barry Sanders James Stewart	2.50	6.00
CS6 John Elway Brian Griese	3.00	8.00
CS7 Peyton Manning Chad Pennington	2.00	5.00
CS8 Terrell Davis Olandis Gary	1.25	3.00
CS9 Emmitt Smith Duce Staley	3.00	8.00
CS10 Troy Aikman Cade McNown	2.00	5.00
CS11 Jerry Rice Isaac Bruce	2.50	6.00
CS12 Fred Taylor Stephen Davis	1.25	3.00
CS13 Drew Bledsoe Brad Johnson	1.25	3.00
CS14 Mark Brunell Shaun King	1.00	2.50
CS15 Steve Young Akili Smith	1.50	4.00
CS16 Eddie George Ricky Williams	1.25	3.00
CS17 Kurt Warner Jon Kitna	2.00	5.00
CS18 Edgerrin James Corey Dillon	1.25	3.00
CS19 Cris Carter Tim Brown	1.25	3.00
CS20 Keyshawn Johnson Plaxico Burress	1.25	3.00
CS21 Marshall Faulk Robert Smith	1.25	3.00
CS22 Antonio Freeman Travis Taylor	1.00	2.50
CS23 Marvin Harrison Kevin Johnson	1.25	3.00
CS24 Dorsey Levens Jamal Lewis	1.25	3.00
CS25 Curtis Martin Shaun Alexander	1.50	4.00
CS26 Steve McNair Daunte Culpepper	1.25	3.00
CS27 Jimmy Smith Peter Warrick	1.25	3.00
CS28 Jerome Bettis Ron Dayne	1.25	3.00
CS29 Joey Galloway Torry Holt	1.25	3.00
CS30 Eric Moulds Terrell Owens	1.25	3.00

2001 Leaf Certified Materials

This 145 card set was issued in five card packs which were issued 12 packs per box and six boxes per case. The SRP on these packs was $11.99 per pack. Cards number 1-100 feature veterans while cards 101-145 feature rookies. Of the rookies, cards number 111-145 feature rookie cards with pieces of memorabilia and are serial numbered to 400. A variety of different swatches were used on some cards with the value being the same on all versions.

COMP.SET w/o SPs (100)	12.50	30.00
1 Aaron Brooks	.30	.75
2 Ahman Green	.40	1.00
3 Akili Smith	.25	.60
4 Amani Toomer	.30	.75
5 Antonio Freeman	.40	1.00
6 Barry Sanders	1.00	2.50
7 Brad Johnson	.30	.75
8 Brett Favre	1.25	3.00
9 Brian Griese	.30	.75
10 Brian Urlacher	.50	1.25
11 Bruce Smith	.40	1.00
12 Cade McNown	.30	.75
13 Chad Pennington	.40	1.00
14 Charlie Batch	.30	.75
15 Charlie Garner	.30	.75
16 Corey Dillon	.30	.75
17 Cris Carter	.40	1.00
18 Curtis Martin	.40	1.00
19 Dan Marino	1.00	2.50
20 Darrell Jackson	.30	.75
21 Daunte Culpepper	.30	.75
22 David Boston	.25	.60
23 Derrick Alexander	.25	.60
24 Donovan McNabb	.40	1.00
25 Dorsey Levens	.30	.75
26 Doug Flutie	.40	1.00
27 Drew Bledsoe	.40	1.00
28 Ed McCaffrey	.30	.75
29 Eddie George	.40	1.00
30 Edgerrin James	.40	1.00
31 Elvis Grbac	.30	.75
32 Emmitt Smith	1.00	2.50
33 Eric Moulds	.30	.75
34 Frank Wycheck	.25	.60
35 Fred Taylor	.40	1.00
36 Ike Hilliard	.30	.75
37 Isaac Bruce	.40	1.00
38 Jacquez Green	.25	.60
39 Jake Plummer	.30	.75
40 Jamal Anderson	.30	.75
41 Jamal Lewis	.40	1.00
42 James Stewart	.25	.60
43 Jay Fiedler	.30	.75
44 Jeff Garcia	.30	.75
45 Jeff George	.30	.75
46 Jerome Bettis	.40	1.00
47 Jerry Rice	.75	2.00
48 Jevon Kearse	.30	.75
49 Jimmy Smith	.30	.75
50 Joe Horn	.30	.75
51 Joey Galloway	.30	.75
52 John Elway	1.00	2.50
53 Junior Seau	.40	1.00
54 Keenan McCardell	.30	.75
55 Kerry Collins	.30	.75
56 Keyshawn Johnson	.30	.75
57 Kurt Warner	.60	1.50
58 Lamar Smith	.30	.75
59 Laveranues Coles	.30	.75
60 Marcus Robinson	.30	.75
61 Mark Brunell	.30	.75
62 Marshall Faulk	.40	1.00
63 Marvin Harrison	.40	1.00
64 Matt Hasselbeck	.40	1.00
65 Mike Alstott	.30	.75
66 Mike Anderson	.30	.75
67 Muhsin Muhammad	.30	.75
68 Peter Warrick	.30	.75
69 Peyton Manning	1.00	2.50
70 Plaxico Burress	.30	.75
71 Randy Moss	.40	1.00
72 Ray Lewis	.40	1.00
73 Rich Gannon	.30	.75
74 Ricky Watters	.30	.75
75 Ricky Williams	.40	1.00
76 Rob Johnson	.30	.75
77 Rod Smith	.30	.75
78 Ron Dayne	.30	.75
79 Shannon Sharpe	.40	1.00
80 Shaun Alexander	.40	1.00
81 Stephen Davis	.30	.75
82 Steve McNair	.40	1.00
83 Steve Young	.50	1.25
84 Sylvester Morris	.25	.60
85 Terrell Davis	.40	1.00
86 Terrell Owens	.40	1.00
87 Terry Glenn	.30	.75
88 Thomas Jones	.30	.75
89 Tiki Barber	.40	1.00
90 Tim Brown	.40	1.00
91 Tim Couch	.25	.60
92 Tony Gonzalez	.40	1.00
93 Torry Holt	.30	.75
94 Travis Taylor	.25	.60
95 Troy Aikman	.60	1.50
96 Tyrone Wheatley	.30	.75
97 Vinny Testaverde	.30	.75
98 Warren Sapp	.30	.75
99 Warrick Dunn	.40	1.00
100 Wayne Chrebet	.30	.75
101 Chris Taylor RC	1.25	3.00
102 Ken-Yon Rambo RC	1.25	3.00
103 Correll Buckhalter RC	2.00	5.00
104 A.J. Feeley RC	1.50	4.00
105 Josh Booty RC	1.50	4.00
106 LaMont Jordan RC	2.00	5.00
107 Alge Crumpler RC	2.00	5.00
108 Jamal Reynolds RC	1.25	3.00
109 Nate Clements RC	1.50	4.00
110 Will Allen RC	2.00	5.00
111 Santana Moss FF RC	4.00	10.00
112 Chad Johnson FF RC	5.00	12.00
113 Chris Chambers FF RC	3.00	8.00
114 David Terrell FF RC	2.50	6.00
115 Freddie Mitchell FF RC	2.00	5.00
116 Koren Robinson FF RC	2.50	6.00
117 Quincy Morgan FF RC	2.50	6.00
118 Reggie Wayne FF RC	6.00	15.00
119 Robert Ferguson FF RC	3.00	8.00
120 Rod Gardner FF RC	2.50	6.00
121 Snoop Minnis FF RC	2.00	5.00
122 Josh Heupel FF RC	3.00	8.00
123 Anthony Thomas FF RC	3.00	8.00
124 Deuce McAllister FF RC	3.00	8.00
125 James Jackson FF RC	2.00	5.00
126 Travis Minor FF RC	2.50	6.00
127 Kevan Barlow FF RC	2.50	6.00
128 LaDainian Tomlinson FF RC	10.00	25.00
129 Todd Heap FF RC	3.00	8.00
130 Michael Bennett FF RC	2.50	6.00
131 Rudi Johnson FF RC	3.00	8.00
132 Travis Henry FF RC	2.50	6.00
133 Michael Vick FF RC	12.00	30.00
134 Drew Brees FF RC	20.00	50.00
135 Chris Weinke FF RC	2.50	6.00
136 Quincy Carter FF RC	2.50	6.00
137 Mike McMahon FF RC	2.50	6.00
138 Jesse Palmer FF RC	2.50	6.00
139 Marques Tuiasosopo FF RC	2.50	6.00
140 Dan Morgan FF RC	2.50	6.00
141 Gerard Warren FF RC	2.50	6.00
142 Leonard Davis FF RC	3.00	8.00
143 Andre Carter FF RC	2.50	6.00
144 Justin Smith FF RC	3.00	8.00
145 Sage Rosenfels FF RC	3.00	8.00

2001 Leaf Certified Materials Mirror Gold

*VETS 1-110: 10X TO 25X BASIC CARDS
*ROOKIES 101-110: 2X TO 5X
*ROOKIE FF 111-145: 2X TO 5X
STATED PRINT RUN 25 SER.#'d SETS
OVERALL INSERT ODDS 1:4

2001 Leaf Certified Materials Mirror Red

*VETS 1-100: 5X TO 12X BASIC CARDS
*ROOKIES 101-110: 1X TO 2.5X
1-110 VET/ROOKIE PRINT RUN 75
111-145 FF AUTO PRINT RUN 150
OVERALL INSERT ODDS 1:4

111 Santana Moss FF AU	12.00	30.00
112 Chad Johnson FF AU	40.00	80.00
113 Chris Chambers FF AU	10.00	25.00
114 David Terrell FF AU	8.00	20.00
115 Freddie Mitchell FF AU	6.00	15.00
116 Koren Robinson FF AU	8.00	20.00
117 Quincy Morgan FF AU	8.00	20.00
118 Reggie Wayne FF AU	40.00	80.00
119 Robert Ferguson FF AU	10.00	25.00
120 Rod Gardner FF AU	8.00	20.00
121 Snoop Minnis FF AU	6.00	15.00
122 Josh Heupel FF AU	10.00	25.00
123 Anthony Thomas FF AU	10.00	25.00
124 Deuce McAllister FF AU	10.00	25.00
125 James Jackson FF AU	6.00	15.00
126 Travis Minor FF AU	8.00	20.00
127 Kevan Barlow FF AU	8.00	20.00
128 LaDainian Tomlinson FF AU	75.00	150.00
129 Todd Heap FF AU	10.00	25.00
130 Michael Bennett FF AU	8.00	20.00
131 Rudi Johnson FF AU	10.00	25.00
132 Travis Henry FF AU	8.00	20.00
133 Michael Vick FF AU	75.00	150.00
134 Drew Brees FF AU	125.00	200.00
135 Chris Weinke FF AU	8.00	20.00
136 Quincy Carter FF AU	8.00	20.00
137 Mike McMahon FF AU	8.00	20.00
138 Jesse Palmer FF AU	8.00	20.00
139 Marques Tuiasosopo FF AU	8.00	20.00
140 Dan Morgan FF AU	8.00	20.00
141 Gerard Warren FF AU	8.00	20.00
143 Andre Carter FF AU	8.00	20.00
144 Justin Smith FF AU	10.00	25.00
145 Sage Rosenfels FF AU	10.00	25.00

2001 Leaf Certified Materials Fabric of the Game

OVERALL INSERT ODDS 1:4

1BA Art Monk	12.50	30.00
1CE Art Monk/21		
1CR Art Monk/68	20.00	50.00
1JN Art Monk/81	20.00	50.00
2BA Barry Sanders	15.00	40.00
2CE Barry Sanders/21 AU		
2CR Barry Sanders/109	20.00	40.00
2JN Barry Sanders/20		
3BA Bart Starr	25.00	50.00
3CE Bart Starr/21 AU	100.00	200.00
3CR Bart Starr/57	30.00	80.00
3SN Bart Starr/105	25.00	60.00
4BA Bob Griese	7.50	20.00
4CE Bob Griese/21		
4CR Bob Griese/56	12.50	30.00
4SN Bob Griese/90	10.00	25.00
5BA Dan Fouts W	7.50	20.00
5CE Dan Fouts W/21		
5CR Dan Fouts W/58	10.00	25.00
5SN Dan Fouts W/93	10.00	25.00
6BA Dan Fouts B	7.50	20.00
6CE Dan Fouts B/21		
6CR Dan Fouts B/58	12.50	30.00
6SN Dan Fouts B/93	10.00	25.00
7BA Dan Marino T	25.00	50.00
7CE Dan Marino T/21 AU		
7CR Dan Marino T/86	25.00	60.00
7SN Dan Marino T/48	30.00	80.00
8BA Dan Marino W	20.00	50.00
8CE Dan Marino W/21		
8CR Dan Marino W/86	25.00	60.00
8SN Dan Marino W/48	30.00	80.00
9BA Deacon Jones	7.50	20.00
9CE Deacon Jones/21		
9JN Deacon Jones/75	10.00	25.00
9SN Deacon Jones/21		
10BA Don Maynard	5.00	12.00
10CE Don Maynard/21		
10CR Don Maynard/88	7.50	20.00
10SN Don Maynard/22		
11BA Earl Campbell	7.50	20.00
11CE Earl Campbell/21		
11CR Earl Campbell/74	10.00	25.00
11JN Earl Campbell/34	20.00	50.00
11SN Earl Campbell/36	20.00	50.00
12BA Eric Dickerson		
12CE Eric Dickerson/21		
12CR Eric Dickerson/96	10.00	25.00
12JN Eric Dickerson/29	25.00	50.00
12SN Eric Dickerson/20		
13BA Fran Tarkenton	15.00	40.00
13CE Fran Tarkenton/21		
13CR Fran Tarkenton/80	20.00	50.00
13SN Fran Tarkenton/31	40.00	80.00
14BA Frank Gifford	7.50	20.00
14CE Frank Gifford/21		
14CR Frank Gifford/77	12.50	30.00
14SN Frank Gifford/51	15.00	40.00
15BA Gale Sayers	20.00	40.00
15CE Gale Sayers/21		
15CR Gale Sayers/56	20.00	50.00
15SN Gale Sayers/37	25.00	60.00
15JNAU Gale Sayers/40 AU	75.00	125.00
16BA George Blanda SP	25.00	50.00
16CE George Blanda/21		
16CR George Blanda/135	7.50	20.00
16SN George Blanda/47	15.00	40.00
17BA Jim Brown SP	25.00	60.00
17CE Jim Brown/21		
17CR Jim Brown/126	20.00	50.00
17JN Jim Brown AU/32	125.00	250.00
17SN Jim Brown/21		
18BA Joe Montana W	25.00	60.00
18CE Joe Montana W/21		
18CR Joe Montana W/63	40.00	100.00
18SN Joe Montana W/87	30.00	80.00
19BA Joe Montana R SP	75.00	150.00
19CE Joe Montana R/21		
19CR Joe Montana R/63	40.00	100.00
19JN Joe Montana R/16 AU		
19SN Joe Montana R/112	25.00	60.00
20BA Joe Namath	20.00	50.00
20CE Joe Namath/21		
20CR Joe Namath/50	30.00	80.00
20JN Joe Namath/12 AU		
20SN Joe Namath/26	100.00	200.00
21BA John Elway O	15.00	40.00
21CE John Elway O/21 AU	125.00	250.00
21CR John Elway O/56	30.00	80.00
21SN John Elway O/93	25.00	60.00
22BA John Elway B	15.00	40.00
22CE John Elway B/21		
22CR John Elway B/56	30.00	80.00
22SN John Elway B/93	25.00	60.00
23BA Johnny Unitas	25.00	50.00
23CE Johnny Unitas/21 AU	300.00	500.00
23CR Johnny Unitas/54	25.00	60.00
23SN Johnny Unitas/97	25.00	60.00
24BA Larry Csonka SP		
24CE Larry Csonka/21		
24CR Larry Csonka/68	15.00	40.00
24JN Larry Csonka/39	25.00	60.00
24SN Larry Csonka/118	12.50	30.00
25BA Lawrence Taylor SP		
25CE Lawrence Taylor/21		
25CR Lawrence Taylor/132	7.50	20.00
25JN Lawrence Taylor/56	15.00	40.00
25SN Lawrence Taylor/20		
27BA Marcus Allen R SP		
27CE Marcus Allen R/21		
27CR Marcus Allen R/123	7.50	20.00
27JN Marcus Allen R/32	20.00	50.00
27SN Marcus Allen R/68	12.50	30.00
28BA Marcus Allen W SP		
28CE Marcus Allen W/21		
28CR Marcus Allen W/123	7.50	20.00
28JN Marcus Allen W/32	30.00	60.00
28SN Marcus Allen W/68	12.50	30.00
29BA Ozzie Newsome SP		
29CE Ozzie Newsome/21		
29CR Ozzie Newsome/47	10.00	25.00
29JN Ozzie Newsome/82	7.50	20.00
29SN Ozzie Newsome/89	7.50	20.00
30BA Raymond Berry SP		
30CE Raymond Berry/21		
30CR Raymond Berry/68	10.00	25.00
30JN Raymond Berry/82	10.00	25.00
30SN Raymond Berry/75	10.00	25.00
31BA Roger Staubach SP		
31CE Roger Staubach/21		
31CR Roger Staubach/153	20.00	50.00
31SN Roger Staubach/62	25.00	60.00
32BA Sonny Jurgensen	7.50	20.00
32CE Sonny Jurgensen/21		
32CR Sonny Jurgensen/57	15.00	40.00
32SN Sonny Jurgensen/32		
33BA Steve Largent SP		
33CE Steve Largent/21		
33CR Steve Largent/100	12.50	30.00
33JN Steve Largent/80	15.00	40.00
34BA Steve Young W	12.50	30.00
34CE Steve Young W/21		
34CR Steve Young W/96	15.00	40.00
34SN Steve Young W/36	25.00	60.00
35BA Steve Young R	12.50	30.00
35CE Steve Young R/21		
35CR Steve Young R/96	15.00	40.00
35SN Steve Young R/36	25.00	60.00
36BA Terry Bradshaw W	15.00	40.00
36CE Terry Bradshaw W/21		
36CR Terry Bradshaw W/51	25.00	60.00
36JN Terry Bradshaw W/12 AU		
36SN Terry Bradshaw W/28	40.00	100.00
37BA Terry Bradshaw PB	15.00	40.00
37CE Terry Bradshaw PB/21		
37CR Terry Bradshaw PB/51	25.00	60.00
37SN Terry Bradshaw PB/28	40.00	100.00
38BA Tony Dorsett	12.50	30.00
38CE Tony Dorsett/21		
38CR Tony Dorsett/91	12.50	30.00
38JN Tony Dorsett/33	30.00	80.00
38SN Tony Dorsett/51	20.00	50.00
39BA Walter Payton W SP	50.00	120.00
39CE Walter Payton W/21		
39CR Walter Payton W/125	30.00	80.00
39JN Walter Payton W/34	60.00	150.00
39SN Walter Payton W/53	40.00	100.00
40BA Walter Payton B SP		
40CE Walter Payton B/21		
40CR Walter Payton B/125	30.00	80.00
40JN Walter Payton B/34	60.00	150.00
40SN Walter Payton B/53	40.00	100.00
41BA Brett Favre G SP		
41CE Brett Favre G/21		
41CR Brett Favre G/266	15.00	40.00
41SN Brett Favre G/20		
42BA Brett Favre W SP		
42CE Brett Favre W/21		
42CR Brett Favre W/266	15.00	40.00
42SN Brett Favre W/20		
43BA Brian Griese	7.50	20.00
43CE Brian Griese/21		
43CR Brian Griese/36	15.00	40.00
43SN Brian Griese/102	7.50	20.00
44BA Charley Taylor	5.00	12.00
44CE Charley Taylor/21		
44CR Charley Taylor/90	7.50	20.00
44JN Charley Taylor/42	10.00	25.00
44SN Charley Taylor/72	7.50	20.00
45BA Daunte Culpepper P	7.50	20.00
45CE Daunte Culpepper P/21		
45CR Daunte Culpepper P/40	12.50	30.00
45SN Daunte Culpepper P/98	10.00	25.00
46BA Daunte Culpepper W	7.50	20.00
46CE Daunte Culpepper W/21		
46CR Daunte Culpepper W/40	12.50	30.00
46SN Daunte Culpepper W/98	10.00	25.00
47BA Donovan McNabb G	12.50	25.00
47CE Donovan McNabb G/21		
47CR Donovan McNabb G/133	10.00	25.00
47SN Donovan McNabb G/77	12.50	30.00
48BA Donovan McNabb W	10.00	25.00
48CE Donovan McNabb W/21		
48CR Donovan McNabb W/133	10.00	25.00
48SN Donovan McNabb W/77	12.50	30.00
49BA Drew Bledsoe	7.50	20.00
49CE Drew Bledsoe/21		
49CR Drew Bledsoe/166	7.50	20.00
49SN Drew Bledsoe/77	12.50	30.00
50BA Eddie George	7.50	20.00
50CE Eddie George/21		
50CR Eddie George/164	7.50	20.00
50JN Eddie George/27	25.00	60.00
51BA Edgerrin James B	10.00	25.00
51CE Edgerrin James B/21		
51CR Edgerrin James B/72	10.00	25.00
51JN Edgerrin James B/32	25.00	50.00
51SN Edgerrin James B/63	12.50	30.00
52BA Edgerrin James W	10.00	25.00
52CE Edgerrin James W/21		
52CR Edgerrin James W/72	10.00	25.00
52JN Edgerrin James W/32	20.00	50.00
52SN Edgerrin James W/63	12.50	30.00
53BA Emmitt Smith W	12.50	30.00
53CE Emmitt Smith W/21		
53CR Emmitt Smith W/145	15.00	40.00
53JN Emmitt Smith W/22		
53SN Emmitt Smith W/79	25.00	50.00
54BA Emmitt Smith B	12.50	30.00
54CE Emmitt Smith B/21		
54CR Emmitt Smith B/145	15.00	40.00
54JN Emmitt Smith B/22		
54SN Emmitt Smith B/79	20.00	50.00
55BA Jamal Lewis	7.50	20.00
55CE Jamal Lewis/21		
55CR Jamal Lewis/27	15.00	40.00
55JN Jamal Lewis/31	15.00	40.00
55SN Jamal Lewis/45	12.50	30.00
56BA Jerry Rice R	15.00	40.00
56CE Jerry Rice R/21		
56CR Jerry Rice R/96	20.00	40.00
56JN Jerry Rice R/80	30.00	80.00
56SN Jerry Rice R/75	25.00	60.00
57BA Jerry Rice W	12.50	25.00
57CE Jerry Rice W/21		
57CR Jerry Rice W/96	20.00	40.00
57JN Jerry Rice W/80	40.00	80.00
57SN Jerry Rice W/75	25.00	60.00
58BA Kurt Warner W	7.50	20.00
58CE Kurt Warner W/21		
58CR Kurt Warner W/104	10.00	25.00
58SN Kurt Warner W/21		
59BA Kurt Warner B	7.50	20.00
59CE Kurt Warner B/21		
59CR Kurt Warner B/104	10.00	25.00
59SN Kurt Warner B/21		
60BA Marshall Faulk W	7.50	20.00
60CE Marshall Faulk W/21		
60CR Marshall Faulk W/89	10.00	25.00
60JN Marshall Faulk W/28	15.00	40.00
60SN Marshall Faulk W/81	10.00	25.00
61BA Marshall Faulk B	7.50	20.00
61CE Marshall Faulk B/21		
61CR Marshall Faulk B/89	10.00	25.00
61JN Marshall Faulk B/28	15.00	40.00
61SN Marshall Faulk B/81	10.00	25.00
62BA Mike Anderson	7.50	20.00
62CE Mike Anderson/21		
62CR Mike Anderson/80	7.50	20.00
62JN Mike Anderson/38	15.00	40.00
63BA Peyton Manning W	12.50	30.00
63CE Peyton Manning W/21		
63CR Peyton Manning W/88	15.00	40.00
63SN Peyton Manning W/94	15.00	40.00
64BA Peyton Manning B	12.50	30.00
64CE Peyton Manning B/21		
64CR Peyton Manning B/88	15.00	40.00
64SN Peyton Manning B/94	15.00	40.00
65BA Randy Moss W	10.00	25.00
65CE Randy Moss W/21		
65CR Randy Moss W/43	20.00	50.00
65JN Randy Moss W/84	15.00	40.00
65SN Randy Moss W/78	15.00	40.00
66BA Randy Moss P	10.00	25.00
66CE Randy Moss P/21		
66CR Randy Moss P/43	25.00	60.00
66JN Randy Moss P/84	15.00	40.00
66SN Randy Moss P/78	15.00	40.00
67BA Ricky Williams SP		
67CE Ricky Williams/21		
67JN Ricky Williams/34	15.00	40.00
67SN Ricky Williams/248	7.50	20.00
68BA Terrell Davis SP	7.50	20.00
68CE Terrell Davis/21		
68CR Terrell Davis/157	7.50	20.00
68JN Terrell Davis/30	15.00	40.00
68SN Terrell Davis/78	10.00	25.00
69BA Troy Aikman	15.00	30.00
69CE Troy Aikman/21		
69CR Troy Aikman/167	12.50	30.00
69SN Troy Aikman/69	20.00	50.00
70BA Warren Moon	7.50	20.00
70CE Warren Moon/21		
70CR Warren Moon/80	10.00	25.00
70SN Warren Moon/33	15.00	40.00
71BA Antonio Freeman W SP		
71CE Antonio Freeman W/21		
71CR Antonio Freeman W/365	6.00	15.00
71JN Antonio Freeman W/86	10.00	25.00
72BA Antonio Freeman G SP		
72CE Antonio Freeman G/21		
72CR Antonio Freeman G/365	6.00	15.00
72JN Antonio Freeman G/86	10.00	25.00
73BA Bernie Kosar	7.50	20.00
73CE Bernie Kosar/21		
73CR Bernie Kosar/124	7.50	20.00
73SN Bernie Kosar/102	7.50	20.00
74BA Boomer Esiason	6.00	15.00
74CE Boomer Esiason/21		
74CR Boomer Esiason/247	7.50	20.00
74SN Boomer Esiason/63	10.00	25.00
75BA Cade McNown	5.00	12.00
75CE Cade McNown/21		
75CR Cade McNown/281	5.00	12.00
75SN Cade McNown/68	6.00	15.00
76BA Charlie Batch	5.00	12.00
76CE Charlie Batch/21		
76CR Charlie Batch/76	6.00	15.00
76SN Charlie Batch/221	5.00	12.00
77BA Corey Dillon SP	7.50	20.00
77CE Corey Dillon/21		
77CR Corey Dillon/104	7.50	20.00
77JN Corey Dillon/28		
77SN Corey Dillon/315	7.50	20.00
78BA Cris Carter	6.00	15.00
78CE Cris Carter/21		
78CR Cris Carter/123	7.50	20.00
78JN Cris Carter/80	15.00	40.00
78SN Cris Carter/96	10.00	25.00
79BA Curtis Martin	6.00	15.00
79CE Curtis Martin/21		
79CR Curtis Martin/275	7.50	20.00
79JN Curtis Martin/28	15.00	40.00
79SN Curtis Martin/55	12.50	30.00
80BA Deion Sanders	10.00	25.00
80CE Deion Sanders/21		
80CR Deion Sanders/48	20.00	40.00
80JN Deion Sanders/21		
80SN Deion Sanders/91	15.00	40.00
81BA Duce Staley	6.00	15.00
81CE Duce Staley/21		
81CR Duce Staley/125	7.50	20.00
81JN Duce Staley/22		
81SN Duce Staley/201	6.00	15.00
82BA Ed McCaffrey	6.00	15.00
82CE Ed McCaffrey/21		
82CR Ed McCaffrey/52	12.50	30.00
82JN Ed McCaffrey/87	10.00	25.00
82SN Ed McCaffrey/101	7.50	20.00
83BA Eric Moulds	6.00	15.00
83CE Eric Moulds/21		
83CR Eric Moulds/84	7.50	20.00
83JN Eric Moulds/80	10.00	25.00
83SN Eric Moulds/94	7.50	20.00
84BA Fred Taylor		
84CE Fred Taylor/21		
84CR Fred Taylor/77		
84JN Fred Taylor/28	15.00	40.00
84SN Fred Taylor/240	7.50	20.00
85BA Isaac Bruce B	6.00	15.00
85CE Isaac Bruce B/21		
85CR Isaac Bruce B/80	7.50	20.00
85JN Isaac Bruce B/80	10.00	25.00
85SN Isaac Bruce B/87	7.50	20.00
86BA Isaac Bruce W	6.00	15.00
86CE Isaac Bruce W/21		
86CR Isaac Bruce W/80	7.50	20.00
86JN Isaac Bruce W/80	10.00	25.00
86SN Isaac Bruce W/87	7.50	20.00
87BA Jake Plummer SP	6.00	15.00
87CE Jake Plummer/21		
87CR Jake Plummer/166	6.00	15.00
87SN Jake Plummer/270	5.00	12.00
88BA Jamal Anderson SP	7.50	20.00
88CE Jamal Anderson/21		
88CR Jamal Anderson/39	10.00	25.00
88JN Jamal Anderson/32		
88SN Jamal Anderson/382	6.00	15.00
89BA Jerome Bettis B SP	10.00	25.00
89CE Jerome Bettis B/21		
89CR Jerome Bettis B/52	15.00	40.00
89JN Jerome Bettis B/36	20.00	50.00
89SN Jerome Bettis B/355	10.00	25.00
90BA Jerome Bettis W SP	10.00	25.00
90CE Jerome Bettis W/21		
90CR Jerome Bettis W/52	15.00	40.00
90JN Jerome Bettis W/36	20.00	50.00
90SN Jerome Bettis W/355	10.00	25.00
91BA Jevon Kearse	6.00	15.00
91CE Jevon Kearse/21		
91CR Jevon Kearse/110	6.00	15.00
91JN Jevon Kearse/90	7.50	20.00
92BA Jim Kelly	10.00	25.00
92CE Jim Kelly/21		
92CR Jim Kelly/237	10.00	25.00
92SN Jim Kelly/64	20.00	40.00
93BA Keyshawn Johnson SP		
93CE Keyshawn Johnson/21		
93CR Keyshawn Johnson/376	7.50	20.00
93SN Keyshawn Johnson/71	10.00	25.00
94BA Mark Brunell W SP	7.50	20.00
94CE Mark Brunell W/21		
94CR Mark Brunell W/119	7.50	20.00
94SN Mark Brunell W/311	6.00	15.00
95BA Mark Brunell T SP	7.50	20.00
95CE Mark Brunell T/21		
95CR Mark Brunell T/119	7.50	20.00
95SN Mark Brunell T/311	6.00	15.00
96BA Marvin Harrison	6.00	15.00
96CE Marvin Harrison/21		
96CR Marvin Harrison/78	10.00	25.00
96JN Marvin Harrison/88	10.00	25.00
96SN Marvin Harrison/102	7.50	20.00
97BA Michael Irvin	7.50	20.00
97CE Michael Irvin/21		
97CR Michael Irvin/65	10.00	25.00
97JN Michael Irvin/88	10.00	25.00
97SN Michael Irvin/111	7.50	20.00
98BA Mike Alstott	6.00	15.00
98CE Mike Alstott/21		
98CR Mike Alstott/130	7.50	20.00
98JN Mike Alstott/40	15.00	40.00
98SN Mike Alstott/131	7.50	20.00
99BA Olandis Gary	6.00	15.00
99CE Olandis Gary/21		
99CR Olandis Gary/289	6.00	15.00
99JN Olandis Gary/22		
99SN Olandis Gary/80	10.00	25.00
100BA Peter Warrick	6.00	15.00
100CE Peter Warrick/21		
100CR Peter Warrick/148	7.50	20.00
100JN Peter Warrick/80	10.00	25.00
100SN Peter Warrick/51	12.50	30.00
101BA Ron Dayne	6.00	15.00
101CE Ron Dayne/21		
101CR Ron Dayne/228	6.00	15.00
101JN Ron Dayne/27	15.00	40.00
101SN Ron Dayne/50	12.50	30.00
102BA Shaun Alexander SP		
102CE Shaun Alexander/21		
102CR Shaun Alexander/313	10.00	25.00
102JN Shaun Alexander/37	25.00	50.00
102SN Shaun Alexander/41	15.00	40.00
103BA Stephen Davis SP	7.50	20.00
103CE Stephen Davis/21		
103CR Stephen Davis/76	10.00	25.00
103JN Stephen Davis/48	12.50	30.00
103SN Stephen Davis/313	6.00	15.00
104BA Steve McNair B SP		
104CE Steve McNair B/21		
104CR Steve McNair B/362	7.50	20.00
104SN Steve McNair B/83	10.00	25.00
105BA Steve McNair W SP		
105CE Steve McNair W/21		
105CR Steve McNair W/362	7.50	20.00
105SN Steve McNair W/83	10.00	25.00
106BA Terrell Owens SP		
106CE Terrell Owens/21		
106CR Terrell Owens/319	7.50	20.00
106JN Terrell Owens/81	12.00	30.00
106SN Terrell Owens/69	12.00	30.00
107BA Tim Brown	7.50	20.00
107CE Tim Brown/21		
107CR Tim Brown/87	10.00	25.00
107JN Tim Brown/81	10.00	25.00
107SN Tim Brown/76	10.00	25.00
108BA Tim Couch	6.00	15.00
108CE Tim Couch/21		
108CR Tim Couch/360	6.00	15.00
108SN Tim Couch/77	7.50	20.00
109BA Torry Holt	7.50	20.00
109CE Torry Holt/21		
109CR Torry Holt/134	7.50	20.00
109JN Torry Holt/88	10.00	25.00
109SN Torry Holt/85	10.00	25.00
110BA Warrick Dunn SP		
110CE Warrick Dunn/21		
110CR Warrick Dunn/191	7.50	20.00
110JN Warrick Dunn/28	15.00	40.00
110SN Warrick Dunn/248	7.50	20.00
111BA Akili Smith	5.00	12.00
111CE Akili Smith/21		
111CR Akili Smith/198	5.00	12.00
111SN Akili Smith/41	7.50	20.00
112BA Amani Toomer	5.00	12.00
112CE Amani Toomer/21		
112CR Amani Toomer/201	5.00	12.00
112JN Amani Toomer/81	7.50	20.00
112SN Amani Toomer/91	6.00	15.00
113BA Az-Zahir Hakim	5.00	12.00
113CE Az-Zahir Hakim/21		
113CR Az-Zahir Hakim/109	6.00	15.00
113JN Az-Zahir Hakim/81	7.50	20.00
113SN Az-Zahir Hakim/80	7.50	20.00
114BA Champ Bailey	5.00	12.00
114CE Champ Bailey/21		
114CR Champ Bailey/123	6.00	15.00
114JN Champ Bailey/24		
114SN Champ Bailey/103	7.50	20.00
115BA Charles Woodson	6.00	15.00
115CE Charles Woodson/21		
115CR Charles Woodson/169	7.50	20.00
115JN Charles Woodson/24		
115SN Charles Woodson/79	10.00	25.00
116BA Chris Redman	5.00	12.00
116CE Chris Redman/21		
116CR Chris Redman/84	6.00	15.00
116SN Chris Redman/66	6.00	15.00
117BA Courtney Brown	5.00	12.00
117CE Courtney Brown/21		
117CR Courtney Brown/69	7.50	20.00
117JN Courtney Brown/92	6.00	15.00
117SN Courtney Brown/61	7.50	20.00
118BA Darrell Green	6.00	15.00
118CE Darrell Green/21		
118CR Darrell Green/121	7.50	20.00
118JN Darrell Green/28	25.00	60.00
118SN Darrell Green/23		
119BA Dorsey Levens	5.00	12.00
119CE Dorsey Levens/21		
119CR Dorsey Levens/247	5.00	12.00
119JN Dorsey Levens/25		
119SN Dorsey Levens/77	10.00	25.00
120BA Frank Sanders	5.00	12.00
120CE Frank Sanders/21		
120CR Frank Sanders/70	6.00	15.00
120JN Frank Sanders/81	6.00	15.00
120SN Frank Sanders/54	7.50	20.00
121BA Herman Moore	5.00	12.00
121CE Herman Moore/21		
121CR Herman Moore/93	6.00	15.00
121JN Herman Moore/84	7.50	20.00
121SN Herman Moore/40	10.00	25.00
122BA J.J. Stokes	5.00	12.00
122CE J.J. Stokes/21		
122CR J.J. Stokes/241	5.00	12.00
122JN J.J. Stokes/83	7.50	20.00
122SN J.J. Stokes/53	7.50	20.00
123BA James Allen	5.00	12.00
123CE James Allen/21		
123CR James Allen/56	7.50	20.00
123JN James Allen/20		
123SN James Allen/290	6.00	15.00
124BA Jason Sehorn	5.00	12.00
124CE Jason Sehorn/21		
124CR Jason Sehorn/163	6.00	15.00
124JN Jason Sehorn/31	12.50	30.00
124SN Jason Sehorn/73	7.50	20.00
125BA Jay Fiedler	6.00	15.00
125CE Jay Fiedler/21		
125CR Jay Fiedler/268	7.50	20.00
125SN Jay Fiedler/74	10.00	25.00
126BA Jimmy Smith	6.00	15.00
126CE Jimmy Smith/21		
126CR Jimmy Smith/75	10.00	25.00
126JN Jimmy Smith/82	10.00	25.00
126SN Jimmy Smith/91	7.50	20.00
127BA Johnnie Morton	5.00	12.00
127CE Johnnie Morton/21		
127CR Johnnie Morton/98	6.00	15.00
127JN Johnnie Morton/87	6.00	15.00
127SN Johnnie Morton/61	10.00	25.00
128BA Junior Seau	7.50	20.00
128CE Junior Seau/21		
128CR Junior Seau/45	10.00	25.00
128JN Junior Seau/55	10.00	25.00
128SN Junior Seau/123	7.50	20.00
129BA Keenan McCardell	5.00	12.00
129CE Keenan McCardell/21		
129CR Keenan McCardell/32	10.00	25.00
129JN Keenan McCardell/87	6.00	15.00
129SN Keenan McCardell/94	6.00	15.00
130BA Kevin Johnson	5.00	12.00
130CE Kevin Johnson/21		
130CR Kevin Johnson/123	6.00	15.00
130JN Kevin Johnson/85	7.50	20.00
130SN Kevin Johnson/79	7.50	20.00
131BA Kordell Stewart SP	6.00	15.00
131CE Kordell Stewart/21		
131CR Kordell Stewart/357	6.00	15.00
131SN Kordell Stewart/73	7.50	20.00
132BA Lamar Smith SP	7.50	20.00
132CE Lamar Smith/21		
132CR Lamar Smith/108	7.50	20.00
132JN Lamar Smith/26	15.00	40.00
132SN Lamar Smith/309	6.00	15.00
133BA Laveranues Coles SP		
133CE Laveranues Coles/21		
133CR Laveranues Coles/370	6.00	15.00
133JN Laveranues Coles/87	7.50	20.00
134BA Michael Strahan	7.50	20.00
134CE Michael Strahan/21		
134CR Michael Strahan/327	6.00	15.00
134JN Michael Strahan/92	7.50	20.00
135BA Rich Gannon SP		
135CE Rich Gannon/21		
135CR Rich Gannon/134	7.50	20.00
135SN Rich Gannon/284	7.50	20.00
136BA Ricky Watters	5.00	12.00
136CE Ricky Watters/21		
136CR Ricky Watters/90	6.00	15.00
136JN Ricky Watters/32	12.50	30.00
136SN Ricky Watters/278	5.00	12.00
137BA Rob Johnson	6.00	15.00
137CE Rob Johnson/21		
137CR Rob Johnson/89	7.50	20.00
137SN Rob Johnson/307	5.00	12.00
138BA Rod Smith	5.00	12.00
138CE Rod Smith/21		
138CR Rod Smith/78	10.00	25.00
138JN Rod Smith/80	10.00	25.00
138SN Rod Smith/100	7.50	20.00
139BA Sebastian Janikowski	5.00	12.00
139CE Sebastian Janikowski/21		
139CR Sebastian Janikowski/112	6.00	15.00
139SN Sebastian Janikowski/68	6.00	15.00
140BA Shaun King	5.00	12.00
140CE Shaun King/21		
140CR Shaun King/322	5.00	12.00
140SN Shaun King/78	6.00	15.00
141BA Terry Glenn SP	5.00	12.00
141CE Terry Glenn/21		
141CR Terry Glenn/315	5.00	12.00
141JN Terry Glenn/86	6.00	15.00
141SN Terry Glenn/39		
142BA Thurman Thomas	6.00	15.00
142CE Thurman Thomas/21		
142CR Thurman Thomas/65	7.50	20.00
142JN Thurman Thomas/34	15.00	40.00
142SN Thurman Thomas/136	6.00	15.00
143BA Tony Gonzalez	6.00	15.00
143CE Tony Gonzalez/21		
143CR Tony Gonzalez/261	7.50	20.00
143JN Tony Gonzalez/88	10.00	25.00
143SN Tony Gonzalez/39	15.00	40.00
144BA Travis Prentice	5.00	12.00
144CE Travis Prentice/21		
144CR Travis Prentice/173	5.00	12.00
144JN Travis Prentice/41	7.50	20.00
144SN Travis Prentice/191	5.00	12.00
145BA Tyrone Wheatley	6.00	15.00
145CE Tyrone Wheatley/21		
145CR Tyrone Wheatley/80	7.50	20.00
145JN Tyrone Wheatley/47	12.50	30.00
145SN Tyrone Wheatley/232	6.00	15.00
146BA Vinny Testaverde	6.00	15.00
146CE Vinny Testaverde/21		
146CR Vinny Testaverde/226	6.00	15.00
146SN Vinny Testaverde/69	10.00	25.00
147BA Warren Sapp	6.00	15.00
147CE Warren Sapp/21		
147CR Warren Sapp/274	6.00	15.00
147JN Warren Sapp/99	10.00	25.00
148BA Wayne Chrebet	6.00	15.00
148CE Wayne Chrebet/21		
148CR Wayne Chrebet/70	10.00	25.00
148JN Wayne Chrebet/80	10.00	25.00
148SN Wayne Chrebet/69	10.00	25.00
149BA Wesley Walls SP		
149CE Wesley Walls/21		
149CR Wesley Walls/368	5.00	12.00
149JN Wesley Walls/85	10.00	25.00
150BA JaJuan Dawson	5.00	12.00
150CE JaJuan Dawson/21		
150CR JaJuan Dawson/97	6.00	15.00
150JN JaJuan Dawson/88	6.00	15.00
150SN JaJuan Dawson/26	10.00	25.00

2001 Leaf Certified Materials Chicago Collection

NOT PRICED DUE TO SCARCITY

2002 Leaf Certified

Released in late September, 2002, this set contains 100 veterans and 32 rookies. Each rookie features a piece of event worn jersey, except for William Green, who features event worn football. The rookies are serial #'d to 800. Each box contained 16 packs of 5 cards. SRP for this product was $9.99 per pack.

COMP.SET w/o SP's (100)	10.00	25.00
ROOKIE JERSEY PRINT RUN 800		
1 David Boston	.25	.60
2 Jake Plummer	.30	.75
3 Michael Vick	.60	1.50
4 Jamal Anderson	.30	.75
5 Chris Redman	.25	.60
6 Ray Lewis	.40	1.00
7 Eric Moulds	.30	.75
8 Travis Henry	.25	.60
9 Nate Clements	.25	.60
10 Chris Weinke	.25	.60
11 Muhsin Muhammad	.30	.75
12 Wesley Walls	.30	.75
13 Anthony Thomas	.30	.75
14 Brian Urlacher	.40	1.00
15 Dez White	.25	.60
16 Corey Dillon	.30	.75
17 Peter Warrick	.30	.75
18 Tim Couch	.25	.60
19 Kevin Johnson	.25	.60
20 James Jackson	.25	.60
21 Emmitt Smith	1.00	2.50
22 Quincy Carter	.25	.60
23 Brian Griese	.30	.75
24 Ed McCaffrey	.30	.75
25 Rod Smith	.30	.75
26 Terrell Davis	.40	1.00
27 Mike Anderson	.30	.75
28 Germane Crowell	.25	.60
29 James Stewart	.25	.60
30 Charlie Batch	.25	.60
31 Antonio Freeman	.40	1.00
32 Brett Favre	1.00	2.50
33 Ahman Green	.30	.75
34 LeRoy Butler	.30	.75
35 Edgerrin James	.30	.75
36 Marvin Harrison	.40	1.00
37 Peyton Manning	.75	2.00
38 Fred Taylor	.30	.75
39 Jimmy Smith	.30	.75
40 Mark Brunell	.30	.75
41 Keenan McCardell	.30	.75
42 Tony Gonzalez	.40	1.00
43 Priest Holmes	.40	1.00
44 Jay Fiedler	.30	.75
45 Chris Chambers	.30	.75
46 Zach Thomas	.40	1.00
47 Travis Minor	.25	.60
48 Cris Carter	.40	1.00
49 Daunte Culpepper	.30	.75
50 Randy Moss	.40	1.00
51 Drew Bledsoe	.40	1.00
52 Tom Brady	1.00	2.50
53 Antowain Smith	.30	.75
54 Troy Brown	.30	.75
55 Aaron Brooks	.30	.75
56 Ricky Williams	.30	.75
57 Ron Dayne	.30	.75
58 Kerry Collins	.30	.75
59 Michael Strahan	.40	1.00
60 Amani Toomer	.30	.75
61 Chad Pennington	.40	1.00
62 Curtis Martin	.40	1.00
63 Vinny Testaverde	.30	.75
64 Wayne Chrebet	.30	.75
65 Charles Woodson	.40	1.00
66 Rich Gannon	.30	.75
67 Tim Brown	.40	1.00
68 Jerry Rice	.75	2.00
69 Tyrone Wheatley	.30	.75
70 Donovan McNabb	.40	1.00
71 Duce Staley	.30	.75
72 Todd Pinkston	.25	.60
73 Correll Buckhalter	.30	.75
74 Jerome Bettis	.40	1.00
75 Kordell Stewart	.30	.75
76 Plaxico Burress	.30	.75
77 Hines Ward	.40	1.00
78 Junior Seau	.40	1.00
79 LaDainian Tomlinson	.50	1.25
80 Doug Flutie	.40	1.00
81 Terrell Owens	.40	1.00
82 Jeff Garcia	.30	.75
83 Ricky Watters	.30	.75
84 Shaun Alexander	.30	.75
85 Koren Robinson	.25	.60
86 Isaac Bruce	.40	1.00
87 Kurt Warner	.40	1.00
88 Marshall Faulk	.40	1.00
89 Torry Holt	.40	1.00
90 Keyshawn Johnson	.30	.75
91 Mike Alstott	.30	.75
92 Warren Sapp	.30	.75
93 Brad Johnson	.30	.75
94 Eddie George	.30	.75
95 Jevon Kearse	.30	.75
96 Steve McNair	.40	1.00
97 Derrick Mason	.30	.75
98 Frank Wycheck	.25	.60
99 Champ Bailey	.40	1.00
100 Stephen Davis	.30	.75
101 Ladell Betts JSY RC	3.00	8.00
102 Antonio Bryant JSY RC	3.00	8.00
103 Reche Caldwell JSY RC	3.00	8.00
104 David Carr JSY RC	3.00	8.00
105 Tim Carter JSY RC	2.50	6.00
106 Eric Crouch JSY RC	3.00	8.00
107 Rohan Davey JSY RC	3.00	8.00
108 Andre Davis JSY RC	2.50	6.00
109 T.J. Duckett JSY RC	3.00	8.00
110 DeShaun Foster JSY RC	3.00	8.00
111 Jabar Gaffney JSY RC	3.00	8.00
112 Daniel Graham JSY RC	2.50	6.00
113 William Green FB RC	2.50	6.00
114 Joey Harrington JSY RC	3.00	8.00
115 David Garrard JSY RC	4.00	10.00
116 Ron Johnson JSY RC	2.50	6.00
117 Ashley Lelie JSY RC	2.50	6.00
118 Josh McCown JSY RC	3.00	8.00
119 Maurice Morris JSY RC	2.50	6.00
120 Julius Peppers JSY RC	6.00	15.00
121 Clinton Portis JSY RC	4.00	10.00
122 Patrick Ramsey JSY RC	3.00	8.00
123 Antwaan Randle El JSY RC	3.00	8.00
124 Josh Reed JSY RC	2.50	6.00
125 Cliff Russell JSY RC	2.00	5.00
126 Jeremy Shockey JSY RC	5.00	12.00
127 Donte Stallworth JSY RC	3.00	8.00
128 Travis Stephens JSY RC	2.00	5.00
129 Javon Walker JSY RC	3.00	8.00
130 Marquise Walker JSY RC	2.00	5.00
131 Roy Williams JSY RC	3.00	8.00
132 Mike Williams JSY RC	2.00	5.00

2002 Leaf Certified Mirror Blue Materials

*VETS 1-100: .6X TO 1.5X MIRROR RED
*ROOKIE 101-132: .6X TO 1.5X MIR.RED
1-100 VET JERSEY PRINT RUN 50
101-132 ROOKIE HELMET PRINT RUN 100

2002 Leaf Certified Mirror Gold Materials

*VETS 1-100: 1X TO 2.5X MIRROR RED
*ROOKIES 101-132: 1X TO 2.5X MIR.RED
MIRROR GOLD PRINT RUN 25

2002 Leaf Certified Mirror Red Materials

1-100 VETERAN PRINT RUN 100
101-132 ROOKIE JSY/FB PRINT RUN 250

1 David Boston	4.00	10.00
2 Jake Plummer	5.00	12.00
3 Michael Vick	10.00	25.00
4 Jamal Anderson	5.00	12.00
5 Chris Redman	4.00	10.00
6 Ray Lewis	6.00	15.00
7 Eric Moulds	5.00	12.00
8 Travis Henry	4.00	10.00
9 Nate Clements	4.00	10.00
10 Chris Weinke	4.00	10.00
11 Muhsin Muhammad	5.00	12.00
12 Wesley Walls	5.00	12.00
13 Anthony Thomas	5.00	12.00
14 Brian Urlacher	6.00	15.00
15 Dez White	4.00	10.00
16 Corey Dillon	5.00	12.00
17 Peter Warrick	5.00	12.00
18 Tim Couch	4.00	10.00
19 Kevin Johnson	4.00	10.00
20 James Jackson	4.00	10.00
21 Emmitt Smith	15.00	40.00
22 Quincy Carter	4.00	10.00
23 Brian Griese	5.00	12.00
24 Ed McCaffrey	5.00	12.00
25 Rod Smith	5.00	12.00
26 Terrell Davis	6.00	15.00
27 Mike Anderson	5.00	12.00
28 Germane Crowell	4.00	10.00
29 James Stewart	4.00	10.00
30 Charlie Batch	4.00	10.00
31 Antonio Freeman	6.00	15.00
32 Brett Favre	15.00	40.00
33 Ahman Green	5.00	12.00
34 LeRoy Butler	5.00	12.00
35 Edgerrin James	5.00	12.00
36 Marvin Harrison	6.00	15.00
37 Peyton Manning	12.00	30.00
38 Fred Taylor	5.00	12.00
39 Jimmy Smith	5.00	12.00
40 Mark Brunell	5.00	12.00
41 Keenan McCardell	5.00	12.00
42 Tony Gonzalez	6.00	15.00
43 Priest Holmes	6.00	15.00
44 Jay Fiedler	5.00	12.00
45 Chris Chambers	5.00	12.00
46 Zach Thomas	6.00	15.00
47 Travis Minor	4.00	10.00
48 Cris Carter	6.00	15.00
49 Daunte Culpepper	5.00	12.00
50 Randy Moss	6.00	15.00
51 Drew Bledsoe	6.00	15.00
52 Tom Brady	15.00	40.00
53 Antowain Smith	5.00	12.00
54 Troy Brown	5.00	12.00
55 Aaron Brooks	5.00	12.00
56 Ricky Williams	5.00	12.00
57 Ron Dayne	5.00	12.00
58 Kerry Collins	5.00	12.00
59 Michael Strahan	6.00	15.00
60 Amani Toomer	5.00	12.00
61 Chad Pennington	6.00	15.00
62 Curtis Martin	6.00	15.00
63 Vinny Testaverde	5.00	12.00
64 Wayne Chrebet	5.00	12.00
65 Charles Woodson	6.00	15.00
66 Rich Gannon	5.00	12.00
67 Tim Brown	6.00	15.00
68 Jerry Rice	12.00	30.00
69 Tyrone Wheatley	5.00	12.00
70 Donovan McNabb	6.00	15.00
71 Duce Staley	5.00	12.00
72 Todd Pinkston	4.00	10.00
73 Correll Buckhalter	5.00	12.00
74 Jerome Bettis	6.00	15.00
75 Kordell Stewart	5.00	12.00
76 Plaxico Burress	5.00	12.00
77 Hines Ward	6.00	15.00
78 Junior Seau	6.00	15.00
79 LaDainian Tomlinson	8.00	20.00
80 Doug Flutie	6.00	15.00
81 Terrell Owens	6.00	15.00
82 Jeff Garcia	5.00	12.00
83 Ricky Watters	5.00	12.00
84 Shaun Alexander	5.00	12.00
85 Koren Robinson	4.00	10.00
86 Isaac Bruce	6.00	15.00
87 Kurt Warner	6.00	15.00
88 Marshall Faulk	6.00	15.00
89 Torry Holt	6.00	15.00
90 Keyshawn Johnson	5.00	12.00
91 Mike Alstott	5.00	12.00
92 Warren Sapp	5.00	12.00
93 Brad Johnson	5.00	12.00
94 Eddie George	5.00	12.00
95 Jevon Kearse	5.00	12.00
96 Steve McNair	6.00	15.00
97 Derrick Mason	5.00	12.00
98 Frank Wycheck	4.00	10.00
99 Champ Bailey	6.00	15.00
100 Stephen Davis	5.00	12.00
101 Ladell Betts	5.00	12.00
102 Antonio Bryant	5.00	12.00
103 Reche Caldwell	5.00	12.00
104 David Carr	5.00	12.00
105 Tim Carter	4.00	10.00
106 Eric Crouch	5.00	12.00
107 Rohan Davey	5.00	12.00
108 Andre Davis	4.00	10.00
109 T.J. Duckett	5.00	12.00
110 DeShaun Foster	5.00	12.00
111 Jabar Gaffney	5.00	12.00
112 Daniel Graham	4.00	10.00
113 William Green	4.00	10.00
114 Joey Harrington	5.00	12.00
115 David Garrard	6.00	15.00
116 Ron Johnson	4.00	10.00
117 Ashley Lelie	4.00	10.00
118 Josh McCown	5.00	12.00
119 Maurice Morris	4.00	10.00
120 Julius Peppers	10.00	25.00
121 Clinton Portis	6.00	15.00
122 Patrick Ramsey	5.00	12.00
123 Antwaan Randle El	5.00	12.00
124 Josh Reed	4.00	10.00
125 Cliff Russell	3.00	8.00
126 Jeremy Shockey	8.00	20.00
127 Donte Stallworth	5.00	12.00
128 Travis Stephens	3.00	8.00
129 Javon Walker	5.00	12.00
130 Marquise Walker	3.00	8.00
131 Roy Williams	5.00	12.00
132 Mike Williams	3.00	8.00

2002 Leaf Certified Fabric of the Game

STATED PRINT RUN 100 SER.#'d SETS
*TEAM LOGO/50: .5X TO 1.2X BASIC JSY
TEAM LOGO PRINT RUN 50 SER.#'d SETS

1 Andre Reed	8.00	20.00
2 Art Monk	8.00	20.00
3 Barry Sanders	15.00	40.00
4 Bert Jones	6.00	15.00
5 Bob Griese	10.00	25.00
6 Craig Morton	8.00	20.00
7 Deacon Jones	8.00	20.00
8 Dick Butkus	15.00	40.00
9 Don Maynard	8.00	20.00
10 Earl Campbell	10.00	25.00
11 Eric Dickerson	8.00	20.00
12 Fran Tarkenton	10.00	25.00
13 Franco Harris	10.00	25.00
14 Gale Sayers	12.00	30.00
15 Henry Ellard	6.00	15.00
16 Herschel Walker	8.00	20.00
17 Howie Long	12.00	30.00
18 Jim McMahon	10.00	25.00
19 Joe Theismann	10.00	25.00
20 John Riggins	10.00	25.00
21 Ken Stabler	12.00	30.00
22 L.C. Greenwood	8.00	20.00
23 Marcus Allen	10.00	25.00
24 Ozzie Newsome	8.00	20.00
25 Raymond Berry	8.00	20.00
26 Roger Staubach	15.00	40.00
27 Sterling Sharpe	8.00	20.00
28 Steve Bartkowski	8.00	20.00
29 Steve Largent	10.00	25.00
30 Terry Bradshaw	15.00	40.00
31 Tony Dorsett	10.00	25.00
32 Joe Montana	30.00	80.00
33 Joe Namath	15.00	40.00
34 Ronnie Lott	10.00	25.00
35 Thurman Thomas	10.00	25.00
36 Boomer Esiason	8.00	20.00
37 Dan Marino	25.00	60.00
38 Jim Kelly	12.00	30.00
39 John Elway	20.00	50.00
40 Phil Simms	8.00	20.00
41 Steve Young	12.00	30.00
42 Troy Aikman	15.00	40.00
43 Warren Moon	10.00	25.00
44 Daunte Culpepper	8.00	20.00
45 Edgerrin James	8.00	20.00
46 Emmitt Smith	25.00	60.00
47 Kurt Warner	10.00	25.00
48 Marshall Faulk	10.00	25.00
49 Tim Brown	10.00	25.00
50 Terrell Owens	10.00	25.00

2002 Leaf Certified Fabric of the Game Autographs

STATED PRINT RUN 1-84

1 Andre Reed/83	25.00	50.00
2 Art Monk/81	30.00	60.00
3 Barry Sanders/20	100.00	200.00
7 Deacon Jones/75	30.00	60.00
8 Dick Butkus/51	60.00	100.00
10 Earl Campbell/34	75.00	125.00
11 Eric Dickerson/29	50.00	120.00
13 Franco Harris/32	75.00	150.00
14 Gale Sayers/40	60.00	120.00
15 Henry Ellard/80	25.00	50.00
16 Herschel Walker/34	40.00	70.00
17 Howie Long/75	60.00	100.00
20 John Riggins/44	40.00	100.00
22 L.C. Greenwood/68	30.00	60.00
23 Marcus Allen/32	40.00	80.00
24 Ozzie Newsome/82	25.00	50.00
25 Raymond Berry/82	30.00	60.00
27 Sterling Sharpe/84	30.00	60.00
29 Steve Largent/80	50.00	100.00
31 Tony Dorsett/33	75.00	135.00
34 Ronnie Lott/42	40.00	80.00
35 Thurman Thomas/34	50.00	100.00
45 Edgerrin James/32	40.00	80.00
46 Emmitt Smith/22	125.00	200.00
48 Marshall Faulk/28	60.00	120.00
49 Tim Brown/81	40.00	80.00
50 Terrell Owens/81	40.00	80.00

2002 Leaf Certified Future

COMPLETE SET (20)	25.00	60.00
STATED ODDS 1:15		
CF1 David Carr	1.00	2.50
CF2 Joey Harrington	1.00	2.50
CF3 Kurt Kittner	.60	1.50
CF4 Patrick Ramsey	1.00	2.50
CF5 William Green	.75	2.00
CF6 T.J. Duckett	1.00	2.50
CF7 Clinton Portis	1.25	3.00
CF8 DeShaun Foster	1.00	2.50
CF9 Brian Westbrook	1.50	4.00
CF10 Javon Walker	1.00	2.50
CF11 Donte Stallworth	1.00	2.50
CF12 Antonio Bryant	1.00	2.50
CF13 Ashley Lelie	.75	2.00
CF14 Jabar Gaffney	1.00	2.50
CF15 Reche Caldwell	1.00	2.50
CF16 Josh Reed	.75	2.00
CF17 Julius Peppers	2.00	5.00
CF18 Albert Haynesworth	1.00	2.50
CF19 Quentin Jammer	1.00	2.50
CF20 Roy Williams	1.00	2.50

2002 Leaf Certified Gold Team

COMPLETE SET (20)	20.00	50.00
STATED ODDS 1:15		
GT1 Kurt Warner	1.25	3.00
GT2 Brett Favre	3.00	8.00
GT3 Jeff Garcia	1.00	2.50
GT4 Rich Gannon	1.00	2.50
GT5 Steve McNair	1.25	3.00
GT6 Torn Brady	3.00	8.00
GT7 Edgerrin James	1.00	2.50
GT8 Curtis Martin	1.25	3.00
GT9 Marshall Faulk	1.25	3.00
GT10 Emmitt Smith	3.00	8.00
GT11 Ricky Williams	1.00	2.50
GT12 Garrison Hearst	1.00	2.50
GT13 David Boston	.75	2.00
GT14 Jerry Rice	2.50	6.00
GT15 Randy Moss	1.25	3.00
GT16 Keyshawn Johnson	1.00	2.50
GT17 Tim Brown	1.25	3.00
GT18 Marvin Harrison	1.25	3.00
GT19 Michael Strahan	1.25	3.00
GT20 Brian Urlacher	1.25	3.00

2002 Leaf Certified Mirror Red Signatures

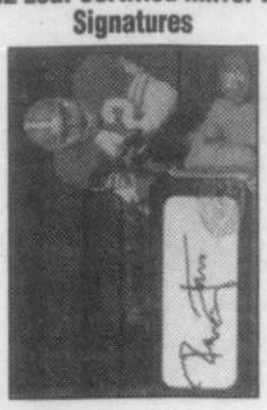

STATED PRINT RUN 50 SER.#'d SETS
*BLUE/25: .6X TO 1.5X RED AUTO/50
BLUE PRINT RUN 25 SER.#'d SETS
UNPRICED GOLD PRINT RUN 10 SETS

1 Joe Montana	50.00	120.00
2 Joe Namath	50.00	100.00
3 Ronnie Lott	20.00	40.00
4 Thurman Thomas	12.00	30.00
5 John Riggins	20.00	50.00
6 Barry Sanders	50.00	100.00
7 Phil Simms	20.00	40.00
8 Steve Young	20.00	40.00
9 Troy Aikman	40.00	80.00
10 Deuce McAllister	10.00	25.00
11 Justin Smith	7.50	20.00
12 Eric Moulds	6.00	15.00
13 Chris Weinke	7.50	20.00
14 Aaron Brooks	7.50	20.00
15 Kurt Warner	25.00	60.00
16 Drew Brees	40.00	80.00
17 Edgerrin James	12.00	30.00
18 Correll Buckhalter	7.50	20.00
19 Jimmy Smith	6.00	15.00
20 Elvis Grbac	6.00	15.00
21 Tim Brown	10.00	25.00
22 Stephen Davis	7.50	20.00
23 Dan Morgan	6.00	15.00
24 Robert Ferguson	10.00	25.00
25 Peter Warrick	10.00	25.00
26 Kerry Collins	10.00	25.00
27 Isaac Bruce	10.00	25.00
28 David Terrell	7.50	20.00
29 Jamal Lewis	10.00	25.00
30 Jeff Blake	6.00	15.00
31 Santana Moss	10.00	25.00
32 Mark Brunell	10.00	25.00
33 Gerard Warren	6.00	15.00
34 Marcus Robinson	6.00	15.00
35 Randall Cunningham	10.00	25.00
36 Quincy Carter	7.50	20.00
37 Marshall Faulk	25.00	50.00
38 LaMont Jordan	10.00	25.00

2002 Leaf Certified Skills

COMPLETE SET (20)	12.50	30.00
STATED ODDS 1:15		
CS1 Donovan McNabb	1.00	2.50
CS2 Kordell Stewart	.75	2.00
CS3 Mark Brunell	.75	2.00
CS4 Peyton Manning	2.00	5.00
CS5 Daunte Culpepper	.75	2.00
CS6 Brian Griese	.75	2.00
CS7 Eddie George	.75	2.00
CS8 Ahman Green	.75	2.00
CS9 Shaun Alexander	.75	2.00
CS10 LaDainian Tomlinson	1.25	3.00
CS11 Anthony Thomas	.75	2.00
CS12 Priest Holmes	1.00	2.50
CS13 Torry Holt	1.00	2.50
CS14 Rod Smith	.75	2.00
CS15 Terrell Owens	1.00	2.50
CS16 Troy Brown	.75	2.00
CS17 Derrick Mason	.75	2.00
CS18 Jimmy Smith	.75	2.00
CS19 Jevon Kearse	.75	2.00
CS20 Zach Thomas	1.00	2.50

2002 Leaf Certified Samples

*SAMPLES: .8X TO 2X BASIC CARDS

2002 Leaf Certified Samples Gold

*GOLD SAMPLES: .6X TO 1.5X SILVER

2003 Leaf Certified Materials

Released in September of 2003, this set consists of 180 cards including 150 veterans and 30 rookies. The rookies were serial numbered to 1250 and featured a swatch of event worn jersey from the 2003 Rookie Photo Shoot. Boxes contained 10 packs of 5 cards.

COMP.SET w/o SP's (150)	12.50	30.00
151-180 ROOKIE PRINT RUN 1250		
1 Jake Plummer	.30	.75
2 David Boston	.25	.60
3 MarTay Jenkins	.25	.60
4 Marcel Shipp	.25	.60
5 Michael Vick	.50	1.25
6 T.J. Duckett	.30	.75
7 Chris Redman	.25	.60
8 Ray Lewis	.40	1.00
9 Jamal Lewis	.30	.75
10 Eric Moulds	.30	.75
11 Nate Clements	.30	.75
12 Travis Henry	.25	.60
13 Drew Bledsoe	.40	1.00
14 Peerless Price	.25	.60
15 Josh Reed	.25	.60
16 Wesley Walls	.30	.75
17 Muhsin Muhammad	.30	.75
18 Julius Peppers	.40	1.00
19 Dez White	.25	.60
20 Mike Brown	.30	.75
21 Brian Urlacher	.40	1.00
22 Anthony Thomas	.30	.75
23 David Terrell	.25	.60
24 Corey Dillon	.30	.75
25 Peter Warrick	.30	.75
26 Josh McCown	.30	.75
27 Dennis Northcutt	.25	.60
28 Kevin Johnson	.25	.60
29 Tim Couch	.25	.60
30 Gerard Warren	.25	.60
31 William Green	.25	.60
32 Antonio Bryant	.25	.60
33 Darren Woodson	.30	.75
34 Emmitt Smith	1.00	2.50
35 Quincy Carter	.25	.60
36 Roy Williams	.30	.75
37 Brian Griese	.30	.75
38 Ed McCaffrey	.30	.75
39 Mike Anderson	.30	.75
40 Rod Smith	.30	.75
41 Clinton Portis	.30	.75
42 Ashley Lelie	.25	.60
43 Cory Schlesinger	.25	.60
44 Germane Crowell	.25	.60
45 James Stewart	.25	.60
46 Scotty Anderson	.25	.60
47 Joey Harrington	.25	.60
48 Brett Favre	1.00	2.50
49 Terry Glenn	.30	.75
50 Ahman Green	.30	.75
51 Donald Driver	.40	1.00
52 Javon Walker	.30	.75
53 David Carr	.30	.75
54 Ron Dayne	.30	.75
55 Terrell Davis	.40	1.00
56 Edgerrin James	.40	1.00
57 Marvin Harrison	.40	1.00
58 Peyton Manning	.75	2.00
59 Fred Taylor	.30	.75
60 Jimmy Smith	.30	.75
61 Kyle Brady	.25	.60
62 Mark Brunell	.30	.75
63 Tony Gonzalez	.40	1.00
64 Priest Holmes	.40	1.00
65 Trent Green	.30	.75
66 Jason Taylor	.30	.75
67 Jay Fiedler	.25	.60
68 Zach Thomas	.40	1.00
69 Chris Chambers	.30	.75
70 Ricky Williams	.30	.75
71 Randy McMichael	.25	.60
72 Daunte Culpepper	.30	.75
73 Randy Moss	.40	1.00
74 Michael Bennett	.30	.75
75 Ty Law	.30	.75
76 Tom Brady	1.00	2.50
77 Troy Brown	.30	.75
78 Antowain Smith	.30	.75
79 Aaron Brooks	.30	.75
80 Donte Stallworth	.25	.60
81 Joe Horn	.30	.75
82 Deuce McAllister	.30	.75
83 Amani Toomer	.30	.75
84 Kerry Collins	.30	.75
85 Michael Strahan	.40	1.00
86 Tiki Barber	.40	1.00
87 Jeremy Shockey	.40	1.00
88 Chad Pennington	.40	1.00
89 Curtis Martin	.40	1.00
90 Laveranues Coles	.25	.60
91 Vinny Testaverde	.30	.75
92 Santana Moss	.30	.75
93 Charles Woodson	.40	1.00
94 Sebastian Janikowski	.30	.75
95 Tim Brown	.40	1.00
96 Rich Gannon	.30	.75
97 Jerry Rice	.75	2.00
98 Donovan McNabb	.40	1.00
99 Duce Staley	.30	.75
100 Todd Pinkston	.25	.60
101 Chad Lewis	.30	.75
102 A.J. Feeley	.25	.60
103 Jerome Bettis	.40	1.00
104 Plaxico Burress	.30	.75
105 Hines Ward	.40	1.00
106 Antwaan Randle El	.30	.75
107 Kendrell Bell	.25	.60
108 Junior Seau	.40	1.00
109 LaDainian Tomlinson	.40	1.00
110 Doug Flutie	.40	1.00
111 Drew Brees	.40	1.00
112 Terrell Owens	.40	1.00
113 Jeff Garcia	.30	.75
114 Garrison Hearst	.30	.75
115 Koren Robinson	.30	.75
116 Shaun Alexander	.30	.75
117 Isaac Bruce	.40	1.00
118 Kurt Warner	.40	1.00
119 Marshall Faulk	.40	1.00
120 Torry Holt	.40	1.00
121 Keyshawn Johnson	.40	1.00
122 Warren Sapp	.30	.75
123 Mike Alstott	.40	1.00
124 Brad Johnson	.30	.75
125 Eddie George	.30	.75
126 Jevon Kearse	.30	.75
127 Steve McNair	.40	1.00
128 Derrick Mason	.30	.75
129 Keith Bulluck	.25	.60
130 Champ Bailey	.40	1.00
131 Darrell Green	.40	1.00
132 Stephen Davis	.30	.75
133 Rod Gardner	.25	.60
134 Barry Sanders	1.00	2.50
135 Cris Carter	.50	1.25
136 Dan Marino	1.25	3.00
137 Deion Sanders	.50	1.25
138 Jim Kelly	.60	1.50
139 Joe Montana	1.25	3.00
140 John Elway	1.25	3.00
141 Marcus Allen	.50	1.25
142 Reggie White	.50	1.25
143 Sterling Sharpe	.50	1.25
144 Steve Young	.60	1.50
145 Thurman Thomas	.50	1.25
146 Troy Aikman	.60	1.50
147 Warren Moon	.40	1.00
148 Drew Bledsoe	.40	1.00
149 Jerry Rice	.75	2.00
150 Ricky Williams	.30	.75
151 Carson Palmer JSY RC	6.00	15.00
152 Byron Leftwich JSY RC	3.00	8.00
153 Kyle Boller JSY RC	3.00	8.00
154 Rex Grossman JSY RC	3.00	8.00
155 Dave Ragone JSY RC	2.00	5.00
156 Kliff Kingsbury JSY RC	2.50	6.00
157 Seneca Wallace JSY RC	3.00	8.00
158 Larry Johnson JSY RC	3.00	8.00
159 Willis McGahee JSY RC	4.00	10.00
160 Justin Fargas JSY RC	3.00	8.00
161 Onterrio Smith JSY RC	2.00	5.00
162 Chris Brown JSY RC	2.00	5.00
163 Musa Smith JSY RC	2.00	5.00
164 Artose Pinner JSY RC	2.00	5.00
165 Andre Johnson JSY RC	8.00	20.00
166 Kelley Washington JSY RC	2.00	5.00
167 Taylor Jacobs JSY RC	2.00	5.00
168 Bryant Johnson JSY RC	3.00	8.00
169 Tyrone Calico JSY RC	2.50	6.00
170 Anquan Boldin JSY RC	5.00	12.00
171 Bethel Johnson JSY RC	2.00	5.00
172 Nate Burleson JSY RC	2.50	6.00
173 Kevin Curtis JSY RC	3.00	8.00
174 Dallas Clark JSY RC	5.00	12.00
175 Teyo Johnson JSY RC	2.50	6.00
176 Terrell Suggs JSY RC	3.00	8.00
177 DeWayne Robertson JSY RC	2.50	6.00
178 Brian St.Pierre JSY RC	2.50	6.00
179 Terence Newman JSY RC	2.50	6.00
180 Marcus Trufant JSY RC	2.50	6.00

2003 Leaf Certified Materials Mirror Black

STATED PRINT RUN 1 SER.#'d SET
NOT PRICED DUE TO SCARCITY

2003 Leaf Certified Materials Mirror Blue

*BLUE VETS: 10X TO 25X BASIC CARDS
*BLUE RETIRED: 8X TO 20X
*BLUE ROOKIES: 1X TO 2.5X
STATED PRINT RUN 50 SER.#'d SETS

2003 Leaf Certified Materials Mirror Emerald

STATED PRINT RUN 5 SER.#'d SETS
NOT PRICED DUE TO SCARCITY

2003 Leaf Certified Materials Mirror Gold

*GOLD VETS: 20X TO 50X BASIC CARDS
*GOLD RETIRED: 15X TO 40X
*GOLD ROOKIES: 2.5X TO 6X
STATED PRINT RUN 25 SER.#'d SETS

2003 Leaf Certified Materials Mirror Red

*RED VETS: 6X TO 15X BASIC CARDS
*RED RETIRED: 5X TO 12X
*RED ROOKIES: .6X TO 1.5X
STATED PRINT RUN 150 SER.#'d SETS

2003 Leaf Certified Materials Fabric of the Game

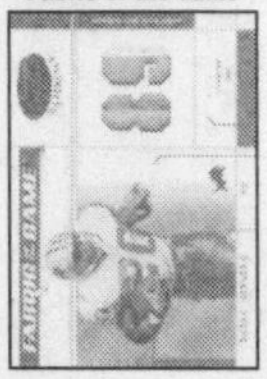

SER.#'d UNDER 25 NOT PRICED

1BA Art Monk/50	8.00	20.00
1DE Art Monk/80	6.00	15.00
1JN Art Monk AU/81	40.00	80.00
1LO Art Monk/25	12.00	30.00
2BA Barry Sanders/50	20.00	50.00
2DE Barry Sanders/89	15.00	40.00
2JN Barry Sanders AU/20	150.00	300.00
2LO Barry Sanders/25	30.00	80.00
3BA Bart Starr/50	15.00	40.00
3DE Bart Starr/56	15.00	40.00
3LO Bart Starr/25	25.00	60.00
4BA Bob Griese/50	10.00	25.00
4DE Bob Griese/67	10.00	25.00
4LO Bob Griese/25	15.00	40.00
5BA Charley Taylor/50	8.00	20.00
5DE Charley Taylor/64	8.00	20.00
5JN Charley Taylor AU/42	25.00	60.00
5LO Charley Taylor/25	12.00	30.00
6BA Cris Carter/50	10.00	25.00
6DE Cris Carter/87	8.00	20.00
6JN Cris Carter AU/80	60.00	120.00
6LO Cris Carter/25	15.00	40.00
7BA Dan Fouts/50	10.00	25.00
7DE Dan Fouts/73	8.00	20.00
7LO Dan Fouts/25	15.00	40.00
8BA Dan Marino/50	25.00	60.00
8DE Dan Marino/83	20.00	50.00
8LO Dan Marino/25	30.00	80.00
9BA Daryl Johnston/50	10.00	25.00
9DE Daryl Johnston/89	8.00	20.00
9JN Daryl Johnston AU/48	100.00	175.00
9LO Daryl Johnston/25	15.00	40.00
10BA Daryle Lamonica/50	6.00	15.00
10DE Daryle Lamonica/63	6.00	15.00
10LO Daryle Lamonica/25	10.00	25.00
11BA Deacon Jones/50	8.00	20.00
11DE Deacon Jones/61	8.00	20.00
11JN Deacon Jones AU/75	25.00	60.00
11LO Deacon Jones/25	12.00	30.00
12BA Deion Sanders/50	10.00	25.00
12DE Deion Sanders/89	8.00	20.00
12JN Deion Sanders AU/21	75.00	150.00
12LO Deion Sanders/25	15.00	40.00
13BA Dick Butkus/50	15.00	40.00
13DE Dick Butkus/65	15.00	40.00
13JN Dick Butkus AU/51	100.00	200.00
13LO Dick Butkus/25	25.00	60.00
14BA Doak Walker BA/50	15.00	40.00
14DE Doak Walker DE/50	15.00	40.00
14JN Doak Walker/37	40.00	80.00
14LO Doak Walker/25	25.00	60.00
15BA Don Maynard/50	8.00	20.00
15DE Don Maynard/58	8.00	20.00
15LO Don Maynard/25	12.00	30.00
16BA Earl Campbell/50	10.00	25.00
16DE Earl Campbell/78	8.00	20.00
16JN Earl Campbell AU/34	40.00	100.00
16LO Earl Campbell/25	15.00	40.00
17BA Eric Dickerson/50	8.00	20.00
17DE Eric Dickerson/83	6.00	15.00
17JN Eric Dickerson AU/29	40.00	100.00
17LO Eric Dickerson/25	12.00	30.00
18BA Franco Harris/50	12.00	30.00
18DE Franco Harris/72	10.00	25.00
18JN Franco Harris AU/32	100.00	200.00
18LO Franco Harris/25	20.00	50.00
19BA Frank Gifford/50	10.00	25.00
19DE Frank Gifford/52	10.00	25.00
19LO Frank Gifford/25	15.00	40.00
20BA Fred Biletnikoff/50	10.00	25.00
20DE Fred Biletnikoff/65	10.00	25.00
20JN Fred Biletnikoff AU/25	30.00	80.00
20LO Fred Biletnikoff/25	15.00	40.00
21BA Gale Sayers/50	15.00	40.00
21DE Gale Sayers/65	15.00	40.00
21JN Gale Sayers AU/40	75.00	150.00
21LO Gale Sayers/25	25.00	60.00
22BA George Blanda/50	10.00	25.00
22DE George Blanda/49	10.00	25.00
22LO George Blanda/25	15.00	40.00
23BA Herman Edwards/50	8.00	20.00
23DE Herman Edwards/77	6.00	15.00
23JN Herman Edwards AU/46	20.00	50.00
23LO Herman Edwards/25	12.00	30.00
24BA Irving Fryar/50	6.00	15.00
24DE Irving Fryar/84	5.00	12.00
24JN Irving Fryar AU/80	20.00	50.00
24LO Irving Fryar/25	10.00	25.00
25BA James Lofton/50	8.00	20.00
25DE James Lofton/78	6.00	15.00
25JN James Lofton AU/80	20.00	50.00
25LO James Lofton/25	12.00	30.00
26BA Jay Novacek/50	8.00	20.00
26DE Jay Novacek/85	6.00	15.00
26JN Jay Novacek AU/84	40.00	100.00
26LO Jay Novacek/25	12.00	30.00
27BA Jim Brown/50	15.00	40.00
27DE Jim Brown/57	15.00	40.00
27JN Jim Brown AU/32	125.00	250.00
27LO Jim Brown/25	25.00	60.00
28BA Jim Kelly/50	12.00	30.00
28DE Jim Kelly/86	10.00	25.00
28LO Jim Kelly/25	20.00	50.00
29BA Jim McMahon/50	10.00	25.00
29DE Jim McMahon/82	8.00	20.00
29LO Jim McMahon/25	15.00	40.00
30BA Jim Plunkett/50	8.00	20.00
30DE Jim Plunkett/71	6.00	15.00
30LO Jim Plunkett/25	12.00	30.00
31BA Jim Thorpe/50	90.00	150.00
31LO Jim Thorpe/25	100.00	200.00
32BA Joe Greene/50	10.00	25.00
32DE Joe Greene/69	10.00	25.00
32JN Joe Greene AU/75	60.00	100.00
32LO Joe Greene/25	15.00	40.00
33BA Joe Montana/50	25.00	60.00
33DE Joe Montana/79	20.00	50.00
33LO Joe Montana/25	40.00	100.00
34BA Joe Theismann/50	10.00	25.00
34DE Joe Theismann/74	8.00	20.00
34LO Joe Theismann/25	15.00	40.00
35BA John Elway/50	25.00	60.00
35DE John Elway/83	20.00	50.00
35LO John Elway/25	40.00	100.00
36BA John Riggins/50	10.00	25.00
36DE John Riggins/71	8.00	20.00
36JN John Riggins AU/44	30.00	80.00
36LO John Riggins/25	15.00	40.00
37BA John Taylor/50	8.00	20.00
37DE John Taylor/87	6.00	15.00
37JN John Taylor AU/82	15.00	40.00
37LO John Taylor/25	12.00	30.00
38BA Johnny Unitas/50	20.00	50.00
38DE Johnny Unitas/56	20.00	50.00
38LO Johnny Unitas/25	30.00	80.00
39BA Ken Stabler/50	12.00	30.00
39DE Ken Stabler/70	10.00	25.00
39LO Ken Stabler/25	20.00	50.00
40BA L.C. Greenwood/50	8.00	20.00
40DE L.C. Greenwood/69	8.00	20.00
40JN L.C. Greenwood AU/68	30.00	80.00
40LO L.C. Greenwood/25	12.00	30.00
41BA Larry Csonka/50	10.00	25.00
41DE Larry Csonka/68	10.00	25.00
41JN Larry Csonka AU/39	75.00	150.00
41LO Larry Csonka/25	15.00	40.00
42BA Lawrence Taylor/50	10.00	25.00
42DE Lawrence Taylor/81	8.00	20.00
42JN Lawrence Taylor AU/56	75.00	150.00
42LO Lawrence Taylor/25	15.00	40.00
43BA Marcus Allen/50	10.00	25.00
43DE Marcus Allen/82	8.00	20.00
43JN Marcus Allen AU/32	40.00	100.00
43LO Marcus Allen/25	15.00	40.00
44BA Mark Bavaro/50	8.00	20.00
44DE Mark Bavaro/85	6.00	15.00
44JN Mark Bavaro AU/89	25.00	60.00
44LO Mark Bavaro/25	12.00	30.00
45BA Mel Blount/50	8.00	20.00
45DE Mel Blount/70	6.00	15.00
45JN Mel Blount AU/47	30.00	80.00
45LO Mel Blount/25	12.00	30.00
46BA Ozzie Newsome/50	8.00	20.00
46DE Ozzie Newsome/78	6.00	15.00
46JN Ozzie Newsome AU/82	20.00	50.00
46LO Ozzie Newsome/25	12.00	30.00
47BA Ray Nitschke/50	20.00	50.00
47DE Ray Nitschke/58	20.00	50.00
47JN Ray Nitschke/66	20.00	50.00
47LO Ray Nitschke/25	25.00	60.00
48BA Raymond Berry/50	8.00	20.00
48DE Raymond Berry/55	8.00	20.00
48JN Raymond Berry AU/82	25.00	60.00
48LO Raymond Berry/25	12.00	30.00
49BA Reggie White/50	15.00	40.00
49DE Reggie White/85	12.00	30.00
49JN Reggie White AU/92	175.00	300.00
49LO Reggie White/25	25.00	60.00
50BA Richard Dent/50	8.00	20.00
50DE Richard Dent/83	6.00	15.00
50JN Richard Dent AU/95	25.00	60.00
50LO Richard Dent/25	12.00	30.00
51BA Roger Staubach/50	15.00	40.00
51DE Roger Staubach/69	15.00	40.00
51LO Roger Staubach/25	25.00	60.00
52BA Sonny Jurgensen/50	8.00	20.00
52DE Sonny Jurgensen/57	8.00	20.00
52LO Sonny Jurgensen/25	12.00	30.00
53BA Sterling Sharpe/50	10.00	25.00
53DE Sterling Sharpe/88	6.00	15.00
53JN Sterling Sharpe AU/84	25.00	60.00
53LO Sterling Sharpe/25	15.00	40.00
54BA Steve Largent/50	10.00	25.00
54DE Steve Largent/76	8.00	20.00
54JN Steve Largent AU/80	25.00	60.00
54LO Steve Largent/25	15.00	40.00
55BA Steve Young/50	12.00	30.00
55DE Steve Young/85	10.00	25.00
55LO Steve Young/25	20.00	50.00
56BA Ted Hendricks/50	8.00	20.00
56DE Ted Hendricks/69	8.00	20.00
56JN Ted Hendricks AU/83	20.00	50.00
56LO Ted Hendricks/25	12.00	30.00
57BA Terrell Davis/50	10.00	25.00
57DE Terrell Davis/95	6.00	15.00
57JN Terrell Davis AU/30	40.00	100.00
57LO Terrell Davis/25	15.00	40.00
58BA Terry Bradshaw/50	15.00	40.00
58DE Terry Bradshaw/70	12.00	30.00
58LO Terry Bradshaw/25	25.00	60.00
59BA Thurman Thomas/50	10.00	25.00
59DE Thurman Thomas/88	6.00	15.00
59JN Thurman Thomas AU/34	40.00	100.00
59LO Thurman Thomas/25	15.00	40.00
60BA Tony Dorsett/50	10.00	25.00
60DE Tony Dorsett/77	8.00	20.00
60JN Tony Dorsett AU/33	40.00	100.00
60LO Tony Dorsett/25	15.00	40.00
61BA Troy Aikman/50	12.00	30.00
61DE Troy Aikman/89	8.00	20.00
61LO Troy Aikman/25	20.00	50.00
62BA Walter Payton/50	30.00	80.00
62DE Walter Payton/75	25.00	60.00
62JN Walter Payton/34	40.00	100.00
62LO Walter Payton/25	50.00	120.00
63BA Warren Moon/50	8.00	20.00
63DE Warren Moon/84	6.00	15.00
63LO Warren Moon/25	12.00	30.00
64BA Michael Vick/50	10.00	25.00
64LO Michael Vick/25	15.00	40.00
65BA Emmitt Smith/50	20.00	50.00
65DE Emmitt Smith/90	15.00	40.00

65JN Emmitt Smith/22	30.00	80.00
65LO Emmitt Smith/25	30.00	80.00
66BA Brett Favre/50	20.00	50.00
66DE Brett Favre/91	15.00	40.00
66LO Brett Favre/25	30.00	80.00
67BA Edgerrin James/50	8.00	20.00
67DE Edgerrin James/99	6.00	15.00
67JN Edgerrin James/32	10.00	25.00
67LO Edgerrin James/25	12.00	30.00
68BA Peyton Manning/50	15.00	40.00
68DE Peyton Manning/98	12.00	30.00
68LO Peyton Manning/25	25.00	60.00
69BA Priest Holmes/50	8.00	20.00
69DE Priest Holmes/98	6.00	15.00
69JN Priest Holmes AU/31	40.00	100.00
69LO Priest Holmes/25	12.00	30.00
70BA Randy Moss/50	8.00	20.00
70DE Randy Moss/98	6.00	15.00
70JN Randy Moss/84	6.00	15.00
70LO Randy Moss/25	12.00	30.00
71BA Jerry Rice/50	15.00	40.00
71DE Jerry Rice/85	12.00	30.00
71JN Jerry Rice/80	12.00	30.00
71LO Jerry Rice/25	25.00	60.00
72BA Donovan McNabb/50	8.00	20.00
72DE Donovan McNabb/99	6.00	15.00
72LO Donovan McNabb/25	12.00	30.00
73BA LaDainian Tomlinson/50	8.00	20.00
73JN LaDainian Tomlinson/21	12.00	30.00
73LO LaDainian Tomlinson/25	12.00	30.00
74BA Marshall Faulk/50	8.00	20.00
74DE Marshall Faulk/94	6.00	15.00
74JN Marshall Faulk/28	12.00	30.00
74LO Marshall Faulk/25	12.00	30.00
75BA Kurt Warner/50	8.00	20.00
75DE Kurt Warner/99	6.00	15.00
75LO Kurt Warner/25	12.00	30.00
76BA David Carr/50	6.00	15.00
76LO David Carr/25	10.00	25.00
77BA Joey Harrington/50	5.00	12.00
77LO Joey Harrington/25	8.00	20.00
78BA Clinton Portis/50	6.00	15.00
78JN Clinton Portis AU/26	30.00	80.00
78LO Clinton Portis/25	10.00	25.00
79BA Roy Williams/50	6.00	15.00
79JN Roy Williams/31	8.00	20.00
79LO Roy Williams/25	10.00	25.00
80BA Jerome Bettis/50	8.00	20.00
80DE Jerome Bettis/93	6.00	15.00
80JN Jerome Bettis AU/36	100.00	200.00
80LO Jerome Bettis/25	12.00	30.00
81BA Tim Brown/50	8.00	20.00
81DE Tim Brown/88	6.00	15.00
81JN Tim Brown/81	6.00	15.00
81LO Tim Brown/25	12.00	30.00
82BA Jeff Garcia/50	6.00	15.00
82DE Jeff Garcia/99	5.00	12.00
82LO Jeff Garcia/25	10.00	25.00
83BA Eddie George/50	6.00	15.00
83DE Eddie George/96	5.00	12.00
83JN Eddie George/27	10.00	25.00
83LO Eddie George/25	10.00	25.00
84BA Ahman Green/50	6.00	15.00
84DE Ahman Green/98	5.00	12.00
84JN Ahman Green/30	8.00	20.00
84LO Ahman Green/25	10.00	25.00
85BA Ed McCaffrey/50	6.00	15.00
85DE Ed McCaffrey/91	5.00	12.00
85JN Ed McCaffrey/87	5.00	12.00
85LO Ed McCaffrey/25	10.00	25.00
86BA Steve McNair/50	8.00	20.00
86DE Steve McNair/95	6.00	15.00
86LO Steve McNair/25	12.00	30.00
87BA Terrell Owens/50	8.00	20.00
87DE Terrell Owens/96	6.00	15.00
87JN Terrell Owens/81	6.00	15.00
87LO Terrell Owens/25	12.00	30.00
88BA Zach Thomas/50	8.00	20.00
88DE Zach Thomas/96	6.00	15.00
88JN Zach Thomas AU/54	30.00	80.00
88LO Zach Thomas/25	12.00	30.00
89BA Michael Bennett/50	6.00	15.00
89JN Michael Bennett AU/23	20.00	50.00
89LO Michael Bennett/25	10.00	25.00
90BA Rich Gannon/50	6.00	15.00
90DE Rich Gannon/87	5.00	12.00
90LO Rich Gannon/25	10.00	25.00
91BA Tony Gonzalez/50	8.00	20.00
91DE Tony Gonzalez/97	6.00	15.00
91JN Tony Gonzalez/88	6.00	15.00
91LO Tony Gonzalez/25	12.00	30.00
92BA Garrison Hearst/50	6.00	15.00
92DE Garrison Hearst/93	5.00	12.00
92JN Garrison Hearst/20	10.00	25.00
92LO Garrison Hearst/25	10.00	25.00
93BA Jevon Kearse/50	6.00	15.00
93DE Jevon Kearse/99	5.00	12.00
93JN Jevon Kearse/90	5.00	12.00
93LO Jevon Kearse/25	10.00	25.00
94BA Santana Moss/50	6.00	15.00
94JN Santana Moss AU/83	15.00	40.00
94LO Santana Moss/25	10.00	25.00
95BA Eric Moulds/50	6.00	15.00
95DE Eric Moulds/96	5.00	12.00
95JN Eric Moulds/80	5.00	12.00
95LO Eric Moulds/25	10.00	25.00
96BA Mike Alstott/50	8.00	20.00
96DE Mike Alstott/96	6.00	15.00
96JN Mike Alstott/40	10.00	25.00
96LO Mike Alstott/25	12.00	30.00
97BA Anthony Thomas/50	6.00	15.00
97JN Anthony Thomas/35	8.00	20.00
97LO Anthony Thomas/25	10.00	25.00
98BA Daunte Culpepper/50	6.00	15.00
98DE Daunte Culpepper/99	5.00	12.00
98LO Daunte Culpepper/25	10.00	25.00
99BA Junior Seau/50	8.00	20.00
99DE Junior Seau/90	6.00	15.00
99JN Junior Seau/55	8.00	20.00
99LO Junior Seau/25	12.00	30.00
100BA Warren Sapp/50	6.00	15.00
100DE Warren Sapp/96	5.00	12.00
100JN Warren Sapp/99	5.00	12.00
100LO Warren Sapp/25	10.00	25.00

2003 Leaf Certified Materials Mirror Signatures

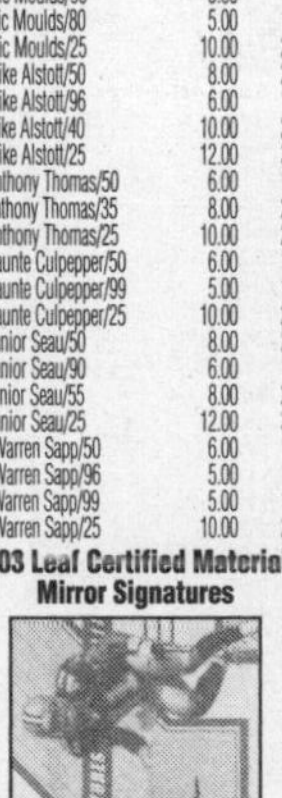

STATED PRINT RUN 25-100

MS1 Jim Brown/100	40.00	80.00
MS2 Joe Montana/100	75.00	150.00
MS3 John Riggins/100	15.00	40.00
MS4 Randy White/100	15.00	40.00
MS5 Terry Bradshaw/100	50.00	80.00
MS6 Deion Branch/50	12.00	30.00
MS7 Jeff Garcia/25	15.00	40.00
MS8 Joe Horn/50	10.00	25.00
MS9 Joey Harrington/25	15.00	40.00
MS10 Kurt Warner/100	20.00	40.00
MS11 Randy Moss/25	50.00	100.00
MS12 Tim Brown/25	20.00	50.00
MS13 Torry Holt/25	15.00	40.00
MS14 Zach Thomas/25	15.00	40.00
MS15 Byron Leftwich/25	25.00	60.00
MS16 Carson Palmer/25	100.00	200.00
MS17 Charles Rogers/25	10.00	25.00
MS18 Larry Johnson/25	25.00	60.00
MS19 Bryant Johnson/50	12.00	30.00
MS20 Kelley Washington/50	12.00	30.00
MS21 Terrell Suggs/50	20.00	40.00
MS22 Terence Newman/100	12.00	30.00
MS23 Musa Smith/100	8.00	20.00
MS24 Dave Ragone/100	8.00	20.00
MS25 Chris Brown/100	8.00	20.00

2003 Leaf Certified Materials Potential

STATED PRINT RUN 125 SER.#'d SETS

CP1 Antonio Bryant	3.00	8.00
CP2 Antwaan Randle El	4.00	10.00
CP3 Ashley Lelie	3.00	8.00
CP4 Chris Chambers	4.00	10.00
CP5 Clinton Portis	4.00	10.00
CP6 David Carr	4.00	10.00
CP7 Drew Brees	5.00	12.00
CP8 Javon Walker	4.00	10.00
CP9 Jeremy Shockey	5.00	12.00
CP10 Joey Harrington	3.00	8.00
CP11 Josh Reed	3.00	8.00
CP12 Julius Peppers	5.00	12.00
CP13 Koren Robinson	4.00	10.00
CP14 LaDainian Tomlinson	5.00	12.00
CP15 Marcel Shipp	3.00	8.00
CP16 Roy Williams	4.00	10.00
CP17 T.J. Duckett	4.00	10.00
CP18 Travis Henry	3.00	8.00

2003 Leaf Certified Materials Skills

STATED PRINT RUN 100 SER.#'d SETS

CS1 Rich Gannon	4.00	10.00
CS2 Drew Bledsoe	5.00	12.00
CS3 Peyton Manning	10.00	25.00
CS4 Kerry Collins	4.00	10.00
CS5 Daunte Culpepper	4.00	10.00
CS6 Tom Brady	12.00	30.00
CS7 Trent Green	4.00	10.00
CS8 Brett Favre	12.00	30.00
CS9 Aaron Brooks	4.00	10.00
CS10 Steve McNair	5.00	12.00
CS11 Jeff Garcia	4.00	10.00
CS12 Drew Brees	5.00	12.00
CS13 Brian Griese	4.00	10.00
CS14 Chad Pennington	5.00	12.00
CS15 Brad Johnson	4.00	10.00
CS16 Ricky Williams	4.00	10.00
CS17 LaDainian Tomlinson	5.00	12.00
CS18 Priest Holmes	5.00	12.00
CS19 Clinton Portis	4.00	10.00
CS20 Travis Henry	3.00	8.00
CS21 Deuce McAllister	4.00	10.00
CS22 Tiki Barber	5.00	12.00
CS23 Jamal Lewis	4.00	10.00
CS24 Fred Taylor	4.00	10.00
CS25 Corey Dillon	4.00	10.00
CS26 Michael Bennett	4.00	10.00
CS27 Ahman Green	4.00	10.00
CS28 Shaun Alexander	4.00	10.00
CS29 Eddie George	4.00	10.00
CS30 Curtis Martin	5.00	12.00
CS31 Duce Staley	4.00	10.00
CS32 James Stewart	3.00	8.00
CS33 Marvin Harrison	5.00	12.00
CS34 Randy Moss	5.00	12.00
CS35 Amani Toomer	4.00	10.00
CS36 Hines Ward	5.00	12.00
CS37 Plaxico Burress	4.00	10.00
CS38 Torry Holt	5.00	12.00
CS39 Terrell Owens	5.00	12.00
CS40 Eric Moulds	4.00	10.00
CS41 Laveranues Coles	3.00	8.00
CS42 Peerless Price	3.00	8.00
CS43 Koren Robinson	4.00	10.00
CS44 Jerry Rice	10.00	25.00
CS45 Emmitt Smith	12.00	30.00
CS46 Keyshawn Johnson	5.00	12.00
CS47 Isaac Bruce	5.00	12.00
CS48 Donald Driver	5.00	12.00
CS49 Jimmy Smith	4.00	10.00
CS50 Rod Smith	4.00	10.00

2003 Leaf Certified Materials Samples

Inserted one per Beckett Football Card Monthly, these cards parallel the basic Certified Materials cards. Each can be noted by the word "Sample" stamped in silver on the back.

*SAMPLES: .8X TO 2X BASIC CARDS

2004 Leaf Certified Materials

Leaf Certified Materials initially released in early October 2004. The base set consists of 233-cards including 50-rookie or rookie autographs serial numbered of 1000 and 33-jersey rookie cards. Hobby boxes contained 10-packs of 5-cards and carried an S.R.P. of $15 per pack. Six parallel sets and a variety of inserts can be found seeded in hobby and retail packs highlighted by the multi-tiered Material game used jerseys and Signatures autographed inserts.

COMP.SET w/o SP's (150) 12.50 30.00
151-200 ROOKIE AU PRINT RUN 1000
201-233 ROOKIE JSY PRINT RUN 1250
UNPRICED MIRROR BLACK PRINT RUN 1
UNPRICED MIRR.EMERALD PRINT RUN 5

1 Anquan Boldin	.40	1.00
2 Emmitt Smith	1.00	2.50
3 Josh McCown	.30	.75
4 Marcel Shipp	.25	.60
5 Michael Vick	.50	1.25
6 Peerless Price	.25	.60
7 T.J. Duckett	.30	.75
8 Warrick Dunn	.30	.75
9 Jamal Lewis	.30	.75
10 Kyle Boller	.30	.75
11 Ray Lewis	.40	1.00
12 Terrell Suggs	.30	.75
13 Todd Heap	.30	.75
14 Drew Bledsoe	.40	1.00
15 Eric Moulds	.30	.75
16 Travis Henry	.25	.60
17 Julius Peppers	.30	.75
18 Muhsin Muhammad	.30	.75
19 Stephen Davis	.30	.75
20 Anthony Thomas	.30	.75
21 Brian Urlacher	.40	1.00
22 Rex Grossman	.30	.75
23 Chad Johnson	.40	1.00
24 Corey Dillon	.30	.75
25 Peter Warrick	.30	.75
26 Jeff Garcia	.30	.75
27 Tim Couch	.30	.75
28 William Green	.25	.60
29 Antonio Bryant	.30	.75
30 Keyshawn Johnson	.30	.75
31 Quincy Carter	.25	.60
32 Roy Williams S	.30	.75
33 Terence Newman	.30	.75
34 Ashley Lelie	.25	.60
35 Ed McCaffrey	.40	1.00
36 Jake Plummer	.30	.75
37 Mike Anderson	.30	.75
38 Rod Smith	.30	.75
39 Charles Rogers	.25	.60
40 Joey Harrington	.30	.75
41 Ahman Green	.30	.75
42 Brett Favre	1.00	2.50
43 Donald Driver	.40	1.00
44 Javon Walker	.25	.60
45 Robert Ferguson	.25	.60
46 Andre Johnson	.40	1.00
47 David Carr	.25	.60
48 Edgerrin James	.30	.75
49 Marvin Harrison	.40	1.00
50 Peyton Manning	.75	2.00
51 Reggie Wayne	.40	1.00
52 Byron Leftwich	.30	.75
53 Fred Taylor	.30	.75
54 Jimmy Smith	.30	.75
55 Dante Hall	.30	.75
56 Priest Holmes	.40	1.00
57 Tony Gonzalez	.40	1.00
58 Trent Green	.30	.75
59 A.J. Feeley	.25	.60
60 Chris Chambers	.30	.75
61 David Boston	.25	.60
62 Jason Taylor	.30	.75
63 Jay Fiedler	.25	.60
64 Junior Seau	.40	1.00
65 Randy McMichael	.25	.60
66 Ricky Williams	.30	.75
67 Zach Thomas	.40	1.00
68 Daunte Culpepper	.30	.75
69 Michael Bennett	.30	.75
70 Randy Moss	.40	1.00
71 Tom Brady	.75	2.00
72 Troy Brown	.30	.75
73 Ty Law	.30	.75
74 Aaron Brooks	.30	.75
75 Deuce McAllister	.30	.75
76 Donte Stallworth	.25	.60
77 Amani Toomer	.30	.75
78 Jeremy Shockey	.30	.75
79 Kerry Collins	.30	.75
80 Michael Strahan	.40	1.00
81 Tiki Barber	.40	1.00
82 Chad Pennington	.40	1.00
83 Curtis Martin	.40	1.00
84 Justin McCareins	.25	.60
85 Santana Moss	.30	.75
86 Charles Woodson	.40	1.00
87 Jerry Rice	.75	2.00
88 Rich Gannon	.30	.75
89 Tim Brown	.40	1.00
90 Warren Sapp	.30	.75
91 Correll Buckhalter	.30	.75
92 Donovan McNabb	.40	1.00
93 Freddie Mitchell	.25	.60
94 Jevon Kearse	.30	.75
95 Terrell Owens	.40	1.00
96 Antwaan Randle El	.30	.75
97 Duce Staley	.30	.75
98 Hines Ward	.40	1.00
99 Jerome Bettis	.40	1.00
100 Plaxico Burress	.30	.75
101 Doug Flutie	.40	1.00
102 LaDainian Tomlinson	.40	1.00
103 Koren Robinson	.25	.60
104 Matt Hasselbeck	.30	.75
105 Shaun Alexander	.30	.75
106 Isaac Bruce	.30	.75
107 Kurt Warner	.40	1.00
108 Marc Bulger	.30	.75
109 Marshall Faulk	.40	1.00
110 Torry Holt	.30	.75
111 Brad Johnson	.30	.75
112 Mike Alstott	.30	.75
113 Derrick Mason	.30	.75
114 Drew Bennett	.30	.75
115 Eddie George	.30	.75
116 Frank Wycheck	.30	.75
117 Keith Bulluck	.25	.60
118 Steve McNair	.40	1.00
119 Tyrone Calico	.30	.75
120 Clinton Portis	.40	1.00
121 LaVar Arrington	.30	.75
122 Laveranues Coles	.25	.60
123 Mark Brunell	.30	.75
124 Patrick Ramsey	.30	.75
125 Rod Gardner	.25	.60
126 Jake Plummer FLB	.30	.75
127 Thomas Jones FLB	.40	1.00
128 Priest Holmes FLB	.40	1.00
129 Jim Kelly FLB	.60	1.50
130 Doug Flutie FLB	.40	1.00
131 Walter Payton FLB	2.50	6.00
132 Troy Aikman FLB	1.00	2.50
133 John Elway FLB	1.50	4.00
134 Barry Sanders FLB	1.25	3.00
135 Mark Brunell FLB	.30	.75
136 Earl Campbell FLB	.60	1.50
137 Joe Montana FLB	1.50	4.00
138 Dan Marino FLB	1.50	4.00
139 Curtis Martin FLB	.40	1.00
140 Drew Bledsoe FLB	.40	1.00
141 Ricky Williams FLB	.30	.75
142 Junior Seau FLB	.40	1.00
143 Charlie Garner FLB	.30	.75
144 Jerry Rice FLB	.75	2.00
145 Ahman Green FLB	.30	.75
146 Jerome Bettis FLB	.40	1.00
147 Trent Green FLB	.30	.75
148 Warrick Dunn FLB	.30	.75
149 Deion Sanders FLB	.40	1.00
150 Stephen Davis FLB	.30	.75
151 Adimchinobe Echemandu AU RC	3.00	8.00
152 Ahmad Carroll RC	1.25	3.00
153 Andy Hall AU RC	2.50	6.00
154 B.J. Johnson AU RC	2.50	6.00
155 B.J. Symons AU RC	2.50	6.00
156 Bradlee Van Pelt AU RC	3.00	8.00
157 Brandon Miree AU RC	2.50	6.00
158 Bruce Perry AU RC	2.50	6.00
159 Carlos Francis AU RC	2.50	6.00
160 Casey Bramlet AU RC	2.50	6.00
161 Chris Gamble RC	1.50	4.00
162 Clarence Moore AU RC	2.50	6.00
163 Cody Pickett AU RC	3.00	8.00
164 Craig Krenzel AU RC	3.00	8.00
165 D.J. Hackett RC	1.50	4.00
166 D.J. Williams RC	2.00	5.00
167 Derrick Ward AU RC	4.00	10.00
168 Drew Carter AU RC	3.00	8.00
169 Ernest Wilford RC	1.50	4.00
170 Drew Henson RC	1.25	3.00
171 Jamaar Taylor AU RC	2.50	6.00
172 Jared Lorenzen AU RC	3.00	8.00
173 Jarrett Payton AU RC	3.00	8.00
174 Jason Babin AU RC	4.00	10.00
175 Jeff Smoker AU RC	3.00	8.00
176 Jeris McIntyre AU RC	2.50	6.00
177 Jerricho Cotchery RC	1.50	4.00
178 Jim Sorgi AU RC	3.00	8.00
179 John Navarre AU RC	2.50	6.00
180 Patrick Crayton AU RC	4.00	10.00
181 Johnnie Morant RC	1.25	3.00
182 Sean Taylor RC	4.00	10.00
183 Jonathan Vilma RC	2.00	5.00
184 Josh Harris RC	1.25	3.00
185 Kenechi Udeze RC	1.50	4.00
186 Mark Jones AU RC	2.50	6.00
187 Matt Mauck AU RC	2.50	6.00
188 Maurice Mann AU RC	2.50	6.00
189 Michael Turner RC	2.50	6.00
190 P.K. Sam RC	1.25	3.00
191 Quincy Wilson RC	1.50	4.00
192 Ran Carthon AU RC	2.50	6.00
193 Ryan Krause AU RC	2.50	6.00
194 Samie Parker RC	1.25	3.00
195 Sloan Thomas AU RC	3.00	8.00
196 Tommie Harris RC	2.00	5.00
197 Triandos Luke AU RC	2.50	6.00
198 Troy Fleming AU RC	2.50	6.00
199 Vince Wilfork RC	2.00	5.00
200 Will Smith RC	1.50	4.00
201 Larry Fitzgerald JSY RC	6.00	15.00
202 DeAngelo Hall JSY RC	2.50	6.00
203 Matt Schaub JSY RC	5.00	12.00
204 Michael Jenkins JSY RC	2.50	6.00
205 Devard Darling JSY RC	1.50	4.00
206 J.P. Losman JSY RC	2.00	5.00
207 Lee Evans JSY RC	2.50	6.00
208 Keary Colbert JSY RC	1.50	4.00
209 Bernard Berrian JSY RC	2.50	6.00
210 Chris Perry JSY RC	2.00	5.00
211 Kellen Winslow JSY RC	2.50	6.00
212 Luke McCown JSY RC	2.00	5.00
213 Julius Jones JSY RC	2.00	5.00
214 Darius Watts JSY RC	1.50	4.00
215 Tatum Bell JSY RC	2.00	5.00
216 Kevin Jones JSY RC	2.00	5.00
217 Roy Williams JSY RC	2.50	6.00
218 Dunta Robinson JSY RC	1.50	4.00
219 Greg Jones JSY RC	1.50	4.00
220 Reggie Williams JSY RC	2.00	5.00
221 Mewelde Moore JSY RC	2.00	5.00
222 Ben Watson JSY RC	2.50	6.00
223 Cedric Cobbs JSY RC	1.50	4.00
224 Devery Henderson JSY RC	2.50	6.00
225 Eli Manning JSY RC	15.00	40.00
226 Robert Gallery JSY RC	2.50	6.00
227 Ben Roethlisberger JSY RC	15.00	40.00
228 Philip Rivers JSY RC	10.00	25.00
229 Derrick Hamilton JSY RC	1.50	4.00
230 Rashaun Woods JSY RC	1.50	4.00
231 Steven Jackson JSY RC	4.00	10.00
232 Michael Clayton JSY RC	2.00	5.00
233 Ben Troupe JSY RC	2.00	5.00

2004 Leaf Certified Materials Mirror Blue

*VETS 1-150: 1X TO 2.5X MIRROR WHITE
*ROOKIES 151-200: 1X TO 2.5X MIR.WHITE
STATED PRINT RUN 50 SER.#'d SETS

2004 Leaf Certified Materials Mirror Gold

*VETS 1-150: 1.5X TO 4X MIRROR WHITE
*ROOKIES 151-200: 1.5X TO 4X MIRR.WHITE
STATED PRINT RUN 25 SER.#'d SETS

2004 Leaf Certified Materials Mirror Red

*VETS 1-150: .5X TO 1.2X MIRROR WHITE
*ROOKIES 151-200: .5X TO 1.2X MIR.WHITE
STATED PRINT RUN 100 SER.#'d SETS

2004 Leaf Certified Materials Mirror White

*VETS 1-150: 2X TO 5X BASIC CARDS

COMMON ROOKIE (151-200)	1.25	3.00
ROOKIE SEMISTARS 151-200	1.50	4.00
ROOKIE UNL.STARS 151-200	2.00	5.00

STATED PRINT RUN 150 SER.#'d SETS

189 Michael Turner	2.50	6.00

2004 Leaf Certified Materials Certified Potential Jersey

STATED PRINT RUN 150 SER.#'d SETS
*INFINITE/75: .5X TO 1.2X BASIC JSY
INFINITE PRINT RUN 75 SER.#'d SETS
*INFINITE PRIME/25: 1.2X TO 3X BASIC JSY
INFIN.PRIME PRINT RUN 25 SER.#'d SETS
UNPRICED BLACK PRINT RUN 1 SET

CP1 A.J. Feeley	2.50	6.00
CP2 Andre Johnson	4.00	10.00
CP3 Anquan Boldin	4.00	10.00
CP4 Antonio Bryant	3.00	8.00
CP5 Antwaan Randle El	3.00	8.00
CP6 Ashley Lelie	2.50	6.00
CP7 Bryant Johnson	2.50	6.00
CP8 Byron Leftwich	3.00	8.00
CP9 Charles Rogers	2.50	6.00
CP10 Correll Buckhalter	3.00	8.00
CP11 Dallas Clark	4.00	10.00
CP12 David Carr	2.50	6.00
CP13 Donte Stallworth	2.50	6.00
CP14 Drew Bennett	3.00	8.00
CP15 Javon Walker	2.50	6.00
CP16 Joey Harrington	3.00	8.00
CP17 Josh McCown	3.00	8.00
CP18 Justin McCareins	2.50	6.00
CP19 Kyle Boller	3.00	8.00
CP20 Marcel Shipp	2.50	6.00
CP21 Nick Barnett	3.00	8.00
CP22 Rex Grossman	3.00	8.00
CP23 Terence Newman	3.00	8.00
CP24 Terrell Suggs	3.00	8.00
CP25 Tyrone Calico	3.00	8.00

2004 Leaf Certified Materials Certified Skills Jersey

STATED PRINT RUN 175 SER.#'d SETS
*POSITION/75: .5X TO 1.2X BASIC JSY
POSITION PRINT RUN 75 SER.#'d SETS
*POSITION PRIME/25: 1.2X TO 3X BASIC JSY
POSIT.PRIME PRINT RUN 25 SER.#'d SETS
UNPRICED BLACK PRINT RUN 1 SET

CS1 Peyton Manning	10.00	25.00
CS2 Trent Green	4.00	10.00
CS3 Marc Bulger	4.00	10.00
CS4 Matt Hasselbeck	4.00	10.00
CS5 Brad Johnson	4.00	10.00
CS6 Tom Brady	10.00	25.00
CS7 Aaron Brooks	4.00	10.00
CS8 Daunte Culpepper	4.00	10.00
CS9 Brett Favre	12.00	30.00
CS10 Quincy Carter	3.00	8.00
CS11 Donovan McNabb	5.00	12.00
CS12 Steve McNair	5.00	12.00
CS13 Kerry Collins	4.00	10.00
CS14 Dan Marino	12.00	30.00
CS15 John Elway	12.00	30.00
CS16 Warren Moon	5.00	12.00
CS17 Fran Tarkenton	5.00	12.00
CS18 Brett Favre	12.00	30.00
CS19 Joe Montana	12.00	30.00
CS20 Jamal Lewis	4.00	10.00
CS21 Ahman Green	4.00	10.00
CS22 LaDainian Tomlinson	5.00	12.00
CS23 Deuce McAllister	4.00	10.00
CS24 Clinton Portis	5.00	12.00
CS25 Fred Taylor	4.00	10.00
CS26 Stephen Davis	4.00	10.00
CS27 Shaun Alexander	4.00	10.00
CS28 Priest Holmes	5.00	12.00
CS29 Ricky Williams	4.00	10.00
CS30 Travis Henry	3.00	8.00
CS31 Curtis Martin	5.00	12.00
CS32 Edgerrin James	4.00	10.00
CS33 Tiki Barber	5.00	12.00
CS34 Eddie George	4.00	10.00
CS35 Anthony Thomas	4.00	10.00
CS36 Emmitt Smith	12.00	30.00
CS37 Walter Payton	20.00	50.00
CS38 Barry Sanders	10.00	25.00
CS39 Torry Holt	4.00	10.00
CS40 Randy Moss	5.00	12.00
CS41 Anquan Boldin	5.00	12.00
CS42 Chad Johnson	5.00	12.00
CS43 Derrick Mason	4.00	10.00
CS44 Marvin Harrison	5.00	12.00
CS45 Laveranues Coles	3.00	8.00
CS46 Hines Ward	5.00	12.00
CS47 Santana Moss	4.00	10.00
CS48 Terrell Owens	5.00	12.00
CS49 Jerry Rice	10.00	25.00
CS50 Tim Brown	5.00	12.00

2004 Leaf Certified Materials Fabric of the Game

STATED PRINT RUN 100 SER.#'d SETS
*21st CENT/21: 1.2X TO 3X BASIC JSY
21st CENTURY PRINT RUN 21
*DEBUT YEAR/70-103: .4X TO 1X
*DEBUT YEAR/50-69: .5X TO 1.2X
*DEBUT YEAR/15: 1.2X TO 3X
UNPRICED TEAM LOGO PRINT RUN 5

FG1 Aaron Brooks	4.00	10.00
FG2 Ahman Green	4.00	10.00
FG3 Andre Johnson	5.00	12.00
FG4 Anquan Boldin	5.00	12.00
FG5 Antwaan Randle El	4.00	10.00
FG6 Barry Sanders	12.00	30.00
FG7 Bart Starr	15.00	40.00
FG8 Bob Griese	6.00	15.00
FG9 Brett Favre	12.00	30.00
FG10 Brian Urlacher	5.00	12.00
FG11 Bruce Smith	6.00	15.00
FG12 Byron Leftwich	4.00	10.00
FG13 Chad Johnson	5.00	12.00
FG14 Chad Pennington	5.00	12.00
FG15 Charles Rogers	3.00	8.00
FG16 Charles Woodson	5.00	12.00
FG17 Chris Chambers	4.00	10.00
FG18 Clinton Portis	5.00	12.00
FG19 Dan Marino	15.00	40.00
FG20 Daryl Johnston	6.00	15.00
FG21 Daunte Culpepper	4.00	10.00
FG22 David Carr	3.00	8.00
FG23 Deacon Jones	5.00	12.00
FG24 Deion Sanders	6.00	15.00
FG25 Derrick Mason	4.00	10.00
FG26 Deuce McAllister	4.00	10.00
FG27 Doak Walker	10.00	25.00
FG28 Don Maynard	5.00	12.00
FG29 Don Shula	6.00	15.00
FG30 Donovan McNabb	5.00	12.00
FG31 Drew Bledsoe	5.00	12.00
FG32 Earl Campbell	6.00	15.00
FG33 Eddie George	4.00	10.00
FG34 Edgerrin James	4.00	10.00
FG35 Emmitt Smith	12.00	30.00
FG36 Fran Tarkenton	6.00	15.00
FG37 Franco Harris	8.00	20.00
FG38 Fred Biletnikoff	6.00	15.00
FG39 George Blanda	6.00	15.00
FG40 Harvey Martin	4.00	10.00
FG41 Herman Edwards	5.00	12.00
FG42 Hines Ward	5.00	12.00
FG43 Jake Plummer	4.00	10.00
FG44 Jamal Lewis	4.00	10.00
FG45 James Lofton	4.00	10.00
FG46 Javon Walker	3.00	8.00
FG47 Jeremy Shockey	4.00	10.00
FG48 Jerry Rice	10.00	25.00
FG49 Jim Brown	10.00	25.00
FG50 Jim Kelly	6.00	15.00
FG51 Jim Plunkett	5.00	12.00
FG52 Jim Thorpe	60.00	120.00
FG53 Joe Greene	6.00	15.00
FG54 Joe Montana	15.00	40.00
FG55 Joe Namath	12.00	30.00
FG56 Joey Harrington	4.00	10.00
FG57 John Elway	15.00	40.00
FG58 John Riggins	6.00	15.00
FG59 Kendrell Bell	3.00	8.00
FG60 L.C. Greenwood	5.00	12.00
FG61 LaDainian Tomlinson	5.00	12.00
FG62 Lawrence Taylor	6.00	15.00
FG63 Leroy Kelly	5.00	12.00
FG64 Lynn Swann	12.00	30.00
FG65 Marc Bulger	4.00	10.00
FG66 Mark Bavaro	4.00	10.00
FG67 Marshall Faulk	5.00	12.00
FG68 Matt Hasselbeck	4.00	10.00
FG69 Mel Blount	5.00	12.00
FG70 Michael Irvin	6.00	15.00
FG71 Michael Vick	8.00	20.00
FG72 Mike Singletary	6.00	15.00
FG73 Ozzie Newsome	5.00	12.00
FG74 Paul Warfield	5.00	12.00
FG75 Peyton Manning	10.00	25.00
FG76 Priest Holmes	5.00	12.00
FG77 Quincy Carter	3.00	8.00
FG78 Randy Moss	5.00	12.00
FG79 Ray Nitschke	12.00	25.00
FG80 Reggie White	6.00	15.00
FG81 Rex Grossman	4.00	10.00
FG82 Richard Dent	4.00	10.00
FG83 Ricky Williams	4.00	10.00
FG84 Roger Staubach	10.00	25.00
FG85 Roy Williams S	4.00	10.00
FG86 Santana Moss	4.00	10.00
FG87 Shaun Alexander	4.00	10.00
FG88 Sterling Sharpe	5.00	12.00
FG89 Steve McNair	5.00	12.00
FG90 Terrell Davis	6.00	15.00
FG91 Terry Bradshaw	10.00	25.00
FG92 Thurman Thomas	5.00	12.00
FG93 Tiki Barber	5.00	12.00
FG94 Todd Heap	4.00	10.00
FG95 Tom Brady	10.00	25.00
FG96 Tony Dorsett	6.00	15.00
FG97 Trent Green	4.00	10.00
FG98 Troy Aikman	10.00	25.00
FG99 Walter Payton	20.00	50.00
FG100 Warren Moon	5.00	12.00

2004 Leaf Certified Materials Fabric of the Game Jersey Number

*JERSEY/66-99: .5X TO 1.2X BASIC INSERTS
*JERSEY/32-37: .8X TO 2X BASIC INSERTS
*JERSEY/22-28: 1X TO 2.5X BASIC INSERTS
*JERSEY/10-18: 1.2X TO 3X BASIC INSERTS
STATED PRINT RUN 1-97
JSY's #'d UNDER 10 NOT PRICED
JSY AU's #'d UNDER 20 NOT PRICED

FG2 Ahman Green AU/30	20.00	50.00
FG4 Anquan Boldin AU/81	15.00	40.00
FG5 Antwaan Randle El AU/82	15.00	40.00
FG6 Barry Sanders AU/20	75.00	150.00
FG10 Brian Urlacher AU/54	30.00	60.00
FG13 Chad Johnson AU/85	20.00	50.00
FG17 Chris Chambers AU/84	15.00	40.00
FG18 Clinton Portis AU/26	25.00	60.00
FG20 Daryl Johnston AU/48	20.00	50.00
FG23 Deacon Jones AU/75	15.00	40.00
FG24 Deion Sanders AU/21	60.00	120.00
FG25 Derrick Mason AU/85	12.00	30.00
FG26 Deuce McAllister AU/26	25.00	60.00
FG29 Don Shula AU/25	30.00	80.00
FG32 Earl Campbell AU/34	30.00	80.00
FG33 Eddie George AU/27	25.00	50.00
FG34 Edgerrin James/32	8.00	20.00
FG35 Emmitt Smith/22	30.00	80.00
FG37 Franco Harris AU/32	50.00	100.00
FG38 Fred Biletnikoff AU/25	30.00	80.00
FG40 Harvey Martin/79	5.00	12.00
FG41 Herman Edwards AU/46	12.00	30.00
FG42 Hines Ward AU/86	40.00	80.00
FG44 Jamal Lewis AU/31	20.00	50.00
FG45 James Lofton AU/80	12.00	30.00
FG46 Javon Walker AU/84	12.00	30.00
FG49 Jim Brown AU/32	60.00	120.00
FG53 Joe Greene AU/75	35.00	60.00
FG58 John Riggins AU/44	25.00	60.00
FG59 Kendrell Bell AU/97	12.00	30.00
FG60 L.C. Greenwood AU/68	40.00	80.00
FG61 LaDainian Tomlinson AU/21	40.00	100.00
FG62 Lawrence Taylor AU/56	60.00	100.00
FG63 Leroy Kelly AU/44	20.00	50.00
FG66 Mark Bavaro AU/89	20.00	50.00
FG69 Mel Blount AU/47	25.00	60.00
FG70 Michael Irvin AU/88	30.00	60.00
FG72 Mike Singletary AU/50	20.00	50.00
FG73 Ozzie Newsome AU/82	15.00	40.00
FG74 Paul Warfield AU/42	25.00	60.00
FG76 Priest Holmes AU/31	20.00	50.00
FG80 Reggie White AU/92	250.00	400.00
FG82 Richard Dent AU/95	12.00	30.00
FG85 Roy Williams S AU/31	20.00	50.00
FG86 Santana Moss AU/83	12.00	30.00
FG87 Shaun Alexander AU/37	25.00	60.00
FG88 Sterling Sharpe AU/84	20.00	50.00
FG90 Terrell Davis AU/30	30.00	80.00
FG92 Thurman Thomas AU/34	30.00	80.00
FG93 Tiki Barber AU/21	30.00	80.00
FG94 Todd Heap AU/86	15.00	40.00
FG96 Tony Dorsett AU/33	30.00	80.00

2004 Leaf Certified Materials Gold Team Jersey

STATED PRINT RUN 150 SER.#'d SETS
*24K/75: .5X TO 1.2X BASIC JSY
24K PRINT RUN 75 SER.#'d SETS
*24K PRIME/25: 1X TO 2.5X BASIC JSY
24K PRIME PRINT RUN 25 SER.#'d SETS
UNPRICED BLACK PRINT RUN 1 SET

GT1 Barry Sanders	10.00	25.00
GT2 Brett Favre	12.00	30.00
GT3 Brian Urlacher	5.00	12.00
GT4 Byron Leftwich	4.00	10.00
GT5 Chad Pennington	5.00	12.00
GT6 Dan Marino	12.00	30.00
GT7 Daunte Culpepper	4.00	10.00
GT8 David Carr	3.00	8.00
GT9 Deuce McAllister	4.00	10.00
GT10 Donovan McNabb	5.00	12.00
GT11 Emmitt Smith	12.00	30.00
GT12 Jerry Rice	10.00	25.00
GT13 Joe Montana	12.00	30.00
GT14 Joey Harrington	4.00	10.00
GT15 John Elway	12.00	30.00
GT16 LaDainian Tomlinson	5.00	12.00
GT17 Michael Vick	6.00	15.00
GT18 Peyton Manning	10.00	25.00
GT19 Priest Holmes	5.00	12.00
GT20 Randy Moss	5.00	12.00
GT21 Ricky Williams	4.00	10.00
GT22 Steve McNair	5.00	12.00
GT23 Tom Brady	10.00	25.00
GT24 Troy Aikman	8.00	20.00
GT25 Walter Payton	20.00	50.00

2004 Leaf Certified Materials Mirror Red Materials

*RED ROOK.201-233: .6X TO 1.5X BASE JSY
MIRROR RED PRINT RUN 150
UNPRICED BLACK PRINT RUN 1
*BLUE/50: .8X TO 2X MIRROR RED
BLUE PRINT RUN 50 SER.#'d SETS
UNPRICED EMERALD PRINT RUN 5
*GOLD/25: 1X TO 2.5X MIRROR RED
MIRROR GOLD PRINT RUN 25
*WHITE/250: .3X TO .8X MIRROR RED
*WHITE/75: .5X TO 1.2X MIRROR RED
MIRROR WHITE PRINT RUN 75-250

1 Anquan Boldin	4.00	10.00
2 Emmitt Smith	10.00	25.00
3 Josh McCown	3.00	8.00
4 Marcel Shipp	2.50	6.00
5 Michael Vick	5.00	12.00
6 Peerless Price	2.50	6.00
7 T.J. Duckett	3.00	8.00
8 Warrick Dunn	3.00	8.00
9 Jamal Lewis	3.00	8.00
10 Kyle Boller	3.00	8.00
11 Ray Lewis	4.00	10.00
12 Terrell Suggs	3.00	8.00
13 Todd Heap	3.00	8.00
14 Drew Bledsoe	4.00	10.00
15 Eric Moulds	3.00	8.00
16 Travis Henry	2.50	6.00
17 Julius Peppers	3.00	8.00
18 Muhsin Muhammad	3.00	8.00
19 Stephen Davis	3.00	8.00
20 Anthony Thomas	3.00	8.00
21 Brian Urlacher	4.00	10.00
22 Rex Grossman	3.00	8.00
23 Chad Johnson	4.00	10.00
24 Corey Dillon	3.00	8.00
25 Peter Warrick	3.00	8.00
26 Jeff Garcia	3.00	8.00
27 Tim Couch	3.00	8.00
28 William Green	2.50	6.00
29 Antonio Bryant	3.00	8.00
30 Keyshawn Johnson	3.00	8.00
31 Quincy Carter	2.50	6.00
32 Roy Williams S	3.00	8.00
33 Terence Newman	3.00	8.00
34 Ashley Lelie	2.50	6.00
35 Ed McCaffrey	4.00	10.00
36 Jake Plummer	3.00	8.00
37 Mike Anderson	3.00	8.00
38 Rod Smith	3.00	8.00
39 Charles Rogers	2.50	6.00
40 Joey Harrington	3.00	8.00
41 Ahman Green	3.00	8.00
42 Brett Favre	10.00	25.00
43 Donald Driver	4.00	10.00
44 Javon Walker	2.50	6.00
45 Robert Ferguson	2.50	6.00
46 Andre Johnson	4.00	10.00
47 David Carr	2.50	6.00
48 Edgerrin James	3.00	8.00
49 Marvin Harrison	4.00	10.00
50 Peyton Manning	8.00	20.00
51 Reggie Wayne	4.00	10.00
52 Byron Leftwich	3.00	8.00
53 Fred Taylor	3.00	8.00
54 Jimmy Smith	3.00	8.00
55 Dante Hall	3.00	8.00
56 Priest Holmes	4.00	10.00
57 Tony Gonzalez	4.00	10.00
58 Trent Green	3.00	8.00
59 A.J. Feeley	2.50	6.00
60 Chris Chambers	3.00	8.00
61 David Boston	2.50	6.00
62 Jason Taylor	3.00	8.00
63 Jay Fiedler	2.50	6.00
64 Junior Seau	4.00	10.00
65 Randy McMichael	2.50	6.00
66 Ricky Williams	3.00	8.00
67 Zach Thomas	4.00	10.00
68 Daunte Culpepper	3.00	8.00
69 Michael Bennett	3.00	8.00
70 Randy Moss	4.00	10.00
71 Tom Brady	8.00	20.00
72 Troy Brown	3.00	8.00
73 Ty Law	3.00	8.00
74 Aaron Brooks	3.00	8.00
75 Deuce McAllister	3.00	8.00
76 Donte Stallworth	2.50	6.00
77 Amani Toomer	3.00	8.00
78 Jeremy Shockey	3.00	8.00
79 Kerry Collins	3.00	8.00
80 Michael Strahan	4.00	10.00
81 Tiki Barber	4.00	10.00
82 Chad Pennington	4.00	10.00
83 Curtis Martin	4.00	10.00
84 Justin McCareins	2.50	6.00
85 Santana Moss	3.00	8.00
86 Charles Woodson	4.00	10.00
87 Jerry Rice	8.00	20.00
88 Rich Gannon	3.00	8.00
89 Tim Brown	4.00	10.00
90 Warren Sapp	3.00	8.00
91 Correll Buckhalter	3.00	8.00
92 Donovan McNabb	4.00	10.00
93 Freddie Mitchell	2.50	6.00
94 Jevon Kearse	3.00	8.00
95 Terrell Owens	4.00	10.00
96 Antwaan Randle El	3.00	8.00
97 Duce Staley	3.00	8.00
98 Hines Ward	4.00	10.00
99 Jerome Bettis	4.00	10.00
100 Plaxico Burress	3.00	8.00
101 Doug Flutie	4.00	10.00
102 LaDainian Tomlinson	4.00	10.00
103 Koren Robinson	2.50	6.00
104 Matt Hasselbeck	3.00	8.00
105 Shaun Alexander	3.00	8.00
106 Isaac Bruce	3.00	8.00
107 Kurt Warner	4.00	10.00
108 Marc Bulger	3.00	8.00
109 Marshall Faulk	4.00	10.00
110 Torry Holt	3.00	8.00
111 Brad Johnson	3.00	8.00
112 Mike Alstott	3.00	8.00
113 Derrick Mason	3.00	8.00
114 Drew Bennett	3.00	8.00
115 Eddie George	3.00	8.00
116 Frank Wycheck	3.00	8.00
117 Keith Bulluck	2.50	6.00
118 Steve McNair	4.00	10.00
119 Tyrone Calico	3.00	8.00
120 Clinton Portis	4.00	10.00
121 LaVar Arrington	3.00	8.00
122 Laveranues Coles	2.50	6.00
123 Mark Brunell	3.00	8.00
124 Patrick Ramsey	3.00	8.00
125 Rod Gardner	2.50	6.00

126 Jake Plummer FLB 3.00 8.00
127 Thomas Jones FLB 4.00 10.00
128 Priest Holmes FLB 4.00 10.00
129 Jim Kelly FLB 5.00 12.00
130 Doug Flutie FLB 4.00 10.00
131 Walter Payton FLB 20.00 50.00
132 Troy Aikman FLB 8.00 20.00
133 John Elway FLB 12.00 30.00
134 Barry Sanders FLB 10.00 25.00
135 Mark Brunell FLB 3.00 8.00
136 Earl Campbell FLB 5.00 12.00
137 Joe Montana FLB 12.00 30.00
138 Dan Marino FLB 12.00 30.00
139 Curtis Martin FLB 4.00 10.00
140 Drew Bledsoe FLB 4.00 10.00
141 Ricky Williams FLB 3.00 8.00
142 Junior Seau FLB 4.00 10.00
143 Charlie Garner FLB 3.00 8.00
144 Jerry Rice FLB 8.00 20.00
145 Ahman Green FLB 3.00 8.00
146 Jerome Bettis FLB 6.00 15.00
147 Trent Green FLB 3.00 8.00
148 Warrick Dunn FLB 3.00 8.00
149 Deion Sanders FLB 6.00 15.00
150 Stephen Davis FLB 3.00 8.00

2004 Leaf Certified Materials Mirror Blue Signatures

BLUE STATED PRINT RUN 15-100
BLUES #'d UNDER 20 NOT PRICED
UNPRICED BLACK PRINT RUN 1 SET
UNPRICED EMERALD PRINT RUN 5 SETS
1 Anquan Boldin/50 12.00 30.00
3 Josh McCown/100 8.00 20.00
5 Michael Vick/100 25.00 50.00
21 Brian Urlacher/40 25.00 60.00
22 Rex Grossman/100 8.00 20.00
30 Keyshawn Johnson/20 12.00 30.00
32 Roy Williams S/89 8.00 20.00
40 Joey Harrington/20 12.00 30.00
41 Ahman Green/60 10.00 25.00
44 Javon Walker/20 10.00 25.00
56 Priest Holmes/25 15.00 40.00
60 Chris Chambers/20 12.00 30.00
69 Michael Bennett/84 8.00 20.00
74 Aaron Brooks/28 12.00 30.00
75 Deuce McAllister/50 10.00 25.00
80 Michael Strahan/25 15.00 40.00
82 Chad Pennington/20 15.00 40.00
85 Santana Moss/100 8.00 20.00
96 Antwaan Randle El/38 12.00 30.00
98 Hines Ward/25 30.00 60.00
102 LaDainian Tomlinson/25 25.00 60.00
104 Matt Hasselbeck/87 8.00 20.00
105 Shaun Alexander/25 12.00 30.00
129 Jim Kelly FLB/25 30.00 80.00
137 Joe Montana FLB/25 60.00 120.00
152 Ahmad Carroll/25 10.00 25.00
161 Chris Gamble/75 8.00 20.00
165 D.J. Hackett/75 8.00 20.00
166 D.J. Williams/100 10.00 25.00
169 Ernest Wilford/25 12.00 30.00
177 Jerricho Cotchery/75 8.00 20.00
181 Johnnie Morant/50 8.00 20.00
183 Jonathan Vilma/75 10.00 25.00
184 Josh Harris/25 10.00 25.00
185 Kenechi Udeze/100 8.00 20.00
189 Michael Turner/100 15.00 40.00
190 P.K. Sam/100 6.00 15.00
191 Quincy Wilson/50 10.00 25.00
194 Samie Parker/75 6.00 15.00
196 Tommie Harris/50 12.00 30.00
199 Vince Wilfork/100 10.00 25.00
200 Will Smith/75 8.00 20.00

2004 Leaf Certified Materials Mirror Gold Signatures

GOLD PRINT RUN 10-25
GOLD SER.#'d LESS THAN 25 UNPRICED
1 Anquan Boldin/25 15.00 40.00
3 Josh McCown/25 12.00 30.00
5 Michael Vick/25 50.00 100.00
22 Rex Grossman/25 12.00 30.00
23 Chad Johnson/25 15.00 40.00
32 Roy Williams S/25 12.00 30.00
41 Ahman Green/25 12.00 30.00
42 Brett Favre/20 150.00 250.00
47 David Carr/25 10.00 25.00
54 Jimmy Smith/20 12.00 30.00
55 Dante Hall/25 12.00 30.00
69 Michael Bennett/25 12.00 30.00
85 Santana Moss/25 12.00 30.00
96 Antwaan Randle El/25 12.00 30.00
104 Matt Hasselbeck/25 12.00 30.00
113 Derrick Mason/25 12.00 30.00
122 Laveranues Coles/25 10.00 25.00
161 Chris Gamble/25 12.00 30.00
165 D.J. Hackett/25 12.00 30.00
166 D.J. Williams/25 15.00 40.00
177 Jerricho Cotchery/25 12.00 30.00
181 Johnnie Morant/25 10.00 25.00
183 Jonathan Vilma/25 15.00 40.00
185 Kenechi Udeze/25 12.00 30.00
189 Michael Turner/25 50.00 100.00
190 P.K. Sam/25 10.00 25.00
191 Quincy Wilson/25 12.00 30.00
194 Samie Parker/25 10.00 25.00
196 Tommie Harris/25 15.00 40.00
199 Vince Wilfork/25 15.00 40.00
200 Will Smith/25 12.00 30.00

2004 Leaf Certified Materials Mirror Red Signatures

RED STATED PRINT RUN 20-250
RED SER. #'d UNDER 20 NOT PRICED
1 Anquan Boldin/89 10.00 25.00
3 Josh McCown/135 6.00 15.00
5 Michael Vick/120 30.00 60.00
14 Drew Bledsoe/20 15.00 40.00
21 Brian Urlacher/50 25.00 60.00
22 Rex Grossman/237 6.00 15.00
30 Keyshawn Johnson/40 10.00 25.00
32 Roy Williams S/125 6.00 15.00
40 Joey Harrington/32 12.00 30.00
41 Ahman Green/60 10.00 25.00
44 Javon Walker/31 10.00 25.00
49 Marvin Harrison/20 15.00 40.00
50 Peyton Manning/20 75.00 150.00
56 Priest Holmes/63 12.00 30.00
60 Chris Chambers/31 12.00 30.00
69 Michael Bennett/125 6.00 15.00
71 Tom Brady/20 125.00 200.00
75 Deuce McAllister/85 8.00 20.00
80 Michael Strahan/60 12.00 30.00
82 Chad Pennington/30 15.00 40.00
85 Santana Moss/250 6.00 15.00
96 Antwaan Randle El/50 10.00 25.00
98 Hines Ward/49 15.00 40.00
102 LaDainian Tomlinson/60 20.00 50.00
105 Shaun Alexander/60 10.00 25.00
115 Eddie George/20 12.00 30.00
120 Clinton Portis/20 15.00 40.00
129 Jim Kelly FLB/48 20.00 50.00
132 Troy Aikman FLB/20 40.00 80.00
136 Earl Campbell FLB/20 20.00 50.00
137 Joe Montana FLB/60 60.00 100.00
145 Ahman Green FLB/100 8.00 20.00
152 Ahmad Carroll/90 6.00 15.00
161 Chris Gamble/100 8.00 20.00
165 D.J. Hackett/90 8.00 20.00
166 D.J. Williams/250 8.00 20.00
169 Ernest Wilford/55 10.00 25.00
177 Jerricho Cotchery/90 8.00 20.00
181 Johnnie Morant/90 6.00 15.00
183 Jonathan Vilma/225 8.00 20.00
185 Kenechi Udeze/165 6.00 15.00
189 Michael Turner/130 10.00 25.00
190 P.K. Sam/215 5.00 12.00
191 Quincy Wilson/90 8.00 20.00
194 Samie Parker/140 5.00 12.00
196 Tommie Harris/75 10.00 25.00
199 Vince Wilfork/225 8.00 20.00
200 Will Smith/100 8.00 20.00

2005 Leaf Certified Materials

This 229-card set was released in September, 2005. The set was issued through the hobby in five-card packs with an $10 SRP which came 10 packs to a box. Cards numbered 151-229 all feature 2005 rookies with cards numbered 201-229 also including a player-worn jersey swatch. Those cards from 151-200 were all issued to a stated print run of 1000 serial numbered sets while the cards 201-229 were issued to stated print runs between 499 and 1499 serial numbered sets.

COMP.SET w/o RCs (150) 15.00 40.00
151-200 PRINT RUN 1000 SER.#'d SETS
UNPRICED MIR.BLACK PRINT RUN 1 SET
UNPRICED MIR.EMERALD PRINT RUN 5 SETS
1 Anquan Boldin .30 .75
2 Josh McCown .30 .75
3 Larry Fitzgerald .40 1.00
4 Michael Vick .40 1.00
5 Peerless Price .25 .60
6 T.J. Duckett .25 .60
7 Warrick Dunn .30 .75
8 Jamal Lewis .30 .75
9 Kyle Boller .30 .75
10 Todd Heap .30 .75
11 Ray Lewis .40 1.00
12 Terrell Suggs .30 .75
13 Drew Bledsoe .40 1.00
14 Eric Moulds .25 .60
15 J.P. Losman .25 .60
16 Lee Evans .30 .75
17 Willis McGahee .40 1.00
18 DeShaun Foster .30 .75
19 Jake Delhomme .30 .75
20 Steve Smith .40 1.00
21 Brian Urlacher .40 1.00
22 Rex Grossman .30 .75
23 Carson Palmer .40 1.00
24 Chad Johnson .30 .75
25 Rudi Johnson .30 .75
26 Kellen Winslow Jr. .30 .75
27 Kelly Holcomb .25 .60
28 Lee Suggs .25 .60
29 William Green .25 .60
30 Julius Jones .25 .60
31 Keyshawn Johnson .30 .75
32 Roy Williams S .25 .60
33 Terence Newman .25 .60
34 Ashley Lelie .25 .60
35 Champ Bailey .30 .75
36 Darius Watts .25 .60
37 Jake Plummer .30 .75
38 Tatum Bell .25 .60
39 Charles Rogers .25 .60
40 Joey Harrington .30 .75
41 Kevin Jones .25 .60
42 Roy Williams WR .30 .75
43 Ahman Green .30 .75
44 Brett Favre 1.00 2.50
45 Javon Walker .25 .60
46 Robert Ferguson .25 .60
47 Andre Johnson .40 1.00
48 David Carr .25 .60
49 Domanick Davis .25 .60
50 Dallas Clark .30 .75
51 Edgerrin James .30 .75
52 Marvin Harrison .40 1.00
53 Peyton Manning .75 2.00
54 Reggie Wayne .40 1.00
55 Byron Leftwich .30 .75
56 Fred Taylor .30 .75
57 Jimmy Smith .30 .75
58 Reggie Williams .25 .60
59 Priest Holmes .30 .75
60 Tony Gonzalez .30 .75
61 Trent Green .30 .75
62 Chris Chambers .30 .75
63 Jason Taylor .30 .75
64 Junior Seau .40 1.00
65 Zach Thomas .40 1.00
66 Daunte Culpepper .30 .75
67 Michael Bennett .30 .75
68 Randy Moss .40 1.00
69 Corey Dillon .30 .75
70 Tom Brady .75 2.00
71 Deion Branch .25 .60
72 Aaron Brooks .25 .60
73 Deuce McAllister .30 .75
74 Donte Stallworth .25 .60
75 Joe Horn .30 .75
76 Eli Manning .60 1.50
77 Jeremy Shockey .40 1.00
78 Michael Strahan .40 1.00
79 Tiki Barber .40 1.00
80 Anthony Becht .25 .60
81 Chad Pennington .40 1.00
82 Curtis Martin .40 1.00
83 Justin McCareins .25 .60
84 Laveranues Coles .25 .60
85 Santana Moss .30 .75
86 Shaun Ellis .25 .60
87 Jerry Porter .25 .60
88 Brian Westbrook .30 .75
89 Chad Lewis .25 .60
90 Donovan McNabb .40 1.00
91 Freddie Mitchell .25 .60
92 Hugh Douglas .25 .60
93 Jevon Kearse .30 .75
94 Terrell Owens .40 1.00
95 Todd Pinkston .25 .60
96 Antwaan Randle El .30 .75
97 Ben Roethlisberger .60 1.50
98 Duce Staley .30 .75
99 Hines Ward .40 1.00
100 Jerome Bettis .40 1.00
101 Antonio Gates .40 1.00
102 Drew Brees .40 1.00
103 LaDainian Tomlinson .40 1.00
104 Kevan Barlow .25 .60
105 Darrell Jackson .25 .60
106 Koren Robinson .25 .60
107 Matt Hasselbeck .30 .75
108 Shaun Alexander .30 .75
109 Marc Bulger .30 .75
110 Steven Jackson .40 1.00
111 Torry Holt .30 .75
112 Michael Clayton .25 .60
113 Chris Brown .25 .60
114 Drew Bennett .30 .75
115 Keith Bulluck .25 .60
116 Steve McNair .40 1.00
117 Clinton Portis .30 .75
118 LaVar Arrington .30 .75
119 John Riggins .50 1.25
120 Sean Taylor .40 1.00
121 Jake Plummer .30 .75
122 Thomas Jones .40 1.00
123 Doug Flutie .40 1.00
124 Walter Payton 1.25 3.00
125 Corey Dillon .30 .75
126 Troy Aikman .60 1.50
127 Terrell Davis .40 1.00
128 Marshall Faulk .40 1.00
129 Dan Marino 1.25 3.00
130 Thurman Thomas .50 1.25
131 Warren Moon .50 1.25
132 Curtis Martin .40 1.00
133 Drew Bledsoe .40 1.00
134 Kerry Collins .30 .75
135 Keyshawn Johnson .30 .75
136 A.J. Feeley .25 .60
137 Duce Staley .30 .75
138 Junior Seau .40 1.00
139 Jerry Rice .75 2.00
140 Steve Young .60 1.50
141 Jerome Bettis .40 1.00
142 Kurt Warner .40 1.00
143 Trent Green .30 .75
144 Keyshawn Johnson .30 .75
145 Warren Sapp .30 .75
146 Warrick Dunn .30 .75
147 Jevon Kearse .30 .75
148 Deion Sanders .60 1.50
149 Laveranues Coles .25 .60
150 Stephen Davis .30 .75
151 Cedric Benson RC 2.00 5.00
152 Mike Williams 2.00 5.00
153 DeMarcus Ware RC 4.00 10.00
154 Shawne Merriman RC 2.00 5.00
155 Thomas Davis RC 1.25 3.00
156 Derrick Johnson RC 1.50 4.00
157 Travis Johnson RC 1.25 3.00
158 David Pollack RC 1.50 4.00
159 Erasmus James RC 1.50 4.00
160 Marcus Spears RC 1.50 4.00
161 Fabian Washington RC 1.50 4.00
162 Aaron Rodgers RC 20.00 40.00
163 Marlin Jackson RC 1.25 3.00
164 Heath Miller RC 2.50 6.00
165 Matt Roth RC 1.50 4.00
166 Dan Cody RC 1.50 4.00
167 Bryant McFadden RC 1.50 4.00
168 Chris Henry RC 2.00 5.00
169 David Greene RC 1.25 3.00
170 Brandon Jones RC 1.50 4.00
171 Marion Barber RC 2.00 5.00
172 Brandon Jacobs RC 2.50 6.00
173 Jerome Mathis RC 2.00 5.00
174 Craphonso Thorpe RC 1.25 3.00
175 Alvin Pearman RC 1.25 3.00
176 Darren Sproles RC 2.00 5.00
177 Fred Gibson RC 1.50 4.00
178 Roydell Williams RC 1.50 4.00
179 Airese Currie RC 1.25 3.00
180 Damien Nash RC 1.50 4.00
181 Dan Orlovsky RC 2.00 5.00
182 Adrian McPherson RC 1.25 3.00
183 Larry Brackins RC 1.25 3.00
184 Rasheed Marshall RC 1.50 4.00
185 Cedric Houston RC 2.00 5.00
186 Chad Owens RC 1.50 4.00
187 Tab Perry RC 1.25 3.00
188 Dante Ridgeway RC 1.25 3.00
189 Craig Bragg RC 1.25 3.00
190 Deandra Cobb RC 1.25 3.00
191 Derek Anderson RC 1.50 4.00
192 Paris Warren RC 1.50 4.00
193 Lionel Gates RC 1.25 3.00
194 Anthony Davis RC 1.25 3.00
195 Ryan Fitzpatrick RC 4.00 10.00
196 J.R. Russell RC 1.25 3.00
197 Jason White RC 2.00 5.00
198 Kay-Jay Harris RC 1.25 3.00
199 T.A. McLendon RC 1.25 3.00
200 Taylor Stubblefield RC 1.25 3.00
201 Adam Jones JSY/1499 RC 2.50 6.00
202 Alex Smith QB JSY/499 RC 12.50 30.00
203 Andrew Walter JSY/1249 RC 2.50 6.00
204 Antrel Rolle JSY/999 RC 3.00 8.00
205 Braylon Edwards JSY/499 RC 10.00 25.00
206 Cadillac Williams JSY/499 RC 8.00 20.00
207 Carlos Rogers JSY/1499 RC 2.00 5.00
208 Charlie Frye JSY/1499 RC 2.00 5.00
209 Ciatrick Fason JSY/1499 RC 2.00 5.00
210 Courtney Roby JSY/1249 RC 2.50 6.00
211 Eric Shelton JSY/999 RC 2.00 5.00
212 Frank Gore JSY/999 RC 5.00 12.00
213 J.J. Arrington JSY/499 RC 4.00 10.00
214 Kyle Orton JSY/1499 RC 3.00 8.00
215 Jason Campbell JSY/749 RC 5.00 12.00
216 Mark Bradley JSY/999 RC 2.00 5.00
217 Mark Clayton JSY/499 RC 4.00 10.00
218 Matt Jones JSY/749 RC 4.00 10.00
219 Maurice Clarett JSY/999 2.50 6.00
220 Reggie Brown JSY/999 RC 2.00 5.00
221 Roddy White JSY/749 RC 4.00 10.00
222 Ronnie Brown JSY/499 RC 12.50 30.00
223 Roscoe Parrish JSY/999 RC 2.00 5.00
224 Ryan Moats JSY/999 RC 2.50 6.00
225 Stefan LeFors JSY/1499 RC 2.00 5.00
226 Terrence Murphy JSY/1499 RC 2.00 5.00
227 Troy Williamson JSY/749 RC 4.00 10.00
228 Vernand Morency JSY/1499 RC 2.50 6.00
229 Vincent Jackson JSY/1499 RC 4.00 10.00

2005 Leaf Certified Materials Mirror Blue

*VETERANS: 5X TO 12X BASIC CARDS
*ROOKIES: 1X TO 2.5X BASIC CARDS
MIRROR BLUE PRINT RUN 50 SER.#'d SETS
162 Aaron Rodgers 100.00 200.00

2005 Leaf Certified Materials Mirror Gold

*VETERANS: 8X TO 20X BASIC CARDS
*ROOKIES: 2X TO 5X BASIC CARDS
MIRROR GOLD PRINT RUN 25 SER.#'d SETS
162 Aaron Rodgers 125.00 200.00

2005 Leaf Certified Materials Mirror Red

*VETERANS: 3X TO 8X BASIC CARDS
*ROOKIES: .8X TO 2X BASIC CARDS
MIRROR RED PRINT RUN 100 SER.#'d SETS
162 Aaron Rodgers 90.00 150.00

2005 Leaf Certified Materials Mirror White

*VETERANS: 2X TO 5X BASIC CARDS
*ROOKIES: .5X TO 1.2X BASIC CARDS
MIRR.WHITE PRINT RUN 150 SER.#'d SETS
162 Aaron Rodgers 60.00 100.00

2005 Leaf Certified Materials Certified Potential

STATED PRINT RUN 750 SER.#'d SETS
UNPRICED BLACK PRINT RUN 10 SETS
*BLUE/100: .8X TO 2X BASIC INSERTS
*EMERALD/25: 2X TO 5X BASIC INSERTS
*GOLD/50: 1.2X TO 3X BASIC INSERTS
*MIRROR/500: .5X TO 1.2X BASIC INSERTS
*RED/250: .6X TO 1.5X BASIC INSERTS
1 Anquan Boldin 1.00 2.50
2 Larry Fitzgerald 1.25 3.00
3 Kyle Boller 1.00 2.50
4 Lee Evans 1.00 2.50
5 Willis McGahee 1.25 3.00
6 DeShaun Foster 1.00 2.50
7 Rex Grossman 1.00 2.50
8 Carson Palmer 1.25 3.00
9 Julius Jones .75 2.00
10 Ashley Lelie .75 2.00
11 Kevin Jones .75 2.00
12 Roy Williams WR 1.00 2.50
13 Javon Walker .75 2.00
14 Andre Johnson 1.25 3.00
15 Domanick Davis .75 2.00
16 Byron Leftwich 1.00 2.50
17 Reggie Williams .75 2.00
18 Nate Burleson .75 2.00
19 Eli Manning 2.00 5.00
20 Ben Roethlisberger 2.00 5.00
21 Antonio Gates 1.25 3.00
22 Steven Jackson 1.25 3.00
23 Michael Clayton .75 2.00
24 Sean Taylor 1.25 3.00
25 Kellen Winslow 1.00 2.50

2005 Leaf Certified Materials Certified Potential Jersey

STATED PRINT RUN 150 SER.#'d SETS
*INFINITE/75: .5X TO 1.2X BASIC JSY/150
*PRIME/25: 1X TO 2.5X BASIC JSY/150
UNPRICED BLACK PRINT RUN 1 SET
1 Anquan Boldin 3.00 8.00
2 Larry Fitzgerald 4.00 10.00
3 Kyle Boller 3.00 8.00
4 Lee Evans 3.00 8.00
5 Willis McGahee 4.00 10.00
6 DeShaun Foster 3.00 8.00
7 Rex Grossman 3.00 8.00
8 Carson Palmer 4.00 10.00
9 Julius Jones 2.50 6.00
10 Ashley Lelie 2.50 6.00
11 Kevin Jones 2.50 6.00
12 Roy Williams WR 3.00 8.00
13 Javon Walker 2.50 6.00
14 Andre Johnson 4.00 10.00
15 Domanick Davis 2.50 6.00
16 Byron Leftwich 3.00 8.00
17 Reggie Williams 2.50 6.00
18 Nate Burleson 2.50 6.00
19 Eli Manning 6.00 15.00
20 Ben Roethlisberger 6.00 15.00
21 Antonio Gates 4.00 10.00
22 Steven Jackson 4.00 10.00
23 Michael Clayton 2.50 6.00
24 Sean Taylor 10.00 25.00
25 Kellen Winslow 3.00 8.00

2005 Leaf Certified Materials Certified Skills

STATED PRINT RUN 750 SER.#'d SETS
UNPRICED BLACK PRINT RUN 10 SETS
*BLUE/100: .8X TO 2X BASIC INSERTS
*EMERALD/25: 2X TO 5X BASIC INSERTS
*GOLD/50: 1.2X TO 3X BASIC INSERTS
*MIRROR/500: .5X TO 1.2X BASIC INSERTS
*RED/250: .6X TO 1.5X BASIC INSERTS
1 Daunte Culpepper 1.00 2.50
2 Trent Green 1.00 2.50
3 Peyton Manning 2.50 6.00
4 Jake Plummer 1.00 2.50
5 Brett Favre 3.00 8.00
6 Marc Bulger 1.00 2.50
7 Jake Delhomme 1.00 2.50
8 Donovan McNabb 1.25 3.00
9 Aaron Brooks .75 2.00
10 Tom Brady 2.50 6.00
11 David Carr .75 2.00
12 Matt Hasselbeck 1.00 2.50
13 Drew Brees 1.25 3.00
14 Joey Harrington 1.00 2.50
15 Curtis Martin 1.25 3.00
16 Shaun Alexander 1.00 2.50
17 Corey Dillon 1.00 2.50
18 Edgerrin James 1.00 2.50
19 Tiki Barber 1.25 3.00
20 Rudi Johnson 1.00 2.50
21 LaDainian Tomlinson 1.25 3.00
22 Clinton Portis 1.00 2.50
23 Domanick Davis .75 2.00
24 Ahman Green 1.00 2.50
25 Kevin Jones .75 2.00
26 Willis McGahee 1.25 3.00
27 Deuce McAllister 1.00 2.50
28 Chris Brown .75 2.00
29 Jamal Lewis 1.00 2.50
30 Jerome Bettis 1.25 3.00
31 Priest Holmes 1.00 2.50
32 Joe Horn 1.00 2.50
33 Javon Walker .75 2.00
34 Torry Holt 1.00 2.50
35 Chad Johnson 1.00 2.50
36 Drew Bennett 1.00 2.50
37 Reggie Wayne 1.25 3.00
38 Terrell Owens 1.25 3.00
39 Darrell Jackson .75 2.00
40 Michael Clayton .75 2.00
41 Jimmy Smith 1.00 2.50
42 Rod Smith 1.00 2.50
43 Andre Johnson 1.25 3.00
44 Marvin Harrison 1.25 3.00
45 Ashley Lelie .75 2.00
46 Eric Moulds .75 2.00
47 Nate Burleson .75 2.00
48 Hines Ward 1.25 3.00
49 Antonio Gates 1.25 3.00
50 Laveranues Coles .75 2.00

2005 Leaf Certified Materials Certified Skills Jersey

STATED PRINT RUN 175 SER.#'d SETS
UNPRICED BLACK PRINT RUN 1 SET
*POSITION/75: .5X TO 1.2X BASIC JSY/175
*PRIME/25: 1X TO 2.5X BASIC JSY/175
1 Daunte Culpepper 3.00 8.00
2 Trent Green 3.00 8.00
3 Peyton Manning 8.00 20.00
4 Jake Plummer 3.00 8.00
5 Brett Favre 10.00 25.00
6 Marc Bulger 3.00 8.00
7 Jake Delhomme 3.00 8.00
8 Donovan McNabb 4.00 10.00
9 Aaron Brooks 2.50 6.00
10 Tom Brady 8.00 20.00
11 David Carr 2.50 6.00
12 Matt Hasselbeck 3.00 8.00
13 Drew Brees 4.00 10.00
14 Joey Harrington 3.00 8.00
15 Curtis Martin 4.00 10.00
16 Shaun Alexander 3.00 8.00
17 Corey Dillon 3.00 8.00
18 Edgerrin James 3.00 8.00
19 Tiki Barber 4.00 10.00
20 Rudi Johnson 3.00 8.00
21 LaDainian Tomlinson 4.00 10.00
22 Clinton Portis 3.00 8.00
23 Domanick Davis 2.50 6.00
24 Ahman Green 3.00 8.00
25 Kevin Jones 2.50 6.00
26 Willis McGahee 4.00 10.00
27 Deuce McAllister 3.00 8.00
28 Chris Brown 2.50 6.00
29 Jamal Lewis 3.00 8.00
30 Jerome Bettis 4.00 10.00
31 Priest Holmes 3.00 8.00
32 Joe Horn 3.00 8.00
33 Javon Walker 2.50 6.00
34 Torry Holt 3.00 8.00
35 Chad Johnson 3.00 8.00
36 Drew Bennett 3.00 8.00
37 Reggie Wayne 4.00 10.00
38 Terrell Owens 4.00 10.00
39 Darrell Jackson 2.50 6.00
40 Michael Clayton 2.50 6.00
41 Jimmy Smith 3.00 8.00
42 Rod Smith 3.00 8.00
43 Andre Johnson 4.00 10.00
44 Marvin Harrison 4.00 10.00
45 Ashley Lelie 2.50 6.00
46 Eric Moulds 2.50 6.00
47 Nate Burleson 2.50 6.00
48 Hines Ward 4.00 10.00
49 Antonio Gates 4.00 10.00
50 Laveranues Coles 2.50 6.00

2005 Leaf Certified Materials Fabric of the Game

STATED PRINT RUN 100 SER.#'d SETS
UNPRICED TEAM LOGO PRINT RUN 5 SETS
1 Barry Sanders 12.00 30.00
2 Bart Starr 12.00 30.00
3 Ben Roethlisberger 8.00 20.00
4 Bo Jackson 10.00 25.00
5 Bob Griese 8.00 20.00
6 Boomer Esiason 6.00 15.00
7 Brett Favre 12.00 30.00
8 Brian Urlacher 5.00 12.00
9 Byron Leftwich 4.00 10.00
10 Carson Palmer 5.00 12.00
11 Chad Johnson 4.00 10.00
12 Chad Pennington 5.00 12.00
13 Clinton Portis 4.00 10.00
14 Corey Dillon 4.00 10.00
15 Cris Collinsworth 6.00 15.00
16 Dan Marino 20.00 50.00
17 Dan Fouts 8.00 20.00
18 Eli Manning 8.00 20.00
19 Daryl Johnston 8.00 20.00
20 David Carr 3.00 8.00
21 Deacon Jones 6.00 15.00
22 Deion Sanders 10.00 25.00
23 Don Maynard 6.00 15.00
24 Don Meredith 15.00 40.00
25 Don Shula 6.00 15.00
26 Donovan McNabb 5.00 12.00
27 Earl Campbell 8.00 20.00
28 Fran Tarkenton 8.00 20.00
29 Gale Sayers 10.00 25.00
30 Gene Upshaw 6.00 15.00
31 Herman Edwards 5.00 12.00
32 Herschel Walker 6.00 15.00
33 Hines Ward 5.00 12.00
34 Ickey Woods 5.00 12.00
35 James Lofton 5.00 12.00
36 Jerry Rice 10.00 25.00
37 Jevon Kearse 4.00 10.00
38 Jim Brown 10.00 25.00
39 Jim Kelly 10.00 25.00
40 Joe Greene 8.00 20.00
41 Joe Montana 20.00 50.00
42 Joe Namath 12.00 30.00
43 John Elway 15.00 40.00
44 John Riggins 8.00 20.00
45 John Taylor 5.00 12.00
46 L.C. Greenwood 6.00 15.00
47 Julius Jones 3.00 8.00
48 Lawrence Taylor 8.00 20.00
49 Leroy Kelly 6.00 15.00
50 Marcus Allen 8.00 20.00
51 Michael Irvin 8.00 20.00
52 Michael Vick 6.00 15.00
53 Mike Ditka 8.00 20.00
54 Mike Singletary 8.00 20.00
55 Ozzie Newsome 6.00 15.00
56 Paul Warfield 6.00 15.00
57 Peyton Manning 10.00 25.00
58 Priest Holmes 4.00 10.00
59 Randall Cunningham 6.00 15.00
60 Roger Craig 8.00 20.00
61 Richard Dent 6.00 15.00
62 Roger Staubach 12.00 30.00
63 Rudi Johnson 4.00 10.00
64 Domanick Davis 3.00 8.00
65 Sonny Jurgensen 6.00 15.00
66 Steve Largent 8.00 20.00
67 Sterling Sharpe 6.00 15.00
68 Steve Young 10.00 25.00
69 Steven Jackson 5.00 12.00
70 Tatum Bell 3.00 8.00
71 Terrell Davis 8.00 20.00
72 Andre Johnson 5.00 12.00
73 Terry Bradshaw 12.00 30.00
74 Thurman Thomas 8.00 20.00
75 Tom Brady 10.00 25.00
76 Tony Dorsett 6.00 15.00
77 Troy Aikman 10.00 25.00
78 Walter Payton 20.00 50.00
79 Warren Moon 8.00 20.00
80 Willis McGahee 5.00 12.00
81 Johnny Unitas 90.00 150.00
Jim Thorpe
82 LaVar Arrington 6.00 15.00
Ray Lewis
83 Tiki Barber 6.00 15.00
Jamal Lewis
84 Aaron Brooks 5.00 12.00
Joey Harrington
85 Brian Westbrook 5.00 12.00
Ahman Green
86 Terrell Owens 6.00 15.00
Anquan Boldin
87 Antonio Gates 6.00 15.00
Todd Heap
88 Matt Hasselbeck 5.00 12.00
Trent Green
89 Curtis Martin 6.00 15.00
Shaun Alexander
90 Michael Clayton 5.00 12.00
Roy Williams
91 Daunte Culpepper 6.00 15.00
Steve McNair
92 Larry Fitzgerald 6.00 15.00
Javon Walker
93 LaDainian Tomlinson 6.00 15.00
Kevin Jones
94 Drew Brees 6.00 15.00
Marc Bulger
95 Ray Nitschke 20.00 50.00
Reggie White
96 Randy Moss 6.00 15.00
Marvin Harrison
97 Jeremy Shockey 6.00 15.00
Tony Gonzalez
98 Steve Smith 6.00 15.00
Torry Holt
99 Chris Brown 5.00 12.00
Deuce McAllister
100 Jake Plummer 5.00 12.00
Jake Delhomme

2005 Leaf Certified Materials Fabric of the Game 21st Century

*21st CENT/21: 1X TO 2.5X BASIC JSY/100
81 Johnny Unitas 125.00 250.00
Jim Thorpe

2005 Leaf Certified Materials Fabric of the Game Debut Year

*DEBUT YEAR/70-104: .4X TO 1X
*DEBUT YEAR/51-69: .5X TO 1.2X
DEBUT YEAR PRINT RUN 51-104
81 Johnny Unitas 90.00 150.00
Jim Thorpe/56

2005 Leaf Certified Materials Fabric of the Game Jersey Number

*JERSEY/56-89: .5X TO 1.2X BASIC JSY
*JERSEY/31-37: .8X TO 2X BASIC JSY
*JERSEY/17-29: 1X TO 2.5X BASIC JSY
SERIAL #'d UNDER 15 NOT PRICED
1 Barry Sanders AU/20 90.00 175.00
2 Bart Starr AU/15 100.00 200.00
4 Bo Jackson AU/34 90.00 150.00
8 Brian Urlacher AU/54 30.00 60.00
11 Chad Johnson AU/85 15.00 40.00
13 Clinton Portis AU/26 15.00 40.00
15 Cris Collinsworth AU/80 12.50 30.00
19 Daryl Johnston AU/48 30.00 60.00
21 Deacon Jones AU/75 12.50 30.00
22 Deion Sanders AU/21 50.00 100.00
24 Don Meredith AU/17 90.00 150.00
25 Don Shula AU/25 30.00 80.00
27 Earl Campbell AU/34 25.00 60.00
29 Gale Sayers AU/40 40.00 80.00
30 Gene Upshaw AU/63 25.00 50.00
31 Herman Edwards AU/46 10.00 25.00
32 Herschel Walker AU/34 15.00 40.00
33 Hines Ward AU/86 50.00 100.00
34 Ickey Woods AU/30 12.50 30.00
35 James Lofton AU/80 12.50 30.00
37 Jevon Kearse AU/93 10.00 25.00
38 Jim Brown AU/32 60.00 120.00
40 Joe Greene AU/75 40.00 80.00
41 Joe Montana AU/16 75.00 150.00
44 John Riggins AU/44 30.00 60.00
45 John Taylor AU/82 15.00 40.00
46 L.C. Greenwood AU/68 25.00 50.00
47 Julius Jones AU/21 12.50 30.00
48 Lawrence Taylor AU/56 50.00 100.00
49 Leroy Kelly AU/44 15.00 40.00
50 Marcus Allen AU/32 75.00 125.00
53 Mike Ditka AU/89 50.00 100.00
54 Mike Singletary AU/50 15.00 40.00
55 Ozzie Newsome AU/82 10.00 25.00
56 Paul Warfield AU/42 20.00 50.00
58 Priest Holmes AU/31 30.00 60.00
60 Roger Craig AU/33 30.00 60.00
61 Richard Dent AU/95 12.50 30.00
63 Rudi Johnson AU/32 15.00 40.00
64 Domanick Davis AU/37 15.00 40.00
66 Steve Largent AU/80 30.00 60.00
67 Sterling Sharpe AU/84 15.00 40.00
69 Steven Jackson AU/39 25.00 60.00
70 Tatum Bell AU/26 15.00 40.00
71 Terrell Davis AU/30 20.00 50.00
72 Andre Johnson AU/80 10.00 25.00
74 Thurman Thomas AU/34 15.00 40.00
76 Tony Dorsett AU/33 40.00 80.00
80 Willis McGahee AU/21 12.50 30.00
81 Johnny Unitas 125.00 250.00
Jim Thorpe/21

2005 Leaf Certified Materials Gold Team

STATED PRINT RUN 750 SER.#'d SETS
*MIRROR/500: .5X TO 1.2X BASIC INSERTS
1 Anquan Boldin 1.00 2.50
2 Antonio Gates 1.25 3.00
3 LaVar Arrington 1.00 2.50
4 Brett Favre 3.00 8.00
5 Brian Urlacher 1.25 3.00
6 Byron Leftwich 1.00 2.50
7 Chad Pennington 1.25 3.00
8 Deuce McAllister 1.00 2.50
9 Dan Marino 3.00 8.00
10 Daunte Culpepper 1.00 2.50
11 Donovan McNabb 1.25 3.00
12 Drew Brees 1.25 3.00
13 Earl Campbell 1.25 3.00
14 Edgerrin James 1.00 2.50
15 Gale Sayers 1.50 4.00
16 Michael Clayton .75 2.00
17 Jerry Rice 2.50 6.00
18 John Elway 2.50 6.00
19 LaDainian Tomlinson 1.25 3.00
20 Larry Fitzgerald 1.25 3.00
21 Michael Vick 1.25 3.00
22 Peyton Manning 2.50 6.00
23 Priest Holmes 1.00 2.50
24 Tom Brady 2.50 6.00
25 Troy Aikman 1.50 4.00

2005 Leaf Certified Materials Gold Team Jersey

STATED PRINT RUN 150 SER.#'d SETS
*24K/75: .5X TO 1.2X BASIC JSY/150
UNPRICED BLACK PRINT RUN 1 SET
*PRIME/25: 1X TO 2.5X BASIC JSY/150
1 Anquan Boldin 3.00 8.00
2 Antonio Gates 4.00 10.00
3 LaVar Arrington 3.00 8.00
4 Brett Favre 10.00 25.00
5 Brian Urlacher 4.00 10.00
6 Byron Leftwich 3.00 8.00
7 Chad Pennington 4.00 10.00
8 Deuce McAllister 3.00 8.00
9 Dan Marino 12.00 30.00
10 Daunte Culpepper 3.00 8.00
11 Donovan McNabb 4.00 10.00
12 Drew Brees 4.00 10.00
13 Earl Campbell 5.00 12.00
14 Edgerrin James 3.00 8.00
15 Gale Sayers 6.00 15.00
16 Michael Clayton 2.50 6.00
17 Jerry Rice 8.00 20.00
18 John Elway 10.00 25.00
19 LaDainian Tomlinson 4.00 10.00
20 Larry Fitzgerald 4.00 10.00
21 Michael Vick 5.00 12.00
22 Peyton Manning 8.00 20.00
23 Priest Holmes 3.00 8.00
24 Tom Brady 8.00 20.00
25 Troy Aikman 6.00 15.00

2005 Leaf Certified Materials Mirror Red Materials

1-150 VET RED PRINT RUN 100
201-229 ROOKIE RED PRINT RUN 150
UNPRICED MIR.BLACK PRINT RUN 1 SET
UNPRICED MIR.EMERALD PRINT RUN 5 SETS
1 Anquan Boldin 3.00 8.00
2 Josh McCown 3.00 8.00
3 Larry Fitzgerald 4.00 10.00
4 Michael Vick 4.00 10.00
5 Peerless Price 2.50 6.00
6 T.J. Duckett 2.50 6.00
7 Warrick Dunn 3.00 8.00
8 Jamal Lewis 3.00 8.00
9 Kyle Boller 3.00 8.00
10 Todd Heap 3.00 8.00
11 Ray Lewis 4.00 10.00
12 Terrell Suggs 3.00 8.00
13 Drew Bledsoe 4.00 10.00
14 Eric Moulds 2.50 6.00
15 J.P. Losman 2.50 6.00
16 Lee Evans 3.00 8.00
17 Willis McGahee 4.00 10.00
18 DeShaun Foster 3.00 8.00
19 Jake Delhomme 3.00 8.00
20 Steve Smith 4.00 10.00
21 Brian Urlacher 4.00 10.00
22 Rex Grossman 3.00 8.00
23 Carson Palmer 4.00 10.00
24 Chad Johnson 3.00 8.00
25 Rudi Johnson 3.00 8.00
26 Kellen Winslow 3.00 8.00
27 Kelly Holcomb 2.50 6.00
28 Lee Suggs 2.50 6.00
29 William Green 2.50 6.00
30 Julius Jones 2.50 6.00
31 Keyshawn Johnson 3.00 8.00
32 Roy Williams S 2.50 6.00
33 Terence Newman 2.50 6.00
34 Ashley Lelie 2.50 6.00
35 Champ Bailey 3.00 8.00
36 Darius Watts 2.50 6.00
37 Jake Plummer 3.00 8.00
38 Tatum Bell 2.50 6.00
39 Charles Rogers 2.50 6.00
40 Joey Harrington 3.00 8.00
41 Kevin Jones 2.50 6.00
42 Roy Williams WR 3.00 8.00
43 Ahman Green 3.00 8.00
44 Brett Favre 10.00 25.00
45 Javon Walker 2.50 6.00
46 Robert Ferguson 2.50 6.00
47 Andre Johnson 4.00 10.00
48 David Carr 2.50 6.00
49 Domanick Davis 2.50 6.00
50 Dallas Clark 3.00 8.00
51 Edgerrin James 3.00 8.00
52 Marvin Harrison 4.00 10.00
53 Peyton Manning 8.00 20.00
54 Reggie Wayne 4.00 10.00
55 Byron Leftwich 3.00 8.00
56 Fred Taylor 3.00 8.00
57 Jimmy Smith 3.00 8.00
58 Reggie Williams 2.50 6.00
59 Priest Holmes 3.00 8.00
60 Tony Gonzalez 3.00 8.00
61 Trent Green 3.00 8.00
62 Chris Chambers 3.00 8.00
63 Jason Taylor 3.00 8.00
64 Junior Seau 4.00 10.00
65 Zach Thomas 4.00 10.00
66 Daunte Culpepper 3.00 8.00
67 Michael Bennett 3.00 8.00
68 Randy Moss 4.00 10.00
69 Corey Dillon 3.00 8.00
70 Tom Brady 8.00 20.00
71 Deion Branch 2.50 6.00
72 Aaron Brooks 2.50 6.00
73 Deuce McAllister 3.00 8.00
74 Donte Stallworth 2.50 6.00
75 Joe Horn 3.00 8.00
76 Eli Manning 6.00 15.00
77 Jeremy Shockey 4.00 10.00
78 Michael Strahan 4.00 10.00

79 Tiki Barber 4.00 10.00
80 Anthony Becht 2.50 6.00
81 Chad Pennington 4.00 10.00
82 Curtis Martin 4.00 10.00
83 Justin McCareins 2.50 6.00
84 Laveranues Coles 2.50 6.00
85 Santana Moss 3.00 8.00
86 Shaun Ellis 2.50 6.00
87 Jerry Porter 2.50 6.00
88 Brian Westbrook 3.00 8.00
89 Chad Lewis 2.50 6.00
90 Donovan McNabb 4.00 10.00
91 Freddie Mitchell 2.50 6.00
92 Hugh Douglas 2.50 6.00
93 Jevon Kearse 3.00 8.00
94 Terrell Owens 4.00 10.00
95 Todd Pinkston 2.50 6.00
96 Antwaan Randle El 3.00 8.00
97 Ben Roethlisberger 6.00 15.00
98 Duce Staley 3.00 8.00
99 Hines Ward 4.00 10.00
100 Jerome Bettis 4.00 10.00
101 Antonio Gates 4.00 10.00
102 Drew Brees 4.00 10.00
103 LaDainian Tomlinson 4.00 10.00
104 Kevan Barlow 2.50 6.00
105 Darrell Jackson 2.50 6.00
106 Koren Robinson 2.50 6.00
107 Matt Hasselbeck 3.00 8.00
108 Shaun Alexander 3.00 8.00
109 Marc Bulger 3.00 8.00
110 Steven Jackson 4.00 10.00
111 Torry Holt 3.00 8.00
112 Michael Clayton 2.50 6.00
113 Chris Brown 2.50 6.00
114 Drew Bennett 3.00 8.00
115 Keith Bulluck 2.50 6.00
116 Steve McNair 4.00 10.00
117 Clinton Portis 3.00 8.00
118 LaVar Arrington 3.00 8.00
119 John Riggins 5.00 12.00
120 Sean Taylor 10.00 25.00
121 Jake Plummer 3.00 8.00
122 Thomas Jones 4.00 10.00
123 Doug Flutie 5.00 12.00
124 Walter Payton 12.00 30.00
125 Corey Dillon 3.00 8.00
126 Troy Aikman 6.00 15.00
127 Terrell Davis 5.00 12.00
128 Marshall Faulk 4.00 10.00
129 Dan Marino 12.00 30.00
130 Thurman Thomas 5.00 12.00
131 Warren Moon 5.00 12.00
132 Curtis Martin 4.00 10.00
133 Drew Bledsoe 4.00 10.00
134 Kerry Collins 3.00 8.00
135 Keyshawn Johnson 3.00 8.00
136 A.J. Feeley 2.50 6.00
137 Duce Staley 3.00 8.00
138 Junior Seau 4.00 10.00
139 Jerry Rice 8.00 20.00
140 Steve Young 6.00 15.00
141 Jerome Bettis 8.00 20.00
142 Kurt Warner 6.00 15.00
143 Trent Green 3.00 8.00
144 Keyshawn Johnson 3.00 8.00
145 Warren Sapp 3.00 8.00
146 Warrick Dunn 3.00 8.00
147 Jevon Kearse 3.00 8.00
148 Deion Sanders 6.00 15.00
149 Laveranues Coles 2.50 6.00
150 Stephen Davis 3.00 8.00
201 Adam Jones 2.00 5.00
202 Alex Smith QB 5.00 12.00
203 Andrew Walter 2.50 6.00
204 Antrel Rolle 3.00 8.00
205 Braylon Edwards 4.00 10.00
206 Cadillac Williams 3.00 8.00
207 Carlos Rogers 3.00 8.00
208 Charlie Frye 3.00 8.00
209 Ciatrick Fason 2.00 5.00
210 Courtney Roby 2.50 6.00
211 Eric Shelton 2.00 5.00
212 Frank Gore 5.00 12.00
213 J.J. Arrington 2.50 6.00
214 Kyle Orton 3.00 8.00
215 Jason Campbell 4.00 10.00
216 Mark Bradley 2.00 5.00
217 Mark Clayton 2.50 6.00
218 Matt Jones 2.50 6.00
219 Maurice Clarett 2.00 5.00
220 Reggie Brown 2.00 5.00
221 Roddy White 4.00 10.00
222 Ronnie Brown 4.00 10.00
223 Roscoe Parrish 2.00 5.00
224 Ryan Moats 2.00 5.00
225 Stefan LeFors 2.00 5.00
226 Terrence Murphy 2.00 5.00
227 Troy Williamson 2.50 6.00
228 Vernand Morency 2.00 5.00
229 Vincent Jackson 4.00 10.00

2005 Leaf Certified Materials Mirror Blue Materials

*VETERANS: .8X TO 2X MIR.RED MATER.
*ROOKIES: 1.2X TO 3X MIRROR RED MATER.
BLUE PRINT RUN 50 SER.#'d SETS

2005 Leaf Certified Materials Mirror Gold Materials

*VETERANS: 1.2X TO 3X MIR.RED MATER.
*ROOKIE: 2X TO 5X MIRROR RED MAT.
GOLD PRINT RUN 25 SER.#'d SETS

2005 Leaf Certified Materials Mirror White Materials

*SINGLES: .3X TO .8X MIRROR RED MATER.
MIR.WHITE PRINT RUN 175 SER.#'d SETS

2005 Leaf Certified Materials Mirror White Signatures

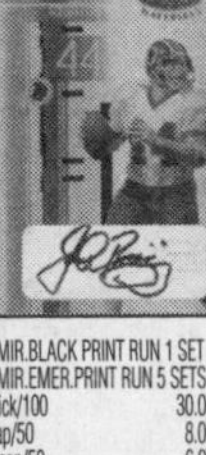

UNPRICED MIR.BLACK PRINT RUN 1 SET
UNPRICED MIR.EMER.PRINT RUN 5 SETS
4 Michael Vick/100 30.00 60.00
10 Todd Heap/50 8.00 20.00
15 J.P. Losman/50 6.00 15.00
16 Lee Evans/50 8.00 20.00
17 Willis McGahee/50 10.00 25.00
20 Steve Smith/100 12.50 30.00
30 Julius Jones/100 5.00 12.00
31 Keyshawn Johnson/25 10.00 25.00
33 Terence Newman/100 5.00 12.00
34 Ashley Lelie/50 6.00 15.00
38 Tatum Bell/50 6.00 15.00
40 Joey Harrington/25 10.00 25.00
54 Reggie Wayne/50 10.00 25.00
55 Byron Leftwich/50 8.00 20.00
57 Jimmy Smith/75 6.00 15.00
71 Deion Branch/75 5.00 12.00
72 Aaron Brooks/100 5.00 12.00
73 Deuce McAllister/50 8.00 20.00
75 Joe Horn/75 6.00 15.00
76 Eli Manning/125 40.00 80.00
79 Tiki Barber/50 20.00 40.00
93 Jevon Kearse/50 8.00 20.00
98 Duce Staley/50 8.00 20.00
99 Hines Ward/39 35.00 60.00
101 Antonio Gates/75 10.00 25.00
107 Matt Hasselbeck/75 6.00 15.00
110 Steven Jackson/79 8.00 20.00
112 Michael Clayton/100 5.00 12.00
113 Chris Brown/100 5.00 12.00
114 Drew Bennett/75 6.00 15.00
119 John Riggins/50 30.00 60.00
131 Warren Moon/50 15.00 40.00
140 Steve Young/50 40.00 80.00
153 DeMarcus Ware/100 25.00 50.00
154 Shawne Merriman/50 25.00 50.00
155 Thomas Davis/100 5.00 12.00
156 Derrick Johnson/50 8.00 20.00
157 Travis Johnson/100 5.00 12.00
158 David Pollack/50 8.00 20.00
159 Erasmus James/50 8.00 20.00
162 Aaron Rodgers/50 350.00 500.00
163 Marlin Jackson/100 5.00 12.00
164 Heath Miller/50 12.50 30.00
165 Matt Roth/100 6.00 15.00
166 Dan Cody/100 6.00 15.00
167 Bryant McFadden/100 6.00 15.00
168 Chris Henry/100 8.00 20.00
169 David Greene/100 5.00 12.00
170 Brandon Jones/100 6.00 15.00
171 Marion Barber/100 8.00 20.00
172 Brandon Jacobs/100 20.00 40.00
173 Jerome Mathis/100 8.00 20.00
174 Craphonso Thorpe/100 5.00 12.00
175 Alvin Pearman/100 5.00 12.00
176 Darren Sproles/100 20.00 40.00
177 Fred Gibson/100 6.00 15.00
178 Roydell Williams/100 6.00 15.00
179 Airese Currie/100 5.00 12.00
180 Damien Nash/100 6.00 15.00
181 Dan Orlovsky/100 8.00 20.00
182 Adrian McPherson/100 5.00 12.00
183 Larry Brackins/100 5.00 12.00
184 Rasheed Marshall/100 6.00 15.00
185 Cedric Houston/100 8.00 20.00
186 Chad Owens/100 6.00 15.00
187 Tab Perry/100 5.00 12.00
188 Dante Ridgeway/100 5.00 12.00
189 Craig Bragg/100 5.00 12.00
190 Deandra Cobb/100 5.00 12.00
191 Derek Anderson/100 6.00 15.00
192 Paris Warren/100 6.00 15.00
193 Lionel Gates/100 5.00 12.00
194 Anthony Davis/100 5.00 12.00
195 Ryan Fitzpatrick/100 20.00 40.00
196 J.R. Russell/100 5.00 12.00
197 Jason White/100 8.00 20.00
198 Kay-Jay Harris/100 5.00 12.00
199 T.A. McLendon/100 5.00 12.00
200 Taylor Stubblefield/100 5.00 12.00

2005 Leaf Certified Materials Mirror Blue Signatures

*VETS/30-50: .6X TO 1.5X MIR.WHITE/100
*VETERANS/30: .6X TO 1.5X MIR.WHITE/75
*VETERANS/25: .6X TO 1.5X MIR.WHITE/100
*ROOKIES/30: .8X TO 2X MIR.WHITE/100
BLUE SER.#'d UNDER 25 NOT PRICED

2005 Leaf Certified Materials Mirror Gold Signatures

*VETERANS/25: .6X TO 1.5X MIR.WHITE/100
GOLD SER.#'d UNDER 25 NOT PRICED

2005 Leaf Certified Materials Mirror Red Signatures

*RED/70-75: .4X TO 1X WHITE/100
*RED/50: .5X TO 1.2X WHITE/75-100
*RED/25: .5X TO 1.2X WHITE/39-50
*RED/25: .6X TO 1.5X WHITE/100
RED STATED PRINT RUN 20-100
9 Kyle Boller/25 10.00 25.00
43 Ahman Green/25 15.00 40.00
71 Deion Branch/50 6.00 15.00
151 Cedric Benson/25 30.00 80.00
162 Aaron Rodgers/25 400.00 700.00

2006 Leaf Certified Materials

This 251-card set was released in September, 2006. The set was issued into the hobby in September, 2006. The set was five-card packs which came 10 packs to a box. Cards numbered 1-150 feature veterans in team alphabetical order while cards numbered 151-231 feature rookies and cards numbered 232-251 feature retired greats. Cards numbered 151-200 were issued to a stated print run of either 500 or 1000 copies, while cards numbered 201-232 all had player-worn swatches and those cards were issued to various print runs, which we have notated in our checklists and cards numbered 233-251 all feature game-worn swatches and those cards were issued to stated print runs of between 75 and 150 serial numbered copies.

COMP.SET w/o SP's (150) 15.00 40.00
1 Anquan Boldin .30 .75
2 Edgerrin James .30 .75
3 Kurt Warner .40 1.00
4 Larry Fitzgerald .40 1.00
5 Alge Crumpler .30 .75
6 Brian Finneran .25 .60
7 Michael Jenkins .30 .75
8 Michael Vick .40 1.00
9 Warrick Dunn .30 .75
10 Derrick Mason .30 .75
11 Jamal Lewis .30 .75
12 Kyle Boller .30 .75
13 Todd Heap .30 .75
14 Mark Clayton .30 .75
15 Eric Moulds .25 .60
16 J.P. Losman .30 .75
17 Josh Reed .25 .60
18 Lee Evans .30 .75
19 Willis McGahee .30 .75
20 DeShaun Foster .30 .75
21 Jake Delhomme .30 .75
22 Stephen Davis .30 .75
23 Keary Colbert .25 .60
24 Steve Smith .40 1.00
25 Brian Urlacher .40 1.00
26 Cedric Benson .30 .75
27 Muhsin Muhammad .30 .75
28 Rex Grossman .30 .75
29 Thomas Jones .30 .75
30 Carson Palmer .40 1.00
31 Chad Johnson .30 .75
32 Rudi Johnson .30 .75
33 T.J. Houshmandzadeh .30 .75
34 Charlie Frye .30 .75
35 Dennis Northcutt .25 .60
36 Braylon Edwards .30 .75
37 Reuben Droughns .30 .75
38 Drew Bledsoe .40 1.00
39 Julius Jones .25 .60
40 Terrell Owens .40 1.00
41 Jason Witten .40 1.00
42 Terry Glenn .30 .75
43 Roy Williams S .30 .75
44 Jake Plummer .30 .75
45 Rod Smith .30 .75
46 Tatum Bell .25 .60
47 Ashley Lelie .25 .60
48 Josh McCown .25 .60
49 Kevin Jones .25 .60
50 Mike Williams .25 .60
51 Roy Williams WR .30 .75
52 Ahman Green .30 .75
53 Brett Favre .75 2.00
54 Aaron Rodgers .75 2.00
55 Samkon Gado .30 .75
56 Donald Driver .40 1.00
57 Robert Ferguson .25 .60
58 Andre Johnson .40 1.00
59 David Carr .25 .60
60 Domanick Davis .25 .60
61 Dallas Clark .30 .75
62 Marvin Harrison .40 1.00
63 Peyton Manning .60 1.50
64 Reggie Wayne .30 .75
65 Brandon Stokley .30 .75
66 Byron Leftwich .30 .75
67 Fred Taylor .30 .75
68 Jimmy Smith .30 .75
69 Matt Jones .25 .60
70 Larry Johnson .30 .75
71 Tony Gonzalez .30 .75
72 Trent Green .30 .75
73 Eddie Kennison .25 .60
74 Samie Parker .25 .60
75 Chris Chambers .30 .75
76 Daunte Culpepper .30 .75
77 Randy McMichael .25 .60
78 Ronnie Brown .40 1.00
79 Marty Booker .25 .60
80 Zach Thomas .40 1.00
81 Brad Johnson .30 .75
82 Mewelde Moore .25 .60
83 Nate Burleson .25 .60
84 Troy Williamson .25 .60
85 Deion Branch .30 .75
86 Tom Brady .60 1.50
87 Corey Dillon .30 .75
88 Daniel Graham .25 .60
89 Troy Brown .25 .60
90 Deuce McAllister .30 .75
91 Donte Stallworth .25 .60
92 Drew Brees .40 1.00
93 Joe Horn .30 .75
94 Devery Henderson .25 .60
95 Eli Manning .50 1.25
96 Jeremy Shockey .40 1.00
97 Plaxico Burress .30 .75
98 Amani Toomer .30 .75
99 Tiki Barber .40 1.00
100 Chad Pennington .30 .75
101 Curtis Martin .40 1.00
102 Laveranues Coles .25 .60
103 Justin McCareins .25 .60
104 Jerry Porter .25 .60
105 LaMont Jordan .30 .75
106 Doug Gabriel .25 .60
107 Randy Moss .40 1.00
108 Brian Westbrook .30 .75
109 Donovan McNabb .40 1.00
110 Reggie Brown .25 .60
111 Chad Lewis .25 .60
112 Ryan Moats .25 .60
113 Jevon Kearse .30 .75
114 Ben Roethlisberger .50 1.25
115 Heath Miller .30 .75
116 Hines Ward .40 1.00
117 Willie Parker .30 .75
118 Troy Polamalu .50 1.25
119 Antonio Gates .40 1.00
120 Eric Parker .25 .60
121 Keenan McCardell .30 .75
122 LaDainian Tomlinson .40 1.00
123 Philip Rivers .40 1.00
124 Alex Smith QB .40 1.00
125 Antonio Bryant .25 .60
126 Frank Gore .40 1.00
127 Kevan Barlow .25 .60
128 Darrell Jackson .30 .75
129 Jerramy Stevens .30 .75
130 Matt Hasselbeck .30 .75
131 Shaun Alexander .30 .75
132 Isaac Bruce .30 .75
133 Marc Bulger .30 .75
134 Marshall Faulk .30 .75
135 Steven Jackson .40 1.00
136 Torry Holt .30 .75
137 Cadillac Williams .30 .75
138 Chris Simms .30 .75
139 Joey Galloway .30 .75
140 Michael Clayton .25 .60
141 Brandon Jones .25 .60
142 Chris Brown .25 .60
143 Drew Bennett .30 .75
144 Tyrone Calico .25 .60
145 Steve McNair .30 .75
146 Antwaan Randle El .30 .75
147 Clinton Portis .40 1.00
148 Mark Brunell .30 .75
149 Santana Moss .30 .75
150 Jason Campbell .30 .75
151 Brodie Croyle/500 RC 3.00 8.00
152 Greg Jennings/500 RC 5.00 12.00
153 Joseph Addai/500 RC 3.00 8.00
154 Bennie Brazell/1000 RC 1.50 4.00
155 David Thomas/500 RC 2.50 6.00
156 Marques Colston/1000 RC 4.00 10.00
157 Reggie McNeal/500 RC 2.50 6.00
158 D.J. Shockley/1000 RC 1.50 4.00
159 Dominique Byrd/500 RC 2.50 6.00
160 Antonio Cromartie/1000 RC 2.00 5.00
161 Donte Whitner/1000 RC 2.00 5.00
162 Anwar Phillips/1000 RC 1.50 4.00
163 A.J. Nicholson/1000 RC 1.25 3.00
164 De'Arrius Howard/500 RC 3.00 8.00
165 Erik Meyer/500 RC 2.50 6.00
166 Darrell Hackney/1000 RC 1.50 4.00
167 Paul Pinegar/500 RC 2.00 5.00
168 Brandon Kirsch/500 RC 2.50 6.00
169 Quinton Ganther/1000 RC 1.25 3.00
170 Andre Hall/1000 RC 1.50 4.00
171 Derrick Ross/1000 RC 1.50 4.00
172 Mike Bell/1000 RC 2.00 5.00
173 Wendell Mathis/500 RC 2.50 6.00
174 Garrett Mills/500 RC 3.00 8.00
175 David Anderson/1000 RC 1.50 4.00
176 Kevin McMahan/1000 RC 1.50 4.00
177 Martin Nance/1000 RC 1.50 4.00
178 Greg Lee/500 RC 2.00 5.00
179 Anthony Mix/500 RC 2.50 6.00
180 D'Brickashaw Ferguson/500 RC 3.00 8.00
181 Tamba Hali/500 RC 3.00 8.00
182 Haloti Ngata/1000 RC 2.00 5.00
183 Claude Wroten/1000 RC 1.25 3.00
184 Gabe Watson/1000 RC 1.25 3.00
185 D'Qwell Jackson/1000 RC 1.50 4.00
186 Abdul Hodge/500 RC 2.00 5.00
187 Chad Greenway/500 RC 3.00 8.00
188 Bobby Carpenter/1000 RC 1.25 3.00
189 DeMeco Ryans/500 RC 3.00 8.00
190 Rocky McIntosh/500 RC 2.50 6.00
191 Thomas Howard/1000 RC 1.50 4.00
192 Jon Alston/500 RC 2.00 5.00
193 Jimmy Williams/1000 RC 2.00 5.00
194 Ashton Youboty/500 RC 2.00 5.00
195 Alan Zemaitis/1000 RC 2.00 5.00
196 Cedric Griffin/500 RC 2.50 6.00
197 Ko Simpson/1000 RC 1.50 4.00
198 Pat Watkins/500 RC 2.50 6.00
199 Bernard Pollard/1000 RC 1.50 4.00
200 Jay Cutler/500 RC 4.00 10.00
201 Chad Jackson JSY/1400 RC 3.00 8.00
202 Laurence Maroney JSY/550 RC 2.50 6.00
203 Tarvaris Jackson JSY/1400 RC 2.50 6.00
204 Michael Huff JSY/1400 RC 2.00 5.00
205 Mario Williams JSY/1400 RC 2.50 6.00
206 Marcedes Lewis JSY/1400 RC 2.50 6.00
207 Maurice Drew JSY/1400 RC 4.00 10.00
208 Vince Young JSY/550 RC 4.00 10.00
209 LenDale White JSY/550 RC 4.00 10.00
210 Reggie Bush JSY/550 RC 6.00 15.00
211 Matt Leinart JSY/550 RC 3.00 8.00
212 Michael Robinson JSY/1400 RC 3.00 8.00
213 Vernon Davis JSY/550 RC 5.00 12.00
214 Brandon Williams JSY/1400 RC 1.50 4.00
215 Derek Hagan JSY/1400 RC 3.00 8.00
216 Jason Avant JSY/1400 RC 1.50 4.00
217 Brandon Marshall JSY/1400 RC 3.00 8.00
218 Omar Jacobs JSY/1400 RC 3.00 8.00
219 Santonio Holmes JSY/550 RC 6.00 15.00
220 Jerious Norwood JSY/1400 RC 2.00 5.00
221 Demetrius Williams JSY/1400 RC 3.00 8.00
222 Sinorice Moss JSY/1400 RC 3.00 8.00
223 Leon Washington JSY/1400 RC 2.00 5.00
224 Kellen Clemens JSY/900 RC 2.00 5.00
225 A.J. Hawk JSY/550 RC 3.00 8.00
226 Maurice Stovall JSY/1400 RC 3.00 8.00
227 DeAngelo Williams JSY/550 RC 4.00 10.00
228 Charlie Whitehurst JSY/1400 RC 2.50 6.00
229 Travis Wilson JSY/1400 RC 3.00 8.00
230 Joe Klopfenstein JSY/1400 RC 3.00 8.00
231 Brian Calhoun JSY/1400 RC 3.00 8.00
232 Barry Sanders JSY/150 10.00 25.00
233 Jerry Rice JSY/150 8.00 20.00
234 Dan Marino JSY/150 12.00 30.00
235 Earl Campbell JSY/150 6.00 15.00
236 Jim Brown JSY/100 10.00 25.00
237 Joe Montana JSY/125 10.00 25.00
238 Troy Aikman JSY/150 8.00 20.00
239 Walter Payton JSY/100 15.00 40.00
240 Terry Bradshaw JSY/150 10.00 25.00
241 John Elway JSY/150 10.00 25.00
242 Fred Biletnikoff JSY/100 6.00 15.00
243 Lance Alworth JSY/125 6.00 15.00
244 Ronnie Lott JSY/150 6.00 15.00
245 Yale Lary JSY/125 6.00 15.00
246 Bart Starr JSY/80 12.00 30.00
247 Doak Walker JSY/75 10.00 25.00
248 Gale Sayers JSY/100 8.00 20.00
249 Bo Jackson JSY/150 6.00 15.00
250 Roger Staubach JSY/125 10.00 25.00
251 Dick Butkus JSY/150 8.00 20.00

2006 Leaf Certified Materials Mirror Red

*RED VETS 1-150: 4X TO 10X BASIC CARDS
*ROOKIES: 1X TO 2.5X BASIC RC/1000
*ROOKIES: .6X TO 1.5X BASIC RC/500
RED PRINT RUN 100 SER.#'d SETS
UNPRICED MIRROR BLACK #'d TO 1
UNPRICED MIRROR EMERALD #'d TO 5

2006 Leaf Certified Materials Mirror Blue

*BLUE VETS 1-150: 5X TO 12X BASIC CARDS
*ROOKIES: 1.2X TO 3X BASIC RC/1000
*ROOKIES: .8X TO 2X BASIC RC/500
BLUE PRINT RUN 50 SER.#'d SETS

2006 Leaf Certified Materials Mirror Gold

*GOLD VETS 1-150: 8X TO 20X BASIC CARDS
*ROOKIES: 2X TO 5X BASIC RC/1000
*ROOKIES: 1.2X TO 3X BASIC RC/500
GOLD PRINT RUN 25 SER.#'d SETS

2006 Leaf Certified Materials Certified Potential Gold

*MIRROR/500: .5X TO 1.2X GOLD/800
MIRROR PRINT RUN 500 SER.#'d SETS
*RED/250: .6X TO 1.5X GOLD/800
RED PRINT RUN 250 SER.#'d SETS
*BLUE/100: .8X TO 2X GOLD/800
BLUE PRINT RUN 100 SER.#'d SETS
*HOLOGOLD/25: 1.2X TO 3X GOLD/800
HOLOGOLD PRINT RUN 25 SER.#'d SETS
UNPRICED EMERALD PRINT RUN 5 SETS
UNPRICED BLACK PRINT RUN 1 SET
1 Alex Smith QB 1.25 3.00
2 Andre Johnson 1.25 3.00
3 Braylon Edwards 1.00 2.50
4 Cadillac Williams 1.00 2.50
5 Cedric Benson 1.00 2.50
6 Charlie Frye 1.00 2.50
7 Chris Brown .75 2.00
8 Chris Chambers 1.00 2.50
9 Darrell Jackson 1.00 2.50
10 Kevin Jones .75 2.00
11 Lee Evans 1.00 2.50
12 Mark Clayton 1.00 2.50
13 Matt Jones .75 2.00
14 Nate Burleson .75 2.00
15 Reggie Brown .75 2.00
16 Ronnie Brown 1.25 3.00
17 Samkon Gado 1.00 2.50
18 Santana Moss 1.00 2.50
19 Steven Jackson 1.25 3.00

2006 Leaf Certified Materials Certified Potential Materials

STATED PRINT RUN 100 SER.#'d SETS
PRIME BLACK PRINT RUN 1 SER.#'d SETS
1 Alex Smith QB 4.00 10.00
2 Andre Johnson 3.00 8.00
3 Braylon Edwards 3.00 8.00
4 Cadillac Williams 4.00 10.00
5 Cedric Benson 3.00 8.00
7 Chris Brown 2.50 6.00
8 Chris Chambers 3.00 8.00
9 Darrell Jackson 3.00 8.00
10 Kevin Jones 4.00 10.00
11 Lee Evans 2.50 6.00
12 Mark Clayton 3.00 8.00
13 Matt Jones 3.00 8.00
14 Nate Burleson 3.00 8.00
15 Reggie Brown 3.00 8.00
16 Ronnie Brown 4.00 10.00
17 Samkon Gado/51 3.00 8.00
18 Santana Moss 3.00 8.00
19 Steven Jackson 4.00 10.00

2006 Leaf Certified Materials Certified Skills Gold

GOLD PRINT RUN 800 SER.#'d SETS
*MIRROR/500: .5X TO 1.2X GOLD/800
MIRROR PRINT RUN 500 SER.#'d SETS
*RED/250: .6X TO 1.5X GOLD/800
RED PRINT RUN 250 SER.#'d SETS
*BLUE/100: .8X TO 2X GOLD/800
BLUE PRINT RUN 100 SER.#'d SETS
*HOLOGOLD/25: 1.2X TO 3X GOLD/800
EMERALD PRINT RUN 5 SER.#'d SETS
BLACK PRINT RUN 1 SER.#'d SETS
1 Anquan Boldin 1.00 2.50
2 Antonio Gates 1.25 3.00
3 Byron Leftwich 1.00 2.50
4 Chad Johnson 1.00 2.50
5 Clinton Portis 1.25 3.00
6 Domanick Davis .75 2.00
7 Donovan McNabb 1.25 3.00
8 Drew Bennett 1.00 2.50
9 Edgerrin James 1.00 2.50
10 Hines Ward 1.25 3.00
11 Javon Walker 1.00 2.50
12 Larry Johnson 1.00 2.50
13 Marvin Harrison 1.25 3.00
14 Roy Williams WR 1.00 2.50
15 Rudi Johnson 1.00 2.50
16 Tatum Bell .75 2.00
17 Tiki Barber 1.25 3.00
18 Torry Holt 1.00 2.50
19 Willie Parker 1.00 2.50
20 Willis McGahee 1.00 2.50

2006 Leaf Certified Materials Certified Skills Materials

STATED PRINT RUN 100 SER.#'d SETS
UNPRICED PRIME PRINT RUN 5 SETS
UNPRICED PRIME BLACK PRINT RUN 1 SET
1 Anquan Boldin 3.00 8.00
2 Antonio Gates 3.00 8.00
3 Byron Leftwich 3.00 8.00
4 Chad Johnson 3.00 8.00
5 Clinton Portis 4.00 10.00
6 Domanick Davis 2.50 6.00
7 Donovan McNabb 4.00 10.00
8 Drew Bennett 2.50 6.00
9 Edgerrin James 4.00 10.00
10 Hines Ward 4.00 10.00
11 Javon Walker 3.00 8.00
12 Larry Johnson 4.00 10.00
14 Roy Williams WR 4.00 10.00
15 Rudi Johnson 3.00 8.00
16 Tatum Bell 3.00 8.00
17 Tiki Barber 4.00 10.00
18 Torry Holt 3.00 8.00
20 Willis McGahee 3.00 8.00

2006 Leaf Certified Materials Fabric of the Game

STATED PRINT RUN 100 SER.#'d SETS
SERIAL #'d UNDER 25 NOT PRICED
1 Barry Sanders 10.00 25.00
2 Bart Starr/75 12.00 30.00
3 Bo Jackson 10.00 25.00
4 Bob Griese 5.00 12.00
5 Deuce McAllister 3.00 8.00
6 Charley Taylor 4.00 10.00
7 Cliff Branch 5.00 12.00
8 Craig Morton 4.00 10.00
9 Cris Carter 6.00 15.00
10 Dan Marino 12.00 30.00
11 Deacon Jones 4.00 10.00
12 Deion Sanders 5.00 12.00
13 Dick Butkus 8.00 20.00
14 Don Maynard 4.00 10.00
15 Earl Campbell 5.00 12.00
16 Eric Dickerson 5.00 12.00
17 Fran Tarkenton 5.00 12.00
18 Fred Biletnikoff 5.00 12.00
19 Gale Sayers/75 8.00 20.00
20 George Blanda 8.00 20.00
21 Harvey Martin 5.00 12.00
22 Henry Ellard 4.00 10.00
23 Herman Edwards 3.00 8.00
24 Ickey Woods 4.00 10.00
25 Jack Lambert 8.00 20.00
26 Jackie Smith 4.00 10.00
27 Jim Brown/50 12.00 30.00
28 Jim Otto 5.00 12.00
29 Joe Montana/80 12.00 30.00
30 Joe Theismann 5.00 12.00
31 John Elway 10.00 25.00
32 John Riggins 5.00 12.00
33 Lance Alworth/75 8.00 20.00
34 Len Dawson 6.00 15.00
35 Marcus Allen 5.00 12.00
36 Mark Gastineau 5.00 12.00
37 Mike Singletary 5.00 12.00
38 Paul Krause 4.00 10.00
39 Paul Warfield 4.00 10.00
40 Phil Simms 5.00 12.00
41 Roger Staubach 10.00 25.00
42 Ronnie Lott 6.00 15.00
43 Steve Largent 5.00 12.00
44 Terrell Davis/75 5.00 12.00
45 Terry Bradshaw 10.00 25.00
46 Thurman Thomas 4.00 10.00
47 Tony Dorsett 6.00 15.00
48 Troy Aikman 8.00 20.00
49 Walter Payton/75 15.00 40.00
50 Warren Moon 5.00 12.00
51 Willie Brown 4.00 10.00
52 Y.A. Tittle 8.00 20.00
53 Yale Lary 4.00 10.00
54 Doak Walker/50 20.00 40.00
55 Jerry Rice 8.00 20.00
57 Red Grange/50 75.00 135.00
60 Ahman Green 4.00 10.00
61 Alex Smith QB 4.00 10.00
62 Alge Crumpler 3.00 8.00
63 Andre Johnson 3.00 8.00
64 Anquan Boldin 3.00 8.00
65 Jimmy Smith 3.00 8.00
66 Antonio Gates 3.00 8.00
67 Ashley Lelie 2.50 6.00
68 Ben Roethlisberger 8.00 20.00
69 Deion Branch 3.00 8.00
70 Brandon Jones 2.50 6.00
71 Braylon Edwards 3.00 8.00
72 Brett Favre 8.00 20.00
73 Brian Urlacher 4.00 10.00
74 Brian Westbrook/75 3.00 8.00
75 Byron Leftwich 3.00 8.00
76 Cadillac Williams 4.00 10.00
77 Carson Palmer 4.00 10.00
78 Cedric Benson 3.00 8.00
79 Chad Johnson 3.00 8.00
80 Chad Pennington 3.00 8.00
82 Chris Brown 2.50 6.00
83 Chris Chambers 3.00 8.00
84 Clinton Portis 4.00 10.00
85 Corey Dillon 3.00 8.00
86 Curtis Martin 4.00 10.00
87 Dallas Clark 2.50 6.00
88 Darrell Jackson 3.00 8.00
89 David Carr 3.00 8.00
91 Domanick Davis 2.50 6.00
93 Donovan McNabb 4.00 10.00
94 Donte Stallworth 3.00 8.00
95 Daunte Culpepper 4.00 10.00
97 Edgerrin James 4.00 10.00
98 Eli Manning 6.00 15.00
99 Fred Taylor 3.00 8.00
100 Hines Ward 4.00 10.00
101 Jake Delhomme 3.00 8.00
102 Javon Walker 3.00 8.00
103 Jeremy Shockey 4.00 10.00
104 Julius Jones 4.00 10.00
105 Keenan McCardell 2.50 6.00
106 Kevin Jones 4.00 10.00
107 LaDainian Tomlinson 4.00 10.00
108 LaMont Jordan 3.00 8.00
109 Larry Fitzgerald 3.00 8.00
110 Larry Johnson 4.00 10.00
111 Laveranues Coles 3.00 8.00
112 Lee Evans 2.50 6.00
113 Marc Bulger/75 3.00 8.00
114 Mark Clayton 3.00 8.00
115 Marvin Harrison 4.00 10.00
116 Matt Hasselbeck 3.00 8.00
117 Matt Jones 3.00 8.00
118 Michael Clayton 2.50 6.00
119 Michael Vick 4.00 10.00
120 Peyton Manning 8.00 20.00
121 Philip Rivers 4.00 10.00
122 Plaxico Burress 3.00 8.00
123 Priest Holmes 3.00 8.00
124 Randy Moss 4.00 10.00
125 Reggie Brown 3.00 8.00
126 Reggie Wayne 3.00 8.00
127 Reuben Droughns 2.50 6.00
128 Robert Ferguson 2.50 6.00
129 Rod Smith 3.00 8.00
130 Ronnie Brown 4.00 10.00
131 Roy Williams S 4.00 10.00
132 Roy Williams WR 4.00 10.00
133 Rudi Johnson 3.00 8.00
134 Samkon Gado 3.00 8.00
135 Santana Moss 3.00 8.00
136 Shaun Alexander 5.00 12.00
137 Steve McNair 3.00 8.00
138 Steve Smith 4.00 10.00
139 Steven Jackson 4.00 10.00
140 Stephen Davis 2.50 6.00
142 Thomas Jones 3.00 8.00
143 Tiki Barber 4.00 10.00
144 Tom Brady 6.00 15.00
145 Tony Gonzalez 3.00 8.00
146 Torry Holt 3.00 8.00
147 Trent Green 3.00 8.00
149 Willis McGahee 3.00 8.00

2006 Leaf Certified Materials Fabric of the Game Prime

*PRIME/15-25: 1X TO 2.5X BASIC JSY/75-100
*PRIME/15-25: .8X TO 2X BASIC JSY/50
59 Aaron Rodgers 25.00 60.00
92 Donald Driver 6.00 15.00
96 Drew Bledsoe 10.00 25.00
141 T.J. Houshmandzadeh 6.00 15.00
148 Willie Parker 10.00 25.00
150 Zach Thomas 10.00 25.00

2006 Leaf Certified Materials Fabric of the Game College

STATED PRINT RUN 100 SER.#'d SETS
*PRIME/25: 1X TO 2.5X BASIC INSERTS
PRIME PRINT RUN 25 SER.#'d SETS
PRIME SER.#'d UNDER 25 NOT PRICED
1 Roy Williams WR 6.00 15.00
2 LenDale White 8.00 20.00
3 Reggie Bush 10.00 25.00
4 Matt Leinart 5.00 12.00
5 Cadillac Williams 6.00 15.00
6 Ronnie Brown 6.00 15.00
7 Reggie Wayne/65 4.00 10.00
8 Braylon Edwards 4.00 10.00
9 Dan Marino 15.00 40.00
10 Eric Dickerson 8.00 20.00
11 Peyton Manning 20.00 50.00
12 A.J. Hawk 10.00 25.00
13 Laurence Maroney 4.00 10.00
14 Maurice Drew 8.00 20.00
15 Maurice Stovall 6.00 15.00
16 Travis Wilson 6.00 15.00
17 Marcedes Lewis 5.00 12.00
18 Jay Cutler 10.00 25.00
19 Mario Williams 5.00 12.00
20 Joseph Addai 5.00 12.00

2006 Leaf Certified Materials Fabric of the Game College Combos

STATED PRINT RUN 50 SER.#'d SETS
UNPRICED PRIME PRINT RUN 10 SETS
1 Roy Williams WR 10.00 25.00
Cedric Benson
2 Peyton Manning 25.00 60.00
Matt Leinart
3 Barry Sanders 25.00 60.00
Thurman Thomas
4 Roger Staubach 15.00 40.00
Terry Bradshaw
5 Mario Williams 10.00 25.00
A.J. Hawk

2006 Leaf Certified Materials Fabric of the Game Combos

STATED PRINT RUN 1-50 SER.#'d SETS
SERIAL #'d UNDER 25 NOT PRICED
UNPRICED PRIME PRINT RUN 10 SETS
1 Bart Starr 30.00 80.00
Aaron Rodgers
2 Thurman Thomas 5.00 12.00
Willis McGahee
3 Ickey Woods 5.00 12.00
Rudi Johnson
5 Doak Walker 50.00 100.00
Dutch Clark/25
6 Eric Dickerson 8.00 20.00
Marcus Allen
7 Tony Gonzalez 5.00 12.00
Jeremy Shockey
8 Ben Roethlisberger 15.00 40.00
Matt Hasselbeck
10 Julius Jones 10.00 25.00
Thomas Jones
11 Cedric Benson 6.00 15.00
Roy Williams WR
12 Peyton Manning 15.00 40.00
Carson Palmer
13 Bo Jackson 8.00 20.00
Samkon Gado
14 Jimmy Smith 5.00 12.00
Steve Smith
15 Joe Montana 25.00 60.00
Brett Favre
16 Ronnie Lott 10.00 25.00
Roy Williams S
18 Tony Dorsett 15.00 40.00
Barry Sanders
19 Cadillac Williams 6.00 15.00
Ronnie Brown
20 Dan Marino 30.00 80.00
Troy Aikman
21 Larry Johnson 8.00 20.00
LaDainian Tomlinson
22 John Elway 15.00 40.00
Tom Brady
24 Terry Bradshaw 12.00 30.00
Joe Theismann
25 Jerry Rice 15.00 40.00
Lance Alworth

2006 Leaf Certified Materials Fabric of the Game Football Die Cut

*FB/66-100: .4X TO 1X BASIC FOTG/75-100
*FB/40-58: .5X TO 1.2X BASIC FOTG/75-100
STATED PRINT RUN 1-100 SER.#'d SETS
SERIAL #'d UNDER 25 NOT PRICED
57 Red Grange/25 90.00 150.00

2006 Leaf Certified Materials Fabric of the Game Jersey Number

*JN/75-99: .4X TO 1X BASIC FOTG/75-100
*JN/40-60: .5X TO 1.2X BASIC FOTG/75-100
*JN/30-39: .6X TO 1.5X BASIC FOTG/75-100
*JN/30-39: .5X TO 1.2X BASIC FOTG/50
*JN/25-29: .8X TO 2X BASIC FOTG/75-100
STATED PRINT RUN 1-99 SER.#'d SETS
SERIAL #'d UNDER 25 NOT PRICED

2006 Leaf Certified Materials Fabric of the Game Jersey Number Autographs

STATED PRINT RUN 1-89 SER.#'d SETS
SERIAL #'d UNDER 25 NOT PRICED
3 Bo Jackson/34 60.00 120.00
6 Charley Taylor/42 15.00 40.00
11 Deacon Jones/75 15.00 30.00
15 Earl Campbell/34 30.00 60.00
16 Eric Dickerson/29 40.00 80.00
18 Fred Biletnikoff/25 30.00 60.00
19 Gale Sayers/40 40.00 80.00
22 Henry Ellard/80 10.00 25.00
23 Herman Edwards/46 10.00 25.00
24 Ickey Woods/30 15.00 30.00
25 Jack Lambert/58 40.00 80.00
27 Jim Brown/32 60.00 120.00
28 Jim Otto/60 25.00 50.00
32 John Riggins/44 30.00 60.00
35 Marcus Allen/32 40.00 80.00
37 Mike Singletary/50 20.00 40.00
39 Paul Warfield/42 20.00 40.00
42 Ronnie Lott/42 40.00 80.00
43 Steve Largent/80 25.00 50.00
44 Terrell Davis/30 20.00 50.00
46 Thurman Thomas/34 15.00 40.00
47 Tony Dorsett/33 30.00 80.00
53 Yale Lary/28 30.00 60.00
55 Jerry Rice/80 90.00 150.00
62 Alge Crumpler/83 10.00 30.00
64 Anquan Boldin/81 12.00 30.00
69 Deion Branch/83 12.00 30.00
78 Cedric Benson/32 20.00 50.00
82 Chris Brown/29 10.00 25.00
87 Dallas Clark/44 12.00 30.00
91 Domanick Davis/37 12.00 30.00
97 Edgerrin James/32 20.00 50.00
100 Hines Ward/86 30.00 60.00
106 Kevin Jones/34 15.00 40.00
108 LaMont Jordan/34 20.00 40.00
110 Larry Johnson/27 20.00 50.00
112 Lee Evans/83 10.00 25.00
118 Michael Clayton/80 10.00 25.00
123 Priest Holmes/31 20.00 50.00
125 Reggie Brown/86 12.00 30.00
126 Reggie Wayne/87 20.00 40.00
131 Roy Williams S/31 30.00 60.00
133 Rudi Johnson/32 15.00 40.00
134 Samkon Gado/35 15.00 40.00
135 Santana Moss/89 20.00 40.00
136 Shaun Alexander/37 40.00 80.00
138 Steve Smith/89 20.00 40.00
139 Steven Jackson/39 20.00 40.00
146 Torry Holt/81 12.00 30.00

2006 Leaf Certified Materials Fabric of the Game Position

*POS/40-50: .5X TO 1.2X FOTG/75-100
*POS/30-39: .6X TO 1.5X FOTG/75-100
STATED PRINT RUN 24-50 SER.#'d SETS
SERIAL #'d UNDER 25 NOT PRICED
59 Aaron Rodgers/30 20.00 40.00

2006 Leaf Certified Materials Fabric of the Game Team Logo

*TL/25: 1X TO 2.5X FOTG/75-100
STATED PRINT RUN 5-25 SER.#'d SETS
SERIAL #'d UNDER 25 NOT PRICED

UNPRICED AUTO PRINT RUN 2-5
58 Aaron Brooks 6.00 15.00
59 Aaron Rodgers 20.00 50.00
90 DeShaun Foster 8.00 20.00
92 Donald Driver 8.00 20.00
141 T.J. Houshmandzadeh 8.00 20.00
148 Willie Parker 10.00 25.00
150 Zach Thomas 8.00 20.00

2006 Leaf Certified Materials Gold Team

STATED PRINT RUN 500 SER.#'d SETS
*MIRROR/100: .6X TO 1.5X GOLD/500
MIRROR PRINT RUN 100 SER.#'d SETS
1 Ben Roethlisberger 2.00 5.00
2 Brett Favre 3.00 8.00
3 Carson Palmer 1.50 4.00
4 Eli Manning 2.00 5.00
5 LaDainian Tomlinson 1.50 4.00
6 Larry Johnson 1.25 3.00
7 Peyton Manning 2.50 6.00
8 Shaun Alexander 1.25 3.00
9 Steve Smith 1.50 4.00
10 Tom Brady 2.50 6.00

2006 Leaf Certified Materials Gold Team Materials

STATED PRINT RUN 85-100 SER.#'d SETS
UNPRICED PRIME PRINT RUN 5 SETS
UNPRICED PRIME BLACK PRINT RUN 1
1 Ben Roethlisberger 8.00 20.00
2 Brett Favre 8.00 20.00
3 Carson Palmer 4.00 10.00
4 Eli Manning 6.00 15.00
5 LaDainian Tomlinson 4.00 10.00
6 Larry Johnson 4.00 10.00
7 Peyton Manning/85 8.00 20.00
8 Shaun Alexander 5.00 12.00
9 Steve Smith 4.00 10.00
10 Tom Brady 6.00 15.00

2006 Leaf Certified Materials Mirror Red Signatures

RED PRINT RUN 30-250 SER.#'d SETS
UNPRICED EMERALD PRINT RUN 5 SETS
UNPRICED BLACK PRINT RUN 1 SET
13 Todd Heap/172 6.00 15.00
18 Lee Evans/75 5.00 12.00
21 Jake Delhomme/75 8.00 20.00
32 Rudi Johnson/50 6.00 15.00
46 Tatum Bell/50 6.00 15.00
60 Domanick Davis/30 8.00 20.00
63 Peyton Manning/50 60.00 100.00
64 Reggie Wayne/50 8.00 20.00
69 Matt Jones/75 6.00 15.00
70 Larry Johnson/100 15.00 40.00
83 Nate Burleson/50 8.00 20.00
110 Reggie Brown/75 8.00 20.00
113 Jevon Kearse/100 6.00 15.00
154 Bennie Brazell/250 4.00 10.00
155 David Thomas/250 5.00 12.00
156 Marques Colston/150 25.00 60.00
157 Reggie McNeal/125 4.00 10.00
158 D.J. Shockley/125 4.00 10.00
159 Dominique Byrd/250 5.00 12.00
160 Antonio Cromartie/125 5.00 12.00
161 Donte Whitner/125 5.00 12.00
162 Anwar Phillips/169 4.00 10.00
163 A.J. Nicholson/194 4.00 10.00
165 Erik Meyer/250 4.00 10.00
166 Darrell Hackney/250 4.00 10.00
167 Paul Pinegar/250 4.00 10.00
168 Brandon Kirsch/244 5.00 12.00
169 Quinton Ganther/250 4.00 10.00
170 Andre Hall/250 5.00 12.00
171 Derrick Ross/250 4.00 10.00
172 Mike Bell/250 8.00 20.00
173 Wendell Mathis/250 4.00 10.00
174 Garrett Mills/250 5.00 12.00
175 David Anderson/250 4.00 10.00
176 Kevin McMahan/118 4.00 10.00
177 Martin Nance/250 4.00 10.00
178 Greg Lee/250 4.00 10.00
180 D'Brickashaw Ferguson/250 5.00 12.00
181 Tamba Hali/250 5.00 12.00
182 Haloti Ngata/250 5.00 12.00
183 Claude Wroten/250 4.00 10.00
184 Gabe Watson/250 4.00 10.00
185 D'Qwell Jackson/250 4.00 10.00
186 Abdul Hodge/250 5.00 12.00
187 Chad Greenway/250 6.00 15.00
188 Bobby Carpenter/250 4.00 10.00
189 DeMeco Ryans/250 6.00 15.00
190 Rocky McIntosh/250 5.00 12.00
191 Thomas Howard/250 5.00 12.00
192 Jon Alston/250 5.00 12.00
193 Jimmy Williams/250 5.00 12.00
194 Ashton Youboty/250 5.00 12.00
195 Alan Zemaitis/234 5.00 12.00
196 Cedric Griffin/250 4.00 10.00
197 Ko Simpson/250 4.00 10.00
198 Pat Watkins/250 5.00 12.00
199 Bernard Pollard/250 5.00 12.00

2006 Leaf Certified Materials Mirror Blue Signatures

13 Todd Heap/100 8.00 20.00
14 Mark Clayton/25 15.00 40.00
18 Lee Evans/25 10.00 25.00
21 Jake Delhomme/50 12.00 30.00
32 Rudi Johnson/50 8.00 20.00
43 Roy Williams S/40 12.00 30.00
46 Tatum Bell/25 12.00 30.00
60 Domanick Davis/25 10.00 25.00
63 Peyton Manning/25 75.00 150.00
64 Reggie Wayne/25 15.00 40.00
69 Matt Jones/50 10.00 25.00
70 Larry Johnson/50 15.00 40.00
83 Nate Burleson/25 12.00 30.00
110 Reggie Brown/25 12.00 30.00
113 Jevon Kearse/75 8.00 20.00
143 Drew Bennett/50 8.00 20.00
151 Brodie Croyle/50 6.00 15.00
152 Greg Jennings/50 40.00 80.00
153 Joseph Addai/75 20.00 50.00
154 Bennie Brazell/100 5.00 12.00
155 David Thomas/100 6.00 15.00
156 Marques Colston/50 30.00 80.00
157 Reggie McNeal/75 5.00 12.00
158 D.J. Shockley/75 6.00 15.00
159 Dominique Byrd/100 6.00 15.00
160 Antonio Cromartie/75 6.00 15.00
161 Donte Whitner/75 6.00 15.00
162 Anwar Phillips/100 5.00 12.00
163 A.J. Nicholson/100 5.00 12.00
164 De'Arrius Howard/70 5.00 12.00
165 Erik Meyer/100 5.00 12.00
166 Darrell Hackney/100 5.00 12.00
167 Paul Pinegar/100 5.00 12.00
168 Brandon Kirsch/100 6.00 15.00
169 Quinton Ganther/100 5.00 12.00
170 Andre Hall/100 6.00 15.00
171 Derrick Ross/100 5.00 12.00
172 Mike Bell/100 6.00 15.00
173 Wendell Mathis/100 5.00 12.00
174 Garrett Mills/100 5.00 12.00
175 David Anderson/100 5.00 12.00
176 Kevin McMahan/100 5.00 12.00
177 Martin Nance/100 5.00 12.00
178 Greg Lee/100 5.00 12.00
179 Anthony Mix/100 5.00 12.00
180 D'Brickashaw Ferguson/100 6.00 15.00
181 Tamba Hali/100 6.00 15.00
182 Haloti Ngata/100 6.00 15.00
183 Claude Wroten/100 5.00 12.00
184 Gabe Watson/100 5.00 12.00
185 D'Qwell Jackson/100 5.00 12.00
186 Abdul Hodge/100 6.00 15.00
187 Chad Greenway/100 6.00 15.00
188 Bobby Carpenter/100 6.00 15.00
189 DeMeco Ryans/100 8.00 20.00
190 Rocky McIntosh/100 6.00 15.00
191 Thomas Howard/100 6.00 15.00
192 Jon Alston/100 6.00 15.00
193 Jimmy Williams/100 6.00 15.00
194 Ashton Youboty/100 6.00 15.00
195 Alan Zemaitis/100 6.00 15.00
196 Cedric Griffin/100 5.00 12.00
197 Ko Simpson/100 5.00 12.00
198 Pat Watkins/100 6.00 15.00
199 Bernard Pollard/100 6.00 15.00
200 Jay Cutler/50 50.00 120.00

2006 Leaf Certified Materials Mirror Gold Signatures

GOLD PRINT RUN 6-25 SER.#'d SETS
SERIAL NUMBERED UNDER 25 NOT PRICED
5 Alge Crumpler/25 10.00 25.00
13 Todd Heap/25 12.00 30.00
21 Jake Delhomme/25 15.00 40.00
29 Thomas Jones/25 12.00 30.00
32 Rudi Johnson/25 12.00 30.00
36 Braylon Edwards/25 12.00 30.00
43 Roy Williams S/24 15.00 40.00
51 Roy Williams WR/25 15.00 40.00
55 Samkon Gado/25 12.00 30.00
62 Marvin Harrison/25 20.00 50.00
66 Byron Leftwich/25 15.00 40.00
68 Jimmy Smith/25 12.00 30.00
69 Matt Jones/25 12.00 30.00
70 Larry Johnson/25 25.00 60.00
113 Jevon Kearse/25 12.00 30.00
117 Willie Parker/25 15.00 40.00
130 Matt Hasselbeck/25 15.00 40.00
138 Chris Simms/25 12.00 30.00
143 Drew Bennett/25 10.00 25.00
151 Brodie Croyle/25 10.00 25.00
152 Greg Jennings/25 60.00 120.00
153 Joseph Addai/25 30.00 80.00
154 Bennie Brazell/25 8.00 20.00
155 David Thomas/25 10.00 25.00
156 Marques Colston/25 50.00 120.00
157 Reggie McNeal/25 8.00 20.00
158 D.J. Shockley/25 8.00 20.00
159 Dominique Byrd/25 10.00 25.00
160 Antonio Cromartie/25 10.00 25.00
161 Donte Whitner/25 10.00 25.00
162 Anwar Phillips/25 8.00 20.00
163 A.J. Nicholson/25 8.00 20.00
164 De'Arrius Howard/25 8.00 20.00
165 Erik Meyer/25 8.00 20.00
166 Darrell Hackney/25 8.00 20.00
167 Paul Pinegar/25 8.00 20.00
168 Brandon Kirsch/25 10.00 25.00
169 Quinton Ganther/25 8.00 20.00
170 Andre Hall/25 12.00 30.00
171 Derrick Ross/25 8.00 20.00
172 Mike Bell/25 10.00 25.00
173 Wendell Mathis/25 8.00 20.00
174 Garrett Mills/25 8.00 20.00
175 David Anderson/25 8.00 20.00
176 Kevin McMahan/25 8.00 20.00
177 Martin Nance/25 8.00 20.00
178 Greg Lee/25 8.00 20.00
179 Anthony Mix/25 8.00 20.00
180 D'Brickashaw Ferguson/25 10.00 25.00
181 Tamba Hali/25 10.00 25.00
182 Haloti Ngata/25 10.00 25.00
183 Claude Wroten/25 8.00 20.00
184 Gabe Watson/25 8.00 20.00
185 D'Qwell Jackson/25 8.00 20.00
186 Abdul Hodge/25 10.00 25.00
187 Chad Greenway/25 10.00 25.00
188 Bobby Carpenter/25 10.00 25.00
189 DeMeco Ryans/25 12.00 30.00
190 Rocky McIntosh/25 10.00 25.00
191 Thomas Howard/25 10.00 25.00
192 Jon Alston/25 10.00 25.00
193 Jimmy Williams/25 10.00 25.00
194 Ashton Youboty/25 10.00 25.00
195 Alan Zemaitis/25 10.00 25.00
196 Cedric Griffin/25 8.00 20.00
197 Ko Simpson/25 8.00 20.00
198 Pat Watkins/25 10.00 25.00
199 Bernard Pollard/25 10.00 25.00
200 Jay Cutler/25 75.00 200.00

2006 Leaf Certified Materials Mirror Red Materials

*RETIRED 232-251: .5X TO 1.2 BASE JSY
RED PRINT RUN 40-150
UNPRICED MIRROR BLACK #'d TO 1
UNPRICED MIRROR EMERALD #'d TO 5
1 Anquan Boldin 3.00 8.00
2 Edgerrin James 3.00 8.00
4 Larry Fitzgerald 4.00 10.00
5 Alge Crumpler 3.00 8.00
7 Michael Jenkins 3.00 8.00
8 Michael Vick 4.00 10.00
9 Warrick Dunn 3.00 8.00
11 Jamal Lewis 3.00 8.00
12 Kyle Boller/125 3.00 8.00
13 Todd Heap 3.00 8.00
14 Mark Clayton 3.00 8.00
16 J.P. Losman 3.00 8.00
17 Josh Reed 2.50 6.00
18 Lee Evans 3.00 8.00
19 Willis McGahee 3.00 8.00
21 Jake Delhomme 3.00 8.00
22 Stephen Davis 3.00 8.00
23 Keary Colbert 2.50 6.00
24 Steve Smith 4.00 10.00
25 Brian Urlacher 4.00 10.00
26 Cedric Benson 3.00 8.00
27 Muhsin Muhammad 3.00 8.00
28 Rex Grossman 3.00 8.00
29 Thomas Jones 3.00 8.00
30 Carson Palmer 4.00 10.00
31 Chad Johnson 3.00 8.00
32 Rudi Johnson 3.00 8.00
35 Dennis Northcutt 2.50 6.00
36 Braylon Edwards 3.00 8.00
37 Reuben Droughns 3.00 8.00
39 Julius Jones 2.50 6.00
42 Terry Glenn 3.00 8.00
43 Roy Williams S 3.00 8.00
44 Jake Plummer 3.00 8.00
45 Rod Smith 3.00 8.00
46 Tatum Bell 2.50 6.00
47 Ashley Lelie 2.50 6.00
49 Kevin Jones 2.50 6.00
50 Mike Williams 2.50 6.00
51 Roy Williams WR 3.00 8.00
52 Ahman Green/81 3.00 8.00
53 Brett Favre/100 8.00 20.00
54 Aaron Rodgers/50 20.00 50.00
55 Samkon Gado 3.00 8.00
57 Robert Ferguson 2.50 6.00
58 Andre Johnson 4.00 10.00
59 David Carr 2.50 6.00
60 Domanick Davis/100 2.50 6.00
61 Dallas Clark 3.00 8.00
62 Marvin Harrison 4.00 10.00
63 Peyton Manning 6.00 15.00
64 Reggie Wayne 3.00 8.00
65 Brandon Stokley 3.00 8.00
66 Byron Leftwich 3.00 8.00
67 Fred Taylor 3.00 8.00
68 Jimmy Smith 3.00 8.00
69 Matt Jones 2.50 6.00
70 Larry Johnson 3.00 8.00
71 Tony Gonzalez 3.00 8.00
72 Trent Green 3.00 8.00
75 Chris Chambers 3.00 8.00
76 Daunte Culpepper 3.00 8.00
78 Ronnie Brown 4.00 10.00
81 Brad Johnson 3.00 8.00
84 Troy Williamson 2.50 6.00
85 Deion Branch 3.00 8.00
86 Tom Brady 6.00 15.00
87 Corey Dillon 3.00 8.00
89 Troy Brown 2.50 6.00
90 Deuce McAllister 3.00 8.00
91 Donte Stallworth 2.50 6.00
93 Joe Horn 3.00 8.00
95 Eli Manning 5.00 12.00
96 Jeremy Shockey 4.00 10.00
97 Plaxico Burress 3.00 8.00
98 Amani Toomer 3.00 8.00
99 Tiki Barber 4.00 10.00
100 Chad Pennington 3.00 8.00
101 Curtis Martin 4.00 10.00
102 Laveranues Coles 2.50 6.00
104 Jerry Porter/100 2.50 6.00
105 LaMont Jordan 3.00 8.00
107 Randy Moss 4.00 10.00
108 Brian Westbrook/75 3.00 8.00
109 Donovan McNabb 4.00 10.00
110 Reggie Brown 2.50 6.00
111 Chad Lewis 2.50 6.00
113 Jevon Kearse 3.00 8.00
114 Ben Roethlisberger 5.00 12.00
116 Hines Ward 4.00 10.00
117 Willie Parker/63 4.00 10.00
118 Troy Polamalu 5.00 12.00
119 Antonio Gates 4.00 10.00
121 Keenan McCardell 3.00 8.00
122 LaDainian Tomlinson 4.00 10.00
123 Philip Rivers 4.00 10.00
124 Alex Smith QB 4.00 10.00
125 Antonio Bryant/40 3.00 8.00
127 Kevan Barlow 2.50 6.00
128 Darrell Jackson 3.00 8.00
130 Matt Hasselbeck 3.00 8.00
131 Shaun Alexander 3.00 8.00
132 Isaac Bruce 3.00 8.00
133 Marc Bulger 3.00 8.00
134 Marshall Faulk 3.00 8.00
135 Steven Jackson 4.00 10.00
136 Torry Holt 3.00 8.00
137 Cadillac Williams 3.00 8.00
138 Chris Simms 3.00 8.00
140 Michael Clayton 2.50 6.00
141 Brandon Jones 2.50 6.00
142 Chris Brown 2.50 6.00
143 Drew Bennett 3.00 8.00
144 Tyrone Calico 2.50 6.00
145 Steve McNair 3.00 8.00
147 Clinton Portis 4.00 10.00
148 Mark Brunell 3.00 8.00
149 Santana Moss 3.00 8.00
150 Jason Campbell 3.00 8.00
201 Chad Jackson 2.50 6.00
202 Laurence Maroney 3.00 8.00
203 Tarvaris Jackson 4.00 10.00
204 Michael Huff 3.00 8.00
205 Mario Williams 4.00 10.00
206 Marcedes Lewis 4.00 10.00
207 Maurice Drew 6.00 15.00
208 Vince Young 5.00 12.00
209 LenDale White 3.00 8.00
210 Reggie Bush 8.00 20.00
211 Matt Leinart 4.00 10.00
212 Michael Robinson 3.00 8.00
213 Vernon Davis 5.00 12.00
214 Brandon Williams 2.50 6.00
215 Derek Hagan 3.00 8.00
216 Jason Avant 2.50 6.00
217 Brandon Marshall 4.00 10.00
218 Omar Jacobs 2.50 6.00
219 Santonio Holmes 5.00 12.00
220 Jerious Norwood 3.00 8.00
221 Demetrius Williams 3.00 8.00
222 Sinorice Moss 4.00 10.00
223 Leon Washington 3.00 8.00
224 Kellen Clemens 3.00 8.00
225 A.J. Hawk 4.00 10.00
226 Maurice Stovall 2.50 6.00
227 DeAngelo Williams 5.00 12.00
228 Charlie Whitehurst 4.00 10.00
229 Travis Wilson 2.50 6.00
230 Joe Klopfenstein 2.50 6.00
231 Brian Calhoun 2.50 6.00

2006 Leaf Certified Materials Mirror Blue Materials

BLUE PRINT RUN 15-50
SERIAL #'d UNDER 25 NOT PRICED
201 Chad Jackson AU 12.00 30.00
202 Laurence Maroney AU 15.00 40.00
203 Tarvaris Jackson AU 20.00 50.00
204 Michael Huff AU 15.00 40.00
205 Mario Williams AU 20.00 50.00
206 Marcedes Lewis AU 20.00 50.00
207 Maurice Drew AU 30.00 80.00
208 Vince Young AU 25.00 60.00
209 LenDale White AU 15.00 40.00
210 Reggie Bush AU 40.00 100.00
211 Matt Leinart AU 20.00 50.00
212 Michael Robinson AU 15.00 40.00
213 Vernon Davis AU 25.00 60.00
214 Brandon Williams AU 12.00 30.00
215 Derek Hagan AU 15.00 40.00
216 Jason Avant AU 12.00 30.00
217 Brandon Marshall AU 20.00 50.00
218 Omar Jacobs AU 12.00 30.00
219 Santonio Holmes AU 25.00 60.00
220 Jerious Norwood AU 15.00 40.00
221 Demetrius Williams AU 15.00 40.00
222 Sinorice Moss AU 20.00 50.00
223 Leon Washington AU 15.00 40.00
224 Kellen Clemens AU 15.00 40.00
225 A.J. Hawk AU 20.00 50.00
226 Maurice Stovall AU 12.00 30.00
227 DeAngelo Williams AU 25.00 60.00
228 Charlie Whitehurst AU 20.00 50.00
229 Travis Wilson ERR AU 12.00 30.00
(Autograph is Tarvaris Jackson)
230 Joe Klopfenstein AU 12.00 30.00
231 Brian Calhoun AU 12.00 30.00

2006 Leaf Certified Materials Mirror Gold Materials

*GOLD/15-25: .8X TO 2X RED MATERIAL
*GOLD AU/25: .6X TO 1.2X BLUE MAT.AU

2007 Leaf Certified Materials

This 253-card set was released in September, 2007. The set was issued into the hobby in five-card packs, with a $10 SRP, which came 10 packs to a box. Cards numbered 1-150 are veterans sequenced in alphabetical team order by division while cards numbered 151-234 feature 2007 NFL rookies and cards numbered 235-254 honor retired greats. Within the Rookie Cards groupings; Cards numbered 151-175 were issued to a stated print run of 1000 serial numbered sets, while cards 176-200, signed by the player, were issued to a stated print run of 399 serial numbered sets and cards numbered 201-234 which had a player-worn jersey swatch were issued to stated print runs between 849 and 1499 serial numbered sets. The retired greats all have game-worn jersey swatches and those cards were issued to a stated print run of 75 serial numbered copies. Card number 245 was never issued for this set.

COMP.SET w/o SP's (150) 15.00 40.00
ROOKIE PRINT RUN 1500 SER.#'d SETS
AU ROOKIE PRINT RUN 399 SER.#'d SETS
JSY ROOKIE PRINT RUN 849-1499
JSY LEGEND PRINT RUN 75 SER.#'d SETS
UNPRICED MIRR.BLACK PRINT RUN 1
UNPRICED MIRR.EMERALD PRINT RUN 5
1 Tony Romo .50 1.25
2 Julius Jones .25 .60
3 Terry Glenn .30 .75
4 Terrell Owens .40 1.00
5 Jason Witten .40 1.00
6 Patrick Crayton .25 .60
7 Eli Manning .40 1.00
8 Plaxico Burress .30 .75
9 Jeremy Shockey .30 .75
10 Brandon Jacobs .30 .75
11 Sinorice Moss .30 .75
12 Donovan McNabb .40 1.00
13 Brian Westbrook .30 .75
14 Reggie Brown .25 .60
15 Hank Baskett .30 .75
16 Jason Campbell .30 .75
17 Clinton Portis .30 .75
18 Santana Moss .30 .75
19 Chris Cooley .30 .75
20 Ladell Betts .25 .60
21 Rex Grossman .30 .75
22 Cedric Benson .30 .75
23 Bernard Berrian .25 .60
24 Devin Hester .40 1.00
25 Brian Urlacher .40 1.00
26 Jon Kitna .25 .60
27 Roy Williams WR .30 .75
28 Mike Furrey .30 .75
29 Tatum Bell .25 .60
30 Brett Favre .75 2.00
31 Donald Driver .40 1.00
32 Greg Jennings .40 1.00
33 Nick Barnett .25 .60
34 Tarvaris Jackson .25 .60
35 Chester Taylor .25 .60
36 Troy Williamson .25 .60
37 Michael Vick .40 1.00
38 Warrick Dunn .30 .75
39 Joe Horn .30 .75
40 Michael Jenkins .30 .75
41 Alge Crumpler .30 .75
42 Jerious Norwood .30 .75
43 Jake Delhomme .30 .75
44 DeShaun Foster .30 .75
45 Steve Smith .30 .75
46 DeAngelo Williams .40 1.00
47 Drew Brees .40 1.00
48 Deuce McAllister .30 .75
49 Marques Colston .40 1.00
50 Devery Henderson .25 .60
51 Reggie Bush .40 1.00
52 Cadillac Williams .30 .75
53 Joey Galloway .30 .75
54 Michael Clayton .25 .60
55 Derrick Brooks .30 .75
56 Matt Leinart .30 .75
57 Edgerrin James .30 .75
58 Anquan Boldin .30 .75
59 Larry Fitzgerald .40 1.00
60 Marc Bulger .30 .75
61 Steven Jackson .40 1.00
62 Torry Holt .30 .75
63 Isaac Bruce .30 .75
64 Randy McMichael .25 .60
65 Drew Bennett .25 .60
66 Alex Smith QB .40 1.00
67 Frank Gore .40 1.00
68 Vernon Davis .30 .75
69 Darrell Jackson .25 .60
70 Matt Hasselbeck .30 .75
71 Shaun Alexander .30 .75
72 Deion Branch .30 .75
73 Nate Burleson .25 .60
74 J.P. Losman .25 .60
75 Anthony Thomas .25 .60
76 Lee Evans .30 .75
77 Josh Reed .25 .60
78 Daunte Culpepper .30 .75
79 Ronnie Brown .30 .75
80 Chris Chambers .30 .75
81 Marty Booker .25 .60
82 Jason Taylor .30 .75
83 Zach Thomas .30 .75
84 Tom Brady .60 1.50
85 Laurence Maroney .30 .75
86 Randy Moss .40 1.00
87 Ben Watson .25 .60
88 Donte Stallworth .30 .75
89 Tedy Bruschi .40 1.00
90 Chad Pennington .30 .75
91 Thomas Jones .30 .75
92 Laveranues Coles .25 .60
93 Jerricho Cotchery .30 .75
94 Leon Washington .30 .75
95 Steve McNair .30 .75
96 Willis McGahee .30 .75
97 Demetrius Williams .25 .60
98 Todd Heap .25 .60
99 Ray Lewis .40 1.00
100 Mark Clayton .30 .75
101 Carson Palmer .30 .75
102 Rudi Johnson .30 .75
103 Chad Johnson .30 .75
104 T.J. Houshmandzadeh .30 .75
105 Charlie Frye .30 .75
106 Braylon Edwards .30 .75
107 Kellen Winslow .30 .75
108 Jamal Lewis .30 .75
109 Ben Roethlisberger .40 1.00
110 Willie Parker .30 .75
111 Hines Ward .40 1.00
112 Heath Miller .25 .60
113 Troy Polamalu .40 1.00
114 Ahman Green .30 .75
115 Andre Johnson .30 .75
116 Matt Schaub .30 .75
117 DeMeco Ryans .30 .75
118 Peyton Manning .60 1.50
119 Joseph Addai .30 .75
120 Marvin Harrison .40 1.00
121 Reggie Wayne .30 .75
122 Dallas Clark .25 .60
123 Byron Leftwich .30 .75
124 Fred Taylor .30 .75
125 Matt Jones .30 .75
126 Reggie Williams .30 .75
127 Marcedes Lewis .25 .60
128 Maurice Jones-Drew .40 1.00
129 Ernest Wilford .25 .60
130 Vince Young .30 .75
131 LenDale White .30 .75
132 Brandon Jones .25 .60
133 Jay Cutler .40 1.00
134 Travis Henry .30 .75
135 Javon Walker .30 .75
136 Rod Smith .30 .75
137 Champ Bailey .30 .75
138 Mike Bell .30 .75
139 Brandon Marshall .30 .75
140 Larry Johnson .25 .60
141 Eddie Kennison .25 .60
142 Tony Gonzalez .30 .75
143 Brodie Croyle .30 .75
144 LaMont Jordan .30 .75
145 Ronald Curry .30 .75
146 Philip Rivers .40 1.00
147 LaDainian Tomlinson .40 1.00
148 Michael Turner .40 1.00
149 Antonio Gates .40 1.00
150 Shawne Merriman .30 .75
151 Aaron Ross RC 2.00 5.00
152 Adam Carriker RC 1.50 4.00
153 Ahmad Bradshaw RC 3.00 8.00
154 Alan Branch RC 1.50 4.00
155 Chansi Stuckey RC 2.00 5.00
156 Charles Johnson RC 1.25 3.00
157 Chris Leak RC 1.50 4.00
158 Jarvis Moss RC 1.50 4.00
159 Dan Bazuin RC 1.50 4.00
160 David Harris RC 1.50 4.00
161 Dwayne Wright RC 1.50 4.00
162 Eric Frampton RC 1.50 4.00
163 Eric Wright RC 2.00 5.00
164 Jared Zabransky RC 1.50 4.00
165 Jason Snelling RC 2.00 5.00
166 Jordan Palmer RC 1.50 4.00
167 Kenneth Darby RC 1.50 4.00
168 LaMarr Woodley RC 2.00 5.00
169 LaRon Landry RC 2.00 5.00
170 Lawrence Timmons RC 2.00 5.00
171 Leon Hall RC 1.50 4.00
172 Michael Griffin RC 2.00 5.00
173 Mike Walker RC 2.00 5.00
174 Paul Posluszny RC 2.00 5.00
175 Thomas Clayton RC 1.50 4.00
176 Amobi Okoye AU RC 5.00 12.00
177 Anthony Spencer AU RC 5.00 12.00
178 Aundrae Allison AU RC 3.00 8.00
179 Ben Patrick AU RC 4.00 10.00
180 Brandon Meriweather AU RC 5.00 12.00
181 Chris Davis AU RC 3.00 8.00
182 Chris Houston AU RC 4.00 10.00
184 Dallas Baker AU RC 3.00 8.00
185 Darius Walker AU RC 3.00 8.00
186 Darrelle Revis AU RC 12.00 30.00
187 David Clowney AU RC 4.00 10.00
188 DeShawn Wynn AU RC 4.00 10.00
189 Ikaika Alama-Francis AU RC 5.00 12.00
190 Isaiah Stanback AU RC 3.00 8.00
191 Jacoby Jones AU RC 5.00 12.00
192 Jamaal Anderson AU RC 4.00 10.00
193 James Jones AU RC 5.00 12.00
194 Courtney Taylor AU RC 4.00 10.00
195 Jon Beason AU RC 4.00 10.00
196 Jonathan Wade AU RC 4.00 10.00
197 Josh Wilson AU RC 4.00 10.00
198 Kolby Smith AU RC 4.00 10.00
199 Laurent Robinson AU RC 7.50 15.00
200 Reggie Nelson AU RC 4.00 10.00
201 Dwayne Jarrett JSY RC 2.50 6.00
202 Johnnie Lee Higgins JSY RC 2.50 6.00
203 Michael Bush JSY RC 3.00 8.00
204 Antonio Pittman JSY RC 2.00 5.00
205 Patrick Willis JSY RC 6.00 15.00
206 Gaines Adams JSY RC 3.00 8.00
207 Tony Hunt JSY RC 2.00 5.00
208 Chris Henry RB JSY RC 2.00 5.00
209 John Beck JSY RC 3.00 8.00
210 Dwayne Bowe JSY RC 4.00 10.00
211 Brian Leonard JSY RC 2.50 6.00
212 Anthony Gonzalez JSY RC 3.00 8.00
213 Trent Edwards JSY RC 3.00 8.00
214 Jason Hill JSY RC 3.00 8.00
215 JaMarcus Russell JSY/849 RC 2.00 5.00
216 Ted Ginn Jr. JSY RC 2.50 6.00
217 Paul Williams JSY RC 2.00 5.00
218 Garrett Wolfe JSY RC 2.00 5.00
219 Adrian Peterson JSY/849 RC 12.00 30.00
220 Kevin Kolb JSY RC 5.00 12.00
221 Marshawn Lynch JSY/849 RC 3.00 8.00
222 Steve Smith USC JSY RC 3.00 8.00
223 Greg Olsen JSY RC 2.50 6.00
224 Kenny Irons JSY RC 2.00 5.00
225 Brandon Jackson JSY RC 2.50 6.00
226 Yamon Figurs JSY RC 2.00 5.00
227 Lorenzo Booker JSY RC 2.50 6.00
228 Drew Stanton JSY RC 2.00 5.00
229 Brady Quinn JSY/849 RC 3.00 8.00
230 Joe Thomas JSY RC 3.00 8.00
231 Robert Meachem JSY RC 3.00 8.00
232 Troy Smith JSY RC 3.00 8.00
233 Sidney Rice JSY RC 4.00 10.00
234 Calvin Johnson JSY/849 RC 10.00 25.00
235 Bart Starr JSY 12.00 30.00
236 Bob Griese JSY 8.00 20.00
237 Bobby Layne JSY/50 10.00 25.00
238 Bulldog Turner JSY 8.00 20.00
239 Earl Campbell JKT 8.00 20.00
240 Franco Harris JSY 8.00 20.00
241 James Lofton JSY 5.00 12.00
242 Jim McMahon JSY 10.00 25.00
243 Jim Thorpe JSY 60.00 100.00
244 Joe Namath JSY 10.00 25.00
246 Lou Groza JSY 6.00 15.00
247 Ray Nitschke JSY 10.00 25.00
248 Ron Mix JSY 5.00 12.00
249 Roosevelt Brown JSY 5.00 12.00
250 Sam Huff JSY 6.00 15.00
251 Sammy Baugh JSY 20.00 40.00
252 Sid Luckman JSY 15.00 30.00
253 Otto Graham JSY 15.00 30.00
254 Y.A. Tittle JSY 8.00 20.00

2007 Leaf Certified Materials Mirror Black

UNPRICED MIRROR BLACK PRINT RUN 1

2007 Leaf Certified Materials Mirror Blue

*VETS 1-150: 5X TO 12X BASIC CARDS
*BLUE ROOKIES: .5X TO 1.2X MIRROR RED
STATED PRINT RUN 50 SER.#'d SETS

2007 Leaf Certified Materials Mirror Emerald

UNPRICED EMERALD PRINT RUN 5

2007 Leaf Certified Materials Mirror Gold

*VET 1-150: 8X TO 20X BASIC CARDS
*GOLD ROOKIES: .8X TO 2X MIRROR RED
STATED PRINT RUN 25 SER.#'d SETS

2007 Leaf Certified Materials Mirror Red

*VETS 1-150: 4X TO 10X BASIC CARDS
COMMON ROOKIE (151-200) 3.00 8.00
ROOKIE SEMISTARS 4.00 10.00
ROOKIE UNL.STARS 5.00 12.00
STATED PRINT RUN 100 SER.#'d SETS
169 LaRon Landry 5.00 12.00
174 Paul Posluszny 5.00 12.00
188 DeShawn Wynn 4.00 10.00
191 Jacoby Jones 5.00 12.00
193 James Jones 5.00 12.00

2007 Leaf Certified Materials Certified Potential

STATED PRINT RUN 1000 SER.#'d SETS
*MIRROR/500: .5X TO 1.2X BASIC INSERTS
MIRROR PRINT RUN 500 SER.#'d SETS
*RED/250: .6X TO 1.5X BASIC INSERTS
RED PRINT RUN 250 SER.#'d SETS
*BLUE/100: .8X TO 2X BASIC INSERTS
BLUE PRINT RUN 100 SER.#'d SETS
*GOLD/25: 1.2X TO 3X BASIC INSERTS
GOLD PRINT RUN 25 SER.#'d SETS
UNPRICED EMERALD PRINT RUN 5
UNPRICED BLACK PRINT RUN 1
1 Brandon Marshall 1.00 2.50
2 DeAngelo Williams 1.25 3.00
3 Demetrius Williams .75 2.00
4 Laurence Maroney 1.00 2.50
5 LenDale White 1.00 2.50
6 Joseph Addai 1.00 2.50
7 Marcedes Lewis .75 2.00
8 Maurice Jones-Drew 1.25 3.00
9 Santonio Holmes 1.00 2.50
10 Sinorice Moss 1.00 2.50
11 Tarvaris Jackson .75 2.00
12 Reggie Bush 1.25 3.00
13 Matt Leinart 1.00 2.50
14 Vince Young 1.00 2.50
15 Vernon Davis 1.00 2.50

2007 Leaf Certified Materials Certified Potential Materials

STATED PRINT RUN 10-250
UNPRICED PRIME PRINT RUN 5
UNPRICED PRIME BLACK PRINT RUN 1
SERIAL #'d UNDER 25 NOT PRICED
1 Brandon Marshall 3.00 8.00
3 Demetrius Williams 2.50 6.00
4 Laurence Maroney 3.00 8.00
5 LenDale White 3.00 8.00
6 Joseph Addai 3.00 8.00
8 Maurice Jones-Drew 4.00 10.00
9 Santonio Holmes 3.00 8.00
10 Sinorice Moss 3.00 8.00
12 Reggie Bush 4.00 10.00
13 Matt Leinart 3.00 8.00
14 Vince Young 3.00 8.00

2007 Leaf Certified Materials Certified Skills

STATED PRINT RUN 1000 SER.#'d SETS
*MIRROR/500: .5X TO 1.2X BASIC INSERTS
MIRROR PRINT RUN 500 SER.#'d SETS
*RED/250: .6X TO 1.5X BASIC INSERTS
RED PRINT RUN 250 SER.#'d SETS
*BLUE/100: .8X TO 2X BASIC INSERTS
BLUE PRINT RUN 100 SER.#'d SETS
*GOLD/25: 1.2X TO 3X BASIC INSERTS
GOLD PRINT RUN 25 SER.#'d SETS
UNPRICED EMERALD PRINT RUN 5
UNPRICED BLACK PRINT RUN 1
1 Carson Palmer 1.00 2.50
2 Brett Favre 2.50 6.00
3 Tom Brady 2.00 5.00
4 Eli Manning 1.25 3.00
5 Tony Romo 1.50 4.00
6 Philip Rivers 1.25 3.00
7 Steven Jackson 1.25 3.00
8 Willie Parker 1.00 2.50
9 Rudi Johnson 1.00 2.50
10 Brian Westbrook 1.00 2.50
11 Edgerrin James 1.00 2.50
12 Deuce McAllister 1.00 2.50
13 Shaun Alexander 1.00 2.50
14 Reggie Wayne 1.00 2.50
15 Donald Driver 1.25 3.00
16 Lee Evans 1.00 2.50
17 Torry Holt 1.00 2.50
18 Steve Smith 1.00 2.50
19 Terrell Owens 1.25 3.00
20 T.J. Houshmandzadeh 1.00 2.50

2007 Leaf Certified Materials Certified Skills Materials

STATED PRINT RUN 5-100
UNPRICED PRIME PRINT RUN 5
UNPRICED PRIME BLACK PRINT RUN 1
SERIAL #'d UNDER 25 NOT PRICED
1 Carson Palmer/60 4.00 10.00
2 Brett Favre 10.00 25.00
3 Tom Brady 8.00 20.00
4 Eli Manning/50 5.00 12.00
5 Tony Romo/50 6.00 15.00
6 Philip Rivers/50 5.00 12.00
7 Steven Jackson 5.00 12.00
8 Willie Parker/50 4.00 10.00
9 Rudi Johnson 4.00 10.00
11 Edgerrin James 4.00 10.00
12 Deuce McAllister 4.00 10.00
13 Shaun Alexander 4.00 10.00
14 Reggie Wayne 4.00 10.00
16 Lee Evans 4.00 10.00
18 Steve Smith 4.00 10.00

2007 Leaf Certified Materials Fabric of the Game

STATED PRINT RUN 1-40
SERIAL #'d UNDER 40 NOT PRICED
3 Andre Johnson 5.00 12.00
5 Antonio Gates 6.00 15.00
9 Brandon Marshall 5.00 12.00
11 Brett Favre 12.00 30.00
12 Brian Urlacher 6.00 15.00
14 Byron Leftwich 5.00 12.00
15 Cadillac Williams 5.00 12.00
16 Carson Palmer 5.00 12.00
17 Cedric Benson 5.00 12.00
18 Chad Johnson 5.00 12.00
19 Chad Pennington 5.00 12.00
21 Clinton Portis 5.00 12.00
25 DeAngelo Williams 6.00 15.00
27 DeShaun Foster 5.00 12.00
28 Deuce McAllister 5.00 12.00
29 Devin Hester 6.00 15.00
30 Donald Driver 6.00 15.00
31 Donovan McNabb 6.00 15.00
32 Drew Brees 6.00 15.00
34 Edgerrin James 5.00 12.00
35 Eli Manning 6.00 15.00
36 Frank Gore 6.00 15.00
38 Hines Ward 6.00 15.00
43 Javon Walker 5.00 12.00
44 Jay Cutler 6.00 15.00
50 Joseph Addai 5.00 12.00
51 Julius Jones 4.00 10.00
52 LaDainian Tomlinson 6.00 15.00
54 Larry Fitzgerald 6.00 15.00
55 Larry Johnson 4.00 10.00
56 Laurence Maroney 5.00 12.00
59 LenDale White 5.00 12.00
60 Leon Washington 5.00 12.00
64 Marques Colston 6.00 15.00
65 Marvin Harrison 6.00 15.00
66 Matt Hasselbeck 5.00 12.00
67 Matt Leinart 5.00 12.00
68 Maurice Jones-Drew 6.00 15.00
71 Mike Bell 5.00 12.00
73 Peyton Manning 10.00 25.00
74 Philip Rivers 6.00 15.00
77 Reggie Bush 6.00 15.00
78 Reggie Wayne 5.00 12.00
79 Rex Grossman 5.00 12.00
80 Ronnie Brown 5.00 12.00
82 Roy Williams WR 5.00 12.00
83 Rudi Johnson 5.00 12.00
85 Shaun Alexander 5.00 12.00
86 Shawne Merriman 5.00 12.00
87 Sinorice Moss 5.00 12.00
89 Steve Smith 5.00 12.00
90 Steven Jackson 6.00 15.00
91 T.J. Houshmandzadeh 5.00 12.00
93 Terrell Owens 6.00 15.00
96 Tom Brady 10.00 25.00
97 Tony Gonzalez 5.00 12.00
99 Torry Holt 5.00 12.00
101 Vince Young 5.00 12.00
103 Warrick Dunn 5.00 12.00
104 Willie Parker 5.00 12.00
106 Jan Stenerud 6.00 15.00
107 Barry Sanders 15.00 40.00
108 Bart Starr 15.00 40.00
109 Bill Bates 8.00 20.00
110 Bob Griese 10.00 25.00
111 Charlie Joiner 8.00 20.00
112 Dan Hampton 8.00 20.00
113 Dan Marino 20.00 50.00
114 Earl Campbell JKT 10.00 25.00
115 Franco Harris 10.00 25.00
116 Cliff Harris 6.00 15.00
117 Gale Sayers 12.00 30.00
118 Jack Lambert 10.00 25.00
119 James Lofton 6.00 15.00
120 Jerry Rice 15.00 40.00
121 Jim Brown 12.00 30.00
122 Jim Kelly 12.00 30.00
124 Joe Montana 20.00 50.00
125 Joe Namath 12.00 30.00
126 Joe Theismann 10.00 25.00
127 John Elway 15.00 40.00
128 John Riggins 8.00 20.00
130 Johnny Unitas 25.00 60.00
131 Lance Alworth 8.00 20.00
132 Lee Roy Selmon 8.00 20.00
133 Len Dawson 10.00 25.00
134 Lou Groza 8.00 20.00
135 Mike Singletary 10.00 25.00
136 Ozzie Newsome 8.00 20.00
138 Paul Warfield 8.00 20.00
139 Ray Nitschke 12.00 30.00
140 Ron Mix 6.00 15.00
141 Roosevelt Brown 6.00 15.00
142 Sam Huff 8.00 20.00
143 Sammy Baugh 20.00 50.00
144 Ted Hendricks 8.00 20.00
145 Tiki Barber 10.00 25.00
146 Troy Aikman 12.00 30.00
147 Walter Payton 20.00 50.00
148 Warren Moon 10.00 25.00
149 Y.A. Tittle 10.00 25.00
150 Sid Luckman 15.00 40.00

2007 Leaf Certified Materials Fabric of the Game NFL Die Cut

COMMON CARD 8.00 20.00
SEMISTARS 10.00 25.00
UNLISTED STARS 12.00 30.00
*NFL DC/20-25: .8X TO 2X BASIC FOTG
STATED PRINT RUN 5-25
6 Ben Roethlisberger 12.00 30.00
98 Tony Romo 15.00 40.00

2007 Leaf Certified Materials Fabric of the Game Jersey Number

*JER.NO/31-99: .4X TO 1X BASE FOTG
*JER.NO/20-29: .5X TO 1.2X BASE FOTG
STATED PRINT RUN 1-99
SERIAL #'d UNDER 20 NOT PRICED

2 Alge Crumpler/83	5.00	12.00
3 Andre Johnson/80	5.00	12.00
4 Anquan Boldin/81	5.00	12.00
5 Antonio Gates/85	6.00	15.00
7 Ben Watson/84	4.00	10.00
8 Bernard Berrian/80	4.00	10.00
12 Brian Urlacher/54	6.00	15.00
15 Cadillac Williams/24	6.00	15.00
17 Cedric Benson/32	5.00	12.00
20 Chris Chambers/84	5.00	12.00
21 Clinton Portis/26	6.00	15.00
22 Correll Buckhalter/28	6.00	15.00
23 Dallas Clark/44	4.00	10.00
25 DeAngelo Williams/34	6.00	15.00
27 DeShaun Foster/26	6.00	15.00
28 Deuce McAllister/26	6.00	15.00
29 Devin Hester/23	8.00	20.00
30 Donald Driver/80	6.00	15.00
34 Edgerrin James/32	5.00	12.00
36 Frank Gore/21	8.00	20.00
37 Fred Taylor/28	6.00	15.00
38 Hines Ward/86	6.00	15.00
39 Isaac Bruce/80	5.00	12.00
43 Javon Walker/84	5.00	12.00
45 Jeremy Shockey/80	5.00	12.00
46 Jerious Norwood/32	5.00	12.00
48 Jerry Porter/84	5.00	12.00
49 Joey Galloway/84	5.00	12.00
50 Joseph Addai/29	6.00	15.00
51 Julius Jones/21	5.00	12.00
52 LaDainian Tomlinson/21	8.00	20.00
53 LaMont Jordan/34	5.00	12.00
55 Larry Johnson/27	5.00	12.00
56 Laurence Maroney/39	5.00	12.00
58 Lee Evans/83	5.00	12.00
59 LenDale White/25	6.00	15.00
60 Leon Washington/29	6.00	15.00
62 Marion Barber/24	8.00	20.00
65 Marvin Harrison/88	6.00	15.00
68 Maurice Jones-Drew/32	6.00	15.00
69 Michael Clayton/80	4.00	10.00
71 Mike Bell/20	6.00	15.00
72 Muhsin Muhammad/87	5.00	12.00
75 Ray Lewis/52	6.00	15.00
77 Reggie Bush/25	8.00	20.00
78 Reggie Wayne/87	5.00	12.00
80 Ronnie Brown/23	6.00	15.00
81 Roy Williams S/31	5.00	12.00
83 Rudi Johnson/32	5.00	12.00
84 Santana Moss/09	5.00	12.00
85 Shaun Alexander/37	5.00	12.00
86 Shawne Merriman/56	5.00	12.00
87 Sinorice Moss/83	5.00	12.00
89 Steve Smith/89	5.00	12.00
90 Steven Jackson/39	6.00	15.00
91 T.J. Houshmandzadeh/84	5.00	12.00
92 Tedy Bruschi/54	6.00	15.00
94 Terry Glenn/83	5.00	12.00
95 Todd Heap/86	4.00	10.00
97 Tony Gonzalez/88	5.00	12.00
102 Vincent Jackson/83	5.00	12.00
103 Warrick Dunn/28	6.00	15.00
104 Willie Parker/39	5.00	12.00
105 Zach Thomas/54	5.00	12.00
107 Barry Sanders/20	20.00	50.00
109 Bill Bates/40	8.00	20.00
112 Dan Hampton/99	8.00	20.00
114 Earl Campbell/34	10.00	25.00
115 Franco Harris/32	10.00	25.00
116 Cliff Harris/43	6.00	15.00
117 Gale Sayers/40	12.00	30.00
118 Jack Lambert/58	10.00	25.00
119 James Lofton/80	6.00	15.00
120 Jerry Rice/80	15.00	40.00
121 Jim Brown/32	8.00	20.00
128 John Riggins/44	8.00	20.00
132 Lee Roy Selmon/63	8.00	20.00
134 Lou Groza/76	8.00	20.00
135 Mike Singletary/50	10.00	25.00
136 Ozzie Newsome/82	5.00	12.00
138 Paul Warfield/42	5.00	12.00
139 Ray Nitschke/66	12.00	30.00
140 Ron Mix/74	6.00	15.00
141 Roosevelt Brown/79	6.00	15.00
142 Sam Huff/70	8.00	20.00
143 Sammy Baugh/33	20.00	50.00
144 Ted Hendricks/83	8.00	20.00
145 Tiki Barber/21	12.00	30.00
147 Walter Payton/34	20.00	50.00
150 Sid Luckman/42	15.00	40.00

2007 Leaf Certified Materials Fabric of the Game Position

*POSITION/40-50: .4X TO 1X BASE FOTG
*POSITION/25-30: .5X TO 1.2X BASE FOTG
STATED PRINT RUN 9-50

1 Alex Smith QB	6.00	15.00
2 Alge Crumpler	5.00	12.00
3 Andre Johnson	5.00	12.00
4 Anquan Boldin	5.00	12.00
5 Antonio Gates	6.00	15.00
7 Ben Watson	4.00	10.00
8 Bernard Berrian	4.00	10.00
9 Brandon Marshall	5.00	12.00
11 Brett Favre	12.00	30.00
12 Brian Urlacher	6.00	15.00
14 Byron Leftwich	5.00	12.00
15 Cadillac Williams	5.00	12.00
16 Carson Palmer	5.00	12.00
18 Chad Johnson	5.00	12.00
19 Chad Pennington	5.00	12.00
20 Chris Chambers	5.00	12.00
21 Clinton Portis	5.00	12.00
22 Correll Buckhalter	5.00	12.00
23 Dallas Clark	4.00	10.00
24 Daunte Culpepper	5.00	12.00
27 DeShaun Foster	5.00	12.00
28 Deuce McAllister	5.00	12.00
29 Devin Hester	6.00	15.00
31 Donovan McNabb	6.00	15.00
32 Drew Brees	6.00	15.00
34 Edgerrin James	5.00	12.00
35 Eli Manning/25	8.00	20.00
36 Frank Gore	6.00	15.00
37 Fred Taylor	5.00	12.00
38 Hines Ward	6.00	15.00
41 Jake Delhomme	5.00	12.00
42 Jason Campbell	5.00	12.00
43 Javon Walker	5.00	12.00
44 Jay Cutler	6.00	15.00
45 Jeremy Shockey	5.00	12.00
46 Jerious Norwood	5.00	12.00
48 Jerry Porter	5.00	12.00
49 Joey Galloway	5.00	12.00
50 Joseph Addai	5.00	12.00
51 Julius Jones	4.00	10.00
52 LaDainian Tomlinson	6.00	15.00
53 LaMont Jordan/25	6.00	15.00
54 Larry Fitzgerald	6.00	15.00
55 Larry Johnson	4.00	10.00
56 Laurence Maroney	5.00	12.00
58 Lee Evans	5.00	12.00
59 LenDale White	5.00	12.00
60 Leon Washington/49	5.00	12.00
61 Marc Bulger	5.00	12.00
62 Marion Barber	6.00	15.00
65 Marvin Harrison	6.00	15.00
66 Matt Hasselbeck	5.00	12.00
67 Matt Leinart	5.00	12.00
68 Maurice Jones-Drew	6.00	15.00
69 Michael Clayton	4.00	10.00
70 Michael Vick	6.00	15.00
71 Mike Bell	5.00	12.00
72 Muhsin Muhammad	5.00	12.00
73 Peyton Manning/25	12.00	30.00
74 Philip Rivers/25	8.00	20.00
75 Ray Lewis	6.00	15.00
77 Reggie Bush	6.00	15.00
78 Reggie Wayne	5.00	12.00
79 Rex Grossman	5.00	12.00
80 Ronnie Brown	5.00	12.00
81 Roy Williams S	5.00	12.00
82 Roy Williams WR	5.00	12.00
83 Rudi Johnson	5.00	12.00
84 Santana Moss/45	5.00	12.00
85 Shaun Alexander	5.00	12.00
87 Sinorice Moss	5.00	12.00
88 Steve McNair/25	6.00	15.00
89 Steve Smith	5.00	12.00
90 Steven Jackson	6.00	15.00
92 Tedy Bruschi	6.00	15.00
94 Terry Glenn	5.00	12.00
95 Todd Heap	4.00	10.00
96 Tom Brady	10.00	25.00
97 Tony Gonzalez/25	6.00	15.00
101 Vince Young/25	6.00	15.00
102 Vincent Jackson/25	6.00	15.00
103 Warrick Dunn	5.00	12.00
105 Zach Thomas	5.00	12.00
106 Jan Stenerud	6.00	15.00
107 Barry Sanders	15.00	40.00
108 Bart Starr	15.00	40.00
109 Bill Bates	8.00	20.00
111 Charlie Joiner	8.00	20.00
112 Dan Hampton	8.00	20.00
113 Dan Marino	20.00	50.00
114 Earl Campbell	10.00	25.00
115 Franco Harris	10.00	25.00
116 Cliff Harris	6.00	15.00
117 Gale Sayers	12.00	30.00
118 Jack Lambert	10.00	25.00
119 James Lofton	6.00	15.00
120 Jerry Rice	15.00	40.00
121 Jim Brown/30	15.00	40.00
122 Jim Kelly/25	15.00	40.00
123 Jim McMahon/25	15.00	40.00
124 Joe Montana	20.00	50.00
125 Joe Namath	12.00	30.00
126 Joe Theismann	10.00	25.00
127 John Elway	15.00	40.00
128 John Riggins	8.00	20.00
130 Johnny Unitas	25.00	60.00
131 Lance Alworth/25	10.00	25.00
132 Lee Roy Selmon	8.00	20.00
133 Len Dawson	10.00	25.00
134 Lou Groza/25	10.00	25.00
135 Mike Singletary/25	12.00	30.00
136 Ozzie Newsome	8.00	20.00
138 Paul Warfield/25	8.00	20.00
139 Ray Nitschke/25	15.00	40.00
140 Ron Mix	6.00	15.00
141 Roosevelt Brown/30	8.00	20.00
142 Sam Huff/25	10.00	25.00
144 Ted Hendricks	8.00	20.00
145 Tiki Barber	10.00	25.00
146 Troy Aikman	12.00	30.00
147 Walter Payton	20.00	50.00
148 Warren Moon	10.00	25.00
149 Y.A. Tittle	10.00	25.00
150 Sid Luckman/25	20.00	50.00

2007 Leaf Certified Materials Fabric of the Game Prime

*PRIME/20-25: .5X TO 1.2X BASE FOTG
PRIME PRINT RUN 1-25

1 Alex Smith QB	8.00	20.00
2 Alge Crumpler	6.00	15.00
3 Andre Johnson	6.00	15.00
5 Antonio Gates	8.00	20.00
6 Ben Roethlisberger	8.00	20.00
7 Ben Watson	5.00	12.00
8 Bernard Berrian	5.00	12.00
9 Brandon Marshall	6.00	15.00
10 Braylon Edwards	6.00	15.00
12 Brian Urlacher	8.00	20.00
13 Brian Westbrook	6.00	15.00
14 Byron Leftwich	6.00	15.00
15 Cadillac Williams	6.00	15.00
16 Carson Palmer	6.00	15.00
17 Cedric Benson	6.00	15.00
18 Chad Johnson	6.00	15.00
19 Chad Pennington	6.00	15.00
20 Chris Chambers	6.00	15.00
21 Clinton Portis	6.00	15.00
22 Correll Buckhalter	6.00	15.00
23 Dallas Clark	5.00	12.00
24 Daunte Culpepper	6.00	15.00
25 DeAngelo Williams	8.00	20.00
26 Deion Branch	6.00	15.00
27 DeShaun Foster	6.00	15.00
28 Deuce McAllister	6.00	15.00
29 Devin Hester	8.00	20.00
30 Donald Driver	8.00	20.00
31 Donovan McNabb	8.00	20.00
32 Drew Brees	8.00	20.00
33 Eddie Kennison	5.00	12.00
34 Edgerrin James	6.00	15.00
35 Eli Manning	8.00	20.00
36 Frank Gore	8.00	20.00
37 Fred Taylor	6.00	15.00
38 Hines Ward	8.00	20.00
40 J.P. Losman	5.00	12.00
41 Jake Delhomme	6.00	15.00
42 Jason Campbell	6.00	15.00
43 Javon Walker	6.00	15.00
44 Jay Cutler	8.00	20.00
45 Jeremy Shockey/20	6.00	15.00
46 Jerious Norwood	6.00	15.00
47 Jerricho Cotchery	6.00	15.00
48 Jerry Porter	6.00	15.00
49 Joey Galloway	6.00	15.00
50 Joseph Addai	6.00	15.00
51 Julius Jones	5.00	12.00
52 LaDainian Tomlinson	8.00	20.00
53 LaMont Jordan	6.00	15.00
55 Larry Johnson	5.00	12.00
56 Laurence Maroney	6.00	15.00
57 Laveranues Coles	5.00	12.00
58 Lee Evans	6.00	15.00
59 LenDale White	6.00	15.00
60 Leon Washington	6.00	15.00
61 Marc Bulger	6.00	15.00
62 Marion Barber	8.00	20.00
63 Mark Clayton	6.00	15.00
64 Marques Colston	8.00	20.00
65 Marvin Harrison	8.00	20.00
66 Matt Hasselbeck	6.00	15.00
68 Maurice Jones-Drew	8.00	20.00
69 Michael Clayton	5.00	12.00
70 Michael Vick	8.00	20.00
71 Mike Bell	6.00	15.00
72 Muhsin Muhammad	6.00	15.00
73 Peyton Manning	12.00	30.00
74 Philip Rivers	8.00	20.00
75 Ray Lewis	8.00	20.00
76 Reggie Brown	5.00	12.00
77 Reggie Bush	8.00	20.00
78 Reggie Wayne	6.00	15.00
79 Rex Grossman	6.00	15.00
80 Ronnie Brown	6.00	15.00
81 Roy Williams S	6.00	15.00
82 Roy Williams WR	6.00	15.00
83 Rudi Johnson	6.00	15.00
84 Santana Moss	6.00	15.00
85 Shaun Alexander	6.00	15.00
86 Shawne Merriman	6.00	15.00
87 Sinorice Moss	6.00	15.00
89 Steve Smith	6.00	15.00
90 Steven Jackson	8.00	20.00
91 T.J. Houshmandzadeh	6.00	15.00
92 Tedy Bruschi	8.00	20.00
93 Terrell Owens	8.00	20.00
94 Terry Glenn	6.00	15.00
95 Todd Heap	5.00	12.00
96 Tom Brady	12.00	30.00
97 Tony Gonzalez	6.00	15.00
98 Tony Romo	10.00	25.00
99 Torry Holt	6.00	15.00
100 Vernon Davis	6.00	15.00
103 Warrick Dunn	6.00	15.00
104 Willie Parker	6.00	15.00
105 Zach Thomas	6.00	15.00
107 Barry Sanders	20.00	50.00
108 Bart Starr	20.00	50.00
109 Bill Bates	10.00	25.00
111 Charlie Joiner	10.00	25.00
112 Dan Hampton	10.00	25.00
113 Dan Marino	25.00	60.00
114 Earl Campbell	12.00	30.00
115 Franco Harris	12.00	30.00
116 Cliff Harris	8.00	20.00
117 Gale Sayers	15.00	40.00
118 Jack Lambert	12.00	30.00
119 James Lofton	8.00	20.00
120 Jerry Rice	20.00	50.00
121 Jim Brown	15.00	40.00
122 Jim Kelly	15.00	40.00
123 Jim McMahon	15.00	40.00
124 Joe Montana	25.00	60.00
125 Joe Namath	15.00	40.00
127 John Elway	20.00	50.00
128 John Riggins	10.00	25.00
130 Johnny Unitas	30.00	80.00
131 Lance Alworth	10.00	25.00
132 Lee Roy Selmon	10.00	25.00
133 Len Dawson	12.00	30.00
135 Mike Singletary	12.00	30.00
136 Ozzie Newsome	10.00	25.00
138 Paul Warfield	10.00	25.00
140 Ron Mix	8.00	20.00
145 Tiki Barber	12.00	30.00
146 Troy Aikman	15.00	40.00
147 Walter Payton	25.00	60.00

2007 Leaf Certified Materials Fabric of the Game Team Logo

*TEAM LOGO/20-25: .5X TO 1.2X BASE FOTG
STATED PRINT RUN 2-25

1 Alex Smith QB	8.00	20.00
2 Alge Crumpler	6.00	15.00
3 Andre Johnson	6.00	15.00
5 Antonio Gates	8.00	20.00
6 Ben Roethlisberger	8.00	20.00
7 Ben Watson	5.00	12.00
8 Bernard Berrian	5.00	12.00
9 Brandon Marshall	6.00	15.00
10 Braylon Edwards	6.00	15.00
12 Brian Urlacher	8.00	20.00
13 Brian Westbrook	6.00	15.00
14 Byron Leftwich	6.00	15.00
15 Cadillac Williams	6.00	15.00
16 Carson Palmer	6.00	15.00
18 Chad Johnson	6.00	15.00
19 Chad Pennington	6.00	15.00
20 Chris Chambers	6.00	15.00
21 Clinton Portis	6.00	15.00
22 Correll Buckhalter	6.00	15.00
23 Dallas Clark	5.00	12.00
25 DeAngelo Williams	8.00	20.00
26 Deion Branch/22	6.00	15.00
27 DeShaun Foster	6.00	15.00
28 Deuce McAllister	6.00	15.00
29 Devin Hester	8.00	20.00
30 Donald Driver	8.00	20.00
31 Donovan McNabb	8.00	20.00
32 Drew Brees	8.00	20.00
33 Eddie Kennison	5.00	12.00
34 Edgerrin James	6.00	15.00
35 Eli Manning	8.00	20.00
36 Frank Gore	8.00	20.00
37 Fred Taylor	6.00	15.00
38 Hines Ward	8.00	20.00
40 J.P. Losman	5.00	12.00
41 Jake Delhomme	6.00	15.00
42 Jason Campbell	6.00	15.00
43 Javon Walker/20	6.00	15.00
44 Jay Cutler	8.00	20.00
45 Jeremy Shockey	6.00	15.00
46 Jerious Norwood	6.00	15.00
47 Jerricho Cotchery	6.00	15.00
48 Jerry Porter	6.00	15.00
49 Joey Galloway	6.00	15.00
51 Julius Jones	5.00	12.00
52 LaDainian Tomlinson	8.00	20.00
53 LaMont Jordan	6.00	15.00
55 Larry Johnson	5.00	12.00
56 Laurence Maroney	6.00	15.00
57 Laveranues Coles	5.00	12.00
58 Lee Evans	6.00	15.00
59 LenDale White	6.00	15.00
60 Leon Washington	6.00	15.00
61 Marc Bulger	6.00	15.00
62 Marion Barber	8.00	20.00
63 Mark Clayton	6.00	15.00
65 Marvin Harrison	8.00	20.00
66 Matt Hasselbeck	6.00	15.00
68 Maurice Jones-Drew	8.00	20.00
69 Michael Clayton	5.00	12.00
71 Mike Bell	6.00	15.00
72 Muhsin Muhammad	6.00	15.00
73 Peyton Manning	12.00	30.00
74 Philip Rivers	8.00	20.00
75 Ray Lewis	8.00	20.00
76 Reggie Brown	5.00	12.00
77 Reggie Bush	8.00	20.00
78 Reggie Wayne	6.00	15.00
79 Rex Grossman	6.00	15.00
80 Ronnie Brown	6.00	15.00
81 Roy Williams S	6.00	15.00
82 Roy Williams WR	6.00	15.00
83 Rudi Johnson	6.00	15.00
84 Santana Moss	6.00	15.00
85 Shaun Alexander	6.00	15.00
86 Shawne Merriman	6.00	15.00
87 Sinorice Moss	6.00	15.00
89 Steve Smith	6.00	15.00
90 Steven Jackson	8.00	20.00
91 T.J. Houshmandzadeh	6.00	15.00
92 Tedy Bruschi	8.00	20.00
93 Terrell Owens	8.00	20.00
94 Terry Glenn	6.00	15.00
95 Todd Heap	5.00	12.00
96 Tom Brady	12.00	30.00
97 Tony Gonzalez	6.00	15.00
98 Tony Romo	10.00	25.00
99 Torry Holt	6.00	15.00
100 Vernon Davis	6.00	15.00
103 Warrick Dunn	6.00	15.00
104 Willie Parker	6.00	15.00
105 Zach Thomas	6.00	15.00
107 Barry Sanders	20.00	50.00
108 Bart Starr	20.00	50.00
109 Bill Bates	10.00	25.00
111 Charlie Joiner	10.00	25.00
112 Dan Hampton	10.00	25.00
113 Dan Marino	25.00	60.00
114 Earl Campbell	12.00	30.00
115 Franco Harris	12.00	30.00
116 Cliff Harris	8.00	20.00
117 Gale Sayers	15.00	40.00
118 Jack Lambert	12.00	30.00
119 James Lofton	8.00	20.00
120 Jerry Rice	20.00	50.00
121 Jim Brown	15.00	40.00
122 Jim Kelly	15.00	40.00
124 Joe Montana	25.00	60.00
125 Joe Namath	15.00	40.00
127 John Elway	20.00	50.00
128 John Riggins	10.00	25.00
129 John Stallworth	12.00	30.00
130 Johnny Unitas	30.00	80.00
131 Lance Alworth	10.00	25.00
132 Lee Roy Selmon	10.00	25.00
133 Len Dawson	12.00	30.00
135 Mike Singletary	12.00	30.00
136 Ozzie Newsome	10.00	25.00
137 Paul Krause/22	8.00	20.00
138 Paul Warfield	10.00	25.00
145 Tiki Barber	12.00	30.00
146 Troy Aikman	15.00	40.00
147 Walter Payton	25.00	60.00

2007 Leaf Certified Materials Fabric of the Game Autographs Jersey Number

STATED PRINT RUN 1-63
UNPRICED BASE AU FOTG SER.#'d 5-10
UNPRICED AU FB DIE CUT SER.#'d 1-10
UNPRICED AU POSITION SER.#'d 4-10
UNPRICED AU TEAM LOGO SER.#'d 4-5

15 Cadillac Williams/24	25.00	50.00
17 Cedric Benson/32	12.00	30.00
25 DeAngelo Williams/34	15.00	40.00
30 Frank Gore/21	20.00	40.00
37 Fred Taylor/28	12.00	30.00
46 Jerious Norwood/32	12.00	30.00
50 Joseph Addai/29	25.00	60.00
52 LaDainian Tomlinson/21		
55 Larry Johnson/27	25.00	50.00
59 LenDale White/25		
62 Marion Barber/24	40.00	80.00
68 Maurice Jones-Drew/32	20.00	40.00
71 Mike Bell/20		
77 Reggie Bush/25	40.00	100.00
80 Ronnie Brown/23	25.00	50.00
83 Rudi Johnson/32	15.00	40.00
90 Steven Jackson/39	20.00	40.00
104 Willie Parker/39	25.00	50.00
107 Barry Sanders/20	100.00	200.00
109 Bill Bates/40	25.00	50.00
114 Earl Campbell/34	25.00	50.00
116 Cliff Harris/43	25.00	50.00
117 Gale Sayers/40	40.00	80.00
121 Jim Brown/32	40.00	80.00
128 John Riggins/44	20.00	50.00
132 Lee Roy Selmon/63	15.00	40.00
138 Paul Warfield/42	15.00	40.00
145 Tiki Barber/21		

2007 Leaf Certified Materials Fabric of the Game College

STATED PRINT RUN 100 SER.#'d SETS
*PRIME/25: 1X TO 2.5X BASIC INSERTS
PRIME PRINT RUN 5-25
UNPRICED AUTO PRINT RUN 5

1 Frank Gore	5.00	12.00
2 Kenny Irons	2.50	6.00
3 Robert Meachem	4.00	10.00
4 Courtney Taylor	3.00	8.00
5 Dwayne Jarrett	3.00	8.00
6 Steve Smith USC	4.00	10.00
7 Adrian Peterson	15.00	40.00
8 Brandon Meriweather	4.00	10.00
9 Greg Olsen	3.00	8.00
10 Brady Quinn	4.00	10.00
11 Jon Beason	3.00	8.00
12 JaMarcus Russell	6.00	15.00
13 Dwayne Bowe	6.00	15.00
14 Craig Buster Davis	3.00	8.00
15 LaRon Landry	4.00	10.00
16 Zach Miller	4.00	10.00
17 Jordan Palmer	3.00	8.00
18 Johnnie Lee Higgins	3.00	8.00
19 Vince Young	5.00	12.00
20 Michael Bush	4.00	10.00

2007 Leaf Certified Materials Fabric of the Game College Combos

STATED PRINT RUN 50 SER.#'d SETS
UNPRICED PRIME PRINT RUN 2-10

1 Vince Young	30.00	60.00
Adrian Peterson		
2 Carson Palmer	10.00	25.00
Jordan Palmer		
3 JaMarcus Russell	12.00	30.00
Dwayne Bowe		
4 Brady Quinn	15.00	40.00
Maurice Stovall		
5 Steve Smith USC	6.00	15.00
Dwayne Jarrett		

2007 Leaf Certified Materials Fabric of the Game Combos

STATED PRINT RUN 1-100
*PRIME/25: .8X TO 2X BASE COMBO/75-100
*PRIME/25: .5X TO 1.2X BASE COMBO/25-45
PRIME PRINT RUN 5-25

2 Bobby Layne	25.00	50.00
Yale Lary/25		
3 Sid Luckman	20.00	40.00
Bulldog Turner/75		
4 Otto Graham	12.00	30.00
Lou Groza		
5 Jim Thorpe	60.00	120.00
Sammy Baugh/75		
6 Johnny Unitas	20.00	40.00
Joe Namath		
7 Jim Otto	15.00	30.00
Ray Nitschke		
9 Walter Payton	20.00	40.00
Doak Walker		
11 Troy Aikman	20.00	40.00
Tony Romo		
12 Warren Moon	15.00	30.00
Vince Young		
13 James Lofton	10.00	25.00
Donald Driver/45		
14 Barry Sanders	20.00	40.00
Reggie Bush		
15 Bill Bates	8.00	20.00
Roy Williams S		
16 Jerry Rice	15.00	30.00
Chad Johnson		
17 Franco Harris	10.00	25.00
Willie Parker		
18 John Elway	15.00	40.00
Jay Cutler		
19 Joe Montana	25.00	60.00
Peyton Manning		
20 Mike Singletary	8.00	20.00
Jack Lambert		
21 Jim Brown	12.00	30.00
LaDainian Tomlinson		
22 Dan Marino	30.00	60.00
Brett Favre		
23 Gale Sayers	15.00	30.00
Cedric Benson		
24 John Riggins	8.00	20.00
Larry Johnson		
25 Tom Brady	12.00	30.00
Matt Leinart		

2007 Leaf Certified Materials Gold Team

STATED PRINT RUN 500 SER.#'d SETS
*MIRROR/100: .5X TO 1.2X BASIC INSERTS
MIRROR PRINT RUN 100 SER.#'d SETS

1 LaDainian Tomlinson	2.50	6.00
2 Larry Johnson	1.50	4.00
3 Frank Gore	2.50	6.00
4 Tiki Barber	2.50	6.00
5 Chad Johnson	2.00	5.00
6 Marvin Harrison	2.50	6.00
7 Roy Williams WR	2.00	5.00
8 Drew Brees	2.50	6.00
9 Peyton Manning	4.00	10.00
10 Marc Bulger	2.00	5.00

2007 Leaf Certified Materials Gold Team Materials

STATED PRINT RUN 50-250
UNPRICED PRIME PRINT RUN 5
UNPRICED PRIME BLK PRINT RUN 1

1 LaDainian Tomlinson	4.00	10.00
2 Larry Johnson	2.50	6.00
3 Frank Gore/180	4.00	10.00
4 Tiki Barber	4.00	10.00
6 Marvin Harrison	4.00	10.00
7 Roy Williams WR/50	4.00	10.00
8 Drew Brees	4.00	10.00
9 Peyton Manning/125	8.00	20.00
10 Marc Bulger	3.00	8.00

2007 Leaf Certified Materials Mirror Blue Materials

*MIRROR BLUE: .5X TO 1.2X MIRROR RED

COMMON ROOKIE JSY AU	12.00	30.00
ROOKIE JSY AU SEMISTARS	15.00	40.00
ROOKIE JSY AU UNL.STARS	20.00	50.00

MIRROR BLUE PRINT RUN 12-50
SERIAL #'d UNDER 25 NOT PRICED

205 Patrick Willis FF AU	40.00	100.00
210 Dwayne Bowe FF AU	25.00	60.00
215 JaMarcus Russell FF AU	12.00	30.00
219 Adrian Peterson FF AU	150.00	300.00
220 Kevin Kolb FF AU	30.00	80.00
221 Marshawn Lynch FF AU	30.00	60.00
222 Steve Smith FF USC AU	20.00	50.00
223 Greg Olsen FF AU	15.00	40.00
229 Brady Quinn FF AU	20.00	50.00
234 Calvin Johnson FF AU	50.00	120.00

2007 Leaf Certified Materials Mirror Gold Materials

*MIRR.GOLD: .8X TO 2X MIRR.RED/90-150
*MIRR.GOLD: .6X TO 1.5X MIRR.RED/30-35
*ROOK.JSY AU/25: .6X TO 1.5X MIRR.BLUE/50
*RETIRED: .6X TO 1.5X MIRR.RED
MIRROR GOLD PRINT RUN 8-25
SERIAL #'d UNDER 20 NOT PRICED

219 Adrian Peterson FF AU	250.00	500.00
234 Calvin Johnson FF AU	100.00	200.00

2007 Leaf Certified Materials Mirror Red Materials

*RETIRED: .5X TO 1.2X BASE JSYs
STATED PRINT RUN 25-250
UNPRICED MIRROR BLACK #'d TO 1
UNPRICED MIRROR EMERALD #'d TO 5

1 Tony Romo/100	5.00	12.00
2 Julius Jones/125	2.50	6.00
3 Terry Glenn/125	3.00	8.00
4 Terrell Owens/100	4.00	10.00
5 Jason Witten/150	4.00	10.00
7 Eli Manning/100	4.00	10.00
8 Plaxico Burress/125	3.00	8.00
9 Jeremy Shockey/125	3.00	8.00
10 Brandon Jacobs/125	3.00	8.00
11 Sinorice Moss/125	3.00	8.00
12 Donovan McNabb/100	4.00	10.00
13 Brian Westbrook/90	3.00	8.00
14 Reggie Brown/125	2.50	6.00
15 Hank Baskett/125	3.00	8.00
16 Jason Campbell/125	3.00	8.00
17 Clinton Portis/100	3.00	8.00
18 Santana Moss/125	3.00	8.00
21 Rex Grossman/125	3.00	8.00
22 Cedric Benson/125	3.00	8.00
23 Bernard Berrian/100	2.50	6.00
24 Devin Hester/125	4.00	10.00
25 Brian Urlacher/125	4.00	10.00
26 Jon Kitna/125	2.50	6.00
27 Roy Williams WR/100	3.00	8.00
29 Tatum Bell/125	2.50	6.00
30 Brett Favre/100	8.00	20.00
31 Donald Driver/100	4.00	10.00
33 Nick Barnett/125	2.50	6.00
35 Chester Taylor/100	2.50	6.00
36 Troy Williamson/125	2.50	6.00
37 Michael Vick/35	5.00	12.00
38 Warrick Dunn/125	3.00	8.00
39 Joe Horn/125	3.00	8.00
40 Michael Jenkins/100	3.00	8.00
41 Alge Crumpler/100	3.00	8.00
42 Jerious Norwood/100	3.00	8.00
43 Jake Delhomme/125	3.00	8.00
44 DeShaun Foster/100	3.00	8.00
45 Steve Smith/100	3.00	8.00
46 DeAngelo Williams/100	4.00	10.00
47 Drew Brees/100	4.00	10.00
48 Deuce McAllister/100	3.00	8.00
49 Marques Colston/100	4.00	10.00
51 Reggie Bush/100	4.00	10.00
52 Cadillac Williams/100	3.00	8.00
53 Joey Galloway/125	3.00	8.00
54 Michael Clayton/125	2.50	6.00
55 Derrick Brooks/125	3.00	8.00
56 Matt Leinart/100	3.00	8.00
57 Edgerrin James/100	3.00	8.00
58 Anquan Boldin/100	3.00	8.00
59 Larry Fitzgerald/100	4.00	10.00
60 Marc Bulger/125	3.00	8.00
61 Steven Jackson/100	4.00	10.00
62 Torry Holt/100	3.00	8.00
63 Isaac Bruce/115	3.00	8.00
66 Alex Smith QB/125	4.00	10.00
67 Frank Gore/100	4.00	10.00
68 Vernon Davis/100	3.00	8.00
70 Matt Hasselbeck/100	3.00	8.00
71 Shaun Alexander/100	3.00	8.00
72 Deion Branch/125	3.00	8.00
74 J.P. Losman/125	2.50	6.00
75 Anthony Thomas/125	2.50	6.00
76 Lee Evans/125	3.00	8.00
77 Josh Reed/125	2.50	6.00
78 Daunte Culpepper/125	3.00	8.00
79 Ronnie Brown/100	3.00	8.00
80 Chris Chambers/100	3.00	8.00
82 Jason Taylor/125	3.00	8.00
83 Zach Thomas/125	3.00	8.00
84 Tom Brady/100	6.00	15.00
85 Laurence Maroney/125	3.00	8.00
86 Randy Moss/100	4.00	10.00
87 Ben Watson/110	2.50	6.00
89 Tedy Bruschi/125	4.00	10.00
90 Chad Pennington/125	3.00	8.00
91 Thomas Jones/125	3.00	8.00
92 Laveranues Coles/125	2.50	6.00
93 Jerricho Cotchery/125	3.00	8.00
94 Leon Washington/100	3.00	8.00
95 Steve McNair/100	3.00	8.00
96 Willis McGahee/125	3.00	8.00
98 Todd Heap/125	2.50	6.00
99 Ray Lewis/125	4.00	10.00
100 Mark Clayton/125	3.00	8.00
101 Carson Palmer/100	3.00	8.00
102 Rudi Johnson/125	3.00	8.00
103 Chad Johnson/100	3.00	8.00
104 T.J. Houshmandzadeh/125	3.00	8.00
105 Charlie Frye/125	3.00	8.00
106 Braylon Edwards/125	3.00	8.00
107 Kellen Winslow/125	3.00	8.00
108 Jamal Lewis/125	3.00	8.00
109 Ben Roethlisberger/125	4.00	10.00
110 Willie Parker/125	3.00	8.00
111 Hines Ward/100	4.00	10.00
112 Heath Miller/125	2.50	6.00
114 Ahman Green/110	3.00	8.00
115 Andre Johnson/125	3.00	8.00
117 DeMeco Ryans/125	3.00	8.00
118 Peyton Manning/100	6.00	15.00
119 Joseph Addai/100	3.00	8.00
120 Marvin Harrison/125	4.00	10.00
121 Reggie Wayne/125	3.00	8.00
122 Dallas Clark/125	2.50	6.00
123 Byron Leftwich/125	3.00	8.00
124 Fred Taylor/125	3.00	8.00
125 Matt Jones/125	3.00	8.00
128 Maurice Jones-Drew/125	4.00	10.00
130 Vince Young/100	3.00	8.00
131 LenDale White/125	3.00	8.00
132 Brandon Jones/100	2.50	6.00
133 Jay Cutler/100	4.00	10.00
135 Javon Walker/30	4.00	10.00
136 Rod Smith/125	3.00	8.00
137 Champ Bailey/100	3.00	8.00
138 Mike Bell/125	3.00	8.00
139 Brandon Marshall/125	3.00	8.00
140 Larry Johnson/125	2.50	6.00
141 Eddie Kennison/125	2.50	6.00
142 Tony Gonzalez/125	3.00	8.00
143 Brodie Croyle/125	3.00	8.00
144 LaMont Jordan/100	3.00	8.00
146 Philip Rivers/125	4.00	10.00
147 LaDainian Tomlinson/125	4.00	10.00
149 Antonio Gates/125	4.00	10.00
150 Shawne Merriman/125	3.00	8.00
201 Dwayne Jarrett/250	2.50	6.00
202 Johnnie Lee Higgins/250	2.50	6.00
203 Michael Bush/250	3.00	8.00
204 Antonio Pittman/250	2.00	5.00
205 Patrick Willis/250	6.00	15.00
206 Gaines Adams/250	3.00	8.00
207 Tony Hunt/250	2.00	5.00
208 Chris Henry RB/250	2.00	5.00
209 John Beck/250	3.00	8.00
210 Dwayne Bowe/250	4.00	10.00
211 Brian Leonard/250	2.50	6.00
212 Anthony Gonzalez/250	3.00	8.00
213 Trent Edwards/250	3.00	8.00
214 Jason Hill/250	3.00	8.00
215 JaMarcus Russell/250	2.00	5.00
216 Ted Ginn Jr./250	2.50	6.00
217 Paul Williams/250	2.00	5.00
218 Garrett Wolfe/250	2.00	5.00
219 Adrian Peterson/250	12.00	30.00
220 Kevin Kolb/250	5.00	12.00
221 Marshawn Lynch/250	3.00	8.00
222 Steve Smith USC/250	3.00	8.00
223 Greg Olsen/250	2.50	6.00
224 Kenny Irons/250	2.00	5.00
225 Brandon Jackson/250	2.50	6.00
226 Yamon Figurs/250	2.00	5.00
227 Lorenzo Booker/250	2.50	6.00
228 Drew Stanton/250	2.00	5.00
229 Brady Quinn/250	3.00	8.00
230 Joe Thomas/250	3.00	8.00
231 Robert Meachem/250	3.00	8.00
232 Troy Smith/250	3.00	8.00
233 Sidney Rice/250	4.00	10.00
234 Calvin Johnson/250	10.00	25.00
235 Bart Starr/50	15.00	40.00
236 Bob Griese/50	10.00	25.00
237 Bobby Layne/25	12.00	30.00
238 Bulldog Turner/50	10.00	25.00
239 Earl Campbell/50	10.00	25.00
240 Franco Harris/50	10.00	25.00
241 James Lofton/50	6.00	15.00
242 Jim McMahon/25	12.00	30.00
243 Jim Thorpe/25	60.00	120.00
244 Joe Namath/50	12.00	30.00
245 John Stallworth/50	8.00	20.00
246 Lou Groza/50	8.00	20.00
247 Ray Nitschke/50	12.00	30.00
248 Ron Mix/50	6.00	15.00
249 Roosevelt Brown/50	6.00	15.00
250 Sam Huff/50	8.00	20.00
251 Sammy Baugh/50	20.00	50.00
252 Sid Luckman/25	15.00	40.00
253 Otto Graham/25	15.00	40.00
254 Y.A. Tittle/50	10.00	25.00

2007 Leaf Certified Materials Mirror Blue Signatures

MIRROR BLUE PRINT RUN 50 SER.#'d SETS
*MIRR.GOLD/25: .5X TO 1.2X MIRR.BLUE/50
MIRROR GOLD PRINT RUN 10-25
*MIRR.RED/100: .3X TO .8X MIRR.BLUE/50
MIRROR RED PRINT RUN 100
UNPRICED MIRROR BLACK PRINT RUN 1
UNPRICED MIRROR EMERALD PRINT RUN 5

151 Aaron Ross	6.00	15.00
153 Ahmad Bradshaw	20.00	50.00
155 Chansi Stuckey	6.00	15.00
159 Dan Bazuin	5.00	12.00
160 David Harris	5.00	12.00
161 Dwayne Wright	5.00	12.00
162 Eric Frampton	5.00	12.00
165 Jason Snelling	6.00	15.00
167 Kenneth Darby	5.00	12.00
168 LaMarr Woodley	10.00	25.00
172 Michael Griffin	6.00	15.00
173 Mike Walker	6.00	15.00
177 Anthony Spencer	6.00	15.00
178 Aundrae Allison	4.00	10.00
179 Ben Patrick	5.00	12.00
180 Brandon Meriweather	6.00	15.00
181 Chris Davis	4.00	10.00
182 Chris Houston	5.00	12.00
184 Dallas Baker	4.00	10.00
187 David Clowney	5.00	12.00
188 DeShawn Wynn	8.00	20.00
189 Ikaika Alama-Francis	6.00	15.00
190 Isaiah Stanback	4.00	10.00
194 Courtney Taylor	5.00	12.00
196 Jonathan Wade	5.00	12.00
197 Josh Wilson	5.00	12.00
198 Kolby Smith	5.00	12.00

2007 Leaf Certified Materials Souvenir Stamps Autographs Pro Team Logos

UNPRICED 1969 STAMP AU PRINT RUN 5-10
UNPRICED PRO TEAM AU PRINT RUN 5-15
UNPRICED USA FLAG AU #'d TO 1

2007 Leaf Certified Materials Souvenir Stamps Material Pro Team Logos

STATED PRINT RUN 50 SER.#'d SETS
*1969 STAMP/25: .5X TO 1.2X TEAM LOGO
UNPRICED POP WARNER PRINT RUN 5
UNPRICED USA FLAG PRINT RUN 10
UNPRICED AUTOs PRINT RUN 1

1 Trent Edwards	5.00	12.00
2 Marshawn Lynch	5.00	12.00
3 Chris Henry RB	3.00	8.00
4 Paul Williams	3.00	8.00
5 Sidney Rice	6.00	15.00
6 Adrian Peterson	20.00	50.00
7 Drew Stanton	3.00	8.00
8 Calvin Johnson	15.00	40.00
9 Yamon Figurs	3.00	8.00
10 Brian Leonard	4.00	10.00
11 Garrett Wolfe	3.00	8.00
12 Kenny Irons	3.00	8.00
13 Joe Thomas	5.00	12.00
14 Brady Quinn	5.00	12.00
15 Brandon Jackson	4.00	10.00
16 Steve Smith USC	5.00	12.00
17 Dwayne Jarrett	4.00	10.00
18 Troy Smith	5.00	12.00
19 Ted Ginn Jr.	4.00	10.00
20 John Beck	5.00	12.00
21 Lorenzo Booker	4.00	10.00
22 Antonio Pittman	3.00	8.00
23 Robert Meachem	5.00	12.00
24 Dwayne Bowe	6.00	15.00
25 Greg Olsen	4.00	10.00
26 Anthony Gonzalez	5.00	12.00
27 JaMarcus Russell	3.00	8.00
28 Michael Bush	5.00	12.00
29 Johnnie Lee Higgins	4.00	10.00
30 Kevin Kolb	8.00	20.00
31 Tony Hunt	3.00	8.00
32 Patrick Willis	10.00	25.00
33 Jason Hill	5.00	12.00
34 Gaines Adams	5.00	12.00

2007 Leaf Certified Materials Souvenir Stamps College Autographs College Logo

UNPRICED AU COLLEGE PRINT RUN 5-9
UNPRICED AU 1969 STAMP PRINT RUN 5
UNPRICED AU USA FLAG PRINT RUN 1

2007 Leaf Certified Materials Souvenir Stamps College Material College Logo

STATED PRINT RUN 50 SER.#'d SETS
*1969 STAMP/25: .5X TO 1.2X BASE INSERTS
UNPRICED AUTOs PRINT RUN 1
UNPRICED POP WARNER PRINT RUN 5
UNPRICED USA FLAG PRINT RUN 10

1 Kenny Irons	6.00	15.00
2 Robert Meachem	8.00	20.00
3 Adrian Peterson	25.00	60.00
4 Greg Olsen	4.00	10.00
5 Michael Bush	5.00	12.00
6 JaMarcus Russell	3.00	8.00
7 Dwayne Bowe	12.00	30.00

2008 Leaf Certified Materials

This set was released on September 24, 2008. The base set consists of 255 cards. Cards 1-150 feature veterans, cards 151-200 are a mix of rookies serial numbered of

1500 and autographed rookie cards serial numbered of 249-999. Cards 201-234 are jersey rookie cards serial numbered of 599, and cards 235-255 are jersey legend cards serial numbered of 100.

COMP.SET w/o SP's (150) 15.00 40.00
UNSIGNED ROOKIE PRINT RUN 1500
AU ROOKIE PRINT RUN 249-999
JSY ROOKIE PRINT RUN 599
JSY LEGEND PRINT RUN 100
1 Matt Leinart .40 1.00
2 Larry Fitzgerald .40 1.00
3 Anquan Boldin .30 .75
4 Edgerrin James .30 .75
5 Jerious Norwood .30 .75
6 Roddy White .30 .75
7 Joe Horn .30 .75
8 Michael Turner .40 1.00
9 Willis McGahee .30 .75
10 Derrick Mason .30 .75
11 Mark Clayton .30 .75
12 Demetrius Williams .25 .60
13 Trent Edwards .25 .60
14 Marshawn Lynch .30 .75
15 Lee Evans .30 .75
16 Steve Smith .30 .75
17 DeAngelo Williams .30 .75
18 Julius Peppers .30 .75
19 Jake Delhomme .30 .75
20 Adrian Peterson .60 1.50
21 Greg Olsen .30 .75
22 Devin Hester .40 1.00
23 Brian Urlacher .40 1.00
24 Rex Grossman .30 .75
25 Carson Palmer .40 1.00
26 Chad Johnson .30 .75
27 T.J. Houshmandzadeh .30 .75
28 Rudi Johnson .30 .75
29 Derek Anderson .25 .60
30 Jamal Lewis .30 .75
31 Kellen Winslow .30 .75
32 Braylon Edwards .30 .75
33 Tony Romo .50 1.25
34 Terrell Owens .40 1.00
35 Marion Barber .30 .75
36 Jason Witten .40 1.00
37 Jay Cutler .40 1.00
38 Selvin Young .25 .60
39 Brandon Marshall .30 .75
40 Brandon Stokley .30 .75
41 Jon Kitna .30 .75
42 Roy Williams WR .30 .75
43 Calvin Johnson .40 1.00
44 Mike Furrey .30 .75
45 Aaron Rodgers .75 2.00
46 Ryan Grant .40 1.00
47 Greg Jennings .40 1.00
48 Donald Driver .30 .75
49 Matt Schaub .30 .75
50 Ahman Green .30 .75
51 Andre Johnson .30 .75
52 Kevin Walter .30 .75
53 DeMeco Ryans .30 .75
54 Peyton Manning .60 1.50
55 Joseph Addai .30 .75
56 Marvin Harrison .40 1.00
57 Reggie Wayne .30 .75
58 Dallas Clark .30 .75
59 Anthony Gonzalez .25 .60
60 David Garrard .30 .75
61 Fred Taylor .30 .75
62 Maurice Jones-Drew .30 .75
63 Reggie Williams .30 .75
64 Marcedes Lewis .25 .60
65 Matt Jones .30 .75
66 Jerry Porter .25 .60
67 Brodie Croyle .30 .75
68 Larry Johnson .30 .75
69 Kolby Smith .25 .60
70 Tony Gonzalez .30 .75
71 Dwayne Bowe .30 .75
72 John Beck .25 .60
73 Ronnie Brown .30 .75
74 Ted Ginn Jr. .30 .75
75 Derek Hagan .25 .60
76 Jason Taylor .30 .75
77 Bernard Berrian .30 .75
78 Tarvaris Jackson .30 .75
79 Adrian Peterson .60 1.50
80 Chester Taylor .25 .60
81 Sidney Rice .40 1.00
82 Tom Brady .60 1.50
83 Randy Moss .40 1.00
84 Laurence Maroney .30 .75
85 Wes Welker .40 1.00
86 Drew Brees .40 1.00
87 Reggie Bush .40 1.00
88 Deuce McAllister .30 .75
89 Marques Colston .30 .75
90 Eli Manning .40 1.00
91 Plaxico Burress .30 .75
92 Brandon Jacobs .30 .75
93 Amani Toomer .30 .75
94 Jeremy Shockey .30 .75
95 Steve Smith USC .30 .75
96 Michael Strahan .30 .75
97 Kellen Clemens .30 .75
98 Leon Washington .30 .75
99 Jerricho Cotchery .30 .75
100 Laveranues Coles .25 .60
101 Thomas Jones .30 .75
102 Javon Walker .30 .75
103 JaMarcus Russell .30 .75
104 Justin Fargas .25 .60
105 Michael Bush .30 .75
106 Zach Miller .30 .75
107 Donovan McNabb .40 1.00
108 Brian Westbrook .30 .75
109 Kevin Curtis .25 .60
110 Reggie Brown .25 .60
111 Greg Lewis .25 .60
112 Ben Roethlisberger .40 1.00
113 Willie Parker .30 .75
114 Hines Ward .30 .75
115 Santonio Holmes .30 .75
116 Philip Rivers .40 1.00
117 LaDainian Tomlinson .40 1.00
118 Vincent Jackson .25 .60
119 Antonio Gates .40 1.00
120 Brett Favre 2.50 6.00
121 Alex Smith QB .40 1.00
122 Frank Gore .30 .75
123 Michael Robinson .25 .60
124 Vernon Davis .30 .75
125 Isaac Bruce .30 .75
126 Patrick Willis .30 .75
127 Matt Hasselbeck .30 .75
128 Nate Burleson .25 .60
129 Deion Branch .30 .75
130 Julius Jones .25 .60
131 Marc Bulger .30 .75
132 Steven Jackson .40 1.00
133 Torry Holt .30 .75
134 Warrick Dunn .30 .75
135 Jeff Garcia .30 .75
136 Cadillac Williams .30 .75
137 Earnest Graham .25 .60
138 Joey Galloway .30 .75
139 Michael Clayton .25 .60
140 Vince Young .30 .75
141 LenDale White .30 .75
142 Justin Gage .25 .60
143 Roydell Williams .25 .60
144 Alge Crumpler .30 .75
145 Brandon Jones .25 .60
146 Jason Campbell .30 .75
147 Clinton Portis .30 .75
148 Ladell Betts .25 .60
149 Santana Moss .25 .60
150 Chris Cooley .30 .75
151 Adrian Arrington AU/999 RC 3.00 8.00
152 Andre Woodson RC 1.50 4.00
153 Antoine Cason AU/749 RC 4.00 10.00
154 Aqib Talib AU/999 RC 4.00 10.00
155 Brad Cottam AU/999 RC 3.00 8.00
156 Brandon Flowers AU/899 RC 4.00 10.00
157 Chauncey Washington AU/799 RC 3.00 8.00
158 Chevis Jackson RC 1.00 2.50
159 Colt Brennan RC 1.50 4.00
160 Curtis Lofton AU/999 RC 3.00 8.00
161 Dan Connor RC 1.50 4.00
162 Dennis Dixon RC 1.50 4.00
163 Derrick Harvey RC 1.00 2.50
164 Dominique Rodgers-Cromartie RC 1.50 4.00
165 Erik Ainge AU/699 RC 4.00 10.00
166 Fred Davis AU/999 RC 4.00 10.00
167 Jacob Hester AU/399 RC 5.00 12.00
168 Jermichael Finley RC 1.50 4.00
169 Jerod Mayo RC 1.50 4.00
170 John Carlson RC 1.50 4.00
171 Josh Johnson RC 1.50 4.00
172 Jordon Dizon AU/299 RC 5.00 12.00
173 Josh Morgan RC 1.50 4.00
174 Justin Forsett AU/649 RC 4.00 10.00
175 Keenan Burton RC 1.00 2.50
176 Keith Rivers RC 1.50 4.00
177 Kenny Phillips RC 1.50 4.00
178 Kevin Robinson AU/999 RC 2.50 6.00
179 Lavelle Hawkins RC 1.00 2.50
180 Leodis McKelvin AU/999 RC 3.00 8.00
181 Marcus Smith RC 1.25 3.00
182 Marcus Thomas AU/499 RC 4.00 10.00
183 Martellus Bennett RC 1.25 3.00
184 Matt Flynn RC 3.00 8.00
185 Mike Jenkins RC 1.50 4.00
186 Mike Hart RC 1.50 4.00
187 Paul Hubbard RC 1.25 3.00
188 Peyton Hillis AU/499 RC 15.00 40.00
189 Quentin Groves AU/275 RC 4.00 10.00
190 Reggie Smith RC 1.25 3.00
191 Ryan Torain AU/299 RC 5.00 12.00
192 Sedrick Ellis RC 1.50 4.00
193 Shawn Crable RC 1.00 2.50
194 Tashard Choice AU/999 RC 3.00 8.00
195 Terrell Thomas AU/999 RC 3.00 8.00
196 Thomas Brown AU/999 RC 3.00 8.00
197 Tim Hightower AU/499 RC 5.00 12.00
198 Tracy Porter AU/999 RC 6.00 15.00
199 Vernon Gholston AU/999 RC 3.00 8.00
200 Will Franklin AU/249 RC 4.00 10.00
201 Andre Caldwell JSY RC 2.00 5.00
202 Dustin Keller JSY RC 2.50 6.00
203 Earl Bennett JSY RC 2.50 6.00
204 Early Doucet JSY RC 2.00 5.00
205 Glenn Dorsey JSY RC 2.50 6.00
206 Harry Douglas JSY RC 2.00 5.00
207 John David Booty JSY RC 2.00 5.00
208 Kevin O'Connell JSY RC 2.00 5.00
209 Darren McFadden JSY RC 8.00 20.00
210 Jonathan Stewart JSY RC 4.00 10.00
211 Felix Jones JSY RC 8.00 20.00
212 Rashard Mendenhall JSY RC 5.00 12.00
213 Chris Johnson JSY RC 6.00 15.00
214 Matt Forte JSY RC 4.00 10.00
215 Ray Rice JSY RC 5.00 12.00
216 Kevin Smith JSY RC 2.50 6.00
217 Jamaal Charles JSY RC 4.00 10.00
218 Steve Slaton JSY RC 2.50 6.00
219 Matt Ryan JSY RC 8.00 20.00
220 Joe Flacco JSY RC 8.00 20.00
221 Brian Brohm JSY RC 2.50 6.00
222 Chad Henne JSY RC 2.50 6.00
223 Donnie Avery JSY RC 2.00 5.00
224 Devin Thomas JSY RC 2.00 5.00
225 Jordy Nelson JSY RC 3.00 8.00
226 James Hardy JSY RC 2.00 5.00
227 Eddie Royal JSY RC 2.50 6.00
228 DeSean Jackson JSY RC 5.00 12.00
229 Malcolm Kelly JSY RC 2.00 5.00
230 Limas Sweed JSY RC 2.50 6.00
231 Mario Manningham JSY RC 2.50 6.00
232 Jerome Simpson JSY RC 2.50 6.00
233 Dexter Jackson JSY RC 2.00 5.00
234 Jake Long JSY RC 2.50 6.00
235 Bart Starr JSY 10.00 25.00
236 Johnny Unitas JSY/75 12.00 30.00
237 Brett Favre JSY 12.00 30.00
238 Tom Landry JSY 12.00 30.00
239 Hank Stram JSY 6.00 15.00
240 Chuck Foreman JSY 4.00 10.00
241 Dan Marino JSY 12.00 30.00
242 Andre Reed JSY 5.00 12.00
243 Frank Gifford JSY/50 6.00 15.00
244 John Riggins JSY 5.00 12.00
245 John Stallworth JSY 5.00 12.00
246 John Elway JSY 10.00 25.00
247 Emmitt Smith JSY 12.00 30.00
248 Randall Cunningham JSY 6.00 15.00
249 Reggie White JSY 6.00 15.00
250 John Matuszak JSY 6.00 15.00
251 Troy Aikman JSY 8.00 20.00
252 Billy Sims JSY 5.00 12.00
253 Willie Brown JSY 4.00 10.00
254 Barry Sanders JSY 10.00 25.00
255 Walter Payton JSY 12.00 30.00

2008 Leaf Certified Materials Mirror Black

UNPRICED MIRROR BLACK PRINT RUN 1

2008 Leaf Certified Materials Mirror Blue

*VETS 1-150: 5X TO 12X BASIC CARDS
*ROOKIES 151-200: .5X TO 1.2X MIRR.RED
STATED PRINT RUN 50 SER.#'d SETS
120 Brett Favre 15.00 40.00

2008 Leaf Certified Materials Mirror Emerald

UNPRICED MIRROR EMERALD PRINT RUN 5

2008 Leaf Certified Materials Mirror Gold

*VETS 1-150: 8X TO 20X BASIC CARDS
*ROOKIES 151-200: .8X TO 2X MIRR.RED
STATED PRINT RUN 25 SER.#'d SETS
120 Brett Favre 25.00 60.00

2008 Leaf Certified Materials Mirror Red

*VETS 1-150: 4X TO 10X BASIC CARDS
COMMON ROOKIE (151-200) 3.00 8.00
ROOKIE UNL.STARS 4.00 10.00
STATED PRINT RUN 100 SER.#'d SETS
120 Brett Favre 12.00 30.00
159 Colt Brennan 4.00 10.00
162 Dennis Dixon 4.00 10.00
165 Erik Ainge 4.00 10.00
169 Jerod Mayo 4.00 10.00
173 Josh Morgan 4.00 10.00
184 Matt Flynn 8.00 20.00
185 Mike Jenkins 4.00 10.00
186 Mike Hart 4.00 10.00
197 Tim Hightower 4.00 10.00

2008 Leaf Certified Materials Certified Potential

STATED PRINT RUN 1000 SER.#'d SETS
*MIRROR/500: .4X TO 1X BASIC INSERTS
MIRROR PRINT RUN 500 SER.#'d SETS
*RED/250: .5X TO 1.2X BASIC INSERTS
RED PRINT RUN 250 SER.#'d SETS
*BLUE/100: .6X TO 1.5X BASIC INSERTS
BLUE PRINT RUN 100 SER.#'d SETS
*GOLD/25: 1X TO 2.5X BASIC INSERTS
GOLD PRINT RUN 25 SER.#'d SETS
UNPRICED EMERALD PRINT RUN 5
UNPRICED BLACK PRINT RUN 1
1 Darren McFadden 2.00 5.00
2 Jonathan Stewart 1.25 3.00
3 Felix Jones 1.25 3.00
4 Rashard Mendenhall 1.50 4.00
5 Chris Johnson 2.00 5.00
6 Matt Forte 1.25 3.00
7 Ray Rice 1.50 4.00
8 Kevin Smith .75 2.00
9 Jamaal Charles 1.25 3.00
10 Steve Slaton .75 2.00
11 Matt Ryan 3.00 8.00
12 Joe Flacco 2.50 6.00
13 Brian Brohm .75 2.00
14 Chad Henne .75 2.00
15 Donnie Avery .60 1.50
16 Devin Thomas .60 1.50
17 Jordy Nelson 1.00 2.50
18 James Hardy .60 1.50
19 Eddie Royal .75 2.00
20 DeSean Jackson 1.50 4.00
21 Malcolm Kelly .60 1.50
22 Limas Sweed .75 2.00
23 Mario Manningham .75 2.00
24 Jerome Simpson .75 2.00
25 Dexter Jackson .60 1.50

2008 Leaf Certified Materials Certified Potential Autographs

STATED PRINT RUN 50-100
1 Darren McFadden/50 30.00 80.00
2 Jonathan Stewart/50 10.00 25.00
3 Felix Jones/50 25.00 60.00
4 Rashard Mendenhall/50 20.00 50.00
5 Chris Johnson 25.00 60.00
6 Matt Forte 25.00 50.00
7 Ray Rice 20.00 40.00
8 Kevin Smith 6.00 15.00
9 Jamaal Charles 10.00 25.00
10 Steve Slaton 6.00 15.00
11 Matt Ryan/50 60.00 120.00
12 Joe Flacco 40.00 80.00
13 Brian Brohm/50 6.00 15.00
14 Chad Henne/50 6.00 15.00
15 Donnie Avery 5.00 12.00
16 Devin Thomas 5.00 12.00
17 Jordy Nelson 15.00 30.00
18 James Hardy 5.00 12.00
19 Eddie Royal 6.00 15.00
20 DeSean Jackson 20.00 40.00
21 Malcolm Kelly 5.00 12.00
22 Limas Sweed 6.00 15.00
23 Mario Manningham 6.00 15.00
24 Jerome Simpson 6.00 15.00
25 Dexter Jackson 5.00 12.00

2008 Leaf Certified Materials Certified Potential Materials

STATED PRINT RUN 250 SER.#'d SETS
*PRIME/25: 1X TO 2.5X BASIC JSY/250
PRIME PRINT RUN 25 SER.#'d SETS
UNPRICED PRIME BLACK PRINT RUN 1
1 Darren McFadden 8.00 20.00
2 Jonathan Stewart 3.00 8.00
3 Felix Jones 6.00 15.00
4 Rashard Mendenhall 4.00 10.00
5 Chris Johnson 5.00 12.00
6 Matt Forte 3.00 8.00
7 Ray Rice 4.00 10.00
8 Kevin Smith 2.00 5.00
9 Jamaal Charles 3.00 8.00
10 Steve Slaton 2.00 5.00
11 Matt Ryan 6.00 15.00
12 Joe Flacco 6.00 15.00
13 Brian Brohm 2.00 5.00
14 Chad Henne 2.00 5.00
15 Donnie Avery 2.00 5.00
16 Devin Thomas 1.50 4.00
17 Jordy Nelson 2.50 6.00
18 James Hardy 1.50 4.00
19 Eddie Royal 2.00 5.00
20 DeSean Jackson 4.00 10.00
21 Malcolm Kelly 1.50 4.00
22 Limas Sweed 2.00 5.00
23 Mario Manningham 2.00 5.00
24 Jerome Simpson 2.50 6.00
25 Dexter Jackson 2.50 6.00

2008 Leaf Certified Materials Certified Skills

STATED PRINT RUN 1000 SER.#'d SETS
*MIRROR/500: .4X TO 1X BASIC INSERTS
MIRROR PRINT RUN 500 SER.#'d SETS
*RED/250: .5X TO 1.2X BASIC INSERTS
RED PRINT RUN 250 SER.#'d SETS
*BLUE/100: .6X TO 1.5X BASIC INSERTS
BLUE PRINT RUN 100 SER.#'d SETS
*GOLD/25: 1X TO 2.5X BASIC INSERTS
GOLD PRINT RUN 25 SER.#'d SETS
UNPRICED EMERALD PRINT RUN 5
UNPRICED BLACK PRINT RUN 1
1 Adrian Peterson 2.00 5.00
2 Greg Jennings 1.25 3.00
3 Marion Barber 1.00 2.50
4 LaRon Landry 1.00 2.50
5 Brandon Marshall 1.00 2.50
6 Brandon Jacobs 1.00 2.50
7 T.J. Houshmandzadeh 1.00 2.50
8 Reggie Wayne 1.00 2.50
9 Braylon Edwards 1.00 2.50
10 Brian Westbrook 1.00 2.50

2008 Leaf Certified Materials Certified Skills Materials Prime

PRIME PRINT RUN 25 SER.#'d SETS
*BASE JSY/250: .2X TO .5X PRIME/25
UNPRICED PRIME BLACK PRINT RUN 1
1 Adrian Peterson/24 12.00 30.00
6 Brandon Jacobs 6.00 15.00
7 T.J. Houshmandzadeh 6.00 15.00
8 Reggie Wayne 6.00 15.00
10 Brian Westbrook 6.00 15.00

2008 Leaf Certified Materials Fabric of the Game

STATED PRINT RUN 25-99
UNPRICED TEAM LOGO AUTO PRINT RUN 1-5
1 Alan Page 5.00 12.00
2 Andre Reed 5.00 12.00
3 Barry Sanders 10.00 25.00
4 Bart Starr 10.00 25.00
5 Billy Sims 5.00 12.00
6 Bo Jackson 8.00 20.00
7 Bob Griese 6.00 15.00
8 Bob Lilly 5.00 12.00
9 Brett Favre 10.00 25.00
11 Charley Taylor 4.00 10.00
12 Charlie Joiner 4.00 10.00
13 Chuck Foreman 4.00 10.00
14 Cliff Harris 4.00 10.00
15 Cris Collinsworth 5.00 12.00
16 Dan Marino 12.00 30.00
17 Danny White 6.00 15.00
18 Daryl Johnston/25 12.00 30.00
19 Daryle Lamonica 5.00 12.00
20 Deacon Jones 5.00 12.00
21 Dick Butkus 8.00 20.00
22 Don Maynard 5.00 12.00
23 Emmitt Smith 10.00 25.00
24 Eric Dickerson 5.00 12.00
25 Fran Tarkenton 6.00 15.00
26 Franco Harris 6.00 15.00
28 Fred Biletnikoff 6.00 15.00
29 Gene Upshaw 4.00 10.00
30 Garo Yepremian 4.00 10.00
31 Hank Stram 5.00 12.00
34 James Lofton 5.00 12.00
35 Jan Stenerud/75 4.00 10.00
36 Jerry Rice 10.00 25.00
37 Jim Brown/50 8.00 20.00
38 Jim Kelly/50 6.00 15.00
39 Jim McMahon 6.00 15.00
40 Jim Otto 4.00 10.00
41 John Matuszak 6.00 15.00
42 Joe Montana 12.00 30.00
43 John Riggins 5.00 12.00
44 John Elway 10.00 25.00
45 John Stallworth 5.00 12.00
46 Ken Stabler 6.00 15.00
47 Lance Alworth/33 8.00 20.00
49 Lenny Moore 5.00 12.00
50 Marcus Allen 6.00 15.00
51 Mark Duper 4.00 10.00
52 Mark Gastineau/50 4.00 10.00
53 Merlin Olsen/35 8.00 20.00
54 Michael Irvin 5.00 12.00
55 Ozzie Newsome 5.00 12.00
56 Paul Warfield/50 5.00 12.00
57 Phil Simms 5.00 12.00
58 Randall Cunningham 6.00 15.00
59 Randy White 5.00 12.00
60 Reggie White 6.00 15.00
61 Ronnie Lott 6.00 15.00
62 Rosey Grier 4.00 10.00
63 Sammy Baugh/50 10.00 25.00
64 Steve Largent 6.00 15.00
66 Steve Young 8.00 20.00
67 Ted Hendricks 4.00 10.00
68 Tiki Barber 5.00 12.00
69 Tom Landry 12.00 30.00
70 Troy Aikman 8.00 20.00
71 Walter Payton 12.00 30.00
72 Warren Moon 6.00 15.00
74 Y.A. Tittle/50 6.00 15.00
75 LaDainian Tomlinson 4.00 10.00
76 Adrian Peterson/40 6.00 15.00
78 Willie Parker 3.00 8.00
79 Clinton Portis 3.00 8.00
80 Edgerrin James 3.00 8.00
81 Willis McGahee 3.00 8.00
82 Fred Taylor/80 3.00 8.00
83 Marshawn Lynch 3.00 8.00
84 Frank Gore 3.00 8.00
85 Joseph Addai 3.00 8.00
86 Marion Barber 3.00 8.00
89 Brandon Jacobs 3.00 8.00
90 Tom Brady/70 6.00 15.00
91 Peyton Manning 6.00 15.00
92 Drew Brees 4.00 10.00
93 Tony Romo 5.00 12.00
94 Carson Palmer 4.00 10.00
95 Jon Kitna 3.00 8.00
96 Matt Hasselbeck 3.00 8.00
98 Jay Cutler 4.00 10.00
99 Eli Manning 4.00 10.00
100 Donovan McNabb 4.00 10.00
103 Philip Rivers 4.00 10.00
106 Chad Johnson 3.00 8.00
107 Larry Fitzgerald 4.00 10.00
111 Marques Colston 3.00 8.00
113 Torry Holt 3.00 8.00
114 Wes Welker 4.00 10.00
117 T.J. Houshmandzadeh/70 3.00 8.00
118 Santonio Holmes 3.00 8.00
119 Derrick Mason 3.00 8.00
121 Steve Smith 3.00 8.00
123 Dwayne Bowe/40 3.00 8.00

2008 Leaf Certified Materials Fabric of the Game Prime

*PRIME/20-25: .6X TO 1.5X BASIC FOTG
PRIME PRINT RUN 1-25
10 Carl Eller 8.00 20.00
65 Sterling Sharpe 8.00 20.00

2008 Leaf Certified Materials Fabric of the Game College

STATED PRINT RUN 6-100
SERIAL #'d UNDER 20 NOT PRICED
UNPRICED AUTO PRINT RUN 10
1 Malcolm Kelly 2.50 6.00
2 Allen Patrick 2.50 6.00
3 Shawn Crable 2.00 5.00
4 Chris Long 3.00 8.00
5 Felix Jones/50 10.00 25.00
6 Darren McFadden 8.00 20.00
7 Marcus Monk 2.50 6.00
8 Matt Ryan/20 12.00 30.00
9 Dan Connor 3.00 8.00
11 Jamaal Charles 5.00 12.00
12 Limas Sweed 3.00 8.00
13 Sedrick Ellis 3.00 8.00
14 Keith Rivers 3.00 8.00
15 Fred Davis 3.00 8.00
16 John David Booty 2.50 6.00
17 Terrell Thomas 2.50 6.00
19 Brandon Flowers 3.00 8.00
21 Colt Brennan 8.00 20.00
22 Aqib Talib 3.00 8.00
23 Brian Brohm 3.00 8.00
24 Glenn Dorsey 3.00 8.00
25 Early Doucet 2.50 6.00
26 Chevis Jackson 2.00 5.00
27 Craig Steltz 2.50 6.00
28 Kenny Phillips 3.00 8.00
29 Calais Campbell 2.50 6.00
30 Mike Hart 3.00 8.00
31 Chad Henne 3.00 8.00
32 Mario Manningham 3.00 8.00
33 Lawrence Jackson 2.50 6.00
34 Steve Largent 5.00 12.00
35 Simeon Castille 2.50 6.00
36 Ali Highsmith 2.50 6.00
37 Ernie Wheelwright 2.50 6.00
38 Jonathan Hefney 2.50 6.00
39 Robert Killebrew 2.50 6.00

2008 Leaf Certified Materials Fabric of the Game College Prime

*PRIME/25: .8X TO 2X FOTG/100
*PRIME/25: .6X TO 1.5X FOTG/50
*PRIME/20: .5X TO 1.2X FOTG/20
PRIME PRINT RUN 20-25
10 Erik Ainge 6.00 15.00
18 Xavier Adibi 4.00 10.00

2008 Leaf Certified Materials Fabric of the Game College Combos

STATED PRINT RUN 25-50
1 Vince Young / Jamaal Charles 8.00 20.00
2 Felix Jones / Darren McFadden/25 15.00 40.00
3 Michael Bush / Harry Douglas 4.00 10.00
4 Mario Manningham / Mike Hart 5.00 12.00
5 Adrian Peterson / Malcolm Kelly 8.00 20.00
6 Matt Leinart / John David Booty 4.00 10.00
7 JaMarcus Russell / Early Doucet 4.00 10.00
9 Steve Smith USC / Fred Davis 5.00 12.00
10 Jeremy Shockey / Kellen Winslow 4.00 10.00

2008 Leaf Certified Materials Fabric of the Game College Combos Prime

*PRIME/25: .5X TO 1.2X BASIC COMBO
PRIME PRINT RUN 5-25
8 Xavier Adibi / Brandon Flowers 6.00 15.00

2008 Leaf Certified Materials Fabric of the Game Combos

STATED PRINT RUN 50-100
3 Eli Manning / Plaxico Burress/80 5.00 12.00
4 Larry Fitzgerald / Edgerrin James 5.00 12.00
6 Tarvaris Jackson / Adrian Peterson 8.00 20.00
9 Jeff Garcia / Joey Galloway/50 4.00 10.00
10 Tom Landry / Hank Stram 12.00 30.00
11 Randy White / Bob Lilly 8.00 20.00
12 Barry Sanders / Adrian Peterson 12.00 30.00

2008 Leaf Certified Materials Fabric of the Game Combos Prime

PRIME PRINT RUN 3-25
1 Tom Brady / Randy Moss 12.00 30.00
2 Philip Rivers / LaDainian Tomlinson 8.00 20.00
3 Eli Manning / Plaxico Burress 8.00 20.00
5 Randy Moss / Terrell Owens 8.00 20.00
7 Clinton Portis / Santana Moss 6.00 15.00
8 Jon Kitna / Roy Williams WR 6.00 15.00
9 Jeff Garcia / Joey Galloway 6.00 15.00
11 Randy White / Bob Lilly 10.00 25.00
12 Barry Sanders / Adrian Peterson 15.00 40.00
13 Eli Manning / Tom Brady 12.00 30.00

2008 Leaf Certified Materials Fabric of the Game Jersey Number

*JER NUM/50-99: .5X TO 1.2X BASIC JSY
*JER NUM/20-44: .6X TO 1.5X BASIC JSY
STATED PRINT RUN 1-99
SERIAL #'d UNDER 20 NOT PRICED
77 Brian Westbrook/36 6.00 15.00

2008 Leaf Certified Materials Fabric of the Game NFL Die Cut

*NFL DC/50: .5X TO 1.2X BASIC FOTG
*NFL DC/25-30: .6X TO 1.5X BASIC FOTG
NFL DIE CUT PRINT RUN 10-50
10 Carl Eller 6.00 15.00
77 Brian Westbrook/25 5.00 12.00

2008 Leaf Certified Materials Fabric of the Game NFL Die Cut Prime

*NFL DC PRIME/20-25: .8X TO 2X BASIC FOTG
NFL DIE CUT PRIME PRINT RUN 1-25
65 Sterling Sharpe 10.00 25.00

2008 Leaf Certified Materials Fabric of the Game Position

*POSITION/25-50: .4X TO 1X BASIC JSY
STATED PRINT RUN 10-50
10 Carl Eller/25 6.00 15.00
27 Frank Gifford/25 8.00 20.00
77 Brian Westbrook/25 4.00 10.00

2008 Leaf Certified Materials Fabric of the Game Team Die Cut

*TEAM DC/15-25: .8X TO 2X BASIC FOTG
TEAM DIE CUT PRINT RUN 10-25
UNPRICED PRIME TEAM DC PRINT RUN 1-10

2008 Leaf Certified Materials Fabric of the Game Team Logo Prime

COMMON ACTIVE/25 5.00 12.00
ACTIVE UNL.STARS/25 6.00 15.00
*TEAM LOGO/25: .6X TO 1.5X BASIC FOTG
STATED PRINT RUN 3-25
65 Sterling Sharpe 8.00 20.00

2008 Leaf Certified Materials Gold Team

STATED PRINT RUN 1000 SER.#'d SETS
*MIRROR/100: .8X TO 2X BASIC INSERTS
MIRROR PRINT RUN 100 SER.#'d SETS
1 Tom Brady 2.00 5.00
2 Peyton Manning 2.00 5.00
3 Tony Romo 1.50 4.00
4 LaDainian Tomlinson 1.25 3.00
5 Terrell Owens 1.25 3.00
6 Randy Moss 1.25 3.00
7 Joseph Addai 1.00 2.50
8 Ben Roethlisberger 1.25 3.00
9 Eli Manning 1.25 3.00
10 Drew Brees 1.25 3.00

2008 Leaf Certified Materials Gold Team Materials

STATED PRINT RUN 10-250
SERIAL #'d UNDER 10 NOT PRICED
UNPRICED PRIME BLACK PRINT RUN 1
1 Tom Brady/125 6.00 15.00
3 Tony Romo/250 5.00 12.00
10 Drew Brees/180 4.00 10.00

2008 Leaf Certified Materials Gold Team Materials Prime

COMMON CARD 8.00 20.00
PRIME PRINT RUN 25 SER.#'d SETS
1 Tom Brady 12.00 30.00
4 LaDainian Tomlinson 8.00 20.00
5 Terrell Owens 8.00 20.00
6 Randy Moss 8.00 20.00
9 Eli Manning 8.00 20.00

2008 Leaf Certified Materials Mirror Blue Materials

COMMON ACTIVE/20-50 3.00 8.00
ACTIVE SEMISTARS/20-50 4.00 10.00
ACTIVE UNL.STARS/20-50 5.00 12.00
*BLUE ROOKIES: .4X TO 1X MIR.RED
*BLUE RETIRED: .5X TO 1.2X MIR.RED
MIRROR BLUE PRINT RUN 20-50
33 Tony Romo 6.00 15.00
54 Peyton Manning 8.00 20.00
79 Adrian Peterson 8.00 20.00
82 Tom Brady 8.00 20.00
87 Reggie Bush 5.00 12.00
112 Ben Roethlisberger 5.00 12.00
117 LaDainian Tomlinson 5.00 12.00

2008 Leaf Certified Materials Mirror Blue Signatures

MIRROR BLUE PRINT RUN 50-100
UNPRICED MIRR.BLACK PRINT RUN 1
UNPRICED MIRR.EMERALD PRINT RUN 5
151 Adrian Arrington/100 4.00 10.00
152 Andre Woodson/50 6.00 15.00
153 Antoine Cason/50 6.00 15.00
154 Aqib Talib/100 5.00 12.00
155 Brad Cottam/100 4.00 10.00
156 Brandon Flowers/50 6.00 15.00
157 Chauncey Washington/50 5.00 12.00
159 Colt Brennan/50 6.00 15.00
160 Curtis Lofton/100 4.00 10.00
161 Dan Connor/50 6.00 15.00
162 Dennis Dixon/50 10.00 25.00
163 Derrick Harvey/50 4.00 10.00
164 Dominique Rodgers-Cromartie/100 5.00 12.00
165 Erik Ainge/50 6.00 15.00
166 Fred Davis/100 5.00 12.00
167 Jacob Hester/50 6.00 15.00
168 Jermichael Finley/100 20.00 40.00
169 Jerod Mayo/100 5.00 12.00
170 John Carlson/100 5.00 12.00
171 Josh Johnson/50 6.00 15.00
172 Jordon Dizon/50 6.00 15.00
173 Josh Morgan/100 5.00 12.00
174 Justin Forsett/50 6.00 15.00
175 Keenan Burton/100 3.00 8.00
176 Keith Rivers/50 6.00 15.00
177 Kenny Phillips/100 5.00 12.00
178 Kevin Robinson/100 3.00 8.00
179 Lavelle Hawkins/100 3.00 8.00
180 Leodis McKelvin/100 4.00 10.00
182 Marcus Thomas/50 5.00 12.00
183 Martellus Bennett/100 4.00 10.00
184 Matt Flynn/50 20.00 50.00
185 Mike Jenkins/100 5.00 12.00
186 Mike Hart/100 5.00 12.00
188 Peyton Hillis/50 40.00 80.00
189 Quentin Groves/50 5.00 12.00
190 Reggie Smith/100 4.00 10.00
191 Ryan Torain/50 6.00 15.00
192 Sedrick Ellis/100 5.00 12.00
194 Tashard Choice/100 4.00 10.00
195 Terrell Thomas/100 4.00 10.00
196 Thomas Brown/100 4.00 10.00
197 Tim Hightower/50 6.00 15.00
198 Tracy Porter/100 5.00 12.00
199 Vernon Gholston/100 4.00 10.00
200 Will Franklin/50 5.00 12.00
201 Andre Caldwell FF 8.00 20.00
202 Dustin Keller FF 10.00 25.00
203 Earl Bennett FF 10.00 25.00
204 Early Doucet FF 8.00 20.00
205 Glenn Dorsey FF EXCH
206 Harry Douglas FF
207 John David Booty FF 8.00 20.00
208 Kevin O'Connell FF 8.00 20.00
209 Darren McFadden FF 30.00 80.00
210 Jonathan Stewart FF 20.00 50.00
211 Felix Jones FF 20.00 50.00
212 Rashard Mendenhall FF 25.00 60.00
213 Chris Johnson FF 30.00 80.00
214 Matt Forte FF 15.00 40.00
215 Ray Rice FF 20.00 50.00
216 Kevin Smith FF 10.00 25.00
217 Jamaal Charles FF 15.00 40.00
218 Steve Slaton FF 10.00 25.00
219 Matt Ryan FF 75.00 150.00
220 Joe Flacco FF 50.00 100.00
221 Brian Brohm FF 12.00 30.00
222 Chad Henne FF 12.00 30.00
223 Donnie Avery FF 8.00 20.00
224 Devin Thomas FF 8.00 20.00
225 Jordy Nelson FF 25.00 50.00
226 James Hardy FF 8.00 20.00
227 Eddie Royal FF 10.00 25.00
228 DeSean Jackson FF 25.00 60.00
229 Malcolm Kelly FF 8.00 20.00
230 Limas Sweed FF 10.00 25.00
231 Mario Manningham FF 12.00 30.00
232 Jerome Simpson FF 10.00 25.00
233 Dexter Jackson FF 8.00 20.00
234 Jake Long FF 10.00 25.00

2008 Leaf Certified Materials Mirror Gold Materials

COMMON ACTIVE/15-25 5.00 12.00
ACTIVE SEMISTARS/15-25 6.00 15.00
ACTIVE UNL.STARS/15-25 8.00 20.00
*GOLD ROOKIES: .8X TO 2X MIR.RED
*GOLD RETIRED: .8X TO 2X MIR.RED
MIRROR GOLD PRINT RUN 15-25
33 Tony Romo 10.00 25.00
54 Peyton Manning 12.00 30.00
79 Adrian Peterson 12.00 30.00
82 Tom Brady 12.00 30.00
87 Reggie Bush 8.00 20.00
117 LaDainian Tomlinson 8.00 20.00

2008 Leaf Certified Materials Mirror Gold Signatures

*FF AU GOLD/25: .8X TO 2X BLUE/100
*FF AU GOLD/25: .6X TO 1.5X BLUE/50
MIRROR GOLD PRINT RUN 10-25
SERIAL #'d UNDER 25 NOT PRICED
168 Jermichael Finley 30.00 60.00
169 Jerod Mayo 8.00 20.00
173 Josh Morgan 8.00 20.00
184 Matt Flynn 25.00 60.00
185 Mike Jenkins 8.00 20.00
186 Mike Hart 8.00 20.00
188 Peyton Hillis 50.00 120.00
197 Tim Hightower 25.00 60.00
209 Darren McFadden FF 50.00 125.00
211 Felix Jones FF 30.00 80.00
213 Chris Johnson FF 75.00 150.00
214 Matt Forte FF 40.00 100.00
215 Ray Rice FF 60.00 120.00
219 Matt Ryan FF 100.00 200.00
220 Joe Flacco FF 75.00 150.00
222 Chad Henne FF 50.00 100.00

2008 Leaf Certified Materials Mirror Red Materials

COMMON ROOKIE/100 3.00 8.00
ROOKIE SEMIS/100 4.00 10.00
ROOKIE UNL.STAR/100 5.00 12.00
*RETIRED: .5X TO 1.2X BASIC JSY
MIRROR RED PRINT RUN 20-150
UNPRICED MIRROR EMERALD PRINT RUN 5
UNPRICED MIRROR BLACK PRINT RUN 1
1 Matt Leinart 4.00 10.00
2 Larry Fitzgerald 4.00 10.00
3 Anquan Boldin 3.00 8.00
4 Edgerrin James 3.00 8.00
5 Jerious Norwood 3.00 8.00
7 Joe Horn/50 4.00 10.00
8 Michael Turner 4.00 10.00
9 Willis McGahee 3.00 8.00
10 Derrick Mason 3.00 8.00
11 Mark Clayton 3.00 8.00
12 Demetrius Williams 2.50 6.00
13 Trent Edwards 2.50 6.00
14 Marshawn Lynch 3.00 8.00
15 Lee Evans 3.00 8.00
16 Steve Smith 3.00 8.00
17 DeAngelo Williams/75 4.00 10.00
18 Julius Peppers 3.00 8.00
22 Devin Hester 4.00 10.00
23 Brian Urlacher/70 5.00 12.00
24 Rex Grossman 3.00 8.00
25 Carson Palmer 4.00 10.00
26 Chad Johnson 3.00 8.00
27 T.J. Houshmandzadeh 3.00 8.00
28 Rudi Johnson 3.00 8.00
29 Derek Anderson/120 2.50 6.00
31 Kellen Winslow Jr/65 4.00 10.00
33 Tony Romo 5.00 12.00
34 Terrell Owens 4.00 10.00
35 Marion Barber 3.00 8.00
36 Jason Witten/125 4.00 10.00
37 Jay Cutler 4.00 10.00
39 Brandon Marshall/100 3.00 8.00
40 Brandon Stokley 3.00 8.00
41 Jon Kitna 3.00 8.00
42 Roy Williams WR 3.00 8.00
43 Calvin Johnson 4.00 10.00
47 Greg Jennings/125 4.00 10.00
48 Donald Driver 3.00 8.00
51 Andre Johnson/50 4.00 10.00
53 DeMeco Ryans 3.00 8.00
54 Peyton Manning 6.00 15.00
55 Joseph Addai 3.00 8.00
56 Marvin Harrison/50 5.00 12.00
57 Reggie Wayne 3.00 8.00
58 Dallas Clark 3.00 8.00
59 Anthony Gonzalez 2.50 6.00
60 David Garrard/75 4.00 10.00
61 Fred Taylor 3.00 8.00
62 Maurice Jones-Drew/110 3.00 8.00
63 Reggie Williams 3.00 8.00
65 Matt Jones 3.00 8.00
67 Brodie Croyle 3.00 8.00
68 Larry Johnson 3.00 8.00
70 Tony Gonzalez/125 3.00 8.00
71 Dwayne Bowe 3.00 8.00
73 Ronnie Brown 3.00 8.00
74 Ted Ginn Jr./105 3.00 8.00
76 Jason Taylor 3.00 8.00
77 Bernard Berrian 3.00 8.00
78 Tarvaris Jackson 3.00 8.00
79 Adrian Peterson 6.00 15.00
80 Chester Taylor 2.50 6.00
82 Tom Brady 6.00 15.00
83 Randy Moss/125 4.00 10.00
84 Laurence Maroney 3.00 8.00
85 Wes Welker 4.00 10.00
86 Drew Brees 4.00 10.00
87 Reggie Bush 4.00 10.00
88 Deuce McAllister 3.00 8.00
89 Marques Colston 3.00 8.00
90 Eli Manning 4.00 10.00
91 Plaxico Burress 3.00 8.00
92 Brandon Jacobs/125 3.00 8.00
93 Amani Toomer 3.00 8.00
94 Jeremy Shockey 3.00 8.00
95 Steve Smith USC/110 3.00 8.00

96 Michael Strahan	3.00	8.00
98 Leon Washington	3.00	8.00
99 Jerricho Cotchery	3.00	8.00
100 Laveranues Coles	2.50	6.00
101 Thomas Jones/20	5.00	12.00
102 Javon Walker	3.00	8.00
104 Justin Fargas/145	2.50	6.00
107 Donovan McNabb	4.00	10.00
108 Brian Westbrook	3.00	8.00
111 Greg Lewis	2.50	6.00
112 Ben Roethlisberger/130	4.00	10.00
113 Willie Parker	3.00	8.00
114 Hines Ward	3.00	8.00
115 Santonio Holmes	3.00	8.00
116 Philip Rivers	4.00	10.00
117 LaDainian Tomlinson	4.00	10.00
118 Vincent Jackson	2.50	6.00
121 Alex Smith QB	4.00	10.00
122 Frank Gore	3.00	8.00
123 Michael Robinson	2.50	6.00
124 Vernon Davis	3.00	8.00
125 Isaac Bruce/60	4.00	10.00
126 Patrick Willis	3.00	8.00
127 Matt Hasselbeck	3.00	8.00
129 Deion Branch/20	5.00	12.00
130 Julius Jones	2.50	6.00
132 Steven Jackson/20	6.00	15.00
133 Torry Holt	3.00	8.00
134 Warrick Dunn	3.00	8.00
135 Jeff Garcia	3.00	8.00
136 Cadillac Williams	3.00	8.00
139 Michael Clayton	2.50	6.00
140 Vince Young	3.00	8.00
141 LenDale White	3.00	8.00
144 Alge Crumpler	3.00	8.00
145 Brandon Jones	2.50	6.00
146 Jason Campbell/65	4.00	10.00
147 Clinton Portis	3.00	8.00
148 Ladell Betts	2.50	6.00
150 Chris Cooley/20	5.00	12.00
201 Andre Caldwell	3.00	8.00
202 Dustin Keller	4.00	10.00
203 Earl Bennett	4.00	10.00
204 Early Doucet	3.00	8.00
205 Glenn Dorsey	4.00	10.00
206 Harry Douglas	3.00	8.00
207 John David Booty	3.00	8.00
208 Kevin O'Connell	3.00	8.00
209 Darren McFadden	10.00	25.00
210 Jonathan Stewart	8.00	20.00
211 Felix Jones	6.00	15.00
212 Rashard Mendenhall	8.00	20.00
213 Chris Johnson	10.00	25.00
214 Matt Forte	8.00	20.00
215 Ray Rice	8.00	20.00
216 Kevin Smith	4.00	10.00
217 Jamaal Charles	6.00	15.00
218 Steve Slaton	4.00	10.00
219 Matt Ryan	12.00	30.00
220 Joe Flacco	8.00	20.00
221 Brian Brohm	4.00	10.00
222 Chad Henne	4.00	10.00
223 Donnie Avery	3.00	8.00
224 Dovin Thomas	3.00	8.00
225 Jordy Nelson	5.00	12.00
226 James Hardy	3.00	8.00
227 Eddie Royal	4.00	10.00
228 DeSean Jackson	8.00	20.00
229 Malcolm Kelly	3.00	8.00
230 Limas Sweed	4.00	10.00
231 Mario Manningham	4.00	10.00
232 Jerome Simpson	4.00	10.00
233 Dexter Jackson	3.00	8.00
234 Jake Long	4.00	10.00
235 Bart Starr	12.00	30.00
236 Johnny Unitas	15.00	40.00
237 Brett Favre	15.00	40.00
238 Tom Landry	10.00	25.00
239 Hank Stram	6.00	15.00
240 Chuck Foreman	5.00	12.00
241 Dan Marino	15.00	40.00
242 Andre Reed	6.00	15.00
243 Frank Gifford/25	10.00	25.00
244 John Riggins	6.00	15.00
245 John Stallworth	6.00	15.00
246 John Elway	12.00	30.00
247 Emmitt Smith	15.00	40.00
248 Randall Cunningham	8.00	20.00
249 Reggie White	8.00	20.00
250 John Matuszak	8.00	20.00
251 Troy Aikman	10.00	25.00
252 Billy Sims	6.00	15.00
253 Willie Brown	5.00	12.00
254 Barry Sanders	12.00	30.00
255 Walter Payton	15.00	40.00

2008 Leaf Certified Materials Mirror Red Signatures

*RED/250: .25X TO .6X MIR.BLUE/100
*RED/100: .3X TO .8X MIR.BLUE/50
MIRROR RED PRINT RUN 100-250

213 Chris Johnson FF/250	30.00	80.00
219 Matt Ryan FF/100	60.00	120.00
220 Joe Flacco FF/100	50.00	100.00

2008 Leaf Certified Materials Rookie Fabric of the Game

STATED PRINT RUN 250 SER.#'d SETS
UNPRICED AUTO PRINT RUN 5
*JER NUM/72-89: .5X TO 1.2X FOTG/250
*JER NUM/34-39: .6X TO 1.5X FOTG/250
*JER NUM/20-29: .8X TO 2X FOTG/250
JERSEY NUMBER PRINT RUN 1-89
*NFL DC/99: .5X TO 1.2X FOTG/250
*POSITION/100: .5X TO 1.2X FOTG/250
*TEAM DC/25: .8X TO 2X FOTG/250
*TEAM PRIME/25: 1X TO 2.5X FOTG/250

1 Earl Bennett	2.50	6.00
2 Harry Douglas	2.00	5.00
3 Dustin Keller	2.50	6.00
4 Jake Long	2.50	6.00
5 Early Doucet	2.00	5.00
6 Malcolm Kelly	2.00	5.00
7 Dexter Jackson	2.00	5.00
8 Rashard Mendenhall	5.00	12.00
9 Steve Slaton	2.50	6.00
10 Joe Flacco	5.00	12.00
11 Donnie Avery	2.00	5.00
12 James Hardy	2.00	5.00
13 Kevin Smith	2.50	6.00
14 DeSean Jackson	5.00	12.00
15 Kevin O'Connell	2.00	5.00
16 Ray Rice	5.00	12.00
17 Andre Caldwell	2.00	5.00
18 Chris Johnson	6.00	15.00
19 Jonathan Stewart	5.00	12.00
20 Matt Ryan	6.00	15.00
21 Matt Forte	5.00	12.00
22 Jamaal Charles	4.00	10.00
23 Eddie Royal	2.50	6.00
24 Darren McFadden	6.00	15.00
25 Brian Brohm	2.50	6.00
26 Felix Jones	4.00	10.00
27 Jordy Nelson	3.00	8.00
28 Jerome Simpson	2.50	6.00
29 Chad Henne	2.50	6.00
30 John David Booty	2.00	5.00
31 Mario Manningham	2.50	6.00
32 Glenn Dorsey	2.50	6.00
33 Devin Thomas	2.00	5.00
34 Limas Sweed	2.50	6.00

2008 Leaf Certified Materials Souvenir Stamps Autographs Pro Team Logos

UNPRICED COLLEGE LOGO PRINT RUN 2-10
UNPRICED PRO LOGO PRINT RUN 1-21
UNPRICED 1969 STAMP PRINT RUN 2-5
UNPRICED USA FLAG PRINT RUN 2-5

2008 Leaf Certified Materials Souvenir Stamps College Material College Logo

COLLEGE LOGO PRINT RUN 20-50
*PRIME/25: .6X TO 1.5X COLL.LOGO/30-50
*PRIME/25: .5X TO 1.2X COLL.LOGO/20
PRIME PRINT RUN 1-25
*1969 STAMP/25: .5X TO 1.2X COLL.LOGO
1969 STAMP PRINT RUN 5-25
UNPRICED POP WARNER PRINT RUN 1-5
UNPRICED USA FLAG PRINT RUN 5-10

1 Brian Brohm	4.00	10.00
2 Chad Henne	8.00	20.00
3 Darren McFadden	12.00	30.00
4 DeSean Jackson/45	8.00	20.00
5 Early Doucet	5.00	12.00
6 Eddie Royal	4.00	10.00
7 Felix Jones	12.00	30.00
8 Glenn Dorsey	6.00	15.00
10 Jamaal Charles	6.00	15.00
11 John David Booty	3.00	8.00
13 Limas Sweed	4.00	10.00
14 Malcolm Kelly	5.00	12.00
15 Mario Manningham	5.00	12.00
16 Matt Ryan	12.00	30.00
18 Sedrick Ellis	4.00	10.00
19 Dan Connor	6.00	15.00
20 Kenny Phillips	4.00	10.00
21 Fred Davis	4.00	10.00
22 Mike Hart	8.00	20.00
23 Allen Patrick	5.00	12.00
24 Erik Ainge	5.00	12.00
25 Dennis Dixon/20	6.00	15.00
26 Matt Flynn/30	8.00	20.00
27 Vernon Gholston	5.00	12.00
28 Aqib Talib	4.00	10.00
29 Chris Long	4.00	10.00
30 Brandon Flowers	5.00	12.00

2008 Leaf Certified Materials Souvenir Stamps Material Pro Team Logos

PRO TEAM LOGO PRINT RUN 50
*PRIME/25: .6X TO 1.5X PRO TEAM/50
PRIME PRINT RUN 25
*1969 STAMP/25: .5X TO 1.2X PRO LOGO
1969 STAMP PRINT RUN 25
UNPRICED POP WARNER PRINT RUN 5
UNPRICED USA FLAG PRINT RUN 10

1 Malcolm Kelly	3.00	8.00
2 Jerome Simpson	4.00	10.00
3 Jamaal Charles	6.00	15.00
4 Limas Sweed	4.00	10.00
5 James Hardy	3.00	8.00
6 Felix Jones	6.00	15.00
7 Rashard Mendenhall	8.00	20.00
8 Devin Thomas	3.00	8.00
9 Dustin Keller	4.00	10.00
10 Brian Brohm	4.00	10.00
11 Jake Long	4.00	10.00
12 John David Booty	3.00	8.00
13 Eddie Royal	4.00	10.00
14 Donnie Avery	3.00	8.00
15 Early Doucet	3.00	8.00
16 Ray Rice	8.00	20.00
17 Chad Henne	4.00	10.00
18 Earl Bennett	4.00	10.00
19 Steve Slaton	4.00	10.00
20 Kevin O'Connell	3.00	8.00
21 Darren McFadden	10.00	25.00
22 Jordy Nelson	5.00	12.00
23 Matt Ryan	15.00	40.00
24 Harry Douglas	3.00	8.00
25 Joe Flacco	12.00	30.00
26 Mario Manningham	4.00	10.00
27 Dexter Jackson	3.00	8.00
28 DeSean Jackson	8.00	20.00
29 Glenn Dorsey	4.00	10.00
30 Matt Forte	6.00	15.00
31 Jonathan Stewart	6.00	15.00
32 Chris Johnson	10.00	25.00
33 Kevin Smith	4.00	10.00
34 Andre Caldwell	3.00	8.00

2008 Leaf Certified Materials Souvenir Stamps Material Autographs Pro Team Logos

UNPRICED PRO LOGO PRINT RUN 2-5
NINE DIFF.UNPRICED PARALLELS
SERIAL NUMBERED FROM 1-5

2011 Leaf Legends of Sport

STATED PRINT RUN 6-50
NO PRICING ON CARDS #'d TO 12 OR LESS

BA18 Cam Newton/15	60.00	120.00
BA39 Joe Greene/6		
BA40 Joe Montana/14	75.00	150.00
BA47 Len Dawson/40	15.00	40.00
BA50 Mark Ingram/50	20.00	50.00
BA52 Mel Renfro/25	10.00	25.00
BA54 Mike Ditka/21	15.00	40.00
BA61 Ozzie Newsome/20	10.00	25.00
BA80 Ted Hendricks/20	10.00	25.00

2011 Leaf Legends of Sport Gold

STATED PRINT RUN 5 SER. #'d SETS
UNPRICED DUE TO SCARCITY

2011 Leaf Legends of Sport Purple

STATED PRINT RUN 1 SER. #'d SET
UNPRICED DUE TO SCARCITY

2011 Leaf Legends of Sport Silver

STATED PRINT RUN 10 SER. #'d SETS
UNPRICED DUE TO SCARCITY

2011 Leaf Legends of Sport Award Winners Autographs Bronze

STATED PRINT RUN 10-50

AW5 Cam Newton/18	60.00	150.00
AW15 Mark Ingram/50	20.00	50.00

2011 Leaf Legends of Sport Award Winners Autographs Gold

STATED PRINT RUN 5 SER. #'d SETS
UNPRICED DUE TO SCARCITY

2011 Leaf Legends of Sport Award Winners Autographs Purple

STATED PRINT RUN 1 SER. #'d SET
UNPRICED DUE TO SCARCITY

2011 Leaf Legends of Sport Award Winners Autographs Silver

STATED PRINT RUN 10 SER. #'d SETS
UNPRICED DUE TO SCARCITY

2011 Leaf Legends of Sport Cut Signatures

GS Gale Sayers	20.00	50.00
JN6 Joe Namath		
RR14 Bert Bell		

2011 Leaf Legends of Sport Moments of Greatness Autographs Bronze

STATED PRINT RUN 10-50

MG7 Cam Newton/18	60.00	150.00
MG19 Mark Ingram/45	20.00	50.00
MG20 Mark Ingram/44	20.00	50.00
MG21 Mike Ditka/20	15.00	40.00
MG24 Ozzie Newsome/19	10.00	25.00

2011 Leaf Legends of Sport Moments of Greatness Autographs Gold

STATED PRINT RUN 5 SER. #'d SETS
UNPRICED DUE TO SCARCITY

2011 Leaf Legends of Sport Moments of Greatness Autographs Purple

STATED PRINT RUN 1 SER. #'d SET
UNPRICED DUE TO SCARCITY

2011 Leaf Legends of Sport Moments of Greatness Autographs Silver

STATED PRINT RUN 10 SER. #'d SET
UNPRICED DUE TO SCARCITY

2011 Leaf Legends of Sport Numeration Autographs

STATED PRINT RUN 4-30
NO PRICING ON CARDS #'d TO 12 OR LESS

NU9 Joe Montana/16	75.00	150.00
NU11 Mark Ingram/22	20.00	50.00
NU25 Mel Renfro/20	10.00	25.00

2011 Leaf Legends of Sport Perennial All-Stars Autographs

STATED PRINT RUN 5-24
NO PRICING ON CARDS #'d TO 13 OR LESS
PE19 Joe Montana/8
PE25 Mike Ditka/5
PE29 Ozzie Newsome/7

2000 Leaf Limited

Released in early February 2001, Leaf Limited features all foil base cards with a player action shot set against a striped background in each respective player's team colors with the team logo in the upper left hand corner. A black bordered diamond is centered behind the player and contains an action photo shaded in the color of the card's background. Card numbers 1-200 picture veteran players and are sequentially numbered as follows: 1-50 are sequentially numbered to 5000, 51-100 are sequentially numbered to 4000, 101-150 are sequentially numbered to 3000, 151-200 are sequentially numbered to 2000. Rookie and prospect cards are numbered in lower quantities as follows: 201-250 are sequentially numbered to 1500, 251-300 are sequentially numbered to 1000, 301-350 are sequentially numbered to 500, and 351-400 are sequentially numbered to 350. Card numbers 401-425 contain both swatches of game worn jerseys and game used footballs. The design differs from the base set in that cards are enhanced with gold foil and feature player action shots on the left side of the card front and two rectangular swatches of memorabilia on the right side of the card. A portrait style shaded photo of the featured player appears in a diamond behind the color action shot, and each respective player's team logo appears above the memorabilia swatches. These cards are inserted in packs at the rate of one in 17.

COMP.SET w/o SPs (200) 60.00 120.00
201-250 ROOKIE PRINT RUN 1500
251-300 ROOKIE PRINT RUN 1000
301-350 ROOKIE PRINT RUN 500
351-400 ROOKIE PRINT RUN 350
401-425 RC JSY-FB/100-1000 ODDS 1:17

1 Ben Coates	.30	.75
2 Joe Horn	.40	1.00
3 Jonathan Linton	.30	.75
4 Derrick Mason	.40	1.00
5 Ray Lucas	.30	.75
6 Brock Huard	.30	.75
7 Frank Wycheck	.40	1.00
8 Michael Strahan	.40	1.00
9 Jessie Armstead	.30	.75
10 Stephen Alexander	.30	.75
11 Larry Centers	.30	.75
12 Michael Pittman	.30	.75
13 Priest Holmes	.50	1.25
14 Jermaine Lewis	.30	.75
15 Jay Riemersma	.30	.75
16 Wesley Walls	.30	.75
17 Curtis Enis	.30	.75
18 Bobby Engram	.40	1.00
19 Jim Miller	.30	.75
20 Eddie Kennison	.30	.75
21 Errict Rhett	.40	1.00
22 Chris Warren	.30	.75
23 Byron Chamberlain	.30	.75
24 Desmond Howard	.40	1.00
25 Lamar Smith	.30	.75
26 Robert Porcher	.30	.75
27 Corey Bradford	.30	.75
28 Donald Driver	.75	2.00
29 Ahman Green	.40	1.00
30 Ken Dilger	.30	.75
31 James McKnight	.30	.75
32 Kimble Anders	.30	.75
33 Zach Thomas	.50	1.25
34 James Johnson	.30	.75
35 Lawyer Milloy	.30	.75
36 Ty Law	.40	1.00
37 Willie McGinest	.40	1.00
38 Jason Sehorn	.30	.75
39 Andre Rison	.40	1.00
40 Rickey Dudley	.30	.75
41 Patrick Jeffers	.40	1.00
42 Darrell Russell	.30	.75
43 Charles Johnson	.30	.75
44 Michael Westbrook	.30	.75
45 Levon Kirkland	.30	.75
46 Ryan Leaf	.40	1.00
47 Sean Dawkins	.30	.75
48 Todd Lyght	.30	.75
49 Kevin Carter	.30	.75
50 Neil O'Donnell	.30	.75
51 Randall Cunningham	.50	1.25
52 Oronde Gadsden	.40	1.00
53 O.J. McDuffie	.40	1.00
54 Jake Reed	.40	1.00
55 Brian Mitchell	.30	.75
56 Kordell Stewart	.40	1.00
57 Derrick Mayes	.30	.75
58 Az-Zahir Hakim	.30	.75
59 Jacquez Green	.30	.75
60 Andre Reed	.50	1.25
61 Deion Sanders	.50	1.25
62 Frank Sanders	.30	.75
63 Rob Moore	.30	.75
64 Shawn Jefferson	.30	.75
65 Pat Johnson	.30	.75
66 Peter Boulware	.30	.75
67 Donald Hayes	.30	.75
68 Marty Booker	.40	1.00
69 Leslie Shepherd	.30	.75
70 Jason Tucker	.30	.75
71 Johnnie Morton	.40	1.00
72 Germane Crowell	.30	.75
73 Herman Moore	.40	1.00
74 Bill Schroeder	.40	1.00
75 E.G. Green	.30	.75
76 Jerome Pathon	.30	.75
77 Tony Brackens	.30	.75
78 Tony Richardson RC	.40	1.00
79 Sam Madison	.30	.75
80 Jeff George	.40	1.00
81 Matthew Hatchette	.30	.75
82 Kevin Faulk	.40	1.00
83 Jeff Blake	.40	1.00
84 Ike Hilliard	.40	1.00
85 Napoleon Kaufman	.40	1.00
86 Charles Woodson	.50	1.25
87 Na Brown	.30	.75
88 Hines Ward	.50	1.25
89 Troy Edwards	.30	.75
90 Curtis Conway	.40	1.00
91 Junior Seau	.50	1.25
92 Jim Harbaugh	.40	1.00
93 J.J. Stokes	.40	1.00
94 Jon Kitna	.40	1.00
95 Reidel Anthony	.30	.75
96 Warrick Dunn	.40	1.00
97 Carl Pickens	.40	1.00
98 Yancey Thigpen	.30	.75
99 Albert Connell	.30	.75
100 Irving Fryar	.40	1.00
101 Qadry Ismail	.50	1.25
102 Shannon Sharpe	.60	1.50
103 Joey Galloway	.50	1.25
104 Ed McCaffrey	.50	1.25
105 Rod Smith	.50	1.25
106 Terrell Owens	.60	1.50
107 Warren Sapp	.50	1.25
108 Jevon Kearse	.50	1.25
109 Bruce Smith	.60	1.50
110 Champ Bailey	.50	1.25
111 David Boston	.40	1.00
112 Tim Dwight	.50	1.25
113 Terance Mathis	.40	1.00
114 Tony Banks	.40	1.00
115 Shawn Bryson	.40	1.00
116 Peerless Price	.50	1.25
117 Muhsin Muhammad	.50	1.25
118 Tim Biakabutuka	.50	1.25
119 Steve Beuerlein	.50	1.25
120 Corey Dillon	.50	1.25
121 Kevin Johnson	.40	1.00
122 Rocket Ismail	.50	1.25
123 Charlie Batch	.50	1.25
124 James Stewart	.40	1.00
125 Terrence Wilkins	.40	1.00
126 Keenan McCardell	.50	1.25
127 Mark Brunell	.50	1.25
128 Fred Taylor	.60	1.50
129 Derrick Alexander	.40	1.00
130 Tony Gonzalez	.60	1.50
131 Warren Moon	.60	1.50
132 Thurman Thomas	.60	1.50
133 Tony Martin	.50	1.25
134 Jay Fiedler	.50	1.25
135 John Randle	.50	1.25
136 Troy Brown	.50	1.25
137 Amani Toomer	.50	1.25
138 Kerry Collins	.50	1.25
139 Tiki Barber	.60	1.50
140 Wayne Chrebet	.50	1.25
141 Tyrone Wheatley	.40	1.00
142 Duce Staley	.50	1.25
143 Jermaine Fazande	.40	1.00
144 Charlie Garner	.50	1.25
145 Torry Holt	.60	1.50
146 Mike Alstott	.60	1.50
147 Shaun King	.40	1.00
148 Darrell Green	.50	1.25
149 Brad Johnson	.50	1.25
150 Olandis Gary	.50	1.25
151 Jake Plummer	.60	1.50
152 Chris Chandler	.60	1.50
153 Jamal Anderson	.60	1.50
154 Eric Moulds	.60	1.50
155 Doug Flutie	.75	2.00
156 Rob Johnson	.60	1.50
157 Marcus Robinson	.60	1.50
158 Cade McNown	.50	1.25
159 Akili Smith	.50	1.25
160 Tim Couch	.60	1.50
161 Emmitt Smith	2.00	5.00
162 Troy Aikman	1.25	3.00
163 Brian Griese	.60	1.50
164 John Elway	2.00	5.00
165 Terrell Davis	.75	2.00
166 Dorsey Levens	.60	1.50
167 Antonio Freeman	.60	1.50
168 Brett Favre	2.50	6.00
169 Marvin Harrison	.75	2.00
170 Peyton Manning	2.00	5.00
171 Edgerrin James	.75	2.00
172 Jimmy Smith	.60	1.50
173 Elvis Grbac	.50	1.25
174 Dan Marino	2.50	6.00
175 Randy Moss	.75	2.00
176 Cris Carter	.75	2.00
177 Robert Smith	.60	1.50
178 Daunte Culpepper	.60	1.50
179 Terry Glenn	.60	1.50
180 Drew Bledsoe	.75	2.00
181 Ricky Williams	.75	2.00
182 Jake Delhomme RC	2.00	5.00
183 Curtis Martin	.75	2.00
184 Vinny Testaverde	.60	1.50
185 Tim Brown	.75	2.00
186 Rich Gannon	.60	1.50
187 Donovan McNabb	.75	2.00
188 Jerome Bettis	.75	2.00
189 Bobby Shaw RC	.60	1.50
190 Jerry Rice	1.50	4.00
191 Steve Young	1.00	2.50
192 Jeff Garcia	.60	1.50
193 Ricky Watters	.60	1.50
194 Isaac Bruce	.75	2.00
195 Marshall Faulk	.75	2.00
196 Kurt Warner	1.25	3.00
197 Keyshawn Johnson	.60	1.50
198 Eddie George	.60	1.50
199 Steve McNair	.75	2.00
200 Stephen Davis	.60	1.50
201 Bobby Brooks RC	1.25	3.00
202 Cornelius Griffin RC	1.25	3.00
203 Danny Clark RC	1.25	3.00
204 Pat Dennis RC	1.25	3.00
205 Tommy Hendricks RC	1.25	3.00
206 Fred Jones RC	1.25	3.00
207 Isaiah Kacyvenski RC	1.25	3.00
208 Keith Miller RC	1.25	3.00
209 Andre O' Neal RC	1.25	3.00
210 Justin Snow RC	1.25	3.00
211 Armegis Spearman RC	1.25	3.00
212 Lester Towns RC	1.25	3.00
213 Antonio Wilson RC	1.25	3.00
214 Greg Wesley RC	1.25	3.00
215 Jabari Issa RC	1.25	3.00
216 Darwin Walker RC	1.25	3.00
217 Reggie Grimes RC	1.25	3.00
218 Rian Lindell RC	1.25	3.00
219 Chris Combs RC	1.25	3.00
220 Rashard Anderson RC	1.25	3.00
221 Erik Flowers RC	1.25	3.00
222 Corey Moore RC	1.25	3.00
223 Rob Meier RC	1.25	3.00
224 John Milem RC	1.25	3.00
225 Jeremiah Parker RC	1.25	3.00
226 Neil Rackers RC	1.25	3.00
227 Josh Taves RC	1.25	3.00
228 Mao Tosi RC	1.25	3.00
229 Gary Berry RC	1.25	3.00
230 Matt Bowen RC	1.25	3.00
231 Ralph Brown RC	1.25	3.00
232 Tony Darden RC	1.25	3.00
233 Arturo Freeman RC	1.25	3.00
234 David Gibson RC	1.25	3.00
235 Demario Brown RC	1.25	3.00
236 Deveron Harper RC	1.25	3.00
237 Johnnie Harris RC	1.25	3.00
238 Marcus Knight RC	1.25	3.00
239 Ronnie Heard RC	1.25	3.00
240 Eric Johnson RC	1.50	4.00
241 John Keith RC	1.25	3.00
242 Anthony Malbrough RC	1.25	3.00
243 Anthony Mitchell RC	1.25	3.00
244 Aric Morris RC	1.25	3.00
245 Bobby Myers RC	1.25	3.00
246 Erik Olson RC	1.25	3.00
247 Lewis Sanders RC	1.25	3.00
248 Tony Scott RC	1.25	3.00
249 David Terrell RC	1.25	3.00
250 Travares Tillman RC	1.25	3.00
251 David Stachelski RC	1.50	4.00
252 Darren Howard RC	1.50	4.00
253 Frank Chamberlin RC	1.50	4.00
254 Na'il Diggs RC	1.50	4.00
255 Orantes Grant RC	1.50	4.00
256 Barrett Green RC	1.50	4.00
257 Kory Minor RC	1.50	4.00
258 Deon Grant RC	1.50	4.00
259 Mark Simoneau RC	1.50	4.00
260 Raynoch Thompson RC	1.50	4.00
261 Kenyatta Wright RC	1.50	4.00
262 Marcus Bell LB RC	1.50	4.00
263 Jack Golden RC	1.50	4.00
264 Thomas Hamner RC	1.50	4.00
265 Sekou Sanyika RC	1.50	4.00
266 Marcus Washington RC	2.00	5.00
267 Tim Seder RC	1.50	4.00
268 Paul Edinger RC	2.50	6.00
269 Michael Boireau RC	1.50	4.00
270 Byron Frisch RC	1.50	4.00
271 Ketric Sanford RC	1.50	4.00
272 Frank Murphy RC	1.50	4.00
273 Robaire Smith RC	1.50	4.00
274 Adalius Thomas RC	5.00	12.00
275 William Bartee RC	1.50	4.00
276 Robert Bean RC	1.50	4.00
277 Tyrone Carter RC	2.00	5.00
278 Ike Charlton RC	1.50	4.00
279 Mario Edwards RC	1.50	4.00
280 Dwayne Goodrich RC	1.50	4.00
281 Michael Hawthorne RC	1.50	4.00
282 Kareem Larrimore RC	1.50	4.00
283 Mark Roman RC	1.50	4.00
284 Jacoby Shepherd RC	1.50	4.00
285 Jason Webster RC	1.50	4.00
286 Jimmy Wyrick RC	1.50	4.00
287 Rashidi Barnes RC	1.50	4.00
288 David Barrett RC	1.50	4.00
289 Ainsley Battles RC	1.50	4.00
290 Lamar Chapman RC	1.50	4.00
291 Todd Franz RC	1.50	4.00
292 Michael Green RC	1.50	4.00
293 Antwan Harris RC	1.50	4.00
294 Brandon Jennings RC	1.50	4.00
295 Darrick Vaughn RC	1.50	4.00
296 David Macklin RC	1.50	4.00
297 Bobby Brown RC	1.50	4.00
298 Reggie Stephens RC	1.50	4.00
299 Kenoy Kennedy RC	1.50	4.00
300 Raion Hill RC	1.50	4.00
301 Windrell Hayes RC	2.50	6.00
302 DaShon Polk RC	2.50	6.00
303 Tywan Mitchell RC	2.50	6.00
304 Casey Crawford RC	2.50	6.00
305 Hank Poteat RC	2.50	6.00
306 Mondriel Fulcher RC	2.50	6.00
307 Cory Geason RC	2.50	6.00
308 James Hill RC	2.50	6.00
309 Brian Jennings RC	2.50	6.00
310 John Jones RC	2.50	6.00
311 Anthony Lucas RC	2.50	6.00
312 Mike Leach RC	2.50	6.00
313 Dustin Lyman RC	2.50	6.00
314 Derek Rackley RC	2.50	6.00
315 Sebastian Janikowski RC	4.00	*10.00
316 Brad St.Louis RC	2.50	6.00
317 Jay Tant RC	2.50	6.00
318 Austin Wheatley RC	2.50	6.00
319 Jermaine Wiggins RC	3.00	8.00
320 Todd Yoder RC	2.50	6.00
321 Deon Dyer RC	2.50	6.00
322 Jim Finn RC	2.50	6.00
323 Herbert Goodman RC	2.50	6.00
324 Mike Green RC	4.00	10.00
325 Dante Hall RC	4.00	10.00
326 Thabiti Davis RC	2.50	6.00
327 Kevin Houser RC	2.50	6.00
328 Jonas Lewis RC	2.50	6.00
329 Chad Morton RC	4.00	10.00
330 Patrick Pass RC	3.00	8.00
331 Maurice Smith RC	2.50	6.00
332 Paul Smith RC	2.50	6.00
333 Terrelle Smith RC	2.50	6.00
334 Craig Walendy RC	2.50	6.00
335 Jamel White RC	2.50	6.00
336 Jarious Jackson RC	3.00	8.00
337 Matt Lytle RC	2.50	6.00
338 Ron Powlus RC	4.00	10.00
339 Ian Gold RC	2.50	6.00
340 Brandon Short RC	2.50	6.00
341 T.J. Slaughter RC	2.50	6.00
342 Nate Webster RC	2.50	6.00
343 John Engelberger RC	2.50	6.00
344 Rogers Beckett RC	2.50	6.00
345 Mike Brown RC	4.00	10.00
346 Anthony Wright RC	4.00	10.00
347 Danny Farmer RC	2.50	6.00
348 Clint Stoerner RC	4.00	10.00
349 Julian Peterson RC	4.00	10.00
350 Ahmed Plummer RC	2.50	6.00
351 Avion Black RC	3.00	8.00
352 Kwame Cavil RC	3.00	8.00
353 Chris Cole RC	4.00	10.00
354 Chris Coleman RC	3.00	8.00
355 Trevor Gaylor RC	3.00	8.00
356 Damon Hodge RC	4.00	10.00
357 Darrell Jackson RC	4.00	10.00
358 Reggie Jones RC	3.00	8.00
359 Charles Lee RC	3.00	8.00
360 Jerry Porter RC	5.00	12.00
361 Bobby Shaw	4.00	10.00
362 Ron Dugans RC	3.00	8.00
363 James Williams RC	3.00	8.00
364 Bashir Yamini RC	3.00	8.00
365 Anthony Becht RC	4.00	10.00
366 Erron Kinney RC	3.00	8.00
367 Aaron Shea RC	4.00	10.00
368 Chris Samuels RC	4.00	10.00
369 Trung Canidate RC	4.00	10.00
370 Obafemi Ayanbadejo RC	4.00	10.00
371 Doug Chapman RC	3.00	8.00
372 Ronney Jenkins RC	3.00	8.00
373 Curtis Keaton RC	3.00	8.00
374 Kevin McDougal RC	3.00	8.00
375 Frank Moreau RC	3.00	8.00
376 Aaron Stecker RC	4.00	10.00
377 Shyrone Stith RC	3.00	8.00
378 Tom Brady RC	200.00	350.00
379 Giovanni Carmazzi RC	3.00	8.00
380 Joe Hamilton RC	3.00	8.00
381 Todd Husak RC	3.00	8.00
382 Doug Johnson RC	4.00	10.00
383 Tee Martin RC	5.00	12.00
384 Chad Pennington RC	8.00	20.00
385 Tim Rattay RC	4.00	10.00
386 Chris Redman RC	4.00	10.00
387 Billy Volek RC	5.00	12.00
388 Spergon Wynn RC	4.00	10.00
389 John Abraham RC	5.00	12.00
390 Keith Bulluck RC	4.00	10.00
391 Rob Morris RC	4.00	10.00
392 JaJuan Dawson RC	3.00	8.00
393 Chris Hovan RC	4.00	10.00
394 Shaun Ellis RC	5.00	12.00
395 Deltha O'Neal RC	4.00	10.00
396 Gari Scott RC	3.00	8.00
397 Dialleo Burks RC	3.00	8.00
398 Shockmain Davis RC	3.00	8.00
399 Brad Hoover RC	4.00	10.00
400 Brian Finneran RC	5.00	12.00
401 Sylvester Morris J FB/750 RC	2.50	6.00
402 Denn Northcutt J FB/500 RC	3.00	8.00
403 Todd Pinkston J FB/100 RC	4.00	10.00
404 Larry Foster J FB/500 RC	2.50	6.00
405 R.Jay Soward J FB/1000 RC	2.50	6.00
406 Travis Taylor J FB/250 RC	5.00	12.00
407 Peter Warrick J FB/1000 RC	4.00	10.00
408 Dez White J FB/1000 RC	3.00	8.00
409 Ron Dayne J FB/1000 RC	4.00	10.00
410 Thomas Jones J FB/500 RC	5.00	12.00
411 Jamal Lewis J FB/1000 RC	4.00	10.00
412 Sammy Morris J FB/500 RC	3.00	8.00
413 Travis Prentice J FB/500 RC	3.00	8.00
414 J.R. Redmond J FB/250 RC	4.00	10.00
415 Michael Wiley FB/1000 RC	2.50	6.00
416 Laver Coles J FB/250 RC	6.00	15.00
417 Bubba Franks J FB/500 RC	4.00	10.00
418 Mike Anderson J FB/250 RC	6.00	15.00
419 Plaxico Burress J FB/250 RC	6.00	15.00
420 Ron Dixon J FB/1000 RC	2.50	6.00
421 Troy Walters J FB/1000 RC	2.50	6.00
422 Sha Alexander J FB/1000 RC	5.00	12.00
423 Brian Urlacher J FB/1000 RC	15.00	40.00
424 Corey Simon J FB/1000 RC	3.00	8.00
425 Courtney Brown J FB/500 RC	3.00	8.00

2000 Leaf Limited Limited Series

*VETS 1-50: 6X TO 15X BASIC CARDS
*VETS 51-100: 6X TO 15X BASIC CARDS
*VETS 101-150: 5X TO 12X BASIC CARDS
*VETS 151-200: 4X TO 10X BASIC CARDS
*ROOKIE 151-200: 2X TO 5X BASIC CARD
1-200 VETERAN LS PRINT RUN 35
*ROOKIES 201-250: 1.5X TO 4X
*ROOKIES 251-300: 1.2X TO 3X
*ROOKIES 301-350: .8X TO 2X
*ROOKIES 351-400: .6X TO 1.5X
201-400 ROOKIE LS PRINT RUN 50
401-425 ROOK. JSY-FB PRINT RUN 25
LIM.SERIES OVERALL STATED ODDS 1:17

378 Tom Brady	350.00	600.00

2000 Leaf Limited Piece of the Game Previews

AKA 4TH DOWN BASE CARDS
*THIRD DOWN/300: .5X TO 1.2X FOURTH
THIRD DOWN PRINT RUN 300
*SECOND DOWN/100: .6X TO 1.5X FOURTH
SECOND DOWN PRINT RUN 100
*FIRST DOWN/25: 1.2X TO 3X FOURTH
FIRST DOWN PRINT RUN 25

BF4G Brett Favre	15.00	40.00
BG14N Brian Griese	4.00	10.00
BS20B Barry Sanders	10.00	25.00
DC11P Daunte Culpepper	4.00	10.00
DF7W Doug Flutie	5.00	12.00
DM5W Donovan McNabb	5.00	12.00
DM13W Dan Marino	15.00	40.00
DS22G Duce Staley	4.00	10.00
EJ32R Edgerrin James	5.00	12.00
EM87N Ed McCaffrey	4.00	10.00
FT28W Fred Taylor	5.00	12.00
IB80W Isaac Bruce	5.00	12.00
JB36B Jerome Bettis	5.00	12.00
JE7W John Elway	12.00	30.00
JK12W Jim Kelly	6.00	15.00
JP16R Jake Plummer	4.00	10.00
JR80R Jerry Rice	10.00	25.00
JS82B Jimmy Smith	4.00	10.00
KW13W Kurt Warner	8.00	20.00
MB8W Mark Brunell	4.00	10.00
RM84P Randy Moss	5.00	12.00
RS26P Robert Smith	4.00	10.00
SD48W Stephen Davis	4.00	10.00
SY8R Steve Young	6.00	15.00
TC2B Tim Couch	4.00	10.00

2003 Leaf Limited

Released in December of 2003, this set features 150 cards, including 100 active and retired veterans and 50 rookies. Cards 1-100 are serial numbered to 999, and rookies 101-125 are serial numbered to 750. Rookies 126-150 are serial numbered to 150, and feature an authentic player autograph on a silver foil sticker. Please note that Charles Rogers, Nate Burleson, Onterrio Smith, and Willis McGahee were issued as exchange cards in packs. The exchange deadline is //1/2006. Boxes contained 4 packs of 4 cards. The pack SRP was $70.

COMP.SET w/o SP's (100) 100.00 250.00
101-125 ROOKIE PRINT RUN 750
126-150 ROOKIE AU PRINT RUN 150

1 Emmitt Smith	4.00	10.00
2 Michael Vick	2.00	5.00
3 Peerless Price	1.00	2.50
4 T.J. Duckett	1.25	3.00
5 Jamal Lewis	1.25	3.00
6 Drew Bledsoe	1.50	4.00
7 Eric Moulds	1.25	3.00
8 Travis Henry	1.00	2.50
9 Jim Kelly	2.00	5.00
10 Julius Peppers	1.50	4.00
11 Dick Butkus	2.50	6.00
12 Mike Singletary	1.50	4.00
13 Walter Payton	5.00	12.00
14 Anthony Thomas	1.25	3.00
15 Brian Urlacher	1.50	4.00
16 Marty Booker	1.25	3.00
17 Corey Dillon	1.25	3.00
18 Jim Thorpe	2.00	5.00
19 Jim Brown	2.50	6.00
20 Tim Couch	1.00	2.50
21 William Green	1.00	2.50
22 Deion Sanders	1.50	4.00
23 Michael Irvin	1.50	4.00
24 Roger Staubach	2.50	6.00
25 Troy Aikman	2.00	5.00
26 Tony Dorsett	1.50	4.00
27 Antonio Bryant	1.00	2.50
28 Clinton Portis	1.25	3.00
29 Jake Plummer	1.25	3.00
30 Rod Smith	1.25	3.00
31 Barry Sanders	3.00	8.00
32 Doak Walker	1.50	4.00
33 Joey Harrington	1.00	2.50
34 Bart Starr	2.50	6.00
35 Ahman Green	1.25	3.00
36 Brett Favre	4.00	10.00
37 Donald Driver	1.50	4.00
38 David Carr	1.25	3.00
39 Don Shula	1.50	4.00
40 Johnny Unitas	3.00	8.00
41 Edgerrin James	1.50	4.00
42 Marvin Harrison	1.50	4.00
43 Peyton Manning	3.00	8.00
44 Fred Taylor	1.25	3.00
45 Jimmy Smith	1.25	3.00
46 Mark Brunell	1.25	3.00
47 Marcus Allen	1.50	4.00
48 Priest Holmes	1.50	4.00
49 Tony Gonzalez	1.50	4.00
50 Trent Green	1.25	3.00
51 Dan Marino	4.00	10.00
52 Bob Griese	1.50	4.00
53 Chris Chambers	1.25	3.00
54 Ricky Williams	1.25	3.00
55 Fran Tarkenton	1.50	4.00
56 Daunte Culpepper	1.25	3.00
57 Michael Bennett	1.25	3.00
58 Randy Moss	1.50	4.00
59 Tom Brady	4.00	10.00
60 Aaron Brooks	1.25	3.00
61 Deuce McAllister	1.25	3.00
62 Donte Stallworth	1.00	2.50
63 Mark Bavaro	1.25	3.00
64 Jeremy Shockey	1.50	4.00
65 Kerry Collins	1.25	3.00

66 Tiki Barber	1.50	4.00
67 Joe Namath	2.50	6.00
68 Chad Pennington	1.50	4.00
69 Curtis Martin	1.50	4.00
70 Jerry Porter	1.00	2.50
71 Jerry Rice	3.00	8.00
72 Rich Gannon	1.25	3.00
73 Tim Brown	1.50	4.00
74 Donovan McNabb	1.50	4.00
75 Terry Bradshaw	2.50	6.00
76 Antwaan Randle El	1.25	3.00
77 Plaxico Burress	1.25	3.00
78 Tommy Maddox	1.25	3.00
79 David Boston	1.00	2.50
80 Drew Brees	1.50	4.00
81 LaDainian Tomlinson	1.50	4.00
82 Joe Montana	4.00	10.00
83 Steve Young	2.00	5.00
84 Jeff Garcia	1.25	3.00
85 Terrell Owens	1.50	4.00
86 Koren Robinson	1.25	3.00
87 Matt Hasselbeck	1.25	3.00
88 Shaun Alexander	1.25	3.00
89 Isaac Bruce	1.50	4.00
90 Kurt Warner	1.50	4.00
91 Marshall Faulk	1.50	4.00
92 Torry Holt	1.50	4.00
93 Brad Johnson	1.25	3.00
94 Keyshawn Johnson	1.50	4.00
95 Earl Campbell	1.50	4.00
96 Eddie George	1.25	3.00
97 Steve McNair	1.50	4.00
98 John Riggins	1.50	4.00
99 Laveranues Coles	1.00	2.50
100 Patrick Ramsey	1.25	3.00
101 LaTarence Dunbar RC	1.50	4.00
102 Sam Aiken RC	2.00	5.00
103 Bobby Wade RC	2.00	5.00
104 Justin Gage RC	2.00	5.00
105 Lee Suggs RC	2.00	5.00
106 Jason Witten RC	6.00	15.00
107 Quentin Griffin RC	2.00	5.00
108 Domanick Davis RC	2.00	5.00
109 LaBrandon Toefield RC	2.00	5.00
110 J.R. Tolver RC	2.00	5.00
111 Kliff Kingsbury RC	2.00	5.00
112 Talman Gardner RC	1.50	4.00
113 Teyo Johnson RC	2.00	5.00
114 Billy McMullen RC	1.50	4.00
115 L.J. Smith RC	2.50	6.00
116 Brian St.Pierre RC	2.00	5.00
117 Brandon Lloyd RC	4.00	10.00
118 Seneca Wallace RC	2.50	6.00
119 Kevin Curtis RC	2.50	6.00
120 Shaun McDonald RC	2.00	5.00
121 Terrell Suggs RC	2.50	6.00
122 Terence Newman RC	2.00	5.00
123 Tony Romo RC	20.00	50.00
124 DeWayne Robertson RC	2.00	5.00
125 Marcus Trufant RC	2.00	5.00
126 Artose Pinner AU RC	6.00	15.00
127 Bryant Johnson AU RC	10.00	25.00
128 Kelley Washington AU RC	6.00	15.00
129 Dallas Clark AU RC	25.00	50.00
130 Onterrio Smith AU RC	6.00	15.00
131 Tony Hollings AU RC	8.00	20.00
132 Tyrone Calico AU RC	8.00	20.00
133 Carson Palmer AU RC	30.00	80.00
134 Byron Leftwich AU RC	10.00	25.00
135 Rex Grossman AU RC	10.00	25.00
136 Kyle Boller AU RC	10.00	25.00
137 Chris Simms AU RC	10.00	25.00
138 Dave Ragone AU RC	6.00	15.00
139 Ken Dorsey AU RC	8.00	20.00
140 Willis McGahee AU RC	12.00	30.00
141 Larry Johnson AU RC	10.00	25.00
142 Musa Smith AU RC	6.00	15.00
143 Chris Brown AU RC	6.00	15.00
144 Charles Rogers AU RC	8.00	20.00
145 Andre Johnson AU RC	40.00	80.00
146 Taylor Jacobs AU RC	6.00	15.00
147 Anquan Boldin AU RC	25.00	60.00
148 Bethel Johnson AU RC	6.00	15.00
149 Justin Fargas AU RC	10.00	25.00
150 Nate Burleson AU RC	8.00	20.00

2003 Leaf Limited Bronze Spotlight

*VETS 1-100: .8X TO 2X BASIC CARDS
*ROOKIES 101-125: .6X TO 1.5X
1-125 STATED PRINT RUN 150
*ROOKIE AU/25 126-150: .6X TO 1.5X
126-150 ROOKIE AU PRINT RUN 25

123 Tony Romo	40.00	100.00

2003 Leaf Limited Gold Spotlight

*VETS 1-100: 3X TO 8X BASIC CARDS
*ROOKIES 101-125: 2.5X TO 6X
1-125 STATED PRINT RUN 25
UNPRICED 126-150 AU PRINT RUN 10

123 Tony Romo	125.00	250.00

2003 Leaf Limited Platinum Spotlight

STATED PRINT RUN 1 SER.#'d SETS
NOT PRICED DUE TO SCARCITY

2003 Leaf Limited Silver Spotlight

*VETS 1-100: 1.2X TO 3X BASIC CARDS
*ROOKIES 101-125: 1X TO 2.5X
1-125 STATED PRINT RUN 75
UNPRICED 126-150 AU PRINT RUN 15

123 Tony Romo	50.00	120.00

2003 Leaf Limited Contenders Preview Autographs

STATED PRINT RUN 10-25
SER.#'d TO 10 NOT PRICED

111 Mike Doss/25	15.00	40.00
112 Chris Simms/25	15.00	40.00
114 Justin Gage/25	12.00	30.00
117 Jason Witten/25	60.00	120.00
126 Carson Palmer/25	200.00	400.00
127 Byron Leftwich/25	15.00	40.00
128 Kyle Boller/25	15.00	40.00
129 Rex Grossman/25	20.00	50.00
133 Seneca Wallace/25	15.00	40.00
134 Larry Johnson/25	25.00	60.00
136 Justin Fargas/25	15.00	40.00
138 Chris Brown/25	10.00	25.00
139 Musa Smith/25	10.00	25.00
140 Artose Pinner/25	10.00	25.00
141 Andre Johnson/25	125.00	200.00
142 Kelley Washington/25	10.00	25.00
143 Taylor Jacobs/25	10.00	25.00
144 Bryant Johnson/25	15.00	40.00
145 Tyrone Calico/25	12.00	30.00
146 Anquan Boldin/25	50.00	120.00
147 Bethel Johnson/25	10.00	25.00
149 Kevin Curtis/25	15.00	40.00
150 Dallas Clark/25	50.00	80.00
151 Teyo Johnson/25	12.00	30.00
152 Terrell Suggs/25	25.00	60.00
154 Terence Newman/25	12.00	30.00
155 Marcus Trufant/25	12.00	30.00
157 Brooks Bollinger/25	12.00	30.00
158 Ken Dorsey/25	12.00	30.00
163 Avon Cobourne/25	10.00	25.00
165 Tony Hollings/25	12.00	30.00
167 Arlen Harris/25	10.00	25.00
170 L.J. Smith/25	15.00	40.00
196 Mike Sherman/25	15.00	40.00
197 Dave Wannstedt/25	12.00	30.00
198 Dick Vermeil/25	15.00	40.00
199 Tony Dungy/25	50.00	100.00
200 Mike Martz/25	12.00	30.00

2003 Leaf Limited Cuts Autographs

LC1 John Elway/75	125.00	225.00
LC2 Michael Vick/94	30.00	60.00
LC3 Warren Moon/100	30.00	60.00
LC4 Aaron Brooks/100	15.00	40.00

2003 Leaf Limited Double Threads

PRINT RUN 100 SER.#'d SETS
UNPRICED PRIME PRINT RUN 10

DT1 Johnny Unitas	60.00	100.00
Peyton Manning/25		
DT2 Don Shula	15.00	40.00
Edgerrin James		
DT3 Jim Kelly	12.00	30.00
Drew Bledsoe		
DT4 Jim Kelly	12.00	30.00
Bruce Smith		
DT5 Dick Butkus	25.00	60.00
Brian Urlacher		
DT6 Walter Payton	30.00	80.00
Mike Singletary		
DT7 Dick Butkus	20.00	50.00
Mike Singletary		
DT8 Jim Brown	15.00	40.00
Bernie Kosar		
DT9 Roger Staubach	20.00	50.00
Troy Aikman		
DT10 Tony Dorsett	25.00	60.00
Emmitt Smith		
DT11 Michael Irvin	10.00	25.00
Antonio Bryant		
DT12 Deion Sanders	10.00	25.00
Roy Williams		
DT13 Terrell Davis	8.00	20.00
Clinton Portis		
DT14 John Elway	25.00	60.00
Terrell Davis		
DT15 Tony Dorsett	10.00	25.00
Clinton Portis		
DT16 Doak Walker	20.00	40.00
Barry Sanders		
DT17 Bart Starr	30.00	80.00
Brett Favre		
DT18 Earl Campbell	10.00	25.00
Eddie George		
DT19 Joe Montana	25.00	60.00
Rich Gannon		
DT20 Marcus Allen	10.00	25.00
Priest Holmes		
DT21 Bob Griese	25.00	60.00
Dan Marino		
DT22 Fran Tarkenton	10.00	25.00
Daunte Culpepper		
DT23 Drew Bledsoe	25.00	60.00
Tom Brady		
DT24 Ricky Williams	8.00	20.00
Deuce McAllister		
DT25 Mark Bavaro	10.00	25.00
Jeremy Shockey		
DT26 Joe Namath	10.00	25.00
Chad Pennington		
DT27 Joe Namath	15.00	40.00
John Riggins		
DT28 Marcus Allen	20.00	50.00
Jerry Rice		
DT29 Terry Bradshaw	15.00	40.00
Antwaan Randle El		
DT30 Drew Brees	10.00	25.00
LaDainian Tomlinson		
DT31 Joe Montana	25.00	60.00
Jeff Garcia		
DT32 Steve Young	20.00	50.00
Jerry Rice		
DT33 Joe Montana	30.00	80.00
Jerry Rice		
DT34 Jerry Rice	20.00	50.00
Terrell Owens		
DT35 Kurt Warner	10.00	25.00
Marshall Faulk		
DT36 John Riggins	10.00	25.00
Deion Sanders		
DT37 Michael Vick	12.00	30.00
Donovan McNabb		
DT38 Joey Harrington	8.00	20.00
David Carr		
DT39 John Elway	30.00	80.00
Brett Favre		
DT40 Jim Kelly	25.00	60.00
Dan Marino		
DT41 Joe Montana	25.00	60.00
Donovan McNabb		
DT42 Steve Young	12.00	30.00
Michael Vick		
DT43 Walter Payton	30.00	80.00
Emmitt Smith		
DT44 Jim Brown	20.00	50.00
Barry Sanders		
DT45 Ricky Williams	10.00	25.00
Priest Holmes		
DT46 Emmitt Smith	25.00	60.00
LaDainian Tomlinson		
DT47 Marshall Faulk	10.00	25.00
Edgerrin James		
DT48 Earl Campbell	10.00	25.00
Ricky Williams		
DT49 Edgerrin James	10.00	25.00
Clinton Portis		
DT50 Jeremy Shockey	12.00	30.00
Andre Johnson		

2003 Leaf Limited Hardwear

STATED PRINT RUN 100 SER.#'d SETS
*LIMITED/25: .8X TO 2X BASIC HEL/100
UNPRICED SHIELD PRINT RUN 1

H1 Jeremy Shockey	10.00	25.00
H2 Dan Marino	25.00	60.00
H3 Joe Montana	25.00	60.00
H4 Emmitt Smith	25.00	60.00
H5 Brian Urlacher	10.00	25.00
H6 Brett Favre	25.00	60.00
H7 Ricky Williams	8.00	20.00
H8 Earl Campbell	10.00	25.00
H9 Jerry Rice	20.00	50.00
H10 John Elway	25.00	60.00
H11 Marcus Allen Chiefs	10.00	25.00
H12 Randy Moss	10.00	25.00
H13 Steve Young	12.00	30.00
H14 Troy Aikman	12.00	30.00
H15 Tony Dorsett	10.00	25.00
H16 Jim Kelly	12.00	30.00
H17 Marshall Faulk	10.00	25.00
H18 Jeff Garcia	8.00	20.00
H19 Tom Brady	25.00	60.00
H20 Chad Pennington	10.00	25.00
H21 Deuce McAllister	8.00	20.00
H22 Marcus Allen Raiders	10.00	25.00
H23 Travis Henry	6.00	15.00
H24 Roger Staubach	15.00	40.00
H25 Terrell Owens	10.00	25.00

2003 Leaf Limited Legends Jerseys

STATED PRINT RUN 50 SER.#'d SETS
UNPRICED PRIME PRINT RUN 5
UNPRICED SEASONS PRINT RUN 6-19

LL1 Barry Sanders	15.00	40.00
LL2 Bart Starr	15.00	40.00
LL3 Brett Favre	20.00	50.00
LL4 Dan Marino	20.00	50.00
LL5 Doak Walker	20.00	50.00
LL6 Don Shula AU	30.00	60.00
LL7 Earl Campbell	10.00	25.00
LL8 Emmitt Smith	20.00	50.00
LL9 Fran Tarkenton AU	30.00	60.00
LL10 Jerry Rice	15.00	40.00
LL11 Jim Brown AU	70.00	120.00
LL12 Jim Kelly	12.00	30.00
LL13 Jim Thorpe	90.00	150.00
LL14 Joe Montana	25.00	60.00
LL15 Joe Namath	15.00	40.00
LL16 John Elway	20.00	50.00
LL17 John Riggins	10.00	25.00
LL18 Roger Staubach	15.00	40.00
LL19 Terry Bradshaw	15.00	40.00
LL20 Walter Payton	30.00	80.00

2003 Leaf Limited Material Monikers

STATED PRINT RUN 5-25
SER.#'d UNDER 15 NOT PRICED
UNPRICED LIMITED PRINT RUN 1

M1 Dan Marino/15	75.00	150.00
M3 Jim Brown/25	60.00	120.00
M4 Jim Kelly/25	60.00	120.00
M5 Joe Montana/25	100.00	200.00
M6 Joe Montana/15	75.00	150.00
M8 John Riggins/25	25.00	60.00
M9 John Riggins/25	25.00	60.00
M10 Mark Bavaro/25	20.00	50.00
M13 Daunte Culpepper/25	20.00	50.00
M14 Troy Aikman/15	50.00	100.00
M16 Michael Vick/25	50.00	100.00
M17 Roger Staubach/25	50.00	100.00
M18 Drew Bledsoe/25	25.00	60.00
M19 Brian Urlacher/25	50.00	100.00
M22 Joey Harrington/20	15.00	40.00
M25 David Carr/20	20.00	50.00
M26 Marvin Harrison/15	25.00	60.00
M28 Priest Holmes/15	25.00	60.00
M30 Ricky Williams/20	20.00	50.00
M31 Earl Campbell/25	25.00	60.00
M33 Tom Brady/20	175.00	300.00
M36 Jerry Rice/20	90.00	150.00
M37 Dick Butkus/25	60.00	100.00
M38 Jeff Garcia/20	20.00	50.00
M39 Joe Namath/15	60.00	120.00
M40 Kurt Warner/25	25.00	60.00
M41 Jim Brown/20	60.00	120.00
Jamal Lewis		
M42 Kurt Warner/20	60.00	100.00
Torry Holt		
M43 Kurt Warner	60.00	100.00
Isaac Bruce/25		
M44 Joe Montana	100.00	200.00
Marcus Allen/25		
M45 Joe Montana	100.00	200.00
Jeff Garcia/25		
M48 Steve McNair	50.00	100.00
Eddie George/25		

2003 Leaf Limited Player Threads

STATED PRINT RUN 34-50
UNPRICED LIMITED PRINT RUN 1
UNPRICED PRIME PRINT RUN 10

PT1 Barry Sanders	20.00	50.00
PT2 Brett Favre	25.00	60.00
PT3 Dan Marino	25.00	60.00
PT4 Donovan McNabb	10.00	25.00
PT5 Earl Campbell/34	10.00	25.00
PT6 Emmitt Smith	25.00	60.00
PT7 Fran Tarkenton	10.00	25.00
PT8 Jeremy Shockey	10.00	25.00
PT9 Jim Kelly	12.00	30.00
PT10 John Riggins	10.00	25.00
PT11 LaDanian Tomlinson	10.00	25.00
PT12 Mike Singletary	10.00	25.00
PT13 Peyton Manning	20.00	50.00
PT14 Priest Holmes	10.00	25.00
PT15 Randy Moss	10.00	25.00
PT16 Roger Staubach	15.00	40.00
PT17 Steve Young	12.00	30.00
PT18 Terry Bradshaw	15.00	40.00
PT19 Tom Brady	25.00	60.00
PT20 Tony Dorsett	10.00	25.00
PT21 Troy Aikman	12.00	30.00
PT22 Walter Payton	30.00	80.00
PT23 Clinton Portis	8.00	20.00
PT24 Drew Bledsoe	10.00	25.00
PT25 Edgerrin James	10.00	25.00
PT26 Jerry Rice	20.00	50.00
PT27 Joe Montana	25.00	60.00
PT28 John Elway	25.00	60.00
PT29 Marshall Faulk	10.00	25.00
PT30 Ricky Williams	8.00	20.00

2003 Leaf Limited Team Trademarks Autographs

STATED PRINT RUN 5-50
*LIMITED/25: .5X TO 1.2X BASE AU/50

LT1 Aaron Brooks	15.00	40.00
LT2 Ahman Green	15.00	40.00
LT4 Bob Griese	20.00	50.00
LT5 Brian Urlacher	25.00	60.00
LT6 Chad Pennington	20.00	50.00
LT7 Chris Chambers	15.00	40.00
LT8 Clinton Portis	15.00	40.00
LT9 Dan Marino	100.00	200.00
LT10 David Carr	15.00	40.00
LT11 Deion Sanders	40.00	80.00
LT12 Deuce McAllister	15.00	40.00
LT13 Dick Butkus	50.00	100.00
LT14 Don Shula	20.00	50.00
LT15 Drew Bledsoe	20.00	50.00
LT16 Earl Campbell	20.00	50.00
LT17 Ashley Lelie	12.00	30.00
LT18 Eric Moulds	15.00	40.00
LT19 Fran Tarkenton	20.00	50.00
LT20 Isaac Bruce	20.00	50.00
LT21 Jamal Lewis	15.00	40.00
LT22 Jim Kelly	40.00	80.00
LT23 Joe Namath	75.00	150.00
LT24 Joey Harrington	12.00	30.00
LT26 Kendrell Bell	12.00	30.00
LT27 Kurt Warner	20.00	50.00
LT28 Antwaan Randle El	15.00	40.00
LT29 Marcus Allen	20.00	50.00
LT30 Marvin Harrison	20.00	50.00
LT31 Michael Irvin	30.00	60.00
LT32 Michael Vick	30.00	60.00
LT33 Mike Alstott	20.00	50.00
LT34 Mike Singletary	20.00	50.00
LT35 Priest Holmes	20.00	50.00
LT36 Ricky Williams	15.00	40.00
LT37 Roger Staubach	60.00	100.00
LT38 Roy Williams	15.00	40.00
LT39 Santana Moss	15.00	40.00
LT40 Shaun Alexander	15.00	40.00
LT41 Steve Largent	20.00	50.00
LT42 Steve McNair	20.00	50.00
LT43 Steve Young	40.00	80.00
LT44 Terrell Owens	20.00	50.00
LT45 Tim Brown	20.00	50.00
LT46 Tom Brady	150.00	300.00
LT47 Tony Dorsett	20.00	50.00
LT48 Quincy Carter	12.00	30.00
LT49 Troy Aikman	60.00	120.00
LT50 Warren Moon	15.00	40.00

2003 Leaf Limited Threads

STATED PRINT RUN 100 SER.#'d SETS
*POSITION/75: .5X TO 1.2X BASIC JSY
POSITION STATED PRINT RUN 75

LT1 Aaron Brooks	5.00	12.00
LT2 Aaron Brooks	5.00	12.00
LT3 Ahman Green	5.00	12.00
LT4 Ahman Green	5.00	12.00
LT5 Barry Sanders	12.00	30.00
LT6 Barry Sanders	12.00	30.00
LT7 Bart Starr	12.00	30.00
LT8 Bob Griese	6.00	15.00
LT9 Brett Favre	15.00	40.00
LT10 Brett Favre	15.00	40.00
LT11 Brian Urlacher	6.00	15.00
LT12 Chad Pennington	6.00	15.00
LT13 Clinton Portis	5.00	12.00
LT14 Clinton Portis	5.00	12.00
LT15 Clinton Portis Miami	5.00	12.00
LT16 Dan Marino	15.00	40.00
LT17 Dan Marino	15.00	40.00
LT18 Daunte Culpepper	5.00	12.00
LT19 Daunte Culpepper	5.00	12.00
LT20 Daunte Culpepper	5.00	12.00
LT21 David Carr	5.00	12.00
LT22 Deion Sanders	6.00	15.00
LT23 Deion Sanders	6.00	15.00
LT24 Deuce McAllister	5.00	12.00
LT25 Dick Butkus	12.00	30.00
LT26 Doak Walker	15.00	40.00
LT27 Don Shula AU	35.00	60.00
LT28 Donovan McNabb	6.00	15.00
LT29 Donovan McNabb	6.00	15.00
LT30 Drew Bledsoe	6.00	15.00
LT31 Drew Bledsoe	6.00	15.00
LT32 Drew Bledsoe	6.00	15.00
LT33 Drew Bledsoe	6.00	15.00
LT34 Drew Brees	6.00	15.00
LT35 Earl Campbell/66*	8.00	20.00
LT35AU Earl Campbell AU/34*	30.00	50.00
LT36 Earl Campbell	8.00	20.00
LT37 Edgerrin James	6.00	15.00
LT38 Edgerrin James	6.00	15.00
LT39 Edgerrin James	6.00	15.00
LT40 Emmitt Smith	15.00	40.00
LT41 Fran Tarkenton AU	25.00	50.00
LT42 Jeff Garcia	5.00	12.00
LT43 Jeff Garcia	5.00	12.00
LT44 Jeremy Shockey	6.00	15.00
LT45 Jeremy Shockey	6.00	15.00
LT46 Jerry Rice	12.00	30.00
LT47 Jerry Rice	12.00	30.00
LT48 Jerry Rice	12.00	30.00
LT49 Jim Brown	12.00	30.00
LT50 Jim Kelly	10.00	25.00
LT51 Jim Thorpe	75.00	150.00
LT52 Joe Montana	20.00	50.00
LT53 Joe Montana	20.00	50.00
LT54 Joe Montana	20.00	50.00
LT55 Joe Namath	12.00	30.00
LT56 Joey Harrington	4.00	10.00
LT57 John Elway	15.00	40.00
LT58 John Elway	15.00	40.00
LT59 John Elway	15.00	40.00
LT60 John Elway	15.00	40.00
LT61 John Riggins Redskins	8.00	20.00
LT62 John Riggins Jets	8.00	20.00
LT63 Johnny Unitas	15.00	40.00
LT64 Kurt Warner AU	30.00	60.00
LT65 LaDainian Tomlinson	6.00	15.00
LT66 Shaun Alexander	5.00	12.00
LT67 Marcus Allen	8.00	20.00
LT68 Marcus Allen	8.00	20.00
LT69 Mark Bavaro	6.00	15.00
LT70 Marshall Faulk	6.00	15.00
LT71 Marshall Faulk	6.00	15.00
LT72 Marshall Faulk SDSU	6.00	15.00
LT73 Marvin Harrison	6.00	15.00
LT74 Marvin Harrison	6.00	15.00
LT75 Michael Vick	8.00	20.00
LT76 Mike Singletary	8.00	20.00
LT77 Mike Singletary	8.00	20.00
LT78 Peyton Manning	12.00	30.00
LT79 Peyton Manning	12.00	30.00
LT80 Peyton Manning	12.00	30.00
LT81 Priest Holmes	6.00	15.00
LT82 Priest Holmes	6.00	15.00
LT83 Randy Moss	6.00	15.00
LT84 Randy Moss	6.00	15.00
LT85 Ricky Williams	5.00	12.00
LT86 Ricky Williams	5.00	12.00
LT87 Ricky Williams	5.00	12.00
LT88 Ricky Williams	5.00	12.00
LT89 Roger Staubach	12.00	30.00
LT90 Steve Young	8.00	20.00
LT91 Terrell Owens	6.00	15.00
LT92 Terry Bradshaw	12.00	30.00
LT93 Tom Brady	15.00	40.00
LT94 Tom Brady	15.00	40.00
LT95 Tony Dorsett	8.00	20.00
LT96 Tony Dorsett	8.00	20.00
LT97 Troy Aikman	8.00	20.00
LT98 Troy Aikman	8.00	20.00
LT99 Walter Payton	25.00	60.00
LT100 Walter Payton	25.00	60.00

2003 Leaf Limited Threads At the Half

*HALF/50: .6X TO 1.5X BASE JSY/100

LT1 Aaron Brooks AU	15.00	40.00
LT2 Aaron Brooks AU	15.00	40.00
LT24 Deuce McAllister AU	20.00	50.00
LT56 Joey Harrington AU	20.00	50.00
LT64 Kurt Warner AU	30.00	80.00
LT67 Marcus Allen AU	30.00	80.00
LT68 Marcus Allen AU	30.00	80.00
LT69 Mark Bavaro AU	25.00	60.00
LT76 Mike Singletary AU	25.00	60.00
LT81 Priest Holmes AU	25.00	60.00
LT82 Priest Holmes AU	25.00	60.00
LT96 Tony Dorsett AU	25.00	60.00

2003 Leaf Limited Threads Jersey Numbers

*JSY/80-89: .4X TO 1X BASE JSY/100
*JSY/44-63: .6X TO 1.5X BASE JSY/100
*JSY/32-37: .8X TO 2X BASE JSY/100
*JSY/21-28: 1X TO 2.5X BASE JSY/100
STATED PRINT RUN 1-89

LT3 Ahman Green AU/30	20.00	50.00
LT4 Ahman Green AU/30	20.00	50.00
LT5 Barry Sanders AU/20	125.00	200.00
LT6 Barry Sanders AU/20	125.00	200.00
LT11 Brian Urlacher AU/54	30.00	80.00
LT13 Clinton Portis AU/26	30.00	80.00
LT14 Clinton Portis AU/26	30.00	80.00
LT15 Clinton Portis AU/28	30.00	80.00
LT22 Deion Sanders AU/21	50.00	100.00
LT23 Deion Sanders AU/21	50.00	100.00
LT24 Deuce McAllister AU/26	30.00	80.00
LT25 Dick Butkus AU/51	60.00	100.00
LT27 Don Shula AU/25	30.00	80.00
LT35 Earl Campbell AU/34	30.00	80.00
LT36 Earl Campbell AU/20	30.00	80.00
LT66 Shaun Alexander AU/37	25.00	60.00
LT69 Mark Bavaro AU/89	20.00	50.00
LT81 Priest Holmes AU/31	30.00	80.00
LT82 Priest Holmes AU/33	30.00	80.00
LT95 Tony Dorsett AU/33	30.00	80.00
LT96 Tony Dorsett AU/33	30.00	80.00

2003 Leaf Limited Threads Prime

*PRIME/25: .8X TO 2X BASE JSY/100

LT1 Aaron Brooks AU	20.00	50.00
LT2 Aaron Brooks AU	20.00	50.00
LT3 Ahman Green AU	20.00	50.00
LT4 Ahman Green AU	20.00	50.00
LT8 Bob Griese AU	25.00	60.00
LT9 Brett Favre AU	150.00	300.00
LT10 Brett Favre AU	150.00	300.00
LT12 Chad Pennington AU	25.00	60.00
LT15 Clinton Portis AU	20.00	50.00
LT19 Daunte Culpepper AU	20.00	50.00
LT30 Drew Bledsoe AU	25.00	60.00
LT31 Drew Bledsoe AU	25.00	60.00
LT32 Drew Bledsoe AU	25.00	60.00
LT33 Drew Bledsoe AU	25.00	60.00
LT41 Fran Tarkenton AU	25.00	60.00
LT56 Joey Harrington AU	15.00	40.00
LT61 John Riggins AU	25.00	60.00
LT62 John Riggins AU	25.00	60.00
LT64 Kurt Warner AU	25.00	60.00
LT66 Shaun Alexander AU	20.00	50.00
LT75 Michael Vick AU	50.00	100.00
LT81 Priest Holmes AU	25.00	60.00
LT85 Ricky Williams AU	20.00	50.00
LT86 Ricky Williams AU	20.00	50.00
LT87 Ricky Williams AU	20.00	50.00
LT88 Ricky Williams AU	20.00	50.00
LT92 Terry Bradshaw AU	75.00	150.00
LT97 Troy Aikman AU	75.00	150.00

2004 Leaf Limited

Leaf Limited initially released in early December 2004 and was one of the most well-received products of the year due to the large number of game used and autographed card inserts. The base set consists of 233-cards including 50-retired players serial numbered of 799, 50-rookies numbered of 350, and 33-rookie jersey autograph cards numbered of 150. Hobby boxes contained 4-packs of 4-cards and carried an S.R.P. of $70 per pack.

201-233 ROOK.JSY AU PRINT RUN 150
UNPRICED PLATINUM PRINT RUN 1

1 A.J. Feeley	1.00	2.50
2 Aaron Brooks	1.25	3.00
3 Ahman Green	1.25	3.00
4 Andre Johnson	1.50	4.00
5 Anquan Boldin	1.50	4.00
6 Antwaan Randle El	1.25	3.00
7 Ashley Lelie	1.00	2.50
8 Brad Johnson	1.25	3.00
9 Brett Favre	4.00	10.00
10 Brian Urlacher	1.50	4.00
11 Brian Westbrook	1.50	4.00
12 Byron Leftwich	1.25	3.00
13 Carson Palmer	1.50	4.00
14 Chad Johnson	1.50	4.00
15 Chad Pennington	1.50	4.00
16 Charlie Garner	1.25	3.00
17 Charles Rogers	1.00	2.50
18 Chris Brown	1.00	2.50
19 Chris Chambers	1.25	3.00
20 Clinton Portis	1.50	4.00
21 Corey Dillon	1.25	3.00
22 Deion Sanders	1.50	4.00
23 Curtis Martin	1.50	4.00
24 Daunte Culpepper	1.25	3.00
25 David Terrell	1.00	2.50
26 David Carr	1.00	2.50
27 Deion Branch	1.25	3.00
28 Derrick Mason	1.25	3.00
29 DeShaun Foster	1.25	3.00
30 Deuce McAllister	1.25	3.00
31 Domanick Davis	1.00	2.50
32 Donovan McNabb	1.50	4.00
33 Donte Stallworth	1.00	2.50
34 Drew Bledsoe	1.50	4.00
35 Duce Staley	1.25	3.00
36 Eddie George	1.25	3.00
37 Edgerrin James	1.25	3.00
38 Emmitt Smith	4.00	10.00
39 Eric Moulds	1.25	3.00
40 Fred Taylor	1.25	3.00
41 Hines Ward	1.50	4.00
42 Isaac Bruce	1.25	3.00
43 Jake Delhomme	1.25	3.00
44 Jake Plummer	1.25	3.00
45 Javon Walker	1.00	2.50
46 Jeff Garcia	1.25	3.00
47 Jeremy Shockey	1.25	3.00
48 Jerome Bettis	1.50	4.00
49 Jerry Porter	1.00	2.50
50 Jerry Rice	3.00	8.00
51 Jevon Kearse	1.25	3.00
52 Jimmy Smith	1.25	3.00
53 Joe Horn	1.25	3.00
54 Joey Harrington	1.25	3.00
55 Josh McCown	1.25	3.00
56 Kevan Barlow	1.00	2.50
57 Koren Robinson	1.00	2.50
58 Kyle Boller	1.25	3.00
59 LaDainian Tomlinson	1.50	4.00
60 LaVar Arrington	1.25	3.00
61 Laveranues Coles	1.00	2.50
62 Lee Suggs	1.25	3.00
63 Marc Bulger	1.25	3.00
64 Mark Brunell	1.25	3.00
65 Marshall Faulk	1.50	4.00
66 Marvin Harrison	1.50	4.00
67 Matt Hasselbeck	1.25	3.00
68 Michael Bennett	1.25	3.00
69 Michael Strahan	1.50	4.00
70 Michael Vick	2.00	5.00
71 Peerless Price	1.00	2.50
72 Peter Warrick	1.25	3.00
73 Peyton Manning	3.00	8.00
74 Priest Holmes	1.50	4.00
75 Quentin Griffin	1.00	2.50
76 Randy Moss	1.50	4.00
77 Ray Lewis	1.50	4.00
78 Rex Grossman	1.25	3.00
79 Lamar Gordon	1.00	2.50
80 Rod Smith	1.25	3.00
81 Roy Williams S	1.25	3.00
82 Rudi Johnson	1.25	3.00
83 Santana Moss	1.25	3.00
84 Shaun Alexander	1.25	3.00
85 Stephen Davis	1.25	3.00
86 Steve McNair	1.50	4.00
87 Steve Smith	1.50	4.00
88 T.J. Duckett	1.25	3.00
89 Terrell Owens	1.50	4.00
90 Thomas Jones	1.50	4.00
91 Tiki Barber	1.50	4.00
92 Tim Brown	1.50	4.00
93 Tom Brady	3.00	8.00
94 Tony Gonzalez	1.50	4.00
95 Torry Holt	1.25	3.00
96 Travis Henry	1.00	2.50
97 Trent Green	1.25	3.00
98 Warren Sapp	1.25	3.00
99 William Green	1.00	2.50
100 Willis McGahee	1.50	4.00
101 Barry Sanders	4.00	10.00
102 Bart Starr	5.00	12.00
103 Bo Jackson	3.00	8.00
104 Bob Griese	2.00	5.00
105 Bronko Nagurski	2.00	5.00
106 Dan Marino	5.00	12.00
107 Deion Sanders	2.00	5.00
108 Dick Butkus	3.00	8.00
109 Doak Walker	2.00	5.00
110 Don Maynard	1.50	4.00
111 Don Shula	2.00	5.00
112 Earl Campbell	2.00	5.00
113 Fran Tarkenton	2.00	5.00
114 Franco Harris	2.50	6.00
115 Fred Biletnikoff	2.00	5.00
116 Gale Sayers	2.50	6.00
117 Herman Edwards	1.50	4.00
118 Jim Brown	3.00	8.00
119 Jim Kelly	2.00	5.00
120 Jim Thorpe	2.00	5.00
121 Jimmy Johnson	1.50	4.00
122 Joe Greene	2.00	5.00
123 Joe Montana	5.00	12.00
124 Joe Namath	3.00	8.00
125 John Elway	5.00	12.00
126 John Riggins	2.00	5.00
127 Johnny Unitas	5.00	12.00
128 Larry Csonka	2.00	5.00
129 Lawrence Taylor	2.00	5.00
130 Marcus Allen	2.00	5.00
131 Mark Bavaro	1.25	3.00
132 Michael Irvin	2.00	5.00
133 Mike Ditka	2.00	5.00
134 Mike Singletary	2.00	5.00
135 Ozzie Newsome	1.50	4.00
136 Paul Warfield	1.50	4.00
137 Randall Cunningham	1.50	4.00
138 Ray Nitschke	2.00	5.00
139 Red Grange	2.00	5.00
140 Reggie White	2.00	5.00
141 Roger Staubach	3.00	8.00
142 Sterling Sharpe	1.50	4.00
143 Steve Largent	2.00	5.00
144 Terrell Davis	2.00	5.00
145 Terry Bradshaw	3.00	8.00
146 Thurman Thomas	1.50	4.00
147 Tony Dorsett	2.00	5.00
148 Troy Aikman	3.00	8.00
149 Walter Payton	8.00	20.00
150 Warren Moon	1.50	4.00
151 Ahmad Carroll RC	2.00	5.00
152 Andy Hall RC	2.00	5.00
153 Antwan Odom RC	2.50	6.00
154 B.J. Symons RC	2.00	5.00
155 Carlos Francis RC	2.00	5.00
156 Casey Bramlet RC	2.00	5.00
157 Chris Cooley RC	3.00	8.00
158 Chris Gamble RC	2.50	6.00
159 Clarence Moore RC	2.00	5.00
160 Cody Pickett RC	2.50	6.00
161 Courtney Watson RC	2.00	5.00
162 Craig Krenzel RC	2.50	6.00
163 D.J. Hackett RC	2.50	6.00
164 D.J. Williams RC	3.00	8.00
165 Derrick Strait RC	2.00	5.00
166 Dontarrious Thomas RC	2.50	6.00
167 Drew Henson RC	2.00	5.00
168 Ernest Wilford RC	2.50	6.00
169 Jamaar Taylor RC	2.00	5.00
170 Jason Babin RC	3.00	8.00
171 Jeff Smoker RC	2.50	6.00
172 Jerricho Cotchery RC	2.50	6.00
173 Jim Sorgi RC	2.50	6.00
174 Joey Thomas RC	2.00	5.00
175 John Navarre RC	2.00	5.00
176 Johnnie Morant RC	2.00	5.00
177 Jonathan Vilma RC	3.00	8.00
178 Josh Harris RC	2.00	5.00
179 Keiwan Ratliff RC	2.00	5.00
180 Kenechi Udeze RC	2.50	6.00
181 Kris Wilson RC	2.50	6.00
182 Marcus Tubbs RC	2.00	5.00
183 Marquise Hill RC	2.00	5.00
184 Matt Mauck RC	2.00	5.00
185 Maurice Mann RC	2.00	5.00
186 Michael Boulware RC	3.00	8.00
187 Michael Turner RC	4.00	10.00
188 P.K. Sam RC	2.00	5.00
189 Patrick Crayton RC	3.00	8.00
190 Ricardo Colclough RC	2.50	6.00
191 Richard Smith RC	2.00	5.00
192 Samie Parker RC	2.00	5.00
193 Sean Taylor RC	6.00	15.00
194 Teddy Lehman RC	2.00	5.00
195 Thomas Tapeh RC	2.50	6.00
196 Tommie Harris RC	3.00	8.00
197 Triandos Luke RC	2.00	5.00
198 Troy Fleming RC	2.00	5.00
199 Vince Wilfork RC	3.00	8.00
200 Will Smith RC	2.50	6.00
201 Larry Fitzgerald JSY AU RC	50.00	100.00
202 DeAngelo Hall JSY AU RC	12.00	30.00
203 Matt Schaub JSY AU RC	25.00	60.00
204 Michael Jenkins JSY AU RC	12.00	30.00
205 Devard Darling JSY AU RC	8.00	20.00
206 J.P. Losman JSY AU RC	10.00	25.00
207 Lee Evans JSY AU RC	12.00	30.00
208 Keary Colbert JSY AU RC	8.00	20.00
209 Bernard Berrian JSY AU RC	12.00	30.00
210 Chris Perry JSY AU RC	10.00	25.00
211 Kellen Winslow JSY AU RC	12.00	30.00
212 Luke McCown JSY AU RC	10.00	25.00
213 Julius Jones JSY AU RC	10.00	25.00
214 Darius Watts JSY AU RC	8.00	20.00
215 Tatum Bell JSY AU RC	10.00	25.00
216 Kevin Jones JSY AU RC	10.00	25.00
217 Roy Williams WR JSY AU RC	12.00	30.00
218 Dunta Robinson JSY AU RC	8.00	20.00
219 Greg Jones JSY AU RC	8.00	20.00
220 Reggie Williams JSY AU RC	10.00	25.00
221 Mewelde Moore JSY AU RC	10.00	25.00
222 Ben Watson JSY AU RC	12.00	30.00
223 Cedric Cobbs JSY AU RC	8.00	20.00
224 Devery Henderson JSY AU RC	12.00	30.00
225 Eli Manning JSY AU RC	90.00	150.00
226 Robert Gallery JSY AU RC	12.00	30.00
227 Ben Roethlisberger JSY AU RC	75.00	150.00
228 Philip Rivers JSY AU RC	60.00	120.00
229 Derrick Hamilton JSY AU RC	8.00	20.00
230 Rashaun Woods JSY AU RC	8.00	20.00
231 Steven Jackson JSY AU RC	20.00	50.00
232 Michael Clayton JSY AU RC	10.00	25.00
233 Ben Troupe JSY AU RC	10.00	25.00

2004 Leaf Limited Bronze Spotlight

*VETS 1-100: .8X TO 2X BASIC CARDS
*RETIRED 101-150: .8X TO 2X
*ROOKIES 151-200: .5X TO 1.2X
1-200 PRINT RUN 100 SER.#'d SETS
*ROOKIE JSY AU: .5X TO 1.2X
201-233 ROOK.JSY AU PRINT RUN 25

225 Eli Manning JSY AU	175.00	300.00
227 Ben Roethlisberger JSY AU	150.00	300.00

2004 Leaf Limited Gold Spotlight

*VETS 1-100: 2X TO 5X BASIC CARDS
*RETIRED 101-150: 2X TO 5X
*ROOKIES 151-200: 1X TO 2.5X
1-200 PRINT RUN 25 SER.#'d SETS
UNPRICED ROOK.JSY AU PRINT RUN 10

2004 Leaf Limited Silver Spotlight

*VETS 1-100: 1.2X TO 3X BASIC CARDS
*RETIRED 101-150: 1.2X TO 3X
*ROOKIES 151-200: .6X TO 1.5X
1-150 PRINT RUN 50 SER.#'d SETS
*ROOKIE JSY AU: .6X TO 1.5X
151-233 ROOK.JSY AU PRINT RUN 15
225 Eli Manning JSY AU 175.00 300.00
227 Ben Roethlisberger JSY AU 150.00 300.00

2004 Leaf Limited Bound by Round Jerseys

STATED PRINT RUN 50 SER.#'d SETS
*PRIME/25: .6X TO 1.5X BASIC DUAL/50
PRIME PRINT RUN 25 SER.#'d SETS
BR1 Brett Favre 20.00 50.00
Anquan Boldin
BR2 Dan Marino 20.00 50.00
Barry Sanders
BR3 John Elway 20.00 50.00
Emmitt Smith
BR4 Walter Payton 25.00 60.00
Jerry Rice
BR5 Bo Jackson 15.00 40.00
Michael Vick
BR6 Marcus Allen 10.00 25.00
Tim Brown
BR7 Joe Montana 20.00 50.00
Terrell Owens
BR8 Tom Brady 15.00 40.00
Matt Hasselbeck
BR9 Donovan McNabb 10.00 25.00
Marvin Harrison
BR10 Ricky Williams 7.50 20.00
Deuce McAllister
BR11 Clinton Portis 7.50 20.00
Antwaan Randle El
BR12 Hines Ward 7.50 20.00
Ahman Green
BR13 Marshall Faulk 7.50 20.00
Edgerrin James
BR14 Terrell Davis 10.00 25.00
Marc Bulger
BR15 Mark Bavaro 6.00 15.00
Stephen Davis
BR16 Aaron Brooks 7.50 20.00
Rudi Johnson
BR17 Ed McCaffrey 10.00 25.00
Steve Largent
BR18 Chad Johnson 7.50 20.00
Travis Henry
BR19 Chris Chambers 10.00 25.00
Fred Biletnikoff
BR20 Mike Singletary 10.00 25.00
Randall Cunningham
BR21 Fran Tarkenton 15.00 40.00
Ray Nitschke
BR22 Trent Green 10.00 25.00
Leroy Kelly
BR23 Michael Irvin 7.50 20.00
Sterling Sharpe
BR24 Jamal Lewis 7.50 20.00
Ray Lewis
BR25 Brian Urlacher 10.00 25.00
Daunte Culpepper
BR26 Joe Namath 15.00 40.00
Chad Pennington
BR27 Byron Leftwich 10.00 25.00
Randy Moss
BR28 Jim Kelly 10.00 25.00
Drew Bledsoe
BR29 Tony Dorsett 10.00 25.00
LaDainian Tomlinson
BR30 Dick Butkus 15.00 40.00
Lawrence Taylor
BR31 Gale Sayers 10.00 25.00
Shaun Alexander
BR32 Earl Campbell 7.50 20.00
David Carr
BR33 Deion Sanders 12.00 30.00
Roy Williams S
BR34 Ozzie Newsome 7.50 20.00
Jeremy Shockey
BR35 Joey Harrington 7.50 20.00
Bob Griese
BR36 Reggie White 15.00 40.00
Peyotn Manning
BR37 John Riggins 10.00 25.00
Larry Csonka
BR38 James Lofton 7.50 20.00
Torry Holt
BR39 Joe Greene 10.00 25.00
Julius Peppers
BR40 Paul Warfield 6.00 15.00
Santana Moss
BR41 Troy Aikman 10.00 25.00
Steve McNair
BR42 Walter Payton 25.00 60.00
Michael Vick
BR43 Clinton Portis 20.00 50.00
Brett Favre
BR44 Dan Marino 20.00 50.00
Emmitt Smith
BR45 Bo Jackson 15.00 40.00
Jerry Rice
BR46 Joe Namath 15.00 40.00
Troy Aikman
BR47 John Elway 20.00 50.00
Barry Sanders
BR48 Peyton Manning 15.00 40.00
David Carr
BR49 Brian Urlacher 12.00 30.00
Randy Moss
BR50 Ricky Williams 10.00 25.00
Donovan McNabb

2004 Leaf Limited Common Threads

STATED PRINT RUN 50 SER.#'d SETS
*PRIME/10: 1.2X TO 3X BASIC DUAL/50
PRIME PRINT RUN 10 SETS
CT1 Daunte Culpepper 8.00 20.00
Steve McNair
CT2 Randall Cunningham 10.00 25.00
Donovan McNabb
CT3 Byron Leftwich 8.00 20.00
Aaron Brooks
CT4 John Elway 15.00 40.00
David Carr
CT5 Joe Montana 49ers 25.00 60.00
Tom Brady
CT6 Joe Montana Chiefs 20.00 50.00
Trent Green
CT7 Troy Aikman 12.00 30.00
Joey Harrington
CT8 Joe Namath 12.00 30.00
Chad Pennington
CT9 Fran Tarkenton 12.00 30.00
Michael Vick
CT10 Marc Bulger 6.00 15.00
Matt Hasselbeck
CT11 Dan Marino 25.00 60.00
Peyton Manning
CT12 Bart Starr 40.00 80.00
Brett Favre
CT13 Jim Kelly 10.00 25.00
Drew Bledsoe
CT14 Earl Campbell 8.00 20.00
Ricky Williams
CT15 Marcus Allen 10.00 25.00
Priest Holmes
CT16 Walter Payton 20.00 50.00
LaDainian Tomlinson
CT17 Barry Sanders 20.00 50.00
Clinton Portis
CT18 Bo Jackson 12.00 30.00
Jamal Lewis
CT19 Terrell Davis 10.00 25.00
Edgerrin James
CT20 Larry Csonka 10.00 25.00
Deuce McAllister
CT21 Gale Sayers 12.00 30.00
Shaun Alexander
CT22 Tony Dorsett 10.00 25.00
Ahman Green
CT23 Leroy Kelly 10.00 25.00
John Riggins
CT24 Emmitt Smith 12.00 30.00
Travis Henry
CT25 Bo Jackson 12.00 30.00
Rudi Johnson
CT26 Jerry Rice 12.00 30.00
Anquan Boldin
CT27 Jerry Rice 12.00 30.00
Marvin Harrison
CT28 Randy Moss 10.00 25.00
Chris Chambers
CT29 Michael Irvin 10.00 25.00
Terrell Owens
CT30 Fred Biletnikoff 8.00 20.00
Tim Brown
CT31 Torry Holt 8.00 20.00
Chad Johnson
CT32 James Lofton 8.00 20.00
Sterling Sharpe
CT33 Steve Largent 10.00 25.00
Laveranues Coles
CT34 Paul Warfield 6.00 15.00
Santana Moss
CT35 Reggie White 10.00 25.00
Julius Peppers
CT36 Mike Singletary 15.00 40.00
Ray Lewis
CT37 Dick Butkus 15.00 40.00
Brian Urlacher
CT38 Lawrence Taylor 10.00 25.00
LaVar Arrington
CT39 Deion Sanders 12.00 30.00
Terence Newman
CT40 Mark Bavaro 8.00 20.00
Jeremy Shockey
CT41 Michael Vick 12.00 30.00
Donovan McNabb
CT42 John Elway 25.00 60.00
Brett Favre
CT43 Joe Montana 49ers 20.00 50.00
Dan Marino
CT44 Troy Aikman 15.00 40.00
Tom Brady
CT45 Joe Montana Chiefs 20.00 50.00
Chad Pennington
CT46 Jim Kelly 15.00 40.00
Peyton Manning
CT47 Dan Marino 25.00 60.00
John Elway
CT48 Walter Payton 25.00 60.00
Barry Sanders
CT49 Walter Payton 25.00 60.00
Emmitt Smith
CT50 Jerry Rice 15.00 40.00
Randy Moss

2004 Leaf Limited Contenders Preview Autographs

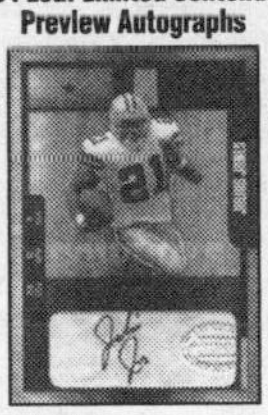

STATED PRINT RUN 15-25
102 Ahmad Carroll/25 10.00 25.00
106 Ben Roethlisberger/15 250.00 400.00
107 Ben Troupe/25 12.00 30.00
108 Ben Watson/25 15.00 40.00
109 Bernard Berrian/25 25.00 50.00
114 Cedric Cobbs/25 10.00 25.00
116 Chris Perry/25 12.00 30.00
117 Clarence Moore/25 10.00 25.00
119 Craig Krenzel/25 12.00 30.00
121 D.J. Williams/25 15.00 40.00
123 DeAngelo Hall/20 15.00 40.00
124 Derrick Hamilton/25 10.00 25.00
126 Devard Darling/25 10.00 25.00
127 Devery Henderson/25 15.00 40.00
129 Drew Henson/15 10.00 25.00
131 Eli Manning/15 250.00 400.00
132 Ernest Wilford/25 12.00 30.00
133 Greg Jones/25 10.00 25.00
134 J.P. Losman/25 12.00 30.00
135 Jamaar Taylor/25 10.00 25.00
138 Jason Babin/25 15.00 40.00
144 Jonathan Vilma/25 15.00 40.00
146 Julius Jones/25 12.00 30.00
147 Keary Colbert/25 10.00 25.00
149 Kenechi Udeze/25 12.00 30.00
150 Kevin Jones/20 12.00 30.00
152 Lee Evans/25 15.00 40.00
153 Luke McCown/25 12.00 30.00
154 Matt Mauck/25 10.00 25.00
155 Matt Schaub/25 50.00 120.00
157 Mewelde Moore/25 12.00 30.00
158 Michael Clayton/25 12.00 30.00
159 Michael Jenkins/25 15.00 40.00
162 Philip Rivers/25 125.00 250.00
165 Rashaun Woods/25 10.00 25.00
166 Reggie Williams/20 12.00 30.00
167 Ricardo Colclough/25 12.00 30.00
169 Roy Williams WR/25 15.00 40.00
174 Steven Jackson/25 50.00 120.00
175 Tatum Bell/25 12.00 30.00
178 Troy Fleming/25 10.00 25.00
182 Michael Boulware/25 15.00 40.00
186 Chris Cooley/20 25.00 50.00
188 Willie Parker/25 25.00 60.00
194 Erik Coleman/25 12.00 30.00
196 Andy Reid CO/15 15.00 40.00
197 Brian Billick CO/15 15.00 40.00
198 Jeff Fisher CO/15 15.00 40.00
199 Jon Gruden CO/15 15.00 40.00
200 Marvin Lewis CO/15 15.00 40.00

2004 Leaf Limited Cuts Autographs

STATED PRINT RUN 25-100
LC1 Tom Brady/50 100.00 200.00
LC2 Priest Holmes/50 20.00 50.00
LC3 Dan Marino/50 125.00 250.00
LC4 LaDainian Tomlinson/50 40.00 80.00
LC5 Jake Plummer/100 15.00 40.00
LC6 Bronko Nagurski/30 200.00 350.00
LC7 Vince Lombardi/25 350.00 550.00
LC8 Aaron Brooks/55 12.00 30.00
LC9 Warren Moon/55 20.00 50.00

2004 Leaf Limited Hardwear

STATED PRINT RUN 100 SER.#'d SETS
UNPRICED SHIELD PRINT RUN 1 SET
H1 Anquan Boldin 8.00 20.00
H2 Ahman Green 6.00 15.00
H3 Brian Urlacher 8.00 20.00
H4 Chad Johnson 8.00 20.00
H5 Chad Pennington 8.00 20.00
H6 Chris Chambers 6.00 15.00
H7 Eddie George 6.00 15.00
H8 Jake Plummer 6.00 15.00
H9 Jerry Rice 15.00 40.00
H10 Larry Csonka 8.00 20.00
H11 LaDainian Tomlinson 8.00 20.00
H12 Lawrence Taylor 8.00 20.00
H13 Marc Bulger 6.00 15.00
H14 Marcus Allen 8.00 20.00
H15 Matt Hasselbeck 6.00 15.00
H16 Michael Bennett 6.00 15.00
H17 Marvin Harrison 8.00 20.00
H18 Michael Irvin 8.00 20.00
H19 Peyton Manning 15.00 40.00
H20 Randy Moss 8.00 20.00
H21 Ray Lewis 8.00 20.00
H22 Ricky Williams 6.00 15.00
H23 Shaun Alexander 6.00 15.00
H24 Steve McNair 8.00 20.00
H25 Torry Holt 6.00 15.00

2004 Leaf Limited Hardwear Limited

*UNSIGNED LIMITED: .8X TO 2X
LIMITED PRINT RUN 25 SER.#'d SETS
H1 Anquan Boldin AU 25.00 60.00
H3 Brian Urlacher AU 60.00 100.00
H15 Matt Hasselbeck AU 30.00 80.00
H23 Shaun Alexander AU 75.00 135.00
H25 Torry Holt AU 30.00 80.00

2004 Leaf Limited Legends Jerseys

STATED PRINT RUN 50 SER.#'d SETS
UNPRICED PRIME PRINT RUN 5 SETS
UNPRICED SEASON PRINT RUN 6-18 SETS
LL1 Barry Sanders 15.00 40.00
LL2 Bart Starr 20.00 50.00
LL3 Brett Favre 20.00 50.00
LL4 Dick Butkus 15.00 40.00
LL5 Doak Walker 10.00 25.00
LL6 Fran Tarkenton 10.00 25.00
LL7 Franco Harris 12.00 30.00
LL8 Fred Biletnikoff 10.00 25.00
LL9 Gale Sayers 12.00 30.00
LL10 Jim Brown AU 60.00 120.00
LL11 Jim Kelly 10.00 25.00
LL12 Jim Thorpe 100.00 200.00
LL13 Joe Montana 49ers 20.00 50.00
LL14 Joe Namath AU 50.00 100.00
LL15 John Elway 15.00 40.00
LL16 John Riggins 10.00 25.00
LL17 Johnny Unitas 20.00 50.00
LL18 Steve Largent 10.00 25.00
LL19 Terry Bradshaw 12.00 30.00
LL20 Walter Payton 25.00 60.00

2004 Leaf Limited Lettermen

UNPRICED LETTERMEN PRINT RUN 4-10

2004 Leaf Limited Material Monikers

CARDS #'d UNDER 20 NOT PRICED
UNPRICED LIMITED PRINT RUN 1 SET
MM1 Ahman Green/25 20.00 50.00
MM2 Barry Sanders/25 125.00 250.00
MM3 Bart Starr/31 90.00 150.00
MM8 Joe Namath/50 50.00 100.00
MM9 Byron Leftwich/25 20.00 50.00
MM10 Donovan McNabb/25 40.00 80.00
MM11 Daunte Culpepper/40 15.00 40.00
MM12 Fran Tarkenton/50 20.00 50.00
MM13 Jamal Lewis/25 20.00 50.00
MM14 Jim Brown/25 60.00 120.00
MM16 Anquan Boldin/25 25.00 60.00
MM20 Tom Brady/25 175.00 300.00
MM22 Jim Kelly/25 40.00 80.00
MM23 Clinton Portis/25 25.00 60.00
MM24 John Riggins/25 25.00 60.00
MM25 Roy Williams S/25 20.00 50.00
MM26 Deion Sanders/25 50.00 100.00
MM27 Earl Campbell/20 25.00 60.00
MM28 Priest Holmes/50 20.00 50.00
MM29 Larry Csonka/25 25.00 60.00
MM31 LaDainian Tomlinson/25 50.00 100.00
MM33 Steve McNair/50 20.00 50.00
MM34 Peyton Manning/45 60.00 120.00
MM36 Terry Bradshaw/50 50.00 100.00
MM37 Bo Jackson/25 75.00 125.00
MM42 Jim Brown/25 60.00 120.00
Jamal Lewis
MM45 John Riggins/25 40.00 80.00
Clinton Portis
MM46 Deion Sanders/25 50.00 100.00
Roy Williams S

2004 Leaf Limited Player Threads

THREADS PRINT RUN 50 SER.#'d SETS
*PRIME/25: .6X TO 1.5X BASIC INSERT
PRIME PRINT RUN 25 SER.#'d SETS
UNPRICED LIMITED PRINT RUN 1 SET
PT1 Ahman Green Tri 8.00 20.00
PT2 Barry Sanders Tri 25.00 60.00
PT3 Brett Favre Dual 20.00 50.00
PT4 Brian Urlacher Dual 10.00 25.00
PT5 Carson Palmer Dual 8.00 20.00
PT6 Clinton Portis Tri 10.00 25.00
PT7 Dan Marino Tri 30.00 80.00
PT8 Daunte Culpepper Tri 8.00 20.00
PT9 Donovan McNabb Dual 8.00 20.00
PT10 Drew Bledsoe Tri 10.00 25.00
PT11 Edgerrin James Tri 8.00 20.00
PT12 Emmitt Smith Tri 25.00 60.00
PT13 Fran Tarkenton Dual 10.00 25.00
PT14 Jeremy Shockey Tri 8.00 20.00
PT15 Jerry Rice Tri 20.00 50.00
PT16 Joe Montana Tri 30.00 80.00
PT17 John Elway Tri 25.00 60.00
PT18 Marcus Allen Tri 12.00 30.00
PT19 Marshall Faulk Tri 10.00 25.00
PT20 Michael Vick Dual 12.00 30.00
PT21 Mike Singletary Dual 10.00 25.00
PT22 Peyton Manning Dual 15.00 40.00
PT23 Priest Holmes Tri 10.00 25.00
PT24 Randy Moss Dual 8.00 20.00
PT25 Ricky Williams Tri 8.00 20.00
PT26 Roger Staubach Dual 15.00 40.00
PT27 Terry Bradshaw Dual 15.00 40.00
PT28 Tom Brady Dual 15.00 40.00
PT29 Troy Aikman Dual 12.00 30.00
PT30 Walter Payton Dual 30.00 80.00

2004 Leaf Limited Team Threads Dual

STATED PRINT RUN 50 SER.#'d SETS
*PRIME/10: .8X TO 2X BASIC DUAL/50
PRIME PRINT RUN 10 SETS
TT1 Anquan Boldin 10.00 25.00
Larry Fitzgerald
TT2 Michael Vick 10.00 25.00
Peerless Price
TT3 Jamal Lewis 8.00 20.00
Ray Lewis
TT4 Drew Bledsoe 10.00 25.00
Jim Kelly
TT5 Brian Urlacher 30.00 80.00
Walter Payton
TT6 Carson Palmer 8.00 20.00
Chad Johnson
TT7 Emmitt Smith 20.00 50.00
Troy Aikman
TT8 John Elway 20.00 50.00
Terrell Davis
TT9 Barry Sanders 15.00 40.00
Joey Harrington
TT10 Brett Favre 20.00 50.00
Sterling Sharpe
TT11 Andre Johnson 8.00 20.00
David Carr
TT12 Edgerrin James 15.00 40.00
Peyton Manning
TT13 Byron Leftwich 6.00 15.00
Fred Taylor
TT14 Priest Holmes 20.00 50.00
Joe Montana
TT15 Dan Marino 20.00 50.00
Ricky Williams
TT16 Daunte Culpepper 8.00 20.00
Randy Moss
TT17 Tom Brady 15.00 40.00
Drew Bledsoe
TT18 Lawrence Taylor 10.00 25.00
Jeremy Shockey
TT19 Chad Pennington 12.00 30.00
Joe Namath
TT20 Jerry Rice 15.00 40.00
Bo Jackson
TT21 Donovan McNabb 8.00 20.00
Randall Cunningham
TT22 Jerry Rice 30.00 80.00
Joe Montana
TT23 Matt Hasselbeck 8.00 20.00
Steve Largent
TT24 Steve McNair 8.00 20.00
Earl Campbell
TT25 Clinton Portis 8.00 20.00
Laveranues Coles

2004 Leaf Limited Team Threads Quad

UNPRICED QUAD PRINT RUN 10
UNPRICED AUTOS PRINT RUN 1

2004 Leaf Limited Team Threads Triple

STATED PRINT RUN 25 SER.#'d SETS
UNPRICED PRIME PRINT RUN 5
TT1 Michael Vick 20.00 50.00
Peerless Price
Warrick Dunn
TT2 Drew Bledsoe 15.00 40.00
Jim Kelly
Bruce Smith
TT3 Brian Urlacher 50.00 120.00
Dick Butkus
Walter Payton
TT4 Emmitt Smith 40.00 100.00
Michael Irvin
Troy Aikman
TT5 Jake Plummer 30.00 80.00
John Elway
Terrell Davis
TT6 Barry Sanders 40.00 100.00
Joey Harrington
Doak Walker
TT7 Ahman Green 50.00 120.00
Brett Favre
Sterling Sharpe
TT8 Edgerrin James 25.00 60.00
Marvin Harrison
Peyton Manning
TT9 Joe Montana 40.00 100.00
Priest Holmes
Marcus Allen
TT10 Bob Griese 40.00 100.00
Dan Marino
Ricky Williams
TT11 Daunte Culpepper 15.00 40.00
Fran Tarkenton
Randy Moss
TT12 Jeremy Shockey 15.00 40.00
Lawrence Taylor
Mark Bavaro
TT13 Joe Namath 25.00 60.00
Chad Pennington
Curtis Martin
TT14 Bo Jackson 30.00 80.00
Marcus Allen
Jerry Rice
TT15 Clinton Portis 15.00 40.00
Laveranues Coles
John Riggins

2004 Leaf Limited Team Trademarks Autographs

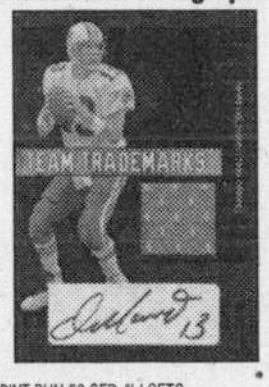

AUTO PRINT RUN 50 SER.#'d SETS
*LIMITED/25: .5X TO 1.2X BASIC AU
LIMITED PRINT RUN 25 SER.#'d SETS
TT1 Ahman Green 12.00 30.00
TT2 Anquan Boldin 15.00 40.00
TT3 Bo Jackson 30.00 80.00
TT4 Bob Griese 15.00 40.00
TT5 Brian Urlacher 25.00 60.00
TT6 Chad Johnson 15.00 40.00
TT7 Chad Pennington 15.00 40.00
TT8 Clinton Portis 15.00 40.00
TT9 Dan Marino 75.00 150.00
TT10 Deuce McAllister 12.00 30.00
TT11 Domanick Davis 10.00 25.00
TT12 Don Shula 20.00 50.00
TT13 Drew Bledsoe 15.00 40.00
TT14 Fran Tarkenton 20.00 50.00
TT15 Franco Harris 25.00 60.00
TT16 Fred Biletnikoff 15.00 40.00
TT17 Gale Sayers 40.00 80.00
TT18 Herman Edwards 12.00 30.00
TT19 Jake Delhomme 12.00 30.00
TT20 Jim Brown 60.00 120.00
TT21 Jimmy Johnson 20.00 50.00
TT22 Joe Montana 49ers 60.00 120.00
TT23 Joe Namath 50.00 100.00
TT24 Joey Harrington 12.00 30.00
TT25 John Riggins 20.00 50.00
TT26 LaDainian Tomlinson 30.00 80.00
TT27 Lawrence Taylor 25.00 60.00
TT28 Marvin Harrison 15.00 40.00
TT29 Matt Hasselbeck 12.00 30.00
TT30 Michael Irvin 15.00 40.00
TT31 Michael Strahan 15.00 40.00
TT32 Michael Vick 30.00 60.00
TT33 Mike Singletary 15.00 40.00
TT34 Ozzie Newsome 12.00 30.00
TT35 Priest Holmes 15.00 40.00
TT36 Steve Smith 15.00 40.00
TT37 Rex Grossman 12.00 30.00
TT38 Earl Campbell 25.00 50.00
TT39 Roger Staubach 40.00 100.00
TT40 Roy Williams S 12.00 30.00
TT41 Santana Moss 12.00 30.00
TT42 Shaun Alexander 12.00 30.00
TT43 Stephen Davis 12.00 30.00
TT44 Steve Largent 30.00 60.00
TT45 Thurman Thomas 12.00 30.00
TT46 Tom Brady 125.00 200.00
TT47 Tony Dorsett 25.00 50.00
TT48 Torry Holt 12.00 30.00
TT49 Trent Green 12.00 30.00
TT50 Troy Aikman 50.00 100.00

2004 Leaf Limited Threads

STATED PRINT RUN 75-100
LT1 Aaron Brooks/75 4.00 10.00
LT2 Ahman Green Sea./75 4.00 10.00
LT3 Ahman Green GB/75 4.00 10.00
LT4 Andre Johnson Mia./75 5.00 12.00
LT5 Andre Johnson/75 5.00 12.00
LT6 Anquan Boldin FSU/75 5.00 12.00
LT7 Anquan Boldin/75 5.00 12.00
LT8 Barry Sanders OSU/100 12.00 30.00
LT9 Barry Sanders/100 12.00 30.00
LT10 Bart Starr/100 15.00 40.00
LT11 Bo Jackson/100 10.00 25.00
LT12 Bob Griese/75 6.00 15.00
LT13 Brett Favre/100 12.00 30.00
LT14 Brian Urlacher/75 8.00 20.00
LT15 Byron Leftwich/75 4.00 10.00
LT16 Carson Palmer USC/75 5.00 12.00
LT17 Carson Palmer/75 5.00 12.00
LT18 Chad Pennington/75 5.00 12.00
LT19 Clinton Portis Mia./75 5.00 12.00
LT20 Clinton Portis/75 5.00 12.00
LT21 David Carr/75 4.00 10.00
LT22 Dan Marino/100 15.00 40.00
LT23 Dan Marino PB/100 15.00 40.00
LT24 Daunte Culpepper/75 4.00 10.00
LT25 Daunte Culpepper PB/75 4.00 10.00
LT26 Deion Sanders 'Boys/75 8.00 20.00
LT27 Deion Sanders 'Skins/75 6.00 15.00
LT28 Deuce McAllister AU/100 10.00 25.00
LT29 Dick Butkus/75 10.00 25.00
LT30 Domanick Davis AU/100 8.00 20.00
LT31 Don Maynard/75 5.00 12.00
LT32 Donovan McNabb/75 8.00 20.00
LT33 Drew Bledsoe WSU/75 6.00 15.00
LT34 Drew Bledsoe/75 5.00 12.00
LT35 Earl Campbell/75 6.00 15.00
LT36 Edgerrin James Mia./75 4.00 10.00
LT37 Edgerrin James/75 4.00 10.00
LT38 Emmitt Smith/100 15.00 40.00
LT39 Fran Tarkenton Vikes/75 6.00 15.00
LT40 Fran Tarkenton NYG/75 6.00 15.00
LT41 George Blanda/75 6.00 15.00
LT42 Jake Delhomme AU/100 10.00 25.00
LT43 Jamal Lewis/75 4.00 10.00
LT44 Jeremy Shockey Mia./75 4.00 10.00
LT45 Jeremy Shockey/75 4.00 10.00
LT46 Jerry Rice/100 10.00 25.00
LT47 Jevon Kearse Flor./75 4.00 10.00
LT48 Jim Kelly/75 8.00 20.00
LT49 Joe Greene/75 6.00 15.00
LT50 Joe Greene SB/75 6.00 15.00
LT51 Joe Montana 49ers/100 15.00 40.00
LT52 Joe Montana Chiefs/100 15.00 40.00
LT53 Joe Namath/100 10.00 25.00
LT54 Joey Harrington/75 4.00 10.00
LT55 John Elway Stan./100 15.00 40.00
LT56 John Elway/100 15.00 40.00
LT57 John Riggins NYJ/75 6.00 15.00
LT58 John Riggins 'Skins/75 6.00 15.00
LT59 Josh McCown/75 4.00 10.00
LT60 Kellen Winslow Jr. Mia./75 5.00 12.00
LT61 Kyle Boller Cal./75 4.00 10.00
LT62 Michael Vick VT/100 8.00 20.00
LT63 LaDainian Tomlinson/75 5.00 12.00
LT64 Larry Fitzgerald/75 12.00 30.00
LT65 Lawrence Taylor/75 6.00 15.00
LT66 Marc Bulger/75 4.00 10.00
LT67 Marcus Allen Raid./75 6.00 15.00
LT68 Marcus Allen Chiefs/75 6.00 15.00
LT69 Marshall Faulk SDSU/75 5.00 12.00
LT70 Marshall Faulk Rams/75 5.00 12.00
LT71 Matt Hasselbeck AU/100 10.00 25.00
LT72 Michael Clayton LSU/75 4.00 10.00
LT73 Michael Irvin/75 6.00 15.00
LT74 Michael Irvin PB/75 6.00 15.00
LT75 Michael Vick/100 8.00 20.00
LT76 Mike Singletary Bay./75 6.00 15.00
LT77 Ozzie Newsome/75 5.00 12.00
LT78 Peyton Manning/75 10.00 25.00
LT79 Peyton Manning PB/75 10.00 25.00
LT80 Priest Holmes Chiefs/75 5.00 12.00
LT81 Priest Holmes Rav./75 5.00 12.00
LT82 Randy Moss/75 5.00 12.00
LT83 Reggie White/75 6.00 15.00
LT84 Reggie Williams Wash./75 4.00 10.00
LT85 Rex Grossman/75 4.00 10.00
LT86 Ricky Williams/75 4.00 10.00
LT87 Roger Staubach/75 10.00 25.00
LT88 Shaun Alexander/75 4.00 10.00
LT89 Steve Largent/75 6.00 15.00
LT90 Steve McNair/75 5.00 12.00
LT91 Sonny Jurgensen/75 5.00 12.00
LT92 Steve Smith AU/100 12.00 30.00
LT93 Terrell Davis/75 6.00 15.00
LT94 Terry Bradshaw/100 10.00 25.00
LT95 Tom Brady/100 10.00 25.00
LT96 Tom Brady PB/100 10.00 25.00
LT97 Tony Dorsett/75 6.00 15.00
LT98 Trent Green/75 4.00 10.00
LT99 Troy Aikman/75 10.00 25.00
LT100 Walter Payton/100 25.00 60.00

2004 Leaf Limited Threads At the Half

*UNSIGNED: .5X TO 1.2X BASIC THREADS
LT3 Ahman Green GB AU/50 12.00 30.00
LT6 Anquan Boldin FSU AU/50 15.00 40.00
LT7 Anquan Boldin AU/50 15.00 40.00
LT28 Deuce McAllister AU/50 12.00 30.00
LT30 Domanick Davis AU/50 10.00 25.00
LT35 Earl Campbell AU/50 20.00 50.00
LT42 Jake Delhomme AU/50 12.00 30.00
LT49 Joe Greene AU/50 20.00 50.00
LT53 Joe Namath AU/50 50.00 100.00
LT63 LaDainian Tomlinson AU/50 30.00 80.00
LT71 Matt Hasselbeck AU/50 12.00 30.00
LT83 Reggie White AU/50 ERR 75.00 150.00
(Autograph is that of
Reggie White the running back)
LT85 Rex Grossman AU/50 12.00 30.00
LT91 Sonny Jurgensen AU/50 15.00 40.00
LT92 Steve Smith AU/50 15.00 40.00
LT98 Trent Green AU/50 12.00 30.00

2004 Leaf Limited Threads Jersey Numbers

*UNSIGNED/63-92: .5X TO 1.2X THREADS
*UNSIGNED/42-56: .6X TO 1.5X THREADS
*UNSIGNED/30-37: .8X TO 2X BASIC THREADS
*UNSIGNED/21-28: 1X TO 2.5X BASIC THREADS
*UNSIGNED/10-19: 1.2X TO 3X BASIC THREADS
STATED PRINT RUN 1-92
AUTOs #'d UNDER 20 NOT PRICED
LT2 Ahman Green Sea. AU/30 20.00 50.00
LT9 Barry Sanders AU/20 100.00 175.00
LT14 Brian Urlacher AU/54 25.00 60.00
LT19 Clinton Portis Mia. AU/28 25.00 60.00
LT20 Clinton Portis AU/26 25.00 60.00
LT26 Deion Sanders 'Boys AU/21 50.00 100.00
LT28 Deuce McAllister AU/26 25.00 60.00
LT30 Domanick Davis AU/37 15.00 40.00
LT35 Earl Campbell AU/34 25.00 60.00
LT57 John Riggins NYJ AU/44 40.00 80.00
LT58 John Riggins 'Skins AU/44 30.00 80.00
LT63 LaDainian Tomlinson AU/21 40.00 80.00
LT80 Priest Holmes Chiefs AU/31 25.00 60.00
LT92 Steve Smith AU/89 15.00 40.00
LT93 Terrell Davis AU/30 15.00 40.00
LT97 Tony Dorsett AU/33 25.00 60.00

2004 Leaf Limited Threads Positions

*UNSIGNED: .5X TO 1.2X BASIC THREADS
LT7 Anquan Boldin AU/75 12.00 30.00
LT28 Deuce McAllister AU/75 10.00 25.00
LT30 Domanick Davis AU/75 8.00 20.00
LT42 Jake Delhomme AU/75 10.00 25.00
LT71 Matt Hasselbeck AU/75 10.00 25.00
LT92 Steve Smith AU/75 12.00 30.00

2004 Leaf Limited Threads Prime

*UNSIGNED: .8X TO 2X BASIC THREADS
PRIME PRINT RUN 25 SER.#'d SETS
LT2 Ahman Green Sea. AU 15.00 40.00
LT3 Ahman Green GB AU 15.00 40.00
LT6 Anquan Boldin FSU AU 20.00 50.00
LT7 Anquan Boldin AU 20.00 50.00
LT8 Barry Sanders OSU AU 100.00 200.00
LT14 Brian Urlacher AU 30.00 80.00
LT15 Byron Leftwich AU 15.00 40.00
LT19 Clinton Portis Mia. AU 20.00 50.00
LT20 Clinton Portis AU 20.00 50.00
LT21 David Carr AU 12.00 30.00
LT28 Deuce McAllister AU 15.00 40.00
LT30 Domanick Davis AU 12.00 30.00
LT35 Earl Campbell AU 40.00 80.00
LT39 Fran Tarkenton Vikes AU 25.00 60.00
LT40 Fran Tarkenton NYG AU 25.00 60.00
LT41 George Blanda AU 40.00 80.00
LT42 Jake Delhomme AU 15.00 40.00
LT46 Jerry Rice AU 150.00 250.00
LT53 Joe Namath AU 60.00 120.00
LT54 Joey Harrington AU 15.00 40.00
LT57 John Riggins NYJ AU 25.00 60.00
LT58 John Riggins 'Skins AU 40.00 80.00
LT63 LaDainian Tomlinson AU 40.00 100.00
LT65 Lawrence Taylor AU 40.00 80.00
LT67 Marcus Allen Raid. AU 40.00 100.00
LT68 Marcus Allen Chiefs AU 40.00 80.00
LT71 Matt Hasselbeck AU 15.00 40.00
LT75 Michael Vick AU 50.00 100.00
LT76 Mike Singletary Bay. AU 25.00 60.00
LT78 Peyton Manning AU 100.00 200.00
LT79 Peyton Manning PB AU 100.00 200.00
LT83A Reggie White AU ERR 30.00 80.00
Autograph is that of
Reggie White the running back)
LT83B Reggie White AU COR 200.00 350.00
LT85 Rex Grossman AU 15.00 40.00
LT87 Roger Staubach AU 60.00 120.00
LT88 Shaun Alexander AU 15.00 40.00
LT89 Steve Largent AU 40.00 80.00
LT92 Steve Smith AU 20.00 50.00
LT93 Terrell Davis AU 25.00 60.00
LT94 Terry Bradshaw AU 75.00 150.00
LT97 Tony Dorsett AU 25.00 60.00

2005 Leaf Limited

This 229-card set was released in November, 2005. The set was issued in the hobby in four-card hobby packs with an $70 SRP. Cards numbered 1-100 feature veterans in team alphabetical order while cards numbered 101-150 feature veterans in first name alphabetical order and the set concludes with rookies from 151-229. Within the rookie subset, the final 29 cards (201-229) feature both autographs and player-worn jersey pieces. All cards 1-150 were issued to a stated print run of 599 serial numbered sets while cards numbered 151-200 were issued to a stated print run of 250 copies and cards numbered 201-229 were issued to a stated print run of 100 copies. A few players did not return their signatures in time for pack out and those cards could be redeemed until June 1, 2007.

1-150 PRINT RUN 599 SER.#'d SETS
151-200 ROOKIE PRINT RUN 250
201-229 JSY AU PRINT RUN 100 SETS
UNPRICED PLATINUM SER.#'d TO 1
1 Anquan Boldin 1.25 3.00
2 Kurt Warner 1.50 4.00
3 Larry Fitzgerald 1.50 4.00
4 Alge Crumpler 1.25 3.00
5 Michael Vick 1.50 4.00
6 Warrick Dunn 1.25 3.00
7 Jamal Lewis 1.25 3.00
8 Kyle Boller 1.25 3.00
9 Ray Lewis 1.50 4.00
10 Derrick Mason 1.25 3.00
11 J.P. Losman 1.00 2.50
12 Lee Evans 1.25 3.00
13 Willis McGahee 1.50 4.00
14 DeShaun Foster 1.25 3.00
15 Jake Delhomme 1.25 3.00
16 Steve Smith 1.50 4.00
17 Brian Urlacher 1.50 4.00
18 Rex Grossman 1.25 3.00
19 Muhsin Muhammad 1.25 3.00
20 Carson Palmer 1.50 4.00
21 Chad Johnson 1.25 3.00
22 Rudi Johnson 1.25 3.00
23 Antonio Bryant 1.00 2.50
24 Lee Suggs 1.00 2.50
25 Trent Dilfer 1.25 3.00
26 Drew Bledsoe 1.50 4.00
27 Julius Jones 1.00 2.50
28 Keyshawn Johnson 1.25 3.00
29 Roy Williams S 1.00 2.50
30 Ashley Lelie 1.00 2.50
31 Jake Plummer 1.25 3.00
32 Tatum Bell 1.00 2.50
33 Rod Smith 1.25 3.00
34 Joey Harrington 1.25 3.00
35 Kevin Jones 1.00 2.50
36 Roy Williams WR 1.25 3.00
37 Ahman Green 1.25 3.00
38 Brett Favre 4.00 10.00
39 Javon Walker 1.00 2.50
40 Andre Johnson 1.50 4.00
41 David Carr 1.00 2.50
42 Domanick Davis 1.00 2.50
43 Edgerrin James 1.25 3.00
44 Marvin Harrison 1.50 4.00
45 Peyton Manning 3.00 8.00
46 Reggie Wayne 1.50 4.00
47 Byron Leftwich 1.25 3.00
48 Fred Taylor 1.25 3.00
49 Jimmy Smith 1.25 3.00
50 Priest Holmes 1.25 3.00
51 Tony Gonzalez 1.25 3.00
52 Trent Green 1.25 3.00
53 Chris Chambers 1.25 3.00
54 Ricky Williams 1.25 3.00
55 Daunte Culpepper 1.25 3.00
56 Nate Burleson 1.00 2.50
57 Michael Bennett 1.25 3.00
58 Corey Dillon 1.25 3.00
59 Deion Branch 1.00 2.50
60 Tom Brady 3.00 8.00
61 Aaron Brooks 1.00 2.50
62 Deuce McAllister 1.25 3.00
63 Joe Horn 1.25 3.00
64 Eli Manning 2.50 6.00
65 Jeremy Shockey 1.50 4.00
66 Plaxico Burress 1.25 3.00
67 Tiki Barber 1.50 4.00
68 Chad Pennington 1.50 4.00
69 Curtis Martin 1.50 4.00
70 Laveranues Coles 1.00 2.50
71 Kerry Collins 1.25 3.00
72 LaMont Jordan 1.25 3.00
73 Randy Moss 1.50 4.00
74 Brian Westbrook 1.25 3.00
75 Donovan McNabb 1.50 4.00
76 Terrell Owens 1.50 4.00
77 Ben Roethlisberger 2.50 6.00
78 Duce Staley 1.25 3.00
79 Hines Ward 1.50 4.00
80 Jerome Bettis 1.50 4.00

81 Antonio Gates 1.50 4.00
82 Drew Brees 1.50 4.00
83 LaDainian Tomlinson 1.50 4.00
84 Brandon Lloyd 1.00 2.50
85 Kevan Barlow 1.00 2.50
86 Darrell Jackson 1.00 2.50
87 Matt Hasselbeck 1.25 3.00
88 Shaun Alexander 1.25 3.00
89 Marc Bulger 1.25 3.00
90 Steven Jackson 1.50 4.00
91 Torry Holt 1.25 3.00
92 Brian Griese 1.25 3.00
93 Michael Clayton 1.00 2.50
94 Chris Brown 1.00 2.50
95 Drew Bennett 1.25 3.00
96 Steve McNair 1.50 4.00
97 Clinton Portis 1.25 3.00
98 LaVar Arrington 1.25 3.00
99 Patrick Ramsey 1.25 3.00
100 Santana Moss 1.25 3.00
101 Barry Sanders 3.00 8.00
102 Bart Starr 3.00 8.00
103 Bo Jackson 2.50 6.00
104 Brian Piccolo 2.50 6.00
105 Bob Griese 2.00 5.00
106 Dan Fouts 2.00 5.00
107 Dan Marino 5.00 12.00
108 Deacon Jones 1.50 4.00
109 Doak Walker 2.00 5.00
110 Don Maynard 1.50 4.00
111 Don Meredith 2.00 5.00
112 Don Shula 1.50 4.00
113 Earl Campbell 2.00 5.00
114 Eric Dickerson 1.50 4.00
115 Fran Tarkenton 2.00 5.00
116 Franco Harris 2.00 5.00
117 Gale Sayers 2.50 6.00
118 Jack Lambert 2.00 5.00
119 James Lofton 1.25 3.00
120 Jim Brown 2.50 6.00
121 Jim Kelly 2.50 6.00
122 Jim Thorpe 2.50 6.00
123 Joe Greene 2.00 5.00
124 Joe Montana 5.00 12.00
125 Joe Namath 3.00 8.00
126 John Elway 4.00 10.00
127 John Riggins 2.00 5.00
128 Johnny Unitas 3.00 8.00
129 Lawrence Taylor 2.00 5.00
130 Leroy Kelly 1.50 4.00
131 Marcus Allen 2.00 5.00
132 Michael Irvin 2.00 5.00
133 Mike Ditka 2.00 5.00
134 Mike Singletary 2.00 5.00
135 Ozzie Newsome 1.50 4.00
136 Paul Hornung 2.00 5.00
137 Paul Warfield 1.50 4.00
138 Randall Cunningham 1.50 4.00
139 Red Grange 2.50 6.00
140 Roger Staubach 3.00 8.00
141 Sammy Baugh 2.00 5.00
142 Sonny Jurgensen 1.50 4.00
143 Steve Largent 2.00 5.00
144 Steve Young 2.50 6.00
145 Terrell Davis 2.00 5.00
146 Terry Bradshaw 3.00 8.00
147 Tony Dorsett 1.50 4.00
148 Troy Aikman 2.50 6.00
149 Walter Payton 5.00 12.00
150 Warren Moon 2.00 5.00
151 Aaron Rodgers RC 50.00 80.00
152 Adrian McPherson RC 2.00 5.00
153 Airese Currie RC 2.00 5.00
154 Alvin Pearman RC 2.00 5.00
155 Anthony Davis RC 2.00 5.00
156 Brandon Jacobs RC 4.00 10.00
157 Brandon Jones RC 2.50 6.00
158 Cedric Benson RC 3.00 8.00
159 Cedric Houston RC 3.00 8.00
160 Chad Owens RC 2.50 6.00
161 Chris Henry RC 3.00 8.00
162 Nate Washington RC 3.00 8.00
163 Craig Bragg RC 2.00 5.00
164 Craphonso Thorpe RC 2.00 5.00
165 Damien Nash RC 2.50 6.00
166 Dan Orlovsky RC 3.00 8.00
167 Dante Ridgeway RC 2.00 5.00
168 Darren Sproles RC 3.00 8.00
169 David Greene RC 2.00 5.00
170 David Pollack RC 2.50 6.00
171 Deandra Cobb RC 2.00 5.00
172 DeMarcus Ware RC 6.00 15.00
173 Derek Anderson RC 2.50 6.00
174 Derrick Johnson RC 2.50 6.00
175 Erasmus James RC 2.50 6.00
176 Fabian Washington RC 2.50 6.00
177 Fred Gibson RC 2.50 6.00
178 Harry Williams RC 2.50 6.00
179 Heath Miller RC 4.00 10.00
180 J.R. Russell RC 2.00 5.00
181 James Kilian RC 2.00 5.00
182 Jerome Mathis RC 3.00 8.00
183 Larry Brackins RC 2.00 5.00
184 LeRon McCoy RC 2.00 5.00
185 Lionel Gates RC 2.00 5.00
186 Marcus Spears RC 2.50 6.00
187 Marion Barber RC 3.00 8.00
188 Marlin Jackson RC 2.00 5.00
189 Matt Cassel RC 6.00 15.00
190 Mike Williams 3.00 8.00
191 Noah Herron RC 2.00 5.00
192 Paris Warren RC 2.50 6.00
193 Rasheed Marshall RC 2.50 6.00
194 Roscoe Crosby RC 2.00 5.00
195 Roydell Williams RC 2.50 6.00
196 Ryan Fitzpatrick RC 5.00 12.00
197 Shawne Merriman RC 3.00 8.00
198 Tab Perry RC 2.00 5.00
199 Thomas Davis RC 2.00 5.00
200 Travis Johnson RC 2.00 5.00
201 Adam Jones JSY AU RC 6.00 15.00
202 Alex Smith QB JSY AU RC 25.00 50.00
203 Andrew Walter JSY AU RC 8.00 20.00
204 Antrel Rolle JSY AU RC 10.00 25.00
205 Braylon Edwards JSY AU RC 12.00 30.00
206 Cadillac Williams JSY AU RC 10.00 25.00
207 Carlos Rogers JSY AU RC 10.00 25.00
208 Charlie Frye JSY AU RC 10.00 25.00
209 Ciatrick Fason JSY AU RC 6.00 15.00
210 Courtney Roby JSY AU RC 8.00 20.00
211 Eric Shelton JSY AU RC 6.00 15.00
212 Frank Gore JSY AU RC 15.00 40.00
213 J.J. Arrington JSY AU RC 8.00 20.00
214 Kyle Orton JSY AU RC 10.00 25.00
215 Jason Campbell JSY AU RC 12.00 30.00
216 Mark Bradley JSY AU RC 6.00 15.00
217 Mark Clayton JSY AU RC 8.00 20.00
218 Matt Jones JSY AU RC 8.00 20.00
219 Maurice Clarett JSY AU 6.00 15.00
220 Reggie Brown JSY AU RC 6.00 15.00
221 Ronnie Brown JSY AU RC 12.00 30.00
222 Roddy White JSY AU RC 12.00 30.00
223 Ryan Moats JSY AU RC 6.00 15.00
224 Roscoe Parrish JSY AU RC 6.00 15.00
225 Stefan LeFors JSY AU RC 6.00 15.00
226 Terrence Murphy JSY AU RC 6.00 15.00
227 Troy Williamson JSY AU RC 8.00 20.00
228 Vernand Morency JSY AU RC 6.00 15.00
229 Vincent Jackson JSY AU RC 12.00 30.00

2005 Leaf Limited Bronze Spotlight

*VETS 1-100: .8X TO 2X BASIC CARDS
*RETIRED 101-150: .6X TO 1.5X BASIC CARD
*ROOKIES 151-200: .4X TO 1X BASIC CARD
1-200 STATED PRINT RUN 100
*ROOKIE AU 201-229: .6X TO 1.5X BASIC AU
201-229 AU STATED PRINT RUN 25
151 Aaron Rodgers 75.00 125.00
202 Alex Smith QB JSY AU 50.00 100.00

2005 Leaf Limited Gold Spotlight

*VETS 1-100: 2X TO 5X BASIC CARDS
*RETIRED 101-150: 1.5X TO 4X BASIC CARD
*ROOKIES 151-200: 1X TO 2.5X BASIC CARD
1-200 STATED PRINT RUN 25
UNPRICED 201-229 AU PRINT RUN 10
142 Sonny Jurgensen AU 15.00 40.00
151 Aaron Rodgers 150.00 250.00

2005 Leaf Limited Silver Spotlight

*VETS 1-100: 1.2X TO 3X BASIC CARDS
*RETIRED 101-150: 1X TO 2.5X BASIC CARD
*ROOKIES 151-200: .6X TO 1.5X BASIC CARD
1-200 STATED PRINT RUN 50
*ROOKIES 201-299: .5X TO 1.2X BASIC AU RC
201-299 AU STATED PRINT RUN 15
142 Sonny Jurgensen AU 12.00 30.00
151 Aaron Rodgers 125.00 200.00
202 Alex Smith QB JSY AU 50.00 100.00

2005 Leaf Limited Bound by Round Jerseys

STATED PRINT RUN 75 SER.#'d SETS
*PRIME/25: .8X TO 2X BASIC DUAL/75
BR1 Peyton Manning / Dan Marino 20.00 50.00
BR2 Lawrence Taylor / Jeremy Shockey 8.00 20.00
BR3 Deion Sanders / Roy Williams S 10.00 25.00
BR4 Steve McNair / Byron Leftwich 8.00 20.00
BR5 Joe Namath / Chad Pennington 12.00 30.00
BR6 LaDainian Tomlinson / Shaun Alexander 6.00 15.00
BR7 Daunte Culpepper / Donovan McNabb 6.00 15.00
BR8 Jerry Rice / Torry Holt 12.00 30.00
BR9 Edgerrin James / Jamal Lewis 5.00 12.00
BR10 Gale Sayers / Tony Dorsett 10.00 25.00
BR11 Earl Campbell / Bo Jackson 10.00 25.00
BR12 John Elway / Michael Vick 15.00 40.00
BR13 Jerry Rice / Steve Young 15.00 40.00
BR14 Ray Lewis / Brian Urlacher 6.00 15.00
BR15 Joe Namath / John Riggins 12.00 30.00
BR16 Troy Aikman / David Carr 10.00 25.00
BR17 Peyton Manning / Marvin Harrison 12.00 30.00
BR18 Marcus Allen / Bo Jackson 10.00 25.00
BR19 Jim Brown / Walter Payton 20.00 50.00
BR20 Ozzie Newsome / Paul Warfield 6.00 15.00
BR21 James Lofton / Javon Walker 5.00 12.00
BR22 Jim Kelly / J.P. Losman 10.00 25.00
BR23 Bob Griese / Dan Marino 20.00 50.00
BR24 Steve Young / Donovan McNabb 10.00 25.00
BR25 Barry Sanders / Walter Payton 25.00 60.00
BR26 Michael Irvin / Troy Aikman 10.00 25.00
BR27 Dan Marino / John Elway 20.00 50.00
BR28 Randy Moss / Roy Williams WR 6.00 15.00
BR29 Michael Irvin / Michael Clayton 8.00 20.00
BR30 Jerry Rice / Larry Fitzgerald 12.00 30.00
BR31 Eli Manning / Peyton Manning 12.00 30.00
BR32 Ben Roethlisberger / Terry Bradshaw 20.00 50.00
BR33 Eric Dickerson / Steven Jackson 8.00 20.00
BR34 Barry Sanders / Kevin Jones 12.00 30.00
BR35 Sterling Sharpe / Javon Walker 6.00 15.00
BR36 Bo Jackson / Willis McGahee 10.00 25.00
BR37 Steve Young / Michael Vick 10.00 25.00
BR38 Eli Manning / Ben Roethlisberger 10.00 25.00
BR39 Mike Singletary / Jack Lambert 8.00 20.00
BR40 Clinton Portis / Randall Cunningham 6.00 15.00
BR41 Antwaan Randle El / Chad Johnson 5.00 12.00
BR42 Anquan Boldin / Jake Plummer 5.00 12.00
BR43 Brett Favre / Julius Jones 15.00 40.00
BR44 Joe Montana / Fran Tarkenton 20.00 50.00
BR45 Terrell Owens / Hines Ward 6.00 15.00
BR46 Ray Nitschke / Ahman Green 10.00 25.00
BR47 Domanick Davis / Rudi Johnson 5.00 12.00
BR48 Steve Largent / Aaron Brooks 8.00 20.00
BR49 Tom Brady / Terrell Davis 12.00 30.00
BR50 Matt Hasselbeck / Marc Bulger 5.00 12.00

2005 Leaf Limited Common Threads

STATED PRINT RUN 25 SER.#'d SETS
UNPRICED PRIME PRINT RUN 10 SETS
CT1 Steve Young / Michael Vick 15.00 40.00
CT2 Dan Marino / Peyton Manning 30.00 80.00
CT3 Terry Bradshaw / Ben Roethlisberger 20.00 50.00
CT4 Joe Montana / Tom Brady 30.00 80.00
CT5 Joe Namath / Chad Pennington 20.00 50.00
CT6 Bart Starr / Brett Favre 30.00 80.00
CT7 Daunte Culpepper / Donovan McNabb 10.00 25.00
CT8 Steve McNair / Warren Moon 12.00 30.00
CT9 John Elway / Jake Plummer 25.00 60.00
CT10 Roger Staubach / Troy Aikman 20.00 50.00
CT11 Jim Kelly / J.P. Losman 15.00 40.00
CT12 Joe Montana / Trent Green 30.00 80.00
CT13 Randall Cunningham / Aaron Brooks 10.00 25.00
CT14 Marc Bulger / Matt Hasselbeck 8.00 20.00
CT15 David Carr / Byron Leftwich 8.00 20.00
CT16 Earl Campbell / Domanick Davis 12.00 30.00
CT17 Tony Dorsett / Julius Jones 10.00 25.00
CT18 Marcus Allen / Priest Holmes 12.00 30.00
CT19 Jim Brown / Leroy Kelly 15.00 40.00
CT20 Barry Sanders / Kevin Jones 20.00 50.00
CT21 John Riggins / Clinton Portis 12.00 30.00
CT22 Walter Payton / Gale Sayers 30.00 80.00
CT23 Terrell Davis / Jamal Lewis 12.00 30.00
CT24 Eric Dickerson / Steven Jackson 12.00 30.00
CT25 Bo Jackson / Willis McGahee 15.00 40.00
CT26 LaDainian Tomlinson / Edgerrin James 10.00 25.00
CT27 Shaun Alexander / Ahman Green 8.00 20.00
CT28 Deuce McAllister / Rudi Johnson 8.00 20.00
CT29 Michael Irvin / Keyshawn Johnson 12.00 30.00
CT30 Terrell Owens / Andre Johnson 10.00 25.00
CT31 Marvin Harrison / Reggie Wayne 10.00 25.00
CT32 Randy Moss / Roy Williams WR 10.00 25.00
CT33 Torry Holt / Chad Johnson 8.00 20.00
CT34 Sterling Sharpe / Javon Walker 10.00 25.00
CT35 Jerry Rice / Larry Fitzgerald 20.00 50.00
CT36 Steve Largent / Paul Warfield 12.00 30.00
CT37 Jack Lambert / Brian Urlacher 12.00 30.00
CT38 Mike Singletary / Ray Lewis 12.00 30.00
CT39 Lawrence Taylor / LaVar Arrington 12.00 30.00
CT40 Ozzie Newsome / Jeremy Shockey 12.00 30.00
CT41 Bart Starr / Johnny Unitas 50.00 120.00
CT42 Peyton Manning / Eli Manning 20.00 50.00
CT43 Joe Montana / Steve Young 30.00 80.00
CT44 Terry Bradshaw / Tom Brady 20.00 50.00
CT45 Joe Montana / Troy Aikman 30.00 80.00
CT46 John Elway / Brett Favre 30.00 80.00
CT47 Dan Marino / Jim Kelly 30.00 80.00
CT48 Michael Vick / Donovan McNabb 12.00 30.00
CT49 Jim Brown / Barry Sanders 20.00 50.00
CT50 Walter Payton / Jerry Rice 30.00 80.00

2005 Leaf Limited Contenders Preview Autographs

102 Adam Jones/25 10.00 25.00
103 Adrian McPherson/25 10.00 25.00
104 Alvin Pearman/25 10.00 25.00
109 Antrel Rolle/25 15.00 40.00
110 Brandon Jacobs/25 20.00 50.00
111 Brandon Jones/25 12.00 30.00
119 Charlie Frye/25 15.00 40.00
121 Ciatrick Fason/25 10.00 25.00
122 Courtney Roby/25 12.00 30.00
127 Dan Orlovsky/25 15.00 40.00
129 Darren Sproles/25 15.00 40.00
130 David Greene/25 10.00 25.00
131 David Pollack/25 12.00 30.00
133 DeMarcus Ware/25 30.00 80.00
135 Derrick Johnson/25 12.00 30.00
137 Eric Shelton/25 10.00 25.00
141 Heath Miller/25 20.00 50.00
146 Jerome Mathis/25 15.00 40.00
152 Marion Barber/25 25.00 60.00
153 Mark Bradley/25 10.00 25.00
162 Reggie Brown/25 10.00 25.00
163 Roddy White/25 20.00 50.00
165 Roscoe Parrish/25 10.00 25.00
168 Ryan Moats/25 12.00 30.00
170 Shawne Merriman/25 20.00 50.00
171 Stefan LeFors/25 10.00 25.00
176 Terrence Murphy/25 10.00 25.00
179 Troy Williamson/25 12.00 30.00
180 Vernand Morency/25 12.00 30.00
181 Vincent Jackson/25 20.00 50.00

2005 Leaf Limited Cuts Autographs

LC1 Brett Favre/25 150.00 250.00
LC2 Jim Brown/50 60.00 120.00
LC3 Joe Montana/50 75.00 150.00
LC5 Terry Bradshaw/25 75.00 150.00
LC6 Willis McGahee/100 15.00 40.00

2005 Leaf Limited Hardwear

STATED PRINT RUN 100 SER.#'d SETS
UNPRICED LIMITED SHIELD #'d TO 1
H1 Boomer Esiason 6.00 15.00
H2 Curtis Martin 6.00 15.00
H3 Daunte Culpepper 5.00 12.00
H4 Donovan McNabb 6.00 15.00
H5 Drew Brees 6.00 15.00
H6 Edgerrin James 5.00 12.00
H7 Eric Dickerson 6.00 15.00
H8 Hines Ward 6.00 15.00
H9 Jake Delhomme 5.00 12.00
H10 Jamal Lewis 5.00 12.00
H11 Jerome Bettis 6.00 15.00
H12 Jerry Rice 12.00 30.00
H13 Marcus Allen 8.00 20.00
H14 Marvin Harrison 6.00 15.00
H15 Michael Vick 8.00 20.00
H16 Priest Holmes 5.00 12.00
H17 Randall Cunningham AU 20.00 40.00
H18 Randy Moss 6.00 15.00
H19 Reggie White 15.00 40.00
H20 Steve Young 10.00 25.00
H21 Tom Brady 12.00 30.00
H22 Eli Manning 10.00 25.00
H23 Clinton Portis 5.00 12.00
H24 Brett Favre 15.00 40.00
H25 Thurman Thomas 8.00 20.00

2005 Leaf Limited Hardwear Limited

*UNSIGNED/25: .8X TO 2X BASIC INSERTS
LIMITED PRINT RUN 25 SER.#'d SETS
H1 Boomer Esiason AU 30.00 80.00
H7 Eric Dickerson AU 40.00 100.00
H9 Jake Delhomme AU 25.00 60.00
H12 Jerry Rice AU 100.00 175.00
H17 Randall Cunningham AU 30.00 80.00
H20 Steve Young AU 75.00 135.00
H23 Clinton Portis AU 30.00 80.00

2005 Leaf Limited Legends Jerseys

STATED PRINT RUN 50 SER.#'d SETS
UNPRICED PRIME SER.#'d TO 5
UNPRICED SEASON PRINT RUN 6-20
LL1 Bart Starr 15.00 40.00
LL2 Brett Favre 20.00 50.00
LL3 Dan Marino 20.00 50.00
LL4 Don Meredith AU 50.00 100.00
LL5 Fran Tarkenton AU 25.00 50.00
LL6 Franco Harris AU 30.00 60.00
LL7 Gale Sayers AU 30.00 60.00
LL8 Jerry Rice 15.00 40.00
LL9 Jack Lambert 10.00 25.00
LL10 Jim Brown 12.00 30.00
LL11 Jim Thorpe 100.00 175.00
LL12 Joe Montana 20.00 50.00
LL13 Joe Namath 15.00 40.00
LL14 John Elway 15.00 40.00
LL15 Johnny Unitas 15.00 40.00
LL16 Terry Bradshaw 15.00 40.00
LL17 Doak Walker 10.00 25.00
LL18 Don Shula AU 20.00 50.00
LL19 John Riggins 10.00 25.00
LL20 Steve Largent 10.00 25.00

2005 Leaf Limited Lettermen

UNPRICED LETTERMEN PRINT RUN 4-14

2005 Leaf Limited Material Monikers

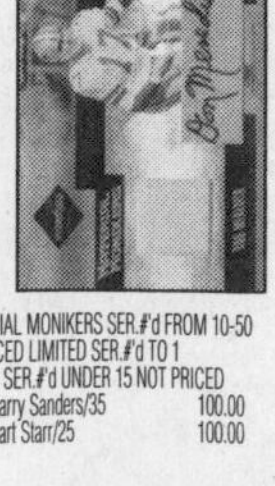

MATERIAL MONIKERS SER.#'d FROM 10-50
UNPRICED LIMITED SER.#'d TO 1
CARDS SER.#'d UNDER 15 NOT PRICED
MM1 Barry Sanders/35 100.00 200.00
MM2 Bart Starr/25 100.00 175.00
MM3 Ben Roethlisberger/35 75.00 150.00
MM4 Bo Jackson/50 40.00 80.00
MM5 Brett Favre/25 125.00 250.00
MM6 Dan Marino/25 100.00 200.00
MM7 Don Meredith/50 50.00 100.00
MM8 Earl Campbell/35 25.00 60.00
MM9 Eli Manning/25 75.00 150.00
MM10 Jack Lambert/50 60.00 100.00
MM11 Jerry Rice/35 100.00 200.00
MM12 Jim Brown/50 60.00 120.00
MM13 Jim Kelly/25 60.00 100.00
MM14 Joe Montana/15 100.00 200.00
MM15 Joe Namath/50 50.00 120.00
MM16 John Elway/50 100.00 200.00
MM17 Julius Jones/25 40.00 80.00
MM18 Marcus Allen/25 40.00 80.00
MM19 Michael Vick/25 40.00 80.00
MM20 Priest Holmes/25 25.00 60.00
MM21 Roger Staubach/15 60.00 120.00
MM22 Steve Young/25 60.00 120.00
MM23 Terry Bradshaw/35 60.00 120.00
MM24 Tom Brady/15 150.00 300.00
MM25 Tony Dorsett/25 40.00 80.00
MM26 Jim Brown / Barry Sanders/15 150.00 250.00
MM27 Bart Starr / Brett Favre/25 175.00 300.00
MM28 Marcus Allen / Bo Jackson/25 100.00 175.00
MM29 Bob Griese / Dan Marino/25 125.00 250.00
MM30 Boomer Esiason / Carson Palmer/17 30.00 80.00
MM31 Dan Marino / Peyton Manning/25 250.00 400.00
MM33 Eric Dickerson / Steven Jackson/50 30.00 80.00
MM34 Jack Lambert / Joe Greene/50 90.00 175.00
MM35 Jim Kelly / J.P. Losman/50 60.00 120.00
MM37 Joe Namath / Chad Pennington/25 60.00 150.00
MM38 John Riggins / Clinton Portis/50 30.00 80.00
MM39 John Elway / Terrell Davis/25 125.00 250.00
MM40 Roger Staubach / Mike Ditka/25 60.00 120.00
MM41 Mike Singletary / Brian Urlacher/50 40.00 80.00
MM42 Joe Montana / Steve Young/25 150.00 300.00
MM43 Terry Bradshaw / Ben Roethlisberger/15 200.00 350.00
MM44 Tony Dorsett / Julius Jones/25 50.00 100.00
MM45 Troy Aikman / Michael Irvin/50 60.00 120.00
MM46 Deion Sanders / Roy Williams S/25 60.00 100.00
MM47 Lawrence Taylor / Eli Manning/40 60.00 120.00
MM48 Jerry Rice / Marvin Harrison/50 150.00 250.00
MM49 Thurman Thomas / Willis McGahee/50 30.00 80.00
MM50 Terrell Davis / Tatum Bell/20 40.00 80.00

2005 Leaf Limited Player Threads

STATED PRINT RUN 50 SER.#'d SETS
*PRIME/25: .6X TO 1.5X BASIC JSY/50
UNPRICED LIMITED PRINT RUN 1
PT1 Ahman Green 8.00 20.00
PT2 Barry Sanders 20.00 50.00
PT3 Brett Favre 25.00 60.00
PT4 Carson Palmer 10.00 25.00
PT5 Clinton Portis 8.00 20.00
PT6 Corey Dillon 8.00 20.00
PT7 Curtis Martin 10.00 25.00
PT8 Dan Marino 30.00 80.00
PT9 Daunte Culpepper 8.00 20.00
PT10 Donovan McNabb 10.00 25.00
PT11 Edgerrin James 8.00 20.00
PT12 Deion Sanders 12.00 30.00
PT13 Jamal Lewis 8.00 20.00
PT14 Joe Montana 30.00 80.00
PT15 Joe Namath 20.00 50.00
PT16 John Elway 25.00 60.00
PT17 Julius Jones 6.00 15.00
PT18 Jerome Bettis 15.00 40.00
PT19 Marcus Allen 12.00 30.00
PT20 Michael Vick 10.00 25.00
PT21 Peyton Manning 20.00 50.00
PT22 Priest Holmes 8.00 20.00
PT23 Terry Bradshaw 20.00 50.00
PT24 Tom Brady 20.00 50.00
PT25 Troy Aikman 15.00 40.00
PT26 Walter Payton 30.00 80.00
PT27 Willis McGahee 10.00 25.00
PT28 Joe Greene 12.00 30.00
PT29 Steven Jackson 10.00 25.00
PT30 Lawrence Taylor 12.00 30.00

2005 Leaf Limited Prime Pairings Autographs

UNPRICED PAIRINGS PRINT RUN 5 SETS

2005 Leaf Limited Team Threads Dual

STATED PRINT RUN 75 SER.#'d SETS
UNPRICED PRIME PRINT RUN 10
TT1 Michael Vick / Warrick Dunn 10.00 25.00
TT2 Jim Kelly / Willis McGahee 12.00 30.00
TT3 Walter Payton / Gale Sayers 25.00 60.00
TT4 Boomer Esiason / Carson Palmer 10.00 25.00
TT5 Jim Brown / Ozzie Newsome 12.00 30.00
TT6 Troy Aikman / Michael Irvin 12.00 30.00
TT7 John Elway / Terrell Davis 20.00 50.00
TT8 Doak Walker / Barry Sanders 15.00 40.00
TT9 Bart Starr / Brett Favre 25.00 60.00
TT10 Earl Campbell / Warren Moon 10.00 25.00
TT11 Johnny Unitas / Peyton Manning 20.00 50.00
TT12 Joe Montana / Marcus Allen 20.00 50.00
TT13 Marcus Allen / Bo Jackson 12.00 30.00
TT14 Eric Dickerson / Steven Jackson 10.00 25.00
TT15 Bob Griese / Dan Marino 25.00 60.00
TT16 Daunte Culpepper / Randy Moss 8.00 20.00
TT17 Tom Brady / Corey Dillon 15.00 40.00
TT18 Lawrence Taylor / Eli Manning 15.00 40.00
TT19 Joe Namath / Chad Pennington 15.00 40.00
TT20 Donovan McNabb / Terrell Owens 8.00 20.00
TT21 Terry Bradshaw / Ben Roethlisberger 15.00 40.00
TT22 Dan Fouts / LaDainian Tomlinson 10.00 25.00
TT23 Joe Montana / Jerry Rice 20.00 50.00
TT24 Steve Largent / Matt Hasselbeck 10.00 25.00
TT25 John Riggins / Clinton Portis 10.00 25.00

2005 Leaf Limited Team Threads Triple

STATED PRINT RUN 50 SER.#'d SETS
UNPRICED PRIME PRINT RUN 5
TT1 Jamal Lewis / Ray Lewis / Kyle Boller 10.00 25.00
TT2 Walter Payton / Gale Sayers / Mike Singletary 25.00 60.00
TT3 Jim Brown / Ozzie Newsome / Paul Warfield 12.00 30.00
TT4 Troy Aikman / Michael Irvin / Tony Dorsett 15.00 40.00
TT5 Doak Walker / Barry Sanders / Kevin Jones 20.00 50.00
TT6 Bart Starr / Brett Favre / Sterling Sharpe 25.00 60.00
TT7 Earl Campbell / Warren Moon / Steve McNair 10.00 25.00
TT8 Johnny Unitas / Peyton Manning / Edgerrin James 25.00 60.00
TT9 Joe Montana / Marcus Allen / Priest Holmes 25.00 60.00
TT10 Marcus Allen / Bo Jackson / Jerry Rice 20.00 50.00
TT11 Eric Dickerson / Steven Jackson / Marc Bulger 10.00 25.00
TT12 Tom Brady / Corey Dillon / Drew Bledsoe 20.00 50.00
TT13 Terry Bradshaw / Ben Roethlisberger / Jack Lambert 25.00 60.00
TT14 Dan Fouts / LaDainian Tomlinson / Drew Brees 10.00 25.00
TT15 Joe Montana / Jerry Rice / Steve Young 25.00 60.00

2005 Leaf Limited Team Threads Quad

STATED PRINT RUN 25 SER.#'d SETS
UNPRICED PRIME PRINT RUN 1 SET
TT1 Michael Vick / Warrick Dunn / Alge Crumpler / T.J. Duckett 20.00 50.00
TT2 Jim Kelly / Willis McGahee / J.P. Losman / Thurman Thomas 25.00 60.00
TT3 Walter Payton / Gale Sayers / Mike Singletary / Brian Urlacher 75.00 125.00
TT4 Troy Aikman / Michael Irvin / Tony Dorsett / Roger Staubach 25.00 60.00
TT5 Doak Walker / Barry Sanders / Kevin Jones / Roy Williams 40.00 100.00
TT6 Johnny Unitas / Payton Manning / Edgerrin James / Marvin Harrison 40.00 100.00
TT7 Daunte Culpepper / Randy Moss / Fran Tarkenton / Michael Bennett 20.00 50.00
TT8 Lawrence Taylor / Tiki Barber / Eli Manning / Jeremy Shockey 25.00 60.00
TT9 Joe Namath / Chad Pennington / Curtis Martin / Laveranues Coles 25.00 60.00
TT10 Terry Bradshaw / Ben Roethlisberger / Jack Lambert / Franco Harris 40.00 100.00

2005 Leaf Limited Team Trademarks Autographs

TT1-TT31 PRINT RUN 50 SER.#'d SETS
TT32-TT46 PRINT RUN 25 SER.#'d SETS
*LIMITED/25: .5X TO 1.2X AUTOS/50
LIMITED SER.#'d TO 10 NOT PRICED
TT1 Barry Sanders 75.00 150.00
TT2 Bo Jackson 40.00 80.00
TT3 Bob Griese 15.00 40.00
TT4 Dan Fouts 15.00 40.00
TT5 Don Maynard 12.00 30.00
TT6 Don Meredith 50.00 100.00
TT7 Don Shula 15.00 40.00
TT8 Earl Campbell 15.00 40.00
TT9 Eric Dickerson 15.00 40.00
TT10 L.C. Greenwood 15.00 40.00
TT11 Franco Harris 25.00 60.00
TT12 Gene Upshaw 15.00 40.00
TT13 Jack Lambert 50.00 100.00
TT14 Jim Brown 50.00 100.00
TT15 Jim Kelly 30.00 80.00
TT16 Joe Montana 75.00 150.00
TT17 Joe Namath 50.00 100.00
TT18 John Riggins 15.00 40.00
TT19 Marcus Allen 15.00 40.00
TT20 Michael Irvin 40.00 80.00
TT21 Mike Ditka 30.00 60.00
TT22 Mike Singletary 15.00 40.00
TT23 Paul Warfield 15.00 40.00
TT24 Richard Dent 12.00 30.00
TT25 Roger Staubach 50.00 100.00
TT26 Sonny Jurgensen 15.00 40.00
TT27 James Lofton 10.00 25.00
TT28 Steve Largent 15.00 40.00
TT29 Steve Young 40.00 80.00
TT30 Tony Dorsett 15.00 40.00
TT31 Warren Moon 15.00 40.00
TT32 Aaron Brooks/25 12.00 30.00
TT33 Ahman Green/25 15.00 40.00
TT34 Ben Roethlisberger/25 75.00 150.00
TT35 Brian Urlacher/25 30.00 80.00
TT37 Chris Brown/25 12.00 30.00
TT38 David Carr/25 12.00 30.00
TT39 Deion Sanders/25 30.00 80.00
TT41 Eli Manning/25 75.00 125.00
TT42 Hines Ward/25 30.00 60.00
TT43 Julius Jones/25 12.00 30.00
TT44 Matt Hasselbeck/25 15.00 40.00
TT45 Michael Clayton/25 12.00 30.00
TT46 Michael Vick/25 50.00 80.00
TT48 Roy Williams S/25 12.00 30.00
TT49 Steven Jackson/25 20.00 50.00

2005 Leaf Limited Threads

STATED PRINT RUN 25-100
LT1 Aaron Brooks/25 6.00 15.00
LT2 Ahman Green 4.00 10.00
LT3 Andre Johnson/25 10.00 25.00
LT4 Barry Sanders 10.00 25.00
LT5 Ben Roethlisberger 8.00 20.00
LT6 Bo Jackson 8.00 20.00
LT7 Bob Griese 6.00 15.00
LT8 Boomer Esiason 5.00 12.00
LT9 Brett Favre 12.00 30.00
LT10 Brian Urlacher 5.00 12.00
LT11 Byron Leftwich 4.00 10.00
LT12 Cadillac Williams 5.00 12.00
LT13 Carson Palmer 5.00 12.00
LT14 Cedric Benson 5.00 12.00
LT15 Chad Johnson 4.00 10.00
LT16 Chad Pennington 5.00 12.00
LT17 Clinton Portis 4.00 10.00
LT18 Corey Dillon 4.00 10.00
LT19 Dan Fouts 6.00 15.00
LT20 Dan Marino Pitt 20.00 50.00
LT21 Dan Marino 12.00 30.00
LT22 Dan Marino 12.00 30.00
LT23 Daunte Culpepper 4.00 10.00
LT24 David Carr 3.00 8.00
LT25 Deuce McAllister 4.00 10.00
LT26 Domanick Davis/25 6.00 15.00
LT27 Don Maynard AU 12.50 30.00
LT28 Donovan McNabb 5.00 12.00
LT29 Earl Campbell 6.00 15.00
LT30 Edgerrin James 4.00 10.00
LT31 Eli Manning 8.00 20.00
LT32 Eric Dickerson Rams 5.00 12.00
LT33 Eric Dickerson Colts 5.00 12.00
LT34 Gale Sayers 8.00 20.00
LT35 Hines Ward 5.00 12.00
LT36 J.P. Losman 3.00 8.00
LT37 Jack Lambert 6.00 15.00
LT38 Jake Delhomme 4.00 10.00
LT39 James Lofton 4.00 10.00
LT40 Jerry Rice 49ers 10.00 25.00
LT41 Jerry Rice Raid. 10.00 25.00
LT42 Jim Kelly 8.00 20.00
LT43 Joe Greene 6.00 15.00
LT44 Joe Montana 49ers 12.00 30.00
LT45 Joe Montana Chiefs 12.00 30.00
LT46 Joe Namath 10.00 25.00
LT47 John Elway 10.00 25.00
LT48 John Elway 10.00 25.00
LT49 John Riggins 6.00 15.00
LT50 Julius Jones 3.00 8.00
LT51 Julius Jones ND 5.00 12.00
LT52 Kevin Jones 3.00 8.00
LT53 Keyshawn Johnson 4.00 10.00
LT54 LaDainian Tomlinson 5.00 12.00
LT55 Larry Fitzgerald 5.00 12.00
LT56 Lawrence Taylor 6.00 15.00
LT57 Lawrence Taylor NC 10.00 25.00
LT58 Marcus Allen Raid. 6.00 15.00
LT59 Marcus Allen Chiefs 6.00 15.00
LT60 Marvin Harrison 5.00 12.00
LT61 Matt Hasselbeck 4.00 10.00
LT62 Michael Clayton 3.00 8.00
LT63 Michael Clayton LSU 3.00 8.00
LT64 Michael Irvin 6.00 15.00
LT65 Michael Vick 6.00 15.00
LT66 Michael Vick VT 6.00 15.00
LT67 Mike Singletary 6.00 15.00
LT68 Mike Singletary Bay. 6.00 15.00
LT69 Ozzie Newsome 5.00 12.00
LT70 Leroy Kelly AU 12.50 30.00
LT71 Peyton Manning 10.00 25.00
LT72 Priest Holmes 4.00 10.00
LT73 Randy Moss 5.00 12.00
LT74 Reggie Wayne AU/25 20.00 40.00
LT75 Roger Staubach 10.00 25.00
LT76 Roy Williams S 3.00 8.00
LT77 Roy Williams S Okl 6.00 15.00

LT78 Roy Williams WR	4.00	10.00
LT79 Rudi Johnson	4.00	10.00
LT80 Sonny Jurgensen AU/100	12.50	30.00
LT81 Sterling Sharpe	5.00	12.00
LT82 Steve Largent	6.00	15.00
LT83 Steve Young	8.00	20.00
LT84 Steven Jackson	5.00	12.00
LT85 Steven Jackson Ore.St.	5.00	12.00
LT86 Tatum Bell	3.00	8.00
LT87 Terrell Davis	6.00	15.00
LT88 Terrell Owens	5.00	12.00
LT89 Terry Bradshaw SB	10.00	25.00
LT90 Terry Bradshaw PB	10.00	25.00
LT91 Tiki Barber AU/25	25.00	50.00
LT92 Tom Brady	10.00	25.00
LT93 Tom Brady PB	10.00	25.00
LT94 Tony Dorsett	5.00	12.00
LT95 Tony Dorsett Pitt	5.00	12.00
LT96 Trent Green AU/25	15.00	40.00
LT97 Troy Aikman	8.00	20.00
LT98 Walter Payton	15.00	40.00
LT99 Warren Moon	6.00	15.00
LT100 Willis McGahee	5.00	12.00

2005 Leaf Limited Threads At the Half

*UNSIGNED/50: .5X TO 1.2X THREADS/75
*UNSIGNED/25: .6X TO 1.5X THREADS/75
STATED PRINT RUN 25-50

LT2 Ahman Green AU/25	20.00	50.00
LT7 Bob Griese AU/50	15.00	40.00
LT8 Boomer Esiason AU/50	15.00	40.00
LT11 Byron Leftwich AU/25	20.00	50.00
LT15 Chad Johnson AU/25	20.00	50.00
LT18 Corey Dillon AU/25	15.00	40.00
LT19 Dan Fouts AU/50	20.00	50.00
LT27 Don Maynard	6.00	15.00
LT53 Keyshawn Johnson AU/25	15.00	40.00
LT61 Matt Hasselbeck AU/25	20.00	50.00
LT69 Ozzie Newsome AU/50	12.00	30.00
LT70 Leroy Kelly AU/50	12.00	30.00
LT74 Reggie Wayne AU/25	20.00	50.00
LT78 Roy Williams WR AU/25	15.00	40.00
LT80 Sonny Jurgensen AU/50	20.00	50.00
LT81 Sterling Sharpe AU/50	15.00	40.00
LT91 Tiki Barber AU/25	20.00	50.00
LT96 Trent Green AU/25	15.00	40.00

2005 Leaf Limited Threads Jersey Numbers

*UNSIGNED/80-88: .4X TO 1X BASE THREADS
*UNSIGNED/32-56: .5X TO 1.2X BASE THREAD
*UNSIGNED/18-29: .6X TO 1.5X
CARDS SER.#'d UNDER 25 NOT PRICED

LT2 Ahman Green AU/30	20.00	50.00
LT6 Bo Jackson AU/34	30.00	80.00
LT10 Brian Urlacher AU/54	60.00	100.00
LT12 Cadillac Williams AU/24	60.00	120.00
LT14 Cedric Benson AU/32	25.00	60.00
LT15 Chad Johnson AU/85	20.00	50.00
LT17 Clinton Portis AU/28	20.00	50.00
LT25 Deuce McAllister AU/26	20.00	50.00
LT29 Earl Campbell AU/34	25.00	60.00
LT34 Gale Sayers AU/40	60.00	120.00
LT35 Hines Ward AU/86	50.00	80.00
L137 Jack Lambert AU/58	60.00	120.00
LT39 James Lofton AU/80	15.00	40.00
LT43 Joe Greene AU/75	30.00	80.00
LT49 John Riggins AU/44	25.00	60.00
LT57 Lawrence Taylor NC AU/98	60.00	120.00
LT58 Marcus Allen Raid.AU/32	40.00	80.00
LT59 Marcus Allen Chiefs AU/32	25.00	60.00
LT62 Michael Clayton AU/80	15.00	40.00
LT67 Mike Singletary AU/50	15.00	40.00
LT68 Mike Singletary Bay.AU/63	15.00	40.00
LT69 Ozzie Newsome AU/82	15.00	30.00
LT70 Leroy Kelly AU/44	15.00	40.00
LT72 Priest Holmes AU/31	30.00	80.00
LT74 Reggie Wayne AU/87	20.00	50.00
LT76 Roy Williams S AU/31	30.00	80.00
LT77 Roy Williams S Okl.AU/38	60.00	100.00
LT79 Rudi Johnson AU/32	20.00	50.00
LT81 Sterling Sharpe AU/84	15.00	40.00
LT84 Steven Jackson AU/39	25.00	60.00
LT85 Steven Jackson Ore.St.AU/34	20.00	50.00
LT86 Tatum Bell AU/26	15.00	40.00
LT87 Terrell Davis AU/30	25.00	60.00
LT95 Tony Dorsett Pitt AU/33	30.00	80.00

2005 Leaf Limited Threads Prime

*PRIME/25: .8X TO 2X BASIC THREAD/75
STATED PRINT RUN 10-25
PRIME SER.#'d UNDER 25 NOT PRICED

LT6 Bo Jackson AU/25	60.00	120.00
LT7 Bob Griese AU/25	25.00	60.00
LT19 Dan Fouts AU/25	25.00	60.00
LT27 Don Maynard AU/25	15.00	40.00
LT29 Earl Campbell AU/25	25.00	60.00
LT34 Gale Sayers AU/25	50.00	100.00
LT37 Jack Lambert AU/25	90.00	150.00
LT39 James Lofton AU/25	20.00	50.00
LT42 Jim Kelly AU/25	40.00	100.00
LT46 Joe Namath AU/25	50.00	120.00
LT57 Lawrence Taylor NC AU/25	100.00	175.00
LT69 Ozzie Newsome AU/25	15.00	40.00
LT70 Leroy Kelly AU/25	15.00	40.00
LT80 Sonny Jurgensen AU/25	25.00	60.00
LT81 Sterling Sharpe AU/25	20.00	50.00
LT82 Steve Largent AU/25	20.00	50.00
LT83 Steve Young AU/25	40.00	100.00
LT87 Terrell Davis AU/25	25.00	60.00
LT99 Warren Moon AU/25	20.00	50.00

2006 Leaf Limited

This 306 card set was released in November, 2006. The set was issued into the hobby in four-card packs with an $70 SRP. Cards numbered 1-150, which include a retired greats subset from cards 118-150, were issued to a stated print run of 799 serial numbered sets. Cards numbered 151-305 feature 2006 rookies and they are broken down into the following subsets: Cards numbered 151-250 were issued to a stated print run of 299 serial numbered sets while cards numbered 251-295 were signed by the player and those cards were issued to a stated print run of 100 serial numbered sets and the set concludes with multi-player signed cards, some of which have player-worn jersey swatches as well. Those cards between 296 and 305 were issed to stated print runs between 25 and 100 serial numbered sets.

1-150 PRINT RUN 799 SER.#'d SETS
151-250 RC PRINT RUN 299 SER.#'d SETS
AU RC PRINT RUN 100 SETS
296-305 JSY AU PRINT RUN 25-100

1 Alex Smith QB	1.50	4.00
2 Antonio Bryant	1.00	2.50
3 Frank Gore	1.50	4.00
4 Rex Grossman	1.25	3.00
5 Thomas Jones	1.25	3.00
6 Cedric Benson	1.25	3.00
7 Carson Palmer	1.50	4.00
8 Chad Johnson	1.25	3.00
9 Rudi Johnson	1.25	3.00
10 T.J. Houshmandzadeh	1.25	3.00
11 J.P. Losman	1.25	3.00
12 Lee Evans	1.25	3.00
13 Willis McGahee	1.25	3.00
14 Jake Plummer	1.25	3.00
15 Javon Walker	1.25	3.00
16 Rod Smith	1.25	3.00
17 Tatum Bell	1.00	2.50
18 Braylon Edwards	1.25	3.00
19 Charlie Frye	1.25	3.00
20 Reuben Droughns	1.25	3.00
21 Cadillac Williams	1.25	3.00
22 Chris Simms	1.25	3.00
23 Joey Galloway	1.25	3.00
24 Anquan Boldin	1.25	3.00
25 Edgerrin James	1.25	3.00
26 Kurt Warner	1.50	4.00
27 Larry Fitzgerald	1.50	4.00
28 Antonio Gates	1.50	4.00
29 Keenan McCardell	1.25	3.00
30 LaDainian Tomlinson	1.50	4.00
31 Philip Rivers	1.50	4.00
32 Eddie Kennison	1.00	2.50
33 Larry Johnson	1.25	3.00
34 Priest Holmes	1.25	3.00
35 Trent Green	1.25	3.00
36 Tony Gonzalez	1.25	3.00
37 Dallas Clark	1.25	3.00
38 Marvin Harrison	1.50	4.00
39 Peyton Manning	2.50	6.00
40 Reggie Wayne	1.25	3.00
41 Drew Bledsoe	1.50	4.00
42 Julius Jones	1.00	2.50
43 Roy Williams S	1.25	3.00
44 Terrell Owens	1.50	4.00
45 Terry Glenn	1.25	3.00
46 Chris Chambers	1.25	3.00
47 Daunte Culpepper	1.25	3.00
48 Marty Booker	1.00	2.50
49 Ronnie Brown	1.50	4.00
50 Brian Westbrook	1.25	3.00
51 Donovan McNabb	1.50	4.00
52 Jevon Kearse	1.25	3.00
53 Reggie Brown	1.00	2.50
54 Alge Crumpler	1.25	3.00
55 Michael Vick	1.50	4.00
56 Warrick Dunn	1.25	3.00
57 Eli Manning	2.00	5.00
58 Jeremy Shockey	1.50	4.00
59 Plaxico Burress	1.25	3.00
60 Tiki Barber	1.50	4.00
61 Byron Leftwich	1.25	3.00
62 Fred Taylor	1.25	3.00
63 Jimmy Smith	1.25	3.00
64 Matt Jones	1.00	2.50
65 Josh McCown	1.00	2.50
66 Roy Williams WR	1.25	3.00
67 Kevin Jones	1.00	2.50
68 Aaron Rodgers	3.00	8.00
69 Brett Favre	3.00	8.00
70 Robert Ferguson	1.00	2.50
71 Samkon Gado	1.25	3.00
72 Ahman Green	1.25	3.00
73 DeShaun Foster	1.25	3.00
74 Jake Delhomme	1.25	3.00
75 Keary Colbert	1.00	2.50
76 Steve Smith	1.50	4.00
77 Corey Dillon	1.25	3.00
78 Deion Branch	1.25	3.00
79 Tedy Bruschi	1.50	4.00
80 Tom Brady	2.50	6.00
81 Jerry Porter	1.00	2.50
82 Randy Moss	1.50	4.00
83 LaMont Jordan	1.25	3.00
84 Isaac Bruce	1.25	3.00
85 Marc Bulger	1.25	3.00
86 Steven Jackson	1.50	4.00
87 Torry Holt	1.25	3.00
88 Derrick Mason	1.25	3.00
89 Mark Clayton	1.25	3.00
90 Steve McNair	1.25	3.00
91 Jamal Lewis	1.25	3.00
92 Antwaan Randle El	1.25	3.00
93 Clinton Portis	1.50	4.00
94 Santana Moss	1.25	3.00
95 Chad Pennington	1.25	3.00
96 Laveranues Coles	1.00	2.50
97 Curtis Martin	1.50	4.00
98 Mewelde Moore	1.00	2.50
99 Troy Williamson	1.00	2.50
100 Brad Johnson	1.25	3.00
101 Darrell Jackson	1.25	3.00
102 Matt Hasselbeck	1.25	3.00
103 Nate Burleson	1.00	2.50
104 Shaun Alexander	1.25	3.00
105 Ben Roethlisberger	2.00	5.00
106 Hines Ward	1.50	4.00
107 Willie Parker	1.25	3.00
108 Donte Stallworth	1.00	2.50
109 Drew Brees	1.50	4.00
110 Deuce McAllister	1.25	3.00
111 Andre Johnson	1.50	4.00
112 David Carr	1.00	2.50
113 Domanick Davis	1.00	2.50
114 Eric Moulds	1.00	2.50
115 David Givens	1.25	3.00
116 Drew Bennett	1.25	3.00
117 Chris Brown	1.00	2.50
118 Bob Griese	2.00	5.00
119 Daryle Lamonica	1.25	3.00
120 Dave Casper	1.25	3.00
121 Don Meredith	2.00	5.00
122 Herschel Walker	1.50	4.00
123 Jack Lambert	2.00	5.00
124 Jackie Smith	1.25	3.00
125 Jim Otto	1.25	3.00
126 John Riggins	2.00	5.00
127 John Stallworth	1.50	4.00
128 Lawrence Taylor	2.00	5.00
129 Lester Hayes	1.25	3.00
130 L.C. Greenwood	1.50	4.00
131 Paul Warfield	1.50	4.00
132 Barry Sanders	3.00	8.00
133 Bart Starr	3.00	8.00
134 Billy Sims	1.50	4.00
135 Bulldog Turner	1.50	4.00
136 Deion Sanders	2.50	6.00
137 Dutch Clark	1.50	4.00
138 Forrest Gregg	1.25	3.00
139 Gale Sayers	2.50	6.00
140 Jim Brown	2.50	6.00
141 Jim Thorpe	2.50	6.00
142 Joe Montana	4.00	10.00
143 John Elway	3.00	8.00
144 Johnny Unitas	3.00	8.00
145 Lance Alworth	1.50	4.00
146 Raymond Berry	1.50	4.00
147 Doak Walker	2.00	5.00
148 Red Grange	2.50	6.00
149 Walter Payton	4.00	10.00
150 Yale Lary	1.25	3.00
151 Adam Jennings RC	2.50	6.00
152 Alan Zemaitis RC	3.00	8.00
153 Patrick Cobbs RC	2.50	6.00
154 Anthony Schlegel RC	2.50	6.00
155 Anthony Smith RC	3.00	8.00
156 Antonio Cromartie RC	3.00	8.00
157 Ashton Youboty RC	2.00	5.00
158 Bennie Brazell RC	2.50	6.00
159 Bernard Pollard RC	2.50	6.00
160 Brodrick Bunkley RC	2.50	6.00
161 Calvin Lowry RC	3.00	8.00
162 Cedric Griffin RC	2.50	6.00
163 Cedric Humes RC	2.00	5.00
164 Charles Davis RC	2.50	6.00
165 Chris Gocong RC	2.50	6.00
166 Claude Wroten RC	2.00	5.00
167 Clint Ingram RC	3.00	8.00
168 D.J. Shockley RC	2.50	6.00
169 Danieal Manning RC	3.00	8.00
170 Daniel Bullocks RC	3.00	8.00
171 Darnell Bing RC	2.50	6.00
172 Chris Hannon RC	2.50	6.00
173 Darryl Tapp RC	2.50	6.00
174 David Anderson RC	2.50	6.00
175 David Kirtman RC	2.50	6.00
176 David Pittman RC	2.50	6.00
177 Davin Joseph RC	2.50	6.00
178 Sam Hurd RC	2.00	5.00
179 Delanie Walker RC	3.00	8.00
180 DeMeco Ryans RC	3.00	8.00
181 Derrick Ross RC	2.50	6.00
182 Devin Hester RC	6.00	15.00
183 Domenik Hixon RC	3.00	8.00
184 Dominique Byrd RC	2.50	6.00
185 Donte Whitner RC	3.00	8.00
186 D'Qwell Jackson RC	2.50	6.00
187 Dusty Dvoracek RC	3.00	8.00
188 Eric Smith RC	2.50	6.00
189 Fred Evans RC	2.50	6.00
190 Ernie Sims RC	2.50	6.00
191 Ethan Kilmer RC	2.50	6.00
192 Freddie Keiaho RC	2.50	6.00
193 Frostee Rucker RC	2.50	6.00
194 Gabe Watson RC	2.00	5.00
195 Garrett Mills RC	3.00	8.00
196 Dawan Landry RC	3.00	8.00
197 Gerris Wilkinson RC	2.00	5.00
198 Jarrad Page RC	3.00	8.00
199 Haloti Ngata RC	3.00	8.00
200 Hank Baskett RC	3.00	8.00
201 Jai Lewis RC	2.50	6.00
202 Jamar Williams RC	2.50	6.00
203 James Anderson RC	2.00	5.00
204 Jason Allen RC	2.50	6.00
205 Jason Hatcher RC	2.50	6.00
206 Chris Barclay RC	2.50	6.00
207 J.D. Runnels RC	2.50	6.00
208 Jeff King RC	2.50	6.00
209 Jeffrey Webb RC	2.50	6.00
210 Jerome Harrison RC	3.00	8.00
211 Jimmy Williams RC	3.00	8.00
212 John David Washington RC	2.50	6.00
213 Jon Alston RC	2.00	5.00
214 Johnathon Joseph RC	2.50	6.00
215 Kamerion Wimbley RC	3.00	8.00
216 Kelly Jennings RC	2.50	6.00
217 Charles Sharon RC	2.50	6.00
218 Ko Simpson RC	2.50	6.00
219 Lawrence Vickers RC	2.50	6.00
220 Leon Williams RC	2.50	6.00
221 Leonard Pope RC	3.00	8.00
222 Marques Colston RC	10.00	25.00
223 Martin Nance RC	2.50	6.00
224 Mathias Kiwanuka RC	3.00	8.00
225 Mike Bell RC	3.00	8.00
226 Mike Hass RC	2.50	6.00
227 Miles Austin RC	6.00	15.00
228 Nate Salley RC	2.50	6.00
229 Nick Mangold RC	2.50	6.00
230 Owen Daniels RC	3.00	8.00
231 Shaun Bodiford RC	2.50	6.00
232 Quinn Sypniewski RC	2.50	6.00
233 Quinton Ganther RC	2.00	5.00
234 Richard Marshall RC	2.00	5.00
235 Rocky McIntosh RC	2.50	6.00
236 Roman Harper RC	2.50	6.00
237 Stephen Tulloch RC	2.50	6.00
238 Brett Basanez RC	3.00	8.00
239 Tamba Hali RC	3.00	8.00
240 Brett Elliott RC	3.00	8.00
241 Thomas Howard RC	2.50	6.00
242 Tim Jennings RC	2.50	6.00
243 Jason Carter RC	2.50	6.00
244 Todd Watkins RC	2.00	5.00
245 Tony Scheffler RC	3.00	8.00
246 Tye Hill RC	2.00	5.00
247 Victor Adeyanju RC	2.50	6.00
248 Wendell Mathis RC	2.50	6.00
249 Will Blackmon RC	2.50	6.00
250 Willie Reid RC	2.50	6.00
251 Mario Williams JSY AU RC	8.00	20.00
252 Reggie Bush JSY AU RC	30.00	80.00
253 Vince Young JSY AU RC	10.00	25.00
254 A.J. Hawk JSY AU RC	8.00	20.00
255 Vernon Davis JSY AU RC	10.00	25.00
256 Michael Huff JSY AU RC	6.00	15.00
257 Matt Leinart JSY AU RC	8.00	20.00
258 Jay Cutler AU RC	40.00	100.00
259 Laurence Maroney JSY AU RC	6.00	15.00
260 Santonio Holmes JSY AU RC	10.00	25.00
261 DeAngelo Williams JSY AU RC	10.00	25.00
262 Marcedes Lewis JSY AU RC	8.00	20.00
263 Joseph Addai AU RC	8.00	20.00
264 Chad Jackson JSY AU RC	5.00	12.00
265 Sinorice Moss JSY AU RC	8.00	20.00
266 LenDale White JSY AU RC	6.00	15.00
267 Kellen Clemens JSY AU RC	6.00	15.00
268 Greg Jennings AU RC	20.00	40.00
269 Joe Klopfenstein JSY AU RC	5.00	12.00
270 Maurice Drew JSY AU RC	12.00	30.00
271 Tarvaris Jackson JSY AU RC	8.00	20.00
272 Brian Calhoun JSY AU RC	5.00	12.00
273 Travis Wilson JSY AU RC	5.00	12.00
274 Jerious Norwood JSY AU RC	6.00	15.00
275 Charlie Whitehurst JSY AU RC	8.00	20.00
276 Derek Hagan JSY AU RC	6.00	15.00
277 Brandon Williams JSY AU RC	5.00	12.00
278 Brodie Croyle AU RC	8.00	20.00
279 Maurice Stovall JSY AU RC	5.00	12.00
280 Michael Robinson JSY AU RC	6.00	15.00
281 Jason Avant JSY AU RC	5.00	12.00
282 Demetrius Williams JSY AU RC	6.00	15.00
283 Leon Washington JSY AU RC	6.00	15.00
284 Brandon Marshall JSY AU RC	8.00	20.00
285 Omar Jacobs JSY AU RC	5.00	12.00
286 Anthony Fasano AU RC	8.00	20.00
287 Ingle Martin AU RC	6.00	15.00
288 Reggie McNeal AU RC	6.00	15.00
289 Brad Smith AU RC	8.00	20.00
290 Jeremy Bloom AU RC	6.00	15.00
291 Bruce Gradkowski AU RC	8.00	20.00
292 P.J. Daniels AU RC	5.00	12.00
293 Cory Rodgers AU RC	6.00	15.00
294 Skyler Green AU RC	5.00	12.00
295 Bobby Carpenter AU RC	5.00	12.00
296 Devin Aromashodu AU/100	10.00	25.00
Ben Obomanu		
Anthony Mix		
297 Abdul Hodge AU/100	10.00	25.00
Chad Greenway		
298 Mario Williams AU/100	20.00	40.00
John McCargo		
Manny Lawson		
299 Anthony Fasano AU/50	20.00	40.00
Maurice Stovall		
300 A.J. Hawk AU/50	20.00	50.00
Bobby Carpenter		
301 Matt Leinart AU/25	100.00	200.00
Reggie Bush		
LenDale White		
302 Vince Young AU/50	30.00	80.00
David Thomas		
303 Drew Olson AU/100	25.00	50.00
Maurice Drew		
Marcedes Lewis		
304 Marques Hagans AU/100	10.00	25.00
Wali Lundy		
D'Brickashaw Ferguson		
305 Brian Calhoun AU/100	10.00	25.00
Brandon Williams		
Jonathan Orr		
TC Steve Smith TC/500	2.50	6.00
TCA Steve Smith TC AU/50	20.00	40.00

2006 Leaf Limited Bronze Spotlight

*VETS/50 1-117: .8X TO 2X BASIC CARDS
*RETIRED/50 118-150: .6X TO 1.5X
*ROOKIE/50 151-250: .6X TO 1.5X
STATED PRINT RUN 50 SER.#'d SETS

2006 Leaf Limited Gold Spotlight

UNPRICED GOLD SPOTLIGHT PRINT RUN 5-10

2006 Leaf Limited Platinum Spotlight

UNPRICED PLATINUM PRINT RUN 1

2006 Leaf Limited Silver Spotlight

*VETS/25 1-117: 1.2X TO 3X BASIC CARDS
*RETIRED/25 118-150: 1X TO 2.5X
*ROOKIE/25 151-250: 1X TO 2.5X
*ROOKIE AU/25 251-295: .6X TO 1.2X
*COMBO AU/25 296-305: .6X TO 1.2X
SILVER PRINT RUN 10-25
SERIAL #'d TO 10 NOT PRICED

2006 Leaf Limited College Phenoms Autographs

*ROOKIES: .4X TO 1X BASIC CARDS
STATED PRINT RUN 50 SER.#'d SETS
UNPRICED GOLD PRINT RUN 10
UNPRICED PLATINUM PRINT RUN 1
*SILVER/25: .5X TO 1.2X BASIC CARDS

2006 Leaf Limited Contenders Preview Autographs

STATED PRINT RUN 50-100

1 Brodie Croyle/100	8.00	20.00
2 Santonio Holmes/100	25.00	50.00
3 Tim Jennings/100	6.00	15.00
4 Travis Wilson/100	5.00	12.00
5 Leon Washington/100	6.00	15.00
6 Brad Smith/100	8.00	20.00
7 Jerome Harrison/100	8.00	20.00
8 Joe Klopfenstein/100	5.00	12.00
9 Matt Leinart/50	15.00	40.00
10 Chad Greenway/100	8.00	20.00
11 Dominique Byrd/100	6.00	15.00
12 A.J. Hawk/50	12.00	30.00
13 Greg Jennings/100	20.00	40.00
14 Johnathan Joseph /100	6.00	15.00
15 Mike Bell/50	12.00	30.00
16 Willie Reid/100	6.00	15.00
17 Haloti Ngata/100	8.00	20.00
18 Marques Hagans/100	5.00	12.00
19 Will Blackmon/100	6.00	15.00
20 Reggie Bush/50	40.00	100.00
21 Domenik Hixon/100	8.00	20.00
22 Leonard Pope /100	8.00	20.00
23 John McCargo/100	5.00	12.00
24 Daniel Bullocks/100	8.00	20.00
25 Rocky McIntosh/100	6.00	15.00
26 Jason Allen/100	6.00	15.00
27 Jay Cutler/50	60.00	120.00
28 Richard Marshall/100	6.00	15.00
29 LenDale White/50	10.00	25.00
30 Roman Harper/100	6.00	15.00
31 Vernon Davis/50	15.00	40.00
32 Danieal Manning/100	8.00	20.00
33 Cory Rodgers/100	6.00	15.00
34 David Thomas/100	6.00	15.00
35 Derek Hagan/100	6.00	15.00
36 Jerious Norwood/100	6.00	15.00
37 Vince Young/50	25.00	60.00
38 Joseph Addai/100	8.00	20.00
39 Skyler Green/100	5.00	12.00
40 Omar Jacobs/100	5.00	12.00

2006 Leaf Limited Cuts Autographs

STATED PRINT RUN 30 SER.#'d SETS

1 A.J. Hawk	25.00	60.00
2 Brandon Marshall	20.00	50.00
3 Brandon Williams	12.00	30.00
4 Brian Calhoun	12.00	30.00
5 Chad Jackson	12.00	30.00
6 Charlie Whitehurst	20.00	50.00
7 DeAngelo Williams	25.00	60.00
8 Demetrius Williams	15.00	40.00
9 Derek Hagan	15.00	40.00
10 Jason Avant	12.00	30.00
11 Jerious Norwood	15.00	40.00
12 Joe Klopfenstein	12.00	30.00
13 Kellen Clemens	15.00	40.00
14 Laurence Maroney	15.00	40.00
15 LenDale White	15.00	40.00
16 Leon Washington	15.00	40.00
17 Marcedes Lewis	20.00	50.00
18 Mario Williams	25.00	60.00
19 Matt Leinart	20.00	50.00
20 Maurice Drew	25.00	60.00
21 Maurice Stovall	12.00	30.00
22 Michael Huff	15.00	40.00
23 Michael Robinson	15.00	40.00
24 Omar Jacobs	12.00	30.00
25 Reggie Bush	60.00	150.00
26 Santonio Holmes	30.00	80.00
27 Sinorice Moss	20.00	50.00
28 Tarvaris Jackson	20.00	50.00
29 Travis Wilson	12.00	30.00
30 Vernon Davis	25.00	60.00
31 Vince Young	20.00	60.00
32 Greg Jennings	30.00	60.00
33 Brodie Croyle	20.00	50.00
34 Joseph Addai	20.00	50.00
35 Jay Cutler	50.00	120.00

2006 Leaf Limited Hardwear

HARDWEAR PRINT RUN 24-100
*LTD/27-39: .6X TO 1.5X HARDWEAR/100
*LTD/27-39: .5X TO 1.2X HARDWEAR/49
LIMITED PRINT RUN 2-39

1 Brian Urlacher/58	8.00	20.00
2 Carson Palmer/24	8.00	20.00
3 Curtis Martin	6.00	15.00
4 Derrick Thomas	15.00	30.00
5 Priest Holmes/28	6.00	15.00
6 Eric Dickerson	5.00	12.00
7 Herman Edwards	5.00	12.00
8 Jerry Rice/49	12.00	30.00
9 Jim Kelly	8.00	20.00
10 John Elway	10.00	25.00
11 Marcus Allen	6.00	15.00
12 Marshall Faulk	5.00	12.00
13 Marvin Harrison	6.00	15.00
14 Michael Vick	6.00	15.00
15 Mike Singletary/86	6.00	15.00
16 Steve Young	8.00	20.00
17 Terrell Davis	6.00	15.00
18 Thurman Thomas	5.00	12.00
19 Reggie White	8.00	20.00
20 Willis McGahee	6.00	15.00

2006 Leaf Limited Legends

STATED PRINT RUN 100 SER.#'d SETS
*HOLOFOIL/50: .5X TO 1.2X BASIC INSERTS
HOLOFOIL PRINT RUN 50 SER.#'d SETS

1 Bart Starr	4.00	10.00
2 Bobby Layne	2.50	6.00
3 Gale Sayers	3.00	8.00
4 Doak Walker	2.50	6.00
5 Red Grange	3.00	8.00
6 Johnny Unitas	4.00	10.00
7 Y.A. Tittle	2.50	6.00
8 Yale Lary	1.50	4.00
9 Walter Payton	5.00	12.00
10 Jim Thorpe	3.00	8.00
11 Jim Brown	3.00	8.00
12 Bulldog Turner	2.00	5.00
13 Lance Alworth	2.00	5.00
14 Sonny Jurgensen	2.00	5.00
15 Ray Nitschke	2.50	6.00
16 Bob Lilly	2.00	5.00
17 Dutch Clark	2.00	5.00
18 Lee Roy Selmon	2.00	5.00
19 Craig Morton	1.50	4.00
20 Forrest Gregg	1.50	4.00

2006 Leaf Limited Legends Materials

STATED PRINT RUN 5-100
*PRIME/25: .6X TO 1.5X BASIC JSYs
PRIME PRINT RUN 2-25
SERIAL #'d UNDER 25 NOT PRICED

1 Bart Starr	12.00	30.00
2 Bobby Layne	8.00	20.00
3 Gale Sayers	8.00	20.00
4 Doak Walker	8.00	20.00
5 Red Grange Hel/75	60.00	120.00
6 Johnny Unitas	12.00	30.00
7 Y.A. Tittle	8.00	20.00
8 Yale Lary	6.00	15.00
9 Walter Payton	12.00	30.00
10 Jim Thorpe	75.00	150.00
11 Jim Brown	10.00	25.00
12 Bulldog Turner	8.00	20.00
13 Lance Alworth/55	10.00	25.00
14 Sonny Jurgensen	6.00	15.00
15 Ray Nitschke	12.00	30.00
16 Bob Lilly	6.00	15.00
18 Lee Roy Selmon	6.00	15.00
19 Craig Morton	6.00	15.00
20 Forrest Gregg	8.00	20.00

2006 Leaf Limited Legends Signature Materials

STATED PRINT RUN 25-100 SER.#'d SETS
*PRIME/25: .6X TO 1.5X BASIC JSY AUTOs
PRIME PRINT RUN 5-25 SER.#'d SETS

1 Bart Starr/50	75.00	135.00
3 Gale Sayers/25	30.00	60.00
7 Y.A. Tittle/100	30.00	60.00
8 Yale Lary/100	12.00	30.00
11 Jim Brown/25	50.00	100.00
13 Lance Alworth/25	40.00	80.00
14 Sonny Jurgensen/100	12.00	30.00
16 Bob Lilly/100	12.00	30.00
18 Lee Roy Selmon/100	15.00	40.00
19 Craig Morton/50	12.00	30.00
20 Forrest Gregg/50	30.00	60.00

2006 Leaf Limited Lettermen

UNPRICED LETTERMEN PRINT RUN 4-12

2006 Leaf Limited Matching Numbers Jerseys

STATED PRINT RUN 100 SER.#'d SETS
*PRIME/25: .6X TO 1.5X BASIC JSYs
PRIME PRINT RUN 10-25
*POSITION/100: .4X TO 1X NUMBER JSYs
*POSIT.PRIME/25: .6X TO 1.5X BASIC JSYs

1 Jim Kelly	12.00	30.00
Tom Brady		
2 Billy Sims	12.00	30.00
Barry Sanders		
3 Roger Staubach	12.00	30.00
Terry Bradshaw		
4 Jim Brown	10.00	25.00
Marcus Allen		
5 Steve Largent	12.00	30.00
Jerry Rice		
6 Raymond Berry/50	6.00	15.00
Ozzie Newsome		
7 Len Dawson	15.00	40.00
Joe Montana		
8 Don Maynard	15.00	40.00
Dan Marino		
9 Forrest Gregg/30	20.00	50.00
Joe Greene		
10 Earl Campbell	15.00	40.00
Walter Payton		
11 Johnny Unitas	15.00	40.00
Lance Alworth		
12 Zach Thomas	8.00	20.00
Brian Urlacher		
13 LaDainian Tomlinson	8.00	20.00
Julius Jones		
14 Peyton Manning	10.00	25.00
Randy Moss		
15 Tiki Barber	6.00	15.00
Willis McGahee		
16 Chad Johnson	6.00	15.00
Antonio Gates		
17 Steve Smith	8.00	20.00
Santana Moss		
18 Larry Fitzgerald	6.00	15.00
Roy Williams WR		
19 Shaun Alexander	8.00	20.00
Domanick Davis		
20 Torry Holt	5.00	12.00
Anquan Boldin		

2006 Leaf Limited Material Monikers Jersey Number

STATED PRINT RUN 1-89
SERIAL #'d UNDER 20 NOT PRICED

6 Chad Johnson/85	15.00	30.00
7 Chris Chambers/84	10.00	25.00
8 Darrell Jackson/82		
9 Domanick Davis/37	10.00	25.00
12 Clinton Portis/26	20.00	40.00
14 Jerry Porter/84	10.00	25.00
15 Julius Jones/21	15.00	30.00
16 Kevin Jones/34	20.00	40.00
17 LaDainian Tomlinson/21	40.00	80.00
18 Larry Johnson/27	20.00	50.00
21 Mark Clayton/89	10.00	25.00
23 Marvin Harrison/88	25.00	50.00
28 Priest Holmes/31	15.00	30.00
30 Reggie Wayne/87	15.00	30.00
31 Ronnie Brown/23	20.00	40.00
33 Rudi Johnson/32	15.00	30.00
34 Samkon Gado/35	10.00	25.00
35 Santana Moss/89	10.00	25.00
36 Shaun Alexander/37	25.00	50.00
37 Steve Smith/89	20.00	40.00
38 T.J. Houshmandzadeh/84	10.00	25.00
39 Tatum Bell/26	15.00	40.00
40 Tiki Barber/21	30.00	60.00
41 Torry Holt/81	15.00	30.00
42 Willie Parker/39	15.00	40.00
43 Willis McGahee/21	15.00	30.00
44 Barry Sanders/20	100.00	175.00
45 Bo Jackson/34	40.00	80.00
46 Charley Taylor/42	15.00	30.00
47 Cliff Branch/21	20.00	40.00
48 Cris Carter/80		
49 Deion Sanders/21	40.00	80.00
51 Henry Ellard/80	10.00	25.00
53 Paul Krause/22		
54 Tony Dorsett/33	25.00	50.00
56 Billy Sims/20	15.00	30.00
58 Deacon Jones/75	15.00	40.00
59 Fred Biletnikoff/25	30.00	60.00
61 Willie Brown/24	20.00	40.00

2006 Leaf Limited Material Monikers Jersey Number Prime

PRIME PRINT RUN 5-25 SER.#'d SETS
SERIAL #'d UNDER 25 NOT PRICED

1 Alex Smith QB/25	40.00	80.00
4 Byron Leftwich/25	15.00	40.00
19 Roger Staubach/25	75.00	135.00
20 Marc Bulger/25	15.00	40.00
42 Willie Parker/25	25.00	60.00
46 Charley Taylor/25	15.00	40.00
47 Cliff Branch/25	15.00	40.00
48 Cris Carter/25	75.00	135.00
49 Deion Sanders/25	30.00	60.00
50 Fran Tarkenton/25	30.00	60.00
51 Henry Ellard/25	15.00	40.00
52 Joe Theismann/25	30.00	60.00
53 Paul Krause/25	15.00	40.00
54 Tony Dorsett/25	30.00	60.00
55 Warren Moon/25	25.00	60.00
56 Billy Sims/25	15.00	40.00
57 Boomer Esiason/25	15.00	40.00
58 Deacon Jones/25	30.00	60.00
59 Fred Biletnikoff/25	30.00	60.00
61 Willie Brown/25	15.00	40.00
62 Troy Aikman/25	60.00	120.00
64 John Elway/25	100.00	175.00
65 Steve Young/25	75.00	135.00

2006 Leaf Limited Monikers Autographs Gold

GOLD STATED PRINT RUN 1-100
UNPRICED PLATINUM PRINT RUN 1

3 Frank Gore/50	15.00	30.00
4 Rex Grossman/50	8.00	20.00
5 Thomas Jones/20	10.00	25.00
9 Rudi Johnson/32	8.00	20.00
10 T.J. Houshmandzadeh/50	8.00	20.00
11 J.P. Losman/50	8.00	20.00
12 Lee Evans/83		
13 Willis McGahee/21	10.00	25.00
19 Charlie Frye/50	8.00	20.00
25 Edgerrin James/32	8.00	20.00
28 Antonio Gates/85	10.00	25.00
30 LaDainian Tomlinson/21	30.00	60.00
34 Priest Holmes/31	10.00	25.00
37 Dallas Clark/44	8.00	20.00
38 Marvin Harrison/25	15.00	40.00
39 Peyton Manning/25	75.00	150.00
46 Chris Chambers/25	10.00	25.00
49 Ronnie Brown/23	12.00	30.00
51 Donovan McNabb/25	20.00	50.00
52 Jevon Kearse/50	8.00	20.00
54 Alge Crumpler/50	8.00	20.00
57 Eli Manning/25	60.00	100.00
61 Byron Leftwich/25	10.00	25.00
63 Jimmy Smith/50	8.00	20.00
64 Matt Jones/50	6.00	15.00
67 Kevin Jones/34	6.00	15.00
71 Samkon Gado/50	8.00	20.00
72 Ahman Green/30	10.00	25.00
76 Steve Smith/50	15.00	30.00
78 Deion Branch/50	8.00	20.00
79 Tedy Bruschi/54	30.00	60.00
81 Jerry Porter/84	5.00	12.00
83 LaMont Jordan/34	8.00	20.00
86 Steven Jackson/39	10.00	25.00
88 Derrick Mason/50	8.00	20.00
93 Clinton Portis/26	12.00	30.00
95 Chad Pennington/50	8.00	20.00
96 Laveranues Coles/22	8.00	20.00
101 Darrell Jackson/82	6.00	15.00
104 Shaun Alexander/37	10.00	25.00
107 Willie Parker/30	10.00	26.00
110 Deuce McAllister/50	8.00	20.00
111 Andre Johnson/50	10.00	25.00
112 David Carr/49	6.00	15.00
113 Domanick Davis/50	6.00	15.00
116 Drew Bennett/50	8.00	20.00
117 Chris Brown/50	6.00	15.00
118 Bob Griese/50	12.00	30.00
119 Daryle Lamonica/100	8.00	20.00
120 Dave Casper/87	12.00	30.00
121 Don Meredith/50	50.00	80.00
122 Herschel Walker/100	8.00	20.00
123 Jack Lambert/58	30.00	50.00
124 Jackie Smith/25	12.00	30.00
125 Jim Otto/50	20.00	40.00
126 John Riggins/44	20.00	40.00
127 John Stallworth/50	20.00	40.00
128 Lawrence Taylor/56	25.00	50.00
129 Lester Hayes/50	12.00	30.00
130 L.C. Greenwood/68	15.00	30.00
131 Paul Warfield/42	15.00	30.00
132 Barry Sanders/20	50.00	100.00
134 Billy Sims/100	8.00	20.00
136 Deion Sanders/21	30.00	60.00
138 Forrest Gregg/75	25.00	50.00
139 Gale Sayers/40	40.00	80.00
140 Jim Brown/32	40.00	80.00
146 Raymond Berry/82	10.00	25.00
150 Yale Lary/75	12.00	30.00
151 Adam Jennings/50	8.00	20.00
152 Alan Zemaitis/25	12.00	30.00
155 Anthony Smith/25	12.00	30.00
156 Antonio Cromartie/50	10.00	25.00
157 Ashton Youboty/25	8.00	20.00
158 Bennie Brazell/25	10.00	25.00
159 Bernard Pollard/25	10.00	25.00
160 Brodrick Bunkley/25	10.00	25.00
161 Calvin Lowry/25	12.00	30.00
162 Cedric Griffin/25	10.00	25.00
163 Cedric Humes/100	5.00	12.00
166 Claude Wroten/25	8.00	20.00
168 D.J. Shockley/25	10.00	25.00
169 Danieal Manning/25	12.00	30.00
170 Daniel Bullocks/25	12.00	30.00
171 Darnell Bing/25	10.00	25.00
173 Darryl Tapp/25	10.00	25.00
174 David Anderson/25	10.00	25.00
175 David Kirtman/25	10.00	25.00
176 David Pittman/25	10.00	25.00
179 Delanie Walker/50	10.00	25.00
180 DeMeco Ryans/25	12.00	30.00
182 Devin Hester/100	30.00	50.00
183 Domenik Hixon/50	10.00	25.00
184 Dominique Byrd/100	6.00	15.00
185 Donte Whitner/50	10.00	25.00
186 D'Qwell Jackson/25	10.00	25.00
187 Dusty Dvoracek/25	12.00	30.00
188 Eric Smith/25	10.00	25.00
190 Ernie Sims/25	10.00	25.00
191 Ethan Kilmer/25	10.00	25.00
194 Gabe Watson/25	8.00	20.00
195 Garrett Mills/50	10.00	25.00
199 Haloti Ngata/25	12.00	30.00
201 Jai Lewis/25	10.00	25.00
204 Jason Allen/50	8.00	20.00
209 Jeffrey Webb/50	8.00	20.00
210 Jerome Harrison/100	8.00	20.00
211 Jimmy Williams/25	12.00	30.00
213 Jon Alston/25	8.00	20.00
214 Johnathan Joseph/50	8.00	20.00
215 Kamerion Wimbley/25	12.00	30.00
216 Kelly Jennings/50	8.00	20.00
218 Ko Simpson/25	10.00	25.00
221 Leonard Pope/50	10.00	25.00
222 Marques Colston/25	50.00	120.00
224 Mathias Kiwanuka/25	12.00	30.00
225 Mike Bell/40	10.00	25.00
226 Mike Hass/100	6.00	15.00
228 Nate Salley/25	10.00	25.00
230 Owen Daniels/50	10.00	25.00

233 Quinton Ganther/100 5.00 12.00
234 Richard Marshall/25 10.00 25.00
235 Rocky McIntosh/25 10.00 25.00
236 Roman Harper/50 8.00 20.00
239 Tamba Hali/25 12.00 30.00
241 Thomas Howard/25 10.00 25.00
242 Tim Jennings/25 10.00 25.00
244 Todd Watkins/25 8.00 20.00
245 Tony Scheffler/100 8.00 20.00
246 Tye Hill/50 6.00 15.00
249 Will Blackmon/50 8.00 20.00
250 Willie Reid/100 6.00 15.00

2006 Leaf Limited Player Threads

STATED PRINT RUN 100 SER.#'d SETS
*PRIME/25-30: .8X TO 2X BASIC INSERTS
PRIME PRINT RUN 5-30
1 Sinorice Moss 4.00 10.00
2 Mario Williams 5.00 12.00
3 Demetrius Williams 4.00 10.00
4 Marcedes Lewis 4.00 10.00
5 Matt Leinart 3.00 8.00
6 Reggie Bush 6.00 15.00
7 LenDale White 6.00 15.00
8 A.J. Hawk 8.00 20.00
9 Laurence Maroney 2.50 6.00
10 Maurice Drew 8.00 20.00
11 Maurice Stovall 4.00 10.00
12 Travis Wilson 4.00 10.00
13 Cedric Benson 5.00 12.00
14 Roy Williams S 4.00 10.00
15 Roy Williams WR 5.00 12.00
16 Ronnie Brown 5.00 12.00
17 Cadillac Williams 4.00 10.00
18 Dan Marino 15.00 40.00
19 Thurman Thomas 6.00 15.00
20 Tony Dorsett 8.00 20.00
21 Peyton Manning 8.00 20.00
22 Laveranues Coles 4.00 10.00
23 Hines Ward 5.00 12.00
24 Michael Clayton 4.00 10.00
25 Andre Johnson 4.00 10.00
26 Jeremy Shockey 5.00 12.00
27 Carson Palmer 5.00 12.00
28 Willis McGahee 5.00 12.00
29 Santana Moss 4.00 10.00
30 Curtis Martin 5.00 12.00
31 Roger Staubach 12.00 30.00
32 Eric Dickerson 6.00 15.00
33 Earl Campbell 8.00 20.00
34 Drew Bledsoe 5.00 12.00
35 Kevin Jones 5.00 12.00
36 Lawrence Taylor 8.00 20.00
37 DeShaun Foster 4.00 10.00
38 Terry Bradshaw 12.00 30.00
39 Terrell Davis 8.00 20.00
40 Mike Singletary 8.00 20.00

2006 Leaf Limited Prime Pairings Autographs

STATED PRINT RUN 25 SER.#'d SETS
1 Vince Young 400.00 700.00
Michael Huff
David Thomas
Matt Leinart
Reggie Bush
LenDale White
2 Don Meredith 250.00 400.00
Roger Staubach
Troy Aikman
Bob Lilly
Tony Dorsett
Craig Morton
3 Fred Biletnikoff 150.00 250.00
Dave Casper
George Blanda
Cliff Branch
Daryle Lamonica
Jim Otto
4 Terry Bradshaw 300.00 450.00
John Stallworth
Jack Lambert
Joe Greene
L.C. Greenwood
Bill Dudley
5 Joe Montana 500.00 750.00
John Elway
Dan Marino
Jim Brown
Earl Campbell
Barry Sanders

2006 Leaf Limited Team Threads Dual

STATED PRINT RUN 100 SER.#'d SETS
*PRIME/30: .8X TO 2X BASIC INSERTS
PRIME PRINT RUN 5-30
1 Thurman Thomas 6.00 15.00
Willis McGahee
2 Bulldog Turner 10.00 25.00
Brian Urlacher
3 Bart Starr 15.00 40.00
Brett Favre
4 Roger Staubach 10.00 25.00
Drew Bledsoe
5 Eric Dickerson 6.00 15.00
Marshall Faulk
6 Y.A. Tittle 10.00 25.00
Steve Young
7 Sonny Jurgensen 8.00 20.00
Joe Theismann
8 Jim Brown 8.00 20.00
Reuben Droughns
9 Len Dawson 15.00 40.00
Joe Montana
10 Paul Warfield 6.00 15.00
Chris Chambers
11 Craig Morton 10.00 25.00
John Elway
12 Marcus Allen 8.00 20.00
LaMont Jordan
13 Henry Ellard 5.00 12.00
Isaac Bruce
14 Don Maynard 5.00 12.00
Chad Pennington
15 Lance Alworth 8.00 20.00
Antonio Gates

2006 Leaf Limited Team Threads Triples

STATED PRINT RUN 100 SER.#'d SETS
*PRIME/25-30: .8X TO 2X BASIC INSERTS
PRIME PRINT RUN 25-30
1 Doak Walker 12.00 30.00
Billy Sims
Barry Sanders
2 Roger Staubach 12.00 30.00
Tony Dorsett
Harvey Martin
3 Y.A. Tittle 20.00 40.00
Joe Montana
Steve Young
4 Terry Bradshaw 12.00 30.00
Jack Lambert
John Stallworth
5 Bart Starr 20.00 40.00
Forrest Gregg
Ray Nitschke
6 Daryle Lamonica 10.00 25.00
George Blanda
Jim Plunkett
7 Bulldog Turner 20.00 40.00
Dick Butkus
Mike Singletary
8 Joe Theismann 10.00 25.00
Charley Taylor
John Riggins
9 John Elway 12.00 30.00
Terrell Davis
Rod Smith
10 Eric Dickerson 6.00 15.00
Henry Ellard
Deacon Jones

2006 Leaf Limited Team Threads Quads

QUAD PRINT RUN 25-50
*PRIME/25: .5X TO 1.2X BASIC INSERTS
PRIME PRINT RUN 5-25
1 Doak Walker 60.00 150.00
Yale Lary
Bobby Layne
Dutch Clark/25
2 Johnny Unitas 40.00 80.00
Raymond Berry
Peyton Manning
Marvin Harrison
3 Red Grange 150.00 250.00
Bulldog Turner
Gale Sayers
Walter Payton/30
4 Bart Starr 40.00 80.00
Ray Nitschke
Forrest Gregg
Reggie White
5 Roger Staubach 40.00 80.00
Tony Dorsett
Bob Lilly
Harvey Martin

2006 Leaf Limited Team Trademarks

STATED PRINT RUN 100 SER.#'d SETS
*HOLOFOIL/50: .5X TO 1.2X BASIC INSERTS
HOLOFOIL PRINT RUN 50 SER.#'d SETS
1 Alex Smith QB 2.00 5.00
2 Anquan Boldin 1.50 4.00
3 Antonio Gates 2.00 5.00
4 Ben Roethlisberger 2.50 6.00
5 Brett Favre 4.00 10.00
6 Michael Vick 2.00 5.00
7 Willis McGahee 1.50 4.00
8 Jake Delhomme 1.50 4.00
9 Cedric Benson 1.50 4.00
10 Chad Johnson 1.50 4.00
11 Drew Bledsoe 2.00 5.00
12 Julius Jones 1.25 3.00
13 Tatum Bell 1.25 3.00
14 Roy Williams WR 1.50 4.00
15 Samkon Gado 1.50 4.00
16 Andre Johnson 2.00 5.00
17 Peyton Manning 3.00 8.00
18 Byron Leftwich 1.50 4.00
19 Larry Johnson 1.50 4.00
20 Ronnie Brown 2.00 5.00
21 Chris Chambers 1.50 4.00
22 Reggie Wayne 1.50 4.00
23 Tom Brady 3.00 8.00
24 Deion Branch 1.50 4.00
25 Donte Stallworth 1.25 3.00
26 Eli Manning 2.50 6.00
27 Tiki Barber 2.00 5.00
28 Curtis Martin 2.00 5.00
29 Randy Moss 2.00 5.00
30 Donovan McNabb 2.00 5.00
31 Reggie Brown 1.25 3.00
32 Willie Parker 1.50 4.00
33 Hines Ward 2.00 5.00
34 Philip Rivers 2.00 5.00
35 LaDainian Tomlinson 2.00 5.00
36 Shaun Alexander 1.50 4.00
37 Marc Bulger 1.50 4.00
38 Torry Holt 1.50 4.00
39 Cadillac Williams 1.50 4.00
40 Clinton Portis 2.00 5.00

2006 Leaf Limited Team Trademarks Materials

STATED PRINT RUN 100 SER.#'d SETS
*PRIME/30: .8X TO 2X BASIC JSYs
PRIME PRINT RUN 30 SER.#'d SETS
1 Alex Smith QB 4.00 10.00
2 Anquan Boldin 3.00 8.00
3 Antonio Gates 4.00 10.00
4 Ben Roethlisberger 6.00 15.00
5 Brett Favre 8.00 20.00
6 Michael Vick 4.00 10.00
7 Willis McGahee 4.00 10.00
8 Jake Delhomme 3.00 8.00
9 Cedric Benson 4.00 10.00
10 Chad Johnson 3.00 8.00
11 Drew Bledsoe 4.00 10.00
12 Julius Jones 4.00 10.00
13 Tatum Bell 3.00 8.00
14 Roy Williams WR 4.00 10.00
15 Samkon Gado 4.00 10.00
16 Andre Johnson 3.00 8.00
17 Peyton Manning 6.00 15.00
18 Byron Leftwich 3.00 8.00
19 Larry Johnson 4.00 10.00
20 Ronnie Brown 4.00 10.00
21 Chris Chambers 3.00 8.00
22 Reggie Wayne 3.00 8.00
23 Tom Brady 6.00 15.00
24 Deion Branch 3.00 8.00
25 Donte Stallworth 3.00 8.00
26 Eli Manning 5.00 12.00
27 Tiki Barber 4.00 10.00
28 Curtis Martin 4.00 10.00
29 Randy Moss 4.00 10.00
30 Donovan McNabb 4.00 10.00
31 Reggie Brown 3.00 8.00
32 Willie Parker 3.00 8.00
33 Hines Ward 4.00 10.00
34 Philip Rivers 4.00 10.00
35 LaDainian Tomlinson 4.00 10.00
36 Shaun Alexander 4.00 10.00
37 Marc Bulger 3.00 8.00
38 Torry Holt 3.00 8.00
39 Cadillac Williams 3.00 8.00
40 Clinton Portis 4.00 10.00

2006 Leaf Limited Team Trademarks Autograph Materials

TRADEMARK AU PRINT RUN 2-100
*PRIME/25: .6X TO 1.5X BASIC JSY AUs
PRIME PRINT RUN 3-25
SERIAL #'d UNDER 25 NOT PRICED
1 Alex Smith QB/50 12.00 30.00
2 Anquan Boldin/30 10.00 25.00
4 Ben Roethlisberger/50 60.00 120.00
7 Willis McGahee/25 10.00 25.00
9 Cedric Benson/40 10.00 25.00
10 Chad Johnson/50 10.00 25.00
11 Drew Bledsoe/50 12.00 30.00
12 Julius Jones/40 8.00 20.00
13 Tatum Bell/25 8.00 20.00
15 Samkon Gado/50 10.00 25.00
16 Andre Johnson/50 12.00 30.00
17 Peyton Manning/40 75.00 125.00
18 Byron Leftwich/100 10.00 25.00
19 Larry Johnson/35 10.00 25.00
21 Chris Chambers/50 10.00 25.00
22 Reggie Wayne/25 10.00 25.00
24 Deion Branch/50 10.00 25.00
26 Eli Manning/45 50.00 80.00
30 Donovan McNabb/40 25.00 50.00
31 Reggie Brown/50 8.00 20.00
32 Willie Parker/50 12.00 30.00
34 Philip Rivers/40 25.00 50.00
35 LaDainian Tomlinson/40 60.00 100.00
36 Shaun Alexander/40 25.00 50.00
39 Cadillac Williams/50 10.00 25.00
40 Clinton Portis/50 12.00 30.00

2006 Leaf Limited Threads

*THREADS/50: .3X TO .8X PRIME/30
THREADS PRINT RUN 5-50
SERIAL #'d UNDER 25 NOT PRICED
119 Daryle Lamonica 5.00 12.00
146 Raymond Berry 6.00 15.00
147 Doak Walker 8.00 20.00

2006 Leaf Limited Threads Prime

*TEAM LOGO/30: .4X TO 1X PRIME/30
1 Alex Smith QB 8.00 20.00
3 Frank Gore 8.00 20.00
4 Rex Grossman 8.00 20.00
5 Thomas Jones 6.00 15.00
6 Cedric Benson 8.00 20.00
7 Carson Palmer 8.00 20.00
8 Chad Johnson 6.00 15.00
9 Rudi Johnson 6.00 15.00
10 T.J. Houshmandzadeh 6.00 15.00
11 J.P. Losman 6.00 15.00
12 Lee Evans 6.00 15.00
13 Willis McGahee 8.00 20.00
14 Jake Plummer 6.00 15.00
16 Rod Smith 6.00 15.00
17 Tatum Bell 6.00 15.00
18 Braylon Edwards 8.00 20.00
19 Charlie Frye 8.00 20.00
20 Reuben Droughns 6.00 15.00
21 Cadillac Williams 6.00 15.00
22 Chris Simms 6.00 15.00
23 Joey Galloway 6.00 15.00
24 Anquan Boldin 6.00 15.00
26 Kurt Warner 6.00 15.00
27 Larry Fitzgerald 8.00 20.00
28 Antonio Gates 8.00 20.00
29 Keenan McCardell 5.00 12.00
30 LaDainian Tomlinson 8.00 20.00
31 Philip Rivers 8.00 20.00
32 Eddie Kennison 5.00 12.00
33 Larry Johnson 8.00 20.00
34 Priest Holmes 6.00 15.00
35 Trent Green 6.00 15.00
36 Tony Gonzalez 6.00 15.00
37 Dallas Clark 5.00 12.00
38 Marvin Harrison 8.00 20.00
39 Peyton Manning 12.00 30.00
40 Reggie Wayne 6.00 15.00
41 Drew Bledsoe 8.00 20.00
42 Julius Jones 8.00 20.00
43 Roy Williams S 6.00 15.00
45 Terry Glenn 6.00 15.00
46 Chris Chambers 6.00 15.00
47 Daunte Culpepper 8.00 20.00
49 Ronnie Brown 8.00 20.00
50 Brian Westbrook 6.00 15.00
51 Donovan McNabb 8.00 20.00
52 Jevon Kearse 6.00 15.00
53 Reggie Brown 6.00 15.00
54 Alge Crumpler 6.00 15.00
55 Michael Vick 8.00 20.00
56 Warrick Dunn 6.00 15.00
57 Eli Manning 10.00 25.00
58 Jeremy Shockey 8.00 20.00
59 Plaxico Burress 6.00 15.00
60 Tiki Barber 8.00 20.00
61 Byron Leftwich 6.00 15.00
62 Fred Taylor 6.00 15.00
63 Jimmy Smith 6.00 15.00
64 Matt Jones 6.00 15.00
66 Roy Williams WR 8.00 20.00
67 Kevin Jones 8.00 20.00
68 Aaron Rodgers 20.00 50.00
69 Brett Favre 15.00 40.00
70 Robert Ferguson 5.00 12.00
72 Ahman Green 6.00 15.00
73 DeShaun Foster 6.00 15.00
74 Jake Delhomme 6.00 15.00
75 Keary Colbert 5.00 12.00
76 Steve Smith 8.00 20.00
77 Corey Dillon 6.00 15.00
79 Tedy Bruschi 10.00 25.00
80 Tom Brady 12.00 30.00
81 Jerry Porter 6.00 15.00
82 Randy Moss 8.00 20.00
83 LaMont Jordan 6.00 15.00
84 Isaac Bruce 6.00 15.00
85 Marc Bulger 6.00 15.00
86 Steven Jackson 8.00 20.00
87 Torry Holt 6.00 15.00
88 Derrick Mason 5.00 12.00
89 Mark Clayton 6.00 15.00
91 Jamal Lewis 6.00 15.00
93 Clinton Portis 8.00 20.00
94 Santana Moss 6.00 15.00
95 Chad Pennington 6.00 15.00
96 Laveranues Coles 6.00 15.00
97 Curtis Martin 8.00 20.00
98 Mewelde Moore 5.00 12.00
99 Troy Williamson 6.00 15.00
101 Darrell Jackson 6.00 15.00
102 Matt Hasselbeck 6.00 15.00
104 Shaun Alexander 8.00 20.00
105 Ben Roethlisberger 12.00 30.00
106 Hines Ward 8.00 20.00
107 Willie Parker 6.00 15.00
110 Deuce McAllister 6.00 15.00
111 Andre Johnson 6.00 15.00
112 David Carr 6.00 15.00
113 Domanick Davis 6.00 15.00
116 Drew Bennett 5.00 12.00
117 Chris Brown 6.00 15.00
118 Bob Griese 8.00 20.00
120 Dave Casper 6.00 15.00
122 Herschel Walker/25 6.00 15.00
123 Jack Lambert 8.00 20.00
124 Jackie Smith 6.00 15.00
125 Jim Otto 8.00 20.00
126 John Riggins 8.00 20.00
127 John Stallworth 8.00 20.00
128 Lawrence Taylor 8.00 20.00
130 L.C. Greenwood 6.00 15.00
131 Paul Warfield 6.00 15.00
132 Barry Sanders 12.00 30.00
133 Bart Starr 12.00 30.00
134 Billy Sims 6.00 15.00
135 Bulldog Turner/25 20.00 40.00
136 Deion Sanders 10.00 25.00
137 Dutch Clark/20 6.00 15.00
138 Forrest Gregg 8.00 20.00
139 Gale Sayers 10.00 25.00
140 Jim Brown 10.00 25.00
142 Joe Montana 15.00 40.00
143 John Elway 12.00 30.00
144 Johnny Unitas 12.00 30.00
145 Lance Alworth 8.00 20.00
149 Walter Payton 15.00 40.00

2007 Leaf Limited

This 355-card set was released in November, 2007. The set was issued into the hobby in a seven-card pack (box) with an $125 SRP. Cards numbered 1-100 feature veterans in alphabetical team order issued to a stated print run of 659 serial numbered sets while cards numbered 101-200 feature retired greats in first name alphabetical order issued to a stated print run of 249 serial numbered sets. The set concludes with 2007 NFL rookies (Cards 201-355). Cards numbered 201-250 were issued to a stated print run of 399 serial numbered sets; cards numbered 251-300 were signed by the player and were issued to stated print runs of between 194 and 299 serial numbered sets and the set concludes with more signed cards from 301-355 all of which were issued to a stated print run of 99 serial numbered sets.

1-100 PRINT RUN 659 SER.#'d SETS
101-200 LEGEND PRINT RUN 249
201-250 ROOKIE PRINT RUN 399
251-300 ROOKIE AU PRINT RUN 194-299
301-355 ROOKIE AU PRINT RUN 99
1 Anquan Boldin 1.25 3.00
2 Edgerrin James 1.25 3.00
3 Larry Fitzgerald 1.50 4.00
4 Matt Leinart 1.25 3.00
5 Alge Crumpler 1.25 3.00
6 Warrick Dunn 1.25 3.00
7 Jerious Norwood 1.25 3.00
8 Willis McGahee 1.25 3.00
9 Steve McNair 1.25 3.00
10 Mark Clayton 1.25 3.00
11 Anthony Thomas 1.00 2.50
12 J.P. Losman 1.00 2.50
13 Lee Evans 1.25 3.00
14 Jake Delhomme 1.25 3.00
15 Steve Smith 1.25 3.00
16 DeAngelo Williams 1.50 4.00
17 Rex Grossman 1.25 3.00
18 Cedric Benson 1.25 3.00
19 Bernard Berrian 1.00 2.50
20 Carson Palmer 1.25 3.00
21 Chad Johnson 1.25 3.00
22 Rudi Johnson 1.25 3.00
23 T.J. Houshmandzadeh 1.25 3.00
24 Kellen Winslow 1.25 3.00
25 Braylon Edwards 1.25 3.00
26 Jamal Lewis 1.25 3.00
27 Julius Jones 1.00 2.50
28 Terrell Owens 1.50 4.00
29 Tony Romo 2.00 5.00
30 Jay Cutler 1.50 4.00
31 Javon Walker 1.25 3.00
32 Travis Henry 1.25 3.00
33 Tatum Bell 1.00 2.50
34 Roy Williams WR 1.25 3.00
35 Jon Kitna 1.00 2.50
36 Brett Favre 3.00 8.00
37 Donald Driver 1.50 4.00
38 Greg Jennings 1.50 4.00
39 Matt Schaub 1.25 3.00
40 Andre Johnson 1.25 3.00
41 Ahman Green 1.25 3.00
42 Peyton Manning 2.50 6.00
43 Marvin Harrison 1.50 4.00
44 Reggie Wayne 1.25 3.00
45 Joseph Addai 1.25 3.00
46 David Garrard 1.25 3.00
47 Fred Taylor 1.25 3.00
48 Maurice Jones-Drew 1.50 4.00
49 Brodie Croyle 1.25 3.00
50 Larry Johnson 1.00 2.50
51 Tony Gonzalez 1.25 3.00
52 Trent Green 1.25 3.00
53 Ronnie Brown 1.25 3.00
54 Chris Chambers 1.25 3.00
55 Tarvaris Jackson 1.00 2.50
56 Troy Williamson 1.00 2.50
57 Chester Taylor 1.00 2.50
58 Tom Brady 2.50 6.00
59 Randy Moss 1.50 4.00
60 Laurence Maroney 1.25 3.00
61 Donte Stallworth 1.25 3.00
62 Drew Brees 1.50 4.00
63 Deuce McAllister 1.25 3.00
64 Reggie Bush 1.50 4.00
65 Marques Colston 1.50 4.00
66 Eli Manning 1.50 4.00
67 Jeremy Shockey 1.25 3.00
68 Brandon Jacobs 1.25 3.00
69 Chad Pennington 1.25 3.00
70 Thomas Jones 1.25 3.00
71 Laveranues Coles 1.00 2.50
72 Jerry Porter 1.25 3.00
73 LaMont Jordan 1.25 3.00
74 Donovan McNabb 1.50 4.00
75 Brian Westbrook 1.25 3.00
76 Reggie Brown 1.00 2.50
77 Ben Roethlisberger 1.50 4.00
78 Hines Ward 1.50 4.00
79 Willie Parker 1.25 3.00
80 Philip Rivers 1.50 4.00
81 Antonio Gates 1.50 4.00
82 LaDainian Tomlinson 1.50 4.00
83 Alex Smith QB 1.50 4.00
84 Darrell Jackson 1.00 2.50
85 Frank Gore 1.50 4.00
86 Matt Hasselbeck 1.25 3.00
87 Shaun Alexander 1.25 3.00
88 Deion Branch 1.25 3.00
89 Marc Bulger 1.25 3.00
90 Steven Jackson 1.50 4.00
91 Torry Holt 1.25 3.00
92 Jeff Garcia 1.25 3.00
93 Cadillac Williams 1.25 3.00
94 Joey Galloway 1.25 3.00
95 Vince Young 1.25 3.00
96 Brandon Jones 1.00 2.50
97 LenDale White 1.25 3.00
98 Jason Campbell 1.25 3.00
99 Clinton Portis 1.25 3.00
100 Santana Moss 1.25 3.00
101 Alan Page 2.00 5.00
102 Barry Sanders 5.00 12.00
103 Bart Starr 5.00 12.00
104 Bill Dudley 2.50 6.00
105 Billy Howton 2.00 5.00
106 Bob Griese 3.00 8.00
107 Bobby Layne 3.00 8.00
108 Boyd Dowler 2.00 5.00
109 Charley Taylor 2.50 6.00
110 Charley Trippi 2.00 5.00
111 Charlie Joiner 2.50 6.00
112 Chuck Bednarik 2.50 6.00
113 Cris Collinsworth 2.50 6.00
114 Dan Fouts 3.00 8.00
115 Dan Hampton 2.50 6.00
116 Dan Marino 6.00 15.00
117 Dante Lavelli 2.00 5.00
118 Darrell Green 2.50 6.00
119 Daryle Lamonica 2.00 5.00
120 Deacon Jones 2.50 6.00
121 Dick Butkus 4.00 10.00
122 Doak Walker 2.50 6.00
123 Don Maynard 2.50 6.00
124 Don Perkins 2.00 5.00
125 Dutch Clark 2.50 6.00
126 Earl Campbell 3.00 8.00
127 Forrest Gregg 2.00 5.00
128 Fran Tarkenton 4.00 10.00
129 Franco Harris 3.00 8.00
130 Fred Biletnikoff 3.00 8.00
131 Gale Sayers 4.00 10.00
132 Gene Upshaw 2.00 5.00
133 George Blanda 2.50 6.00
134 Harlon Hill 2.00 5.00
135 Jack Lambert 3.00 8.00
136 Jack Youngblood 2.50 6.00
137 James Lofton 2.00 5.00
138 Jan Stenerud 2.00 5.00
139 Jethro Pugh 2.00 5.00
140 Jim Brown 4.00 10.00
141 Jim Kelly 4.00 10.00
142 Jim McMahon 4.00 10.00
143 Jim Otto 2.00 5.00
144 Jim Thorpe 4.00 10.00
145 Jimmy Orr 2.00 5.00
146 Joe Greene 3.00 8.00
147 Joe Montana 6.00 15.00
148 Joe Namath 4.00 10.00
149 Joe Theismann 3.00 8.00
150 John Elway 5.00 12.00
151 John Mackey 2.50 6.00
152 John Riggins 2.50 6.00
153 John Stallworth 2.50 6.00
154 Johnny Morris 2.00 5.00
155 Johnny Unitas 5.00 12.00
156 Kellen Winslow Sr. 2.50 6.00
157 Ken Stabler 4.00 10.00
158 Lance Alworth 2.50 6.00
159 Larry Csonka 3.00 8.00
160 Larry Little 2.00 5.00
161 Lee Roy Selmon 2.50 6.00
162 Len Dawson 3.00 8.00
163 Lou Groza 2.50 6.00
164 Lydell Mitchell 2.00 5.00
165 Marcus Allen 3.00 8.00
166 Mark Duper 2.00 5.00
167 Merlin Olsen 2.50 6.00
168 Mike Singletary 3.00 8.00
169 Ollie Matson 2.50 6.00
170 Otto Graham 3.00 8.00
171 Ozzie Newsome 2.50 6.00
172 Paul Hornung 3.00 8.00
173 Paul Warfield 2.50 6.00
174 Phil Simms 2.50 6.00
175 Randall Cunningham 2.50 6.00
176 Ray Nitschke 3.00 8.00
177 Raymond Berry 2.50 6.00
178 Red Grange 4.00 10.00
179 Rick Casares 2.00 5.00
180 Ron Mix 2.00 5.00
181 Roger Craig 2.50 6.00
182 Roger Staubach 5.00 12.00
183 Rosey Brown 2.00 5.00
184 Rosey Grier 2.00 5.00
185 Ronnie Lott 2.50 6.00
186 Sam Huff 2.50 6.00
187 Sammy Baugh 3.00 8.00
188 Sid Luckman 3.00 8.00
189 Sonny Jurgensen 2.50 6.00
190 Sterling Sharpe 2.50 6.00
191 Steve Largent 3.00 8.00
192 Steve Young 4.00 10.00
193 Ted Hendricks 2.50 6.00
194 Thurman Thomas 2.50 6.00
195 Tim Brown 3.00 8.00
196 Tiki Barber 3.00 8.00
197 Troy Aikman 4.00 10.00
198 Walter Payton 6.00 15.00
199 Willie Brown 2.50 6.00
200 Elroy Hirsch 2.50 6.00
201 Brandon McDonald RC 2.00 5.00
202 David Irons RC 2.00 5.00
203 Fred Bennett RC 2.00 5.00
204 Nick Graham RC 2.50 6.00
205 Rashad Barksdale RC 2.00 5.00
206 Tanard Jackson RC 2.00 5.00
207 Tarell Brown RC 3.00 8.00
208 Usama Young RC 2.50 6.00
209 William Gay RC 2.50 6.00
210 Jarvis Moss RC 2.50 6.00
211 Le'Ron McClain RC 3.00 8.00
212 Kevin Payne RC 2.00 5.00
213 Adam Hayward RC 2.50 6.00
214 Brandon Siler RC 2.00 5.00
215 Chad Nkang RC 2.00 5.00
216 Clint Session RC 2.50 6.00
217 Desmond Bishop RC 3.00 8.00
218 Edmond Miles RC 2.50 6.00
219 H.B. Blades RC 2.00 5.00
220 Justin Durant RC 2.50 6.00
221 Justin Rogers RC 3.00 8.00
222 Nate Harris RC 2.50 6.00
223 Quincy Black RC 3.00 8.00
224 Quinton Culberson RC 2.00 5.00
225 Ramon Guzman RC 2.00 5.00
226 Stephen Nicholas RC 2.50 6.00
227 Tim Shaw RC 2.50 6.00
228 Tony Taylor RC 2.50 6.00
229 Zak DeOssie RC 2.50 6.00
230 Mason Crosby RC 2.50 6.00
231 Nick Folk RC 3.00 8.00
232 Matt Gutierrez RC 3.00 8.00
233 Matt Moore RC 3.00 8.00
234 Tyler Thigpen RC 3.00 8.00
235 Clifton Dawson RC 3.00 8.00
236 Gary Russell RC 2.50 6.00
237 Kenton Keith RC 3.00 8.00
238 Pierre Thomas RC 12.00 30.00
239 Gerald Alexander RC 2.00 5.00
240 John Wendling RC 2.50 6.00
241 Eric Frampton RC 2.50 6.00
242 Eric Weddle RC 3.00 8.00
243 Daniel Coats RC 2.50 6.00
244 Michael Matthews RC 2.50 6.00
245 Biren Ealy RC 2.50 6.00
246 Bobby Sippio RC 2.50 6.00
247 Glenn Holt RC 2.50 6.00
248 John Broussard RC 2.50 6.00
249 Legedu Naanee RC 3.00 8.00
250 Syndric Steptoe RC 2.50 6.00
251 Levi Brown AU RC 5.00 12.00
252 Jamaal Anderson AU RC 4.00 10.00
253 Amobi Okoye AU RC 5.00 12.00
254 Adam Carriker AU RC 4.00 10.00
255 Darrelle Revis AU RC 15.00 30.00
256 Michael Griffin AU RC 5.00 12.00
257 Aaron Ross AU RC 5.00 12.00
258 Brandon Meriweather AU RC 5.00 12.00
259 Jon Beason AU RC 4.00 10.00
260 Anthony Spencer AU RC 5.00 12.00
261 Alan Branch No AU RC 2.50 6.00
262 Chris Houston AU RC 4.00 10.00
263 LaMarr Woodley AU RC 10.00 20.00
264 David Harris AU RC 4.00 10.00
265 Eric Wright No AU RC 3.00 8.00
266 Josh Wilson AU RC 4.00 10.00
267 Tim Crowder AU RC 5.00 12.00
268 Victor Abiamiri AU RC 5.00 12.00
269 Ikaika Alama-Francis AU RC 5.00 12.00
270 Dan Bazuin AU RC 4.00 10.00
271 Sabby Piscitelli AU RC 5.00 12.00
272 Quentin Moses AU RC 4.00 10.00
273 Buster Davis AU RC 4.00 10.00
274 Marcus McCauley AU RC 4.00 10.00
275 Matt Spaeth AU RC 5.00 12.00
276 Demarcus Tank Tyler No AU RC 2.00 5.00
277 Charles Johnson No AU RC 2.00 5.00
278 Jonathan Wade AU RC 4.00 10.00
279 Stewart Bradley AU RC 4.00 10.00
280 Aaron Rouse AU RC 4.00 10.00
281 Michael Okwo AU RC 4.00 10.00
282 Daymeion Hughes AU RC 4.00 10.00
283 Ray McDonald AU RC 4.00 10.00
284 Thomas Clayton AU RC 4.00 10.00
285 DeShawn Wynn AU RC 4.00 10.00
286 Jason Snelling AU RC 6.00 15.00
287 Kenneth Darby AU RC 4.00 10.00
288 Ahmad Bradshaw AU/291 RC 15.00 40.00
289 Nate Ilaoa AU/203 RC 4.00 10.00
290 Joel Filani AU RC 4.00 10.00
291 Courtney Taylor AU RC 4.00 10.00
292 Jordan Kent AU/245 RC 4.00 10.00
293 Dallas Baker AU RC 3.00 8.00
294 Roy Hall AU RC 5.00 12.00
295 Chansi Stuckey AU RC 5.00 12.00
296 Scott Chandler AU RC 5.00 12.00
297 Ben Patrick AU RC 4.00 10.00
298 Chris Leak AU RC 4.00 10.00
299 Jared Zabransky AU RC 4.00 10.00
300 Selvin Young AU/194 RC 12.00 30.00
301 Adrian Peterson JSY AU RC 125.00 250.00
302 Anthony Gonzalez JSY AU RC 8.00 20.00
303 Antonio Pittman JSY AU RC 5.00 12.00
304 Aundrae Allison AU RC 5.00 12.00
305 Brady Quinn JSY AU RC 15.00 40.00
306 Brandon Jackson JSY AU RC 6.00 15.00
307 Brian Leonard JSY AU RC 6.00 15.00
308 Calvin Johnson JSY AU RC 50.00 100.00
309 Chris Davis AU RC 5.00 12.00
310 Chris Henry RB JSY AU RC 5.00 12.00
312 David Clowney AU RC 6.00 15.00
313 Drew Stanton JSY AU RC 5.00 12.00
314 Dwayne Bowe JSY AU RC 25.00 50.00
315 Dwayne Jarrett JSY AU RC 6.00 15.00
316 Dwayne Wright AU RC 6.00 15.00
317 Gaines Adams JSY AU RC 8.00 20.00
318 Garrett Wolfe JSY AU RC 5.00 12.00
319 Greg Olsen JSY AU RC 6.00 15.00
320 Isaiah Stanback AU RC 5.00 12.00
321 Jacoby Jones AU RC 8.00 20.00
322 JaMarcus Russell JSY AU RC 5.00 12.00
323 James Jones AU RC 8.00 20.00
324 Jason Hill JSY AU RC 8.00 20.00
325 Jeff Rowe AU RC 5.00 12.00
327 John Beck JSY AU RC 10.00 25.00
328 Johnnie Lee Higgins JSY AU RC 6.00 15.00
329 Jordan Palmer AU RC 6.00 15.00
330 Kenny Irons JSY No AU RC 5.00 12.00
331 Kevin Kolb JSY AU RC 15.00 40.00
332 Kolby Smith AU RC 6.00 15.00
333 LaRon Landry AU RC 8.00 20.00
334 Laurent Robinson AU RC 10.00 25.00
335 Lawrence Timmons AU RC 8.00 20.00
336 Leon Hall AU RC 6.00 15.00
337 Lorenzo Booker JSY AU RC 6.00 15.00
338 Marshawn Lynch JSY AU RC 20.00 50.00
339 Michael Bush JSY AU RC 8.00 20.00
340 Mike Walker AU RC 8.00 20.00
341 Patrick Willis JSY AU RC 20.00 50.00
342 Paul Posluszny AU RC 8.00 20.00
343 Paul Williams JSY AU RC 5.00 12.00
344 Reggie Nelson AU RC 6.00 15.00
345 Robert Meachem JSY AU RC 8.00 20.00
346 Ryne Robinson AU RC 6.00 15.00
347 Sidney Rice JSY AU RC 10.00 25.00
348 Steve Breaston AU RC 8.00 20.00
349 Steve Smith USC JSY AU RC 12.00 30.00
350 Ted Ginn Jr. JSY AU RC 12.00 30.00
351 Tony Hunt JSY AU RC 5.00 12.00
352 Trent Edwards JSY AU RC 8.00 20.00
353 Troy Smith JSY AU RC 8.00 20.00
354 Yamon Figurs JSY AU RC 5.00 12.00
355 Zach Miller AU RC 8.00 20.00

2007 Leaf Limited Bronze Spotlight

*VETS 1-100: 1X TO 2.5X BASIC CARDS
*LEGENDS 101-200: .8X TO 2X BASIC CARDS
COMMON ROOKIE (201-300) 4.00 10.00
ROOKIE SEMISTARS 5.00 12.00
ROOKIE UNL.STARS 6.00 15.00
STATED PRINT RUN 32 SER.#'d SETS
238 Pierre Thomas 30.00 80.00
285 DeShawn Wynn 5.00 12.00
300 Selvin Young 5.00 12.00

2007 Leaf Limited Gold Spotlight

*VETS 1-100: 2.5X TO 6X BASIC CARDS
*LEGENDS 101-200: 1.5X TO 4X BASIC CARDS
COMMON ROOKIE (201-300) 6.00 15.00
ROOKIE SEMISTARS 8.00 20.00
ROOKIE UNL.STARS 10.00 25.00
1-300 UNPRICED GOLD PRINT RUN 10
*ROOKIE AU: .5X TO 1.2X BASIC CARDS
301-355 AU PRINT RUN 25
238 Pierre Thomas 75.00 150.00
301 Adrian Peterson JSY AU 175.00 350.00
305 Brady Quinn JSY AU 30.00 80.00
308 Calvin Johnson JSY AU 75.00 150.00
322 JaMarcus Russell JSY AU 15.00 40.00
338 Marshawn Lynch JSY AU 40.00 80.00

2007 Leaf Limited Platinum Spotlight

UNPRICED PLATINUM PRINT RUN 1

2007 Leaf Limited Silver Spotlight

*VETS 1-100: 1.5X TO 4X BASIC CARDS
*LEGENDS 101-200: 1.2X TO 3X BASIC CARDS
COMMON ROOKIE (201-300) 5.00 12.00
ROOKIE SEMISTARS 6.00 15.00
ROOKIE UNL.STARS 8.00 20.00
1-300 PRINT RUN 20 SER.#'d SETS
*ROOKIE AU: .4X TO 1X BASIC CARDS
301-355 AU PRINT RUN 49
234 Tyler Thigpen 8.00 20.00
238 Pierre Thomas 30.00 80.00
300 Selvin Young 6.00 15.00
301 Adrian Peterson JSY AU 125.00 250.00
305 Brady Quinn JSY AU 20.00 50.00
308 Calvin Johnson JSY AU 60.00 120.00
322 JaMarcus Russell JSY AU 12.00 30.00
338 Marshawn Lynch JSY AU 25.00 60.00

2007 Leaf Limited Banner Season Materials

STATED PRINT RUN 100 SER.#'d SETS
*PRIME/25: 1X TO 2.5X BASIC JSYs
PRIME PRINT RUN 25 SER.#'d SETS
1 LaDainian Tomlinson 4.00 10.00
2 Larry Johnson 2.50 6.00
3 Frank Gore 4.00 10.00
4 Tiki Barber 4.00 10.00
5 Steven Jackson 4.00 10.00
6 Willie Parker 3.00 8.00
7 Drew Brees 4.00 10.00
8 Peyton Manning 6.00 15.00
9 Carson Palmer 3.00 8.00
10 Brett Favre 8.00 20.00
11 Tom Brady 6.00 15.00
12 Ben Roethlisberger 4.00 10.00
13 Philip Rivers 4.00 10.00
14 Chad Johnson 3.00 8.00
15 Marvin Harrison 4.00 10.00
16 Reggie Wayne 3.00 8.00
17 Roy Williams WR 3.00 8.00
18 Lee Evans 3.00 8.00
19 Anquan Boldin 3.00 8.00
20 Torry Holt 3.00 8.00
21 Terrell Owens 4.00 10.00
22 Steve Smith 3.00 8.00
23 Reggie Bush 4.00 10.00
24 Vince Young 3.00 8.00
25 Maurice Jones-Drew 4.00 10.00

2007 Leaf Limited Banner Season Autograph Materials

STATED PRINT RUN 25 SER.#'d SETS
UNPRICED PRIME AU PRINT RUN 5-15
1 LaDainian Tomlinson 50.00 100.00
2 Larry Johnson 20.00 50.00
3 Frank Gore 15.00 40.00
4 Tiki Barber
5 Steven Jackson 20.00 50.00
6 Willie Parker 20.00 50.00
7 Drew Brees 40.00 80.00
8 Peyton Manning 75.00 150.00
10 Brett Favre 125.00 200.00
12 Ben Roethlisberger 50.00 100.00
14 Chad Johnson 15.00 40.00
15 Marvin Harrison 20.00 50.00
16 Reggie Wayne 15.00 40.00
17 Roy Williams WR 15.00 40.00
19 Anquan Boldin 12.00 30.00
20 Torry Holt 15.00 40.00
22 Steve Smith 15.00 40.00
23 Reggie Bush 40.00 100.00
24 Vince Young 30.00 80.00
25 Maurice Jones-Drew 15.00 40.00

2007 Leaf Limited College Phenoms Autographs

STATED PRINT RUN 25 SER.#'d SETS
UNPRICED SILVER PRINT RUN 10
UNPRICED GOLD PRINT RUN 5
UNPRICED PLATINUM PRINT RUN 1
301 Adrian Peterson 150.00 300.00
302 Anthony Gonzalez 10.00 25.00
303 Antonio Pittman 6.00 15.00
304 Aundrae Allison 6.00 15.00
305 Brady Quinn JSY 75.00 150.00
306 Brandon Jackson 8.00 20.00
307 Brian Leonard 8.00 20.00
308 Calvin Johnson 75.00 150.00
313 Drew Stanton 6.00 15.00
314 Dwayne Bowe 12.00 30.00
315 Dwayne Jarrett JSY 8.00 20.00
317 Gaines Adams 10.00 25.00
318 Garrett Wolfe 6.00 15.00
319 Greg Olsen 8.00 20.00
321 Jacoby Jones 10.00 25.00
322 JaMarcus Russell JSY 6.00 15.00
323 James Jones 10.00 25.00
324 Jason Hill 10.00 25.00
327 John Beck 10.00 25.00
328 Johnnie Lee Higgins 8.00 20.00
329 Jordan Palmer JSY 8.00 20.00
331 Kevin Kolb 25.00 60.00
332 Kolby Smith 8.00 20.00
333 LaRon Landry 10.00 25.00
335 Lawrence Timmons 10.00 25.00
336 Leon Hall 8.00 20.00
337 Lorenzo Booker 8.00 20.00
338 Marshawn Lynch 25.00 60.00
339 Michael Bush JSY 10.00 25.00
341 Patrick Willis 20.00 50.00
342 Paul Posluszny 10.00 25.00
344 Reggie Nelson 8.00 20.00
345 Robert Meachem 10.00 25.00
347 Sidney Rice 25.00 50.00
348 Steve Breaston 10.00 25.00
349 Steve Smith USC 10.00 25.00

350 Ted Ginn Jr. 8.00 20.00
351 Tony Hunt 6.00 15.00
352 Trent Edwards 10.00 25.00
353 Troy Smith 10.00 25.00
354 Yamon Figurs 6.00 15.00
355 Zach Miller 10.00 25.00

2007 Leaf Limited Contenders Preview Autographs

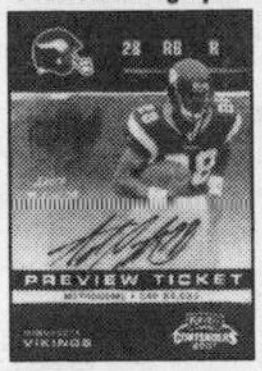

STATED PRINT RUN 25-50
RTP1 Marshawn Lynch/25 30.00 60.00
RTP2 Adrian Peterson/25 250.00 400.00
RTP3 Sidney Rice/50 25.00 50.00
RTP4 Brandon Jackson/50 8.00 20.00
RTP5 Kenny Irons/50 6.00 15.00
RTP6 Brady Quinn/25 20.00 50.00
RTP7 Calvin Johnson/25 75.00 150.00
RTP8 Steve Smith USC/25 15.00 40.00
RTP9 Dwayne Jarrett/50 8.00 20.00
RTP10 Ted Ginn/50 8.00 20.00
RTP11 Dwayne Bowe/50 30.00 60.00
RTP12 Greg Olsen/50 8.00 20.00
RTP13 Anthony Gonzalez/50 10.00 25.00
RTP14 JaMarcus Russell/25 8.00 20.00
RTP15 Michael Bush/50 10.00 25.00
RTP16 Kevin Kolb/50 15.00 40.00
RTP17 Patrick Willis/50 40.00 80.00
RTP18 Jason Hill/50 10.00 25.00

2007 Leaf Limited Cuts Autographs

STATED PRINT RUN 5-150
SER.#'d UNDER 20 NOT PRICED
1 Red Badgro/60 50.00 120.00
2 Tony Canadeo/150 40.00 100.00
3 George Connor/100 40.00 100.00
4 Weeb Ewbank/50 40.00 100.00
5 Ray Flaherty/74 40.00 100.00
6 Lou Groza/68 40.00 100.00
7 Mel Hein/75 50.00 120.00
8 Bulldog Turner/75 60.00 150.00
9 Roosevelt Brown/150 30.00 80.00
10 Ernie Stautner/150 30.00 80.00
11 Ken Strong/100 50.00 120.00
12 Elroy Hirsch/50 40.00 100.00
13 Doak Walker/30 200.00 400.00
15 Sammy Baugh/33 75.00 200.00
18 Otto Graham/30 125.00 250.00
23 Jim Parker/73 40.00 100.00
24 Ace Parker/50 50.00 120.00

2007 Leaf Limited Hardwear

STATED PRINT RUN 93-150
*LIMITED/22-44: 1X TO 2.5X BASIC INSERTS
LIMITED PRINT RUN 22-44
1 Phil Simms/110 8.00 20.00
2 Roger Craig/100 10.00 25.00
3 Ted Hendricks/150 6.00 15.00
4 Ronnie Lott/105 8.00 20.00
5 Darrell Green/93 10.00 25.00

2007 Leaf Limited Hardwear Autographs

STATED PRINT RUN 25 SER.#'d SETS
*LIMITED/25: .8X TO 2X BASIC AUTOs
LIMITED PRINT RUN 25 SER.#'d SETS
1 Phil Simms 40.00 80.00
2 Roger Craig 40.00 80.00
4 Ronnie Lott 50.00 100.00
5 Darrell Green 60.00 120.00

2007 Leaf Limited Jumbo Jerseys

STATED PRINT RUN 50 SER.#'d SETS
*PRIME/10: 1.2X TO 3X BASIC JSY/50
PRIME PRINT RUN 10 SER.#'d SETS
*NUMBERS/80-87: .3X TO .8X BASIC JSY/50
*NUMBERS/32-39: .5X TO 1.2X BASIC JSY/50
*NUMBERS/21-25: .6X TO 1.5X BASIC JSY/50
*NUMBERS/10-18: 1X TO 2.5X BASIC JSY/50
NUMBERS STATED PRINT RUN 4-87
*NUM.PRIME/10: 1.2X TO 3X BASIC JSY/50
NUMBERS PRIME STATED PRINT RUN 10
*TEAM LOGO/50: .4X TO 1X BASIC JSY/50
TEAM LOGO PRINT RUN 50 SER.#'d SETS
*TM LOGO PRIME/10: 1.2X TO 3X BASIC JSY/50
TEAM LOGO PRIME PRINT RUN 10
1 Carson Palmer 5.00 12.00
2 Tom Brady 10.00 25.00
3 Marc Bulger 5.00 12.00
4 Chad Pennington 5.00 12.00
5 J.P. Losman 4.00 10.00
6 Alex Smith QB 6.00 15.00
7 Matt Hasselbeck 5.00 12.00
8 Edgerrin James 5.00 12.00
9 Shaun Alexander 5.00 12.00
10 Lee Evans 5.00 12.00
11 Terrell Owens 6.00 15.00
12 Andre Johnson 5.00 12.00
13 Laveranues Coles 4.00 10.00
14 Brett Favre 12.00 30.00
15 Peyton Manning 10.00 25.00
16 Donovan McNabb 6.00 15.00
17 Drew Brees 6.00 15.00
18 LaDainian Tomlinson 6.00 15.00
19 Frank Gore 6.00 15.00
20 Steven Jackson 6.00 15.00
21 Brian Westbrook 5.00 12.00
22 Reggie Bush 6.00 15.00
23 Vince Young 5.00 12.00
24 Torry Holt 5.00 12.00
25 Eli Manning 6.00 15.00

2007 Leaf Limited Lettermen

UNPRICED LETTERMEN PRINT RUN 4-9

2007 Leaf Limited Matching Numbers Jerseys

STATED PRINT RUN 100 SER.#'d SETS
*PRIME/25: 1X TO 2.5X BASIC JSYs
PRIME PRINT RUN 25 SER.#'d SETS
*POSITION/100: .4X TO 1X BASIC JSYs
POSITIONS PRINT RUN 100 SER.#'d SETS
*POS.PRIME/25: 1X TO 2.5X BASIC JSYs
POSITIONS PRIME PRINT RUN 25
1 Marc Bulger 6.00 15.00
Vince Young
2 Jim McMahon 6.00 15.00
Drew Brees
3 Joe Namath 15.00 40.00
Tom Brady
4 John Elway 10.00 25.00
Matt Leinart
5 Bob Griese 5.00 12.00
Randall Cunningham
6 Tim Brown 5.00 12.00
Terrell Owens
7 Franco Harris 5.00 12.00
Maurice Jones-Drew
8 Tiki Barber 5.00 12.00
LaDainian Tomlinson
9 Tony Gonzalez 5.00 12.00
Marvin Harrison
10 Matt Hasselbeck 6.00 15.00
Steve Young
11 Laveranues Coles 4.00 10.00
Reggie Wayne
12 Steve Largent 5.00 12.00
Donald Driver
13 Reggie Bush 5.00 12.00
LenDale White
14 Sonny Jurgensen 10.00 25.00
Tony Romo
15 Paul Hornung 5.00 12.00
Donovan McNabb
16 Fran Tarkenton 6.00 15.00
Eli Manning
17 Charlie Joiner 8.00 20.00
Peyton Manning
18 Larry Csonka 6.00 15.00
Willie Parker
19 Antonio Gates 5.00 12.00
Vernon Davis
20 Brandon Jacobs 4.00 10.00
Larry Johnson

2007 Leaf Limited Material Monikers Jersey Number

*MAT.MONIKER/66-99: .25X TO .6X PRIME/25
*MAT.MONIKER/34-60: .3X TO .8X PRIME/25
*MAT.MONIKER/21-32: .4X TO 1X PRIME/25
*MAT.MONIKER/10-18: .5X TO 1.2X PRIME/25
STATED PRINT RUN 1-99 SER.#'d SETS
1 Marques Colston/12 25.00 60.00
2 Larry Johnson/27 20.00 50.00
3 Raymond Berry/82 12.00 30.00
4 Cedric Benson/32 20.00 50.00
5 Dan Fouts/14 30.00 80.00
6 Maurice Jones-Drew/32 15.00 40.00
7 Peyton Manning/18 100.00 200.00
8 Frank Gore/21 20.00 50.00
9 Steven Jackson/39 15.00 40.00
10 Rudi Johnson/32 15.00 40.00
11 Joe Montana/16 150.00 300.00
12 Joe Namath/12 60.00 150.00
13 Steve Largent/80 15.00 40.00
15 Jim Brown/32 50.00 120.00
16 John Riggins/44 15.00 40.00
17 Marion Barber/24 25.00 60.00
18 Chuck Bednarik/60 20.00 50.00
19 Cris Collinsworth/80 12.00 30.00
20 Randall Cunningham/12 25.00 60.00
22 A.J. Hawk/50 15.00 40.00
24 Ladell Betts/46 10.00 25.00
25 Thurman Thomas/34 15.00 40.00
26 Reggie Bush/25 25.00 60.00
27 Roger Staubach/12 60.00 150.00
28 Tim Brown/81 15.00 40.00
29 Dan Marino/13 150.00 300.00
30 Dan Hampton/99 12.00 30.00
31 Larry Little/66 10.00 25.00
34 Deacon Jones/75 12.00 30.00
36 Charley Taylor/42 15.00 40.00
37 Hank Baskett/84 10.00 25.00
38 Charlie Joiner/18 20.00 50.00
39 Don Maynard/13 25.00 60.00
40 Gale Sayers/40 30.00 80.00
41 Steve Smith/89 10.00 25.00
42 James Lofton/80 10.00 25.00
43 Chad Johnson/85 10.00 25.00
44 Bart Starr/15 150.00 300.00
46 Brian Westbrook/36 12.00 30.00
47 Ozzie Newsome/82 12.00 30.00
48 LaDainian Tomlinson/21 40.00 100.00
49 Reggie Wayne/87 10.00 25.00

2007 Leaf Limited Material Monikers Jersey Number Prime

PRIME PRINT RUN 4-25
1 Marques Colston 20.00 50.00
2 Larry Johnson 12.00 30.00
4 Cedric Benson 15.00 40.00
5 Dan Fouts 25.00 60.00
6 Maurice Jones-Drew 15.00 40.00
7 Peyton Manning 75.00 150.00
8 Frank Gore 20.00 50.00
9 Steven Jackson 20.00 50.00
10 Rudi Johnson 15.00 40.00
11 Joe Montana 125.00 250.00
12 Joe Namath 60.00 120.00
13 Steve Largent 25.00 60.00
15 Jim Brown 60.00 120.00
16 John Riggins 20.00 50.00
17 Marion Barber 15.00 40.00
18 Chuck Bednarik 25.00 60.00
19 Cris Collinsworth 20.00 50.00
20 Randall Cunningham 20.00 50.00
21 Sonny Jurgensen 20.00 50.00
22 A.J. Hawk 15.00 40.00
23 Eli Manning 20.00 50.00
24 Ladell Betts 12.00 30.00
25 Thurman Thomas 20.00 50.00
26 Reggie Bush 40.00 100.00
27 Roger Staubach 60.00 120.00
28 Tim Brown 25.00 60.00
29 Dan Marino 125.00 250.00
30 Dan Hampton 20.00 50.00
31 Larry Little 15.00 40.00
33 Jan Stenerud 15.00 40.00
34 Deacon Jones 20.00 50.00
35 Steve Young 50.00 100.00
36 Charley Taylor 20.00 50.00
37 Hank Baskett 15.00 40.00
39 Don Maynard 20.00 50.00
40 Gale Sayers 50.00 100.00
41 Steve Smith 15.00 40.00
42 James Lofton 15.00 40.00
43 Chad Johnson 15.00 40.00
44 Bart Starr 125.00 250.00
45 Brett Favre 125.00 200.00
46 Brian Westbrook 15.00 40.00
47 Ozzie Newsome 20.00 50.00
48 LaDainian Tomlinson 50.00 100.00
49 Reggie Wayne 15.00 40.00

2007 Leaf Limited Monikers Autographs Silver

*SILVER/99: .5X TO 1.2X BASIC AU/194-299
SILVER PRINT RUN 99 SER.#'d SETS
*GOLD/49: .6X TO 1.5X BASIC AU/194-299
GOLD PRINT RUN 49 SER.#'d SETS
UNPRICED PLATINUM PRINT RUN 1

2007 Leaf Limited Prime Pairings Autographs

STATED PRINT RUN 10-100
SERIAL #'d UNDER 25 NOT PRICED
1 Franco Harris/25 75.00 125.00
Willie Parker
2 Peyton Manning/25 100.00 200.00
Eli Manning
3 Jim McMahon/25 30.00 60.00
Rex Grossman
4 Jim Kelly/25 60.00 100.00
Thurman Thomas
5 Roger Craig/25
Frank Gore
6 Dan Marino/25 125.00 250.00
Mark Duper
7 Joe Namath/25 60.00 100.00
Don Maynard
10 Bob Griese/25 60.00 100.00
Larry Csonka
11 Cris Collinsworth/25 30.00 60.00
Chad Johnson
12 Harlon Hill/100 30.00 60.00
Rick Casares
Johnny Morris
13 Dan Fouts/25 60.00 100.00
Charlie Joiner
Kellen Winslow Sr.
14 Marcus Allen/25
Larry Johnson
15 John Mackey/25 20.00 50.00
Jimmy Orr
16 John Stallworth/25 75.00 125.00
Hines Ward
17 Marvin Harrison/25 50.00 100.00
Reggie Wayne
19 Phil Simms/25 50.00 100.00
Jim Kelly
20 Sonny Jurgensen/25 40.00 80.00
Joe Theismann
21 Tim Brown/25 30.00 60.00
James Lofton
22 Ronnie Lott/25 60.00 120.00
Darrell Green
24 Deacon Jones/25 60.00 100.00
Merlin Olsen
Rosey Grier
25 Billy Howton/25 75.00 150.00
Boyd Dowler
James Lofton
Sterling Sharpe
26 Jim Brown 150.00 250.00
Barry Sanders
LaDainian Tomlinson/15

2007 Leaf Limited Rookie Jumbo Jersey Numbers

STATED PRINT RUN 2-90
UNPRICED PRIME PRINT RUN 2-10
SERIAL #'d UNDER 15 NOT PRICED
1 Sidney Rice/18 6.00 15.00
2 Kenny Irons/30 2.00 5.00
4 Calvin Johnson/81 8.00 20.00
6 Joe Thomas/73 2.50 6.00
7 Marshawn Lynch/23 4.00 10.00
9 Antonio Pittman/24 2.50 6.00
11 Adrian Peterson/28 15.00 40.00
12 Brandon Jackson/32 2.50 6.00
13 Chris Henry RB/42 2.00 5.00
14 Yamon Figurs/16 3.00 8.00
15 Robert Meachem/17 5.00 12.00
16 Garrett Wolfe/25 2.50 6.00
17 Brian Leonard/23 3.00 8.00
18 Tony Hunt/29 2.50 6.00
21 Greg Olsen/82 2.00 5.00
24 Dwayne Jarrett/80 2.00 5.00
25 Johnnie Lee Higgins/15 4.00 10.00
27 Ted Ginn Jr./19 4.00 10.00
28 Patrick Willis/52 5.00 12.00
29 Lorenzo Booker/20 3.00 8.00
31 Gaines Adams/90 2.50 6.00
32 Jason Hill/89 2.50 6.00
33 Dwayne Bowe/82 3.00 8.00
34 Michael Bush/43 3.00 8.00

2007 Leaf Limited Rookie Jumbo Jersey Numbers Autographs

STATED PRINT RUN 25 SER.#'d SETS
UNPRICED PRIME PRINT RUN 5
1 Sidney Rice 12.00 30.00
2 Kenny Irons No AU 6.00 15.00
3 Trent Edwards 10.00 25.00
4 Calvin Johnson 60.00 120.00
5 Drew Stanton 6.00 15.00
6 Joe Thomas 10.00 25.00
7 Marshawn Lynch 30.00 80.00
8 Brady Quinn 30.00 80.00
9 Antonio Pittman 6.00 15.00
10 Paul Williams 6.00 15.00
11 Adrian Peterson 250.00 400.00
12 Brandon Jackson 8.00 20.00
13 Chris Henry RB 6.00 15.00
14 Yamon Figurs 6.00 15.00
15 Robert Meachem 10.00 25.00
16 Garrett Wolfe 6.00 15.00
17 Brian Leonard 8.00 20.00
18 Tony Hunt 6.00 15.00
19 Kevin Kolb 25.00 60.00
20 Steve Smith USC 15.00 40.00
21 Greg Olsen 8.00 20.00
22 JaMarcus Russell 15.00 40.00
23 Anthony Gonzalez 10.00 25.00
24 Dwayne Jarrett 8.00 20.00
25 Johnnie Lee Higgins 8.00 20.00
26 Troy Smith 10.00 25.00
27 Ted Ginn Jr. 15.00 40.00
28 Patrick Willis 40.00 100.00
29 Lorenzo Booker 8.00 20.00
30 John Beck 10.00 25.00
31 Gaines Adams 10.00 25.00
32 Jason Hill 10.00 25.00
33 Dwayne Bowe 20.00 50.00
34 Michael Bush 10.00 25.00

2007 Leaf Limited Slideshow Autographs

STATED PRINT RUN 30 SER.#'d SETS
1 Trent Edwards 10.00 25.00
2 Marshawn Lynch 15.00 30.00
3 Chris Henry RB 6.00 15.00
4 Paul Williams 6.00 15.00
5 Sidney Rice 12.00 30.00
6 Adrian Peterson 250.00 400.00
7 Drew Stanton 6.00 15.00
8 Calvin Johnson 60.00 150.00
9 Yamon Figurs 6.00 15.00
10 Brian Leonard 8.00 20.00
11 Garrett Wolfe 6.00 15.00
12 Kenny Irons 6.00 15.00
13 Joe Thomas 10.00 25.00
14 Brady Quinn 30.00 80.00
15 Brandon Jackson 8.00 20.00
16 Steve Smith USC 12.00 30.00
17 Dwayne Jarrett 8.00 20.00
18 Troy Smith 10.00 25.00
19 Ted Ginn Jr. 8.00 20.00
20 John Beck 10.00 25.00
21 Lorenzo Booker 8.00 20.00
22 Antonio Pittman 6.00 15.00
23 Robert Meachem 10.00 25.00
24 Dwayne Bowe 12.00 30.00
25 Greg Olsen 8.00 20.00
26 Anthony Gonzalez 10.00 25.00
27 JaMarcus Russell 6.00 15.00
28 Michael Bush 10.00 25.00
29 Johnnie Lee Higgins 8.00 20.00
30 Kevin Kolb 15.00 40.00
31 Tony Hunt 6.00 15.00
32 Patrick Willis 30.00 80.00
33 Jason Hill 10.00 25.00
34 Gaines Adams 10.00 25.00

2007 Leaf Limited Team Threads Dual

STATED PRINT RUN 100 SER.#'d SETS
*PRIME/20-25: .8X TO 2X BASIC DUAL/100
PRIME PRINT RUN 4-25
1 Steve Young 10.00 25.00
Ronnie Lott
2 Dick Butkus 10.00 25.00
Mike Singletary
3 Jim Kelly 10.00 25.00
Thurman Thomas
4 Jim Brown 10.00 25.00
Lou Groza
5 Dan Fouts 8.00 20.00
Kellen Winslow Sr.
6 Len Dawson 8.00 20.00
Jan Stenerud
7 Bob Griese 8.00 20.00
Larry Csonka
8 Rosey Brown 6.00 15.00
Sam Huff
9 Joe Namath 10.00 25.00
Don Maynard
10 Bart Starr 15.00 40.00
Paul Hornung
11 George Blanda 8.00 20.00
Fred Biletnikoff
12 Marcus Allen 8.00 20.00
Tim Brown
13 Merlin Olsen 6.00 15.00
Rosey Grier
14 Joe Theismann 8.00 20.00
John Riggins
15 Jack Lambert 12.00 30.00
Joe Greene

2007 Leaf Limited Team Threads Triples

STATED PRINT RUN 65-100
*PRIME/25: .8X TO 2X BASIC TRIPLE/65-100
PRIME PRINT RUN 5-25
1 Steve Young 12.00 30.00
Ronnie Lott
Roger Craig/65
2 Jim McMahon 12.00 30.00
Mike Singletary
Dan Hampton
3 Jim Brown 12.00 30.00
Otto Graham
Lou Groza
4 Dan Fouts 12.00 30.00
Lance Alworth
Kellen Winslow Sr.
5 Bob Griese 10.00 25.00
Larry Csonka
Larry Little
6 Bart Starr 15.00 40.00
Paul Hornung
Ray Nitschke
7 George Blanda 12.00 30.00
Daryle Lamonica
Ken Stabler
8 Merlin Olsen 8.00 20.00
Rosey Grier
Jack Youngblood
9 Sammy Baugh 20.00 50.00
Sonny Jurgensen
Joe Theismann
10 Franco Harris 15.00 40.00
Joe Greene
Jack Lambert
11 Roger Staubach 15.00 40.00
Troy Aikman
Tony Romo

2007 Leaf Limited Team Threads Quads

STATED PRINT RUN 100 SER.#'d SETS
*PRIME/25: .6X TO 1.5X BASIC QUAD/100
PRIME PRINT RUN 1-25
1 Steve Young 20.00 50.00
Ronnie Lott
Alex Smith QB
Frank Gore
2 Dick Butkus 25.00 60.00
Mike Singletary
Dan Hampton
Brian Urlacher
3 Jim Kelly 15.00 40.00
Thurman Thomas
J.P. Losman
Lee Evans
4 Dan Fouts 12.00 30.00
Kellen Winslow Sr.
Philip Rivers
Antonio Gates
5 Bob Griese 12.00 30.00
Larry Csonka
Chris Chambers
Ronnie Brown
6 Rosey Brown 12.00 30.00
Sam Huff
Eli Manning
Jeremy Shockey
7 Joe Namath 15.00 40.00
Don Maynard
Chad Pennington
Laveranues Coles
8 Bart Starr 25.00 60.00
Paul Hornung
Brett Favre
Donald Driver
9 George Blanda 12.00 30.00
Fred Biletnikoff
Marcus Allen
Tim Brown
10 Jack Lambert 20.00 50.00
Joe Greene
Hines Ward
Willie Parker

2007 Leaf Limited Team Trademarks

STATED PRINT RUN 100 SER.#'d SETS
*HOLOFOIL/25: .8X TO 2X BASIC INSERTS
HOLOFOIL PRINT RUN 25 SER.#'d SETS
1 John Elway 5.00 12.00
2 Vince Young 2.00 5.00
3 Merlin Olsen 2.50 6.00
4 Brandon Jacobs 2.00 5.00
5 Vernon Davis 2.00 5.00
6 Mark Duper 2.00 5.00
7 Chester Taylor 1.50 4.00
8 Sterling Sharpe 2.50 6.00
9 Carson Palmer 2.00 5.00
10 T.J. Houshmandzadeh 2.00 5.00
11 Lee Roy Selmon 2.50 6.00
12 Torry Holt 2.00 5.00
13 Jack Youngblood 2.50 6.00
14 Barry Sanders 5.00 12.00
15 Cadillac Williams 2.00 5.00
16 Matt Leinart 2.00 5.00
17 Kellen Winslow Sr. 2.50 6.00
18 Jim Kelly 4.00 10.00
19 Ron Mix 2.00 5.00
20 Sam Huff 2.50 6.00
21 Franco Harris 3.00 8.00
22 Dick Butkus 4.00 10.00
23 Joe Greene 3.00 8.00
24 Paul Hornung 3.00 8.00
25 Rosey Grier 2.00 5.00
26 Fran Tarkenton 4.00 10.00
27 Marvin Harrison 2.50 6.00
28 George Blanda 2.50 6.00
29 Ronnie Lott 2.50 6.00
30 Jack Lambert 3.00 8.00
31 Bob Griese 3.00 8.00
32 Daryle Lamonica 2.00 5.00
33 Len Dawson 3.00 8.00
34 Mike Singletary 3.00 8.00
35 Tom Brady 4.00 10.00
36 Larry Csonka 3.00 8.00
37 Jim McMahon 4.00 10.00
38 Marcus Allen 3.00 8.00
39 Earl Campbell 3.00 8.00
40 Drew Brees 2.50 6.00

2007 Leaf Limited Team Trademarks Materials

STATED PRINT RUN 99 SER.#'d SETS
*PRIME/50: .6X TO 1.5X BASIC JSY/99
*PRIME/25: .8X TO 2X BASIC JSY/99
PRIME PRINT RUN 25-50
*TEAM LOGO/50: .5X TO 1.2X BASIC JSY/99
TEAM LOGO PRINT RUN 50
1 John Elway 10.00 25.00
2 Vince Young 4.00 10.00
3 Merlin Olsen 5.00 12.00
4 Brandon Jacobs 4.00 10.00
5 Vernon Davis 4.00 10.00
6 Mark Duper 4.00 10.00
7 Chester Taylor 3.00 8.00
8 Sterling Sharpe 5.00 12.00
9 Carson Palmer 4.00 10.00
10 T.J. Houshmandzadeh 4.00 10.00
11 Lee Roy Selmon 5.00 12.00
12 Torry Holt 4.00 10.00
13 Jack Youngblood 5.00 12.00
14 Barry Sanders 10.00 25.00
15 Cadillac Williams 4.00 10.00
16 Matt Leinart 4.00 10.00
17 Kellen Winslow Sr. 5.00 12.00
18 Jim Kelly 8.00 20.00
19 Ron Mix 4.00 10.00
20 Sam Huff 5.00 12.00
21 Franco Harris 6.00 15.00
22 Dick Butkus 8.00 20.00
23 Joe Greene 6.00 15.00
24 Paul Hornung 6.00 15.00
25 Rosey Grier 4.00 10.00
26 Fran Tarkenton 8.00 20.00
27 Marvin Harrison 5.00 12.00
28 George Blanda 5.00 12.00
30 Jack Lambert 6.00 15.00
31 Bob Griese 6.00 15.00
32 Daryle Lamonica 4.00 10.00
33 Len Dawson 6.00 15.00
34 Mike Singletary 6.00 15.00
35 Tom Brady 8.00 20.00
36 Larry Csonka 6.00 15.00
37 Jim McMahon 8.00 20.00
38 Marcus Allen 6.00 15.00
39 Earl Campbell 6.00 15.00
40 Drew Brees 5.00 12.00

2007 Leaf Limited Team Trademarks Autograph Materials

STATED PRINT RUN 25 SER.#'d SETS
*PRIME/15: .6X TO 1.5X BASIC JSY AU/25
PRIME PRINT RUN 5-15
*TEAM LOGO/25: .4X TO 1X BASE JSY AU/25
TEAM LOGO PRINT RUN 25 SER.#'d SETS
1 John Elway 75.00 150.00
2 Vince Young 25.00 60.00
3 Merlin Olsen 15.00 40.00
4 Brandon Jacobs 12.00 30.00
5 Vernon Davis 15.00 40.00
6 Mark Duper 15.00 40.00
7 Chester Taylor 12.00 30.00
8 Sterling Sharpe 20.00 50.00
10 T.J. Houshmandzadeh 15.00 40.00
11 Lee Roy Selmon 25.00 60.00
12 Torry Holt 15.00 40.00
13 Jack Youngblood 20.00 50.00
14 Barry Sanders 75.00 150.00
15 Cadillac Williams 15.00 40.00
17 Kellen Winslow Sr. 20.00 50.00
18 Jim Kelly 25.00 60.00
19 Ron Mix 15.00 40.00
20 Sam Huff 20.00 50.00
21 Franco Harris 25.00 60.00
23 Joe Greene 25.00 60.00
24 Paul Hornung 30.00 80.00
25 Rosey Grier 15.00 40.00
26 Fran Tarkenton 25.00 60.00
27 Marvin Harrison 20.00 50.00
28 George Blanda 25.00 60.00
29 Ronnie Lott 20.00 50.00
30 Jack Lambert 40.00 80.00
31 Bob Griese 20.00 50.00
32 Daryle Lamonica 15.00 40.00
33 Len Dawson 20.00 50.00
34 Mike Singletary 20.00 50.00
36 Larry Csonka 25.00 60.00
37 Jim McMahon 20.00 50.00
38 Marcus Allen 25.00 60.00
39 Earl Campbell 20.00 50.00
40 Drew Brees 50.00 100.00

2007 Leaf Limited Threads

STATED PRINT RUN 100 SER.#'d SETS
*PRIME/25: .8X TO 2X BASIC JSY/100
*PRIME/10-15: 1.2X TO 3X BASIC JSY/100
PRIME PRINT RUN 2-25
*PRIM JSY #/58-99: .6X TO 1.5X BASIC JSY/100
*PRIM JSY #/32-51: 1X TO 2.5X BASIC JSY/100
*PRIM JSY #/20-29: 1.2X TO 3X BASIC JSY/100
*PRIM JSY #/10-19: 1.5X TO 4X BASIC JSY/100
PRIME JERSEY NUMBER PRINT RUN 1-99
*PRIME TEAM LOGO/10: 1.2X TO 3X BASIC JSY/100
PRIME TEAM LOGO PRINT RUN 5-10
UNPRICED SUPER PRIME PRINT RUN 1
1 Anquan Boldin 3.00 8.00
2 Edgerrin James 3.00 8.00
3 Larry Fitzgerald 4.00 10.00
4 Matt Leinart 3.00 8.00
5 Alge Crumpler 3.00 8.00
6 Warrick Dunn 3.00 8.00
7 Jerious Norwood 3.00 8.00
9 Steve McNair 3.00 8.00
10 Mark Clayton 3.00 8.00
12 J.P. Losman 2.50 6.00
13 Lee Evans 3.00 8.00
14 Jake Delhomme 3.00 8.00
15 Steve Smith 3.00 8.00
16 DeAngelo Williams 4.00 10.00
17 Rex Grossman 3.00 8.00
18 Cedric Benson 3.00 8.00
19 Bernard Berrian 2.50 6.00
20 Carson Palmer 3.00 8.00
21 Chad Johnson 3.00 8.00
22 Rudi Johnson 3.00 8.00
23 T.J. Houshmandzadeh 3.00 8.00
24 Kellen Winslow 3.00 8.00
25 Braylon Edwards 3.00 8.00
27 Julius Jones 2.50 6.00
28 Terrell Owens 4.00 10.00
29 Tony Romo 5.00 12.00
30 Jay Cutler 4.00 10.00
31 Javon Walker 3.00 8.00
34 Roy Williams WR 3.00 8.00
35 Jon Kitna 2.50 6.00
36 Brett Favre 8.00 20.00
37 Donald Driver 4.00 10.00
38 Greg Jennings 4.00 10.00
40 Andre Johnson 3.00 8.00
42 Peyton Manning 8.00 20.00
43 Marvin Harrison 4.00 10.00
44 Reggie Wayne 3.00 8.00
45 Joseph Addai 3.00 8.00
47 Fred Taylor 3.00 8.00
48 Maurice Jones-Drew 4.00 10.00
49 Brodie Croyle 3.00 8.00
50 Larry Johnson 2.50 6.00
51 Tony Gonzalez 3.00 8.00
53 Ronnie Brown 3.00 8.00
54 Chris Chambers 3.00 8.00
55 Tarvaris Jackson 2.50 6.00
56 Troy Williamson 2.50 6.00
57 Chester Taylor 2.50 6.00
58 Tom Brady 8.00 20.00
59 Randy Moss 6.00 15.00
60 Laurence Maroney 3.00 8.00
62 Drew Brees 4.00 10.00
63 Deuce McAllister 3.00 8.00
64 Reggie Bush 4.00 10.00
65 Marques Colston 4.00 10.00
66 Eli Manning 4.00 10.00
67 Jeremy Shockey 3.00 8.00
68 Brandon Jacobs 3.00 8.00
69 Chad Pennington 3.00 8.00
71 Laveranues Coles 2.50 6.00
72 Jerry Porter 3.00 8.00
73 LaMont Jordan 3.00 8.00
74 Donovan McNabb 4.00 10.00
75 Brian Westbrook 3.00 8.00
76 Reggie Brown 2.50 6.00
77 Ben Roethlisberger 4.00 10.00
78 Hines Ward 4.00 10.00
79 Willie Parker 3.00 8.00
80 Philip Rivers 4.00 10.00
81 Antonio Gates 4.00 10.00
82 LaDainian Tomlinson 4.00 10.00
83 Alex Smith QB 4.00 10.00
85 Frank Gore 4.00 10.00
86 Matt Hasselbeck 3.00 8.00
87 Shaun Alexander 3.00 8.00
88 Deion Branch 3.00 8.00
89 Marc Bulger 3.00 8.00
90 Steven Jackson 4.00 10.00
91 Torry Holt 3.00 8.00
93 Cadillac Williams 3.00 8.00
94 Joey Galloway 3.00 8.00
95 Vince Young 3.00 8.00
96 Brandon Jones 2.50 6.00
97 LenDale White 3.00 8.00
98 Jason Campbell 3.00 8.00
99 Clinton Portis 3.00 8.00
100 Santana Moss 3.00 8.00
101 Alan Page 4.00 10.00
102 Barry Sanders 10.00 25.00
103 Bart Starr 10.00 25.00
106 Bob Griese 6.00 15.00
107 Bobby Layne 6.00 15.00
109 Charley Taylor 5.00 12.00
111 Charlie Joiner 5.00 12.00
112 Chuck Bednarik 8.00 20.00
113 Cris Collinsworth 5.00 12.00
114 Dan Fouts 6.00 15.00
115 Dan Hampton 6.00 15.00
116 Dan Marino 12.00 30.00
118 Darrell Green 5.00 12.00
119 Daryle Lamonica 4.00 10.00
120 Deacon Jones 5.00 12.00
121 Dick Butkus 8.00 20.00
122 Doak Walker 6.00 15.00
123 Don Maynard 5.00 12.00
126 Earl Campbell 6.00 15.00
127 Forrest Gregg 5.00 12.00
128 Fran Tarkenton 8.00 20.00
129 Franco Harris 6.00 15.00
130 Fred Biletnikoff 6.00 15.00
131 Gale Sayers 8.00 20.00
133 George Blanda 5.00 12.00
135 Jack Lambert 8.00 20.00
136 Jack Youngblood 5.00 12.00
137 James Lofton 4.00 10.00
138 Jan Stenerud 4.00 10.00
140 Jim Brown 8.00 20.00
141 Jim Kelly 8.00 20.00
142 Jim McMahon 6.00 15.00
143 Jim Otto 4.00 10.00
144 Jim Thorpe 60.00 100.00
146 Joe Greene 6.00 15.00
147 Joe Montana 12.00 30.00
148 Joe Namath 8.00 20.00
149 Joe Theismann 6.00 15.00
150 John Elway 10.00 25.00
152 John Riggins 5.00 12.00
155 Johnny Unitas 12.00 30.00
156 Kellen Winslow Sr. 5.00 12.00
157 Ken Stabler 8.00 20.00
158 Lance Alworth 8.00 20.00
159 Larry Csonka 6.00 15.00
160 Larry Little 4.00 10.00
161 Lee Roy Selmon 5.00 12.00
162 Len Dawson 6.00 15.00
163 Lou Groza 5.00 12.00
165 Marcus Allen 6.00 15.00
166 Mark Duper 4.00 10.00
167 Merlin Olsen 5.00 12.00
168 Mike Singletary 6.00 15.00
170 Otto Graham 8.00 20.00
171 Ozzie Newsome 5.00 12.00
172 Paul Hornung 6.00 15.00
173 Paul Warfield 5.00 12.00
174 Phil Simms 5.00 12.00
175 Randall Cunningham 5.00 12.00
176 Ray Nitschke 8.00 20.00
177 Raymond Berry 5.00 12.00
180 Ron Mix 4.00 10.00
182 Roger Staubach 10.00 25.00
183 Rosey Brown 4.00 10.00
184 Rosey Grier 4.00 10.00
186 Sam Huff 5.00 12.00
187 Sammy Baugh 12.00 30.00
188 Sid Luckman 12.00 30.00
189 Sonny Jurgensen 5.00 12.00
190 Sterling Sharpe 5.00 12.00
191 Steve Largent 6.00 15.00
192 Steve Young 8.00 20.00
193 Ted Hendricks 5.00 12.00
194 Thurman Thomas 5.00 12.00
195 Tim Brown 6.00 15.00
196 Tiki Barber 6.00 15.00
197 Troy Aikman 8.00 20.00
198 Walter Payton 15.00 40.00
199 Willie Brown 5.00 12.00
200 Elroy Hirsch 12.00 30.00

2008 Leaf Limited

This set was released on October 29, 2008. The base set consists of 333 cards. Cards 1-100 feature veterans, while cards 101-200 feature legends serial numbered of 499. Cards 201-300 have rookies serial numbered of 999 as well as some autographed rookies serial numbered of 99-299. Cards 301-334 are rookie jersey cards serial numbered of 99.

COMP.SET w/o SP's (100) 8.00 20.00
101-200 LEGEND PRINT RUN 499
BASE ROOKIE PRINT RUN 999
AU ROOKIE PRINT RUN 99-299
JSY ROOKIE PRINT RUN 99 SER.#'d SETS
1 Anquan Boldin .30 .75
2 Edgerrin James .30 .75
3 Larry Fitzgerald .40 1.00
4 Kurt Warner .40 1.00
5 Michael Turner .40 1.00
6 Roddy White .30 .75
7 Joe Horn .30 .75
8 Derrick Mason .30 .75
9 Mark Clayton .30 .75
10 Willis McGahee .30 .75
11 Trent Edwards .25 .60
12 Marshawn Lynch .30 .75
13 Lee Evans .30 .75
14 Jake Delhomme .30 .75
15 Steve Smith .30 .75
16 DeAngelo Williams .30 .75
17 Rex Grossman .30 .75
18 Adrian Peterson Bears .25 .60
19 Devin Hester .40 1.00
20 Carson Palmer .40 1.00
21 Chris Perry .25 .60
22 T.J. Houshmandzadeh .30 .75
23 Chad Johnson .30 .75
24 Braylon Edwards .30 .75
25 Derek Anderson .25 .60
26 Jamal Lewis .30 .75
27 Tony Romo .50 1.25
28 Terrell Owens .40 1.00
29 Marion Barber .30 .75
30 Jason Witten .40 1.00
31 Jay Cutler .40 1.00
32 Selvin Young .25 .60
33 Brandon Marshall .30 .75
34 Jon Kitna .30 .75
35 Calvin Johnson .40 1.00
36 Roy Williams WR .30 .75
37 Aaron Rodgers .75 2.00
38 Donald Driver .30 .75
39 Greg Jennings .40 1.00
40 Matt Schaub .30 .75
41 Andre Johnson .30 .75
42 Kevin Walter .30 .75
43 Peyton Manning .60 1.50
44 Joseph Addai .30 .75
45 Reggie Wayne .30 .75
46 David Garrard .30 .75
47 Fred Taylor .30 .75
48 Maurice Jones-Drew .30 .75
49 Reggie Williams .30 .75
50 Brodie Croyle .30 .75
51 Larry Johnson .30 .75
52 Tony Gonzalez .30 .75
53 Chad Pennington .30 .75
54 Ronnie Brown .30 .75
55 Ted Ginn Jr. .30 .75
56 Tarvaris Jackson .30 .75
57 Adrian Peterson .60 1.50
58 Chester Taylor .25 .60
59 Tom Brady .60 1.50
60 Randy Moss .40 1.00
61 Laurence Maroney .30 .75
62 Drew Brees .40 1.00
63 Marques Colston .30 .75
64 Reggie Bush .40 1.00
65 Eli Manning .40 1.00
66 Plaxico Burress .30 .75
67 Brandon Jacobs .30 .75
68 Brett Favre 3.00 8.00
69 Jerricho Cotchery .30 .75
70 Laveranues Coles .25 .60
71 JaMarcus Russell .30 .75
72 Justin Fargas .25 .60
73 Ronald Curry .30 .75
74 Donovan McNabb .40 1.00
75 Brian Westbrook .30 .75
76 Kevin Curtis .25 .60
77 Ben Roethlisberger .40 1.00

78 Willie Parker	.30	.75
79 Santonio Holmes	.30	.75
80 Philip Rivers	.40	1.00
81 LaDainian Tomlinson	.40	1.00
82 Antonio Gates	.40	1.00
83 J.T. O'Sullivan	.25	.60
84 Frank Gore	.30	.75
85 Isaac Bruce	.30	.75
86 Matt Hasselbeck	.30	.75
87 Julius Jones	.25	.60
88 Deion Branch	.30	.75
89 Marc Bulger	.30	.75
90 Steven Jackson	.40	1.00
91 Torry Holt	.30	.75
92 Jeff Garcia	.30	.75
93 Earnest Graham	.25	.60
94 Joey Galloway	.30	.75
95 Vince Young	.30	.75
96 LenDale White	.30	.75
97 Roydell Williams	.25	.60
98 Jason Campbell	.30	.75
99 Santana Moss	.25	.60
100 Clinton Portis	.30	.75
101 Alan Page	1.50	4.00
102 Bart Starr	3.00	8.00
103 Bert Jones	1.25	3.00
104 Bill Dudley	1.25	3.00
105 Billy Howton	1.25	3.00
106 Red Grange	2.50	6.00
107 Billy Sims	1.50	4.00
108 Bo Jackson	2.50	6.00
109 Bob Griese	2.00	5.00
110 Bob Lilly	1.50	4.00
111 Bob Waterfield	1.50	4.00
112 Bobby Bell	1.25	3.00
113 Brett Favre	5.00	12.00
114 Carl Eller	1.25	3.00
115 Charley Taylor	1.25	3.00
116 Charley Trippi	1.25	3.00
117 Chuck Foreman	1.25	3.00
118 Cliff Harris	1.25	3.00
119 Cris Collinsworth	1.50	4.00
120 Danny White	1.25	3.00
121 Dante Lavelli	1.25	3.00
122 Daryl Johnston	2.00	5.00
123 Daryle Lamonica	1.50	4.00
124 Deacon Jones	1.50	4.00
125 Del Shofner	1.25	3.00
126 Dick Butkus	2.50	6.00
127 Doak Walker	2.00	5.00
128 Don Perkins	1.25	3.00
129 Dub Jones	1.25	3.00
130 Forrest Gregg	1.25	3.00
131 Fran Tarkenton	2.00	5.00
132 Frank Gifford	2.00	5.00
133 Fred Biletnikoff	2.00	5.00
134 Fred Dryer	1.25	3.00
135 Fred Williamson	1.25	3.00
136 Gale Sayers	2.50	6.00
137 Gary Collins	1.25	3.00
138 Hugh McElhenny	1.25	3.00
139 Jack Lambert	2.00	5.00
140 James Lofton	1.25	3.00
141 Jan Stenerud	1.25	3.00
142 Jim McMahon	2.00	5.00
143 Jim Otto	1.25	3.00
144 Jim Taylor	2.00	5.00
145 Jim Thorpe	2.50	6.00
146 Joe Montana	4.00	10.00
147 John Riggins	1.50	4.00
148 John Matuszak	2.00	5.00
149 Johnny Unitas	3.00	8.00
150 Ken Stabler	2.00	5.00
152 Lance Alworth	1.50	4.00
153 Larry Little	1.25	3.00
154 Lee Roy Selmon	1.50	4.00
155 Lem Barney	1.25	3.00
156 Len Dawson	2.00	5.00
157 Lenny Moore	1.50	4.00
158 Leroy Kelly	1.50	4.00
159 Lydell Mitchell	1.25	3.00
160 Marcus Allen	2.00	5.00
161 Mark Duper	1.25	3.00
162 Mark Gastineau	1.25	3.00
163 Merlin Olsen	1.50	4.00
164 Mike Curtis	1.25	3.00
165 Norm Van Brocklin	1.50	4.00
166 Ollie Matson	1.50	4.00
167 Ozzie Newsome	1.50	4.00
168 Paul Hornung	2.00	5.00
169 Paul Krause	1.25	3.00
170 Paul Warfield	1.50	4.00
171 Pete Retzlaff	1.25	3.00
172 Phil Simms	1.50	4.00
173 Ace Parker	1.25	3.00
174 Randy White	1.50	4.00
175 Reggie White	2.00	5.00
176 Roger Craig	1.50	4.00
177 Ronnie Lott	2.00	5.00
178 Rosey Grier	1.25	3.00
179 Sammy Baugh	2.00	5.00
180 Sid Luckman	1.50	4.00
181 Sonny Jurgensen	1.50	4.00
182 Sterling Sharpe	1.50	4.00
183 Steve Largent	2.00	5.00
184 Ted Hendricks	1.25	3.00
185 Tiki Barber	1.50	4.00
186 Tim Brown	2.00	5.00
187 Tom Fears	1.25	3.00
188 Tommy McDonald	1.50	4.00
189 Tony Canadeo	1.25	3.00
190 Tony Dorsett	2.00	5.00
191 Troy Aikman	2.50	6.00
192 Walter Payton	4.00	10.00
193 Warren Moon	2.00	5.00
194 William Perry	1.25	3.00
195 Willie Lanier	1.25	3.00
196 Willie Brown	1.25	3.00
197 Willie Davis	1.25	3.00
198 Willie Wood	1.25	3.00
199 Y.A. Tittle	2.00	5.00
200 Yale Lary	1.25	3.00
201 Adrian Arrington AU/99 RC	4.00	10.00
202 Alex Brink RC	2.50	6.00
203 Ali Highsmith AU/99 RC	3.00	8.00
204 Allen Patrick RC	2.00	5.00
205 Andre Woodson AU/99 RC	5.00	12.00
206 Anthony Alridge RC	2.00	5.00
207 Antoine Cason AU/99 RC	5.00	12.00
208 Aqib Talib AU/199 RC	4.00	10.00
209 Arman Shields RC	2.00	5.00
210 Brad Cottam AU/99 RC	4.00	10.00
211 Brandon Flowers RC	2.50	6.00
212 Bruce Davis RC	2.00	5.00
213 Calais Campbell AU/299 RC	3.00	8.00
214 Caleb Campbell AU/99 RC	5.00	12.00
215 Chauncey Washington RC	2.00	5.00
216 Chevis Jackson RC	1.50	4.00
217 Chris Long AU/99 RC	10.00	25.00
218 Colt Brennan AU/99 RC	10.00	25.00
219 Cory Boyd RC	1.50	4.00
220 Craig Steltz RC	2.00	5.00
221 Craig Stevens RC	1.50	4.00
222 Curtis Lofton AU/99 RC	4.00	10.00
223 Dan Connor AU/299 RC	4.00	10.00
224 Dantrell Savage RC	2.00	5.00
225 Darius Reynaud AU/99 RC	3.00	8.00
226 Darrell Strong RC	2.00	5.00
227 Davone Bess AU/299 RC	6.00	15.00
228 Dennis Dixon AU/99 RC	8.00	20.00
229 Derek Fine RC	2.00	5.00
230 Derrick Harvey AU/299 RC	2.50	6.00
231 DJ Hall RC	2.00	5.00
232 Dominique Rodgers-Cromartie/ AU/299 RC	4.00	
10.00		
233 Erik Ainge AU/299 RC	4.00	10.00
234 Erin Henderson AU/99 RC	5.00	12.00
235 Ernie Wheelwright RC	2.00	5.00
236 Fred Davis AU/299 RC	4.00	10.00
237 Joe Jon Finley RC	2.00	5.00
238 Jacob Hester AU/99 RC	5.00	12.00
239 Jacob Tamme AU/299 RC	4.00	10.00
240 Jalen Parmele RC	2.00	5.00
241 Jamar Adams RC	2.00	5.00
242 Jason Rivers RC	2.00	5.00
243 Jaymar Johnson RC	1.50	4.00
244 Jed Collins RC	2.00	5.00
245 Jermichael Finley AU/99 RC	12.50	25.00
246 Jerod Mayo AU/99 RC	5.00	12.00
247 John Carlson AU/299 RC	4.00	10.00
248 Jonathan Hefney RC	2.00	5.00
249 Jordon Dizon AU/99 RC	5.00	12.00
250 Josh Johnson AU/299 RC	4.00	10.00
251 Josh Morgan RC	2.50	6.00
252 Justin Forsett RC	2.50	6.00
253 Kalvin McRae RC	1.50	4.00
254 Keenan Burton AU/299 RC	2.50	6.00
255 Keith Rivers AU/299 RC	4.00	10.00
256 Kellen Davis AU/99 RC	3.00	8.00
257 Kenneth Moore RC	2.00	5.00
258 Kenny Phillips AU/299 RC	4.00	10.00
259 Kentwan Balmer AU/299 RC	3.00	8.00
260 Kevin Robinson RC	1.50	4.00
261 Lavelle Hawkins AU/299 RC	2.50	6.00
262 Lawrence Jackson AU/299 RC	3.00	8.00
263 Leodis McKelvin AU/299 RC	3.00	8.00
264 Marcus Henry RC	2.00	5.00
265 Marcus Monk RC	2.00	5.00
266 Marcus Smith RC	2.00	5.00
267 Marcus Thomas RC	2.00	5.00
268 Mark Bradford RC	1.50	4.00
269 Martellus Bennett AU/299 RC	5.00	12.00
270 Martin Rucker AU/299 RC	3.00	8.00
271 Matt Flynn AU/299 RC	25.00	50.00
272 Mike Jenkins AU/299 RC	4.00	10.00
273 Mike Hart AU/299 RC	4.00	10.00
274 Owen Schmitt RC	2.50	6.00
275 Pat Sims AU/299 RC	3.00	8.00
276 Patrick Lee RC	2.00	5.00
277 Paul Hubbard RC	2.00	5.00
278 Paul Smith RC	2.50	6.00
279 Peyton Hillis RC	3.00	8.00
280 Phillip Merling AU/299 RC	3.00	8.00
281 Pierre Garcon RC	5.00	12.00
282 Quentin Groves RC	2.00	5.00
283 Reggie Smith AU/99 RC	4.00	10.00
284 Ryan Grice-Mullen RC	1.50	4.00
285 Ryan Torain AU/99 RC	5.00	12.00
286 Sam Keller RC	2.00	5.00
287 Sedrick Ellis AU/299 RC	4.00	10.00
288 Shawn Crable RC	1.50	4.00
289 Simeon Castille RC	2.00	5.00
290 Tashard Choice AU/299 RC	3.00	8.00
291 Tavares Gooden RC	2.00	5.00
292 Terrell Thomas AU/99 RC	4.00	10.00
293 Terrence Wheatley RC	1.50	4.00
294 Thomas Brown AU/99 RC	4.00	10.00
295 Tim Hightower RC	2.50	6.00
296 Tracy Porter RC	2.50	6.00
297 Vernon Gholston AU/299 RC	3.00	8.00
298 Will Franklin RC	2.00	5.00
299 Xavier Adibi AU/299 RC	2.50	6.00
300 Xavier Omon RC	2.50	6.00
301 Andre Caldwell JSY AU RC	8.00	20.00
302 Brian Brohm JSY AU RC	10.00	25.00
303 Chad Henne JSY AU RC	10.00	25.00
304 Chris Johnson JSY AU RC	30.00	80.00
305 Darren McFadden JSY AU RC	25.00	60.00
306 DeSean Jackson JSY AU RC	30.00	60.00
307 Devin Thomas JSY AU RC	8.00	20.00
308 Dexter Jackson JSY AU RC	8.00	20.00
309 Donnie Avery JSY AU RC	8.00	20.00
310 Dustin Keller JSY AU RC	12.00	30.00
311 Earl Bennett JSY AU RC	10.00	25.00
312 Early Doucet JSY AU RC	8.00	20.00
313 Eddie Royal JSY AU RC	10.00	25.00
314 Felix Jones JSY AU RC	25.00	60.00
315 Glenn Dorsey JSY AU RC EXCH	10.00	25.00
316 Harry Douglas JSY AU RC	8.00	20.00
317 Jake Long JSY AU RC	10.00	25.00
318 Jamaal Charles JSY AU RC	15.00	40.00
319 James Hardy JSY AU RC	8.00	20.00
320 Jerome Simpson JSY AU RC	10.00	25.00
321 Joe Flacco JSY AU RC	50.00	100.00
322 John David Booty JSY AU RC	8.00	20.00
323 Jonathan Stewart JSY AU RC	15.00	40.00
324 Jordy Nelson JSY AU RC	20.00	40.00
325 Kevin O'Connell JSY AU RC	8.00	20.00
326 Kevin Smith JSY AU RC	10.00	25.00
327 Limas Sweed JSY AU RC	10.00	25.00
328 Malcolm Kelly JSY AU RC	8.00	20.00
329 Mario Manningham JSY AU RC	15.00	30.00
330 Matt Forte JSY AU RC	25.00	60.00
331 Matt Ryan JSY AU RC	60.00	120.00
332 Rashard Mendenhall JSY AU RC	20.00	50.00
333 Ray Rice JSY AU RC	25.00	50.00
334 Steve Slaton JSY AU RC	10.00	25.00

2008 Leaf Limited Bronze Spotlight

*VETS 1-100: 2.5X TO 6X BASIC CARDS
*LEGENDS 101-200: .6X TO 1.5X BASIC CARDS

COMMON ROOKIE (201-300)	1.50	4.00
ROOKIE SEMISTARS	2.00	5.00
ROOKIE UNL.STARS	2.50	6.00

STATED PRINT RUN 125 SER.#'d SETS

68 Brett Favre	6.00	15.00
217 Chris Long	2.50	6.00
218 Colt Brennan	2.50	6.00
227 Davone Bess	2.50	6.00
246 Jerod Mayo	2.50	6.00
271 Matt Flynn	5.00	12.00
273 Mike Hart	2.50	6.00
279 Peyton Hillis	3.00	8.00
295 Tim Hightower	2.50	6.00

2008 Leaf Limited Gold Spotlight

*VETS 1-100: 3X TO 8X BASIC CARDS
*LEGENDS 101-200: .8X TO 2X BASIC CARDS
*ROOKIES 201-300: .5X TO 1.2X BASIC CARDS
1-300 PRINT RUN 49 SER.#'d SETS
*JSY AU 301-334: .5X TO 1.2X BASE JSY AU
301-334 PRINT RUN 25 SER.#'d SETS

68 Brett Favre	8.00	20.00
304 Chris Johnson JSY AU	60.00	150.00
321 Joe Flacco JSY AU	60.00	120.00
331 Matt Ryan JSY AU	100.00	200.00

2008 Leaf Limited Platinum Spotlight

UNPRICED PLATINUM PRINT RUN 1

2008 Leaf Limited Silver Spotlight

*VETS 1-100: 2.5X TO 6X BASIC CARDS
*LEGENDS 101-200: .6X TO 1.5X BASIC CARDS
*ROOKIES 201-300: .4X TO 1X BRONZE
1-300 PRINT RUN 99 SER.#'d SETS
*JSY AU 301-334: .4X TO 1X BASE JSY AU
301-334 PRINT RUN 49 SER.#'d SETS

68 Brett Favre	6.00	15.00
304 Chris Johnson JSY AU	60.00	120.00
331 Matt Ryan JSY AU	75.00	150.00

2008 Leaf Limited Banner Season

STATED PRINT RUN 999 SER.#'d SETS
*HOLOFOIL/100: .6X TO 1.5X BASIC INSERTS
HOLOFOIL PRINT RUN 100 SER.#'d SETS

1 Adrian Peterson	2.00	5.00
2 Anthony Gonzalez	.75	2.00
3 Brandon Jacobs	1.00	2.50
4 Brandon Marshall	1.00	2.50
5 Brian Westbrook	1.00	2.50
6 Willie Parker	1.00	2.50
7 LaDainian Tomlinson	1.25	3.00
8 Reggie Wayne	1.00	2.50
9 Randy Moss	1.25	3.00
10 Chad Johnson	1.00	2.50
11 Larry Fitzgerald	1.25	3.00
12 Terrell Owens	1.25	3.00
13 Braylon Edwards	1.00	2.50
14 Marques Colston	1.00	2.50
15 Roddy White	1.00	2.50
16 Santonio Holmes	1.00	2.50
17 Tom Brady	2.00	5.00
18 Drew Brees	1.25	3.00
19 Tony Romo	1.50	4.00
20 Eli Manning	1.25	3.00
21 Joseph Addai	1.00	2.50
22 Patrick Crayton	1.00	2.50
23 Tony Gonzalez	1.00	2.50
24 Clinton Portis	1.00	2.50
25 Greg Jennings	1.25	3.00

2008 Leaf Limited Banner Season Autograph Materials

STATED PRINT RUN 5-25
*PRIME/16-25: .5X TO 1.2X BASIC JSY AU/25
PRIME PRINT RUN 1-25
SERIAL #'d UNDER 15 NOT PRICED

2 Anthony Gonzalez	10.00	25.00
3 Brandon Jacobs	12.00	30.00
4 Brandon Marshall	12.00	30.00
5 Brian Westbrook	12.00	30.00
6 Willie Parker	12.00	30.00
8 Reggie Wayne	12.00	30.00
10 Chad Johnson	12.00	30.00
13 Braylon Edwards	12.00	30.00
14 Marques Colston	12.00	30.00
15 Roddy White	12.00	30.00
18 Drew Brees	40.00	80.00
19 Tony Romo	50.00	100.00
21 Joseph Addai	12.00	30.00
22 Patrick Crayton	12.00	30.00
25 Greg Jennings	15.00	40.00

2008 Leaf Limited Banner Season Materials

STATED PRINT RUN 60-100
*PRIME/25: .8X TO 2X BASIC JSY
PRIME PRINT RUN 25 SER.#'d SETS

1 Adrian Peterson	6.00	15.00
2 Anthony Gonzalez	2.50	6.00
3 Brandon Jacobs	3.00	8.00
4 Brandon Marshall	3.00	8.00
5 Brian Westbrook	3.00	8.00
6 Willie Parker	3.00	8.00
7 LaDainian Tomlinson	4.00	10.00
8 Reggie Wayne	3.00	8.00
9 Randy Moss	4.00	10.00
10 Chad Johnson	3.00	8.00
11 Larry Fitzgerald/78	4.00	10.00
12 Terrell Owens	4.00	10.00
13 Braylon Edwards	3.00	8.00
14 Marques Colston	3.00	8.00
15 Roddy White	3.00	8.00
16 Santonio Holmes	3.00	8.00
17 Tom Brady	6.00	15.00
18 Drew Brees	4.00	10.00
19 Tony Romo	5.00	12.00
20 Eli Manning	4.00	10.00
21 Joseph Addai	3.00	8.00
22 Patrick Crayton/60	3.00	8.00
23 Tony Gonzalez	3.00	8.00
24 Clinton Portis	3.00	8.00
25 Greg Jennings	4.00	10.00

2008 Leaf Limited College Phenoms Jersey Autographs

STATED PRINT RUN 45-99
*SILVER/25-50: .5X TO 1.2X BASIC JSY AU
SILVER SPOTLIGHT PRINT RUN 25-50
*GOLD-10-25: .6X TO 1.5X BASIC JSY AU
GOLD SPOTLIGHT PRINT RUN 10-25
UNPRICED PLATINUM PRINT RUN 1

204 Allen Patrick/99	6.00	15.00
218 Colt Brennan/99	12.00	30.00
223 Dan Connor/99	8.00	20.00
233 Erik Ainge/99	12.00	30.00
255 Keith Rivers/99	8.00	20.00
273 Mike Hart/99	8.00	20.00
297 Vernon Gholston/50	8.00	20.00
302 Brian Brohm/99	8.00	20.00
305 Darren McFadden/50	30.00	80.00
312 Early Doucet/50	8.00	20.00
314 Felix Jones/45	20.00	50.00
315 Glenn Dorsey/50 EXCH	10.00	25.00
316 Harry Douglas/50	8.00	20.00
318 Jamaal Charles/50	15.00	40.00
327 Limas Sweed/50	10.00	25.00
328 Malcolm Kelly/50	8.00	20.00

2008 Leaf Limited Cuts Autographs

STATED PRINT RUN 1-100
SERIAL #'d UNDER 15 NOT PRICED

1 Bert Bell/50	40.00	80.00
2 Ace Parker/29	40.00	80.00
4 Tom Fears/15	60.00	120.00
5 Bulldog Turner/75	40.00	80.00
6 Bob Waterfield/40	60.00	120.00
7 Doak Walker/25	150.00	250.00
9 Ernie Stautner/100	30.00	60.00
10 Bruiser Kinard/40	100.00	200.00
11 Hank Stram/85	60.00	100.00
15 Sammy Baugh/30	60.00	120.00
17 Tony Canadeo/72	40.00	80.00
18 Walter Payton/100	150.00	300.00
20 Elroy Hirsch/23	50.00	100.00
21 Otto Graham/21		
22 Jim Brown/25	60.00	100.00
23 Gale Sayers/25	40.00	80.00
24 Hugh McElhenny/25	40.00	80.00
25 Ozzie Newsome/25	30.00	60.00

2008 Leaf Limited Jumbo Jerseys

STATED PRINT RUN 25-50
*PRIME/10: 1X TO 2.5X BASIC JSY
PRIME PRINT RUN 10
*JER NUM/25-30: .4X TO 1X BASIC JSY
JERSEY NUMBER PRINT RUN 25-30
*JER NUM PRIME/10: 1X TO 2.5X BASIC JSY
JSY NUMBER PRIME PRINT RUN 5-10
*TEAM LOGO/25-50: .4X TO 1X BASIC JSY
TEAM LOGO PRINT RUN 4-50
*TM LOGO PRIME/2-10: 1X TO 2.5X BASIC JSY
TEAM LOGO PRIME PRINT RUN 2-10

1 Philip Rivers	5.00	12.00
2 Torry Holt/45	4.00	10.00
3 Steven Jackson	5.00	12.00
4 Adrian Peterson	8.00	20.00
5 Brandon Jacobs	4.00	10.00
6 Calvin Johnson	5.00	12.00
7 DeAngelo Williams	4.00	10.00
8 Derrick Mason	4.00	10.00
9 Marion Barber	6.00	15.00
10 Steve Smith	4.00	10.00
11 LaRon Landry	4.00	10.00
12 Marques Colston	4.00	10.00
13 Larry Johnson/30	4.00	10.00
14 Ronnie Brown	4.00	10.00
15 Rudi Johnson	4.00	10.00
16 Sidney Rice/25	5.00	12.00
17 Randy Moss	5.00	12.00
18 Tony Romo	6.00	15.00
19 Clinton Portis	4.00	10.00
20 LaDainian Tomlinson	5.00	12.00
21 Brian Westbrook	4.00	10.00
22 Laurence Maroney	4.00	10.00
23 T.J. Houshmandzadeh	4.00	10.00
24 Antonio Gates	5.00	12.00
25 Andre Johnson	4.00	10.00

2008 Leaf Limited Jumbo Jerseys Autographs

STATED PRINT RUN 5-25
UNPRICED PRIME PRINT RUN 1-5
*JSY NUM AU/15-25: .4X TO 1X BASIC JSY AU
JERSEY NUMBER PRINT RUN 5-25
UNPRICED JSY NUM PRIME PRINT RUN 1-5
*TM LOGO AU/15-25: .4X TO 1X BASE JSY AU
TEAM LOGO PRINT RUN 5-25
UNPRICED TEAM LOGO PRIME PRINT RUN 1-5

7 DeAngelo Williams/15	12.00	30.00
11 LaRon Landry/25	12.00	30.00
12 Marques Colston/25	12.00	30.00
14 Ronnie Brown/25	12.00	30.00
21 Brian Westbrook/25	15.00	40.00

2008 Leaf Limited Lettermen

UNPRICED LETTERMEN PRINT RUN 4-10

2008 Leaf Limited Matching Numbers Jerseys

STATED PRINT RUN 100 SER.#'d SETS
*PRIME/25: .8X TO 2X BASIC DUAL/100
PRIME PRINT RUN 25
*POSITION/100: .4X TO 1X BASIC DUAL/100
POSITION PRINT RUN 100 SER.#'d SETS
*POS.PRIME/25: .8X TO 2X BASIC DUAL/100
POSITION PRIME PRINT RUN 25

1 Trent Edwards	5.00	12.00
Donovan McNabb		
2 Ben Roethlisberger	5.00	12.00
Matt Leinart		
3 Matt Schaub	4.00	10.00
Matt Hasselbeck		
4 Carson Palmer	8.00	20.00
Tony Romo		
5 Santonio Holmes	4.00	10.00
Vince Young		
6 Larry Fitzgerald	5.00	12.00
Roy Williams WR		
7 Aaron Rodgers	10.00	25.00
Marques Colston		
8 Braylon Edwards	4.00	10.00
Plaxico Burress		
9 Philip Rivers	5.00	12.00
Jason Campbell		
10 Marshawn Lynch	6.00	15.00
Devin Hester		
11 Fred Taylor	8.00	20.00
Adrian Peterson		
12 Joseph Addai	4.00	10.00
Chester Taylor		
13 Edgerrin James	4.00	10.00
Rudi Johnson		
14 Willie Parker	4.00	10.00
Laurence Maroney		
15 Donald Driver	4.00	10.00
Andre Johnson		
16 Terrell Owens	5.00	12.00
Randy Moss		
17 Lee Evans	4.00	10.00
Deion Branch		
18 T.J. Houshmandzadeh	4.00	10.00
Joey Galloway		
19 Chad Johnson	5.00	12.00
Greg Jennings		
20 Steve Smith	4.00	10.00
Jerricho Cotchery		

2008 Leaf Limited Material Monikers Jersey Number

STATED PRINT RUN 15-50
*PRIME/25: .6X TO 1.5X JSY AU/45-50
*PRIME/15-25: .5X TO 1.2X JSY AU/45-50
PRIME PRINT RUN 4-25

1 Ben Roethlisberger	50.00	100.00
2 A.J. Hawk	10.00	25.00
3 Calvin Johnson/20	25.00	50.00
4 Chris Henry RB	10.00	25.00
5 Dallas Clark/16	12.00	30.00
6 DeAngelo Williams	10.00	25.00
7 DeMeco Ryans	10.00	25.00
8 Derrick Mason/15	12.00	30.00
9 Derrick Ward	8.00	20.00
10 Donald Driver	10.00	25.00
11 Frank Gore	10.00	25.00
12 Fred Taylor	10.00	25.00
13 Greg Lewis	8.00	20.00
14 James Jones	8.00	20.00
15 Jerious Norwood/25	12.00	30.00
17 Justin Fargas	8.00	20.00
19 Kevin Curtis	8.00	20.00
21 Ladell Betts	8.00	20.00
22 LaMont Jordan	10.00	25.00
23 LaRon Landry	10.00	25.00
24 Larry Johnson	10.00	25.00
25 Marion Barber	20.00	40.00
26 Marques Colston	10.00	25.00
27 Mike Bell	8.00	20.00
28 Mike Furrey	10.00	25.00
29 Patrick Crayton	10.00	25.00
30 Patrick Willis/15	12.00	30.00
31 Peyton Manning/18	50.00	100.00
32 Jason Witten	20.00	40.00
33 Hank Baskett	8.00	20.00
34 Ronnie Brown	10.00	25.00
35 Rudi Johnson/24	12.00	30.00
36 Ryan Grant	12.00	30.00
37 Santonio Holmes	10.00	25.00
38 Selvin Young/44	8.00	20.00
39 Sidney Rice	12.00	30.00
40 Tarvaris Jackson/15	12.00	30.00
41 T.J. Houshmandzadeh	10.00	25.00
42 Tony Romo	50.00	80.00
43 Trent Edwards	8.00	20.00
44 Vincent Jackson	8.00	20.00
45 Wes Welker	20.00	40.00
46 Willie Parker	12.00	30.00
47 Jim Brown	40.00	80.00
49 Adrian Peterson/25	60.00	120.00
50 Braylon Edwards	10.00	25.00

2008 Leaf Limited Monikers Autographs Gold

UNPRICED GOLD AU PRINT RUN 10
UNPRICED PLATINUM AU PRINT RUN 1

2008 Leaf Limited Prime Pairings Autographs

STATED PRINT RUN 25-75

PP1 Joe Klecko/25	15.00	40.00
Mark Gastineau		
PP3 Raymond Berry	25.00	50.00
Lenny Moore/75		
PP4 Jim McMahon	25.00	50.00
William Perry/50		
PP5 Dub Jones/25	12.00	30.00
Bert Jones		
PP6 Howie Long/25	60.00	100.00
Ken Stabler		
Gene Upshaw		
PP7 Fran Tarkenton/25	25.00	50.00
Chuck Foreman		
PP8 Deacon Jones/25	30.00	60.00
Merlin Olsen		
Rosey Grier		
PP9 Fred Williamson/25	40.00	80.00
Bobby Bell		
Willie Lanier		
PP10 Tommy McDonald/25	12.00	30.00
Pete Retzlaff		
PP11 Darren McFadden/25	50.00	120.00
Justin Fargas		
Michael Bush		
PP12 Larry Johnson	15.00	40.00
Kolby Smith/75		
PP13 Tony Romo/25	40.00	100.00
Marion Barber		
PP14 Alan Page/25	25.00	50.00
Carl Eller		
PP15 Rudi Johnson/25	10.00	25.00
Kenny Watson		
PP16 Ben Roethlisberger/25	60.00	120.00
Santonio Holmes		
PP17 Marshawn Lynch/25	40.00	80.00
Fred Jackson		
PP18 Willie Davis/25	50.00	100.00
Willie Wood		
PP19 Bart Starr/25	125.00	200.00
Jim Taylor		
Forrest Gregg		
PP20 Lem Barney/25	15.00	40.00
Alex Karras		
PP21 Gary Collins/25	25.00	50.00
Paul Warfield		
PP22 Y.A. Tittle/25	25.00	50.00
Del Shofner		
PP23 Willie Brown/25	60.00	120.00
Daryle Lamonica		
Fred Biletnikoff		
PP24 Sonny Jurgensen/25	30.00	60.00
Charley Taylor		
PP25 Bo Jackson/25	75.00	135.00
Marcus Allen		
PP26 Jim Brown/25	60.00	100.00
Leroy Kelly		

2008 Leaf Limited Rookie Jumbo Jerseys

STATED PRINT RUN 50 SER.#'d SETS
*PRIME/10: 1.2X TO 3X BASIC JSY
PRIME PRINT RUN 10 SER.#'d SETS
*JSY NUM/50: .4X TO 1X BASIC JSY
JERSEY NUMBER PRINT RUN 50
*JSY NUM PRIME/10: 1.2X TO 3X BASIC JSY
JERSEY NUMBER PRIME PRINT RUN 2-10
*TEAM LOGO/50: .4X TO 1X BASIC JSY
TEAM LOGO PRINT RUN 50
*TEAM LOGO PRIME/10: 1.2X TO 3X BASIC JSY
TEAM LOGO PRIME PRINT RUN 2-10

1 Jordy Nelson	3.00	8.00
2 Rashard Mendenhall	5.00	12.00
3 Steve Slaton	2.50	6.00
4 DeSean Jackson	5.00	12.00
5 Donnie Avery	2.00	5.00
6 Felix Jones	4.00	10.00
7 Dustin Keller	2.50	6.00
8 Earl Bennett	2.50	6.00
9 Devin Thomas	2.00	5.00
10 Kevin O'Connell	2.00	5.00
11 John David Booty	2.00	5.00
12 Joe Flacco	8.00	20.00
13 Darren McFadden	6.00	15.00
14 Malcolm Kelly	2.00	5.00
15 Jake Long	2.50	6.00
16 Jerome Simpson	2.50	6.00
17 Brian Brohm	2.50	6.00
18 Glenn Dorsey	2.50	6.00
19 Mario Manningham	2.50	6.00
20 Limas Sweed	2.50	6.00
21 Matt Ryan	8.00	20.00
22 Eddie Royal	2.50	6.00
23 Jonathan Stewart	4.00	10.00
24 Jamaal Charles	4.00	10.00
25 Dexter Jackson	2.00	5.00
26 Harry Douglas	2.00	5.00
27 James Hardy	2.00	5.00
28 Chris Johnson	6.00	15.00
29 Early Doucet	2.00	5.00
30 Kevin Smith	2.50	6.00
31 Ray Rice	4.00	10.00
32 Chad Henne	2.50	6.00
33 Andre Caldwell	2.50	6.00
34 Matt Forte	4.00	10.00

2008 Leaf Limited Rookie Jumbo Jerseys Autographs

STATED PRINT RUN 5-15
UNPRICED PRIME PRINT RUN 1-5
*JSY NUM/15: .4X TO 1X BASIC JSY AU/15
JERSEY NUMBER PRINT RUN 2-15
UNPRICED JSY NUM.PRIME PRINT RUN 1-5
*TEAM LOGO/15: .4X TO 1X BASIC JSY AU/15
TEAM LOGO PRINT RUN 3-15
UNPRICED TEAM LOGO PRIME PRINT RUN 1-5

1 Jordy Nelson	25.00	50.00
2 Rashard Mendenhall	25.00	60.00
3 Steve Slaton	12.00	30.00
4 DeSean Jackson	25.00	60.00
5 Donnie Avery	10.00	25.00
6 Felix Jones	20.00	50.00
7 Dustin Keller	12.00	30.00
8 Earl Bennett	12.00	30.00
9 Devin Thomas/10	10.00	25.00
10 Kevin O'Connell	10.00	25.00
11 John David Booty	10.00	25.00
12 Joe Flacco	50.00	120.00
13 Darren McFadden	30.00	80.00
15 Jake Long	12.00	30.00
16 Jerome Simpson	12.00	30.00
17 Brian Brohm	12.00	30.00
19 Mario Manningham	12.00	30.00
20 Limas Sweed	12.00	30.00
21 Matt Ryan	75.00	200.00
22 Eddie Royal	12.00	30.00
23 Jonathan Stewart	20.00	50.00
24 Jamaal Charles	20.00	50.00
25 Dexter Jackson	10.00	25.00
27 James Hardy	10.00	25.00
28 Chris Johnson	50.00	120.00
29 Early Doucet	10.00	25.00
30 Kevin Smith	12.00	30.00
31 Ray Rice	25.00	60.00
32 Chad Henne/10	12.00	30.00
33 Andre Caldwell	10.00	25.00
34 Matt Forte	20.00	50.00

2008 Leaf Limited Slideshow Autographs

STATED PRINT RUN 50 SER.#'d SETS

1 Steve Slaton	12.00	30.00
2 Ray Rice	25.00	60.00
3 Rashard Mendenhall	25.00	60.00
4 Matt Ryan	50.00	100.00
5 Matt Forte	20.00	50.00
6 Mario Manningham	15.00	40.00
7 Malcolm Kelly	10.00	25.00
8 Limas Sweed	12.00	30.00
9 Kevin Smith	12.00	30.00
10 Kevin O'Connell	10.00	25.00
11 Jordy Nelson	25.00	50.00
12 Jonathan Stewart	15.00	40.00
13 John David Booty	10.00	25.00
14 Joe Flacco	40.00	80.00
15 Jerome Simpson	12.00	30.00
16 James Hardy	10.00	25.00
17 Jamaal Charles	20.00	50.00
18 Jake Long	12.00	30.00
19 Harry Douglas	10.00	25.00
20 Glenn Dorsey	12.00	30.00
21 Felix Jones	20.00	50.00
22 Eddie Royal	12.00	30.00
23 Early Doucet	10.00	25.00
24 Earl Bennett	12.00	30.00
25 Dustin Keller	12.00	30.00
26 Donnie Avery	10.00	25.00
27 Dexter Jackson	10.00	25.00
28 Devin Thomas	10.00	25.00
29 DeSean Jackson	25.00	60.00
30 Darren McFadden	30.00	60.00
31 Chris Johnson	40.00	80.00
32 Chad Henne	12.00	30.00
33 Brian Brohm	12.00	30.00
34 Andre Caldwell	10.00	25.00

2008 Leaf Limited Team Threads Dual

STATED PRINT RUN 100 SER.#'d SETS
*PRIME/25: .8X TO 2X BASIC DUAL JSY
PRIME PRINT RUN 25 SER.#'d SETS

1 Lee Evans	4.00	10.00
Marshawn Lynch		
2 Derek Anderson	4.00	10.00
Braylon Edwards		
3 Matt Schaub	4.00	10.00
Andre Johnson		
4 Fred Taylor	4.00	10.00
Maurice Jones-Drew		
5 Vince Young	4.00	10.00
LenDale White		
6 Jay Cutler	5.00	12.00
Brandon Stokley		
7 Larry Johnson	4.00	10.00
Tony Gonzalez		
8 Brian Westbrook	4.00	10.00
Correll Buckhalter		
9 Roy Williams WR	5.00	12.00
Calvin Johnson		
10 Steven Jackson	5.00	12.00
Torry Holt		

2008 Leaf Limited Team Threads Triples

STATED PRINT RUN 100 SER.#'d SETS
*PRIME/25: .8X TO 2X BASIC TRIO JSY
PRIME PRINT RUN 25 SER.#'d SETS

1 David Garrard	5.00	12.00
Fred Taylor		
Matt Jones		
2 Jeff Garcia	5.00	12.00
Cadillac Williams		
Joey Galloway		
3 Jake Delhomme	5.00	12.00
Steve Smith		
DeAngelo Williams		
4 Eli Manning	6.00	15.00
Plaxico Burress		
Brandon Jacobs		
5 Alex Smith QB	6.00	15.00
Frank Gore		
Vernon Davis		
6 Willis McGahee	6.00	15.00
Mark Clayton		
Ray Lewis		
7 Matt Hasselbeck	5.00	12.00
Deion Branch		
Nate Burleson		
8 Thomas Jones	5.00	12.00
Jerricho Cotchery		
Laveranues Coles		
9 Tarvaris Jackson	10.00	25.00
Adrian Peterson		
Chester Taylor		
10 Donovan McNabb	6.00	15.00
Brian Westbrook		
Reggie Brown		

2008 Leaf Limited Team Threads Quads

STATED PRINT RUN 100 SER.#'d SETS
*PRIME/25: .6X TO 1.5X BASIC QUAD JSY
PRIME PRINT RUN 25 SER.#'d SETS

1 Tom Brady	12.00	30.00
Randy Moss		
Laurence Maroney		
Wes Welker		
2 Peyton Manning	12.00	30.00
Joseph Addai		
Reggie Wayne		
Dallas Clark		
3 Aaron Rodgers	15.00	40.00
Donald Driver		
Greg Jennings		
Ryan Grant		
4 Carson Palmer	8.00	20.00
Rudi Johnson		
Chad Johnson		
T.J. Houshmandzadeh		
5 Ben Roethlisberger	8.00	20.00
Willie Parker		
Santonio Holmes		
Hines Ward		
6 Drew Brees	8.00	20.00
Deuce McAllister		
Reggie Bush		
Marques Colston		
7 Matt Leinart	8.00	20.00
Edgerrin James		
Anquan Boldin		
Larry Fitzgerald		
8 Philip Rivers	8.00	20.00
LaDainian Tomlinson		
Antonio Gates		
Vincent Jackson		
9 Jason Campbell	8.00	20.00
Clinton Portis		
Chris Cooley		
Santana Moss		
10 Tony Romo	10.00	25.00
Terrell Owens		
Marion Barber		
Jason Witten		

2008 Leaf Limited Team Trademarks

STATED PRINT RUN 999 SER.#'d SETS
*HOLOFOIL/100: .5X TO 1.2X BASIC INSERTS
HOLOFOIL PRINT RUN 100 SER.#'d SETS

1 Alex Karras	1.25	3.00
2 Dan Marino	3.00	8.00
3 Emmitt Smith	3.00	8.00
4 Gene Upshaw	1.00	2.50
5 Joe Klecko	1.00	2.50
6 Roger Staubach	2.00	5.00
7 Raymond Berry	1.25	3.00
8 Eric Dickerson	1.25	3.00
9 Earl Campbell	1.50	4.00
10 Howie Long	1.50	4.00
11 John Mackey	1.00	2.50
12 Jim Brown	2.00	5.00
13 Franco Harris	1.50	4.00
14 Steve Young	2.00	5.00
15 Barry Sanders	2.50	6.00
16 Billy Sims	1.25	3.00
17 Brett Favre	3.00	8.00
18 Carl Eller	1.00	2.50
19 Charley Taylor	1.00	2.50
20 Chuck Foreman	1.00	2.50
21 Dallas Clark	1.00	2.50
22 Alan Page	1.25	3.00
23 Danny White	1.00	2.50
24 Deacon Jones	1.25	3.00
25 Dick Butkus	2.00	5.00
26 Fran Tarkenton	1.50	4.00
27 Fred Dryer	1.00	2.50
28 Hank Baskett	.75	2.00
29 John Matuszak	1.50	4.00
30 Len Dawson	1.50	4.00
31 Mark Gastineau	1.00	2.50
32 Ladell Betts	.75	2.00
33 Paul Warfield	1.25	3.00
34 Randall Cunningham	1.50	4.00
35 Ronnie Lott	1.50	4.00
36 Sonny Jurgensen	1.25	3.00
37 Tiki Barber	1.25	3.00
38 Willie Brown	1.00	2.50
39 Willie Lanier	1.00	2.50
40 Kenny Watson	.75	2.00

2008 Leaf Limited Team Trademarks Autograph Materials Prime

STATED PRINT RUN 1-25
SERIAL #'d UNDER 15 NOT PRICED

2 Dan Marino	90.00	150.00
5 Joe Klecko	12.00	30.00
6 Roger Staubach	40.00	80.00
7 Raymond Berry	15.00	40.00
10 Howie Long	30.00	60.00
11 John Mackey	12.00	30.00
12 Jim Brown	50.00	100.00
13 Franco Harris	40.00	80.00
14 Steve Young	30.00	60.00

15 Barry Sanders/15	60.00	120.00
16 Billy Sims	15.00	40.00
17 Brett Favre	100.00	175.00
18 Carl Eller	12.00	30.00
22 Alan Page	15.00	40.00
28 Hank Baskett	10.00	25.00
30 Len Dawson	20.00	50.00
31 Mark Gastineau	12.00	30.00
32 Ladell Betts	10.00	25.00
34 Randall Cunningham	30.00	60.00
35 Ronnie Lott	20.00	50.00
37 Tiki Barber	15.00	40.00
38 Willie Brown	12.00	30.00
39 Willie Lanier	12.00	30.00

2008 Leaf Limited Team Trademarks Materials

STATED PRINT RUN 100 SER.#'d SETS
*PRIME/50: .6X TO 1.5X BASIC JSY/100
*PRIME/50: .4X TO 1X BASIC JSY/44
*PRIME/20-30: .8X TO 2X BASIC JSY/100
PRIME PRINT RUN 5-50
*TEAM LOGO/50: .4X TO 1X BASIC JSY/100
*TEAM LOGO/15-25: .5X TO 1.2X BASIC JSY/100
TEAM LOGO PRINT RUN 15-50

1 Alex Karras	4.00	10.00
2 Dan Marino	10.00	25.00
3 Emmitt Smith Pants/44	12.00	30.00
4 Gene Upshaw	3.00	8.00
5 Joe Klecko	3.00	8.00
6 Roger Staubach	6.00	15.00
7 Raymond Berry	4.00	10.00
8 Eric Dickerson	4.00	10.00
9 Earl Campbell	5.00	12.00
10 Howie Long	5.00	12.00
11 John Mackey	3.00	8.00
12 Jim Brown	6.00	15.00
13 Franco Harris	5.00	12.00
14 Steve Young	6.00	15.00
15 Barry Sanders	8.00	20.00
17 Brett Favre	10.00	25.00
18 Carl Eller	3.00	8.00
19 Charley Taylor	3.00	8.00
20 Chuck Foreman	5.00	12.00
22 Alan Page	4.00	10.00
23 Danny White	4.00	10.00
24 Deacon Jones	4.00	10.00
25 Dick Butkus	6.00	15.00
26 Fran Tarkenton	5.00	12.00
27 Fred Dryer	3.00	8.00
28 Hank Baskett	3.00	8.00
29 John Matuszak	5.00	12.00
30 Len Dawson	5.00	12.00
31 Mark Gastineau	3.00	8.00
32 Ladell Betts	3.00	8.00
33 Paul Warfield	4.00	10.00
34 Randall Cunningham	5.00	12.00
35 Ronnie Lott	5.00	12.00
36 Sonny Jurgensen	4.00	10.00
37 Tiki Barber	4.00	10.00
38 Willie Brown	3.00	8.00
39 Willie Lanier	3.00	8.00

2008 Leaf Limited Threads

STATED PRINT RUN 15-100
UNPRICED SUPER PRIME PRINT RUN 1

1 Anquan Boldin	3.00	8.00
2 Edgerrin James	3.00	8.00
3 Larry Fitzgerald	4.00	10.00
5 Michael Turner/55	4.00	10.00
6 Roddy White	3.00	8.00
8 Derrick Mason	3.00	8.00
9 Mark Clayton	3.00	8.00
10 Willis McGahee	3.00	8.00
11 Trent Edwards	2.50	6.00
12 Marshawn Lynch	3.00	8.00
13 Lee Evans	3.00	8.00
15 Steve Smith	3.00	8.00
16 DeAngelo Williams	3.00	8.00
17 Rex Grossman/35	4.00	10.00
19 Devin Hester	4.00	10.00
20 Carson Palmer	4.00	10.00
22 T.J. Houshmandzadeh	3.00	8.00
23 Chad Johnson	3.00	8.00
24 Braylon Edwards	3.00	8.00
25 Derek Anderson	2.50	6.00
26 Jamal Lewis	3.00	8.00
27 Tony Romo	5.00	12.00
28 Terrell Owens	4.00	10.00
29 Marion Barber	3.00	8.00
30 Jason Witten	4.00	10.00
31 Jay Cutler	4.00	10.00
32 Selvin Young	2.50	6.00
33 Brandon Marshall	3.00	8.00
34 Jon Kitna	3.00	8.00
35 Calvin Johnson	4.00	10.00
36 Roy Williams WR	3.00	8.00
37 Aaron Rodgers	8.00	20.00
38 Donald Driver	3.00	8.00
39 Greg Jennings	4.00	10.00
40 Matt Schaub	3.00	8.00
41 Andre Johnson	3.00	8.00
43 Peyton Manning	6.00	15.00
44 Joseph Addai	3.00	8.00
45 Reggie Wayne	3.00	8.00
46 David Garrard	3.00	8.00
47 Fred Taylor	3.00	8.00
48 Maurice Jones-Drew	3.00	8.00
49 Reggie Williams	3.00	8.00
50 Brodie Croyle/33	4.00	10.00
51 Larry Johnson	3.00	8.00
52 Tony Gonzalez/25	4.00	10.00
54 Ronnie Brown	3.00	8.00
56 Tarvaris Jackson	3.00	8.00
57 Adrian Peterson	6.00	15.00
58 Chester Taylor	2.50	6.00
59 Tom Brady	6.00	15.00
60 Randy Moss	4.00	10.00
61 Laurence Maroney	3.00	8.00
62 Drew Brees	4.00	10.00
63 Marques Colston	3.00	8.00
64 Reggie Bush/65	4.00	10.00
65 Eli Manning	4.00	10.00
66 Plaxico Burress	3.00	8.00
67 Brandon Jacobs	3.00	8.00
69 Jerricho Cotchery	3.00	8.00
70 Laveranues Coles/50	2.50	6.00
71 JaMarcus Russell	3.00	8.00
72 Justin Fargas	2.50	6.00
74 Donovan McNabb	4.00	10.00
75 Brian Westbrook	3.00	8.00
76 Kevin Curtis	2.50	6.00
77 Ben Roethlisberger	4.00	10.00
78 Willie Parker	3.00	8.00
79 Santonio Holmes	3.00	8.00
80 Philip Rivers	4.00	10.00
81 LaDainian Tomlinson	4.00	10.00
82 Antonio Gates	4.00	10.00
84 Frank Gore	3.00	8.00
86 Matt Hasselbeck	3.00	8.00
87 Julius Jones/60	2.50	6.00
88 Deion Branch	3.00	8.00
89 Marc Bulger	3.00	8.00
90 Steven Jackson	4.00	10.00
91 Torry Holt	3.00	8.00
92 Jeff Garcia	3.00	8.00
94 Joey Galloway	3.00	8.00
95 Vince Young	3.00	8.00
96 LenDale White	3.00	8.00
97 Roydell Williams	2.50	6.00
98 Jason Campbell	3.00	8.00
99 Santana Moss	2.50	6.00
100 Clinton Portis	3.00	8.00
101 Alan Page	5.00	12.00
102 Bart Starr	10.00	25.00
103 Bert Jones	4.00	10.00
108 Bo Jackson	8.00	20.00
109 Bob Griese	6.00	15.00
110 Bob Lilly	5.00	12.00
111 Bob Waterfield	8.00	20.00
113 Brett Favre	10.00	25.00
114 Carl Eller	6.00	15.00
115 Charley Taylor	4.00	10.00
117 Chuck Foreman	4.00	10.00
118 Cliff Harris/40	6.00	15.00
119 Cris Collinsworth/40	6.00	15.00
120 Danny White	4.00	10.00
124 Deacon Jones	5.00	12.00
126 Dick Butkus	8.00	20.00
127 Doak Walker	8.00	20.00
130 Forrest Gregg	4.00	10.00
131 Fran Tarkenton/30	8.00	20.00
132 Frank Gifford	6.00	15.00
133 Fred Biletnikoff	6.00	15.00
134 Fred Dryer	4.00	10.00
136 Gale Sayers	8.00	20.00
139 Jack Lambert	6.00	15.00
140 James Lofton	4.00	10.00
141 Jan Stenerud/15	6.00	15.00
142 Jim McMahon	6.00	15.00
143 Jim Otto	4.00	10.00
145 Jim Thorpe/24	100.00	175.00
146 Joe Montana	12.00	30.00
147 John Riggins	5.00	12.00
148 John Matuszak	6.00	15.00
149 Johnny Unitas	10.00	25.00
152 Lance Alworth/40	8.00	20.00
153 Larry Little	4.00	10.00
154 Lee Roy Selmon	5.00	12.00
155 Lem Barney	4.00	10.00
156 Len Dawson	6.00	15.00
157 Lenny Moore	5.00	12.00
160 Marcus Allen	6.00	15.00
162 Mark Gastineau	4.00	10.00
165 Norm Van Brocklin	5.00	12.00
166 Ollie Matson	5.00	12.00
167 Ozzie Newsome	5.00	12.00
168 Paul Hornung	6.00	15.00
170 Paul Warfield	5.00	12.00
172 Phil Simms	5.00	12.00
174 Randy White	5.00	12.00
175 Reggie White	8.00	20.00
176 Roger Craig/85	5.00	12.00
177 Ronnie Lott	6.00	15.00
178 Rosey Grier/49	4.00	10.00
179 Sammy Baugh	10.00	25.00
180 Sid Luckman	8.00	20.00
181 Sonny Jurgensen	6.00	15.00
183 Steve Largent	6.00	15.00
184 Ted Hendricks	4.00	10.00
185 Tiki Barber	5.00	12.00
186 Tim Brown	6.00	15.00
187 Tom Fears	4.00	10.00
188 Tommy McDonald	5.00	12.00
190 Tony Dorsett	6.00	15.00
191 Troy Aikman	8.00	20.00
192 Walter Payton	12.00	30.00
193 Warren Moon	6.00	15.00
194 William Perry/19	6.00	15.00
195 Willie Lanier	4.00	10.00
196 Willie Brown	4.00	10.00
199 Y.A. Tittle	6.00	15.00

2008 Leaf Limited Threads Prime

*PRIME/35-50: .6X TO 1.5X BASIC JSY/49-100
*PRIME/50: .5X TO 1.2X BASIC JSY/25-35
*PRIME/15-29: .8X TO 2X BASIC JSY/49-100
*PRIME/25: .6X TO 1.5X BASIC JSY/30 40
PRIME PRINT RUN 1-50 SER.#'d SETS

14 Jake Delhomme/50	5.00	12.00
55 Ted Ginn Jr./29	6.00	15.00
161 Mark Duper/35	6.00	15.00
182 Sterling Sharpe/25	10.00	25.00

2008 Leaf Limited Threads Prime Jersey Number

COMMON ACTIVE/80-89	3.00	8.00
ACTIVE SEMISTARS/80-89	4.00	10.00
ACTIVE UNL.STARS/80-89	5.00	12.00
COMMON ACTIVE/31-39	5.00	12.00
ACTIVE UNL.STARS/31-39	6.00	15.00
COMMON ACTIVE/15-29	5.00	12.00
ACTIVE SEMISTARS/15-29	6.00	15.00
ACTIVE UNL.STARS/15-29	8.00	20.00
COMMON RETIRED/54-84	6.00	15.00
COMMON RETIRED/32-42	8.00	20.00
RETIRED UNL.STARS/32-42	10.00	25.00
COMMON RETIRED/15-24	8.00	20.00
RETIRED SEMISTARS/15-24	10.00	25.00
RETIRED UNL.STARS/15-24	12.00	30.00

STATED PRINT RUN 2-89
SERIAL #'d UNDER 15 NOT PRICED

14 Jake Delhomme/17	6.00	15.00
43 Peyton Manning/18	12.00	30.00
55 Ted Ginn Jr./19	6.00	15.00
57 Adrian Peterson/28	12.00	30.00
64 Reggie Bush/25	8.00	20.00
81 LaDainian Tomlinson/21	8.00	20.00
102 Bart Starr/15	20.00	50.00
136 Gale Sayers/40	12.00	30.00
146 Joe Montana/16	25.00	60.00
149 Johnny Unitas/19	20.00	50.00
182 Sterling Sharpe/84	6.00	15.00
192 Walter Payton/34	20.00	50.00

2008 Leaf Limited Threads Prime Team Logo

*PRIME/25: .8X TO 2X BASIC JSY/49-100
*PRIME/25: .6X TO 1.5X BASIC JSY/25-35
STATED PRINT RUN 1-25
SERIAL #'d UNDER 25 NOT PRICED

55 Ted Ginn Jr./25	6.00	15.00

2011 Leaf Metal National Convention

STATED PRINT RUN 300 SER. #'d SETS
*PRISM BLUE/25: 1.5X TO 4X BASIC CARDS
*PRISM SILVER/70: 1X TO 2.5X BASIC CARDS

PR2 Cam Newton	4.00	10.00
PR4 Vince Lombardi	2.50	6.00

2011 Leaf Metal National Convention Prismatic Silver

*PRISM SILVER/70: 1X TO 2.5X BASIC CARDS
STATED PRINT RUN 70 SER. #'d SETS

2011 Leaf Muhammad Ali Metal Fans of Ali Autographs

FAUM7 Joe Montana	35.00	70.00

2011 Leaf Muhammad Ali Metal Fans of Ali Autographs Printing Plates Black

STATED PRINT RUN 1 SER. #'d SET
UNPRICED DUE TO SCARCITY

2011 Leaf Muhammad Ali Metal Fans of Ali Autographs Printing Plates Cyan

STATED PRINT RUN 1 SER. #'d SET
UNPRICED DUE TO SCARCITY

2011 Leaf Muhammad Ali Metal Fans of Ali Autographs Printing Plates Magenta

STATED PRINT RUN 1 SER. #'d SET
UNPRICED DUE TO SCARCITY

2011 Leaf Muhammad Ali Metal Fans of Ali Autographs Printing Plates Yellow

STATED PRINT RUN 1 SER. #'d SET
UNPRICED DUE TO SCARCITY

2011 Leaf Muhammad Ali Metal Fans of Ali Autographs Prismatic Blue

STATED PRINT RUN 10 SER. #'d SETS
UNPRICED DUE TO SCARCITY

2011 Leaf Muhammad Ali Metal Fans of Ali Autographs Prismatic Gold

STATED PRINT RUN 1 SER. #'d SET
UNPRICED DUE TO SCARCITY

2011 Leaf Muhammad Ali Metal Fans of Ali Autographs Prismatic Red

STATED PRINT RUN 5 SER. #'d SETS
UNPRICED DUE TO SCARCITY

2012 Leaf National Convention

BG2 Bob Griese	.30	.75
BL1 Bob Lilly	.25	.60
BS2 Barry Sanders	.50	1.25
DD1 Dan Dierdorf	.20	.50
DH1 Dan Hampton	.20	.50
DM2 Don Maynard	.25	.60
DS2 Deion Sanders	.30	.75
DS3 Don Shula	.30	.75
EC1 Earl Campbell	.30	.75
ED1 Eric Dickerson	.25	.60
FG1 Frank Gifford	.25	.60
JK1 Jim Kelly	.40	1.00
JL1 James Lofton	.25	.60
JM1 Joe Montana	.60	1.50
JO1 Jim Otto	.20	.50
JR1 Jerry Rice	.50	1.25
LD1 Len Dawson	.30	.75
MD1 Mike Ditka	.30	.75
MF1 Marshall Faulk	.30	.75
MR1 Mel Renfro	.25	.60
ON1 Ozzie Newsome	.25	.60
RL1 Ronnie Lott	.30	.75
SY1 Steve Young	.40	1.00
TH1 Ted Hendricks	.20	.50
TT1 Thurman Thomas	.30	.75
WM1 Warren Moon	.30	.75
YAT Y.A. Tittle	.25	.60

2012 Leaf National Convention VIP

COMPLETE SET (5)	5.00	12.00
VIP2 Robert Griffin III	2.00	5.00

2011 Leaf Previews National Convention

PR2 Cam Newton	2.50	6.00
PR4 Vince Lombardi	1.50	4.00
PR6 Mark Ingram	1.50	4.00

1998 Leaf Rookies and Stars

The 1998 Leaf Rookies and Stars set was issued in one series totalling 300 cards. The fronts feature color action palyer photos. The backs carry player information. The set includes the following short-printed subsets with an insertion rate of 1:2: Rookies (171-240) and Power Tools (241-270). Also inclued in the set are Team Lineup cards (271-300).

COMPLETE SET (300)	125.00	250.00
1 Keyshawn Johnson	.25	.60
2 Marvin Harrison	.25	.60
3 Eddie Kennison	.15	.40
4 Bryant Young	.08	.25
5 Darren Woodson	.08	.25
6 Tyrone Wheatley	.15	.40
7 Michael Westbrook	.15	.40
8 Charles Way	.08	.25
9 Ricky Watters	.15	.40
10 Chris Warren	.15	.40
11 Wesley Walls	.15	.40
12 Tamarick Vanover	.08	.25
13 Zach Thomas	.25	.60
14 Derrick Thomas	.25	.60
15 Yancey Thigpen	.08	.25
16 Vinny Testaverde	.15	.40
17 Dana Stubblefield	.08	.25
18 J.J. Stokes	.15	.40
19 James Stewart	.15	.40
20 Jeff George	.15	.40
21 John Randle	.15	.40
22 Gary Brown	.08	.25
23 Ed McCaffrey	.15	.40
24 James Jett	.15	.40
25 Rob Johnson	.15	.40
26 Daryl Johnston	.15	.40
27 Jermaine Lewis	.15	.40
28 Tony Martin	.15	.40
29 Derrick Mayes	.15	.40
30 Keenan McCardell	.15	.40
31 O.J. McDuffie	.15	.40
32 Chris Chandler	.15	.40
33 Doug Flutie	.25	.60
34 Scott Mitchell	.15	.40
35 Warren Moon	.25	.60
36 Rob Moore	.15	.40
37 Johnnie Morton	.15	.40
38 Neil O'Donnell	.15	.40
39 Rich Gannon	.25	.60
40 Andre Reed	.15	.40
41 Jake Reed	.15	.40
42 Errict Rhett	.15	.40
43 Simeon Rice	.15	.40
44 Andre Rison	.15	.40
45 Eric Moulds	.25	.60
46 Frank Sanders	.15	.40
47 Darnay Scott	.15	.40
48 Junior Seau	.25	.60
49 Shannon Sharpe	.15	.40
50 Bruce Smith	.15	.40
51 Jimmy Smith	.15	.40
52 Robert Smith	.25	.60
53 Derrick Alexander	.15	.40
54 Kimble Anders	.15	.40
55 Jamal Anderson	.25	.60
56 Mario Bates	.15	.40
57 Edgar Bennett	.08	.25
58 Tim Biakabutuka	.15	.40
59 Ki-Jana Carter	.08	.25
60 Larry Centers	.08	.25
61 Mark Chmura	.15	.40
62 Wayne Chrebet	.25	.60
63 Ben Coates	.15	.40
64 Curtis Conway	.15	.40
65 Randall Cunningham	.25	.60
66 Rickey Dudley	.08	.25
67 Bert Emanuel	.15	.40
68 Bobby Engram	.15	.40
69 William Floyd	.08	.25
70 Irving Fryar	.15	.40
71 Elvis Grbac	.15	.40
72 Kevin Greene	.15	.40
73 Jim Harbaugh	.15	.40
74 Raymont Harris	.08	.25
75 Garrison Hearst	.25	.60
76 Greg Hill	.08	.25
77 Desmond Howard	.15	.40
78 Bobby Hoying	.15	.40
79 Michael Jackson	.08	.25
80 Terry Allen	.25	.60
81 Jerome Bettis	.25	.60
82 Jeff Blake	.15	.40
83 Robert Brooks	.15	.40
84 Tim Brown	.25	.60
85 Isaac Bruce	.25	.60
86 Cris Carter	.25	.60
87 Ty Detmer	.15	.40
88 Trent Dilfer	.25	.60
89 Marshall Faulk	.30	.75
90 Antonio Freeman	.25	.60
91 Gus Frerotte	.08	.25
92 Joey Galloway	.15	.40
93 Michael Irvin	.25	.60
94 Brad Johnson	.25	.60
95 Danny Kanell	.15	.40
96 Napoleon Kaufman	.25	.60
97 Dorsey Levens	.25	.60
98 Natrone Means	.15	.40
99 Herman Moore	.15	.40
100 Adrian Murrell	.15	.40
101 Carl Pickens	.15	.40
102 Rod Smith	.15	.40
103 Thurman Thomas	.25	.60
104 Reggie White	.25	.60
105 Jim Druckenmiller	.08	.25
106 Antowain Smith	.25	.60
107 Reidel Anthony	.15	.40
108 Ike Hilliard	.15	.40
109 Rae Carruth	.08	.25
110 Troy Davis	.08	.25
111 Terance Mathis	.15	.40
112 Brett Favre	1.00	2.50
113 Dan Marino	1.00	2.50
114 Emmitt Smith	.75	2.00
115 Barry Sanders	.75	2.00
116 Eddie George	.25	.60
117 Drew Bledsoe	.40	1.00
118 Troy Aikman	.50	1.25
119 Terrell Davis	.25	.60
120 John Elway	1.00	2.50
121 Mark Brunell	.25	.60
122 Jerry Rice	.50	1.25
123 Kordell Stewart	.25	.60
124 Steve McNair	.25	.60
125 Curtis Martin	.25	.60
126 Steve Young	.30	.75
127 Kerry Collins	.15	.40
128 Terry Glenn	.25	.60
129 Deion Sanders	.25	.60
130 Mike Alstott	.25	.60
131 Tony Banks	.15	.40
132 Karim Abdul-Jabbar	.25	.60
133 Terrell Owens	.25	.60
134 Yatil Green	.08	.25
135 Tony Gonzalez	.25	.60
136 Byron Hanspard	.08	.25
137 David LaFleur	.08	.25
138 Danny Wuerffel	.15	.40
139 Tiki Barber	.25	.60
140 Peter Boulware	.08	.25
141 Will Blackwell	.08	.25
142 Warrick Dunn	.25	.60
143 Corey Dillon	.25	.60
144 Jake Plummer	.25	.60
145 Neil Smith	.15	.40
146 Charles Johnson	.08	.25
147 Fred Lane	.08	.25
148 Dan Wilkinson	.08	.25
149 Ken Norton	.08	.25
150 Stephen Davis	.08	.25
151 Gilbert Brown	.08	.25
152 Kenny Bynum RC	.08	.25
153 Derrick Cullors	.08	.25
154 Charlie Garner	.15	.40
155 Jeff Graham	.08	.25
156 Warren Sapp	.15	.40
157 Jerald Moore	.08	.25
158 Sean Dawkins	.08	.25
159 Charlie Jones	.08	.25
160 Kevin Lockett	.08	.25
161 James McKnight	.25	.60
162 Chris Penn	.08	.25
163 Leslie Shepherd	.08	.25
164 Karl Williams	.08	.25
165 Mark Bruener	.08	.25
166 Ernie Conwell	.08	.25
167 Ken Dilger	.08	.25
168 Troy Drayton	.08	.25
169 Freddie Jones	.08	.25
170 Dale Carter	.08	.25
171 Charles Woodson RC	3.00	8.00
172 Alonzo Mayes RC	1.00	2.50
173 Andre Wadsworth RC	1.50	4.00
174 Grant Wistrom RC	1.50	4.00
175 Greg Ellis RC	1.00	2.50
176 Chris Howard RC	1.00	2.50
177 Keith Brooking RC	2.50	6.00
178 Takeo Spikes RC	2.50	6.00
179 Anthony Simmons RC	1.50	4.00
180 Brian Simmons RC	1.50	4.00
181 Sam Cowart RC	1.50	4.00
182 Ken Oxendine RC	1.00	2.50
183 Vonnie Holliday RC	1.50	4.00
184 Terry Fair RC	1.50	4.00
185 Shaun Williams RC	1.50	4.00
186 Tremayne Stephens RC	1.00	2.50
187 Duane Starks RC	1.00	2.50
188 Jason Peter RC	1.00	2.50
189 Tebucky Jones RC	1.00	2.50
190 Donovin Darius RC	1.50	4.00
191 R.W. McQuarters RC	1.50	4.00
192 Corey Chavous RC	2.50	6.00
193 Cameron Cleeland RC	1.00	2.50
194 Stephen Alexander RC	1.50	4.00
195 Rod Rutledge RC	1.00	2.50
196 Scott Frost RC	1.00	2.50
197 Fred Beasley RC	1.00	2.50
198 Dorian Boose RC	1.00	2.50
199 Randy Moss RC	10.00	25.00
200 Jacquez Green RC	1.50	4.00
201 Marcus Nash RC	1.00	2.50
202 Hines Ward RC	12.50	25.00
203 Kevin Dyson RC	2.50	6.00
204 E.G. Green RC	1.50	4.00
205 Germane Crowell RC	1.50	4.00
206 Joe Jurevicius RC	2.50	6.00
207 Tony Simmons RC	1.50	4.00
208 Tim Dwight RC	2.50	6.00
209 Az-Zahir Hakim RC	2.50	6.00
210 Jerome Pathon RC	2.50	6.00
211 Pat Johnson RC	1.50	4.00
212 Mikhael Ricks RC	1.50	4.00
213 Donald Hayes RC	1.50	4.00
214 Jammi German RC	1.00	2.50
215 Larry Shannon RC	1.00	2.50
216 Brian Alford RC	1.00	2.50
217 Curtis Enis RC	1.00	2.50
218 Fred Taylor RC	4.00	10.00
219 Robert Edwards RC	1.50	4.00
220 Ahman Green RC	5.00	12.00
221 Tavian Banks RC	1.50	4.00
222 Skip Hicks RC	1.50	4.00
223 Robert Holcombe RC	1.50	4.00
224 John Avery RC	1.50	4.00
225 C.Fuamatu-Ma'afala RC	1.50	4.00
226 Michael Pittman RC	4.00	8.00
227 Rashaan Shehee RC	1.50	4.00
228 Jonathan Linton RC	1.50	4.00
229 Jon Ritchie RC	1.50	4.00
230 Chris Floyd RC	1.00	2.50
231 Wilmont Perry RC	1.00	2.50
232 Raymond Priester RC	1.00	2.50
233 Peyton Manning RC	25.00	50.00
234 Ryan Leaf RC	2.50	6.00
235 Brian Griese RC	5.00	12.00
236 Jeff Ogden RC	2.50	6.00
237 Charlie Batch RC	2.50	6.00
238 Moses Moreno RC	1.00	2.50
239 Jonathan Quinn RC	2.50	6.00
UER back Jonathon		
240 Flozell Adams RC	1.00	2.50
241 Brett Favre PT	5.00	12.00
242 Dan Marino PT	5.00	12.00
243 Emmitt Smith PT	4.00	10.00
244 Barry Sanders PT	4.00	10.00
245 Eddie George PT	1.00	2.50
246 Drew Bledsoe PT	2.00	5.00
247 Troy Aikman PT	2.50	6.00
248 Terrell Davis PT	1.00	2.50
249 John Elway PT	5.00	12.00
250 Carl Pickens PT	1.00	2.50
251 Jerry Rice PT	2.50	6.00
252 Kordell Stewart PT	1.00	2.50
253 Steve McNair PT	1.00	2.50
254 Curtis Martin PT	1.00	2.50
255 Steve Young PT	1.50	4.00
256 Herman Moore PT	1.00	2.50
257 Dorsey Levens PT	1.00	2.50
258 Deion Sanders PT	1.00	2.50
259 Napoleon Kaufman PT	1.00	2.50
260 Warrick Dunn PT	1.00	2.50
261 Corey Dillon PT	1.00	2.50
262 Jerome Bettis PT	1.00	2.50
263 Tim Brown PT	1.00	2.50
264 Cris Carter PT	1.00	2.50
265 Antonio Freeman PT	1.00	2.50
266 Randy Moss PT	6.00	15.00
267 Curtis Enis PT	1.00	2.50
268 Fred Taylor PT	1.50	4.00
269 Robert Edwards PT	1.00	2.50
270 Peyton Manning PT	12.50	25.00
271 Barry Sanders TL	.40	1.00
272 Eddie George TL	.15	.40
273 Troy Aikman TL	.25	.60
274 Mark Brunell TL	.25	.60
275 Kordell Stewart TL	.25	.60
276 Tim Biakabutuka TL	.08	.25
277 Terry Glenn TL	.08	.25
278 Mike Alstott TL	.08	.25
279 Tony Banks TL	.08	.25
280 Karim Abdul-Jabbar TL	.08	.25
281 Terrell Owens TL	.15	.40
282 Byron Hanspard TL	.08	.25
283 Jake Plummer TL	.15	.40
284 Terry Allen TL	.08	.25
285 Jeff Blake TL	.08	.25
286 Brad Johnson TL	.08	.25
287 Danny Kanell TL	.08	.25
288 Natrone Means TL	.08	.25
289 Rod Smith TL	.08	.25
290 Thurman Thomas TL	.08	.25
291 Reggie White TL	.08	.25
292 Troy Davis TL	.08	.25
293 Curtis Conway TL	.08	.25
294 Irving Fryar TL	.08	.25
295 Jim Harbaugh TL	.08	.25
296 Andre Rison TL	.08	.25
297 Ricky Watters TL	.08	.25
298 Keyshawn Johnson TL	.08	.25
299 Jeff George TL	.08	.25
300 Marshall Faulk TL	.25	.60

1998 Leaf Rookies and Stars Longevity

*LONGEVITY STARS: 20X TO 50X BASIC
*LONGEVITY RC STARS: 1.5X TO 4X BASIC
*LONGEV.PT STARS: 4X TO 10X BASIC PT's
*LONGEV.PT ROOKIES: 1.2X TO 3X PT's
STATED PRINT RUN 50 SERIAL #'d SETS

202 Hines Ward	75.00	150.00
233 Peyton Manning	175.00	300.00

1998 Leaf Rookies and Stars Longevity Holofoil

STATED PRINT RUN 1 SERIAL #'d SET

1998 Leaf Rookies and Stars True Blue

COMPLETE SET (300)	400.00	800.00

*TRUE BLUE STARS: 4X TO 10X BASIC CARDS
*TRUE BLUE RCs: .3X TO .8X BASIC CARDS
*TRUE BLUE POWER TOOLS: .8X TO 2X BASIC CARDS
STATED PRINT RUN 500 SETS

1998 Leaf Rookies and Stars Cross Training

COMPLETE SET (10)	40.00	80.00
STATED PRINT RUN 1000 SERIAL #'d SETS		
1 Brett Favre	10.00	25.00
2 Mark Brunell	2.50	6.00
3 Barry Sanders	8.00	20.00
4 John Elway	10.00	25.00
5 Jerry Rice	5.00	12.00
6 Kordell Stewart	2.50	6.00
7 Steve McNair	2.50	6.00
8 Deion Sanders	2.50	6.00
9 Jake Plummer	2.50	6.00
10 Steve Young	3.00	8.00

1998 Leaf Rookies and Stars Crusade Green

COMPLETE SET (30)	250.00	500.00

GREEN PRINT RUN 250 SERIAL #'d SETS
*PURPLE/100: .8X TO 2X GREEN/250
PURPLE PRINT RUN 100 SERIAL #'d SETS
*RED/25: 1.5X TO 4X GREEN/250
RED PRINT RUN 25 SERIAL #'d SETS

1 Brett Favre	20.00	50.00
2 Dan Marino	20.00	50.00
3 Emmitt Smith	15.00	40.00
4 Barry Sanders	15.00	40.00
5 Eddie George	4.00	12.00
6 Drew Bledsoe	6.00	15.00
7 Troy Aikman	10.00	25.00
8 Terrell Davis	5.00	12.00
9 John Elway	20.00	50.00
10 Mark Brunell	4.00	10.00
11 Jerry Rice	10.00	25.00
12 Kordell Stewart	4.00	10.00
13 Steve McNair	5.00	12.00
14 Curtis Martin	5.00	12.00
16 Steve Young	6.00	15.00
18 Deion Sanders	5.00	12.00
22 Terrell Owens	5.00	12.00
23 Jamal Anderson	4.00	10.00
25 Jerome Bettis	5.00	12.00
30 Cris Carter	5.00	12.00
32 Marshall Faulk	6.00	15.00
33 Antonio Freeman	4.00	10.00
40 Dorsey Levens	3.00	8.00
49 Garrison Hearst	3.00	8.00
57 Warrick Dunn	4.00	10.00
59 Jake Plummer	4.00	10.00
66 Peyton Manning	50.00	120.00
69 Randy Moss	12.00	30.00
77 Fred Taylor	5.00	12.00
78 Robert Edwards	3.00	8.00

1998 Leaf Rookies and Stars Extreme Measures

COMPLETE SET (10)	60.00	120.00
OVERALL PRINT RUN 1000 SER.#'d SETS		
1 Barry Sanders/918*	7.50	20.00
2 Warrick Dunn/941*	2.50	6.00
3 Curtis Martin/930*	2.50	6.00
4 Terrell Davis/419*	2.50	6.00
5 Troy Aikman/929*	5.00	12.00
6 Drew Bledsoe/972*	4.00	10.00
7 Eddie George/191*	6.00	15.00
8 Emmitt Smith/888*	7.50	20.00
9 Dan Marino/615*	12.50	30.00
10 Brett Favre/965*	10.00	25.00

1998 Leaf Rookies and Stars Extreme Measures Die Cuts

COMPLETE SET (10)	300.00	600.00
1 Barry Sanders/82*	40.00	100.00
2 Warrick Dunn/59*	10.00	25.00
3 Curtis Martin/70*	10.00	25.00
4 Terrell Davis/581*	5.00	12.00
5 Troy Aikman/71*	15.00	40.00
6 Drew Bledsoe/28*	40.00	100.00
7 Eddie George/809*	5.00	12.00
8 Emmitt Smith/112*	30.00	80.00
9 Dan Marino/385*	20.00	50.00
10 Brett Favre/35*	75.00	200.00

1998 Leaf Rookies and Stars Freshman Orientation

COMPLETE SET (20)	30.00	80.00
STATED PRINT RUN 2500 SERIAL #'d SETS		
1 Peyton Manning	15.00	30.00
2 Kevin Dyson	1.25	3.00
3 Joe Jurevicius	1.25	3.00
4 Tony Simmons	1.00	2.50
5 Marcus Nash	.60	1.50
6 Ryan Leaf	1.25	3.00
7 Curtis Enis	.60	1.50
8 Skip Hicks	1.25	3.00
9 Brian Griese	2.50	6.00
10 Jerome Pathon	1.25	3.00
11 John Avery	1.00	2.50
12 Fred Taylor	2.00	5.00
13 Robert Edwards	1.00	2.50
14 Robert Holcombe	1.00	2.50
15 Ahman Green	3.00	8.00
16 Hines Ward	6.00	12.00
17 Jacquez Green	1.25	3.00
18 Germane Crowell	1.25	3.00
19 Randy Moss	8.00	20.00
20 Charles Woodson	1.50	4.00

1998 Leaf Rookies and Stars Game Plan

COMPLETE SET (20)	15.00	40.00

STATED PRINT RUN 5000 SERIAL #'d SETS
*MASTERS: 1.2X TO 3X BASIC INSERTS
MASTERS PRINT RUN FIRST 500 SER.#'d SETS

1 Ryan Leaf	.60	1.25
2 Peyton Manning	5.00	10.00
3 Brett Favre	2.50	6.00
4 Mark Brunell	.60	1.50
5 Isaac Bruce	.60	1.50
6 Dan Marino	2.50	6.00
7 Jerry Rice	1.25	3.00
8 Cris Carter	.60	1.50
9 Emmitt Smith	2.00	5.00
10 Kordell Stewart	.60	1.50
11 Corey Dillon	.60	1.50
12 Barry Sanders	2.00	5.00
13 Curtis Martin	.60	1.50
14 Carl Pickens	.40	1.00
15 Eddie George	.60	1.50
16 Warrick Dunn	.60	1.50
17 Jake Plummer	.60	1.50
18 Curtis Enis	.20	.50
19 Drew Bledsoe	1.00	2.50
20 Terrell Davis	.60	1.50

1998 Leaf Rookies and Stars Great American Heroes

COMPLETE SET (20)	40.00	80.00
STATED PRINT RUN 2500 SERIAL #'d SETS		
1 Brett Favre	4.00	10.00
2 Dan Marino	4.00	10.00
3 Emmitt Smith	3.00	8.00
4 Barry Sanders	3.00	8.00
5 Eddie George	1.00	2.50
6 Drew Bledsoe	1.50	4.00
7 Troy Aikman	2.00	5.00
8 Terrell Davis	1.00	2.50
9 John Elway	4.00	10.00
10 Mark Brunell	1.00	2.50
11 Jerry Rice	2.00	5.00
12 Kordell Stewart	1.00	2.50
13 Steve McNair	1.00	2.50
14 Curtis Martin	1.00	2.50
15 Steve Young	1.25	3.00
16 Dorsey Levens	1.00	2.50
17 Herman Moore	.60	1.50
18 Deion Sanders	1.00	2.50
19 Thurman Thomas	1.00	2.50
20 Peyton Manning	6.00	12.00

1998 Leaf Rookies and Stars Greatest Hits

COMPLETE SET (20)	25.00	60.00
STATED PRINT RUN 2500 SERIAL #'d SETS		
1 Brett Favre	4.00	10.00
2 Eddie George	1.00	2.50
3 John Elway	4.00	10.00
4 Steve Young	1.25	3.00
5 Napoleon Kaufman	1.00	2.50
6 Dan Marino	4.00	10.00
7 Drew Bledsoe	1.50	4.00
8 Mark Brunell	1.00	2.50
9 Warrick Dunn	1.00	2.50
10 Dorsey Levens	1.00	2.50
11 Emmitt Smith	3.00	8.00
12 Troy Aikman	2.00	5.00
13 Jerry Rice	2.00	5.00
14 Jake Plummer	1.00	2.50
15 Herman Moore	.60	1.50
16 Barry Sanders	3.00	8.00
17 Terrell Davis	1.00	2.50
18 Kordell Stewart	1.00	2.50
19 Jerome Bettis	1.00	2.50
20 Isaac Bruce	1.00	2.50

1998 Leaf Rookies and Stars MVP Contenders

COMPLETE SET (20)	25.00	60.00
STATED PRINT RUN 2500 SERIAL #'d SETS		
1 Tim Brown	1.00	2.50
2 Herman Moore	.60	1.50
3 Jake Plummer	1.00	2.50
4 Warrick Dunn	1.00	2.50
5 Dorsey Levens	1.00	2.50
6 Steve McNair	1.00	2.50
7 John Elway	4.00	10.00
8 Troy Aikman	2.00	5.00
9 Steve Young	1.25	3.00
10 Curtis Martin	1.00	2.50
11 Kordell Stewart	1.00	2.50
12 Jerry Rice	2.00	5.00
13 Mark Brunell	1.00	2.50
14 Terrell Davis	1.00	2.50
15 Drew Bledsoe	1.50	4.00
16 Eddie George	1.00	2.50
17 Barry Sanders	3.00	8.00
18 Emmitt Smith	3.00	8.00
19 Dan Marino	4.00	10.00
20 Brett Favre	4.00	10.00

1998 Leaf Rookies and Stars Standing Ovation

COMPLETE SET (10)	12.50	30.00
STATED PRINT RUN 5000 SERIAL #'d SETS		
1 Brett Favre	2.50	6.00
2 Dan Marino	2.50	6.00
3 Emmitt Smith	2.00	5.00
4 Barry Sanders	2.00	5.00
5 Terrell Davis	.60	1.50
6 Jerry Rice	1.25	3.00
7 Steve Young	.75	2.00
8 Reggie White	.60	1.50
9 John Elway	2.50	6.00
10 Eddie George	.60	1.50

1998 Leaf Rookies and Stars Ticket Masters

COMPLETE SET (20)	50.00	100.00

STATED PRINT RUN 2500 SERIAL #'d SETS
*DIE CUT/250: 1.2X TO 3X BASIC INSERT

1 Brett Favre / Dorsey Levens	5.00	12.00
2 Dan Marino / Karim Abdul-Jabbar	5.00	12.00
3 Troy Aikman / Deion Sanders	2.50	6.00
4 Barry Sanders / Herman Moore	4.00	10.00
5 Steve McNair / Eddie George	1.50	4.00
6 Drew Bledsoe / Robert Edwards	2.00	5.00
7 Terrell Davis / John Elway	5.00	12.00
8 Jerry Rice / Steve Young	3.00	8.00
9 Kordell Stewart / Jerome Bettis	1.50	4.00
10 Curtis Martin / Keyshawn Johnson	1.00	2.50
11 Warrick Dunn / Trent Dilfer	1.50	4.00
12 Corey Dillon / Carl Pickens	1.50	4.00
13 Tim Brown / Napoleon Kaufman	1.50	4.00
14 Jake Plummer / Frank Sanders	1.50	4.00
15 Ryan Leaf / Natrone Means	1.50	4.00
16 Peyton Manning / Marshall Faulk	15.00	30.00
17 Mark Brunell / Fred Taylor	1.50	4.00
18 Curtis Enis / Curtis Conway	1.00	2.50
19 Cris Carter / Randy Moss	10.00	25.00
20 Isaac Bruce / Tony Banks	1.00	2.50

1998 Leaf Rookies and Stars Touchdown Club

COMPLETE SET (20)	20.00	50.00
STATED PRINT RUN 5000 SERIAL #'d SETS		
1 Brett Favre	2.50	6.00
2 Dan Marino	2.50	6.00
3 Emmitt Smith	2.00	5.00
4 Barry Sanders	2.00	5.00
5 Eddie George	.60	1.50
6 Drew Bledsoe	1.00	2.50
7 Terrell Davis	.60	1.50
8 Mark Brunell	.60	1.50
9 Jerry Rice	1.25	3.00
10 Kordell Stewart	.60	1.50
11 Curtis Martin	.60	1.50
12 Karim Abdul-Jabbar	.60	1.50
13 Warrick Dunn	.60	1.50
14 Corey Dillon	.60	1.50
15 Jerome Bettis	.60	1.50
16 Antonio Freeman	.60	1.50
17 Keyshawn Johnson	.60	1.50
18 John Elway	2.50	6.00
19 Steve Young	.75	2.00
20 Jake Plummer	.60	1.50

1999 Leaf Rookies and Stars

Released as a 300-card set, 1999 Leaf Rookies and Stars features 200 veteran players and 100 rookies inserted at one in two packs. Base cards are highlighted with silver foil and rookie cards are highlighted with blue foil.

COMPLETE SET (300)	75.00	150.00
COMP.SET w/o SP's (200)	15.00	30.00
1 Frank Sanders	.15	.40
2 Adrian Murrell	.20	.50
3 Rob Moore	.15	.40
4 Simeon Rice	.15	.40
5 Michael Pittman	.15	.40
6 Jake Plummer	.20	.50
7 Chris Chandler	.20	.50
8 Tim Dwight	.20	.50
9 Chris Calloway	.15	.40
10 Terance Mathis	.15	.40
11 Jamal Anderson	.20	.50
12 Byron Hanspard	.15	.40
13 O.J. Santiago	.15	.40
14 Ken Oxendine	.15	.40
15 Priest Holmes	.25	.60
16 Scott Mitchell	.15	.40
17 Tony Banks	.20	.50
18 Patrick Johnson	.15	.40
19 Rod Woodson	.25	.60
20 Jermaine Lewis	.15	.40
21 Errict Rhett	.15	.40
22 Stoney Case	.15	.40
23 Andre Reed	.25	.60
24 Eric Moulds	.20	.50
25 Rob Johnson	.20	.50
26 Doug Flutie	.25	.60
27 Bruce Smith	.25	.60
28 Jay Riemersma	.15	.40
29 Antowain Smith	.15	.40
30 Thurman Thomas	.25	.60
31 Jonathan Linton	.15	.40
32 Muhsin Muhammad	.20	.50
33 Rae Carruth	.15	.40
34 Wesley Walls	.20	.50
35 Fred Lane	.15	.40
36 Kevin Greene	.20	.50
37 Tim Biakabutuka	.20	.50
38 Curtis Enis	.15	.40
39 Shane Matthews	.15	.40
40 Bobby Engram	.20	.50
41 Curtis Conway	.20	.50
42 Marcus Robinson	.20	.50
43 Darnay Scott	.15	.40
44 Carl Pickens	.20	.50
45 Corey Dillon	.20	.50
46 Jeff Blake	.20	.50
47 Terry Kirby	.15	.40
48 Ty Detmer	.20	.50
49 Leslie Shepherd	.15	.40
50 Karim Abdul-Jabbar	.20	.50
51 Emmitt Smith	.60	1.50
52 Deion Sanders	.25	.60
53 Michael Irvin	.25	.60
54 Rocket Ismail	.20	.50
55 David LaFleur	.15	.40
56 Troy Aikman	.40	1.00
57 Ed McCaffrey	.20	.50
58 Rod Smith	.20	.50
59 Shannon Sharpe	.25	.60
60 Brian Griese	.20	.50
61 John Elway	.75	2.00
62 Bubby Brister	.15	.40
63 Neil Smith	.15	.40
64 Terrell Davis	.25	.60
65 John Avery	.15	.40
66 Derek Loville	.15	.40
67 Ron Rivers	.15	.40
68 Herman Moore	.20	.50
69 Johnnie Morton	.20	.50
70 Charlie Batch	.20	.50
71 Barry Sanders	.60	1.50
72 Germane Crowell	.15	.40
73 Greg Hill	.15	.40
74 Gus Frerotte	.15	.40
75 Corey Bradford	.20	.50
76 Dorsey Levens	.20	.50
77 Antonio Freeman	.20	.50
78 Mark Chmura	.15	.40
79 Brett Favre	.75	2.00
80 Bill Schroeder	.20	.50
81 Matt Hasselbeck	.25	.60
82 E.G. Green	.15	.40
83 Ken Dilger	.15	.40
84 Jerome Pathon	.15	.40
85 Marvin Harrison	.25	.60
86 Peyton Manning	.75	2.00
87 Tavian Banks	.15	.40
88 Keenan McCardell	.20	.50
89 Mark Brunell	.20	.50
90 Fred Taylor	.20	.50
91 Jimmy Smith	.20	.50
92 James Stewart	.15	.40
93 Kyle Brady	.15	.40
94 Derrick Thomas	.25	.60
95 Rashaan Shehee	.15	.40
96 Derrick Alexander WR	.15	.40
97 Byron Bam Morris	.15	.40
98 Andre Rison	.20	.50
99 Elvis Grbac	.15	.40
100 Tony Gonzalez	.25	.60
101 Donnell Bennett	.15	.40
102 Warren Moon	.25	.60
103 Zach Thomas	.25	.60
104 Oronde Gadsden	.15	.40
105 Dan Marino	.75	2.00
106 O.J. McDuffie	.20	.50
107 Tony Martin	.20	.50
108 Randy Moss	.25	.60
109 Cris Carter	.25	.60
110 Robert Smith	.20	.50
111 Randall Cunningham	.25	.60
112 Jake Reed	.20	.50
113 John Randle	.20	.50
114 Leroy Hoard	.15	.40
115 Jeff George	.15	.40
116 Ty Law	.20	.50
117 Shawn Jefferson	.15	.40
118 Troy Brown	.20	.50
119 Robert Edwards	.15	.40
120 Tony Simmons	.15	.40
121 Terry Glenn	.20	.50
122 Ben Coates	.20	.50
123 Drew Bledsoe	.25	.60
124 Terry Allen	.20	.50
125 Cameron Cleeland	.15	.40
126 Eddie Kennison	.20	.50
127 Amani Toomer	.20	.50
128 Kerry Collins	.20	.50
129 Joe Jurevicius	.15	.40
130 Tiki Barber	.25	.60
131 Ike Hilliard	.20	.50
132 Michael Strahan	.20	.50
133 Gary Brown	.15	.40
134 Jason Sehorn	.20	.50
135 Curtis Martin	.25	.60
136 Vinny Testaverde	.20	.50
137 Dedric Ward	.15	.40
138 Keyshawn Johnson	.20	.50
139 Wayne Chrebet	.20	.50
140 Tyrone Wheatley	.20	.50
141 Napoleon Kaufman	.15	.40
142 Tim Brown	.25	.60
143 Rickey Dudley	.15	.40
144 Jon Ritchie	.15	.40
145 James Jett	.15	.40
146 Rich Gannon	.20	.50
147 Charles Woodson	.25	.60
148 Charles Johnson	.15	.40
149 Duce Staley	.20	.50
150 Will Blackwell	.15	.40
151 Kordell Stewart	.20	.50
152 Jerome Bettis	.25	.60
153 Hines Ward	.25	.60
154 Richard Huntley	.15	.40
155 Natrone Means	.20	.50
156 Mikhael Ricks	.15	.40
157 Junior Seau	.25	.60
158 Jim Harbaugh	.20	.50
159 Ryan Leaf	.20	.50
160 Erik Kramer	.20	.50
161 Terrell Owens	.25	.60
162 J.J. Stokes	.15	.40
163 Lawrence Phillips	.20	.50
164 Charlie Garner	.20	.50
165 Jerry Rice	.50	1.25
166 Garrison Hearst	.20	.50
167 Steve Young	.30	.75
168 Derrick Mayes	.15	.40
169 Ahman Green	.20	.50
170 Joey Galloway	.20	.50
171 Ricky Watters	.20	.50
172 Jon Kitna	.20	.50
173 Sean Dawkins	.15	.40
174 Az-Zahir Hakim	.15	.40
175 Robert Holcombe	.15	.40
176 Isaac Bruce	.25	.60
177 Amp Lee	.15	.40
178 Marshall Faulk	.25	.60
179 Trent Green	.20	.50
180 Eric Zeier	.15	.40
181 Bert Emanuel	.20	.50
182 Jacquez Green	.15	.40
183 Reidel Anthony	.15	.40
184 Warren Sapp	.20	.50
185 Mike Alstott	.25	.60
186 Warrick Dunn	.20	.50
187 Trent Dilfer	.20	.50
188 Neil O'Donnell	.20	.50
189 Eddie George	.20	.50
190 Yancey Thigpen	.15	.40
191 Steve McNair	.25	.60
192 Kevin Dyson	.15	.40
193 Frank Wycheck	.20	.50
194 Stephen Davis	.20	.50
195 Stephen Alexander	.15	.40
196 Darrell Green	.25	.60
197 Skip Hicks	.15	.40
198 Brad Johnson	.20	.50
199 Michael Westbrook	.15	.40
200 Albert Connell	.15	.40
201 David Boston RC	1.00	2.50
202 Joel Makovicka RC	.75	2.00
203 Chris Greisen RC	.75	2.00
204 Jeff Paulk RC	.75	2.00
205 Reginald Kelly RC	.75	2.00
206 Chris McAlister RC	1.00	2.50
207 Brandon Stokley RC	1.25	3.00
208 Antoine Winfield RC	.75	2.00
209 Bobby Collins RC	.75	2.00
210 Peerless Price RC	1.00	2.50
211 Shawn Bryson RC	.75	2.00
212 Sheldon Jackson RC	.75	2.00
213 Kamil Loud RC	.75	2.00
214 D'Wayne Bates RC	.75	2.00
215 Jerry Azumah RC	.75	2.00
216 Marty Booker RC	1.00	2.50
217 Cade McNown RC	1.00	2.50
218 James Allen RC	.75	2.00
219 Nick Williams RC	.75	2.00
220 Akili Smith RC	1.00	2.50
221 Craig Yeast RC	.75	2.00
222 Damon Griffen RC	1.25	3.00
223 Scott Covington RC	.75	2.00
224 Michael Basnight RC	.75	2.00
225 Ronnie Powell RC	.75	2.00
226 Rahim Abdullah RC	.75	2.00
227 Tim Couch RC	1.25	3.00
228 Kevin Johnson RC	1.00	2.50
229 Darrin Chiaverini RC	.75	2.00
230 Mark Campbell RC	.75	2.00
231 Mike Lucky RC	.75	2.00
232 Robert Thomas RC	.75	2.00
233 Ebenezer Ekuban RC	.75	2.00
234 Dat Nguyen RC	1.25	3.00
235 Wane McGarity RC	.75	2.00
236 Jason Tucker RC	1.00	2.50
237 Olandis Gary RC	1.25	3.00
238 Al Wilson RC	1.25	3.00
239 Travis McGriff RC	.75	2.00
240 Desmond Clark RC	1.00	2.50
241 Andre Cooper RC	.75	2.00
242 Chris Watson RC	.75	2.00
243 Sedrick Irvin RC	.75	2.00
244 Chris Claiborne RC	.75	2.00
245 Cory Sauter RC	.75	2.00
246 Brock Olivo RC	.75	2.00
247 De'Mond Parker RC	.75	2.00
248 Aaron Brooks RC	1.25	3.00
249 Antuan Edwards RC	.75	2.00
250 Basil Mitchell RC	.75	2.00
251 Terrence Wilkins RC	1.00	2.50
252 Edgerrin James RC	1.50	4.00
253 Fernando Bryant RC	.75	2.00
254 Mike Cloud RC	.75	2.00
255 Larry Parker RC	1.00	2.50
256 Rob Konrad RC	.75	2.00
257 Cecil Collins RC	.75	2.00
258 James Johnson RC	.75	2.00
259 Jim Kleinsasser RC	1.25	3.00
260 Daunte Culpepper RC	1.25	3.00
261 Michael Bishop RC	1.00	2.50
262 Andy Katzenmoyer RC	1.00	2.50
263 Kevin Faulk RC	1.25	3.00
264 Brett Bech RC	.75	2.00
265 Ricky Williams RC	2.00	5.00
266 Sean Bennett RC	.75	2.00
267 Joe Montgomery RC	.75	2.00
268 Dan Campbell RC	1.25	3.00
269 Ray Lucas RC	1.00	2.50
270 Scott Dreisbach RC	.75	2.00
271 Jed Weaver RC	.75	2.00
272 Dameane Douglas RC	.75	2.00
273 Cecil Martin RC	.75	2.00
274 Donovan McNabb RC	6.00	15.00
275 Na Brown RC	.75	2.00
276 Jerame Tuman RC	.75	2.00
277 Amos Zereoue RC	1.00	2.50
278 Troy Edwards RC	1.00	2.50
279 Jermaine Fazande RC	.75	2.00
280 Steve Heiden RC	.75	2.00
281 Jeff Garcia RC	5.00	12.00
282 Terry Jackson RC	.75	2.00
283 Charlie Rogers RC	.75	2.00
284 Brock Huard RC	1.00	2.50
285 Karsten Bailey RC	.75	2.00
286 Lamar King RC	.75	2.00
287 Justin Watson RC	.75	2.00
288 Kurt Warner RC	6.00	15.00
289 Torry Holt RC	2.00	5.00
290 Joe Germaine RC	1.00	2.50
291 Dre Bly RC	1.25	3.00
292 Martin Gramatica RC	.75	2.00
293 Rabih Abdullah RC	.75	2.00
294 Shaun King RC	1.00	2.50
295 Anthony McFarland RC	1.00	2.50
296 Darnell McDonald RC	.75	2.00
297 Kevin Daft RC	.75	2.00
298 Jevon Kearse RC	1.25	3.00
299 Mike Sellers	1.00	2.50
300 Champ Bailey RC	2.50	6.00

1999 Leaf Rookies and Stars Longevity

*STARS: 20X TO 50X BASIC CARDS
1-200 STATED PRINT RUN 50 SER.#'d SETS
*RCs: 2X TO 5X
201-300 STATED PRINT RUN 30 SER.#'d SETS

1999 Leaf Rookies and Stars Cross Training

COMPLETE SET (25)	60.00	120.00
STATED PRINT RUN 1250 SER.#'d SETS		
CT1 Champ Bailey	2.00	5.00
CT2 Mark Brunell	2.00	5.00
CT3 Daunte Culpepper	5.00	12.00
CT4 Randall Cunningham	2.00	5.00
CT5 Terrell Davis	2.00	5.00
CT6 Charlie Batch	2.00	5.00
CT7 Dorsey Levens	2.00	5.00
CT8 John Elway	6.00	15.00
CT9 Marshall Faulk	2.50	6.00
CT10 Brett Favre	6.00	15.00
CT11 Doug Flutie	2.00	5.00
CT12 Edgerrin James	5.00	12.00
CT13 Curtis Martin	2.00	5.00
CT14 Donovan McNabb	6.00	15.00
CT15 Steve McNair	2.00	5.00
CT16 Cade McNown	.75	2.00
CT17 Randy Moss	5.00	12.00
CT18 Jake Plummer	1.25	3.00
CT19 Barry Sanders	6.00	15.00
CT20 Deion Sanders	2.00	5.00
CT21 Akili Smith	.75	2.00
CT22 Kordell Stewart	1.25	3.00
CT23 Ricky Williams	2.50	6.00
CT24 Charles Woodson	2.00	5.00
CT25 Steve Young	2.50	6.00

1999 Leaf Rookies and Stars Dress For Success

SINGLE JERSEY PRINT RUN 200 SER.#'d SETS		
DUAL JERSEYS PRINT RUN 100 SER.#'d SETS		
1 Barry Sanders	30.00	80.00
2 Emmitt Smith	30.00	80.00
3 Barry Sanders Emmitt Smith	60.00	150.00
4 Eddie George	10.00	25.00
5 Terrell Davis	10.00	25.00
6 Eddie George Terrell Davis	15.00	40.00
7 Tim Couch	10.00	25.00
8 Dan Marino	40.00	100.00
9 Tim Couch Dan Marino	50.00	120.00
10 Brett Favre	40.00	100.00
11 Troy Aikman	20.00	50.00
12 Brett Favre Troy Aikman	60.00	120.00
13 Drew Bledsoe	12.50	30.00
14 Mark Brunell	10.00	25.00
15 Drew Bledsoe Mark Brunell	15.00	40.00
16 Randy Moss	25.00	60.00
17 Jerry Rice	25.00	60.00
18 Randy Moss Jerry Rice	40.00	100.00
19 Antonio Freeman	7.50	20.00
20 Terry Glenn	7.50	20.00
21 Antonio Freeman Terry Glenn	12.00	30.00
22 Steve Young	15.00	40.00
23 Kordell Stewart	7.50	20.00
24 Steve Young Kordell Stewart	25.00	60.00
25 Fred Taylor	10.00	25.00
26 Dorsey Levens	6.00	15.00
27 Fred Taylor Dorsey Levens	10.00	25.00
28 Keyshawn Johnson	10.00	25.00
29 Herman Moore	6.00	15.00
30 Keyshawn Johnson Herman Moore	10.00	25.00

1999 Leaf Rookies and Stars John Elway Collection

HELMET/SHOES PRINT RUN 125 CARDS		
JERSEY PRINT RUN 300 SERIAL #'d CARDS		
JEC1 John Elway Home Jer.	25.00	60.00
JEC2 John Elway Away Jer.	25.00	60.00
JEC3 John Elway Shoe	50.00	125.00
JEC4 J.Elway Blue Helmet	60.00	150.00
JEC5 J.Elway Orange Hel.	60.00	150.00

1999 Leaf Rookies and Stars Freshman Orientation

COMPLETE SET (25)	40.00	80.00
STATED PRINT RUN 2500 SER.#'d SETS		
FO1 Champ Bailey	1.25	3.00
FO2 D'Wayne Bates	.50	1.25
FO3 David Boston	.60	1.50
FO4 Kurt Warner	4.00	10.00
FO5 Cecil Collins	.30	.75
FO6 Tim Couch	.60	1.50
FO7 Daunte Culpepper	3.00	8.00
FO8 Troy Edwards	.50	1.25
FO9 Kevin Faulk	.60	1.50
FO10 Joe Germaine	.50	1.25
FO11 Torry Holt	2.50	6.00
FO12 Brock Huard	.60	1.50
FO13 Sedrick Irvin	.30	.75
FO14 Edgerrin James	3.00	8.00
FO15 Kevin Johnson	.60	1.50
FO16 Shaun King	.50	1.25
FO17 Rob Konrad	.60	1.50
FO18 Sean Bennett	.30	.75
FO19 Donovan McNabb	4.00	10.00
FO20 Cade McNown	.50	1.25
FO21 Peerless Price	.60	1.50
FO22 Akili Smith	.50	1.25
FO23 Ricky Williams	1.50	4.00
FO24 James Johnson	.50	1.25
FO25 Olandis Gary	.60	1.50

1999 Leaf Rookies and Stars Game Plan

COMPLETE SET (25)	40.00	80.00
STATED PRINT RUN 2500 SER.#'d SETS		
*MASTERS: 3X TO 8X BASIC INSERTS		
MASTERS PRINT RUN 50 SER.#'d SETS		
GP1 Jamal Anderson	1.25	3.00
GP2 Jerome Bettis	1.25	3.00
GP3 Drew Bledsoe	1.50	4.00
GP4 Tim Brown	1.25	3.00
GP5 Mark Brunell	1.25	3.00
GP6 Tim Couch	.60	1.50
GP7 Terrell Davis	1.25	3.00
GP8 Corey Dillon	1.25	3.00
GP9 Warrick Dunn	1.25	3.00
GP10 Brad Johnson	1.25	3.00
GP11 Brett Favre	4.00	10.00
GP12 Doug Flutie	1.25	3.00
GP13 Joey Galloway	.75	2.00
GP14 Eddie George	1.25	3.00
GP15 Keyshawn Johnson	1.25	3.00
GP16 Peyton Manning	4.00	10.00
GP17 Dan Marino	4.00	10.00
GP18 Donovan McNabb	4.00	10.00
GP19 Cade McNown	.50	1.25
GP20 Randy Moss	3.00	8.00
GP21 Jake Plummer	.75	2.00
GP22 Barry Sanders	4.00	10.00
GP23 Emmitt Smith	2.50	6.00
GP24 Ricky Williams	1.50	4.00
GP25 Steve Young	1.50	4.00

1999 Leaf Rookies and Stars Great American Heroes

COMPLETE SET (25)	40.00	80.00
STATED PRINT RUN 2500 SER.#'d SETS		
1 Troy Aikman	2.50	6.00
2 Jamal Anderson	1.25	3.00
3 Drew Bledsoe	1.50	4.00
4 Mark Brunell	1.25	3.00
5 Cris Carter	1.25	3.00
6 Randall Cunningham	1.25	3.00
7 Terrell Davis	1.25	3.00
8 John Elway	4.00	10.00
9 Brett Favre	4.00	10.00
10 Doug Flutie	1.25	3.00
11 Antonio Freeman	1.25	3.00
12 Eddie George	1.25	3.00
13 Peyton Manning	4.00	10.00
14 Dan Marino	4.00	10.00
15 Curtis Martin	1.25	3.00
16 Warren Moon	1.25	3.00
17 Randy Moss	3.00	8.00
18 Jake Plummer	.75	2.00
19 Jerry Rice	2.50	6.00
20 Barry Sanders	4.00	10.00
21 Deion Sanders	1.25	3.00
22 Emmitt Smith	2.50	6.00
23 Fred Taylor	1.25	3.00
24 Ricky Williams	4.00	10.00
25 Steve Young	1.50	4.00

1999 Leaf Rookies and Stars Greatest Hits

COMPLETE SET (25)	30.00	60.00
STATED PRINT RUN 2500 SER.#'d SETS		
GH1 Troy Aikman	2.50	6.00
GH2 Terry Glenn	1.25	3.00
GH3 Jamal Anderson	1.25	3.00
GH4 Drew Bledsoe	1.50	4.00
GH5 Cris Carter	1.25	3.00
GH6 Terrell Davis	1.25	3.00
GH7 John Elway	4.00	10.00
GH8 Brett Favre	4.00	10.00
GH9 Antonio Freeman	1.25	3.00
GH10 Eddie George	1.25	3.00
GH11 Priest Holmes	2.00	5.00
GH12 Keyshawn Johnson	1.25	3.00
GH13 Dorsey Levens	1.25	3.00
GH14 Dan Marino	4.00	10.00
GH15 Curtis Martin	1.25	3.00
GH16 Randy Moss	3.00	8.00
GH17 Eric Moulds	.75	2.00
GH18 Terrell Owens	1.25	3.00
GH19 Carl Pickens	.75	2.00
GH20 Jake Plummer	.75	2.00
GH21 Jerry Rice	2.50	6.00
GH22 Barry Sanders	4.00	10.00
GH23 Marvin Harrison	1.25	3.00
GH24 Robert Smith	1.25	3.00
GH25 Fred Taylor	1.25	3.00

1999 Leaf Rookies and Stars Prime Cuts

PC1 Tim Couch	20.00	50.00
PC2 Fred Taylor	20.00	50.00
PC3 Terry Glenn	15.00	40.00
PC4 Drew Bledsoe	25.00	60.00
PC5 Dan Marino	60.00	150.00
PC6 Jerry Rice	40.00	100.00
PC7 Barry Sanders	40.00	100.00
PC8 Mark Brunell	20.00	50.00
PC9 Brett Favre	60.00	150.00
PC10 Steve Young	30.00	80.00
PC11 Keyshawn Johnson	20.00	50.00
PC12 Antonio Freeman	20.00	50.00
PC13 Randy Moss	30.00	80.00
PC14 Troy Aikman	30.00	80.00
PC15 Emmitt Smith	50.00	120.00

1999 Leaf Rookies and Stars Signature Series

SINGLE SIGNED PRINT RUN 150 SER.#'d SETS		
DUAL SIGNED PRINT RUN 50 SER.#'d SETS		
SS1 Terrell Davis	15.00	40.00
SS2 Edgerrin James	15.00	40.00
SS3 Terrell Davis Edgerrin James	60.00	120.00
SS4 Eddie George	15.00	40.00
SS5 Ricky Williams	15.00	40.00
SS6 Eddie George AUTO/90 Ricky Williams (Williams did not sign)	20.00	50.00
SS7 Jake Plummer	15.00	40.00
SS8 Donovan McNabb	40.00	80.00
SS9 Jake Plummer Donovan McNabb	40.00	80.00
SS10 Randall Cunningham	15.00	40.00
SS11 Daunte Culpepper	15.00	40.00
SS12 Randall Cunningham Daunte Culpepper	40.00	100.00
SS13 Fred Taylor	12.00	30.00
SS14 Cecil Collins	10.00	25.00
SS15 Fred Taylor Olandis Gary	15.00	40.00
SS16 Randy Moss	30.00	60.00
SS17 Torry Holt	15.00	40.00
SS18 Randy Moss Torry Holt	40.00	80.00
SS19 Steve Young	40.00	80.00
SS20 Cade McNown	12.00	30.00
SS21 Steve Young Cade McNown	40.00	100.00
SS22 Jerry Rice	60.00	120.00
SS23 David Boston	12.00	30.00
SS24 Jerry Rice David Boston	40.00	100.00
SS25 Doug Flutie	15.00	40.00
SS26 Akili Smith	10.00	25.00
SS27 Doug Flutie Akili Smith	30.00	60.00
SS28 Dan Marino	75.00	150.00
SS29 Tim Couch	12.00	30.00
SS30 Dan Marino Tim Couch	75.00	150.00

1999 Leaf Rookies and Stars SlideShow

COMP.RED SET (25)	250.00	500.00
RED STATED PRINT RUN 100 SER.#'d CARDS		
*GREEN STARS: .8X TO 2X REDS		
*GREEN ROOKIES: .6X TO 1.5X REDS		
GREEN STATED PRINT RUN 50 SER.#'d CARDS		
*BLUE STARS: 1.5X TO 4X REDS		
*BLUE ROOKIES: 1X TO 2.5X REDS		
BLUE STATED PRINT RUN 25 SER.#'d CARDS		
UNPRICED STUDIOS SERIAL #'d OF 1 SET		
1 Troy Aikman	12.50	30.00
2 Drew Bledsoe	7.50	20.00
3 Mark Brunell	6.00	15.00
4 Tim Couch	6.00	15.00
5 Terrell Davis	6.00	15.00
6 John Elway	20.00	50.00
7 Brett Favre	20.00	50.00
8 Antonio Freeman	6.00	15.00
9 Eddie George	6.00	15.00
10 Torry Holt	7.50	20.00
11 Edgerrin James	15.00	40.00
12 Keyshawn Johnson	6.00	15.00
13 Jon Kitna	6.00	15.00
14 Dorsey Levens	6.00	15.00
15 Peyton Manning	15.00	40.00
16 Dan Marino	20.00	50.00
17 Randy Moss	12.50	30.00
18 Jake Plummer	6.00	15.00
19 Jerry Rice	12.50	30.00
20 Barry Sanders	20.00	50.00
21 Marvin Harrison	6.00	15.00
22 Emmitt Smith	12.50	30.00
23 Fred Taylor	6.00	15.00
24 Ricky Williams	7.50	20.00
25 Steve Young	7.50	20.00

1999 Leaf Rookies and Stars Statistical Standouts

COMPLETE SET (25)	50.00	100.00
STATED PRINT RUN 1250 SER.#'d SETS		
SS1 Jamal Anderson	1.50	4.00
SS2 Jerome Bettis	1.50	4.00
SS3 Drew Bledsoe	2.00	5.00
SS4 Cris Carter	1.50	4.00
SS5 Randall Cunningham	1.50	4.00
SS6 Terrell Davis	1.50	4.00
SS7 John Elway	5.00	12.00
SS8 Marshall Faulk	2.00	5.00
SS9 Brett Favre	5.00	12.00
SS10 Antonio Freeman	1.50	4.00
SS11 Joey Galloway	1.00	2.50
SS12 Eddie George	1.50	4.00
SS13 Garrison Hearst	1.00	2.50
SS14 Keyshawn Johnson	1.50	4.00
SS15 Peyton Manning	5.00	12.00
SS16 Steve McNair	1.50	4.00
SS17 Randy Moss	4.00	10.00
SS18 Eric Moulds	1.00	2.50
SS19 Terrell Owens	1.50	4.00
SS20 Jake Plummer	1.00	2.50
SS21 Barry Sanders	5.00	12.00
SS22 Emmitt Smith	3.00	8.00
SS23 Fred Taylor	1.50	4.00
SS24 Vinny Testaverde	1.00	2.50
SS25 Steve Young	2.00	5.00

1999 Leaf Rookies and Stars Statistical Standouts Die Cuts

COMPLETE SET (25)	600.00	1,200.00
CARDS #'d UNDER 26 NOT PRICED		
SS2 Jerome Bettis/71	6.00	15.00
SS3 Drew Bledsoe/37	15.00	40.00
SS5 Randall Cunningham/52	10.00	25.00
SS7 John Elway/47	30.00	80.00
SS8 Marshall Faulk/86	10.00	25.00
SS9 Brett Favre/63	30.00	80.00
SS12 Eddie George/76	7.50	20.00
SS13 Garrison Hearst/51	6.00	15.00
SS14 Keyshawn Johnson/60	6.00	15.00
SS15 Peyton Manning/26	40.00	100.00
SS16 Steve McNair/71	7.50	20.00
SS17 Randy Moss/17	60.00	150.00
SS21 Barry Sanders/76	25.00	60.00
SS22 Emmitt Smith/25	40.00	100.00
SS23 Fred Taylor/77	7.50	20.00
SS24 Vinny Testaverde/29	7.50	20.00
SS25 Steve Young/34	20.00	50.00

1999 Leaf Rookies and Stars Ticket Masters

COMPLETE SET (25)	50.00	100.00
STATED PRINT RUN 2500 SER.#'d SETS		
*EXECUTIVES: 4X TO 10X BASIC INSERTS		
TM1 Randy Moss Cris Carter	5.00	12.00
TM2 Brett Favre Antonio Freeman	5.00	12.00
TM3 Cecil Collins Dan Marino	5.00	12.00
TM4 Brian Griese Terrell Davis	2.00	5.00
TM5 Edgerrin James Peyton Manning	12.50	25.00
TM6 Emmitt Smith Troy Aikman	3.00	8.00
TM7 Jerry Rice Steve Young	3.00	8.00
TM8 Mark Brunell Fred Taylor	1.25	3.00
TM9 David Boston Jake Plummer	1.25	3.00
TM10 Terry Glenn Drew Bledsoe	2.00	5.00
TM11 Charlie Batch Herman Moore	1.25	3.00
TM12 Mike Alstott Warrick Dunn	1.25	3.00
TM13 Eddie George Steve McNair	1.25	3.00
TM14 Kordell Stewart Jerome Bettis	1.25	3.00
TM15 Chris Chandler Jamal Anderson	1.25	3.00
TM16 Akili Smith Corey Dillon	1.25	3.00
TM17 Curtis Enis Cade McNown	1.25	3.00
TM18 Isaac Bruce Marshall Faulk	1.25	3.00
TM19 Eric Moulds Doug Flutie	1.25	3.00
TM20 Joey Galloway Ricky Watters	1.25	3.00
TM21 Michael Westbrook Brad Johnson	1.25	3.00
TM22 Curtis Martin Keyshawn Johnson	1.25	3.00
TM23 Napoleon Kaufman Tim Brown	1.25	3.00
TM24 Kevin Johnson Tim Couch	1.25	3.00
TM25 Duce Staley Donovan McNabb	4.00	10.00

1999 Leaf Rookies and Stars Touchdown Club

COMPLETE SET (20)	75.00	150.00
STATED PRINT RUN 1000 SER.#'d SETS		
*DIE CUTS: 2X TO 5X BASIC INSERTS		
DIE CUT STATED PRINT RUN 60 SER.#'d SETS		
TC1 Randy Moss	6.00	15.00
TC2 Brett Favre	8.00	20.00
TC3 Dan Marino	8.00	20.00
TC4 Barry Sanders	8.00	20.00
TC5 John Elway	8.00	20.00
TC6 Terrell Davis	2.50	6.00
TC7 Peyton Manning	8.00	20.00
TC8 Emmitt Smith	5.00	12.00
TC9 Jerry Rice	5.00	12.00
TC10 Fred Taylor	2.50	6.00
TC11 Drew Bledsoe	3.00	8.00
TC12 Steve Young	3.00	8.00
TC13 Eddie George	2.50	6.00
TC14 Cris Carter	2.50	6.00
TC15 Antonio Freeman	2.50	6.00
TC16 Marvin Harrison	2.50	6.00
TC17 Kurt Warner	6.00	15.00
TC18 Stephen Davis	2.50	6.00
TC19 Terry Glenn	2.50	6.00
TC20 Brad Johnson	2.50	6.00

2000 Leaf Rookies and Stars

Released in late December 2000, Leaf Rookies and Stars features a 300-card base set divided up into 100 veteran cards, 160 rookies sequentially numbered to 1000, and 40 NFL Europe Prospects sequentially numbered to 3000. Base cards showcase full color player action shots with a border along the left side and bottom of the card. Rookie cards have the word "Rookie" along the left card border, and the words "NFLE Prospects" appear along the left edge of the NFL Europe Prospect cards. In addition, several rookies and all of the NFL Europe Prospects autographed the first 200 serial numbered sets out of the stated print run which are broken out into a separate listing. Leaf Rookies and Stars was packaged five cards per pack and carried a suggested retail price of $2.99.

COMP.SET w/o SP's (100)	6.00	15.00
1 Jake Plummer	.20	.50
2 David Boston	.15	.40
3 Tim Dwight	.20	.50
4 Jamal Anderson	.20	.50
5 Chris Chandler	.20	.50
6 Tony Banks	.15	.40
7 Qadry Ismail	.20	.50
8 Eric Moulds	.20	.50
9 Doug Flutie	.25	.60
10 Lamar Smith	.15	.40
11 Peerless Price	.20	.50
12 Rob Johnson	.20	.50
13 Reggie White	.25	.60
14 Muhsin Muhammad	.20	.50
15 Steve Beuerlein	.20	.50
16 Cade McNown	.15	.40
17 Derrick Alexander	.15	.40
18 Marcus Robinson	.20	.50
19 Corey Dillon	.20	.50
20 Akili Smith	.15	.40
21 Tim Couch	.20	.50
22 Kevin Johnson	.15	.40
23 Emmitt Smith	.60	1.50
24 Troy Aikman	.40	1.00
25 Joey Galloway	.20	.50
26 Rocket Ismail	.20	.50
27 John Elway	.60	1.50
28 Terrell Davis	.25	.60
29 Brian Griese	.20	.50
30 Olandis Gary	.20	.50
31 Ed McCaffrey	.20	.50
32 Rod Smith	.20	.50
33 Barry Sanders	.50	1.25
34 Charlie Batch	.20	.50
35 Germane Crowell	.15	.40
36 James Stewart	.15	.40
37 Brett Favre	.75	2.00
38 Dorsey Levens	.20	.50
39 Antonio Freeman	.20	.50
40 Peyton Manning	.60	1.50
41 Edgerrin James	.25	.60
42 Marvin Harrison	.25	.60
43 Fred Taylor	.25	.60
44 Mark Brunell	.20	.50
45 Jimmy Smith	.20	.50
46 Elvis Grbac	.15	.40
47 Tony Gonzalez	.25	.60
48 Dan Marino	.75	2.00
49 Joe Horn	.20	.50
50 Jay Fiedler	.20	.50
51 James Allen	.15	.40
52 Randy Moss	.25	.60
53 Daunte Culpepper	.20	.50
54 Cris Carter	.25	.60
55 Robert Smith	.20	.50
56 Drew Bledsoe	.25	.60
57 Terry Glenn	.20	.50
58 Ricky Williams	.25	.60
59 Amani Toomer	.20	.50
60 Kerry Collins	.20	.50
61 Curtis Martin	.25	.60
62 Vinny Testaverde	.20	.50
63 Wayne Chrebet	.20	.50
64 Tim Brown	.25	.60
65 Tyrone Wheatley	.15	.40
66 Rich Gannon	.20	.50
67 Donovan McNabb	.25	.60
68 Duce Staley	.20	.50
69 Jerome Bettis	.25	.60
70 Donald Hayes	.15	.40
71 Junior Seau	.25	.60
72 Jermaine Fazande	.15	.40
73 Jerry Rice	.50	1.25
74 Steve Young	.30	.75
75 Terrell Owens	.25	.60
76 Charlie Garner	.20	.50
77 Jeff Garcia	.20	.50
78 Tim Biakabutuka	.20	.50
79 Tiki Barber	.25	.60
80 Ricky Watters	.20	.50
81 Kurt Warner	.40	1.00
82 Marshall Faulk	.25	.60
83 Isaac Bruce	.25	.60
84 Torry Holt	.25	.60
85 Mike Alstott	.25	.60
86 Warrick Dunn	.20	.50
87 Shaun King	.15	.40
88 Keyshawn Johnson	.20	.50
89 Warren Sapp	.20	.50
90 Eddie George	.20	.50
91 Jevon Kearse	.20	.50
92 Steve McNair	.25	.60
93 Carl Pickens	.20	.50
94 Deion Sanders	.25	.60
95 Stephen Davis	.20	.50
96 Brad Johnson	.20	.50
97 Bruce Smith	.25	.60
98 Michael Westbrook	.15	.40
99 Albert Connell	.15	.40
100 Jeff George	.20	.50
101 Thomas Jones RC	4.00	10.00
102 Bashir Yamini RC	2.00	5.00
103 Jamal Lewis RC	3.00	8.00
104 Travis Taylor RC	2.50	6.00
105 Chris Redman RC	2.50	6.00
106 Avion Black RC	2.00	5.00
107 Sammy Morris RC	2.50	6.00
108 Dez White RC	2.50	6.00
109 Peter Warrick RC	3.00	8.00
110 Ron Dugans RC	2.00	5.00
111 Curtis Keaton RC	2.00	5.00
112 Danny Farmer RC	2.00	5.00
113 Courtney Brown RC	2.50	6.00
114 Dennis Northcutt RC	2.50	6.00
115 Travis Prentice RC	2.50	6.00
116 JaJuan Dawson RC	2.00	5.00
117 Spergon Wynn RC	2.50	6.00
118 Michael Wiley RC	2.00	5.00
119 Chris Cole RC	2.50	6.00
120 Mike Anderson RC	3.00	8.00
121 Muneer Moore RC	2.00	5.00
122 Reuben Droughns RC	3.00	8.00
123 Bubba Franks RC	3.00	8.00
124 Anthony Lucas RC	2.00	5.00
125 Charles Lee RC	2.00	5.00
126 R.Jay Soward RC	2.00	5.00
127 Shyrone Stith RC	2.00	5.00
128 Sylvester Morris RC	2.00	5.00
129 Frank Moreau RC	2.00	5.00
130 Dante Hall RC	3.00	8.00
131 Doug Chapman RC	2.00	5.00
132 Troy Walters RC	2.00	5.00
133 J.R. Redmond RC	2.00	5.00
134 Tom Brady RC	125.00	225.00
135 Terrelle Smith RC	2.00	5.00
136 Chad Morton RC	3.00	8.00
137 Ron Dayne RC	3.00	8.00
138 Ron Dixon RC	2.00	5.00
139 Chad Pennington RC	5.00	12.00
140 Anthony Becht RC	2.50	6.00
141 Laveranues Coles RC	3.00	8.00
142 Windrell Hayes RC	2.00	5.00
143 Sebastian Janikowski RC	3.00	8.00
144 Jerry Porter RC	3.00	8.00
145 Corey Simon RC	2.50	6.00
146 Todd Pinkston RC	2.00	5.00
147 Gari Scott RC	2.00	5.00
148 Plaxico Burress RC	3.00	8.00
149 Tee Martin RC	3.00	8.00
150 Trevor Gaylor RC	2.00	5.00
151 Ronney Jenkins RC	2.00	5.00
152 Giovanni Carmazzi RC	2.00	5.00
153 Tim Rattay RC	2.50	6.00
154 Shaun Alexander RC	4.00	10.00
155 Darrell Jackson RC	2.50	6.00
156 James Williams RC	2.00	5.00
157 Trung Canidate RC	2.50	6.00
158 Joe Hamilton RC	2.00	5.00
159 Erron Kinney RC	2.00	5.00
160 Todd Husak RC	2.00	5.00
161 Raynoch Thompson RC	2.00	5.00
162 Darwin Walker RC	2.00	5.00
163 Jay Tant RC	2.00	5.00
164 Doug Johnson RC	2.50	6.00
165 Robert Bean RC	2.00	5.00

166 Mark Simoneau RC 2.00 5.00
167 John Jones RC 2.00 5.00
168 Obafemi Ayanbadejo RC 2.50 6.00
169 Mike Brown RC 3.00 8.00
170 Shockmain Davis RC 2.00 5.00
171 Erik Flowers RC 2.00 5.00
172 Corey Moore RC 2.00 5.00
173 Drew Haddad RC 2.00 5.00
174 Kwame Cavil RC 2.00 5.00
175 Pat Dennis RC 2.00 5.00
176 Rashard Anderson RC 2.00 5.00
177 Brian Finneran RC 3.00 8.00
178 Na'il Diggs RC 2.00 5.00
179 Marc Bulger RC 3.00 8.00
180 Mondriel Fulcher RC 2.00 5.00
181 Dwayne Carswell 2.00 5.00
182 Brian Urlacher RC 12.00 30.00
183 Paul Edinger RC 3.00 8.00
184 Karon Coleman RC 2.00 5.00
185 Aaron Shea RC 2.50 6.00
186 Fabien Bownes RC 2.00 5.00
187 Damon Hodge RC 2.50 6.00
188 Dwayne Goodrich RC 2.00 5.00
189 Clint Stoerner RC 3.00 8.00
190 James Whalen RC 2.00 5.00
191 Deltha O'Neal RC 2.50 6.00
192 Ian Gold RC 2.00 5.00
193 Kenoy Kennedy RC 2.00 5.00
194 Jarious Jackson RC 2.50 6.00
195 Leroy Fields RC 2.00 5.00
196 Barrett Green RC 2.00 5.00
197 Joey Jamison RC 2.00 5.00
198 Rondell Mealey RC 2.00 5.00
199 Rob Morris RC 2.50 6.00
200 Marcus Washington RC 2.50 6.00
201 Trevor Insley RC 2.00 5.00
202 Jamel White RC 2.00 5.00
203 Kevin McDougal RC 2.00 5.00
204 Ibn Green RC 2.00 5.00
205 T.J. Slaughter RC 2.00 5.00
206 Emanuel Smith RC 2.00 5.00
207 Herbert Goodman RC 2.00 5.00
208 William Bartee RC 2.00 5.00
209 Orantes Grant RC 2.00 5.00
210 Brad Hoover RC 2.50 6.00
211 Deon Dyer RC 2.00 5.00
212 Jonas Lewis RC 2.00 5.00
213 Chris Hovan RC 2.50 6.00
214 Fred Robbins RC 2.00 5.00
215 Michael Boireau RC 2.00 5.00
216 Giles Cole RC 2.00 5.00
217 Dave Stachelski RC 2.00 5.00
218 Patrick Pass RC 2.50 6.00
219 Darren Howard RC 2.00 5.00
220 Austin Wheatley RC 2.00 5.00
221 Kevin Houser RC 2.00 5.00
222 Rian Lindell RC 2.00 5.00
223 Jake Delhomme RC 8.00 20.00
224 Cornelius Griffin RC 2.00 5.00
225 Shaun Ellis RC 3.00 8.00
226 John Abraham RC 3.00 8.00
227 Travares Tillman RC 2.00 5.00
228 Julian Peterson RC 3.00 8.00
229 Marcus Knight RC 2.00 5.00
230 Thomas Hamner RC 2.00 5.00
231 Hank Poteat RC 2.00 5.00
232 Neil Rackers RC 2.00 5.00
233 Bobby Shaw RC 2.50 6.00
234 Rogers Beckett RC 2.00 5.00
235 Reggie Jones RC 2.00 5.00
236 Tim Seder RC 2.00 5.00
237 Durell Price RC 2.00 5.00
238 Ahmed Plummer RC 2.00 5.00
239 John Engelberger RC 2.00 5.00
240 Paul Smith RC 2.00 5.00
241 Chofic Fieldo RC 2.00 6.00
242 Kevin Feterik RC 2.00 5.00
243 Jacoby Shepherd RC 2.00 5.00
244 Nate Webster RC 2.00 5.00
245 Ketric Sanford RC 2.00 5.00
246 Tavarus Hogans RC 2.00 5.00
247 Keith Bulluck RC 2.50 6.00
248 Mike Green RC 3.00 8.00
249 Chris Coleman RC 2.00 5.00
250 Demario Brown RC 2.00 5.00
251 Billy Volek RC 3.00 8.00
252 Mareno Philyaw RC 2.00 5.00
253 Ethan Howell RC 2.00 5.00
254 Chris Samuels RC 2.50 6.00
255 Brandon Short RC 2.00 5.00
256 Maurice Smith RC 2.50 6.00
257 Frank Murphy RC 2.00 5.00
258 Darrick Vaughn RC 2.00 5.00
259 Payton Williams RC 2.00 5.00
260 JaJuan Seider RC 2.00 5.00
261 Antonio Banks EP RC .60 1.50
262 Jonathan Brown EP RC .60 1.50
263 Ontiwaun Carter EP RC .60 1.50
264 Jeremaine Copeland EP .60 1.50
265 Ralph Dawkins EP RC .60 1.50
266 Marques Douglas EP RC .60 1.50
267 Kevin Drake EP RC .60 1.50
268 Damon Dunn EP RC .60 1.50
269 Todd Floyd EP RC .60 1.50
270 Tony Graziani EP .75 2.00
271 Derrick Ham EP RC .75 2.00
272 Duane Hawthorne EP RC .60 1.50
273 Alonzo Johnson EP RC .60 1.50
274 Mark Kacmarynski EP RC .60 1.50
275 Eric Kresser EP .60 1.50
276 Jim Kubiak EP RC .60 1.50
277 Blaine McElmurry EP RC .60 1.50
278 Scott Milanovich EP .60 1.50
279 Norman Miller EP RC .60 1.50
280 Sean Morey EP RC .60 1.50
281 Jeff Ogden EP .60 1.50
282 Pepe Pearson EP RC .60 1.50
283 Ron Powlus EP RC 1.00 2.50
284 Jason Shelley EP RC .60 1.50
285 Ben Snell EP RC .60 1.50
286 Aaron Stecker EP RC .75 2.00
287 L.C. Stevens EP .60 1.50
288 Mike Sutton EP RC .60 1.50
289 Damian Vaughn EP RC .60 1.50
290 Ted White EP .60 1.50
291 Marcus Crandell EP RC .60 1.50
292 Darryl Daniel EP RC .60 1.50
293 Jesse Haynes EP .60 1.50
294 Matt Lytle EP RC .60 1.50
295 Deon Mitchell EP RC .75 2.00
296 Kendrick Nord EP RC .60 1.50
297 Ronnie Powell EP .60 1.50
298 Selucio Sanford EP RC .60 1.50
299 Corey Thomas EP .60 1.50
300 Vershan Jackson EP RC .60 1.50
301 Michael Vick XRC 10.00 25.00
302 Drew Brees XRC 20.00 40.00
303 Quincy Carter XRC 3.00 8.00
304 Marques Tuiasosopa XRC 3.00 8.00
305 Chris Weinke XRC 3.00 8.00
306 LaDainian Tomlinson XRC 8.00 20.00
307 Deuce McAllister XRC 4.00 10.00
308 Michael Bennett XRC 4.00 10.00
309 Anthony Thomas XRC 4.00 10.00
310 LaMont Jordan XRC 4.00 10.00
311 David Terrell XRC 3.00 8.00
312 Koren Robinson XRC 3.00 8.00
313 Rod Gardner XRC 3.00 8.00
314 Santana Moss XRC 4.00 10.00
315 Freddie Mitchell XRC 2.50 6.00
316 Gerard Warren XRC 2.50 6.00
317 Justin Smith XRC 4.00 10.00
318 Richard Seymour XRC 3.00 8.00
319 Andre Carter XRC 2.50 6.00
320 Jamal Reynolds XRC 2.50 6.00

2000 Leaf Rookies and Stars Longevity

*VETS 1-100: 10X TO 25X BASIC CARDS
1-100 VETERAN PRINT RUN 50
*ROOKIES 101-200: 1X TO 2.5X
*EP 261-300: 2X TO 5X BASIC CARDS
*ROOKIES 301-320: .8X TO 2X
101-320 ROOKIE/EP PRINT RUN 30
134 Tom Brady 450.00 800.00
302 Drew Brees 75.00 125.00
306 LaDainian Tomlinson 30.00 80.00

2000 Leaf Rookies and Stars Rookie Autographs

FIRST 200 SER.#'d ROOKIE CARDS SIGNED
103 Jamal Lewis 8.00 20.00
104 Travis Taylor 6.00 15.00
105 Chris Redman 6.00 15.00
108 Dez White 6.00 15.00
109 Peter Warrick 8.00 20.00
112 Danny Farmer 5.00 12.00
113 Courtney Brown 6.00 15.00
115 Travis Prentice 6.00 15.00
116 JaJuan Dawson 5.00 12.00
120 Mike Anderson 8.00 20.00
123 Bubba Franks 8.00 20.00
126 R.Jay Soward 5.00 12.00
127 Shyrone Stith 5.00 12.00
128 Sylvester Morris 5.00 12.00
137 Ron Dayne 8.00 20.00
139 Chad Pennington 12.00 30.00
141 Laveranues Coles 8.00 20.00
144 Jerry Porter 8.00 20.00
145 Corey Simon 6.00 15.00
146 Todd Pinkston 5.00 12.00
140 Plaxico Burress 15.00 30.00
154 Shaun Alexander 10.00 25.00
155 Darrell Jackson 6.00 15.00
157 Trung Canidate 6.00 15.00
261 Antonio Banks 5.00 12.00
262 Jonathan Brown 5.00 12.00
263 Ontiwaun Carter 5.00 12.00
264 Jeremaine Copeland 5.00 12.00
266 Marques Douglas 5.00 12.00
267 Kevin Drake 5.00 12.00
268 Damon Dunn 5.00 12.00
269 Todd Floyd 5.00 12.00
270 Tony Graziani 6.00 15.00
272 Duane Hawthorne 5.00 12.00
273 Alonzo Johnson 5.00 12.00
274 Mark Kacmarynski 5.00 12.00
275 Eric Kresser 5.00 12.00
276 Jim Kubiak 5.00 12.00
277 Blaine McElmurry 5.00 12.00
278 Scott Milanovich 5.00 12.00
279 Norman Miller 5.00 12.00
280 Sean Morey 5.00 12.00
281 Jeff Ogden 5.00 12.00
282 Pepe Pearson 5.00 12.00
283 Ron Powlus 8.00 20.00
284 Jason Shelley 5.00 12.00
285 Ben Snell 5.00 12.00
286 Aaron Stecker 6.00 15.00
287 L.C. Stevens 5.00 12.00
288 Mike Sutton 5.00 12.00
290 Ted White 5.00 12.00
292 Darryl Daniel 5.00 12.00
293 Jesse Haynes 5.00 12.00
294 Matt Lytle 5.00 12.00
295 Deon Mitchell 6.00 15.00
296 Kendrick Nord 5.00 12.00
298 Selucio Sanford 5.00 12.00
299 Corey Thomas 5.00 12.00
300 Vershan Jackson 5.00 12.00
114 Dennis Northcutt 6.00 15.00

2000 Leaf Rookies and Stars Dress Four Success

STATED PRINT RUN 25-300
1C Jerry Rice Combo/25 50.00 125.00
1H Jerry Rice Helmet/100 20.00 50.00
1J Jerry Rice Jersey/300 12.00 30.00
1P Jerry Rice Pants/300 12.00 30.00
1S Jerry Rice Shoe/50 25.00 60.00
2C Eddie George Combo/25 20.00 50.00
2F Eddie George FB/100 8.00 20.00
2J Eddie George Jersey/200 5.00 12.00
2S Eddie George Shoe/50 10.00 25.00
3C Troy Aikman Combo/25 40.00 100.00
3F Troy Aikman FB/100 15.00 40.00
3H Troy Aikman Helmet/100 15.00 40.00
3J Troy Aikman Jersey/300 10.00 25.00
3S Troy Aikman Shoe/50 20.00 50.00
4F Mark Brunell FB/100 8.00 20.00
4J Mark Brunell Jersey/300 5.00 12.00
4S Mark Brunell Shoe/50 10.00 25.00
5C Barry Sanders Combo/25 50.00 125.00
5F Barry Sanders FB/100 20.00 50.00
5H Barry Sanders Helmet 20.00 50.00
5J Barry Sanders Jersey/300 12.00 30.00
5S Barry Sanders Shoe/50 25.00 60.00
6C Marshall Faulk Combo/25 25.00 60.00
6J Marshall Faulk Jersey/300 6.00 15.00
6P Marshall Faulk Pants/300 6.00 15.00
6S Marshall Faulk Shoe/50 12.00 30.00
7C Dan Marino Combo/25 80.00 200.00
7H Dan Marino Helmet/100 30.00 80.00
7J Dan Marino Jersey/300 20.00 50.00
7P Dan Marino Pants/300 20.00 50.00
7S Dan Marino Shoe/50 40.00 100.00
8C Stephen Davis Combo/25 20.00 50.00
8F Stephen Davis FB/100 8.00 20.00
8H Stephen Davis Helmet 8.00 20.00
8J Stephen Davis Jersey/300 5.00 12.00
8S Stephen Davis Shoe/50 10.00 25.00
9C Terrell Davis Combo/25 25.00 60.00
9H Terrell Davis Helmet/100 10.00 25.00
9J Terrell Davis Jersey/225 6.00 15.00
9S Terrell Davis Shoe/50 12.00 30.00
10C Brett Favre Combo/25 80.00 200.00
10F Brett Favre FB/100 30.00 80.00
10H Brett Favre Helmet/100 30.00 80.00
10J Brett Favre Jersey/175 25.00 60.00
10S Brett Favre Shoe/50 40.00 100.00

2000 Leaf Rookies and Stars Freshman Orientation

COMPLETE SET (30) 50.00 100.00
STATED PRINT RUN 2000 SER.#'d SETS
FO1 Peter Warrick 1.25 3.00
FO2 Jamal Lewis 1.25 3.00
FO3 Thomas Jones 1.50 4.00
FO4 Plaxico Burress 1.25 3.00
FO5 Travis Taylor 1.00 2.50
FO6 Ron Dayne 1.25 3.00
FO7 Bubba Franks 1.25 3.00
FO8 Chad Pennington 2.00 5.00
FO9 Shaun Alexander 1.50 4.00
FO10 Sylvester Morris .75 2.00
FO11 R.Jay Soward .75 2.00
FO12 Trung Canidate 1.00 2.50
FO13 Dennis Northcutt 1.00 2.50
FO14 Todd Pinkston .75 2.00
FO15 Jerry Porter 1.25 3.00
FO16 Travis Prentice 1.00 2.50
FO17 Giovanni Carmazzi .75 2.00
FO18 Ron Dugans .75 2.00
FO19 Dez White 1.00 2.50
FO20 Mike Anderson 1.25 3.00
FO21 Ron Dixon .75 2.00
FO22 Chris Redman 1.00 2.50
FO23 J.R. Redmond .75 2.00
FO24 Laveranues Coles 1.25 3.00
FO25 JaJuan Dawson .75 2.00
FO26 Darrell Jackson 1.00 2.50
FO27 Sammy Morris 1.00 2.50
FO28 Doug Chapman .75 2.00
FO29 Tim Rattay 1.00 2.50
FO30 Gari Scott .75 2.00

2000 Leaf Rookies and Stars Game Plan

COMPLETE SET (30) 30.00 60.00
STATED PRINT RUN 2000 SER.#'d SETS
*MASTERS/50: 2X TO 5X BASIC INSERTS
MASTERS PRINT RUN 50 SER.#'d SETS
GP1 Jerome Bettis .75 2.00
GP2 Charlie Garner .60 1.50
GP3 Jamal Lewis .75 2.00
GP4 Eric Moulds .60 1.50
GP5 Cade McNown .50 1.25
GP6 Peter Warrick .75 2.00
GP7 Tim Couch .60 1.50
GP8 Emmitt Smith 2.00 5.00
GP9 Troy Aikman 1.25 3.00
GP10 Terrell Davis .75 2.00
GP11 Brett Favre 2.50 6.00
GP12 Peyton Manning 2.00 5.00
GP13 Edgerrin James .75 2.00
GP14 Fred Taylor .75 2.00
GP15 Randy Moss .75 2.00
GP16 Daunte Culpepper .60 1.50
GP17 Drew Bledsoe .75 2.00
GP18 Ricky Williams .75 2.00
GP19 Ron Dayne .75 2.00
GP20 Curtis Martin .75 2.00
GP21 Donovan McNabb .75 2.00
GP22 Plaxico Burress .75 2.00
GP23 Jerry Rice 1.50 4.00
GP24 Shaun Alexander 1.00 2.50
GP25 Kurt Warner 1.25 3.00
GP26 Marshall Faulk .75 2.00
GP27 Keyshawn Johnson .60 1.50
GP28 Eddie George .60 1.50
GP29 Steve McNair .75 2.00
GP30 Stephen Davis .60 1.50

2000 Leaf Rookies and Stars Great American Heroes

COMPLETE SET (10) 20.00 40.00
STATED PRINT RUN 1000 SER.#'d SETS
GAH1 John Elway 2.50 6.00
GAH2 Terrell Davis 1.00 2.50
GAH3 Barry Sanders 2.00 5.00
GAH4 Edgerrin James 1.00 2.50
GAH5 Dan Marino 3.00 8.00
GAH6 Randy Moss 1.00 2.50
GAH7 Ricky Williams 1.00 2.50
GAH8 Jerry Rice 2.00 5.00
GAH9 Steve Young 1.25 3.00
GAH10 Kurt Warner 1.50 4.00

2000 Leaf Rookies and Stars Great American Signatures

AUTO.PRINT RUN 100 SER.#'d SETS
GAS1 John Elway 60.00 120.00
GAS2 Terrell Davis 20.00 50.00
GAS3 Barry Sanders 50.00 100.00
GAS4 Edgerrin James 20.00 50.00
GAS5 Dan Marino 75.00 150.00
GAS7 Ricky Williams 20.00 50.00
GAS8 Jerry Rice 60.00 120.00
GAS10 Kurt Warner 30.00 60.00

2000 Leaf Rookies and Stars Great American Treasures

JERSEY PRINT RUN 100 SER.#'d SETS
GAT1 John Elway 25.00 60.00
GAT2 Terrell Davis 10.00 25.00
GAT3 Barry Sanders 20.00 50.00
GAT4 Edgerrin James 10.00 25.00
GAT5 Dan Marino 30.00 80.00
GAT6 Randy Moss 10.00 25.00
GAT7 Ricky Williams 10.00 25.00
GAT8 Jerry Rice 20.00 50.00
GAT9 Steve Young 12.00 30.00
GAT10 Kurt Warner 15.00 40.00

2000 Leaf Rookies and Stars Great American Treasures Autographs

GATA1 John Elway 100.00 200.00
GATA2 Terrell Davis 30.00 80.00
GATA3 Barry Sanders 100.00 200.00
GATA4 Edgerrin James 30.00 80.00
GATA5 Dan Marino 125.00 250.00
GATA7 Ricky Williams 30.00 80.00
GATA8 Jerry Rice 125.00 200.00
GATA9 Steve Young 75.00 150.00
GATA10 Kurt Warner 60.00 120.00

2000 Leaf Rookies and Stars Joe Montana Collection

STATED PRINT RUN 125-300
MC1 Joe Montana/49ers Jersey/300 25.00 60.00
MC2 Joe Montana Chiefs Jersey/300 25.00 60.00
MC3 Joe Montana Helmet/125 30.00 80.00
MC4 Joe Montana Football/125 30.00 80.00
MC5 Joe Montana Shoe/125 30.00 80.00

2000 Leaf Rookies and Stars Joe Montana Collection Autographs

COMMON CARD (MC1-MC5) 75.00 200.00
FIRST 25 SER.#'d SETS SIGNED
MC1 Joe Montana/49ers Jersey 75.00 200.00
MC2 Joe Montana Chiefs Jersey 75.00 200.00
MC3 Joe Montana Helmet 75.00 200.00
MC4 Joe Montana Football 75.00 200.00
MC5 Joe Montana Shoe 75.00 200.00

2000 Leaf Rookies and Stars Prime Cuts

STATED PRINT RUN 25 SER.#'d SETS
PC1 Eric Moulds 12.00 30.00
PC2 Cade McNown 10.00 25.00
PC3 Tim Couch 12.00 30.00
PC4 Emmitt Smith 40.00 100.00
PC5 John Elway 50.00 120.00
PC6 Terrell Davis 15.00 40.00
PC7 Brian Griese 12.00 30.00
PC8 Barry Sanders 30.00 80.00
PC9 Brett Favre 60.00 150.00
PC10 Antonio Freeman 12.00 30.00
PC11 Peyton Manning 50.00 120.00
PC12 Edgerrin James 15.00 40.00
PC13 Marvin Harrison 15.00 40.00
PC14 Fred Taylor 15.00 40.00
PC15 Mark Brunell 12.00 30.00
PC16 Jimmy Smith 12.00 30.00
PC17 Dan Marino 60.00 150.00
PC18 Randy Moss 15.00 40.00
PC19 Cris Carter 15.00 40.00
PC20 Ricky Williams 15.00 40.00
PC21 Curtis Martin 15.00 40.00
PC22 Donovan McNabb 15.00 40.00
PC23 Jerry Rice 40.00 100.00
PC24 Steve Young 20.00 50.00
PC25 Kurt Warner 25.00 60.00
PC26 Marshall Faulk 15.00 40.00
PC27 Isaac Bruce 15.00 40.00
PC28 Shaun King
PC29 Eddie George 12.00 30.00
PC30 Steve McNair 15.00 40.00

2000 Leaf Rookies and Stars SlideShow

COMPLETE SET (60) 60.00 120.00
STATED PRINT RUN 1000 SER.#'d SETS
*STUDIO/20: 3X TO 8X BASIC INSERTS
STUDIO PRINT RUN 20 SER.#'d SETS
S1 Jake Plummer .75 2.00
S2 Thomas Jones 1.00 2.50
S3 Jamal Anderson .75 2.00
S4 Jamal Lewis .75 2.00
S5 Travis Taylor .60 1.50
S6 Eric Moulds .75 2.00
S7 Cade McNown .60 1.50
S8 Marcus Robinson .75 2.00
S9 Corey Dillon .75 2.00
S10 Akili Smith .60 1.50
S11 Peter Warrick .75 2.00
S12 Tim Couch .75 2.00
S13 Travis Prentice .60 1.50
S14 Emmitt Smith 2.50 6.00
S15 Troy Aikman 1.50 4.00
S16 Mike Anderson .75 2.00
S17 John Elway 2.50 6.00
S18 Terrell Davis 1.00 2.50
S19 Brian Griese .75 2.00
S20 Terrell Owens 1.00 2.50
S21 Barry Sanders 2.00 5.00
S22 Charlie Batch .75 2.00
S23 Brett Favre 3.00 8.00
S24 Dorsey Levens .75 2.00
S25 Antonio Freeman .75 2.00
S26 Peyton Manning 2.50 6.00
S27 Edgerrin James 1.00 2.50
S28 Marvin Harrison 1.00 2.50
S29 Fred Taylor 1.00 2.50
S30 Mark Brunell .75 2.00
S31 Jimmy Smith .75 2.00
S32 Sylvester Morris .60 1.50
S33 Dan Marino 3.00 8.00
S34 Randy Moss 1.00 2.50
S35 Daunte Culpepper .75 2.00
S36 Cris Carter 1.00 2.50
S37 Robert Smith .75 2.00
S38 Drew Bledsoe 1.00 2.50
S39 Ricky Williams 1.00 2.50
S40 Ron Dayne .75 2.00
S41 Curtis Martin 1.00 2.50
S42 Chad Pennington 1.25 3.00
S43 Tim Brown 1.00 2.50
S44 Donovan McNabb 1.00 2.50
S45 Torry Holt 1.00 2.50
S46 Plaxico Burress .75 2.00
S47 Jerry Rice 2.00 5.00
S48 Steve Young 1.25 3.00
S49 Shaun Alexander 1.00 2.50
S50 Kurt Warner 1.50 4.00
S51 Marshall Faulk 1.00 2.50
S52 Isaac Bruce 1.00 2.50
S53 Shaun King .60 1.50
S54 Keyshawn Johnson .75 2.00
S55 Mike Alstott 1.00 2.50
S56 Eddie George .75 2.00
S57 Steve McNair 1.00 2.50
S58 Jevon Kearse .75 2.00
S59 Stephen Davis .75 2.00
S60 Brad Johnson .75 2.00

2000 Leaf Rookies and Stars Statistical Standouts

COMPLETE SET (40) 75.00 150.00
STATED PRINT RUN 500 SER.#'d SETS
SS1 Thomas Jones 1.50 4.00
SS2 Jamal Lewis 1.25 3.00
SS3 Travis Taylor 1.00 2.50
SS4 Cade McNown 1.00 2.50
SS5 Corey Dillon 1.25 3.00
SS6 Akili Smith 1.00 2.50
SS7 Peter Warrick 1.25 3.00
SS8 Tim Couch 1.25 3.00
SS9 Emmitt Smith 4.00 10.00
SS10 Troy Aikman 2.50 6.00
SS11 John Elway 4.00 10.00
SS12 Terrell Davis 1.50 4.00
SS13 Barry Sanders 3.00 8.00
SS14 Brett Favre 5.00 12.00
SS15 Dorsey Levens 1.25 3.00
SS16 Antonio Freeman 1.25 3.00
SS17 Peyton Manning 4.00 10.00
SS18 Edgerrin James 1.25 3.00
SS19 Marvin Harrison 1.50 4.00
SS20 Fred Taylor 1.50 4.00
SS21 Dan Marino 5.00 12.00
SS22 Randy Moss 1.50 4.00
SS23 Daunte Culpepper 1.25 3.00
SS24 Cris Carter 1.50 4.00
SS25 Drew Bledsoe 1.50 4.00
SS26 Ricky Williams 1.50 4.00
SS27 Ron Dayne 1.25 3.00
SS28 Curtis Martin 1.50 4.00
SS29 Chad Pennington 2.00 5.00
SS30 Plaxico Burress 1.25 3.00
SS31 Jerry Rice 3.00 8.00
SS32 Steve Young 2.00 5.00
SS33 Shaun Alexander 2.00 5.00
SS34 Kurt Warner 2.50 6.00
SS35 Marshall Faulk 1.50 4.00
SS36 Isaac Bruce 1.50 4.00
SS37 Eddie George 1.25 3.00
SS38 Steve McNair 1.50 4.00
SS39 Stephen Davis 1.25 3.00
SS40 Brad Johnson 1.25 3.00

2000 Leaf Rookies and Stars Ticket Masters

COMPLETE SET (30) 30.00 60.00
STATED PRINT RUN 2000 SER.#'d SETS
TM1 Thomas Jones / Jake Plummer 1.00 2.50
TM2 Jamal Anderson / Chris Chandler .60 1.50
TM3 Travis Taylor / Jamal Lewis .75 2.00
TM4 Eric Moulds / Rob Johnson .60 1.50
TM5 Muhsin Muhammad / Steve Beuerlein .60 1.50
TM6 Cade McNown / Marcus Robinson .60 1.50
TM7 Peter Warrick / Akili Smith .75 2.00
TM8 Tim Couch / Kevin Johnson .60 1.50
TM9 Emmitt Smith / Troy Aikman 2.00 5.00
TM10 Terrell Davis / Brian Griese .75 2.00
TM11 Charlie Batch / James Stewart .60 1.50
TM12 Brett Favre / Antonio Freeman 2.50 6.00
TM13 Peyton Manning / Edgerrin James 2.00 5.00
TM14 Mark Brunell / Fred Taylor .75 2.00
TM15 Jay Fiedler / Lamar Smith .60 1.50
TM16 Randy Moss / Daunte Culpepper .75 2.00
TM17 Drew Bledsoe / Terry Glenn .75 2.00
TM18 Ricky Williams / Jeff Blake .75 2.00
TM19 Kerry Collins / Ron Dayne .75 2.00
TM20 Chad Pennington / Curtis Martin 1.25 3.00
TM21 Tim Brown / Rich Gannon .75 2.00
TM22 Donovan McNabb / Duce Staley .75 2.00
TM23 Plaxico Burress / Jerome Bettis .75 2.00
TM24 Ryan Leaf / Jermaine Fazande .60 1.50
TM25 Jerry Rice / Terrell Owens 1.50 4.00
TM26 Shaun Alexander / Ricky Watters 1.00 2.50
TM27 Kurt Warner / Marshall Faulk 1.25 3.00
TM28 Shaun King / Keyshawn Johnson .60 1.50
TM29 Eddie George / Steve McNair .75 2.00
TM30 Stephen Davis / Brad Johnson .60 1.50

2001 Leaf Rookies and Stars Chicago Collection

NOT PRICED DUE TO SCARCITY

2001 Leaf Rookies and Stars

This 300 card set was issued in December, 2001. The cards were issued in five card packs which came 24 to a box. Cards numbered 1-100 honored leading veterans while cards numbered 101-300 featured rookies.

COMP.SET w/o SP's (100) 7.50 20.00
201-300 ROOKIE ODDS 1:24
1 Aaron Brooks .20 .50
2 Ahman Green .25 .60
3 Antonio Freeman .25 .60
4 Brad Johnson .20 .50
5 Brett Favre .75 2.00
6 Brian Griese .20 .50
7 Brian Urlacher .30 .75
8 Bruce Smith .25 .60
9 Cade McNown .20 .50
10 Chad Pennington .25 .60
11 Champ Bailey .25 .60
12 Charles Woodson .25 .60
13 Charlie Batch .20 .50
14 Charlie Garner .20 .50
15 Corey Dillon .20 .50
16 Cris Carter .25 .60
17 Curtis Martin .25 .60
18 Dan Marino .60 1.50
19 Daunte Culpepper .20 .50
20 David Boston .15 .40
21 Deion Sanders .25 .60
22 Donovan McNabb .25 .60
23 Doug Flutie .25 .60
24 Drew Bledsoe .25 .60
25 Duce Staley .20 .50
26 Ed McCaffrey .20 .50
27 Eddie George .25 .60
28 Edgerrin James .25 .60
29 Elvis Grbac .20 .50
30 Emmitt Smith .60 1.50
31 Eric Moulds .20 .50
32 Fred Taylor .25 .60
33 Germane Crowell .15 .40
34 Ike Hilliard .20 .50
35 Isaac Bruce .25 .60
36 Jake Plummer .20 .50
37 Jamal Anderson .20 .50
38 Jamal Lewis .25 .60
39 James Allen .15 .40
40 James Stewart .15 .40
41 Jay Fiedler .20 .50
42 Jeff Garcia .20 .50
43 Jeff George .20 .50
44 Jeff Lewis .15 .40
45 Jerome Bettis .25 .60
46 Jerry Rice .50 1.25
47 Jevon Kearse .20 .50
48 Jimmy Smith .20 .50
49 Joey Galloway .20 .50
50 John Elway .60 1.50
51 Junior Seau .25 .60
52 Keenan McCardell .20 .50
53 Kerry Collins .20 .50
54 Kevin Johnson .15 .40
55 Keyshawn Johnson .20 .50
56 Kordell Stewart .20 .50
57 Kurt Warner .40 1.00
58 Lamar Smith .20 .50
59 Marcus Robinson .20 .50
60 Mark Brunell .20 .50
61 Marshall Faulk .25 .60
62 Marvin Harrison .25 .60
63 Matt Hasselbeck .25 .60
64 Mike Alstott .20 .50
65 Mike Anderson .20 .50
66 Muhsin Muhammad .20 .50
67 Peter Warrick .20 .50
68 Peyton Manning .60 1.50
69 Priest Holmes .25 .60
70 Randy Moss .25 .60
71 Ray Lewis .25 .60
72 Rich Gannon .20 .50
73 Ricky Watters .20 .50
74 Ricky Williams .25 .60
75 Rob Johnson .20 .50
76 Rod Smith .20 .50
77 Ron Dayne .20 .50
78 Shannon Sharpe .25 .60
79 Shaun Alexander .25 .60
80 Stephen Davis .20 .50
81 Steve McNair .25 .60
82 Steve Young .30 .75
83 Sylvester Morris .15 .40
84 Terrell Davis .25 .60
85 Terrell Owens .25 .60
86 Thomas Jones .20 .50
87 Tim Brown .25 .60
88 Tim Couch .15 .40
89 Tony Banks .15 .40
90 Tony Gonzalez .25 .60
91 Torry Holt .20 .50
92 Travis Taylor .15 .40
93 Trent Green .25 .60
94 Troy Aikman .40 1.00
95 Tyrone Wheatley .20 .50
96 Vinny Testaverde .20 .50
97 Warren Sapp .20 .50
98 Warrick Dunn .25 .60
99 Wayne Chrebet .20 .50
100 Zach Thomas .25 .60
101 A.J. Feeley RC 1.50 4.00
102 Josh Booty RC 1.50 4.00
103 Roderick Robinson RC 1.25 3.00
104 Renaldo Hill RC 1.50 4.00
105 Harold Blackmon RC 1.25 3.00
106 Rudi Johnson RC 2.00 5.00
107 Curtis Fuller RC 1.25 3.00
108 Dan Alexander RC 1.50 4.00
109 Anthony Thomas RPS 2.00 5.00
110 Travis Minor RPS 1.50 4.00
111 Heath Evans RC 1.50 4.00
112 Joe Walker RC 1.25 3.00
113 Moran Norris RC 1.25 3.00
114 Quincy Carter RPS 1.50 4.00
115 Michael Vick RPS 5.00 12.00
116 Vinny Sutherland RC 1.25 3.00
117 Scotty Anderson RC 1.25 3.00
118 Eddie Berlin RC 1.25 3.00
119 Jonathan Carter RC 1.25 3.00
120 Monty Beisel RC 1.25 3.00
121 T.J. Houshmandzadeh RC 2.50 6.00
122 Rodney Bailey RC 1.25 3.00
123 Reggie Germany RC 1.25 3.00
124 Ellis Wyms RC 1.25 3.00
125 Koren Robinson RPS 1.50 4.00
126 Antonio Pierce RC 4.00 10.00
127 Arnold Jackson RC 1.25 3.00
128 Andre Rone RC 1.25 3.00
129 Richard Newsome RC 1.25 3.00
130 Ifeanyi Ohalete RC 1.25 3.00
131 Dan O'Leary RC 1.25 3.00
132 Shad Meier RC 1.25 3.00
133 Jay Feely RC 2.00 5.00
134 Brandon Manumaleuna RC 1.50 4.00
135 Riall Johnson RC 1.25 3.00
136 Snoop Minnis RPS 1.25 3.00
137 Jermaine Hampton RC 1.25 3.00
138 Johnny Huggins RC 1.25 3.00
139 Marcellus Rivers RC 1.25 3.00
140 Andre Carter RPS 1.50 4.00
141 Michael Stone RC 1.25 3.00
142 Tony Dixon RC 1.25 3.00
143 Bhawoh Jue RC 1.50 4.00
144 Will Peterson RC 1.50 4.00
145 Anthony Henry RC 2.00 5.00
146 Marques Tuiasosopo RPS 1.50 4.00
147 Reggie Swinton RC 1.25 3.00
148 Robert Carswell RC 1.25 3.00
149 Freddie Mitchell RPS 1.25 3.00
150 Idrees Bashir RC 1.25 3.00
151 James Boyd RC 1.25 3.00
152 Chris Chambers RPS 1.25 3.00
153 Aaron Schobel RC 2.00 5.00
154 Dominic Raiola RC 1.25 3.00
155 Derrick Burgess RC 2.00 5.00
156 DeLawrence Grant RC 1.25 3.00
157 Karon Riley RC 1.25 3.00
158 Cedric Scott RC 1.25 3.00
159 Patrick Washington RC 1.25 3.00
160 Eric Johnson RC 2.00 5.00
161 Tevita Ofahengaue RC 1.25 3.00
162 Chris Cooper RC 1.25 3.00
163 Fred Wakefield RC 1.25 3.00
164 Kenny Smith RC 1.25 3.00
165 Marcus Bell RC 1.25 3.00
166 Mario Fatafehi RC 1.25 3.00
167 Anthony Herron RC 1.25 3.00
168 Joe Tafoya RC 1.25 3.00
169 Morlon Greenwood RC 1.25 3.00
170 Orlando Huff RC 1.25 3.00
171 Carlos Polk RC 1.25 3.00
172 Edgerton Hartwell RC 1.25 3.00
173 Zeke Moreno RC 1.50 4.00
174 Alex Lincoln RC 1.25 3.00
175 Quinton Caver RC 1.25 3.00
176 Matt Stewart RC 1.25 3.00
177 Markus Steele RC 1.25 3.00
178 Dwight Smith RC 1.25 3.00
179 Reggie Wayne RPS 2.50 6.00
180 Jeramethrius Butler RC 1.25 3.00
181 Jason Doering RC 1.25 3.00
182 John Howell RC 1.25 3.00
183 Alvin Porter RC 1.25 3.00
184 Eric Downing RC 1.25 3.00
185 John Nix RC 1.25 3.00
186 Tim Baker RC 1.25 3.00
187 Robert Garza RC 1.25 3.00
188 Randy Chevrier RC 1.25 3.00
189 Drew Brees RPS 8.00 20.00
190 Shawn Worthen RC 1.25 3.00
191 Drew Bennett RC 2.00 5.00
192 Marlon McCree RC 1.25 3.00
193 David Terrell RPS 1.50 4.00
194 Jeff Backus RC 1.25 3.00
195 Otis Leverette RC 1.25 3.00
196 Jason Glenn RC 1.25 3.00
197 Rashad Holman RC 1.25 3.00
198 T.J. Turner RC 1.25 3.00
199 Lynn Scott RC 1.25 3.00
200 Bill Gramatica RC 1.25 3.00
201 Michael Vick RC 12.00 30.00
202 Drew Brees RC 20.00 50.00
203 Quincy Carter RC 2.50 6.00
204 Jesse Palmer RC 2.50 6.00
205 Mike McMahon RC 2.50 6.00
206 Dave Dickenson RC 2.50 6.00
207 Jameel Cook RC 2.50 6.00
208 Marques Tuiasosopo RC 2.50 6.00
209 Chris Weinke RC 2.50 6.00
210 Sage Rosenfels RC 3.00 8.00
211 Josh Heupel RC 3.00 8.00
212 LaDainian Tomlinson RC 10.00 25.00
213 Michael Bennett RC 2.50 6.00
214 Anthony Thomas RC 3.00 8.00
215 Travis Henry RC 2.50 6.00
216 James Jackson RC 2.00 5.00
217 Correll Buckhalter RC 3.00 8.00
218 Derrick Blaylock RC 2.50 6.00
219 Dee Brown RC 2.00 5.00
220 LeVar Woods RC 2.50 6.00
221 Deuce McAllister RC 3.00 8.00
222 LaMont Jordan RC 3.00 8.00
223 Kevan Barlow RC 2.50 6.00
224 Travis Minor RC 2.50 6.00
225 David Terrell RC 2.50 6.00
226 Koren Robinson RC 2.50 6.00
227 Rod Gardner RC 2.50 6.00
228 Santana Moss RC 4.00 10.00
229 Freddie Mitchell RC 2.00 5.00
230 Reggie Wayne RC 6.00 15.00
231 Quincy Morgan RC 2.50 6.00
232 Chris Chambers RC 3.00 8.00
233 Steve Smith RC 6.00 15.00
234 Snoop Minnis RC 2.00 5.00
235 Justin McCareins RC 2.50 6.00
236 Onome Ojo RC 2.00 5.00
237 Damerien McCants RC 2.50 6.00
238 Mike McMahon RPS 2.50 6.00
239 Cedrick Wilson RC 2.50 6.00
240 Kevin Kasper RC 2.00 5.00
241 Chris Taylor RC 2.00 5.00
242 Ken-Yon Rambo RC 2.00 5.00
243 Richmond Flowers RC 2.00 5.00
244 Andre King RC 2.00 5.00
245 Boo Williams RC 2.00 5.00
246 Adrian Wilson RC 8.00 20.00
247 Cory Bird RC 2.50 6.00
248 Alex Bannister RC 2.00 5.00
249 Elvis Joseph RC 2.00 5.00
250 Chad Johnson RC 5.00 12.00
251 Robert Ferguson RC 3.00 8.00
252 David Martin RC 2.00 5.00
253 Quentin McCord RC 2.50 6.00
254 Todd Heap RC 3.00 8.00

255 Alge Crumpler RC 3.00 8.00
256 Nate Clements RC 2.50 6.00
257 Will Allen RC 3.00 8.00
258 Willie Middlebrooks RC 2.50 6.00
259 Fred Smoot RC 3.00 8.00
260 Andre Dyson RC 2.00 5.00
261 Gary Baxter RC 2.00 5.00
262 Jamar Fletcher RC 2.00 5.00
263 Ken Lucas RC 2.50 6.00
264 Tay Cody RC 2.00 5.00
265 Eric Kelly RC 2.00 5.00
266 Adam Archuleta RC 2.50 6.00
267 Derrick Gibson RC 2.00 5.00
268 Jarrod Cooper RC 2.50 6.00
269 Hakim Akbar RC 2.00 5.00
270 Tony Driver RC 2.50 6.00
271 Justin Smith RC 3.00 8.00
272 Andre Carter RC 2.50 6.00
273 Jamal Reynolds RC 2.00 5.00
274 Gerard Warren RC 2.50 6.00
275 Richard Seymour RC 3.00 8.00
276 Damione Lewis RC 2.50 6.00
277 Casey Hampton RC 3.00 8.00
278 Marcus Stroud RC 2.50 6.00
279 Benjamin Gay RC 2.50 6.00
280 Shaun Rogers RC 3.00 8.00
281 Dan Morgan RC 2.50 6.00
282 Kendrell Bell RC 3.00 8.00
283 Tommy Polley RC 2.00 5.00
284 Jamie Winborn RC 2.50 6.00
285 Sedrick Hodge RC 2.00 5.00
286 Torrance Marshall RC 2.00 5.00
287 Eric Westmoreland RC 2.00 5.00
288 Brian Allen RC 2.00 5.00
289 Brandon Spoon RC 2.50 6.00
290 Henry Burris RC 3.00 8.00
291 Leonard Davis RC 3.00 8.00
292 Kenyatta Walker RC 2.00 5.00
293 Cedric James RC 2.00 5.00
294 Sean Brewer RC 2.00 5.00
295 Jason Brookins RC 3.00 8.00
296 Kyle Vanden Bosch RC 3.00 8.00
297 Nick Goings RC 3.00 8.00
298 Kris Jenkins RC 3.00 8.00
299 Dominic Rhodes RC 3.00 8.00
300 Leonard Myers RC 2.00 5.00

2001 Leaf Rookies and Stars Longevity

*VETS 1-100: 10X TO 25X BASIC CARDS
1-100 VETERAN PRINT RUN 50
*ROOKIES 101-200: 2.5X TO 6X
*ROOKIES 201-300: 1.5X TO 4X
101-200 ROOKIE PRINT RUN 25

2001 Leaf Rookies and Stars Rookie Autographs

ANNOUNCED PRINT RUN 230 SETS
106 Rudi Johnson 10.00 25.00
111 Heath Evans 8.00 20.00
113 Moran Norris 6.00 15.00
118 Eddie Berlin 6.00 15.00
119 Jonathan Carter 6.00 15.00
121 T.J. Houshmandzadeh 12.00 30.00
123 Reggie Germany 6.00 15.00
201 Michael Vick 100.00 200.00
202 Drew Brees 125.00 200.00
204 Jesse Palmer 8.00 20.00
205 Mike McMahon 8.00 20.00
206 Dave Dickenson 8.00 20.00
209 Chris Weinke 8.00 20.00
212 LaDainian Tomlinson 75.00 150.00
213 Michael Bennett 8.00 20.00
214 Anthony Thomas 10.00 25.00
215 Travis Henry 8.00 20.00
216 James Jackson 6.00 15.00
217 Correll Buckhalter 10.00 25.00
218 Derrick Blaylock 8.00 20.00
219 Dee Brown 6.00 15.00
221 Deuce McAllister 10.00 25.00
222 LaMont Jordan 10.00 25.00
223 Kevan Barlow 8.00 20.00
224 Travis Minor 8.00 20.00
225 David Terrell 8.00 20.00
226 Koren Robinson 8.00 20.00
228 Santana Moss 12.00 30.00
229 Freddie Mitchell 6.00 15.00
231 Quincy Morgan 8.00 20.00
233 Steve Smith 40.00 80.00
234 Snoop Minnis 6.00 15.00
235 Justin McCareins 8.00 20.00
236 Onome Ojo 6.00 15.00
239 Cedrick Wilson 8.00 20.00
240 Kevin Kasper 6.00 15.00
242 Ken-Yon Rambo 6.00 15.00
248 Alex Bannister 6.00 15.00
250 Chad Johnson 40.00 80.00
251 Robert Ferguson 10.00 25.00
254 Todd Heap 10.00 25.00
255 Alge Crumpler 10.00 25.00
256 Nate Clements No Auto 8.00 20.00
257 Will Allen 10.00 25.00
271 Justin Smith 10.00 25.00
273 Jamal Reynolds 6.00 15.00
275 Richard Seymour No Auto 10.00 25.00
276 Damione Lewis 8.00 20.00
277 Casey Hampton No Auto 10.00 25.00
280 Shaun Rogers 10.00 25.00

2001 Leaf Rookies and Stars Crosstraining

STATED PRINT RUN 100 SER.#'d SETS
CT1 Terrell Davis 8.00 20.00
Michael Bennett
CT2 Troy Aikman 12.00 30.00
Quincy Carter
CT3 Donovan McNabb 30.00 80.00
Michael Vick
CT4 Randy Moss 8.00 20.00
Rod Gardner
CT5 Corey Dillon 6.00 15.00
Kevan Barlow
CT6 Warren Sapp 6.00 15.00
Gerard Warren
CT7 Marshall Faulk 8.00 20.00
Deuce McAllister
CT8 Edgerrin James 8.00 20.00
James Jackson
CT9 Cris Carter 10.00 25.00
Reggie Wayne
CT10 Barry Sanders 15.00 40.00
LaDainian Tomlinson
CT11 Tim Couch 30.00 80.00
Drew Brees
CT12 Peter Warrick 6.00 15.00
Snoop Minnis
CT13 Torry Holt 6.00 15.00
Koren Robinson
CT14 Isaac Bruce 6.00 15.00
Santana Moss
CT15 Jerry Rice 15.00 40.00
David Terrell
CT16 Tim Brown 8.00 20.00
Chris Chambers
CT17 Emmitt Smith 20.00 50.00
Travis Henry
CT18 Eddie George 8.00 20.00
Anthony Thomas
CT19 Drew Bledsoe 8.00 20.00
Chris Weinke
CT20 Dan Marino 20.00 50.00
Josh Heupel
CT21 Jerome Bettis 8.00 20.00
Rudi Johnson
CT22 Keyshawn Johnson 12.00 30.00
Chad Johnson
CT23 Mark Brunell 6.00 15.00
Marques Tuiasosopo
CT24 Jevon Kearse 6.00 15.00
Andre Carter
CT25 Steve Young 10.00 25.00
Mike McMahon

2001 Leaf Rookies and Stars Dress For Success

STATED ODDS 1:96
*PRIME CUT/50: .8X TO 2X BASIC INSERT
PRIME CUT PRINT RUN 50 SER.#'d SETS
DFS1 Tim Brown 8.00 20.00
DFS2 Lamar Smith 6.00 15.00
DFS3 Boomer Esiason 8.00 20.00
DFS4 Dan Marino 20.00 50.00
DFS5 Lawrence Taylor 10.00 25.00
DFS6 Marshall Faulk 8.00 20.00
DFS7 Isaac Bruce 8.00 20.00
DFS8 Stephen Davis 6.00 15.00
DFS9 Marvin Harrison 8.00 20.00
DFS10 Michael Strahan 8.00 20.00
DFS11 Jerome Bettis 8.00 20.00
DFS12 Cris Carter 8.00 20.00
DFS13 Emmitt Smith 20.00 50.00
DFS14 Jevon Kearse 6.00 15.00
DFS15 Eric Moulds 6.00 15.00
DFS16 Curtis Martin 8.00 20.00
DFS17 Randy Moss 8.00 20.00
DFS18 Peyton Manning 20.00 50.00
DFS19 John Elway 20.00 50.00
DFS20 Warrick Dunn 8.00 20.00
DFS21 Steve Young 12.00 30.00
DFS22 Donovan McNabb 8.00 20.00
DFS23 Keyshawn Johnson 6.00 15.00
DFS24 Ron Dayne 6.00 15.00
DFS25 Rich Gannon 6.00 15.00

2001 Leaf Rookies and Stars Dress For Success Autographs

ANNOUNCED PRINT RUN 25 SETS
DFS1 Tim Brown 40.00 100.00
DFS4 Dan Marino 175.00 300.00
DFS6 Marshall Faulk 50.00 125.00
DFS7 Isaac Bruce 50.00 125.00
DFS8 Stephen Davis 40.00 100.00
DFS9 Marvin Harrison 50.00 125.00
DFS12 Cris Carter 50.00 125.00
DFS13 Emmitt Smith 175.00 300.00
DFS15 Eric Moulds
DFS19 John Elway 125.00 250.00
DFS21 Steve Young 75.00 150.00
DFS24 Ron Dayne 40.00 100.00

2001 Leaf Rookies and Stars Freshman Orientation

STATED ODDS 1:96
*CLASS OFFICER/50: .8X TO 2X BASIC INSERTS
CLASS OFFICERS PRINT RUN 50 SER.#'d SETS
FO1 Michael Vick 20.00 50.00
FO2 Drew Brees 30.00 80.00
FO3 Quincy Carter 4.00 10.00
FO4 Chris Weinke 4.00 10.00
FO5 Santana Moss 6.00 15.00
FO6 Mike McMahon 4.00 10.00
FO7 Jesse Palmer 4.00 10.00
FO8 Deuce McAllister 5.00 12.00
FO9 LaDainian Tomlinson 20.00 50.00
FO10 Anthony Thomas 5.00 12.00
FO11 Michael Bennett 4.00 10.00
FO12 Travis Henry 4.00 10.00
FO13 James Jackson 3.00 8.00
FO14 Kevan Barlow 4.00 10.00
FO15 Rudi Johnson 5.00 12.00
FO16 Travis Minor 4.00 10.00
FO17 David Terrell 4.00 10.00
FO18 Rod Gardner 4.00 10.00
FO19 Quincy Morgan 4.00 10.00
FO20 Freddie Mitchell 3.00 8.00
FO21 Reggie Wayne 10.00 25.00
FO22 Koren Robinson 4.00 10.00
FO23 Chris Chambers 5.00 12.00
FO24 Snoop Minnis 3.00 8.00
FO25 Chad Johnson 8.00 20.00

2001 Leaf Rookies and Stars Freshman Orientation Autographs

ANNOUNCED PRINT RUN 25 SETS
FO4 Chris Weinke 25.00 60.00
FO9 LaDainian Tomlinson 200.00 400.00
FO19 Quincy Morgan 25.00 60.00
FO25 Chad Johnson 40.00 80.00

2001 Leaf Rookies and Stars Player's Collection

SINGLE MEM PRINT RUN 100
COMBO PRINT RUN 25
PC1 Eddie George Glove 12.50 30.00
PC2 Eddie George JSY 12.50 30.00
PC3 Eddie George Helmet 12.50 30.00
PC4 Eddie George Shoes 12.50 30.00
PC5 Eddie George Combo 30.00 80.00
Glove-Jersey-Helmet-Shoes
PC6 Troy Aikman FB 20.00 50.00
PC7 Troy Aikman JSY 20.00 50.00
PC8 Troy Aikman Helmet 25.00 60.00
PC9 Troy Aikman Shoes 20.00 50.00
PC10 Troy Aikman Combo 75.00 150.00
Football-Jersey-Helmet-Shoes
PC11 Kurt Warner Pants 15.00 40.00
PC12 Kurt Warner JSY 15.00 40.00
PC13 Kurt Warner Helmet 15.00 40.00
PC14 Kurt Warner Shoes 15.00 40.00
PC15 Kurt Warner Combo 40.00 100.00
Pants-Jersey-Helmet-Shoes

2001 Leaf Rookies and Stars Player's Collection Autographs

STATED PRINT RUN 25 SER.#'d SETS
PC8 Troy Aikman 60.00 120.00
PC13 Kurt Warner 50.00 100.00

2001 Leaf Rookies and Stars Slideshow

STATED PRINT RUN 100 SER.#'d SETS
*VIEWMASTER/25: .6X TO 1.5X BASIC INSERTS
VIEWMASTER PRINT RUN 25 SER.#'d SETS
SS1 Barry Sanders 20.00 50.00
SS2 Brett Favre 25.00 60.00
SS3 Brian Griese 6.00 15.00
SS4 Cris Carter 8.00 20.00
SS5 Dan Marino 20.00 50.00
SS6 Daunte Culpepper 6.00 15.00
SS7 Donovan McNabb 8.00 20.00
SS8 Drew Bledsoe 8.00 20.00
SS9 Eddie George 8.00 20.00
SS10 Edgerrin James 8.00 20.00
SS11 Emmitt Smith 20.00 50.00
SS12 Fred Taylor 8.00 20.00
SS13 John Elway 20.00 50.00
SS14 Kurt Warner 12.00 30.00
SS15 Marshall Faulk 8.00 20.00
SS16 Peyton Manning 20.00 50.00
SS17 Randy Moss 8.00 20.00
SS18 Ricky Williams 8.00 20.00
SS19 Ron Dayne 6.00 15.00
SS20 Steve McNair 8.00 20.00
SS21 Steve Young 10.00 25.00
SS22 Terrell Davis 8.00 20.00
SS23 Tim Brown 8.00 20.00
SS24 Tim Couch 5.00 12.00
SS25 Troy Aikman 12.00 30.00

2001 Leaf Rookies and Stars Slideshow Autographs

STATED PRINT RUN 25 SER.#'d SETS
UNPRICED VIEW MASTER AU PRINT RUN 5
SS3 Brian Griese 25.00 60.00
SS4 Cris Carter 50.00 120.00
SS18 Ricky Williams 40.00 100.00
SS21 Steve Young 125.00 250.00
SS23 Tim Brown 50.00 120.00

2001 Leaf Rookies and Stars Statistical Standouts

STATED ODDS 1:96
*SUPER/50: .8X TO 2X BASIC INSERTS
SUPER SS PRINT RUN 50 SER.#'d SETS
SS1 Peyton Manning 12.00 30.00
SS2 Jeff Garcia 4.00 10.00
SS3 Donovan McNabb 5.00 12.00
SS4 Daunte Culpepper 4.00 10.00
SS5 Kurt Warner 8.00 20.00
SS6 Vinny Testaverde 4.00 10.00
SS7 Mark Brunell 4.00 10.00
SS8 Edgerrin James 5.00 12.00
SS9 Eddie George 5.00 12.00
SS10 Mike Anderson 4.00 10.00
SS11 Corey Dillon 4.00 10.00
SS12 Fred Taylor 5.00 12.00
SS13 Marshall Faulk 5.00 12.00
SS14 Stephen Davis 4.00 10.00
SS15 Torry Holt 4.00 10.00
SS16 Rod Smith 4.00 10.00
SS17 Isaac Bruce 5.00 12.00
SS18 Terrell Owens 5.00 12.00
SS19 Randy Moss 5.00 12.00
SS20 Marvin Harrison 5.00 12.00
SS21 Kerry Collins 4.00 10.00
SS22 Junior Seau 5.00 12.00
SS23 Warren Sapp 4.00 10.00
SS24 Donnie Abraham 3.00 8.00
SS25 Dexter McCleon 3.00 8.00

2001 Leaf Rookies and Stars Statistical Standouts Autographs

STATED PRINT RUN 25 SER.#'d SETS
SS4 Daunte Culpepper 25.00 60.00
SS5 Kurt Warner 50.00 100.00
SS6 Vinny Testaverde 25.00 60.00
SS7 Mark Brunell 25.00 60.00
SS8 Edgerrin James 30.00 80.00
SS10 Mike Anderson 25.00 60.00
SS11 Corey Dillon 25.00 60.00
SS13 Marshall Faulk 30.00 80.00
SS14 Stephen Davis 25.00 60.00
SS15 Torry Holt 25.00 60.00
SS17 Isaac Bruce 30.00 80.00
SS18 Terrell Owens 30.00 80.00
SS20 Marvin Harrison 30.00 80.00

2001 Leaf Rookies and Stars Triple Threads

STATED PRINT RUN 100 SER.#'d SETS
TT1 Cris Carter 15.00 40.00
Daunte Culpepper
Randy Moss
TT2 Fred Taylor 15.00 40.00
Jimmy Smith
Mark Brunell
TT3 Edgerrin James 30.00 80.00
Marvin Harrison
Peyton Manning
TT4 Antonio Freeman 30.00 80.00
Brett Favre
Dorsey Levens
TT5 Brian Griese 15.00 40.00
Ed McCaffrey
Terrell Davis
TT6 Isaac Bruce 25.00 60.00
Kurt Warner
Marshall Faulk
TT7 Troy Aikman 25.00 60.00
Emmitt Smith
Michael Irvin
TT8 Keyshawn Johnson 15.00 40.00
Warren Sapp
Warrick Dunn
TT9 Jim Kelly 20.00 50.00
Thurman Thomas
Andre Reed
TT10 Eddie George 15.00 40.00
Jevon Kearse
Steve McNair

2002 Leaf Rookies and Stars

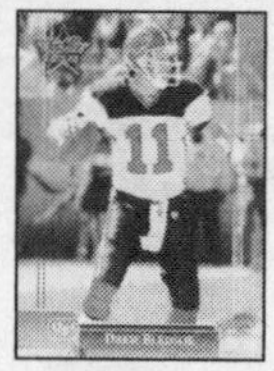

Released in December 2002, this set contains 100 veterans and 200 rookies. Rookies were inserted approximately one per pack. Boxes contained 24 packs of 6 cards.

COMPLETE SET (300) 100.00 250.00
COMP.SET w/o SP's (100) 10.00 25.00
1 Jake Plummer .25 .60
2 David Boston .20 .50
3 Thomas Jones .30 .75
4 Michael Vick .50 1.25
5 Warrick Dunn .25 .60
6 Jamal Lewis .25 .60
7 Chris Redman .20 .50
8 Ray Lewis .30 .75
9 Drew Bledsoe .30 .75
10 Travis Henry .20 .50
11 Eric Moulds .25 .60
12 Steve Smith .30 .75
13 Chris Weinke .20 .50
14 Lamar Smith .25 .60
15 Anthony Thomas .25 .60
16 David Terrell .20 .50
17 Brian Urlacher .30 .75
18 Corey Dillon .25 .60
19 Michael Westbrook .20 .50
20 Peter Warrick .25 .60
21 Tim Couch .20 .50
22 James Jackson .20 .50
23 Kevin Johnson .20 .50
24 Quincy Carter .20 .50
25 Joey Galloway .25 .60
26 Emmitt Smith .75 2.00
27 Terrell Davis .30 .75
28 Brian Griese .25 .60
29 Ed McCaffrey .25 .60
30 Rod Smith .25 .60
31 Mike McMahon .20 .50
32 Germane Crowell .20 .50
33 Az-Zahir Hakim .20 .50
34 Terry Glenn .25 .60
35 Brett Favre .75 2.00
36 Ahman Green .25 .60
37 James Allen .20 .50
38 Corey Bradford .20 .50
39 Peyton Manning .60 1.50
40 Edgerrin James .25 .60
41 Marvin Harrison .30 .75
42 Qadry Ismail .25 .60
43 Fred Taylor .25 .60
44 Mark Brunell .25 .60
45 Jimmy Smith .25 .60
46 Priest Holmes .30 .75
47 Tony Gonzalez .30 .75
48 Trent Green .25 .60
49 Johnnie Morton .25 .60
50 Chris Chambers .25 .60
51 Ricky Williams .25 .60
52 Zach Thomas .30 .75
53 Randy Moss .30 .75
54 Michael Bennett .25 .60
55 Derrick Alexander .20 .50
56 Daunte Culpepper .25 .60
57 Tom Brady .75 2.00
58 Troy Brown .25 .60
59 Antowain Smith .25 .60
60 Joe Horn .25 .60
61 Aaron Brooks .25 .60
62 Deuce McAllister .25 .60
63 Kerry Collins .25 .60
64 Amani Toomer .25 .60
65 Michael Strahan .30 .75
66 Laveranues Coles .25 .60
67 Vinny Testaverde .25 .60
68 Curtis Martin .30 .75
69 Rich Gannon .25 .60
70 Tim Brown .30 .75
71 Jerry Rice .60 1.50
72 Donovan McNabb .30 .75
73 Freddie Mitchell .20 .50
74 Duce Staley .25 .60
75 Kordell Stewart .25 .60
76 Jerome Bettis .30 .75
77 Plaxico Burress .25 .60
78 Drew Brees .50 1.25
79 LaDainian Tomlinson .40 1.00
80 Junior Seau .30 .75
81 Jeff Garcia .25 .60
82 Garrison Hearst .25 .60
83 Terrell Owens .30 .75
84 Shaun Alexander .25 .60
85 Koren Robinson .20 .50
86 Kurt Warner .30 .75
87 Marshall Faulk .30 .75
88 Isaac Bruce .30 .75
89 Torry Holt .30 .75
90 Rob Johnson .25 .60
91 Brad Johnson .25 .60
92 Keyshawn Johnson .25 .60
93 Mike Alstott .25 .60
94 Eddie George .25 .60
95 Steve McNair .30 .75
96 Derrick Mason .25 .60
97 Jevon Kearse .25 .60
98 Stephen Davis .25 .60
99 Sage Rosenfels .25 .60
100 Rod Gardner .20 .50
101 Adrian Peterson RC 1.50 4.00
102 Nick Rolovich RC 1.00 2.50
103 Lew Thomas RC 1.00 2.50
104 David Carr RC 1.50 4.00
105 Daryl Jones RC 1.00 2.50
106 Brandon Doman RC 1.00 2.50
107 Ed Reed RC 6.00 15.00
108 Tellis Redmon RC 1.00 2.50
109 Andra Davis RC 1.00 2.50
110 Kendall Newson RC 1.00 2.50
111 Joe Burns RC 1.00 2.50
112 Maurice Morris RC 1.25 3.00
113 Craig Nall RC 1.25 3.00
114 Phillip Buchanon RC 1.50 4.00
115 Mike Echols RC 1.00 2.50
116 Terry Jones Jr. RC 1.00 2.50
117 Anthony Weaver RC 1.00 2.50
118 Jeb Putzier RC 1.50 4.00
119 Tony Fisher RC 1.25 3.00
120 Joey Harrington RC 1.50 4.00
121 Lamar Gordon RC 1.25 3.00
122 Tracey Wistrom RC 1.25 3.00
123 Ashley Lelie RC 1.25 3.00
124 Will Witherspoon RC 1.50 4.00
125 Travis Stephens RC 1.00 2.50
126 J.T. O'Sullivan RC 1.25 3.00
127 Brian Westbrook RC 2.50 6.00
128 James Mungro RC 1.50 4.00
129 Lamont Thompson RC 1.25 3.00
130 Jarrod Baxter RC 1.00 2.50
131 Andre Lott RC 1.00 2.50
132 Steve Bellisari RC 1.00 2.50
133 David Garrard RC 2.00 5.00
134 Michael Lewis RC 1.50 4.00
135 James Allen RC 1.00 2.50
136 Bryant McKinnie RC 1.00 2.50
137 Marques Anderson RC 1.25 3.00
138 Rohan Davey RC 1.50 4.00
139 Kyle Johnson RC 1.00 2.50
140 Dusty Bonner RC 1.00 2.50
141 DeShaun Foster RC 1.50 4.00
142 Chad Hutchinson RC 1.00 2.50
143 Jack Brewer RC 1.00 2.50
144 Eddie Freeman RC 1.00 2.50
145 Seth Burford RC 1.00 2.50
146 Roosevelt Williams RC 1.00 2.50
147 Jamin Elliott RC 1.00 2.50
148 Charles Grant RC 1.50 4.00
149 Jeff Kelly RC 1.00 2.50
150 Cliff Russell RC 1.00 2.50
151 Josh Scobey RC 1.25 3.00
152 Tank Williams RC 1.25 3.00
153 Larry Tripplett RC 1.00 2.50
154 Clinton Portis RC 2.00 5.00
155 Javin Hunter RC 1.00 2.50
156 Deveren Johnson RC 1.00 2.50
157 Reche Caldwell RC 1.50 4.00
158 Ronald Curry RC 1.25 3.00
159 Chris Hope RC 1.50 4.00
160 Damien Anderson RC 1.00 2.50
161 Saleem Rasheed RC 1.00 2.50
162 Albert Haynesworth RC 1.50 4.00
163 Bryan Gilmore RC 1.00 2.50
164 Wes Pate RC 1.00 2.50
165 Deion Branch RC 1.50 4.00
166 Ben Leber RC 1.00 2.50
167 Andre Davis RC 1.25 3.00
168 Darrell Hill RC 1.00 2.50
169 Rodney Wright RC 1.00 2.50
170 Demontray Carter RC 1.00 2.50
171 Zak Kustok RC 1.00 2.50
172 James Wofford RC 1.00 2.50
173 David Priestley RC 1.00 2.50
174 Donte Stallworth RC 1.50 4.00
175 Marc Boerigter RC 1.50 4.00
176 Freddie Milons RC 1.00 2.50
177 John Simon RC 1.00 2.50
178 Josh Norman RC 1.00 2.50
179 Jabar Gaffney RC 1.50 4.00
180 Doug Jolley RC 1.00 2.50
181 Preston Parsons RC 1.00 2.50
182 Chris Baker RC 1.00 2.50
183 Javon Walker RC 1.50 4.00
184 Justin Peelle RC 1.00 2.50
185 Josh Reed RC 1.25 3.00
186 Omar Easy RC 1.25 3.00
187 Jerramy Stevens RC 1.50 4.00
188 Shaun Hill RC 2.00 5.00
189 David Thornton RC 1.00 2.50
190 John Henderson RC 1.25 3.00
191 Verron Haynes RC 1.00 2.50
192 Dennis Johnson RC 1.00 2.50
193 Napoleon Harris RC 1.25 3.00
194 Jonathan Wells RC 1.50 4.00
195 Howard Green RC 1.00 2.50
196 Travis Fisher RC 1.25 3.00
197 Anton Palepoi RC 1.00 2.50
198 Ed Stansbury RC 1.00 2.50
199 Josh McCown RC 1.50 4.00
200 Alex Brown RC 1.50 4.00
201 Joseph Jefferson RC 1.00 2.50
202 Julius Peppers RC 3.00 8.00
203 Larry Ned RC 1.00 2.50
204 Rock Cartwright RC 1.50 4.00
205 Kalimba Edwards RC 1.25 3.00
206 Matt Schobel RC 1.50 4.00
207 Maurice Jackson RC 1.00 2.50
208 Kelly Campbell RC 1.25 3.00
209 Mel Mitchell RC 1.00 2.50
210 Ken Simonton RC 1.00 2.50
211 Brian Allen RC 1.00 2.50
212 Darnell Sanders RC 1.00 2.50
213 Jesse Chatman RC 1.00 2.50
214 Keyuo Craver RC 1.00 2.50
215 Chester Taylor RC 1.50 4.00
216 Kurt Kittner RC 1.00 2.50
217 Derek Ross RC 1.25 3.00
218 Charles Hill RC 1.00 2.50
219 Jarvis Green RC 1.00 2.50
220 Mike Jenkins RC 1.00 2.50
221 Robert Royal RC 1.50 4.00
222 Ladell Betts RC 1.50 4.00
223 Antwoine Womack RC 1.00 2.50
224 Raonall Smith RC 1.00 2.50
225 Charles Stackhouse RC 1.00 2.50
226 Quinn Gray RC 1.25 3.00
227 Lito Sheppard RC 1.50 4.00
228 Ryan Van Dyke RC 1.00 2.50
229 Will Overstreet RC 1.00 2.50
230 Leonard Henry RC 1.00 2.50
231 Dorsett Davis RC 1.00 2.50
232 Marquand Manuel RC 1.00 2.50
233 Luke Staley RC 1.00 2.50
234 Carlos Hall RC 1.00 2.50
235 Marcus Brady RC 1.00 2.50
236 Ryan Denney RC 1.00 2.50
237 Eric McCoo RC 1.00 2.50
238 Major Applewhite RC 1.50 4.00
239 Adam Tate RC 1.00 2.50
240 Marquise Walker RC 1.00 2.50
241 John Flowers RC 1.00 2.50
242 Levar Fisher RC 1.00 2.50
243 Ricky Williams RC 1.25 3.00
244 Mike Rumph RC 1.00 2.50
245 Delvin Joyce RC 1.00 2.50
246 Bryan Thomas RC 1.00 2.50
247 Mike Williams RC 1.00 2.50
248 Sam Brandon RC 1.00 2.50
249 Eddie Drummond RC 1.00 2.50
250 Najeh Davenport RC 1.50 4.00
251 Brian Williams RC 1.00 2.50
252 Scott Fujita RC 1.50 4.00
253 Dwight Freeney RC 2.00 5.00
254 Herb Haygood RC 1.00 2.50
255 Patrick Ramsey RC 1.50 4.00
256 Atnaf Harris RC 1.00 2.50
257 Jason McAddley RC 1.25 3.00
258 Pete Rebstock RC 1.00 2.50
259 Quentin Jammer RC 1.50 4.00
260 Luke Butkus RC 1.00 2.50
261 Jeremy Allen RC 1.00 2.50
262 Jake Schifino RC 1.00 2.50
263 Randy Fasani RC 1.25 3.00
264 Bryan Fletcher RC 1.00 2.50
265 Jeremy Shockey RC 2.50 6.00
266 Kevin Bentley RC 1.00 2.50
267 Jon McGraw RC 1.00 2.50
268 Robert Thomas RC 1.00 2.50
269 Coy Wire RC 1.25 3.00
270 Brian Poli-Dixon RC 1.00 2.50
271 Willie Offord RC 1.00 2.50
272 Rocky Calmus RC 1.25 3.00
273 Sheldon Brown RC 1.50 4.00
274 Terry Charles RC 1.00 2.50
275 Ron Johnson RC 1.25 3.00
276 Roy Williams RC 1.50 4.00
277 Sam Simmons RC 1.00 2.50
278 Andre Goodman RC 1.00 2.50
279 Ryan Sims RC 1.50 4.00
280 Antwaan Randle El RC 1.50 4.00
281 Alan Harper RC 1.00 2.50
282 Tavon Mason RC 1.00 2.50
283 Kahlil Hill RC 1.00 2.50
284 Antonio Bryant RC 1.50 4.00
285 Akin Ayodele RC 1.25 3.00
286 T.J. Duckett RC 1.50 4.00
287 Kenyon Coleman RC 1.00 2.50
288 Tim Carter RC 1.25 3.00
289 Lamont Brightful RC 1.00 2.50
290 Trev Faulk RC 1.00 2.50
291 Randy McMichael RC 1.50 4.00
292 Daniel Graham RC 1.25 3.00
293 Wendell Bryant RC 1.00 2.50
294 Jamar Martin RC 1.25 3.00
295 Chris Luzar RC 1.00 2.50
296 William Green RC 1.25 3.00
297 Lee Mays RC 1.00 2.50
298 Eric Crouch RC 1.50 4.00
299 Steve Smith RC 1.00 2.50
300 Woody Dantzler RC 1.25 3.00

2002 Leaf Rookies and Stars Longevity

*VETS 1-100: 10X TO 25X BASIC CARDS
*ROOKIES 101-200: 2X TO 5X
STATED PRINT RUN 50 SER.#'d SETS

2002 Leaf Rookies and Stars Rookie Autographs

ANNOUNCED PRINT RUN 150
101 Adrian Peterson 10.00 25.00
109 Andra Davis 6.00 15.00
117 Anthony Weaver 6.00 15.00
123 Ashley Lelie 8.00 20.00
127 Brian Westbrook 15.00 40.00
131 Andre Lott 6.00 15.00
136 Bryant McKinnie 6.00 15.00
142 Chad Hutchinson 6.00 15.00
148 Charles Grant 10.00 25.00
150 Cliff Russell 6.00 15.00
154 Clinton Portis 12.00 30.00
160 Damien Anderson 6.00 15.00
165 Deion Branch 12.50 30.00
170 Demontray Carter 6.00 15.00
174 Donte Stallworth 10.00 25.00
176 Freddie Milons 6.00 15.00
179 Jabar Gaffney 10.00 25.00
183 Javon Walker 10.00 25.00
190 John Henderson 8.00 20.00
199 Josh McCown 10.00 25.00
202 Julius Peppers 40.00 100.00
205 Kalimba Edwards 8.00 20.00
208 Kelly Campbell 8.00 20.00
210 Ken Simonton 6.00 15.00
214 Keyuo Craver 6.00 15.00
216 Kurt Kittner 6.00 15.00
222 Ladell Betts 10.00 25.00
227 Lito Sheppard 10.00 25.00
233 Luke Staley 6.00 15.00
240 Marquise Walker 6.00 15.00
244 Mike Rumph 6.00 15.00
247 Mike Williams 6.00 15.00
250 Najeh Davenport 10.00 25.00
255 Patrick Ramsey 10.00 25.00
259 Quentin Jammer 10.00 25.00
263 Randy Fasani 8.00 20.00
268 Robert Thomas 6.00 15.00
272 Rocky Calmus 8.00 20.00
275 Ron Johnson 8.00 20.00
276 Roy Williams 10.00 25.00
282 Tavon Mason 6.00 15.00
284 Antonio Bryant 10.00 25.00
286 T.J. Duckett 10.00 25.00
288 Tim Carter 8.00 20.00
290 Trev Faulk 6.00 15.00
293 Wendall Bryant 6.00 15.00
296 William Green 8.00 20.00
300 Woody Dantzler 8.00 20.00

2002 Leaf Rookies and Stars Action Packed Bronze

COMPLETE SET (20) 25.00 60.00
BRONZE PRINT RUN 1850 SER.#'d SETS
*SILVER/500: .8X TO 2X BRONZE/1850
SILVER PRINT RUN 500 SER.#'d SETS
*GOLD/150: 1.5X TO 4X BRONZE/1850
GOLD PRINT RUN 150 SER.#'d SETS
1 Brian Urlacher 1.00 2.50
2 Randy Moss 1.00 2.50
3 T.J. Duckett 1.00 2.50
4 Peyton Manning 2.00 5.00
5 Edgerrin James .75 2.00
6 Donte Stallworth 1.00 2.50
7 Joey Harrington 1.00 2.50
8 Drew Brees 1.50 4.00
9 Anthony Thomas .75 2.00
10 William Green .75 2.00
11 LaDainian Tomlinson 1.25 3.00
12 Donovan McNabb 1.00 2.50
13 Patrick Ramsey 1.00 2.50
14 Shaun Alexander .75 2.00
15 Kurt Warner 1.00 2.50
16 Michael Vick 1.50 4.00
17 Antonio Bryant 1.00 2.50
18 Jeff Garcia .75 2.00
19 David Carr 1.00 2.50
20 Chris Chambers .75 2.00

2002 Leaf Rookies and Stars Dress for Success

STATED PRINT RUN 400 SER.#'d SETS
DS1 LaDainian Tomlinson 6.00 15.00
DS2 Quincy Carter 3.00 8.00
DS3 Freddie Mitchell 3.00 8.00
DS4 Anthony Thomas 4.00 10.00
DS5 Quincy Morgan 3.00 8.00
DS6 Chris Weinke 3.00 8.00

2002 Leaf Rookies and Stars Freshman Orientation Jerseys

STATED PRINT RUN 650 SER.#'d SETS
FO1 Ashley Lelie 4.00 10.00
FO2 David Garrard 6.00 15.00
FO3 Javon Walker 5.00 12.00
FO4 Jeremy Shockey 8.00 20.00
FO5 Josh McCown 5.00 12.00
FO6 Josh Reed 4.00 10.00
FO7 Ladell Betts 5.00 12.00
FO8 Patrick Ramsey 5.00 12.00
FO9 Tim Carter 4.00 10.00
FO10 Joey Harrington 5.00 12.00
FO11 Roy Williams 5.00 12.00
FO12 David Carr 5.00 12.00
FO13 Antonio Bryant 5.00 12.00
FO14 T.J. Duckett 5.00 12.00
FO15 Reche Caldwell 5.00 12.00
FO16 Julius Peppers 10.00 25.00
FO17 Maurice Morris 4.00 10.00
FO18 Clinton Portis 6.00 15.00
FO19 DeShaun Foster 5.00 12.00
FO20 Donte Stallworth 5.00 12.00
FO21 Eric Crouch 5.00 12.00
FO22 Andre Davis 4.00 10.00
FO23 Marquise Walker 3.00 8.00
FO24 Rohan Davey 5.00 12.00
FO25 Antwaan Randle El 5.00 12.00
FO26 Jabar Gaffney 5.00 12.00
FO27 Travis Stephens 3.00 8.00
FO28 Ron Johnson 4.00 10.00
FO29 Daniel Graham 4.00 10.00
FO30 Cliff Russell 3.00 8.00
FO31 Mike Williams 3.00 8.00
FO32 William Green 4.00 10.00

2002 Leaf Rookies and Stars Freshman Orientation Autographs

STATED PRINT RUN 25 SER.#'d SETS
FO1 Ashley Lelie 15.00 40.00
FO2 David Garrard 75.00 150.00
FO4 Jeremy Shockey 30.00 80.00
FO5 Josh McCown 20.00 50.00
FO6 Josh Reed 15.00 40.00
FO7 Ladell Betts 20.00 50.00
FO8 Patrick Ramsey 20.00 50.00
FO9 Tim Carter
FO10 Joey Harrington 20.00 50.00

2002 Leaf Rookies and Stars Great American Heroes

COMPLETE SET (40) 40.00 100.00
STATED PRINT RUN 2000 SER.#'d SETS
GAH1 Steve Young 2.00 5.00
GAH2 Troy Aikman 2.50 6.00
GAH3 Daunte Culpepper 1.25 3.00
GAH4 Correll Buckhalter 1.25 3.00

GAH5 Marshall Faulk	1.50	4.00
GAH6 Kevan Barlow	1.00	2.50
GAH7 Marvin Harrison	1.50	4.00
GAH8 Peter Warrick	1.25	3.00
GAH9 LaMont Jordan	1.25	3.00
GAH10 Rod Gardner	1.00	2.50
GAH11 Charlie Batch	1.00	2.50
GAH12 Reggie Wayne	1.50	4.00
GAH13 Ricky Watters	1.25	3.00
GAH14 Ken-Yon Rambo	1.00	2.50
GAH15 Kurt Warner	1.50	4.00
GAH16 Ahman Green	1.25	3.00
GAH17 Dan Morgan	1.00	2.50
GAH18 Isaac Bruce	1.50	4.00
GAH19 Chad Pennington	1.50	4.00
GAH20 Josh Heupel	1.25	3.00
GAH21 Tony Stewart	1.00	2.50
GAH22 Rudi Johnson	1.50	4.00
GAH23 Michael Bennett	1.25	3.00
GAH24 Quincy Carter	1.00	2.50
GAH25 Aaron Brooks	1.25	3.00
GAH26 Jesse Palmer	1.00	2.50
GAH27 Cade McNown	1.25	3.00
GAH28 Jeff Garcia	1.25	3.00
GAH29 Jevon Kearse	1.25	3.00
GAH30 Justin Smith	1.00	2.50
GAH31 Kerry Collins	1.25	3.00
GAH32 Kordell Stewart	1.25	3.00
GAH33 Michael Vick	2.50	6.00
GAH34 Ricky Williams	1.25	3.00
GAH35 Vinny Testaverde	1.25	3.00
GAH36 Terrell Davis	1.50	4.00
GAH37 Jake Plummer	1.25	3.00
GAH38 Drew Bledsoe	1.50	4.00
GAH39 Santana Moss	1.25	3.00
GAH40 Elvis Grbac	1.00	2.50

2002 Leaf Rookies and Stars Great American Heroes Autographs

STATED PRINT RUN 10-242		
GAH3 Daunte Culpepper/33		
GAH5 Marshall Faulk/67	20.00	40.00
GAH6 Kevan Barlow/30	12.00	30.00
GAH7 Marvin Harrison/25	20.00	50.00
GAH8 Peter Warrick/110	6.00	15.00
GAH9 LaMont Jordan/40	15.00	40.00
GAH10 Rod Gardner/25		
GAH11 Charlie Batch/20		
GAH12 Reggie Wayne/35	20.00	40.00
GAH13 Ricky Watters/100	7.50	20.00
GAH14 Ken-Yon Rambo/20		
GAH18 Isaac Bruce/25	15.00	40.00
GAH19 Chad Pennington/50	25.00	60.00
GAH20 Josh Heupel/120	10.00	25.00
GAH21 Tony Stewart/199	6.00	15.00
GAH22 Rudi Johnson/59	10.00	25.00
GAH23 Michael Bennett/242	7.50	20.00
GAH24 Quincy Carter/106	10.00	25.00
GAH25 Aaron Brooks/25	12.00	30.00
GAH26 Jesse Palmer/25		
GAH27 Cade McNown/25		
GAH28 Jeff Garcia/25	15.00	40.00
GAH29 Jevon Kearse/25		
GAH30 Justin Smith/40		
GAH31 Kerry Collins/25	15.00	40.00
GAH32 Kordell Stewart/25	12.00	30.00
GAH33 Michael Vick/57	30.00	80.00
GAH34 Ricky Williams/25		
GAH37 Jake Plummer/25	15.00	40.00
GAH38 Drew Bledsoe/25	15.00	40.00
GAH39 Santana Moss/200	7.50	20.00
GAH40 Elvis Grbac/40	10.00	25.00

2002 Leaf Rookies and Stars Initial Steps

STATED PRINT RUN 125 SER.#'d SETS		
IS1 Jabar Gaffney	6.00	15.00
IS2 Cliff Russell	4.00	10.00
IS3 T.J. Duckett	6.00	15.00
IS4 Josh Reed	5.00	12.00
IS5 Daniel Graham	5.00	12.00
IS6 Antonio Bryant	6.00	15.00
IS7 Ashley Lelie	5.00	12.00
IS8 Mike Williams	4.00	10.00
IS9 Ladell Betts	6.00	15.00
IS10 Jeremy Shockey	10.00	25.00
IS11 Josh McCown	6.00	15.00
IS12 Andre Davis	5.00	12.00
IS13 Travis Stephens	4.00	10.00
IS14 Roy Williams	6.00	15.00
IS15 Rohan Davey	6.00	15.00
IS16 Julius Peppers	12.00	30.00
IS17 Javon Walker	6.00	15.00
IS18 Reche Caldwell	6.00	15.00
IS19 Clinton Portis	8.00	20.00
IS20 Antwaan Randle El	6.00	15.00
IS21 Eric Crouch	6.00	15.00
IS22 Patrick Ramsey	6.00	15.00
IS23 Marquise Walker	4.00	10.00
IS24 David Garrard	8.00	20.00
IS25 David Carr	6.00	15.00

2002 Leaf Rookies and Stars Pinnacle

STATED ODDS 1:670 RETAIL		
1 Brett Favre	8.00	20.00
2 Emmitt Smith	8.00	20.00
3 Kurt Warner	3.00	8.00
4 Jerry Rice	6.00	15.00
5 Michael Vick	5.00	12.00
6 LaDainian Tomlinson	4.00	10.00
7 Eddie George	2.50	6.00
8 Tom Brady	8.00	20.00
9 Marshall Faulk	3.00	8.00
10 Peyton Manning	6.00	15.00

2002 Leaf Rookies and Stars Rookie Masks

STATED PRINT RUN 250 SER.#'d SETS		
RM1 Ladell Betts	6.00	15.00
RM2 Antonio Bryant	6.00	15.00
RM3 Reche Caldwell	6.00	15.00
RM4 David Carr	6.00	15.00
RM5 Tim Carter	5.00	12.00
RM6 Eric Crouch	6.00	15.00
RM7 Rohan Davey	6.00	15.00
RM8 Andre Davis	5.00	12.00
RM9 T.J. Duckett	6.00	15.00
RM10 DeShaun Foster	6.00	15.00
RM11 Jabar Gaffney	6.00	15.00
RM12 Daniel Graham	5.00	12.00
RM13 William Green	5.00	12.00
RM14 Joey Harrington	6.00	15.00
RM15 Ron Johnson	5.00	12.00
RM16 Ashley Lelie	5.00	12.00
RM17 Josh McCown	6.00	15.00
RM18 Maurice Morris	5.00	12.00
RM19 Julius Peppers	12.00	30.00
RM20 Clinton Portis	8.00	20.00
RM21 Patrick Ramsey	6.00	15.00
RM22 Antwaan Randle El	6.00	15.00
RM23 Josh Reed	5.00	12.00
RM24 Cliff Russell	4.00	10.00
RM25 Jeremy Shockey	10.00	25.00
RM26 Donte Stallworth	6.00	15.00
RM27 Travis Stephens	4.00	10.00
RM28 Javon Walker	6.00	15.00
RM29 Marquise Walker	4.00	10.00
RM30 Roy Williams	6.00	15.00
RM31 Mike Williams	4.00	10.00
RM32 David Garrard	8.00	20.00

2002 Leaf Rookies and Stars Run With History

RH1 Emmitt Smith/937	12.00	30.00
RH2 Emmitt Smith/1563	12.00	30.00
RH3 Emmitt Smith/1713	12.00	30.00
RH4 Emmitt Smith/1486	12.00	30.00
RH5 Emmitt Smith/1484	12.00	30.00
RH6 Emmitt Smith/1773	12.00	30.00
RH7 Emmitt Smith/1204	12.00	30.00
RH8 Emmitt Smith/1074	12.00	30.00
RH9 Emmitt Smith/1332	12.00	30.00
RH10 Emmitt Smith/1397	12.00	30.00
RH11 Emmitt Smith/1203	12.00	30.00
RH12 Emmitt Smith/1021	12.00	30.00

2002 Leaf Rookies and Stars Run With History Autographs

STATED PRINT RUN 22 SERIAL #'d SETS		
RH1 Emmitt Smith	175.00	300.00
RH3 Emmitt Smith	175.00	300.00
RH4 Emmitt Smith	175.00	300.00
RH6 Emmitt Smith	175.00	300.00

2002 Leaf Rookies and Stars Slideshow

STATED PRINT RUN 1500 SER.#'d SETS		
SS1 Anthony Thomas	1.00	2.50
SS2 Eddie George	1.00	2.50
SS3 Kurt Warner	1.25	3.00
SS4 Ricky Williams	1.00	2.50
SS5 Donovan McNabb	1.25	3.00
SS6 Jeff Garcia	1.00	2.50
SS7 Randy Moss	1.25	3.00
SS8 Shaun Alexander	1.00	2.50
SS9 Brett Favre	3.00	8.00
SS10 Jerry Rice	2.50	6.00
SS11 Emmitt Smith	3.00	8.00
SS12 Marshall Faulk	1.25	3.00
SS13 Michael Vick	2.00	5.00
SS14 Zach Thomas	1.25	3.00
SS15 Peyton Manning	2.50	6.00

2002 Leaf Rookies and Stars Standing Ovation

COMPLETE SET (13)	10.00	25.00
STATED PRINT RUN 2500 SER.#'d SETS		
SO1 Tom Brady	2.50	6.00
SO2 Kordell Stewart	.75	2.00
SO3 Kurt Warner	1.00	2.50
SO4 Jeff Garcia	.75	2.00
SO5 Priest Holmes	1.00	2.50
SO6 Shaun Alexander	.75	2.00
SO7 Marshall Faulk	1.00	2.50
SO8 Anthony Thomas	.75	2.00
SO9 Jerry Rice	2.00	5.00
SO10 David Boston	.60	1.50
SO11 Terrell Owens	1.00	2.50
SO12 Michael Strahan	1.00	2.50
SO13 New England Patriots	.75	2.50

2002 Leaf Rookies and Stars Ticket Masters

COMPLETE SET (20)	25.00	60.00
STATED PRINT RUN 2500 SER.#'d SETS		
TM1 Michael Vick	1.50	4.00
T.J. Duckett		
TM2 Jamal Lewis	1.00	2.50
Ray Lewis		
TM3 Drew Bledsoe	1.00	2.50
Travis Henry		
TM4 Chris Weinke	1.00	2.50
DeShaun Foster		
TM5 Anthony Thomas	1.00	2.50
Brian Urlacher		
TM6 Tim Couch	.75	2.00
William Green		
TM7 Quincy Carter	2.50	6.00
Emmitt Smith		
TM8 Brian Griese	.75	2.00
Ashley Lelie		
TM9 Joey Harrington	1.00	2.50
Germane Crowell		
TM10 Brett Favre	2.50	6.00
Ahman Green		
TM11 David Carr	1.00	2.50
Jabar Gaffney		
TM12 Peyton Manning	2.00	5.00
Edgerrin James		
TM13 Ricky Williams	.75	2.00
Chris Chambers		
TM14 Randy Moss	1.00	2.50
Daunte Culpepper		
TM15 Aaron Brooks	1.00	*2.50
Donte Stallworth		
TM16 Jerry Rice	2.00	5.00
Tim Brown		
TM17 Drew Brees	1.50	4.00
LaDainian Tomlinson		
TM18 Jeff Garcia	.75	2.00
Garrison Hearst		
TM19 Kurt Warner	1.00	2.50
Marshall Faulk		
TM20 Steve McNair	1.00	2.50
Eddie George		

2002 Leaf Rookies and Stars Triple Threads

STATED PRINT RUN 50 SER.#'d SETS		
TT1 Kordell Stewart	15.00	40.00
Jerome Bettis		
Plaxico Burress		
TT2 Jeff Garcia	10.00	25.00
Terrell Owens		
Garrison Hearst		
TT3 Tim Brown	50.00	80.00
Jerry Rice		
Rich Gannon		
TT4 Anthony Thomas	20.00	50.00
Brian Urlacher		
David Terrell		
TT5 Brett Favre	50.00	100.00
Ahman Green		
Terry Glenn		

2003 Leaf Rookies and Stars

Released in December of 2003, this set contains 295 cards, including 96 veterans and 199 rookies. Rookies 201-250 are serial numbered to 750. Rookies 251-280 feature event worn jersey swatches and are serial numbered to 550. Rookies 281-295 feature event worn jersey swatches and are serial numbered to 400. Boxes contained 24 packs of 6 cards. SRP was $4.

COMP.SET w/o SP's (100)	7.50	20.00
201-250 PRINT RUN 750 SER.#'d SETS		
1 Emmitt Smith	.75	2.00
2 Michael Vick	.40	1.00
3 Peerless Price	.20	.50
4 T.J. Duckett	.25	.60
5 Warrick Dunn	.25	.60
6 Jamal Lewis	.25	.60
7 Ray Lewis	.30	.75
8 Drew Bledsoe	.30	.75
9 Eric Moulds	.25	.60
10 Josh Reed	.20	.50
11 Travis Henry	.20	.50
12 Julius Peppers	.30	.75
13 Anthony Thomas	.25	.60
14 Brian Urlacher	.30	.75
15 Marty Booker	.25	.60
16 Kordell Stewart	.25	.60
17 Corey Dillon	.25	.60
18 Chad Johnson	.30	.75
19 Tim Couch	.20	.50
20 William Green	.20	.50
21 Antonio Bryant	.20	.50
22 Roy Williams	.25	.60
23 Ashley Lelie	.20	.50
24 Clinton Portis	.25	.60
25 Ed McCaffrey	.25	.60
26 Jake Plummer	.25	.60
27 Rod Smith	.25	.60
28 Joey Harrington	.20	.50
29 Ahman Green	.25	.60
30 Brett Favre	.75	2.00
31 Donald Driver	.30	.75
32 Javon Walker	.25	.60
33 David Carr	.25	.60
34 Edgerrin James	.30	.75
35 Marvin Harrison	.30	.75
36 Peyton Manning	.60	1.50
37 Fred Taylor	.25	.60
38 Jimmy Smith	.25	.60
39 Mark Brunell	.25	.60
40 Priest Holmes	.30	.75
41 Tony Gonzalez	.30	.75
42 Trent Green	.25	.60
43 Chris Chambers	.25	.60
44 Jay Fiedler	.20	.50
45 Junior Seau	.30	.75
46 Ricky Williams	.25	.60
47 Zach Thomas	.30	.75
48 Daunte Culpepper	.25	.60
49 Michael Bennett	.25	.60
50 Randy Moss	.30	.75
51 Tom Brady	.75	2.00
52 Troy Brown	.25	.60
53 Aaron Brooks	.25	.60
54 Deuce McAllister	.25	.60
55 Donte Stallworth	.20	.50
56 Joe Horn	.25	.60
57 Jeremy Shockey	.30	.75
58 Kerry Collins	.25	.60
59 Michael Strahan	.30	.75
60 Tiki Barber	.30	.75
61 Chad Pennington	.30	.75
62 Curtis Martin	.30	.75
63 Santana Moss	.25	.60
64 Charles Woodson	.30	.75
65 Jerry Rice	.60	1.50
66 Rich Gannon	.25	.60
67 Tim Brown	.30	.75
68 Donovan McNabb	.30	.75
69 Antwaan Randle El	.25	.60
70 Tommy Maddox	.25	.60
71 Jerome Bettis	.30	.75
72 Kendrell Bell	.20	.50
73 Plaxico Burress	.25	.60
74 David Boston	.20	.50
75 Drew Brees	.30	.75
76 LaDainian Tomlinson	.30	.75
77 Kevan Barlow	.20	.50
78 Jeff Garcia	.25	.60
79 Terrell Owens	.30	.75
80 Matt Hasselbeck	.25	.60
81 Koren Robinson	.25	.60
82 Shaun Alexander	.25	.60
83 Isaac Bruce	.30	.75
84 Kurt Warner	.30	.75
85 Marshall Faulk	.30	.75
86 Torry Holt	.30	.75
87 Brad Johnson	.25	.60
88 Keyshawn Johnson	.30	.75
89 Mike Alstott	.30	.75
90 Warren Sapp	.25	.60
91 Eddie George	.25	.60
92 Jevon Kearse	.25	.60
93 Steve McNair	.30	.75
94 Laveranues Coles	.20	.50
95 Rod Gardner	.20	.50
96 Patrick Ramsey	.25	.60
97 Kyle Boller	.20	.50
Terrell Suggs		
Musa Smith CL		
98 Rex Grossman	.05	.15
Taylor Jacobs CL		
99 Anquan Boldin	.15	.40
Bryant Johnson CL		
100 Tyrone Calico	.15	.40
Chris Brown CL		
101 Charles Tillman RC	2.00	5.00
102 Justin Griffith RC	1.25	3.00
103 Ovie Mughelli RC	1.25	3.00
104 Chris Edmonds RC	1.00	2.50
105 Jeremi Johnson RC	1.00	2.50
106 Malaefou MacKenzie RC	1.00	2.50
107 James Lynch RC	1.00	2.50
108 B.J. Askew RC	1.25	3.00
109 Andrew Pinnock RC	1.25	3.00
110 Chris Davis RC	1.25	3.00
111 Dan Curley RC	1.00	2.50
112 Lenny Walls RC	1.00	2.50
113 Travis Fisher RC	1.25	3.00
114 Ahmaad Galloway RC	1.25	3.00
115 Joe Smith RC	1.25	3.00
116 Reno Mahe RC	1.25	3.00
117 Torrie Cox RC	1.00	2.50
118 Kerry Carter RC	1.00	2.50
119 Dwone Hicks RC	1.00	2.50
120 Cato June RC	2.00	5.00
121 Terry Pierce RC	1.00	2.50
122 Eddie Moore RC	1.00	2.50
123 Mike Seidman RC	1.00	2.50
124 Michael Nattiel RC	1.00	2.50
125 Casey Fitzsimmons RC	1.25	3.00
126 George Wrighster RC	1.00	2.50
127 Mike Pinkard RC	1.00	2.50
128 Donald Lee RC	1.25	3.00
129 Sean Berton RC	1.00	2.50
130 Soloman Bates RC	1.00	2.50
131 Zach Hilton RC	1.25	3.00
132 Antonio Gates RC	12.00	30.00
133 Aaron Walker RC	1.25	3.00
134 Richard Angulo RC	1.00	2.50
135 Will Heller RC	1.25	3.00
136 Theo Sanders RC	1.00	2.50
137 Jimmy Farris RC	1.00	2.50
138 Ryan Nece RC	1.25	3.00
139 Antonio Brown RC	1.00	2.50
140 Clarence Coleman RC	1.00	2.50
141 Lawrence Hamilton RC	1.00	2.50
142 C.J. Jones RC	1.00	2.50
143 Frisman Jackson RC	1.25	3.00
144 Antonio Chatman RC	1.50	4.00
145 Rocky Boiman RC	1.25	3.00
146 Tron LaFavor RC	1.00	2.50
147 Derick Armstrong RC	1.25	3.00
148 J.J. Moses RC	1.00	2.50
149 Aaron Moorehead RC	1.25	3.00
150 Brad Pyatt RC	1.00	2.50
151 Arland Bruce RC	1.00	2.50
152 Chris Horn RC	1.25	3.00
153 Kareem Kelly RC	1.00	2.50
154 Talman Gardner RC	1.00	2.50
155 David Tyree RC	1.50	4.00
156 Willie Ponder RC	1.00	2.50
157 Greg Lewis RC	3.00	8.00
158 Eric Parker RC	1.50	4.00
159 Kassim Osgood RC	1.50	4.00
160 Jason Willis RC	1.00	2.50
161 Akbar Gbaja-Biamila RC	1.25	3.00
162 Mike Furrey RC	4.00	10.00
163 Chris Kelsay RC	1.25	3.00
164 Cory Redding RC	1.25	3.00
165 Kenny Peterson RC	1.25	3.00
166 Osi Umenyiora RC	2.00	5.00
167 Tyler Brayton RC	1.25	3.00
168 DeWayne White RC	1.00	2.50
169 Kevin Williams RC	1.50	4.00
170 Dan Klecko RC	1.25	3.00
171 Johnathan Sullivan RC	1.00	2.50
172 William Joseph RC	1.00	2.50
173 Rien Long RC	1.00	2.50
174 Angelo Crowell RC	1.25	3.00
175 Chaun Thompson RC	1.00	2.50
176 Bradie James RC	1.50	4.00
177 Antwan Peek RC	1.00	2.50
178 Kawika Mitchell RC	1.50	4.00
179 Cie Grant RC	1.25	3.00
180 E.J. Henderson RC	1.25	3.00
181 Victor Hobson RC	1.00	2.50
182 Alonzo Jackson RC	1.00	2.50
183 Matt Wilhelm RC	1.25	3.00
184 Pisa Tinoisamoa RC	1.50	4.00
185 Ricky Manning RC	1.25	3.00
186 Dennis Weathersby RC	1.00	2.50
187 Donald Strickland RC	1.00	2.50
188 Asante Samuel RC	3.00	8.00
189 Eugene Wilson RC	1.50	4.00
190 Nnamdi Asomugha RC	3.00	8.00
191 Ike Taylor RC	3.00	8.00
192 Drayton Florence RC	1.50	4.00
193 DeJuan Groce RC	1.50	4.00
194 Shane Walton RC	1.00	2.50
195 Terrence Holt RC	1.25	3.00
196 Rashean Mathis RC	1.25	3.00
197 Julian Battle RC	1.25	3.00
198 Hanik Milligan RC	1.00	2.50
199 Terrence Kiel RC	1.25	3.00
200 David Kircus RC	1.50	4.00
201 Lee Suggs RC	1.50	4.00
202 Charles Rogers RC	1.50	4.00
203 Brandon Lloyd RC	3.00	8.00
204 Terrence Edwards RC	1.25	3.00
205 Tony Romo RC	20.00	50.00
206 Brooks Bollinger RC	1.50	4.00
207 Jerome McDougle RC	1.25	3.00
208 Jimmy Kennedy RC	1.50	4.00
209 Ken Dorsey RC	1.50	4.00
210 Kirk Farmer RC	1.50	4.00
211 Mike Doss RC	2.00	5.00
212 Chris Simms RC	2.00	5.00
213 Cecil Sapp RC	1.25	3.00
214 Justin Gage RC	1.50	4.00
215 Sam Aiken RC	1.50	4.00
216 Doug Gabriel RC	1.50	4.00
217 Jason Witten RC	5.00	12.00
218 Bennie Joppru RC	1.25	3.00
219 Jason Gesser RC	1.50	4.00
220 Brock Forsey RC	1.50	4.00
221 Quentin Griffin RC	1.50	4.00
222 Avon Cobourne RC	1.25	3.00
223 Domanick Davis RC	1.50	4.00
224 Boss Bailey RC	1.50	4.00
225 Tony Hollings RC	1.50	4.00
226 LaBrandon Toefield RC	1.50	4.00
227 Arlen Harris RC	1.25	3.00
228 Sultan McCullough RC	1.25	3.00
229 Visanthe Shiancoe RC	2.00	5.00
230 L.J. Smith RC	2.00	5.00
231 LaTarence Dunbar RC	1.25	3.00
232 Walter Young RC	1.25	3.00
233 Bobby Wade RC	1.50	4.00
234 Zuriel Smith RC	1.25	3.00
235 Adrian Madise RC	1.25	3.00
236 Ken Hamlin RC	2.00	5.00
237 Carl Ford RC	1.25	3.00
238 Cortez Hankton RC	1.50	4.00
239 J.R. Tolver RC	1.50	4.00
240 Keenan Howry RC	1.25	3.00
241 Billy McMullen RC	1.25	3.00
242 Arnaz Battle RC	2.00	5.00
243 Shaun McDonald RC	1.50	4.00
244 Andre Woolfolk RC	1.50	4.00
245 Sammy Davis RC	1.50	4.00
246 Calvin Pace RC	1.50	4.00
247 Michael Haynes RC	1.25	3.00
248 Ty Warren RC	1.50	4.00
249 Nick Barnett RC	2.00	5.00
250 Troy Polamalu RC	15.00	30.00
251 Carson Palmer JSY RC	6.00	15.00
252 Byron Leftwich JSY RC	3.00	8.00
253 Kyle Boller JSY RC	3.00	8.00
254 Rex Grossman JSY RC	3.00	8.00
255 Dave Ragone JSY RC	2.00	5.00
256 Brian St.Pierre JSY RC	2.50	6.00
257 Kliff Kingsbury JSY RC	2.50	6.00
258 Seneca Wallace JSY RC	3.00	8.00
259 Larry Johnson JSY RC	3.00	8.00
260 Willis McGahee JSY RC	4.00	10.00
261 Justin Fargas JSY RC	3.00	8.00
262 Onterrio Smith JSY RC	2.00	5.00
263 Chris Brown JSY RC	2.00	5.00
264 Musa Smith JSY RC	2.00	5.00
265 Artose Pinner JSY RC	2.00	5.00
266 Andre Johnson JSY RC	8.00	20.00
267 Kelley Washington JSY RC	2.00	5.00
268 Taylor Jacobs JSY RC	2.00	5.00
269 Bryant Johnson JSY RC	3.00	8.00
270 Tyrone Calico JSY RC	2.50	6.00
271 Anquan Boldin JSY RC	5.00	12.00
272 Bethel Johnson JSY RC	2.00	5.00
273 Nate Burleson JSY RC	2.50	6.00
274 Kevin Curtis JSY RC	3.00	8.00
275 Dallas Clark JSY RC	5.00	12.00
276 Teyo Johnson JSY RC	2.50	6.00
277 Terrell Suggs JSY RC	3.00	8.00
278 DeWayne Robertson JSY RC	2.50	6.00
279 Terence Newman JSY RC	2.50	6.00
280 Marcus Trufant JSY RC	2.50	6.00
281 Carson Palmer	6.00	15.00
Byron Leftwich JSY		
282 Rex Grossman	3.00	8.00
Brian St.Pierre JSY		
283 Kyle Boller	3.00	8.00
Dave Ragone JSY		
284 Kliff Kingsbury	3.00	8.00
Seneca Wallace JSY		
285 Larry Johnson	4.00	10.00
Willis McGahee JSY		
286 Justin Fargas	2.00	5.00
Onterrio Smith JSY		
287 Chris Brown	2.00	5.00
Musa Smith JSY		
288 Artose Pinner	8.00	20.00
Andre Johnson JSY		
289 Kelley Washington	2.00	5.00
Taylor Jacobs JSY		
290 Bryant Johnson	3.00	8.00
Tyrone Calico JSY		
291 Anquan Boldin	5.00	12.00
Bryant Johnson JSY		
292 Nate Burleson	3.00	8.00
Kevin Curtis JSY		
293 Dallas Clark	5.00	12.00
Teyo Johnson JSY		
294 Terrell Suggs	3.00	8.00
DeWayne Robertson JSY		
295 Terence Newman	2.50	6.00
Marcus Trufant JSY		

2003 Leaf Rookies and Stars Longevity

*VETS 1-100: 5X TO 12X BASIC CARDS		
1-100 PRINT RUN 100 SER.#'d SETS		
*ROOKIES 101-200: 2.5X TO 6X		
101-200 PRINT RUN 50		
201-250 AUTO PRINT RUN 25		
UNPRICED 251-280 JSY AU PRINT RUN 10		
*DUAL JSY 181-295: .6X TO 1.5X		
281-295 DUAL JSY PRINT RUN 25		
SERIAL #'d UNDER 25 NOT PRICED		
201 Lee Suggs AU	15.00	40.00
202 Charles Rogers AU	15.00	40.00
203 Brandon Lloyd AU	30.00	80.00
204 Terrence Edwards AU	12.00	30.00
205 Tony Romo AU	800.00	1,200.00
206 Brooks Bollinger AU	15.00	40.00
207 Jerome McDougle AU	12.00	30.00
208 Jimmy Kennedy AU	15.00	40.00
209 Ken Dorsey AU	15.00	40.00
210 Kirk Farmer AU	15.00	40.00
211 Mike Doss AU	20.00	50.00
212 Chris Simms AU	20.00	50.00
213 Cecil Sapp AU	12.00	30.00
214 Justin Gage AU	15.00	40.00
215 Sam Aiken AU	15.00	40.00
216 Doug Gabriel AU	15.00	40.00
217 Jason Witten AU	75.00	125.00
218 Bennie Joppru AU	12.00	30.00
219 Jason Gesser AU	15.00	40.00
220 Brock Forsey AU	15.00	40.00
222 Avon Cobourne AU	12.00	30.00
223 Domanick Davis AU	15.00	40.00
224 Boss Bailey AU	15.00	40.00
225 Tony Hollings AU	15.00	40.00
227 Arlen Harris AU	12.00	30.00
228 Sultan McCullough AU	12.00	30.00
229 Visanthe Shiancoe AU	20.00	50.00
230 L.J. Smith AU	20.00	50.00
231 LaTarence Dunbar AU	12.00	30.00
232 Walter Young AU	12.00	30.00
234 Zuriel Smith AU	12.00	30.00
235 Adrian Madise AU	12.00	30.00
236 Ken Hamlin AU	20.00	50.00
237 Carl Ford AU	12.00	30.00
238 Cortez Hankton AU	15.00	40.00
239 J.R. Tolver AU	15.00	40.00
242 Arnaz Battle AU	20.00	50.00
243 Shaun McDonald AU	15.00	40.00
244 Andre Woolfolk AU	15.00	40.00
245 Sammy Davis AU	15.00	40.00
246 Calvin Pace AU	15.00	40.00
247 Michael Haynes AU	12.00	30.00
248 Ty Warren AU	15.00	40.00
249 Nick Barnett AU	20.00	50.00
250 Troy Polamalu AU	300.00	500.00

2003 Leaf Rookies and Stars Rookie Autographs

201-250 AUTO PRINT RUN 150		
201-250 FIRST 150 BASE CARDS SIGNED		
251-280 JSY AUTO PRINT RUN 50		
251-280 FIRST 50 BASE CARDS SIGNED		
201 Lee Suggs	8.00	20.00
202 Charles Rogers	8.00	20.00
203 Brandon Lloyd	15.00	40.00
204 Terrence Edwards	6.00	15.00
205 Tony Romo	450.00	800.00
206 Brooks Bollinger	8.00	20.00
207 Jerome McDougle	6.00	15.00
208 Jimmy Kennedy	8.00	20.00
209 Ken Dorsey	8.00	20.00
210 Kirk Farmer	8.00	20.00
211 Mike Doss	10.00	25.00
212 Chris Simms	10.00	25.00
213 Cecil Sapp	6.00	15.00
214 Justin Gage	8.00	20.00
215 Sam Aiken	8.00	20.00
216 Doug Gabriel	8.00	20.00
217 Jason Witten	40.00	80.00
218 Bennie Joppru	6.00	15.00
219 Jason Gesser	8.00	20.00
220 Brock Forsey	8.00	20.00
221 Quentin Griffin	8.00	20.00
222 Avon Cobourne	6.00	15.00
223 Domanick Davis	8.00	20.00
224 Boss Bailey	8.00	20.00
225 Tony Hollings	8.00	20.00
226 LaBrandon Toefield	8.00	20.00
227 Arlen Harris	6.00	15.00
228 Sultan McCullough	6.00	15.00
229 Visanthe Shiancoe	10.00	25.00
230 L.J. Smith	10.00	25.00
231 LaTarence Dunbar	6.00	15.00
232 Walter Young	6.00	15.00
233 Bobby Wade	8.00	20.00
234 Zuriel Smith	6.00	15.00
235 Adrian Madise	6.00	15.00
236 Ken Hamlin	10.00	25.00
237 Carl Ford	6.00	15.00
238 Cortez Hankton	8.00	20.00
239 J.R. Tolver	8.00	20.00
242 Arnaz Battle	10.00	25.00
243 Shaun McDonald	8.00	20.00
244 Andre Woolfolk	8.00	20.00
245 Sammy Davis	8.00	20.00
246 Calvin Pace	8.00	20.00
247 Michael Haynes	6.00	15.00
248 Ty Warren	8.00	20.00
249 Nick Barnett	10.00	25.00
250 Troy Polamalu	200.00	400.00
251 Carson Palmer JSY	90.00	150.00
252 Byron Leftwich JSY	15.00	40.00
253 Kyle Boller JSY	15.00	40.00
254 Rex Grossman JSY	15.00	40.00
255 Dave Ragone JSY	10.00	25.00
256 Brian St.Pierre JSY	12.00	30.00
257 Kliff Kingsbury JSY	12.00	30.00
258 Seneca Wallace JSY	15.00	40.00
259 Larry Johnson JSY	15.00	40.00
260 Willis McGahee JSY	20.00	50.00
261 Justin Fargas JSY	15.00	40.00
262 Onterrio Smith JSY	10.00	25.00
263 Chris Brown JSY	10.00	25.00
264 Musa Smith JSY	10.00	25.00
265 Artose Pinner JSY	10.00	25.00
266 Andre Johnson JSY	50.00	100.00
267 Kelley Washington JSY	10.00	25.00
268 Taylor Jacobs JSY	10.00	25.00
269 Bryant Johnson JSY	15.00	40.00
270 Tyrone Calico JSY	12.00	30.00
271 Anquan Boldin JSY	25.00	60.00
272 Bethel Johnson JSY	10.00	25.00
273 Nate Burleson JSY	12.00	30.00
274 Kevin Curtis JSY	15.00	40.00
275 Dallas Clark JSY	25.00	50.00
276 Teyo Johnson JSY	12.00	30.00
277 Terrell Suggs JSY	25.00	60.00
279 Terence Newman JSY	12.00	30.00
280 Marcus Trufant JSY	12.00	30.00

2003 Leaf Rookies and Stars Freshman Orientation Jersey

PRINT RUN 600 SERIAL #'d SETS		
*CLASS OFFICER/25: 1.2X TO 3X JSY/600		
CL.OFFICERS PRINT RUN 25 SER.#'d SETS		
FO1 Carson Palmer	5.00	12.00
FO2 Byron Leftwich	2.50	6.00
FO3 Kyle Boller	2.50	6.00
FO4 Rex Grossman	2.50	6.00
FO5 Dave Ragone	1.50	4.00
FO6 Brian St.Pierre	2.00	5.00
FO7 Kliff Kingsbury	2.00	5.00
FO8 Seneca Wallace	2.50	6.00
FO9 Larry Johnson	2.50	6.00
FO10 Willis McGahee	3.00	8.00
FO11 Justin Fargas	2.50	6.00
FO12 Onterrio Smith	1.50	4.00
FO13 Chris Brown	1.50	4.00
FO14 Musa Smith	1.50	4.00
FO15 Artose Pinner	1.50	4.00
FO16 Andre Johnson	6.00	15.00
FO17 Kelley Washington	1.50	4.00
FO18 Taylor Jacobs	1.50	4.00
FO19 Bryant Johnson	2.50	6.00
FO20 Tyrone Calico	2.00	5.00
FO21 Anquan Boldin	4.00	10.00
FO22 Bethel Johnson	1.50	4.00
FO23 Nate Burleson	2.00	5.00
FO24 Kevin Curtis	2.50	6.00
FO25 Dallas Clark	4.00	10.00
FO26 Teyo Johnson	2.00	5.00
FO27 Terrell Suggs	2.50	6.00
FO28 DeWayne Robertson	2.00	5.00
FO29 Terence Newman	2.00	5.00
FO30 Marcus Trufant	2.00	5.00

2003 Leaf Rookies and Stars Great American Heroes

COMPLETE SET (20)	20.00	50.00
PRINT RUN 1325 SERIAL #'d SETS		
GA1 Brian Urlacher	1.25	3.00
GA2 Bob Griese	1.25	3.00
GA3 Mel Blount	1.00	2.50
GA4 Ahman Green	1.00	2.50
GA5 Aaron Brooks	1.00	2.50
GA6 Chad Pennington	1.25	3.00
GA7 Clinton Portis	1.00	2.50
GA8 Isaac Bruce	1.25	3.00
GA9 Jamal Lewis	1.00	2.50
GA10 Jeff Garcia	1.00	2.50
GA11 Jerry Rice	2.50	6.00
GA12 Joey Harrington	.75	2.00
GA13 Kurt Warner	1.25	3.00
GA14 LaDainian Tomlinson	1.25	3.00
GA15 Rod Smith	1.00	2.50
GA16 Tommy Maddox	1.00	2.50
GA17 Rex Grossman	1.25	3.00
GA18 Cecil Sapp	.75	2.00
GA19 Byron Leftwich	1.25	3.00
GA20 Kenny Peterson	1.00	2.50

2003 Leaf Rookies and Stars Great American Heroes Autographs

RANDOM INSERTS IN PACKS		
SERIAL #'d UNDER 25 NOT PRICED		
GA1 Brian Urlacher/25	30.00	80.00
GA3 Mel Blount/53	15.00	40.00
GA4 Ahman Green/25	25.00	60.00
GA5 Aaron Brooks/75	10.00	25.00
GA7 Clinton Portis/30	30.00	80.00
GA8 Isaac Bruce/75	12.50	30.00
GA9 Jamal Lewis/25	25.00	60.00
GA10 Jeff Garcia/25	25.00	60.00
GA11 Jerry Rice/25	100.00	200.00
GA12 Joey Harrington/30	25.00	60.00
GA13 Kurt Warner/25	30.00	80.00
GA14 LaDainian Tomlinson/25	75.00	125.00
GA15 Rod Smith/150	12.50	30.00
GA16 Tommy Maddox/50	12.50	30.00
GA17 Rex Grossman/50	25.00	60.00
GA18 Cecil Sapp/100	6.00	15.00
GA19 Byron Leftwich/25	25.00	60.00
GA20 Kenny Peterson No Auto	6.00	15.00

2003 Leaf Rookies and Stars Initial Steps Shoe

PRINT RUN 100 SERIAL #'d SETS		
IS1 Carson Palmer	8.00	20.00
IS2 Byron Leftwich	4.00	10.00
IS3 Kyle Boller	4.00	10.00
IS4 Rex Grossman	4.00	10.00
IS5 Dave Ragone	2.50	6.00
IS6 Brian St.Pierre	3.00	8.00
IS7 Kliff Kingsbury	3.00	8.00
IS8 Seneca Wallace	4.00	10.00
IS9 Larry Johnson	4.00	10.00
IS10 Willis McGahee	5.00	12.00
IS11 Justin Fargas	4.00	10.00
IS12 Onterrio Smith	2.50	6.00
IS13 Chris Brown	2.50	6.00
IS14 Musa Smith	2.50	6.00
IS15 Artose Pinner	2.50	6.00
IS16 Andre Johnson	10.00	25.00
IS17 Kelley Washington	2.50	6.00
IS18 Taylor Jacobs	2.50	6.00
IS19 Bryant Johnson	4.00	10.00
IS20 Tyrone Calico	3.00	8.00
IS21 Anquan Boldin	6.00	15.00
IS22 Bethel Johnson	2.50	6.00
IS23 Nate Burleson	3.00	8.00
IS24 Kevin Curtis	4.00	10.00
IS25 Dallas Clark	6.00	15.00
IS26 Teyo Johnson	3.00	8.00
IS27 Terrell Suggs	4.00	10.00
IS28 DeWayne Robertson	3.00	8.00
IS29 Terence Newman	3.00	8.00
IS30 Marcus Trufant	3.00	8.00

2003 Leaf Rookies and Stars Masks

STATED PRINT RUN 350 SER. #'d SETS		
*DUAL MASK/100: .8X TO 2X FO JSY/600		
DUAL PRINT RUN 100 SER.#'d SETS		
FIRST 100 CARDS FEATURE DUAL SWATCHES		
RM1 Carson Palmer	6.00	15.00
RM2 Byron Leftwich	3.00	8.00
RM3 Kyle Boller	3.00	8.00
RM4 Rex Grossman	3.00	8.00
RM5 Dave Ragone	2.00	5.00
RM6 Brian St.Pierre	2.50	6.00
RM7 Kliff Kingsbury	2.50	6.00
RM8 Seneca Wallace	3.00	8.00
RM9 Larry Johnson	3.00	8.00
RM10 Willis McGahee	4.00	10.00
RM11 Justin Fargas	3.00	8.00
RM12 Onterrio Smith	2.00	5.00
RM13 Chris Brown	2.00	5.00
RM14 Musa Smith	2.00	5.00
RM15 Artose Pinner	2.00	5.00
RM16 Andre Johnson	8.00	20.00
RM17 Kelley Washington	2.00	5.00
RM18 Taylor Jacobs	2.00	5.00
RM19 Bryant Johnson	3.00	8.00
RM20 Tyrone Calico	2.50	6.00

RM21 Anquan Boldin 5.00 12.00
RM22 Bethel Johnson 2.00 5.00
RM23 Nate Burleson 2.50 6.00
RM24 Kevin Curtis 3.00 8.00
RM25 Dallas Clark 5.00 12.00
RM26 Teyo Johnson 2.50 6.00
RM27 Terrell Suggs 3.00 8.00
RM28 DeWayne Robertson 2.50 6.00
RM29 Terence Newman 2.50 6.00
RM30 Marcus Trufant 2.50 6.00

2003 Leaf Rookies and Stars Prime Cuts

STATED PRINT RUN 25 SER.#'d SETS
PC1 Aaron Brooks 10.00 25.00
PC2 Ahman Green 10.00 25.00
PC3 Antonio Bryant 8.00 20.00
PC4 Antwaan Randle El 10.00 25.00
PC5 Ashley Lelie 8.00 20.00
PC6 Brett Favre 30.00 80.00
PC7 Brian Urlacher 12.00 30.00
PC8 Chad Pennington 12.00 30.00
PC9 Chris Chambers 10.00 25.00
PC10 Clinton Portis 10.00 25.00
PC11 Daunte Culpepper 10.00 25.00
PC12 David Carr 10.00 25.00
PC13 Deuce McAllister 10.00 25.00
PC14 Donovan McNabb 12.00 30.00
PC15 Donte Stallworth 8.00 20.00
PC16 Drew Bledsoe 12.00 30.00
PC17 Drew Brees 12.00 30.00
PC18 Edgerrin James 12.00 30.00
PC19 Jeff Garcia 10.00 25.00
PC20 Jeremy Shockey 12.00 30.00
PC21 Jerry Rice 25.00 60.00
PC22 Joey Harrington 8.00 20.00
PC23 Julius Peppers 12.00 30.00
PC24 Kurt Warner 12.00 30.00
PC25 LaDainian Tomlinson 12.00 30.00
PC26 Marshall Faulk 12.00 30.00
PC27 Marvin Harrison 12.00 30.00
PC28 Michael Vick 15.00 40.00
PC29 Peyton Manning 25.00 60.00
PC30 Priest Holmes 12.00 30.00
PC31 Randy Moss 12.00 30.00
PC32 Ricky Williams 10.00 25.00
PC33 Shaun Alexander 10.00 25.00
PC34 Steve McNair 12.00 30.00
PC35 Tom Brady 30.00 80.00
PC36 William Green 8.00 20.00

2003 Leaf Rookies and Stars Slideshow

COMPLETE SET (10) 10.00 25.00
PRINT RUN 1500 SER. #'d SETS
SS1 Clinton Portis 1.00 2.50
SS2 Drew Bledsoe 1.25 3.00
SS3 Michael Vick 1.50 4.00
SS4 Donovan McNabb 1.25 3.00
SS5 Brett Favre 3.00 8.00
SS6 Deuce McAllister 1.00 2.50
SS7 Ricky Williams 1.00 2.50
SS8 Jeremy Shockey 1.25 3.00
SS9 Brian Urlacher 1.25 3.00
SS10 Chad Pennington 1.25 3.00

2003 Leaf Rookies and Stars Ticket Masters

COMPLETE SET (20) 25.00 60.00
STATED PRINT RUN 1325 SER.#'d SETS
TM1 Brett Favre 3.00 8.00
Ahman Green
TM2 Joey Harrington 1.00 2.50
Charles Rogers
TM3 Brian Urlacher 1.25 3.00
Anthony Thomas
TM4 Randy Moss 1.25 3.00
Daunte Culpepper
TM5 Kurt Warner 1.25 3.00
Marshall Faulk
TM6 Jeff Garcia 1.25 3.00
Terrell Owens
TM7 Ricky Williams 1.25 3.00
Zach Thomas
TM8 LaDainian Tomlinson 1.25 3.00
Drew Brees
TM9 Jerry Rice 2.50 6.00
Rich Gannon
TM10 Priest Holmes 1.25 3.00
Tony Gonzalez
TM11 Clinton Portis 1.00 2.50
Rod Smith
TM12 Drew Bledsoe 1.25 3.00
Travis Henry
TM13 Chad Johnson 2.00 5.00
Carson Palmer
TM14 Chad Pennington 1.25 3.00
Curtis Martin
TM15 Steve McNair 1.25 3.00
Eddie George
TM16 Peyton Manning 2.50 6.00
Marvin Harrison
TM17 Deuce McAllister 1.00 2.50
Aaron Brooks
TM18 Donovan McNabb 1.25 3.00
Duce Staley
TM19 Michael Vick 1.50 4.00
Peerless Price
TM20 Jeremy Shockey 1.25 3.00
Tiki Barber

2003 Leaf Rookies and Stars Triple Threads

STATED PRINT RUN 100 SER.#'d SETS
TT1 Michael Vick 10.00 25.00
T.J. Duckett
Warrick Dunn
TT2 Kurt Warner 8.00 20.00
Marshall Faulk
Torry Holt
TT3 Drew Bledsoe 8.00 20.00
Eric Moulds
Travis Henry
TT4 Brian Urlacher 15.00 40.00
Anthony Thomas
Mike Brown
TT5 Clinton Portis 6.00 15.00
Ed McCaffrey
Musa Smith
TT6 Brett Favre 20.00 50.00
Ahman Green
Donald Driver
TT7 Peyton Manning 15.00 40.00
Edgerrin James
Marvin Harrison
TT8 Mark Brunell 6.00 15.00
Fred Taylor
Jimmy Smith
TT9 Trent Green 8.00 20.00
Priest Holmes
Tony Gonzalez
TT10 Ricky Williams 8.00 20.00
Chris Chambers
Zach Thomas
TT11 Daunte Culpepper 8.00 20.00
Michael Bennett
Randy Moss
TT12 Tom Brady 20.00 50.00
Antowain Smith
Tim Brown
TT13 Aaron Brooks 6.00 15.00
Deuce McAllister
Donte Stallworth
TT14 Kerry Collins 8.00 20.00
Jeremy Shockey
Michael Strahan
TT15 Chad Pennington 8.00 20.00
Curtis Martin
Santana Moss
TT16 Rich Gannon 15.00 40.00
Jerry Rice
Tim Brown
TT17 Donovan McNabb 8.00 20.00
Duce Staley
Todd Pinkston
TT18 Jerome Bettis 8.00 20.00
Kendrell Bell
Plaxico Burress
TT19 Drew Brees 8.00 20.00
Doug Flutie
LaDainian Tomlinson
TT20 Jeff Garcia 8.00 20.00
Garrison Hearst
Terrell Owens

2004 Leaf Rookies and Stars

Leaf Rookies and Stars initially released in mid-November 2004. The base set consists of 299-cards including 100-rookies non-serial numbered, 50-rookies numbered of 750, 33-rookie jersey cards numbered of 750, and 16-dual rookie jersey cards numbered of 500. Hobby boxes contained 24-packs of 6-cards and carried an S.R.P. of $4 per pack. Three parallel sets and a variety of inserts can be found seeded in hobby and retail packs highlighted by the Fans of the Game Autograph and Rookie Autograph inserts.

COMP.SET w/o SP's (200) 30.00 60.00
COMP.SET w/o RC's (100) 7.50 20.00
201-250 RC PRINT RUN 750 SER.#'d SETS
251-283 JSY PRINT RUN 750 SER.#'d SETS
284-299 PRINT RUN 500 SER.#'d SETS
1 Anquan Boldin .30 .75
2 Emmitt Smith .75 2.00
3 Josh McCown .25 .60
4 Michael Vick .40 1.00
5 Peerless Price .20 .50
6 T.J. Duckett .25 .60
7 Warrick Dunn .25 .60
8 Jamal Lewis .25 .60
9 Kyle Boller .25 .60
10 Ray Lewis .30 .75
11 Drew Bledsoe .30 .75
12 Eric Moulds .25 .60
13 Travis Henry .20 .50
14 Jake Delhomme .25 .60
15 Stephen Davis .25 .60
16 Steve Smith .30 .75
17 Brian Urlacher .30 .75
18 Rex Grossman .25 .60
19 Thomas Jones .30 .75
20 Carson Palmer .30 .75
21 Chad Johnson .30 .75
22 Rudi Johnson .25 .60
23 Jeff Garcia .25 .60
24 William Green .20 .50
25 Keyshawn Johnson .25 .60
26 Terence Newman .25 .60
27 Roy Williams S .25 .60
28 Jake Plummer .25 .60
29 Quentin Griffin .20 .50
30 Rod Smith .25 .60
31 Charles Rogers .20 .50
32 Joey Harrington .25 .60
33 Ahman Green .25 .60
34 Brett Favre .75 2.00
35 Javon Walker .20 .50
36 Andre Johnson .30 .75
37 David Carr .20 .50
38 Domanick Davis .20 .50
39 Edgerrin James .25 .60
40 Marvin Harrison .30 .75
41 Peyton Manning .60 1.50
42 Byron Leftwich .25 .60
43 Fred Taylor .25 .60
44 Jimmy Smith .25 .60
45 Priest Holmes .30 .75
46 Tony Gonzalez .30 .75
47 Trent Green .25 .60
48 A.J. Feeley .20 .50
49 Chris Chambers .25 .60
50 Deion Sanders .30 .75
51 Daunte Culpepper .25 .60
52 Michael Bennett .25 .60
53 Randy Moss .30 .75
54 Corey Dillon .25 .60
55 Deion Branch .25 .60
56 Tom Brady .60 1.50
57 Aaron Brooks .25 .60
58 Deuce McAllister .25 .60
59 Joe Horn .25 .60
60 Jeremy Shockey .25 .60
61 Michael Strahan .30 .75
62 Tiki Barber .30 .75
63 Chad Pennington .30 .75
64 Curtis Martin .30 .75
65 Santana Moss .25 .60
66 Jerry Porter .20 .50
67 Jerry Rice .60 1.50
68 Warren Sapp .25 .60
69 Donovan McNabb .30 .75
70 Jevon Kearse .25 .60
71 Terrell Owens .30 .75
72 Duce Staley .25 .60
73 Hines Ward .30 .75
74 Jerome Bettis .30 .75
75 LaDainian Tomlinson .30 .75
76 Kevan Barlow .20 .50
77 Tim Rattay .20 .50
78 Koren Robinson .20 .50
79 Matt Hasselbeck .25 .60
80 Shaun Alexander .25 .60
81 Isaac Bruce .25 .60
82 Marc Bulger .25 .60
83 Marshall Faulk .30 .75
84 Torry Holt .25 .60
85 Brad Johnson .25 .60
86 Derrick Brooks .25 .60
87 Chris Brown .20 .50
88 Derrick Mason .25 .60
89 Eddie George .25 .60
90 Steve McNair .30 .75
91 Clinton Portis .30 .75
92 LaVar Arrington .25 .60
93 Laveranues Coles .20 .50
94 Mark Brunell .25 .60
95 DeAngelo Hall CL .40 1.00
Matt Schaub
Michael Jenkins
96 J.P. Losman CL .20 .50
Lee Evans
97 Kellen Winslow Jr. CL .20 .50
Luke McCown
98 Darius Watts CL .15 .40
Tatum Bell
99 Kevin Jones CL .20 .50
Roy Williams WR
100 Greg Jones CL .15 .40
Reggie Williams
101 Darnell Dockett RC 1.00 2.50
102 Karlos Dansby RC 1.50 4.00
103 Larry Croom RC 1.00 2.50
104 Chad Lavalais RC 1.00 2.50
105 Demorrio Williams RC 1.50 4.00
106 B.J. Sams RC 1.00 2.50
107 Dwan Edwards RC 1.00 2.50
108 Jason Peters RC 1.25 3.00
109 Shaud Williams RC 1.25 3.00
110 Tim Anderson RC 1.25 3.00
111 Tim Euhus RC 1.00 2.50
112 Michael Gaines RC 1.00 2.50
113 Rod Rutherford RC 1.00 2.50
114 Leon Joe RC 1.00 2.50
115 Nathan Vasher RC 1.50 4.00
116 Caleb Miller RC 1.00 2.50
117 Jamall Broussard RC 1.00 2.50
118 Keiwan Ratliff RC 1.00 2.50
119 Landon Johnson RC 1.00 2.50
120 Madieu Williams RC 1.00 2.50
121 Matthias Askew RC 1.00 2.50
122 Robert Geathers RC 1.00 2.50
123 Richard Alston RC 1.00 2.50
124 Bruce Thornton RC 1.00 2.50
125 Patrick Crayton RC 1.50 4.00
126 Bradlee Van Pelt RC 1.25 3.00
127 Charlie Adams RC 1.00 2.50
128 Nate Jackson RC 1.00 2.50
129 Roc Alexander RC 1.00 2.50
130 Romar Crenshaw RC 1.00 2.50
131 Keith Smith RC 1.00 2.50
132 Joey Thomas RC 1.00 2.50
133 Kelvin Kight RC 1.00 2.50
134 Scott McBrien RC 1.25 3.00
135 Andrae Thurman RC 1.00 2.50
136 Derick Armstrong 1.00 2.50
137 Glenn Earl RC 1.00 2.50
138 Kendrick Starling RC 1.00 2.50
139 Ben Hartsock RC 1.00 2.50
140 Gilbert Gardner RC 1.00 2.50
141 Jason David RC 1.00 2.50
142 Daryl Smith RC 1.00 2.50
143 Jared Allen RC 4.00 10.00
144 Jeris McIntyre RC 1.00 2.50
145 John Booth RC 1.00 2.50
146 Jonathan Smith RC 1.00 2.50
147 Junior Siavii RC 1.00 2.50
148 Keyaron Fox RC 1.25 3.00
149 Kris Wilson RC 1.25 3.00
150 Doug Easlick RC 1.00 2.50
151 Fred Russell RC 1.25 3.00
152 Tony Bua RC 1.00 2.50
153 Will Poole RC 1.50 4.00
154 Ben Nelson RC 1.00 2.50
155 Brock Lesnar RC 5.00 12.00
156 Butchie Wallace RC 1.00 2.50
157 Darrion Scott RC 1.25 3.00
158 Dontarrious Thomas RC 1.25 3.00
159 Richard Owens RC 1.00 2.50
160 Rod Davis RC 1.00 2.50
161 Dexter Reid RC 1.00 2.50
162 Kory Chapman RC 1.00 2.50
163 Marquise Hill RC 1.00 2.50
164 Courtney Watson RC 1.00 2.50
165 Mike Karney RC 1.25 3.00
166 Gibril Wilson RC 1.50 4.00
167 Reggie Torbor RC 1.00 2.50
168 Darrell McClover RC 1.00 2.50
169 Derrick Strait RC 1.00 2.50
170 Erik Coleman RC 1.25 3.00
171 Johnathan Reese RC 1.00 2.50
172 Rashad Washington RC 1.00 2.50
173 Courtney Anderson RC 1.00 2.50
174 Stuart Schweigert RC 1.25 3.00
175 J.R. Reed RC 1.00 2.50
176 Justin Jenkins RC 1.00 2.50
177 Matt Ware RC 1.50 4.00
178 Nate Lawrie RC 1.00 2.50
179 Thomas Tapeh RC 1.25 3.00
180 Matt Kranchick RC 1.25 3.00
181 Willie Parker RC 2.00 5.00
182 Igor Olshansky RC 1.25 3.00
183 Ryan Krause RC 1.00 2.50
184 Shaun Phillips RC 1.50 4.00
185 Wes Welker RC 5.00 12.00
186 Richard Seigler RC 1.00 2.50
187 Shawntae Spencer RC 1.00 2.50
188 Marcus Tubbs RC 1.00 2.50
189 Niko Koutouvides RC 1.00 2.50
190 Brandon Chillar RC 1.25 3.00
191 Tony Hargrove RC 1.00 2.50
192 Mark Jones RC 1.00 2.50
193 Marquis Cooper RC 1.00 2.50
194 Antwan Odom RC 1.25 3.00
195 Michael Waddell RC 1.00 2.50
196 Randy Starks RC 1.00 2.50
197 Rich Gardner RC 1.25 3.00
198 Travis Laboy RC 1.25 3.00
199 Vick King RC 1.00 2.50
200 Chris Cooley RC 1.50 4.00
201 Adimchinobe Echemandu RC 2.00 5.00
202 Ahmad Carroll RC 1.50 4.00
203 Andy Hall RC 1.50 4.00
204 B.J. Johnson RC 1.50 4.00
205 B.J. Symons RC 1.50 4.00
206 Brandon Miree RC 1.50 4.00
207 Bruce Perry RC 1.50 4.00
208 Carlos Francis RC 1.50 4.00
209 Casey Bramlet RC 1.50 4.00
210 Chris Gamble RC 2.00 5.00
211 Clarence Moore RC 1.50 4.00
212 Cody Pickett RC 2.00 5.00
213 Craig Krenzel RC 2.00 5.00
214 D.J. Hackett RC 2.00 5.00
215 D.J. Williams RC 2.50 6.00
216 Derrick Ward RC 2.50 6.00
217 Drew Carter RC 2.00 5.00
218 Drew Henson RC 1.50 4.00
219 Ernest Wilford RC 2.00 5.00
220 Jamaar Taylor RC 1.50 4.00
221 Jared Lorenzen RC 2.00 5.00
222 Jarrett Payton RC 2.00 5.00
223 Jason Babin RC 2.50 6.00
224 Jeff Smoker RC 2.00 5.00
225 Jerricho Cotchery RC 2.00 5.00
226 Jim Sorgi RC 2.00 5.00
227 John Navarre RC 1.50 4.00
228 Johnnie Morant RC 1.50 4.00
229 Jonathan Vilma RC 2.50 6.00
230 Josh Harris RC 1.50 4.00
231 Kenechi Udeze RC 2.00 5.00
232 Matt Mauck RC 1.50 4.00
233 Maurice Mann RC 1.50 4.00
234 Michael Turner RC 3.00 8.00
235 P.K. Sam RC 1.50 4.00
236 Quincy Wilson RC 2.00 5.00
237 Ran Carthon RC 1.50 4.00
238 Ricardo Colclough RC 2.00 5.00
239 Samie Parker RC 1.50 4.00
240 Sean Jones RC 2.00 5.00
241 Sean Taylor RC 5.00 12.00
242 Sloan Thomas RC 2.00 5.00
243 Tommie Harris RC 2.50 6.00
244 Triandos Luke RC 1.50 4.00
245 Troy Fleming RC 1.50 4.00
246 Vince Wilfork RC 2.50 6.00
247 Will Smith RC 2.00 5.00
248 Michael Boulware RC 2.50 6.00
249 Richard Smith RC 1.50 4.00
250 Teddy Lehman RC 1.50 4.00
251 Larry Fitzgerald JSY RC 8.00 20.00
252 DeAngelo Hall JSY RC 3.00 8.00
253 Matt Schaub JSY RC 6.00 15.00
254 Michael Jenkins JSY RC 3.00 8.00
255 Devard Darling JSY RC 2.00 5.00
256 J.P. Losman JSY RC 2.50 6.00
257 Lee Evans JSY RC 3.00 8.00
258 Keary Colbert JSY RC 2.00 5.00
259 Bernard Berrian JSY RC 3.00 8.00
260 Chris Perry JSY RC 2.50 6.00
261 Kellen Winslow Jr. JSY RC 3.00 8.00
262 Luke McCown JSY RC 2.50 6.00
263 Julius Jones JSY RC 2.50 6.00
264 Darius Watts JSY RC 2.00 5.00
265 Tatum Bell JSY RC 2.50 6.00
266 Kevin Jones JSY RC 2.50 6.00
267 Roy Williams JSY RC 3.00 8.00
268 Dunta Robinson JSY RC 2.00 5.00
269 Greg Jones JSY RC 2.00 5.00
270 Reggie Williams JSY RC 2.50 6.00
271 Mewelde Moore JSY RC 2.50 6.00
272 Ben Watson JSY RC 3.00 8.00
273 Cedric Cobbs JSY RC 2.00 5.00
274 Devery Henderson JSY RC 3.00 8.00
275 Eli Manning JSY RC 15.00 40.00
276 Robert Gallery JSY RC 3.00 8.00
277 Ben Roethlisberger JSY RC 15.00 40.00
278 Philip Rivers JSY RC 12.00 30.00
279 Derrick Hamilton JSY RC 2.00 5.00
280 Rashaun Woods JSY RC 2.00 5.00
281 Steven Jackson JSY RC 5.00 12.00
282 Michael Clayton JSY RC 2.50 6.00
283 Ben Troupe JSY RC 2.50 6.00
284 Eli Manning JSY 15.00 40.00
Philip Rivers JSY
285 Larry Fitzgerald JSY 8.00 20.00
Roy Williams WR JSY
286 Kellen Winslow Jr. JSY 3.00 8.00
Greg Jones JSY
287 DeAngelo Hall JSY 3.00 8.00
Dunta Robinson JSY
288 Reggie Williams JSY 2.50 6.00
Devard Darling JSY
289 Ben Roethlisberger JSY 15.00 40.00
J.P. Losman JSY
290 Michael Clayton JSY 3.00 8.00
Devery Henderson JSY
291 Steven Jackson JSY 5.00 12.00
Chris Perry JSY
292 Lee Evans JSY 3.00 8.00
Michael Jenkins JSY
293 Rashaun Woods JSY 2.50 6.00
Tatum Bell JSY
294 Kevin Jones JSY 3.00 8.00
Bernard Berrian JSY
295 Ben Watson JSY 3.00 8.00
Ben Troupe JSY
296 Julius Jones JSY 2.50 6.00
Mewelde Moore JSY
297 Matt Schaub JSY 6.00 15.00
Derrick Hamilton JSY
298 Luke McCown JSY 2.50 6.00
Darius Watts JSY
299 Keary Colbert JSY 2.00 5.00
Cedric Cobbs JSY

2004 Leaf Rookies and Stars Longevity Parallel

*VETS 1-100: 3X TO 8X BASIC CARDS
1-100 PRINT RUN 125
*ROOKIES 101-200: 2X TO 5X
101-200 STATED PRINT RUN 75
201-250 AU PRINT RUN 50
UNPRICED 251-283 AU PRINT RUN 10
*ROOKIES JSY 284-299: 1.2X TO 3X
284-299 JSY PRINT RUN 25
216 Derrick Ward AU 12.00 30.00
234 Michael Turner AU 30.00 80.00
241 Sean Taylor No Auto 6.00 15.00

2004 Leaf Rookies and Stars Longevity Holofoil Parallel

*VETS 1-100: 4X TO 10X BASE CARD HI
1-100 PRINT RUN 75 SER.#'d SETS
*ROOKIES 101-200: 2.5X TO 6X
101-200 PRINT RUN 25 SER.#'d SETS
UNPRICED 201-250 AU PRINT RUN 10 SETS
UNPRICED 251-283 JSY AU PRINT RUN 5
UNPRICED 284-299 JSY PRINT RUN 10 SETS

2004 Leaf Rookies and Stars Longevity True Blue Parallel

*VETS 1-100: 2X TO 5X BASE CARD HI
1-100 PRINT RUN 249 SER.#'d SETS
*ROOKIES 101-200: 2X TO 5X
101-200 PRINT RUN 75 SER.#'d SETS
*ROOKIES 201-250: 2.5X TO 6X
201-250 PRINT RUN 25 SER.#'d SETS

2004 Leaf Rookies and Stars Crusade Red

RED PRINT RUN 1250 SER.#'d SETS
*GREEN/750: .5X TO 1.2X RED/1250
GREEN PRINT RUN 750 SER.#'d SETS
*GREEN DC/25: 2X TO 5X RED/1250
GREEN DIE CUT PRINT RUN 25
*PURPLE/250: .6X TO 1.5X RED/1250
PURPLE PRINT RUN 250 SER.#'d SETS
*PRPL DC/50: 1.2X TO 3X RED/1250
PURPLE DIE CUT PRINT RUN 50
*RED DC/10: 3X TO 8X RED/1250
RED DC PRINT RUN 10 SETS
C1 Brett Favre 3.00 8.00
C2 Brian Urlacher 1.25 3.00
C3 Byron Leftwich 1.00 2.50
C4 Carson Palmer 1.25 3.00
C5 Chad Pennington 1.25 3.00
C6 Clinton Portis 1.25 3.00
C7 Daunte Culpepper 1.00 2.50
C8 David Carr .75 2.00
C9 Deuce McAllister 1.00 2.50
C10 Donovan McNabb 1.25 3.00
C11 Emmitt Smith 3.00 8.00
C12 Jamal Lewis 1.00 2.50
C13 Jeremy Shockey 1.00 2.50
C14 Jerry Rice 2.50 6.00
C15 Joe Namath 2.00 5.00
C16 Joey Harrington 1.00 2.50
C17 LaDainian Tomlinson 1.25 3.00
C18 LaVar Arrington 1.00 2.50
C19 Michael Vick 1.50 4.00
C20 Peyton Manning 2.50 6.00
C21 Priest Holmes 1.25 3.00
C22 Randy Moss 1.25 3.00
C23 Ricky Williams 1.00 2.50
C24 Steve McNair 1.25 3.00
C25 Tom Brady 2.50 6.00

2004 Leaf Rookies and Stars Fans of the Game

COMPLETE SET (6) 12.00 30.00
STATED ODDS 1:24 HOBBY
FG1 Tony Hawk 1.00 2.50
FG2 Michael Phelps 10.00 25.00
FG3 Damien Fahey .75 2.00
FG4 Jackie Mason .75 2.00
FG5 Bob Saget .75 2.00
FG6 Linda Cohn 1.00 2.50

2004 Leaf Rookies and Stars Fans of the Game Autographs

FG1 Tony Hawk SP 50.00 100.00
FG2 Michael Phelps SP 250.00 450.00
FG3 Damien Fahey 8.00 20.00
FG4 Jackie Mason 12.00 30.00
FG5 Bob Saget 12.00 30.00
FG6 Linda Cohn 12.00 30.00

2004 Leaf Rookies and Stars Freshman Orientation Jersey

STATED PRINT RUN 500 SER.#'d SETS
*CLASS OFFICERS/100: .6X TO 1.5X
CLASS OFFICERS PRINT RUN 100 SETS
FO1 Eli Manning 15.00 40.00
FO2 Robert Gallery 2.50 6.00
FO3 Larry Fitzgerald 6.00 15.00
FO4 Philip Rivers 10.00 25.00
FO5 Kellen Winslow Jr. 2.50 6.00
FO6 Roy Williams WR 2.50 6.00
FO7 DeAngelo Hall 2.50 6.00
FO8 Reggie Williams 2.00 5.00
FO9 Dunta Robinson 1.50 4.00
FO10 Ben Roethlisberger 12.00 30.00
FO11 Lee Evans 2.50 6.00
FO12 Michael Clayton 2.00 5.00
FO13 J.P. Losman 2.00 5.00
FO14 Steven Jackson 4.00 10.00
FO15 Chris Perry 2.00 5.00
FO16 Michael Jenkins 2.50 6.00
FO17 Kevin Jones 2.00 5.00
FO18 Rashaun Woods 1.50 4.00
FO19 Ben Watson 2.50 6.00
FO20 Ben Troupe 2.00 5.00
FO21 Tatum Bell 2.00 5.00
FO22 Julius Jones 2.00 5.00
FO23 Devery Henderson 2.50 6.00
FO24 Darius Watts 1.50 4.00
FO25 Greg Jones 1.50 4.00
FO26 Keary Colbert 1.50 4.00
FO27 Derrick Hamilton 1.50 4.00
FO28 Bernard Berrian 2.50 6.00
FO29 Devard Darling 1.50 4.00
FO30 Matt Schaub 5.00 12.00
FO31 Luke McCown 2.00 5.00
FO32 Mewelde Moore 2.00 5.00
FO33 Cedric Cobbs 1.50 4.00

2004 Leaf Rookies and Stars Great American Heroes Red

RED PRINT RUN 1250 SER.#'d SETS
*BLUE/250: .6X TO 1.5X RED/1250
BLUE PRINT RUN 250 SER.#'d SETS
*WHITE/750: .5X TO 1.2X RED/1250
WHITE PRINT RUN 750 SER.#'d SETS
GAH1 Anquan Boldin 1.25 3.00
GAH2 Chad Pennington 1.25 3.00
GAH3 Christian Okoye .75 2.00
GAH4 Dante Hall 1.00 2.50
GAH5 Derrick Mason 1.00 2.50
GAH6 Domanick Davis .75 2.00
GAH7 Hines Ward 1.25 3.00
GAH8 Joe Horn 1.00 2.50
GAH9 Joe Namath 2.00 5.00
GAH10 Laveranues Coles .75 2.00
GAH11 Matt Hasselbeck 1.00 2.50
GAH12 Patrick Ramsey 1.00 2.50
GAH13 Rex Grossman 1.00 2.50
GAH14 Rudi Johnson 1.00 2.50
GAH15 Sammy Baugh 1.25 3.00
GAH16 Steve Smith 1.25 3.00
GAH17 Terrell Suggs 1.00 2.50
GAH18 Todd Heap 1.00 2.50
GAH19 Tom Brady 2.50 6.00
GAH20 Adam Vinatieri 1.25 3.00
GAH21 Craig Krenzel .75 2.00
GAH22 DeAngelo Hall 1.00 2.50
GAH23 Matt Mauck .60 1.50
GAH24 Philip Rivers 4.00 10.00
GAH25 Tatum Bell .75 2.00

2004 Leaf Rookies and Stars Great American Heroes Autographs

STATED PRINT RUN 25-100
GAH1 Anquan Boldin/50 10.00 25.00
GAH2 Chad Pennington/25 15.00 40.00
GAH3 Christian Okoye/100 6.00 15.00
GAH4 Dante Hall/50 8.00 20.00
GAH5 Derrick Mason/50 8.00 20.00
GAH6 Domanick Davis/75 6.00 15.00
GAH7 Hines Ward/50 25.00 60.00
GAH8 Joe Horn/100 8.00 20.00
GAH9 Joe Namath/100 50.00 100.00
GAH10 Laveranues Coles/25 10.00 25.00
GAH11 Matt Hasselbeck/25 12.00 30.00
GAH12 Patrick Ramsey/25 12.00 30.00
GAH13 Rex Grossman/25 12.00 30.00
GAH14 Rudi Johnson/50 8.00 20.00
GAH16 Steve Smith/75 10.00 25.00
GAH19 Tom Brady/25 175.00 300.00
GAH20 Adam Vinatieri/75 30.00 60.00
GAH21 Craig Krenzel/25 12.00 30.00
GAH22 DeAngelo Hall/25 15.00 40.00
GAH23 Matt Mauck/25 10.00 25.00
GAH24 Philip Rivers/25 50.00 80.00

2004 Leaf Rookies and Stars Initial Steps Shoe

STATED PRINT RUN 100 SER.#'d SETS
IS1 Eli Manning 15.00 40.00
IS2 Robert Gallery 2.50 6.00
IS3 Larry Fitzgerald 6.00 15.00
IS4 Philip Rivers 10.00 25.00
IS5 Kellen Winslow Jr. 2.50 6.00
IS6 Roy Williams WR 2.50 6.00
IS7 DeAngelo Hall 2.50 6.00
IS8 Reggie Williams 2.00 5.00
IS9 Dunta Robinson 1.50 4.00
IS10 Ben Roethlisberger 12.00 30.00
IS11 Lee Evans 2.50 6.00
IS12 Michael Clayton 2.00 5.00
IS13 J.P. Losman 2.00 5.00
IS14 Steven Jackson 4.00 10.00
IS15 Chris Perry 2.00 5.00
IS16 Michael Jenkins 2.50 6.00
IS17 Kevin Jones 2.00 5.00
IS18 Rashaun Woods 1.50 4.00
IS19 Ben Watson 2.50 6.00
IS20 Ben Troupe 2.00 5.00
IS21 Tatum Bell 2.00 5.00
IS22 Julius Jones 2.00 5.00
IS23 Devery Henderson 2.50 6.00
IS24 Darius Watts 1.50 4.00
IS25 Greg Jones 1.50 4.00
IS26 Keary Colbert 1.50 4.00
IS27 Derrick Hamilton 1.50 4.00
IS28 Bernard Berrian 2.50 6.00
IS29 Devard Darling 1.50 4.00
IS30 Matt Schaub 5.00 12.00
IS31 Luke McCown 2.00 5.00
IS32 Mewelde Moore 2.00 5.00
IS33 Cedric Cobbs 1.50 4.00

2004 Leaf Rookies and Stars Masks

STATED PRINT RUN 325 SER.#'d SETS
M1 Eli Manning 15.00 40.00
M2 Robert Gallery 2.50 6.00
M3 Larry Fitzgerald 6.00 15.00
M4 Philip Rivers 10.00 25.00
M5 Kellen Winslow Jr. 2.50 6.00
M6 Roy Williams WR 2.50 6.00
M7 DeAngelo Hall 2.50 6.00
M8 Reggie Williams 2.00 5.00
M9 Dunta Robinson 1.50 4.00
M10 Ben Roethlisberger 12.00 30.00
M11 Lee Evans 2.50 6.00
M12 Michael Clayton 2.00 5.00
M13 J.P. Losman 2.00 5.00
M14 Steven Jackson 4.00 10.00
M15 Chris Perry 2.00 5.00
M16 Michael Jenkins 2.50 6.00
M17 Kevin Jones 2.00 5.00
M18 Rashaun Woods 1.50 4.00
M19 Ben Watson 2.50 6.00
M20 Ben Troupe 2.00 5.00
M21 Tatum Bell 2.00 5.00
M22 Julius Jones 2.00 5.00
M23 Devery Henderson 2.50 6.00
M24 Darius Watts 1.50 4.00
M25 Greg Jones 1.50 4.00
M26 Keary Colbert 1.50 4.00
M27 Derrick Hamilton 1.50 4.00
M28 Bernard Berrian 2.50 6.00
M29 Devard Darling 1.50 4.00
M30 Matt Schaub 5.00 12.00
M31 Luke McCown 2.00 5.00
M32 Mewelde Moore 2.00 5.00
M33 Cedric Cobbs 1.50 4.00

2004 Leaf Rookies and Stars Prime Cuts

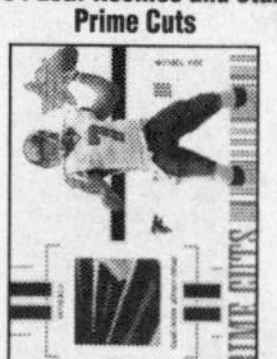

STATED PRINT RUN 25 SER.#'d SETS
PC1 Brett Favre 40.00 100.00
PC2 Brian Urlacher 15.00 40.00
PC3 Byron Leftwich 12.00 30.00
PC4 Chad Pennington 15.00 40.00
PC5 Daunte Culpepper 12.00 30.00
PC6 David Carr 10.00 25.00
PC7 Deuce McAllister 12.00 30.00
PC8 Donovan McNabb 15.00 40.00
PC9 Emmitt Smith 40.00 100.00
PC10 Jamal Lewis 12.00 30.00
PC11 Jeremy Shockey 12.00 30.00
PC12 Jerry Rice 30.00 80.00
PC13 Joe Namath 30.00 80.00
PC14 Joey Harrington 12.00 30.00
PC15 LaDainian Tomlinson 15.00 40.00
PC16 LaVar Arrington 15.00 40.00
PC17 Marc Bulger 12.00 30.00
PC18 Matt Hasselbeck 12.00 30.00
PC19 Michael Vick 20.00 50.00
PC20 Peyton Manning 30.00 80.00
PC21 Priest Holmes 15.00 40.00
PC22 Randy Moss 15.00 40.00
PC23 Ricky Williams 12.00 30.00
PC24 Steve McNair 15.00 40.00
PC25 Tom Brady 30.00 80.00

2004 Leaf Rookies and Stars Rookie Autographs

201-250 PRINT RUN 150 SER.#'d SETS
251-283 PRINT RUN 50 SER.#'d SETS
CARDS SER.#'d UNDER 20 NOT PRICED
201 Adimchinobe Echemandu 6.00 15.00
202 Ahmad Carroll 5.00 12.00
203 Andy Hall 5.00 12.00
204 B.J. Johnson 5.00 12.00
205 B.J. Symons 5.00 12.00
206 Brandon Miree 5.00 12.00
207 Bruce Perry 5.00 12.00
208 Carlos Francis 5.00 12.00
209 Casey Bramlet 5.00 12.00
210 Chris Gamble 6.00 15.00
211 Clarence Moore 5.00 12.00
212 Cody Pickett 6.00 15.00
213 Craig Krenzel 6.00 15.00
214 D.J. Hackett 6.00 15.00
215 D.J. Williams 8.00 20.00
216 Derrick Ward 8.00 20.00
217 Drew Carter 6.00 15.00
218 Drew Henson 5.00 12.00
219 Ernest Wilford 6.00 15.00
220 Jamaar Taylor 5.00 12.00
221 Jared Lorenzen 6.00 15.00
222 Jarrett Payton 6.00 15.00
223 Jason Babin 8.00 20.00
224 Jeff Smoker 6.00 15.00
225 Jerricho Cotchery 6.00 15.00
226 Jim Sorgi 6.00 15.00
227 John Navarre 5.00 12.00
228 Johnnie Morant 5.00 12.00
229 Jonathan Vilma 8.00 20.00
230 Josh Harris 5.00 12.00
231 Kenechi Udeze 6.00 15.00
232 Matt Mauck 5.00 12.00
233 Maurice Mann 5.00 12.00
234 Michael Turner 15.00 40.00
235 P.K. Sam 5.00 12.00
236 Quincy Wilson 6.00 15.00
237 Ran Carthon 5.00 12.00
238 Ricardo Colclough 6.00 15.00
239 Samie Parker 5.00 12.00
240 Sean Jones 6.00 15.00
241 Sean Taylor No Auto 4.00 10.00
242 Sloan Thomas 6.00 15.00
243 Tommie Harris 8.00 20.00
244 Triandos Luke 5.00 12.00
245 Troy Fleming 5.00 12.00
246 Vince Wilfork 8.00 20.00
247 Will Smith 6.00 15.00
248 Michael Boulware 8.00 20.00
249 Richard Smith 5.00 12.00
250 Teddy Lehman 5.00 12.00
252 DeAngelo Hall JSY 12.00 30.00
253 Matt Schaub JSY 25.00 60.00
254 Michael Jenkins JSY 12.00 30.00
255 Devard Darling JSY 8.00 20.00
256 J.P. Losman JSY 10.00 25.00
257 Lee Evans JSY 12.00 30.00
258 Keary Colbert JSY 8.00 20.00
259 Bernard Berrian JSY 12.00 30.00
260 Chris Perry JSY 10.00 25.00
261 Kellen Winslow JSY 12.00 30.00
262 Luke McCown JSY 10.00 25.00
263 Julius Jones JSY 10.00 25.00
264 Darius Watts JSY 8.00 20.00
265 Tatum Bell JSY 10.00 25.00
266 Kevin Jones JSY 10.00 25.00
267 Roy Williams WR JSY 12.00 30.00
268 Dunta Robinson JSY 8.00 20.00
269 Greg Jones JSY 8.00 20.00
270 Reggie Williams JSY 10.00 25.00
271 Mewelde Moore JSY 10.00 25.00
272 Ben Watson JSY 12.00 30.00
273 Cedric Cobbs JSY 8.00 20.00
274 Devery Henderson JSY 12.00 30.00
275 Eli Manning JSY 175.00 300.00
276 Robert Gallery JSY 12.00 30.00
277 Ben Roethlisberger JSY 125.00 250.00
278 Philip Rivers JSY 75.00 150.00
279 Derrick Hamilton JSY 8.00 20.00
280 Rashaun Woods JSY 8.00 20.00
281 Steven Jackson JSY 40.00 100.00
282 Michael Clayton JSY 10.00 25.00
283 Ben Troupe JSY 10.00 25.00

2004 Leaf Rookies and Stars Slideshow Bronze

BRONZE PRINT RUN 1250 SER.#'d SETS
*VIEW MASTER/250: .6X TO 1.5X BRNZ
VIEW MASTER PRINT RUN 250
*SILVER STUDIO/750: .5X TO 1.2X BRNZ
SILVER STUDIO PRINT RUN 750
SS1 Aaron Brooks 1.00 2.50
SS2 Ahman Green 1.00 2.50
SS3 Anquan Boldin 1.25 3.00
SS4 Chad Johnson 1.25 3.00
SS5 Chris Chambers 1.00 2.50
SS6 Drew Bledsoe 1.25 3.00
SS7 Edgerrin James 1.00 2.50
SS8 Jake Delhomme 1.00 2.50
SS9 Jake Plummer 1.00 2.50
SS10 Joe Namath 2.00 5.00
SS11 Kevan Barlow .75 2.00
SS12 Kyle Boller 1.00 2.50
SS13 LaVar Arrington 1.00 2.50
SS14 Marc Bulger 1.00 2.50
SS15 Marshall Faulk 1.25 3.00
SS16 Marvin Harrison 1.25 3.00
SS17 Matt Hasselbeck 1.00 2.50
SS18 Roy Williams S 1.00 2.50
SS19 Rudi Johnson 1.00 2.50

SS20 Shaun Alexander 1.00 2.50
SS21 Stephen Davis 1.00 2.50
SS22 Tom Brady 2.50 6.00
SS23 Travis Henry .75 2.00
SS24 Trent Green 1.00 2.50
SS25 Donovan McNabb 1.25 3.00

2004 Leaf Rookies and Stars Ticket Masters Bronze

BRONZE PRINT RUN 1250 SER.#'d SETS
*GOLD/250: .6X TO 1.5X BRONZE/1250
GOLD CHAMPIONSHIP PRINT RUN 250
*SILVER/750: .5X TO 1.2X BRONZE/1250
SILVER STATED PRINT RUN 750
TM1 Emmitt Smith 3.00 8.00
Anquan Boldin
TM2 Michael Vick 1.50 4.00
Michael Jenkins
TM3 Jamal Lewis 1.25 3.00
Ray Lewis
TM4 Drew Bledsoe 1.25 3.00
Travis Henry
TM5 Jake Delhomme 1.00 2.50
Julius Peppers
TM6 Brian Urlacher 1.25 3.00
Rex Grossman
TM7 Carson Palmer 1.25 3.00
Chad Johnson
TM8 Kellen Winslow Jr. 1.25 3.00
Jeff Garcia
TM9 Joey Harrington .75 2.00
Roy Williams WR
TM10 Brett Favre 3.00 8.00
Ahman Green
TM11 David Carr 1.25 3.00
Andre Johnson
TM12 Peyton Manning 2.50 6.00
Edgerrin James
TM13 Byron Leftwich 1.00 2.50
Fred Taylor
TM14 Priest Holmes 1.25 3.00
Trent Green
TM15 Ricky Williams 1.00 2.50
Chris Chambers
TM16 Daunte Culpepper 1.25 3.00
Randy Moss
TM17 Tom Brady 2.50 6.00
Corey Dillon
TM18 Eli Manning 5.00 12.00
Jeremy Shockey
TM19 Chad Pennington 1.25 3.00
Curtis Martin
TM20 Jerry Rice 2.50 6.00
Tim Brown
TM21 Donovan McNabb 1.25 3.00
Terrell Owens
TM22 Ben Roethlisberger 5.00 12.00
Hines Ward
TM23 Philip Rivers 3.00 8.00
LaDainian Tomlinson
TM24 Marc Bulger 1.25 3.00
Marshall Faulk
TM25 Clinton Portis 1.25 3.00
LaVar Arrington

2004 Leaf Rookies and Stars Triple Threads

STATED PRINT RUN 100 SER.#'d SETS
1 Anquan Boldin 10.00 25.00
Josh McCown
Larry Fitzgerald
2 Michael Vick 10.00 25.00
Warrick Dunn
Peerless Price
3 Jamal Lewis 8.00 20.00
Kyle Boller
Ray Lewis
4 Drew Bledsoe 8.00 20.00
Eric Moulds
Travis Henry
5 Jake Delhomme 8.00 20.00
Stephen Davis
Steve Smith
6 Brian Urlacher 8.00 20.00
Rex Grossman
Anthony Thomas
7 Chad Johnson 8.00 20.00
Rudi Johnson
Peter Warrick
8 Darren Woodson 10.00 25.00
Roy Williams
Terence Newman
9 Jake Plummer 8.00 20.00
Rod Smith
Shannon Sharpe
10 Brett Favre 25.00 50.00
Ahman Green
Javon Walker
11 Patrick Ramsey 10.00 25.00
Laveranues Coles
LaVar Arrington
12 Peyton Manning 15.00 40.00
Edgerrin James
Marvin Harrison
13 Byron Leftwich 6.00 15.00
Fred Taylor
Jimmy Smith
14 Trent Green 8.00 20.00
Priest Holmes
Dante Hall
15 Ricky Williams 8.00 20.00
Chris Chambers
Zach Thomas
16 Daunte Culpepper 8.00 20.00
Michael Bennett
Randy Moss
17 Tom Brady 15.00 40.00
Bethel Johnson
Ty Law
18 Aaron Brooks 6.00 15.00
Deuce McAllister
Donte Stallworth
19 Tiki Barber 8.00 20.00
Jeremy Shockey
Amani Toomer
20 Chad Pennington 8.00 20.00
Curtis Martin
Santana Moss
21 Jerry Rice 15.00 40.00
Rich Gannon
Tim Brown
22 Jerome Bettis 8.00 20.00
Hines Ward
Plaxico Burress
23 Matt Hasselbeck 6.00 15.00
Shaun Alexander
Koren Robinson
24 Marc Bulger 8.00 20.00
Marshall Faulk
Isaac Bruce
25 Steve McNair 8.00 20.00
Chris Brown
Derrick Mason
26 David Carr 8.00 20.00
Domanick Davis
Andre Johnson

2004 Leaf Rookies and Stars Longevity

COMP.SET w/o RCs (100) 10.00 25.00
*VETS 1-100: .6X TO 1.5X BASIC CARDS
*ROOKIES 101-200: .5X TO 1.2X
101-200 RC PRINT RUN 999
*ROOKIES 201-250: .5X TO 1.2X
201-250 RC STATED PRINT RUN 499
*ROOKIES 251-283: .5X TO 1.2X
251-283 JSY RC PRINT RUN 299

2004 Leaf Rookies and Stars Longevity Black

*VETS 1-100: 3X TO 8X BASIC CARDS
1-100 PRINT RUN 75 SER.#'d SETS
*ROOKIES 101-200: 1.5X TO 4X BASIC CARDS
101-200 PRINT RUN 50 SER.#'d SETS
*ROOKIES 201-250: 1.5X TO 4X BASIC CARDS
201-250 PRINT RUN 25 SER.#'d SETS
251-283 UNPRICED JSY PRINT RUN 10 SETS

2004 Leaf Rookies and Stars Longevity Emerald

*VETS 1-100: 2.5X TO 6X BASIC CARDS
1-100 PRINT RUN 99 SER.#'d SETS
*ROOKIES 101-200: 1.2X TO 3X BASIC CARDS
101-200 PRINT RUN 75 SER.#'d SETS
*ROOKIES 201-250: 1X TO 2.5X BASIC CARDS
201-250 PRINT RUN 50 SER.#'d SETS
*ROOKIES 251-283: 1.2X TO 3X BASIC CARDS
251-283 JSY PRINT RUN 25 SER.#'d SETS

2004 Leaf Rookies and Stars Longevity Gold

*VETS 1-100: 1.5X TO 4X BASIC CARDS
1-100 STATED PRINT RUN 150
*ROOKIES*101-200: 1X TO 2.5X BASIC CARDS
101-200 STATED PRINT RUN 99
*ROOKIES 201-250: .8X TO 2X BASIC CARDS
201-250 STATED PRINT RUN 75
*ROOKIES 251-283: .6X TO 1.5X BASIC JSY
251-283 JSY PRINT RUN 50

2004 Leaf Rookies and Stars Longevity Ruby

*VETS 1-100: 1X TO 2.5X BASIC CARDS
1-100 STATED PRINT RUN 250
*ROOKIES 101-200: .6X TO 1.5X BASIC CARDS
101-200 STATED PRINT RUN 199
*ROOKIES 201-250: .5X TO 1.2X BASIC CARDS
201-250 STATED PRINT RUN 150
*ROOKIES 251-283: .5X TO 1.2X BASIC JSY
251-283 JSY PRINT RUN 100

2004 Leaf Rookies and Stars Longevity Sapphire

*VETS 1-100: 1.2X TO 3X BASIC CARDS
1-100 STATED PRINT RUN 199
*ROOKIES 101-200: .8X TO 2X BASIC CARDS
101-200 STATED PRINT RUN 150
*ROOKIES 201-250: .6X TO 1.5X BASIC CARDS
201-250 STATED PRINT RUN 99
*ROOKIES 251-283: .5X TO 1.2X BASIC JSY
251-283 JSY PRINT RUN 75

2004 Leaf Rookies and Stars Longevity Draft Class of 2001 Autographs

STATED ODDS 1:233
301 Michael Vick 35.00 60.00
302 Drew Brees 50.00 100.00
304 Marques Tuiasosopo 7.50 20.00
305 Chris Weinke 7.50 20.00
307 Deuce McAllister 50.00 100.00
309 Anthony Thomas 6.00 15.00
311 David Terrell 7.50 20.00
312 Koren Robinson 7.50 20.00
314 Santana Moss 7.50 20.00
315 Freddie Mitchell 7.50 20.00
316 Gerard Warren 7.50 20.00
317 Justin Smith 7.50 20.00
320 Jamal Reynolds 6.00 15.00

2004 Leaf Rookies and Stars Longevity Materials Black

COMMON CARD/20-25 8.00 20.00
SEMISTARS/20-25 10.00 25.00
UNL.STARS/20-25 12.00 30.00
BLACK SER.#'d TO 5 OR 10 NOT PRICED

2004 Leaf Rookies and Stars Longevity Materials Emerald

1 Anquan Boldin/35 10.00 25.00
2 Emmitt Smith/50 20.00 50.00
3 Josh McCown/35 8.00 20.00
4 Michael Vick/50 10.00 25.00
5 Peerless Price/25 8.00 20.00
6 T.J. Duckett/35 8.00 20.00
7 Warrick Dunn/35 8.00 20.00
8 Jamal Lewis/25 10.00 25.00
9 Kyle Boller/50 8.00 20.00
10 Ray Lewis/25 12.00 30.00
11 Drew Bledsoe/25 12.00 30.00
12 Eric Moulds/35 8.00 20.00
13 Travis Henry/35 6.00 15.00
14 Jake Delhomme/35 8.00 20.00
15 Stephen Davis/35 8.00 20.00
16 Steve Smith/35 10.00 25.00
17 Brian Urlacher/35 10.00 25.00
18 Rex Grossman/35 8.00 20.00
19 Thomas Jones/35 10.00 25.00
20 Carson Palmer/25 12.00 30.00
21 Chad Johnson/35 10.00 25.00
22 Rudi Johnson/35 8.00 20.00
23 Jeff Garcia/35 8.00 20.00
24 William Green/25 8.00 20.00
25 Keyshawn Johnson/35 8.00 20.00
26 Terence Newman/25 10.00 25.00
27 Roy Williams S/35 8.00 20.00
28 Jake Plummer/35 8.00 20.00
29 Quentin Griffin/25 8.00 20.00
30 Rod Smith/25 10.00 25.00
31 Charles Rogers/35 6.00 15.00
32 Joey Harrington/35 8.00 20.00
33 Ahman Green/35 10.00 25.00
34 Brett Favre/50 20.00 50.00
35 Javon Walker/35 6.00 15.00
36 Andre Johnson/35 10.00 25.00
37 David Carr/25 8.00 20.00
38 Domanick Davis/35 6.00 15.00
39 Edgerrin James/35 8.00 20.00
40 Marvin Harrison/35 10.00 25.00
41 Peyton Manning/50 15.00 40.00
43 Fred Taylor/35 8.00 20.00
44 Jimmy Smith/25 10.00 25.00
45 Priest Holmes/40 10.00 25.00
46 Tony Gonzalez/35 10.00 25.00
47 Trent Green/35 8.00 20.00
49 Chris Chambers/35 8.00 20.00
51 Daunte Culpepper/40 8.00 20.00
52 Michael Bennett/35 8.00 20.00
53 Randy Moss/40 10.00 25.00
54 Corey Dillon/40 10.00 25.00
56 Tom Brady/50 15.00 40.00
57 Aaron Brooks/35 8.00 20.00
58 Deuce McAllister/35 8.00 20.00
60 Jeremy Shockey/35 8.00 20.00
61 Michael Strahan/35 10.00 25.00
62 Tiki Barber/35 10.00 25.00
63 Chad Pennington/35 10.00 25.00
64 Curtis Martin/35 10.00 25.00
65 Santana Moss/35 8.00 20.00
66 Jerry Porter/35 6.00 15.00
67 Jerry Rice/50 15.00 40.00
69 Donovan McNabb/50 8.00 20.00
70 Jevon Kearse/25 10.00 25.00
71 Terrell Owens/35 10.00 25.00
72 Duce Staley/25 10.00 25.00
73 Hines Ward/35 10.00 25.00
74 Jerome Bettis/35 10.00 25.00
75 LaDainian Tomlinson/40 10.00 25.00
78 Koren Robinson/35 6.00 15.00
79 Matt Hasselbeck/35 8.00 20.00
80 Shaun Alexander/35 8.00 20.00
81 Isaac Bruce/25 10.00 25.00
82 Marc Bulger/35 8.00 20.00
83 Marshall Faulk/35 10.00 25.00
84 Torry Holt/35 8.00 20.00
85 Brad Johnson/25 10.00 25.00
87 Chris Brown/35 6.00 15.00
88 Derrick Mason/25 10.00 25.00
89 Eddie George/35 8.00 20.00
90 Steve McNair/35 10.00 25.00
91 Clinton Portis/35 10.00 25.00
92 LaVar Arrington/35 8.00 20.00
93 Laveranues Coles/25 8.00 20.00

2004 Leaf Rookies and Stars Longevity Materials Gold

1 Anquan Boldin/75 8.00 20.00
4 Michael Vick/75 10.00 25.00
6 T.J. Duckett/75 6.00 15.00
8 Jamal Lewis/75 6.00 15.00
9 Kyle Boller/65 6.00 15.00
10 Ray Lewis/50 8.00 20.00
11 Drew Bledsoe/75 6.00 15.00
13 Travis Henry/75 5.00 12.00
14 Jake Delhomme/50 6.00 15.00
16 Steve Smith/75 8.00 20.00
17 Brian Urlacher/75 8.00 20.00
18 Rex Grossman/75 6.00 15.00
19 Thomas Jones/75 6.00 15.00
21 Chad Johnson/50 8.00 20.00
23 Jeff Garcia/50 6.00 15.00
24 William Green/75 5.00 12.00
25 Keyshawn Johnson/50 6.00 15.00
26 Terence Newman/75 6.00 15.00
28 Jake Plummer/50 6.00 15.00
29 Quentin Griffin/50 5.00 12.00
32 Joey Harrington/50 6.00 15.00
36 Andre Johnson/50 8.00 20.00
37 David Carr/75 6.00 15.00
38 Domanick Davis/75 5.00 12.00
40 Marvin Harrison/75 8.00 20.00
42 Byron Leftwich/75 8.00 20.00
43 Fred Taylor/25 8.00 20.00
46 Tony Gonzalez/75 6.00 15.00
48 A.J. Feeley/50 5.00 12.00
50 Deion Sanders/50 8.00 20.00
53 Randy Moss/50 8.00 20.00
54 Corey Dillon/75 6.00 15.00
57 Aaron Brooks/75 6.00 15.00
58 Deuce McAllister/50 8.00 20.00
59 Joe Horn/25 8.00 20.00
60 Jeremy Shockey/75 6.00 15.00
61 Michael Strahan/75 6.00 15.00
62 Tiki Barber/75 8.00 20.00
63 Chad Pennington/75 6.00 15.00
64 Curtis Martin/75 8.00 20.00
65 Santana Moss/75 5.00 12.00
66 Jerry Porter/75 5.00 12.00
67 Jerry Rice/75 15.00 40.00
68 Warren Sapp/75 6.00 15.00
69 Donovan McNabb/75 8.00 20.00
70 Jevon Kearse/75 6.00 15.00
72 Duce Staley/60 6.00 15.00
73 Hines Ward/75 8.00 20.00
78 Koren Robinson/75 5.00 12.00
79 Matt Hasselbeck/75 6.00 15.00
81 Isaac Bruce/75 6.00 15.00
82 Marc Bulger/75 6.00 15.00
83 Marshall Faulk/75 8.00 20.00
84 Torry Holt/50 8.00 20.00
85 Brad Johnson/50 6.00 15.00
88 Derrick Mason/50 6.00 15.00
89 Eddie George/50 6.00 15.00
93 Laveranues Coles/50 5.00 12.00
94 Mark Brunell/50 6.00 15.00

2004 Leaf Rookies and Stars Longevity Materials Ruby

4 Michael Vick/150 6.00 15.00
6 T.J. Duckett/125 4.00 10.00
11 Drew Bledsoe/150 5.00 12.00
14 Jake Delhomme/150 4.00 10.00
15 Stephen Davis/99 4.00 10.00
16 Steve Smith/150 5.00 12.00
18 Rex Grossman/150 4.00 10.00
19 Thomas Jones/150 4.00 10.00
20 Carson Palmer/99 5.00 12.00
23 Jeff Garcia/99 4.00 10.00
24 William Green/125 3.00 8.00
26 Terence Newman/125 4.00 10.00
29 Quentin Griffin/99 3.00 8.00
32 Joey Harrington/99 4.00 10.00
36 Andre Johnson/99 5.00 12.00
37 David Carr/150 4.00 10.00
38 Domanick Davis/150 3.00 8.00
40 Marvin Harrison/150 5.00 12.00
42 Byron Leftwich/150 5.00 12.00
43 Fred Taylor/135 4.00 10.00
44 Jimmy Smith/99 4.00 10.00
46 Tony Gonzalez/150 4.00 10.00
48 A.J. Feeley/99 3.00 8.00
50 Deion Sanders/150 5.00 12.00
52 Michael Bennett/99 4.00 10.00
53 Randy Moss/125 5.00 12.00
54 Corey Dillon/99 4.00 10.00
57 Aaron Brooks/150 4.00 10.00
58 Deuce McAllister/99 4.00 10.00
60 Jeremy Shockey/125 4.00 10.00
61 Michael Strahan/125 5.00 12.00
62 Tiki Barber/125 5.00 12.00
63 Chad Pennington/150 5.00 12.00
64 Curtis Martin/125 5.00 12.00
66 Jerry Porter/150 3.00 8.00
67 Jerry Rice/150 10.00 25.00
68 Warren Sapp/125 4.00 10.00
69 Donovan McNabb/150 5.00 12.00
70 Jevon Kearse/150 4.00 10.00
72 Duce Staley/99 4.00 10.00
73 Hines Ward/150 5.00 12.00
74 Jerome Bettis/150 6.00 15.00
75 LaDainian Tomlinson/150 6.00 15.00
78 Koren Robinson/150 3.00 8.00
79 Matt Hasselbeck/150 4.00 10.00
80 Shaun Alexander/50 5.00 12.00
81 Isaac Bruce/75 5.00 12.00
82 Marc Bulger/150 4.00 10.00
85 Brad Johnson/99 4.00 10.00
87 Chris Brown/80 4.00 10.00
88 Derrick Mason/99 4.00 10.00
90 Steve McNair/150 5.00 12.00
92 LaVar Arrington/99 4.00 10.00
93 Laveranues Coles/125 3.00 8.00
94 Mark Brunell/125 4.00 10.00

2004 Leaf Rookies and Stars Longevity Materials Sapphire

1 Anquan Boldin/99 6.00 15.00
3 Josh McCown/84 5.00 12.00
4 Michael Vick/99 8.00 20.00
6 T.J. Duckett/99 5.00 12.00
8 Jamal Lewis/75 6.00 15.00
9 Kyle Boller/99 5.00 12.00
11 Drew Bledsoe/99 6.00 15.00
13 Travis Henry/99 4.00 10.00
14 Jake Delhomme/75 6.00 15.00
16 Steve Smith/99 6.00 15.00
17 Brian Urlacher/99 6.00 15.00
18 Rex Grossman/99 5.00 12.00
19 Thomas Jones/99 6.00 15.00
24 William Green/99 4.00 10.00
25 Keyshawn Johnson/50 6.00 15.00
26 Terence Newman/99 5.00 12.00
27 Roy Williams S/50 6.00 15.00
28 Jake Plummer/50 6.00 15.00
29 Quentin Griffin/75 5.00 12.00
36 Andre Johnson/75 8.00 20.00
37 David Carr/99 4.00 10.00
38 Domanick Davis/99 4.00 10.00
40 Marvin Harrison/99 6.00 15.00
41 Peyton Manning/50 15.00 40.00
42 Byron Leftwich/99 5.00 12.00
44 Jimmy Smith/50 6.00 15.00
46 Tony Gonzalez/99 5.00 12.00
48 A.J. Feeley/75 5.00 12.00
50 Deion Sanders/99 6.00 15.00
51 Daunte Culpepper/50 6.00 15.00
52 Michael Bennett/50 6.00 15.00
53 Randy Moss/75 8.00 20.00
54 Corey Dillon/99 6.00 15.00
56 Tom Brady/75 15.00 40.00
57 Aaron Brooks/99 5.00 12.00
58 Deuce McAllister/75 6.00 15.00
60 Jeremy Shockey/99 5.00 12.00
61 Michael Strahan/99 6.00 15.00
62 Tiki Barber/90 6.00 15.00
63 Chad Pennington/99 6.00 15.00
64 Curtis Martin/99 6.00 15.00
65 Santana Moss/50 10.00 25.00
66 Jerry Porter/99 4.00 10.00
67 Jerry Rice/99 12.00 30.00
68 Warren Sapp/99 6.00 15.00
69 Donovan McNabb/99 6.00 15.00
70 Jevon Kearse/99 5.00 12.00
72 Duce Staley/75 6.00 15.00
73 Hines Ward/99 6.00 15.00
78 Koren Robinson/99 4.00 10.00
79 Matt Hasselbeck/99 6.00 15.00
81 Isaac Bruce/50 6.00 15.00
82 Marc Bulger/99 5.00 12.00
85 Brad Johnson/75 5.00 12.00
89 Eddie George/50 6.00 15.00
91 Clinton Portis/50 8.00 20.00
92 LaVar Arrington/50 8.00 20.00
93 Laveranues Coles/75 5.00 12.00
94 Mark Brunell/75 5.00 12.00

2005 Leaf Rookies and Stars

This 293-card set was released in December, 2005. The set was issued in six-card packs with an $4 SRP which came 24 packs to a box. The set begins with veterans in alphabetical order by team (Cards 1-96); Checklists (97-100); Rookies (101-250); Rookies with a player-worn jersey piece (251-279) and concludes with multi-player rookie jersey cards (280-293). Cards numbered 201 through 250 were issued to a stated print run of 799 serial numbered sets, while cards numbered 251-279 were issued to a stated print run of 750 serial numbered sets and cards numbered 280-293 were issued to a stated print run of 500 serial numbered sets.

COMP.SET w/o RC's (100) 7.50 20.00
201-250 RC PRINT RUN 799 SER.#'d SETS
251-279 JSY PRINT RUN 750 SER.#'d SETS
280-293 JSY DUAL PRINT RUN 500 SER.#'d SETS
1 Anquan Boldin .25 .60
2 Kurt Warner .30 .75
3 Larry Fitzgerald .30 .75
4 Michael Vick .30 .75
5 T.J. Duckett .20 .50
6 Warrick Dunn .25 .60
7 Jamal Lewis .25 .60
8 Kyle Boller .25 .60
9 Ray Lewis .30 .75
10 Derrick Mason .25 .60
11 J.P. Losman .25 .60
12 Lee Evans .25 .60
13 Willis McGahee .30 .75
14 DeShaun Foster .25 .60
15 Jake Delhomme .25 .60
16 Steve Smith .30 .75
17 Brian Urlacher .30 .75
18 Rex Grossman .25 .60
19 Muhsin Muhammad .25 .60
20 Carson Palmer .30 .75
21 Chad Johnson .25 .60
22 Rudi Johnson .25 .60
23 Lee Suggs .20 .50
24 Drew Bledsoe .30 .75
25 Julius Jones .20 .50
26 Keyshawn Johnson .25 .60
27 Roy Williams S .25 .60
28 Ashley Lelie .20 .50
29 Jake Plummer .25 .60
30 Rod Smith .25 .60
31 Tatum Bell .20 .50
32 Joey Harrington .20 .50
33 Kevin Jones .20 .50
34 Roy Williams WR .25 .60
35 Ahman Green .25 .60
36 Brett Favre .75 2.00
37 Javon Walker .20 .50
38 Andre Johnson .30 .75
39 David Carr .30 .75
40 Domanick Davis .20 .50
41 Edgerrin James .25 .60
42 Marvin Harrison .25 .60
43 Peyton Manning .60 1.50
44 Reggie Wayne .30 .75
45 Byron Leftwich .25 .60
46 Fred Taylor .25 .60
47 Jimmy Smith .25 .60
48 Priest Holmes .25 .60
49 Tony Gonzalez .25 .60
50 Trent Green .25 .60
51 Chris Chambers .25 .60
52 Daunte Culpepper .25 .60
53 Michael Bennett .20 .50
54 Nate Burleson .20 .50
55 Corey Dillon .20 .50
56 Deion Branch .20 .50
57 Tom Brady .60 1.50
58 Aaron Brooks .20 .50
59 Deuce McAllister .25 .60
60 Joe Horn .25 .60
61 Eli Manning .50 1.25
62 Jeremy Shockey .30 .75
63 Tiki Barber .30 .75
64 Plaxico Burress .25 .60
65 Chad Pennington .25 .60
66 Curtis Martin .30 .75
67 Laveranues Coles .20 .50
68 Jerry Porter .20 .50
69 Kerry Collins .25 .60
70 LaMont Jordan .25 .60
71 Randy Moss .30 .75
72 Brian Westbrook .30 .75
73 Donovan McNabb .30 .75
74 Terrell Owens .30 .75
75 Ben Roethlisberger .50 1.25
76 Duce Staley .25 .60
77 Hines Ward .30 .75
78 Jerome Bettis .30 .75
79 Antonio Gates .30 .75
80 Drew Brees .30 .75
81 LaDainian Tomlinson .30 .75
82 Kevan Barlow .20 .50
83 Darrell Jackson .20 .50
84 Matt Hasselbeck .20 .50
85 Shaun Alexander .25 .60
86 Marc Bulger .25 .60
87 Steven Jackson .30 .75
88 Torry Holt .25 .60
89 Brian Griese .20 .50
90 Michael Clayton .20 .50
91 Chris Brown .20 .50
92 Drew Bennett .25 .60
93 Steve McNair .30 .75
94 Clinton Portis .25 .60
95 LaVar Arrington .25 .60
96 Santana Moss .25 .60
97 Alex Smith QB CL .50 1.25
Frank Gore
98 Braylon Edwards CL .40 1.00
Charlie Frye
99 Ciatrick Fason CL .25 .60
Troy Williamson
100 Carlos Rogers CL .40 1.00
Jason Campbell
101 Travis Johnson RC 1.00 2.50
102 Alex Smith TE RC 1.00 2.50
103 Channing Crowder RC 1.25 3.00
104 Craig Bragg RC 1.00 2.50
105 Darrent Williams RC 1.25 3.00
106 Derrick Wimbush RC 1.25 3.00
107 Josh Cribbs RC 5.00 12.00
108 Luis Castillo RC 1.25 3.00
109 Matt Roth RC 1.25 3.00
110 Mike Patterson RC 1.00 2.50
111 Fred Gibson RC 1.25 3.00
112 Marcus Spears RC 1.25 3.00
113 Brodney Pool RC 1.50 4.00
114 Barrett Ruud RC 1.50 4.00
115 Stanford Routt RC 1.25 3.00
116 Josh Bullocks RC 1.25 3.00
117 Kevin Burnett RC 1.25 3.00
118 Corey Webster RC 1.25 3.00
119 Lofa Tatupu RC 1.50 4.00
120 Mike Nugent RC 1.25 3.00
121 Jim Leonhard RC 1.25 3.00
122 Ronald Bartell RC 1.25 3.00
123 Nick Collins RC 1.50 4.00
124 Justin Miller RC 1.25 3.00
125 Jonathan Babineaux RC 1.25 3.00
126 Kelvin Hayden RC 1.25 3.00
127 Matt McCoy RC 1.25 3.00
128 Oshiomogho Atogwe RC 1.50 4.00
129 Stanley Wilson RC 1.25 3.00
130 Justin Tuck RC 2.00 5.00
131 Eric Green RC 1.25 3.00
132 Karl Paymah RC 1.25 3.00
133 Kirk Morrison RC 1.50 4.00
134 Dustin Fox RC 1.50 4.00
135 Alfred Fincher RC 1.25 3.00
136 Chris Henry RC 1.50 4.00
137 Ellis Hobbs RC 1.50 4.00
138 Scott Starks RC 1.25 3.00
139 Jordan Beck RC 1.25 3.00
140 Vincent Burns RC 1.25 3.00
141 Darryl Blackstock RC 1.25 3.00
142 Domonique Foxworth RC 1.25 3.00
143 Leroy Hill RC 1.25 3.00
144 Cedric Killings RC 1.00 2.50
145 Leonard Weaver RC 1.50 4.00
146 Sean Considine RC 1.00 2.50
147 Antonio Perkins RC 1.00 2.50
148 Travis Daniels RC 1.25 3.00
149 Vincent Fuller RC 1.25 3.00
150 Manuel White RC 1.25 3.00
151 Kerry Rhodes RC 1.50 4.00
152 Brady Poppinga RC 1.50 4.00
153 Chris Canty RC 1.50 4.00
154 James Sanders RC 1.25 3.00
155 Matt Giordano RC 1.25 3.00
156 Boomer Grigsby RC 1.50 4.00
157 Donte Nicholson RC 1.00 2.50
158 Jerome Collins RC 1.25 3.00
159 Trent Cole RC 1.50 4.00
160 Alphonso Hodge RC 1.00 2.50
161 Jonathan Welsh RC 1.00 2.50
162 Adam Seward RC 1.25 3.00
163 Robert McCune RC 1.25 3.00
164 Eric King RC 1.00 2.50
165 Gerald Sensabaugh RC 1.50 4.00
166 Justin Green RC 1.50 4.00
167 Jeb Huckeba RC 1.25 3.00
168 Michael Boley RC 1.50 4.00
169 Andre Maddox RC 1.00 2.50
170 Rian Wallace RC 1.00 2.50
171 Michael Hawkins RC 1.00 2.50
172 Lance Mitchell RC 1.25 3.00
173 Ryan Claridge RC 1.00 2.50
174 James Butler RC 1.25 3.00
175 Ryan Riddle RC 1.00 2.50
176 Bo Scaife RC 1.25 3.00
177 Chris Harris RC 1.25 3.00
178 C.C. Brown RC 1.00 2.50
179 Pat Thomas RC 1.00 2.50
180 Derrick Johnson CB RC 1.00 2.50
181 Joel Dreessen RC 1.25 3.00
182 Rick Razzano RC 1.00 2.50
183 Nehemiah Broughton RC 1.25 3.00
184 Marcus Maxwell RC 1.00 2.50
185 Harry Williams RC 1.00 2.50
186 Patrick Estes RC 1.00 2.50
187 Billy Bajema RC 1.00 2.50
188 Madison Hedgecock RC 1.50 4.00
189 Manuel Wright RC 1.25 3.00
190 Roscoe Crosby RC 1.00 2.50
191 Wesley Duke RC 1.25 3.00
192 Ronnie Cruz RC 1.00 2.50
193 Adam Bergen RC 1.00 2.50
194 B.J. Ward RC 1.00 2.50
195 Stephen Spach RC 1.00 2.50
196 Marviel Underwood RC 1.25 3.00
197 John Bronson RC 1.00 2.50
198 Zak Keasey RC 1.25 3.00
199 Gregg Guenther RC 1.25 3.00
200 Jerome Carter RC 1.00 2.50
201 Aaron Rodgers RC 30.00 60.00
202 Adrian McPherson RC 1.25 3.00
203 Alvin Pearman RC 1.25 3.00
204 Airese Currie RC 1.25 3.00
205 Anthony Davis RC 1.25 3.00
206 Brandon Jacobs RC 2.50 6.00
207 Brandon Jones RC 1.50 4.00
208 Bryant McFadden RC 1.50 4.00
209 Cedric Benson RC 2.00 5.00
210 Cedric Houston RC 2.00 5.00
211 Chad Owens RC 1.50 4.00
212 Chris Henry 2.00 5.00
213 Craphonso Thorpe RC 1.25 3.00
214 Damien Nash RC 1.50 4.00
215 Dan Cody RC 1.50 4.00
216 Dan Orlovsky RC 2.00 5.00
217 Dante Ridgeway RC 1.25 3.00
218 Darren Sproles RC 2.00 5.00
219 David Greene RC 1.25 3.00
220 David Pollack RC 1.25 3.00
221 Deandra Cobb RC 1.25 3.00
222 DeMarcus Ware RC 4.00 10.00
223 Derek Anderson RC 1.50 4.00
224 Derrick Johnson RC 1.50 4.00
225 Fabian Washington RC 1.50 4.00
226 Roydell Williams RC 1.50 4.00
227 Heath Miller RC 2.50 6.00
228 J.R. Russell RC 1.25 3.00
229 James Kilian RC 1.25 3.00
230 Jerome Mathis RC 2.00 5.00
231 Larry Brackins RC 1.25 3.00
232 LeRon McCoy RC 1.25 3.00
233 Lionel Gates RC 1.25 3.00
234 Marion Barber RC 2.00 5.00
235 Marlin Jackson RC 1.25 3.00
236 Matt Cassel RC 4.00 10.00
237 Mike Williams 2.00 5.00
238 Nate Washington RC 2.00 5.00
239 Noah Herron RC 1.25 3.00
240 Fred Amey RC 1.50 4.00
241 Paris Warren RC 1.50 4.00
242 Rasheed Marshall RC 1.50 4.00
243 Ryan Fitzpatrick RC 3.00 8.00
244 Shaun Cody RC 1.50 4.00
245 Shawne Merriman RC 2.00 5.00
246 Tab Perry RC 1.25 3.00
247 Thomas Davis RC 1.50 4.00
248 Tyson Thompson RC 2.00 5.00
249 Chris Carr RC 1.50 4.00
250 Odell Thurman RC 2.00 5.00
251 Adam Jones JSY RC 2.00 5.00
252 Alex Smith QB JSY RC 4.00 10.00
253 Andrew Walter JSY RC 2.00 5.00
254 Antrel Rolle JSY RC 2.50 6.00
255 Braylon Edwards JSY RC 3.00 8.00
256 Carlos Rogers JSY RC 2.50 6.00
257 Cadillac Williams JSY RC 2.50 6.00
258 Charlie Frye JSY RC 2.50 6.00
259 Ciatrick Fason JSY RC 1.50 4.00
260 Courtney Roby JSY RC 1.50 4.00
261 Eric Shelton JSY RC 1.50 4.00
262 Frank Gore JSY RC 4.00 10.00
263 J.J. Arrington JSY RC 2.00 5.00
264 Jason Campbell JSY RC 3.00 8.00
265 Kyle Orton JSY RC 2.50 6.00
266 Mark Clayton JSY RC 2.00 5.00
267 Mark Bradley JSY RC 1.50 4.00
268 Matt Jones JSY RC 2.00 5.00
269 Maurice Clarett JSY 2.00 5.00
270 Reggie Brown JSY RC 1.50 4.00
271 Roddy White JSY RC 3.00 8.00
272 Ronnie Brown JSY RC 3.00 8.00
273 Roscoe Parrish JSY RC 1.50 4.00
274 Ryan Moats JSY RC 2.00 5.00
275 Stefan LeFors JSY RC 1.50 4.00
276 Terrence Murphy JSY RC 2.00 5.00
277 Troy Williamson JSY RC 2.00 5.00
278 Vernand Morency JSY RC 2.00 5.00
279 Vincent Jackson JSY RC 3.00 8.00
280 Alex Smith QB Jsy 4.00 10.00
Jason Campbell Jsy
281 Ronnie Brown Jsy 3.00 8.00
Cadillac Williams Jsy
282 Braylon Edwards Jsy 3.00 8.00
Troy Williamson Jsy
283 Adam Jones Jsy 2.50 6.00
Antrelle Rolle Jsy
284 Roscoe Parrish Jsy 4.00 10.00
Frank Gore Jsy
285 Charlie Frye Jsy 2.50 6.00
Andrew Walter Jsy
286 J.J. Arrington Jsy 2.00 5.00
Eric Shelton Jsy
287 Carlos Rogers Jsy 2.50 6.00
Kyle Orton Jsy
288 Mark Clayton Jsy 2.00 5.00
Mark Bradley Jsy
289 Roddy White Jsy 3.00 8.00
Reggie Brown Jsy
290 Terrence Murphy Jsy 2.00 5.00
Courtney Roby Jsy
291 Maurice Clarett Jsy 1.50 4.00
Ciatrick Fason Jsy
292 Ryan Moats Jsy 1.50 4.00
Stefan LeFors Jsy
293 Matt Jones Jsy 3.00 8.00
Vincent Jackson Jsy

2005 Leaf Rookies and Stars Longevity Parallel

*VETERANS: 2.5X TO 6X BASIC CARDS
1-100 VET PRINT RUN 150 SER.#'d SETS
*ROOKIES 101-200: 1X TO 2.5X BASIC CARDS
101-200 ROOKIE PRINT RUN 99 SER.#'d SETS
201-250 ROOKIE AUTO PRINT RUN 50
UNPRICED 251-279 JSY AU PRINT RUN 10
*DUAL JSY: 1X TO 2.5X BASIC CARDS
280-293 DUAL JSY PRINT RUN 25 SETS
201 Aaron Rodgers AU 350.00 500.00
202 Adrian McPherson AU 6.00 15.00
203 Alvin Pearman AU 6.00 15.00
204 Airese Currie AU 6.00 15.00
205 Anthony Davis AU 6.00 15.00
206 Brandon Jacobs AU 12.00 30.00
207 Brandon Jones AU 8.00 20.00
208 Bryant McFadden AU 8.00 20.00
209 Cedric Benson AU 15.00 40.00
210 Cedric Houston AU 10.00 25.00
211 Chad Owens AU 8.00 20.00
212 Chris Henry AU 10.00 25.00
213 Craphonso Thorpe AU 6.00 15.00
214 Damien Nash AU 8.00 20.00
215 Dan Cody AU 8.00 20.00
216 Dan Orlovsky AU 10.00 25.00
217 Dante Ridgeway AU 6.00 15.00
218 Darren Sproles AU 20.00 50.00
219 David Greene AU 6.00 15.00
220 David Pollack AU 8.00 20.00
221 Deandra Cobb AU 6.00 15.00
222 DeMarcus Ware AU 30.00 60.00
223 Derek Anderson AU 8.00 20.00
224 Derrick Johnson AU 8.00 20.00
225 Fabian Washington AU 8.00 20.00
226 Roydell Williams AU 8.00 20.00
227 Heath Miller AU 12.00 30.00
228 J.R. Russell AU 6.00 15.00
229 James Kilian AU 6.00 15.00
230 Jerome Mathis AU 10.00 25.00
231 Larry Brackins AU 6.00 15.00
232 LeRon McCoy AU 6.00 15.00
233 Lionel Gates AU 6.00 15.00
234 Marion Barber AU 15.00 40.00
235 Marlin Jackson AU 6.00 15.00
236 Matt Cassel AU 30.00 80.00
237 Mike Williams AU 10.00 25.00
238 Nate Washington AU 15.00 30.00
239 Noah Herron AU 6.00 15.00
240 Fred Amey AU 6.00 15.00
241 Paris Warren AU 8.00 20.00
242 Rasheed Marshall AU 8.00 20.00
243 Ryan Fitzpatrick AU 20.00 50.00
244 Shaun Cody AU 8.00 20.00
245 Shawne Merriman AU 10.00 25.00
246 Tab Perry AU 6.00 15.00
247 Thomas Davis AU 6.00 15.00
248 Tyson Thompson AU 6.00 15.00
249 Chris Carr AU 6.00 15.00
250 Odell Thurman AU 10.00 25.00

2005 Leaf Rookies and Stars Longevity Holofoil Parallel

*VETERANS: 3X TO 8X BASIC CARDS
1-100 VET PRINT RUN 99 SER.#'d SETS
*ROOKIES 101-200: 2.5X TO 6X BASIC CARDS
101-200 ROOKIE PRINT RUN 25 SER.#'d SETS
UNPRICED 201-250 AU PRINT RUN 5
UNPRICED 251-279 JSY AU PRINT RUN 5
UNPRICED 280-293 DUAL JSY PRINT RUN 10

2005 Leaf Rookies and Stars Longevity True Blue Parallel

*VETERANS 1-100: 3X TO 8X BASIC CARDS
1-100 PRINT RUN 99 SER.#'d SETS
*ROOKIES 101-200: 1.5X TO 4X BASIC CARDS
101-200 ROOKIE PRINT RUN 50 SER.#'d SETS
UNPRICED 201-250 PRINT RUN 10 SETS
INSERTS IN SPECIAL RETAIL BOXES

2005 Leaf Rookies and Stars Longevity True Green Parallel

*VETERANS 1-100: 2.5X TO 6X BASIC CARDS
1-100 PRINT RUN 200 SER.#'d SETS
*ROOKIES 101-200: 1X TO 2.5X BASIC CARDS
101-200 ROOKIE PRINT RUN 100 SER.#'d SETS
*ROOKIES 201-250: 1.5X TO 4X BASIC CARDS
201-250 ROOKIE PRINT RUN 25 SER.#'d SETS
201 Aaron Rodgers 150.00 250.00

2005 Leaf Rookies and Stars Crusade Red

RED PRINT RUN 1250 SER.#'d SETS
*GREEN: .5X TO 1.2X RED
GREEN PRINT RUN 750 SER.#'d SETS
*GREEN DIE CUT: 2X TO 5X RED
GREEN DIE CUT PRINT RUN 25 SER.#'d SETS
*PURPLE: .6X TO 1.5X RED
PURPLE PRINT RUN 250 SER.#'d SETS
*PURPLE DIE CUT: 1.2X TO 3X RED
PURPLE DIE CUT PRINT RUN 50 SER.#'d SETS
UNPRICED RED DIE CUT PRINT RUN 10 SETS
C1 Aaron Brooks .75 2.00
C2 Ahman Green 1.00 2.50
C3 Andre Johnson 1.00 2.50
C4 Ben Roethlisberger 2.00 5.00
C5 Brian Urlacher 1.25 3.00
C6 Byron Leftwich 1.00 2.50
C7 Carson Palmer 1.25 3.00
C8 Chad Pennington 1.25 3.00
C9 Domanick Davis .75 2.00
C10 Donovan McNabb 1.25 3.00
C11 Eli Manning 2.00 5.00
C12 Jake Plummer 1.00 2.50
C13 Jamal Lewis 1.00 2.50
C14 Julius Jones .75 2.00
C15 Jerome Bettis 1.25 3.00
C16 Larry Fitzgerald 1.25 3.00
C17 Marvin Harrison 1.25 3.00
C18 Michael Vick 1.25 3.00
C19 Peyton Manning 2.50 6.00
C20 Priest Holmes 1.00 2.50
C21 Ray Lewis 1.25 3.00
C22 Steve McNair 1.25 3.00
C23 Terrell Owens 1.25 3.00
C24 Tiki Barber 1.25 3.00
C25 Willis McGahee 1.25 3.00

2005 Leaf Rookies and Stars Crusade Materials

MATERIAL PRINT RUN 250 SER.#'d SETS
*DIE CUT: .5X TO 1.2X BASIC JSY INSERTS

DIE CUT PRINT RUN 150 SER.#'d SETS
*PRIME: 1X TO 2.5X BASIC JSY INSERTS
PRIME PRINT RUN 25 SER.#'d SETS
UNPRICED PRIME DC PRINT RUN 10 SETS
C1 Aaron Brooks 3.00 8.00
C2 Ahman Green 4.00 10.00
C3 Andre Johnson 3.00 8.00
C4 Ben Roethlisberger 8.00 20.00
C5 Brian Urlacher 4.00 10.00
C6 Byron Leftwich 4.00 10.00
C7 Carson Palmer 4.00 10.00
C8 Chad Pennington 4.00 10.00
C9 Domanick Davis 3.00 8.00
C10 Donovan McNabb 5.00 12.00
C11 Eli Manning 8.00 20.00
C12 Jake Plummer 3.00 8.00
C13 Jamal Lewis 3.00 8.00
C14 Julius Jones 5.00 12.00
C15 Jerome Bettis 4.00 10.00
C16 Larry Fitzgerald 3.00 8.00
C17 Marvin Harrison 4.00 10.00
C18 Michael Vick 6.00 15.00
C19 Peyton Manning 7.50 20.00
C20 Priest Holmes 4.00 10.00
C21 Ray Lewis 4.00 10.00
C22 Steve McNair 4.00 10.00
C23 Terrell Owens 4.00 10.00
C24 Tiki Barber 4.00 10.00
C25 Willis McGahee 3.00 8.00

2005 Leaf Rookies and Stars Freshman Orientation Jersey

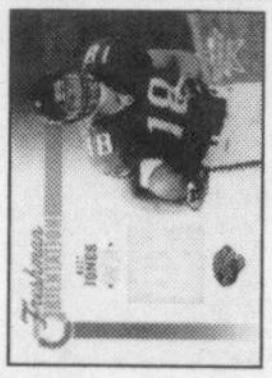

STATED PRINT RUN 350 SER.#'d SETS
*CLASS OFFICE: .6X TO 1.5X BASIC JSYs
CLASS OFFICER PRINT RUN 100 SER.#'d SETS
FO1 Adam Jones 2.00 5.00
FO2 Alex Smith QB 4.00 10.00
FO3 Andrew Walter 2.00 5.00
FO4 Antrel Rolle 2.50 6.00
FO5 Braylon Edwards 3.00 8.00
FO6 Carlos Rogers 2.50 6.00
FO7 Cadillac Williams 2.50 6.00
FO8 Charlie Frye 2.50 6.00
FO9 Ciatrick Fason 1.50 4.00
FO10 Courtney Roby 2.00 5.00
FO11 Eric Shelton 1.50 4.00
FO12 Frank Gore 4.00 10.00
FO13 J.J. Arrington 2.00 5.00
FO14 Jason Campbell 3.00 8.00
FO15 Kyle Orton 2.50 6.00
FO16 Mark Clayton 2.50 6.00
FO17 Mark Bradley 1.50 4.00
FO18 Matt Jones 2.50 6.00
FO19 Maurice Clarett 2.00 5.00
FO20 Reggie Brown 1.50 4.00
FO21 Roddy White 3.00 8.00
FO22 Ronnie Brown 3.00 8.00
FO23 Roscoe Parrish 1.50 4.00
FO24 Ryan Moats 2.00 5.00
FO25 Stefan LeFors 1.50 4.00
FO26 Terrence Murphy 2.00 5.00
FO27 Troy Williamson 2.00 5.00
FO28 Vernand Morency 2.00 5.00
FO29 Vincent Jackson 3.00 8.00

2005 Leaf Rookies and Stars Great American Heroes Red

RED PRINT RUN 1250 SER.#'d SETS
*BLUE: .6X TO 1.5X RED
BLUE PRINT RUN 250 SER.#'d SETS
*WHITE: .5X TO 1.2X RED
WHITE PRINT RUN 750 SER.#'d SETS
GAH1 Aaron Brooks 1.00 2.50
GAH2 Alge Crumpler 1.25 3.00
GAH3 Antonio Gates 1.50 4.00
GAH4 Jevon Kearse 1.25 3.00
GAH5 Byron Leftwich 1.25 3.00
GAH6 Chad Johnson 1.25 3.00
GAH7 Chad Pennington 1.50 4.00
GAH8 Chris Brown 1.00 2.50
GAH9 Cris Collinsworth 1.50 4.00
GAH10 Daryl Johnston 1.50 4.00
GAH11 Derrick Brooks 1.25 3.00
GAH12 Domanick Davis 1.00 2.50
GAH13 Herschel Walker 1.50 4.00
GAH14 J.P. Losman 1.00 2.50
GAH15 Jim Plunkett 1.50 4.00
GAH16 John Taylor 1.25 3.00
GAH17 Julius Jones 1.00 2.50
GAH18 Leroy Kelly 1.50 4.00
GAH19 Michael Vick 1.50 4.00
GAH20 Nate Burleson 1.00 2.50
GAH21 Richard Dent 1.50 4.00
GAH22 Roger Craig 2.00 5.00
GAH23 Rudi Johnson 1.25 3.00
GAH24 Steve Smith 1.50 4.00
GAH25 Terence Newman 1.00 2.50

2005 Leaf Rookies and Stars Great American Heroes Autographs

STATED PRINT RUN 50-300
GAH1 Aaron Brooks/150 6.00 15.00
GAH2 Alge Crumpler/100 7.50 20.00
GAH3 Antonio Gates/100 20.00 40.00
GAH4 Jevon Kearse/100 7.50 20.00
GAH5 Byron Leftwich/50 12.50 30.00
GAH6 Chad Johnson/50 15.00 40.00
GAH7 Chad Pennington/50 12.50 30.00
GAH8 Chris Brown/150 7.50 20.00
GAH9 Cris Collinsworth/70 7.50 20.00
GAH10 Daryl Johnston/202 15.00 40.00
GAH11 Derrick Brooks/300 12.50 30.00
GAH12 Domanick Davis/50 7.50 20.00
GAH13 Herschel Walker/100 15.00 40.00
GAH14 J.P. Losman/75 7.50 20.00
GAH15 Jim Plunkett/100 12.50 30.00
GAH16 John Taylor/75 7.50 20.00
GAH17 Julius Jones/50 25.00 50.00
GAH18 Leroy Kelly/75 12.50 30.00
GAH19 Michael Vick/50 30.00 60.00
GAH20 Nate Burleson/100 7.50 20.00
GAH21 Richard Dent/105 15.00 40.00
GAH22 Roger Craig/212 12.50 30.00
GAH23 Rudi Johnson/100 12.50 30.00
GAH24 Steve Smith/100 12.50 30.00
GAH25 Terence Newman/150 12.50 30.00

2005 Leaf Rookies and Stars Great American Heroes Jerseys

JERSEY PRINT RUN 250 SER.#'d SETS
*PRIME: 1X TO 2.5X BASIC JERSEYS
PRIME PRINT RUN 25 SER.#'d SETS
GAH1 Aaron Brooks 3.00 8.00
GAH2 Alge Crumpler 3.00 8.00
GAH3 Antonio Gates 4.00 10.00
GAH4 Jevon Kearse 3.00 8.00
GAH5 Byron Leftwich 4.00 10.00
GAH6 Chad Johnson 4.00 10.00
GAH7 Chad Pennington 4.00 10.00
GAH8 Chris Brown 3.00 8.00
GAH9 Cris Collinsworth 4.00 10.00
GAH10 Daryl Johnston/135 6.00 15.00
GAH11 Derrick Brooks 4.00 10.00
GAH12 Domanick Davis 3.00 8.00
GAH13 Herschel Walker 4.00 10.00
GAH14 J.P. Losman 3.00 8.00
GAH15 Jim Plunkett 5.00 12.00
GAH16 John Taylor 4.00 10.00
GAH17 Julius Jones 5.00 12.00
GAH18 Leroy Kelly 4.00 10.00
GAH19 Michael Vick 6.00 15.00
GAH20 Nate Burleson 3.00 8.00
GAH21 Richard Dent 4.00 10.00
GAH22 Roger Craig 5.00 12.00
GAH23 Rudi Johnson 3.00 8.00
GAH24 Steve Smith 3.00 8.00
GAH25 Terence Newman 3.00 8.00

2005 Leaf Rookies and Stars Initial Steps Shoe

STATED PRINT RUN 100 SER.#'d SETS
IS1 Adam Jones 5.00 12.00
IS2 Alex Smith QB 12.50 30.00
IS3 Andrew Walter 5.00 12.00
IS4 Antrel Rolle 5.00 12.00
IS5 Braylon Edwards 10.00 25.00
IS6 Carlos Rogers 5.00 12.00
IS7 Cadillac Williams 8.00 20.00
IS8 Charlie Frye 5.00 12.00
IS9 Ciatrick Fason 5.00 12.00
IS10 Courtney Roby 5.00 12.00
IS11 Eric Shelton 5.00 12.00
IS12 Frank Gore 8.00 20.00
IS13 J.J. Arrington 5.00 12.00
IS14 Jason Campbell 6.00 15.00
IS15 Kyle Orton 5.00 12.00
IS16 Mark Clayton 5.00 12.00
IS17 Mark Bradley 5.00 12.00
IS18 Matt Jones
IS19 Maurice Clarett 5.00 12.00
IS20 Reggie Brown 5.00 12.00
IS21 Roddy White 6.00 15.00
IS22 Ronnie Brown 12.50 30.00
IS23 Roscoe Parrish 5.00 12.00
IS24 Ryan Moats 5.00 12.00
IS25 Stefan LeFors 5.00 12.00
IS26 Terrence Murphy 5.00 12.00
IS27 Troy Williamson 5.00 12.00
IS28 Vernand Morency 5.00 12.00
IS29 Vincent Jackson 6.00 15.00

2005 Leaf Rookies and Stars Masks

STATED PRINT RUN 325 SER.#'d SETS
M1 Adam Jones 4.00 10.00
M2 Alex Smith QB 10.00 25.00
M3 Andrew Walter 4.00 10.00
M4 Antrel Rolle 4.00 10.00
M5 Braylon Edwards 8.00 20.00
M6 Carlos Rogers 5.00 12.00
M7 Cadillac Williams 8.00 20.00
M8 Charlie Frye 4.00 10.00
M9 Ciatrick Fason 4.00 10.00
M10 Courtney Roby 4.00 10.00
M11 Eric Shelton 4.00 10.00
M12 Frank Gore 6.00 15.00
M13 J.J. Arrington 4.00 10.00
M14 Jason Campbell 5.00 12.00
M15 Kyle Orton 5.00 12.00
M16 Mark Clayton 4.00 10.00
M17 Mark Bradley 4.00 10.00
M18 Matt Jones 4.00 10.00
M19 Maurice Clarett 4.00 10.00
M20 Reggie Brown 4.00 10.00
M21 Roddy White 5.00 12.00
M22 Ronnie Brown 10.00 25.00
M23 Roscoe Parrish 4.00 10.00
M24 Ryan Moats 4.00 10.00
M25 Stefan LeFors 4.00 10.00
M26 Terrence Murphy 4.00 10.00
M27 Troy Williamson 4.00 10.00
M28 Vernand Morency 4.00 10.00
M29 Vincent Jackson 5.00 12.00

2005 Leaf Rookies and Stars Prime Cuts

STATED PRINT RUN 25 SER.#'d SETS
PC1 Peyton Manning 25.00 60.00
PC2 Michael Vick 25.00 60.00
PC3 Tom Brady 30.00 60.00
PC4 Daunte Culpepper 15.00 40.00
PC5 Brett Favre 30.00 80.00
PC6 Ben Roethlisberger 30.00 80.00
PC7 Byron Leftwich 12.50 30.00
PC8 Steve McNair 15.00 40.00
PC9 Chad Pennington 12.50 30.00
PC10 Eli Manning 40.00 80.00
PC11 LaDainian Tomlinson 15.00 40.00
PC12 Priest Holmes 15.00 40.00
PC13 Shaun Alexander 20.00 50.00
PC14 Clinton Portis 15.00 40.00
PC15 Julius Jones 20.00 50.00
PC16 Ahman Green 15.00 40.00
PC17 Corey Dillon 12.50 30.00
PC18 Edgerrin James 15.00 40.00
PC19 Marvin Harrison 15.00 40.00
PC20 Chad Johnson 12.50 30.00
PC21 Hines Ward 15.00 40.00
PC22 Torry Holt 12.50 30.00
PC23 Andre Johnson 12.50 30.00
PC24 Michael Clayton 12.50 30.00
PC25 Randy Moss 15.00 40.00

2005 Leaf Rookies and Stars Rookie Autographs

201-250 AUTO PRINT RUN 150
251-279 JSY AUTO PRINT RUN 50
201 Aaron Rodgers 250.00 400.00
202 Adrian McPherson 5.00 12.00
203 Alvin Pearman 5.00 12.00
204 Airese Currie 5.00 12.00
205 Anthony Davis 5.00 12.00
206 Brandon Jacobs 25.00 50.00
207 Brandon Jones 6.00 15.00
208 Bryant McFadden 6.00 15.00
209 Cedric Benson 8.00 20.00
210 Cedric Houston 8.00 20.00
211 Chad Owens 6.00 15.00
212 Chris Henry 8.00 20.00
213 Craphonso Thorpe 5.00 12.00
214 Damien Nash 6.00 15.00
215 Dan Cody 6.00 15.00
216 Dan Orlovsky 8.00 20.00
217 Dante Ridgeway 5.00 12.00
218 Darren Sproles 8.00 20.00
219 David Greene 5.00 12.00
220 David Pollack 6.00 15.00
221 Deandra Cobb 5.00 12.00
222 DeMarcus Ware 25.00 50.00
223 Derek Anderson 6.00 15.00
224 Derrick Johnson 6.00 15.00
225 Fabian Washington 6.00 15.00
226 Roydell Williams 6.00 15.00
227 Heath Miller 10.00 25.00
228 J.R. Russell 5.00 12.00
229 James Kilian 5.00 12.00
230 Jerome Mathis 8.00 20.00
231 Larry Brackins 5.00 12.00
232 LeRon McCoy 5.00 12.00
233 Lionel Gates 5.00 12.00
234 Marion Barber 12.00 30.00
235 Marlin Jackson 5.00 12.00
236 Matt Cassel 25.00 60.00
237 Mike Williams 10.00 25.00
238 Nate Washington 8.00 20.00
239 Noah Herron 5.00 12.00
240 Fred Amey 5.00 12.00
241 Paris Warren 6.00 15.00
242 Rasheed Marshall 6.00 15.00
243 Ryan Fitzpatrick 20.00 40.00
244 Shaun Cody 6.00 15.00
245 Shawne Merriman 8.00 20.00
246 Tab Perry 5.00 12.00
247 Thomas Davis 5.00 12.00
248 Tyson Thompson 8.00 20.00
249 Chris Carr 5.00 12.00
250 Odell Thurman 8.00 20.00
251 Adam Jones JSY 10.00 25.00
252 Alex Smith QB JSY 40.00 80.00
253 Andrew Walter JSY 12.00 30.00
254 Antrel Rolle JSY 15.00 40.00
255 Braylon Edwards JSY 40.00 80.00
256 Carlos Rogers JSY 15.00 40.00
257 Cadillac Williams JSY 20.00 50.00
258 Charlie Frye JSY 15.00 40.00
259 Ciatrick Fason JSY 10.00 25.00
260 Courtney Roby JSY 12.00 30.00
261 Eric Shelton JSY 10.00 25.00
262 Frank Gore JSY 30.00 60.00
263 J.J. Arrington JSY 12.00 30.00
264 Jason Campbell JSY 30.00 60.00
265 Kyle Orton JSY 25.00 50.00
266 Mark Clayton JSY 12.00 30.00
267 Mark Bradley JSY 10.00 25.00
268 Matt Jones JSY 12.00 30.00
269 Maurice Clarett JSY 10.00 25.00
270 Reggie Brown JSY 10.00 25.00
271 Roddy White JSY 20.00 50.00
272 Ronnie Brown JSY 40.00 100.00
273 Roscoe Parrish JSY 10.00 25.00
274 Ryan Moats JSY 10.00 25.00
275 Stefan LeFors JSY 10.00 25.00
276 Terrence Murphy JSY 10.00 25.00
277 Troy Williamson JSY 12.00 30.00
278 Vernand Morency JSY 10.00 25.00
279 Vincent Jackson JSY 20.00 50.00

2005 Leaf Rookies and Stars Slideshow Bronze

BRONZE PRINT RUN 1250 SER.#'d SETS
*SILVER: .5X TO 1.2X BRONZE
SILVER PRINT RUN 750 SER.#'d SETS
*VIEW MASTER: .6X TO 1.5X BRONZE
VIEW MASTER PRINT RUN 250 SER.#'d SETS
SS1 Brett Favre 3.00 8.00
SS2 Michael Vick 1.25 3.00
SS3 Deion Sanders 1.50 4.00
SS4 J.P. Losman .75 2.00
SS5 Julius Jones .75 2.00
SS6 Eli Manning 2.00 5.00
SS7 Kevin Jones .75 2.00
SS8 Domanick Davis .75 2.00
SS9 Edgerrin James 1.00 2.50
SS10 Byron Leftwich 1.00 2.50
SS11 Priest Holmes 1.00 2.50
SS12 Tom Brady 2.50 6.00
SS13 Tedy Bruschi 1.25 3.00
SS14 Deuce McAllister 1.00 2.50
SS15 Jeremy Shockey 1.25 3.00
SS16 Chad Pennington 1.25 3.00
SS17 Randy Moss 1.25 3.00
SS18 Terrell Owens 1.25 3.00
SS19 Ben Roethlisberger 2.00 5.00
SS20 Antonio Gates 1.25 3.00
SS21 Alex Smith QB 2.00 5.00
SS22 Steven Jackson 1.25 3.00
SS23 Clinton Portis 1.00 2.50
SS24 Steve McNair 1.25 3.00
SS25 Willis McGahee 1.25 3.00

2005 Leaf Rookies and Stars Ticket Masters Bronze

BRONZE PRINT RUN 1250 SER.#'d SETS
*GOLD: .6X TO 1.5X BRONZE
GOLD PRINT RUN 250 SER.#'d SETS
*SILVER: .5X TO 1.2X BRONZE
SILVER PRINT RUN 750 SER.#'d SETS
TM1 Larry Fitzgerald 2.00 5.00
Anquan Boldin
TM2 Alge Crumpler 3.00 8.00
Michael Vick
TM3 Willis McGahee 2.00 5.00
J.P. Losman
TM4 Shaun Alexander 2.50 6.00
Matt Hasselbeck
TM5 Brian Urlacher 2.00 5.00
Cedric Benson
TM6 Carson Palmer 2.00 5.00
Rudi Johnson
TM7 Julius Jones 2.50 6.00
Drew Bledsoe
TM8 Jake Plummer 3.00 8.00
Jerry Rice
TM9 Kevin Jones 2.00 5.00
Roy Williams WR
TM10 Brett Favre 5.00 12.00
Javon Walker
TM11 David Carr 2.00 5.00
Domanik Davis
TM12 Peyton Manning 3.00 8.00
Marvin Harrison
TM13 Tony Gonzalez 2.00 5.00
Priest Holmes
TM14 Ronnie Brown 3.00 8.00
Chris Chambers
TM15 Troy Williamson 2.00 5.00
Daunte Culpepper
TM16 Tom Brady 5.00 12.00
Deion Branch
TM17 Eli Manning 4.00 10.00
Plaxico Burress
TM18 Chad Pennington 2.00 5.00
Laveranues Coles
TM19 Randy Moss 2.00 5.00
LaMont Jordan
TM20 Donovan McNabb 2.50 6.00
Jevon Kearse
TM21 Ben Roethlisberger 5.00 12.00
Jerome Bettis
TM22 LaDainian Tomlinson 2.50 6.00
Antonio Gates
TM23 Torry Holt 2.50 6.00
Steven Jackson
TM24 Steve McNair 2.00 5.00
Drew Bennett
TM25 Micheal Clayton 2.50 6.00
Cadillac Williams

2005 Leaf Rookies and Stars Triple Threads

STATED PRINT RUN 150 SER.#'d SETS
*PRIME: .8X TO 2X BASIC JERSEYS
PRIME PRINT RUN 25 SER.#'d SETS
TT1 J.P. Losman 7.50 20.00
Eric Moulds
Willis McGahee
TT2 Rex Grossman 12.50 30.00
Thomas Jones
Brian Urlacher
TT3 Carson Palmer 12.50 30.00
Rudi Johnson
Chad Johnson
TT4 Julius Jones 12.50 30.00
Roy Williams S
Keyshawn Johnson
TT5 Jake Plummer 7.50 20.00
Tatum Bell
Ashley Lelie
TT6 Joey Harrington 7.50 20.00
Kevin Jones
Roy Williams WR
TT7 Brett Favre 15.00 40.00
Ahman Green
Javon Walker
TT8 David Carr 7.50 20.00
Domanik Davis
Andre Johnson
TT9 Peyton Manning 20.00 40.00
Reggie Wayne
Marvin Harrison
TT10 Byron Leftwich 7.50 20.00
Fred Taylor
JImmy Smith
TT11 Trent Green 10.00 25.00
Priest Holmes
Tony Gonzalez
TT12 Daunte Culpepper 10.00 25.00
Michael Bennett
Nate Burleson
TT13 Tom Brady 12.50 30.00
Corey Dillon
Deion Branch
TT14 Aaron Brooks 7.50 20.00
Deuce McAllister
Joe Horn
TT15 Eli Manning 20.00 40.00
Jeremy Shockey
Tiki Barber
TT16 Chad Pennington 10.00 25.00
Curtis Martin
Laveranues Coles
TT17 Jake Delhomme 10.00 25.00
Stephen Davis
Julius Peppers
TT18 Donovan McNabb 12.50 30.00
Brian Westbrook
Terrell Owens
TT19 Ben Roethlisberger 20.00 50.00
Jerome Bettis
Hines Ward
TT20 Drew Brees 12.50 30.00
LaDainian Tomlinson
Antonio Gates
TT21 Matt Hasselbeck 15.00 30.00
Shaun Alexander
Darrell Jackson
TT22 Marc Bulger 10.00 25.00
Steven Jackson
Torry Holt
TT23 Steve McNair 10.00 25.00
Chris Brown
Drew Bennett
TT24 Clinton Portis 10.00 25.00
Lavar Arrington
Rod Gardner
TT25 Kyle Boller 7.50 20.00
Jamal Lewis
Ray Lewis

2005 Leaf Rookies and Stars Longevity

This 279-card set was released in January, 2006. The set was issued in the hobby in five-card packs which came 24 packs to a box. The first 96 cards in the set feature veterans sequenced in team alphabetical order while cards numbered 97-100 feature two rookie teammate checklists and cards 101-279 all feature rookies. In the rookie subset, cards numbered 251-279 all have a player-worn relic piece attached. Cards numbered 101-200 were issued to a stated print run of 999 serial numbered sets while cards numbered 201-250 were issued to a stated print run of 599 serial numbered sets and cards numbered 251-279 were issued to a stated print run of 299 serial numbered sets.

COMP.SET w/o RC's (100) 10.00 25.00
*VETS 1-100: .5X TO 1.2X BASIC LR&S
*ROOKIES 101-200: .4X TO 1X
101-200 PRINT RUN 999 SER.#'d SETS
*ROOKIES 201-250: .4X TO 1X
201-250 PRINT RUN 599 SER.#'d SETS
*ROOKIE JSYs 251-279: .4X TO 1X
251-279 JSY PRINT RUN 299 SER.#'d SETS

2005 Leaf Rookies and Stars Longevity Black

*VETERANS 1-100: 2.5X TO 6X BASIC CARDS
1-100 PRINT RUN 99 SER.#'d SETS
*ROOKIES 101-200: 1.5X TO 4X BASIC CARDS
101-200 PRINT RUN 50 SER.#'d SETS
*ROOKIES 201-250: 1.5X TO 4X BASIC CARDS
201-250 PRINT RUN 25 SER.#'d SETS
251-279 UNPRICED JSY PRINT RUN 10 SETS
201 Aaron Rodgers 150.00 250.00

2005 Leaf Rookies and Stars Longevity Emerald

*VETERANS 1-100: 2X TO 5X BASIC CARDS
1-100 PRINT RUN 150 SER.#'d SETS
*ROOKIES: 1X TO 2.5X BASIC CARDS
101-200 PRINT RUN 99 SER.#'d SETS
*ROOKIES 201-250: 1.2X TO 3X BASIC CARDS
201-250 PRINT RUN 50 SER.#'d SETS
*ROOKIE JSYs 251-279: 1.2X TO 3X
251-279 JSY PRINT RUN 25 SER.#'d SETS
201 Aaron Rodgers 125.00 200.00

2005 Leaf Rookies and Stars Longevity Gold

*VETS 1-100: 1.5X TO 4X BASIC CARDS
1-100 PRINT RUN 199 SER.#'d SETS
*ROOKIES 101-200: .8X TO 2X BASIC CARDS
101-200 PRINT RUN 150 SER.#'d SETS
*ROOKIES 201-250: .8X TO 2X BASIC CARDS
201-250 PRINT RUN 99 SER.#'d SETS
*ROOKIE JSYs 201-250: .8X TO 2X
251-279 JSY PRINT RUN 50 SER.#'d SETS
201 Aaron Rodgers 100.00 175.00

2005 Leaf Rookies and Stars Longevity Ruby

*VETERANS 1-100: 1.2X TO 3X BASIC CARDS
1-100 PRINT RUN 299 SER.#'d SETS
*ROOKIES 101-200: .6X TO 1.5X
101-200 PRINT RUN 250 SER.#'d SETS
*ROOKIES 201-250: .6X TO 1.5X
201-250 PRINT RUN 199 SER.#'d SETS
*ROOKIE JSYs 251-2790: .6X TO 1.5X
251-279 JSY PRINT RUN 99 SER.#'d SETS
201 Aaron Rodgers 90.00 150.00

2005 Leaf Rookies and Stars Longevity Sapphire

*VETERANS 1-100: 1.2X TO 3X BASIC CARDS
1-100 PRINT RUN 250 SER.#'d SETS
*ROOKIES 101-200: .8X TO 2X
101-200 PRINT RUN 199 SER.#'d SETS
*ROOKIES 201-250: .8X TO 2X
201-250 PRINT RUN 150 SER.#'d SETS
*ROOKIE JSYs 251-279: .8X TO 2X
251-279 JSY PRINT RUN 75 SER.#'d SETS
201 Aaron Rodgers 90.00 150.00

2005 Leaf Rookies and Stars Longevity Materials Black

COMMON CARD/25 7.50 20.00
SEMISTARS/25 10.00 25.00
UNL.STARS/25 12.50 30.00
BLACK STATED PRINT RUN 5-25
36 Brett Favre/15 30.00 80.00
43 Peyton Manning/25 25.00 60.00
57 Tom Brady/25 25.00 60.00
78 Jerome Bettis/25 20.00 50.00

2005 Leaf Rookies and Stars Longevity Materials Emerald

COMMON CARD/39-50 5.00 12.00
SEMISTARS/39-50 6.00 15.00
UNL.STARS/39-50 8.00 20.00
COMMON CARD/20-30 8.00 20.00
UNL.STARS/20-30 10.00 25.00
EMERALD STATED PRINT RUN 9-50
4 Michael Vick/20 10.00 25.00
36 Brett Favre/30 25.00 60.00
43 Peyton Manning/50 15.00 40.00
57 Tom Brady/50 15.00 40.00
61 Eli Manning/25 15.00 40.00
78 Jerome Bettis/50 12.00 30.00

2005 Leaf Rookies and Stars Longevity Materials Gold

COMMON CARD/80-99 4.00 10.00
SEMISTARS/80-99 5.00 12.00
UNL.STARS/80-99 6.00 15.00
COMMON CARD/55-79 6.00 15.00
UNL.STARS/55-79 8.00 20.00
COMMON CARD/30-50 6.00 15.00
SEMISTARS/30-50 8.00 20.00
UNL.STARS/30-50 10.00 25.00
COMMON CARD/15-25 10.00 25.00
UNL.STARS/15-25 12.00 30.00
GOLD STATED PRINT RUN 13-99
36 Brett Favre/99 15.00 40.00
43 Peyton Manning/99 12.00 30.00
57 Tom Brady/99 12.00 30.00
61 Eli Manning/99 10.00 25.00
75 Ben Roethlisberger/99 10.00 25.00
78 Jerome Bettis/99 10.00 25.00

2005 Leaf Rookies and Stars Longevity Materials Ruby

COMMON CARD/150-199 2.50 6.00
SEMISTARS/150-199 3.00 8.00
UNL.STARS/150-199 4.00 10.00
COMMON CARD/100-130 3.00 8.00
SEMISTARS/100-130 4.00 10.00
UNL.STARS/100-130 5.00 12.00
COMMON CARD/50-79 5.00 12.00
UNL.STARS/50-79 7.50 20.00
RUBY STATED PRINT RUN 55-199
36 Brett Favre/199 10.00 25.00
43 Peyton Manning/199 8.00 20.00
61 Eli Manning/165 6.00 15.00
75 Ben Roethlisberger/199 6.00 15.00

2005 Leaf Rookies and Stars Longevity Materials Sapphire

COMMON CARD/90-150 3.00 8.00
SEMISTARS/90-150 4.00 10.00
UNL.STARS/90-150 5.00 12.00
COMMON CARD/50-77 4.00 10.00
SEMISTARS/50-77 5.00 12.00
UNL.STARS/50-77 6.00 15.00
COMMON CARD/25 6.00 15.00
SAPPHIRE STATED PRINT RUN 25-150
36 Brett Favre/150 12.00 30.00
43 Peyton Manning/150 10.00 25.00
61 Eli Manning/105 8.00 20.00
75 Ben Roethlisberger/150 8.00 20.00
78 Jerome Bettis/77 10.00 25.00

2005 Leaf Rookies and Stars Longevity Sunday Signatures

*GOLD: .5X TO 1.2X BASIC AUTOS
GOLDS SER.#'d UNDER 20 NOT PRICED
1 Aaron Brooks/150 6.00 15.00
3 Antonio Gates/75 10.00 25.00
4 Ashley Lelie/175 10.00 25.00
6 Chris Brown/125
7 Christian Okoye/50 10.00 25.00
8 Daryl Johnston/175 15.00 40.00
9 Deion Branch/100 10.00 25.00
11 Derrick Brooks/299 10.00 25.00
12 Nate Burleson/251 6.00 15.00
13 Donnie Edwards/299 6.00 15.00
14 Drew Bennett/276 6.00 15.00
15 Domanick Davis/75 6.00 15.00
17 Fran Tarkenton/99 15.00 40.00
19 Gene Upshaw/107 10.00 25.00
20 Herschel Walker/99 15.00 40.00
21 Hines Ward/63 20.00 50.00
23 Jevon Kearse/299 10.00 25.00
24 Jimmy Smith/100 6.00 15.00
25 John Taylor/99 10.00 25.00
27 L.C. Greenwood/50 15.00 40.00
28 LaMont Jordan/299 10.00 25.00
29 Lee Evans/299 6.00 15.00
30 Leroy Kelly/57 12.50 30.00
33 Mike Ditka/150 20.00 40.00
35 Paul Hornung/75 12.50 30.00
36 Paul Warfield/179 10.00 25.00
37 Randall Cunningham/75 15.00 40.00
38 Reggie Wayne/150 12.50 30.00
39 Rex Grossman/125 15.00 30.00
40 Richard Dent/95 10.00 25.00
41 Rudi Johnson/50 10.00 25.00
42 Sonny Jurgensen/79 15.00 40.00
43 Sterling Sharpe/75 12.50 30.00
45 Tatum Bell/97 10.00 25.00
49 Warren Moon/50 12.50 30.00
50 Y.A. Tittle/100 15.00 40.00

2006 Leaf Rookies and Stars

This 281-card set was released in October, 2006. The set was issued into the hobby in five-card packs which came 24 to a box. Cards numbered 1-100 feature players in team alphabetical order while cards numbered 101-281 feature 2006 rookies. The Rookie Cards are broken into the following subsets: Cards numbered 101-200 were issued to a stated print run of 999 serial numbered sets, while cards 201-250 were issued to a stated print run of 599 serial numbered sets. Cards numbered 251-270 have a player-worn jersey swatch and those cards were issued to a stated print run of 799 serial numbered sets and the set concludes with cards numbered 271-281 which have both player-worn swatches and an autograph and those cards were issued to stated print runs betwwn 99 and 449 serial numbered copies. For those cards, we have explicitly notated the print runs in our checklist.

COMP.SET w/o RC's (100) 8.00 20.00
101-200 ROOKIE PRINT RUN 999
201-250 ROOKIE PRINT RUN 599
251-270 JSY ROOKIE PRINT RUN 799
JSY AU ROOKIE PRINT RUN 99-449
1 Anquan Boldin .20 .50
2 Edgerrin James .20 .50
3 Kurt Warner .25 .60
4 Larry Fitzgerald .25 .60
5 Alge Crumpler .20 .50
6 Michael Vick .25 .60
7 Warrick Dunn .20 .50
8 Derrick Mason .20 .50
9 Jamal Lewis .20 .50
10 Mike Anderson .20 .50
11 Josh Reed .15 .40
12 Lee Evans .20 .50
13 Willis McGahee .20 .50
14 DeShaun Foster .20 .50
15 Jake Delhomme .20 .50
16 Keyshawn Johnson .20 .50
17 Steve Smith .25 .60
18 Cedric Benson .20 .50
19 Muhsin Muhammad .20 .50
20 Rex Grossman .20 .50
21 Carson Palmer .25 .60
22 Chad Johnson .20 .50
23 Rudi Johnson .20 .50
24 T.J. Houshmandzadeh .20 .50
25 Charlie Frye .20 .50
26 Joe Jurevicius .15 .40
27 Reuben Droughns .20 .50
28 Drew Bledsoe .25 .60
29 Julius Jones .15 .40
30 Terrell Owens .25 .60
31 Terry Glenn .20 .50
32 Jake Plummer .20 .50
33 Rod Smith .20 .50
34 Tatum Bell .15 .40
35 Josh McCown .15 .40
36 Kevin Jones .15 .40
37 Roy Williams WR .20 .50
38 Ahman Green .20 .50
39 Brett Favre .50 1.25
40 Donald Driver .25 .60
41 Robert Ferguson .15 .40
42 Samkon Gado .20 .50
43 Andre Johnson .25 .60
44 David Carr .15 .40
45 Domanick Davis .15 .40
46 Eric Moulds .15 .40
47 Marvin Harrison .25 .60
48 Peyton Manning .40 1.00
49 Reggie Wayne .20 .50
50 Dallas Clark .20 .50
51 Fred Taylor .20 .50
52 Byron Leftwich .20 .50
53 Jimmy Smith .20 .50
54 Larry Johnson .20 .50
55 Tony Gonzalez .20 .50
56 Trent Green .20 .50
57 Eddie Kennison .15 .40
58 Chris Chambers .20 .50
59 Daunte Culpepper .20 .50
60 Ronnie Brown .25 .60
61 Chester Taylor .20 .50
62 Brad Johnson .20 .50
63 Deion Branch .20 .50
64 Corey Dillon .20 .50
65 Tom Brady .40 1.00
66 Deuce McAllister .20 .50
67 Donte Stallworth .15 .40
68 Drew Brees .25 .60
69 Eli Manning .30 .75
70 Plaxico Burress .20 .50
71 Tiki Barber .25 .60
72 Chad Pennington .20 .50
73 Curtis Martin .25 .60
74 Laveranues Coles .15 .40
75 Aaron Brooks .20 .50
76 LaMont Jordan .20 .50
77 Randy Moss .25 .60
78 Brian Westbrook .20 .50
79 Donovan McNabb .25 .60
80 Jabar Gaffney .15 .40
81 Hines Ward .25 .60
82 Ben Roethlisberger .30 .75
83 Willie Parker .20 .50
84 Antonio Gates .25 .60
85 LaDainian Tomlinson .25 .60
86 Philip Rivers .25 .60
87 Alex Smith QB .25 .60
88 Antonio Bryant .15 .40
89 Kevan Barlow .15 .40
90 Darrell Jackson .20 .50
91 Matt Hasselbeck .20 .50
92 Shaun Alexander .20 .50
93 Torry Holt .20 .50
94 Steven Jackson .25 .60
95 Cadillac Williams .20 .50
96 Joey Galloway .20 .50
97 David Givens .20 .50
98 Drew Bennett .20 .50
99 Antwaan Randle El .20 .50
100 Clinton Portis .25 .60
101 Kamerion Wimbley RC 1.50 4.00
102 Mathias Kiwanuka RC 1.50 4.00
103 Reggie McNeal RC 1.25 3.00
104 Claude Wroten RC 1.00 2.50
105 Gabe Watson RC 1.00 2.50
106 D'Qwell Jackson RC 1.25 3.00
107 Todd Watkins RC 1.00 2.50
108 Bennie Brazell RC 1.25 3.00
109 David Anderson RC 1.25 3.00
110 John David Washington RC 1.25 3.00
111 Marques Hagans RC 1.00 2.50
112 Kevin Youngblood RC 1.00 2.50
113 Ben Obomanu RC 1.50 4.00
114 Jamal Jones RC 1.00 2.50
115 Nick Mangold RC 1.25 3.00
116 Davin Joseph RC 1.25 3.00
117 Erik Meyer RC 1.25 3.00
118 Taurean Henderson RC 1.50 4.00
119 A.J. Nicholson RC 1.00 2.50
120 Thomas Howard RC 1.25 3.00
121 Jon Alston RC 1.00 2.50
122 Ashton Youboty RC 1.00 2.50
123 Alan Zemaitis RC 1.50 4.00
124 Lawrence Vickers RC 1.25 3.00
125 J.D. Runnels RC 1.25 3.00
126 Ray Perkins RC 1.25 3.00
127 Jeff King RC 1.25 3.00
128 Quinn Sypniewski RC 1.25 3.00
129 Jason Carter RC 1.25 3.00
130 Malcom Floyd RC 2.00 5.00
131 Mike Jennings RC 1.25 3.00
132 Chris Gocong RC 1.25 3.00
133 Frostee Rucker RC 1.25 3.00
134 Jason Hatcher RC 1.25 3.00
135 Victor Adeyanju RC 1.25 3.00
136 Elvis Dumervil RC 1.50 4.00
137 Ray Edwards RC 1.50 4.00
138 Anthony Schlegel RC 1.25 3.00
139 Freddie Keiaho RC 1.25 3.00
140 Gerris Wilkinson RC 1.00 2.50
141 Leon Williams RC 1.25 3.00
142 Stephen Tulloch RC 1.25 3.00
143 Jamar Williams RC 1.25 3.00
144 Clint Ingram RC 1.50 4.00
145 James Anderson RC 1.00 2.50
146 Darrell Hackney RC 1.25 3.00
147 Paul Pinegar RC 1.00 2.50
148 Brandon Kirsch RC 1.25 3.00
149 Andre Hall RC 1.25 3.00
150 De'Arrius Howard RC 1.50 4.00
151 Cedric Humes RC 1.00 2.50
152 Wendell Mathis RC 1.25 3.00
153 Gerald Riggs RC 1.25 3.00
154 Quinton Ganther RC 1.00 2.50
155 Martin Nance RC 1.25 3.00
156 Greg Lee RC 1.00 2.50
157 Jai Lewis RC 1.25 3.00
158 Cory Rodgers RC 1.25 3.00
159 Mike Espy RC 1.50 4.00
160 Chris Barclay RC 1.25 3.00
161 DeMeco Ryans RC 1.50 4.00
162 Rocky McIntosh RC 1.25 3.00
163 David Kirtman RC 1.25 3.00
164 Skyler Green RC 1.00 2.50
165 Will Blackmon RC 1.25 3.00
166 Darryl Tapp RC 1.25 3.00
167 Dusty Dvoracek RC 1.50 4.00
168 Richard Marshall RC 1.25 3.00
169 Tim Jennings RC 1.25 3.00
170 David Pittman RC 1.25 3.00
171 DeMario Minter RC 1.25 3.00
172 Marcus Maxey RC 1.25 3.00
173 Roman Harper RC 1.25 3.00
174 Anthony Smith RC 1.50 4.00
175 Nate Salley RC 1.25 3.00
176 Mike Hass RC 1.25 3.00
177 Greg Blue RC 1.25 3.00
178 Daniel Bullocks RC 1.50 4.00
179 Danieal Manning RC 1.50 4.00
180 Calvin Lowry RC 1.50 4.00
181 Eric Smith RC 1.25 3.00
182 Jimmy Williams RC 1.50 4.00
183 Cedric Griffin RC 1.25 3.00
184 Ko Simpson RC 1.25 3.00
185 Pat Watkins RC 1.25 3.00
186 Marcus Vick RC 1.00 2.50
187 Bernard Pollard RC 1.25 3.00
188 Darnell Bing RC 1.25 3.00
189 Cory Ross RC 1.50 4.00
190 Patrick Cobbs RC 1.25 3.00
191 Montell Owens RC 1.25 3.00
192 Chris Hannon RC 1.25 3.00
193 John Madsen RC 1.50 4.00
194 Shaun Bodiford RC 1.25 3.00
195 Fred Evans RC 1.25 3.00
196 Cletis Gordon RC .75 2.00
197 Jarrad Page RC 1.50 4.00
198 Brett Elliott RC 1.50 4.00
199 Brett Basanez RC 1.50 4.00
200 Drew Olson RC 1.00 2.50
201 Jay Cutler RC 4.00 10.00
202 Brodie Croyle RC 2.00 5.00
203 Ingle Martin RC 1.50 4.00
204 Derrick Ross RC 1.50 4.00
205 Bruce Gradkowski RC 2.00 5.00
206 D.J. Shockley RC 1.50 4.00
207 Joseph Addai RC 2.00 5.00

208 P.J. Daniels RC 1.25 3.00
209 Marques Colston RC 4.00 10.00
210 Jerome Harrison RC 2.00 5.00
211 Wali Lundy RC 1.50 4.00
212 Mike Bell RC 2.00 5.00
213 Miles Austin RC 5.00 12.00
214 Anthony Fasano RC 2.00 5.00
215 Tony Scheffler RC 2.00 5.00
216 Leonard Pope RC 2.00 5.00
217 David Thomas RC 1.50 4.00
218 Dominique Byrd RC 1.50 4.00
219 Garrett Mills RC 2.00 5.00
220 Hank Baskett RC 2.00 5.00
221 Greg Jennings RC 3.00 8.00
222 Devin Hester RC 3.00 8.00
223 Willie Reid RC 1.50 4.00
224 Brad Smith RC 2.00 5.00
225 Sam Hurd RC 1.25 3.00
226 Owen Daniels RC 2.00 5.00
227 Domenik Hixon RC 2.00 5.00
228 Jeremy Bloom RC 1.50 4.00
229 Dawan Landry RC 2.00 5.00
230 Jonathan Orr RC 1.50 4.00
231 Delanie Walker RC 2.00 5.00
232 Adam Jennings RC 1.50 4.00
233 Jeffrey Webb RC 1.50 4.00
234 Ethan Kilmer RC 1.50 4.00
235 Tye Hill RC 1.25 3.00
236 Jason Allen RC 1.50 4.00
237 Antonio Cromartie RC 2.00 5.00
238 D'Brickashaw Ferguson RC 2.00 5.00
239 Tamba Hali RC 2.00 5.00
240 Haloti Ngata RC 2.00 5.00
241 Brodrick Bunkley RC 1.50 4.00
242 John McCargo RC 1.25 3.00
243 Johnathan Joseph RC 1.50 4.00
244 Kelly Jennings RC 1.50 4.00
245 Donte Whitner RC 2.00 5.00
246 Abdul Hodge RC 1.25 3.00
247 Ernie Sims RC 1.50 4.00
248 Chad Greenway RC 2.00 5.00
249 Bobby Carpenter RC 1.25 3.00
250 Manny Lawson RC 1.50 4.00
251 Matt Leinart JSY/599 RC 3.00 8.00
252 Kellen Clemens JSY RC 2.00 5.00
253 Tarvaris Jackson JSY RC 2.50 6.00
254 Charlie Whitehurst JSY RC 2.50 6.00
255 DeAngelo Williams JSY/599 RC 4.00 10.00
256 Maurice Drew JSY RC 4.00 10.00
257 Brian Calhoun JSY RC 1.50 4.00
258 Jerious Norwood JSY RC 2.00 5.00
259 Vernon Davis JSY RC 3.00 8.00
260 Joe Klopfenstein JSY RC 1.50 4.00
261 Sinorice Moss JSY RC 2.50 6.00
262 Derek Hagan JSY RC 2.00 5.00
263 Brandon Williams JSY RC 1.50 4.00
264 Michael Robinson JSY RC 2.00 5.00
265 Jason Avant JSY RC 1.50 4.00
266 Brandon Marshall JSY RC 2.50 6.00
267 Demetrius Williams JSY RC 2.00 5.00
268 Mario Williams JSY RC 2.50 6.00
269 Michael Huff JSY RC 2.00 5.00
270 Chad Jackson JSY RC 1.50 4.00
271 Vince Young JSY AU/249 RC 25.00 60.00
272 Omar Jacobs JSY AU/449 RC 6.00 15.00
273 Reggie Bush JSY AU/99 RC 50.00 120.00
274 Laurence Maroney JSY AU/99 RC 15.00 40.00
275 LenDale White JSY AU/249 RC 15.00 40.00
276 Leon Washington JSY AU/199 RC 12.00 30.00
277 Marcedes Lewis JSY AU/449 RC 6.00 15.00
278 Santonio Holmes JSY AU/449 RC 25.00 40.00
279 Travis Wilson JSY AU/449 RC 4.00 10.00
280 Maurice Stovall JSY AU/99 RC 5.00 12.00
281 A.J. Hawk JSY AU/99 RC 20.00 50.00

2006 Leaf Rookies and Stars Gold

*VETERANS 1-100: 2X TO 5X BASIC CARDS
*ROOKIES 101-200: 1X TO 2.5X BASIC CARDS
*ROOKIES 201-250: .8X TO 2X BASIC CARDS
STATED PRINT RUN 299 SER.#'d SETS

2006 Leaf Rookies and Stars Longevity Black Parallel

*VETS 1-100: 10X TO 25X BASIC CARDS
VETERANS PRINT RUN 25 SER.#'d SETS
UNPRICED ROOKIE 101-250 PRINT RUN 10
UNPRICED ROOKIE JSY PRINT RUN 10

2006 Leaf Rookies and Stars Longevity Gold Parallel

*VETS 1-100: 6X TO 15X BASIC CARDS
VETERANS PRINT RUN 49 SER.#'d SETS
*ROOKIES 101-200: 2.5X TO 6X BASIC CARDS
*ROOKIES 201-250: 2X TO 5X BASIC CARDS
101-250 PRINT RUN 25 SER.#'d SETS
*JSY ROOKIES 251-270: 1X TO 2.5X
JSY ROOKIES PRINT RUN 25 SER.#'d SETS

2006 Leaf Rookies and Stars Longevity Holofoil Parallel

*VETS 1-100: 4X TO 10X BASIC CARDS
VETERANS PRINT RUN 99 SER.#'d SETS
*ROOKIES 101-250: 1.5X TO 4X BASIC CARDS
*ROOKIES 201-250: 1.2X TO 3X BASIC CARDS
101-250 PRINT RUN 49 SER.#'d SETS
*JSY ROOKIES 251-270: .6X TO 1.5X
JSY ROOKIES PRINT RUN 50 SER.#'d SETS

2006 Leaf Rookies and Stars Longevity Silver Parallel

*VETS 1-100: 2.5X TO 6X BASIC CARDS
VETERANS PRINT RUN 199 SER.#'d SETS
*ROOKIES 101-200: 1.2X TO 3X BASIC CARDS
*ROOKIES 201-250: 1X TO 2.5X BASIC CARDS
101-250 PRINT RUN 99 SER.#'d SETS
*JSY ROOKIES 251-270: .5X TO 1.2X
JSY ROOKIES PRINT RUN 100 SER.#'d SETS

2006 Leaf Rookies and Stars 1948 Leaf Blue

*ORANGE: .5X TO 1.2X BASIC INSERTS
*YELLOW: .8X TO 2X BASIC INSERTS
INSERTS IN WALMART BLASTER BOXES
1 Vince Young 1.50 4.00
2 LenDale White 1.00 2.50
3 Reggie Bush 2.50 6.00
4 Matt Leinart 1.25 3.00
5 Michael Robinson 1.00 2.50
6 Vernon Davis 1.50 4.00
7 Chad Jackson .75 2.00
8 Tarvaris Jackson 1.25 3.00
9 Jason Avant .75 2.00
10 Brandon Marshall 1.25 3.00
11 Santonio Holmes 1.50 4.00
12 Jerious Norwood 1.00 2.50
13 Sinorice Moss 1.25 3.00
14 Leon Washington 1.00 2.50
15 Charlie Whitehurst 1.25 3.00
16 Travis Wilson .75 2.00
17 Joe Klopfenstein .75 2.00
18 Brian Calhoun .75 2.00
19 Mario Williams 1.25 3.00
20 Maurice Stovall .75 2.00
21 Brodie Croyle 1.25 3.00
22 Greg Jennings 2.00 5.00
23 Demetrius Williams 1.00 2.50
24 A.J. Hawk 1.25 3.00
25 Omar Jacobs .75 2.00
26 Brandon Williams .75 2.00
27 Kellen Clemens 1.00 2.50
28 Maurice Drew 2.00 5.00
29 Michael Huff 1.00 2.50
30 Jay Cutler 2.50 6.00
31 Laurence Maroney 1.00 2.50
32 Derek Hagan 1.00 2.50
33 Joseph Addai 1.25 3.00
34 DeAngelo Williams 1.50 4.00
35 Marcedes Lewis 1.25 3.00

2006 Leaf Rookies and Stars Crosstraining Red

RED PRINT RUN 1000 SER.#'d SETS
*BLUE/500: .5X TO 1.2X RED/1000
BLUE PRINT RUN 500 SER.#'d SETS
*GREEN/100: .8X TO 2X RED/1000
GREEN PRINT RUN 100 SER.#'d SETS
*PURPLE/25: 1.5X TO 4X RED/1000
PURPLE PRINT RUN 25 SER.#'d SETS
1 Laurence Maroney .60 1.50
2 Brandon Marshall .75 2.00
3 Santonio Holmes 1.00 2.50
4 DeAngelo Williams 1.00 2.50
5 Leon Washington .60 1.50
6 Mario Williams .75 2.00
7 LenDale White .60 1.50
8 Brian Calhoun .50 1.25
9 Charlie Whitehurst .75 2.00
10 Kellen Clemens .60 1.50
11 A.J. Hawk .75 2.00
12 Joe Klopfenstein .50 1.25
13 Maurice Drew 1.25 3.00
14 Omar Jacobs .50 1.25
15 Jason Avant .50 1.25
16 Matt Leinart .75 2.00
17 Marcedes Lewis .75 2.00
18 Jerious Norwood .60 1.50
19 Demetrius Williams .60 1.50
20 Vince Young 1.00 2.50
21 Brandon Williams .50 1.25
22 Maurice Stovall .50 1.25
23 Sinorice Moss .75 2.00
24 Michael Huff .60 1.50
25 Reggie Bush 1.50 4.00
26 Michael Robinson .60 1.50
27 Chad Jackson .50 1.25
28 Derek Hagan .60 1.50
29 Vernon Davis 1.00 2.50

2006 Leaf Rookies and Stars Crosstraining Materials

STATED PRINT RUN 125 SER.#'d SETS
*PRIME/25: .6X TO 1.5X BASIC INSERTS
PRIME PRINT RUN 25 SER.#'d SETS
1 Laurence Maroney 1.50 4.00
2 Brandon Marshall 2.50 6.00
3 Santonio Holmes 4.00 10.00
4 DeAngelo Williams 2.50 6.00
5 Leon Washington 3.00 8.00
6 Mario Williams 2.00 5.00
7 LenDale White 4.00 10.00
8 Brian Calhoun 2.50 6.00
9 Charlie Whitehurst 2.50 6.00
10 Kellen Clemens 3.00 8.00
11 A.J. Hawk 6.00 15.00
12 Joe Klopfenstein 2.50 6.00
13 Maurice Drew 5.00 12.00
14 Omar Jacobs 2.50 6.00
15 Jason Avant 1.25 3.00
16 Matt Leinart 2.00 5.00
17 Marcedes Lewis 2.50 6.00
18 Jerious Norwood 3.00 8.00
19 Demetrius Williams 2.50 6.00
20 Vince Young 2.50 6.00
21 Brandon Williams 2.50 6.00
22 Maurice Stovall 2.50 6.00
23 Sinorice Moss 2.50 6.00
24 Michael Huff 1.50 4.00
25 Reggie Bush 4.00 10.00
26 Michael Robinson 2.50 6.00
27 Chad Jackson 2.50 6.00
28 Derek Hagan 2.50 6.00
29 Vernon Davis 2.50 6.00

2006 Leaf Rookies and Stars Crusade Red

RED PRINT RUN 1000 SER.#'d SETS
*BLUE/500: .5X TO 1.2X RED/1000
BLUE PRINT RUN 500 SER.#'d SETS
*GREEN/100: 1X TO 2.5X RED/1000
GREEN PRINT RUN 100 SER.#'d SETS
*PURPLE/25: 1.5X TO 4X RED/1000
PURPLE PRINT RUN 25 SER.#'d SETS
UNPRICED AUTO PRINT RUN 1-5
1 Ben Roethlisberger 1.50 4.00
2 Brett Favre 2.50 6.00
3 LaDainian Tomlinson 1.25 3.00
4 Michael Vick 1.25 3.00
5 Peyton Manning 2.00 5.00
6 Chad Johnson 1.00 2.50
7 Eli Manning 1.50 4.00
8 Marvin Harrison 1.25 3.00
9 Steve Smith 1.25 3.00
10 Shaun Alexander 1.00 2.50
11 Philip Rivers 1.25 3.00
12 Willie Parker 1.00 2.50
13 Tom Brady 2.00 5.00
14 Donovan McNabb 1.25 3.00
15 Larry Johnson 1.00 2.50

2006 Leaf Rookies and Stars Crusade Materials

STATED PRINT RUN 250 SER.#'d SETS
*PRIME/25: 1X TO 2.5X JSY/250
PRIME PRINT RUN 25 SER.#'d SETS
1 Ben Roethlisberger 6.00 15.00
2 Brett Favre 8.00 20.00
3 LaDainian Tomlinson 4.00 10.00
4 Michael Vick 4.00 10.00
5 Peyton Manning 6.00 15.00
6 Chad Johnson 3.00 8.00
7 Eli Manning 5.00 12.00
8 Marvin Harrison 4.00 10.00
9 Steve Smith 4.00 10.00
10 Shaun Alexander/200 4.00 10.00
11 Philip Rivers 4.00 10.00
12 Willie Parker 3.00 8.00
13 Tom Brady 6.00 15.00
14 Donovan McNabb 4.00 10.00
15 Larry Johnson 4.00 10.00

2006 Leaf Rookies and Stars Dress for Success Jerseys

BASE JSY PRINT RUN 100 SER.#'d SETS
*PRIME/25: .6X TO 1.5X JSY/100
PRIME PRINT RUN 25 SER.#'d SETS
*SHOES/115: .4X TO 1X BASIC JSYs
SHOE PRINT RUN 115 SER.#'d SETS
*HELMET/110: .5X TO 1.2X JSY/100
HELMET PRINT RUN 110 SER.#'d SETS
*FACE MASK/335-350: .4X TO 1X JSY/100
PRINT RUN 335-350 SER.#'d SETS
UNPRICED JSY AU PRINT RUN 10
UNPRICED PRIME AU PRINT RUN 5
1 Demetrius Williams 2.50 6.00
2 Leon Washington 1.50 4.00
3 A.J. Hawk 6.00 15.00
4 Brian Calhoun 2.50 6.00
5 Omar Jacobs 2.50 6.00
6 Reggie Bush 10.00 25.00
7 Michael Robinson 2.50 6.00
8 Brandon Williams 2.50 6.00
9 Jason Avant 1.25 3.00
10 Jerious Norwood 3.00 8.00
11 Kellen Clemens 3.00 8.00
12 Sinorice Moss 2.50 6.00
13 Maurice Stovall 2.50 6.00
14 Mario Williams 2.00 5.00
15 Maurice Drew 5.00 12.00
16 LenDale White 4.00 10.00
17 Matt Leinart 4.00 10.00
18 Vernon Davis 2.50 6.00
19 Derek Hagan 2.50 6.00
20 Brandon Marshall 2.50 6.00
21 Santonio Holmes 4.00 10.00
22 DeAngelo Williams 6.00 15.00
23 Joe Klopfenstein 2.50 6.00
24 Charlie Whitehurst 2.50 6.00
25 Travis Wilson 2.50 6.00
26 Marcedes Lewis 2.50 6.00
27 Chad Jackson 2.50 6.00
28 Vince Young 8.00 20.00
29 Michael Huff 1.50 4.00
30 Tarvaris Jackson 2.00 5.00
31 Laurence Maroney 1.50 4.00

2006 Leaf Rookies and Stars Elements

*FOIL: .6X TO 1.5X BASIC INSERTS
*HOLOFOIL: .8X TO 2X BASIC INSERTS
1 Ben Roethlisberger 2.00 5.00
2 Zach Thomas 1.50 4.00
3 Troy Polamalu 2.00 5.00
4 Tedy Bruschi 1.50 4.00
5 Ray Lewis 1.50 4.00
6 Tom Brady 2.50 6.00
7 Chad Johnson 1.25 3.00
8 Fred Taylor 1.25 3.00
9 Byron Leftwich 1.25 3.00
10 Rudi Johnson 1.25 3.00
11 Chad Pennington 1.25 3.00
12 Hines Ward 1.50 4.00
13 Brian Urlacher 1.50 4.00
14 Peyton Manning 2.50 6.00
15 LaDainian Tomlinson 1.50 4.00
16 Shaun Alexander 1.25 3.00
17 Trent Green 1.25 3.00
18 Curtis Martin 1.50 4.00
19 Willis McGahee 1.25 3.00

2006 Leaf Rookies and Stars Elements Materials

STATED PRINT RUN 250 SER.#'d SETS
*FOIL/100: .5X TO 1.2X JSY/250
FOIL PRINT RUN 100 SER.#'d SETS
*HOLOFOIL/25: 1X TO 2.5X JSY/250
HOLOFOIL PRINT RUN 25 SER.#'d SETS
1 Ben Roethlisberger 6.00 15.00
2 Zach Thomas 4.00 10.00
3 Troy Polamalu 5.00 12.00
4 Tedy Bruschi 4.00 10.00
5 Ray Lewis 4.00 10.00
6 Tom Brady 6.00 15.00
7 Chad Johnson 3.00 8.00
8 Fred Taylor 3.00 8.00
9 Byron Leftwich 3.00 8.00
10 Rudi Johnson 3.00 8.00
11 Chad Pennington 3.00 8.00
12 Hines Ward 4.00 10.00
13 Brian Urlacher 4.00 10.00
14 Peyton Manning 6.00 15.00
15 LaDainian Tomlinson 4.00 10.00
16 Shaun Alexander 4.00 10.00
17 Trent Green 3.00 8.00
18 Curtis Martin 4.00 10.00
19 Willis McGahee 4.00 10.00

2006 Leaf Rookies and Stars Freshman Orientation Materials Jerseys

STATED PRINT RUN 125 SER.#'d SETS
*PRIME/25: .6X TO 1.5X JSY/125
PRIME PRINT RUN 25 SER.#'d SETS
*FOOTBALL/150-175: .4X TO 1X JSY/125
FOOTBALLS PRINT RUN 150-175
UNPRICED JSY AU PRINT RUN 10
UNPRICED JSY PRIME AU PRINT RUN 5
1 DeAngelo Williams 2.50 6.00
2 Reggie Bush 4.00 10.00
3 LenDale White 4.00 10.00
4 Charlie Whitehurst 3.00 8.00
5 Travis Wilson 2.50 6.00
6 Vince Young 2.50 6.00
7 Brandon Marshall 2.50 6.00
8 Joe Klopfenstein 2.50 6.00
9 Mario Williams 2.00 5.00
10 Omar Jacobs 2.50 6.00
11 Michael Huff 1.50 4.00
12 Sinorice Moss 2.50 6.00
13 Brian Calhoun 2.50 6.00
14 Demetrius Williams 2.50 6.00
15 Brandon Williams 3.00 8.00
16 Maurice Drew 4.00 10.00
17 Derek Hagan 2.50 6.00
18 Jerious Norwood 3.00 8.00
19 Leon Washington 1.50 4.00
20 Kellen Clemens 3.00 8.00
21 Santonio Holmes 4.00 10.00
22 Jason Avant 1.25 3.00
23 A.J. Hawk 6.00 15.00
24 Maurice Stovall 2.50 6.00
25 Vernon Davis 2.50 6.00
26 Marcedes Lewis 2.50 6.00
27 Tarvaris Jackson 2.00 5.00
28 Laurence Maroney 1.50 4.00
29 Chad Jackson 2.50 6.00
30 Michael Robinson 2.50 6.00
31 Matt Leinart 2.00 5.00

2006 Leaf Rookies and Stars Materials Gold

*LONG.GOLD/250: .5X TO 1.2X BASIC JSYs
LONG.GOLD PRINT RUN 250 SER.#'d SETS
*LONG.BLACK/25: 1.2X TO 3X BASIC JSYs
LONG.BLACK PRINT RUN 25 SER.#'d SETS
1 Anquan Boldin 2.50 6.00
3 Kurt Warner 2.50 6.00
4 Larry Fitzgerald 3.00 8.00
5 Alge Crumpler 2.50 6.00
6 Michael Vick 3.00 8.00
7 Warrick Dunn 2.50 6.00
11 Josh Reed 2.00 5.00
12 Lee Evans 2.50 6.00
13 Willis McGahee 3.00 8.00
14 DeShaun Foster 2.50 6.00
15 Jake Delhomme 2.50 6.00
17 Steve Smith 3.00 8.00
18 Cedric Benson 3.00 8.00
20 Rex Grossman 3.00 8.00
21 Carson Palmer 3.00 8.00
25 Charlie Frye 3.00 8.00
27 Reuben Droughns 2.50 6.00
28 Drew Bledsoe 3.00 8.00
29 Julius Jones 3.00 8.00
31 Terry Glenn 2.50 6.00
32 Jake Plummer 2.50 6.00
33 Rod Smith 2.50 6.00
34 Tatum Bell 2.50 6.00
36 Kevin Jones 3.00 8.00
37 Roy Williams WR 3.00 8.00
38 Ahman Green 2.50 6.00
39 Brett Favre 6.00 15.00
40 Donald Driver 2.50 6.00
41 Robert Ferguson 2.00 5.00
42 Samkon Gado 3.00 8.00
43 Andre Johnson 2.50 6.00
44 David Carr 2.50 6.00
45 Domanick Davis 2.50 6.00
47 Marvin Harrison 3.00 8.00
48 Peyton Manning 5.00 12.00
49 Reggie Wayne 2.50 6.00
50 Dallas Clark 2.00 5.00
51 Fred Taylor 2.50 6.00
52 Byron Leftwich 2.50 6.00
53 Jimmy Smith 2.50 6.00
54 Larry Johnson 3.00 8.00
57 Eddie Kennison 2.00 5.00
58 Chris Chambers 2.50 6.00
60 Ronnie Brown 3.00 8.00
63 Deion Branch 2.50 6.00
64 Corey Dillon 2.50 6.00
65 Tom Brady 5.00 12.00
69 Eli Manning 4.00 10.00
71 Tiki Barber 3.00 8.00
72 Chad Pennington 2.50 6.00
73 Curtis Martin 3.00 8.00
74 Laveranues Coles 2.50 6.00
76 LaMont Jordan 2.50 6.00
78 Brian Westbrook 2.50 6.00
79 Donovan McNabb 3.00 8.00
81 Hines Ward 3.00 8.00
82 Ben Roethlisberger 5.00 12.00
83 Willie Parker 2.50 6.00
84 Antonio Gates 3.00 8.00
85 LaDainian Tomlinson 3.00 8.00
86 Philip Rivers 3.00 8.00
87 Alex Smith QB 3.00 8.00
90 Darrell Jackson 2.50 6.00
91 Matt Hasselbeck 2.50 6.00
92 Shaun Alexander 3.00 8.00
93 Torry Holt 2.50 6.00
94 Steven Jackson 3.00 8.00
95 Cadillac Williams 2.50 6.00
96 Joey Galloway 2.50 6.00
98 Drew Bennett 2.00 5.00
100 Clinton Portis 3.00 8.00

2006 Leaf Rookies and Stars NFL Kickoff Classic

1 Brett Favre 3.00 8.00
2 Ben Roethlisberger 2.00 5.00
3 Peyton Manning 2.50 6.00
4 Tom Brady 2.50 6.00
5 Eli Manning 2.00 5.00
6 Shaun Alexander 1.25 3.00
7 LaDainian Tomlinson 1.50 4.00
8 Larry Johnson 1.25 3.00
9 Ronnie Brown 1.50 4.00
10 Cadillac Williams 1.25 3.00

2006 Leaf Rookies and Stars Rookie Material Autographs

STATED PRINT RUN 25-85
UNPRICED LONG.HOLOFOIL PRINT RUN 10
UNPRICED LONG.GOLD PRINT RUN 5
UNPRICED BLACK PRIME PRINT RUN 1
251 Matt Leinart/85 20.00 50.00
252 Kellen Clemens/25 8.00 20.00
253 Tarvaris Jackson/25 10.00 25.00
254 Charlie Whitehurst/25 10.00 25.00
255 DeAngelo Williams/25 30.00 80.00
256 Maurice Drew/85 25.00 60.00
257 Brian Calhoun/25 6.00 15.00
258 Jerious Norwood/25 8.00 20.00
259 Vernon Davis/25 12.00 30.00
260 Joe Klopfenstein/85 5.00 12.00
261 Sinorice Moss/25 10.00 25.00
262 Derek Hagan/85 6.00 15.00
263 Brandon Williams/25 6.00 15.00
264 Michael Robinson/25 8.00 20.00
265 Jason Avant/85 5.00 12.00
266 Brandon Marshall/25 10.00 25.00
267 Demetrius Williams/25 8.00 20.00
268 Mario Williams/25 10.00 25.00
269 Michael Huff/25 8.00 20.00
270 Chad Jackson/85 5.00 12.00

2006 Leaf Rookies and Stars Rookie Material Autographs Longevity

LONGEVITY PRINT RUN 15-25 SER.#'d SETS
271 Vince Young/25 50.00 120.00
272 Omar Jacobs/25 8.00 20.00
273 Reggie Bush/25 50.00 120.00
274 Laurence Maroney/25 20.00 50.00
276 LenDale White/25 20.00 50.00
276 Leon Washington/25 20.00 50.00
277 Marcedes Lewis/25 8.00 20.00
278 Santonio Holmes/25 30.00 60.00
279 Travis Wilson/25 8.00 20.00
280 Maurice Stovall/25 8.00 20.00
281 A.J. Hawk/25 40.00 80.00

2006 Leaf Rookies and Stars Prime Cuts

STATED PRINT RUN 50 SER.#'d SETS
*COMBO/25: .6X TO 1.5X PRIME CUT/50
COMBO PRINT RUN 25 SER.#'d SETS
1 Alge Crumpler 6.00 15.00
2 Antonio Gates 8.00 20.00
3 Peyton Manning 12.00 30.00
4 Chad Johnson 6.00 15.00
5 Julius Jones 8.00 20.00
6 Shaun Alexander 8.00 20.00
7 Marvin Harrison 8.00 20.00
8 Larry Johnson 8.00 20.00
9 Torry Holt 6.00 15.00
10 Curtis Martin 8.00 20.00
11 Tom Brady 12.00 30.00
12 Anquan Boldin 6.00 15.00
13 Michael Vick 8.00 20.00

2006 Leaf Rookies and Stars Rookie Autographs Longevity

STATED PRINT RUN 15-50 SETS
*HOLOFOIL/19-25: .6X TO 1.5X BASIC AU/50
HOLOFOIL PRINT RUN 7-25 SER.#'d SETS
SER.#'d UNDER 25 NOT PRICED
103 Reggie McNeal/25 8.00 20.00
104 Claude Wroten 4.00 10.00
105 Gabe Watson 4.00 10.00
107 Todd Watkins 4.00 10.00
108 Bennie Brazell 5.00 12.00
109 David Anderson 5.00 12.00
110 John David Washington 5.00 12.00
111 Marques Hagans/25 6.00 15.00
117 Erik Meyer 5.00 12.00
118 Taurean Henderson 6.00 15.00
119 A.J. Nicholson 4.00 10.00
122 Ashton Youboty 4.00 10.00
123 Alan Zemaitis 6.00 15.00
146 Darrell Hackney 5.00 12.00
147 Paul Pinegar 4.00 10.00
148 Brandon Kirsch/40 5.00 12.00
149 Andre Hall 5.00 12.00
151 Cedric Humes/25 6.00 15.00
152 Wendell Mathis/45 5.00 12.00
153 Gerald Riggs 5.00 12.00
154 Quinton Ganther/25 6.00 15.00
155 Martin Nance/25 8.00 20.00
156 Greg Lee/25 6.00 15.00
157 Jai Lewis 5.00 12.00
158 Cory Rodgers 5.00 12.00
161 DeMeco Ryans 6.00 15.00
162 Rocky McIntosh 5.00 12.00
163 David Kirtman 5.00 12.00
164 Skyler Green 4.00 10.00
165 Will Blackmon 5.00 12.00
166 Darryl Tapp 5.00 12.00
167 Dusty Dvoracek 6.00 15.00
168 Richard Marshall 4.00 10.00
169 Tim Jennings 5.00 12.00
170 David Pittman 5.00 12.00
171 DeMario Minter 5.00 12.00
172 Marcus Maxey 5.00 12.00
173 Roman Harper 5.00 12.00
174 Anthony Smith 6.00 15.00
175 Nate Salley 5.00 12.00
176 Mike Hass 5.00 12.00
177 Greg Blue 5.00 12.00
178 Daniel Bullocks 6.00 15.00
179 Danieal Manning 6.00 15.00
180 Calvin Lowry 6.00 15.00
181 Eric Smith 5.00 12.00
182 Jimmy Williams 6.00 15.00
183 Cedric Griffin 5.00 12.00
184 Ko Simpson 5.00 12.00
185 Pat Watkins 5.00 12.00
187 Bernard Pollard 5.00 12.00
188 Darnell Bing/34 5.00 12.00
201 Jay Cutler/25 100.00 200.00
202 Brodie Croyle/25 10.00 25.00
203 Ingle Martin/25 8.00 20.00
204 Derrick Ross 5.00 12.00
205 Bruce Gradkowski/25 10.00 25.00
206 D.J. Shockley/25 8.00 20.00
207 Joseph Addai/25 10.00 25.00
208 P.J. Daniels/25 6.00 15.00
209 Marques Colston 25.00 60.00
210 Jerome Harrison/25 10.00 25.00
211 Wali Lundy/25 8.00 20.00
212 Mike Bell/40 6.00 15.00
213 Miles Austin/25 125.00 200.00
214 Anthony Fasano 6.00 15.00
215 Tony Scheffler 6.00 15.00
216 Leonard Pope 6.00 15.00
217 David Thomas 5.00 12.00
218 Dominique Byrd 5.00 12.00
219 Garrett Mills 6.00 15.00
220 Hank Baskett 6.00 15.00
221 Greg Jennings 12.00 30.00
222 Devin Hester 15.00 40.00
223 Willie Reid 5.00 12.00
224 Brad Smith 6.00 15.00
225 Sam Hurd 4.00 10.00
226 Owen Daniels 6.00 15.00
227 Domenik Hixon 6.00 15.00
228 Jeremy Bloom 5.00 12.00
229 Dawan Landry 6.00 15.00
230 Jonathan Orr 5.00 12.00
231 Delanie Walker 6.00 15.00
232 Adam Jennings 5.00 12.00
233 Jeffrey Webb 5.00 12.00
234 Ethan Kilmer 5.00 12.00
235 Tye Hill 4.00 10.00
236 Jason Allen 5.00 12.00
237 Antonio Cromartie 6.00 15.00
238 D'Brickashaw Ferguson 6.00 15.00
239 Tamba Hali 6.00 15.00
240 Haloti Ngata 6.00 15.00
241 Brodrick Bunkley 5.00 12.00
242 John McCargo 4.00 10.00
243 Johnathan Joseph 5.00 12.00
244 Kelly Jennings 5.00 12.00
245 Donte Whitner 6.00 15.00
246 Abdul Hodge 4.00 10.00
247 Ernie Sims 5.00 12.00
248 Chad Greenway 6.00 15.00
249 Bobby Carpenter 4.00 10.00
250 Manny Lawson 5.00 12.00

2006 Leaf Rookies and Stars Rookie Crusade Red

RED PRINT RUN 1000 SER.#'d SETS
*BLUE/500: .5X TO 1.2X RD/1000
BLUE PRINT RUN 500 SER.#'d SETS
*GREEN/100: .8X TO 2X RED/1000
GREEN PRINT RUN 100 SER.#'d SETS
*PURPLE/25: 1.5X TO 4X RED/1000
PURPLE PRINT RUN 25 SER.#'d SETS
1 Chad Jackson .50 1.25
2 Laurence Maroney .60 1.50
3 Tarvaris Jackson .75 2.00
4 Michael Huff .60 1.50
5 Mario Williams .75 2.00
6 Marcedes Lewis .75 2.00
7 Maurice Drew 1.25 3.00
8 Vince Young 1.00 2.50
9 LenDale White .60 1.50
10 Reggie Bush 1.50 4.00
11 Matt Leinart .75 2.00
12 Michael Robinson .60 1.50
13 Vernon Davis 1.00 2.50
14 Brandon Williams .50 1.25
15 Derek Hagan .60 1.50
16 Jason Avant .50 1.25
17 Brandon Marshall .75 2.00
18 Omar Jacobs .50 1.25
19 Santonio Holmes 1.00 2.50
20 Jerious Norwood .60 1.50
21 Demetrius Williams .60 1.50
22 Sinorice Moss .75 2.00
23 Leon Washington .60 1.50
24 Kellen Clemens .60 1.50
25 A.J. Hawk .75 2.00
26 Maurice Stovall .50 1.25
27 DeAngelo Williams 1.00 2.50
28 Charlie Whitehurst .75 2.00
29 Travis Wilson .50 1.25
30 Joe Klopfenstein .50 1.25
31 Brian Calhoun .50 1.25

2006 Leaf Rookies and Stars Rookie Crusade Materials

STATED PRINT RUN 175 SER.#'d SETS
*PRIME/25: .6X TO 1.5X JSY/175
PRIME PRINT RUN 25 SER.#'d SETS
1 Chad Jackson 2.50 6.00
2 Laurence Maroney 1.50 4.00
3 Tarvaris Jackson 3.00 8.00
4 Michael Huff 3.00 8.00
5 Mario Williams 2.00 5.00
6 Marcedes Lewis 2.50 6.00
7 Maurice Drew 5.00 12.00
8 Vince Young 2.50 6.00
9 LenDale White 4.00 10.00
10 Reggie Bush 4.00 10.00
11 Matt Leinart 2.00 5.00
12 Michael Robinson 2.50 6.00
13 Vernon Davis 4.00 10.00
14 Brandon Williams 2.50 6.00
15 Derek Hagan 2.50 6.00
16 Jason Avant 2.50 6.00
17 Brandon Marshall 2.50 6.00
18 Omar Jacobs 2.50 6.00
19 Santonio Holmes 4.00 10.00
20 Jerious Norwood 3.00 8.00
21 Demetrius Williams 2.50 6.00
22 Sinorice Moss 2.50 6.00
23 Leon Washington 1.50 4.00
24 Kellen Clemens 3.00 8.00
25 A.J. Hawk 6.00 15.00
26 Maurice Stovall 2.50 6.00
27 DeAngelo Williams 2.50 6.00
28 Charlie Whitehurst 2.50 6.00
29 Travis Wilson 2.50 6.00
30 Joe Klopfenstein 2.50 6.00
31 Brian Calhoun 2.50 6.00

2006 Leaf Rookies and Stars Standing Ovation Red

RED/1000 PRINT RUN 1000 SER.#'d SETS
*BLUE/500: .5X TO 1.2X RED/1000
BLUE PRINT RUN 500 SER.#'d SETS
*GREEN/100: 1X TO 2.5X RED/1000
GREEN PRINT RUN 100 SER.#'d SETS
*PURPLE/25: 1.5X TO 4X RED/1000
PURPLE PRINT RUN 25 SER.#'d SETS
1 Alex Smith QB 1.25 3.00
2 Brian Urlacher 1.25 3.00
3 Chris Brown .75 2.00
4 Darrell Jackson 1.00 2.50
5 Domanick Davis .75 2.00
6 Jerry Porter .75 2.00
7 Jevon Kearse 1.00 2.50
8 LaMont Jordan 1.00 2.50
9 Lee Evans 1.00 2.50
10 Mark Clayton 1.00 2.50
11 Marc Bulger 1.00 2.50
12 Reggie Brown .75 2.00
13 Reggie Wayne 1.00 2.50
14 Roy Williams S 1.00 2.50
15 Rudi Johnson 1.00 2.50
16 T.J. Houshmandzadeh 1.00 2.50
17 Tedy Bruschi 1.25 3.00
18 Willis McGahee 1.00 2.50
19 Torry Holt 1.00 2.50
20 Alge Crumpler 1.00 2.50
21 Andre Johnson 1.25 3.00
22 Zach Thomas 1.25 3.00
23 Warrick Dunn 1.00 2.50
24 Priest Holmes 1.00 2.50
25 Derrick Mason 1.00 2.50

2006 Leaf Rookies and Stars Standing Ovation Autographs

STATED PRINT RUN 25 SER.#'d SETS
SER.#'d UNDER 25 NOT PRICED
5 Domanick Davis 8.00 20.00
7 Jevon Kearse 8.00 20.00
8 LaMont Jordan 8.00 20.00
12 Reggie Brown 8.00 20.00
13 Reggie Wayne 12.00 30.00
14 Roy Williams S 12.00 30.00
15 Rudi Johnson 15.00 40.00
16 T.J. Houshmandzadeh 12.00 30.00
17 Tedy Bruschi 40.00 80.00
18 Willis McGahee 12.00 30.00

2006 Leaf Rookies and Stars Standing Ovation Materials

STATED PRINT RUN 250 SER.#'d SETS
*PRIME/25: 1X TO 2.5X JSY/250
PRIME PRINT RUN 25 SER.#'d SETS
1 Alex Smith QB 5.00 12.00
2 Brian Urlacher 4.00 10.00
3 Chris Brown 3.00 8.00
4 Darrell Jackson 3.00 8.00
5 Domanick Davis 3.00 8.00
6 Jerry Porter 3.00 8.00
7 Jevon Kearse 3.00 8.00
8 LaMont Jordan 3.00 8.00
9 Lee Evans 3.00 8.00
10 Mark Clayton 3.00 8.00
11 Marc Bulger 3.00 8.00
12 Reggie Brown 3.00 8.00
13 Reggie Wayne 3.00 8.00
14 Roy Williams S 3.00 8.00
15 Rudi Johnson 3.00 8.00
16 T.J. Houshmandzadeh 3.00 8.00
17 Tedy Bruschi 4.00 10.00
18 Willis McGahee 4.00 10.00
19 Torry Holt 3.00 8.00
20 Alge Crumpler 3.00 8.00
21 Andre Johnson 3.00 8.00
22 Zach Thomas 4.00 10.00
23 Warrick Dunn 3.00 8.00
24 Priest Holmes 3.00 8.00
25 Derrick Mason 2.50 6.00

2006 Leaf Rookies and Stars Statistical Standouts Autographs

UNPRICED AUTO PRINT RUN 2-10

2006 Leaf Rookies and Stars Statistical Standouts Materials

STATED PRINT RUN 250 SER.#'d SETS
*PRIME/25: 1X TO 2.5X JSY/250
PRIME PRINT RUN 25 SER.#'d SETS
1 Tom Brady 6.00 15.00
2 Trent Green 3.00 8.00
3 Brett Favre 8.00 20.00
4 Carson Palmer 4.00 10.00
5 Eli Manning 5.00 12.00
6 Peyton Manning 6.00 15.00
7 Drew Bledsoe 4.00 10.00
8 Matt Hasselbeck 3.00 8.00
9 Jake Delhomme 3.00 8.00
10 Steve Smith 4.00 10.00
11 Santana Moss 3.00 8.00
12 Chad Johnson 3.00 8.00
13 Larry Fitzgerald 4.00 10.00
14 Torry Holt 3.00 8.00
15 Joey Galloway 3.00 8.00
16 Marvin Harrison 4.00 10.00
17 Shaun Alexander 4.00 10.00
18 Tiki Barber 4.00 10.00
19 Larry Johnson 4.00 10.00
20 Clinton Portis 4.00 10.00
21 LaDainian Tomlinson 4.00 10.00
22 Rudi Johnson 3.00 8.00
23 Warrick Dunn 3.00 8.00
24 Willie Parker 3.00 8.00
25 Chris Chambers 3.00 8.00

2006 Leaf Rookies and Stars Statistical Standouts Material Autographs Prime

PRIME PRINT RUN 4-27 SER.#'d SETS
UNPRICED JSY AU PRINT RUN 5-20
SER.#'d UNDER 25 NOT PRICED
11 Santana Moss/25 12.00 30.00
12 Chad Johnson/25 12.00 30.00
16 Marvin Harrison/25 25.00 50.00
17 Shaun Alexander/25 15.00 40.00
18 Tiki Barber/21
19 Larry Johnson/27 20.00 50.00
20 Clinton Portis/26 15.00 40.00
21 LaDainian Tomlinson/21
24 Willie Parker/25 15.00 40.00
25 Chris Chambers/25 12.00 30.00

2006 Leaf Rookies and Stars Longevity Target

COMP.SET w/o RC's (100) 8.00 20.00
*VETERANS 1-100: .4X TO 1X BASIC CARDS
*ROOKIES/999 101-200: .4X TO 1X
101-200 PRINT RUN 999 SER.#'d SETS
*ROOKIES/599 201-250: .4X TO 1X
201-250 PRINT RUN 599 SER.#'d SETS

2006 Leaf Rookies and Stars Longevity Target Emerald Parallel

*VETS 1-100: 6X TO 15X BASIC CARDS
VETERANS PRINT RUN 49 SER.#'d SETS
*ROOKIES 101-200: 2.5X TO 6X BASIC CARDS
*ROOKIES 201-250: 2X TO 5X BASIC CARDS
101-250 PRINT RUN 29 SER.#'d SETS

2006 Leaf Rookies and Stars Longevity Target Ruby Parallel

*VETS 1-100: 2X TO 5X BASIC CARDS
VETERANS PRINT RUN 249 SER.#'d SETS
*ROOKIES 101-200: 1X TO 2.5X BASIC CARDS
*ROOKIES 201-250: .8X TO 2X BASIC CARDS
ROOKIES PRINT RUN 199 SER.#'d SETS
*ROOKIE JSY 251-270: .4X TO 1X
JSY ROOKIES PRINT RUN 499 SER.#'d SETS

2006 Leaf Rookies and Stars Longevity Target Sapphire Parallel

*VETS 1-100: 3X TO 8X BASIC CARDS
1-100 PRINT RUN 149 SER.#'d SETS
*ROOKIES 101-200: 1.22X TO 3X
*ROOKIES 201-250: 1X TO 2.5X BASIC CARDS
101-200 PRINT RUN 99 SER.#'d SETS
*ROOKIE JSY 251-270: .5X TO 1.2X
JSY ROOKIES PRINT RUN 249 SER.#'d SETS

2006 Leaf Rookies and Stars Longevity Target Materials Ruby

*LONG.RUBY/150-250: .5X TO 1.2X
*LONG.RUBY/82-100: .6X TO 1.5X MAT.GOLD
*LONG.RUBY/55: .8X TO 2X MAT.GOLD
*LONG.RUBY/25: 1.2X TO 3X MAT.GOLD
STATED PRINT RUN 1-250 SER.#'d SETS
*EMER.PRIME/25: 1.2X TO 3X MAT.GOLD
EMERALD PRIME PRINT RUN 10-25
*SAPPHIRE/88-100: .6X TO 1.5X MAT.GOLD
*SAPPHIRE/50: .8X TO 2X MAT.GOLD
SAPPHIRE PRINT RUN 100 SER.#'d SETS
SER.#'d UNDER 25 NOT PRICED
1 Anquan Boldin/250 3.00 8.00
4 Larry Fitzgerald/250 4.00 10.00
6 Michael Vick/250 5.00 12.00
9 Jamal Lewis/250 3.00 8.00
15 Jake Delhomme/250 3.00 8.00
19 Muhsin Muhammad/82 4.00 10.00
32 Jake Plummer/250 3.00 8.00
38 Ahman Green/175 3.00 8.00
39 Brett Favre/55 12.00 30.00
44 David Carr/250 3.00 8.00
48 Peyton Manning/250 6.00 15.00
52 Byron Leftwich/250 3.00 8.00
53 Jimmy Smith/250 3.00 8.00
55 Tony Gonzalez/100 4.00 10.00
64 Corey Dillon/150 3.00 8.00
67 Donte Stallworth/180 3.00 8.00
69 Eli Manning/250 5.00 12.00
72 Chad Pennington/250 3.00 8.00
73 Curtis Martin/250 4.00 10.00
79 Donovan McNabb/100 5.00 12.00
82 Ben Roethlisberger/25 15.00 40.00
98 Drew Bennett/250 2.50 6.00
100 Clinton Portis/250 4.00 10.00

2006 Leaf Rookies and Stars Longevity Target Rookie Autographs

STATED PRINT RUN 5-250 SER.#'d SETS
SER.#'d UNDER 25 NOT PRICED
104 Claude Wroten/125 3.00 8.00
105 Gabe Watson/70 5.00 12.00
107 Todd Watkins/125 4.00 10.00
108 Bennie Brazell/125 4.00 10.00
109 David Anderson/125 4.00 10.00
110 John David Washington/125 4.00 10.00
111 Marques Hagans/90 4.00 10.00
117 Erik Meyer/250 3.00 8.00
118 Taurean Henderson/59 6.00 15.00
121 Jon Alston/50 6.00 15.00
122 Ashton Youboty/95 5.00 12.00
146 Darrell Hackney/54 5.00 12.00
147 Paul Pinegar/61 5.00 12.00

148 Brandon Kirsch/45	8.00	20.00
149 Andre Hall/100	6.00	15.00
150 De'Arrius Howard/100	5.00	12.00
152 Wendell Mathis/100	4.00	10.00
154 Quinton Ganther/40	6.00	15.00
155 Martin Nance/104	4.00	10.00
156 Greg Lee/102	4.00	10.00
157 Jai Lewis/142	3.00	8.00
162 Rocky McIntosh/125	5.00	12.00
163 David Kirtman/125	4.00	10.00
164 Skyler Green/40	8.00	20.00
165 Will Blackmon/125	4.00	10.00
166 Darryl Tapp/125	4.00	10.00
167 Dusty Dvoracek/125	5.00	12.00
168 Richard Marshall/125	4.00	10.00
169 Tim Jennings/125	4.00	10.00
170 David Pittman/125	4.00	10.00
171 DeMario Minter/125	4.00	10.00
172 Marcus Maxey/125	4.00	10.00
173 Roman Harper/125	4.00	10.00
174 Anthony Smith/125	6.00	15.00
175 Nate Salley/125	4.00	10.00
176 Mike Hass/40	8.00	20.00
177 Greg Blue/125	4.00	10.00
178 Daniel Bullocks/125	5.00	12.00
179 Danieal Manning/125	5.00	12.00
180 Calvin Lowry/125	5.00	12.00
181 Eric Smith/125	4.00	10.00
182 Jimmy Williams/62	8.00	20.00
183 Cedric Griffin/125	4.00	10.00
185 Pat Watkins/125	5.00	12.00
187 Bernard Pollard/125	4.00	10.00
204 Derrick Ross/125	5.00	12.00
207 Joseph Addai/50	25.00	60.00
211 Wali Lundy/40	8.00	20.00
213 Miles Austin/105	50.00	100.00
219 Garrett Mills/40	8.00	20.00
225 Sam Hurd/125	3.00	8.00
226 Owen Daniels/125	5.00	12.00
227 Domenik Hixon/40	8.00	20.00
229 Dawan Landry/125	5.00	12.00
230 Jonathan Orr/40	6.00	15.00
231 Delanie Walker/40	6.00	15.00
233 Jeffrey Webb/40	6.00	15.00
234 Ethan Kilmer/125	5.00	12.00
236 Jason Allen/40	8.00	20.00
240 Haloti Ngata/125	6.00	15.00
241 Brodrick Bunkley/40	8.00	20.00
242 John McCargo/125	4.00	10.00
246 Abdul Hodge/25	1.00	25.00
248 Chad Greenway/125	5.00	12.00
250 Manny Lawson/125	5.00	12.00

2006 Leaf Rookies and Stars Longevity Target Rookie Material Autographs Ruby

STATED PRINT RUN 25-50 SER.#'d SETS
UNPRICED TARGET EMERALD PRINT RUN 1
UNPRICED TARGET SAPP.PRINT RUN 5-10

251 Matt Leinart/25	30.00	80.00
252 Kellen Clemens/50	12.00	30.00
253 Tarvaris Jackson/50	10.00	25.00
254 Charlie Whitehurst/50	8.00	20.00
255 DeAngelo Williams/25	30.00	80.00
256 Maurice Drew/50	35.00	60.00
257 Brian Calhoun/25	10.00	25.00
258 Jerious Norwood/50	15.00	40.00
259 Vernon Davis/25	15.00	40.00
260 Joe Klopfenstein/50	6.00	15.00
261 Sinorice Moss/25	10.00	25.00
262 Derek Hagan/50	8.00	20.00
263 Brandon Williams/50	8.00	20.00
264 Michael Robinson/50	8.00	20.00
265 Jason Avant/50	8.00	20.00
266 Brandon Marshall/50	15.00	30.00
267 Demetrius Williams/50	8.00	20.00
268 Mario Williams/50	12.00	30.00
269 Michael Huff/50	10.00	25.00
270 Chad Jackson/25	10.00	25.00
271 Vince Young/25	50.00	120.00
272 Omar Jacobs/50	6.00	15.00
273 Reggie Bush/25	60.00	150.00
274 Laurence Maroney/25	20.00	50.00
275 LenDale White/25	30.00	60.00
276 Leon Washington/50	20.00	40.00
277 Marcedes Lewis/50	8.00	20.00
278 Santonio Holmes/25	25.00	60.00
279 Travis Wilson/50	8.00	20.00
280 Maurice Stovall/50	8.00	20.00
281 A.J. Hawk/25	40.00	80.00

2007 Leaf Rookies and Stars

This 266-card set was released in November, 2007. The set was issued into the hobby in five-card packs, with a $4 SRP, which came 24 packs to a box. Cards 1-115 feature veterans while cards 116-266 feature 2007 NFL rookies. The Rookie Cards are broken down thusly: Cards numbered 116-200 were issued to a stated print run of 999 serial numbered sets while cards numbered 201-266 were all signed by the player and were issued to stated print runs of between 99 and 299 serial numbered sets. A few players did not return their cards in time for pack out and those cards could be redeemed until June 1, 2009.

COMP.SET w/o SP's (100)	10.00	25.00
116-200 ROOKIE PRINT RUN 999		
201-266 ROOKIE AU PRINT RUN 99-299		
1 Tony Romo	.40	1.00
2 Julius Jones	.20	.50
3 Terrell Owens	.30	.75
4 Eli Manning	.30	.75
5 Plaxico Burress	.25	.60
6 Jeremy Shockey	.25	.60
7 Brandon Jacobs	.25	.60
8 Donovan McNabb	.30	.75
9 Brian Westbrook	.25	.60
10 Reggie Brown	.20	.50
11 Jason Campbell	.25	.60
12 Clinton Portis	.25	.60
13 Santana Moss	.25	.60
14 Rex Grossman	.25	.60
15 Cedric Benson	.25	.60
16 Muhsin Muhammad	.25	.60
17 Jon Kitna	.20	.50
18 Roy Williams WR	.25	.60
19 Tatum Bell	.20	.50
20 Brett Favre	.60	1.50
21 Vernand Morency	.25	.60
22 Donald Driver	.30	.75
23 Tarvaris Jackson	.20	.50
24 Chester Taylor	.20	.50
25 Troy Williamson	.20	.50
26 Jerious Norwood	.25	.60
27 Warrick Dunn	.25	.60
28 Alge Crumpler	.25	.60
29 Jake Delhomme	.25	.60
30 DeShaun Foster	.25	.60
31 Steve Smith	.25	.60
32 Drew Brees	.30	.75
33 Deuce McAllister	.25	.60
34 Marques Colston	.30	.75
35 Reggie Bush	.30	.75
36 Jeff Garcia	.25	.60
37 Cadillac Williams	.25	.60
38 Joey Galloway	.25	.60
39 Matt Leinart	.25	.60
40 Edgerrin James	.25	.60
41 Anquan Boldin	.25	.60
42 Larry Fitzgerald	.30	.75
43 Marc Bulger	.25	.60
44 Steven Jackson	.30	.75
45 Torry Holt	.25	.60
46 Alex Smith QB	.30	.75
47 Frank Gore	.30	.75
48 Vernon Davis	.25	.60
49 Matt Hasselbeck	.25	.60
50 Shaun Alexander	.25	.60
51 Deion Branch	.25	.60
52 J.P. Losman	.20	.50
53 Anthony Thomas	.20	.50
54 Lee Evans	.25	.60
55 Trent Green	.25	.60
56 Ronnie Brown	.25	.60
57 Chris Chambers	.25	.60
58 Tom Brady	.50	1.25
59 Laurence Maroney	.25	.60
60 Randy Moss	.30	.75
61 Chad Pennington	.25	.60
62 Jerricho Cotchery	.25	.60
63 Leon Washington	.25	.60
64 Steve McNair	.25	.60
65 Willis McGahee	.25	.60
66 Mark Clayton	.25	.60
67 Carson Palmer	.25	.60
68 Rudi Johnson	.25	.60
69 Chad Johnson	.25	.60
70 T.J. Houshmandzadeh	.25	.60
71 Charlie Frye	.25	.60
72 Braylon Edwards	.25	.60
73 Jamal Lewis	.25	.60
74 Ben Roethlisberger	.30	.75
75 Willie Parker	.25	.60
76 Hines Ward	.30	.75
77 Ahman Green	.25	.60
78 Andre Johnson	.25	.60
79 Matt Schaub	.25	.60
80 Peyton Manning	.50	1.25
81 Joseph Addai	.25	.60
82 Marvin Harrison	.30	.75
83 Reggie Wayne	.25	.60
84 Byron Leftwich	.25	.60
85 Fred Taylor	.25	.60
86 Maurice Jones-Drew	.30	.75
87 Vince Young	.25	.60
88 LenDale White	.25	.60
89 Brandon Jones	.20	.50
90 Jay Cutler	.30	.75
91 Javon Walker	.25	.60
92 Mike Bell	.25	.60
93 Larry Johnson	.20	.50
94 Tony Gonzalez	.25	.60
95 Brodie Croyle	.25	.60
96 LaMont Jordan	.25	.60
97 Dominic Rhodes	.25	.60
98 Philip Rivers	.30	.75
99 LaDainian Tomlinson	.30	.75
100 Antonio Gates	.30	.75
101 Drew Brees ELE	1.50	4.00
102 Reggie Bush ELE	1.50	4.00
103 Brett Favre ELE	3.00	8.00
104 Marvin Harrison ELE	1.50	4.00
105 Eli Manning ELE	1.50	4.00
106 Willie Parker ELE	1.25	3.00
107 Brian Westbrook ELE	1.25	3.00
108 Tom Brady ELE	2.50	6.00
109 Jay Cutler ELE	1.50	4.00
110 Rudi Johnson ELE	1.25	3.00
111 J.P. Losman ELE	1.00	2.50
112 Laurence Maroney ELE	1.25	3.00
113 Carson Palmer ELE	1.25	3.00
114 Ben Roethlisberger ELE	1.50	4.00
115 Brian Urlacher ELE	1.50	4.00
116 A.J. Davis RC	1.25	3.00
117 Usama Young RC	1.50	4.00
118 Aaron Rouse RC	1.50	4.00
119 Ahmad Bradshaw RC	3.00	8.00
120 Alan Branch RC	1.50	4.00
121 Alonzo Coleman RC	1.50	4.00
122 Amobi Okoye RC	2.00	5.00
123 Anthony Spencer RC	2.00	5.00
124 Deon Anderson RC	1.50	4.00
125 Justin Durant RC	1.50	4.00
126 Brandon Siler RC	1.25	3.00
127 Buster Davis RC	1.50	4.00
128 Charles Johnson RC	1.25	3.00
129 Courtney Taylor RC	1.50	4.00
130 Dallas Baker RC	1.25	3.00
131 Dan Bazuin RC	1.50	4.00
132 Danny Ware RC	2.00	5.00
133 Darius Walker RC	1.25	3.00
134 David Ball RC	1.50	4.00
135 David Harris RC	1.50	4.00
136 David Irons RC	1.25	3.00
137 Daymeion Hughes RC	1.50	4.00
138 Anthony Waters RC	1.50	4.00
139 Antwan Barnes RC	2.00	5.00
140 Eric Frampton RC	1.50	4.00
141 Eric Weddle RC	2.00	5.00
142 Eric Wright RC	2.00	5.00
143 Fred Bennett RC	1.25	3.00
144 Gary Russell RC	1.50	4.00
145 H.B. Blades RC	1.25	3.00
146 Jacoby Jones RC	2.00	5.00
147 Clifton Dawson RC	2.00	5.00
148 Kevin Boss RC	3.00	8.00
149 Jarvis Moss RC	1.50	4.00
150 Gerald Alexander RC	1.25	3.00
151 Jeff Rowe RC	1.25	3.00
152 Tanard Jackson RC	1.25	3.00
153 Joel Filani RC	1.50	4.00
154 Jon Abbate RC	1.25	3.00
155 Jon Beason RC	1.50	4.00
156 Marcus Mason RC	2.00	5.00
157 Jonathan Wade RC	1.50	4.00
158 Dante Rosario RC	2.00	5.00
159 Josh Wilson RC	1.50	4.00
160 Kenneth Darby RC	1.50	4.00
161 Biren Ealy RC	1.50	4.00
162 LaMarr Woodley RC	2.00	5.00
163 Levi Brown RC	2.00	5.00
164 Marcus McCauley RC	1.50	4.00
165 Matt Spaeth RC	2.00	5.00
166 Michael Okwo RC	1.50	4.00
167 Mike Walker RC	2.00	5.00
168 Quentin Moses RC	1.50	4.00
169 Ray McDonald RC	1.50	4.00
170 Reggie Ball RC	1.50	4.00
171 Justin Harrell RC	1.50	4.00
172 Ed Johnson RC	1.50	4.00
173 Rufus Alexander RC	1.50	4.00
174 Ryan McBean RC	2.00	5.00
175 Ryne Robinson RC	1.50	4.00
176 Sabby Piscitelli RC	2.00	5.00
177 Scott Chandler RC	2.00	5.00
178 Selvin Young RC	1.50	4.00
179 Steve Breaston RC	2.00	5.00
180 Stewart Bradley RC	1.50	4.00
181 Turk McBride RC	1.50	4.00
182 Demarcus Tank Tyler RC	1.25	3.00
183 Tim Crowder RC	2.00	5.00
184 Tim Shaw RC	1.50	4.00
185 Kenton Keith RC	2.00	5.00
186 Tyler Palko RC	1.50	4.00
187 Mason Crosby RC	1.50	4.00
188 Pierre Thomas RC	5.00	12.00
189 Victor Abiamiri RC	2.00	5.00
190 Zak DeOssie RC	1.50	4.00
191 Tyler Thigpen RC	2.00	5.00
192 Tony Ugoh RC	1.50	4.00
193 Michael Allan RC	1.25	3.00
194 Martrez Milner RC	1.25	3.00
195 John Broussard RC	1.50	4.00
196 Roy Hall RC	2.00	5.00
197 Matt Gutierrez RC	2.00	5.00
198 Legedu Naanee RC	2.00	5.00
199 Derek Stanley RC	1.50	4.00
200 Quincy Black RC	2.00	5.00
201 Trent Edwards/99 AU RC	12.00	30.00
202 Marshawn Lynch/99 AU RC	20.00	40.00
203 Chris Henry/99 AU RC	8.00	20.00
204 Paul Williams/299 AU RC	5.00	12.00
205 Sidney Rice/99 AU RC	15.00	40.00
206 Adrian Peterson/99 AU RC	150.00	300.00
207 Drew Stanton/99 AU RC	8.00	20.00
208 Calvin Johnson/99 AU RC	75.00	150.00
209 Yamon Figurs/99 AU RC	8.00	20.00
210 Troy Smith/99 AU RC	12.00	30.00
211 Garrett Wolfe/249 AU RC	5.00	12.00
212 Greg Olsen/99 AU RC	10.00	25.00
213 Joe Thomas/99 AU RC	12.00	30.00
214 Brady Quinn/99 AU RC	15.00	40.00
215 Ted Ginn Jr./99 AU RC	10.00	25.00
216 John Beck/99 AU RC	12.00	30.00
218 Robert Meachem/99 AU RC	12.00	30.00
219 JaMarcus Russell/99 AU RC	8.00	20.00
220 Michael Bush/99 AU RC		
221 Kevin Kolb/99 AU RC	20.00	50.00
223 Patrick Willis/99 AU RC	25.00	60.00
224 Jason Hill/249 AU RC	8.00	20.00
225 Brandon Jackson/99 AU RC	10.00	25.00
226 David Clowney/299 AU RC	6.00	15.00
228 Leon Hall/99 AU RC	10.00	25.00
229 Dwayne Bowe/99 AU RC	15.00	40.00
230 Kolby Smith/299 AU RC	8.00	20.00
232 Dwayne Jarrett/99 AU RC	10.00	25.00
233 Lorenzo Booker/99 AU RC	10.00	25.00
234 Anthony Gonzalez/99 AU RC	12.00	30.00
235 Johnnie Lee Higgins/99 AU RC	10.00	25.00
236 Isaiah Stanback/299 AU RC	5.00	12.00
237 LaRon Landry/249 AU RC	8.00	20.00
238 Paul Posluszny/99 AU RC	12.00	30.00
239 Brian Leonard/99 AU RC	10.00	25.00
242 Aundrae Allison/249 AU RC	5.00	12.00
244 Jamaal Anderson/249 AU RC	6.00	15.00
245 Adam Carriker/99 AU RC	10.00	25.00
246 Darrelle Revis/99 AU RC	20.00	50.00
247 Lawrence Timmons/99 AU RC	12.00	30.00
248 Michael Griffin/299 AU RC	8.00	20.00
250 Reggie Nelson/99 AU RC	10.00	25.00
252 Zach Miller/99 AU RC	12.00	30.00
253 Chris Houston/299 AU RC	6.00	15.00
255 Laurent Robinson/299 AU RC	10.00	25.00
256 James Jones/246 AU RC	8.00	20.00
258 Chris Davis/249 AU RC	5.00	12.00
259 Thomas Clayton/299 AU RC	6.00	15.00
260 Jordan Palmer/99 AU RC	10.00	25.00
261 Jordan Kent/299 AU RC	6.00	15.00
262 Chansi Stuckey/299 AU RC	8.00	20.00
263 Nate Ilaoa/299 AU RC	6.00	15.00
264 Chris Leak/99 AU RC	10.00	25.00
265 Jared Zabransky/99 AU RC	10.00	25.00
266 Syndric Steptoe/299 AU RC	6.00	15.00

2007 Leaf Rookies and Stars Gold Retail

*1-100 VETS/349: 1.5X TO 4X BASIC CARDS
*101-115 VETS/349: .4X TO 1X BASIC CARDS
*ROOKIES/349: .5X TO 1.2X BASIC CARDS
STATED PRINT RUN 349 SER.#'d SETS

2007 Leaf Rookies and Stars Black Holofoil

*1-100 VETS/25: 8X TO 20X BASIC CARDS
*101-115 VETS/10: 2.5X TO 6X BASIC CARDS
1-100 VETERAN PRINT RUN 25
*117-200 ROOKIE/10: 2.5X TO 6X BASIC CARD
101-200 STATED PRINT RUN 10

2007 Leaf Rookies and Stars Gold

*1-100 VETS/49: 5X TO 12X BASIC CARDS
*101-115 VETS/25: 1.5X TO 4X BASIC CARDS
1-115 VETERAN STATED PRINT RUN 49
*ROOKIES/25: 1.5X TO 4X BASIC CARDS
116-200 ROOKIE STATED PRINT RUN 25

2007 Leaf Rookies and Stars Silver Holofoil

*1-100 VETS/99: 3X TO 8X BASIC CARDS
*101-115 VETS/49: .8X TO 2X BASIC CARDS
1-115 VETERAN PRINT RUN 99
*ROOKIES/49: 1X TO 2.5X BASIC CARDS
116-200 ROOKIE PRINT RUN 49

2007 Leaf Rookies and Stars Silver

*1-100 VETS/249: 2X TO 5X BASIC CARDS
*101-115 VETS/199: .6X TO 1.5X BASIC CARDS
1-115 VETERAN PRINT RUN 199-249
*ROOKIES/199: .8X TO 2X BASIC CARDS
116-200 ROOKIE PRINT RUN 199

2007 Leaf Rookies and Stars Crosstraining Red

RED PRINT RUN 1000 SER.#'d SETS
*BLUE/500: .5X TO 1.2X RED/1000
BLUE PRINT RUN 500 SER.#'d SETS
*GREEN/100: .6X TO 1.5X RED/1000
GREEN PRINT RUN 100 SER.#'d SETS
*PURPLE/25: 1.5X TO 4X RED/1000
PURPLE PRINT RUN 25 SER.#'d SETS

1 Yamon Figurs	.50	1.25
2 Marshawn Lynch	.75	2.00
3 Dwayne Jarrett	.60	1.50
4 Greg Olsen	.60	1.50
5 Brady Quinn	.75	2.00
6 Calvin Johnson	2.50	6.00
7 Drew Stanton	.50	1.25
8 Brandon Jackson	.60	1.50
9 Anthony Gonzalez	.75	2.00
10 Dwayne Bowe	1.00	2.50
11 John Beck	.75	2.00
12 Ted Ginn Jr.	.60	1.50
13 Adrian Peterson	3.00	8.00
14 Robert Meachem	.75	2.00
15 JaMarcus Russell	.50	1.25
16 Michael Bush	.75	2.00
17 Kevin Kolb	1.25	3.00
18 Jason Hill	.75	2.00
19 Brian Leonard	.60	1.50
20 Paul Williams	.50	1.25

2007 Leaf Rookies and Stars Crosstraining Materials Green

STATED PRINT RUN 250 SER.#'d SETS
*PURPLE PRIME/25: .8X TO 2X BASIC JSYs
PURPLE PRIME PRINT RUN 25 SER.#'d SETS

1 Yamon Figurs	2.50	6.00
2 Marshawn Lynch	2.00	5.00
3 Dwayne Jarrett	1.50	4.00
4 Greg Olsen	1.50	4.00
5 Brady Quinn	2.00	5.00
6 Calvin Johnson	6.00	15.00
7 Drew Stanton	1.25	3.00
8 Brandon Jackson	1.50	4.00
9 Anthony Gonzalez	2.00	5.00
10 Dwayne Bowe	2.50	6.00
11 John Beck	2.00	5.00
12 Ted Ginn Jr.	1.50	4.00
13 Adrian Peterson	8.00	20.00
14 Robert Meachem	2.50	6.00
15 JaMarcus Russell	1.25	3.00
16 Michael Bush	2.00	5.00
17 Kevin Kolb	3.00	8.00
18 Jason Hill	2.50	6.00
19 Brian Leonard	2.50	6.00
20 Paul Williams	2.50	6.00

2007 Leaf Rookies and Stars Crusade Red

RED PRINT RUN 1000 SER.#'d SETS
*BLUE/500: .5X TO 1.2X RED/1000
BLUE PRINT RUN 500 SER.#'d SETS
*GREEN/100: .8X TO 2X RED/1000
GREEN PRINT RUN 100 SER.#'d SETS
*PURPLE/25: 1.5X TO 4X RED/1000
PURPLE PRINT RUN 25 SER.#'d SETS

1 Hines Ward	1.25	3.00
2 Andre Johnson	1.00	2.50
3 Joey Galloway	1.00	2.50
4 Terry Glenn	1.00	2.50
5 Jerricho Cotchery	1.00	2.50
6 Mark Clayton	1.00	2.50
7 Brandon Marshall	1.00	2.50
8 Braylon Edwards	1.00	2.50
9 Brett Favre	2.50	6.00
10 Tom Brady	2.00	5.00
11 LaDainian Tomlinson	1.25	3.00
12 Larry Johnson	.75	2.00
13 Chad Johnson	1.00	2.50
14 Torry Holt	1.00	2.50
15 Vincent Jackson	1.00	2.50

2007 Leaf Rookies and Stars Crusade Materials Green

STATED PRINT RUN 250 SER.#'d SETS
*PURPLE PRIME/25: 1X TO 2.5X BASIC JSYs
PURPLE PRIME PRINT RUN 8-25

1 Hines Ward	4.00	10.00
2 Andre Johnson	3.00	8.00
3 Joey Galloway	3.00	8.00
4 Terry Glenn	3.00	8.00
5 Jerricho Cotchery	3.00	8.00
6 Mark Clayton	3.00	8.00
7 Brandon Marshall	3.00	8.00
8 Braylon Edwards	3.00	8.00
9 Brett Favre	8.00	20.00
10 Tom Brady	6.00	15.00
11 LaDainian Tomlinson	4.00	10.00
12 Larry Johnson	2.50	6.00
13 Chad Johnson	3.00	8.00
14 Torry Holt	3.00	8.00
15 Vincent Jackson	3.00	8.00

2007 Leaf Rookies and Stars Dress for Success Jerseys

STATED PRINT RUN 175 SER.#'d SETS
*PRIME/25: .8X TO 2X JSY/175
*FACE MASK/287-300: .4X TO 1X JSY/175
*HELMET/55: .8X TO 2X JSY/175
*SHOE/55: .6X TO 1.5X JSY/175
*LONGEVITY JSY/100: .5X TO 1.2X BASIC JSY/175
*LONG.HELMET/55: .6X TO 1.5X JSY/175
*LONG.SHOE/55: .6X TO 1.5X JSY/175
*LONG.FACE MASK/50: .6X TO 1.5X JSY/175
UNPRICED AUTO PRINT RUN 10
UNPRICED PRIME AU PRINT RUN 5

1 Troy Smith	2.00	5.00
2 Yamon Figurs	1.25	3.00
3 Trent Edwards	2.00	5.00
4 Marshawn Lynch	2.00	5.00
5 Dwayne Jarrett	1.50	4.00
6 Garrett Wolfe	1.25	3.00
7 Greg Olsen	1.50	4.00
8 Kenny Irons	1.25	3.00
9 Joe Thomas	2.00	5.00
10 Brady Quinn	2.00	5.00
11 Calvin Johnson	6.00	15.00
12 Drew Stanton	1.25	3.00
13 Brandon Jackson	1.50	4.00
14 Anthony Gonzalez	2.00	5.00
15 Dwayne Bowe	2.50	6.00
16 John Beck	2.00	5.00
17 Lorenzo Booker	1.50	4.00
18 Ted Ginn Jr.	1.50	4.00
19 Adrian Peterson	8.00	20.00
20 Sidney Rice	2.50	6.00
21 Antonio Pittman	1.25	3.00
22 Robert Meachem	2.00	5.00
23 Steve Smith USC	2.00	5.00
24 JaMarcus Russell	1.25	3.00
25 Johnnie Lee Higgins	2.00	5.00
26 Michael Bush	2.00	5.00
27 Kevin Kolb	3.00	8.00
28 Tony Hunt	1.25	3.00
29 Patrick Willis	4.00	10.00
30 Jason Hill	2.00	5.00
31 Brian Leonard	1.50	4.00
32 Gaines Adams	2.00	5.00
33 Chris Henry RB	1.25	3.00
34 Paul Williams	1.25	3.00

2007 Leaf Rookies and Stars Elements Materials

STATED PRINT RUN 250 SER.#'d SETS
*FOIL/100: .5X TO 1.2X BASIC JSYs
FOIL PRINT RUN 100 SER.#'d SETS
*HOLOFOIL/25: 1X TO 2.5X BASIC JSYs
HOLOFOIL PRINT RUN 25 SER.#'d SETS

101 Drew Brees	4.00	10.00
102 Reggie Bush	4.00	10.00
103 Brett Favre	8.00	20.00
104 Marvin Harrison	4.00	10.00
105 Eli Manning	4.00	10.00
106 Willie Parker	3.00	8.00
107 Brian Westbrook	3.00	8.00
108 Tom Brady	6.00	15.00
109 Jay Cutler	4.00	10.00
110 Rudi Johnson	3.00	8.00
111 J.P. Losman	2.50	6.00
112 Laurence Maroney	3.00	8.00
113 Carson Palmer	3.00	8.00
114 Ben Roethlisberger	4.00	10.00
115 Brian Urlacher	4.00	10.00

2007 Leaf Rookies and Stars Freshman Orientation Materials Jerseys

JERSEY PRINT RUN 175 SER.#'d SETS
*PRIME/25: .8X TO 2X BASIC JSY/175
*FOOTBALL/49-107: .6X TO 1.5X JSY/175
*LONG.JSY/100: .5X TO 1.2X BASIC JSY/175
*LONG.BALL/25: .8X TO 2X BASIC JSY/175
UNPRICED AUTO PRINT RUN 10
UNPRICED PRIME AU PRINT RUN 5

1 Yamon Figurs	1.25	3.00
2 Marshawn Lynch	2.00	5.00
3 Garrett Wolfe	1.25	3.00
4 Kenny Irons	1.25	3.00
5 Brady Quinn	2.00	5.00
6 Drew Stanton	1.25	3.00
7 Anthony Gonzalez	2.00	5.00
8 John Beck	2.00	5.00
9 Ted Ginn Jr.	1.50	4.00
10 Sidney Rice	2.50	6.00
11 Robert Meachem	2.00	5.00
12 JaMarcus Russell	1.25	3.00
13 Michael Bush	2.00	5.00
14 Tony Hunt	1.25	3.00
15 Jason Hill	2.00	5.00
16 Gaines Adams	2.00	5.00
17 Paul Williams	1.25	3.00
18 Troy Smith	2.00	5.00
19 Trent Edwards	2.00	5.00
20 Dwayne Jarrett	1.50	4.00
21 Greg Olsen	1.50	4.00
22 Joe Thomas	2.00	5.00
23 Calvin Johnson	6.00	15.00
24 Brandon Jackson	1.50	4.00
25 Dwayne Bowe	2.50	6.00
26 Lorenzo Booker	1.50	4.00
27 Adrian Peterson	8.00	20.00
28 Antonio Pittman	1.25	3.00
29 Steve Smith USC	2.00	5.00
30 Johnnie Lee Higgins	2.00	5.00
31 Kevin Kolb	3.00	8.00
32 Patrick Willis	4.00	10.00
33 Brian Leonard	1.50	4.00
34 Chris Henry RB	1.25	3.00

2007 Leaf Rookies and Stars Materials Gold Retail

UNNUMBERED INSERTS IN RETAIL PACKS
*GOLD HOB/185-200: .4X TO 1X GOLD RET
*GOLD HOB/100-125: .5X TO 1.2X GOLD RET
*GOLD HOB/50-65: .6X TO 1.5X GOLD RET
*GOLD HOB/15-25: .8X TO 2X GOLD RET
GOLD HOBBY PRINT RUN 1-250
*BLACK PRIME/10: 1.5X TO 4X GOLD RET
BLACK PRIME PRINT RUN 10
*EMERALD PRIME/25: 1X TO 2.5X GOLD RET
EMERALD PRIME PRINT RUN 25
*LONG.RUBY/150-250: .4X TO 1X GOLD RET
LONGEVITY RUBY PRINT RUN 150-250
*LONG.SAPPHIRE/100: .5X TO 1.2X GOLD RET
*LONG.SAPPHIRE/15: .8X TO 2X GOLD RET
LONGEVITY SAPPHIRE PRINT RUN 15-100

1 Tony Romo	5.00	12.00
2 Julius Jones	2.50	6.00
4 Eli Manning	4.00	10.00
5 Plaxico Burress	3.00	8.00
6 Jeremy Shockey	3.00	8.00
7 Brandon Jacobs	3.00	8.00
8 Donovan McNabb	4.00	10.00
9 Brian Westbrook	3.00	8.00
10 Reggie Brown	2.50	6.00
11 Jason Campbell	3.00	8.00
12 Clinton Portis	3.00	8.00
13 Santana Moss	3.00	8.00
14 Rex Grossman	3.00	8.00
15 Cedric Benson	3.00	8.00
16 Muhsin Muhammad	3.00	8.00
17 Jon Kitna	2.50	6.00
18 Roy Williams WR	3.00	8.00
19 Tatum Bell	2.50	6.00
20 Brett Favre	8.00	20.00
22 Donald Driver	4.00	10.00
23 Tarvaris Jackson	2.50	6.00
24 Chester Taylor	2.50	6.00
25 Troy Williamson	2.50	6.00
26 Jerious Norwood	3.00	8.00
27 Warrick Dunn	3.00	8.00
28 Alge Crumpler	3.00	8.00
29 Jake Delhomme	3.00	8.00
30 DeShaun Foster	3.00	8.00
31 Steve Smith	3.00	8.00
32 Drew Brees	4.00	10.00
33 Deuce McAllister	3.00	8.00
34 Marques Colston	4.00	10.00
35 Reggie Bush	4.00	10.00
36 Jeff Garcia	3.00	8.00
37 Cadillac Williams	3.00	8.00
38 Joey Galloway	3.00	8.00
39 Matt Leinart	3.00	8.00
40 Edgerrin James	3.00	8.00
41 Anquan Boldin	3.00	8.00
42 Larry Fitzgerald	4.00	10.00
43 Marc Bulger	3.00	8.00
44 Steven Jackson	4.00	10.00
45 Torry Holt	3.00	8.00
46 Alex Smith QB	4.00	10.00
47 Frank Gore	4.00	10.00
48 Vernon Davis	3.00	8.00
49 Matt Hasselbeck	3.00	8.00
50 Shaun Alexander	3.00	8.00
51 Deion Branch	3.00	8.00
52 J.P. Losman	2.50	6.00
53 Anthony Thomas	2.50	6.00
54 Lee Evans	3.00	8.00
55 Trent Green	3.00	8.00
56 Ronnie Brown	3.00	8.00
57 Chris Chambers	3.00	8.00
58 Tom Brady	6.00	15.00
59 Laurence Maroney	3.00	8.00
60 Randy Moss	4.00	10.00
61 Chad Pennington	3.00	8.00
62 Jerricho Cotchery	3.00	8.00
63 Leon Washington	3.00	8.00
64 Steve McNair	3.00	8.00
65 Willis McGahee	3.00	8.00
66 Mark Clayton	3.00	8.00
67 Carson Palmer	3.00	8.00
68 Rudi Johnson	3.00	8.00
69 Chad Johnson	3.00	8.00
70 T.J. Houshmandzadeh	3.00	8.00
71 Charlie Frye	3.00	8.00
72 Braylon Edwards	3.00	8.00
73 Jamal Lewis	3.00	8.00
74 Ben Roethlisberger	4.00	10.00
75 Willie Parker	3.00	8.00
76 Hines Ward	4.00	10.00
78 Andre Johnson	3.00	8.00
80 Peyton Manning	6.00	15.00
81 Joseph Addai	3.00	8.00
82 Marvin Harrison	4.00	10.00
83 Reggie Wayne	3.00	8.00
84 Byron Leftwich	3.00	8.00
86 Maurice Jones-Drew	4.00	10.00
87 Vince Young	3.00	8.00
88 LenDale White	3.00	8.00
89 Brandon Jones	2.50	6.00
90 Jay Cutler	4.00	10.00
91 Javon Walker	3.00	8.00
92 Mike Bell	3.00	8.00
93 Larry Johnson	2.50	6.00
94 Tony Gonzalez	3.00	8.00
95 Brodie Croyle	3.00	8.00
96 LaMont Jordan	3.00	8.00
98 Philip Rivers	4.00	10.00
99 LaDainian Tomlinson	4.00	10.00
100 Antonio Gates	4.00	10.00

2007 Leaf Rookies and Stars Prime Cuts

STATED PRINT RUN 50 SER.#'d SETS
*COMBOS/25: .6X TO 1.5X BASIC JSYs
COMBOS PRINT RUN 25 SER.#'d SETS

1 Vince Young	6.00	15.00
2 LaDainian Tomlinson	8.00	20.00
3 Chad Johnson	6.00	15.00
4 Tom Brady	12.00	30.00
5 Brett Favre	15.00	40.00
6 Marvin Harrison	8.00	20.00
7 Larry Johnson	5.00	12.00

2007 Leaf Rookies and Stars Rookie Autographs Holofoil

HOLOFOIL PRINT RUN 50-75
UNPRICED GOLD AUTO PRINT RUN 8-20
UNPRICED EMERALD AUTO PRINT RUN 5
UNPRICED BLACK AUTO PRINT RUN 1
*LONGEVITY/50: .4X TO 1X HOLO.AU/50-75
*LONGEVITY/25: .5X TO 1.2X HOLO.AU/50-75
LONGEVITY PRINT RUN 9-50
UNPRICED LONG.RUBY PRINT RUN 5-10
UNPRICED LONG.SAPPHIRE PRINT RUN 1

116 A.J. Davis	5.00	12.00
118 Aaron Rouse	6.00	15.00
121 Alonzo Coleman	6.00	15.00
122 Amobi Okoye	8.00	20.00
123 Anthony Spencer	8.00	20.00
129 Courtney Taylor	6.00	15.00
130 Dallas Baker	5.00	12.00
131 Dan Bazuin	6.00	15.00
132 Danny Ware	8.00	20.00
133 Darius Walker	5.00	12.00
134 David Ball	6.00	15.00
135 David Harris	6.00	15.00
136 David Irons	5.00	12.00
137 Daymeion Hughes	6.00	15.00
140 Eric Frampton	6.00	15.00
143 Fred Bennett	5.00	12.00
144 Gary Russell	6.00	15.00
145 H.B. Blades	5.00	12.00
146 Jacoby Jones	8.00	20.00
149 Jarvis Moss	6.00	15.00
151 Jeff Rowe	5.00	12.00
153 Joel Filani	6.00	15.00
155 Jon Beason	6.00	15.00
157 Jonathan Wade	6.00	15.00
159 Josh Wilson	6.00	15.00
160 Kenneth Darby	6.00	15.00
162 LaMarr Woodley	12.00	30.00
163 Levi Brown	8.00	20.00
164 Marcus McCauley	6.00	15.00
165 Matt Spaeth	8.00	20.00
166 Michael Okwo	6.00	15.00
167 Mike Walker	8.00	20.00
168 Quentin Moses	6.00	15.00
169 Ray McDonald	6.00	15.00
170 Reggie Ball	6.00	15.00
173 Rufus Alexander	6.00	15.00
174 Ryan McBean	8.00	20.00
175 Ryne Robinson	6.00	15.00
176 Sabby Piscitelli/75	8.00	20.00
177 Scott Chandler	8.00	20.00
179 Steve Breaston	8.00	20.00
180 Stewart Bradley	6.00	15.00
183 Tim Crowder	8.00	20.00
184 Tim Shaw/75	6.00	15.00
186 Tyler Palko	6.00	15.00
189 Victor Abiamiri	8.00	20.00

2007 Leaf Rookies and Stars Rookie Autographs College

*COLLEGE/12-25: .8X TO 2X BASIC AU/246-299
*COLLEGE/12-25: .5X TO 1.2X BASIC AU/99
COLLEGE SWATCH PRINT RUN 12-25
UNPRICED GOLD PRINT RUN 10
UNPRICED EMERALD PRINT RUN 5
UNPRICED BLACK PRINT RUN 1
UNPRICED LONGEVITY PRINT RUN 10
UNPRICED LONGEVITY RUBY PRINT RUN 5
UNPRICED LONG.SAPPHIRE PRINT RUN 1

206 Adrian Peterson/15	150.00	300.00
208 Calvin Johnson/15	100.00	200.00
214 Brady Quinn/15	75.00	150.00

2007 Leaf Rookies and Stars Rookie Crusade Red

STATED PRINT RUN 1000 SER.#'d SETS
*BLUE: .5X TO 1.2X BASIC INSERTS
BLUE PRINT RUN 500 SER.#'d SETS
*GREEN: .6X TO 1.5X BASIC INSERTS
GREEN PRINT RUN 100 SER.#'d SETS
*PURPLE: 1.5X TO 4X BASIC INSERTS
PURPLE PRINT RUN 25 SER.#'d SETS

1 Troy Smith	.75	2.00
2 Yamon Figurs	.50	1.25
3 Trent Edwards	.75	2.00
4 Marshawn Lynch	.75	2.00
5 Dwayne Jarrett	.60	1.50
6 Garrett Wolfe	.50	1.25
7 Greg Olsen	.60	1.50
8 Kenny Irons	.50	1.25
9 Joe Thomas	.75	2.00
10 Brady Quinn	.75	2.00
11 Calvin Johnson	2.50	6.00
12 Drew Stanton	.50	1.25
13 Brandon Jackson	.60	1.50
14 Anthony Gonzalez	.75	2.00
15 Dwayne Bowe	1.00	2.50
16 John Beck	.75	2.00
17 Lorenzo Booker	.60	1.50
18 Ted Ginn Jr.	.60	1.50
19 Adrian Peterson	3.00	8.00
20 Sidney Rice	1.00	2.50
21 Antonio Pittman	.50	1.25
22 Robert Meachem	.75	2.00
23 Steve Smith USC	.75	2.00
24 JaMarcus Russell	.50	1.25
25 Johnnie Lee Higgins	.60	1.50
26 Michael Bush	.75	2.00
27 Kevin Kolb	1.25	3.00
28 Tony Hunt	.50	1.25
29 Patrick Willis	1.50	4.00
30 Jason Hill	.75	2.00
31 Brian Leonard	.60	1.50
32 Gaines Adams	.75	2.00
33 Chris Henry RB	.50	1.25
34 Paul Williams	.50	1.25

2007 Leaf Rookies and Stars Rookie Crusade Materials Green

STATED PRINT RUN 250 SER.#'d SETS
*PURPLE/25: .8X TO 2X GREEN/250
PURPLE PRIME PRINT RUN 25 SER.#'d SETS

1 Troy Smith	2.00	5.00
2 Yamon Figurs	1.25	3.00
3 Trent Edwards	2.00	5.00
4 Marshawn Lynch	2.00	5.00
5 Dwayne Jarrett	1.50	4.00
6 Garrett Wolfe	1.25	3.00
7 Greg Olsen	1.50	4.00
8 Kenny Irons	1.25	3.00
9 Joe Thomas	2.00	5.00
10 Brady Quinn	2.00	5.00
11 Calvin Johnson	6.00	15.00
12 Drew Stanton	1.25	3.00
13 Brandon Jackson	1.50	4.00
14 Anthony Gonzalez	2.00	5.00
15 Dwayne Bowe	2.50	6.00
16 John Beck	2.00	5.00
17 Lorenzo Booker	1.50	4.00
18 Ted Ginn Jr.	1.50	4.00
19 Adrian Peterson	8.00	20.00
20 Sidney Rice	2.50	6.00
21 Antonio Pittman	1.25	3.00
22 Robert Meachem	2.00	5.00
23 Steve Smith USC	2.00	5.00
24 JaMarcus Russell	1.25	3.00
25 Johnnie Lee Higgins	2.00	5.00
26 Michael Bush	2.00	5.00
27 Kevin Kolb	3.00	8.00
28 Tony Hunt	1.25	3.00
29 Patrick Willis	4.00	10.00
30 Jason Hill	2.00	5.00
31 Brian Leonard	1.50	4.00
32 Gaines Adams	2.00	5.00
33 Chris Henry RB	1.25	3.00
34 Paul Williams	1.25	3.00

2007 Leaf Rookies and Stars Rookie Jerseys Jumbo Swatch

STATED PRINT RUN 50 SER.#'d SETS
*GOLD/25: .6X TO 1.5X BASIC JSY/50
GOLD PRINT RUN 25 SER.#'d SETS
UNPRICED EMERALD PRINT RUN 2-5
UNPRICED BLACK PRINT RUN 1
*LONGEVITY/50: .4X TO 1X BASIC JUMBO/50
LONGEVITY PRINT RUN 50 SER.#'d SETS
UNPRICED LONGEVITY RUBY PRINT RUN 2-5
UNPRICED LONGEVITY SAPPHIRE PRINT RUN 1

201 Trent Edwards	4.00	10.00
202 Marshawn Lynch	4.00	10.00
203 Chris Henry RB	2.50	6.00
204 Paul Williams	2.50	6.00
205 Sidney Rice	5.00	12.00
206 Adrian Peterson	15.00	40.00
207 Drew Stanton	2.50	6.00
208 Calvin Johnson	12.00	30.00
209 Yamon Figurs	2.50	6.00
210 Troy Smith	4.00	10.00
211 Garrett Wolfe	2.50	6.00
212 Greg Olsen	3.00	8.00
213 Joe Thomas	4.00	10.00
214 Brady Quinn	4.00	10.00
215 Ted Ginn Jr.	3.00	8.00
216 John Beck	4.00	10.00
217 Antonio Pittman	2.50	6.00
218 Robert Meachem	4.00	10.00
219 JaMarcus Russell	2.50	6.00
220 Michael Bush	4.00	10.00
221 Kevin Kolb	6.00	15.00
222 Tony Hunt	2.50	6.00
223 Patrick Willis	8.00	20.00
224 Jason Hill	4.00	10.00
225 Brandon Jackson	3.00	8.00
227 Kenny Irons	2.50	6.00
229 Dwayne Bowe	5.00	12.00
231 Steve Smith USC	4.00	10.00
232 Dwayne Jarrett	3.00	8.00
233 Lorenzo Booker	3.00	8.00
234 Anthony Gonzalez	4.00	10.00
235 Johnnie Lee Higgins	3.00	8.00
239 Brian Leonard	3.00	8.00
240 Gaines Adams	4.00	10.00

2007 Leaf Rookies and Stars Rookie Jerseys Jumbo Swatch College

COLLEGE PRINT RUN 5-15
*GOLD/10: .5X TO 1.2X BASIC JSY/15
COLLEGE GOLD PRINT RUN 2-10
UNPRICED EMERALD PRINT RUN 2-3
UNPRICED BLACK PRINT RUN 1

206 Adrian Peterson	100.00	200.00
212 Greg Olsen	8.00	20.00
214 Brady Quinn	50.00	100.00
219 JaMarcus Russell	6.00	15.00
220 Michael Bush	10.00	25.00
229 Dwayne Bowe	12.00	30.00
232 Dwayne Jarrett	8.00	20.00
237 LaRon Landry	10.00	25.00
241 Craig Buster Davis	8.00	20.00

2007 Leaf Rookies and Stars Standing Ovation Red

RED PRINT RUN 1000 SER.#'d SETS
*BLUE/500: .5X TO 1.2X RED/1000
BLUE PRINT RUN 500 SER.#'d SETS
*GREEN/100: .8X TO 2X RED/1000
GREEN PRINT RUN 100 SER.#'d SETS
*PURPLE/25: 1.5X TO 4X RED/1000
PURPLE PRINT RUN 25 SER.#'d SETS

1 Tiki Barber	1.25	3.00
2 Ladell Betts	.75	2.00
3 Fred Taylor	1.00	2.50
4 Warrick Dunn	1.00	2.50
5 Julius Jones	.75	2.00
6 Deuce McAllister	1.00	2.50
7 Ronnie Brown	1.00	2.50
8 Maurice Jones-Drew	1.25	3.00
9 Shaun Alexander	1.00	2.50
10 Steve Smith	1.00	2.50
11 Isaac Bruce	1.00	2.50

12 T.J. Houshmandzadeh 1.00 2.50
13 Marques Colston 1.25 3.00
14 Devin Hester 1.25 3.00
15 Larry Fitzgerald 1.25 3.00
16 Antonio Gates 1.25 3.00
17 Tony Gonzalez 1.00 2.50
18 Muhsin Muhammad 1.00 2.50
19 Eli Manning 1.25 3.00
20 Rex Grossman 1.00 2.50
21 Peyton Manning 2.00 5.00
22 Steve McNair 1.00 2.50
23 Tony Romo 1.50 4.00
24 Alex Smith QB 1.25 3.00
25 Donovan McNabb 1.25 3.00
26 Matt Leinart 1.00 2.50
27 Lee Evans 1.00 2.50
28 Matt Hasselbeck 1.00 2.50
29 Jay Cutler 1.25 3.00
30 Vince Young 1.00 2.50
31 Reggie Bush 1.25 3.00

2007 Leaf Rookies and Stars Standing Ovation Materials Green

GREEN PRINT RUN 150-250
*PURPLE PRIME/25: 1X TO 2.5X GRN/150-250
PURPLE PRIME PRINT RUN 25 SER.#'d SETS
1 Tiki Barber/150 4.00 10.00
2 Ladell Betts 2.50 6.00
3 Fred Taylor/192 3.00 8.00
4 Warrick Dunn/245 3.00 8.00
5 Julius Jones 2.50 6.00
6 Deuce McAllister 3.00 8.00
7 Ronnie Brown 3.00 8.00
8 Maurice Jones-Drew 4.00 10.00
9 Shaun Alexander 3.00 8.00
10 Steve Smith 3.00 8.00
11 Isaac Bruce 3.00 8.00
12 T.J. Houshmandzadeh 3.00 8.00
13 Marques Colston 4.00 10.00
14 Devin Hester 6.00 15.00
15 Larry Fitzgerald 4.00 10.00
16 Antonio Gates 4.00 10.00
17 Tony Gonzalez 3.00 8.00
18 Muhsin Muhammad 3.00 8.00
19 Eli Manning 4.00 10.00
20 Rex Grossman 3.00 8.00
21 Peyton Manning 6.00 15.00
22 Steve McNair 3.00 8.00
23 Tony Romo 5.00 12.00
24 Alex Smith QB 4.00 10.00
25 Donovan McNabb 4.00 10.00
26 Matt Leinart 3.00 8.00
27 Lee Evans 3.00 8.00
28 Matt Hasselbeck 3.00 8.00
29 Jay Cutler 4.00 10.00
30 Vince Young 3.00 8.00
31 Reggie Bush 4.00 10.00

2007 Leaf Rookies and Stars Statistical Standouts Materials

STATED PRINT RUN 245-250
*PRIME/25: 1X TO 2.5X BASIC JSYs
UNPRICED AUTO PRINT RUN 5
UNPRICED PRIME AU PRINT RUN 1
1 Drew Brees 4.00 10.00
2 Peyton Manning 6.00 15.00
3 Marc Bulger 3.00 8.00
4 Carson Palmer 3.00 8.00
5 Brett Favre 8.00 20.00
6 Tom Brady 6.00 15.00
7 Philip Rivers 4.00 10.00
8 Chad Johnson 3.00 8.00
9 Marvin Harrison 4.00 10.00
10 Reggie Wayne 3.00 8.00
11 Roy Williams WR 3.00 8.00
12 Donald Driver 4.00 10.00
13 Anquan Boldin 3.00 8.00
14 Torry Holt 3.00 8.00
15 Terrell Owens/245 4.00 10.00
16 LaDainian Tomlinson 4.00 10.00
17 Larry Johnson 2.50 6.00
18 Frank Gore 4.00 10.00
19 Steven Jackson 4.00 10.00
20 Willie Parker 3.00 8.00
21 Rudi Johnson 3.00 8.00
22 Brian Westbrook 3.00 8.00
23 Joseph Addai 3.00 8.00
24 Reggie Bush 4.00 10.00
25 Vince Young 3.00 8.00

2007 Leaf Rookies and Stars Studio Rookies

INSERTS IN WAL-MART BLASTER BOXES
1 Adrian Peterson 3.00 8.00
2 Anthony Gonzalez .75 2.00
3 Antonio Pittman .50 1.25
4 Brady Quinn .75 2.00
5 Brandon Jackson .60 1.50
6 Brian Leonard .60 1.50
7 Calvin Johnson 2.50 6.00
8 Chris Henry RB .50 1.25
9 Drew Stanton .50 1.25
10 Dwayne Bowe 1.00 2.50
11 Dwayne Jarrett .60 1.50
12 Gaines Adams .75 2.00
13 Garrett Wolfe .50 1.25
14 Greg Olsen .60 1.50
15 JaMarcus Russell .50 1.25
16 Jason Hill .75 2.00
17 Joe Thomas .75 2.00
18 John Beck .75 2.00
19 Johnnie Lee Higgins .60 1.50
20 Kenny Irons .50 1.25
21 Kevin Kolb 1.25 3.00
22 Lorenzo Booker .60 1.50
23 Marshawn Lynch .75 2.00
24 Michael Bush .75 2.00
25 Patrick Willis 1.50 4.00
26 Paul Williams .50 1.25
27 Robert Meachem .75 2.00
28 Sidney Rice 1.00 2.50
29 Steve Smith USC .75 2.00
30 Ted Ginn Jr. .60 1.50
31 Tony Hunt .50 1.25
32 Trent Edwards .75 2.00
33 Troy Smith .75 2.00
34 Yamon Figurs .50 1.25
35 JaMarcus Russell 1.00 2.50
Dwayne Bowe
36 Steve Smith USC .75 2.00
Dwayne Jarrett
37 Troy Smith .75 2.00
Yamon Figurs
38 Marshawn Lynch .75 2.00
Trent Edwards
39 Garrett Wolfe .60 1.50
Greg Olsen
40 Brady Quinn .75 2.00
Joe Thomas
41 Drew Stanton 2.50 6.00
Calvin Johnson
42 Adrian Peterson 3.00 8.00
Sidney Rice
43 Antonio Pittman .75 2.00
Robert Meachem
44 Tony Hunt 1.25 3.00
Kevin Kolb
45 Jason Hill 1.50 4.00
Patrick Willis
46 Chris Henry RB .50 1.25
Paul Williams
47 Marshawn Lynch 3.00 8.00
Adrian Peterson
48 Patrick Willis 1.50 4.00
Gaines Adams
49 JaMarcus Russell .75 2.00
Brady Quinn
50 Dwayne Bowe 1.00 2.50
Tony Hunt
51 Lorenzo Booker .75 2.00
John Beck
Ted Ginn Jr.
52 Michael Bush .75 2.00
JaMarcus Russell
Johnnie Lee Higgins
53 Brady Quinn 8.00 20.00
Adrian Peterson
Calvin Johnson
JaMarcus Russell
54 Antonio Pittman .50 1.25
Ted Ginn Jr.
Troy Smith
Anthony Gonzalez

2007 Leaf Rookies and Stars Thanksgiving Classic

INSERTS IN DICK'S SPORTING GOODS PACKS
TC1 Tony Romo 1.00 2.50
TC2 Calvin Johnson 2.50 6.00
TC3 Warrick Dunn .60 1.50
TC4 Brett Favre 1.50 4.00
TC5 Chad Pennington .60 1.50
TC6 Peyton Manning 1.25 3.00
TC7 Adrian Peterson 2.50 6.00
TC8 Vince Young .60 1.50
TC9 Reggie Bush .75 2.00
TC10 Brady Quinn .60 1.50
TC11 JaMarcus Russell .40 1.00
TC12 Marshawn Lynch .75 2.00

2007 Leaf Rookies and Stars Longevity

COMP.SET w/o RC's (115) 8.00 20.00
*1-115 VETS: .4X TO 1X BASIC CARDS
*ROOKIES/999: .4X TO 1X BASIC CARDS
116-200 ROOKIE PRINT RUN 999

2007 Leaf Rookies and Stars Longevity Emerald

*1-100 VETS/49: 6X TO 15X BASIC CARDS
*101-115 VETS/29: 1.5X TO 4X BASIC CARDS
1-115 VETERAN PRINT RUN 49
*ROOKIES/29: 2X TO 5X BASIC CARDS
116-200 ROOKIE PRINT RUN 29

2007 Leaf Rookies and Stars Longevity Ruby

*1-100 VETS/249: 2X TO 5X BASIC CARDS
*101-115 VETS/199: .6X TO 1.5X BASIC CARDS
1-115 VETERAN PRINT RUN 199-249
*ROOKIES/199: .8X TO 2X BASIC CARDS
161-200 ROOKIE PRINT RUN 199

2007 Leaf Rookies and Stars Longevity Sapphire

*1-100 VETS/149: 2.5X TO 6X BASIC CARDS
*101-115 VETS/99: .8X TO 2X BASIC CARDS
1-115 VETERAN PRINT RUN 99-149
*ROOKIES/99: 1.2X TO 3X BASIC CARDS
116-200 ROOKIE PRINT RUN 99

2008 Leaf Rookies and Stars

This set was released on November 12, 2008. The base set consists of 249 cards. Cards 1-115 feature veterans, and cards 116-200 are rookies serial numbered of 999. Cards 201-250 are autographed rookie cards, with serial numbers ranging from 52-273.

COMP.SET w/o SP's (100) 10.00 25.00
116-200 ROOKIE PRINT RUN 999
AU ROOKIE PRINT RUN 52-273
1 Matt Leinart .30 .75
2 Larry Fitzgerald .30 .75
3 Anquan Boldin .25 .60
4 Edgerrin James .25 .60
5 Roddy White .25 .60
6 Michael Turner .30 .75
7 Willis McGahee .25 .60
8 Derrick Mason .25 .60
9 Demetrius Williams .20 .50
10 Trent Edwards .20 .50
11 Marshawn Lynch .25 .60
12 Lee Evans .25 .60
13 Steve Smith .25 .60
14 DeAngelo Williams .25 .60
15 Julius Peppers .25 .60
16 Greg Olsen .25 .60
17 Devin Hester .30 .75
18 Rex Grossman .25 .60
19 Carson Palmer .30 .75
20 Chad Johnson .25 .60
21 T.J. Houshmandzadeh .25 .60
22 Chris Perry .20 .50
23 Derek Anderson .20 .50
24 Kellen Winslow .25 .60
25 Braylon Edwards .25 .60
26 Tony Romo .40 1.00
27 Terrell Owens .30 .75
28 Marion Barber .25 .60
29 Jay Cutler .30 .75
30 Brandon Stokley .25 .60
31 Jon Kitna .25 .60
32 Roy Williams WR .25 .60
33 Calvin Johnson .30 .75
34 Aaron Rodgers .60 1.50
35 Ryan Grant .30 .75
36 Donald Driver .25 .60
37 Matt Schaub .25 .60
38 Andre Johnson .25 .60
39 Kevin Walter .25 .60
40 Peyton Manning .50 1.25
41 Joseph Addai .25 .60
42 Reggie Wayne .25 .60
43 Dallas Clark .25 .60
44 David Garrard .25 .60
45 Fred Taylor .25 .60
46 Maurice Jones-Drew .25 .60
47 Reggie Williams .25 .60
48 Brodie Croyle .25 .60
49 Larry Johnson .25 .60
50 Tony Gonzalez .25 .60
51 Chad Pennington .25 .60
52 Ronnie Brown .25 .60
53 Ted Ginn Jr. .25 .60
54 Tarvaris Jackson .25 .60
55 Adrian Peterson .50 1.25
56 Sidney Rice .30 .75
57 Tom Brady .50 1.25
58 Randy Moss .30 .75
59 Laurence Maroney .25 .60
60 Drew Brees .30 .75
61 Reggie Bush .30 .75
62 Deuce McAllister .25 .60
63 Eli Manning .30 .75
64 Plaxico Burress .25 .60
65 Brandon Jacobs .25 .60
66 Brett Favre 2.00 5.00
67 Leon Washington .25 .60
68 Laveranues Coles .20 .50
69 JaMarcus Russell .25 .60
70 Justin Fargas .20 .50
71 Zach Miller .25 .60
72 Donovan McNabb .30 .75
73 Brian Westbrook .25 .60
74 Reggie Brown .20 .50
75 Ben Roethlisberger .30 .75
76 Willie Parker .25 .60
77 Santonio Holmes .25 .60
78 Philip Rivers .30 .75
79 LaDainian Tomlinson .30 .75
80 Vincent Jackson .20 .50
81 Antonio Gates .30 .75
82 J.T. O'Sullivan .20 .50
83 Frank Gore .25 .60
84 Vernon Davis .25 .60
85 Matt Hasselbeck .25 .60
86 Deion Branch .25 .60
87 Julius Jones .20 .50
88 Marc Bulger .25 .60
89 Steven Jackson .30 .75
90 Torry Holt .25 .60
91 Warrick Dunn .25 .60
92 Jeff Garcia .25 .60
93 Joey Galloway .25 .60
94 Vince Young .25 .60
95 LenDale White .25 .60
96 Roydell Williams .20 .50
97 Jason Campbell .25 .60
98 Clinton Portis .25 .60
99 Santana Moss .20 .50
100 Ladell Betts .20 .50
101 Trent Edwards ELE 1.00 2.50
102 Marshawn Lynch ELE 1.25 3.00
103 Braylon Edwards ELE 1.25 3.00
104 Carson Palmer ELE 1.50 4.00
105 Tom Brady ELE 2.50 6.00
106 Matt Hasselbeck ELE 1.25 3.00
107 Nate Burleson ELE 1.00 2.50
108 Fred Taylor ELE 1.25 3.00
109 David Garrard ELE 1.25 3.00
110 Maurice Jones-Drew ELE 1.25 3.00
111 Devin Hester ELE 1.50 4.00
112 Willie Parker ELE 1.25 3.00
113 Ben Roethlisberger ELE 1.50 4.00
114 Ryan Grant ELE 1.50 4.00
115 Eli Manning ELE 1.50 4.00
116 Adrian Arrington RC 1.50 4.00
117 Ali Highsmith RC 1.25 3.00
118 Anthony Alridge RC 1.50 4.00
119 Antoine Cason RC 2.00 5.00
120 Aqib Talib RC 2.00 5.00
121 Brad Cottam RC 1.50 4.00
122 Brandon Flowers RC 2.00 5.00
123 Calais Campbell RC 1.50 4.00
124 Chauncey Washington RC 1.50 4.00
125 Chevis Jackson RC 1.25 3.00
126 Cory Boyd RC 1.25 3.00
127 Craig Steltz RC 1.50 4.00
128 Curtis Lofton RC 1.50 4.00
129 DJ Hall RC 1.50 4.00
130 Dantrell Savage RC 1.50 4.00
131 Darius Reynaud RC 1.25 3.00
132 Darrell Strong RC 1.50 4.00
133 Davone Bess RC 2.00 5.00
134 Derrick Harvey RC 1.25 3.00
135 Dominique Rodgers-Cromartie RC 2.00 5.00
136 Erin Henderson RC 2.00 5.00
137 Ernie Wheelwright RC 1.50 4.00
138 Fred Davis RC 2.00 5.00
139 Joe Jon Finley RC 1.50 4.00
140 Jacob Hester RC 2.00 5.00
141 Jacob Tamme RC 2.00 5.00
142 Jamar Adams RC 1.50 4.00
143 Jason Rivers RC 1.50 4.00
144 Jed Collins RC 1.50 4.00
145 Jermichael Finley RC 2.00 5.00
146 John Carlson RC 2.00 5.00
147 Jonathan Hefney RC 1.50 4.00
148 Jordon Dizon RC 2.00 5.00
149 Josh Morgan RC 2.00 5.00
150 Justin Forsett RC 2.00 5.00
151 Kalvin McRae RC 1.25 3.00
152 Keenan Burton RC 1.25 3.00
153 Kellen Davis RC 1.25 3.00
154 Kentwan Balmer RC 1.50 4.00
155 Kevin Robinson RC 1.25 3.00
156 Lawrence Jackson RC 1.50 4.00
157 Leodis McKelvin RC 1.50 4.00
158 Marcus Monk RC 1.50 4.00
159 Marcus Smith RC 1.50 4.00
160 Marcus Thomas RC 1.50 4.00
161 Mark Bradford RC 1.25 3.00
162 Martellus Bennett RC 1.50 4.00
163 Martin Rucker RC 1.50 4.00
164 Mike Jenkins RC 2.00 5.00
165 Owen Schmitt RC 2.00 5.00
166 Pat Sims RC 1.50 4.00
167 Paul Hubbard RC 1.50 4.00
168 Paul Smith RC 2.00 5.00
169 Peyton Hillis RC 2.50 6.00
170 Phillip Merling RC 1.50 4.00
171 Quentin Groves RC 1.50 4.00
172 Reggie Smith RC 1.50 4.00
173 Ryan Grice-Mullen RC 1.25 3.00
174 Ryan Torain RC 2.00 5.00
175 Sam Keller RC 1.50 4.00
176 Sedrick Ellis RC 2.00 5.00
177 Shawn Crable RC 1.25 3.00
178 Simeon Castille RC 1.50 4.00
179 Terrell Thomas RC 1.50 4.00
180 Thomas Brown RC 1.50 4.00
181 Tim Hightower RC 2.00 5.00
182 Tracy Porter RC 2.00 5.00
183 Vernon Gholston RC 1.50 4.00
184 Will Franklin RC 1.50 4.00
185 Xavier Adibi RC 1.25 3.00
186 Alex Brink RC 2.00 5.00
187 Jalen Parmele RC 1.50 4.00
188 Xavier Omon RC 2.00 5.00
189 Craig Stevens RC 1.25 3.00
190 Derek Fine RC 1.50 4.00
191 Gary Barnidge RC 1.25 3.00
192 Arman Shields RC 1.50 4.00
193 Kenneth Moore RC 1.50 4.00
194 Marcus Henry RC 1.50 4.00
195 Jaymar Johnson RC 1.25 3.00
196 Pierre Garcon RC 2.50 6.00
197 Patrick Lee RC 1.50 4.00
198 Terrence Wheatley RC 1.25 3.00
199 Tavares Gooden RC 1.50 4.00
200 Bruce Davis RC 1.50 4.00
201 Allen Patrick AU/268 RC 6.00 15.00
202 Andre Caldwell AU/116 RC 8.00 20.00
203 Andre Woodson AU/219 RC 8.00 20.00
204 Brian Brohm AU/99 RC 12.00 30.00
206 Chad Henne AU/99 RC 20.00 50.00
207 Chris Johnson AU/166 RC 40.00 100.00
208 Chris Long AU/99 RC EXCH 12.00 30.00
209 Colt Brennan AU/213 RC 8.00 20.00
210 Dan Connor AU/270 RC 8.00 20.00
211 Darren McFadden AU/99 RC 30.00 80.00
212 Dennis Dixon AU/218 RC 8.00 20.00
213 DeSean Jackson AU/119 RC 30.00 60.00
214 Devin Thomas AU/118 RC 8.00 20.00
215 Dexter Jackson AU/132 RC 8.00 20.00
216 Donnie Avery AU/129 RC 8.00 20.00
217 Dustin Keller AU/115 RC 10.00 25.00
218 Earl Bennett AU/118 RC 15.00 30.00
219 Early Doucet AU/106 RC 8.00 20.00
220 Eddie Royal AU/126 RC 10.00 25.00
221 Erik Ainge AU/271 RC 8.00 20.00
222 Felix Jones AU/99 RC 30.00 80.00
223 Glenn Dorsey AU/99 RC 12.00 30.00
224 Harry Douglas AU/99 RC 10.00 25.00
225 Jake Long AU/99 RC 12.00 30.00
226 Jamaal Charles AU/118 RC 15.00 40.00
227 James Hardy AU/118 RC 8.00 20.00
228 Jerod Mayo AU/52 RC 30.00 60.00
229 Jerome Simpson AU/117 RC 10.00 25.00
230 Joe Flacco AU/99 RC 60.00 120.00
231 John David Booty AU/118 RC 8.00 20.00
232 Jonathan Stewart AU/99 RC 30.00 60.00
233 Jordy Nelson AU/99 RC 30.00 60.00
234 Josh Johnson AU/268 RC 8.00 20.00
235 Keith Rivers AU/263 RC 6.00 15.00
236 Kenny Phillips AU/99 RC 10.00 25.00
237 Kevin O'Connell AU/142 RC 8.00 20.00
238 Kevin Smith AU/117 RC 10.00 25.00
239 Lavelle Hawkins AU/273 RC 5.00 12.00
240 Limas Sweed AU/103 RC 10.00 25.00
241 Malcolm Kelly AU/108 RC 8.00 20.00
242 Mario Manningham AU/118 RC 15.00 30.00
243 Matt Flynn AU/263 RC 30.00 60.00
244 Matt Forte AU/107 RC 30.00 80.00
245 Matt Ryan AU/99 RC 75.00 150.00
246 Mike Hart AU/263 RC 8.00 20.00
247 Rashard Mendenhall AU/99 RC 30.00 60.00
248 Ray Rice AU/105 RC 20.00 50.00
249 Steve Slaton AU/118 RC 10.00 25.00
250 Tashard Choice AU/270 RC 6.00 15.00

2008 Leaf Rookies and Stars Gold Retail

*VETS 1-100: 1.5X TO 4X BASIC CARDS
*ELEMENTS 101-115: .4X TO 1X BASIC CARDS
*ROOKIES 116-200: .5X TO 1.2X BASIC CARDS
STATED PRINT RUN 349 SER.#'d SETS
66 Brett Favre 4.00 10.00

2008 Leaf Rookies and Stars Longevity Parallel Silver

*VETS 1-100: 2X TO 5X BASIC CARDS
*ELEMENT 101-115: .5X TO 1.2X BASIC ELE
*ROOKIES 116-200: .6X TO 1.5X BASIC CARDS
STATED PRINT RUN 249 SER.#'d SETS
66 Brett Favre 4.00 10.00

2008 Leaf Rookies and Stars Longevity Parallel Black

*VETS 1-100: 5X TO 12X BASIC CARDS
*ELEMENTS 101-115: 1.2X TO 3X BASIC CARDS
*ROOKIES 116-200: 1.2X TO 3X BASIC CARDS
STATED PRINT RUN 25 SER.#'d SETS

2008 Leaf Rookies and Stars Longevity Parallel Gold

*VETS 1-100: 4X TO 10X BASIC CARDS
*ELEMENTS 101-115: 1X TO 2.5X BASIC CARDS
*ROOKIES 116-200: 1X TO 2.5X BASIC CARDS
STATED PRINT RUN 49 SER.#'d SETS
66 Brett Favre 8.00 20.00

2008 Leaf Rookies and Stars Longevity Parallel Silver Holofoil

*VETS 1-100: 3X TO 8X BASIC CARDS
*ELEMENTS 101-115: .8X TO 2X BASIC CARDS
*ROOKIES 116-200: .8X TO 2X BASIC CARDS
STATED PRINT RUN 99 SER.#'d SETS
66 Brett Favre 6.00 15.00

2008 Leaf Rookies and Stars Crosstraining

STATED PRINT RUN 1000 SER.#'d SETS
*GOLD/500: .5X TO 1.2X BASIC INSERTS
GOLD PRINT RUN 500 SER.#'d SETS
*BLACK/100: .6X TO 1.5X BASIC INSERTS
BLACK PRINT RUN 100 SER.#'d SETS
1 Andre Caldwell .60 1.50
2 Brian Brohm .75 2.00
3 Chad Henne .75 2.00
4 Chris Johnson 2.00 5.00
5 Darren McFadden 2.00 5.00
6 DeSean Jackson 1.50 4.00
7 Devin Thomas .60 1.50
8 Dexter Jackson .60 1.50
9 Donnie Avery .60 1.50
10 Dustin Keller .75 2.00
11 Earl Bennett .75 2.00
12 Early Doucet .60 1.50
13 Eddie Royal .75 2.00
14 Felix Jones 1.25 3.00
15 Glenn Dorsey .75 2.00
16 Harry Douglas .60 1.50
17 Jake Long .75 2.00
18 Jamaal Charles 1.25 3.00
19 James Hardy .60 1.50
20 Jerome Simpson .75 2.00
21 Joe Flacco 2.50 6.00
22 John David Booty .60 1.50
23 Jonathan Stewart 1.25 3.00
24 Jordy Nelson 1.00 2.50
25 Kevin O'Connell .60 1.50
26 Kevin Smith .75 2.00
27 Limas Sweed .75 2.00
28 Malcolm Kelly .60 1.50
29 Mario Manningham .75 2.00
30 Matt Forte 1.25 3.00
31 Matt Ryan 3.00 8.00
32 Rashard Mendenhall 1.50 4.00
33 Ray Rice 1.50 4.00
34 Steve Slaton .75 2.00

2008 Leaf Rookies and Stars Crosstraining Autographs

STATED PRINT RUN 25 SER.#'d SETS
1 Andre Caldwell 5.00 12.00
2 Brian Brohm 6.00 15.00
3 Chad Henne 15.00 40.00
4 Chris Johnson 50.00 100.00
5 Darren McFadden 30.00 60.00
6 DeSean Jackson 20.00 50.00
7 Devin Thomas 5.00 12.00
8 Dexter Jackson 5.00 12.00
9 Donnie Avery 5.00 12.00
10 Dustin Keller 6.00 15.00
11 Earl Bennett 6.00 15.00
12 Early Doucet 5.00 12.00
13 Eddie Royal 6.00 15.00
14 Felix Jones 20.00 50.00
15 Glenn Dorsey EXCH
16 Harry Douglas 5.00 12.00
17 Jake Long 6.00 15.00
18 Jamaal Charles 15.00 40.00
19 James Hardy 5.00 12.00
20 Jerome Simpson 6.00 15.00
21 Joe Flacco 50.00 100.00
22 John David Booty 5.00 12.00
23 Jonathan Stewart 10.00 25.00
24 Jordy Nelson 12.00 30.00
25 Kevin O'Connell 5.00 12.00
26 Kevin Smith 6.00 15.00
27 Limas Sweed 6.00 15.00
28 Malcolm Kelly 5.00 12.00
29 Mario Manningham 6.00 15.00
30 Matt Forte 20.00 50.00
31 Matt Ryan 60.00 120.00
32 Rashard Mendenhall 20.00 50.00
33 Ray Rice 20.00 50.00
34 Steve Slaton 6.00 15.00

2008 Leaf Rookies and Stars Crosstraining Materials

STATED PRINT RUN 250 SER.#'d SETS
*PRIME/25: .8X TO 2X BASIC JSY/250
PRIME PRINT RUN 5-25
1 Andre Caldwell 2.00 5.00
2 Brian Brohm 2.50 6.00
3 Chad Henne 2.50 6.00
4 Chris Johnson 6.00 15.00
5 Darren McFadden 6.00 15.00
6 DeSean Jackson 5.00 12.00
7 Devin Thomas 2.00 5.00
8 Dexter Jackson 2.00 5.00
9 Donnie Avery 2.00 5.00
10 Dustin Keller 2.50 6.00
11 Earl Bennett 2.50 6.00
12 Early Doucet 2.00 5.00
13 Eddie Royal 2.50 6.00
14 Felix Jones 4.00 10.00
15 Glenn Dorsey 2.50 6.00
16 Harry Douglas 2.00 5.00
17 Jake Long 2.50 6.00
18 Jamaal Charles 4.00 10.00
19 James Hardy 2.00 5.00
20 Jerome Simpson 2.50 6.00
21 Joe Flacco 8.00 20.00
22 John David Booty 2.00 5.00
23 Jonathan Stewart 5.00 12.00
24 Jordy Nelson 3.00 8.00
25 Kevin O'Connell 2.00 5.00
26 Kevin Smith 2.50 6.00
27 Limas Sweed 2.50 6.00
28 Malcolm Kelly 2.00 5.00
29 Mario Manningham 2.50 6.00
30 Matt Forte 4.00 10.00
31 Matt Ryan 10.00 25.00
32 Rashard Mendenhall 5.00 12.00
33 Ray Rice 5.00 12.00
34 Steve Slaton 2.50 6.00

2008 Leaf Rookies and Stars Dress for Success Jersey Autographs

STATED PRINT RUN 25 SER.#'d SETS
UNPRICED PRIME AU PRINT RUN 10
1 Jake Long 8.00 20.00
2 Jamaal Charles 15.00 40.00
3 James Hardy 6.00 15.00
4 Jerome Simpson 8.00 20.00
5 Joe Flacco 50.00 100.00
6 John David Booty 6.00 15.00
7 Jonathan Stewart 12.00 30.00
8 Jordy Nelson 15.00 40.00
9 Kevin O'Connell 6.00 15.00
10 Kevin Smith 8.00 20.00
11 Limas Sweed 8.00 20.00
12 Malcolm Kelly 6.00 15.00
13 Mario Manningham 8.00 20.00
14 Matt Forte 20.00 50.00
15 Matt Ryan 75.00 150.00
16 Rashard Mendenhall 20.00 50.00
17 Ray Rice 20.00 50.00
18 Steve Slaton 8.00 20.00
19 Andre Caldwell 6.00 15.00
20 Brian Brohm 8.00 20.00
21 Chad Henne 15.00 40.00
22 Chris Johnson 50.00 100.00
23 Darren McFadden 30.00 60.00
24 DeSean Jackson 20.00 50.00
25 Devin Thomas 6.00 15.00
26 Dexter Jackson 6.00 15.00
27 Donnie Avery 6.00 15.00
28 Dustin Keller 8.00 20.00
29 Earl Bennett 8.00 20.00
30 Early Doucet 6.00 15.00
31 Eddie Royal 8.00 20.00
32 Felix Jones 20.00 50.00
33 Glenn Dorsey No AU 6.00 15.00
34 Harry Douglas 6.00 15.00

2008 Leaf Rookies and Stars Dress for Success Jerseys

STATED PRINT RUN 250 SER.#'d SETS
*PRIME/25: .8X TO 2X BASIC JSY/250
PRIME PRINT RUN 25 SER.#'d SETS
*SHOE/24-25: .8X TO 2X BASIC JSY/250
SHOE PRINT RUN 24-25
*LONGEVITY/100: .5X TO 1.2X BASIC JSY/250
*LONG SHOE/20-25: .8X TO 2X BASIC JSY/250
1 Jake Long 2.50 6.00
2 Jamaal Charles 4.00 10.00
3 James Hardy 2.00 5.00
4 Jerome Simpson 2.50 6.00
5 Joe Flacco 8.00 20.00
6 John David Booty 2.00 5.00
7 Jonathan Stewart 4.00 10.00
8 Jordy Nelson 3.00 8.00
9 Kevin O'Connell 2.00 5.00
10 Kevin Smith 2.50 6.00
11 Limas Sweed 2.50 6.00
12 Malcolm Kelly 2.00 5.00
13 Mario Manningham 2.50 6.00
14 Matt Forte 4.00 10.00
15 Matt Ryan 10.00 25.00
16 Rashard Mendenhall 5.00 12.00
17 Ray Rice 5.00 12.00
18 Steve Slaton 2.50 6.00
19 Andre Caldwell 2.00 5.00
20 Brian Brohm 2.50 6.00
21 Chad Henne 2.50 6.00
22 Chris Johnson 6.00 15.00
23 Darren McFadden 6.00 15.00
24 DeSean Jackson 5.00 12.00
25 Devin Thomas 2.00 5.00
26 Dexter Jackson 2.00 5.00
27 Donnie Avery 2.00 5.00
28 Dustin Keller 2.50 6.00
29 Earl Bennett 2.50 6.00
30 Early Doucet 2.00 5.00
31 Eddie Royal 2.50 6.00
32 Felix Jones 4.00 10.00
33 Glenn Dorsey 2.50 6.00
34 Harry Douglas 2.00 5.00

2008 Leaf Rookies and Stars Elements Materials

STATED PRINT RUN 250 SER.#'d SETS
*FOIL/100: .5X TO 1.2X BASIC JSY/250
FOIL PRINT RUN 100 SER.#'d SETS
*HOLOFOIL/25: .8X TO 2X BASIC JSY/250
HOLOFOIL PRINT RUN 25 SER.#'d SETS
101 Trent Edwards 2.50 6.00
102 Marshawn Lynch 3.00 8.00
103 Braylon Edwards 3.00 8.00
104 Carson Palmer 4.00 10.00
105 Tom Brady 6.00 15.00
106 Matt Hasselbeck 3.00 8.00
108 Fred Taylor 3.00 8.00
109 David Garrard 3.00 8.00
110 Maurice Jones-Drew 3.00 8.00
111 Devin Hester 4.00 10.00
112 Willie Parker 3.00 8.00
113 Ben Roethlisberger 4.00 10.00
114 Ryan Grant 4.00 10.00
115 Eli Manning 4.00 10.00

2008 Leaf Rookies and Stars Freshman Orientation Materials Jersey Autographs

STATED PRINT RUN 25 SER.#'d SETS
UNPRICED PRIME PRINT RUN 10
1 Kevin O'Connell 6.00 15.00
2 Jordy Nelson 15.00 40.00
3 Jonathan Stewart 12.00 30.00
4 John David Booty 6.00 15.00
5 Joe Flacco 40.00 100.00
6 Jerome Simpson EXCH
7 James Hardy 6.00 15.00
8 Jamaal Charles 15.00 40.00
9 Jake Long
10 Harry Douglas 6.00 15.00
11 Glenn Dorsey EXCH
12 Felix Jones 20.00 50.00
13 Eddie Royal 8.00 20.00
14 Early Doucet 6.00 15.00
15 Earl Bennett 8.00 20.00
16 Dustin Keller 8.00 20.00
17 Donnie Avery 6.00 15.00
18 Dexter Jackson 6.00 15.00
19 Devin Thomas 6.00 15.00
20 DeSean Jackson 20.00 50.00
21 Darren McFadden 30.00 60.00
22 Chris Johnson 30.00 80.00
23 Chad Henne 15.00 40.00
24 Brian Brohm 8.00 20.00
25 Andre Caldwell 6.00 15.00
26 Steve Slaton 8.00 20.00
27 Ray Rice 20.00 50.00
28 Rashard Mendenhall 20.00 50.00
29 Matt Ryan 60.00 150.00
30 Matt Forte 20.00 50.00
31 Mario Manningham 8.00 20.00
32 Malcolm Kelly 6.00 15.00
33 Limas Sweed 8.00 20.00
34 Kevin Smith 8.00 20.00

2008 Leaf Rookies and Stars Freshman Orientation Materials Jerseys

STATED PRINT RUN 250 SER.#'d SETS
*PRIME: .8X TO 2X BASIC JSY/250
PRIME PRINT RUN 25 SER.#'d SETS
*LONGEVITY/100: .5X TO 1.2X BASIC JSY/250
*LONG FB/25: 1X TO 2.5X BASIC JSY/250
LONGEVITY FB PRINT RUN 7-25
1 Kevin O'Connell 2.00 5.00
2 Jordy Nelson 3.00 8.00
3 Jonathan Stewart 4.00 10.00
4 John David Booty 2.00 5.00
5 Joe Flacco 5.00 12.00
6 Jerome Simpson 2.50 6.00
7 James Hardy 2.00 5.00
8 Jamaal Charles 4.00 10.00
9 Jake Long 2.50 6.00
10 Harry Douglas 2.00 5.00
11 Glenn Dorsey 2.50 6.00
12 Felix Jones 4.00 10.00
13 Eddie Royal 2.50 6.00
14 Early Doucet 2.00 5.00
15 Earl Bennett 2.50 6.00
16 Dustin Keller 2.50 6.00
17 Donnie Avery 2.00 5.00
18 Dexter Jackson 2.00 5.00
19 Devin Thomas 2.00 5.00
20 DeSean Jackson 5.00 12.00
21 Darren McFadden 6.00 15.00
22 Chris Johnson 6.00 15.00
23 Chad Henne 2.50 6.00
24 Brian Brohm 2.50 6.00
25 Andre Caldwell 2.00 5.00
26 Steve Slaton 2.50 6.00
27 Ray Rice 5.00 12.00
28 Rashard Mendenhall 5.00 12.00
29 Matt Ryan 10.00 25.00
30 Matt Forte 4.00 10.00
31 Mario Manningham 2.50 6.00
32 Malcolm Kelly 2.00 5.00
33 Limas Sweed 2.50 6.00
34 Kevin Smith 2.50 6.00

2008 Leaf Rookies and Stars Gold Stars

STATED PRINT RUN 1000 SER.#'d SETS
*BLACK/500: .5X TO 1.2X BASIC INSERTS
BLACK PRINT RUN 500 SER.#'d SETS
*HOLOFOIL/100: .6X TO 1.5X BASIC INSERTS
HOLOFOIL PRINT RUN 100 SER.#'d SETS
*BLACK HOLO/50: .8X TO 2X BASIC INSERTS
BLACK HOLOFOIL PRINT RUN 50 SER.#'d SETS
1 Eli Manning 1.00 2.50
2 Vince Young .75 2.00
3 Chad Johnson .75 2.00
4 Brandon Jacobs .75 2.00
5 Donald Driver .75 2.00
6 Ryan Grant 1.00 2.50
7 Trent Edwards .60 1.50
8 Laurence Maroney .75 2.00
9 Santonio Holmes .75 2.00
10 Jerious Norwood .75 2.00

2008 Leaf Rookies and Stars Gold Stars Autographs

STATED PRINT RUN 5-25
SERIAL #'d UNDER 20 NOT PRICED
3 Chad Johnson/25 10.00 25.00
4 Brandon Jacobs/25 15.00 30.00
5 Donald Driver/25 15.00 30.00
6 Ryan Grant/25 20.00 40.00
7 Trent Edwards/20 15.00 30.00
9 Santonio Holmes/25 10.00 25.00
10 Jerious Norwood/25 EXCH 10.00 25.00

2008 Leaf Rookies and Stars Gold Stars Materials

STATED PRINT RUN 250 SER.#'d SETS
*BLK PRIME/25-50: .8X TO 2X BASIC JSY/250
BLACK PRIME PRINT RUN 7-50
1 Eli Manning 4.00 10.00
2 Vince Young 3.00 8.00
3 Chad Johnson 3.00 8.00
4 Brandon Jacobs 3.00 8.00
5 Donald Driver 3.00 8.00
6 Ryan Grant 4.00 10.00
7 Trent Edwards 2.50 6.00
8 Laurence Maroney 3.00 8.00
9 Santonio Holmes 3.00 8.00
10 Jerious Norwood 3.00 8.00

2008 Leaf Rookies and Stars Materials Emerald Prime

EMERALD PRIME PRINT RUN 4-50
*BLACK/20-25: .5X TO 1.2X EMER/35-50
*BLACK/20-25: .4X TO 1X EMER/13-60
*BLACK/10-15: .5X TO 1.2X EMER/13-30
BLACK PRIME PRINT RUN 1-25
SERIAL #'d UNDER 13 NOT PRICED
2 Larry Fitzgerald/25 8.00 20.00
3 Anquan Boldin/50 5.00 12.00
4 Edgerrin James/25 6.00 15.00
7 Willis McGahee/50 5.00 12.00
8 Derrick Mason/25 6.00 15.00
9 Demetrius Williams/25 5.00 12.00
10 Trent Edwards/25 5.00 12.00
11 Marshawn Lynch/25 6.00 15.00
12 Lee Evans/50 5.00 12.00
13 Steve Smith/50 5.00 12.00
14 DeAngelo Williams/25 6.00 15.00
15 Julius Peppers/50 5.00 12.00
17 Devin Hester/25 8.00 20.00
18 Rex Grossman/50 5.00 12.00
19 Carson Palmer/25 8.00 20.00
20 Chad Johnson/50 5.00 12.00
21 T.J. Houshmandzadeh/50 5.00 12.00
23 Derek Anderson/25 5.00 12.00
24 Kellen Winslow/25 6.00 15.00
25 Braylon Edwards/50 5.00 12.00
26 Tony Romo/25 10.00 25.00
27 Terrell Owens/25 8.00 20.00
28 Marion Barber/25 6.00 15.00
30 Brandon Stokley/13 6.00 15.00
31 Jon Kitna/50 5.00 12.00
32 Roy Williams WR/50 5.00 12.00
33 Calvin Johnson/50 6.00 15.00
34 Aaron Rodgers/25 15.00 40.00
35 Ryan Grant/25 8.00 20.00
36 Donald Driver/50 5.00 12.00
37 Matt Schaub/25 6.00 15.00
38 Andre Johnson/40 5.00 12.00
40 Peyton Manning/25 12.00 30.00
41 Joseph Addai/25 6.00 15.00
42 Reggie Wayne/25 6.00 15.00
43 Dallas Clark/25 6.00 15.00
44 David Garrard/25 6.00 15.00
45 Fred Taylor/50 5.00 12.00
46 Maurice Jones-Drew/25 6.00 15.00
47 Reggie Williams/50 5.00 12.00
49 Larry Johnson/50 5.00 12.00
50 Tony Gonzalez/50 5.00 12.00
52 Ronnie Brown/50 5.00 12.00
54 Tarvaris Jackson/25 6.00 15.00
55 Adrian Peterson/30 20.00 50.00
57 Tom Brady/50 10.00 25.00
58 Randy Moss/25 8.00 20.00
59 Laurence Maroney/50 5.00 12.00
60 Drew Brees/25 8.00 20.00
61 Reggie Bush/25 8.00 20.00
62 Deuce McAllister/50 5.00 12.00
63 Eli Manning/25 8.00 20.00
64 Plaxico Burress/25 6.00 15.00
65 Brandon Jacobs/25 6.00 15.00
67 Leon Washington/50 5.00 12.00
68 Laveranues Coles/20 5.00 12.00
70 Justin Fargas/25 5.00 12.00
72 Donovan McNabb/25 8.00 20.00
73 Brian Westbrook/25 6.00 15.00
74 Reggie Brown/50 4.00 10.00
75 Ben Roethlisberger/25 8.00 20.00
76 Willie Parker/50 5.00 12.00
77 Santonio Holmes/25 6.00 15.00
78 Philip Rivers/25 8.00 20.00
79 LaDainian Tomlinson/50 6.00 15.00
80 Vincent Jackson/30 5.00 12.00
81 Antonio Gates/50 6.00 15.00
83 Frank Gore/50 5.00 12.00
84 Vernon Davis/50 5.00 12.00
85 Matt Hasselbeck/50 5.00 12.00
86 Deion Branch/50 5.00 12.00
88 Marc Bulger/40 5.00 12.00
89 Steven Jackson/50 6.00 15.00
90 Torry Holt/50 5.00 12.00
91 Warrick Dunn/50 5.00 12.00
93 Joey Galloway/25 6.00 15.00
94 Vince Young/35 5.00 12.00
95 LenDale White/25 6.00 15.00
96 Roydell Williams/25 5.00 12.00
97 Jason Campbell/25 6.00 15.00
98 Clinton Portis/50 5.00 12.00
99 Santana Moss/50 4.00 10.00
100 Ladell Betts/50 4.00 10.00

2008 Leaf Rookies and Stars Materials Gold Longevity

LONGEVITY PRINT RUN 2-250
1 Matt Leinart/250 4.00 10.00

2 Larry Fitzgerald/250 4.00 10.00
3 Anquan Boldin/250 3.00 8.00
4 Edgerrin James/250 3.00 8.00
9 Demetrius Williams/250 2.50 6.00
13 Steve Smith/250 3.00 8.00
15 Julius Peppers/65 4.00 10.00
19 Carson Palmer/250 4.00 10.00
23 Derek Anderson/210 2.50 6.00
25 Braylon Edwards/250 3.00 8.00
27 Terrell Owens/250 4.00 10.00
28 Marion Barber/250 3.00 8.00
29 Jay Cutler/250 4.00 10.00
30 Brandon Stokley/250 3.00 8.00
33 Calvin Johnson/40 5.00 12.00
34 Aaron Rodgers/250 8.00 20.00
38 Andre Johnson/250 3.00 8.00
41 Joseph Addai/250 3.00 8.00
44 David Garrard/250 3.00 8.00
47 Reggie Williams/250 3.00 8.00
48 Brodie Croyle/250 3.00 8.00
50 Tony Gonzalez/25 5.00 12.00
52 Ronnie Brown/115 3.00 8.00
56 Sidney Rice/60 5.00 12.00
60 Drew Brees/250 4.00 10.00
61 Reggie Bush/145 4.00 10.00
62 Deuce McAllister/135 3.00 8.00
63 Eli Manning/45 5.00 12.00
65 Brandon Jacobs/250 3.00 8.00
66 Brett Favre/250 15.00 40.00
67 Leon Washington/250 3.00 8.00
72 Donovan McNabb/250 4.00 10.00
73 Brian Westbrook/55 4.00 10.00
75 Ben Roethlisberger/55 5.00 12.00
76 Willie Parker/30 5.00 12.00
80 Vincent Jackson/250 2.50 6.00
81 Antonio Gates/49 5.00 12.00
83 Frank Gore/60 4.00 10.00
84 Vernon Davis/80 3.00 8.00
86 Deion Branch/18 5.00 12.00
88 Marc Bulger/250 3.00 8.00
91 Warrick Dunn/215 3.00 8.00
92 Jeff Garcia/250 3.00 8.00
94 Vince Young/250 3.00 8.00
95 LenDale White/250 3.00 8.00
96 Roydell Williams/100 2.50 6.00
97 Jason Campbell/250 3.00 8.00
100 Ladell Betts/250 2.50 6.00

2008 Leaf Rookies and Stars Prime Cuts

STATED PRINT RUN 50 SER.#'d SETS
*COMBO/25: .6X TO 1.5X BASIC PRIME/50
COMBOS PRINT RUN 25 SER.#'d SETS
1 Peyton Manning 12.00 30.00
2 Carson Palmer 8.00 20.00
3 Donovan McNabb 8.00 20.00
4 Marshawn Lynch 6.00 15.00
5 Terrell Owens 8.00 20.00
6 Ronnie Brown 6.00 15.00
7 Wes Welker 8.00 20.00
8 Clinton Portis 6.00 15.00
9 Edgerrin James 6.00 15.00
10 Randy Moss 8.00 20.00
11 Derrick Mason 6.00 15.00
12 Frank Gore 6.00 15.00
13 DeAngelo Williams 6.00 15.00
14 Tarvaris Jackson 6.00 15.00

2008 Leaf Rookies and Stars Prime Cuts Autographs

STATED PRINT RUN 10-25
UNPRICED COMBO AU PRINT RUN 5-10
1 Peyton Manning/10 125.00 200.00
4 Marshawn Lynch 15.00 40.00
6 Ronnie Brown/20
7 Wes Welker 25.00 50.00
12 Frank Gore 15.00 40.00
13 DeAngelo Williams 12.00 30.00

2008 Leaf Rookies and Stars Rookie Autographs Holofoil

HOLOFOIL PRINT RUN 1-250
UNPRICED BLACK PRINT RUN 1
UNPRICED BLUE PRINT RUN 5
UNPRICED GOLD PRINT RUN 15
UNPRICED EMERALD PRINT RUN 5
SERIAL #'d UNDER 25 NOT PRICED
116 Adrian Arrington/50 5.00 12.00
117 Ali Highsmith/250 2.50 6.00
121 Brad Cottam/25 5.00 12.00
126 Cory Boyd/242 2.50 6.00
128 Curtis Lofton/50 5.00 12.00
133 Davone Bess/100 5.00 12.00
134 Derrick Harvey/50 4.00 10.00
135 Dominique Rodgers-Cromartie/50 6.00 15.00
136 Erin Henderson/154 4.00 10.00
138 Fred Davis/50 6.00 15.00
141 Jacob Tamme/100 5.00 12.00
143 Jason Rivers/250 3.00 8.00
145 Jermichael Finley/50 15.00 30.00
146 John Carlson/100 5.00 12.00
152 Keenan Burton/50 4.00 10.00
153 Kellen Davis/50 4.00 10.00
154 Kentwan Balmer/50 5.00 12.00
156 Lawrence Jackson/100 4.00 10.00
157 Leodis McKelvin/50 5.00 12.00
161 Mark Bradford/250 2.50 6.00
162 Martellus Bennett/50 5.00 12.00
163 Martin Rucker/100 4.00 10.00
164 Mike Jenkins/100 5.00 12.00
166 Pat Sims/250 3.00 8.00
172 Reggie Smith/50 5.00 12.00
173 Ryan Grice-Mullen/250 2.50 6.00
175 Sam Keller/250 3.00 8.00
176 Sedrick Ellis/100 5.00 12.00
179 Terrell Thomas/50 5.00 12.00
183 Vernon Gholston/50 5.00 12.00
185 Xavier Adibi/250 2.50 6.00

2008 Leaf Rookies and Stars Rookie Patch Autographs College

COLLEGE AUTO PRINT RUN 25-130
UNPRICED BLACK PRINT RUN 1
UNPRICED EMERALD PRINT RUN 5
UNPRICED GOLD PRINT RUN 10
201 Allen Patrick/31 10.00 25.00
202 Andre Caldwell/29 10.00 25.00
203 Andre Woodson/29 12.00 30.00
204 Brian Brohm/27 12.00 30.00
205 Caleb Campbell/88 10.00 25.00
206 Chad Henne/30 12.00 30.00
207 Chris Johnson/29 50.00 100.00
208 Chris Long/27 EXCH
209 Colt Brennan/29 12.00 30.00
210 Dan Connor/31 12.00 30.00
211 Darren McFadden/27 25.00 60.00
212 Dennis Dixon/30 12.00 30.00
213 DeSean Jackson/32 25.00 60.00
214 Devin Thomas/29 10.00 25.00
215 Dexter Jackson/27 10.00 25.00
216 Donnie Avery/29 10.00 25.00
217 Dustin Keller/29 20.00 40.00
218 Earl Bennett/29 12.00 30.00
219 Early Doucet/29 10.00 25.00
220 Eddie Royal/29 12.00 30.00
221 Erik Ainge/29 12.00 30.00
222 Felix Jones/30 25.00 60.00
223 Glenn Dorsey/27 12.00 30.00
224 Harry Douglas/29 10.00 25.00
225 Jake Long/29 12.00 30.00
226 Jamaal Charles/29 20.00 50.00
227 James Hardy/31 10.00 25.00
228 Jerod Mayo/29 12.00 30.00
230 Joe Flacco/30 60.00 100.00
231 John David Booty/30 10.00 25.00
232 Jonathan Stewart/29 20.00 50.00
233 Jordy Nelson/29 25.00 60.00
234 Josh Johnson/32 12.00 30.00
235 Keith Rivers/27 12.00 30.00
236 Kenny Phillips/28 12.00 30.00
238 Kevin Smith/29 12.00 30.00
239 Lavelle Hawkins/29 8.00 20.00
240 Limas Sweed/130 10.00 25.00
241 Malcolm Kelly/30 10.00 25.00
242 Mario Manningham/36 25.00 50.00
243 Matt Flynn/28 40.00 80.00
244 Matt Forte/29 25.00 60.00
245 Matt Ryan/29 75.00 135.00
246 Mike Hart/30 12.00 30.00
247 Rashard Mendenhall/32 25.00 60.00
248 Ray Rice/30 25.00 60.00
249 Steve Slaton/29 12.00 30.00
250 Tashard Choice/25 10.00 25.00

2008 Leaf Rookies and Stars Rookie Jersey Jumbo Swatch

STATED PRINT RUN 25-50
*GOLD/15-25: .6X TO 1.5X JSY/25-50
GOLD PRINT RUN 15-25
*EMERALD/10: 1X TO 2.5X JSY/25-50
EMERALD PRINT RUN 2-10
UNPRICED BLACK PRINT RUN 1
*LONGEVITY/25-50: .4X TO 1X BASIC JSY
LONGEVITY PRINT RUN 25-50
UNPRICED LONG.RUBY PRINT RUN 2-5
UNPRICED LONG.SAPPHIRE PRINT RUN 1
202 Andre Caldwell 3.00 8.00
204 Brian Brohm 4.00 10.00
206 Chad Henne 4.00 10.00
207 Chris Johnson 10.00 25.00
211 Darren McFadden 10.00 25.00
213 DeSean Jackson 8.00 20.00
214 Devin Thomas 3.00 8.00
215 Dexter Jackson 3.00 8.00
216 Donnie Avery 3.00 8.00
217 Dustin Keller 4.00 10.00
218 Earl Bennett 4.00 10.00
219 Early Doucet/25 3.00 8.00
220 Eddie Royal 4.00 10.00
222 Felix Jones 6.00 15.00
223 Glenn Dorsey 4.00 10.00
224 Harry Douglas 3.00 8.00
225 Jake Long 4.00 10.00
226 Jamaal Charles 6.00 15.00
227 James Hardy 3.00 8.00
229 Jerome Simpson 4.00 10.00
230 Joe Flacco 8.00 20.00
231 John David Booty 3.00 8.00
232 Jonathan Stewart 8.00 20.00
233 Jordy Nelson 5.00 12.00
237 Kevin O'Connell 3.00 8.00
238 Kevin Smith 4.00 10.00
240 Limas Sweed 4.00 10.00
241 Malcolm Kelly 3.00 8.00
242 Mario Manningham 4.00 10.00
244 Matt Forte 8.00 20.00
245 Matt Ryan 10.00 25.00
247 Rashard Mendenhall 8.00 20.00
248 Ray Rice 8.00 20.00
249 Steve Slaton 4.00 10.00

2008 Leaf Rookies and Stars Rookie Jersey Jumbo Swatch College

STATED PRINT RUN 6-25
*GOLD/10: .6X TO 1.5X JSY/15-25
GOLD PRINT RUN 5-10
UNPRICED EMERALD PRINT RUN 3-5
UNPRICED BLACK PRINT RUN 1
201 Allen Patrick 8.00 20.00
204 Brian Brohm 6.00 15.00
206 Chad Henne 10.00 25.00
208 Chris Long/15 6.00 15.00
209 Colt Brennan 10.00 25.00
210 Dan Connor 6.00 15.00
211 Darren McFadden 15.00 40.00
219 Early Doucet/15 5.00 12.00
221 Erik Ainge 10.00 25.00
222 Felix Jones 10.00 25.00
223 Glenn Dorsey 6.00 15.00
224 Harry Douglas 5.00 12.00
226 Jamaal Charles 10.00 25.00
231 John David Booty 5.00 12.00
235 Keith Rivers 6.00 15.00
236 Kenny Phillips 6.00 15.00
240 Limas Sweed 6.00 15.00
241 Malcolm Kelly 5.00 12.00

2008 Leaf Rookies and Stars Statistical Standouts Materials

STATED PRINT RUN 250 SER.#'d SETS
*PRIME/25-50: .8X TO 2X BASIC JSY/250
PRIME PRINT RUN 25-50
UNPRICED AUTO PRINT RUN 5
UNPRICED PRIME AU PRINT RUN 1
1 Adrian Peterson 6.00 15.00
2 Joseph Addai 3.00 8.00
3 LaDainian Tomlinson 4.00 10.00
4 Braylon Edwards 3.00 8.00
5 T.J. Houshmandzadeh 3.00 8.00
6 Marques Colston 3.00 8.00
7 Tom Brady 6.00 15.00
8 Tony Romo 5.00 12.00
9 Ben Roethlisberger 4.00 10.00
10 Brian Westbrook 3.00 8.00
11 Willie Parker 3.00 8.00
12 Marion Barber 3.00 8.00
13 Reggie Wayne 3.00 8.00
14 Drew Brees 4.00 10.00
15 Maurice Jones-Drew 3.00 8.00

2008 Leaf Rookies and Stars Studio Rookies

STATED PRINT RUN 1000 SER.#'d SETS
*GOLD/500: .5X TO 1.2X BASIC INSERTS
GOLD PRINT RUN 500 SER.#'d SETS
*BLACK/100: .6X TO 1.5X BASIC INSERTS
BLACK PRINT RUN 100 SER.#'d SETS
1 Steve Slaton .75 2.00
2 Ray Rice 1.50 4.00
3 Rashard Mendenhall 1.50 4.00
4 Matt Ryan 3.00 8.00
5 Matt Forte 1.25 3.00
6 Mario Manningham .75 2.00
7 Malcolm Kelly .60 1.50
8 Limas Sweed .75 2.00
9 Kevin Smith .75 2.00
10 Kevin O'Connell .60 1.50
11 Jordy Nelson 1.00 2.50
12 Jonathan Stewart 1.25 3.00
13 John David Booty .60 1.50
14 Joe Flacco 2.50 6.00
15 Jerome Simpson .75 2.00
16 James Hardy .60 1.50
17 Jamaal Charles 1.25 3.00
18 Jake Long .75 2.00
19 Harry Douglas .60 1.50
20 Glenn Dorsey .75 2.00
21 Felix Jones 1.25 3.00
22 Eddie Royal .75 2.00
23 Early Doucet .60 1.50
24 Earl Bennett .75 2.00
25 Dustin Keller .75 2.00
26 Donnie Avery .60 1.50
27 Dexter Jackson .60 1.50
28 Devin Thomas .60 1.50
29 DeSean Jackson 1.50 4.00
30 Darren McFadden 2.00 5.00
31 Chris Johnson 2.00 5.00
32 Chad Henne .75 2.00
33 Brian Brohm .75 2.00
34 Andre Caldwell .60 1.50

2008 Leaf Rookies and Stars Studio Rookies Autographs

STATED PRINT RUN 25 SER.#'d SETS
1 Steve Slaton 6.00 15.00
2 Ray Rice 15.00 40.00
3 Rashard Mendenhall 20.00 50.00
4 Matt Ryan 60.00 120.00
5 Matt Forte 20.00 50.00
6 Mario Manningham EXCH
7 Malcolm Kelly 5.00 12.00
8 Limas Sweed 6.00 15.00
9 Kevin Smith 6.00 15.00
10 Kevin O'Connell 5.00 12.00
11 Jordy Nelson 15.00 30.00
12 Jonathan Stewart 10.00 25.00
13 John David Booty 5.00 12.00
14 Joe Flacco 40.00 100.00
15 Jerome Simpson 6.00 15.00
16 James Hardy 5.00 12.00
17 Jamaal Charles 15.00 40.00
18 Jake Long 6.00 15.00
19 Harry Douglas 5.00 12.00
20 Glenn Dorsey EXCH
21 Felix Jones 20.00 50.00
22 Eddie Royal 6.00 15.00
23 Early Doucet 5.00 12.00
24 Earl Bennett 6.00 15.00
25 Dustin Keller 6.00 15.00
26 Donnie Avery 5.00 12.00
27 Dexter Jackson 5.00 12.00
28 Devin Thomas 5.00 12.00
29 DeSean Jackson 20.00 50.00
30 Darren McFadden 25.00 60.00
31 Chris Johnson 50.00 100.00
32 Chad Henne 20.00 50.00
33 Brian Brohm 6.00 15.00
34 Andre Caldwell 5.00 12.00

2008 Leaf Rookies and Stars Studio Rookies Materials

STATED PRINT RUN 250 SER.#'d SETS
*PRIME/25: .8X TO 2X BASIC JSY/250
PRIME PRINT RUN 5-25
1 Steve Slaton 2.50 6.00
2 Ray Rice 5.00 12.00
3 Rashard Mendenhall 5.00 12.00
4 Matt Ryan 10.00 25.00
5 Matt Forte 4.00 10.00
6 Mario Manningham 2.50 6.00
7 Malcolm Kelly 2.00 5.00
8 Limas Sweed 2.50 6.00
9 Kevin Smith 2.50 6.00
10 Kevin O'Connell 2.00 5.00
11 Jordy Nelson 3.00 8.00
12 Jonathan Stewart 4.00 10.00
13 John David Booty 2.00 5.00
14 Joe Flacco 8.00 20.00
15 Jerome Simpson 2.50 6.00
16 James Hardy 2.00 5.00
17 Jamaal Charles 4.00 10.00
18 Jake Long 2.50 6.00
19 Harry Douglas 2.00 5.00
20 Glenn Dorsey 2.50 6.00
21 Felix Jones 4.00 10.00
22 Eddie Royal 2.50 6.00
23 Early Doucet 2.00 5.00
24 Earl Bennett 2.50 6.00
25 Dustin Keller 2.50 6.00
26 Donnie Avery 2.00 5.00
27 Dexter Jackson 2.00 5.00
28 Devin Thomas 2.00 5.00
29 DeSean Jackson 5.00 12.00
30 Darren McFadden 6.00 15.00
31 Chris Johnson 6.00 15.00
32 Chad Henne 2.50 6.00
33 Brian Brohm 2.50 6.00
34 Andre Caldwell 2.00 5.00

2008 Leaf Rookies and Stars Studio Rookies Combos

STATED PRINT RUN 1000 SER.#'d SETS
*GOLD/500: .5X TO 1.2X BASIC INSERTS
GOLD PRINT RUN 500 SER.#'d SETS
*BLACK/100: .6X TO 1.5X BASIC INSERTS
BLACK PRINT RUN 100 SER.#'d SETS
1 Matt Ryan 3.00 8.00
Harry Douglas
2 Brian Brohm 1.00 2.50
Jordy Nelson
3 Jamaal Charles 1.25 3.00
Glenn Dorsey
4 Matt Forte 1.25 3.00
Earl Bennett
5 Rashard Mendenhall 1.50 4.00
Limas Sweed
6 Andre Caldwell .75 2.00
Jerome Simpson
7 Joe Flacco 2.50 6.00
Ray Rice
8 Chad Henne .75 2.00
Jake Long
9 Malcolm Kelly .60 1.50
Devin Thomas
10 Darren McFadden 2.00 5.00
Felix Jones

2008 Leaf Rookies and Stars Studio Rookies Combos Autographs

STATED PRINT RUN 25 SER.#'d SETS
1 Matt Ryan 60.00 120.00
Harry Douglas
2 Brian Brohm 30.00 60.00
Jordy Nelson
3 Jamaal Charles AU 20.00 40.00
Glenn Dorsey No AU
4 Matt Forte 25.00 50.00
Earl Bennett
5 Rashard Mendenhall 25.00 50.00
Limas Sweed
6 Andre Caldwell 20.00 40.00
Jerome Simpson
7 Joe Flacco 60.00 100.00
Ray Rice
8 Chad Henne 25.00 50.00
Jake Long
9 Malcolm Kelly
Devin Thomas EXCH
10 Darren McFadden 50.00 120.00
Felix Jones

2008 Leaf Rookies and Stars Studio Rookies Combos Materials

STATED PRINT RUN 250 SER.#'d SETS
*PRIME/10-25: .8X TO 2X BASIC JSY/250
PRIME PRINT RUN 10-25
1 Matt Ryan 8.00 20.00
Harry Douglas
2 Brian Brohm 4.00 10.00
Jordy Nelson
3 Jamaal Charles 4.00 10.00
Glenn Dorsey
4 Matt Forte 6.00 15.00
Earl Bennett
5 Rashard Mendenhall 6.00 15.00
Limas Sweed
6 Andre Caldwell 3.00 8.00
Jerome Simpson
7 Joe Flacco 6.00 15.00
Ray Rice
8 Chad Henne 3.00 8.00
Jake Long
9 Malcolm Kelly 4.00 10.00
Devin Thomas
10 Darren McFadden 8.00 20.00
Felix Jones

2008 Leaf Rookies and Stars Team Chemistry Autographs

UNPRICED DUAL AUTO PRINT RUN 11

2008 Leaf Rookies and Stars Longevity

This set was released on December 5, 2008. The base set consists of 248 cards. Cards 1-115 feature veterans, and cards 116-200 are rookies serial numbered of 999. Cards 201-250 are autographed rookie cards serial numbered of 10.

COMP.SET w/o SP's (100) 10.00 25.00
*1-100 VETS: .4X TO 1X BASIC CARDS
116-200 ROOKIE PRINT RUN 999
UNPRICED 201-250 AU RC PRINT RUN 10
1 Matt Leinart .30 .75
2 Larry Fitzgerald .30 .75
3 Anquan Boldin .25 .60
4 Edgerrin James .25 .60
5 Roddy White .25 .60
6 Michael Turner .30 .75
7 Willis McGahee .25 .60
8 Derrick Mason .25 .60
9 Demetrius Williams .20 .50
10 Trent Edwards .20 .50
11 Marshawn Lynch .25 .60
12 Lee Evans .25 .60
13 Steve Smith .25 .60
14 DeAngelo Williams .25 .60
15 Julius Peppers .25 .60
16 Greg Olsen .25 .60
17 Devin Hester .30 .75
18 Rex Grossman .25 .60
19 Carson Palmer .30 .75
20 Chad Johnson .25 .60
21 T.J. Houshmandzadeh .25 .60
22 Chris Perry .20 .50
23 Derek Anderson .20 .50
24 Kellen Winslow .25 .60
25 Braylon Edwards .25 .60
26 Tony Romo .40 1.00
27 Terrell Owens .30 .75
28 Marion Barber .25 .60
29 Jay Cutler .30 .75
30 Brandon Stokley .25 .60
31 Jon Kitna .25 .60
32 Roy Williams WR .25 .60
33 Calvin Johnson .30 .75
34 Aaron Rodgers .60 1.50
35 Ryan Grant .30 .75
36 Donald Driver .25 .60
37 Matt Schaub .25 .60
38 Andre Johnson .25 .60
39 Kevin Walter .25 .60
40 Peyton Manning .50 1.25
41 Joseph Addai .25 .60
42 Reggie Wayne .25 .60
43 Dallas Clark .25 .60
44 David Garrard .25 .60
45 Fred Taylor .25 .60
46 Maurice Jones-Drew .25 .60
47 Reggie Williams .25 .60
48 Brodie Croyle .25 .60
49 Larry Johnson .25 .60
50 Tony Gonzalez .25 .60
51 Chad Pennington .25 .60
52 Ronnie Brown .25 .60
53 Ted Ginn Jr. .25 .60
54 Tarvaris Jackson .25 .60
55 Adrian Peterson .50 1.25
56 Sidney Rice .30 .75
57 Tom Brady .50 1.25
58 Randy Moss .30 .75
59 Laurence Maroney .25 .60
60 Drew Brees .30 .75
61 Reggie Bush .30 .75
62 Deuce McAllister .25 .60
63 Eli Manning .30 .75
64 Plaxico Burress .25 .60
65 Brandon Jacobs .25 .60
66 Brett Favre 2.00 5.00
67 Leon Washington .25 .60
68 Laveranues Coles .20 .50
69 JaMarcus Russell .25 .60
70 Justin Fargas .20 .50
71 Zach Miller .25 .60
72 Donovan McNabb .30 .75
73 Brian Westbrook .25 .60
74 Reggie Brown .20 .50
75 Ben Roethlisberger .30 .75
76 Willie Parker .25 .60
77 Santonio Holmes .25 .60
78 Philip Rivers .30 .75
79 LaDainian Tomlinson .30 .75
80 Vincent Jackson .20 .50
81 Antonio Gates .30 .75
82 J.T. O'Sullivan .20 .50
83 Frank Gore .25 .60
84 Vernon Davis .25 .60
85 Matt Hasselbeck .25 .60
86 Deion Branch .25 .60
87 Julius Jones .20 .50
88 Marc Bulger .25 .60
89 Steven Jackson .30 .75
90 Torry Holt .25 .60
91 Warrick Dunn .25 .60
92 Jeff Garcia .25 .60
93 Joey Galloway .25 .60
94 Vince Young .25 .60
95 LenDale White .25 .60
96 Roydell Williams .20 .50
97 Jason Campbell .25 .60
98 Clinton Portis .25 .60
99 Santana Moss .20 .50
100 Ladell Betts .20 .50
101 Trent Edwards ELE .60 1.50
102 Marshawn Lynch ELE .75 2.00
103 Braylon Edwards ELE .75 2.00
104 Carson Palmer ELE 1.00 2.50
105 Tom Brady ELE 1.50 4.00
106 Matt Hasselbeck ELE .75 2.00
107 Nate Burleson ELE .60 1.50
108 Fred Taylor ELE .75 2.00
109 David Garrard ELE .75 2.00
110 Maurice Jones-Drew ELE .75 2.00
111 Devin Hester ELE 1.00 2.50
112 Willie Parker ELE .75 2.00
113 Ben Roethlisberger ELE 1.00 2.50
114 Ryan Grant ELE 1.00 2.50
115 Eli Manning ELE 1.00 2.50
116 Adrian Arrington RC 1.50 4.00
117 Ali Highsmith RC 1.25 3.00
118 Anthony Alridge RC 1.50 4.00
119 Antoine Cason RC 2.00 5.00
120 Aqib Talib RC 2.00 5.00
121 Brad Cottam RC 1.50 4.00
122 Brandon Flowers RC 2.00 5.00
123 Calais Campbell RC 1.50 4.00
124 Chauncey Washington RC 1.50 4.00
125 Chevis Jackson RC 1.25 3.00
126 Cory Boyd RC 1.25 3.00
127 Craig Steltz RC 1.50 4.00
128 Curtis Lofton RC 1.50 4.00
129 DJ Hall RC 1.50 4.00
130 Dantrell Savage RC 1.50 4.00
131 Darius Reynaud RC 1.25 3.00
132 Darrell Strong RC 1.50 4.00
133 Davone Bess RC 2.00 5.00
134 Derrick Harvey RC 1.25 3.00
135 Dominique Rodgers-Cromartie RC 2.00 5.00
136 Erin Henderson RC 2.00 5.00
137 Ernie Wheelwright RC 1.50 4.00
138 Fred Davis RC 2.00 5.00
139 Joe Jon Finley RC 1.50 4.00
140 Jacob Hester RC 2.00 5.00
141 Jacob Tamme RC 2.00 5.00
142 Jamar Adams RC 1.50 4.00
143 Jason Rivers RC 1.50 4.00
144 Jed Collins RC 1.50 4.00
145 Jermichael Finley RC 2.00 5.00
146 John Carlson RC 2.00 5.00
147 Jonathan Hefney RC 1.50 4.00
148 Jordon Dizon RC 2.00 5.00
149 Josh Morgan RC 2.00 5.00
150 Justin Forsett RC 2.00 5.00
151 Kalvin McRae RC 1.25 3.00
152 Keenan Burton RC 1.25 3.00
153 Kellen Davis RC 1.25 3.00
154 Kentwan Balmer RC 1.50 4.00
155 Kevin Robinson RC 1.25 3.00
156 Lawrence Jackson RC 1.50 4.00
157 Leodis McKelvin RC 1.50 4.00
158 Marcus Monk RC 1.50 4.00
159 Marcus Smith RC 1.50 4.00
160 Marcus Thomas RC 1.50 4.00
161 Mark Bradford RC 1.25 3.00
162 Martellus Bennett RC 1.50 4.00
163 Martin Rucker RC 1.50 4.00
164 Mike Jenkins RC 2.00 5.00
165 Owen Schmitt RC 2.00 5.00
166 Pat Sims RC 1.50 4.00
167 Paul Hubbard RC 1.50 4.00
168 Paul Smith RC 2.00 5.00
169 Peyton Hillis RC 2.50 6.00
170 Phillip Merling RC 1.50 4.00
171 Quentin Groves RC 1.50 4.00
172 Reggie Smith RC 1.50 4.00
173 Ryan Grice-Mullen RC 1.25 3.00
174 Ryan Torain RC 2.00 5.00
175 Sam Keller RC 1.50 4.00
176 Sedrick Ellis RC 2.00 5.00
177 Shawn Crable RC 1.25 3.00
178 Simeon Castille RC 1.50 4.00
179 Terrell Thomas RC 1.50 4.00
180 Thomas Brown RC 1.50 4.00
181 Tim Hightower RC 2.00 5.00
182 Tracy Porter RC 2.00 5.00
183 Vernon Gholston RC 1.50 4.00
184 Will Franklin RC 1.50 4.00
185 Xavier Adibi RC 1.25 3.00
186 Alex Brink RC 2.00 5.00
187 Jalen Parmele RC 1.50 4.00
188 Xavier Omon RC 2.00 5.00
189 Craig Stevens RC 1.25 3.00
190 Derek Fine RC 1.50 4.00
191 Gary Barnidge RC 1.25 3.00
192 Arman Shields RC 1.50 4.00
193 Kenneth Moore RC 1.50 4.00
194 Marcus Henry RC 1.50 4.00
195 Jaymar Johnson RC 1.25 3.00
196 Pierre Garcon RC 2.50 6.00
197 Patrick Lee RC 1.50 4.00
198 Terrence Wheatley RC 1.25 3.00
199 Tavares Gooden RC 1.50 4.00
200 Bruce Davis RC 1.50 4.00

2008 Leaf Rookies and Stars Longevity Emerald

*VETS 1-100: 4X TO 10X BASIC CARDS
*ELEMENTS 101-115: 1.5X TO 4X BASIC CARDS
*ROOKIES 116-200: 1X TO 2.5X BASIC CARDS
EMERALD PRINT RUN 49 SER.#'d SETS
66 Brett Favre 8.00 20.00

2008 Leaf Rookies and Stars Longevity Ruby

*VETS 1-100: 2X TO 5X BASIC CARDS
*ELEMENTS 101-115: .8X TO 2X BASIC CARDS
*ROOKIES 116-200: .5X TO 1.2X BASIC CARDS
RUBY PRINT RUN 249 SER.#'d SETS
66 Brett Favre 4.00 10.00

2008 Leaf Rookies and Stars Longevity Sapphire

*VETS 1-100: 2.5X TO 6X BASIC CARDS
*ELEMENT 101-115: 1X TO 2.5X BASIC CARDS
*ROOKIES 116-200: .6X TO 1.5X BASIC CARDS
SAPPHIRE PRINT RUN 149 SER.#'d SETS
66 Brett Favre 5.00 12.00

2008 Leaf Rookies and Stars Longevity Materials Sapphire

SAPPHIRE PRINT RUN 100 SER.#'d SETS
*RUBY/250-350: .3X TO .8X BASIC INSERTS
*RUBY/97-175: .4X TO 1X BASIC INSERTS
RUBY PRINT RUN 97-350
1 Matt Leinart 5.00 12.00
2 Larry Fitzgerald 5.00 12.00
3 Anquan Boldin 4.00 10.00
4 Edgerrin James 4.00 10.00
7 Willis McGahee 4.00 10.00
8 Derrick Mason 4.00 10.00
9 Demetrius Williams 3.00 8.00
10 Trent Edwards 3.00 8.00
11 Marshawn Lynch 4.00 10.00
12 Lee Evans 4.00 10.00
13 Steve Smith 4.00 10.00
14 DeAngelo Williams 4.00 10.00
15 Julius Peppers 4.00 10.00
17 Devin Hester 5.00 12.00
19 Carson Palmer 5.00 12.00
20 Chad Johnson 4.00 10.00
21 T.J. Houshmandzadeh 4.00 10.00
23 Derek Anderson 3.00 8.00
24 Kellen Winslow 4.00 10.00
25 Braylon Edwards 4.00 10.00
26 Tony Romo 6.00 15.00
27 Terrell Owens 5.00 12.00
28 Marion Barber 4.00 10.00
29 Jay Cutler 5.00 12.00
30 Brandon Stokley 4.00 10.00
31 Jon Kitna 4.00 10.00
32 Roy Williams WR 4.00 10.00
34 Aaron Rodgers 10.00 25.00
35 Ryan Grant 5.00 12.00
36 Donald Driver 4.00 10.00
37 Matt Schaub 4.00 10.00
38 Andre Johnson 4.00 10.00
40 Peyton Manning 8.00 20.00
41 Joseph Addai 4.00 10.00
42 Reggie Wayne 4.00 10.00
43 Dallas Clark 4.00 10.00
44 David Garrard 4.00 10.00
45 Fred Taylor 4.00 10.00
46 Maurice Jones-Drew 4.00 10.00
47 Reggie Williams 4.00 10.00
48 Brodie Croyle 4.00 10.00
49 Larry Johnson 4.00 10.00
50 Tony Gonzalez 4.00 10.00
54 Tarvaris Jackson 4.00 10.00
55 Adrian Peterson 8.00 20.00
57 Tom Brady 8.00 20.00
58 Randy Moss 5.00 12.00
59 Laurence Maroney 4.00 10.00
60 Drew Brees 5.00 12.00
61 Reggie Bush 5.00 12.00
63 Eli Manning 5.00 12.00
64 Plaxico Burress 4.00 10.00
65 Brandon Jacobs 4.00 10.00
67 Leon Washington/60 4.00 10.00
68 Laveranues Coles 3.00 8.00
70 Justin Fargas 3.00 8.00
72 Donovan McNabb 5.00 12.00
73 Brian Westbrook 4.00 10.00
74 Reggie Brown 3.00 8.00
75 Ben Roethlisberger 5.00 12.00
76 Willie Parker 4.00 10.00
77 Santonio Holmes 4.00 10.00
78 Philip Rivers 5.00 12.00
79 LaDainian Tomlinson 5.00 12.00
81 Antonio Gates 5.00 12.00
83 Frank Gore 4.00 10.00
85 Matt Hasselbeck 4.00 10.00
86 Deion Branch 4.00 10.00
88 Marc Bulger/50 4.00 10.00
89 Steven Jackson 5.00 12.00
90 Torry Holt 4.00 10.00
92 Jeff Garcia 4.00 10.00
93 Joey Galloway 4.00 10.00
94 Vince Young 4.00 10.00
95 LenDale White 4.00 10.00
96 Roydell Williams 3.00 8.00
97 Jason Campbell 4.00 10.00
98 Clinton Portis 4.00 10.00
99 Santana Moss 3.00 8.00
100 Ladell Betts 3.00 8.00

2008 Leaf Rookies and Stars Longevity Rookie Autographs

LONGEVITY PRINT RUN 9-500
UNPRICED RUBY PRINT RUN 5
UNPRICED SAPPHIRE PRINT RUN 1
UNPRICED COLLEGE PRINT RUN 5
UNPRICED COLLEGE RUBY PRINT RUN 1
UNPRICED COLL.SAPPHIRE PRINT RUN 1
117 Ali Highsmith/500 2.00 5.00
123 Calais Campbell/250 3.00 8.00
126 Cory Boyd/500 2.00 5.00
130 Dantrell Savage/314 3.00 8.00
131 Darius Reynaud/50 3.00 8.00
136 Erin Henderson/500 3.00 8.00
143 Jason Rivers/500 2.50 6.00
145 Jermichael Finley/100 8.00 20.00
153 Kellen Davis/125 3.00 8.00
154 Kentwan Balmer/250 3.00 8.00
161 Mark Bradford/500 2.00 5.00
166 Pat Sims/450 2.50 6.00
173 Ryan Grice-Mullen/500 2.00 5.00
175 Sam Keller/500 2.50 6.00
185 Xavier Adibi/450 2.00 5.00

1997 Leaf Signature

The 1997 Leaf Signature set was issued in one series totalling 117 cards and features UV coated borderless color player photos measuring approximately 8" by 10". The cards are unnumberd and checklisted below alphabetically.

COMPLETE SET (117) 90.00 150.00
1 Karim Abdul-Jabbar 1.00 2.50
2 Troy Aikman 2.00 5.00
3 Derrick Alexander WR .60 1.50
4 Terry Allen 1.00 2.50
5 Mike Alstott 1.00 2.50
6 Jamal Anderson 1.00 2.50
7 Reidel Anthony RC 1.00 2.50
8 Darnell Autry RC .60 1.50
9 Tony Banks .60 1.50
10 Tiki Barber RC 4.00 10.00
11 Pat Barnes RC 1.00 2.50
12 Jerome Bettis 1.00 2.50
13 Tim Biakabutuka .60 1.50
14 Will Blackwell RC .60 1.50
15 Jeff Blake .60 1.50
16 Drew Bledsoe 1.25 3.00
17 Peter Boulware RC 1.00 2.50
18 Robert Brooks .60 1.50
19 Dave Brown .60 1.50
20 Tim Brown 1.00 2.50
21 Isaac Bruce 1.00 2.50
22 Mark Brunell 1.25 3.00
23 Rae Carruth RC .40 1.00
24 Ki-Jana Carter .40 1.00
25 Cris Carter 1.00 2.50
26 Larry Centers .60 1.50
27 Ben Coates .60 1.50
28 Kerry Collins 1.00 2.50
29 Todd Collins .40 1.00
30 Albert Connell RC 1.00 2.50
31 Curtis Conway .60 1.50
32 Terrell Davis 1.25 3.00
33 Troy Davis RC .60 1.50
34 Corey Dillon RC 2.50 6.00
35 Jim Druckenmiller RC .60 1.50
36 Warrick Dunn RC 2.00 5.00
37 John Elway 4.00 10.00
38 Bert Emanuel .60 1.50
39 Bobby Engram .60 1.50
40 Boomer Esiason .60 1.50
41 Jim Everett .40 1.00
42 Marshall Faulk 1.25 3.00
43 Brett Favre 4.00 10.00
44 Antonio Freeman 1.00 2.50
45 Gus Frerotte .40 1.00
46 Irving Fryar .60 1.50
47 Joey Galloway .60 1.50
48 Eddie George 1.00 2.50
49 Jeff George .60 1.50
50 Tony Gonzalez RC 2.50 6.00
51 Jay Graham .60 1.50
52 Elvis Grbac .60 1.50
53 Darrell Green .60 1.50
54 Yatil Green RC .60 1.50
55 Rodney Hampton .60 1.50
56 Byron Hanspard RC .60 1.50
57 Jim Harbaugh .60 1.50
58 Marvin Harrison 1.00 2.50
59 Garrison Hearst .60 1.50
60 Greg Hill .40 1.00
61 Ike Hilliard RC 1.00 2.50
62 Jeff Hostetler .40 1.00
63 Brad Johnson 1.00 2.50
64 Keyshawn Johnson 1.00 2.50
65 Daryl Johnston .60 1.50
66 Napoleon Kaufman 1.00 2.50
67 Jim Kelly 1.00 2.50
68 Eddie Kennison .60 1.50
69 Joey Kent 1.00 2.50
70 Bernie Kosar .40 1.00
71 Erik Kramer .40 1.00
72 Dorsey Levens 1.00 2.50
73 Kevin Lockett RC .60 1.50
74 Dan Marino 4.00 10.00
75 Curtis Martin 1.25 3.00
76 Tony Martin .60 1.50
77 Leeland McElroy .40 1.00
78 Steve McNair 1.25 3.00
79 Natrone Means .60 1.50
80 Eric Metcalf .60 1.50
81 Anthony Miller .60 1.50
82 Rick Mirer .40 1.00
83 Scott Mitchell .60 1.50
84 Warren Moon 1.00 2.50
85 Herman Moore .60 1.50
86 Muhsin Muhammad .60 1.50
87 Adrian Murrell .60 1.50
88 Neil O'Donnell .60 1.50
89 Terrell Owens 1.25 3.00
90 Brett Perriman .40 1.00
91 Lawrence Phillips .40 1.00
92 Jake Plummer RC 2.50 6.00
93 Andre Reed .60 1.50
94 Jerry Rice 2.00 5.00
95 Darrell Russell RC .40 1.00
96 Rashaan Salaam .40 1.00
97 Barry Sanders 3.00 8.00
98 Chris Sanders .40 1.00
99 Deion Sanders 1.00 2.50
100 Frank Sanders .60 1.50
101 Darnay Scott .60 1.50
102 Junior Seau 1.00 2.50
103 Shannon Sharpe .60 1.50
104 Sedrick Shaw RC .60 1.50
105 Heath Shuler .40 1.00
106 Antowain Smith RC 1.50 4.00
107 Bruce Smith .60 1.50
108 Emmitt Smith 3.00 8.00
109 Kordell Stewart 1.00 2.50
110 J.J. Stokes .60 1.50
111 Vinny Testaverde .60 1.50
112 Thurman Thomas 1.00 2.50
113 Tamarick Vanover .60 1.50
114 Herschel Walker .60 1.50
115 Michael Westbrook .60 1.50
116 Danny Wuerffel RC 1.00 2.50
117 Steve Young 1.25 3.00

1997 Leaf Signature Autographs

UNL.STARS/1000-2500 10.00 25.00
ONE AUTOGRAPH PER PACK
*FD MARKERS/1000-5000: .8X TO 2X
*FD MARKERS/200-500: .6X TO 1.5X
*FD MARK SP #64/87: 1X TO 2.5X
FIRST DOWN PRINT RUN 100 SETS
1 Karim Abdul-Jabbar/2500 6.00 15.00
2 Derrick Alexander WR/4000 5.00 12.00
3 Terry Allen/3000 5.00 12.00
4 Mike Alstott/4000 8.00 20.00
5 Jamal Anderson/4000 8.00 20.00
6 Reidel Anthony/2000 6.00 15.00
7 Darnell Autry/4000 3.00 8.00
8 Tony Banks/500 15.00 40.00
9 Tiki Barber/4000 12.00 30.00
10 Pat Barnes/4000 3.00 8.00
11 Jerome Bettis/500 40.00 80.00
12 Tim Biakabutuka/3000 5.00 12.00

13 Will Blackwell/2500	4.00	10.00
14 Jeff Blake/500	12.50	25.00
15 Drew Bledsoe/500	30.00	60.00
16 Peter Boulware/4000	8.00	20.00
17 Robert Brooks/1000	6.00	15.00
18 Dave Brown/500	12.50	25.00
19 Tim Brown/2500	15.00	30.00
20 Isaac Bruce/2500	10.00	25.00
21 Mark Brunell/500	15.00	40.00
22 Rae Carruth/5000	8.00	20.00
23 Cris Carter/2500	12.50	30.00
24 Larry Centers/4000	5.00	12.00
25 Ben Coates/4000	3.00	8.00
26 Todd Collins/4000	10.00	20.00
27 Albert Connell/4000	3.00	8.00
28 Curtis Conway/3000	5.00	12.00
29 Terrell Davis/2500	15.00	30.00
30 Troy Davis/4000	3.00	8.00
31 Trent Dilfer/500	20.00	50.00
32 Corey Dillon/4000	15.00	30.00
33 Jim Druckenmiller/5000	3.00	8.00
34 Warrick Dunn/2000	15.00	40.00
35 John Elway/500	60.00	120.00
36 Bert Emanuel/4000	5.00	12.00
37 Bobby Engram/3000	5.00	12.00
38 Boomer Esiason/500	20.00	50.00
39 Jim Everett/500	12.50	25.00
40 Marshall Faulk/3000	15.00	30.00
41 Antonio Freeman/2000	10.00	25.00
42 Gus Frerotte/500	15.00	40.00
43 Irving Fryar/3000	5.00	12.00
44 Joey Galloway/3000	5.00	12.00
45 Eddie George/300	20.00	50.00
46 Jeff George/500	12.50	25.00
47 Tony Gonzalez/4000	15.00	40.00
48 Jay Graham/1000	4.00	10.00
49 Elvis Grbac/500	15.00	40.00
50 Darrell Green/2500	30.00	60.00
51 Yatil Green/5000	3.00	8.00
52 Rodney Hampton/4000	3.00	8.00
53 Byron Hanspard/4000	3.00	8.00
54 Jim Harbaugh/500	15.00	40.00
55 Marvin Harrison/3000	25.00	40.00
56 Garrison Hearst/4000	8.00	20.00
57 Greg Hill/4000	3.00	8.00
58 Ike Hilliard/2000	6.00	15.00
59 Jeff Hostetler/500	12.50	25.00
60 Brad Johnson/2000	6.00	15.00
61 Keyshawn Johnson/1000	10.00	25.00
62 Daryl Johnston/3000	8.00	20.00
63 Jim Kelly/500	40.00	80.00
64 Eddie Kennison/3000	5.00	12.00
65 Joey Kent/4000	3.00	8.00
66 Bernie Kosar/500	15.00	40.00
67 Erik Kramer/500	12.50	25.00
68 Dorsey Levens/3000	8.00	20.00
69 Kevin Lockett/4000	3.00	8.00
70 Tony Martin/4000	5.00	12.00
71 Leeland McElroy/4000	3.00	8.00
72 Natrone Means/3000	5.00	12.00
73 Eric Metcalf/4000	5.00	12.00
74 Anthony Miller/3000	3.00	8.00
75 Rick Mirer/500	12.50	25.00
76 Scott Mitchell/500	15.00	40.00
77 Warren Moon/500	20.00	50.00
78 Herman Moore/2500	5.00	12.00
79 Muhsin Muhammad/3000	8.00	20.00
80 Adrian Murrell/3000	3.00	8.00
81 Neil O'Donnell/500	12.50	25.00
82 Terrell Owens/3000	20.00	40.00
83 Brett Perriman/1000	4.00	10.00
84 Lawrence Phillips/1000	4.00	10.00
85 Jake Plummer/5000	15.00	30.00
86 Andre Reed/3000	8.00	20.00
87 Jerry Rice	60.00	120.00
88 Darrell Russell/2000	4.00	10.00
89 Rashaan Salaam/3000	3.00	8.00
90 Barry Sanders/400	60.00	120.00
91 Chris Sanders/3000	3.00	8.00
92 Frank Sanders/3000	5.00	12.00
93 Darnay Scott/2000	5.00	12.00
94 Junior Seau/500	30.00	60.00
95 Shannon Sharpe/1000	20.00	40.00
96 Sedrick Shaw/4000	3.00	8.00
97 Heath Shuler/500	12.50	25.00
98 Antowain Smith/5000	8.00	20.00
99 Emmitt Smith/200	150.00	250.00
100 Kordell Stewart/500	15.00	40.00
101 J.J. Stokes/3000	5.00	12.00
102 Vinny Testaverde/200	20.00	50.00
103 Thurman Thomas/2500	15.00	30.00
104 Tamarick Vanover/4000	5.00	12.00
105 Herschel Walker/3000	15.00	30.00
106 Michael Westbrook/3000	5.00	12.00
107 Danny Wuerffel/4000	5.00	12.00
108 Steve Young/500	50.00	100.00

1997 Leaf Signature Old School Drafts Autographs

STATED PRINT RUN 1000 SERIAL #'d SETS

1 Joe Theismann	15.00	40.00
2 Archie Manning	20.00	50.00
3 Len Dawson	15.00	40.00
4 Sammy Baugh	40.00	80.00
5 Dan Fouts	15.00	40.00
6 Danny White	15.00	40.00
7 Ron Jaworski	12.00	30.00
8 Jim Plunkett	12.00	30.00
9 Y.A. Tittle	20.00	50.00
11 Ken Stabler	20.00	50.00
12 Billy Kilmer	12.00	30.00

2012 Leaf Vince Lombardi Legacy

COMPLETE SET (40)	75.00	150.00
COMMON CARD	2.00	5.00

2012 Leaf Vince Lombardi Legacy Jacket Swatches

COMMON CARD
ONE JACKET SWATCH PER BOX
UNPRICED GOLD PRINT RUN 5
UNPRICED SILVER PRINT RUN 10
UNPRICED PURPLE PRINT RUN 1

1993-94 Legendary Foils

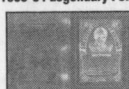

The Legendary Foils Sport Series was intended to be a monthly series featuring Pro Football Hall of Famers. The cards measure approximately 3 1/2" by 5" and were issued in a green and black custom designed folder. The embossed fronts carry the players portrait and a short career summary. The gold edition cards are completely gold foil layered on a matte gold background, while the colored edition cards have a green background. Production was limited to no more than 95,000 for the colored edition and 5,000 for the gold edition. The serial number also appears on the front. The backs are silver and carry Legendary Foil logos. There were no card numbers. We've included single card prices below for the colored version.

1 Morris Red Badgro	.80	2.00
2 Terry Bradshaw	1.60	4.00
P1 Terry Bradshaw Promo	1.60	4.00

2006 Lehigh Valley Outlawz GLIFL

COMPLETE SET (36)	6.00	12.00
1 Corey Adderley	.20	.50
2 Mark Barrionnette	.20	.50
3 Lloyd C. Brooks Jr.	.20	.50
4 Damien Ciecwisz	.20	.50
5 Steve Cook	.20	.50
6 Doug Folger	.20	.50
7 Drew DeRogatis	.20	.50
8 T.K. Ford	.20	.50
9 Larry Koch	.20	.50
10 Keith McConnell	.20	.50
11 Sean McGinley	.20	.50
12 Andrew Nelson	.20	.50
13 Billy Parker	.20	.50
14 Mike Ramos	.20	.50
15 Chris Reed	.20	.50
16 Chad Schwenk	.20	.50
17 Brian Smith	.20	.50
18 James Spence	.20	.50
19 Keeno Theadford	.20	.50
20 Joe Wooten	.20	.50
21 Coaches	.20	.50
Owner		
Jim DePaul Own		
Mike DePaul GM		
Al Forsythe Asst.CO		
Clayton		
22 Outkast Mascot	.20	.50
23 Lady Outlawz - Amber	.20	.50
24 Lady Outlawz - Andrea	.20	.50
25 Lady Outlawz - Brittany	.20	.50
26 Lady Outlawz - Chrissy	.20	.50
27 Lady Outlawz - Gabrielle	.20	.50
28 Lady Outlawz - Genie	.20	.50
29 Lady Outlawz - Jessie	.20	.50
30 Lady Outlawz - Kate	.20	.50
31 Lady Outlawz - Kelly	.20	.50
32 Lady Outlawz - Amanda	.20	.50
33 Lady Outlawz - Michele	.20	.50
34 Lady Outlawz - Monica	.20	.50
35 Lady Outlawz - Valerie	.20	.50
36 Lady Outlawz Group Photo	.20	.50

2007 Lehigh Valley Outlawz CIFL

COMPLETE SET (40)	6.00	12.00
1 Marc Barionnette	.20	.50
2 Kevin Bliss	.20	.50
3 Lloyd Brooks	.20	.50
4 Ed Chan	.20	.50
5 Phil DeCecco	.20	.50
6 Joe DeLuise	.20	.50
7 Drew DeRogatis	.20	.50
8 Ryan Harrison	.20	.50
9 Barry Helverson	.20	.50
10 Omar Johnson	.20	.50
11 Collis Martin	.20	.50
12 Keith McConnell	.20	.50
13 Mike Merritt	.20	.50
14 Allen Neal	.20	.50
15 Billy Parker	.20	.50
16 Mike Ramos	.20	.50
17 Zikoma Richards	.20	.50
18 Eddie Scipio	.20	.50
19 Ray Simmons	.20	.50
20 Brian Smith	.20	.50
21 Dom Stewart	.20	.50
22 Al Stokes	.20	.50
23 Sal Tubbs	.20	.50
24 Joe Wooten	.20	.50
25 Devon White	.20	.50
26 Coaches	.20	.50
Mike DePaul Asst.CO		
James DePaul CO		
Al Forsythe Ast.CO		
Trev Mar		
27 Team Card	.20	.50
28 Lady Outlawz - Amber	.20	.50
29 Lady Outlawz - Genie	.20	.50
30 Lady Outlawz - Jes	.20	.50
31 Lady Outlawz - Julie	.20	.50
32 Lady Outlawz - Kasey	.20	.50
33 Lady Outlawz - Kate	.20	.50
34 Lady Outlawz - Michele	.20	.50
35 Lady Outlawz - Robyn	.20	.50
36 Lady Outlawz - Sarah	.20	.50
37 Lady Outlawz - Shaina	.20	.50
38 Lady Outlawz - Shannon	.20	.50
39 Lady Outlawz - Valerie	.20	.50
40 Lady Outlawz Group Photo	.20	.50

2008 Lehigh Valley Outlawz CIFL

COMPLETE SET (40)	6.00	12.00
1 Dom Stewart	.20	.50
2 Desmond Maul	.20	.50
3 Joe Wooten	.20	.50
4 Steve Cook	.20	.50
5 BJ Hall	.20	.50
6 Brandon Simmons	.20	.50
7 Dave Carter	.20	.50
8 Eddie Scipio	.20	.50
9 Billy Parker	.20	.50
10 Mark Sedlock	.20	.50
11 Jermaine Thaxton	.20	.50
12 Mark Barrionette	.20	.50
13 Jaime Sellers	.20	.50
14 Adwela Dawes	.20	.50
15 Sal Byron	.20	.50
16 Devon White	.20	.50
17 Brian Smith	.20	.50
18 Scott Blum	.20	.50
19 Greg Hammond	.20	.50
20 Wendell Bates	.20	.50
21 Sal Tubbs	.20	.50
22 Drew DeRogotis	.20	.50
23 Mike Ramos	.20	.50
24 Gene Rich	.20	.50
25 Al Stokes	.20	.50
26 Outlawz Team CL	.20	.50
27 Outkast Mascot	.20	.50
28 Bethany CHEER	.20	.50
29 Gabrielle CHEER	.20	.50
30 Genie CHEER	.20	.50
31 Jackie CHEER	.20	.50
32 Jes CHEER	.20	.50
33 Julie CHEER	.20	.50
34 Kate CHEER	.20	.50
35 Marci CHEER	.20	.50
36 Michele CHEER	.20	.50
37 Robyn CHEER	.20	.50
38 Shannon CHEER	.20	.50
39 Valerie CHEER	.20	.50
40 Lady Outlawz Photo	.20	.50

2009 Limited

1-150 STATED PRINT RUN 399
AUTO ROOKIE PRINT RUN 99-399
JSY AUTO ROOKIE PRINT RUN 149

1 Kurt Warner	1.50	4.00
2 Larry Fitzgerald	1.50	4.00
3 Tim Hightower	1.00	2.50
4 Matt Ryan	1.50	4.00
5 Michael Turner	1.25	3.00
6 Roddy White	1.25	3.00
7 Tony Gonzalez	1.25	3.00
8 Mark Clayton	1.00	2.50
9 Joe Flacco	1.50	4.00
10 Willis McGahee	1.25	3.00
11 Lee Evans	1.25	3.00
12 Marshawn Lynch	1.25	3.00
13 Terrell Owens	1.50	4.00
14 DeAngelo Williams	1.50	4.00
15 Jake Delhomme	1.25	3.00
16 Steve Smith	1.25	3.00
17 Brian Urlacher	1.50	4.00
18 Greg Olsen	1.00	2.50
19 Jay Cutler	1.50	4.00
20 Matt Forte	1.50	4.00
21 Carson Palmer	1.50	4.00
22 Cedric Benson	1.25	3.00
23 Chad Ochocinco	1.25	3.00
24 Brady Quinn	1.25	3.00
25 Braylon Edwards	1.25	3.00
26 Jamal Lewis	1.25	3.00
27 Marion Barber	1.25	3.00
28 Roy Williams WR	1.25	3.00
29 Tony Romo	2.50	6.00
30 Eddie Royal	1.25	3.00
31 Kyle Orton	1.25	3.00
32 LaMont Jordan	1.00	2.50
33 Calvin Johnson	1.50	4.00
34 Daunte Culpepper	1.25	3.00
35 Kevin Smith	1.25	3.00
36 Aaron Rodgers	3.00	8.00
37 Greg Jennings	1.50	4.00
38 Ryan Grant	1.25	3.00
39 Andre Johnson	1.25	3.00
40 Matt Schaub	1.25	3.00
41 Steve Slaton	1.25	3.00
42 Anthony Gonzalez	1.00	2.50
43 Joseph Addai	1.50	4.00
44 Peyton Manning	2.50	6.00
45 Reggie Wayne	1.25	3.00
46 David Garrard	1.25	3.00
47 Maurice Jones-Drew	1.25	3.00
48 Torry Holt	1.25	3.00
49 Dwayne Dowe	1.25	3.00
50 Larry Johnson	1.25	3.00
51 Matt Cassel	1.25	3.00
52 Chad Pennington	1.25	3.00
53 Ronnie Brown	1.25	3.00
54 Ricky Williams	1.25	3.00
55 Adrian Peterson	2.50	6.00
56 Bernard Berrian	1.25	3.00
57 Brett Favre Vikings	8.00	20.00
58 Laurence Maroney	1.25	3.00
59 Randy Moss	1.50	4.00
60 Tom Brady	2.50	6.00
61 Wes Welker	1.50	4.00
62 Drew Brees	1.50	4.00
63 Marques Colston	1.25	3.00
64 Reggie Bush	1.50	4.00
65 Brandon Jacobs	1.25	3.00
66 Eli Manning	1.50	4.00
67 Kevin Boss	1.25	3.00
68 Jerricho Cotchery	1.25	3.00
69 Leon Washington	1.25	3.00
70 Darren McFadden	1.50	4.00
71 JaMarcus Russell	1.00	2.50
72 Zach Miller	1.00	2.50
73 Brian Westbrook	1.25	3.00
74 DeSean Jackson	1.25	3.00
75 Donovan McNabb	1.50	4.00
76 Ben Roethlisberger	1.50	4.00
77 Santonio Holmes	1.25	3.00
78 Willie Parker	1.00	2.50
79 Antonio Gates	1.25	3.00
80 LaDainian Tomlinson	1.50	4.00
81 Philip Rivers	1.50	4.00
82 Vincent Jackson	1.25	3.00
83 Frank Gore	1.25	3.00
84 Isaac Bruce	1.25	3.00
85 Vernon Davis	1.25	3.00
86 Julius Jones	1.00	2.50
87 Matt Hasselbeck	1.25	3.00
88 T.J. Houshmandzadeh	1.25	3.00
89 Donnie Avery	1.25	3.00
90 Marc Bulger	1.25	3.00
91 Steven Jackson	1.25	3.00
92 Antonio Bryant	1.00	2.50
93 Derrick Ward	1.00	2.50
94 Kellen Winslow Jr.	1.25	3.00
95 Chris Johnson	1.50	4.00
96 Kerry Collins	1.25	3.00
97 LenDale White	1.25	3.00
98 Chris Cooley	1.25	3.00
99 Clinton Portis	1.25	3.00
100 Jason Campbell	1.00	2.50
101 Archie Manning	2.00	5.00
102 Bart Starr	3.00	8.00
103 Billy Howton	1.25	3.00
104 Bob Griese	2.00	5.00
105 Bob Lilly	1.50	4.00
106 Brett Favre Jets	4.00	10.00
107 Carl Eller	1.25	3.00
108 Charley Taylor	1.25	3.00
109 Charley Trippi	1.25	3.00
110 Chuck Bednarik	1.50	4.00
111 Dan Fouts	2.00	5.00
112 Dan Marino	3.00	8.00
113 Deacon Jones	1.50	4.00
114 Don Maynard	1.50	4.00
115 Emmitt Smith	2.50	6.00
116 Fran Tarkenton	2.00	5.00
117 Fred Biletnikoff	2.00	5.00
118 Garo Yepremian	1.25	3.00
119 George Blanda	1.50	4.00
120 Hugh McElhenny	1.25	3.00
121 Jack Lambert	2.00	5.00
122 James Lofton	1.25	3.00
123 Jan Stenerud	1.25	3.00
124 Jerry Rice	2.50	6.00
125 Jethro Pugh	1.25	3.00
126 Jim Brown	2.50	6.00
127 Jim Otto	1.25	3.00
128 Joe Greene	2.00	5.00
129 Joe Montana	3.00	8.00
130 Joe Namath	2.50	6.00
131 John Elway	2.50	6.00
132 John Stallworth	1.50	4.00
133 Lance Alworth	1.50	4.00
134 Lenny Moore	1.50	4.00
135 Phil Simms	1.50	4.00
136 Raymond Berry	1.50	4.00
137 Roger Staubach	2.50	6.00
138 Ted Hendricks	1.25	3.00
139 Tiki Barber	1.25	3.00
140 Troy Aikman	2.00	5.00
141 Willie Brown	1.25	3.00
142 Walter Payton	4.00	10.00
143 Jim Thorpe	2.50	6.00
144 Doak Walker	2.00	5.00
145 Ace Parker	1.25	3.00
146 Don Perkins	1.25	3.00
147 Sammy Baugh	2.00	5.00
148 Jim McMahon	1.50	4.00
149 Jim Kelly	1.50	4.00
150 Barry Sanders	2.50	6.00
151 Aaron Brown RC/399	2.00	5.00
152 Aaron Kelly AU/399 RC	4.00	10.00
153 Aaron Maybin AU/99 RC	5.00	12.00
154 Austin Collie AU/399 RC	6.00	15.00
155 B.J. Raji AU/399 RC	5.00	12.00
156 Bernard Scott RC/399	2.00	5.00
157 Brandon Gibson AU/399 RC	5.00	12.00
158 Brandon Tate AU/399 RC	5.00	12.00
159 Brian Cushing AU/199 RC	5.00	12.00
160 Brian Hartline RC/399	2.00	5.00
161 Brian Orakpo AU/249 RC	5.00	12.00
162 Brooks Foster AU/399 RC	3.00	8.00
163 Cameron Morrah AU/399 RC	3.00	8.00
164 Cedric Peerman AU/199 RC	4.00	10.00
165 Chase Coffman AU/399 RC	4.00	10.00
166 Chris Ogbonnaya RC/399	1.50	4.00
167 Clay Matthews AU/299 RC	35.00	60.00
168 Clint Sintim AU/149 RC	6.00	15.00
169 Cornelius Ingram AU/399 RC	3.00	8.00
170 Demetrius Byrd AU/99 RC	5.00	12.00
171 Devin Moore AU/299 RC	4.00	10.00
172 Dominique Edison AU/399 RC	3.00	8.00
173 Everette Brown AU/399 RC	4.00	10.00
174 Gartrell Johnson RC/399	1.25	3.00
175 Hunter Cantwell AU/149 RC	6.00	15.00
176 James Casey AU/399 RC	4.00	10.00
177 James Laurinaitis AU/299 RC	5.00	12.00
178 Jared Cook AU/399 RC	5.00	12.00
179 Jarett Dillard AU/399 RC	5.00	12.00
180 Johnny Knox AU/399 RC	8.00	20.00
181 Kenny McKinley AU/399 RC	5.00	12.00
182 Kevin Ogletree AU/249 RC	6.00	15.00
183 Kory Sheets AU/99 RC	5.00	12.00
184 Larry English AU/249 RC	5.00	12.00
185 Louis Murphy AU/99 RC	12.00	30.00
186 Malcolm Jenkins AU/249 RC	5.00	12.00
187 Mike Goodson AU/299 RC	5.00	12.00
188 Nathan Brown AU/399 RC	4.00	10.00
189 P.J. Hill AU/399 RC	4.00	10.00
190 Quan Cosby AU/249 RC	4.00	10.00
191 Quinn Johnson AU/399 RC	4.00	10.00
192 Rashad Jennings AU/199 RC	5.00	12.00
193 Rey Maualuga AU/399 RC	5.00	12.00
194 Shawn Nelson AU/99 RC EXCH	5.00	12.00
195 Tiquan Underwood RC/399	1.50	4.00
196 Tom Brandstater AU/149 RC	6.00	15.00
197 Tony Fiammetta AU/399 RC	4.00	10.00
198 Travis Beckum AU/399 RC	4.00	10.00
199 Tyrell Sutton AU/399 RC	4.00	10.00
200 Vontae Davis AU/399 RC	5.00	12.00
201 Glen Coffee JSY AU RC	6.00	15.00
202 Michael Crabtree JSY AU RC	30.00	80.00
203 Nate Davis JSY AU RC	6.00	15.00
204 Javon Ringer JSY AU RC	8.00	20.00
205 Kenny Britt JSY AU RC	10.00	25.00
206 Mike Wallace JSY AU RC	30.00	60.00
207 Jeremy Maclin JSY AU RC	12.00	30.00
208 LeSean McCoy JSY AU RC	20.00	50.00
209 Donald Brown JSY AU RC	8.00	20.00
210 Mike Thomas JSY AU RC	8.00	20.00
211 Tyson Jackson JSY AU RC	6.00	15.00
212 Josh Freeman JSY AU RC	40.00	80.00
213 Darrius Heyward-Bey JSY AU RC	8.00	20.00
214 Aaron Curry JSY AU RC	8.00	20.00
215 Deon Butler JSY AU RC	6.00	15.00
216 Jason Smith JSY AU RC	6.00	15.00
217 Juaquin Iglesias JSY AU RC	6.00	15.00
218 Stephen McGee JSY AU RC	8.00	20.00
219 Andre Brown JSY AU RC	5.00	12.00
220 Hakeem Nicks JSY AU RC	12.00	30.00
221 Ramses Barden JSY AU RC	5.00	12.00
222 Rhett Bomar JSY AU RC	6.00	15.00
223 Percy Harvin JSY AU RC	40.00	100.00
224 Pat White JSY AU RC	8.00	20.00
225 Patrick Turner JSY AU RC	6.00	15.00
226 Chris Wells JSY AU RC	25.00	60.00
227 Mark Sanchez JSY AU RC	60.00	120.00
228 Shonn Greene JSY AU RC	12.00	30.00
229 Brian Robiskie JSY AU RC	8.00	20.00
230 Mohamed Massaquoi JSY AU RC	6.00	15.00
231 Brandon Pettigrew JSY AU RC	8.00	20.00
232 Derrick Williams JSY AU RC	6.00	15.00
233 Matthew Stafford JSY AU RC	75.00	135.00
234 Knowshon Moreno JSY AU RC	15.00	40.00

2009 Limited Gold Spotlight

1-200 UNPRICED GOLD PRINT RUN 5
201-234 UNPRICED GOLD JSY AU PRINT RUN 10

2009 Limited Silver Spotlight

1-200 UNPRICED SILVER PRINT RUN 10
*201-234 JSY AU/25: .5X TO 1.2X BASE JSY AU
201-234 ROOKIE JSY AU PRINT RUN 25

212 Josh Freeman JSY AU	60.00	120.00
227 Mark Sanchez JSY AU	100.00	200.00
233 Matthew Stafford JSY AU	150.00	250.00

2009 Limited Banner Season Autograph Materials

JSY AUTO PRINT RUN 2-25

4 Bernard Berrian/20	10.00	25.00
12 Drew Brees/25	40.00	80.00
19 Matt Ryan/25	30.00	60.00

2009 Limited Banner Season Autograph Materials Prime

PRIME AUTO PRINT RUN 1-25

19 Matt Ryan/25	40.00	80.00

2009 Limited Banner Season Materials

STATED PRINT RUN 50 SER.#'d SETS

4 Bernard Berrian	4.00	10.00
7 Brian Westbrook	4.00	10.00
12 Drew Brees	5.00	12.00
19 Matt Ryan	5.00	12.00
25 Willis McGahee	4.00	10.00

2009 Limited Banner Season Materials Prime

STATED PRINT RUN 2-25

2 Andre Johnson/25	5.00	12.00
7 Brian Westbrook/25	5.00	12.00
10 Clinton Portis/25	5.00	12.00
11 DeAngelo Williams/25	6.00	15.00
17 LenDale White/25	5.00	12.00
19 Matt Ryan/25	6.00	15.00
20 Maurice Jones-Drew/25	5.00	12.00
22 Steve Smith/25	5.00	12.00

2009 Limited Cuts Autographs

CUT AUTO STATED PRINT RUN 3-26

2 Bert Bell/20	25.00	50.00
4 Dante Lavelli/22	25.00	50.00
7 Frank Gatski/25	25.00	50.00
10 George McAfee/26	25.00	50.00
11 Jay Berwanger/16	30.00	60.00
16 Red Badgro/25	25.00	50.00
17 Ollie Matson/16	30.00	60.00
20 Roosevelt Brown/25	30.00	60.00
21 Sammy Baugh/25	50.00	80.00
23 Tony Canadeo/25	30.00	60.00
25 Weeb Ewbank/25	25.00	50.00

2009 Limited Draft Day Jerseys Autographs Prime

PRIME AUTO PRINT RUN 25

1 Josh Freeman	30.00	60.00
2 Brian Cushing	8.00	20.00
3 Aaron Curry	8.00	20.00
4 Michael Crabtree	30.00	60.00
5 Jason Smith	6.00	15.00

2009 Limited Draft Day Lids

STATED PRINT RUN 50 SER.#'d SETS
*JSY/100: .3X TO .8X BASIC LID/50
*JSY PRIME/84-100: 4X TO 1X LID/50
*COMBO/50: .4X TO 1X BASIC LID/50
*COMBO PRIME/17-25: .6X TO 1.5X LID/50

1 Josh Freeman	6.00	15.00
2 Brian Cushing	3.00	8.00
3 Matthew Stafford	15.00	40.00
4 Aaron Curry	3.00	8.00
5 Michael Crabtree	6.00	15.00
6 Jason Smith	2.50	6.00
7 Eugene Monroe	2.00	5.00
8 Michael Oher	12.50	25.00
9 Brian Orakpo	3.00	8.00

2009 Limited Jumbo Jerseys Jersey Number

JUMBO JSY NUMBER PRINT RUN 10-50
*JUMBO JSY/10-50: .4X TO 1X JUM.JSY NUMTS

2 Antonio Gates/25	4.00	10.00
4 Brian Urlacher/50	5.00	12.00
9 Mark Clayton/50	3.00	8.00
12 Earnest Graham/50	3.00	8.00
14 Jamal Lewis/50	4.00	10.00
15 Jim Brown/10	15.00	40.00
19 Ray Lewis/50	5.00	12.00
20 Reggie Brown/15	4.00	10.00
22 Ricky Williams/50	4.00	10.00

2009 Limited Jumbo Jerseys Autographs

JUMBO JSY AUTO PRINT RUN 1-25
*JSY NUM AU/25: .4X TO 1X BASIC JSY AU/25

15 Jim Brown/25	50.00	100.00
23 Ryan Grant/25	20.00	40.00

2009 Limited Material Monikers

STATED PRINT RUN 9-50
SERIAL #'d UNDER 15 NOT PRICED

1 Andre Johnson/25	12.00	30.00
2 Barry Sanders/15	60.00	120.00
4 Chuck Bednarik/50	12.00	30.00
6 Dan Fouts/25	20.00	50.00
7 Dan Marino/25	100.00	175.00
8 Deacon Jones/50	12.00	30.00
13 Fran Tarkenton/25	20.00	50.00
16 Jack Lambert/20	40.00	80.00
20 Jerry Rice/25	75.00	150.00
21 Jim Brown/50	30.00	80.00
22 Jim Kelly/25	25.00	50.00
23 Jim McMahon/50	12.00	30.00
25 Joe Montana/15	100.00	175.00
26 Joe Namath/50	40.00	80.00
31 LaRon Landry/50	8.00	20.00
32 Larry Johnson/20	12.00	30.00
38 Joe Greene/25	25.00	50.00
39 Phil Simms/25	15.00	40.00
42 Santonio Holmes/20	12.00	30.00
43 Raymond Berry/50	12.00	30.00
44 Steve Slaton/50	10.00	25.00
45 Roger Staubach/25	30.00	60.00
46 Ryan Grant/50	12.00	30.00
47 Tiki Barber/25	12.00	30.00
48 Tony Romo/15	40.00	80.00
49 Vincent Jackson/50	10.00	25.00

2009 Limited Monikers Autographs Gold

GOLD STATED PRINT RUN 4-50
SERIAL #'d UNDER 16 NOT PRICED

3 Tim Hightower/28	6.00	15.00
4 Matt Ryan/25	30.00	60.00
20 Matt Forte/25	10.00	25.00
22 Cedric Benson/19	8.00	20.00
30 Eddie Royal/33	6.00	15.00
41 Steve Slaton/25	8.00	20.00
62 Drew Brees/30	40.00	80.00
82 Vincent Jackson/33	6.00	15.00
88 T.J. Houshmandzadeh/22	8.00	20.00
93 Derrick Ward/50	5.00	12.00
101 Archie Manning/25	15.00	40.00
103 Billy Howton/50	8.00	20.00
104 Bob Griese/25	15.00	40.00
105 Bob Lilly/50	12.00	30.00
106 Brett Favre/25	100.00	200.00
107 Carl Eller/50	8.00	20.00
108 Charley Taylor/50	8.00	20.00
109 Charley Trippi/50	10.00	25.00
110 Chuck Bednarik/50	10.00	25.00
111 Dan Fouts/25	30.00	60.00
112 Dan Marino/25	100.00	175.00
113 Deacon Jones/50	12.00	30.00
114 Don Maynard/50	10.00	25.00
115 Emmitt Smith/22	75.00	150.00
116 Fran Tarkenton/25	15.00	40.00
117 Fred Biletnikoff/25	15.00	40.00
118 Garo Yepremian/50	8.00	20.00
119 George Blanda/25	25.00	50.00
120 Hugh McElhenny/50	8.00	20.00
122 James Lofton/50	8.00	20.00
123 Jan Stenerud/50	8.00	20.00
125 Jethro Pugh/50	8.00	20.00
126 Jim Brown/50	30.00	60.00
127 Jim Otto/50	8.00	20.00
129 Joe Montana/16	75.00	150.00
132 John Stallworth/25	12.00	30.00
133 Lance Alworth/25	25.00	50.00
134 Lenny Moore/50	10.00	25.00
136 Raymond Berry/50	10.00	25.00
138 Ted Hendricks/25	10.00	25.00
139 Tiki Barber/25	12.00	30.00
141 Willie Brown/50	8.00	20.00
145 Ace Parker/25	10.00	25.00
146 Don Perkins/50	8.00	20.00
148 Jim McMahon/25	12.00	30.00

2009 Limited NFL Draft Rookie Helmet Autographs

1 Matthew Stafford	75.00	135.00
2 Mark Sanchez	50.00	120.00
3 Chris Wells	15.00	40.00
4 Percy Harvin	30.00	60.00
5 Jeremy Maclin	20.00	50.00
6 Knowshon Moreno	15.00	40.00
7 Michael Crabtree	30.00	60.00

2009 Limited Prime Pairings Autographs

STATED PRINT RUN 5-20
SERIAL #'d UNDER 15 NOT PRICED

1 Jan Stenerud/50	12.00	30.00
Garo Yepremian		
2 Billy Howton/25	60.00	120.00
Bart Starr		
3 George Blanda/25	30.00	60.00
Jim Otto		
4 Fran Tarkenton/31	40.00	80.00
Carl Eller		
5 Charley Trippi/25	25.00	50.00
Ace Parker		
6 Willie Brown/25	15.00	40.00
Ted Hendricks		
7 Joe Montana/15	60.00	120.00
Phil Simms		
8 Joe Namath/50	100.00	200.00
Mark Sanchez		
9 Hugh McElhenny/50	40.00	80.00
Jim Brown		
10 Emmitt Smith/25	75.00	150.00
Tiki Barber		
12 Don Maynard/25	30.00	60.00
Lance Alworth		
13 Raymond Berry/50	12.00	30.00
Lenny Moore		
14 Jim McMahon/25	75.00	150.00
John Elway		
15 Fred Biletnikoff/25	20.00	50.00
Willie Brown		
16 Deacon Jones/20	25.00	50.00
Joe Greene		
17 Roger Staubach/25	50.00	100.00
Bob Griese		
19 Archie Manning/25	40.00	80.00
Dan Fouts		
21 James Lofton/25	20.00	40.00
John Stallworth		
22 Charley Taylor/25	20.00	50.00
Fred Biletnikoff		
23 Don Perkins/50	30.00	60.00
Bob Lilly		
Jethro Pugh		
25 Chuck Bednarik/50	20.00	40.00
Aaron Maybin		
26 Tyson Jackson/50	10.00	25.00
Brian Orakpo		
27 Malcolm Jenkins/50	8.00	20.00
Vontae Davis		
28 Brian Cushing/50	40.00	80.00
Clay Matthews		
Rey Maualuga		
29 Percy Harvin/50	40.00	80.00
Louis Murphy		
30 Derrick Williams/50	12.00	30.00
Deon Butler		

2009 Limited Pro Bowl Materials

STATED PRINT RUN 100
*PRIME/25: .6X TO 1.5X BASIC JSY/100

1 Chris Cooley	4.00	10.00
2 DeMarcus Ware	4.00	10.00
3 Anquan Boldin	3.00	8.00
4 Kurt Warner	4.00	10.00
5 Wes Welker	4.00	10.00

2009 Limited Pro Bowl Materials Combo

STATED PRINT RUN 100 SER.#'d SETS
*PRIME/25: .6X TO 1.5X BASIC COMBO/100

1 Peyton Manning	8.00	20.00
Jay Cutler		
2 Peyton Manning	10.00	25.00
Eli Manning		
3 Michael Turner	8.00	20.00
Adrian Peterson		
4 Thomas Jones	4.00	10.00
Ronnie Brown		
5 Peyton Manning	8.00	20.00
Drew Brees		
6 Peyton Manning	8.00	20.00
Tony Gonzalez		
7 Drew Brees	5.00	12.00
Larry Fitzgerald		
8 Eli Manning	5.00	12.00
Larry Fitzgerald		
9 Michael Turner	4.00	10.00
Roddy White		
10 Mike Sellers	4.00	10.00
Chris Cooley		
11 Adrian Peterson	12.00	30.00
Jared Allen		
12 Thomas Jones	4.00	10.00
Alan Faneca		
13 Andre Johnson	4.00	10.00
Mario Williams		
14 Julius Peppers	6.00	15.00
Jared Allen		
15 Troy Polamalu	8.00	20.00
Adrian Wilson		

2009 Limited Pro Bowl Materials Quad

STATED PRINT RUN 100 SER.#'d SETS
*PRIME/25: .6X TO 1.5X BASIC QUAD/100

1 Michael Turner	10.00	25.00
Adrian Peterson		
Thomas Jones		
Ronnie Brown		
2 Larry Fitzgerald	6.00	15.00
Steve Smith		
Anquan Boldin		
Roddy White		
3 Andre Johnson	6.00	15.00
Reggie Wayne		
Wes Welker		
Tony Gonzalez		
4 Steve Smith	6.00	15.00
Larry Fitzgerald		
Tony Gonzalez		
Reggie Wayne		
5 Adrian Peterson	10.00	25.00
Larry Fitzgerald		
Le'Ron McClain		
Tony Gonzalez		
6 Kurt Warner	10.00	25.00
Larry Fitzgerald		
Anquan Boldin		
Adrian Wilson		
7 Peyton Manning	15.00	40.00
Reggie Wayne		
Robert Mathis		
Dwight Freeney		
8 Mario Williams	5.00	12.00
Dwight Freeney		
Robert Mathis		
Albert Haynesworth		
9 DeMarcus Ware	5.00	12.00
Lance Briggs		
Patrick Willis		
Jon Beason		
10 James Harrison	12.00	30.00
Terrell Suggs		
Ray Lewis		
James Farrior		

2009 Limited Pro Bowl Materials Trios

TRIO JSY STATED PRINT RUN 100
*PRIME/25: .6X TO 1.5X BASIC TRIO/100

1 Kurt Warner	6.00	15.00
Eli Manning		
Drew Brees		
2 Peyton Manning	10.00	25.00
Drew Brees		
Eli Manning		
3 Steve Smith	4.00	10.00
Julius Peppers		
Jon Beason		
4 Le'Ron McClain	8.00	20.00
Ray Lewis		
Terrell Suggs		
5 James Farrior	15.00	40.00
James Harrison		
Troy Polamalu		

2009 Limited Rookie Jumbo Jerseys

STATED PRINT RUN 50 SER.#'d SETS
*JSY NUM/50: .4X TO 1X BASIC JSY/50
*JSY NUM PRIME/25: .6X TO 1.5X BASIC JSY/50
*PRIME/25: .6X TO 1.5X BASIC JSY/50

1 Knowshon Moreno	2.50	6.00
2 Derrick Williams	2.00	5.00
3 Brandon Pettigrew	2.50	6.00
4 Mark Sanchez	10.00	25.00
5 Brian Robiskie	2.50	6.00
6 Patrick Turner	2.00	5.00
7 Percy Harvin	4.00	10.00
8 Ramses Barden	2.00	5.00
9 Andre Brown	1.50	4.00
10 Matthew Stafford	8.00	20.00
11 Juaquin Iglesias	2.00	5.00
12 Deon Butler	2.00	5.00
13 Darrius Heyward-Bey	2.50	6.00
14 Tyson Jackson	2.00	5.00
15 Donald Brown	2.50	6.00
16 Jeremy Maclin	4.00	10.00
17 Kenny Britt	3.00	8.00
18 Michael Crabtree	5.00	12.00
19 Josh Freeman	5.00	12.00
20 Mike Wallace	5.00	12.00
21 Hakeem Nicks	4.00	10.00
22 Rhett Bomar	2.00	5.00
23 Mohamed Massaquoi	2.00	5.00
24 Aaron Curry	2.50	6.00
25 Pat White	2.50	6.00
26 Jason Smith	2.00	5.00
27 Mike Thomas	2.50	6.00
28 Chris Wells	4.00	10.00
29 Stephen McGee	2.50	6.00
30 Shonn Greene	4.00	10.00
31 LeSean McCoy	5.00	12.00
32 Javon Ringer	2.50	6.00
33 Nate Davis	2.00	5.00
34 Glen Coffee	2.00	5.00

2009 Limited Rookie Jumbo Jerseys Autographs Prime

PRIME AUTO PRINT RUN 25 SER.#'d SETS

1 Knowshon Moreno	40.00	80.00
2 Derrick Williams	8.00	20.00
3 Brandon Pettigrew	10.00	25.00
4 Mark Sanchez	60.00	120.00
5 Brian Robiskie	10.00	25.00
6 Patrick Turner	8.00	20.00
7 Percy Harvin	50.00	100.00
8 Ramses Barden	6.00	15.00
9 Andre Brown	6.00	15.00
10 Matthew Stafford	75.00	150.00
11 Juaquin Iglesias	8.00	20.00
12 Deon Butler	8.00	20.00
13 Darrius Heyward-Bey	10.00	25.00
14 Tyson Jackson	8.00	20.00
15 Donald Brown	10.00	25.00
16 Jeremy Maclin	15.00	40.00
17 Kenny Britt	12.00	30.00
18 Michael Crabtree	40.00	80.00
19 Josh Freeman	20.00	50.00
20 Mike Wallace	20.00	50.00
21 Hakeem Nicks	15.00	40.00
22 Rhett Bomar	8.00	20.00
23 Mohamed Massaquoi	8.00	20.00
24 Aaron Curry	10.00	25.00
25 Pat White	10.00	25.00
26 Jason Smith	8.00	20.00
27 Mike Thomas	10.00	25.00
28 Chris Wells	15.00	40.00
29 Stephen McGee	10.00	25.00
30 Shonn Greene	15.00	40.00
31 LeSean McCoy	30.00	80.00
32 Javon Ringer	10.00	25.00
33 Nate Davis	8.00	20.00
34 Glen Coffee	8.00	20.00

2009 Limited Slideshow Autographs

STATED PRINT RUN 50 SER.#'d SETS
1 Donald Brown 8.00 20.00
2 Tyson Jackson 6.00 15.00
3 Darrius Heyward-Bey 8.00 20.00
4 Deon Butler 6.00 15.00
5 Juaquin Iglesias 6.00 15.00
6 Andre Brown 5.00 12.00
7 Ramses Barden 5.00 12.00
8 Percy Harvin 40.00 80.00
9 Patrick Turner 6.00 15.00
10 Mark Sanchez 50.00 100.00
11 Brian Robiskie 8.00 20.00
12 Brandon Pettigrew 8.00 20.00
13 Matthew Stafford 50.00 100.00
14 Knowshon Moreno 25.00 50.00
15 LeSean McCoy 20.00 50.00
16 Mike Wallace 15.00 40.00
17 Javon Ringer 8.00 20.00
18 Michael Crabtree 30.00 60.00
19 Glen Coffee 6.00 15.00
20 Nate Davis 6.00 15.00
21 Derrick Williams 6.00 15.00
22 Mohamed Massaquoi 6.00 15.00
23 Shonn Greene 12.00 30.00
24 Chris Wells 12.00 30.00
25 Pat White 8.00 20.00
26 Rhett Bomar 6.00 15.00
27 Hakeem Nicks 12.00 30.00
28 Stephen McGee 8.00 20.00
29 Jason Smith 6.00 15.00
30 Aaron Curry 8.00 20.00
31 Josh Freeman 15.00 40.00
32 Jeremy Maclin 12.00 30.00
33 Mike Thomas 8.00 20.00
34 Kenny Britt 10.00 25.00

2009 Limited Super Bowl Materials Combo

COMBO PRINT RUN 50 SER.#'d SETS
*BASE MATERIAL/35: .4X TO 1X COMBO MAT/50
1 Kurt Warner 8.00 20.00
2 Larry Fitzgerald 8.00 20.00
3 Anquan Boldin 6.00 15.00
4 Ben Patrick 5.00 12.00
5 Steve Breaston 6.00 15.00
6 Ben Roethlisberger 15.00 40.00
7 Santonio Holmes 10.00 25.00
8 Willie Parker 5.00 12.00
9 James Harrison 15.00 40.00
10 Gary Russell 5.00 12.00

2009 Limited Team Trademarks Autograph Materials

STATED PRINT RUN 4-25
*PRIME/18: .5X TO 1.2X JSY AU/25
SERIAL #'d UNDER 25 NOT PRICED
9 Donald Driver/25 20.00 40.00

2009 Limited Team Trademarks Materials

STATED PRINT RUN 30-50
7 Carson Palmer/50 5.00 12.00
10 Donovan McNabb/50 5.00 12.00
11 Felix Jones/50 5.00 12.00
13 Jake Delhomme/50 4.00 10.00
18 Marshawn Lynch/50 4.00 10.00
20 Matt Schaub/30 4.00 10.00
21 Peyton Manning/50 8.00 20.00
24 Tom Brady/50 8.00 20.00
25 Walter Payton/50 15.00 40.00

2009 Limited Team Trademarks Materials Prime

STATED PRINT RUN 25 SER.#'d SETS
6 Cadillac Williams 6.00 15.00
9 Donald Driver 6.00 15.00
11 Felix Jones 8.00 20.00
12 Hines Ward 6.00 15.00
13 Jake Delhomme 6.00 15.00
14 Jason Campbell 5.00 12.00
15 Jason Witten 8.00 20.00
17 Marion Barber 6.00 15.00
18 Marshawn Lynch 6.00 15.00
19 Matt Hasselbeck 6.00 15.00
22 Reggie Bush 8.00 20.00
24 Tom Brady 12.00 30.00
25 Walter Payton 25.00 60.00

2009 Limited Threads Prime

PRIME STATED PRINT RUN 1-50
4 Matt Ryan/15 8.00 20.00
8 Mark Clayton/50 4.00 10.00
11 Lee Evans/50 5.00 12.00
12 Marshawn Lynch/50 5.00 12.00
14 DeAngelo Williams/50 6.00 15.00
16 Steve Smith/50 5.00 12.00
17 Brian Urlacher/49 6.00 15.00
23 Chad Ochocinco/50 5.00 12.00
24 Brady Quinn/50 5.00 12.00
26 Jamal Lewis/25 6.00 15.00
27 Marion Barber/50 5.00 12.00
38 Ryan Grant/25 6.00 15.00
39 Andre Johnson/50 5.00 12.00
47 Maurice Jones-Drew/50 5.00 12.00
49 Dwayne Bowe/20 6.00 15.00
50 Larry Johnson/50 5.00 12.00
53 Ronnie Brown/50 5.00 12.00
54 Ricky Williams/50 5.00 12.00
58 Laurence Maroney/50 5.00 12.00
60 Tom Brady/50 10.00 25.00
64 Reggie Bush/50 6.00 15.00
73 Brian Westbrook/50 5.00 12.00
77 Santonio Holmes/50 5.00 12.00
78 Willie Parker/50 4.00 10.00
79 Antonio Gates/50 5.00 12.00
82 Vincent Jackson/50 5.00 12.00
83 Frank Gore/50 5.00 12.00
87 Matt Hasselbeck/50 5.00 12.00
90 Marc Bulger/50 5.00 12.00
91 Steven Jackson/50 5.00 12.00
97 LenDale White/25 6.00 15.00
98 Chris Cooley/50 5.00 12.00
99 Clinton Portis/50 5.00 12.00
100 Jason Campbell/50 4.00 10.00
105 Bob Lilly/15 10.00 25.00
106 Brett Favre/35 15.00 40.00
108 Charley Taylor/50 6.00 15.00
111 Dan Fouts/50 10.00 25.00
112 Dan Marino/50 15.00 40.00
113 Deacon Jones/25 10.00 25.00
114 Don Maynard/25 10.00 25.00
116 Fran Tarkenton/50 10.00 25.00
117 Fred Biletnikoff/50 10.00 25.00
121 Jack Lambert/25 12.00 30.00
122 James Lofton/50 6.00 15.00
123 Jan Stenerud/50 6.00 15.00
124 Jerry Rice/50 12.00 30.00
126 Jim Brown/25 15.00 40.00
127 Jim Otto/25 8.00 20.00
129 Joe Montana/25 20.00 50.00
132 John Stallworth/25 10.00 25.00
136 Raymond Berry/50 8.00 20.00
137 Roger Staubach/50 12.00 30.00
138 Ted Hendricks/50 6.00 15.00
139 Tiki Barber/50 6.00 15.00
141 Willie Brown/50 6.00 15.00
142 Walter Payton/50 20.00 50.00
149 Jim Kelly/50 8.00 20.00
150 Barry Sanders/50 12.00 30.00

2010 Limited

1-150 STATED PRINT RUN 499
151-200 ROOKIE PRINT RUN 499
201-235 JSY AU RC PRINT RUN 199
EXCH EXPIRATION: 5/24/2012
1 Chris Wells 1.25 3.00
2 Larry Fitzgerald 1.50 4.00
3 Steve Breaston 1.00 2.50
4 Matt Ryan 1.50 4.00
5 Michael Turner 1.00 2.50
6 Roddy White 1.25 3.00
7 Anquan Boldin 1.25 3.00
8 Joe Flacco 1.50 4.00
9 Ray Rice 1.25 3.00
10 Ryan Fitzpatrick 1.50 4.00
11 Lee Evans 1.25 3.00
12 Marshawn Lynch 1.25 3.00
13 DeAngelo Williams 1.25 3.00
14 Jonathan Stewart 1.25 3.00
15 Steve Smith 1.25 3.00
16 Devin Hester 1.50 4.00
17 Jay Cutler 1.50 4.00
18 Matt Forte 1.25 3.00
19 Carson Palmer 1.25 3.00
20 Cedric Benson 1.25 3.00
21 Chad Ochocinco 1.25 3.00
22 Terrell Owens 1.50 4.00
23 Mohamed Massaquoi 1.25 3.00
24 Jerome Harrison 1.00 2.50
25 Josh Cribbs 1.50 4.00
26 Jason Witten 1.50 4.00
27 Miles Austin 1.50 4.00
28 Tony Romo 2.00 5.00
29 Eddie Royal 1.00 2.50
30 Knowshon Moreno 1.25 3.00
31 Kyle Orton 1.25 3.00
32 Calvin Johnson 1.50 4.00
33 Matthew Stafford 1.50 4.00
34 Nate Burleson 1.00 2.50
35 Aaron Rodgers 3.00 8.00
36 Greg Jennings 1.25 3.00
37 Ryan Grant 1.25 3.00
38 Andre Johnson 1.25 3.00
39 Matt Schaub 1.25 3.00
40 Owen Daniels 1.00 2.50
41 Dallas Clark 1.25 3.00
42 Peyton Manning 2.50 6.00
43 Joseph Addai 1.25 3.00
44 Reggie Wayne 1.25 3.00
45 David Garrard 1.25 3.00
46 Maurice Jones-Drew 1.25 3.00
47 Mike Sims-Walker 1.25 3.00
48 Dwayne Bowe 1.25 3.00
49 Jamaal Charles 1.25 3.00
50 Matt Cassel 1.25 3.00
51 Chad Henne 1.25 3.00
52 Ronnie Brown 1.25 3.00
53 Brandon Marshall 1.25 3.00
54 Adrian Peterson 2.50 6.00
55 Brett Favre 4.00 10.00
56 Percy Harvin 1.50 4.00
57 Visanthe Shiancoe 1.25 3.00
58 Randy Moss 1.50 4.00
59 Tom Brady 2.50 6.00
60 Wes Welker 1.50 4.00
61 Devery Henderson 1.00 2.50
62 Drew Brees 1.50 4.00
63 Reggie Bush 1.50 4.00
64 Brandon Jacobs 1.25 3.00
65 Eli Manning 1.50 4.00
66 Steve Smith USC 1.25 3.00
67 Braylon Edwards 1.25 3.00
68 Mark Sanchez 1.50 4.00
69 Shonn Greene 1.25 3.00
70 Darren McFadden 1.25 3.00
71 Jason Campbell 1.25 3.00
72 Louis Murphy 1.25 3.00
73 Kevin Kolb 1.25 3.00
74 DeSean Jackson 1.25 3.00
75 LeSean McCoy 1.25 3.00
76 Ben Roethlisberger 1.50 4.00
77 Rashard Mendenhall 1.25 3.00
78 Hines Ward 1.25 3.00
79 Antonio Gates 1.25 3.00
80 Darren Sproles 1.25 3.00
81 Philip Rivers 1.50 4.00
82 Alex Smith QB 1.25 3.00
83 Frank Gore 1.25 3.00
84 Vernon Davis 1.25 3.00
85 Leon Washington 1.25 3.00
86 Matt Hasselbeck 1.00 2.50
87 Deion Branch 1.00 2.50
88 James Laurinaitis 1.25 3.00
89 Steven Jackson 1.25 3.00
90 Donnie Avery 1.25 3.00
91 Cadillac Williams 1.25 3.00
92 Josh Freeman 1.50 4.00
93 Kellen Winslow Jr. 1.25 3.00
94 Chris Johnson 1.50 4.00
95 Kenny Britt 1.25 3.00
96 Vince Young 1.00 2.50
97 Donovan McNabb 1.50 4.00
98 Chris Cooley 1.25 3.00
99 Clinton Portis 1.25 3.00
100 Santana Moss 1.25 3.00
101 Alan Page 1.50 4.00
102 Alex Karras 1.50 4.00
103 Andre Reed 1.50 4.00
104 Archie Manning 2.00 5.00
105 Art Monk 2.00 5.00
106 Billy Howton 1.25 3.00
107 Bobby Bell 1.25 3.00
108 Boyd Dowler 1.25 3.00
109 Charley Taylor 1.25 3.00
110 Charley Trippi 1.25 3.00
111 Charlie Joiner 1.25 3.00
112 Dante Lavelli 1.25 3.00
113 Daryle Lamonica 1.25 3.00
114 Dave Casper 1.25 3.00
115 Deacon Jones 1.50 4.00
116 Del Shofner 1.25 3.00
117 Doug Flutie 1.50 4.00
118 Dub Jones 1.25 3.00
119 Earl Campbell 2.00 5.00
120 Ernie Davis 4.00 10.00
121 Floyd Little 1.25 3.00
122 Forrest Gregg 1.25 3.00
123 Jan Stenerud 1.25 3.00
124 George Blanda 1.50 4.00
125 Harlon Hill 1.25 3.00
126 Hank Jordan 1.25 3.00
127 Jack Youngblood 1.25 3.00
128 Jackie Slater 1.25 3.00
129 Jim McMahon 1.50 4.00
130 Jim Otto 1.25 3.00
131 Jim Plunkett 1.50 4.00
132 Jim Taylor 2.00 5.00
133 Jimmy Orr 1.25 3.00
134 Larry Little 1.25 3.00
135 Lee Roy Selmon 1.50 4.00
136 Lem Barney 1.25 3.00
137 Lenny Moore 1.50 4.00
138 Leroy Kelly 1.50 4.00
139 Lydell Mitchell 1.25 3.00
140 Mark Duper 1.25 3.00
141 Merlin Olsen 1.50 4.00
142 Mike Curtis 1.25 3.00
143 Ozzie Newsome 1.50 4.00
144 Paul Krause 1.25 3.00
145 Priest Holmes 1.25 3.00
146 Randy White 1.50 4.00
147 Raymond Berry 1.50 4.00
148 Roger Craig 1.50 4.00
149 Ronnie Lott 2.00 5.00
150 Walter Payton 4.00 10.00
151 Aaron Hernandez RC 3.00 8.00
152 Anthony Dixon RC 2.00 5.00
153 Anthony McCoy RC 1.50 4.00
154 Antonio Brown RC 3.00 8.00
155 Brandon Graham RC 1.50 4.00
156 Brandon Spikes RC 2.00 5.00
157 Bryan Bulaga RC 2.00 5.00
158 Carlos Dunlap RC 2.00 5.00
159 Carlton Mitchell RC 1.50 4.00
160 Chris Cook RC 2.00 5.00
161 Corey Wootton RC 1.50 4.00
162 David Gettis RC 2.00 5.00
163 David Reed RC 1.50 4.00
164 Deji Karim RC 2.00 5.00
165 Derrick Morgan RC 1.50 4.00
166 Devin McCourty RC 2.00 5.00
167 Dominique Franks RC 1.25 3.00
168 Earl Thomas RC 2.00 5.00
169 Ed Dickson RC 2.00 5.00
170 Everson Griffen RC 2.00 5.00
171 Garrett Graham RC 1.50 4.00
172 Jacoby Ford RC 2.00 5.00
173 Jason Pierre-Paul RC 3.00 8.00
174 Jason Worilds RC 2.00 5.00
175 Javier Arenas RC 2.00 5.00
176 Jerry Hughes RC 2.00 5.00
177 Jimmy Graham RC 4.00 10.00
178 Joe Haden RC 2.00 5.00
179 Joe Webb RC 2.00 5.00
180 John Skelton RC 2.00 5.00
181 Kareem Jackson RC 2.00 5.00
182 Marc Mariani RC 2.00 5.00
183 Max Hall RC 2.00 5.00
184 Michael Hoomanawanui RC 2.00 5.00
185 Morgan Burnett RC 2.00 5.00
186 Nate Allen RC 2.00 5.00
187 NaVorro Bowman RC 2.00 5.00
188 Patrick Robinson RC 2.00 5.00
189 Perrish Cox RC 1.50 4.00
190 Ricky Sapp RC 1.50 4.00
191 Riley Cooper RC 2.00 5.00
192 Russell Okung RC 2.00 5.00
193 Sean Lee RC 2.00 5.00
194 Sean Weatherspoon RC 2.00 5.00
195 Stephen Williams RC 2.00 5.00
196 Taylor Mays RC 2.00 5.00
197 Tony Moeaki RC 2.00 5.00
198 Tony Pike RC 2.00 5.00
199 Trent Williams RC 2.00 5.00
200 Victor Cruz RC 6.00 15.00
201 Sam Bradford JSY AU RC 60.00 120.00
202 Ndamukong Suh JSY AU RC 30.00 60.00
203 Gerald McCoy JSY AU RC 8.00 20.00
204 Eric Berry JSY AU RC 20.00 50.00
205 Rolando McClain JSY AU RC 8.00 20.00
206 C.J. Spiller JSY AU RC 12.00 30.00
207 Ryan Mathews JSY AU RC 25.00 60.00
208 Jermaine Gresham JSY AU RC 12.00 30.00
209 Demaryius Thomas JSY AU RC 12.00 30.00
210 Dez Bryant JSY AU RC 30.00 80.00
211 Tim Tebow JSY AU RC 75.00 135.00
212 Jahvid Best JSY AU RC 12.00 30.00
214 Arrelious Benn JSY AU RC 10.00 25.00
215 Rob Gronkowski JSY AU RC 25.00 50.00
216 Jimmy Clausen JSY AU RC 8.00 20.00
217 Toby Gerhart JSY AU RC 8.00 20.00
218 Ben Tate JSY AU RC 10.00 25.00
219 Montario Hardesty JSY AU RC 8.00 20.00
220 Golden Tate JSY AU RC 8.00 20.00
221 Damian Williams JSY AU RC 8.00 20.00
222 Brandon LaFell JSY AU RC 8.00 20.00
223 Emmanuel Sanders JSY AU RC 8.00 20.00
224 Jordan Shipley JSY AU RC 8.00 20.00
225 Colt McCoy JSY AU RC 25.00 60.00
226 Eric Decker JSY AU RC 12.00 30.00
227 Andre Roberts JSY AU RC 8.00 20.00
228 Armanti Edwards JSY AU RC 8.00 20.00
229 Taylor Price JSY AU RC 8.00 20.00
230 Mardy Gilyard JSY AU RC 8.00 20.00
231 Mike Williams JSY AU RC 15.00 40.00
232 Marcus Easley JSY AU RC 6.00 15.00
233 Joe McKnight JSY AU RC 8.00 20.00
234 Mike Kafka JSY AU RC 8.00 20.00
235 Jonathan Dwyer JSY AU RC EXCH 8.00 20.00

2010 Limited Gold Spotlight

*VETS 1-100: 1X TO 2.5X BASIC CARDS
*LEGENDS 101-150: .8X TO 2X BASIC CARDS
*ROOKIES 151-200: .8X TO 2X BASIC CARDS
1-200 STATED PRINT RUN 25
201-235 UNPRICED JSY AU PRINT RUN 10

2010 Limited Silver Spotlight

*VETS 1-100: .8X TO 2X BASIC CARDS
*LEGENDS 101-150: .6X TO 1.5X BASIC CARDS
*ROOKIES 151-200: .6X TO 1.5X BASIC CARDS
1-200 STATED PRINT RUN 50
*ROOK.JSY AU 201-235: .5X TO 1.2X JSY AU RC
201-235 JSY AU PRINT RUN 25
201 Sam Bradford JSY AU 100.00 200.00
210 Dez Bryant JSY AU 60.00 100.00
211 Tim Tebow JSY AU 125.00 200.00

2010 Limited America's Team

STATED PRINT RUN 50 SER.#'d SETS
1 Bill Bates 4.00 10.00
2 Bob Hayes 6.00 15.00
3 Bob Lilly 5.00 12.00
4 Chuck Howley 4.00 10.00
5 Cliff Harris 4.00 10.00
6 D.D. Lewis 4.00 10.00
7 Danny White 5.00 12.00
8 Darren Woodson 5.00 12.00
9 Deion Sanders 6.00 15.00
10 DeMarcus Ware 4.00 10.00
11 Don Perkins 4.00 10.00
12 Ed Too Tall Jones 5.00 12.00
13 Emmitt Smith 8.00 20.00
14 Everson Walls 4.00 10.00
15 Felix Jones 4.00 10.00
16 Harvey Martin 4.00 10.00
17 Jason Witten 4.00 10.00
18 Lee Roy Jordan 5.00 12.00
19 Mark Stepnoski 4.00 10.00
20 Mel Renfro 4.00 10.00
21 Michael Irvin 5.00 12.00
22 Rayfield Wright 4.00 10.00
23 Roger Staubach 8.00 20.00
24 Tony Dorsett 6.00 15.00
25 Tony Romo 5.00 12.00

2010 Limited America's Team Autographs

STATED PRINT RUN 1-50
EXCH EXPIRATION: 5/24/2012
1 Bill Bates/50 15.00 40.00
3 Bob Lilly/50 15.00 40.00
5 Cliff Harris/50 15.00 40.00
6 D.D. Lewis/20 20.00 50.00
8 Darren Woodson/50 15.00 40.00
9 Deion Sanders/21 30.00 60.00
10 DeMarcus Ware/50 15.00 40.00
11 Don Perkins/50 15.00 40.00
14 Everson Walls/50 15.00 40.00
18 Lee Roy Jordan/50 15.00 40.00
19 Mark Stepnoski/50 15.00 40.00
20 Mel Renfro/50 20.00 50.00
21 Michael Irvin/15 30.00 60.00
22 Rayfield Wright/50 20.00 50.00
24 Tony Dorsett/33 30.00 60.00

2010 Limited America's Team Threads

STATED PRINT RUN 50 SER.#'d SETS
*PRIME/15-25: .5X TO 1.2X BASIC JSY/50
1 Bill Bates 8.00 20.00
2 Bob Hayes 8.00 20.00
3 Bob Lilly 8.00 20.00
4 Chuck Howley 8.00 20.00
5 Cliff Harris 6.00 15.00
6 D.D. Lewis 6.00 15.00
7 Danny White 8.00 20.00
8 Darren Woodson 8.00 20.00
9 Deion Sanders 8.00 20.00
10 DeMarcus Ware 6.00 15.00
12 Ed Too Tall Jones 8.00 20.00
13 Emmitt Smith 12.00 30.00
15 Felix Jones 6.00 15.00
16 Harvey Martin 8.00 20.00
17 Jason Witten 8.00 20.00
21 Michael Irvin 8.00 20.00
23 Roger Staubach 12.00 30.00
24 Tony Dorsett 8.00 20.00
25 Tony Romo 10.00 25.00

2010 Limited America's Team Threads Autographs

STATED PRINT RUN 5-25
*PRME/15: .5X TO 1.2X JSY AU/22-25
1 Bill Bates/25 25.00 50.00
3 Bob Lilly/25 25.00 50.00
4 Chuck Howley/25 25.00 50.00
6 D.D. Lewis/25 25.00 50.00
7 Danny White/25 25.00 50.00
8 Darren Woodson/25 25.00 50.00
9 Deion Sanders/25 40.00 80.00
10 DeMarcus Ware/25 25.00 50.00
12 Ed Too Tall Jones/25 30.00 60.00
13 Emmitt Smith/22 100.00 175.00
21 Michael Irvin/25 40.00 80.00
24 Tony Dorsett/25 30.00 60.00

2010 Limited Banner Season Autograph Materials

STATED PRINT RUN 15-25
1 LeSean McCoy/25 12.00 30.00
2 Aaron Rodgers/15 150.00 250.00
3 Vernon Davis/25 12.00 25.00
4 Mark Sanchez/25 40.00 80.00
7 Calvin Johnson/25 15.00 40.00
8 Maurice Jones-Drew/25 12.00 30.00
10 Matt Ryan/25 30.00 60.00
13 DeSean Jackson/25 12.00 30.00
14 Andre Johnson/15 EXCH
15 Brett Favre/25 125.00 200.00
16 Dallas Clark/25 15.00 40.00
18 Rashard Mendenhall/25 12.00 30.00
19 Philip Rivers/15 15.00 40.00
20 Percy Harvin/15
21 Matt Forte/25 12.00 30.00
22 Vince Young/15 10.00 25.00
23 Knowshon Moreno/25 12.00 30.00
24 Visanthe Shiancoe/25 EXCH 12.00 30.00
25 Brent Celek/25 12.00 30.00

2010 Limited Banner Season Autograph Materials Prime

STATED PRINT RUN 5-15
1 LeSean McCoy/15 15.00 40.00
3 Vernon Davis/15 15.00 40.00
4 Mark Sanchez/15 50.00 100.00
6 Chad Ochocinco/15 15.00 40.00
7 Calvin Johnson/15 20.00 50.00
8 Maurice Jones-Drew/15 15.00 40.00
10 Matt Ryan/15 40.00 80.00
13 DeSean Jackson/15 15.00 40.00
15 Brett Favre/15 150.00 250.00
16 Dallas Clark/14 15.00 40.00
17 Lee Evans/15 15.00 40.00
18 Rashard Mendenhall/15 15.00 40.00
21 Matt Forte/15 15.00 40.00
23 Knowshon Moreno/15 15.00 40.00
24 Visanthe Shiancoe/10 EXCH 15.00 40.00
25 Brent Celek/15 15.00 40.00

2010 Limited Banner Season Materials

STATED PRINT RUN 100 SER.#'d SETS
1 LeSean McCoy 3.00 8.00
2 Aaron Rodgers 12.50 25.00
3 Vernon Davis 3.00 8.00
4 Mark Sanchez 4.00 10.00
7 Calvin Johnson 4.00 10.00
8 Maurice Jones-Drew 3.00 8.00
9 Chris Johnson 4.00 10.00
10 Matt Ryan 4.00 10.00
13 DeSean Jackson 3.00 8.00
14 Andre Johnson 3.00 8.00
15 Brett Favre 10.00 25.00
16 Dallas Clark 3.00 8.00
18 Rashard Mendenhall 3.00 8.00
19 Philip Rivers 4.00 10.00
20 Percy Harvin 4.00 10.00
21 Matt Forte 3.00 8.00
22 Vince Young 2.50 6.00
23 Knowshon Moreno 3.00 8.00
24 Visanthe Shiancoe 3.00 8.00
25 Brent Celek 3.00 8.00

2010 Limited Banner Season Materials Prime

*PRIME/45-50: .6X TO 1.5X BASIC JSY/100
*PRIME/25: .8X TO 2X BASIC JSY/100
PRIEM STATED PRINT RUN 25-50
6 Chad Ochocinco/50 5.00 12.00
17 Lee Evans/45 5.00 12.00

2010 Limited Cuts Autographs

STATED PRINT RUN 1-50
4 Bill Dudley/50 15.00 40.00
10 Bulldog Turner/20 40.00 80.00

2010 Limited Draft Day Duos

STATED PRINT RUN 25-75
*PRIME/25: .8X TO 2X BASIC DUO/75-100
1 C.J. Spiller/100 5.00 12.00
Jahvid Best
2 Eric Berry/75 3.00 8.00
Dan Williams
3 Demaryius Thomas/100 4.00 10.00
Derrick Morgan
4 Sam Bradford/25 15.00 40.00
Ndamukong Suh
5 Trent Williams/100 3.00 8.00
Russell Okung

2010 Limited Draft Day Quads

STATED PRINT RUN 25-100
*PRIME/25: .8X TO 2X BASIC QUAD/100
1 Sam Bradford/25 20.00 50.00
Ndamukong Suh
Gerald McCoy
Trent Williams
2 Eric Berry/100 10.00 25.00
Russell Okung
Joe Haden
C.J. Spiller
3 Sam Bradford/25 20.00 50.00
C.J. Spiller
Demaryius Thomas
Jahvid Best
4 Ndamukong Suh/100 8.00 20.00
Gerald McCoy
Dan Williams
Jared Odrick

2010 Limited Draft Day Lids

LIDS PRINT RUN 50 SER.#'d SETS
*COMBO/50: .4X TO 1X LID/50
*COMBO PRIME/18-25: .8X TO 2X LID/50
*JERSEY/100: .3X TO .8X LID/50
*JSY PRIME/50: .5X TO 1.2X LID/50
1 Bryan Bulaga 3.00 8.00
2 C.J. Spiller 5.00 12.00
3 Demaryius Thomas 4.00 10.00
4 Derrick Morgan 2.50 6.00
5 Eric Berry 6.00 15.00
6 Gerald McCoy 3.00 8.00
7 Jahvid Best 6.00 15.00
8 Joe Haden 3.00 8.00
9 Ndamukong Suh 6.00 15.00
10 Russell Okung 3.00 8.00
11 Trent Williams 3.00 8.00
12 Sam Bradford 12.00 30.00
13 Dan Williams 2.50 6.00
14 Jared Odrick 3.00 8.00

2010 Limited Draft Day Trios

STATED PRINT RUN 25-100
*PRIME/25: .8X TO 2X BASIC TRIO/100
1 Sam Bradford/25 20.00 50.00
Ndamukong Suh
Gerald McCoy
2 Trent Williams/100 4.00 10.00
Eric Berry
Russell Okung
3 C.J. Spiller/100 8.00 20.00
Jahvid Best
Demaryius Thomas
4 Sam Bradford/25 20.00 50.00
Gerald McCoy
Trent Williams

2010 Limited Initial Steps Autographs

STATED PRINT RUN 10-99
EXCH EXPIRATION: 5/24/2012
1 Eric Berry/99 6.00 15.00
2 Montario Hardesty/99 6.00 15.00
3 Joe McKnight/99 6.00 15.00
5 Demaryius Thomas/99 8.00 20.00
6 Jonathan Dwyer EXCH/99 6.00 15.00
7 Colt McCoy/99 25.00 50.00
8 Rob Gronkowski/99 20.00 40.00
9 Jermaine Gresham/99 8.00 20.00
10 Sam Bradford/99 40.00 100.00
11 Eric Decker/99 8.00 20.00
12 Toby Gerhart/99 6.00 15.00
13 Mike Williams/99 10.00 25.00
16 Brandon LaFell/99 6.00 15.00
17 Mike Kafka/99 6.00 15.00
18 Armanti Edwards/99 6.00 15.00
19 Ryan Mathews/99 12.00 30.00
20 Tim Tebow/99 60.00 120.00
21 Emmanuel Sanders/99 6.00 15.00
22 Taylor Price/99 6.00 15.00
23 C.J. Spiller/10
24 Jahvid Best/99 10.00 25.00
25 Golden Tate/99 6.00 15.00
26 Jordan Shipley/99 6.00 15.00
27 Dez Bryant/99 30.00 60.00
28 Rolando McClain/99 6.00 15.00
29 Arrelious Benn/99 6.00 15.00
30 Ben Tate/99 8.00 20.00
31 Jimmy Clausen/99 6.00 15.00
32 Damian Williams/99 6.00 15.00
33 Andre Roberts/99 6.00 15.00
34 Marcus Easley/99 5.00 12.00
35 Mardy Gilyard/99 6.00 15.00

2010 Limited Initial Steps Jerseys

JERSEY PRINT RUN 99 SER.#'d SETS
*PRIME/25: .8X TO 2X BASIC JSY/99
*SHOES/80: .5X TO 1.2X BASIC JSY/99
1 Eric Berry 2.50 6.00
2 Montario Hardesty 2.50 6.00
3 Joe McKnight 2.50 6.00
4 Ndamukong Suh 5.00 12.00
5 Demaryius Thomas 3.00 8.00
6 Jonathan Dwyer 2.50 6.00
7 Colt McCoy 5.00 12.00
8 Rob Gronkowski 6.00 15.00
9 Jermaine Gresham 3.00 8.00
10 Sam Bradford 10.00 25.00
11 Eric Decker 3.00 8.00
12 Toby Gerhart 2.50 6.00
13 Mike Williams 4.00 10.00
14 Gerald McCoy 2.50 6.00
15 Dexter McCluster 2.50 6.00
16 Brandon LaFell 2.50 6.00
17 Mike Kafka 2.50 6.00
18 Armanti Edwards 2.50 6.00
19 Ryan Mathews 5.00 12.00
20 Tim Tebow 10.00 25.00
21 Emmanuel Sanders 2.50 6.00
22 Taylor Price 2.50 6.00
23 C.J. Spiller 4.00 10.00
24 Jahvid Best 5.00 12.00
25 Golden Tate 2.50 6.00
26 Jordan Shipley 2.50 6.00
27 Dez Bryant 8.00 20.00
28 Rolando McClain 2.50 6.00
29 Arrelious Benn 2.50 6.00
30 Ben Tate 3.00 8.00
31 Jimmy Clausen 2.50 6.00
32 Damian Williams 2.50 6.00
33 Andre Roberts 2.50 6.00
34 Marcus Easley 2.00 5.00
35 Mardy Gilyard 2.50 6.00

2010 Limited Jumbo Jerseys

STATED PRINT RUN 25 SER.#'d SETS
3 Willis McGahee 5.00 12.00
4 Clinton Portis 5.00 12.00
6 Brian Orakpo 4.00 10.00
8 Marion Barber 5.00 12.00
9 Heath Miller 5.00 12.00
10 Patrick Willis 5.00 12.00
11 Darrelle Revis 6.00 15.00
12 Eddie Royal 4.00 10.00
13 Dwayne Bowe 5.00 12.00
14 Sidney Rice 5.00 12.00
15 Randy Moss 6.00 15.00
16 Shonn Greene 5.00 12.00
19 Darren McFadden 5.00 12.00
20 Kyle Orton 5.00 12.00
21 Will Smith 4.00 10.00
22 Joseph Addai 5.00 12.00
23 Bernard Berrian 4.00 10.00
24 Santana Moss 5.00 12.00
25 Ray Lewis 8.00 20.00
26 Felix Jones 5.00 12.00
28 Jay Cutler 6.00 15.00
29 Steven Jackson 5.00 12.00
30 Devin Hester 6.00 15.00
31 Cedric Benson 5.00 12.00
33 Reggie Bush 6.00 15.00
34 DeMarcus Ware 5.00 12.00
35 Devery Henderson 4.00 10.00

2010 Limited Jumbo Jerseys Jersey Number

STATED PRINT RUN 12-25
1 Greg Jennings/25 5.00 12.00
2 Charles Woodson/10
3 Willis McGahee/25 5.00 12.00
4 Clinton Portis/25 5.00 12.00
6 Brian Orakpo/25 4.00 10.00
8 Marion Barber/25 5.00 12.00
9 Heath Miller/25 5.00 12.00
10 Patrick Willis/25 5.00 12.00
11 Darrelle Revis/25 6.00 15.00
12 Eddie Royal/25 4.00 10.00
13 Dwayne Bowe/25 5.00 12.00
14 Sidney Rice/25 5.00 12.00
15 Randy Moss/25 6.00 15.00
16 Shonn Greene/25 5.00 12.00
19 Darren McFadden/25 5.00 12.00
20 Kyle Orton/25 5.00 12.00
21 Will Smith/25 4.00 10.00
22 Joseph Addai/25 5.00 12.00
23 Bernard Berrian/25 4.00 10.00
24 Santana Moss/25 5.00 12.00
25 Ray Lewis/25 8.00 20.00
26 Felix Jones/25 5.00 12.00
28 Jay Cutler/25 6.00 15.00
29 Steven Jackson/25 5.00 12.00
30 Devin Hester/10
31 Cedric Benson/25 5.00 12.00
33 Reggie Bush/12
34 DeMarcus Ware/25 5.00 12.00
35 Devery Henderson/25 4.00 10.00

2010 Limited Jumbo Jerseys Jersey Number Prime

STATED PRINT RUN 1-15
1 Greg Jennings/15 8.00 20.00
4 Clinton Portis/15 8.00 20.00
5 Hines Ward/15 8.00 20.00
6 Brian Orakpo/15 6.00 15.00
7 Cadillac Williams/15 8.00 20.00
8 Marion Barber/15 8.00 20.00
9 Heath Miller/15 8.00 20.00
10 Patrick Willis/15 8.00 20.00
11 Darrelle Revis/15 8.00 20.00
12 Eddie Royal/15 6.00 15.00
13 Dwayne Bowe/15 8.00 20.00
14 Sidney Rice/15 8.00 20.00
15 Randy Moss/15 10.00 25.00
17 Donald Driver/15 8.00 20.00
19 Darren McFadden/15 8.00 20.00
21 Will Smith/15 6.00 15.00
22 Joseph Addai/15 8.00 20.00
23 Bernard Berrian/15 6.00 15.00
24 Santana Moss/15 8.00 20.00
25 Ray Lewis/15 12.00 30.00
26 Felix Jones/15 8.00 20.00
28 Jay Cutler/15 10.00 25.00
29 Steven Jackson/15 8.00 20.00
30 Devin Hester/15 10.00 25.00
31 Cedric Benson/15 8.00 20.00
34 DeMarcus Ware/15 8.00 20.00
35 Devery Henderson/15 6.00 15.00

2010 Limited Jumbo Jerseys Prime

STATED PRINT RUN 1-15
1 Greg Jennings/15 8.00 20.00
2 Charles Woodson/15 10.00 25.00
3 Willis McGahee/15 8.00 20.00
4 Clinton Portis/15 8.00 20.00
5 Hines Ward/15 8.00 20.00
6 Brian Orakpo/15 6.00 15.00
7 Cadillac Williams/15 8.00 20.00
8 Marion Barber/15 8.00 20.00
9 Heath Miller/15 8.00 20.00
10 Patrick Willis/15 8.00 20.00
11 Darrelle Revis/15 10.00 25.00
12 Eddie Royal/15 6.00 15.00
13 Dwayne Bowe/15 8.00 20.00
14 Sidney Rice/15 8.00 20.00
15 Randy Moss/15 10.00 25.00
17 Donald Driver/15 8.00 20.00
19 Darren McFadden/15 8.00 20.00
21 Will Smith/15 6.00 15.00
22 Joseph Addai/15 8.00 20.00
23 Bernard Berrian/15 6.00 15.00
24 Santana Moss/15 8.00 20.00
25 Ray Lewis/15 12.00 30.00
26 Felix Jones/15 8.00 20.00
28 Jay Cutler/15 10.00 25.00
29 Steven Jackson/15 8.00 20.00
30 Devin Hester/15 10.00 25.00
31 Cedric Benson/15 8.00 20.00
33 Reggie Bush/15 10.00 25.00
34 DeMarcus Ware/15 8.00 20.00
35 Devery Henderson/15 6.00 15.00

2010 Limited Material Monikers

STATED PRINT RUN 15-50
*PRIME/15: .6X TO 1.5X JSY AU/50
*PRIME/14-15: .5X TO 1.2X JSY AU/15-25
1 Barry Sanders/25 60.00 120.00
2 Bart Starr/25 90.00 150.00
3 Bernie Kosar/25 20.00 50.00
4 Bo Jackson/25 40.00 80.00
5 Bob Griese/25 EXCH 20.00 50.00
6 Boomer Esiason/25 30.00 60.00
7 Bruce Smith/25 20.00 50.00
8 Chuck Bednarik/15 15.00 40.00
9 Craig James/25 12.00 30.00
10 Curtis Martin/25 20.00 50.00
11 Dan Marino/50 60.00 120.00
12 Dick Butkus/25 30.00 60.00
13 Don Maynard/25 15.00 40.00
14 Ed McCaffrey/25 30.00 60.00
15 Eddie George/12 15.00 40.00
16 Fran Tarkenton/25 20.00 50.00
17 Fred Biletnikoff/25 20.00 50.00
18 Gale Sayers/25 25.00 60.00
19 Henry Ellard/25 12.00 30.00
20 Howie Long/25 20.00 50.00
21 Irving Fryar/25 15.00 40.00
23 Jerry Rice/25 75.00 150.00
24 Jim Brown/25 40.00 80.00
25 Jim Kelly/25 20.00 50.00
27 Joe Montana/50 60.00 100.00
28 Joe Namath/50 40.00 80.00
29 John Elway/50 60.00 120.00
30 John Randle/25 15.00 40.00
31 Junior Seau/25 50.00 100.00
32 Keyshawn Johnson/25 12.00 30.00
33 L.C. Greenwood/25 20.00 50.00
34 Len Dawson/25 20.00 50.00
35 Michael Strahan/25 15.00 40.00
36 Mike Alstott/25 15.00 40.00
37 Mike Singletary/25 20.00 50.00
38 Paul Warfield/25 15.00 40.00
39 Phil Simms/25 15.00 40.00
40 Randall Cunningham/25 25.00 50.00
41 Rod Smith/25 12.00 30.00
42 Steve Largent/25 20.00 50.00
43 Steve Young/25 40.00 80.00
44 Terry Bradshaw/25 60.00 120.00
45 Tiki Barber/25 15.00 40.00
46 Wayne Chrebet/25 15.00 40.00
47 Brent Jones/25 12.00 30.00
48 Terrell Davis/25 20.00 50.00
49 Thurman Thomas/25 20.00 50.00
50 Tom Rathman/25 15.00 40.00

2010 Limited Monikers Autographs Gold

1-100 GOLD VET PRINT RUN 4-25
101-150 GOLD LEGEND PRINT RUN 5-25
151-199 GOLD ROOKIE PRINT RUN 25
*SILVER/199: .25X TO .6X GOLD/25
1 Chris Wells/25
6 Roddy White/25 10.00 25.00
9 Ray Rice/25 15.00 40.00
13 DeAngelo Williams/25
14 Jonathan Stewart/25 10.00 25.00
15 Steve Smith/25
20 Cedric Benson/15 10.00 25.00
25 Josh Cribbs/25 20.00 40.00
33 Matthew Stafford/25 25.00 50.00
39 Matt Schaub/25 10.00 25.00
41 Dallas Clark/15 20.00 40.00
42 Peyton Manning/18 60.00 120.00
49 Jamaal Charles/25 10.00 25.00
67 Braylon Edwards/25 10.00 25.00
68 Mark Sanchez/25 30.00 60.00
72 Louis Murphy/25 10.00 25.00
73 Kevin Kolb/25 10.00 25.00
77 Rashard Mendenhall/25 12.00 30.00
80 Darren Sproles/25 10.00 25.00
81 Philip Rivers/17
95 Kenny Britt/25 10.00 25.00
97 Donovan McNabb/25 25.00 50.00
101 Alan Page/25 10.00 25.00
102 Alex Karras/25 10.00 25.00
103 Andre Reed/15 10.00 25.00
104 Archie Manning/25 15.00 40.00
105 Art Monk/25 50.00 80.00
106 Billy Howton/25 8.00 20.00
107 Bobby Bell/25 8.00 20.00
108 Boyd Dowler/25 8.00 20.00
109 Charley Taylor/25 8.00 20.00
110 Charley Trippi/25 10.00 25.00
111 Charlie Joiner/25 10.00 25.00
113 Daryle Lamonica/25 8.00 20.00
114 Dave Casper/25 10.00 25.00
115 Deacon Jones/25 10.00 25.00
116 Del Shofner/25 8.00 20.00
117 Doug Flutie/25 EXCH 12.00 30.00
118 Dub Jones/25 8.00 20.00
119 Earl Campbell/25 EXCH 12.00 30.00
121 Floyd Little/25 8.00 20.00
122 Forrest Gregg/25 12.00 30.00
123 Jan Stenerud/25 8.00 20.00
124 George Blanda/25 25.00 50.00
125 Harlon Hill/25 8.00 20.00
127 Jack Youngblood/25 8.00 20.00
128 Jackie Slater/25 EXCH 8.00 20.00
129 Jim McMahon/25 10.00 25.00
130 Jim Otto/25 8.00 20.00
131 Jim Plunkett/25 12.00 30.00
132 Jim Taylor/25 25.00 50.00
133 Jimmy Orr/25 8.00 20.00
134 Larry Little/25 8.00 20.00
135 Lee Roy Selmon/25 12.00 30.00
136 Lem Barney/25 8.00 20.00
137 Lenny Moore/25 10.00 25.00
138 Leroy Kelly/25 12.00 30.00
139 Lydell Mitchell/25 8.00 20.00
140 Mark Duper/25 10.00 25.00
142 Mike Curtis/25 10.00 25.00
143 Ozzie Newsome/25 10.00 25.00
144 Paul Krause/25 10.00 25.00
145 Priest Holmes/25 10.00 25.00
146 Randy White/25 12.00 30.00
147 Raymond Berry/25 12.00 30.00
149 Ronnie Lott/25 20.00 40.00
151 Aaron Hernandez/25 12.00 30.00
152 Anthony Dixon/25 8.00 20.00
153 Anthony McCoy/25 6.00 15.00
154 Antonio Brown/25 25.00 50.00
155 Brandon Graham/25 6.00 15.00
156 Brandon Spikes/25 8.00 20.00
157 Bryan Bulaga/25 8.00 20.00
158 Carlos Dunlap/25 8.00 20.00
159 Carlton Mitchell/25 6.00 15.00
160 Chris Cook/25 8.00 20.00
161 Corey Wootton/25 6.00 15.00
162 David Gettis/25 8.00 20.00
165 Derrick Morgan/25 6.00 15.00
166 Devin McCourty/25 8.00 20.00
167 Dominique Franks/25 5.00 12.00
168 Earl Thomas/25 8.00 20.00
169 Ed Dickson/25 8.00 20.00
170 Everson Griffen/25 8.00 20.00
171 Garrett Graham/25 6.00 15.00
172 Jacoby Ford/25 20.00 40.00
173 Jason Pierre-Paul/25 12.00 30.00
174 Jason Worilds/25 8.00 20.00
176 Jerry Hughes/25 8.00 20.00

177 Jimmy Graham/25 25.00 50.00
178 Joe Haden/25 8.00 20.00
180 John Skelton/25 8.00 20.00
181 Kareem Jackson/25 8.00 20.00
185 Morgan Burnett/25 8.00 20.00
186 Nate Allen/25 8.00 20.00
187 NaVorro Bowman/25 8.00 20.00
188 Patrick Robinson/25 EXCH 8.00 20.00
189 Perrish Cox/25 6.00 15.00
190 Ricky Sapp/25 6.00 15.00
191 Riley Cooper/25 10.00 25.00
192 Russell Okung/25 10.00 25.00
193 Sean Lee/25 8.00 20.00
194 Sean Weatherspoon/25 8.00 20.00
196 Taylor Mays/25 8.00 20.00
198 Tony Pike/25 8.00 20.00
199 Trent Williams/25 EXCH 8.00 20.00

2010 Limited Rookie Jumbo Jerseys

STATED PRINT RUN 100 SER.#'d SETS
*JSY NUMBER/50: .5X TO 1.2X JSY/100
1 C.J. Spiller 4.00 10.00
2 Tim Tebow 10.00 25.00
3 Brandon LaFell 2.50 6.00
4 Jonathan Dwyer 2.50 6.00
5 Damian Williams 2.50 6.00
6 Sam Bradford 10.00 25.00
7 Andre Roberts 2.50 6.00
8 Mike Williams 4.00 10.00
9 Jermaine Gresham 3.00 8.00
10 Rob Gronkowski 6.00 15.00
11 Taylor Price 2.50 6.00
12 Gerald McCoy 2.50 6.00
13 Jahvid Best 5.00 12.00
14 Eric Decker 3.00 8.00
15 Toby Gerhart 2.50 6.00
16 Joe McKnight 2.50 6.00
17 Dexter McCluster 2.50 6.00
18 Ndamukong Suh 5.00 12.00
19 Marcus Easley 2.00 5.00
20 Jordan Shipley 2.50 6.00
21 Dez Bryant 8.00 20.00
22 Golden Tate 2.50 6.00
23 Mardy Gilyard 2.50 6.00
24 Jimmy Clausen 2.50 6.00
25 Rolando McClain 2.50 6.00
26 Mike Kafka 2.50 6.00
27 Colt McCoy 5.00 12.00
28 Ben Tate 3.00 8.00
29 Emmanuel Sanders 2.50 6.00
30 Eric Berry 2.50 6.00
31 Ryan Mathews 5.00 12.00
32 Montario Hardesty 2.50 6.00
33 Armanti Edwards 2.50 6.00
34 Demaryius Thomas 3.00 8.00
35 Arrelious Benn 2.50 6.00

2010 Limited Rookie Jumbo Jerseys Autographs Prime

PRIME PRINT RUN 25 SER.#'d SETS
*BASIC JSY AU/10: .5X TO 1.2X PRIME AU/25
*JSY # AU/10: .5X TO 1.2X PRIME AU/25
EXCH EXPIRATION: 5/24/2012
1 C.J. Spiller 15.00 40.00
2 Tim Tebow 100.00 175.00
3 Brandon LaFell 10.00 25.00
4 Jonathan Dwyer 10.00 25.00
5 Damian Williams 10.00 25.00
6 Sam Bradford 75.00 150.00
7 Andre Roberts 10.00 25.00
8 Mike Williams 15.00 40.00
9 Jermaine Gresham 12.00 30.00
10 Rob Gronkowski 40.00 80.00
11 Taylor Price 10.00 25.00
12 Gerald McCoy 10.00 25.00
13 Jahvid Best 15.00 40.00
14 Eric Decker 12.00 30.00
15 Toby Gerhart 10.00 25.00
16 Joe McKnight 10.00 25.00
18 Ndamukong Suh 30.00 60.00
19 Marcus Easley 8.00 20.00
20 Jordan Shipley 10.00 25.00
21 Dez Bryant 50.00 100.00
22 Golden Tate 10.00 25.00
23 Mardy Gilyard 10.00 25.00
24 Jimmy Clausen 10.00 25.00
25 Rolando McClain 10.00 25.00
26 Mike Kafka 10.00 25.00
27 Colt McCoy 40.00 80.00
28 Ben Tate 12.00 30.00
29 Emmanuel Sanders 10.00 25.00
30 Eric Berry 10.00 25.00
31 Ryan Mathews 20.00 50.00
32 Montario Hardesty 10.00 25.00
33 Armanti Edwards 10.00 25.00
34 Demaryius Thomas 12.00 30.00
35 Arrelious Benn 10.00 25.00

2010 Limited Team Trademarks Autograph Materials

STATED PRINT RUN 5-15
1 Kevin Kolb/15
2 Brandon Jacobs/15
3 Adrian Peterson/15 75.00 150.00
5 Darren Sproles/15 12.00 30.00
6 Drew Brees/15 40.00 80.00
8 Chris Cooley/15 30.00 60.00
10 Eli Manning/15 40.00 80.00
12 Jamaal Charles/15 15.00 40.00
13 Peyton Manning/15
14 Ryan Grant/15 15.00 40.00
16 Carson Palmer/15 12.00 30.00
18 Ben Roethlisberger/15 50.00 100.00
20 Tom Brady/15 125.00 200.00
22 Frank Gore/15 12.00 30.00
24 Antonio Gates/15 12.00 30.00
25 Joe Flacco/15 30.00 60.00

2010 Limited Team Trademarks Materials

STATED PRINT RUN 100 SER.#'d SETS
1 Kevin Kolb 3.00 8.00
2 Brandon Jacobs 3.00 8.00
3 Adrian Peterson 6.00 15.00
5 Darren Sproles 3.00 8.00
6 Drew Brees 4.00 10.00
8 Chris Cooley 3.00 8.00
9 Jason Witten 4.00 10.00
12 Jamaal Charles 3.00 8.00
13 Peyton Manning 6.00 15.00
14 Ryan Grant 3.00 8.00
15 Larry Fitzgerald 4.00 10.00
16 Carson Palmer 3.00 8.00
17 Wes Welker 4.00 10.00
18 Ben Roethlisberger 4.00 10.00
20 Tom Brady 6.00 15.00
21 Jeremy Shockey 3.00 8.00
22 Frank Gore 3.00 8.00
23 Brian Urlacher 4.00 10.00
24 Antonio Gates 3.00 8.00
25 Joe Flacco 4.00 10.00

2010 Limited Team Trademarks Materials Prime

*PRIME/30-50: .6X TO 1.5X BASIC JSY
*PRIME/25: .8X TO 2X BASIC JSY
PRIME PRINT RUN 10-50
7 Troy Polamalu/50 10.00 25.00
19 Ronnie Brown/50 5.00 12.00

2010 Limited Threads

STATED PRINT RUN 1-199
1 Chris Wells/199 3.00 8.00
2 Larry Fitzgerald/199 4.00 10.00
4 Matt Ryan/199 4.00 10.00
6 Roddy White/199 3.00 8.00
11 Lee Evans/199 3.00 8.00
16 Devin Hester/199 4.00 10.00
17 Jay Cutler/199 4.00 10.00
18 Matt Forte/199 3.00 8.00
19 Carson Palmer/199 3.00 8.00
20 Cedric Benson/199 3.00 8.00
21 Chad Ochocinco/199 3.00 8.00
22 Terrell Owens/199 4.00 10.00
26 Jason Witten/95 4.00 10.00
28 Tony Romo/199 5.00 12.00
29 Eddie Royal/199 2.50 6.00
30 Knowshon Moreno/199 3.00 8.00
31 Kyle Orton/199 3.00 8.00
32 Calvin Johnson/199 4.00 10.00
33 Matthew Stafford/199 4.00 10.00
35 Aaron Rodgers/199 12.00 30.00
36 Greg Jennings/199 3.00 8.00
37 Ryan Grant/115 3.00 8.00
38 Andre Johnson/199 3.00 8.00
39 Matt Schaub/199 3.00 8.00
40 Owen Daniels/195 2.50 6.00
41 Dallas Clark/115 3.00 8.00
42 Peyton Manning/199 6.00 15.00
43 Joseph Addai/199 3.00 8.00
45 David Garrard/199 3.00 8.00
46 Maurice Jones-Drew/199 3.00 8.00
47 Mike Sims-Walker/199 3.00 8.00
48 Dwayne Bowe/199 3.00 8.00
49 Jamaal Charles/199 3.00 8.00
50 Matt Cassel/199 3.00 8.00
54 Adrian Peterson/199 6.00 15.00
55 Brett Favre/199 10.00 25.00
57 Visanthe Shiancoe/199 3.00 8.00
59 Tom Brady/199 6.00 15.00
61 Devery Henderson/100 2.50 6.00
62 Drew Brees/199 4.00 10.00
63 Reggie Bush/199 4.00 10.00
64 Brandon Jacobs/199 3.00 8.00
65 Eli Manning/199 4.00 10.00
66 Steve Smith USC/199 3.00 8.00
67 Braylon Edwards/199 3.00 8.00
68 Mark Sanchez/199 4.00 10.00
69 Shonn Greene/185 3.00 8.00
70 Darren McFadden/199 3.00 8.00
71 Jason Campbell/199 3.00 8.00
72 Louis Murphy/199 3.00 8.00
73 Kevin Kolb/199 3.00 8.00
74 DeSean Jackson/100 3.00 8.00
75 LeSean McCoy/199 3.00 8.00
76 Ben Roethlisberger/199 4.00 10.00
77 Rashard Mendenhall/100 3.00 8.00
79 Antonio Gates/199 3.00 8.00
80 Darren Sproles/199 3.00 8.00
81 Philip Rivers/199 4.00 10.00
82 Alex Smith QB/150 3.00 8.00
83 Frank Gore/199 3.00 8.00
84 Vernon Davis/199 3.00 8.00
86 Matt Hasselbeck/199 2.50 6.00
89 Steven Jackson/85 3.00 8.00
94 Chris Johnson/195 4.00 10.00
96 Vince Young/199 2.50 6.00
97 Donovan McNabb/199 4.00 10.00
98 Chris Cooley/199 3.00 8.00
99 Clinton Portis/199 3.00 8.00
100 Santana Moss/199 3.00 8.00
101 Alan Page/199 5.00 12.00
102 Alex Karras/199 5.00 12.00
103 Andre Reed/199 5.00 12.00
104 Archie Manning/100 6.00 15.00
105 Art Monk/199 6.00 15.00
109 Charley Taylor/199 4.00 10.00
111 Charlie Joiner/199 4.00 10.00
113 Daryle Lamonica/199 4.00 10.00
115 Deacon Jones/199 5.00 12.00
117 Doug Flutie/199 5.00 12.00
119 Earl Campbell/199 6.00 15.00
120 Ernie Davis/199 25.00 50.00
122 Forrest Gregg/199 5.00 12.00
124 George Blanda/199 5.00 12.00
126 Hank Jordan/199 6.00 15.00
127 Jack Youngblood/199 4.00 10.00
128 Jackie Slater/199 4.00 10.00
129 Jim McMahon/199 5.00 12.00
130 Jim Otto/199 4.00 10.00
131 Jim Plunkett/199 5.00 12.00
134 Larry Little/199 4.00 10.00
135 Lee Roy Selmon/199 5.00 12.00
137 Lenny Moore/30 8.00 20.00
140 Mark Duper/130 4.00 10.00
141 Merlin Olsen/199 5.00 12.00
143 Ozzie Newsome/199 5.00 12.00
145 Priest Holmes/199 4.00 10.00
147 Raymond Berry/199 5.00 12.00
148 Roger Craig/199 5.00 12.00
149 Ronnie Lott/199 6.00 15.00
150 Walter Payton/199 12.00 30.00

2010 Limited Threads Prime

PRIME STATED PRINT RUN 2-50
1 Chris Wells/25 5.00 12.00
2 Larry Fitzgerald/25 6.00 15.00
4 Matt Ryan/25 6.00 15.00
6 Roddy White/50 4.00 10.00
11 Lee Evans/50 4.00 10.00
14 Jonathan Stewart/50 4.00 10.00
16 Devin Hester/50 5.00 12.00
17 Jay Cutler/30 5.00 12.00
18 Matt Forte/50 4.00 10.00
19 Carson Palmer/50 4.00 10.00
20 Cedric Benson/50 4.00 10.00
21 Chad Ochocinco/50 4.00 10.00
26 Jason Witten/50 5.00 12.00
28 Tony Romo/50 6.00 15.00
29 Eddie Royal/50 3.00 8.00
30 Knowshon Moreno/50 4.00 10.00
31 Kyle Orton/40 4.00 10.00
32 Calvin Johnson/50 5.00 12.00
35 Aaron Rodgers/50 15.00 40.00
36 Greg Jennings/50 4.00 10.00
38 Andre Johnson/50 4.00 10.00
42 Peyton Manning/50 8.00 20.00
43 Joseph Addai/50 4.00 10.00
45 David Garrard/50 4.00 10.00
46 Maurice Jones-Drew/50 4.00 10.00
47 Mike Sims-Walker/50 4.00 10.00
48 Dwayne Bowe/50 4.00 10.00
49 Jamaal Charles/50 4.00 10.00
50 Matt Cassel/50 4.00 10.00
52 Ronnie Brown/50 4.00 10.00
54 Adrian Peterson/50 8.00 20.00
55 Brett Favre/25 15.00 40.00
56 Percy Harvin/50 5.00 12.00
58 Randy Moss/35 5.00 12.00
59 Tom Brady/50 8.00 20.00
60 Wes Welker/50 5.00 12.00
61 Devery Henderson/50 3.00 8.00
64 Brandon Jacobs/50 4.00 10.00
67 Braylon Edwards/50 4.00 10.00
68 Mark Sanchez/50 5.00 12.00
70 Darren McFadden/50 4.00 10.00
72 Louis Murphy/50 4.00 10.00
73 Kevin Kolb/50 4.00 10.00
74 DeSean Jackson/50 4.00 10.00
75 LeSean McCoy/50 4.00 10.00
76 Ben Roethlisberger/25 6.00 15.00
77 Rashard Mendenhall/50 4.00 10.00
78 Hines Ward/50 4.00 10.00
79 Antonio Gates/50 4.00 10.00
80 Darren Sproles/50 4.00 10.00
81 Philip Rivers/50 5.00 12.00
82 Alex Smith QB/50 4.00 10.00
83 Frank Gore/30 4.00 10.00
84 Vernon Davis/50 4.00 10.00
89 Steven Jackson/50 4.00 10.00
91 Cadillac Williams/50 4.00 10.00
94 Chris Johnson/50 5.00 12.00
95 Kenny Britt/20 5.00 12.00
98 Chris Cooley/50 4.00 10.00
99 Clinton Portis/50 4.00 10.00
100 Santana Moss/50 4.00 10.00
101 Alan Page/50 6.00 15.00
105 Art Monk/50 8.00 20.00
109 Charley Taylor/25 8.00 20.00
113 Daryle Lamonica/20 8.00 20.00
117 Doug Flutie/50 6.00 15.00
120 Ernie Davis/25 40.00 80.00
126 Hank Jordan/15 10.00 25.00
128 Jackie Slater/50 5.00 12.00
129 Jim McMahon/50 6.00 15.00
130 Jim Otto/50 5.00 12.00
131 Jim Plunkett/15 10.00 25.00
134 Larry Little/50 5.00 12.00
135 Lee Roy Selmon/50 6.00 15.00
140 Mark Duper/30 5.00 12.00
145 Priest Holmes/50 5.00 12.00
148 Roger Craig/25 10.00 25.00
149 Ronnie Lott/50 8.00 20.00
150 Walter Payton/50 15.00 40.00

2011 Limited

1-200 STATED PRINT RUN 499
201-236 ROOKJSY AU PRINT RUN 199-299
EXCH EXPIRATION: 6/28/2013
1 Beanie Wells 1.25 3.00
2 Kevin Kolb 1.25 3.00
3 Larry Fitzgerald 1.25 3.00
4 Matt Ryan 1.50 4.00
5 Michael Turner 1.25 3.00
6 Roddy White 1.25 3.00
7 Anquan Boldin 1.25 3.00
8 Joe Flacco 1.50 4.00
9 Ray Rice 1.25 3.00
10 C.J. Spiller 1.25 3.00
11 Ryan Fitzpatrick 1.25 3.00
12 Steve Johnson 1.25 3.00
13 DeAngelo Williams 1.25 3.00
14 Jonathan Stewart 1.25 3.00
15 Steve Smith 1.25 3.00
16 Jay Cutler 1.25 3.00
17 Matt Forte 1.25 3.00
18 Roy Williams WR 1.25 3.00
19 Bo Scaife 1.00 2.50
20 Cedric Benson 1.25 3.00
21 Jordan Shipley 1.25 3.00
22 Colt McCoy 1.25 3.00
23 Josh Cribbs 1.25 3.00
24 Peyton Hillis 1.25 3.00
25 Felix Jones 1.25 3.00
26 Jason Witten 1.50 4.00
27 Miles Austin 1.25 3.00
28 Tony Romo 1.50 4.00
29 Brandon Lloyd 1.25 3.00
30 Knowshon Moreno 1.25 3.00
31 Kyle Orton 1.25 3.00
32 Calvin Johnson 1.50 4.00
33 Jahvid Best 1.25 3.00
34 Matthew Stafford 1.50 4.00
35 Aaron Rodgers 2.50 6.00
36 Greg Jennings 1.25 3.00
37 Jordy Nelson 1.25 3.00
38 Andre Johnson 1.25 3.00
39 Arian Foster 1.25 3.00
40 Matt Schaub 1.25 3.00
41 Dallas Clark 1.25 3.00
42 Peyton Manning 2.50 6.00
43 Reggie Wayne 1.25 3.00
44 Mike Thomas 1.25 3.00
45 Marcedes Lewis 1.00 2.50
46 Maurice Jones-Drew 1.25 3.00
47 Dwayne Bowe 1.25 3.00
48 Jamaal Charles 1.25 3.00
49 Matt Cassel 1.25 3.00
50 Brian Hartline 1.00 2.50
51 Chad Henne 1.25 3.00
52 Reggie Bush 1.25 3.00
53 Adrian Peterson 2.00 5.00
54 Donovan McNabb 1.50 4.00
55 Percy Harvin 1.25 3.00
56 BenJarvus Green-Ellis 1.25 3.00
57 Chad Ochocinco 1.25 3.00
58 Tom Brady 2.50 6.00
59 Wes Welker 1.50 4.00
60 Devery Henderson 1.00 2.50
61 Drew Brees 1.50 4.00
62 Marques Colston 1.25 3.00
63 Ahmad Bradshaw 1.25 3.00
64 Eli Manning 1.50 4.00
65 Hakeem Nicks 1.25 3.00
66 Mark Sanchez 1.50 4.00
67 Santonio Holmes 1.25 3.00
68 Shonn Greene 1.25 3.00
69 Darren McFadden 1.25 3.00
70 Jacoby Ford 1.25 3.00
71 Jason Campbell 1.25 3.00
72 DeSean Jackson 1.25 3.00
73 LeSean McCoy 1.25 3.00
74 Michael Vick 1.50 4.00
75 Nnamdi Asomugha 1.25 3.00
76 Ben Roethlisberger 1.50 4.00
77 Mike Wallace 1.50 4.00
78 Rashard Mendenhall 1.25 3.00
79 Antonio Gates 1.25 3.00
80 Philip Rivers 1.50 4.00
81 Ryan Mathews 1.25 3.00
82 Frank Gore 1.25 3.00
83 Michael Crabtree 1.25 3.00
84 Vernon Davis 1.25 3.00
85 Marshawn Lynch 1.25 3.00
86 Zach Miller 1.25 3.00
87 Sidney Rice 1.25 3.00
88 Tarvaris Jackson 1.00 2.50
89 Danny Amendola 1.25 3.00
90 Sam Bradford 1.50 4.00
91 Steven Jackson 1.25 3.00
92 Josh Freeman 1.50 4.00
93 LeGarrette Blount 1.25 3.00
94 Mike Williams 1.25 3.00
95 Chris Johnson 1.25 3.00
96 Kenny Britt 1.25 3.00
97 Matt Hasselbeck 1.25 3.00
98 Chris Cooley 1.25 3.00
99 Rex Grossman 1.25 3.00
100 Ryan Torain 1.00 2.50
101 Ozzie Newsome 1.50 4.00
102 Andre Reed 1.50 4.00
103 Doug Flutie 1.50 4.00
104 Franco Harris 2.00 5.00
105 Jack Lambert 2.00 5.00
106 Jay Novacek 1.50 4.00
107 Jerry Rice 3.00 8.00
108 Jim Kelly 2.00 5.00
109 Jim Otto 1.25 3.00
110 Ken Stabler 2.00 5.00
111 Terrell Davis 2.00 5.00
112 Willie Brown 1.25 3.00
113 Joe Namath 2.50 6.00
114 Junior Seau 2.00 5.00
115 Rod Woodson 1.50 4.00
116 Sam Huff 1.50 4.00
117 Steve Bartkowski 1.50 4.00
118 Steve Young 2.50 6.00
119 Troy Aikman 2.50 6.00
120 Y.A. Tittle 2.00 5.00
121 Cris Collinsworth 1.50 4.00
122 Dick Butkus 2.50 6.00
123 Earl Campbell 2.00 5.00
124 Fred Biletnikoff 1.50 4.00
125 Jerome Bettis 2.00 5.00
126 Bo Jackson 2.50 6.00
127 Brett Favre 4.00 10.00
128 Alan Page 1.50 4.00
129 Art Monk 1.50 4.00
130 Barry Sanders 3.00 8.00
131 Bernie Kosar 1.50 4.00
132 Bob Griese 2.00 5.00
133 Bob Hayes 2.00 5.00
134 Boyd Dowler 1.25 3.00
135 Bruce Smith 1.50 4.00
136 Charley Taylor 1.25 3.00
137 Charlie Joiner 1.50 4.00
138 Billy Sims 1.50 4.00
139 Boomer Esiason 1.50 4.00
140 Chuck Bednarik 1.50 4.00
141 Chuck Foreman 1.25 3.00
142 Cliff Harris 1.25 3.00
143 Dan Fouts 2.00 5.00
144 Dave Casper 1.25 3.00
145 Derrick Thomas 5.00 12.00
146 Don Maynard 1.50 4.00
147 Doug Williams 1.25 3.00
148 Eddie George 1.50 4.00
149 Emmitt Smith 3.00 8.00
150 Fred Williamson 1.25 3.00
151 Aaron Williams RC 1.50 4.00
152 Adrian Clayborn RC 2.00 5.00
153 Akeem Ayers RC 1.50 4.00
154 Aldon Smith RC 3.00 8.00
155 Terrelle Pryor RC 2.50 6.00
156 Brandon Harris RC 1.25 3.00
157 Cameron Heyward RC 2.00 5.00
158 Cameron Jordan RC 1.50 4.00
159 Cecil Shorts RC 1.50 4.00
160 Corey Liuget RC 1.25 3.00
161 D.J. Williams RC 2.00 5.00
162 Da'Quan Bowers RC 2.00 5.00
163 Denarius Moore RC 2.50 6.00
164 Dion Lewis RC 2.00 5.00
165 Dwayne Harris RC 2.00 5.00
166 Evan Royster RC 2.00 5.00
167 Greg McElroy RC 2.00 5.00
168 Greg Salas RC 2.00 5.00
169 J.J. Watt RC 2.50 6.00
170 Jacquizz Rodgers RC 2.00 5.00
171 Jeremy Kerley RC 2.00 5.00
172 Jimmy Smith RC 2.00 5.00
173 Johnny White RC 1.50 4.00
174 Jordan Cameron RC 1.50 4.00
175 Julius Thomas RC 1.50 4.00
176 Justin Houston RC 2.00 5.00
177 Kealoha Pilares RC 2.00 5.00
178 Kris Durham RC 1.50 4.00
179 Lance Kendricks RC 1.50 4.00
180 Luke Stocker RC 1.50 4.00
181 Martez Wilson RC 2.00 5.00
182 Chris Neild RC 3.00 8.00
183 Niles Paul RC 2.00 5.00
184 Owen Marecic RC 2.00 5.00
185 Patrick Peterson RC 3.00 8.00
186 Phil Taylor RC 1.50 4.00
187 Prince Amukamara RC 2.00 5.00
188 Quinton Carter RC 1.25 3.00
189 Rahim Moore RC 1.50 4.00
190 Ricky Stanzi RC 2.50 6.00
191 Robert Housler RC 1.50 4.00
192 Robert Quinn RC 2.00 5.00
193 Roy Helu RC 4.00 10.00
194 Ryan Kerrigan RC 2.00 5.00
195 Ryan Whalen RC 1.50 4.00
196 Stephen Paea RC 2.00 5.00
197 T.J. Yates RC 2.50 6.00
198 Tandon Doss RC 1.50 4.00
199 Tyrod Taylor RC 2.00 5.00
200 Tyron Smith RC 2.50 6.00
201 Cam Newton JSY AU/199 RC 150.00 300.00
202 Von Miller JSY AU/299 RC EXCH 12.00 30.00
203 Marcell Dareus JSY AU/299 RC EXCH 10.00 25.00
204 A.J. Green JSY AU/199 RC 30.00 80.00
205 Julio Jones JSY AU/299 RC EXCH 30.00 80.00
206 Jake Locker JSY AU/199 RC 40.00 100.00
207 Blaine Gabbert JSY AU/199 RC 15.00 40.00
208 Christian Ponder JSY AU/199 RC 30.00 60.00
209 Jonathan Baldwin JSY AU/299 RC 10.00 25.00
210 Mark Ingram JSY AU/199 RC 25.00 60.00
211 Andy Dalton JSY AU/299 RC 50.00 100.00
212 Colin Kaepernick JSY AU/299 RC 12.00 30.00
213 Ryan Williams JSY AU/299 RC 12.00 30.00
214 Kyle Rudolph JSY AU/299 RC EXCH 10.00 25.00
215 Titus Young JSY AU/299 RC 12.00 30.00
216 Shane Vereen JSY AU/299 RC 10.00 25.00
217 Mikel Leshoure JSY AU/299 RC 15.00 30.00
218 Torrey Smith JSY AU/299 RC 15.00 40.00
219 Greg Little JSY AU/299 RC 10.00 25.00
220 Daniel Thomas JSY AU/299 RC EXCH 10.00 25.00
221 Randall Cobb JSY AU/299 RC 12.00 30.00
222 DeMarco Murray JSY AU/299 RC 40.00 80.00
223 Stevan Ridley JSY AU/299 RC EXCH 10.00 25.00
224 Ryan Mallett JSY AU/199 RC 30.00 60.00
225 Austin Pettis JSY AU/299 RC 8.00 20.00
226 Leonard Hankerson JSY AU/299 RC 10.00 25.00
227 Vincent Brown JSY AU/299 RC 10.00 25.00
228 Jerrel Jernigan JSY AU/299 RC 8.00 20.00
229 Alex Green JSY AU/299 RC 8.00 20.00
230 Clyde Gates JSY AU/299 RC 8.00 20.00
231 Kendall Hunter JSY AU/299 RC 10.00 25.00
232 Delone Carter JSY AU/299 RC 8.00 20.00
233 Taiwan Jones JSY AU/299 RC 10.00 25.00
234 Bilal Powell JSY AU/299 RC 6.00 15.00
235 Jamie Harper JSY AU/299 RC EXCH 8.00 20.00
236 Jordan Todman JSY AU/299 RC 6.00 15.00

2011 Limited Gold Spotlight

*1-100 VETS/25: 1X TO 2.5X BASIC CARDS
*101-150 LEGEND/25: 1X TO 2.5X BASIC CARDS
*151-200 ROOKIES/25: .8X TO 2X BASIC RC
1-200 STATED PRINT RUN 25
UNPRICED 201-236 JSY AU PRINT RUN 10

2011 Limited Silver Spotlight

*1-100 VETS/50: .8X TO 2X BASIC CARDS
*101-150 LEGEND/50: .8X TO 2X BASIC CARDS
*151-200 ROOKIES/50: .6X TO 1.5X BASIC RC
1-200 STATED PRINT RUN 50
*201-236 ROOKIE JSY AU/25: .5X TO 1.2X
201-236 STATED PRINT RUN 25
EXCH EXPIRATION: 6/28/2013
201 Cam Newton JSY AU 200.00 350.00
206 Jake Locker JSY AU 75.00 135.00
210 Mark Ingram JSY AU 60.00 120.00
211 Andy Dalton JSY AU 60.00 120.00
222 DeMarco Murray JSY AU 75.00 135.00

2011 Limited Banner Season Materials Prime

STATED PRINT RUN 4-50
3 Dwayne Bowe/50 5.00 12.00
4 Aaron Rodgers/50 15.00 40.00
5 Matt Ryan/50 6.00 15.00
6 Ed Reed/50 6.00 15.00
7 Maurice Jones-Drew/50 5.00 12.00
8 Philip Rivers/50 6.00 15.00
9 Santana Moss/50 5.00 12.00
10 Roddy White/50 5.00 12.00
11 DeMarcus Ware/50 5.00 12.00
13 Brandon Lloyd/50 5.00 12.00
14 Michael Vick/44 6.00 15.00
15 Jamaal Charles/50 5.00 12.00
16 Eli Manning/50 6.00 15.00
17 Calvin Johnson/50 6.00 15.00
18 Michael Turner/50 5.00 12.00
20 Chris Johnson/50 5.00 12.00
22 Matt Schaub/50 5.00 12.00
23 Adrian Peterson/50 8.00 20.00

2011 Limited Cuts Autographs

UNPRICED CUT AUTO PRINT RUN 1-15

2011 Limited Draft Day Duos

STATED PRINT RUN 100 SER.#'d SETS
*PRIME/25: .8X TO 2X BASIC DUO/100
1 Cam Newton 12.00 30.00
Blaine Gabbert
2 A.J. Green 6.00 15.00
Julio Jones
3 Von Miller 5.00 12.00
Aldon Smith
4 A.J. Green 6.00 15.00
Mark Ingram
5 Julio Jones 6.00 15.00
Mark Ingram

2011 Limited Draft Day Jerseys

STATED PRINT RUN 100 SER.#'d SETS
*PRIME/50: .5X TO 1.2X JSY/100
*LIDC/60: .6X TO 1.2X JCY/100
*COMBOS/50: .5X TO 1.2X JSY/100
*COMBO PRIME/25: .8X TO 2X JSY/100
1 Cam Newton 12.00 30.00
2 Von Miller 4.00 10.00
3 A.J. Green 6.00 15.00
4 Julio Jones 6.00 15.00
5 Aldon Smith 5.00 12.00
6 Tyron Smith 5.00 12.00
7 Blaine Gabbert 5.00 12.00
8 J.J. Watt 4.00 10.00
9 Nick Fairley 4.00 10.00
10 Corey Liuget 2.00 5.00
11 Adrian Clayborn 4.00 10.00
12 Phil Taylor 2.50 6.00
13 Mark Ingram 6.00 15.00

2011 Limited Draft Day Jerseys Autographs Prime

STATED PRINT RUN 15 SER.#'d SETS
*BASE JSY AU/10: .4X TO 1X PRIME/15
1 Cam Newton 150.00 250.00
2 Von Miller 25.00 50.00
3 A.J. Green 60.00 120.00
4 Julio Jones 60.00 120.00
5 Aldon Smith EXCH 50.00 100.00
6 Tyron Smith 30.00 60.00
7 Blaine Gabbert 30.00 80.00
8 J.J. Watt 25.00 50.00
10 Corey Liuget 10.00 25.00
11 Adrian Clayborn 15.00 40.00
12 Phil Taylor 12.00 30.00
13 Mark Ingram 60.00 120.00

2011 Limited Draft Day Quads

STATED PRINT RUN 100 SER.#'d SETS
*PRIME/25: .8X TO 2X BASIC QUAD/100
1 Cam Newton 15.00 40.00
Von Miller
A.J. Green
Julio Jones
2 Cam Newton 15.00 40.00
A.J. Green
Julio Jones
Blaine Gabbert
3 Von Miller 8.00 20.00
Aldon Smith
J.J. Watt
Nick Fairley
4 Tyron Smith 6.00 15.00
Corey Liuget
Adrian Clayborn
Phil Taylor

2011 Limited Draft Day Trios

STATED PRINT RUN 100 SER.#'d SETS
*PRIME/25: .8X TO 2X BASIC TRIO/100
1 Mark Ingram 8.00 20.00
A.J. Green
Julio Jones
2 Nick Fairley 5.00 12.00
Corey Liuget
Phil Taylor
3 Von Miller 6.00 15.00
Aldon Smith
Blaine Gabbert
4 Cam Newton 15.00 40.00
A.J. Green
Mark Ingram

2011 Limited Initial Steps Autographs

STATED PRINT RUN 25-50
1 Mikel Leshoure/50 6.00 15.00
4 Vincent Brown/50 5.00 12.00
6 Jerrel Jernigan/50 5.00 12.00
7 Mark Ingram/25 25.00 50.00
8 Von Miller/50 8.00 20.00
9 Titus Young/50 8.00 20.00
10 Leonard Hankerson/50 6.00 15.00
11 Cam Newton/25 100.00 175.00
13 Alex Green/50 6.00 15.00
14 Christian Ponder/25 15.00 40.00
15 Colin Kaepernick/50 8.00 20.00
17 Jonathan Baldwin/50 6.00 15.00
20 Jake Locker/25 30.00 60.00
21 DeMarco Murray/50 25.00 50.00
22 Randall Cobb/50 8.00 20.00
23 A.J. Green/25 15.00 40.00
25 Ryan Mallett/25 15.00 40.00
26 Delone Carter/50 5.00 12.00
27 Blaine Gabbert/25 12.00 30.00
28 Austin Pettis/50 5.00 12.00
32 Torrey Smith/50 8.00 20.00
33 Andy Dalton/50 25.00 50.00
34 Shane Vereen/50 6.00 15.00
36 Jordan Todman/50 4.00 10.00

2011 Limited Initial Steps Jerseys

JERSEY PRINT RUN 99 SER.#'d SETS
*PRIME/25: .6X TO 1.5X BASIC JSY/99
SHOE/99: .4X TO 1X BASIC JSY/99
1 Mikel Leshoure/99 3.00 8.00
2 Bilal Powell/99 2.00 5.00
3 Jamie Harper/99 3.00 8.00
4 Vincent Brown/99 3.00 8.00
5 Clyde Gates/99 2.50 6.00
6 Jerrel Jernigan/99 2.50 6.00
7 Mark Ingram/99 6.00 15.00
8 Von Miller/99 4.00 10.00
9 Titus Young/99 4.00 10.00
10 Leonard Hankerson/99 3.00 8.00
11 Cam Newton/99 15.00 40.00
12 Julio Jones/99 6.00 15.00
13 Alex Green/99 3.00 8.00
14 Christian Ponder/99 6.00 15.00
15 Colin Kaepernick/99 4.00 10.00
16 Taiwan Jones/99 3.00 8.00
17 Jonathan Baldwin/99 3.00 8.00
18 Ryan Williams/99 4.00 10.00
19 Marcell Dareus/99 3.00 8.00
20 Jake Locker/99 8.00 20.00
21 DeMarco Murray/99 6.00 15.00
22 Randall Cobb/99 4.00 10.00
23 A.J. Green/75 6.00 15.00
24 Daniel Thomas/99 3.00 8.00
25 Ryan Mallett/99 6.00 15.00
26 Delone Carter/99 2.50 6.00
27 Blaine Gabbert/99 5.00 12.00
28 Austin Pettis/99 2.50 6.00
29 Stevan Ridley/99 3.00 8.00
30 Kyle Rudolph/99 3.00 8.00
31 Greg Little/99 3.00 8.00
32 Torrey Smith/99 4.00 10.00
33 Andy Dalton/99 8.00 20.00
34 Shane Vereen/99 3.00 8.00
35 Kendall Hunter/99 3.00 8.00
36 Jordan Todman/99 2.00 5.00

2011 Limited Jumbo Jerseys Autographs

UNPRICED JUMBO AU PRINT RUN 10

2011 Limited Jumbo Jerseys Jersey Number

STATED PRINT RUN 25 SER.#'d SETS
*PRIME/13-15: .6X TO 1.5X JUMBO JSY/25
*JSY # PRIME/15: .6X TO 1.5X JUM.JSY/25
1 Johnny Knox 5.00 12.00
2 Jordan Shipley 5.00 12.00
3 Steve Johnson 5.00 12.00
4 Dexter McCluster 4.00 10.00
5 Santana Moss 5.00 12.00
6 Brian Hartline 5.00 12.00
7 Marcedes Lewis 4.00 10.00
8 Jason Campbell 5.00 12.00
9 London Fletcher 4.00 10.00
10 Jon Beason 4.00 10.00
11 Jared Allen 8.00 20.00
12 Jacoby Ford 5.00 12.00
13 Jermaine Gresham 5.00 12.00
14 James Harrison 8.00 20.00
16 DeAngelo Hall 4.00 10.00
17 Marc Mariani 5.00 12.00
18 Cedric Benson 5.00 12.00
19 Patrick Willis 5.00 12.00
20 Matt Cassel 5.00 12.00
21 Antonio Gates 5.00 12.00
23 Shonn Greene 5.00 12.00
24 Marques Colston 5.00 12.00
25 Tamba Hali 6.00 15.00
26 Tony Romo 6.00 15.00
27 Tony Gonzalez 5.00 12.00
28 Julius Peppers 5.00 12.00
29 Chad Greenway 10.00 25.00
30 Knowshon Moreno 5.00 12.00
32 Chris Cooley 5.00 12.00
34 Eddie Royal 4.00 10.00
35 Brian Orakpo 5.00 12.00

2011 Limited Limitless

STATED PRINT RUN 249 SER.#'d SETS
1 Colt McCoy 1.25 3.00
2 Tim Tebow 4.00 10.00
3 Michael Vick 1.50 4.00
4 Danny Woodhead 2.00 5.00
5 Darren McFadden 1.25 3.00
6 DeAngelo Williams 1.25 3.00
7 Jacoby Ford 1.25 3.00
8 Vernon Davis 1.25 3.00
9 Ryan Mathews 1.25 3.00
10 DeSean Jackson 1.25 3.00
11 Dez Bryant 1.50 4.00
12 Mark Sanchez 1.50 4.00
13 Steven Jackson 1.25 3.00
14 Joe Flacco 1.50 4.00
15 Sam Bradford 1.50 4.00
16 Darrelle Revis 1.25 3.00
17 Miles Austin 1.25 3.00
18 Adrian Peterson 2.00 5.00
19 Tom Brady 2.50 6.00
20 Kenny Britt 1.25 3.00
21 Percy Harvin 1.25 3.00
22 Ryan Torain 1.00 2.50
23 Jason Witten 1.50 4.00
24 Devin Hester 1.50 4.00
25 Santonio Holmes 1.25 3.00

2011 Limited Limitless Threads Autographs

STATED PRINT RUN 10-25
*PRIME/10-20: .5X TO 1.2X JSY AU/15-25
1 Colt McCoy/25 12.00 30.00
2 Tim Tebow/25 60.00 120.00
3 Michael Vick/15 30.00 60.00
5 Darren McFadden/20 15.00 40.00
6 DeAngelo Williams/20 12.00 30.00
7 Jacoby Ford/10 EXCH
8 Vernon Davis/20 12.00 30.00
9 Ryan Mathews/25 EXCH
10 DeSean Jackson/20 12.00 30.00
11 Dez Bryant/20
12 Mark Sanchez/20 25.00 50.00
13 Steven Jackson/25 12.00 30.00
14 Joe Flacco/20 25.00 50.00
15 Sam Bradford/25 40.00 80.00
16 Darrelle Revis/20 15.00 40.00
17 Miles Austin/20 15.00 40.00
18 Adrian Peterson/10
19 Tom Brady/15 EXCH
21 Percy Harvin/20 15.00 40.00
22 Ryan Torain/25 12.00 30.00
23 Jason Witten/20 15.00 40.00
25 Santonio Holmes/25 12.00 30.00

2011 Limited Material Monikers

STATED PRINT RUN 10-50
*PRIME/10: .6X TO 1.5X JSY AU/30-50
*PRIME/10: .5X TO 1.2X JSY AU/20-25
1 Arian Foster/50 25.00 50.00
2 Jim Kelly/35 25.00 50.00
3 Dwayne Bowe/20 EXCH
4 Aaron Rodgers/20 175.00 300.00
5 Matt Ryan/20 20.00 50.00
6 Jim Otto/50
7 Maurice Jones-Drew/30 12.00 30.00
8 Doug Flutie/25
9 Terrell Davis/35 25.00 50.00
10 Andre Reed/25 15.00 40.00
12 Jack Lambert/25 30.00 60.00
13 Brandon Lloyd/25 12.00 30.00
14 Willie Brown/50 10.00 25.00
15 Jamaal Charles/20 12.00 30.00
16 Ken Stabler/50 15.00 40.00
17 Calvin Johnson/25
18 Michael Turner/20 12.00 30.00
20 Dan Marino/30 100.00 175.00
21 Drew Brees/10
22 Franco Harris/25 EXCH 20.00 50.00
23 Adrian Peterson/10
24 Jerry Rice/25 75.00 150.00
25 Mike Wallace/25 15.00 40.00
26 Cris Collinsworth/25 EXCH 15.00 40.00
27 Junior Seau/35 30.00 60.00
28 Fred Biletnikoff/25 EXCH 15.00 40.00
29 Michael Vick/20 40.00 80.00
30 Earl Campbell/25 EXCH 20.00 50.00
31 Bo Jackson/25 40.00 80.00
32 Steve Young/30 30.00 60.00
33 Philip Rivers/25 15.00 40.00
35 Jerome Bettis/25 90.00 150.00
36 Roddy White/25 12.00 30.00
37 Steve Bartkowski/35 12.00 30.00
38 Brett Favre/20
39 Danny White/50
40 Rod Woodson/25 50.00 100.00
41 Y.A. Tittle/30 EXCH 20.00 50.00
42 Peyton Hillis/25 15.00 40.00
44 Joe Namath/35 50.00 100.00
45 Chuck Howley/50 EXCH 12.00 30.00
46 Dick Butkus/30 40.00 80.00
47 Eli Manning/20 50.00 100.00
48 Troy Aikman/30 EXCH 30.00 60.00
49 Jan Stenerud/50 10.00 25.00
50 Peyton Manning/20 60.00 120.00

2011 Limited Monikers Autographs Gold

GOLD STATED PRINT RUN 4-25
EXCH EXPIRATION: 6/28/2013
10 C.J. Spiller/25 10.00 25.00
19 Bo Scaife/25 8.00 20.00
25 Felix Jones/15 10.00 25.00
33 Jahvid Best/25 10.00 25.00
34 Matthew Stafford/25 30.00 60.00
36 Greg Jennings/15 12.00 30.00
39 Arian Foster/25 30.00 60.00
40 Matt Schaub/25 12.00 30.00
51 Chad Henne/25 10.00 25.00
54 Donovan McNabb/15 25.00 50.00
56 BenJarvus Green-Ellis/25 25.00 50.00
57 Chad Ochocinco/25 12.00 30.00
75 Nnamdi Asomugha/25 15.00 40.00
76 Ben Roethlisberger/25 40.00 80.00
83 Michael Crabtree/25 12.00 30.00
87 Sidney Rice/25 10.00 25.00
89 Danny Amendola/25 12.00 30.00
92 Josh Freeman/25 12.00 30.00
99 Rex Grossman/25 12.00 30.00
100 Ryan Torain/25 12.00 30.00
101 Ozzie Newsome/25 12.00 30.00
103 Doug Flutie/15 15.00 40.00
108 Jim Kelly/15 20.00 40.00
109 Jim Otto/25 10.00 25.00
112 Willie Brown/25 10.00 25.00
125 Jerome Bettis/15 50.00 100.00
128 Alan Page/15 12.00 30.00
129 Art Monk/25 30.00 60.00
130 Barry Sanders/25 60.00 120.00
131 Bernie Kosar/25 15.00 40.00
132 Bob Griese/25 25.00 50.00
134 Boyd Dowler/25 8.00 20.00
136 Charley Taylor/25 8.00 20.00
137 Charlie Joiner/25 10.00 25.00
139 Boomer Esiason/25 20.00 40.00
140 Chuck Bednarik/25 10.00 25.00
142 Cliff Harris/25 12.00 30.00
144 Dave Casper/25 12.00 30.00
147 Doug Williams/25 15.00 40.00
148 Eddie George/25 25.00 50.00
149 Emmitt Smith/22 100.00 200.00
150 Fred Williamson/25 12.00 30.00
151 Aaron Williams/25 6.00 15.00
152 Adrian Clayborn/25 8.00 20.00
153 Akeem Ayers/25 6.00 15.00
154 Aldon Smith/25 EXCH 25.00 50.00
155 Terrelle Pryor/25
156 Brandon Harris/25 5.00 12.00
157 Cameron Heyward/25 8.00 20.00
158 Cameron Jordan/25 6.00 15.00
159 Cecil Shorts/25 6.00 15.00
160 Corey Liuget/25 5.00 12.00
161 D.J. Williams/25 8.00 20.00
162 Da'Quan Bowers/25 8.00 20.00
163 Denarius Moore/25 10.00 25.00
164 Dion Lewis/25 8.00 20.00
165 Dwayne Harris/25 8.00 20.00
166 Evan Royster/25 12.00 30.00
167 Greg McElroy/25 12.00 30.00
168 Greg Salas/25 8.00 20.00
169 J.J. Watt/25 12.00 30.00
170 Jacquizz Rodgers/25 8.00 20.00
171 Jeremy Kerley/25 EXCH 8.00 20.00
172 Jimmy Smith/25 8.00 20.00
173 Johnny White/25 EXCH 6.00 15.00
174 Jordan Cameron/25 6.00 15.00
175 Julius Thomas/25 6.00 15.00
176 Justin Houston/25 8.00 20.00
177 Kealoha Pilares/25 8.00 20.00
178 Kris Durham/25 6.00 15.00
179 Lance Kendricks/25 6.00 15.00
180 Luke Stocker/25 6.00 15.00
181 Martez Wilson/25 8.00 20.00
183 Niles Paul/25 EXCH 8.00 20.00
185 Patrick Peterson/25 40.00 100.00
186 Phil Taylor/25 6.00 15.00
187 Prince Amukamara/25 8.00 20.00
188 Quinton Carter/25 5.00 12.00
189 Rahim Moore/25 6.00 15.00
190 Ricky Stanzi/25 12.00 30.00
191 Robert Housler/25 6.00 15.00
193 Roy Helu/25 15.00 40.00
194 Ryan Kerrigan/25 8.00 20.00
195 Ryan Whalen/25 6.00 15.00

196 Stephen Paea/25 8.00 20.00
197 T.J. Yates/25 15.00 40.00
198 Tandon Doss/25 6.00 15.00
199 Tyrod Taylor/25 12.00 30.00

2011 Limited Monikers Autographs Silver

VETERAN/LEGEND PRINT RUN 10-50
*SILVER ROOKIE/199: .25X TO .6X GOLD
ROOKIE STATED PRINT RUN 199
EXCH EXPIRATION: 6/28/2013
4 Matt Ryan/10
6 Roddy White/25 10.00 25.00
7 Anquan Boldin/35 8.00 20.00
8 Joe Flacco/10
10 C.J. Spiller/50 8.00 20.00
13 DeAngelo Williams/25 10.00 25.00
14 Jonathan Stewart/50.
17 Matt Forte/25 12.00 30.00
19 Bo Scaife/50 6.00 15.00
22 Colt McCoy/25 10.00 25.00
24 Peyton Hillis/25 12.00 30.00
25 Felix Jones/35 8.00 20.00
26 Jason Witten/25 15.00 40.00
27 Miles Austin/25 12.00 30.00
29 Brandon Lloyd/25 10.00 25.00
30 Knowshon Moreno/50 8.00 20.00
33 Jahvid Best/50 8.00 20.00
34 Matthew Stafford/50 25.00 50.00
35 Aaron Rodgers/10
36 Greg Jennings/50 10.00 25.00
39 Arian Foster/50 25.00 50.00
40 Matt Schaub/50 10.00 25.00
42 Peyton Manning/25 60.00 120.00
43 Reggie Wayne/25 10.00 25.00
48 Jamaal Charles/25 10.00 25.00
49 Matt Cassel/25 10.00 25.00
50 Brian Hartline/25 8.00 20.00
51 Chad Henne/50 8.00 20.00
54 Donovan McNabb/25 25.00 50.00
55 Percy Harvin/25 10.00 25.00
56 BenJarvus Green-Ellis/50 25.00 50.00
57 Chad Ochocinco/50 10.00 25.00
61 Drew Brees/15 40.00 80.00
64 Eli Manning/15 75.00 125.00
66 Mark Sanchez/15 20.00 40.00
67 Santonio Holmes/25 10.00 25.00
68 Shonn Greene/50 8.00 20.00
69 Darren McFadden/25 12.00 30.00
72 DeSean Jackson/15
73 LeSean McCoy/25 12.00 30.00
80 Philip Rivers/15 15.00 40.00
83 Michael Crabtree/50 10.00 25.00
84 Vernon Davis/15
87 Sidney Rice/50 8.00 20.00
89 Danny Amendola/50 10.00 25.00
90 Sam Bradford/15 25.00 50.00
92 Josh Freeman/50 10.00 25.00
98 Chris Cooley/25 12.00 30.00
99 Rex Grossman/50 10.00 25.00
101 Ozzie Newsome/30 10.00 25.00
102 Andre Reed/15 12.00 30.00
104 Franco Harris/10
105 Jack Lambert/25 30.00 60.00
108 Jim Kelly/25 20.00 40.00
109 Jim Otto/30 10.00 25.00
111 Terrell Davis/20 15.00 40.00
112 Willie Brown/35
113 Joe Namath/25 50.00 100.00
117 Steve Bartkowski/50 8.00 20.00
128 Alan Page/50 10.00 25.00
132 Bob Griese/35 15.00 40.00
134 Boyd Dowler/50 12.00 30.00
139 Boomer Esiason/40 12.00 30.00
142 Cliff Harris/50 10.00 25.00
144 Dave Casper/50 10.00 25.00
147 Doug Williams/50 10.00 25.00
150 Fred Williamson/50 10.00 25.00

2011 Limited Rookie Jumbo Jerseys

STATED PRINT RUN 43-99
*JUMBO PRIME/10: 1.2X TO 3X JUM.JSY/43-99
*JSY #/36-49: .5X TO 1.2X JUM.JSY/43-99
*JSY # PRIME/10: 1.2X TO 3X JUM.JSY/43-99
1 Cam Newton/99 12.00 30.00
2 Jonathan Baldwin/99 2.50 6.00
3 Von Miller/99 3.00 8.00
4 Ryan Mallett/99 5.00 12.00
5 A.J. Green/60 5.00 12.00
6 Bilal Powell/99 1.50 4.00
7 Greg Little/99 2.50 6.00
8 Leonard Hankerson/99 2.50 6.00
9 Taiwan Jones/99 2.50 6.00
10 Shane Vereen/99 2.50 6.00
11 Jamie Harper/99 2.50 6.00
12 Daniel Thomas/99 2.50 6.00
13 Andy Dalton/99 6.00 15.00
14 Clyde Gates/99 2.00 5.00
15 Kendall Hunter/99 2.50 6.00
16 Mikel Leshoure/99 2.50 6.00
17 Torrey Smith/99 3.00 8.00
18 Blaine Gabbert/99 4.00 10.00
19 Alex Green/99 2.50 6.00
20 Delone Carter/99 2.00 5.00
22 Mark Ingram/99 5.00 12.00
23 Austin Pettis/99 2.00 5.00
24 Marcell Dareus/99 2.50 6.00
25 Titus Young/99 3.00 8.00
26 Randall Cobb/99 3.00 8.00
27 Christian Ponder/99 5.00 12.00
28 Julio Jones/99 5.00 12.00
29 Stevan Ridley/99 2.50 6.00
30 Vincent Brown/99 2.50 6.00
31 Jake Locker/99 6.00 15.00
32 Jordan Todman/99 1.50 4.00
33 Jerrel Jernigan/99 2.00 5.00
34 DeMarco Murray/99 5.00 12.00
35 Kyle Rudolph/43 2.50 6.00
36 Colin Kaepernick/99 3.00 8.00

2011 Limited Rookie Jumbo Jerseys Autographs Prime

STATED PRINT RUN 25 SER.#'d SETS
*BASIC JSY AU/10: .4X TO 1X PRIME AU/25
*JSY # AU/10: .4X TO 1X PRIME AU/25
EXCH EXPIRATION: 6/28/2013
1 Cam Newton 125.00 250.00
2 Jonathan Baldwin 12.00 30.00
3 Von Miller 15.00 40.00
4 Ryan Mallett 30.00 60.00
5 A.J. Green 40.00 80.00
6 Bilal Powell 8.00 20.00
7 Greg Little 12.00 30.00
8 Leonard Hankerson 12.00 30.00
9 Taiwan Jones 12.00 30.00
10 Shane Vereen 12.00 30.00
11 Jamie Harper EXCH 12.00 30.00
12 Daniel Thomas 12.00 30.00
13 Andy Dalton 50.00 100.00
14 Clyde Gates 10.00 25.00
15 Kendall Hunter 12.00 30.00
16 Mikel Leshoure 12.00 30.00
17 Torrey Smith 20.00 50.00
18 Blaine Gabbert 30.00 60.00
19 Alex Green 12.00 30.00
20 Delone Carter 10.00 25.00
21 Ryan Williams EXCH 15.00 40.00
22 Mark Ingram 40.00 80.00
23 Austin Pettis 10.00 25.00
24 Marcell Dareus EXCH 12.00 30.00
25 Titus Young 15.00 40.00
26 Randall Cobb 15.00 40.00
27 Christian Ponder 30.00 60.00
28 Julio Jones 40.00 80.00
29 Stevan Ridley 12.00 30.00
30 Vincent Brown 12.00 30.00
31 Jake Locker 50.00 100.00
32 Jordan Todman 8.00 20.00
33 Jerrel Jernigan 10.00 25.00
34 DeMarco Murray 40.00 80.00
35 Kyle Rudolph EXCH 12.00 30.00
36 Colin Kaepernick 20.00 50.00

2011 Limited Rookie Lettermen

UNPRICED LETTERMEN PRINT RUN 4-10

2011 Limited Team Trademarks Autograph Materials

STATED PRINT RUN 6-25
*PRIME/10: .5X TO 1.2X JSY AU/15-25
1 Larry Fitzgerald/20 15.00 40.00
2 Michael Turner/15 12.00 30.00
3 Anquan Boldin/20 12.00 30.00
4 Jonathan Stewart/6
5 Steve Smith/20 EXCH 12.00 30.00
7 Troy Polamalu/25 75.00 150.00
8 Matt Forte/20 15.00 40.00
9 Hakeem Nicks/20 12.00 30.00
10 Reggie Wayne/25 12.00 30.00
11 Matthew Stafford/25 40.00 80.00
12 Jay Cutler/20 12.00 30.00
14 Ray Rice/25 EXCH
15 Hines Ward/20 40.00 80.00
17 Dallas Clark/25 12.00 30.00
18 LaDainian Tomlinson/25
19 LeSean McCoy/20 15.00 40.00
22 Frank Gore/25 12.00 30.00
23 Jeremy Maclin/25 EXCH

2011 Limited Team Trademarks Materials Prime

STATED PRINT RUN 5-50
2 Michael Turner/50 5.00 12.00
3 Anquan Boldin/50 5.00 12.00
5 Steve Smith/50 5.00 12.00
6 Brian Urlacher/50 6.00 15.00
8 Matt Forte/50 5.00 12.00
9 Hakeem Nicks/50 5.00 12.00
10 Reggie Wayne/50 5.00 12.00
11 Matthew Stafford/50 6.00 15.00
12 Jay Cutler/50 5.00 12.00
13 Mike Thomas/50 5.00 12.00
14 Ray Rice/50 5.00 12.00
17 Dallas Clark/50 5.00 12.00
18 LaDainian Tomlinson/50 6.00 15.00
20 Ray Lewis/50 8.00 20.00
21 Wes Welker/50 8.00 20.00
22 Frank Gore/25 6.00 15.00
23 Jeremy Maclin/50 5.00 12.00
24 Chris Johnson/50 5.00 12.00
25 Visanthe Shiancoe/43 5.00 12.00

2011 Limited Threads

STATED PRINT RUN 13-99
1 Beanie Wells/99 3.00 8.00
2 Kevin Kolb/99 3.00 8.00
3 Larry Fitzgerald/48 3.00 8.00
4 Matt Ryan/99 4.00 10.00
5 Michael Turner/99 3.00 8.00
7 Anquan Boldin/99 3.00 8.00
8 Joe Flacco/99 4.00 10.00
9 Ray Rice/99 4.00 10.00
10 C.J. Spiller/99 3.00 8.00
11 Ryan Fitzpatrick/99 3.00 8.00
12 Steve Johnson/99 3.00 8.00
13 DeAngelo Williams/99 3.00 8.00
16 Jay Cutler/99 3.00 8.00
17 Matt Forte/99 3.00 8.00
18 Roy Williams WR/99 3.00 8.00
20 Cedric Benson/99 3.00 8.00
21 Jordan Shipley/99 3.00 8.00
22 Colt McCoy/99 3.00 8.00
23 Josh Cribbs/99 3.00 8.00
25 Felix Jones/99 3.00 8.00
26 Jason Witten/99 4.00 10.00
27 Miles Austin/99 3.00 8.00
28 Tony Romo/99 4.00 10.00
29 Brandon Lloyd/99 3.00 8.00
30 Knowshon Moreno/99 3.00 8.00
31 Kyle Orton/99 3.00 8.00
32 Calvin Johnson/99 4.00 10.00
33 Jahvid Best/99 3.00 8.00
34 Matthew Stafford/99 4.00 10.00
35 Aaron Rodgers/99 10.00 25.00
38 Andre Johnson/99 3.00 8.00
40 Matt Schaub/99 3.00 8.00
41 Dallas Clark/99 3.00 8.00
43 Reggie Wayne/99 3.00 8.00
45 Marcedes Lewis/50 2.50 6.00
46 Maurice Jones-Drew/99 3.00 8.00
47 Dwayne Bowe/99 3.00 8.00
48 Jamaal Charles/99 3.00 8.00
49 Matt Cassel/99 3.00 8.00
50 Brian Hartline/99 3.00 8.00
51 Chad Henne/99 3.00 8.00
54 Donovan McNabb/99 4.00 10.00
55 Percy Harvin/99 3.00 8.00
56 BenJarvus Green-Ellis/99 6.00 10.00
58 Tom Brady/99 6.00 15.00
59 Wes Welker/99 4.00 10.00
60 Devery Henderson/99 2.50 6.00
61 Drew Brees/99 4.00 10.00
62 Marques Colston/99 3.00 8.00
64 Eli Manning/99 4.00 10.00
65 Hakeem Nicks/99 3.00 8.00
66 Mark Sanchez/99 4.00 10.00
67 Santonio Holmes/99 3.00 8.00
68 Shonn Greene/99 3.00 8.00
69 Darren McFadden/99 3.00 8.00
70 Jacoby Ford/99 3.00 8.00
71 Jason Campbell/99 3.00 8.00
72 DeSean Jackson/99 3.00 8.00
73 LeSean McCoy/99 3.00 8.00
74 Michael Vick/99 4.00 10.00
76 Ben Roethlisberger/99 4.00 10.00
77 Mike Wallace/99 4.00 10.00
78 Rashard Mendenhall/25 4.00 10.00
79 Antonio Gates/99 3.00 8.00
80 Philip Rivers/99 4.00 10.00
81 Ryan Mathews/99 3.00 8.00
82 Frank Gore/99 3.00 8.00
83 Michael Crabtree/65 3.00 8.00
84 Vernon Davis/99 3.00 8.00
86 Zach Miller/99 3.00 8.00
89 Danny Amendola/99 3.00 8.00
90 Sam Bradford/99 4.00 10.00
91 Steven Jackson/99 3.00 8.00
95 Chris Johnson/99 3.00 8.00
96 Kenny Britt/99 3.00 8.00
97 Matt Hasselbeck/99 3.00 8.00
98 Chris Cooley/99 4.00 10.00
100 Ryan Torain/99 2.50 6.00
101 Ozzie Newsome/99 5.00 12.00
102 Andre Reed/30 6.00 15.00
103 Doug Flutie/99 5.00 12.00
104 Franco Harris/99 6.00 15.00
105 Jack Lambert/99 6.00 15.00
106 Jay Novacek/99 6.00 15.00
107 Jerry Rice/99 8.00 20.00
108 Jim Kelly/99 6.00 15.00
109 Jim Otto/99 4.00 10.00
110 Ken Stabler/99 6.00 15.00
111 Terrell Davis/99 6.00 15.00
112 Willie Brown/99 4.00 10.00
113 Joe Namath/23 10.00 25.00
114 Junior Seau/99 6.00 15.00
115 Rod Woodson/99 6.00 15.00
116 Sam Huff/99 5.00 12.00
117 Steve Bartkowski/99 5.00 12.00
118 Steve Young/99 8.00 20.00
119 Troy Aikman/99 8.00 20.00
120 Y.A. Tittle/99 6.00 15.00
121 Cris Collinsworth/99 5.00 12.00
122 Dick Butkus/99 8.00 20.00
123 Earl Campbell/93 6.00 15.00
124 Fred Biletnikoff/99 5.00 12.00
126 Bo Jackson/99 8.00 20.00
127 Brett Favre/99 12.00 30.00
128 Alan Page/99 5.00 12.00
131 Bernie Kosar/99 5.00 12.00
132 Bob Griese/99 6.00 15.00
133 Bob Hayes/99 8.00 20.00
135 Bruce Smith/99 5.00 12.00
136 Charley Taylor/99 4.00 10.00
137 Charlie Joiner/13 6.00 15.00
138 Billy Sims/46 5.00 12.00
139 Boomer Esiason/99 5.00 12.00
141 Chuck Foreman/99 5.00 12.00
143 Dan Fouts/99 6.00 15.00
145 Derrick Thomas/25 40.00 100.00
146 Don Maynard/99 5.00 12.00
148 Eddie George/99 5.00 12.00
149 Emmitt Smith/99 10.00 25.00

2011 Limited Threads Prime

STATED PRINT RUN 1-50
1 Beanie Wells/15 5.00 12.00
4 Matt Ryan/50 5.00 12.00
5 Michael Turner/50 4.00 10.00
6 Roddy White/50 4.00 10.00
7 Anquan Boldin/50 4.00 10.00
8 Joe Flacco/50 5.00 12.00
9 Ray Rice/50 5.00 12.00
10 C.J. Spiller/50 4.00 10.00
11 Ryan Fitzpatrick/50 4.00 10.00
12 Steve Johnson/50 4.00 10.00
13 DeAngelo Williams/50 4.00 10.00
15 Steve Smith/50 4.00 10.00
16 Jay Cutler/50 4.00 10.00
17 Matt Forte/50 4.00 10.00
20 Cedric Benson/25 5.00 12.00
21 Jordan Shipley/50 4.00 10.00
22 Colt McCoy/50 4.00 10.00
23 Josh Cribbs/50 4.00 10.00
25 Felix Jones/50 4.00 10.00
26 Jason Witten/50 5.00 12.00
27 Miles Austin/50 4.00 10.00
28 Tony Romo/50 5.00 12.00
29 Brandon Lloyd/50 4.00 10.00
30 Knowshon Moreno/40 4.00 10.00
32 Calvin Johnson/50 5.00 12.00
33 Jahvid Best/32 4.00 10.00
34 Matthew Stafford/50 5.00 12.00
35 Aaron Rodgers/50 12.00 30.00
40 Matt Schaub/50 4.00 10.00
41 Dallas Clark/21 5.00 12.00
43 Reggie Wayne/19 5.00 12.00
45 Marcedes Lewis/34 3.00 8.00
46 Maurice Jones-Drew/50 4.00 10.00
47 Dwayne Bowe/50 4.00 10.00
48 Jamaal Charles/50 4.00 10.00
49 Matt Cassel/50 4.00 10.00
50 Brian Hartline/50 4.00 10.00
53 Adrian Peterson/50 6.00 15.00
55 Percy Harvin/50 4.00 10.00
56 BenJarvus Green-Ellis/50 8.00 20.00
59 Wes Welker/50 5.00 12.00
60 Devery Henderson/50 3.00 8.00
62 Marques Colston/25 5.00 12.00
63 Ahmad Bradshaw/50 4.00 10.00
64 Eli Manning/50 5.00 12.00
65 Hakeem Nicks/50 4.00 10.00
66 Mark Sanchez/25 6.00 15.00
67 Santonio Holmes/50 4.00 10.00
68 Shonn Greene/50 4.00 10.00
69 Darren McFadden/50 4.00 10.00
70 Jacoby Ford/50 4.00 10.00
72 DeSean Jackson/50 4.00 10.00
79 Antonio Gates/50 4.00 10.00
80 Philip Rivers/50 5.00 12.00
81 Ryan Mathews/50 4.00 10.00
82 Frank Gore/25 5.00 12.00
86 Zach Miller/50 4.00 10.00
89 Danny Amendola/50 4.00 10.00
90 Sam Bradford/50 5.00 12.00
91 Steven Jackson/50 4.00 10.00
95 Chris Johnson/50 4.00 10.00
96 Kenny Britt/30 4.00 10.00
97 Matt Hasselbeck/25 5.00 12.00
98 Chris Cooley/50 5.00 12.00
100 Ryan Torain/50 3.00 8.00
101 Ozzie Newsome/50 6.00 15.00
103 Doug Flutie/50 6.00 15.00
104 Franco Harris/20 10.00 25.00
105 Jack Lambert/50 8.00 20.00
106 Jay Novacek/50 8.00 20.00
107 Jerry Rice/24 12.00 30.00
108 Jim Kelly/50 8.00 20.00
109 Jim Otto/50 5.00 12.00
111 Terrell Davis/50 8.00 20.00
114 Junior Seau/15 10.00 25.00
115 Rod Woodson/50 8.00 20.00
116 Sam Huff/50 6.00 15.00
117 Steve Bartkowski/50 6.00 15.00
118 Steve Young/50 10.00 25.00
119 Troy Aikman/50 10.00 25.00
120 Y.A. Tittle/50 8.00 20.00
121 Cris Collinsworth/50 6.00 15.00
125 Jerome Bettis/50 8.00 20.00
128 Alan Page/50 6.00 15.00
130 Barry Sanders/50 12.00 30.00
131 Bernie Kosar/50 6.00 15.00
132 Bob Griese/50 8.00 20.00
133 Bob Hayes/50 10.00 25.00
135 Bruce Smith/50 6.00 15.00
139 Boomer Esiason/50 6.00 15.00
141 Chuck Foreman/25 8.00 20.00
145 Derrick Thomas/50 40.00 100.00
146 Don Maynard/35 6.00 15.00
148 Eddie George/50 6.00 15.00
149 Emmitt Smith/50 12.00 30.00

1950 Lions Matchbooks

Universal Match Corp. produced these Detroit Lions matchcovers. Each measures approximately 1 1/2" by 4 1/2" (when completely folded out) and features a blue bordered front with the player's photo in black and white along with an advertisement for either Mello Crisp Potato Chips or Ray Whyte Chevy. Backs contain the 1950 Lions' sesaon schedule. The prices given are for full covers (with strikers) missing the actual matches. This is the form in which the matchbooks are most commonly found. Complete books with matches typically carry a 50% premium. Books missing the striker are considered VG at best.

1 Leon Hart 12.50 25.00
(Ray Whyte ad on back)
2 Doak Walker 15.00 30.00
(Mello Crisp ad on back)

1953-59 Lions McCarthy Postcards

Photographer J.D. McCarthy released a number of postcards throughout the 1950s to the early 1980s with many issued over a number of years. This group was most likely released during the 1950s as most feature older photographs and follow the same format of featuring a facsimile autograph on the cardfronts. Several players are featured on more than one card type with the differences noted below. Most also include a typical postcard style cardback, but some were printed blankbacked and many do contain back variations. There are two slightly different sizes that were used as well: larger 3 5/8" by 5 1/2" and smaller 3 1/4" by 5 1/2". It is thought that many of the postcards were reprinted from time to time, thus the reasoning behind what may seem like undervalued prices.

COMPLETE SET (108) 500.00 1,000.00
1A Charlie Ane 6.00 12.00
(three point stance)
1B Charlie Ane 6.00 12.00
(standing)
2A Vince Banonis 4.00 8.00
Oversized postcard,
no facsimile
2B Vince Banonis 4.00 8.00
Oversized postcard,
facsimile Autograph
2C Vince Banonis 4.00 8.00
smaller card
no logo on front
2D Vince Banonis 4.00 8.00
(smaller card
McCarthy logo on front)
3 Terry Barr 6.00 12.00
4A Les Bingaman 6.00 12.00
(larger postcard,
with helmet)
4B Les Bingaman 6.00 12.00
(larger card, no helmet)
4C Les Bingaman 6.00 12.00
(smaller card, no helmet)
5 Bill Bowman 4.00 8.00
6 Cloyce Box 7.50 15.00
7 Jim Cain DE 4.00 8.00
8 Stan Campbell 4.00 8.00
9 Lew Carpenter 4.00 8.00
10A Howard Cassady 7.50 15.00
(With ball)
10B Howard Cassady 7.50 15.00
(Standing)
11A Jack Christiansen 10.00 20.00
(kneeling pose)
11B Jack Christiansen 10.00 20.00
(running pose,
smaller card)
11C Jack Christiansen 10.00 20.00
(running pose,
larger card)
12A Ollie Cline 4.00 8.00
(all of left foot showing)
12B Ollie Cline 4.00 8.00
(left foot slightly cut out)
13A Lou Creekmur 10.00 20.00
(larger card)
13B Lou Creekmur 10.00 20.00
(smaller card)
14 Gene Cronin 4.00 8.00
15A Jim David 6.00 12.00
(larger card)
15B Jim David 6.00 12.00
(smaller card)
16A Dorne Dibble 4.00 8.00
(running pose)
16B Dorne Dibble 4.00 8.00
(kneeling pose)
17A Don Doll 6.00 12.00
(larger card)
17B Don Doll 4.00 8.00
(smaller card)
18A Jim Doran 6.00 12.00
(kneeling pose)
18B Jim Doran 6.00 12.00
(catching pass)
18C Jim Doran 6.00 12.00
(standing pose)
19 Bob Dove 4.00 8.00
20 Tom Dublinski 4.00 8.00
21 Sonny Gandee 4.00 8.00
22 Gene Gedman 4.00 8.00
23A Jim Gibbons 4.00 8.00
(kneeling pose,
black and white photo)
23B Jim Gibbons 4.00 8.00
(kneeling pose,
sepia photo)
23C Jim Gibbons 4.00 8.00
(catching pass)
24 Jug Girard 6.00 12.00
25 Bill Glass 4.00 8.00
26 Pat Harder 7.50 15.00
27 Leon Hart 12.50 25.00
28 Bob Hoernschemeyer 6.00 12.00
29 Doug Hogland 4.00 8.00
30A John Henry Johnson 12.50 25.00
(no greeting on back)
30B John Henry Johnson 12.50 25.00
(printed greeting on back)
31 Steve Junker 4.00 8.00
32 Carl Karilivacz 4.00 8.00
33 Alex Karras 12.50 25.00
34 Ray Krouse 4.00 8.00
35A Dick Lane 10.00 20.00
(no ad on back)
35B Dick Lane 10.00 20.00
(liquor ad on back)
36A Yale Lary 10.00 20.00
(larger card)
36B Yale Lary 10.00 20.00
(smaller card,
blankbacked)
36C Yale Lary 10.00 20.00
(smaller card,
postcard back)
37A Bobby Layne 20.00 40.00
(larger card)
37B Bobby Layne 20.00 40.00
(smaller card)
38 Dan Lewis 4.00 8.00
39 Gary Lowe 4.00 8.00
40A Gil Mains 4.00 8.00
(no ad on back)
40B Gil Mains 4.00 8.00
(realty ad on back)
41A Jim Martin 6.00 12.00
(punting pose)
41B Jim Martin 6.00 12.00
(kneeling pose,
larger card)
41C Jim Martin 6.00 12.00
(kneeling pose,
smaller card)
42 Darris McCord 4.00 8.00
43A Thurman McGraw 4.00 8.00
(larger card, with
facsimile autograph)
43B Thurman McGraw 6.00 12.00
(larger card, no
facsimile autograph)
43C Thurman McGraw 6.00 12.00
(smaller card)
44 Don McIlhenny 6.00 12.00
45 Andy Miketa 4.00 8.00
46A Dave Middleton 4.00 8.00
(kneeling pose)
46B Dave Middleton 4.00 8.00
(running pose)
47 Bob Miller 4.00 8.00
48A Earl Morrall 7.50 15.00
(black and white photo)
48B Earl Morrall 7.50 15.00
(sepia photo)
49 Buddy Parker CO 6.00 12.00
50 Gerry Perry 4.00 8.00
51 Nick Pietrosante 6.00 12.00
52A John Prchlik 4.00 8.00
(facsimile autograph)
53B John Prchlik 4.00 8.00
(no facsimile)
54 Jerry Reichow 4.00 8.00
55 Perry Richards 4.00 8.00
56 Lee Riley 4.00 8.00
57 Ken Russell 4.00 8.00
58 Tobin Rote 7.50 15.00
59 Tom Rychlec 4.00 8.00
60 Jim Salsbury 4.00 8.00
61A Joe Schmidt 12.50 25.00
(hands on knees)
61B Joe Schmidt 12.50 25.00
(kneeling pose)
62 Harley Sewell 6.00 12.00
63 Bob Smith RB 6.00 12.00
64 Oliver Spencer 4.00 8.00
65 Dick Stanfel 4.00 8.00
66 Bill Stits 4.00 8.00
67 Lavern Torgeson 4.00 8.00
68A Tom Tracy 4.00 8.00
(no ad on back)
68B Tom Tracy 4.00 8.00
(Pontiac ad on back)
69A Doak Walker 17.50 35.00
(larger card, Laughead photo)
69B Doak Walker 17.50 35.00
(smaller card, Laughead photo)
70A Wayne Walker 6.00 12.00
(running pose)
70B Wayne Walker 6.00 12.00
(portrait)
71 Ken Webb 4.00 8.00
72 Dave Whitsell 4.00 8.00
73A George Wilson CO 6.00 12.00
(no team name on front)
73B George Wilson CO 6.00 12.00
(team name on front)
74 Roger Zatkoff 4.00 8.00

1960-85 Lions McCarthy Postcards

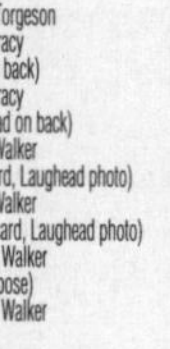

Photographer J.D. McCarthy released a number of postcards throughout the 1950s to the mid-1980s with many issued over a number of years. This group was most likely released gradually between 1960-1980 as most feature newer photographs and follow the similar format of including the player's name within a name plate below the photo. Several players are featured on more than one card type with the differences noted below. Most also include a typical postcard style cardback, but some were printed blankbacked and many do contain back variations. It is thought that many of the postcards were reprinted from time to time, thus the reasoning behind what may seem like undervalued prices.

COMPLETE SET (92) 200.00 400.00
1 Jimmy Allen 2.00 4.00
2 Al Baker 4.00 8.00
3 Larry Ball 2.00 4.00
4A Lem Barney 7.50 15.00
((portrait)
4B Lem Barney 7.50 15.00
(kneeling pose)
5A Lynn Boden 2.00 4.00
(standing)
5B Lynn Boden 2.00 4.00
(kneeling)
6 Craig Cotton 2.00 4.00
7 Leon Crosswhite 2.00 4.00
8A Gary Danielson 3.00 6.00
(facing straight ahead)
8B Gary Danielson 3.00 6.00
(facing straight with
Golling Datsun ad on back)
8C Gary Danielson 2.00 4.00
(facing straight with
multiple Datsun ads on back)
8D Gary Danielson 3.00 6.00
(facing slightly to right)
9 Nick Eddy 2.00 4.00
10A Doug English 3.00 6.00
(action photos)
10B Doug English 3.00 6.00
(kneeling pose)
11A Mel Farr 3.00 6.00
(standing)
11B Mel Farr 3.00 6.00
(kneeling)
12 Bobby Felts 2.00 4.00
13 Ed Flanagan 2.00 4.00
14 Rockne Freitas 2.00 4.00
15 Frank Gallagher 2.00 4.00
16 Billy Gambrell 2.00 4.00
17A Jim Gibbons 2.00 4.00
(White name box
barely visible,
no ad on back)
17B Jim Gibbons 3.00 6.00
(White name box
barely visible, Palmer
Moving ad on back)
18 Bob Grottkau 2.00 4.00
19 Larry Hand 3.00 6.00
20 R.W. Hicks 2.00 4.00
21 Billy Howard 2.00 4.00
22 James Hunter 2.00 4.00
23 Ray Jarvis 2.00 4.00
24 Dick Jauron 4.00 8.00
25A Ron Jessie UER 3.00 6.00
name misspelled Jessi
25B Ron Jessie 3.00 6.00
26 Levi Johnson 2.00 4.00
27 Horace King 2.00 4.00
28A Bob Kowalkowski 2.00 4.00
('Guard' listed below photo)
28B Bob Kowalkowski 2.00 4.00
(wall in background)
28C Bob Kowalkowski 2.00 4.00
(trees in background)
29A Greg Landry 4.00 8.00
(with helmet and football)
29B Greg Landry 4.00 8.00
(with helmet only in stadium)
29C Greg Landry 4.00 8.00
(with helmet only
at training camp)
30 Dick Lane 5.00 10.00
(kneeling pose)
31A Dick Lebeau 3.00 6.00
(McCarthy logo on right)
31B Dick Lebeau 3.00 6.00
(McCarthy logo on left)
32A Mike Lucci 3.00 6.00
(portrait with McCarthy
logo on left)
32B Mike Lucci 3.00 6.00
(large face portrait)
32C Mike Lucci 3.00 6.00
(portrait with helmet
in left hand)
32D Mike Lucci 3.00 6.00
(kneeling with McCarthy
logo at right)
32E Mike Lucci 3.00 6.00
(kneeling with McCarthy
logo at left)
33 Bruce Maher 2.00 4.00
34A Errol Mann 2.00 4.00
(hands on hips)
34B Errol Mann 2.00 4.00
(standing holding helmet)
35 Amos Marsh 2.00 4.00
36 Earl McCullouch 2.00 4.00
37 Jim Mitchell 2.00 4.00
38 Bill Munson 3.00 6.00
39 Eddie Murray 3.00 6.00
40 Paul Naumoff 2.00 4.00
41 Orlando Nelson 2.00 4.00
42 Herb Orvis 2.00 4.00
43A Steve Owens 5.00 10.00
(right hand on helmet)
43B Steve Owens 5.00 10.00
(Reynolds Aluminum
sign in view)
43C Steve Owens 5.00 10.00
(facing straight ahead)
43D Steve Owens 5.00 10.00
(facing left)
43E Steve Owens 5.00 10.00
(white letter name
without box)
43F Steve Owens 2.00 4.00
(wearing black arm band)
44 Ernie Price 2.00 4.00
45 Wayne Rasmussen 2.00 4.00
46 Rudy Redmond 2.00 4.00
47A Charlie Sanders 4.00 8.00
(standing pose, no
clock in view)
47B Charlie Sanders 4.00 8.00
(standing pose,/3:24 on clock)
47C Charlie Sanders 4.00 8.00
(squatting pose)
47D Charlie Sanders 4.00 8.00
(kneeling pose, with
football and helmet)
47E Charlie Sanders 4.00 8.00
(kneeling pose
in training camp)
47F Charlie Sanders 4.00 8.00
(kneeling pose
in Tiger Stadium)
47G Charlie Sanders 4.00 8.00
(kneeling pose, left
hand under chin)
48 Freddie Scott 3.00 6.00
49 Bobby Thompson 2.00 4.00
50 Leonard Thompson 3.00 6.00
51A Bill Triplett 2.00 4.00
(McCarthy logo on left)
51B Bill Triplett 2.00 4.00
(McCarthy logo on right)
52A Wayne Walker 3.00 6.00
kneeling pose
with helmet)
52B Wayne Walker 3.00 6.00
kneeling pose
without helmet)
53 Jim Weatherall 2.00 4.00
54 Charlie Weaver 2.00 4.00
55 Herman Weaver 2.00 4.00
56A Mike Weger 2.00 4.00
(McCarthy logo on left)
56B Mike Weger 2.00 4.00
(McCarthy logo on right)
57 Bobby Williams 2.00 4.00
58 Jim Yarbrough 2.00 4.00
59 Garo Yepremian 4.00 8.00

1961 Lions Jay Publishing

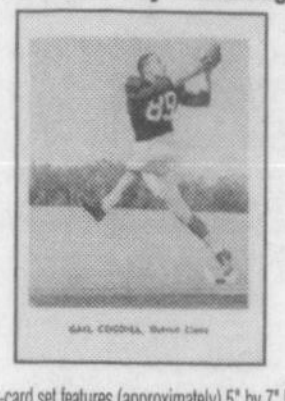

This 12-card set features (approximately) 5" by 7" black-and-white player photos. The photos show players in traditional poses with the quarterback preparing to throw, the runner heading downfield, and the defenseman ready for the tackle. These cards were packaged 12 to a packet and originally sold for 25 cents. The backs are blank. The cards are unnumbered and checklisted below in alphabetical order.

COMPLETE SET (12) 50.00 100.00
1 Carl Brettschneider 4.00 8.00
2 Howard Cassady 5.00 10.00
3 Gail Cogdill 4.00 8.00
4 Jim Gibbons 4.00 8.00
5 Alex Karras 6.00 12.00
6 Yale Lary 6.00 12.00
7 Jim Martin 4.00 8.00
8 Earl Morrall 5.00 10.00
9 Jim Ninowski 5.00 10.00
10 Nick Pietrosante 4.00 8.00
11 Joe Schmidt 6.00 12.00
12 George Wilson CO 4.00 8.00

1961 Lions Team Issue

The Lions issued these photos around 1961. Each features a black and white player image, measures roughly 7 3/4" by 9 1/2" and is surrounded by a thin white border. The player's name and position is printed in a small box within the photo. The backs are blank and we've listed the photos alphabetically below.

COMPLETE SET (12) 75.00 125.00
1 Terry Barr 5.00 10.00
2 Howard Cassady 6.00 12.00
3 Gail Cogdill 5.00 10.00
4 Jim Gibbons 6.00 12.00
5 Dick Lane 7.50 15.00
6 Yale Lary 7.50 15.00
7 Dan Lewis 5.00 10.00
8 Jim Martin 5.00 10.00
9 Earl Morrall 7.50 15.00
10 Jim Ninowski 6.00 12.00
11 Nick Pietrosante 5.00 10.00
12 Joe Schmidt 10.00 20.00

1961-62 Lions Falstaff Beer Team Photos

These oversized (roughly 6 1/4" by 9") color team photos were sponsored by Falstaff Beer and distributed in the Detroit area. Each was printed on card stock and included advertising messages and the Lions season schedule on the back.

1961 Lions Team 18.00 30.00
1962 Lions Team 18.00 30.00

1963-67 Lions Team Issue 8x10

The Detroit Lions issued these photos printed on glossy photographic stock. Each measures approximately 8" by 10" and features a black and white photo. The player's name, position, and team name appear below the photo on most of the pictures. However, a few photos catalogued below do not include the player's position. Therefore it is likely that the photos were released over a period of years. A photographer's imprint can often be found on the backs.

COMPLETE SET (23) 100.00 200.00
1 Lem Barney 7.50 15.00
2 Charley Bradshaw 5.00 10.00
3 Roger Brown DT 5.00 10.00
4 Ernie Clark 5.00 10.00
5 Gail Cogdill 5.00 10.00
6 John Gordy 5.00 10.00
7 Wally Hilgenberg 6.00 12.00
8 Alex Karras 7.50 15.00
(facing straight ahead)
9 Alex Karras 7.50 15.00
(facing to his left)
10 Bob Kowalkowski 5.00 10.00
11 Dick LeBeau 5.00 10.00
12 Joe Don Looney 6.00 12.00
13 Mike Lucci 6.00 12.00
14 Bruce Maher 5.00 10.00
15 Paul Naumoff 5.00 10.00
16 Tom Nowatzke 5.00 10.00
17 Milt Plum 6.00 12.00
18 Pat Studstill 5.00 10.00
(football at chest)
19 Pat Studstill 5.00 10.00
(football on right hip)
20 Pat Studstill 5.00 10.00
(football tucked under arm)
21 Karl Sweetan 5.00 10.00
22 Bobby Thompson 5.00 10.00
23 Wayne Walker 5.00 10.00

1964-65 Lions Team Issue

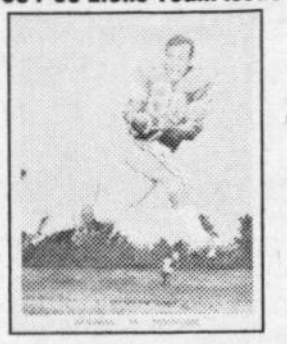

The Lions issued single photos and photo packs to fans throughout the mid 1960s. Each photo in this set is a black and white 7 3/8" by 9 3/8" posed action shot surrounded by a white border. The player's name, position, and team name are printed on a single line below the photo. The print type, style, and size are identical on each photo. However, some of the players were issued in one or more years as some of the cards can be found with a date (either Oct. 1, 1964 or Sep. 24, 1965) stamped in blue ink on the cardback while others have no stamp. Of those known to be stamped, we've included the year(s) below. The cards also look identical to the 1966 issue. Players found in both sets have the specific differences noted below.

COMPLETE SET (40)	150.00	300.00
1 Terry Barr 65	5.00	10.00
2 Roger Brown DT 65	5.00	10.00
(jersey number hidden)		
3 Gail Cogdill 64	5.00	10.00
(OE listed as position)		
4 Dick Compton 64/65	5.00	10.00
5 Larry Ferguson 65	5.00	10.00
6 Dennis Gaubatz 64/65	5.00	10.00
7 Jim Gibbons 64/65	6.00	12.00
(OE listed as position)		
8 John Gonzaga 64/65	5.00	10.00
9 John Gordy 64/65	5.00	10.00
(OG-T listed as position)		
10 Tom Hall 65	5.00	10.00
11 Ron Kramer	5.00	10.00
(head shot photo)		
12 Roger LaLonde 65	5.00	10.00
13 Dick Lane 64	7.50	15.00
14 Dan LaRose 65	5.00	10.00
15 Yale Lary 64/65	7.50	15.00
16 Dick LeBeau 65	5.00	10.00
(DHB listed as position)		
17 Monte Lee 65	5.00	10.00
18 Dan Lewis 64/65	5.00	10.00
19 Gary Lowe 65	5.00	10.00
20 Bruce Maher 64	5.00	10.00
(DHB listed as position)		
21 Darris McCord 64/65	5.00	10.00
(both feet on ground in photo)		
22 Hugh McInnis 65	5.00	10.00
23 Max Messner 65	5.00	10.00
24 Floyd Peters 65	5.00	10.00
25 Nick Pietrosante 65	5.00	10.00
26 Milt Plum 65	6.00	12.00
(passing with ball above head)		
27 Bill Quinlan 65	5.00	10.00
28 Nick Ryder 65	5.00	10.00
29 Daryl Sanders 65	5.00	10.00
(OT listed as position)		
30 Joe Schmidt 64/65	7.50	15.00
31 Bob Scholtz 65	5.00	10.00
32 James Simon 64	5.00	10.00
33 J.D. Smith T 65	5.00	10.00
(running right)		
34 Pat Studstill 65	5.00	10.00
(HB listed as position)		
35 Larry Vargo 65	5.00	10.00
36 Wayne Walker 64/65	5.00	10.00
(facing right)		
37 Tom Watkins 64/65	5.00	10.00
(OHB listed as position)		
38 Warren Wells 65	5.00	10.00
39 Bob Whitlow 65	5.00	10.00
40 Sam Williams 64	5.00	10.00

1966 Lions Marathon Oil

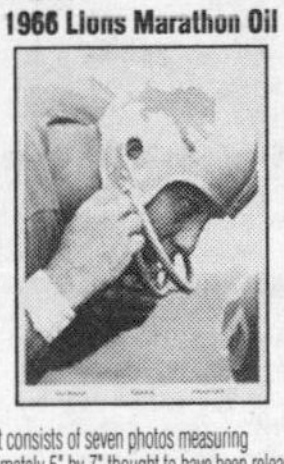

This set consists of seven photos measuring approximately 5" by 7" thought to have been released by Marathon Oil. The fronts feature black-and-white photos with white borders. The player's name, position, and team name are printed in the bottom border. The backs are blank. The cards are unnumbered and checklisted below in alphabetical order.

COMPLETE SET (7)	30.00	60.00
1 Gail Cogdill	5.00	10.00
2 John Gordy	5.00	10.00
3 Alex Karras	7.50	15.00
4 Ron Kramer	5.00	10.00
5 Milt Plum	6.00	12.00
6 Wayne Rasmussen	5.00	10.00
7 Daryl Sanders	5.00	10.00

1966 Lions Team Issue

The Detroit Lions issued this set of large photos to Lions' fans who requested player pictures in 1966. Each measures approximately 7 1/2" by 9 1/2" and features a black and white photo. The player's name, position, and team name appear below the photo. The cards look identical to the 1964-65 issue. Players found in both sets have the specific differences noted below.

COMPLETE SET (41)	150.00	300.00
1 Mike Alford	5.00	10.00
2 Roger Brown	5.00	10.00
(jersey number in view)		
3 Ernie Clark	5.00	10.00
4 Bill Cody	5.00	10.00
5 Gail Cogdill	5.00	10.00
(E listed as position)		
6 Ed Flanagan	5.00	10.00
7 Jim Gibbons	5.00	10.00
(E listed as position)		
8 John Gordy	5.00	10.00
(G listed as position)		
9 Larry Hand	5.00	10.00
10 John Henderson	5.00	10.00
11 Wally Hilgenberg	6.00	12.00
12 Alex Karras	7.50	15.00
13 Bob Kowalkowski	5.00	10.00
14 Ron Kramer	5.00	10.00
(action shot photo)		
15 Dick LeBeau	5.00	10.00
(DB listed as position)		
16 Joe Don Looney	6.00	12.00
17 Mike Lucci	6.00	12.00
18 Bruce Maher	5.00	10.00
(DB listed as position)		
19 Bill Malinchak	5.00	10.00
20 Amos Marsh	5.00	10.00
21 Jerry Mazzanti	5.00	10.00
22 Darris McCord	5.00	10.00
(one foot on ground in photo)		
23 Bruce McLenna	5.00	10.00
24 Tom Nowatzke	5.00	10.00
25 Milt Plum	6.00	12.00
(passing with ball to his side)		
26 Wayne Rasmussen	5.00	10.00
27 Johnnie Robinson DB	5.00	10.00
28 Jerry Rush	5.00	10.00
29 Daryl Sanders	5.00	10.00
(T listed as position)		
30 Bobby Smith	5.00	10.00
31 J.D. Smith	5.00	10.00
(running left)		
32 Pat Studstill	5.00	10.00
(FL listed as position)		
33 Karl Sweetan	5.00	10.00
34 Bobby Thompson	5.00	10.00
35 Jim Todd	5.00	10.00
36 Doug Van Horn	5.00	10.00
37 Tom Vaughn	5.00	10.00
38 Wayne Walker	5.00	10.00
(facing forward)		
39 Willie Walker	5.00	10.00
40 Tom Watkins	5.00	10.00
(HB listed as position)		
41 Coaching Staff	10.00	20.00
John North		
Lou Rymkus		
Harry Gilmer		
Carl Taseff		
Carl Brettschneider		
Sammy Baugh		
Joe Schmidt		

1968 Lions Tasco Prints

Tasco Associates produced this set of Detroit Lions prints. The fronts feature a large color artist's rendering of the player along with the player's name and position. The backs are blank. The prints measure approximately 11 1/2" by 16."

COMPLETE SET (7)	50.00	100.00
1 Lem Barney	7.50	15.00
2 Mel Farr	5.00	10.00
3 Alex Karras	15.00	25.00
4 Dick LeBeau	5.00	10.00
5 Mike Lucci	6.00	12.00
6 Earl McCullouch	5.00	10.00
7 Bill Munson	6.00	12.00
8 Wayne Rasmussen	5.00	10.00
9 Jerry Rush	5.00	10.00

1986 Lions Police

This 14-card set of Detroit Lions is numbered on the card backs, which are printed in black ink on white card stock. Cards measure approximately 2 5/8" by 4 1/8". The set was sponsored by the Detroit Lions, Oscar Mayer, Claussen, WJR/WHYT, the Detroit Crime Prevention Section, and the Pontiac Police Athletic League. Uniform numbers are printed on the card front along with the player's name and position.

COMPLETE SET (14)	2.50	6.00
1 William Gay	.20	.50
2 Pontiac Silverdome	.20	.50
3 Leonard Thompson	.25	.60
4 Eddie Murray	.30	.75
5 Eric Hipple	.30	.75
6 James Jones	.30	.75
7 Darryl Rogers CO	.20	.50
8 Chuck Long	.30	.75
9 Garry James	.25	.60
10 Michael Cofer	.25	.60
11 Jeff Chadwick	.25	.60
12 Jimmy Williams	.20	.50
13 Keith Dorney	.20	.50
14 Bobby Watkins	.20	.50

1987 Lions Ace Fact Pack

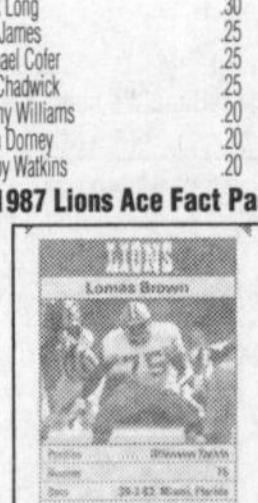

This 33 card set measures approximately 2 1/4" by 3 5/8". This set features members of the Detroit Lions and has rounded corners. The back of the cards features a design for "Ace" like a playing card. These cards were manufactured in West Germany (by Ace Fact Pack) and we have checklisted this set alphabetically.

COMPLETE SET (33)	30.00	80.00
1 Carl Bland	1.25	3.00
2 Lomas Brown	2.00	5.00
3 Jeff Chadwick	1.25	3.00
4 Michael Cofer	1.25	3.00
5 Keith Dorney	1.25	3.00
6 Keith Ferguson	1.25	3.00
7 William Gay	1.25	3.00
8 James Harrell	1.25	3.00
9 Eric Hipple	2.00	5.00
10 Garry James	2.00	5.00
11 Demetrious Johnson	1.25	3.00
12 James Jones	2.00	5.00
13 Chuck Long	2.00	5.00
14 Vernon Maxwell	1.25	3.00
15 Bruce McNorton	1.25	3.00
16 Devon Mitchell	1.25	3.00
17 Steve Mott	1.25	3.00
18 Eddie Murray	2.00	5.00
19 Harvey Salem	1.25	3.00
20 Rich Stenger	1.25	3.00
21 Eric Williams	2.00	5.00
22 Jimmy Williams	1.25	3.00
23 Lions Helmet	1.25	3.00
24 Lions Information	1.25	3.00
25 Lions Uniform	1.25	3.00
26 Game Record Holders	1.25	3.00
27 Season Record Holders	1.25	3.00
28 Career Record Holders	1.25	3.00
29 Record 1967-86	1.25	3.00
30 1986 Team Statistics	1.25	3.00
31 All-Time Greats	1.25	3.00
32 Championship Seasons	1.25	3.00
33 Pontiac Silverdome	1.25	3.00

1987 Lions Police

This 14-card set of Detroit Lions is numbered on the back. The card backs are printed in blue ink on white card stock and contain a safety tip entitled "Little Oscar Says". Cards measure approximately 2 5/8" by 4 1/8". The set was sponsored by the Detroit Lions, Oscar Mayer, Claussen Pickles, WJR/WHYT, the Detroit Crime Prevention Section, and the Pontiac Police Athletic League. Uniform numbers are printed on the card front along with the player's name and position. Reportedly, nearly three million cards were distributed through the participating police agencies. The Lions team name appears above the player photo which differentiates this set from the 1988 Police Lions set.

COMPLETE SET (14)	2.50	6.00
1 Michael Cofer	.20	.50
Vernon Maxwell		
William Gay		
2 Rich Strenger	.15	.40
3 Keith Ferguson	.15	.40
4 James Jones	.25	.60
5 Jeff Chadwick	.20	.50
6 Devon Mitchell	.15	.40
7 Eddie Murray	.25	.60
8 Reggie Rogers	.20	.50
9 Chuck Long	.25	.60
10 Jimmie Giles	.25	.60
11 Eric Williams	.15	.40
12 Lomas Brown	.20	.50
13 Jimmy Williams	.15	.40
14 Garry James	.20	.50

1988 Lions Police

The 1988 Police Detroit Lions set contains 14 numbered cards measuring approximately 2 5/8" by 4 1/8". There are 13 single player cards plus one for Detroit's top three 1988 draft picks. The backs have career highlights and safety tips. The Lions team name appears below the player photo which differentiates this set from the similar-looking 1987 Police Lions set.

COMPLETE SET (14)	2.00	5.00
1 Rob Rubick	.20	.50
2 Paul Butcher	.20	.50
3 Pete Mandley	.25	.60
4 Jimmy Williams	.20	.50
5 Harvey Salem	.20	.50
6 Chuck Long	.25	.60
7 Pat Carter	.25	.60
Bennie Blades		
Chris Spielman		
8 Jerry Ball	.30	.75
9 Lomas Brown	.25	.60
10 Dennis Gibson	.20	.50
11 Jim Arnold	.20	.50
12 Michael Cofer	.20	.50
13 James Jones	.25	.60
14 Steve Mott	.20	.50

1989 Lions Police

The 1989 Police Detroit Lions set contains 12 numbered cards measuring approximately 2 5/8" by 4 1/8". The set was also sponsored by Oscar Mayer. The fronts have white borders and color action photos; some are horizontally oriented, others are vertically oriented. The horizontally oriented backs have safety tips and brief career highlights. These cards were printed on very thin stock. The set is notable for a card of Barry Sanders, showing a photo of him at his postdraft press conference. It has been reported that three million cards were given away during this program by police officers in Michigan and Ontario.

COMPLETE SET (12)	5.00	12.00
1 George Jamison	.15	.40
2 Wayne Fontes CO	.20	.50
3 Kevin Glover	.15	.40
4 Chris Spielman	.40	1.00
5 Eddie Murray	.20	.50
6 Bennie Blades	.30	.75
7 Joe Milinichik	.15	.40
8 Michael Cofer	.15	.40
9 Jerry Ball	.20	.50
10 Dennis Gibson	.15	.40
11 Barry Sanders	4.00	10.00
12 Jim Arnold	.15	.40

1990 Lions Police

This 12 card set was issued by Oscar Mayer in conjunction with the Detroit Lions, Claussen, WWJ radio station, the Detroit Crime Prevention Society, and the Crime Prevention Association of Michigan. The fronts of the cards feature an action photo of the player on the front and a drawing of the player along with a brief note about the player on the back. In addition there is a safety tip from Little Oscar (the symbol for Oscar Mayer) on the back. The cards measure approximately 2 5/8" by 4 1/8".

COMPLETE SET (12)	3.20	8.00
1 William White	.14	.35
2 Chris Spielman	.30	.75
3 Rodney Peete	.40	1.00
4 Jimmy Williams	.14	.35
5 Bennie Blades	.20	.50
6 Barry Sanders	2.00	5.00
7 Jerry Ball	.20	.50
8 Richard Johnson	.20	.50
9 Michael Cofer	.14	.35
10 Lomas Brown	.20	.50
11 Joe Schmidt GM	.30	.75
Andre Ware		
Wayne Fontes CO		
12 Eddie Murray	.20	.50

1991 Lions Police

This 12-card Police Lions set was distributed during the season by participating Michigan police departments. The cards measure approximately 2 5/8" by 4 1/8" and feature color action shots of each player enclosed in a yellow border on thin card stock. Oscar Mayer's logo, player's name, and team helmet appearing at the bottom of each card are highlighted by blue lines above and below. Card backs, printed vertically, carry a black and white head shot of the player, player information, while a safety tip from the main sponsor appears at the bottom left half of card. The bottom right half lists card numbers and other sponsor names.

COMPLETE SET (12)	2.40	6.00
1 Mel Gray	.25	.60
2 Ken Dallafior	.14	.35
3 Chris Spielman	.25	.60
4 Bennie Blades	.20	.50
5 Robert Clark	.20	.50
6 Eric Andolsek	.20	.50
7 Rodney Peete	.30	.75
8 William White	.14	.35
9 Lomas Brown	.20	.50
10 Jerry Ball	.20	.50
11 Michael Cofer	.14	.35
12 Barry Sanders	1.20	3.00

1993 Lions 60th Season Commemorative

These 16 standard-size 60th-season commemorative cards feature borderless player photos on their fronts. Some photos are color, others are black-and-white; some are action shots, others are posed. The player's name (or the card's title), the rectangle it appears in, and the 60th season logo, all appear in team colors. The white backs carry black-and-white head shots of the players. Also appearing are the players' names, the years they played for the Lions, position, and career highlights. The team color-coded 60th season logo reappears in a lower corner. The cards came with their own approximately 6" by 8" four-page black vinyl card holder emblazoned with the Lions' 60th season logo.

COMPLETE SET (16)	10.00	25.00
1 Barry Sanders	4.80	12.00
2 Joe Schmidt	.60	1.50
3 The Fearsome Foursome	.30	.75
Sam Williams		
Roger Brown		
Alex Karras		
Darris McCord		
4 Chris Spielman	.30	.75
5 Billy Sims	.30	.75
6 '40s Phenoms	.30	.75
Alex Wojciechowicz		
Byron(Whizzer) White		
7 Thunder and Lightning	.20	.50
Bennie Blades		
Mel Gray		
8 Bobby Layne	1.20	3.00
9 Dutch Clark	.30	.75
10 Great Games	.20	.50
Thanksgiving 1962		
11 Charlie Sanders	.30	.75
12 Lomas Brown	.20	.50
13 Doug English	.30	.75
14 Doak Walker	.80	2.00
15 Roaring '20s	1.60	4.00
Lem Barney		
Billy Sims		
Barry Sanders		
16 Anniversary Card	.20	.50

2005 Lions Activa Medallions

COMPLETE SET (21)	30.00	60.00
1 Jeff Backus	1.25	3.00
2 Boss Bailey	1.25	3.00
3 Dre Bly	1.25	3.00
4 Shaun Cody	1.25	3.00
5 Eddie Drummond	1.25	3.00
6 Jeff Garcia	1.50	4.00
7 James Hall	1.25	3.00
8 Jason Hanson	1.25	3.00
9 Joey Harrington	1.50	4.00
10 Kevin Jones	1.50	4.00
11 Kenoy Kennedy	1.25	3.00
12 Teddy Lehman	1.25	3.00
13 Marcus Pollard	1.25	3.00
14 Cory Redding	1.25	3.00
15 Charles Rogers	1.25	3.00
16 Shaun Rogers	1.25	3.00
17 Cory Schlesinger	1.25	3.00
18 Mike Williams	.75	2.00
19 Roy Williams WR	1.50	4.00
20 Damien Woody	1.25	3.00
21 Lions Logo	1.00	2.50

2006 Lions Donruss Thanksgiving Classic

COMPLETE SET (7)	6.00	12.00
DT1 Jon Kitna	.60	1.50
DT2 Kevin Jones	.50	1.25
DT3 Roy Williams WR	.60	1.50
DT4 Brian Calhoun	.50	1.25
DT5 Ernie Sims	.60	1.50
DT6 Billy Sims	.75	2.00
NNO Cover Card CL	.20	.50

2006 Lions Super Bowl XL

Each card manufacturer produced 3-cards to be distributed at the Super Bowl XL Card Show in Detroit via wrapper redemption programs. The design varies from manufacturer and slightly from card-to-card but each is numbered on the back as part of the 9-card set.

COMPLETE SET (9)	6.00	15.00
1 Barry Sanders	1.25	3.00
Topps		
2 Roy Williams WR	.60	1.50
Topps		
3 Kevin Jones	.60	1.50
Topps		
4 Joey Harrington	.60	1.50
Upper Deck		
5 Dan Orlovsky	.75	2.00
Upper Deck		
6 Boss Bailey	.50	1.25
Upper Deck		
7 Mike Williams	.75	2.00
Donruss/Playoff		
8 Shaun Rogers	.50	1.25
Donruss/Playoff		
9 Marcus Pollard	.50	1.25
Donruss/Playoff		

2006 Lions Topps

COMPLETE SET (12)	3.00	6.00
DET1 Charles Rogers	.25	.60
DET2 Kevin Jones	.20	.50
DET3 Roy Williams WR	.25	.60
DET4 Mike Williams	.20	.50
DET5 Scottie Vines	.20	.50
DET6 Daniel Bullocks	.30	.75
DET7 Dre Bly	.20	.50
DET8 Marcus Pollard	.20	.50
DET9 Josh McCown	.20	.50
DET10 Jon Kitna	.25	.60
DET11 Brian Calhoun	.20	.50
DET12 Ernie Sims	.25	.60

2007 Lions Donruss Thanksgiving Classic

COMPLETE SET (4)	3.00	8.00
1 Calvin Johnson	2.50	6.00
2 Roy Williams WR	.50	1.25
3 Jon Kitna	.40	1.00
4 Barry Sanders	1.00	2.50

2007 Lions Topps

COMPLETE SET (12)	3.00	6.00
1 Roy Williams WR	.25	.60
2 Kevin Jones	.20	.50
3 Mike Furrey	.25	.60
4 Jason Hanson	.20	.50
5 Ernie Sims	.20	.50
6 Jon Kitna	.20	.50
7 Shaun McDonald	.20	.50
8 T.J. Duckett	.20	.50
9 Tatum Bell	.20	.50
10 Shaun Rogers	.20	.50
11 Calvin Johnson	1.50	4.00
12 Drew Stanton	.20	.50

2008 Lions Topps

COMPLETE SET (12)	2.50	5.00
1 Roy Williams WR	.25	.60
2 Jon Kitna	.25	.60
3 Shaun McDonald	.20	.50
4 Ernie Sims	.20	.50
5 Kevin Jones	.20	.50
6 Calvin Johnson	.30	.75
7 Mike Furrey	.25	.60
8 Leigh Bodden	.20	.50
9 Tatum Bell	.20	.50
10 Paris Lenon	.20	.50
11 Kevin Smith	.40	1.00
12 Jordon Dizon	.40	1.00

1990 Little Big Leaguers

This 95-page book/album was published by Simon and Schuster and includes boyhood stories of today's pro football players. Moreover, five 8 1/2" by 11" sheets of cards (nine cards per sheet) are inserted at the end of the album; after perforation, the cards measure the standard size. The fronts feature black and white photos of these players as kids. The cards have blue and white borders, and in the thicker blue borders above and below the picture, one finds the player's name and the words "Little Football Big Leaguers" respectively. The backs have the same design, only with biography and career summary in place of the picture. The cards are unnumbered and checklisted below in alphabetical order.

COMPLETE SET (45)	24.00	60.00
1 Troy Aikman	4.00	10.00
2 Morten Andersen	.30	.75
3 Jerry Ball	.30	.75
4 Carl Banks	.30	.75
5 Bennie Blades	.30	.75
6 Brian Blades	.40	1.00
7 Joey Browner	.30	.75
8 Keith Byars	.40	1.00
9 Anthony Carter	.30	.75
10 Deron Cherry	.30	.75
11 Roger Craig	.40	1.00
12 John Elway	6.00	15.00
13 Doug Flutie	2.00	5.00
14 Tim Goad	.30	.75
15 Bob Golic	.30	.75
16 Dino Hackett	.30	.75
17 Dan Hampton	.30	.75
18 Bobby Hebert	.30	.75
19 Darryl Henley	.30	.75
20 Wes Hopkins	.30	.75
21 Hank Ilesic	.30	.75
22 Tunch Ilkin	.30	.75
23 Perry Kemp	.30	.75
24 Bernie Kosar	.40	1.00
25 Mike Lansford	.30	.75
26 Shawn Lee	.30	.75
27 Charles Mann	.30	.75
28 Dan Marino	6.00	15.00
29 Bruce Matthews	.40	1.00
30 Clay Matthews	.30	.75
31 Freeman McNeil	.30	.75
32 Warren Moon	1.00	2.50
33 Anthony Munoz	.40	1.00
34 Andre Reed	.40	1.00
35 Andre Rison	.40	1.00
36 Phil Simms	1.00	2.50
37 Mike Singletary	.40	1.00
38 Rohn Stark	.30	.75
39 Kelly Stouffer	.30	.75
40 Vinny Testaverde	.40	1.00
41 Doug Williams	.30	.75
42 Marc Wilson	.30	.75
43 Craig Wolfley	.30	.75
44 Ron Wolfley	.30	.75
45 Steve Young	3.20	8.00

2004 Los Angeles Avengers AFL

This 12-card set was issued by the team in a perforated sheet format and features several different sponsor logos on the cardfronts. The player's image is in color within a red border that features the words "Avenger Football" running down the left side.

COMPLETE SET (12)	6.00	12.00
1 Remy Hamilton	.50	1.25
2 Chris Butterfield	.50	1.25
3 Chris Jackson	1.00	2.50
4 Sean McNamara	.50	1.25
5 Greg Hopkins	1.00	2.50
6 Damen Wheeler	.50	1.25
7 Kevin Ingram	.60	1.50
8 Henry Douglas	.60	1.50
9 Lonnie Ford	.60	1.50
10 Carlos Fowler	.50	1.25
11 Al Lucas	.50	1.25
12 Tony Graziani	1.00	2.50

2007 Los Angeles Avengers AFL

COMPLETE SET (12)	6.00	12.00
1 Sonny Cumbie	.60	1.50
2 Silas Demary	.40	1.00
3 Lonnie Ford	.40	1.00
4 Remy Hamilton	.50	1.25
5 Kevin Ingram	.40	1.00
6 Lenzie Jackson	.40	1.00
7 Sean McNamara	.40	1.00
8 Brandon Perkins	.40	1.00
9 Robert Quiroga	.40	1.00
10 Jason Stewart	.40	1.00
11 Rob Turner	.40	1.00
12 Damen Wheeler	.40	1.00

2008 Los Angeles Avengers AFL

COMPLETE SET (12)	5.00	10.00
1 Sonny Cumbie	.60	1.50
2 Lonnie Ford	.40	1.00
3 Tim Hicks	.40	1.00
4 Kevin Ingram	.40	1.00
5 Josh Jeffries	.40	1.00
6 Ken Jones	.40	1.00
7 Timon Marshall	.40	1.00
8 Sean McNamara	.40	1.00
9 Brandon Perkins	.40	1.00
10 Jason Stewart	.40	1.00
11 Lashaun Ward	.40	1.00
12 Damen Wheeler	.40	1.00

2001 Louisville Fire AF2

This set was produced for and distributed by the Louisville Fire Arena Football 2 team. The unnumbered cards are sponsored by SunCom and feature a color photo of the player on the front and a black and white cardback.

COMPLETE SET (12)	6.00	12.00
1 Alan Campos	.40	1.00
2 Leroy Frederick	.40	1.00
3 John Fuqua	.50	1.25
4 Brian McDonald	.40	1.00
5 Anthony Payton	.40	1.00
6 Matt Pike	.60	1.50
7 Ron Selesky CO	.40	1.00
8 Charles Sheffield	.40	1.00
9 Leland Taylor	.40	1.00
10 Jabir Walker	.40	1.00
11 Bobby Washington	.50	1.25
12 Team Photo CL	.40	1.00

2004 Louisville Fire AF2

This set was issued by the team and sponsored by Speedway. Each card was printed in full color and produced on very thin card stock. No year of issue or card number is provided on the cards. They are arranged alphabetically below for ease in cataloging.

COMPLETE SET (20)	10.00	20.00
1 Marvin Constant	.40	1.00
2 Sam Crenshaw	.50	1.25
3 Jason Fergueson	.40	1.00
4 Demetrius Forney	.40	1.00
5 Dennis Fryzel	.40	1.00
6 Takuya Furutani	.40	1.00
7 Tommy Johnson CO	.50	1.25
8 Antwan Lawrence	.40	1.00
9 Nick Myers	.40	1.00
10 Anthony Payton	.40	1.00
11 Marc Samuel	.40	1.00
12 Matt Sauk	.50	1.25
13 James Scott	.40	1.00
14 Derrick Shephard	.40	1.00
15 Tony Stallings	.40	1.00
16 Vic Vrabel	.40	1.00
17 Saru Wantanbe	.40	1.00
18 Kenta Yagi	.40	1.00
19 Axe (Mascot)	.40	1.00
20 Team Photo	.40	1.00
(Checklist)		

1968 MacGregor Advisory Staff

MacGregor released a number of player photos during the 1960s. Each measures roughly 8" by 10 1/2" and carries a black and white photo of the player. Included below the photo is a note that the player is a member of MacGregor's advisory staff. The photos are blankbacked and unnumbered and checklisted below in alphabetical order. Any additions to the list below are appreciated.

1 Mike Ditka	15.00	30.00
2 Joe Namath	30.00	60.00
3 Bart Starr	15.00	30.00
4 Johnny Unitas	20.00	40.00

1973-87 Mardi Gras Parade Doubloons

These Mardi Gras Parade Doubloons or coins were thrown into the crowds by passing floats during the celebration each year in New Orleans. Although many different subject matters appear on these types of coins, we've only listed the football players below. Each includes a sculpted portrait of the player on one side and the parade logo on the other on a gold or bronze colored coin; all are from the Gladiators Parade unless noted below. We've listed the coins by their year of issue. Any additions to the list below are appreciated.

COMPLETE SET (16)	15.00	30.00
1973 Danny Abramowicz (Romulus and Remus Parade)	1.00	2.00
1974 George Blanda	1.50	3.00
1975 Ken Stabler	2.50	5.00
1977 Bert Jones	1.00	2.00
1978 Joe Ferguson	1.00	2.00
1979 Ray Guy	1.00	2.00
1980 Norris Weese	1.00	2.00
1981 Billy Kilmer	1.00	2.00
1982 Sonny Jurgensen	1.50	3.00
1983 Danny Abramowicz	1.00	2.00
1984 Archie Manning	1.50	3.00
1985 Richard Todd	1.00	2.00
1986 Brian Hansen	1.00	2.00
1987 Morten Andersen	1.00	2.00
1995 Jim Finks Green (Jefferson)	1.00	2.00
1995 Jim Finks Silver (Jefferson)	1.00	2.00

1997 Mark Brunell Tracard

This set of six-cards was printed specifically for Mark Brunell for use during signing sessions and fan mail requests. Each card was hand signed by Brunell and features a different photo on the front and religious message on the back along with the card number. No print year is given, but they were released throughout the late 1990s.

COMPLETE SET (6)	54.00	135.00
COMMON CARD (1-6)	10.00	25.00

1977 Marketcom Test

The 1977 Marketcom Test checklist below includes known mini-posters with each measuring approximately 5 1/2" by 8 1/2". They were printed on paper-thin stock and are virtually always found with fold creases. Marketcom is credited at the bottom of most of them along with the year 1977. Some are blankbacked while others include an advertisement for obtaining a large version of the poster. These posters are unnumbered and listed below in alphabetical order.

1 Otis Armstrong (large poster ad on back)	20.00	40.00
2 Ken Burrough (large poster ad on back)	20.00	40.00
3 Greg Pruitt (blankbacked)	20.00	40.00
4 Jack Youngblood (blankbacked)	20.00	40.00

1978-79 Marketcom Test

The 1978-79 Marketcom set includes mini-posters measuring approximately 5 1/2" by 8 1/2". They were printed on paper-thin stock and are virtually always found with fold creases. Marketcom is credited at the bottom of each poster front and some include a year designation while others do not. Most poster backs are blank but others have been found with an advertisement on the back for full sized posters. Finally, another version of many of the posters was also printed on thin cardboard stock without any folds. These cardboard versions are blankbacked and thicker than the paper version but slightly thinner than the 1980 posters. The posters are unnumbered and listed below in alphabetical order.

COMPLETE SET (34)	250.00	450.00
1 Otis Armstrong SP	5.00	10.00
2 Steve Bartkowski SP	6.00	12.00
3 Terry Bradshaw SP	20.00	40.00
4 Ken Burrough	3.00	6.00
5 Earl Campbell	15.00	30.00
6 Dave Casper	4.00	8.00
7 Gary Danielson	3.00	6.00
8 Dan Dierdorf SP	6.00	12.00
9 Tony Dorsett SP	20.00	40.00
10 Dan Fouts SP	12.50	25.00
11 Wallace Francis	4.00	8.00
12 Tony Galbreath	3.00	6.00
13 Randy Gradishar SP	5.00	10.00
14 Bob Griese SP	12.50	25.00
15 Steve Grogan	4.00	8.00
16 Ray Guy	4.00	8.00
17 Pat Haden SP	6.00	12.00
18 Jack Ham	6.00	12.00
19 Cliff Harris SP	5.00	10.00
20 Franco Harris	7.50	15.00
21 Jim Hart	4.00	8.00
22 Ron Jaworski	4.00	8.00
23 John Jefferson	5.00	10.00
24 Bert Jones SP	6.00	12.00
25 Jack Lambert SP	10.00	20.00
26 Archie Manning	6.00	12.00
27 Harvey Martin SP	5.00	10.00
28 Reggie McKenzie	3.00	6.00
29 Karl Mecklenburg SP	5.00	10.00
30 Craig Morton	4.00	8.00
31 Dan Pastorini	3.00	6.00
32 Walter Payton SP	20.00	40.00
33 Lee Roy Selmon	5.00	10.00
34 Roger Staubach SP	20.00	40.00
35 Joe Theismann UER (Misspelled Theisman on card)	6.00	12.00
36 Wesley Walker SP	5.00	10.00
37 Randy White	6.00	12.00
38 Jack Youngblood SP	5.00	10.00
39 Jim Zorn	4.00	8.00

1980 Marketcom

In 1980, Marketcom issued a set of 50 Football Mini-Posters. These 5 1/2" by 8 1/2" cards are very attractive, featuring a large full color (action scene) picture of each player with a white border. The cards have the player's name on front at top and have a facsimile autograph on the picture as well; cards are numbered on the back at the bottom as "x of 50". A very tough to find Rocky Bleier card (numbered 51) was produced as well, but is not listed below due to lack of market information.

COMPLETE SET (50)	30.00	60.00
1 Ottis Anderson	.75	2.00
2 Brian Sipe	.40	1.00
3 Lawrence McCutcheoh	.40	1.00
4 Ken Anderson	.75	2.00
5 Roland Harper	.40	1.00
6 Chuck Foreman	.40	1.00
7 Gary Danielson	.40	1.00
8 Wallace Francis	.40	1.00
9 John Jefferson	.50	1.25
10 Charlie Waters	.50	1.25
11 Jack Ham	.75	2.00
12 Jack Lambert	.75	2.00
13 Walter Payton	5.00	12.00
14 Bert Jones	.50	1.25
15 Harvey Martin	.50	1.25
16 Jim Hart	.40	1.00
17 Craig Morton	.50	1.25
18 Reggie McKenzie	.40	1.00
19 Keith Wortman	.40	1.00
20 Otis Armstrong	.40	1.00
21 Steve Grogan	.50	1.25
22 Jim Zorn	.40	1.00
23 Bob Griese	1.25	3.00
24 Tony Dorsett	2.00	5.00
25 Wesley Walker	.40	1.00
26 Dan Fouts	1.00	2.50
27 Dan Dierdorf	.75	2.00
28 Steve Bartkowski	.50	1.25
29 Archie Manning	.50	1.25
30 Randy Gradishar	.50	1.25
31 Randy White	.75	2.00
32 Joe Theismann	.75	2.00
33 Tony Galbreath	.40	1.00
34 Cliff Harris	.50	1.25
35 Ray Guy	.50	1.25
36 Dave Casper	.50	1.25
37 Ron Jaworski	.50	1.25
38 Greg Pruitt	.40	1.00
39 Ken Burrough	.40	1.00
40 Robert Brazile	.40	1.00
41 Pat Haden	.50	1.25
42 Dan Pastorini	.40	1.00
43 Lee Roy Selmon	.75	2.00
44 Franco Harris	1.25	3.00
45 Jack Youngblood	.50	1.25
46 Terry Bradshaw	4.00	8.00
47 Roger Staubach	4.00	8.00
48 Earl Campbell	2.50	5.00
49 Phil Simms	1.50	3.00
50 Delvin Williams	.40	1.00

1981 Marketcom

In 1981, Marketcom issued a set of 50 Football Mini-Posters. These 5 1/2" by 8 1/2" cards are very attractive, featuring a large full color (action scene) picture of each player with a white border. The cards have player's name on front at top and have a facsimile autograph on the picture as well; cards are numbered on the back at the bottom. This set can be distinguished from the set of the previous year by the presence of statistics and text on the backs of this issue.

COMPLETE SET (50)	25.00	50.00
1 Ottis Anderson	.60	1.50
2 Brian Sipe	.40	1.00
3 Rocky Bleier	.60	1.50
4 Ken Anderson	.75	2.00
5 Roland Harper	.30	.75
6 Steve Furness	.30	.75
7 Gary Danielson	.30	.75
8 Wallace Francis	.40	1.00
9 John Jefferson	.40	1.00
10 Charlie Waters	.40	1.00
11 Jack Ham	.60	1.50
12 Jack Lambert	.75	2.00
13 Walter Payton	3.00	8.00
14 Bert Jones	.60	1.50
15 Harvey Martin	.40	1.00
16 Jim Hart	.40	1.00
17 Craig Morton	.60	1.50
18 Reggie McKenzie	.30	.75
19 Keith Wortman	.30	.75
20 Joe Greene	.75	2.00
21 Steve Grogan	.60	1.50
22 Jim Zorn	.40	1.00
23 Bob Griese	1.00	2.50
24 Tony Dorsett	1.50	4.00
25 Wesley Walker	.40	1.00
26 Dan Fouts	1.00	2.50
27 Dan Dierdorf	.60	1.50
28 Steve Bartkowski	.60	1.50
29 Archie Manning	.60	1.50
30 Randy Gradishar	.40	1.00
31 Randy White	.75	2.00
32 Joe Theismann	.75	2.00
33 Tony Galbreath	.30	.75
34 Cliff Harris	.40	1.00
35 Ray Guy	.60	1.50
36 Joe Ferguson	.40	1.00
37 Ron Jaworski	.60	1.50
38 Greg Pruitt	.40	1.00
39 Ken Burrough	.30	.75
40 Robert Brazile	.30	.75
41 Pat Haden	.40	1.00
42 Ken Stabler	1.50	4.00
43 Lee Roy Selmon	.60	1.50
44 Franco Harris	1.00	2.50
45 Jack Youngblood	.60	1.50
46 Terry Bradshaw	2.50	6.00
47 Roger Staubach	2.50	6.00
48 Earl Campbell	1.50	4.00
49 Phil Simms	.75	2.00
50 Delvin Williams	.30	.75

1982 Marketcom

In 1982, Marketcom issued a set of 48 Football Mini-Posters. These 5 1/2" by 8 1/2" cards are very attractive, featuring a large full color (action scene) picture of each player with a white border. The cards have player's name on front at top and have a facsimile autograph on the picture as well; cards are numbered on the back at the bottom. The back carries biographical information, player profile, and statistics. The lower right corner of the card back indicates "St. Louis - Marketcom - Series C".

COMPLETE SET (48)	300.00	500.00
1 Joe Ferguson	3.00	6.00
2 Kellen Winslow	4.00	8.00
3 Jim Hart	3.00	6.00
4 Archie Manning	3.00	6.00
5 Earl Campbell	15.00	25.00
6 Wallace Francis	3.00	6.00
7 Randy Gradishar	3.00	6.00
8 Ken Stabler	15.00	25.00
9 Danny White	4.00	8.00
10 Jack Ham	4.00	8.00
11 Lawrence Taylor	15.00	30.00
12 Eric Hipple	2.50	5.00
13 Ron Jaworski	3.00	6.00
14 George Rogers	3.00	6.00
15 Jack Lambert	7.50	15.00
16 Randy White	6.00	12.00
17 Terry Bradshaw	25.00	40.00
18 Ray Guy	3.00	6.00
19 Rob Carpenter	2.50	5.00
20 Reggie McKenzie	2.50	5.00
21 Tony Dorsett	15.00	25.00
22 Wesley Walker	3.00	6.00
23 Tommy Kramer	3.00	6.00
24 Dwight Clark	3.00	6.00
25 Franco Harris	10.00	20.00
26 Craig Morton	3.00	6.00
27 Harvey Martin	3.00	6.00
28 Jim Zorn	3.00	6.00
29 Steve Bartkowski	3.00	6.00
30 Joe Theismann	5.00	10.00
31 Dan Dierdorf	4.00	8.00
32 Walter Payton	30.00	60.00
33 John Jefferson	3.00	6.00
34 Phil Simms	4.00	8.00
35 Lee Roy Selmon	5.00	10.00
36 Joe Montana	50.00	100.00
37 Robert Brazile	3.00	6.00
38 Steve Grogan	3.00	6.00
39 Dave Logan	2.50	5.00
40 Ken Anderson	4.00	8.00
41 Richard Todd	3.00	6.00
42 Jack Youngblood	4.00	8.00
43 Ottis Anderson	3.00	6.00
44 Brian Sipe	3.00	6.00
45 Mark Gastineau	3.00	6.00
46 Mike Pruitt	2.50	5.00
47 Cris Collinsworth	3.00	6.00
48 Dan Fouts	6.00	12.00

1987 Marketcom/Sports Illustrated

This 20-card white-bordered, multi-sport set measures approximately 3 1/16" by 4 14/16" and features color action photos of players in various sports produced by Marketcom. Cards #1-13 display Baseball players; cards #14-17, Basketball players; cards #18-10, Football players. The backs are blank. The set was issued to promote the Sports Illustrated sticker line. The cards are unnumbered and checklisted below alphabetically within each sport.

COMPLETE SET (20)	60.00	150.00
18 John Elway	10.00	25.00
19 Lawrence Taylor	1.25	3.00
20 Herschel Walker	1.25	3.00

1971 Mattel Mini-Records

This 18-disc set was designed to be played on a special Mattel mini-record player, which is not included in the complete set price. Each black plastic disc, approximately 2 1/2" in diameter, features a recording on one side and a color drawing of the player on the other. The picture appears on a paper disk that is glued onto the smooth unrecorded side of the mini-record. On the recorded side, the player's name and the set's subtitle appear in arcs stamped in the central portion of the mini-record. The hand-engraved player's name appears again along with a production number, copyright symbol, and the Mattel name and year of production in the ring between the central portion of the record and the grooves. The ivory discs are the ones which are double sided and are considered to be much tougher than the black discs. They are currently valued at 2X the regular records. They were also known as "Mattel Show 'N Tell". The discs are unnumbered and checklisted below in alphabetical order according to sport.

COMPLETE SET (18)	200.00	400.00
FB1 Donny Anderson	1.25	3.00
FB2 Lem Barney	1.50	4.00
FB3 John Brodie DP	1.50	4.00
FB4 Dick Butkus DP	3.00	8.00
FB5 Bob Hayes DP	1.50	4.00
FB6 Sonny Jurgensen	2.50	6.00
FB7 Alex Karras	2.50	6.00
FB8 Leroy Kelly	2.00	5.00
FB9 Daryle Lamonica DP	1.25	3.00
FB10 John Mackey DP	1.50	4.00
FB11 Earl Morrall	1.25	3.00
FB12 Joe Namath	15.00	30.00
FB13 Merlin Olsen DP	1.50	4.00
FB14 Alan Page	2.00	5.00
FB15 Gale Sayers DP	3.00	8.00
FB16 O.J. Simpson DP	3.00	8.00
FB17 Bart Starr	12.50	25.00

1937 Mayfair Candies Touchdown 100 Yards

Mayfair Candies produced this perforated card set in 1937. Each unnumbered card features an unidentified football action photo on the front and a football play description on the back. The set involved a contest whereby the collector tried to accumulate "100 Yards" based on football plays described on the cardbacks. The offer expired on February 15, 1938 and winners could exchange the cards for an official sized football. The ACC designation is R343 and each card measures approximately 1 3/4" by 2 3/4" and was unnumbered. Since there are no card numbers and no identification of players, we have cataloged the cards below using the first several words found at the top of the cardbacks. We have also included the cardfront photo's background color and number of players featured in the image for each card to help catalog the cardfronts. Note that four cardfronts exist with two different cardbacks each. Red Grange is the only player of note that has been positively identified.

COMPLETE SET (24)	5,000.00	8,000.00
1 2 Yards to go!... (Orange/10)	200.00	350.00
2 3 Yards to go... (Green/10)	200.00	350.00
3 Again the off tackle... (Orange/10)	200.00	350.00
4 Being in perfect position... (Red/7)	200.00	350.00
5 Changing quickly from... (Blue/4)	200.00	350.00
6 Charging hard... (Gray/6)	200.00	350.00
7 Coming from in front... (Green/6)	200.00	350.00
8 Coming out of a.... (Blue/11)	200.00	350.00
9 Digging in their heels... (Brown/5)	200.00	350.00
10 Early in the third... (Green/16)	200.00	350.00
11 Flipping a underhand.... (Orange/2)	200.00	350.00
12 Giving every ounce... (Green-Gray/12)	200.00	350.00
13 In a play that fizzled... (Yellow/8)	200.00	350.00
14 Indecision on the part... (Green/15)	200.00	350.00
15 Late in the same... (Orange/7)	200.00	350.00
16 Left Tackle is called.... (Orange/10)	200.00	350.00
17 Line holds beautifully... (Orange/4)/(Red Grange pictured)	900.00	1,500.00
18 Only intense rivalry... (Orange/11)	200.00	350.00
19 Outmaneuvered.... (Green/4)	200.00	350.00
20 Quarterback runs... (Orange/11)	200.00	350.00
21 Revealing for the first... (Orange/6)	200.00	350.00
22 Same old story... (Yellow/14)	200.00	350.00
23 Smashing close behind... (Brown/5)	200.00	350.00
24 Snapping out of their... (Orange/9)	200.00	350.00
25 The fullback driving... (Yellow/3)	200.00	350.00
26 Three unsuccessful... (Green/15)	200.00	350.00
27 Trying the old... (Orange/9)	200.00	350.00
28 What have we here?... (Orange/2)	200.00	350.00

1894 Mayo

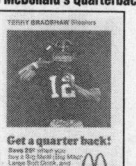

The 1894 Mayo college football series contains 35-cards of top Ivy League players. The cards feature sepia photos of the player surrounded by a black border, in which the player's name, his college, and a Mayo Cut Plug ad appears. The cards have solid black backs and measure approximately 1 5/8" by 2 7/8". Each card is unnumbered, but we've assigned card numbers alphabetically in the checklist below for your convenience. One of the cards has no specific identification of the player (John Dunlop of Harvard) and is listed below as being anonymous. It's one of the most highly sought after of all football cards and seldom seen. We've not included it in the complete set price due to its scarcity. Those players who were All-American selections are listed below with the year(s) of selection. The Poe (likely Neilson Poe) in the set is a direct descendant of the famous writer Edgar Allan Poe.

COMPLETE SET (34)	15,000.00	25,000.00
1 Robert Acton Harvard	500.00	800.00
2 George Adee Yale AA94	500.00	800.00
3 Richard Armstrong Yale	500.00	800.00
4 H.W.Barnett Princeton	500.00	800.00
5 Art Beale Harvard	500.00	800.00
6 Anson Beard Yale	500.00	800.00
7 Charles Brewer Harvard AA92/93/95	500.00	800.00
8 Harry Brown Princeton	500.00	800.00
9 C.D. Burt Princeton	500.00	800.00
10 Frank Butterworth Yale AA93/94	550.00	850.00
11 Eddie Crowdis Princeton	500.00	800.00
12 Robert Emmons Harvard	500.00	800.00
13 Madison Gonterman UER Harvard (Misspelled Gouterman)	500.00	800.00
14 George Gray UER Harvard (misspelled Grey)	500.00	800.00
15 John Greenway Yale	550.00	850.00
16 William Hickok Yale AA93/94	550.00	850.00
17 Frank Hinkey Yale AA91/92/93/94	800.00	1,200.00
18 Augustus Holly Princeton	500.00	800.00
19 Langdon Lea Princeton AA93/94/95	550.00	850.00
20 William Mackie Harvard	500.00	800.00
21 Tom Manahan Harvard	500.00	800.00
22 Jim McCrea Yale	500.00	800.00
23 Frank Morse Princeton AA93	500.00	800.00
24 Fred Murphy Yale AA95/96	550.00	850.00
25 Neilson Poe Princeton	800.00	1,200.00
26 Dudley Riggs Princeton AA95	550.00	850.00
27 Phillip Stillman Yale AA94	500.00	800.00
28 Knox Taylor Princeton	500.00	800.00
29 Brinck Thorne Yale AA95	500.00	800.00
30 Thomas Trenchard Princeton AA93	550.00	850.00
31 William Ward Princeton	500.00	800.00
32 Bert Waters Harvard AA92/94	550.00	850.00
33 Arthur Wheeler Princeton AA92/93/94	550.00	850.00
34 Edgar Wrightington Harvard AA96	500.00	800.00
35 Anonymous John Dunlop Harvard	12,000.00	18,000.00

1975 McDonald's Quarterbacks

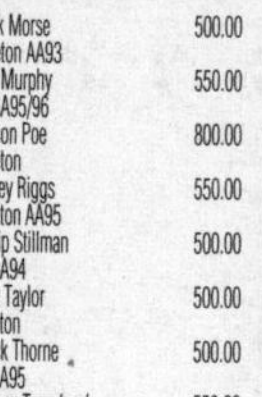

The 1975 McDonald's Quarterbacks set contains four cards, each of which was used as a promotion for McDonald's hamburger restaurants. The cards measure 2 1/2" by 3 7/16". One might get a quarter back if the coupon at the bottom of the card were presented at one of McDonald's retail establishments. Each coupon was valid for only one week, that particular week clearly marked on the coupon. The cards themselves are in color with yellow borders on the front and statistics on the back. The back of each card is a different color. Statistics are given for each of the quarterback's previous seasons record passing and rushing. The prices below are for the cards with coupons intact as that is the way they are usually found.

COMPLETE SET (4)	12.50	25.00
1 Terry Bradshaw	7.50	15.00
2 Joe Ferguson	2.00	5.00
3 Ken Stabler	4.00	10.00
4 Al Woodall	1.50	4.00

1985 McDonald's Bears Orange Tab

This set of 32 cards featuring the Chicago Bears was available with three different tab colors. Yellow tabs referenced the Super Bowl. Orange tabs referenced the NFC Championship Game. Blue tabs referenced the Divisional Playoff game. All three sets contain the same 32 players. The cards measure approximately 4 1/2" by 5 7/8" with the tab intact and 4 1/2" by 4 3/8" without the tab, noticeably larger than the McDonald's cards of 1986. Apparently this set was a test market which evidently was successful enough for McDonald's to distribute all 28 teams (plus All-Stars) in 1986. The promotion was intended to last until the Bears were eliminated from the playoffs, but they never were; they won the Super Bowl in convincing fashion. Prices listed are for cards with tabs intact.

COMPLETE ORANGE SET (32)	12.00	30.00
COMP.BLUE SET (32)	15.00	40.00
*BLUE TAB: .5X TO 1.2X ORANGE		
COMP.YELLOW SET (32)	12.00	30.00
*YELLOW TAB: .4X TO 1X ORANGE		
4 Steve Fuller	.30	.75
6 Kevin Butler	.30	.75
8 Maury Buford	.20	.50
9 Jim McMahon	.75	2.00
21 Leslie Frazier	.20	.50
22 Dave Duerson	.20	.50
26 Matt Suhey	.30	.75
27 Mike Richardson	.20	.50
29 Dennis Gentry	.20	.50
33 Calvin Thomas	.20	.50
34 Walter Payton	3.00	8.00
45 Gary Fencik	.30	.75
50 Mike Singletary	1.00	2.50
55 Otis Wilson	.20	.50
58 Wilber Marshall	.40	1.00
62 Mark Bortz	.20	.50
63 Jay Hilgenberg	.30	.75
72 William Perry	.40	1.00
73 Mike Hartenstine	.20	.50
74 Jim Covert	.30	.75
75 Stefan Humphries	.20	.50
76 Steve McMichael	.40	1.00
78 Keith Van Horne	.20	.50
80 Tim Wrightman	.20	.50
82 Ken Margerum	.20	.50
83 Willie Gault	.40	1.00
85 Dennis McKinnon	.30	.75
87 Emery Moorehead	.20	.50
95 Richard Dent	.75	2.00
99 Dan Hampton	.75	2.00
NNO Mike Ditka CO	.75	2.00
NNO Buddy Ryan ACO	.40	1.00

1986 McDonald's All-Stars Green Tab

This 30-card set was issued in all of the cities that were not near NFL cities and hence is the easiest of the McDonald's subsets to find. The set was issued over a four-week period with blue tabs the first week, black (or gray) tabs the second week, gold (or orange) tabs the third week, and green tabs the fourth week. The cards measure approximately 3 1/16" by 4 11/16" with the tab intact and 3 1/16" by 3 5/8" without the tab. The value of cards without tabs or tabs scratched off is F-G at best. All-Stars were printed on a 30-card sheet; hence, there are no DP cards, unlike the situation with the team subsets, where six cards were double printed. Since the cards are unnumbered, they are listed below by uniform number; in several instances, players on different teams have the same number.

COMP.GREEN SET (30)	2.50	6.00
COMP.BLACK SET (30)	2.50	6.00
*BLACK: .4X TO 1X GREEN		
COMP.BLUE SET (30)	2.50	6.00
*BLUE: .4X TO 1X GREEN		
COMP.GOLD SET (30)	2.50	6.00
*GOLD: .4X TO 1X GREEN		
9 Jim McMahon	.15	.40
11 Phil Simms	.15	.40
13 Dan Marino	1.00	2.50
14 Dan Fouts	.15	.40
16 Joe Montana	1.00	2.50
20A Deron Cherry	.05	.15
20B Joe Morris	.05	.15
32 Marcus Allen	.15	.40
33 Roger Craig	.08	.25
34A Kevin Mack	.05	.15
34B Walter Payton	.60	1.50
42 Gerald Riggs	.05	.15
45 Kenny Easley	.05	.15
47A Joey Browner	.05	.15
47B LeRoy Irvin	.05	.15
52 Mike Webster	.08	.25
54A E.J. Junior	.05	.15
54B Randy White	.08	.25
56 Lawrence Taylor	.15	.40
63 Mike Munchak	.05	.15
66 Joe Jacoby	.05	.15
73 John Hannah	.08	.25
75A Chris Hinton	.05	.15
75B Rulon Jones	.05	.15
75C Howie Long	.08	.25
78 Anthony Munoz	.08	.25
81 Art Monk	.15	.40
82A Ozzie Newsome	.15	.40
82B Mike Quick	.05	.15
99 Mark Gastineau	.05	.15

1986 McDonald's Bears Green Tab

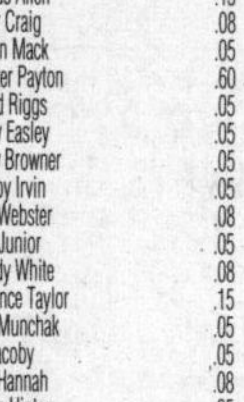

This 24-card set was issued in McDonald's Hamburger restaurants around Chicago. The set was issued over a four-week period with blue tabs the first week, black (or gray) tabs the second week, gold (or orange) tabs the third week, and green tabs the fourth week. The cards measure approximately 3 1/16" by 4 11/16" with the tab intact and 3 1/16" by 3 5/8" without the tab. The cards are numbered below by uniform number. The value of cards without tabs or tabs scratched off is F-G at best. The cards were printed on a 30-card sheet; hence, there are six double-printed cards listed DP in the checklist below. For individual prices on the more expensive color tabs, merely apply the ratio of that color's set price to the base (cheapest) color set price and use the resulting multiple on the individual prices for that color.

COMP.GREEN SET (24)	3.00	8.00
COMP.BLACK SET (24)	3.00	8.00
*BLACK: .4X TO 1X GREEN		
COMP.BLUE SET (24)	6.00	15.00
*BLUE: .8X TO 2X GREEN		
COMP.GOLD SET (24)	3.00	8.00
*GOLD: .4X TO 1X GREEN		
6 Kevin Butler DP	.15	.40
8 Maury Buford	.10	.30
9 Jim McMahon DP	.40	1.00
22 Dave Duerson	.10	.30
26 Matt Suhey	.15	.40
27 Mike Richardson	.10	.30
34 Walter Payton DP	1.00	2.50
45 Gary Fencik	.15	.40
50 Mike Singletary DP	.40	1.00
55 Otis Wilson	.10	.30
57 Tom Thayer	.10	.30
58 Wilber Marshall	.20	.50
62 Mark Bortz DP	.10	.30
63 Jay Hilgenberg	.15	.40
72 William Perry DP	.20	.50
74 Jim Covert	.15	.40
76 Steve McMichael	.20	.50
78 Keith Van Horne	.10	.30
80 Tim Wrightman	.10	.30
82 Ken Margerum	.10	.30
83 Willie Gault	.20	.50
87 Emery Moorehead	.10	.30
95 Richard Dent	.40	1.00
99 Dan Hampton	.40	1.00

1986 McDonald's Bengals Green Tab

This 24-card set was issued in McDonald's Hamburger restaurants around Cincinnati. The set was issued over a four-week period with blue tabs the first week, black (or gray) tabs the second week, gold (or orange) tabs the third week, and green tabs the fourth week. The cards measure approximately 3 1/16" by 4 11/16" with the tab intact and 3 1/16" by 3 5/8" without the tab. The cards are numbered below by uniform number. The value of cards without tabs or tabs scratched off is F-G at best. The cards were printed on a 30-card sheet; hence, there are six double-printed cards listed DP in the checklist below. For individual prices on the more expensive color tabs, merely apply the ratio of that color's set price to the base (cheapest) color set price and use the resulting multiple on the individual prices for that color. Boomer Esiason appears in his Rookie Card year.

COMP.GREEN SET (24)	5.00	12.00
COMP.BLACK SET (24)	5.00	12.00
*BLACK: .4X TO 1X GREEN		
COMP.BLUE SET (24)	10.00	25.00
*BLUE: .8X TO 2X GREEN		
COMP.GOLD SET (24)	5.00	12.00
*GOLD: .4X TO 1X GREEN		
7 Boomer Esiason	1.25	3.00
14 Ken Anderson DP	.50	1.25
20 Ray Horton	.25	.60
21 James Brooks DP	.40	1.00
22 James Griffin	.20	.50
28 Larry Kinnebrew	.25	.60
34 Louis Breeden DP	.20	.50
37 Robert Jackson	.20	.50
40 Charles Alexander DP	.20	.50
52 Dave Rimington	.25	.60
57 Reggie Williams	.40	1.00
65 Max Montoya	.25	.60
69 Tim Krumrie	.30	.75
73 Eddie Edwards	.25	.60
74 Brian Blados DP	.20	.50
77 Mike Wilson	.20	.50
78 Anthony Munoz	.60	1.50
79 Ross Browner	.25	.60
80 Cris Collinsworth	.40	1.00
81 Eddie Brown DP	.30	.75
82 Rodney Holman	.25	.60
83 M.L. Harris	.20	.50
90 Emanuel King	.20	.50
91 Carl Zander	.20	.50

1986 McDonald's Bills Green Tab

This 24-card set was issued in McDonald's Hamburger restaurants around Buffalo. The set was issued over a four-week period with blue tabs the first week, black (or gray) tabs the second week, gold (or orange) tabs the third week, and green tabs the fourth week. The cards measure approximately 3 1/16" by 4 11/16" with the tab intact and 3 1/16" by 3 5/8" without the tab. The cards are numbered below by uniform number. The value of cards without tabs or tabs scratched off is F-G at best. The cards were printed on a 30-card sheet; hence, there are six double-printed cards listed DP in the checklist below. For individual prices on the more expensive color tabs, merely apply the ratio of that color's set price to the base (cheapest) color set price and use the resulting multiple on the individual prices for that color. Andre Reed and Bruce Smith appear in their Rookie Card year.

COMP.GREEN SET (24)	6.00	15.00
COMP.BLACK SET (24)	12.00	30.00
*BLACK: .8X TO 2X GREEN		
COMP.BLUE SET (24)	50.00	120.00
*BLUE: 3X TO 8X GREEN		
COMP.GOLD SET (24)	6.00	15.00
*GOLD: .4X TO 1X GREEN		
4 John Kidd	.30	.75
7 Bruce Mathison	.30	.75
11 Scott Norwood	.40	1.00
22 Steve Freeman	.30	.75
26 Charles Romes	.30	.75
28 Greg Bell DP	.40	1.00
29 Derrick Burroughs DP	.30	.75
43 Martin Bayless DP	.30	.75
51 Jim Ritcher	.40	1.00
54 Eugene Marve	.30	.75
55 Jim Haslett	.30	.75
57 Lucius Sanford	.30	.75
63 Justin Cross DP	.30	.75
65 Tim Vogler	.30	.75
70 Joe Devlin	.30	.75
72 Ken Jones	.30	.75
76 Fred Smerlas	.40	1.00
77 Ben Williams	.40	1.00
78 Bruce Smith	1.50	4.00
80 Jerry Butler DP	.40	1.00
83 Andre Reed	1.50	4.00
85 Chris Burkett DP	.40	1.00
87 Eason Ramson	.30	.75
95 Sean McNanie	.30	.75

1986 McDonald's Broncos Green Tab

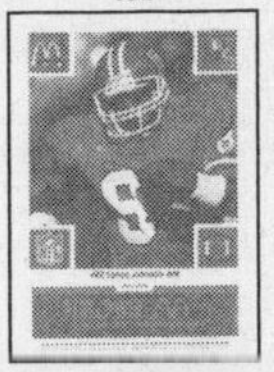

This 24-card set was issued in McDonald's Hamburger restaurants around Denver. The set was issued over a four-week period with blue tabs the first week, black (or gray) tabs the second week, gold (or orange) tabs the third week, and green tabs the fourth week. The cards measure approximately 3 1/16" by 4 11/16" with the tab intact and 3 1/16" by 3 5/8" without the tab. The cards are numbered below by uniform number. The value of cards without tabs or tabs scratched off is F-G at best. The cards were printed on a 30-card sheet; hence, there are six double-printed cards listed DP in the checklist below. For individual prices on the more expensive color tabs, merely apply the ratio of that color's set price to the base (cheapest) color set price and use the resulting multiple on the individual prices for that color.

COMP.GREEN SET (24)	8.00	20.00
COMP.BLACK SET (24)	8.00	20.00
*BLACK: .4X TO 1X GREEN		
COMP.BLUE SET (24)	15.00	40.00
*BLUE: .8X TO 2X GREEN		
COMP.GOLD SET (24)	8.00	20.00
*GOLD: .4X TO 1X GREEN		
3 Rich Karlis	.20	.50
7 John Elway DP	4.00	10.00
20 Louis Wright	.30	.75
22 Tony Lilly	.20	.50
23 Sammy Winder	.30	.75
30 Steve Sewell	.30	.75
31 Mike Harden	.30	.75
43 Steve Foley	.30	.75
47 Gerald Willhite	.30	.75
49 Dennis Smith	.30	.75
50 Jim Ryan	.20	.50
54 Keith Bishop DP	.20	.50
55 Rick Dennison DP	.20	.50
57 Tom Jackson	.50	1.25
60 Paul Howard	.20	.50
64 Bill Bryan DP	.20	.50
68 Rubin Carter DP	.20	.50
70 Dave Studdard	.20	.50
75 Rulon Jones	.30	.75
77 Karl Mecklenburg	.20	.50
79 Barney Chavous DP	.20	.50
81 Steve Watson	.30	.75
82 Vance Johnson	.20	.50
84 Clint Sampson	.20	.50

1986 McDonald's Browns Green Tab

This 24 card set was issued in McDonald's Hamburger restaurants around Cleveland. The set was issued over a four-week period with blue tabs the first week, black (or gray) tabs the second week, gold (or orange) tabs the third week, and green tabs the fourth week. The cards measure approximately 3 1/16" by 4 11/16" with the tab intact and 3 1/16" by 3 5/8" without the tab. The cards are numbered below by uniform number. The value of cards without tabs or tabs scratched off is F-G at best. The cards were printed on a 30-card sheet; hence, there are six double-printed cards listed DP in the checklist below. For individual prices on the more expensive color tabs, merely apply the ratio of that color's set price to the base (cheapest) color set price and use the resulting multiple on the individual prices for that color. Bernie Kosar appears in his Rookie Card year.

COMP.GREEN SET (24)	2.50	6.00
COMP.BLACK SET (24)	3.00	8.00
*BLACK: .5X TO 1.2X GREEN		
COMP.BLUE SET (24)	5.00	12.00
*BLUE .8X TO 2X GREEN		
COMP.GOLD SET (24)	2.50	6.00
*GOLD: .4X TO 1X GREEN		
9 Matt Bahr DP	.08	.25
18 Gary Danielson	.08	.25
19 Bernie Kosar DP	.75	2.00
27 Al Gross	.08	.25
29 Hanford Dixon	.15	.40
31 Frank Minnifield	.15	.40
34 Kevin Mack	.20	.50
37 Chris Rockins	.08	.25
44 Earnest Byner	.30	.75
51 Eddie Johnson	.08	.25
55 Curtis Weathers	.08	.25
56 Chip Banks DP	.08	.25
57 Clay Matthews	.20	.50
60 Tom Cousineau	.08	.25
61 Mike Baab DP	.08	.25
63 Cody Risien	.15	.40
77 Rickey Bolden DP	.08	.25
78 Carl Hairston	.08	.25
79 Bob Golic	.15	.40
82 Ozzie Newsome	.40	1.00
84 Glen Young	.08	.25
85 Clarence Weathers	.08	.25
86 Brian Brennan DP	.15	.40
96 Reggie Camp	.08	.25

1986 McDonald's Buccaneers Green Tab

This 24-card set was issued in McDonald's Hamburger restaurants in the Tampa Bay area. The set was issued over a four-week period with blue tabs the first week, black (or gray) tabs the second week, gold (or orange) tabs the third week, and green tabs the fourth week. The cards measure approximately 3 1/16" by 4 11/16" with the tab intact and 3 1/16" by 3 5/8" without the tab. The cards are numbered below by uniform number. The value of cards without tabs or tabs scratched off is F-G at best. The cards were printed on a 30-card sheet; hence, there are six double-printed cards listed DP in the checklist below. For individual prices on the more expensive color tabs, merely apply the ratio of that color's set price to the base (cheapest) color set price and use the resulting multiple on the individual prices for that color. Steve Young appears in his NFL Rookie Card year.

COMP.GREEN SET (24)	8.00	20.00
COMP.BLACK SET (24)	8.00	20.00
*BLACK: .4X TO 1X GREEN		
COMP.BLUE SET (24)	8.00	20.00
*BLUE: .4X TO 1X GREEN		
COMP.GOLD SET (24)	8.00	20.00
*GOLD: .4X TO 1X GREEN		
1 Donald Igwebuike	.10	.30
8 Steve Young	4.00	10.00
17 Steve DeBerg	.30	.75
21 John Holt	.10	.30
23 Jeremiah Castille DP	.10	.30
30 David Greenwood	.10	.30
32 James Wilder	.20	.50
44 Ivory Sully	.10	.30
51 Chris Washington	.10	.30
52 Scot Brantley DP	.10	.30
54 Ervin Randle	.10	.30
58 Jeff Davis DP	.10	.30
60 Randy Grimes	.10	.30
62 Sean Farrell	.15	.40
66 George Yarno	.10	.30
73 Ron Heller	.10	.30
76 David Logan	.10	.30
78 John Cannon DP	.10	.30
82 Jerry Bell DP	.10	.30
86 Calvin Magee	.10	.30
87 Gerald Carter DP	.10	.30
88 Jimmie Giles	.20	.50
89 Kevin House	.20	.50
90 Ron Holmes	.15	.40

1986 McDonald's Cardinals Green Tab

This 24-card set was issued in McDonald's Hamburger restaurants around St. Louis. The set was issued over a four-week period with blue tabs the first week, black (or gray) tabs the second week, gold (or orange) tabs the third week, and green tabs the fourth week. The cards measure approximately 3 1/16" by 4 11/16" with the tab intact and 3 1/16" by 3 5/8" without the tab. The cards are numbered below by uniform number. The value of cards without tabs or tabs scratched off is F-G at best. The cards were printed on a 30-card sheet; hence, there are six double-printed cards listed DP in the checklist below. For individual prices on the more expensive color tabs, merely apply the ratio of that color's set price to the base (cheapest) color set price and use the resulting multiple on the individual prices for that color.

COMP.GREEN SET (24)	2.50	6.00
COMP.BLACK SET (24)	2.50	6.00
*BLACK: .4X TO 1X GREEN		
COMP.BLUE SET (24)	4.00	10.00
*BLUE: .6X TO 1.5X GREEN		
COMP.GOLD SET (24)	2.50	6.00
*GOLD: .4X TO 1X GREEN		
15 Neil Lomax	.20	.50
18 Carl Birdsong DP	.08	.25
30 Stump Mitchell	.15	.40
32 Ottis Anderson DP	.30	.75
43 Lonnie Young	.08	.25
45 Leonard Smith	.08	.25
47 Cedric Mack	.08	.25
48 Lionel Washington	.08	.25
53 Freddie Joe Nunn	.15	.40
54 E.J. Junior	.15	.40
57 Niko Noga	.08	.25
60 Al Bubba Baker DP	.15	.40
63 Tootie Robbins	.08	.25
65 David Galloway	.08	.25
66 Doug Dawson DP	.08	.25
67 Luis Sharpe	.08	.25
71 Joe Bostic DP	.08	.25
73 Mark Duda DP	.08	.25
75 Curtis Greer	.08	.25
80 Doug Marsh	.08	.25
81 Roy Green	.20	.50
83 Pat Tilley	.08	.25
84 J.T. Smith	.15	.40
89 Greg LaFleur	.08	.25

1986 McDonald's Chargers Green Tab

This 24-card set was issued in McDonald's Hamburger restaurants around San Diego. The set was issued over a four-week period with blue tabs the first week, black (or gray) tabs the second week, gold (or orange) tabs the third week, and green tabs the fourth week. The cards measure approximately 3 1/16" by 4 11/16" with the tab intact and 3 1/16" by 3 5/8" without the tab. The cards are numbered below by uniform number. The value of cards without tabs or tabs scratched off is F-G at best. The cards were printed on a 30-card sheet; hence, there are six double-printed cards listed DP in the checklist below. For individual prices on the more expensive color tabs, merely apply the ratio of that color's set price to the base (cheapest) color set price and use the resulting multiple on the individual prices for that color.

COMP.GREEN SET (24)	5.00	12.00
COMP.BLACK SET (24)	8.00	20.00
*BLACK: .6X TO 1.5X GREEN		
COMP.BLUE SET (24)	10.00	25.00
*BLUE: .8X TO 2X GREEN		
COMP.GOLD SET (24)	5.00	12.00
*GOLD: .4X TO 1X GREEN		
9 Mark Herrmann	.15	.40
14 Dan Fouts DP	.60	1.50
18 Charlie Joiner	.50	1.25
21 Buford McGee	.15	.40
22 Gill Byrd DP	.20	.50
26 Lionel James	.20	.50
29 John Hendy	.15	.40
37 Jeffery Dale DP	.15	.40
40 Gary Anderson RB DP	.30	.75
43 Tim Spencer	.15	.40
51 Woodrow Lowe	.15	.40
54 Billy Ray Smith	.20	.50
60 Dennis McKnight	.15	.40
62 Don Macek	.15	.40
67 Ed White	.15	.40
74 Jim Lachey	.40	1.00
78 Chuck Ehin DP	.15	.40
80 Kellen Winslow	.60	1.50
83 Trumaine Johnson	.15	.40
85 Eric Sievers	.15	.40
88 Pete Holohan	.20	.50
89 Wes Chandler DP	.20	.50
93 Earl Wilson	.15	.40
99 Lee Williams	.20	.50

1986 McDonald's Chiefs Green Tab

This 24-card set was issued in McDonald's Hamburger restaurants around Kansas City. The set was issued over a four-week period with blue tabs the first week, black (or gray) tabs the second week, gold (or orange) tabs the third week, and green tabs the fourth week. The cards measure approximately 3 1/16" by 4 11/16" with the tab intact and 3 1/16" by 3 5/8" without the tab. The cards are numbered below by uniform number. The value of cards without tabs or tabs scratched off is F-G at best. The cards were printed on a 30-card sheet; hence, there are six double-printed cards listed DP in the checklist below. For individual prices on the more expensive color tabs, merely apply the ratio of that color's set price to the base (cheapest) color set price and use the resulting multiple on the individual prices for that color.

COMP.GREEN SET (24)	8.00	20.00
COMP.BLACK SET (24)	12.00	30.00
*BLACK: .6X TO 1.5X GREEN		
COMP.BLUE SET (24)	8.00	20.00
*BLUE: .4X TO 1X GREEN		
COMP.GOLD SET (24)	8.00	20.00
*GOLD: .4X TO 1X GREEN		
6 Jim Arnold DP	.30	.75
8 Nick Lowery	.40	1.00
9 Bill Kenney	.30	.75
14 Todd Blackledge DP	.40	1.00
20 Deron Cherry DP	.50	1.25
29 Albert Lewis	.50	1.25
31 Kevin Ross	.50	1.25
34 Lloyd Burruss DP	.30	.75
41 Garcia Lane	.30	.75
42 Jeff Smith	.30	.75
43 Mike Pruitt	.40	1.00
44 Herman Heard	.30	.75
50 Calvin Daniels	.30	.75
59 Gary Spani	.30	.75
63 Bill Maas	.30	.75
64 Bob Olderman	.30	.75
66 Brad Budde DP	.30	.75
67 Art Still	.30	.75
72 David Lutz	.30	.75
83 Stephone Paige	.50	1.25
85 Jonathan Hayes	.40	1.00
88 Carlos Carson DP	.40	1.00
89 Henry Marshall	.30	.75
97 Scott Radecic	.30	.75

1986 McDonald's Colts Green Tab

This 24-card set was issued in McDonald's Hamburger restaurants around Indianapolis. The set was issued over a four-week period with blue tabs the first week, black (or gray) tabs the second week, gold (or orange) tabs the third week, and green tabs the fourth week. The cards measure approximately 3 1/16" by 4 11/16" with the tab intact and 3 1/16" by 3 5/8" without the tab. The cards are numbered below by uniform number. The value of cards without tabs or tabs scratched off is F-G at best. The cards were printed on a 30-card sheet; hence, there are six double-printed cards listed DP in the checklist below. For individual prices on the more expensive color tabs, merely apply the ratio of that color's set price to the base (cheapest) color set price and use the resulting multiple on the individual prices for that color.

COMP.GREEN SET (24)	8.00	20.00
COMP.BLACK SET (24)	8.00	20.00
*BLACK: .4X TO 1X GREEN		
COMP.BLUE SET (24)	40.00	80.00
*BLUE: 1.5X TO 4X GREEN		
COMP.GOLD SET (24)	6.00	15.00
*GOLD: .3X TO .8X GREEN		
2 Raul Allegre DP	.25	.60
3 Rohn Stark	.30	.75
25 Nesby Glasgow	.25	.60
27 Preston Davis	.25	.60
32 Randy McMillan	.30	.75
34 George Wonsley	.25	.60
38 Eugene Daniel	.30	.75
44 Owen Gill	.25	.60
47 Leonard Coleman	.25	.60
50 Duane Bickett DP	.40	1.00
53 Ray Donaldson	.30	.75
55 Barry Krauss	.25	.60
64 Ben Utt	.25	.60
66 Ron Solt	.25	.60
72 Karl Baldischwiler DP	.25	.60
75 Chris Hinton	.30	.75
81 Pat Beach DP	.25	.60
85 Matt Bouza DP	.25	.60
87 Wayne Capers DP	.25	.60
88 Robbie Martin	.25	.60
92 Brad White	.25	.60
93 Cliff Odom	.25	.60
96 Blaise Winter	.25	.60
98 Johnie Cooks	.25	.60

1986 McDonald's Cowboys Green Tab

This 25-card set was issued in McDonald's Hamburger restaurants around Dallas. The set was issued over a four-week period with blue tabs the first week, black (or gray) tabs the second week, gold (or orange) tabs the third week, and green tabs the fourth week. The cards measure approximately 3 1/16" by 4 11/16" with the tab intact and 3 1/16" by 3 5/8" without the tab. The cards are numbered below by uniform number. The Herschel Walker card was produced later due to his popularity. Walker's card was produced only with a green tab without any coating on the tab to be scratched off; hence his cards are typically found in nice condition. The value of cards without tabs or tabs scratched off is F-G at best. The cards (other than Herschel Walker) were printed on a 30-card sheet; hence, there are six double-printed cards listed DP in the checklist below. For individual prices on the more expensive color tabs, merely apply the ratio of that color's set price to the base (cheapest) color set price and use the resulting multiple on the individual prices for that color.

COMP.GREEN SET (24)	4.00	10.00
COMP.BLACK SET (24)	4.00	10.00
*BLACK: .4X TO 1X GREEN		
COMP.BLUE SET (24)	4.00	10.00
*BLUE: .4X TO 1X GREEN		
COMP.GOLD SET (24)	4.00	10.00
*GOLD: .4X TO 1X GREEN		
1 Rafael Septien	.08	.25
11 Danny White	.20	.50
24 Everson Walls	.15	.40
26 Michael Downs DP	.08	.25
27 Ron Fellows	.08	.25
30 Timmy Newsome	.08	.25
33 Tony Dorsett DP	.50	1.25
34 Herschel Walker	.75	2.00
40 Bill Bates DP	.20	.50
47 Dextor Clinkscale DP	.08	.25
50 Jeff Rohrer	.08	.25
54 Randy White	.30	.75
56 Eugene Lockhart	.15	.40
58 Mike Hegman	.08	.25
61 Jim Cooper DP	.08	.25
63 Glen Titensor	.08	.25
64 Tom Rafferty	.08	.25
65 Kurt Petersen	.08	.25
72 Ed Too Tall Jones	.30	.75
75 Phil Pozderac	.08	.25
77 Jim Jeffcoat	.20	.50
78 John Dutton	.15	.40
80 Tony Hill	.15	.40
82 Mike Renfro	.08	.25
84 Doug Cosbie DP	.08	.25

1986 McDonald's Dolphins Green Tab

This 25-card set was issued in McDonald's Hamburger restaurants around Miami. The set was issued over a four-week period with blue tabs the first week, black (or gray) tabs the second week, gold (or orange) tabs the third week, and green tabs the fourth week. The cards measure approximately 3 1/16" by 4 11/16" with the tab intact and 3 1/16" by 3 5/8" without the tab. The cards are numbered below by uniform number. Joe Carter and Tony Nathan have photos reversed so that there are 25 different cards, but since this error happened on a double-printed player, no additional value is assigned. The value of cards without tabs or tabs scratched off is F-G at best. The cards were printed on a 30-card sheet; hence, there are five double-printed cards listed DP in the checklist below. For individual prices on the more expensive color tabs, merely apply the ratio of that color's set price to the base (cheapest) color set price and use the resulting multiple on the individual prices for that color.

COMP.GREEN SET (24)	10.00	25.00
COMP.BLACK SET (24)	10.00	25.00
*BLACK: .4X TO 1X GREEN		
COMP.BLUE SET (24)	15.00	40.00
*BLUE: .6X TO 1.5X GREEN		
COMP.GOLD SET (24)	10.00	25.00
*GOLD: .4X TO 1X GREEN		
4 Reggie Roby	.40	1.00
7 Fuad Reveiz	.25	.60
10 Don Strock	.40	1.00
13 Dan Marino	4.00	10.00
22 Tony Nathan	.40	1.00
23A Joe Carter ERR (Photo actually Tony Nathan 22)	.40	1.00
23B Joe Carter COR	.25	.60
27 Lorenzo Hampton	.25	.60
30 Ron Davenport	.25	.60
43 Bud Brown DP	.25	.60
47 Glenn Blackwood DP	.25	.60
49 William Judson	.25	.60
55 Hugh Green	.40	1.00
57 Dwight Stephenson	.75	2.00
58 Kim Bokamper DP	.25	.60
59 Bob Brudzinski DP	.25	.60
61 Roy Foster	.25	.60
71 Mike Charles	.25	.60
75 Doug Betters DP	.25	.60
79 Jon Giesler	.25	.60
83 Mark Clayton	.60	1.50
84 Bruce Hardy	.25	.60
85 Mark Duper	.50	1.25
89 Nat Moore	.40	1.00
91 Mack Moore	.25	.60

1986 McDonald's Eagles Green Tab

This 24-card set was issued in McDonald's Hamburger restaurants around Philadelphia. The set was issued over a four-week period with blue tabs the first week, black (or gray) tabs the second week, gold (or orange) tabs the third week, and green tabs the fourth week. The cards measure approximately 3 1/16" by 4 11/16" with the tab intact and 3 1/16" by 3 5/8" without the tab. The cards are numbered below by uniform number. The value of cards without tabs or tabs scratched off is F-G at best. The cards were printed on a 30-card sheet; hence, there are six double-printed cards listed DP in the checklist below. For individual prices on the more expensive color tabs, merely apply the ratio of that color's set price to the base (cheapest) color set price and use the resulting multiple on the individual prices for that color. Randall Cunningham appears in this set, a year before his Topps Rookie Card.

COMP.GREEN SET (24)	6.00	15.00
COMP.BLACK SET (24)	8.00	20.00
*BLACK: .5X TO 1.2X GREEN		
COMP.BLUE SET (24)	25.00	60.00
*BLUE: 1.5X TO 4X GREEN		
COMP.GOLD SET (24)	6.00	15.00
*GOLD: .4X TO 1X GREEN		
7 Ron Jaworski	.20	.50
8 Paul McFadden	.08	.25
12 Randall Cunningham DP	2.00	5.00
22 Brenard Wilson	.08	.25
24 Ray Ellis	.08	.25
29 Elbert Foules	.08	.25
36 Herman Hunter	.08	.25
41 Earnest Jackson	.15	.40
43 Roynell Young	.15	.40
48 Wes Hopkins	.15	.40
50 Garry Cobb DP	.08	.25
63 Ron Baker DP	.08	.25
66 Ken Reeves	.08	.25
71 Ken Clarke DP	.08	.25
73 Steve Kenney	.08	.25
74 Leonard Mitchell	.08	.25
81 Kenny Jackson	.15	.40
82 Mike Quick	.15	.40
85 Ron Johnson	.08	.25
88 John Spagnola	.08	.25
91 Reggie White	2.00	5.00
93 Tom Strauthers	.08	.25
94 Byron Darby DP	.08	.25
98 Greg Brown DP	.08	.25

1986 McDonald's Falcons Green Tab

This 24-card set was issued in McDonald's Hamburger restaurants around Atlanta. The set was issued over a four-week period with blue tabs the first week, black (or gray) tabs the second week, gold (or orange) tabs the third week, and green tabs the fourth week. The cards measure approximately 3 1/16" by 4 11/16" with the tab intact and 3 1/16" by 3 5/8" without the tab. The cards are numbered below by uniform number. The value of cards without tabs or tabs scratched off is F-G at best. The cards were printed on a 30-card sheet; hence, there are six double-printed cards listed DP in the checklist below. For individual prices on the more expensive color tabs, merely apply the ratio of that color's set price to the base (cheapest) color set price and use the resulting multiple on the individual prices for that color.

COMP.GREEN SET (24)	6.00	15.00
COMP.BLACK SET (24)	75.00	150.00
*BLACK: 4X TO 10X GREEN		
COMP.BLUE SET (24)	20.00	50.00
*BLUE: 1.2X TO 3X GREEN		
COMP.GOLD SET (24)	12.00	30.00
*GOLD: .8X TO 2X GREEN		
3 Rick Donnelly	.25	.60
16 David Archer DP	.50	1.25
18 Mick Luckhurst	.25	.60
23 Bobby Butler	.25	.60
26 James Britt DP	.25	.60
37 Kenny Johnson	.25	.60
39 Cliff Austin DP	.25	.60
42 Gerald Riggs	.30	.75
50 Buddy Curry	.25	.60
56 Al Richardson	.25	.60
57 Jeff Van Note	.30	.75
58 David Frye	.25	.60
61 John Scully	.25	.60
62 Brett Miller	.25	.60
74 Mike Pitts	.25	.60
76 Mike Gann	.25	.60
77 Rick Bryan	.25	.60
78 Mike Kenn	.30	.75
79 Bill Fralic	.30	.75
81 Billy Johnson	.30	.75
82 Stacey Bailey DP	.25	.60
87 Cliff Benson DP	.25	.60
88 Arthur Cox	.25	.60
89 Charlie Brown DP	.30	.75

1986 McDonald's 49ers Green Tab

This 24-card set was issued in McDonald's Hamburger restaurants around San Francisco. The set was issued over a four-week period with blue tabs the first week, black (or gray) tabs the second week, gold (or orange) tabs the third week, and green tabs the fourth week. The cards measure approximately 3 1/16" by 4 11/16" with the tab intact and 3 1/16" by 3 5/8" without the tab. The cards are numbered below by uniform number. The value of cards without tabs or tabs scratched off is F-G at best. The cards were printed on a 30-card sheet; hence, there are six double-printed cards listed DP in the checklist below. For individual prices on the more expensive color tabs, merely apply the ratio of that color's set price to the base (cheapest) color set price and use the resulting multiple on the individual prices for that color. Jerry Rice appears in his Rookie Card year.

COMP.GREEN SET (24)	12.00	30.00
COMP.BLACK SET (24)	12.00	30.00
*BLACK: .4X TO 1X GREEN		
COMP.BLUE SET (24)	20.00	50.00
*BLUE: .6X TO 1.5X GREEN		
COMP.GOLD SET (24)	12.00	30.00
*GOLD: .4X TO 1X GREEN		
16 Joe Montana	5.00	12.00
21 Eric Wright	.40	1.00
26 Wendell Tyler	.40	1.00
27 Carlton Williamson	.25	.60
33 Roger Craig DP	.50	1.25
42 Ronnie Lott	.75	2.00
49 Jeff Fuller	.25	.60
50 Riki Ellison	.25	.60
51 Randy Cross DP	.40	1.00
56 Fred Quillan	.25	.60
58 Keena Turner	.25	.60
62 Guy McIntyre	.25	.60
68 John Ayers DP	.25	.60
71 Keith Fahnhorst	.25	.60
72 Jeff Stover	.25	.60
76 Dwaine Board DP	.25	.60
77 Bubba Paris	.25	.60
78 Manu Tuiasosopo	.25	.60
80 Jerry Rice	6.00	15.00
81 Russ Francis	.40	1.00
86 John Frank	.25	.60
87 Dwight Clark DP	.40	1.00
90 Todd Shell	.25	.60
95 Michael Carter DP	.40	1.00

1986 McDonald's Giants Green Tab

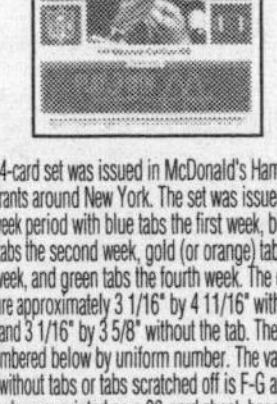

This 24-card set was issued in McDonald's Hamburger restaurants around New York. The set was issued over a four-week period with blue tabs the first week, black (or gray) tabs the second week, gold (or orange) tabs the third week, and green tabs the fourth week. The cards measure approximately 3 1/16" by 4 11/16" with the tab intact and 3 1/16" by 3 5/8" without the tab. The cards are numbered below by uniform number. The value of cards without tabs or tabs scratched off is F-G at best. The cards were printed on a 30-card sheet; hence, there are six double-printed cards listed DP in the checklist below. For individual prices on the more expensive color tabs, merely apply the ratio of that color's set price to the base (cheapest) color set price and use the resulting multiple on the individual prices for that color.

COMP.GREEN SET (24)	2.50	6.00
COMP.BLACK SET (24)	3.00	8.00
*BLACK: .5X TO 1.2X GREEN		
COMP.BLUE SET (24)	5.00	12.00
*BLUE: .8X TO 2X GREEN		
COMP.GOLD SET (24)	2.50	6.00
*GOLD: .4X TO 1X GREEN		
5 Sean Landeta	.15	.40
11 Phil Simms	.60	1.50
20 Joe Morris	.20	.50
23 Perry Williams	.08	.25
26 Rob Carpenter DP	.08	.25
33 George Adams DP	.08	.25
34 Elvis Patterson	.15	.40
43 Terry Kinard	.08	.25
44 Maurice Carthon	.08	.25
48 Kenny Hill	.08	.25
53 Harry Carson	.15	.40
54 Andy Headen	.08	.25
56 Lawrence Taylor	.60	1.50
60 Brad Benson DP	.08	.25
63 Karl Nelson	.08	.25
64 Jim Burt DP	.15	.40
67 Billy Ard DP	.08	.25
70 Leonard Marshall	.15	.40
75 George Martin	.15	.40
80 Phil McConkey	.15	.40
84 Zeke Mowatt	.08	.25
85 Don Hasselbeck	.08	.25
86 Lionel Manuel	.15	.40
89 Mark Bavaro DP	.15	.40

1986 McDonald's Jets Green Tab

This 24-card set was issued in McDonald's Hamburger restaurants around New York. The set was issued over a four-week period with blue tabs the first week, black (or gray) tabs the second week, gold (or orange) tabs the third week, and green tabs the fourth week. The cards measure approximately 3 1/16" by 4 11/16" with the tab intact and 3 1/16" by 3 5/8" without the tab. The cards are numbered below by uniform number. The value of cards without tabs or tabs scratched off is F-G at best. The cards were printed on a 30-card sheet; hence, there are six double-printed cards listed DP in the checklist below. For individual prices on the more expensive color tabs, merely apply the ratio of that color's set price to the base (cheapest) color set price and use the resulting multiple on the individual prices for that color.

COMP.GREEN SET (24)	15.00	40.00
COMP.BLACK SET (24)	40.00	80.00
*BLACK: .8X TO 2X GREEN		
COMP.BLUE SET (24)	40.00	80.00
*BLUE: .8X TO 2X GREEN		
COMP.GOLD SET (24)	15.00	40.00
*GOLD: .4X TO 1X GREEN		
5 Pat Leahy	.60	1.50
7 Ken O'Brien	.75	2.00
21 Kirk Springs	.60	1.50
24 Freeman McNeil	1.00	2.50
27 Russell Carter DP	.60	1.50
29 Johnny Lynn	.60	1.50
34 Johnny Hector	.75	2.00
39 Harry Hamilton	.60	1.50
49 Tony Paige	.75	2.00
53 Jim Sweeney	.60	1.50
56 Lance Mehl	.60	1.50
59 Kyle Clifton DP	.75	2.00
60 Dan Alexander DP	.60	1.50
65 Joe Fields DP	.60	1.50
73 Joe Klecko	.75	2.00
78 Barry Bennett DP	.60	1.50
80 Johnny Lam Jones	.60	1.50
82 Mickey Shuler	.60	1.50
85 Wesley Walker	.75	2.00
87 Kurt Sohn	.60	1.50
88 Al Toon	1.00	2.50
89 Rocky Klever	.60	1.50
93 Marty Lyons	.75	2.00
99 Mark Gastineau DP	.75	2.00

1986 McDonald's Lions Green Tab

This 24-card set was issued in McDonald's Hamburger restaurants around Detroit. The set was issued over a four-week period with blue tabs the first week, black (or gray) tabs the second week, gold (or orange) tabs the third week, and green tabs the fourth week. The cards measure approximately 3 1/16" by 4 11/16" with the tab intact and 3 1/16" by 3 5/8" without the tab. The cards are numbered below by uniform number. The value of cards without tabs or tabs scratched off is F-G at best. The cards were printed on a 30-card sheet; hence, there are six double-printed cards listed DP in the checklist below. For individual prices on the more expensive color tabs, merely apply the ratio of that color's set price to the base (cheapest) color set price and use the resulting multiple on the individual prices for that color.

COMP.GREEN SET (24)	2.50	6.00
COMP.BLACK SET (24)	2.50	6.00
*BLACK: .4X TO 1X GREEN		
COMP.BLUE SET (24)	2.50	6.00
*BLUE: .4X TO 1X GREEN		
COMP.GOLD SET (24)	2.50	6.00
*GOLD: .4X TO 1X GREEN		
3 Eddie Murray	.15	.40
11 Mike Black DP	.08	.25
17 Eric Hipple	.15	.40
20 Billy Sims	.20	.50
21 Demetrious Johnson	.08	.25
27 Bobby Watkins	.08	.25
29 Bruce McNorton	.08	.25
30 James Jones	.15	.40
33 William Graham	.08	.25
35 Alvin Hall	.08	.25
39 Leonard Thompson	.15	.40
50 August Curley DP	.08	.25
52 Steve Mott	.08	.25
55 Mike Cofer DP	.15	.40
59 Jimmy Williams	.08	.25
70 Keith Dorney DP	.08	.25
71 Rich Strenger	.08	.25
75 Lomas Brown DP	.15	.40
76 Eric Williams	.08	.25
79 William Gay	.08	.25
82 Pete Mandley	.08	.25
86 Mark Nichols	.08	.25
87 David Lewis TE	.08	.25
89 Jeff Chadwick DP	.08	.25

1986 McDonald's Oilers Green Tab

This 24-card set was issued in McDonald's Hamburger restaurants around Houston. The set was issued over a four-week period with blue tabs the first week, black (or gray) tabs the second week, gold (or orange) tabs the third week, and green tabs the fourth week. The cards measure approximately 3 1/16" by 4 11/16" with the tab intact and 3 1/16" by 3 5/8" without the tab. The cards are numbered below by uniform number. The value of cards without tabs or tabs scratched off is F-G at best. The cards were printed on a 30-card sheet; hence, there are six double-printed cards listed DP in the checklist below. For individual prices on the more expensive color tabs, merely apply the ratio of that color's set price to the base (cheapest) color set price and use the resulting multiple on the individual prices for that color.

COMP.GREEN SET (24)	3.00	8.00
COMP.BLACK SET (24)	3.00	8.00
*BLACK: .4X TO 1X GREEN		
COMP.BLUE SET (24)	5.00	12.00
*BLUE: .6X TO 1.5X GREEN		
COMP.GOLD SET (24)	3.00	8.00
*GOLD: .4X TO 1X GREEN		
1 Warren Moon	1.50	4.00
7 Tony Zendejas	.10	.30
10 Oliver Luck	.10	.30
21 Bo Eason	.10	.30
23 Richard Johnson	.10	.30
24 Steve Brown DP	.10	.30
25 Keith Bostic DP	.10	.30
29 Patrick Allen DP	.10	.30
33 Mike Rozier	.20	.50
40 Butch Woolfolk	.10	.30
53 Avon Riley	.10	.30
56 Robert Abraham DP	.10	.30
63 Mike Munchak	.40	1.00
67 Mike Stensrud	.10	.30
70 Dean Steinkuhler	.10	.30
71 Richard Byrd DP	.10	.30
73 Harvey Salem	.10	.30
74 Bruce Matthews	.30	.75
79 Ray Childress	.30	.75
83 Tim Smith	.10	.30
85 Drew Hill	.30	.75
87 Jamie Williams	.10	.30
91 Johnny Meads	.10	.30
94 Frank Bush DP	.10	.30

1986 McDonald's Packers Green Tab

This 24-card set was issued in McDonald's Hamburger restaurants around Green Bay and Milwaukee. The set was issued over a four-week period with blue tabs the first week, black (or gray) tabs the second week, gold (or orange) tabs the third week, and green tabs the fourth week. The cards measure approximately 3 1/16" by 4 11/16" with the tab intact and 3 1/16" by 3 5/8" without the tab. The cards are numbered below by uniform number. The value of cards without tabs or tabs scratched off is F-G at best. The cards were printed on a 30-card sheet; hence, there are six double-printed cards listed DP in the checklist below. For individual prices on the more expensive color tabs, merely apply the ratio of that color's set price to the base (cheapest) color set price and use the resulting multiple on the individual prices for that color.

COMP.GREEN SET (24)	2.50	6.00
COMP.BLACK SET (24)	2.50	6.00
*BLACK: .4X TO 1X GREEN		
COMP.BLUE SET (24)	2.50	6.00
*BLUE: .4X TO 1X GREEN		
COMP.GOLD SET (24)	2.50	6.00
*GOLD: .4X TO 1X GREEN		
10 Al Del Greco DP	.08	.25
12 Lynn Dickey	.15	.40
16 Randy Wright	.15	.40
18 Jim Zorn	.15	.40
22 Mark Lee	.08	.25
26 Tim Lewis	.08	.25
31 Gerry Ellis	.08	.25
33 Jessie Clark DP	.08	.25
37 Mark Murphy	.15	.40
41 Tom Flynn	.08	.25
42 Gary Ellerson	.08	.25
53 Mike Douglass	.08	.25
55 Randy Scott	.08	.25
59 John Anderson DP	.08	.25
67 Karl Swanke	.08	.25
75 Ken Ruettgers	.08	.25
76 Alphonso Carreker DP	.08	.25
77 Mike Butler DP	.08	.25
79 Donnie Humphrey	.08	.25
82 Paul Coffman DP	.08	.25
85 Phillip Epps	.15	.40
90 Ezra Johnson	.08	.25
91 Brian Noble	.15	.40
94 Charles Martin	.08	.25

1986 McDonald's Patriots Green Tab

This 24-card set was issued in McDonald's Hamburger restaurants around New England. The set was issued over a four-week period with blue tabs the first week, black (or gray) tabs the second week, gold (or orange) tabs the third week, and green tabs the fourth week. The cards measure approximately 3 1/16" by 4 11/16" with the tab intact and 3 1/16" by 3 5/8" without the tab. The cards are numbered below by uniform number. The value of cards without tabs or tabs scratched off is F-G at best. The cards were printed on a 30-card sheet; hence, there are six double-printed cards listed DP in the checklist below. For individual prices on the more expensive color tabs, merely apply the ratio of that color's set price to the base (cheapest) color set price and use the resulting multiple on the individual prices for that color.

COMP.GREEN SET (24)	2.50	6.00
COMP.BLACK SET (24)	2.50	6.00
*BLACK: .4X TO 1X GREEN		
COMP.BLUE SET (24)	2.50	6.00
*BLUE: .4X TO 1X GREEN		
COMP.GOLD SET (24)	2.50	6.00
*GOLD: .4X TO 1X GREEN		
3 Rich Camarillo DP	.08	.25
11 Tony Eason DP	.15	.40
14 Steve Grogan	.20	.50
24 Robert Weathers	.08	.25
26 Raymond Clayborn DP	.08	.25
30 Mosi Tatupu	.08	.25
31 Fred Marion	.08	.25
32 Craig James	.20	.50
33 Tony Collins DP	.15	.40
38 Roland James	.08	.25
42 Ronnie Lippett	.08	.25
50 Larry McGrew	.08	.25
55 Don Blackmon DP	.08	.25
56 Andre Tippett	.20	.50
57 Steve Nelson	.08	.25
58 Pete Brock DP	.08	.25
60 Garin Veris	.08	.25
61 Ron Wooten	.08	.25
73 John Hannah	.20	.50
77 Kenneth Sims	.08	.25
80 Irving Fryar	.40	1.00
81 Stephen Starring	.08	.25
83 Cedric Jones	.08	.25
86 Stanley Morgan	.20	.50

1986 McDonald's Raiders Green Tab

This 24-card set was issued in McDonald's Hamburger restaurants around Los Angeles. The set was issued over a four-week period with blue tabs the first week, black (or gray) tabs the second week, gold (or orange) tabs the third week, and green tabs the fourth week. The cards measure approximately 3 1/16" by 4 11/16" with the tab intact and 3 1/16" by 3 5/8" without the tab. The cards are numbered below by uniform number. The value of cards without tabs or tabs scratched off is F-G at best. The cards were printed on a 30-card sheet; hence, there are six double-printed cards listed DP in the checklist below. For individual prices on the more expensive color tabs, merely apply the ratio of that color's set price to the base (cheapest) color set price and use the resulting multiple on the individual prices for that color.

COMP.GREEN SET (24)	3.00	8.00
COMP.BLACK SET (24)	5.00	12.00
*BLACK: .6X TO 1.5X GREEN		
COMP.BLUE SET (24)	6.00	15.00
*BLUE: .8X TO 2X GREEN		
COMP.GOLD SET (24)	3.00	8.00
*GOLD: .4X TO 1X GREEN		
1 Marc Wilson	.15	.40
8 Ray Guy DP	.20	.50
10 Chris Bahr DP	.08	.25
16 Jim Plunkett	.20	.50
22 Mike Haynes	.15	.40
26 Vann McElroy	.08	.25
27 Frank Hawkins	.08	.25
32 Marcus Allen DP	1.00	2.50
36 Mike Davis DP	.08	.25
37 Lester Hayes	.15	.40
46 Todd Christensen DP	.20	.50
53 Rod Martin	.15	.40
54 Reggie McKenzie	.08	.25
55 Matt Millen	.15	.40
70 Henry Lawrence	.08	.25
71 Bill Pickel	.08	.25
72 Don Mosebar	.15	.40
73 Charley Hannah	.08	.25
75 Howie Long	.60	1.50
79 Bruce Davis DP	.08	.25
84 Jessie Hester	.15	.40
85 Dokie Williams	.08	.25
91 Brad Van Pelt	.08	.25
99 Sean Jones	.20	.50

1986 McDonald's Rams Green Tab

This 24-card set was issued in McDonald's Hamburger restaurants around Los Angeles. The set was issued over a four-week period with blue tabs the first week, black (or gray) tabs the second week, gold (or orange) tabs the third week, and green tabs the fourth week. The cards measure approximately 3 1/16" by 4 11/16" with the tab intact and 3 1/16" by 3 5/8" without the tab. The cards are numbered below by uniform number. The value of cards without tabs or tabs scratched off is F-G at best. The cards were printed on a 30-card sheet; hence, there are six double-printed cards listed DP in the checklist below. For individual prices on the more expensive color tabs, merely apply the ratio of that color's set price to the base (cheapest) color set price and use the resulting multiple on the individual prices for that color.

COMP.GREEN SET (24)	2.50	6.00
COMP.BLACK SET (24)	2.50	6.00
*BLACK: .4X TO 1X GREEN		
COMP.BLUE SET (24)	3.00	8.00
*BLUE: .5X TO 1.2X GREEN		
COMP.GOLD SET (24)	2.50	6.00
*GOLD: .4X TO 1X GREEN		
1 Mike Lansford	.08	.25
3 Dale Hatcher	.08	.25
5 Dieter Brock DP	.08	.25
20 Johnnie Johnson	.08	.25
21 Nolan Cromwell DP	.15	.40
22 Vince Newsome	.08	.25
27 Gary Green	.08	.25
29 Eric Dickerson DP	.60	1.50
44 Mike Guman	.08	.25
47 LeRoy Irvin	.15	.40
50 Jim Collins DP	.08	.25
54 Mike Wilcher	.08	.25
55 Carl Ekern	.08	.25
56 Doug Smith	.08	.25
58 Mel Owens	.08	.25
60 Dennis Harrah	.08	.25
71 Reggie Doss DP	.08	.25
72 Kent Hill	.08	.25
75 Irv Pankey	.08	.25
78 Jackie Slater	.20	.50
80 Henry Ellard	.40	1.00
81 David Hill	.08	.25
87 Tony Hunter	.08	.25
89 Ron Brown DP	.15	.40

1986 McDonald's Redskins Green Tab

This 24-card set was issued in McDonald's Hamburger restaurants around Washington. The set was issued over a four-week period with blue tabs the first week, black (or gray) tabs the second week, gold (or orange) tabs the third week, and green tabs the fourth week. The cards measure approximately 3 1/16" by 4 11/16" with the tab intact and 3 1/16" by 3 5/8" without the tab. The cards are numbered below by uniform number. The value of cards without tabs or tabs scratched off is F-G at best. The cards were printed on a 30-card sheet; hence, there are six double-printed cards listed DP in the checklist below. For individual prices on the more expensive color tabs, merely apply the ratio of that color's set price to the base (cheapest) color set price and use the resulting multiple on the individual prices for that color.

COMP.GREEN SET (24)	2.50	6.00
COMP.BLACK SET (24)	2.50	6.00
*BLACK: .4X TO 1X GREEN		
COMP.BLUE SET (24)	2.50	6.00
*BLUE: .4X TO 1X GREEN		
COMP.GOLD SET (24)	2.50	6.00
*GOLD: .4X TO 1X GREEN		
3 Mark Moseley	.08	.25
10 Jay Schroeder	.20	.50
22 Curtis Jordan	.08	.25
28 Darrell Green	.20	.50
32 Vernon Dean DP	.08	.25
35 Keith Griffin	.08	.25
37 Raphel Cherry DP	.08	.25
38 George Rogers	.15	.40
51 Monte Coleman DP	.15	.40
52 Neal Olkewicz	.08	.25
53 Jeff Bostic DP	.08	.25
55 Mel Kaufman	.08	.25
57 Rich Milot	.08	.25
65 Dave Butz DP	.15	.40
66 Joe Jacoby	.15	.40
68 Russ Grimm	.15	.40
71 Charles Mann	.20	.50
72 Dexter Manley	.15	.40
73 Mark May	.15	.40
77 Darryl Grant	.08	.25
81 Art Monk	.60	1.50
84 Gary Clark DP	.40	1.00
85 Don Warren	.15	.40
86 Clint Didier	.08	.25

1986 McDonald's Saints Green Tab

This 24-card set was issued in McDonald's Hamburger restaurants around New Orleans. The set was issued over a four-week period with blue tabs the first week, black (or gray) tabs the second week, gold (or orange) tabs the third week, and green tabs the fourth week. The cards measure approximately 3 1/16" by 4 11/16" with the tab intact and 3 1/16" by 3 5/8" without the tab. The cards are numbered below by uniform number. The value of cards without tabs or tabs scratched off is F-G at best. The cards were printed on a 30-card sheet; hence, there are six double-printed cards listed DP in the checklist below. For individual prices on the more expensive color tabs, merely apply the ratio of that color's set price to the base (cheapest) color set price and use the resulting multiple on the individual prices for that color.

COMP.GREEN SET (24)	8.00	20.00
COMP.BLACK SET (24)	12.00	30.00
*BLACK: .6X TO 1.5X GREEN		
COMP.BLUE SET (24)	30.00	80.00
*BLUE: 1.5X TO 4X GREEN		
COMP.GOLD SET (24)	6.00	15.00
*GOLD: .3X TO .8X GREEN		
3 Bobby Hebert	.50	1.25
7 Morten Andersen DP	.60	1.50
10 Brian Hansen	.30	.75
18 Dave Wilson	.30	.75
20 Russell Gary	.30	.75
25 Johnnie Poe	.30	.75
30 Wayne Wilson	.30	.75
44 Dave Waymer	.40	1.00
46 Hokie Gajan	.30	.75
49 Frank Wattelett	.30	.75
50 Jack Del Rio DP	.50	1.25
57 Rickey Jackson	.50	1.25
60 Steve Korte	.30	.75
61 Joel Hilgenberg	.30	.75
63 Brad Edelman DP	.30	.75
64 Dave Lafary	.30	.75
67 Stan Brock DP	.30	.75
73 Frank Warren	.30	.75
75 Bruce Clark DP	.30	.75
84 Eric Martin	.50	1.25
85 Hoby Brenner DP	.30	.75
88 Eugene Goodlow	.30	.75
89 Tyrone Young	.30	.75
99 Tony Elliott	.30	.75

1986 McDonald's Seahawks Green Tab

This 24-card set was issued in McDonald's Hamburger restaurants around Seattle. The set was issued over a four-week period with blue tabs the first week, black (or gray) tabs the second week, gold (or orange) tabs the third week, and green tabs the fourth week. The cards measure approximately 3 1/16" by 4 11/16" with the tab intact and 3 1/16" by 3 5/8" without the tab. The cards are numbered below by uniform number. The value of cards without tabs or tabs scratched off is F-G at best. The cards were printed on a 30-card sheet; hence, there are six double-printed cards listed DP in the checklist below. For individual prices on the more expensive color tabs, merely apply the ratio of that color's set price to the base (cheapest) color set price and use the resulting multiple on the individual prices for that color.

COMP.GREEN SET (24)	2.50	6.00
COMP.BLACK SET (24)	2.50	6.00
*BLACK: .4X TO 1X GREEN		
COMP.BLUE SET (24)	3.00	8.00
*BLUE: .5X TO 1.2X GREEN		
COMP.GOLD SET (24)	2.50	6.00
*GOLD: .4X TO 1X GREEN		
9 Norm Johnson	.15	.40
17 Dave Krieg	.20	.50
20 Terry Taylor	.08	.25
22 Dave Brown DP	.08	.25
28 Curt Warner	.20	.50
33 Dan Doornink	.08	.25
44 John Harris	.08	.25
45 Kenny Easley	.15	.40
46 David Hughes	.08	.25
50 Fredd Young	.08	.25
53 Keith Butler DP	.08	.25
55 Michael Jackson	.08	.25
58 Bruce Scholtz	.08	.25
59 Blair Bush DP	.08	.25
61 Robert Pratt	.08	.25
64 Ron Essink	.08	.25
65 Edwin Bailey DP	.08	.25
72 Joe Nash	.08	.25
77 Jeff Bryant DP	.08	.25
78 Bob Cryder DP	.08	.25
79 Jacob Green	.15	.40
80 Steve Largent	.75	2.00
81 Daryl Turner	.08	.25
82 Paul Skansi	.08	.25

1986 McDonald's Steelers Green Tab

This 24-card set was issued in McDonald's Hamburger restaurants around Pittsburgh. The set was issued over a four-week period with blue tabs the first week, black (or gray) tabs the second week, gold (or orange) tabs the third week, and green tabs the fourth week. The cards measure approximately 3 1/16" by 4 11/16" with the tab intact and 3 1/16" by 3 5/8" without the tab. The cards are numbered below by uniform number. The value of cards without tabs or tabs scratched off is F-G at best. The cards were printed on a 30-card sheet; hence, there are six double-printed cards listed DP in the checklist below. For individual prices on the more expensive color tabs, merely apply the ratio of that color's set price to the base (cheapest) color set price and use the resulting multiple on the individual prices for that color.

COMP.GREEN SET (24)	4.00	10.00
COMP.BLACK SET (24)	6.00	15.00
*BLACK: .6X TO 1.5X GREEN		
COMP.BLUE SET (24)	10.00	25.00
*BLUE: 1X TO 2.5X GREEN		
COMP.GOLD SET (24)	4.00	10.00
*GOLD: .4X TO 1X GREEN		
1 Gary Anderson K DP	.20	.50
16 Mark Malone	.20	.50
21 Eric Williams	.15	.40
24 Rich Erenberg DP	.15	.40
30 Frank Pollard	.15	.40
31 Donnie Shell	.20	.50
34 Walter Abercrombie DP	.15	.40
49 Dwayne Woodruff	.15	.40
50 David Little	.15	.40
52 Mike Webster	.20	.50
53 Bryan Hinkle	.20	.50
56 Robin Cole DP	.15	.40
57 Mike Merriweather	.20	.50
62 Tunch Ilkin	.15	.40
65 Ray Pinney	.15	.40
67 Gary Dunn DP	.15	.40
73 Craig Wolfley	.15	.40
74 Terry Long	.15	.40
82 John Stallworth	.40	1.00
83 Louis Lipps	.30	.75
87 Weegie Thompson	.15	.40
92 Keith Gary DP	.15	.40
93 Keith Willis	.15	.40
99 Darryl Sims	.15	.40

1986 McDonald's Vikings Green Tab

This 24-card set was issued in McDonald's Hamburger restaurants around Minneapolis and St. Paul. The set was issued over a four-week period with blue tabs the first week, black (or gray) tabs the second week, gold (or orange) tabs the third week, and green tabs the fourth week. The cards measure approximately 3 1/16" by 4 11/16" with the tab intact and 3 1/16" by 3 5/8" without the tab. The cards are numbered below by uniform number. The value of cards without tabs or tabs scratched off is F-G at best. The cards were printed on a 30-card sheet; hence, there are six double-printed cards listed DP in the checklist below. For individual prices on the more expensive color tabs, merely apply the ratio of that color's set price to the base (cheapest) color set price and use the resulting multiple on the individual prices for that color.

COMP.GREEN SET (24)	6.00	15.00
COMP.BLACK SET (24)	12.00	30.00
*BLACK: .8X TO 2X GREEN		
COMP.BLUE SET (24)	15.00	40.00
*BLUE: 1X TO 2.5X GREEN		
COMP.GOLD SET (24)	6.00	15.00
*GOLD: .4X TO 1X GREEN		
8 Greg Coleman DP	.25	.60
9 Tommy Kramer	.30	.75
11 Wade Wilson	.40	1.00
20 Darrin Nelson	.30	.75
23 Ted Brown DP	.25	.60
37 Willie Teal	.25	.60
39 Carl Lee	.30	.75
46 Alfred Anderson DP	.25	.60
47 Joey Browner DP	.40	1.00
55 Scott Studwell	.25	.60
56 Chris Doleman	.40	1.00
59 Matt Blair DP	.30	.75
67 Dennis Swilley	.25	.60
68 Curtis Rouse	.25	.60
75 Keith Millard	.40	1.00
76 Tim Irwin	.25	.60
77 Mark Mullaney	.25	.60
79 Doug Martin	.25	.60
81 Anthony Carter DP	.50	1.25
83 Steve Jordan	.40	1.00
87 Leo Lewis	.30	.75
89 Mike Jones	.25	.60
96 Tim Newton	.25	.60
99 David Howard	.25	.60

1993 McDonald's GameDay

As part of the "McDonald's/NFL Kickoff Payoff" promotion, customers could win NFL Fantasy prizes, such as trips to Super Bowl XXVII, and McDonald's/GameDay trading cards featuring local NFL teams. Customers received a pull-tab gamepiece on packages of large and extra-large french fries, hash browns, 21- and 32-oz. soft drinks, and 16-oz. coffee. Every gamepiece won free food, an instant-win NFL Fantasy prize, or NFL Point Values of six (touchdown), three (field goal), or one (extra point). The Point Values could be collected and redeemed for trading cards or special discounts on merchandise. For ten points, customers received a six-card sheet at participating McDonald's restaurants while supplies lasted. Measuring approximately 2 1/2" by 4 3/4", the GameDay cards are similar to the regular issues, except that they have McDonald's logos on both sides, and on the backs are renumbered with a "McD" prefix. Three sheets make a complete team set. Most McDonald's restaurants in a region offered cards of the local NFL team(s). In addition, many restaurants offered an All-Star set of 18 NFL superstars. Each NFL team has 18 cards in total on three different sheets (A, B, and C), and the cards are listed below in alphabetical team order, preceded by the All-Star set. One sheet was distributed per week for three weeks during the promotion.

COMPLETE SET (87)	20.00	50.00
1 All-Stars A	.80	2.00
Deion Sanders		
Thurman Thomas		
Troy Aikman		
John Elway		
Barry Sanders		
Sterling Sharpe		
2 All-Stars B	.80	2.00
Derrick Thomas		
Howie Long		
Dan Marino		
Chris Doleman		
Vaughan Johnson		
Phil Simms		
3 All-Stars C	.40	1.00
Randall Cunningham		
Barry Foster		
Jerry Rice		
Junior Seau		
Cortez Kennedy		
Mark Rypien		
4 Atlanta Falcons A	.60	1.50
Deion Sanders		
Moe Gardner		
Tim Green		
Michael Haynes		
Chris Hinton		
Tim McKyer		
5 Atlanta Falcons B	.40	1.00
Chris Miller		
Bruce Pickens		
Mike Pritchard		
Andre Rison		
Darion Conner		
Jessie Tuggle		
6 Atlanta Falcons C	.30	.75
Drew Hill		
Pierce Holt		
Elbert Shelley		
Jesse Solomon		
Bobby Hebert		
Lincoln Kennedy		
7 Buffalo Bills A	.40	1.00
Howard Ballard		
Don Beebe		
Cornelius Bennett		
Phil Hansen		
Henry Jones		
Jim Kelly		
8 Buffalo Bills B	.40	1.00
Nate Odomes		
Andre Reed		
Frank Reich		
Bruce Smith		
Darryl Talley		
Steve Tasker		
9 Buffalo Bills C	.50	1.25
Bill Brooks		
Jim Ritcher		
Thurman Thomas		
Kenneth Davis		
Jeff Wright		
Thomas Smith		
10 Chicago Bears A	.30	.75
Neal Anderson		
Trace Armstrong		
Mark Carrier DB		
Wendell Davis		
Richard Dent		
Shaun Gayle		
11 Chicago Bears B	.30	.75
Jim Harbaugh		
Darren Lewis		
Jim Morrissey		
William Perry		
Alonzo Spellman		
Tom Waddle		
12 Chicago Bears C	.40	1.00
Steve McMichael		
Craig Heyward		
Lemuel Stinson		
Keith Van Horne		
Donnell Woolford		
Curtis Conway		
13 Cincinnati Bengals A	.30	.75
Derrick Fenner		
James Francis		
David Fulcher		
Harold Green		
Rod Jones CB		
David Klingler		
14 Cincinnati Bengals B	.50	1.25
Bruce Kozerski		
Tim Krumrie		
Ricardo McDonald		
Carl Pickens		
Reggie Rembert		
Daniel Stubbs		
15 Cincinnati Bengals C	.30	.75
Eddie Brown		
Gary Reasons		
Lamar Rogers		
Alfred Williams		
Darryl Williams		
John Copeland		
16 Cleveland Browns A	.40	1.00
Rob Burnett		
Jay Hilgenberg		
Leroy Hoard		
Michael Jackson		
Mike Johnson		
Bernie Kosar		
17 Cleveland Browns B	.40	1.00
Eric Metcalf		
Michael Dean Perry		
Clay Matthews		
Lawyer Tillman		
Eric Turner		
Tommy Vardell		
18 Cleveland Browns C	.30	.75
David Brandon		
Tony Jones T		
Scott Galbraith		
James Jones DT		
Vinny Testaverde		
Steve Everitt		
19 Dallas Cowboys A	.60	1.50
Troy Aikman		
Tony Casillas		
Thomas Everett		
Charles Haley		
Alvin Harper		
Michael Irvin		
20 Dallas Cowboys B	.40	1.00
Jim Jeffcoat		
Daryl Johnston		
Robert Jones		
Nate Newton		
Ken Norton Jr.		
Jay Novacek		
21 Dallas Cowboys C	1.00	2.50
Russell Maryland		
Emmitt Smith		
Kevin Smith		
Mark Stepnoski		
Tony Tolbert		
Larry Brown DB		
22 Denver Broncos A	1.00	2.50
Steve Atwater		
Mike Croel		
Shane Dronett		
John Elway		
Simon Fletcher		
Reggie Rivers		
23 Denver Broncos B	.30	.75
Vance Johnson		
Greg Lewis		
Tommy Maddox		
Arthur Marshall		
Shannon Sharpe		
Dennis Smith		
24 Denver Broncos C	.30	.75
Rod Bernstine		
Michael Brooks		
Wymon Henderson		
Greg Kragen		
Karl Mecklenburg		
Dan Williams		
25 Detroit Lions A	.30	.75
Bennie Blades		
Michael Cofer		
Ray Crockett		
Mel Gray		
Willie Green		
Jason Hanson		
26 Detroit Lions B	.60	1.50
Herman Moore		
Rodney Peete		
Brett Perriman		
Kelvin Pritchett		
Barry Sanders		
Tracy Scroggins		
27 Detroit Lions C	.40	1.00
Pat Swilling		
Lomas Brown		
Erik Kramer		
Chris Spielman		
Andre Ware		
William White		
28 Green Bay Packers A	1.00	2.50
Tony Bennett		
Matt Brock		
Terrell Buckley		
LeRoy Butler		
Chris Jacke		
Brett Favre		
29 Green Bay Packers B	.40	1.00
Jackie Harris		
Brian Noble		
Bryce Paup		
Sterling Sharpe		
Ed West		
Johnny Holland		
30 Green Bay Packers C	.50	1.25
Tunch Ilkin		
George Teague		
Reggie White		
Ken O'Brien		
John Stephens		
Wayne Simmons		
31 Houston Oilers A	.30	.75
Cody Carlson		
Ray Childress		
Curtis Duncan		
William Fuller		
Haywood Jeffires		
Lamar Lathon		
32 Houston Oilers B	.40	1.00
Bruce Matthews		
Bubba McDowell		
Warren Moon		
Mike Munchak		
Eddie Robinson		
Webster Slaughter		
33 Houston Oilers C	.30	.75
Ernest Givins		
Cris Dishman		
Al Smith		
Lorenzo White		
Lee Williams		
Brad Hopkins		
34 Indianapolis Colts A	.30	.75
Chip Banks		
Kerry Cash		
Quentin Coryatt		
Rodney Culver		
Steve Emtman		
Reggie Langhorne		
35 Indianapolis Colts B	.40	1.00
Jeff Herrod		
Anthony Johnson		
Jeff George		
Rohn Stark		
Jack Trudeau		
Clarence Verdin		
36 Indianapolis Colts C	.30	.75
Duane Bickett		
Eugene Daniel		
Jessie Hester		
Chris Goode		
Kirk Lowdermilk		
Sean Dawkins		
37 Kansas City Chiefs A	.30	.75
Dale Carter		
Willie Davis		
Dave Krieg		
Albert Lewis		
Nick Lowery		
J.J. Birden		
38 Kansas City Chiefs B	.30	.75
Charles Mincy		
Christian Okoye		
Kevin Ross		
Dan Saleaumua		
Tracy Simien		
Harvey Williams		
39 Kansas City Chiefs C	.60	1.50
Todd McNair		
Neil Smith		
Derrick Thomas		
Leonard Griffin		
Barry Word		
Joe Montana		
40 Los Angeles Raiders A	.30	.75
Eddie Anderson		
Jeff Gossett		
Ethan Horton		
Jeff Jaeger		
Howie Long		
Todd Marinovich		
41 Los Angeles Raiders B	.30	.75
Terry McDaniel		
Don Mosebar		
Anthony Smith		
Greg Townsend		
Aaron Wallace		
Steve Wisniewski		
42 Los Angeles Raiders C	.40	1.00
Nick Bell		
Tim Brown		
Eric Dickerson		
James Lofton		
Jeff Hostetler		
Patrick Bates		
43 Los Angeles Rams A	.30	.75
Flipper Anderson		
Marc Boutte		
Henry Ellard		
Bill Hawkins		
Cleveland Gary		
David Lang		
44 Los Angeles Rams B	.40	1.00
Jim Everett		
Darryl Henley		
Todd Lyght		
Anthony Newman		
Roman Phifer		
Jim Price		
45 Los Angeles Rams C	.60	1.50
Shane Conlan		
Henry Rolling		
Larry Kelm		
Jackie Slater		
Fred Stokes		
Jerome Bettis		
46 Miami Dolphins A	.30	.75
Marco Coleman		
Bryan Cox		
Jeff Cross		
Mark Duper		
Keith Sims		
Mark Higgs		
47 Miami Dolphins B	1.00	2.50
Keith Jackson		
Dan Marino		
John Offerdahl		
Louis Oliver		
Tony Paige		
Pete Stoyanovich		
48 Miami Dolphins C	.40	1.00
Tony Martin		
Irving Fryar		
Troy Vincent		
Richmond Webb		
Jarvis Williams		
O.J. McDuffie		
49 Minnesota Vikings A	.40	1.00
Terry Allen		
Anthony Carter		
Cris Carter		
Jack Del Rio		
Chris Doleman		
Rich Gannon		
50 Minnesota Vikings B	.30	.75
Steve Jordan		
Carl Lee		
Randall McDaniel		
John Randle		
Sean Salisbury		
Todd Scott		
51 Minnesota Vikings C	.30	.75
Jim McMahon		
Audray McMillian		
Mike Merriweather		
Henry Thomas		
Gary Zimmerman		
Robert Smith		
52 New England Patriots A	.30	.75
Ray Agnew		
Bruce Armstrong		
Vincent Brown		
Eugene Chung		
Marv Cook		
Maurice Hurst		
53 New England Patriots B	.40	1.00
Pat Harlow		
Eugene Lockhart		
Greg McMurtry		
Scott Zolak		
Leonard Russell		
Andre Tippett		
54 New England Patriots C	1.00	2.50
David Howard		
Johnny Rembert		
Jon Vaughn		
Brent Williams		
Scott Secules		
Drew Bledsoe		
55 New Orleans Saints A	.30	.75
Morten Andersen		
Gene Atkins		
Toi Cook		
Richard Cooper		
Jim Dombrowski		
Vaughn Dunbar		
56 New Orleans Saints B	.30	.75
Joel Hilgenberg		
Rickey Jackson		
Vaughan Johnson		
Wayne Martin		
Renaldo Turnbull		
Frank Warren		
57 New Orleans Saints C	.30	.75
Irv Smith		
Brad Muster		
Dalton Hilliard		
Eric Martin		
Sam Mills		
Willie Roaf		
58 New York Giants A	.40	1.00
Jarrod Bunch		
Mark Collins		
Howard Cross		
Rodney Hampton		
Erik Howard		
Greg Jackson		
59 New York Giants B	.40	1.00
Pepper Johnson		
Sean Landeta		
Ed McCaffrey		
Dave Meggett		
Bart Oates		
Phil Simms		
60 New York Giants C	.40	1.00
Carton Bailey		
Carl Banks		
John Elliott		
Eric Dorsey		
Lawrence Taylor		
Mike Sherrard		
61 New York Jets A	.30	.75
Brad Baxter		
Scott Mersereau		
Chris Burkett		
Kyle Clifton		
Jeff Lageman		
Mo Lewis		
62 New York Jets B	.30	.75
Johnny Mitchell		
Rob Moore		
Browning Nagle		
Blair Thomas		
Brian Washington		
Marvin Washington		
63 New York Jets C	.40	1.00
Boomer Esiason		
James Hasty		
Ronnie Lott		
Leonard Marshall		
Terance Mathis		
Marvin Jones		
64 Philadelphia Eagles A	.40	1.00
Eric Allen		
Fred Barnett		
Randall Cunningham		
Byron Evans		
Andy Harmon		
Seth Joyner		
65 Philadelphia Eagles B	.40	1.00
Heath Sherman		
Vai Sikahema		
Clyde Simmons		
Herschel Walker		
Andre Waters		
Calvin Williams		
66 Philadelphia Eagles C	.30	.75
Keith Byars		
Mike Golic		
Leonard Renfro		
William Thomas		
Antone Davis		
Lester Holmes		
67 Phoenix Cardinals A	.30	.75
Johnny Bailey		
Rich Camarillo		
Larry Centers		
Chris Chandler		
Ken Harvey		
Randal Hill		
68 Phoenix Cardinals B	.40	1.00
Mark May		
Robert Massey		
Freddie Joe Nunn		
Ricky Proehl		
Eric Hill		
Eric Swann		
69 Phoenix Cardinals C	.50	1.25
Gary Clark		
John Booty		
Chuck Cecil		
Steve Beuerlein		
Ernest Dye		
Garrison Hearst		
70 Pittsburgh Steelers A	.40	1.00
Dermontti Dawson		
Barry Foster		
Jeff Graham		
Eric Green		
Carlton Haselrig		
Bryan Hinkle		
71 Pittsburgh Steelers B	.40	1.00
Merril Hoge		
D.J. Johnson		
Carnell Lake		
David Little		
Neil O'Donnell		
Darren Perry		
72 Pittsburgh Steelers C	.40	1.00
Bubby Brister		
Kevin Greene		
Greg Lloyd		
Leon Searcy		
Rod Woodson		
Deon Figures		
73 San Diego Chargers A	.30	.75
Eric Bieniemy		
Marion Butts		
Burt Grossman		
Ronnie Harmon		
Stan Humphries		
Nate Lewis		
74 San Diego Chargers B	.40	1.00
Chris Mims		
Leslie O'Neal		
Stanley Richard		
Junior Seau		
Harry Swayne		
Derrick Walker		
75 San Diego Chargers C	.40	1.00
Jerrol Williams		
Gill Byrd		
John Friesz		
Anthony Miller		
Gary Plummer		
Darrien Gordon		
76 San Francisco 49ers A	.40	1.00
Ricky Watters		
Michael Carter		
Don Griffin		
Dana Hall		
Brent Jones		
Harris Barton		
77 San Francisco 49ers B	.60	1.50
Tom Rathman		
Jerry Rice		
Bill Romanowski		
John Taylor		
Steve Wallace		
Michael Walter		
78 San Francisco 49ers C	.60	1.50
Kevin Fagan		
Todd Kelly		
Guy McIntyre		
Tim McDonald		
Steve Young		
Dana Stubblefield		
79 Seattle Seahawks A	.30	.75
Robert Blackmon		
Brian Blades		
Jeff Bryant		
Dwayne Harper		
Andy Heck		
Tommy Kane		
80 Seattle Seahawks B	.40	1.00
Cortez Kennedy		
Dan McGwire		
Rufus Porter		
Ray Roberts		
Eugene Robinson		
Chris Warren		
81 Seattle Seahawks C	.40	1.00
Ferrell Edmunds		
Kelvin Martin		
John L. Williams		
Tony Woods		
David Wyman		
Rick Mirer		
82 Tampa Bay Buccaneers A	.30	.75
Gary Anderson RB		
Tyji Armstrong		
Reggie Cobb		
Lawrence Dawsey		
Steve DeBerg		
Santana Dotson		
83 Tampa Bay Buccaneers B	.30	.75
Ron Hall		
Courtney Hawkins		
Keith McCants		
Charles McRae		
Ricky Reynolds		
Broderick Thomas		
84 Tampa Bay Buccaneers C	.30	.75
Vince Workman		
Paul Gruber		
Hardy Nickerson		
Marty Carter		
Mark Wheeler		
Eric Curry		

85 Washington Redskins A	.40	1.00
Earnest Byner		
Andre Collins		
Brad Edwards		
Ricky Ervins		
Darrell Green		
Desmond Howard		
86 Washington Redskins B	.40	1.00
Tim Johnson		
Jim Lachey		
Chip Lohmiller		
Mark Rypien		
Ricky Sanders		
Mark Schlereth		
87 Washington Redskins C	.40	1.00
Al Noga		
Kurt Gouveia		
Charles Mann		
Wilber Marshall		
Art Monk		
Tom Carter		

1996 McDonald's Looney Tunes Cups

These cups were available at participating McDonald's restaurants during the 1996 Season. Each player cup has a corresponding Looney Tunes character on the cup with them.

COMPLETE SET (4)	2.40	6.00
1 Drew Bledsoe	.50	1.25
Wile E. Coyote		
2 Dan Marino	.80	2.00
Daffy Duck		
3 Barry Sanders	.50	1.25
Tazmanian Devil		
4 Emmitt Smith	.80	2.00
Bugs Bunny		

2003 Merrick Mint Laser Line Gold

The Merrick Mint produced these licensed etched cards printed on gold foil stock in 2003. The set is commonly referred to as Laser Line Gold cards since that name is printed on the cardbacks.

1 Jerome Bettis	4.00	10.00
2 Drew Bledsoe	4.00	10.00
3 Tom Brady	6.00	15.00
4 David Carr	4.00	10.00
5 Daunte Culpepper	4.00	10.00
6 Marshall Faulk	4.00	10.00
7 Brett Favre	6.00	15.00
8 Rich Gannon	4.00	10.00
9 Eddie George	4.00	10.00
10 Edgerrin James	4.00	10.00
11 Peyton Manning	6.00	15.00
12 Donovan McNabb	4.00	10.00
13 Randy Moss	4.00	10.00
14 Chad Pennington	4.00	10.00
15 Carson Palmer	4.00	10.00
16 Jerry Rice	5.00	12.00
17 Warren Sapp	4.00	10.00
18 Jeremy Shockey	4.00	10.00
19 Emmitt Smith	6.00	15.00
20 Michael Strahan	4.00	10.00
21 LaDainian Tomlinson	4.00	10.00
22 Brian Urlacher	4.00	10.00
23 Kurt Warner	4.00	10.00
24 Ricky Williams	4.00	10.00
25 Michael Vick	5.00	12.00

2005 Merrick Mint Sculpted Gold Cards

1 Tom Brady	7.50

2006 Merrick Mint Draft Picks Silver Sig

This series of laser line foil cards was produced by Merrick Mint and relased in June 2006. Each card features a gold foil front and back etched in black with a player image from the 2006 NFL Draft. The backs include information about the laser line printing process as well as a stamped serial number. The cardfronts included a facsimile player autograph printed in one of three different foil colors. The Silver Sig version was produced in quantities of 2006, the Gold Sig version was 499-copies, and the Holographic Gold was printed in a quantity of 99-cards.

*GOLD SIG: .5X TO 1.2X SILVER SIG
*HOLO.GOLD: .6X TO 1.5X SILVER SIG

1 Reggie Bush	12.00	20.00
2 Jay Cutler	10.00	15.00
3 Matt Leinart	10.00	15.00
4 Vince Young	10.00	15.00

2006 Merrick Mint Feel the Game Sculpted Gold Cards

1 Brett Favre	7.50	15.00
2 Ben Roethlisberger	7.50	15.00
3 Brian Urlacher	7.50	15.00

2006 Merrick Mint Reggie Bush

This 3-card set issued by Merrick Mint in June 2006. Each card was printed in an all-gold foil front and back with a black etched design. The player's name and team name appear below the image and the backs are identical for the 3-cards. The cardfronts also feature a gold holofoil facsimile signature. Each is serial numbered of 619-cards made.

COMPLETE SET (3)	15.00	30.00
1 Reggie Bush	6.00	12.00
Wearing Saints jersey		
2 Reggie Bush	6.00	12.00
Holding up Saints jersey		
3 Reggie Bush	6.00	12.00
Holding Heisman trophy		

2007 Merrick Mint Laser Line Gold

1 Adrian Peterson	6.00	12.00
2 Brady Quinn	5.00	10.00
3 JaMarcus Russell	4.00	8.00

1995 Metal

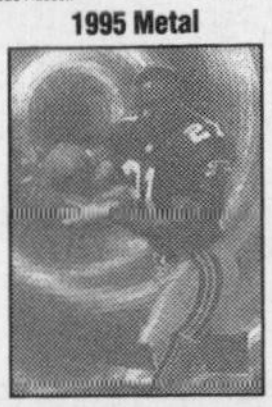

This set marked the debut season for the 200 card all foil-etched standard-size set. Cards were available in 8 card packs for the suggested retail price of $2.49. Card fronts feature different silver-etched backgrounds with the player's name and "Fleer Metal" logo at the bottom. Card backs are "machine-like" with player statistics and biographical information. The set is ordered by teams. Rookie Cards include Jeff Blake, Ki-Jana Carter, Kerry Collins, Joey Galloway, Steve McNair, Rashaan Salaam, J.J. Stokes and Michael Westbrook. Also included in random packs was an instant winner card for a trip to Super Bowl XXX. A Trent Dilfer Sample card was produced and priced below.

COMPLETE SET (200)	7.50	20.00
1 Garrison Hearst	.15	.40
2 Seth Joyner	.02	.10
3 Dave Krieg	.02	.10
4 Lorenzo Lynch	.02	.10
5 Rob Moore	.07	.20
6 Eric Swann	.07	.20
7 Aeneas Williams	.02	.10
8 Chris Doleman	.02	.10
9 Bert Emanuel	.15	.40
10 Jeff George	.07	.20
11 Craig Heyward	.07	.20
12 Terance Mathis	.07	.20
13 Eric Metcalf	.07	.20
14 Cornelius Bennett	.07	.20
15 Bucky Brooks	.02	.10
16 Jeff Burris	.02	.10
17 Jim Kelly	.15	.40
18 Andre Reed	.07	.20
19 Bruce Smith	.15	.40
20 Don Beebe	.02	.10
21 Kerry Collins RC	.75	2.00
22 Barry Foster	.07	.20
23 Lamar Lathon	.02	.10
24 Sam Mills	.07	.20
25 Tyrone Poole RC	.15	.40
26 Frank Reich	.02	.10
27 Joe Cain	.02	.10
28 Curtis Conway	.15	.40
29 Jeff Graham	.02	.10
30 Erik Kramer	.02	.10
31 Rashaan Salaam RC	.07	.20
32 Lewis Tillman	.02	.10
33 Chris Zorich	.02	.10
34 Jeff Blake RC	.30	.75
35 Ki-Jana Carter RC	.15	.40
36 Carl Pickens	.07	.20
37 Corey Sawyer	.02	.10
38 Darnay Scott	.07	.20
39 Dan Wilkinson	.07	.20
40 Darryl Williams	.02	.10
41 Derrick Alexander WR	.15	.40
42 Leroy Hoard	.02	.10
43 Michael Jackson	.07	.20
44 Antonio Langham	.02	.10
45 Andre Rison	.07	.20
46 Vinny Testaverde	.07	.20
47 Eric Turner	.02	.10
48 Troy Aikman	.40	1.00
49 Charles Haley	.07	.20
50 Michael Irvin	.15	.40
51 Daryl Johnston	.07	.20
52 Jay Novacek	.07	.20
53 Emmitt Smith	.60	1.50
54 Kevin Williams WR	.07	.20
55 Steve Atwater	.02	.10
56 Rod Bernstine	.02	.10
57 John Elway	.75	2.00
58 Glyn Milburn	.02	.10
59 Anthony Miller	.07	.20
60 Mike Pritchard	.02	.10
61 Shannon Sharpe	.07	.20
62 Mike Johnson	.02	.10
63 Scott Mitchell	.07	.20
64 Herman Moore	.15	.40
65 Brett Perriman	.07	.20
66 Barry Sanders	.60	1.50
67 Chris Spielman	.07	.20
68 Edgar Bennett	.07	.20
69 Robert Brooks	.15	.40
70 Brett Favre	.75	2.00
71 LeShon Johnson	.07	.20
72 George Koonce	.02	.10
73 Reggie White	.15	.40
74 Gary Brown	.02	.10
75 Cris Dishman	.02	.10
76 Mel Gray	.02	.10
77 Steve McNair RC	1.25	3.00
78 Webster Slaughter	.02	.10
79 Rodney Thomas RC	.07	.20
80 Trev Alberts	.02	.10
81 Quentin Coryatt	.07	.20
82 Sean Dawkins	.07	.20
83 Craig Erickson	.02	.10
84 Marshall Faulk	.50	1.25
85 Stephen Grant RC	.02	.10
86 Steve Beuerlein	.07	.20
87 Tony Boselli RC	.15	.40
88 Desmond Howard	.07	.20
89 James O. Stewart RC	.50	1.25
90 Marcus Allen	.15	.40
91 Kimble Anders	.07	.20
92 Steve Bono	.07	.20
93 Lake Dawson	.07	.20
94 Greg Hill	.07	.20
95 Neil Smith	.07	.20
96 William White	.02	.10
97 Tim Bowens	.02	.10
98 Bryan Cox	.02	.10
99 Irving Fryar	.07	.20
100 Eric Green	.02	.10
101 Dan Marino	.75	2.00
102 O.J. McDuffie	.15	.40
103 Bernie Parmalee	.07	.20
104 Cris Carter	.15	.40
105 Jack Del Rio	.02	.10
106 Rocket Ismail	.07	.20
107 Warren Moon	.07	.20
108 Jake Reed	.07	.20
109 Dewayne Washington	.07	.20
110 Bruce Armstrong	.02	.10
111 Drew Bledsoe	.25	.60
112 Vincent Brisby	.02	.10
113 Ben Coates	.07	.20
114 Willie McGinest	.07	.20
115 Dave Meggett	.02	.10
116 Chris Slade	.02	.10
117 Mario Bates	.07	.20
118 Quinn Early	.07	.20
119 Jim Everett	.02	.10
120 Michael Haynes	.07	.20
121 Tyrone Hughes	.07	.20
122 Renaldo Turnbull	.02	.10
123 Ray Zellers RC	.07	.20
124 Dave Brown	.07	.20
125 Chris Calloway	.02	.10
126 Rodney Hampton	.07	.20
127 Thomas Lewis	.07	.20
128 Phillippi Sparks	.02	.10
129 Tyrone Wheatley RC	.50	1.25
130 Kyle Brady RC	.15	.40
131 Boomer Esiason	.07	.20
132 Aaron Glenn	.02	.10
133 Bobby Houston	.02	.10
134 Mo Lewis	.02	.10
135 Johnny Mitchell	.02	.10
136 Ronald Moore	.02	.10
137 Greg Biekert	.02	.10
138 Tim Brown	.15	.40
139 Jeff Hostetler	.07	.20
140 Rocket Ismail	.07	.20
141 Napoleon Kaufman RC	.50	1.25
142 Chester McGlockton	.07	.20
143 Harvey Williams	.02	.10
144 Fred Barnett	.07	.20
145 Randall Cunningham	.15	.40
146 William Fuller	.02	.10
147 Charlie Garner	.15	.40
148 Andy Harmon	.02	.10
149 Ricky Watters	.07	.20
150 Calvin Williams	.07	.20
151 Kevin Greene	.07	.20
152 Charles Johnson	.07	.20
153 Greg Lloyd	.07	.20
154 Byron Bam Morris	.02	.10
155 Neil O'Donnell	.07	.20
156 Darren Perry	.02	.10
157 Rod Woodson	.07	.20
158 Jerome Bettis	.15	.40
159 Isaac Bruce	.25	.60
160 Troy Drayton	.02	.10
161 Sean Gilbert	.07	.20
162 Todd Lyght	.02	.10
163 Chris Miller	.02	.10
164 Andre Coleman	.02	.10
165 Stan Humphries	.07	.20
166 Shawn Jefferson	.02	.10
167 Natrone Means	.07	.20
168 Leslie O'Neal	.07	.20
169 Junior Seau	.15	.40
170 Mark Seay	.07	.20
171 William Floyd	.07	.20
172 Merton Hanks	.02	.10
173 Brent Jones	.02	.10
174 Jerry Rice	.40	1.00
175 Deion Sanders UER	.25	.60
Card lists him as a linebacker		
176 J.J. Stokes RC	.15	.40
177 Lee Woodall	.02	.10
178 Bryant Young	.07	.20
179 Steve Young	.30	.75
180 Brian Blades	.07	.20
181 Joey Galloway RC	.60	1.50
182 Cortez Kennedy	.07	.20
183 Kevin Mawae	.02	.10
184 Rick Mirer	.07	.20
185 Chris Warren	.07	.20
186 Lawrence Dawsey	.02	.10
187 Trent Dilfer	.15	.40
188 Paul Gruber	.02	.10
189 Hardy Nickerson	.02	.10
190 Errict Rhett	.07	.20
191 Warren Sapp RC	.60	1.50
192 Tom Carter	.02	.10
193 Henry Ellard	.07	.20
194 Darrell Green	.02	.10
195 Brian Mitchell	.02	.10
196 Heath Shuler	.07	.20
197 Michael Westbrook RC	.15	.40
198 Checklist 1-96	.02	.10
199 Checklist 97-200	.02	.10
200 Checklist Inserts	.02	.10
S1 Trent Dilfer Sample	.40	1.00

1995 Metal Gold Blasters

COMPLETE SET (18)	12.00	30.00
STATED ODDS 1:6		
1 Troy Aikman	1.00	2.50
2 Jerome Bettis	.40	1.00
3 Tim Brown	.40	1.00
4 Ben Coates	.20	.50
5 John Elway	2.00	5.00
6 Brett Favre	2.00	5.00
7 William Floyd	.20	.50
8 Joey Galloway	.75	1.50
9 Rodney Hampton	.20	.50
10 Dan Marino	2.00	5.00
11 Steve McNair	1.50	3.00
12 Herman Moore	.40	1.00
13 Errict Rhett	.20	.50
14 Rashaan Salaam	.07	.20
15 Chris Warren	.20	.50
16 Michael Westbrook	.15	.40
17 Rod Woodson	.20	.50
18 Steve Young	.75	2.00

1995 Metal Platinum Portraits

COMPLETE SET (12)	7.50	20.00
STATED ODDS 1:9		
1 Drew Bledsoe	1.00	2.00
2 Ki-Jana Carter	.60	1.25
3 Marshall Faulk	2.00	4.00
4 Natrone Means	.25	.60
5 Byron Bam Morris	.10	.30
6 Jerry Rice	1.50	3.00
7 Andre Rison	.25	.60
8 Barry Sanders	2.50	5.00
9 Deion Sanders	1.00	2.00
10 Emmitt Smith	2.50	5.00
11 J.J. Stokes	.60	1.25
12 Ricky Watters	.25	.60

1995 Metal Silver Flashers

COMPLETE SET (50)	12.50	30.00
STATED ODDS 1:2		
1 Troy Aikman	1.00	2.00
2 Marcus Allen	.30	.75
3 Jerome Bettis	.30	.75
4 Drew Bledsoe	.60	1.25
5 Tim Brown	.30	.75
6 Cris Carter	.30	.75
7 Ki-Jana Carter	.15	.40
8 Ben Coates	.15	.40
9 Kerry Collins	.75	2.00
10 Randall Cunningham	.30	.75
11 Lake Dawson	.15	.40
12 Trent Dilfer	.30	.75
13 John Elway	2.00	4.00
14 Jim Everett	.07	.20
15 Marshall Faulk	1.25	2.50
16 Brett Favre	2.00	4.00
17 William Floyd	.15	.40
18 Jeff George	.15	.40
19 Rodney Hampton	.15	.40
20 Jeff Hostetler	.15	.40
21 Stan Humphries	.15	.40
22 Michael Irvin	.30	.75
23 Cortez Kennedy	.15	.40
24 Dan Marino	2.00	4.00
25 Terance Mathis	.15	.40
26 Willie McGinest	.15	.40
27 Natrone Means	.15	.40
28 Rick Mirer	.15	.40
29 Warren Moon	.15	.40
30 Herman Moore	.30	.75
31 Byron Bam Morris	.07	.20
32 Carl Pickens	.15	.40
33 Errict Rhett	.15	.40
34 Jerry Rice	1.00	2.00
35 Andre Rison	.15	.40
36 Rashaan Salaam	.07	.20
37 Barry Sanders	1.50	3.00
38 Deion Sanders	.60	1.25
39 Junior Seau	.30	.75
40 Shannon Sharpe	.15	.40
41 Heath Shuler	.15	.40
42 Emmitt Smith	1.50	3.00
43 J.J. Stokes	.15	.40
44 Chris Warren	.15	.40
45 Ricky Watters	.15	.40
46 Michael Westbrook	.15	.40
47 Tyrone Wheatley	.60	1.25
48 Reggie White	.30	.75
49 Rod Woodson	.15	.40
50 Steve Young	.75	1.50

1996 Metal Samples

COMPLETE SET (3)	1.50	4.00
S1 Trent Dilfer	.30	.75
S2 Brett Favre	1.00	2.50
S3 Dave Meggett	.30	.75
NNO Uncut Panel	1.50	4.00

1996 Metal

The 1996 Fleer Metal set was issued in one series totalling 150 cards and features metallized foil engraved by hand on each card front making no two player cards alike. The eight-card packs retail for $2.49 each. The set contains the subset Rookies (124-148).

COMPLETE SET (150)	10.00	25.00
1 Garrison Hearst	.07	.20
2 Rob Moore	.07	.20
3 Frank Sanders	.07	.20
4 Eric Swann	.02	.10
5 Jeff George	.07	.20
6 Craig Heyward	.02	.10
7 Terance Mathis	.02	.10
8 Eric Metcalf	.02	.10
9 Derrick Alexander WR	.07	.20
10 Andre Rison	.07	.20
11 Vinny Testaverde	.07	.20
12 Eric Turner	.02	.10
13 Jim Kelly	.15	.40
14 Bryce Paup	.02	.10
15 Bruce Smith	.07	.20
16 Thurman Thomas	.15	.40
17 Bob Christian	.02	.10
18 Kerry Collins	.15	.40
19 Lamar Lathon	.02	.10
20 Tyrone Poole	.02	.10
21 Curtis Conway	.15	.40
22 Bryan Cox	.02	.10
23 Erik Kramer	.02	.10
24 Rashaan Salaam	.07	.20
25 Jeff Blake	.15	.40
26 Ki-Jana Carter	.07	.20
27 Carl Pickens	.07	.20
28 Darnay Scott	.07	.20
29 Troy Aikman	.40	1.00
30 Michael Irvin	.15	.40
31 Daryl Johnston	.07	.20
32 Deion Sanders	.25	.60
33 Emmitt Smith	.60	1.50
34 Terrell Davis	.30	.75
35 John Elway	.75	2.00
36 Anthony Miller	.07	.20
37 Shannon Sharpe	.07	.20
38 Scott Mitchell	.07	.20
39 Herman Moore	.07	.20
40 Brett Perriman	.02	.10
41 Barry Sanders	.60	1.50
42 Edgar Bennett	.07	.20
43 Robert Brooks	.15	.40
44 Mark Chmura	.07	.20
45 Brett Favre	.75	2.00
46 Reggie White	.15	.40
47 Mel Gray	.02	.10
48 Steve McNair	.30	.75
49 Chris Sanders	.07	.20
50 Rodney Thomas	.02	.10
51 Quentin Coryatt	.02	.10
52 Sean Dawkins	.02	.10
53 Ken Dilger	.07	.20
54 Marshall Faulk	.20	.50
55 Jim Harbaugh	.07	.20
56 Tony Boselli	.02	.10
57 Mark Brunell	.25	.60
58 Natrone Means	.07	.20
59 James O.Stewart	.07	.20
60 Marcus Allen	.15	.40
61 Steve Bono	.02	.10
62 Neil Smith	.07	.20
63 Tamarick Vanover	.07	.20
64 Eric Green	.02	.10
65 Terry Kirby	.07	.20
66 Dan Marino	.75	2.00
67 O.J. McDuffie	.07	.20
68 Cris Carter	.15	.40
69 Qadry Ismail	.07	.20
70 Warren Moon	.07	.20
71 Jake Reed	.07	.20
72 Drew Bledsoe	.25	.60
73 Ben Coates	.07	.20
74 Curtis Martin	.30	.75
75 Dave Meggett	.02	.10
76 Mario Bates	.07	.20
77 Jim Everett	.02	.10
78 Michael Haynes	.02	.10
79 Tyrone Hughes	.02	.10
80 Dave Brown	.02	.10
81 Rodney Hampton	.07	.20
82 Thomas Lewis	.02	.10
83 Tyrone Wheatley	.07	.20
84 Kyle Brady	.02	.10
85 Hugh Douglas	.07	.20
86 Adrian Murrell	.07	.20
87 Neil O'Donnell	.07	.20
88 Tim Brown	.15	.40
89 Jeff Hostetler	.02	.10
90 Napoleon Kaufman	.15	.40
91 Harvey Williams	.02	.10
92 Charlie Garner	.07	.20
93 Rodney Peete	.02	.10
94 Ricky Watters	.07	.20
95 Calvin Williams	.02	.10
96 Jerome Bettis	.15	.40
97 Greg Lloyd	.07	.20
98 Kordell Stewart	.15	.40
99 Yancey Thigpen	.07	.20
100 Rod Woodson	.07	.20
101 Isaac Bruce	.15	.40
102 Kevin Carter	.02	.10
103 Steve Walsh	.02	.10
104 Aaron Hayden	.02	.10
105 Stan Humphries	.07	.20
106 Junior Seau	.15	.40
107 William Floyd	.07	.20
108 Brent Jones	.02	.10
109 Jerry Rice	.40	1.00
110 J.J. Stokes	.15	.40
111 Steve Young	.30	.75
112 Brian Blades	.02	.10
113 Joey Galloway	.15	.40
114 Rick Mirer	.07	.20
115 Chris Warren	.07	.20
116 Trent Dilfer	.15	.40
117 Alvin Harper	.02	.10
118 Hardy Nickerson	.02	.10
119 Errict Rhett	.07	.20
120 Terry Allen	.07	.20
121 Brian Mitchell	.02	.10
122 Heath Shuler	.07	.20
123 Michael Westbrook	.15	.40
124 Karim Abdul-Jabbar RC	.15	.40
125 Tim Biakabutuka RC	.15	.40
126 Duane Clemons RC	.02	.10
127 Stephen Davis RC	.75	2.00
128 Rickey Dudley RC	.15	.40
129 Bobby Engram RC	.15	.40
130 Daryl Gardener RC	.02	.10
131 Eddie George RC	.60	1.50
132 Terry Glenn RC	.50	1.25
133 Kevin Hardy RC	.15	.40
134 Walt Harris RC	.02	.10
135 Marvin Harrison RC	1.25	3.00
136 Keyshawn Johnson RC	.50	1.25
137 Cedric Jones RC	.02	.10
138 Eddie Kennison RC	.15	.40
139 Sam Manuel RC	.02	.10
Sean Manuel RC		
140 Leeland McElroy RC	.07	.20
141 Ray Mickens RC	.02	.10
142 Johathan Ogden RC	.15	.40
143 Lawrence Phillips RC	.15	.40
144 Kavika Pittman RC	.02	.10
145 Simeon Rice RC	.40	1.00
146 Regan Upshaw RC	.02	.10
147 Alex Van Dyke RC	.07	.20
148 Stepfret Williams RC	.07	.20
149 Checklist	.02	.10
150 Checklist	.02	.10

1996 Metal Precious Metal

COMPLETE SET (148)	250.00	500.00
*VETS: 10X TO 25X BASIC CARDS		
*ROOKIES: 6X TO 15X BASIC CARDS		
ONE PER BOX		

1996 Metal Freshly Forged

COMPLETE SET (10)	15.00	40.00
STATED ODDS 1:80 HOBBY		
1 Tim Biakabutuka	.75	2.00
2 Jeff Blake	2.50	6.00
3 Ki-Jana Carter	1.25	3.00
4 Eddie George	3.00	8.00
5 Terry Glenn	2.50	6.00
6 Keyshawn Johnson	2.50	6.00
7 Curtis Martin	5.00	12.00
8 Leeland McElroy	.40	1.00
9 Lawrence Phillips	.75	2.00
10 Kordell Stewart	2.50	6.00

1996 Metal Goldfingers

COMPLETE SET (12)	7.50	20.00
STATED ODDS 1:8		
1 Isaac Bruce	1.25	3.00
2 Joey Galloway	1.25	3.00
3 Michael Irvin	1.25	3.00
4 Herman Moore	.60	1.50
5 Carl Pickens	.60	1.50
6 Jerry Rice	3.00	8.00
7 Chris Sanders	.60	1.50
8 Frank Sanders	.60	1.50
9 J.J. Stokes	1.25	3.00
10 Yancey Thigpen	.60	1.50
11 Tamarick Vanover	.60	1.50
12 Michael Westbrook	1.25	3.00

1996 Metal Goldflingers

COMPLETE SET (12)	10.00	25.00
STATED ODDS 1:12 RETAIL		
1 Troy Aikman	1.50	4.00
2 Steve Bono	.15	.40
3 Kerry Collins	.60	1.50
4 Trent Dilfer	.60	1.50
5 Brett Favre	3.00	8.00
6 Gus Frerotte	.30	.75
7 Stan Humphries	.30	.75
8 Dan Marino	3.00	8.00
9 Steve McNair	1.25	3.00
10 Scott Mitchell	.30	.75
11 Steve Young	1.25	3.00
12 Eric Zeier	.60	1.50

1996 Metal Molten Metal

COMPLETE SET (10)	30.00	80.00
STATED ODDS 1:120		
1 Troy Aikman	5.00	12.00
2 Ki-Jana Carter	1.00	2.50
3 Kerry Collins	2.00	5.00
4 Terrell Davis	4.00	10.00
5 Marshall Faulk	2.50	6.00
6 Brett Favre	10.00	25.00
7 Keyshawn Johnson	2.00	5.00
8 Curtis Martin	4.00	10.00
9 Deion Sanders	3.00	8.00
10 Emmitt Smith	8.00	20.00

1996 Metal Platinum Portraits

COMPLETE SET (10)	35.00	80.00
1-10: STATED ODDS 1:50		
11-12: AVAIL.VIA WRAPPER OFFER		
1 Isaac Bruce	1.50	4.00
2 Terrell Davis	3.00	8.00
3 John Elway	8.00	20.00
4 Joey Galloway	1.50	4.00
5 Steve McNair	3.00	8.00
6 Errict Rhett	.75	2.00
7 Rashaan Salaam	.75	2.00
8 Barry Sanders	6.00	15.00
9 Chris Warren	.75	2.00
10 Steve Young	3.00	8.00
11 Eddie George	3.00	8.00
12 Simeon Rice	2.00	5.00

1997 Metal Universe

The 1997 Metal Universe set was issued in one series totalling 200-cards and was distributed in eight-card packs with a suggested retail price of $2.49. The fronts feature action photography with Marvel comic art backgrounds on etched foil card stock. The backs carry player information and career statistics with the player's best statistical category highlighted.

COMPLETE SET (200)	7.50	20.00
1 Terry Glenn	.10	.30
2 Terry Kirby	.10	.30
3 Thomas Lewis	.07	.20
4 Tim Biakabutuka	.10	.30
5 Tim Brown	.20	.50
6 Todd Collins	.07	.20
7 Tony Banks	.10	.30
8 Tony Brackens	.07	.20
9 Tony Martin	.07	.20
10 Trent Dilfer	.20	.50
11 Troy Aikman	.40	1.00
12 Ty Detmer	.10	.30
13 Tyrone Wheatley	.10	.30
14 Vinny Testaverde	.10	.30
15 Wayne Chrebet	.20	.50
16 Wesley Walls	.10	.30
17 William Floyd	.10	.30
18 Willie McGinest	.10	.30
19 Yancey Thigpen	.10	.30
20 Zach Thomas	.20	.50
21 Terry Allen	.20	.50
22 Terrell Owens	.25	.60
23 Terrell Davis	.25	.60
24 Terance Mathis	.10	.30
25 Ted Johnson	.07	.20
26 Tamarick Vanover	.07	.20
27 Steve Young	.25	.60
28 Steve McNair	.25	.60
29 Stan Humphries	.10	.30
30 Simeon Rice	.10	.30
31 Shannon Sharpe	.20	.50
32 Sean Jones	.07	.20
33 Scott Mitchell	.10	.30
34 Sam Mills	.10	.30
35 Rodney Hampton	.10	.30
36 Rod Woodson	.20	.50
37 Robert Smith	.10	.30
38 Rob Moore	.10	.30
39 Ricky Watters	.10	.30
40 Rickey Dudley	.10	.30
41 Rick Mirer	.07	.20
42 Reggie White	.20	.50
43 Ray Zellars	.07	.20
44 Ray Lewis	.30	.75
45 Rashaan Salaam	.07	.20
46 Quentin Coryatt	.07	.20
47 Qadry Ismail	.10	.30
48 O.J. McDuffie	.10	.30
49 Nilo Silvan	.07	.20
50 Neil Smith	.10	.30
51 Neil O'Donnell	.10	.30
52 Natrone Means	.10	.30
53 Napoleon Kaufman	.10	.30
54 Mike Tomczak	.07	.20
55 Mike Alstott	.20	.50
56 Michael Westbrook	.10	.30
57 Michael Jackson	.10	.30
58 Michael Irvin	.20	.50
59 Michael Haynes	.07	.20
60 Michael Bates	.07	.20
61 Mel Gray	.07	.20
62 Marvin Harrison	.20	.50
63 Marshall Faulk	.20	.50
64 Mark Brunell	.20	.50
65 Mario Bates	.07	.20
66 Marcus Allen	.20	.50
67 Lorenzo Neal	.07	.20
68 Levon Kirkland	.07	.20
69 Leonard Russell	.07	.20
70 Leeland McElroy	.07	.20
71 Lawyer Milloy	.10	.30
72 Lawrence Phillips	.07	.20
73 Larry Centers	.10	.30
74 Lamar Lathon	.07	.20
75 Kordell Stewart	.20	.50
76 Kimble Anders	.10	.30
77 Ki-Jana Carter	.10	.30
78 Keyshawn Johnson	.20	.50
79 Kevin Turner	.07	.20
80 Jermaine Lewis	.10	.30
81 Jerome Bettis	.20	.50
82 Jerris McPhail	.07	.20
83 Joey Galloway	.10	.30
84 Jerry Rice	.40	1.00
85 Jim Everett	.07	.20
86 Jimmy Smith	.10	.30
87 Jim Harbaugh	.20	.50
88 John Elway	.75	2.00
89 John Friesz	.07	.20
90 John Mobley	.07	.20
91 Johnnie Morton	.10	.30
92 Junior Seau	.20	.50
93 Karim Abdul-Jabbar	.10	.30
94 Keenan McCardell	.10	.30
95 Ken Dilger	.07	.20
96 Ken Norton	.07	.20
97 Kent Graham	.07	.20
98 Kerry Collins	.20	.50
99 Kevin Greene	.10	.30
100 Kevin Hardy	.07	.20
101 Jeff Lewis	.07	.20
102 Jeff George	.10	.30
103 Jeff Graham	.07	.20
104 Jeff Blake	.10	.30
105 Jason Sehorn	.10	.30
106 Jason Dunn	.07	.20
107 Jamie Asher	.07	.20
108 Jamal Anderson	.10	.30
109 Jake Reed	.10	.30
110 Isaac Bruce	.20	.50
111 Irving Fryar	.10	.30
112 Iheanyi Uwaezuoke	.07	.20
113 Hugh Douglas	.07	.20
114 Herman Moore	.10	.30
115 Harvey Williams	.07	.20
116 Hardy Nickerson	.07	.20
117 Gus Frerotte	.07	.20
118 Greg Hill	.07	.20
119 Glyn Milburn	.07	.20
120 Frank Wycheck	.07	.20
121 Frank Sanders	.10	.30
122 Errict Rhett	.07	.20
123 Erik Kramer	.07	.20
124 Eric Moulds	.10	.30
125 Eric Metcalf	.10	.30
126 Emmitt Smith	.60	1.50
127 Edgar Bennett	.10	.30
128 Eddie Kennison	.10	.30
129 Eddie George	.20	.50
130 Drew Bledsoe	.20	.50
131 Dorsey Levens	.10	.30
132 Desmond Howard	.10	.30
133 Derrick Thomas	.20	.50
134 Derrick Alexander WR	.10	.30
135 Deion Sanders	.20	.50
136 Dave Brown	.07	.20
137 Daryl Johnston	.20	.50
138 Darnay Scott	.10	.30
139 Darick Holmes	.07	.20
140 Dan Marino	.75	2.00
141 Curtis Martin	.20	.50
142 Curtis Conway	.10	.30
143 Cris Carter	.20	.50
144 Chris Warren	.10	.30
145 Chris T. Jones	.07	.20
146 Chris Slade	.07	.20
147 Chris Sanders	.07	.20
148 Chester McGlockton	.07	.20
149 Charlie Jones	.07	.20
150 Charles Way	.07	.20
151 Carl Pickens	.10	.30
152 Bryan Still	.07	.20
153 Bruce Smith	.20	.50
154 Brian Mitchell	.07	.20
155 Brett Perriman	.07	.20
156 Brett Favre	1.00	2.50
157 Brad Johnson	.10	.30
158 Thurman Thomas	.20	.50
159 Bobby Engram	.10	.30
160 Bert Emanuel	.10	.30
161 Ben Coates	.10	.30
162 Barry Sanders	.60	1.50
163 Byron Bam Morris	.07	.20
164 Ashley Ambrose	.07	.20
165 Antonio Freeman	.20	.50
166 Anthony Miller	.07	.20
167 Anthony Johnson	.07	.20
168 Andre Rison	.10	.30
169 Andre Reed	.10	.30
170 Alex Molden	.07	.20
171 Aeneas Williams	.07	.20
172 Adrian Murrell	.10	.30
173 Aaron Hayden	.07	.20
174 Darnell Autry RC	.10	.30
175 Orlando Pace RC	.20	.50
176 Darrell Russell RC	.07	.20
177 Peter Boulware RC	.20	.50
178 Shawn Springs RC	.10	.30
179 Bryant Westbrook RC	.07	.20
180 Dwayne Rudd RC	.10	.30
181 Rae Carruth RC	.07	.20
182 Troy Davis RC	.10	.30
183 Antowain Smith RC	.20	.50
184 James Farrior RC	.20	.50
185 Walter Jones RC	.10	.30
186 Sam Madison RC	.20	.50
187 Tom Knight RC	.07	.20
188 Reidel Anthony RC	.20	.50
189 Warrick Dunn RC	.50	1.25
190 Reinard Wilson RC	.10	.30
191 Tyrus McCloud RC	.07	.20
192 Michael Booker RC	.07	.20
193 Tony Gonzalez RC	.75	2.00
194 Pat Barnes RC	.07	.20
195 Tiki Barber RC	.75	2.00
196 Sedrick Shaw RC	.10	.30
197 Corey Dillon RC	.50	1.25
198 Danny Wuerffel RC	.20	.50
199 Checklist (1-152)	.07	.20
200 Checklist/153-200	.07	.20
inserts		
S1 Terrell Davis Sample	.75	2.00

1997 Metal Universe Precious Metal Gems

*PREC.METAL/150: 25X TO 60X BASIC CARDS
STATED PRINT RUN 150 SER.#'d SETS

1997 Metal Universe Precious Metal Gems Green

*VETS 1-173: 125X TO 250X BASIC CARDS
*ROOKIES 174-198: 100X TO 200X
FIRST 15 SERIAL #'d CARDS ARE GREEN

84 Jerry Rice	175.00	300.00
88 John Elway	250.00	500.00
126 Emmitt Smith	250.00	400.00
140 Dan Marino	250.00	500.00
156 Brett Favre	300.00	600.00
162 Barry Sanders	250.00	400.00
193 Tony Gonzalez	200.00	400.00
195 Tiki Barber	200.00	400.00

1997 Metal Universe Body Shop

COMPLETE SET (15)	50.00	120.00
STATED ODDS 1:96		
1 Zach Thomas	6.00	15.00
2 Steve Young	8.00	20.00
3 Steve McNair	8.00	20.00
4 Simeon Rice	4.00	10.00
5 Shannon Sharpe	4.00	10.00
6 Napoleon Kaufman	6.00	15.00
7 Mike Alstott	6.00	15.00
8 Michael Westbrook	4.00	10.00
9 Kordell Stewart	6.00	15.00
10 Kevin Hardy	2.50	6.00
11 Kerry Collins	6.00	15.00
12 Junior Seau	6.00	15.00
13 Jamal Anderson	6.00	15.00
14 Drew Bledsoe	8.00	20.00
15 Deion Sanders	6.00	15.00

1997 Metal Universe Gold Universe

COMPLETE SET (10)	50.00	120.00
STATED ODDS 1:120 RETAIL		
1 Dan Marino	20.00	50.00
2 Deion Sanders	5.00	12.00
3 Drew Bledsoe	6.00	15.00
4 Isaac Bruce	5.00	12.00
5 Joey Galloway	3.00	8.00
6 Karim Abdul-Jabbar	3.00	8.00
7 Lawrence Phillips	2.00	5.00
8 Marshall Faulk	6.00	15.00
9 Marvin Harrison	5.00	12.00
10 Steve Young	6.00	15.00

1997 Metal Universe Iron Rookies

COMPLETE SET (15)	40.00	80.00
STATED ODDS 1:24		
1 Darnell Autry	1.50	3.00
2 Orlando Pace	2.00	4.00
3 Peter Boulware	2.00	4.00
4 Shawn Springs	1.50	3.00

5 Bryant Westbrook .60 1.50
6 Rae Carruth .60 1.50
7 Troy Davis 1.50 3.00
8 Antowain Smith 5.00 12.00
9 James Farrior 2.00 4.00
10 Dwayne Rudd .60 1.50
11 Darrell Russell .60 1.50
12 Warrick Dunn 6.00 15.00
13 Sedrick Shaw 1.50 3.00
14 Danny Wuerffel 2.00 4.00
15 Sam Madison 1.50 3.00

1997 Metal Universe Marvel Metal

COMPLETE SET (20) 20.00 50.00
STATED ODDS 1:6
1 Barry Sanders 3.00 8.00
2 Bruce Smith .60 1.50
3 Desmond Howard .60 1.50
4 Eddie George 1.00 2.50
5 Eddie Kennison .60 1.50
6 Jerry Rice 2.00 5.00
7 Joey Galloway .60 1.50
8 John Elway 4.00 10.00
9 Karim Abdul-Jabbar .60 1.50
10 Kerry Collins 1.00 2.50
11 Kevin Hardy .40 1.00
12 Kordell Stewart 1.00 2.50
13 Mark Brunell 1.25 3.00
14 Marshall Faulk 1.25 3.00
15 Michael Westbrook .60 1.50
16 Simeon Rice .60 1.50
17 Steve McNair 1.25 3.00
18 Terry Glenn 1.00 2.50
19 Tony Brackens .40 1.00
20 Tony Martin .60 1.50

1997 Metal Universe Platinum Portraits

COMPLETE SET (10) 60.00 150.00
STATED ODDS 1:288
1 Troy Aikman 8.00 20.00
2 Terrell Davis 5.00 12.00
3 Marvin Harrison 4.00 10.00
4 Keyshawn Johnson 4.00 10.00
5 Jerry Rice 8.00 20.00
6 Emmitt Smith 12.50 30.00
7 Dan Marino 15.00 40.00
8 Curtis Martin 5.00 12.00
9 Brett Favre 15.00 40.00
10 Barry Sanders 12.50 30.00

1997 Metal Universe Titanium

COMPLETE SET (20) 60.00 150.00
STATED ODDS 1:72 HOBBY
1 Barry Sanders 8.00 20.00
2 Brett Favre 10.00 25.00
3 Curtis Martin 3.00 8.00
4 Eddie George 2.50 6.00
5 Eddie Kennison 1.50 4.00
6 Emmitt Smith 8.00 20.00
7 Herman Moore 1.50 4.00
8 Isaac Bruce 2.50 6.00
9 Jerry Rice 5.00 12.00
10 John Elway 10.00 25.00
11 Keyshawn Johnson 2.50 6.00
12 Lawrence Phillips 1.00 2.50
13 Mark Brunell 3.00 8.00
14 Mike Alstott 2.50 6.00
15 Steve McNair 3.00 8.00
16 Steve Young 3.00 8.00
17 Terrell Davis 3.00 8.00
18 Terry Glenn 2.50 6.00
19 Tony Banks 1.50 4.00
20 Troy Aikman 5.00 12.00

1998 Metal Universe Samples

1 Jake Plummer .40 1.00
2 Shannon Sharpe .50 1.25

1998 Metal Universe

The 1998 Metal Universe set was issued in one series totalling 200 cards. The 8-card packs retail for $2.69 each. The set contains the subset: Rookies (173-197), and Checklists (198-200). The fronts feature color action photography on flat foil and placed on a scenic background of the featured player's team state.

COMPLETE SET (200) 15.00 40.00
1 Jerry Rice .40 1.00
2 Muhsin Muhammad .15 .40
3 Ed McCaffrey .15 .40
4 Brett Favre 1.00 2.50
5 Troy Brown .15 .40
6 Brad Johnson .15 .40
7 John Elway .75 2.00
8 Herman Moore .15 .40
9 O.J. McDuffie .15 .40
10 Tim Brown .20 .50
11 Byron Hanspard .10 .30
12 Rae Carruth .10 .30
13 Rod Smith WR .15 .40
14 John Randle .15 .40
15 Karim Abdul-Jabbar .15 .40
16 Bobby Hoying .15 .40
17 Steve Young .25 .60
18 Andre Hastings .10 .30
19 Chidi Ahanotu .10 .30
20 Barry Sanders .60 1.50
21 Bruce Smith .15 .40
22 Kimble Anders .10 .30
23 Troy Davis .10 .30
24 Jamal Anderson .15 .40
25 Curtis Conway .15 .40
26 Mark Chmura .10 .30
27 Reggie White .20 .50
28 Jake Reed .15 .40
29 Willie McGinest .10 .30
30 Terrell Davis .20 .50
31 Joey Galloway .15 .40
32 Leslie Shepherd .10 .30
33 Peter Boulware .10 .30
34 Chad Lewis .10 .30
35 Marcus Allen .20 .50
36 Randal Hill .10 .30
37 Jerome Bettis .20 .50
38 William Floyd .10 .30
39 Warren Moon .20 .50
40 Mike Alstott .20 .50
41 Jay Graham .10 .30
42 Emmitt Smith .60 1.50
43 James O. Stewart .15 .40
44 Charlie Garner .15 .40
45 Merton Hanks .10 .30
46 Shawn Springs .10 .30
47 Chris Calloway .10 .30
48 Larry Centers .10 .30
49 Michael Jackson .10 .30
50 Deion Sanders .20 .50
51 Jimmy Smith .15 .40
52 Jason Sehorn .15 .40
53 Charles Johnson .10 .30
54 Garrison Hearst .15 .40
55 Chris Warren .15 .40
56 Warren Sapp .15 .40
57 Corey Dillon .15 .40
58 Marvin Harrison .20 .50
59 Chris Sanders .10 .30
60 Jamie Asher .10 .30
61 Yancey Thigpen .10 .30
62 Freddie Jones .10 .30
63 Rob Moore .15 .40
64 Jermaine Lewis .10 .30
65 Michael Irvin .20 .50
66 Natrone Means .15 .40
67 Charles Way .10 .30
68 Terry Kirby .10 .30
69 Tony Banks .15 .40
70 Steve McNair .20 .50
71 Vinny Testaverde .15 .40
72 Dexter Coakley .10 .30
73 Keenan McCardell .15 .40
74 Glenn Foley .10 .30
75 Isaac Bruce .20 .50
76 Terry Allen .15 .40
77 Todd Collins .10 .30
78 Troy Aikman .40 1.00
79 Damon Jones .10 .30
80 Leon Johnson .10 .30
81 James Jett .10 .30
82 Frank Wycheck .10 .30
83 Andre Reed .15 .40
84 Derrick Alexander WR .15 .40
85 Jason Taylor .15 .40
86 Wayne Chrebet .20 .50
87 Napoleon Kaufman .15 .40
88 Eddie George .20 .50
89 Ernie Conwell .10 .30
90 Antowain Smith .15 .40
91 Johnnie Morton .15 .40
92 Jerris McPhail .10 .30
93 Cris Carter .20 .50
94 Danny Kanell .10 .30
95 Stan Humphries .10 .30
96 Terrell Owens .20 .50
97 Willie Davis .10 .30
98 David Dunn .10 .30
99 Tony Brackens .10 .30
100 Kordell Stewart .15 .40
101 Rodney Thomas .10 .30
102 Keyshawn Johnson .20 .50
103 Carl Pickens .15 .40
104 Mark Brunell .20 .50
105 Jeff George .15 .40
106 Bert Emanuel .10 .30
107 Wesley Walls .15 .40
108 Bryant Westbrook .10 .30
109 Dorsey Levens .15 .40
110 Drew Bledsoe .20 .50
111 Adrian Murrell .10 .30
112 Aeneas Williams .10 .30
113 Raymont Harris .10 .30
114 Tony Gonzalez .20 .50
115 Sean Dawkins .10 .30
116 Billy Joe Hobert .10 .30
117 James McKnight .15 .40
118 Reidel Anthony .10 .30
119 Terance Mathis .10 .30
120 Darrien Gordon .10 .30
121 Dale Carter .10 .30
122 Duce Staley .20 .50
123 Jerald Moore .10 .30
124 Eric Swann .10 .30
125 Antonio Freeman .20 .50
126 Chris Penn .10 .30
127 Ken Dilger .10 .30
128 Robert Smith .15 .40
129 Tiki Barber .20 .50
130 Mark Bruener .10 .30
131 Junior Seau .20 .50
132 Trent Dilfer .20 .50
133 Gus Frerotte .10 .30
134 Jake Plummer .15 .40
135 Jeff Blake .15 .40
136 Jim Harbaugh .15 .40
137 Michael Strahan .15 .40
138 Gary Brown .10 .30
139 Tony Martin .15 .40
140 Stephen Davis .15 .40
141 Thurman Thomas .20 .50
142 Scott Mitchell .15 .40
143 Dan Marino .75 2.00
144 David Palmer .10 .30
145 J.J. Stokes .10 .30
146 Chris Chandler .15 .40
147 Darnell Autry .10 .30
148 Robert Brooks .15 .40
149 Derrick Mayes .10 .30
150 Curtis Martin .20 .50
151 Steve Broussard .10 .30
152 Eddie Kennison UER .15 .40
('97 stats incorrect)
153 Kerry Collins .15 .40
154 Shannon Sharpe .20 .50
155 Andre Rison .15 .40
156 Dwayne Rudd .10 .30
157 Orlando Pace .10 .30
158 Terry Glenn .15 .40
159 Frank Sanders .10 .30
160 Ricky Proehl .10 .30
161 Marshall Faulk .20 .50
162 Irving Fryar .15 .40
163 Courtney Hawkins .10 .30
164 Eric Metcalf .10 .30
165 Warrick Dunn .20 .50
166 Cris Dishman .10 .30
167 Fred Lane .10 .30
168 John Mobley .10 .30
169 Elvis Grbac .15 .40
170 Ben Coates .15 .40
171 Rickey Dudley .10 .30
172 Ricky Watters .15 .40
173 Alonzo Mayes RC .10 .30
174 Andre Wadsworth RC .15 .40
175 Brian Simmons RC .10 .30
176 Charles Woodson RC .60 1.50
177 Curtis Enis RC .15 .40
178 Fred Taylor RC .60 1.50
179 Germane Crowell RC .15 .40
180 Greg Ellis RC .10 .30
181 Jacquez Green RC .15 .40
182 Jason Peter RC .10 .30
183 John Dutton RC .10 .30
184 Kevin Dyson RC .20 .50
185 Kivuusama Mays RC .10 .30
186 Marcus Nash RC .10 .30
187 Michael Myers RC .10 .30
188 Ahman Green RC .75 2.00
189 Peyton Manning RC 7.50 15.00
190 Randy Moss RC 2.00 5.00
191 Robert Edwards RC .15 .40
192 Robert Holcombe RC .10 .30
193 Ryan Leaf RC .20 .50
194 Takeo Spikes RC .30 .75
195 Tavian Banks RC .15 .40
196 Tim Dwight RC .20 .50
197 Vonnie Holliday RC .15 .40
198 Dorsey Levens CL .10 .30
199 Jerry Rice CL .20 .50
200 Dan Marino CL .30 .75

1998 Metal Universe Precious Metal Gems

*VETS: 60X TO 120X BASIC CARDS
*ROOKIE STARS: 25X TO 60X
STATED PRINT RUN 50 SER.#'d SETS
189 Peyton Manning 500.00 800.00

1998 Metal Universe Decided Edge

COMPLETE SET (10) 150.00 300.00
STATED ODDS 1:288
1 Terrell Davis 5.00 12.00
2 Brett Favre 20.00 50.00
3 John Elway 20.00 50.00
4 Barry Sanders 15.00 40.00
5 Eddie George 5.00 12.00
6 Jerry Rice 10.00 25.00
7 Emmitt Smith 15.00 40.00
8 Dan Marino 20.00 50.00
9 Troy Aikman 10.00 25.00
10 Marcus Allen 5.00 12.00

1998 Metal Universe E-X2001 Previews

COMPLETE SET (15) 125.00 250.00
STATED ODDS 1:144
1 Barry Sanders 15.00 40.00
2 Brett Favre 20.00 50.00
3 Corey Dillon 5.00 12.00
4 John Elway 20.00 50.00
5 Drew Bledsoe 8.00 20.00
6 Eddie George 5.00 12.00
7 Emmitt Smith 15.00 40.00
8 Joey Galloway 3.00 8.00
9 Karim Abdul-Jabbar 5.00 12.00
10 Kordell Stewart 5.00 12.00
11 Mark Brunell 5.00 12.00
12 Mike Alstott 5.00 12.00
13 Warrick Dunn 5.00 12.00
14 Antonio Freeman 5.00 12.00
15 Terrell Davis 5.00 12.00

1998 Metal Universe Planet Football

COMPLETE SET (15) 25.00 50.00
STATED ODDS 1:8
1 Barry Sanders 3.00 8.00
2 Corey Dillon 1.00 2.50
3 Warrick Dunn 1.00 2.50
4 Jake Plummer 1.00 2.50
5 John Elway 4.00 10.00
6 Kordell Stewart 1.00 2.50
7 Curtis Martin 1.00 2.50
8 Mark Brunell 1.00 2.50
9 Dorsey Levens 1.00 2.50
10 Troy Aikman 2.00 5.00
11 Terry Glenn 1.00 2.50
12 Eddie George 1.00 2.50
13 Keyshawn Johnson 1.00 2.50
14 Steve McNair 1.00 2.50
15 Jerry Rice 2.00 5.00

1998 Metal Universe Quasars

COMPLETE SET (15) 25.00 60.00
STATED ODDS 1:20
1 Peyton Manning 15.00 40.00
2 Ryan Leaf 1.25 3.00
3 Charles Woodson 1.50 4.00
4 Randy Moss 10.00 25.00
5 Curtis Enis .60 1.50
6 Tavian Banks 1.00 2.50
7 Germane Crowell 1.00 2.50
8 Kevin Dyson 1.25 3.00
9 Robert Edwards 1.00 2.50
10 Jacquez Green 1.00 2.50
11 Alonzo Mayes .60 1.50
12 Brian Simmons 1.00 2.50
13 Takeo Spikes 1.25 3.00
14 Andre Wadsworth 1.00 2.50
15 Ahman Green 4.00 10.00

1998 Metal Universe Titanium

COMPLETE SET (10) 30.00 80.00
STATED ODDS 1:96
1 Corey Dillon 2.50 6.00
2 Emmitt Smith 8.00 20.00
3 Terrell Davis 2.50 6.00
4 Brett Favre 10.00 25.00
5 Mark Brunell 2.50 6.00
6 Dan Marino 10.00 25.00
7 Curtis Martin 2.50 6.00
8 Kordell Stewart 2.50 6.00
9 Warrick Dunn 2.50 6.00
10 Steve McNair 2.50 6.00

1999 Metal Universe

This 250 card set was issued in eight card packs with a SRP of $2.69 and released in July, 1999. Subsets include Prominent and Dominant (183-207), Rookies (208-247) and Checklist (248-250). Notable Rookie Cards include Tim Couch, Edgerrin James and Ricky Williams. Before the set was released, a Promo Card of Doug Flutie was issued. This card is listed and priced at the end of these listings.

COMPLETE SET (250) 15.00 40.00
1 Eric Moulds .15 .40
2 David Palmer .12 .30
3 Ricky Watters .15 .40
4 Antonio Freeman .15 .40
5 Hugh Douglas .15 .40
6 Johnnie Morton .15 .40
7 Corey Fuller .12 .30
8 J.J. Stokes .12 .30
9 Keith Poole .12 .30
10 Steve Beuerlein .15 .40
11 Keenan McCardell .15 .40
12 Carl Pickens .15 .40
13 Mark Bruener .12 .30
14 Warren Sapp .15 .40
15 Rich Gannon .15 .40
16 Bruce Smith .20 .50
17 Mark Chmura .12 .30
18 Drew Bledsoe .20 .50
19 Charles Woodson .20 .50
20 Ahman Green .15 .40
21 Ricky Proehl .12 .30
22 Corey Dillon .15 .40
23 Terry Fair .12 .30
24 Mark Brunell .15 .40
25 Leroy Hoard .12 .30
26 La'Roi Glover RC .20 .50
27 Tim Brown .20 .50
28 Kevin Turner .12 .30
29 Terrell Owens .20 .50
30 Mike Alstott .20 .50
31 Rob Moore .12 .30
32 Troy Aikman .30 .75
33 Derrick Alexander .12 .30
34 Chris Calloway .12 .30
35 Kordell Stewart .15 .40
36 Reidel Anthony .12 .30
37 Michael Westbrook .12 .30
38 Ray Lewis .20 .50
39 Alonzo Mayes .12 .30
40 Rod Smith .15 .40
41 Reggie Barlow .12 .30
42 Sean Dawkins .12 .30
43 Duce Staley .15 .40
44 R.W. McQuarters .12 .30
45 Robert Holcombe .12 .30
46 Priest Holmes .20 .50
47 Erik Kramer .15 .40
48 Shannon Sharpe .20 .50
49 Mike Vanderjagt .12 .30
50 Cris Carter .20 .50
51 Billy Joe Tolliver .12 .30
52 Vinny Testaverde .15 .40
53 Antonio Langham .12 .30
54 Damon Gibson .12 .30
55 Garrison Hearst .15 .40
56 Brad Johnson .15 .40
57 Randall Cunningham .20 .50
58 Jim Harbaugh .15 .40
59 Curtis Enis .12 .30
60 Bill Romanowski .15 .40
61 Marcus Pollard .12 .30
62 Zach Thomas .20 .50
63 Cameron Cleeland .12 .30
64 Curtis Martin .20 .50
65 Charlie Garner .15 .40
66 Jerris McPhail .12 .30
67 Jon Kitna .15 .40
68 Chris Chandler .15 .40
69 Emmitt Smith .50 1.25
70 Andre Rison .15 .40
71 Wayne Chrebet .15 .40
72 Mikhael Ricks .12 .30
73 Yancey Thigpen .12 .30
74 Peter Boulware .12 .30
75 Bobby Engram .15 .40
76 John Mobley .12 .30
77 Peyton Manning .60 1.50
78 O.J. McDuffie .15 .40
79 Tony Simmons .12 .30
80 Mo Lewis .12 .30
81 Bryan Still .12 .30
82 Eugene Robinson .15 .40
83 Curtis Conway .15 .40
84 Ed McCaffrey .15 .40
85 Marvin Harrison .20 .50
86 Dan Marino .60 1.50
87 Ty Law .15 .40
88 Leon Johnson .12 .30
89 Junior Seau .20 .50
90 Terance Mathis .12 .30
91 Wesley Walls .15 .40
92 John Elway .60 1.50
93 Marshall Faulk .20 .50
94 Oronde Gadsden .12 .30
95 Keyshawn Johnson .15 .40
96 Muhsin Muhammad .15 .40
97 Dorsey Levens .15 .40
98 Shawn Jefferson .12 .30
99 Rocket Ismail .15 .40
100 Vonnie Holliday .12 .30
101 Terry Glenn .15 .40
102 Shawn Springs .12 .30
103 Tim Dwight .15 .40
104 Terrell Davis .20 .50
105 Karim Abdul-Jabbar .15 .40
106 Bryan Cox .15 .40
107 Steve McNair .20 .50
108 Tony Martin .15 .40
109 Jason Elam .12 .30
110 John Avery .12 .30
111 Aaron Glenn .12 .30
112 Eddie George .15 .40
113 Larry Centers .15 .40
114 Darnay Scott .12 .30
115 Jimmy Smith .15 .40
116 Tiki Barber .20 .50
117 Charles Johnson .12 .30
118 Mike Archie RC .20 .50
119 Adrian Murrell .15 .40
120 Dexter Coakley .12 .30
121 Dale Carter .12 .30
122 Kent Graham .12 .30
123 Hines Ward .20 .50
124 Greg Hill .12 .30
125 Skip Hicks .12 .30
126 Doug Flutie .20 .50
127 Leslie Shepherd .12 .30
128 Neil O'Donnell .15 .40
129 Herman Moore .15 .40
130 Kevin Hardy .12 .30
131 Randy Moss .20 .50
132 Andre Hastings .12 .30
133 Rickey Dudley .12 .30
134 Jerome Bettis .20 .50
135 Jerry Rice .40 1.00
136 Jake Plummer .15 .40
137 Billy Davis .12 .30
138 Tony Gonzalez .20 .50
139 Ike Hilliard .15 .40
140 Freddie Jones .12 .30
141 Isaac Bruce .20 .50
142 Darrell Green .20 .50
143 Trent Green .15 .40
144 Jamal Anderson .15 .40
145 Deion Sanders .20 .50
146 Byron Bam Morris .12 .30
147 Charles Way .12 .30
148 Natrone Means .15 .40
149 Frank Wycheck .15 .40
150 Brett Favre .60 1.50
151 Michael Bates .12 .30
152 Ben Coates .15 .40
153 Koy Detmer .12 .30
154 Eddie Kennison .15 .40
155 Eric Metcalf .12 .30
156 Takeo Spikes .12 .30
157 Fred Taylor .15 .40
158 Gary Brown .12 .30
159 Levon Kirkland .12 .30
160 Trent Dilfer .15 .40
161 Antowain Smith .12 .30
162 Robert Brooks .15 .40
163 Robert Smith .15 .40
164 Napoleon Kaufman .12 .30
165 Chad Brown .12 .30
166 Warrick Dunn .15 .40
167 Joey Galloway .15 .40
168 Frank Sanders .12 .30
169 Michael Irvin .20 .50
170 Elvis Grbac .12 .30
171 Michael Strahan .15 .40
172 Ryan Leaf .15 .40
173 Stephen Alexander .12 .30
174 Andre Reed .20 .50
175 Barry Sanders .50 1.25
176 Jake Reed .15 .40
177 James Jett .12 .30
178 Steve Young .25 .60
179 Jermaine Lewis .12 .30
180 Charlie Batch .15 .40
181 Jacquez Green .12 .30
182 Kevin Dyson .12 .30
183 Roell Preston PD .12 .30
184 Randall Cunningham PD .20 .50
185 Charlie Batch PD .15 .40
186 Kordell Stewart PD .15 .40
187 Bennie Thompson PD .12 .30
188 Deion Sanders PD .20 .50
189 Jake Plummer PD .15 .40
190 Eric Moulds PD .15 .40
191 Derrick Brooks PD .20 .50
192 Steve McNair PD .20 .50
193 Ryan Leaf PD .15 .40
194 Keyshawn Johnson PD .15 .40
195 Eddie George PD .15 .40
196 Warrick Dunn PD .15 .40
197 Jessie Tuggle PD .12 .30
198 Rodney Harrison PD .15 .40
199 Vinny Testaverde PD .15 .40
200 Marshall Faulk PD .20 .50
201 Ray Buchanan PD .12 .30
202 Garrison Hearst PD .15 .40
203 John Randle PD .15 .40
204 Drew Bledsoe PD .20 .50
205 Sam Gash PD .12 .30
206 Troy Aikman PD .30 .75
207 Michael McCrary .12 .30
208 Chris Claiborne RC .20 .50
209 Ricky Williams RC .50 1.25
210 Tim Couch RC .30 .75
211 Champ Bailey RC .60 1.50
212 Torry Holt RC .50 1.25
213 Donovan McNabb RC 1.50 4.00
214 David Boston RC .25 .60
215 Chris McAlister RC .25 .60
216 Aaron Gibson RC .20 .50
217 Daunte Culpepper RC .30 .75
218 Matt Stinchcomb RC .20 .50
219 Edgerrin James RC .40 1.00
220 Jevon Kearse RC .30 .75
221 Ebenezer Ekuban RC .20 .50
222 Kris Farris RC .20 .50
223 Chris Terry RC .20 .50
224 Cecil Collins RC .20 .50
225 Akili Smith RC .25 .60
226 Shaun King RC .25 .60
227 Rahim Abdullah RC .20 .50
228 Peerless Price RC .25 .60
229 Antoine Winfield RC .20 .50
230 Antuan Edwards RC .20 .50
231 Rob Konrad RC .20 .50
232 Troy Edwards RC .25 .60
233 John Thornton RC .20 .50
234 Fred Vinson RC .20 .50
235 Gary Stills RC .20 .50
236 Desmond Clark RC .25 .60
237 Lamar King RC .20 .50
238 Jared DeVries RC .20 .50
239 Martin Gramatica RC .20 .50
240 Montae Reagor RC .20 .50
241 Andy Katzenmoyer RC .25 .60
242 Rufus French RC .20 .50
243 D'Wayne Bates RC .20 .50
244 Amos Zereoue RC .25 .60
245 Dre Bly RC .30 .75
246 Kevin Johnson RC .25 .60
247 Cade McNown RC .25 .60
248 Kordell Stewart CL .15 .40
249 Deion Sanders CL .20 .50
250 Vinny Testaverde CL .15 .40
P1 Doug Flutie Promo .40 1.00

1999 Metal Universe Precious Metal Gems

*VETS 40X TO 100X
*ROOKIE STARS: 15X TO 40X
STATED PRINT RUN 50 SER.#'d SETS

1999 Metal Universe Linchpins

STATED ODDS 1:360 HOB, 1:480 RET
LP1 Emmitt Smith 20.00 50.00
LP2 Charlie Batch 6.00 15.00
LP3 Fred Taylor 8.00 20.00
LP4 Jake Plummer 8.00 20.00
LP5 Brett Favre 30.00 80.00
LP6 Barry Sanders 20.00 50.00
LP7 Mark Brunell 8.00 20.00
LP8 Peyton Manning 25.00 60.00
LP9 Randy Moss 12.00 30.00
LP10 Terrell Davis 10.00 25.00

1999 Metal Universe Planet Metal

COMPLETE SET (15) 75.00 150.00
STATED ODDS 1:36 HOB, 1:48 RET
PM1 Terrell Davis 2.50 6.00
PM2 Troy Aikman 5.00 12.00
PM3 Peyton Manning 8.00 20.00
PM4 Mark Brunell 2.50 6.00
PM5 John Elway 8.00 20.00
PM6 Doug Flutie 2.50 6.00
PM7 Dan Marino 8.00 20.00
PM8 Brett Favre 8.00 20.00
PM9 Barry Sanders 8.00 20.00
PM10 Emmitt Smith 5.00 12.00
PM11 Fred Taylor 2.50 6.00
PM12 Jerry Rice 5.00 12.00
PM13 Jamal Anderson 2.50 6.00
PM14 Randall Cunningham 2.50 6.00
PM15 Randy Moss 6.00 15.00

1999 Metal Universe Quasars

COMPLETE SET (15) 40.00 80.00
STATED ODDS 1:18 HOB, 1:24 RET
*PRISMS: .75X TO 2X BASIC INSERT
PRISMS PRINT RUN 99 SERIAL #'d SETS
QS1 Ricky Williams 2.00 5.00
QS2 Tim Couch 1.00 2.50
QS3 Shaun King .60 1.50
QS4 Champ Bailey 1.25 3.00
QS5 Torry Holt 2.50 6.00
QS6 Donovan McNabb 5.00 12.00
QS7 David Boston 1.00 2.50
QS8 Andy Katzenmoyer .60 1.50
QS9 Daunte Culpepper 4.00 10.00
QS10 Edgerrin James 4.00 10.00
QS11 Cade McNown .60 1.50
QS12 Troy Edwards .60 1.50
QS13 Akili Smith .60 1.50
QS14 Peerless Price 1.00 2.50
QS15 Amos Zereoue 1.00 2.50

1999 Metal Universe Starchild

COMPLETE SET (20) 10.00 25.00
STATED ODDS 1:6 HOB, 1:8 RET
SC1 Skip Hicks .50 1.25
SC2 Mike Alstott 1.25 3.00
SC3 Joey Galloway .75 2.00
SC4 Tony Simmons .50 1.25
SC5 Jamal Anderson 1.25 3.00
SC6 John Avery .50 1.25
SC7 Charles Woodson 1.25 3.00
SC8 Jon Kitna 1.25 3.00
SC9 Marshall Faulk 1.50 4.00
SC10 Eric Moulds 1.25 3.00
SC11 Keyshawn Johnson 1.25 3.00
SC12 Ryan Leaf .50 1.25
SC13 Curtis Enis .50 1.25
SC14 Steve McNair 1.25 3.00
SC15 Corey Dillon 1.25 3.00
SC16 Tim Dwight 1.25 3.00
SC17 Brian Griese 1.25 3.00
SC18 Drew Bledsoe 1.50 4.00
SC19 Eddie George 1.25 3.00
SC20 Terrell Owens 1.25 3.00

2000 Metal

Released in early December 2000, Metal features a 300-card base set consisting of 200 veteran player cards, 50 rookie cards in vertical format, and 50 shortprinted rookies in horizontal format inserted in packs at the rate of one in two. Base cards feature a textured card with player names in silver ink and rookie cards with the same card stock but player names printed in bronze ink. Metal was packaged in 28-pack boxes with packs containing 10 cards each and carried a suggested retail price of $1.99.

COMPLETE SET (300) 40.00 80.00
COMP.SET w/o SP's (250) 6.00 15.00
251-300 ROOKIE SP ODDS 1:2
1 Tim Couch .15 .40
2 Olandis Gary .15 .40
3 Andre Hastings .12 .30
4 Donovan McNabb .20 .50
5 Bobby Engram .15 .40
6 Bert Emanuel .12 .30
7 Levon Kirkland .12 .30
8 Chris Chandler .15 .40
9 Herman Moore .15 .40
10 Jeff Blake .15 .40
11 Cortez Kennedy .12 .30
12 Antowain Smith .15 .40
13 Marvin Harrison .20 .50
14 Bryant Young .12 .30
15 Peerless Price .15 .40
16 Peyton Manning .50 1.25
17 Darrell Russell .12 .30
18 Darrell Green .15 .40
19 James Allen .12 .30
20 Tedy Bruschi .30 .75
21 Jon Kitna .15 .40
22 Doug Flutie .20 .50
23 Bill Schroeder .15 .40
24 Curtis Martin .20 .50
25 Kevin Lockett .12 .30
26 Errict Rhett .15 .40
27 Kevin Faulk .15 .40
28 J.J. Stokes .15 .40
29 Jonathan Linton .12 .30
30 Jimmy Smith .15 .40
31 Brian Dawkins .20 .50
32 Michael Westbrook .12 .30
33 Randall Cunningham .20 .50
34 Oronde Gadsden .15 .40
35 Shawn Springs .12 .30
36 Shannon Sharpe .20 .50
37 Terrence Wilkins .12 .30
38 Aaron Glenn .12 .30
39 Torrance Small .12 .30
40 Sean Dawkins .12 .30
41 Terrell Davis .20 .50
42 Ike Hilliard .15 .40
43 Warrick Dunn .15 .40
44 Jeremiah Trotter RC .40 1.00
45 O.J. McDuffie .15 .40
46 Richard Huntley .12 .30
47 Aeneas Williams .12 .30
48 Rocket Ismail .15 .40
49 Terry Glenn .15 .40
50 Derrick Mayes .12 .30
51 Wayne Chrebet .15 .40
52 Kevin Dyson .15 .40
53 Takeo Spikes .12 .30
54 Matthew Hatchette .12 .30
55 Shawn Bryson .12 .30
56 Qadry Ismail .15 .40
57 Jerome Pathon .12 .30
58 Rich Gannon .15 .40
59 Stephen Davis .15 .40
60 Marcus Robinson .15 .40
61 Damon Huard .15 .40
62 Junior Seau .20 .50
63 Curtis Enis .12 .30
64 Tony Richardson RC .15 .40
65 Troy Edwards .12 .30
66 Robert Brooks .15 .40
67 Antonio Freeman .15 .40
68 Kerry Collins .15 .40
69 Jacquez Green .12 .30
70 Akili Smith .12 .30
71 Zach Thomas .20 .50
72 Kordell Stewart .15 .40
73 Deion Sanders .20 .50
74 David Patten .12 .30
75 Drew Bledsoe .20 .50
76 Shaun King .12 .30
77 Eddie Kennison .12 .30
78 Stacey Mack .12 .30
79 Jim Harbaugh .15 .40
80 Shawn Jefferson .12 .30
81 James Stewart .12 .30
82 Pete Mitchell .12 .30
83 Mike Alstott .20 .50
84 Marty Booker .15 .40
85 Hardy Nickerson .12 .30
86 Charles Johnson .12 .30
87 Jeff George .15 .40
88 Jermaine Lewis .12 .30
89 Edgerrin James .20 .50
90 Rickey Dudley .12 .30
91 Eddie George .15 .40
92 Darren Woodson .12 .30
93 Willie McGinest .15 .40
94 Jeff Garcia .15 .40
95 Eric Moulds .15 .40
96 Tony Brackens .12 .30
97 Charles Woodson .20 .50
98 Warren Sapp .15 .40
99 Corey Dillon .15 .40
100 Tony Martin .15 .40
101 Bruce Smith .20 .50
102 Troy Aikman .30 .75
103 Daunte Culpepper .15 .40
104 Christian Fauria .12 .30
105 Steve Beuerlein .15 .40
106 Fred Taylor .20 .50
107 Ricky Watters .15 .40
108 Brian Mitchell .12 .30
109 Emmitt Smith .50 1.25
110 Robert Smith .15 .40
111 Jerry Rice .40 1.00
112 Priest Holmes .20 .50
113 Jay Fiedler .15 .40
114 Curtis Conway .15 .40
115 Jamal Anderson .15 .40
116 E.G. Green .12 .30
117 Kent Graham .12 .30
118 Frank Wycheck .15 .40
119 Jake Plummer .15 .40
120 Randy Moss .20 .50
121 Charlie Garner .15 .40
122 Frank Sanders .12 .30
123 Germane Crowell .12 .30
124 Jason Sehorn .12 .30
125 Marshall Faulk .20 .50
126 David Sloan .12 .30
127 Cris Carter .20 .50
128 Robert Chancey .12 .30
129 Tony Banks .12 .30
130 Ken Dilger .12 .30
131 Dedric Ward .12 .30
132 Yancey Thigpen .12 .30
133 Jeremy McDaniel .12 .30
134 John Randle .15 .40
135 Jerome Bettis .20 .50
136 Tim Dwight .15 .40
137 Charlie Batch .15 .40
138 Mark Brunell .15 .40
139 Tyrone Wheatley .15 .40
140 Champ Bailey .15 .40
141 Brian Griese .15 .40
142 Keith Poole .12 .30
143 Kurt Warner .30 .75
144 Tim Biakabutuka .15 .40
145 Elvis Grbac .12 .30
146 Cade McNown .12 .30
147 Albert Connell .12 .30
148 Donald Driver .30 .75
149 Donald Hayes .12 .30
150 Terrell Owens .20 .50
151 Johnnie Morton .15 .40
152 Tiki Barber .20 .50
153 Keyshawn Johnson .15 .40
154 Carl Pickens .15 .40
155 Thurman Thomas .20 .50
156 Jeff Graham .12 .30
157 Peter Boulware .12 .30
158 Brett Favre .60 1.50
159 Vinny Testaverde .15 .40
160 Derrick Brooks .20 .50
161 Wesley Walls .12 .30
162 Derrick Alexander .12 .30
163 Duce Staley .15 .40
164 Troy Brown .15 .40
165 Keenan McCardell .15 .40
166 James Jett .15 .40
167 Simeon Rice .15 .40
168 Rod Smith .15 .40
169 Ricky Williams .20 .50
170 Az-Zahir Hakim .12 .30
171 Muhsin Muhammad .15 .40
172 Andre Rison .15 .40
173 Tim Brown .20 .50
174 Brad Johnson .15 .40
175 Darrin Chiaverini .12 .30
176 Jake Reed .15 .40
177 Kevin Carter .12 .30
178 Jay Riemersma .12 .30
179 Tony Gonzalez .20 .50
180 Hines Ward .20 .50
181 David Boston .12 .30
182 Ed McCaffrey .15 .40
183 Amani Toomer .15 .40
184 Torry Holt .20 .50
185 Rob Johnson .15 .40
186 Kevin Hardy .12 .30
187 Napoleon Kaufman .15 .40
188 Jevon Kearse .15 .40
189 Terance Mathis .12 .30
190 Dorsey Levens .15 .40
191 Kyle Brady .12 .30
192 Steve McNair .20 .50
193 Kevin Johnson .12 .30
194 Lamar Smith .12 .30
195 Ryan Leaf .15 .40
196 Rod Woodson .20 .50
197 Corey Bradford .12 .30
198 Joe Horn .15 .40
199 Isaac Bruce .20 .50
200 Steve Young .60 1.50
Dan Marino
201 DeMario Brown RC .25 .60
202 Chad Morton RC .40 1.00
203 Quinton Spotwood RC .25 .60
204 Mike Anderson RC .40 1.00
205 Jarious Jackson RC .30 .75
206 Hank Poteat RC .25 .60
207 Rogers Beckett RC .25 .60
208 Deon Dyer RC .25 .60
209 Charles Lee RC .25 .60
210 Barrett Green RC .25 .60
211 T.J. Slaughter RC .25 .60
212 Chris Hovan RC .30 .75
213 Mark Simoneau RC .25 .60
214 Rashard Anderson RC .25 .60
215 Trevor Insley RC .25 .60
216 Paul Smith RC .25 .60
217 Doug Johnson RC .30 .75
218 Dwayne Goodrich RC .25 .60
219 Julian Peterson RC .40 1.00
220 Keith Bulluck RC .30 .75
221 Chris Samuels RC .30 .75
222 Shaun Ellis RC .40 1.00

223 Na'il Diggs RC .25 .60
224 William Bartee RC .25 .60
225 John Abraham RC .40 1.00
226 Trevor Gaylor RC .25 .60
227 Dante Hall RC .40 1.00
228 Marcus Knight RC .25 .60
229 Patrick Pass RC .30 .75
230 Bashir Yamini RC .25 .60
231 Deltha O'Neal RC .30 .75
232 Vaughn Sanders RC .25 .60
233 Todd Husak RC .25 .60
234 Thomas Hamner RC .25 .60
235 Chafie Fields RC .25 .60
236 Orantes Grant RC .25 .60
237 Muneer Moore RC .25 .60
238 Kwame Cavil RC .25 .60
239 Spergon Wynn RC .30 .75
240 Leon Murray RC .25 .60
241 Rob Morris RC .30 .75
242 Ben Kelly RC .25 .60
243 Darren Howard RC .25 .60
244 Raynoch Thompson RC .25 .60
245 Mike Green RC .40 1.00
246 Sammy Morris RC .30 .75
247 Ahmed Plummer RC .25 .60
248 Ian Gold RC .25 .60
249 Chris Coleman RC .25 .60
250 Ron Dixon RC .25 .60
251 Peter Warrick RC .75 2.00
252 Joe Hamilton RC .50 1.25
253 Dennis Northcutt RC .60 1.50
254 Laveranues Coles RC .75 2.00
255 Michael Wiley RC .50 1.25
256 Plaxico Burress RC .75 2.00
257 Danny Farmer RC .50 1.25
258 Aaron Shea RC .60 1.50
259 Sebastian Janikowski RC .75 2.00
260 Corey Simon RC .60 1.50
261 Frank Murphy RC .50 1.25
262 JaJuan Dawson RC .50 1.25
263 Ron Dayne RC .75 2.00
264 Tim Rattay RC .60 1.50
265 Troy Walters RC .50 1.25
266 J.R. Redmond RC .50 1.25
267 Tom Brady RC 25.00 50.00
268 Jamal Lewis RC .75 2.00
269 Anthony Lucas RC .50 1.25
270 Reuben Droughns RC .75 2.00
271 James Williams RC .50 1.25
272 Shyrone Stith RC .50 1.25
273 Jerry Porter RC .75 2.00
274 Brian Urlacher RC 3.00 8.00
275 Avion Black RC .50 1.25
276 Thomas Jones RC 1.00 2.50
277 Chad Pennington RC 1.25 3.00
278 Travis Prentice RC .60 1.50
279 Chris Redman RC .60 1.50
280 Travis Taylor RC .60 1.50
281 Giovanni Carmazzi RC .50 1.25
282 Sherrod Gideon RC .50 1.25
283 Bubba Franks RC .75 2.00
284 Sylvester Morris RC .50 1.25
285 Curtis Keaton RC .50 1.25
286 Frank Moreau RC .50 1.25
287 Terrelle Smith RC .50 1.25
288 Shaun Alexander RC 1.00 2.50
289 Tee Martin RC .75 2.00
290 R.Jay Soward RC .50 1.25
291 Dez White RC .60 1.50
292 Trung Canidate RC .60 1.50
293 Darrell Jackson RC .60 1.50
294 Marc Bulger RC .75 2.00
295 Courtney Brown RC .60 1.50
296 Todd Pinkston RC .50 1.25
297 Anthony Becht RC .60 1.50
298 Doug Chapman RC .50 1.25
299 Gari Scott RC .50 1.25
300 Chris Cole RC .60 1.50

2000 Metal Emerald

*VETS 1-200: 1.2X TO 3X BASIC CARDS
1-200 EMERALD VETERAN ODDS 1:4
*ROOKIES 201-250: .8X TO 2X RCs
*ROOKIES 251-300: .4X TO 1X RC SPs
201-300 EMERALD ROOKIE ODDS 1:7
267 Tom Brady 50.00 120.00

2000 Metal Heavy Metal

COMPLETE SET (10) 10.00 25.00
STATED ODDS 1:20
1 Emmitt Smith 2.00 5.00
2 Randy Moss .75 2.00
3 Kurt Warner 1.25 3.00
4 Keyshawn Johnson .60 1.50
5 Ricky Williams .75 2.00
6 Peyton Manning 2.00 5.00
7 Edgerrin James .75 2.00
8 Peter Warrick .75 2.00
9 Brett Favre 2.50 6.00
10 Tim Couch .60 1.50

2000 Metal Hot Commodities

COMPLETE SET (10) 7.50 20.00
STATED ODDS 1:14
1 Kurt Warner 1.00 2.50
2 Jerry Rice 1.25 3.00
3 Terrell Davis .60 1.50
4 Peyton Manning 1.50 4.00
5 Stephen Davis .50 1.25
6 Brett Favre 2.00 5.00
7 Ron Dayne .60 1.50
8 Troy Aikman 1.00 2.50
9 Edgerrin James .60 1.50
10 Eddie George .50 1.25

2000 Metal Steel of the Draft

COMPLETE SET (10) 6.00 15.00
STATED ODDS 1:28
1 Peter Warrick .60 1.50
2 Ron Dayne .60 1.50
3 Plaxico Burress .60 1.50
4 Thomas Jones .75 2.00
5 Jamal Lewis .60 1.50
6 Shaun Alexander .75 2.00
7 Chad Pennington 1.00 2.50
8 Travis Taylor .50 1.25
9 Chris Redman .50 1.25
10 J.R. Redmond .40 1.00

2000 Metal Sunday Showdown

COMPLETE SET (15) 7.50 20.00
STATED ODDS 1:4
1 Emmitt Smith 1.25 3.00
Stephen Davis
2 Mark Brunell .40 1.00
Tim Couch
3 Randy Moss .50 1.25
Isaac Bruce
4 Shaun King .30 .75
Akili Smith
5 Peter Warrick .50 1.25
Plaxico Burress
6 Chad Pennington .75 2.00
Peyton Manning
7 Ricky Williams .50 1.25
Edgerrin James
8 Marshall Faulk .50 1.25
Jamal Anderson
9 Troy Aikman .75 2.00
Donovan McNabb
10 Daunte Culpepper .40 1.00
Cade McNown
11 Terrell Davis .60 1.50
Shaun Alexander
12 Brett Favre 1.50 4.00
Brad Johnson
13 Jevon Kearse .50 1.25
Fred Taylor
14 Thomas Jones .50 1.25
Ron Dayne
15 Jerry Rice 1.00 2.50
Keyshawn Johnson

1992 Metallic Images Tins

Designed by Metallic Images Inc. and sold through participating 7-Eleven stores, these four collector tins each contained two decks of playing cards. The tins are unumbered and listed below alphabetically.

COMPLETE SET (4) 12.50 30.00
1 Dan Marino 5.00 12.00
2 Warren Moon 2.00 5.00
3 Y.A. Tittle 2.00 5.00
4 Johnny Unitas 3.00 8.00

1993 Metallic Images QB Legends

An offshoot of CUI, a Wilmington-based maker of collectible ceramic and glassware products, Metallic Images Inc. produced these 20 metal cards to honor outstanding NFL quarterbacks. Only 49,000 numbered sets were produced, each accompanied by a certificate of authenticity and packaged in a collectors tin featuring graphics on the sides and lid. These metallic cards measure approximately 2 9/16" by 3 9/16" and have rolled metal edges. The fronts display a color action shot cutout and superimposed on a team color-coded background with gold pinstripes. A black-and-white headshot appears in an oval at the upper left corner, while the team logo and uniform number are below. On a pinstripe panel inside a team color-coded border, the backs present career summary.

COMPLETE SET (20) 20.00 50.00
1 Steve Bartkowski 2.50 6.00
2 John Brodie 2.50 6.00
3 Charley Conerly 2.00 5.00
4 Lynn Dickey 2.00 5.00
5 Tom Flores 2.00 5.00
6 Roman Gabriel 2.00 5.00
7 Bob Griese 2.50 6.00
8 Steve Grogan 2.50 6.00
9 James Harris 2.00 5.00
10 Jim Hart 2.00 5.00
11 Sonny Jurgensen 2.50 6.00
12 Billy Kilmer 2.50 6.00
13 Daryle Lamonica 2.50 6.00
14 Archie Manning 2.50 6.00
15 Craig Morton 2.50 6.00
16 Dan Pastorini 2.00 5.00
17 Jim Plunkett 2.50 6.00
18 Y.A. Tittle 2.50 6.00
19 Johnny Unitas 4.00 10.00
20 Danny White 2.50 6.00

1996 Metallic Impressions Golden Arm Greats

Released as a 5-card set, Metallic Impressions Golden Arm Greats showcases some of the best quarterbacks of the century. Base cards are thin metal and feature full color oval portrait shots in one of the upper corners and action shots across the majority of the card front. The set was released in factory set form within a colorful tin box.

COMPLETE SET (5) 12.50 25.00
1 Sonny Jurgensen 2.00 5.00
2 Jim Plunkett 2.00 5.00
3 Y.A. Tittle 2.00 5.00
4 Johnny Unitas 5.00 10.00
5 Danny White 2.00 5.00

2005 Mid Mon Valley Hall of Fame

This set was released in 2005 by the Mid Mon Valley Sports Hall of Fame. Each card features a local sport legend printed on white card stock with a black and white artist's rendering of the featured subject on the front. The cover card proclaims the set as "Series 1 (2001-2005)" inductees.

COMPLETE SET (36) 10.00 20.00
124 Henry Adams FB .30 .75
125 Tom Ballaban CO FB .30 .75
126 Gene Belczyk CO FB .30 .75
127 Dale Hamer Official FB .30 .75
129 Joe Sarra CO FB .40 1.00
130 Jack Scarvel CO FB .30 .75
132 Bernie Galiffa FB .30 .75
133 Fred Mazurek FB .50 1.25
134 Bill Parkinson Official FB .30 .75
135 Pete Rostosky FB .30 .75
136 Joe Rudolph FB .40 1.00
137 James Simms FB .30 .75
138 Bill Urbanik FB .50 1.25
139 John Bruno CO FB .30 .75
140 Don Croftcheck FB .50 1.25
141 Tony Romantino FB .30 .75
145 Fred Yuss FB .30 .75
146 Ron Yuss FB .30 .75
147 Melvin Bassi Official FB .30 .75
149 Craig Cotton FB .50 1.25
152 Scott Zolak FB .50 1.25
154 Craig Fayak FB .30 .75
155 Steve Garban FB .40 1.00
156 Stan Kemp FB .30 .75

2006 Mid Mon Valley Hall of Fame

This set was released in 2006 by the Mid Mon Valley Sports Hall of Fame. Each card features a local sport legend printed on white card stock with a black and white artist's rendering of the featured subject on the front. The cover card proclaims the set as "Series 2 (1997-2000/2006)" inductees.

COMPLETE SET (36) 10.00 20.00
94 Rudy Andabaker FB .30 .75
98 Carl Crawley FB .30 .75
99 Doug Crusan FB .30 .75
100 Frank Lignelli FB .30 .75
101 Bill Malinchak FB .30 .75
102 Eric Crabtree FB .40 1.00
103 Dick Fields FB .30 .75
104 Pappy Johnson FB .30 .75
107 Jeff Petrucci FB .30 .75
111 Mike Buccianeri FB .30 .75
112 Bill Contz FB .40 1.00
113 Angelo DaBiero FB .30 .75
115 Sam Havrilak FB .40 1.00
116 John Popovich FB .30 .75
118 Tony Benjamin FB .30 .75
119 Auggie Bossu FB .30 .75
120 Julius Dawkins FB .30 .75
121 Val Jansante FB .30 .75
122 Joe Montana FB 2.00 5.00
159 Greg Paterra FB .30 .75
100 Anthony Peterson FB .30 .75

1985 Miller Lite Beer

These oversized cards measure approximately 4 3/4" by 7" and feature on their fronts white-bordered posed player photos. The player's name and position, along with logos for his team and Miller Lite appear within the wide bottom margin. The logos reappear on the white backs, along with the player's career highlights. The cards are unnumbered and checklisted below in alphabetical order.

COMPLETE SET (6) 60.00 150.00
1 Larry Csonka 10.00 25.00
2 John Hadl CO 6.00 15.00
3 Freeman McNeil 6.00 15.00
NFL Man of the Year
4 Jack Reynolds 6.00 15.00
Lite Beer All-Stars
5 Steve Young 30.00 75.00
USFL Man of the Year
6 1985 LA Express 6.00 15.00
Cheerleaders

2005 Montgomery Maulers NIFL

This set was issued by the Montgomery Maulers of the National Indoor Football League. Each card features one or more players or coaches from the team.

COMPLETE SET (32) 5.00 10.00
1 Fred Barnett OL .20 .50
Jamaal Fletcher DB
2 Darian Chestnut .20 .50
3 Chrys Chukwuma .30 .75
4 Cliff Clark AC .20 .50
Mike Williams AC
Carlos Clayton AC
Kelvin Stokes AC
5 Undrae Crosby .20 .50
6 Cliff Darrington .20 .50
7 Pat Epkins .20 .50
8 Ray Fleming .20 .50
9 Eric Hall .20 .50
Corey Sears
10 Jonathan Harrell .20 .50
11 Antoine Hill .20 .50
12 Shaun Holmes .20 .50
13 Eric Hudson .20 .50
14 Kevin Jones K .20 .50
15 Jamie LaMunyon Owner .20 .50
16 Jesse Marsh .20 .50
17 Quincy McCall .20 .50
18 Nathan McDaniel .20 .50
19 David Philyaw .20 .50
20 Mareno Philyaw .30 .75
21 Andre Reed DL .20 .50
22 J.R. Richardson .20 .50
23 Richard Rowe .20 .50
24 Everette Rosette .20 .50
25 Machion Sanders .20 .50
26 James Shiver .20 .50
27 Archie Smith .20 .50
28 Tarsus Thomas .20 .50
29 Duke Vaiga .20 .50
30 Buffalo Wild Wings .20 .50
store photo
31 Buffalo Wild Wings Coupon/5 free wings .20 .50
32 Buffalo Wild Wings Coupon/10% off .20 .50

1988 Monty Gum

This 100-card set was made in Europe by Monty Gum. The cards measure approximately 1 15/16" by 2 3/4" and contain thick yellow borders around a color photo. There was also an album issued with the set. The cards do not feature specific players, only generic team action scenes; hence they are not very popular with collectors. The cards have blank backs. Each is numbered and subtitled at the bottom inside a black box. There is a blank-backed sticker version, a thin paper version and a white cardboard version of each card in the set. The sticker backs actually have a white paper cover that is removable. Otherwise, they are the same as the card versions; the stickers are considered the toughest version to find.

COMPLETE SET (100) 50.00 125.00
*STICKERS: 1X TO 2X CARDS
1 Atlanta Falcons .60 1.50
Atlanta Stadium
2 Atlanta Falcons .50 1.25
Defense
3 Atlanta Falcons .50 1.25
Offense
4 Buffalo Bills .50 1.25
Blocked Punt
5 Chicago Bears .50 1.25
At the Scrimmage Line
6 Chicago Bears .50 1.25
(Action shot)
7 Cincinnati Bengals .50 1.25
Riverfront Stadium
8 Cincinnati Bengals .50 1.25
Inside the Stadium
9 Cincinnati Bengals 2.50 6.00
Goal Line Stand
(Walter Payton diving)
10 Cincinnati Bengals .50 1.25
(Action shot)
11 Cincinnati Bengals .60 1.50
Cheerleader
12 Cleveland Browns .50 1.25
Cleveland Stadium
13 Cleveland Browns .60 1.50
QB Rollout
(Bernie Kosar)
14 Cleveland Browns .50 1.25
Head Coach
15 Cleveland Browns .50 1.25
Fans
16 Dallas Cowboys .60 1.50
Texas Stadium
17 Dallas Cowboys .60 1.50
Touchdown Reception
18 Dallas Cowboys .60 1.50
Cheerleader
19 Denver Broncos .50 1.25
Mile High Stadium
20 Denver Broncos .50 1.25
Swarming Defense
21 Denver Broncos .60 1.50
(Randy Gradishar)
22 Detroit Lions .50 1.25
QB Sack Celebration
23 Green Bay Packers .50 1.25
On the Run
24 Green Bay Packers .50 1.25
(Action shot)
25 Houston Oilers .50 1.25
Houston Astrodome
26 Houston Oilers .50 1.25
Tackled from behind
27 Indianapolis Colts .50 1.25
Field Goal Attempt
28 Kansas City Chiefs .50 1.25
Up the Middle
29 Kansas City Chiefs .50 1.25
(Action shot)
30 Kansas City Chiefs .60 1.50
Cheerleader
31 Los Angeles Raiders .60 1.50
L.A. Memorial Coliseum
32 Los Angeles Raiders .60 1.50
Inside the Stadium
33 Los Angeles Raiders .60 1.50
In the Pocket
34 Los Angeles Raiders 1.25 3.00
(Marcus Allen;
Super Bowl shot)
35 Los Angeles Rams .50 1.25
Anaheim Stadium
36 Los Angeles Rams .60 1.50
Power Blocking
(Eric Dickerson running)
37 Los Angeles Rams .50 1.25
(Action shot)
38 Miami Dolphins 6.00 15.00
Attacking the Zone
Dan Marino
39 Miami Dolphins .60 1.50
(Action shot)
40 Minnesota Vikings .50 1.25
(Metrodome)
41 Minnesota Vikings .50 1.25
Halfback Handoff
42 New England Patriots .50 1.25
Sullivan Stadium
43 New England Patriots .60 1.50
Throwing Deep
(Steve Grogan)
44 New England Patriots 2.00 5.00
(Earl Campbell running)
45 New Orleans Saints .75 2.00
Swarming Linebackers
(Roger Craig running)
46 New Orleans Saints UER .60 1.50
(Photo actually shows
Washington and Michigan
in '81 Rose Bowl game)
47 New York Giants .60 1.50
Turning the Corner
48 New York Giants .50 1.25
(Action shot)
49 New York Jets .50 1.25
Breaking Loose
50 New York Jets .50 1.25
(Line photo)
51 Philadelphia Eagles .50 1.25
Veterans Stadium
52 Philadelphia Eagles .50 1.25
Power Right
53 Philadelphia Eagles .50 1.25
(Action shot)
54 Philadelphia Eagles .50 1.25
Fans
55 Pittsburgh Steelers .60 1.50
Three Rivers Stadium
56 Pittsburgh Steelers .60 1.50
Swarming to the Ball
57 Pittsburgh Steelers .75 2.00
(Action shot)
Jack Lambert and Donnie Shell
58 St.Louis Cardinals .50 1.25
Busch Stadium
59 St.Louis Cardinals .50 1.25
Setting Up
60 St.Louis Cardinals .50 1.25
(Action shot)
61 St.Louis Cardinals UER .50 1.25
(Photo actually shows
Saints vs. Browns game)
62 San Diego Chargers .50 1.25
Jack Murphy Stadium
(Outside of stadium)
63 San Diego Chargers .50 1.25
Jack Murphy Stadium
(Inside of stadium)
64 San Diego Chargers 1.00 2.50
Going for the Bomb; Dan Fouts
65 San Diego Chargers .50 1.25
Fans
66 San Francisco 49ers .60 1.50
Candlestick Park
67 San Francisco 49ers .60 1.50
Nose Guard on Attack
68 San Francisco 49ers 6.00 15.00
(Joe Montana)
69 San Francisco 49ers 6.00 15.00
(Joe Montana)
70 Seattle Seahawks .50 1.25
Shutting down the run
71 Seattle Seahawks .50 1.25
(Action shot)
72 Tampa Bay Buccaneers .50 1.25
Tampa Stadium
73 Tampa Bay Buccaneers .50 1.25
Tampa Stadium
74 Tampa Bay Buccaneers .60 1.25
Breaking Free
75 Tampa Bay Buccaneers .50 1.25
Defense
76 Washington Redskins .60 1.50
R.F.Kennedy Stadium
77 Washington Redskins .60 1.50
Redskins at the 50
78 Washington Redskins .60 1.50
(Action shot)
79 Washington Redskins .60 1.50
Fans
80 Official NFL Football .40 1.00
81 Helmets:Falcons .40 1.00
Bills
82 Helmets:Bears .40 1.00
Bengals
83 Helmets:Browns/ .40 1.00
Cowboys
84 Helmets:Broncos .40 1.00
Lions
85 Helmets:Packers/ .40 1.00
Oilers
86 Helmets:Colts .40 1.00
Chiefs
87 Helmets:Raiders .40 1.00
Rams
88 Helmets:Dolphins/ .40 1.00
Vikings
89 Helmets:Patriots/ .40 1.00
Saints
90 Helmets:Giants .40 1.00
Jets
91 Philadelphia Eagles .40 1.00
Helmet
92 Pittsburgh Steelers .40 1.00
Helmet
93 St. Louis Cardinals .40 1.00
Helmet
94 San Diego Chargers .40 1.00
Helmet
95 San Francisco 49ers .40 1.00
Helmet
96 Seattle Seahawks .40 1.00
Helmet
97 Tampa Bay Buccaneers .40 1.00
Helmet
98 Washington Redskins .40 1.00
Helmet
99 National Football .40 1.00
League Logo
100 American Football Fans .50 1.25

1996 MotionVision

The 1996 MotionVision set was issued in two series of 12 cards each for a total of 24 cards and was distributed in one-card packs with a suggested retail price of $5.99 each. Only 25,000 of each player card was produced. Created on thick plastic, the cards feature Digital Film imaging technology which takes live actual game day footage from the NFL films, transfers them to a film emulsion, and plays back the action sequence on the card with the flick of a wrist. Each Digital Replay was individually packaged in its own see-through custom designed CD jewel case for maximum protection. A Super Bowl XXXI Promo card was distributed at the Super Bowl in New Orleans. It features NFC and AFC helmets crashing in action. An unnumbered Troy Aikman promo card was also distributed.

COMPLETE SET (24) 20.00 50.00
COMP.SERIES 1 (12) 10.00 25.00
COMP.SERIES 2 (12) 10.00 25.00
1 Troy Aikman 1.25 3.00
2 Dan Marino 2.50 6.00
3 Steve Young .75 2.00
4 Emmitt Smith 2.00 5.00
5 Drew Bledsoe 1.25 3.00
6 Kordell Stewart .75 2.00
7 Jerry Rice 1.25 3.00
8 Warren Moon .40 1.00
9 Junior Seau .75 2.00
10 Barry Sanders 2.00 5.00
11 Jim Harbaugh .30 .75
12 John Elway 2.50 6.00
13 Brett Favre 2.50 6.00
14 Brett Favre 2.50 6.00
15 Troy Aikman 1.25 3.00
16 Emmitt Smith 2.00 5.00
17 Dan Marino 2.50 6.00
18 Kordell Stewart .75 2.00
19 John Elway 2.50 6.00
20 Kerry Collins .40 1.00
21 Jim Kelly .40 1.00
22 Drew Bledsoe 1.25 3.00
23 Mark Brunell 1.25 3.00
24 Jerry Rice 1.25 3.00
P1 Troy Aikman Promo 1.20 3.00
NNO Super Bowl XXXI Promo 8.00 20.00
(issued at the game)

1996 MotionVision Limited Digital Replays

COMPLETE SET (10) 40.00 100.00
COMPLETE SERIES 1 (6) 20.00 50.00
COMPLETE SERIES 2 (4) 20.00 50.00
LDR1-LDR6: RANDOM INSERTS IN SER.1
LDR1-LDR6 PRINT RUN 2500 SETS
LDR7-LDR10: RANDOM INSERTS IN SER.2
LDR7-LDR10 PRINT RUN 3500 SETS
LDR1 Troy Aikman 4.00 10.00
LDR1A Troy Aikman AU 60.00 120.00
LDR2 Dan Marino 10.00 20.00
LDR3 Steve Young 3.00 8.00
LDR3A Steve Young AU 50.00 100.00
LDR4 Emmitt Smith 7.50 15.00
LDR5 Drew Bledsoe 3.00 8.00
LDR5A Drew Bledsoe AU 50.00 100.00
LDR6 Kordell Stewart 3.00 8.00
LDR6A Kordell Stewart AU 40.00 80.00
LDR7 Brett Favre 10.00 20.00
LDR8 Brett Favre 10.00 20.00
LDR9 Emmitt Smith 7.50 15.00
LDR10 Kerry Collins 2.50 6.00

1997 MotionVision

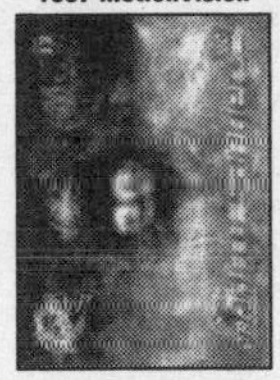

The 1997 MotionVision series one football set consisted of 20-cards and was distributed in one-card packs with a suggested retail price of $6.99. Series two was released later after the season and contained just 8-cards. Printed on thick plastic, the cards feature Digital Film imaging technology which takes live actual game day footage from NFL Films, transfers them to a film emulsion, and plays back the action sequence on the card with the flick of a wrist.

COMPLETE SET (28) 25.00 60.00
COMP.SERIES 1 (20) 12.50 30.00
COMP.SERIES 2 (8) 15.00 30.00
1 Terrell Davis .60 1.50
2 Curtis Martin .60 1.50
3 Joey Galloway .50 1.25
4 Eddie George .75 2.00
5 Isaac Bruce .75 2.00
6 Antonio Freeman .75 2.00
7 Terry Glenn .40 1.00
8 Deion Sanders .75 2.00
9 Jerome Bettis .75 2.00
10 Reggie White .75 2.00
11 Brett Favre 2.00 5.00
12 Dan Marino 2.00 5.00
13 Emmitt Smith 1.50 4.00
14 Mark Brunell .60 1.50
15 John Elway 2.00 5.00
16 Drew Bledsoe .60 1.50
17 Barry Sanders 1.50 4.00
18 Jeff Blake .40 1.00
19 Kerry Collins .75 2.00
20 Jerry Rice 1.00 2.50
21 Dan Marino 2.00 5.00
22 Troy Aikman 1.00 2.50
23 Brett Favre 2.00 5.00
24 Emmitt Smith 1.50 4.00
25 Kordell Stewart .75 2.00
26 Terrell Davis .60 1.50
27 Eddie George .75 2.00
28 Drew Bledsoe .60 1.50

1997 MotionVision Jumbos

COMPLETE SET (4) 10.00 25.00
SS1 Brett Favre 3.00 8.00
SS2 Dan Marino 3.00 8.00
SS3 John Elway 3.00 8.00
SS4 Steve Young 2.50 3.00

1997 MotionVision Limited Digital Replays

COMPLETE SET (8) 25.00 60.00
COMP.SERIES 1 (4) 50.00 50.00
COMP.SERIES 2 (4) 25.00 20.00
STATED ODDS 1:25
LDR1 Terrell Davis 6.00 15.00
LDR1A Terrell Davis AUTO 75.00 150.00
LDR2 Curtis Martin 3.00 8.00
LDR3 Brett Favre 7.50 20.00
LDR4 Barry Sanders 7.50 20.00
LDR5 Warrick Dunn 4.00 10.00
LDR6 Antowain Smith 3.00 8.00
XVRR Warrick Dunn EXCH 3.00 8.00
XVRR Antowain Smith EXCH 2.50 6.00

1997 MotionVision Super Bowl XXXI

These four cards were made available via a redemption offer in 1996 MotionVision series 2 packs, as well as 1997 series 1 packs. There was one card made commemorating each Conference Championship game and one for Super Bowl XXXI. The fourth card features Favre during the Super Bowl using a jumbo format (roughly 5 5/8" by 3 3/4"). Each is numbered of 5000 cards produced.

COMPLETE SET (4) 30.00 75.00
1 Drew Bledsoe 0.00 15.00
AFC Championship Game
2 Brett Favre 8.00 20.00
3 Brett Favre 8.00 20.00
4 Brett Favre Jumbo 8.00 20.00

1976 MSA Cups

This set of cups was produced by MSA and distributed at various outlets and stores in 1976. Each features a photo of the player without the use of team logos. It is thought that two different 20-cup sets were released throughout the country. Any additions to this list are appreciated.

1 Ken Anderson 4.00 8.00
2 Lem Barney 4.00 8.00
3 Steve Bartkowski 3.00 6.00
4 Fred Biletnikoff 5.00 10.00
5 Terry Bradshaw 12.00 25.00
(gold uniform)
6 Gary Danielson 2.50 5.00
7 Joe Ferguson 3.00 6.00
8 Chuck Foreman 3.00 6.00
9 Dan Fouts 6.00 12.00
10 Randy Gradishar 3.00 6.00
11 Bob Griese 6.00 12.00
12 Archie Griffin 3.00 6.00
13 Steve Grogan 3.00 6.00
14 Pat Haden 3.00 6.00
15 Jim Hart 2.50 5.00
16 Gary Huff 2.50 5.00
17 Ron Jaworski 3.00 6.00
18 Billy Johnson 2.50 5.00
19 Essex Johnson 2.50 5.00
20 Bert Jones 3.00 6.00
21 Billy Kilmer 3.00 6.00
22 Mike Livingston 2.50 5.00
23 Archie Manning 2.50 5.00
24 Ed Marinaro 4.00 8.00
25 Lawrence McCutchen 2.50 5.00
26 Craig Morton 3.00 6.00
27 Dan Pastorini 3.00 6.00
28 Walter Payton 25.00 40.00
29 Jim Plunkett 5.00 10.00
30 Greg Pruitt 2.50 5.00
31 John Riggins 6.00 12.00
32 Brian Sipe 3.00 6.00
33 Steve Spurrier 10.00 20.00
34 Roger Staubach 12.50 25.00
35 Mark Van Eeghen 3.00 6.00
36 Brad Van Pelt 2.50 5.00
37 David Whitehurst 2.50 5.00

1981 MSA Holsum Discs

This 32-disc set was produced by MSA, but apparently not widely distributed. Several brands of bread (including Holsum and Gardner's in Wisconsin) carried one football disc per specially marked loaf during the promotion. The discs are blank backed and are approximately 2 3/4" in diameter. Since they are unnumbered, they are listed below in alphabetical order. The discs are licensed only by the NFL Players Association and carry no sponsor logos or identification. There were also two different posters (Holsum and Gardner's) produced for holding and displaying the set. The key card in the set depicts Joe Montana in his rookie year for cards.

COMPLETE SET (32) 125.00 250.00
1 Ken Anderson 2.00 5.00
2 Ottis Anderson 1.50 4.00
3 Steve Bartkowski 1.50 4.00
4 Ricky Bell 1.25 3.00
5 Terry Bradshaw 10.00 20.00
6 Harold Carmichael 1.50 4.00
7 Joe Cribbs 1.25 3.00
8 Gary Danielson 1.25 3.00
9 Lynn Dickey 1.25 3.00
10 Dan Doornink 1.25 3.00
11 Vince Evans 1.25 3.00
12 Joe Ferguson 1.50 4.00
13 Vagas Ferguson 1.25 3.00
14 Dan Fouts 4.00 8.00
15 Steve Fuller 1.25 3.00
16 Archie Griffin 1.50 4.00
17 Steve Grogan 1.50 4.00
18 Bruce Harper 1.25 3.00
19 Jim Hart 1.50 4.00
20 Jim Jensen 1.25 3.00
21 Bert Jones 1.50 4.00
22 Archie Manning 2.00 5.00
23 Ted McKnight 1.25 3.00
24 Joe Montana 80.00 175.00
25 Craig Morton 1.50 4.00
26 Robert Newhouse 1.50 4.00
27 Phil Simms 5.00 10.00
28 Billy Taylor 1.25 3.00
29 Joe Theismann 2.50 6.00
30 Mark Van Eeghen 1.25 3.00
31 Delvin Williams 1.25 3.00
32 Tim Wilson 1.25 3.00
NNO Display Poster 10.00 25.00

1982 MSA QB Super Series Icee Cups

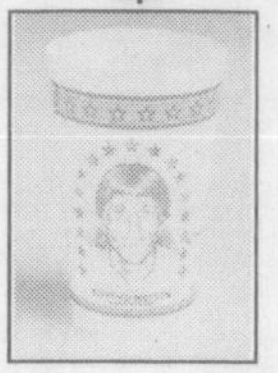

This series of cups was licensed through MSA and features one quarterback from each NFL team - although not always the starting QB. They were sponsored by Icee and Coca-Cola and include a black and white photo of the player surrounded by a star design. There is an artist's rendering of a football scene on the back of the cups.

COMPLETE SET (28)	150.00	300.00
1 Craig Morton	6.00	12.00
2 Dan Fouts	12.50	25.00
3 Danny White	7.50	15.00
4 Gary Danielson	5.00	10.00
5 Tommy Kramer	6.00	12.00
6 Matt Robinson	5.00	10.00
7 Ken Anderson	7.50	15.00
8 Tom Flick	5.00	10.00
9 Pat Ryan	5.00	10.00
10 Phil Simms	7.50	15.00
11 Gifford Nielsen	5.00	10.00
12 Steve Grogan	6.00	12.00
13 Brian Sipe	6.00	12.00
14 Bob Avellini	5.00	10.00
15 Joe Pisarcik	5.00	10.00
16 Cliff Stoudt	5.00	10.00
17 Steve Fuller	5.00	10.00
18 Archie Manning	7.50	15.00
19 Bert Jones	6.00	12.00
20 Dave Krieg	5.00	10.00
21 Don Strock	6.00	12.00
22 Marc Wilson	6.00	12.00
23 Lynn Dickey	5.00	10.00
24 Steve Bartkowski	7.50	15.00
25 Guy Benjamin	5.00	10.00
26 Art Schlichter	5.00	10.00
27 Jim Hart	6.00	12.00
28 Doug Williams	7.50	15.00

1990 MSA Superstars

This 12-card, 2 1/2" by 3 3/8", set was issued in boxes of (Ralston Purina) Staff and Food Club Frosted Flakes cereal. The cards were released as two cards in every box and a coupon was also inserted that enabled collectors to mail away and receive the set for 2 UPC symbol codes and postage and handling. These cards are unnumbered so we have checklisted them alphabetically. The fronts of the cards have the word "Superstars" on top of the players photo and his name and team underneath. The back of the card features personal information about the player and statistical information in a textual style. There are no team logos on the card as the cards apparently were issued with only the permission of the National Football League Players Association. There is no mention of MSA on the cards, but they are very similar to the Mike Schechter baseball issue for Ralston Purina so they have been cataloged as such.

COMPLETE SET (12)	20.00	40.00
1 Carl Banks	.60	1.50
2 Cornelius Bennett	.80	2.00
3 Roger Craig	.80	2.00
4 Jim Everett	.80	2.00
5 Bo Jackson	1.50	4.00
6 Ronnie Lott	.80	2.00
7 Don Majkowski	.60	1.50
8 Dan Marino	12.50	25.00
9 Karl Mecklenburg	.60	1.50
10 Christian Okoye	.60	1.50
11 Mike Singletary	1.00	2.50
12 Herschel Walker	1.00	2.50

2000 MTA MetroCard

These 4-cards are actually New York subway tickets to be used at MTA. Each features a color image of the player printed on a thin plastic stock. The backs feature the MTA logo and an electronic strip.

COMPLETE SET (4)	2.40	6.00
1 Kevin Mawae	.60	1.50
2 Wayne Chrebet	.80	2.00
3 Jason Sehorn	.60	1.50
4 Michael Strahan	.80	2.00

1990 MVP Pins

This set of pins was produced by Ace Novelties and distributed along with a regular issue 1990 Score football card. Each die cut pin includes a color photo of the player along with the pin number and "Ace 1990" notation on the back. The pins were mounted on a thick backer board that featured the team's helmet logo and "MVP" at the top of the card.

COMPLETE PIN SET (67)	25.00	50.00
1 Troy Aikman	.75	2.00
2 Flipper Anderson	.30	.75
3 Neal Anderson	.30	.75
4 Ottis Anderson	.30	.75
5 Mark Bavaro	.30	.75
6 Cornelius Bennett	.30	.75
7 Albert Bentley	.30	.75
8 Duane Bickett	.30	.75
9 Brian Blades	.30	.75
10 Bubby Brister	.40	1.00
11 James Brooks	.30	.75
12 Tim Brown	.50	1.25
13 Mark Carrier WR	.40	1.00
14 Anthony Carter	.30	.75
15 Deron Cherry	.30	.75
16 Mark Clayton	.30	.75
17 Roger Craig	.40	1.00
18 Henry Ellard	.40	1.00
19 John Elway	1.25	3.00
20 Boomer Esiason	.50	1.25
21 Jim Everett	.40	1.00
22 Roy Green	.30	.75
23 Drew Hill	.30	.75
24 Dalton Hilliard	.30	.75
25 Bobby Humphrey	.30	.75
26 Bo Jackson	.50	1.25
27 Keith Jackson	.30	.75
28 Bernie Kosar	.40	1.00
29 Louis Lipps	.30	.75
30 Eugene Lockhart	.30	.75
31 Howie Long	.40	1.00
32 Ronnie Lott	.40	1.00
33 Don Majkowski	.30	.75
34 Charles Mann	.30	.75
35 Dan Marino	1.25	3.00
36 Freeman McNeil	.30	.75
37 Karl Mecklenburg	.30	.75
38 Eric Metcalf	.30	.75
39 Keith Millard	.30	.75
40 Anthony Miller	.40	1.00
41 Chris Miller	.40	1.00
42 Art Monk	.40	1.00
43 Joe Montana	1.50	4.00
44 Warren Moon	.50	1.25
45 Ozzie Newsome	.40	1.00
46 Christian Okoye	.30	.75
47 Mike Quick	.30	.75
48 Jerry Rice	.75	2.00
49 Mark Rypien	.40	1.00
50 Barry Sanders	1.25	3.00
51 Deion Sanders	.60	1.50
52 Sterling Sharpe	.50	1.25
53 Phil Simms	.50	1.25
54 Mike Singletary	.40	1.00
55 Billy Ray Smith	.30	.75
56 Bruce Smith	.40	1.00
57 Chris Spielman	.30	.75
58 John Stephens	.30	.75
59 Lawrence Taylor	.50	1.25
60 Vinny Testaverde	.50	1.25
61 Andre Tippett	.30	.75
62 Mike Tomczak	.30	.75
63 Al Toon	.40	1.00
64 Herschel Walker	.40	1.00
65 Reggie White	.50	1.25
66 John L. Williams	.30	.75
67 Ickey Woods	.30	.75
L1 Bears Logo	.08	.25
L2 Bengals Logo	.08	.25
L3 Bills Logo	.08	.25
L4 Broncos Logo	.20	.50
L5 Browns Logo	.08	.25
L6 Buccaneers Logo	.08	.25
L7 Cardinals Logo	.08	.25
L8 Chargers Logo	.08	.25
L9 Chiefs Logo	.08	.25
L10 Colts Logo	.08	.25
L11 Cowboys Logo	.20	.50
L12 Dolphins Logo	.20	.50
L13 Eagles Logo	.08	.25
L14 Falcons Logo	.08	.25
L15 49ers Logo	.20	.50
L16 Giants Logo	.08	.25
L17 Jets Logo	.08	.25
L18 Lions Logo	.08	.25
L19 Oilers Logo	.08	.25
L20 Packers Logo	.20	.50
L21 Patriots Logo	.08	.25
L22 Raiders Logo	.20	.50
L23 Rams Logo	.08	.25
L24 Redskins Logo	.20	.50
L25 Saints Logo	.08	.25
L26 Seahawks Logo	.08	.25
L27 Steelers Logo	.08	.25
L28 Vikings Logo	.08	.25

1974 Nabisco Sugar Daddy

This set of 25 tiny (approximately 1 1/16" by 2 3/4") cards features athletes from a variety of popular pro sports. One card was included in specially marked Sugar Daddy and Sugar Mama candy bars. The cards were designed to be placed on a 18" by 24" poster, which could only be obtained through a mail-in offer direct from Nabisco. The set is referred to as "Pro Faces" as the cards show an enlarged head photo with a small caricature body. Cards 1-10 are football players, cards 11-16 and 22 are hockey players, and cards 17-21 and 23-25 are basketball players. Each card was produced in two printings. The first printing has a copyright date of 1973 printed on the backs (although the cards are thought to have been released in early 1974) and the second printing is missing a copyright date altogether.

COMPLETE SET (25)	75.00	150.00
1 Roger Staubach	15.00	30.00
2 Floyd Little	2.50	6.00
3 Steve Owens	2.50	6.00
4 Roman Gabriel	2.50	6.00
5 Bobby Douglass	2.00	5.00
6 John Gilliam	2.00	5.00
7 Bob Lilly	5.00	10.00
8 John Brockington	2.00	5.00
9 Jim Plunkett	2.50	6.00
10 Greg Landry	2.00	5.00

1975 Nabisco Sugar Daddy

This set of 25 tiny (approximately 1 1/16" by 2 3/4") cards features athletes from a variety of popular pro sports. One card was included in specially marked Sugar Daddy and Sugar Mama candy bars. The cards were designed to be placed on a 18" by 24" poster, which could only be obtained through a mail-in offer direct from Nabisco. The set is referred to as "Sugar Daddy All-Stars". As with the set of the previous year, the cards show an enlarged head photo with a small caricature body with a flag background of stars and stripes. This set is referred on the back as Series No. 2 and has a red, white, and blue background behind the picture on the front of the card. Cards 1-10 are pro football players and the remainder are pro basketball (17-21, 23-25) and hockey (11-16, 22) players.

COMPLETE SET (25)	75.00	150.00
1 Roger Staubach	15.00	30.00
2 Floyd Little	2.50	6.00
3 Alan Page	2.50	6.00
4 Merlin Olsen	4.00	8.00
5 Wally Chambers	2.00	5.00
6 John Gilliam	2.00	5.00
7 Bob Lilly	5.00	10.00
8 John Brockington	2.00	5.00
9 Jim Plunkett	2.50	6.00
10 Willie Lanier	2.50	6.00

1976 Nabisco Sugar Daddy 1

This set of 25 tiny (approximately 1 1/16" by 2 3/4") cards features action scenes from a variety of popular sports from around the world. One card was included in specially marked Sugar Daddy and Sugar Mama candy bars. The set is referred to as "Sugar Daddy Sports World - Series 1" on the backs of the cards. The cards are in color with a relatively wide white border around the front of the cards.

COMPLETE SET (25)	40.00	80.00
6 Football Charley Johnson	5.00	12.00

1976 Nabisco Sugar Daddy 2

This set of 25 tiny (approximately 1 1/16" by 2 3/4") cards features action scenes from a variety of popular sports from around the world. One card was included in specially marked Sugar Daddy and Sugar Mama candy bars. The set is referred to as "Sugar Daddy Sports World - Series 2" on the backs of the cards. The cards are in color with a relatively wide white border around the front of the cards.

COMPLETE SET (25)	40.00	80.00
4 Football (Sonny Jurgensen)	7.50	15.00

1935 National Chicle

The 1935 National Chicle set was the first nationally distributed bubble gum set dedicated exclusively to football players. The cards measure 2 3/8" by 2 7/8". Card numbers 25 to 36 are more difficult to obtain than other cards in this set. The Knute Rockne and Bronko Nagurski cards are two of the most valuable football cards in existence. The set features NFL players except for the Rockne card. There are variations on the back of nearly every card with respect to the size of Eddie Casey's facsimile signature. It was printed in either small or large letters with the large letter version thought to be slightly more difficult to find. Please note that many different reprints of these cards exist (particularly Rockne and Nagurski) so caution should be taken before paying a large sum for a card. The original cards were printed with blue ink on the back not green. Some reprints feature the word "reprint" on the front or back while others do not. A close look at the dot pattern on the front of the card is a tell tale sign of a reprint card. The originals do not show a dot pattern under magnification.

COMPLETE SET (36)	10,000.00	15,000.00
COMMON CARD (1-24)	100.00	175.00
COMMON CARD (25-36)	400.00	600.00
WRAPPER (1-CENT)	200.00	400.00
1 Dutch Clark RC	300.00	600.00
2 Bo Molenda RC	100.00	175.00
3 George Kenneally RC	100.00	175.00
4 Ed Matesic RC	100.00	175.00
5 Glenn Presnell RC	100.00	175.00
6 Pug Rentner RC	100.00	175.00
7 Ken Strong RC	250.00	400.00
8 Jim Zyntell RC	100.00	175.00
9 Knute Rockne CO	1,000.00	1,600.00
10 Cliff Battles RC	250.00	400.00
11 Turk Edwards RC	250.00	400.00
12 Tom Hupke RC	100.00	175.00
13 Homer Griffiths RC	100.00	175.00
14 Phil Sarboe UER RC	100.00	175.00
15 Ben Ciccone RC	100.00	175.00
16 Ben Smith RC	100.00	175.00
17 Tom Jones RC	100.00	175.00
18 Mike Mikulak RC	100.00	175.00
19 Ralph Kercheval RC	100.00	175.00
20 Warren Heller RC	100.00	175.00
21 Cliff Montgomery RC	100.00	175.00
22 Shipwreck Kelly UER RC	100.00	175.00
23 Beattie Feathers RC	175.00	300.00
24 Clarke Hinkle RC	350.00	600.00
25 Dale Burnett RC	400.00	600.00
26 John Dell Isola RC	400.00	600.00
27 Bull Tosi RC	400.00	600.00
28 Stan Kostka RC	400.00	600.00
29 Jim MacMurdo RC	400.00	600.00
30 Ernie Caddel RC	400.00	600.00
31 Nic Niccola RC	400.00	600.00
32 Swede Johnston RC	400.00	600.00
33 Ernie Smith RC	400.00	600.00
34 Bronko Nagurski RC	3,500.00	5,000.00
35 Luke Johnsos RC	400.00	600.00
36 Bernie Masterson RC	350.00	800.00

2004 National Trading Card Day

This 53-card set (49 basic cards plus four cover cards) was given out in five separate sealed packs (one from each of the following manufacturers: Donruss, Fleer, Press Pass, Topps and Upper Deck). One of the five packs was distributed at no cost to each patron that visited a participating sports card shop on April 3rd, 2004 as part of the National Trading Card Day promotion in an effort to increase awareness of collecting sports cards. The 50-card set is composed of 16 baseball, 9 basketball, 10 football, 4 golf, 5 hockey and 4 NASCAR cards. Of note, first year cards of NBA rookie stars LeBron James and Carmelo Anthony were included respectively within the UD and Fleer packs. An early Alex Rodriguez Yankees card was also highlighted within the Fleer pack.

F1-F9 ISSUED IN FLEER PACK
T1-T12 ISSUED IN TOPPS PACK
DP1-DP6 ISSUED IN DONRUSS PACK
PP1-PP7 ISSUED IN PRESS PASS PACK
UD1-UD15 ISSUED IN UPPER DECK PACK

F5 Brett Favre	.75	2.00
F6 Marshall Faulk	.30	.75
T5 Michael Vick	.50	1.25
T6 Charles Rogers	.20	.50
DP5 Anquan Boldin	.20	.50
DP6 Ricky Williams	.30	.75
PP6 Eli Manning	1.50	4.00
PP7 Roy Williams WR	.40	1.00
UD9 Michael Vick	.50	1.25
UD11 Peyton Manning	.75	2.00

1999 New Jersey Red Dogs AFL

COMPLETE SET (33)	7.50	15.00
1 Alvin Ashley	.30	.75
2 Henry Baker	.30	.75
3 Wilke Bazile	.30	.75
4 Jerome Brown	.30	.75
5 Kevin Clemens	.30	.75
6 Keita Crespina	.30	.75
7 Rickey Foggie	.30	.75
8 Harvie Herrington	.30	.75
9 Pierre Hixon	.30	.75
10 Latish Kinsler	.30	.75
11 Willie Latta	.30	.75
12 Chad Lindsey	.30	.75
13 Adrian Lunsford	.30	.75
14 Ron Perry	.30	.75
15 Manny Pina	.30	.75
16 Charles Puleri	.30	.75
17 John Robinson	.30	.75
18 Dimitrious Stanley	.30	.75
19 Matthew Steeple	.30	.75
20 Robert Stewart	.30	.75
21 Larry Thompson	.30	.75
22 Steve Videtich	.30	.75
23 Jason Walters	.30	.75
24 Jermaine Younger	.30	.75
25 Frank Mattiace CO	.30	.75
26 Frank Haege AHC	.30	.75
27 Pete Costanza AC	.30	.75
28 Amod Field AC	.30	.75
29 Jeff Hoffman AC	.30	.75
30 Joe Moss AC	.30	.75
31 Team Mascot	.30	.75
32 Fans	.30	.75
33 Dance Team	.30	.75

1992 NewSport

This set of 32 glossy player photos was sponsored by NewSport and issued in France. The month when each card was issued is printed as a tagline on the card back; four cards were issued per month from November 1991 to June 1992. The set was also available in four-card uncut strips. The cards measure approximately 4" by 6" and display glossy color player photos with white borders. The player's name and position appear in the top border, while the NewSport and NFL logos adorn the bottom of the card face. In French, the backs present biography, complete statistics, and career summary. The cards are unnumbered and checklisted below in alphabetical order.

COMPLETE SET (32)	50.00	120.00
1 Bubby Brister	1.25	3.00
2 James Brooks	.75	2.00
3 Joey Browner	.75	2.00
4 Gill Byrd	.75	2.00
5 Eric Dickerson	1.25	3.00
6 Henry Ellard	1.25	3.00
7 John Elway	7.50	20.00
8 Mervyn Fernandez	.75	2.00
9 David Fulcher	.75	2.00
10 Ernest Givins	.75	2.00
11 Jay Hilgenberg	.75	2.00
12 Michael Irvin	2.00	5.00
13 Dave Krieg	.75	2.00
14 Albert Lewis	.75	2.00
15 James Lofton	1.25	3.00
16 Dan Marino	7.50	20.00
17 Wilber Marshall	.75	2.00
18 Freeman McNeil	.75	2.00
19 Karl Mecklenburg	.75	2.00
20 Joe Montana	10.00	25.00
21 Christian Okoye	.75	2.00
22 Michael Dean Perry	.75	2.00
23 Tom Rathman	.75	2.00
24 Mark Rypien	.75	2.00
25 Barry Sanders	6.00	15.00
26 Deion Sanders	2.50	6.00
27 Sterling Sharpe	1.25	3.00
28 Pat Swilling	.75	2.00
29 Lawrence Taylor	1.25	3.00
30 Vinny Testaverde	1.25	3.00
31 Andre Tippett	.75	2.00
32 Reggie White	2.00	5.00

2008 New York Dragons AFL Donruss

This set was produced by Donruss and issued at a regular season Dragons game in 2008.

NYD1 Aaron Garcia	.50	1.25
NYD2 Kevin Swayne	.40	1.00
NYD3 Joe Laudano	.40	1.00
NYD4 Chris Anthony	.40	1.00
NYD5 Billy Parker	.40	1.00
NYD6 Jason Willis	.40	1.00
NYD7 Greg Randall	.40	1.00
NYD8 Weylan Harding CO	.40	1.00

1974 New York News This Day in Sports

These cards are newspaper clippings of drawings by Hollreiser and are accompanied by textual description highlighting a player's unique sports feat. Cards are approximately 2" X 4 1/4". These are multisport cards and aranged in chronological order.

COMPLETE SET (40)	50.00	120.00
25 Doc Blanchard Glenn Davis Sept. 30, 1944	1.50	3.00
27 Archie Manning Oct. 4, 1969	1.50	3.00
31 Harold Jackson Oct. 14, 1973	1.00	2.00
32 O.J. Simpson Oct. 21, 1967	1.50	3.00
33 Doc Blanchard Nov. 11, 1944	1.00	2.00
35 Bronko Nagurski Nov. 23, 1929	1.50	3.00
37 New York Giants Dec. 9, 1934	1.00	2.00
38 John Brodie Dec. 20, 1970	1.00	2.00
39 Roger Staubach Dec. 23, 1972	2.00	4.00
40 Paul Brown Otto Graham Dec. 26, 1954	1.50	3.00

1974 New York Stars WFL Team Issue 8X10

The photos measure roughly 8" x 10" and include black and white images with the player's name centered below the photo, the team logo to the left and the player's position to the right. The backs are blank.

1 Howard Baldwin Pres.	5.00	10.00
2 Robert Keating VP	5.00	10.00
3 Babe Parilli CO	7.50	15.00

1991-92 NFL Experience

This 28-card set measures approximately 2 1/2" by 4 3/4" and has black borders around each picture. Produced by the NFL, this stylized card set highlights Super Bowl players and scenes. Card fronts run either horizontally or vertically and carry the NFL Experience logo at the bottom center. The backs are printed horizontally with the words "The NFL Experience" and card number appearing in black in a light pink bar at the top. The bottom pink bar carries a description of front artwork, while the center portion describes some aspect of NFL life. Sponsors' logos appear on the right portion of each back.

COMPLETE SET (28)	1.60	4.00
1 NFL Experience Theme Art	.10	.30
2 Super Bowl I Max McGee	.07	.20
3 Super Bowl II Vince Lombardi Bart Starr	.20	.50
4 Super Bowl III Don Shula Joe Namath	.30	.75
5 Super Bowl IV	.07	.20
6 Super Bowl V Colts Cowboys	.07	.20
7 Super Bowl VI Duane Thomas Bob Lilly Roger Staubach Tom Landry Tex Schramm	.25	.60
8 Super Bowl VII	.07	.20
9 Super Bowl VIII Larry Csonka	.10	.30
10 Super Bowl IX	.07	.20
11 Super Bowl X Lynn Swann Jack Lambert	.10	.30
12 Super Bowl XI John Madden Raiders Vikings	.10	.30
13 Super Bowl XIII Randy White Harvey Martin Craig Morton	.10	.30
14 Super Bowl XIII Steelers Cowboys	.07	.20
15 Super Bowl XIV Terry Bradshaw	.25	.60
16 Super Bowl XV Raiders Eagles	.07	.20
17 Super Bowl XVI/49ers Bengals	.07	.20
18 Super Bowl XVII John Riggins	.10	.30
19 Super Bowl XVIII Marcus Allen	.10	.30
20 Super Bowl XIX/49ers Dolphins	.07	.20
21 Super Bowl XX Richard Dent	.10	.30
22 Super Bowl XXI	.07	.20
23 Super Bowl XXII John Elway Doug Williams	.30	.75
24 Super Bowl XXIII/49ers Bengals	.07	.20
25 Super Bowl XXIV Joe Montana	.50	1.25
26 Super Bowl XXV Collage of 25 Super Bowls	.07	.20
27 Super Bowl XXVI Lombardi Trophy	.07	.20
28 Joe Theismann	.10	.30

1998 NFL Films Magic Motion 5x7

1 Troy Aikman	3.00	8.00
2 Peyton Manning	5.00	12.00
3 Jerry Rice	4.00	10.00
4 Barry Sanders	4.00	10.00
5 Emmitt Smith	4.00	10.00
6 Steve Young	2.50	6.00

1997 NFL-Opoly

This set of cards was issued as part of a Monopoly style board game using the NFL and it's players as the pieces. Each card features a color player photo on the cardfront with basic team information and game point value on the cardbacks. The cards were not numbered.

COMPLETE SET (14)	10.00	25.00
1 Troy Aikman	1.60	4.00
2 Jeff Blake	.40	1.00
3 Drew Bledsoe	1.20	3.00
4 Dave Brown	.20	.50
5 Mark Brunell	1.20	3.00
6 Kerry Collins	.40	1.00
7 John Elway	3.20	8.00
8 Brett Favre	3.20	8.00
9 Jim Harbaugh	.40	1.00
10 Dan Marino	3.20	8.00
11 Neil O'Donnell	.20	.50
12 Jerry Rice	1.60	4.00
13 Barry Sanders	3.20	8.00
14 Kordell Stewart	1.20	3.00

2005 NFL Players Inc

These cards were issued by Players Inc at various events to promote the players they represent. Each oversized (roughly 3 1/4" by 4 1/8") card includes a posed photo shoot image of a player with variations in the photography for some players. The cardbacks include specific information about the Players Inc and their licensees.

1 Chad Johnson Player Marketing, close-up photo Holding a football in both hands	1.00	2.50
2 Ben Roethlisberger Fantasy Football Photo crushing a football	4.00	10.00
3 Ben Roethlisberger Reebok, full body photo	4.00	10.00
4 Roy Williams S Marketing and Appearances Holding up his hands	1.00	2.50
5 Roy Williams S Trading Card Licensees Full body photo	1.00	2.50
6 Brian Westbrook Fantasy Football Full body photo	1.00	2.50

1972 NFL Properties Cloth Patches

This set of team logos and team helmet stickers was produced by NFL Properties in 1972. Each measures roughly 1 1/2" by 1 3/4" and was printed on cloth sticker stock with a blank back. The stickers closely resemble the early cloth patches used in many of the Fleer releases from that era. It is thought by many hobbyists that this set was actually released in Schwebel Bread products in 1975.

COMPLETE SET (52)	150.00	300.00
1 Chicago Bears (logo)	3.00	6.00
2 Chicago Bears (helmet)	3.00	6.00
3 Cincinnati Bengals (logo)	3.00	6.00
4 Cincinnati Bengals (helmet)	3.00	6.00
5 Buffalo Bills (logo)	3.00	6.00
6 Buffalo Bills (helmet)	3.00	6.00
7 Denver Broncos (logo)	3.00	6.00
8 Denver Broncos (helmet)	3.00	6.00
9 Cleveland Browns (logo)	5.00	10.00
10 Cleveland Browns (helmet)	4.00	8.00
11 St.Louis Cardinals (logo)	3.00	6.00
12 St.Louis Cardinals (helmet)	3.00	6.00
13 San Diego Chargers (logo)	3.00	6.00
14 San Diego Chargers (helmet)	3.00	6.00
15 Kansas City Chiefs (logo)	3.00	6.00
16 Kansas City Chiefs (helmet)	3.00	6.00
17 Baltimore Colts (logo)	3.00	6.00
18 Baltimore Colts (helmet)	3.00	6.00
19 Dallas Cowboys (logo)	5.00	10.00
20 Dallas Cowboys (helmet)	5.00	10.00
21 Miami Dolphins (logo)	5.00	10.00
22 Miami Dolphins (helmet)	5.00	10.00
23 Philadelphia Eagles (logo)	3.00	6.00
24 Philadelphia Eagles (helmet)	3.00	6.00
25 Atlanta Falcons (logo)	3.00	6.00
26 Atlanta Falcons (helmet)	3.00	6.00
27 San Francisco 49ers (logo)	4.00	8.00
28 San Francisco 49ers (helmet)	4.00	8.00
29 New York Giants (logo)	4.00	8.00
30 New York Giants (helmet)	4.00	8.00
31 New York Jets (logo)	3.00	6.00
32 New York Jets (helmet)	3.00	6.00
33 Detroit Lions (logo)	3.00	6.00
34 Detroit Lions (helmet)	3.00	6.00
35 Houston Oilers (logo)	3.00	6.00
36 Houston Oilers (helmet)	3.00	6.00
37 Green Bay Packers (logo)	4.00	8.00
38 Green Bay Packers (helmet)	4.00	8.00
39 New England Patriots (logo)	3.00	6.00
40 New England Patriots (helmet)	3.00	6.00
41 Oakland Raiders (logo)	5.00	10.00
42 Oakland Raiders (helmet)	5.00	10.00
43 Los Angeles Rams (logo)	3.00	6.00
44 Los Angeles Rams (helmet)	3.00	6.00
45 Washington Redskins (logo)	5.00	10.00
46 Washington Redskins (helmet)	5.00	10.00
47 New Orleans Saints (logo)	3.00	6.00
48 New Orleans Saints (helmet)	3.00	6.00
49 Pittsburgh Steelers (logo)	4.00	8.00
50 Pittsburgh Steelers (helmet)	4.00	8.00
51 Minnesota Vikings (logo)	4.00	8.00
52 Minnesota Vikings (helmet)	4.00	8.00

1983 NFL Properties Huddles

These cards were produced by NFL Properties and distributed in various licensed products including Avon soaps. Each card features the Huddle character on the front along with the 1983 copyright line. The cardbacks provide a brief team history.

COMPLETE SET (28)	20.00	50.00
1 Atlanta Falcons	.60	1.50
2 Buffalo Bills	.75	2.00
3 Chicago Bears	.75	2.00
4 Cincinnati Bengals	.60	1.50
5 Cleveland Browns	.75	2.00
6 Dallas Cowboys	1.25	3.00
7 Denver Broncos	.75	2.00
8 Detroit Lions	.60	1.50
9 Green Bay Packers	1.25	3.00
10 Houston Oilers	.60	1.50
11 Indianapolis Colts	.60	1.50
12 Kansas City Chiefs	.60	1.50
13 Los Angeles Raiders	1.25	3.00
14 Los Angeles Rams	.60	1.50
15 Miami Dolphins	1.25	3.00
16 Minnesota Vikings	.75	2.00
17 New England Patriots	.60	1.50
18 New Orleans Saints	.60	1.50
19 New York Giants	.75	2.00
20 New York Jets	.75	2.00
21 Philadelphia Eagles	.60	1.50
22 Pittsburgh Steelers	1.25	3.00
23 St. Louis Cardinals	.60	1.50
24 San Diego Chargers	.60	1.50
25 San Francisco 49ers	1.25	3.00
26 Seattle Seahawks	.60	1.50
27 Tampa Bay Buccaneers	.60	1.50
28 Washington Redskins	.75	2.00

1993 NFL Properties Santa Claus

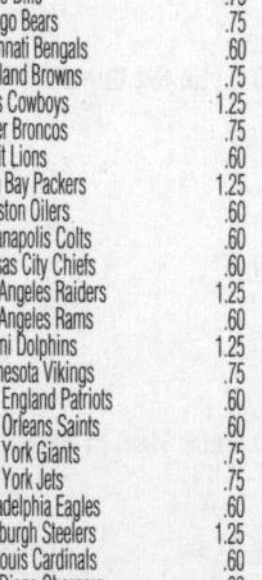

The first Santa Claus card produced by an NFL trading card licensee was in 1989. In 1993, each of the 12 trading card licensees produced an NFL Santa Claus Card, and the entire set, which included a checklist card issued by NFL Properties, was offered through a special mail-away offer for any 30 1993 NFL trading card wrappers and 1.50 for postage and handling. The cards were sent out to dealers along with a season's greeting card. All the cards measure the standard size and feature different artistic renderings of Santa Claus on their fronts and season's greetings on their backs. Although some cards are numbered while others are not, the cards are checklisted below alphabetically according to the licensee's name.

COMPLETE SET (13)	6.00	15.00
1 Santa Claus	.50	1.25
Action Packed		
2 Santa Claus	.50	1.25
Classic		
3 Santa Claus	.50	1.25
Collector's Edge		
4 Santa Claus	.50	1.25
Fleer		
5 Santa Claus	.50	1.25
Pacific		
6 Santa Claus	.50	1.25
Pinnacle		
7 Santa Claus	.50	1.25
Playoff		
8 Santa Claus	.50	1.25
Pro Set		
9 Santa Claus	.50	1.25
SkyBox		
10 Santa Claus	.50	1.25
Topps		
11 Santa Claus	2.00	5.00
Upper Deck		
(Joe Montana in background)		
12 Santa Claus	.50	1.25
Wild Card		
13 Checklist Card	.50	1.25
NFL Properties		

1993-95 NFL Properties Show Redemption Cards

Produced by NFL Properties and handed out to attendees at card shows, these oversized cards measure approximately 3 1/2" by 5" and feature on their fronts collages of player portraits and/or photos. A banner at the top of each card carries the city and dates that the show was held. On the card given out at the National in Chicago, each of the honored players has signed the card in silver ink. The card given out in St. Louis, listed below as 4B, replaced 4A, which was done to commemorate the St. Louis Stallions NFL franchise that never materialized and so was not released. One thousand of 4B were distributed each of the three days of the show, making a total of 3,000. The white back of each card carries text about the players depicted on the front (except card number 2, the back of which carries the 49ers 1993 schedule) and the individual serial number out of the total produced. Card 4B also carries the date that the card was distributed next to the "X of 1000" production figure. Except for the first card, the cards are numbered on the back in Roman numerals. The 49ers card was available at the Team NFL booth at the 1993 San Francisco Labor Day Sports Collector's Convention in exchange for ten wrappers from any licensed 1993 NFL card product. Card number 6A was given to attendees of the Cocktail Reception sponsored by NFL Properties at the 15th National Sports Collectors Convention. The three featured players autographed the card in blue ink. Card number 6B was issued as part of a Back-to-School promotion; collectors redeemed two proofs-of-purchase for this oversized Elway card and an NFL FACT card.

COMPLETE SET (9)	360.00	900.00
1 Chicago Bears	60.00	150.00
Saluting Hall of Famers/7/24/93 (200)		
Dick Butkus		
Mike Ditka		
Gale Sayers		
(Signed in silver ink)		
2 San Francisco 49ers	12.00	30.00
Labor Day Weekend/9/93 (1,000)		
NFL Kickoff '93		
Ricky Watters		
Steve Young		
Keith DeLong		
Jerry Rice		
John Taylor		
Tim McDonald		
(1993 49er schedule		
on card back)		
3 San Francisco 49ers	10.00	25.00
Labor Day Weekend/9/93 (1,000)		
Saluting Bay		
Area Legends		
Y.A. Tittle		
Ken Stabler		
(Career summaries		
on back)		
3AU San Francisco/49ers AUTO	80.00	200.00
Labor Day Weekend/9/93 (100)		
Saluting Bay		
Area Legends		
Y.A. Tittle		
Ken Stabler		
Signed by both players		
4B St. Louis Cardinals	4.00	10.00
Saluting Three Decades of		
Gateway City QBs/10/29-31/93 (3000)		
Jim Hart		
Charley Johnson		
Neil Lomax		
5 Dallas Cowboys Champs	8.00	20.00
6A Houston Oilers	80.00	200.00
Saluting a Trio of		
Oilers Legends (Autographed)/8/4-7/94 (200)		
Earl Campbell		
Dan Pastorini		
Ken Stabler		
6B John Elway/1995 Spokesman NFL	80.00	200.00
Trading Cards		
Autographed (300)		
7 Joe Namath	100.00	250.00
John Elway		
Autographed (300)		

1994 NFL Properties Back-to-School

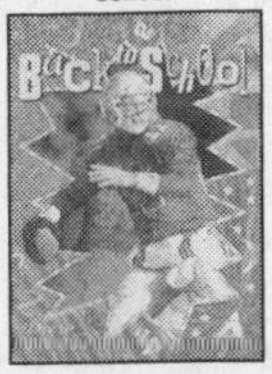

The NFL developed this 11-card standard-size set for football fans and card collectors. The set was available to collectors who sent 20 wrappers from any NFL-licensed trading cards to the NFL '94 Back-to-School Offer address in Minnesota by Nov. 30, 1994. The set features one standard-size card from each of the major licensed football card manufacturers. As originally conceived, the set included a Brett Favre card by Pro Set, but NFL Properties was unable to include this card in the set since Pro Set went out of business. All cards feature on their backs the NFL Back-to-School logo and a message on the importance of staying in school. Only the Action Packed (BS1) and Upper Deck (#19) cards are numbered on the backs. The cards are checklisted below alphabetically according to card manufacturers.

COMPLETE SET (11)	6.00	15.00
1 NFL Quarterback Club	.30	.75
Action Packed		
2 Emmitt Smith	1.20	3.00
Classic		
3 John Elway	1.20	3.00
Collector's Edge		
4 Jerome Bettis	.40	1.00
Fleer		
5 Sterling Sharpe	.30	.75
Pacific		
6 Drew Bledsoe	.80	2.00
Pinnacle		
7 Dana Stubblefield	.20	.50
Playoff		
8 Jim Kelly	.30	.75
SkyBox		
9 Jerry Rice	.80	2.00
Topps		
10 Joe Montana	1.20	3.00
Upper Deck		
11 Checklist	.20	.50
NFL Properties		

1994 NFL Properties Santa Claus

In 1994, each of the ten trading card licensees produced an NFL Santa Claus card. Collectors could obtain the set by sending in 20 wrappers of any participating football card manufacturer and 1.50 for postage and handling. The offer expired on March 31, 1995, or earlier should NFL Properties run out of cards. All the cards measure the standard-size and feature different artistic renderings of Santa Claus on their fronts and season's greetings on their backs. Though some cards are numbered while others are not, all the cards are listed below alphabetically according to licensee's name.

COMPLETE SET (11)	4.00	10.00
1 Santa Claus	.50	1.25
Action Packed		
2 Santa Claus	.50	1.25
Classic		
3 Santa Claus	.50	1.25
Collector's Edge		
4 Santa Claus	.50	1.25
Fleer		
5 Santa Claus	.50	1.25
Pacific		
6 Santa Claus	.50	1.25
Pinnacle		
7 Santa Claus	.50	1.25
Playoff		
8 Santa Claus	1.00	2.50
SkyBox		
(Jim Kelly featured)		
9 Santa Claus	.50	1.25
Topps		
10 Santa Claus	.50	1.25
Upper Deck		
11 Checklist Card	.50	1.25
NFL Properties		

1995 NFL Properties Back-to-School

NFL Properties developed this set for football fans and card collectors. The set was available to collectors via a wrapper redemption prgram just like the 1994 set. The set features one standard-size card from each of the major licensed football card manufacturers. All cards feature on their backs the NFL Back-to-School logo and a message on the importance of staying in school. Some of the cards are numbered on the backs similar to that player's base set card. We've cataloged the cards below in alphabetical oder.

COMPLETE SET (9)	4.80	12.00
1 Troy Aikman	.60	1.50
Drew Bledsoe		
(Pinnacle)		
2 John Elway	1.20	3.00
(NFL Properties)		
3 Michael Irvin	.30	.75
(Fleer)		
4 Natrone Means	.20	.50
(Pacific)		
5 Rick Mirer	.20	.50
(Playoff)		
6 Joe Montana	1.20	3.00
(Collector's Choice)		
7 Junior Seau	.30	.75
(Collector's Edge)		
8 Emmitt Smith	1.00	2.50
(Pro Line)		
9 Steve Young	.40	1.00
(Topps)		

1995 NFL Properties Santa Claus

This nine-card set consists of Santa Claus cards produced by the eight NFL trading card licensees and features different artistic renderings of Santa Claus and season's greetings. The cards are listed below alphabetically according to the licensee's name. Collectors could obtain the set by sending in 20 wrappers of any participating football card manufacturer and $1.50 for postage and handling. The offer expired on March 31, 1996.

COMPLETE SET (9)	4.00	10.00
1 Title Card	.40	1.00
Santa and friend		
2 Santa Claus	1.00	2.50
Classic Proline		
with Emmitt Smith		
and Drew Bledsoe		
3 Santa Claus	.40	1.00
Collector's Edge		
4 Santa Claus	.40	1.00
Pacific		
5 Santa Claus	1.20	3.00
Pinnacle		
with Dan Marino		
Emmitt Smith		
Steve Young		
6 Santa Claus	.40	1.00
Playoff		
7 Santa Claus	.40	1.00
Skybox		
8 Santa Claus	.40	1.00
Topps		
9 Santa Claus	.40	1.00
Upper Deck		

1996 NFL Properties Back-to-School

The NFL developed this 9-card standard-size set to promote football card collecting. The set was available to collectors who sent 20 wrappers from any NFL-licensed trading card set and $1.50 postage to the NFL '96 Back-to-School Collector's Set address in Minnesota by Nov. 30, 1996. The set features one standard-size card from each of the major licensed football card manufacturers. The cards are checklisted below alphabetically

COMPLETE SET (9)	4.80	12.00
1 Steve Bono	.30	.75
Collector's Edge		
2 John Elway	1.00	2.50
NFL Properties		
3 Brett Favre	1.00	2.50
4 Dan Marino	1.00	2.50
Upper Deck		
5 Dan Marino	.80	2.00
Steve Young		
Pinnacle		
6 Deion Sanders	.40	1.00
Playoff		
7 Emmitt Smith	.80	2.00
Classic		
8 Chris Warren	.20	.50
Pacific		
9 Steve Young	.40	1.00
Topps		

1996 NFL Properties Santa Claus

This nine-card set consists of Santa Claus cards produced by the eight NFL trading card licensees and features different artistic renderings of Santa Claus and season's greetings. The cards are listed below alphabetically according to the licensee's name. Collectors could obtain the set by sending in 20 wrappers of any participating football card manufacturer and $1.50 for postage and handling. The offer expired on March 31, 1997.

COMPLETE SET (9)	4.00	10.00
1 Title Card	.30	.75
Santa Claus		
2 Santa Claus	.30	.75
Collector's Edge		
with Jeff Blake		
and Steve Bono		
3 Santa Claus	1.20	3.00
Fleer		
Skybox		
with Brett Favre		
4 Santa Claus	.30	.75
Pacific		
5 Santa Claus	.80	2.00
Pinnacle		
with Drew Bledsoe		
and Jim Harbaugh		
6 Santa Claus	.30	.75
Playoff		
7 Santa Claus	.80	2.00
Score Board		
with Troy Aikman		
8 Santa Claus	.30	.75
Topps		
9 Santa Claus	.30	.75
Upper Deck		

1996 NFL Properties 7-Eleven

NFL Properties and 7-Eleven stores teamed to distribute this 9-card set promoting football card collecting. Each card was available through 7-Eleven stores three per month (October-December) during the 1996 NFL season. A collector was required to send in two football card wrappers and a sales receipt from the 7-Eleven store along with $1 postage to receive one of the nine cards. A different NFL licensed trading card manufacturer produced each card.

COMPLETE SET (9)	10.00	25.00
1 John Elway	2.00	5.00
2 Jerry Rice	1.00	2.50
3 Dan Marino	2.00	5.00
4 Barry Sanders	2.00	5.00
5 Kordell Stewart	.60	1.50
6 Steve Young	.80	2.00
7 Joe Namath	1.00	2.50
8 Brett Favre	2.00	5.00
9 Trent Dilfer	.30	.75

1997 NFL Properties Santa Claus

This eight card standard-size set continued the tradition of all the NFL card manufacturers combining to make a special holiday set. As with previous sets, one could receive this set in return for sending in wrappers and a small amount of money for a redemption.

COMPLETE SET (8)	3.20	8.00
1 Title Card	.20	.50
Santa Claus		
2 Santa Claus	.20	.50
Collector's Edge		
with Jeff Blake		
Steve Bono		
3 Santa Claus	1.00	2.50
Pinnacle		
with Drew Bledsoe		
Kerry Collins		
Dan Marino		
Jim Harbaugh		
4 Santa Claus	.30	.75
Playoff		
Reggie White		
5 Santa Claus	1.20	3.00
Score Board		
with Brett Favre		
6 Santa Claus	.20	.50
Topps		
7 Santa Claus	.30	.75
Ultra		
Steve McNair painted over		
8 Santa Claus	.60	1.50
Upper Deck		
Troy Aikman		

2002 NFL Properties Punt, Pass, and Kick

This 10-card set was distributed as prizes at the NFL Properties Punt, Pass and Kick contest. Each card features color action photos, and the PPK logo. Each of the five major football manufacturors produced two cards for the set.

COMPLETE SET (10)	7.50	20.00
1 Troy Aikman/Fleer	1.25	3.00
2 Drew Bledsoe/Pacific	1.25	3.00
3 Randall Cunningham/Donruss	.75	2.00
4 Brett Favre/Donruss	2.50	6.00
5 Bert Jones/Fleer	.75	2.00
6 Jim Kelly/Topps	.75	2.00
7 Bernie Kosar/Upper Deck	.75	2.00
8 Dan Marino/Upper Deck	3.00	8.00
9 Vinny Testaverde/Topps	.75	2.00
10 Danny White/Pacific	.75	2.00

2001 NFL Showdown 1st Edition

The 2001 NFL Showdown product was released in mid-2001 as a 462-card football strategy game. Although the packaging and the cardbacks identifies the year of release as 2002, it is considered a 2001 year set. The 1st Edition cards were printed with a silver stamp on the front of the card reading 1st Edition. The set features 400-regular player cards and 62-foil cards that were short printed. The 1st Edition packs were released as eleven-card packs with seven player cards, two Strategy cards, and two Play cards per pack. The packs carried a suggested retail price of $2.99.

COMP.SET w/o FOILS (400)	20.00	50.00
1 Cary Blanchard	.25	.60
2 David Boston	.25	.60
3 Rob Fredrickson	.25	.60
4 MarTay Jenkins	.25	.60
5 Thomas Jones	.30	.75
6 Tom Knight	.25	.60
7 Kwamie Lassiter	.25	.60
8 Ronald McKinnon FOIL	.50	1.25
9 Michael Pittman	.30	.75
10 Jake Plummer	.30	.75
11 Frank Sanders	.25	.60
12 L.J. Shelton	.25	.60
13 Pat Tillman RC	6.00	15.00
14 Aeneas Williams	.30	.75
15 Ashley Ambrose	.25	.60
16 Morten Andersen	.25	.60
17 Jamal Anderson	.30	.75
18 Ronnie Bradford	.25	.60
19 Ray Buchanan FOIL	.50	1.25
20 Chris Chandler	.30	.75
21 Henri Crockett	.25	.60
22 Travis Hall	.25	.60
23 Edward Jasper RC	.25	.60
24 Shawn Jefferson	.25	.60
25 Terance Mathis	.25	.60
26 Ephraim Salaam RC	.25	.60
27 Brady Smith	.25	.60
28 Bob Whitfield	.25	.60
29 Sam Adams	.25	.60
30 Tony Banks	.25	.60
31 Rob Burnett	.25	.60
32 Trent Dilfer	.30	.75
33 Kim Herring	.25	.60
34 Priest Holmes	.40	1.00
35 Qadry Ismail	.30	.75
36 Jamal Lewis FOIL	.75	2.00
37 Ray Lewis FOIL	.75	2.00
38 Michael McCrary FOIL	.50	1.25
39 Edwin Mulitalo RC	.25	.60
40 Jonathan Ogden FOIL	.60	1.50
41 Shannon Sharpe	.40	1.00
42 Jamie Sharper	.25	.60
43 Matt Stover	.25	.60
44 Rod Woodson	.40	1.00
45 Ruben Brown	.25	.60
46 Keion Carpenter RC	.25	.60
47 Steve Christie	.25	.60
48 Sam Cowart FOIL	.50	1.25
49 Doug Flutie FOIL	.75	2.00
50 Rob Johnson	.30	.75
51 Henry Jones	.25	.60
52 Sammy Morris	.30	.75
53 Eric Moulds	.30	.75
54 Keith Newman RC	.25	.60
55 Jay Riemersma	.25	.60
56 Sam Rogers	.25	.60
57 Ted Washington	.25	.60
58 Marcellus Wiley	.25	.60
59 Steve Beuerlein	.30	.75
60 Tim Biakabutuka	.25	.60
61 Isaac Byrd	.25	.60
62 Eric Davis	.25	.60
63 Doug Evans	.25	.60
64 Sean Gilbert	.25	.60
65 Donald Hayes	.25	.60
66 Mike Minter FOIL RC	.60	1.50
67 Muhsin Muhammad FOIL	.60	1.50
68 Joe Nedney	.25	.60
69 Chris Terry	.25	.60
70 Wesley Walls	.25	.60
71 Reggie White	.40	1.00
72 Lee Woodall	.25	.60
73 James Allen	.25	.60
74 Mike Brown	.25	.60
75 Phillip Daniels	.25	.60
76 Paul Edinger	.25	.60
77 Jim Flanigan	.25	.60
78 Walt Harris	.25	.60
79 Eddie Kennison	.30	.75
80 Cade McNown	.30	.75
81 Glyn Milburn	.25	.60
82 Tony Parrish	.25	.60
83 Marcus Robinson	.30	.75
84 Brian Urlacher FOIL	1.00	2.50
85 Chris Villarrial RC	.25	.60
86 James Williams	.25	.60
87 Willie Anderson	.25	.60
88 Chris Carter RC	.25	.60
89 Tom Carter	.25	.60
90 John Copeland	.25	.60
91 Corey Dillon	.30	.75
92 Steve Foley RC	.25	.60
93 Oliver Gibson	.25	.60
94 Tony McGee	.25	.60
95 Matt O'Dwyer	.25	.60
96 Akili Smith	.25	.60
97 Armegis Spearman	.25	.60
98 Takeo Spikes FOIL	.50	1.25
99 Peter Warrick	.30	.75
100 Darryl Williams	.25	.60
101 Jim Bundren RC	.25	.60
102 Stalin Colinet	.25	.60
103 Tim Couch FOIL	.50	1.25
104 Phil Dawson	.25	.60
105 Percy Ellsworth	.25	.60
106 Kevin Johnson	.25	.60
107 Daylon McCutcheon	.25	.60
108 Keith McKenzie	.25	.60
109 Jamir Miller	.25	.60
110 Roman Oben	.25	.60
111 Doug Pederson	.25	.60
112 Travis Prentice	.25	.60
113 Wali Rainer	.25	.60
114 Aaron Shea	.25	.60
115 Troy Aikman	.60	1.50
116 Larry Allen	.30	.75
117 Randall Cunningham	.40	1.00
118 Ebenezer Ekuban	.25	.60
119 Jackie Harris	.30	.75
120 Leon Lett	.25	.60
121 James McKnight	.25	.60
122 Solomon Page RC	.25	.60
123 Izell Reese RC	.25	.60
124 Tim Seder	.25	.60
125 Emmitt Smith FOIL	2.00	5.00
126 Phillippi Sparks	.25	.60
127 Mark Stepnoski	.25	.60
128 Barron Wortham	.25	.60
129 Mike Anderson FOIL	.60	1.50
130 Eric Brown	.25	.60
131 Dwayne Carswell FOIL	.50	1.25
132 Desmond Clark	.30	.75
133 Brian Griese FOIL	.60	1.50
134 Billy Jenkins	.25	.60
135 Tony Jones	.25	.60
136 Ed McCaffrey	.30	.75
137 John Mobley	.25	.60
138 Tom Nalen	.25	.60
139 Kavika Pittman	.25	.60
140 Trevor Pryce	.25	.60
141 Bill Romanowski	.30	.75
142 Rod Smith	.30	.75
143 Jimmy Spencer	.25	.60
144 Al Wilson	.25	.60
145 Charlie Batch	.30	.75
146 Stephen Boyd	.25	.60
147 Germane Crowell	.25	.60
148 Luther Elliss	.25	.60
149 Aaron Gibson	.25	.60
150 Desmond Howard FOIL	.60	1.50
151 James Jones	.25	.60
152 Herman Moore	.30	.75
153 Johnnie Morton	.30	.75
154 Robert Porcher	.25	.60
155 Kurt Schulz	.25	.60
156 David Sloan	.25	.60
157 James Stewart	.25	.60
158 Bryant Westbrook	.25	.60
159 LeRoy Butler	.30	.75
160 Santana Dotson	.25	.60
161 Brett Favre FOIL	2.50	6.00
162 Mike Flanagan RC	.25	.60
163 Bubba Franks	.30	.75
164 Antonio Freeman	.40	1.00
165 Ahman Green	.40	1.00
166 Bernardo Harris	.25	.60
167 Ryan Longwell	.30	.75
168 Marco Rivera RC	.25	.60
169 Bill Schroeder	.30	.75
170 Darren Sharper FOIL	.60	1.50
171 Nate Wayne RC	.25	.60
172 Tyrone Williams	.25	.60
173 Jason Belser	.25	.60
174 Chad Bratzke	.25	.60
175 Jeff Burris	.25	.60
176 Ken Dilger	.25	.60
177 Tarik Glenn	.25	.60
178 Marvin Harrison FOIL	.75	2.00
179 Waverly Jackson RC	.25	.60
180 Edgerrin James FOIL	.75	2.00
181 Ellis Johnson	.25	.60
182 Peyton Manning FOIL	2.00	5.00
183 Adam Meadows RC	.25	.60
184 Jerome Pathon	.25	.60
185 Mike Peterson	.25	.60
186 Marcus Pollard	.25	.60
187 Terrence Wilkins	.25	.60
188 Josh Williams RC	.25	.60
189 Aaron Beasley	.25	.60
190 Tony Boselli	.30	.75
191 Tony Brackens	.25	.60
192 Kyle Brady	.25	.60
193 Mark Brunell	.30	.75
194 Donovin Darius	.25	.60
195 Todd Fordham RC	.25	.60
196 Kevin Hardy	.25	.60
197 Mike Hollis	.25	.60
198 Keenan McCardell	.30	.75
199 Jimmy Smith FOIL	.60	1.50
200 Brendan Stai	.25	.60
201 Fred Taylor FOIL	.75	2.00
202 Gary Walker RC	.25	.60
203 Derrick Alexander	.25	.60
204 Kimble Anders	.25	.60
205 Duane Clemons FOIL	.50	1.25
206 Donnie Edwards	.25	.60
207 Tony Gonzalez FOIL	.75	2.00
208 Elvis Grbac	.30	.75
209 James Hasty	.25	.60
210 Eric Hicks RC	.40	1.00
211 Sylvester Morris	.25	.60
212 Marvcus Patton	.25	.60
213 Tony Richardson	.25	.60
214 John Tait	.25	.60
215 Greg Wesley	.25	.60
216 Dan Williams	.25	.60
217 Trace Armstrong	.25	.60
218 Mark Dixon RC	.25	.60
219 Kevin Donnalley	.25	.60
220 Jay Fiedler	.30	.75
221 Oronde Gadsden	.25	.60
222 Larry Izzo	.25	.60
223 Sam Madison	.25	.60
224 Olindo Mare	.25	.60
225 Brock Marion	.25	.60
226 Tim Ruddy	.25	.60
227 Leslie Shepherd	.25	.60
228 Lamar Smith	.30	.75
229 Patrick Surtain	.25	.60
230 Jason Taylor FOIL	.75	2.00
231 Zach Thomas FOIL	.75	2.00
232 Brian Walker	.25	.60
233 Gary Anderson	.25	.60
234 Matt Birk RC	.25	.60
235 Cris Carter	.40	1.00
236 Daunte Culpepper FOIL	.60	1.50
237 Cris Dishman	.25	.60
238 Robert Griffith	.25	.60
239 Corbin Lacina	.25	.60
240 Ed McDaniel	.25	.60
241 Randy Moss FOIL	.75	2.00
242 John Randle	.30	.75
243 Talance Sawyer RC	.25	.60
244 Robert Smith FOIL	.60	1.50
245 Todd Steussie FOIL	.50	1.25
246 Robert Tate	.25	.60
247 Orlando Thomas	.25	.60
248 Kailee Wong	.25	.60
249 Drew Bledsoe	.40	1.00
250 Troy Brown	.30	.75
251 Chad Eaton	.25	.60
252 Kevin Faulk	.30	.75
253 Terry Glenn	.30	.75
254 Ty Law	.30	.75
255 Willie McGinest FOIL	.50	1.25
256 Lawyer Milloy	.30	.75
257 J.R. Redmond	.25	.60
258 Chris Slade	.25	.60
259 Greg Spires RC	.25	.60
260 Henry Thomas	.25	.60
261 Adam Vinatieri	.40	1.00
262 Grant Williams RC	.25	.60
263 Jeff Blake FOIL	.60	1.50
264 Andrew Glover	.25	.60
265 La'Roi Glover FOIL	.50	1.25
266 Joe Horn	.30	.75
267 Darren Howard	.25	.60
268 Willie Jackson	.25	.60
269 Joe Johnson	.25	.60
270 Sammy Knight	.25	.60
271 Keith Mitchell RC	.25	.60
272 Alex Molden	.25	.60
273 Chris Naeole	.25	.60
274 William Roaf	.30	.75
275 Darrin Smith	.25	.60
276 Kyle Turley	.25	.60
277 Fred Weary	.25	.60
278 Ricky Williams	.40	1.00
279 Jessie Armstead FOIL	.50	1.25
280 Tiki Barber	.40	1.00
281 Micheal Barrow	.25	.60
282 Lomas Brown	.25	.60
283 Kerry Collins	.30	.75
284 Ron Dayne	.30	.75
285 Keith Hamilton	.25	.60
286 Ike Hilliard	.30	.75
287 Emmanuel McDaniel RC	.25	.60
288 Pete Mitchell	.25	.60
289 Ryan Phillips RC	.25	.60
290 Jason Sehorn FOIL	.60	1.50
291 Michael Strahan FOIL	.75	2.00
292 Amani Toomer	.30	.75
293 Shaun Williams	.25	.60
294 Dusty Zeigler RC	.25	.60
295 Richie Anderson	.25	.60
296 Wayne Chrebet	.30	.75
297 Marcus Coleman	.25	.60
298 Bryan Cox	.30	.75
299 Shaun Ellis	.25	.60
300 Aaron Glenn	.30	.75
301 Victor Green	.25	.60
302 John Hall	.25	.60
303 Marvin Jones	.25	.60
304 Mo Lewis	.25	.60
305 Curtis Martin	.40	1.00
306 Kevin Mawae	.25	.60
307 Vinny Testaverde	.30	.75
308 Randy Thomas RC	.25	.60
309 Dedric Ward	.25	.60
310 Ryan Young FOIL RC	.50	1.25
311 Eric Allen	.30	.75
312 Greg Biekert	.25	.60
313 Tim Brown FOIL	.75	2.00
314 Tony Bryant	.25	.60
315 Mo Collins	.25	.60
316 Rich Gannon FOIL	.60	1.50
317 Grady Jackson RC	.25	.60
318 Marquez Pope	.25	.60
319 Andre Rison	.30	.75
320 Barrett Robbins	.25	.60
321 Darrell Russell	.25	.60
322 Matt Stinchcomb	.25	.60
323 William Thomas	.25	.60
324 Tyrone Wheatley	.30	.75
325 Steve Wisniewski	.25	.60
326 Charles Woodson FOIL	.75	2.00
327 Darnell Autry	.25	.60
328 Mike Caldwell	.25	.60
329 Brian Dawkins	.30	.75
330 Hugh Douglas FOIL	.50	1.25
331 Carlos Emmons	.25	.60
332 Charles Johnson	.25	.60
333 Chad Lewis	.25	.60
334 Jermane Mayberry	.25	.60
335 Donovan McNabb FOIL	.75	2.00
336 Jon Runyan	.25	.60
337 Corey Simon	.25	.60
338 Torrance Small	.25	.60
339 Bobby Taylor	.25	.60
340 Hollis Thomas	.25	.60
341 Jeremiah Trotter	.25	.60
342 Troy Vincent FOIL	.60	1.50
343 Brent Alexander	.25	.60
344 Jerome Bettis	.40	1.00
345 Kris Brown	.25	.60
346 Mark Bruener	.30	.75
347 Lethon Flowers	.25	.60
348 Jason Gildon FOIL	.50	1.25
349 Kent Graham	.30	.75
350 Joey Porter RC	.75	2.00
351 Chad Scott	.25	.60
352 Bobby Shaw	.25	.60
353 Kordell Stewart	.30	.75
354 Rich Tylski	.25	.60
355 Hines Ward	.40	1.00
356 Dewayne Washington	.25	.60
357 Ben Coleman	.25	.60
358 Curtis Conway	.30	.75
359 Gerald Dixon	.25	.60
360 Mike Dumas	.25	.60
361 Terrell Fletcher	.25	.60
362 Jeff Graham	.25	.60
363 Jim Harbaugh	.30	.75
364 Rodney Harrison FOIL	.60	1.50
365 Freddie Jones	.25	.60
366 Ryan Leaf	.25	.60
367 John Parrella	.25	.60
368 Raleigh Roundtree RC	.25	.60
369 Orlando Ruff RC	.25	.60
370 Junior Seau FOIL	.75	2.00
371 Ray Brown	.25	.60
372 Brentson Buckner	.25	.60
373 Jeff Garcia	.30	.75
374 Charlie Garner FOIL	.60	1.50
375 Monty Montgomery RC	.25	.60
376 Terrell Owens	.40	1.00
377 Julian Peterson	.25	.60
378 Jerry Rice FOIL	1.50	4.00
379 Lance Schulters	.25	.60
380 J.J. Stokes	.25	.60
381 Winfred Tubbs	.25	.60
382 Jason Webster	.25	.60
383 Matt Willig	.25	.60
384 Bryant Young	.30	.75
385 Jay Bellamy	.25	.60
386 Chad Brown	.25	.60
387 Sean Dawkins	.25	.60
388 Darrell Jackson	.30	.75
389 Pete Kendall	.25	.60
390 Cortez Kennedy	.25	.60
391 Jon Kitna	.30	.75
392 George Koonce	.25	.60
393 Itula Mili	.25	.60
394 Anthony Simmons	.25	.60
395 Michael Sinclair	.25	.60
396 Ricky Watters FOIL	.60	1.50
397 Floyd Wedderburn RC	.25	.60
398 Willie Williams	.25	.60
399 Dre Bly	.25	.60
400 Isaac Bruce	.40	1.00
401 Marshall Faulk FOIL	.75	2.00
402 London Fletcher FOIL	.50	1.25
403 Trent Green	.40	1.00
404 Az-Zahir Hakim	.25	.60
405 Torry Holt	.30	.75
406 Mike A. Jones	.25	.60
407 Keith Lyle	.25	.60
408 Dexter McCleon	.25	.60
409 Orlando Pace	.30	.75
410 Ricky Proehl	.25	.60
411 Ryan Tucker RC	.25	.60
412 Kurt Warner FOIL	1.25	3.00
413 Grant Wistrom	.25	.60
414 Jeff Zgonina RC	.25	.60
415 Donnie Abraham	.25	.60
416 Mike Alstott	.30	.75
417 Ronde Barber FOIL	.60	1.50
418 Derrick Brooks FOIL	.75	2.00
419 Jeff Christy	.25	.60
420 Jamie Duncan	.25	.60
421 Warrick Dunn	.40	1.00
422 Martin Gramatica	.25	.60
423 Jacquez Green	.25	.60
424 Keyshawn Johnson	.30	.75
425 Shaun King	.25	.60
426 John Lynch	.30	.75
427 Randall McDaniel	.30	.75
428 Anthony McFarland	.25	.60
429 Dave Moore	.25	.60
430 Warren Sapp FOIL	.60	1.50
431 Blaine Bishop	.25	.60
432 Al Del Greco	.25	.60
433 Eddie George FOIL	.75	2.00
434 Randall Godfrey	.25	.60
435 Kenny Holmes	.25	.60
436 Brad Hopkins	.25	.60
437 Jevon Kearse	.30	.75
438 Derrick Mason FOIL	.60	1.50
439 Bruce Matthews FOIL	.60	1.50
440 Steve McNair	.40	1.00
441 Marcus Robertson	.25	.60
442 Eddie Robinson	.25	.60
443 Samari Rolle	.25	.60
444 Chris Sanders	.25	.60
445 John Thornton	.25	.60
446 Frank Wycheck	.25	.60
447 Stephen Alexander	.25	.60
448 Champ Bailey	.40	1.00
449 Shawn Barber RC	.25	.60
450 Marco Coleman	.25	.60
451 Albert Connell	.25	.60
452 Stephen Davis	.30	.75
453 Irving Fryar	.30	.75
454 Jeff George	.30	.75
455 Andy Heck	.25	.60
456 Brad Johnson	.30	.75
457 Deion Sanders	.40	1.00
458 Sam Shade	.25	.60
459 Keith Sims	.25	.60
460 Bruce Smith FOIL	.75	2.00
461 Dana Stubblefield	.25	.60
462 James Thrash	.30	.75

2001 NFL Showdown 1st Edition Monochrome

COMPLETE SET (62)	2.00	5.00

*MONOCHROMES: .1X TO .25X BASIC CARDS

2001 NFL Showdown 1st Edition Plays

COMPLETE SET (70)	1.50	4.00
COMMON CARD (1-70)	.02	.10

2001 NFL Showdown 1st Edition Showdown Stars

These 9-cards were released as a promo set for the 2001 NFL Showdown 1ST Edition product. Each card includes a gold foil "Showdown Stars" notation on the front.

COMPLETE SET (9)	3.00	8.00
L1 Ray Lewis	.30	.75
L2 Brian Urlacher	.40	1.00
L3 Brett Favre	1.00	2.50
L4 Peyton Manning	.75	2.00
L5 Tony Gonzalez	.30	.75
L6 Randy Moss	.30	.75
L7 Donovan McNabb	.30	.75
L8 Marshall Faulk	.30	.75
L9 Warren Sapp	.25	.60

2001 NFL Showdown 1st Edition Strategy

COMPLETE SET (50)	5.00	12.00
S1 Keenan McCardell	.15	.40
Afterburners		
S2 Mark Brunell	.25	.60
Air It Out		
S3 Packers vs. Eagles	.15	.40
Between the Hashes		
S4 Browns vs. Titans	.08	.25
Big Man		
S5 Jackie Harris	.08	.25
Big Play		
S6 Panthers vs. Rams	.08	.25
Great Block		
S7 Brad Maynard	.08	.25
Lucky Bounce		
S8 Curtis Martin	.25	.60
Second Effort		
S9 Panthers vs. 49ers	.08	.25
Thread the Needle		
S10 Tiki Barber	.15	.40
Tuck the Ball In		
S11 Chiefs vs. Seahawks	.08	.25
Back and Forth		
S12 Kerry Collins	.15	.40
Coverage Sack		
S13 Bears vs. Lions	.08	.25
Deep Blitz		
S14 Warren Sapp	.15	.40
Spy		
S15 Jonathan Ogden	.08	.25
Collision		
S16 Browns Lineman	.08	.25
Leg Trapped		
S17 Buccaneers Lineman	.08	.25
Speed Bump		
S18 Falcons vs. Panthers	.08	.25
Tangled Up		
S19 Bears vs. Saints	.08	.25
Defensive Holding		
S20 Keyshawn Johnson	.25	.60
Defensive Pass Interference		
S21 Steve McNair	.25	.60
Titans offensive line		
False Start		
S22 Tony Gonzalez	.15	.40
Offensive Holding		
S23 Colts vs. Jaguars	.08	.25
Offsides		
S24 Junior Seau	.25	.60
Bert Emanuel		
Bad Pass		
S25 Sam Shade	.08	.25
David LaFleur		
Force Fumble		
S26 Bears vs. Jaguars	.08	.25
Battle for the Ball		
S27 Emmitt Smith	.60	1.50
Big Hole		
S28 Derrick Alexander WR	.15	.40
Burned		
S29 Dave Wohlabaugh	.08	.25
Clear the Middle		
S30 Hines Ward	.15	.40
Fingertips		
S31 Marshall Faulk	.40	1.00
Power Back		
S32 Corey Dillon	.25	.60
Spin Move		
S33 Michael Westbrook	.08	.25
Timing Pattern		
S34 Colts vs. Packers	.25	.60
Under Pressure		
S35 Titans huddle	.15	.40
Work the Clock		
S36 Colts vs. Packers	.08	.25
Deep Coverage		
S37 Drew Bledsoe	.30	.75
Deep in the Backfield		
S38 Walt Harris	.08	.25
Tony Parrish		
Interceptor		
S39 Stephen Davis	.15	.40
Stuff		
S40 Wesley Walls	.08	.25
Gamer		
S41 Tim Couch	.25	.60
Walk It Off		
S42 Chiefs vs. Seahawks	.08	.25
Facemask		
S43 Lions vs. Bears	.08	.25
Personal Foul		
S44 Browns vs. Titans	.08	.25
Piling On		
S45 Charlie Batch	.15	.40
Roughing the Passer		
S46 Redskins vs. Eagles	.15	.40
Tripping		
S47 Patriots vs. Buccaneers	.08	.25
Blown Route		
S48 Brett Favre	1.00	2.50
Piledriver		
S49 Rams vs. Seahawks	.08	.25
Quick Return		
S50 Levon Kirkland	.15	.40
Eric Warfield		
Runback		

2001 NFL Showdown First and Goal

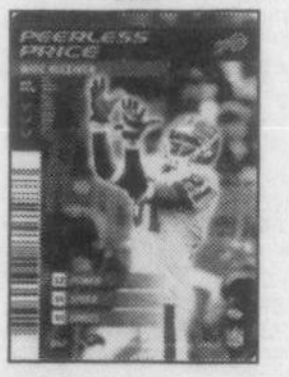

This set marked the second release of NFL Showdown for 2001 and includes many of the top draft picks. Card #48 was intended to be Andy Katzenmoyer, but the card was never produced. The regular base cards do not feature the set name on the fronts but can be identified by the lack of the silver foil logo found on the "1st Edition" set. The foil cards feature the player's name printed in holofoil along with a holofoil printed set name "1st and Goal" near the bottom of the cardfront.

COMP.SET w/o FOILS (149)	15.00	40.00
1 Jason Elam	.30	.75
2 Aaron Brooks FOIL	.60	1.50
3 Anthony Wright	.25	.60
4 David Akers RC	.25	.60
5 John Kasay	.25	.60
6 Chris Redman	.40	1.00
7 Jeff Lewis	.25	.60
8 Shane Matthews	.25	.60
9 Chad Pennington	.40	1.00
10 Mike Vanderjagt	.25	.60
11 Jeff Wilkins	.25	.60
12 Todd Collins	.25	.60
13 Dave Brown	.25	.60
14 Autry Denson	.25	.60
15 Chris Watson	.25	.60
16 Duce Staley	.30	.75
17 Aaron Stecker	.25	.60
18 Rodney Heath	.25	.60
19 Gerald McBurrows RC	.25	.60
20 Deltha O'Neal	.25	.60
21 Fakhir Brown RC	.25	.60
22 Dorsey Levens	.30	.75
23 Antoine Winfield	.25	.60
24 Paul Smith	.25	.60
25 Darren Woodson	.30	.75
26 Chad Morton	.25	.60
27 Brian Mitchell	.30	.75
28 Terrell Davis	.40	1.00
29 George Teague	.25	.60
30 Shyrone Stith	.25	.60
31 Mike Cloud	.25	.60
32 Tebucky Jones	.25	.60
33 Brandon Bennett	.25	.60
34 Shaun Alexander	.40	1.00
35 Carnell Lake	.25	.60
36 Dainon Sidney RC	.25	.60
37 Jon Witman	.25	.60
38 Frank Moreau	.25	.60
39 Zack Walz RC	.25	.60
40 Ian Gold	.25	.60
41 Warrick Holdman RC	.25	.60
42 T.J. Slaughter	.25	.60
43 Hardy Nickerson	.25	.60
44 Brian Simmons	.25	.60
45 Keith Brooking	.30	.75
46 Peter Boulware	.25	.60
47 Jessie Tuggle	.25	.60
49 Kevin Long RC	.25	.60
50 Damien Woody	.25	.60
51 Shane Dronett	.25	.60
52 Matt Lepsis RC	.25	.60
53 Kenny Mixon RC	.25	.60
54 Greg Jefferson	.25	.60
55 Plaxico Burress	.30	.75
56 Terry Hardy	.25	.60
57 Troy Edwards	.25	.60
58 Rocket Ismail	.30	.75
59 O.J. McDuffie	.25	.60
60 Tyrone Davis	.25	.60
61 Bobby Engram	.30	.75
62 Peerless Price	.25	.60
63 Jed Weaver	.25	.60
64 Michael Westbrook	.25	.60
65 Patrick Jeffers FOIL	.50	1.25
66 Jerry Porter	.25	.60
67 Joey Galloway	.30	.75
68 Rob Moore	.25	.60
69 Cory Geason	.25	.60
70 Cam Cleeland	.25	.60
71 Andrew Jordan	.25	.60
72 Greg Clark FOIL	.50	1.25
73 Dennis Northcutt	.25	.60
74 Jeremy McDaniel	.25	.60
75 Ron Dixon	.25	.60
76 Darnay Scott	.30	.75
77 Kevin Dyson	.25	.60
78 David Dunn	.25	.60
79 JaJuan Dawson	.25	.60
80 Damon Jones	.25	.60
81 Travis Taylor	.25	.60
82 David LaFleur	.25	.60
83 Tai Streets	.25	.60
84 Junior Bryant RC	.25	.60
85 Chuck Smith	.25	.60
86 Dimitrius Underwood	.25	.60
87 Courtney Brown FOIL	.50	1.25
88 Gilbert Brown	.25	.60
89 John Abraham FOIL	.50	1.25
90 Rob Morris	.25	.60
91 Rick Lyle	.25	.60
92 Brandon Whiting RC	.25	.60
93 Raylee Johnson	.25	.60
94 Alge Crumpler RC	.75	2.00
95 Michael Vick FOIL RC	6.00	15.00
96 Todd Heap RC	.75	2.00
97 Chris Weinke FOIL RC	1.25	3.00
98 David Terrell RC	.60	1.50
99 Anthony Thomas RC	.75	2.00
100 Chad Johnson RC	1.25	3.00
101 Justin Smith RC	.75	2.00
102 Jeff Backus RC	.50	1.25
103 Shaun Rogers RC	.75	2.00
104 Reggie Wayne RC	1.50	4.00
105 Jamal Reynolds FOIL RC	1.00	2.50
106 Robert Ferguson RC	.75	2.00
107 Chris Chambers RC	.75	2.00
108 Jamar Fletcher RC	.50	1.25
109 Deuce McAllister RC	.75	2.00
110 Will Allen FOIL RC	.75	2.00
111 Lamont Jordan RC	.75	2.00
112 Santana Moss RC	1.00	2.50
113 Freddie Mitchell RC	.50	1.25
114 Andre Carter FOIL RC	1.25	3.00
115 LaDainian Tomlinson FOIL RC	5.00	12.00
116 Drew Brees FOIL RC	10.00	25.00
117 Rod Gardner RC	.60	1.50
118 Fred Smoot RC	.75	2.00
119 Derrick Gibson RC	.50	1.25
120 Adam Archuleta FOIL RC	1.25	3.00
121 Damione Lewis RC	.60	1.50
122 Michael Bennett RC	.60	1.50
123 Leonard Davis FOIL RC	1.50	4.00
124 Quincy Morgan RC	.60	1.50
125 Marcus Stroud FOIL RC	1.25	3.00
126 Kenyatta Walker RC	.50	1.25
127 Willie Middlebrooks RC	.60	1.50
128 Kendrell Bell RC	.75	2.00
129 Casey Hampton RC	.75	2.00
130 Nate Clements RC	.60	1.50
131 Steve Hutchinson RC	1.25	3.00
132 Koren Robinson FOIL RC	1.25	3.00
133 Brandon Stokley	.30	.75
134 Jake Reed	.30	.75
135 Kevin Donnalley	.25	.60
136 Todd Steussie FOIL	.25	.60
137 Ted Washington	.25	.60
138 Jon Kitna	.30	.75
139 Todd Lyght		
140 Tony Horne	.25	.60
141 Priest Holmes	.40	1.00
142 James McKnight	.25	.60
143 Albert Connell	.25	.60
144 Jay Bellamy	.25	.60
145 James Darling		
146 Matthew Hatchette	.25	.60
147 James Thrash FOIL	.30	.75
148 Alex Molden	.25	.60
149 Ryan McNeil		
150 Brad Johnson FOIL	.30	.75
151 Simeon Rice	.30	.75
152 Charlie Garner FOIL	.30	.75
153 Trace Armstrong	.25	.60
154 Mark Fields		
155 Kim Herring	.25	.60
156 Aeneas Williams	.30	.75
157 Lance Johnstone	.20	.50
158 Dwayne Rudd	.20	.50
159 Rickey Dudley FOIL	.40	1.00
160 Kenny Holmes	.20	.50
161 Doug Flutie FOIL	1.00	2.50
162 Chester McGlockton	.20	.50
163 Eddie Kennison	.20	.50
164 Elvis Grbac FOIL	.60	1.50
165 Ray Crockett	.20	.50
166 Trent Green FOIL	1.00	2.50
167 Chad Eaton	.20	.50
168 Matt Hasselbeck	.30	.75
169 Levon Kirkland	.20	.50
170 John Randle	.30	.75
171 Marcus Robertson	.20	.50
172 Pete Kendall	.20	.50
173 Keith Traylor	.20	.50
174 Jerry Rice FOIL	2.00	5.00
175 Dana Stubblefield	.20	.50
CL1 Checklist Card 1	.02	.10
CL2 Checklist Card 2	.02	.10
CL3 Checklist Card 3	.02	.10

2001 NFL Showdown First and Goal Plays

COMPLETE SET (20)	.60	1.50
COMMON CARD (P1-P20)	.02	.10

2001 NFL Showdown First and Goal Strategy

COMPLETE SET (10)	1.25	3.00
S1 Fake Handoff	.10	.30
Akili Smith		
S2 Force of Will	.10	.30
S3 In Motion	.30	.75
Tim Brown		
S4 Long Routes	.20	.50
Frank Sanders		
S5 Shrug Them Off	.10	.30
S6 Textbook Play	.30	.75
Drew Bledsoe		
Kenny Holmes		
S7 Aggressive Coverage	.10	.30
Darnay Scott		
S8 Blind Side Rush	.30	.75
S9 Support The Weak Side	.10	.30
Browns vs. Colts		
S10 Trick Plays	.30	.75
Oakland Raiders sideline		
Jon Gruden		

2002 NFL Showdown

This 356-card set was available in packs found in starter kits and in 11-card booster packs. Despite the 2003 logo on the packaging and the cardbacks, this product was released in the Fall of 2002. The foil cards were produced with a gold foil player name at the top instead of a holofoil design like the 2001 release. A cover card featuring Brian Urlacher was also seeded into packs to promote the upcoming 1st and Goal second series.

COMP.SET w/o FOILS (300)	20.00	50.00
1 David Boston FOIL	.60	1.50
2 Leonard Davis	.25	.60
3 Rob Fredrickson	.25	.60
4 MarTay Jenkins	.25	.60
5 Kwamie Lassiter	.25	.60
6 Ronald McKinnon	.25	.60
7 Michael Pittman	.30	.75
8 Scott Player	.25	.60
9 Jake Plummer	.30	.75
10 Frank Sanders	.25	.60
11 Lonnie Shelton	.25	.60
12 LeVar Woods	.25	.60
13 Ashley Ambrose	.25	.60
14 Ray Buchanan	.25	.60
15 Chris Chandler	.30	.75
16 Henri Crockett	.25	.60
17 Kynan Forney	.25	.60
18 Travis Hall	.25	.60
19 Patrick Kerney	.25	.60
20 Brady Smith	.25	.60
21 Maurice Smith	.25	.60
22 Darrick Vaughn	.25	.60
23 Michael Vick FOIL	1.50	4.00
24 Bob Whitfield	.25	.60
25 Peter Boulware	.25	.60
26 Elvis Grbac	.25	.60
27 Corey Harris	.25	.60
28 Jermaine Lewis	.25	.60
29 Ray Lewis FOIL	1.00	2.50
30 Chris McAlister	.25	.60
31 Michael McCrary	.25	.60
32 Edwin Mulitalo	.25	.60
33 Jonathan Ogden	.30	.75
34 Jamie Sharper	.30	.75
35 Travis Taylor	.25	.60
36 Rod Woodson FOIL	1.00	2.50
37 Ruben Brown	.25	.60
38 Larry Centers	.30	.75
39 Jay Foreman RC	.25	.60
40 Phil Hansen	.25	.60
41 Travis Henry	.25	.60
42 Peerless Price FOIL	.60	1.50
43 Brandon Spoon	.25	.60
44 Alex Van Pelt	.25	.60
45 Pat Williams RC	.60	1.50
46 Doug Evans	.25	.60
47 Richard Huntley	.25	.60
48 Dan Morgan	.25	.60
49 Muhsin Muhammad	.30	.75
50 Todd Sauerbrun	.25	.60
51 Steve Smith FOIL	1.00	2.50
52 Todd Steussie	.25	.60
53 Chris Weinke	.25	.60
54 Marty Booker	.30	.75
55 Phillip Daniels	.25	.60
56 Paul Edinger	.25	.60
57 Warrick Holdman	.25	.60
58 Olin Kreutz RC	.50	1.25
59 Brad Maynard RC	.25	.60
60 R.W. McQuarters FOIL	.60	1.50
61 Jim Miller	.25	.60
62 Tony Parrish	.25	.60
63 Anthony Thomas FOIL	.75	2.00
64 Keith Traylor	.25	.60
65 Brian Urlacher FOIL	1.00	2.50
66 Larry Whigham	.25	.60
67 James Williams	.25	.60
68 Corey Dillon	.30	.75
69 Oliver Gibson	.25	.60
70 Jon Kitna	.30	.75
71 Matt O'Dwyer	.25	.60
72 Darnay Scott	.30	.75
73 Brian Simmons	.25	.60
74 Justin Smith	.25	.60
75 Takeo Spikes FOIL	.60	1.50
76 Roger Chanoine RC	.25	.60
77 Tim Couch	.25	.60
78 Corey Fuller	.25	.60
79 Kevin Johnson	.25	.60
80 Daylon McCutcheon	.25	.60
81 Keith McKenzie	.25	.60
82 Jamir Miller FOIL	.60	1.50
83 Roman Oben	.25	.60
84 Orpheus Roye	.25	.60
85 Dwayne Rudd	.25	.60
86 Gerard Warren	.25	.60
87 Jamel White	.25	.60
88 Larry Allen	.25	.60
89 Quincy Carter	.25	.60
90 Michael Myers	.25	.60
91 Dat Nguyen	.25	.60
92 Emmitt Smith FOIL	2.50	6.00
93 Mark Stepnoski	.25	.60
94 Reggie Swinton	.25	.60
95 Darren Woodson	.30	.75
96 Mike Anderson	.30	.75
97 Eric Brown	.25	.60
98 Desmond Clark	.30	.75
99 Chris Cole	.25	.60
100 Jason Elam	.30	.75
101 Ian Gold	.25	.60
102 Brian Griese	.30	.75
103 Matt Lepsis	.25	.60
104 John Mobley	.25	.60
105 Deltha O'Neal FOIL	.60	1.50
106 Trevor Pryce	.25	.60
107 Rod Smith FOIL	.75	2.00
108 Jeff Backus	.25	.60
109 Charlie Batch	.25	.60
110 Desmond Howard	.30	.75
111 Johnnie Morton	.30	.75
112 Robert Porcher	.25	.60
113 Shaun Rogers FOIL	.60	1.50
114 Brendan Stai	.25	.60
115 James Stewart	.25	.60
116 Corey Bradford	.25	.60
117 Gilbert Brown	.25	.60
118 LeRoy Butler	.30	.75
119 Brett Favre FOIL	2.50	6.00
120 Mike Flanagan	.25	.60
121 Bubba Franks	.30	.75
122 Antonio Freeman	.40	1.00
123 Ahman Green FOIL	.75	2.00
124 Bernardo Harris	.25	.60
125 Vonnie Holliday	.25	.60
126 Mike McKenzie	.25	.60
127 Marco Rivera	.25	.60
128 Bill Schroeder	.25	.60
129 Darren Sharper FOIL	.75	2.00
130 Idrees Bashir	.25	.60
131 Jeff Burris	.25	.60
132 Ken Dilger	.30	.75
133 Tarik Glenn	.25	.60
134 Marvin Harrison FOIL	1.00	2.50
135 Peyton Manning	.75	2.00
136 Mike Vanderjagt	.25	.60
137 Terrence Wilkins	.25	.60
138 Tony Brackens	.25	.60
139 Mark Brunell	.30	.75
140 Keenan McCardell	.30	.75
141 Hardy Nickerson	.25	.60
142 Seth Payne RC	.25	.60
143 Jimmy Smith FOIL	.75	2.00
144 Gary Walker	.25	.60
145 Maurice Williams	.25	.60
146 Donnie Edwards	.25	.60
147 Tony Gonzalez	.40	1.00
148 Trent Green	.30	.75
149 Priest Holmes FOIL	1.00	2.50
150 Marvcus Patton	.25	.60
151 Will Shields	.25	.60
152 John Tait	.25	.60
153 Greg Wesley	.25	.60
154 Chris Chambers FOIL	.75	2.00
155 Jay Fiedler	.30	.75
156 Oronde Gadsden	.25	.60
157 Sam Madison	.25	.60
158 Olindo Mare	.25	.60
159 Brock Marion FOIL	.60	1.50
160 James McKnight	.25	.60
161 Kenny Mixon	.25	.60
162 Derrick Rodgers	.25	.60
163 Tim Ruddy	.25	.60
164 Lamar Smith	.30	.75
165 Patrick Surtain	.25	.60
166 Jason Taylor	.30	.75
167 Zach Thomas FOIL	1.00	2.50
168 Gary Anderson	.25	.60
169 Matt Birk	.25	.60
170 Todd Bouman	.25	.60
171 Cris Carter	.40	1.00
172 Byron Chamberlain	.25	.60
173 Daunte Culpepper FOIL	.75	2.00
174 Chris Hovan	.25	.60
175 Ed McDaniel	.25	.60
176 Randy Moss	.40	1.00
177 Tom Brady	1.00	2.50
178 Troy Brown FOIL	.75	2.00
179 Tedy Bruschi	.40	1.00
180 Mike Compton	.25	.60
181 Bryan Cox	.30	.75
182 Tebucky Jones	.25	.60
183 Ty Law	.30	.75
184 Lawyer Milloy FOIL	.60	1.50
185 David Patten	.25	.60
186 Roman Phifer	.25	.60
187 Richard Seymour	.30	.75
188 Antowain Smith FOIL	.75	2.00
189 Adam Vinatieri	.40	1.00
190 Grant Williams	.25	.60
191 Jay Bellamy	.25	.60
192 Aaron Brooks FOIL	.75	2.00
193 John Carney	.25	.60
194 Charlie Clemons	.25	.60
195 Jerry Fontenot	.25	.60
196 La'Roi Glover	.25	.60
197 Joe Horn	.30	.75
198 Darren Howard	.25	.60
199 Willie Jackson	.25	.60
200 Sammy Knight	.25	.60
201 Deuce McAllister	.30	.75
202 Kyle Turley	.25	.60
203 Ricky Williams	.30	.75
204 Will Allen	.25	.60
205 Morten Andersen	.25	.60
206 Tiki Barber	.40	1.00
207 Micheal Barrow	.25	.60
208 Kerry Collins	.30	.75
209 Ron Dayne	.30	.75
210 Keith Hamilton	.25	.60
211 Luke Petitgout	.25	.60
212 Jason Sehorn	.30	.75
213 Michael Strahan FOIL	1.00	2.50
214 Amani Toomer	.30	.75
215 Shaun Williams	.25	.60
216 John Abraham FOIL	.75	2.00
217 Anthony Becht	.25	.60
218 Wayne Chrebet	.30	.75
219 Shaun Ellis	.25	.60
220 Victor Green	.25	.60
221 Marvin Jones	.25	.60
222 LaMont Jordan	.30	.75
223 Mo Lewis	.25	.60
224 Curtis Martin FOIL	1.00	2.50
225 Steve Martin RC	.25	.60
226 Chad Pennington	.40	1.00
227 Vinny Testaverde	.30	.75
228 Craig Yeast	.25	.60
229 Greg Biekert	.25	.60
230 Tim Brown FOIL	1.00	2.50
231 Tony Bryant	.25	.60
232 David Dunn	.25	.60
233 Rich Gannon FOIL	.75	2.00
234 Charlie Garner	.30	.75
235 Grady Jackson	.25	.60
236 Lincoln Kennedy	.25	.60
237 Shane Lechler	.25	.60
238 Marquez Pope	.25	.60
239 Jerry Rice FOIL	2.00	5.00
240 William Thomas	.25	.60
241 Tyrone Wheatley	.30	.75
242 Charles Woodson	.40	1.00
243 David Akers	.25	.60
244 Brian Dawkins	.30	.75
245 Hugh Douglas FOIL	.60	1.50
246 Carlos Emmons	.25	.60
247 Chad Lewis	.25	.60
248 Jermane Mayberry	.25	.60
249 Donovan McNabb	.40	1.00
250 Jon Runyan	.25	.60
251 Corey Simon	.25	.60
252 Duce Staley	.30	.75
253 Hollis Thomas	.25	.60
254 James Thrash	.30	.75
255 Jeremiah Trotter FOIL	.60	1.50
256 Troy Vincent FOIL	.75	2.00
257 Brent Alexander	.25	.60
258 Kendrell Bell FOIL	.60	1.50
259 Jerome Bettis FOIL	1.00	2.50
260 Kris Brown	.25	.60
261 Troy Edwards	.25	.60
262 Lethon Flowers	.25	.60
263 Jason Gildon	.30	.75
264 Jeff Hartings	.25	.60
265 Earl Holmes	.25	.60
266 Josh Miller RC	.25	.60
267 Kordell Stewart FOIL	.75	2.00
268 Hines Ward	.40	1.00
269 Dewayne Washington	.25	.60
270 Amos Zereoue	.25	.60
271 Drew Brees	.60	1.50
272 Curtis Conway	.30	.75
273 Doug Flutie	.40	1.00
274 Rodney Harrison	.30	.75
275 Vaughn Parker	.25	.60
276 Junior Seau	.40	1.00
277 LaDainian Tomlinson FOIL	1.25	3.00
278 Marcellus Wiley	.25	.60
279 Kevan Barlow	.25	.60
280 Ray Brown	.25	.60
281 Jose Cortez RC	.25	.60
282 Dave Fiore	.25	.60
283 Jeff Garcia FOIL	.75	2.00
284 Garrison Hearst FOIL	.75	2.00
285 Eric Johnson	.25	.60
286 Terrell Owens FOIL	1.00	2.50
287 Ahmed Plummer	.25	.60
288 Lance Schulters	.25	.60
289 J.J. Stokes	.25	.60
290 Dana Stubblefield	.25	.60
291 Jeff Ulbrich	.25	.60
292 Bryant Young	.25	.60
293 Shaun Alexander FOIL	.75	2.00
294 Chad Brown	.25	.60
295 Trent Dilfer	.30	.75
296 Chad Eaton	.25	.60
297 Jeff Feagles	.25	.60
298 Matt Hasselbeck	.40	1.00
299 Steve Hutchinson	.30	.75
300 Darrell Jackson	.30	.75
301 Walter Jones	.25	.60
302 John Randle FOIL	.75	2.00
303 Koren Robinson	.25	.60
304 Anthony Simmons	.25	.60
305 Reggie Tongue	.25	.60
306 Dre Bly	.25	.60
307 Isaac Bruce	.40	1.00
308 Trung Canidate	.25	.60
309 Ernie Conwell	.25	.60
310 Marshall Faulk FOIL	1.00	2.50
311 Mark Fields	.25	.60
312 London Fletcher	.25	.60
313 Az-Zahir Hakim	.25	.60
314 Torry Holt	.40	1.00
315 Orlando Pace	.30	.75
316 Ryan Tucker	.25	.60
317 Kurt Warner FOIL	1.00	2.50
318 Jeff Wilkins	.25	.60
319 Aeneas Williams FOIL	.75	2.00
320 Donnie Abraham	.25	.60
321 Mike Alstott FOIL	.75	2.00
322 Ronde Barber FOIL	.75	2.00
323 Derrick Brooks	.40	1.00
324 Jamie Duncan	.25	.60
325 Martin Gramatica	.25	.60
326 Brad Johnson	.30	.75
327 Keyshawn Johnson	.30	.75
328 John Lynch	.30	.75
329 Randall McDaniel	.30	.75
330 Simeon Rice	.25	.60
331 Warren Sapp	.30	.75
332 Kevin Carter	.25	.60
333 Kevin Dyson	.30	.75
334 Eddie George	.30	.75
335 Randall Godfrey	.25	.60
336 Brad Hopkins	.25	.60
337 Jevon Kearse	.30	.75
338 Derrick Mason FOIL	.75	2.00
339 Bruce Matthews	.30	.75
340 Steve McNair FOIL	1.00	2.50
341 Joe Nedney	.25	.60
342 Eddie Robinson	.25	.60
343 Frank Wycheck	.25	.60
344 Champ Bailey	.40	1.00
345 Tony Banks	.25	.60
346 Bryan Barker	.25	.60
347 Marco Coleman	.25	.60
348 Stephen Davis	.30	.75
349 Kenard Lang FOIL	.60	1.50
350 Eric Metcalf	.25	.60
351 Kevin Mitchell	.25	.60
352 Chris Samuels	.25	.60
353 Sam Shade	.25	.60
354 Bruce Smith	.40	1.00
355 Fred Smoot	.30	.75
356 David Terrell	.25	.60
NNO Brian Urlacher Cover	.40	1.00

2002 NFL Showdown Plays

COMPLETE SET (70)	2.00	5.00
COMMON CARD (P1-P70)	.02	.10

2002 NFL Showdown Showdown Stars

These 6-cards were released as a promo set for the 2002 NFL Showdown product. Each card includes a gold foil "Showdown Stars" notation on the front. A "Training Camp" version of each card was also produced.

COMPLETE SET (6)	2.50	6.00
1 Brian Urlacher	.40	1.00
2 Curtis Martin	.40	1.00
3 LaDainian Tomlinson	.50	1.25
4 Shaun Alexander	.30	.75
5 Michael Vick	.60	1.50
6 Sammy Knight	.25	.60

2002 NFL Showdown Strategy

COMPLETE SET (50)	3.00	8.00
S1 Trung Canidate	.10	.30
Burst of Speed		
S2 Kurt Warner	.30	.75
Clumsy Handoff		
S3 Brian Griese	.20	.50
Coverage Sack		
S4 Dorsey Levens	.10	.30
Deep Blitz		
S5 Colts vs. Packers	.07	.20
Deep in the Backfield		
S6 49ers vs. Saints	.07	.20
Great Coverage		
S7 Bengals vs. Ravens	.07	.20
Keepaway		
S8 Quarterback Hurry	.07	.20
S9 Matt Hasselbeck	.10	.30
Concussion		
S10 Falcons vs. Panthers	.07	.20
Deafening Collision		
S11 Steve Beuerlein	.10	.30
Leg Trapped		
S12 Stinger	.10	.30
S13 Thurman Thomas	.10	.30
Tangled Up		
S14 Muhsin Muhammad	.10	.30
Champ Bailey		
Afterburners		
S15 Chris Chandler	.10	.30
Aggressive Blocking		
S16 Giants vs. Chiefs	.07	.20
Battle for the Ball		
S17 Vinny Testaverde	.10	.30
Beat the Blitz		
S18 Matt Stover	.07	.20
Between the Hashes		
S19 Bengals vs. Ravens	.07	.20
Big Hole		
S20 Shaun Alexander	.10	.30
Burned		
S21 Germane Crowell	.07	.20
Cannon		
S22 Lamar Smith	.10	.30
Dodge		
S23 Bears vs. Panthers	.07	.20
Escape the Pressure		
S24 Jacquez Green	.07	.20
Fingertips		
S25 David Patten	.07	.20
Good Hands		
S26 Brett Favre	.20	.50
Marco Rivera		
William Henderson		
Great Block		
S27 Brad Johnson	.20	.50
Mike Alstott		
Grind the Clock		
S28 Shane Lechler	.07	.20
Hang Time		
S29 Cowboys vs. Raiders	.07	.20
Lucky Bounce		
S30 Brandon Bennett	.07	.20
Make Em Miss		
S31 Steve Christie	.07	.20
Off the Crossbar		
S32 Jets vs. Bills	.07	.20
Second Effort		
S33 Brian Griese	.20	.50
Thread the Needle		
S34 Doug Flutie	.20	.50
Work the Clock		
S35 Jeff Graham	.07	.20
Deltha O'Neal		
Yards After Catch		
S36 Curtis Conway	.07	.20
Defensive Holding		
S37 Bears vs. Jaguars	.07	.20
Defensive Pass Interference		
S38 49ers vs. Saints	.07	.20
Facemask		
S39 Cowboys vs. Raiders	.07	.20
False Start		
S40 Buccaneers vs. Vikings	.10	.30
Intentional Grounding		
(Brad Johnson)		
S41 Tony Gonzalez	.10	.30
Offensive Holding		
S42 Browns vs. Steelers	.07	.20
Offsides		
S43 Alex Van Pelt	.07	.20
Roughing the Passer		
S44 Cardinals vs. Redskins	.07	.20
Tripping		
S45 Todd Pinkston	.10	.30
James Thrash		
Bad Pass		
S46 Ty Law	.10	.30
Jacquez Green		
Blown Route		
S47 Forced Fumble	.07	.20
S48 Cardinals vs. Redskins	.07	.20
Into Traffic		
S49 Aeneas Williams	.07	.20
Open-Field Recovery		
S50 Buccaneers vs. Vikings	.07	.20
Pile Driver		

2002 NFL Showdown Training Camp

These 6-cards were released as a promo set for the 2002 NFL Showdown product. Each card includes a gold foil "Training Camp" notation on the front.

COMPLETE SET (6)	2.50	6.00
1 Brian Urlacher	.40	1.00
2 Curtis Martin	.40	1.00
3 LaDainian Tomlinson	.50	1.25
4 Shaun Alexander	.30	.75
5 Michael Vick	.60	1.50
6 Sammy Knight	.25	.60

2002 NFL Showdown First and Goal

This set marked the second series for 2002 which includes many of the top draft picks for that year. A total of 25-Foil cards were produced.

COMP.SET w/o FOILS (125)	20.00	40.00
1 John Henderson FOIL RC	1.25	3.00
2 Sean Moran	.25	.60
3 Bill Schroeder	.25	.60
4 Tony Simmons	.25	.60
5 Travis Fisher RC	.60	1.50
6 James Allen	.25	.60
7 Javon Walker FOIL RC	1.50	4.00
8 Robert Edwards	.25	.60
9 Jerome Pathon	.25	.60
10 Ryan Sims FOIL RC	1.50	4.00
11 Levar Fisher RC	.50	1.25
12 Bryant McKinnie FOIL RC	1.00	2.50
13 Larry Tripplett RC	.50	1.25
14 T.J. Duckett FOIL RC	1.50	4.00
15 Chris Sanders	.25	.60
16 Levi Jones RC	.50	1.25
17 Jon McGraw RC	.50	1.25
18 Quentin Jammer FOIL RC	1.50	4.00
19 Shannon Sharpe	.40	1.00
20 Lito Sheppard FOIL RC	1.50	4.00
21 Mike Caldwell	.25	.60
22 Napoleon Harris RC	.60	1.50
23 Aaron Beasley	.25	.60
24 Brandon Mitchell RC	.50	1.25
25 Qadry Ismail	.30	.75
26 Wendell Bryant FOIL RC	1.00	2.50
27 Rabih Abdullah	.25	.60
28 Mike Pearson RC	.50	1.25
29 DeMingo Graham RC	.50	1.25
30 Steve White	.25	.60
31 Bryan Cox	.30	.75
32 Najeh Davenport RC	.75	2.00
33 Joey Harrington FOIL RC	1.50	4.00
34 Dennis Johnson RC	.50	1.25
35 Stalin Colinet	.25	.60
36 James Farrior FOIL	.30	.75
37 Marco Battaglia	.25	.60
38 Jerramy Stevens RC	.75	2.00
39 Duane Starks	.25	.60
40 Dorsett Davis RC	.50	1.25
41 James Cannida RC	.50	1.25
42 Ricky Williams FOIL	.75	2.00
43 Tank Williams RC	.60	1.50
44 Michael Lewis RC	.75	2.00
45 Omar Easy RC	.60	1.50
46 Sam Cowart	.25	.60
47 Albert Haynesworth FOIL RC	1.50	4.00
48 Tim Carter RC	.60	1.50
49 Chris Chandler	.30	.75
50 Freddie Jones	.25	.60
51 Brock Huard	.30	.75
52 Phillip Buchanon FOIL RC	1.50	4.00
53 Patrick Ramsey RC	.75	2.00
54 Jabar Gaffney RC	.75	2.00
55 Josh McCown RC	.75	2.00
56 Mikhael Ricks	.25	.60
57 William Roaf	.25	.60
58 Stephen Alexander	.25	.60
59 Reidel Anthony	.25	.60
60 Rick Mirer	.30	.75
61 William Green FOIL RC	1.25	3.00
62 Will Overstreet RC	.50	1.25
63 Dwight Freeney FOIL RC	2.00	5.00
64 Michael Pittman FOIL	.75	2.00
65 Spencer Folau RC	.50	1.25
66 Jamie Duncan	.25	.60
67 Robert Griffith	.25	.60
68 Rob Moore	.25	.60
69 Marquise Walker RC	.50	1.25
70 Doug Evans FOIL	.60	1.50
71 Ron Stone RC	.50	1.25
72 Ed Reed FOIL RC	6.00	15.00
73 Az-Zahir Hakim	.25	.60
74 Josh Reed RC	.60	1.50
75 Leonard Henry RC	.50	1.25
76 Rocky Calmus RC	.60	1.50
77 Jeremy Newberry RC	.50	1.25
78 Marques Anderson RC	.60	1.50
79 Kurt Kittner RC	.50	1.25
80 Clinton Portis RC	1.00	2.50
81 Craig Nall RC	.60	1.50
82 Terrence Wilkins	.25	.60
83 Lance Schulters	.25	.60
84 Chris Carter	.25	.60
85 Raonall Smith	.25	.60
86 David Carr FOIL RC	1.50	4.00
87 Kerry Jenkins RC	.50	1.25
88 Bryan Thomas RC	.50	1.25
89 Alex Brown RC	.75	2.00
90 Donte Stallworth FOIL RC	1.50	4.00
91 Donnie Abraham	.25	.60
92 Rob Johnson	.30	.75
93 Donnie Edwards	.25	.60
94 Anthony Weaver RC	.50	1.25
95 Bill Romanowski	.30	.75
96 Pete Mitchell	.25	.60
97 Danny Wuerffel	.30	.75
98 Daryl Jones RC	.50	1.25
99 Chester Taylor RC	.75	2.00
100 Jamar Martin RC	.60	1.50
101 Robert Thomas RC	.50	1.25

102 Joe Jurevicius	.25	.60
103 Greg Comella	.25	.60
104 Eddie Freeman RC	.50	1.25
105 Drew Bledsoe	.40	1.00
106 Andre Davis RC	.60	1.50
107 Kaseem Sinceno	.25	.60
108 Jumbo Elliott	.25	.60
109 Terrance Shaw	.25	.60
110 Barry Stokes RC	.50	1.25
111 Ken Dilger	.30	.75
112 Marc Colombo FOIL RC	1.00	2.50
113 Ashley Lelie FOIL RC	1.25	3.00
114 Brian Westbrook RC	1.25	3.00
115 Jeremiah Trotter FOIL	.60	1.50
116 Reche Caldwell RC	.75	2.00
117 Leon Searcy	.25	.60
118 Ryan Tucker	.25	.60
119 Corey Harris	.25	.60
120 Terry Glenn	.30	.75
121 Dale Carter	.25	.60
122 Blaine Bishop	.25	.60
123 Jamie Nails RC	.50	1.25
124 Ladell Betts RC	.75	2.00
125 Freddie Milons RC	.50	1.25
126 Corey Bradford	.25	.60
127 Kalimba Edwards RC	.60	1.50
128 Greg Favors	.25	.60
129 Walt Harris	.25	.60
130 Henri Crockett	.25	.60
131 Jeremy Shockey FOIL RC	2.50	6.00
132 Maurice Morris RC	.60	1.50
133 Antwaan Randle El RC	.75	2.00
134 Greg Jones	.25	.60
135 Chester Pitts RC	.50	1.25
136 Roosevelt Williams RC	.50	1.25
137 David Sloan	.25	.60
138 Sam Garnes	.25	.60
139 Jimmy Herndon RC	.50	1.25
140 Charles Grant RC	.75	2.00
141 Cory Raymer	.25	.60
142 D'Wayne Bates	.25	.60
143 Sam Simmons RC	.50	1.25
144 Victor Riley	.25	.60
145 Mike Rumph RC	.50	1.25
146 Kris Brown	.25	.60
147 Johnnie Morton FOIL	.75	2.00
148 Bobby Shaw	.25	.60
149 David Loverne RC	.50	1.25
150 Jake Schifino RC	.50	1.25

2002 NFL Showdown First and Goal Plays

COMPLETE SET (20)	.60	1.50
COMMON CARD (P1-P20)	.02	.10

2002 NFL Showdown First and Goal Strategy

COMPLETE SET (10)	1.25	3.00
S1 Broncos vs. Dolphins	.07	.20
Bad Break		
S2 Broncos vs. Dolphins	.07	.20
Blocked Field Goal		
S3 Kevin Dyson	.10	.30
Serious Jets		
S4 Ray Lewis	.20	.50
Shadow		
S5 Tim Seder	.07	.20
Fake Field Goal		
S6 Jay Fiedler	.10	.30
Flushed from the Pocket		
S7 Kurt Warner	.30	.75
Golden Arm		
S8 Kurt Warner	.30	.75
Hurry-up Offense		
S9 Giants vs. Redskins	.07	.20
In the Trenches		
S10 Tom Brady	.40	1.00
Take a Chance		

1971 NFLPA Wonderful World Stamps

This set of 390 stamps was issued in both 1971 and 1972 under the auspices of the NFL Players Association in conjunction with an album entitled "The Wonderful World of Pro Football USA." The album features a photo of Earl Morrall and Mark Washington from Super Bowl V. The stamps are numbered and measure approximately 1 15/16" by 2 7/8". The team order of the album is arranged alphabetically according to the city name and then alphabetically by player name within each team The picture stamp album contains 30 pages measuring approximately 9 1/2" by 13 1/4". The text narrates the story of pro football in the United States. The album includes spaces for 390 color player stamps. The checklist and stamp numbering below is according to the album. There are some numbering and very slight text variations between the 1971 and 1972 issues on some stamps, as noted below.

COMPLETE SET (390)	350.00	600.00
1 Bob Berry	.40	1.00
2 Greg Brezina	.40	1.00
3 Ken Burrow	.40	1.00
4 Jim Butler	.40	1.00
5 Paul Gipson	.40	1.00
6 Claude Humphrey	.50	1.25
7 George Kunz	.40	1.00
8 Tom McCauley	.40	1.00
9 Jim Mitchell	.40	1.00
10 Tommy Nobis	.75	1.50
11 Ken Reaves	.40	1.00
12 Rudy Redmond	.40	1.00
13 John Small	.40	1.00
14 Harmon Wages	.40	1.00
15 John Zook	.40	1.00
16 Norm Bulaich	.40	1.00
17 Mike Curtis	.50	1.25
18 Jim Duncan	.40	1.00
19 Ted Hendricks	1.00	2.00
20 Roy Hilton	.40	1.00
21 Eddie Hinton	.40	1.00
22 David Lee	.40	1.00
23 Jerry Logan	.40	1.00
24 John Mackey	1.00	2.00
25 Tom Matte	.50	1.25
26 Jim O'Brien	.40	1.00
27 Glenn Ressler	.40	1.00
28 Johnny Unitas	6.00	12.00
29 Bob Vogel	.40	1.00
30 Rick Volk	.40	1.00
31 Butch Byrd	.40	1.00
32 Edgar Chandler	.40	1.00
33 Paul Costa	.40	1.00
34 Jim Dunaway	.40	1.00
35 Paul Guidry	.40	1.00
36 Jim Harris	.40	1.00
37 Robert James	.40	1.00
38 Mike McBath	.40	1.00
39 Haven Moses	.40	1.00
40 John Pitts	.40	1.00
41 Jim Reilly	.40	1.00
42 Dennis Shaw	.40	1.00
43 O.J. Simpson	5.00	10.00
44 Mike Stratton	.40	1.00
45 Bob Tatarek	.40	1.00
46 Craig Baynham	.40	1.00
47 Dick Butkus	5.00	10.00
48 Jim Cadile	.40	1.00
49 Lee Roy Caffey	.40	1.00
50 Jack Concannon	.50	1.25
51 Bobby Douglass	.50	1.25
52 Dick Cordon	.40	1.00
53 Bobby Joe Green	.40	1.00
54 Bob Hyland	.40	1.00
55 Ed O'Bradovich	.40	1.00
56 Mac Percival	.40	1.00
57 Gale Sayers	5.00	10.00
58 George Seals	.40	1.00
59 Bill Staley	.40	1.00
60 Cecil Turner	.40	1.00
61 Al Beauchamp	.40	1.00
62 Virgil Carter	.40	1.00
63 Vernon Holland	.40	1.00
64 Bob Johnson TE	.40	1.00
65 Ron Lamb	.40	1.00
66 Dave Lewis	.40	1.00
67 Rufus Mayes	.40	1.00
68 Horst Muhlmann	.40	1.00
69 Lemar Parrish	.50	1.25
70 Jess Phillips	.40	1.00
71 Mike Reid	.75	1.50
72 Ken Riley	.50	1.25
73 Paul Robinson	.40	1.00
74 Bob Trumpy	.50	1.25
75 Ernie Wright	.40	1.00
76 Don Cockroft	.40	1.00
77 Gary Collins	.50	1.25
78 Gene Hickerson	.40	1.00
79 Jim Houston	.40	1.00
80 Walter Johnson	.40	1.00
81 Joe Jones DE	.40	1.00
82 Leroy Kelly	1.00	2.00
83 Bob Matheson	.40	1.00
84 Milt Morin	.40	1.00
85 Bill Nelsen	.50	1.25
86 Mike Phipps	.50	1.25
87 Dick Schafrath	.50	1.25
88 Bo Scott	.50	1.25
89 Jerry Sherk	.40	1.00
90 Ron Snidow	.40	1.00
91 Herb Adderley	1.00	2.00
92 George Andrie	.40	1.00
93 Mike Clark	.40	1.00
94 Dave Edwards	.40	1.00
95 Walt Garrison	.50	1.25
96 Cornell Green	.50	1.25
97 Bob Hayes	1.00	2.00
98 Calvin Hill	.75	1.50
99 Chuck Howley	.50	1.25
100 Lee Roy Jordan	.75	1.50
101 Dave Manders	.40	1.00
102 Craig Morton	.75	1.50
103 Ralph Neely	.40	1.00
104 Mel Renfro	1.00	2.00
105 Roger Staubach	10.00	20.00
106 Bob Anderson	.40	1.00
107 Sam Brunelli	.40	1.00
108 Dave Costa	.40	1.00
109 Mike Current	.40	1.00
110 Pete Duranko	.40	1.00
111 Cornell Gordon	.40	1.00
112 Mike Haffner	.40	1.00
113 Don Horn	.40	1.00
114 Rich Jackson	.40	1.00
115 Floyd Little	.75	1.50
116 Dick Post	.50	1.25
117 Paul Smith	.40	1.00
118 Billy Thompson	.50	1.25
119 Dave Washington	.40	1.00
120 Jim Whalen	.40	1.00
121 Lem Barney	1.00	2.00
122 Nick Eddy	.40	1.00
123 Mel Farr	.40	1.00
124 Ed Flanagan	.40	1.00
125 Larry Hand	.40	1.00
126 Alex Karras	1.50	3.00
127 Greg Landry	.50	1.25
128 Dick LeBeau	.40	1.00
129 Mike Lucci	.50	1.25
130 Earl McCullouch	.40	1.00
131 Bill Munson	.50	1.25
132 Joe Robb	.40	1.00
133 Jerry Rush	.40	1.00
134 Altie Taylor	.40	1.00
135 Wayne Walker	.50	1.25
136 Lionel Aldridge	.40	1.00
137 Ken Bowman	.40	1.00
138 Fred Carr	.40	1.00
139 Carroll Dale	.50	1.25
140 Ken Ellis	.40	1.00
141 Gale Gillingham	.40	1.00
142 Dave Hampton	.40	1.00
143 Doug Hart	.40	1.00
144 John Hilton	.40	1.00
145 Mike McCoy	.40	1.00
146 Ray Nitschke	1.00	2.00
147 Frank Patrick	.40	1.00
148 Francis Peay	.40	1.00
149 Dave Robinson	.50	1.25
150 Bart Starr	6.00	12.00
name spelled correctly		
151 Elvin Bethea	.75	1.50
152 Garland Boyette	.40	1.00
153 Ken Burrough	.50	1.25
154 Woody Campbell	.40	1.00
155 Joe Dawkins	.40	1.00
156 Lynn Dickey	.50	1.25
157 Elbert Drungo	.40	1.00
158 Gene Ferguson	.40	1.00
159 Willie Frazier	.40	1.00
160 Charley Johnson	.50	1.25
161 Charlie Joiner	1.25	2.50
162 Dan Pastorini	.75	1.50
163 Dave Rowe	.40	1.00
164 Walt Suggs	.40	1.00
165 Mike Tilleman	.40	1.00
166 Bobby Bell	1.00	2.00
167 Aaron Brown	.40	1.00
168 Buck Buchanan	1.00	2.00
169 Ed Budde	.40	1.00
170 Curley Culp	.50	1.25
171 Len Dawson	2.50	5.00
172 Robert Holmes	.40	1.00
173 Jim Lynch	.40	1.00
174 Jim Marsalis	.40	1.00
175 Mo Moorman	.40	1.00
176 Ed Podolak	.50	1.25
177 Johnny Robinson	.50	1.25
178 Jan Stenerud	.75	1.50
179 Otis Taylor	.75	1.50
180 Jim Tyrer	.40	1.00
181 Kermit Alexander	.40	1.00
182 Coy Bacon	.40	1.00
183 Roman Gabriel	.75	1.50
184 Ken Iman	.40	1.00
185 Deacon Jones	1.25	2.50
186 Les Josephson	.40	1.00
187 Marlin McKeever	.40	1.00
188 Merlin Olsen	2.00	4.00
189 Phil Olsen	.40	1.00
190 Richie Petitbon	.50	1.25
191 David Ray	.40	1.00
192 Lance Rentzel	.50	1.25
193 Isiah Robertson	.50	1.25
194 Larry Smith	.40	1.00
195 Jack Snow	.50	1.25
196 Nick Buoniconti	.75	1.50
197 Doug Crusan	.40	1.00
198 Larry Csonka	5.00	10.00
199 Bob DeMarco	.40	1.00
200 Marv Fleming	.50	1.25
201 Bob Griese	4.00	8.00
202 Jim Kiick	.75	1.50
203 Mercury Morris	.75	1.50
204 John Richardson	.40	1.00
205 Jim Riley	.40	1.00
206 Jake Scott	.75	1.50
207 Howard Twilley	.40	1.00
208 Paul Warfield	2.00	4.00
209 Ed Weisacosky	.40	1.00
210 Garo Yepremian	.50	1.25
211 Grady Alderman	.50	1.25
212 John Beasley	.40	1.00
213 Gary Cuozzo	.50	1.25
214 John Henderson	.40	1.00
215 Wally Hilgenberg	.40	1.00
216 Clinton Jones	.40	1.00
217 Karl Kassulke	.40	1.00
218 Paul Krause	.75	1.50
219 Dave Osborn	.50	1.25
220 Alan Page	1.00	2.00
221 Ed Sharockman	.40	1.00
222 Norm Snead	.50	1.25
223 Mick Tingelhoff	.50	1.25
224 Lon Warwick	.40	1.00
225 Gene Washington Vik	.50	1.25
226 Hank Barton	.40	1.00
227 Larry Carwell	.40	1.00
228 Tom Funchess	.40	1.00
229 Carl Garrett	.50	1.25
230 Jim Hunt	.40	1.00
231 Daryle Johnson	.40	1.00
232 Joe Kapp	.50	1.25
233 Tim Kelly	.40	1.00
234 Jon Morris	.40	1.00
235 Jim Nance	.50	1.25
236 Jim Plunkett	1.50	3.00
237 Dan Schneiss	.40	1.00
238 Ron Sellers	.40	1.00
No jersey number		
239 Ed Toner	.40	1.00
240 Gerald Warren	.40	1.00
241 Dan Abramowicz	.50	1.25
242 Tony Baker	.50	1.25
243 Leo Carroll	.40	1.00
244 Dick Davis	.40	1.00
245 Tom Dempsey	.50	1.25
246 Al Dodd	.40	1.00
247 Jim Flanigan LB	.40	1.00
248 Hoyle Granger	.40	1.00
249 Edd Hargett	.40	1.00
250 Gene Howard	.40	1.00
251 Jake Kupp	.40	1.00
252 Dave Long	.40	1.00
253 Dick Lyons	.40	1.00
254 Mike Morgan	.40	1.00
255 Del Williams	.40	1.00
256 Fred Dryer	.75	1.50
257 Bobby Duhon	.40	1.00
258 Jim Files	.40	1.00
259 Tucker Frederickson	.50	1.25
260 Pete Gogolak	.40	1.00
261 Don Herrmann	.40	1.00
262 Ron Johnson	.40	1.00
263 Jim Kanicki	.40	1.00
264 Ernie Koy	.40	1.00
265 Spider Lockhart	.40	1.00
266 Clifton McNeil	.40	1.00
267 Joe Morrison	.40	1.00
268 Fran Tarkenton	4.00	8.00
269 Willie Williams	.40	1.00
270 Willie Young	.40	1.00
271 Al Atkinson	.40	1.00
272 Ralph Baker	.40	1.00
273 Emerson Boozer UER	.50	1.25
Photo is Mike Battle		
274 Mike Battle UER	.40	1.00
Photo is Emerson Boozer		
275 John Elliott	.40	1.00
276 Dave Herman	.40	1.00
277 Winston Hill	.40	1.00
278 Gus Hollomon	.40	1.00
279 Bobby Howfield	.40	1.00
280 Pete Lammons	.40	1.00
281 Joe Namath	10.00	20.00
282 Gerry Philbin UER	.40	1.00
Spelled Jerry		
283 Matt Snell	.50	1.25
284 Steve Tannen	.40	1.00
285 Al Woodall	.40	1.00
286 Fred Biletnikoff	2.00	4.00
287 George Blanda	3.00	6.00
288 Willie Brown	1.00	2.00
289 Raymond Chester	.50	1.25
290 Tony Cline	.40	1.00
291 Dan Conners	.40	1.00
292 Ben Davidson	.50	1.25
293 Hewritt Dixon	.40	1.00
294 Bill Enyart	.40	1.00
295 Daryle Lamonica	.75	1.50
296 Gus Otto	.40	1.00
297 Jim Otto	1.00	2.00
298 Charlie Smith	.40	1.00
299 Gene Upshaw	1.00	2.00
300 Warren Wells	.40	1.00
301 Rick Arrington	.40	1.00
302 Gary Ballman	.40	1.00
303 Lee Bouggess	.40	1.00
304 Bill Bradley	.50	1.25
305 Richard Harris	.40	1.00
306 Ben Hawkins	.40	1.00
307 Harold Jackson	.75	1.50
308 Pete Liske	.40	1.00
309 Al Nelson	.40	1.00
310 Gary Pettigrew	.40	1.00
311 Cyril Pinder	.40	1.00
312 Tim Rossovich	.50	1.25
313 Tom Woodeshick	.50	1.25
314 Adrian Young	.40	1.00
315 Steve Zabel	.40	1.00
316 Chuck Allen	.40	1.00
317 Warren Bankston	.40	1.00
318 Chuck Beatty	.40	1.00
319 Terry Bradshaw	10.00	20.00
320 John Fuqua	.40	1.00
321 Terry Hanratty	.50	1.25
322 Chuck Hinton	.40	1.00
323 Ray Mansfield	.40	1.00
324 Ben McGee	.40	1.00
325 Andy Russell	.50	1.25
326 Ron Shanklin	.40	1.00
327 Bruce Van Dyke	.40	1.00
328 Lloyd Voss	.40	1.00
329 Bobby Walden	.40	1.00
330 Allen Watson	.40	1.00
331 Jim Bakken	.50	1.25
332 Pete Beathard	.40	1.00
333 Miller Farr	.40	1.00
334 Mel Gray	.75	1.50
335 Jim Hart	.75	1.50
336 MacArthur Lane	.50	1.25
337 Chuck Latourette	.40	1.00
338 Ernie McMillan	.40	1.00
339 Bob Reynolds	.40	1.00
340 Jackie Smith	1.00	2.00
341 Larry Stallings	.40	1.00
342 Jerry Stovall	.40	1.00
343 Chuck Walker	.40	1.00
344 Roger Wehrli	.50	1.25
345 Larry Wilson	1.00	2.00
346 Bob Babich	.40	1.00
347 Pete Barnes	.40	1.00
348 Marty Domres	.40	1.00
349 Steve DeLong	.40	1.00
350 Gary Garrison	.50	1.25
351 Walker Gillette	.40	1.00
352 Dave Grayson	.40	1.00
353 John Hadl	.75	1.50
354 Jim Hill	.40	1.00
355 Bob Howard	.40	1.00
356 Tony Liscio	.40	1.00
357 Dennis Partee	.40	1.00
358 Andy Rice	.40	1.00
359 Russ Washington	.40	1.00
360 Doug Wilkerson	.40	1.00
361 John Brodie	1.25	2.50
362 Doug Cunningham	.40	1.00
363 Bruce Gossett	.40	1.00
364 Stan Hindman	.40	1.00
365 John Isenbarger	.40	1.00
366 Charlie Krueger	.40	1.00
367 Frank Nunley	.40	1.00
368 Woody Peoples	.40	1.00
369 Len Rohde	.40	1.00
370 Steve Spurrier	6.00	12.00
371 Gene Washington 49er	.50	1.25
372 Dave Wilcox	.50	1.25
373 Ken Willard	.40	1.00
374 Bob Windsor	.40	1.00
375 Dick Witcher	.40	1.00
376 Maxie Baughan	.40	1.00
377 Larry Brown RB	.75	1.50
378 Boyd Dowler	.50	1.25
379 Chris Hanburger	.50	1.25
380 Charlie Harraway	.40	1.00
381 Rickie Harris	.40	1.00
382 Sonny Jurgensen	2.00	4.00
383 Billy Kilmer	.75	1.50
384 Tommy Mason	.50	1.25
385 Brig Owens	.40	1.00
386 Jack Pardee	.50	1.25
387 Myron Pottios	.40	1.00
388 Jerry Smith	.40	1.00
389 Diron Talbert	.40	1.00
390 Charley Taylor	1.50	3.00
NNO Wonderful World Album	50.00	100.00
(Earl Morrall and Mark Washington pictured)		

1972 NFLPA Wonderful World Stamps

This set of 390 stamps was issued in both 1971 and 1972 under the auspices of the NFL Players Association in conjunction with an album entitled "The Wonderful World of Pro Football USA." The album pictures Walt Garrison being tackled during Super Bowl VI. The stamps are numbered and are approximately 1 15/16" by 2 7/8". The team order of the album is arranged alphabetically according to the city name and then alphabetically by player name within each team The picture stamp album contains 30 pages measuring approximately 9 1/2" by 13 1/4". The text narrates the story of pro football in the United States. The album includes spaces for 390 color player stamps. The checklist and stamp numbering below is according to the album. There are some numbering and very slight text variations between the 1971 and 1972 issues on some stamps, as noted below.

COMPLETE SET (390)	250.00	400.00
1 Bob Berry	.50	1.25
2 Greg Brezina	.40	1.00
3 Ken Burrow	.40	1.00
4 Jim Butler	.40	1.00
5 Wes Chesson	.40	1.00
6 Claude Humphrey	.40	1.00
7 George Kunz	.40	1.00
8 Tom McCauley	.40	1.00
9 Jim Mitchell	.40	1.00
10 Tommy Nobis	.75	1.50
11 Ken Reaves	.40	1.00
12 Bill Sandeman	.40	1.00
13 John Small	.40	1.00
14 Harmon Wages	.40	1.00
15 John Zook	.40	1.00
16 Norm Bulaich	.50	1.25
17 Bill Curry	.50	1.25
18 Mike Curtis	.50	1.25
19 Ted Hendricks	1.00	2.00
20 Roy Hilton	.40	1.00
21 Eddie Hinton	.40	1.00
22 David Lee	.40	1.00
23 Jerry Logan	.40	1.00
24 John Mackey	1.00	2.00
25 Tom Matte	.50	1.25
26 Jim O'Brien	.50	1.25
27 Glenn Ressler	.40	1.00
28 Johnny Unitas	6.00	12.00
29 Bob Vogel	.40	1.00
30 Rick Volk	.40	1.00
31 Paul Costa	.40	1.00
32 Jim Dunaway	.40	1.00
33 Paul Guidry	.40	1.00
34 Jim Harris	.40	1.00
35 Robert James	.40	1.00
36 Mike McBath	.40	1.00
37 Haven Moses	.50	1.25
38 Wayne Patrick	.40	1.00
39 John Pitts	.40	1.00
40 Jim Reilly	.40	1.00
41 Pete Richardson	.40	1.00
42 Dennis Shaw	.50	1.25
43 O.J. Simpson	4.00	8.00
44 Mike Stratton	.40	1.00
45 Bob Tatarek	.40	1.00
46 Dick Butkus	5.00	10.00
47 Jim Cadile	.40	1.00
48 Jack Concannon	.50	1.25
49 Bobby Douglass	.50	1.25
50 George Farmer	.40	1.00
51 Dick Gordon	.40	1.00
52 Bobby Joe Green	.40	1.00
53 Ed O'Bradovich	.40	1.00
54 Mac Percival	.40	1.00
55 Gale Sayers	5.00	10.00
56 George Seals	.40	1.00
57 Jim Seymour	.40	1.00
58 Ron Smith	.40	1.00
59 Bill Staley	.40	1.00
60 Cecil Turner	.40	1.00
61 Al Beauchamp	.40	1.00
62 Virgil Carter	.40	1.00
63 Vern Holland	.40	1.00
64 Bob Johnson	.50	1.25
65 Ron Lamb	.40	1.00
66 Dave Lewis	.40	1.00
67 Rufus Mayes	.40	1.00
68 Horst Muhlmann	.40	1.00
69 Lemar Parrish	.50	1.25
70 Jess Phillips	.40	1.00
71 Mike Reid	1.00	2.00
72 Ken Riley	.50	1.25
73 Paul Robinson	.40	1.00
74 Bob Trumpy	.50	1.25
75 Fred Willis	.50	1.25
76 Don Cockroft	.40	1.00
77 Gary Collins	.40	1.00
78 Gene Hickerson	.40	1.00
79 Fair Hooker	.40	1.00
80 Jim Houston	.40	1.00
81 Walter Johnson	.40	1.00
82 Joe Jones	.40	1.00
83 Leroy Kelly	1.00	2.00
84 Milt Morin	.40	1.00
85 Reece Morrison	.40	1.00
86 Bill Nelsen	.50	1.25
87 Mike Phipps	.50	1.25
88 Bo Scott	.40	1.00
89 Jerry Sherk	.40	1.00
90 Ron Snidow	.40	1.00
91 Herb Adderley	1.00	2.00
92 George Andrie	.40	1.00
93 Mike Clark	.40	1.00
94 Dave Edwards	.40	1.00
95 Walt Garrison	.50	1.25
96 Cornell Green	.50	1.25
97 Bob Hayes	1.00	2.00
98 Calvin Hill	.75	1.50
99 Chuck Howley	.50	1.25
100 Lee Roy Jordan	1.00	2.00
101 Dave Manders	.40	1.00
102 Craig Morton	.75	1.50
103 Ralph Neely	.40	1.00
104 Mel Renfro	1.00	2.00
105 Roger Staubach	10.00	20.00
106 Bob Anderson	.40	1.00
107 Sam Brunelli	.40	1.00
108 Dave Costa	.40	1.00
109 Mike Current	.40	1.00
110 Pete Duranko	.40	1.00
111 George Goeddeke	.40	1.00
112 Cornell Gordon	.40	1.00
113 Don Horn	.40	1.00
114 Rich Jackson	.40	1.00
115 Larry Kaminski	.40	1.00
116 Floyd Little	.75	1.50
117 Marv Montgomery	.40	1.00
118 Steve Ramsey	.40	1.00
119 Paul Smith	.40	1.00
120 Bill Thompson	.40	1.00
121 Lem Barney	1.00	2.00
122 Nick Eddy	.40	1.00
123 Mel Farr	.40	1.00
124 Ed Flanagan	.40	1.00
125 Larry Hand	.40	1.00
126 Greg Landry	.50	1.25
127 Dick LeBeau	.50	1.25
128 Mike Lucci	.50	1.25
129 Earl McCullouch	.40	1.00
130 Bill Munson	.50	1.25
131 Wayne Rasmussen	.40	1.00
132 Joe Robb	.40	1.00
133 Jerry Rush	.40	1.00
134 Altie Taylor	.40	1.00
135 Wayne Walker	.50	1.25
136 Ken Bowman	.40	1.00
137 John Brockington	.50	1.25
138 Fred Carr	.40	1.00
139 Carroll Dale	.50	1.25
140 Ken Ellis	.40	1.00
141 Gale Gillingham	.40	1.00
142 Dave Hampton	.40	1.00
143 Doug Hart	.40	1.00
144 MacArthur Lane	.50	1.25
145 Mike McCoy	.40	1.00
146 Ray Nitschke	1.00	2.00
147 Frank Patrick	.40	1.00
148 Francis Peay	.40	1.00
149 Dave Robinson	.50	1.25
150 Bart Starr	6.00	12.00
name misspelled Part		
151 Bob Atkins	.40	1.00
152 Elvin Bethea	.75	1.50
153 Garland Boyette	.40	1.00
154 Ken Burrough	.50	1.25
155 Woody Campbell	.40	1.00
156 John Charles	.40	1.00
157 Lynn Dickey	.50	1.25
158 Elbert Drungo	.40	1.00
159 Gene Ferguson	.40	1.00
160 Charley Johnson	.50	1.25
161 Charlie Joiner	1.25	2.50
162 Dan Pastorini	.75	1.50
163 Ron Pritchard	.40	1.00
164 Walt Suggs	.40	1.00
165 Mike Tilleman	.40	1.00
166 Bobby Bell	1.00	2.00
167 Aaron Brown	.40	1.00
168 Buck Buchanan	1.00	2.00
169 Ed Budde	.40	1.00
170 Curley Culp	.40	1.00
171 Len Dawson	2.50	5.00
172 Willie Lanier	1.25	2.50
173 Jim Lynch	.40	1.00
174 Jim Marsalis	.40	1.00
175 Mo Moorman	.40	1.00
176 Ed Podolak	.50	1.25
177 Johnny Robinson	.50	1.25
178 Jan Stenerud	.75	1.50
179 Otis Taylor	.75	1.50
180 Jim Tyrer	.40	1.00
181 Kermit Alexander	.40	1.00
182 Coy Bacon	.40	1.00
183 Dick Buzin	.40	1.00
184 Roman Gabriel	.75	1.50
185 Gene Howard	.40	1.00
186 Ken Iman	.40	1.00
187 Les Josephson	.40	1.00
188 Marlin McKeever	.40	1.00
189 Merlin Olsen	2.00	4.00
190 Phil Olsen	.40	1.00
191 David Ray	.40	1.00
192 Lance Rentzel	.50	1.25
193 Isiah Robertson	.50	1.25
194 Larry Smith	.40	1.00
195 Jack Snow	.50	1.25
196 Nick Buoniconti	.75	1.50
197 Doug Crusan	.40	1.00
198 Larry Csonka	5.00	10.00
199 Bob DeMarco	.40	1.00
200 Marv Fleming	.50	1.25
201 Bob Griese	4.00	8.00
202 Jim Kiick	.75	1.50
203 Bob Kuechenberg	.50	1.25
204 Mercury Morris	.75	1.50
205 John Richardson	.40	1.00
206 Jim Riley	.40	1.00
207 Jake Scott	.50	1.25
208 Howard Twilley	.50	1.25
209 Paul Warfield	2.00	4.00
210 Garo Yepremian	.50	1.25
211 Grady Alderman	.40	1.00
212 John Beasley	.40	1.00
213 John Henderson	.40	1.00
214 Wally Hilgenberg	.40	1.00
215 Clint Jones	.40	1.00
216 Karl Kassulke	.40	1.00
217 Paul Krause	.75	1.50
218 Dave Osborn	.40	1.00
219 Alan Page	1.00	2.00
220 Ed Sharockman	.40	1.00
221 Fran Tarkenton	4.00	8.00
222 Mick Tingelhoff	.50	1.25
223 Charlie West	.40	1.00
224 Lonnie Warwick	.40	1.00
225 Gene Washington Vik	.50	1.25
226 Hank Barton	.40	1.00
227 Ron Berger	.40	1.00
228 Larry Carwell	.40	1.00
229 Jim Cheyunski	.40	1.00
230 Carl Garrett	.40	1.00
231 Rickie Harris	.40	1.00
232 Daryle Johnson	.40	1.00
233 Steve Kiner	.40	1.00
234 Jon Morris	.40	1.00
235 Jim Nance	.50	1.25
236 Tom Neville	.40	1.00
237 Jim Plunkett	1.25	2.50
238 Ron Sellers	.40	1.00
239 Len St. Jean	.40	1.00
240 Don Webb	.40	1.00
241 Dan Abramowicz	.50	1.25
242 Dick Absher	.40	1.00
243 Leo Carroll	.40	1.00
244 Jim Duncan	.40	1.00
245 Al Dodd	.40	1.00
246 Jim Flanigan	.40	1.00
247 Hoyle Granger	.40	1.00
248 Edd Hargett	.40	1.00
249 Glen Ray Hines	.40	1.00
250 Hugo Hollas	.40	1.00
251 Jake Kupp	.40	1.00
252 Dave Long	.40	1.00
253 Mike Morgan	.40	1.00
254 Tom Roussel	.40	1.00
255 Del Williams	.40	1.00
256 Otto Brown	.40	1.00
257 Bobby Duhon	.40	1.00
258 Scott Eaton	.40	1.00
259 Jim Files	.40	1.00
260 Tucker Frederickson	.50	1.25
261 Pete Gogolak	.40	1.00
262 Bob Grim	.40	1.00
263 Don Herrmann	.40	1.00
264 Ron Johnson	.50	1.25
265 Jim Kanicki	.40	1.00
266 Spider Lockhart	.50	1.25
267 Joe Morrison	.50	1.25
268 Bob Tucker	.50	1.25
269 Willie Williams	.40	1.00
270 Willie Young	.40	1.00
271 Al Atkinson	.40	1.00
272 Ralph Baker	.40	1.00
273 Emerson Boozer	.50	1.25
274 John Elliott	.40	1.00
275 Dave Herman	.40	1.00
276 Winston Hill	.40	1.00
277 Gus Hollomon	.40	1.00
278 Bobby Howfield	.40	1.00
279 Pete Lammons	.40	1.00
280 Joe Namath	10.00	20.00
281 Gerry Philbin	.40	1.00
282 Matt Snell	.50	1.25
283 Steve Tannen	.40	1.00
284 Earlie Thomas	.40	1.00
285 Al Woodall	.40	1.00
286 Fred Biletnikoff	2.00	4.00
287 George Blanda	3.00	6.00
288 Willie Brown	1.00	2.00
289 Raymond Chester	.50	1.25
290 Tony Cline	.40	1.00
291 Dan Conners	.40	1.00
292 Ben Davidson	.50	1.25
293 Hewritt Dixon	.40	1.00
294 Tom Keating	.40	1.00
295 Daryle Lamonica	.75	1.50
296 Gus Otto	.40	1.00
297 Jim Otto	1.00	2.00
298 Rod Sherman	.40	1.00
299 Charlie Smith	.40	1.00
300 Gene Upshaw	1.00	2.00
301 Rick Arrington	.40	1.00
302 Gary Ballman	.40	1.00
303 Lee Bouggess	.40	1.00
304 Bill Bradley	.50	1.25
305 Happy Feller	.40	1.00
306 Richard Harris	.40	1.00
307 Ben Hawkins	.40	1.00
308 Harold Jackson	.50	1.25
309 Pete Liske	.40	1.00
310 Al Nelson	.40	1.00
311 Gary Pettigrew	.40	1.00
312 Tim Rossovich	.40	1.00
313 Tom Woodeshick	.40	1.00
314 Adrian Young	.40	1.00
315 Steve Zabel	.40	1.00
316 Chuck Allen	.50	1.25
317 Warren Bankston	.40	1.00
318 Chuck Beatty	.40	1.00
319 Terry Bradshaw	10.00	20.00
320 John Fuqua	.40	1.00
321 Terry Hanratty	.50	1.25
322 Ray Mansfield	.40	1.00
323 Ben McGee	.40	1.00
324 John Rowser	.40	1.00
325 Andy Russell	.50	1.25
326 Ron Shanklin	.40	1.00
327 Dave Smith	.40	1.00
328 Bruce Van Dyke	.40	1.00
329 Lloyd Voss	.40	1.00
330 Bobby Walden	.40	1.00
331 Donny Anderson	.50	1.25
332 Jim Bakken	.50	1.25
333 Pete Beathard	.40	1.00
334 Miller Farr	.40	1.00
335 Mel Gray	.50	1.25
336 Jim Hart	.75	1.50
337 Rolf Krueger	.40	1.00
338 Chuck Latourette	.40	1.00
339 Ernie McMillan	.40	1.00
340 Bob Reynolds	.40	1.00
341 Jackie Smith	1.00	2.00
342 Larry Stallings	.40	1.00
343 Chuck Walker	.40	1.00
344 Roger Wehrli	.50	1.25
345 Larry Wilson	1.00	2.00
346 Bob Babich	.40	1.00
347 Pete Barnes	.40	1.00
348 Steve DeLong	.40	1.00
349 Marty Domres	.40	1.00
350 Gary Garrison	.50	1.25
351 John Hadl	.75	1.50
352 Kevin Hardy	.40	1.00
353 Bob Howard	.40	1.00
354 Deacon Jones	1.25	2.50
355 Terry Owens	.40	1.00
356 Dennis Partee	.40	1.00
357 Jeff Queen	.40	1.00
358 Jim Tolbert	.40	1.00
359 Russ Washington	.40	1.00
360 Doug Wilkerson	.40	1.00
361 John Brodie	1.25	2.50
362 Doug Cunningham	.40	1.00
363 Bruce Gossett	.40	1.00
364 Stan Hindman	.40	1.00
365 John Isenbarger	.40	1.00
366 Charlie Krueger	.40	1.00
367 Frank Nunley	.40	1.00
368 Woody Peoples	.40	1.00
369 Len Rohde	.40	1.00
370 Steve Spurrier	6.00	12.00
371 Gene Washington 49er	.50	1.25
372 Dave Wilcox	.50	1.25
373 Ken Willard	.50	1.25
374 Bob Windsor	.40	1.00
375 Dick Witcher	.40	1.00
376 Verlon Biggs	.40	1.00
377 Larry Brown	.75	1.50
378 Speedy Duncan	.50	1.25
379 Chris Hanburger	.50	1.25
380 Charlie Harraway	.40	1.00
381 Sonny Jurgensen	2.00	4.00
382 Billy Kilmer	.75	1.50
383 Tommy Mason	.50	1.25
384 Ron McDole	.40	1.00
385 Brig Owens	.40	1.00
386 Jack Pardee	.50	1.25
387 Myron Pottios	.40	1.00
388 Jerry Smith	.40	1.00
389 Diron Talbert	.40	1.00
390 Charley Taylor	1.50	3.00
NNO Wonderful World Album	10.00	20.00
(Walt Garrison tackled)		

1972 NFLPA Fabric Cards

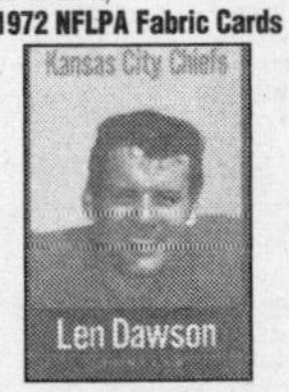

The 1972 NFLPA Fabric Cards set includes 35 cards printed on cloth. These thin fabric cards measure approximately 2 1/4" by 3 1/2" and are blank backed. The cards are sometimes referred to as "Iron Ons" as they were intended to be semi-permanently ironed on to clothes. The full color portrait of the player is surrounded by a black border. Below the player's name at the bottom of the card is indicated copyright by the NFL Players Association in 1972. The cards may have been illegally reprinted. There is some additional interest in the Staubach card due to the fact that his 1972 Topps card (that same year) is considered his Rookie Card. Since they are unnumbered, they are listed below in alphabetical order according to the player's name. These fabric cards were originally available in vending machines at retail stores and other outlets.

COMPLETE SET (35)	75.00	150.00
1 Donny Anderson	1.00	2.50
2 George Blanda	3.00	6.00
3 Terry Bradshaw	7.50	15.00
4 John Brockington	1.00	2.50
5 John Brodie	2.00	4.00
6 Dick Butkus	5.00	10.00
7 Larry Csonka	3.00	6.00
8 Mike Curtis	1.00	2.50
9 Len Dawson	2.50	5.00
10 Carl Eller	1.25	3.00
11 Mike Garrett	1.00	2.50
12 Joe Greene	4.00	8.00
13 Bob Griese	3.00	6.00
14 Dick Gordon	1.00	2.50
15 John Hadl	1.25	3.00
16 Bob Hayes	1.50	4.00
17 Ron Johnson	1.00	2.50
18 Deacon Jones	1.50	4.00
19 Sonny Jurgensen	2.50	5.00
20 Leroy Kelly	1.50	4.00
21 Jim Kiick	1.25	3.00
22 Greg Landry	1.00	2.50
23 Floyd Little	1.25	3.00
24 Mike Lucci	1.00	2.50
25 Archie Manning	2.00	4.00
26 Joe Namath	10.00	20.00
27 Tommy Nobis	1.25	3.00
28 Alan Page	1.50	4.00
29 Jim Plunkett	2.00	4.00
30 Gale Sayers	5.00	10.00
31 O.J. Simpson	5.00	10.00
32 Roger Staubach	10.00	20.00
33 Duane Thomas	1.25	3.00
34 Johnny Unitas	10.00	20.00
35 Paul Warfield	3.00	6.00

1972 NFLPA Vinyl Stickers

The 1972 NFLPA Vinyl Stickers set contains 20 stand-up type stickers depicting the players in a caricature-like style with big heads. These irregularly shaped stickers are approximately 2 3/4" by 4 3/4". Below the player's name at the bottom of the card is indicated copyright by the NFL Players Association in 1972. The set is sometimes offered as a short set excluding the shorter-printed cards, i.e., those listed by SP in the checklist below. Since they are unnumbered, they are listed below in alphabetical order according to the player's name. The Roger Staubach card holds special interest in that 1972 represents Roger's rookie year for cards. These stickers were originally available in vending machines at retail stores and other outlets. The Dick Butkus and Joe Namath stickers exist as reverse negatives. The set is considered complete with either Butkus or Namath variation.

COMPLETE SET (20) 100.00 175.00
1 Donny Anderson 1.50 4.00
2 George Blanda 3.00 6.00
3 Terry Bradshaw 7.50 15.00
4 John Brockington 1.50 4.00
5 John Brodie 2.50 6.00
6A Dick Butkus Reversed Negative 5.00 10.00
6B Dick Butkus 5.00 10.00
7 Dick Gordon 1.50 4.00
8 Joe Greene 2.50 6.00
9 John Hadl 2.00 5.00
10 Bob Hayes 2.50 6.00
11 Ron Johnson SP 4.00 8.00
12 Floyd Little 1.50 4.00
13A Joe Namath Reversed Negative 10.00 20.00
13B Joe Namath 10.00 20.00
14 Tommy Nobis 2.00 5.00
15 Alan Page SP 6.00 12.00
16 Jim Plunkett 2.50 5.00
17 Gale Sayers 5.00 10.00
18 Roger Staubach 10.00 20.00
19 Johnny Unitas 10.00 20.00
20 Paul Warfield 2.50 6.00

1972 NFLPA Woodburning Kit

This Woodburning set was sold as an arts and crafts kit with 16-individual player wooden plaques measuring roughly 4" by 4 1/4", 2-generic football player plaques measuring 2 3/8" by 4 1/2" and two larger (roughly 8" by 10") plaques featuring 5-players on each. Each plaque is unnumbered and blankbacked with bright red or maroon printing on the front featuring a drawing of an NFL player. It is thought that each can be found with either the bright red printing or the darker maroon printing. The player image was supposed to be burning out with a tool and then painted by the collector.

1 Lance Alworth 10.00 25.00
2 Terry Bradshaw 15.00 40.00
3 Nick Buoniconti 8.00 20.00
4 Dick Butkus 12.00 30.00
5 Roy Jefferson 6.00 15.00
6 Ron Johnson 6.00 15.00
7 Sonny Jurgensen 10.00 25.00
8 Daryle Lamonica 8.00 20.00
9 Alan Page 8.00 20.00
10 O.J. Simpson 10.00 25.00
11 Matt Snell 8.00 20.00
12 Gene Washington Minn. 6.00 15.00
17 Generic Player (with NFL Players logo) 4.00 10.00
18 Quarterbacks 8.00 20.00
Jim Plunkett
Roman Gabriel
Bill Munson
Marty Domres
John Hadl
19 Running Backs 8.00 20.00
Mike Garrett
MacArthur Lane
Steve Owens
Garo Yepremian
Emerson Boozer

1979 NFLPA Pennant Stickers

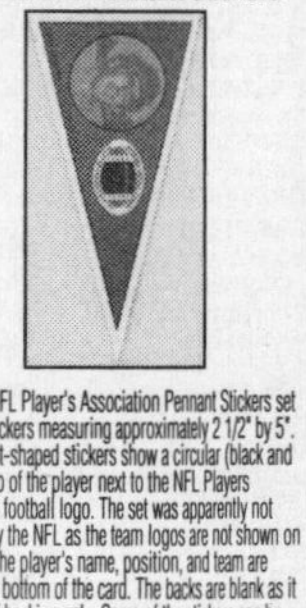

The 1979 NFL Player's Association Pennant Stickers set contains stickers measuring approximately 2 1/2" by 5". The pennant-shaped stickers show a circular (black and white) photo of the player next to the NFL Players Association football logo. The set was apparently not approved by the NFL as the team logos are not shown on the cards. The player's name, position, and team are given at the bottom of the card. The backs are blank as it is a peel-off backing only. Some of the stickers can be found with more than one color background and have been listed accordingly below. The complete set price includes just one sticker for each player.

COMPLETE SET (54) 300.00 600.00
1 Lyle Alzado (Red) 3.00 6.00
2 Ken Anderson (Blue) 4.00 8.00
3 Steve Bartkowski SP (Yellow) 12.50 25.00
4 Ricky Bell (Red) 3.00 6.00
5 Elvin Bethea (Blue) 3.00 6.00
6A Tom Blanchard (Blue) 2.50 5.00
6B Tom Blanchard (Red) 2.50 5.00
6C Tom Blanchard (Yellow) 2.50 5.00
7A Terry Bradshaw (Red) 25.00 50.00
7B Terry Bradshaw (Yellow) 25.00 50.00
8A Bob Breunig (Red) 2.50 5.00
8B Bob Breunig (Yellow) 2.50 5.00
9A Greg Brezina (Purple) 2.50 5.00
9B Greg Brezina (Red) 2.50 5.00
9C Greg Brezina (Yellow) 2.50 5.00
10 Doug Buffone SP (Green) 12.50 25.00
11 Earl Campbell (Yellow) 15.00 30.00
12 John Cappelletti (Green) 4.00 8.00
13 Harold Carmichael (Blue) 3.00 6.00
14 Chuck Crist SP (Green) 12.50 25.00
15 Sam Cunningham (Green) 2.50 5.00
16 Isaac Curtis SP (Blue) 12.50 25.00
17 Joe DeLamielleure (Blue) 4.00 8.00
18A Tom Dempsey (Blue) 2.50 5.00
18B Tom Dempsey (Red) 2.50 5.00
18C Tom Dempsey (Yellow) 2.50 5.00
19 Tony Dorsett (Yellow) 10.00 20.00
20 Dan Fouts SP (Red) 15.00 30.00
21A Roy Gerela (Red) 2.50 5.00
21B Roy Gerela (Yellow) 2.50 5.00
22 Bob Griese UER (Purple; Greise) 10.00 20.00
23A Franco Harris (Red) 10.00 20.00
23B Franco Harris (Yellow) 10.00 20.00
23C Franco Harris SP (Green) 25.00 50.00
24 Jim Hart SP (Green) 12.50 25.00
25 Charlie Joiner (Green) 4.00 8.00
26 Doug Kotar SP (Green) 25.00 50.00
27 Paul Krause (Green) 4.00 8.00
28 Bob Kuechenberg (Purple) 2.50 5.00
29 Greg Landry (Purple) 3.00 6.00
30 Archie Manning (Blue) 3.00 6.00
31 Chester Marcol (Purple) 2.50 5.00
32A Harvey Martin (Red) 3.00 6.00
32B Harvey Martin (Yellow) 3.00 6.00
33 Lawrence McCutcheon SP (Yellow) 12.50 25.00
34 Craig Morton (Green) 3.00 6.00
35 Haven Moses (Green) 2.50 5.00
36 Steve Odom (Green) 2.50 5.00
37 Morris Owens (Green) 2.50 5.00
38 Dan Pastorini SP (Red) 12.50 25.00
39 Walter Payton (Yellow) 25.00 50.00
40 Greg Pruitt SP (Green) 12.50 25.00
41 John Riggins (Purple) 6.00 12.00
42 Jake Scott (Red) 2.50 5.00
43 Jerry Sherk SP 12.50 25.00
44 Ken Stabler SP (Blue) 30.00 60.00
45 Roger Staubach (Yellow) 25.00 50.00
46 Jan Stenerud (Purple) 3.00 6.00
47 Art Still SP (Yellow) 12.50 25.00
48 Mick Tingelhoff (Blue) 2.50 5.00
49 Richard Todd (Yellow) 2.50 5.00
50 Brad Van Pelt SP (Purple) 30.00 50.00
51 Phil Villapiano SP (Purple) 12.50 25.00
52A Wesley Walker (Red) 3.00 6.00
52B Wesley Walker (Yellow) 3.00 6.00
53 Roger Wehrli SP (Yellow) 12.50 25.00
54 Jim Zorn SP (Red) 12.50 25.00

1983 NFLPA Player Pencils Series 1

This set was produced by NAPPCO and licensed by the NFL Player's Association. Each is an actual wooden pencil produced in the team colors with a one-color player image. Each pencil is numbered of 36-pencils in series 1.

COMPLETE SET (36) 125.00 200.00
1 Dan Fouts 4.00 8.00
2 LeRoy Irvin 2.00 4.00
3 Ray Guy 2.50 5.00
4 Steve Largent 4.00 8.00
5 Dwight Clark 2.50 5.00
6 Tom Jackson 2.50 5.00
7 Chuck Muncie 2.00 4.00
8 Ed Too Tall Jones 3.00 6.00
9 Joe Ferguson 2.00 4.00
10 Mark Gastineau 2.00 4.00
11 Stanley Morgan 2.00 4.00
12 Lawrence Taylor 3.00 6.00
13 Terry Bradshaw 10.00 20.00
14 Franco Harris 5.00 10.00
15 Vince Ferragamo 2.00 4.00
16 Mark Moseley 2.00 4.00
17 Mike Pagel 2.00 4.00
18 Ron Jaworski 2.50 5.00
19 Ozzie Newsome 3.00 6.00
20 Ken Anderson 2.50 5.00
21 Jack Lambert 3.00 6.00
22 Joe Klecko 2.00 4.00
23 Lee Roy Selmon 2.50 5.00
24 Steve Bartkowski 2.50 5.00
25 Tommy Vigorito 2.00 4.00
26 Russell Erxleben 2.00 4.00
27A Archie Manning 3.00 6.00
27B Carl Roaches 3.00 6.00
28 Danny White 3.00 6.00
29 William Andrews 2.50 5.00
30 Walter Payton 12.50 25.00
31 Billy Sims 2.50 5.00
32 Tommy Kramer 2.00 4.00
33 John Jefferson 2.50 5.00
34 Brad Budde 2.00 4.00
35 Ottis Anderson 2.50 5.00
36 Tony Dorsett 7.50 15.00

1983 NFLPA Player Pencils Series 2

This set was produced by NAPPCO and licensed by the NFL Player's Association. Each is an actual wooden pencil produced in the team colors with a one-color player image. Each pencil is numbered of 18-pencils in series 2.

3 Steve Largent 4.00 8.00
4 Ed Too Tall Jones 3.00 6.00
5 Lawrence Taylor 3.00 6.00
6 Franco Harris 5.00 10.00
7 Vince Ferragamo 2.00 4.00
9 Walter Payton 12.50 25.00
10 Billy Sims 2.50 5.00
13 Tony Dorsett 7.50 15.00
14 Joe Klecko 2.00 4.00

1986 NFLPA Player Pencils Series 3

13 William Perry 2.50 5.00

1987 NFLPA Player Pencils Series 3

This set was produced by Nappco and licensed by the NFL Player's Association. Each is an actual wooden pencil produced in the team colors with a one-color player image. Each pencil is numbered of 12 in the set and noted as part of the series 3. The year of issue is also included on the pencil.

1 John Elway 15.00 30.00
2 Jim McMahon 7.50 15.00
3 Dan Hampton 6.00 12.00
7 Marcus Allen 7.50 15.00
10 Joe Montana 15.00 30.00

1988 NFLPA Player Pencils

This set was licensed by the NFL Player's Association. Each is an actual wooden pencil produced with metallic paint highlights and a black and white player image. Most of the pencils were released in a numbered version (with NAPPCO logo) as well as unnumbered version. We've listed them below alphabetically. The year of issue is included on each pencil.

COMPLETE SET (18) 100.00 200.00
1 Eric Dickerson 5.00 10.00
2 John Elway 12.50 25.00
3 Jim Everett 4.00 8.00
4 Bobby Hebert 3.00 6.00
5 Jim Kelly 7.50 15.00
6 Bernie Kosar 4.00 8.00
7 Steve Largent 5.00 10.00
8 Howie Long 5.00 10.00
9 Dan Marino 12.50 25.00
10 Jim McMahon 4.00 8.00
11 Freeman McNeil 3.00 6.00
12 Joe Montana 20.00 40.00
13 Jerry Rice 10.00 20.00
14 Lawrence Taylor 5.00 10.00
15 Andre Tippett 3.00 6.00
16 Herschel Walker 4.00 8.00
17 Reggie White 5.00 10.00
18 Doug Williams 4.00 8.00

1995 NFLPA Super Bowl Player's Party

These ten standard-size cards were given away at a NFLPA Super Bowl XXIX player's party. Each card company produced one card; reportedly, the set was limited to 500 of each card. The cards are unnumbered and checklisted below in alphabetical order.

COMPLETE SET (10) 40.00 100.00
1 Marcus Allen Pinnacle 4.80 12.00
2 Jerome Bettis Fleer 4.80 12.00
3 Tim Brown Collector's Edge 3.20 8.00
4 Trent Dilfer SkyBox 3.20 8.00
5 Marshall Faulk Pacific 6.00 15.00
6 Ronnie Lott Classic 2.40 6.00
7 Dan Marino Upper Deck 16.00 40.00
8 Junior Seau Stadium Club 2.40 6.00
9 Sterling Sharpe Action Packed 2.40 6.00
10 Heath Shuler Playoff 2.40 6.00

1996 NFLPA Super Bowl Player's Party

This 12-card set was given away at a NFLPA Super Bowl XXX player's party. Each card company produced a card for one or more of their brands and each card carries the Players, Inc. logo. The cards are unnumbered and checklisted below in alphabetical order.

COMPLETE SET (12) 6.00 15.00
1 Marcus Allen Ronnie Lott Collector's Edge .40 1.00
2 Steve Beuerlein Topps .30 .75
3 Jeff Blake Pacific .60 1.50
4 Tim Brown Action Packed .40 1.00
5 Kerry Collins Classic .40 1.00
6 Kevin Greene Playoff .30 .75
7 Garrison Hearst Fleer Metal .40 1.00
8 Daryl Johnston SkyBox Impact .30 .75
9 Joe Montana Upper Deck 2.00 5.00
10 Deion Sanders Donruss Red Zone .60 1.50
11 Herschel Walker Pinnacle .30 .75
12 Logo Card Checklist back .30 .75

1997 NFLPA Super Bowl Player's Party

This 11-card set was distributed at the NFL Player's Association Super Bowl XXXI player's party in New Orleans. Each card company produced one or two cards for the set with each carrying the Player's Party logo. The cards are unnumbered and checklisted below in alphabetical order.

COMPLETE SET (11) 6.00 15.00
1 Morten Andersen SkyBox .30 .75
2 Steve Bono Collector's Edge .30 .75
3 Robert Brooks Pacific .40 1.00
4 Tony Dorsett Topps .50 1.25
5 Gus Frerotte Donruss .40 1.00
6 Kevin Hardy Pinnacle .30 .75
7 Tyrone Hughes Score Board .30 .75
8 Dan Marino Upper Deck 2.00 5.00
9 Curtis Martin SkyBox 1.00 2.50
10 Deion Sanders Playoff .50 1.25
11 Tim Brown Schedule Card not release by a manufacturer .40 1.00
12 Checklist Card Upper Deck .30 .75

1998 NFLPA Super Bowl Player's Party

This set was distributed at the NFL Player's Association Super Bowl player's party in San Diego. Each card company produced cards for the set with each carrying the Player's Party logo. The cards are unnumbered (except for the two Score Board issues) and checklisted below in alphabetical order.

COMPLETE SET (13) 4.00 10.00
1 Troy Aikman (Collector's Choice) .80 2.00
2 Jerome Bettis (Fleer) .40 1.00
3 Tim Brown (SkyBox) .40 1.00
4 Mark Brunell (Pacific) .60 1.50
5 Terrell Davis (Playoff) 1.20 3.00
6 Tony Dorsett (Score Board) .30 .75
7 Warrick Dunn (Pinnacle) .50 1.25
8 Eddie George (Pinnacle) .80 2.00
9 Stan Humphries (Upper Deck) .30 .75
10 Brent Jones (Score Board) .20 .50
11 Neil Smith (Collector's Edge) .20 .50
12 Reggie White (Topps) .40 1.00
13 Checklist Card (Playoff) .20 .50

1999 NFLPA Super Bowl Player's Party

This set was distributed at the NFL Player's Association Super Bowl Player's Party in Miami. Each card company produced cards for the set with each carrying the Player's Party logo. The cards feature various numbering schemes but have been listed below according to the checklist card order. Note that some of the cards carry a 1998 copyright line. The Daunte Culpepper card was issued by Press Pass and was signed by Culpepper at the event.

COMPLETE SET (11) 4.80 12.00
1 Cover Checklist Card .20 .50
2 Shannon Sharpe .30 .75
3 Mark Brunell (Pacific) .80 2.00
4 Warrick Dunn .40 1.00
5 Ray Lewis .20 .50
6 Trace Armstrong .20 .50
7 Zach Thomas .30 .75
8 Fuad Reveiz .20 .50
9 Jerome Bettis .40 1.00
10 Jacquez Green .20 .50
11 Emmitt Smith (Topps) 1.60 4.00
NNO Daunte Culpepper AUTO (Press Pass) 30.00 60.00

2000 NFLPA Super Bowl Player's Party

This set was distributed at the NFL Player's Association Super Bowl Player's Party in Atlanta in January 2000 in complete set form. The Tim Couch Press Pass card was inadvertently left out of the wrapped set and was distributed by hand later on. Each card company produced cards for the set with each carrying the Player's Inc. logo on the cardfronts. Each card is unnumbered but has been listed below according to the checklist card order. Note that some of the cards do carry a 1999 copyright line instead of 2000.

COMPLETE SET (14) 6.00 15.00
1 Edgerrin James Playoff Inc. 1.20 3.00
2 Curtis Martin SkyBox Dominion .30 .75
3 Kurt Warner Pacific Paramount 2.00 5.00
4 Randy Moss Upper Deck .80 2.00
5 Tim Couch Topps .80 2.00
6 Tim Couch Press Pass .80 2.00
7 Emmitt Smith Collector's Edge .60 1.50
8 Kevin Greene Playoff Inc. .10 .25
9 Dorsey Levens Fleer .16 .40
10 Mark Brunell Pacific .40 1.00
11 Herschel Walker Upper Deck .10 .25
12 Tim Dwight Topps .16 .40
13 John Randle Collector's Edge .16 .40
14 Checklist Card .10 .25

2001 NFLPA Stay Cool in School

This 11-card set was produced for the NFL Player's Association and sponsored by each of the licensed NFL card manufacturers. Cards and sets were given away during the 2001 NFL season to students in the New Orleans area as part of a larger Stay Cool in School program, sponsored by the NFL, that included a variety of prizes rewarding students for good grades and other achievements.

COMPLETE SET (11) 6.00 12.00
1 Mike Anderson (Topps) .50 1.25
2 Corey Dillon (Pacific) .30 .75
3 Ahman Green (Donruss Playoff) .30 .75
4 Marvin Harrison .30 .75
5 Donovan McNabb (Fleer) .50 1.25
6 Shannon Sharpe (Fleer) .14 .40
7 LaDainian Tomlinson (Upper Deck) 1.25 3.00
8 Michael Vick 1.25 3.00
9 Kurt Warner (Donruss Playoff) 1.00 2.50
10 Chris Weinke (Topps) .50 1.25
11 Cover Card CL .08 .25

2001 NFLPA Super Bowl Player's Party

This set was distributed at the NFL Player's Association Super Bowl Player's Party in Tampa in January 2001 in complete set form. Each card company produced cards for the set with each carrying the Player's Inc. logo on the cardfronts. Each card is unnumbered but has been listed below alphabetically. Note that some of the cards do carry a year 2000 copyright line instead of 2001.

COMPLETE SET (13) 4.00 10.00
1 Tony Boselli (Topps) .10 .25
2 Derrick Brooks (Collector's Edge) .30 .75
3 Isaac Bruce (Fleer) .30 .75
4 Plaxico Burress (Donruss) .16 .40
5 Tim Couch (Fleer) .40 1.00
6 Daunte Culpepper .60 1.50
7 Ron Dayne (Pacific) .60 1.50
8 Marshall Faulk (Collector's Edge) .30 .75
9 Edgerrin James .80 2.00
10 Jon Kitna (Pacific) .16 .40
11 Kurt Warner (Playoff) .80 2.00
12 Peter Warrick (Upper Deck) .60 1.50
13 Cover Checklist Card .10 .25

2002 NFLPA Player of the Day

This set was released by the NFL Players Association to hobby shops participating in the Player of the Day contest in Fall 2002. Each NFL Players' licensed manufacturer issued one card representing one of their football brands. Each card featured the Player of the Day logo on the front.

COMPLETE SET (6) 6.00 15.00
1 Checklist Card .40 1.00
2 Jeff Garcia (Donruss/Playoff) .75 2.00
3 Donovan McNabb (Fleer Maximum) 1.00 2.50
4 Michael Vick (Pacific) 1.00 2.50
5 Brett Favre (Topps) 2.00 5.00
6 Peyton Manning (UD Game Gear) 1.50 4.00

2003 NFLPA Player of the Day

This set was released by the NFL Players Association to hobby shops participating in the Player of the Day contest in the Fall 2003. Each NFL Players' licensed manufacturer issued one card representing one of their football brands. Each card featured the Player of the Day logo on the front.

COMPLETE SET (4) 4.00 10.00
1 Peyton Manning 1.50 4.00
2 Jeff Garcia (Gridiron Kings) .75 2.00
3 David Carr (Fleer Platinum) 1.50 4.00
4 Clinton Portis (Topps) 1.25 3.00

2003 NFLPA Scholastic

This 6-card set was issued by the NFL Player's Association for the benefit of the national Scolastic education program. Each card was produced by one of the major NFL licensed trading card partners complete with a unique card number on the backs.

COMPLETE SET (6) 5.00 10.00
1 Brian Urlacher 1.00 2.50
2 Donovan McNabb (Ultra) 1.00 2.50
3 Jeff Garcia (Score) .75 2.00
4 Peyton Manning 1.50 4.00
5 Michael Vick 1.25 3.00
NNO Cover Card .20 .50

2004 NFLPA Player of the Day

This 5-card set was released by NFL Players to hobby shops participating in the Player of the Day contest in Fall 2004. Each NFL Players' licensed manufacturer issued one card representing one of their 2004 football brands. Each card featured the 2004 Player of the Day logo on the front.

COMPLETE SET (5) 2.50 6.00
POD1 Eli Manning 1.50 4.00
POD2 Michael Vick .50 1.25
POD3 Larry Fitzgerald (Topps) .50 1.25
POD4 Tom Brady (SP Game Used Edition) .50 1.25
NNO Cover Card Checklist .08 .25

2005 NFLPA Player of the Day

This 4-card set was released by NFL Players to hobby shops participating in the Player of the Day contest in Fall 2005. Each NFL Players' licensed manufacturer issued one card representing one of their 2005 football brands. The cards feature the 2005 Player of the Day logo on the front.

COMPLETE SET (4) 2.00 4.00
POD1 Tom Brady (Topps) .50 1.25
POD2 Michael Vick (Playoff Prestige) .50 1.25
POD3 Cover Card CL .08 .25
POD4 Peyton Manning (Upper Deck) .60 1.50

2006 NFLPA Player of the Day

This 4-card set was released by NFL Players to hobby shops participating in the Player of the Day contest in Fall 2006. Each NFL Players' licensed manufacturer issued one card representing one of their 2006 football brands. The cards feature the 2006 Player of the Day logo on the front.

COMPLETE SET (4) 2.50 6.00
POD1 Tom Brady (Donruss Classics) .75 2.00
POD2 Peyton Manning (Topps) .75 2.00
POD3 Reggie Bush (Upper Deck) .75 2.00
POD4 Checklist Card .08 .25

2008 NFLPA Player of the Day

This 4-card set was released by NFL Players to hobby shops participating in the Player of the Day contest in Fall 2008. Each of the three NFL Players' licensed manufacturers issued one card representing one of their football brands. The cards feature the 2008 Player of the Day logo on the front.

COMPLETE SET (4) 2.50 6.00
POD1 Darren McFadden (Donruss Prestige) 1.00 2.50
POD2 Adrian Peterson (Topps) .75 2.00
POD3 Tom Brady (Upper Deck) .75 2.00
POD4 Checklist .08 .25

2009 NFLPA Player of the Day

This set was released by NFL Players to hobby shops participating in the Player of the Day contest in Fall 2009. Each of the three NFL Players' licensed manufacturers issued one card representing one of their football brands. The cards feature the 2009 Player of the Day logo on the front.

COMPLETE SET (3) 2.00 5.00
POD1 Larry Fitzgerald (Prestige) .50 1.25
POD2 Adrian Peterson (Topps) .75 2.00
POD3 Peyton Manning (Upper Deck) .75 2.00

1983-85 Nike Poster Cards

The cards in this set measure approximately 5" by 7" and were produced for use by retailers of Nike full-size posters as a promotional counter display. The cards are plastic coated and feature color pictures of players posed in unique settings. The hole at the top was designed so that dealers could attach the cards to the display with a soft plastic fastener provided by Nike. The borders are black. Originally, 27-cards were issued together and others were added later as new posters were created. The backs are plain white and carry the poster name, item number, and the player names (except on group photos). The cards are numbered only by the item number on back and have been listed below according to the final two digits of that number.

COMPLETE SET (43) 125.00 225.00
26 Field Generals (Eight NFL quarter-backs dressed in military garb) 5.00 10.00
27 Speedsters (Thirteen NFL players) 6.00 12.00
40 Steeler Pounder 10.00 20.00
Franco Harris
41 Atlanta Arsenal 3.00 6.00
Alfred Jackson
Steve Bartkowski
Alfred Jenkins
42 Texas Thunder 6.00 12.00
Ed(Too Tall) Jones
Harvey Martin
46 No Passing 1.25 3.00
Mike Haynes
Vann McElroy
Mike Davis
Lester Hayes
47 Lofton 2.00 5.00
James Lofton
59 Football 1.25 3.00
Lester Hayes
Louis Lipps
61 The Judge 1.25 3.00
Lester Hayes

1985 Nike

This oversized (slightly larger than 3x5 cards) multisport set was issued by Nike to promote athletic shoe sales. Although the set contains an attractive rookie-season card of Michael Jordan, the fairly plentiful supply has kept the market value quite affordable. Sets were distributed in shrinkwrapped form. The cards are unnumbered and are listed here in alphabetical order.

COMP.FACTORY SET (5)	50.00	125.00
COMPLETE SET (5)	30.00	75.00
3 James Lofton	.60	1.50

1984 Oakland Invaders Smokey

This five-card set features the Oakland Invaders of the USFL. The theme of the set is Forestry, i.e., Smokey the Bear is pictured on each card. The set commemorates the 40th birthday of Smokey Bear and is sponsored by the California Forestry Department in conjunction with the U.S. Forest Service. The cards measure approximately 5" by 7". The front features a color posed photo of the football player with Smokey Bear. The player's signature, jersey number, and a public service announcement concerning wildfire prevention occur below the picture. Biographical information is provided on the back.

COMPLETE SET (5)	30.00	60.00
1 Dupre Marshall	6.00	15.00
2 Gary Plummer	6.00	15.00
3 David Shaw	6.00	15.00
4 Kevin Shea	6.00	15.00
5 Smokey Bear (With all four players)	6.00	15.00

1985 Oakland Invaders Team Issue

These 5" by 7" black and white photos were issued by the Oakland Invaders USFL team. Each is blankbacked and features a player photo on the front with his name, position, and team name below the photo.

COMPLETE SET (15)	25.00	60.00
1 Ray Bentley	2.00	5.00
2 Fred Besana	1.50	4.00
3 Novo Dojovic	1.50	4.00
4 Anthony Carter	3.00	8.00
5 David Greenwood	1.50	4.00
6 Bobby Hebert	2.00	5.00
7 Derek Holloway	1.50	4.00
8 Jim Leonard	1.50	4.00
9 Ray Pinney	1.50	4.00
10 Gary Plummer	3.00	8.00
11 Charlie Sumner CO	1.50	4.00
12 Stan Talley	1.50	4.00
13 Ruben Vaughan	1.50	4.00
14 John Williams	2.00	5.00
15 Steve Wright	1.50	4.00

1992 Ocean Spray Frito Lay Posters

This set of posters, measuring 14 1/2"x 22" was sponsored by Ocean Spray and Frito Lay. Each includes a photo of one or more NFL stars as well as a brief list of all-time statistical leaders.

COMPLETE SET (5)	25.00	50.00
1 Bombs Away	7.50	15.00
Troy Aikman		
Steve Young		
Dan Marino		
2 Trench Warfare	6.00	12.00
Joe Montana		
3 Ground Assault	6.00	12.00
Barry Sanders		
4 Air Strike	6.00	12.00
Andre Rison		
Jerry Rice		
Michael Irvin		
5 Sackers	4.00	8.00

2006 Odessa Roughnecks IFL

COMPLETE SET (28)	7.50	15.00
1 Ezequiel Arevalo	.30	.75
2 Anthony Armstrong	.30	.75
3 Joel Babb	.30	.75
4 Arthur Berlanga	.30	.75
5 Jermaine Blakley	.30	.75
6 Andre Burns	.30	.75
7 Ahmad Childress	.30	.75
8 Marcus Dawson	.30	.75
9 Aaron Dunklin	.30	.75
10 Derin Graham	.30	.75
11 Dewayne Hogan	.30	.75
12 Tommy Jones	.30	.75
13 Clint McNutt	.30	.75
14 Jermaine Mills	.30	.75
15 Sean Parker	.30	.75
16 Jadhai Pickett	.30	.75
17 David Robertson	.30	.75
18 Joey Robinson	.30	.75
19 Anthony Sapa	.30	.75
20 Ryan Schneider	.30	.75
21 Dominique Steamer	.30	.75
22 Larry Thompson	.30	.75
23 Keith Turner	.30	.75
24 Sikoti Uipi	.30	.75
25 Chris Williams CO	.30	.75
26 Levron Williams	.30	.75
27 Digger - Mascot	.30	.75
28 Roughneck Dancers	.30	.75

2008 Odessa Roughnecks IFL

COMPLETE SET (15)	5.00	10.00
1 Rodney Allen	.30	.75
2 Leonard Bell	.30	.75
3 Jimmy Connor	.30	.75
4 Brandon Douglas	.30	.75
5 Shomari Earls	.30	.75
6 Peter Fields	.30	.75
7 Dennis Gile	.30	.75
8 Mike Glover	.30	.75
9 Sam Griffin	.30	.75
10 DeWayne Hogan	.30	.75
11 Michael Moore	.30	.75
12 Thomas Parker	.30	.75
13 Cameron Rodgers	.30	.75
14 Earl Stephens	.30	.75
15 Cover Card	.30	.75

1960 Oilers Matchbooks

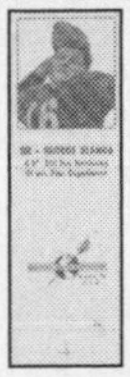

The 1960 Oilers Matchbook set was produced by Universal Match Corp. and features the team's logo and mascot on one side when flattened. The other side includes a small black and white player photo along with the Universal Match Corporation logo.

COMPLETE SET (10)	100.00	175.00
1 George Blanda	20.00	40.00
2 Johnny Carson	10.00	20.00
3 Doug Cline	10.00	20.00
4 Don Hitt	10.00	20.00
5 Mark Johnston	10.00	20.00
6 Dan Lanphear	10.00	20.00
7 Jacky Lee	10.00	20.00
8 Bill Mathis	10.00	20.00
9 Hogan Wharton	10.00	20.00
10 Bob White	10.00	20.00

1961 Oilers Jay Publishing

This 24-card set features (approximately) 5" by 7" black-and-white player photos. The photos show players in traditional poses with the quarterback preparing to throw, the runner heading downfield, and the defenseman ready for the tackle. These cards were packaged 12 to a packet and originally sold for 25 cents. The backs are blank. The cards are unnumbered and checklisted below in alphabetical order.

COMPLETE SET (24)	100.00	175.00
1 Dalva Allen	4.00	8.00
2 Tony Banfield	4.00	8.00
3 George Blanda	15.00	30.00
4 Billy Cannon	6.00	12.00
5 Doug Cline	4.00	8.00
6 Willard Dewveall	4.00	8.00
7 Mike Dukes	4.00	8.00
8 Don Floyd	4.00	8.00
9 Freddy Glick	4.00	8.00
10 Bill Groman	4.00	8.00
11 Charlie Hennigan	5.00	10.00
12 Ed Husmann	4.00	8.00
13 Al Jamison	4.00	8.00
14 Mark Johnston	4.00	8.00
15 Jacky Lee	4.00	8.00
16 Bob McLeod	4.00	8.00
17 Rich Michael	4.00	8.00
18 Dennit Morris	4.00	8.00
19 Jim Norton	4.00	8.00
20 Bob Schmidt	4.00	8.00
21 Dave Smith	4.00	8.00
22 Bob Talamini	4.00	8.00
23 Charley Tolar	4.00	8.00
24 Hogan Wharton	4.00	8.00

1965 Oilers Team Issue 8X10

These photos measure 8" by 10" and feature black-and-white player images with white borders. Most of the photos feature posed action shots. The player's position (spelled out completely), name, and team name are printed in the bottom white border in all caps. The backs are blank and the photos are unnumbered and checklisted below in alphabetical order.

COMPLETE SET (38)	200.00	350.00
1 Scott Appleton	6.00	12.00
2 Johnny Baker (diving pose)	6.00	12.00
3 Johnny Baker (cutting to his right)	6.00	12.00
4 Tony Banfield	6.00	12.00
5 Sonny Bishop	6.00	12.00
6A Sid Blanks (position: Halfback)	6.00	12.00
6B Sid Blanks (position: Offensive Halfback)	6.00	12.00
7 Danny Brabham	6.00	12.00
8 Ode Burrell	6.00	12.00
9 Doug Cline	6.00	12.00
10 Gary Cutsinger	6.00	12.00
11 Norm Evans	6.00	12.00
12 Don Floyd	6.00	12.00
13 Wayne Frazier	6.00	12.00
14 Willie Frazier	6.00	12.00
15 John Frongillo	6.00	12.00
16 Freddy Glick	6.00	12.00
17 Tom Goode	6.00	12.00
18 Jim Hayes	6.00	12.00
19 Charlie Hennigan	6.00	12.00
20 W.K. Hicks (looking to his right)	6.00	12.00
21 W.K. Hicks (looking to his left)	6.00	12.00
22 Ed Husmann	6.00	12.00
23 Bobby Jancik	6.00	12.00
24 Pete Jacques	6.00	12.00
25 Bobby Maples	6.00	12.00
26 Bud McFadin	6.00	12.00
27 Bob McLeod (catching pass from his right)	6.00	12.00
28 Bob McLeod (catching pass from his left)	6.00	12.00
29 Jim Norton	6.00	12.00
30 Larry Onesti	6.00	12.00
31 Jack Spikes	6.00	12.00
32 Walt Suggs	6.00	12.00
33 Bob Talamini	6.00	12.00
34 Charley Tolar	6.00	12.00
35 Don Trull (AFL logo showing on ball)	6.00	12.00
36 Don Trull (no AFL logo showing on ball)	6.00	12.00
37 Maxie Williams	6.00	12.00
38 John Wittenborn	6.00	12.00

1965 Oilers Team Issue Color

This team-issued set of 16 player photos measures approximately 7 3/4" by 9 3/4" and features color posed shots of players in uniform. Eight photos were grouped together as a set and packaged in plastic bags; set 1 and 2 each originally sold for 50 cents. The photos were printed on thin paper stock and white borders frame each picture. A facsimile autograph is inscribed across the pictures in black ink. The backs are blank. The photos are unnumbered and checklisted below in alphabetical order.

COMPLETE SET (16)	75.00	150.00
1 Scott Appleton	5.00	10.00
2 Tony Banfield	5.00	10.00
3 Sonny Bishop	5.00	10.00
4 George Blanda	15.00	30.00
5 Sid Blanks	5.00	10.00
6 Danny Brabham	5.00	10.00
7 Ode Burrell	5.00	10.00
8 Doug Cline	5.00	10.00
9 Don Floyd	5.00	10.00
10 Freddy Glick	5.00	10.00
11 Charlie Hennigan	5.00	10.00
12 Ed Husmann	5.00	10.00
13 Walt Suggs	5.00	10.00
14 Bob Talamini	5.00	10.00
15 Charley Tolar	5.00	10.00
16 Don Trull	5.00	10.00

1966 Oilers Team Issue 8X10

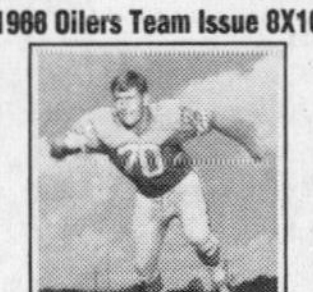

These photos measure 8" by 10" and feature black-and-white player images with white borders. Most of the photos feature posed action shots. The player's position (initials), name, and team name are printed in the bottom white border in all caps. The backs are blank and the photos are unnumbered and checklisted below in alphabetical order.

COMPLETE SET (5)	25.00	50.00
1 Scott Appleton	6.00	12.00
2 Ode Burrell	6.00	12.00
3 Jacky Lee	6.00	12.00
4 Walt Suggs	6.00	12.00
5 Charley Tolar	6.00	12.00

1967 Oilers Team Issue 5X7

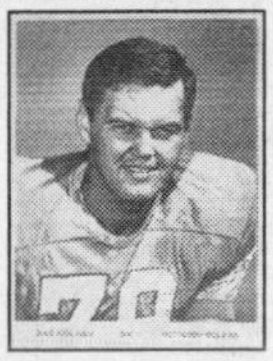

This 14-card set of the Houston Oilers measures approximately 5 1/8" by 7" and features black-and-white player photos. The backs are blank. The cards are unnumbered and checklisted below in alphabetical order.

COMPLETE SET (14)	50.00	100.00
1 Pete Barnes	4.00	8.00
2 Sonny Bishop	4.00	8.00
3 Ode Burrell	4.00	8.00
4 Ronnie Caveness	4.00	8.00
5 Joe Childress CO	4.00	8.00
6 Glen Ray Hines	4.00	8.00
7 Pat Holmes	4.00	8.00
8 Bobby Jancik	4.00	8.00
9 Pete Johns	4.00	8.00
10 Jim Norton	4.00	8.00
11 Willie Parker	4.00	8.00
12 Bob Poole	4.00	8.00
13 Alvin Reed	4.00	8.00
14 Olen Underwood	4.00	8.00

1968 Oilers Team Issue 5X7

These 5" by 7" black-and-white photos have a 3/8" white border and include a facsimile signature of the featured player. The player's name, position (initials), and team name are printed in the bottom white border. The backs are blank and the photos are unnumbered, thus checklisted below in alphabetical order.

COMPLETE SET (12)	40.00	80.00
1 Pete Beathard	5.00	10.00
2 Garland Boyette	4.00	8.00
3 Ode Burrell	4.00	8.00
4 Miller Farr	4.00	8.00
5 Hoyle Granger	4.00	8.00
6 Pat Holmes	4.00	8.00
7 Bobby Maples	4.00	8.00
8 Jim Norton	4.00	8.00
9 George Rice	4.00	8.00
10 Walt Suggs	4.00	8.00
11 Bob Talamini	4.00	8.00
12 George Webster	5.00	10.00

1968-69 Oilers Team Issue 8X10

These approximately 8" by 10" black-and-white photos have white borders. Most of the photos feature posed action shots. The player's name, position (initials), and team name are printed in the bottom white border in all caps. The coaches photos feature a slightly different text style. The backs are blank and the photos are unnumbered and checklisted below in alphabetical order.

COMPLETE SET (40)	150.00	300.00
1A Jim Beirne (position WR)	6.00	12.00
1B Jim Beirne position SE		
2 Elvin Bethea	7.50	15.00
3 Sonny Bishop	6.00	12.00
4 Garland Boyette	6.00	12.00
5 Ode Burrell	6.00	12.00
6 Fd Carrington	6.00	12.00
7 Joe Childress CO	6.00	12.00
8 Bob Davis QB	6.00	12.00
9 Hugh Devore CO	6.00	12.00
10 Tom Domres	6.00	12.00
11 F.A. Dry CO	6.00	12.00
12 Miller Farr	6.00	12.00
13 Charles Frazier	6.00	12.00
14 Hoyle Granger	6.00	12.00
15 Mac Haik (Portrait)	6.00	12.00
16 W.K. Hicks	6.00	12.00
17 Glen Ray Hines	6.00	12.00
18A Pat Holmes (position: DE)	6.00	12.00
18B Pat Holmes (position: DT)	6.00	12.00
19 Roy Hopkins	6.00	12.00
20 Wally Lemm CO	6.00	12.00
21 Jim LeMoine	6.00	12.00
22 Bobby Maples	6.00	12.00
23 Richard Marshall	6.00	12.00
24 Bud McFadin CO	6.00	12.00
25 Zeke Moore	6.00	12.00
26 Willie Parker DT	6.00	12.00
27 Johnny Peacock	6.00	12.00
28 Fran Polsfoot CO	6.00	12.00
29 Ron Pritchard (Preparing to fend off blocker)	6.00	12.00
30 Alvin Reed	6.00	12.00
31 Tom Regner	6.00	12.00
32 George Rice	6.00	12.00
33 Bob Robertson	6.00	12.00
34 Walt Suggs	6.00	12.00
35 Don Trull	6.00	12.00
36 Olen Underwood	6.00	12.00
37 Loyd Wainscott	6.00	12.00
38 Wayne Walker	7.50	15.00
39 George Webster	7.50	15.00
40 Glenn Woods	6.00	12.00

1969 Oilers Postcards

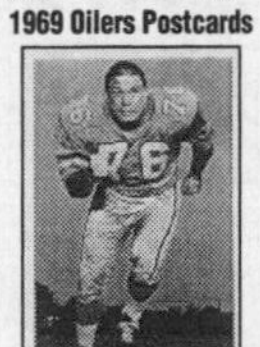

These postcards were issued in the late 1960s or possibly early 1970s. Each features a black and white photo of an Oilers player on the front along with his name printed below the photo and to the left. The backs feature a postcard format with most also including a list of Oiler's souvenir items that could be ordered from the team. The postcards measure roughly 3 1/4" by 5 1/2." Any additions to this list are appreciated.

COMPLETE SET (6)	20.00	40.00
1 Jim Beirne	4.00	8.00
2 Woody Campbell	4.00	8.00
3 Alvin Reed	4.00	8.00
4 Tom Regner	4.00	8.00
5 Walt Suggs	4.00	8.00
6 George Webster	5.00	10.00

1971 Oilers Team Issue 4X5

This 23 card set measures approximately 4" by 5 1/2" and features black-and-white, close-up, player photos, bordered in white and printed on a textured paper stock. The team name appears at the top between an Oilers helmet and the NFL logo, while the player's name and position are printed in the bottom border. The cards are unnumbered and checklisted below in alphabetical order. The set's date is defined by the fact that Willie Alexander, Ron Billingsley, Ken Burrough, Lynn Dickey, Robert Holmes, Dan Pastorini, Floyd Rice, Mike Tilleman's first year with the Houston Oilers was 1971, and Charlie Johnson's last year with the Oilers was 1971.

COMPLETE SET (23)	75.00	150.00
1 Willie Alexander	4.00	8.00
2 Jim Beirne	4.00	8.00
3 Elvin Bethea	6.00	12.00
4 Ron Billingsley	4.00	8.00
5 Garland Boyette	4.00	8.00
6 Leo Brooks	4.00	8.00
7 Ken Burrough	5.00	10.00
8 Woody Campbell	4.00	8.00
9 Lynn Dickey	5.00	10.00
10 Elbert Drungo	4.00	8.00
11 Pat Holmes	4.00	8.00
12 Robert Holmes	4.00	8.00
13 Ken Houston	6.00	12.00
14 Charley Johnson	5.00	10.00
15 Charlie Joiner	10.00	20.00
16 Zeke Moore	4.00	8.00
17 Mark Moseley	5.00	10.00
18 Dan Pastorini	5.00	10.00
19 Alvin Reed	4.00	8.00
20 Tom Regner	4.00	8.00
21 Floyd Rice	4.00	8.00
22 Mike Tilleman	4.00	8.00
23 George Webster	5.00	10.00

1971 Oilers Team Issue 5X7

This set of the Houston Oilers measures approximately 5" by 7" and features borderless black-and-white player photos. The photos are very similar to the 1972 release but can be differentiated by the slight difference in the positioning of the player's name and team name below the photo. The 1972 photos feature both names much closer to the photos edge than the 1971 set. The cards are unnumbered and checklisted below in alphabetical order.

COMPLETE SET (15)	50.00	100.00
1 Allen Aldridge	4.00	8.00
2 Jim Beirne	4.00	8.00
3 Elvin Bethea	5.00	10.00
4 Ron Billingsley (no moustache in photo)	4.00	8.00
5 Ken Burrough	5.00	10.00
6 John Charles	4.00	8.00
7 Joe Dawkins	4.00	8.00
8 Calvin Fox	4.00	8.00
9 Johnny Gonzalez Eq.Mgr.	4.00	8.00
10 Cleo Johnson	4.00	8.00
11 Spike Jones	4.00	8.00
12 Alvin Reed	4.00	8.00
13 Floyd Rice	4.00	8.00
14 Mike Tilleman (half of jersey number shown)	4.00	8.00
15 George Webster (facing slightly right)	5.00	10.00

1972 Oilers Team Issue 5X7

This set of the Houston Oilers measures approximately 5" by 7" and features borderless black-and-white player photos. The backs are blank. The cards are unnumbered and checklisted below in alphabetical order. The photos are very similar to the 1971 release but can be differentiated by the slight difference in the positioning of player's name and team name below the photo. The 1972 photos feature both names much closer to the photos edge than the 1971 set

COMPLETE SET (12)	40.00	80.00
1 Ron Billingsley (moustache in photo)	4.00	8.00
2 Garland Boyette	4.00	8.00
3 Levert Carr	4.00	8.00
4 Walter Highsmith	4.00	8.00
5 Al Johnson	4.00	8.00
6 Benny Johnson	4.00	8.00
7 Guy Murdock	4.00	8.00
8 Willie Rodgers	4.00	8.00
9 Ron Saul	4.00	8.00
10 Mike Tilleman (only 1/4 of jersey number shown)	4.00	8.00
11 Ward Walsh	4.00	8.00
12 George Webster (facing straight)	5.00	10.00

1973 Oilers McDonald's

This set of photos was sponsored by McDonald's. Each photo measures approximately 8" by 10" and features a posed color close-up photo bordered in white. The player's name and team name are printed in black in the bottom white border. The top portion of the back has biographical information, career summary, and career statistics. The bottom portion carries the Oilers 1973 game schedule. The photos are unnumbered and are checklisted below alphabetically.

COMPLETE SET (4)	25.00	50.00
1 Bill Curry	5.00	10.00
2 John Matuszak	7.50	15.00
3 Zeke Moore	5.00	10.00
4 Dan Pastorini	7.50	15.00

1973 Oilers Team Issue

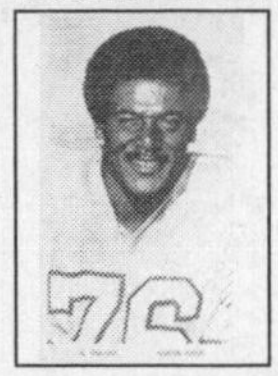

This 17-card set of the Houston Oilers measures approximately 5" by 8" and features black-and-white player photos with a white border. The backs are blank. The cards are unnumbered and checklisted below in alphabetical order.

COMPLETE SET (17)	50.00	100.00
1 Mack Alston	4.00	8.00
2 Bob Atkins	4.00	8.00
3 Skip Butler	4.00	8.00
4 Al Cowlings	4.00	8.00
5 Lynn Dickey	5.00	10.00
6 Mike Fanucci	4.00	8.00
7 Edd Hargett	4.00	8.00
8 Lewis Jolley	4.00	8.00
9 Clifton McNeil	4.00	8.00
10 Ralph Miller	4.00	8.00
11 Zeke Moore	4.00	8.00
12 Dave Parks	4.00	8.00
13 Willie Rodgers	4.00	8.00
14 Greg Sampson	4.00	8.00
15 Finn Seemann	4.00	8.00
16 Jeff Severson	4.00	8.00
17 Fred Willis	4.00	8.00

1974 Oilers Team Issue

These photos measure approximately 5" by 7" and contain black and white player shots on heavy paper stock. Each carries a facsimile signature and was produced around 1974. These cardbacks are blank. The Bethea, Bingham, Gresham, and Smith card are smaller in size than the rest of the series (approximately 5" by 6 1/2") and could possibly have been issued in another year.

COMPLETE SET (15)	50.00	100.00
1 Mack Alston	4.00	8.00
2 George Amundson	4.00	8.00
3 Elvin Bethea	6.00	12.00
4 Gregg Bingham UER	4.00	8.00
5 Ken Burrough	5.00	10.00
6 Skip Butler	4.00	8.00
7 Al Cowlings	4.00	8.00
8 Lynn Dickey	5.00	10.00
9 Bob Gresham	4.00	8.00
10 Zeke Moore	4.00	8.00
11 Billy Parks	4.00	8.00
12 Dan Pastorini	5.00	10.00
13 Greg Sampson	4.00	8.00
14 Jeff Severson	4.00	8.00
15 Tody Smith	4.00	8.00

1975 Oilers Team Issue

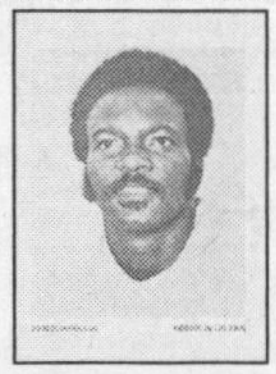

These photos measure approximately 5" by 7" and contain black and white player shots printed on heavy paper stock. Unlike the 1974 issue, these photos do not carry a facsimile signature. The cardbacks are blank and some of the photos are cropped smaller than others.

COMPLETE SET (12)	50.00	100.00
1 Willie Alexander	4.00	8.00
2 Elvin Bethea	6.00	12.00
3 Ken Burrough	5.00	10.00
4 Lynn Dickey	5.00	10.00
5 Fred Hoaglin	4.00	8.00
6 Billy Johnson	6.00	12.00
7 Steve Kiner	4.00	8.00
8 Zeke Moore	4.00	8.00
9 Guy Roberts	4.00	8.00
10 Willie Rodgers	4.00	8.00
11 Ted Washington	4.00	8.00
12 Fred Willis	4.00	8.00

1975 Oilers Team Sheets

This set consists of three 8" by 10" sheets that display a group of black-and-white player photos on each. The player's name is printed below each photo and the backs are blank. The sheets are unnumbered and checklisted below alphabetically according to the player featured in the upper left corner.

COMPLETE SET (3)	10.00	20.00
1 Bud Adams	4.00	8.00
Bum Phillips		
Ron Saul		
Greg Sampson		
Mack Alston		
Skip Butler		
Curley Culp		
2 Duane Benson	4.00	8.00
Ed Fischer		
Steve Kiner		
Gregg Bingham		
Kevin Hunt		
Zeke Moore		
Bob Atkins		
Elbert Drungo		
Dan Pastorini		
Ted Washington		
3 Fred Hoaglin	3.00	6.00
Ken Burrough		
Billy Johnson		
Tody Smith		
C.L. Whittington		
Lynn Dickey		
Billy Parks		
Ronnie Coleman		
Robert Brazille		
Don Hardeman		

1980 Oilers Police

The 14-card set of the 1980 Houston Oilers is unnumbered and checklist below in alphabetical order. The cards measure approximately 2 5/8" by 4 1/8". The Kiwanis Club, the local law enforcement agency, and the Houston Oilers sponsored this set. The backs feature "Oilers Tips" and a Kiwanis logo. The fronts feature logos of the Kiwanis and the City of Houston.

COMPLETE SET (14)	10.00	20.00
1 Gregg Bingham	.40	1.00
2 Robert Brazile	.50	1.25
3 Ken Burrough	.60	1.50
4 Rob Carpenter	.50	1.25
5 Ronnie Coleman	.40	1.00
6 Curley Culp	.50	1.25
7 Carter Hartwig	.40	1.00
8 Billy Johnson	.60	1.50
9 Carl Mauck	.40	1.00
10 Gifford Nielsen	.40	1.00
11 Cliff Parsley	.40	1.00
12 Bum Phillips CO	.75	2.00
13 Mike Renfro	.40	1.00
14 Ken Stabler	4.00	8.00

1985 Oklahoma Outlaws Team Sheets

These 8" by 10" sheets were issued by the Oklahoma Outlaws primarily to the media for use as player images for print. Each features 8-players or coaches with the player's jersey number, name, and position beneath his picture. The sheets are blankbacked and unnumbered.

COMPLETE SET (6)	12.00	30.00
1 Selwyn Drain	2.50	6.00
Kelvin Middleton		
Lance Shields		
Fred Sims		
Reggie Brown		
Carl Allen		
Kevin Long		
Ernest Anderson		
2 John Gillen	2.00	5.00
Ed Smith		
Bruce Gheesling		
Tom Thayer		
Don Hickman		
Mark Buben		
Dave Tipton		
John Stadnik		
3 Bruce Laird	2.00	5.00
Allan Clark		
Mack Boatner		
Daryl Goodlow		
Mike Katolin		
Gerry Sullivan		
Jimmie Carter		
Vic Koenning		
4 Johnny Lewis	2.00	5.00
Kit Lathrop		
Karl Lorch		
Alvin Powell		
John Mistler		
Al Williams		
Ron Wheeler		
Motrandy Taylor		
5 W.R. Tatham Sr. CO	2.00	5.00
W.R. Tatham Jr. CO		
Frank Kush CO		
Roger Theder CO		
Deek Pollard CCO		
Mike Westhoff CO		
Ben Hawkins CO		
Skip Stress CO		
6 John Teerlinck	3.00	8.00
Tim Mills		
Lonnie Harris		
Case DeBruijn		
Alan Risher		
Luis Zendejas		
Doug Williams		
Rick Johnson		

2001 Oklahoma Wranglers AFL

These cards were released in 2001 by the Oklahoma Wranglers of the Arena Football League and sponsored by KWTV News. The cards are printed in color on the front and back and include the year of issue in the lower right hand corner of the cardfronts.

COMPLETE SET (22)	7.50	15.00
1 Kusanti Abdul-Salaam	.40	1.00
2 Britt Bowen	.40	1.00
3 Tom Briggs	.40	1.00
4 Wes Caswell	.40	1.00
5 Antonio Chandler	.40	1.00
6 Lamart Cooper	.50	1.25
7 Demetrius Crowder	.40	1.00
8 Akaba Delaney	.40	1.00
9 Barry Dillard	.40	1.00
10 Shawn Foreman	.40	1.00
11 Brian Goolsby	.40	1.00
12 Lindsay Hassell	.40	1.00
13 Josh Heskew	.40	1.00
14 Carlos Johnson	.40	1.00
15 Ron Lopez	.75	2.00
16 Mike Mari	.40	1.00
17 Travis McDonald	.40	1.00
18 Bobby McGowins	.40	1.00
19 Eric Miller	.40	1.00
20 Tyrone Peace	.40	1.00
21 Joe Phears	.50	1.25
(No Photo on Front)		
22 Chuck Reed	.40	1.00

2008 Omaha Beef UIF

COMPLETE SET (30)	6.00	12.00
1 Javon Bell	.20	.50
2 Reicko Jones	.20	.50
3 James McNear	.20	.50
4 Brent Hafford	.20	.50
5 Chris Eads	.20	.50
6 David Horne	.20	.50
7 Kyle Whitehurst	.20	.50
8 Ken Horton	.20	.50
9 Ricky Lebeda	.20	.50
10 Dustin Creager	.20	.50
11 Chad Schmigel	.20	.50
12 Jamar Day	.20	.50
13 Diezeas Calbert	.20	.50
14 R.J. Rollins	.20	.50
15 James Poynter	.20	.50
16 Dan Potmesil	.20	.50
17 Ron Jackson	.20	.50
18 Robert Moore	.20	.50
19 Mike Nizzi	.20	.50
20 Blake Fuchtman	.20	.50
21 James Head	.20	.50
22 Colin Bryant	.20	.50
23 Demoine Adams	.20	.50
24 Marques Salmond	.20	.50
25 Steve Martin CO	.20	.50
26 James Kerwin Asst. CO	.20	.50
27 Tony Veland Def. Coor.	.20	.50
28 Tommie Williams Off.Coor.	.20	.50
29 Rival Game	.20	.50
30 Schedule CL	.20	.50

2010 Omaha Nighthawks UFL

COMPLETE SET (10)	15.00	30.00
1 Justin Brantly	1.00	2.50
2 Dusty Dvoracek	1.00	2.50
3 Robert Ferguson	1.50	4.00
4 George Foster	1.00	2.50
5 Jeff Garcia	2.50	6.00
6 Ahman Green	2.00	5.00
7 Cato June	1.50	4.00
8 Jay Moore	1.00	2.50
9 Gary Stills	1.00	2.50
10 Shaud Williams	1.00	2.50

1979 Open Pantry

This set is an unnumbered, 12-card issue featuring players from Milwaukee area professional sports teams with five Brewers baseball (1-5), five Bucks basketball (6-10), and two Packers football (11-12). Cards are black and white with red trim and measure approximately 5" by 6". Cards were sponsored by Open Pantry, Lake to Lake, and MACC (Milwaukee Athletes against Childhood Cancer). The cards are unnumbered and hence are listed and numbered below alphabetically within sport.

COMPLETE SET (12)	12.50	25.00
11 Rich McGeorge	1.00	2.00
12 Steve Wagner	1.00	2.00

1994 Orlando Predators AFL

The Orlando Predators of the Arena Football League issued this set for distribution through their consession stands and gift shop. Each card is unnumbered and measures the standard size. Reportedly, the set was limited to a production run of 2000.

COMPLETE SET (27)	6.00	12.00
1 Ben Bennett	.30	.75
2 Henry Brown	.20	.50
3 Webbie Burnett	.20	.50
4 Jorge Cimadevilla	.20	.50
5 Bernard Clark	.20	.50
6 Wayne Dickson	.20	.50
7 Eric Drakes	.20	.50
8 Chris Ford	.20	.50
9 Victor Hall	.20	.50
10 Paul McGowan	.20	.50
11 Perry Moss CO	.30	.75
12 Jerry Odom	.20	.50
13 Billy Owens WR	.20	.50
14 Marshall Roberts	.20	.50
15 Durwood Roquemore	.20	.50
16 Rusty Russell DL	.20	.50
17 Tony Scott	.20	.50
18 Ricky Shaw	.20	.50
19 Alex Shell	.20	.50
20 Bill Stewart	.20	.50
21 Duke Tobin	.20	.50
22 Barry Wagner	.40	1.00
23 Jackie Walker	.20	.50
24 Herkie Walls	.20	.50
25 Isaac Williams	.20	.50
26 Coaches	.30	.75
27 The Klaw (mascot)	.20	.50

1998 Orlando Predators AFL

This set was released by the Predators in sealed factory set form. Each card includes a colorful border surrounding the player photo on the front with the players' name and jersey number above the image.

COMPLETE SET (28)	6.00	15.00
1 Chris Barber	.20	.50
2 Webbie Burnett	.20	.50
3 John Clark	.20	.50
4 David Cool	.20	.50
5 Bret Cooper	.20	.50
6 Tommy Dorsey	.20	.50
7 Eric Drakes	.20	.50
8 Corris Ervin	.20	.50
9 Kevin Gaines	.20	.50
10 Robert Gordon	.20	.50
11 Bill Hall	.20	.50
12 Victor Hall	.20	.50
13 Rick Hamilton	.30	.75
14 Kelvin Ingram	.20	.50
15 Chad Johnston	.20	.50
16 Bruce LaSane	.20	.50
17 Ty Law	.20	.50
18 Reggie Lee	.20	.50
James Crockett		
19 Damon Mason	.20	.50
20 Connell Maynor	.20	.50
21 Rich McKenzie	.20	.50
22 Jerry Odom	.20	.50
23 Pat O'Hara	.30	.75
24 Howard Smothers	.20	.50
25 Connell Spain	.20	.50
26 Matt Storm	.20	.50
27 Barry Wagner	.50	1.25
28 Jay Gruden CO	.50	1.25

1998 Orlando Predators AFL Champions

COMPLETE SET (27)	6.00	15.00
1 Connell Maynor	.20	.50
2 Chris Barber	.20	.50
3 Bruce Lasane	.20	.50
4 Bret Cooper	.20	.50
5 Bill Hall	.20	.50
6 Barry Wagner	.50	1.25
7 Howard Smothers	.20	.50
8 Eric Drakes	.20	.50
9 David Cool	.20	.50
10 Damon Mason	.20	.50
11 Corris Ervin	.20	.50
12 Connell Spain	.20	.50
13 Pat O'Hara	.30	.75
14 Matt Storm	.20	.50
15 Kevin Gaines	.20	.50
16 Kenny McEntyre	.20	.50
17 Kelvin Ingram	.20	.50
18 Jay Gruden CO	.50	1.25
19 Ty Law	.20	.50
20 Tommy Dorsey	.20	.50
21 Robert Gordon	.20	.50
22 Rick Hamilton	.30	.75
23 Rich McKenzie	.20	.50
24 Reggie Lee	.20	.50
25 Webbie Burnett	.20	.50
26 Victor Hall	.20	.50
27 Cover Card CL	.20	.50

1999 Orlando Predators AFL

This set was produced by Mercury Printers Publications and released by the Predators in sealed factory set form. Each card includes a colorful border surrounding the player photo on the front with a bio on the back.

COMPLETE SET (27)	6.00	15.00
1 Keif Bryant	.20	.50
2 Webbie Burnett	.20	.50
3 William Carr	.20	.50
4 B.J. Cohen	.20	.50
5 David Cool	.20	.50
6 Bret Cooper	.20	.50
7 Jeff Cothran	.20	.50
8 Cliff Dell	.30	.75
9 Tommy Dorsey	.20	.50
10 Eric Drakes	.20	.50
11 Kevin Gaines	.20	.50
12 Jay Gruden CO	.50	1.25
13 Bill Hall	.20	.50
14 Victor Hall	.20	.50
15 Rick Hamilton	.30	.75
16 Kevin Johnson OL	.20	.50
17 Ty Law WR	.20	.50
18 Reggie Lee	.20	.50
19 Damon Mason	.20	.50
20 Connell Maynor	.20	.50
21 Kenny McEntyre	.20	.50
22 Rich McKenzie	.20	.50
23 Browning Nagle	.50	1.25
24 Pat O'Hara	.30	.75
25 Matt Storm	.20	.50
26 Barry Wagner	.50	1.25
27 Antwuan Wyatt	.20	.50

2000 Orlando Predators AFL

COMPLETE SET (28)	10.00	20.00
1 Ernest Allen	.40	1.00
2 Braniff Bonaventure	.40	1.00
3 Rodney Brown	.40	1.00
4 Webbie Burnett	.40	1.00
5 B.J. Cohen	.40	1.00
6 David Cool	.40	1.00
7 Bret Cooper	.40	1.00
8 Clif Dell	.40	1.00
9 Tommy Dorsey	.40	1.00
10 Joe Douglass	.40	1.00
11 Curtis Eason	.40	1.00
12 Jay Gruden CO	.60	1.50
13 Bill Hall	.40	1.00
14 Rick Hamilton	.40	1.00
15 Ty Law	.40	1.00
16 Reggie Lee	.40	1.00
17 Damon Mason	.40	1.00
18 Dedric Mathis	.40	1.00
19 Connell Maynor	.40	1.00
20 Kenny McEntyre	.40	1.00
21 Rich McKenzie	.40	1.00
22 Mark Nonsant	.40	1.00
23 Pat O'Hara	.60	1.50
24 Mike Osuna	.40	1.00
25 Frederick Ray	.40	1.00
26 Matt Storm	.40	1.00
27 Team Card	.40	1.00

1938-42 Overland All American Roll Candy Wrappers

These unnumbered candy wrappers measure roughly 5" by 5 1/4" and were issued over a period of time in the late 1930's and early 1940's. A drawing of the player is at the top of the wrapper with his name, team name, and a short biography below. All players known thus far are post college athletes with some playing in the NFL and some on the military teams which were so popular during World War II. The product name and price "All American Football Roll 1-cent" appears at the bottom with the Overland Candy Corporation mentioned below that. The backs are blank and the wrappers are nearly always found with multiple creases. Any additions to this list are appreciated.

1 Sammy Baugh	800.00	1,200.00
2 Bill DeCorrevont	350.00	600.00
3 Rudy Mucha	350.00	600.00
4 Bruce Smith	500.00	800.00

1984 Pacific Legends

This 30-card set (produced by Pacific Trading Cards in 1984) has a yellowish tone to the front of the cards, similar to Cramer's Baseball Legends, but is entitled "Football Legends." The cards measure approximately 2 1/2" by 3 1/2". The set features prominent individuals who played football at universities in the Pac 10 conference (and its predecessors).

COMPLETE SET (30)	30.00	60.00
1 O.J. Simpson	2.50	6.00
2 Mike Garrett	.75	2.00
3 Pop Warner CO	.75	2.00
4 Bob Schloredt	.60	1.50
5 Pat Haden	.75	2.00
6 Ernie Nevers	.75	2.00
7 Jackie Robinson	2.50	6.00
8 Arnie Weinmeister	.75	2.00
9 Gary Beban	1.50	4.00
10 Jim Plunkett	1.50	4.00
11 Bobby Grayson	.60	1.50
12 Craig Morton	.75	2.00
13 Ben Davidson	.75	2.00
14 Jim Hardy	.60	1.50
15 Vern Burke	.60	1.50
16 Hugh McElhenny	1.00	2.50
17 John Wayne	2.50	6.00
18 Ricky Bell UER	.75	2.00
Name spelled Rickey on both sides		
19 George Wildcat Wilson	.60	1.50
20 Bob Waterfield	1.00	2.50
21 Charlie Mitchell	.60	1.50
22 Donn Moomaw	.60	1.50
23 Don Heinrich	.60	1.50
24 Terry Baker	1.50	4.00
25 Jack Thompson	.75	2.00
26 Charles White	1.00	2.50
27 Frank Gifford	1.50	4.00
28 Lynn Swann	3.00	8.00
29 Brick Muller	.60	1.50
30 Ron Yary	.75	2.00

1989 Pacific Steve Largent

The 1989 Pacific Trading Cards Steve Largent set contains 110 standard-size cards, 85 of which are numbered. The numbered cards have silver borders on the fronts with photos of various career highlights; some are horizontally oriented, others are vertically oriented. The backs all are horizontally oriented and have light blue borders with information about the highlight shown on the front. The other 25 unnumbered cards are actually puzzle pieces which form a 12 1/2" by 17 1/2" poster of Largent in action. The cards were distributed as factory sets and in ten-card wax packs.

COMPLETE SET (110)	10.00	25.00
COMMON CARD (1-85)	.08	.25
1 Title Card	.30	.75
(checklist 1-42 on back)		
9 Coach Patera and	.15	.40
Coach Jerry Rhome		
10 Rookie 1976	.30	.75
13 First Team All-Rookie	.15	.40
16 Captains Largent and	.15	.40
Norm Evans		
19 Jerry Rhome and Largent	.30	.75
22 Zorn Connection	.15	.40
23 Steve Largent and	.15	.40
Jim Zorn (in jeans)		
25 Seahawks MVP 1981	.15	.40
28 Chuck Knox Head Coach	.15	.40
31 Tilley and Largent UER	.30	.75
Two Greats From Tulsa		
(card back refers to		
Howard Twilley)		
42 Seattle Sports Star	.15	.40
of the Year		
45 Steve and Eugene	.15	.40
Robinson		
51 Captains Lane, Brown,	.15	.40
and Largent		
53 Krieg Connection	.15	.40
55 NFL All-Time Leading	.15	.40
Receiver		
57 Steve and Coach Knox	.15	.40
58 1987 Seahawks MVP	.15	.40
59 Largent at Quarterback	.30	.75
60 NFL All-Time Great	.15	.40
61 Travelers' NFL Man of	.15	.40
the Year 1988		
63 Holding for Norm	.15	.40
Johnson		
67 Agee, Largent, and	.15	.40
Paul Skansi		
70 Pro Bowl Greats,	1.25	3.00
Largent and John Elway		
74 Jim Zorn and Largent	.15	.40
in Hawaii		
75 Mr. Seahawk	.15	.40
76 Sets NFL Career	.15	.40
Yardage Record		
77 Two of the Greatest	.30	.75
(with Charlie Joiner)		
78 Steve Largent,	.30	.75
Jerry Rhome, and		
Charlie Joiner		
79 NFL All-Time Leader	.15	.40
in Receptions		
80 NFL All-Time Leader	.15	.40
in Consecutive		
Game Receptions		
82 NFL All-Time Leader	.15	.40
1000 Yard Seasons		
83 First Recipient of the	.30	.75
Bart Starr Trophy		
84 Steve Largent,	.15	.40
Wide Receiver		
85 Future Hall of Famer	.40	1.00

1991 Pacific Prototypes

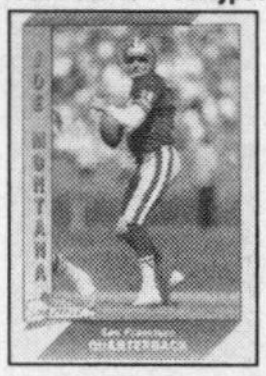

This five-card standard-size set was sent out by Pacific Trading Cards to prospective dealers prior to the general release of their debut set of NFL football cards. The cards are styled almost exactly like the regular issue Pacific cards that followed shortly thereafter. These prototype cards are distinguished from the regular issue cards by their different card numbers and the presence of zeroes for the stat totals on the prototype card backs. The cards are numbered on the back. The production run reportedly was approximately 5,000 sets, and these sets were distributed to dealers in the Pacific network with the rest being used as sales samples.

COMPLETE SET (5)	60.00	100.00
1 Joe Montana	25.00	40.00
(Different border		
from regular card)		
32 Bo Jackson	4.00	8.00
66 Eric Metcalf	1.60	4.00
100 Barry Sanders	25.00	40.00
232 Troy Aikman	15.00	25.00

1991 Pacific

This 660-card standard size set was the first full football set issued by Pacific Trading Cards. The cards were issued in two series of 550 and 110 cards with packs containing 10 cards. Factory sets were also produced for each series. The cards feature a full-color glossy front with the name on the left hand side of the card. Rookie Cards include Mike Croel, Lawrence Dawsey, Craig Erickson (his only Rookie Card), Ricky Ervins, Brett Favre, Jeff Graham, Mark Higgs, Randal Hill, Michael Jackson, Herman Moore, Erric Pegram, Mike Pritchard, Leonard Russell and Harvey Williams.

COMPLETE SET (660)	7.50	15.00
COMP.SERIES 1 (550)	4.00	8.00
COMP.FACT.SER.1 (550)	5.00	10.00
COMP.SERIES 2 (110)	4.00	8.00
COMP.FACT.SER.2 (110)	6.00	12.00
COMP.CHECKLIST SET (5)	7.50	15.00
1 Deion Sanders	.15	.40
2 Steve Broussard	.01	.05
3 Aundray Bruce	.01	.05
4 Rick Bryan	.01	.05
5 John Rade	.01	.05
6 Scott Case	.01	.05
7 Tony Casillas	.01	.05
8 Shawn Collins	.01	.05
9 Darion Conner	.01	.05
10 Tory Epps	.01	.05
11 Bill Fralic	.01	.05
12 Mike Gann	.01	.05
13 Tim Green UER	.01	.05
(Listed as DT instead of DE)		
14 Chris Hinton	.01	.05
15 Houston Hoover UER	.01	.05
(misspelled Deon on back)		
16 Chris Miller	.02	.10
17 Andre Rison	.02	.10
18 Mike Rozier	.01	.05
19 Jessie Tuggle	.01	.05
20 Don Beebe	.01	.05
21 Ray Bentley	.01	.05
22 Shane Conlan	.01	.05
23 Kent Hull	.01	.05
24 Mark Kelso	.01	.05
25 James Lofton UER	.02	.10
(Photo on front is Flip Johnson)		
26 Scott Norwood	.01	.05
27 Andre Reed	.02	.10
28 Leonard Smith	.01	.05
29 Bruce Smith	.08	.25
30 Leon Seals	.01	.05
31 Darryl Talley	.01	.05
32 Steve Tasker	.02	.10
33 Thurman Thomas	.08	.25
34 James Williams	.01	.05
35 Will Wolford	.01	.05
36 Frank Reich	.02	.10
37 Jeff Wright RC	.01	.05
38 Neal Anderson	.02	.10
39 Trace Armstrong	.01	.05
40 Johnny Bailey UER	.01	.05
(Gained 5320 yards in		
college, should be 6320)		
41 Mark Bortz UER	.01	.05
(misspelled Johnny on back)		
42 Cap Boso RC	.01	.05
43 Kevin Butler	.01	.05
44 Mark Carrier DB	.02	.10
45 Jim Covert	.01	.05
46 Wendell Davis	.01	.05
47 Richard Dent	.02	.10
48 Shaun Gayle	.01	.05
49 Jim Harbaugh	.08	.25
50 Jay Hilgenberg	.01	.05
51 Brad Muster	.01	.05
52 William Perry	.02	.10
53 Mike Singletary UER	.02	.10
54 Peter Tom Willis	.01	.05
55 Donnell Woolford	.01	.05
56 Steve McMichael	.02	.10
57 Eric Ball	.01	.05
58 Lewis Billups	.01	.05
59 Jim Breech	.01	.05
60 James Brooks	.02	.10
61 Eddie Brown	.01	.05
62 Rickey Dixon	.01	.05
63 Boomer Esiason	.02	.10
64 James Francis	.01	.05
65 David Fulcher	.01	.05
66 David Grant	.01	.05
67 Harold Green UER	.01	.05
(Misplaced apostrophe in Gamecocks)		
68 Rodney Holman	.01	.05
69 Stanford Jennings	.01	.05
70A Tim Krumrie ERR	.20	.50
(Misspelled Krumprie on front)		
70B Tim Krumrie COR	.10	.30
71 Tim McGee	.01	.05
72 Anthony Munoz	.02	.10
73 Mitchell Price RC	.01	.05
74 Eric Thomas	.01	.05
75 Ickey Woods	.01	.05
76 Mike Baab	.01	.05
77 Thane Gash	.01	.05
78 David Grayson	.01	.05
79 Mike Johnson	.01	.05
80 Reggie Langhorne	.01	.05
81 Kevin Mack	.01	.05
82 Clay Matthews	.02	.10
83A Eric Metcalf ERR	.20	.50
(reads "Terry is the son of Terry")		
83B Eric Metcalf COR	.10	.30
(reads "Eric is the son of Terry")		
84 Frank Minnifield	.01	.05
85 Mike Oliphant	.01	.05
86 Mike Pagel	.01	.05
87 John Talley	.01	.05
88 Lawyer Tillman	.01	.05
89 Gregg Rakoczy UER	.01	.05
(Misspelled Greg on both sides)		
90 Bryan Wagner	.01	.05
91 Rob Burnett RC	.02	.10
92 Tommie Agee	.01	.05
93 Troy Aikman UER	.30	.75
(4328 yards is career		
total not season; text		
has him breaking passing		
record which is not true)		
94A Bill Bates ERR	.20	.50
(Black line on cardfront)		
94B Bill Bates COR	.10	.30
(No black line on front)		
95 Jack Del Rio	.02	.10
96 Issiac Holt UER	.01	.05
(Photo on back Timmy Newsome)		
97 Michael Irvin	.08	.25
98 Jim Jeffcoat UER	.01	.05
(red line has Jeff on back)		
99 Jimmie Jones	.01	.05
100 Kelvin Martin	.01	.05
101 Nate Newton	.02	.10
102 Danny Noonan	.01	.05
103 Ken Norton Jr.	.02	.10
104 Jay Novacek	.08	.25
105 Mike Saxon	.01	.05
106 Derrick Shepard	.01	.05
107 Emmitt Smith	1.00	2.50
108 Daniel Stubbs	.01	.05
109 Tony Tolbert	.01	.05
110 Alexander Wright	.01	.05
111 Steve Atwater	.01	.05
112 Melvin Bratton	.01	.05
113 Tyrone Braxton UER	.01	.05
(Went to North Dakota		
State, not South Dakota)		
114 Alphonso Carreker	.01	.05
115 John Elway	.50	1.25
116 Simon Fletcher	.01	.05
117 Bobby Humphrey	.01	.05
118 Mark Jackson	.01	.05
119 Vance Johnson	.01	.05
120 Greg Kragen UER	.01	.05
(Recovered 20 fumbles		
in '89, yet 11 in career)		
121 Karl Mecklenburg UER	.01	.05
(Misspelled Mecklenberg on front)		
122A Orson Mobley ERR	.20	.50
(Misspelled Orsen)		
122B Orson Mobley COR	.02	.10
123 Alton Montgomery	.01	.05
124 Ricky Nattiel	.01	.05
125 Steve Sewell	.01	.05
126 Shannon Sharpe	.20	.50
127 Dennis Smith	.01	.05
128A Andre Townsend ERR RC	.20	.50
(Misspelled Andie on front)		
128B Andrew Townsend COR RC	.02	.10
129 Mike Horan	.01	.05
130 Jerry Ball	.01	.05
131 Bennie Blades	.01	.05
132 Lomas Brown	.01	.05
133 Jeff Campbell UER	.01	.05
(No NFL totals line)		
134 Robert Clark	.01	.05
135 Michael Cofer	.01	.05
136 Dennis Gibson	.01	.05
137 Mel Gray	.02	.10
138 LeRoy Irvin UER	.01	.05
(Misspelled LEROY; spent 10		
years with Rams, not 11)		
139 George Jamison RC	.01	.05
140 Richard Johnson	.01	.05
141 Eddie Murray	.01	.05
142 Dan Owens	.01	.05
143 Rodney Peete	.02	.10
144 Barry Sanders	.50	1.25
145 Chris Spielman	.02	.10
146 Marc Spindler	.01	.05
147 Andre Ware	.02	.10
148 William White	.01	.05
149 Tony Bennett	.02	.10
150 Robert Brown	.01	.05
151 LeRoy Butler	.02	.10
152 Anthony Dilweg	.01	.05
153 Michael Haddix	.01	.05
154 Ron Hallstrom	.01	.05
155 Tim Harris	.01	.05
156 Johnny Holland	.01	.05
157 Chris Jacke	.01	.05
158 Perry Kemp	.01	.05
159 Mark Lee	.01	.05
160 Don Majkowski	.01	.05
161 Tony Mandarich UER	.01	.05
(United Stated on back)		
162 Mark Murphy	.01	.05
163 Brian Noble	.01	.05
164 Shawn Patterson	.01	.05
165 Jeff Query	.01	.05
166 Sterling Sharpe	.08	.25
167 Darrell Thompson	.01	.05
168 Ed West	.01	.05
169 Ray Childress UER	.01	.05
(Front DE, back DT)		
170A Cris Dishman RC ERR	.02	.10
(Misspelled Chris on both sides)		
170B C.Dishman RC COR	.02	.10
ERR		
Misspelled Chris on back only		
170C Cris Dishman COR RC	.02	.10
(name correct on both sides)		
171 Curtis Duncan	.01	.05
172 William Fuller	.02	.10
173 Ernest Givins UER	.02	.10
(Missing a highlight		
line on back)		
174 Drew Hill	.01	.05
175A Haywood Jeffires ERR	.08	.25
(Misspelled Jeffries on both sides)		
175B Haywood Jeffires COR	.08	.25
176 Sean Jones	.02	.10
177 Lamar Lathon	.01	.05
178 Bruce Matthews	.02	.10
179 Bubba McDowell	.01	.05
180 Johnny Meads	.01	.05
181 Warren Moon UER	.08	.25
(Birth listed as '65,		
should be '56)		
182 Mike Munchak	.02	.10
183 Allen Pinkett	.01	.05
184 Dean Steinkuhler UER	.01	.05
(Oakland should be Outland)		
185 Lorenzo White UER	.01	.05
(Rout misspelled on card back)		
186A John Grimsley ERR	.20	.50
(Misspelled Grimsby)		
186B John Grimsley COR	.02	.10
187 Pat Beach	.01	.05
188 Albert Bentley	.01	.05
189 Dean Biasucci	.01	.05
190 Duane Bickett	.01	.05
191 Bill Brooks	.01	.05
192 Eugene Daniel	.01	.05
193 Jeff George	.08	.25
194 Jon Hand	.01	.05
195 Jeff Herrod	.01	.05
196A Jessie Hester ERR	.10	.30
(Misspelled Jesse)		
196B Jessie Hester ERR	.02	.10
(Name corrected;		
6-year player, not 7;		
no NFL total line)		
197 Mike Prior	.01	.05
198 Stacey Simmons	.01	.05
199 Rohn Stark	.01	.05
200 Pat Tomberlin	.01	.05
201 Clarence Verdin	.01	.05
202 Keith Taylor	.01	.05
203 Jack Trudeau	.01	.05
204 Chip Banks	.01	.05
205 John Alt	.01	.05
206 Deron Cherry	.01	.05
207 Steve DeBerg	.01	.05
208 Tim Grunhard	.01	.05
209 Albert Lewis	.01	.05
210 Nick Lowery UER	.01	.05
(12 years exp., should be 13)		
211 Bill Maas	.01	.05
212 Chris Martin	.01	.05
213 Todd McNair	.01	.05
214 Christian Okoye	.01	.05
215 Stephone Paige	.01	.05
216 Steve Pelluer	.01	.05
217 Kevin Porter	.01	.05
218 Kevin Ross	.01	.05
219 Dan Saleaumua	.01	.05
220 Neil Smith	.08	.25
221 David Szott RC UER	.01	.05
(Listed as Off. Guard)		
222 Derrick Thomas	.08	.25
223 Barry Word	.01	.05
224 Percy Snow	.01	.05
225 Marcus Allen	.08	.25
226 Eddie Anderson UER	.01	.05
(Began career with		
Seahawks, not Raiders)		
227 Steve Beuerlein UER	.02	.10
(Not injured during '90		
season, but was inactive)		
228A Tim Brown ERR	.08	.25
(No position on card)		
228B Tim Brown COR	.08	.25
229 Scott Davis	.01	.05
230 Mike Dyal	.01	.05
231 Mervyn Fernandez UER	.01	.05
(Card says free agent in '87		
but was drafted in '83)		
232 Willie Gault UER	.01	.05
(Text says 60 catches		
in '90, stats say 50)		
233 Ethan Horton UER	.01	.05
(No height and weight listings)		
234 Bo Jackson UER	.10	.30
(Drafted in '87, not '86)		
235 Howie Long	.08	.25
236 Terry McDaniel	.01	.05
237 Max Montoya	.01	.05
238 Don Mosebar	.01	.05
239 Jay Schroeder	.01	.05
240 Steve Smith	.01	.05
241 Greg Townsend	.01	.05
242 Aaron Wallace	.01	.05
243 Lionel Washington	.01	.05
244A Steve Wisniewski ERR	.02	.10
(Misspelled Winsniewski on both sides;		
Drafted, should be traded)		
244B Steve Wisniewski ERR	.30	.75
(Misspelled Winsniewsk on back)		
244C Steve Wisniewski COR	.02	.10
245 Flipper Anderson	.01	.05
246 Latin Berry RC	.01	.05
247 Robert Delpino	.01	.05
248 Marcus Dupree	.08	.25
249 Henry Ellard	.02	.10
250 Jim Everett	.02	.10
251 Cleveland Gary	.01	.05
252 Jerry Gray	.01	.05
253 Kevin Greene	.02	.10
254 Pete Holohan UER	.01	.05
(Photo on back Kevin Greene)		
255 Buford McGee	.01	.05
256 Tom Newberry	.01	.05
257A Irv Pankey ERR	.20	.50
(Misspelled Panky on both sides)		
257B Irv Pankey COR	.02	.10
258 Jackie Slater	.01	.05
259 Doug Smith	.01	.05
260 Frank Stams	.01	.05
261 Michael Stewart	.01	.05
262 Fred Strickland	.01	.05
263 J.B. Brown UER	.01	.05
(No periods after		
initials on card front)		
264 Mark Clayton	.02	.10
265 Jeff Cross	.01	.05
266 Mark Dennis RC	.01	.05
267 Mark Duper	.02	.10
268 Ferrell Edmunds	.01	.05
269 Dan Marino	.50	1.25
270 John Offerdahl	.01	.05
271 Louis Oliver	.01	.05
272 Tony Paige	.01	.05
273 Reggie Roby	.01	.05
274 Sammie Smith	.01	.05
275 Keith Sims	.01	.05
276 Brian Sochia	.01	.05
277 Pete Stoyanovich	.01	.05
278 Richmond Webb	.01	.05
279 Jarvis Williams	.01	.05
280 Tim McKyer	.01	.05
281A Jim C. Jensen ERR	.20	.50
(Misspelled Jenson on back)		
281B Jim C. Jensen COR	.02	.10
(Plays skill position not skilled)		
282 Scott Secules RC	.01	.05
283 Ray Berry	.01	.05
284 Joey Browner UER	.01	.05
(Safetys, sic)		
285 Anthony Carter	.02	.10
286A Cris Carter ERR	.20	.50
(Misspelled Chris on both sides)		
286B Cris Carter ERR	.60	1.50
COR		
(Misspelled Chris on back only)		
286C Cris Carter COR	.20	.50
287 Chris Doleman	.01	.05
288 Mark Dusbabek UER	.01	.05
(Front DT, back LB)		
289 Hassan Jones	.01	.05
290 Steve Jordan	.01	.05
291 Carl Lee	.01	.05
292 Kirk Lowdermilk	.01	.05
293 Randall McDaniel	.02	.10
294 Mike Merriweather	.01	.05
295A Keith Millard UER	.07	.20
(No position on card)		
295B Keith Millard COR	1.00	2.50
296 Al Noga UER	.01	.05
(reads DT, should be DE)		
297 Scott Studwell UER	.01	.05
(83 career tackles,		
but bio says 156		
tackles in '81 season)		
298 Henry Thomas	.01	.05
299 Herschel Walker	.02	.10
300 Gary Zimmerman	.02	.10
301 Rich Gannon	.08	.25
302 Wade Wilson UER	.02	.10
(Led AFC, should be NFC)		
303 Vincent Brown	.01	.05
304 Marv Cook	.01	.05
305 Hart Lee Dykes	.01	.05
306 Irving Fryar	.02	.10
307 Tommy Hodson UER	.01	.05
(No NFL totals line)		
308 Maurice Hurst	.01	.05
309 Ronnie Lippett UER	.01	.05
(reads reserves on back)		
310 Fred Marion	.01	.05
311 Greg McMurtry	.01	.05
312 Johnny Rembert	.01	.05
313 Chris Singleton	.01	.05
314 Ed Reynolds	.01	.05
315 Andre Tippett	.01	.05
316 Garin Veris	.01	.05
317 Brent Williams	.01	.05
318A John Stephens ERR	.02	.10
(Misspelled Stevens on both sides)		
318B John Stephens COR	.30	.75
ERR		
(Misspelled Stevens on back only)		
318C John Stephens COR	.02	.10
319 Sammy Martin	.01	.05
320 Bruce Armstrong	.01	.05
321A Morten Andersen ERR	.10	.30
(Misspelled Anderson on both sides)		
321B Morten Andersen ERR	.30	.75
COR		
Misspelled Anderson only on back		
321C Morten Andersen COR	.02	.10
(Andersen correct on both sides)		
322 Gene Atkins UER	.01	.05
(No NFL Exp. line)		
323 Vince Buck	.01	.05
324 John Fourcade	.01	.05
325 Kevin Haverdink	.01	.05
326 Bobby Hebert	.01	.05

327 Craig Heyward .02 .10
328 Dalton Hilliard .01 .05
329 Rickey Jackson .01 .05
330A Vaughan Johnson ERR .07 .20
(Misspelled Vaughn)
330B Vaughan Johnson COR 1.00 2.50
331 Eric Martin .01 .05
332 Wayne Martin .01 .05
333 Rueben Mayes UER .01 .05
(Misspelled Reuben on back)
334 Sam Mills .01 .05
335 Brett Perriman .08 .25
336 Pat Swilling .02 .10
337 Renaldo Turnbull .01 .05
338 Lonzell Hill .01 .05
339 Steve Walsh UER .01 .05
(19 of 20 for 70.3, should be 95 percent)
340 Carl Banks UER .01 .05
(Led defensive in tackles should say defense)
341 Mark Bavaro UER .01 .05
(incorrect weight on back: 145)
342 Maurice Carthon .01 .05
343 Pat Harlow RC .01 .05
344 Eric Dorsey .01 .05
345 John Elliott .01 .05
346 Rodney Hampton .08 .25
347 Jeff Hostetler .02 .10
348 Erik Howard UER .01 .05
(listed as DT instead of NT)
349 Pepper Johnson .01 .05
350A Sean Landeta ERR .02 .10
(Misspelled Landetta on both sides)
350B Sean Landeta COR .20 .50
351 Leonard Marshall .01 .05
352 Dave Meggett .02 .10
353A Bart Oates ERR .02 .10
(Misspelled Oats on both sides; misspelled Megget on back)
353B Bart Oates COR .30 .75
ERR
(Misspelled Oats on back only; misspelled Megget on back)
353C Bart Oates COR .02 .10
(Oates corrected, Meggett misspelled on back)
354 Gary Reasons .01 .05
355 Phil Simms .02 .10
356 Lawrence Taylor .08 .25
357 Reyna Thompson .01 .05
358 Brian Williams OL UER .01 .05
(Front C-G, back G)
359 Matt Bahr .01 .05
360 Mark Ingram .02 .10
361 Brad Baxter .01 .05
362 Mark Boyer .01 .05
363 Dennis Byrd .01 .05
364 Dave Cadigan UER .01 .05
(Terance misspelled as Terrance on back)
365 Kyle Clifton .01 .05
366 James Hasty .01 .05
367 Joe Kelly UER .01 .05
(Front 50, back 58)
368 Jeff Lageman .01 .05
369 Pat Leahy UER .01 .05
(Career-best FG in/'65, should say '85)
370 Terance Mathis .02 .10
371 Erik McMillan .01 .05
372 Rob Moore .08 .25
373 Ken O'Brien .01 .05
374 Tony Stargell .01 .05
375 Jim Sweeney UER .01 .05
(Landetta, sic)
376 Al Toon .02 .10
377 Johnny Hector .01 .05
378 Jeff Criswell .01 .05
379 Mike Haight RC .01 .05
380 Troy Benson .01 .05
381 Eric Allen .01 .05
382 Fred Barnett .08 .25
383 Jerome Brown .01 .05
384 Keith Byars .01 .05
385 Randall Cunningham .08 .25
386 Byron Evans .01 .05
387 Wes Hopkins .01 .05
388 Keith Jackson .02 .10
389 Seth Joyner UER .02 .10
(Fumble recovery line not aligned)
390 Bobby Wilson RC .01 .05
391 Heath Sherman .01 .05
392 Clyde Simmons UER .01 .05
(Listed as DT instead of DE)
393 Ben Smith .01 .05
394 Andre Waters .01 .05
395 Reggie White UER .08 .25
(Derrick Thomas holds NFL record with 7 sacks)
396 Calvin Williams .02 .10
397 Al Harris .01 .05
398 Anthony Toney .01 .05
399 Mike Quick .01 .05
400 Anthony Bell .01 .05
401 Rich Camarillo .01 .05
402 Roy Green .01 .05
403 Ken Harvey .02 .10
404 Eric Hill .01 .05
405 Garth Jax RC UER .01 .05
(Should have comma before 'the' and after/'Cowboys' on cardback)
406 Ernie Jones .01 .05
407A Cedric Mack ERR .07 .20
(Misspelled Cedrick onfront)
407B Cedric Mack COR 1.00 2.50
(Cedric corrected, NFL Exp. line is red instead of black)
408 Dexter Manley .01 .05
409 Tim McDonald .01 .05
410 Freddie Joe Nunn .01 .05
411 Ricky Proehl .01 .05
412 Moe Gardner RC .01 .05
413 Timm Rosenbach .01 .05
414 Luis Sharpe UER .01 .05
(Lomiller, sic)
415 Vai Sikahema UER .01 .05
(Front RB, back PR)
416 Anthony Thompson .01 .05
417 Ron Wolfley UER .01 .05
(Missing NFL fact line under vital stats)
418 Lonnie Young .01 .05
419 Gary Anderson K .01 .05
420 Bubby Brister .01 .05
421 Thomas Everett .01 .05
422 Eric Green .01 .05
423 Delton Hall .01 .05
424 Bryan Hinkle .01 .05
425 Merril Hoge .01 .05
426 Carnell Lake .01 .05
427 Louis Lipps .01 .05
428 David Little .01 .05
429 Greg Lloyd .08 .25
430 Mike Mularkey .01 .05
431 Keith Willis UER .01 .05
(No period after C in L.C. Greenwood on back)
432 Dwayne Woodruff .01 .05
433 Rod Woodson UER .08 .25
(No NFL experience listed on card)
434 Tim Worley .01 .05
435 Warren Williams .01 .05
436 Terry Long UER .01 .05
(Not 5th NFL team, tied for 7th)
437 Martin Bayless .01 .05
438 Jarrod Bunch RC .01 .05
439 Marion Butts .02 .10
440 Gill Byrd UER .01 .05
(Pickoffs misspelled as two words)
441 Arthur Cox .01 .05
442 John Friesz .08 .25
443 Leo Goeas .01 .05
444 Burt Grossman .01 .05
445 Courtney Hall UER .01 .05
(In DYK section, is should be in)
446 Ronnie Harmon .01 .05
447 Nate Lewis RC .01 .05
448 Anthony Miller .02 .10
449 Leslie O'Neal .02 .10
450 Gary Plummer .01 .05
451 Junior Seau .08 .25
452 Billy Ray Smith .01 .05
453 Billy Joe Tolliver .01 .05
454 Broderick Thompson .01 .05
455 Lee Williams .01 .05
456 Michael Carter .01 .05
457 Mike Cofer .01 .05
458 Kevin Fagan .01 .05
459 Charles Haley .02 .10
460 Pierce Holt .01 .05
461 Johnnie Jackson RC UER .01 .05
Johnny on front
462 Brent Jones .08 .25
463 Guy McIntyre .01 .05
464 Joe Montana .50 1.25
465A Bubba Paris ERR .02 .10
(Misspelled Parris; reversed negative)
465B Bubba Paris ERR .20 .50
COR
(Misspelled Parris; photo corrected
465C Bubba Paris COR .02 .10
466 Tom Rathman UER .01 .05
(Born 10/7/62, not 11/7/62)
467 Jerry Rice UER .30 .75
(4th to catch 100, should say 2nd)
468 Mike Sherrard .01 .05
469 John Taylor UER .02 .10
(AL1-Time, sic)
470 Steve Young .30 .75
471 Dennis Brown .01 .05
472 Dexter Carter .01 .05
473 Bill Romanowski .01 .05
474 Dave Waymer .01 .05
475 Robert Blackmon .01 .05
476 Derrick Fenner .01 .05
477 Nesby Glasgow UER .01 .05
(Missing fumbles totals)
478 Jacob Green .01 .05
479 Andy Heck .01 .05
480 Norm Johnson UER .01 .05
(They own and operate card store, not run)
481 Tommy Kane .01 .05
482 Cortez Kennedy .08 .25
483A Dave Krieg ERR .07 .20
(Misspelled Kreig on both sides)
483B Dave Krieg COR 1.00 2.50
484 Bryan Millard .01 .05
485 Joe Nash .01 .05
486 Rufus Porter .01 .05
487 Eugene Robinson .01 .05
488 Mike Tice RC .01 .05
489 Chris Warren .08 .25
490 John L. Williams UER .01 .05
(No period after L on card front)
491 Terry Wooden .01 .05
492 Tony Woods .01 .05
493 Brian Blades .02 .10
494 Paul Skansi .01 .05
495 Gary Anderson RB .01 .05
496 Mark Carrier WR .08 .25
497 Chris Chandler .08 .25
498 Steve Christie .01 .05
499 Reggie Cobb .01 .05
500 Reuben Davis .01 .05
501 Willie Drewrey UER .01 .05
(Misspelled Drewery on both sides of card)
502 Randy Grimes .01 .05
503 Paul Gruber .01 .05
504 Wayne Haddix .01 .05
505 Ron Hall .01 .05
506 Harry Hamilton .01 .05
507 Bruce Hill .01 .05
508 Eugene Marve .01 .05
509 Keith McCants .01 .05
510 Winston Moss .01 .05
511 Kevin Murphy .01 .05
512 Mark Robinson .01 .05
513 Vinny Testaverde .02 .10
514 Broderick Thomas .01 .05
515A Jeff Bostic UER .02 .10
(Lomiller, sic; on back, word goal touches lower border)
515B Jeff Bostic UER .02 .10
(Lomiller, sic; on back, word goal is away from border)
516 Todd Bowles .01 .05
517 Earnest Byner .01 .05
518 Gary Clark .08 .25
519 Craig Erickson RC .08 .25
520 Darryl Grant .01 .05
521 Darrell Green .01 .05
522 Russ Grimm .02 .10
523 Stan Humphries .08 .25
524 Joe Jacoby UER .01 .05
(Lomiller, sic)
525 Jim Lachey .01 .05
526 Chip Lohmiller .01 .05
527 Charles Mann .01 .05
528 Wilber Marshall .01 .05
529A Art Monk .02 .10
(On back, y in history touches copyright symbol)
529B Art Monk .02 .10
(On back, y in history is away from symbol)
530 Tracy Rocker .01 .05
531 Mark Rypien .02 .10
532 Ricky Sanders UER .01 .05
(Stats say caught 56, text says 57)
533 Alvin Walton UER .01 .05
(Listed as WR, should be S)
534 Todd Marinovich RC UER .01 .05
17 percent, should be 71 percent
535 Mike Dumas RC .01 .05
536A Russell Maryland ERR RC .08 .25
No Highlight Line
536B Russell Maryland COR RC .08 .25
Highlight Line Added
537 Eric Turner RC UER .02 .10
(Don Rogers misspelled as Rodgers)
538 Ernie Mills RC .02 .10
539 Ed King RC .01 .05
540 Mike Stonebreaker .01 .05
541 Chris Zorich RC .08 .25
542A Mike Croel RC UER .01 .05
(Missing highlight line under bio notes; front photo reversed negative; on back, y in weekly inside copyright)
542B Mike Croel RC UER .01 .05
(Missing highlight line under bio notes; front photo reversed negative; on back, y in weekly barely touches copyright)
543 Eric Moten RC .01 .05
544 Dan McGwire RC .01 .05
545 Keith Cash RC .01 .05
546 Kenny Walker RC UER .01 .05
(Drafted 8th round, not 7th)
547 Leroy Hoard UER .02 .10
(LeROY on card; not a draft pick)
548 Luis Cristobal UER .01 .05
(front LB, back G)
549 Stacy Danley .01 .05
550 Todd Lyght RC .01 .05
551 Brett Favre RC 3.00 8.00
552 Mike Pritchard RC .08 .25
553 Moe Gardner .01 .05
554 Tim McKyer .01 .05
555 Erric Pegram RC .08 .25
556 Norm Johnson .01 .05
557 Bruce Pickens RC .01 .05
558 Henry Jones RC .02 .10
559 Phil Hansen RC .01 .05
560 Cornelius Bennett .02 .10
561 Stan Thomas .01 .05
562 Chris Zorich .02 .10
563 Anthony Morgan RC .01 .05
564 Darren Lewis RC .01 .05
565 Mike Stonebreaker .01 .05
566 Alfred Williams RC .01 .05
567 Lamar Rogers RC .01 .05
568 Erik Wilhelm RC UER .01 .05
(No NFL Experience line on card back)
569 Ed King .01 .05
570 Michael Jackson WR RC .08 .25
571 James Jones RC .01 .05
572 Russell Maryland .08 .25
573 Dixon Edwards RC .01 .05
574 Darrick Brownlow RC .01 .05
575 Larry Brown DB RC .02 .10
576 Mike Croel .01 .05
577 Keith Traylor RC .01 .05
578 Kenny Walker .01 .05
579 Reggie Johnson RC .01 .05
580 Herman Moore RC .08 .25
581 Kelvin Pritchett RC .02 .10
582 Kevin Scott RC .01 .05
583 Vinnie Clark RC .01 .05
584 Esera Tuaolo RC .01 .05
585 Don Davey .01 .05
586 Blair Kiel RC .01 .05
587 Mike Dumas .01 .05
588 Darryll Lewis RC .02 .10
589 John Flannery RC .01 .05
590 Kevin Donnalley RC .01 .05
591 Shane Curry .01 .05
592 Mark Vander Poel RC .01 .05
593 Dave McCloughan .01 .05
594 Mel Agee RC .01 .05
595 Kerry Cash RC .01 .05
596 Harvey Williams RC .08 .25
597 Joe Valerio RC .01 .05
598 Tim Barnett RC UER .01 .05
(Harvey Williams pictured on front)
599 Todd Marinovich .02 .10
600 Nick Bell RC .01 .05
601 Roger Craig .02 .10
602 Ronnie Lott .02 .10
603 Mike Jones RC LB .01 .05
604 Todd Lyght .01 .05
605 Roman Phifer RC .01 .05
606 David Lang RC .01 .05
607 Aaron Craver RC .01 .05
608 Mark Higgs RC .01 .05
609 Chris Green .01 .05
610 Randy Baldwin RC .01 .05
611 Pat Harlow .01 .05
612 Leonard Russell RC .08 .25
613 Jerome Henderson RC .01 .05
614 Scott Zolak RC UER .01 .05
(Bio says drafted in/1984, should be 1991)
615 Jon Vaughn RC .01 .05
616 Harry Colon RC .01 .05
617 Wesley Carroll RC .01 .05
618 Quinn Early .02 .10
619 Reginald Jones RC .01 .05
620 Jarrod Bunch .01 .05
621 Kanavis McGhee RC .01 .05
622 Ed McCaffrey RC .75 2.00
623 Browning Nagle RC .01 .05
624 Mo Lewis RC .02 .10
625 Blair Thomas .01 .05
626 Antone Davis RC .01 .05
627 Jim McMahon .02 .10
628 Scott Kowalkowski RC .01 .05
629 Brad Goebel RC .01 .05
630 William Thomas RC .01 .05
631 Eric Swann RC .08 .25
632 Mike Jones DE RC .01 .05
633 Aeneas Williams RC .08 .25
634 Dexter Davis RC .01 .05
635 Tom Tupa UER .01 .05
(Did play in 1990, but not as QB)
636 Johnny Johnson .01 .05
637 Randal Hill RC .02 .10
638 Jeff Graham RC .08 .25
639 Ernie Mills .01 .05
640 Adrian Cooper RC .01 .05
641 Stanley Richard RC .01 .05
642 Eric Bieniemy RC .01 .05
643 Eric Moten .01 .05
644 Shawn Jefferson RC .02 .10
645 Ted Washington RC .01 .05
646 John Johnson RC .01 .05
647 Dan McGwire .01 .05
648 Doug Thomas RC .01 .05
649 David Daniels RC .01 .05
650 John Kasay RC .02 .10
651 Jeff Kemp .01 .05
652 Charles McRae RC .01 .05
653 Lawrence Dawsey RC .02 .10
654 Robert Wilson RC .01 .05
655 Dexter Manley .01 .05
656 Chuck Weatherspoon .01 .05
657 Tim Ryan G RC .01 .05
658 Bobby Wilson .01 .05
659 Ricky Ervins RC .02 .10
660 Matt Millen .02 .10

1991 Pacific Picks The Pros

COMPLETE SET (25) 20.00 50.00
*GOLD/SILVER: SAME PRICE
GOLDS RANDOM INSERTS IN HOB/RET
SILVERS RANDOM INSERTS IN JUMBO
STATED PRINT RUN 10,000 SETS
1 Russell Maryland 1.00 2.50
2 Andre Reed .40 1.00
3 Jerry Rice 3.00 8.00
4 Keith Jackson .40 1.00
5 Jim Lachey .20 .50
6 Anthony Munoz .40 1.00
7 Randall McDaniel .20 .50
8 Bruce Matthews .40 1.00
9 Kent Hull .20 .50
10 Joe Montana 5.00 12.00
11 Barry Sanders 5.00 12.00
12 Thurman Thomas 1.00 2.50
13 Morten Andersen .40 1.00
14 Jerry Ball .20 .50
15 Jerome Brown .20 .50
16 Reggie White 1.00 2.50
17 Bruce Smith 1.00 2.50
18 Derrick Thomas 1.00 2.50
19 Lawrence Taylor 1.00 2.50
20 Charles Haley .40 1.00
21 Albert Lewis .20 .50
22 Rod Woodson 1.00 2.50
23 David Fulcher .20 .50
24 Joey Browner .20 .50
25 Sean Landeta .40 1.00

1991 Pacific Flash Cards

The 1991 Pacific Flash Cards football set contains 110 standard-size cards. The front design has brightly colored triangles on a white card face and a math problem involving addition, subtraction, multiplication, or division. By performing one of these operations on the two numbers, one arrives at the uniform number of the player featured on the backs. The back design is similar to the front but has a glossy color game shot of the player, with either career summary or last year's highlights below the picture.

COMPLETE SET (110) 4.00 10.00
1 Steve Young .30 .75
2 Hart Lee Dykes .01 .05
3 Timm Rosenbach .01 .05
4 Andre Collins .01 .05
5 Johnny Johnson .01 .05
6 Nick Lowery .01 .05
7 John Stephens .01 .05
8 Jim Arnold .01 .05
9 Steve DeBerg .01 .05
10 Christian Okoye .01 .05
11 Eric Swann .02 .10
12 Jerry Robinson .01 .05
13 Steve Wisniewski .01 .05
14 Jim Harbaugh .02 .10
15 Steve Broussard .01 .05
16 Mike Singletary UER .02 .10
17 Tim Green .01 .05
18 Roger Craig .02 .10
19 Maury Buford .01 .05
20 Marcus Allen .07 .20
21 Deion Sanders .20 .50
22 Chris Miller .02 .10
23 Joey Browner .01 .05
24 Bubby Brister .02 .10
25 Buford McGee .01 .05
26 Ed West .01 .05
27 Mark Murphy .01 .05
28 Tim Worley .01 .05
29 Keith Willis .01 .05
30 Rich Gannon .07 .20
31 Jim Everett .02 .10
32 Duval Love .01 .05
33 Bob Nelson .01 .05
34 Anthony Munoz .02 .10
35 Boomer Esiason .02 .10
36 Kenny Walker .01 .05
37 Mike Horan .01 .05
38 Gary Kubiak .01 .05
39 David Treadwell .01 .05
40 Robert Wilson .01 .05
41 Lewis Billups .01 .05
42 Kevin Mack .01 .05
43 John Elway .60 1.50
44 Lee Johnson .01 .05
45 Ken Willis .01 .05
46 Herman Moore .30 .75
47 Eddie Murray .01 .05
48 Mike Saxon .01 .05
49 John L. Williams .01 .05
50 Barry Sanders .60 1.50
51 Andre Ware .02 .10
52 Dave Krieg .02 .10
53 Cortez Kennedy .01 .05
54 Bo Jackson .07 .20
55 Derrick Fenner .01 .05
56 Steve Walsh .01 .05
57 Brett Maxie .01 .05
58 Stan Brock .01 .05
59 DeMond Winston .01 .05
60 Sam Mills .01 .05
61 Eric Martin .01 .05
62 Michael Carter .01 .05
63 Steve Wallace .01 .05
64 Jesse Sapolu .01 .05
65 Bill Romanowski .01 .05
66 Joe Montana .80 2.00
67 Sean Landeta .01 .05
68 Doug Riesenberg .01 .05
69 Myron Guyton .01 .05
70 Andre Reed .02 .10
71 John Elliott .01 .05
72 Jeff Hostetler .02 .10
73 Rohn Stark .01 .05
74 Jeff George .02 .10
75 Duane Bickett .01 .05
76 Emmitt Smith .75 2.00
77 Michael Irvin .07 .20
78 Tony Stargell .01 .05
79 Kyle Clifton .01 .05
80 John Booty .01 .05
81 Fred Barnett .02 .10
82 Blair Thomas .01 .05
83 Erik McMillan .01 .05
84 Broderick Thomas .01 .05
85 Jim Skow .01 .05
86 Gary Anderson RB .01 .05
87 Mark Robinson .01 .05
88 Steve Christie .01 .05
89 Cody Carlson .01 .05
90 Warren Moon .07 .20
91 Lorenzo White .01 .05
92 Reggie Roby .01 .05
93 Jim C. Jensen .01 .05
94 Mark Clayton .02 .10
95 Willie Gault .02 .10
96 Don Mosebar .01 .05
97 Gary Plummer .01 .05
98 Leslie O'Neal .01 .05
99 Neal Anderson .02 .10
100 Derrick Thomas .02 .10
101 Luis Sharpe .01 .05
102 D.J. Dozier .01 .05
103 Jarrod Bunch .01 .05
104 Mark Ingram .01 .05
105 James Lofton .02 .10
106 Jay Schroeder .01 .05
107 Ronnie Lott .07 .20
108 Todd Marinovich .01 .05
109 Chris Zorich .01 .05
110 Charles McRae .01 .05

1992 Pacific Prototypes

The 1992 Pacific prototypes were given away at the Super Bowl card show in Minneapolis and used as sales samples. The cards measure the standard size. The cards were intended to be a preview for the upcoming 1992 Pacific set since they used the new card design. The production run was approximately 5,000 sets. The fronts feature glossy color action player photos enclosed by white borders. The player's name is printed vertically in a color stripe running down the left side of the picture, with the team helmet in the lower left corner. In a horizontal format, the backs have a second color photo and player profile.

COMPLETE SET (6) 10.00 25.00
1 Warren Moon 2.00 5.00
2 Pat Swilling 1.60 4.00
3 Michael Irvin 2.00 5.00
4 Haywood Jeffires 1.60 4.00
5 Thurman Thomas 2.00 5.00
6 Leonard Russell 1.60 4.00

1992 Pacific

The 1992 Pacific set consists of 660 standard-size cards. The set was issued in two series of 330 cards. A factory set consisted of every card. Cards were issued in 14-card packs and 24-card jumbo packs for each series. Factory sets included a 30-card Statistical Leaders set. The cards are checklisted alphabetically according to teams. Cards 320-330 and 649-660 are Draft Picks. Rookie Cards include Steve Bono and Ben Coates (exclusive to Pacific). Separately numbered checklist cards were also randomly inserted in packs.

COMPLETE SET (660) 6.00 15.00
COMP.FACT.SET (690) 10.00 25.00
COMP.SERIES 1 (330) 3.00 8.00
COMP.SERIES 2 (330) 3.00 8.00
COMP.CHECKLIST SET (5) 1.50 3.00
1 Steve Broussard .01 .05
2 Darion Conner .01 .05
3 Tory Epps .01 .05
4 Michael Haynes .02 .10
5 Chris Hinton .01 .05
6 Mike Kenn .01 .05
7 Tim McKyer .01 .05
8 Chris Miller .02 .10
9 Erric Pegram .02 .10
10 Mike Pritchard .02 .10
11 Moe Gardner .01 .05
12 Tim Green .01 .05
13 Norm Johnson .01 .05
14 Don Beebe .01 .05
15 Cornelius Bennett .02 .10
16 Al Edwards .01 .05
17 Mark Kelso .01 .05
18 James Lofton .02 .10
19 Frank Reich .02 .10
20 Leon Seals .01 .05
21 Darryl Talley .01 .05
22 Thurman Thomas .08 .25
23 Kent Hull .01 .05
24 Jeff Wright .01 .05
25 Nate Odomes .01 .05
26 Carwell Gardner .01 .05
27 Neal Anderson .01 .05
28 Mark Carrier DB .01 .05
29 Johnny Bailey .01 .05
30 Jim Harbaugh .08 .25
31 Jay Hilgenberg .01 .05
32 William Perry .02 .10
33 Wendell Davis .01 .05
34 Donnell Woolford .01 .05
35 Keith Van Horne .01 .05
36 Shaun Gayle .01 .05
37 Tom Waddle .01 .05
38 Chris Zorich .02 .10
39 Tom Thayer .01 .05
40 Rickey Dixon .01 .05
41 James Francis .01 .05
42 David Fulcher .01 .05
43 Reggie Rembert .01 .05
44 Anthony Munoz .02 .10
45 Harold Green .01 .05
46 Mitchell Price .01 .05
47 Rodney Holman .01 .05
48 Bruce Kozerski .01 .05
49 Bruce Reimers .01 .05
50 Erik Wilhelm .01 .05
51 Harlon Barnett .01 .05
52 Mike Johnson .01 .05
53 Brian Brennan .01 .05
54 Ed King .01 .05
55 Reggie Langhorne .01 .05
56 James Jones .01 .05
57 Mike Baab .01 .05
58 Dan Fike .01 .05
59 Frank Minnifield .01 .05
60 Clay Matthews .02 .10
61 Kevin Mack .01 .05
62 Tony Casillas .01 .05
63 Jay Novacek .02 .10
64 Larry Brown DB .01 .05
65 Michael Irvin .08 .25
66 Jack Del Rio .01 .05
67 Ken Willis .01 .05
68 Emmitt Smith .60 1.50
69 Alan Veingrad .01 .05
70 John Gesek .01 .05
71 Steve Beuerlein .02 .10
72 Vinson Smith RC .01 .05
73 Steve Atwater .01 .05
74 Mike Croel .01 .05
75 John Elway .50 1.25
76 Gaston Green .01 .05
77 Mike Horan .01 .05
78 Vance Johnson .01 .05
79 Karl Mecklenburg .01 .05
80 Shannon Sharpe .08 .25
81 David Treadwell .01 .05
82 Kenny Walker .01 .05
83 Greg Lewis .01 .05
84 Shawn Moore .01 .05
85 Alton Montgomery .01 .05
86 Michael Young .01 .05
87 Jerry Ball .01 .05
88 Bennie Blades .01 .05
89 Mel Gray .02 .10
90 Herman Moore .08 .25
91 Erik Kramer .02 .10
92 Willie Green .01 .05
93 George Jamison .01 .05
94 Chris Spielman .02 .10
95 Kelvin Pritchett .01 .05
96 William White .01 .05
97 Mike Utley .02 .10
98 Tony Bennett .01 .05
99 LeRoy Butler .01 .05
100 Vinnie Clark .01 .05
101 Ron Hallstrom .01 .05
102 Chris Jacke .01 .05
103 Tony Mandarich .01 .05
104 Sterling Sharpe .08 .25
105 Don Majkowski .01 .05
106 Johnny Holland .01 .05
107 Esera Tuaolo .01 .05
108 Darrell Thompson .01 .05
109 Bubba McDowell .01 .05
110 Curtis Duncan .01 .05
111 Lamar Lathon .01 .05
112 Drew Hill .01 .05
113 Bruce Matthews .01 .05
114 Bo Orlando RC .01 .05
115 Don Maggs .01 .05
116 Lorenzo White .01 .05
117 Ernest Givins .02 .10
118 Tony Jones .01 .05
119 Dean Steinkuhler .01 .05
120 Dean Biasucci .01 .05
121 Duane Bickett .01 .05
122 Bill Brooks .01 .05
123 Ken Clark .01 .05
124 Jessie Hester .01 .05
125 Anthony Johnson .02 .10
126 Chip Banks .01 .05
127 Mike Prior .01 .05
128 Rohn Stark .01 .05
129 Jeff Herrod .01 .05
130 Clarence Verdin .01 .05
131 Tim Manoa .01 .05
132 Brian Baldinger RC .01 .05
133 Tim Barnett .01 .05
134 J.J. Birden .01 .05
135 Deron Cherry .01 .05
136 Steve DeBerg .01 .05
137 Nick Lowery .01 .05
138 Todd McNair .01 .05
139 Christian Okoye .01 .05
140 Mark Vlasic .01 .05
141 Dan Saleaumua .01 .05
142 Neil Smith .08 .25
143 Robb Thomas .01 .05
144 Eddie Anderson .01 .05
145 Nick Bell .01 .05
146 Tim Brown .08 .25
147 Roger Craig .02 .10
148 Jeff Gossett .01 .05
149 Ethan Horton .01 .05
150 Jamie Holland .01 .05
151 Jeff Jaeger .01 .05
152 Todd Marinovich .01 .05
153 Marcus Allen .08 .25
154 Steve Smith .01 .05
155 Flipper Anderson .01 .05
156 Robert Delpino .01 .05
157 Cleveland Gary .01 .05
158 Kevin Greene .02 .10
159 Dale Hatcher .01 .05
160 Duval Love .01 .05
161 Ron Brown .01 .05
162 Jackie Slater .01 .05
163 Doug Smith .01 .05
164 Aaron Cox .01 .05
165 Larry Kelm .01 .05
166 Mark Clayton .02 .10
167 Louis Oliver .01 .05
168 Mark Higgs .01 .05
169 Aaron Craver .01 .05
170 Sammie Smith .01 .05
171 Tony Paige .01 .05
172 Jeff Cross .01 .05
173 David Griggs .01 .05
174 Richmond Webb .01 .05
175 Vestee Jackson .01 .05
176 Jim C. Jensen .01 .05
177 Anthony Carter .02 .10
178 Cris Carter .20 .50
179 Chris Doleman .01 .05
180 Rich Gannon .08 .25
181 Al Noga .01 .05
182 Randall McDaniel .02 .10
183 Todd Scott .01 .05
184 Henry Thomas .01 .05
185 Felix Wright .01 .05
186 Gary Zimmerman .01 .05
187 Herschel Walker .02 .10
188 Vincent Brown .01 .05
189 Harry Colon .01 .05
190 Irving Fryar .02 .10
191 Marv Cook .01 .05
192 Leonard Russell .02 .10
193 Hugh Millen .01 .05
194 Pat Harlow .01 .05
195 Jon Vaughn .01 .05
196 Ben Coates RC .30 .75
197 Johnny Rembert .01 .05
198 Greg McMurtry .01 .05
199 Morten Andersen .01 .05
200 Tommy Barnhardt .01 .05
201 Bobby Hebert .01 .05
202 Dalton Hilliard .01 .05
203 Sam Mills .01 .05
204 Pat Swilling .01 .05
205 Rickey Jackson .01 .05
206 Stan Brock .01 .05
207 Reginald Jones .01 .05
208 Gill Fenerty .01 .05
209 Eric Martin .01 .05
210 Matt Bahr .01 .05
211 Rodney Hampton .02 .10
212 Jeff Hostetler .02 .10
213 Pepper Johnson .01 .05
214 Leonard Marshall .01 .05
215 Doug Riesenberg .01 .05
216 Stephen Baker .01 .05
217 Mike Fox .01 .05
218 Bart Oates .01 .05
219 Everson Walls .01 .05
220 Gary Reasons .01 .05
221 Jeff Lageman .01 .05
222 Joe Kelly .01 .05
223 Mo Lewis .01 .05
224 Tony Stargell .01 .05
225 Jim Sweeney .01 .05
226 Freeman McNeil .02 .10
227 Brian Washington .01 .05
228 Johnny Hector .01 .05
229 Terance Mathis .02 .10
230 Rob Moore .02 .10
231 Brad Baxter .01 .05
232 Eric Allen .01 .05
233 Fred Barnett .02 .10
234 Jerome Brown .01 .05
235 Keith Byars .01 .05
236 William Thomas .01 .05
237 Jessie Small .01 .05
238 Robert Drummond .01 .05
239 Reggie White .08 .25
240 James Joseph .01 .05
241 Brad Goebel .01 .05
242 Clyde Simmons .01 .05
243 Rich Camarillo .01 .05
244 Ken Harvey .01 .05
245 Garth Jax .01 .05
246 Johnny Johnson UER .01 .05
(Photo on back not him)
247 Mike Jones .01 .05
248 Ernie Jones .01 .05
249 Tom Tupa .01 .05
250 Ron Wolfley .01 .05
251 Luis Sharpe .01 .05
252 Eric Swann .02 .10
253 Anthony Thompson .01 .05
254 Gary Anderson K .01 .05
255 Dermontti Dawson .01 .05
256 Jeff Graham .08 .25
257 Eric Green .01 .05
258 Louis Lipps .01 .05
259 Neil O'Donnell .02 .10
260 Rod Woodson .08 .25
261 Dwight Stone .01 .05
262 Aaron Jones .01 .05
263 Keith Willis .01 .05
264 Ernie Mills .01 .05
265 Martin Bayless .01 .05
266 Rod Bernstine .01 .05
267 John Carney .01 .05
268 John Friesz .02 .10
269 Nate Lewis .01 .05
270 Shawn Jefferson .01 .05
271 Burt Grossman .01 .05
272 Eric Moten .01 .05
273 Gary Plummer .01 .05
274 Henry Rolling .01 .05
275 Steve Hendrickson RC .01 .05
276 Michael Carter .01 .05
277 Steve Bono RC .08 .25
278 Dexter Carter .01 .05
279 Mike Cofer .01 .05
280 Charles Haley .02 .10
281 Tom Rathman .01 .05
282 Guy McIntyre .01 .05
283 John Taylor .02 .10
284 Dave Waymer .01 .05
285 Steve Wallace .01 .05
286 Jamie Williams .01 .05
287 Brian Blades .02 .10
288 Jeff Bryant .01 .05
289 Grant Feasel .01 .05
290 Jacob Green .01 .05
291 Andy Heck .01 .05
292 Kelly Stouffer .01 .05
293 John Kasay .01 .05
294 Cortez Kennedy .02 .10
295 Bryan Millard .01 .05
296 Eugene Robinson .01 .05
297 Tony Woods .01 .05
298 Jesse Anderson UER .01 .05
(Should have Tight End, not TIGHT END)
299 Gary Anderson RB .01 .05
300 Mark Carrier WR .02 .10
301 Reggie Cobb .01 .05
302 Robert Wilson .01 .05
303 Jesse Solomon .01 .05
304 Broderick Thomas .01 .05
305 Lawrence Dawsey .02 .10
306 Charles McRae .01 .05
307 Paul Gruber .01 .05
308 Vinny Testaverde .02 .10
309 Brian Mitchell .02 .10
310 Darrell Green .01 .05
311 Art Monk .02 .10
312 Russ Grimm .02 .10
313 Mark Rypien .01 .05
314 Bobby Wilson .01 .05
315 Wilber Marshall .01 .05
316 Gerald Riggs .01 .05
317 Chip Lohmiller .01 .05
318 Joe Jacoby .01 .05
319 Martin Mayhew .01 .05
320 Amp Lee RC .01 .05
321 Terrell Buckley RC .01 .05
322 Tommy Vardell RC .01 .05
323 Ricardo McDonald RC .01 .05
324 Joe Bowden RC .01 .05
325 Darryl Williams RC .01 .05
326 Carlos Huerta .01 .05
327 Patrick Rowe RC .01 .05
328 Siran Stacy RC .01 .05
329 Dexter McNabb RC .01 .05

330 Willie Clay RC	.01	.05
331 Oliver Barnett	.01	.05
332 Aundray Bruce	.01	.05
333 Ken Tippins RC	.01	.05
334 Jessie Tuggle	.01	.05
335 Brian Jordan	.02	.10
336 Andre Rison	.02	.10
337 Houston Hoover	.01	.05
338 Bill Fralic	.01	.05
339 Pat Chaffey RC	.01	.05
340 Keith Jones	.01	.05
341 Jamie Dukes RC	.01	.05
342 Chris Mohr	.01	.05
343 John Davis	.01	.05
344 Ray Bentley	.01	.05
345 Scott Norwood	.01	.05
346 Shane Conlan	.01	.05
347 Steve Tasker	.02	.10
348 Will Wolford	.01	.05
349 Gary Baldinger RC	.01	.05
350 Kirby Jackson	.01	.05
351 Jamie Mueller	.01	.05
352 Pete Metzelaars	.01	.05
353 Richard Dent	.02	.10
354 Ron Rivera	.01	.05
355 Jim Morrissey	.01	.05
356 John Roper	.01	.05
357 Steve McMichael	.02	.10
358 Ron Morris	.01	.05
359 Darren Lewis	.01	.05
360 Anthony Morgan	.01	.05
361 Stan Thomas	.01	.05
362 James Thornton	.01	.05
363 Brad Muster	.01	.05
364 Tim Krumrie	.01	.05
365 Lee Johnson	.01	.05
366 Eric Ball	.01	.05
367 Alonzo Mitz RC	.01	.05
368 David Grant	.01	.05
369 Lynn James	.01	.05
370 Lewis Billups	.01	.05
371 Jim Breech	.01	.05
372 Alfred Williams	.01	.05
373 Wayne Haddix	.01	.05
374 Tim McGee	.01	.05
375 Michael Jackson	.02	.10
376 Leroy Hoard	.02	.10
377 Tony Jones	.01	.05
378 Vince Newsome	.01	.05
379 Todd Philcox RC	.01	.05
380 Eric Metcalf	.02	.10
381 John Rienstra	.01	.05
382 Matt Stover	.01	.05
383 Brian Hansen	.01	.05
384 Joe Morris	.01	.05
385 Anthony Pleasant	.01	.05
386 Mark Stepnoski	.01	.05
387 Erik Williams	.01	.05
388 Jimmie Jones	.01	.05
389 Kevin Gogan	.01	.05
390 Manny Hendrix RC	.01	.05
391 Issiac Holt	.01	.05
392 Ken Norton	.02	.10
393 Tommie Agee	.01	.05
394 Alvin Harper	.02	.10
395 Alexander Wright	.01	.05
396 Mike Saxon	.01	.05
397 Michael Brooks	.01	.05
398 Bobby Humphrey	.01	.05
399 Ken Lanier	.01	.05
400 Steve Sewell	.01	.05
401 Robert Perryman	.01	.05
402 Wymon Henderson	.01	.05
403 Keith Kartz	.01	.05
404 Clarence Kay	.01	.05
405 Keith Traylor	.01	.05
406 Doug Widell	.01	.05
407 Dennis Smith	.01	.05
408 Marc Spindler	.01	.05
409 Lomas Brown	.01	.05
410 Robert Clark	.01	.05
411 Eric Andolsek	.01	.05
412 Mike Farr	.01	.05
413 Ray Crockett	.01	.05
414 Jeff Campbell	.01	.05
415 Dan Owens	.01	.05
416 Jim Arnold	.01	.05
417 Barry Sanders	.50	1.25
418 Eddie Murray	.01	.05
419 Vince Workman	.01	.05
420 Ed West	.01	.05
421 Charles Wilson	.01	.05
422 Perry Kemp	.01	.05
423 Chuck Cecil	.01	.05
424 James Campen	.01	.05
425 Robert Brown	.01	.05
426 Brian Noble	.01	.05
427 Rich Moran	.01	.05
428 Vai Sikahema	.01	.05
429 Allen Rice	.01	.05
430 Haywood Jeffires	.02	.10
431 Warren Moon	.08	.25
432 Greg Montgomery	.01	.05
433 Sean Jones	.01	.05
434 Richard Johnson	.01	.05
435 Al Smith	.01	.05
436 Johnny Meads	.01	.05
437 William Fuller	.01	.05
438 Mike Munchak	.02	.10
439 Ray Childress	.01	.05
440 Cody Carlson	.01	.05
441 Scott Radecic	.01	.05
442 Quintus McDonald RC	.01	.05
443 Eugene Daniel	.01	.05
444 Mark Herrmann RC	.01	.05
445 John Baylor RC	.01	.05
446 Dave McCloughan	.01	.05
447 Mark Vander Poel	.01	.05
448 Randy Dixon	.01	.05
449 Keith Taylor	.01	.05
450 Alan Grant	.01	.05
451 Tony Siragusa	.01	.05
452 Rich Baldinger	.01	.05
453 Derrick Thomas	.08	.25
454 Bill Jones RC	.01	.05
455 Troy Stradford	.01	.05
456 Barry Word	.01	.05
457 Tim Grunhard	.01	.05
458 Chris Martin	.01	.05
459 Jayice Pearson RC	.01	.05
460 Dino Hackett	.01	.05
461 David Lutz	.01	.05
462 Albert Lewis	.01	.05
463 Fred Jones RC	.01	.05
464 Winston Moss	.01	.05
465 Sam Graddy RC	.01	.05
466 Steve Wisniewski	.01	.05
467 Jay Schroeder	.01	.05
468 Ronnie Lott	.02	.10
469 Willie Gault	.02	.10
470 Greg Townsend	.01	.05
471 Max Montoya	.01	.05
472 Howie Long	.08	.25
473 Lionel Washington	.01	.05
474 Riki Ellison	.01	.05
475 Tom Newberry	.01	.05
476 Damone Johnson	.01	.05
477 Pat Terrell	.01	.05
478 Marcus Dupree	.08	.25
479 Todd Lyght	.01	.05
480 Buford McGee	.01	.05
481 Bern Brostek	.01	.05
482 Jim Price	.01	.05
483 Robert Young	.01	.05
484 Tony Zendejas	.01	.05
485 Robert Bailey RC	.01	.05
486 Alvin Wright	.01	.05
487 Pat Carter	.01	.05
488 Pete Stoyanovich	.01	.05
489 Reggie Roby	.01	.05
490 Harry Galbreath	.01	.05
491 Mike McGruder RC	.01	.05
492 J.B. Brown	.01	.05
493 E.J. Junior	.01	.05
494 Ferrell Edmunds	.01	.05
495 Scott Secules	.01	.05
496 Greg Baty RC	.01	.05
497 Mike Iaquaniello	.01	.05
498 Keith Sims	.01	.05
499 John Randle	.02	.10
500 Joey Browner	.01	.05
501 Steve Jordan	.01	.05
502 Darrin Nelson	.01	.05
503 Audray McMillian	.01	.05
504 Harry Newsome	.01	.05
505 Hassan Jones	.01	.05
506 Ray Berry	.01	.05
507 Mike Merriweather	.01	.05
508 Leo Lewis	.01	.05
509 Tim Irwin	.01	.05
510 Kirk Lowdermilk	.01	.05
511 Alfred Anderson	.01	.05
512 Michael Timpson RC	.01	.05
513 Jerome Henderson	.01	.05
514 Andre Tippett	.01	.05
515 Chris Singleton	.01	.05
516 John Stephens	.01	.05
517 Ronnie Lippett	.01	.05
518 Bruce Armstrong	.01	.05
519 Marion Hobby RC	.01	.05
520 Tim Goad	.01	.05
521 Mickey Washington RC	.01	.05
522 Fred Smerlas	.01	.05
523 Wayne Martin	.01	.05
524 Frank Warren	.01	.05
525 Floyd Turner	.01	.05
526 Wesley Carroll	.01	.05
527 Gene Atkins	.01	.05
528 Vaughan Johnson	.01	.05
529 Hoby Brenner	.01	.05
530 Renaldo Turnbull	.01	.05
531 Joel Hilgenberg	.01	.05
532 Craig Heyward	.02	.10
533 Vince Buck	.01	.05
534 Jim Dombrowski	.01	.05
535 Fred McAfee RC	.01	.05
536 Phil Simms	.02	.10
537 Lewis Tillman	.01	.05
538 John Elliott	.01	.05
539 Dave Meggett	.02	.10
540 Mark Collins	.01	.05
541 Ottis Anderson	.02	.10
542 Bobby Abrams RC	.01	.05
543 Sean Landeta	.01	.05
544 Brian Williams OL	.01	.05
545 Erik Howard	.01	.05
546 Mark Ingram	.01	.05
547 Kanavis McGhee	.01	.05
548 Kyle Clifton	.01	.05
549 Marvin Washington	.01	.05
550 Jeff Criswell	.01	.05
551 Dave Cadigan	.01	.05
552 Chris Burkett	.01	.05
553 Erik McMillan	.01	.05
554 James Hasty	.01	.05
555 Louie Aguiar RC	.01	.05
556 Troy Johnson RC	.01	.05
557 Troy Taylor RC	.01	.05
558 Pat Kelly RC	.01	.05
559 Heath Sherman	.01	.05
560 Roger Ruzek	.01	.05
561 Andre Waters	.01	.05
562 Izel Jenkins	.01	.05
563 Keith Jackson	.02	.10
564 Byron Evans	.01	.05
565 Wes Hopkins	.01	.05
566 Rich Miano	.01	.05
567 Seth Joyner	.01	.05
568 Thomas Sanders	.01	.05
569 David Alexander	.01	.05
570 Jeff Kemp	.01	.05
571 Jock Jones RC	.01	.05
572 Craig Patterson RC	.01	.05
573 Robert Massey	.01	.05
574 Bill Lewis	.01	.05
575 Freddie Joe Nunn	.01	.05
576 Aeneas Williams	.02	.10
577 John Jackson	.01	.05
578 Tim McDonald	.01	.05
579 Michael Zordich RC	.01	.05
580 Eric Hill	.01	.05
581 Lorenzo Lynch	.01	.05
582 Vernice Smith RC	.01	.05
583 Greg Lloyd	.02	.10
584 Carnell Lake	.01	.05
585 Hardy Nickerson	.02	.10
586 Delton Hall	.01	.05
587 Gerald Williams	.01	.05
588 Bryan Hinkle	.01	.05
589 Barry Foster	.02	.10
590 Bubby Brister	.02	.10
591 Rick Strom RC	.01	.05
592 David Little	.01	.05
593 Leroy Thompson	.01	.05
594 Eric Bieniemy	.01	.05
595 Courtney Hall	.01	.05
596 George Thornton	.01	.05
597 Donnie Elder	.01	.05
598 Billy Ray Smith	.01	.05
599 Gill Byrd	.01	.05
600 Marion Butts	.01	.05
601 Ronnie Harmon	.01	.05
602 Anthony Shelton	.01	.05
603 Mark May	.01	.05
604 Craig McEwen RC	.01	.05
605 Steve Young	.25	.60
606 Keith Henderson	.01	.05
607 Pierce Holt	.01	.05
608 Roy Foster	.01	.05
609 Don Griffin	.01	.05
610 Harry Sydney	.01	.05
611 Todd Bowles	.01	.05
612 Ted Washington	.01	.05
613 Johnnie Jackson	.01	.05
614 Jesse Sapolu	.01	.05
615 Brent Jones	.02	.10
616 Travis McNeal	.01	.05
617 Darrick Brilz RC	.01	.05
618 Terry Wooden	.01	.05
619 Tommy Kane	.01	.05
620 Nesby Glasgow	.01	.05
621 Dwayne Harper	.01	.05
622 Rick Tuten	.01	.05
623 Chris Warren	.02	.10
624 John L. Williams	.01	.05
625 Rufus Porter	.01	.05
626 David Daniels	.01	.05
627 Keith McCants	.01	.05
628 Reuben Davis	.01	.05
629 Mark Royals	.01	.05
630 Marty Carter RC	.01	.05
631 Ian Beckles	.01	.05
632 Ron Hall	.01	.05
633 Eugene Marve	.01	.05
634 Willie Drewrey	.01	.05
635 Tom McHale RC	.01	.05
636 Kevin Murphy	.01	.05
637 Robert Hardy RC	.01	.05
638 Ricky Sanders	.01	.05
639 Gary Clark	.02	.10
640 Andre Collins	.01	.05
641 Brad Edwards	.01	.05
642 Monte Coleman	.01	.05
643 Clarence Vaughn RC	.01	.05
644 Fred Stokes	.01	.05
645 Charles Mann	.01	.05
646 Earnest Byner	.01	.05
647 Jim Lachey	.01	.05
648 Jeff Bostic	.01	.05
649 Chris Mims RC	.01	.05
650 George Williams RC	.01	.05
651 Ed Cunningham RC	.01	.05
652 Tony Smith WR RC	.01	.05
653 Will Furrer RC	.01	.05
654 Matt Elliott RC	.01	.05
655 Mike Mooney RC	.01	.05
656 Eddie Blake RC	.01	.05
657 Leon Searcy RC	.01	.05
658 Kevin Turner RC	.01	.05
659 Keith Hamilton RC	.02	.10
660 Alan Haller RC	.01	.05

1992 Pacific Bob Griese

COMPLETE SET (9)	2.00	5.00
COMMON GRIESE (10-18)	.25	.60
AU Bob Griese AUTO	20.00	50.00
(Certified autograph card)		

1992 Pacific Steve Largent

COMPLETE SET (9)	2.00	5.00
COMMON LARGENT (1-9)	.25	.60
AU Steve Largent AUTO	30.00	60.00
(Certified autograph card)		

1992 Pacific Picks The Pros

COMPLETE SET (25)	8.00	20.00
*GOLD/SILVER: SAME PRICE		
1 Mark Rypien	.10	.30
2 Marv Cook	.10	.30
3 Jim Lachey	.10	.30
4 Darrell Green	.10	.30
5 Derrick Thomas	.60	1.50
6 Thurman Thomas	.60	1.50
7 Kent Hull	.10	.30
8 Tim McDonald	.10	.30
9 Mike Croel	.10	.30
10 Anthony Munoz	.25	.60
11 Jerome Brown	.10	.30
12 Reggie White	.60	1.50
13 Gill Byrd	.10	.30
14 Jessie Tuggle	.10	.30
15 Randall McDaniel	.10	.30
16 Sam Mills	.10	.30
17 Pat Swilling	.10	.30
18 Eugene Robinson	.10	.30
19 Michael Irvin	.60	1.50
20 Emmitt Smith	4.00	10.00
21 Jeff Gossett	.10	.30
22 Jeff Jaeger	.10	.30
23 William Fuller	.10	.30
24 Mike Munchak	.25	.60
25 Andre Rison	.25	.60

1992 Pacific Prism Inserts

COMPLETE SET (10)	5.00	12.00
1 Thurman Thomas	.40	1.00
2 Gaston Green	.07	.20
3 Christian Okoye	.07	.20
4 Leonard Russell	.15	.40
5 Mark Higgs	.07	.20
6 Emmitt Smith	2.50	6.00
7 Barry Sanders	2.00	5.00
8 Rodney Hampton	.15	.40
9 Earnest Byner	.07	.20
10 Herschel Walker	.15	.40

1992 Pacific Statistical Leaders

COMPLETE SET (30)	5.00	10.00
ONE SET PER FACTORY SET		
1 Chris Miller	.07	.20
2 Thurman Thomas	.20	.50
3 Jim Harbaugh	.20	.50
4 Jim Breech	.02	.10
5 Kevin Mack	.02	.10
6 Emmitt Smith	1.50	3.00
7 Gaston Green	.02	.10
8 Barry Sanders	1.25	2.50
9 Tony Bennett	.02	.10
10 Warren Moon	.20	.50
11 Bill Brooks	.02	.10
12 Christian Okoye	.02	.10
13 Jay Schroeder	.02	.10
14 Robert Delpino	.02	.10
15 Mark Higgs	.02	.10
16 John Randle	.07	.20
17 Leonard Russell	.07	.20
18 Pat Swilling	.02	.10
19 Rodney Hampton	.07	.20
20 Terance Mathis	.07	.20
21 Fred Barnett	.07	.20
22 Aeneas Williams	.07	.20
23 Neil O'Donnell	.07	.20
24 Marion Butts	.02	.10
25 Steve Young	.60	1.25
26 John L. Williams	.02	.10
27 Reggie Cobb	.02	.10
28 Mark Rypien	.02	.10
29 Thurman Thomas	.20	.50
AFC Rushing Leaders		
30 Emmitt Smith	1.50	3.00
NFC Rushing Leaders		

1993 Pacific Prototypes

COMPLETE SET (5)	6.00	15.00
1 Emmitt Smith	2.40	6.00
2 Barry Sanders	2.40	6.00
3 Derrick Thomas	.60	1.50
4 Jim Everett	.60	1.50
5 Steve Young	1.20	3.00

1993 Pacific

The 1993 Pacific football set consists of 440 standard-size cards. Just 5,000 cases or 99,000 of each card were reportedly produced. Randomly inserted throughout the 12-card foil packs were a 25-card Pacific Picks the Pros gold foil set and a 20-card Prism set. The production run on the insert sets was 8,000 each. The cards are checklisted according to NFC and AFC divisional alignments. The set closes with the following topical subsets: NFL Stars (393-417) and Rookies (418-440). Rookie Cards include Jerome Bettis, Drew Bledsoe, Reggie Brooks, Curtis Conway, Garrison Hearst, O.J. McDuffie, Natrone Means, Glyn Milburn, Rick Mirer, Robert Smith and Kevin Williams. Separately numbered checklist cards were also randomly inserted into packs.

COMPLETE SET (440)	10.00	20.00
1 Emmitt Smith	.60	1.50
2 Troy Aikman	.30	.75
3 Larry Brown DB	.01	.05
4 Tony Casillas	.01	.05
5 Thomas Everett	.01	.05
6 Alvin Harper	.02	.10
7 Michael Irvin	.08	.25
8 Charles Haley	.02	.10
9 Leon Lett RC	.02	.10
10 Kevin Smith	.02	.10
11 Robert Jones	.01	.05
12 Jimmy Smith	.08	.25
13 Derrick Gainer RC	.01	.05
14 Lin Elliott	.01	.05
15 William Thomas	.01	.05
16 Clyde Simmons	.01	.05
17 Seth Joyner	.01	.05
18 Randall Cunningham	.08	.25
19 Byron Evans	.01	.05
20 Fred Barnett	.02	.10
21 Calvin Williams	.02	.10
22 James Joseph	.01	.05
23 Heath Sherman	.01	.05
24 Siran Stacy	.01	.05
25 Andy Harmon	.02	.10
26 Eric Allen	.01	.05
27 Herschel Walker	.02	.10
28 Vai Sikahema	.01	.05
29 Earnest Byner	.01	.05
30 Jeff Bostic	.01	.05
31 Monte Coleman	.01	.05
32 Ricky Ervins	.01	.05
33 Darrell Green	.01	.05
34 Mark Schlereth	.01	.05
35 Mark Rypien	.01	.05
36 Art Monk	.02	.10
37 Brian Mitchell	.02	.10
38 Chip Lohmiller	.01	.05
39 Charles Mann	.01	.05
40 Shane Collins	.01	.05
41 Jim Lachey	.01	.05
42 Desmond Howard	.02	.10
43 Rodney Hampton	.02	.10
44 Dave Brown RC	.08	.25
45 Mark Collins	.01	.05
46 Jarrod Bunch	.01	.05
47 William Roberts	.01	.05
48 Sean Landeta	.01	.05
49 Lawrence Taylor	.08	.25
50 Ed McCaffrey	.08	.25
51 Bart Oates	.01	.05
52 Pepper Johnson	.01	.05
53 Eric Dorsey	.01	.05
54 Erik Howard	.01	.05
55 Phil Simms	.02	.10
56 Derek Brown TE	.01	.05
57 Johnny Bailey	.01	.05
58 Rich Camarillo	.01	.05
59 Larry Centers RC	.08	.25
60 Chris Chandler	.02	.10
61 Randal Hill	.01	.05
62 Ricky Proehl	.01	.05
63 Freddie Joe Nunn	.01	.05
64 Robert Massey	.01	.05
65 Aeneas Williams	.01	.05
66 Luis Sharpe	.01	.05
67 Eric Swann	.02	.10
68 Timm Rosenbach	.01	.05
69 Anthony Edwards RC	.01	.05
70 Greg Davis	.01	.05
71 Terry Allen	.08	.25
72 Anthony Carter	.02	.10
73 Cris Carter	.08	.25
74 Roger Craig	.02	.10
75 Jack Del Rio	.01	.05
76 Chris Doleman	.01	.05
77 Rich Gannon	.08	.25
78 Hassan Jones	.01	.05
79 Steve Jordan	.01	.05
80 Randall McDaniel	.02	.10
81 Sean Salisbury	.01	.05
82 Harry Newsome	.01	.05
83 Carlos Jenkins	.01	.05
84 Jake Reed	.08	.25
85 Edgar Bennett	.08	.25
86 Tony Bennett	.01	.05
87 Terrell Buckley	.01	.05
88 Ty Detmer	.08	.25
89 Brett Favre	.75	2.00
90 Chris Jacke	.01	.05
91 Sterling Sharpe	.08	.25
92 James Campen	.01	.05
93 Brian Noble	.01	.05
94 Lester Archambeau RC	.01	.05
95 Harry Sydney	.01	.05
96 Corey Harris	.01	.05
97 Don Majkowski	.01	.05
98 Ken Ruettgers	.01	.05
99 Lomas Brown	.01	.05
100 Jason Hanson	.01	.05
101 Robert Porcher	.01	.05
102 Chris Spielman	.02	.10
103 Erik Kramer	.02	.10
104 Tracy Scroggins	.01	.05
105 Rodney Peete	.01	.05
106 Barry Sanders	.50	1.25
107 Herman Moore	.08	.25
108 Brett Perriman	.08	.25
109 Mel Gray	.02	.10
110 Dennis Gibson	.01	.05
111 Bennie Blades	.01	.05
112 Andre Ware	.01	.05
113 Gary Anderson RB	.01	.05
114 Tyji Armstrong	.01	.05
115 Reggie Cobb	.01	.05
116 Marty Carter	.01	.05
117 Lawrence Dawsey	.01	.05
118 Steve DeBerg	.01	.05
119 Ron Hall	.01	.05
120 Courtney Hawkins	.01	.05
121 Broderick Thomas	.01	.05
122 Keith McCants	.01	.05
123 Bruce Reimers	.01	.05
124 Darrick Brownlow	.01	.05
125 Mark Wheeler	.01	.05
126 Ricky Reynolds	.01	.05
127 Neal Anderson	.01	.05
128 Trace Armstrong	.01	.05
129 Mark Carrier DB	.01	.05
130 Richard Dent	.02	.10
131 Wendell Davis	.01	.05
132 Darren Lewis	.01	.05
133 Tom Waddle	.01	.05
134 Jim Harbaugh	.08	.25
135 Steve McMichael	.02	.10
136 William Perry	.02	.10
137 Alonzo Spellman	.01	.05
138 John Roper	.01	.05
139 Peter Tom Willis	.01	.05
140 Dante Jones	.01	.05
141 Harris Barton	.01	.05
142 Michael Carter	.01	.05
143 Eric Davis	.01	.05
144 Dana Hall	.01	.05
145 Amp Lee	.01	.05
146 Don Griffin	.01	.05
147 Jerry Rice	.40	1.00
148 Ricky Watters	.08	.25
149 Steve Young	.30	.75
150 Bill Romanowski	.01	.05
151 Klaus Wilmsmeyer	.01	.05
152 Steve Bono	.02	.10
153 Tom Rathman	.01	.05
154 Odessa Turner	.01	.05
155 Morten Andersen	.01	.05
156 Richard Cooper	.01	.05
157 Toi Cook	.01	.05
158 Quinn Early	.02	.10
159 Vaughn Dunbar	.01	.05
160 Rickey Jackson	.01	.05
161 Wayne Martin	.01	.05
162 Hoby Brenner	.01	.05
163 Joel Hilgenberg	.01	.05
164 Mike Buck	.01	.05
165 Torrance Small	.01	.05
166 Eric Martin	.01	.05
167 Vaughan Johnson	.01	.05
168 Sam Mills	.01	.05
169 Steve Broussard	.01	.05
170 Darion Conner	.01	.05
171 Drew Hill	.01	.05
172 Chris Hinton	.01	.05
173 Chris Miller	.02	.10
174 Tim McKyer	.01	.05
175 Norm Johnson	.01	.05
176 Mike Pritchard	.02	.10
177 Andre Rison	.02	.10
178 Deion Sanders	.20	.50
179 Tony Smith	.01	.05
180 Bruce Pickens	.01	.05
181 Michael Haynes	.02	.10
182 Jessie Tuggle	.01	.05
183 Marc Boutte	.01	.05
184 Don Bracken	.01	.05
185 Bern Brostek	.01	.05
186 Henry Ellard	.02	.10
187 Jim Everett	.02	.10
188 Sean Gilbert	.02	.10
189 Cleveland Gary	.01	.05
190 Todd Kinchen	.01	.05
191 Pat Terrell	.01	.05
192 Jackie Slater	.01	.05
193 David Lang	.01	.05
194 Flipper Anderson	.01	.05
195 Tony Zendejas	.01	.05
196 Roman Phifer	.01	.05
197 Steve Christie	.01	.05
198 Cornelius Bennett	.02	.10
199 Phil Hansen	.01	.05
200 Don Beebe	.01	.05
201 Mark Kelso	.01	.05
202 Bruce Smith	.08	.25
203 Darryl Talley	.01	.05
204 Andre Reed	.02	.10
205 Mike Lodish	.01	.05
206 Jim Kelly	.08	.25
207 Thurman Thomas	.08	.25
208 Kenneth Davis	.01	.05
209 Frank Reich	.02	.10
210 Kent Hull	.01	.05
211 Marco Coleman	.01	.05
212 Bryan Cox	.01	.05
213 Jeff Cross	.01	.05
214 Mark Higgs	.01	.05
215 Keith Jackson	.02	.10
216 Scott Miller	.01	.05
217 John Offerdahl	.01	.05
218 Dan Marino	.60	1.50
219 Keith Sims	.01	.05
220 Chuck Klingbeil	.01	.05
221 Troy Vincent	.01	.05
222 Mike Williams WR RC	.01	.05
223 Pete Stoyanovich	.01	.05
224 J.B. Brown	.01	.05
225 Ashley Ambrose	.01	.05
226 Jason Belser RC	.01	.05
227 Jeff George	.08	.25
228 Quentin Coryatt	.02	.10
229 Duane Bickett	.01	.05
230 Steve Emtman	.01	.05
231 Anthony Johnson	.02	.10
232 Rohn Stark	.01	.05
233 Jessie Hester	.01	.05
234 Reggie Langhorne	.01	.05
235 Clarence Verdin	.01	.05
236 Dean Biasucci	.01	.05
237 Jack Trudeau	.01	.05
238 Tony Siragusa	.01	.05
239 Chris Burkett	.01	.05
240 Brad Baxter	.01	.05
241 Rob Moore	.02	.10
242 Browning Nagle	.01	.05
243 Jim Sweeney	.01	.05
244 Kurt Barber	.01	.05
245 Siupeli Malamala RC	.01	.05
246 Mike Brim	.01	.05
247 Mo Lewis	.01	.05
248 Johnny Mitchell	.01	.05
249 Ken Whisenhunt RC	.10	.30
250 James Hasty	.01	.05
251 Kyle Clifton	.01	.05
252 Terance Mathis	.02	.10
253 Ray Agnew	.01	.05
254 Eugene Chung	.01	.05
255 Marv Cook	.01	.05
256 Johnny Rembert	.01	.05
257 Maurice Hurst	.01	.05
258 Jon Vaughn	.01	.05
259 Leonard Russell	.02	.10
260 Pat Harlow	.01	.05
261 Andre Tippett	.01	.05
262 Michael Timpson	.01	.05
263 Greg McMurtry	.01	.05
264 Chris Singleton	.01	.05
265 Reggie Redding RC	.01	.05
266 Walter Stanley	.01	.05
267 Gary Anderson K	.01	.05
268 Merril Hoge	.01	.05
269 Barry Foster	.02	.10
270 Charles Davenport	.01	.05
271 Jeff Graham	.02	.10
272 Adrian Cooper	.01	.05
273 David Little	.01	.05
274 Neil O'Donnell	.08	.25
275 Rod Woodson	.08	.25
276 Ernie Mills	.01	.05
277 Dwight Stone	.01	.05
278 Darren Perry	.01	.05
279 Dermontti Dawson	.01	.05
280 Carlton Haselrig	.01	.05
281 Pat Coleman	.01	.05
282 Ernest Givins	.02	.10
283 Warren Moon	.08	.25
284 Haywood Jeffires	.02	.10
285 Cody Carlson	.01	.05
286 Ray Childress	.01	.05
287 Bruce Matthews	.01	.05
288 Webster Slaughter	.01	.05
289 Bo Orlando	.01	.05
290 Lorenzo White	.01	.05
291 Eddie Robinson	.01	.05
292 Bubba McDowell	.01	.05
293 Bucky Richardson	.01	.05
294 Sean Jones	.01	.05
295 David Brandon	.01	.05
296 Shawn Collins	.01	.05
297 Lawyer Tillman	.01	.05
298 Bob Dahl	.01	.05
299 Kevin Mack	.01	.05
300 Bernie Kosar	.02	.10
301 Tommy Vardell	.01	.05
302 Jay Hilgenberg	.01	.05
303 Michael Dean Perry	.02	.10
304 Michael Jackson	.02	.10
305 Eric Metcalf	.02	.10
306 Rico Smith RC	.01	.05
307 Stevon Moore RC	.01	.05
308 Leroy Hoard	.02	.10
309 Eric Ball	.01	.05
310 Derrick Fenner	.01	.05
311 James Francis	.01	.05
312 Ricardo McDonald	.01	.05
313 Tim Krumrie	.01	.05
314 Carl Pickens	.02	.10
315 David Klingler	.01	.05
316 Donald Hollas RC	.01	.05
317 Harold Green	.01	.05
318 Daniel Stubbs	.01	.05
319 Alfred Williams	.01	.05
320 Darryl Williams	.01	.05
321 Mike Arthur RC	.01	.05
322 Leonard Wheeler	.01	.05
323 Gill Byrd	.01	.05
324 Eric Bieniemy	.01	.05
325 Marion Butts	.01	.05
326 John Carney	.01	.05
327 Stan Humphries	.02	.10
328 Ronnie Harmon	.01	.05
329 Junior Seau	.08	.25
330 Nate Lewis	.01	.05
331 Harry Swayne	.01	.05
332 Leslie O'Neal	.02	.10
333 Eric Moten	.01	.05
334 Blaise Winter RC	.01	.05
335 Anthony Miller	.02	.10
336 Gary Plummer	.01	.05
337 Willie Davis	.08	.25
338 J.J. Birden	.01	.05
339 Tim Barnett	.01	.05
340 Dave Krieg	.02	.10
341 Barry Word	.01	.05
342 Tracy Simien	.01	.05
343 Christian Okoye	.01	.05
344 Todd McNair	.01	.05
345 Dan Saleaumua	.01	.05
346 Derrick Thomas	.08	.25
347 Harvey Williams	.02	.10
348 Kimble Anders RC	.08	.25
349 Tim Grunhard	.01	.05
350 Tony Hargain RC UER	.01	.05
(Hargrain on front)		
351 Simon Fletcher	.01	.05
352 John Elway	.60	1.50
353 Mike Croel	.01	.05
354 Steve Atwater	.01	.05
355 Tommy Maddox	.08	.25
356 Karl Mecklenburg	.01	.05
357 Shane Dronett	.01	.05
358 Kenny Walker	.01	.05
359 Reggie Rivers RC	.01	.05
360 Cedric Tillman RC	.01	.05
361 Arthur Marshall RC	.01	.05
362 Greg Lewis	.01	.05
363 Shannon Sharpe	.08	.25
364 Doug Widell	.01	.05
365 Todd Marinovich	.01	.05
366 Nick Bell	.01	.05
367 Eric Dickerson	.02	.10
368 Max Montoya	.01	.05
369 Winston Moss	.01	.05
370 Howie Long	.08	.25
371 Willie Gault	.01	.05
372 Tim Brown	.08	.25
373 Steve Smith	.01	.05
374 Steve Wisniewski	.01	.05
375 Alexander Wright	.01	.05
376 Ethan Horton	.01	.05
377 Napoleon McCallum	.01	.05
378 Terry McDaniel	.01	.05
379 Patrick Hunter	.01	.05
380 Robert Blackmon	.01	.05
381 John Kasay	.01	.05
382 Cortez Kennedy	.02	.10
383 Andy Heck	.01	.05
384 Bill Hitchcock RC	.01	.05
385 Rick Mirer RC	.08	.25
386 Jeff Bryant	.01	.05
387 Eugene Robinson	.01	.05
388 John L. Williams	.01	.05
389 Chris Warren	.02	.10
390 Rufus Porter	.01	.05
391 Joe Tofflemire RC	.01	.05
392 Dan McGwire	.01	.05
393 Boomer Esiason	.02	.10
394 Brad Muster	.01	.05
395 James Lofton	.02	.10
396 Tim McGee	.01	.05
397 Steve Beuerlein	.02	.10
398 Gaston Green	.01	.05
399 Bill Brooks	.01	.05
400 Ronnie Lott	.02	.10
401 Jay Schroeder	.01	.05
402 Marcus Allen	.08	.25
403 Kevin Greene	.02	.10
404 Kirk Lowdermilk	.01	.05
405 Hugh Millen	.01	.05
406 Pat Swilling	.01	.05
407 Bobby Hebert	.01	.05
408 Carl Banks	.01	.05
409 Jeff Hostetler	.02	.10
410 Leonard Marshall	.01	.05
411 Ken O'Brien	.01	.05
412 Joe Montana	.60	1.50
413 Reggie White	.08	.25
414 Gary Clark	.02	.10
415 Johnny Johnson	.01	.05
416 Tim McDonald	.01	.05
417 Pierce Holt	.01	.05
418 Gino Torretta RC	.02	.10
419 Glyn Milburn RC	.08	.25
420 O.J. McDuffie RC	.08	.25
421 Coleman Rudolph RC	.01	.05
422 Reggie Brooks RC	.02	.10
423 Garrison Hearst RC	.25	.60
424 Leonard Renfro RC	.01	.05
425 Kevin Williams RC	.08	.25
426 Demetrius DuBose RC	.01	.05
427 Elvis Grbac RC	.50	1.25
428 Lincoln Kennedy RC	.01	.05
429 Carlton Gray RC	.01	.05
430 Micheal Barrow RC	.08	.25
431 George Teague RC	.02	.10
432 Curtis Conway RC	.15	.40
433 Natrone Means RC	.08	.25
434 Jerome Bettis RC	2.00	5.00
435 Drew Bledsoe RC	.75	2.00
436 Robert Smith RC	.40	1.00
437 Deon Figures RC	.01	.05
438 Qadry Ismail RC	.08	.25
439 Chris Slade RC	.02	.10
440 Dana Stubblefield RC	.08	.25

1993 Pacific Picks the Pros Gold

COMPLETE SET (25)	15.00	40.00
1 Jerry Rice	4.00	8.00
2 Sterling Sharpe	1.00	2.00
3 Richmond Webb	.15	.40
4 Harris Barton	.15	.40
5 Randall McDaniel	.15	.40
6 Steve Wisniewski	.15	.40
7 Mark Stepnoski	.15	.40
8 Steve Young	3.00	6.00
9 Emmitt Smith	6.00	12.00
10 Barry Foster	.30	.75
11 Nick Lowery	.15	.40
12 Reggie White	1.00	2.00
13 Leslie O'Neal	.30	.75
14 Cortez Kennedy	.30	.75
15 Ray Childress	.15	.40
16 Vaughan Johnson	.15	.40
17 Wilber Marshall	.15	.40
18 Junior Seau	1.00	2.00
19 Sam Mills	.15	.40
20 Rod Woodson	1.00	2.00
21 Ricky Reynolds	.15	.40
22 Steve Atwater	.15	.40
23 Chuck Cecil	.15	.40
24 Rich Camarillo	.15	.40
25 Dale Carter	.15	.40

1993 Pacific Silver Prism Inserts

COMPLETE SET (20)	25.00	60.00
*CIRCULAR BACKGROUND: SAME PRICE		
CIRCULAR:ONE PER SPEC.RET.PACK		
1 Troy Aikman	2.00	5.00
2 Jerome Bettis	6.00	15.00
3 Drew Bledsoe	2.50	6.00
4 Reggie Brooks	.10	.30
5 Brett Favre	5.00	12.00
6 Barry Foster	.25	.60
7 Garrison Hearst	.75	2.00
8 Michael Irvin	.60	1.50
9 Cortez Kennedy	.25	.60
10 David Klingler	.10	.30
11 Dan Marino	4.00	10.00
12 Rick Mirer	.30	.75
13 Joe Montana	4.00	10.00
14 Jay Novacek	.10	.30
15 Jerry Rice	2.50	6.00
16 Barry Sanders	3.00	8.00
17 Sterling Sharpe	.60	1.50
18 Emmitt Smith	4.00	10.00
19 Thurman Thomas	.60	1.50
20 Steve Young	2.00	5.00

1994 Pacific

This set consists of 450 standard size cards featuring full-bleed color photos. The player's name and position are in gold foil at the bottom. The backs are dominated by a color with statistics at the bottom. The players are grouped alphabetically within their team subsets. The set closes with a Rookies (417-450) subset. Rookie Cards in this set include Mario Bates, Lake Dawson, Trent Dilfer, Marshall Faulk, William Floyd, Greg Hill. Charles Johnson, Errict Rhett, Darnay Scott, and Heath Shuler. A Sterling Sharpe Promo card was produced and priced at the end of our listings.

COMPLETE SET (450)	15.00	30.00
1 Troy Aikman	.40	1.00
2 Charles Haley	.02	.10
3 Alvin Harper	.02	.10
4 Michael Irvin	.08	.25
5 Jim Jeffcoat	.01	.05
6 Daryl Johnston	.02	.10
7 Robert Jones	.01	.05
8 Brock Marion RC	.08	.25
9 Russell Maryland	.01	.05
10 Ken Norton	.02	.10
11 Jay Novacek	.02	.10
12 Emmitt Smith	.60	1.50
13 Kevin Smith	.01	.05
14 Tony Tolbert	.01	.05
15 Kevin Williams WR	.02	.10
16 Don Beebe	.01	.05
17 Cornelius Bennett	.02	.10
18 Bill Brooks	.01	.05
19 Steve Christie	.01	.05
20 Russell Copeland	.01	.05
21 Kenneth Davis	.01	.05
22 Kent Hull	.01	.05

23 Jim Kelly	.08	.25
24 Pete Metzelaars	.01	.05
25 Andre Reed	.02	.10
26 Frank Reich	.02	.10
27 Bruce Smith	.08	.25
28 Darryl Talley	.01	.05
29 Steve Tasker	.02	.10
30 Thurman Thomas	.08	.25
31 Steve Bono	.02	.10
32 Dexter Carter	.01	.05
33 Kevin Fagan	.01	.05
34 Dana Hall	.01	.05
35 Brent Jones	.02	.10
36 Amp Lee	.01	.05
37 Marc Logan	.01	.05
38 Tim McDonald	.01	.05
39 Guy McIntyre	.01	.05
40 Tom Rathman	.01	.05
41 Jerry Rice	.40	1.00
42 Dana Stubblefield	.02	.10
43 Steve Wallace	.01	.05
44 Ricky Watters	.02	.10
45 Steve Young	.30	.75
46 Marcus Allen	.08	.25
47 Kimble Anders	.02	.10
48 Tim Barnett	.01	.05
49 J.J. Birden	.01	.05
50 Dale Carter	.01	.05
51 Jonathan Hayes	.01	.05
52 Dave Krieg	.02	.10
53 Albert Lewis	.01	.05
54 Nick Lowery	.01	.05
55 Joe Montana	.75	2.00
56 Neil Smith	.02	.10
57 John Stephens	.01	.05
58 Derrick Thomas	.08	.25
59 Harvey Williams	.02	.10
60 Micheal Barrow	.01	.05
61 Gary Brown	.01	.05
62 Cody Carlson	.01	.05
63 Ray Childress	.01	.05
64 Curtis Duncan	.01	.05
65 Ernest Givins	.02	.10
66 Haywood Jeffires	.02	.10
67 Wilber Marshall	.01	.05
68 Bubba McDowell	.01	.05
69 Warren Moon	.08	.25
70 Mike Munchak	.02	.10
71 Marcus Robertson	.01	.05
72 Webster Slaughter	.01	.05
73 Gary Wellman RC	.01	.05
74 Lorenzo White	.01	.05
75 Ray Crockett	.01	.05
76 Jason Hanson	.01	.05
77 Rodney Holman	.01	.05
78 George Jamison	.01	.05
79 Erik Kramer	.02	.10
80 Ryan McNeil	.01	.05
81 Derrick Moore	.01	.05
82 Herman Moore	.08	.25
83 Rodney Peete	.01	.05
84 Brett Perriman	.02	.10
85 Barry Sanders	.60	1.50
86 Chris Spielman	.02	.10
87 Pat Swilling	.01	.05
88 Vernon Turner	.01	.05
89 Andre Ware	.01	.05
90 Michael Brooks	.01	.05
91 Dave Brown	.02	.10
92 Derek Brown TE	.01	.05
93 Jarrod Bunch	.01	.05
94 Chris Calloway	.01	.05
95 Kent Graham	.02	.10
96 Rodney Hampton	.02	.10
97 Mark Jackson	.01	.05
98 Ed McCaffrey	.08	.25
99 Dave Meggett	.01	.05
100 Aaron Pierce	.01	.05
101 Mike Sherrard	.01	.05
102 Phil Simms	.02	.10
103 Lewis Tillman	.01	.05
104 Eddie Anderson	.01	.05
105 Patrick Bates	.01	.05
106 Nick Bell	.01	.05
107 Tim Brown	.08	.25
108 Willie Gault	.01	.05
109 Jeff Gossett	.01	.05
110 Ethan Horton	.01	.05
111 Jeff Hostetler	.02	.10
112 Rocket Ismail	.02	.10
113 Chester McGlockton	.01	.05
114 Anthony Smith	.01	.05
115 Steve Smith	.01	.05
116 Greg Townsend	.01	.05
117 Steve Wisniewski	.01	.05
118 Alexander Wright	.01	.05
119 Steve Atwater	.01	.05
120 Rod Bernstine	.01	.05
121 Mike Croel	.01	.05
122 Shane Dronett	.01	.05
123 Jason Elam	.02	.10
124 John Elway	.75	2.00
125 Brian Habib	.01	.05
126 Rondell Jones	.01	.05
127 Tommy Maddox	.08	.25
128 Karl Mecklenburg	.01	.05
129 Glyn Milburn	.02	.10
130 Derek Russell	.01	.05
131 Shannon Sharpe	.02	.10
132 Dennis Smith	.01	.05
133 Edgar Bennett	.08	.25
134 Tony Bennett	.01	.05
135 Robert Brooks	.08	.25
136 Terrell Buckley	.01	.05
137 LeRoy Butler	.01	.05
138 Mark Clayton	.01	.05
139 Ty Detmer	.02	.10
140 Brett Favre	.75	2.00
141 John Jurkovic RC	.02	.10
142 Bryce Paup	.02	.10
143 Sterling Sharpe	.02	.10
144 George Teague	.01	.05
145 Darrell Thompson	.01	.05
146 Ed West	.01	.05
147 Reggie White	.08	.25
148 Terry Allen	.02	.10
149 Anthony Carter	.02	.10
150 Cris Carter	.20	.50
151 Roger Craig	.02	.10
152 Jack Del Rio	.01	.05
153 Chris Doleman	.01	.05
154 Scottie Graham RC	.02	.10
155 Eric Guliford RC	.01	.05
156 Qadry Ismail	.08	.25
157 Steve Jordan	.01	.05
158 Randall McDaniel	.02	.10
159 Jim McMahon	.02	.10
160 Audray McMillian	.01	.05
161 Sean Salisbury	.01	.05
162 Robert Smith	.08	.25
163 Henry Thomas	.01	.05
164 Gary Anderson K	.01	.05
165 Deon Figures	.01	.05
166 Barry Foster	.01	.05
167 Jeff Graham	.01	.05
168 Kevin Greene	.02	.10
169 Dave Hoffman	.01	.05
170 Merril Hoge	.01	.05
171 Gary Jones	.01	.05
172 Greg Lloyd	.02	.10
173 Ernie Mills	.01	.05
174 Neil O'Donnell	.08	.25
175 Darren Perry	.01	.05
176 Leon Searcy	.01	.05
177 Leroy Thompson	.01	.05
178 Willie Williams RC	.01	.05
179 Rod Woodson	.02	.10
180 Keith Byars	.01	.05
181 Marco Coleman	.01	.05
182 Bryan Cox	.01	.05
183 Irving Fryar	.02	.10
184 John Grimsley	.01	.05
185 Mark Higgs	.01	.05
186 Mark Ingram	.01	.05
187 Keith Jackson	.01	.05
188 Terry Kirby	.08	.25
109 Dan Marino	.75	2.00
190 O.J. McDuffie	.08	.25
191 Scott Mitchell	.02	.10
192 Pete Stoyanovich	.01	.05
193 Troy Vincent	.01	.05
194 Richmond Webb	.01	.05
195 Brad Baxter	.01	.05
196 Chris Burkett	.01	.05
197 Rob Carpenter	.01	.05
198 Boomer Esiason	.02	.10
199 Johnny Johnson	.01	.05
200 Jeff Lageman	.01	.05
201 Mo Lewis	.01	.05
202 Ronnie Lott	.02	.10
203 Leonard Marshall	.01	.05
204 Terance Mathis	.02	.10
205 Johnny Mitchell	.01	.05
206 Rob Moore	.02	.10
207 Anthony Prior	.01	.05
208 Blair Thomas	.01	.05
209 Brian Washington	.01	.05
210 Eric Bieniemy	.01	.05
211 Marion Butts	.01	.05
212 Gill Byrd	.01	.05
213 John Carney	.01	.05
214 Darren Carrington	.01	.05
215 John Friesz	.02	.10
216 Ronnie Harmon	.01	.05
217 Stan Humphries	.02	.10
218 Nate Lewis	.01	.05
219 Natrone Means	.08	.25
220 Anthony Miller	.02	.10
221 Chris Mims	.01	.05
222 Eric Moten	.01	.05
223 Leslie O'Neal	.01	.05
224 Junior Seau	.08	.25
225 Morten Andersen	.01	.05
226 Gene Atkins	.01	.05
227 Derek Brown RBK	.01	.05
228 Toi Cook	.01	.05
229 Vaughn Dunbar	.01	.05
230 Quinn Early	.02	.10
231 Reggie Freeman	.01	.05
232 Tyrone Hughes	.02	.10
233 Rickey Jackson	.01	.05
234 Eric Martin	.01	.05
235 Sam Mills	.01	.05
236 Brad Muster	.01	.05
237 Torrance Small	.01	.05
238 Irv Smith	.01	.05
239 Wade Wilson	.01	.05
240 Eric Allen	.01	.05
241 Victor Bailey	.01	.05
242 Fred Barnett	.02	.10
243 Mark Bavaro	.01	.05
244 Bubby Brister	.02	.10
245 Randall Cunningham	.08	.25
246 Antone Davis	.01	.05
247 Britt Hager RC	.01	.05
248 Vaughn Hebron	.01	.05
249 James Joseph	.01	.05
250 Seth Joyner	.01	.05
251 Rich Miano	.01	.05
252 Heath Sherman	.01	.05
253 Clyde Simmons	.01	.05
254 Herschel Walker	.02	.10
255 Calvin Williams	.02	.10
256 Jerry Ball	.01	.05
257 Mark Carrier WR	.02	.10
258 Michael Jackson	.02	.10
259 Mike Johnson	.01	.05
260 James Jones	.01	.05
261 Brian Kinchen	.01	.05
262 Clay Matthews	.01	.05
263 Eric Metcalf	.02	.10
264 Stevon Moore	.01	.05
265 Michael Dean Perry	.02	.10
266 Todd Philcox	.01	.05
267 Anthony Pleasant	.01	.05
268 Vinny Testaverde	.02	.10
269 Eric Turner	.01	.05
270 Tommy Vardell	.01	.05
271 Neal Anderson	.01	.05
272 Trace Armstrong	.01	.05
273 Mark Carrier DB	.01	.05
274 Bob Christian	.01	.05
275 Curtis Conway	.08	.25
276 Richard Dent	.02	.10
277 Robert Green	.01	.05
278 Jim Harbaugh	.08	.25
279 Craig Heyward	.02	.10
280 Terry Obee	.01	.05
281 Alonzo Spellman	.01	.05
282 Tom Waddle	.01	.05
283 Peter Tom Willis	.01	.05
284 Donnell Woolford	.01	.05
285 Tim Worley	.01	.05
286 Chris Zorich	.01	.05
287 Steve Broussard	.01	.05
288 Darion Conner	.01	.05
289 Jumpy Geathers	.01	.05
290 Michael Haynes	.02	.10
291 Bobby Hebert	.01	.05
292 Lincoln Kennedy	.01	.05
293 Chris Miller	.01	.05
294 David Mims RC	.01	.05
295 Erric Pegram	.01	.05
296 Mike Pritchard	.01	.05
297 Andre Rison	.02	.10
298 Deion Sanders	.20	.50
299 Chuck Smith	.01	.05
300 Tony Smith	.01	.05
301 Johnny Bailey	.01	.05
302 Steve Beuerlein	.02	.10
303 Chuck Cecil	.01	.05
304 Chris Chandler	.02	.10
305 Gary Clark	.02	.10
306 Rick Cunningham RC	.01	.05
307 Ken Harvey	.01	.05
308 Garrison Hearst	.08	.25
309 Randal Hill	.01	.05
310 Robert Massey	.01	.05
311 Ronald Moore	.01	.05
312 Ricky Proehl	.01	.05
313 Eric Swann	.02	.10
314 Aeneas Williams	.01	.05
315 Michael Bates	.01	.05
316 Brian Blades	.02	.10
317 Carlton Gray	.01	.05
318 Paul Green RC	.01	.05
319 Patrick Hunter	.01	.05
320 John Kasay	.01	.05
321 Cortez Kennedy	.02	.10
322 Kelvin Martin	.01	.05
323 Dan McGwire	.01	.05
324 Rick Mirer	.08	.25
325 Eugene Robinson	.01	.05
326 Rick Tuten	.01	.05
327 Chris Warren	.02	.10
328 John L. Williams	.01	.05
329 Reggie Cobb	.01	.05
330 Horace Copeland	.01	.05
331 Lawrence Dawsey	.01	.05
332 Santana Dotson	.02	.10
333 Craig Erickson	.01	.05
334 Ron Hall	.01	.05
335 Courtney Hawkins	.01	.05
336 Keith McCants	.01	.05
337 Hardy Nickerson	.02	.10
338 Mazio Royster RC	.01	.05
339 Broderick Thomas	.01	.05
340 Casey Weldon RC	.08	.25
341 Mark Wheeler	.01	.05
342 Vince Workman	.01	.05
343 Flipper Anderson	.01	.05
344 Jerome Bettis	.20	.50
345 Richard Buchanan	.01	.05
346 Shane Conlan	.01	.05
347 Troy Drayton	.01	.05
348 Henry Ellard	.02	.10
349 Jim Everett	.02	.10
350 Cleveland Gary	.01	.05
351 Sean Gilbert	.01	.05
352 David Lang	.01	.05
353 Todd Lyght	.01	.05
354 T.J. Rubley	.01	.05
355 Jackie Slater	.01	.05
356 Russell White	.02	.10
357 Bruce Armstrong	.01	.05
358 Drew Bledsoe	.30	.75
359 Vincent Brisby	.02	.10
360 Vincent Brown	.01	.05
361 Ben Coates	.02	.10
362 Marv Cook	.01	.05
363 Ray Crittenden RC	.01	.05
364 Corey Croom RC	.01	.05
365 Pat Harlow	.01	.05
366 Dion Lambert	.01	.05
367 Greg McMurtry	.01	.05
368 Leonard Russell	.01	.05
369 Scott Secules	.01	.05
370 Chris Slade	.01	.05
371 Michael Timpson	.01	.05
372 Kevin Turner	.01	.05
373 Ashley Ambrose	.01	.05
374 Dean Biasucci	.01	.05
375 Duane Bickett	.01	.05
376 Quentin Coryatt	.01	.05
377 Rodney Culver	.01	.05
378 Sean Dawkins RC	.08	.25
379 Jeff George	.08	.25
380 Jeff Herrod	.01	.05
301 Jessie Hester	.01	.05
382 Anthony Johnson	.02	.10
383 Reggie Langhorne	.01	.05
384 Roosevelt Potts	.01	.05
385 William Schultz RC	.01	.05
386 Rohn Stark	.01	.05
387 Clarence Verdin	.01	.05
388 Carl Banks	.01	.05
389 Reggie Brooks	.02	.10
390 Earnest Byner	.01	.05
391 Tom Carter	.01	.05
392 Cary Conklin	.01	.05
393 Pat Eilers RC	.01	.05
394 Ricky Ervins	.01	.05
395 Rich Gannon	.08	.25
396 Darrell Green	.01	.05
397 Desmond Howard	.02	.10
398 Chip Lohmiller	.01	.05
399 Sterling Palmer RC	.01	.05
400 Mark Rypien	.01	.05
401 Ricky Sanders	.01	.05
402 Johnny Thomas	.01	.05
403 John Copeland	.01	.05
404 Derrick Fenner	.01	.05
405 Alex Gordon	.01	.05
406 Harold Green	.01	.05
407 Lance Gunn	.01	.05
408 David Klingler	.01	.05
409 Ricardo McDonald	.01	.05
410 Tim McGee	.01	.05
411 Reggie Rembert	.01	.05
412 Patrick Robinson	.01	.05
413 Jay Schroeder	.01	.05
414 Erik Wilhelm	.01	.05
415 Alfred Williams	.01	.05
416 Darryl Williams	.01	.05
417 Sam Adams RC	.02	.10
418 Mario Bates RC	.08	.25
419 James Bostic RC	.08	.25
420 Bucky Brooks RC	.01	.05
421 Jeff Burris RC	.02	.10
422 Shante Carver RC	.01	.05
423 Jeff Cothran RC	.01	.05
424 Lake Dawson RC	.02	.10
425 Trent Dilfer RC	.50	1.25
426 Marshall Faulk RC	2.00	5.00
427 Cory Fleming RC	.01	.05
428 William Floyd RC	.08	.25
429 Glenn Foley RC	.08	.25
430 Rob Fredrickson RC	.02	.10
431 Charlie Garner RC	.50	1.25
432 Greg Hill RC	.08	.25
433 Charles Johnson RC	.08	.25
434 Calvin Jones RC	.01	.05
435 Jimmy Klingler RC	.01	.05
436 Antonio Langham RC	.02	.10
437 Kevin Lee RC	.01	.05
438 Chuck Levy RC	.01	.05
439 Willie McGinest RC	.08	.25
440 Jamir Miller RC	.02	.10
441 Johnnie Morton RC	.20	.50
442 David Palmer RC	.08	.25
443 Errict Rhett RC	.08	.25
444 Cory Sawyer RC	.02	.10
445 Darnay Scott RC	.20	.50
446 Heath Shuler RC	.08	.25
447 Lamar Smith RC	.50	1.25
448 Dan Wilkinson RC	.02	.10
449 Bernard Williams RC	.01	.05
450 Bryant Young RC	.15	.40
P1 Sterling Sharpe Promo Numbered 000	.30	.75

1994 Pacific Crystalline

COMPLETE SET (20)	40.00	75.00
STATED ODDS 1:7		
STATED PRINT RUN 7000 SETS		
1 Emmitt Smith	12.50	25.00
2 Jerome Bettis	4.00	8.00
3 Thurman Thomas	2.00	4.00
4 Erric Pegram	.30	.75
5 Barry Sanders	12.50	25.00
6 Leonard Russell	.30	.75
7 Rodney Hampton	.75	1.50
8 Chris Warren	.75	1.50
9 Reggie Brooks	.75	1.50
10 Ronald Moore	.30	.75
11 Gary Brown	.30	.75
12 Ricky Watters	.75	1.50
13 Johnny Johnson	.30	.75
14 Rod Bernstine	.30	.75
15 Marcus Allen	2.00	4.00
16 Leroy Thompson	.30	.75
17 Marion Butts	.30	.75
18 Herschel Walker	.75	1.50
19 Barry Foster	.30	.75
20 Roosevelt Potts	.30	.75

1994 Pacific Gems of the Crown

COMPLETE SET (36)	50.00	100.00
STATED ODDS 1:7		
STATED PRINT RUN 7000 SETS		
1 Troy Aikman	2.50	6.00
2 Marcus Allen	.60	1.50
3 Jerome Bettis	1.25	3.00
4 Drew Bledsoe	2.00	5.00
5 Reggie Brooks	.25	.60
6 Gary Brown	.10	.30
7 Tim Brown	.60	1.50
8 Cody Carlson	.10	.30
9 John Elway	5.00	12.00
10 Boomer Esiason	.25	.60
11 Brett Favre	5.00	12.00
12 Rodney Hampton	.25	.60
13 Alvin Harper	.25	.60
14 Jeff Hostetler	.25	.60
15 Jim Kelly	.60	1.50
16 Dan Marino	5.00	12.00
17 Eric Martin	.10	.30
18 O.J. McDuffie	.60	1.50
19 Natrone Means	.60	1.50
20 Rick Mirer	.60	1.50
21 Joe Montana	5.00	12.00
22 Herman Moore	.60	1.50
23 Ronald Moore	.10	.30
24 Neil O'Donnell	.60	1.50
25 Erric Pegram	.10	.30
26 Roosevelt Potts	.10	.30
27 Jerry Rice	2.50	6.00
28 Barry Sanders	4.00	10.00
29 Shannon Sharpe	.25	.60
30 Sterling Sharpe	.25	.60
31 Emmitt Smith	4.00	10.00
32 Thurman Thomas	.60	1.50
33 Herschel Walker	.25	.60
34 Chris Warren	.25	.60
35 Ricky Watters	.25	.60
36 Steve Young	2.00	5.00
9AU John Elway AUTO/50	75.00	150.00
Inserted in '95 Prisms packs		

1994 Pacific Knights of the Gridiron

COMPLETE SET (20)	30.00	60.00
STATED ODDS 1:7		
STATED PRINT RUN 7000 SETS		
1 Mario Bates	.30	.75
2 Jerome Bettis	2.50	6.00
3 Drew Bledsoe	4.00	10.00
4 Vincent Brisby	.50	1.25
5 Reggie Brooks	.10	.30
6 Derek Brown RBK	.25	.60
7 Jeff Burris	.10	.30
8 Trent Dilfer	1.50	4.00
9 Troy Drayton	.25	.60
10 Marshall Faulk	6.00	15.00
11 William Floyd	.30	.75
12 Rocket Ismail	.50	1.25
13 Terry Kirby	1.25	3.00
14 Thomas Lewis	.25	.60
15 Natrone Means	1.25	3.00
16 Rick Mirer	1.25	3.00
17 David Palmer	.30	.75
18 Errict Rhett	.30	.75
19 Darnay Scott	.60	1.50
20 Heath Shuler	.30	.75

1994 Pacific Marquee Prisms

COMPLETE SET (36)	10.00	25.00
ONE GOLD OR SILVER PER MARQUEE		
*GOLDS: 2.5X to 6X BASIC INSERTS		
GOLD STATED ODDS 1:18		
1 Troy Aikman	1.00	2.00
2 Marcus Allen	.20	.50
3 Jerome Bettis	.40	1.00
4 Drew Bledsoe	.75	1.50
5 Reggie Brooks	.07	.20
6 Dave Brown	.07	.20
7 Ben Coates	.07	.20
8 Reggie Cobb	.02	.10
9 Curtis Conway	.20	.50
10 John Elway	2.00	4.00
11 Marshall Faulk	2.50	5.00
12 Brett Favre	2.00	4.00
13 Barry Foster	.02	.10
14 Rodney Hampton	.07	.20
15 Michael Irvin	.20	.50
16 Terry Kirby	.20	.50
17 Dan Marino	2.00	4.00
18 Natrone Means	.20	.50
19 Rick Mirer	.20	.50
20 Joe Montana	2.00	4.00
21 Warren Moon	.20	.50
22 Ronald Moore	.02	.10
23 David Palmer	.08	.25
24 Errict Rhett	.08	.25
25 Jerry Rice	1.00	2.00
26 Bucky Richardson	.02	.10
27 Barry Sanders	1.50	3.00
28 Shannon Sharpe	.07	.20
29 Sterling Sharpe	.07	.20
30 Heath Shuler	.08	.25
31 Emmitt Smith	1.50	3.00
32 Irving Spikes	.02	.10
33 Thurman Thomas	.20	.50
34 Chris Warren	.07	.20
35 Ricky Watters	.07	.20
36 Steve Young	.75	1.50

1995 Pacific

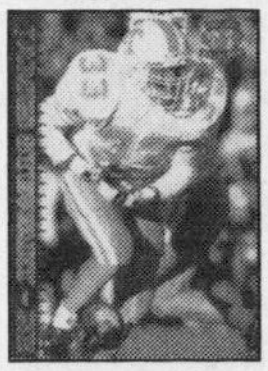

This 450 card set was issued in one series and featured 12 cards per pack. Rookie Cards in this set include Jeff Blake, Kerry Collins, Joey Galloway, Steve McNair, Rashaan Salaam, Kordell Stewart, J.J Stokes, Yancey Thigpen and Michael Westbrook. Natrone Means standard sized and jumbo (7" by 9 3/4") promo cards were produced and are included below.

COMPLETE SET (450)	10.00	25.00
1 Randy Baldwin	.02	.10
2 Tommy Barnhardt	.02	.10
3 Tim McKyer	.02	.10
4 Sam Mills	.07	.20
5 Brian O'Neal	.02	.10
6 Frank Reich	.02	.10
7 Jack Trudeau	.02	.10
8 Vernon Turner	.02	.10
9 Kerry Collins RC	.75	2.00
10 Shawn King	.02	.10
11 Steve Beuerlein	.07	.20
12 Derek Brown	.02	.10
13 Reggie Clark	.02	.10
14 Reggie Cobb	.02	.10
15 Desmond Howard	.07	.20
16 Jeff Lageman	.02	.10
17 Kelvin Pritchett	.02	.10
18 Cedric Tillman	.02	.10
19 Tony Boselli RC	.10	.30
20 James O. Stewart RC	.50	1.25
21 Eric Davis	.02	.10
22 William Floyd	.07	.20
23 Elvis Grbac	.10	.30
24 Brent Jones	.02	.10
25 Ken Norton, Jr.	.07	.20
26 Bart Oates	.02	.10
27 Jerry Rice	.40	1.00
28 Deion Sanders	.15	.40
29 John Taylor	.02	.10
30 Adam Walker RC	.02	.10
31 Steve Wallace	.02	.10
32 Ricky Watters	.07	.20
33 Lee Woodall	.02	.10
34 Bryant Young	.07	.20
35 Steve Young	.30	.75
36 J.J. Stokes RC	.10	.30
37 Troy Aikman	.40	1.00
38 Larry Allen	.07	.20
39 Chris Boniol RC	.02	.10
40 Lincoln Coleman	.02	.10
41 Charles Haley	.07	.20
42 Alvin Harper	.02	.10
43 Chad Hennings	.07	.20
44 Michael Irvin	.10	.30
45 Daryl Johnston	.07	.20
46 Leon Lett	.02	.10
47 Nate Newton	.07	.20
48 Jay Novacek	.07	.20
49 Emmitt Smith	.60	1.50
50 James Washington	.02	.10
51 Kevin Williams	.07	.20
52 Sherman Williams RC	.02	.10
53 Barry Foster	.07	.20
54 Eric Green	.02	.10
55 Kevin Greene	.07	.20
56 Andre Hastings	.07	.20
57 Charles Johnson	.07	.20
58 Greg Lloyd	.07	.20
59 Ernie Mills	.02	.10
60 Byron Bam Morris	.02	.10
61 Neil O'Donnell	.07	.20
62 Darren Perry	.02	.10
63 Yancey Thigpen RC	.07	.20
64 Mike Tomczak	.02	.10
65 John L. Williams	.02	.10
66 Rod Woodson	.07	.20
67 Mark Bruener RC	.07	.20
68 Kordell Stewart RC	.60	1.50
69 Jeff Brohm RC	.02	.10
70 Andre Coleman	.02	.10
71 Reuben Davis	.02	.10
72 Dennis Gibson	.02	.10
73 Darrien Gordon	.02	.10
74 Stan Humphries	.07	.20
75 Shawn Jefferson	.02	.10
76 Tony Martin	.07	.20
77 Natrone Means	.07	.20
78 Shannon Mitchell RC	.02	.10
79 Leslie O'Neal	.07	.20
80 Alfred Pupunu	.02	.10
81 Stanley Richard	.02	.10
82 Junior Seau	.10	.30
83 Mark Seay	.07	.20
84 Derrick Alexander WR	.10	.30
85 Carl Banks	.02	.10
86 Isaac Booth	.02	.10
87 Rob Burnett	.02	.10
88 Earnest Byner	.02	.10
89 Steve Everitt	.02	.10
90 Leroy Hoard	.02	.10
91 Pepper Johnson	.02	.10
92 Antonio Langham	.02	.10
93 Eric Metcalf	.07	.20
94 Anthony Pleasant	.02	.10
95 Frank Stams	.02	.10
96 Vinny Testaverde	.07	.20
97 Eric Turner	.02	.10
98 Mike Miller RC	.02	.10
99 Craig Powell RC	.02	.10
100 Gene Atkins	.02	.10
101 Aubrey Beavers	.02	.10
102 Tim Bowens	.02	.10
103 Keith Byars	.02	.10
104 Bryan Cox	.02	.10
105 Aaron Craver	.02	.10
106 Jeff Cross	.02	.10
107 Irving Fryar	.07	.20
108 Dan Marino	.75	2.00
109 O.J. McDuffie	.10	.30
110 Bernie Parmalee	.07	.20
111 James Saxon	.02	.10
112 Keith Sims	.02	.10
113 Irving Spikes	.07	.20
114 Pete Mitchell RC	.07	.20
115 Terry Allen	.07	.20
116 Cris Carter	.10	.30
117 Adrian Cooper	.02	.10
118 Bernard Dafney	.02	.10
119 Jack Del Rio	.02	.10
120 Vencie Glenn	.02	.10
121 Qadry Ismail	.07	.20
122 Carlos Jenkins	.02	.10
123 Andrew Jordan	.02	.10
124 Ed McDaniel	.02	.10
125 Warren Moon	.07	.20
126 David Palmer	.07	.20
127 John Randle	.07	.20
128 Jake Reed	.07	.20
129 Derrick Alexander DE RC	.02	.10
130 Chad May RC	.02	.10
131 Korey Stringer RC	.10	.30
132 Bruce Armstrong	.02	.10
133 Drew Bledsoe	.25	.60
134 Vincent Brisby	.02	.10
135 Troy Brown	.10	.30
136 Vincent Brown	.02	.10
137 Marion Butts	.02	.10
138 Ben Coates	.07	.20
139 Ray Crittenden	.02	.10
140 Maurice Hurst	.02	.10
141 Aaron Jones	.02	.10
142 Willie McGinest	.07	.20
143 Marty Moore RC	.10	.30
144 Mike Pitts	.02	.10
145 Leroy Thompson	.02	.10
146 Michael Timpson	.02	.10
147 Bennie Blades	.02	.10
148 Jocelyn Borgella	.02	.10
149 Anthony Carter	.07	.20
150 Willie Clay	.02	.10
151 Mel Gray	.02	.10
152 Mike Johnson	.02	.10
153 Dave Krieg	.02	.10
154 Robert Massey	.02	.10
155 Scott Mitchell	.07	.20
156 Herman Moore	.10	.30
157 Johnnie Morton	.07	.20
158 Barry Sanders	.60	1.50
159 Chris Spielman	.07	.20
160 Broderick Thomas	.02	.10
161 Cory Schlesinger RC	.07	.20
162 Marcus Allen	.10	.30
163 Donnell Bennett	.07	.20
164 J.J. Birden	.02	.10
165 Matt Blundin RC	.02	.10
166 Steve Bono	.07	.20
167 Dale Carter	.07	.20
168 Lake Dawson	.07	.20
169 Ron Dickerson RC	.02	.10
170 Lin Elliott	.02	.10
171 Jaime Fields	.02	.10
172 Greg Hill	.07	.20
173 Danan Hughes	.02	.10
174 Neil Smith	.07	.20
175 Steve Stenstrom RC	.02	.10
176 Edgar Bennett	.07	.20
177 Robert Brooks	.10	.30
178 Mark Brunell	.25	.60
179 Doug Evans RC	.10	.30
180 Brett Favre	.75	2.00
181 Corey Harris	.02	.10
182 LeShon Johnson	.07	.20
183 Sean Jones	.02	.10
184 Lenny McGill RC	.02	.10
185 Terry Mickens	.02	.10
186 Sterling Sharpe	.07	.20
187 Joe Sims	.02	.10
188 Darrell Thompson	.02	.10
189 Reggie White	.10	.30
190 Craig Newsome RC	.02	.10
191 Tim Brown	.10	.30
192 Vince Evans	.02	.10
193 Rob Fredrickson	.02	.10
194 Andrew Glover RC	.02	.10
195 Jeff Hostetler	.07	.20
196 Rocket Ismail	.07	.20
197 Jeff Jaeger	.02	.10
198 James Jett	.07	.20
199 Chester McGlockton	.07	.20
200 Don Mosebar	.02	.10
201 Tom Rathman	.02	.10
202 Harvey Williams	.02	.10
203 Steve Wisniewski	.02	.10
204 Alexander Wright	.02	.10
205 Napoleon Kaufman RC	.50	1.25
206 Trace Armstrong	.02	.10
207 Curtis Conway	.10	.30
208 Raymont Harris	.02	.10
209 Erik Kramer	.02	.10
210 Nate Lewis	.02	.10
211 Shane Matthews RC	.10	.30
212 John Thierry	.02	.10
213 Lewis Tillman	.02	.10
214 Tom Waddle	.02	.10
215 Steve Walsh	.02	.10
216 James Williams T RC	.02	.10
217 Donnell Woolford	.02	.10
218 Chris Zorich	.02	.10
219 Rashaan Salaam RC	.07	.20
220 John Booty	.02	.10
221 Michael Brooks	.02	.10
222 Dave Brown	.07	.20
223 Chris Calloway	.02	.10
224 Gary Downs	.02	.10
225 Kent Graham	.07	.20
226 Keith Hamilton	.02	.10
227 Rodney Hampton	.07	.20
228 Brian Kozlowski	.02	.10
229 Thomas Lewis	.07	.20
230 Dave Meggett	.02	.10
231 Aaron Pierce	.02	.10
232 Mike Sherrard	.02	.10
233 Phillippi Sparks	.02	.10
234 Tyrone Wheatley RC	.50	1.25
235 Trev Alberts	.02	.10
236 Aaron Bailey RC	.02	.10
237 Jason Belser	.02	.10
238 Tony Bennett	.02	.10
239 Kerry Cash	.02	.10
240 Marshall Faulk	.50	1.25
241 Stephen Grant	.02	.10
242 Jeff Herrod	.02	.10
243 Ronald Humphrey	.02	.10
244 Kirk Lowdermilk	.02	.10
245 Don Majkowski	.02	.10
246 Tony McCoy	.02	.10
247 Floyd Turner	.02	.10
248 Lamont Warren	.02	.10
249 Zack Crockett RC	.07	.20
250 Michael Bankston	.02	.10
251 Larry Centers	.07	.20
252 Gary Clark	.02	.10
253 Ed Cunningham	.02	.10
254 Garrison Hearst	.10	.30
255 Eric Hill	.02	.10
256 Terry Irving	.02	.10
257 Lorenzo Lynch	.02	.10
258 Jamir Miller	.02	.10
259 Ronald Moore	.02	.10
260 Terry Samuels	.02	.10
261 Jay Schroeder	.02	.10
262 Eric Swann	.07	.20
263 Aeneas Williams	.02	.10
264 Frank Sanders RC	.10	.30
265 Morten Andersen	.02	.10
266 Mario Bates	.07	.20
267 Derek Brown RBK	.02	.10
268 Darion Conner	.02	.10
269 Quinn Early	.07	.20
270 Jim Everett	.02	.10
271 Michael Haynes	.07	.20
272 Wayne Martin	.02	.10
273 Derrell Mitchell RC	.02	.10
274 Lorenzo Neal	.02	.10
275 Jimmy Spencer	.02	.10
276 Winfred Tubbs	.02	.10
277 Renaldo Turnbull	.02	.10
278 Jeff Uhlenhake	.02	.10
279 Steve Atwater	.02	.10
280 Keith Burns RC	.02	.10
281 Butler By'Not'e RC	.07	.20
282 Jeff Campbell	.02	.10
283 Derrick Clark RC	.02	.10
284 Shane Dronett	.02	.10
285 Jason Elam	.07	.20
286 John Elway	.75	2.00
287 Jerry Evans	.02	.10
288 Karl Mecklenburg	.02	.10
289 Glyn Milburn	.02	.10
290 Anthony Miller	.07	.20
291 Tom Rouen	.02	.10
292 Leonard Russell	.02	.10
293 Shannon Sharpe	.07	.20
294 Steve Russ RC	.02	.10
295 Mel Agee	.02	.10
296 Lester Archambeau	.02	.10
297 Bert Emanuel	.10	.30
298 Jeff George	.07	.20
299 Craig Heyward	.07	.20
300 Bobby Hebert	.02	.10
301 D.J. Johnson	.02	.10
302 Mike Kenn	.02	.10
303 Terance Mathis	.07	.20
304 Clay Matthews	.07	.20
305 Erric Pegram	.07	.20
306 Andre Rison	.07	.20
307 Chuck Smith	.02	.10
308 Jessie Tuggle	.02	.10
309 Lorenzo Styles RC	.02	.10
310 Cornelius Bennett	.07	.20
311 Bill Brooks	.02	.10
312 Jeff Burris	.02	.10
313 Carwell Gardner	.02	.10
314 Kent Hull	.02	.10
315 Yonel Jourdain	.02	.10
316 Jim Kelly	.10	.30
317 Vince Marrow	.02	.10
318 Pete Metzelaars	.02	.10
319 Andre Reed	.07	.20
320 Kurt Schulz RC	.02	.10
321 Bruce Smith	.10	.30
322 Darryl Talley	.02	.10
323 Matt Darby	.02	.10
324 Justin Armour RC	.02	.10
325 Todd Collins RC	.50	1.25
326 David Alexander DE	.02	.10
327 Eric Allen	.02	.10
328 Fred Barnett	.07	.20
329 Randall Cunningham	.10	.30
330 William Fuller	.02	.10
331 Charlie Garner	.10	.30
332 Vaughn Hebron	.02	.10
333 James Joseph	.02	.10
334 Bill Romanowski	.02	.10
335 Kon Rose	.02	.10
336 Jeff Snyder	.02	.10
337 William Thomas	.02	.10
338 Herschel Walker	.07	.20
339 Calvin Williams	.07	.20
340 Dave Barr RC	.02	.10
341 Chidi Ahanotu	.02	.10
342 Barney Bussey	.02	.10
343 Horace Copeland	.02	.10
344 Trent Dilfer	.10	.30
345 Craig Erickson	.02	.10
346 Paul Gruber	.02	.10
347 Courtney Hawkins	.02	.10
348 Lonnie Marts	.02	.10
349 Martin Mayhew	.02	.10
350 Hardy Nickerson	.02	.10
351 Errict Rhett	.07	.20
352 Lamar Thomas	.02	.10
353 Charles Wilson	.02	.10
354 Vince Workman	.02	.10
355 Derrick Brooks RC	.60	1.50
356 Warren Sapp RC	.60	1.50
357 Sam Adams	.02	.10
358 Michael Bates	.02	.10
359 Brian Blades	.07	.20
360 Carlton Gray	.02	.10
361 Bill Hitchcock	.02	.10
362 Cortez Kennedy	.07	.20
363 Rick Mirer	.07	.20
364 Eugene Robinson	.02	.10
365 Michael Sinclair	.02	.10
366 Steve Smith	.02	.10
367 Bob Spitulski	.02	.10
368 Rick Tuten	.02	.10
369 Chris Warren	.07	.20
370 Terrence Warren	.02	.10
371 Christian Fauria RC	.07	.20
372 Joey Galloway RC	.60	1.50
373 Boomer Esiason	.07	.20
374 Aaron Glenn	.02	.10
375 Victor Green RC	.02	.10
376 Johnny Johnson	.02	.10
377 Mo Lewis	.02	.10
378 Ronnie Lott	.07	.20
379 Nick Lowery	.02	.10
380 Johnny Mitchell	.02	.10
381 Rob Moore	.07	.20
382 Adrian Murrell	.07	.20
383 Anthony Prior	.02	.10
384 Brian Washington	.02	.10
385 Matt Willig RC	.02	.10
386 Kyle Brady RC	.10	.30
387 Flipper Anderson	.02	.10
388 Johnny Bailey	.02	.10
389 Jerome Bettis	.10	.30
390 Isaac Bruce	.20	.50
391 Shane Conlan	.02	.10
392 Troy Drayton	.02	.10
393 D'Marco Farr	.02	.10
394 Jessie Hester	.02	.10
395 Todd Kinchen	.02	.10
396 Ron Middleton	.02	.10
397 Chris Miller	.02	.10
398 Marquez Pope	.02	.10
399 Robert Young	.02	.10
400 Tony Zendejas	.02	.10
401 Kevin Carter RC	.10	.30
402 Reggie Brooks	.07	.20
403 Tom Carter	.02	.10
404 Andre Collins	.02	.10
405 Pat Eilers	.02	.10
406 Henry Ellard	.07	.20
407 Ricky Ervins	.02	.10

408 Gus Frerotte	.07	.20
409 Ken Harvey	.02	.10
410 Jim Lachey	.02	.10
411 Brian Mitchell	.02	.10
412 Reggie Roby	.02	.10
413 Heath Shuler	.07	.20
414 Tyronne Stowe	.02	.10
415 Tydus Winans	.02	.10
416 Cory Raymer RC	.02	.10
417 Michael Westbrook RC	.10	.30
418 Jeff Blake RC	.30	.75
419 Steve Broussard	.02	.10
420 Dave Cadigan	.02	.10
421 Jeff Cothran	.02	.10
422 Derrick Fenner	.02	.10
423 James Francis	.02	.10
424 Lee Johnson	.02	.10
425 Louis Oliver	.02	.10
426 Carl Pickens	.07	.20
427 Jeff Query	.02	.10
428 Corey Sawyer	.02	.10
429 Darnay Scott	.07	.20
430 Dan Wilkinson	.07	.20
431 Alfred Williams	.02	.10
432 Ki-Jana Carter RC	.10	.30
433 David Dunn RC	.02	.10
434 John Walsh RC	.02	.10
435 Gary Brown	.02	.10
436 Pat Carter	.02	.10
437 Ray Childress	.02	.10
438 Ernest Givins	.02	.10
439 Haywood Jeffires	.02	.10
440 Lamar Lathon	.02	.10
441 Bruce Matthews	.02	.10
442 Marcus Robertson	.02	.10
443 Eddie Robinson	.02	.10
444 Malcolm Seabron RC	.02	.10
445 Webster Slaughter	.02	.10
446 Al Smith	.02	.10
447 Billy Joe Tolliver	.02	.10
448 Lorenzo White	.02	.10
449 Steve McNair RC	1.25	3.00
450 Rodney Thomas RC	.07	.20
P1 Natrone Means Promo	.40	1.00
P1J Natrone Means Promo	.40	1.00
Jumbo card 7-in by 9 3/4-in		

1995 Pacific Blue

COMPLETE BLUE SET (450)	100.00	200.00
*STARS: 3.5X TO 7X BASIC CARDS		
*RCs: 2X TO 4X BASIC CARDS		
STATED ODDS 9:37 RETAIL		

1995 Pacific Platinum

COMPLETE SET (450)	100.00	200.00
*STARS: 3X TO 6X BASIC CARDS		
*RCs: 1.5X TO 3X BASIC CARDS		
STATED ODDS 9:37 HOBBY		

1995 Pacific Cramer's Choice

COMPLETE SET (6)	30.00	80.00
STATED ODDS 1:720		
CC1 Ki-Jana Carter	2.50	6.00
CC2 Emmitt Smith	12.50	30.00
CC3 Marshall Faulk	10.00	25.00
CC4 Jerry Rice	8.00	20.00
CC5 Deion Sanders	3.00	8.00
CC6 Steve Young	6.00	15.00

1995 Pacific Gems of the Crown

COMPLETE SET (36)	50.00	100.00
STATED ODDS 2:37		
GC1 Jim Kelly	1.25	3.00
GC2 Kerry Collins	3.00	8.00
GC3 Darnay Scott	.75	2.00
GC4 Jeff Blake	1.25	3.00
GC5 Terry Allen	.75	2.00
GC6 Emmitt Smith	6.00	15.00
GC7 Michael Irvin	1.25	3.00
GC8 Troy Aikman	4.00	10.00
GC9 John Elway	8.00	20.00
GC10 Dave Krieg	.40	1.00
GC11 Barry Sanders	6.00	15.00
GC12 Brett Favre	8.00	20.00
GC13 Marshall Faulk	5.00	12.00
GC14 Marcus Allen	1.25	3.00
GC15 Tim Brown	1.25	3.00
GC16 Bernie Parmalee	.75	2.00
GC17 Dan Marino	8.00	20.00
GC18 Cris Carter	1.25	3.00
GC19 Drew Bledsoe	2.50	6.00
GC20 Mario Bates	.75	2.00
GC21 Rodney Hampton	.75	2.00
GC22 Ben Coates	.75	2.00
GC23 Charles Johnson	.75	2.00
GC24 Byron Bam Morris	.40	1.00
GC25 Stan Humphries	.75	2.00
GC26 Deion Sanders	1.50	4.00
GC27 Jerry Rice	4.00	10.00
GC28 Ricky Watters	.75	2.00
GC29 Steve Young	3.00	8.00
GC30 Natrone Means	.75	2.00
GC31 William Floyd	.75	2.00
GC32 Chris Warren	.75	2.00
GC33 Rick Mirer	.75	2.00
GC34 Jerome Bettis	1.25	3.00
GC35 Errict Rhett	.75	2.00
GC36 Heath Shuler	.75	2.00

1995 Pacific G-Force

COMPLETE SET (10)	12.50	30.00
STATED ODDS 1:37		
GF1 Marcus Allen	1.25	2.50
GF2 Terry Allen	.75	1.50
GF3 Emmitt Smith	6.00	12.00
GF4 Barry Sanders	6.00	12.00
GF5 Marshall Faulk	5.00	10.00
GF6 Rodney Hampton	.75	1.50
GF7 Natrone Means	.75	1.50
GF8 Chris Warren	.75	1.50
GF9 Jerome Bettis	1.25	2.50
GF10 Errict Rhett	.75	1.50

1995 Pacific Gold Crown Die Cuts

COMP.HOLOFOIL SET (20)	50.00	100.00
*FLAT GOLDS: .6X TO 1.5X BASIC INSERTS		
STATED ODDS 1:37		
DC1 Ki-Jana Carter	1.25	3.00
DC2 Michael Irvin	1.25	3.00
DC3 Emmitt Smith	6.00	15.00
DC4 Troy Aikman	4.00	10.00
DC5 John Elway	8.00	20.00
DC6 Barry Sanders	6.00	15.00
DC7 Marshall Faulk	5.00	12.00
DC8 Dan Marino	8.00	20.00
DC9 Ben Coates	.75	2.00
DC10 Drew Bledsoe	2.50	6.00
DC11 Byron Bam Morris	.40	1.00
DC12 Jerry Rice	4.00	10.00
DC13 William Floyd	.75	2.00
DC14 Steve Young	3.00	8.00
DC15 Natrone Means	.75	2.00
DC16 Deion Sanders	1.50	4.00
DC17 Rick Mirer	.75	2.00
DC18 Chris Warren	.75	2.00
DC19 Jerome Bettis	1.25	3.00
DC20 Errict Rhett	.75	2.00

1995 Pacific Hometown Heroes

COMPLETE SET (10)	20.00	40.00
STATED ODDS 1:37		
HH1 Emmitt Smith	4.00	8.00
HH2 Troy Aikman	2.50	5.00
HH3 Barry Sanders	4.00	8.00
HH4 Marshall Faulk	3.00	6.00
HH5 Dan Marino	5.00	10.00
HH6 Drew Bledsoe	1.50	3.00
HH7 Natrone Means	.40	1.00
HH8 Steve Young	2.00	4.00
HH9 Jerry Rice	2.50	5.00
HH10 Errict Rhett	.40	1.00

1995 Pacific Rookies

COMPLETE SET (20)	20.00	40.00
STATED ODDS 2:37		
1 Dave Barr	.08	.25
2 Kyle Brady	.30	.75
3 Mark Bruener	.20	.50
4 Ki-Jana Carter	.30	.75
5 Kerry Collins	2.00	5.00
6 Todd Collins	.75	2.00
7 Christian Fauria	.20	.50
8 Joey Galloway	1.50	4.00
9 Chris T. Jones	.08	.25
10 Napoleon Kaufman	1.25	3.00
11 Chad May	.08	.25
12 Steve McNair	3.00	8.00
13 Rashaan Salaam	.20	.50
14 Warren Sapp	1.50	4.00
15 James O. Stewart	1.25	3.00
16 Kordell Stewart	1.50	4.00
17 J.J. Stokes	.30	.75
18 Michael Westbrook	.30	.75
19 Tyrone Wheatley	1.25	3.00
20 Sherman Williams	.08	.25

1995 Pacific Young Warriors

COMPLETE SET (20)	15.00	30.00
STATED ODDS 2:37		
1 Bert Emanuel	1.50	3.00
2 Darnay Scott	1.00	2.00
3 Dan Wilkinson	1.00	2.00
4 Derrick Alexander WR	1.50	3.00
5 Willie McGinest	1.00	2.00
6 Marshall Faulk	6.00	12.00
7 Lake Dawson	1.00	2.00
8 Greg Hill	1.00	2.00
9 Tim Bowens	.40	1.00
10 David Palmer	1.00	2.00
11 Aaron Glenn	.40	1.00
12 Mario Bates	1.00	2.00
13 Charles Johnson	1.00	2.00
14 Byron Bam Morris	.40	1.00
15 William Floyd	1.00	2.00
16 Adam Walker	.40	1.00
17 Bryant Young	1.00	2.00
18 Trent Dilfer	1.50	3.00
19 Errict Rhett	1.00	2.00
20 Heath Shuler	1.00	2.00

1996 Pacific

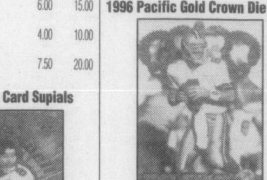

This 450-card set was issued in one series and distributed in 12-card packs.The set features borderless color action player photos with gold foil highlights. Two parallel sets were also issued: Red Foil and Blue Foil. The scorching red foil version was inserted in retail only packs at the rate of nine in 37. The electric blue foil version was inserted at the same rate in hobby only packs. The cards are grouped alphabetically within teams and checklisted below alphabetically according to teams. Two different Chris Warren Promo cards were also produced.

COMPLETE SET (450)	20.00	40.00
1 Jeff Feagles	.02	.10
2 Rob Moore	.07	.20
3 Clyde Simmons	.02	.10
4 Mike Buck	.02	.10
5 Aeneas Williams	.02	.10
6 Simeon Rice RC	.40	1.00
7 Garrison Hearst	.07	.20
8 Eric Swann	.02	.10
9 Dave Krieg	.02	.10
10 Leeland McElroy RC	.07	.20
11 Oscar McBride	.02	.10
12 Frank Sanders	.07	.20
13 Larry Centers	.07	.20
14 Seth Joyner	.02	.10
15 Stevie Anderson	.02	.10
16 Craig Heyward	.02	.10
17 Devin Bush	.02	.10
18 Eric Metcalf	.02	.10
19 Jeff George	.07	.20
20 Richard Huntley RC	.07	.20
21 Jamal Anderson RC	.20	.50
22 Bert Emanuel	.07	.20
23 Terance Mathis	.02	.10
24 Roman Fortin	.02	.10
25 Jessie Tuggle	.02	.10
26 Morten Andersen	.02	.10
27 Chris Doleman	.02	.10
28 D.J. Johnson	.02	.10
29 Kevin Ross	.02	.10
30 Michael Jackson	.07	.20
31 Eric Zeier	.02	.10
32 Jonathan Ogden RC	.15	.40
33 Eric Turner	.02	.10
34 Andre Rison	.07	.20
35 Lorenzo White	.02	.10
36 Earnest Byner	.02	.10
37 Derrick Alexander WR	.07	.20
38 Brian Kinchen	.02	.10
39 Anthony Pleasant	.02	.10
40 Vinny Testaverde	.07	.20
41 Pepper Johnson	.02	.10
42 Frank Hartley	.02	.10
43 Craig Powell	.02	.10
44 Leroy Hoard	.02	.10
45 Kent Hull	.02	.10
46 Bryce Paup	.02	.10
47 Andre Reed	.07	.20
48 Darick Holmes	.02	.10
49 Russell Copeland	.02	.10
50 Jerry Ostroski RC	.02	.10
51 Chris Green	.02	.10
52 Eric Moulds RC	.50	1.25
53 Justin Armour	.02	.10
54 Jim Kelly	.15	.40
55 Cornelius Bennett	.02	.10
56 Steve Tasker	.02	.10
57 Thurman Thomas	.15	.40
58 Bruce Smith	.07	.20
59 Todd Collins	.07	.20
60 Shawn King	.02	.10
61 Don Beebe	.02	.10
62 John Kasay	.02	.10
63 Tim McKyer	.02	.10
64 Darion Conner	.02	.10
65 Pete Metzelaars	.02	.10
66 Derrick Moore	.02	.10
67 Blake Brockermeyer	.02	.10
68 Tim Biakabutuka RC	.15	.40
69 Sam Mills	.02	.10
70 Vince Workman	.02	.10
71 Kerry Collins	.15	.40
72 Carlton Bailey	.02	.10
73 Mark Carrier WR	.02	.10
74 Donnell Woolford	.02	.10
75 Walt Harris RC	.02	.10
76 John Thierry	.02	.10
77 Al Fontenot RC	.02	.10
78 Lewis Tillman	.02	.10
79 Curtis Conway	.15	.40
80 Chris Zorich	.02	.10
81 Mark Carrier DB	.02	.10
82 Bobby Engram RC	.15	.40
83 Alonzo Spellman	.02	.10
84 Rashaan Salaam	.07	.20
85 Michael Timpson	.02	.10
86 Nate Lewis	.02	.10
87 James Williams T	.02	.10
88 Jeff Graham	.02	.10
89 Erik Kramer	.02	.10
90 Willie Anderson	.02	.10
91 Tony McGee	.02	.10
92 Marco Battaglia	.02	.10
93 Dan Wilkinson	.02	.10
94 John Walsh	.02	.10
95 Eric Bieniemy	.02	.10
96 Ricardo McDonald	.02	.10
97 Carl Pickens	.07	.20
98 Kevin Sargent	.02	.10
99 David Dunn	.02	.10
100 Jeff Blake	.15	.40
101 Harold Green	.02	.10
102 James Francis	.02	.10
103 John Copeland	.02	.10
104 Darnay Scott	.07	.20
105 Darren Woodson	.07	.20
106 Jay Novacek	.02	.10
107 Charles Haley	.07	.20
108 Mark Tuinei	.02	.10
109 Michael Irvin	.15	.40
110 Troy Aikman	.40	1.00
111 Chris Boniol	.02	.10
112 Sherman Williams	.02	.10
113 Deion Sanders	.25	.60
114 Emmitt Smith	.60	1.50
115 Eric Bjornson	.02	.10
116 Nate Newton	.02	.10
117 Larry Allen	.02	.10
118 Kevin Williams	.02	.10
119 Leon Lett	.02	.10
120 John Mobley	.02	.10
121 Anthony Miller	.07	.20
122 Brian Habib	.02	.10
123 Aaron Craver	.02	.10
124 Glyn Milburn	.02	.10
125 Shannon Sharpe	.07	.20
126 Steve Atwater	.02	.10
127 Jason Elam	.07	.20
128 John Elway	.75	2.00
129 Reggie Rivers	.02	.10
130 Mike Pritchard	.02	.10
131 Vance Johnson	.02	.10
132 Terrell Davis	.30	.75
133 Tyrone Braxton	.02	.10
134 Ed McCaffrey	.07	.20
135 Brett Perriman	.02	.10
136 Chris Spielman	.02	.10
137 Luther Elliss	.02	.10
138 Johnnie Morton	.07	.20
139 Zefross Moss	.02	.10
140 Barry Sanders	.60	1.50
141 Lomas Brown	.02	.10
142 Cory Schlesinger	.02	.10
143 Jason Hanson	.02	.10
144 Kevin Glover	.02	.10
145 Ron Rivers RC	.07	.20
146 Aubrey Matthews	.02	.10
147 Reggie Brown LB RC	.02	.10
148 Herman Moore	.07	.20
149 Scott Mitchell	.07	.20
150 Brett Favre	.75	2.00
151 Sean Jones	.02	.10
152 LeRoy Butler	.02	.10
153 Mark Chmura	.07	.20
154 Derrick Mayes RC	.15	.40
155 Mark Ingram	.02	.10
156 Antonio Freeman	.15	.40
157 Chris Darkins RC	.02	.10
158 Robert Brooks	.15	.40
159 William Henderson	.15	.40
160 George Koonce	.02	.10
161 Craig Newsome	.02	.10
162 Darius Holland	.02	.10
163 George Teague	.02	.10
164 Edgar Bennett	.07	.20
165 Reggie White	.15	.40
166 Micheal Barrow	.02	.10
167 Mel Gray	.02	.10
168 Anthony Dorsett	.02	.10
169 Roderick Lewis	.02	.10
170 Henry Ford	.02	.10
171 Mark Stepnoski	.02	.10
172 Chris Sanders	.07	.20
173 Anthony Cook	.02	.10
174 Eddie Robinson	.02	.10
175 Steve McNair	.30	.75
176 Haywood Jeffires	.02	.10
177 Eddie George RC	.50	1.25
178 Marion Butts	.02	.10
179 Malcolm Seabron	.02	.10
180 Rodney Thomas	.02	.10
181 Ken Dilger	.07	.20
182 Zack Crockett	.02	.10
183 Tony Bennett	.02	.10
184 Quentin Coryatt	.02	.10
185 Marshall Faulk	.20	.50
186 Sean Dawkins	.02	.10
187 Jim Harbaugh	.07	.20
188 Eugene Daniel	.02	.10
189 Roosevelt Potts	.02	.10
190 Lamont Warren	.02	.10
191 Will Wolford	.02	.10
192 Tony Siragusa	.02	.10
193 Aaron Bailey	.02	.10
194 Trev Alberts	.02	.10
195 Kevin Hardy	.07	.20
196 Greg Spann	.02	.10
197 Steve Beuerlein	.07	.20
198 Steve Taneyhill	.02	.10
199 Vaughn Dunbar	.02	.10
200 Mark Brunell	.25	.60
201 Bernard Carter	.02	.10
202 James O. Stewart	.07	.20
203 Tony Boselli	.02	.10
204 Chris Doering	.02	.10
205 Willie Jackson	.07	.20
206 Tony Brackens RC	.15	.40
207 Ernest Givins	.02	.10
208 Le'Shai Maston	.02	.10
209 Pete Mitchell	.07	.20
210 Desmond Howard	.07	.20
211 Vinnie Clark	.02	.10
212 Jeff Lageman	.02	.10
213 Derrick Walker	.02	.10
214 Dan Saleaumua	.02	.10
215 Derrick Thomas	.15	.40
216 Neil Smith	.07	.20
217 Willie Davis	.02	.10
218 Mark Collins	.02	.10
219 Lake Dawson	.02	.10
220 Greg Hill	.07	.20
221 Anthony Davis	.02	.10
222 Kimble Anders	.07	.20
223 Webster Slaughter	.02	.10
224 Tamarick Vanover	.07	.20
225 Marcus Allen	.15	.40
226 Steve Bono	.02	.10
227 Will Shields	.02	.10
228 Karim Abdul-Jabbar RC	.15	.40
229 Tim Bowens	.02	.10
230 Keith Sims	.02	.10
231 Terry Kirby	.07	.20
232 Gene Atkins	.02	.10
233 Dan Marino	.75	2.00
234 Richmond Webb	.02	.10
235 Gary Clark	.02	.10
236 O.J. McDuffie	.07	.20
237 Marco Coleman	.02	.10
238 Bernie Parmalee	.02	.10
239 Randal Hill	.02	.10
240 Bryan Cox	.02	.10
241 Irving Fryar	.07	.20
242 Derrick Alexander DE	.02	.10
243 Qadry Ismail	.07	.20
244 Warren Moon	.07	.20
245 Cris Carter	.15	.40
246 Chad May	.02	.10
247 Robert Smith	.07	.20
248 Fuad Reveiz	.02	.10
249 Orlando Thomas	.02	.10
250 Chris Hinton	.02	.10
251 Jack Del Rio	.02	.10
252 Moe Williams RC	.40	1.00
253 Roy Barker	.02	.10
254 Jake Reed	.07	.20
255 Adrian Cooper	.02	.10
256 Curtis Martin	.30	.75
257 Ben Coates	.07	.20
258 Drew Bledsoe	.25	.60
259 Maurice Hurst	.02	.10
260 Troy Brown	.15	.40
261 Bruce Armstrong	.02	.10
262 Myron Guyton	.02	.10
263 Dave Meggett	.02	.10
264 Terry Glenn RC	.40	1.00
265 Chris Slade	.02	.10
266 Vincent Brisby	.02	.10
267 Willie McGinest	.02	.10
268 Vincent Brown	.02	.10
269 Will Moore	.02	.10
270 Jay Barker	.02	.10
271 Ray Zellars	.02	.10
272 Derek Brown RBK	.02	.10
273 William Roaf	.02	.10
274 Quinn Early	.02	.10
275 Michael Haynes	.02	.10
276 Rufus Porter	.02	.10
277 Renaldo Turnbull	.02	.10
278 Wayne Martin	.02	.10
279 Tyrone Hughes	.02	.10
280 Irv Smith	.02	.10
281 Eric Allen	.02	.10
282 Mark Fields	.02	.10
283 Mario Bates	.07	.20
284 Jim Everett	.02	.10
285 Vince Buck	.02	.10
286 Alex Molden RC	.02	.10
287 Tyrone Wheatley	.07	.20
288 Chris Calloway	.02	.10
289 Jessie Armstead	.02	.10
290 Arthur Marshall	.02	.10
291 Aaron Pierce	.02	.10
292 Dave Brown	.02	.10
293 Rodney Hampton	.07	.20
294 Jumbo Elliott	.02	.10
295 Mike Sherrard	.02	.10
296 Howard Cross	.02	.10
297 Michael Brooks	.02	.10
298 Herschel Walker	.07	.20
299 Danny Kanell RC	.15	.40
300 Keith Elias	.02	.10
301 Bobby Houston	.02	.10
302 Dexter Carter	.02	.10
303 Tony Casillas	.02	.10
304 Kyle Brady	.02	.10
305 Glenn Foley	.07	.20
306 Ronald Moore	.02	.10
307 Ryan Yarborough	.02	.10
308 Aaron Glenn	.02	.10
309 Adrian Murrell	.07	.20
310 Boomer Esiason	.07	.20
311 Kyle Clifton	.02	.10
312 Wayne Chrebet	.25	.60
313 Erik Howard	.02	.10
314 Keyshawn Johnson RC	.40	1.00
315 Marvin Washington	.02	.10
316 Johnny Mitchell	.02	.10
317 Alex Van Dyke RC	.07	.20
318 Billy Joe Hobert	.07	.20
319 Andrew Glover	.02	.10
320 Vince Evans	.02	.10
321 Chester McGlockton	.02	.10
322 Pat Swilling	.02	.10
323 Rocket Ismail	.02	.10
324 Eddie Anderson	.02	.10
325 Rickey Dudley RC	.15	.40
326 Steve Wisniewski	.02	.10
327 Harvey Williams	.02	.10
328 Napoleon Kaufman	.15	.40
329 Tim Brown	.15	.40
330 Jeff Hostetler	.02	.10
331 Anthony Smith	.02	.10
332 Terry McDaniel	.02	.10
333 Charlie Garner	.07	.20
334 Ricky Watters	.07	.20
335 Brian Dawkins RC	.50	1.25
336 Randall Cunningham	.15	.40
337 Gary Anderson	.02	.10
338 Calvin Williams	.02	.10
339 Chris T. Jones	.07	.20
340 Bobby Hoying RC	.15	.40
341 William Fuller	.02	.10
342 William Thomas	.02	.10
343 Mike Mamula	.02	.10
344 Fred Barnett	.02	.10
345 Rodney Peete	.02	.10
346 Mark McMillian	.02	.10
347 Bobby Taylor	.02	.10
348 Yancey Thigpen	.07	.20
349 Neil O'Donnell	.07	.20
350 Rod Woodson	.07	.20
351 Kordell Stewart	.15	.40
352 Dermontti Dawson	.02	.10
353 Norm Johnson	.02	.10
354 Ernie Mills	.02	.10
355 Byron Bam Morris	.02	.10
356 Mark Bruener	.02	.10
357 Kevin Greene	.07	.20
358 Greg Lloyd	.07	.20
359 Andre Hastings	.02	.10
360 Eric Pegram	.02	.10
361 Carnell Lake	.02	.10
362 Dwayne Harper	.02	.10
363 Ronnie Harmon	.02	.10
364 Leslie O'Neal	.02	.10
365 John Carney	.02	.10
366 Stan Humphries	.07	.20
367 Brian Roche RC	.02	.10
368 Terrell Fletcher	.02	.10
369 Shaun Gayle	.02	.10
370 Alfred Pupunu	.02	.10
371 Shawn Jefferson	.02	.10
372 Junior Seau	.15	.40
373 Mark Seay	.02	.10
374 Aaron Hayden	.02	.10
375 Tony Martin	.07	.20
376 Steve Young	.30	.75
377 J.J. Stokes	.15	.40
378 Jerry Rice	.40	1.00
379 Derek Loville	.02	.10
380 Lee Woodall	.02	.10
381 Terrell Owens RC	1.00	2.50
382 Elvis Grbac	.07	.20
383 Ricky Ervins	.02	.10
384 Eric Davis	.02	.10
385 Dana Stubblefield	.07	.20
386 Gary Plummer	.02	.10
387 Tim McDonald	.02	.10
388 William Floyd	.07	.20
389 Ken Norton Jr.	.02	.10
390 Merton Hanks	.02	.10
391 Bart Oates	.02	.10
392 Brent Jones	.02	.10
393 Steve Broussard	.02	.10
394 Robert Blackmon	.02	.10
395 Rick Tuten	.02	.10
396 Pete Kendall	.02	.10
397 John Friesz	.02	.10
398 Terry Wooden	.02	.10
399 Rick Mirer	.07	.20
400 Chris Warren	.07	.20
401 Joey Galloway	.15	.40
402 Howard Ballard	.02	.10
403 Jason Kyle	.02	.10
404 Kevin Mawae	.02	.10
405 Mack Strong	.15	.40
406 Reggie Brown RBK RC	.02	.10
407 Cortez Kennedy	.02	.10
408 Sean Gilbert	.02	.10
409 J.T. Thomas	.02	.10
410 Shane Conlan	.02	.10
411 Johnny Bailey	.02	.10
412 Mark Rypien	.02	.10
413 Leonard Russell	.02	.10
414 Troy Drayton	.02	.10
415 Jerome Bettis	.15	.40
416 Jessie Hester	.02	.10
417 Isaac Bruce	.15	.40
418 Roman Phifer	.02	.10
419 Todd Kinchen	.02	.10
420 Alexander Wright	.02	.10
421 Marcus Jones RC	.02	.10
422 Horace Copeland	.02	.10
423 Eric Curry	.02	.10
424 Courtney Hawkins	.02	.10
425 Alvin Harper	.02	.10
426 Derrick Brooks	.15	.40
427 Errict Rhett	.07	.20
428 Trent Dilfer	.15	.40
429 Hardy Nickerson	.02	.10
430 Brad Culpepper	.02	.10
431 Warren Sapp	.02	.10
432 Reggie Roby	.02	.10
433 Santana Dotson	.02	.10
434 Jerry Ellison	.02	.10
435 Lawrence Dawsey	.02	.10
436 Heath Shuler	.07	.20
437 Stanley Richard	.07	.20
438 Rod Stephens	.02	.10
439 Stephen Davis RC	.60	1.50
440 Terry Allen	.07	.20
441 Michael Westbrook	.15	.40
442 Ken Harvey	.02	.10
443 Coleman Bell	.02	.10
444 Marvcus Patton	.02	.10
445 Gus Frerotte	.07	.20
446 Leslie Shepherd	.02	.10
447 Tom Carter	.02	.10
448 Brian Mitchell	.02	.10
449 Darrell Green	.02	.10
450A Tony Woods (issued in packs)	.02	.10
450B Chris Warren Promo	.20	.50
CW1 Chris Warren Promo (Gold Crown Die Cut style)	.40	1.00

1996 Pacific Blue

COMPLETE SET (450)	150.00	300.00
*STARS: 3X TO 6X BASIC CARDS		
*RCs: 1.5X TO 3X BASIC CARDS		
STATED ODDS 9:37		

1996 Pacific Red

COMPLETE SET (450)	200.00	400.00
*STARS: 4X TO 8X BASIC CARDS		
*RCs: 2X TO 4X BASIC CARDS		
STATED ODDS 9:37		

1996 Pacific Silver

COMPLETE SET (450)	150.00	300.00
*STARS: 3X TO 6X BASIC CARDS		
*RCs: 1.5X TO 3X BASIC CARDS		
RANDOM INSERTS IN SPECIAL RETAIL		

1996 Pacific Bomb Squad

COMPLETE SET (10)	40.00	100.00
STATED ODDS 1:73		
1 Jeff Blake / Carl Pickens	2.50	6.00
2 John Elway / Anthony Miller	12.50	30.00
3 Scott Mitchell / Herman Moore	4.00	10.00
4 Troy Aikman / Jay Novacek	5.00	12.00
5 Brett Favre / Robert Brooks	12.50	30.00
6 Steve McNair / Chris Sanders	4.00	10.00
7 Dan Marino / Irving Fryar	12.50	30.00
8 Drew Bledsoe / Terry Glenn	6.00	15.00
9 Kordell Stewart / Kordell Stewart	4.00	10.00
10 Steve Young / Jerry Rice	7.50	20.00

1996 Pacific Card Supials

COMPLETE SET (72)	150.00	300.00
COMP.LARGE SET (36)	100.00	200.00
COMP.SMALL SET (36)	50.00	125.00
LARGE CARDS PRICED BELOW		
*SMALL CARDS: .3X TO .7X LARGE		
STATED ODDS 1:37		
1 Garrison Hearst	.75	2.00
2 Jeff George	.75	2.00
3 Eric Zeier	.40	1.00
4 Jim Kelly	1.50	4.00
5 Kerry Collins	1.50	4.00
6 Rashaan Salaam	.75	2.00
7 Jeff Blake	1.50	4.00
8 Troy Aikman	4.00	10.00
9 Emmitt Smith	6.00	15.00
10 Terrell Davis	3.00	8.00
11 John Elway	8.00	20.00
12 Deion Sanders	2.50	6.00
13 Barry Sanders	6.00	15.00
14 Brett Favre	8.00	20.00
15 Steve McNair	3.00	8.00
16 Marshall Faulk	2.00	5.00
17 Mark Brunell	2.50	6.00
18 Tamarick Vanover	.75	2.00
19 Dan Marino	8.00	20.00
20 Cris Carter	1.50	4.00
21 Keyshawn Johnson	4.00	10.00
22 Rodney Hampton	.75	2.00
23 Curtis Martin	3.00	8.00
24 Drew Bledsoe	2.50	6.00
25 Mario Bates	.75	2.00
26 Napoleon Kaufman	1.50	4.00
27 Ricky Watters	.75	2.00
28 Kordell Stewart	1.50	4.00
29 Junior Seau	1.50	4.00
30 Steve Young	3.00	8.00
31 Jerry Rice	4.00	10.00
32 Isaac Bruce	1.50	4.00
33 Joey Galloway	1.50	4.00
34 Chris Warren	.75	2.00
35 Errict Rhett	.75	2.00
36 Michael Westbrook	1.50	4.00

1996 Pacific Cramer's Choice

COMPLETE SET (10)	60.00	150.00
STATED ODDS 1:721		
CC1 Emmitt Smith	10.00	25.00
CC2 John Elway	12.50	30.00
CC3 Barry Sanders	10.00	25.00
CC4 Brett Favre	12.50	30.00
CC5 Reggie White	2.50	6.00
CC6 Dan Marino	12.50	30.00
CC7 Curtis Martin	5.00	12.00
CC8 Keyshawn Johnson	6.00	15.00
CC9 Kordell Stewart	2.50	6.00
CC10 Jerry Rice	6.00	15.00

1996 Pacific Gems of the Crown

COMPLETE SET (36)	125.00	250.00
COMP.SERIES 1 SET (18)	60.00	100.00
COMP.SERIES 2 SET (18)	90.00	150.00
1-18: STATED ODDS 2:37 DYNAGON		
19-36: STATED ODDS 1:37 PACIFIC		
GC1 Kerry Collins	1.50	4.00
GC2 Rashaan Salaam	.75	2.00
GC3 Steve Young	3.00	8.00
GC4 Rodney Thomas	.40	1.00
GC5 Michael Westbrook	1.50	4.00
GC6 Cris Carter	1.50	4.00
GC7 Jerry Rice	4.00	10.00
GC8 Drew Bledsoe	2.50	6.00
GC9 Steve McNair	3.00	8.00
GC10 Terrell Davis	3.00	8.00
GC11 Barry Sanders	6.00	15.00
GC12 Robert Brooks	1.50	4.00
GC13 Chris Warren	.75	2.00
GC14 Marshall Faulk	2.00	5.00
GC15 John Elway	8.00	20.00
GC16 Isaac Bruce	1.50	4.00
GC17 Emmitt Smith	6.00	15.00
GC18 Thurman Thomas	1.50	4.00
GC19 Garrison Hearst	.75	2.00
GC20 Jeff Blake	1.50	4.00
GC21 Troy Aikman	4.00	10.00
GC22 Deion Sanders	2.50	6.00
GC23 Brett Favre	8.00	20.00
GC24 Robert Smith	.75	2.00
GC25 Mario Bates	.75	2.00
GC26 Napoleon Kaufman	1.50	4.00
GC27 Kordell Stewart	1.50	4.00
GC28 Jim Kelly	1.50	4.00
GC29 Jim Harbaugh	.75	2.00
GC30 Tamarick Vanover	.75	2.00
GC31 Dan Marino	8.00	20.00
GC32 Warren Moon	.75	2.00
GC33 Curtis Martin	3.00	8.00
GC34 Rodney Hampton	.75	2.00
GC35 Ricky Watters	.75	2.00
GC36 Joey Galloway	1.50	4.00

1996 Pacific Gold Crown Die Cuts

COMPLETE SET (20)	60.00	150.00
GOLD STATED ODDS 1:37		
*PLATINUMS: 1X TO 2.5X GOLDS		
PLAT: INSERTS IN SPECIAL RETAIL PACKS		
1 Emmitt Smith	8.00	20.00
2 Troy Aikman	5.00	12.00
3 Barry Sanders	8.00	20.00
4 Kerry Collins	2.00	5.00
5 Jeff Blake	2.00	5.00
6 John Elway	10.00	25.00
7 Terrell Davis	4.00	10.00
8 Deion Sanders	3.00	8.00
9 Brett Favre	10.00	25.00
10 Dan Marino	10.00	25.00
11 Eddie George	2.50	6.00
12 Curtis Martin	4.00	10.00
13 Drew Bledsoe	3.00	8.00
14 Keyshawn Johnson	2.00	5.00
15 Napoleon Kaufman	2.00	5.00
16 Kordell Stewart	2.00	5.00
17 Steve Young	4.00	10.00
18 Jerry Rice	5.00	12.00
19 Joey Galloway	2.00	5.00
20 Chris Warren	1.00	2.50

1996 Pacific Power Corps

COMPLETE SET (20)	40.00	75.00
STATED ODDS 6:21 SPECIAL RETAIL		
*FOIL PARAL (1/11/14/17-19): 1X to 2.5X		
ONLY SIX FOIL CARDS MADE		
PC1 Troy Aikman	2.50	5.00
PC2 Jeff Blake	1.00	2.00
PC3 Drew Bledsoe	1.50	3.00
PC4 Kerry Collins	1.00	2.00
PC5 Terrell Davis	2.00	4.00
PC6 John Elway	5.00	10.00
PC7 Marshall Faulk	1.25	2.50
PC8 Brett Favre	5.00	10.00
PC9 Joey Galloway	1.00	2.00
PC10 Garrison Hearst	.40	1.00
PC11 Dan Marino	5.00	10.00
PC12 Curtis Martin	2.00	4.00
PC13 Steve McNair	2.00	4.00
PC14 Jerry Rice	2.50	5.00
PC15 Rashaan Salaam	.40	1.00
PC16 Barry Sanders	4.00	8.00
PC17 Emmitt Smith	4.00	8.00
PC18 Kordell Stewart	1.00	2.00
PC19 Chris Warren	.40	1.00
PC20 Steve Young	2.00	4.00

1996 Pacific The Zone

COMPLETE SET (20)	60.00	150.00
STATED ODDS 1:145		
1 Jim Kelly	1.50	4.00
2 Rashaan Salaam	.75	2.00
3 Carl Pickens	.75	2.00
4 Jeff Blake	1.50	4.00
5 Kerry Collins	1.50	4.00
6 Emmitt Smith	6.00	15.00
7 Troy Aikman	4.00	10.00
8 John Elway	8.00	20.00
9 Barry Sanders	6.00	15.00
10 Herman Moore	.75	2.00
11 Scott Mitchell	.75	2.00
12 Brett Favre	8.00	20.00
13 Robert Brooks	1.50	4.00
14 Marshall Faulk	2.00	5.00
15 Dan Marino	8.00	20.00
16 Drew Bledsoe	2.50	6.00
17 Curtis Martin	3.00	8.00
18 Steve Young	3.00	8.00
19 Jerry Rice	4.00	10.00
20 Chris Warren	.75	2.00

1996 Pacific Super Bowl

This six-card set was produced with both a gold and bronze foil border. The bronze set was made available through a special wrapper redemption program at the 1996 Super Bowl Card Show in Phoenix. Collectors with five wrappers would receive one card and 30-pack wrappers were good for a complete set. The fronts feature color action player photos with a bronze foil overlay going up the sides of the card along with the Super Bowl Card Show logo. The gold foil set was available via a wrapper redemption program with 1995 Triple Folders. Collectors could receive a complete set by sending 18 Triple Folders wrappers to Pacific along with $5.95. The gold cards are basically a parallel to the bronze issue, but contain a Super Bowl XXX logo on the cardfronts.

COMP.GOLD SET (6)	4.00	10.00
*BRONZE CARDS: SAME PRICE		
1 Chris Warren	.40	1.00
2 Kordell Stewart	.80	2.00
3 Curtis Martin	.80	2.00
4 Errict Rhett	.40	1.00
5 Neil O'Donnell	.40	1.00
6 Barry Sanders	1.60	4.00

1997 Pacific

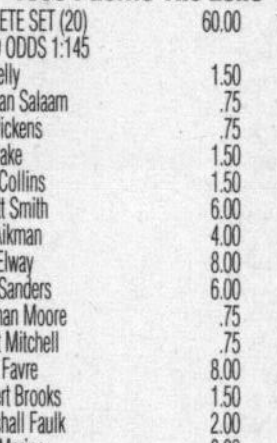

The 1997 Pacific set was issued in one series totalling 450 cards and distributed in 12-card packs with a suggested retail price of $2.49. The fronts feature borderless action color player photos with gold foil printing. The backs carry player information and career statistics. The cards are grouped alphabetically within teams. Four different parallels sets were released in various forms of packaging. The Platinum Blue foil parallel was the toughest to pull with, reportedly, only 67-sets produced.

COMPLETE SET (450)	15.00	30.00
1 Lomas Brown	.07	.20
2 Pat Carter	.07	.20
3 Larry Centers	.10	.30

4 Matt Darby	.07	.20
5 Marcus Dowdell	.07	.20
6 Aaron Graham	.07	.20
7 Kent Graham	.07	.20
8 LeShon Johnson	.07	.20
9 Seth Joyner	.07	.20
10 Leeland McElroy	.07	.20
11 Rob Moore	.10	.30
12 Simeon Rice	.10	.30
13 Eric Swann	.07	.20
14 Aeneas Williams	.07	.20
15 Morten Andersen	.07	.20
16 Jamal Anderson	.20	.50
17 Lester Archambeau	.07	.20
18 Cornelius Bennett	.07	.20
19 J.J. Birden	.07	.20
20 Antone Davis	.07	.20
21 Bert Emanuel	.10	.30
22 Travis Hall RC	.07	.20
23 Bobby Hebert	.07	.20
24 Craig Heyward	.07	.20
25 Terance Mathis	.10	.30
26 Tim McKyer	.07	.20
27 Eric Metcalf	.10	.30
28 Jessie Tuggle	.07	.20
29 Derrick Alexander WR	.10	.30
30 Orlando Brown	.07	.20
31 Rob Burnett	.07	.20
32 Earnest Byner	.07	.20
33 Ray Ethridge	.07	.20
34 Steve Everitt	.07	.20
35 Carwell Gardner	.07	.20
36 Michael Jackson	.10	.30
37 Jermaine Lewis	.20	.50
38 Stevon Moore	.07	.20
39 Byron Bam Morris	.07	.20
40 Jonathan Ogden	.07	.20
41 Vinny Testaverde	.10	.30
42 Todd Collins	.07	.20
43 Russell Copeland	.07	.20
44 Quinn Early	.07	.20
45 John Fina	.07	.20
46 Phil Hansen	.07	.20
47 Eric Moulds	.20	.50
48 Bryce Paup	.07	.20
49 Andre Reed	.10	.30
50 Kurt Schulz	.07	.20
51 Bruce Smith	.10	.30
52 Chris Spielman	.07	.20
53 Steve Tasker	.07	.20
54 Thurman Thomas	.20	.50
55 Carlton Bailey	.07	.20
56 Michael Bates	.07	.20
57 Blake Brockermeyer	.07	.20
58 Mark Carrier WR	.07	.20
59 Kerry Collins	.20	.50
60 Eric Davis	.07	.20
61 Kevin Greene	.10	.30
62 Rocket Ismail	.10	.30
63 Anthony Johnson	.07	.20
64 Shawn King	.07	.20
65 Greg Kragen	.07	.20
66 Sam Mills	.07	.20
67 Tyrone Poole	.07	.20
68 Wesley Walls	.10	.30
69 Mark Carrier DB	.07	.20
70 Curtis Conway	.10	.30
71 Bobby Engram	.10	.30
72 Jim Flanigan	.07	.20
73 Al Fontenot	.07	.20
74 Raymont Harris	.07	.20
75 Walt Harris	.07	.20
76 Andy Heck	.07	.20
77 Dave Krieg	.07	.20
78 Rashaan Salaam	.07	.20
79 Vinson Smith	.07	.20
80 Alonzo Spellman	.07	.20
81 Michael Timpson	.07	.20
82 James Williams	.07	.20
83 Ashley Ambrose	.07	.20
84 Eric Bieniemy	.07	.20
85 Jeff Blake	.10	.30
86 Ki-Jana Carter	.07	.20
87 John Copeland	.07	.20
88 David Dunn	.07	.20
89 Jeff Hill	.07	.20
90 Ricardo McDonald	.07	.20
91 Tony McGee	.07	.20
92 Greg Myers	.07	.20
93 Carl Pickens	.10	.30
94 Corey Sawyer	.07	.20
95 Darnay Scott	.10	.30
96 Dan Wilkinson	.07	.20
97 Troy Aikman	.40	1.00
98 Larry Allen	.07	.20
99 Eric Bjornson	.07	.20
100 Ray Donaldson	.07	.20
101 Michael Irvin	.20	.50
102 Daryl Johnston	.10	.30
103 Nate Newton	.07	.20
104 Deion Sanders	.20	.50
105 Jim Schwantz RC	.07	.20
106 Emmitt Smith	.60	1.50
107 Broderick Thomas	.07	.20
108 Tony Tolbert	.07	.20
109 Erik Williams	.07	.20
110 Sherman Williams	.07	.20
111 Darren Woodson	.07	.20
112 Steve Atwater	.07	.20
113 Aaron Craver	.07	.20
114 Ray Crockett	.07	.20
115 Terrell Davis	.25	.60
116 Jason Elam	.10	.30
117 John Elway	.75	2.00
118 Todd Kinchen	.07	.20
119 Ed McCaffrey	.10	.30
120 Anthony Miller	.07	.20
121 John Mobley	.07	.20
122 Michael Dean Perry	.07	.20
123 Reggie Rivers	.07	.20
124 Shannon Sharpe	.10	.30
125 Alfred Williams	.07	.20
126 Reggie Brown LB	.10	.30
127 Luther Elliss	.07	.20
128 Kevin Glover	.07	.20
129 Jason Hanson	.07	.20
130 Pepper Johnson	.07	.20
131 Glyn Milburn	.07	.20
132 Scott Mitchell	.10	.30
133 Herman Moore	.10	.30
134 Johnnie Morton	.10	.30
135 Brett Perriman	.07	.20
136 Robert Porcher	.07	.20
137 Ron Rivers	.07	.20
138 Barry Sanders	.60	1.50
139 Henry Thomas	.07	.20
140 Don Beebe	.07	.20
141 Edgar Bennett	.10	.30
142 Robert Brooks	.10	.30
143 LeRoy Butler	.07	.20
144 Mark Chmura	.10	.30
145 Brett Favre	.75	2.00
146 Antonio Freeman	.20	.50
147 Chris Jacke	.07	.20
148 Travis Jervey	.10	.30
149 Sean Jones	.07	.20
150 Dorsey Levens	.20	.50
151 John Michels	.07	.20
152 Craig Newsome	.07	.20
153 Eugene Robinson	.07	.20
154 Reggie White	.20	.50
155 Micheal Barrow	.07	.20
156 Blaine Bishop	.07	.20
157 Chris Chandler	.10	.30
158 Anthony Cook	.07	.20
159 Malcolm Floyd	.07	.20
160 Eddie George	.20	.50
161 Roderick Lewis	.07	.20
162 Steve McNair	.25	.60
163 John Henry Mills RC	.07	.20
164 Derek Russell	.07	.20
165 Chris Sanders	.07	.20
166 Mark Stepnoski	.07	.20
167 Frank Wycheck	.07	.20
168 Robert Young	.07	.20
169 Trev Alberts	.07	.20
170 Aaron Bailey	.07	.20
171 Tony Bennett	.07	.20
172 Ray Buchanan	.07	.20
173 Quentin Coryatt	.07	.20
174 Eugene Daniel	.07	.20
175 Sean Dawkins	.07	.20
176 Ken Dilger	.07	.20
177 Marshall Faulk	.25	.60
178 Jim Harbaugh	.10	.30
179 Marvin Harrison	.20	.50
180 Paul Justin	.07	.20
181 Lamont Warren	.07	.20
182 Bernard Whittington	.07	.20
183 Tony Boselli	.07	.20
184 Tony Brackens	.07	.20
185 Mark Brunell	.25	.60
186 Brian DeMarco	.07	.20
187 Rich Griffith	.07	.20
188 Kevin Hardy	.07	.20
189 Willie Jackson	.07	.20
190 Jeff Lageman	.07	.20
191 Keenan McCardell	.10	.30
192 Natrone Means	.10	.30
193 Pete Mitchell	.07	.20
194 Joel Smeenge	.07	.20
195 Jimmy Smith	.10	.30
196 James O.Stewart	.10	.30
197 Marcus Allen	.20	.50
198 John Alt	.07	.20
199 Kimble Anders	.10	.30
200 Steve Bono	.10	.30
201 Vaughn Booker RC	.07	.20
202 Dale Carter	.07	.20
203 Mark Collins	.07	.20
204 Greg Hill	.07	.20
205 Joe Horn	.20	.50
206 Dan Saleaumua	.07	.20
207 Will Shields	.07	.20
208 Neil Smith	.10	.30
209 Derrick Thomas	.20	.50
210 Tamarick Vanover	.10	.30
211 Karim Abdul-Jabbar	.10	.30
212 Fred Barnett	.07	.20
213 Tim Bowens	.07	.20
214 Kirby Dar Dar RC	.10	.30
215 Troy Drayton	.07	.20
216 Craig Erickson	.07	.20
217 Daryl Gardener	.07	.20
218 Randal Hill	.07	.20
219 Dan Marino	.75	2.00
220 O.J. McDuffie	.10	.30
221 Bernie Parmalee	.07	.20
222 Stanley Pritchett	.07	.20
223 Daniel Stubbs	.07	.20
224 Zach Thomas	.20	.50
225 Derrick Alexander DE	.07	.20
226 Cris Carter	.20	.50
227 Jeff Christy	.07	.20
228 Qadry Ismail	.10	.30
229 Brad Johnson	.20	.50
230 Andrew Jordan	.07	.20
231 Randall McDaniel	.07	.20
232 David Palmer	.07	.20
233 John Randle	.10	.30
234 Jake Reed	.10	.30
235 Scott Sisson	.07	.20
236 Korey Stringer	.07	.20
237 Darryl Talley	.07	.20
238 Orlando Thomas	.07	.20
239 Bruce Armstrong	.07	.20
240 Drew Bledsoe	.25	.60
241 Willie Clay	.07	.20
242 Ben Coates	.10	.30
243 Ferric Collons RC	.07	.20
244 Terry Glenn	.20	.50
245 Jerome Henderson	.07	.20
246 Shawn Jefferson	.07	.20
247 Dietrich Jells	.07	.20
248 Ty Law	.10	.30
249 Curtis Martin	.25	.60
250 Willie McGinest	.07	.20
251 Dave Meggett	.07	.20
252 Lawyer Milloy	.10	.30
253 Chris Slade	.07	.20
254 Je'rod Cherry	.07	.20
255 Jim Everett	.07	.20
256 Mark Fields	.07	.20
257 Michael Haynes	.07	.20
258 Tyrone Hughes	.07	.20
259 Haywood Jeffires	.07	.20
260 Wayne Martin	.07	.20
261 Mark McMillian	.07	.20
262 Rufus Porter	.07	.20
263 William Roaf	.07	.20
264 Torrance Small	.07	.20
265 Renaldo Turnbull	.07	.20
266 Ray Zellars	.07	.20
267 Jessie Armstead	.07	.20
268 Chad Bratzke	.07	.20
269 Dave Brown	.07	.20
270 Chris Calloway	.07	.20
271 Howard Cross	.07	.20
272 Lawrence Dawsey	.07	.20
273 Rodney Hampton	.10	.30
274 Danny Kanell	.07	.20
275 Arthur Marshall	.07	.20
276 Aaron Pierce	.07	.20
277 Phillippi Sparks	.07	.20
278 Amani Toomer	.10	.30
279 Charles Way	.07	.20
280 Richie Anderson	.10	.30
281 Fred Baxter	.07	.20
282 Wayne Chrebet	.20	.50
283 Kyle Clifton	.07	.20
284 Jumbo Elliott	.07	.20
285 Aaron Glenn	.07	.20
286 Jeff Graham	.07	.20
287 Bobby Hamilton RC	.07	.20
288 Keyshawn Johnson	.20	.50
289 Adrian Murrell	.10	.30
290 Neil O'Donnell	.10	.30
291 Webster Slaughter	.07	.20
292 Alex Van Dyke	.07	.20
293 Marvin Washington	.07	.20
294 Joe Aska	.07	.20
295 Jerry Ball	.07	.20
296 Tim Brown	.20	.50
297 Rickey Dudley	.10	.30
298 Pat Harlow	.07	.20
299 Nolan Harrison	.07	.20
300 Billy Joe Hobert	.10	.30
301 James Jett	.10	.30
302 Napoleon Kaufman	.20	.50
303 Lincoln Kennedy	.07	.20
304 Albert Lewis	.07	.20
305 Chester McGlockton	.07	.20
306 Pat Swilling	.07	.20
307 Steve Wisniewski	.07	.20
308 Darion Conner	.07	.20
309 Ty Detmer	.10	.30
310 Jason Dunn	.07	.20
311 Irving Fryar	.10	.30
312 James Fuller	.07	.20
313 William Fuller	.07	.20
314 Charlie Garner	.10	.30
315 Bobby Hoying	.10	.30
316 Tom Hutton	.07	.20
317 Chris T. Jones	.07	.20
318 Mike Mamula	.07	.20
319 Mark Seay	.07	.20
320 Bobby Taylor	.07	.20
321 Ricky Watters	.10	.30
322 Jahine Arnold	.07	.20
323 Jerome Bettis	.20	.50
324 Chad Brown	.07	.20
325 Mark Bruener	.07	.20
326 Andre Hastings	.07	.20
327 Norm Johnson	.07	.20
328 Levon Kirkland	.07	.20
329 Carnell Lake	.07	.20
330 Greg Lloyd	.07	.20
331 Ernie Mills	.07	.20
332 Orpheus Roye RC	.07	.20
333 Kordell Stewart	.20	.50
334 Yancey Thigpen	.10	.30
335 Mike Tomczak	.07	.20
336 Rod Woodson	.10	.30
337 Tony Banks	.10	.30
338 Bern Brostek	.07	.20
339 Isaac Bruce	.20	.50
340 Ernie Conwell	.07	.20
341 Keith Crawford RC	.07	.20
342 Wayne Gandy	.07	.20
343 Harold Green	.07	.20
344 Carlos Jenkins	.07	.20
345 Jimmie Jones	.07	.20
346 Eddie Kennison	.10	.30
347 Todd Lyght	.07	.20
348 Leslie O'Neal	.07	.20
349 Lawrence Phillips	.07	.20
350 Greg Robinson	.07	.20
351 Darren Bennett	.07	.20
352 Lewis Bush	.07	.20
353 Eric Castle	.07	.20
354 Terrell Fletcher	.07	.20
355 Darrien Gordon	.07	.20
356 Kurt Gouveia	.07	.20
357 Aaron Hayden	.07	.20
358 Stan Humphries	.10	.30
359 Tony Martin	.10	.30
360 Vaughn Parker RC	.07	.20
361 Brian Roche	.07	.20
362 Leonard Russell	.07	.20
363 Junior Seau	.20	.50
364 Roy Barker	.07	.20
365 Harris Barton	.07	.20
366 Dexter Carter	.07	.20
367 Chris Doleman	.07	.20
368 Tyronne Drakeford	.07	.20
369 Elvis Grbac	.10	.30
370 Derek Loville	.07	.20
371 Tim McDonald	.07	.20
372 Ken Norton	.07	.20
373 Terrell Owens	.25	.60
374 Gary Plummer	.07	.20
375 Jerry Rice	.40	1.00
376 Dana Stubblefield	.07	.20
377 Lee Woodall	.07	.20
378 Steve Young	.25	.60
379 Robert Blackmon	.07	.20
380 Brian Blades	.07	.20
381 Carlester Crumpler	.07	.20
382 Christian Fauria	.07	.20
383 John Friesz	.07	.20
384 Joey Galloway	.10	.30
385 Derrick Graham	.07	.20
386 Cortez Kennedy	.07	.20
387 Warren Moon	.20	.50
388 Winston Moss	.07	.20
389 Mike Pritchard	.07	.20
390 Michael Sinclair	.07	.20
391 Lamar Smith	.20	.50
392 Chris Warren	.10	.30
393 Chidi Ahanotu	.07	.20
394 Mike Alstott	.20	.50
395 Reggie Brooks	.07	.20
396 Trent Dilfer	.20	.50
397 Jerry Ellison	.07	.20
398 Paul Gruber	.07	.20
399 Alvin Harper	.07	.20
400 Courtney Hawkins	.07	.20
401 Dave Moore	.07	.20
402 Errict Rhett	.07	.20
403 Warren Sapp	.10	.30
404 Nilo Silvan	.07	.20
405 Regan Upshaw	.07	.20
406 Casey Weldon	.07	.20
407 Terry Allen	.20	.50
408 Jamie Asher	.07	.20
409 Bill Brooks	.07	.20
410 Tom Carter	.07	.20
411 Henry Ellard	.07	.20
412 Gus Frerotte	.07	.20
413 Darrell Green	.10	.30
414 Ken Harvey	.07	.20
415 Tre Johnson	.07	.20
416 Brian Mitchell	.07	.20
417 Rich Owens	.07	.20
418 Heath Shuler	.07	.20
419 Michael Westbrook	.10	.30
420 Tony Woods RC	.07	.20
421 Reidel Anthony RC	.20	.50
422 Darnell Autry RC	.10	.30
423 Tiki Barber RC	1.25	3.00
424 Pat Barnes RC	.20	.50
425 Terry Battle RC	.07	.20
426 Will Blackwell RC	.10	.30
427 Peter Boulware RC	.20	.50
428 Rae Carruth RC	.07	.20
429 Troy Davis RC	.10	.30
430 Jim Druckenmiller RC	.10	.30
431 Warrick Dunn RC	.60	1.50
432 Marc Edwards RC	.07	.20
433 James Farrior RC	.20	.50
434 Yatil Green RC	.10	.30
435 Byron Hanspard RC	.10	.30
436 Ike Hilliard RC	.30	.75
437 David LaFleur RC	.07	.20
438 Kevin Lockett RC	.10	.30
439 Sam Madison RC	.20	.50
440 Brian Manning RC	.10	.30
441 Orlando Pace RC	.20	.50
442 Jake Plummer RC	1.00	2.50
443 Chad Scott RC	.10	.30
444 Sedrick Shaw RC	.10	.30
445 Antowain Smith RC	.50	1.25
446 Shawn Springs RC	.10	.30
447 Ross Verba RC	.07	.20
448 Bryant Westbrook RC	.07	.20
449 Renaldo Wynn RC	.07	.20
450 Jimmy Johnson CO	.10	.30
S1 Mark Brunell Sample	.40	1.00

1997 Pacific Copper

COMPLETE SET (450)	100.00	200.00
*STARS: 3X TO 6X BASIC CARDS		
*RCs: 1.5X TO 3X BASIC CARDS		
ONE PER HOBBY PACK		

1997 Pacific Platinum Blue

*STARS: 10X TO 25X BASIC CARDS
*RCs: 5X TO 12X BASIC CARDS
STATED ODDS 1:73
STATED PRINT RUN 67 SETS

1997 Pacific Red

COMPLETE SET (450)	150.00	300.00
*STARS: 5X TO 10X BASIC CARDS		
*RCs: 2.5X TO 5X BASIC CARDS		
REDS ONE PER SPECIAL RETAIL PACK		

1997 Pacific Silver

COMPLETE SET (450)	125.00	250.00
*STARS: 4X TO 8X BASIC CARDS		
*RCs: 2X TO 4X BASIC CARDS		
ONE PER RETAIL PACK		

1997 Pacific Big Number Die Cuts

COMPLETE SET (20)	25.00	60.00
STATED ODDS 1:37		
1 Jamal Anderson	1.50	4.00
2 Kerry Collins	1.50	4.00
3 Troy Aikman	3.00	8.00
4 Emmitt Smith	5.00	12.00
5 Terrell Davis	2.00	5.00
6 John Elway	6.00	16.00
7 Barry Sanders	5.00	12.00
8 Brett Favre	6.00	15.00
9 Eddie George	1.50	4.00
10 Mark Brunell	2.00	5.00
11 Marcus Allen	1.50	4.00
12 Karim Abdul-Jabbar	1.00	2.50
13 Dan Marino	6.00	15.00
14 Drew Bledsoe	2.00	5.00
15 Curtis Martin	2.00	5.00
16 Napoleon Kaufman	1.50	4.00
17 Jerome Bettis	1.50	4.00
18 Eddie Kennison	1.00	2.50
19 Jerry Rice	3.00	8.00
20 Steve Young	2.00	5.00

1997 Pacific Mark Brunell

COMPLETE SET (8)	12.50	30.00
COMMON CARD (1-8)	1.50	4.00
INSERTS IN VARIOUS PACIFIC PRODUCTS		

1997 Pacific Card Supials

COMPLETE SET (72)	60.00	150.00
COMP.LARGE SET (36)	40.00	100.00
COMP.SMALL SET (36)	25.00	60.00
*SMALL CARDS: .3X TO .8X LARGE		
STATED ODDS 1:37		
1 Todd Collins	1.00	2.50
2 Kerry Collins	1.25	3.00
3 Wesley Walls	1.00	2.50
4 Jeff Blake	1.00	2.50
5 Troy Aikman	2.50	6.00
6 Emmitt Smith	4.00	10.00
7 Terrell Davis	1.50	4.00
8 John Elway	5.00	12.00
9 Herman Moore	1.25	3.00
10 Barry Sanders	4.00	10.00
11 Brett Favre	5.00	12.00
12 Dorsey Levens	1.25	3.00
13 Eddie George	1.25	3.00
14 Steve McNair	1.50	4.00
15 Marshall Faulk	1.50	4.00
16 Mark Brunell	1.25	3.00
17 Natrone Means	1.25	3.00
18 Marcus Allen	1.50	4.00
19 Karim Abdul-Jabbar	1.00	2.50
20 Dan Marino	5.00	12.00
21 Brad Johnson	1.25	3.00
22 Drew Bledsoe	1.50	4.00
23 Terry Glenn	1.25	3.00
24 Curtis Martin	1.50	4.00
25 Napoleon Kaufman	1.00	2.50
26 Ricky Watters	1.25	3.00
27 Jerome Bettis	1.50	4.00
28 Kordell Stewart	1.25	3.00
29 Tony Banks	1.00	2.50
30 Isaac Bruce	1.50	4.00
31 Eddie Kennison	1.00	2.50
32 Jerry Rice	3.00	8.00
33 Steve Young	2.00	5.00
34 Joey Galloway	1.25	3.00
35 Chris Warren	1.00	2.50
36 Gus Frerotte	1.00	2.50

1997 Pacific Cramer's Choice

COMPLETE SET (10)	100.00	250.00
STATED ODDS 1:721		
1 Kevin Greene	2.50	6.00
2 Emmitt Smith	12.50	30.00
3 Terrell Davis	5.00	12.00
4 John Elway	15.00	40.00
5 Barry Sanders	12.50	30.00
6 Brett Favre	15.00	40.00
7 Eddie George	4.00	10.00
8 Mark Brunell	5.00	12.00
9 Terry Glenn	4.00	10.00
10 Jerry Rice	8.00	20.00

1997 Pacific Gold Crown Die Cuts

COMPLETE SET (36)	50.00	120.00
STATED ODDS 1:37		
1 Larry Centers	1.00	2.50
2 Vinny Testaverde	1.00	2.50
3 Kerry Collins	1.50	4.00
4 Kevin Greene	1.00	2.50
5 Anthony Johnson	.60	1.50
6 Jeff Blake	1.00	2.50
7 Troy Aikman	3.00	8.00
8 Emmitt Smith	5.00	12.00
9 Terrell Davis	2.00	5.00
10 John Elway	6.00	15.00
11 Barry Sanders	5.00	12.00
12 Brett Favre	6.00	15.00
13 Antonio Freeman	1.50	4.00
14 Eddie George	1.50	4.00
15 Marshall Faulk	2.00	5.00
16 Mark Brunell	2.00	5.00
17 Jimmy Smith	1.00	2.50
18 Marcus Allen	1.50	4.00
19 Karim Abdul-Jabbar	1.00	2.50
20 Dan Marino	6.00	15.00
21 Brad Johnson	1.50	4.00
22 Drew Bledsoe	2.00	5.00
23 Terry Glenn	1.50	4.00
24 Curtis Martin	2.00	5.00
25 Adrian Murrell	1.00	2.50
26 Tim Brown	1.50	4.00
27 Jerome Bettis	1.50	4.00
28 Kordell Stewart	1.50	4.00
29 Tony Banks	1.00	2.50
30 Terrell Owens	2.00	5.00
31 Jerry Rice	3.00	8.00
32 Steve Young	2.00	5.00
33 Chris Warren	1.00	2.50
34 Terry Allen	1.50	4.00
35 Gus Frerotte	.60	1.50
36 Jim Druckenmiller	1.00	2.50

1997 Pacific Team Checklists

COMPLETE SET (30)	40.00	100.00
STATED ODDS 1:37		
1 Larry Centers	1.00	2.50
Kent Graham		
LeShon Johnson		
2 Jamal Anderson	2.50	6.00
Bert Emanuel		
Morten Andersen		
3 Vinny Testaverde	1.50	4.00
Derrick Alexander WR		
Michael Jackson		
4 Todd Collins	1.00	2.50
Steve Tasker		
Bruce Smith		
5 Kerry Collins	2.50	6.00
Wesley Walls		
Kevin Greene		
6 Rashaan Salaam	1.00	2.50
Raymont Harris		
Curtis Conway		
7 Jeff Blake	1.00	2.50
Carl Pickens		
Ki-Jana Carter		
8 Emmitt Smith	6.00	15.00
Troy Aikman		
Michael Irvin		
9 John Elway	5.00	12.00
Terrell Davis		
Steve Atwater		
10 Barry Sanders	5.00	12.00
Herman Moore		
Scott Mitchell		
11 Brett Favre	7.50	20.00
Reggie White		
Antonio Freeman		
12 Steve McNair	5.00	12.00
Eddie George		
Chris Sanders		
13 Marshall Faulk	1.50	4.00
Jim Harbaugh		
Marvin Harrison		
14 Mark Brunell	3.00	8.00
Keenan McCardell		
Natrone Means		
15 Marcus Allen	2.50	6.00
Dale Carter		
Derrick Thomas		
16 Dan Marino	7.50	20.00
Karim Abdul-Jabbar		
Zach Thomas		
17 Brad Johnson	2.50	6.00
Cris Carter		
Jake Reed		
18 Drew Bledsoe	5.00	12.00
Curtis Martin		
Terry Glenn		
19 Jim Everett	1.00	2.50
Wayne Martin		
Ray Zellars		
20 Dave Brown	1.00	2.50
Rodney Hampton		
Amani Toomer		
21 Keyshawn Johnson	2.50	6.00
Adrian Murrell		
Neil O'Donnell		
22 Napoleon Kaufman	2.50	6.00
Tim Brown		
Chester McGlockton		
23 Ricky Watters	1.50	4.00
Ty Detmer		
Irving Fryar		
24 Jerome Bettis	3.00	8.00
Kordell Stewart		
Will Blackwell		
25 Tony Banks	1.50	4.00
Eddie Kennison		
Isaac Bruce		
26 Tony Martin	1.00	2.50
Stan Humphries		
Junior Seau		
27 Steve Young	5.00	12.00
Jerry Rice		
Terrell Owens		
28 Chris Warren	2.50	6.00
Joey Galloway		
Cortez Kennedy		
29 Trent Dilfer	1.50	4.00
Errict Rhett		
Mike Alstott		
30 Gus Frerotte	2.50	6.00
Terry Allen		
Michael Westbrook		

1997 Pacific The Zone

COMPLETE SET (20)	40.00	100.00
STATED ODDS 1:73		
1 Kerry Collins	2.00	5.00
2 Jeff Blake	1.25	3.00
3 Emmitt Smith	6.00	15.00
4 Terrell Davis	2.50	6.00
5 John Elway	8.00	20.00
6 Barry Sanders	6.00	15.00
7 Brett Favre	8.00	20.00
8 Mark Brunell	2.50	6.00
9 Karim Abdul-Jabbar	1.25	3.00
10 Dan Marino	8.00	20.00
11 Drew Bledsoe	2.50	6.00
12 Terry Glenn	2.00	5.00
13 Curtis Martin	2.50	6.00
14 Napoleon Kaufman	2.00	5.00
15 Jerome Bettis	2.00	5.00
16 Eddie Kennison	1.25	3.00
17 Tony Martin	1.25	3.00
18 Jerry Rice	4.00	10.00
19 Steve Young	2.50	6.00
20 Terry Allen	2.00	5.00

1997 Pacific Roy Firestone

This 6-card set was issued to promote Roy Firestone's involvement with Pacific Trading Cards. Each card includes Roy in a similar card design to various 1997 Pacific football products.

COMPLETE SET (6)	1.20	3.00
COMMON CARD (1-6)	.20	.50

1998 Pacific

The 1998 Pacific set was issued in one series totalling 450 cards and was distributed in ten-card packs with a suggested retail price of $2.19. The fronts feature color action player photos with silver foil highlights. The backs carry player information and career statistics.

COMPLETE SET (450)	25.00	60.00
1 Mario Bates	.15	.40
2 Lomas Brown	.08	.25
3 Larry Centers	.08	.25
4 Chris Gedney	.08	.25
5 Terry Irving	.08	.25
6 Tom Knight	.08	.25
7 Eric Metcalf	.08	.25
8 Jamir Miller	.08	.25
9 Rob Moore	.15	.40
10 Joe Nedney	.08	.25
11 Jake Plummer	.25	.60
12 Simeon Rice	.15	.40
13 Frank Sanders	.15	.40
14 Eric Swann	.08	.25
15 Aeneas Williams	.08	.25
16 Morten Andersen	.08	.25
17 Jamal Anderson	.25	.60
18 Michael Booker	.08	.25
19 Keith Brooking RC	.60	1.50
20 Ray Buchanan	.08	.25
21 Devin Bush	.08	.25
22 Chris Chandler	.15	.40
23 Tony Graziani	.08	.25
24 Harold Green	.08	.25
25 Byron Hanspard	.08	.25
26 Todd Kinchen	.08	.25
27 Tony Martin	.15	.40
28 Terance Mathis	.15	.40
29 Eugene Robinson	.08	.25
30 O.J. Santiago	.08	.25
31 Chuck Smith	.08	.25
32 Jessie Tuggle	.08	.25
33 Bob Whitfield	.08	.25
34 Peter Boulware	.08	.25
35 Jay Graham	.08	.25
36 Eric Green	.08	.25
37 Jim Harbaugh	.15	.40
38 Michael Jackson	.08	.25
39 Jermaine Lewis	.15	.40
40 Ray Lewis	.25	.60
41 Michael McCrary	.08	.25
42 Stevon Moore	.08	.25
43 Jonathan Ogden	.08	.25
44 Errict Rhett	.15	.40
45 Matt Stover	.08	.25
46 Rod Woodson	.15	.40
47 Eric Zeier	.15	.40
48 Ruben Brown	.08	.25
49 Steve Christie	.08	.25
50 Quinn Early	.08	.25
51 John Fina	.08	.25
52 Doug Flutie	.25	.60
53 Phil Hansen	.08	.25
54 Lonnie Johnson	.08	.25
55 Rob Johnson	.15	.40
56 Henry Jones	.08	.25
57 Eric Moulds	.25	.60
58 Andre Reed	.15	.40
59 Antowain Smith	.25	.60
60 Bruce Smith	.15	.40
61 Thurman Thomas	.25	.60
62 Ted Washington	.08	.25
63 Michael Bates	.08	.25
64 Tim Biakabutuka	.15	.40
65 Blake Brockermeyer	.08	.25
66 Mark Carrier	.08	.25
67 Rae Carruth	.08	.25
68 Kerry Collins	.15	.40
69 Doug Evans	.08	.25
70 William Floyd	.08	.25
71 Sean Gilbert	.08	.25
72 Rocket Ismail	.08	.25
73 John Kasay	.08	.25
74 Fred Lane	.08	.25
75 Lamar Lathon	.08	.25
76 Muhsin Muhammad	.15	.40
77 Wesley Walls	.15	.40
78 Edgar Bennett	.08	.25
79 Tom Carter	.08	.25
80 Curtis Conway	.15	.40
81 Bobby Engram	.15	.40
82 Curtis Enis RC	.30	.75
83 Jim Flanigan	.08	.25
84 Walt Harris	.08	.25
85 Jeff Jaeger	.08	.25
86 Erik Kramer	.08	.25
87 John Mangum	.08	.25
88 Glyn Milburn	.08	.25
89 Barry Minter	.08	.25
90 Chris Penn	.08	.25
91 Todd Sauerbrun	.08	.25
92 James Williams	.08	.25
93 Ashley Ambrose	.08	.25
94 Willie Anderson	.08	.25
95 Eric Bieniemy	.08	.25
96 Jeff Blake	.15	.40
97 Ki-Jana Carter	.08	.25
98 John Copeland	.08	.25
99 Corey Dillon	.25	.60
100 Tony McGee	.08	.25
101 Neil O'Donnell	.15	.40
102 Carl Pickens	.15	.40
103 Kevin Sargent	.08	.25
104 Darnay Scott	.15	.40
105 Takeo Spikes RC	.60	1.50
106 Troy Aikman	.50	1.25
107 Larry Allen	.08	.25
108 Eric Bjornson	.08	.25
109 Billy Davis	.08	.25
110 Jason Garrett RC	.50	1.25
111 Michael Irvin	.25	.60
112 Daryl Johnston	.15	.40
113 David LaFleur	.08	.25
114 Everett McIver	.08	.25
115 Ernie Mills	.08	.25
116 Nate Newton	.08	.25
117 Deion Sanders	.25	.60
118 Emmitt Smith	.75	2.00
119 Kevin Smith	.08	.25
120 Erik Williams	.08	.25
121 Steve Atwater	.08	.25
122 Tyrone Braxton	.08	.25
123 Ray Crockett	.08	.25
124 Terrell Davis	.25	.60
125 Jason Elam	.08	.25
126 John Elway	1.00	2.50
127 Willie Green	.08	.25
128 Brian Griese RC	1.25	3.00
129 Tony Jones	.08	.25
130 Ed McCaffrey	.15	.40
131 John Mobley	.08	.25
132 Tom Nalen	.08	.25
133 Marcus Nash RC	.30	.75
134 Bill Romanowski	.08	.25
135 Shannon Sharpe	.15	.40
136 Neil Smith	.15	.40
137 Rod Smith	.15	.40
138 Keith Traylor	.08	.25
139 Stephen Boyd	.08	.25
140 Mark Carrier DB	.08	.25
141 Charlie Batch RC	.60	1.50
142 Jason Hanson	.08	.25
143 Scott Mitchell	.15	.40
144 Herman Moore	.15	.40
145 Johnnie Morton	.15	.40
146 Robert Porcher	.08	.25
147 Ron Rivers	.08	.25
148 Barry Sanders	.75	2.00
149 Tracy Scroggins	.08	.25
150 David Sloan	.08	.25
151 Tommy Vardell	.08	.25
152 Kerwin Waldroup	.08	.25
153 Bryant Westbrook	.08	.25
154 Robert Brooks	.15	.40
155 Gilbert Brown	.08	.25
156 LeRoy Butler	.08	.25
157 Mark Chmura	.15	.40
158 Earl Dotson	.08	.25
159 Santana Dotson	.08	.25
160 Brett Favre	1.00	2.50
161 Antonio Freeman	.25	.60
162 Raymont Harris	.08	.25
163 William Henderson	.15	.40
164 Vonnie Holliday RC	.50	1.25
165 George Koonce	.08	.25
166 Dorsey Levens	.25	.60
167 Derrick Mayes	.15	.40
168 Craig Newsome	.08	.25
169 Ross Verba	.08	.25
170 Reggie White	.25	.60
171 Elijah Alexander	.08	.25
172 Aaron Bailey	.08	.25
173 Jason Belser	.08	.25
174 Robert Blackmon	.08	.25
175 Zack Crockett	.08	.25
176 Ken Dilger	.08	.25
177 Marshall Faulk	.30	.75
178 Tarik Glenn	.08	.25
179 Marvin Harrison	.25	.60
180 Tony Mandarich	.08	.25
181 Peyton Manning RC	7.50	15.00
182 Marcus Pollard	.08	.25
183 Lamont Warren	.08	.25
184 Tavian Banks RC	.50	1.25
185 Reggie Barlow	.08	.25
186 Tony Boselli	.08	.25
187 Tony Brackens	.08	.25
188 Mark Brunell	.25	.60
189 Kevin Hardy	.08	.25
190 Mike Hollis	.08	.25
191 Jeff Lageman	.08	.25
192 Keenan McCardell	.15	.40
193 Pete Mitchell	.08	.25
194 Bryce Paup	.08	.25
195 Leon Searcy	.08	.25
196 Jimmy Smith	.15	.40
197 James Stewart	.15	.40
198 Fred Taylor RC	1.00	2.50
199 Renaldo Wynn	.08	.25
200 Derrick Alexander WR	.15	.40
201 Kimble Anders	.15	.40
202 Donnell Bennett	.08	.25
203 Dale Carter	.08	.25
204 Anthony Davis	.08	.25
205 Rich Gannon	.25	.60
206 Tony Gonzalez	.25	.60
207 Elvis Grbac	.15	.40
208 James Hasty	.08	.25
209 Leslie O'Neal	.08	.25
210 Andre Rison	.15	.40
211 Rashaan Shehee RC	.50	1.25
212 Will Shields	.08	.25
213 Pete Stoyanovich	.08	.25
214 Derrick Thomas	.25	.60
215 Tamarick Vanover	.08	.25
216 Karim Abdul-Jabbar	.25	.60
217 Trace Armstrong	.08	.25
218 John Avery RC	.50	1.25
219 Tim Bowens	.08	.25
220 Terrell Buckley	.08	.25
221 Troy Drayton	.08	.25
222 Daryl Gardener	.08	.25
223 Damon Huard RC	1.25	3.00
224 Charles Jordan	.08	.25
225 Dan Marino	1.00	2.50
226 O.J. McDuffie	.15	.40
227 Bernie Parmalee	.08	.25
228 Stanley Pritchett	.08	.25
229 Derrick Rodgers	.08	.25
230 Lamar Thomas	.08	.25
231 Zach Thomas	.25	.60
232 Richmond Webb	.08	.25
233 Derrick Alexander DE	.08	.25
234 Jerry Ball	.08	.25
235 Cris Carter	.25	.60
236 Randall Cunningham	.25	.60
237 Charles Evans	.08	.25
238 Corey Fuller	.08	.25
239 Andrew Glover	.08	.25
240 Leroy Hoard	.08	.25
241 Brad Johnson	.25	.60
242 Ed McDaniel	.08	.25
243 Randall McDaniel	.08	.25
244 Randy Moss RC	4.00	10.00
245 John Randle	.15	.40
246 Jake Reed	.15	.40
247 Dwayne Rudd	.08	.25
248 Robert Smith	.25	.60
249 Bruce Armstrong	.08	.25
250 Drew Bledsoe	.40	1.00
251 Vincent Brisby	.08	.25

252 Tedy Bruschi .50 1.25
253 Ben Coates .15 .40
254 Derrick Cullors .08 .25
255 Terry Glenn .25 .60
256 Shawn Jefferson .08 .25
257 Ted Johnson .08 .25
258 Ty Law .15 .40
259 Willie McGinest .08 .25
260 Lawyer Milloy .15 .40
261 Sedrick Shaw .08 .25
262 Chris Slade .08 .25
263 Troy Davis .08 .25
264 Mark Fields .08 .25
265 Andre Hastings .08 .25
266 Billy Joe Hobert .08 .25
267 Qadry Ismail .15 .40
268 Tony Johnson .08 .25
269 Sammy Knight RC .25 .60
270 Wayne Martin .08 .25
271 Chris Naeole .08 .25
272 Keith Poole .08 .25
273 William Roaf .08 .25
274 Pio Sagapolutele .08 .25
275 Danny Wuerffel .15 .40
276 Ray Zellars .08 .25
277 Jessie Armstead .08 .25
278 Tiki Barber .25 .60
279 Chris Calloway .08 .25
280 Percy Ellsworth .08 .25
281 Sam Garnes RC .30 .75
282 Kent Graham .08 .25
283 Ike Hilliard .15 .40
284 Danny Kanell .15 .40
285 Corey Miller .08 .25
286 Phillippi Sparks .08 .25
287 Michael Strahan .15 .40
288 Amani Toomer .15 .40
289 Charles Way .08 .25
290 Tyrone Wheatley .15 .40
291 Tito Wooten .08 .25
292 Kyle Brady .08 .25
293 Keith Byars .08 .25
294 Wayne Chrebet .25 .60
295 John Elliott .08 .25
296 Glenn Foley .15 .40
297 Aaron Glenn .08 .25
298 Keyshawn Johnson .25 .60
299 Curtis Martin .25 .60
300 Otis Smith .08 .25
301 Vinny Testaverde .15 .40
302 Alex Van Dyke .08 .25
303 Dedric Ward .08 .25
304 Greg Biekert .08 .25
305 Tim Brown .25 .60
306 Rickey Dudley .08 .25
307 Jeff George .15 .40
308 Pat Harlow .08 .25
309 Desmond Howard .15 .40
310 James Jett .15 .40
311 Napoleon Kaufman .25 .60
312 Lincoln Kennedy .08 .25
313 Russell Maryland .08 .25
314 Darrell Russell .08 .25
315 Eric Turner .08 .25
316 Steve Wisniewski .08 .25
317 Charles Woodson RC .75 2.00
318 James Darling RC .30 .75
319 Jason Dunn .08 .25
320 Irving Fryar .15 .40
321 Charlie Garner .15 .40
322 Jeff Graham .08 .25
323 Bobby Hoying .15 .40
324 Chad Lewis .15 .40
325 Rodney Peete .08 .25
326 Freddie Solomon .08 .25
327 Duce Staley .30 .75
328 Bobby Taylor .08 .25
329 William Thomas .08 .25
330 Kevin Turner .08 .25
331 Troy Vincent .08 .25
332 Jerome Bettis .25 .60
333 Will Blackwell .08 .25
334 Mark Bruener .08 .25
335 Andre Coleman .08 .25
336 Dermontti Dawson .08 .25
337 Jason Gildon .08 .25
338 Courtney Hawkins .08 .25
339 Charles Johnson .08 .25
340 Levon Kirkland .08 .25
341 Carnell Lake .08 .25
342 Tim Lester .08 .25
343 Joel Steed .08 .25
344 Kordell Stewart .25 .60
345 Will Wolford .08 .25
346 Tony Banks .15 .40
347 Isaac Bruce .25 .60
348 Ernie Conwell .08 .25
349 D'Marco Farr .08 .25
350 Wayne Gandy .08 .25
351 Jerome Pathon RC .60 1.50
352 Eddie Kennison .15 .40
353 Amp Lee .08 .25
354 Keith Lyle .08 .25
355 Ryan McNeil .08 .25
356 Jerald Moore .08 .25
357 Orlando Pace .08 .25
358 Roman Phifer .08 .25
359 David Thompson RC .30 .75
360 Darren Bennett .08 .25
361 John Carney .08 .25
362 Marco Coleman .08 .25
363 Terrell Fletcher .08 .25
364 William Fuller .08 .25
365 Charlie Jones .08 .25
366 Freddie Jones .08 .25
367 Ryan Leaf RC .60 1.50
368 Natrone Means .15 .40
369 Junior Seau .25 .60
370 Terrance Shaw .08 .25
371 Tremayne Stephens RC .30 .75
372 Bryan Still .08 .25
373 Aaron Taylor .08 .25
374 Greg Clark .08 .25
375 Ty Detmer .15 .40
376 Jim Druckenmiller .08 .25
377 Marc Edwards .08 .25
378 Merton Hanks .08 .25
379 Garrison Hearst .25 .60
380 Chuck Levy .08 .25
381 Ken Norton .08 .25
382 Terrell Owens .25 .60
383 Marquez Pope .08 .25
384 Jerry Rice .50 1.25
385 Irv Smith .08 .25
386 J.J. Stokes .15 .40
387 Iheanyi Uwaezuoke .08 .25
388 Bryant Young .08 .25
389 Steve Young .30 .75
390 Sam Adams .08 .25
391 Chad Brown .08 .25
392 Christian Fauria .08 .25
393 Joey Galloway .15 .40
394 Ahman Green RC 1.50 4.00
395 Walter Jones .08 .25
396 Cortez Kennedy .08 .25
397 Jon Kitna .25 .60
398 James McKnight .25 .60
399 Warren Moon .25 .60
400 Mike Pritchard .08 .25
401 Michael Sinclair .08 .25
402 Shawn Springs .08 .25
403 Ricky Watters .15 .40
404 Darryl Williams .08 .25
405 Mike Alstott .25 .60
406 Reidel Anthony .15 .40
407 Derrick Brooks .25 .60
408 Brad Culpepper .08 .25
409 Trent Dilfer .25 .60
410 Warrick Dunn .25 .60
411 Bert Emanuel .15 .40
412 Jacquez Green RC .50 1.25
413 Paul Gruber .08 .25
414 Patrick Hape RC .50 1.25
415 Dave Moore .08 .25
416 Hardy Nickerson .08 .25
417 Warren Sapp .15 .40
418 Robb Thomas .08 .25
419 Regan Upshaw .08 .25
420 Karl Williams .08 .25
421 Blaine Bishop .08 .25
422 Anthony Cook .08 .25
423 Willie Davis .08 .25
424 Al Del Greco .08 .25
425 Kevin Dyson .25 .60
426 Henry Ford .08 .25
427 Eddie George .25 .60
428 Jackie Harris .08 .25
429 Steve McNair .25 .60
430 Chris Sanders .08 .25
431 Mark Stepnoski .08 .25
432 Yancey Thigpen .08 .25
433 Barron Wortham .08 .25
434 Frank Wycheck .08 .25
435 Stephen Alexander RC .50 1.25
436 Terry Allen .25 .60
437 Jamie Asher .08 .25
438 Bob Dahl .08 .25
439 Stephen Davis .08 .25
440 Cris Dishman .08 .25
441 Gus Frerotte .08 .25
442 Darrell Green .15 .40
443 Trent Green .30 .75
444 Ken Harvey .08 .25
445 Skip Hicks RC .50 1.25
446 Jeff Hostetler .08 .25
447 Brian Mitchell .08 .25
448 Leslie Shepherd .08 .25
449 Michael Westbrook .15 .40
450 Dan Wilkinson .08 .25
S1 Warrick Dunn Sample .40 1.00

1998 Pacific Platinum Blue

*STARS: 8X TO 20X BASIC CARDS
*ROOKIES: 2.5X TO 6X BASIC CARDS
STATED ODDS 1:73 HOB/RET

1998 Pacific Red

COMPLETE SET (450) 100.00 200.00
*STARS: 1.2X TO 3X BASIC CARDS
*RC'S: .5X TO 1X BASIC CARDS
ONE PER SPECIAL RETAIL PACK

1998 Pacific Cramer's Choice

COMPLETE SET (10) 75.00 200.00
STATED ODDS 1:721
1 Terrell Davis 5.00 12.00
2 John Elway 15.00 40.00
3 Barry Sanders 12.50 30.00
4 Brett Favre 15.00 40.00
5 Peyton Manning 30.00 80.00
6 Mark Brunell 4.00 10.00
7 Dan Marino 15.00 40.00
8 Ryan Leaf 4.00 10.00
9 Jerry Rice 8.00 20.00
10 Warrick Dunn 4.00 10.00

1998 Pacific Dynagon Turf

COMPLETE SET (20) 50.00 100.00
STATED ODDS 4:37
*TITANIUM/99: 2.5X TO 6X BASIC INSERT
TITANIUM STATED PRINT RUN 99
1 Corey Dillon 1.25 3.00
2 Troy Aikman 2.50 6.00
3 Emmitt Smith 4.00 10.00
4 Terrell Davis 1.25 3.00
5 John Elway 5.00 12.00
6 Barry Sanders 4.00 10.00
7 Brett Favre 5.00 12.00
8 Peyton Manning 12.50 25.00
9 Mark Brunell 1.25 3.00
10 Dan Marino 5.00 12.00
11 Drew Bledsoe 2.00 5.00
12 Curtis Martin 1.25 3.00
13 Napoleon Kaufman 1.25 3.00
14 Jerome Bettis 1.25 3.00
15 Kordell Stewart 1.25 3.00
16 Ryan Leaf 1.00 2.50
17 Jerry Rice 2.50 6.00
18 Steve Young 1.50 4.00
19 Warrick Dunn 1.25 3.00
20 Eddie George 1.25 3.00

1998 Pacific Gold Crown Die Cuts

COMPLETE SET (36) 50.00 120.00
STATED ODDS 1:37
1 Jake Plummer 1.50 4.00
2 Antowain Smith 1.00 2.50
3 Curtis Enis .50 1.25
4 Corey Dillon 1.50 4.00
5 Troy Aikman 3.00 8.00
6 Deion Sanders 1.50 4.00
7 Emmitt Smith 5.00 12.00
8 Terrell Davis 1.50 4.00
9 John Elway 6.00 15.00
10 Barry Sanders 5.00 12.00
11 Brett Favre 6.00 15.00
12 Dorsey Levens .50 1.25
13 Marshall Faulk 2.00 5.00
14 Peyton Manning 12.50 25.00
15 Mark Brunell 1.50 4.00
16 Fred Taylor 1.50 4.00
17 Derrick Thomas 1.50 4.00
18 Dan Marino 6.00 15.00
19 Brad Johnson 1.00 2.50
20 Robert Smith .50 1.25
21 Drew Bledsoe 2.50 6.00
22 Glenn Foley .50 1.25
23 Curtis Martin 1.50 4.00
24 Napoleon Kaufman 1.00 2.50
25 Charles Woodson 1.00 2.50
26 Jerome Bettis 1.50 4.00
27 Kordell Stewart 1.50 4.00
28 Ryan Leaf .50 1.25
29 Garrison Hearst 1.00 2.50
30 Jerry Rice 3.00 8.00
31 J.J. Stokes .50 1.25
32 Steve Young 2.00 5.00
33 Joey Galloway 1.00 2.50
34 Ricky Watters 1.00 2.50
35 Warrick Dunn 1.50 4.00
36 Eddie George 1.50 4.00

1998 Pacific Team Checklists

COMPLETE SET (30) 75.00 150.00
STATED ODDS 2:37
1 Jake Plummer 2.00 5.00
2 Jamal Anderson 2.00 5.00
3 Eric Zeier 1.25 3.00
4 Rob Johnson 1.25 3.00
5 Fred Lane .75 2.00
6 Curtis Enis .60 1.50
7 Corey Dillon 2.00 5.00
8 Troy Aikman 4.00 10.00
9 John Elway 8.00 20.00
10 Barry Sanders 6.00 15.00
11 Brett Favre 8.00 20.00
12 Peyton Manning 15.00 30.00
13 Mark Brunell 2.00 5.00
14 Elvis Grbac 1.25 3.00
15 Dan Marino 8.00 20.00
16 Robert Smith 2.00 5.00
17 Drew Bledsoe 3.00 8.00
18 Danny Wuerffel 1.25 3.00
19 Tiki Barber 2.00 5.00
20 Curtis Martin 2.00 5.00
21 Napoleon Kaufman 2.00 5.00
22 Duce Staley 2.50 6.00
23 Kordell Stewart 2.00 5.00
24 Tony Banks 1.25 3.00
25 Ryan Leaf 1.25 3.00
26 Jerry Rice 4.00 10.00
27 Warren Moon 2.00 5.00
28 Warrick Dunn 2.00 5.00
29 Eddie George 2.00 5.00
30 Terry Allen 2.00 5.00

1998 Pacific Timelines

COMPLETE SET (20) 125.00 300.00
STATED ODDS 1:181 HOBBY
1 Troy Aikman 8.00 20.00
2 Deion Sanders 4.00 10.00
3 Emmitt Smith 12.50 30.00
4 Terrell Davis 4.00 10.00
5 John Elway 15.00 40.00
6 Barry Sanders 12.50 30.00
7 Brett Favre 15.00 40.00
8 Peyton Manning 40.00 80.00
9 Mark Brunell 4.00 10.00
10 Dan Marino 15.00 40.00
11 Drew Bledsoe 6.00 15.00
12 Curtis Martin 4.00 10.00
13 Jerome Bettis 4.00 10.00
14 Kordell Stewart 4.00 10.00
15 Ryan Leaf 3.00 8.00
16 Jerry Rice 8.00 20.00
17 Steve Young 5.00 12.00
18 Ricky Watters 2.50 6.00
19 Warrick Dunn 4.00 10.00
20 Eddie George 4.00 10.00

1999 Pacific

The 1999 Pacific set was issued in one series totalling 450 cards and was distributed in 12-card packs with a suggested retail price of $2.49. The fronts feature color action player photos. The backs carry player information and career statistics.

COMPLETE SET (450) 30.00 80.00
1 Mario Bates .15 .40
2 Larry Centers .20 .50
3 Chris Gedney .15 .40
4 Kwamie Lassiter RC .30 .75
5 Johnny McWilliams .15 .40
6 Eric Metcalf .15 .40
7 Rob Moore .15 .40
8 Adrian Murrell .20 .50
9 Jake Plummer .20 .50
10 Simeon Rice .15 .40
11 Frank Sanders .15 .40
12 Andre Wadsworth .15 .40
13 Aeneas Williams .15 .40
14 Michael Pittman .30 .75
Ronnie Anderson RC
15 Morten Andersen .15 .40
16 Jamal Anderson .20 .50
17 Lester Archambeau .15 .40
18 Chris Chandler .20 .50
19 Bob Christian .15 .40
20 Steve DeBerg .20 .50
21 Tim Dwight .20 .50
22 Tony Martin .20 .50
23 Terance Mathis .15 .40
24 Eugene Robinson .20 .50
25 O.J. Santiago .15 .40
26 Chuck Smith .15 .40
27 Jessie Tuggle .15 .40
28 Jammi German .15 .40
Ken Oxendine
29 Peter Boulware .15 .40
30 Jay Graham .15 .40
31 Jim Harbaugh .20 .50
32 Priest Holmes .25 .60
33 Michael Jackson .15 .40
34 Jermaine Lewis .15 .40
35 Ray Lewis .25 .60
36 Michael McCrary .15 .40
37 Jonathan Ogden .15 .40
38 Errict Rhett .15 .40
39 James Roe RC .30 .75
40 Floyd Turner .15 .40
41 Rod Woodson .25 .60
42 Eric Zeier .15 .40
43 Wally Richardson .15 .40
Patrick Johnson
44 Ruben Brown .15 .40
45 Quinn Early .15 .40
46 Doug Flutie .25 .60
47 Sam Gash .15 .40
48 Phil Hansen .15 .40
49 Lonnie Johnson .15 .40
50 Rob Johnson .20 .50
51 Eric Moulds .20 .50
52 Andre Reed .25 .60
53 Jay Riemersma .15 .40
54 Antowain Smith .15 .40
55 Bruce Smith .25 .60
56 Thurman Thomas .25 .60
57 Ted Washington .15 .40
58 Jonathan Linton .30 .75
Kamil Loud RC
59 Michael Bates .15 .40
60 Steve Beuerlein .20 .50
61 Tim Biakabutuka .20 .50
62 Mark Carrier WR .20 .50
63 Eric Davis .15 .40
64 William Floyd .20 .50
65 Sean Gilbert .15 .40
66 Kevin Greene .20 .50
67 Rocket Ismail .20 .50
68 Anthony Johnson .15 .40
69 Fred Lane .15 .40
70 Muhsin Muhammad .20 .50
71 Winslow Oliver .15 .40
72 Wesley Walls .20 .50
73 Dameyune Craig RC .50 1.25
Shane Matthews
74 Edgar Bennett .20 .50
75 Curtis Conway .20 .50
76 Bobby Engram .20 .50
77 Curtis Enis .15 .40
78 Ty Hallock RC .30 .75
79 Walt Harris .15 .40
80 Jeff Jaeger .15 .40
81 Erik Kramer .20 .50
82 Glyn Milburn .15 .40
83 Chris Penn .15 .40
84 Steve Stenstrom .15 .40
85 Ryan Wetnight .15 .40
86 James Allen RC .40 1.00
Moses Moreno
87 Ashley Ambrose .15 .40
88 Brandon Bennett RC .30 .75
89 Eric Bieniemy .15 .40
90 Jeff Blake .20 .50
91 Corey Dillon .20 .50
92 Paul Justin .15 .40
93 Eric Kresser RC .30 .75
94 Tremain Mack .15 .40
95 Tony McGee .15 .40
96 Neil O'Donnell .20 .50
97 Carl Pickens .20 .50
98 Darnay Scott .15 .40
99 Takeo Spikes .15 .40
100 Ty Detmer .20 .50
101 Chris Gardocki .15 .40
102 Damon Gibson .15 .40
103 Antonio Langham .15 .40
104 Jerris McPhail .15 .40
105 Irv Smith .15 .40
106 Freddie Solomon .15 .40
107 Scott Milanovich .30 .75
Fred Brock RC
108 Troy Aikman .40 1.00
109 Larry Allen .20 .50
110 111 .15 .40
111 Billy Davis .15 .40
112 Michael Irvin .25 .60
113 David LaFleur .15 .40
114 Ernie Mills .15 .40
115 Nate Newton .20 .50
116 Deion Sanders .25 .60
117 Emmitt Smith .60 1.50
118 Chris Warren .20 .50
119 Bubby Brister .15 .40
120 Terrell Davis .25 .60
121 Jason Elam .15 .40
122 John Elway .75 2.00
123 Willie Green .15 .40
124 Howard Griffith .15 .40
125 Vaughn Hebron .15 .40
126 Ed McCaffrey .20 .50
127 John Mobley .15 .40
128 Bill Romanowski .20 .50
129 Shannon Sharpe .25 .60
130 Neil Smith .15 .40
131 Rod Smith .20 .50
132 Brian Griese .20 .50
Marcus Nash
133 Charlie Batch .20 .50
134 Stephen Boyd .15 .40
135 Mark Carrier DB .15 .40
136 Germane Crowell .15 .40
137 Terry Fair .15 .40
138 Jason Hanson .15 .40
139 Greg Jeffries RC .30 .75
140 Herman Moore .20 .50
141 Johnnie Morton .20 .50
142 Robert Porcher .15 .40
143 Ron Rivers .15 .40
144 Barry Sanders .60 1.50
145 Tommy Vardell .20 .50
146 Bryant Westbrook .15 .40
147 Robert Brooks .20 .50
148 LeRoy Butler .20 .50
149 Mark Chmura .15 .40
150 Tyrone Davis .15 .40
151 Brett Favre .75 2.00
152 Antonio Freeman .20 .50
153 Raymont Harris .20 .50
154 Vonnie Holliday .15 .40
155 Darick Holmes .15 .40
156 Dorsey Levens .20 .50
157 Brian Manning .15 .40
158 Derrick Mayes .15 .40
159 Roell Preston .15 .40
160 Jeff Thomason .15 .40
161 Tyrone Williams .20 .50
162 Corey Bradford .40 1.00
Michael Blair RC
163 Aaron Bailey .15 .40
164 Ken Dilger .15 .40
165 Marshall Faulk .25 .60
166 E.G. Green .15 .40
167 Marvin Harrison .25 .60
168 Craig Heyward .20 .50
169 Peyton Manning .75 2.00
170 Jerome Pathon .15 .40
171 Marcus Pollard .15 .40
172 Torrance Small .15 .40
173 Mike Vanderjagt .15 .40
174 Lamont Warren .20 .50
175 Tavian Banks .15 .40
176 Reggie Barlow .15 .40
177 Tony Boselli .20 .50
178 Tony Brackens .15 .40
179 Mark Brunell .20 .50
180 Kevin Hardy .15 .40
181 Damon Jones .15 .40
182 Jamie Martin .15 .40
183 Keenan McCardell .20 .50
184 Pete Mitchell .15 .40
185 Bryce Paup .15 .40
186 Jimmy Smith .20 .50
187 Fred Taylor .20 .50
188 Alvis Whitted .15 .40
Chris Howard
189 Derrick Alexander WR .15 .40
190 Kimble Anders .15 .40
191 Donnell Bennett .15 .40
192 Dale Carter .15 .40
193 Rich Gannon .20 .50
194 Tony Gonzalez .25 .60
195 Elvis Grbac .15 .40
196 Joe Horn .20 .50
197 Kevin Lockett .15 .40
198 Byron Bam Morris .15 .40
199 Andre Rison .20 .50
200 Derrick Thomas .25 .60
201 Tamarick Vanover .20 .50
202 Gregory Favors .15 .40
Rashaan Shehee
203 Karim Abdul-Jabbar .20 .50
204 Trace Armstrong .15 .40
205 John Avery .15 .40
206 Lorenzo Bromell RC .30 .75
207 Terrell Buckley .20 .50
208 Oronde Gadsden .15 .40
209 Sam Madison .15 .40
210 Dan Marino .75 2.00
211 O.J. McDuffie .20 .50
212 Ed Perry RC .30 .75
213 Jason Taylor .20 .50
214 Lamar Thomas .15 .40
215 Zach Thomas .25 .60
216 Henry Lusk .30 .75
Nate Jacquet RC
217 Damon Huard .30 .75
Todd Doxzon RC
218 Gary Anderson .15 .40
219 Cris Carter .25 .60
220 Randall Cunningham .25 .60
221 Andrew Glover .15 .40
222 Matthew Hatchette .20 .50
223 Brad Johnson .20 .50
224 Ed McDaniel .15 .40
225 Randall McDaniel .25 .60
226 Randy Moss .25 .60
227 David Palmer .15 .40
228 John Randle .20 .50
229 Jake Reed .20 .50
230 Robert Smith .20 .50
231 Todd Steussie .15 .40
232 Stalin Colinet RC .30 .75
Kivuusama Mays
233 Jay Fiedler RC 1.50 4.00
Todd Bouman RC
234 Drew Bledsoe .25 .60
235 Troy Brown .20 .50
236 Ben Coates .20 .50
237 Derrick Cullors .15 .40
238 Robert Edwards .15 .40
239 Terry Glenn .20 .50
240 Shawn Jefferson .15 .40
241 Ty Law .20 .50
242 Lawyer Milloy .20 .50
243 Lovett Purnell RC .30 .75
244 Sedrick Shaw .15 .40
245 Tony Simmons .15 .40
246 Chris Slade .15 .40
247 Rod Rutledge .30 .75
Anthony Ladd RC
248 Chris Floyd .15 .40
Harold Shaw
249 Ink Aleaga RC .30 .75
250 Cameron Cleeland .15 .40
251 Kerry Collins .20 .50
252 Troy Davis .15 .40
253 Sean Dawkins .15 .40
254 Mark Fields .15 .40
255 Andre Hastings .15 .40
256 Sammy Knight .15 .40
257 Keith Poole .15 .40
258 William Roaf .20 .50
259 Lamar Smith .15 .40
260 Danny Wuerffel .20 .50
261 Josh Wilcox RC .30 .75
Brett Bech RC
262 Chris Bordano RC .30 .75
Wilmont Perry
263 Jessie Armstead .20 .50
264 Tiki Barber .25 .60
265 Chad Bratzke .15 .40
266 Gary Brown .15 .40
267 Chris Calloway .15 .40
268 Howard Cross .15 .40
269 Kent Graham .15 .40
270 Ike Hilliard .20 .50
271 Danny Kanell .15 .40
272 Michael Strahan .20 .50
273 Amani Toomer .20 .50
274 Charles Way .15 .40
275 Mike Cherry .30 .75
Greg Comella RC
276 Kyle Brady .15 .40
277 Keith Byars .15 .40
278 Chad Cascadden .20 .50
279 Wayne Chrebet .20 .50
280 Bryan Cox .20 .50
281 Glenn Foley .15 .40
282 Aaron Glenn .15 .40
283 Keyshawn Johnson .20 .50
284 Leon Johnson .15 .40
285 Mo Lewis .15 .40
286 Curtis Martin .25 .60
287 Otis Smith .15 .40
288 Vinny Testaverde .20 .50
289 Dedric Ward .15 .40
290 Tim Brown .25 .60
291 Rickey Dudley .15 .40
292 Jeff George .15 .40
293 Desmond Howard .20 .50
294 James Jett .15 .40
295 Lance Johnstone .15 .40
296 Randy Jordan .15 .40
297 Napoleon Kaufman .15 .40
298 Lincoln Kennedy .15 .40
299 Terry Mickens .15 .40
300 Darrell Russell .15 .40
301 Harvey Williams .15 .40
302 Jon Ritchie .25 .60
Charles Woodson
303 Rodney Williams .30 .75
Jermaine Williams RC
304 Koy Detmer .15 .40
305 Hugh Douglas .20 .50
306 Jason Dunn .15 .40
307 Irving Fryar .20 .50
308 Charlie Garner .20 .50
309 Jeff Graham .15 .40
310 Bobby Hoying .15 .40
311 Rodney Peete .20 .50
312 Allen Rossum .20 .50
313 Duce Staley .20 .50
314 William Thomas .15 .40
315 Kevin Turner .15 .40
316 Kaseem Sinceno RC .30 .75
Corey Walker RC
317 Jahine Arnold .15 .40
318 Jerome Bettis .25 .60
319 Will Blackwell .15 .40
320 Mark Bruener .15 .40
321 Dermontti Dawson .20 .50
322 Chris Fuamatu-Ma'afala .15 .40
323 Courtney Hawkins .15 .40
324 Richard Huntley .15 .40
325 Charles Johnson .15 .40
326 Levon Kirkland .15 .40
327 Kordell Stewart .20 .50
328 Hines Ward .25 .60
329 Dewayne Washington .15 .40
330 Tony Banks .20 .50
331 Steve Bono .15 .40
332 Isaac Bruce .25 .60
333 June Henley RC .30 .75
334 Robert Holcombe .15 .40
335 Mike Jones LB .15 .40
336 Eddie Kennison .20 .50
337 Amp Lee .15 .40
338 Jerald Moore .15 .40
339 Ricky Proehl .15 .40
340 J.T. Thomas .15 .40
341 Derrick Harris .15 .40
Az-Zahir Hakim
342 Roland Williams .15 .40
Grant Wistrom
343 Kurt Warner RC 5.00 12.00
Tony Horne
344 Terrell Fletcher .15 .40
345 Greg Jackson .15 .40
346 Charlie Jones .15 .40
347 Freddie Jones .15 .40
348 Ryan Leaf .20 .50
349 Natrone Means .20 .50
350 Mikhael Ricks .15 .40
351 Junior Seau .25 .60
352 Bryan Still .15 .40
353 Tremayne Stephens .30 .75
Ryan Thelwell RC
354 Greg Clark .15 .40
355 Marc Edwards .20 .50
356 Merton Hanks .15 .40
357 Garrison Hearst .20 .50
358 R.W. McQuarters .15 .40
359 Ken Norton Jr. .15 .40
360 Terrell Owens .25 .60
361 Jerry Rice .50 1.25
362 J.J. Stokes .15 .40
363 Bryant Young .20 .50
364 Steve Young .30 .75
365 Chad Brown .15 .40
366 Christian Fauria .15 .40
367 Joey Galloway .20 .50
368 Ahman Green .20 .50
369 Cortez Kennedy .15 .40
370 Jon Kitna .20 .50
371 James McKnight .15 .40
372 Mike Pritchard .15 .40
373 Michael Sinclair .15 .40
374 Shawn Springs .15 .40
375 Ricky Watters .20 .50
376 Darryl Williams .15 .40
377 Robert Wilson .50 1.25
Kerry Joseph RC
378 Mike Alstott .25 .60
379 Reidel Anthony .15 .40
380 Derrick Brooks .25 .60
381 Trent Dilfer .20 .50
382 Warrick Dunn .20 .50
383 Bert Emanuel .20 .50
384 Jacquez Green .15 .40
385 Patrick Hape .15 .40
386 John Lynch .20 .50
387 Dave Moore .15 .40
388 Hardy Nickerson .15 .40
389 Warren Sapp .20 .50
390 Karl Williams .15 .40
391 Blaine Bishop .15 .40
392 Joe Bowden .15 .40
393 Isaac Byrd RC .30 .75
394 Willie Davis .15 .40
395 Al Del Greco .15 .40
396 Kevin Dyson .15 .40
397 Eddie George .20 .50
398 Jackie Harris .20 .50
399 Dave Krieg .20 .50
400 Steve McNair .25 .60
401 Michael Roan .15 .40
402 Yancey Thigpen .15 .40
403 Frank Wycheck .20 .50
404 Derrick Mason .20 .50
Steve Matthews
405 Stephen Alexander .15 .40
406 Terry Allen .20 .50
407 Jamie Asher .15 .40
408 Stephen Davis .20 .50
409 Darrell Green .25 .60
410 Trent Green .20 .50
411 Skip Hicks .15 .40
412 Brian Mitchell .20 .50
413 Leslie Shepherd .15 .40
414 Michael Westbrook .15 .40
415 Terry Hardy .30 .75
Rabih Abdullah RC
416 Corey Thomas RC .40 1.00
Mike Quinn RC
417 Jonathan Quinn 2.50 6.00
Kelly Holcomb RC
418 Brian Alford .15 .40
Blake Spence
419 Andy Haase RC .30 .75
Carlos King
420 James Thrash RC .50 1.25
Karl Hankton
421 Fred Beasley .40 1.00
Itula Mili RC
422 Champ Bailey RC 1.00 2.50
423 D'Wayne Bates RC .30 .75
424 Michael Bishop RC .40 1.00
425 David Boston RC .40 1.00
426 Shawn Bryson RC .30 .75
427 Tim Couch RC .50 1.25
428 Scott Covington RC .30 .75
429 Daunte Culpepper RC .50 1.25
430 Autry Denson RC .30 .75
431 Troy Edwards RC .40 1.00
432 Kevin Faulk RC .50 1.25
433 Joe Germaine RC .40 1.00
434 Torry Holt RC .75 2.00
435 Brock Huard RC .40 1.00
436 Sedrick Irvin RC .30 .75
437 Edgerrin James RC .60 1.50
438 Andy Katzenmoyer RC .40 1.00
439 Shaun King RC .40 1.00
440 Rob Konrad RC .30 .75
441 Donovan McNabb RC 2.00 5.00
442 Cade McNown RC .40 1.00
443 Billy Miller RC .30 .75
444 Dee Miller RC .30 .75
445 Sirr Parker RC .30 .75
446 Peerless Price RC .40 1.00
447 Akili Smith RC .40 1.00
448 Tai Streets RC .40 1.00
449 Ricky Williams RC .75 2.00
450 Amos Zereoue RC .40 1.00
S1 Warrick Dunn Sample .25 .60

1999 Pacific Copper

*COPPER STARS: 12.5X TO 30X
*COPPER RCs: 2.5X TO 6X
COPPER PRINT RUN 99 SERIAL #'d SETS
343 Kurt Warner 30.00 80.00
Tony Horne

1999 Pacific Gold

*GOLD STARS: 10X TO 25X BASIC CARDS
*GOLD RCs: 2X TO 5X
GOLD PRINT RUN 199 SER.#'d SETS
343 Kurt Warner 25.00 60.00
Tony Horne

1999 Pacific Opening Day

*OPEN.DAY STARS: 20X TO 50X
*OPEN.DAY RCs: 5X TO 12X
OPENING DAY PRINT RUN 45 SERIAL #'d SETS
343 Kurt Warner 60.00 150.00
Tony Horne

1999 Pacific Platinum Blue

*PLAT.BLUE STARS: 12X TO 30X HI COL.
*PLAT.BLUE RCs: 2.5X TO 6X
PLAT.BLUE PRINT RUN 75 SERIAL #'d SETS
343 Kurt Warner 40.00 100.00
Tony Horne

1999 Pacific Red

*RED STARS: 10X TO 25X BASIC CARDS
*RED RCs: 2X TO 5X
RED STATED ODDS 4:25 SPECIAL RETAIL
343 Kurt Warner 25.00 60.00
Tony Horne

1999 Pacific Cramer's Choice

COMPLETE SET (10) 75.00 200.00
STATED PRINT RUN 299 SERIAL #'d SETS
1 Jamal Anderson 6.00 15.00
2 Terrell Davis 6.00 15.00
3 John Elway 20.00 50.00
4 Barry Sanders 20.00 50.00
5 Brett Favre 20.00 50.00
6 Peyton Manning 20.00 50.00
7 Fred Taylor 6.00 15.00
8 Dan Marino 20.00 50.00
9 Randall Cunningham 6.00 15.00
10 Randy Moss 15.00 40.00

1999 Pacific Dynagon Turf

COMPLETE SET (20) 40.00 80.00
STATED ODDS 2:25
*TITANIUMS: 3X TO 8X BASIC INSERTS
TITANIUM PRINT RUN 99 SERIAL #'d SETS
1 Jake Plummer .75 2.00
2 Jamal Anderson 1.25 3.00
3 Doug Flutie 1.25 3.00
4 Emmitt Smith 2.50 6.00
5 Terrell Davis 1.25 3.00
6 John Elway 4.00 10.00
7 Barry Sanders 4.00 10.00
8 Brett Favre 4.00 10.00
9 Peyton Manning 4.00 10.00
10 Mark Brunell 1.25 3.00
11 Fred Taylor 1.25 3.00
12 Dan Marino 4.00 10.00
13 Randall Cunningham 1.25 3.00
14 Randy Moss 3.00 8.00
15 Drew Bledsoe 1.50 4.00
16 Curtis Martin 1.25 3.00
17 Jerome Bettis 1.25 3.00
18 Jerry Rice 2.50 6.00
19 Jon Kitna 1.25 3.00
20 Eddie George 1.25 3.00

1999 Pacific Gold Crown Die Cuts

COMPLETE SET (36) 75.00 200.00
STATED ODDS 1:25
1 Jake Plummer 1.50 4.00
2 Jamal Anderson 2.50 6.00
3 Priest Holmes 4.00 10.00
4 Doug Flutie 2.50 6.00
5 Antowain Smith 2.50 6.00
6 Corey Dillon 2.50 6.00
7 Troy Aikman 5.00 12.00
8 Emmitt Smith 5.00 12.00
9 Terrell Davis 2.50 6.00
10 John Elway 8.00 20.00
11 Brian Griese 2.50 6.00
12 Charlie Batch 2.50 6.00
13 Barry Sanders 8.00 20.00
14 Brett Favre 8.00 20.00
15 Antonio Freeman 2.50 6.00
16 Marshall Faulk 3.00 8.00
17 Peyton Manning 8.00 20.00
18 Mark Brunell 2.50 6.00
19 Fred Taylor 2.50 6.00
20 Dan Marino 8.00 20.00
21 Randall Cunningham 2.50 6.00
22 Randy Moss 6.00 15.00
23 Drew Bledsoe 3.00 8.00
24 Keyshawn Johnson 2.50 6.00
25 Curtis Martin 2.50 6.00
26 Napoleon Kaufman 2.50 6.00
27 Jerome Bettis 2.50 6.00
28 Kordell Stewart 1.50 4.00
29 Terrell Owens 2.50 6.00
30 Jerry Rice 5.00 12.00
31 Steve Young 3.00 8.00
32 Joey Galloway 1.50 4.00
33 Jon Kitna 2.50 6.00
34 Trent Dilfer 2.50 6.00

35 Warrick Dunn 2.50 6.00
36 Eddie George 2.50 6.00

1999 Pacific Pro Bowl Die Cuts

COMPLETE SET (20) 50.00 120.00
STATED ODDS 1:49
1 Jamal Anderson 3.00 8.00
2 Chris Chandler 2.00 5.00
3 Doug Flutie 3.00 8.00
4 Deion Sanders 3.00 8.00
5 Emmitt Smith 6.00 15.00
6 Terrell Davis 3.00 8.00
7 John Elway 10.00 25.00
8 Barry Sanders 10.00 25.00
9 Antonio Freeman 3.00 8.00
10 Marshall Faulk 4.00 10.00
11 Randall Cunningham 3.00 8.00
12 Randy Moss 8.00 20.00
13 Robert Smith 3.00 8.00
14 Ty Law 2.00 5.00
15 Keyshawn Johnson 3.00 8.00
16 Curtis Martin 3.00 8.00
17 Jerry Rice 6.00 15.00
18 Steve Young 4.00 10.00
19 Mike Alstott 3.00 8.00
20 Eddie George 3.00 8.00

1999 Pacific Record Breakers

COMPLETE SET (20) 200.00 400.00
STATED PRINT RUN 199 SERIAL #'d SETS
1 Jake Plummer 3.00 8.00
2 Jamal Anderson 5.00 12.00
3 Doug Flutie 5.00 12.00
4 Troy Aikman 10.00 25.00
5 Emmitt Smith 10.00 25.00
6 Terrell Davis 5.00 12.00
7 John Elway 15.00 40.00
8 Barry Sanders 15.00 40.00
9 Brett Favre 15.00 40.00
10 Marshall Faulk 6.00 15.00
11 Peyton Manning 15.00 40.00
12 Mark Brunell 5.00 12.00
13 Fred Taylor 5.00 12.00
14 Dan Marino 15.00 40.00
15 Randall Cunningham 5.00 12.00
16 Randy Moss 12.50 30.00
17 Drew Bledsoe 6.00 15.00
18 Curtis Martin 5.00 12.00
19 Jerry Rice 10.00 25.00
20 Steve Young 6.00 15.00

1999 Pacific Team Checklists

COMPLETE SET (31) 25.00 60.00
STATED ODDS 2:25
1 Jake Plummer .60 1.50
2 Jamal Anderson 1.00 2.50
3 Priest Holmes 1.50 4.00
4 Doug Flutie 1.00 2.50
5 Muhsin Muhammad .60 1.50
6 Curtis Enis .40 1.00
7 Corey Dillon 1.00 2.50
8 Ty Detmer .40 1.00
9 Emmitt Smith 2.00 5.00
10 John Elway 3.00 8.00
11 Barry Sanders 3.00 8.00
12 Brett Favre 3.00 8.00
13 Peyton Manning 3.00 8.00
14 Fred Taylor 1.00 2.50
15 Andre Rison .60 1.50
16 Dan Marino 3.00 8.00
17 Randy Moss 2.50 6.00
18 Drew Bledsoe 1.25 3.00
19 Cameron Cleeland .40 1.00
20 Ike Hilliard .40 1.00
21 Curtis Martin 1.00 2.50
22 Napoleon Kaufman 1.00 2.50
23 Duce Staley 1.00 2.50
24 Jerome Bettis 1.00 2.50
25 Isaac Bruce 1.00 2.50
26 Ryan Leaf 1.00 2.50
27 Steve Young 1.25 3.00
28 Joey Galloway .60 1.50
29 Warrick Dunn 1.00 2.50
30 Eddie George 1.00 2.50
31 Michael Westbrook .60 1.50

1999 Pacific Backyard Football

This set was distributed through the Backyard Football computer software package. The NFL player cards utilize the cardfronts of the base 1999 Pacific football cards with a slightly redesigned cardback and new card number. Additionally, there are 10-unnumbered cards featuring the animated characters from the game.

COMPLETE SET (18) 4.00 10.00
1 Drew Bledsoe .40 1.00
2 Randall Cunningham .30 .75
3 John Elway .80 2.00
4 Brett Favre .80 2.00
5 Dan Marino .80 2.00
6 Jerry Rice .50 1.25
7 Barry Sanders .80 2.00
8 Steve Young .40 1.00
NNO Lisa Crocket .08 .25
NNO Angela Delvecchio .08 .25
NNO Marky Dubois .08 .25
NNO Gretchen Hasselhoff .08 .25
NNO Ricky Johnson .08 .25
NNO Achmed Khan .08 .25
NNO Maria Luna .08 .25
NNO Pablo Sanchez .08 .25
NNO Jocinda Smith .08 .25
NNO Reese Worthington .08 .25

2000 Pacific

Released as a 450-card set, 2000 Pacific consists of 400 regular cards and 50 rookie cards. Cards feature full-color action shots and silver foil highlights. 2000 Pacific was packaged in 36-pack boxes containing 12 cards each and carried a suggested retail price of $2.79.

COMPLETE SET (450) 25.00 60.00
1 Mario Bates .15 .40
2 David Boston .15 .40
3 Rob Fredrickson .15 .40
4 Terry Hardy .15 .40
5 Rob Moore .15 .40
6 Adrian Murrell .15 .40
7 Michael Pittman .15 .40
8 Jake Plummer .20 .50
9 Simeon Rice .20 .50
10 Frank Sanders .15 .40
11 Aeneas Williams .15 .40
12 Mac Cody .15 .40
Andy McCullough
13 Dennis McKinley RC .15 .40
Joel Makovicka
14 Jamal Anderson .20 .50
15 Chris Calloway .15 .40
16 Chris Chandler .20 .50
17 Bob Christian .15 .40
18 Tim Dwight .20 .50
19 Jammi German .15 .40
20 Ronnie Harris .15 .40
21 Terance Mathis .15 .40
22 Ken Oxendine .15 .40
23 O.J. Santiago .15 .40
24 Bob Whitfield .15 .40
25 Eugene Baker .15 .40
Reggie Kelly
26 Justin Armour .15 .40
27 Tony Banks .15 .40
28 Peter Boulware .15 .40
29 Stoney Case .15 .40
30 Priest Holmes .25 .60
31 Qadry Ismail .20 .50
32 Patrick Johnson .15 .40
33 Michael McCrary .15 .40
34 Jonathan Ogden .15 .40
35 Errict Rhett .20 .50
36 Duane Starks .15 .40
37 Doug Flutie .25 .60
38 Rob Johnson .20 .50
39 Jonathan Linton .15 .40
40 Eric Moulds .20 .50
41 Peerless Price .20 .50
42 Andre Reed .25 .60
43 Jay Riemersma .15 .40
44 Antowain Smith .20 .50
45 Bruce Smith .25 .60
46 Thurman Thomas .25 .60
47 Kevin Williams .15 .40
48 Bobby Collins .15 .40
Sheldon Jackson
49 Michael Bates .15 .40
50 Steve Beuerlein .20 .50
51 Tim Biakabutuka .20 .50
52 Antonio Edwards .15 .40
53 Donald Hayes .15 .40
54 Patrick Jeffers .20 .50
55 Anthony Johnson .15 .40
56 Jeff Lewis .15 .40
57 Eric Metcalf .15 .40
58 Muhsin Muhammad .20 .50
59 Jason Peter .15 .40
60 Wesley Walls .15 .40
61 John Allred .15 .40
62 Marty Booker .20 .50
63 Curtis Conway .20 .50
64 Bobby Engram .20 .50
65 Curtis Enis .15 .40
66 Shane Matthews .15 .40
67 Cade McNown .15 .40
68 Glyn Milburn .15 .40
69 Jim Miller .15 .40
70 Marcus Robinson .20 .50
71 Ryan Wetnight .15 .40
72 James Allen .15 .40
Macey Brooks
73 Jeff Blake .20 .50
74 Corey Dillon .20 .50
75 Rodney Heath RC .15 .40
76 Willie Jackson .15 .40
77 Tremain Mack .15 .40
78 Tony McGee .15 .40
79 Carl Pickens .20 .50
80 Darnay Scott .20 .50
81 Akili Smith .15 .40
82 Takeo Spikes .15 .40
83 Craig Yeast .15 .40
84 Michael Basnight .15 .40
Nick Williams
85 Karim Abdul-Jabbar .15 .40
86 Darrin Chiaverini .15 .40
87 Tim Couch .20 .50
88 Marc Edwards .15 .40
89 Kevin Johnson .15 .40
90 Terry Kirby .15 .40
91 Daylon McCutcheon .15 .40
92 Jamir Miller .15 .40
93 Leslie Shepherd .15 .40
94 Irv Smith .15 .40
95 Mark Campbell .15 .40
James Dearth
96 Zola Davis RC .15 .40
Damon Dunn RC
97 Madre Hill .15 .40
Tarek Saleh RC
98 Troy Aikman .40 1.00
99 Eric Bjornson .15 .40
100 Dexter Coakley .15 .40
101 Greg Ellis .15 .40
102 Rocket Ismail .20 .50
103 David LaFleur .15 .40
104 Ernie Mills .15 .40
105 Jeff Ogden .15 .40
106 Ryan Neufeld RC .15 .40
Robert Thomas
107 Deion Sanders .25 .60
108 Emmitt Smith .60 1.50
109 Chris Warren .15 .40
110 Mike Lucky .15 .40
Jason Tucker
111 Byron Chamberlain .15 .40
112 Terrell Davis .25 .60
113 Jason Elam .15 .40
114 Olandis Gary .20 .50
115 Brian Griese .20 .50
116 Ed McCaffrey .20 .50
117 Trevor Pryce .15 .40
118 Bill Romanowski .15 .40
119 Shannon Sharpe .25 .60
120 Rod Smith .20 .50
121 Al Wilson .15 .40
122 Andre Cooper .15 .40
Chris Watson
123 Charlie Batch .20 .50
124 Stephen Boyd .15 .40
125 Chris Claiborne .15 .40
126 Germane Crowell .15 .40
127 Terry Fair .15 .40
128 Gus Frerotte .20 .50
129 Jason Hanson .15 .40
130 Greg Hill .15 .40
131 Herman Moore .20 .50
132 Johnnie Morton .20 .50
133 Barry Sanders .50 1.25
134 David Sloan .15 .40
135 Brock Olivo .15 .40
Cory Sauter
136 Corey Bradford .15 .40
137 Tyrone Davis .15 .40
138 Brett Favre .75 2.00
139 Antonio Freeman .20 .50
140 Vonnie Holliday .15 .40
141 Dorsey Levens .20 .50
142 Keith McKenzie .15 .40
143 Mike McKenzie .15 .40
144 Bill Schroeder .20 .50
145 Jeff Thomason .15 .40
146 Frank Winters RC .15 .40
147 Cornelius Bennett .15 .40
148 Tony Blevins RC .15 .40
149 Chad Bratzke .15 .40
150 Ken Dilger .15 .40
151 Tarik Glenn .15 .40
152 E.G. Green .15 .40
153 Marvin Harrison .25 .60
154 Edgerrin James .25 .60
155 Peyton Manning .60 1.50
156 Jerome Pathon .15 .40
157 Marcus Pollard .15 .40
158 Terrence Wilkins .15 .40
159 Isaac Jones RC .15 .40
Paul Shields RC
160 Reggie Barlow .15 .40
161 Aaron Beasley .15 .40
162 Tony Boselli .20 .50
163 Tony Brackens .15 .40
164 Kyle Brady .15 .40
165 Mark Brunell .20 .50
166 Jay Fiedler .20 .50
167 Kevin Hardy .15 .40
168 Carnell Lake .15 .40
169 Keenan McCardell .20 .50
170 Jonathan Quinn .15 .40
171 Jimmy Smith .20 .50
172 James Stewart .15 .40
173 Fred Taylor .25 .60
174 Lenzie Jackson RC .15 .40
Stacey Mack
175 Derrick Alexander .15 .40
176 Donnell Bennett .15 .40
177 Donnie Edwards .15 .40
178 Tony Gonzalez .25 .60
179 Elvis Grbac .15 .40
180 James Hasty .15 .40
181 Joe Horn .20 .50
182 Lonnie Johnson .15 .40
183 Kevin Lockett .15 .40
184 Larry Parker .15 .40
185 Tony Richardson RC .20 .50
186 Rashaan Shehee .15 .40
187 Tamarick Vanover .15 .40
188 Trace Armstrong .15 .40
189 Oronde Gadsden .20 .50
190 Damon Huard .20 .50
191 Nate Jacquet .15 .40
192 James Johnson .15 .40
193 Rob Konrad .15 .40
194 Sam Madison .15 .40
195 Dan Marino .75 2.00
196 Tony Martin .20 .50
197 O.J. McDuffie .20 .50
198 Stanley Pritchett .15 .40
199 Tim Ruddy .15 .40
200 Patrick Curtain .15 .40
201 Zach Thomas .25 .60
202 Cris Carter .25 .60
203 Duane Clemons .15 .40
204 Carlester Crumpler .15 .40
205 Daunte Culpepper .20 .50
206 Jeff George .20 .50
207 Matthew Hatchette .15 .40
208 Leroy Hoard .15 .40
209 Randy Moss .25 .60
210 John Randle .20 .50
211 Jake Reed .20 .50
212 Robert Smith .20 .50
213 Robert Tate .15 .40
214 Terry Allen .20 .50
215 Bruce Armstrong .15 .40
216 Drew Bledsoe .25 .60
217 Ben Coates .15 .40
218 Kevin Faulk .20 .50
219 Terry Glenn .20 .50
220 Shawn Jefferson .15 .40
221 Andy Katzenmoyer .15 .40
222 Ty Law .20 .50
223 Willie McGinest .20 .50
224 Lawyer Milloy .15 .40
225 Tony Simmons .15 .40
226 Michael Bishop .15 .40
Sean Morey RC
227 Cameron Cleeland .15 .40
228 Troy Davis .15 .40
229 Jake Delhomme RC .60 1.50
230 Andre Hastings .15 .40
231 Eddie Kennison .15 .40
232 Wilmont Perry .15 .40
233 Dino Philyaw .15 .40
234 Keith Poole .15 .40
235 William Roaf .15 .40
236 Billy Joe Tolliver .15 .40
237 Fred Weary .15 .40
238 Ricky Williams .25 .60
239 P.J. Franklin RC .15 .40
Marvin Powell RC
240 Jessie Armstead .15 .40
241 Tiki Barber .25 .60
242 Dan Campbell .15 .40
243 Kerry Collins .20 .50
244 Percy Ellsworth .15 .40
245 Kent Graham .15 .40
246 Ike Hilliard .20 .50
247 Cedric Jones .15 .40
248 Bashir Levingston RC .15 .40
249 Pete Mitchell .15 .40
250 Michael Strahan .20 .50
251 Amani Toomer .20 .50
252 Charles Way .15 .40
253 Andre Weathers RC .15 .40
254 Richie Anderson .15 .40
255 Wayne Chrebet .20 .50
256 Marcus Coleman .15 .40
257 Bryan Cox .15 .40
258 Jason Fabini RC .15 .40
259 Robert Farmer RC .15 .40
260 Keyshawn Johnson .20 .50
261 Ray Lucas .15 .40
262 Curtis Martin .25 .60
263 Kevin Mawae .15 .40
264 Eric Ogbogu .15 .40
265 Bernie Parmalee .15 .40
266 Vinny Testaverde .20 .50
267 Dedric Ward .15 .40
268 Eric Barton RC .15 .40
269 Tim Brown .25 .60
270 Tony Bryant .15 .40
271 Rickey Dudley .15 .40
272 Rich Gannon .20 .50
273 Bobby Hoying .15 .40
274 James Jett .20 .50
275 Napoleon Kaufman .20 .50
276 Jon Ritchie .15 .40
277 Darrell Russell .15 .40
278 Kenny Shedd .15 .40
279 Marquis Walker RC .15 .40
280 Tyrone Wheatley .15 .40
281 Charles Woodson .25 .60
282 Luther Broughton RC .15 .40
283 Al Harris RC .25 .60
284 Greg Jefferson .15 .40
285 Dietrich Jells .15 .40
286 Charles Johnson .15 .40
287 Chad Lewis .15 .40
288 Mike Mamula .15 .40
289 Donovan McNabb .25 .60
290 Doug Pederson .15 .40
291 Allen Rossum .15 .40
292 Torrance Small .15 .40
293 Duce Staley .20 .50
294 Jerome Bettis .25 .60
295 Kris Brown .15 .40
296 Mark Bruener .20 .50
297 Troy Edwards .15 .40
298 Jason Gildon .15 .40
299 Richard Huntley .15 .40
300 Bobby Shaw RC .20 .50
301 Scott Shields RC .15 .40
302 Kordell Stewart .20 .50
303 Hines Ward .25 .60
304 Amos Zereoue .15 .40
305 Matt Cushing RC .15 .40
Jerame Tuman
306 Pete Gonzalez .25 .60
Anthony Wright RC
307 Isaac Bruce .25 .60
308 Kevin Carter .15 .40
309 Marshall Faulk .25 .60
310 London Fletcher RC .25 .60
311 Joe Germaine .15 .40
312 Az-Zahir Hakim .15 .40
313 Torry Holt .25 .60
314 Tony Horne .15 .40
315 Mike Jones LB .15 .40
316 Dexter McCleon .20 .50
317 Orlando Pace .20 .50
318 Ricky Proehl .15 .40
319 Kurt Warner .40 1.00
320 Roland Williams .15 .40
321 Grant Wistrom .15 .40
322 James Hodgins RC .15 .40
Justin Watson
323 Jermaine Fazande .15 .40
324 Jeff Graham .15 .40
325 Jim Harbaugh .20 .50
326 Raylee Johnson .15 .40
327 Charlie Jones .15 .40
328 Freddie Jones .15 .40
329 Natrone Means .20 .50
330 Chris Penn .15 .40
331 Mikhael Ricks .15 .40
332 Junior Seau .25 .60
333 Reggie Davis RC .15 .40
Robert Reed RC
334 Fred Beasley .15 .40
335 Brentson Buckner .15 .40
336 Greg Clark .15 .40
337 Dave Fiore RC .15 .40
338 Charlie Garner .20 .50
339 Mark Harris RC .15 .40
340 Ramos McDonald RC .15 .40
341 Terrell Owens .25 .60
342 Jerry Rice .50 1.25
343 Lance Schulters .15 .40
344 J.J. Stokes .20 .50
345 Bryant Young .15 .40
346 Steve Young .30 .75
347 Jeff Garcia .20 .50
348 Fabien Bownes RC .15 .40
349 Chad Brown .15 .40
350 Reggie Brown .15 .40
351 Sean Dawkins .15 .40
352 Christian Fauria .15 .40
353 Ahman Green .20 .50
354 Walter Jones .15 .40
355 Cortez Kennedy .15 .40
356 Jon Kitna .20 .50
357 Derrick Mayes .15 .40
358 Charlie Rogers .15 .40
359 Shawn Springs .15 .40
360 Ricky Watters .20 .50
361 Donnie Abraham .15 .40
362 Mike Alstott .25 .60
363 Reidel Anthony .15 .40
364 Ronde Barber .20 .50
365 Derrick Brooks .25 .60
366 Warrick Dunn .20 .50
367 Jacquez Green .15 .40
368 Marcus Jones .15 .40
369 Shaun King .15 .40
370 John Lynch .20 .50
371 Warren Sapp .20 .50
372 Steve White RC .15 .40
373 Martin Gramatica .15 .40
Kevin McLeod RC
374 Blaine Bishop .15 .40
375 Al Del Greco .15 .40
376 Kevin Dyson .20 .50
377 Eddie George .20 .50
378 Jevon Kearse .20 .50
379 Derrick Mason .20 .50
380 Bruce Matthews .20 .50
381 Steve McNair .25 .60
382 Neil O'Donnell .15 .40
383 Yancey Thigpen .15 .40
384 Frank Wycheck .20 .50
385 Devin Daft .15 .40
Larry Brown
386 Stephen Alexander .15 .40
387 Champ Bailey .20 .50
388 Larry Centers .15 .40
389 Marco Coleman .15 .40
390 Albert Connell .15 .40
391 Stephen Davis .20 .50
392 Irving Fryar .20 .50
393 Skip Hicks .15 .40
394 Brad Johnson .20 .50
395 Michael Westbrook .15 .40
396 Obafemi Ayanbadejo RC .20 .50
Lennox Gordon RC
397 Donald Driver .40 1.00
Ronnie Powell
398 Todd Bouman .15 .40
Jeremy Brigham RC
399 Brock Huard .15 .40
Sherdrick Bonner
400 Mike Sellers .15 .40
Spencer George RC
401 Shaun Alexander RC .50 1.25
402 LaVar Arrington RC .60 1.50
403 Tom Brady RC 10.00 25.00
404 Demario Brown RC .25 .60
405 Plaxico Burress RC .40 1.00
406 Trung Canidate RC .30 .75
407 Giovanni Carmazzi RC .25 .60
408 Kwame Cavil RC .25 .60
409 Chrys Chukwuma RC .25 .60
410 Ron Dayne RC .40 1.00
411 Reuben Droughns RC .40 1.00
412 Ron Dugans RC .25 .60
413 Deon Dyer RC .25 .60
414 Danny Farmer RC .25 .60
415 Chafie Fields RC .25 .60
416 Trevor Gaylor RC .25 .60
417 Sherrod Gideon RC .25 .60
418 Joey Goodspeed RC .25 .60
419 Joe Hamilton RC .25 .60
420 Tony Hartley RC .25 .60
421 Todd Husak RC .25 .60
422 Trevor Insley RC .25 .60
423 Thomas Jones RC .50 1.25
424 Marcus Knight RC .25 .60
425 Jamal Lewis RC .40 1.00
426 Anthony Lucas RC .25 .60
427 Tee Martin RC .40 1.00
428 Rondell Mealey RC .25 .60
429 Sylvester Morris RC .25 .60
430 Chad Morton RC .40 1.00
431 Dennis Northcutt RC .30 .75
432 Chad Pennington RC .60 1.50
433 Rodnick Phillips RC .25 .60
434 Mareno Philyaw RC .25 .60
435 Jerry Porter RC .40 1.00
436 Travis Prentice RC .30 .75
437 Tim Rattay RC .30 .75
438 Chris Redman RC .30 .75
439 J.R. Redmond RC .25 .60
440 Gari Scott RC .25 .60
441 Keith Smith RC .25 .60
442 Terrelle Smith RC .25 .60
443 R.Jay Soward RC .25 .60
444 Q.Spotwood RC UER .25 .60
yardage totals reads 3080
445 Shyrone Stith RC .25 .60
446 Travis Taylor RC .30 .75
447 Troy Walters RC .25 .60
448 Peter Warrick RC .40 1.00
449 Dez White RC .30 .75
450 Michael Wiley RC .25 .60

2000 Pacific Copper

*COPPER STARS: 8X TO 20X BASIC CARDS
*COPPER ROOKIES: 4X TO 10X
STATED PRINT RUN 75 SERIAL #'d SETS
403 Tom Brady 125.00 250.00

2000 Pacific Gold

*VETS 1-400: 4X TO 10X BASIC CARDS
*ROOKIES 401-450: 2.5X TO 6X
RETAIL GOLD PRINT RUN 199
403 Tom Brady 125.00 200.00

2000 Pacific Platinum Blue Draft Picks

*PLAT.BLUE ROOKIES: 2X TO 5X
STATED PRINT RUN 399 SER.#'d SETS
403 Tom Brady 100.00 200.00

2000 Pacific Premiere Date

*VETS 1-400: 6X TO 15X BASIC CARDS
*ROOKIES 401-450: 4X TO 10X
STATED PRINT RUN 78 SER.#'d SETS
403 Tom Brady 200.00 350.00

2000 Pacific Draft Picks 999

*ROOKIES/999: 1.2X TO 3X BASIC RC
STATED PRINT RUN 999 SER.#'d SETS

2000 Pacific AFC Leaders

COMPLETE SET (10) 7.50 20.00
STATED ODDS 1:37
1 Tim Couch .75 2.00
2 Olandis Gary .75 2.00
3 Marvin Harrison 1.00 2.50
4 Edgerrin James 1.00 2.50
5 Peyton Manning 2.50 6.00
6 Mark Brunell .75 2.00
7 Jimmy Smith .75 2.00
8 Drew Bledsoe 1.00 2.50
9 Keyshawn Johnson .75 2.00
10 Eddie George .75 2.00

2000 Pacific Autographs

PACIFIC ANNC'D PRINT RUNS BELOW
51 Tim Biakabutuka/200* 6.00 15.00
70 Marcus Robinson/200* 6.00 15.00
87 Tim Couch/100* 8.00 20.00
154 Edgerrin James/50* 20.00 50.00
229 Jake Delhomme/500* 15.00 40.00
307 Isaac Bruce/100* 10.00 25.00
319 Kurt Warner/253* 25.00 50.00
344 J.J. Stokes/100* 8.00 20.00
362 Mike Alstott/100* 10.00 25.00
377 Eddie George/60* 15.00 40.00
391 Stephen Davis/100* 8.00 20.00
401 Shaun Alexander/150* 25.00 60.00
403 Tom Brady/200* 350.00 500.00
404 Demario Brown/300* 5.00 12.00
405 Plaxico Burress/300* 15.00 30.00
406 Trung Canidate/300* 6.00 15.00
407 Giovanni Carmazzi/200* 5.00 12.00
408 Kwame Cavil/300* 5.00 12.00
410 Ron Dayne/200* 8.00 20.00
411 Reuben Droughns/200* 8.00 20.00
412 Ron Dugans/400* 5.00 12.00
414 Danny Farmer/250* 5.00 12.00
415 Chafie Fields/400* 5.00 12.00
417 Sherrod Gideon/200* 5.00 12.00
419 Joe Hamilton/200* 5.00 12.00
420 Tony Hartley/200* 5.00 12.00
421 Todd Husak/300* 5.00 12.00
423 Thomas Jones/300* 10.00 25.00
424 Marcus Knight/200* 5.00 12.00
425 Jamal Lewis/100* 10.00 25.00
426 Anthony Lucas/200* 5.00 12.00
427 Tee Martin/200* 8.00 20.00
428 Rondell Mealey/200* 5.00 12.00
429 Sylvester Morris/100* 6.00 15.00
431 Dennis Northcutt/200* 6.00 15.00
432 Chad Pennington/150* 12.50 30.00
434 Mareno Philyaw/200* 5.00 12.00
435 Jerry Porter/200* 8.00 20.00
436 Travis Prentice/300* 6.00 15.00
437 Tim Rattay/200* 6.00 15.00
438 Chris Redman/150* 8.00 20.00
439 J.R. Redmond/200* 5.00 12.00
443 R.Jay Soward/400* 5.00 12.00
445 Shyrone Stith/200* 5.00 12.00
446 Travis Taylor/200* 6.00 15.00
447 Troy Walters/300* 5.00 12.00
448 Peter Warrick/288* 8.00 20.00
449 Dez White/300* 6.00 15.00
450 Michael Wiley/300* 5.00 12.00

2000 Pacific Cramer's Choice

COMPLETE SET (10) 75.00 200.00
STATED ODDS 1:721
1 Tim Couch 5.00 12.00
2 Emmitt Smith 15.00 40.00
3 Brett Favre 20.00 50.00
4 Edgerrin James 6.00 15.00
5 Peyton Manning 15.00 40.00
6 Randy Moss 6.00 15.00
7 Marshall Faulk 6.00 15.00
8 Kurt Warner 10.00 25.00
9 Eddie George 5.00 12.00
10 Peter Warrick 6.00 15.00

2000 Pacific Finest Hour

STATED ODDS 1:73
1 Terrell Davis 1.25 3.00
2 Barry Sanders 2.50 6.00
3 Brett Favre 4.00 10.00
4 Edgerrin James 1.25 3.00
5 Drew Bledsoe 1.25 3.00
6 Damon Huard 1.00 2.50
7 Randy Moss 1.25 3.00
8 Kurt Warner 2.00 5.00
9 Jerry Rice 2.50 6.00
10 Stephen Davis 1.00 2.50
11 Shaun Alexander 1.50 4.00
12 Peter Warrick 1.25 3.00
13 Chris Redman 1.00 2.50
14 Chad Pennington 2.00 5.00
15 Tom Brady 40.00 80.00
16 Plaxico Burress 1.25 3.00
17 Todd Husak .75 2.00
18 Jamal Lewis 1.25 3.00
19 Thomas Jones 1.50 4.00
20 Ron Dayne 1.25 3.00

2000 Pacific Game Worn Jerseys

STATED ODDS 1:5 BOXES
1 Kurt Warner 10.00 25.00
2 Fred Taylor 6.00 15.00
3 Ricky Williams 6.00 15.00
4 Ike Hilliard 5.00 12.00
5 Tim Brown 6.00 15.00
6 Brett Favre 20.00 50.00
7 Jon Kitna 5.00 12.00
8 Kordell Stewart 5.00 12.00
9 Natrone Means 6.00 12.00

2000 Pacific Gold Crown Die Cuts

COMPLETE SET (36) 40.00 100.00
STATED ODDS 1:37
1 Jake Plummer 1.00 2.50
2 Cade McNown .75 2.00
3 Corey Dillon 1.00 2.50
4 Akili Smith .75 2.00
5 Tim Couch 1.00 2.50
6 Kevin Johnson .75 2.00
7 Olandis Gary 1.00 2.50
8 Brian Griese 1.00 2.50
9 Marvin Harrison 1.25 3.00
10 Edgerrin James 1.25 3.00
11 Mark Brunell 1.00 2.50
12 Fred Taylor 1.25 3.00
13 Damon Huard 1.00 2.50
14 Dan Marino 4.00 10.00
15 Randy Moss 1.25 3.00
16 Drew Bledsoe 1.25 3.00
17 Ricky Williams 1.25 3.00
18 Keyshawn Johnson 1.00 2.50
19 Donovan McNabb 1.25 3.00
20 Marshall Faulk 1.25 3.00
21 Kurt Warner 2.00 5.00
22 Jon Kitna 1.00 2.50
23 Jerry Rice 2.50 6.00
24 Shaun King .75 2.00
25 Eddie George 1.00 2.50
26 Steve McNair 1.25 3.00
27 Stephen Davis 1.00 2.50
28 Brad Johnson 1.00 2.50
29 Shaun Alexander 1.50 4.00
30 Plaxico Burress 1.25 3.00
31 Ron Dayne 1.25 3.00
32 Joe Hamilton .75 2.00
33 Thomas Jones 1.50 4.00
34 Chad Pennington 2.00 5.00
35 Chris Redman 1.00 2.50
36 Peter Warrick 1.25 3.00

2000 Pacific NFC Leaders

COMPLETE SET (10) 10.00 25.00
STATED ODDS 1:37
1 Marcus Robinson .75 2.00
2 Troy Aikman 1.50 4.00
3 Emmitt Smith 2.50 6.00
4 Cris Carter 1.00 2.50
5 Randy Moss 1.00 2.50
6 Isaac Bruce 1.00 2.50
7 Marshall Faulk 1.00 2.50
8 Kurt Warner 1.50 4.00
9 Stephen Davis .75 2.00
10 Brad Johnson .75 2.00

2000 Pacific Pro Bowl Die Cuts

COMPLETE SET (20) 20.00 50.00
STATED ODDS 1:37
1 Steve Beuerlein 1.00 2.50
2 Corey Dillon 1.00 2.50
3 Emmitt Smith 3.00 8.00
4 Marvin Harrison 1.25 3.00
5 Edgerrin James 1.25 3.00
6 Peyton Manning 3.00 8.00
7 Mark Brunell 1.00 2.50
8 Jimmy Smith 1.00 2.50
9 Tony Gonzalez 1.25 3.00
10 Cris Carter 1.25 3.00
11 Randy Moss 1.25 3.00
12 Rich Gannon 1.00 2.50
13 Keyshawn Johnson 1.00 2.50
14 Terry Glenn 1.00 2.50
15 Marshall Faulk 1.25 3.00
16 Kurt Warner 2.00 5.00
17 Mike Alstott 1.25 3.00
18 Eddie George 1.00 2.50
19 Stephen Davis 1.00 2.50
20 Brad Johnson 1.00 2.50

2000 Pacific Reflections

COMPLETE SET (20) 30.00 80.00
STATED ODDS 1:145
1 Cade McNown 1.00 2.50
2 Tim Couch 1.25 3.00
3 Troy Aikman 2.50 6.00
4 Emmitt Smith 4.00 10.00
5 Terrell Davis 1.50 4.00
6 Barry Sanders 3.00 8.00
7 Brett Favre 5.00 12.00
8 Marvin Harrison 1.50 4.00
9 Edgerrin James 1.50 4.00
10 Mark Brunell 1.25 3.00
11 Fred Taylor 1.50 4.00
12 Dan Marino 5.00 12.00
13 Randy Moss 1.50 4.00
14 Ricky Williams 1.50 4.00
15 Marshall Faulk 1.50 4.00
16 Kurt Warner 2.50 6.00
17 Jon Kitna 1.25 3.00
18 Shaun King 1.00 2.50
19 Eddie George 1.25 3.00
20 Stephen Davis 1.25 3.00

2001 Pacific

Released as a 530-card set, 2001 Pacific consists of 450 regular veteran cards and 80 serial numbered rookie cards. The cards feature full-color action shots and silver foil highlights. 2001 Pacific was packaged in 36-pack boxes containing 10 cards each and carried a suggested retail price of $2.99. Some rookies were issued as redemption cards which carried an expiration date of 12/31/2001.

COMP.SET w/o SP's (450) 25.00 50.00
ROOKIE QB PRINT RUN 1000
ROOKIE RB PRINT RUN 1500
ROOKIE WR PRINT RUN 1750
ROOKIE DEF/OTHER PRINT RUN 2500
1 David Boston .15 .40
2 Mac Cody .15 .40
3 Chris Gedney .15 .40
4 Chris Greisen .15 .40
5 Terry Hardy .15 .40
6 MarTay Jenkins .15 .40
7 Thomas Jones .20 .50
8 Joel Makovicka .15 .40
9 Tywan Mitchell .15 .40
10 Rob Moore .15 .40
11 Michael Pittman .20 .50
12 Jake Plummer .20 .50
13 Frank Sanders .15 .40
14 Aeneas Williams .20 .50
15 Jamal Anderson .20 .50
16 Eugene Baker .15 .40
17 Chris Chandler .20 .50
18 Tim Dwight .20 .50
19 Brian Finneran .20 .50
20 Jammi German .15 .40
21 Shawn Jefferson .15 .40
22 Doug Johnson .15 .40
23 Danny Kanell .20 .50
24 Reggie Kelly .15 .40
25 Terance Mathis .15 .40
26 Derek Rackley .15 .40
27 Ron Rivers .15 .40
28 Maurice Smith .15 .40
29 Sam Adams .15 .40
30 Obafemi Ayanbadejo .15 .40
31 Tony Banks .15 .40
32 Trent Dilfer .20 .50
33 Sam Gash .15 .40
34 Priest Holmes .25 .60
35 Qadry Ismail .20 .50
36 Pat Johnson .15 .40
37 Jamal Lewis .25 .60
38 Jermaine Lewis .15 .40
39 Ray Lewis .25 .60
40 Chris Redman .25 .60
41 Shannon Sharpe .25 .60
42 Brandon Stokley .20 .50
43 Travis Taylor .15 .40
44 Shawn Bryson .15 .40
45 Kwame Cavil .15 .40
46 Sam Cowart .15 .40
47 Doug Flutie .25 .60
48 Rob Johnson .20 .50
49 Jonathan Linton .15 .40
50 Jeremy McDaniel .15 .40
51 Sammy Morris .20 .50
52 Eric Moulds .20 .50
53 Peerless Price .15 .40
54 Jay Riemersma .15 .40
55 Antowain Smith .20 .50
56 Chris Watson .15 .40
57 Marcellus Wiley .15 .40
58 Michael Bates .15 .40
59 Steve Beuerlein .20 .50
60 Tim Biakabutuka .15 .40
61 Isaac Byrd .15 .40
62 Dameyune Craig .15 .40
63 William Floyd .15 .40
64 Karl Hankton .15 .40
65 Donald Hayes .15 .40
66 Chris Hetherington RC .15 .40
67 Brad Hoover .20 .50
68 Patrick Jeffers .15 .40
69 Muhsin Muhammad .20 .50
70 Iheanyi Uwaezuoke .15 .40
71 Wesley Walls .15 .40
72 James Allen .15 .40
73 Marlon Barnes .15 .40
74 D'Wayne Bates .15 .40
75 Marty Booker .20 .50
76 Macey Brooks .15 .40
77 Bobby Engram .20 .50
78 Curtis Enis .15 .40
79 Mark Hartsell RC .15 .40
80 Eddie Kennison .20 .50
81 Shane Matthews .15 .40
82 Cade McNown .20 .50
83 Jim Miller .20 .50
84 Marcus Robinson .20 .50
85 Brian Urlacher .30 .75
86 Dez White .20 .50
87 Brandon Bennett .15 .40
88 Steve Bush RC .15 .40
89 Corey Dillon .20 .50
90 Ron Dugans .15 .40
91 Danny Farmer .15 .40
92 Damon Griffin .15 .40
93 Clif Groce .15 .40
94 Curtis Keaton .15 .40
95 Scott Mitchell .15 .40
96 Darnay Scott .20 .50

97 Akili Smith .15 .40
98 Peter Warrick .20 .50
99 Nick Williams .15 .40
100 Craig Yeast .15 .40
101 Bobby Brown .15 .40
102 Darrin Chiaverini .15 .40
103 Tim Couch .15 .40
104 JaJuan Dawson .15 .40
105 Marc Edwards .15 .40
106 Kevin Johnson .15 .40
107 Dennis Northcutt .15 .40
108 David Patten .15 .40
109 Doug Pederson .15 .40
110 Travis Prentice .15 .40
111 Errict Rhett .20 .50
112 Aaron Shea .15 .40
113 Kevin Thompson .15 .40
114 Jamel White .15 .40
115 Spergon Wynn .15 .40
116 Troy Aikman .40 1.00
117 Chris Brazzell .15 .40
118 Randall Cunningham .25 .60
119 Jackie Harris .20 .50
120 Damon Hodge .15 .40
121 Rocket Ismail .20 .50
122 David LaFleur .15 .40
123 Wane McGarity .15 .40
124 James McKnight .15 .40
125 Emmitt Smith .60 1.50
126 Clint Stoerner .20 .50
127 Jason Tucker .15 .40
128 Michael Wiley .15 .40
129 Anthony Wright .15 .40
130 Mike Anderson .20 .50
131 Dwayne Carswell .15 .40
132 Byron Chamberlain .15 .40
133 Desmond Clark .20 .50
134 Chris Cole .15 .40
135 KaRon Coleman .15 .40
136 Terrell Davis .25 .60
137 Gus Frerotte .20 .50
138 Olandis Gary .15 .40
139 Brian Griese .20 .50
140 Howard Griffith .15 .40
141 Jarious Jackson .15 .40
142 Ed McCaffrey .20 .50
143 Scottie Montgomery RC .15 .40
144 Rod Smith .20 .50
145 Charlie Batch .20 .50
146 Stoney Case .15 .40
147 Germane Crowell .15 .40
148 Larry Foster .15 .40
149 Desmond Howard .20 .50
150 Sedrick Irvin .15 .40
151 Herman Moore .20 .50
152 Johnnie Morton .20 .50
153 Robert Porcher .15 .40
154 Cory Sauter .15 .40
155 Cory Schlesinger .15 .40
156 David Sloan .15 .40
157 Brian Stablein .15 .40
158 James Stewart .15 .40
159 Corey Bradford .15 .40
160 Tyrone Davis .15 .40
161 Donald Driver .25 .60
162 Brett Favre .75 2.00
163 Bubba Franks .20 .50
164 Antonio Freeman .25 .60
165 Herbert Goodman .15 .40
166 Ahman Green .25 .60
167 Matt Hasselbeck .25 .60
168 William Henderson .20 .50
169 Charles Lee .15 .40
170 Dorsey Levens .20 .50
171 Bill Schroeder .20 .50
172 Darren Sharper .20 .50
173 Matt Snider .15 .40
174 Danny Wuerffel .20 .50
175 Ken Dilger .15 .40
176 Jim Finn .15 .40
177 Lennox Gordon .15 .40
178 E.G. Green .15 .40
179 Marvin Harrison .25 .60
180 Kelly Holcomb .20 .50
181 Trevor Insley .15 .40
182 Edgerrin James .25 .60
183 Peyton Manning .60 1.50
184 Kevin McDougal .15 .40
185 Jerome Pathon .15 .40
186 Marcus Pollard .15 .40
187 Justin Snow .15 .40
188 Terrence Wilkins .15 .40
189 Reggie Barlow .15 .40
190 Kyle Brady .15 .40
191 Mark Brunell .20 .50
192 Kevin Hardy .15 .40
193 Anthony Johnson .15 .40
194 Stacey Mack .15 .40
195 Jamie Martin .15 .40
196 Keenan McCardell .20 .50
197 Daimon Shelton .15 .40
198 Jimmy Smith .20 .50
199 R.Jay Soward .15 .40
200 Shyrone Stith .15 .40
201 Fred Taylor .25 .60
202 Alvis Whitted .15 .40
203 Jermaine Williams .15 .40
204 Derrick Alexander .15 .40
205 Kimble Anders .15 .40
206 Donnell Bennett .15 .40
207 Mike Cloud .15 .40
208 Todd Collins .15 .40
209 Tony Gonzalez .25 .60
210 Elvis Grbac .20 .50
211 Dante Hall .25 .60
212 Kevin Lockett .15 .40
213 Warren Moon .25 .60
214 Frank Moreau .15 .40
215 Sylvester Morris .15 .40
216 Larry Parker .15 .40
217 Tony Richardson .15 .40
218 Trace Armstrong .15 .40
219 Autry Denson .15 .40
220 Bert Emanuel .15 .40
221 Jay Fiedler .20 .50
222 Oronde Gadsden .15 .40
223 Damon Huard .20 .50
224 James Johnson .15 .40
225 Rob Konrad .15 .40
226 Tony Martin .20 .50
227 O.J. McDuffie .15 .40
228 Mike Quinn .15 .40
229 Lamar Smith .20 .50
230 Jason Taylor .25 .60
231 Thurman Thomas .25 .60
232 Zach Thomas .25 .60
233 Todd Bouman .15 .40
234 Bubby Brister .20 .50
235 Cris Carter .25 .60
236 Daunte Culpepper .20 .50
237 John Davis RC .15 .40
238 Robert Griffith .15 .40
239 Matthew Hatchette .15 .40
240 Jim Kleinsasser .20 .50
241 Randy Moss .25 .60
242 John Randle .20 .50
243 Robert Smith .20 .50
244 Chris Walsh RC .15 .40
245 Troy Walters .15 .40
246 Moe Williams .15 .40
247 Michael Bishop .20 .50
248 Drew Bledsoe .25 .60
249 Troy Brown .20 .50
250 Tedy Bruschi .25 .60
251 Tony Carter .15 .40
252 Shockmain Davis .15 .40
253 Kevin Faulk .20 .50
254 Terry Glenn .20 .50
255 Ty Law .20 .50
256 Lawyer Milloy .20 .50
257 J.R. Redmond .15 .40
258 Harold Shaw .15 .40
259 Tony Simmons .15 .40
260 Jermaine Wiggins .15 .40
261 Jeff Blake .20 .50
262 Aaron Brooks .20 .50
263 Cam Cleeland .15 .40
264 Andrew Glover .15 .40
265 La'Roi Glover .15 .40
266 Joe Horn .20 .50
267 Kevin Houser .15 .40
268 Willie Jackson .15 .40
269 Jerald Moore .15 .40
270 Chad Morton .15 .40
271 Keith Poole .15 .40
272 Terrelle Smith .15 .40
273 Ricky Williams .25 .60
274 Robert Wilson .15 .40
275 Jessie Armstead .15 .40
276 Tiki Barber .25 .60
277 Mike Cherry .15 .40
278 Kerry Collins .20 .50
279 Greg Comella .15 .40
280 Thabiti Davis .15 .40
281 Ron Dayne .20 .50
282 Ron Dixon .15 .40
283 Ike Hilliard .20 .50
284 Joe Jurevicius .15 .40
285 Jason Sehorn .20 .50
286 Michael Strahan .25 .60
287 Amani Toomer .20 .50
288 Craig Walendy .15 .40
289 Damon Washington RC .15 .40
290 Richie Anderson .15 .40
291 Anthony Becht .15 .40
292 Wayne Chrebet .20 .50
293 Laveranues Coles .20 .50
294 Bryan Cox .20 .50
295 Marvin Jones .15 .40
296 Mo Lewis .15 .40
297 Ray Lucas .15 .40
298 Curtis Martin .25 .60
299 Bernie Parmalee .15 .40
300 Chad Pennington .25 .60
301 Jerald Sowell .15 .40
302 Dwight Stone .15 .40
303 Vinny Testaverde .20 .50
304 Dedric Ward .15 .40
305 Tim Brown .25 .60
306 Zack Crockett .15 .40
307 Scott Dreisbach .15 .40
308 Rickey Dudley .15 .40
309 David Dunn .15 .40
310 Mondriel Fulcher .15 .40
311 Rich Gannon .20 .50
312 James Jett .15 .40
313 Randy Jordan .20 .50
314 Napoleon Kaufman .15 .40
315 Rodney Peete .15 .40
316 Jerry Porter .15 .40
317 Andre Rison .20 .50
318 Tyrone Wheatley .20 .50
319 Charles Woodson .25 .60
320 Darnell Autry .15 .40
321 Na Brown .15 .40
322 Hugh Douglas .15 .40
323 Charles Johnson .15 .40
324 Chad Lewis .15 .40
325 Cecil Martin .15 .40
326 Donovan McNabb .25 .60
327 Brian Mitchell .20 .50
328 Todd Pinkston .15 .40
329 Ron Powlus .20 .50
330 Stanley Pritchett .15 .40
331 Torrance Small .15 .40
332 Duce Staley .20 .50
333 Troy Vincent .20 .50
334 Chris Warren .20 .50
335 Jerome Bettis .25 .60
336 Plaxico Burress .20 .50
337 Troy Edwards .15 .40
338 Chris Fuamatu-Ma'afala .15 .40
339 Cory Geason .15 .40
340 Kent Graham .20 .50
341 Courtney Hawkins .15 .40
342 Richard Huntley .15 .40
343 Tee Martin .20 .50
344 Bobby Shaw .15 .40
345 Kordell Stewart .20 .50
346 Hines Ward .25 .60
347 Destry Wright RC .15 .40
348 Amos Zereoue .15 .40
349 Isaac Bruce .25 .60
350 Trung Canidate .15 .40
351 Marshall Faulk .25 .60
352 London Fletcher .15 .40
353 Joe Germaine .15 .40
354 Trent Green .25 .60
355 Az-Zahir Hakim .15 .40
356 James Hodgins .15 .40
357 Robert Holcombe .15 .40
358 Torry Holt .20 .50
359 Tony Horne .15 .40
360 Ricky Proehl .15 .40
361 Chris Thomas RC .15 .40
362 Kurt Warner .40 1.00
363 Justin Watson .15 .40
364 Kenny Bynum .15 .40
365 Robert Chancey .15 .40
366 Curtis Conway .20 .50
367 Jermaine Fazande .15 .40
368 Terrell Fletcher .15 .40
369 Trevor Gaylor .15 .40
370 Jeff Graham .15 .40
371 Jim Harbaugh .20 .50
372 Rodney Harrison .20 .50
373 Ronney Jenkins .15 .40
374 Freddie Jones .15 .40
375 Reggie Jones .15 .40
376 Ryan Leaf .15 .40
377 Junior Seau .25 .60
378 Fred Beasley .15 .40
379 Greg Clark .15 .40
380 Jeff Garcia .20 .50
381 Charlie Garner .20 .50
382 Terry Jackson .15 .40
383 Brian Jennings .15 .40
384 Travis Jervey .15 .40
385 Jonas Lewis .15 .40
386 Terrell Owens .25 .60
387 Jerry Rice .50 1.25
388 Paul Smith .15 .40
389 J.J. Stokes .15 .40
390 Tai Streets .15 .40
391 Justin Swift .15 .40
392 Shaun Alexander .25 .60
393 Karsten Bailey .15 .40
394 Chad Brown .15 .40
395 Sean Dawkins .15 .40
396 Christian Fauria .15 .40
397 Brock Huard .15 .40
398 Darrell Jackson .20 .50
399 Jon Kitna .20 .50
400 Derrick Mayes .15 .40
401 Itula Mili .15 .40
402 Charlie Rogers .15 .40
403 Mack Strong .20 .50
404 Ricky Watters .20 .50
405 James Williams WR .15 .40
406 Rabih Abdullah .15 .40
407 Mike Alstott .20 .50
408 Reidel Anthony .15 .40
409 Derrick Brooks .25 .60
410 Warrick Dunn .25 .60
411 Jacquez Green .15 .40
412 Joe Hamilton .15 .40
413 Keyshawn Johnson .20 .50
414 Shaun King .15 .40
415 Charles Kirby RC .15 .40
416 Warren Sapp .20 .50
417 Aaron Stecker .15 .40
418 Todd Yoder .15 .40
419 Eric Zeier .15 .40
420 Chris Coleman .15 .40
421 Kevin Dyson .15 .40
422 Eddie George .25 .60
423 Jevon Kearse .20 .50
424 Erron Kinney .15 .40
425 Mike Leach .15 .40
426 Derrick Mason .20 .50
427 Steve McNair .25 .60
428 Lorenzo Neal .20 .50
429 Carl Pickens .20 .50
430 Chris Sanders .15 .40
431 Yancey Thigpen .15 .40
432 Rodney Thomas .15 .40
433 Frank Wycheck .15 .40
434 Stephen Alexander .15 .40
435 Champ Bailey .25 .60
436 Larry Centers .20 .50
437 Albert Connell .15 .40
438 Stephen Davis .20 .50
439 Zeron Flemister RC .15 .40
440 Irving Fryar .20 .50
441 Jeff George .20 .50
442 Skip Hicks .15 .40
443 Todd Husak .15 .40
444 Brad Johnson .20 .50
445 Adrian Murrell .20 .50
446 Deion Sanders .25 .60
447 Mike Sellers .15 .40
448 Derrius Thompson .15 .40
449 James Thrash .20 .50
450 Michael Westbrook .15 .40
451 Alex Bannister AU/1750 RC 4.00 10.00
452 Kevan Barlow AU/1500 RC 5.00 12.00
453 Drew Brees AU/1000 RC 60.00 120.00
454 Travis Henry AU/1500 RC 5.00 12.00
455 Chad Johnson AU/1750 RC 12.50 30.00
456 Mike McMahon AU/1000 RC 5.00 12.00
457 Bobby Newcombe AU/1750 RC 5.00 12.00
458 Sage Rosenfels AU/1000 RC 6.00 15.00
459 LaDainian Tomlinson AU/1500 RC 40.00 80.00
460 Chris Weinke AU/1000 RC 5.00 12.00
461 Tay Cody RC .75 2.00
462 Adam Archuleta RC 1.00 2.50
463 Will Allen RC 1.25 3.00
464 Moran Norris RC .75 2.00
465 Tommy Polley RC .75 2.00
466 Ennis Davis RC .75 2.00
467 Jamar Fletcher RC .75 2.00
468 Derrick Gibson RC .75 2.00
469 Sedrick Hodge RC .75 2.00
470 Willie Howard RC .75 2.00
471 Steve Hutchinson RC 2.00 5.00
472 Michael Stone RC .75 2.00
473 Vinny Sutherland/1750 RC 1.00 2.50
474 Joe Tafoya RC .75 2.00
475 Maurice Williams RC .75 2.00
476 Pork Chop Womack RC .75 2.00
477 Chad Ward RC .75 2.00
478 Scotty Anderson/1750 RC 1.00 2.50
479 Gary Baxter RC .75 2.00
480 Marques Tuiasosopo/1000 RC 2.00 5.00
481 Tim Hasselbeck/1000 RC 2.00 5.00
482 Clevan Thomas RC .75 2.00
483 Marcus Stroud RC 1.00 2.50
484 John Schlecht RC .75 2.00
485 Brandon Spoon RC 1.00 2.50
486 Alex Lincoln RC .75 2.00
487 Anthony Thomas/1750 RC 1.50 4.00
488 Freddie Mitchell/1750 RC 1.00 2.50
489 Brian Allen RC .75 2.00
490 Zeke Moreno RC 1.00 2.50
491 Tony Driver RC 1.00 2.50
492 Kynan Forney RC .75 2.00
493 Reggie Wayne/1750 RC 3.00 8.00
494 Larry Casher RC .75 2.00
495 Fred Wakefield RC .75 2.00
496 Jeff Backus RC .75 2.00
497 Jarrod Cooper RC 1.00 2.50
498 Heath Evans RC 1.00 2.50
499 James Jackson/1500 RC 1.00 2.50
500 Jabari Holloway RC .75 2.00
501 Quincy Morgan/1750 RC 1.25 3.00
502 Josh Booty/1000 RC 2.00 5.00
503 Ja'Mar Toombs RC .75 2.00
504 Jason McKinley/1000 RC 1.50 4.00
505 Reggie White/1500 RC 1.00 2.50
506 Todd Heap/1750 RC 1.50 4.00
507 Rudi Johnson/1500 RC 1.50 4.00
508 Snoop Minnis/1750 RC 1.00 2.50
509 David Terrell/1750 RC 1.25 3.00
510 Torrance Marshall RC .75 2.00
511 Michael Bennett/1500 RC 1.25 3.00
512 Chris Chambers/1750 RC 1.50 4.00
513 Ben Leard/1000 RC 1.50 4.00
514 Rod Gardner/1750 RC 1.25 3.00
515 Michael Vick/1000 RC 10.00 25.00
516 Josh Heupel/1000 RC 2.50 6.00
517 Jesse Palmer/1000 RC 2.00 5.00
518 Quincy Carter/1000 RC 2.00 5.00
519 A.J. Feeley/1000 RC 2.00 5.00
520 David Rivers/1000 RC 1.50 4.00
521 Deuce McAllister/1500 RC 1.50 4.00
522 LaMont Jordan/1500 RC 1.50 4.00
523 David Allen/1500 RC 1.00 2.50
524 Correll Buckhalter/1500 RC 1.50 4.00
525 Travis Minor/1500 1.25 3.00
526 Koren Robinson/1750 RC 1.25 3.00
527 Santana Moss/1750 RC 2.00 5.00
528 Robert Ferguson/1750 RC 1.50 4.00
529 T.J. Houshmandzadeh/1750 RC 2.00 5.00
530 Cedrick Wilson/1750 RC 1.25 3.00

2001 Pacific Hobby LTD

*VETERANS: 6X TO 15X BASIC CARDS
STATED PRINT RUN 99 SER.#'d SETS

2001 Pacific Premiere Date

*VETERANS: 12X TO 30X BASIC CARDS
STATED PRINT RUN 45 SER.#'d SETS

2001 Pacific Retail LTD

*VETERANS: 4X TO 10X BASIC CARDS
STATED PRINT RUN 299 SER.#'d SETS

2001 Pacific All-Rookie Team

COMPLETE SET (10) 12.50 30.00
STATED ODDS 1:37
1 Kevan Barlow .60 1.50
2 Drew Brees 5.00 12.00
3 Travis Henry .60 1.50
4 Chad Johnson 1.25 3.00
5 Freddie Mitchell .50 1.25
6 Anthony Thomas .75 2.00
7 LaDainian Tomlinson 2.50 6.00
8 Marques Tuiasosopo .60 1.50
9 Reggie Wayne 1.50 4.00
10 Chris Weinke .60 1.50

2001 Pacific Cramer's Choice

COMPLETE SET (10) 100.00 200.00
STATED PRINT RUN 99 SER.#'d SETS
1 Trent Dilfer 5.00 12.00
2 Jamal Lewis 6.00 15.00
3 Emmitt Smith 15.00 40.00
4 Brett Favre 20.00 50.00
5 Edgerrin James 6.00 15.00
6 Peyton Manning 15.00 40.00
7 Randy Moss 6.00 15.00
8 Marshall Faulk 6.00 15.00
9 Kurt Warner 10.00 25.00
10 Eddie George 6.00 15.00

2001 Pacific Game Gear

STATED PRINT RUN 20-99
1 Thomas Jones J 8.00 20.00
2 Jake Plummer J 8.00 20.00
3 Rod Woodson J 10.00 25.00
4 Rob Johnson J 8.00 20.00
5 Corey Dillon J 8.00 20.00
6 Akili Smith J 6.00 15.00
7 Peter Warrick J 8.00 20.00
8 Mark Brunell J 8.00 20.00
9 Keenan McCardell J/20 15.00 40.00
10 Fred Taylor J 10.00 25.00
11 Dan Marino J 25.00 60.00
12 Trent Green J 10.00 25.00
13 Kurt Warner J 15.00 40.00
14 Jerry Rice J/20 60.00 120.00
15 Brock Huard J/20 12.00 30.00
16 Jamal Lewis F 10.00 25.00
17 Peter Warrick F 8.00 20.00
18 Mike Anderson F 8.00 20.00
19 Edgerrin James F 10.00 25.00
20 Daunte Culpepper F 8.00 20.00
21 Randy Moss F 10.00 25.00
22 Ron Dayne F 8.00 20.00
23 Marshall Faulk F 10.00 25.00
24 Kurt Warner F 15.00 40.00
25 Eddie George F 10.00 25.00

2001 Pacific Gold Crown Die Cuts

COMPLETE SET (30) 30.00 80.00
STATED ODDS 1:73
1 Jamal Lewis 1.50 4.00
2 Corey Dillon 1.25 3.00
3 Peter Warrick 1.25 3.00
4 Troy Aikman 2.50 6.00
5 Emmitt Smith 4.00 10.00
6 Mike Anderson 1.25 3.00
7 Terrell Davis 1.50 4.00
8 Brian Griese 1.25 3.00
9 Brett Favre 5.00 12.00
10 Marvin Harrison 1.50 4.00
11 Edgerrin James 1.50 4.00
12 Peyton Manning 4.00 10.00
13 Mark Brunell 1.25 3.00
14 Fred Taylor 1.50 4.00
15 Cris Carter 1.50 4.00
16 Daunte Culpepper 1.25 3.00
17 Randy Moss 1.50 4.00
18 Drew Bledsoe 1.50 4.00
19 Ricky Williams 1.50 4.00
20 Kerry Collins 1.25 3.00
21 Ron Dayne 1.25 3.00
22 Curtis Martin 1.50 4.00
23 Donovan McNabb 1.50 4.00
24 Jerome Bettis 1.50 4.00
25 Isaac Bruce 1.50 4.00
26 Marshall Faulk 1.50 4.00
27 Kurt Warner 2.50 6.00
28 Jeff Garcia 1.25 3.00
29 Jerry Rice 3.00 8.00
30 Steve McNair 1.50 4.00

2001 Pacific Impact Zone

COMPLETE SET (20) 12.50 30.00
STATED ODDS 1:37
1 Jamal Lewis .60 1.50
2 Corey Dillon .50 1.25
3 Peter Warrick .50 1.25
4 Emmitt Smith 1.50 4.00
5 Mike Anderson .50 1.25
6 Brian Griese .50 1.25
7 Edgerrin James .60 1.50
8 Mark Brunell .50 1.25
9 Fred Taylor .60 1.50
10 Randy Moss .60 1.50
11 Ricky Williams .60 1.50
12 Ron Dayne .50 1.25
13 Curtis Martin .60 1.50
14 Rich Gannon .50 1.25
15 Donovan McNabb .60 1.50
16 Marshall Faulk .60 1.50
17 Jerry Rice 1.25 3.00
18 Mike Alstott .50 1.25
19 Warrick Dunn .60 1.50
20 Eddie George .60 1.50

2001 Pacific Pro Bowl Die Cuts

COMPLETE SET (20) 12.50 30.00
STATED ODDS 1:37
1 Eric Moulds .75 2.00
2 Corey Dillon .75 2.00
3 Marvin Harrison 1.00 2.50
4 Edgerrin James 1.00 2.50
5 Peyton Manning 2.50 6.00
6 Jimmy Smith .75 2.00
7 Tony Gonzalez 1.00 2.50
8 Elvis Grbac .75 2.00
9 Cris Carter 1.00 2.50
10 Daunte Culpepper .75 2.00
11 Joe Horn .75 2.00
12 Rich Gannon .75 2.00
13 Donovan McNabb 1.00 2.50
14 Torry Holt .75 2.00
15 Jeff Garcia .75 2.00
16 Terrell Owens 1.00 2.50
17 Warrick Dunn 1.00 2.50
18 Eddie George 1.00 2.50
19 Derrick Mason .75 2.00
20 Stephen Davis .75 2.00

2001 Pacific War Room

COMPLETE SET (20) 20.00 50.00
STATED ODDS 2:37
1 Alex Bannister .60 1.50
2 Kevan Barlow .75 2.00
3 Josh Booty .75 2.00
4 Drew Brees 6.00 15.00
5 Tim Hasselbeck .75 2.00
6 Travis Henry .75 2.00
7 James Jackson .60 1.50
8 Chad Johnson 1.50 4.00
9 Rudi Johnson 1.00 2.50
10 Mike McMahon .75 2.00
11 Snoop Minnis .60 1.50
12 Freddie Mitchell .60 1.50
13 Quincy Morgan .75 2.00
14 Bobby Newcombe .75 2.00
15 Sage Rosenfels 1.00 2.50
16 Anthony Thomas 1.00 2.50
17 LaDainian Tomlinson 3.00 8.00
18 Marques Tuiasosopo .75 2.00
19 Reggie Wayne 2.00 5.00
20 Chris Weinke .75 2.00

2001 Pacific Brown Royale

This 9-card die cut set was distributed at the 2001 National Sports Collector's Convention in Cleveland. Each features a Cleveland Browns player on the front and a 2001 NFL rookie on the back. The dog bone shaped cards were serial numbered of 1000.

COMPLETE SET (18) 20.00 50.00
1 Spergon Wynn 3.00 8.00
Drew Brees
2 Tim Couch 2.00 5.00
Marques Tuiasosopo
3 Errict Rhett 5.00 12.00
Anthony Thomas
4 Jamel White 2.00 5.00
James Jackson
5 Travis Prentice 3.00 8.00
LaDainian Tomlinson
6 Dennis Northcutt 2.00 5.00
Koren Robinson
7 JaJuan Dawson 2.00 5.00
Rod Gardner
8 Kevin Johnson 2.50 6.00
David Terrell
9 Quincy Morgan 2.00 5.00
Santana Moss

2002 Pacific

This 500-card set includes 450 veterans and 50 rookies. Product was released in late spring/early summer 2002. Boxes contained 36 packs of 10 cards. Pack SRP was $2.99. Please note that cards 501-525 were only available in packs of 2002 Pacific Heads Update.

COMPLETE SET (500) 50.00 100.00
ROOKIE STATED ODDS ONE PER PACK
1 David Boston .15 .40
2 Arnold Jackson .15 .40
3 MarTay Jenkins .15 .40
4 Thomas Jones .25 .60
5 Kwamie Lassiter .15 .40
6 Joel Makovicka .15 .40
7 Ronald McKinnon .15 .40
8 Tywan Mitchell .15 .40
9 Michael Pittman .20 .50
10 Jake Plummer .20 .50
11 Frank Sanders .15 .40
12 Kyle Vanden Bosch .20 .50
13 Jamal Anderson .20 .50
14 Keith Brooking .15 .40
15 Chris Chandler .20 .50
16 Bob Christian .15 .40
17 Alge Crumpler .20 .50
18 Brian Finneran .15 .40
19 Shawn Jefferson .15 .40
20 Patrick Kerney .15 .40
21 Terance Mathis .15 .40
22 Maurice Smith .15 .40
23 Rodney Thomas .20 .50
24 Darrick Vaughn .15 .40
25 Michael Vick .40 1.00
26 Sam Adams .15 .40
27 Terry Allen .20 .50
28 Obafemi Ayanbadejo .15 .40
29 Peter Boulware .15 .40
30 Jason Brookins .15 .40
31 Randall Cunningham .25 .60
32 Elvis Grbac .15 .40
33 Todd Heap .20 .50
34 Qadry Ismail .20 .50
35 Jamal Lewis .20 .50
36 Ray Lewis .25 .60
37 Chris Redman .15 .40
38 Shannon Sharpe .25 .60
39 Brandon Stokley .20 .50
40 Travis Taylor .15 .40
41 Moe Williams .15 .40
42 Rod Woodson .25 .60
43 Shawn Bryson .15 .40
44 Larry Centers .20 .50
45 Nate Clements .15 .40
46 London Fletcher .15 .40
47 Reggie Germany .15 .40
48 Travis Henry .15 .40
49 Jeremy McDaniel .15 .40
50 Sammy Morris .20 .50
51 Eric Moulds .20 .50
52 Peerless Price .15 .40
53 Jay Riemersma .15 .40
54 Alex Van Pelt .15 .40
55 Tim Biakabutuka .20 .50
56 Isaac Byrd .15 .40
57 Doug Evans .15 .40
58 Donald Hayes .15 .40
59 Chris Hetherington .15 .40
60 Brad Hoover .15 .40
61 Richard Huntley .15 .40
62 Patrick Jeffers .20 .50
63 Matt Lytle .15 .40
64 Dan Morgan .15 .40
65 Muhsin Muhammad .20 .50
66 Mike Rucker RC .25 .60
67 Steve Smith .25 .60
68 Wesley Walls .20 .50
69 Chris Weinke .15 .40
70 James Allen .15 .40
71 Fred Baxter .15 .40
72 Marty Booker .20 .50
73 Mike Brown .20 .50
74 Rosevelt Colvin RC .30 .75
75 Phillip Daniels .15 .40
76 Leon Johnson .15 .40
77 Shane Matthews .15 .40
78 Jim Miller .15 .40
79 Tony Parrish .15 .40
80 Marcus Robinson .20 .50
81 David Terrell .15 .40
82 Anthony Thomas .20 .50
83 Brian Urlacher .25 .60
84 Ted Washington .15 .40
85 Dez White .15 .40
86 Brandon Bennett .15 .40
87 Corey Dillon .20 .50
88 Ron Dugans .15 .40
89 Danny Farmer .15 .40
90 T.J. Houshmandzadeh .25 .60
91 Chad Johnson .25 .60
92 Curtis Keaton .15 .40
93 Jon Kitna .20 .50
94 Tony McGee .20 .50
95 Lorenzo Neal .20 .50
96 Darnay Scott .20 .50
97 Akili Smith .20 .50
98 Justin Smith .15 .40
99 Takeo Spikes .15 .40
100 Peter Warrick .20 .50
101 Tim Couch .15 .40
102 JaJuan Dawson .15 .40
103 Benjamin Gay .15 .40
104 Anthony Henry .15 .40
105 James Jackson .15 .40
106 Kevin Johnson .15 .40
107 Andre King .15 .40
108 Jamir Miller .15 .40
109 Quincy Morgan .15 .40
110 Dennis Northcutt .15 .40
111 O.J. Santiago .15 .40
112 Jamel White .15 .40
113 Quincy Carter .15 .40
114 Darrin Chiaverini .15 .40
115 Dexter Coakley .15 .40
116 Joey Galloway .20 .50
117 Troy Hambrick .15 .40
118 Rocket Ismail .20 .50
119 Dat Nguyen .15 .40
120 Ken-Yon Rambo .15 .40
121 Emmitt Smith .60 1.50
122 Reggie Swinton .15 .40
123 Robert Thomas .15 .40
124 Michael Wiley .15 .40
125 Anthony Wright .15 .40
126 Mike Anderson .20 .50
127 Dwayne Carswell .15 .40
128 Desmond Clark .20 .50
129 Chris Cole .15 .40
130 Terrell Davis .25 .60
131 Gus Frerotte .20 .50
132 Olandis Gary .20 .50
133 Brian Griese .20 .50
134 Kevin Kasper .15 .40
135 Ed McCaffrey .20 .50
136 Phil McGeoghan RC .15 .40
137 John Mobley .15 .40
138 Scottie Montgomery .15 .40
139 Deltha O'Neal .15 .40
140 Trevor Pryce .15 .40
141 Rod Smith .20 .50
142 Al Wilson .20 .50
143 Scotty Anderson .15 .40
144 Charlie Batch .15 .40
145 Aveion Cason .15 .40
146 Germane Crowell .15 .40
147 Reuben Droughns .20 .50
148 Bert Emanuel .20 .50
149 Larry Foster .15 .40
150 Az-Zahir Hakim .15 .40
151 Desmond Howard .20 .50
152 Mike McMahon .15 .40
153 Herman Moore .20 .50
154 Johnnie Morton .20 .50
155 Robert Porcher .15 .40
156 Cory Schlesinger .15 .40
157 David Sloan .15 .40
158 James Stewart .15 .40
159 Lamont Warren .15 .40
160 Donald Driver .25 .60
161 Brett Favre .60 1.50
162 Bubba Franks .20 .50
163 Antonio Freeman .25 .60
164 Kabeer Gbaja-Biamila .20 .50
165 Terry Glenn .20 .50
166 Ahman Green .20 .50
167 William Henderson .20 .50
168 Dorsey Levens .20 .50
169 David Martin .15 .40
170 Rondell Mealey .15 .40
171 Bill Schroeder .15 .40
172 Darren Sharper .20 .50
173 Avion Black .15 .40
174 Tony Boselli .20 .50
175 Corey Bradford .15 .40
176 Marcus Coleman .15 .40
177 Leomont Evans .15 .40
178 Aaron Glenn .15 .40
179 Trevor Insley .15 .40
180 Jermaine Lewis .15 .40
181 Anthony Malbrough .15 .40
182 Frank Moreau .15 .40
183 Mike Quinn .15 .40
184 Charlie Rogers .15 .40
185 Jamie Sharper .20 .50
186 Matt Snider .15 .40
187 Gary Walker .15 .40
188 Kevin Williams RC .40 1.00
189 Kailee Wong .15 .40
190 Chad Bratzke .15 .40
191 Ken Dilger .20 .50
192 Marvin Harrison .25 .60
193 Edgerrin James .20 .50
194 Kevin McDougal .15 .40
195 Rob Morris .15 .40
196 Jerome Pathon .15 .40
197 Marcus Pollard .15 .40
198 Dominic Rhodes .20 .50
199 Marcus Washington .15 .40
200 Reggie Wayne .25 .60
201 Terrence Wilkins .15 .40
202 Tony Brackens .15 .40
203 Kyle Brady .15 .40
204 Mark Brunell .20 .50
205 Donovin Darius .15 .40
206 Sean Dawkins .20 .50
207 Damon Gibson .15 .40
208 Elvis Joseph .15 .40
209 Stacey Mack .15 .40
210 Keenan McCardell .20 .50
211 Hardy Nickerson .15 .40
212 Jonathan Quinn .15 .40
213 Micah Ross RC .15 .40
214 Jimmy Smith .20 .50
215 Fred Taylor .20 .50
216 Patrick Washington .15 .40
217 Derrick Alexander .15 .40
218 Mike Cloud .15 .40
219 Donnie Edwards .15 .40
220 Tony Gonzalez .25 .60
221 Trent Green .20 .50
222 Dante Hall .20 .50
223 Priest Holmes .25 .60
224 Eddie Kennison .20 .50
225 Snoop Minnis .15 .40
226 Larry Parker .15 .40
227 Marvcus Patton .15 .40
228 Tony Richardson .15 .40
229 Mikhael Ricks .15 .40
230 Chris Chambers .20 .50
231 Jay Fiedler .20 .50
232 Oronde Gadsden .15 .40
233 Rob Konrad .15 .40
234 Sam Madison .15 .40
235 Brock Marion .15 .40
236 James McKnight .15 .40
237 Travis Minor .15 .40
238 Jeff Ogden .20 .50
239 Lamar Smith .20 .50
240 Jason Taylor .20 .50
241 Zach Thomas .25 .60
242 Dedric Ward .15 .40
243 Ricky Williams .20 .50
244 Michael Bennett .20 .50
245 Todd Bouman .15 .40
246 Cris Carter .25 .60
247 Byron Chamberlain .15 .40
248 Doug Chapman .15 .40
249 Kenny Clark RC .15 .40
250 Daunte Culpepper .20 .50
251 Nate Jacquet .15 .40
252 Jim Kleinsasser .25 .60
253 Harold Morrow .15 .40
254 Randy Moss .25 .60
255 Jake Reed .20 .50
256 Spergon Wynn .15 .40
257 Drew Bledsoe .25 .60
258 Tom Brady .60 1.50
259 Troy Brown .20 .50
260 Fred Coleman .15 .40
261 Marc Edwards .15 .40
262 Kevin Faulk .20 .50
263 Bobby Hamilton .15 .40
264 Ty Law .20 .50
265 Lawyer Milloy .15 .40
266 David Patten .15 .40
267 J.R. Redmond .15 .40
268 Antowain Smith .20 .50
269 Adam Vinatieri .25 .60
270 Jermaine Wiggins .15 .40
271 Aaron Brooks .20 .50
272 Cam Cleeland .15 .40
273 Charlie Clemons RC .15 .40
274 James Fenderson RC .15 .40
275 La'Roi Glover .15 .40
276 Joe Horn .20 .50
277 Willie Jackson .15 .40
278 Sammy Knight .15 .40
279 Michael Lewis RC .25 .60
280 Deuce McAllister .20 .50
281 Terrelle Smith .15 .40
282 Boo Williams .15 .40
283 Robert Wilson .15 .40
284 Tiki Barber .25 .60
285 Micheal Barrow .15 .40
286 Kerry Collins .20 .50
287 Greg Comella .15 .40
288 Thabiti Davis .15 .40
289 Ron Dayne .20 .50
290 Ron Dixon .15 .40
291 Ike Hilliard .20 .50
292 Joe Jurevicius .15 .40
293 Michael Strahan .25 .60
294 Amani Toomer .20 .50
295 Damon Washington .15 .40
296 John Abraham .20 .50
297 Richie Anderson .15 .40
298 Anthony Becht .15 .40
299 Wayne Chrebet .20 .50
300 Laveranues Coles .20 .50
301 James Farrior .20 .50
302 Marvin Jones .15 .40
303 LaMont Jordan .20 .50
304 Curtis Martin .25 .60
305 Santana Moss .20 .50
306 Chad Pennington .25 .60
307 Kevin Swayne .15 .40
308 Vinny Testaverde .20 .50
309 Craig Yeast .15 .40
310 Greg Biekert .15 .40
311 Tim Brown .25 .60
312 Zack Crockett .15 .40
313 Rich Gannon .20 .50
314 Charlie Garner .20 .50
315 Sebastian Janikowski .15 .40
316 Randy Jordan .15 .40
317 Terry Kirby .15 .40
318 Jerry Porter .15 .40
319 Jerry Rice .50 1.25
320 Jon Ritchie .15 .40
321 Tyrone Wheatley .20 .50
322 Roland Williams .15 .40
323 Charles Woodson .25 .60
324 Correll Buckhalter .20 .50
325 Brian Dawkins .20 .50
326 Hugh Douglas .15 .40

327 A.J. Feeley	.15	.40
328 Chad Lewis	.15	.40
329 Cecil Martin	.15	.40
330 Brian Mitchell	.20	.50
331 Freddie Mitchell	.15	.40
332 Todd Pinkston	.15	.40
333 Rod Smart RC	.20	.50
334 Duce Staley	.20	.50
335 James Thrash	.20	.50
336 Jeremiah Trotter	.15	.40
337 Troy Vincent	.20	.50
338 Kendrell Bell	.15	.40
339 Jerome Bettis	.25	.60
340 Demetrius Brown RC	.15	.40
341 Plaxico Burress	.20	.50
342 Troy Edwards	.15	.40
343 Chris Fuamatu-Ma'afala	.15	.40
344 Jason Gildon	.20	.50
345 Earl Holmes	.15	.40
346 Joey Porter	.20	.50
347 Chad Scott	.15	.40
348 Bobby Shaw	.15	.40
349 Kordell Stewart	.20	.50
350 Hines Ward	.25	.60
351 Amos Zereoue	.15	.40
352 Adam Archuleta	.15	.40
353 Dre Bly	.15	.40
354 Isaac Bruce	.25	.60
355 Trung Canidate	.15	.40
356 Ernie Conwell	.15	.40
357 Marshall Faulk	.25	.60
358 Torry Holt	.25	.60
359 Leonard Little	.20	.50
360 Yo Murphy	.15	.40
361 Ricky Proehl	.20	.50
362 Kurt Warner	.25	.60
363 Aeneas Williams	.20	.50
364 Drew Brees	.40	1.00
365 Curtis Conway	.20	.50
366 Tim Dwight	.15	.40
367 Terrell Fletcher	.15	.40
368 Doug Flutie	.25	.60
369 Jeff Graham	.15	.40
370 Rodney Harrison	.20	.50
371 Ronney Jenkins	.15	.40
372 Raylee Johnson	.15	.40
373 Freddie Jones	.15	.40
374 Ryan McNeil	.15	.40
375 Junior Seau	.25	.60
376 LaDainian Tomlinson	.30	.75
377 Marcellus Wiley	.15	.40
378 Kevan Barlow	.15	.40
379 Fred Beasley	.15	.40
380 Zack Bronson RC	.15	.40
381 Andre Carter	.15	.40
382 Jeff Garcia	.20	.50
383 Garrison Hearst	.20	.50
384 Terry Jackson	.15	.40
385 Eric Johnson	.15	.40
386 Saladin McCullough RC	.15	.40
387 Terrell Owens	.25	.60
388 Ahmed Plummer	.15	.40
389 J.J. Stokes	.15	.40
390 Tai Streets	.15	.40
391 Vinny Sutherland	.15	.40
392 Bryant Young	.15	.40
393 Shaun Alexander	.20	.50
394 Chad Brown	.15	.40
395 Kerwin Cook RC	.15	.40
396 Trent Dilfer	.20	.50
397 Bobby Engram	.20	.50
398 Christian Fauria	.15	.40
399 Matt Hasselbeck	.25	.60
400 Darrell Jackson	.20	.50
401 John Randle	.20	.50
402 Koren Robinson	.15	.40
403 Anthony Simmons	.15	.40
404 Mack Strong	.15	.40
405 Ricky Watters	.20	.50
406 James Williams WR	.15	.40
407 Mike Alstott	.20	.50
408 Ronde Barber	.20	.50
409 Derrick Brooks	.25	.60
410 Jameel Cook	.15	.40
411 Warrick Dunn	.20	.50
412 Jacquez Green	.15	.40
413 Brad Johnson	.20	.50
414 Keyshawn Johnson	.20	.50
415 Rob Johnson	.20	.50
416 John Lynch	.20	.50
417 Dave Moore	.15	.40
418 Warren Sapp	.20	.50
419 Aaron Stecker	.15	.40
420 Karl Williams	.15	.40
421 Drew Bennett	.20	.50
422 Eddie Berlin	.15	.40
423 Rafael Cooper RC	.15	.40
424 Kevin Dyson	.20	.50
425 Eddie George	.20	.50
426 Mike Green	.15	.40
427 Skip Hicks	.15	.40
428 Jevon Kearse	.20	.50
429 Erron Kinney	.15	.40
430 Derrick Mason	.20	.50
431 Justin McCareins	.20	.50
432 Steve McNair	.25	.60
433 Neil O'Donnell	.20	.50
434 Frank Wycheck	.15	.40
435 Reidel Anthony	.15	.40
436 Jessie Armstead	.15	.40
437 Champ Bailey	.25	.60
438 Tony Banks	.15	.40
439 Michael Bates	.15	.40
440 Donnell Bennett	.15	.40
441 Ki-Jana Carter	.20	.50
442 Stephen Davis	.20	.50
443 Zeron Flemister	.15	.40
444 Rod Gardner	.15	.40
445 Kevin Lockett	.15	.40
446 Eric Metcalf	.15	.40
447 Sage Rosenfels	.20	.50
448 Fred Smoot	.20	.50
449 Michael Westbrook	.15	.40
450 Danny Wuerffel	.20	.50
451 Jason McAddley RC	.50	1.25
452 Freddie Milons RC	.40	1.00
453 Bryan Thomas RC	.40	1.00
454 Levi Jones RC	.40	1.00
455 William Green RC	.50	1.25
456 Luke Staley RC	.40	1.00
457 Daniel Graham RC	.50	1.25
458 David Garrard RC	.75	2.00
459 Reche Caldwell RC	.60	1.50
460 Andra Davis RC	.40	1.00
461 Lito Sheppard RC	.60	1.50
462 Chris Hope RC	.60	1.50
463 Javon Walker RC	.60	1.50
464 David Carr RC	.60	1.50
465 Alan Harper RC	.40	1.00
466 Adrian Peterson RC	.60	1.50
467 Kelly Campbell RC	.50	1.25
468 Ashley Lelie RC	.50	1.25
469 Kurt Kittner RC	.40	1.00
470 Antwaan Randle El RC	.60	1.50
471 Ladell Betts RC	.60	1.50
472 Josh Reed RC	.50	1.25
473 Clinton Portis RC	.75	2.00
474 Ron Johnson RC	.50	1.25
475 Eric Crouch RC	.60	1.50
476 Tracey Wistrom RC	.50	1.25
477 David Neill RC	.40	1.00
478 Ronald Curry RC	.50	1.25
479 Lamar Gordon RC	.50	1.25
480 Damien Anderson RC	.40	1.00
481 Napoleon Harris RC	.50	1.25
482 Zak Kustok RC	.40	1.00
483 Rocky Calmus RC	.50	1.25
484 Roy Williams RC	.60	1.50
485 Joey Harrington RC	.60	1.50
486 Maurice Morris RC	.50	1.25
487 Antonio Bryant RC	.60	1.50
488 Josh McCown RC	.60	1.50
489 John Henderson RC	.50	1.25
490 Quentin Jammer RC	.60	1.50
491 Mike Williams RC	.40	1.00
492 Patrick Ramsey RC	.60	1.50
493 Kenyon Coleman RC	.40	1.00
494 DeShaun Foster RC	.60	1.50
495 Brian Poli-Dixon RC	.40	1.00
496 Cliff Russell RC	.40	1.00
497 Brian Westbrook RC	1.00	2.50
498 Andre Davis RC	.50	1.25
499 Larry Tripplett RC	.40	1.00
500 Lamont Thompson RC	.50	1.25
501 T.J. Duckett RC	.60	1.50
502 Dameon Hunter RC	.40	1.00
503 Javin Hunter RC	.40	1.00
504 Tellis Redmon RC	.40	1.00
505 Chester Taylor RC	.60	1.50
506 Randy Fasani RC	.50	1.25
507 Julius Peppers RC	1.25	3.00
508 Jamin Elliott RC	.40	1.00
509 Chad Hutchinson RC	.40	1.00
510 Eddie Drummond RC	.40	1.00
511 Craig Nall RC	.50	1.25
512 Jabar Gaffney RC	.60	1.50
513 Jonathan Wells RC	.60	1.50
514 Shaun Hill RC	.75	2.00
515 Deion Branch RC	.60	1.50
516 Rohan Davey RC	.60	1.50
517 J.T. O'Sullivan RC	.50	1.25
518 Tim Carter RC	.50	1.25
519 Daryl Jones RC	.40	1.00
520 Jeremy Shockey RC	1.00	2.50
521 Seth Burford RC	.40	1.00
522 Brandon Doman RC	.40	1.00
523 Jerramy Stevens RC	.60	1.50
524 Travis Stephens RC	.40	1.00
525 Marquise Walker RC	.40	1.00

2002 Pacific Chicago National

Available via a wrapper redemption at the Pacific booth during the 2002 Chicago National Convention, this 8-card set was serial numbered to just 500 copies. Collectors had to open a box of 2002 Pacific football or 2001-02 Pacific hockey product to receive the set. Each card featured an NHL player and an NFL player on either side.

COMPLETE SET (8)	12.00	30.00
1 Ilya Kovalchuk Michael Vick	2.00	5.00
2 Joe Thornton Tom Brady	4.00	10.00
3 Eric Daze Anthony Thomas	2.00	5.00
4 Peter Forsberg Brian Griese	2.00	5.00
5 Mike Modano Emmitt Smith	2.50	6.00
6 Steve Yzerman Joey Harrington	2.00	5.00
7 Eric Lindros Ron Dayne	1.50	4.00
8 Chris Pronger Kurt Warner	2.00	5.00

2002 Pacific Extreme LTD

*VETS 1-450: 20X TO 50X BASIC CARDS
*ROOKIES 451-500: 8X TO 20X BASIC CARDS
STATED ODDS 1:145
STATED PRINT RUN 24 SER.#'d SETS

2002 Pacific LTD

*VETS 1-450: 8X TO 20X BASIC CARDS
*ROOKIES 451-500: 3X TO 8X
STATED ODDS 1:37
STATED PRINT RUN 71 SER.#'d SETS

2002 Pacific Premiere Date

*VETS 1-450: 12X TO 30X BASIC CARDS
*ROOKIES 451-500: 5X TO 12X
STATED ODDS 1:37 HOBBY
STATED PRINT RUN 36 SER.#'d SETS

2002 Pacific Cramer's Choice

STATED ODDS 1:721
STATED PRINT RUN 120 SER.#'d SETS

1 David Boston	5.00	12.00
2 Anthony Thomas	6.00	15.00
3 Emmitt Smith	20.00	50.00
4 Brett Favre	20.00	50.00
5 Priest Holmes	8.00	20.00
6 Tom Brady	20.00	50.00
7 Marshall Faulk	8.00	20.00
8 Kurt Warner	8.00	20.00
9 Terrell Owens	8.00	20.00
10 Shaun Alexander	6.00	15.00

2002 Pacific Draft Force

COMPLETE SET (20)	30.00	80.00
STATED ODDS 1:145		
1 William Green	1.50	4.00
2 Luke Staley	1.25	3.00
3 Reche Caldwell	2.00	5.00
4 David Carr	2.00	5.00
5 Ashley Lelie	1.50	4.00
6 Kurt Kittner	1.25	3.00
7 Antwaan Randle El	2.00	5.00
8 Ladell Betts	2.00	5.00
9 Josh Reed	1.50	4.00
10 Clinton Portis	2.50	6.00
11 Eric Crouch	2.00	5.00
12 Lamar Gordon	1.50	4.00
13 Joey Harrington	2.00	5.00
14 Maurice Morris	1.50	4.00
15 Antonio Bryant	2.00	5.00
16 Josh McCown	2.00	5.00
17 Patrick Ramsey	2.00	5.00
18 DeShaun Foster	2.00	5.00
19 Brian Westbrook	3.00	8.00
20 Andre Davis	1.50	4.00

2002 Pacific Feature Attractions

COMPLETE SET (20)	25.00	60.00
STATED ODDS 1:37		
1 Michael Vick	1.50	4.00
2 Anthony Thomas	.75	2.00
3 Emmitt Smith	2.50	6.00
4 Brett Favre	2.50	6.00
4 Brian Griese	.75	2.00
6 Ahman Green	.75	2.00
7 Edgerrin James	.75	2.00
8 Priest Holmes	1.00	2.50
9 Ricky Williams	.75	2.00
10 Daunte Culpepper	.75	2.00
11 Tom Brady	2.50	6.00
12 Ron Dayne	.75	2.00
13 Curtis Martin	1.00	2.50
14 Jerry Rice	2.00	5.00
15 Marshall Faulk	1.00	2.50
16 Torry Holt	1.00	2.50
17 Kurt Warner	1.00	2.50
18 LaDainian Tomlinson	1.25	3.00
19 Warrick Dunn	.75	2.00
20 Eddie George	.75	2.00

2002 Pacific Game Worn Jerseys

STATED ODDS 2:37 HOBBY BOXES
STATED ODDS ONE PER RETAIL BOX

1 David Boston	2.50	6.00
2 MarTay Jenkins	2.50	6.00
3 Jake Plummer	3.00	8.00
4 Michael Vick	6.00	15.00
5 Jamal Lewis	3.00	8.00
6 Travis Henry	2.50	6.00
7 Steve Smith	4.00	10.00
8 Anthony Thomas	3.00	8.00
9 Peter Warrick	3.00	8.00
10 Quincy Carter	2.50	6.00
11 Terrell Davis	4.00	10.00
12 Mike McMahon	2.50	6.00
13 Brett Favre	10.00	25.00
14 Antonio Freeman	4.00	10.00
15 Ahman Green	3.00	8.00
16 Marvin Harrison	4.00	10.00
17 Reggie Wayne	4.00	10.00
18 Mark Brunell	3.00	8.00
19 Priest Holmes	4.00	10.00
20 Snoop Minnis	2.50	6.00
21 Chris Chambers	3.00	8.00
22 Ricky Williams	3.00	8.00
23 Daunte Culpepper	3.00	8.00
24 Randy Moss	4.00	10.00
25 Spergon Wynn	2.50	6.00
26 Drew Bledsoe	4.00	10.00
27 Tom Brady	10.00	25.00
28 Aaron Brooks	3.00	8.00
29 Jesse Palmer	2.50	6.00
30 Curtis Martin	4.00	10.00
31 Santana Moss	3.00	8.00
32 Tim Brown	4.00	10.00
33 Jerry Rice	8.00	20.00
34 Marques Tuiasosopo	2.50	6.00
35 Correll Buckhalter	3.00	8.00
36 Jerome Bettis	4.00	10.00
37 Marshall Faulk	4.00	10.00
38 Kurt Warner	4.00	10.00
39 Aeneas Williams	3.00	8.00
40 LaDainian Tomlinson	5.00	12.00
41 Kevan Barlow	2.50	6.00
42 Terrell Owens	4.00	10.00
43 Shaun Alexander	3.00	8.00
44 Trent Dilfer	3.00	8.00
45 Matt Hasselbeck	4.00	10.00
46 Warrick Dunn	3.00	8.00
47 Justin McCareins	3.00	8.00
48 Steve McNair	4.00	10.00
49 Tony Banks	2.50	6.00
50 Sage Rosenfels	3.00	8.00

2002 Pacific Pro Bowl Die Cuts

COMPLETE SET (20)	25.00	60.00
STATED ODDS 1:37		
1 David Boston	1.25	3.00
2 Brian Urlacher	2.00	5.00
3 Corey Dillon	1.50	4.00
4 Ahman Green	1.50	4.00
5 Marvin Harrison	2.00	5.00
6 Priest Holmes	2.00	5.00
7 Troy Brown	1.50	4.00
8 Curtis Martin	2.00	5.00
9 Tim Brown	2.00	5.00
10 Rich Gannon	1.50	4.00
11 Kordell Stewart	1.50	4.00
12 Hines Ward	2.00	5.00
13 Marshall Faulk	2.00	5.00
14 Torry Holt	2.00	5.00
15 Kurt Warner	2.00	5.00
16 Jeff Garcia	1.50	4.00
17 Garrison Hearst	1.50	4.00
18 Terrell Owens	2.00	5.00
19 Mike Alstott	1.50	4.00
20 Keyshawn Johnson	1.50	4.00

2002 Pacific Rocket Launchers

COMPLETE SET (20)	12.50	30.00
STATED ODDS 2:37		
1 Jake Plummer	.60	1.50
2 Michael Vick	1.25	3.00
3 Chris Weinke	.50	1.25
4 Tim Couch	.50	1.25
5 Quincy Carter	.50	1.25
6 Brian Griese	.60	1.50
7 Mark Brunell	.60	1.50
8 Daunte Culpepper	.60	1.50
9 Drew Bledsoe	.75	2.00
10 Tom Brady	2.00	5.00
11 Aaron Brooks	.60	1.50
12 Kerry Collins	.60	1.50
13 Kordell Stewart	.60	1.50
14 Drew Brees	1.25	3.00
15 Jeff Garcia	.60	1.50
16 Brad Johnson	.60	1.50
17 Steve McNair	.75	2.00
18 David Carr	.75	2.00
19 Joey Harrington	.75	2.00
20 Patrick Ramsey	.75	2.00

2002 Pacific War Room

COMPLETE SET (10)	12.00	30.00
STATED ODDS 1:73		
1 William Green	1.00	2.50
2 David Carr	1.25	3.00
3 Ashley Lelie	1.00	2.50
4 Kurt Kittner	.75	2.00
5 Josh Reed	1.00	2.50
6 Clinton Portis	1.50	4.00
7 Joey Harrington	1.25	3.00
8 Josh McCown	1.25	3.00
9 Patrick Ramsey	1.25	3.00
10 DeShaun Foster	1.25	3.00

2002 Pacific Adrenaline

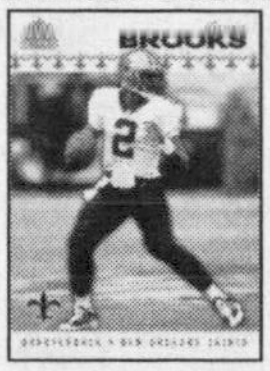

Released in September, 2002, this set features 288 cards including over 100 rookies. Boxes contained 36 packs, 10 cards per pack. There were 20 boxes per case. SRP was $2.99 per pack.

COMPLETE SET (288)	25.00	50.00
1 Damien Anderson RC	.40	1.00
2 David Boston	.20	.50
3 Wendell Bryant RC	.40	1.00
4 Thomas Jones	.30	.75
5 Jason McAddley RC	.50	1.25
6 Josh McCown RC	.60	1.50
7 Jake Plummer	.25	.60
8 Frank Sanders	.20	.50
9 Josh Scobey RC	.50	1.25
10 Keith Brooking	.20	.50
11 T.J. Duckett RC	.60	1.50
12 Warrick Dunn	.25	.60
13 Brian Finneran	.20	.50
14 Kahlil Hill RC	.40	1.00
15 Shawn Jefferson	.20	.50
16 Kurt Kittner RC	.40	1.00
17 Will Overstreet RC	.40	1.00
18 Michael Vick	.50	1.25
19 Ron Johnson RC	.50	1.25
20 Jamal Lewis	.25	.60
21 Ray Lewis	.30	.75
22 Chris Redman	.20	.50
23 Tellis Redmon RC	.40	1.00
24 Brandon Stokley	.25	.60
25 Chester Taylor RC	.60	1.50
26 Travis Taylor	.20	.50
27 Anthony Weaver RC	.40	1.00
28 Drew Bledsoe	.30	.75
29 Shawn Bryson	.20	.50
30 Larry Centers	.25	.60
31 Ryan Denney RC	.40	1.00
32 Travis Henry	.20	.50
33 Richard Huntley	.20	.50
34 Eric Moulds	.25	.60
35 Peerless Price	.20	.50
36 Josh Reed RC	.50	1.25
37 Isaac Byrd	.20	.50
38 Randy Fasani RC	.50	1.25
39 DeShaun Foster RC	.60	1.50
40 Kyle Johnson RC	.40	1.00
41 Muhsin Muhammad	.25	.60
42 Julius Peppers RC	1.25	3.00
43 Lamar Smith	.25	.60
44 Steve Smith	.30	.75
45 Chris Weinke	.20	.50
46 Marty Booker	.25	.60
47 Chris Chandler	.25	.60
48 Eric McCoo RC	.40	1.00
49 Jim Miller	.20	.50
50 Adrian Peterson RC	.60	1.50
51 Marcus Robinson	.25	.60
52 David Terrell	.20	.50
53 Anthony Thomas	.25	.60
54 Brian Urlacher	.30	.75
55 Corey Dillon	.25	.60
56 Gus Frerotte	.25	.60
57 Chad Johnson	.30	.75
58 Jon Kitna	.25	.60
59 Justin Smith	.20	.50
60 Takeo Spikes	.20	.50
61 Lamont Thompson RC	.50	1.25
62 Peter Warrick	.25	.60
63 Michael Westbrook	.20	.50
64 Tim Couch	.20	.50
65 Andre Davis RC	.50	1.25
66 JaJuan Dawson	.20	.50
67 William Green RC	.50	1.25
68 James Jackson	.20	.50
69 Kevin Johnson	.20	.50
70 Jamir Miller	.20	.50
71 Quincy Morgan	.20	.50
72 Jamel White	.20	.50
73 Antonio Bryant RC	.60	1.50
74 Quincy Carter	.20	.50
75 Woody Dantzler RC	.50	1.25
76 Joey Galloway	.25	.60
77 Ennis Haywood RC	.40	1.00
78 Chad Hutchinson RC	.40	1.00
79 Rocket Ismail	.25	.60
80 Emmitt Smith	.75	2.00
81 Roy Williams RC	.60	1.50
82 Mike Anderson	.25	.60
83 Terrell Davis	.30	.75
84 Brian Griese	.25	.60
85 Herb Haygood RC	.40	1.00
86 Ashley Lelie RC	.50	1.25
87 Ed McCaffrey	.25	.60
88 Deltha O'Neal	.20	.50
89 Clinton Portis RC	.75	2.00
90 Rod Smith	.25	.60
91 Scotty Anderson	.20	.50
92 Eddie Drummond RC	.40	1.00
93 Az-Zahir Hakim	.20	.50
94 Joey Harrington RC	.60	1.50
95 Mike McMahon	.20	.50
96 James Mungro RC	.60	1.50
97 Bill Schroeder	.20	.50
98 Luke Staley RC	.40	1.00
99 James Stewart	.20	.50
100 Marques Anderson RC	.50	1.25
101 Najeh Davenport RC	.60	1.50
102 Brett Favre	.75	2.00
103 Robert Ferguson	.25	.60
104 Bubba Franks	.25	.60
105 Terry Glenn	.25	.60
106 Ahman Green	.25	.60
107 Craig Nall RC	.50	1.25
108 Javon Walker RC	.60	1.50
109 James Allen	.20	.50
110 Jarrod Baxter RC	.40	1.00
111 Corey Bradford	.20	.50
112 David Carr RC	.60	1.50
113 Delvon Flowers RC	.40	1.00
114 Jabar Gaffney RC	.60	1.50
115 Jermaine Lewis	.20	.50
116 Travis Prentice	.20	.50
117 Jonathan Wells RC	.60	1.50
118 Brian Allen RC	.40	1.00
119 Chad Bratzke	.20	.50
120 Marvin Harrison	.30	.75
121 Qadry Ismail	.25	.60
122 Edgerrin James	.25	.60
123 Peyton Manning	.60	1.50
124 Rob Morris	.20	.50
125 Dominic Rhodes	.25	.60
126 Reggie Wayne	.30	.75
127 Tony Brackens	.20	.50
128 Mark Brunell	.25	.60
129 Donovin Darius	.20	.50
130 David Garrard RC	.75	2.00
131 John Henderson RC	.50	1.25
132 Stacey Mack	.20	.50
133 Bobby Shaw	.20	.50
134 Jimmy Smith	.25	.60
135 Fred Taylor	.25	.60
136 Omar Easy RC	.50	1.25
137 Eddie Freeman RC	.40	1.00
138 Tony Gonzalez	.30	.75
139 Trent Green	.25	.60
140 Priest Holmes	.30	.75
141 Eddie Kennison	.25	.60
142 Snoop Minnis	.20	.50
143 Johnnie Morton	.25	.60
144 Ryan Sims RC	.60	1.50
145 Chris Chambers	.25	.60
146 Jay Fiedler	.25	.60
147 Oronde Gadsden	.20	.50
148 Leonard Henry RC	.40	1.00
149 James McKnight	.20	.50
150 Travis Minor	.20	.50
151 Sam Simmons RC	.40	1.00
152 Zach Thomas	.30	.75
153 Ricky Williams	.25	.60
154 Derrick Alexander	.20	.50
155 Jeremy Allen RC	.40	1.00
156 Atrews Bell RC	.40	1.00
157 Michael Bennett	.25	.60
158 Kelly Campbell RC	.50	1.25
159 Byron Chamberlain	.20	.50
160 Doug Chapman	.20	.50
161 Daunte Culpepper	.25	.60
162 Randy Moss	.30	.75
163 Tom Brady	.75	2.00
164 Deion Branch RC	.60	1.50
165 Troy Brown	.25	.60
166 Rohan Davey RC	.60	1.50
167 Kevin Faulk	.25	.60
168 Daniel Graham RC	.50	1.25
169 David Patten	.20	.50
170 Antowain Smith	.25	.60
171 Antwoine Womack RC	.40	1.00
172 Aaron Brooks	.25	.60
173 Charlie Clemons	.20	.50
174 Joe Horn	.25	.60
175 Sammy Knight	.20	.50
176 Deuce McAllister	.25	.60
177 J.T. O'Sullivan RC	.50	1.25
178 Jerome Pathon	.20	.50
179 Donte Stallworth RC	.60	1.50
180 Ricky Williams RC	.50	1.25
181 Tiki Barber	.30	.75
182 Tim Carter RC	.50	1.25
183 Kerry Collins	.25	.60
184 Ron Dayne	.25	.60
185 Ike Hilliard	.25	.60
186 Daryl Jones RC	.40	1.00
187 Jeremy Shockey RC	1.00	2.50
188 Michael Strahan	.30	.75
189 Amani Toomer	.25	.60
190 Wayne Chrebet	.25	.60
191 Laveranues Coles	.25	.60
192 Alan Harper RC	.40	1.00
193 LaMont Jordan	.25	.60
194 Curtis Martin	.30	.75
195 Chad Morton	.20	.50
196 Santana Moss	.25	.60
197 Vinny Testaverde	.25	.60
198 Bryan Thomas RC	.40	1.00
199 Tim Brown	.30	.75
200 Ronald Curry RC	.50	1.25
201 Rich Gannon	.25	.60
202 Charlie Garner	.25	.60
203 Napoleon Harris RC	.50	1.25
204 Larry Ned RC	.40	1.00
205 Jerry Rice	.60	1.50
206 Tyrone Wheatley	.25	.60
207 Charles Woodson	.30	.75
208 Michael Lewis RC	.60	1.50
209 Donovan McNabb	.30	.75
210 Freddie Milons RC	.40	1.00
211 Freddie Mitchell	.20	.50
212 Todd Pinkston	.20	.50
213 Lito Sheppard RC	.60	1.50
214 Duce Staley	.25	.60
215 James Thrash	.25	.60
216 Brian Westbrook RC	1.00	2.50
217 Kendrell Bell	.20	.50
218 Jerome Bettis	.30	.75
219 Plaxico Burress	.25	.60
220 Verron Haynes RC	.40	1.00
221 Chris Hope RC	.60	1.50
222 Lee Mays RC	.40	1.00
223 Antwaan Randle El RC	.60	1.50
224 Kordell Stewart	.25	.60
225 Hines Ward	.30	.75
226 Isaac Bruce	.30	.75
227 Eric Crouch RC	.60	1.50
228 Marshall Faulk	.30	.75
229 Lamar Gordon RC	.50	1.25
230 Torry Holt	.30	.75
231 Leonard Little	.25	.60
232 Robert Thomas RC	.40	1.00
233 Kurt Warner	.30	.75
234 Terrence Wilkins	.20	.50
235 Drew Brees	.50	1.25
236 Seth Burford RC	.40	1.00
237 Reche Caldwell RC	.60	1.50
238 Curtis Conway	.25	.60
239 Doug Flutie	.30	.75
240 Quentin Jammer RC	.60	1.50
241 Brian Poli-Dixon RC	.40	1.00
242 Junior Seau	.30	.75
243 LaDainian Tomlinson	.40	1.00
244 Kevan Barlow	.20	.50
245 Andre Carter	.20	.50
246 Brandon Doman RC	.40	1.00
247 Jeff Garcia	.25	.60
248 Garrison Hearst	.25	.60
249 Terrell Owens	.30	.75
250 Derek Smith RC	.50	1.25
251 J.J. Stokes	.20	.50
252 Vinny Sutherland	.20	.50
253 Shaun Alexander	.25	.60
254 Chad Brown	.20	.50
255 Trent Dilfer	.25	.60
256 Bobby Engram	.25	.60
257 Darrell Jackson	.25	.60
258 Nakoa McElrath RC	.40	1.00
259 Maurice Morris RC	.50	1.25
260 Koren Robinson	.20	.50
261 Jerramy Stevens RC	.60	1.50
262 Mike Alstott	.25	.60
263 Derrick Brooks	.30	.75
264 Brad Johnson	.25	.60
265 Keyshawn Johnson	.25	.60
266 Keenan McCardell	.25	.60
267 Michael Pittman	.25	.60
268 Warren Sapp	.25	.60
269 Travis Stephens RC	.40	1.00
270 Marquise Walker RC	.40	1.00
271 Rocky Calmus RC	.50	1.25
272 Kevin Dyson	.25	.60
273 Eddie George	.25	.60
274 Albert Haynesworth RC	.60	1.50
275 Derrick Mason	.25	.60
276 Steve McNair	.30	.75
277 Dicenzo Miller RC	.40	1.00
278 Jake Schifino RC	.40	1.00
279 Tank Williams RC	.50	1.25
280 Champ Bailey	.30	.75
281 Ladell Betts RC	.60	1.50
282 Stephen Davis	.25	.60
283 Rod Gardner	.20	.50
284 Jacquez Green	.20	.50
285 Shane Matthews	.20	.50
286 Patrick Ramsey RC	.60	1.50
287 Cliff Russell RC	.40	1.00
288 Jeremiah Trotter	.20	.50

2002 Pacific Adrenaline Blue

*ROOKIES: 1.5X TO 4X BASIC CARDS
STATED ODDS 2:37
STATED PRINT RUN 165 SER.#'d SETS

2002 Pacific Adrenaline Red

*VETS: 1X TO 2.5X BASIC CARDS
*ROOKIES: .5X TO 1.2X
ONE PER PACK

2002 Pacific Adrenaline Driven

COMPLETE SET (27)	20.00	50.00
STATED ODDS 1:5		
1 T.J. Duckett	.75	2.00
2 Michael Vick	1.25	3.00
3 Drew Bledsoe	.75	2.00
4 DeShaun Foster	.75	2.00
5 Anthony Thomas	.60	1.50
6 William Green	.60	1.50
7 Emmitt Smith	2.00	5.00
8 Ashley Lelie	.60	1.50
9 Clinton Portis	1.00	2.50
10 Joey Harrington	.75	2.00
11 Brett Favre	2.00	5.00
12 Javon Walker	.75	2.00
13 David Carr	.75	2.00
14 Edgerrin James	.60	1.50
15 Ricky Williams	.60	1.50
16 Daunte Culpepper	.60	1.50
17 Randy Moss	.75	2.00
18 Tom Brady	2.00	5.00
19 Donte Stallworth	.75	2.00
20 Jerry Rice	1.50	4.00
21 Antwaan Randle El	.75	2.00
22 Eric Crouch	.75	2.00
23 Marshall Faulk	.75	2.00
24 Kurt Warner	.75	2.00
25 Drew Brees	1.25	3.00
26 LaDainian Tomlinson	1.00	2.50
27 Patrick Ramsey	.75	2.00

2002 Pacific Adrenaline Game Worn Jerseys

STATED ODDS 2:37
*GOLD/25: 1.2X TO 3X BASIC JSY
GOLD STATED PRINT RUN 25 SETS

1 Thomas Jones	5.00	12.00
2 Jake Plummer	4.00	10.00
3 Michael Vick	8.00	20.00
4 Chris Redman	3.00	8.00
5 Drew Bledsoe	5.00	12.00
6 Peerless Price	3.00	8.00
7 Brian Urlacher	5.00	12.00
8 Corey Dillon	4.00	10.00
9 Takeo Spikes	3.00	8.00
10 Tim Couch	3.00	8.00
11 Ken-Yon Rambo	3.00	8.00
12 Emmitt Smith	12.00	30.00
13 Mike Anderson	4.00	10.00
14 Brett Favre	12.00	30.00
15 Terry Glenn	4.00	10.00
16 Edgerrin James	4.00	10.00
17 Peyton Manning	10.00	25.00
18 Mark Brunell	4.00	10.00
19 Stacey Mack	3.00	8.00
20 Fred Taylor	4.00	10.00
21 Tony Richardson	3.00	8.00
22 Ricky Williams	4.00	10.00
23 Daunte Culpepper	4.00	10.00
24 Jim Kleinsasser	5.00	12.00
25 Randy Moss	5.00	12.00
26 Christian Fauria	3.00	8.00
27 Patrick Pass	3.00	8.00
28 Ron Dayne	4.00	10.00
29 Anthony Becht	3.00	8.00
30 LaMont Jordan	4.00	10.00
31 Curtis Martin	5.00	12.00
32 Jerry Rice	10.00	25.00
33 Jon Ritchie	3.00	8.00
34 Donovan McNabb	5.00	12.00
35 Brian Mitchell	4.00	10.00
36 Jerome Bettis	5.00	12.00
37 Mark Bruener	4.00	10.00
38 Kordell Stewart	4.00	10.00
39 Marshall Faulk	5.00	12.00
40 Kurt Warner	5.00	12.00
41 Terrence Wilkins	3.00	8.00
42 Drew Brees	8.00	20.00
43 Trevor Gaylor	3.00	8.00
44 LaDainian Tomlinson	6.00	15.00
45 Jeff Garcia	4.00	10.00
46 Terrell Owens	5.00	12.00
47 Shaun Alexander	4.00	10.00
48 Eddie George	4.00	10.00
49 Steve McNair	5.00	12.00
50 Shane Matthews	3.00	8.00

2002 Pacific Adrenaline Playmakers

COMPLETE SET (18)	10.00	25.00
STATED ODDS 1:5		
1 T.J. Duckett	.60	1.50
2 Michael Vick	1.00	2.50
3 Anthony Thomas	.50	1.25
4 William Green	.50	1.25
5 Emmitt Smith	1.50	4.00
6 Ashley Lelie	.50	1.25
7 Joey Harrington	.60	1.50
8 Brett Favre	1.50	4.00
9 David Carr	.60	1.50
10 Randy Moss	.60	1.50
11 Tom Brady	1.50	4.00
12 Donte Stallworth	.60	1.50
13 Jerry Rice	1.25	3.00
14 Donovan McNabb	.60	1.50
15 Eric Crouch	.60	1.50
16 Marshall Faulk	.60	1.50
17 Kurt Warner	.60	1.50
18 LaDainian Tomlinson	.75	2.00

2002 Pacific Adrenaline Power Surge

COMPLETE SET (6)	10.00	25.00
STATED ODDS 2:37		
1 Michael Vick	1.50	4.00
2 Emmitt Smith	2.50	6.00
3 Joey Harrington	1.00	2.50
4 Brett Favre	2.50	6.00
5 David Carr	1.00	2.50
6 Tom Brady	2.50	6.00

2002 Pacific Adrenaline Rookie Report

COMPLETE SET (12)	10.00	25.00
STATED ODDS 1:7		
1 T.J. Duckett	.50	1.25
2 DeShaun Foster	.50	1.25
3 William Green	.40	1.00
4 Ashley Lelie	.40	1.00
5 Clinton Portis	.60	1.50
6 Joey Harrington	.50	1.25
7 Javon Walker	.50	1.25
8 David Carr	.50	1.25
9 Jabar Gaffney	.50	1.25
10 Donte Stallworth	.50	1.25
11 Antwaan Randle El	.50	1.25
12 Patrick Ramsey	.50	1.25

2002 Pacific Adrenaline Rush

COMPLETE SET (18)	10.00	25.00
STATED ODDS 1:5		
1 T.J. Duckett	.60	1.50
2 DeShaun Foster	.60	1.50
3 Anthony Thomas	.50	1.25
4 Corey Dillon	.50	1.25
5 William Green	.50	1.25
6 Emmitt Smith	1.50	4.00
7 Terrell Davis	.60	1.50
8 Clinton Portis	.75	2.00
9 Ahman Green	.50	1.25
10 Edgerrin James	.50	1.25
11 Priest Holmes	.60	1.50
12 Ricky Williams	.50	1.25
13 Curtis Martin	.60	1.50
14 Jerome Bettis	.50	1.25
15 Marshall Faulk	.60	1.50
16 LaDainian Tomlinson	.75	2.00
17 Shaun Alexander	.50	1.25
18 Eddie George	.50	1.25

1996 Pacific Dynagon

The 1996 Dynagon Prism set was issued in one series totalling 144 cards. The set was issued in two card packs with 36 packs in a box and 20 boxes in a case. Against a gold background which includes a NFL football, the player's photo is shown. The player's name is printed on the right. The horizontal backs include another photo as well as some text. The set is sequenced in alphabetical order within alphabetical team order. Rookie Cards include Tim Biakabutuka, Eddie George, Terry Glenn, Keyshawn Johnson and Lawrence Phillips.

COMPLETE SET (144)	25.00	60.00
1 Larry Centers	.30	.75
2 Garrison Hearst	.30	.75
3 Dave Krieg	.15	.40
4 Frank Sanders	.30	.75
5 Jeff George	.30	.75
6 Craig Heyward	.15	.40
7 Terance Mathis	.15	.40
8 Eric Metcalf	.15	.40
9 Todd Collins	.30	.75
10 Darick Holmes	.15	.40
11 Jim Kelly	.60	1.50
12 Eric Moulds RC	1.50	4.00
13 Bryce Paup	.15	.40
14 Thurman Thomas	.60	1.50
15 Tim Biakabutuka RC	.60	1.50
16 Blake Brockermeyer	.15	.40
17 Mark Carrier WR	.15	.40
18 Kerry Collins	.60	1.50
19 Derrick Moore	.15	.40
20 Bobby Engram RC	.60	1.50
21 Jeff Graham	.15	.40
22 Erik Kramer	.15	.40
23 Rashaan Salaam	.30	.75
24 Steve Stenstrom	.15	.40
25 Chris Zorich	.15	.40
26 Jeff Blake	.60	1.50
27 David Dunn	.15	.40
28 Carl Pickens	.30	.75
29 Darnay Scott	.30	.75
30 Earnest Byner	.15	.40
31 Leroy Hoard	.15	.40
32 Keenan McCardell	.60	1.50
33 Eric Zeier	.15	.40
34 Troy Aikman	1.25	3.00
35 Chris Boniol	.15	.40
36 Michael Irvin	.60	1.50
37 Daryl Johnston	.30	.75
38 Deion Sanders	.75	2.00
39 Emmitt Smith	2.00	5.00
40 Stepfret Williams	.15	.40
41 John Elway	2.50	6.00
42 Terrell Davis	1.00	2.50
*43 Anthony Miller	.30	.75
44 Shannon Sharpe	.30	.75
45 Scott Mitchell	.30	.75

46 Herman Moore	.30	.75
47 Brett Perriman	.15	.40
48 Barry Sanders	2.00	5.00
49 Cory Schlesinger	.15	.40
50 Edgar Bennett	.30	.75
51 Robert Brooks	.60	1.50
52 Mark Chmura	.30	.75
53 Brett Favre	2.50	6.00
54 Reggie White	.60	1.50
55 Eddie George RC	1.50	4.00
56 Steve McNair	1.00	2.50
57 Chris Sanders	.30	.75
58 Rodney Thomas	.15	.40
59 Ben Bronson RC	.15	.40
60 Zack Crockett	.15	.40
61 Marshall Faulk	.75	2.00
62 Jim Harbaugh	.30	.75
63 Mark Brunell	.75	2.00
64 Kevin Hardy RC	.60	1.50
65 Willie Jackson	.30	.75
66 Pete Mitchell	.30	.75
67 James O.Stewart	.30	.75
68 Marcus Allen	.60	1.50
69 Steve Bono	.15	.40
70 Lake Dawson	.15	.40
71 Neil Smith	.30	.75
72 Tamarick Vanover	.30	.75
73 Irving Fryar	.30	.75
74 Terry Kirby	.30	.75
75 Dan Marino	2.50	6.00
76 O.J. McDuffie	.30	.75
77 Bernie Parmalee	.15	.40
78 Stanley Pritchett RC	.30	.75
79 Cris Carter	.60	1.50
80 Qadry Ismail	.30	.75
81 Chad May	.15	.40
82 Warren Moon	.30	.75
83 Robert Smith	.30	.75
84 Drew Bledsoe	.75	2.00
85 Ben Coates	.30	.75
86 Terry Glenn RC	1.25	3.00
87 Curtis Martin	1.00	2.50
88 Willie McGinest	.15	.40
89 Mario Bates	.30	.75
90 Jim Everett	.15	.40
91 Wayne Martin	.15	.40
92 Shane Pahukoa RC	.15	.40
93 Ray Zellars	.15	.40
94 Dave Brown	.15	.40
95 Chris Calloway	.15	.40
96 Rodney Hampton	.30	.75
97 Tyrone Wheatley	.30	.75
98 Wayne Chrebet	.75	2.00
99 Glenn Foley	.30	.75
100 Keyshawn Johnson RC	1.25	3.00
101 Adrian Murrell	.30	.75
102 Alex Van Dyke RC	.30	.75
103 Tim Brown	.60	1.50
104 Billy Joe Hobert	.30	.75
105 Rocket Ismail	.15	.40
106 Napoleon Kaufman	.60	1.50
107 Harvey Williams	.15	.40
108 Charlie Garner	.30	.75
109 Rodney Peete	.15	.40
110 Ricky Watters	.30	.75
111 Calvin Williams	.15	.40
112 Mark Bruener	.15	.40
113 Kevin Greene	.30	.75
114 Ernie Mills	.15	.40
115 Kordell Stewart	.60	1.50
116 Yancey Thigpen	.30	.75
117 Dave Barr	.15	.40
118 Jerome Bettis	.60	1.50
119 Isaac Bruce	.60	1.50
120 Lawrence Phillips RC	.60	1.50
121 J.T. Thomas	.15	.40
122 Ronnie Harmon	.15	.40
123 Aaron Hayden RC	.15	.40
124 Stan Humphries	.30	.75
125 Junior Seau	.60	1.50
126 William Floyd	.30	.75
127 Elvis Grbac	.30	.75
128 Jerry Rice	1.25	3.00
129 J.J. Stokes	.60	1.50
130 Steve Young	1.00	2.50
131 Joey Galloway	.60	1.50
132 Cortez Kennedy	.15	.40
133 Kevin Mawae	.15	.40
134 Rick Mirer	.30	.75
135 Chris Warren	.30	.75
136 Trent Dilfer	.60	1.50
137 Jerry Ellison	.15	.40
138 Alvin Harper	.15	.40
139 Errict Rhett	.30	.75
140 Terry Allen	.30	.75
141 Brian Mitchell	.15	.40
142 Gus Frerotte	.30	.75
143 Michael Westbrook	.60	1.50
144 Heath Shuler	.30	.75

1996 Pacific Dynagon Best Kept Secrets

COMPLETE SET (100)	15.00	30.00
ONE PER PACK		
1 Wendall Gaines	.07	.20
2 Randy Kirk	.07	.20
3 Anthony Redmon	.07	.20
4 Bernard Wilson	.07	.20
5 Ron Davis	.07	.20
6 Roell Preston	.15	.40
7 Robbie Tobeck	.07	.20
8 Harold Bishop	.07	.20
9 Dan Footman	.07	.20
10 Ernest Hunter	.07	.20
11 Tony Cline	.07	.20
12 Kurt Schulz	.07	.20
13 Alex Van Pelt	.50	1.25
14 Howard Griffith	.07	.20
15 Mark Thomas	.07	.20
16 Keshon Johnson	.07	.20
17 Kevin Miniefield	.07	.20
18 Steve Stenstrom	.15	.40
19 Jeff Cothran	.07	.20
20 Jeff Hill	.07	.20
21 Alundis Brice	.07	.20
22 Cory Fleming	.07	.20
23 Kendell Watkins	.07	.20
24 Charlie Williams	.07	.20
25 Byron Chamberlain	.60	1.50
26 Jerry Evans	.07	.20
27 Rod Smith WR	1.25	3.00
28 Kevin Hickman	.07	.20
29 Ron Rivers	.15	.40
30 Henry Thomas	.07	.20
31 Keith Crawford	.07	.20
32 Doug Evans	.15	.40
33 William Henderson	.25	.60
34 John Jurkovic	.07	.20
35 Blaine Bishop	.07	.20
36 Kenny Davidson	.07	.20
37 Erik Norgard	.07	.20
38 Derwin Gray	.07	.20
39 Ellis Johnson	.07	.20
40 Tony McCoy	.07	.20
41 Glen Sanders	.07	.20
42 Bernard Whittington	.07	.20
43 Travis Davis	.07	.20
44 Rogerick Green	.07	.20
45 Rob Johnson	.25	.60
46 Curtis Marsh	.07	.20
47 Matt Blundin	.15	.40
48 Lin Elliott	.07	.20
49 Pellom McDaniels	.07	.20
50 Kirby Dar Dar	.15	.40
51 Jeff Kopp	.07	.20
52 Billy Milner	.07	.20
53 Tuineau Alipate	.07	.20
54 Jeff Brady	.07	.20
55 David Dixon	.07	.20
56 Mike Morris	.07	.20
57 Max Lane	.07	.20
58 Tim Roberts	.07	.20
59 Reggie E.White	.07	.20
60 Tommy Hodson	.07	.20
61 Joe Johnson	.15	.40
62 Gary Downs	.07	.20
63 Gary Harrell	.07	.20
64 Robert Harris	.07	.20
65 Kenyon Rasheed	.07	.20
66 Richie Anderson	.25	.60
67 Matt Brock	.07	.20
68 Hugh Douglas	.15	.40
69 Jeff Gossett	.07	.20
70 Mike Jones	.07	.20
71 Mike Morton	.07	.20
72 Anthony Smith	.07	.20
73 Jay Fiedler	1.50	4.00
74 Frank Wainright	.07	.20
75 Marc Woodard	.07	.20
76 Eric Zomalt	.07	.20
77 Chad Brown	.07	.20
78 James Parrish	.07	.20
79 Justin Strzelczyk	.07	.20
80 Darryl Ashmore	.07	.20
81 Gerald McBurrows	.07	.20
82 Lovell Pinkney	.07	.20
83 Lewis Bush	.07	.20
84 Eric Castle	.07	.20
85 Terrance Shaw	.07	.20
86 Frank Pollack	.07	.20
87 Kirk Scrafford	.07	.20
88 Alfred Williams	.07	.20
89 Carlton Gray	.07	.20
90 James McKnight	.60	1.50
91 Todd Peterson	.07	.20
92 Dean Wells	.07	.20
93 Curtis Buckley	.07	.20
94 Thomas Everett	.07	.20
95 Pete Pierson	.07	.20
96 Jamie Asher	.15	.40
97 William Bell	.07	.20
98 Trent Green	.75	2.00
99 Richard Huntley	.15	.40
100 Terrell Owens	2.00	5.00

1996 Pacific Dynagon Dynamic Duos

COMPLETE SET (24)	60.00	120.00
DD1-DD12: STATED ODDS 1:37 HOBBY		
DD13-DD24: STATED ODDS 1:37 RETAIL		
DD1 Troy Aikman	3.00	8.00
DD2 Jerry Rice	3.00	8.00
DD3 Brett Favre	6.00	15.00
DD4 Marshall Faulk	2.00	5.00
DD5 Carl Pickens	.75	2.00
DD6 Terrell Davis	2.50	6.00
DD7 Curtis Martin	2.50	6.00
DD8 Dan Marino	6.00	15.00
DD9 Herman Moore	.75	2.00
DD10 Kordell Stewart	1.50	4.00
DD11 Emmitt Smith	5.00	12.00
DD12 Trent Dilfer	1.50	4.00
DD13 Deion Sanders	2.00	5.00
DD14 Steve Young	2.50	6.00
DD15 Robert Brooks	1.50	4.00
DD16 Jim Harbaugh	.75	2.00
DD17 Jeff Blake	1.50	4.00
DD18 John Elway	6.00	15.00
DD19 Drew Bledsoe	2.00	5.00
DD20 Bernie Parmalee	.40	1.00
DD21 Barry Sanders	5.00	12.00
DD22 Kevin Greene	.75	2.00
DD23 Sherman Williams	.40	1.00
DD24 Errict Rhett	.75	2.00

1996 Pacific Dynagon Kings of the NFL

COMPLETE SET (10)	60.00	150.00
STATED ODDS 1:361		
K1 Emmitt Smith	8.00	20.00
K2 Dan Marino	10.00	25.00
K3 Barry Sanders	8.00	20.00
K4 Curtis Martin	4.00	10.00
K5 Brett Favre	10.00	25.00
K6 Kordell Stewart	2.50	6.00
K7 Emmitt Smith	8.00	20.00
K8 Jerry Rice	5.00	12.00
K9 John Elway	10.00	25.00
K10 Dan Marino	10.00	25.00

1996 Pacific Dynagon Tandems

COMPLETE SET (72)	150.00	400.00
STATED ODDS 1:37		
1 Dan Marino Troy Aikman	12.50	30.00
2 Emmitt Smith Rashaan Salaam	10.00	25.00
3 Jim Kelly John Elway	12.50	30.00
4 Steve Young Brett Favre	12.50	30.00
5 Curtis Martin Terrell Davis	7.50	20.00
6 Kordell Stewart Napoleon Kaufman	4.00	10.00
7 Barry Sanders Jerry Rice	12.50	30.00
8 Joey Galloway J.J.Stokes	4.00	10.00
9 Kerry Collins Jeff Blake	4.00	10.00
10 Deion Sanders Reggie White	6.00	15.00
11 Herman Moore Mark Chmura	2.50	6.00
12 Eric Zeier Tyrone Wheatley	2.50	6.00
13 Errict Rhett Robert Brooks	2.50	6.00
14 Trent Dilfer Steve McNair	6.00	15.00
15 Marshall Faulk Drew Bledsoe	6.00	15.00
16 Tamarick Vanover Michael Westbrook	2.50	6.00
17 Heath Shuler Jerome Bettis	4.00	10.00
18 Isaac Bruce Tim Brown	4.00	10.00
19 Terry Allen Chris Warren	2.50	6.00
20 Brian Mitchell Alex Van Dyke	2.50	6.00
21 Jerry Ellison Kevin Mawae	1.50	4.00
22 Alvin Harper Stanley Pritchett	2.50	6.00
23 Rick Mirer Elvis Grbac	2.50	6.00
24 Cortez Kennedy Junior Seau	4.00	10.00
25 William Floyd Aaron Hayden	2.50	6.00
26 Stan Humphries Dave Barr	2.50	6.00
27 J.T.Thomas Stepfret Williams	1.50	4.00
28 Ronnie Harmon Yancey Thigpen	2.50	6.00
29 Ernie Mills Calvin Williams	1.50	4.00
30 Mark Bruener Eddie George	4.00	10.00
31 Kevin Greene Eric Moulds	4.00	10.00
32 Ricky Watters Harvey Williams	2.50	6.00
33 Rodney Peete Keyshawn Johnson	4.00	10.00
34 Charlie Garner Adrian Murrell	2.50	6.00
35 Rocket Ismail Wayne Chrebet	4.00	10.00
36 Billy Joe Hobert Glenn Foley	1.50	4.00
37 Rodney Hampton Ben Coates	2.50	6.00
38 Chris Calloway Qadry Ismail	2.50	6.00
39 Dave Brown Warren Moon	4.00	10.00
40 Ray Zellars Robert Smith	2.50	6.00
41 Shane Pahukoa Bernie Parmalee	1.50	4.00
42 Wayne Martin Neil Smith	1.50	4.00
43 Jim Everett Steve Bono	2.50	6.00
44 Mario Bates Terry Kirby	2.50	6.00
45 Willie McGinest Lawrence Phillips	4.00	10.00
46 Chad May Mark Brunell	2.50	6.00
47 Cris Carter O.J. McDuffie	4.00	10.00
48 Irving Fryar Lake Dawson	2.50	6.00
49 Marcus Allen James O.Stewart	4.00	10.00
50 Willie Jackson Terry Glenn	2.50	6.00
51 Pete Mitchell Kevin Hardy	2.50	6.00
52 Jim Harbaugh Scott Mitchell	2.50	6.00
53 Zack Crockett Rodney Thomas	2.50	6.00
54 Ben Bronson Chris Sanders	2.50	6.00
55 Edgar Bennett Tim Biakabutuka	2.50	6.00
56 Brett Perriman Anthony Miller	2.50	6.00
57 Cory Schlesinger Daryl Johnston	2.50	6.00
58 Shannon Sharpe Michael Irvin	4.00	10.00
59 Chris Boniol Thurman Thomas	4.00	10.00
60 Keenan McCardell Darnay Scott	2.50	6.00
61 Leroy Hoard Chris Zorich	1.50	4.00
62 Earnest Byner Jeff Graham	2.50	6.00
63 Carl Pickens Darick Holmes	1.50	4.00
64 David Dunn Mark Carrier WR	2.50	6.00
65 Steve Stenstrom Todd Collins	2.50	6.00
66 Erik Kramer Derrick Moore	2.50	6.00
67 Larry Centers Bobby Engram	2.50	6.00
68 Garrison Hearst Jeff George	2.50	6.00
69 Dave Krieg Craig Heyward	2.50	6.00
70 Frank Sanders Terance Mathis	2.50	6.00
71 Gus Frerotte Eric Metcalf	2.50	6.00
72 Bryce Paup Blake Brockermeyer	1.50	4.00

1997 Pacific Dynagon

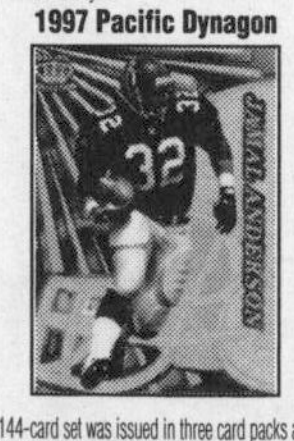

This 144-card set was issued in three card packs and recognizes some of the hottest players in the NFL. The fronts feature action color player images on a background of a football helmet and rays foiled in gold. The backs carry player information.

COMPLETE SET (144)	40.00	80.00
1 Larry Centers	.40	1.00
2 Kent Graham	.25	.60
3 Leeland McElroy	.25	.60
4 Frank Sanders	.40	1.00
5 Jamal Anderson	.50	1.25
6 Bert Emanuel	.40	1.00
7 Bobby Hebert	.25	.60
8 Terance Mathis	.40	1.00
9 Eric Metcalf	.40	1.00
10 Derrick Alexander WR	.40	1.00
11 Earnest Byner	.25	.60
12 Michael Jackson	.40	1.00
13 Vinny Testaverde	.40	1.00
14 Quinn Early	.25	.60
15 Jim Kelly	.50	1.25
16 Eric Moulds	.50	1.25
17 Andre Reed	.40	1.00
18 Bruce Smith	.40	1.00
19 Thurman Thomas	.50	1.25
20 Tim Biakabutuka	.40	1.00
21 Mark Carrier WR	.25	.60
22 Kerry Collins	.50	1.25
23 Kevin Greene	.40	1.00
24 Anthony Johnson	.25	.60
25 Wesley Walls	.40	1.00
26 Curtis Conway	.40	1.00
27 Bobby Engram	.40	1.00
28 Raymont Harris	.25	.60
29 Dave Krieg	.25	.60
30 Rashaan Salaam	.25	.60
31 Jeff Blake	.40	1.00
32 Ki-Jana Carter	.25	.60
33 Garrison Hearst	.40	1.00
34 Carl Pickens	.40	1.00
35 Darnay Scott	.40	1.00
36 Troy Aikman	1.00	2.50
37 Chris Boniol	.25	.60
38 Michael Irvin	.50	1.25
39 Deion Sanders	.50	1.25
40 Emmitt Smith	1.50	4.00
41 Herschel Walker	.40	1.00
42 Terrell Davis	.60	1.50
43 John Elway	2.00	5.00
44 Ed McCaffrey	.40	1.00
45 Shannon Sharpe	.40	1.00
46 Alfred Williams	.25	.60
47 Scott Mitchell	.40	1.00
48 Herman Moore	.40	1.00
49 Brett Perriman	.25	.60
50 Barry Sanders	1.50	4.00
51 Edgar Bennett	.40	1.00
52 Robert Brooks	.40	1.00
53 Mark Chmura	.40	1.00
54 Brett Favre	2.00	5.00
55 Antonio Freeman	.50	1.25
56 Desmond Howard	.40	1.00
57 Reggie White	.50	1.25
58 Chris Chandler	.40	1.00
59 Eddie George	.50	1.25
60 James McKeehan	.25	.60
61 Steve McNair	.60	1.50
62 Chris Sanders	.25	.60
63 Sean Dawkins	.25	.60
64 Ken Dilger	.25	.60
65 Marshall Faulk	.60	1.50
66 Jim Harbaugh	.40	1.00
67 Marvin Harrison	.50	1.25
68 Tony Boselli	.25	.60
69 Mark Brunell	.60	1.50
70 Keenan McCardell	.40	1.00
71 Natrone Means	.40	1.00
72 Jimmy Smith	.40	1.00
73 Marcus Allen	.50	1.25
74 Kimble Anders	.40	1.00
75 Dale Carter	.25	.60
76 Greg Hill	.25	.60
77 Derrick Thomas	.50	1.25
78 Tamarick Vanover	.40	1.00
79 Karim Abdul-Jabbar	.50	1.25
80 Dan Marino	2.00	5.00
81 O.J. McDuffie	.40	1.00
82 Jerris McPhail	.25	.60
83 Zach Thomas	.50	1.25
84 Cris Carter	.50	1.25
85 Brad Johnson	.50	1.25
86 Jake Reed	.40	1.00
87 Robert Smith	.40	1.00
88 Drew Bledsoe	.60	1.50
89 Ben Coates	.40	1.00
90 Terry Glenn	.50	1.25
91 Curtis Martin	.60	1.50
92 Willie McGinest	.25	.60
93 Jim Everett	.25	.60
94 Michael Haynes	.25	.60
95 Haywood Jeffires	.25	.60
96 Ray Zellars	.25	.60
97 Dave Brown	.25	.60
98 Rodney Hampton	.40	1.00
99 Danny Kanell	.40	1.00
100 Thomas Lewis	.25	.60
101 Wayne Chrebet	.50	1.25
102 Keyshawn Johnson	.50	1.25
103 Adrian Murrell	.40	1.00
104 Neil O'Donnell	.40	1.00
105 Tim Brown	.50	1.25
106 Rickey Dudley	.40	1.00
107 Jeff Hostetler	.25	.60
108 Napoleon Kaufman	.50	1.25
109 Ty Detmer	.40	1.00
110 Jason Dunn	.25	.60
111 Irving Fryar	.40	1.00
112 Chris T. Jones	.25	.60
113 Ricky Watters	.40	1.00
114 Jerome Bettis	.50	1.25
115 Chad Brown	.25	.60
116 Kordell Stewart	.50	1.25
117 Mike Tomczak	.25	.60
118 Rod Woodson	.40	1.00
119 Tony Banks	.40	1.00
120 Isaac Bruce	.50	1.25
121 Eddie Kennison	.40	1.00
122 Lawrence Phillips	.25	.60
123 Terrell Fletcher	.25	.60
124 Stan Humphries	.40	1.00
125 Tony Martin	.40	1.00
126 Junior Seau	.50	1.25
127 Elvis Grbac	.40	1.00
128 Terrell Owens	.60	1.50
129 Ted Popson RC	.25	.60
130 Jerry Rice	1.00	2.50
131 Steve Young	.60	1.50
132 John Friesz	.25	.60
133 Joey Galloway	.40	1.00
134 Michael McCrary	.25	.60
135 Lamar Smith	.50	1.25
136 Chris Warren	.40	1.00
137 Mike Alstott	.50	1.25
138 Trent Dilfer	.50	1.25
139 Courtney Hawkins	.25	.60
140 Errict Rhett	.25	.60
141 Terry Allen	.50	1.25
142 Henry Ellard	.25	.60
143 Gus Frerotte	.25	.60
144 Leslie Shepherd	.25	.60
C Mark Brunell Sample	.75	2.00

1997 Pacific Dynagon Copper

COMPLETE SET (144)	300.00	600.00
*COPPER STARS: 2X TO 5X BASIC CARDS		
STATED ODDS 2:37 HOBBY		

1997 Pacific Dynagon Red

COMPLETE SET (144)	300.00	600.00
*RED CARDS: 4X TO 8X BASIC CARDS		
STATED ODDS 4:21 SPECIAL RETAIL		

1997 Pacific Dynagon Silver

COMPLETE SET (144)	400.00	800.00
*SILVER CARDS: 3.5X TO 7X BASIC CARDS		
STATED ODDS 2:37 RETAIL		

1997 Pacific Dynagon Best Kept Secrets

COMPLETE SET (110)	10.00	25.00
ONE OR TWO PER PACK		
1 Mark Brunell	.30	.75
2 Bob Dahl	.08	.25
3 Tommy Bennett	.08	.25
4 Jamal Anderson	.25	.60
5 Jermaine Lewis	.25	.60
6 Chris Brantley	.08	.25
7 Mathew Campbell	.08	.25
8 Jeff Jaeger	.08	.25
9 Marco Battaglia	.08	.25
10 Troy Aikman	.50	1.25
11 Terrell Davis	.30	.75
12 Jeff Hartings	.25	.60
13 Brett Favre	1.25	2.50
14 Eddie George	.25	.60
15 Elijah Alexander	.08	.25
16 Bryan Barker	.08	.25
17 Louie Aguiar	.08	.25
18 Karim Abdul-Jabbar	.25	.60
19 Greg DeLong	.08	.25
20 Drew Bledsoe	.30	.75
21 Jim Everett	.08	.25
22 Keith Elias	.08	.25
23 Richie Anderson	.15	.40
24 Joe Aska	.08	.25
25 Barrett Brooks	.08	.25
26 Jerome Bettis	.25	.60
27 Darryl Ashmore	.08	.25
28 Tony Berti	.08	.25
29 Frank Pollack	.08	.25
30 Joey Galloway	.15	.40
31 Jason Maniecki	.08	.25
32 Trent Green	.30	.75
33 Pat Carter	.08	.25
34 Ruben Brown	.08	.25
35 Kerry Collins	.25	.60
36 Keith Jennings	.08	.25
37 Randall Godfrey	.08	.25
38 David Diaz-Infante	.08	.25
39 Derek Price	.08	.25
40 William Henderson	.15	.40
41 James Ritchey	.08	.25
42 Richard Dent	.08	.25
43 Ben Coleman	.08	.25
44 Shane Burton	.15	.40
45 Dixon Edwards	.08	.25
46 Ted Johnson	.25	.60
47 Harry Boatswain	.08	.25
48 Derrick Fenner	.08	.25
49 Ty Detmer	.15	.40
50 Corey Holliday	.08	.25
51 Jerry Rice	.50	1.25
52 Boomer Esiason	.15	.40
53 Jeff Pahukoa	.08	.25
54 Scott Otis	.08	.25
55 Darick Holmes	.08	.25
56 Frank Garcia	.08	.25
57 Michael Lowery	.08	.25
58 Jeff Blake	.15	.40
59 Dale Hellestrae	.08	.25
60 John Elway	1.00	2.50
61 Barry Sanders	.75	2.00
62 Dorsey Levens	.25	.60
63 James Roberson	.08	.25
64 Jim Harbaugh	.15	.40
65 Travis Davis	.08	.25
66 Marcus Allen	.25	.60
67 Steve Emtman	.08	.25
68 Martin Harrison	.08	.25
69 Curtis Martin	.30	.75
70 Anthony Newman	.08	.25
71 Ron Stone	.08	.25
72 Reggie Cobb	.08	.25
73 Robert Jenkins	.08	.25
74 Morris Unutoa	.08	.25
75 Kordell Stewart	.25	.60
76 Raylee Johnson	.15	.40
77 Tommy Thompson	.08	.25
78 Dou Innocent	.08	.25
79 Jim Pyne	.08	.25
80 Jim Kelly	.25	.60
81 Leeland McElroy	.08	.25
82 Dan Stryzinski	.08	.25
83 James Roe	.08	.25
84 Anthony Johnson	.08	.25
85 Chris Villarrial	.08	.25
86 Kerry Joseph	.25	.60
87 Emmitt Smith	.75	2.00
88 Jeff Lewis	.08	.25
89 Kerwin Waldroup	.08	.25
90 Aaron Taylor	.08	.25
91 Sheddrick Wilson	.08	.25
92 Chris Hetherington	.15	.40
93 Bryan Schwartz	.08	.25
94 Reggie Tongue	.08	.25
95 Dan Marino	1.00	2.50
96 Warren Moon	.25	.60
97 Pio Sagapolutele	.08	.25
98 Austin Robbins	.08	.25
99 Stan White	.08	.25
100 Keyshawn Johnson	.25	.60
101 Napoleon Kaufman	.25	.60
102 Ricky Watters	.15	.40
103 Jon Witman	.15	.40
104 Jermaine Ross	.08	.25
105 Leonard Russell	.08	.25
106 Iheanyi Uwaezuoke	.15	.40
107 Gino Torretta	.08	.25
108 Robb Thomas	.08	.25
109 Shar Pourdanesh	.08	.25
110 Gabe Northern	.08	.25

1997 Pacific Dynagon Careers

COMPLETE SET (10)	40.00	100.00
STATED ODDS: 2:721		
*HOLO.GOLDS: 1.2X TO 3X BASIC INSERTS		
*SILVERS: 2X TO 4X BASIC INSERTS		
*PURPLES: 2X TO 4X BASIC INSERTS		
STATED PRINT RUN 30 EACH COLOR		
1 Jim Kelly	2.00	5.00
2 Emmitt Smith	6.00	15.00
3 John Elway	8.00	20.00
4 Barry Sanders	6.00	15.00
5 Brett Favre	8.00	20.00
6 Reggie White	2.00	5.00
7 Dan Marino	8.00	20.00
8 Drew Bledsoe	2.50	6.00
9 Jerry Rice	4.00	10.00
10 Steve Young	2.50	6.00

1997 Pacific Dynagon Player of the Week

COMPLETE SET (20)	30.00	80.00
STATED ODDS 1:37		
1 Karim Abdul-Jabbar	1.25	3.00
2 Eddie George	1.25	3.00
3 Curtis Martin	1.50	4.00
4 Mark Brunell	1.50	4.00
5 John Elway	5.00	12.00
6 Drew Bledsoe	1.50	4.00
7 Emmitt Smith	4.00	10.00
8 Terrell Davis	1.50	4.00
9 Troy Aikman	2.50	6.00
10 Jerry Rice	2.50	6.00
11 Dan Marino	5.00	12.00
12 Barry Sanders	4.00	10.00
13 Brett Favre	5.00	12.00
14 Steve Young	1.50	4.00
15 Kerry Collins	1.25	3.00
16 Eddie Kennison	1.00	2.50
17 Terry Allen	1.25	3.00
18 Brett Favre	5.00	12.00
19 Desmond Howard	1.00	2.50
20 Mark Brunell	1.50	4.00

1997 Pacific Dynagon Royal Connections

COMPLETE SET (30)	100.00	200.00
STATED ODDS: 1:73		
1A Kent Graham	1.25	3.00
1B Larry Centers	2.00	5.00
2A Jim Kelly	2.50	6.00
2B Andre Reed	2.00	5.00
3A Kerry Collins	2.50	6.00
3B Wesley Walls	2.00	5.00
4A Jeff Blake	2.00	5.00
4B Carl Pickens	2.00	5.00
5A Troy Aikman	5.00	12.00
5B Michael Irvin	2.50	6.00
6A John Elway	10.00	25.00
6B Shannon Sharpe	2.00	5.00
7A Brett Favre	10.00	25.00
7B Antonio Freeman	2.50	6.00
8A Mark Brunell	2.50	6.00
8B Keenan McCardell	2.00	5.00
9A Dan Marino	10.00	25.00
9B O.J. McDuffie	2.00	5.00
10A Brad Johnson	2.50	6.00
10B Jake Reed	2.00	5.00
11A Drew Bledsoe	3.00	8.00
11B Terry Glenn	2.50	6.00
12A Ty Detmer	2.00	5.00
12B Irving Fryar	2.00	5.00
13A Kordell Stewart	2.50	6.00
13B Charles Johnson	2.00	5.00
14A Tony Banks	2.00	5.00
14B Isaac Bruce	2.50	6.00
15A Steve Young	3.00	8.00
15B Jerry Rice	5.00	12.00

1997 Pacific Dynagon Tandems

COMPLETE SET (72)	50.00	120.00
STATED ODDS: 1:37		
1 Jerome Bettis Eddie George	1.50	4.00
2 Jamal Anderson Eric Moulds	1.50	4.00
3 Kerry Collins Kordell Stewart	1.50	4.00
4 Jeff Blake Ty Detmer	1.25	3.00
5 Michael Irvin Tim Brown	1.50	4.00
6 Deion Sanders Ray Zellars	1.50	4.00
7 Emmitt Smith Steve Young	5.00	12.00
8 Terrell Davis Barry Sanders	5.00	12.00
9 John Elway Dan Marino	6.00	15.00
10 Robert Brooks Eddie Kennison	1.25	3.00
11 Mark Chmura Shannon Sharpe	1.25	3.00
12 Brett Favre Mark Brunell	5.00	12.00
13 Antonio Freeman Isaac Bruce	1.50	4.00
14 Desmond Howard Natrone Means	1.25	3.00
15 Reggie White Keyshawn Johnson	1.50	4.00
16 Edgar Bennett Chris Sanders	.75	2.00
17 Terry Glenn Jerry Rice	4.00	10.00
18 Steve McNair Karim Abdul-Jabbar	1.50	4.00
19 Marshall Faulk Tamarick Vanover	2.00	5.00
20 Gus Frerotte Brad Johnson	1.25	3.00
21 Jim Kelly Tim Biakabutuka	1.50	4.00
22 Lawrence Phillips Ben Coates	.75	2.00
23 Napoleon Kaufman Terrell Owens	3.00	8.00
24 Elvis Grbac Junior Seau	1.50	4.00
25 Drew Bledsoe Tony Banks	1.50	4.00
26 Curtis Martin Troy Aikman	4.00	10.00
27 Curtis Conway Brett Perriman	1.25	3.00
28 Bobby Engram Larry Centers	.75	2.00
29 Raymont Harris Eric Metcalf	.75	2.00
30 Dave Krieg Derrick Alexander	.75	2.00
31 Rashaan Salaam Leeland McElroy	1.25	3.00
32 Ki-Jana Carter Herman Moore	1.25	3.00
33 Garrison Hearst Earnest Byner	1.25	3.00
34 Carl Pickens Frank Sanders	1.25	3.00
35 Darnay Scott Michael Jackson	1.25	3.00
36 Chris Boniol Kent Graham	.75	2.00
37 Herschel Walker Thurman Thomas	1.50	4.00
38 Ed McCaffrey Quinn Early	1.25	3.00
39 Aeneas Williams Mike Alstott	1.25	3.00
40 Scott Mitchell Mark Carrier	.75	2.00
41 Bert Emanuel Henry Ellard	.75	2.00
42 Bobby Hebert Trent Dilfer	1.25	3.00
43 Terence Mathis Andre Reed	1.25	3.00
44 Vinny Testaverde Chris Warren	1.25	3.00
45 Bruce Smith Kevin Greene	1.50	4.00
46 Anthony Johnson Terry Allen	1.25	3.00
47 Wesley Walls Errict Rhett	1.25	3.00
48 John Friesz Jeff Hostetler	.75	2.00
49 Joey Galloway Leslie Shepherd	1.25	3.00
50 Michael McCrary Cedric Jones	.75	2.00
51 Lamar Smith Courtney Hawkins	1.25	3.00
52 Rickey Dudley Jason Dunn	1.25	3.00
53 Irving Fryar Tony Martin	1.25	3.00
54 Ted Popson Ricky Watters	1.25	3.00
55 Chad Brown Zach Thomas	1.50	4.00
56 Mike Tomczak Stan Humphries	1.25	3.00
57 Rod Woodson Willie McGinest	1.25	3.00
58 Terrell Fletcher Jerris McPhail	.75	2.00
59 O.J. McDuffie Cris Carter	1.50	4.00
60 Jake Reed Marcus Allen	1.50	4.00
61 Robert Smith Greg Hill	1.25	3.00
62 Jim Everett Dave Brown	.75	2.00
63 Michael Haynes James McKeehan	.75	2.00
64 Haywood Jeffires Sean Dawkins	.75	2.00
65 Rodney Hampton Adrian Murrell	1.25	3.00
66 Danny Kanell Marvin Harrison	1.50	4.00
67 Thomas Lewis Dale Carter	.75	2.00
68 Wayne Chrebet Ken Dilger	1.50	4.00
69 Neil O'Donnell Chris Chandler	1.25	3.00
70 Jim Harbaugh Jimmy Smith	1.25	3.00
71 Derrick Thomas Tony Boselli	1.50	4.00
72 Keenan McCardell Kimble Anders	1.25	3.00

2001 Pacific Dynagon

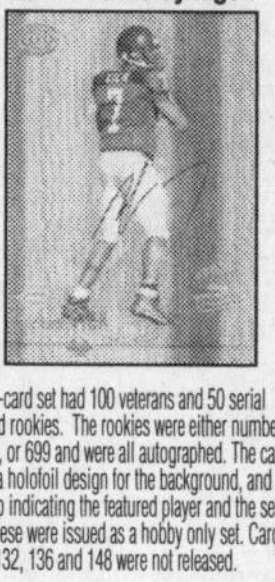

This 150-card set had 100 veterans and 50 serial numbered rookies. The rookies were either numbered to 199, 499, or 699 and were all autographed. The cards featured a holofoil design for the background, and a gold foil stamp indicating the featured player and the set name. These were issued as a hobby only set. Cards number 132, 136 and 148 were not released.

COMP.SET w/o SP's (100)	15.00	40.00
127-150 ROOKIE AU PRINT RUN 699		
1 David Boston	.25	.60
2 Thomas Jones	.30	.75
3 Jake Plummer	.30	.75
4 Jamal Anderson	.30	.75
5 Tim Dwight	.30	.75
6 Elvis Grbac	.30	.75
7 Jamal Lewis	.40	1.00
8 Ray Lewis	.40	1.00
9 Shannon Sharpe	.40	1.00
10 Rob Johnson	.30	.75
11 Eric Moulds	.30	.75
12 Peerless Price	.25	.60
13 Tim Biakabutuka	.25	.60
14 Patrick Jeffers	.25	.60
15 Muhsin Muhammad	.30	.75
16 James Allen	.25	.60
17 Cade McNown	.30	.75
18 Marcus Robinson	.30	.75
19 Brian Urlacher	.50	1.25
20 Corey Dillon	.30	.75
21 Akili Smith	.25	.60
22 Peter Warrick	.30	.75
23 Tim Couch	.25	.60
24 Kevin Johnson	.25	.60
25 Randall Cunningham	.40	1.00
26 Emmitt Smith	1.00	2.50
27 Mike Anderson	.30	.75
28 Terrell Davis	.40	1.00
29 Brian Griese	.30	.75
30 Ed McCaffrey	.30	.75
31 Rod Smith	.30	.75
32 Charlie Batch	.30	.75
33 Johnnie Morton	.30	.75
34 James Stewart	.25	.60
35 Brett Favre	1.25	3.00
36 Antonio Freeman	.40	1.00
37 Ahman Green	.40	1.00
38 Marvin Harrison	.40	1.00
39 Edgerrin James	.40	1.00
40 Peyton Manning	1.00	2.50
41 Mark Brunell	.30	.75
42 Keenan McCardell	.30	.75
43 Jimmy Smith	.30	.75
44 Fred Taylor	.40	1.00
45 Derrick Alexander	.25	.60
46 Tony Gonzalez	.40	1.00
47 Sylvester Morris	.25	.60
48 Jay Fiedler	.30	.75
49 Oronde Gadsden	.25	.60
50 Lamar Smith	.30	.75
51 Cris Carter	.40	1.00
52 Daunte Culpepper	.30	.75
53 Randy Moss	.40	1.00

1996 Pacific Dynagon Best Kept Secrets

54 Drew Bledsoe	.40	1.00
55 Terry Glenn	.30	.75
56 J.R. Redmond	.25	.60
57 Aaron Brooks	.30	.75
58 Joe Horn	.30	.75
59 Ricky Williams	.40	1.00
60 Tiki Barber	.40	1.00
61 Kerry Collins	.30	.75
62 Ron Dayne	.30	.75
63 Amani Toomer	.30	.75
64 Wayne Chrebet	.30	.75
65 Curtis Martin	.40	1.00
66 Vinny Testaverde	.30	.75
67 Tim Brown	.40	1.00
68 Rich Gannon	.30	.75
69 Tyrone Wheatley	.30	.75
70 Charles Johnson	.25	.60
71 Donovan McNabb	.40	1.00
72 Duce Staley	.30	.75
73 Jerome Bettis	.40	1.00
74 Plaxico Burress	.30	.75
75 Kordell Stewart	.30	.75
76 Isaac Bruce	.40	1.00
77 Marshall Faulk	.40	1.00
78 Torry Holt	.30	.75
79 Kurt Warner	.60	1.50
80 Curtis Conway	.30	.75
81 Doug Flutie	.40	1.00
82 Jeff Garcia	.30	.75
83 Charlie Garner	.30	.75
84 Terrell Owens	.40	1.00
85 Jerry Rice	.75	2.00
86 Shaun Alexander	.40	1.00
87 Matt Hasselbeck	.40	1.00
88 Darrell Jackson	.30	.75
89 Mike Alstott	.30	.75
90 Warrick Dunn	.40	1.00
91 Brad Johnson	.30	.75
92 Keyshawn Johnson	.30	.75
93 Shaun King	.25	.60
94 Eddie George	.40	1.00
95 Jevon Kearse	.30	.75
96 Derrick Mason	.30	.75
97 Steve McNair	.40	1.00
98 Stephen Davis	.30	.75
99 Jeff George	.30	.75
100 Deion Sanders	.40	1.00
101 Michael Bennett AU RC	8.00	20.00
102 Drew Brees AU RC	125.00	200.00
103 Chris Chambers AU RC	10.00	25.00
104 LaMont Jordan AU RC	10.00	25.00
105 Deuce McAllister AU RC	10.00	25.00
106 Koren Robinson AU RC	8.00	20.00
107 David Terrell AU RC	8.00	20.00
108 LaDainian Tomlinson AU RC	50.00	100.00
109 Marques Tuiasosopo AU RC	8.00	20.00
110 Michael Vick AU RC	60.00	120.00
111 Chris Weinke AU RC	8.00	20.00
112 Kevan Barlow AU RC	5.00	12.00
113 Josh Booty AU RC	5.00	12.00
114 Rod Gardner AU RC	5.00	12.00
115 Todd Heap AU RC	6.00	15.00
116 Travis Henry AU RC	5.00	12.00
117 James Jackson AU RC	4.00	10.00
118 Chad Johnson AU RC	20.00	40.00
119 Rudi Johnson AU RC	6.00	15.00
120 Ben Leard AU RC	4.00	10.00
121 Quincy Morgan AU RC	5.00	12.00
122 Snoop Minnis AU RC	4.00	10.00
123 Freddie Mitchell AU RC	4.00	10.00
124 Sage Rosenfels AU RC	6.00	15.00
125 Anthony Thomas AU RC	6.00	15.00
126 Reggie Wayne AU RC	20.00	40.00
127 Dan Alexander AU RC	4.00	10.00
128 Will Allen AU RC	5.00	12.00
129 Scotty Anderson AU RC	3.00	8.00
130 Adam Archuleta AU RC	4.00	10.00
131 Alex Bannister AU RC	3.00	8.00
133 Tay Cody AU RC	3.00	8.00
134 Tony Dixon AU RC	3.00	8.00
135 Heath Evans AU RC	4.00	10.00
137 Derrick Gibson AU RC	3.00	8.00
138 Edgerton Hartwell AU RC	3.00	8.00
139 Tim Hasselbeck AU RC	4.00	10.00
140 Jabari Holloway AU RC	3.00	8.00
141 Torrance Marshall AU RC	3.00	8.00
142 Jason McKinley AU RC	3.00	8.00
143 Mike McMahon AU RC	4.00	10.00
144 Bobby Newcombe AU RC	4.00	10.00
145 Moran Norris AU RC	3.00	8.00
146 Tommy Polley AU RC	3.00	8.00
147 Vinny Sutherland AU RC	3.00	8.00
149 Reggie White AU RC	3.00	8.00
150 Cedrick Wilson AU RC	4.00	10.00

2001 Pacific Dynagon Premiere Date

*VETERANS: 3X TO 8X BASIC CARDS
STATED PRINT RUN 135 SER.#'d SETS

2001 Pacific Dynagon Red

*VETERANS: 4X TO 10X BASIC CARDS
STATED PRINT RUN 99 SERIAL #'d SETS

2001 Pacific Dynagon Retail

This 150-card set parallels the base Dynagon hobby set. Each ard has a white background instead of the silver foilboard look of the hobby release. The rookies (#101-150) were randomly seeded at the rate of 1:4 packs.

COMP.SET w/o RC's (100)	12.50	25.00
*RETAIL VETS 1-100: .3X TO .8X HOB		
101-150 ROOKIE ODDS 1:4 RET		
102 Drew Brees RC	5.00	12.00
103 Chris Chambers RC	.75	2.00
104 LaMont Jordan RC	.75	2.00
105 Deuce McAllister RC	.75	2.00
106 Koren Robinson RC	.60	1.50
107 David Terrell RC	.60	1.50
108 LaDainian Tomlinson RC	2.50	6.00
109 Marques Tuiasosopo RC	.60	1.50
110 Michael Vick RC	3.00	8.00
111 Chris Weinke RC	.60	1.50
112 Kevan Barlow RC	.60	1.50
113 Josh Booty RC	.60	1.50
114 Rod Gardner RC	.60	1.50
115 Todd Heap RC	.75	2.00
116 Travis Henry RC	.60	1.50
117 James Jackson RC	.50	1.25
118 Chad Johnson RC	1.25	3.00
119 Rudi Johnson RC	.75	2.00
120 Ben Leard RC	.50	1.25
121 Quincy Morgan RC	.60	1.50
122 Snoop Minnis RC	.50	1.25
123 Freddie Mitchell RC	.50	1.25
124 Sage Rosenfels RC	.75	2.00
125 Anthony Thomas RC	.75	2.00
126 Reggie Wayne RC	1.50	4.00
127 Dan Alexander RC	.60	1.50
128 Will Allen RC	.75	2.00
129 Scotty Anderson RC	.50	1.25
130 Adam Archuleta RC	.60	1.50
131 Alex Bannister RC	.50	1.25
132 Gary Baxter RC	.50	1.25
133 Tay Cody RC	.50	1.25
134 Tony Dixon RC	.50	1.25
135 Heath Evans RC	.60	1.50
136 Jamar Fletcher RC	.50	1.25
137 Derrick Gibson RC	.50	1.25
138 Edgerton Hartwell RC	.50	1.25
139 Tim Hasselbeck RC	.60	1.50
140 Jabari Holloway RC	.50	1.25
141 Torrance Marshall RC	.50	1.25
142 Jason McKinley RC	.50	1.25
143 Mike McMahon RC	.60	1.50
144 Bobby Newcombe RC	.60	1.50
145 Moran Norris RC	.50	1.25
146 Tommy Polley RC	.50	1.25
147 Vinny Sutherland RC	.50	1.25
148 Ja'Mar Toombs RC	.50	1.25
149 Reggie White RC	.50	1.25
150 Cedrick Wilson RC	.60	1.50

2001 Pacific Dynagon Retail Silver

*VETERANS: 2.5X TO 6X BASIC RETAIL
STATED PRINT RUN 199 SER.#'d SETS

2001 Pacific Dynagon Big Numbers

COMPLETE SET (20)	20.00	50.00
STATED PRINT RUN 799 SER.#'d SETS		
1 Cade McNown	1.25	3.00
2 Peter Warrick	1.25	3.00
3 Tim Couch	1.00	2.50
4 Mike Anderson	1.25	3.00
5 Brian Griese	1.25	3.00
6 Cris Carter	1.50	4.00
7 Mark Brunell	1.25	3.00
8 Drew Bledsoe	1.50	4.00
9 Ricky Williams	1.50	4.00
10 Ron Dayne	1.25	3.00
11 Curtis Martin	1.50	4.00
12 Rich Gannon	1.25	3.00
13 Jerome Bettis	1.50	4.00
14 Torry Holt	1.25	3.00
15 Jeff Garcia	1.25	3.00
16 Jerry Rice	3.00	8.00
17 Warrick Dunn	1.50	4.00
18 Eddie George	1.50	4.00
19 Steve McNair	1.50	4.00
20 Stephen Davis	1.25	3.00

2001 Pacific Dynagon Canton Bound

COMPLETE SET (10)	50.00	120.00
STATED PRINT RUN 99 SER.#'d SETS		
1 Emmitt Smith	10.00	25.00
2 Brett Favre	12.00	30.00
3 Edgerrin James	4.00	10.00
4 Peyton Manning	10.00	25.00
5 Dan Marino	10.00	25.00
6 Cris Carter	4.00	10.00
7 Randy Moss	4.00	10.00
8 Marshall Faulk	4.00	10.00
9 Kurt Warner	6.00	15.00
10 Jerry Rice	8.00	20.00

2001 Pacific Dynagon Dynamic Duos

COMPLETE SET (20)	20.00	50.00
STATED PRINT RUN 1499 SER.#'d SETS		
1 Jake Plummer David Boston	.75	2.00
2 Jamal Lewis Priest Holmes	1.00	2.50
3 Rob Johnson Eric Moulds	.75	2.00
4 Cade McNown Marcus Robinson	.75	2.00
5 Corey Dillon Peter Warrick	.75	2.00
6 Tim Couch Kevin Johnson	.60	1.50
7 Mike Anderson Terrell Davis	1.00	2.50
8 Brian Griese Rod Smith	.75	2.00
9 Brett Favre Antonio Freeman	3.00	8.00
10 Peyton Manning Marvin Harrison	2.50	6.00
11 Mark Brunell Fred Taylor	1.00	2.50
12 Daunte Culpepper Randy Moss	1.00	2.50
13 Drew Bledsoe Terry Glenn	1.00	2.50
14 Tiki Barber Ron Dayne	1.00	2.50
15 Rich Gannon Tim Brown	1.00	2.50
16 Donovan McNabb Duce Staley	1.00	2.50
17 Kurt Warner Torry Holt	1.50	4.00
18 Jeff Garcia Terrell Owens	1.00	2.50
19 Mike Alstott Warrick Dunn	1.00	2.50
20 Steve McNair Derrick Mason	1.00	2.50

2001 Pacific Dynagon Freshman Phenoms

COMPLETE SET (10)	40.00	80.00
STATED PRINT RUN 599 SER.#'d SETS		
1 Michael Bennett	1.50	4.00
2 Drew Brees	12.00	30.00
3 Josh Heupel	2.00	5.00
4 Deuce McAllister	2.00	5.00
5 Santana Moss	2.50	6.00
6 Ken-Yon Rambo	1.25	3.00
7 Koren Robinson	1.50	4.00
8 David Terrell	1.50	4.00
9 LaDainian Tomlinson	6.00	15.00
10 Michael Vick	8.00	20.00

2001 Pacific Dynagon Game Used Footballs

STATED ODDS 1:82 HOB 1:481 RET		
STATED PRINT RUN 214 SER.#'d SETS		
1 Jamal Lewis	6.00	15.00
2 Peter Warrick	5.00	12.00
3 Tim Couch	4.00	10.00
4 Emmitt Smith	15.00	40.00
5 Mike Anderson	5.00	12.00
6 Terrell Davis	6.00	15.00
7 Brett Favre	20.00	50.00
8 Edgerrin James	6.00	15.00
9 Peyton Manning	15.00	40.00
10 Mark Brunell	5.00	12.00
11 Fred Taylor	6.00	15.00
12 Daunte Culpepper	5.00	12.00
13 Randy Moss	6.00	15.00
14 Drew Bledsoe	6.00	15.00
15 Ricky Williams	6.00	15.00
16 Donovan McNabb	6.00	15.00
17 Marshall Faulk	6.00	15.00
18 Kurt Warner	10.00	25.00
19 Jerry Rice	12.00	30.00
20 Eddie George	6.00	15.00

2001 Pacific Dynagon Logo Optics

COMPLETE SET (20)	15.00	40.00
STATED PRINT RUN 499 SER.#'d SETS		
1 Jamal Lewis	1.25	3.00
2 Eric Moulds	1.00	2.50
3 Corey Dillon	1.00	2.50
4 Emmitt Smith	3.00	8.00
5 Terrell Davis	1.25	3.00
6 Brian Griese	1.00	2.50
7 Edgerrin James	1.25	3.00
8 Fred Taylor	1.25	3.00
9 Lamar Smith	1.00	2.50
10 Daunte Culpepper	1.00	2.50
11 Ricky Williams	1.25	3.00
12 Curtis Martin	1.25	3.00
13 Tyrone Wheatley	1.00	2.50
14 Donovan McNabb	1.25	3.00
15 Jerome Bettis	1.25	3.00
16 Marshall Faulk	1.25	3.00
17 Jeff Garcia	1.00	2.50
18 Warrick Dunn	1.25	3.00
19 Eddie George	1.25	3.00
20 Stephen Davis	1.00	2.50

2001 Pacific Dynagon Premiere Players

COMPLETE SET (20)	30.00	80.00
STATED PRINT RUN 999 SER.#'d SETS		
1 David Allen	.75	2.00
2 Kevan Barlow	1.00	2.50
3 Michael Bennett	1.00	2.50
4 Drew Brees	8.00	20.00
5 Chris Chambers	1.25	3.00
6 Josh Heupel	1.25	3.00
7 James Jackson	.75	2.00
8 LaMont Jordan	1.25	3.00
9 Deuce McAllister	1.25	3.00
10 Freddie Mitchell	.75	2.00
11 Santana Moss	1.50	4.00
12 Ken-Yon Rambo	.75	2.00
13 Koren Robinson	1.00	2.50
14 David Terrell	1.00	2.50
15 Anthony Thomas	1.25	3.00
16 LaDainian Tomlinson	4.00	10.00
17 Marques Tuiasosopo	1.00	2.50
18 Michael Vick	5.00	12.00
19 Reggie Wayne	2.50	6.00
20 Chris Weinke	1.00	2.50

2001 Pacific Dynagon Top of the Class

COMPLETE SET (25)	15.00	40.00
STATED ODDS 1:1 HOB 1:4 RET		
1 Kevan Barlow	.50	1.25
2 Michael Bennett	.50	1.25
3 Drew Brees	4.00	10.00
4 Chris Chambers	.60	1.50
5 Rod Gardner	.50	1.25
6 Travis Henry	.50	1.25
7 Josh Heupel	.60	1.50
8 James Jackson	.40	1.00
9 Chad Johnson	1.00	2.50
10 LaMont Jordan	.60	1.50
11 Deuce McAllister	.60	1.50
12 Mike McMahon	.50	1.25
13 Snoop Minnis	.40	1.00
14 Travis Minor	.50	1.25
15 Freddie Mitchell	.40	1.00
16 Santana Moss	.75	2.00
17 Ken-Yon Rambo	.40	1.00
18 Koren Robinson	.50	1.25
19 David Terrell	.50	1.25
20 Anthony Thomas	.60	1.50
21 LaDainian Tomlinson	2.00	5.00
22 Marques Tuiasosopo	.50	1.25
23 Michael Vick	2.50	6.00
24 Reggie Wayne	1.25	3.00
25 Chris Weinke	.50	1.25

2002 Pacific Exclusive

Released in late-October, 2002, this 200 card set contains a good mix of veterans and rookies, along with several autographed rookie cards. Boxes contained 18 packs of 6 cards. Boxes were packed 16 per case. Each box contained an authentic bobble head doll. Also available in packs were rookie updates for 2002 Pacific, Pacific Atomic, and Pacific Heads Up.

ROOKIE AU/100-1045 ODDS 1:21		
1 David Boston	.30	.75
2 Thomas Jones	.50	1.25
3 Jake Plummer	.40	1.00
4 Frank Sanders	.30	.75
5 Josh Scobey RC	.60	1.50
6 Warrick Dunn	.40	1.00
7 Brian Finneran	.30	.75
8 Kahlil Hill RC	.50	1.25
9 Shawn Jefferson	.30	.75
10 Kurt Kittner RC	.50	1.25
11 Michael Vick	.75	2.00
12 Ron Johnson RC	.60	1.50
13 Jamal Lewis	.40	1.00
14 Ray Lewis	.50	1.25
15 Chris Redman	.30	.75
16 Brandon Stokley	.40	1.00
17 Chester Taylor RC	.75	2.00
18 Travis Taylor	.30	.75
19 Drew Bledsoe	.50	1.25
20 Travis Henry	.30	.75
21 Eric Moulds	.40	1.00
22 Peerless Price	.30	.75
23 Randy Fasani RC	.60	1.50
24 Muhsin Muhammad	.40	1.00
25 Lamar Smith	.40	1.00
26 Steve Smith	.50	1.25
27 Chris Weinke	.30	.75
28 Marty Booker	.40	1.00
29 Jim Miller	.30	.75
30 Adrian Peterson RC	.75	2.00
31 Marcus Robinson	.40	1.00
32 David Terrell	.30	.75
33 Anthony Thomas	.40	1.00
34 Brian Urlacher	.50	1.25
35 Corey Dillon	.40	1.00
36 Chad Johnson	.50	1.25
37 Jon Kitna	.40	1.00
38 Michael Westbrook	.30	.75
39 Peter Warrick	.40	1.00
40 Tim Couch	.30	.75
41 JaJuan Dawson	.30	.75
42 James Jackson	.30	.75
43 Kevin Johnson	.30	.75
44 Quincy Morgan	.30	.75
45 Quincy Carter	.30	.75
46 Joey Galloway	.40	1.00
47 Troy Hambrick	.30	.75
48 Chad Hutchinson RC	.50	1.25
49 Rocket Ismail	.40	1.00
50 Emmitt Smith	1.25	3.00
51 Mike Anderson	.40	1.00
52 Terrell Davis	.50	1.25
53 Brian Griese	.40	1.00
54 Herb Haygood RC	.50	1.25
55 Ed McCaffrey	.40	1.00
56 Rod Smith	.40	1.00
57 Germane Crowell	.30	.75
58 Az-Zahir Hakim	.30	.75
59 Mike McMahon	.30	.75
60 Bill Schroeder	.30	.75
61 Luke Staley RC	.50	1.25
62 James Stewart	.30	.75
63 Brett Favre	1.25	3.00
64 Robert Ferguson	.40	1.00
65 Bubba Franks	.40	1.00
66 Terry Glenn	.40	1.00
67 Ahman Green	.40	1.00
68 Craig Nall RC	.60	1.50
69 James Allen	.30	.75
70 Corey Bradford	.30	.75
71 Jermaine Lewis	.30	.75
72 Travis Prentice	.30	.75
73 Brian Allen RC	.50	1.25
74 Marvin Harrison	.50	1.25
75 Edgerrin James	.40	1.00
76 Peyton Manning	1.00	2.50
77 Reggie Wayne	.50	1.25
78 Mark Brunell	.40	1.00
79 Patrick Johnson	.30	.75
80 Jimmy Smith	.40	1.00
81 Fred Taylor	.40	1.00
82 Tony Gonzalez	.50	1.25
83 Trent Green	.40	1.00
84 Priest Holmes	.50	1.25
85 Johnnie Morton	.40	1.00
86 Chris Chambers	.40	1.00
87 Jay Fiedler	.40	1.00
88 Oronde Gadsden	.30	.75
89 Leonard Henry RC	.50	1.25
90 Travis Minor	.30	.75
91 Sam Simmons RC	.50	1.25
92 Ricky Williams	.40	1.00
93 Derrick Alexander	.30	.75
94 Michael Bennett	.40	1.00
95 Daunte Culpepper	.40	1.00
96 Randy Moss	.50	1.25
97 Tom Brady	1.25	3.00
98 Deion Branch RC	.75	2.00
99 Troy Brown	.40	1.00
100 Rohan Davey RC	.75	2.00
101 Donald Hayes	.30	.75
102 David Patten	.30	.75
103 Antowain Smith	.40	1.00
104 Antwoine Womack RC	.50	1.25
105 Aaron Brooks	.40	1.00
106 Joe Horn	.40	1.00
107 Deuce McAllister	.40	1.00
108 J.T. O'Sullivan RC	.60	1.50
109 Jerome Pathon	.30	.75
110 Tiki Barber	.50	1.25
111 Tim Carter RC	.60	1.50
112 Kerry Collins	.40	1.00
113 Ron Dayne	.40	1.00
114 Ike Hilliard	.40	1.00
115 Amani Toomer	.40	1.00
116 Wayne Chrebet	.40	1.00
117 Laveranues Coles	.40	1.00
118 Curtis Martin	.50	1.25
119 Santana Moss	.40	1.00
120 Vinny Testaverde	.40	1.00
121 Tim Brown	.50	1.25
122 Ronald Curry RC	.60	1.50
123 Rich Gannon	.40	1.00
124 Charlie Garner	.40	1.00
125 Larry Ned RC	.50	1.25
126 Jerry Rice	1.00	2.50
127 Tyrone Wheatley	.40	1.00
128 Donovan McNabb	.50	1.25
129 Freddie Mitchell	.30	.75
130 Todd Pinkston	.30	.75
131 Duce Staley	.40	1.00
132 James Thrash	.40	1.00
133 Jerome Bettis	.50	1.25
134 Plaxico Burress	.40	1.00
135 Kordell Stewart	.40	1.00
136 Hines Ward	.50	1.25
137 Amos Zereoue	.30	.75
138 Isaac Bruce	.50	1.25
139 Trung Canidate	.30	.75
140 Eric Crouch RC	.75	2.00
141 Marshall Faulk	.50	1.25
142 Lamar Gordon RC	.60	1.50
143 Torry Holt	.50	1.25
144 Kurt Warner	.50	1.25
145 Terrence Wilkins	.30	.75
146 Drew Brees	.75	2.00
147 Seth Burford RC	.50	1.25
148 Reche Caldwell RC	.75	2.00
149 Curtis Conway	.40	1.00
150 Tim Dwight	.30	.75
151 Doug Flutie	.50	1.25
152 LaDainian Tomlinson	.60	1.50
153 Kevan Barlow	.30	.75
154 Brandon Doman RC	.50	1.25
155 Jeff Garcia	.40	1.00
156 Garrison Hearst	.40	1.00
157 Terrell Owens	.50	1.25
158 J.J. Stokes	.30	.75
159 Shaun Alexander	.40	1.00
160 Trent Dilfer	.40	1.00
161 Darrell Jackson	.40	1.00
162 Koren Robinson	.30	.75
163 Mike Alstott	.40	1.00
164 Brad Johnson	.40	1.00
165 Keyshawn Johnson	.40	1.00
166 Keenan McCardell	.40	1.00
167 Michael Pittman	.40	1.00
168 Travis Stephens RC	.50	1.25
169 Marquise Walker RC	.50	1.25
170 Kevin Dyson	.40	1.00
171 Eddie George	.40	1.00
172 Derrick Mason	.40	1.00
173 Steve McNair	.50	1.25
174 Reidel Anthony	.30	.75
175 Ladell Betts RC	.75	2.00
176 Stephen Davis	.40	1.00
177 Rod Gardner	.30	.75
178 Jacquez Green	.30	.75
179 Shane Matthews	.30	.75
180 Cliff Russell RC	.50	1.25
181 Josh McCown AU/779 RC	8.00	20.00
182 T.J. Duckett RC	.75	2.00
183 Josh Reed RC	.60	1.50
184 DeShaun Foster AU/105 RC	10.00	25.00
185 Andre Davis AU/770 RC	6.00	16.00
186 William Green RC	.60	1.50
187 Antonio Bryant AU/575 RC	8.00	20.00
188 Ashley Lelie AU/100 RC	8.00	20.00
189 Clinton Portis AU/524 RC	10.00	25.00
190 Joey Harrington RC	.75	2.00
191 Javon Walker AU/519 RC	8.00	20.00
192 David Carr AU/100 RC	10.00	25.00
193 Jabar Gaffney AU/103 RC	10.00	25.00
194 Jonathan Wells AU/615 RC	8.00	20.00
195 David Garrard AU/787 RC	10.00	25.00
196 Donte Stallworth RC	.75	2.00
197 Brian Westbrook AU/930 RC	12.00	30.00
198 Antwaan Randle El AU/788 RC	8.00	20.00
199 Maurice Morris AU/1045 RC	6.00	15.00
200 Patrick Ramsey RC	.75	2.00

2002 Pacific Exclusive Blue

BLUE PRINT RUN 299 SER.#'d SETS		
5 Josh Scobey	1.50	4.00
8 Kahlil Hill	1.25	3.00
10 Kurt Kittner	1.25	3.00
12 Ron Johnson	1.50	4.00
17 Chester Taylor	2.00	5.00
23 Randy Fasani	1.50	4.00
30 Adrian Peterson	2.00	5.00
48 Chad Hutchinson	1.25	3.00
54 Herb Haygood	1.25	3.00
61 Luke Staley	1.25	3.00
68 Craig Nall	1.50	4.00
73 Brian Allen	1.25	3.00
89 Leonard Henry	1.25	3.00
91 Sam Simmons	1.25	3.00
98 Deion Branch	2.00	5.00
100 Rohan Davey	2.00	5.00
104 Antwoine Womack	1.25	3.00
108 J.T. O'Sullivan	1.50	4.00
111 Tim Carter	1.50	4.00
122 Ronald Curry	1.50	4.00
125 Larry Ned	1.25	3.00
140 Eric Crouch	2.00	5.00
142 Lamar Gordon	1.50	4.00
147 Seth Burford	1.25	3.00
148 Reche Caldwell	2.00	5.00
154 Brandon Doman	1.25	3.00
168 Travis Stephens	1.25	3.00
169 Marquise Walker	1.25	3.00
175 Ladell Betts	2.00	5.00
180 Cliff Russell	1.25	3.00
181 Josh McCown	2.00	5.00
182 T.J. Duckett	2.00	5.00
183 Josh Reed	1.50	4.00
184 DeShaun Foster	2.00	5.00
185 Andre Davis	1.50	4.00
186 William Green	1.50	4.00
187 Antonio Bryant	2.00	5.00
188 Ashley Lelie	1.50	4.00
189 Clinton Portis	2.50	6.00
190 Joey Harrington	2.00	5.00
191 Javon Walker	2.00	5.00
192 David Carr	2.00	5.00
193 Jabar Gaffney	2.00	5.00
194 Jonathan Wells	2.00	5.00
195 David Garrard	2.50	6.00
196 Donte Stallworth	2.00	5.00
197 Brian Westbrook	3.00	8.00
198 Antwaan Randle El	2.00	5.00
199 Maurice Morris	1.50	4.00
200 Patrick Ramsey	2.00	5.00

2002 Pacific Exclusive Gold

*VETS: 1.2X TO 3X BASIC CARDS
ONE GOLD PER PACK

2002 Pacific Exclusive Retail

Retail packs of Pacific Exclusive featured the same 200 cards as the hobby version except that each of the 14-Autographed Rookie Cards from hobby were replaced with unsigned versions in the retail packs. We've included only listings for those 14-replacement cards.

181 Josh McCown RC	.75	2.00
184 DeShaun Foster RC	.75	2.00
185 Andre Davis RC	.60	1.50
187 Antonio Bryant RC	.75	2.00
188 Ashley Lelie RC	.60	1.50
189 Clinton Portis RC	1.00	2.50
191 Javon Walker RC	.75	2.00
192 David Carr RC	.75	2.00
193 Jabar Gaffney RC	.75	2.00
194 Jonathan Wells RC	.75	2.00
195 David Garrard RC	1.00	2.50
197 Brian Westbrook RC	1.25	3.00
198 Antwaan Randle El RC	.75	2.00
199 Maurice Morris RC	.60	1.50

2002 Pacific Exclusive Advantage

COMPLETE SET (20)	20.00	50.00
STATED ODDS 1:6		
1 Michael Vick	1.50	4.00
2 Drew Bledsoe	1.00	2.50
3 Anthony Thomas	.75	2.00
4 Corey Dillon	.75	2.00
5 Tim Couch	.60	1.50
6 Emmitt Smith	2.50	6.00
7 Brett Favre	2.50	6.00
8 Edgerrin James	.75	2.00
9 Peyton Manning	2.00	5.00
10 Ricky Williams	.75	2.00
11 Daunte Culpepper	.75	2.00
12 Randy Moss	1.00	2.50
13 Tom Brady	2.50	6.00
14 Jerry Rice	2.00	5.00
15 Donovan McNabb	1.00	2.50
16 Marshall Faulk	1.00	2.50
17 Kurt Warner	1.00	2.50
18 Drew Brees	1.50	4.00
19 LaDainian Tomlinson	1.25	3.00
20 Shaun Alexander	.75	2.00

2002 Pacific Exclusive Destined for Greatness

COMPLETE SET (10)	10.00	25.00
STATED ODDS 1:11		
1 T.J. Duckett	.75	2.00
2 DeShaun Foster	.75	2.00
3 William Green	.60	1.50
4 Ashley Lelie	.60	1.50
5 Clinton Portis	1.00	2.50
6 Joey Harrington	.75	2.00
7 David Carr	.75	2.00
8 Donte Stallworth	.75	2.00
9 Antwaan Randle El	.75	2.00
10 Patrick Ramsey	.75	2.00

2002 Pacific Exclusive Etched in Stone

COMPLETE SET (10)	12.50	30.00
STATED ODDS 1:21		
1 Michael Vick	1.50	4.00
2 Anthony Thomas	.75	2.00
3 Emmitt Smith	2.50	6.00
4 Brett Favre	2.50	6.00
5 Peyton Manning	2.00	5.00
6 Randy Moss	1.00	2.50
7 Tom Brady	2.50	6.00
8 Jerry Rice	2.00	5.00
9 Marshall Faulk	1.00	2.50
10 Kurt Warner	1.00	2.50

2002 Pacific Exclusive Game Worn Jerseys

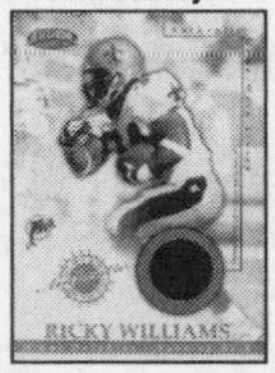

STATED ODDS 2:21		
*GOLD/25: 1.2X TO 3X BASIC JSY		
GOLD JSY PRINT RUN 25 SETS		
1 Frank Sanders	3.00	8.00
2 Jamal Anderson	4.00	10.00
3 Quentin McCord	3.00	8.00
4 Michael Vick	8.00	20.00
5 Jeremy McDaniel	3.00	8.00
6 Jay Riemersma	3.00	8.00
7 Charlie Rogers	3.00	8.00
8 Marcus Robinson	4.00	10.00
9 Brian Urlacher	5.00	12.00
10 Corey Dillon	4.00	10.00
11 Michael Westbrook	3.00	8.00
12 Tim Couch	3.00	8.00
13 Aaron Shea	3.00	8.00
14 Emmitt Smith	12.00	30.00
15 Kevin Kasper	3.00	8.00
16 Rob Moore	3.00	8.00
17 Brett Favre	12.00	30.00
18 Robert Ferguson	4.00	10.00
19 Ahman Green	4.00	10.00
20 Avion Black	3.00	8.00
21 Clif Groce	3.00	8.00
22 Brock Huard	4.00	10.00
23 Peyton Manning	10.00	25.00
24 Troy Walters	3.00	8.00
25 Mark Brunell	4.00	10.00
26 Bobby Shaw	3.00	8.00
27 Jimmy Smith	4.00	10.00
28 Ricky Williams	4.00	10.00
29 Daunte Culpepper	4.00	10.00
30 Randy Moss	5.00	12.00
31 Aaron Brooks	4.00	10.00
32 Terrelle Smith	3.00	8.00
33 Laveranues Coles	4.00	10.00
34 Curtis Martin	5.00	12.00
35 Rich Gannon	4.00	10.00
36 Jerry Rice	10.00	25.00
37 Donovan McNabb	5.00	12.00
38 James Thrash	4.00	10.00
39 Jerome Bettis	5.00	12.00
40 Plaxico Burress	4.00	10.00
41 Chris Fuamatu-Ma'afala	3.00	8.00
42 Marshall Faulk	5.00	12.00
43 Kurt Warner	5.00	12.00
44 Drew Brees	8.00	20.00
45 Terrell Fletcher	3.00	8.00
46 Shaun Alexander	4.00	10.00
47 Brad Johnson	4.00	10.00
48 Michael Pittman	4.00	10.00
49 Aaron Stecker	3.00	8.00
50 Erron Kinney	3.00	8.00

2002 Pacific Exclusive Great Expectations

COMPLETE SET (20)	12.50	30.00
STATED ODDS 1:6		
1 Josh McCown	.60	1.50
2 T.J. Duckett	.60	1.50
3 Josh Reed	.50	1.25
4 DeShaun Foster	.60	1.50
5 Andre Davis	.50	1.25
6 William Green	.50	1.25
7 Antonio Bryant	.60	1.50
8 Ashley Lelie	.50	1.25
9 Clinton Portis	.75	2.00
10 Joey Harrington	.60	1.50
11 Javon Walker	.60	1.50
12 David Carr	.60	1.50
13 Jabar Gaffney	.60	1.50
14 Jonathan Wells	.60	1.50
15 David Garrard	.75	2.00
16 Donte Stallworth	.60	1.50
17 Brian Westbrook	1.00	2.50
18 Antwaan Randle El	.60	1.50
19 Maurice Morris	.50	1.25
20 Patrick Ramsey	.60	1.50

2002 Pacific Exclusive Maximum Overdrive

COMPLETE SET (30)	20.00	50.00
STATED ODDS 1:6		
1 T.J. Duckett	.60	1.50
2 Michael Vick	1.00	2.50
3 DeShaun Foster	.60	1.50
4 Anthony Thomas	.50	1.25
5 Tim Couch	.40	1.00
6 Andre Davis	.50	1.25
7 William Green	.50	1.25
8 Antonio Bryant	.60	1.50
9 Emmitt Smith	1.50	4.00
10 Ashley Lelie	.50	1.25
11 Clinton Portis	.75	2.00
12 Joey Harrington	.60	1.50
13 Brett Favre	1.50	4.00
14 Javon Walker	.60	1.50
15 David Carr	.60	1.50
16 Jabbar Gaffney	.60	1.50
17 Peyton Manning	1.25	3.00
18 Ricky Williams	.50	1.25
19 Daunte Culpepper	.50	1.25
20 Randy Moss	.60	1.50
21 Tom Brady	1.50	4.00
22 Donte Stallworth	.60	1.50
23 Jerry Rice	1.25	3.00
24 Donovan McNabb	.60	1.50
25 Antwaan Randle El	.60	1.50
26 Marshall Faulk	.60	1.50
27 Kurt Warner	.60	1.50
28 Drew Brees	1.00	2.50
29 LaDainian Tomlinson	.75	2.00
30 Patrick Ramsey	.60	1.50

1995 Pacific Gridiron

Pacific produced 750 hobby cases (blue foil) and 750 retail cases (red foil). Each set also had a parallel set representing 10 percent of the sets produced. Just 30 "Gold" sets were produced, with two gold cards seeded per hobby or retail case.This 100-card set measures 3 1/2" by 5". The fronts feature full-color action shots which bleed to the borders. The backs have a write-up of the player's performance in the game pictured in the front photo. The back also has an inset photo. Pacific founders Mike and Cheryl Cramer took many of the photos used in this set. Rookie Cards in this set include Jeff Blake, Ki-Jana Carter, and Steve McNair. Natrone Means appears on four different promo cards as listed below.

COMP.BLUE SET (100)	20.00	50.00
1 Natrone Means	.20	.50
2 Dave Meggett	.10	.30
3 Curtis Conway	.20	.50
4 Sam Adams	.10	.30
5 Qadry Ismail	.20	.50
6 Steve Young	.75	2.00
7 Errict Rhett	.20	.50
8 Nate Lewis	.10	.30
9 Barry Sanders	2.00	5.00
10 Sterling Sharpe	.20	.50
11 Steve Beuerlein	.20	.50
12 Irving Spikes	.20	.50
13 Byron Bam Morris	.10	.30
14 Eric Metcalf	.20	.50
15 Michael Irvin	.40	1.00
16 Dan Marino	2.00	5.00
17 Stan Humphries	.20	.50
18 Leroy Hoard	.20	.50
19 Marcus Allen	.40	1.00
20 Barry Foster	.20	.50
21 Ronald Moore	.10	.30
22 Rodney Hampton	.20	.50
23 Ben Coates	.20	.50
24 Vernon Turner	.10	.30
25 Shannon Sharpe	.20	.50
26 Larry Centers	.20	.50
27 Mack Strong RC	.75	2.00
28 Reggie White	.40	1.00
29 Harvey Williams	.10	.30
30 Darnay Scott	.20	.50
31 Drew Bledsoe	1.00	2.50
32 Marshall Faulk	.75	2.00
33 Troy Aikman	1.00	2.50
34 Boomer Esiason	.20	.50
35 Bobby Hebert	.10	.30
36 Brian Mitchell	.10	.30
37 Andre Rison	.20	.50
38 Brett Favre	2.00	5.00
39 Don Majkowski	.10	.30
40 Johnny Johnson	.10	.30
41 Mark Carrier WR	.20	.50
42 James Joseph	.10	.30
43 Mario Bates	.20	.50
44 Craig Heyward	.20	.50
45 Henry Ellard	.20	.50
46 Thurman Thomas	.40	1.00
47 Jerome Bettis	.40	1.00
48 Dave Brown	.20	.50
49 Lorenzo White	.10	.30
50 Joe Montana	2.00	5.00
51 Vinny Testaverde	.20	.50
52 Lake Dawson	.20	.50
53 Michael Timpson	.10	.30
54 Ricky Ervins	.10	.30
55 Cris Carter	.40	1.00
56 Raymont Harris	.10	.30
57 Andre Coleman	.10	.30
58 Craig Erickson	.10	.30
59 Jeff Hostetler	.20	.50
60 Deion Sanders	.60	1.50
61 Eric Turner	.10	.30
62 Daryl Johnston	.20	.50
63 Bernie Parmalee	.20	.50
64 Ricky Watters	.20	.50
65 David Palmer	.20	.50
66 Aaron Glenn	.10	.30
67 Todd Kinchen	.10	.30
68 Edgar Bennett	.20	.50
69 Mel Gray	.10	.30
70 Randall Cunningham	.40	1.00
71 Michael Haynes	.20	.50
72 Chris Miller	.10	.30
73 Glyn Milburn	.10	.30
74 Steve McNair RC	2.50	6.00
75 Lewis Tillman	.10	.30
76 Chuck Levy	.10	.30
77 Carl Pickens	.20	.50
78 Michael Bates	.10	.30
79 Jeff Blake RC	.60	1.50
80 O.J. McDuffie	.40	1.00
81 Tim Brown	.40	1.00
82 Haywood Jeffires	.10	.30
83 Jeff Burris	.10	.30
84 John Elway	2.00	5.00
85 Charles Johnson	.20	.50
86 Emmitt Smith	2.00	5.00
87 William Floyd	.20	.50
88 Herschel Walker	.20	.50
89 Rick Mirer	.20	.50
90 Roosevelt Potts	.10	.30
91 Rod Woodson	.20	.50
92 Greg Hill	.20	.50
93 Junior Seau	.40	1.00
94 Dave Krieg	.10	.30
95 Jim Kelly	.40	1.00
96 Warren Moon	.40	1.00
97 Leroy Thompson	.10	.30
98 Ki-Jana Carter RC	.40	1.00
99 Herman Moore	.40	1.00
100 Jerry Rice	1.00	2.50
P1 Natrone Means Bronze Foil Numbered 100	.40	1.00
P2 Natrone Means Gold Foil Numbered 100	.40	1.00
P3 Natrone Means Red Foil Numbered 100	.40	1.00

P4 Natrone Means Blue Foil Numbered 100	.40	1.00
P5 Natrone Means Platinum Foil Numbered 100	.40	1.00

1995 Pacific Gridiron Copper

COMP.COPPER SET (100)	100.00	200.00

*COPPER STARS: 1.2X TO 3X BASIC CARDS
*COPPER RCs: .8X TO 2X BASIC CARDS

1995 Pacific Gridiron Gold

*GOLD STARS: 20X TO 50X BASIC CARDS
*GOLD RCs: 12X TO 30X BASIC CARDS

1995 Pacific Gridiron Platinum

COMP.PLATINUM SET (100)	100.00	200.00

*PLATINUM STARS: 1.2X TO 3X BASIC CARDS
*PLATINUM RCs: .8X TO 2X BASIC CARDS

1995 Pacific Gridiron Red

COMP.RED SET (100)	20.00	50.00

*RED CARDS: SAME PRICE AS BLUES

1996 Pacific Gridiron

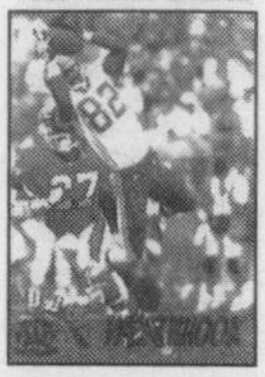

The 1996 Pacific Gridiron set was issued in one series totalling 125 cards in 2-card packs with 36 packs per box and 20 boxes per case. The was a hobby version with each printed with blue foil highlights on the front and a red foil retail version. The oversized cards measure roughly 3 1/2" by 5". The set is sequenced in alphabetical order within alphabetical team order.

COMPLETE SET (125)	12.50	30.00
1 Larry Centers	.15	.40
2 Garrison Hearst	.15	.40
3 Dave Krieg	.08	.25
4 Frank Sanders	.15	.40
5 Jamal Anderson RC	.40	1.00
6 J.J. Birden	.08	.25
7 Eric Metcalf	.08	.25
8 Jeff George	.15	.40
9 Cornelius Bennett	.08	.25
10 Todd Collins	.15	.40
11 Darick Holmes	.08	.25
12 Jim Kelly	.30	.75
13 Bryce Paup	.08	.25
14 Bob Christian	.08	.25
15 Kerry Collins	.30	.75
16 Pete Metzelaars	.08	.25
17 Derrick Moore	.08	.25
18 Curtis Conway	.30	.75
19 Jim Flanigan	.08	.25
20 Erik Kramer	.08	.25
21 Rashaan Salaam	.15	.40
22 Eric Bieniemy	.08	.25
23 Jeff Blake	.30	.75
24 Tony McGee	.08	.25
25 Darnay Scott	.15	.40
26 Vashone Adams RC	.08	.25
27 Leroy Hoard	.08	.25
28 Andre Rison	.15	.40
29 Tommy Vardell	.08	.25
30 Troy Aikman	.75	2.00
31 Michael Irvin	.30	.75
32 Daryl Johnston	.15	.40
33 Deion Sanders	.40	1.00
34 Emmitt Smith	1.25	3.00
35 Terrell Davis	.60	1.50
36 John Elway	1.50	4.00
37 Ed McCaffrey	.15	.40
38 Anthony Miller	.15	.40
39 Scott Mitchell	.15	.40
40 Brett Perriman	.08	.25
41 Barry Sanders	1.25	3.00
42 Chris Spielman	.08	.25
43 Edgar Bennett	.15	.40
44 Robert Brooks	.30	.75
45 Brett Favre	1.50	4.00
46 Antonio Freeman	.30	.75
47 Reggie White	.30	.75
48 Haywood Jeffires	.08	.25
49 Steve McNair	.60	1.50
50 Rodney Thomas	.08	.25
51 Frank Wycheck	.08	.25
52 Ashley Ambrose	.08	.25
53 Mark Brunell	.50	1.25
54 Ken Dilger	.15	.40
55 Marshall Faulk	.40	1.00
56 Jim Harbaugh	.15	.40
57 Tony Boselli	.08	.25
58 Pete Mitchell	.15	.40
59 James O.Stewart	.15	.40
60 Marcus Allen	.30	.75
61 Steve Bono	.08	.25
62 Lake Dawson	.08	.25
63 Tamarick Vanover	.15	.40
64 Bryan Cox	.08	.25
65 Dan Marino	1.50	4.00
66 O.J. McDuffie	.15	.40
67 Bernie Parmalee	.08	.25
68 Cris Carter	.30	.75
69 Rocket Ismail	.08	.25
70 Warren Moon	.15	.40
71 Robert Smith	.15	.40
72 Drew Bledsoe	.50	1.25
73 Vincent Brisby	.08	.25
74 Ben Coates	.15	.40
75 Curtis Martin	.60	1.50
76 Mario Bates	.15	.40
77 Derek Brown RBK	.08	.25
78 Jim Everett	.08	.25
79 Dave Brown	.08	.25
80 Chris Calloway	.08	.25
81 Rodney Hampton	.15	.40
82 Tyrone Wheatley	.15	.40
83 Kyle Brady	.08	.25
84 Wayne Chrebet	.40	1.00
85 Adrian Murrell	.15	.40
86 Tim Brown	.30	.75
87 Rob Carpenter	.08	.25
88 Charlie Garner	.15	.40
89 Daryl Hobbs RC	.08	.25
90 Napoleon Kaufman	.30	.75
91 Rodney Peete	.08	.25
92 Ricky Watters	.15	.40
93 Calvin Williams	.08	.25
94 Kevin Greene	.15	.40
95 Greg Lloyd	.15	.40
96 Neil O'Donnell	.15	.40
97 Erric Pegram	.08	.25
98 Kordell Stewart	.30	.75
99 Yancey Thigpen	.15	.40
100 Rod Woodson	.15	.40
101 Isaac Bruce	.30	.75
102 Jerome Bettis	.30	.75
103 J.T. Thomas	.08	.25
104 Ronnie Harmon	.08	.25
105 Aaron Hayden RC	.08	.25
106 Stan Humphries	.15	.40
107 Alfred Pupunu	.08	.25
108 William Floyd	.15	.40
109 Brent Jones	.08	.25
110 Jerry Rice	.75	2.00
111 J.J. Stokes	.30	.75
112 John Taylor	.08	.25
113 Steve Young	.50	1.25
114 Harvey Williams	.08	.25
115 John Friesz	.08	.25
116 Joey Galloway	.30	.75
117 Cortez Kennedy	.08	.25
118 Rick Mirer	.15	.40
119 Chris Warren	.15	.40
120 Trent Dilfer	.30	.75
121 Alvin Harper	.08	.25
122 Errict Rhett	.15	.40
123 Terry Allen	.15	.40
124 Gus Frerotte	.15	.40
125 Michael Westbrook	.30	.75
S1 Chris Warren Sample	.40	1.00

1996 Pacific Gridiron Copper

COMP.COPPER SET (125)	100.00	200.00

*COPPER STARS: 2X TO 5X BASIC CARDS
*COPPER RCs: 1.2X TO 3X BASIC CARDS
STATED ODDS 4:37 HOBBY

1996 Pacific Gridiron Gold

*GOLD STARS: 20X TO 50X BASIC CARDS
*GOLD RCs: 12X TO 30X BASIC CARDS

1996 Pacific Gridiron Platinum

COMP.PLATINUM SET (125)	100.00	200.00

*PLATINUM STARS: 2X TO 5X BASIC CARDS
*PLATINUM RCs: 1.2X TO 3X BASIC CARDS
STATED ODDS 4:37 RETAIL

1996 Pacific Gridiron Red

*RED: .4X TO 1X BLUE CARDS

1996 Pacific Gridiron Driving Force

COMPLETE SET (10)	15.00	40.00
STATED ODDS 1:73		
DF1 Chris Warren	.75	2.00
DF2 Emmitt Smith	6.00	15.00
DF3 Barry Sanders	6.00	15.00
DF4 Rashaan Salaam	.75	2.00
DF5 Errict Rhett	.75	2.00
DF6 Curtis Martin	3.00	8.00
DF7 Garrison Hearst	.75	2.00
DF8 Marshall Faulk	2.00	5.00
DF9 Terrell Davis	3.00	8.00
DF10 Edgar Bennett	.75	2.00

1996 Pacific Gridiron Gems

COMPLETE SET (50)	12.00	30.00
STATED ODDS 27:37		
GG1 J.J. Birden	.08	.25
GG2 Garrison Hearst	.15	.40
GG3 Bryce Paup	.08	.25
GG4 Kerry Collins	.30	.75
GG5 Alonzo Spellman	.08	.25
GG6 Chris Zorich	.08	.25
GG7 Harold Green	.08	.25
GG8 Lee Johnson	.08	.25
GG9 Eric Zeier	.15	.40
GG10 Troy Aikman	.75	2.00
GG11 Deion Sanders	.40	1.00
GG12 Emmitt Smith	1.25	3.00
GG13 John Elway	1.50	4.00
GG14 Mike Pritchard	.08	.25
GG15 Shane Bonham	.08	.25
GG16 Barry Sanders	1.25	3.00
GG17 Edgar Bennett	.15	.40
GG18 Brett Favre	1.50	4.00
GG19 Reggie White	.30	.75
GG20 Eddie Robinson	.08	.25
GG21 Marshall Faulk	.40	1.00
GG22 Brian Stablein	.08	.25
GG23 Don Davey	.08	.25
GG24 Neil Smith	.15	.40
GG25 Derrick Thomas	.30	.75
GG26 Eric Green	.08	.25
GG27 Jake Reed	.15	.40
GG28 Troy Brown	.20	.50
GG29 Will Moore	.08	.25
GG30 Wesley Walls	.15	.40
GG31 Herschel Walker	.15	.40
GG32 Keyshawn Johnson	.50	1.25
GG33 Billy Joe Hobert	.08	.25
GG34 Ricky Watters	.15	.40
GG35 Ernie Mills	.08	.25
GG36 Kordell Stewart	.30	.75
GG37 Terrell Fletcher	.08	.25
GG38 Junior Seau	.30	.75
GG39 Elvis Grbac	.15	.40
GG40 Gary Plummer	.08	.25
GG41 Jerry Rice	.75	2.00
GG42 Steve Young	.50	1.25
GG43 Carlester Crumpler	.08	.25
GG44 Joey Galloway	.30	.75
GG45 Cortez Kennedy	.08	.25
GG46 Chris Warren	.15	.40
GG47 Greg Robinson	.08	.25
GG48 Errict Rhett	.15	.40
GG49 Terry Allen	.15	.40
GG50 Stanley Richard	.08	.25

1996 Pacific Gridiron Gold Crown Die Cuts

COMPLETE SET (20)	75.00	150.00
STATED ODDS 1:37		
LISTED PRICES ARE FOR PRIZE CARDS		
GC1 Barry Sanders	8.00	20.00
GC2 Ricky Watters	1.00	2.50
GC3 Troy Aikman	5.00	12.00
GC4 Deion Sanders	2.50	6.00
GC5 Kerry Collins	2.00	5.00
GC6 Dan Marino	10.00	25.00
GC7 Steve Young	3.00	8.00
GC8 Drew Bledsoe	3.00	8.00
GC9 Jerry Rice	5.00	12.00
GC10 Steve McNair	4.00	10.00
GC11 Joey Galloway	2.00	5.00
GC12 John Elway	10.00	25.00
GC13 Terrell Davis	4.00	10.00
GC14 Rashaan Salaam	1.00	2.50
GC15 Kordell Stewart	2.00	5.00
GC16 Emmitt Smith	8.00	20.00
GC17 Curtis Martin	4.00	10.00
GC18 Marshall Faulk	2.50	6.00
GC19 Brett Favre	10.00	25.00
GC20 Chris Warren	1.00	2.50

1996 Pacific Gridiron Rock Solid Rookies

COMPLETE SET (6)	40.00	80.00
STATED ODDS 1:121		
RP1 Joey Galloway	6.00	15.00
RP2 Napoleon Kaufman	6.00	15.00
RP3 Michael Westbrook	4.00	10.00
RP4 Kerry Collins	6.00	15.00
RP5 Aaron Hayden	2.50	6.00
RP6 Kordell Stewart	6.00	15.00

2002 Pacific Heads Up

This 175-card base set includes 125 veterans and 50 rookies. The rookie cards are serially numbered to 1090. The cards were distributed as both a hobby and retail product. Please note that cards 176-195 were only available in packs of 2002 Pacific Heads Update.

COMP.SET w/o SP's (100)	10.00	25.00
ROOKIE PRINT RUN 1090 SER.#'d SETS		
1 David Boston	.25	.60
2 Thomas Jones	.40	1.00
3 Jake Plummer	.30	.75
4 Jamal Anderson	.30	.75
5 Warrick Dunn	.30	.75
6 Shawn Jefferson	.25	.60
7 Michael Vick	.60	1.50
8 Jamal Lewis	.30	.75
9 Chris Redman	.25	.60
10 Brandon Stokley	.30	.75
11 Travis Taylor	.25	.60
12 Drew Bledsoe	.40	1.00
13 Travis Henry	.25	.60
14 Eric Moulds	.30	.75
15 Peerless Price	.25	.60
16 Alex Van Pelt	.25	.60
17 Muhsin Muhammad	.30	.75
18 Lamar Smith	.30	.75
19 Steve Smith	.40	1.00
20 Chris Weinke	.25	.60
21 Marty Booker	.30	.75
22 Jim Miller	.25	.60
23 David Terrell	.25	.60
24 Anthony Thomas	.30	.75
25 Corey Dillon	.30	.75
26 Chad Johnson	.40	1.00
27 Jon Kitna	.30	.75
28 Peter Warrick	.30	.75
29 Tim Couch	.25	.60
30 James Jackson	.25	.60
31 Kevin Johnson	.25	.60
32 Quincy Morgan	.25	.60
33 Quincy Carter	.25	.60
34 Joey Galloway	.30	.75
35 Rocket Ismail	.30	.75
36 Emmitt Smith	1.00	2.50
37 Terrell Davis	.40	1.00
38 Brian Griese	.30	.75
39 Ed McCaffrey	.30	.75
40 Rod Smith	.30	.75
41 Scotty Anderson	.25	.60
42 Az-Zahir Hakim	.25	.60
43 Mike McMahon	.25	.60
44 Bill Schroeder	.25	.60
45 Brett Favre	1.00	2.50
46 Robert Ferguson	.30	.75
47 Terry Glenn	.30	.75
48 Ahman Green	.30	.75
49 James Allen	.25	.60
50 Corey Bradford	.25	.60
51 Jermaine Lewis	.25	.60
52 Marvin Harrison	.40	1.00
53 Edgerrin James	.30	.75
54 Peyton Manning	.75	2.00
55 Reggie Wayne	.40	1.00
56 Mark Brunell	.30	.75
57 Keenan McCardell	.30	.75
58 Jimmy Smith	.30	.75
59 Fred Taylor	.30	.75
60 Derrick Alexander	.25	.60
61 Tony Gonzalez	.40	1.00
62 Trent Green	.30	.75
63 Priest Holmes	.40	1.00
64 Chris Chambers	.30	.75
65 Jay Fiedler	.30	.75
66 James McKnight	.25	.60
67 Ricky Williams	.30	.75
68 Michael Bennett	.30	.75
69 Daunte Culpepper	.30	.75
70 Randy Moss	.40	1.00
71 Tom Brady	1.00	2.50
72 Troy Brown	.30	.75
73 Antowain Smith	.30	.75
74 Aaron Brooks	.30	.75
75 Joe Horn	.30	.75
76 Willie Jackson	.25	.60
77 Deuce McAllister	.30	.75
78 Tiki Barber	.40	1.00
79 Kerry Collins	.30	.75
80 Ron Dayne	.30	.75
81 Ike Hilliard	.30	.75
82 Wayne Chrebet	.30	.75
83 Laveranues Coles	.30	.75
84 Curtis Martin	.40	1.00
85 Vinny Testaverde	.30	.75
86 Tim Brown	.40	1.00
87 Rich Gannon	.30	.75
88 Charlie Garner	.30	.75
89 Jerry Rice	.75	2.00
90 Correll Buckhalter	.30	.75
91 Donovan McNabb	.40	1.00
92 Duce Staley	.30	.75
93 James Thrash	.30	.75
94 Jerome Bettis	.40	1.00
95 Plaxico Burress	.30	.75
96 Kordell Stewart	.30	.75
97 Hines Ward	.40	1.00
98 Isaac Bruce	.40	1.00
99 Marshall Faulk	.40	1.00
100 Torry Holt	.40	1.00
101 Kurt Warner	.40	1.00
102 Drew Brees	.60	1.50
103 Tim Dwight	.25	.60
104 Doug Flutie	.40	1.00
105 LaDainian Tomlinson	.50	1.25
106 Jeff Garcia	.30	.75
107 Garrison Hearst	.30	.75
108 Terrell Owens	.40	1.00
109 J.J. Stokes	.25	.60
110 Shaun Alexander	.30	.75
111 Trent Dilfer	.30	.75
112 Darrell Jackson	.30	.75
113 Koren Robinson	.25	.60
114 Mike Alstott	.30	.75
115 Brad Johnson	.30	.75
116 Keyshawn Johnson	.30	.75
117 Michael Pittman	.30	.75
118 Kevin Dyson	.30	.75
119 Eddie George	.30	.75
120 Derrick Mason	.30	.75
121 Steve McNair	.40	1.00
122 Reidel Anthony	.25	.60
123 Stephen Davis	.30	.75
124 Rod Gardner	.25	.60
125 Jacquez Green	.25	.60
126 Jason McAddley RC	1.25	3.00
127 Josh McCown RC	1.50	4.00
128 T.J. Duckett RC	1.50	4.00
129 Kahlil Hill RC	1.00	2.50
130 Kurt Kittner RC	1.00	2.50
131 Ron Johnson RC	1.25	3.00
132 Chester Taylor RC	1.50	4.00
133 Josh Reed RC	1.25	3.00
134 Randy Fasani RC	1.25	3.00
135 DeShaun Foster RC	1.50	4.00
136 Julius Peppers RC	3.00	8.00
137 Eric McCoo RC	1.00	2.50
138 Adrian Peterson RC	1.50	4.00
139 Andre Davis RC	1.25	3.00
140 William Green RC	1.25	3.00
141 Antonio Bryant RC	1.50	4.00
142 Roy Williams RC	1.50	4.00
143 Ashley Lelie RC	1.25	3.00
144 Clinton Portis RC	2.00	5.00
145 Joey Harrington RC	1.50	4.00
146 Luke Staley RC	1.00	2.50
147 Javon Walker RC	1.50	4.00
148 David Carr RC	1.50	4.00
149 Jabar Gaffney RC	1.50	4.00
150 Jonathan Wells RC	1.50	4.00
151 David Garrard RC	2.00	5.00
152 Leonard Henry RC	1.00	2.50
153 Major Applewhite RC	1.50	4.00
154 Deion Branch RC	1.50	4.00
155 Rohan Davey RC	1.50	4.00
156 Daniel Graham RC	1.25	3.00
157 Antwoine Womack RC	1.00	2.50
158 J.T. O'Sullivan RC	1.25	3.00
159 Donte Stallworth RC	1.50	4.00
160 Jeremy Shockey RC	2.50	6.00
161 Ronald Curry RC	1.25	3.00
162 Larry Ned RC	1.00	2.50
163 Freddie Milons RC	1.00	2.50
164 Brian Westbrook RC	2.50	6.00
165 Lee Mays RC	1.00	2.50
166 Antwaan Randle El RC	1.50	4.00
167 Eric Crouch RC	1.50	4.00
168 Lamar Gordon RC	1.25	3.00
169 Reche Caldwell RC	1.50	4.00
170 Maurice Morris RC	1.25	3.00
171 Travis Stephens RC	1.00	2.50
172 Marquise Walker RC	1.00	2.50
173 Ladell Betts RC	1.50	4.00
174 Patrick Ramsey RC	1.50	4.00
175 Cliff Russell RC	1.00	2.50
176 Dameon Hunter RC	1.00	2.50
177 Javin Hunter RC	1.00	2.50
178 Tellis Redmon RC	1.00	2.50
179 Ed Reed RC	6.00	15.00
180 Jamin Elliott RC	1.00	2.50
181 Chad Hutchinson RC	1.00	2.50
182 Eddie Drummond RC	1.00	2.50
183 Najeh Davenport RC	1.50	4.00
184 Craig Nall RC	1.25	3.00
185 Jarrod Baxter RC	1.00	2.50
186 Marc Boerigter RC	1.50	4.00
187 Kelly Campbell RC	1.25	3.00
188 Shaun Hill RC	2.00	5.00
189 Tim Carter RC	1.25	3.00
190 Daryl Jones RC	1.00	2.50
191 Phillip Buchanon RC	1.50	4.00
192 Napoleon Harris RC	1.25	3.00
193 Seth Burford RC	1.00	2.50
194 Brandon Doman RC	1.00	2.50
195 Jerramy Stevens RC	1.50	4.00

2002 Pacific Heads Up Blue

*VETS 1-125: 2X TO 5X BASIC CARDS
*ROOKIES 126-175: .5X TO 1.2X
BLUE/210 ODDS 2:19 HOB, 1:25 RET
STATED PRINT RUN 210 SER.#'d SETS

2002 Pacific Heads Up Purple

*VETS 1-125: 10X TO 25X BASIC CARDS
*ROOKIES 126-175: 2X TO 5X
PURPLE PRINT RUN 25 SER.#'d SETS

2002 Pacific Heads Up Red

*VETS 1-125: 4X TO 10X BASIC CARDS
*ROOKIES 126-175: 1X TO 2.5X
RED/65 STATED ODDS 1:19 HOB
STATED PRINT RUN 65 SER.#'d SETS

2002 Pacific Heads Up Bobble Head Dolls

STATED ODDS 1 PER BOX		
1 Jerome Bettis	6.00	15.00
2 Tom Brady	15.00	40.00
3 David Carr	6.00	15.00
4 Daunte Culpepper	5.00	12.00
5 Marshall Faulk	6.00	15.00
6 Brett Favre	15.00	40.00
7 Randy Moss	6.00	15.00
8 Jerry Rice	12.00	30.00
9 Emmitt Smith	15.00	40.00
10 Anthony Thomas	5.00	12.00
11 LaDainian Tomlinson	8.00	20.00
12 Michael Vick	10.00	25.00
13 Kurt Warner	6.00	15.00
14 Ricky Williams	5.00	12.00

2002 Pacific Heads Up Game Worn Jersey Quads

STATED ODDS 2:19 HOB, 1:97 RET
*GOLD/45: .8X TO 2X BASIC QUAD
GOLD PRINT RUN 45 SER.#'d SETS

1 David Boston	8.00	20.00
Thomas Jones		
Jake Plummer		
Frank Sanders		
2 Bill Gramatica	5.00	12.00
Mar Tay Jenkins		
Joel Makovicka		
Tywan Mitchell		
3 Obafemi Ayanbadejo	6.00	15.00
Todd Heap		
Chris Redman		
Travis Taylor		
4 Shawn Bryson	6.00	15.00
Reggie Germany		
Sammy Morris		
Jay Riemersma		
5 Isaac Byrd	6.00	15.00
Muhsin Muhammad		
Wesley Walls		
Chris Weinke		
6 Marty Booker	8.00	20.00
Jim Miller		
David Terrell		
Brian Urlacher		
7 Corey Dillon	8.00	20.00
Chad Johnson		
Darnay Scott		
Peter Warrick		
8 Curtis Keaton	6.00	15.00
Scott Mitchell		
Brad St. Louis		
Nick Williams		
9 Tim Couch	5.00	12.00
JaJuan Dawson		
Kevin Johnson		
Jamel White		
10 Cris Carter	15.00	40.00
Joey Galloway		
Rocket Ismail		
Emmitt Smith		
11 Troy Hambrick	6.00	15.00
Michael Wiley		
Darren Woodson		
Anthony Wright		
12 Mike Anderson	6.00	15.00
Olandis Gary		
Brian Griese		
Rod Smith		
13 Brett Favre	20.00	50.00
Antonio Freeman		
Ahman Green		
David Martin		
14 Tyrone Davis	6.00	15.00
Robert Ferguson		
Bubba Franks		
William Henderson		
15 Marvin Harrison	15.00	40.00
Edgerrin James		
Peyton Manning		
Marcus Pollard		
16 Mark Brunell	6.00	15.00
Keenan McCardell		
Jimmy Smith		
Fred Taylor		
17 Tony Gonzalez	8.00	20.00
Trent Green		
Sylvester Morris		
Tony Richardson		
18 Jay Fiedler	8.00	20.00
Oronde Gadsden		
Travis Minor		
Zach Thomas		
19 Michael Bennett	8.00	20.00
Cris Carter		
Daunte Culpepper		
Randy Moss		
20 Drew Bledsoe	20.00	50.00
Tom Brady		
Troy Brown		
Patrick Pass		
21 Aaron Brooks	6.00	15.00
Joe Horn		
Deuce McAllister		
Robert Wilson		
22 Tiki Barber	8.00	20.00
Kerry Collins		
Ron Dayne		
Amani Toomer		
23 Jonathan Carter	6.00	15.00
Ron Dixon		
Ike Hilliard		
Jason Sehorn		
24 Anthony Becht	8.00	20.00
Laveranues Coles		
Curtis Martin		
Chad Pennington		
25 Tim Brown	15.00	40.00
Zack Crockett		
Jerry Rice		
Charles Woodson		
26 David Dunn	6.00	15.00
James Jett		
Randy Jordan		
Jerry Porter		
27 Chad Lewis	8.00	20.00
Donovan McNabb		
Brian Mitchell		
Todd Pinkston		
28 Jerome Bettis	10.00	25.00
Plaxico Burress		
Kordell Stewart		
Hines Ward		
29 Isaac Bruce	8.00	20.00
Marshall Faulk		
Torry Holt		
Kurt Warner JSY		
30 Drew Brees	12.00	30.00
Doug Flutie		
Junior Seau		
LaDainian Tomlinson		
31 Terrell Fletcher	5.00	12.00
Trevor Gaylor		
Ronney Jenkins		
Fred McCrary		
32 Jeff Garcia	8.00	20.00
Terrell Owens		
Tim Rattay		
J.J. Stokes		
33 Fred Beasley	6.00	15.00
Greg Clark		
Paul Smith		
Cedrick Wilson		
34 Shaun Alexander	8.00	20.00
Alex Bannister		
Matt Hasselbeck		
Darrell Jackson		
35 Brock Huard	6.00	15.00
Itula Mili		
Mack Strong		
James Williams		
36 Joe Hamilton	6.00	15.00
Brad Johnson		
Rob Johnson		
Shaun King		
37 Mike Alstott	6.00	15.00
Keyshawn Johnson		
Warren Sapp		
Aaron Stecker		
38 Kevin Dyson	8.00	20.00
Eddie George		
Derrick Mason		
Steve McNair		
39 David Boston	6.00	15.00
Jake Plummer		
Corey Dillon		
Peter Warrick		
40 Isaac Bruce	8.00	20.00
Marshall Faulk		
Torry Holt		
Kurt Warner P		
41 Terry Hardy	5.00	12.00
Chris Greisen		
Dennis McKinley		
Brian Gilmore		
42 Marcel Shipp	6.00	15.00
Jamal Anderson		
Skip Hicks		
Lamont Jordan		
43 Rob Moore	5.00	12.00
Quentin McCord		
Avion Black		
Patrick Johnson		
44 Elvis Grbac	6.00	15.00
KevinThompson		
Tee Martin		
Todd Husak		
45 Aaron Shea	6.00	15.00
David Sloan		
Pete Mitchell		
Mark Breuner		
46 Chris Hetherington	8.00	20.00
Stanley Pritchett		
Frank Moreau		
Jim Kleinsasser		
47 Tony Simmons	5.00	12.00
Na Brown		
Charles Johnson		
Bobby Shaw		
48 Daunte Culpepper	12.00	30.00
Steve McNair		
Mark Brunell		
Michael Vick		
49 Emmitt Smith	20.00	50.00
Ricky Williams		
Curtis Martin		
Ahman Green		
50 Tim Couch	20.00	50.00
Brett Favre		
Donovan McNabb		
Drew Brees		

2002 Pacific Heads Up Head First

STATED ODDS 1:19 HOB, 1:49 RET		
1 Michael Vick	2.00	5.00
2 Brian Urlacher	1.25	3.00
3 Tim Couch	.75	2.00
4 William Green	1.00	2.50
5 Emmitt Smith	3.00	8.00
6 Joey Harrington	1.25	3.00
7 David Carr	1.25	3.00
8 Edgerrin James	1.00	2.50
9 Peyton Manning	2.50	6.00
10 Ricky Williams	1.00	2.50
11 Randy Moss	1.25	3.00
12 Jerry Rice	2.50	6.00
13 Donovan McNabb	1.25	3.00
14 Marshall Faulk	1.25	3.00
15 LaDainian Tomlinson	1.50	4.00
16 Shaun Alexander	1.00	2.50

2002 Pacific Heads Up Inside the Numbers

STATED ODDS 2:19 HOB, 2:25 RET		
1 T.J. Duckett	1.00	2.50
2 Michael Vick	1.50	4.00
3 DeShaun Foster	1.00	2.50
4 Anthony Thomas	.75	2.00
5 William Green	.75	2.00
6 Emmitt Smith	2.50	6.00
7 Terrell Davis	1.00	2.50
8 Joey Harrington	1.00	2.50
9 Brett Favre	2.50	6.00
10 David Carr	1.00	2.50
11 Jabar Gaffney	1.00	2.50
12 Edgerrin James	.75	2.00
13 Peyton Manning	2.00	5.00
14 Ricky Williams	.75	2.00
15 Daunte Culpepper	.75	2.00
16 Randy Moss	1.00	2.50
17 Tom Brady	2.50	6.00
18 Donte Stallworth	1.00	2.50
19 Jerry Rice	2.00	5.00
20 Donovan McNabb	1.00	2.50
21 Marshall Faulk	1.00	2.50
22 Kurt Warner	1.00	2.50
23 LaDainian Tomlinson	1.25	3.00
24 Patrick Ramsey	1.00	2.50

2002 Pacific Heads Up Prime Picks

STATED ODDS 1:37 HOB, 1:97 RET		
1 T.J. Duckett	1.00	2.50
2 DeShaun Foster	1.00	2.50
3 William Green	.75	2.00
4 Ashley Lelie	.75	2.00
5 Joey Harrington	1.00	2.50
6 Javon Walker	1.00	2.50
7 David Carr	1.00	2.50
8 Jabar Gaffney	1.00	2.50
9 Donte Stallworth	1.00	2.50
10 Patrick Ramsey	1.00	2.50

2002 Pacific Heads Update

Released in late November 2002, this set contains 175 cards including over 70 rookies. Boxes contained 18 packs of 6 cards, and were packed 6 boxes per case. Each box also contained one bobble head doll. Retail boxes contained 24 packs of 3 cards. There were 20 boxes per retail case.

COMPLETE SET (175)	40.00	80.00
1 David Boston	.25	.60
2 Wendell Bryant RC	.50	1.25
3 Thomas Jones	.40	1.00
4 Jason McAddley RC	.60	1.50
5 Josh McCown RC	.75	2.00
6 Jake Plummer	.30	.75
7 T.J. Duckett RC	.75	2.00
8 Warrick Dunn	.30	.75
9 Shawn Jefferson	.25	.60
10 Kurt Kittner RC	.50	1.25
11 Michael Vick	.60	1.50
12 Dameon Hunter RC	.50	1.25
13 Javin Hunter RC	.50	1.25
14 Ron Johnson RC	.60	1.50
15 Jamal Lewis	.30	.75
16 Ray Lewis	.40	1.00
17 Chris Redman	.25	.60
18 Tellis Redmon RC	.50	1.25
19 Ed Reed RC	4.00	10.00
20 Chester Taylor RC	.75	2.00
21 Drew Bledsoe	.40	1.00
22 Travis Henry	.25	.60
23 Eric Moulds	.30	.75
24 Josh Reed RC	.60	1.50
25 Randy Fasani RC	.60	1.50
26 DeShaun Foster RC	.75	2.00
27 Muhsin Muhammad	.30	.75
28 Julius Peppers RC	1.50	4.00
29 Lamar Smith	.30	.75
30 Chris Weinke	.25	.60
31 Marty Booker	.30	.75
32 Jamin Elliott RC	.50	1.25
33 Jim Miller	.25	.60
34 Adrian Peterson RC	.75	2.00
35 Anthony Thomas	.30	.75
36 Brian Urlacher	.40	1.00
37 Corey Dillon	.30	.75
38 Gus Frerotte	.30	.75
39 Peter Warrick	.30	.75
40 Michael Westbrook	.25	.60
41 Tim Couch	.25	.60
42 Andre Davis RC	.60	1.50
43 William Green RC	.60	1.50
44 Kevin Johnson	.25	.60
45 Quincy Morgan	.25	.60
46 Antonio Bryant RC	.75	2.00
47 Quincy Carter	.25	.60
48 Joey Galloway	.30	.75
49 Chad Hutchinson RC	.50	1.25
50 Emmitt Smith	1.00	2.50
51 Roy Williams RC	.75	2.00
52 Terrell Davis	.40	1.00
53 Brian Griese	.30	.75
54 Ashley Lelie RC	.60	1.50
55 Clinton Portis RC	1.00	2.50
56 Rod Smith	.30	.75
57 Eddie Drummond RC	.50	1.25
58 Joey Harrington RC	.75	2.00
59 Mike McMahon	.25	.60
60 Bill Schroeder	.25	.60
61 James Stewart	.25	.60
62 Najeh Davenport RC	.75	2.00
63 Brett Favre	1.00	2.50
64 Tony Fisher RC	.60	1.50
65 Terry Glenn	.30	.75
66 Ahman Green	.30	.75
67 Craig Nall RC	.60	1.50
68 Javon Walker RC	.75	2.00
69 James Allen	.25	.60
70 Jarrod Baxter RC	.50	1.25
71 Corey Bradford	.25	.60
72 David Carr RC	.75	2.00
73 Jabar Gaffney RC	.75	2.00
74 Jermaine Lewis	.25	.60
75 Ed Stansbury RC	.50	1.25
76 Jonathan Wells RC	.75	2.00
77 Dwight Freeney RC	1.00	2.50
78 Marvin Harrison	.40	1.00
79 Edgerrin James	.30	.75
80 Peyton Manning	.75	2.00
81 Ricky Williams RC	.60	1.50
82 Mark Brunell	.30	.75
83 David Garrard RC	1.00	2.50
84 John Henderson RC	.60	1.50
85 Jimmy Smith	.30	.75
86 Fred Taylor	.30	.75
87 Marc Boerigter RC	.75	2.00
88 Omar Easy RC	.60	1.50
89 Tony Gonzalez	.40	1.00
90 Trent Green	.30	.75
91 Priest Holmes	.40	1.00
92 Chris Chambers	.30	.75
93 Jay Fiedler	.30	.75
94 Ricky Williams	.30	.75
95 Michael Bennett	.30	.75
96 Kelly Campbell RC	.60	1.50
97 Daunte Culpepper	.30	.75
98 Shaun Hill RC	1.00	2.50
99 Randy Moss	.40	1.00
100 Tom Brady	1.00	2.50
101 Deion Branch RC	.75	2.00
102 Troy Brown	.30	.75
103 Rohan Davey RC	.75	2.00
104 Daniel Graham RC	.60	1.50
105 Antowain Smith	.30	.75
106 Aaron Brooks	.30	.75
107 Joe Horn	.30	.75
108 Deuce McAllister	.30	.75
109 J.T. O'Sullivan RC	.60	1.50
110 Donte Stallworth RC	.75	2.00
111 Tiki Barber	.40	1.00
112 Tim Carter RC	.60	1.50
113 Kerry Collins	.30	.75
114 Daryl Jones RC	.50	1.25
115 Jeremy Shockey RC	1.25	3.00
116 Amani Toomer	.30	.75
117 Laveranues Coles	.30	.75
118 Curtis Martin	.40	1.00
119 Vinny Testaverde	.30	.75
120 Bryan Thomas RC	.50	1.25

121 Tim Brown	.40	1.00
122 Phillip Buchanon RC	.75	2.00
123 Rich Gannon	.30	.75
124 Napoleon Harris RC	.60	1.50
125 Jerry Rice	.75	2.00
126 Donovan McNabb	.40	1.00
127 Freddie Milons RC	.50	1.25
128 Lito Sheppard RC	.75	2.00
129 Duce Staley	.30	.75
130 James Thrash	.30	.75
131 Brian Westbrook RC	1.25	3.00
132 Jerome Bettis	.40	1.00
133 Verron Haynes RC	.50	1.25
134 Lee Mays RC	.50	1.25
135 Antwaan Randle El RC	.75	2.00
136 Kordell Stewart	.30	.75
137 Hines Ward	.40	1.00
138 Isaac Bruce	.40	1.00
139 Marshall Faulk	.40	1.00
140 Lamar Gordon RC	.60	1.50
141 Torry Holt	.40	1.00
142 Robert Thomas RC	.50	1.25
143 Kurt Warner	.40	1.00
144 Drew Brees	.60	1.50
145 Seth Burford RC	.50	1.25
146 Reche Caldwell RC	.75	2.00
147 Doug Flutie	.40	1.00
148 Quentin Jammer RC	.75	2.00
149 LaDainian Tomlinson	.50	1.25
150 Brandon Doman RC	.50	1.25
151 Jeff Garcia	.30	.75
152 Garrison Hearst	.30	.75
153 Terrell Owens	.40	1.00
154 Mike Rumph RC	.50	1.25
155 Shaun Alexander	.30	.75
156 Trent Dilfer	.30	.75
157 Darrell Jackson	.30	.75
158 Maurice Morris RC	.60	1.50
159 Koren Robinson	.25	.60
160 Jerramy Stevens RC	.75	2.00
161 Brad Johnson	.30	.75
162 Keyshawn Johnson	.30	.75
163 Keenan McCardell	.30	.75
164 Travis Stephens RC	.50	1.25
165 Marquise Walker RC	.50	1.25
166 Eddie George	.30	.75
167 Albert Haynesworth RC	.75	2.00
168 Derrick Mason	.30	.75
169 Steve McNair	.40	1.00
170 Ladell Betts RC	.75	2.00
171 Stephen Davis	.30	.75
172 Rod Gardner	.25	.60
173 Shane Matthews	.25	.60
174 Patrick Ramsey RC	.75	2.00
175 Cliff Russell RC	.50	1.25

2002 Pacific Heads Update Blue

*VETS: 2X TO 5X BASIC CARDS
*ROOKIES: 1X TO 2.5X
FOUR PER HOBBY BOX

2002 Pacific Heads Update Red

*VETS: 1.2X TO 3X BASIC CARDS
*ROOKIES: .6X TO 1.5X
STATED ODDS 1:2 RETAIL

2002 Pacific Heads Update Big Numbers

COMPLETE SET (20)	25.00	60.00
STATED ODDS 1:5 HOB, 1:13 RET		
1 Michael Vick	2.00	5.00
2 Anthony Thomas	1.00	2.50
3 Tim Couch	.75	2.00
4 William Green	1.00	2.50
5 Antonio Bryant	1.25	3.00
6 Emmitt Smith	3.00	8.00
7 Ashley Lelie	1.00	2.50
8 Joey Harrington	1.25	3.00
9 Brett Favre	3.00	8.00
10 David Carr	1.25	3.00
11 Peyton Manning	2.50	6.00
12 Ricky Williams	1.00	2.50
13 Daunte Culpepper	1.00	2.50
14 Randy Moss	1.25	3.00
15 Tom Brady	3.00	8.00
16 Donte Stallworth	1.25	3.00
17 Jerry Rice	2.50	6.00
18 Marshall Faulk	1.25	3.00
19 Kurt Warner	1.25	3.00
20 LaDainian Tomlinson	1.50	4.00

2002 Pacific Heads Update Bobble Head Dolls

STATED ODDS ONE PER BOX		
1 Drew Bledsoe	6.00	15.00
2 T.J. Duckett	6.00	15.00
3 Eddie George	5.00	12.00
4 Ahman Green	5.00	12.00
5 William Green	5.00	12.00
6 Joey Harrington	6.00	15.00
7 Peyton Manning	12.00	30.00

2002 Pacific Heads Update Command Performance

COMPLETE SET (20)	25.00	60.00
STATED ODDS 1:5 HOB, 1:13 RET		
1 David Boston	.75	2.00
2 Anthony Thomas	1.00	2.50
3 Corey Dillon	1.00	2.50
4 Tim Couch	.75	2.00
5 Emmitt Smith	3.00	8.00
6 Brett Favre	3.00	8.00
7 Ahman Green	1.00	2.50
8 Ricky Williams	1.00	2.50
9 Daunte Culpepper	1.00	2.50
10 Randy Moss	1.25	3.00
11 Tom Brady	3.00	8.00
12 Curtis Martin	1.25	3.00
13 Jerry Rice	2.50	6.00
14 Donovan McNabb	1.25	3.00
15 Marshall Faulk	1.25	3.00
16 Kurt Warner	1.25	3.00
17 Drew Brees	2.00	5.00
18 LaDainian Tomlinson	1.50	4.00
19 Shaun Alexander	1.00	2.50
20 Steve McNair	1.25	3.00

2002 Pacific Heads Update Game Worn Jerseys

JERSEY/50-450 ODDS 2:19 HOB
*GOLD/25: .8X TO 2X BASIC JSY/100-450
*GOLD/25: .6X TO 1.5X BASIC JSY/50-95

GOLD PRINT RUN 25 SER.#'d SETS

1 David Boston/215	3.00	8.00
2 Bryan Gilmore/250	3.00	8.00
3 Thomas Jones/350	5.00	12.00
4 Jake Plummer/215	4.00	10.00
5 Frank Sanders/335	3.00	8.00
6 Warrick Dunn/315	4.00	10.00
7 Michael Vick/250	8.00	20.00
8 Drew Bledsoe/160	5.00	12.00
9 Corey Dillon/350	4.00	10.00
10 Peter Warrick/410	4.00	10.00
11 Tim Couch/50	4.00	10.00
12 Jamel White/105	3.00	8.00
13 Emmitt Smith/270	12.00	30.00
14 Mike Anderson/215	4.00	10.00
15 Terrell Davis/250	5.00	12.00
16 Brian Griese/115	4.00	10.00
17 Ed McCaffrey/225	4.00	10.00
18 Brett Favre/50	15.00	40.00
19 Ahman Green/95	5.00	12.00
20 Marvin Harrison/150	5.00	12.00
21 Qadry Ismail/95	5.00	12.00
22 Peyton Manning/180	10.00	25.00
23 Mark Brunell/390	4.00	10.00
24 Jimmy Smith/200	4.00	10.00
25 Fred Taylor/425	4.00	10.00
26 Tony Gonzalez/305	5.00	12.00
27 Desmond Clark/275	4.00	10.00
28 Zach Thomas/195	5.00	12.00
29 Ricky Williams/125	4.00	10.00
30 Derrick Alexander/225	3.00	8.00
31 Cris Carter/305	5.00	12.00
32 Randy Moss/350	5.00	12.00
33 Tom Brady/85	15.00	40.00
34 Christian Fauria/255	3.00	8.00
35 Deuce McAllister/95	5.00	12.00
36 Curtis Martin/175	5.00	12.00
37 Tim Brown/375	5.00	12.00
38 Rich Gannon/165	4.00	10.00
39 Jerry Rice/255	10.00	25.00
40 Jon Ritchie/450	3.00	8.00
41 Correll Buckhalter/305	4.00	10.00
42 Donovan McNabb/315	5.00	12.00
43 Marshall Faulk/225	5.00	12.00
44 Kurt Warner/185	5.00	12.00
45 Terrence Wilkins/225	3.00	8.00
46 Shaun Alexander/400	4.00	10.00
47 Trent Dilfer/115	4.00	10.00
48 Itula Mili/185	3.00	8.00
49 Joe Jurevicius/100	3.00	8.00
50 Michael Pittman/145	4.00	10.00

2002 Pacific Heads Update Generations

COMPLETE SET (20)	25.00	60.00
STATED ODDS 1:5 HOB, 1:13 RET		
1 Brett Favre	2.50	6.00
David Carr		
2 Peyton Manning	2.00	5.00
Joey Harrington		
3 Kurt Warner	1.00	2.50
Patrick Ramsey		
4 Emmitt Smith	2.50	6.00
William Green		
5 Jerome Bettis	1.00	2.50
T.J. Duckett		
6 Randy Moss	1.00	2.50
Ashley Lelie		
7 Jerry Rice	2.00	5.00
Donte Stallworth		
8 Tom Brady	2.50	6.00
Josh McCown		
9 Anthony Thomas	1.00	2.50
DeShaun Foster		
10 Michael Vick	1.50	4.00
David Garrard		
11 Marshall Faulk	.75	2.00
Maurice Morris		
12 Daunte Culpepper	1.00	2.50
Rohan Davey		
13 Tim Couch	.75	2.00
Randy Fasani		
14 LaDainian Tomlinson	1.25	3.00
Clinton Portis		
15 Isaac Bruce	1.00	2.50
Jabar Gaffney		
16 Marvin Harrison	1.00	2.50
Javon Walker		
17 Kordell Stewart	1.00	2.50
Antwaan Randle El		
18 David Boston	1.00	2.50
Antonio Bryant		
19 Terrell Owens	1.00	2.50
Andre Davis		
20 Ricky Williams	1.00	2.50
Jonathan Wells		

2001 Pacific Impressions

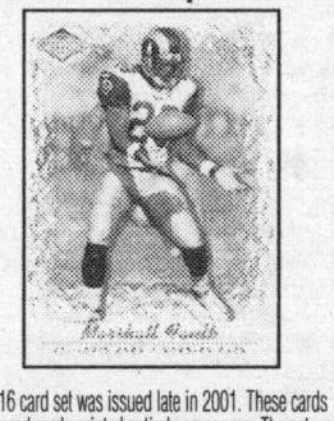

This 216 card set was issued late in 2001. These cards all featured cards printed entirely on canvas. The set was issued in three card packs with an SRP of $5.99 per pack which were issued 16 packs to a box. Cards numbered 145-216 featured rookies and were inserted at stated odds of one in 17 and were serial numbered to 117.

COMP.SET w/o RC's (144)	40.00	80.00
ROOKIE/117 STATED ODDS 1:17		
1 David Boston	.30	.75
2 Thomas Jones	.40	1.00
3 Rob Moore	.30	.75
4 Michael Pittman	.40	1.00
5 Jake Plummer	.40	1.00
6 Jamal Anderson	.40	1.00
7 Chris Chandler	.40	1.00
8 Shawn Jefferson	.30	.75
9 Terance Mathis	.30	.75
10 Elvis Grbac	.40	1.00
11 Qadry Ismail	.40	1.00
12 Jamal Lewis	.50	1.25
13 Ray Lewis	.50	1.25
14 Shannon Sharpe	.50	1.25
15 Shawn Bryson	.30	.75
16 Rob Johnson	.40	1.00
17 Sammy Morris	.40	1.00
18 Eric Moulds	.40	1.00
19 Peerless Price	.30	.75
20 Tim Biakabutuka	.30	.75
21 Richard Huntley	.30	.75
22 Patrick Jeffers	.30	.75
23 Dameyune Craig	.30	.75
24 Muhsin Muhammad	.40	1.00
25 James Allen	.30	.75
26 Marcus Robinson	.40	1.00
27 Brian Urlacher	.60	1.50
28 Corey Dillon	.40	1.00
29 Jon Kitna	.40	1.00
30 Akili Smith	.30	.75
31 Peter Warrick	.40	1.00
32 Tim Couch	.30	.75
33 Kevin Johnson	.30	.75
34 Dennis Northcutt	.30	.75
35 JaJuan Dawson	.30	.75
36 Joey Galloway	.40	1.00
37 Rocket Ismail	.40	1.00
38 Emmitt Smith	1.25	3.00
39 Mike Anderson	.40	1.00
40 Terrell Davis	.50	1.25
41 Brian Griese	.40	1.00
42 Ed McCaffrey	.40	1.00
43 Rod Smith	.40	1.00
44 Charlie Batch	.40	1.00
45 Germane Crowell	.30	.75
46 Herman Moore	.40	1.00
47 Johnnie Morton	.40	1.00
48 James Stewart	.30	.75
49 Brett Favre	1.50	4.00
50 Antonio Freeman	.50	1.25
51 Ahman Green	.50	1.25
52 Dorsey Levens	.40	1.00
53 Bill Schroeder	.40	1.00
54 Marvin Harrison	.50	1.25
55 Edgerrin James	.50	1.25
56 Peyton Manning	1.25	3.00
57 Jerome Pathon	.30	.75
58 Terrence Wilkins	.30	.75
59 Mark Brunell	.40	1.00
60 Keenan McCardell	.40	1.00
61 Jimmy Smith	.40	1.00
62 Fred Taylor	.50	1.25
63 Derrick Alexander	.30	.75
64 Tony Gonzalez	.50	1.25
65 Trent Green	.50	1.25
66 Priest Holmes	.50	1.25
67 Jay Fiedler	.40	1.00
68 Oronde Gadsden	.30	.75
69 O.J. McDuffie	.30	.75
70 Cade McNown	.40	1.00
71 Lamar Smith	.40	1.00
72 Zach Thomas	.50	1.25
73 Cris Carter	.50	1.25
74 Daunte Culpepper	.40	1.00
75 Randy Moss	.50	1.25
76 Travis Prentice	.30	.75
77 Drew Bledsoe	.50	1.25
78 Kevin Faulk	.40	1.00
79 Charles Johnson	.30	.75
80 J.R. Redmond	.30	.75
81 Jeff Blake	.40	1.00
82 Aaron Brooks	.40	1.00
83 Albert Connell	.30	.75
84 Joe Horn	.40	1.00
85 Ricky Williams	.50	1.25
86 Tiki Barber	.50	1.25
87 Kerry Collins	.40	1.00
88 Ron Dayne	.40	1.00
89 Ike Hilliard	.40	1.00
90 Amani Toomer	.40	1.00
91 Richie Anderson	.30	.75
92 Wayne Chrebet	.40	1.00
93 Laveranues Coles	.40	1.00
94 Curtis Martin	.50	1.25
95 Chad Pennington	.50	1.25
96 Vinny Testaverde	.40	1.00
97 Tim Brown	.50	1.25
98 Rich Gannon	.40	1.00
99 Charlie Garner	.40	1.00
100 Jerry Rice	1.00	2.50
101 Tyrone Wheatley	.40	1.00
102 Charles Woodson	.50	1.25
103 Todd Pinkston	.30	.75
104 Donovan McNabb	.50	1.25
105 Duce Staley	.40	1.00
106 James Thrash	.40	1.00
107 Jerome Bettis	.50	1.25
108 Plaxico Burress	.40	1.00
109 Bobby Shaw	.30	.75
110 Kordell Stewart	.40	1.00
111 Hines Ward	.50	1.25
112 Isaac Bruce	.50	1.25
113 Marshall Faulk	.50	1.25
114 Az-Zahir Hakim	.30	.75
115 Torry Holt	.40	1.00
116 Kurt Warner	.75	2.00
117 Curtis Conway	.40	1.00
118 Tim Dwight	.40	1.00
119 Doug Flutie	.50	1.25
120 Jeff Graham	.30	.75
121 Jeff Garcia	.40	1.00
122 Garrison Hearst	.40	1.00
123 Terrell Owens	.50	1.25
124 J.J. Stokes	.30	.75
125 Tai Streets	.30	.75
126 Shaun Alexander	.50	1.25
127 Matt Hasselbeck	.50	1.25
128 Darrell Jackson	.40	1.00
129 Ricky Watters	.40	1.00
130 Mike Alstott	.40	1.00
131 Warrick Dunn	.50	1.25
132 Jacquez Green	.30	.75
133 Brad Johnson	.40	1.00
134 Keyshawn Johnson	.40	1.00
135 Warren Sapp	.40	1.00
136 Kevin Dyson	.30	.75
137 Eddie George	.50	1.25
138 Jevon Kearse	.40	1.00
139 Derrick Mason	.40	1.00
140 Steve McNair	.50	1.25
141 Champ Bailey	.50	1.25
142 Stephen Davis	.40	1.00
143 Jeff George	.40	1.00
144 Michael Westbrook	.30	.75
145 Bobby Newcombe RC	3.00	8.00
146 Corey Brown RC	2.50	6.00
147 Quentin McCord RC	3.00	8.00
148 Vinny Sutherland RC	2.50	6.00
149 Michael Vick RC	15.00	40.00
150 Chris Barnes RC	2.50	6.00
151 Tim Hasselbeck RC	3.00	8.00
152 Todd Heap RC	4.00	10.00
153 Nate Clements RC	3.00	8.00
154 Reggie Germany RC	2.50	6.00
155 Travis Henry RC	3.00	8.00
156 Dee Brown RC	2.50	6.00
157 Dan Morgan RC	3.00	8.00
158 Steve Smith RC	8.00	20.00
159 Chris Weinke RC	3.00	8.00
160 David Terrell RC	3.00	8.00
161 Anthony Thomas RC	4.00	10.00
162 T.J. Houshmandzadeh RC	5.00	12.00
163 Chad Johnson RC	6.00	15.00
164 Rudi Johnson RC	4.00	10.00
165 James Jackson RC	2.50	6.00
166 Andre King RC	2.50	6.00
167 Quincy Morgan RC	3.00	8.00
168 Quincy Carter RC	3.00	8.00
169 Kevin Kasper RC	2.50	6.00
170 Scotty Anderson RC	2.50	6.00
171 Mike McMahon RC	3.00	8.00
172 Robert Ferguson RC	4.00	10.00
173 Jamal Reynolds RC	2.50	6.00
174 Reggie Wayne RC	8.00	20.00
175 Marcus Stroud RC	3.00	8.00
176 Derrick Blaylock RC	3.00	8.00
177 Ryan Helming RC	2.50	6.00
178 Snoop Minnis RC	2.50	6.00
179 Chris Chambers RC	4.00	10.00
180 Josh Heupel RC	4.00	10.00
181 Travis Minor RC	3.00	8.00
182 Michael Bennett RC	3.00	8.00
183 Deuce McAllister RC	4.00	10.00
184 Onome Ojo RC	2.50	6.00
185 Will Allen RC	4.00	10.00
186 Jonathan Carter RC	2.50	6.00
187 Jesse Palmer RC	3.00	8.00
188 Corey Alston RC	2.50	6.00
189 LaMont Jordan RC	4.00	10.00
190 Santana Moss RC	5.00	12.00
191 Derek Combs RC	2.50	6.00
192 Derrick Gibson RC	2.50	6.00
193 Ken-Yon Rambo RC	2.50	6.00
194 Marques Tuiasosopo RC	3.00	8.00
195 Correll Buckhalter RC	4.00	10.00
196 Freddie Mitchell RC	2.50	6.00
197 Chris Taylor RC	2.50	6.00
198 Adam Archuleta RC	3.00	8.00
199 Damione Lewis RC	3.00	8.00
200 Francis St.Paul RC	2.50	6.00
201 Milton Wynn RC	2.50	6.00
202 Drew Brees RC	25.00	60.00
203 LaDainian Tomlinson RC	12.00	30.00
204 Kevan Barlow RC	3.00	8.00
205 Andre Carter RC	3.00	8.00
206 Cedrick Wilson RC	3.00	8.00
207 Alex Bannister RC	2.50	6.00
208 Josh Booty RC	3.00	8.00
209 Heath Evans RC	3.00	8.00
210 Ken Lucas RC	3.00	8.00
211 Koren Robinson RC	3.00	8.00
212 Dan Alexander RC	3.00	8.00
213 Eddie Berlin RC	2.50	6.00
214 Rod Gardner RC	3.00	8.00
215 Darnerien McCants RC	3.00	8.00
216 Sage Rosenfels RC	4.00	10.00

2001 Pacific Impressions Hobby Red Backs

*VETS 1-144: 1.5X TO 4X BASIC CARDS
*ROOKIES 145-216: .25X TO .6X
RED BACK/280 ODDS 2:4 HOBBY
STATED PRINT RUN 280 SER.#'d SETS

2001 Pacific Impressions Premiere Date

*VETS 1-144: 5X TO 12X BASIC CARDS
*ROOKIES 145-216: .8X TO 2X
PREMIERE DATE/50 ODDS 1:17 HOB
STATED PRINT RUN 50 SER.#'d SETS

2001 Pacific Impressions Retail

The Retail version is essentially a parallel to the hobby canvas Impressions set except that the retail have blue cardbacks. The rookies were inserted at a stated rate of one in four retail packs.

COMP.SET w/o SPs (144)	30.00	60.00
*RETAIL VETS 1-144: .25X TO .6X HOBBY		
RETAIL ROOKIE STATED ODDS 1:4		
145 Bobby Newcombe RC	.60	1.50
146 Corey Brown RC	.50	1.25
147 Quentin McCord RC	.60	1.50
148 Vinny Sutherland RC	.50	1.25
149 Michael Vick RC	3.00	8.00
150 Chris Barnes RC	.50	1.25
151 Tim Hasselbeck RC	.60	1.50
152 Todd Heap RC	.75	2.00
153 Nate Clements RC	.60	1.50
154 Reggie Germany RC	.50	1.25
155 Travis Henry RC	.60	1.50
156 Dee Brown RC	.50	1.25
157 Dan Morgan RC	.60	1.50
158 Steve Smith RC	1.50	4.00
159 Chris Weinke RC	.60	1.50
160 David Terrell RC	.60	1.50
161 Anthony Thomas RC	.75	2.00
162 T.J. Houshmandzadeh RC	1.00	2.50
163 Chad Johnson RC	1.25	3.00
164 Rudi Johnson RC	.75	2.00
165 James Jackson RC	.50	1.25
166 Andre King RC	.50	1.25
167 Quincy Morgan RC	.60	1.50
168 Quincy Carter RC	.60	1.50
169 Kevin Kasper RC	.50	1.25
170 Scotty Anderson RC	.50	1.25
171 Mike McMahon RC	.60	1.50
172 Robert Ferguson RC	.75	2.00
173 Jamal Reynolds RC	.50	1.25
174 Reggie Wayne RC	1.50	4.00
175 Marcus Stroud RC	.60	1.50
176 Derrick Blaylock RC	.60	1.50
177 Ryan Helming RC	.50	1.25
178 Snoop Minnis RC	.50	1.25
179 Chris Chambers RC	.75	2.00
180 Josh Heupel RC	.75	2.00
181 Travis Minor RC	.60	1.50
182 Michael Bennett RC	.60	1.50
183 Deuce McAllister RC	.75	2.00
184 Onome Ojo RC	.50	1.25
185 Will Allen RC	.75	2.00
186 Jonathan Carter RC	.50	1.25
187 Jesse Palmer RC	.60	1.50
188 Corey Alston RC	.50	1.25
189 LaMont Jordan RC	.75	2.00
190 Santana Moss RC	1.00	2.50
191 Derek Combs RC	.50	1.25
192 Derrick Gibson RC	.50	1.25
193 Ken-Yon Rambo RC	.50	1.25
194 Marques Tuiasosopo RC	.60	1.50
195 Correll Buckhalter RC	.75	2.00
196 Freddie Mitchell RC	.50	1.25
197 Chris Taylor RC	.50	1.25
198 Adam Archuleta RC	.60	1.50
199 Damione Lewis RC	.60	1.50
200 Francis St.Paul RC	.50	1.25
201 Milton Wynn RC	.50	1.25
202 Drew Brees RC	5.00	12.00
203 LaDainian Tomlinson RC	2.50	6.00
204 Kevan Barlow RC	.60	1.50
205 Andre Carter RC	.60	1.50
206 Cedrick Wilson RC	.60	1.50
207 Alex Bannister RC	.50	1.25
208 Josh Booty RC	.60	1.50
209 Heath Evans RC	.60	1.50
210 Ken Lucas RC	.60	1.50
211 Koren Robinson RC	.60	1.50
212 Dan Alexander RC	.60	1.50
213 Eddie Berlin RC	.50	1.25
214 Rod Gardner RC	.60	1.50
215 Darnerien McCants RC	.60	1.50
216 Sage Rosenfels RC	.75	2.00

2001 Pacific Impressions Shadow

*VETS 1-144: 6X TO 15X BASIC CARDS
*ROOKIES 101-216: .8X TO 2X
SHADOW/25 ODDS 1:65 HOB, 1:193 RET
STATED PRINT RUN 25 SER.#'d SETS

2001 Pacific Impressions Classic Images

COMPLETE SET (10)	20.00	50.00
STATED ODDS 1:65 HOB, 1:97 RET		
1 Emmitt Smith	4.00	10.00
2 Terrell Davis	1.50	4.00
3 Brett Favre	5.00	12.00
4 Edgerrin James	1.50	4.00
5 Peyton Manning	4.00	10.00
6 Daunte Culpepper	1.25	3.00
7 Randy Moss	1.50	4.00
8 Jerry Rice	3.00	8.00
9 Donovan McNabb	1.50	4.00
10 Kurt Warner	2.50	6.00

2001 Pacific Impressions First Impressions

COMPLETE SET (20)	30.00	80.00
STATED ODDS 1:33 HOB, 1:97 RET		
1 Michael Vick	4.00	10.00
2 Travis Henry	.75	2.00
3 Chris Weinke	.75	2.00
4 David Terrell	.75	2.00
5 Anthony Thomas	1.00	2.50
6 Chad Johnson	1.50	4.00
7 Quincy Carter	.75	2.00
8 Reggie Wayne	2.00	5.00
9 Chris Chambers	1.00	2.50
10 Michael Bennett	.75	2.00
11 Deuce McAllister	1.00	2.50
12 Jesse Palmer	.75	2.00
13 LaMont Jordan	1.00	2.50
14 Santana Moss	1.25	3.00
15 Marques Tuiasosopo	.75	2.00
16 Freddie Mitchell	.60	1.50
17 Drew Brees	6.00	15.00
18 LaDainian Tomlinson	3.00	8.00
19 Rod Gardner	.75	2.00
20 Sage Rosenfels	1.00	2.50

2001 Pacific Impressions Future Foundations

STATED ODDS 1:257 HOBBY		
STATED PRINT RUN 50 SER.#'d SETS		
1 Michael Vick	15.00	40.00
2 Chris Weinke	3.00	8.00
3 David Terrell	3.00	8.00
4 Michael Bennett	3.00	8.00
5 Deuce McAllister	4.00	10.00
6 Santana Moss	5.00	12.00
7 Freddie Mitchell	2.50	6.00
8 Drew Brees	25.00	60.00
9 LaDainian Tomlinson	12.00	30.00
10 Koren Robinson	3.00	8.00

2001 Pacific Impressions Lasting Impressions

COMPLETE SET (20)	20.00	50.00
STATED ODDS 1:17 HOB, 1:25 RET		
1 Jamal Lewis	1.00	2.50
2 Peter Warrick	.75	2.00
3 Emmitt Smith	2.50	6.00
4 Mike Anderson	.75	2.00
5 Terrell Davis	1.00	2.50
6 Brian Griese	.75	2.00
7 Brett Favre	3.00	8.00
8 Edgerrin James	1.00	2.50
9 Peyton Manning	2.50	6.00
10 Mark Brunell	.75	2.00
11 Daunte Culpepper	.75	2.00
12 Randy Moss	1.00	2.50
13 Drew Bledsoe	1.00	2.50
14 Ricky Williams	1.00	2.50
15 Ron Dayne	.75	2.00
16 Jerry Rice	2.00	5.00
17 Donovan McNabb	1.00	2.50
18 Marshall Faulk	1.00	2.50
19 Kurt Warner	1.50	4.00
20 Eddie George	1.00	2.50

2001 Pacific Impressions Renderings

COMPLETE SET (20)	12.50	30.00
STATED ODDS 2:17 HOB, 2:25 RET		
1 Michael Vick	1.50	4.00
2 Travis Henry	.30	.75
3 Chris Weinke	.30	.75
4 David Terrell	.30	.75
5 Anthony Thomas	.40	1.00
6 Chad Johnson	.60	1.50
7 James Jackson	.25	.60
8 Quincy Carter	.30	.75
9 Reggie Wayne	.75	2.00
10 Chris Chambers	.40	1.00
11 Michael Bennett	.30	.75
12 Deuce McAllister	.40	1.00
13 LaMont Jordan	.40	1.00
14 Santana Moss	.50	1.25
15 Marques Tuiasosopo	.30	.75
16 Freddie Mitchell	.25	.60
17 Drew Brees	2.50	6.00
18 LaDainian Tomlinson	1.25	3.00
19 Kevan Barlow	.30	.75
20 Rod Gardner	.30	.75

2001 Pacific Impressions Triple Threads

STATED ODDS 3:17 HOB,1:97 RET		
1 David Boston	5.00	12.00
Thomas Jones		
Jake Plummer		
2 Joel Makovicka	4.00	10.00
Dennis McKinley		
Tywan Mitchell		
3 Jamal Anderson	5.00	12.00
Mike Alstott		
Stephen Davis		
4 Qadry Ismail	5.00	12.00
Pat Johnson		
Brandon Stokley		
5 Tim Biakabutuka	5.00	12.00
Brad Hoover		
Muhsin Muhammad		
6 Chris Weinke	15.00	40.00
Marques Tuiasosopo		
Drew Brees		
7 Richard Huntley	12.00	30.00
Dan Kreider		
Amos Zereoue		
8 Shane Matthews	5.00	12.00
Cade McNown		
Jim Miller		
9 Bobby Engram	5.00	12.00
Marcus Robinson		
Dez White		
10 Ron Dugans	4.00	10.00
Danny Farmer		
Craig Yeast		
11 Steve Bush	4.00	10.00
Tony McGee		
Brad St. Louis		
12 Corey Dillon	6.00	15.00
Ricky Watters		
Eddie George		
13 JaJuan Dawson	5.00	12.00
Travis Prentice		
Errict Rhett		
14 Tim Couch	10.00	25.00
Troy Aikman		
Kurt Warner		
15 Desmond Clark	5.00	12.00
KaRon Coleman		
Howard Griffith		
16 Gus Frerotte	5.00	12.00
Ed McCaffrey		
Rod Smith		
17 Brian Griese	20.00	50.00
Brett Favre		
Drew Bledsoe		
18 Terrell Davis	15.00	40.00
Curtis Martin		
LaDainian Tomlinson		
19 Charlie Batch	5.00	12.00
Johnnie Morton		
James Stewart		
20 Herbert Goodman	6.00	15.00
Ahman Green		
Dorsey Levens		
21 Marvin Harrison	15.00	40.00
Edgerrin James		
Peyton Manning UER		
(Harrison pictured twice on front)		
22 Ken Dilger	4.00	10.00
Lennox Gordon		
Terrence Wilkins		
23 Mark Brunell	6.00	15.00
Jimmy Smith		
Fred Taylor		
24 Jay Fiedler	5.00	12.00
Oronde Gadsden		
Lamar Smith		
25 Cris Carter	6.00	15.00
Daunte Culpepper		
Randy Moss		
26 Shockmain Davis	5.00	12.00
Kevin Faulk		
Terry Glenn		
27 Jeff Blake	5.00	12.00
Aaron Brooks		
Joe Horn		
28 Tiki Barber	6.00	15.00
Kerry Collins		
Ron Dayne		
29 Wayne Chrebet	5.00	12.00
Dwight Stone		
Vinny Testaverde		
30 Tim Brown	6.00	15.00
Rich Gannon		
Tyrone Wheatley		
31 Plaxico Burress	5.00	12.00
Troy Edwards		
Courtney Hawkins		
32 Giovanni Carmazzi	4.00	10.00
Rick Mirer		
Tim Rattay		
33 Shaun Alexander	6.00	15.00
Darrell Jackson		
James Williams		
34 Reggie Brown	5.00	12.00
Charlie Rogers		
Mack Strong		
35 Reidel Anthony	5.00	12.00
(Jacquez Green		
Keyshawn Johnson		

1996 Pacific Invincible

The 1996 Pacific Invincible set was issued in one series totalling 150 cards and distributed in three-card packs. The set offers a "cel" inlay in each of the 150 cards. Each card carried an "I" prefix on the card number. Jeff Blake #31 was inserted later in the production run due to the Braille embossing causing it to be short-printed versus the rest of the set. Several parallel card versions were also produced: bronze foil for hobby and silver foil for retail. There was a Platinum Blue series made which parallels both hobby and retail that was more difficult to pull. A Chris Warren Promo card was produced and modeled after the Pro Bowl insert set.

COMPLETE SET (150)	25.00	60.00
1 Larry Centers	.40	1.00
2 Garrison Hearst	.40	1.00
3 Seth Joyner	.25	.60
4 Simeon Rice RC	2.00	5.00
5 Eric Swann	.25	.60
6 Bert Emanuel	.40	1.00
7 Jeff George	.40	1.00
8 Craig Heyward	.25	.60
9 Terance Mathis	.25	.60
10 Eric Metcalf	.25	.60
11 Derrick Alexander WR	.40	1.00
12 Leroy Hoard	.25	.60
13 Andre Rison	.40	1.00
14 Tommy Vardell	.25	.60
15 Eric Zeier	.25	.60
16 Jim Kelly	.75	2.00
17 Eric Moulds RC	2.00	5.00
18 Bryce Paup	.25	.60
19 Bruce Smith	.40	1.00
20 Thurman Thomas	.75	2.00
21 Tim Biakabutuka RC	.75	2.00
22 Blake Brockermeyer	.25	.60
23 Kerry Collins	.75	2.00
24 Howard Griffith	.25	.60
25 Lamar Lathon	.25	.60
26 Mark Carrier DB	.25	.60
27 Curtis Conway	.75	2.00
28 Erik Kramer	.25	.60
29 Rashaan Salaam	.40	1.00
30 Alonzo Spellman	.25	.60
31 Jeff Blake SP	2.00	5.00
(Braille cardback)		
32 Harold Green	.25	.60
33 Carl Pickens	.40	1.00
34 Darnay Scott	.40	1.00
35 Dan Wilkinson	.25	.60
36 Troy Aikman	1.25	3.00
37 Jay Novacek	.25	.60
38 Deion Sanders	1.00	2.50
39 Emmitt Smith	2.00	5.00
40 Kevin Williams	.25	.60
41 Terrell Davis	1.00	2.50
42 John Elway	2.50	6.00
43 Anthony Miller	.40	1.00
44 Michael Dean Perry	.25	.60
45 Shannon Sharpe	.40	1.00
46 Scott Mitchell	.40	1.00
47 Herman Moore	.40	1.00
48 Brett Perriman	.25	.60
49 Barry Sanders	2.00	5.00
50 Chris Spielman	.25	.60
51 Edgar Bennett	.40	1.00
52 Robert Brooks	.75	2.00
53 Brett Favre	2.50	6.00
54 Derrick Mayes RC	.75	2.00
55 Reggie White	.75	2.00
56 Eddie George RC	2.00	5.00
57 Haywood Jeffires	.25	.60
58 Steve McNair	1.00	2.50
59 Chris Sanders	.40	1.00
60 Rodney Thomas	.25	.60
61 Tony Bennett	.25	.60
62 Quentin Coryatt	.25	.60
63 Ken Dilger	.40	1.00
64 Marshall Faulk	1.00	2.50
65 Jim Harbaugh	.40	1.00
66 Tony Boselli	.25	.60
67 Mark Brunell	.75	2.00
68 Kevin Hardy RC	.75	2.00
69 Desmond Howard	.40	1.00
70 James O.Stewart	.40	1.00
71 Marcus Allen	.75	2.00
72 Steve Bono	.25	.60
73 Neil Smith	.40	1.00
74 Derrick Thomas	.75	2.00
75 Tamarick Vanover	.40	1.00
76 Karim Abdul-Jabbar RC	.75	2.00
77 Irving Fryar	.40	1.00
78 Eric Green	.25	.60
79 Dan Marino	2.50	6.00
80 Bernie Parmalee	.25	.60
81 Cris Carter	.75	2.00
82 Warren Moon	.40	1.00
83 Jake Reed	.40	1.00
84 Robert Smith	.40	1.00
85 Moe Williams RC	2.00	5.00
86 Drew Bledsoe	1.00	2.50
87 Ben Coates	.40	1.00
88 Terry Glenn RC	1.50	4.00
89 Curtis Martin	1.00	2.50
90 Dave Meggett	.25	.60
91 Mario Bates	.40	1.00
92 Jim Everett	.25	.60
93 Michael Haynes	.25	.60
94 Torrance Small	.25	.60
95 Ray Zellars	.25	.60
96 Kyle Brady	.25	.60
97 Wayne Chrebet	.75	2.00
98 Keyshawn Johnson RC	1.50	4.00
99 Adrian Murrell	.40	1.00
100 Alex Van Dyke RC	.40	1.00
101 Michael Brooks	.25	.60
102 Dave Brown	.25	.60
103 Chris Calloway	.25	.60
104 Rodney Hampton	.40	1.00
105 Amani Toomer RC	1.50	4.00
106 Tyrone Wheatley	.40	1.00
107 Tim Brown	.75	2.00
108 Rickey Dudley RC	.75	2.00
109 Billy Joe Hobert	.40	1.00
110 Rocket Ismail	.40	1.00
111 Napoleon Kaufman	.75	2.00
112 Harvey Williams	.25	.60
113 Charlie Garner	.40	1.00
114 Bobby Hoying RC	.75	2.00
115 Rodney Peete	.25	.60
116 Ricky Watters	.40	1.00
117 Greg Lloyd	.40	1.00
118 Erric Pegram	.25	.60
119 Kordell Stewart	.75	2.00
120 Yancey Thigpen	.40	1.00
121 Jon Witman RC	.40	1.00
122 Aaron Hayden	.25	.60
123 Stan Humphries	.40	1.00
124 Tony Martin	.40	1.00
125 Leslie O'Neal	.25	.60
126 Junior Seau	.75	2.00
127 Jerome Bettis	.75	2.00
128 Isaac Bruce	.75	2.00
129 Ernie Conwell RC	.25	.60
130 Lawrence Phillips RC	.75	2.00
131 William Floyd	.40	1.00
132 Terrell Owens RC	4.00	10.00
133 Jerry Rice	1.25	3.00
134 J.J. Stokes	.75	2.00
135 Steve Young	1.00	2.50
136 Brian Blades	.25	.60
137 Christian Fauria	.25	.60
138 Joey Galloway	.75	2.00
139 Rick Mirer	.40	1.00
140 Chris Warren	.40	1.00
141 Horace Copeland	.25	.60
142 Trent Dilfer	.75	2.00
143 Alvin Harper	.25	.60
144 Dave Moore	.25	.60
145 Errict Rhett	.40	1.00
146 Terry Allen	.40	1.00
147 Gus Frerotte	.40	1.00
148 Brian Mitchell	.25	.60
149 Heath Shuler	.40	1.00
150 Michael Westbrook	.75	2.00
PCC1 Chris Warren Promo	.60	1.50
(Pro Bowl styled card)		

1996 Pacific Invincible Bronze

COMPLETE SET (149)	150.00	300.00

*STARS: 1.5X TO 4X BASIC CARDS
*RCs: .8X TO 2X BASIC CARDS
STATED ODDS 4:25 HOBBY

1996 Pacific Invincible Platinum Blue

*STARS: 2X TO 5X BASIC CARDS
STATED ODDS 1:25
*RCs: 1X TO 2.5X BASIC CARDS

1996 Pacific Invincible Silver

COMPLETE SET (149)	125.00	250.00

*STARS: 1.2X TO 3X BASIC CARDS
*RCs: .6X TO 1.5X BASIC CARDS
STATED ODDS 4:25 RETAIL

1996 Pacific Invincible Kick Starter Die Cuts

COMPLETE SET (20)	40.00	100.00
STATED ODDS 1:49		
KS1 Jeff Blake	2.50	6.00
KS2 Tim Brown	2.50	6.00
KS3 Kerry Collins	2.50	6.00
KS4 John Elway	8.00	20.00
KS5 Marshall Faulk	3.00	8.00
KS6 Brett Favre	8.00	20.00
KS7 Keyshawn Johnson	2.50	6.00
KS8 Dan Marino	8.00	20.00

KS9 Curtis Martin	3.00	8.00
KS10 Steve McNair	3.00	8.00
KS11 Errict Rhett	1.25	3.00
KS12 Jerry Rice	4.00	10.00
KS13 Rashaan Salaam	1.25	3.00
KS14 Barry Sanders	6.00	15.00
KS15 Deion Sanders	3.00	8.00
KS16 Emmitt Smith	6.00	15.00
KS17 Kordell Stewart	2.50	6.00
KS18 Tamarick Vanover	1.25	3.00
KS19 Chris Warren	1.25	3.00
KS20 Ricky Watters	1.25	3.00

1996 Pacific Invincible Pro Bowl

COMPLETE SET (20)	25.00	60.00
STATED ODDS 1:25		
1 Jeff Blake	2.00	5.00
2 Steve Bono	.60	1.50
3 Tim Brown	2.00	5.00
4 Cris Carter	2.00	5.00
5 Ben Coates	1.00	2.50
6 Brett Favre	6.00	15.00
7 Jim Harbaugh	1.00	2.50
8 Curtis Martin	2.50	6.00
9 Warren Moon	1.00	2.50
10 Herman Moore	1.00	2.50
11 Carl Pickens	1.00	2.50
12 Jerry Rice	3.00	8.00
13 Barry Sanders	5.00	12.00
14 Shannon Sharpe	1.00	2.50
15 Emmitt Smith	5.00	12.00
16 Yancey Thigpen	1.00	2.50
17 Chris Warren	1.00	2.50
18 Ricky Watters	1.00	2.50
19 Reggie White	2.00	5.00
20 Steve Young	2.50	6.00

1996 Pacific Invincible Smash Mouth

COMPLETE SET (180)	10.00	20.00
TWO PER PACK		
1 Marcus Dowdell	.05	.15
2 Karl Dunbar	.05	.15
3 Eric England	.05	.15
4 Garrison Hearst	.07	.20
5 Bryan Reeves	.05	.15
6 Simeon Rice	.15	.40
7 Jeff George	.07	.20
8 Bobby Hebert	.05	.15
9 Craig Heyward	.05	.15
10 David Richards	.05	.15
11 Elbert Shelley	.05	.15
12 Lonnie Johnson	.05	.15
13 Jim Kelly	.15	.40
14 Corbin Lacina	.05	.15
15 Bryce Paup	.05	.15
16 Sam Rogers	.05	.15
17 Bruce Smith	.07	.20
18 Thurman Thomas	.15	.40
19 Carl Banks	.05	.15
20 Dan Footman	.05	.15
21 Louis Riddick	.05	.15
22 Matt Stover	.05	.15
23 Tommy Barnhardt	.05	.15
24 Kerry Collins	.15	.40
25 Mark Dennis	.05	.15
26 Matt Elliott	.05	.15
27 Eric Guliford	.05	.15
28 Lamar Lathon	.05	.15
29 Joe Cain	.05	.15
30 Marty Carter	.05	.15
31 Robert Green	.05	.15
32 Erik Kramer	.05	.15
33 Todd Perry	.05	.15
34 Rashaan Salaam	.07	.20
35 Alonzo Spellman	.05	.15
36 Jeff Blake	.15	.40
37 Andre Collins	.05	.15
38 Todd Kelly	.05	.15
39 Carl Pickens	.07	.20
40 Kevin Sargent	.05	.15
41 Troy Aikman	.40	1.00
42 Charles Haley	.07	.20
43 Daryl Johnston	.07	.20
44 Nate Newton	.05	.15
45 Deion Sanders	.25	.60
46 Emmitt Smith	.60	1.50
47 Steve Atwater	.05	.15
48 Terrell Davis	.30	.75
49 John Elway	.75	2.00
50 Michael Dean Perry	.05	.15
51 Shannon Sharpe	.07	.20
52 David Wyman	.05	.15
53 Bennie Blades	.05	.15
54 Kevin Glover	.05	.15
55 Herman Moore	.07	.20
56 Robert Porcher	.05	.15
57 Barry Sanders	.60	1.50
58 Henry Thomas	.05	.15
59 Edgar Bennett	.07	.20
60 Robert Brooks	.15	.40
61 Brett Favre	.75	2.00
62 Harry Galbreath	.05	.15
63 Sean Jones	.05	.15
64 Reggie White	.15	.40
65 Blaine Bishop	.05	.15
66 Chuck Cecil	.05	.15
67 Cris Dishman	.05	.15
68 Steve McNair	.30	.75
69 Rodney Thomas	.05	.15
70 Jason Belser	.05	.15
71 Ray Buchanan	.05	.15
72 Quentin Coryatt	.05	.15
73 Marshall Faulk	.20	.50
74 Jim Harbaugh	.07	.20
75 Devon McDonald	.05	.15
76 Tony Boselli	.05	.15
77 Tony Brackens	.07	.20
78 Mark Brunell	.25	.60
79 Don Davey	.05	.15
80 Rich Griffith	.05	.15
81 Kevin Hardy	.07	.20
82 Mickey Washington	.05	.15
83 Louie Aguiar	.05	.15
84 Dan Saleaumua	.05	.15
85 Will Shields	.05	.15
86 Neil Smith	.05	.15
87 Derrick Thomas	.07	.20
88 Tamarick Vanover	.07	.20
89 Gene Atkins	.05	.15
90 Bryan Cox	.05	.15
91 Steve Emtman	.05	.15
92 Chris Gray	.05	.15
93 Dan Marino	.75	2.00
94 Derrick Alexander DE	.05	.15
95 Cris Carter	.15	.40
96 Jeff Christy	.05	.15
97 Robert Smith	.07	.20
98 Korey Stringer	.08	.25
99 Orlando Thomas	.05	.15
100 Esera Tuaolo	.05	.15
101 Drew Bledsoe	.25	.60
102 Eddie Cade	.05	.15
103 Mike Jones	.05	.15
104 Curtis Martin	.30	.75
105 Willie McGinest	.05	.15
106 Chris Slade	.05	.15
107 Eric Allen	.05	.15
108 Mario Bates	.07	.20
109 Jim Dombrowski	.05	.15
110 Wayne Martin	.05	.15
111 William Roaf	.05	.15
112 Irv Smith	.05	.15
113 Michael Brooks	.05	.15
114 Stacey Dillard	.05	.15
115 Rodney Hampton	.07	.20
116 Doug Riesenberg	.05	.15
117 Coleman Rudolph	.05	.15
118 Tyrone Wheatley	.07	.20
119 Kyle Brady	.05	.15
120 Roger Duffy	.05	.15
121 Keyshawn Johnson	.30	.75
122 Gary Jones	.05	.15
123 Eddie Anderson	.05	.15
124 Rickey Dudley	.15	.40
125 Napoleon Kaufman	.15	.40
126 Greg Skrepenak	.05	.15
127 Pat Swilling	.05	.15
128 Steve Wisniewski	.05	.15
129 William Fuller	.05	.15
130 Kurt Gouveia	.05	.15
131 Andy Harmon	.05	.15
132 Mike Mamula	.05	.15
133 Guy McIntyre	.05	.15
134 Ricky Watters	.07	.20
135 Kevin Greene	.07	.20
136 Bill Johnson	.05	.15
137 Carnell Lake	.05	.15
138 Greg Lloyd	.07	.20
139 Erric Pegram	.05	.15
140 Leon Searcy	.05	.15
141 Shane Conlan	.05	.15
142 Troy Drayton	.05	.15
143 Wayne Gandy	.05	.15
144 Sean Gilbert	.05	.15
145 Carlos Jenkins	.05	.15
146 Lawrence Phillips	.07	.20
147 Aaron Hayden	.05	.15
148 Stan Humphries	.07	.20
149 Leslie O'Neal	.05	.15
150 Bo Orlando	.05	.15
151 Junior Seau	.07	.20
152 Harry Swayne	.05	.15
153 Harris Barton	.05	.15
154 Merton Hanks	.05	.15
155 Rod Milstead	.05	.15
156 Ken Norton Jr.	.05	.15
157 Gary Plummer	.05	.15
158 Jerry Rice	.40	1.00
159 Steve Wallace	.05	.15
160 Steve Young	.30	.75
161 James Atkins	.05	.15
162 Brian Blades	.05	.15
163 Matt Joyce	.05	.15
164 Cortez Kennedy	.05	.15
165 Kevin Mawae	.05	.15
166 Winston Moss	.05	.15
167 Chris Warren	.07	.20
168 Derrick Brooks	.05	.15
169 Trent Dilfer	.15	.40
170 Santana Dotson	.05	.15
171 Alvin Harper	.05	.15
172 Hardy Nickerson	.05	.15
173 Errict Rhett	.07	.20
174 Warren Sapp	.25	.60
175 Terry Allen	.07	.20
176 John Gesek	.05	.15
177 Ken Harvey	.05	.15
178 Tre Johnson	.05	.15
179 Rod Stephens	.05	.15
180 Michael Westbrook	.15	.40

1996 Pacific Invincible Chris Warren

COMPLETE SET (10)	1.50	4.00
COMMON CARD (CW1-CW10)	.20	.50

1997 Pacific Invincible

The 1997 Pacific Invincible set was issued in one series totalling 150 cards and distributed in three-card packs. The fronts feature color player images on a gold, green, yellow stripe-design background with a "cel" inlay of the player's head. The backs carry player information. Several parallel versions were also produced: copper foil for hobby and silver foil for retail. There was a Platinum Blue series made which parallels both hobby and retail and was more difficult to pull.

COMPLETE SET (150)	40.00	100.00
1 Larry Centers	.40	1.00
2 Kent Graham	.25	.60
3 LeShon Johnson	.25	.60
4 Leeland McElroy	.25	.60
5 Jake Plummer RC	4.00	10.00
6 Frank Sanders	.40	1.00
7 Morten Andersen	.25	.60
8 Jamal Anderson	.60	1.50
9 Bert Emanuel	.40	1.00
10 Bobby Hebert	.25	.60
11 Roell Preston	.25	.60
12 Derrick Alexander WR	.40	1.00
13 Michael Jackson	.40	1.00
14 Byron Bam Morris	.25	.60
15 Vinny Testaverde	.40	1.00
16 Todd Collins	.25	.60
17 Andre Reed	.40	1.00
18 Antowain Smith RC	2.00	5.00
19 Steve Tasker	.25	.60
20 Thurman Thomas	.60	1.50
21 Tim Biakabutuka	.40	1.00
22 Rae Carruth RC	.25	.60
23 Kerry Collins	.60	1.50
24 Kevin Greene	.40	1.00
25 Anthony Johnson	.25	.60
26 Wesley Walls	.40	1.00
27 Darnell Autry RC	.40	1.00
28 Curtis Conway	.40	1.00
29 Raymont Harris	.25	.60
30 Rashaan Salaam	.25	.60
31 Jeff Blake	.40	1.00
32 Ki-Jana Carter	.25	.60
33 David Dunn	.25	.60
34 Carl Pickens	.40	1.00
35 Darnay Scott	.40	1.00
36 Troy Aikman	1.25	3.00
37 Michael Irvin	.60	1.50
38 Deion Sanders	.60	1.50
39 Emmitt Smith	2.00	5.00
40 Herschel Walker	.40	1.00
41 Kevin Williams	.25	.60
42 Steve Atwater	.25	.60
43 Terrell Davis	.75	2.00
44 John Elway	2.50	6.00
45 Ed McCaffrey	.40	1.00
46 Shannon Sharpe	.40	1.00
47 Scott Mitchell	.40	1.00
48 Herman Moore	.40	1.00
49 Brett Perriman	.25	.60
50 Barry Sanders	2.00	5.00
51 Edgar Bennett	.40	1.00
52 Robert Brooks	.40	1.00
53 Brett Favre	2.50	6.00
54 Antonio Freeman	.60	1.50
55 Dorsey Levens	.60	1.50
56 Reggie White	.60	1.50
57 Eddie George	.60	1.50
58 Steve McNair	.75	2.00
59 Chris Sanders	.40	1.00
60 Sean Dawkins	.25	.60
61 Marshall Faulk	.75	2.00
62 Jim Harbaugh	.40	1.00
63 Marvin Harrison	.60	1.50
64 Brian Stablein	.25	.60
65 Mark Brunell	.75	2.00
66 Keenan McCardell	.40	1.00
67 Natrone Means	.40	1.00
68 Pete Mitchell	.25	.60
69 Jimmy Smith	.40	1.00
70 Marcus Allen	.60	1.50
71 Kimble Anders	.40	1.00
72 Greg Hill	.25	.60
73 Kevin Lockett RC	.40	1.00
74 Derrick Thomas	.60	1.50
75 Tamarick Vanover	.40	1.00
76 Karim Abdul-Jabbar	.40	1.00
77 Yatil Green RC	.40	1.00
78 Randal Hill	.25	.60
79 Dan Marino	2.50	6.00
80 Stanley Pritchett	.25	.60
81 Irving Spikes	.25	.60
82 Cris Carter	.60	1.50
83 Brad Johnson	.60	1.50
84 Robert Smith	.40	1.00
85 Darryl Talley	.25	.60
86 Drew Bledsoe	.75	2.00
87 Ben Coates	.40	1.00
88 Terry Glenn	.60	1.50
89 Curtis Martin	.75	2.00
90 Sedrick Shaw RC	.40	1.00
91 Mario Bates	.25	.60
92 Troy Davis RC	.40	1.00
93 Jim Everett	.25	.60
94 Michael Haynes	.25	.60
95 Tiki Barber RC	5.00	12.00
96 Dave Brown	.25	.60
97 Rodney Hampton	.40	1.00
98 Ike Hilliard RC	1.25	3.00
99 Danny Kanell	.25	.60
100 Wayne Chrebet	.60	1.50
101 Keyshawn Johnson	.60	1.50
102 Adrian Murrell	.40	1.00
103 Neil O'Donnell	.40	1.00
104 Alex Van Dyke	.25	.60
105 Joe Aska	.25	.60
106 Tim Brown	.60	1.50
107 Rickey Dudley	.40	1.00
108 Napoleon Kaufman	.60	1.50
109 Carl Kidd RC	.25	.60
110 Ty Detmer	.40	1.00
111 Jason Dunn	.25	.60
112 Irving Fryar	.40	1.00
113 Bobby Hoying	.40	1.00
114 Ricky Watters	.40	1.00
115 Jerome Bettis	.60	1.50
116 Charles Johnson	.40	1.00
117 Greg Lloyd	.25	.60
118 Kordell Stewart	.60	1.50
119 Rod Woodson	.40	1.00
120 Tony Banks	.40	1.00
121 Isaac Bruce	.60	1.50
122 Eddie Kennison	.40	1.00
123 Lawrence Phillips	.25	.60
124 Stan Humphries	.40	1.00
125 Tony Martin	.40	1.00
126 Corey Dillon RC	5.00	12.00
127 Leonard Russell	.25	.60
128 Junior Seau	.60	1.50
129 Jim Druckenmiller RC	.40	1.00
130 Marc Edwards RC	.40	1.00
131 Ken Norton Jr.	.25	.60
132 Terrell Owens	.75	2.00
133 Jerry Rice	1.25	3.00
134 Iheanyi Uwaezuoke	.25	.60
135 Steve Young	.75	2.00
136 John Friesz	.25	.60
137 Joey Galloway	.40	1.00
138 Warren Moon	.60	1.50
139 Todd Peterson RC	.25	.60
140 Chris Warren	.40	1.00
141 Mike Alstott	.60	1.50
142 Reidel Anthony RC	.60	1.50
143 Trent Dilfer	.60	1.50
144 Warrick Dunn RC	2.50	6.00
145 Errict Rhett	.25	.60
146 Terry Allen	.60	1.50
147 Henry Ellard	.25	.60
148 Gus Frerotte	.25	.60
149 Brian Mitchell	.25	.60
150 Leslie Shepherd	.25	.60
S1 Mark Brunell Sample	1.25	3.00

1997 Pacific Invincible Copper

COMPLETE SET (150)	250.00	600.00
*COPPER STARS: 2.5X TO 6X BASIC CARDS		
*COPPER RCs: 1.2X TO 3X BASIC CARDS		
STATED ODDS 2:37 HOBBY		

1997 Pacific Invincible Platinum Blue

*PLAT.BLUE VETS: 3X TO 8X BASIC CARDS
*PLAT.BLUE RCs: 1X TO 2.5X BASIC CARDS
STATED ODDS 1:73

1997 Pacific Invincible Red

COMPLETE SET (150)	250.00	600.00
*RED STARS: 2.5X TO 6X BASIC CARDS		
*RED RCs: 1.2X TO 3X BASIC CARDS		
STATED ODDS 2:37		

1997 Pacific Invincible Silver

COMPLETE SET (150)	200.00	500.00
*SILVER STARS: 2X TO 5X BASIC CARDS		
*SILVER RCs: 1X TO 2.5X BASIC CARDS		
STATED ODDS 2:37 RETAIL		

1997 Pacific Invincible Canton, OH

COMPLETE SET (10)	40.00	100.00
STATED ODDS 1:361		
1 Troy Aikman	4.00	10.00
2 Emmitt Smith	8.00	20.00
3 John Elway	8.00	20.00
4 Barry Sanders	6.00	15.00
5 Brett Favre	8.00	20.00
6 Reggie White	2.50	6.00
7 Marcus Allen	2.50	6.00
8 Dan Marino	8.00	20.00
9 Jerry Rice	5.00	12.00
10 Steve Young	3.00	8.00

1997 Pacific Invincible Moments in Time

COMPLETE SET (20)	30.00	80.00
STATED ODDS 1:73		
1 Kerry Collins	1.50	4.00
2 Troy Aikman	3.00	8.00
3 Emmitt Smith	5.00	12.00
4 Terrell Davis	2.00	5.00
5 John Elway	6.00	15.00
6 Barry Sanders	5.00	12.00
7 Brett Favre	6.00	15.00
8 Reggie White	1.50	4.00
9 Eddie George	1.50	4.00
10 Mark Brunell	1.50	4.00
11 Marcus Allen	1.50	4.00
12 Karim Abdul-Jabbar	1.00	2.50
13 Dan Marino	6.00	15.00
14 Drew Bledsoe	2.00	5.00
15 Terry Glenn	1.50	4.00
16 Curtis Martin	2.00	5.00
17 Jerome Bettis	1.50	4.00
18 Eddie Kennison	1.00	2.50
19 Jerry Rice	3.00	8.00
20 Steve Young	2.00	5.00

1997 Pacific Invincible Pop Cards

COMPLETE SET (10)	25.00	60.00
OVERALL STATED ODDS 2:37		
*PUZZLE PIECES: .2X TO .5X BASIC INSERTS		
*GOLD PRIZES: 1X TO 2.5X BASIC INSERTS		
1 Kerry Collins	1.50	4.00
2 Troy Aikman	3.00	8.00
3 Emmitt Smith	5.00	12.00
4 John Elway	6.00	15.00
5 Barry Sanders	5.00	12.00
6 Brett Favre	6.00	15.00
7 Mark Brunell	1.50	4.00
8 Dan Marino	6.00	15.00
9 Drew Bledsoe	2.00	5.00
10 Jerry Rice	4.00	10.00

1997 Pacific Invincible Smash Mouth

COMPLETE SET (220)	10.00	20.00
ONE OR TWO PER PACK		
1 Don Majkowski	.07	.20
2 Leo Araguz	.07	.20
3 John Carney	.07	.20
4 Brett Favre	.75	2.00
5 Cole Ford	.07	.20
6 Marty Carter	.07	.20
7 John Elway	.75	2.00
8 Mark Brunell	.25	.60
9 Rodney Peete	.07	.20
10 Jeff Feagles	.07	.20
11 Drew Bledsoe	.25	.60
12 Kerry Collins	.20	.50
13 Dan Marino	.75	2.00
14 Torrian Gray	.07	.20
15 Reidel Anthony	.20	.50
16 Jim Druckenmiller	.10	.30
17 Jim Everett	.07	.20
18 Pat Barnes	.20	.50
19 Ike Hilliard	.20	.50
20 Barry Sanders	.60	1.50
21 Terry Allen	.20	.50
22 Emmitt Smith	.60	1.50
23 Antowain Smith	.30	.75
24 Robert Griffith	.07	.20
25 Mickey Washington	.07	.20
26 Napoleon Kaufman	.20	.50
27 Eddie George	.20	.50
28 Curtis Martin	.25	.60
29 Anthony Lynn	.07	.20
30 Terrell Davis	.25	.60
31 Steve Broussard	.07	.20
32 Ricky Watters	.10	.30
33 Karim Abdul-Jabbar	.20	.50
34 Thurman Thomas	.20	.50
35 Ross Verba	.07	.20
36 Jerome Bettis	.20	.50
37 Chad Cota	.07	.20
38 Antonio Langham	.07	.20
39 Brett Maxie	.07	.20
40 James Hasty	.07	.20
41 Conrad Hamilton	.07	.20
42 Chris Warren	.10	.30
43 George Jones	.10	.30
44 Byron Hanspard	.10	.30
45 Henri Crockett	.07	.20
46 Brent Alexander	.07	.20
47 John Lynch	.10	.30
48 Renaldo Wynn	.07	.20
49 Jared Tomich	.07	.20
50 James Francis	.07	.20
51 Brian Williams LB	.07	.20
52 Kevin Mawae	.07	.20
53 Marvcus Patton	.07	.20
54 Michael Barber	.07	.20
55 Robert Jones	.07	.20
56 Ernest Dixon	.07	.20
57 Mo Lewis	.07	.20
58 Peter Boulware	.20	.50
59 Wayne Simmons	.07	.20
60 Anthony Redmon	.07	.20
61 Tim Ruddy	.07	.20
62 Victor Green	.07	.20
63 Kirk Lowdermilk	.07	.20
64 John Jurkovic	.07	.20
65 John Jackson	.07	.20
66 Kevin Gogan	.07	.20
67 Adam Schreiber	.07	.20
68 Mike Morris	.07	.20
69 Albert Connell	.20	.50
70 Tony Mayberry	.07	.20
71 Mark Tuinei	.07	.20
72 Harry Swayne	.07	.20
73 Todd Steussie	.07	.20
74 Glenn Parker	.07	.20
75 D'Marco Farr	.07	.20
76 Ed Simmons	.07	.20
77 Tarik Glenn	.20	.50
78 Rick Hamilton	.07	.20
79 Dave Szott	.07	.20
80 Jerry Rice	.40	1.00
81 Tim Brown	.20	.50
82 Charlie Jones	.10	.30
83 Jerry Wunsch	.07	.20
84 Lonnie Johnson	.07	.20
85 Reggie Johnson	.07	.20
86 Willie Davis	.07	.20
87 Greg Clark	.07	.20
88 Deems May	.07	.20
89 J.J.Birden	.07	.20
90 Chuck Smith	.07	.20
91 Coleman Rudolph	.07	.20
92 Leon Johnson	.10	.30
93 Trace Armstrong	.07	.20
94 John Thierry	.07	.20
95 Dean Wells	.07	.20
96 Mike Jones DE	.07	.20
97 Mike Lodish	.07	.20
98 Tony Siragusa	.07	.20
99 Daved Benefield	.07	.20
100 Michael Bankston	.07	.20
101 Jamal Anderson	.20	.50
102 Greg Montgomery	.07	.20
103 Mark Maddox	.07	.20
104 Matt Elliott	.07	.20
105 Joe Cain	.07	.20
106 Jeff Blake	.10	.30
107 Troy Aikman	.40	1.00
108 Brian Habib	.07	.20
109 Pete Chryplewicz	.07	.20
110 Earl Dotson	.07	.20
111 Joe Bowden	.07	.20
112 Marshall Faulk	.25	.60
113 Reggie Barlow	.07	.20
114 Marcus Allen	.20	.50
115 Jeff Buckey	.07	.20
116 Mitch Berger	.07	.20
117 Corwin Brown	.07	.20
118 Troy Davis	.10	.30
119 Rodney Hampton	.10	.30
120 Tom Knight	.07	.20
121 Michael Booker	.07	.20
122 Matt Stover	.07	.20
123 Mark Pike	.07	.20
124 Rohn Stark	.07	.20
125 Todd Sauerbrun	.07	.20
126 Corey Dillon	.75	2.00
127 Tyji Armstrong	.07	.20
128 Vaughn Hebron	.07	.20
129 Antonio London	.07	.20
130 Santana Dotson	.07	.20
131 Cris Dishman	.07	.20
132 Stephen Grant	.07	.20
133 Mike Hollis	.07	.20
134 Martin Bayless	.07	.20
135 Sam Madison	.20	.50
136 Esera Tuaolo	.07	.20
137 Hason Graham	.07	.20
138 Jim Dombrowski	.07	.20
139 Bernard Holsey	.07	.20
140 Kyle Brady	.07	.20
141 David Klingler	.07	.20
142 Don Griffin	.07	.20
143 Bernard Dafney	.07	.20
144 Derrick Harris	.07	.20
145 Charles Johnson	.10	.30
146 Dedrick Dodge	.07	.20
147 Antonio Edwards	.07	.20
148 Jorge Diaz	.07	.20
149 Marc Logan	.07	.20
150 Lou D'Agostino	.07	.20
151 Lance Johnstone	.07	.20
152 Ray Farmer	.07	.20
153 Brentson Buckner	.07	.20
154 Tony Banks	.10	.30
155 Omar Ellison	.07	.20
156 Derrick Deese	.07	.20
157 Howard Ballard	.07	.20
158 Ronde Barber	.30	.75
159 Gus Frerotte	.07	.20
160 Leeland McElroy	.07	.20
161 Devin Bush	.07	.20
162 Eddie Sutter	.07	.20
163 Sam Rogers	.07	.20
164 Carl Simpson	.07	.20
165 Lee Johnson	.07	.20
166 Tony Casillas	.07	.20
167 Randy Hilliard	.07	.20
168 Ryan McNeil	.07	.20
169 William Henderson	.10	.30
170 Irv Eatman	.07	.20
171 Derwin Gray	.07	.20
172 Rob Johnson	.20	.50
173 Derrick Walker	.07	.20
174 Chris Singleton	.07	.20
175 Chris Walsh	.07	.20
176 Marty Moore	.20	.50
177 Paul Green	.07	.20
178 Brian Williams OL	.07	.20
179 Robert Farmer	.07	.20
180 Derrick Witherspoon	.07	.20
181 Jim Miller	.20	.50
182 James Harris DE	.07	.20
183 Shannon Mitchell	.07	.20
184 Steve Young	.25	.60
185 Ronnie Harris	.07	.20
186 Trent Dilfer	.20	.50
187 Joe Patton	.07	.20
188 Jake Plummer	.60	1.50
189 Ron George	.07	.20
190 Vinny Testaverde	.10	.30
191 Ryan Wetnight	.07	.20
192 Steve Tovar	.07	.20
193 Godfrey Myles	.07	.20
194 Rod Smith WR	.20	.50
195 Zefross Moss	.07	.20
196 Jerald Sowell	.07	.20
197 Jason Layman	.07	.20
198 Ray McElroy	.07	.20
199 Tom McManus	.07	.20
200 Shawn Wooden	.07	.20
201 Tony Johnson	.07	.20
202 James Farrior	.20	.50
203 Marc Woodard	.07	.20
204 Chad Scott	.10	.30
205 Dwayne White	.07	.20
206 Warrick Dunn	.40	1.00
207 Joe Wolf	.07	.20
208 Dedric Ward	.10	.30
209 Bennie Thompson	.07	.20
210 Bracy Walker	.07	.20
211 Tracy Scroggins	.07	.20
212 Derrick Mason	.30	.75
213 Ed King	.07	.20
214 Harry Galbreath	.07	.20
215 Joel Steed	.07	.20
216 Jackie Harris	.07	.20
217 Craig Sauer	.07	.20
218 Reinard Wilson	.10	.30
219 Barron Wortham	.07	.20
220 Errict Rhett	.07	.20

1997 Pacific Invincible Smash Mouth X-tra

COMPLETE SET (59)	7.50	15.00
ONE OR TWO PER PACK		
1 Steve Young	.25	.60
2 Jeff Blake	.10	.30
3 Troy Aikman	.40	1.00
4 Brett Favre	.75	2.00
5 Gus Frerotte	.07	.20
6 Tony Banks	.10	.30
7 John Elway	.75	2.00
8 Mark Brunell	.25	.60
9 Rodney Peete	.07	.20
10 Trent Dilfer	.20	.50
11 Drew Bledsoe	.25	.60
12 Kerry Collins	.20	.50
13 Dan Marino	.75	2.00
14 Vinny Testaverde	.10	.30
15 Reidel Anthony	.20	.50
16 Jim Druckenmiller	.10	.30
17 Jim Everett	.07	.20
18 Pat Barnes	.20	.50
19 Ike Hilliard	.20	.50
20 Barry Sanders	.60	1.50
21 Terry Allen	.20	.50
22 Emmitt Smith	.60	1.50
23 Antowain Smith	.30	.75
24 Jake Plummer	.60	1.50
25 Vaughn Hebron	.07	.20
26 Napoleon Kaufman	.20	.50
27 Eddie George	.20	.50
28 Curtis Martin	.25	.60
29 Rodney Hampton	.10	.30
30 Terrell Davis	.25	.60
31 Marshall Faulk	.25	.60
32 Ricky Watters	.10	.30
33 Karim Abdul-Jabbar	.20	.50
34 Thurman Thomas	.20	.50
35 Troy Davis	.10	.30
36 Jerome Bettis	.20	.50
37 Warrick Dunn	.40	1.00
38 Leeland McElroy	.07	.20
39 William Henderson	.10	.30
40 Jamal Anderson	.20	.50
41 Errict Rhett	.07	.20
42 Chris Warren	.10	.30
43 George Jones	.10	.30
44 Byron Hanspard	.10	.30
45 Jerald Sowell	.07	.20
46 Marcus Allen	.20	.50
47 Kirk Lowdermilk	.07	.20
48 Brian Habib	.07	.20
49 Derrick Mason	.30	.75
50 Jerry Rice	.40	1.00
51 Albert Connell	.20	.50
52 Kyle Brady	.07	.20
53 Tim Brown	.20	.50
54 Charles Johnson	.10	.30
55 Jackie Harris	.07	.20
56 Lonnie Johnson	.07	.20
57 Deems May	.07	.20
58 Peter Boulware	.20	.50
59 Wayne Simmons	.07	.20

2001 Pacific Invincible

In July of 2001 Pacific released Invincible. The 300-card set featured 44 short printed rookies numbered to 299 and six rookie jersey cards serial numberd to 250. The base set design had a gold background with the player photo and a small clear cell with the player's head shot in the bottom left corner. The veteran player cards were serial numbered to 1000.

COMP.SET w/o SP's (250)	90.00	150.00
251-300 ROOKIE PRINT RUN 299		
1 David Boston	.50	1.25
2 MarTay Jenkins	.50	1.25
3 Thomas Jones	.60	1.50
4 Rob Moore	.50	1.25
5 Michael Pittman	.60	1.50
6 Jake Plummer	.60	1.50
7 Frank Sanders	.50	1.25
8 Jamal Anderson	.60	1.50
9 Chris Chandler	.60	1.50
10 Jammi German	.50	1.25
11 Shawn Jefferson	.50	1.25
12 Doug Johnson	.50	1.25
13 Terance Mathis	.50	1.25
14 Rodney Thomas	.50	1.25
15 Elvis Grbac	.60	1.50
16 Qadry Ismail	.60	1.50
17 Jamal Lewis	.75	2.00
18 Jermaine Lewis	.50	1.25
19 Ray Lewis	.75	2.00
20 Chris Redman	.75	2.00
21 Shannon Sharpe	.75	2.00
22 Travis Taylor	.50	1.25
23 Shawn Bryson	.50	1.25
24 Larry Centers	.60	1.50
25 Rob Johnson	.60	1.50
26 Jeremy McDaniel	.50	1.25
27 Sammy Morris	.60	1.50
28 Eric Moulds	.60	1.50
29 Peerless Price	.50	1.25
30 Antowain Smith	.60	1.50
31 Michael Bates	.50	1.25
32 Tim Biakabutuka	.50	1.25
33 Isaac Byrd	.50	1.25
34 Brad Hoover	.60	1.50
35 Patrick Jeffers	.50	1.25
36 Jeff Lewis	.50	1.25
37 Muhsin Muhammad	.60	1.50
38 Wesley Walls	.50	1.25
39 James Allen	.50	1.25
40 Marty Booker	.60	1.50
41 Macey Brooks	.50	1.25
42 Bobby Engram	.60	1.50
43 Cade McNown	.60	1.50
44 Marcus Robinson	.60	1.50
45 Brian Urlacher	1.00	2.50
46 Dez White	.60	1.50
47 Brandon Bennett	.50	1.25
48 Corey Dillon	.60	1.50
49 Danny Farmer	.50	1.25
50 Jon Kitna	.60	1.50
51 Darnay Scott	.60	1.50
52 Akili Smith	.50	1.25
53 Peter Warrick	.60	1.50
54 Craig Yeast	.50	1.25
55 Tim Couch	.50	1.25
56 JaJuan Dawson	.50	1.25
57 Curtis Enis	.50	1.25
58 Kevin Johnson	.50	1.25
59 Dennis Northcutt	.50	1.25
60 Travis Prentice	.50	1.25
61 Errict Rhett	.60	1.50
62 Tony Banks	.50	1.25
63 Randall Cunningham	.75	2.00
64 Rocket Ismail	.60	1.50
65 Wane McGarity	.50	1.25
66 Carl Pickens	.60	1.50
67 Emmitt Smith	2.00	5.00
68 Jason Tucker	.50	1.25
69 Michael Wiley	.50	1.25
70 Mike Anderson	.60	1.50
71 Terrell Davis	.75	2.00
72 Gus Frerotte	.60	1.50
73 Olandis Gary	.50	1.25
74 Brian Griese	.60	1.50
75 Eddie Kennison	.60	1.50
76 Ed McCaffrey	.60	1.50
77 Rod Smith	.60	1.50
78 Charlie Batch	.60	1.50
79 Germane Crowell	.50	1.25
80 Larry Foster	.50	1.25
81 Desmond Howard	.60	1.50
82 Herman Moore	.60	1.50
83 Johnnie Morton	.60	1.50
84 Robert Porcher	.50	1.25
85 James Stewart	.50	1.25
86 Donald Driver	.75	2.00
87 Brett Favre	2.50	6.00
88 Bubba Franks	.60	1.50
89 Antonio Freeman	.75	2.00
90 Ahman Green	.75	2.00
91 William Henderson	.60	1.50
92 Dorsey Levens	.60	1.50
93 Bill Schroeder	.60	1.50
94 Ken Dilger	.50	1.25
95 E.G. Green	.50	1.25
96 Marvin Harrison	.75	2.00
97 Edgerrin James	.75	2.00
98 Peyton Manning	2.00	5.00
99 Jerome Pathon	.50	1.25
100 Marcus Pollard	.50	1.25
101 Terrence Wilkins	.50	1.25
102 Kyle Brady	.50	1.25
103 Mark Brunell	.60	1.50
104 Stacey Mack	.50	1.25
105 Keenan McCardell	.60	1.50
106 Jimmy Smith	.60	1.50
107 R. Jay Soward	.50	1.25
108 Shyrone Stith	.50	1.25
109 Fred Taylor	.75	2.00
110 Derrick Alexander WR	.50	1.25
111 Kimble Anders	.50	1.25
112 Todd Collins	.50	1.25
113 Tony Gonzalez	.75	2.00
114 Trent Green	.75	2.00
115 Priest Holmes	.75	2.00
116 Tony Horne	.50	1.25
117 Frank Moreau	.50	1.25
118 Sylvester Morris	.50	1.25
119 Tony Richardson	.50	1.25
120 Jay Fiedler	.60	1.50
121 Oronde Gadsden	.50	1.25
122 James Johnson	.50	1.25
123 Ray Lucas	.50	1.25
124 Tony Martin	.60	1.50
125 O.J. McDuffie	.50	1.25
126 James McKnight	.50	1.25
127 Lamar Smith	.60	1.50
128 Jason Taylor	.75	2.00
129 Zach Thomas	.75	2.00
130 Dedric Ward	.50	1.25
131 Cris Carter	.75	2.00
132 Daunte Culpepper	.60	1.50
133 Randy Moss	.75	2.00
134 Chris Walsh RC	.50	1.25
135 Troy Walters	.50	1.25
136 Moe Williams	.50	1.25
137 Drew Bledsoe	.75	2.00
138 Troy Brown	.60	1.50
139 Kevin Faulk	.60	1.50
140 Terry Glenn	.60	1.50
141 Ty Law	.60	1.50
142 Lawyer Milloy	.60	1.50
143 David Patten	.50	1.25
144 J.R. Redmond	.50	1.25
145 Tony Simmons	.50	1.25
146 Jeff Blake	.60	1.50
147 Aaron Brooks	.60	1.50
148 Albert Connell	.50	1.25
149 Joe Horn	.60	1.50
150 Willie Jackson	.50	1.25
151 Chad Morton	.50	1.25
152 Keith Poole	.50	1.25
153 Ricky Williams	.75	2.00
154 Robert Wilson	.50	1.25
155 Jessie Armstead	.50	1.25
156 Tiki Barber	.75	2.00
157 Kerry Collins	.60	1.50
158 Ron Dayne	.60	1.50
159 Ron Dixon	.50	1.25
160 Ike Hilliard	.60	1.50
161 Jason Sehorn	.60	1.50
162 Michael Strahan	.75	2.00
163 Amani Toomer	.60	1.50
164 Richie Anderson	.50	1.25
165 Wayne Chrebet	.60	1.50
166 Laveranues Coles	.60	1.50
167 Matthew Hatchette	.50	1.25
168 Marvin Jones	.50	1.25
169 Curtis Martin	.75	2.00
170 Chad Pennington	.75	2.00
171 Vinny Testaverde	.60	1.50
172 Tim Brown	.75	2.00
173 Zack Crockett	.50	1.25
174 Rich Gannon	.60	1.50
175 Charlie Garner	.60	1.50
176 James Jett	.50	1.25
177 Randy Jordan	.60	1.50
178 Andre Rison	.60	1.50
179 Tyrone Wheatley	.60	1.50
180 Charles Woodson	.75	2.00
181 Darnell Autry	.50	1.25
182 Charles Johnson	.50	1.25
183 Chad Lewis	.50	1.25
184 Donovan McNabb	.75	2.00
185 Todd Pinkston	.50	1.25
186 Stanley Pritchett	.50	1.25
187 Torrance Small	.50	1.25
188 Duce Staley	.60	1.50
189 James Thrash	.60	1.50
190 Jerome Bettis	.75	2.00
191 Plaxico Burress	.60	1.50
192 Troy Edwards	.50	1.25
193 Courtney Hawkins	.50	1.25
194 Richard Huntley	.50	1.25
195 Bobby Shaw	.50	1.25
196 Kordell Stewart	.60	1.50
197 Hines Ward	.75	2.00
198 Isaac Bruce	.75	2.00

199 Trung Canidate	.50	1.25
200 Marshall Faulk	.75	2.00
201 Az-Zahir Hakim	.50	1.25
202 Torry Holt	.60	1.50
203 Ricky Proehl	.50	1.25
204 Kurt Warner	1.25	3.00
205 Aeneas Williams	.60	1.50
206 Curtis Conway	.60	1.50
207 Tim Dwight	.60	1.50
208 Jermaine Fazande	.50	1.25
209 Terrell Fletcher	.50	1.25
210 Doug Flutie	.75	2.00
211 Jeff Graham	.50	1.25
212 Freddie Jones	.50	1.25
213 Reggie Jones	.50	1.25
214 Junior Seau	.75	2.00
215 Fred Beasley	.50	1.25
216 Jeff Garcia	.60	1.50
217 Terrell Owens	.75	2.00
218 Jerry Rice	1.50	4.00
219 Paul Smith	.50	1.25
220 J.J. Stokes	.50	1.25
221 Tai Streets	.50	1.25
222 Shaun Alexander	.75	2.00
223 Karsten Bailey	.50	1.25
224 Matt Hasselbeck	.75	2.00
225 Brock Huard	.50	1.25
226 Darrell Jackson	.60	1.50
227 Shawn Springs	.50	1.25
228 Ricky Watters	.60	1.50
229 James Williams WR	.50	1.25
230 Mike Alstott	.60	1.50
231 Reidel Anthony	.50	1.25
232 Warrick Dunn	.75	2.00
233 Jacquez Green	.50	1.25
234 Brad Johnson	.60	1.50
235 Keyshawn Johnson	.60	1.50
236 Shaun King	.50	1.25
237 Warren Sapp	.60	1.50
238 Kevin Dyson	.50	1.25
239 Eddie George	.75	2.00
240 Jevon Kearse	.60	1.50
241 Derrick Mason	.60	1.50
242 Steve McNair	.75	2.00
243 Chris Sanders	.50	1.25
244 Frank Wycheck	.50	1.25
245 Stephen Alexander	.50	1.25
246 Stephen Davis	.60	1.50
247 Irving Fryar	.60	1.50
248 Jeff George	.60	1.50
249 Kevin Lockett	.50	1.25
250 Michael Westbrook	.50	1.25
251 Bobby Newcombe RC	1.50	4.00
252 Alge Crumpler RC	2.00	5.00
253 Vinny Sutherland RC	1.25	3.00
254 Michael Vick RC	8.00	20.00
255 Travis Henry RC	1.50	4.00
256 Dan Morgan RC	1.50	4.00
257 Chris Weinke JSY/250 RC	4.00	10.00
258 David Terrell RC	1.50	4.00
259 Anthony Thomas JSY/250 RC	5.00	12.00
260 T.J. Houshmandzadeh RC	2.50	6.00
261 Chad Johnson RC	3.00	8.00
262 Rudi Johnson RC	2.00	5.00
263 James Jackson RC	1.25	3.00
264 Quincy Morgan RC	1.50	4.00
265 Scotty Anderson RC	1.25	3.00
266 Mike McMahon RC	1.50	4.00
267 Robert Ferguson RC	2.00	5.00
268 Reggie Wayne RC	4.00	10.00
269 Snoop Minnis RC	1.25	3.00
270 Chris Chambers RC	2.00	5.00
271 Josh Heupel RC	2.00	5.00
272 Travis Minor RC	1.50	4.00
273 Michael Bennett RC	1.50	4.00
274 Ben Leard RC	1.25	3.00
275 Deuce McAllister RC	2.00	5.00
276 Moran Norris RC	1.25	3.00
277 Jesse Palmer RC	1.50	4.00
278 LaMont Jordan RC	2.00	5.00
279 Santana Moss RC	2.50	6.00
280 Ken-Yon Rambo RC	1.25	3.00
281 Marques Tuiasosopo JSY/250 RC	4.00	10.00
282 Correll Buckhalter RC	2.00	5.00
283 A.J. Feeley RC	1.50	4.00
284 Freddie Mitchell JSY/250 RC	3.00	8.00
285 Joey Getherall RC	1.25	3.00
286 Chris Taylor RC	1.25	3.00
287 Adam Archuleta RC	1.50	4.00
288 David Rivers RC	1.25	3.00
289 Drew Brees JSY/250 RC	30.00	60.00
290 LaDainian Tomlinson JSY/250 RC	15.00	40.00
291 David Allen RC	1.25	3.00
292 Kevan Barlow RC	1.50	4.00
293 Cedrick Wilson RC	1.50	4.00
294 Alex Bannister RC	1.25	3.00
295 Josh Booty RC	1.50	4.00
296 Heath Evans RC	1.50	4.00
297 Koren Robinson RC	1.50	4.00
298 Dan Alexander RC	1.50	4.00
299 Rod Gardner RC	1.50	4.00
300 Sage Rosenfels RC	2.00	5.00

2001 Pacific Invincible Blue

*VETS 1-250: 1.2X TO 3X BASIC CARDS
*VET JSY 1-250: 2.5X TO 6X BASIC CARDS
1-250 VETERAN PRINT RUN 250
*ROOKIES: .8X TO 2X BASIC RC
*ROOKIES: .4X TO 1X BASIC JSY
251-300 ROOKIE PRINT RUN 99

2001 Pacific Invincible Premiere Date

*VETS 1-250: 2.5X TO 6X BASIC CARDS
*ROOKIES 251-300: 1X TO 2.5X BASE RC
*ROOKIES: .5X TO 1.2X BASE JSY RC
STATED PRINT RUN 55 SERIAL #'d SETS

2001 Pacific Invincible Red

*VETS: .5X TO 1.2X BASIC CARDS
*VET JSY: 1.5X TO 4X BASIC CARDS
1-250 VETERAN PRINT RUN 750
*ROOKIES: .4X TO 1X BASE RC
*ROOKIES: .2X TO .5X BASE JSY RC
251-300 ROOKIE PRINT RUN 199

2001 Pacific Invincible Retail

Pacific released a retail set for Invincible in July of 2001 which was a 300-card set that paralleled the hobby base set. The card design is similar to the base set except it has a silver background instead of the gold, and the cards are not serial numbered.

COMP.SET w/o RC's (250)	30.00	60.00
251 Bobby Newcombe RC	.60	1.50
252 Alge Crumpler RC	.75	2.00
253 Vinny Sutherland RC	.50	1.25
254 Michael Vick RC	3.00	8.00
255 Travis Henry RC	.60	1.50
256 Dan Morgan RC	.60	1.50
257 Chris Weinke RC	.60	1.50
258 David Terrell RC	.60	1.50
259 Anthony Thomas RC	.75	2.00
260 T.J. Houshmandzadeh RC	1.00	2.50
261 Chad Johnson RC	1.25	3.00
262 Rudi Johnson RC	.75	2.00
263 James Jackson RC	.50	1.25
264 Quincy Morgan RC	.60	1.50
265 Scotty Anderson RC	.50	1.25
266 Mike McMahon RC	.60	1.50
267 Robert Ferguson RC	.75	2.00
268 Reggie Wayne RC	1.50	4.00
269 Snoop Minnis RC	.50	1.25
270 Chris Chambers RC	.75	2.00
271 Josh Heupel RC	.75	2.00
272 Travis Minor RC	.60	1.50
273 Michael Bennett RC	.60	1.50
274 Ben Leard RC	.50	1.25
275 Deuce McAllister RC	.75	2.00
276 Moran Norris RC	.50	1.25
277 Jesse Palmer RC	.60	1.50
278 LaMont Jordan RC	.75	2.00
279 Santana Moss RC	1.00	2.50
280 Ken-Yon Rambo RC	.50	1.25
281 Marques Tuiasosopo RC	.60	1.50
282 Correll Buckhalter RC	.75	2.00
283 A.J. Feeley RC	.60	1.50
284 Freddie Mitchell RC	.50	1.25
285 Joey Getherall RC	.50	1.25
286 Chris Taylor RC	.50	1.25
287 Adam Archuleta RC	.60	1.50
288 David Rivers RC	.50	1.25
289 Drew Brees RC	5.00	12.00
290 LaDainian Tomlinson RC	2.50	6.00
291 David Allen RC	.50	1.25
292 Kevan Barlow RC	.60	1.50
293 Cedrick Wilson RC	.60	1.50
294 Alex Bannister RC	.50	1.25
295 Josh Booty RC	.60	1.50
296 Heath Evans RC	.60	1.50
297 Koren Robinson RC	.60	1.50
298 Dan Alexander RC	.60	1.50
299 Rod Gardner RC	.60	1.50
300 Sage Rosenfels RC	.75	2.00

2001 Pacific Invincible Afterburners

COMPLETE SET (20)	15.00	40.00
STATED PRINT RUN 2000 SER.#'d SETS		
1 Jamal Lewis	1.25	3.00
2 Eric Moulds	1.00	2.50
3 David Terrell	1.00	2.50
4 Corey Dillon	1.00	2.50
5 Peter Warrick	1.00	2.50
6 Marvin Harrison	1.25	3.00
7 Edgerrin James	1.25	3.00
8 Jimmy Smith	1.00	2.50
9 Fred Taylor	1.25	3.00
10 Sylvester Morris	.75	2.00
11 Chris Chambers	1.00	2.50
12 Michael Bennett	.75	2.00
13 Randy Moss	1.25	3.00
14 Santana Moss	1.25	3.00
15 Tim Brown	1.25	3.00
16 Isaac Bruce	1.25	3.00
17 Marshall Faulk	1.25	3.00
10 Torry Holt	1.00	2.50
19 LaDainian Tomlinson	3.00	8.00
20 Warrick Dunn	1.25	3.00

2001 Pacific Invincible Fast Forward

COMPLETE SET (20)	30.00	80.00
STATED PRINT RUN 1000 SER.#'d SETS		
1 Jamal Lewis	1.50	4.00
2 Eric Moulds	1.25	3.00
3 Emmitt Smith	4.00	10.00
4 Mike Anderson	1.25	3.00
5 Marvin Harrison	1.50	4.00
6 Jimmy Smith	1.25	3.00
7 Cris Carter	1.50	4.00
8 Daunte Culpepper	1.25	3.00
9 Randy Moss	1.50	4.00
10 Ricky Williams	1.50	4.00
11 Ron Dayne	1.25	3.00
12 Curtis Martin	1.50	4.00
13 Rich Gannon	1.25	3.00
14 Jerome Bettis	1.50	4.00
15 Isaac Bruce	1.50	4.00
16 Marshall Faulk	1.50	4.00
17 Torry Holt	1.25	3.00
18 Kurt Warner	2.50	6.00
19 Jeff Garcia	1.25	3.00
20 Jerry Rice	3.00	8.00

2001 Pacific Invincible Heat Seekers

COMPLETE SET (20)	30.00	80.00
STATED PRINT RUN 750 SER.#'d SETS		
1 Jake Plummer	1.25	3.00
2 Michael Vick	6.00	15.00
3 Rob Johnson	1.25	3.00
4 Cade McNown	1.25	3.00
5 Akili Smith	1.00	2.50
6 Tim Couch	1.00	2.50
7 Brian Griese	1.25	3.00
8 Charlie Batch	1.25	3.00
9 Brett Favre	5.00	12.00
10 Peyton Manning	4.00	10.00
11 Mark Brunell	1.25	3.00
12 Daunte Culpepper	1.25	3.00
13 Drew Bledsoe	1.50	4.00
14 Aaron Brooks	1.25	3.00
15 Rich Gannon	1.25	3.00
16 Marques Tuiasosopo	1.25	3.00
17 Kurt Warner	2.50	6.00
18 Jeff Garcia	1.25	3.00
19 Steve McNair	1.50	4.00
20 Jeff George	1.25	3.00

2001 Pacific Invincible New Sensations

COMPLETE SET (30)	20.00	50.00
STATED PRINT RUN 1250 SER.#'d SETS		
1 Vinny Sutherland	.40	1.00
2 Michael Vick	2.50	6.00
3 Travis Henry	.50	1.25
4 Chris Weinke	.50	1.25
5 David Terrell	.50	1.25
6 Anthony Thomas	.60	1.50
7 Chad Johnson	1.00	2.50
8 James Jackson	.40	1.00
9 Quincy Morgan	.50	1.25
10 Mike McMahon	.50	1.25
11 Reggie Wayne	1.25	3.00
12 Snoop Minnis	.40	1.00
13 Chris Chambers	.60	1.50
14 Josh Heupel	.60	1.50
15 Travis Minor	.50	1.25
16 Michael Bennett	.50	1.25
17 Deuce McAllister	.60	1.50
18 LaMont Jordan	.60	1.50
19 Santana Moss	.75	2.00
20 Ken-Yon Rambo	.40	1.00
21 Marques Tuiasosopo	.50	1.25
22 Correll Buckhalter	.60	1.50
23 Freddie Mitchell	.40	1.00
24 Drew Brees	4.00	10.00
25 LaDainian Tomlinson	2.00	5.00
26 Kevan Barlow	.50	1.25
27 Josh Booty	.50	1.25
28 Koren Robinson	.50	1.25
29 Rod Gardner	.50	1.25
30 Sage Rosenfels	.60	1.50

2001 Pacific Invincible Rookie Die Cuts

COMPLETE SET (10)	30.00	80.00
STATED PRINT RUN 100 SER.#'d SETS		
1 Michael Vick	10.00	25.00
2 Chris Weinke	2.00	5.00
3 David Terrell	2.00	5.00
4 Michael Bennett	2.00	5.00
5 Deuce McAllister	2.50	6.00
6 Freddie Mitchell	1.50	4.00
7 Drew Brees	15.00	40.00
8 LaDainian Tomlinson	8.00	20.00
9 Koren Robinson	2.00	5.00
10 Rod Gardner	2.00	5.00

2001 Pacific Invincible School Colors

COMPLETE SET (60)	30.00	80.00
STATED PRINT RUN 2750 SER.#'d SETS		
1 Doug Flutie	.75	2.00
2 Tim Hasselbeck	.60	1.50
3 Darrell Jackson	.60	1.50
4 Jesse Palmer	.60	1.50
5 Emmitt Smith	2.00	5.00
6 Fred Taylor	.75	2.00
7 Warrick Dunn	.75	2.00
8 Snoop Minnis	.50	1.25
9 Travis Minor	.60	1.50
10 Peter Warrick	.60	1.50
11 Chris Weinke	.60	1.50
12 Terrell Davis	.75	2.00
13 Olandis Gary	.50	1.25
14 Randy Moss	.75	2.00
15 Chad Pennington	.75	2.00
16 James Jackson	.50	1.25
17 Edgerrin James	.75	2.00
18 Santana Moss	.75	2.00
19 Reggie Wayne	1.25	3.00
20 Brian Griese	.60	1.50
21 David Terrell	.60	1.50
22 Anthony Thomas	.75	2.00
23 Tyrone Wheatley	.60	1.50
24 Ahman Green	.75	2.00
25 Dan Alexander	.60	1.50
26 Correll Buckhalter	.75	2.00
27 Bobby Newcombe	.60	1.50
28 Torry Holt	.60	1.50
29 Koren Robinson	.60	1.50
30 Jerome Bettis	.75	2.00
31 Tim Brown	.75	2.00
32 Joey Getherall	.50	1.25
33 Jahari Holloway	.50	1.25
34 David Boston	.50	1.25
35 Cris Carter	.75	2.00
36 Eddie George	.75	2.00
37 Ken-Yon Rambo	.50	1.25
38 Kevan Barlow	.60	1.50
39 Curtis Martin	.75	2.00
40 Mike Alstott	.60	1.50
41 Drew Brees	4.00	10.00
42 Vinny Sutherland	.50	1.25
43 Marvin Harrison	.75	2.00
44 Kevin Johnson	.50	1.25
45 Donovan McNabb	.75	2.00
46 Travis Henry	.60	1.50
47 Jamal Lewis	.75	2.00
48 Peyton Manning	2.00	5.00
49 Troy Aikman	1.25	3.00
50 Cade McNown	.60	1.50
51 Freddie Mitchell	.50	1.25
52 Keyshawn Johnson	.60	1.50
53 Junior Seau	.75	2.00
54 Rob Johnson	.60	1.50
55 Mark Brunell	.60	1.50
56 Corey Dillon	.60	1.50
57 Marques Tuiasosopo	.60	1.50
58 Ron Dayne	.60	1.50
59 Michael Bennett	.60	1.50
60 Chris Chambers	.60	1.50

2001 Pacific Invincible Widescreen

COMPLETE SET (20)	15.00	40.00
STATED PRINT RUN 2500 SER.#'d SETS		
1 Corey Dillon	1.00	2.50
2 Peter Warrick	1.00	2.50
3 Tim Couch	.75	2.00
4 Kevin Johnson	.75	2.00
5 Brian Griese	1.00	2.50
6 Brett Favre	4.00	10.00
7 Peyton Manning	3.00	8.00
8 Fred Taylor	1.25	3.00
9 Sylvester Morris	.75	2.00
10 Drew Bledsoe	1.25	3.00
11 Tyrone Wheatley	1.00	2.50
12 Donovan McNabb	1.25	3.00
13 Jerome Bettis	1.25	3.00
14 Plaxico Burress	1.00	2.50
15 Jeff Garcia	1.00	2.50
16 Terrell Owens	1.25	3.00
17 Shaun Alexander	1.25	3.00
18 Eddie George	1.25	3.00
19 Derrick Mason	1.00	2.50
20 Steve McNair	1.25	3.00

2001 Pacific Invincible XXXVI

COMPLETE SET (20)	40.00	100.00
STATED PRINT RUN 499 SER.#'d SETS		
1 Jamal Lewis	1.50	4.00
2 Rob Johnson	1.25	3.00
3 Mike Anderson	1.25	3.00
4 Terrell Davis	1.50	4.00
5 Brett Favre	5.00	12.00
6 Marvin Harrison	1.50	4.00
7 Edgerrin James	1.50	4.00
8 Mark Brunell	1.25	3.00
9 Cris Carter	1.50	4.00
10 Daunte Culpepper	1.25	3.00
11 Ricky Williams	1.50	4.00
12 Ron Dayne	1.25	3.00
13 Curtis Martin	1.50	4.00
14 Rich Gannon	1.25	3.00
15 Donovan McNabb	1.50	4.00
16 Marshall Faulk	1.50	4.00
17 Kurt Warner	2.50	6.00
18 Warrick Dunn	1.50	4.00
19 Eddie George	1.50	4.00
20 Steve McNair	1.50	4.00

1996 Pacific Litho-Cel

This 100-card set was distributed in three-card packs with a mixture of "litho" cards and "cel" cards. Action player photos are featured on the front of the Litho card in limited color with a different action photo of the same player on the back in full color. The Cel version of each card was produced in 1-color and made to be combined with a Litho card to make the front photo of the player magically appear in full color. The prices below refer to the basic "litho" cards.

COMPLETE SET (100)	15.00	40.00
*CEL CARDS: .4X TO 1X LITHO		
1 Kent Graham	.20	.50
2 LeShon Johnson	.20	.50
3 Leeland McElroy RC	.30	.75
4 Frank Sanders	.30	.75
5 Jamal Anderson RC	.50	1.25
6 Cornelius Bennett	.20	.50
7 Bobby Hebert	.20	.50
8 Earnest Byner	.20	.50
9 Michael Jackson	.30	.75
10 Vinny Testaverde	.30	.75
11 Jim Kelly	.40	1.00
12 Andre Reed	.30	.75
13 Bruce Smith	.30	.75
14 Thurman Thomas	.40	1.00
15 Kerry Collins	.40	1.00
16 Lamar Lathon	.20	.50
17 Kevin Greene	.30	.75
18 Bobby Engram RC	.40	1.00
19 Erik Kramer	.20	.50
20 Rashaan Salaam	.30	.75
21 Jeff Blake	.40	1.00
22 Garrison Hearst	.30	.75
23 Carl Pickens	.30	.75
24 Darnay Scott	.30	.75
25 Troy Aikman	.60	1.50
26 Eric Bjornson	.20	.50
27 Deion Sanders	.50	1.25
28 Emmitt Smith	1.00	2.50
29 Terrell Davis	.50	1.25
30 John Elway	1.25	3.00
31 Anthony Miller	.30	.75
32 John Mobley	.20	.50
33 Scott Mitchell	.30	.75
34 Herman Moore	.30	.75
35 Brett Perriman	.20	.50
36 Barry Sanders	1.00	2.50
37 Edgar Bennett	.30	.75
38 Robert Brooks	.40	1.00
39 Brett Favre	1.25	3.00
40 Reggie White	.40	1.00
41 Chris Chandler	.30	.75
42 Eddie George RC	1.00	2.50
43 Steve McNair	.50	1.25
44 Chris Sanders	.30	.75
45 Ken Dilger	.30	.75
46 Marshall Faulk	.50	1.25
47 Jim Harbaugh	.30	.75
48 Mark Brunell	.50	1.25
49 Keenan McCardell	.40	1.00
50 James O.Stewart	.30	.75
51 Marcus Allen	.40	1.00
52 Steve Bono	.20	.50
53 Greg Hill	.30	.75
54 Tamarick Vanover	.30	.75
55 Karim Abdul-Jabbar RC	.40	1.00
56 Dan Marino	1.25	3.00
57 Zach Thomas RC	.75	2.00
58 Cris Carter	.40	1.00
59 Warren Moon	.30	.75
60 Robert Smith	.30	.75
61 Drew Bledsoe	.50	1.25
62 Terry Glenn RC	.75	2.00
63 Curtis Martin	.50	1.25
64 Mario Bates	.30	.75
65 Jim Everett	.20	.50
66 Haywood Jeffires	.20	.50
67 Dave Brown	.20	.50
68 Rodney Hampton	.30	.75
69 Amani Toomer RC	.75	2.00
70 Adrian Murrell	.30	.75
71 Neil O'Donnell	.30	.75
72 Alex Van Dyke RC	.30	.75
73 Tim Brown	.40	1.00
74 Jeff Hostetler	.20	.50
75 Napoleon Kaufman	.40	1.00
76 Irving Fryar	.30	.75
77 Chris T. Jones	.30	.75
78 Ricky Watters	.30	.75
79 Jerome Bettis	.40	1.00
80 Kordell Stewart	.40	1.00
81 Tony Banks RC	.40	1.00
82 Eddie Kennison RC	.40	1.00
83 Lawrence Phillips RC	.40	1.00
84 Stan Humphries	.30	.75
85 Tony Martin	.30	.75
86 Leonard Russell	.20	.50
87 Junior Seau	.40	1.00
88 Jerry Rice	.60	1.50
89 J.J. Stokes	.40	1.00
90 Tommy Vardell	.20	.50
91 Steve Young	.50	1.25
92 Joey Galloway	.40	1.00
93 Rick Mirer	.30	.75
94 Chris Warren	.30	.75
95 Mike Alstott RC	.75	2.00
96 Trent Dilfer	.40	1.00
97 Nilo Silvan	.20	.50
98 Terry Allen	.30	.75
99 Gus Frerotte	.30	.75
100 Michael Westbrook	.40	1.00
P1 Chris Warren Promo Blue Litho Card	.40	1.00
P2 Chris Warren Promo Red Litho Card	.40	1.00
P3 Chris Warren Promo Blue Cel Card	.40	1.00
P4 Chris Warren Promo Red Cel Card	.40	1.00

1996 Pacific Litho-Cel Bronze

COMPLETE SET (100)	150.00	300.00
*VETS: 2.5X TO 6X BASIC LITHO		
*ROOKIES: 1.2X TO 3X BASIC LITHO		
STATED ODDS 3:25 RETAIL		

1996 Pacific Litho-Cel Silver

COMPLETE SET (100)	125.00	250.00
*VETS: 2X TO 5X BASIC LITHO		
*ROOKIES 1X TO 2.5X BASIC LITHO		
STATED ODDS 3:25 HOBBY		

1996 Pacific Litho-Cel Feature Performers

COMPLETE SET (20)	40.00	100.00
STATED ODDS 1:25		
FP1 Jim Kelly	2.00	5.00
FP2 Troy Aikman	3.00	8.00
FP3 Deion Sanders	2.50	6.00
FP4 Emmitt Smith	5.00	12.00
FP5 Terrell Davis	2.50	6.00
FP6 John Elway	6.00	15.00
FP7 Herman Moore	1.00	2.50
FP8 Barry Sanders	5.00	12.00
FP9 Robert Brooks	2.00	5.00
FP10 Brett Favre	6.00	15.00
FP11 Eddie George	2.50	6.00
FP12 Jim Harbaugh	1.00	2.50
FP13 Marcus Allen	2.00	5.00
FP14 Karim Abdul-Jabbar	1.00	2.50
FP15 Dan Marino	6.00	15.00
FP16 Joey Galloway	2.00	5.00
FP17 Curtis Martin	2.50	6.00
FP18 Jerome Bettis	2.00	5.00
FP19 Jerry Rice	3.00	8.00
FP20 Steve Young	2.50	6.00

1996 Pacific Litho-Cel Game Time

COMPLETE SET (100)	7.50	20.00
ONLY #GT97-GT100 PRINTED IN GOLD FOIL		
ONE GAME TIME PER PACK		
GT1 Eddie George	.25	.60
GT2 Larry Bowie	.02	.10
GT3 Jarius Hayes	.02	.10
GT4 Jamal Anderson	.15	.40
GT5 Ernest Hunter	.02	.10
GT6 Darick Holmes	.02	.10
GT7 Kerry Collins	.15	.40
GT8 Raymont Harris	.02	.10
GT9 Jeff Blake	.15	.40
GT10 Troy Aikman	.40	1.00
GT11 Terrell Davis	.30	.75
GT12 Kevin Glover	.02	.10
GT13 Brett Favre	.75	2.00
GT14 Al Del Greco	.02	.10
GT15 Marshall Faulk	.25	.60
GT16 Bryan Barker	.02	.10
GT17 Rich Gannon	.15	.40
GT18 Dwight Hollier	.02	.10
GT19 Dixon Edwards	.02	.10
GT20 Drew Bledsoe	.25	.60
GT21 Paul Green	.02	.10
GT22 Lawrence Dawsey	.02	.10
GT23 Ron Carpenter DB	.02	.10
GT24 Joe Aska	.02	.10
GT25 Joe Panos	.02	.10
GT26 Norm Johnson	.02	.10
GT27 Tony Banks	.15	.40
GT28 Darren Bennett	.02	.10
GT29 Steve Israel	.02	.10
GT30 Michael Barber	.02	.10
GT31 Dexter Nottage	.02	.10
GT32 Kwamie Lassiter	.15	.40
GT33 Travis Hall	.02	.10
GT34 Greg Montgomery	.02	.10
GT35 Jim Kelly	.15	.40
GT36 Matt Elliott	.02	.10
GT37 Jack Jackson	.02	.10
GT38 Ki-Jana Carter	.07	.20
GT39 Deion Sanders	.25	.60
GT40 Jason Elam	.07	.20
GT41 Johnnie Morton	.07	.20
GT42 Darius Holland	.02	.10
GT43 Sheddrick Wilson	.02	.10
GT44 Derrick Frazier	.02	.10
GT45 Travis Davis	.02	.10
GT46 Pellom McDaniels	.02	.10
GT47 Dan Marino	.75	2.00
GT48 Ben Hanks	.02	.10
GT49 Tedy Bruschi	2.50	6.00
GT50 Tommy Hodson	.02	.10
GT51 Amani Toomer	.20	.50
GT52 Brian Hansen	.02	.10
GT53 Paul Butcher	.02	.10
GT54 Kevin Turner	.02	.10
GT55 Darren Perry	.02	.10
GT56 Mike Gruttadauria	.02	.10
GT57 Charlie Jones	.02	.10
GT58 Iheanyi Uwaezuoke	.02	.10
GT59 Glenn Montgomery	.02	.10
GT60 Mike Alstott	.20	.50
GT61 Joe Patton	.02	.10
GT62 Leeland McElroy	.07	.20
GT63 Robbie Tobeck	.02	.10
GT64 Vinny Testaverde	.07	.20
GT65 Chris Spielman	.02	.10
GT66 Anthony Johnson	.07	.20
GT67 Todd Sauerbrun	.02	.10
GT68 Jeff Hill	.02	.10
GT69 Emmitt Smith	.60	1.50
GT70 John Elway	.75	2.00
GT71 Barry Sanders	.60	1.50
GT72 Brian Williams LB	.02	.10
GT73 Chris Gardocki	.02	.10
GT74 Jimmy Smith	.15	.40
GT75 Ricky Siglar	.02	.10
GT76 Tim Ruddy	.02	.10
GT77 Moe Williams	.40	1.00
GT78 Willie Clay	.02	.10
GT79 Henry Lusk	.02	.10
GT80 Brian Williams OL	.02	.10
GT81 Ronald Moore	.02	.10
GT82 Trey Junkin	.02	.10
GT83 James Willis	.02	.10
GT84 Joel Steed	.02	.10
GT85 Jamie Martin	.75	2.00
GT86 Shawn Lee	.02	.10
GT87 Steve Young	.30	.75
GT88 Barrett Robbins	.02	.10
GT89 Charles Dimry	.02	.10
GT90 Darryl Pounds	.02	.10
GT91 Herschel Walker	.07	.20
GT92 Bill Romanowski	.02	.10
GT93 David Tate	.02	.10
GT94 Marrio Grier	.02	.10
GT95 Rodney Young	.02	.10
GT96 Lamar Smith	.15	.40
GT97 Don Beebe	.10	.30
GT98 Ty Detmer	.25	.60
GT99 Ted Popson	.10	.30
GT100 Natrone Means	.25	.60

1996 Pacific Litho-Cel Litho-Proof

COMPLETE SET (36)	150.00	300.00
STATED PRINT RUN 360 SERIAL #'d SETS		
STATED ODDS 1:97		
*CERTIFIED CARDS: .8X TO 2X BASIC INSERTS		
CERTIFIED STATED ODDS 1:481		
1 Jim Kelly	5.00	12.00
2 Kerry Collins	4.00	10.00
3 Rashaan Salaam	2.50	6.00
4 Jeff Blake	3.00	8.00
5 Carl Pickens	2.50	6.00
6 Troy Aikman	6.00	15.00
7 Deion Sanders	5.00	12.00
8 Emmitt Smith	10.00	25.00
9 Terrell Davis	5.00	12.00
10 John Elway	12.00	30.00
11 Herman Moore	2.50	6.00
12 Barry Sanders	10.00	25.00
13 Robert Brooks	3.00	8.00
14 Brett Favre	12.00	30.00
15 Reggie White	4.00	10.00
16 Eddie George	4.00	10.00
17 Marshall Faulk	5.00	12.00
18 Jim Harbaugh	3.00	8.00
19 Mark Brunell	4.00	10.00
20 Marcus Allen	4.00	10.00
21 Steve Bono	2.50	6.00
22 Karim Abdul-Jabbar	2.50	6.00
23 Dan Marino	12.00	30.00
24 Warren Moon	3.00	8.00
25 Drew Bledsoe	4.00	10.00
26 Curtis Martin	5.00	12.00
27 Amani Toomer	3.00	8.00
28 Tim Brown	4.00	10.00
29 Napoleon Kaufman	2.50	6.00
30 Ricky Watters	3.00	8.00
31 Jerome Bettis	4.00	10.00
32 Kordell Stewart	3.00	8.00
33 Jerry Rice	6.00	15.00
34 Steve Young	5.00	12.00
35 Joey Galloway	3.00	8.00
36 Terry Allen	3.00	8.00

1996 Pacific Litho-Cel Moments in Time

COMPLETE SET (20)	75.00	200.00
STATED ODDS 1:49		
MT1 Jim Kelly	3.00	8.00
MT2 Kerry Collins	3.00	8.00
MT3 Rashaan Salaam	1.50	4.00
MT4 Troy Aikman	5.00	12.00
MT5 Deion Sanders	4.00	10.00
MT6 Emmitt Smith	8.00	20.00
MT7 Terrell Davis	4.00	10.00
MT8 John Elway	10.00	25.00
MT9 Barry Sanders	8.00	20.00
MT10 Robert Brooks	3.00	8.00
MT11 Brett Favre	10.00	25.00
MT12 Marshall Faulk	4.00	10.00
MT13 Jim Harbaugh	1.50	4.00
MT14 Steve Bono	1.00	2.50
MT15 Dan Marino	10.00	25.00
MT16 Drew Bledsoe	4.00	10.00
MT17 Curtis Martin	4.00	10.00
MT18 Jerry Rice	5.00	12.00
MT19 Steve Young	4.00	10.00
MT20 Terry Allen	1.50	4.00

1998 Pacific Omega

The 1998 Pacific Omega set was issued in one series totalling 250 standard size cards and distributed in eight-card packs with a suggested retail price of $1.99. The fronts feature color action player photos etched with silver foil. The backs carry player information and career statistics.

COMPLETE SET (250)	15.00	40.00
1 Larry Centers	.08	.25
2 Rob Moore	.15	.40
3 Michael Pittman RC	.75	1.50
4 Jake Plummer	.25	.60
5 Simeon Rice	.15	.40
6 Frank Sanders	.15	.40
7 Eric Swann	.08	.25
8 Morten Andersen	.08	.25
9 Jamal Anderson	.25	.60
10 Chris Chandler	.15	.40
11 Harold Green	.08	.25
12 Byron Hanspard	.08	.25
13 Terance Mathis	.15	.40
14 O.J. Santiago	.08	.25
15 Peter Boulware	.08	.25
16 Jay Graham	.08	.25
17 Eric Green	.08	.25
18 Michael Jackson	.08	.25
19 Jermaine Lewis	.15	.40
20 Ray Lewis	.25	.60
21 Jonathan Ogden	.08	.25
22 Eric Zeier	.15	.40
23 Steve Christie	.08	.25
24 Todd Collins	.08	.25
25 Quinn Early	.08	.25
26 Eric Moulds	.25	.60
27 Andre Reed	.15	.40
28 Antowain Smith	.25	.60
29 Bruce Smith	.15	.40
30 Thurman Thomas	.25	.60
31 Ted Washington	.08	.25
32 Michael Bates	.08	.25
33 Tim Biakabutuka	.15	.40
34 Mark Carrier	.08	.25
35 Rae Carruth	.08	.25
36 Kerry Collins	.15	.40
37 Kevin Greene	.15	.40
38 Fred Lane	.08	.25
39 Muhsin Muhammad	.15	.40
40 Wesley Walls	.15	.40
41 Curtis Conway	.15	.40
42 Bobby Engram	.15	.40
43 Curtis Enis RC	.20	.50
44 Walt Harris	.08	.25
45 Erik Kramer	.08	.25
46 Chris Penn	.08	.25
47 Ryan Wetnight RC	.08	.25
48 Jeff Blake	.15	.40
49 Ki-Jana Carter	.08	.25
50 John Copeland	.08	.25
51 Corey Dillon	.25	.60
52 Tony McGee	.08	.25
53 Carl Pickens	.15	.40
54 Darnay Scott	.15	.40
55 Takeo Spikes RC	.50	1.25
56 Troy Aikman	.50	1.25
57 Eric Bjornson	.08	.25
58 Greg Ellis RC	.20	.50
59 Michael Irvin	.25	.60
60 Daryl Johnston	.15	.40
61 David LaFleur	.08	.25
62 Deion Sanders	.25	.60
63 Emmitt Smith	.75	2.00
64 Jason Garrett RC	.40	1.00
65 Nicky Sualua RC	.15	.40
66 Steve Atwater	.08	.25
67 Terrell Davis	.25	.60
68 John Elway	1.00	2.50
69 Brian Griese RC	1.00	2.50
70 Ed McCaffrey	.15	.40
71 John Mobley	.08	.25
72 Marcus Nash RC	.20	.50
73 Shannon Sharpe	.15	.40
74 Neil Smith	.15	.40
75 Rod Smith	.15	.40
76 Charlie Batch RC	.50	1.25
77 Germane Crowell RC	.30	.75
78 Jason Hanson	.08	.25
79 Scott Mitchell	.15	.40
80 Herman Moore	.15	.40
81 Johnnie Morton	.15	.40
82 Barry Sanders	.75	2.00
83 Tommy Vardell	.08	.25
84 Robert Brooks	.15	.40
85 Gilbert Brown	.08	.25
86 LeRoy Butler	.08	.25
87 Mark Chmura	.15	.40
88 Brett Favre	1.00	2.50
89 Antonio Freeman	.25	.60
90 William Henderson	.15	.40
91 Vonnie Holliday RC	.30	.75
92 Dorsey Levens	.25	.60
93 Reggie White	.25	.60
94 Aaron Bailey	.08	.25
95 Quentin Coryatt	.08	.25
96 Zack Crockett	.08	.25
97 Ken Dilger	.08	.25
98 Marshall Faulk	.30	.75
99 E.G. Green RC	.30	.75
100 Marvin Harrison	.25	.60
101 Peyton Manning RC	7.50	15.00
102 Jerome Pathon RC	.50	1.25
103 Tavian Banks RC	.30	.75
104 Tony Boselli	.08	.25
105 Tony Brackens	.08	.25
106 Mark Brunell	.25	.60
107 Kevin Hardy	.08	.25
108 Keenan McCardell	.15	.40
109 Pete Mitchell	.08	.25
110 Jimmy Smith	.15	.40
111 James Stewart	.15	.40
112 Fred Taylor RC	.75	2.00
113 Kimble Anders	.15	.40
114 Dale Carter	.08	.25
115 Tony Gonzalez	.25	.60
116 Elvis Grbac	.15	.40
117 Donnell Bennett	.08	.25
118 Andre Rison	.15	.40
119 Rashaan Shehee RC	.30	.75
120 Derrick Thomas	.25	.60
121 Tamarick Vanover	.08	.25
122 Karim Abdul-Jabbar	.25	.60
123 John Avery RC	.30	.75
124 Troy Drayton	.08	.25
125 John Dutton RC	.20	.50
126 Craig Erickson	.08	.25
127 Dan Marino	1.00	2.50
128 O.J. McDuffie	.15	.40
129 Jerris McPhail	.08	.25
130 Stanley Pritchett	.08	.25
131 Larry Shannon RC	.20	.50
132 Zach Thomas	.25	.60
133 Cris Carter	.25	.60
134 Randall Cunningham	.25	.60
135 Andrew Glover	.08	.25
136 Brad Johnson	.25	.60
137 Randall McDaniel	.08	.25
138 David Palmer	.08	.25
139 John Randle	.15	.40
140 Jake Reed	.15	.40
141 Robert Smith	.25	.60
142 Drew Bledsoe	.40	1.00
143 Ben Coates	.15	.40
144 Robert Edwards RC	.30	.75
145 Terry Glenn	.25	.60
146 Shawn Jefferson	.08	.25
147 Willie McGinest	.08	.25
148 Tony Simmons RC	.30	.75
149 Chris Slade	.08	.25
150 Troy Davis	.08	.25
151 Mark Fields	.08	.25
152 Andre Hastings	.08	.25
153 Billy Joe Hobert	.08	.25
154 William Roaf	.08	.25
155 Heath Shuler	.08	.25
156 Danny Wuerffel	.15	.40
157 Ray Zellars	.08	.25
158 Jessie Armstead	.08	.25
159 Tiki Barber	.25	.60
160 Chris Calloway	.08	.25
161 Mike Cherry	.08	.25
162 Danny Kanell	.15	.40
163 Amani Toomer	.15	.40
164 Charles Way	.08	.25
165 Tyrone Wheatley	.15	.40
166 Kyle Brady	.08	.25
167 Wayne Chrebet	.25	.60
168 Glenn Foley	.15	.40
169 Scott Frost RC	.20	.50
170 Keyshawn Johnson	.25	.60
171 Leon Johnson	.08	.25
172 Alex Van Dyke	.08	.25
173 Dedric Ward	.08	.25
174 Tim Brown	.25	.60
175 Rickey Dudley	.08	.25
176 Jeff George	.15	.40
177 Desmond Howard	.15	.40
178 James Jett	.15	.40
179 Napoleon Kaufman	.25	.60
180 Darrell Russell	.08	.25
181 Charles Woodson RC	.60	1.50
182 Jason Dunn	.08	.25
183 Irving Fryar	.15	.40
184 Charlie Garner	.15	.40
185 Bobby Hoying	.15	.40
186 Chris T. Jones	.08	.25
187 Michael Timpson	.08	.25
188 Kevin Turner	.08	.25
189 Jerome Bettis	.25	.60
190 Will Blackwell	.08	.25
191 Mark Bruener	.08	.25
192 Charles Johnson	.08	.25
193 George Jones	.08	.25
194 Levon Kirkland	.08	.25
195 Kordell Stewart	.25	.60
196 Hines Ward RC	2.50	5.00
197 Tony Banks	.15	.40
198 Isaac Bruce	.25	.60
199 Ernie Conwell	.08	.25
200 Robert Holcombe RC	.30	.75
201 Eddie Kennison	.15	.40
202 Amp Lee	.08	.25
203 Orlando Pace	.08	.25
204 Charlie Jones	.08	.25

205 Freddie Jones .08 .25
206 Ryan Leaf RC .50 1.25
207 Natrone Means .15 .40
208 Junior Seau .25 .60
209 Bryan Still .08 .25
210 Greg Clark .08 .25
211 Jim Druckenmiller .08 .25
212 Marc Edwards .08 .25
213 Garrison Hearst .25 .60
214 Terrell Owens .25 .60
215 Jerry Rice .50 1.25
216 J.J. Stokes .15 .40
217 Bryant Young .08 .25
218 Steve Young .30 .75
219 Chad Brown .08 .25
220 Joey Galloway .15 .40
221 Cortez Kennedy .08 .25
222 Jon Kitna .25 .60
223 James McKnight .25 .60
224 Warren Moon .25 .60
225 Michael Sinclair .08 .25
226 Ricky Watters .15 .40
227 Mike Alstott .25 .60
228 Reidel Anthony .15 .40
229 Derrick Brooks .25 .60
230 Trent Dilfer .25 .60
231 Warrick Dunn .25 .60
232 Dave Moore .08 .25
233 Hardy Nickerson .08 .25
234 Warren Sapp .15 .40
235 Karl Williams .08 .25
236 Willie Davis .08 .25
237 Kevin Dyson RC .50 1.25
238 Eddie George .25 .60
239 Derrick Mason .15 .40
240 Steve McNair .25 .60
241 Chris Sanders .08 .25
242 Frank Wycheck .08 .25
243 Terry Allen .25 .60
244 Jamie Asher .08 .25
245 Gus Frerotte .08 .25
246 Darrell Green .15 .40
247 Skip Hicks RC .30 .75
248 Brian Mitchell .08 .25
249 Leslie Shepherd .08 .25
250 Michael Westbrook .15 .40

1998 Pacific Omega EO Portraits

COMPLETE SET (20) 50.00 120.00
STATED ODDS 1:73
1 Jake Plummer 2.00 5.00
2 Corey Dillon 2.00 5.00
3 Troy Aikman 4.00 10.00
4 Emmitt Smith 6.00 15.00
5 Terrell Davis 2.00 5.00
6 John Elway 8.00 20.00
7 Barry Sanders 6.00 15.00
8 Brett Favre 8.00 20.00
9 Dorsey Levens 2.00 5.00
10 Peyton Manning 10.00 20.00
11 Mark Brunell 2.00 5.00
12 Dan Marino 8.00 20.00
13 Drew Bledsoe 3.00 8.00
14 Jerome Bettis 2.00 5.00
15 Kordell Stewart 2.00 5.00
16 Ryan Leaf .60 1.50
17 Jerry Rice 4.00 10.00
18 Steve Young 2.50 6.00
19 Warrick Dunn 2.00 5.00
20 Eddie George 2.00 5.00

1998 Pacific Omega Face To Face

COMPLETE SET (10) 125.00 250.00
STATED ODDS 1:145
1 Peyton Manning 12.50 25.00
Ryan Leaf
2 Barry Sanders 12.50 30.00
Warrick Dunn
3 Dan Marino 15.00 40.00
John Elway
4 Jerry Rice 7.50 20.00
Antonio Freeman
5 Jake Plummer 6.00 15.00
Drew Bledsoe
6 Corey Dillon 6.00 15.00
Eddie George
7 Emmitt Smith 12.50 30.00
Terrell Davis
8 Steve Young 6.00 15.00
Mark Brunell
9 Kordell Stewart 6.00 15.00
Steve McNair
10 Troy Aikman 15.00 40.00
Brett Favre

1998 Pacific Omega Online

COMPLETE SET (36) 30.00 80.00
STATED ODDS 4:37
1 Jake Plummer 1.25 3.00
2 Antowain Smith .75 2.00
3 Curtis Enis .40 1.00
4 Corey Dillon 1.25 3.00
5 Troy Aikman 2.50 6.00
6 Emmitt Smith 4.00 10.00
7 Terrell Davis 1.25 3.00
8 John Elway 5.00 12.00
9 Shannon Sharpe .75 2.00
10 Herman Moore .40 1.00
11 Barry Sanders 4.00 10.00
12 Brett Favre 5.00 12.00
13 Antonio Freeman .75 2.00
14 Dorsey Levens .40 1.00
15 Peyton Manning 10.00 20.00
16 Marshall Faulk 1.50 4.00
17 Mark Brunell 1.25 3.00
18 Fred Taylor 1.25 3.00
19 Dan Marino 5.00 12.00
20 Robert Smith .40 1.00
21 Drew Bledsoe 2.00 5.00
22 Tiki Barber 1.25 3.00
23 Danny Kanell .40 1.00
24 Tim Brown 1.25 3.00
25 Napoleon Kaufman .75 2.00
26 Charles Woodson .75 2.00
27 Jerome Bettis 1.25 3.00
28 Kordell Stewart 1.25 3.00
29 Ryan Leaf .40 1.00
30 Jerry Rice 2.50 6.00
31 Steve Young 1.50 4.00
32 Joey Galloway .75 2.00
33 Trent Dilfer .75 2.00
34 Warrick Dunn 1.25 3.00
35 Eddie George 1.25 3.00
36 Steve McNair 1.25 3.00

1998 Pacific Omega Prisms

COMPLETE SET (20) 60.00 150.00
STATED ODDS 1:37
1 Jake Plummer 1.50 4.00
2 Corey Dillon 1.50 4.00
3 Troy Aikman 3.00 8.00
4 Emmitt Smith 5.00 12.00
5 Terrell Davis 1.50 4.00
6 John Elway 6.00 15.00
7 Barry Sanders 5.00 12.00
8 Brett Favre 6.00 15.00
9 Peyton Manning 15.00 30.00
10 Mark Brunell 1.50 4.00
11 Dan Marino 6.00 15.00
12 Drew Bledsoe 2.50 6.00
13 Napoleon Kaufman 1.50 4.00
14 Jerome Bettis 1.50 4.00
15 Kordell Stewart 1.50 4.00
16 Ryan Leaf 1.00 2.50
17 Jerry Rice 3.00 8.00
18 Steve Young 2.00 5.00
19 Warrick Dunn 1.50 4.00
20 Eddie George 1.50 4.00

1998 Pacific Omega Rising Stars

COMPLETE SET (30) 40.00 80.00
STATED ODDS 4:37 HOBBY
*BLUE/100: 3X TO 8X SILVER
*GREEN/50: 5X TO 12X SILVER
*PURPLE/25: 8X TO 20X SILVER
*RED/75: 4X TO 10X SILVER
UNPRICED GOLD PRINT RUN 1
1 Michael Pittman .75 2.00
2 Keith Brooking .30 .75
3 Duane Starks .30 .75
4 Curtis Enis .30 .75
5 Marcus Nash .30 .75
6 Brian Griese 1.50 4.00
7 Terry Fair .30 .75
8 Germane Crowell .50 1.25
9 Charlie Batch .75 2.00
10 E.G. Green .50 1.25
11 Peyton Manning 12.50 25.00
12 Jerome Pathon .75 2.00
13 Fred Taylor 1.25 3.00
14 Tavian Banks .50 1.25
15 Rashaan Shehee .50 1.25
16 John Avery .50 1.25
17 John Dutton .30 .75
18 Robert Edwards .50 1.25
19 Tony Simmons .50 1.25
20 Joe Jurevicius .50 1.25
21 Scott Frost .30 .75
22 Charles Woodson 1.00 2.50
23 Hines Ward 3.00 8.00
24 Robert Holcombe .50 1.25
25 Az-Zahir Hakim .75 2.00
26 Ryan Leaf .75 2.00
27 Ahman Green .75 2.00
28 Kevin Dyson .75 2.00
29 Stephen Alexander .50 1.25
30 Skip Hicks .50 1.25

1999 Pacific Omega

Released as a 250-card set, the 1999 Pacific Omega football features single and dual prospect cards, and base set cards sporting three action photos of each player and are accentuated by foil highlights. Packaged in 36-pack boxes with packs contain six cards, Pacific Omega carried a suggested retail price of $1.99.

COMPLETE SET (250) 20.00 40.00
1 Mario Bates .12 .30
2 David Boston RC .25 .60
3 Rob Moore .12 .30
4 Adrian Murrell .15 .40
5 Jake Plummer .15 .40
6 Frank Sanders .12 .30
7 Aeneas Williams .12 .30
8 Joel Makovicka RC .20 .50
Lonnie Shelton RC
9 Jamal Anderson .15 .40
10 Ray Buchanan .12 .30
11 Chris Chandler .15 .40
12 Tim Dwight .15 .40
13 Byron Hanspard .12 .30
14 Terance Mathis .12 .30
15 O.J. Santiago .12 .30
16 Danny Kanell .12 .30
Chris Calloway
17 Peter Boulware .12 .30
18 Priest Holmes .20 .50
19 Patrick Johnson .12 .30
20 Jermaine Lewis .12 .30
21 Ray Lewis .20 .50
22 Michael McCrary .12 .30
23 Jonathan Ogden .12 .30
24 Tony Banks .15 .40
Scott Mitchell
25 Doug Flutie .20 .50
26 Rob Johnson .15 .40
27 Eric Moulds .15 .40
28 Andre Reed .20 .50
29 Antowain Smith .12 .30
30 Bruce Smith .20 .50
31 Kevin Williams .12 .30
32 Shawn Bryson RC .25 .60
Peerless Price RC
33 Steve Beuerlein .15 .40
34 Tim Biakabutuka .15 .40
35 Rae Carruth .12 .30
36 Dameyune Craig RC .30 .75
37 William Floyd .15 .40
38 Kevin Greene .15 .40
39 Muhsin Muhammad .15 .40
40 Wesley Walls .15 .40
41 Edgar Bennett .15 .40
42 Robert Chancey RC .20 .50
43 Curtis Conway .15 .40
44 Bobby Engram .15 .40
45 Curtis Enis .12 .30
46 Cade McNown RC .25 .60
47 Ryan Wetnight .12 .30
48 D'Wayne Bates RC .25 .60
Marty Booker RC
49 Jeff Blake .15 .40
50 Scott Covington RC .20 .50
51 Corey Dillon .15 .40
52 James Hundon .12 .30
53 Carl Pickens .15 .40
54 Darnay Scott .12 .30
55 Akili Smith RC .25 .60
56 Craig Yeast RC .20 .50
57 Tim Couch RC .30 .75
58 Ty Detmer .15 .40
59 Marc Edwards .15 .40
60 Kevin Johnson RC .25 .60
61 Terry Kirby .12 .30
62 Sedrick Shaw .12 .30
63 Leslie Shepherd .12 .30
64 Darrin Chiaverini RC .20 .50
Daylon McCutcheon RC
65 Troy Aikman .30 .75
66 Michael Irvin .20 .50
67 David LaFleur .12 .30
68 Wane McGarity RC .20 .50
69 Ernie Mills .12 .30
70 Deion Sanders .20 .50
71 Emmitt Smith .50 1.25
72 Rocket Ismail .15 .40
James McKnight
73 Bubby Brister .12 .30
74 Byron Chamberlain RC .25 .60
75 Terrell Davis .20 .50
76 Olandis Gary RC .30 .75
77 Brian Griese .15 .40
78 Ed McCaffrey .15 .40
79 Shannon Sharpe .20 .50
80 Rod Smith .15 .40
81 Travis McGriff RC .30 .75
Al Wilson RC
82 Charlie Batch .15 .40
83 Chris Claiborne RC .20 .50
84 Germane Crowell .12 .30
85 Terry Fair .12 .30
86 Sedrick Irvin RC .20 .50
87 Herman Moore .15 .40
88 Johnnie Morton .15 .40
89 Barry Sanders .50 1.25
90 Mark Chmura .12 .30
91 Brett Favre .60 1.50
92 Antonio Freeman .15 .40
93 Desmond Howard .15 .40
94 Dorsey Levens .15 .40
95 Derrick Mayes .12 .30
96 Bill Schroeder .15 .40
97 Aaron Brooks RC .30 .75
Dee Miller RC
98 E.G. Green .12 .30
99 Marvin Harrison .20 .50
100 Edgerrin James RC .40 1.00
101 Peyton Manning .60 1.50
102 Jerome Pathon .12 .30
103 Marcus Pollard .12 .30
104 Ken Dilger .12 .30
105 Derrick Alexander WR .12 .30
106 Reggie Barlow .12 .30
107 Tony Boselli .15 .40
108 Mark Brunell .15 .40
109 George Jones .12 .30
110 Keenan McCardell .15 .40
111 Jimmy Smith .15 .40
112 James Stewart .12 .30
113 Fred Taylor .15 .40
114 Kimble Anders .12 .30
115 Mike Cloud RC .20 .50
116 Tony Gonzalez .20 .50
117 Elvis Grbac .12 .30
118 Byron Bam Morris .12 .30
119 Andre Rison .15 .40
120 Derrick Thomas .20 .50
121 Karim Abdul-Jabbar .15 .40
122 Oronde Gadsden .12 .30
123 James Johnson RC .20 .50
124 Rob Konrad RC .20 .50
125 Dan Marino .60 1.50
126 O.J. McDuffie .15 .40
127 Lamar Thomas .12 .30
128 Zach Thomas .20 .50
129 Cris Carter .20 .50
130 Daunte Culpepper RC .30 .75
131 Randall Cunningham .20 .50
132 Matthew Hatchette .15 .40
133 Leroy Hoard .12 .30
134 David Palmer .12 .30
135 John Randle .15 .40
136 Randy Moss .20 .50
137 Robert Smith .15 .40
138 Drew Bledsoe .20 .50
139 Ben Coates .15 .40
140 Kevin Faulk RC .30 .75
141 Terry Glenn .15 .40
142 Shawn Jefferson .12 .30
143 Ty Law .15 .40
144 Tony Simmons .12 .30
145 Michael Bishop RC .25 .60
Andy Katzenmoyer RC
146 Cameron Cleeland .12 .30
147 Andre Hastings .12 .30
148 Billy Joe Hobert .12 .30
149 Joe Johnson .12 .30
150 Keith Poole .12 .30
151 William Roaf .15 .40
152 Billy Joe Tolliver .12 .30
153 Ricky Williams RC .50 1.25
154 Tiki Barber .20 .50
155 Gary Brown .12 .30
156 Kent Graham .12 .30
157 Ike Hilliard .15 .40
158 David Patten .15 .40
159 Jason Sehorn .15 .40
160 Amani Toomer .15 .40
161 Joe Montgomery RC .20 .50
Luke Petitgout RC
162 Wayne Chrebet .15 .40
163 Bryan Cox .15 .40
164 Aaron Glenn .12 .30
165 Keyshawn Johnson .15 .40
166 Leon Johnson .12 .30
167 Curtis Martin .20 .50
168 Vinny Testaverde .15 .40
169 Dedric Ward .12 .30
170 Tim Brown .20 .50
171 Rickey Dudley .12 .30
172 James Jett .12 .30
173 Napoleon Kaufman .12 .30
174 Jon Ritchie .12 .30
175 Darrell Russell .12 .30
176 Charles Woodson .20 .50
177 Rich Gannon .15 .40
Heath Shuler
178 Hugh Douglas .15 .40
179 Donovan McNabb RC 1.50 4.00
180 Allen Rossum .15 .40
181 Duce Staley .15 .40
182 Kevin Turner .12 .30
183 Charles Johnson .12 .30
Doug Pederson
184 Barry Gardner RC .20 .50
Cecil Martin RC
185 Jerome Bettis .20 .50
186 Mark Bruener .12 .30
187 Troy Edwards RC .25 .60
188 Courtney Hawkins .12 .30
189 Levon Kirkland .12 .30
190 Kordell Stewart .15 .40
191 Hines Ward .20 .50
192 Malcolm Johnson RC .25 .60
Amos Zereoue RC
193 Greg Clark .12 .30
194 Terrell Fletcher .12 .30
195 Charlie Jones .12 .30
196 Cecil Collins RC .20 .50
197 Natrone Means .15 .40
198 Mikhael Ricks .12 .30
199 Junior Seau .20 .50
200 Bryan Still .12 .30
201 Ryan Thelwell RC .20 .50
202 Garrison Hearst .15 .40
203 Terry Jackson RC .20 .50
204 R.W. McQuarters .12 .30
205 Terrell Owens .20 .50
206 Jerry Rice .40 1.00
207 J.J. Stokes .12 .30
208 Lawrence Phillips .15 .40
Tommy Vardell
209 Steve Young .25 .60
210 Karsten Bailey RC .20 .50
211 Chad Brown .12 .30
212 Christian Fauria .12 .30
213 Joey Galloway .15 .40
214 Ahman Green .15 .40
215 Brock Huard RC .25 .60
216 Cortez Kennedy .12 .30
217 Jon Kitna .15 .40
218 Ricky Watters .15 .40
219 Isaac Bruce .20 .50
220 Az-Zahir Hakim .12 .30
221 June Henley RC .20 .50
222 Greg Hill .12 .30
223 Torry Holt RC .50 1.25
224 Amp Lee .12 .30
225 Ricky Proehl .12 .30
226 Marshall Faulk .20 .50
Trent Green
227 Mike Alstott .20 .50
228 Reidel Anthony .12 .30
229 Trent Dilfer .15 .40
230 Warrick Dunn .15 .40
231 Bert Emanuel .15 .40
232 Jacquez Green .12 .30
233 Warren Sapp .15 .40
234 Shaun King RC .25 .60
Anthony McFarland RC
235 Mike Archie RC .30 .75
236 Kevin Dyson .12 .30
237 Eddie George .15 .40
238 Derrick Mason .15 .40
239 Steve McNair .20 .50
240 Yancey Thigpen .12 .30
241 Frank Wycheck .15 .40
242 Darran Hall .30 .75
Jevon Kearse RC
243 Stephen Alexander .12 .30
244 Champ Bailey RC .60 1.50
245 Stephen Davis .15 .40
246 Skip Hicks .12 .30
247 James Thrash RC .30 .75
248 Michael Westbrook .12 .30
249 Dan Wilkinson .15 .40
250 Brad Johnson .15 .40
Larry Centers

1999 Pacific Omega Copper

*COPPER STARS: 8X TO 20X BASIC CARDS
*COPPER RCs: 3X TO 8X
COPPER STATED PRINT RUN 99 SER.#'d SETS
RANDOM INSERTS IN HOBBY PACKS

1999 Pacific Omega Gold

COMPLETE SET (250) 200.00 400.00
*GOLD STARS: 4X TO 10X BASIC CARDS
*GOLD ROOKIES: 1.5X TO 4X
GOLD STATED PRINT RUN 299 SER.#'d SETS
RANDOM INSERTS IN RETAIL PACKS

1999 Pacific Omega Platinum Blue

*PLAT.BLUE STARS: 8X TO 20X BASIC CARDS
*PLAT.BLUE ROOKIES: 3X TO 8X
PLATINUM BLUE PRINT RUN 75 SER.#'d SETS
RANDOM INSERTS IN HOBBY/RETAIL

1999 Pacific Omega Premiere Date

*PREM.DATE STARS: 10X TO 25X BASIC CARDS
*PREMIERE DATE ROOKIES: 4X TO 10X
PREMIERE DATE PRINT RUN 60 SER.#'d SETS

1999 Pacific Omega 5-Star Attack

COMPLETE SET (30) 25.00 60.00
STATED ODDS 4:37
*BLUE FOILS: 2.5X TO 6X BASIC INSERTS
BLUE STATED PRINT RUN 100 SER.#'d SETS
*GREEN FOILS: 4X TO 10X BASIC INSERTS
GREEN STATED PRINT RUN 50 SER.#'d SETS
*PURPLE FOILS: 6X TO 15X BASIC INSERTS
PURPLE STATED PRINT RUN 25 SER.#'d SETS
*RED FOILS: 3X TO 8X BASIC INSERTS
RED STATED PRINT RUN 75 SER.#'d SETS
1 Chris Chandler .50 1.25
2 Tim Couch .50 1.25
3 Peyton Manning 2.50 6.00
4 Dan Marino 2.50 6.00
5 Drew Bledsoe 1.00 2.50
6 Vinny Testaverde .50 1.25
7 Randall Cunningham .75 2.00
8 Doug Flutie .75 2.00
9 Charlie Batch .75 2.00
10 Mark Brunell .75 2.00
11 Steve Young 1.00 2.50
12 Jon Kitna .75 2.00
13 Jamal Anderson .75 2.00
14 Priest Holmes 1.25 3.00
15 Emmitt Smith 1.50 4.00
16 Fred Taylor .75 2.00
17 Curtis Martin .75 2.00
18 Eddie George .75 2.00
19 Ed McCaffrey .50 1.25
20 Antonio Freeman .75 2.00
21 Randy Moss 2.00 5.00
22 Keyshawn Johnson .75 2.00
23 Terrell Owens .75 2.00
24 Joey Galloway .50 1.25
25 Cade McNown .40 1.00
26 Akili Smith .40 1.00
27 Edgerrin James 2.00 5.00
28 Daunte Culpepper 2.00 5.00
29 Ricky Williams 1.00 2.50
30 Donovan McNabb 2.50 6.00

1999 Pacific Omega Draft Class

COMPLETE SET (10) 25.00 60.00
STATED ODDS 1:145
1 Darrell Green 5.00 12.00
Dan Marino
2 Jerry Rice 3.00 8.00
Bruce Smith
3 Troy Aikman 6.00 15.00
Barry Sanders
4 Shannon Sharpe 3.00 8.00
Emmitt Smith
5 Brett Favre 5.00 12.00
Herman Moore
6 Drew Bledsoe 2.00 5.00
Mark Brunell
7 Terrell Davis 2.00 5.00
Curtis Martin
8 Warrick Dunn 2.00 5.00
Jake Plummer
9 Peyton Manning 4.00 10.00
Randy Moss
10 Tim Couch 2.50 6.00
Ricky Williams

1999 Pacific Omega EO Portraits

COMPLETE SET (20) 40.00 100.00
STATED ODDS 1:73
1 Jake Plummer 1.25 3.00
2 Jamal Anderson 1.25 3.00
3 Akili Smith .60 1.50
4 Tim Couch .60 1.50
5 Troy Aikman 4.00 10.00
6 Emmitt Smith 4.00 10.00
7 Terrell Davis 2.00 5.00
8 Barry Sanders 6.00 15.00
9 Brett Favre 6.00 15.00
10 Peyton Manning 6.00 15.00
11 Mark Brunell 2.00 5.00
12 Fred Taylor 1.25 3.00
13 Dan Marino 6.00 15.00
14 Randy Moss 5.00 12.00
15 Ricky Williams 2.00 5.00
16 Curtis Martin 2.00 5.00
17 Jerry Rice 4.00 10.00
18 Jon Kitna 2.00 5.00
19 Warrick Dunn 2.00 5.00
20 Eddie George 2.00 5.00

1999 Pacific Omega Gridiron Masters

COMPLETE SET (36) 20.00 50.00
STATED ODDS 4:37
1 David Boston .40 1.00
2 Jake Plummer .40 1.00
3 Jamal Anderson .60 1.50
4 Chris Chandler .40 1.00
5 Priest Holmes 1.00 2.50
6 Doug Flutie .60 1.50
7 Akili Smith .30 .75
8 Cade McNown .30 .75
9 Tim Couch .40 1.00
10 Deion Sanders .60 1.50
11 Emmitt Smith 1.25 3.00
12 Rod Smith .40 1.00
13 Charlie Batch .60 1.50
14 Herman Moore .40 1.00
15 Barry Sanders 2.00 5.00
16 Antonio Freeman .60 1.50
17 Edgerrin James 1.50 4.00
18 Mark Brunell .60 1.50
19 Fred Taylor .60 1.50
20 Randall Cunningham .60 1.50
21 Randy Moss 1.50 4.00
22 Terry Glenn .60 1.50
23 Keyshawn Johnson .60 1.50
24 Curtis Martin .60 1.50
25 Vinny Testaverde .40 1.00
26 Donovan McNabb 2.00 5.00
27 Jerome Bettis .60 1.50
28 Terrell Owens .60 1.50
29 Jerry Rice 1.25 3.00
30 Steve Young .75 2.00
31 Joey Galloway .40 1.00
32 Jon Kitna .60 1.50
33 Warrick Dunn .60 1.50
34 Shaun King .40 1.00
35 Eddie George .60 1.50
36 Steve McNair .60 1.50

1999 Pacific Omega TD 99

COMPLETE SET (20) 25.00 50.00
STATED ODDS 1:37
1 Jamal Anderson 1.00 2.50
2 Priest Holmes 1.50 4.00
3 Doug Flutie 1.00 2.50
4 Tim Couch .60 1.50
5 Troy Aikman 2.00 5.00
6 Emmitt Smith 2.00 5.00
7 Terrell Davis 1.00 2.50
8 Herman Moore .60 1.50
9 Brett Favre 3.00 8.00
10 Antonio Freeman 1.00 2.50
11 Mark Brunell 1.00 2.50
12 Fred Taylor 1.00 2.50
13 Randall Cunningham 1.00 2.50
14 Randy Moss 2.50 6.00
15 Drew Bledsoe 1.25 3.00
16 Terrell Owens 1.00 2.50
17 Steve Young 1.25 3.00
18 Jon Kitna 1.00 2.50
19 Warrick Dunn 1.00 2.50
20 Eddie George 1.00 2.50

2000 Pacific Omega

Released in late October 2000, Pacific Omega features a 250-card base set comprised of 150 veteran cards, 75 rookie cards sequentially numbered to 500, and 25 dual player prospect cards sequentially numbered to 500. Omega was packaged in 36-pack boxes with each pack containing six cards.

COMP.SET w/o SP's (150) 7.50 20.00
1 David Boston .15 .40
2 Dave Brown .15 .40
3 Rob Moore .15 .40
4 Jake Plummer .20 .50
5 Simeon Rice .20 .50
6 Frank Sanders .15 .40
7 Jamal Anderson .20 .50
8 Chris Chandler .20 .50
9 Tim Dwight .20 .50
10 Terance Mathis .15 .40
11 Tony Banks .15 .40
12 Peter Boulware .15 .40
13 Priest Holmes .25 .60
14 Qadry Ismail .20 .50
15 Doug Flutie .25 .60
16 Rob Johnson .20 .50
17 Jonathan Linton .15 .40
18 Eric Moulds .20 .50
19 Peerless Price .20 .50
20 Antowain Smith .20 .50
21 Steve Beuerlein .20 .50
22 Tim Biakabutuka .20 .50
23 Patrick Jeffers .20 .50
24 Muhsin Muhammad .20 .50
25 Wesley Walls .15 .40
26 Bobby Engram .20 .50
27 Curtis Enis .15 .40
28 Cade McNown .15 .40
29 Marcus Robinson .20 .50
30 Willie Anderson .15 .40
31 Michael Basnight .15 .40
32 Corey Dillon .20 .50
33 Akili Smith .15 .40
34 Tim Couch .20 .50
35 Kevin Johnson .15 .40
36 Wali Rainer .15 .40
37 Troy Aikman .40 1.00
38 Dexter Coakley .15 .40
39 Rocket Ismail .20 .50
40 Emmitt Smith .60 1.50
41 Chris Warren .15 .40
42 Terrell Davis .25 .60
43 Olandis Gary .20 .50
44 Brian Griese .20 .50
45 Ed McCaffrey .20 .50
46 Rod Smith .20 .50
47 Charlie Batch .20 .50
48 Germane Crowell .15 .40
49 Herman Moore .20 .50
50 Johnnie Morton .20 .50
51 Barry Sanders .50 1.25
52 Corey Bradford .15 .40
53 Brett Favre .75 2.00
54 Antonio Freeman .20 .50
55 Dorsey Levens .20 .50
56 Bill Schroeder .20 .50
57 Ken Dilger .15 .40
58 Marvin Harrison .25 .60
59 Edgerrin James .25 .60
60 Peyton Manning .60 1.50
61 Jerome Pathon .15 .40
62 Terrence Wilkins .15 .40
63 Mark Brunell .20 .50
64 Keenan McCardell .20 .50
65 Jimmy Smith .20 .50
66 Fred Taylor .25 .60
67 Derrick Alexander .15 .40
68 Donnell Bennett .15 .40
69 Tony Gonzalez .25 .60
70 Elvis Grbac .15 .40
71 Tony Richardson RC .20 .50
72 Oronde Gadsden .20 .50
73 Damon Huard .20 .50
74 James Johnson .15 .40
75 Dan Marino .75 2.00
76 Tony Martin .20 .50
77 O.J. McDuffie .20 .50
78 Cris Carter .25 .60
79 Daunte Culpepper .20 .50
80 Randy Moss .25 .60
81 Robert Smith .20 .50
82 Drew Bledsoe .25 .60
83 Kevin Faulk .20 .50
84 Terry Glenn .20 .50
85 P.J. Franklin RC .15 .40
86 Keith Poole .15 .40
87 Ricky Williams .25 .60
88 Tiki Barber .25 .60
89 Kerry Collins .20 .50
90 Ike Hilliard .20 .50
91 Amani Toomer .20 .50
92 Wayne Chrebet .20 .50
93 Ray Lucas .15 .40
94 Curtis Martin .25 .60
95 Vinny Testaverde .20 .50
96 Tim Brown .25 .60
97 Rich Gannon .20 .50
98 James Jett .20 .50
99 Napoleon Kaufman .20 .50
100 Tyrone Wheatley .15 .40
101 Charles Woodson .25 .60
102 Brian Dawkins .25 .60
103 Charles Johnson .15 .40
104 Donovan McNabb .25 .60
105 Torrance Small .15 .40
106 Duce Staley .20 .50
107 Jerome Bettis .25 .60
108 Troy Edwards .15 .40
109 Richard Huntley .15 .40
110 Kordell Stewart .20 .50
111 Hines Ward .25 .60
112 Isaac Bruce .25 .60
113 Marshall Faulk .25 .60
114 Az-Zahir Hakim .15 .40
115 Torry Holt .25 .60
116 Tony Horne .15 .40
117 Kurt Warner .40 1.00
118 Jermaine Fazande .15 .40
119 Jeff Graham .15 .40
120 Jim Harbaugh .20 .50
121 Mikhael Ricks .15 .40
122 Junior Seau .25 .60
123 Jeff Garcia .20 .50
124 Charlie Garner .20 .50
125 Terrell Owens .25 .60
126 Jerry Rice .50 1.25
127 J.J. Stokes .20 .50
128 Jon Kitna .20 .50
129 Derrick Mayes .15 .40
130 Charlie Rogers .15 .40
131 Shawn Springs .15 .40
132 Ricky Watters .20 .50
133 Mike Alstott .25 .60
134 Reidel Anthony .15 .40
135 Warrick Dunn .20 .50
136 Jacquez Green .15 .40
137 Shaun King .15 .40
138 Warren Sapp .20 .50
139 Kevin Dyson .20 .50
140 Eddie George .20 .50
141 Jevon Kearse .20 .50
142 Steve McNair .25 .60
143 Yancey Thigpen .15 .40
144 Frank Wycheck .20 .50
145 Champ Bailey .20 .50
146 Larry Centers .15 .40
147 Albert Connell .15 .40
148 Stephen Davis .20 .50
149 Brad Johnson .20 .50
150 Michael Westbrook .15 .40
151 Thomas Jones RC 4.00 10.00
152 Jay Tant RC 2.00 5.00
153 Doug Johnson RC 2.50 6.00
154 Mareno Philyaw RC 2.00 5.00
155 Jamal Lewis RC 3.00 8.00
156 Chris Redman RC 2.50 6.00
157 Travis Taylor RC 2.50 6.00
158 Kwame Cavil RC 2.00 5.00
159 Corey Moore RC 2.00 5.00
160 Deon Grant RC 2.00 5.00
161 Frank Murphy RC 2.00 5.00
162 Dez White RC 2.50 6.00
163 Ron Dugans RC 2.00 5.00
164 Tony Hartley RC 2.00 5.00
165 Curtis Keaton RC 2.00 5.00
166 Peter Warrick RC 3.00 8.00
167 Courtney Brown RC 2.50 6.00
168 JaJuan Dawson RC 2.00 5.00
169 Dennis Northcutt RC 2.50 6.00
170 Travis Prentice RC 2.50 6.00
171 Aaron Shea RC 2.50 6.00
172 Michael Wiley RC 2.00 5.00
173 Chris Cole RC 2.50 6.00
174 Jarious Jackson RC 2.50 6.00
175 Deltha O'Neal RC 2.50 6.00
176 Reuben Droughns RC 3.00 8.00
177 Bubba Franks RC 3.00 8.00
178 Anthony Lucas RC 2.00 5.00
179 Rondell Mealey RC 2.00 5.00
180 Ibn Green RC 2.00 5.00
181 Kevin McDougal RC 2.00 5.00
182 R.Jay Soward RC 2.00 5.00
183 Shyrone Stith RC 2.00 5.00
184 Dante Hall RC 3.00 8.00
185 Frank Moreau RC 2.00 5.00
186 Sylvester Morris RC 2.00 5.00
187 Deon Dyer RC 2.00 5.00
188 Ben Kelly RC 2.00 5.00
189 Quinton Spotwood RC 2.00 5.00
190 Troy Walters RC 2.00 5.00
191 Tom Brady RC 100.00 200.00
192 J.R. Redmond RC 2.00 5.00
193 David Stachelski RC 2.00 5.00
194 Marc Bulger RC 3.00 8.00
195 Sherrod Gideon RC 2.00 5.00
196 Chad Morton RC 3.00 8.00
197 Ron Dayne RC 3.00 8.00
198 Anthony Becht RC 2.50 6.00
199 Laveranues Coles RC 3.00 8.00
200 Chad Pennington RC 5.00 12.00
201 Sebastian Janikowski RC 3.00 8.00
202 Marcus Knight RC 2.00 5.00
203 Jerry Porter RC 3.00 8.00
204 Todd Pinkston RC 2.00 5.00
205 Gari Scott RC 2.00 5.00
206 Plaxico Burress RC 3.00 8.00
207 Danny Farmer RC 2.00 5.00
208 Tee Martin RC 3.00 8.00
209 Hank Poteat RC 2.00 5.00
210 Trung Canidate RC 2.50 6.00
211 Patrick Batteaux RC 2.00 5.00
212 Trevor Gaylor RC 2.00 5.00
213 Ronney Jenkins RC 2.00 5.00
214 Terrence McCaskey RC 2.00 5.00
215 JaJuan Seider RC 2.00 5.00
216 Giovanni Carmazzi RC 2.00 5.00
217 Chafie Fields RC 2.00 5.00
218 Jonas Lewis RC 2.00 5.00
219 Tim Rattay RC 2.50 6.00
220 Shaun Alexander RC 4.00 10.00
221 Darrell Jackson RC 2.50 6.00
222 James Williams RC 2.00 5.00
223 Joe Hamilton RC 2.00 5.00
224 Erron Kinney RC 2.00 5.00
225 Todd Husak RC 2.00 5.00
226 Plaxico Burress 1.00 2.50
Danny Farmer
227 Ron Dayne 1.50 4.00
Joe Hamilton
228 Peter Warrick 1.50 4.00
Ron Dugans
229 Thomas Jones 1.00 2.50
Curtis Keaton
230 Shaun Alexander 1.50 4.00
Reuben Droughns
231 Travis Taylor 1.25 3.00
Darrell Jackson
232 Giovanni Carmazzi 1.25 3.00
Tim Rattay
233 Trung Canidate 1.00 2.50
J.R. Redmond
234 Sylvester Morris 1.00 2.50
R.Jay Soward
235 Travis Prentice 1.25 3.00
Trevor Gaylor
236 Todd Pinkston 1.00 2.50
Sherrod Gideon
237 Frank Murphy 1.25 3.00
Dez White
238 Chris Redman 40.00 80.00
Tom Brady
239 Jamal Lewis 1.50 4.00
Tee Martin
240 Rondell Mealey 1.00 2.50
Shyrone Stith
241 Michael Wiley 1.00 2.50
Chad Morton
242 Laveranues Coles 1.50 4.00
Sebastian Janikowski
243 Troy Walters 1.00 2.50
Todd Husak
244 Marc Bulger 1.50 4.00
Jerry Porter
245 Mareno Philyaw 1.25 3.00
Doug Johnson
246 Dennis Northcutt 1.25 3.00
Courtney Brown
247 Jarious Jackson 1.25 3.00
Chris Cole
248 JaJuan Dawson 1.00 2.50
Gari Scott
249 Quinton Spotwood 1.00 2.50
Chafie Fields
250 Chad Pennington 2.50 6.00
James Williams

2000 Pacific Omega Copper

*COPPER VETS: 10X TO 25X BASIC CARDS

2000 Pacific Omega Gold

*GOLD VETS: 6X TO 15X BASIC CARDS
GOLD/95 ODDS 1:37 RETAIL
GOLD PRINT RUN 95 SER.#'d SETS

2000 Pacific Omega Platinum Blue

*BLUE VETS: 12X TO 30X BASIC CARDS
BLUE/51 STATED ODDS 1:145
BLUE PRINT RUN 51 SER.#'d SETS

2000 Pacific Omega Premiere Date

*PREM.DATE VETS: 6X TO 15X BASIC CARD
PREMIERE DATE PRINT RUN 92 SER.#'d SETS
PREMIERE DATE/92 ODDS 1:37 HOBBY

2000 Pacific Omega AFC Conference Contenders

COMPLETE SET (18) 10.00 25.00
STATED ODDS 2:37
1 Jamal Lewis .75 2.00
2 Akili Smith .50 1.25
3 Peter Warrick .75 2.00
4 Tim Couch .60 1.50
5 Terrell Davis .75 2.00
6 Brian Griese .60 1.50
7 Marvin Harrison .75 2.00
8 Edgerrin James .75 2.00
9 Mark Brunell .60 1.50
10 Fred Taylor .75 2.00
11 Jimmy Smith .60 1.50
12 Curtis Martin .75 2.00
13 Tim Brown .75 2.00
14 Jerome Bettis .75 2.00
15 Plaxico Burress .75 2.00
16 Jon Kitna .60 1.50
17 Eddie George .60 1.50
18 Steve McNair .75 2.00

2000 Pacific Omega Autographs

STATED ODDS 1:4 HOB.BOX,1:10 RET.BOX		
1 Drew Bledsoe	20.00	40.00
2 Mark Brunell	6.00	15.00
3 Stephen Davis	6.00	15.00
4 Torry Holt	8.00	20.00
5 Edgerrin James	12.00	30.00
6 Kurt Warner	25.00	60.00
7 Tyrone Wheatley	5.00	12.00

2000 Pacific Omega EO Portraits

COMPLETE SET (20)	20.00	50.00
STATED ODDS 1:73		
UNPRICED PARALLEL #'d OF 1 SET		
1 Jake Plummer	.75	2.00
2 Peter Warrick	1.00	2.50
3 Tim Couch	.75	2.00
4 Troy Aikman	1.50	4.00
5 Emmitt Smith	2.50	6.00
6 Terrell Davis	1.00	2.50
7 Brett Favre	3.00	8.00
8 Edgerrin James	1.00	2.50
9 Peyton Manning	2.50	6.00
10 Mark Brunell	.75	2.00
11 Fred Taylor	1.00	2.50
12 Randy Moss	1.00	2.50
13 Drew Bledsoe	1.00	2.50
14 Ricky Williams	1.00	2.50
15 Ron Dayne	1.00	2.50
16 Chad Pennington	1.50	4.00
17 Marshall Faulk	1.00	2.50
18 Kurt Warner	1.50	4.00
19 Jerry Rice	2.00	5.00
20 Eddie George	.75	2.00

2000 Pacific Omega Fourth and Goal

COMPLETE SET (36)	10.00	25.00
STATED ODDS 4:37 HOBBY		
*1-9 PARA/100: 2X TO 5X BASIC INSERT		
1-9 PARALLEL PRINT RUN 100 SETS		
*10-18 PARA/50: 2.5X TO 6X BASIC INSERT		
10-18 PARALLEL PRINT RUN 50 SETS		
*19-27 PARA/25: 4X TO 10X BASIC INSERT		
19-27 PARALLEL PRINT RUN 25 SETS		
*28-36 PARA/10: 10X TO 15X BASIC INSERT		
28-36 PARALLEL PRINT RUN 10 SETS		
1 Eric Moulds	.50	1.25
2 Marcus Robinson	.50	1.25
3 Antonio Freeman	.50	1.25
4 Marvin Harrison	.60	1.50
5 Jimmy Smith	.50	1.25
6 Cris Carter	.60	1.50
7 Randy Moss	.60	1.50
8 Tim Brown	.60	1.50
9 Isaac Bruce	.60	1.50
10 Emmitt Smith	1.50	4.00
11 Edgerrin James	.60	1.50
12 Fred Taylor	.60	1.50
13 Robert Smith	.50	1.25
14 Curtis Martin	.60	1.50
15 Marshall Faulk	.60	1.50
16 Warrick Dunn	.50	1.25
17 Eddie George	.50	1.25
18 Stephen Davis	.50	1.25
19 Steve Beuerlein	.50	1.25
20 Akili Smith	.40	1.00
21 Tim Couch	.50	1.25
22 Brian Griese	.50	1.25
23 Mark Brunell	.50	1.25
24 Daunto Culpepper	.50	1.25
25 Kurt Warner	1.00	2.50
26 Jon Kitna	.50	1.25
27 Shaun King	.40	1.00
28 Thomas Jones	.60	1.50
29 Jamal Lewis	.50	1.25
30 Travis Taylor	.40	1.00
31 Peter Warrick	.50	1.25
32 Ron Dayne	.50	1.25
33 Chad Pennington	.75	2.00
34 Plaxico Burress	.50	1.25
35 Giovanni Carmazzi	.40	1.00
36 Shaun Alexander	.60	1.50

2000 Pacific Omega Game Worn Jerseys

COMPLETE SET (10)	75.00	150.00
1 Keenan McCardell	6.00	15.00
2 Fred Taylor	8.00	20.00
3 Dan Marino	20.00	50.00
4 Wayne Chrebet	6.00	15.00
5 Jerome Bettis	8.00	20.00
6 Charles Johnson	5.00	12.00
7 Donovan McNabb	8.00	20.00
8 Kevin Turner	6.00	15.00
9 Brock Huard	5.00	12.00
10 Cortez Kennedy	5.00	12.00

2000 Pacific Omega Generations

COMPLETE SET (20)	20.00	50.00
STATED ODDS 1:145		
1 Cade McNown	1.00	2.50
Dez White		
2 Tim Couch	1.00	2.50
Dennis Northcutt		
3 Troy Aikman	2.00	5.00
Chad Pennington		
4 Emmitt Smith	1.50	4.00
Thomas Jones		
5 Terrell Davis	1.25	3.00
Jamal Lewis		
6 Brett Favre	4.00	10.00
Giovanni Carmazzi		
7 Marvin Harrison	1.25	3.00
Travis Taylor		
8 Edgerrin James	1.50	4.00
Shaun Alexander		
9 Peyton Manning	1.25	3.00
Tee Martin		
10 Mark Brunell	.75	2.00
R.Jay Soward		
11 Cris Carter	.75	2.00
Sylvester Morris		
12 Randy Moss	1.25	3.00
Peter Warrick		
13 Drew Bledsoe	30.00	60.00
Tom Brady		
14 Jerome Bettis	1.25	3.00
Ron Dayne		
15 Marshall Faulk	1.25	3.00
Trung Canidate		
16 Kurt Warner	1.00	2.50
Chris Redman		
17 Jerry Rice	2.50	6.00
Plaxico Burress		
18 Warrick Dunn	.75	2.00
J.R. Redmond		
19 Eddie George	1.25	3.00
Reuben Droughns		
20 Stephen Davis	1.00	2.50
Travis Prentice		

2000 Pacific Omega NFC Conference Contenders

COMPLETE SET (18)	10.00	25.00
STATED ODDS 2:37		
1 Thomas Jones	1.00	2.50
2 Cade McNown	.50	1.25
3 Ron Dayne	.75	2.00
4 Donovan McNabb	.75	2.00
5 Emmitt Smith	2.00	5.00
6 Jake Plummer	.60	1.50
7 Randy Moss	.75	2.00
8 Marshall Faulk	.75	2.00
9 Kurt Warner	1.25	3.00
10 Ricky Williams	.75	2.00
11 Marcus Robinson	.60	1.50
12 Warrick Dunn	.60	1.50
13 Jerry Rice	1.50	4.00
14 Jamal Anderson	.60	1.50
15 Cris Carter	.75	2.00
16 Brad Johnson	.60	1.50
17 Stephen Davis	.60	1.50
18 Shaun King	.50	1.25

2000 Pacific Omega Stellar Performers

COMPLETE SET (20)	10.00	25.00
STATED ODDS 1:37		
1 Tim Couch	.50	1.25
2 Troy Aikman	1.00	2.50
3 Emmitt Smith	1.50	4.00
4 Brian Griese	.50	1.25
5 Brett Favre	2.00	5.00
6 Edgerrin James	.60	1.50
7 Peyton Manning	1.50	4.00
8 Mark Brunell	.50	1.25
9 Fred Taylor	.60	1.50
10 Randy Moss	.60	1.50
11 Drew Bledsoe	.60	1.50
12 Isaac Bruce	.60	1.50
13 Marshall Faulk	.60	1.50
14 Kurt Warner	1.00	2.50
15 Jerry Rice	1.25	3.00
16 Jon Kitna	.50	1.25
17 Shaun King	.40	1.00
18 Eddie George	.50	1.25
19 Steve McNair	.60	1.50
20 Stephen Davis	.50	1.25

1997 Pacific Philadelphia

The 1997 Pacific Philadelphia set was issued in one series totaling 330 cards and was distributed in eight-card packs with a suggested retail of $1.49. Each pack contained five regular series cards with either three bonus cards or two bonus and one insert card. The fronts feature color action player photos in a white border. The backs carry player information and career statistics.

COMPLETE SET (330)	25.00	50.00
1 Kevin Butler	.07	.20
2 Larry Centers	.10	.30
3 Kent Graham	.07	.20
4 Leeland McElroy	.07	.20
5 Ronald McKinnon RC	.10	.30
6 Johnny McWilliams	.07	.20
7 Brad Otis	.07	.20
8 Frank Sanders	.10	.30
9 Rob Selby	.07	.20
10 Cedric Smith	.07	.20
11 Joe Staysniak RC	.07	.20
12 Cornelius Bennett	.07	.20
13 David Brandon	.07	.20
14 Tyrone Brown	.07	.20
15 John Burrough	.07	.20
16 Browning Nagle	.07	.20
17 Dan Owens	.07	.20
18 Anthony Phillips	.07	.20
19 Roell Preston	.07	.20
20 Darnell Walker	.07	.20
21 Bob Whitfield	.07	.20
22 Mike Zandofsky	.07	.20
23 Vashone Adams	.07	.20
24 Derrick Alexander WR	.10	.30
25 Harold Bishop	.07	.20
26 Jeff Blackshear	.07	.20
27 Donald Brady RC	.07	.20
28 Mike Frederick	.07	.20
29 Tim Goad	.07	.20
30 DeRon Jenkins	.07	.20
31 Ray Lewis	.30	.75
32 Rick Lyle	.07	.20
33 Byron Bam Morris	.07	.20
34 Chris Brantley	.07	.20
35 Jeff Burris	.07	.20
36 Todd Collins	.07	.20
37 Rob Coons	.07	.20
38 Corbin Lacina RC	.07	.20
39 Emanuel Martin	.07	.20
40 Marlo Perry	.07	.20
41 Shawn Price	.07	.20
42 Thomas Smith	.07	.20
43 Matt Stevens RC	.07	.20
44 Thurman Thomas	.20	.50
45 Jay Barker	.07	.20
46 Tim Biakabutuka	.10	.30
47 Kerry Collins	.20	.50
48 Matt Elliott	.07	.20
49 Howard Griffith	.07	.20
50 Anthony Johnson	.07	.20
51 John Kasay	.07	.20
52 Muhsin Muhammad	.10	.30
53 Winslow Oliver	.07	.20
54 Walter Rasby	.07	.20
55 Gerald Williams	.07	.20
56 Mark Butterfield	.07	.20
57 Bryan Cox	.07	.20
58 Mike Faulkerson	.07	.20
59 Paul Grasmanis	.07	.20
60 Robert Green	.07	.20
61 Jack Jackson	.07	.20
62 Bobby Neely	.07	.20
63 Todd Perry	.07	.20
64 Evan Pilgrim	.07	.20
65 Octus Polk	.07	.20
66 Rashaan Salaam	.07	.20
67 Willie Anderson	.07	.20
68 Jeff Blake	.10	.30
69 Scott Brumfield	.07	.20
70 Jeff Cothran	.07	.20
71 Gerald Dixon	.07	.20
72 Garrison Hearst	.10	.30
73 James Hundon RC	.20	.50
74 Brian Milne	.07	.20
75 Troy Sadowski	.07	.20
76 Tom Tumulty	.07	.20
77 Kimo von Oelhoffen RC	1.25	3.00
78 Troy Aikman	.40	1.00
79 Dale Hellestrae	.07	.20
80 Roger Harper	.07	.20
81 Michael Irvin	.20	.50
82 John Jett	.07	.20
83 Kelvin Martin	.07	.20
84 Deion Sanders	.20	.50
85 Darrin Smith	.07	.20
86 Emmitt Smith	.60	1.50
87 Herschel Walker	.10	.30
88 Charlie Williams	.07	.20
89 Glenn Cadrez	.07	.20
90 Dwayne Carswell RC	.20	.50
91 Terrell Davis	.25	.60
92 David Diaz-infante	.07	.20
93 John Elway	.75	2.00
94 Harald Hasselback	.07	.20
95 Tory James	.07	.20
96 Bill Musgrave	.07	.20
97 Ralph Tamm	.07	.20
98 Maa Tanuvasa RC	.07	.20
99 Gary Zimmerman	.07	.20
100 Shane Bonham	.07	.20
101 Stephen Boyd RC	.07	.20
102 Jeff Hartings RC	.40	1.00
103 Hessley Hempstead	.07	.20
104 Scott Kowalkowski	.07	.20
105 Herman Moore	.10	.30
106 Barry Sanders	.60	1.50
107 Tony Semple	.07	.20
108 Ryan Stewart	.07	.20
109 Mike Wells	.07	.20
110 Richard Woodley	.07	.20
111 Brett Favre	.75	2.00
112 Bernardo Harris RC	.10	.30
113 Keith McKenzie RC	.07	.20
114 Terry Mickens	.07	.20
115 Doug Pederson RC	.20	.50
116 Jeff Thomason RC	.07	.20
117 Adam Timmerman RC	.07	.20
118 Reggie White	.20	.50
119 Bruce Wilkerson	.07	.20
120 Gabe Wilkins RC	.07	.20
121 Tyrone Williams RC	.07	.20
122 Al Del Greco	.07	.20
123 Anthony Dorsett	.07	.20
124 Josh Evans	.07	.20
125 Eddie George	.20	.50
126 Lemanski Hall RC	.07	.20
127 Ronnie Harmon	.07	.20
128 Steve McNair	.25	.60
129 Michael Roan	.07	.20
130 Marcus Robertson	.07	.20
131 Jon Runyan	.07	.20
132 Chris Sanders	.07	.20
133 Korwin Boll	.07	.20
134 Marshall Faulk	.25	.60
135 Clif Groce RC	.07	.20
136 Jim Harbaugh	.10	.30
137 Marvin Harrison	.20	.50
138 Eric Mahlum	.07	.20
139 Tony Mandarich	.07	.20
140 Dedric Mathis	.07	.20
141 Marcus Pollard RC	.07	.20
142 Scott Slutzker	.07	.20
143 Mark Stock	.07	.20
144 Bucky Brooks	.07	.20
145 Mark Brunell	.25	.60
146 Kendricke Bullard	.07	.20
147 Randy Jordan	.07	.20
148 Jeff Kopp	.07	.20
149 Le'Shai Maston	.07	.20
150 Keenan McCardell	.10	.30
151 Clyde Simmons	.07	.20
152 Jimmy Smith	.10	.30
153 Rich Tylski RC	.07	.20
154 Dave Widell	.07	.20
155 Marcus Allen	.20	.50
156 Keith Cash	.07	.20
157 Donnie Edwards	.10	.30
158 Trezelle Jenkins	.07	.20
159 Sean LaChapelle	.07	.20
160 Greg Manusky RC	.07	.20
161 Steve Matthews RC	.07	.20
162 Pellom McDaniels RC	.07	.20
163 Chris Penn	.07	.20
164 Danny Villa	.07	.20
165 Jerome Woods	.07	.20
166 Karim Abdul-Jabbar	.20	.50
167 John Bock	.07	.20
168 O.J. Brigance RC	.07	.20
169 Norman Hand RC	.07	.20
170 Anthony Harris	.07	.20
171 Larry Izzo RC	.07	.20
172 Charles Jordan	.07	.20
173 Dan Marino	.75	2.00
174 Everett McIver	.07	.20
175 Joe Nedney RC	.07	.20
176 Robert Wilson RC	.07	.20
177 David Dixon	.07	.20
178 Charles Evans	.07	.20
179 Hunter Goodwin RC	.07	.20
180 Ben Hanks	.07	.20
181 Warren Moon	.20	.50
182 Harold Morrow RC	.20	.50
183 Fernando Smith	.07	.20
184 Robert Smith	.10	.30
185 Sean Vanhorse	.07	.20
186 Jay Walker	.07	.20
187 Dewayne Washington	.07	.20
188 Moe Williams	.20	.50
189 Mike Bartrum RC	.07	.20
190 Drew Bledsoe	.25	.60
191 Troy Brown	.10	.30
192 Chad Eaton RC	.07	.20
193 Sam Gash	.07	.20
194 Mike Gisler	.07	.20
195 Curtis Martin	.25	.60
196 David Richards	.07	.20
197 Todd Rucci	.07	.20
198 Chris Sullivan	.07	.20
199 Adam Vinatieri RC	10.00	25.00
200 Doug Brien	.07	.20
201 Derek Brown RBK	.07	.20
202 Lee DeRamus	.07	.20
203 Jim Everett	.07	.20
204 Mercury Hayes	.07	.20
205 Joe Johnson	.07	.20
206 Henry Lusk RC	.07	.20
207 Andy McCollum	.07	.20
208 Alex Molden	.07	.20
209 Ray Zellars	.07	.20
210 Marcus Buckley	.07	.20
211 Doug Coleman RC	.07	.20
212 Percy Ellsworth RC	.07	.20
213 Rodney Hampton	.10	.30
214 Brian Saxton	.07	.20
215 Jason Sehorn	.10	.30
216 Stan White	.07	.20
217 Corey Widmer	.07	.20
218 Rodney Young	.07	.20
219 Rob Zatechka	.07	.20
220 Henry Bailey	.07	.20
221 Chad Cascadden RC	.07	.20
222 Wayne Chrebet	.20	.50
223 Tyrone Davis	.07	.20
224 Kwame Ellis	.07	.20
225 Glenn Foley	.10	.30
226 Erik Howard	.07	.20
227 Gary Jones	.07	.20
228 Adrian Murrell	.10	.30
229 Marc Spindler	.07	.20
230 Lonnie Young	.07	.20
231 Eric Zomalt	.07	.20
232 Tim Brown	.20	.50
233 Aundray Bruce	.07	.20
234 Darren Carrington	.07	.20
235 Rick Cunningham	.07	.20
236 Rob Homberg	.07	.20
237 Jeff Hostetler	.07	.20
238 Lorenzo Lynch	.07	.20
239 Barrett Robbins	.07	.20
240 Dan Turk	.07	.20
241 Harvey Williams	.07	.20
242 Brian Dawkins	.20	.50
243 Ty Detmer	.10	.30
244 Troy Drake	.07	.20
245 Rhett Hall	.07	.20
246 Joe Panos	.07	.20
247 Johnny Thomas	.07	.20
248 Kevin Turner	.07	.20
249 Ricky Watters	.10	.30
250 Derrick Witherspoon RC	.07	.20
251 Sylvester Wright	.07	.20
252 Jerome Bettis	.20	.50
253 Carlos Emmons RC	.07	.20
254 Jason Gildon	.07	.20
255 Jonathan Hayes	.07	.20
256 Kevin Henry	.07	.20
257 Jerry Olsavsky	.07	.20
258 Erric Pegram	.07	.20
259 Brendan Stai	.07	.20
260 Justin Strzelczyk	.07	.20
261 Mike Tomczak	.07	.20
262 Tony Banks	.10	.30
263 Hayward Clay	.07	.20
264 Percell Gaskins	.07	.20
265 Eddie Kennison	.10	.30
266 Aaron Laing	.07	.20
267 Keith Lyle	.07	.20
268 Jamie Martin RC	1.00	2.50
269 Lawrence Phillips	.07	.20
270 Zach Wiegert	.07	.20
271 Toby Wright	.07	.20
272 Darren Bennett	.07	.20
273 Tony Berti	.07	.20
274 Freddie Bradley	.07	.20
275 Joe Cocozzo	.07	.20
276 Andre Coleman	.07	.20
277 Marco Coleman	.07	.20
278 Rodney Harrison RC	.40	1.00
279 David Hendrix	.07	.20
280 Leonard Russell	.07	.20
281 Sean Salisbury	.07	.20
282 Dennis Brown	.07	.20
283 Chris Dalman	.07	.20
284 Brent Jones	.10	.30
285 Sean Manuel	.07	.20
286 Marquez Pope	.07	.20
287 Jerry Rice	.40	1.00
288 Kirk Scrafford	.07	.20
289 Iheanyi Uwaezuoke	.10	.30
290 Tommy Vardell	.07	.20
291 Steve Young	.25	.60
292 James Atkins	.07	.20
293 T.J. Cunningham	.07	.20
294 Stan Gelbaugh	.07	.20
295 James Logan	.07	.20
296 James McKnight RC	.60	1.50
297 Rick Mirer	.07	.20
298 Todd Peterson RC	.07	.20
299 Fred Thomas	.07	.20
300 Rick Tuten	.07	.20
301 Chris Warren	.10	.30
302 Donnie Abraham RC	.20	.50
303 Trent Dilfer	.20	.50
304 Kenneth Gant	.07	.20
305 Jeff Gooch	.10	.30
306 Courtney Hawkins	.07	.20
307 Tyoka Jackson RC	.07	.20
308 Melvin Johnson RC	.07	.20
309 Lonnie Marts	.07	.20
310 Hardy Nickerson	.07	.20
311 Errict Rhett	.07	.20
312 Terry Allen	.20	.50
313 Flipper Anderson	.07	.20
314 William Bell	.07	.20
315 Scott Blanton RC	.07	.20
316 Leomont Evans RC	.07	.20
317 Gus Frerotte	.07	.20
318 Darryl Morrison	.07	.20
319 Matt Turk	.07	.20
320 Jeff Uhlenhake	.07	.20
321 Brian Walker RC	.07	.20
322 Mark Brunell LL	.20	.50
323 Barry Sanders LL	.30	.75
324 Isaac Bruce LL	.20	.50
325 Terry Allen LL	.10	.30
326 Steve Young LL	.20	.50
327 Jerry Rice LL	.20	.50
328 Ricky Watters LL	.10	.30
329 Kevin Greene LL	.07	.20
330 Brett Favre LL	.40	1.00
S1 Mark Brunell Sample	.75	2.00

1997 Pacific Philadelphia Gold

Inserted in packs at the rate of three per pack, this 200-card bonus set features borderless color player action photos with gold foil highlights. The backs carry player information. Copper (hobby), Red (special retail) and Silver (retail) parallel sets were also produced and randomly inserted at the rate of 2:37 in their respective pack types.

COMPLETE SET (200)	15.00	30.00
1 Ryan Christopherson	.05	.15
2 James Dexter	.05	.15
3 Boomer Esiason	.08	.25
4 Jarius Hayes	.05	.15
5 Eric Hill	.05	.15
6 Trey Junkin	.05	.15
7 Kwamie Lassiter	.15	.40
8 Patrick Bates	.05	.15
9 Brad Edwards	.05	.15
10 Roman Fortin	.05	.15
11 Harper Le Bel	.05	.15
12 Lorenzo Styles	.05	.15
13 Robbie Tobeck	.05	.15
14 Mike Caldwell	.05	.15
15 Eric Green	.05	.15
16 Brian Kinchen	.05	.15
17 Eric Turner	.05	.15
18 Jerrol Williams	.05	.15
19 Eric Zeier	.08	.25
20 Darick Holmes	.05	.15
21 Ken Irvin	.05	.15
22 Jerry Ostroski	.05	.15
23 Andre Reed	.08	.25
24 Steve Tasker	.05	.15
25 Thurman Thomas	.15	.40
26 Steve Beuerlein	.08	.25
27 Kerry Collins	.15	.40
28 Eric Davis	.05	.15
29 Norberto Garrido	.05	.15
30 Lamar Lathon	.05	.15
31 Andre Royal	.05	.15
32 Tony Carter	.05	.15
33 Jerry Fontenot	.05	.15
34 Raymont Harris	.05	.15
35 Anthony Marshall	.05	.15
36 Barry Minter	.05	.15
37 Steve Stenstrom	.05	.15
38 Donnell Woolford	.05	.15
39 Ken Blackman	.05	.15
40 Jeff Blake	.08	.25
41 Carl Pickens	.08	.25
42 Artie Smith	.05	.15
43 Ramondo Stallings	.05	.15
44 Melvin Tuten	.05	.15
45 Joe Walter	.05	.15
46 Troy Aikman	.40	1.00
47 Billy Davis	.05	.15
48 Chad Hennings	.05	.15
49 Emmitt Smith	.60	1.50
50 George Teague	.05	.15
51 Kevin Williams	.05	.15
52 Terrell Davis	.25	.60
53 John Elway	.75	2.00
54 Tom Nalen	.05	.15
55 Bill Romanowski	.05	.15
56 Rod Smith WR	.15	.40
57 Dan Williams	.05	.15
58 Mike Compton	.05	.15
59 Eric Lynch	.05	.15
60 Aubrey Matthews	.05	.15
61 Pete Metzelaars	.05	.15
62 Herman Moore	.08	.25
63 Barry Sanders	.60	1.50
64 Keith Washington	.05	.15
65 Edgar Bennett	.08	.25
66 Brett Favre	.75	2.00
67 Lamont Hollinquest	.05	.15
68 Keith Jackson	.05	.15
69 Derrick Mayes	.08	.25
70 Andre Rison	.08	.25
71 Eddie George	.15	.40
72 Mel Gray	.05	.15
73 Darryll Lewis	.05	.15
74 John Henry Mills	.05	.15
75 Rodney Thomas	.05	.15
76 Gary Walker	.05	.15
77 Troy Auzenne	.05	.15
78 Sammie Burroughs	.05	.15
79 Jim Harbaugh	.08	.25
80 Tony McCoy	.05	.15
81 Brian Stablein	.05	.15
82 Kipp Vickers	.05	.15
83 Aaron Beasley	.05	.15
84 Mark Brunell	.25	.60
85 Don Davey	.05	.15
86 Chris Hudson	.05	.15
87 Greg Huntington	.05	.15
88 Ernie Logan	.05	.15
89 Donnell Bennett	.05	.15
90 Anthony Davis	.05	.15
91 Tim Grunhard	.05	.15
92 Danan Hughes	.05	.15
93 Tony Richardson	.08	.25
94 Tracy Simien	.05	.15
95 Karim Abdul-Jabbar	.15	.40
96 Dwight Hollier	.05	.15
97 John Kidd	.05	.15
98 Dan Marino	.75	2.00
99 Jerris McPhail	.05	.15
100 Irving Spikes	.05	.15
101 Richmond Webb	.05	.15
102 Jeff Brady	.05	.15
103 Richard Brown	.05	.15
104 Corey Fuller	.05	.15
105 John Gerak	.05	.15
106 Scottie Graham	.05	.15
107 Amp Lee	.05	.15
108 Drew Bledsoe	.25	.60
109 Tedy Bruschi	.30	.75
110 Todd Collins	.05	.15
111 Bob Kratch	.05	.15
112 Curtis Martin	.25	.60
113 Dave Meggett	.05	.15
114 Tom Tupa	.05	.15
115 Eric Allen	.05	.15
116 Mario Bates	.05	.15
117 Clarence Jones	.05	.15
118 Sean Lumpkin	.05	.15
119 Doug Nussmeier	.05	.15
120 Irv Smith	.05	.15
121 Winfred Tubbs	.05	.15
122 Willie Beamon	.05	.15
123 Greg Bishop	.05	.15
124 Dave Brown	.05	.15
125 Gary Downs	.05	.15
126 Thomas Lewis	.05	.15
127 Michael Strahan	.08	.25
128 Tyrone Wheatley	.08	.25
129 Matt Brock	.05	.15
130 Mike Chalenski	.05	.15
131 Roger Duffy	.05	.15
132 John Hudson	.05	.15
133 Frank Reich	.05	.15
134 David Williams	.05	.15
135 Greg Biekert	.05	.15
136 Mike Jones	.05	.15
137 Napoleon Kaufman	.15	.40
138 Carl Kidd	.05	.15
139 Terry McDaniel	.05	.15
140 Mike Morton	.05	.15
141 Olanda Truitt	.05	.15
142 Gary Anderson	.05	.15
143 Richard Cooper	.05	.15
144 Jimmie Johnson	.05	.15
145 Joe Kelly	.05	.15
146 William Thomas	.05	.15
147 Ricky Watters	.08	.25
148 Ed West	.05	.15
149 Michael Zordich	.05	.15
150 Jerome Bettis	.15	.40
151 Dermontti Dawson	.05	.15
152 Lethon Flowers	.05	.15
153 Charles Johnson	.08	.25
154 Darren Perry	.05	.15
155 Kordell Stewart	.15	.40
156 Will Wolford	.05	.15
157 Isaac Bruce	.15	.40
158 Kevin Carter	.05	.15
159 Torin Dorn	.05	.15
160 Leo Goeas	.05	.15
161 Gerald McBurrows	.05	.15
162 Chuck Osborne	.05	.15
163 J.T. Thomas	.05	.15
164 Dwayne Gordon	.05	.15
165 Stan Humphries	.08	.25
166 Shawn Lee	.05	.15
167 Chris Mims	.05	.15
168 John Parrella	.05	.15
169 Junior Seau	.15	.40
170 Bryan Still	.05	.15
171 Curtis Buckley	.05	.15
172 William Floyd	.08	.25
173 Merton Hanks	.05	.15
174 Terry Kirby	.08	.25
175 Jerry Rice	.40	1.00
176 J.J. Stokes	.08	.25
177 Jeff Wilkins	.05	.15
178 Bryant Young	.05	.15
179 Sam Adams	.05	.15
180 John Friesz	.05	.15
181 Joey Galloway	.08	.25
182 Pete Kendall	.05	.15
183 Jason Kyle	.05	.15
184 Darryl Williams	.05	.15
185 Ronnie Williams	.05	.15
186 Mike Alstott	.15	.40
187 Trent Dilfer	.15	.40
188 Tyrone Legette	.05	.15
189 Martin Mayhew	.05	.15
190 Jason Odom	.05	.15
191 Warren Sapp	.08	.25
192 Karl Williams	.05	.15
193 Terry Allen	.15	.40
194 Romeo Bandison	.05	.15
195 Alcides Catanho	.05	.15
196 Gus Frerotte	.05	.15
197 William Gaines	.05	.15
198 Ken Harvey	.05	.15
199 Trevor Matich	.05	.15
200 Scott Turner	.05	.15
S1 Mark Brunell Sample	.40	1.00

1997 Pacific Philadelphia Copper

COMPLETE SET (200)	60.00	120.00
*COPPER: 2X TO 4X GOLD		
STATED ODDS 2:37 HOBBY		

1997 Pacific Philadelphia Red

COMPLETE SET (200)	40.00	80.00
*REDS: 1.2X TO 2.5X GOLDS		

1997 Pacific Philadelphia Silver

COMPLETE SET (200)	125.00	250.00
*SILVERS: 3.5X TO 7X GOLDS		
STATED ODDS 2:37 RETAIL		

1997 Pacific Philadelphia Heart of the Game

COMPLETE SET (20)	40.00	100.00
STATED ODDS 1:73		
1 Thurman Thomas	1.50	4.00
2 Kerry Collins	1.50	4.00
3 Troy Aikman	3.00	8.00
4 Emmitt Smith	5.00	12.00
5 Terrell Davis	2.00	5.00
6 John Elway	6.00	15.00
7 Barry Sanders	5.00	12.00
8 Brett Favre	6.00	15.00
9 Antonio Freeman	1.50	4.00
10 Marshall Faulk	2.00	5.00
11 Mark Brunell	2.00	5.00
12 Marcus Allen	1.50	4.00
13 Dan Marino	6.00	15.00
14 Drew Bledsoe	2.00	5.00
15 Curtis Martin	2.00	5.00
16 Napoleon Kaufman	1.50	4.00
17 Jerome Bettis	1.50	4.00
18 Isaac Bruce	1.50	4.00
19 Jerry Rice	3.00	8.00
20 Steve Young	2.00	5.00

1997 Pacific Philadelphia Milestones

COMPLETE SET (20)	100.00	200.00
STATED ODDS 1:37		
1 Simeon Rice	3.00	8.00
2 Thurman Thomas	3.00	8.00
3 Troy Aikman	6.00	15.00
4 Emmitt Smith	10.00	25.00
5 Terrell Davis	4.00	10.00
6 John Elway	12.50	30.00
7 Brett Favre	12.50	30.00
8 Desmond Howard	2.00	5.00
9 Reggie White	3.00	8.00
10 Mark Brunell	4.00	10.00
11 Marcus Allen	3.00	8.00
12 Karim Abdul-Jabbar	3.00	8.00
13 Dan Marino	12.50	30.00
14 Drew Bledsoe	4.00	10.00
15 Terry Glenn	3.00	8.00
16 Curtis Martin	4.00	10.00
17 Tony Banks	2.00	5.00
18 Jerry Rice	6.00	15.00
19 Steve Young	4.00	10.00
20 Terry Allen	3.00	8.00

1997 Pacific Philadelphia Photoengravings

COMPLETE SET (36)	40.00	100.00
STATED ODDS 2:37		
1 Thurman Thomas	1.25	3.00
2 Kerry Collins	1.25	3.00
3 Jeff Blake	.75	2.00
4 Troy Aikman	2.50	6.00
5 Deion Sanders	1.25	3.00
6 Emmitt Smith	4.00	10.00
7 Terrell Davis	1.50	4.00
8 John Elway	5.00	12.00
9 Herman Moore	.75	2.00
10 Barry Sanders	4.00	10.00
11 Brett Favre	5.00	12.00
12 Desmond Howard	.75	2.00
13 Dorsey Levens	1.25	3.00
14 Eddie George	1.25	3.00
15 Marshall Faulk	1.50	4.00
16 Jim Harbaugh	.75	2.00
17 Marvin Harrison	1.25	3.00
18 Mark Brunell	1.50	4.00
19 Keenan McCardell	.75	2.00
20 Karim Abdul-Jabbar	1.25	3.00
21 Dan Marino	5.00	12.00
22 Brad Johnson	1.25	3.00
23 Drew Bledsoe	1.50	4.00
24 Terry Glenn	1.25	3.00
25 Curtis Martin	1.50	4.00
26 Keyshawn Johnson	1.25	3.00
27 Tim Brown	1.25	3.00
28 Napoleon Kaufman	1.25	3.00
29 Ricky Watters	.75	2.00
30 Jerome Bettis	1.25	3.00
31 Kordell Stewart	1.50	4.00
32 Eddie Kennison	.75	2.00
33 Jerry Rice	2.50	6.00
34 Steve Young	1.50	4.00
35 Chris Warren	.75	2.00
36 Terry Allen	1.25	3.00

1993 Pacific Prisms

After debuting as an insert set in the 1992 Pacific NFL series, Pacific decided to release a 108-card (plus one checklist) set of Prism cards. The standard-size cards comprising this set were issued in one-card packs and feature on their fronts color player action cut-outs over borderless triangular prismatic foil backgrounds. Seventeen thousand of each card were produced. The cards are checklisted alphabetically according to teams. Rookie Cards include Jerome Bettis, Drew Bledsoe, Reggie Brooks, Garrison Hearst, Rick Mirer and Robert Smith. Two promo cards (Emmitt Smith and Drew Bledsoe) were produced and are listed below. They were released primarily at the Chicago National Card Collectors Convention and each looks very similar to its regular issue card. The promos however differ slightly on the backs in relation to the small player and helmet photos. The player photo is touching the helmet and the helmet photo is smaller on the promo cards. Reportedly 5,500 of each promo was produced.

COMPLETE SET (109)	15.00	40.00
1 Chris Miller	.30	.75
2 Mike Pritchard	.30	.75
3 Andre Rison	.30	.75
4 Deion Sanders	1.00	2.50
5 Tony Smith	.20	.50
6 Jim Kelly	.60	1.50
7 Andre Reed	.40	1.00
8 Thurman Thomas	.60	1.50
9 Neal Anderson	.20	.50
10 Jim Harbaugh	.40	1.00
11 Donnell Woolford	.20	.50
12 David Klingler	.20	.50
13 Carl Pickens	.30	.75
14 Alfred Williams	.20	.50
15 Michael Jackson	.30	.75
16 Bernie Kosar	.30	.75
17 Tommy Vardell	.20	.50
18 Troy Aikman	1.25	3.00
19 Alvin Harper	.30	.75
20 Michael Irvin	.60	1.50
21 Russell Maryland	.20	.50
22 Emmitt Smith	2.50	6.00
23 John Elway	2.50	6.00
24 Tommy Maddox	.40	1.00
25 Shannon Sharpe	.60	1.50
26 Herman Moore	.40	1.00
27 Rodney Peete	.20	.50
28 Barry Sanders	2.00	5.00
29 Pat Swilling	.20	.50
30 Terrell Buckley	.20	.50
31 Brett Favre	3.00	8.00
32 Sterling Sharpe	.40	1.00
33 Reggie White	.60	1.50
34 Ernest Givins	.30	.75
35 Haywood Jeffires	.30	.75
36 Warren Moon	.60	1.50
37 Lorenzo White	.20	.50
38 Steve Emtman	.20	.50
39 Jeff George	.40	1.00
40 Reggie Langhorne	.20	.50
41 Dale Carter	.20	.50
42 Joe Montana	2.50	6.00
43 Derrick Thomas	.60	1.50
44 Barry Word	.20	.50
45 Nick Bell	.20	.50
46 Eric Dickerson	.30	.75
47 Jeff Jaeger	.20	.50
48 Jerome Bettis RC	4.00	10.00
49 Henry Ellard	.30	.75
50 Jim Everett	.30	.75
51 Cleveland Gary	.20	.50
52 Marco Coleman	.20	.50
53 Mark Higgs	.20	.50
54 Keith Jackson	.30	.75
55 Dan Marino	2.50	6.00
56 Troy Vincent	.20	.50
57 Terry Allen	.40	1.00
58 Jack Del Rio	.20	.50
59 Sean Salisbury	.20	.50
60 Robert Smith RC	1.25	3.00
61 Drew Bledsoe RC	3.00	8.00
62 Marv Cook	.20	.50
63 Irving Fryar	.30	.75
64 Leonard Russell	.30	.75
65 Andre Tippett	.20	.50
66 Morten Andersen	.20	.50

67 Vaughn Dunbar .20 .50
68 Eric Martin .20 .50
69 David Brown RC .40 1.00
70 Rodney Hampton .30 .75
71 Phil Simms .30 .75
72 Lawrence Taylor .60 1.50
73 Ronnie Lott .30 .75
74 Johnny Mitchell .20 .50
75 Rob Moore .30 .75
76 Browning Nagle .20 .50
77 Fred Barnett .30 .75
78 Randall Cunningham .60 1.50
79 Herschel Walker .30 .75
80 Gary Clark .30 .75
81 Ken Harvey .20 .50
82 Garrison Hearst RC 1.00 2.50
83 Ricky Proehl .20 .50
84 Barry Foster .30 .75
85 Ernie Mills .20 .50
86 Neil O'Donnell .60 1.50
87 Stan Humphries .30 .75
88 Leslie O'Neal .30 .75
89 Junior Seau .60 1.50
90 Amp Lee .20 .50
91 Jerry Rice 1.50 4.00
92 Ricky Watters .60 1.50
93 Steve Young 1.25 3.00
94 Cortez Kennedy .30 .75
95 Rick Mirer RC .60 1.50
96 Eugene Robinson .20 .50
97 Chris Warren .30 .75
98 John L. Williams .20 .50
99 Reggie Cobb .20 .50
100 Lawrence Dawsey .20 .50
101 Santana Dotson .30 .75
102 Courtney Hawkins .20 .50
103 Reggie Brooks RC .30 .75
104 Ricky Ervins .20 .50
105 Desmond Howard .40 1.00
106 Art Monk .40 1.00
107 Mark Rypien .20 .50
108 Ricky Sanders .20 .50
NNO Checklist Card .15 .40
P22 Emmitt Smith Promo 2.50 6.00
P61 Drew Bledsoe Promo 1.25 3.00

1994 Pacific Prisms

These 128 standard-size cards feature borderless fronts with color action player photos cut out and superimposed on a prism-patterned background. There were reportedly 16,000 of each card produced in silver foil and 1,138 of each card produced in gold foil. Each pack contained either a silver or gold Prism card. Rookie Cards include Mario Bates, Marshall Faulk, William Floyd, Greg Hill, Charles Johnson, Errict Rhett and Heath Shuler.

COMPLETE SET (128) 20.00 50.00
1 Troy Aikman UER 1.50 4.00
(Text on back indicates he led Cowboys to victory in Super Bowl XXV. The Giants won SB XXV)
2 Marcus Allen .50 1.25
3 Morten Andersen .15 .40
4 Fred Barnett .30 .75
5 Mario Bates RC .50 1.25
6 Edgar Bennett .50 1.25
7 Rod Bernstine .15 .40
8 Jerome Bettis .75 2.00
9 Steve Beuerlein .30 .75
10 Brian Blades .30 .75
11 Drew Bledsoe 1.25 3.00
12 Vincent Brisby .30 .75
13 Reggie Brooks .30 .75
14 Derek Brown RBK .15 .40
15 Gary Brown .15 .40
16 Tim Brown .50 1.25
17 Marion Butts .15 .40
18 Keith Byars .15 .40
19 Cody Carlson .15 .40
20 Anthony Carter .30 .75
21 Tom Carter .15 .40
22 Gary Clark .30 .75
23 Ben Coates .30 .75
24 Reggie Cobb .15 .40
25 Curtis Conway .30 .75
26 John Copeland .15 .40
27 Randall Cunningham .50 1.25
28 Willie Davis .30 .75
29 Sean Dawkins RC .50 1.25
30 Lawrence Dawsey .15 .40
31 Richard Dent .30 .75
32 Trent Dilfer RC 1.25 3.00
33 Troy Drayton .15 .40
34 Vaughn Dunbar .15 .40
35 Henry Ellard .30 .75
36 John Elway 3.00 8.00
37 Craig Erickson .15 .40
38 Boomer Esiason .30 .75
39 Marshall Faulk RC 5.00 10.00
40 Brett Favre 3.00 8.00
41 William Floyd RC .50 1.25
42 Glenn Foley RC .50 1.25
43 Barry Foster .15 .40
44 Irving Fryar .30 .75
45 Jeff George .50 1.25
46 Scottie Graham RC .30 .75
47 Rodney Hampton .30 .75
48 Jim Harbaugh .50 1.25
49 Alvin Harper .30 .75
50 Courtney Hawkins .15 .40
51 Garrison Hearst .50 1.25
52 Vaughn Hebron .15 .40
53 Greg Hill RC .50 1.25
54 Jeff Hostetler .30 .75
55 Michael Irvin .50 1.25
56 Qadry Ismail .30 .75
57 Rocket Ismail .30 .75
58 Anthony Johnson .30 .75
59 Charles Johnson RC .50 1.25
60 Johnny Johnson .15 .40
61 Brent Jones .30 .75
62 Kyle Clifton .15 .40
63 Jim Kelly .30 .75
64 Cortez Kennedy .30 .75
65 Terry Kirby .50 1.25
66 David Klingler .15 .40
67 Erik Kramer .30 .75
68 Reggie Langhorne .15 .40
69 Chuck Levy RC .15 .40
70 Dan Marino 3.00 8.00
71 O.J. McDuffie .50 1.25
72 Natrone Means .50 1.25
73 Eric Metcalf .30 .75
74 Glyn Milburn .30 .75
75 Anthony Miller .30 .75
76 Rick Mirer .50 1.25
77 Johnny Mitchell .15 .40
78 Scott Mitchell .30 .75
79 Joe Montana 3.00 8.00
80 Warren Moon .30 .75
81 Derrick Moore .15 .40
82 Herman Moore .50 1.25
83 Rob Moore .30 .75
84 Ronald Moore .15 .40
85 Johnnie Morton RC 1.50 4.00
86 Neil O'Donnell .30 .75
87 David Palmer RC .50 1.25
88 Erric Pegram .15 .40
89 Carl Pickens .30 .75
90 Anthony Pleasant .15 .40
91 Roosevelt Potts .15 .40
92 Mike Pritchard .15 .40
93 Andre Reed .30 .75
94 Errict Rhett RC .50 1.25
95 Jerry Rice 1.50 4.00
96 Andre Rison .30 .75
97 Greg Robinson .15 .40
98 T.J. Rubley RC .15 .40
99 Leonard Russell .15 .40
100 Barry Sanders 2.50 6.00
101 Deion Sanders 1.00 2.50
102 Ricky Sanders .15 .40
103 Junior Seau .50 1.25
104 Shannon Sharpe .30 .75
105 Sterling Sharpe .30 .75
106 Heath Shuler RC .50 1.25
107 Phil Simms .30 .75
108 Webster Slaughter .15 .40
109 Bruce Smith .50 1.25
110 Emmitt Smith 3.00 8.00
111 Irv Smith .15 .40
112 Robert Smith .50 1.25
113 Vinny Testaverde .30 .75
114 Derrick Thomas .50 1.25
115 Thurman Thomas .30 .75
116 Leroy Thompson .15 .40
117 Lewis Tillman .15 .40
118 Michael Timpson .15 .40
119 Herschel Walker .30 .75
120 Chris Warren .30 .75
121 Ricky Watters .30 .75
122 Lorenzo White .15 .40
123 Reggie White .50 1.25
124 Dan Wilkinson RC .30 .75
125 Kevin Williams .30 .75
126 Steve Young 1.25 3.00
CL1 Checklist 1 .10 .30
CL2 Checklist 2 .10 .30
S1 Sterling Sharpe Promo .40 1.00

1994 Pacific Prisms Gold

COMPLETE SET (126) 125.00 250.00
*STARS: 1.2X TO 3X BASIC CARDS
*GOLD RCs: .8X TO 2X BASIC CARDS
ANNOUNCED PRINT RUN 1138 SETS

1994 Pacific Prisms Team Helmets

COMPLETE SET (30) 2.00 5.00
1 Arizona Cardinals .08 .25
2 Atlanta Falcons .08 .25
3 Buffalo Bills .08 .25
4 Carolina Panthers .10 .30
5 Chicago Bears .08 .25
6 Cincinnati Bengals .08 .25
7 Cleveland Browns .08 .25
8 Dallas Cowboys .20 .50
9 Denver Broncos .08 .25
10 Detroit Lions .08 .25
11 Green Bay Packers .20 .50
12 Houston Oilers .08 .25
13 Indianapolis Colts .08 .25
14 Jacksonville Jaguars .08 .25
15 Kansas City Chiefs .08 .25
16 Los Angeles Raiders .10 .30
17 Los Angeles Rams .08 .25
18 Miami Dolphins .20 .50
19 Minnesota Vikings .08 .25
20 New England Patriots .08 .25
21 New Orleans Saints .08 .25
22 New York Giants .08 .25
23 New York Jets .08 .25
24 Philadelphia Eagles .08 .25
25 Pittsburgh Steelers .20 .50
26 San Diego Chargers .08 .25
27 San Francisco 49ers .20 .50
28 Seattle Seahawks .08 .25
29 Tampa Bay Buccaneers .08 .25
30 Washington Redskins .20 .50

1995 Pacific Prisms

This 216 card standard-size set was issued in two-card packs including one player card and either a Super Bowl information card, a team card or a uniform card. The set was issued in two series, both containing 108 cards each. A John Elway autograph card, featuring an embossed Pacific logo, was also randomly inserted in the series 2 product. The card was hand signed and hand numbered of 50 and was from the 1994 Pacific Gems of the Crown insert set. It could be found approximately one in every 43,200 packs. We've included this card with the 1994 Pacific Gems of the Crown listings. Finally, a two card unnumbered expansion set was issued in regular packs that contain a red foil-etched background. A Natrone Means Promo card (#1) was produced in both silver and gold foil and priced below.

COMPLETE SET (216) 30.00 80.00
COMP.SERIES 1 (108) 15.00 40.00
COMP.SERIES 2 (108) 15.00 40.00
1 Chuck Levy .08 .25
2 Ronald Moore .08 .25
3 Jay Schroeder .08 .25
4 Bert Emanuel .40 1.00
5 Terance Mathis .20 .50
6 Andre Rison .20 .50
7 Bucky Brooks .08 .25
8 Jeff Burris .08 .25
9 Jim Kelly .40 1.00
10 Lewis Tillman .08 .25
11 Steve Walsh .08 .25
12 Chris Zorich .08 .25
13 Jeff Blake RC 1.00 2.50
14 Steve Broussard .08 .25
15 Jeff Cothran .08 .25
16 Earnset Byner .08 .25
17 Leroy Hoard .08 .25
18 Vinny Testaverde .20 .50
19 Troy Aikman 1.00 2.50
20 Alvin Harper .08 .25
21 Leon Lett .08 .25
22 Jay Novacek .20 .50
23 John Elway 2.00 5.00
24 Karl Mecklenburg .08 .25
25 Leonard Russell .08 .25
26 Mel Gray .08 .25
27 Dave Krieg .08 .25
28 Barry Sanders 1.50 4.00
29 Chris Spielman .20 .50
30 Robert Brooks .40 1.00
31 LeShon Johnson .20 .50
32 Sterling Sharpe .20 .50
33 Ernest Givins .08 .25
34 Billy Joe Tolliver .08 .25
35 Lorenzo White .08 .25
36 Charles Arbuckle .08 .25
37 Sean Dawkins .20 .50
38 Marshall Faulk 1.25 3.00
39 Marcus Allen .40 1.00
40 Donnell Bennett .20 .50
41 Matt Blundin RC .08 .25
42 Greg Hill .20 .50
43 Tim Brown .40 1.00
44 Billy Joe Hobert .20 .50
45 Rocket Ismail .20 .50
46 James Jett .20 .50
47 Tim Bowens .08 .25
48 Irving Fryar .20 .50
49 O.J. McDuffie .40 1.00
50 Irving Spikes .20 .50
51 Terry Allen .20 .50
52 Cris Carter .40 1.00
53 Amp Lee .08 .25
54 Drew Bledsoe .60 1.50
55 Willie McGinest .20 .50
56 Leroy Thompson .08 .25
57 Michael Timpson .08 .25
58 Michael Haynes .20 .50
59 Derrell Mitchell RC .08 .25
60 Dave Brown .20 .50
61 Thomas Lewis .20 .50
62 Dave Meggett .08 .25
63 Boomer Esiason .20 .50
64 Aaron Glenn .08 .25
65 Ronnie Lott .20 .50
66 Randall Cunningham .40 1.00
67 Charlie Garner .40 1.00
68 Herschel Walker .20 .50
69 Barry Foster .20 .50
70 Charles Johnson .20 .50
71 Jim Miller RC 1.25 3.00
72 Rod Woodson .20 .50
73 Andre Coleman .08 .25
74 Natrone Means .20 .50
75 Shannon Mitchell RC .08 .25
76 Junior Seau .40 1.00
77 Elvis Grbac .40 1.00
78 Deion Sanders .60 1.50
79 Adam Walker RC .08 .25
80 Ricky Watters .20 .50
81 Michael Bates .08 .25
82 Brian Blades .20 .50
83 Eugene Robinson .08 .25
84 Chris Warren .20 .50
85 Jerome Bettis .40 1.00
86 Troy Drayton .08 .25
87 Chris Miller .08 .25
88 Trent Dilfer .40 1.00
89 Hardy Nickerson .08 .25
90 Errict Rhett .20 .50
91 Henry Ellard .20 .50
92 Gus Frerotte .20 .50
93 Ricky Ervins .08 .25
94 Dave Barr RC .08 .25
95 Kyle Brady RC .40 1.00
96 Mark Bruener RC .20 .50
97 Ki-Jana Carter RC .40 1.00
98 Kerry Collins RC 2.00 5.00
99 Joey Galloway RC 2.00 5.00
100 Napoleon Kaufman RC 1.50 4.00
101 Steve McNair RC 4.00 10.00
102 Craig Newsome RC .08 .25
103 Rashaan Salaam RC .20 .50
104 Kordell Stewart RC 2.00 5.00
105 J.J. Stokes RC .40 1.00
106 Rodney Thomas RC .20 .50
107 Michael Westbrook RC .40 1.00
108 Tyrone Wheatley RC 1.50 4.00
109 Larry Centers .20 .50
110 Garrison Hearst .40 1.00
111 Jamir Miller .08 .25
112 Jeff George .20 .50
113 Craig Heyward .20 .50
114 Cornelius Bennett .20 .50
115 Andre Reed .20 .50
116 Randy Baldwin .08 .25
117 Tommy Barnhardt .08 .25
118 Sam Mills .20 .50
119 Brian O'Neal .08 .25
120 Frank Reich .08 .25
121 Tony Smith .08 .25
122 Lawyer Tillman .08 .25
123 Jack Trudeau .08 .25
124 Vernon Turner .08 .25
125 Curtis Conway .40 1.00
126 Erik Kramer .08 .25
127 Nate Lewis .08 .25
128 Carl Pickens .20 .50
129 Darnay Scott .20 .50
130 Dan Wilkinson .20 .50
131 Derrick Alexander WR .40 1.00
132 Carl Banks .08 .25
133 Michael Irvin .40 1.00
134 Emmitt Smith 1.50 4.00
135 Kevin Williams WR .20 .50
136 Glyn Milburn .08 .25
137 Anthony Miller .20 .50
138 Shannon Sharpe .20 .50
139 Scott Mitchell .20 .50
140 Herman Moore .40 1.00
141 Edgar Bennett .20 .50
142 Brett Favre 2.00 5.00
143 Reggie White .40 1.00
144 Gary Brown .08 .25
145 Haywood Jeffires .08 .25
146 Webster Slaughter .08 .25
147 Craig Erickson .08 .25
148 Paul Justin .08 .25
149 Lamont Warren .08 .25
150 Steve Beuerlein .20 .50
151 Derek Brown TE .08 .25
152 Mark Brunell .60 1.50
153 Reggie Cobb .08 .25
154 Desmond Howard .20 .50
155 Kelvin Pritchett .08 .25
156 James O. Stewart RC 1.50 4.00
157 Cedric Tillman .08 .25
158 Kimble Anders .20 .50
159 Lake Dawson .20 .50
160 Keith Byars .08 .25
161 Dan Marino 2.00 5.00
162 Bernie Parmalee .20 .50
163 Qadry Ismail .20 .50
164 Warren Moon .20 .50
165 Jake Reed .20 .50
166 Marion Butts .08 .25
167 Ben Coates .20 .50
168 Mario Bates .20 .50
169 Quinn Early .20 .50
170 Jim Everett .08 .25
171 Rodney Hampton .20 .50
172 Mike Horan .08 .25
173 Mike Sherrard .08 .25
174 Johnny Johnson .08 .25
175 Adrian Murrell .20 .50
176 Andrew Glover RC .08 .25
177 Jeff Hostetler .20 .50
178 Harvey Williams .08 .25
179 Fred Barnett .20 .50
180 Vaughn Hebron .08 .25
181 Jeff Sydner .08 .25
182 Kevin Greene .20 .50
183 Byron Bam Morris .08 .25
184 Neil O'Donnell .20 .50
185 Stan Humphries .20 .50
186 Tony Martin .20 .50
187 Mark Seay .20 .50
188 William Floyd .20 .50
189 Rickey Jackson .08 .25
190 Jerry Rice 1.00 2.50
191 Steve Young .75 2.00
192 Cortez Kennedy .20 .50
193 Rick Mirer .20 .50
194 Jessie Hester .08 .25
195 Curtis Martin RC 4.00 10.00
196 Horace Copeland .08 .25
197 Charles Wilson .08 .25
198 Reggie Brooks .20 .50
199 Brian Mitchell .08 .25
200 Heath Shuler .20 .50
201 Justin Armour RC .08 .25
202 Jay Barker RC .08 .25
203 Zack Crockett RC .20 .50
204 Christian Fauria RC .20 .50
205 Antonio Freeman RC 1.50 4.00
206 Chad May RC .08 .25
207 Frank Sanders RC .40 1.00
208 Steve Stenstrom RC .08 .25
209 Lorenzo Styles RC .08 .25
210 Sherman Williams RC .08 .25
211 Ray Zellars RC .20 .50
212 Eric Zeier RC .40 1.00
213 Joey Galloway .75 2.00
214 Napoleon Kaufman .60 1.50
215 Rashaan Salaam .20 .50
216 J.J. Stokes .40 1.00
NNO Steve Beuerlein EE .40 1.00
NNO Barry Foster EE .40 1.00
P1 Natrone Means Promo .40 1.00
Silver foil
P2 Natrone Means Promo .40 1.00
Gold foil

1995 Pacific Prisms Gold

COMPLETE SET (216) 125.00 250.00
*STARS: 1.5X TO 3X BASIC CARDS
*RCs: 1X TO 2X BASIC CARDS
STATED ODDS 2:37

1995 Pacific Prisms Connections

COMPLETE SET (20) 40.00 80.00
1A-10A: STATED ODDS 1:73 SER.2 RET.
1B-10B: STATED ODDS 1:73 SER.2 HOB.
*BLUE HOLOFOILS: 2X TO 5X BASIC INSERTS
BLUE HOLO:10% OF TOTAL PRINT RUN
1A Steve Young 2.50 6.00
1B Jerry Rice 3.00 8.00
2A Dan Marino 6.00 15.00
2B Irving Fryar .60 1.50
3A Drew Bledsoe 2.00 5.00
3B Ben Coates .60 1.50
4A John Elway 6.00 15.00
4B Shannon Sharpe .60 1.50
5A Jeff Hostetler .60 1.50
5B Tim Brown 1.25 3.00
6A Warren Moon .60 1.50
6B Cris Carter 1.25 3.00
7A Neil O'Donnell .60 1.50
7B Charles Johnson .60 1.50
8A Troy Aikman 3.00 8.00
8B Michael Irvin 1.25 3.00
9A Stan Humphries .60 1.50
9B Shawn Jefferson .30 .75
10A Jim Kelly 1.25 3.00
10B Andre Reed .60 1.50

1995 Pacific Prisms Kings of the NFL

COMPLETE SET (10) 60.00 150.00
SER.2 STATED ODDS 1:361
1 Emmitt Smith 8.00 20.00
2 Steve Young 4.00 10.00
3 Jerry Rice 5.00 12.00
4 Deion Sanders 3.00 8.00
5 Emmitt Smith 8.00 20.00
6 Dan Marino 10.00 25.00
7 Drew Bledsoe 3.00 8.00
8 Barry Sanders 8.00 20.00
9 Marshall Faulk 6.00 15.00
10 Marshall Faulk 6.00 15.00
Natrone Means

1995 Pacific Prisms Red Hot Rookies

COMPLETE SET (9) 30.00 80.00
STATED ODDS 1:73 SER.1 HOBBY
1 Ki-Jana Carter 1.25 3.00
2 Joey Galloway 6.00 15.00
3 Steve McNair 12.50 30.00
4 Tyrone Wheatley 5.00 12.00
5 Kerry Collins 6.00 15.00
6 Rashaan Salaam .60 1.50
7 Michael Westbrook 1.25 3.00
8 J.J. Stokes 1.25 3.00
9 Napoleon Kaufman 5.00 12.00

1995 Pacific Prisms Red Hot Stars

COMPLETE SET (9) 40.00 100.00
STATED ODDS 1:73 SER.1 RETAIL
1 Barry Sanders 8.00 20.00
2 Steve Young 4.00 10.00
3 Emmitt Smith 8.00 20.00
4 Drew Bledsoe 3.00 8.00
5 Natrone Means 1.00 2.50
6 Dan Marino 10.00 25.00
7 Marshall Faulk 6.00 15.00
8 Jerry Rice 5.00 12.00
9 Errict Rhett 1.00 2.50

1995 Pacific Prisms Super Bowl Logos

COMPLETE SET (30) 1.60 4.00
COMMON CARD (1-30) .06 .15

1995 Pacific Prisms Team Helmets

COMPLETE SET (30) 1.60 4.00
1 Arizona Cardinals .05 .15
2 Atlanta Falcons .05 .15
3 Buffalo Bills .05 .15
4 Carolina Panthers .07 .20
5 Chicago Bears .05 .15
6 Cincinnati Bengals .05 .15
7 Cleveland Browns .05 .15
8 Dallas Cowboys .08 .25
9 Denver Broncos .05 .15
10 Detroit Lions .05 .15
11 Green Bay Packers .08 .25
12 Houston Oilers .05 .15
13 Indianapolis Colts .05 .15
14 Jacksonville Jaguars .05 .15
15 Kansas City Chiefs .05 .15
16 Los Angeles Raiders .07 .20
17 Miami Dolphins .08 .25
18 Minnesota Vikings .05 .15
19 New England Patriots .05 .15
20 New Orleans Saints .05 .15
21 New York Giants .05 .15
22 New York Jets .05 .15
23 Philadelphia Eagles .05 .15
24 Pittsburgh Steelers .08 .25
25 San Diego Chargers .05 .15
26 San Francisco 49ers .08 .25
27 Seattle Seahawks .05 .15
28 St.Louis Rams .05 .15
29 Tampa Bay Buccaneers .05 .15
30 Washington Redskins .08 .25

1995 Pacific Prisms Team Uniforms

COMPLETE SET (30) 1.60 4.00
1 Arizona Cardinals .05 .15
2 Atlanta Falcons .05 .15
3 Buffalo Bills .05 .15
4 Carolina Panthers .07 .20
5 Chicago Bears .05 .15
6 Cincinnati Bengals .05 .15
7 Cleveland Browns .05 .15
8 Dallas Cowboys .08 .25
9 Denver Broncos .05 .15
10 Detroit Lions .05 .15
11 Green Bay Packers .08 .25
12 Houston Oilers .05 .15
13 Indianapolis Colts .05 .15
14 Jacksonville Jaguars .05 .15
15 Kansas City Chiefs .05 .15
16 Los Angeles Raiders .07 .20
17 Miami Dolphins .08 .25
18 Minnesota Vikings .05 .15
19 New England Patriots .05 .15
20 New Orleans Saints .05 .15
21 New York Giants .05 .15
22 New York Jets .05 .15
23 Philadelphia Eagles .05 .15
24 Pittsburgh Steelers .08 .25
25 San Diego Chargers .05 .15
26 San Francisco 49ers .08 .25
27 Seattle Seahawks .05 .15
28 St.Louis Rams .05 .15
29 Tampa Bay Buccaneers .05 .15
30 Washington Redskins .08 .25

1999 Pacific Prisms

This 150 card set was released in mid November of 1999. Notable rookies found within the set include Tim Couch, Donovan Mcnabb, and Ricky Williams. Also veteran stars such as Dan Marino and Emmitt Smith. Hobby packs carried a suggested retail price of $4.99 per pack with 5 cards per pack and the Retail only version carried a $2.99 suggested retail price per pack containing 3 cards.

COMPLETE SET (150) 30.00 80.00
1 David Boston RC .40 1.00
2 Rob Moore .20 .50
3 Adrian Murrell .25 .60
4 Jake Plummer .25 .60
5 Frank Sanders .20 .50
6 Jamal Anderson .25 .60
7 Chris Chandler .25 .60
8 Tim Dwight .25 .60
9 Terance Mathis .20 .50
10 Peter Boulware .20 .50
11 Priest Holmes .30 .75
12 Pat Johnson .20 .50
13 Jermaine Lewis .20 .50
14 Doug Flutie .30 .75
15 Eric Moulds .25 .60
16 Peerless Price RC .40 1.00
17 Antowain Smith .20 .50
18 Bruce Smith .30 .75
19 Steve Beuerlein .25 .60
20 Tim Biakabutuka .25 .60
21 Muhsin Muhammad .25 .60
22 Wesley Walls .25 .60
23 Edgar Bennett .25 .60
24 Curtis Conway .25 .60
25 Bobby Engram .25 .60
26 Curtis Enis .20 .50
27 Cade McNown RC .40 1.00
28 Jeff Blake .25 .60
29 Scott Covington RC .30 .75
30 Corey Dillon .25 .60
31 Carl Pickens .25 .60
32 Akili Smith RC .40 1.00
33 Craig Yeast RC .30 .75
34 Tim Couch RC .50 1.25
35 Ty Detmer .25 .60
36 Kevin Johnson RC .40 1.00
37 Terry Kirby .20 .50
38 Leslie Shepherd .20 .50
39 Troy Aikman .50 1.25
40 Michael Irvin .30 .75
41 Deion Sanders .30 .75
42 Emmitt Smith .75 2.00
43 Bubby Brister .20 .50
44 Terrell Davis .30 .75
45 Brian Griese .25 .60
46 Ed McCaffrey .25 .60
47 Shannon Sharpe .30 .75
48 Rod Smith .25 .60
49 Charlie Batch .25 .60
50 Germane Crowell .20 .50
51 Sedrick Irvin RC .30 .75
52 Herman Moore .25 .60
53 Johnnie Morton .25 .60
54 Barry Sanders .75 2.00
55 Mark Chmura .20 .50
56 Brett Favre 1.00 2.50
57 Antonio Freeman .25 .60
58 Dorsey Levens .25 .60
59 Ken Dilger .20 .50
60 Marvin Harrison .30 .75
61 Edgerrin James RC .60 1.50
62 Peyton Manning 1.00 2.50
63 Jerome Pathon .20 .50
64 Mark Brunell .25 .60
65 Keenan McCardell .25 .60
66 Jimmy Smith .25 .60
67 Fred Taylor .25 .60
68 Derrick Alexander .20 .50
69 Mike Cloud RC .30 .75
70 Tony Gonzalez .30 .75
71 Elvis Grbac .20 .50
72 Andre Rison .25 .60
73 Cecil Collins RC .30 .75
74 Oronde Gadsden .20 .50
75 James Johnson RC .30 .75
76 Dan Marino 1.00 2.50
77 O.J. McDuffie .25 .60
78 Lamar Thomas .20 .50
79 Cris Carter .30 .75
80 Daunte Culpepper RC .50 1.25
81 Randall Cunningham .30 .75
82 Matthew Hatchette .25 .60
83 Randy Moss .30 .75
84 John Randle .25 .60
85 Robert Smith .25 .60
86 Drew Bledsoe .30 .75
87 Ben Coates .25 .60
88 Kevin Faulk RC .50 1.25
89 Terry Glenn .25 .60
90 Shawn Jefferson .20 .50
91 Cam Cleeland .20 .50
92 Billy Joe Hobert .20 .50
93 Keith Poole .20 .50
94 Ricky Williams RC .75 2.00
95 Gary Brown .20 .50
96 Kent Graham .20 .50
97 Ike Hilliard .25 .60
98 Amani Toomer .25 .60
99 Wayne Chrebet .25 .60
100 Keyshawn Johnson .25 .60
101 Curtis Martin .30 .75
102 Vinny Testaverde .25 .60
103 Tim Brown .30 .75
104 James Jett .20 .50
105 Napoleon Kaufman .20 .50
106 Charles Woodson .30 .75
107 Koy Detmer .20 .50
108 Donovan McNabb RC 2.50 6.00
109 Duce Staley .25 .60
110 Kevin Turner .20 .50
111 Jerome Bettis .30 .75
112 Mark Bruener .20 .50
113 Troy Edwards RC .40 1.00
114 Levon Kirkland .20 .50
115 Kordell Stewart .25 .60
116 Amos Zereoue RC .40 1.00
117 Isaac Bruce .30 .75
118 Marshall Faulk .30 .75
119 Joe Germaine RC .40 1.00
120 Trent Green .25 .60
121 Torry Holt RC .75 2.00
122 Ryan Leaf .25 .60
123 Natrone Means .25 .60
124 Mikhael Ricks .20 .50
125 Junior Seau .30 .75
126 Garrison Hearst .25 .60
127 Terrell Owens .30 .75
128 Jerry Rice .60 1.50
129 J.J. Stokes .20 .50
130 Steve Young .40 1.00
131 Chad Brown .20 .50
132 Joey Galloway .25 .60
133 Brock Huard RC .40 1.00
134 Jon Kitna .25 .60
135 Ricky Watters .25 .60
136 Mike Alstott .30 .75
137 Reidel Anthony .20 .50
138 Trent Dilfer .25 .60
139 Warrick Dunn .25 .60
140 Jacquez Green .20 .50
141 Shaun King RC .40 1.00
142 Darnell McDonald RC .30 .75
143 Eddie George .25 .60
144 Steve McNair .30 .75
145 Yancey Thigpen .20 .50
146 Frank Wycheck .25 .60
147 Champ Bailey RC 1.00 2.50
148 Albert Connell .20 .50
149 Skip Hicks .20 .50
150 Michael Westbrook .20 .50

1999 Pacific Prisms Holographic Blue

*STARS: 10X TO 25X BASIC CARDS
*RCs: 2.5X TO 6X
STATED PRINT RUN 80 SER.#'d SETS
RANDOM INSERTS IN HOBBY/RETAIL

1999 Pacific Prisms Holographic Gold

COMPLETE SET (150) 150.00 300.00
*STARS: 2X TO 5X BASIC CARDS
*RCs: .8X TO 2X
STATED PRINT RUN 480 SERIAL #'d SETS
RANDOM INSERTS IN HOBBY/RETAIL

1999 Pacific Prisms Holographic Mirror

*STARS: 6X TO 15X BASIC CARDS
*RCs: 2X TO 5X
STATED PRINT RUN 150 SERIAL #'d SETS
RANDOM INSERT IN HOBBY/RETAIL

1999 Pacific Prisms Holographic Purple

*STARS: 3X TO 8X BASIC CARDS
*RCs: 1.2X TO 3X
STATED ODDS 320 SERIAL #'d SETS
RANDOM INSERTS IN HOBBY

1999 Pacific Prisms Premiere Date

*STARS: 8X TO 20X BASIC CARDS
*RCs: 2X TO 5X
STATED PRINT RUN 61 SERIAL #'d SETS
ONE PER HOBBY BOX

1999 Pacific Prisms Dial-a-Stats

COMPLETE SET (10) 40.00 100.00
STATED ODDS 1:193
1 Tim Couch 2.00 5.00
2 Emmitt Smith 6.00 15.00
3 Terrell Davis 3.00 8.00
4 Barry Sanders 10.00 25.00
5 Brett Favre 10.00 25.00
6 Mark Brunell 3.00 8.00
7 Dan Marino 10.00 25.00
8 Ricky Williams 3.00 8.00
9 Curtis Martin 3.00 8.00
10 Terrell Owens 3.00 8.00

1999 Pacific Prisms Ornaments

COMPLETE SET (20) 75.00 150.00
STATED ODDS 1:25
1 Jake Plummer 1.50 4.00
2 Jamal Anderson 2.50 6.00
3 Cade McNown .75 2.00
4 Tim Couch 1.50 4.00
5 Troy Aikman 5.00 12.00
6 Deion Sanders 2.50 6.00
7 Emmitt Smith 5.00 12.00
8 Terrell Davis 2.50 6.00
9 Barry Sanders 8.00 20.00
10 Brett Favre 8.00 20.00
11 Peyton Manning 8.00 20.00
12 Mark Brunell 2.50 6.00
13 Fred Taylor 2.50 6.00
14 Dan Marino 8.00 20.00
15 Randy Moss 6.00 15.00
16 Drew Bledsoe 3.00 8.00
17 Terrell Owens 2.50 6.00
18 Jerry Rice 5.00 12.00
19 Steve Young 3.00 8.00
20 Jon Kitna 2.50 6.00

1999 Pacific Prisms Prospects

COMPLETE SET (10) 40.00 80.00
STATED ODDS 1:97 HOBBY
1 David Boston 1.25 3.00
2 Cade McNown .60 1.50
3 Akili Smith .60 1.50
4 Tim Couch 1.25 3.00
5 Edgerrin James 4.00 10.00
6 Cecil Collins 1.00 2.50
7 Daunte Culpepper 4.00 10.00
8 Ricky Williams 2.00 5.00
9 Donovan McNabb 5.00 12.00
10 Torry Holt 3.00 8.00

1999 Pacific Prisms Sunday's Best

COMPLETE SET (20) 40.00 80.00
STATED ODDS 2:25
1 Jake Plummer .75 2.00
2 Akili Smith .40 1.00
3 Tim Couch .75 2.00
4 Emmitt Smith 2.50 6.00
5 Terrell Davis 1.25 3.00
6 Barry Sanders 4.00 10.00
7 Brett Favre 4.00 10.00
8 Peyton Manning 4.00 10.00
9 Mark Brunell 1.25 3.00
10 Fred Taylor 1.25 3.00
11 Dan Marino 4.00 10.00
12 Randy Moss 3.00 8.00
13 Drew Bledsoe 1.50 4.00
14 Ricky Williams 1.25 3.00
15 Curtis Martin 1.25 3.00
16 Terrell Owens 1.25 3.00
17 Jerry Rice 2.50 6.00
18 Steve Young 1.50 4.00
19 Jon Kitna 1.25 3.00
20 Eddie George 1.25 3.00

2001 Pacific Prism Atomic

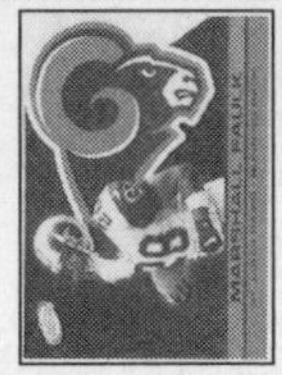

This 198 card set was issued in November, 2001. The cards were issued in five card packs which came 24 packs to a box and 16 boxes to a case. The SRP on the packs were $5.99 for hobby and $2.99 for retail packs. The rookie cards were issued at stated odds of two in 25 and were serial numbered to 506.

COMP.SET w/o RC's (148) 30.00 60.00
149-198 ROOKIE/506 ODDS 2:25
ROOKIE PRINT RUN 506 SER.#'d SETS
1 David Boston .25 .60
2 Thomas Jones .30 .75
3 Rob Moore .25 .60
4 Michael Pittman .30 .75
5 Jake Plummer .30 .75
6 Jamal Anderson .30 .75
7 Chris Chandler .30 .75
8 Shawn Jefferson .25 .60
9 Terance Mathis .25 .60
10 Elvis Grbac .30 .75
11 Qadry Ismail .30 .75
12 Jamal Lewis .40 1.00
13 Ray Lewis .40 1.00
14 Shannon Sharpe .40 1.00
15 Shawn Bryson .25 .60
16 Rob Johnson .30 .75
17 Sammy Morris .30 .75
18 Eric Moulds .30 .75
19 Peerless Price .25 .60
20 Tim Biakabutuka .25 .60
21 Richard Huntley .25 .60
22 Patrick Jeffers .25 .60
23 Jeff Lewis .25 .60
24 Muhsin Muhammad .30 .75
25 James Allen .25 .60
26 Cade McNown .30 .75
27 Marcus Robinson .30 .75
28 Brian Urlacher .50 1.25
29 Corey Dillon .30 .75
30 Jon Kitna .30 .75
31 Akili Smith .25 .60
32 Peter Warrick .30 .75
33 Tim Couch .25 .60
34 Kevin Johnson .25 .60
35 Dennis Northcutt .25 .60
36 Travis Prentice .25 .60
37 Tony Banks .25 .60
38 Joey Galloway .30 .75
39 Rocket Ismail .30 .75
40 Emmitt Smith 1.00 2.50
41 Anthony Wright .25 .60
42 Mike Anderson .30 .75
43 Terrell Davis .40 1.00
44 Olandis Gary .25 .60
45 Brian Griese .30 .75
46 Ed McCaffrey .30 .75
47 Rod Smith .30 .75
48 Charlie Batch .30 .75
49 Germane Crowell .25 .60
50 Herman Moore .30 .75
51 Johnnie Morton .30 .75
52 James Stewart .25 .60
53 Brett Favre 1.25 3.00

54 Antonio Freeman	.40	1.00
55 Ahman Green	.40	1.00
56 Dorsey Levens	.30	.75
57 Bill Schroeder	.30	.75
58 Marvin Harrison	.40	1.00
59 Edgerrin James	.40	1.00
60 Peyton Manning	1.00	2.50
61 Jerome Pathon	.25	.60
62 Terrence Wilkins	.25	.60
63 Mark Brunell	.30	.75
64 Keenan McCardell	.30	.75
65 Jimmy Smith	.30	.75
66 Fred Taylor	.40	1.00
67 Derrick Alexander	.25	.60
68 Tony Gonzalez	.40	1.00
69 Trent Green	.40	1.00
70 Priest Holmes	.40	1.00
71 Sylvester Morris	.25	.60
72 Jay Fiedler	.30	.75
73 Oronde Gadsden	.25	.60
74 O.J. McDuffie	.25	.60
75 Lamar Smith	.30	.75
76 Zach Thomas	.40	1.00
77 Daunte Culpepper	.30	.75
78 Cris Carter	.40	1.00
79 Randy Moss	.40	1.00
80 Chris Walsh RC	.25	.60
81 Moe Williams	.25	.60
82 Drew Bledsoe	.40	1.00
83 Kevin Faulk	.30	.75
84 Terry Glenn	.30	.75
85 Charles Johnson	.25	.60
86 J.R. Redmond	.25	.60
87 Jeff Blake	.30	.75
88 Aaron Brooks	.30	.75
89 Albert Connell	.25	.60
90 Joe Horn	.30	.75
91 Ricky Williams	.40	1.00
92 Tiki Barber	.40	1.00
93 Kerry Collins	.30	.75
94 Ron Dayne	.30	.75
95 Ike Hilliard	.30	.75
96 Amani Toomer	.30	.75
97 Richie Anderson	.25	.60
98 Wayne Chrebet	.30	.75
99 Curtis Martin	.40	1.00
100 Chad Pennington	.40	1.00
101 Vinny Testaverde	.30	.75
102 Tim Brown	.40	1.00
103 Rich Gannon	.30	.75
104 Charlie Garner	.30	.75
105 Jerry Rice	.75	2.00
106 Tyrone Wheatley	.30	.75
107 Charles Woodson	.40	1.00
108 Darnell Autry	.25	.60
109 Donovan McNabb	.40	1.00
110 Duce Staley	.30	.75
111 James Thrash	.30	.75
112 Jerome Bettis	.40	1.00
113 Plaxico Burress	.30	.75
114 Bobby Shaw	.25	.60
115 Kordell Stewart	.30	.75
116 Hines Ward	.40	1.00
117 Isaac Bruce	.40	1.00
118 Marshall Faulk	.40	1.00
119 Az-Zahir Hakim	.25	.60
120 Torry Holt	.30	.75
121 Kurt Warner	.60	1.50
122 Curtis Conway	.30	.75
123 Tim Dwight	.30	.75
124 Doug Flutie	.40	1.00
125 Dave Dickenson RC	1.00	2.50
126 Jeff Garcia	.30	.75
127 Terrell Owens	.40	1.00
128 J.J. Stokes	.25	.60
129 Tai Streets	.25	.60
130 Shaun Alexander	.40	1.00
131 Trent Dilfer	.30	.75
132 Matt Hasselbeck	.40	1.00
133 Darrell Jackson	.30	.75
134 Ricky Watters	.30	.75
135 Mike Alstott	.30	.75
136 Warrick Dunn	.40	1.00
137 Brad Johnson	.30	.75
138 Keyshawn Johnson	.30	.75
139 Warren Sapp	.30	.75
140 Kevin Dyson	.25	.60
141 Eddie George	.40	1.00
142 Jevon Kearse	.30	.75
143 Derrick Mason	.30	.75
144 Steve McNair	.40	1.00
145 Champ Bailey	.40	1.00
146 Stephen Davis	.30	.75
147 Jeff George	.30	.75
148 Michael Westbrook	.25	.60
149 Quentin McCord RC	2.50	6.00
150 Vinny Sutherland RC	2.00	5.00
151 Michael Vick RC	12.00	30.00
152 Chris Barnes RC	2.00	5.00
153 Reggie Germany RC	2.00	5.00
154 Travis Henry RC	2.50	6.00
155 Dee Brown RC	2.00	5.00
156 Dan Morgan RC	2.50	6.00
157 Steve Smith RC	6.00	15.00
158 Chris Weinke RC	2.50	6.00
159 David Terrell RC	2.50	6.00
160 Anthony Thomas RC	3.00	8.00
161 Chad Johnson RC	5.00	12.00
162 Rudi Johnson RC	3.00	8.00
163 James Jackson RC	2.00	5.00
164 Andre King RC	2.00	5.00
165 Quincy Morgan RC	2.50	6.00
166 Quincy Carter RC	2.50	6.00
167 Kevin Kasper RC	2.00	5.00
168 Scotty Anderson RC	2.00	5.00
169 Mike McMahon RC	2.50	6.00
170 Robert Ferguson RC	3.00	8.00
171 Reggie Wayne RC	6.00	15.00
172 Derrick Blaylock RC	2.50	6.00
173 Snoop Minnis RC	2.00	5.00
174 Chris Chambers RC	3.00	8.00
175 Josh Heupel RC	3.00	8.00
176 Travis Minor RC	2.50	6.00
177 Michael Bennett RC	2.50	6.00
178 Deuce McAllister RC	3.00	8.00
179 Jonathan Carter RC	2.00	5.00
180 Jesse Palmer RC	2.50	6.00
181 LaMont Jordan RC	3.00	8.00
182 Santana Moss RC	4.00	10.00
183 Ken-Yon Rambo RC	2.00	5.00
184 Marques Tuiasosopo RC	2.50	6.00
185 Correll Buckhalter RC	3.00	8.00
186 Freddie Mitchell RC	2.00	5.00
187 Milton Wynn RC	2.00	5.00
188 Drew Brees RC	20.00	50.00
189 LaDainian Tomlinson RC	10.00	25.00
190 Kevan Barlow RC	2.50	6.00
191 Cedrick Wilson RC	2.50	6.00
192 Alex Bannister RC	2.00	5.00
193 Josh Booty RC	2.50	6.00
194 Koren Robinson RC	2.50	6.00
195 Eddie Berlin RC	2.00	5.00
196 Rod Gardner RC	2.50	6.00
197 Darnerien McCants RC	2.50	6.00
198 Sage Rosenfels RC	3.00	8.00
NNO Jamal Lewis SAMPLE	.75	2.00
NNO Emmitt Smith SAMPLE	1.00	2.50
NNO Eddie George SAMPLE	.50	1.25
NNO Randy Moss SAMPLE	.60	1.50

2001 Pacific Prism Atomic Blue

*VETS 1-148: 12X TO 30X BASIC CARDS
1-148 VETERAN/29 ODDS 1:193
1-148 VETERAN PRINT RUN 29
149-198 ROOKIE/19 ODDS 1:1153
149-198 ROOKIE PRINT RUN 19

2001 Pacific Prism Atomic Gold

*VETS 1-148: 3X TO 8X BASIC CARDS
*149-196 ROOKIES: .5X TO 1.2X
GOLD/116 ODDS 2:25 HOBBY
STATED PRINT RUN 116 SER.#'d SETS

2001 Pacific Prism Atomic Premiere Date

*VETERANS: 3X TO 8X BASIC CARDS
PREMIERE DATE/86 ODDS 1:25
STATED PRINT RUN 86 SER.#'d SETS

2001 Pacific Prism Atomic Red

*VETS 1-148: 2.5X TO 6X BASIC CARDS
*ROOKIES 149-198: .4X TO 1X
RED/310 ODDS 4:25 RETAIL
STATED PRINT RUN 310 SER.#'d SETS

2001 Pacific Prism Atomic Core Players

COMPLETE SET (20)	15.00	40.00
STATED ODDS 1:25		
1 Jamal Lewis	.75	2.00
2 Peter Warrick	.60	1.50
3 Tim Couch	.50	1.25
4 Emmitt Smith	2.00	5.00
5 Mike Anderson	.60	1.50
6 Terrell Davis	.75	2.00
7 Brett Favre	2.50	6.00
8 Edgerrin James	.75	2.00
9 Peyton Manning	2.00	5.00
10 Fred Taylor	.75	2.00
11 Randy Moss	.75	2.00
12 Ricky Williams	.75	2.00
13 Ron Dayne	.60	1.50
14 Jerry Rice	1.50	4.00
15 Donovan McNabb	.75	2.00
16 Marshall Faulk	.75	2.00
17 Kurt Warner	1.25	3.00
18 Jeff Garcia	.60	1.50
19 Eddie George	.75	2.00
20 Steve McNair	.75	2.00

2001 Pacific Prism Atomic Energy

COMPLETE SET (20)	15.00	40.00
STATED ODDS 1:49		
1 Michael Vick	2.50	6.00
2 Travis Henry	.50	1.25
3 Chris Weinke	.50	1.25
4 David Terrell	.50	1.25
5 Anthony Thomas	.60	1.50
6 Quincy Carter	.50	1.25
7 Reggie Wayne	1.25	3.00
8 Josh Heupel	.60	1.50
9 Michael Bennett	.50	1.25
10 Deuce McAllister	.60	1.50
11 Jesse Palmer	.50	1.25
12 LaMont Jordan	.60	1.50
13 Santana Moss	.75	2.00
14 Marques Tuiasosopo	.50	1.25
15 Freddie Mitchell	.40	1.00
16 Drew Brees	4.00	10.00
17 LaDainian Tomlinson	2.00	5.00
18 Koren Robinson	.50	1.25
19 Rod Gardner	.50	1.25
20 Sage Rosenfels	.60	1.50

2001 Pacific Prism Atomic Jerseys

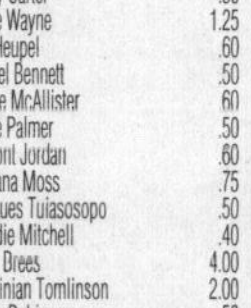

STATED ODDS 4:25 HOBBY		
1 Mac Cody	3.00	8.00
2 MarTay Jenkins	3.00	8.00
3 Thomas Jones	4.00	10.00
4 Rob Moore	3.00	8.00
5 Chris Chandler	4.00	10.00
6 Bob Christian	3.00	8.00
7 Jamal Lewis	5.00	12.00
8 Larry Centers	4.00	10.00
9 Rob Johnson	4.00	10.00
10 Peerless Price	3.00	8.00
11 Brad Hoover	4.00	10.00
12 Muhsin Muhammad	4.00	10.00
13 Chris Weinke	4.00	10.00
14 James Allen	3.00	8.00
15 Macey Brooks	3.00	8.00
16 Bobby Engram	4.00	10.00
17 Anthony Thomas	5.00	12.00
18 Brian Urlacher	6.00	15.00
19 Corey Dillon SP	5.00	12.00
20 Bobby Brown	3.00	8.00
21 Tim Couch	3.00	8.00
22 Curtis Enis	3.00	8.00
23 Emmitt Smith	12.00	30.00
24 Anthony Wright	3.00	8.00
25 Mike Anderson SP	5.00	12.00
26 Eddie Kennison	4.00	10.00
27 James Stewart	3.00	8.00
28 Brett Favre	15.00	40.00
29 Bubba Franks	4.00	10.00
30 William Henderson	4.00	10.00
31 Marvin Harrison	5.00	12.00
32 Edgerrin James	5.00	12.00
33 Peyton Manning SP	15.00	40.00
34 Mark Brunell	4.00	10.00
35 Keenan McCardell	4.00	10.00
36 Jimmy Smith	4.00	10.00
37 R.Jay Soward	3.00	8.00
38 Fred Taylor	5.00	12.00
39 Sylvester Morris	3.00	8.00
40 Autry Denson	3.00	8.00
41 Jay Fiedler	4.00	10.00
42 James Johnson	3.00	8.00
43 Zach Thomas	5.00	12.00
44 Cris Carter	5.00	12.00
45 Daunte Culpepper	4.00	10.00
46 Randy Moss	5.00	12.00
47 Drew Bledsoe	5.00	12.00
48 Aaron Brooks	4.00	10.00
49 Joe Horn	4.00	10.00
50 Terrelle Smith	3.00	8.00
51 Tiki Barber	5.00	12.00
52 Kerry Collins	4.00	10.00
53 Greg Comella	3.00	8.00
54 Ron Dixon	3.00	8.00
55 Ike Hilliard	4.00	10.00
56 Joe Jurevicius	3.00	8.00
57 Richie Anderson	3.00	8.00
58 Laveranues Coles	4.00	10.00
59 Matthew Hatchette	3.00	8.00
60 Curtis Martin	5.00	12.00
61 Dwight Stone	3.00	8.00
62 Vinny Testaverde	4.00	10.00
63 David Dunn	3.00	8.00
64 Napoleon Kaufman	3.00	8.00
65 Jerry Porter	3.00	8.00
66 Jerry Rice	10.00	25.00
67 Andre Rison	4.00	10.00
68 Marques Tuiasosopo	4.00	10.00
69 Tyrone Wheatley	4.00	10.00
70 Charles Woodson	5.00	12.00
71 Donovan McNabb	5.00	12.00
72 Freddie Mitchell	3.00	8.00
73 Duce Staley	4.00	10.00
74 Ernie Conwell	3.00	8.00
75 Marshall Faulk	5.00	12.00
76 Az-Zahir Hakim	3.00	8.00
77 Torry Holt	4.00	10.00
78 Ricky Proehl	3.00	8.00
79 Drew Brees	15.00	40.00
80 Curtis Conway	4.00	10.00
81 Freddie Jones	3.00	8.00
82 Junior Seau	5.00	12.00
83 LaDainian Tomlinson	8.00	20.00
84 Jeff Garcia	4.00	10.00
85 Terrell Owens	5.00	12.00
86 J.J. Stokes	3.00	8.00
87 Tai Streets	3.00	8.00
88 Karsten Bailey	3.00	8.00
89 Brock Huard	3.00	8.00
90 James Williams	3.00	8.00
91 Reidel Anthony	3.00	8.00
92 Jacquez Green	3.00	8.00
93 Joe Hamilton	3.00	8.00
94 Keyshawn Johnson	4.00	10.00
95 Warren Sapp	4.00	10.00
96 Kevin Dyson	3.00	8.00
97 Jevon Kearse	4.00	10.00
98 Derrick Mason	4.00	10.00
99 Stephen Alexander	3.00	8.00
100 Kevin Lockett	3.00	8.00

2001 Pacific Prism Atomic Jersey Patches

COMMON CARD	5.00	12.00
SEMISTARS	6.00	15.00
UNLISTED STARS	8.00	20.00
STATED ODDS 2:25 HOBBY		
18 Brian Urlacher	10.00	25.00
23 Emmitt Smith	20.00	50.00
33 Peyton Manning	20.00	50.00
66 Jerry Rice	15.00	40.00
71 Donovan McNabb	8.00	20.00
125 Tom Brady	50.00	100.00
140 Dan Kreider	25.00	50.00

2001 Pacific Prism Atomic Rookie Reaction

COMPLETE SET (20)	15.00	40.00
STATED ODDS 1:49		
1 Michael Vick	2.50	6.00
2 Travis Henry	.50	1.25
3 Chris Weinke	.50	1.25
4 David Terrell	.50	1.25
5 Anthony Thomas	.60	1.50
6 James Jackson	.40	1.00
7 Quincy Carter	.50	1.25
8 Reggie Wayne	1.25	3.00
9 Josh Heupel	.60	1.50
10 Michael Bennett	.50	1.25
11 Deuce McAllister	.60	1.50
12 LaMont Jordan	.60	1.50
13 Santana Moss	.75	2.00
14 Marques Tuiasosopo	.50	1.25
15 Freddie Mitchell	.40	1.00
16 Drew Brees	4.00	10.00
17 LaDainian Tomlinson	2.00	5.00
18 Kevan Barlow	.50	1.25
19 Koren Robinson	.50	1.25
20 Rod Gardner	.50	1.25

2001 Pacific Prism Atomic Statosphere

COMPLETE SET (20)	15.00	40.00
STATED ODDS 1:25		
1-10 FOUND IN HOBBY		
11-20 FOUND IN RETAIL		
1 Chris Weinke	.60	1.50
2 Tim Couch	.50	1.25
3 Brian Griese	.60	1.50
4 Peyton Manning	2.00	5.00
5 Mark Brunell	.60	1.50
6 Daunte Culpepper	.60	1.50
7 Drew Bledsoe	.75	2.00
8 Kurt Warner	1.25	3.00
9 Jeff Garcia	.60	1.50
10 Steve McNair	.75	2.00
11 Jamal Lewis	.75	2.00
12 Peter Warrick	.60	1.50
13 Emmitt Smith	2.00	5.00
14 Terrell Davis	.75	2.00
15 Edgerrin James	.75	2.00
16 Fred Taylor	.75	2.00
17 Randy Moss	.75	2.00
18 Ricky Williams	.75	2.00
19 Jerry Rice	1.50	4.00
20 Marshall Faulk	.75	2.00

2001 Pacific Prism Atomic Strategic Arms

COMPLETE SET (10)	75.00	150.00
STATED ODDS 1:769		
STATED PRINT RUN 86 SER.#'d SETS		
1 Michael Vick	20.00	50.00
2 Tim Couch	3.00	8.00
3 Brian Griese	4.00	10.00
4 Brett Favre	15.00	40.00
5 Peyton Manning	12.00	30.00
6 Mark Brunell	4.00	10.00
7 Daunte Culpepper	4.00	10.00
8 Drew Bledsoe	5.00	12.00
9 Donovan McNabb	5.00	12.00
10 Kurt Warner	8.00	20.00

2001 Pacific Prism Atomic Team Nucleus

COMPLETE SET (10)	10.00	25.00
STATED ODDS 1:25		
1 Brian Urlacher	1.50	4.00
Anthony Thomas		
David Terrell		
2 Chad Johnson	2.00	5.00
Corey Dillon		
Peter Warrick		
3 Brian Griese	1.25	3.00
Terrell Davis		
Mike Anderson		
4 Reggie Wayne	2.50	6.00
Edgerrin James		
Marvin Harrison		
5 Mark Brunell	1.25	3.00
Fred Taylor		
Jimmy Smith		
6 Daunte Culpepper	1.25	3.00
Michael Bennett		
Randy Moss		
7 Chad Pennington	1.50	4.00
LaMont Jordan		
Santana Moss		
8 Kurt Warner	2.00	5.00
Marshall Faulk		
Isaac Bruce		
9 Doug Flutie	8.00	20.00
Drew Brees		
LaDainian Tomlinson		
10 Steve McNair	1.25	3.00
Eddie George		
Derrick Mason		

2000 Pacific Prism Prospects

Released as a 200-card base set consisting of 100 veteran cards an 100 rookie cards sequentially numbered to 1000, Prism Prospects features full color player action photography set against a holofoil background which is embossed to represent a football field. A black line across the bottom of the card contains the player's name and position. Prism Prospects was packaged in six pack boxes with packs containing three cards each and carried a suggested retail price of $34.99. Each Hobby box also contained a special pack with one Beckett Grading Services graded card.

COMP.SET w/o SP's (100)	10.00	25.00
1 David Boston	.15	.40
2 Jake Plummer	.20	.50
3 Jamal Anderson	.20	.50
4 Chris Chandler	.20	.50
5 Tim Dwight	.20	.50
6 Terance Mathis	.15	.40
7 Tony Banks	.15	.40
8 Priest Holmes	.25	.60
9 Doug Flutie	.25	.60
10 Rob Johnson	.20	.50
11 Eric Moulds	.20	.50
12 Antowain Smith	.20	.50
13 Steve Beuerlein	.20	.50
14 Tim Biakabutuka	.20	.50
15 Muhsin Muhammad	.20	.50
16 Bobby Engram	.20	.50
17 Curtis Enis	.15	.40
18 Cade McNown	.15	.40
19 Marcus Robinson	.20	.50
20 Corey Dillon	.20	.50
21 Akili Smith	.15	.40
22 Tim Couch	.20	.50
23 Kevin Johnson	.15	.40
24 Troy Aikman	.40	1.00
25 Joey Galloway	.20	.50
26 Rocket Ismail	.20	.50
27 Emmitt Smith	.60	1.50
28 Terrell Davis	.25	.60
29 Olandis Gary	.20	.50
30 Brian Griese	.20	.50
31 Charlie Batch	.20	.50
32 Herman Moore	.20	.50
33 Johnnie Morton	.20	.50
34 Brett Favre	.75	2.00
35 Antonio Freeman	.20	.50
36 Dorsey Levens	.20	.50
37 Marvin Harrison	.25	.60
38 Edgerrin James	.25	.60
39 Peyton Manning	.60	1.50
40 Mark Brunell	.20	.50
41 Keenan McCardell	.20	.50
42 Jimmy Smith	.20	.50
43 Fred Taylor	.25	.60
44 Donnell Bennett	.15	.40
45 Tony Gonzalez	.25	.60
46 Elvis Grbac	.15	.40
47 Damon Huard	.20	.50
48 James Johnson	.15	.40
49 Cris Carter	.25	.60
50 Daunte Culpepper	.20	.50
51 Randy Moss	.25	.60
52 Robert Smith	.20	.50
53 Drew Bledsoe	.25	.60
54 Kevin Faulk	.20	.50
55 Terry Glenn	.20	.50
56 Jeff Blake	.20	.50
57 Ricky Williams	.25	.60
58 Kerry Collins	.20	.50
59 Ike Hilliard	.20	.50
60 Amani Toomer	.20	.50
61 Wayne Chrebet	.20	.50
62 Curtis Martin	.25	.60
63 Vinny Testaverde	.20	.50
64 Tim Brown	.25	.60
65 Rich Gannon	.20	.50
66 Napoleon Kaufman	.20	.50
67 Tyrone Wheatley	.15	.40
68 Donovan McNabb	.25	.60
69 Duce Staley	.20	.50
70 Jerome Bettis	.25	.60
71 Troy Edwards	.15	.40
72 Kordell Stewart	.20	.50
73 Isaac Bruce	.25	.60
74 Torry Holt	.25	.60
75 Marshall Faulk	.25	.60
76 Kurt Warner	.40	1.00
77 Jermaine Fazande	.15	.40
78 Jim Harbaugh	.20	.50
79 Ryan Leaf	.20	.50
80 Junior Seau	.25	.60
81 Jeff Garcia	.20	.50
82 J.J. Stokes	.20	.50
83 Terrell Owens	.25	.60
84 Jerry Rice	.50	1.25
85 Jon Kitna	.20	.50
86 Derrick Mayes	.15	.40
87 Ricky Watters	.20	.50
88 Mike Alstott	.25	.60
89 Warrick Dunn	.20	.50
90 Jacquez Green	.15	.40
91 Shaun King	.15	.40
92 Eddie George	.20	.50
93 Jevon Kearse	.20	.50
94 Steve McNair	.25	.60
95 Carl Pickens	.20	.50
96 Stephen Davis	.20	.50
97 Jeff George	.20	.50
98 Brad Johnson	.20	.50
99 Deion Sanders	.25	.60
100 Michael Westbrook	.15	.40
101 Jabari Issa RC	1.50	4.00
102 Thomas Jones RC	3.00	8.00
103 Sekou Sanyika RC	1.50	4.00
104 Jay Tant RC	1.50	4.00
105 Raynoch Thompson RC	1.50	4.00
106 Doug Johnson RC	2.00	5.00
107 Mark Simoneau RC	1.50	4.00
108 Jamal Lewis RC	2.50	6.00
109 Chris Redman RC	2.00	5.00
110 Travis Taylor RC	2.00	5.00
111 Kwame Cavil RC	1.50	4.00
112 Corey Moore RC	1.50	4.00
113 Rashard Anderson RC	1.50	4.00
114 Lester Towns RC	1.50	4.00
115 Paul Edinger RC	2.50	6.00
116 Brian Urlacher RC	10.00	25.00
117 Dez White RC	2.00	5.00
118 Ron Dugans RC	1.50	4.00
119 Danny Farmer RC	1.50	4.00
120 Curtis Keaton RC	1.50	4.00
121 Peter Warrick RC	2.50	6.00
122 Courtney Brown RC	2.00	5.00
123 Lamar Chapman RC	1.50	4.00
124 JaJuan Dawson RC	1.50	4.00
125 Dennis Northcutt RC	2.00	5.00
126 Travis Prentice RC	2.00	5.00
127 Aaron Shea RC	2.00	5.00
128 Spergon Wynn RC	2.00	5.00
129 Dwayne Goodrich RC	1.50	4.00
130 Orantes Grant RC	1.50	4.00
131 Kareem Larrimore RC	1.50	4.00
132 Michael Wiley RC	1.50	4.00
133 Mike Anderson RC	2.50	6.00
134 Chris Cole RC	2.00	5.00
135 Jarious Jackson RC	2.00	5.00
136 Jerry Johnson RC	1.50	4.00
137 Kenoy Kennedy RC	1.50	4.00
138 Deltha O'Neal RC	2.00	5.00
139 Reuben Droughns RC	2.50	6.00
140 Barrett Green RC	1.50	4.00
141 Bubba Franks RC	2.50	6.00
142 Kevin McDougal RC	1.50	4.00
143 Marcus Washington RC	2.00	5.00
144 T.J. Slaughter RC	1.50	4.00
145 R.Jay Soward RC	1.50	4.00
146 Shyrone Stith RC	1.50	4.00
147 William Bartee RC	1.50	4.00
148 Dante Hall RC	2.50	6.00
149 Frank Moreau RC	1.50	4.00
150 Sylvester Morris RC	1.50	4.00
151 Deon Dyer RC	1.50	4.00
152 Ben Kelly RC	1.50	4.00
153 Tyrone Carter RC	2.00	5.00
154 Doug Chapman RC	1.50	4.00
155 Troy Walters RC	1.50	4.00
156 Tom Brady RC	90.00	150.00
157 Patrick Pass RC	2.00	5.00
158 J.R. Redmond RC	1.50	4.00
159 Marc Bulger RC	2.50	6.00
160 Darren Howard RC	1.50	4.00
161 Chad Morton RC	2.50	6.00
162 Mareno Philyaw RC	1.50	4.00
163 Terrelle Smith RC	1.50	4.00
164 Ralph Brown RC	1.50	4.00
165 Ron Dayne RC	2.50	6.00
166 Brandon Short RC	1.50	4.00
167 John Abraham RC	2.50	6.00
168 Anthony Becht RC	2.00	5.00
169 Laveranues Coles RC	2.50	6.00
170 Shaun Ellis RC	2.50	6.00
171 Chad Pennington RC	4.00	10.00
172 Sebastian Janikowski RC	2.50	6.00
173 Jerry Porter RC	2.50	6.00
174 Todd Pinkston RC	1.50	4.00
175 Gari Scott RC	1.50	4.00
176 Corey Simon RC	2.00	5.00
177 Plaxico Burress RC	2.50	6.00
178 Tee Martin RC	2.50	6.00
179 Hank Poteat RC	1.50	4.00
180 Rogers Beckett RC	1.50	4.00
181 Trevor Gaylor RC	1.50	4.00
182 Ronney Jenkins RC	1.50	4.00
183 Giovanni Carmazzi RC	1.50	4.00
184 Chafie Fields RC	1.50	4.00
185 Ahmed Plummer RC	1.50	4.00
186 Tim Rattay RC	2.00	5.00
187 Jeff Ulbrich RC	1.50	4.00
188 Shaun Alexander RC	3.00	8.00
189 Darrell Jackson RC	2.00	5.00
190 Rodnick Phillips RC	1.50	4.00
191 James Williams RC	1.50	4.00
192 Trung Canidate RC	2.00	5.00
193 Joe Hamilton RC	1.50	4.00
194 DeMario Brown RC	1.50	4.00
195 Keith Bulluck RC	2.00	5.00
196 Chris Coleman RC	1.50	4.00
197 Erron Kinney RC	1.50	4.00
198 Billy Volek RC	2.50	6.00
199 Todd Husak RC	1.50	4.00
200 Chris Samuels RC	2.00	5.00

2000 Pacific Prism Prospects Holographic Blue

*HOLOBLUE VETS: 5X TO 12X BASIC CARDS
HOLO.BLUE PRINT RUN 100 SER.#'d SETS

2000 Pacific Prism Prospects Holographic Mirror

*HOLO.MIRROR: 6X TO 15X BASIC CARDS
HOLO.MIRROR PRINT RUN 75 SER.#'d SETS

2000 Pacific Prism Prospects Premiere Date

*PREM.DATE: 3X TO 8X BASIC CARDS
PREM.DATE PRINT RUN 138 SER.#'d SETS

2000 Pacific Prism Prospects Fortified With Stars

COMPLETE SET (10)	30.00	80.00
STATED ODDS 1:97 HOB, 1:241 RET		
1 Jake Plummer	2.50	6.00
2 Peerless Price	2.50	6.00
3 Tim Couch	2.50	6.00
4 Brett Favre	10.00	25.00
5 Drew Bledsoe	3.00	8.00
6 Tyrone Wheatley	2.00	5.00
7 Plaxico Burress	3.00	8.00
8 Jerome Bettis	3.00	8.00
9 Jerry Rice	6.00	15.00
10 Jon Kitna	2.50	6.00

2000 Pacific Prism Prospects Game Worn Jerseys

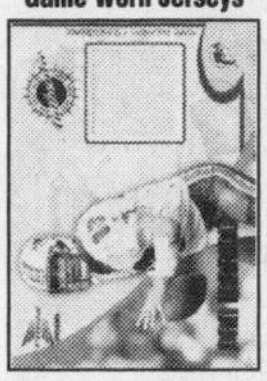

COMPLETE SET (10)	75.00	150.00
*PATCH/78-100: .6X TO 1.5X BASIC JSY		
*PATCH/35: 1X TO 2.5X BASIC JSY		
*PATCH/15-23: 1.2X TO 3X BASIC JSY		
PATCH PRINT RUN 15-100		
1 Randall Cunningham	6.00	15.00
2 Mark Brunell	5.00	12.00
3 Fred Taylor	6.00	15.00
4 Dan Marino	20.00	50.00
5 Drew Bledsoe	6.00	15.00
6 Wayne Chrebet	5.00	12.00
7 Kordell Stewart	5.00	12.00
8 Jerry Rice	12.00	30.00
9 Steve Young	8.00	20.00
10 Jon Kitna	5.00	12.00

2000 Pacific Prism Prospects MVP Candidates

COMPLETE SET (10)	12.50	30.00
STATED ODDS 1:25 HOB, 1:49 RET		
1 Peter Warrick	1.00	2.50
2 Emmitt Smith	2.50	6.00
3 Brett Favre	3.00	8.00
4 Edgerrin James	1.00	2.50
5 Peyton Manning	2.50	6.00
6 Randy Moss	1.00	2.50
7 Ricky Williams	1.00	2.50
8 Marshall Faulk	1.00	2.50
9 Kurt Warner	1.50	4.00
10 Eddie George	.75	2.00

2000 Pacific Prism Prospects Rookie Dial-A-Stats

COMPLETE SET (10)	25.00	50.00
STATED ODDS 1:193 HOB, 1;481 RET		
1 Thomas Jones	2.50	6.00
2 Jamal Lewis	2.00	5.00
3 Chris Redman	1.50	4.00
4 Peter Warrick	2.00	5.00
5 R.Jay Soward	1.25	3.00
6 Ron Dayne	2.00	5.00
7 Laveranues Coles	2.00	5.00
8 Chad Pennington	3.00	8.00
9 Plaxico Burress	2.00	5.00
10 Shaun Alexander	2.50	6.00

2000 Pacific Prism Prospects ROY Candidates

COMPLETE SET (10)	10.00	25.00
STATED ODDS 1:25 HOB, 1:49 RET		
1 Thomas Jones	.75	2.00
2 Jamal Lewis	.60	1.50
3 Travis Taylor	.50	1.25
4 Peter Warrick	.60	1.50
5 Sylvester Morris	.40	1.00
6 Doug Chapman	.40	1.00
7 Ron Dayne	.60	1.50
8 Chad Pennington	1.00	2.50
9 Plaxico Burress	.60	1.50
10 Shaun Alexander	.75	2.00

2000 Pacific Prism Prospects Sno-Globe Die Cuts

COMPLETE SET (20)	40.00	100.00
STATED ODDS 1:25 HOB, 1:49 RET		
1 Cade McNown	1.25	3.00
2 Tim Couch	1.50	4.00
3 Troy Aikman	3.00	8.00
4 Emmitt Smith	5.00	12.00
5 Terrell Davis	2.00	5.00
6 Brian Griese	1.50	4.00
7 Brett Favre	6.00	15.00
8 Peyton Manning	5.00	12.00
9 Edgerrin James	2.00	5.00
10 Mark Brunell	1.50	4.00
11 Damon Huard	1.50	4.00
12 Daunte Culpepper	1.50	4.00
13 Randy Moss	2.00	5.00
14 Drew Bledsoe	2.00	5.00
15 Jon Kitna	1.50	4.00
16 Marshall Faulk	2.00	5.00
17 Kurt Warner	3.00	8.00
18 Eddie George	1.50	4.00
19 Steve McNair	2.00	5.00
20 Stephen Davis	1.50	4.00

1992 Pacific Triple Folders

The 28 cards in this set measure 3 1/2" by 5" when folded and display a glossy action color player photo on the front. The player's name and position are printed in block letters. The two panels that make up the front photo are split down the center and can be opened to reveal three separate photos on the inside. The center panel carries an action color player photo and the player's name in block letters. The left inside panel has an action player photo while the right inside panel has a posed close-up shot. The backs carry career highlights and statistics. The background and lettering are team color-coded. The players chosen represent each of the 28 NFL teams, and the cards are arranged alphabetically according to team name. Each triple folder card pack contained a bonus card from one of the following insert sets: Steve Largent subset, Bob Griese subset, team Statistical Leader subset, gold and silver foil subset, Rushing Leader Prism subset, or Checklist Card subset.

COMPLETE SET (28)	8.00	20.00
1 Chris Miller	.25	.60
2 Thurman Thomas	.40	1.00
3 Neal Anderson	.25	.60
4 Tim McGee	.10	.30
5 Kevin Mack	.10	.30
6 Emmitt Smith	2.00	5.00
7 John Elway	2.00	5.00
8 Barry Sanders	2.00	5.00
9 Sterling Sharpe	.40	1.00
10 Warren Moon	.40	1.00
11 Bill Brooks	.10	.30
12 Christian Okoye	.10	.30
13 Nick Bell	.10	.30
14 Robert Delpino	.10	.30
15 Mark Higgs	.10	.30
16 Rich Gannon	.40	1.00
17 Leonard Russell	.10	.30
18 Pat Swilling	.25	.60
19 Rodney Hampton	.25	.60
20 Rob Moore	.25	.60
21 Reggie White	.40	1.00
22 Johnny Johnson	.10	.30
23 Neil O'Donnell	.25	.60
24 Marion Butts	.10	.30
25 Steve Young	.80	2.00
26 John L. Williams	.10	.30
27 Reggie Cobb	.10	.30
28 Mark Rypien	.10	.30

1993 Pacific Triple Folders

These 30 cards measure approximately 3 1/2" by 10 1/8" when folded out and feature gray-bordered color player action shots on all of their panels, except the backs. When the front panels are closed they merge into a single color player action photo, with the player's name and position printed in team color-coded marbleized lettering down the left side and along the bottom. On a team color-coded marbleized background, the back carries the player's name, position, team, career highlights, and 1992 stats. There were reportedly only 2,500 cases of Triple Folders produced by Pacific.

COMPLETE SET (30)	10.00	25.00
1 Thurman Thomas	.40	1.00
2 Carl Pickens	.25	.60
3 Glyn Milburn	.25	.60
4 Lorenzo White	.10	.30
5 Anthony Johnson	.10	.30
6 Joe Montana	2.00	5.00
7 Nick Bell	.10	.30
8 Dan Marino	1.60	4.00
9 Anthony Carter	.10	.30
10 Drew Bledsoe	1.20	3.00
11 Rob Moore	.25	60
12 Barry Foster	.10	.30
13 Stan Humphries	25	.00
14 Cortez Kennedy	.25	.60
15 Rick Mirer	.25	.60
16 Deion Sanders	.50	1.25
17 Curtis Conway	.25	.60
18 Tommy Vardell	.10	.30
19 Emmitt Smith	1.60	4.00
20 Barry Sanders	1.60	4.00
21 Brett Favre	1.60	4.00
22 Cleveland Gary	.10	.30
23 Morten Andersen	.10	.30
24 Marcus Buckley	.10	.30
25 Rodney Hampton	.25	.60
26 Herschel Walker	.10	.30
27 Garrison Hearst	.40	1.00
28 Jerry Rice	.80	2.00
29 Lawrence Dawsey	.10	.30
30 Desmond Howard	.25	.60

1993 Pacific Triple Folders Gold Prism Inserts

COMPLETE SET (20)	80.00	200.00
*GOLD CARDS: 1.2X TO 3X PACIFIC SILVERS		

1993 Pacific Triple Folders Rookies and Stars

COMPLETE SET (20)	8.00	20.00
1 Troy Aikman	.80	2.00
2 Victor Bailey	.10	.30
3 Jerome Bettis	.60	1.50
4 Drew Bledsoe	1.20	3.00
5 Reggie Brooks	.10	.30
6 Derek Brown RBK	.10	.30
7 Marcus Buckley	.10	.30
8 Curtis Conway	.30	.75
9 Brett Favre	1.60	4.00
10 Barry Foster	.10	.30
11 Garrison Hearst	.40	1.00
12 Cortez Kennedy	.10	.30
13 Rick Mirer	.20	.50
14 Joe Montana	1.60	4.00
15 Jerry Rice	.80	2.00
16 Barry Sanders	1.60	4.00
17 Sterling Sharpe	.20	.50
18 Emmitt Smith	1.60	4.00
19 Robert Smith	.40	1.00
20 Thurman Thomas	.20	.50

1994 Pacific Triple Folders

These 33 cards measure approximately 3 1/2" by 5" when folded and feature white-bordered color action player shots on all of their panels. When the front panels are closed, they merge into a single color action player photo with the player's first name printed on the bottom. When opened, the inside reveals another color action player photo. The player's last name is printed on the bottom with a team helmet on the left and right. On a team color-coded background, the backs carry the player's name and position and a career highlight. The set is arranged in alphabetical order by teams. In addition to a Triple Folder card, each pack included one bonus card from either the Gems of the Crown, Crown Collection Crystalline, or Knights of the Gridiron subsets. Also, randomly inserted in Triple Folder packs only were the Rookies and Stars 40-card insert. Less than 2,999 individually-numbered cases were produced.

COMPLETE SET (33)	10.00	25.00
1 Ronald Moore	.30	.75
2 Erric Pegram	.20	.50
3 Jim Kelly	.40	1.00
4 Thurman Thomas	.40	1.00
5 Curtis Conway	.40	1.00
6 Vinny Testaverde	.20	.50
7 Troy Aikman	.80	2.00
8 Emmitt Smith	1.20	3.00
9 John Elway	1.60	4.00
10 Shannon Sharpe	.30	.75
11 Barry Sanders	1.60	4.00
12 Brett Favre	1.60	4.00
13 Sterling Sharpe	.30	.75
14 Gary Brown	.20	.50
15 Marshall Faulk	1.20	3.00
16 Joe Montana	1.60	4.00
17 Rocket Ismail	.30	.75
18 Jerome Bettis	.40	1.00
19 Dan Marino	1.60	4.00
20 David Palmer	.20	.50
21 Drew Bledsoe	.80	2.00
22 Ben Coates	.30	.75
23 Derrick Ned	.20	.50
24 Rodney Hampton	.30	.75
25 Boomer Esiason	.30	.75
26 Barry Foster	.20	.50
27 Charles Johnson	.30	.75
28 Natrone Means	.30	.75
29 Steve Young	.60	1.50
30 Rick Mirer	.30	.75
31 Chris Warren	.20	.50
32 Trent Dilfer	.40	1.00
33 Heath Shuler	.30	.75

1994 Pacific Triple Folders Rookies and Stars

COMPLETE SET (40)	10.00	25.00
1 Ronald Moore	.20	.50
2 Jeff George	.20	.50
3 Jim Kelly	.30	.75
4 Thurman Thomas	.20	.50
5 Curtis Conway	.30	.75
6 Darnay Scott	.30	.75
7 Vinny Testaverde	.10	.30
8 Troy Aikman	.80	2.00
9 Emmitt Smith	1.20	3.00
10 John Elway	1.60	4.00
11 Shannon Sharpe	.20	.50
12 Barry Sanders	1.60	4.00
13 LeShon Johnson	.10	.30
14 Sterling Sharpe	.20	.50
15 Gary Brown	.10	.30
16 Marshall Faulk	1.60	4.00
17 Lake Dawson	.20	.50
18 Greg Hill	.20	.50
19 Joe Montana	1.60	4.00
20 Tim Brown	.30	.75
21 Jerome Bettis	.40	1.00
22 Dan Marino	1.60	4.00
23 Terry Allen	.30	.75
24 David Palmer	.20	.50
25 Drew Bledsoe	.80	2.00
26 Ben Coates	.20	.50
27 Michael Haynes	.10	.30
28 Rodney Hampton	.20	.50
29 Thomas Lewis	.10	.30
30 Aaron Glenn	.30	.75
31 Charlie Garner	.20	.50
32 Charles Johnson	.20	.50
33 Byron Bam Morris	.10	.30
34 Natrone Means	.30	.75
35 Ricky Watters	.20	.50
36 Steve Young	.50	1.25
37 Rick Mirer	.20	.50
38 Trent Dilfer	.30	.75
39 Errict Rhett	.20	.50
40 Heath Shuler	.30	.75

1995 Pacific Triple Folders

This 48 card set was issued late in 1995 by Pacific and is the first Triple Folder set that features cards that are standard sized when folded. When opened, the length of the cards double in size while the width remains the same as a standard card. The card fronts are full bleed horizontal game shots of the player with the player's name in the lower left hand corner. When opened, the card forms three panels. The left and right panel both feature individual player shots, while the middle shows another full bleed shot showing the completion of the play the folded shot showed. Card backs feature a field in the background with a shot of the player and a brief commentary. Packs include one insert each. In addition, a Super Bowl XXX Wrapper Redemption was offered. Collectors could get a special six-card set by sending in 18 1995 Triple Folder wrappers plus $5.95 for shipping and handling. A Natrone Means promo card was produced and priced below.

COMPLETE SET (48)	10.00	30.00
1 Garrison Hearst	.20	.50
2 Kerry Collins	.60	1.50
3 Jeff George	.10	.30
4 Herschel Walker	.07	.20
5 Lake Dawson	.10	.30
6 Cris Carter	.20	.50
7 Byron Bam Morris	.07	.20
8 Jim Kelly	.20	.50
9 Rashaan Salaam	.10	.30
10 Eric Zeier	.10	.30
11 Curtis Martin	1.00	2.50
12 Jerry Rice	.75	2.00
13 Chris Warren	.10	.30
14 Trent Dilfer	.20	.50
15 Terry Allen	.20	.50
16 Jeff Blake	.40	1.00
17 Drew Bledsoe	.75	2.00
18 Tim Brown	.20	.50
19 Wayne Chrebet	1.50	4.00
20 Bernie Parmalee	.07	.20
21 Stan Humphries	.10	.30
22 Jerome Bettis	.20	.50
23 Michael Westbrook	.40	1.00
24 Charlie Garner	.07	.20
25 Mario Bates	.10	.30
26 Marcus Allen	.20	.50
27 James O. Stewart	.60	1.50
28 Ben Coates	.10	.30
29 Tyrone Wheatley	.40	1.00
30 Steve Young	.60	1.50
31 Natrone Means	.10	.30
32 Terrell Davis	2.50	6.00
33 Napoleon Kaufman	.60	1.50
34 Charles Johnson	.10	.30
35 Barry Sanders	1.50	4.00
36 John Elway	1.50	4.00
37 Joey Galloway	.75	2.00
38 Brett Favre	1.50	4.00
39 Errict Rhett	.10	.30
40 Gary Brown	.07	.20
41 Reggie White	.20	.50
42 Steve Bono	.20	.50
43 Marshall Faulk	.75	2.00
44 Dan Marino	1.50	4.00
45 Emmitt Smith	1.25	3.00
46 Troy Aikman	.75	2.00
47 Ricky Watters	.10	.30
48 Michael Irvin	.20	.50
P1 Natrone Means Promo	.40	1.00

1995 Pacific Triple Folders Big Guns

COMPLETE SET (12)	20.00	50.00
BG1 Drew Bledsoe	2.50	6.00
BG2 Dan Marino	5.00	12.00
BG3 Warren Moon	2.00	4.00
BG4 John Elway	5.00	12.00
BG5 Jeff Blake	2.00	4.00
BG6 Brett Favre	5.00	12.00
BG7 Steve Young	2.50	6.00
BG8 Boomer Esiason	1.50	2.50
BG9 Jim Everett	1.50	2.50
BG10 Jim Kelly	2.00	4.00
BG11 Jeff George	1.50	2.50
BG12 Dave Krieg	1.50	2.50

1995 Pacific Triple Folders Careers

COMPLETE SET (8)	50.00	120.00
C1 Troy Aikman	6.00	15.00
C2 Marcus Allen	4.00	10.00
C3 John Elway	10.00	25.00
C4 Dan Marino	10.00	25.00
C5 Jerry Rice	6.00	15.00
C6 Barry Sanders	10.00	25.00
C7 Emmitt Smith	7.50	20.00
C8 Steve Young	5.00	12.00

1995 Pacific Triple Folders Crystalline

COMPLETE SET (20)	15.00	40.00
CR1 Troy Aikman	1.50	4.00
CR2 Jeff Blake	.50	1.25
CR3 Drew Bledsoe	1.25	3.00
CR4 Kerry Collins	.75	2.00
CR5 John Elway	2.50	6.00
CR6 Marshall Faulk	.75	2.00
CR7 Gus Frerotte	.30	.75
CR8 Joey Galloway	1.00	2.50
CR9 Garrison Hearst	.30	.75
CR10 Jeff Hostetler	.30	.75
CR11 Dan Marino	2.50	6.00
CR12 Natrone Means	.50	1.25
CR13 Errict Rhett	.30	.75
CR14 Rashaan Salaam	.60	1.50
CR15 Barry Sanders	2.50	6.00
CR16 Deion Sanders	.75	2.00
CR17 Emmitt Smith UER	2.00	5.00
All Vital Statistics are Wrong		
CR18 J.J. Stokes	.50	1.25
CR19 Steve Young	1.25	3.00
CR20 Eric Zeier	.30	.75

1995 Pacific Triple Folders Rookies and Stars

COMPLETE GOLD SET (36)	12.50	30.00
*BLUE CARDS: SAME PRICE AS GOLD		
*RASPBERRY: 1.5X TO 4X BASIC INSERTS		
*SILVERS: 1.5X TO 4X BASIC INSERTS		
RS1 Garrison Hearst	.20	.50
RS2 Darick Holmes	.10	.30
RS3 Kerry Collins	.75	2.00
RS4 Rashaan Salaam	.20	.50
RS5 Jeff Blake	.40	1.00
RS6 Eric Zeier	.20	.50
RS7 Troy Aikman	.50	1.25
RS8 Eric Bjornson	.10	.30
RS9 Deion Sanders	.30	.75
RS10 Emmitt Smith	.75	2.00
RS11 Sherman Williams	.10	.30
RS12 Terrell Davis	2.00	5.00
RS13 John Elway	1.00	2.50
RS14 Barry Sanders	1.00	2.50
RS15 Steve McNair	1.00	2.50
RS16 Marshall Faulk	.40	1.00
RS17 James O. Stewart	.60	1.50
RS18 Steve Bono	.10	.30
RS19 Tamarick Vanover	.20	.50
RS20 Dan Marino	1.00	2.50
RS21 Drew Bledsoe	.50	1.25
RS22 Curtis Martin	.75	2.00
RS23 Tyrone Wheatley	.40	1.00
RS24 Tim Brown	.20	.50
RS25 Napoleon Kaufman	.60	1.50
RS26 Ricky Watters	.10	.30
RS27 Natrone Means	.10	.30
RS28 Jerry Rice	.50	1.25
RS29 J.J. Stokes	.40	1.00
RS30 Steve Young	.40	1.00
RS31 Joey Galloway	.60	1.50
RS32 Chris Warren	.10	.30
RS33 Jerome Bettis	.20	.50
RS34 Errict Rhett	.10	.30
RS35 Terry Allen	.20	.50
RS36 Michael Westbrook	.50	1.25

1995 Pacific Triple Folders Teams

COMPLETE SET (30)	20.00	40.00
1 Garrison Hearst	.40	1.00
Dave Krieg		
Rob Moore		
2 Jeff George	.40	1.00
Terance Mathis		
Eric Metcalf		
3 Darick Holmes	.40	1.00
Jim Kelly		
Andre Reed		
4 Edgar Bennett	2.00	5.00
Brett Favre		
Reggie White		
5 Haywood Jeffires	.60	1.50
Chris Chandler		
Steve McNair		
6 Marshall Faulk	.60	1.50
Jim Harbaugh		
Sean Dawkins		
7 Bob Christian	.60	1.50
Tim McKyer		
Kerry Collins		
8 Rashaan Salaam	.40	1.00
Erik Kramer		
Michael Timpson		
9 Carl Pickens	.40	1.00
Jeff Blake		
Darnay Scott		
10 Leroy Hoard	.30	.75
Andre Rison		
Vinny Testaverde		
11 Troy Aikman	1.50	4.00
Michael Irvin		
Emmitt Smith		
12 John Elway	3.00	8.00
Terrell Davis		
Shannon Sharpe		
13 Scott Mitchell	2.00	5.00
Herman Moore		
Barry Sanders		
14 James O.Stewart	.60	1.50
Mark Brunell		
Desmond Howard		
15 Marcus Allen	.40	1.00
Steve Bono		
Greg Hill		
16 Bernie Parmalee	2.00	5.00
Dan Marino		
Irving Fryar		
17 Robert Smith	.60	1.50
Warren Moon		
Cris Carter		
18 Curtis Martin	1.50	4.00
Drew Bledsoe		
Ben Coates		
19 Mario Bates	.30	.75
Jim Everett		
Michael Haynes		
20 Rodney Hampton	.30	.75
Dave Brown		
Herschel Walker		
21 Wayne Chrebet	1.25	3.00
Kyle Brady		
Adrian Murrell		
22 Napoleon Kaufman	1.00	2.50
Jeff Hostetler		
Tim Brown		
23 Ricky Watters	.30	.75
Charlie Garner		
Mike Mamula		
24 Byron Bam Morris	.30	.75
Mike Tomczak		
Charles Johnson		
25 Natrone Means	.40	1.00
Stan Humphries		
Tony Martin		
26 Jerry Rice	1.25	3.00
Steve Young		
J.J. Stokes		
27 Chris Warren	1.00	2.50
Rick Mirer		
Joey Galloway		
28 Jerome Bettis	.60	1.50
Kevin Carter		
Isaac Bruce		
29 Errict Rhett	.40	1.00
Trent Dilfer		
Alvin Harper		
30 Terry Allen	.60	1.50
Gus Frerotte		
Michael Westbrook		

1932 Packers Walker's Cleaners

This set of photos was issued in early 1932 by Walker's Cleaners in the Green Bay area to commemorate the 1929-1931 3-time World Champions. Each large photo was printed in sepia tone and included a facsimile autograph of the featured player as well as the photographer's notation. Each photo also includes a strip on the left side with two holes punched in order to fit into an album that was made available to anyone who built a complete set.. The photos are often found with the two-hole section trimmed off. Lastly a small cover sheet was included with each photo that featured a photo number, sponsorship mentions, a bio of the player and information about obtaining the album. Photos with the cover sheet still attached are valued at roughly double photos without. We've listed the blank backed photos below according to the photo number on the small cover sheets.

COMPLETE SET (27)	8,000.00	12,000.00
1 Curly Lambeau	1,000.00	1,500.00
2 Frank Baker	250.00	400.00
3 Russ Saunders	250.00	400.00
4 Wuert Engelmann	250.00	400.00
5 Hank Bruder	350.00	500.00
6 Waldo Don Carlos	250.00	400.00
7 Roger Grove	250.00	400.00
8 Mike Michalske	400.00	600.00
9 Milt Gantenbein	250.00	400.00
10 Lavie Dilweg	350.00	500.00
11 Verne Lewellen	350.00	500.00
12 Red Dunn	250.00	400.00
13 Johnny Blood McNally	500.00	800.00
14 Jug Earp	350.00	500.00
15 Arnie Herber	500.00	800.00
16 Dick Stahlman	250.00	400.00
17 Red Sleight	250.00	400.00
18 Rudy Comstock	250.00	400.00
19 Jim Bowdoin	250.00	400.00
20 Hurdis McCrary	250.00	400.00
21 Bo Molenda	250.00	400.00
22 Cal Hubbard	600.00	1,000.00
23 Paul Fitzgibbon	250.00	400.00
24 Tom Nash	250.00	400.00
25 Mule Wilson	350.00	500.00
26 Howard Woodin	250.00	400.00
27 Nate Barragar	250.00	400.00
NNO Album	300.00	500.00

1955 Packers Miller Brewing Postcards

1 Tobin Rote	20.00	40.00

1955 Packers Team Issue

This set of large (roughly 8 1/2" by 10 1/2") black and while photos was issued by the Packers around 1955. Each photo was printed on thick stock and includes the player's name and team name within a white box on the front. The photos are blankbacked. Any additions to the list below are appreciated.

1 Charlie Brackens	10.00	20.00
2 Al Carmichael	10.00	20.00
3 Howard Ferguson	10.00	20.00
4 Billy Howton	12.50	25.00
5 Gary Knafelc	10.00	20.00
6 Veryl Switzer	10.00	20.00

1959 Packers Team Issue

The Packers released this set of photos to fans in 1959. They were commonly released in a Green Bay Packers envelope with each measuring roughly 5" by 7" featuring a black and white player photo. The team name appears above the photo and the player's name, position, college, height, and weight is included below the photo. Some photos vary slightly in size and style of print type used while others have sponsor logos on the fronts as noted below. All photos, except Nitschke, feature action shots and a facsimile autograph. The photos were also printed on thin paper stock, are blankbacked, and listed below alphabetically.

COMPLETE SET (30)	400.00	700.00
1 Tom Bettis	7.50	15.00
2 Nate Borden	7.50	15.00
3 Lew Carpenter	7.50	15.00
4 Dan Currie	7.50	15.00
(printer noted in lower border)		
5 Bill Forester	7.50	15.00
6 Bob Freeman	7.50	15.00
7 Forrest Gregg	20.00	35.00
8 Hank Gremminger	7.50	15.00
9 Dave Hanner	7.50	15.00
10 Jerry Helluin	7.50	15.00
11 Paul Hornung	35.00	60.00
12 Gary Knafelc	7.50	15.00
(printer noted in lower border)		
13 Jerry Kramer	20.00	35.00
14 Vince Lombardi CO	125.00	200.00
15 Norm Masters	7.50	15.00
16 Lamar McHan	7.50	15.00
17 Max McGee	10.00	20.00
18 Don McIlhenny	7.50	15.00
19 Steve Meilinger	7.50	15.00
20 Ray Nitschke	30.00	50.00
(portrait; no facsimile auto)		
21 Babe Parilli	10.00	20.00
Channel 5 logo on front)		
22 Bill Quinlan	7.50	15.00
23 Jim Ringo	20.00	35.00
24 Al Romine	7.50	15.00
25 Bob Skoronski	10.00	20.00
26 Bart Starr	40.00	75.00
Channel 5 logo on front)		
27 John Symank	7.50	15.00
28 Jim Taylor	30.00	50.00
29 Jim Temp	7.50	15.00
30 Emlen Tunnell	20.00	35.00

1961 Packers Lake to Lake

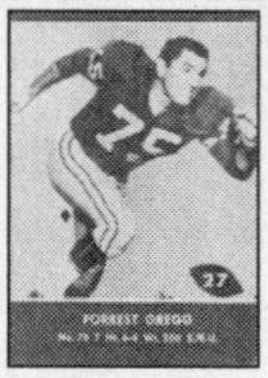

The 1961 Lake to Lake Green Bay Packers set consists of 36 unnumbered, green and white cards each measuring approximately 2 1/2" by 3 1/4". The fronts contain the card number, the player's uniform number, his position, and his height, weight, and college. The backs contain advertisements for the Packer fans to obtain Lake to Lake premiums. Card numbers 1-8 and 17-24 are the most difficult cards to obtain and cards #33-36 are also in shorter supply than #9-16 and #25-32 which are the easiest cards in the set. Lineman Ken Iman's card was issued ten years before his Rookie Card; Defensive back Herb Adderley's card was issued three years before his Rookie Card.

COMPLETE SET (36)	1,500.00	2,800.00
1 Jerry Kramer SP	100.00	175.00
2 Norm Masters SP	60.00	100.00
3 Willie Davis SP	100.00	175.00
4 Bill Quinlan SP	60.00	100.00
5 Jim Temp SP	60.00	100.00
6 Emlen Tunnell SP	75.00	125.00
7 Gary Knafelc SP	60.00	100.00
8 Hank Jordan SP	125.00	200.00
9 Bill Forester	1.50	4.00
10 Paul Hornung	10.00	20.00
11 Jesse Whittenton	1.50	4.00
12 Andy Cvercko	1.50	4.00
13 Jim Taylor	7.50	15.00
14 Hank Gremminger	1.50	4.00
15 Tom Moore	1.50	4.00
16 John Symank	1.50	4.00
17 Max McGee SP	75.00	125.00
18 Bart Starr SP	250.00	400.00
19 Ray Nitschke SP	150.00	250.00
20 Dave Hanner SP	60.00	100.00
21 Tom Bettis SP	60.00	100.00
22 Fuzzy Thurston SP	75.00	125.00
23 Lew Carpenter SP	60.00	100.00
24 Boyd Dowler SP	75.00	125.00
25 Ken Iman	1.50	4.00
26 Bob Skoronski	1.50	4.00
27 Forrest Gregg	5.00	12.00
28 Jim Ringo	5.00	12.00
29 Ron Kramer	1.50	4.00
30 Herb Adderley	7.50	15.00
31 Dan Currie	1.50	4.00
32 John Roach	1.50	4.00
33 Dale Hackbart SP	60.00	100.00
34 Larry Hickman SP	60.00	100.00
35 Nelson Toburen SP	60.00	100.00
36 Willie Wood SP	100.00	175.00

1965 Packers Team Issue

This set of small (5" by 7") black and white photos was issued by the Packers around 1965. Each photo was printed on thick stock, includes the player name, position, and team name below the photo and are blankbacked. Any additions to the list below are appreciated.

1 Herb Adderley	7.50	15.00
2 Lionel Aldridge	6.00	12.00
3 Jim Taylor	15.00	25.00
4 Fuzzy Thurston	7.50	15.00

1966 Packers Mobil Posters

This eight-poster set of the Green Bay Packers measures approximately 11" by 14" and features art prints suitable for framing of various game action pictures. The fronts carry a color action art piece and the backs are blank. The posters were distributed in envelopes that included the title of the artwork and the poster number. Although players are not specifically identified, we've made attempts to identify some key players. The prints are listed below according to the number and title on the envelope.

COMPLETE SET (8)	125.00	250.00
1 The Pass	30.00	60.00
Bart Starr back to pass		
2 The Block	15.00	30.00
Jerry Kramer blocking		
for Elijah Pitts		
3 The Punt	12.50	25.00
Don Chandler punting		
4 The Sweep	18.00	30.00
Jim Taylor following blocking		
5 The Catch	15.00	30.00
Boyd Dowler		
6 The Tackle/	12.50	25.00
7 The Touchdown	12.50	25.00
Tom Moore scoring		
8 The Extra Point	20.00	40.00
Don Chandler with		
Bart Starr holding		

1966 Packers Team Issue

The Green Bay Packers issued player photos over a number of years in the late 1960s. Most of the 8" by 10" photos may have even been issued across a number of years. This set was most likely released in 1966 and can be differentiated by the text included below the black and while player photo. Included (reading left to right) are the player's position (initials), his name in all caps, and full team name in all caps. Any additions to this list are appreciated.

1 Donny Anderson	7.50	15.00
2 Gale Gillingham	6.00	12.00
3 Jim Grabowski	6.00	12.00

1967 Packers Socka-Tumee Prints

These large (roughly 9' x 10 1/2") art prints feature a Packers player in contact with another NFL player in an exagerated action scene that includes a portion of the picture's frame being broken away. While the player is not specifically identified, the artwork is detailed enough to identify a specific player as noted below.

1 Jim Grabowski	25.00	50.00
(with an L.A. Rams player)		
2 Ray Nitschke	60.00	100.00
(Tackling a Chicago Bear)		
3 Don Chandler	25.00	50.00
(punting a Cleveland Brown)		

1967 Packers Team Issue 5x7

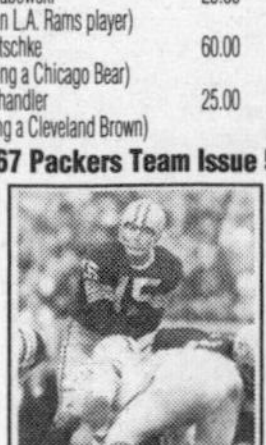

These black and white player photos were released by the Green Bay Packers around 1967. Each measures approximately 5" by 7" and includes the player's name, his position (spelled out in full) and team name below the photo. They are blankbacked and unnumbered. Any additions to this list are appreciated.

COMPLETE SET (13)	100.00	175.00
1 Donny Anderson	6.00	12.00
2 Zeke Bratkowski	6.00	12.00
3 Willie Davis	7.50	15.00
4 Gale Gillingham	5.00	10.00
5 Bob Jeter	5.00	10.00
6 Hank Jordan	7.50	15.00
7 Ron Kostelnik	5.00	10.00
8 Jerry Kramer	7.50	15.00
9 Ray Nitschke	10.00	20.00
10 Dave Robinson	6.00	12.00
11 Bob Skoronski	5.00	10.00
12 Bart Starr	20.00	40.00
13 Travis Williams	5.00	10.00

1967 Packers Team Issue 8x10

The Green Bay Packers issued roughly 8" by 10" player photos over a number of years in the late 1960s. Most of the photos were issued across a number of years. This set was most likely released in 1967 and can be differentiated by the text included below the black and white player photo. Included (reading left to right) are the player's name in all caps, position spelled out in caps, and the city "GREEN BAY" in all caps. Any additions to this list are appreciated.

1 Boyd Dowler	7.50	15.00
2 Bart Starr	20.00	40.00
3 Bart Starr	20.00	40.00
(Best Wishes! inscription)		
4 Bart Starr	20.00	40.00
(Best Wishes for many... inscription)		

1968-69 Packers Team Issue

This team-issued set consists of black-and-white player photos with each measuring approximately 8" by 10". They were printed on thin glossy paper and likely released over a number of years. The player's name, position, and team name are printed in black in the bottom white border. Although they are very similar to the 1971-72 release, the printing used for the text is generally larger. The team name is approximately 1 3/4" to 2" long. The cardbacks are blank. The photos are unnumbered and checklisted below in alphabetical order.

COMPLETE SET (51)	250.00	500.00
1 Herb Adderley	7.50	15.00
(cutting to his left)		
2 Herb Adderley	7.50	15.00
(jumping)		
3 Larry Agajanian	6.00	12.00
4 Lionel Aldridge	6.00	12.00
5 Phil Bengston CO	6.00	12.00
6 Ken Bowman	6.00	12.00
7 Dave Bradley	6.00	12.00
8 Zeke Bratkowski	7.50	15.00
9 Bob Brown	6.00	12.00
(position listed as DL)		
10 Lee Roy Caffey	6.00	12.00
11 Fred Carr	6.00	12.00
(jersey #53)		
12 Fred Carr	6.00	12.00
(jersey #83)		
13 Don Chandler	6.00	12.00
14 Carroll Dale	7.50	15.00
(position listed as FL)		
15 Willie Davis	7.50	15.00
(small signature; 2 7/8-in long)		
16 Willie Davis	7.50	15.00
(large signature; 3 3/8-in long)		
17 Boyd Dowler	7.50	15.00
18 Jim Flanigan	6.00	12.00
19 Marv Fleming	7.50	15.00
20 Forrest Gregg	7.50	15.00
21 Dave Hampton	6.00	12.00
22 Leon Harden	6.00	12.00
23 Doug Hart	6.00	12.00
24 Bill Hayhoe	6.00	12.00
25 Dick Himes	6.00	12.00
(position listed as OT)		
26 Don Horn	6.00	12.00
27 Bob Hyland	6.00	12.00
28 Claudis James	6.00	12.00
29 Bob Jeter	6.00	12.00
30 Ron Jones	6.00	12.00
31 Jerry Kramer	7.50	15.00
32 Vince Lombardi CO	15.00	30.00
33 Bill Lueck	6.00	12.00
(position listed as OG)		
34 Max McGee	7.50	15.00
35 Mike Mercer	6.00	12.00
36 Rich Moore	6.00	12.00
37 Ray Nitschke	10.00	20.00
(same pose as 71-72 set;		
team name 1-3/4-inch long)		
38 Francis Peay	6.00	12.00
39 Elijah Pitts	6.00	12.00
40 Dave Robinson LB	7.50	15.00
41 John Rowser	6.00	12.00
42 Gordon Rule	6.00	12.00
43 John Spilis	6.00	12.00
44 Bart Starr	15.00	30.00
45 Bill Stevens	6.00	12.00
46 Phil Vandersea	6.00	12.00
47 Jim Weatherwax	6.00	12.00
48 Perry Williams	6.00	12.00
(signature on right side)		
49 Travis Williams	6.00	12.00
50 Francis Winkler	6.00	12.00
51 Willie Wood	7.50	15.00

1969 Packers Drenks Potato Chip Pins

The 1969 Packers Drenks Potato Chip set contains 20 pins, each measuring approximately 1 1/8" in diameter. The fronts have a green and white background, with a black and white headshot in the center of the white football-shaped area. The team name at the top and player information at the bottom follow the curve of the pin. The pins are unnumbered and checklisted below in alphabetical order.

COMPLETE SET (20)	75.00	150.00
1 Herb Adderley	5.00	10.00
2 Lionel Aldridge	3.00	6.00
3 Donny Anderson	4.00	8.00
4 Ken Bowman	3.00	6.00
5 Carroll Dale	3.00	6.00
6 Willie Davis	5.00	10.00
7 Boyd Dowler	4.00	8.00
8 Marv Fleming	4.00	8.00
9 Gale Gillingham	3.00	6.00
10 Jim Grabowski	3.00	6.00
11 Forrest Gregg	5.00	10.00
12 Don Horn	3.00	6.00
13 Bob Jeter	3.00	6.00
14 Hank Jordan	5.00	10.00
15 Ray Nitschke	7.50	15.00
16 Elijah Pitts	3.00	6.00
17 Dave Robinson	4.00	8.00
18 Bart Starr	12.50	25.00
19 Travis Williams	3.00	6.00
20 Willie Wood	5.00	10.00

1969 Packers Tasco Prints

Tasco Associates produced this set of Green Bay Packers prints. The fronts feature a large color artist's rendering of the player along with the player's name and position. The backs are blank and unnumbered. The prints measure approximately 11" by 16."

COMPLETE SET (8)	175.00	300.00
1 Donny Anderson	20.00	35.00
2 Willie Davis	25.00	40.00
3 Boyd Dowler	20.00	35.00
4 Jim Grabowski	18.00	30.00
5 Hank Jordan	25.00	40.00
6 Ray Nitschke	30.00	50.00
7 Bart Starr	50.00	80.00
8 Willie Wood	25.00	40.00

1970 Packers Volpe Tumblers

1 Ray Nitschke	20.00	40.00
2 Dave Robinson	10.00	20.00
3 Carroll Dale	10.00	20.00
4 Donny Anderson	10.00	20.00
5 Willie Wood	12.50	25.00

1971-72 Packers Team Issue

This team-issued set consists of black-and-white player photos with each measuring approximately 8" by 10". They were printed on thin glossy paper. The player's name, position, and team name are printed in black in the bottom white border. Although they are very similar to the 1968-69 release, the printing used for the text is generally smaller. The team name is approximately 1 1/2" long. The cardbacks are blank. Several players have two photos in the set. Furthermore, Napper never played in the NFL, and Pittman never played for the Packers, suggesting that these photos may have been taken during training camp or preseason. The photos are unnumbered and checklisted below in alphabetical order.

COMPLETE SET (44)	150.00	300.00
1 John Brockington	6.00	12.00
2 Bob Brown	5.00	10.00
(position listed as DT)		
3 Willie Buchanon	6.00	12.00
4 Jim Carter	5.00	10.00
5 Carroll Dale	6.00	12.00
(position listed as FL)		
6 Dan Devine CO	6.00	12.00
GM		
7 Ken Ellis	5.00	10.00
8 Len Garrett	5.00	10.00
9 Gale Gillingham	5.00	10.00
10 Leland Glass	5.00	10.00
11 Charlie Hall	5.00	10.00
12 Jim Hill	5.00	10.00
13 Dick Himes	5.00	10.00
(position listed as T)		
14 Bob Hudson	5.00	10.00
(Head shot)		
15 Bob Hudson	5.00	10.00
(Kneeling pose)		
16 Kevin Hunt	5.00	10.00
17 Scott Hunter	6.00	12.00
Passing action posed		
18 Scott Hunter	6.00	12.00
Arm raised to pass		
Thin paper stock, non-glossy		
19 Dave Kopay	5.00	10.00
20 Bob Kroll	5.00	10.00
21 Pete Lammons	5.00	10.00
22 MacArthur Lane	6.00	12.00
23 Bill Lueck	5.00	10.00
(position listed as G)		
24 Al Matthews	5.00	10.00
25 Mike McCoy	5.00	10.00
26 Rich McGeorge	5.00	10.00
27 Lou Michaels	6.00	12.00
28 Charlie Napper	5.00	10.00
29 Ray Nitschke	7.50	15.00
(same pose as 68-69 set;		
team name 1-1/2-inch long)		
30 Charlie Pittman	5.00	10.00
31 Alden Roche	5.00	10.00
32 Malcolm Snider	5.00	10.00
(Action pose;		
Falcons' uniform)		
33 Malcolm Snider	5.00	10.00
(Kneeling pose)		
34 Jon Staggers	5.00	10.00
35 Jerry Tagge	5.00	10.00
36 Isaac Thomas	5.00	10.00
(Action pose)/(Cowboys uniform)		
37 Isaac Thomas	5.00	10.00
(Kneeling pose)		
38 Vern Vanoy	5.00	10.00
39 Ron Widby	5.00	10.00
(Action pose)/(Cowboys' uniform)		
40 Ron Widby	5.00	10.00
(Kneeling pose)		
41 Clarence Williams	5.00	10.00
42 Perry Williams	5.00	10.00
(signature on left side)		
43 Keith Wortman	5.00	10.00
44 Coaching Staff	7.50	15.00
Bart Starr		
Hank Kuhlmann		
Dave Hanner		
Burt Gustafson		
John Polonchek		
Don Doll		
Red Cochran		
Dan Devine		
Rollie Dotsch		

1972 Packers Coke Cap Liners

This set of cap liners were issued inside the caps of bottles of Coca-Cola in the Green Bay area in 1972. Each clear plastic liner features a black and white photo of the featured player. They were to be attached to a saver sheet that could be partially or completely filled in order to be exchanged for various prizes from Coke.

COMPLETE SET (22)	50.00	100.00
1 Ken Bowman	2.50	5.00
2 John Brockington	3.00	6.00
3 Bob Brown	2.50	5.00
4 Fred Carr	2.50	5.00
5 Jim Carter	2.50	5.00
6 Carroll Dale	3.00	6.00
7 Ken Ellis	2.50	5.00
8 Gale Gillingham	2.50	5.00
9 Dave Hampton	2.50	5.00
10 Doug Hart	2.50	5.00
11 Jim Hill	2.50	5.00
12 Dick Himes	2.50	5.00
13 Scott Hunter	2.50	5.00
14 MacArthur Lane	3.00	6.00
15 Bill Lueck	2.50	5.00
16 Al Matthews	2.50	5.00
17 Rich McGeorge	2.50	5.00
18 Ray Nitschke	6.00	12.00
19 Francis Peay	2.50	5.00
20 Dave Robinson	4.00	8.00
21 Alden Roche	2.50	5.00
22 Bart Starr	10.00	20.00

1975 Packers Pizza Hut Glasses

This set of glasses was issued by Pizza Hut in the mid-1970s to honor past Green Bay Packers greats. Each glass includes Packer green and gold colored highlights with a black and white picture of the featured player.

COMPLETE SET (6)	50.00	100.00
1 Willie Davis	5.00	10.00
2 Paul Hornung	10.00	20.00
3 Jerry Kramer	5.00	10.00
4 Vince Lombardi	20.00	40.00
5 Ray Nitschke	7.50	15.00
6 Bart Starr	12.50	25.00

1975 Packers Team Issue

The Green Bay Packers issued this set of 15-photos along with a saver album sponsored by Roundy's Food Store. Each measures approximately 6" by 9". The fronts feature posed color photos of the players kneeling with their right hand resting on their helmets. Facsimile autographs are inscribed across the pictures. The backs are blank. The cards are unnumbered and checklisted below in alphabetical order.

COMPLETE SET (15)	50.00	100.00
1 John Brockington	5.00	10.00
2 Willie Buchanon	5.00	10.00
3 Fred Carr	4.00	8.00
4 Jim Carter	4.00	8.00
5 Jack Concannon	4.00	8.00
6 Bill Curry	5.00	10.00
7 John Hadl	6.00	12.00
8 Bill Lueck	4.00	8.00
9 Chester Marcol	4.00	8.00
10 Al Matthews	4.00	8.00
11 Rich McGeorge	4.00	8.00
12 Alden Roche	4.00	8.00
13 Barry Smith	4.00	8.00
14 Barty Smith	4.00	8.00
15 Clarence Williams	4.00	8.00
NNO Saver Album	10.00	20.00

1976-77 Packers Team Issue 5x7

These photos were issued by the Packers, feature black-and-white player images, and measure approximately 5" by 7". They were printed on thin glossy paper with the player's name and position initials on the top line and the team name on the bottom line of type printed below the player's image. The photos are blankbacked, unnumbered and checklisted below in alphabetical order.

COMPLETE SET (28)	75.00	125.00
1 Bert Askson	3.00	6.00
2 John Brockington	4.00	8.00
3 Willie Buchanon	4.00	8.00
4 Mike Butler	3.00	6.00
5 Fred Carr	3.00	6.00
6 Jim Carter	3.00	6.00
7 Charlie Hall	3.00	6.00
8 Willard Harrell 1	3.00	6.00
9 Willard Harrell 2	3.00	6.00
10 Bob Hyland	3.00	6.00
11 Melvin Jackson	3.00	6.00
12 Ezra Johnson	3.00	6.00
13 Mark Koncar	3.00	6.00
14 Steve Luke	3.00	6.00
15 Chester Marcol	3.00	6.00
16 Mike McCoy DB	3.00	6.00
17 Mike Mccoy DT	3.00	6.00
18 Rich Mcgeorge	3.00	6.00
19 Steve Odom	3.00	6.00
20 Ken Payne	3.00	6.00
21 Tom Perko	3.00	6.00
22 Dave Pureifory	3.00	6.00
23 Alden Roche	3.00	6.00
24 Barty Smith 1	3.00	6.00
25 Barty Smith 2	3.00	6.00
26 Perry Smith	3.00	6.00
27 Cliff Taylor	3.00	6.00
28 Tom Toner	3.00	6.00

1976-77 Packers Team Issue 8x10

These team-issued photos feature black-and-white player images with each measuring approximately 8" by 10". They were printed on thin glossy paper with the player's name, position (initials), and team name printed in black in the bottom white border. Most feature the player in a kneeling pose with his hand on his helmet. The photos are blankbacked, unnumbered and checklisted below in alphabetical order.

COMPLETE SET (33)	125.00	250.00
1 Dave Beverly	4.00	8.00
2 Mike Butler	4.00	8.00
3 Jim Culbreath	4.00	8.00
4 Lynn Dickey	5.00	10.00
5 Derrel Gofourth	4.00	8.00
6 Johnnie Gray	4.00	8.00
7 Will Harrell	4.00	8.00
8 Dennis Havig	4.00	8.00
9 Melvin Jackson	4.00	8.00
10 Greg Koch	4.00	8.00
11 Mark Koncar	4.00	8.00
12 Larry McCarren	4.00	8.00
13 Mike McCoy DB	4.00	8.00
14 Mike McCoy DT	4.00	8.00
15 Terdell Middleton	4.00	8.00
16 Tim Moresco	4.00	8.00
17 Steve Okoniewski	4.00	8.00
18 Tom Perko	4.00	8.00
19 Terry Randolph	4.00	8.00
20 Alden Roche	4.00	8.00
21 Dave Roller	4.00	8.00
22 Barty Smith	4.00	8.00
23 Ollie Smith	4.00	8.00
24 Clifton Taylor	4.00	8.00
25 Aundra Thompson	4.00	8.00
26 Tom Toner	4.00	8.00
27 Eric Torkelson	4.00	8.00
28 Bruce Van Dyke	4.00	8.00
29 Randy Vataha	4.00	8.00
30 Steve Wagner	4.00	8.00
31 David Whitehurst	5.00	10.00
32 Clarence Williams	4.00	8.00
33 Keith Wortman	4.00	8.00

1981 Packers Team Sheets

These 2-sheets measure roughly 8" by 10" and feature 16-small black and white player photos on the fronts. The backs are blank and unnumbered.

COMPLETE SET (2)	4.00	10.00
1 Defense Rich Wingo Mike Douglass George Cumby John Anderson LB Guy Prather Kurt Allerman Byron Braggs Terry Jones Casey Merrill Mike Butler Ezra Johnson Bill Whitaker Estus Hood Mike McCoy Mark Lee Johnnie Gray	2.00	5.00
2 Offense Lynn Dickey David Whitehurst Rich Campbell Greg Koch Leotis Harris Karl Swanke Mark Koncar Derrel Gofourth Larry McCarren Syd Kitson Paul Coffman Aundra Thompson John Thompson TE Fred Nixon James Lofton Gary Lewis	2.00	5.00

1983 Packers Police

This 19-card set is somewhat more difficult to find than the other Packers Police sets. Reportedly, there were just 11,000 total sets distributed. There are three different types of backs: First Wisconsin Banks, without First Wisconsin Banks, and Waukesha P.D. The hardest to get of these three is the set without First Wisconsin Banks. All cards are approximately 2 5/8" by 4 1/8". Card backs are printed in green ink on white card stock. A safety tip ("Packer Tips") is given on the back. Cards are unnumbered except for uniform number.

COMPLETE SET (19)	18.00	30.00
10 Jan Stenerud	1.25	3.00
12 Lynn Dickey	.75	2.00
24 Johnnie Gray	.40	1.00
29 Mike McCoy	.40	1.00
31 Gerry Ellis	.40	1.00
40 Eddie Lee Ivery	.75	2.00
52 George Cumby	.40	1.00
53 Mike Douglass	.60	1.50
54 Larry McCarren	.40	1.00
59 John Anderson	.60	1.50
63 Terry Jones	.40	1.00
64 Syd Kitson	.40	1.00
68 Greg Koch	.40	1.00
80 James Lofton	2.00	5.00
82 Paul Coffman	.60	1.50
83 John Jefferson	1.00	2.50
85 Phillip Epps	.75	2.00
87 Ezra Johnson	.40	1.00
NNO Bart Starr CO	3.00	8.00

1984 Packers Police

This 25-card set is numbered on the back. The card backs were printed in green ink. Cards were sponsored by First Wisconsin banks, the local law enforcement agency, and the Green Bay Packers. The cards measure approximately 2 5/8" by 4".

COMPLETE SET (25)	5.00	12.00
1 John Jefferson	.40	1.00
2 Forrest Gregg CO	.75	2.00
3 John Anderson	.25	.60
4 Eddie Garcia	.15	.40
5 Tim Lewis	.15	.40
6 Jessie Clark	.15	.40
7 Karl Swanke	.15	.40
8 Lynn Dickey	.40	1.00
9 Eddie Lee Ivery	.25	.60
10 Dick Modzelewski CO (Defensive Coord.)	.15	.40
11 Mark Murphy	.15	.40
12 David Drechsler	.15	.40
13 Mike Douglass	.15	.40
14 James Lofton	1.25	3.00
15 Bucky Scribner	.15	.40
16 Randy Scott	.15	.40
17 Mark Lee	.25	.60
18 Gerry Ellis	.15	.40
19 Terry Jones	.15	.40
20 Greg Koch	.15	.40
21 Bob Schnelker CO (Offensive Coord.)	.15	.40
22 George Cumby	.15	.40
23 Larry McCarren	.15	.40
24 Syd Kitson	.15	.40
25 Paul Coffman	.25	.60

1984 Packers Team Issue

These team-issued photos feature black-and-white player images with each measuring approximately 8" by 10". They were printed on thin glossy paper with the player's name, position (initials), and team name printed in black in the bottom white border. Most feature the player in a kneeling pose with his hand on his helmet. The photos are blankbacked, unnumbered and checklisted below in alphabetical order.

COMPLETE SET (9)	15.00	25.00
1 Mark Cannon	1.50	3.00
2 Al Del Greco	2.00	4.00
3 Mike Douglass	1.50	3.00
4 Ron Hallstrom	1.50	3.00
5 Estus Hood	1.50	3.00
6 Tim Lewis	1.50	3.00
7 Mike Meade	1.50	3.00
8 Mark Murphy	1.50	3.00
9 Bucky Scribner	1.50	3.00

1985 Packers Police

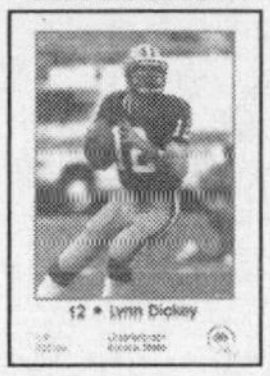

This 25-card set of Green Bay Packers is numbered on the back. Cards measure approximately 2 3/4" by 4". The backs contain a "1985 Packer Tip". Each player's uniform number is given on the card front.

COMPLETE SET (25)	3.00	8.00
1 Forrest Gregg CO	.60	1.50
2 Paul Coffman	.25	.60
3 Terry Jones	.15	.40
4 Ron Hallstrom	.15	.40
5 Eddie Lee Ivery	.25	.60
6 John Anderson	.25	.60
7 Tim Lewis	.15	.40
8 Bob Schnelker CO (Offensive Coord.)	.15	.40
9 Al Del Greco	.15	.40
10 Mark Murphy	.25	.60
11 Tim Huffman	.15	.40
12 Del Rodgers	.15	.40
13 Mark Lee	.25	.60
14 Tom Flynn	.15	.40
15 Dick Modzelewski CO (Defensive Coord.)	.15	.40
16 Randy Scott	.15	.40
17 Bucky Scribner	.15	.40
18 George Cumby	.15	.40
19 James Lofton	.75	2.00
20 Mike Douglass	.15	.40
21 Alphonso Carreker	.15	.40
22 Greg Koch	.15	.40
23 Gerry Ellis	.15	.40
24 Ezra Johnson	.15	.40
25 Lynn Dickey	.40	1.00

1986 Packers Police

This 25-card set of Green Bay Packers is unnumbered except for uniform number. Cards measure approximately 2 3/4" by 4" and the backs contain a "Safety Tip". The fronts features the prominent heading "1986 Packers". Card backs are written in green ink on white card stock.

COMPLETE SET (25)	3.00	8.00
10 Al Del Greco	.15	.40
12 Lynn Dickey	.40	1.00
16 Randy Wright	.40	1.00
26 Tim Lewis	.15	.40
31 Gerry Ellis	.15	.40
33 Jessie Clark	.15	.40
37 Mark Murphy	.25	.60
40 Eddie Lee Ivery	.25	.60
41 Tom Flynn	.15	.40
42 Gary Ellerson	.15	.40
55 Randy Scott	.15	.40
58 Mark Cannon	.15	.40
59 John Anderson	.25	.60
65 Ron Hallstrom	.15	.40
67 Karl Swanke	.15	.40
76 Alphonso Carreker	.15	.40
80 James Lofton	.75	2.00
82 Paul Coffman	.25	.60
85 Phillip Epps	.25	.60
90 Ezra Johnson	.15	.40
91 Brian Noble	.25	.60
93 Robert Brown	.15	.40
94 Charles Martin	.15	.40
99 John Dorsey	.15	.40
NNO Forrest Gregg CO	.50	1.25

1986 Packers Team Sheets

These 8" by 10" sheets were issued primarily to the media for use as player images for print. Each features 10-players with the player's jersey number, name, and position beneath his picture. The sheets are blankbacked and unnumbered.

COMPLETE SET (5)	12.00	30.00
1 Vince Ferragamo Al Del Greco Robbie Bosco Randy Wright Don Bracken Ed Berry Mark Lee DB Mossy Cade Tim Lewis DB Gary Hayes	3.00	8.00
2 Tom Neville Alan Veingrad Dan Knight Ken Ruettgers Alphonso Carreker Donnie Humphrey James Lofton Nolan Franz Phillip Epps Ed West	5.00	12.00
3 Walter Stanley Mark Lewis Ezra Johnson Brian Noble Matt Koart Robert Brown Charles Martin Tim Harris Brent Moore John Dorsey	2.50	6.00
4 Ken Stills Gerry Ellis Jessie Clark Mike Moffitt Kenneth Davis Mark Murphy S John Sullivan Eddie Lee Ivery Tom Flynn Gary Ellerson	2.50	6.00
5 Miles Turpin Randy Scott Burnell Dent Rich Moran Mark Cannon John Anderson Ron Hallstrom Karl Swanke Bill Cherry Keith Uecker	2.50	6.00

1987 Packers Ace Fact Pack

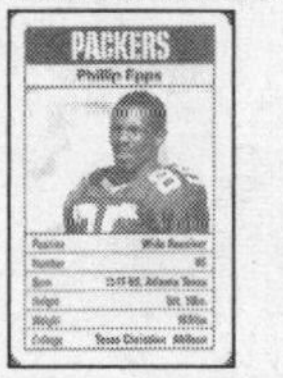

This 33-card set measures approximately 2 1/4" by 3 5/8". These cards feature rounded corners and a playing card type design on the back. There were 22 player cards issued which we have checklisted alphabetically. These cards were made in West Germany (by Ace Fact Pack) for release in Great Britain to capitalize on the popularity of American Football overseas. The set contains members of the Green Bay Packers.

COMPLETE SET (33)	30.00	80.00
1 John Anderson	1.25	3.00
2 Robbie Bosco UER (photo shows Tim Harris chasing Jim McMahon)	1.25	3.00
3 Don Bracken	1.25	3.00
4 John Cannon	1.25	3.00
5 Alphonso Carreker	1.25	3.00
6 Kenneth Davis	2.00	5.00
7 Al Del Greco	2.00	5.00
8 Gary Ellerson	1.25	3.00
9 Gerry Ellis	1.25	3.00
10 Phillip Epps	2.00	5.00
11 Ron Hallstrom	1.25	3.00
12 Mark Lee	1.25	3.00
13 Bobby Leopold	1.25	3.00
14 Charles Martin	1.25	3.00
15 Brian Noble	1.25	3.00
16 Ken Ruettgers	2.00	5.00
17 Randy Scott	1.25	3.00
18 Walter Stanley	1.25	3.00
19 Ken Stills	1.25	3.00
20 Keith Uecker	1.25	3.00
21 Ed West	2.00	5.00
22 Randy Wright	1.25	3.00
23 Packers Helmet	1.25	3.00
24 Packers Information	1.25	3.00
25 Packers Uniform	1.25	3.00
26 Game Record Holders	1.25	3.00
27 Season Record Holders	1.25	3.00
28 Career Record Holders	1.25	3.00
29 Record 1967-86	1.25	3.00
30 1986 Team Statistics	1.25	3.00
31 All-Time Greats	1.25	3.00
32 Roll of Honour	1.25	3.00
33 Lambeau Field/ Milwaukee County Stadium	2.00	5.00

1987 Packers Police

This 22-card set of Green Bay Packers is numbered on the front in the lower right corner below the photo. Sponsors were the Employers Health Insurance Company, Arson Task Force, local law enforcement agencies, and the Green Bay Packers. Cards measure 2 3/4" by 4". The backs contain a "Safety Tip". The fronts features the prominent heading "1987 Packers". Card backs are written in green ink on white card stock. Cards 5, 6, and 20 were never issued as apparently they were scheduled to be players who were later cut and released from the team. Reportedly 35,000 sets were distributed.

COMPLETE SET (22)	3.00	8.00
1 Forrest Gregg CO	.60	1.50
2 Tiger Greene	.15	.40
3 Ron Hallstrom	.15	.40
4 Ezra Johnson	.15	.40
7 Robert Brown	.15	.40
8 Tom Neville	.15	.40
9 Rich Moran	.15	.40
10 Ken Ruettgers	.15	.40
11 Alan Veingrad	.15	.40
12 Mark Lee	.15	.40
13 John Dorsey	.15	.40
14 Paul Ott Carruth	.15	.40
15 Randy Wright	.15	.40
16 Phillip Epps	.25	.60
17 Al Del Greco	.15	.40
18 Tim Harris	.40	1.00
19 Kenneth Davis	.40	1.00
21 John Anderson	.25	.60
22 Mark Murphy	.25	.60
23 Ken Stills	.15	.40
24 Brian Noble	.25	.60
25 Mark Cannon	.15	.40

1988 Packers Police

The 1988 Police Green Bay Packers set contains 25 cards measuring approximately 2 3/4" by 4". There are 24 player cards and one coach card. The backs have football tips and safety tips. The cards are unnumbered so they are listed below in alphabetical order.

COMPLETE SET (25)	4.00	10.00
1 John Anderson	.15	.40
2 Jerry Boyarsky	.15	.40
3 Don Bracken	.15	.40
4 Dave Brown	.15	.40
5 Mark Cannon	.15	.40
6 Alphonso Carreker	.15	.40
7 Paul Ott Carruth	.15	.40
8 Kenneth Davis	.40	1.00
9 John Dorsey	.15	.40
10 Brent Fullwood	.15	.40
11 Tiger Greene	.15	.40
12 Ron Hallstrom	.15	.40
13 Tim Harris	.40	1.00
14 Johnny Holland	.25	.60
15 Lindy Infante CO	.25	.60
16 Mark Lee	.15	.40
17 Don Majkowski	.40	1.00
18 Rich Moran	.15	.40
19 Mark Murphy	.25	.60
20 Ken Ruettgers	.25	.60
21 Walter Stanley	.25	.60
22 Keith Uecker	.15	.40
23 Ed West	.15	.40
24 Randy Wright	.15	.40
25 Max Zendejas	.15	.40

1989 Packers Police

The 1989 Police Green Bay Packers set contains 15 numbered cards measuring approximately 2 3/4" by 4". The fronts have white borders and color action photos bordered in Packers yellow; the vertically oriented backs have safety tips. These cards were printed on very thin stock. Sterling Sharpe appears in his Rookie Card year.

COMPLETE SET (15)	2.50	6.00
1 Lindy Infante CO	.25	.60
2 Don Majkowski	.40	1.00
3 Brent Fullwood	.15	.40
4 Mark Lee	.25	.60
5 Dave Brown	.15	.40
6 Mark Murphy	.25	.60
7 Johnny Holland	.25	.60
8 John Anderson	.25	.60
9 Ken Ruettgers	.25	.60
10 Sterling Sharpe	.75	2.00
11 Ed West	.15	.40
12 Walter Stanley	.25	.60
13 Brian Noble	.25	.60
14 Shawn Patterson	.15	.40
15 Tim Harris	.25	.60

1990 Packers Police

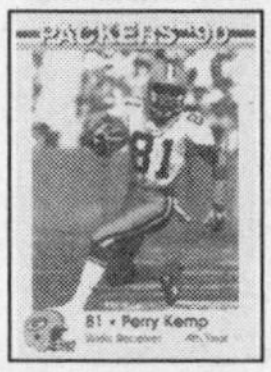

This 20-card set, which measures approximately 2 3/4" by 4", was issued by police departments in Wisconsin and featured members of the 1990 Green Bay Packers. The fronts have white borders with a "Packers '90" title on the front and the name of the subject along with their position and NFL experience. The backs of the card feature a safety tip and small ads for the sponsors of the set.

COMPLETE SET (20)	5.00	12.00
1 Lindy Infante CO	.30	.75
2 Keith Woodside	.20	.50
3 Chris Jacke	.30	.75
4 Chuck Cecil	.30	.75
5 Tony Mandarich	.20	.50
6 Brent Fullwood	.20	.50
7 Robert Brown	.20	.50
8 Scott Stephen	.20	.50
9 Anthony Dilweg	.20	.50
10 Mark Murphy	.20	.50
11 Johnny Holland	.30	.75
12 Sterling Sharpe	.75	2.00
13 Tim Harris	.30	.75
14 Ed West	.20	.50
15 Jeff Query	.20	.50
16 Mark Lee	.20	.50
17 Rich Moran	.20	.50
18 Perry Kemp	.30	.75
19 Brian Noble	.30	.75
20 Don Majkowski	.40	1.00

1990 Packers Shultz

In 1990 the Shultz Say-O-Stores of Wisconsin featured a 15-week Flashback Game. Game tickets were given out at Piggly Wiggly and Sav-U Food stores. The tickets measured approximately 2" by 3 3/8" and were printed on thin white cardboard stock. The fronts displayed a picture of a Packer in a TV set framework, while the back had the rules governing the game. There were 13 players per week, and each week the cards had a different-colored border (apparently by error, the 14th week had 14 cards). On each Wednesday, the stores displayed a poster of the winning player, and customers who had a ticket matching the player on the poster could win the dollar amount specified in the TV set. The cards are checklisted by weeks as follows: 1 (1-13), 2 (14-26), 3 (27-39), 4 (40-52), 5 (53-65), 6 (66-78), 7 (79-91), 8 (92-104), 9 (105-17), 10 (118-30), 11 (131-43), 12 (144-56), 13 (157-69), 14 (170-83), and 15 (184-96). The winning card for each week is indicated by "WIN" after the player's name.

COMPLETE SET (181)	300.00	500.00
1 Carl Bland WIN		
2 Robert Brown	1.50	3.00
3 Burnell Dent	1.50	3.00
4 Herman Fontenot	1.50	3.00
5 Brent Fullwood	1.50	3.00
6 Michael Haddix	1.50	4.00
7 Perry Kemp	1.50	3.00
8 Don Majkowski	2.00	5.00
9 Mark Murphy	1.50	3.00
10 Jeff Query	1.50	3.00
11 Sterling Sharpe	3.20	8.00
12 Ed West	1.50	3.00
13 Keith Woodside	1.50	3.00
14 Jerry Boyarsky	1.50	3.00
15 Robert Brown	1.50	3.00
16 Chuck Cecil	1.50	3.00
17 Brent Fullwood	1.50	3.00
18 Ron Hallstrom	1.50	3.00
19 Perry Kemp	1.50	3.00
20 Don Majkowski	2.00	5.00
21 Rich Moran WIN		
22 Bob Nelson	1.50	3.00
23 Brian Noble	1.50	3.00
24 Jeff Query	1.50	3.00
25 Ed West	1.50	3.00
26 Blaise Winter	1.50	3.00
27 Billy Ard	1.50	3.00
28 Dave Brown	1.50	3.00
29 Burnell Dent	1.50	3.00
30 Tiger Greene	1.50	3.00
31 Mark Lee	1.50	3.00
32 Don Majkowski	2.00	5.00
33 Rich Moran	1.50	3.00
34 Brian Noble WIN		
35 Ron Pitts	1.50	3.00
36 Ken Ruettgers	1.50	3.00
37 Keith Uecker	1.50	3.00
38 Keith Woodside	1.50	3.00
39 Vince Workman	1.50	3.00
40 Carl Bland	1.50	3.00
41 Don Bracken	1.50	3.00
42 Blair Bush	1.50	3.00
43 Michael Haddix	1.50	4.00
44 Johnny Holland	1.50	3.00
45 Chris Jacke	1.50	4.00
46 Don Majkowski	2.00	5.00
47 Perry Kemp WIN		
48 Tony Mandarich	1.50	3.00
49 Shawn Patterson	1.50	3.00
50 Sterling Sharpe	3.20	8.00
51 Scott Stephens	1.50	3.00
52 Alan Veingrad	1.50	3.00
53 Jerry Boyarsky	1.50	3.00
54 Robert Brown	1.50	3.00
55 Chuck Cecil	1.50	3.00
56 Ron Hallstrom	1.50	3.00
57 Herman Fontenot WIN		
58 Tim Harris	1.50	4.00
59 Mark Lee	1.50	3.00
60 Don Majkowski	2.00	5.00
61 Mark Murphy	1.50	3.00
62 Bob Nelson	1.50	3.00
63 Jeff Query	1.50	3.00
64 Blaise Winter	1.50	3.00
65 Vince Workman	1.50	3.00
66 Billy Ard	1.50	3.00
67 Don Bracken	1.50	3.00
68 Robert Brown WIN		
69 Brent Fullwood	1.50	3.00
70 Tiger Greene	1.50	3.00
71 Chris Jacke	1.50	4.00
72 Don Majkowski	2.00	5.00
73 Rich Moran	1.50	3.00
74 Shawn Patterson	1.50	3.00
75 Sterling Sharpe	3.20	8.00
76 Keith Uecker	1.50	3.00
77 Alan Veingrad	1.50	3.00
78 Keith Woodside	1.50	3.00
79 Carl Bland	1.50	3.00
80 Dave Brown	1.50	3.00
81 Blair Bush	1.50	3.00
82 Herman Fontenot	1.50	3.00
83 Michael Haddix	1.50	4.00
84 Tim Harris	1.50	4.00
85 Johnny Holland	1.50	3.00
86 Perry Kemp	1.50	3.00
87 Don Majkowski	2.00	5.00
88 Tony Mandarich	1.50	3.00
89 Ron Pitts	1.50	3.00
90 Vince Workman	1.50	3.00
91 Sterling Sharpe WIN		
92 Billy Ard	1.50	3.00
93 Don Bracken	1.50	3.00
94 Burnell Dent	1.50	3.00
95 Brent Fullwood	1.50	3.00
96 Ron Hallstrom	1.50	3.00
97 Tim Harris WIN		
98 Chris Jacke	1.50	4.00
99 Don Majkowski	2.00	5.00
100 Mark Murphy	1.50	3.00
101 Brian Noble	1.50	3.00
102 Scott Stephens	1.50	3.00
103 Ed West	1.50	3.00
104 Keith Woodside	1.50	3.00
105 Jerry Boyarsky	1.50	3.00
106 Robert Brown	1.50	3.00
107 Herman Fontenot	1.50	3.00
108 Michael Haddix	1.50	4.00
109 Johnny Holland	1.50	3.00
110 Mark Lee	1.50	3.00
111 Don Majkowski WIN		
112 Bob Nelson	1.50	3.00
113 Shawn Patterson	1.50	3.00
114 Jeff Query	1.50	3.00
115 Alan Veingrad	1.50	3.00
116 Blaise Winter	1.50	3.00
117 Vince Workman	1.50	3.00
118 Carl Bland	1.50	3.00
119 Dave Brown	1.50	3.00
120 Blair Bush	1.50	3.00
121 Chuck Cecil	1.50	3.00
122 Herman Fontenot	1.50	3.00
123 Tiger Greene	1.50	3.00
124 Perry Kemp	1.50	3.00
125 Don Majkowski	2.00	5.00
126 Mark Murphy WIN		
127 Brian Noble	1.50	3.00
128 Ken Ruettgers	1.50	3.00
129 Keith Uecker	1.50	3.00
130 Vince Workman	1.50	3.00
131 Jerry Boyarsky	1.50	3.00
132 Burnell Dent	1.50	3.00
133 Brent Fullwood	1.50	3.00
134 Michael Haddix	1.50	4.00
135 Tim Harris	1.50	4.00
136 Chris Jacke	1.50	4.00
137 Don Majkowski WIN		
138 Tony Mandarich	1.50	3.00
139 Rich Moran	1.50	3.00
140 Ron Pitts	1.50	3.00
141 Ken Ruettgers	1.50	3.00
142 Sterling Sharpe	3.20	8.00
143 Ed West	1.50	3.00
144 Billy Ard	1.50	3.00
145 Dave Brown WIN		
146 Tiger Greene	1.50	3.00
147 Tim Harris	1.50	4.00
148 Johnny Holland	1.50	3.00
149 Mark Lee	1.50	3.00
150 Don Majkowski	2.00	5.00
151 Bob Nelson	1.50	3.00
152 Jeff Query	1.50	3.00
153 Scott Stephens	1.50	3.00
154 Alan Veingrad	1.50	3.00
155 Blaise Winter	1.50	3.00
156 Vince Workman	1.50	3.00
157 Carl Bland	1.50	3.00
158 Robert Brown	1.50	3.00
159 Blair Bush	1.50	3.00
160 Herman Fontenot	1.50	3.00
161 Brent Fullwood	1.50	3.00
162 Chris Jacke WIN		
163 Don Majkowski	2.00	5.00
164 Mark Murphy	1.50	3.00
165 Brian Noble	1.50	3.00
166 Shawn Patterson	1.50	3.00
167 Sterling Sharpe	3.20	8.00
168 Ed West	1.50	3.00
169 Keith Woodside	1.50	3.00
170 Don Bracken	1.50	3.00
171 Dave Brown	1.50	3.00
172 Chuck Cecil	1.50	3.00
173 Burnell Dent	1.50	3.00
174 Michael Haddix	1.50	4.00
175 Tim Harris WIN		
176 Johnny Holland	1.50	3.00
177 Ron Hallstrom	1.50	3.00
178 Don Majkowski	2.00	5.00
179 Tony Mandarich	1.50	3.00
180 Rich Moran	1.50	3.00
181 Ron Pitts	1.50	3.00
182 Ken Ruettgers	1.50	3.00
183 Keith Uecker	1.50	3.00
184 Jerry Boyarsky	1.50	3.00
185 Herman Fontenot	1.50	3.00
186 Brent Fullwood	1.50	3.00
187 Ron Hallstrom WIN		
188 Tim Harris	1.50	4.00
189 Chris Jacke	1.50	4.00
190 Perry Kemp	1.50	3.00
191 Don Majkowski	2.00	5.00
192 Bob Nelson	1.50	3.00
193 Jeff Query	1.50	3.00
194 Scott Stephens	1.50	3.00
195 Alan Veingrad	1.50	3.00
196 Vince Workman	1.50	3.00

1990 Packers Super Bowl I 25th Anniversary

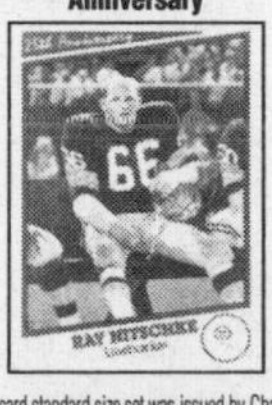

This 45-card standard size set was issued by Champion Cards of Owosso, Michigan and produced by Pacific Trading Cards, Inc. This set celebrated the 25th anniversary of the 1966 Green Bay Packers, the first team to win the Super Bowl. This set has a mix of color and sepia-toned photos and a mix of action and portrait shots on the front with a biography of the player on the back of the card. The only member of the 1966 Packers not featured in this set is Paul Hornung.

COMPLETE SET (45)	6.00	15.00
1 Introduction Card	.20	.50
2 Bart Starr	.80	2.00
3 Herb Adderley	.30	.75
4 Bob Skoronski	.08	.25
5 Tom Brown	.14	.35
6 Lee Roy Caffey	.14	.35
7 Ray Nitschke	.40	1.00
8 Carroll Dale	.14	.35
9 Jim Taylor	.50	1.25
10 Ken Bowman	.08	.25
11 Gale Gillingham	.14	.35
12 Jim Grabowski	.20	.50
13 Dave Robinson	.20	.50
14 Donny Anderson	.20	.50
15 Willie Wood	.30	.75
16 Zeke Bratkowski	.20	.50
17 Doug Hart	.08	.25
18 Jerry Kramer	.30	.75
19 Marv Fleming	.14	.35
20 Lionel Aldridge	.14	.35
21 Bill Red Mack UER	.08	.25
(Text reads returned to football before the following season& should be retired)		
22 Ron Kostelnik	.08	.25
23 Boyd Dowler	.20	.50
24 Vince Lombardi CO	.80	2.00
25 Forrest Gregg	.30	.75
26 Max McGee	.14	.35
Superstar		
27 Fuzzy Thurston	.20	.50
28 Bob Brown DT	.14	.35
29 Willie Davis	.30	.75
30 Elijah Pitts	.20	.50
31 Hank Jordan	.30	.75
32 Bart Starr	.80	2.00
33 Super Bowl I	.30	.75
(Jim Taylor)		
34 1966 Packers	.20	.50
35 Max McGee	.20	.50
36 Jim Weatherwax	.08	.25
37 Bob Long	.08	.25
38 Don Chandler	.14	.35
39 Bill Anderson	.08	.25
40 Tommy Crutcher	.14	.35
41 Dave Hathcock	.08	.25
42 Steve Wright	.08	.25
43 Phil Vandersea	.08	.25
44 Bill Curry	.20	.50
45 Bob Jeter	.14	.35

1991 Packers Police

This 20-card standard-size set was printed on white card stock. These cards feature player action shots on the fronts enclosed by yellow and green borders. A yellow banner design in the top left corner has "1991 Packers" printed in black. Player's name and position appear in gold in the top right green border. College team and years played with Packers are noted in a gold band at bottom. The backs are printed in green ink and have Packer (safety) tips based on the player's position. Sponsor names appear at the bottom of card. Only card number 1 is printed horizontally front and back.

COMPLETE SET (20)	2.80	7.00
1 Lambeau Field	.10	.30
2 Sterling Sharpe	.60	1.50
3 James Campen	.10	.30
4 Chuck Cecil	.20	.50
5 Lindy Infante CO	.20	.50
6 Keith Woodside	.10	.30
7 Perry Kemp	.10	.30
8 Johnny Holland	.20	.50
9 Don Majkowski	.20	.50
10 Tony Bennett	.40	1.00
11 LeRoy Butler	.20	.50
12 Tony Mandarich	.10	.30
13 Darrell Thompson	.20	.50
14 Matt Brock	.10	.30
15 Charles Wilson	.40	1.00
16 Brian Noble	.20	.50
17 Ed West	.10	.30
18 Chris Jacke	.10	.30
19 Blair Kiel	.20	.50
20 Mark Murphy	.10	.30

1991 Packers Super Bowl II

This 50-card Green Bay Packers set was released by Sportscards of Michigan and commemorates the 25th anniversary of the team's win in Super Bowl II. The cards are printed on thin card stock and measure the standard size (2 1/2" by 3 1/2"). The fronts feature either black and white or color player photos with dark green borders. The player's name, team logo, and "Super Bowl II" appear in a yellow stripe below the picture. The backs have biography and career highlights. The cards are numbered on the back.

COMPLETE SET (50)	4.80	12.00
1 Intro Card	.20	.50
Super Bowl Trophy		
2 Steve Wright	.08	.25
3 Jim Flanigan	.08	.25
4 Tom Brown	.14	.35
5 Tommy Joe Crutcher	.14	.35
6 Doug Hart	.14	.35
7 Bob Hyland	.08	.25
8 John Rowser	.08	.25
9 Bob Skoronski	.08	.25
10 Jim Weatherwax	.08	.25
11 Ben Wilson	.08	.25
12 Don Horn	.14	.35
13 Allen Brown	.08	.25
14 Dick Capp	.08	.25
15 Super Bowl II Action	.20	.50
Donny Anderson		
16 Ice Bowl: The Play	.60	1.50
Bart Starr		
17 Chuck Mercein	.14	.35
18 Herb Adderley	.30	.75
19 Ken Bowman	.08	.25
20 Lee Roy Caffey	.14	.35
21 Carroll Dale	.14	.35
22 Marv Fleming	.14	.35
23 Jim Grabowski	.20	.50
24 Bob Jeter	.14	.35
25 Jerry Kramer	.30	.75
26 Max McGee	.20	.50
27 Elijah Pitts	.20	.50
28 Bart Starr	.80	2.00
29 Fuzzy Thurston	.20	.50
30 Willie Wood	.30	.75
31 Lionel Aldridge	.14	.35
32 Donny Anderson	.20	.50
33 Zeke Bratkowski	.20	.50
34 Bob Brown DT	.14	.35
35 Don Chandler	.14	.35
36 Willie Davis	.30	.75
37 Boyd Dowler	.20	.50
38 Gale Gillingham	.14	.35
39 Hank Jordan	.30	.75
40 Ron Kostelnik	.08	.25
41 Vince Lombardi CO	.80	2.00
42 Bob Long	.08	.25
43 Ray Nitschke	.40	1.00
44 Dave Robinson	.20	.50
45 Bart Starr MVP	.60	1.50
46 Travis Williams	.14	.35
47 1967 Packers Team	.20	.50
48 Ice Bowl Game Summary	.08	.25
49 Ice Bowl	.08	.25
NNO Packer Pro Shop	.08	.25

1992 Packers Hall of Fame

This 110-card standard-size set features all 106 Packer Hall of Fame inductees. It was available to collectors exclusively at the Packer Hall of Fame gift shop, and yearly updates will be issued as new members are selected for induction to the Hall of Fame. The cards are printed on thin cardboard stock. The fronts display black and white or color player photos enclosed by an oval gold border on a dark green card face. The player's name, position, and jersey number are in a gold band beneath the picture. The horizontally oriented backs carry biography and career highlights. The player's name appears in green in a gold banner at the top, while the card number is printed on a small helmet at the bottom center. The initial release had no #1 card, but two #45 cards. The Lavern Dilweg card was corrected in later printings as #1.

COMPLETE SET (110)	15.00	40.00
1 Lavern Dilweg COR	.15	.40
2 Red Dunn	.08	.25
3 Mike Michalske	.15	.40
4 Cal Hubbard	.15	.40
5 Johnny Blood McNally	.15	.40
6 Verne Lewellen	.07	.20
7 Cub Buck	.07	.20
8 Whitey Woodin	.07	.20
9 Jug Earp	.07	.20
10 Charlie Mathys	.07	.20
11 Andrew Turnbull PRES	.07	.20
12 Curly Lambeau	.40	1.00
Founder		
Coach		
13 George Calhoun PUB	.07	.20
14 Boob Darling	.07	.20
15 Eddie Jankowski	.07	.20
16 Swede Johnston	.07	.20
17 George Svendsen	.07	.20
18 Bob Monnett	.07	.20
19 Joe Laws	.07	.20
20 Tiny Engebretsen	.07	.20
21 Milt Gantenbein	.07	.20
22 Hank Bruder	.07	.20
23 Clarke Hinkle	.20	.50
24 Lon Evans	.07	.20
25 Buckets Goldenberg	.07	.20
26 Nate Barrager	.07	.20
27 Arnie Herber	.15	.40
28 Lee Joannes PRES	.07	.20
29 Jerry Clifford VP	.07	.20
30 Pete Tinsley	.07	.20
31 Buford Ray	.07	.20
32 Andy Uram	.07	.20
33 Larry Craig	.07	.20
34 Charles Brock	.07	.20
35 Ted Fritsch Sr.	.08	.25
36 Lou Brock	.07	.20
37 Carl Mulleneaux	.07	.20
38 Harry Jacunski	.07	.20
39 Cecil Isbell	.15	.40
40 Bud Svendsen	.07	.20
41 Russ Letlow	.07	.20
42 Don Hutson	.50	1.25
43 Irv Comp	.07	.20
44 John Martinkovic	.07	.20
45A Bobby Dillon	.08	.25
45B Lavern Dilweg UER	.15	.40
(Back is #45 Bobby Dillon)		
46 Wilner Burke	.07	.20
Band Director		
47 Dick Wildung	.07	.20
48 Bill Howton	.15	.40
49 Tobin Rote	.15	.40
50 Jim Ringo	.20	.50
51 Deral Teteak	.07	.20
52 Bob Forte	.07	.20
53 Tony Canadeo	.20	.50
54 Al Carmichael	.07	.20
55 Bob Mann	.07	.20
56 Jack Vainisi	.07	.20
Scout		
57 Ken Bowman	.07	.20
58 Bob Skoronski	.07	.20
59 Dave Hanner	.08	.25
60 Bill Forester	.08	.25
61 Fred Cone	.07	.20
62 Lionel Aldridge	.08	.25
63 Carroll Dale	.08	.25
64 Howard Ferguson	.07	.20
65 Gary Knafelc	.07	.20
66 Ron Kramer	.08	.25
67 Forrest Gregg	.20	.50
68 Phil Bengtson CO	.07	.20
69 Dan Currie	.07	.20
70 Al Schneider	.07	.20
Contributor		
71 Bob Jeter	.08	.25
72 Jesse Whittenton	.08	.25
73 Hank Gremminger	.07	.20
74 Ron Kostelnik	.07	.20
75 Gale Gillingham	.08	.25
76 Lee Roy Caffey	.08	.25
77 Hank Jordan	.20	.50
78 Boyd Dowler	.15	.40
79 Fred Carr	.08	.25
80 Bud Jorgensen TR	.07	.20
81 Eugene Brusky	.07	.20
Team Physician		
82 Fred Trowbridge	.07	.20
Executive Committee		
83 Jan Stenerud	.20	.50
84 Jerry Atkinson	.07	.20
Contributor		
85 Larry McCarren	.07	.20
86 Fred Leicht	.07	.20
Executive Committee		
87 Max McGee	.15	.40
88 Zeke Bratkowski	.15	.40
89 Dave Robinson	.15	.40
90 Herb Adderley	.20	.50
91 Dominic Olejniczak	.08	.25
President		
92 Jerry Kramer	.20	.50
93 Super Bowl I	.08	.25
94 Don Chandler	.07	.20
95 John Brockington	.15	.40
96 Lynn Dickey	.08	.25
97 Bart Starr	1.50	4.00
98 Willie Wood	.30	.75
99 Packer Hall of Fame	.08	.25
100 Donny Anderson	.08	.25
101 Chester Marcol	.08	.25
102 Fuzzy Thurston	.08	.25
103 Paul Hornung	.60	1.50
104 Jim Taylor	.60	1.50
105 Vince Lombardi CO	1.50	4.00
106 Willie Davis	.20	.50
107 Ray Nitschke	.30	.75
108 Elijah Pitts	.08	.25
NNO Honor Roll	.08	.25
Checklist Card		
NNO Packer Hall of Fame	.08	.25
Catalog Order Form		

1992 Packers Police

This 20-card set features players of the Packers. The cards were printed with a green border and color player photograph on front. Cardbacks are white with green printing. We've assigned numbers to the unnumbered issue according to alphabetical order.

COMPLETE SET (20)	10.00	25.00
1 Tony Bennett	.40	1.00
2 Matt Brock	.10	.30
3 LeRoy Butler	.10	.30
4 Vinnie Clark	.20	.50
5 Brett Favre	7.50	20.00
6 Jackie Harris	.40	1.00
7 Johnny Holland	.10	.30
8 Mike Holmgren CO	1.00	2.50
9 Chris Jacke	.10	.30
10 Sherman Lewis CO	.40	1.00
11 Don Majkowski	.20	.50
12 Tony Mandarich	.10	.30
13 Paul McJulien	.10	.30
14 Bryce Paup	.40	1.00
14 Brian Noble	.20	.50
16 Ray Rhodes CO	.40	1.00
17 Tootie Robbins	.10	.30
18 Sterling Sharpe	.60	1.50
19 Darrell Thompson	.10	.30
20 Ron Wolf GM	.20	.50

1993 Packers Archives Postcards

These 40 postcards were made by Champion Cards of Green Bay to commemorate the Packers' 75th anniversary and, except for the unnumbered title card, measure approximately 3 1/2" by 5 1/2". The white-bordered postcards are framed by team color-coded lines and feature mostly black-and-white archival photos of Packer players and teams of yesteryear. Most of the cards display the Packers' 75th anniversary logo in the lower left. The horizontal white backs carry on their left sides information about the subject depicted on the front. On the right side is a ghosted Champion Cards logo. The postcards are numbered on the back within a football icon that appears at the bottom.

COMPLETE SET (40)	12.50	25.00
1 The First Team 1919	.40	1.00
2 The 1920s	.30	.75
3 The 1930s	.30	.75
4 The 1940s	.30	.75
5 The 1950s	.30	.75
6 The 1960s	.30	.75
7 The 1970s	.30	.75
8 The 1980s	.30	.75
9 The 1990s	.30	.75
10 Curly Lambeau 1919	.40	1.00
11 Jim Ringo 1953	.40	1.00
12 Ice Bowl 1967	.40	1.00
13 Jerry Kramer 1958	.40	1.00
14 Ray Nitschke 1958	.50	1.25
15 Fuzzy Thurston 1959	.40	1.00
16 James Lofton 1978-86	.40	1.00
17 Super Bowl I Action	.40	1.00
18 Don Hutson 1935-45	.50	1.25
19 Tony Canadeo '41-43/46-52	.40	1.00
20 Bobby Dillon 1952-59	.30	.75
21 The Quarterback	.40	1.00
22 Willie Wood 1960-71	.40	1.00
23 Dave Beverly 1975-80	.30	.75
24 James Lofton 1978	.40	1.00
25 Tim Harris 1986-90	.40	1.00
26 1929 Championship Team	.30	.75
27 1930 Championship Team	.30	.75
28 1931 Championship Team	.30	.75
29 1936 Championship Team	.30	.75
30 1939 Championship Team	.30	.75
31 1944 Championship Team	.30	.75
32 1961 Championship Team	.40	1.00
33 1962 Championship Team	.40	1.00
34 1965 Championship Team	.40	1.00
35 1966 Championship Team	.40	1.00
36 1967 Championship Team	.40	1.00
37 Old City Stadium	.30	.75
38 New City Stadium	.30	.75
39 Lambeau Field - 1992	.30	.75
NNO Title card	.40	1.00
(3 3/4" by 5 3/4")		

1993 Packers Police

These 20 standard-size cards were issued to commemorate the Packers' 75th anniversary and feature on their fronts white-bordered color player photos. Two team color-coded stripes edge the pictures at the bottom. The 75th anniversary logo appears at the upper left, and the words "Celebrating 75 Years of Pro Football 1919-1993" appear below the photo. The white back carries the player's name, position, years in the NFL, alma mater, and Packers helmet at the upper left. Below are safety messages written by area grade schoolers.

COMPLETE SET (20)	6.00	15.00
1 Ron Wolf GM	.10	.30
2 Wayne Simmons	.20	.50
3 James Campen	.10	.30
4 Matt Brock	.10	.30
5 Mike Holmgren CO	.50	1.25
6 Brian Noble	.20	.50
7 Ken O'Brien	.20	.50
8 George Teague	.20	.50
9 Brett Favre	4.00	10.00
10 LeRoy Butler	.20	.50
11 Harry Galbreath	.10	.30
12 Chris Jacke	.20	.50
13 Sterling Sharpe	.40	1.00
14 Terrell Buckley	.20	.50
15 Ken Ruettgers	.20	.50
16 Johnny Holland	.20	.50
17 Edgar Bennett	.40	1.00
18 Jackie Harris	.30	.75
19 Tony Bennett	.30	.75
20 Reggie White	.60	1.50

1994 Packers Police

This 20-card standard-size set was issued courtesy of the Alma Fire Department and the Green Bay Packer Organization. The fronts display color player photos accented by team color-coded borders. The player's name and uniform number are printed in the green bar beneath the picture. On a white background in dark green print, the backs carry a student tip by Fond du Lac elementary school children and list the set's sponsors.

COMPLETE SET (20)	4.00	10.00
1 Sherman Lewis CO	.30	.75
2 Sterling Sharpe	.30	.75
3 Ken Ruettgers	.20	.50
4 Reggie White	.50	1.25
5 Edgar Bennett	.40	1.00
6 Fritz Shurmur CO	.20	.50
7 Brett Favre	1.50	4.00
8 John Jurkovic	.30	.75
9 Robert Brooks	.40	1.00
10 Reggie Cobb	.08	.25
11 Bryce Paup	.30	.75
12 Harry Galbreath	.08	.25
13 Mike Holmgren CO	.50	1.25
14 Ed West	.08	.25
15 Sean Jones	.30	.75
16 Ron Wolf GM	.08	.25
17 Chris Jacke	.20	.50
18 Wayne Simmons	.20	.50
19 LeRoy Butler	.08	.25
20 George Teague	.20	.50

1995 Packers Safety Fritsch

This 20-card set of the Green Pay Packers features color action player photos in a thin green border. The set was produced by Larry Fritsch Cards and sponsored by the local Fire Department. The backs carry a student safety tip.

COMPLETE SET (20)	3.20	8.00
1 Mike Holmgren CO	.40	1.00
2 Ron Wolf VP	.08	.25
GM		
3 Brett Favre	1.20	3.00
4 Ty Detmer	.40	1.00
5 Chris Jacke	.20	.50
6 Craig Hentrich	.08	.25
7 Craig Newsome	.08	.25
8 George Teague	.20	.50
9 Edgar Bennett	.30	.75
10 LeRoy Butler	.08	.25
11 George Koonce	.08	.25
12 John Jurkovic	.20	.50
13 Aaron Taylor	.08	.25
14 Ken Ruettgers	.08	.25
15 Robert Brooks	.40	1.00
16 Mark Chmura	.50	1.25
17 Reggie White	.40	1.00
18 Doug Evans	.20	.50
19 Sean Jones	.20	.50
20 Wayne Simmons	.20	.50

1995 Packers Sentry Brett Favre

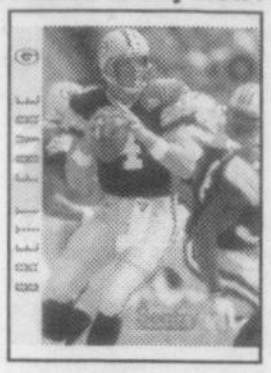

This roughly 8-5/8" by 6-3/4" card was distributed at a Green Bay Packers game during the 1995 season. The unnumbered card was included as part of a perforated sheet that contained an assortment of advertisements. The price below reflects that of the card in uncut sheet form.

1 Brett Favre	.80	2.00

1996 Packers Collector's Choice ShopKo

This 90-card standard-sized set was distributed and produced by Upper Deck for ShopKo, a retailer with stores in the Wisconsin area. The cards feature a unique Collector's Choice design and card numbering and include the following subsets: Season to Remember (#GB31-GB50), Legends of the Green and Gold (#GB51-GB69), and Leaders of the Pack (#GB70-GB90).

COMPLETE SET (90)	16.00	40.00
GB1 Brett Favre	1.60	4.00
GB2 Mark Chmura	.15	.40
GB3 Edgar Bennett	.30	.75
GB4 Robert Brooks	.30	.75
GB5 Antonio Freeman	.60	1.50
GB6 Travis Jervey	.15	.40
GB7 Craig Newsome	.08	.25
GB8 Reggie White	.30	.75
GB9 Sean Jones	.08	.25
GB10 LeRoy Butler	.15	.40
GB11 Chris Jacke	.08	.25
GB12 Derrick Mayes	.30	.75
GB13 Chris Darkins	.15	.40
GB14 Keith Jackson	.08	.25
GB15 Terry Mickens	.08	.25
GB16 Dorsey Levens	.60	1.50
GB17 Jim McMahon	.15	.40
GB18 Craig Hentrich	.08	.25
GB19 George Koonce	.08	.25
GB20 William Henderson	.08	.25
GB21 Doug Evans	.15	.40
GB22 Mike Prior	.08	.25
GB23 Wayne Simmons	.08	.25
GB24 Darius Holland	.08	.25
GB25 Gilbert Brown	.30	.75
GB26 Aaron Taylor	.08	.25
GB27 Frank Winters	.08	.25
GB28 Ken Ruettgers	.08	.25
GB29 Earl Dotson	.08	.25
GB30 Eugene Robinson	.08	.25
GB31 Brett Favre SR	1.00	2.50
GB32 Brett Favre SR	1.00	2.50
GB33 Brett Favre SR	1.00	2.50
GB34 Edgar Bennett SR	.15	.40
GB35 Edgar Bennett SR	.15	.40
GB36 Robert Brooks SR	.15	.40
GB37 Robert Brooks SR	.15	.40
GB38 Mark Chmura SR	.15	.40
GB39 Mark Chmura SR	.15	.40
GB40 LeRoy Butler SR	.08	.25
GB41 LeRoy Butler SR	.08	.25
GB42 Craig Newsome SR	.08	.25
GB43 Craig Newsome SR	.08	.25
GB44 Reggie White SR	.15	.40
GB45 Reggie White SR	.15	.40
GB46 Sean Jones SR	.08	.25
GB47 Sean Jones SR	.08	.25
GB48 Antonio Freeman SR	.30	.75
GB49 Chris Jacke SR	.08	.25
GB50 Offensive Line SR	.08	.25
Aaron Taylor		
Frank Winters		
Earl Dotson		
Mark Chmura		
Harry Galbreath		
Ken Ruettgers		
GB51 Forrest Gregg LGG	.15	.40
GB52 Paul Hornung LGG	.30	.75
GB53 Willie Davis LGG	.15	.40
GB54 Vince Lombardi CO LGG	.30	.75
GB55 Ray Nitschke LGG	.15	.40
GB56 Willie Wood LGG	.15	.40
GB57 Don Hutson LGG	.15	.40
GB58 Don Majkowski LGG	.08	.25
GB59 Bryce Paup LGG	.08	.25
GB60 Sterling Sharpe LGG	.08	.25
GB61 Ted Hendricks LGG	.08	.25
GB62 Lynn Dickey LGG	.08	.25
GB63 James Lofton LGG	.08	.25
GB64 Brett Favre LGG	1.00	2.50
GB65 Edgar Bennett LGG	.15	.40
GB66 Reggie White LGG	.15	.40
GB67 John Jurkovic LGG	.08	.25
GB68 Mike Holmgren CO LGG	.15	.40
GB69 Ron Wolf LGG	.08	.25
GB70 Forrest Gregg LP	.15	.40
GB71 Paul Hornung LP	.15	.40
*GB72 Willie Davis LP	.15	.40
GB73 Ray Nitschke LP	.15	.40
GB74 Willie Wood LP	.15	.40
GB75 Don Hutson LP	.15	.40
GB76 Sterling Sharpe LP	.08	.25
GB77 Don Majkowski LP	.08	.25
GB78 Ted Hendricks LP	.08	.25
GB79 Lynn Dickey LP	.08	.25
GB80 Brett Favre LP	1.00	2.50
GB81 James Lofton LP	.08	.25
GB82 Edgar Bennett LP	.15	.40
GB83 Robert Brooks LP	.15	.40
GB84 Mark Chmura LP	.15	.40
GB85 Reggie White LP	.08	.25
GB86 Sean Jones LP	.08	.25
GB87 Chris Jacke LP	.08	.25
GB88 LeRoy Butler LP	.08	.25
GB89 Craig Newsome LP	.08	.25
GB90 Checklist Card	.08	.25

1996 Packers Police

The Green Bay Packers issued this set in 1996 sponsored by Citgo. The cards feature a green border with the team and year "Packers 1996" at the top of the cardfront. The cardbacks feature green text on white card stock.

COMPLETE SET (20)	3.00	8.00
1 Edgar Bennett	.30	.75
2 Robert Brooks	.30	.75
3 Gilbert Brown	.30	.75
4 LeRoy Butler	.20	.50
5 Mark Chmura	.30	.75
6 Earl Dotson	.08	.25
7 Doug Evans	.20	.50
8 Brett Favre	1.50	4.00
9 Antonio Freeman	.80	2.00
10 Craig Hentrich	.08	.25
11 Chris Jacke	.20	.50
12 Wayne Simmons	.20	.50
13 George Koonce	.08	.25
14 Craig Newsome	.08	.25
15 Ken Ruettgers	.08	.25
16 Keith Jackson	.20	.50
17 Aaron Taylor	.08	.25
18 Reggie White	.40	1.00
19 Mike Holmgren CO	.30	.75
20 Ron Wolf GM	.08	.25

1996 Packers Sentry

This set was issued as a perforated sheet along with a group of advertisements at a 1996 Packers home game. The set was sponsored by Sentry Foods and highlights various games of the 1995 season.

COMPLETE SET (8)	2.40	6.00
1 Sept. 11, 1995	.30	.75
(Reggie White)		
2 Sept. 17, 1995	.80	2.00
(Brett Favre)		
3 Oct. 15, 1995	.80	2.00
(Brett Favre)		
4 Oct. 22, 1995	.08	.25
(Wayne Simmons)		
5 Nov. 12, 1995	.15	.40
(Edgar Bennett)		
6 Nov. 26, 1995	.08	.25
(Errict Rhett)		
7 Dec. 3, 1995	.30	.75
(Reggie White, John Jurkovic, Sean Jones, Jeff Blake)		
8 Team Photo	.15	.40

1997 Packers Collector's Choice

Upper Deck released several team sets in 1997 in a blister pack wrapper. Each of the 14-cards in this set are very similar to the base Collector's Choice cards except for the card numbering on the cardback. A cover/checklist card was added featuring the team helmet.

COMPLETE SET (14)	1.60	4.00
GB1 Robert Brooks	.05	.15
GB2 Antonio Freeman	.08	.25
GB3 Keith Jackson	.02	.10
GB4 Mark Chmura	.05	.15
GB5 Brett Favre	.80	2.00
GB6 Sean Jones	.02	.10
GB7 Reggie White	.08	.25
GB8 LeRoy Butler	.02	.10
GB9 Craig Newsome	.02	.10
GB10 Edgar Bennett	.05	.15
GB11 William Henderson	.02	.10
GB12 Dorsey Levens	.08	.25
GB13 Gilbert Brown	.05	.15
GB14 Packers Logo	.40	1.00
Checklist		
(Brett Favre on back)		

1997 Packers Collector's Choice ShopKo

For the second straight year, a 90-card standard-sized Upper Deck set was distributed and produced for ShopKo, a retailer with stores in the Wisconsin area. The fronts of cards 1-59 feature action color player photos within a white border. The backs carry another smaller player photo with biographical information, statistics, and a "Did You Know" fact about the pictured player. The fronts of the various subset cards (#60-90) feature borderless color action player photos with player information on the backs. All cards have gold foil highlights. The cards were issued in foil pack and factory set form and feature a Collector's Choice logo. Each factory set box included one randomly inserted Road to the Super Bowl Jumbo card.

COMP.FACT.SET (91)	16.00	40.00
GB1 Robert Brooks	.30	.75
GB2 Antonio Freeman	.50	1.25
GB3 Keith Jackson	.15	.40
GB4 Mark Chmura	.15	.40
GB5 Brett Favre	1.60	4.00
GB6 Reggie White	.30	.75
GB7 LeRoy Butler	.08	.25
GB8 Craig Newsome	.08	.25
GB9 Sean Jones	.08	.25
GB10 Edgar Bennett	.15	.40
GB11 William Henderson	.08	.25
GB12 Dorsey Levens	.50	1.25
GB13 Travis Jervey	.15	.40
GB14 Jim McMahon	.15	.40
GB15 Aaron Taylor	.08	.25
GB16 Frank Winters	.08	.25
GB17 Earl Dotson	.08	.25
GB18 Adam Timmerman	.08	.25
GB19 Bruce Wilkerson	.08	.25
GB20 John Michels	.08	.25
GB21 Don Beebe	.08	.25
GB22 Andre Rison	.15	.40
GB23 Desmond Howard	.15	.40
GB24 Terry Mickens	.08	.25
GB25 Derrick Mayes	.15	.40
GB26 Chris Jacke	.08	.25
GB27 Gilbert Brown	.15	.40
GB28 Santana Dotson	.08	.25
GB29 George Koonce	.08	.25
GB30 Wayne Simmons	.08	.25
GB31 Brian Williams	.08	.25
GB32 Ron Cox	.08	.25
GB33 Doug Evans	.08	.25
GB34 Eugene Robinson	.08	.25
GB35 Mike Prior	.08	.25
GB36 Tyrone Williams	.08	.25
GB37 Sherman Lewis CO	.15	.40
GB38 Fritz Shurmur CO	.15	.40
GB39 Gordon(Red) Batty	.08	.25
GB40 Lambeau Field	.15	.40
(crowd scene)		
GB41 Brett Favre SR	1.00	2.50
GB42 Brett Favre SR	1.00	2.50
GB43 Edgar Bennett SR	.15	.40
GB44 Edgar Bennett SR	.15	.40
GB45 Antonio Freeman SR	.30	.75
GB46 Antonio Freeman SR	.30	.75
GB47 Dorsey Levens SR	.30	.75
GB48 Andre Rison SR	.15	.40
GB49 Keith Jackson SR	.08	.25
GB50 Don Beebe SR	.08	.25
GB51 Reggie White SR	.30	.75
GB52 Packer Defense SR	.15	.40
Reggie White, Sean Jones, and Brian Williams		
GB53 Craig Newsome SR	.08	.25
GB54 Eugene Robinson SR	.08	.25
GB55 Desmond Howard SR	.15	.40
GB56 Robert Brooks SR	.30	.75
GB57 Chris Jacke SR	.08	.25
GB58 Mike Holmgren SR	.15	.40
GB59 Ron Wolf SR	.08	.25
GB60 Brett Favre RSB	1.00	2.50
GB61 Brett Favre RSB	1.00	2.50
GB62 Edgar Bennett RSB	.15	.40
GB63 Edgar Bennett RSB	.15	.40
GB64 Dorsey Levens RSB	.30	.75
GB65 Dorsey Levens RSB	.30	.75
GB66 Antonio Freeman RSB	.30	.75
GB67 Antonio Freeman RSB	.30	.75
GB68 Andre Rison RSB	.15	.40
GB69 Don Beebe RSB	.08	.25
GB70 Mark Chmura RSB	.15	.40
GB71 Reggie White RSB	.30	.75
GB72 Eugene Robinson RSB	.08	.25
GB73 Desmond Howard RSB	.15	.40
GB74 Desmond Howard RSB	.15	.40
GB75 Craig Newsome RSB	.08	.25
GB76 Tyrone Williams RSB	.08	.25
GB77 Chris Jacke RSB	.15	.40
GB78 Wayne Simmons RSB	.08	.25
GB79 Offensive Line RSB	.08	.25
Adam Timmerman		
GB80 Brett Favre BB	1.00	2.50
GB81 Antonio Freeman BB	.30	.75
GB82 Reggie White BB	.30	.75
GB83 Wayne Simmons BB	.08	.25
GB84 Edgar Bennett BB	.15	.40
GB85 Andre Rison BB	.15	.40
GB86 Dorsey Levens BB	.30	.75
GB87 Chris Jacke BB	.08	.25
GB88 The Secondary BB	.08	.25
Leroy Butler, Craig Newsome		
GB89 Desmond Howard BB	.15	.40
GB90 Team Logo CL	.08	.25

1997 Packers Playoff

This 50-card set honors the 1997 Super Bowl XXXI World Champions, the Green Bay Packers. The fronts feature borderless color action player photos with the Super Bowl logo printed at the bottom and player's name on one side. The backs carry the score of the championship game with the New England Patriots and player information on a faint background of the dome in New Orleans.

COMPLETE SET (50)	6.00	15.00
1 Super Bowl XXXI Champions	.07	.20
Scoreboard Photo		
2 Brett Favre MVP	1.60	4.00
3 Reggie White	.30	.75
Minister of Defense		
4 Desmond Howard MVP	.15	.40
5 NFC Championship	.07	.20
Trophy Presentation		
6 Mike Holmgren CO	.15	.40
7 Brett Favre	1.60	4.00
8 Chris Jacke	.07	.20
9 Craig Hentrich	.07	.20
10 Craig Newsome	.07	.20
11 Dorsey Levens	.60	1.50
12 Doug Evans	.07	.20
13 Edgar Bennett	.30	.75
14 LeRoy Butler	.07	.20
15 Eugene Robinson	.07	.20
16 Brian Williams LB	.07	.20
17 Frank Winters	.07	.20
18 Ron Cox	.07	.20
19 Wayne Simmons	.07	.20
20 Adam Timmerman	.07	.20
21 Bruce Wilkerson	.07	.20
22 Santana Dotson	.07	.20
23 Earl Dotson	.07	.20
24 Aaron Taylor	.07	.20
25 Desmond Howard	.15	.40
26 Don Beebe	.07	.20
27 Andre Rison	.15	.40
28 Antonio Freeman	.60	1.50
29 Terry Mickens	.07	.20
30 Keith Jackson	.15	.40
31 Mark Chmura	.30	.75
32 Reggie White	.30	.75
33 Gilbert Brown	.15	.40
34 Sean Jones	.07	.20
35 Robert Brooks	.30	.75
George Koonce		
36 Derrick Mayes	.15	.40
Gary Brown		
37 Jim McMahon	.15	.40
38 William Henderson	.07	.20
39 Travis Jervey	.15	.40
Roderick Mullen		
40 Tyrone Williams	.07	.20
41 John Michels	.07	.20
42 Mike Prior	.07	.20
43 Calvin Jones	.07	.20
Jeff Thomason		
44 Brett Favre	1.60	4.00
45 Jeff Dellenbach	.07	.20
46 Bernardo Harris	.07	.20
47 Darius Holland	.07	.20
48 Lamont Hollinquest	.07	.20
49 Lindsay Knapp	.07	.20
50 Gabe Wilkins	.07	.20

1997 Packers Police

The Packers, along with a host of sponsors, produced this set for the 1997 Super Bowl Championship club. The cardfronts feature a colorful design along with a color photo, while the backs were produced simply in green on white card stock.

COMPLETE SET (20)	3.00	8.00
1 Super Bowl XXXI Trophy	.08	.25
2 Mike Holmgren CO	.20	.50
3 Ron Wolf GM	.08	.25
4 Brett Favre	1.50	4.00
5 Reggie White	.40	1.00
6 LeRoy Butler	.08	.25
7 Frank Winters	.08	.25
8 Aaron Taylor	.08	.25
9 Robert Brooks	.20	.50
10 Gilbert Brown	.20	.50
11 Mark Chmura	.20	.50
12 Earl Dotson	.08	.25
13 Santana Dotson	.08	.25
14 Doug Evans	.08	.25
15 Antonio Freeman	.40	1.00
16 William Henderson	.08	.25
17 Craig Hentrich	.08	.25
18 Dorsey Levens	.30	.75
19 Craig Newsome	.08	.25
20 Edgar Bennett	.20	.50

1997 Packers Score

This 15-card set of the Green Bay Packers was distributed in five-card packs with a suggested retail price of $1.99. The fronts feature color action player photos with white borders and the player's name and team logo printed in team color foil at the bottom. The backs carry player information and career statistics. Platinum Team parallel cards were randomly seeded in packs featuring all foil cardfronts.

COMPLETE SET (15)	3.20	8.00
*PLATINUM TEAMS: 1X TO 2X		
1 Brett Favre	1.25	3.00
2 Andre Rison	.15	.40
3 Robert Brooks	.15	.40
4 Keith Jackson	.08	.25
5 Edgar Bennett	.15	.40
6 Reggie White	.30	.75
7 Dorsey Levens	.40	1.00
8 Antonio Freeman	.40	1.00
9 Mark Chmura	.15	.40
10 Wayne Simmons	.08	.25
11 Eugene Robinson	.08	.25
12 Brian Williams LB	.08	.25
13 Doug Evans	.08	.25
14 LeRoy Butler	.08	.25
15 Gilbert Brown	.15	.40

1997 Packers Upper Deck Legends

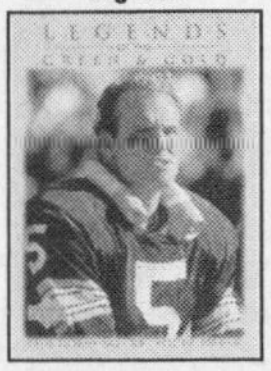

This oversized (roughly 3 1/2" by 5") set was produced by Upper Deck for distributiion through larger retail chains. The cards were sold in complete factory set form in a specially designed display box. Each card features a top "Legends of the Green and Gold" color photo surrounded by an antique style beige border.

COMPLETE SET (20)	8.00	20.00
GB1 Forrest Gregg	.50	1.25
GB2 Paul Hornung	.80	2.00
GB3 Willie Davis	.50	1.25
GB4 Ray Nitschke	.50	1.25
GB5 Willie Wood	.50	1.25
GB6 Don Hutson	.50	1.25
GB7 Don Majkowski	.30	.75
GB8 Bryce Paup	.30	.75
GB9 Sterling Sharpe	.50	1.25
GB10 Ted Hendricks	.30	.75
GB11 Lynn Dickey	.30	.75
GB12 James Lofton	.30	.75
GB13 Brett Favre	2.00	5.00
GB14 Edgar Bennett	.80	2.00
GB15 Reggie White	.80	2.00
GB16 LeRoy Butler	.30	.75
GB17 John Jurkovic	.30	.75
GB18 Mike Holmgren CO	.50	1.25
GB19 Ron Wolf GM	.30	.75
GB20 Packer Helmet CL	.30	.75

1997 Packers vs. Bears Sentry

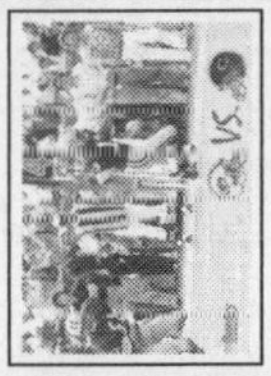

Issued at a Packers home game with the Bears in 1997, Sentry Foods sponsored this set. The cards were released as an uncut sheet of 6-cards and six different smaller ad cards. Each card includes a color photo from one historic Packers vs. Bears game with no particular players identified. We've included names of some of the top featured players below. The cards are unnumbered and listed below in chronological order.

COMPLETE SET (6)	1.60	4.00
1 Dec.16, 1973	.20	.50
(John Brockington)		
2 Sept. 7, 1980	.20	.50
(Chester Marcol)		
3 Nov. 5, 1989	.20	.50
(Sterling Sharpe)		
4 Oct. 31, 1994	.30	.75
(Edgar Bennett,		
Trace Armstrong)		
5 Nov. 12, 1995	1.00	2.50
(Brett Favre,		
Edgar Bennett)		
6 Oct. 6, 1996	.30	.75
(Reggie White,		
Rashaan Salaam)		

1997 Packers vs. Vikings Sentry

Issued at a game with the Vikings in 1997, Sentry Foods sponsored this set for Packers' fans. The cards were released as an uncut sheet of 9-cards and one ad-card for the Junior Power Pack kids club. Each card includes a color photo from one historic Packers vs. Vikings game with no particular players identified. We've included names of some of the top featured players below. The cards are unnumbered and listed below in chronological order.

COMPLETE SET (9)	2.40	6.00
1 Dec. 3, 1967	.40	1.00
(Dave Robinson,		
Willie Davis, Carl Eller,		
Bart Starr, Don Chandler)		
2 Dec. 10, 1972	.40	1.00
(Scott Hunter, Carl Eller)		
3 Nov. 26, 1978	.30	.75
(Chuck Foreman)		
4 Nov. 11, 1979	.30	.75
5 Oct. 26, 1980	.40	1.00
(Lynn Dickey)		
6 Nov. 13, 1983	.30	.75
7 Dec. 13, 1987	.30	.75
(Paul Ott Carruth)		
8 Nov. 26, 1989	.30	.75
(Don Majkowski)		
9 Sept. 4, 1994	.40	1.00
(Edgar Bennett, Brett Favre,		
Jack Del Rio, Henry Thomas,		
John Randle, Ed McDaniel)		

1998 Packers Police

With the sponsorship of local crime prevention authorities, the Packers produced this set for the 1998 team. The cardfronts feature a colorful design along with a color player photo, while the backs were produced simply in green on white card stock.

COMPLETE SET (20)	3.20	8.00
1 Ron Wolf GM	.08	.25
2 Robert Brooks	.20	.50
3 Gilbert Brown	.08	.25
4 Mike Holmgren CO	.20	.50
5 LeRoy Butler	.08	.25
6 Mark Chmura	.20	.50
7 Earl Dotson	.08	.25
8 Santana Dotson	.08	.25
9 Brett Favre	1.50	4.00
10 Antonio Freeman	.40	1.00
11 Bernardo Harris	.08	.25
12 William Henderson	.08	.25
13 Dorsey Levens	.40	1.00
14 Craig Newsome	.08	.25
15 Adam Timmerman	.08	.25
16 Ross Verba	.08	.25
17 Reggie White	.40	1.00
18 Brian Williams LB	.08	.25
19 Tyrone Williams	.08	.25
20 Frank Winters	.08	.25

1998 Packers Upper Deck ShopKo

This 90-card set produced by Upper Deck for ShopKo, a retailer with stores in the Wisconsin area, was distributed in 10-card packs. The cards feature a partial yellow border and gold foil highlights on the cardfronts. The card numbering includes a GR prefix on the first 55-cards and the set includes the following subsets: Leaders of the Pack (P1-P15) and Tundra Titans (T1-T20). A Title Defense parallel set was also produced and randomly inserted in packs (1:4 packs ratio).

COMPLETE SET (90)	10.00	25.00
1 Brett Favre	1.20	3.00
2 Ryan Longwell	.08	.25
3 Steve Bono	.30	.75
4 Craig Hentrich	.08	.25
5 Doug Pederson	.08	.25
6 Craig Newsome	.08	.25
7 Aaron Hayden	.08	.25
8 Dorsey Levens	.40	1.00
9 Mark Collins	.08	.25
10 Roderick Mullen	.08	.25
11 William Henderson	.08	.25
12 Travis Jervey	.15	.40
13 Doug Evans	.08	.25
14 Edgar Bennett	.15	.40
15 LeRoy Butler	.15	.40
16 Tyrone Williams	.08	.25
17 Emory Smith	.08	.25
18 Mike Prior	.08	.25
19 Eugene Robinson	.15	.40
20 Darren Sharper	.40	1.00
21 Chris Darkins	.15	.40
22 Brian Williams	.08	.25
23 Frank Winters	.08	.25
24 George Koonce	.08	.25
25 Seth Joyner	.08	.25
26 Bernardo Harris	.08	.25
27 Lamont Hollinquest	.08	.25
28 Anthony Fogle	.08	.25
29 Marco Rivera	.30	.75
30 Adam Timmerman	.08	.25
31 Bruce Wilkerson	.08	.25
32 Jeff Dellenbach	.08	.25
33 Joe Andruzzi	.08	.25
34 Santana Dotson	.08	.25
35 Earl Dotson	.08	.25
36 Aaron Taylor	.08	.25
37 John Michels	.08	.25
38 Ross Verba	.08	.25
39 Derrick Mayes	.15	.40
40 Tyrone Davis	.08	.25
41 Don Beebe	.15	.40
42 Jeff Thomason	.08	.25
43 Bill Schroeder	.30	.75
44 Terry Mickens	.08	.25
45 Antonio Freeman	.50	1.25
46 Robert Brooks	.15	.40
47 Mark Chmura	.30	.75
48 Darius Holland	.08	.25
49 Reggie White	.30	.75
50 Gilbert Brown	.08	.25
51 Bob Kuberski	.08	.25
52 Keith McKenzie	.08	.25
53 Paul Frase	.08	.25
54 Gabe Wilkins	.08	.25
55 Jermaine Smith	.08	.25
P1 Mike Holmgren CO LP	.15	.40
P2 Sherman Lewis CO LP	.15	.40
P3 Fritz Shurmur CO LP	.08	.25
P4 Ron Wolf GM LP	.08	.25
P5 Brett Favre LP	.80	2.00
P6 Reggie White LP	.15	.40
P7 Dorsey Levens LP	.30	.75
P8 Gilbert Brown LP	.08	.25
P9 Eugene Robinson LP	.08	.25
P10 Antonio Freeman LP	.30	.75
P11 Mark Chmura LP	.15	.40
P12 Seth Joyner LP	.08	.25
P13 LeRoy Butler LP	.08	.25
P14 Robert Brooks LP	.15	.40
P15 Travis Jervey LP	.08	.25
T1 Brett Favre TT	.80	2.00
T2 Reggie White TT	.15	.40
T3 Dorsey Levens TT	.30	.75
T4 Antonio Freeman TT	.30	.75
T5 LeRoy Butler TT	.08	.25
T6 Santana Dotson TT	.08	.25
T7 Frank Winters TT	.08	.25
T8 Robert Brooks TT	.15	.40
T9 Mark Chmura TT	.15	.40
T10 Travis Jervey TT	.08	.25
T11 Gilbert Brown TT	.08	.25
T12 Seth Joyner TT	.08	.25
T13 William Henderson TT	.08	.25
T14 Derrick Mayes TT	.15	.40
T15 Doug Evans TT	.08	.25
T16 Ross Verba TT	.08	.25
T17 Tyrone Williams TT	.08	.25
T18 Gabe Wilkins TT	.08	.25
T19 Eugene Robinson TT	.08	.25
T20 Darren Sharper TT	.25	.60

1998 Packers Upper Deck ShopKo Title Defense

COMP.TITLE DEF.SET (90)	24.00	60.00
*TITLE DEFENSE CARDS: 1.5X TO 3X		

1998 Packers Upper Deck ShopKo II

This 90-card set was produced by Upper Deck for ShopKo, a retailer with stores in the Wisconsin area. It was distributed in late 1998 as a second series set to the original Upper Deck Shopko set released earlier in the year. The fronts features color action player photos with green foil highlights, and the backs carry player information. Unlike series one, the cards contain no prefixes on the card numbers. The set also contains the topical subsets: Game Dated (51-65), and Pack Comeback (66-90). The Ray Nitschke tribute card is listed at the bottom of the checklist.

COMPLETE SET (90)	8.00	20.00
1 Brett Favre	1.20	3.00
2 Ryan Longwell	.08	.25
3 Doug Pederson	.08	.25
4 Craig Newsome	.08	.25
5 Emory Smith	.08	.25
6 Aaron Hayden	.08	.25
7 Dorsey Levens	.40	1.00
8 Roderick Mullen	.08	.25
9 Travis Jervey	.15	.40
10 William Henderson	.08	.25
11 LeRoy Butler	.15	.40
12 Tyrone Williams	.08	.25
13 Mike Prior	.08	.25
14 Darren Sharper	.25	.60
15 Chris Darkins	.15	.40
16 Anthony Hicks	.08	.25
17 Brian Williams	.08	.25
18 Frank Winters	.08	.25
19 George Koonce	.08	.25
20 Bernardo Harris	.08	.25
21 Lamont Hollinquest	.08	.25
22 Seth Joyner	.08	.25
23 Marco Rivera	.30	.75
24 Adam Timmerman	.08	.25
25 Bruce Wilkerson	.08	.25
26 Jeff Dellenbach	.08	.25
27 Joe Andruzzi	.08	.25
28 Santana Dotson	.08	.25
29 Earl Dotson	.08	.25
30 John Michels	.08	.25
31 Ross Verba	.08	.25
32 Derrick Mayes	.15	.40
33 Tyrone Davis	.08	.25
34 Jeff Thomason	.08	.25
35 Bill Schroeder	.08	.25
36 Antonio Freeman	.50	1.25
37 Robert Brooks	.15	.40
38 Mark Chmura	.30	.75
39 Reggie White	.30	.75
40 Gilbert Brown	.08	.25
41 Bob Kuberski	.08	.25
42 Keith McKenzie	.08	.25
43 Jermaine Smith	.08	.25
44 Eric Curry	.08	.25
45 Doug Widell	.08	.25
46 Vaughn Booker	.08	.25
47 Vonnie Holliday	.08	.25
48 Glyn Milburn	.08	.25
49 Antonio London	.08	.25
50 Jonathan Brown	.08	.25
51 Brett Favre GD	.80	2.00
52 Robert Brooks GD	.15	.40
53 Antonio Freeman GD	.30	.75
54 Dorsey Levens GD	.30	.75
55 Mark Chmura GD	.15	.40
56 Reggie White GD	.15	.40
57 LeRoy Butler GD	.08	.25
58 Travis Jervey GD	.08	.25
59 Gilbert Brown GD	.08	.25
60 William Henderson GD	.08	.25
61 Ryan Longwell GD	.08	.25
62 Seth Joyner GD	.08	.25
63 Derrick Mayes GD	.08	.25
64 Ross Verba GD	.08	.25
65 Santana Dotson GD	.08	.25
66 Brett Favre PC	.80	2.00
67 Mark Chmura PC	.15	.40
68 Dorsey Levens PC	.30	.75
69 Robert Brooks PC	.15	.40
70 Antonio Freeman PC	.30	.75
71 Derrick Mayes PC	.08	.25
72 Frank Winters PC	.08	.25
73 Anthony Fogle PC	.08	.25
74 Emory Smith PC	.08	.25
75 Mike Prior PC	.08	.25
76 Adam Timmerman PC	.08	.25
77 Ross Verba PC	.08	.25
78 Reggie White PC	.15	.40
79 Gilbert Brown PC	.08	.25
80 Seth Joyner PC	.08	.25
81 LeRoy Butler PC	.08	.25
82 Craig Newsome PC	.08	.25
83 Ryan Longwell PC	.08	.25
84 Travis Jervey PC	.08	.25
85 William Henderson PC	.08	.25
86 Darren Sharper PC	.15	.40
87 Bernardo Harris PC	.08	.25
88 Bruce Wilkerson PC	.08	.25
89 Earl Dotson PC	.08	.25
90 John Michels PC	.08	.25
RN1 Ray Nitschke	.40	1.00

1998 Packers Upper Deck ShopKo II Lambeau Lineups

COMPLETE SET (30)	4.00	10.00
LL1 Brett Favre	1.20	3.00
LL2 Dorsey Levens	.40	1.00
LL3 Reggie White	.30	.75
LL4 Doug Widell	.08	.25
LL5 William Henderson	.08	.25
LL6 Aaron Hayden	.08	.25
LL7 Robert Brooks	.15	.40
LL8 Antonio Freeman	.40	1.00
LL9 Mark Chmura	.15	.40
LL10 Derrick Mayes	.08	.25
LL11 Seth Joyner	.08	.25
LL12 Darren Sharper	.15	.40
LL13 LeRoy Butler	.08	.25
LL14 Craig Newsome	.08	.25
LL15 Travis Jervey	.08	.25
LL16 Bill Schroeder	.08	.25
LL17 Ross Verba	.08	.25
LL18 Frank Winters	.08	.25
LL19 Jermaine Smith	.08	.25
LL20 Jonathan Brown	.08	.25
LL21 Adam Timmerman	.08	.25
LL22 Santana Dotson	.08	.25
LL23 Gilbert Brown	.08	.25
LL24 Pat Terrell	.08	.25
LL25 Lamont Hollinquest	.08	.25
LL26 Tyrone Williams	.08	.25
LL27 Glyn Milburn	.08	.25
LL28 Roderick Mullen	.08	.25
LL29 Ryan Longwell	.08	.25
LL30 Sean Landeta	.08	.25

1998 Packers Upper Deck ShopKo II Super Pack

COMPLETE SET (30)	10.00	25.00
S1 Brett Favre	3.00	8.00
S2 Dorsey Levens	.75	2.00
S3 Antonio Freeman	1.00	2.50
S4 Robert Brooks	.50	1.25
S5 Ryan Longwell	.30	.75
S6 William Henderson	.50	1.25
S7 Aaron Hayden	.30	.75
S8 Derrick Mayes	.30	.75
S9 Frank Winters	.30	.75
S10 Bill Schroeder	.30	.75
S11 Ross Verba	.30	.75
S12 Travis Jervey	.30	.75
S13 John Michels	.30	.75
S14 Adam Timmerman	.30	.75
S15 Earl Dotson	.30	.75
S16 Lamont Hollinquest	.30	.75
S17 Santana Dotson	.30	.75
S18 Reggie White	1.25	3.00
S19 Gilbert Brown	.30	.75
S20 LeRoy Butler	.30	.75
S21 Craig Newsome	.30	.75
S22 Roderick Mullen	.30	.75
S23 Mike Prior	.30	.75
S24 Brian Williams	.30	.75
S25 Keith McKenzie	.30	.75
S26 Tyrone Williams	.30	.75
S27 Jonathan Brown	.30	.75
S28 Darren Sharper	.75	2.00
S29 George Koonce	.30	.75
S30 Mark Chmura	.50	1.25

1999 Packers Police

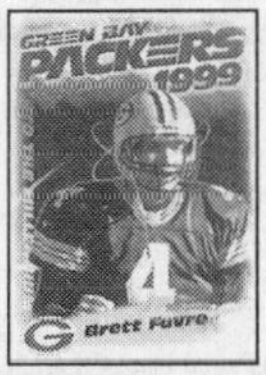

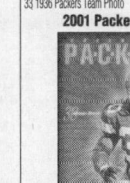

With the sponsorship of the Town of Hull Fire Dept. and Larry Fritsch Cards, this set was produced for the 1999 Packers team. The cardfronts feature a colorful "Green Bay Packers 1999" design along with a color player photo, while the backs were produced simply in green on white card stock. Variations in the sponsor and the law enforcement region on the unnumbered cardbacks can be found.

COMPLETE SET (20)	3.20	8.00
1 Gilbert Brown	.08	.25
2 LeRoy Butler	.08	.25
3 Mark Chmura	.15	.40
4 Earl Dotson	.08	.25
5 Santana Dotson	.08	.25
6 Brett Favre	1.20	3.00
7 Antonio Freeman	.30	.75
8 Bernardo Harris	.08	.25
9 William Henderson	.08	.25
10 Vonnie Holliday	.30	.75
11 George Koonce	.08	.25
12 Dorsey Levens	.30	.75
13 Ryan Longwell	.08	.25
14 Marco Rivera	.15	.40
15 Darren Sharper	.20	.50
16 Ross Verba	.08	.25
17 Brian Williams LB	.08	.25
18 Tyrone Williams	.08	.25
19 Ron Wolf GM	.08	.25
20 Ray Rhodes CO	.15	.40

2000 Packers Police

The Packers continued the longest running series of Police sponsored cards in 2000. Each features a color photo, year, and player name on the cardfronts along with a simple green and white cardback. Variations in the sponsor on the unnumbered cardbacks can be found.

COMPLETE SET (20)	4.00	8.00
1 Ron Wolf GM	.08	.25
2 Mike Sherman CO	.08	.25
3 LeRoy Butler	.15	.40
4 Earl Dotson	.08	.25
5 Santana Dotson	.08	.25
6 Brett Favre	1.25	3.00
7 Antonio Freeman	.30	.75
8 Bernardo Harris	.08	.25
9 William Henderson	.08	.25
10 Vonnie Holliday	.15	.40
11 Dorsey Levens	.30	.75
12 Russell Maryland	.08	.25
13 Mike McKenzie	.08	.25
14 Bill Schroeder	.30	.75
15 Darren Sharper	.20	.50
16 Ross Verba	.08	.25
17 Mike Wahle	.08	.25
18 Brian Williams LB	.08	.25
19 Tyrone Williams	.08	.25
20 Frank Winters	.08	.25

2001 Packers 1936 Champion Series

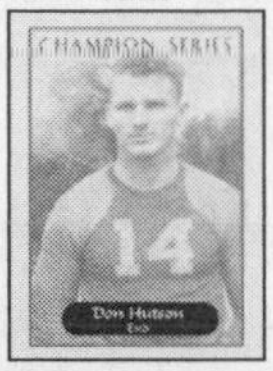

This 33-card set was made by Champion Series to commemorate the Packers' 1936 NFL Championship. Each standard-sized card was printed in an antique orange color on the front with a simple white and maroon cardback. The cardbacks also include the card number.

COMPLETE SET (33)	8.00	12.00
1 Curly Lambeau CO	1.25	3.00
2 Red Smith CO	.20	.50
3 Don Hutson	.75	2.00
4 Clarke Hinkle	.50	1.25
5 Arnie Herber	.30	.75
6 Charles Goldenberg	.30	.75
7 Johnny Blood McNally	.50	1.25
8 Joe Laws	.20	.50
9 Walt Kiesling	.30	.75
10 Russ Letlow	.20	.50
11 George Sauer	.30	.75
12 Al Rose	.20	.50
13 Lon Evans	.20	.50
14 Bob Monnett	.20	.50
15 Henry Bruder	.20	.50
16 Milt Gantenbein	.20	.50
17 Chester Johnston	.20	.50
18 Frank Butler	.20	.50
19 George Svendsen	.20	.50
20 Ernie Smith	.20	.50
21 Adolph Schwammel	.20	.50
22 Herman Schneidman	.20	.50
23 Paul Engebretsen	.20	.50
24 Paul Miller	.20	.50
25 Bernard Scherer	.20	.50
26 Lou Gordon	.20	.50
27 Harry Mattos	.20	.50
28 Cal Clemens	.20	.50
29 Wayland Becker	.20	.50
30 Tony Paulekas	.20	.50
31 Champ Seibold	.20	.50
32 1936 Championship Program	.20	.50
33 1936 Packers Team Photo	.30	.75

2001 Packers Police

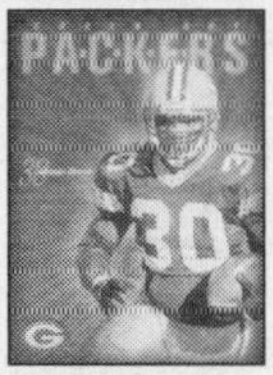

The 2001 Packers Police set features the team name "Green Bay Packers 2001" at the top of the cardfronts along with a player photo produced with a halo effect. The backs were produced simply in green on white card stock. The card number appears in the lower right hand corner. Variations in the sponsor on the cardbacks can be found.

COMPLETE SET (20)	4.00	8.00
1 Mike Sherman CO	.08	.25
2 Brett Favre	1.25	3.00
3 Bill Schroeder	.15	.40
4 Antonio Freeman	.30	.75
5 Marco Rivera	.15	.40
6 Ahman Green	.30	.75
7 William Henderson	.08	.25
8 Mike Flanagan	.08	.25
9 Russell Maryland	.08	.25
10 Santana Dotson	.08	.25
11 John Thierry	.08	.25
12 Vonnie Holliday	.15	.40
13 Na'il Diggs	.08	.25
14 Bernardo Harris	.08	.25
15 Nate Wayne	.08	.25
16 Tyrone Williams	.08	.25
17 LeRoy Butler	.15	.40
18 Darren Sharper	.08	.25
19 Ryan Longwell	.08	.25
20 Allen Rossum	.08	.25

2002 Packers Police

The 2002 Packers Police was sponsored by the Fox River Mall, Grand Chute Police Department, and the Grand Chute Lions Club. The cardfronts feature the team name "Green Bay Packers" at the top and the year near the bottom of the card. The backs were produced simply in green on white card stock. The card number is included in the lower right hand corner. Variations in the sponsor on the cardbacks (such as Larry Fritsch Cards) can be found.

COMPLETE SET (20)	4.00	8.00
1 Ahman Green	.40	1.00
2 Brett Favre	1.25	3.00
3 Bubba Franks	.30	.75
4 Chad Clifton	.08	.25
5 Darren Sharper	.15	.40
6 Gilbert Brown	.08	.25
7 Kabeer Gbaja-Biamila	.30	.75
8 Tyrone Williams	.08	.25
9 Mark Tauscher	.08	.25
10 Mike McKenzie	.08	.25
11 Mike Sherman CO	.08	.25
12 Mike Wahle	.08	.25
13 Na'il Diggs	.08	.25
14 Nate Wayne	.08	.25
15 Robert Ferguson	.15	.40
16 Ryan Longwell	.08	.25
17 Vonnie Holliday	.15	.40
18 William Henderson	.15	.40
19 Joe Johnson	.08	.25
20 Terry Glenn	.15	.40

2003 Packers Police

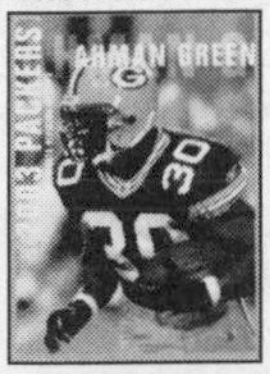

The 2003 Packers Police set was again sponsored by Larry Fritsch Cards, Inc. Another version was sponsored by Doyles Farm and distributed by the New Richmond Police Dept. The cards feature the team name "Packers 2003" along the left border of the cardfronts. The backs were produced simply with green printing on white card stock. The card numbers appear in the upper right hand corner. Variations in the sponsor on the cardbacks can be found. Reportedly, over 125,000 total sets were produced.

COMPLETE SET (20)	4.00	8.00
1 Mike Sherman CO	.08	.25
2 Brett Favre	1.25	3.00
3 Ryan Longwell	.08	.25
4 Ahman Green	.40	1.00
5 William Henderson	.15	.40
6 Mike McKenzie	.08	.25
7 Darren Sharper	.15	.40
8 Mike Flanagan	.08	.25
9 Na'il Diggs	.08	.25
10 Marco Rivera	.08	.25
11 Mark Truscher	.08	.25
12 Chad Clifton	.08	.25
13 Donald Driver	.30	.75
14 Javon Walker	.30	.75
15 Bubba Franks	.15	.40
16 Robert Ferguson	.15	.40
17 Joe Johnson	.08	.25
18 Kabeer Gbaja-Biamila	.15	.40
19 Rod Walker	.08	.25
20 Cletidus Hunt	.08	.25

2004 Packers Police

The Packers continued their streak of issuing a Police set in 2004. This set was again sponsored by Larry Fritsch Cards, Inc. in conjunction with Stevens Point and the Town of Hull as noted on the cardbacks. Another version was sponsored by Doyles Farm and distributed by the New Richmond Police Dept. The cardfronts on this version are the same but the sponsorship information differs on the cardbacks. The cards feature the team name "Green Bay Packers 2004" along the right border of the cardfronts. The backs were produced simply with green printing on white card stock. The card numbers appear in the lower left hand corner.

COMPLETE SET (20)	4.00	8.00
1 Mike Sherman CO	.08	.25
2 Brett Favre	1.25	3.00
3 Ryan Longwell	.08	.25
4 Ahman Green	.40	1.00
5 Al Harris	.15	.40
6 Darren Sharper	.15	.40
7 Najeh Davenport	.15	.40
8 Hannibal Navies	.08	.25
9 Nick Barnett	.08	.25
10 Na'il Diggs	.08	.25
11 Mark Tauscher	.08	.25
12 Mike Wahle	.08	.25
13 Aaron Kampman	.40	1.00
14 Grady Jackson	.08	.25
15 Chad Clifton	.08	.25
16 Donald Driver	.30	.75
17 Javon Walker	.30	.75
18 Bubba Franks	.15	.40
19 Robert Ferguson	.15	.40
20 Kabeer Gbaja-Biamila	.15	.40

2005 Packers Activa Medallions

COMPLETE SET (22)	30.00	60.00
1 Nick Barnett	1.25	3.00
2 Ahmad Carroll	1.25	3.00
3 Chad Clifton	1.25	3.00
4 Najeh Davenport	1.25	3.00
5 Nail Diggs	1.25	3.00
6 Donald Driver	1.25	3.00
7 Brett Favre	2.00	5.00
8 Robert Ferguson	1.25	3.00
9 Tony Fisher	1.25	3.00
10 Mike Flanagan	1.25	3.00
11 Bubba Franks	1.25	3.00
12 Kabeer Gbaja-Biamila	1.25	3.00
13 Ahman Green	1.50	4.00
14 Al Harris	1.25	3.00
15 William Henderson	1.25	3.00
16 Grady Jackson	1.25	3.00
17 Aaron Kampman	1.25	3.00
18 Ryan Longwell	1.25	3.00
19 Aaron Rodgers	2.50	6.00
20 Mark Tauscher	1.25	3.00
21 Javon Walker	1.25	3.00
22 Packers Logo	1.00	2.50

2005 Packers Police

The Packers continued their long tradition by issuing a Police set again in 2005. This set was again sponsored by Larry Fritsch Cards with another version sponsored by Fox River Mall distributed by the Grand Chute Police Dept. The cardfronts on the versions are the same but the sponsorship information differs on the backs. The cards feature the team helmet below the image and the year of issue above the photo on the cardfronts. The backs were produced simply with green printing on white card stock. The card numbers appear in the lower left hand corner.

COMPLETE SET (20)	3.00	8.00
1 Mike Sherman CO	.08	.25
2 Ted Thompson GM	.08	.25
3 Brett Favre	1.25	3.00
4 Ryan Longwell	.08	.25
5 Ahman Green	.30	.75
6 Al Harris	.08	.25
7 William Henderson	.15	.40
8 Nick Barnett	.15	.40
9 Mike Flanagan	.08	.25
10 Na'il Diggs	.08	.25
11 Mark Tauscher	.08	.25
12 Aaron Kampman	.30	.75
13 Grady Jackson	.08	.25
14 Chad Clifton	.08	.25
15 Donald Driver	.15	.40
16 Javon Walker	.30	.75
17 Bubba Franks	.15	.40
18 Robert Ferguson	.15	.40
19 Kabeer Gbaja-Biamila	.15	.40
20 Corey Williams	.15	.40

2005 Packers Topps XXL

COMPLETE SET (4)	6.00	15.00
1 Brett Favre	1.25	3.00
2 Aaron Rodgers	6.00	15.00
3 Ahman Green	.50	1.25
4 Javon Walker	.30	.75

2006 Packers Police

The Packers continued their tradition in football cards by issuing a Police set for 2006. This set was again sponsored by Larry Fritsch Cards as well as a variety of regional law enforcement agencies. The cardfronts on each version are the same but the sponsorship information differs on the backs. The cards feature a thin black border on the front along with the year of issue ghosted into the background. The backs were produced simply with green printing on white card stock.

COMPLETE SET (20)	3.00	8.00
1 Ted Thompson GM	.30	.75
2 Mike McCarthy CO	.30	.75
3 Brett Favre	1.00	2.50
4 Aaron Rodgers	1.00	2.50
5 Charles Woodson	.50	1.25
6 Marquand Manuel	.30	.75
7 Ahman Green	.40	1.00
8 Al Harris	.40	1.00
9 William Henderson	.30	.75
10 Samkon Gado	.40	1.00
11 Nick Collins	.40	1.00
12 A.J. Hawk	.50	1.25
13 Nick Barnett	.40	1.00
14 Mark Tauscher	.30	.75
15 Aaron Kampman	.40	1.00
16 Chad Clifton	.30	.75
17 Donald Driver	.50	1.25
18 Bubba Franks	.30	.75
19 Robert Ferguson	.30	.75
20 Kabeer Gbaja-Biamila	.40	1.00

2006 Packers Topps

COMPLETE SET (12)	3.00	6.00
GB1 Aaron Rodgers	.60	1.50
GB2 Robert Ferguson	.20	.50
GB3 Sam Gado	.25	.60
GB4 Donald Driver	.30	.75
GB5 Nick Barnett	.25	.60
GB6 A.J. Hawk	.30	.75
GB7 Najeh Davenport	.25	.60
GB8 Brett Favre	.60	1.50
GB9 Ahman Green	.25	.60
GB10 Bubba Franks	.20	.50
GB11 Charles Woodson	.30	.75
GB12 Greg Jennings	.50	1.25

2007 Packers Police

The Packers continued the longest running tradition in football cards by issuing a Police set for 2007. This set was again sponsored by Larry Fritsch Cards as well as a variety of regional law enforcement agencies including: Altoona Police Dept. and Campbellsport Police Dept. The cardfronts on each version are the same but the sponsorship information differs on the backs. The cards feature a green border on the front along with the year of issue and a special "25-Years" logo to celebrate the Packers Police set run. The backs were produced simply with green printing on white card stock.

COMPLETE SET (20)	4.00	10.00
1 Ted Thompson GM	.25	.60
2 Mike McCarthy CO	.25	.60
3 Brett Favre	.75	2.00
4 Aaron Rodgers	.75	2.00
5 Donald Driver	.40	1.00
6 Greg Jennings	.40	1.00
7 Chad Clifton	.25	.60
8 Mark Tauscher	.25	.60
9 Daryn Colledge	.25	.60
10 Scott Wells	.25	.60
11 Aaron Kampman	.30	.75
12 Kabeer Gbaja-Biamila	.30	.75
13 Cullen Jenkins	.25	.60
14 Ryan Pickett	.25	.60
15 Justin Harrell	.30	.75
16 A.J. Hawk	.30	.75
17 Nick Barnett	.25	.60
18 Al Harris	.25	.60
19 Charles Woodson	.40	1.00
20 Nick Collins	.25	.60

2007 Packers Topps

COMPLETE SET (12)	3.00	6.00
1 Donald Driver	.30	.75
2 Brett Favre	.60	1.50
3 AJ Hawk	.25	.60
4 Brandon Jackson	.25	.60
5 Greg Jennings	.30	.75
6 Vernand Morency	.25	.60
7 Charles Woodson	.30	.75
8 Aaron Kampman	.25	.60
9 Bubba Franks	.20	.50
10 Nick Barnett	.20	.50
11 Kabeer Gbaja-Biamila	.25	.60
12 Justin Harrell	.25	.60

2008 Packers Police

The Packers continued one of the longest running traditions in football cards by issuing a Police set again for 2008. This set was sponsored by a variety of regional law enforcement agencies including: Amery Police Dept. The cardfronts on each version are the same but the sponsorship information differs on the backs. The cards feature a green border on the front along with the year of issue. The backs were produced simply with green printing on white card stock.

COMPLETE SET (20)	4.00	8.00
1 Ted Thompson GM	.20	.50
2 Mike McCarthy CO	.20	.50
3 Aaron Rodgers	.60	1.50
4 Ryan Grant	.30	.75
5 Donald Driver	.25	.60
6 Donald Lee	.25	.60
7 Greg Jennings	.30	.75
8 Cullen Jenkins	.20	.50
9 Brandon Jackson	.25	.60
10 Al Harris	.20	.50
11 Mark Tauscher	.20	.50
12 Jason Spitz	.20	.50
13 Ryan Pickett	.20	.50
14 Aaron Kampman	.25	.60
15 John Jolly	.20	.50
16 Mason Crosby	.20	.50
17 Nick Barnett	.20	.50
18 Chad Clifton	.20	.50
19 A.J. Hawk	.25	.60
20 Charles Woodson	.30	.75

2008 Packers Topps

COMPLETE SET (12)	2.50	5.00
1 Greg Jennings	.30	.75
2 Donald Driver	.25	.60
3 Ryan Grant	.30	.75
4 Donald Lee	.25	.60
5 James Jones	.20	.50
6 Al Harris	.20	.50
7 Aaron Rodgers	.60	1.50
8 A.J. Hawk	.25	.60
9 Aaron Kampman	.25	.60
10 Nick Barnett	.20	.50
11 Brian Brohm	.40	1.00
12 Jordy Nelson	.50	1.25

2009 Packers Police

COMPLETE SET (20)	4.00	8.00
1 Ted Thompson GM	.20	.50
2 Mike McCarthy CO	.20	.50
3 Aaron Rodgers	.75	2.00
4 Donald Driver	.25	.60
5 Greg Jennings	.30	.75
6 Mason Crosby	.20	.50
7 Ryan Grant	.25	.60
8 Daryn Colledge	.20	.50
9 Chad Clifton	.20	.50
10 Jason Spitz	.20	.50
11 Cullen Jenkins	.20	.50
12 Aaron Kampman	.25	.60
13 Nick Barnett	.20	.50
14 A.J. Hawk	.25	.60
15 Al Harris	.20	.50
16 Charles Woodson	.30	.75
17 Nick Collins	.20	.50
18 Ryan Pickett	.20	.50
19 B.J. Raji	.30	.75
20 Clay Matthews	.75	2.00

2010 Packers Police

COMPLETE SET (20)	4.00	8.00
1 Ted Thompson GM	.20	.50
2 Mike McCarthy CO	.20	.50
3 Aaron Rodgers	.75	2.00
4 Donald Driver	.25	.60
5 Greg Jennings	.25	.60
6 Jermichael Finley	.25	.60
7 Ryan Grant	.25	.60
8 Mark Tauscher	.20	.50
9 Chad Clifton	.20	.50
10 Scott Wells	.20	.50
11 Cullen Jenkins	.20	.50
12 Ryan Pickett	.20	.50
13 B.J. Raji	.25	.60
14 Nick Barnett	.20	.50
15 Brandon Chillar	.20	.50
16 A.J. Hawk	.25	.60
17 Clay Matthews	.30	.75
18 Charles Woodson	.30	.75
19 Nick Collins	.20	.50
20 Mason Crosby	.20	.50

2011 Packers Panini Super Bowl XLV

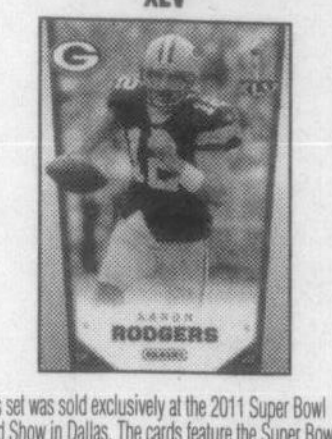

This set was sold exclusively at the 2011 Super Bowl Card Show in Dallas. The cards feature the Super Bowl XLV logo on the fronts and the backs are numbered.

COMPLETE SET (9)	8.00	20.00
1 Aaron Rodgers	2.00	5.00
2 John Kuhn	1.25	3.00
3 Charles Woodson	1.25	3.00
4 Donald Driver	1.00	2.50
5 Greg Jennings	1.00	2.50
6 James Jones	.75	2.00
7 Jordy Nelson	1.00	2.50
8 Clay Matthews	1.25	3.00
9 James Starks	1.00	2.50

2011 Packers Topps Super Bowl XLV

COMPLETE SET (27)	6.00	12.00
1 Aaron Rodgers	.75	2.00
2 Greg Jennings	.30	.75
3 James Jones	.25	.60
4 Donald Driver	.30	.75
5 Jordy Nelson	.30	.75
6 James Starks	.30	.75
7 Brandon Jackson	.25	.60
8 John Kuhn	.40	1.00
9 Andrew Quarless	.25	.60
10 Jermichael Finley	.30	.75
11 Charles Woodson	.40	1.00
12 Clay Matthews	.40	1.00
13 A.J. Hawk	.30	.75
14 B.J. Raji	.30	.75
15 Nick Collins	.25	.60
16 Tramon Williams	.40	1.00
17 Desmond Bishop	.25	.60
18 Sam Shields	.25	.60
19 Chad Clifton	.25	.60
20 Green Bay Packers Aaron Rodgers Greg Jennings	.60	1.50
21 Wild Card Weekend Tramon Williams	.30	.75
22 Divisional Playoffs Aaron Rodgers	.60	1.50
23 NFC Championship Aaron Rodgers	.60	1.50
24 NFC Championship B.J. Raji	.30	.75
25 Super Bowl XLV#Aaron Rodgers Jordy Nelson	.60	1.50
26 Super Bowl XLV Nick Collins	.25	.60
27 Super Bowl XLV Champs Aaron Rodgers Clay Matthews	.60	1.50

2011 Panini Black Friday

COMPLETE SET		
1 Aaron Rodgers	1.25	3.00
2 Tom Brady	1.00	2.50
3 Adrian Peterson	.75	2.00
4 Ray Rice	.50	1.25
5 Jamaal Charles	.50	1.25
6 Andre Johnson	.50	1.25
7 Calvin Johnson	.60	1.50

2011 Panini Black Friday Rookies

COMPLETE SET		
RC6 Cam Newton	6.00	12.00
RC7 Mark Ingram	2.00	5.00
RC8 Julio Jones	2.00	5.00
RC9 Andy Dalton	2.50	6.00
RC10 A.J. Green	2.00	5.00

2011 Panini Black Friday

BW Beanie Wells	.60	1.50
CM Colt McCoy	.60	1.50
DJ DeSean Jackson	.60	1.50
DM Donovan McNabb	.75	2.00
DW DeAngelo Williams	.60	1.50
EM Eli Manning	.75	2.00
JB Jahvid Best	.60	1.50
JJW J.J. Watt	.75	2.00
LB LeGarrette Blount	.60	1.50
MA Miles Austin	.60	1.50
MS Matt Stafford	.75	2.00
PM Peyton Manning	1.25	3.00
RW Roddy White	.60	1.50
SB Sam Bradford	.75	2.00

2011 Panini Black Friday Autographs

40 Tim Tebow Breast Cancer Awareness	60.00	100.00
BW Beanie Wells/25	10.00	25.00
CM Colt McCoy/20	10.00	25.00
JB Jahvid Best/22	10.00	25.00
JJW J.J. Watt/20	10.00	25.00
LB LeGarrette Blount/25	10.00	25.00
MF Marshall Faulk EA Madden 2011	10.00	25.00
TT Tim Tebow Everything in Between	60.00	100.00

2011 Panini Black Friday Autograph Patches

CN Cam Newton/24*	150.00	250.00

2011 Panini Black Friday Draft Day Materials

DDBG Blaine Gabbert/25*	5.00	12.00
DDCN Cam Newton/40*	15.00	40.00
DDJJ Julio Jones/20*	6.00	15.00
DDMI Mark Ingram/25*	6.00	15.00
DDMP Mike Pouncey/25*	3.00	8.00
DDPP Patrick Peterson/20*	5.00	12.00
DDAJG A.J. Green/20*	6.00	15.00

2011 Panini Black Friday Draft Day Materials Autographs

DDCJ Cameron Jordan/25	10.00	25.00
DDMD Marcell Dareus/20	12.00	30.00
DDPA Prince Amukamara/20	12.00	30.00
DDRK Ryan Kerrigan/20	15.00	40.00
DDVM Von Miller/25	15.00	40.00

2011 Panini Black Friday Pro Bowl Materials Footballs

PBAF Arian Foster/19*	6.00	15.00
PBAP Adrian Peterson/22*	10.00	25.00
PBCJ Chris Johnson/20*	6.00	15.00
PBCJ Calvin Johnson/24*	8.00	20.00
PBDB Drew Brees/20*	8.00	20.00
PBDH DeAngelo Hall/18*	5.00	12.00
PBJC Jamaal Charles/18*	6.00	15.00
PBLF Larry Fitzgerald/21*	6.00	15.00
PBMR Matt Ryan/20*	8.00	20.00
PBMV Michael Vick/23*	8.00	20.00
PBPR Philip Rivers/19*	8.00	20.00
PBRL Ray Lewis/24*	8.00	20.00

2011 Panini Black Friday Pro Bowl Materials Jerseys

PBAF Arian Foster/23*	6.00	15.00
PBAP Adrian Peterson/45*	8.00	20.00
PBDB Dwayne Bowe/24*	6.00	15.00
PBDB Drew Brees/21*	8.00	20.00
PBJC Jamaal Charles/22*	6.00	15.00
PBLF Larry Fitzgerald/24*	6.00	15.00
PBMV Michael Vick/8*		
PBRL Ray Lewis/20*	8.00	20.00
PBRW Reggie Wayne/7*		
PBSJ Steven Jackson/24*	6.00	15.00

2011 Panini Black Friday Pro Bowl Materials Pylons

PBAF Arian Foster/24*	6.00	15.00
PBAP Adrian Peterson/44*	10.00	25.00
PBCJ Calvin Johnson/44*	8.00	20.00
PBCJ Chris Johnson/23*	6.00	15.00
PBDB Drew Brees/24*	8.00	20.00
PBJC Jamaal Charles/24*	6.00	15.00
PBLF Larry Fitzgerald/24*	6.00	15.00
PBMR Matt Ryan/23*	8.00	20.00
PBMV Michael Vick/24*	8.00	20.00
PBPR Philip Rivers/24*	8.00	20.00

2011 Panini Black Friday Super Bowl Materials Pylons

*FOOTBALL/24-30: .4X TO 1X PYLON

SB1 Aaron Rodgers/32*	25.00	60.00
SB2 A.J. Hawk/23*	12.00	30.00
SB3 Ben Roethlisberger/19*	15.00	40.00
SB4 Charles Woodson/24*	15.00	40.00
SB5 Clay Matthews/23*	15.00	40.00
SB6 Greg Jennings/18*	15.00	40.00
SB7 Hines Ward/19*	15.00	40.00
SB8 James Jones/21*	10.00	25.00
SB9 James Starks/21*	12.00	30.00
SB10 Jordy Nelson/18*	12.00	30.00
SB11 Mason Crosby/20*	10.00	25.00
SB12 Mike Wallace/15*	15.00	40.00
SB13 Nick Collins/18*	10.00	25.00
SB14 Rashard Mendenhall/18*	12.00	30.00
SB15 Troy Polamalu/18*	15.00	40.00

2010 Panini Century Sports Dual Stamp Combo Dual Memorabilia

STATED PRINT RUN 50-100

1 Knute Rockne Paul Bear Bryant/100	15.00	40.00

2010 Panini Century Sports Dual Stamp Combo Dual Memorabilia Prime

STATED PRINT RUN 100 SER.#'d SETS

1 Knute Rockne Paul Bear Bryant/100	15.00	40.00

2010 Panini Century Sports Dual Stamp Combo Memorabilia

STATED PRINT RUN 49-100

1 Paul Bear Bryant Knute Rockne/100	20.00	40.00

2010 Panini Century Sports Dual Stamp Memorabilia

STATED PRINT RUN 50 SER.#'d SETS

1 Jim Thorpe Jim Thorpe/50	100.00	150.00

2010 Panini Century Sports Dual Stamp Memorabilia Prime

STATED PRINT RUN 1 SER.#'d SET
NO PRICING DUE TO SCARCITY
1 Jim Thorpe
Jim Thorpe/1

2010 Panini Century Sports Stamp Materials

STATED PRINT RUN 1-250
NO PRICING ON QTY 25 OR LESS

6A Knute Rockne/250 22c	15.00	40.00
6B Knute Rockne/250 32c	15.00	40.00

2012 Panini Father's Day

RANDOM INSERTS IN FATHER'S DAY PACKS
CRACKED ICE/25: 5X TO 12X BASE HI

15 Eli Manning	.40	1.00
16 Aaron Rodgers	.75	2.00
17 Tom Brady	.60	1.50
18 Cam Newton	.60	1.50
19 Calvin Johnson	.40	1.00
20 Maurice Jones-Drew	.30	.75
21 Arian Foster	.40	1.00
22 Andy Dalton	.40	1.00

2012 Panini Father's Day 9/11 Tribute Footballs

RANDOM INSERTS IN FATHERS DAY PACKS

AG Antonio Gates	4.00	10.00
AP Adrian Peterson	6.00	15.00
MT Mike Tolbert	4.00	10.00
PH Percy Harvin	4.00	10.00
PR Philip Rivers	5.00	12.00
RM Ryan Mathews	4.00	10.00

2012 Panini Father's Day Draft Day Jumbo Patch

RANDOM INSERTS IN FATHERS DAY PACKS

1 Blaine Gabbert	6.00	15.00
2 Mark Ingram	8.00	20.00
3 A.J. Green	8.00	20.00

2012 Panini Father's Day Elements

RANDOM INSERTS IN FATHERS DAY PACKS
CRACKED ICE/25: 5X TO 12X BASE HI

1 Tom Brady	.60	1.50
2 Brian Urlacher	.40	1.00

2012 Panini Father's Day Elite Series

RANDOM INSERTS IN FATHERS DAY PACKS
CRACKED ICE/25: 5X TO 12X BASE HI

1 Peyton Manning	.75	2.00
2 Tim Tebow	.75	2.00

2012 Panini Father's Day Legends

RANDOM INSERTS IN FATHERS DAY PACKS
CRACKED ICE/25: 5X TO 12X BASE HI

5 John Elway	.60	1.50
6 Joe Montana	.75	2.00
7 Troy Aikman	.50	1.25

2012 Panini Father's Day Manufactured Patch Autographs

RANDOM INSERTS IN FATHERS DAY PACKS

AD Andy Dalton (Bengals logo swatch)	15.00	40.00
AL Andrew Luck (NFL shield swatch)	175.00	300.00
CN Cam Newton (rookie debut swatch)	125.00	200.00
JB Justin Blackmon (NFL shield swatch)	30.00	60.00
TR Trent Richardson (NFL shield swatch)	75.00	150.00
VM Von Miller (Broncos logo swatch)	15.00	40.00

2012 Panini Father's Day Pro Bowl Jerseys

RANDOM INSERTS IN FATHERS DAY PACKS

1 Adrian Peterson	10.00	25.00
2 Larry Fitzgerald	5.00	12.00
3 Alex Mack	5.00	12.00
4 Billy Cundiff	4.00	10.00
5 Brian Waters	5.00	12.00
6 Carl Nicks	5.00	12.00
7 David Akers	5.00	12.00
8 Eric Weems	5.00	12.00
9 Jahri Evans	5.00	12.00
10 Jay Ratliff	6.00	15.00
11 Jeff Saturday	5.00	12.00
12 Mat McBriar	6.00	15.00
13 Montell Owens	5.00	12.00
14 Ovie Mughelli	5.00	12.00
15 Vonta Leach	5.00	12.00
AD Andy Dalton	8.00	20.00
PP Patrick Peterson	6.00	15.00
VM Von Miller	8.00	20.00
AJG A.J. Green	8.00	20.00

2012 Panini Father's Day Rookie of the Year Jerseys

RANDOM INSERTS IN FATHERS DAY PACKS

1 Cam Newton	25.00	50.00
2 Von Miller	8.00	20.00

2012 Panini Father's Day Rookies

STATED PRINT RUN 499 SER.#'d SETS

1 Andrew Luck	12.00	30.00
2 Robert Griffin III	12.00	30.00
3 Ryan Tannehill	4.00	10.00
4 Justin Blackmon	2.50	6.00
5 Trent Richardson	5.00	12.00
6 Michael Floyd	2.50	6.00

2012 Panini Father's Day Rookies Cracked Ice

CRACKED ICE/25: 2.5X TO 6X BASE HI
ANNOUNCED PRINT RUN 25

1 Andrew Luck	125.00	200.00
2 Robert Griffin III	125.00	200.00

2012 Panini Father's Day Season Highlights

RANDOM INSERTS IN FATHERS DAY PACKS
CRACKED ICE/25: 5X TO 12X BASE HI

4 Eli Manning	.40	1.00
5 Aaron Rodgers	.75	2.00
6 Cam Newton	.60	1.50
7 Drew Brees	.40	1.00
8 Peyton Manning	.60	1.50
9 Tim Tebow	.60	1.50

2012 Panini Father's Day Thick Portraits

RANDOM INSERTS IN FATHERS DAY PACKS
ANNOUNCED PRINT RUN 50

1 Andrew Luck	15.00	30.00
2 Robert Griffin III	10.00	25.00
4 Peyton Manning	6.00	15.00
5 Tim Tebow	5.00	12.00

2011 Panini Gold Standard

1-250 STATED PRINT RUN 299
251-286 ROOK.JSY AU PRINT RUN 325-525
EXCH EXPIRATION: 6/7/2013

1 Tom Brady	3.00	8.00
2 Peyton Manning	3.00	8.00
3 Adrian Peterson	2.50	6.00
4 Troy Polamalu	3.00	8.00
5 Andre Johnson	1.50	4.00
6 Darrelle Revis	1.50	4.00
7 Drew Brees	2.00	5.00
8 Aaron Rodgers	4.00	10.00
9 Chris Johnson	1.50	4.00
10 Larry Fitzgerald	1.50	4.00
11 Charles Woodson	2.00	5.00
12 Nnamdi Asomugha	1.50	4.00
13 Clay Matthews	2.00	5.00
14 Michael Vick	2.00	5.00
15 Antonio Gates	1.50	4.00
16 Patrick Willis	1.50	4.00
17 Roddy White	1.50	4.00
18 Arian Foster	1.50	4.00
19 Philip Rivers	2.00	5.00
20 Calvin Johnson	2.00	5.00
21 DeSean Jackson	1.50	4.00
22 Maurice Jones-Drew	1.50	4.00
23 Reggie Wayne	1.50	4.00
24 Devin Hester	2.00	5.00
25 Jamaal Charles	1.50	4.00
26 Jason Witten	2.00	5.00
27 Steven Jackson	1.50	4.00
28 Ben Roethlisberger	2.50	6.00
29 Michael Turner	1.50	4.00
30 Dwayne Bowe	1.50	4.00
31 Tony Gonzalez	1.50	4.00
32 Champ Bailey	1.50	4.00
33 Brian Urlacher	2.00	5.00
34 Wes Welker	2.00	5.00
35 Ndamukong Suh	2.00	5.00
36 Matt Ryan	2.00	5.00
37 Marques Colston	1.50	4.00
38 Asante Samuel	1.25	3.00
39 Ray Rice	1.50	4.00
40 Brandon Lloyd	1.50	4.00
41 Brandon Marshall	1.50	4.00
42 Jerod Mayo	1.25	3.00
43 Miles Austin	1.50	4.00
44 Tony Romo	2.00	5.00
45 Greg Jennings	1.50	4.00
46 Santonio Holmes	1.50	4.00
47 Dallas Clark	1.50	4.00
48 Jared Allen	1.50	4.00
49 Mike Williams	1.50	4.00
50 Josh Freeman	2.00	5.00
51 Vernon Davis	1.50	4.00
52 Joe Flacco	2.00	5.00
53 Frank Gore	1.50	4.00
54 Darren McFadden	1.50	4.00
55 Donovan McNabb	2.00	5.00
56 Ahmad Bradshaw	1.50	4.00
57 Anquan Boldin	1.50	4.00
58 Braylon Edwards	1.50	4.00
59 Carson Palmer	1.50	4.00
60 Chad Henne	1.50	4.00
61 Chris Cooley	1.50	4.00
62 Colt McCoy	1.50	4.00
63 Marcedes Lewis	1.25	3.00
64 DeAngelo Williams	1.50	4.00
65 Dez Bryant	2.00	5.00
66 Donald Driver	1.50	4.00
67 Eli Manning	2.00	5.00
68 Felix Jones	1.50	4.00
69 Greg Olsen	1.25	3.00
70 Hakeem Nicks	1.50	4.00
71 Heath Miller	1.50	4.00
72 Hines Ward	1.50	4.00
73 Jahvid Best	1.50	4.00
74 Jay Cutler	1.50	4.00
75 Jeremy Maclin	1.50	4.00
76 Jonathan Stewart	1.50	4.00
77 Knowshon Moreno	1.50	4.00
78 LaDainian Tomlinson	2.00	5.00
79 Lee Evans	1.50	4.00
80 LeSean McCoy	1.50	4.00
81 Malcom Floyd	1.50	4.00
82 Mark Sanchez	2.00	5.00
83 Matt Cassel	1.50	4.00
84 Matt Forte	1.50	4.00
85 Matt Schaub	1.50	4.00
86 Matthew Stafford	2.00	5.00
87 Michael Crabtree	1.50	4.00
88 Mike Wallace	2.00	5.00
89 Percy Harvin	1.50	4.00
90 Peyton Hillis	1.50	4.00
91 Kenny Britt	1.50	4.00
92 Rashard Mendenhall	1.50	4.00
93 Ray Lewis	2.00	5.00
94 Reggie Bush	1.50	4.00
95 Ryan Mathews	1.50	4.00
96 Sam Bradford	2.00	5.00
97 Sidney Rice	1.50	4.00
98 Steve Smith	1.50	4.00
99 Tim Tebow	4.00	10.00
100 Tony Moeaki	1.25	3.00
101 Jerry Rice	4.00	10.00
102 Jim Brown	3.00	8.00
103 Joe Montana	5.00	12.00
104 Walter Payton	5.00	12.00
105 Dick Butkus	3.00	8.00
106 Barry Sanders	4.00	10.00
107 Brett Favre	6.00	15.00
108 Dan Marino	5.00	12.00
109 John Elway	4.00	10.00
110 Emmitt Smith	4.00	10.00
111 Joe Greene	2.50	6.00
112 Ronnie Lott	2.00	5.00
113 Deacon Jones	2.00	5.00
114 Gale Sayers	2.50	6.00
115 Deion Sanders	2.50	6.00
116 Raymond Berry	2.00	5.00
117 Roger Staubach	3.00	8.00
118 Bart Starr	4.00	10.00
119 Eric Dickerson	2.00	5.00
120 Forrest Gregg	1.50	4.00
121 Marshall Faulk	2.00	5.00
122 Paul Warfield	2.00	5.00
123 Marcus Allen	2.50	6.00
124 Fran Tarkenton	2.50	6.00
125 Michael Irvin	2.50	6.00
126 Lenny Moore	2.00	5.00
127 Joe Namath	3.00	8.00
128 Bo Jackson	3.00	8.00
129 Bob Griese	2.50	6.00
130 Franco Harris	2.50	6.00
131 Jim Kelly	2.50	6.00
132 Jim Taylor	2.00	5.00
133 Len Dawson	2.50	6.00
134 Paul Hornung	2.50	6.00
135 Richard Dent	1.50	4.00
136 Sonny Jurgensen	2.00	5.00
137 Tommy McDonald	2.00	5.00
138 Y.A. Tittle	2.50	6.00
139 Alan Page	2.00	5.00
140 Bob Lilly	2.00	5.00
141 Charlie Joiner	2.00	5.00
142 Chuck Bednarik	2.00	5.00
143 Don Maynard	2.00	5.00
144 Earl Campbell	2.50	6.00
145 Frank Gifford	2.00	5.00
146 Brett Favre	6.00	15.00
147 Dan Fouts	2.50	6.00
148 Warren Moon	2.00	5.00
149 Terrell Davis	2.50	6.00
150 Troy Aikman	3.00	8.00
151 Aaron Williams RC	2.00	5.00
152 Adrian Clayborn RC	2.50	6.00
153 Ahmad Black RC	2.00	5.00
154 Akeem Ayers RC	2.00	5.00
155 Aldon Smith RC	4.00	10.00
156 Aldrick Robinson RC	1.50	4.00
157 Allen Bradford RC	2.00	5.00
158 Anthony Allen RC	1.50	4.00
159 Anthony Castonzo RC	1.50	4.00
160 Anthony Sherman RC	2.00	5.00
161 Baron Batch RC	2.50	6.00
162 Brandon Harris RC	1.50	4.00
163 Brooks Reed RC	2.50	6.00
164 Bruce Carter RC	2.50	6.00
165 Cameron Heyward RC	2.50	6.00
166 Cameron Jordan RC	2.00	5.00
167 Cecil Shorts RC	2.00	5.00
168 Charles Clay RC	2.00	5.00
169 Chris Culliver RC	2.00	5.00
170 Corey Liuget RC	1.50	4.00
171 D.J. Williams RC	2.50	6.00
172 Daniel Hardy RC	2.00	5.00
173 Danny Watkins RC	2.00	5.00
174 Da'Quan Bowers RC	2.50	6.00
175 Da'Rel Scott RC	2.00	5.00
176 David Ausberry RC	2.00	5.00
177 DeMarco Sampson RC	1.50	4.00
178 DeMarcus Van Dyke RC	2.00	5.00
179 Denarius Moore RC	3.00	8.00
180 Derek Sherrod RC	2.50	6.00
181 Dion Lewis RC	2.50	6.00
182 Dwayne Harris RC	2.50	6.00
183 Evan Royster RC	2.50	6.00
184 Gabe Carimi RC	2.50	6.00
185 Greg Jones RC	2.00	5.00
186 Greg McElroy RC	2.50	6.00
187 Greg Salas RC	2.50	6.00
188 J.J. Watt RC	3.00	8.00
189 Jabaal Sheard RC	2.50	6.00
190 Jacquizz Rodgers RC	2.50	6.00
191 Jaiquawn Jarrett RC	2.00	5.00
192 James Carpenter RC	2.50	6.00
193 Jarvis Jenkins RC	1.50	4.00
194 Jay Finley RC	2.00	5.00
195 Jeremy Kerley RC	2.50	6.00
196 Jimmy Smith RC	2.50	6.00
197 Johnny Patrick RC	2.00	5.00
198 Johnny White RC	2.00	5.00
199 Jonas Mouton RC	2.00	5.00
200 Jordan Cameron RC	2.00	5.00
201 Julius Thomas RC	2.00	5.00
202 Justin Houston RC	2.50	6.00
203 Kealoha Pilares RC	2.50	6.00
204 Kelvin Sheppard RC	2.50	6.00
205 Kris Durham RC	2.00	5.00
206 Lance Kendricks RC	2.00	5.00
207 Lee Smith RC	2.00	5.00
208 Luke Stocker RC	2.00	5.00
209 Terrelle Pryor RC	3.00	8.00
210 Marcus Gilchrist RC	1.50	4.00
211 Martez Wilson RC	2.50	6.00
212 Marvin Austin RC	2.00	5.00
213 Mason Foster RC	2.50	6.00
214 Mike Pouncey RC	2.50	6.00
215 Muhammad Wilkerson RC	2.50	6.00
216 Nate Irving RC	2.00	5.00
217 Nate Solder RC	2.50	6.00
218 Nathan Enderle RC	2.50	6.00
219 Nick Fairley RC	3.00	8.00
220 Niles Paul RC	2.50	6.00
221 Owen Marecic RC	2.50	6.00
222 Patrick Peterson RC	4.00	10.00
223 Phil Taylor RC	2.00	5.00
224 Prince Amukamara RC	2.50	6.00
225 Quinton Carter RC	1.50	4.00
226 Rahim Moore RC	2.00	5.00
227 Ras-I Dowling RC	2.50	6.00
228 Richard Gordon RC	2.00	5.00
229 Ricky Stanzi RC	3.00	8.00
230 Robert Housler RC	2.00	5.00
231 Robert Quinn RC	2.50	6.00
232 Ronald Johnson RC	2.00	5.00
233 Roy Helu RC	6.00	15.00
234 Ryan Kerrigan RC	2.50	6.00
235 Ryan Taylor RC	2.00	5.00
236 Ryan Whalen RC	2.00	5.00
237 Scotty McKnight RC	2.00	5.00
238 Shane Bannon RC	1.50	4.00
239 Doug Baldwin RC	12.50	25.00
240 Shaun Chapas RC	2.00	5.00
241 Stanley Havili RC	1.50	4.00
242 Stephen Burton RC	1.50	4.00
243 Stephen Paea RC	2.50	6.00
244 T.J. Yates RC	3.00	8.00
245 Tandon Doss RC	2.00	5.00
246 Terrell McClain RC	2.00	5.00
247 Tyler Sash RC	2.50	6.00
248 Tyrod Taylor RC	2.50	6.00
249 Tyron Smith RC	3.00	8.00
250 Virgil Green RC	2.00	5.00
251 Cam Newton JSY AU/325 RC	125.00	250.00
252 Von Miller JSY AU/525 RC	15.00	30.00
253 Marcell Dareus JSY AU/525 RC EXCH	8.00	20.00
254 A.J. Green JSY AU/325 RC	30.00	80.00
255 Julio Jones JSY AU/525 RC	30.00	80.00
256 Jake Locker JSY AU/325 RC	60.00	120.00
257 Blaine Gabbert JSY AU/325 RC	20.00	50.00
258 Christian Ponder JSY AU/325 RC	40.00	80.00
259 Jonathan Baldwin JSY AU/525 RC	10.00	25.00
260 Mark Ingram JSY AU/325 RC	30.00	80.00
261 Andy Dalton JSY AU/525 RC	50.00	120.00
262 Colin Kaepernick JSY AU/525 RC	12.00	30.00
263 Ryan Williams JSY AU/525 RC	10.00	25.00
264 Kyle Rudolph JSY AU/525 RC	8.00	20.00
265 Titus Young JSY AU/525 RC	10.00	25.00
266 Shane Vereen JSY AU/525 RC	8.00	20.00
267 Mikel Leshoure JSY AU/525 RC	10.00	25.00
268 Torrey Smith JSY AU/525 RC	15.00	40.00
269 Greg Little JSY AU/525 RC	8.00	20.00
270 Daniel Thomas JSY AU/525 RC EXCH	8.00	20.00
271 Randall Cobb JSY AU/525 RC	10.00	25.00
272 DeMarco Murray JSY AU/525 RC	30.00	80.00
273 Stevan Ridley JSY AU/525 RC EXCH	8.00	20.00
274 Ryan Mallett JSY AU/325 RC	20.00	50.00
275 Austin Pettis JSY AU/525 RC	6.00	15.00
276 Leonard Hankerson JSY AU/525 RC	8.00	20.00
277 Vincent Brown JSY AU/525 RC	8.00	20.00
278 Jerrel Jernigan JSY AU/525 RC	6.00	15.00
279 Alex Green JSY AU/525 RC	8.00	20.00
280 Clyde Gates JSY AU/525 RC	8.00	20.00
281 Kendall Hunter JSY AU/525 RC	10.00	25.00
282 Delone Carter JSY AU/525 RC	6.00	15.00
283 Taiwan Jones JSY AU/525 RC	8.00	20.00
284 Bilal Powell JSY AU/525 RC	5.00	12.00
285 Jamie Harper JSY AU/525 RC EXCH	8.00	20.00
286 Jordan Todman JSY AU/525 RC	5.00	12.00

2011 Panini Gold Standard Black Gold

UNPRICED BLACK GOLD PRINT RUN 10

2011 Panini Gold Standard Platinum Gold

*1-100 VETS/25: 1X TO 2.5X BASIC CARDS
*101-150 LEGEND/25: 1X TO 2.5X BASIC CARDS
*151-250 ROOKIE/25: 1X TO 2.5X BASIC CARDS
STATED PRINT RUN 25 SER.#'d SETS

2011 Panini Gold Standard Autographs Silver

UNPRICED VET/LEG AU PRINT RUN 1-5
151-250 ROOKIE AU PRINT RUN 299-499
*GOLD ROOKIE/25: .8X TO 2X SILVER AU/499
*GOLD ROOKIE/25: .6X TO 1.5X SILVER AU/299

151 Aaron Williams/499	4.00	10.00
152 Adrian Clayborn/499	5.00	12.00
153 Ahmad Black/499	4.00	10.00
154 Akeem Ayers/499	4.00	10.00
156 Aldrick Robinson/499	5.00	12.00
157 Allen Bradford/499	4.00	10.00
158 Anthony Allen/499	3.00	8.00
159 Anthony Castonzo/499	3.00	8.00
162 Brandon Harris/499	3.00	8.00
165 Cameron Heyward/499	5.00	12.00
166 Cameron Jordan/499	4.00	10.00
167 Cecil Shorts/499	4.00	10.00
170 Corey Liuget/499	3.00	8.00
171 D.J. Williams/499	5.00	12.00
174 Da'Quan Bowers/499	5.00	12.00
175 Da'Rel Scott/499	4.00	10.00
179 Denarius Moore/499	12.00	30.00
181 Dion Lewis/499	5.00	12.00
182 Dwayne Harris/499	5.00	12.00
183 Evan Royster/499	6.00	15.00
185 Greg Jones/499	4.00	10.00
186 Greg McElroy/499	5.00	12.00
187 Greg Salas/499	5.00	12.00
188 J.J. Watt/499	6.00	15.00
190 Jacquizz Rodgers/499	5.00	12.00
195 Jeremy Kerley/499	5.00	12.00
196 Jimmy Smith/499	5.00	12.00
198 Johnny White/499	4.00	10.00
200 Jordan Cameron/499	4.00	10.00
201 Julius Thomas/499	4.00	10.00
202 Justin Houston/499	5.00	12.00
203 Kealoha Pilares/499	8.00	20.00
205 Kris Durham/499	4.00	10.00
206 Lance Kendricks/499	4.00	10.00
208 Luke Stocker/499	4.00	10.00
209 Terrelle Pryor/299	20.00	40.00

211 Martez Wilson/499 5.00 12.00
220 Niles Paul/499 5.00 12.00
223 Phil Taylor/499 4.00 10.00
224 Prince Amukamara/499 6.00 15.00
225 Quinton Carter/499 3.00 8.00
226 Rahim Moore/499 4.00 10.00
229 Ricky Stanzi/499 8.00 20.00
232 Ronald Johnson/499 4.00 10.00
233 Roy Helu/499 10.00 25.00
234 Ryan Kerrigan/499 5.00 12.00
236 Ryan Whalen/499 4.00 10.00
237 Scotty McKnight/499 4.00 10.00
241 Stanley Havili/499 3.00 8.00
242 Stephen Burton/499 4.00 10.00
243 Stephen Paea/499 5.00 12.00
244 T.J. Yates/499 15.00 30.00
245 Tandon Doss/499 4.00 10.00
247 Tyler Sash/499 5.00 12.00
248 Tyrod Taylor/499 5.00 12.00
249 Tyron Smith/499 6.00 15.00

2011 Panini Gold Standard Gold Leaf Rookies

STATED PRINT RUN 299 SER.#'d SETS
UNPRICED 14K PRINT RUN 6-10
UNPRICED AUTO PRINT RUN 5
1 Cam Newton 8.00 20.00
2 Von Miller 2.00 5.00
3 Marcell Dareus 1.50 4.00
4 A.J. Green 3.00 8.00
5 Julio Jones 3.00 8.00
6 Jake Locker 4.00 10.00
7 Blaine Gabbert 2.50 6.00
8 Christian Ponder 3.00 8.00
9 Jonathan Baldwin 1.50 4.00
10 Mark Ingram 3.00 8.00
11 Andy Dalton 4.00 10.00
12 Colin Kaepernick 2.00 5.00
13 Ryan Williams 2.00 5.00
14 Kyle Rudolph 1.50 4.00
15 Titus Young 2.00 5.00
16 Shane Vereen 1.50 4.00
17 Mikel Leshoure 1.50 4.00
18 Torrey Smith 2.00 5.00
19 Greg Little 1.50 4.00
20 Daniel Thomas 1.50 4.00
21 Randall Cobb 2.00 5.00
22 DeMarco Murray 3.00 8.00
23 Stevan Ridley 1.50 4.00
24 Ryan Mallett 3.00 8.00
25 Austin Pettis 1.25 3.00
26 Leonard Hankerson 1.50 4.00
27 Vincent Brown 1.50 4.00
28 Jerrel Jernigan 1.25 3.00
29 Alex Green 1.50 4.00
30 Clyde Gates 1.25 3.00
31 Kendall Hunter 1.50 4.00
32 Delone Carter 1.25 3.00
33 Taiwan Jones 1.50 4.00
34 Bilal Powell 1.00 2.50
35 Jamie Harper 1.50 4.00
36 Jordan Todman 1.00 2.50

2011 Panini Gold Standard Gold Leaf Rookies Materials

STATED PRINT RUN 299 SER.#'d SETS
*PRIME/25: .8X TO 2X BASIC JSY/299
1 Cam Newton 12.00 30.00
2 Von Miller 4.00 10.00
3 Marcell Dareus 2.50 6.00
4 A.J. Green 5.00 12.00
5 Julio Jones 5.00 12.00
6 Jake Locker 6.00 15.00
7 Blaine Gabbert 4.00 10.00
8 Christian Ponder 5.00 12.00
9 Jonathan Baldwin 2.50 6.00
10 Mark Ingram 5.00 12.00
11 Andy Dalton 6.00 15.00
12 Colin Kaepernick 3.00 8.00
13 Ryan Williams 3.00 8.00
14 Kyle Rudolph 2.50 6.00
15 Titus Young 3.00 8.00
16 Shane Vereen 2.50 6.00
17 Mikel Leshoure 2.50 6.00
18 Torrey Smith 3.00 8.00
19 Greg Little 2.50 6.00
20 Daniel Thomas 2.50 6.00
21 Randall Cobb 3.00 8.00
22 DeMarco Murray 5.00 12.00
23 Stevan Ridley 2.50 6.00
24 Ryan Mallett 5.00 12.00
25 Austin Pettis 2.00 5.00
26 Leonard Hankerson 2.50 6.00
27 Vincent Brown 2.50 6.00
28 Jerrel Jernigan 2.00 5.00
29 Alex Green 3.00 8.00
30 Clyde Gates 2.00 5.00
31 Kendall Hunter 2.50 6.00
32 Delone Carter 2.00 5.00
33 Taiwan Jones 2.50 6.00
34 Bilal Powell 1.50 4.00
35 Jamie Harper 2.50 6.00
36 Jordan Todman 1.50 4.00

2011 Panini Gold Standard Gold Leaf Rookies Materials Autographs

STATED PRINT RUN 50 SER.#'d SETS
1 Cam Newton 90.00 150.00
2 Von Miller 15.00 40.00
4 A.J. Green 40.00 80.00
5 Julio Jones 40.00 80.00
6 Jake Locker 50.00 100.00
7 Blaine Gabbert 20.00 50.00
8 Christian Ponder 30.00 60.00
9 Jonathan Baldwin 8.00 20.00
10 Mark Ingram 30.00 60.00
11 Andy Dalton 40.00 80.00
12 Colin Kaepernick 12.00 30.00
13 Ryan Williams 10.00 25.00
14 Kyle Rudolph 8.00 20.00
15 Titus Young 10.00 25.00
16 Shane Vereen 8.00 20.00
17 Mikel Leshoure 8.00 20.00
18 Torrey Smith 12.00 30.00
19 Greg Little
20 Daniel Thomas 8.00 20.00
21 Randall Cobb 10.00 25.00
22 DeMarco Murray 30.00 60.00
24 Ryan Mallett 20.00 40.00
26 Leonard Hankerson 8.00 20.00
27 Vincent Brown 8.00 20.00
28 Jerrel Jernigan 6.00 15.00
29 Alex Green 8.00 20.00
33 Taiwan Jones 8.00 20.00
34 Bilal Powell 5.00 12.00
35 Jamie Harper 8.00 20.00
36 Jordan Todman 5.00 12.00

2011 Panini Gold Standard Gold Leaf Rookies Materials Autographs Prime

*PRIME/25: .6X TO 1.5X JSY AU/50
PRIME PRINT RUN 25 SER.#'d SETS
1 Cam Newton/25 150.00 250.00
3 Marcell Dareus/25 12.00 30.00
30 Clyde Gates/25 10.00 25.00

2011 Panini Gold Standard Gold Leaf Stars

STATED PRINT RUN 299 SER.#'d SETS
1 Tom Brady 2.50 6.00
2 Philip Rivers 1.50 4.00
3 Aaron Rodgers 2.50 6.00
4 Michael Vick 1.50 4.00
5 Ben Roethlisberger 1.50 4.00
6 Chris Johnson 1.25 3.00
7 Joe Flacco 1.50 4.00
8 Matt Cassel 1.25 3.00
9 Adrian Peterson 2.00 5.00
10 Peyton Manning 2.50 6.00
11 Matt Ryan 1.50 4.00
12 Brandon Lloyd 1.25 3.00
13 Drew Brees 1.50 4.00
14 Dwayne Bowe 1.25 3.00
15 David Garrard 1.25 3.00
16 Roddy White 1.25 3.00
17 Jay Cutler 1.25 3.00
18 Andre Johnson 1.25 3.00
19 Eli Manning 1.50 4.00
20 Reggie Wayne 1.25 3.00
21 Arian Foster 1.25 3.00
22 Larry Fitzgerald 1.25 3.00
23 Maurice Jones-Drew 1.25 3.00
24 Greg Jennings 1.25 3.00
25 Matt Schaub 1.25 3.00

2011 Panini Gold Standard Gold Leaf Stars Materials

STATED PRINT RUN 49-99
*PRIME/25: .6X TO 1.5X BASIC JSY/49-99
1 Tom Brady/99 8.00 20.00
2 Philip Rivers/49 5.00 12.00
3 Aaron Rodgers/49 12.00 30.00
4 Michael Vick/99 5.00 12.00
6 Chris Johnson/49 4.00 10.00
7 Joe Flacco/49 5.00 12.00
8 Matt Cassel/99 4.00 10.00
9 Adrian Peterson/49 6.00 15.00
10 Peyton Manning/99 8.00 20.00
11 Matt Ryan/99 5.00 12.00
12 Brandon Lloyd/99 4.00 10.00
13 Drew Brees/49 5.00 12.00
14 Dwayne Bowe/49 4.00 10.00
15 David Garrard/49 4.00 10.00
16 Roddy White/49 4.00 10.00
17 Jay Cutler/99 4.00 10.00
18 Andre Johnson/49 4.00 10.00
19 Eli Manning/99 5.00 12.00
20 Reggie Wayne/49 4.00 10.00
22 Larry Fitzgerald/99 4.00 10.00
23 Maurice Jones-Drew/99 4.00 10.00
25 Matt Schaub/99 4.00 10.00

2011 Panini Gold Standard Gold Reserve Materials

STATED PRINT RUN 99-299
*PRIME/18-25: .8X TO 2X BASIC JSY
*PRIME/18-25: .6X TO 1.5X BASIC JSY
1 Sam Bradford/299 4.00 10.00
2 Percy Harvin/150 3.00 8.00
3 Josh Freeman/99 5.00 12.00
5 Tim Tebow/99 12.00 30.00
6 Colt McCoy/99 4.00 10.00
7 Darrelle Revis/299 3.00 8.00
8 Dez Bryant/99 5.00 12.00
9 Malcom Floyd/299 3.00 8.00
10 Hakeem Nicks/299 3.00 8.00
11 Jerod Mayo/99 4.00 10.00
13 Jeremy Maclin/299 3.00 8.00
14 Vernon Davis/299 3.00 8.00
15 Darren McFadden/299 3.00 8.00
16 Patrick Willis/299 3.00 8.00
17 Mark Sanchez/299 4.00 10.00
18 Michael Crabtree/99 4.00 10.00
19 DeSean Jackson/299 3.00 8.00
20 Matthew Stafford/299 4.00 10.00

2011 Panini Gold Standard Gold Reserve Materials Autographs

STATED PRINT RUN 10-25
UNPRICED PRIME AU PRINT RUN 5-10
3 Josh Freeman/25 20.00 50.00
6 Colt McCoy/25 15.00 40.00
7 Darrelle Revis/25 15.00 40.00
9 Malcom Floyd/25
10 Hakeem Nicks/25 15.00 40.00
14 Vernon Davis/25 15.00 40.00
16 Patrick Willis/25 20.00 50.00
18 Michael Crabtree/25 15.00 40.00
19 DeSean Jackson/25 15.00 40.00
20 Matthew Stafford/25 40.00 80.00

2011 Panini Gold Standard Gold Rush

STATED PRINT RUN 299 SER.#'d SETS
1 Arian Foster 1.25 3.00
2 Jamaal Charles 1.25 3.00
3 Michael Turner 1.25 3.00
4 Maurice Jones-Drew 1.25 3.00
5 Rashard Mendenhall 1.25 3.00
6 Adrian Peterson 2.00 5.00
7 Chris Johnson 1.25 3.00
8 Steven Jackson 1.25 3.00
9 Ahmad Bradshaw 1.25 3.00
10 Ray Rice 1.25 3.00
11 Peyton Hillis 1.25 3.00
12 Darren McFadden 1.25 3.00
13 Cedric Benson 1.25 3.00
14 LeSean McCoy 1.25 3.00
15 BenJarvus Green-Ellis 1.25 3.00
16 Matt Forte 1.25 3.00
17 LaDainian Tomlinson 1.50 4.00
18 Frank Gore 1.25 3.00
19 Felix Jones 1.25 3.00
20 Knowshon Moreno 1.25 3.00
21 LeGarrette Blount 1.25 3.00
22 DeAngelo Williams 1.25 3.00
23 Ryan Torain 1.00 2.50
24 Ryan Mathews 1.25 3.00
25 Michael Vick 1.50 4.00

2011 Panini Gold Standard Gold Rush Materials

STATED PRINT RUN 49-99
*PRIME/20-25: .8X TO 2X BASIC JSY/49-99
1 Arian Foster/49 4.00 10.00
2 Jamaal Charles/49 3.00 8.00
3 Michael Turner/99 3.00 8.00
4 Maurice Jones-Drew/99 3.00 8.00
5 Rashard Mendenhall/49 3.00 8.00
6 Adrian Peterson/49 5.00 12.00
7 Chris Johnson/49 3.00 8.00
8 Steven Jackson/99 3.00 8.00
9 Ahmad Bradshaw/49 3.00 8.00
10 Ray Rice/99 3.00 8.00
11 Peyton Hillis/99 3.00 8.00
12 Darren McFadden/99 3.00 8.00
13 Cedric Benson/99 3.00 8.00
14 LeSean McCoy/99 3.00 8.00
15 BenJarvus Green-Ellis/99 5.00 12.00
16 Matt Forte/99 4.00 10.00
17 LaDainian Tomlinson/49 4.00 10.00
18 Frank Gore/99 3.00 8.00
19 Felix Jones/99 3.00 8.00
20 Knowshon Moreno/99 3.00 8.00
22 DeAngelo Williams/99 3.00 8.00
23 Ryan Torain/99 2.50 6.00
24 Ryan Mathews/49 3.00 8.00
25 Michael Vick/99 4.00 10.00

2011 Panini Gold Standard Golden Age

STATED PRINT RUN 299 SER.#'d SETS
1 Jim Brown 2.50 6.00
2 Deacon Jones 1.50 4.00
3 Gale Sayers 2.00 5.00
4 Raymond Berry 1.50 4.00
5 Bart Starr 3.00 8.00
6 Forrest Gregg 1.25 3.00
7 Paul Warfield 1.50 4.00
8 Fran Tarkenton 2.00 5.00
9 Lenny Moore 1.50 4.00
10 Joe Namath 2.50 6.00
11 Bob Griese 2.00 5.00
12 Walter Payton 4.00 10.00
13 Dick Butkus 2.50 6.00
14 Joe Greene 2.00 5.00
15 Franco Harris 2.00 5.00
16 Jim Taylor 1.50 4.00
17 Len Dawson 2.00 5.00
18 Sid Luckman 1.50 4.00
19 Sammy Baugh 2.00 5.00
20 Don Maynard 1.50 4.00
21 Chuck Bednarik 1.50 4.00
22 Jim Thorpe 2.50 6.00
23 Frank Gifford 1.50 4.00
24 Red Grange 3.00 6.00
25 Dutch Clark 1.25 3.00

2011 Panini Gold Standard Golden Age Materials

STATED PRINT RUN 25-99
*PRIME/25: .8X TO 2X BASIC JSY/99
*PRIME/25: .6X TO 1.5X BASIC JSY/25
1 Jim Brown/25 10.00 25.00
2 Deacon Jones/25 6.00 15.00
3 Gale Sayers/99 6.00 15.00
4 Raymond Berry/99 5.00 12.00
5 Bart Starr/99 10.00 25.00
6 Forrest Gregg/99 6.00 15.00
7 Paul Warfield/99 5.00 12.00
8 Fran Tarkenton/99 6.00 15.00
9 Lenny Moore/99 5.00 12.00
10 Joe Namath/5
11 Bob Griese/99 6.00 15.00
12 Walter Payton/99 12.00 30.00
13 Dick Butkus/99 8.00 20.00
14 Joe Greene/99 6.00 15.00
15 Franco Harris/99 6.00 15.00
17 Len Dawson/25 8.00 20.00
18 Sid Luckman/30 8.00 20.00
19 Sammy Baugh/25 8.00 20.00
20 Don Maynard/99 5.00 12.00
22 Jim Thorpe/25 60.00 120.00

2011 Panini Gold Standard Golden Anniversary

STATED PRINT RUN 299 SER.#'d SETS
1 Tom Brady 2.50 6.00
2 Wes Welker 1.50 4.00
3 BenJarvus Green-Ellis 1.25 3.00
4 Jerod Mayo 1.00 2.50
5 Curtis Martin 1.50 4.00
6 Adrian Peterson 2.00 5.00
7 Brett Favre 4.00 10.00
8 Jared Allen 1.25 3.00
9 Percy Harvin 1.25 3.00
10 Fran Tarkenton 2.00 5.00
11 Antonio Gates 1.25 3.00
12 Philip Rivers 1.50 4.00
13 Vincent Jackson 1.25 3.00
14 Ryan Mathews 1.25 3.00
15 Dan Fouts 2.00 5.00
16 Darrelle Revis 1.25 3.00
17 Joe Namath 2.50 6.00
18 Mark Sanchez 1.50 4.00
19 Santonio Holmes 1.25 3.00
20 Braylon Edwards 1.25 3.00
21 Charles Woodson 1.50 4.00
22 Darren McFadden 1.25 3.00
23 Nnamdi Asomugha 1.25 3.00
24 Jerry Rice 3.00 8.00
25 Rolando McClain 1.00 2.50
26 Dwayne Bowe 1.25 3.00
27 Jamaal Charles 1.25 3.00
28 Len Dawson 2.00 5.00
29 Priest Holmes 1.25 3.00
30 Matt Cassel 1.25 3.00
31 Earl Campbell 2.00 5.00
32 Warren Moon 1.50 4.00
33 Chris Johnson 1.25 3.00
34 Eddie George 1.50 4.00
35 Kenny Britt 1.25 3.00
36 Brandon Lloyd 1.25 3.00
37 John Elway 3.00 8.00
38 Knowshon Moreno 1.25 3.00
39 Terrell Davis 2.00 5.00
40 Tim Tebow 3.00 8.00
41 C.J. Spiller 1.25 3.00
42 Jim Kelly 2.00 5.00
43 Lee Evans 1.25 3.00
44 Thurman Thomas 2.00 5.00
45 Bruce Smith 1.50 4.00
46 Troy Aikman 2.50 6.00
47 Emmitt Smith 3.00 8.00
48 Miles Austin 1.25 3.00
49 Tony Romo 1.50 4.00
50 Dez Bryant 1.50 4.00

2011 Panini Gold Standard Golden Anniversary Materials

STATED PRINT RUN 25-99
*PRIME/20-25: .6X TO 1.5X BASIC JSY/49-99
*PRIME/25: .5X TO 1.2X BASIC JSY/25
1 Tom Brady/99 8.00 20.00
2 Wes Welker/99 5.00 12.00
3 BenJarvus Green-Ellis/99 6.00 15.00
4 Jerod Mayo/49 3.00 8.00
5 Curtis Martin/10
6 Adrian Peterson/49 6.00 15.00
7 Brett Favre/99 20.00 40.00
8 Jared Allen/49 5.00 12.00
9 Percy Harvin/99 4.00 10.00
10 Fran Tarkenton/99 6.00 15.00
11 Antonio Gates/99 4.00 10.00
12 Philip Rivers/99 6.00 15.00
14 Ryan Mathews/49 4.00 10.00
15 Dan Fouts/99 6.00 15.00
16 Darrelle Revis/99 4.00 10.00
17 Joe Namath/25 12.00 30.00
18 Mark Sanchez/99 5.00 12.00
19 Santonio Holmes/99 4.00 10.00
20 Braylon Edwards/99 4.00 10.00
22 Darren McFadden/99 4.00 10.00
23 Nnamdi Asomugha/49 5.00 12.00
24 Jerry Rice/99 10.00 25.00
26 Dwayne Bowe/49 4.00 10.00
27 Jamaal Charles/49 4.00 10.00
28 Len Dawson/99 6.00 15.00
29 Priest Holmes/99 4.00 10.00
30 Matt Cassel/99 4.00 10.00
31 Earl Campbell/25 8.00 20.00
32 Warren Moon/99 5.00 12.00
33 Chris Johnson/49 4.00 10.00
34 Eddie George/99 5.00 12.00
35 Kenny Britt/99 4.00 10.00
36 Brandon Lloyd/99 4.00 10.00
37 John Elway/99 10.00 25.00
38 Knowshon Moreno/99 4.00 10.00
39 Terrell Davis/25 8.00 20.00
40 Tim Tebow/10 12.00 30.00
41 C.J. Spiller/49 4.00 10.00
42 Jim Kelly/99 6.00 15.00
43 Lee Evans/49 4.00 10.00
44 Thurman Thomas/99 6.00 15.00
45 Bruce Smith/99 5.00 12.00
46 Troy Aikman/99 8.00 20.00
47 Emmitt Smith/99 10.00 25.00
48 Miles Austin/99 4.00 10.00
49 Tony Romo/99 5.00 12.00
50 Dez Bryant/49 5.00 12.00

2011 Panini Gold Standard Golden Anniversary 1961 Autographs

AUTO STATED PRINT RUN 3-99
4 Boyd Dowler/99 12.00 30.00

2011 Panini Gold Standard Golden Anniversary 1961 Materials

STATED PRINT RUN 25-50
*PRIME/25: .6X TO 1.5X BASIC JSY/50
*PRIME/25: .5X TO 1.2X BASIC JSY/20-25
1 Paul Hornung/25 8.00 20.00
2 Y.A. Tittle/50 6.00 15.00
3 Bart Starr/25 12.00 30.00
6 Fran Tarkenton/25 8.00 20.00
7 Jim Brown/20 10.00 25.00
8 Tommy McDonald/25 6.00 15.00
10 Hugh McElhenny/50

2011 Panini Gold Standard Golden Anniversary 1961 Materials Autographs

JERSEY AUTO PRINT RUN 10-25
UNPRICED PRIME AU PRINT RUN 1-10
3 Bart Starr/15 125.00 200.00
6 Fran Tarkenton/15 30.00 60.00
10 Hugh McElhenny/25 25.00 50.00

2011 Panini Gold Standard Gridiron Gold Materials

STATED PRINT RUN 30-299
*PRIME/25: .8X TO 2X BASIC JSY/299
*PRIME/25: .6X TO 1.5X BASIC JSY/55-99
*PRIME/25: .5X TO 1.2X BASIC JSY/30
1 Calvin Johnson/299 4.00 10.00
2 Antonio Gates/299 3.00 8.00
3 Tony Romo/299 4.00 10.00
4 DeMarcus Ware/299 4.00 10.00
5 Miles Austin/299 3.00 8.00
6 Tom Brady/99 8.00 20.00
7 Marques Colston/299 3.00 8.00
8 Philip Rivers/299 4.00 10.00
9 Jason Witten/299 4.00 10.00
10 Charles Woodson/30 12.00 30.00
11 Clay Matthews/99 6.00 15.00
12 Brian Urlacher/299 5.00 12.00
13 Adrian Peterson/99 6.00 15.00
14 Troy Polamalu/299 8.00 20.00
16 Drew Brees/99 5.00 12.00
17 Jared Allen/99 5.00 12.00
18 Chris Johnson/99 4.00 10.00
19 Hines Ward/55 6.00 15.00
20 Peyton Manning/299 6.00 15.00

2011 Panini Gold Standard Gridiron Gold Materials Autographs

JERSEY AUTO PRINT RUN 5-20
19 Hines Ward/20 50.00 100.00

2011 Panini Gold Standard Hall of Gold Materials

STATED PRINT RUN 25-299
*PRIME/25: .8X TO 2X JSY/140-299
*PRIME/25: .6X TO 1.5X JSY/50-99
*PRIME/25: .5X TO 1.2X JSY/25-35
1 Emmitt Smith/299 8.00 20.00
2 Marshall Faulk/25 6.00 15.00
3 Deion Sanders/140 6.00 15.00
4 Jerry Rice/55 12.00 30.00
5 Richard Dent/299 4.00 10.00
6 Joe Montana/299 10.00 25.00
7 Barry Sanders/35 12.00 30.00
8 Dan Marino/299 10.00 25.00
9 John Elway/299 8.00 20.00
11 Michael Irvin/220 5.00 12.00
12 Jim Kelly/299 5.00 12.00
13 Roger Staubach/99 8.00 20.00
14 Sonny Jurgensen/50 5.00 12.00
15 Y.A. Tittle/50 6.00 15.00
16 Joe Namath/25 10.00 25.00
17 Jim Brown/25 10.00 25.00
18 Warren Moon/299 4.00 10.00
19 Thurman Thomas/150 5.00 12.00
20 Troy Aikman/299 6.00 15.00

2011 Panini Gold Standard Hall of Gold Materials Autographs

STATED PRINT RUN 3-25
3 Deion Sanders/25 40.00 80.00
7 Barry Sanders/25
8 Dan Marino/25 75.00 150.00
10 Eric Dickerson/25 25.00 50.00

2010 Panini Gridiron Gear

COMP.SET w/o RC's (150) 8.00 20.00
251-285 ROOK.JSY AU PRINT RUN 164-326
1 Chris Wells .25 .60
2 Larry Fitzgerald .30 .75
3 Steve Breaston .20 .50
4 Tim Hightower .20 .50
5 Curtis Lofton .20 .50
6 Matt Ryan .30 .75
7 Michael Turner .20 .50
8 Roddy White .25 .60
9 Anquan Boldin .25 .60
10 Joe Flacco .30 .75
11 Ray Lewis .30 .75
12 Ray Rice .25 .60
13 T.J. Houshmandzadeh .25 .60
14 Willis McGahee .25 .60
15 Lee Evans .25 .60
16 Marshawn Lynch .25 .60
17 Roscoe Parrish .20 .50
18 Ryan Fitzpatrick .30 .75
19 DeAngelo Williams .25 .60
20 Dwayne Jarrett .20 .50
21 Jonathan Stewart .25 .60
22 Steve Smith .25 .60
23 Brian Urlacher .30 .75
24 Devin Aromashodu .20 .50
25 Devin Hester .30 .75
26 Jay Cutler .30 .75
27 Julius Peppers .25 .60
28 Matt Forte .25 .60
29 Carson Palmer .25 .60
30 Cedric Benson .25 .60
31 Chad Ochocinco .25 .60
32 Terrell Owens .30 .75
33 Benjamin Watson .20 .50
34 Jerome Harrison .20 .50
35 Josh Cribbs .30 .75
36 Mohamed Massaquoi .25 .60
37 DeMarcus Ware .25 .60
38 Felix Jones .25 .60
39 Jason Witten .30 .75
40 Miles Austin .30 .75
41 Tony Romo .40 1.00
42 Brandon Lloyd .25 .60
43 Eddie Royal .20 .50
44 Knowshon Moreno .25 .60
45 Kyle Orton .25 .60
46 Brandon Pettigrew .20 .50
47 Calvin Johnson .30 .75
48 Matthew Stafford .30 .75
49 Nate Burleson .20 .50
50 Aaron Rodgers .60 1.50
51 Clay Matthews .30 .75
52 Donald Driver .25 .60
53 Greg Jennings .25 .60
54 Jermichael Finley .25 .60
55 Andre Johnson .25 .60
56 Arian Foster .25 .60
57 Kevin Walter .25 .60
58 Matt Schaub .25 .60
59 Owen Daniels .20 .50
60 Austin Collie .25 .60
61 Dallas Clark .25 .60
62 Joseph Addai .25 .60
63 Peyton Manning .50 1.25
64 Reggie Wayne .25 .60
65 David Garrard .25 .60
66 Marcedes Lewis .20 .50
67 Maurice Jones-Drew .25 .60
68 Mike Sims-Walker .25 .60
69 Chris Chambers .25 .60
70 Dwayne Bowe .25 .60
71 Jamaal Charles .25 .60
72 Matt Cassel .25 .60
73 Thomas Jones .25 .60
74 Anthony Fasano .20 .50
75 Brandon Marshall .25 .60
76 Brian Hartline .25 .60
77 Chad Henne .25 .60
78 Ronnie Brown .25 .60
79 Adrian Peterson .50 1.25
80 Bernard Berrian .20 .50
81 Brett Favre .75 2.00
82 Percy Harvin .30 .75
83 Sidney Rice .25 .60
84 Visanthe Shiancoe .25 .60
85 Brandon Meriweather .20 .50
86 Fred Taylor .25 .60
87 Randy Moss .30 .75
88 Tom Brady .50 1.25
89 Wes Welker .30 .75
90 Devery Henderson .20 .50
91 Drew Brees .30 .75
92 Marques Colston .25 .60
93 Pierre Thomas .25 .60
94 Reggie Bush .30 .75
95 Robert Meachem .25 .60
96 Ahmad Bradshaw .25 .60
97 Brandon Jacobs .25 .60
98 Eli Manning .30 .75
99 Hakeem Nicks .25 .60
100 Steve Smith USC .25 .60
101 Braylon Edwards .25 .60
102 Darrelle Revis .25 .60
103 LaDainian Tomlinson .30 .75
104 Mark Sanchez .30 .75
105 Shonn Greene .25 .60
106 Darren McFadden .25 .60
107 Darrius Heyward-Bey .25 .60
108 Bruce Gradkowski .20 .50
109 Louis Murphy .25 .60
110 Zach Miller .25 .60
111 DeSean Jackson .25 .60
112 Jeremy Maclin .25 .60
113 Kevin Kolb .25 .60
114 LeSean McCoy .25 .60
115 Michael Vick UER .40 1.00
(Vikings incorrectly listed on back)
116 Ben Roethlisberger .30 .75
117 Heath Miller .25 .60
118 Hines Ward .25 .60
119 Mike Wallace .25 .60
120 Rashard Mendenhall .25 .60
121 Troy Polamalu .30 .75
122 Antonio Gates .25 .60
123 Darren Sproles .25 .60
124 Malcom Floyd .25 .60
125 Philip Rivers .30 .75
126 Frank Gore .25 .60
127 Michael Crabtree .30 .75
128 Patrick Willis .25 .60
129 Vernon Davis .25 .60
130 John Carlson .20 .50
131 Leon Washington .25 .60
132 Matt Hasselbeck .20 .50
133 Mike Williams USC .50 1.25
134 Danny Amendola .30 .75
135 James Laurinaitis .25 .60
136 Mark Clayton .20 .50
137 Steven Jackson .25 .60
138 Cadillac Williams .25 .60
139 Josh Freeman .30 .75
140 Kellen Winslow Jr. .25 .60
141 Reggie Brown .20 .50
142 Bo Scaife .20 .50
143 Chris Johnson .30 .75
144 Justin Gage .20 .50
145 Nate Washington .20 .50
146 Vince Young .20 .50
147 Chris Cooley .25 .60
148 Clinton Portis .25 .60
149 Donovan McNabb .30 .75
150 Santana Moss .25 .60
151 Aaron Hernandez RC 2.00 5.00
152 Andrew Quarless RC 1.25 3.00
153 Anthony Dixon RC 1.25 3.00
154 Anthony McCoy RC 1.00 2.50
155 Antonio Brown RC 2.00 5.00
156 Blair White RC 1.25 3.00
157 Brandon Banks RC 4.00 10.00
158 Brandon Graham RC 1.00 2.50
159 Brandon Spikes RC 1.25 3.00
160 Brian Price RC 1.25 3.00
161 Brody Eldridge RC 1.25 3.00
162 Bryan Bulaga RC 1.25 3.00
163 Carlos Dunlap RC 1.25 3.00
164 Carlton Mitchell RC 1.00 2.50
165 Chris Cook RC 1.25 3.00
166 Chris Gronkowski RC 1.25 3.00
167 Chris Ivory RC 1.50 4.00
168 Chris McGaha RC .75 2.00
169 Clay Harbor RC 1.25 3.00
170 Corey Wootton RC 1.00 2.50
171 Dan LeFevour RC 1.25 3.00
172 Dan Williams RC 1.00 2.50
173 Danario Alexander RC 1.25 3.00
174 Daryl Washington RC 1.00 2.50
175 David Gettis RC 1.25 3.00
176 David Nelson RC 1.25 3.00
177 David Reed RC 1.00 2.50
178 Deji Karim RC 1.25 3.00
179 Dennis Pitta RC 1.25 3.00
180 Derrick Morgan RC 1.00 2.50
181 Devin McCourty RC 1.25 3.00
182 Dezmon Briscoe RC 1.00 2.50
183 Dominique Curry RC 1.00 2.50
184 Dominique Franks RC .75 2.00
185 Donald Jones RC 1.25 3.00
186 Dorin Dickerson RC .75 2.00
187 Duke Calhoun RC 1.00 2.50
188 Earl Thomas RC 1.25 3.00
189 Ed Dickson RC 1.25 3.00
190 Ed Wang RC 1.25 3.00
191 Everson Griffen RC 1.25 3.00
192 Fendi Onobun RC 1.00 2.50
193 Garrett Graham RC 1.00 2.50
194 Jacoby Ford RC 1.25 3.00
195 Jared Odrick RC 1.25 3.00
196 Jason Pierre-Paul RC 2.00 5.00
197 Jason Worilds RC 1.25 3.00
198 Javier Arenas RC 1.25 3.00
199 Jeff Cumberland RC 1.00 2.50
200 Jeremy Horne RC 1.00 2.50
201 Jeremy Williams RC .75 2.00
202 Jerry Hughes RC 1.25 3.00
203 Jim Dray RC 1.00 2.50
204 Jimmy Graham RC 2.50 6.00
205 Joe Haden RC 1.25 3.00
206 Joe Webb RC 1.25 3.00
207 John Conner RC 1.25 3.00
208 John Skelton RC 1.25 3.00
209 Joique Bell RC 1.00 2.50
210 Kareem Jackson RC 1.25 3.00
211 Keiland Williams RC 1.25 3.00
212 Koith Toston RC 1.25 3.00
213 Kerry Meier RC 1.00 2.50
214 Koa Misi RC 1.25 3.00
215 Kyle Williams RC 1.25 3.00
216 Kyle Wilson RC 1.25 3.00
217 LeGarrette Blount RC 2.00 5.00
218 Lamarr Houston RC 1.25 3.00
219 Logan Paulsen RC 1.00 2.50
220 Marc Mariani RC 1.25 3.00
221 Marlon Moore RC 1.25 3.00
222 Max Hall RC 1.25 3.00
223 Max Komar RC 1.25 3.00
224 Michael Hoomanawanui RC 1.25 3.00
225 Michael Palmer RC 1.00 2.50
226 Mickey Shuler RC 1.25 3.00
227 Morgan Burnett RC 1.25 3.00
228 Nate Allen RC 1.25 3.00
229 Nate Byham RC 1.00 2.50
230 NaVorro Bowman RC 1.25 3.00
231 Patrick Robinson RC 1.25 3.00
232 Perrish Cox RC 1.00 2.50
233 Preston Parker RC 1.00 2.50
234 Ricky Sapp RC 1.00 2.50
235 Riley Cooper RC 1.25 3.00
236 Roberto Wallace RC 1.00 2.50
237 Russell Okung RC 1.25 3.00
238 Rusty Smith RC 1.25 3.00
239 Sean Lee RC 1.25 3.00
240 Sean Weatherspoon RC 1.25 3.00
241 Sergio Kindle RC 1.25 3.00
242 Stephen Williams RC 1.25 3.00
243 T.J. Ward RC 1.25 3.00
244 Taylor Mays RC 1.25 3.00
245 Thaddeus Lewis RC 1.00 2.50
246 Tony Moeaki RC 1.25 3.00
247 Tony Pike RC 1.25 3.00
248 Trent Williams RC 1.25 3.00
249 Tyson Alualu RC 1.00 2.50
250 Victor Cruz RC 4.00 10.00
251 Sam Bradford JSY AU/244 RC 40.00 100.00
252 Ndamukong Suh JSY AU/196 RC 20.00 50.00
253 Gerald McCoy JSY AU/209 RC 8.00 20.00
254 Eric Berry JSY AU/199 RC 8.00 20.00
255 Rolando McClain JSY AU/197 RC 8.00 20.00
256 C.J. Spiller JSY AU/228 RC 12.00 30.00
257 Ryan Mathews JSY AU/263 RC 15.00 40.00
258 Jermaine Gresham JSY AU/167 RC 10.00 25.00
259 Demaryius Thomas JSY AU/173 RC 10.00 25.00
260 Dez Bryant JSY AU/293 RC 25.00 60.00
261 Tim Tebow JSY AU/259 RC 60.00 120.00
262 Jahvid Best JSY AU/204 RC 12.00 30.00
263 Dexter McCluster JSY AU/185 RC 8.00 20.00
264 Arrelious Benn JSY AU/186 RC 8.00 20.00
265 Rob Gronkowski JSY AU/164 RC 25.00 60.00
266 Jimmy Clausen JSY AU/223 RC 8.00 20.00
267 Toby Gerhart JSY AU/171 RC 8.00 20.00
268 Ben Tate JSY AU/205 RC 10.00 25.00
269 Montario Hardesty JSY AU/186 RC 8.00 20.00
270 Golden Tate JSY AU/326 RC 8.00 20.00
271 Damian Williams JSY AU/206 RC 8.00 20.00
272 Brandon LaFell JSY AU/188 RC 8.00 20.00
273 Emmanuel Sanders JSY AU/182 RC 8.00 20.00
274 Jordan Shipley JSY AU/177 RC 8.00 20.00
275 Colt McCoy JSY AU/255 RC 12.00 30.00
276 Eric Decker JSY AU/167 RC 10.00 25.00
277 Andre Roberts JSY AU/207 RC 8.00 20.00
278 Armanti Edwards JSY AU/183 RC 8.00 20.00
279 Taylor Price JSY AU/104 RC 8.00 20.00
280 Mardy Gilyard JSY AU/173 RC 8.00 20.00
281 Mike Williams JSY AU/170 RC 15.00 40.00
282 Marcus Easley JSY AU/178 RC 6.00 15.00
283 Joe McKnight JSY AU/167 RC 8.00 20.00
284 Mike Kafka JSY AU/169 RC 8.00 20.00
285 Jonathan Dwyer JSY AU/269 RC 8.00 20.00

2010 Panini Gridiron Gear Gold O's

*VETS: 2.5X TO 6X BASIC CARDS
*ROOKIES: .8X TO 2X BASIC CARDS
STATED PRINT RUN 100 SER.#'d SETS

2010 Panini Gridiron Gear Gold X's

*VETS: 2.5X TO 6X BASIC CARDS
*ROOKIES: .8X TO 2X BASIC CARDS
STATED PRINT RUN 100 SER.#'d SETS

2010 Panini Gridiron Gear Platinum O's

*VETS: 5X TO 12X BASIC CARDS
*ROOKIES: 1.5X TO 4X BASIC CARDS
STATED PRINT RUN 25 SER.#'d SETS

2010 Panini Gridiron Gear Platinum X's

*VETS: 5X TO 12X BASIC CARDS
*ROOKIES: 1.5X TO 4X BASIC CARDS
STATED PRINT RUN 25 SER.#'d SETS

2010 Panini Gridiron Gear Silver O's

*VETS: 2X TO 5X BASIC CARDS
*ROOKIES: .6X TO 1.5X BASIC CARDS
STATED PRINT RUN 250 SER.#'d SETS

2010 Panini Gridiron Gear Silver X's

*VETS: 2X TO 5X BASIC CARDS
*ROOKIES: .6X TO 1.5X BASIC CARDS
STATED PRINT RUN 250 SER.#'d SETS

2010 Panini Gridiron Gear Autographs Gold X's

STATED PRINT RUN 99-299
EXCH EXPIRATION: 6/1/2012
151 Aaron Hernandez/299 8.00 20.00
153 Anthony Dixon/199 5.00 12.00
154 Anthony McCoy/199 4.00 10.00
155 Antonio Brown/199 15.00 30.00
156 Blair White/99 6.00 15.00
157 Brandon Banks/99 15.00 30.00
158 Brandon Graham/199 4.00 10.00
159 Brandon Spikes/299 5.00 12.00
162 Bryan Bulaga/299 5.00 12.00
164 Carlton Mitchell/99 5.00 12.00
167 Chris Ivory/99 15.00 40.00
168 Chris McGaha/99 4.00 10.00
170 Corey Wootton/299 4.00 10.00
171 Dan LeFevour/99 6.00 15.00
173 Danario Alexander/299 5.00 12.00
175 David Gettis/99 6.00 15.00
176 David Nelson/99 6.00 15.00
177 David Reed/99 5.00 12.00
178 Deji Karim/99 6.00 15.00
179 Dennis Pitta/99 6.00 15.00
180 Derrick Morgan/299 4.00 10.00
181 Devin McCourty/299 5.00 12.00
183 Dominique Curry/99 5.00 12.00
184 Dominique Franks/299 3.00 8.00
185 Donald Jones/99 6.00 15.00
188 Earl Thomas/299 5.00 12.00
189 Ed Dickson/299 5.00 12.00
190 Ed Wang/99 6.00 15.00
191 Everson Griffen/299 5.00 12.00
192 Fendi Onobun/99 5.00 12.00
193 Garrett Graham/299 4.00 10.00
194 Jacoby Ford/299 6.00 15.00
196 Jason Pierre-Paul/299 12.50 25.00
197 Jason Worilds/299 5.00 12.00
198 Javier Arenas/99 6.00 15.00
201 Jeremy Williams/99 4.00 10.00
202 Jerry Hughes/299 5.00 12.00
204 Jimmy Graham/299 20.00 40.00
205 Joe Haden/299 5.00 12.00
206 Joe Webb/99 6.00 15.00
207 John Conner/99 6.00 15.00
208 John Skelton/299 5.00 12.00
209 Joique Bell/99 5.00 12.00
211 Keiland Williams/99 6.00 15.00
213 Kerry Meier/99 5.00 12.00
214 Koa Misi/99 6.00 15.00
217 LeGarrette Blount/99 30.00 60.00
218 Lamarr Houston/99 6.00 15.00
220 Marc Mariani/99 6.00 15.00
221 Marlon Moore/99 6.00 15.00
222 Max Hall/99 6.00 15.00
223 Max Komar/99 EXCH 6.00 15.00
224 Michael Hoomanawanui/99 6.00 15.00
225 Michael Palmer/99 5.00 12.00
226 Mickey Shuler/99 6.00 15.00
227 Morgan Burnett/299 5.00 12.00
228 Nate Allen/299 5.00 12.00
231 Patrick Robinson/299 5.00 12.00
232 Perrish Cox/299 4.00 10.00
233 Preston Parker/99 5.00 12.00
234 Ricky Sapp/299 4.00 10.00
235 Riley Cooper/99 6.00 15.00
238 Rusty Smith/99 6.00 15.00
239 Sean Lee/299 5.00 12.00
240 Sean Weatherspoon/299 5.00 12.00
241 Sergio Kindle/299 5.00 12.00
242 Stephen Williams/99 6.00 15.00
243 T.J. Ward/99 6.00 15.00
244 Taylor Mays/299 5.00 12.00
245 Thaddeus Lewis/99 5.00 12.00
246 Tony Moeaki/99 10.00 25.00
247 Tony Pike/99 6.00 15.00
249 Tyson Alualu/99 5.00 12.00
250 Victor Cruz/99 50.00 100.00

2010 Panini Gridiron Gear Autographs Platinum O's

1-149 UNPRICED PLAT.PRINT RUN 1
COMMON ROOKIE 6.00 15.00
ROOKIE SEMISTARS 8.00 20.00
ROOKIE UNL.STARS 10.00 25.00
151-250 ROOKIE PLAT.PRINT RUN 25
EXCH EXPIRATION: 6/1/2012
151 Aaron Hernandez/25 15.00 40.00
152 Andrew Quarless/25 10.00 25.00
155 Antonio Brown/25 20.00 40.00
157 Brandon Banks/25 12.00 30.00
159 Brandon Spikes/25 10.00 25.00
167 Chris Ivory/25 25.00 60.00
169 Clay Harbor/25 10.00 25.00
176 David Nelson/25 10.00 25.00
181 Devin McCourty/25 10.00 25.00
187 Duke Calhoun/25 8.00 20.00
194 Jacoby Ford/25 12.00 30.00
196 Jason Pierre-Paul/25 20.00 50.00
204 Jimmy Graham/25 40.00 80.00
211 Keiland Williams/25 10.00 25.00
217 LeGarrette Blount/25
220 Marc Mariani/25 10.00 25.00
222 Max Hall/25 10.00 25.00
223 Max Komar/25 EXCH 10.00 25.00
226 Mickey Shuler/25 10.00 25.00
246 Tony Moeaki/25 15.00 40.00
248 Trent Williams/25 EXCH 10.00 25.00
250 Victor Cruz/25 75.00 150.00

2010 Panini Gridiron Gear Crash Course

*GOLD/100: .6X TO 1.5X BASIC INSERTS
*PLATINUM/25: .8X TO 2X BASIC INSERTS
*SILVER/250: .5X TO 1.2X BASIC INSERTS
1 Ray Lewis 1.00 2.50
Dustin Keller
2 Darrelle Revis 1.00 2.50
Randy Moss
3 Peyton Manning 1.50 4.00
Mario Williams

4 Eli Manning 1.00 2.50
DeMarcus Ware
5 Aaron Rodgers 1.25 3.00
Jared Allen
6 Chad Ochocinco 1.00 2.50
Troy Polamalu
7 Larry Fitzgerald 1.00 2.50
Patrick Willis
8 Tom Brady 1.50 4.00
Jason Taylor
9 Jason Witten 1.00 2.50
Aaron Ross
10 Brian Orakpo .75 2.00
LeSean McCoy

2010 Panini Gridiron Gear Crash Course Jerseys

STATED PRINT RUN 100-250
*PRIME/25: .8X TO 2X BASIC JSY
1 Ray Lewis/250 5.00 12.00
Dustin Keller
2 Darrelle Revis/250 4.00 10.00
Randy Moss
3 Peyton Manning/250 6.00 15.00
Mario Williams
4 Eli Manning/250 4.00 10.00
DeMarcus Ware
5 Aaron Rodgers/100 6.00 15.00
Jared Allen
6 Chad Ochocinco/100 6.00 15.00
Troy Polamalu
7 Larry Fitzgerald/100 5.00 12.00
Patrick Willis
9 Jason Witten/250 4.00 10.00
Aaron Ross
10 Brian Orakpo/250 3.00 8.00
LeSean McCoy

2010 Panini Gridiron Gear Gamebreakers

*GOLD/100: .6X TO 1.5X BASIC INSERTS
*SILVER/250: .5X TO 1.2X BASIC INSERTS
*PLATINUM/25: .8X TO 2X BASIC INSERTS
1 Larry Fitzgerald 1.00 2.50
2 Dallas Clark .75 2.00
3 Arian Foster .75 2.00
4 Adrian Peterson 1.50 4.00
5 Visanthe Shiancoe .75 2.00
6 Chris Johnson 1.00 2.50
7 Reggie Wayne .75 2.00
8 Brent Celek .75 2.00
9 Peyton Manning 1.50 4.00
10 DeAngelo Williams .75 2.00
11 Darren McFadden .75 2.00
12 Aaron Rodgers 2.00 5.00
13 Miles Austin 1.00 2.50
14 Maurice Jones-Drew .75 2.00
15 Jamaal Charles .75 2.00
16 Ronnie Brown .75 2.00
17 Matt Forte .75 2.00
18 Drew Brees 1.00 2.50
19 Calvin Johnson 1.00 2.50
20 Ray Lewis 1.00 2.50
21 Wes Welker 1.00 2.50
22 DeSean Jackson .75 2.00
23 Percy Harvin 1.00 2.50
24 Michael Crabtree 1.00 2.50
25 Vernon Davis .75 2.00
26 Devery Henderson .60 1.50
27 Devin Hester 1.00 2.50
28 Vince Young .60 1.50
29 Frank Gore .75 2.00
30 Rashard Mendenhall .75 2.00

2010 Panini Gridiron Gear Gamebreakers Jerseys

STATED PRINT RUN 10-250
1 Larry Fitzgerald/100 4.00 10.00
4 Adrian Peterson/250 6.00 15.00
5 Visanthe Shiancoe/250 3.00 8.00
6 Chris Johnson/75 4.00 10.00
8 Brent Celek/250 3.00 8.00
9 Peyton Manning/250 6.00 15.00
11 Darren McFadden/250 3.00 8.00
12 Aaron Rodgers/100 6.00 15.00
14 Maurice Jones-Drew/250 3.00 8.00
15 Jamaal Charles/250 3.00 8.00
17 Matt Forte/250 3.00 8.00
18 Drew Brees/145 4.00 10.00
19 Calvin Johnson/180 4.00 10.00
20 Ray Lewis/150 5.00 12.00
22 DeSean Jackson/250 3.00 8.00
24 Michael Crabtree/35 5.00 12.00
25 Vernon Davis/100 3.00 8.00
27 Devin Hester/175 4.00 10.00
28 Vince Young/250 2.50 6.00
29 Frank Gore/35 4.00 10.00

2010 Panini Gridiron Gear Gamebreakers Jerseys Combos

STATED PRINT RUN 12-100
1 Larry Fitzgerald/100 4.00 10.00
2 Dallas Clark/44 4.00 10.00
4 Adrian Peterson/100 6.00 15.00
5 Visanthe Shiancoe/100 3.00 8.00
6 Chris Johnson/100 4.00 10.00
8 Brent Celek/100 3.00 8.00
9 Peyton Manning/100 6.00 15.00
10 DeAngelo Williams/15 5.00 12.00
11 Darren McFadden/100 3.00 8.00
13 Miles Austin/20 6.00 15.00
14 Maurice Jones-Drew/100 3.00 8.00
15 Jamaal Charles/100 3.00 8.00
17 Matt Forte/100 3.00 8.00
18 Drew Brees/100 4.00 10.00
19 Calvin Johnson/100 4.00 10.00
20 Ray Lewis/100 5.00 12.00
22 DeSean Jackson/100 3.00 8.00
25 Vernon Davis/50 4.00 10.00
27 Devin Hester/100 4.00 10.00
28 Vince Young/100 2.50 6.00

2010 Panini Gridiron Gear Gamebreakers Jerseys Prime

PRIME STATED PRINT RUN 11-50
4 Adrian Peterson/50 10.00 25.00
5 Visanthe Shiancoe/50 5.00 12.00
6 Chris Johnson/50 6.00 15.00
8 Brent Celek/50 5.00 12.00
9 Peyton Manning/50 10.00 25.00
11 Darren McFadden/50 5.00 12.00
14 Maurice Jones-Drew/50 5.00 12.00
15 Jamaal Charles/50 5.00 12.00
16 Ronnie Brown/50 5.00 12.00
17 Matt Forte/50 5.00 12.00
19 Calvin Johnson/50 6.00 15.00
20 Ray Lewis/25 10.00 25.00
21 Wes Welker/50 6.00 15.00
22 DeSean Jackson/50 5.00 12.00
23 Percy Harvin/50 6.00 15.00
25 Vernon Davis/50 5.00 12.00
26 Devery Henderson/50 4.00 10.00
27 Devin Hester/50 6.00 15.00
30 Rashard Mendenhall/50 5.00 12.00

2010 Panini Gridiron Gear Gamebreakers Jerseys Combos Prime

COMBO PRIME PRINT RUN 5-25
4 Adrian Peterson/25 12.00 30.00
5 Visanthe Shiancoe/25 6.00 15.00
6 Chris Johnson/25 8.00 20.00
8 Brent Celek/25 6.00 15.00
9 Peyton Manning/25 12.00 30.00
11 Darren McFadden/25 6.00 15.00
13 Miles Austin/15 8.00 20.00
14 Maurice Jones-Drew/25 6.00 15.00
15 Jamaal Charles/25 6.00 15.00
16 Ronnie Brown/25 6.00 15.00
17 Matt Forte/25 6.00 15.00
19 Calvin Johnson/25 8.00 20.00
20 Ray Lewis/25 10.00 25.00
21 Wes Welker/25 8.00 20.00
22 DeSean Jackson/25 6.00 15.00
23 Percy Harvin/25 8.00 20.00
25 Vernon Davis/25 6.00 15.00
26 Devery Henderson/25 5.00 12.00
27 Devin Hester/25 8.00 20.00
30 Rashard Mendenhall/25 6.00 15.00

2010 Panini Gridiron Gear Jerseys O's

STATED PRINT RUN 30-199
2 Larry Fitzgerald/199 4.00 10.00
11 Ray Lewis/30 6.00 15.00
14 Willis McGahee/199 3.00 8.00
15 Lee Evans/65 3.00 8.00
23 Brian Urlacher/100 4.00 10.00
26 Jay Cutler/199 4.00 10.00
28 Matt Forte/199 3.00 8.00
29 Carson Palmer/199 3.00 8.00
30 Cedric Benson/199 3.00 8.00
37 DeMarcus Ware/199 3.00 8.00
38 Felix Jones/199 3.00 8.00
41 Tony Romo/199 5.00 12.00
44 Knowshon Moreno/130 3.00 8.00
45 Kyle Orton/100 3.00 8.00
50 Aaron Rodgers/100 5.00 12.00
58 Matt Schaub/100 3.00 8.00
62 Joseph Addai/199 3.00 8.00
63 Peyton Manning/199 6.00 15.00
65 David Garrard/30 4.00 10.00
67 Maurice Jones-Drew/199 3.00 8.00
68 Mike Sims-Walker/50 4.00 10.00
70 Dwayne Bowe/199 3.00 8.00
71 Jamaal Charles/199 3.00 8.00
72 Matt Cassel/199 3.00 8.00
79 Adrian Peterson/199 6.00 15.00
80 Bernard Berrian/199 2.50 6.00
81 Brett Favre/199 10.00 25.00
83 Sidney Rice/199 3.00 8.00
86 Fred Taylor/100 3.00 8.00
88 Tom Brady/199 6.00 15.00
92 Marques Colston/199 3.00 8.00
95 Robert Meachem/125 3.00 8.00
97 Brandon Jacobs/199 3.00 8.00
101 Braylon Edwards/199 3.00 8.00
102 Darrelle Revis/55 4.00 10.00
106 Darren McFadden/199 3.00 8.00
109 Louis Murphy/199 3.00 8.00
111 DeSean Jackson/199 3.00 8.00
113 Kevin Kolb/199 3.00 8.00
117 Heath Miller/199 3.00 8.00
122 Antonio Gates/199 3.00 8.00
123 Darren Sproles/150 3.00 8.00
125 Philip Rivers/199 4.00 10.00
128 Patrick Willis/199 3.00 8.00
129 Vernon Davis/199 3.00 8.00
142 Bo Scaife/199 2.50 6.00
143 Chris Johnson/100 4.00 10.00
146 Vince Young/199 2.50 6.00
148 Clinton Portis/70 3.00 8.00

2010 Panini Gridiron Gear Jerseys Prime

STATED PRINT RUN 1-50
2 Larry Fitzgerald/30 6.00 15.00
6 Matt Ryan/40 6.00 15.00
8 Roddy White/50 5.00 12.00
11 Ray Lewis/50 8.00 20.00
14 Willis McGahee/30 5.00 12.00
15 Lee Evans/50 5.00 12.00
21 Jonathan Stewart/50 5.00 12.00
23 Brian Urlacher/50 6.00 15.00
25 Devin Hester/50 6.00 15.00
26 Jay Cutler/50 6.00 15.00
28 Matt Forte/50 5.00 12.00
29 Carson Palmer/50 5.00 12.00
30 Cedric Benson/50 5.00 12.00
31 Chad Ochocinco/50 5.00 12.00
37 DeMarcus Ware/50 5.00 12.00
38 Felix Jones/50 5.00 12.00
39 Jason Witten/50 6.00 15.00
41 Tony Romo/50 8.00 20.00
43 Eddie Royal/50 4.00 10.00
44 Knowshon Moreno/50 5.00 12.00
47 Calvin Johnson/50 6.00 15.00
52 Donald Driver/50 5.00 12.00
62 Joseph Addai/50 5.00 12.00
63 Peyton Manning/50 10.00 25.00
65 David Garrard/50 5.00 12.00
67 Maurice Jones-Drew/50 5.00 12.00
68 Mike Sims-Walker/50 5.00 12.00
70 Dwayne Bowe/50 5.00 12.00
71 Jamaal Charles/50 5.00 12.00
72 Matt Cassel/50 5.00 12.00
78 Ronnie Brown/50 5.00 12.00
79 Adrian Peterson/50 10.00 25.00
80 Bernard Berrian/50 4.00 10.00
81 Brett Favre/25 20.00 50.00
83 Sidney Rice/50 5.00 12.00
84 Visanthe Shiancoe/50 5.00 12.00
87 Randy Moss/25 8.00 20.00
88 Tom Brady/50 10.00 25.00
89 Wes Welker/50 6.00 15.00
92 Marques Colston/50 5.00 12.00
95 Robert Meachem/45 5.00 12.00
97 Brandon Jacobs/50 5.00 12.00
101 Braylon Edwards/50 5.00 12.00
102 Darrelle Revis/50 5.00 12.00
104 Mark Sanchez/25 8.00 20.00
106 Darren McFadden/50 5.00 12.00
109 Louis Murphy/50 5.00 12.00
111 DeSean Jackson/50 5.00 12.00
113 Kevin Kolb/50 5.00 12.00
114 LeSean McCoy/50 5.00 12.00
117 Heath Miller/50 5.00 12.00
120 Rashard Mendenhall/40 5.00 12.00
122 Antonio Gates/50 5.00 12.00
123 Darren Sproles/50 5.00 12.00
125 Philip Rivers/50 6.00 15.00
128 Patrick Willis/50 5.00 12.00
129 Vernon Davis/50 5.00 12.00
137 Steven Jackson/50 5.00 12.00
138 Cadillac Williams/50 5.00 12.00
142 Bo Scaife/50 4.00 10.00
143 Chris Johnson/50 6.00 15.00
147 Chris Cooley/50 5.00 12.00
148 Clinton Portis/50 5.00 12.00
150 Santana Moss/50 5.00 12.00

2010 Panini Gridiron Gear NFL Gridiron Signatures

STATED PRINT RUN 14-30
1 Aaron Rodgers/15 150.00 250.00
2 Reggie Wayne/14 15.00 40.00
3 Felix Jones/15 15.00 40.00
4 Donald Driver/15 20.00 50.00
5 Calvin Johnson/15 20.00 50.00
6 Fran Tarkenton/15 20.00 50.00
7 Rashard Mendenhall/15 15.00 40.00
8 Brandon Jacobs/15 15.00 40.00
9 Barry Sanders/15 75.00 135.00
10 Thurman Thomas/15 20.00 50.00
11 Jim Kelly/15 20.00 50.00
12 Cadillac Williams/15 15.00 40.00
13 LeSean McCoy/15 15.00 40.00
14 Michael Turner/15 12.00 30.00
15 Darren Sproles/30 20.00 50.00
16 Chris Cooley/15 20.00 50.00
17 Kevin Kolb/15 15.00 40.00
18 Maurice Jones-Drew/15 15.00 40.00
19 Ryan Grant/15 15.00 40.00
20 Tony Gonzalez/15 15.00 40.00
23 Junior Seau/15 40.00 80.00

2010 Panini Gridiron Gear NFL Nation

*GOLD/100: .6X TO 1.5X BASIC INSERTS
*PLATINUM/25: .8X TO 2X BASIC INSERTS
*SILVER/250: .5X TO 1.2X BASIC INSERTS
1 Steve Smith .75 2.00
2 Donald Driver .75 2.00
3 Kyle Orton .75 2.00
4 Cadillac Williams .75 2.00
5 Ray Rice .75 2.00
6 Matt Schaub .75 2.00
7 Brian Urlacher 1.00 2.50
8 Chad Ochocinco .75 2.00
9 Shonn Greene .75 2.00
10 Andre Johnson .75 2.00
11 Jay Cutler 1.00 2.50
12 Michael Turner .60 1.50
13 Eli Manning 1.00 2.50
14 Dwayne Bowe .75 2.00
15 Antonio Gates .75 2.00
16 Pierre Thomas .75 2.00
17 Matt Ryan 1.00 2.50
18 Jason Witten 1.00 2.50
19 Brett Favre 2.50 6.00
20 Tony Gonzalez .75 2.00
21 LaDainian Tomlinson 1.00 2.50
22 Knowshon Moreno .75 2.00
23 Patrick Willis .75 2.00
24 Donovan McNabb 1.00 2.50
25 Ben Roethlisberger 1.00 2.50
26 Lee Evans .75 2.00
27 Steven Jackson .75 2.00
28 LeSean McCoy .75 2.00
29 Reggie Bush 1.00 2.50
30 Matthew Stafford 1.00 2.50

2010 Panini Gridiron Gear NFL Nation Jerseys

STATED PRINT RUN 15-250
3 Kyle Orton/245 3.00 8.00
6 Matt Schaub/230 3.00 8.00
7 Brian Urlacher/85 4.00 10.00
11 Jay Cutler/250 4.00 10.00
14 Dwayne Bowe/250 3.00 8.00
15 Antonio Gates/250 3.00 8.00
17 Matt Ryan/35 5.00 12.00
19 Brett Favre/250 10.00 25.00
22 Knowshon Moreno/80 3.00 8.00
23 Patrick Willis/100 3.00 8.00
26 Lee Evans/100 3.00 8.00
28 LeSean McCoy/15 5.00 12.00
30 Matthew Stafford/85 4.00 10.00

2010 Panini Gridiron Gear NFL Nation Jerseys Combos

STATED PRINT RUN 50-100
3 Kyle Orton/100 3.00 8.00
6 Matt Schaub/100 3.00 8.00
7 Brian Urlacher/100 4.00 10.00
11 Jay Cutler/100 4.00 10.00
14 Dwayne Bowe/100 3.00 8.00
15 Antonio Gates/100 3.00 8.00
17 Matt Ryan/100 4.00 10.00
19 Brett Favre/100 10.00 25.00
22 Knowshon Moreno/100 3.00 8.00
23 Patrick Willis/100 3.00 8.00
26 Lee Evans/100 3.00 8.00
28 LeSean McCoy/50 4.00 10.00

2010 Panini Gridiron Gear NFL Nation Jerseys Combos Prime

STATED PRINT RUN 10-25
2 Donald Driver/25 6.00 15.00
4 Cadillac Williams/25 6.00 15.00
7 Brian Urlacher/25 8.00 20.00
8 Chad Ochocinco/25 6.00 15.00
11 Jay Cutler/25 8.00 20.00
14 Dwayne Bowe/25 6.00 15.00
15 Antonio Gates/25 6.00 15.00
18 Jason Witten/25 8.00 20.00
22 Knowshon Moreno/25 6.00 15.00
23 Patrick Willis/25 6.00 15.00
26 Lee Evans/25 6.00 15.00
27 Steven Jackson/25 6.00 15.00
28 LeSean McCoy/25 6.00 15.00

2010 Panini Gridiron Gear NFL Nation Jerseys Prime

PRIME STATED PRINT RUN 10-50
2 Donald Driver/50 5.00 12.00
4 Cadillac Williams/50 5.00 12.00
7 Brian Urlacher/50 6.00 15.00
8 Chad Ochocinco/50 5.00 12.00
11 Jay Cutler/50 6.00 15.00
14 Dwayne Bowe/50 5.00 12.00
15 Antonio Gates/50 5.00 12.00
18 Jason Witten/50 6.00 15.00
19 Brett Favre/20 30.00 60.00
22 Knowshon Moreno/50 5.00 12.00
23 Patrick Willis/50 5.00 12.00
26 Lee Evans/50 5.00 12.00
27 Steven Jackson/50 5.00 12.00
28 LeSean McCoy/50 5.00 12.00

2010 Panini Gridiron Gear NFL Nation Jerseys Autographs

JERSEY AUTO PRINT RUN 5-15
EXCH EXPIRATION: 6/1/2012
1 Steve Smith/15 12.00 30.00
2 Donald Driver/15
3 Kyle Orton/15 12.00 30.00
6 Matt Schaub/15 12.00 30.00
12 Michael Turner/15 10.00 25.00
17 Matt Ryan/15 30.00 60.00
20 Tony Gonzalez/15 15.00 40.00
28 LeSean McCoy/15 12.00 30.00

2010 Panini Gridiron Gear NFL Pro Gridiron Signatures

STATED PRINT RUN 10-50
EXCH EXPIRATION: 6/1/2012
1 Jim Brown/25 40.00 80.00
2 Joe Namath/25 50.00 100.00
3 Floyd Little/25 15.00 40.00
4 John Randle/25 25.00 50.00
5 Michael Strahan/25 15.00 40.00
6 Rickey Jackson/25 15.00 40.00
9 Don Maynard/25 12.00 30.00
13 Jim Otto/50 12.00 30.00
14 Joe Klecko/50 12.00 30.00
15 Jimmy Orr/50 10.00 25.00
20 William Perry/50 12.00 30.00
21 Bernard Berrian/25
23 Pierre Garcon/25 15.00 40.00
24 Chris Wells/25 12.00 30.00
25 Austin Collie/25 15.00 40.00
26 Daryle Lamonica/50 12.00 30.00
27 Ed McCaffrey/25 15.00 40.00
28 Bill Bates/50 12.00 30.00
29 Charley Taylor/50 12.00 30.00
30 Keyshawn Johnson/25 15.00 40.00
31 L.C. Greenwood/25 15.00 40.00
32 Leroy Kelly/50 12.00 30.00
33 Lydell Mitchell/50 10.00 25.00
34 Willie Lanier/25 12.00 30.00
35 Pete Retzlaff/50
36 Rod Smith/25 15.00 40.00
37 Russ Grimm/50 15.00 40.00
39 Todd Christensen/50 10.00 25.00
41 Craig James/25 15.00 40.00
42 Heath Miller/25 12.00 30.00
43 Roddy White/25 12.00 30.00
45 Cedric Benson/25
46 Darren Sproles/25 15.00 40.00
48 Josh Cribbs/25 15.00 40.00
49 Jeremy Maclin/25 12.00 30.00
50 Ryan Grant/25 15.00 40.00

2010 Panini Gridiron Gear Plates and Patches

STATED PRINT RUN 50 SER.#'d SETS
1 Hines Ward 6.00 15.00
2 Carson Palmer 6.00 15.00
3 Randy Moss 8.00 20.00
4 Adrian Peterson 12.00 30.00
5 Troy Polamalu 12.00 30.00
6 Maurice Jones-Drew 6.00 15.00
7 Clinton Portis 6.00 15.00
8 Mark Sanchez 8.00 20.00
9 Chris Cooley 6.00 15.00
10 Brett Favre 20.00 50.00
11 Tony Romo 10.00 25.00
12 Chris Johnson 8.00 20.00
13 Philip Rivers 8.00 20.00
14 Sidney Rice 8.00 20.00
15 Vernon Davis 6.00 15.00

2010 Panini Gridiron Gear Rookie Gridiron Gems Jerseys Prime

STATED PRINT RUN 50 SER.#'d SETS
*BASE JSY/25: .4X TO 1X PRIME/50
*COMBO/25: .5X TO 1.2X PRIME/50
*COMBO PRIME/50: .5X TO 1.2X PRM/50
*JUMBO/25: .5X TO 1.2X PRIME/50
*JUMBO PRIME/10: 1X TO 2.5X PRM/50
*RETAIL/50: .4X TO 1X PRIME/50
*TRIO/50: .5X TO 1.2X PRIME/50
*TRIO PRIME/50: .6X TO 1.5X PRIME/50
251 Sam Bradford 10.00 25.00
252 Ndamukong Suh 5.00 12.00
253 Gerald McCoy 2.50 6.00
254 Eric Berry 2.50 6.00
255 Rolando McClain 2.50 6.00
256 C.J. Spiller 4.00 10.00
257 Ryan Mathews 5.00 12.00
258 Jermaine Gresham 3.00 8.00
259 Demaryius Thomas 3.00 8.00
260 Dez Bryant 10.00 25.00
261 Tim Tebow 10.00 25.00
262 Jahvid Best 4.00 10.00
263 Dexter McCluster 2.50 6.00
264 Arrelious Benn 2.50 6.00
265 Rob Gronkowski 6.00 15.00
266 Jimmy Clausen 2.50 6.00
267 Toby Gerhart 2.50 6.00
268 Ben Tate 3.00 8.00
269 Montario Hardesty 2.50 6.00
270 Golden Tate 2.50 6.00
271 Damian Williams 3.00 8.00
272 Brandon LaFell 2.50 6.00
273 Emmanuel Sanders 2.50 6.00
274 Jordan Shipley 2.50 6.00
275 Colt McCoy 5.00 12.00
276 Eric Decker 3.00 8.00
277 Andre Roberts 2.50 6.00
278 Armanti Edwards 2.50 6.00
279 Taylor Price 2.50 6.00
280 Mardy Gilyard 2.50 6.00
281 Mike Williams 4.00 10.00
282 Marcus Easley 2.00 5.00
283 Joe McKnight 2.50 6.00
284 Mike Kafka 2.50 6.00
285 Jonathan Dwyer 2.50 6.00

2010 Panini Gridiron Gear Rookie Gridiron Gems Jerseys Trios Autographs Prime

*TRIO AU/20: .6X TO 1.5X BASIC JSY AU
TRIO AUTO STATED PRINT RUN 20
*CMB PRIME AU/15: .6X TO 1.5X BASIC JSY AU
*PRIME AU/10: .6X TO 1.5X BASIC JSY AU
EXCH EXPIRATION: 6/1/2012
251 Sam Bradford 60.00 150.00
261 Tim Tebow 75.00 150.00

2010 Panini Gridiron Gear Rookie Orientation

*GOLD/100: .6X TO 1.5X BASIC INSERTS
*PLATINUM/25: .8X TO 2X BASIC INSERTS
*SILVER/250: .5X TO 1.2X BASIC INSERTS
1 Demaryius Thomas 1.00 2.50
2 Jordan Shipley .75 2.00
3 Sam Bradford 3.00 8.00
4 Jonathan Dwyer .75 2.00
5 Eric Berry .75 2.00
6 Montario Hardesty .75 2.00
7 Arrelious Benn .75 2.00
8 Joe McKnight .75 2.00
9 Colt McCoy 1.50 4.00
10 Rolando McClain .75 2.00
11 Dexter McCluster .75 2.00
12 Jermaine Gresham 1.00 2.50
13 Eric Decker 1.00 2.50
14 Ndamukong Suh 1.50 4.00
15 Mike Kafka .75 2.00
16 Andre Roberts .75 2.00
17 Rob Gronkowski 2.00 5.00
18 Dez Bryant 2.50 6.00
19 Gerald McCoy .75 2.00
20 Taylor Price .75 2.00
21 Jahvid Best 1.25 3.00
22 Armanti Edwards .75 2.00
23 C.J. Spiller 1.25 3.00
24 Brandon LaFell .75 2.00
25 Mardy Gilyard .75 2.00
26 Tim Tebow 3.00 8.00
27 Ben Tate 1.00 2.50
28 Golden Tate .75 2.00
29 Emmanuel Sanders .75 2.00
30 Jimmy Clausen .75 2.00
31 Ryan Mathews 1.50 4.00
32 Toby Gerhart .75 2.00
33 Damian Williams .75 2.00
34 Mike Williams 1.25 3.00
35 Marcus Easley .60 1.50

2010 Panini Gridiron Gear Rookie Orientation Jerseys

STATED PRINT RUN 299 SER.#'d SETS
*PRIME/25: 1X TO 2.5X BASIC JSY/299
1 Demaryius Thomas/299 2.50 6.00
2 Jordan Shipley/299 2.00 5.00
3 Sam Bradford/299 8.00 20.00
4 Jonathan Dwyer/299 2.00 5.00
5 Eric Berry/299 2.00 5.00
6 Montario Hardesty/299 2.00 5.00
7 Arrelious Benn/299 2.00 5.00
8 Joe McKnight/299 2.00 5.00
9 Colt McCoy/299 4.00 10.00
10 Rolando McClain/299 2.00 5.00
11 Dexter McCluster/299 2.00 5.00
12 Jermaine Gresham/299 2.50 6.00
13 Eric Decker/299 2.50 6.00
14 Ndamukong Suh/299 4.00 10.00
15 Mike Kafka/299 2.00 5.00
16 Andre Roberts/299 2.00 5.00
17 Rob Gronkowski/299 5.00 12.00
18 Dez Bryant/299 6.00 15.00
19 Gerald McCoy/299 2.00 5.00
20 Taylor Price/299 2.00 5.00
21 Jahvid Best/299 4.00 10.00
22 Armanti Edwards/299 2.00 5.00
23 C.J. Spiller/299 3.00 8.00
24 Brandon LaFell/299 2.00 5.00
25 Mardy Gilyard/299 2.00 5.00
26 Tim Tebow/299 8.00 20.00
27 Ben Tate/299 2.50 6.00
28 Golden Tate/299 2.00 5.00
29 Emmanuel Sanders/299 2.00 5.00
30 Jimmy Clausen/299 2.00 5.00
31 Ryan Mathews/100 4.00 10.00
32 Toby Gerhart/299 2.00 5.00
33 Damian Williams/299 2.00 5.00
34 Mike Williams/299 3.00 8.00
35 Marcus Easley/299 1.50 4.00

2010 Panini Gridiron Gear Rookie Orientation Jerseys Autographs

STATED PRINT RUN 50 SER.#'d SETS
*PRIME/15: .6X TO 1.5X BASIC JSY AU/50
EXCH EXPIRATION: 6/1/2012
1 Demaryius Thomas 8.00 20.00
2 Jordan Shipley 6.00 15.00
3 Sam Bradford 50.00 120.00
4 Jonathan Dwyer EXCH 6.00 15.00
5 Eric Berry 6.00 15.00
6 Montario Hardesty 6.00 15.00
7 Arrelious Benn 6.00 15.00
8 Joe McKnight 6.00 15.00
9 Colt McCoy 12.00 30.00
10 Rolando McClain 6.00 15.00
12 Jermaine Gresham 8.00 20.00
13 Eric Decker 8.00 20.00
15 Mike Kafka 6.00 15.00
16 Andre Roberts 6.00 15.00
17 Rob Gronkowski 25.00 50.00
18 Dez Bryant 25.00 60.00
20 Taylor Price 6.00 15.00
21 Jahvid Best 10.00 25.00
22 Armanti Edwards 6.00 15.00
23 C.J. Spiller 10.00 25.00
24 Brandon LaFell 6.00 15.00
25 Mardy Gilyard 6.00 15.00
26 Tim Tebow 60.00 120.00
27 Ben Tate 8.00 20.00
28 Golden Tate 6.00 15.00
29 Emmanuel Sanders 6.00 15.00
30 Jimmy Clausen 6.00 15.00
31 Ryan Mathews 20.00 50.00
32 Toby Gerhart 6.00 15.00
33 Damian Williams 6.00 15.00
34 Mike Williams 10.00 25.00
35 Marcus Easley 5.00 12.00

2010 Panini Gridiron Gear Rookie Orientation Materials Quad

STATED PRINT RUN 150 SER.#'d SETS
*PRIME/25: .8X TO 2X BASIC QUAD/150
1 Sam Bradford 8.00 20.00
Ndamukong Suh
Gerald McCoy
Eric Berry
2 Sam Bradford 10.00 25.00
Tim Tebow
Jimmy Clausen
Colt McCoy
3 C.J. Spiller 5.00 12.00
Ryan Mathews
Jahvid Best
Toby Gerhart
4 Demaryius Thomas 6.00 15.00
Dez Bryant
Dexter McCluster
Arrelious Benn
5 Golden Tate 2.50 6.00
Damian Williams
Brandon LaFell
Emmanuel Sanders
6 Jordan Shipley 3.00 8.00
Eric Decker
Andre Roberts
Armanti Edwards
7 Taylor Price 4.00 10.00
Mardy Gilyard
Mike Williams
Marcus Easley
8 Montario Hardesty 4.00 10.00
Joe McKnight
Jermaine Gresham
Rob Gronkowski
9 Sam Bradford 10.00 25.00
Tim Tebow
C.J. Spiller
Ryan Mathews
10 Ndamukong Suh 5.00 12.00
Gerald McCoy
Eric Berry
Rolando McClain

2010 Panini Gridiron Gear Rookie Orientation Materials Triple

STATED PRINT RUN 250 SER.#'d SETS
*PRIME/25: .8X TO 2X BASIC TRIPLE/250
1 Jimmy Clausen 2.50 6.00
Brandon LaFell
Armanti Edwards
2 Gerald McCoy 4.00 10.00
Arrelious Benn
Mike Williams
3 Demaryius Thomas 12.00 30.00
Tim Tebow
Eric Decker
4 C.J. Spiller 5.00 12.00
Ryan Mathews
Jahvid Best
5 Sam Bradford 8.00 20.00
Gerald McCoy
Jermaine Gresham
6 Toby Gerhart 3.00 8.00
Ben Tate
Montario Hardesty
7 Arrelious Benn 2.50 6.00
Golden Tate
Damian Williams
8 Ndamukong Suh 5.00 12.00
Eric Berry
Rolando McClain
9 Demaryius Thomas 6.00 15.00
Dez Bryant
Dexter McCluster
10 Sam Bradford 10.00 25.00
Tim Tebow
Jimmy Clausen

2011 Panini Gridiron Gear

COMP.SET w/o RC's (150) 8.00 20.00
ROOKIE JSY AU PRINT RUN 197-317
1 Deion Branch .20 .50
2 Devin McCourty .20 .50
3 Jerod Mayo .20 .50
4 Tom Brady .50 1.25
5 Wes Welker .30 .75
6 Darrelle Revis .25 .60
7 Dustin Keller .25 .60
8 LaDainian Tomlinson .30 .75
9 Mark Sanchez .30 .75
10 Shonn Greene .25 .60
11 Brandon Marshall .25 .60
12 Chad Henne .25 .60
13 Davone Bess .20 .50
14 Karlos Dansby .20 .50
15 Fred Jackson .30 .75
16 Ryan Fitzpatrick .25 .60
17 Steve Johnson .25 .60
18 Lee Evans .25 .60
19 Ben Roethlisberger .30 .75
20 Hines Ward .25 .60
21 Lawrence Timmons .20 .50
22 Mike Wallace .30 .75
23 Rashard Mendenhall .25 .60
24 Anquan Boldin .25 .60
25 Ed Reed .25 .60
26 Joe Flacco .30 .75
27 Ray Lewis .30 .75
28 Ray Rice .25 .60
29 Colt McCoy .25 .60
30 Mohamed Massaquoi .25 .60
31 Peyton Hillis .25 .60
32 T.J. Ward .20 .50
33 Cedric Benson .25 .60
34 Dhani Jones .20 .50
35 Jermaine Gresham .25 .60
36 Jordan Shipley .25 .60
37 Antoine Bethea .20 .50
38 Dallas Clark .25 .60
39 Peyton Manning .50 1.25
40 Pierre Garcon .25 .60
41 Reggie Wayne .25 .60
42 Paul Posluszny .20 .50
43 Marcedes Lewis .20 .50
44 Maurice Jones-Drew .25 .60
45 Mike Thomas .25 .60
46 Andre Johnson .25 .60
47 Arian Foster .25 .60
48 Kevin Walter .25 .60
49 Matt Schaub .25 .60
50 Chris Hope .20 .50
51 Chris Johnson .25 .60
52 Nate Washington .20 .50
53 Derrick Johnson .20 .50
54 Dwayne Bowe .25 .60
55 Jamaal Charles .25 .60
56 Matt Cassel .25 .60
57 Thomas Jones .25 .60
58 Antonio Gates .25 .60
59 Mike Tolbert .25 .60
60 Philip Rivers .30 .75
61 Ryan Mathews .25 .60
62 Vincent Jackson .25 .60
63 Darren McFadden .25 .60
64 Darrius Heyward-Bey .20 .50
65 Jason Campbell .25 .60
66 Tyvon Branch .20 .50
67 Brandon Lloyd .25 .60
68 Champ Bailey .25 .60
69 D.J. Williams .30 .75
70 Knowshon Moreno .25 .60
71 Tim Tebow .60 1.50
72 DeSean Jackson .25 .60
73 Jeremy Maclin .25 .60
74 Kevin Kolb .25 .60
75 LeSean McCoy .25 .60
76 Michael Vick .30 .75
77 Brandon Jacobs .25 .60
78 Eli Manning .30 .75
79 Hakeem Nicks .25 .60
80 Mario Manningham .25 .60
81 DeMarcus Ware .25 .60
82 Dez Bryant .30 .75
83 Felix Jones .25 .60
84 Miles Austin .25 .60
85 Tony Romo .30 .75
86 DeAngelo Hall .20 .50
87 Donovan McNabb .30 .75
88 London Fletcher .20 .50
89 Ryan Torain .20 .50
90 Brian Urlacher .30 .75
91 Jay Cutler .25 .60
92 Johnny Knox .25 .60
93 Matt Forte .25 .60
94 Aaron Rodgers .50 1.25
95 A.J. Hawk .25 .60
96 Charles Woodson .30 .75
97 Greg Jennings .25 .60
98 Jermichael Finley .25 .60
99 Calvin Johnson .30 .75
100 Jahvid Best .25 .60
101 Matthew Stafford .30 .75
102 Ndamukong Suh .30 .75
103 Adrian Peterson .40 1.00
104 Chad Greenway .25 .60
105 Percy Harvin .25 .60
106 Visanthe Shiancoe .25 .60
107 Curtis Lofton .20 .50
108 Matt Ryan .30 .75
109 Michael Turner .25 .60
110 Roddy White .25 .60
111 Tony Gonzalez .25 .60
112 Drew Brees .30 .75
113 Jonathan Vilma .20 .50
114 Marques Colston .25 .60
115 Pierre Thomas .25 .60
116 Reggie Bush .25 .60
117 Josh Freeman .30 .75
118 Kellen Winslow Jr. .25 .60
119 LeGarrette Blount .25 .60
120 Mike Williams .25 .60
121 Ronde Barber .20 .50
122 DeAngelo Williams .25 .60
123 Jonathan Stewart .25 .60
124 Steve Smith .25 .60
125 Marshawn Lynch .25 .60
126 Matt Hasselbeck .25 .60
127 Mike Williams USC .25 .60
128 Brandon Gibson .20 .50
129 Danny Amendola .25 .60
130 James Laurinaitis .20 .50
131 Sam Bradford .30 .75
132 Steven Jackson .25 .60
133 Alex Smith QB .25 .60
134 Frank Gore .25 .60
135 Michael Crabtree .25 .60
136 Patrick Willis .25 .60
137 Vernon Davis .25 .60
138 Beanie Wells .25 .60
139 Larry Fitzgerald .25 .60
140 Paris Lenon .20 .50
141 Ahmad Bradshaw .25 .60
142 Ronnie Brown .25 .60
143 Santonio Holmes .25 .60
144 Sidney Rice .25 .60
145 Santana Moss .25 .60
146 Asante Samuel .20 .50
147 Nnamdi Asomugha .25 .60
148 Brandon Meriweather .20 .50
149 Jared Allen .25 .60
150 Jared Cook .25 .60
151 Aaron Williams RC 1.00 2.50
152 Adrian Clayborn RC 1.25 3.00
153 Ahmad Black RC 1.00 2.50
154 Akeem Ayers RC 1.00 2.50
155 Aldon Smith RC 2.00 5.00
156 Aldrick Robinson RC .75 2.00
157 Allen Bradford RC 1.00 2.50
158 Anthony Allen RC .75 2.00
159 Anthony Castonzo RC .75 2.00
160 Brandon Harris RC .75 2.00
161 Cameron Heyward RC 1.25 3.00
162 Cameron Jordan RC 1.00 2.50
163 Cecil Shorts RC 1.00 2.50
164 Corey Liuget RC .75 2.00
165 D.J. Williams RC 1.25 3.00
166 Da'Quan Bowers RC 1.25 3.00
167 Da'Rel Scott RC 1.00 2.50
168 Denarius Moore RC 1.50 4.00
169 Dion Lewis RC 1.25 3.00
170 Dwayne Harris RC 1.25 3.00
171 Evan Royster RC 1.25 3.00
172 Greg Jones RC 1.00 2.50
173 Greg McElroy RC 1.25 3.00
174 Greg Salas RC 1.25 3.00
175 J.J. Watt RC 1.50 4.00
176 Jacquizz Rodgers RC 1.25 3.00
177 Jeremy Kerley RC 1.25 3.00
178 Jimmy Smith RC 1.25 3.00
179 Johnny White RC 1.00 2.50
180 Jordan Cameron RC 1.00 2.50
181 Julius Thomas RC 1.00 2.50
182 Justin Houston RC 1.25 3.00
183 Kealoha Pilares RC 1.25 3.00
184 Kris Durham RC 1.00 2.50
185 Lance Kendricks RC 1.00 2.50
186 Luke Stocker RC 1.00 2.50
187 Marcus Cannon RC .75 2.00
188 Martez Wilson RC 1.25 3.00
189 Nathan Enderle RC 1.25 3.00
190 Nick Fairley RC 1.50 4.00
191 Niles Paul RC 1.25 3.00
192 Owen Marecic RC 1.25 3.00
193 Patrick Peterson RC 2.00 5.00
194 Phil Taylor RC 1.00 2.50
195 Prince Amukamara RC 1.25 3.00
196 Quinton Carter RC .75 2.00
197 Rahim Moore RC 1.00 2.50
198 Ricky Stanzi RC 1.50 4.00
199 Robert Housler RC 1.00 2.50
200 Robert Quinn RC 1.25 3.00
201 Ronald Johnson RC 1.00 2.50
202 Roy Helu RC 2.50 6.00
203 Ryan Kerrigan RC 1.25 3.00
204 Ryan Whalen RC 1.00 2.50
205 Scotty McKnight RC 1.00 2.50
206 Shane Bannon RC .75 2.00
207 Stanley Havili RC .75 2.00
208 Stephen Burton RC .75 2.00
209 Stephen Paea RC 1.25 3.00
210 T.J. Yates RC 1.50 4.00
211 Tandon Doss RC 1.00 2.50
212 Tyler Sash RC 1.25 3.00
213 Tyrod Taylor RC 1.25 3.00
214 Tyron Smith RC 1.50 4.00
215 Baron Batch RC 1.25 3.00
216 Damien Berry RC 1.00 2.50
217 Derrick Locke RC 1.00 2.50
218 Jay Finley RC 1.00 2.50
219 John Clay RC 1.25 3.00
220 Terrelle Pryor RC 1.50 4.00
221 Pat Devlin RC 1.25 3.00
222 Darvin Adams RC 1.00 2.50
223 David Ausberry RC 1.00 2.50
224 DeAndre Brown RC 1.25 3.00
225 DeMarco Sampson RC .75 2.00
226 Mark Dell RC 1.00 2.50
227 O.J. Murdock RC 1.00 2.50
228 Brooks Reed RC 1.25 3.00
229 Bruce Carter RC 1.25 3.00
230 Jabaal Sheard RC 1.25 3.00
231 Jaiquawn Jarrett RC 1.00 2.50
232 Jarvis Jenkins RC .75 2.00
233 Jonas Mouton RC 1.00 2.50
234 Marcus Gilchrist RC .75 2.00
235 Marvin Austin RC 1.00 2.50
236 Muhammad Wilkerson RC 1.25 3.00
237 Ras-I Dowling RC 1.25 3.00
238 Akeem Dent RC 1.00 2.50
239 Dontay Moch RC .75 2.00
240 Mason Foster RC 1.25 3.00
241 Kelvin Sheppard RC 1.25 3.00
242 Darryl Gamble RC .75 2.00
243 Chris Matthews RC .75 2.00
244 Courtney Smith RC 1.00 2.50
245 Dane Sanzenbacher RC 1.25 3.00
246 Jock Sanders RC 1.00 2.50
247 Lestar Jean RC 1.00 2.50
248 Marcus Harris RC .75 2.00

249 Terrence Toliver RC 1.00 2.50
250 Tori Gurley RC 1.00 2.50
R1 Von Miller JSY AU/299 RC 12.00 30.00
R2 Vincent Brown JSY AU/299 RC 8.00 20.00
R3 Torrey Smith JSY AU/303 RC 10.00 25.00
R4 Titus Young JSY AU/287 RC 10.00 25.00
R5 Taiwan Jones JSY AU/304 RC 8.00 20.00
R6 Stevan Ridley JSY AU/303 RC 8.00 20.00
R7 Shane Vereen JSY AU/317 RC 8.00 20.00
R8 Ryan Williams JSY AU/202 RC 10.00 25.00
R9 Ryan Mallett JSY AU/197 RC 25.00 50.00
R10 Randall Cobb JSY AU/304 RC 10.00 25.00
R11 Mikel Leshoure JSY AU/199 RC 8.00 20.00
R12 Mark Ingram JSY AU/201 RC 25.00 50.00
R13 Marcell Dareus JSY AU/200 RC 8.00 20.00
R14 Leonard Hankerson JSY AU/304 RC 8.00 20.00
R15 Kyle Rudolph JSY AU/299 RC 8.00 20.00
R16 Kendall Hunter JSY AU/304 RC 8.00 20.00
R17 Julio Jones JSY AU/204 RC 25.00 50.00
R18 Jordan Todman JSY AU/309 RC 5.00 12.00
R19 Jonathan Baldwin JSY AU/302 RC 8.00 20.00
R20 Jerrel Jernigan JSY AU/298 RC 6.00 15.00
R21 Jamie Harper JSY AU/304 RC 8.00 20.00
R22 Jake Locker JSY AU/204 RC 30.00 60.00
R23 Greg Little JSY AU/300 RC 8.00 20.00
R24 DeMarco Murray JSY AU/304 RC 25.00 50.00
R25 Delone Carter JSY AU/304 RC 6.00 15.00
R26 Daniel Thomas JSY AU/300 RC 8.00 20.00
R27 Colin Kaepernick JSY AU/205 RC 10.00 25.00
R28 Clyde Gates JSY AU/305 RC 6.00 15.00
R29 Christian Ponder JSY AU/210 RC 20.00 40.00
R30 Cam Newton JSY AU/204 RC 90.00 150.00
R31 Blaine Gabbert JSY AU/204 RC 12.00 30.00
R32 Bilal Powell JSY AU/303 RC 5.00 12.00
R33 Austin Pettis JSY AU/299 RC 6.00 15.00
R34 Andy Dalton JSY AU/204 RC 30.00 60.00
R35 Alex Green JSY AU/304 RC 8.00 20.00
R36 A.J. Green JSY AU/199 RC 25.00 50.00

2011 Panini Gridiron Gear Gold O's

*1-150 VETS/100: 2.5X TO 6X BASIC CARDS
*151-250 ROOKIE/100: .6X TO 1.5X BASIC RC
STATED PRINT RUN 100 SER.#'d SETS

2011 Panini Gridiron Gear Gold X's

*1-150 VETS/100: 2.5X TO 6X BASIC CARDS
*151-250 ROOKIE/100: .6X TO 1.5X BASIC RC
STATED PRINT RUN 100 SER.#'d SETS

2011 Panini Gridiron Gear Platinum O's

*1-150 VETS/25: 5X TO 12X BASIC CARDS
*151-250 ROOKIE/25: 1.2X TO 3X BASIC RC
STATED PRINT RUN 25 SER.#'d SETS

2011 Panini Gridiron Gear Platinum X's

*1-150 VETS/25: 5X TO 12X BASIC CARDS
*151-250 ROOKIE/25: 1.2X TO 3X BASIC RC
STATED PRINT RUN 25 SER.#'d SETS

2011 Panini Gridiron Gear Silver O's

*1-150 VETS/250: 2X TO 5X BASIC CARDS
*151-250 ROOKIE/250: .5X TO 1.2X BASIC RC
STATED PRINT RUN 250 SER.#'d SETS

2011 Panini Gridiron Gear Silver X's

*1-150 VETS/250: 2X TO 5X BASIC CARDS
*151-250 ROOKIE/250: .5X TO 1.2X BASIC RC
STATED PRINT RUN 250 SER.#'d SETS

2011 Panini Gridiron Gear Autographs Gold

UNPRICED VETERAN PRINT RUN 5
ROOKIE STATED PRINT RUN 290-299
*PLATINUM/25: .6X TO 1.5X GOLD/290-299
151 Aaron Williams/299 4.00 10.00
152 Adrian Clayborn/299 5.00 12.00
153 Ahmad Black/299 4.00 10.00
154 Akeem Ayers/299 4.00 10.00
155 Aldon Smith/299 EXCH 8.00 20.00
156 Aldrick Robinson/299 3.00 8.00
157 Allen Bradford/299 4.00 10.00
158 Anthony Allen/299 3.00 8.00
159 Anthony Castonzo/299 3.00 8.00
160 Brandon Harris/299 3.00 8.00
161 Cameron Heyward/299 5.00 12.00
162 Cameron Jordan/299 4.00 10.00
163 Cecil Shorts/299 4.00 10.00
164 Corey Liuget/299 3.00 8.00
165 D.J. Williams/299 5.00 12.00
166 Da'Quan Bowers/299 5.00 12.00
167 Da'Rel Scott/299 4.00 10.00
168 Denarius Moore/299 10.00 25.00
169 Dion Lewis/299 5.00 12.00
170 Dwayne Harris/299 5.00 12.00
171 Evan Royster/299 5.00 12.00
172 Greg Jones/299 4.00 10.00
173 Greg McElroy/299 5.00 12.00
174 Greg Salas/299 5.00 12.00
175 J.J. Watt/299 6.00 15.00
176 Jacquizz Rodgers/299 5.00 12.00
177 Jeremy Kerley/290 5.00 12.00
178 Jimmy Smith/299 5.00 12.00
179 Johnny White/299 EXCH 4.00 10.00
180 Jordan Cameron/299 4.00 10.00
181 Julius Thomas/299 4.00 10.00
182 Justin Houston/299 5.00 12.00
183 Kealoha Pilares/299 5.00 12.00
184 Kris Durham/299 EXCH 4.00 10.00
185 Lance Kendricks/299 4.00 10.00
186 Luke Stocker/299 4.00 10.00
187 Marcus Cannon/299 3.00 8.00
188 Martez Wilson/299 5.00 12.00
191 Niles Paul/299 5.00 12.00
194 Phil Taylor/299 4.00 10.00
195 Prince Amukamara/299 5.00 12.00
196 Quinton Carter/299 3.00 8.00
197 Rahim Moore/299 4.00 10.00
198 Ricky Stanzi/299 6.00 15.00
201 Ronald Johnson/299 4.00 10.00
202 Roy Helu/299 10.00 25.00
203 Ryan Kerrigan/299 5.00 12.00
204 Ryan Whalen/299 4.00 10.00
205 Scotty McKnight/299 4.00 10.00
207 Stanley Havili/299 3.00 8.00
209 Stephen Paea/299 5.00 12.00
210 T.J. Yates/299 12.00 30.00
212 Tyler Sash/299 5.00 12.00
213 Tyrod Taylor/299 5.00 12.00
214 Tyron Smith/299 6.00 15.00
220 Terrelle Pryor/299 15.00 30.00

2011 Panini Gridiron Gear Crash Course

RANDOM INSERTS IN PACKS
*GOLD/100: .6X TO 1.5X BASIC INSERTS
*PLATINUM/25: 1X TO 2.5X BASIC INSERTS
*SILVER/250: .5X TO 1.2X BASIC INSERTS
1 Jon Beason .75 2.00
Michael Turner
2 Patrick Willis .75 2.00
Steven Jackson
3 Cortland Finnegan .75 2.00
Arian Foster
4 Ray Lewis 1.00 2.50
Rashard Mendenhall
5 Terrell Suggs .75 2.00
Cedric Benson
6 Dwight Freeney .75 2.00
Chris Johnson
7 James Harrison 1.00 2.50
Ray Rice
8 DeMeco Ryans .75 2.00
Maurice Jones-Drew
9 Brian Urlacher 1.25 3.00
Adrian Peterson
10 DeMarcus Ware .75 2.00
Ahmad Bradshaw

2011 Panini Gridiron Gear Crash Course Jerseys

STATED PRINT RUN 10-250
*PRIME/25: .8X TO 2X BASIC JSY/100-250
*PRIME/25: .6X TO 1.5X BASIC JSY/50
*PRIME/25: .5X TO 1.2X BASIC JSY/25
1 Jon Beason
Michael Turner
2 Patrick Willis 3.00 8.00
Steven Jackson
3 Cortland Finnegan 4.00 10.00
Arian Foster
4 Ray Lewis 8.00 20.00
Rashard Mendenhall
5 Terrell Suggs 3.00 8.00
Cedric Benson
6 Dwight Freeney 3.00 8.00
Chris Johnson
7 James Harrison 5.00 12.00
Ray Rice
8 DeMeco Ryans 4.00 10.00
Maurice Jones-Drew
9 Brian Urlacher 8.00 20.00
Adrian Peterson
10 DeMarcus Ware 4.00 10.00
Ahmad Bradshaw

2011 Panini Gridiron Gear Gamebreakers

*GOLD/100: .6X TO 1.5X BASIC INSERTS
*PLATINUM/25: 1X TO 2.5X BASIC INSERTS
*SILVER/250: .5X TO 1.2X BASIC INSERTS
1 Arian Foster .75 2.00
2 Dwayne Bowe .75 2.00
3 BenJarvus Green-Ellis .75 2.00
4 Adrian Peterson 1.25 3.00
5 Peyton Hillis .75 2.00
6 Rashard Mendenhall .75 2.00
7 Greg Jennings .75 2.00
8 Calvin Johnson 1.00 2.50
9 Chris Johnson .75 2.00
10 Michael Turner .75 2.00
11 Hakeem Nicks .75 2.00
12 Mike Tolbert .75 2.00
13 Brandon Lloyd .75 2.00
14 Mike Williams .75 2.00
15 Mike Wallace 1.00 2.50
16 Rob Gronkowski 1.00 2.50
17 Roddy White .75 2.00
18 Steve Johnson .75 2.00
19 Antonio Gates .75 2.00
20 Marcedes Lewis .60 1.50
21 Darren McFadden .75 2.00
22 Jeremy Maclin .75 2.00
23 Kenny Britt .75 2.00
24 LeSean McCoy .75 2.00
25 Mario Manningham .75 2.00
26 Matt Forte .75 2.00
27 Michael Vick 1.00 2.50
28 Brandon Jacobs .75 2.00
29 Jason Witten 1.00 2.50
30 Austin Collie .75 2.00

2011 Panini Gridiron Gear Gamebreakers Jerseys

STATED PRINT RUN 25-250
*PRIME/50: .6X TO 1.5X BASIC JSY/99-250
*PRIME/50: .5X TO 1.2X BASIC JSY/50
1 Arian Foster/250 4.00 10.00
2 Dwayne Bowe/250 3.00 8.00
4 Adrian Peterson/25 8.00 20.00
5 Peyton Hillis/100 3.00 8.00
6 Rashard Mendenhall/250 3.00 8.00
9 Chris Johnson/250 3.00 8.00
10 Michael Turner/250 3.00 8.00
11 Hakeem Nicks/250 3.00 8.00
13 Brandon Lloyd/250 3.00 8.00
15 Mike Wallace/250 4.00 10.00
17 Roddy White/50 4.00 10.00
18 Steve Johnson/100 4.00 10.00
19 Antonio Gates/250 3.00 8.00
20 Marcedes Lewis/99 2.50 6.00
21 Darren McFadden/250 3.00 8.00
22 Jeremy Maclin/250 3.00 8.00
23 Kenny Britt/250 3.00 8.00
24 LeSean McCoy/250 3.00 8.00
26 Matt Forte/100 3.00 8.00
27 Michael Vick/250 4.00 10.00
28 Brandon Jacobs/250 3.00 8.00
29 Jason Witten/250 4.00 10.00

2011 Panini Gridiron Gear Gamebreakers Jerseys Autographs

STATED PRINT RUN 5-15
3 BenJarvus Green-Ellis/15 30.00 60.00
23 Kenny Britt/15 EXCH
29 Jason Witten/15 25.00 50.00

2011 Panini Gridiron Gear Gamebreakers Jerseys Combos

STATED PRINT RUN 25-100
*PRIME/25: .8X TO 2X BASIC JSY/100
*PRIME/25: .6X TO 1.5X BASIC JSY/50
1 Arian Foster/100 5.00 12.00
2 Dwayne Bowe/100 4.00 10.00
3 BenJarvus Green-Ellis/100 4.00 10.00
4 Adrian Peterson/25 10.00 25.00
5 Peyton Hillis/50 5.00 12.00
6 Rashard Mendenhall/100 4.00 10.00
8 Calvin Johnson/100 5.00 12.00
9 Chris Johnson/100 4.00 10.00
10 Michael Turner/100 4.00 10.00
11 Hakeem Nicks/100 4.00 10.00
13 Brandon Lloyd/100 4.00 10.00
15 Mike Wallace/100 5.00 12.00
17 Roddy White/50 5.00 12.00
18 Steve Johnson/50 5.00 12.00
19 Antonio Gates/100 4.00 10.00
20 Marcedes Lewis/50 4.00 10.00
21 Darren McFadden/100 4.00 10.00
22 Jeremy Maclin/100 4.00 10.00
23 Kenny Britt/100 4.00 10.00
24 LeSean McCoy/100 4.00 10.00
26 Matt Forte/100 4.00 10.00
27 Michael Vick/100 5.00 12.00
28 Brandon Jacobs/100 4.00 10.00
29 Jason Witten/100 5.00 12.00

2011 Panini Gridiron Gear Jerseys O's

STATED PRINT RUN 25-299
4 Tom Brady/49 8.00 20.00
5 Wes Welker/49 5.00 12.00
6 Darrelle Revis/49 4.00 10.00
8 LaDainian Tomlinson/299 4.00 10.00
9 Mark Sanchez/49 5.00 12.00
10 Shonn Greene/49 4.00 10.00
11 Brandon Marshall/49 4.00 10.00
12 Chad Henne/49 4.00 10.00
15 Fred Jackson/49 5.00 12.00
16 Ryan Fitzpatrick/49 4.00 10.00
17 Steve Johnson/49 4.00 10.00
18 Ben Roethlisberger/49 5.00 12.00
22 Mike Wallace/49 5.00 12.00
23 Rashard Mendenhall/49 4.00 10.00
24 Anquan Boldin/49 4.00 10.00
26 Joe Flacco/299 4.00 10.00
27 Ray Lewis/49 5.00 12.00
28 Ray Rice/49 4.00 10.00
29 Colt McCoy/49 4.00 10.00
33 Cedric Benson/49 4.00 10.00
35 Jermaine Gresham/49 4.00 10.00
36 Jordan Shipley/49 4.00 10.00
38 Dallas Clark/49 4.00 10.00
39 Peyton Manning/249 6.00 15.00
41 Reggie Wayne/299 3.00 8.00
43 Marcedes Lewis/49 3.00 8.00
44 Maurice Jones-Drew/25 5.00 12.00
45 Mike Thomas/49 4.00 10.00
46 Andre Johnson/299 3.00 8.00
47 Arian Foster/299 4.00 10.00
49 Matt Schaub/49 4.00 10.00
51 Chris Johnson/49 4.00 10.00
54 Dwayne Bowe/49 4.00 10.00
55 Jamaal Charles/49 4.00 10.00
56 Matt Cassel/49 4.00 10.00
58 Antonio Gates/49 4.00 10.00
60 Philip Rivers/49 5.00 12.00
61 Ryan Mathews/49 4.00 10.00
63 Darren McFadden/49 4.00 10.00
65 Jason Campbell/49 4.00 10.00
67 Brandon Lloyd/49 4.00 10.00
70 Knowshon Moreno/49 4.00 10.00
71 Tim Tebow/49 10.00 25.00
72 DeSean Jackson/49 4.00 10.00
73 Jeremy Maclin/49 4.00 10.00
75 LeSean McCoy/299 3.00 8.00
76 Michael Vick/49 5.00 12.00
77 Brandon Jacobs/299 3.00 8.00
78 Eli Manning/49 5.00 12.00
79 Hakeem Nicks/299 3.00 8.00
81 DeMarcus Ware/49 5.00 12.00
82 Dez Bryant/249 4.00 10.00
83 Felix Jones/49 4.00 10.00
84 Miles Austin/49 5.00 12.00
85 Tony Romo/49 5.00 12.00
86 DeAngelo Hall/49 3.00 8.00
88 London Fletcher/49 4.00 10.00
89 Ryan Torain/49 3.00 8.00
90 Brian Urlacher/49 5.00 12.00
91 Jay Cutler/49 4.00 10.00
92 Johnny Knox/49 4.00 10.00
93 Matt Forte/99 3.00 8.00
94 Aaron Rodgers/25 15.00 40.00
95 A.J. Hawk/299 3.00 8.00
99 Calvin Johnson/49 5.00 12.00
100 Jahvid Best/49 4.00 10.00
101 Matthew Stafford/49 5.00 12.00
102 Ndamukong Suh/49 5.00 12.00
103 Adrian Peterson/25 8.00 20.00
104 Chad Greenway/49 4.00 10.00
105 Percy Harvin/49 4.00 10.00
106 Visanthe Shiancoe/49 4.00 10.00
108 Matt Ryan/49 5.00 12.00
109 Michael Turner/49 4.00 10.00
110 Roddy White/49 4.00 10.00
111 Tony Gonzalez/49 4.00 10.00
114 Marques Colston/49 4.00 10.00
115 Pierre Thomas/49 4.00 10.00
118 Kellen Winslow Jr./49 4.00 10.00
122 DeAngelo Williams/136 3.00 8.00
123 Jonathan Stewart/249 3.00 8.00
124 Steve Smith/49 4.00 10.00
129 Danny Amendola/49 4.00 10.00
131 Sam Bradford/49 5.00 12.00
132 Steven Jackson/49 4.00 10.00
134 Frank Gore/299 3.00 8.00
135 Michael Crabtree/99 3.00 8.00
136 Patrick Willis/49 4.00 10.00
137 Vernon Davis/49 4.00 10.00
138 Beanie Wells/49 4.00 10.00
141 Ahmad Bradshaw/299 3.00 8.00
143 Santonio Holmes/49 4.00 10.00
145 Santana Moss/49 4.00 10.00
149 Jared Allen/49 5.00 12.00

2011 Panini Gridiron Gear Jerseys Prime

STATED PRINT RUN 2-50
4 Tom Brady/50 10.00 25.00
5 Wes Welker/50 6.00 15.00
6 Darrelle Revis/50 5.00 12.00
7 Dustin Keller/50 5.00 12.00
8 LaDainian Tomlinson/50 6.00 15.00
10 Shonn Greene/50 5.00 12.00
11 Brandon Marshall/50 5.00 12.00
12 Chad Henne/50 5.00 12.00
15 Fred Jackson/25 8.00 20.00
16 Ryan Fitzpatrick/50 5.00 12.00
17 Steve Johnson/50 5.00 12.00
22 Mike Wallace/50 6.00 15.00
24 Anquan Boldin/50 5.00 12.00
25 Ed Reed/50 5.00 12.00
26 Joe Flacco/50 6.00 15.00
27 Ray Lewis/50 6.00 15.00
28 Ray Rice/50 5.00 12.00
29 Colt McCoy/50 5.00 12.00
33 Cedric Benson/50 5.00 12.00
35 Jermaine Gresham/50 5.00 12.00
36 Jordan Shipley/50 5.00 12.00
38 Dallas Clark/50 5.00 12.00
39 Peyton Manning/50 10.00 25.00
40 Pierre Garcon/50 5.00 12.00
43 Marcedes Lewis/50 4.00 10.00
44 Maurice Jones-Drew/50 5.00 12.00
45 Mike Thomas/50 5.00 12.00
46 Andre Johnson/50 5.00 12.00
49 Matt Schaub/50 5.00 12.00
51 Chris Johnson/50 5.00 12.00
52 Nate Washington/50 4.00 10.00
54 Dwayne Bowe/50 5.00 12.00
55 Jamaal Charles/50 5.00 12.00
56 Matt Cassel/50 5.00 12.00
58 Antonio Gates/50 5.00 12.00
60 Philip Rivers/50 6.00 15.00
61 Ryan Mathews/50 5.00 12.00
62 Vincent Jackson/50 5.00 12.00
63 Darren McFadden/50 5.00 12.00
65 Jason Campbell/39 5.00 12.00
67 Brandon Lloyd/50 5.00 12.00
70 Knowshon Moreno/50 5.00 12.00
71 Tim Tebow/50 12.00 30.00
72 DeSean Jackson/50 5.00 12.00
73 Jeremy Maclin/50 5.00 12.00
78 Eli Manning/50 6.00 15.00
79 Hakeem Nicks/50 5.00 12.00
81 DeMarcus Ware/50 5.00 12.00
82 Dez Bryant/50 6.00 15.00
83 Felix Jones/50 5.00 12.00
84 Miles Austin/50 6.00 15.00
85 Tony Romo/50 6.00 15.00
86 DeAngelo Hall/50 4.00 10.00
88 London Fletcher/50 5.00 12.00
89 Ryan Torain/50 4.00 10.00
90 Brian Urlacher/50 6.00 15.00
91 Jay Cutler/50 5.00 12.00
92 Johnny Knox/50 5.00 12.00
93 Matt Forte/50 5.00 12.00
95 A.J. Hawk/50 5.00 12.00
99 Calvin Johnson/50 6.00 15.00
101 Matthew Stafford/50 6.00 15.00
102 Ndamukong Suh/50 6.00 15.00
104 Chad Greenway/50 5.00 12.00
105 Percy Harvin/50 5.00 12.00
106 Visanthe Shiancoe/50 5.00 12.00
108 Matt Ryan/50 6.00 15.00
109 Michael Turner/50 5.00 12.00
110 Roddy White/50 5.00 12.00
111 Tony Gonzalez/50 5.00 12.00
114 Marques Colston/50 5.00 12.00
118 Kellen Winslow Jr./50 5.00 12.00
122 DeAngelo Williams/50 5.00 12.00
123 Jonathan Stewart/50 5.00 12.00
124 Steve Smith/50 5.00 12.00
129 Danny Amendola/50 5.00 12.00
130 James Laurinaitis/50 4.00 10.00
131 Sam Bradford/50 6.00 15.00
132 Steven Jackson/50 5.00 12.00
133 Alex Smith QB/50 5.00 12.00
135 Michael Crabtree/17 6.00 15.00
136 Patrick Willis/50 5.00 12.00
137 Vernon Davis/50 5.00 12.00
138 Beanie Wells/50 5.00 12.00
141 Ahmad Bradshaw/25 6.00 15.00
143 Santonio Holmes/50 5.00 12.00
145 Santana Moss/50 5.00 12.00
146 Asante Samuel/50 4.00 10.00
149 Jared Allen/50 6.00 15.00

2011 Panini Gridiron Gear NFL Gridiron Signatures

STATED PRINT RUN 5-25
3 Troy Polamalu/20 90.00 150.00
19 Aaron Rodgers/21 200.00 300.00
20 Ben Roethlisberger/20 60.00 120.00
21 Calvin Johnson/25 EXCH
22 Drew Brees/25 40.00 80.00
23 Dwayne Bowe/25 EXCH
24 Larry Fitzgerald/25

2011 Panini Gridiron Gear NFL Nation

GOLD/100: .6X TO 1.5X BASIC INSERTS
*PLATINUM/25: 1X TO 2.5X BASIC INSERTS
*SILVER/250: .5X TO 1.2X BASIC INSERTS
1 Adrian Peterson 1.25 3.00
2 Braylon Edwards .75 2.00
3 Patrick Willis .75 2.00
4 DeMarcus Ware .75 2.00
5 Darren McFadden .75 2.00
6 Maurice Jones-Drew .75 2.00
7 Drew Brees 1.00 2.50
8 Bob Sanders .60 1.50
9 Hines Ward .75 2.00
10 Roy Williams .75 2.00
11 Santana Moss .75 2.00
12 Jonathan Vilma .60 1.50
13 Shawne Merriman .60 1.50
14 T.J. Houshmandzadeh .75 2.00
15 Steven Jackson .75 2.00
16 Devin Hester 1.00 2.50
17 Reggie Wayne .75 2.00
18 Vince Young .60 1.50
19 Antonio Gates .75 2.00
20 Mario Williams .60 1.50
21 Reggie Bush .75 2.00
22 Carson Palmer .75 2.00
23 Willis McGahee .60 1.50
24 Dwight Freeney .75 2.00
25 Ben Roethlisberger 1.00 2.50
26 Tony Gonzalez .75 2.00
27 Larry Fitzgerald .75 2.00
28 Michael Vick 1.00 2.50
29 Chad Ochocinco .75 2.00
30 Ed Reed .75 2.00

2011 Panini Gridiron Gear NFL Nation Jerseys

STATED PRINT RUN 25-250
1 Adrian Peterson/25 8.00 20.00
3 Patrick Willis/250 3.00 8.00
4 DeMarcus Ware/250 4.00 10.00
5 Darren McFadden/250 3.00 8.00
6 Maurice Jones-Drew/100 3.00 8.00
7 Drew Brees/250 4.00 10.00
9 Hines Ward/250 4.00 10.00
11 Santana Moss/250 3.00 8.00
15 Steven Jackson/250 3.00 8.00
16 Devin Hester/250 4.00 10.00
17 Reggie Wayne/250 3.00 8.00
19 Antonio Gates/250 3.00 8.00
22 Carson Palmer/250 3.00 8.00
24 Dwight Freeney/250 3.00 8.00
26 Tony Gonzalez/250 3.00 8.00
27 Larry Fitzgerald/250 3.00 8.00
28 Michael Vick/250 4.00 10.00
30 Ed Reed/225 3.00 8.00

2011 Panini Gridiron Gear NFL Nation Jerseys Prime

*PRIME/50: .6X TO 1.5X BASIC JSY/100-250
PRIME STATED PRINT RUN 5-50
25 Ben Roethlisberger/25 8.00 20.00

2011 Panini Gridiron Gear NFL Nation Jerseys Autographs

JSY AU PRINT RUN 5-15
11 Santana Moss/15 12.00 30.00

2011 Panini Gridiron Gear NFL Nation Jerseys Combos

STATED PRINT RUN 25-100
*PRIME/25: .8X TO 2X BASIC COMBO
1 Adrian Peterson/25 8.00 20.00
3 Patrick Willis/100 4.00 10.00
4 DeMarcus Ware/100 5.00 12.00
5 Darren McFadden/100 4.00 10.00
6 Maurice Jones-Drew/100 4.00 10.00
9 Hines Ward/75 5.00 12.00
11 Santana Moss/100 4.00 10.00
15 Steven Jackson/100 4.00 10.00
16 Devin Hester/100 5.00 12.00
17 Reggie Wayne/100 4.00 10.00
19 Antonio Gates/100 4.00 10.00
22 Carson Palmer/100 4.00 10.00
24 Dwight Freeney/100 4.00 10.00
25 Ben Roethlisberger/100 5.00 12.00
26 Tony Gonzalez/100 4.00 10.00
27 Larry Fitzgerald/100 4.00 10.00
28 Michael Vick/100 5.00 12.00
30 Ed Reed/100 4.00 10.00

2011 Panini Gridiron Gear NFL Pro Gridiron Signatures

STATED PRINT RUN 10-30
1 Alan Page/30 12.00 30.00
3 Bo Jackson/15 50.00 100.00
6 Danny White/15 15.00 40.00
7 Ed Too Tall Jones/30 10.00 25.00
9 Forrest Gregg/30
10 Franco Harris/15 30.00 60.00
12 Jim McMahon/15 20.00 50.00
13 Jim Plunkett/30 15.00 40.00
14 Joe Greene/30 15.00 40.00
15 Lenny Moore/30 12.00 30.00
16 Marcus Allen/15 20.00 50.00
17 Mark Duper/30 10.00 25.00
18 Michael Irvin/30 25.00 50.00
19 Paul Hornung/30 15.00 40.00
20 Paul Warfield/30 12.00 30.00
21 Priest Holmes/30 10.00 25.00
22 Randall Cunningham/15 20.00 50.00
23 Raymond Berry/30 12.00 30.00
24 Steve Bartkowski/30
25 Alex Karras/30 12.00 30.00
26 Billy Howton/30 10.00 25.00
27 Bobby Bell/30 10.00 25.00
28 Boyd Dowler/30 15.00 40.00
29 Cliff Harris/30 12.00 30.00
30 Don Perkins/30 12.00 30.00
31 Dub Jones/30 12.00 30.00
32 Frank Gifford/25
33 Fred Williamson/30 12.00 30.00
34 Harlon Hill/30 10.00 25.00
35 Keyshawn Johnson/30
36 Lee Roy Selmon/30 12.00 30.00
37 Leroy Kelly/30 12.00 30.00
38 Lydell Mitchell/30 10.00 25.00
39 Mike Curtis/30 10.00 25.00
40 Ozzie Newsome/30 12.00 30.00
41 Paul Krause/30 12.00 30.00
42 Rick Casares/30 12.00 30.00
43 Ron Mix/30 10.00 25.00
44 Russ Grimm/30 12.00 30.00
45 Sterling Sharpe/30 15.00 40.00
46 Willie Brown/30 10.00 25.00
47 Charley Taylor/30 10.00 25.00
48 Deacon Jones/30
49 James Lofton/30 15.00 40.00
50 Michael Strahan/25 15.00 40.00

2011 Panini Gridiron Gear Plates and Patches

STATED PRINT RUN 10-100
UNPRICED AUTO PRINT RUN 1-10
1 Eli Manning/100 8.00 20.00
3 Antonio Gates/100 6.00 15.00
4 Chris Cooley/100 6.00 15.00
5 Colt McCoy/100 6.00 15.00
6 DeAngelo Williams/50 6.00 15.00
7 DeSean Jackson/100 6.00 15.00
8 Heath Miller/100 6.00 15.00
9 Jamaal Charles/100 6.00 15.00
10 James Laurinaitis/50 5.00 12.00
11 Marques Colston/50 6.00 15.00
12 Miles Austin/100 8.00 20.00
13 Roddy White/100 6.00 15.00
14 Santana Moss/100 6.00 15.00
15 Vernon Davis/100 6.00 15.00

2011 Panini Gridiron Gear Rookie Gridiron Gems Jerseys Retail

STATED PRINT RUN 99 SER.#'d SETS
*HOBBY JSY/25: .5X TO 1.2X RETAIL/99
*JUMBO/25: .6X TO 1.5X RETAIL JSY/99
*JUM.PRIME/10: 1.2X TO 3X RET.JSY/99
*PRIME/50: .5X TO 1.2X RETAIL JSY/99
*COMBO/25: .6X TO 1.5X RETAIL JSY/99
*CMB.PRIME/50: .8X TO 2X RETAIL/99
*TRIO/50: .6X TO 1.5X RETAIL JSY/99
*TRIO PRIME/50: 1X TO 2.5X RETAIL/99
1 Von Miller 2.50 6.00
2 Vincent Brown 2.00 5.00
3 Torrey Smith 2.50 6.00
4 Titus Young 2.50 6.00
5 Taiwan Jones 2.00 5.00
6 Stevan Ridley 2.00 5.00
7 Shane Vereen 2.00 5.00
8 Ryan Williams 2.50 6.00
9 Ryan Mallett 4.00 10.00
10 Randall Cobb 2.50 6.00
11 Mikel Leshoure 2.00 5.00
12 Mark Ingram 4.00 10.00
13 Marcell Dareus 2.00 5.00
14 Leonard Hankerson 2.00 5.00
15 Kyle Rudolph 2.00 5.00
16 Kendall Hunter 2.00 5.00
17 Julio Jones 4.00 10.00
18 Jordan Todman 1.25 3.00
19 Jonathan Baldwin 2.00 5.00
20 Jerrel Jernigan 1.50 4.00
21 Jamie Harper 2.00 5.00
22 Jake Locker 5.00 12.00
23 Greg Little 2.00 5.00
24 DeMarco Murray 4.00 10.00
25 Delone Carter 1.50 4.00
26 Daniel Thomas 2.00 5.00
27 Colin Kaepernick 2.50 6.00
28 Clyde Gates 1.50 4.00
29 Christian Ponder 4.00 10.00
30 Cam Newton 10.00 25.00
31 Blaine Gabbert 3.00 8.00
32 Bilal Powell 1.50 4.00
33 Austin Pettis 1.50 4.00
34 Andy Dalton 5.00 12.00
35 Alex Green 2.00 5.00
36 A.J. Green 4.00 10.00

2011 Panini Gridiron Gear Rookie Gridiron Gems Jerseys Trios Autographs Prime

*TRIO PRIME/20: .6X TO 1.5X BASE JSY AU RC
TRIO PRINT RUN 20 SER.#'d SETS
*COMBO PRIME/15: .4X TO 1X TRIO AU/20
30 Cam Newton 175.00 300.00

2011 Panini Gridiron Gear Rookie Orientation

*GOLD/100: .6X TO 1.5X BASIC INSERTS
*PLATINUM/25: 1X TO 2.5X BASIC INSERTS
*SILVER/250: .5X TO 1.2X BASIC INSERTS
1 A.J. Green 1.50 4.00
2 Austin Pettis .60 1.50
3 Clyde Gates .60 1.50
4 Greg Little .75 2.00
5 Jerrel Jernigan .60 1.50
6 Jonathan Baldwin .75 2.00
7 Julio Jones 1.50 4.00
8 Leonard Hankerson .75 2.00
9 Randall Cobb 1.00 2.50
10 Titus Young 1.00 2.50
11 Torrey Smith 1.00 2.50
12 Vincent Brown .75 2.00
13 Bilal Powell .50 1.25
14 Daniel Thomas .75 2.00
15 Delone Carter .60 1.50
16 DeMarco Murray 1.50 4.00
17 Jamie Harper .75 2.00
18 Alex Green .75 2.00
19 Jordan Todman .50 1.25
20 Ryan Williams 1.00 2.50
21 Shane Vereen .75 2.00
22 Stevan Ridley .75 2.00
23 Taiwan Jones .75 2.00
24 Mark Ingram 1.50 4.00
25 Mikel Leshoure .75 2.00
26 Kendall Hunter .75 2.00
27 Kyle Rudolph .75 2.00
28 Andy Dalton 2.00 5.00
29 Blaine Gabbert 1.25 3.00
30 Cam Newton 4.00 10.00
31 Christian Ponder 1.50 4.00
32 Colin Kaepernick 1.00 2.50
33 Jake Locker 2.00 5.00
34 Ryan Mallett 1.50 4.00
35 Marcell Dareus .75 2.00
36 Von Miller 1.00 2.50

2011 Panini Gridiron Gear Rookie Orientation Jerseys

STATED PRINT RUN 299 SER.#'d SETS
*PRIME/25: 1X TO 2.5X BASIC JSY/299
1 A.J. Green 4.00 10.00
2 Austin Pettis 1.50 4.00
3 Clyde Gates 1.50 4.00
4 Greg Little 2.00 5.00
5 Jerrel Jernigan 1.50 4.00
6 Jonathan Baldwin 2.00 5.00
7 Julio Jones 4.00 10.00
8 Leonard Hankerson 2.00 5.00
9 Randall Cobb 2.50 6.00
10 Titus Young 2.50 6.00
11 Torrey Smith 2.50 6.00
12 Vincent Brown 2.00 5.00
13 Bilal Powell 1.50 4.00
14 Daniel Thomas 2.00 5.00
15 Delone Carter 1.50 4.00
16 DeMarco Murray 4.00 10.00
17 Jamie Harper 2.00 5.00
18 Alex Green 2.00 5.00
19 Jordan Todman 1.25 3.00
20 Ryan Williams 2.50 6.00
21 Shane Vereen 2.00 5.00
22 Stevan Ridley 2.00 5.00
23 Taiwan Jones 2.00 5.00
24 Mark Ingram 4.00 10.00
25 Mikel Leshoure 2.00 5.00
26 Kendall Hunter 2.00 5.00
27 Kyle Rudolph 2.00 5.00
28 Andy Dalton 5.00 12.00
29 Blaine Gabbert 3.00 8.00
30 Cam Newton 10.00 25.00
31 Christian Ponder 4.00 10.00
32 Colin Kaepernick 2.50 6.00
33 Jake Locker 5.00 12.00
34 Ryan Mallett 4.00 10.00
35 Marcell Dareus 2.00 5.00
36 Von Miller 2.50 6.00

2011 Panini Gridiron Gear Rookie Orientation Jerseys Autographs

STATED PRINT RUN 50 SER.#'d SETS
*PRIME/15: .6X TO 1.5X JSY AU/50
1 A.J. Green 15.00 40.00
2 Austin Pettis 5.00 12.00
3 Clyde Gates 5.00 12.00
4 Greg Little 6.00 15.00
5 Jerrel Jernigan 5.00 12.00
6 Jonathan Baldwin 6.00 15.00
7 Julio Jones 15.00 40.00
8 Leonard Hankerson 6.00 15.00
9 Randall Cobb 8.00 20.00
10 Titus Young 8.00 20.00
11 Torrey Smith 8.00 20.00
12 Vincent Brown 6.00 15.00
13 Bilal Powell 4.00 10.00
14 Daniel Thomas 6.00 15.00
15 Delone Carter 5.00 12.00
16 DeMarco Murray EXCH 12.00 30.00
17 Jamie Harper EXCH 6.00 15.00
18 Alex Green 6.00 15.00
19 Jordan Todman 4.00 10.00
20 Ryan Williams EXCH 8.00 20.00
21 Shane Vereen 6.00 15.00
22 Stevan Ridley 6.00 15.00
23 Taiwan Jones 6.00 15.00
24 Mark Ingram 12.00 30.00
25 Mikel Leshoure 6.00 15.00
26 Kendall Hunter 6.00 15.00
27 Kyle Rudolph EXCH 6.00 15.00
28 Andy Dalton 15.00 40.00
29 Blaine Gabbert 10.00 25.00
30 Cam Newton 75.00 150.00
31 Christian Ponder 12.00 30.00
32 Colin Kaepernick 8.00 20.00
33 Jake Locker 20.00 50.00
34 Ryan Mallett 15.00 40.00
35 Marcell Dareus EXCH 6.00 15.00
36 Von Miller 10.00 25.00

2011 Panini Gridiron Gear Rookie Orientation Materials Quad

STATED PRINT RUN 150 SER.#'d SETS
*PRIME/25: .8X TO 2X BASIC QUAD/150
1 Cam Newton 10.00 25.00
Von Miller
Marcell Dareus
A.J. Green
2 Jake Locker 6.00 15.00
Blaine Gabbert
Christian Ponder
Andy Dalton
3 A.J. Green 5.00 12.00
Julio Jones
Jonathan Baldwin
Titus Young
4 Mark Ingram 5.00 12.00
Ryan Williams
Shane Vereen
Daniel Thomas
5 Christian Ponder 5.00 12.00
Kyle Rudolph
Alex Green
Randall Cobb
6 Torrey Smith 4.00 10.00
Greg Little
Austin Pettis
Leonard Hankerson
7 DeMarco Murray 5.00 12.00
Stevan Ridley
Delone Carter
Taiwan Jones
8 Kendall Hunter 3.00 8.00
Bilal Powell
Jamie Harper
Jordan Todman

2011 Panini Gridiron Gear Rookie Orientation Materials Triple

STATED PRINT RUN 250 SER.#'d SETS
*PRIME/25: .8X TO 2X BASIC TRIO/250
1 Cam Newton 10.00 25.00
A.J. Green
Mark Ingram
2 Julio Jones 6.00 15.00
Jake Locker
Ryan Williams
3 Blaine Gabbert 4.00 10.00
Jonathan Baldwin
Shane Vereen
4 Christian Ponder 5.00 12.00
Titus Young
Mikel Leshoure
5 Andy Dalton 6.00 15.00
Colin Kaepernick
Ryan Mallett
6 Daniel Thomas 2.50 6.00
Stevan Ridley
Bilal Powell
7 DeMarco Murray 5.00 12.00
Leonard Hankerson
Jerrel Jernigan
8 Austin Pettis 3.00 8.00
Greg Little
Torrey Smith

2010 Panini Hall of Fame

This 8-card set, featuring members of the 2010 Pro Football Hall of Fame class, was created by Panini and issued at the induction ceremony in Canton in August 2010.

COMPLETE SET (8) 5.00 12.00
1 Emmitt Smith 1.50 4.00
2 Jerry Rice 1.50 4.00
3 Russ Grimm .60 1.50
4 Rickey Jackson .60 1.50
5 Floyd Little .60 1.50
6 John Randle .60 1.50
7 Dick LeBeau .60 1.50
NNO Cover Card .40 1.00

2012 Panini Hall of Fame Class of 2012 Enshrinement National VIP

COMPLETE SET (7) 5.00 12.00
ISSUED TO VIP ATTENDEES
1 Curtis Martin 1.00 2.50
2 Dermontti Dawson .75 2.00
3 Chris Doleman .75 2.00
4 Cortez Kennedy .75 2.00
5 Willie Roaf .75 2.00
6 Jack Butler .75 2.00
NNO Cover Card .20 .50

2011 Panini Headliners National Convention

HL2 Green Bay Packers SB Win
Aaron Rodgers

2011 Panini Madden 12 Marshall Faulk Autographs

One of these four cards was inserted into each EA Sports Madden 12 Hall of Fame edition video game released in 2011. Each card is hand signed and measures larger than standard size.

COMMON FAULK AU 20.00 40.00

2011 Panini National Convention Patch Autographs

CN Cam Newton

2012 Panini National Convention

1-20 CRACKED ICE/25: 5X TO 12X BASE HI
21-40 CRACKED ICE/25: 1.5X TO 4X BASE HI
UNPRICED PLATE ANNCD PRINT RUN 5 SETS
1 Peyton Manning .60 1.50
2 Adrian Peterson .50 1.25
3 Tom Brady .60 1.50
4 Tim Tebow .60 1.50
5 Aaron Rodgers .75 2.00
17 Bo Jackson .40 1.00
19 Curtis Martin .40 1.00
21 Andrew Luck/499 8.00 20.00
22 Robert Griffin III/499 8.00 20.00
23 Trent Richardson/499 5.00 12.00
24 Justin Blackmon/499 2.50 6.00
25 Ryan Tannehill/499 4.00 10.00
26 Michael Floyd/499 2.50 6.00

2012 Panini National Convention Draft Day Materials

1 Andrew Luck 20.00 50.00
2 Trent Richardson 10.00 25.00
3 Matt Kalil 4.00 10.00
4 Morris Claiborne 6.00 15.00
5 Justin Blackmon 6.00 15.00
6 Mark Barron 5.00 12.00
7 Ryan Tannehill 8.00 20.00
8 Stephon Gilmore 3.00 8.00
9 Michael Floyd 6.00 15.00
10 Kendall Wright 4.00 10.00
11 Ryan Kerrigan 5.00 12.00
12 Patrick Peterson 6.00 15.00

2012 Panini National Convention Art Collection

1 Andrew Luck 2.50 6.00
2 Robert Griffin III 2.00 5.00
3 Trent Richardson 1.25 3.00

2012 Panini National Convention Rookie Manufactured Autographs

*CRACKED ICE: X TO X BASE HI
AL Andrew Luck 150.00 250.00
BW Brandon Weeden 40.00 80.00
CU Courtney Upshaw 12.00 30.00
DM Davin Meggett 8.00 20.00
DP Dontari Poe 10.00 25.00
JR Josh Robinson 8.00 20.00
KB Kelvin Beachum 8.00 20.00
KW Kendall Wright 12.00 30.00
MK Matt Kalil 12.00 30.00
RGIII Robert Griffin III 150.00 250.00

2012 Panini National Convention Team Colors Baltimore

CRACKED ICE/25: 4X TO 10X BASE HI
4 Ray Lewis .75 2.00
5 Courtney Upshaw .75 2.00

2012 Panini National Convention Team Colors Washington

CRACKED ICE/25: 4X TO 10X BASE HI
2 Robert Griffin III 3.00 8.00

2012 Panini National Convention Tools of the Trade Towels

1 Andrew Luck 40.00 100.00
2 Robert Griffin III 30.00 80.00
3 Doug Martin 10.00 25.00
4 Michael Floyd 12.00 30.00
5 Ryan Tannehill 15.00 40.00
6 Trent Richardson 20.00 50.00

2012 Panini National Convention VIP

COMPLETE SET (6) 12.00 30.00
1 Robert Griffin III 4.00 10.00
2 Andrew Luck 4.00 10.00

2011 Panini Team Colors National Convention Autographs

TC1 Jay Cutler/5
TC2 Brian Urlacher
TC3 Devin Hester
TC4 Matt Forte

2010 Panini Plates and Patches

101-200 ROOKIE AU PRINT RUN 99-849
201-235 ROOK.JSY AU PRINT RUN 199-699
EXCH EXPIRATION: 7/26/2012
1 Larry Fitzgerald 1.50 4.00
2 Steve Breaston 1.00 2.50
3 Tim Hightower 1.00 2.50
4 Matt Ryan 1.50 4.00
5 Michael Turner 1.00 2.50
6 Roddy White 1.25 3.00
7 Anquan Boldin 1.25 3.00
8 Joe Flacco 1.50 4.00
9 Ray Rice 1.25 3.00
10 Lee Evans 1.25 3.00
11 Marshawn Lynch 1.25 3.00
12 Ryan Fitzpatrick 1.50 4.00
13 DeAngelo Williams 1.25 3.00
14 Jonathan Stewart 1.25 3.00
15 Steve Smith 1.25 3.00
16 Jay Cutler 1.50 4.00
17 Johnny Knox 1.25 3.00
18 Matt Forte 1.25 3.00
19 Carson Palmer 1.25 3.00
20 Cedric Benson 1.25 3.00
21 Chad Ochocinco 1.25 3.00
22 Ben Watson 1.00 2.50
23 Josh Cribbs 1.50 4.00
24 Peyton Hillis 1.50 4.00
25 Jason Witten 1.50 4.00
26 Marion Barber 1.25 3.00
27 Tony Romo 2.00 5.00
28 Eddie Royal 1.00 2.50
29 Knowshon Moreno 1.25 3.00
30 Kyle Orton 1.25 3.00
31 Calvin Johnson 1.50 4.00
32 Matthew Stafford 1.50 4.00
33 Nate Burleson 1.00 2.50
34 Aaron Rodgers 3.00 8.00
35 Brandon Jackson 1.00 2.50
36 Donald Driver 1.25 3.00
37 Andre Johnson 1.25 3.00
38 Arian Foster 1.25 3.00
39 Matt Schaub 1.25 3.00
40 Dallas Clark 1.25 3.00
41 Peyton Manning 2.50 6.00
42 Reggie Wayne 1.25 3.00
43 David Garrard 1.25 3.00
44 Maurice Jones-Drew 1.25 3.00
45 Mike Sims-Walker 1.25 3.00
46 Dwayne Bowe 1.25 3.00
47 Jamaal Charles 1.25 3.00
48 Matt Cassel 1.25 3.00
49 Brandon Marshall 1.25 3.00
50 Chad Henne 1.25 3.00
51 Ronnie Brown 1.25 3.00
52 Adrian Peterson 2.50 6.00
53 Brett Favre 4.00 10.00
54 Percy Harvin 1.50 4.00
55 Visanthe Shiancoe 1.25 3.00
56 BenJarvus Green-Ellis 1.50 4.00
57 Randy Moss 1.50 4.00
58 Tom Brady 2.50 6.00
59 Wes Welker 1.50 4.00
60 Drew Brees 1.50 4.00
61 Marques Colston 1.25 3.00
62 Reggie Bush 1.50 4.00
63 Ahmad Bradshaw 1.25 3.00
64 Eli Manning 1.50 4.00
65 Hakeem Nicks 1.25 3.00
66 Braylon Edwards 1.25 3.00
67 Mark Sanchez 1.50 4.00
68 Shonn Greene 1.25 3.00
69 Bruce Gradkowski 1.00 2.50
70 Darren McFadden 1.25 3.00
71 Darrius Heyward-Bey 1.25 3.00
72 DeSean Jackson 1.25 3.00
73 Jeremy Maclin 1.25 3.00
74 LeSean McCoy 1.25 3.00
75 Michael Vick 2.00 5.00
76 Ben Roethlisberger 1.50 4.00
77 Mike Wallace 1.25 3.00
78 Rashard Mendenhall 1.25 3.00
79 Troy Polamalu 1.50 4.00
80 Antonio Gates 1.25 3.00
81 Malcom Floyd 1.25 3.00
82 Philip Rivers 1.50 4.00
83 Frank Gore 1.25 3.00
84 Michael Crabtree 1.50 4.00
85 Vernon Davis 1.25 3.00
86 John Carlson 1.00 2.50
87 Leon Washington 1.25 3.00
88 Matt Hasselbeck 1.00 2.50
89 Danny Amendola 1.50 4.00
90 Mark Clayton 1.00 2.50
91 Steven Jackson 1.25 3.00
92 Cadillac Williams 1.25 3.00
93 Josh Freeman 1.50 4.00
94 Kellen Winslow Jr. 1.25 3.00
95 Chris Johnson 1.50 4.00
96 Nate Washington 1.00 2.50
97 Vince Young 1.00 2.50
98 Chris Cooley 1.25 3.00
99 Donovan McNabb 1.50 4.00
100 Santana Moss 1.25 3.00
101 Aaron Hernandez AU/549 RC 8.00 20.00
102 Andrew Quarless AU/249 RC 5.00 12.00
103 Anthony Dixon AU/449 RC 5.00 12.00
104 Anthony McCoy AU/449 RC 4.00 10.00
105 Antonio Brown AU/449 RC 12.00 25.00
106 Blair White AU/99 RC 6.00 15.00
107 Brandon Banks AU/249 RC 6.00 15.00
108 Brandon Graham AU/449 RC 4.00 10.00
109 Brandon Spikes AU/649 RC 5.00 12.00
110 Brody Eldridge AU/249 RC 5.00 12.00
111 Bryan Bulaga AU/449 RC 5.00 12.00
112 Carlos Dunlap AU/99 RC 6.00 15.00
113 Carlton Mitchell AU/199 RC 5.00 12.00
114 Chris Cook AU/849 RC 5.00 12.00
115 Chris Ivory AU/249 RC 6.00 15.00
116 Chris McGaha AU/449 RC 3.00 8.00
117 Clay Harbor AU/249 RC 5.00 12.00
118 Corey Wootton AU/449 RC 4.00 10.00
119 Dan LeFevour AU/299 RC 5.00 12.00
120 Dan Williams AU/99 RC 5.00 12.00
121 Daryl Washington AU/99 RC EXCH 5.00 12.00
122 David Gettis AU/449 RC 5.00 12.00
123 David Nelson AU/249 RC 7.50 15.00
124 David Reed AU/249 RC 4.00 10.00
125 Deji Karim AU/249 RC 5.00 12.00
126 Dennis Pitta AU/249 RC 5.00 12.00
127 Derrick Morgan AU/649 RC 4.00 10.00
128 Devin McCourty AU/549 RC 6.00 15.00
129 Dezmon Briscoe AU/99 RC EXCH 5.00 12.00
130 Dominique Curry AU/249 RC 4.00 10.00
131 Dominique Franks AU/449 RC 3.00 8.00
132 Donald Jones AU/249 RC 7.50 15.00
133 Dorin Dickerson AU/249 RC 3.00 8.00
134 Duke Calhoun AU/99 RC 5.00 12.00
135 Earl Thomas AU/449 RC 5.00 12.00
136 Ed Dickson AU/449 RC 5.00 12.00
137 Ed Wang AU/249 RC 5.00 12.00
138 Everson Griffen AU/449 RC 5.00 12.00
139 Fendi Onobun AU/249 RC 4.00 10.00
140 Garrett Graham AU/449 RC 4.00 10.00
141 Jacoby Ford AU/449 RC 6.00 15.00
142 James Starks AU/449 RC 15.00 30.00
143 Jared Odrick AU/249 RC 5.00 12.00
144 Jarrett Brown AU/268 RC 5.00 12.00
145 Jason Pierre-Paul AU/449 RC 12.50 25.00
146 Jason Worilds AU/449 RC 5.00 12.00
147 Javier Arenas AU/249 RC 5.00 12.00
148 Jeremy Horne AU/99 RC 5.00 12.00
149 Jeremy Williams AU/349 RC 3.00 8.00
150 Jerry Hughes AU/549 RC 5.00 12.00
151 Jim Dray AU/249 RC 4.00 10.00
152 Jimmy Graham AU/649 RC 15.00 30.00
153 Joe Haden AU/449 RC 5.00 12.00
154 Joe Webb AU/249 RC 8.00 20.00
155 John Conner AU/249 RC 5.00 12.00
156 John Skelton AU/649 RC 5.00 12.00
157 Joique Bell AU/99 RC 5.00 12.00
158 Kareem Jackson AU/99 RC 6.00 15.00
159 Keiland Williams AU/249 RC 5.00 12.00
160 Keith Toston AU/249 RC 5.00 12.00
161 Kerry Meier AU/249 RC 4.00 10.00
162 Koa Misi AU/249 RC 5.00 12.00
163 Kyle Williams AU/99 RC 6.00 15.00
164 Kyle Wilson AU/449 RC 5.00 12.00
165 Lamarr Houston AU/249 RC 5.00 12.00
166 LeGarrette Blount AU/449 RC 15.00 30.00
167 Lonyae Miller AU/199 RC 5.00 12.00
168 Marc Mariani AU/249 RC 5.00 12.00
169 Marlon Moore AU/249 RC 5.00 12.00
170 Max Hall AU/249 RC 5.00 12.00
171 Max Komar AU/99 RC EXCH 5.00 12.00
172 Michael Hoomanawanui AU/249 RC 5.00 12.00
173 Mickey Shuler AU/249 RC 5.00 12.00
174 Morgan Burnett AU/449 RC 5.00 12.00
175 Nate Allen AU/99 RC 6.00 15.00
176 NaVorro Bowman AU/99 RC 6.00 15.00
177 Patrick Robinson AU/449 RC 5.00 12.00
178 Perrish Cox AU/449 RC 4.00 10.00
179 Preston Parker AU/249 RC 4.00 10.00
180 Ricky Sapp AU/549 RC 4.00 10.00
181 Riley Cooper AU/449 RC 5.00 12.00
182 Roberto Wallace AU/249 RC 4.00 10.00
183 Russell Okung AU/249 RC 5.00 12.00
184 Rusty Smith AU/249 RC 5.00 12.00
185 Michael Palmer AU/449 RC 4.00 10.00
186 Sean Lee AU/549 RC 6.00 15.00
187 Sean Weatherspoon AU/649 RC 5.00 12.00
188 Chris Gronkowski AU/449 RC 5.00 12.00
189 Seyi Ajirotutu AU/199 RC 6.00 15.00
190 Shay Hodge AU/449 RC 4.00 10.00
191 Stephen Williams AU/249 RC 5.00 12.00
192 T.J. Ward AU/249 RC 5.00 12.00
193 Taylor Mays AU/649 RC 5.00 12.00
194 Thaddeus Lewis AU/249 RC UER 4.00 10.00
(name misspelled Lexis)
195 Tony Moeaki AU/249 RC 5.00 12.00
196 Tony Pike AU/449 RC 5.00 12.00
197 Trent Williams AU/99 RC EXCH 6.00 15.00
198 Tyson Alualu AU/249 RC 4.00 10.00
199 Victor Cruz AU/249 RC 40.00 80.00
200 Zac Robinson AU/549 RC 4.00 10.00
201 Andre Roberts JSY AU/499 RC 8.00 20.00
202 Armanti Edwards JSY AU/699 RC 8.00 20.00
203 Arrelious Benn JSY AU/699 RC 8.00 20.00
204 Ben Tate JSY AU/699 RC 10.00 25.00
205 Brandon LaFell JSY AU/599 RC 8.00 20.00
206 C.J. Spiller JSY AU/399 RC 20.00 40.00
207 Colt McCoy JSY AU/399 RC 15.00 40.00
208 Damian Williams JSY AU/699 RC 8.00 20.00
209 Demaryius Thomas JSY AU/699 RC 12.00 30.00
210 Dexter McCluster JSY AU/599 RC 8.00 20.00
211 Dez Bryant JSY AU/599 RC 25.00 60.00
212 Emmanuel Sanders JSY AU/699 RC 8.00 20.00
213 Eric Berry JSY AU/699 RC 8.00 20.00
214 Eric Decker JSY AU/699 RC 10.00 25.00
215 Gerald McCoy JSY AU/199 RC 10.00 25.00
216 Golden Tate JSY AU/599 RC 8.00 20.00
217 Jahvid Best JSY AU/699 RC 12.00 30.00
218 Jermaine Gresham JSY AU/699 RC 10.00 25.00
219 Jimmy Clausen JSY AU/499 RC 8.00 20.00
220 Joe McKnight JSY AU/699 RC 8.00 20.00
221 Jonathan Dwyer JSY AU/699 RC 8.00 20.00
222 Jordan Shipley JSY AU/699 RC 8.00 20.00
223 Marcus Easley JSY AU/699 RC 6.00 15.00
224 Mardy Gilyard JSY AU/699 RC 8.00 20.00
225 Mike Kafka JSY AU/699 RC 8.00 20.00
226 Mike Williams JSY AU/899 RC 15.00 30.00
227 Montario Hardesty JSY AU/699 RC 8.00 20.00
228 Ndamukong Suh JSY AU/199 RC 40.00 80.00
229 Rob Gronkowski JSY AU/699 RC 25.00 50.00
230 Rolando McClain JSY AU/699 RC 8.00 20.00
231 Ryan Mathews JSY AU/699 RC 15.00 40.00
232 Sam Bradford JSY AU/399 RC 50.00 120.00
233 Taylor Price JSY AU/699 RC 8.00 20.00
234 Tim Tebow JSY AU/499 RC 75.00 135.00
235 Toby Gerhart JSY AU/699 RC 8.00 20.00

2010 Panini Plates and Patches Gold

*VETS 1-100: 1.2X TO 3X BASIC CARDS
*ROOKIES 101-200: .6X TO 1.5X SILVER/100
GOLD PRINT RUN 50 SER.#'d SETS

2010 Panini Plates and Patches Rookie Prime Signatures Nameplate

*NP/25: .6X TO 1.5X BASE JSY AU/399-699
*NP/25: .5X TO 1.2X BASE JSY AU/199
NAMEPLATE PRINT RUN 25
EXCH EXPIRATION: 7/26/2012
232 Sam Bradford 125.00 250.00
234 Tim Tebow 150.00 250.00

2010 Panini Plates and Patches Silver

*VETS 1-100: .8X TO 2X BASIC CARDS
SILVER PRINT RUN 100 SER.#'d SETS
101 Aaron Hernandez 5.00 12.00
102 Andrew Quarless 3.00 8.00
103 Anthony Dixon 3.00 8.00
104 Anthony McCoy 2.50 6.00
105 Antonio Brown 5.00 12.00
106 Blair White 3.00 8.00
107 Brandon Banks 4.00 10.00
108 Brandon Graham 2.50 6.00
109 Brandon Spikes 3.00 8.00
110 Brody Eldridge 3.00 8.00
111 Bryan Bulaga 3.00 8.00
112 Carlos Dunlap 3.00 8.00
113 Carlton Mitchell 2.50 6.00
114 Chris Cook 3.00 8.00
115 Chris Ivory 4.00 10.00
116 Chris McGaha 2.00 5.00
117 Clay Harbor 3.00 8.00
118 Corey Wootton 2.50 6.00
119 Dan LeFevour 3.00 8.00
120 Dan Williams 2.50 6.00
121 Daryl Washington 2.50 6.00
122 David Gettis 3.00 8.00
123 David Nelson 3.00 8.00
124 David Reed 2.50 6.00
125 Deji Karim 3.00 8.00
126 Dennis Pitta 3.00 8.00
127 Derrick Morgan 2.50 6.00
128 Devin McCourty 3.00 8.00
129 Dezmon Briscoe 2.50 6.00
130 Dominique Curry 2.50 6.00
131 Dominique Franks 2.00 5.00
132 Donald Jones 3.00 8.00
133 Dorin Dickerson 2.00 5.00
134 Duke Calhoun 2.50 6.00
135 Earl Thomas 3.00 8.00
136 Ed Dickson 3.00 8.00
137 Ed Wang 3.00 8.00
138 Everson Griffen 3.00 8.00
139 Fendi Onobun 2.50 6.00
140 Garrett Graham 2.50 6.00
141 Jacoby Ford 3.00 8.00
142 James Starks 5.00 12.00
143 Jared Odrick 3.00 8.00
144 Jarrett Brown 3.00 8.00
145 Jason Pierre-Paul 5.00 12.00
146 Jason Worilds 3.00 8.00
147 Javier Arenas 3.00 8.00
148 Jeremy Horne 2.50 6.00
149 Jeremy Williams 2.00 5.00
150 Jerry Hughes 3.00 8.00
151 Jim Dray 2.50 6.00
152 Jimmy Graham 6.00 15.00
153 Joe Haden 3.00 8.00
154 Joe Webb 3.00 8.00
155 John Conner 3.00 8.00
156 John Skelton 3.00 8.00
157 Joique Bell 2.50 6.00
158 Kareem Jackson 3.00 8.00
159 Keiland Williams 3.00 8.00
160 Keith Toston 3.00 8.00
161 Kerry Meier 2.50 6.00
162 Koa Misi 3.00 8.00
163 Kyle Williams 3.00 8.00
164 Kyle Wilson 3.00 8.00
165 Lamarr Houston 3.00 8.00
166 LeGarrette Blount 5.00 12.00
167 Lonyae Miller 2.50 6.00
168 Marc Mariani 3.00 8.00
169 Marlon Moore 3.00 8.00
170 Max Hall 3.00 8.00
171 Max Komar 3.00 8.00
172 Michael Hoomanawanui 3.00 8.00
173 Mickey Shuler 3.00 8.00
174 Morgan Burnett 3.00 8.00
175 Nate Allen 3.00 8.00
176 NaVorro Bowman 3.00 8.00
177 Patrick Robinson 3.00 8.00
178 Perrish Cox 2.50 6.00
179 Preston Parker 2.50 6.00
180 Ricky Sapp 2.50 6.00
181 Riley Cooper 3.00 8.00
182 Roberto Wallace 2.50 6.00
183 Russell Okung 3.00 8.00
184 Rusty Smith 3.00 8.00
185 Michael Palmer 2.50 6.00
186 Sean Lee 3.00 8.00
187 Sean Weatherspoon 3.00 8.00
188 Chris Gronkowski 3.00 8.00
189 Seyi Ajirotutu 3.00 8.00
190 Shay Hodge 2.50 6.00
191 Stephen Williams 3.00 8.00
192 T.J. Ward 3.00 8.00
193 Taylor Mays 3.00 8.00
194 Thaddeus Lewis 2.50 6.00
195 Tony Moeaki 3.00 8.00
196 Tony Pike 3.00 8.00
197 Trent Williams 3.00 8.00
198 Tyson Alualu 2.50 6.00
199 Victor Cruz 10.00 25.00
200 Zac Robinson 2.50 6.00

2010 Panini Plates and Patches City Limits

STATED PRINT RUN 299 SER.#'d SETS
1 DeMarcus Ware 1.50 4.00
2 Aaron Rodgers 4.00 10.00
3 Matt Ryan 2.00 5.00
4 Carson Palmer 1.50 4.00
5 Vernon Davis 1.50 4.00
6 Mark Sanchez 2.00 5.00
7 Brett Favre 5.00 12.00
8 Adrian Peterson 3.00 8.00
9 Maurice Jones-Drew 1.50 4.00
10 Drew Brees 2.00 5.00
11 Peyton Manning 3.00 8.00
12 Steve Smith 1.50 4.00
13 Ray Lewis 2.00 5.00
14 Eli Manning 2.00 5.00
15 Troy Polamalu 2.00 5.00
16 Chris Johnson 2.00 5.00
17 Larry Fitzgerald 2.00 5.00
18 Andre Johnson 1.50 4.00
19 Philip Rivers 2.00 5.00
20 Tom Brady 3.00 8.00
21 Chad Henne 1.50 4.00
22 Brian Urlacher 2.00 5.00
23 Chris Cooley 1.50 4.00
24 Kyle Orton 1.50 4.00
25 Steven Jackson 1.50 4.00

2010 Panini Plates and Patches City Limits Autographs

AUTO STATED PRINT RUN 1-15
1 DeMarcus Ware/15
14 Eli Manning/15 40.00 80.00

2010 Panini Plates and Patches City Limits Autograph Materials Prime

PRIME AU PRINT RUN 1-15
1 DeMarcus Ware/15 20.00 40.00

2010 Panini Plates and Patches City Limits Materials

STATED PRINT RUN 95-299
*PRIME/50: .6X TO 1.5X BASIC JSY
*PRIME/25: .8X TO 2X BASIC JSY
1 DeMarcus Ware/200 3.00 8.00
2 Aaron Rodgers/100 8.00 20.00
4 Carson Palmer/299 3.00 8.00
5 Vernon Davis/200 3.00 8.00
7 Brett Favre/299 10.00 25.00
8 Adrian Peterson/200 6.00 15.00
9 Maurice Jones-Drew/200 3.00 8.00
11 Peyton Manning/200 6.00 15.00
13 Ray Lewis/155 4.00 10.00
16 Chris Johnson/190 4.00 10.00
17 Larry Fitzgerald/145 4.00 10.00
18 Andre Johnson/299 3.00 8.00
19 Philip Rivers/200 4.00 10.00
20 Tom Brady/200 6.00 15.00
22 Brian Urlacher/105 4.00 10.00
23 Chris Cooley/200 4.00 10.00
24 Kyle Orton/95 4.00 10.00

2010 Panini Plates and Patches Gridiron Cut Autographs

STATED PRINT RUN 1-100
1 Red Badgro/18 20.00 50.00
2 Sammy Baugh/63 40.00 80.00
3 Bert Bell/6
4 Paul Brown/100 30.00 80.00
5 Roosevelt Brown/36 20.00 50.00
6 Tony Canadeo/37 40.00 80.00
7 Dutch Clark/9
8 George Connor/23 15.00 40.00
9 Lou Creekmur/66 20.00 50.00
10 Ernie Davis/1
11 Bill Dudley/100 15.00 40.00
12 Weeb Ewbank/100 15.00 40.00
13 Tom Fears/9
14 Ray Flaherty/3
15 Otto Graham/15 40.00 80.00
16 Red Grange/3
17 Lou Groza/69 20.00 50.00
18 George Halas/15 100.00 200.00
19 Mel Hein/16 30.00 60.00
20 Bill George/3
21 Elroy Hirsch/23 20.00 50.00
22 Lamar Hunt/6
23 Don Hutson/21 75.00 150.00
24 Vic Janowicz/19 30.00 60.00
25 Stan Jones/39 20.00 50.00
26 Tom Landry/8
27 Dick Lane/27 20.00 50.00
28 Dante Lavelli/58 15.00 40.00
31 Wellington Mara/6
32 Ollie Matson/26 30.00 60.00
33 George McAfee/61 15.00 40.00
34 Marion Motley/67 15.00 40.00
35 Jim Parker/12
36 Walter Payton/75 150.00 300.00
37 Pete Pihos/56 15.00 40.00
38 Andy Robustelli/52 15.00 40.00
39 Art Rooney/11
40 Kyle Rote/80 15.00 40.00
41 Tobin Rote/31 25.00 60.00
42 Hank Soar/33 20.00 50.00
43 Hank Stram/27
44 Ken Strong/18 30.00 80.00
45 Jim Thorpe/1
46 Bulldog Turner/6
47 Johnny Unitas/36 175.00 300.00
48 Gene Upshaw/10
49 Doak Walker/3

2010 Panini Plates and Patches Honors

STATED PRINT RUN 299 SER.#'d SETS
1 DeAngelo Williams 1.50 4.00
2 Wes Welker 2.00 5.00
3 Calvin Johnson 2.00 5.00
4 Devin Hester 2.00 5.00
5 Marques Colston 1.50 4.00
6 Randy Moss 2.00 5.00
7 Josh Cribbs 2.00 5.00
8 Dallas Clark 1.50 4.00
9 Ray Rice 1.50 4.00
10 DeSean Jackson 1.50 4.00
11 Austin Collie 1.50 4.00
12 Donald Driver 1.50 4.00
13 Reggie Wayne 1.50 4.00
14 Jay Cutler 2.00 5.00
15 Pierre Thomas 1.50 4.00
16 Chad Ochocinco 1.50 4.00
17 Matt Schaub 1.50 4.00
18 Tony Romo 2.50 6.00
19 Rashard Mendenhall 1.50 4.00
20 Antonio Gates 1.50 4.00
21 Percy Harvin 2.00 5.00
22 Tony Gonzalez 1.50 4.00
23 Frank Gore 1.50 4.00
24 Miles Austin 2.00 5.00
25 Hines Ward 1.50 4.00

2010 Panini Plates and Patches Honors Autographs

STATED PRINT RUN 5-25
11 Austin Collie/25 12.00 30.00
22 Tony Gonzalez/25
23 Frank Gore/15

2010 Panini Plates and Patches Honors Materials

STATED PRINT RUN 100-299
5 Marques Colston/175 3.00 8.00
6 Randy Moss/175 4.00 10.00
10 DeSean Jackson/175 3.00 8.00
13 Reggie Wayne/100 3.00 8.00
14 Jay Cutler/299 4.00 10.00
18 Tony Romo/175 5.00 12.00
20 Antonio Gates/299 3.00 8.00

2010 Panini Plates and Patches Honors Materials Prime

PRIME STATED PRINT RUN 20-50
2 Wes Welker 6.00 15.00
4 Devin Hester 6.00 15.00
5 Marques Colston 5.00 12.00
10 DeSean Jackson 5.00 12.00
12 Donald Driver 6.00 15.00
13 Reggie Wayne/20 5.00 12.00
14 Jay Cutler 6.00 15.00
16 Chad Ochocinco 5.00 12.00
18 Tony Romo 8.00 20.00
20 Antonio Gates 5.00 12.00

2010 Panini Plates and Patches Jerseys

STATED PRINT RUN 20-299
6 Roddy White/120 3.00 8.00
10 Lee Evans/100 3.00 8.00
16 Jay Cutler/299 4.00 10.00
17 Johnny Knox/299 3.00 8.00
18 Matt Forte/299 3.00 8.00
19 Carson Palmer/299 3.00 8.00
20 Cedric Benson/299 3.00 8.00
26 Marion Barber/299 3.00 8.00
27 Tony Romo/299 5.00 12.00
31 Calvin Johnson/299 4.00 10.00
34 Aaron Rodgers/200 8.00 20.00
37 Andre Johnson/299 3.00 8.00
41 Peyton Manning/299 6.00 15.00
43 David Garrard/100 3.00 8.00
44 Maurice Jones-Drew/210 3.00 8.00
45 Mike Sims-Walker/100 3.00 8.00
46 Dwayne Bowe/299 3.00 8.00
47 Jamaal Charles/270 3.00 8.00
48 Matt Cassel/299 3.00 8.00
52 Adrian Peterson/299 6.00 15.00
53 Brett Favre/299 10.00 25.00
57 Randy Moss/299 4.00 10.00
58 Tom Brady/155 6.00 15.00
61 Marques Colston/299 3.00 8.00
63 Ahmad Bradshaw/270 3.00 8.00
67 Mark Sanchez/20 10.00 25.00
70 Darren McFadden/299 3.00 8.00
72 DeSean Jackson/245 3.00 8.00
76 Ben Roethlisberger/299 4.00 10.00
80 Antonio Gates/299 3.00 8.00
82 Philip Rivers/270 4.00 10.00
85 Vernon Davis/105 3.00 8.00
88 Matt Hasselbeck/95 2.50 6.00
97 Vince Young/299 2.50 6.00
98 Chris Cooley/150 4.00 10.00
99 Donovan McNabb/299 4.00 10.00
100 Santana Moss/120 3.00 8.00

2010 Panini Plates and Patches Jerseys Prime

PRIME PRINT RUN 4-50
10 Lee Evans/15 6.00 15.00
16 Jay Cutler/50 6.00 15.00
17 Johnny Knox/40 5.00 12.00
18 Matt Forte/50 5.00 12.00
19 Carson Palmer/50 5.00 12.00
20 Cedric Benson/50 5.00 12.00
21 Chad Ochocinco/50 5.00 12.00
25 Jason Witten/50 6.00 15.00
26 Marion Barber/50 5.00 12.00
27 Tony Romo/50 8.00 20.00
31 Calvin Johnson/50 6.00 15.00
34 Aaron Rodgers/45 12.00 30.00
36 Donald Driver/50 6.00 15.00
41 Peyton Manning/50 10.00 25.00
46 Dwayne Bowe/20 6.00 15.00
55 Visanthe Shiancoe/50 5.00 12.00
58 Tom Brady/20 12.00 30.00
59 Wes Welker/50 6.00 15.00
61 Marques Colston/20 6.00 15.00
63 Ahmad Bradshaw/15 6.00 15.00
76 Ben Roethlisberger/25 8.00 20.00
80 Antonio Gates/45 5.00 12.00
85 Vernon Davis/50 5.00 12.00
91 Steven Jackson/35 5.00 12.00
95 Chris Johnson/20 8.00 20.00
98 Chris Cooley/25 8.00 20.00
100 Santana Moss/50 5.00 12.00

2010 Panini Plates and Patches Jerseys Prime Jersey Number

PRIME JSY # PRINT RUN 1-50
6 Roddy White/50 5.00 12.00
10 Lee Evans/50 5.00 12.00
13 DeAngelo Williams/25 6.00 15.00
14 Jonathan Stewart/35 5.00 12.00
16 Jay Cutler/50 6.00 15.00
18 Matt Forte/50 5.00 12.00
19 Carson Palmer/50 5.00 12.00
20 Cedric Benson/50 5.00 12.00
21 Chad Ochocinco/50 5.00 12.00
25 Jason Witten/50 6.00 15.00
26 Marion Barber/50 5.00 12.00
27 Tony Romo/50 8.00 20.00
29 Knowshon Moreno/50 5.00 12.00
31 Calvin Johnson/50 6.00 15.00
34 Aaron Rodgers/50 10.00 25.00
36 Donald Driver/50 6.00 15.00
37 Andre Johnson/50 5.00 12.00
39 Matt Schaub/25 6.00 15.00
40 Dallas Clark/25 6.00 15.00
41 Peyton Manning/50 10.00 25.00
42 Reggie Wayne/25 6.00 15.00
43 David Garrard/25 6.00 15.00
44 Maurice Jones-Drew/50 5.00 12.00
46 Dwayne Bowe/50 5.00 12.00
47 Jamaal Charles/50 5.00 12.00
48 Matt Cassel/50 5.00 12.00
52 Adrian Peterson/50 10.00 25.00
55 Visanthe Shiancoe/35 5.00 12.00
58 Tom Brady/50 10.00 25.00
59 Wes Welker/50 6.00 15.00
61 Marques Colston/50 5.00 12.00
63 Ahmad Bradshaw/45 5.00 12.00
70 Darren McFadden/35 5.00 12.00
72 DeSean Jackson/50 5.00 12.00
80 Antonio Gates/50 5.00 12.00
82 Philip Rivers/50 6.00 15.00
85 Vernon Davis/50 5.00 12.00
88 Matt Hasselbeck/25 5.00 12.00
92 Cadillac Williams/50 5.00 12.00
95 Chris Johnson/50 6.00 15.00
98 Chris Cooley/50 6.00 15.00
100 Santana Moss/50 5.00 12.00

2010 Panini Plates and Patches Jerseys Prime Nameplate

STATED PRINT RUN 1-25
6 Roddy White/25 6.00 15.00
10 Lee Evans/15 6.00 15.00
13 DeAngelo Williams/15 6.00 15.00
16 Jay Cutler/25 8.00 20.00
18 Matt Forte/25 6.00 15.00
19 Carson Palmer/25 6.00 15.00
20 Cedric Benson/25 6.00 15.00
21 Chad Ochocinco/25 6.00 15.00
25 Jason Witten/25 8.00 20.00
26 Marion Barber/25 6.00 15.00
27 Tony Romo/25 10.00 25.00
29 Knowshon Moreno/25 6.00 15.00
31 Calvin Johnson/25 8.00 20.00
34 Aaron Rodgers/25 15.00 40.00
36 Donald Driver/25 8.00 20.00
41 Peyton Manning/25 12.00 30.00
42 Reggie Wayne/15 6.00 15.00
43 David Garrard/25 6.00 15.00
44 Maurice Jones-Drew/25 6.00 15.00
46 Dwayne Bowe/25 6.00 15.00
47 Jamaal Charles/25 6.00 15.00
48 Matt Cassel/25 6.00 15.00
52 Adrian Peterson/25 12.00 30.00
55 Visanthe Shiancoe/25 6.00 15.00
58 Tom Brady/25 12.00 30.00
59 Wes Welker/25 8.00 20.00
61 Marques Colston/25 6.00 15.00
67 Mark Sanchez/15 8.00 20.00
70 Darren McFadden/25 6.00 15.00
72 DeSean Jackson/25 6.00 15.00
74 LeSean McCoy/25 6.00 15.00
80 Antonio Gates/25 6.00 15.00
82 Philip Rivers/25 8.00 20.00
85 Vernon Davis/25 6.00 15.00
88 Matt Hasselbeck/15 5.00 12.00
91 Steven Jackson/25 6.00 15.00
92 Cadillac Williams/25 6.00 15.00
95 Chris Johnson/25 8.00 20.00
98 Chris Cooley/25 8.00 20.00
100 Santana Moss/25 6.00 15.00

2010 Panini Plates and Patches NFL Equipment

STATED PRINT RUN 20-150
*COMBO/50-100: .5X TO 1.2X BASIC JSY
1 Willis McGahee/150 3.00 8.00
2 Darren McFadden/150 3.00 8.00
5 Braylon Edwards/125 3.00 8.00
10 David Garrard/130 3.00 8.00
11 Greg Jennings/150 3.00 8.00
12 Ben Roethlisberger/140 4.00 10.00
13 Knowshon Moreno/80 3.00 8.00
14 Vince Young/150 2.50 6.00
15 Marion Barber/150 3.00 8.00
16 Darren Sproles/130 3.00 8.00
19 Visanthe Shiancoe/20 5.00 12.00
20 Jared Allen/150 4.00 10.00
22 Matt Forte/150 3.00 8.00
23 Heath Miller/150 3.00 8.00
24 Patrick Willis/130 3.00 8.00

2010 Panini Plates and Patches NFL Equipment Prime

STATED PRINT RUN 5-50
2 Darren McFadden/15 6.00 15.00
3 Jason Witten/50 6.00 15.00
11 Greg Jennings/25 6.00 15.00
12 Ben Roethlisberger/15 8.00 20.00
13 Knowshon Moreno/35 5.00 12.00
15 Marion Barber/50 5.00 12.00
16 Darren Sproles/50 5.00 12.00
19 Visanthe Shiancoe/5
20 Jared Allen/25 8.00 20.00
21 Ronnie Brown/10
22 Matt Forte/50 5.00 12.00
23 Heath Miller/50 5.00 12.00
24 Patrick Willis/50 5.00 12.00

2010 Panini Plates and Patches NFL Equipment Combos Prime

STATED PRINT RUN 1-25
3 Jason Witten/25 8.00 20.00
9 LeSean McCoy/25 6.00 15.00
10 David Garrard/25 6.00 15.00
11 Greg Jennings/25 6.00 15.00
13 Knowshon Moreno/25 6.00 15.00
15 Marion Barber/25 6.00 15.00
16 Darren Sproles/25 6.00 15.00
20 Jared Allen/25 8.00 20.00
22 Matt Forte/25 6.00 15.00
23 Heath Miller/25 6.00 15.00
24 Patrick Willis/25 6.00 15.00

2010 Panini Plates and Patches Rookie Autographed Jumbo Materials Prime

STATED PRINT RUN 25 SER.#'d SETS
*JUMBO AU/10: .5X TO 1.2X PRIME AU/25
EXCH EXPIRATION: 7/26/2012
1 Jahvid Best 20.00 50.00
2 Golden Tate 12.00 30.00
3 Gerald McCoy 12.00 30.00
4 Eric Decker 15.00 40.00
5 Eric Berry 12.00 30.00
6 Emmanuel Sanders 12.00 30.00
7 Dez Bryant 50.00 100.00
9 Demaryius Thomas 15.00 40.00
10 Damian Williams 12.00 30.00
11 Colt McCoy 30.00 80.00
12 C.J. Spiller 20.00 50.00
13 Brandon LaFell 12.00 30.00
14 Ben Tate 15.00 40.00
15 Arrelious Benn 12.00 30.00
16 Armanti Edwards 12.00 30.00
17 Andre Roberts 12.00 30.00
18 Toby Gerhart 12.00 30.00
19 Tim Tebow 100.00 200.00
20 Taylor Price 12.00 30.00
21 Sam Bradford 100.00 200.00
22 Ryan Mathews 40.00 80.00
23 Rolando McClain 12.00 30.00
24 Rob Gronkowski 40.00 80.00
25 Ndamukong Suh 40.00 80.00
26 Montario Hardesty 12.00 30.00
27 Mike Williams 20.00 50.00
28 Mike Kafka 12.00 30.00
29 Mardy Gilyard 12.00 30.00
30 Marcus Easley 10.00 25.00
31 Jordan Shipley 12.00 30.00
32 Jonathan Dwyer EXCH 12.00 30.00
33 Joe McKnight 12.00 30.00
34 Jimmy Clausen 15.00 40.00
35 Jermaine Gresham 15.00 40.00

2010 Panini Plates and Patches Rookie Blitz

STATED PRINT RUN 299 SER.#'d SETS
1 Demaryius Thomas 2.00 5.00
2 C.J. Spiller 2.50 6.00
3 Jordan Shipley 1.50 4.00
4 Eric Decker 2.00 5.00
5 Andre Roberts 1.50 4.00
6 Toby Gerhart 1.50 4.00
7 Ndamukong Suh 3.00 8.00
8 Sam Bradford 6.00 15.00
9 Arrelious Benn 1.50 4.00
10 Eric Berry 1.50 4.00
11 Jahvid Best 2.50 6.00
12 Rolando McClain 1.50 4.00
13 Tim Tebow 6.00 15.00
14 Dexter McCluster 1.50 4.00
15 Golden Tate 1.50 4.00
16 Jonathan Dwyer 1.50 4.00
17 Mike Williams 2.50 6.00
18 Ryan Mathews 3.00 8.00
19 Rob Gronkowski 4.00 10.00
20 Taylor Price 1.50 4.00
21 Armanti Edwards 1.50 4.00
22 Jimmy Clausen 1.50 4.00
23 Jermaine Gresham 2.00 5.00
24 Brandon LaFell 1.50 4.00
25 Colt McCoy 3.00 8.00
26 Mardy Gilyard 1.50 4.00
27 Dez Bryant 5.00 12.00
28 Damian Williams 1.50 4.00
29 Gerald McCoy 1.50 4.00
30 Emmanuel Sanders 1.50 4.00

2010 Panini Plates and Patches Rookie Blitz Autograph Materials

JSY AUTO PRINT RUN 25
*PRIME/15-25: .5X TO 1.2X JSY AU/25
*AUTO/10: .4X TO 1X JSY AU/25
EXCH EXPIRATION: 7/26/2012
1 Demaryius Thomas 12.00 30.00
2 C.J. Spiller 15.00 40.00
3 Jordan Shipley 10.00 25.00
4 Eric Decker 12.00 30.00
5 Andre Roberts 10.00 25.00
6 Toby Gerhart 10.00 25.00
7 Ndamukong Suh 25.00 60.00
8 Sam Bradford 75.00 150.00
9 Arrelious Benn 10.00 25.00
10 Eric Berry 10.00 25.00
11 Jahvid Best 15.00 40.00
12 Rolando McClain 10.00 25.00
13 Tim Tebow 100.00 175.00
15 Golden Tate 10.00 25.00
16 Jonathan Dwyer EXCH 10.00 25.00
17 Mike Williams 15.00 40.00
18 Ryan Mathews 30.00 80.00
19 Rob Gronkowski 30.00 60.00
20 Taylor Price 10.00 25.00
21 Armanti Edwards 10.00 25.00
22 Jimmy Clausen 15.00 40.00
23 Jermaine Gresham 12.00 30.00
24 Brandon LaFell 10.00 25.00
25 Colt McCoy 30.00 80.00
26 Mardy Gilyard 10.00 25.00
27 Dez Bryant 40.00 100.00
28 Damian Williams 10.00 25.00
29 Gerald McCoy 10.00 25.00
30 Emmanuel Sanders 10.00 25.00

2010 Panini Plates and Patches Rookie Blitz Materials

STATED PRINT RUN 299 SER.#'d SETS
1 Demaryius Thomas 3.00 8.00
2 C.J. Spiller 4.00 10.00
3 Jordan Shipley 2.50 6.00
4 Eric Decker 3.00 8.00
5 Andre Roberts 2.50 6.00
6 Toby Gerhart 2.50 6.00
7 Ndamukong Suh 5.00 12.00
8 Sam Bradford 10.00 25.00
9 Arrelious Benn 2.50 6.00
10 Eric Berry 2.50 6.00
11 Jahvid Best 4.00 10.00
12 Rolando McClain 2.50 6.00
13 Tim Tebow 10.00 25.00
14 Dexter McCluster 2.50 6.00
15 Golden Tate 2.50 6.00
16 Jonathan Dwyer 2.50 6.00
17 Mike Williams 4.00 10.00
18 Ryan Mathews 5.00 12.00
19 Rob Gronkowski 6.00 15.00
20 Taylor Price 2.50 6.00
21 Armanti Edwards 2.50 6.00
22 Jimmy Clausen 2.50 6.00
23 Jermaine Gresham 3.00 8.00
24 Brandon LaFell 2.50 6.00
25 Colt McCoy 5.00 12.00
26 Mardy Gilyard 2.50 6.00
27 Dez Bryant 8.00 20.00
28 Damian Williams 2.50 6.00
29 Gerald McCoy 2.50 6.00
30 Emmanuel Sanders 2.50 6.00

2010 Panini Plates and Patches Rookie Jumbo Materials

STATED PRINT RUN 50 SER.#'d SETS
*PRIME/15: .8X TO 2X BASIC JSY/50
1 Jahvid Best 6.00 15.00
2 Golden Tate 4.00 10.00
3 Gerald McCoy 4.00 10.00
4 Eric Decker 5.00 12.00
5 Eric Berry 4.00 10.00
6 Emmanuel Sanders 4.00 10.00
7 Dez Bryant 12.00 30.00
8 Dexter McCluster 4.00 10.00
9 Demaryius Thomas 5.00 12.00
10 Damian Williams 4.00 10.00
11 Colt McCoy 8.00 20.00
12 C.J. Spiller 6.00 15.00
13 Brandon LaFell 4.00 10.00
14 Ben Tate 5.00 12.00
15 Arrelious Benn 4.00 10.00
16 Armanti Edwards 4.00 10.00
17 Andre Roberts 4.00 10.00
18 Toby Gerhart 4.00 10.00
19 Tim Tebow 15.00 40.00
20 Taylor Price 4.00 10.00
21 Sam Bradford 15.00 40.00
22 Ryan Mathews 8.00 20.00
23 Rolando McClain 4.00 10.00
24 Rob Gronkowski 10.00 25.00
25 Ndamukong Suh 8.00 20.00
26 Montario Hardesty 4.00 10.00
27 Mike Williams 6.00 15.00
28 Mike Kafka 4.00 10.00
29 Mardy Gilyard 4.00 10.00
30 Marcus Easley 3.00 8.00
31 Jordan Shipley 4.00 10.00
32 Jonathan Dwyer 4.00 10.00
33 Joe McKnight 4.00 10.00
34 Jimmy Clausen 4.00 10.00
35 Jermaine Gresham 5.00 12.00

2010 Panini Plates and Patches Signatures Gold

1-100 UNPRICED VET PRINT RUN 5
*GOLD/25: .8X TO 2X BASIC AU/249-849
*GOLD/25: .6X TO 1.5X BASIC AU/99-199
EXCH EXPIRATION: 7/26/2012

2010 Panini Plates and Patches Signatures Silver

*SLVR/50: .5X TO 1.2X BASE AU/249-849
*SLVR/50: .4X TO 1X BASE AU/99-199
SILVER PRINT RUN 50 SER.#'d SETS
EXCH EXPIRATION: 7/26/2012

2010 Panini Plates and Patches Team Supreme Materials

STATED PRINT RUN 2-50
1 Wes Welker/50 6.00 15.00
2 LeSean McCoy/50 5.00 12.00
3 Chad Ochocinco/50 5.00 12.00
4 Cedric Benson/50 5.00 12.00
5 Terrell Suggs/45 4.00 10.00
6 DeSean Jackson/50 5.00 12.00
7 Brandon Jacobs/50 5.00 12.00
8 Devery Henderson/50 4.00 10.00
9 Greg Jennings/40 5.00 12.00
10 Felix Jones/50 5.00 12.00
11 Reggie Wayne/50 5.00 12.00
12 Bo Scaife/35 4.00 10.00
13 Dwayne Bowe/50 5.00 12.00
14 Matthew Stafford/19 8.00 20.00
15 Darrelle Revis/7
16 Sidney Rice/50 5.00 12.00
17 Bernard Berrian/50 4.00 10.00
18 Brian Orakpo/45 4.00 10.00
19 Eddie Royal/23 5.00 12.00
20 Heath Miller/2
21 Will Smith/45 4.00 10.00
22 Calvin Johnson/50 6.00 15.00
23 Shonn Greene/50 5.00 12.00
24 Louis Murphy/50 5.00 12.00
25 Frank Gore/50 5.00 12.00
26 Adrian Peterson/50 10.00 25.00
27 Matt Cassel/45 5.00 12.00
28 Brent Celek/50 5.00 12.00
29 Darren McFadden/50 5.00 12.00
30 Lee Evans/50 5.00 12.00
31 Cadillac Williams/50 5.00 12.00
33 Vernon Davis/50 5.00 12.00
34 Marshawn Lynch/30 5.00 12.00
35 Jamaal Charles/50 5.00 12.00
36 Santana Moss/50 5.00 12.00
37 Dustin Keller/13

38 Steve Slaton/50 4.00 10.00
39 Mark Sanchez/20 8.00 20.00
40 Greg Olsen/50 4.00 10.00
41 Tom Brady/50 10.00 25.00
42 Clinton Portis/50 5.00 12.00
43 Maurice Jones-Drew/50 5.00 12.00
44 Joseph Addai/50 5.00 12.00
45 Roddy White/50 5.00 12.00
46 Tony Romo/50 8.00 20.00
47 Kevin Kolb/50 5.00 12.00
48 Darren Sproles/50 5.00 12.00
50 Brian Urlacher/45 6.00 15.00

2011 Panini Plates and Patches

1-100 VETERAN PRINT RUN 299
100-200 ROOKIE AU PRINT RUN 49-405
201-235 ROOK.JSY AU PRINT RUN 299-499
EXCH EXPIRATION: 8/1/2013
1 Joe Flacco 1.50 4.00
2 Matt Ryan 1.50 4.00
3 Josh Freeman 1.50 4.00
4 Kevin Kolb 1.25 3.00
5 Donovan McNabb 1.50 4.00
6 Jay Cutler 1.25 3.00
7 Michael Vick 1.50 4.00
8 Matt Schaub 1.25 3.00
9 Drew Brees 1.50 4.00
10 Eli Manning 1.50 4.00
11 Larry Fitzgerald 1.25 3.00
12 Tom Brady 2.50 6.00
13 Steve Johnson 1.25 3.00
14 Ryan Fitzpatrick 1.25 3.00
15 Matt Cassel 1.25 3.00
16 Chad Henne 1.25 3.00
17 Philip Rivers 1.50 4.00
18 Peyton Manning 2.50 6.00
19 Brandon Marshall 1.25 3.00
20 Darren McFadden 1.25 3.00
21 Frank Gore 1.25 3.00
22 Matt Forte 1.25 3.00
23 Arian Foster 1.25 3.00
24 Nnamdi Asomugha 1.25 3.00
25 Jamaal Charles 1.25 3.00
26 Beanie Wells 1.25 3.00
27 Ray Rice 1.25 3.00
28 Adrian Peterson 2.00 5.00
29 Joseph Addai 1.25 3.00
30 Ben Roethlisberger 1.50 4.00
31 Montario Hardesty 1.25 3.00
32 Maurice Jones-Drew 1.25 3.00
33 Michael Turner 1.25 3.00
34 Rashard Mendenhall 1.25 3.00
35 Tarvaris Jackson 1.00 2.50
36 Sam Bradford 1.50 4.00
37 Matt Hasselbeck 1.25 3.00
38 Jason Campbell 1.25 3.00
39 Steven Jackson 1.25 3.00
40 Peyton Hillis 1.25 3.00
41 Kyle Orton 1.25 3.00
42 BenJarvus Green-Ellis 1.25 3.00
43 Troy Polamalu 1.50 4.00
44 Ahmad Bradshaw 1.25 3.00
45 Mark Sanchez 1.50 4.00
46 Matthew Stafford 1.50 4.00
47 Tony Romo 1.50 4.00
48 Santonio Holmes 1.25 3.00
49 Mike Sims-Walker 1.25 3.00
50 DeSean Jackson 1.25 3.00
51 Alex Smith 1.25 3.00
52 Jordan Shipley 1.25 3.00
53 Aaron Rodgers 3.00 8.00
54 Colt McCoy 1.25 3.00
55 Terrell Suggs 1.00 2.50
56 Marques Colston 1.25 3.00
57 Percy Harvin 1.25 3.00
58 Rex Grossman 1.25 3.00
59 Nate Burleson 1.00 2.50
60 Johnny Knox 1.25 3.00
61 Plaxico Burress 1.25 3.00
62 Mike Wallace 1.50 4.00
63 Sidney Rice 1.25 3.00
64 Kenny Britt 1.25 3.00
65 Mike Williams 1.25 3.00
66 Reggie Bush 1.25 3.00
67 Fred Jackson 1.50 4.00
68 Shonn Greene 1.25 3.00
69 Rashad Jennings 1.00 2.50
70 Ryan Mathews 1.25 3.00
71 Marshawn Lynch 1.25 3.00
72 LeSean McCoy 1.25 3.00
73 Knowshon Moreno 1.25 3.00
74 Felix Jones 1.25 3.00
75 Jonathan Stewart 1.25 3.00
76 Chris Johnson 1.25 3.00
77 Michael Bush 1.00 2.50
78 Cedric Benson 1.25 3.00
79 DeAngelo Williams 1.25 3.00
80 Andre Johnson 1.25 3.00
81 Calvin Johnson 1.50 4.00
82 Dwayne Bowe 1.25 3.00
83 Wes Welker 1.50 4.00
84 Roddy White 1.25 3.00
85 Chad Ochocinco 1.25 3.00
86 Tim Hightower 1.00 2.50
87 Reggie Wayne 1.25 3.00
88 Dez Bryant 1.50 4.00
89 Steve Smith 1.25 3.00
90 Darren Sproles 1.25 3.00
91 Kellen Winslow Jr. 1.25 3.00
92 Vincent Jackson 1.25 3.00
93 Bo Scaife 1.00 2.50
94 Brandon Lloyd 1.25 3.00
95 Greg Jennings 1.25 3.00
96 Vernon Davis 1.25 3.00
97 Hakeem Nicks 1.25 3.00
98 Jermichael Finley 1.25 3.00
99 Marcedes Lewis 1.00 2.50
100 Santana Moss 1.25 3.00
101 Terrelle Pryor AU/299 RC 8.00 20.00
102 Aaron Williams AU/49 RC EXCH 6.00 15.00
103 Adrian Clayborn AU/49 RC EXCH 8.00 20.00
104 Ahmad Black AU/49 RC EXCH 6.00 15.00
105 Akeem Ayers AU/360 RC 4.00 10.00
106 Aldon Smith AU/49 RC EXCH 20.00 40.00
107 Aldrick Robinson AU/199 RC 4.00 10.00
108 Alex Henery AU/199 RC 15.00 30.00
109 Allen Bradford AU/273 RC 4.00 10.00
110 Anthony Allen AU/49 RC EXCH 5.00 12.00
111 Anthony Castonzo AU/405 RC 3.00 8.00
112 Anthony Sherman AU/199 RC 5.00 12.00
113 Brandon Harris AU/49 RC EXCH 5.00 12.00
114 Cameron Heyward AU/49 RC EXCH 8.00 20.00
115 Cameron Jordan AU/150 RC 5.00 12.00
116 Casey Matthews AU/199 RC 6.00 15.00
117 Cecil Shorts AU/49 RC EXCH 6.00 15.00
118 Charles Clay AU/49 RC EXCH 6.00 15.00
119 Corey Liuget AU/150 RC 4.00 10.00
120 D.J. Williams AU/183 RC 6.00 15.00
121 Da'Quan Bowers AU/150 RC 6.00 15.00
122 Da'Rel Scott AU/199 RC 5.00 12.00
123 Dane Sanzenbacher AU/199 RC 8.00 20.00
124 Darren Evans AU/49 RC EXCH 6.00 15.00
125 David Ausberry AU/49 RC EXCH 6.00 15.00
126 DeMarco Sampson AU/49 RC EXCH 5.00 12.00
127 Denarius Moore AU/106 RC 8.00 20.00
128 Dion Lewis AU/49 RC EXCH 8.00 20.00
129 Dwayne Harris AU/405 RC 5.00 12.00
130 Evan Royster AU/49 RC EXCH 8.00 20.00
131 Greg Jones AU/150 RC 5.00 12.00
132 Greg McElroy AU/49 RC EXCH 8.00 20.00
133 Greg Salas AU/150 RC 6.00 15.00
134 J.J. Watt AU/150 RC 8.00 20.00
135 Jacquizz Rodgers AU/150 RC 6.00 15.00
136 Jamar Newsome AU/49 RC 5.00 12.00
137 Jeremy Kerley AU/49 RC EXCH 8.00 20.00
138 Jimmy Smith AU/49 RC EXCH 8.00 20.00
139 Joe Lefeged AU/199 RC 5.00 12.00
140 Johnny White AU/49 RC EXCH 6.00 15.00
141 Jordan Cameron AU/199 RC 5.00 12.00
142 Josh Portis AU/49 RC EXCH 8.00 20.00
143 Julius Thomas AU/49 RC EXCH 6.00 15.00
144 Justin Houston AU/405 RC 5.00 12.00
145 Kealoha Pilares AU/49 RC EXCH 8.00 20.00
146 Kris Durham AU/199 RC 5.00 12.00
147 Kyle Adams AU/199 RC 4.00 10.00
148 Lance Kendricks AU/405 RC 4.00 10.00
149 Lee Smith AU/199 RC 6.00 15.00
150 Luke Stocker AU/150 RC 5.00 12.00
151 Marcus Cannon AU/199 RC 4.00 10.00
152 Marcus Gilchrist AU/49 RC 5.00 12.00
153 Martez Wilson AU/99 RC 6.00 15.00
154 Mason Foster AU/199 RC 6.00 15.00
155 Dan Bailey AU/199 RC 10.00 25.00
156 Nathan Enderle AU/49 RC EXCH 8.00 20.00
157 Niles Paul AU/49 RC EXCH 8.00 20.00
158 Owen Marecic AU/49 RC EXCH 8.00 20.00
159 Phil Taylor AU/405 RC 4.00 10.00
160 Prince Amukamara AU/50 RC 8.00 20.00
161 Quinton Carter AU/199 RC 4.00 10.00
162 Rahim Moore AU/405 RC 4.00 10.00
163 Richard Gordon AU/99 RC 5.00 12.00
164 Ricky Stanzi AU/150 RC 8.00 20.00
165 Robert Housler AU/199 RC 5.00 12.00
166 Ronald Johnson AU/150 RC 5.00 12.00
167 Roy Helu AU/150 RC 12.00 30.00
168 Ryan Kerrigan AU/150 RC 6.00 15.00
169 Ryan Taylor AU/199 RC 5.00 12.00
170 Ryan Whalen AU/405 RC 4.00 10.00
171 Andrew Hawkins AU/49 RC EXCH 10.00 25.00
172 Shane Bannon AU/99 RC 6.00 15.00
173 Stanley Havili AU/199 RC 4.00 10.00
174 Stephen Burton AU/49 RC EXCH 5.00 12.00
175 Stephen Paea AU/150 RC 6.00 15.00
176 T.J. Yates AU/49 RC 10.00 25.00
177 Tandon Doss AU/150 RC 5.00 12.00
178 Tyler Sash AU/49 RC EXCH 8.00 20.00
179 Tyrod Taylor AU/199 RC 6.00 15.00
180 Tyron Smith AU/49 RC EXCH 15.00 30.00
181 Virgil Green AU/199 RC 5.00 12.00
182 Weslye Saunders AU/49 RC EXCH 20.00 40.00
183 Zack Pianalto AU/199 RC 5.00 12.00
184 Armond Smith AU/49 RC EXCH 6.00 15.00
185 Colin Cochart AU/99 RC 6.00 15.00
186 Doug Baldwin AU/199 RC 10.00 25.00
187 LaQuan Williams AU/49 RC EXCH 6.00 15.00
188 Phillip Tanner AU/99 RC 10.00 25.00
189 Brian Rolle AU/49 RC EXCH
190 Bruce Miller AU/199 RC 8.00 20.00
191 Buster Skrine AU/199 RC 5.00 12.00
192 Chimdi Chekwa AU/199 RC 5.00 12.00
193 Chris Harris AU/199 RC 6.00 15.00
194 Chris White AU/199 RC 5.00 12.00
195 Henry Hynoski AU/199 RC 15.00 40.00
196 Jacquian Williams AU/49 RC EXCH 8.00 20.00
197 K.J. Wright AU/199 RC 8.00 20.00
199 Robert Quinn AU/199 RC 6.00 15.00
200 Patrick Peterson AU/199 RC 25.00 60.00
201 Cam Newton JSY AU/299 RC 75.00 150.00
202 Von Miller JSY AU/499 RC EXCH 12.00 30.00
203 Marcell Dareus JSY AU/499 RC EXCH 8.00 20.00
204 A.J. Green JSY AU/299 RC 30.00 60.00
205 Julio Jones JSY AU/299 RC EXCH 25.00 60.00
206 Jake Locker JSY AU/299 RC 30.00 80.00
207 Blaine Gabbert JSY AU/299 RC 20.00 50.00
208 Christian Ponder JSY AU/299 RC 30.00 60.00
209 Jonathan Baldwin JSY AU/499 RC 8.00 20.00
210 Mark Ingram JSY AU/299 RC 20.00 50.00
211 Andy Dalton JSY AU/499 RC 30.00 80.00
212 Colin Kaepernick JSY AU/499 RC 12.00 30.00
213 Ryan Williams JSY AU/499 RC 10.00 25.00
214 Kyle Rudolph JSY AU/499 RC EXCH 8.00 20.00
215 Titus Young JSY AU/499 RC 10.00 25.00
216 Shane Vereen JSY AU/499 RC 8.00 20.00
217 Mikel Leshoure JSY AU/499 RC 10.00 25.00
218 Torrey Smith JSY AU/499 RC 12.00 30.00
219 Greg Little JSY AU/499 RC 8.00 20.00
220 Daniel Thomas JSY AU/499 RC EXCH 8.00 20.00
221 Randall Cobb JSY AU/499 RC 10.00 25.00
222 DeMarco Murray JSY AU/499 RC 25.00 60.00
223 Stevan Ridley JSY AU/499 RC EXCH 8.00 20.00
224 Ryan Mallett JSY AU/299 RC 20.00 50.00
225 Austin Pettis JSY AU/499 RC 6.00 15.00
226 Leonard Hankerson JSY AU/499 RC 8.00 20.00
227 Vincent Brown JSY AU/499 RC 8.00 20.00
228 Jerrel Jernigan JSY AU/499 RC 5.00 12.00
229 Alex Green JSY AU/499 RC 8.00 20.00
230 Clyde Gates JSY AU/499 RC 6.00 15.00
231 Kendall Hunter JSY AU/499 RC 10.00 25.00
232 Delone Carter JSY AU/499 RC 6.00 15.00
233 Taiwan Jones JSY AU/499 RC 8.00 20.00
234 Bilal Powell JSY AU/499 RC 5.00 12.00
235 Jamie Harper JSY AU/499 RC EXCH 6.00 15.00
236 Jordan Todman JSY AU/499 RC 5.00 12.00

2011 Panini Plates and Patches Gold

*1-100 VETS/50: 1.2X TO 3X BASIC CARDS
*101-200 ROOKIES/50: .6X TO 1.5X SILVER/100
STATED PRINT RUN 50 SER.#'d SETS

2011 Panini Plates and Patches Rookie Autographed Jumbo Materials

BASE JUMBO AUTO PRINT RUN 10
*PRIME/25: .4X TO 1X JUMBO AU/10
1 A.J. Green 50.00 100.00
2 Alex Green 20.00 50.00
4 Austin Pettis 12.00 30.00
6 Blaine Gabbert 40.00 80.00
7 Cam Newton 125.00 250.00
8 Christian Ponder 50.00 100.00
9 Clyde Gates 12.00 30.00
10 Colin Kaepernick 25.00 60.00
12 Delone Carter 12.00 30.00
14 Greg Little 15.00 40.00
15 Jake Locker 75.00 150.00
16 Jamie Harper 15.00 40.00
17 Jerrel Jernigan 12.00 30.00
18 Jonathan Baldwin 15.00 40.00
19 Jordan Todman 10.00 25.00
20 Julio Jones 50.00 100.00
21 Kendall Hunter 25.00 50.00
22 Kyle Rudolph 15.00 40.00
23 Leonard Hankerson 15.00 40.00
25 Mark Ingram 50.00 100.00
26 Mikel Leshoure 15.00 40.00
27 Randall Cobb 20.00 50.00
28 Ryan Mallett 30.00 80.00
30 Shane Vereen 15.00 40.00
32 Taiwan Jones 15.00 40.00
33 Titus Young 20.00 50.00
34 Torrey Smith 20.00 50.00
35 Vincent Brown 15.00 40.00
36 Von Miller 20.00 50.00

2011 Panini Plates and Patches Silver

*1-100 VETS/100: .8X TO 2X BASIC CARDS
COMMON ROOKIE (101-200) 2.00 5.00
ROOKIE SEMISTARS 2.50 6.00
ROOKIE UNL.STARS 3.00 8.00
STATED PRINT RUN 100 SER.#'d SETS
101 Terrelle Pryor 4.00 10.00
106 Aldon Smith 5.00 12.00
127 Denarius Moore 4.00 10.00
134 J.J. Watt 4.00 10.00
164 Ricky Stanzi 4.00 10.00
167 Roy Helu 6.00 15.00
169 Ryan Taylor 2.50 6.00
171 Andrew Hawkins 4.00 10.00
176 T.J. Yates 4.00 10.00
180 Tyron Smith 4.00 10.00
186 Doug Baldwin 5.00 12.00
195 Henry Hynoski 4.00 10.00
196 Jacquian Williams 3.00 8.00
198 Nick Fairley 4.00 10.00
200 Patrick Peterson 5.00 12.00

2011 Panini Plates and Patches City Limits

STATED PRINT RUN 249 SER.#'d SETS
1 Larry Fitzgerald 1.50 4.00
2 Michael Turner 1.50 4.00
3 Joe Flacco 2.00 5.00
4 DeAngelo Williams 1.50 4.00
5 Julius Peppers 1.50 4.00
6 Peyton Hillis 1.50 4.00
7 Miles Austin 1.50 4.00
8 Brandon Lloyd 1.50 4.00
9 Jahvid Best 1.50 4.00
10 Donald Driver 1.50 4.00
11 Matt Schaub 1.50 4.00
12 Peyton Manning 3.00 8.00
13 Maurice Jones-Drew 1.50 4.00
14 Tony Moeaki 1.25 3.00
15 Percy Harvin 1.50 4.00
16 Danny Woodhead 3.00 8.00
17 Devery Henderson 1.25 3.00
18 Ahmad Bradshaw 1.50 4.00
19 Jeremy Maclin 1.50 4.00
20 Heath Miller 1.50 4.00
21 Philip Rivers 2.00 5.00
22 Patrick Willis 1.50 4.00
23 Steven Jackson 1.50 4.00
24 Mike Williams 1.50 4.00
25 Santana Moss 1.50 4.00

2011 Panini Plates and Patches City Limits Autograph Materials Prime

STATED PRINT RUN 1-15
7 Miles Austin/15 30.00 60.00
9 Jahvid Best/15

2011 Panini Plates and Patches City Limits Autographs

STATED PRINT RUN 5-15
7 Miles Austin/15 15.00 40.00
9 Jahvid Best/15 12.00 30.00
10 Donald Driver/15 30.00 60.00
14 Tony Moeaki/15 10.00 25.00
20 Heath Miller/15

2011 Panini Plates and Patches City Limits Materials

STATED PRINT RUN 10-299
*PRIME/50: .8X TO 2X BASIC JSY/299
*PRIME/25: 1X TO 2.5X BASIC JSY/99
*PRIME/25: .8X TO 2X BASIC JSY/49
*PRIME/25: .6X TO 1.5X BASIC JSY/25
1 Larry Fitzgerald/10
2 Michael Turner/49 4.00 10.00
3 Joe Flacco/299 4.00 10.00
4 DeAngelo Williams/99 3.00 8.00
5 Julius Peppers/299 4.00 10.00
6 Peyton Hillis/99 4.00 10.00
7 Miles Austin/299 3.00 8.00
8 Brandon Lloyd/25 5.00 12.00
9 Jahvid Best/99 3.00 8.00
11 Matt Schaub/99 3.00 8.00
13 Maurice Jones-Drew/99 3.00 8.00
15 Percy Harvin/50 4.00 10.00
17 Devery Henderson/299 2.50 6.00
18 Ahmad Bradshaw/99 3.00 8.00
19 Jeremy Maclin/25 5.00 12.00
20 Heath Miller/15 5.00 12.00
21 Philip Rivers/99 4.00 10.00
22 Patrick Willis/99 3.00 8.00
23 Steven Jackson/99 3.00 8.00
25 Santana Moss/31 4.00 10.00

2011 Panini Plates and Patches Gridiron Cut Autographs

STATED PRINT RUN 1-50
1 Sammy Baugh/10
2 Otto Graham/49 30.00 60.00
3 Bob Waterfield/10
4 Bobby Layne/1
5 Norm Van Brocklin/1
6 Jim Finks/1
7 Charley Conerly/5
8 Joe Perry/49 25.00 50.00
9 Ernie Nevers/1
10 Clark Shaughnessy/1
11 Doc Blanchard/2
12 Tuffy Leemans/1
13 Red Grange/1
14 Bill Dudley/49 20.00 40.00
15 Ken Strong/5
16 Arnie Herber/1
17 Les Horvath/4
18 Tony Canadeo/20 30.00 60.00
19 Glenn Davis/10
20 Dick Hoak/1
21 Kyle Rote/1
22 Don Hutson/1
23 Bob Hayes/1
24 Red Cochran/15 30.00 60.00
25 John Mackey/15
26 Frank Gatski/15 25.00 50.00
27 Alex Wojciechowicz/10
28 Ray Beck/30 20.00 40.00
29 Frank Kinard/1
30 Ed Healey/4
31 Turk Edwards/1
32 Lou Groza/16
33 Emlen Tunnell/4
34 Dick Lynch/20 20.00 40.00
35 George Connor/25 25.00 50.00
36 Bill Forester/20 25.00 50.00
37 Bob Pellegrini/25 25.00 50.00
38 Ernie Holmes/15 30.00 60.00
39 Stan Jones/6
40 Henry Jordan/5
41 Andy Robustelli/49 20.00 40.00
42 Wayne Millner/1
43 Morris Badgro/23 20.00 40.00
44 Hank Stram/25 25.00 50.00
45 Weeb Ewbank/49 20.00 40.00
46 Bert Bell/16 20.00 40.00
47 Wellington Mara/1
48 Art Rooney/1
49 Pete Rozelle/1
50 Joe Foss/1

2011 Panini Plates and Patches Honors

STATED PRINT RUN 249 SER.#'d SETS
1 Drew Brees 2.00 5.00
2 Peyton Manning 3.00 8.00
3 Tom Brady 3.00 8.00
4 Michael Vick 2.00 5.00
5 Ed Reed 1.50 4.00
6 James Harrison 2.00 5.00
7 Charles Woodson 2.00 5.00
8 Troy Polamalu 2.00 5.00
9 Chris Johnson 1.50 4.00
10 Carson Palmer 1.50 4.00
11 Adrian Peterson 2.50 6.00
12 Larry Fitzgerald 1.50 4.00
13 Matt Schaub 1.50 4.00
14 DeAngelo Hall 1.25 3.00
15 Patrick Willis 1.50 4.00
16 Jerod Mayo 1.25 3.00
17 Brian Cushing 1.25 3.00
18 Ben Roethlisberger 2.00 5.00
19 Matt Ryan 2.00 5.00
20 Percy Harvin 1.50 4.00
21 Sam Bradford 2.00 5.00
22 Deion Branch 1.25 3.00
23 Hines Ward 1.50 4.00
24 Eli Manning 2.00 5.00
25 Aaron Rodgers 3.00 8.00

2011 Panini Plates and Patches Honors Autographs

STATED PRINT RUN 5-25
7 Charles Woodson/25 150.00 250.00
14 DeAngelo Hall/25 12.00 30.00
16 Jerod Mayo/25 12.00 30.00
17 Brian Cushing/25 10.00 25.00
23 Hines Ward/25 40.00 80.00

2011 Panini Plates and Patches Honors Materials

STATED PRINT RUN 10-299
*PRIME/50: .8X TO 2X BASIC JSY/199-299
*PRIME/25: 1X TO 2.5X BASIC JSY/99-299
1 Drew Brees/99 4.00 10.00
2 Peyton Manning/89 6.00 15.00
3 Tom Brady/99 6.00 15.00
4 Michael Vick/10
5 Ed Reed/99 3.00 8.00
6 James Harrison/199 4.00 10.00
7 Charles Woodson/40 15.00 30.00
9 Chris Johnson/299 3.00 8.00
10 Carson Palmer/299 3.00 8.00
12 Larry Fitzgerald/10
13 Matt Schaub/99 3.00 8.00
14 DeAngelo Hall/199 2.50 6.00
15 Patrick Willis/99 4.00 10.00
18 Ben Roethlisberger/25 6.00 15.00
19 Matt Ryan/99 4.00 10.00
20 Percy Harvin/50 4.00 10.00
21 Sam Bradford/199 4.00 10.00
23 Hines Ward/99 4.00 10.00
24 Eli Manning/199 4.00 10.00
25 Aaron Rodgers/49 12.00 30.00

2011 Panini Plates and Patches Jerseys

STATED PRINT RUN 7-299
1 Joe Flacco/299 4.00 10.00
2 Matt Ryan/99 4.00 10.00
3 Josh Freeman/7
6 Jay Cutler/299 3.00 8.00
8 Matt Schaub/99 3.00 8.00
9 Drew Brees/99 4.00 10.00
10 Eli Manning/199 4.00 10.00
11 Larry Fitzgerald/25 5.00 12.00
12 Tom Brady/99 6.00 15.00
13 Steve Johnson/82 4.00 10.00
14 Ryan Fitzpatrick/199 3.00 8.00
15 Matt Cassel/299 3.00 8.00
16 Chad Henne/99 3.00 8.00
17 Philip Rivers/99 4.00 10.00
19 Brandon Marshall/199 3.00 8.00
20 Darren McFadden/299 3.00 8.00
21 Frank Gore/199 3.00 8.00
22 Matt Forte/99 3.00 8.00
23 Arian Foster/99 6.00 15.00
25 Jamaal Charles/299 3.00 8.00
26 Beanie Wells/99 3.00 8.00
27 Ray Rice/199 4.00 10.00
29 Joseph Addai/299 3.00 8.00
30 Ben Roethlisberger/25 6.00 15.00
32 Maurice Jones-Drew/99 3.00 8.00
33 Michael Turner/49 4.00 10.00
34 Rashard Mendenhall/99 3.00 8.00
36 Sam Bradford/199 4.00 10.00
38 Jason Campbell/199 3.00 8.00
39 Steven Jackson/99 3.00 8.00
40 Peyton Hillis/99 4.00 10.00
41 Kyle Orton/199 3.00 8.00
42 BenJarvus Green-Ellis/49 8.00 20.00
44 Ahmad Bradshaw/99 3.00 8.00
45 Mark Sanchez/299 4.00 10.00
46 Matthew Stafford/99 4.00 10.00
47 Tony Romo/299 4.00 10.00
48 Santonio Holmes/94 3.00 8.00
52 Jordan Shipley/99 3.00 8.00
53 Aaron Rodgers/49 12.00 30.00
54 Colt McCoy/299 3.00 8.00
55 Terrell Suggs/299 2.50 6.00
56 Marques Colston/99 3.00 8.00
57 Percy Harvin/32 4.00 10.00
60 Johnny Knox/99 3.00 8.00
62 Mike Wallace/99 4.00 10.00
64 Kenny Britt/299 3.00 8.00
68 Shonn Greene/299 3.00 8.00
73 Knowshon Moreno/299 3.00 8.00
74 Felix Jones/299 3.00 8.00
75 Jonathan Stewart/99 3.00 8.00
76 Chris Johnson/299 3.00 8.00
79 DeAngelo Williams/99 3.00 8.00
80 Andre Johnson/99 3.00 8.00
83 Wes Welker/99 4.00 10.00
87 Reggie Wayne/99 3.00 8.00
88 Dez Bryant/199 4.00 10.00
89 Steve Smith/99 3.00 8.00
92 Vincent Jackson/99 3.00 8.00
94 Brandon Lloyd/25 5.00 12.00
96 Vernon Davis/199 3.00 8.00
97 Hakeem Nicks/199 3.00 8.00

2011 Panini Plates and Patches Jerseys Prime

STATED PRINT RUN 1-50

2011 Panini Plates and Patches Jerseys Prime Jersey Number

STATED PRINT RUN 1-50

2011 Panini Plates and Patches Jerseys Prime Nameplate

STATED PRINT RUN 1-25
19 Brandon Marshall/25 6.00 15.00
20 Darren McFadden/25 6.00 15.00
25 Jamaal Charles/25 6.00 15.00
32 Maurice Jones-Drew/25 6.00 15.00
33 Michael Turner/25 6.00 15.00
45 Mark Sanchez/25 8.00 20.00
55 Terrell Suggs/25 5.00 12.00
56 Marques Colston/25 6.00 15.00
60 Johnny Knox/25 6.00 15.00
68 Shonn Greene/25 6.00 15.00
70 Ryan Mathews/25 6.00 15.00
73 Knowshon Moreno/25 6.00 15.00
76 Chris Johnson/25 6.00 15.00
81 Calvin Johnson/25 8.00 20.00
83 Wes Welker/25 8.00 20.00
84 Roddy White/25 6.00 15.00
88 Dez Bryant/25 8.00 20.00

2011 Panini Plates and Patches NFL Equipment

STATED PRINT RUN 20-150
*PRIME/50: .5X TO 1.2X BASIC JSY/150
*PRIME/50: .3X TO .8X BASIC JSY/25
*PRIME/25: .6X TO 1.5X BASIC JSY/150
*PRIME/25: .5X TO 1.2X BASIC JSY/50
*PRIME/25: .4X TO 1X BASIC JSY/25
*COMOBS/50: .5X TO 1.2X BASIC JSY/99-150
*COMOBS/25: .6X TO 1.5X BASIC JSY/150
*CMBO PRIME/25: .8X TO 2X BASIC JSY/150
*CMBO PRIME/25: .5X TO 1.2X BASIC JSY/25
1 Anquan Boldin/25 6.00 15.00
2 Cedric Benson/50 5.00 12.00
3 Chris Cooley/150 5.00 12.00
4 DeMarcus Ware/150 5.00 12.00
5 Devin Hester/150 5.00 12.00
6 Dexter McCluster/99 3.00 8.00
7 Eddie Royal/150 3.00 8.00
8 Jacoby Ford/150 4.00 10.00
9 Jared Allen/150 5.00 12.00
10 Jason Campbell/150 4.00 10.00
11 Jay Cutler/150 4.00 10.00
12 Jermaine Gresham/20 6.00 15.00
13 Joe Flacco/150 5.00 12.00
14 Johnny Knox/50 5.00 12.00
15 Jon Beason/150 3.00 8.00
16 Knowshon Moreno/150 4.00 10.00
17 London Fletcher/150 4.00 10.00
18 Marcedes Lewis/48 4.00 10.00
19 Matt Cassel/150 4.00 10.00
20 Matt Forte/50 5.00 12.00
21 Ryan Mathews/25 6.00 15.00
22 Steve Johnson/99 5.00 12.00
23 Tim Tebow/150 10.00 25.00
24 Tony Gonzalez/150 4.00 10.00
25 Tony Romo/150 5.00 12.00

2011 Panini Plates and Patches Rookie Blitz

STATED PRINT RUN 249 SER.#'d SETS
1 Ryan Mallett 3.00 8.00
2 Shane Vereen 1.50 4.00
3 Stevan Ridley 1.50 4.00
4 A.J. Green 3.00 8.00
5 Andy Dalton 4.00 10.00
6 Clyde Gates 1.25 3.00
7 Daniel Thomas 1.50 4.00
8 Jake Locker 4.00 10.00
9 Jamie Harper 1.50 4.00
10 Jordan Todman 1.00 2.50
11 Vincent Brown 1.50 4.00
12 Bilal Powell 1.00 2.50
13 Blaine Gabbert 2.50 6.00
14 Delone Carter 1.25 3.00
15 Greg Little 1.50 4.00
16 Jonathan Baldwin 1.50 4.00
17 Taiwan Jones 1.50 4.00
18 Torrey Smith 2.00 5.00
19 Marcell Dareus 1.50 4.00
20 Von Miller 2.00 5.00
21 Alex Green 1.50 4.00
22 Randall Cobb 2.00 5.00
23 Christian Ponder 3.00 8.00
24 Kyle Rudolph 1.50 4.00
25 Colin Kaepernick 2.00 5.00
26 Kendall Hunter 1.50 4.00
27 Mikel Leshoure 1.50 4.00
28 Titus Young 2.00 5.00
29 Austin Pettis 1.25 3.00
30 Cam Newton 8.00 20.00
31 DeMarco Murray 3.00 8.00
32 Julio Jones 3.00 8.00
33 Leonard Hankerson 1.50 4.00
34 Mark Ingram 3.00 8.00
35 Ryan Williams 2.00 5.00
36 Jerrel Jernigan 1.25 3.00

2011 Panini Plates and Patches Rookie Blitz Autograph Materials Prime

PRIME PRINT RUN 25 SER.#'d SETS
*JERSEY AU/25: .3X TO .8X PRIME AU/25
1 Ryan Mallett 25.00 60.00
2 Shane Vereen 12.00 30.00
4 A.J. Green 40.00 80.00
6 Clyde Gates 10.00 25.00
8 Jake Locker 60.00 120.00
10 Jordan Todman 8.00 20.00
11 Vincent Brown 12.00 30.00
13 Blaine Gabbert 25.00 60.00
14 Delone Carter 10.00 25.00
16 Jonathan Baldwin 12.00 30.00
17 Taiwan Jones 12.00 30.00
18 Torrey Smith 15.00 40.00
20 Von Miller 15.00 40.00
21 Alex Green 15.00 40.00
22 Randall Cobb 15.00 40.00
23 Christian Ponder 30.00 80.00
25 Colin Kaepernick 20.00 50.00
26 Kendall Hunter 15.00 40.00
27 Mikel Leshoure 12.00 30.00
28 Titus Young 15.00 40.00
29 Austin Pettis 10.00 25.00
30 Cam Newton 125.00 250.00
33 Leonard Hankerson 12.00 30.00
34 Mark Ingram 40.00 80.00
35 Ryan Williams 15.00 40.00
36 Jerrel Jernigan 10.00 25.00

2011 Panini Plates and Patches Rookie Blitz Materials

STATED PRINT RUN 99-299
1 Ryan Mallett/299 4.00 10.00
2 Shane Vereen/299 2.50 6.00
3 Stevan Ridley/299 2.50 6.00
4 A.J. Green/299 5.00 12.00
5 Andy Dalton/299 6.00 15.00
6 Clyde Gates/299 2.00 5.00
7 Daniel Thomas/299 2.50 6.00
8 Jake Locker/299 6.00 15.00
9 Jamie Harper/299 2.50 6.00
10 Jordan Todman/299 2.00 5.00
11 Vincent Brown/299 2.50 6.00
12 Bilal Powell/299 2.00 5.00
13 Blaine Gabbert/299 4.00 10.00
14 Delone Carter/299 2.00 5.00
15 Greg Little/299 2.50 6.00
16 Jonathan Baldwin/299 2.50 6.00
17 Taiwan Jones/299 2.50 6.00
18 Torrey Smith/299 3.00 8.00
19 Marcell Dareus/299 2.50 6.00
20 Von Miller/299 3.00 8.00
21 Alex Green/299 2.50 6.00
22 Randall Cobb/299 3.00 8.00
23 Christian Ponder/99 5.00 12.00
25 Colin Kaepernick/299 3.00 8.00
26 Kendall Hunter/299 2.50 6.00
27 Mikel Leshoure/299 2.50 6.00
28 Titus Young/299 3.00 8.00
29 Austin Pettis/299 2.00 5.00
30 Cam Newton/299 12.00 30.00
31 DeMarco Murray/299 5.00 12.00
32 Julio Jones/299 5.00 12.00
33 Leonard Hankerson/299 2.50 6.00
34 Mark Ingram/299 5.00 12.00
35 Ryan Williams/299 3.00 8.00
36 Jerrel Jernigan/299 2.00 5.00

2011 Panini Plates and Patches Rookie Jumbo Materials

STATED PRINT RUN 25-50
*PRIME/15: .8X TO 2X BASIC JUMBO/50
*PRIME/15: .6X TO 1.5X BASIC JUMBO/25
1 A.J. Green/50 8.00 20.00
2 Alex Green/50 4.00 10.00
3 Andy Dalton/50 10.00 25.00
4 Austin Pettis/50 3.00 8.00
5 Bilal Powell/50 2.50 6.00
6 Blaine Gabbert/50 6.00 15.00
7 Cam Newton/50 20.00 50.00
8 Christian Ponder/25 10.00 25.00
9 Clyde Gates/50 3.00 8.00
10 Colin Kaepernick/50 5.00 12.00
11 Daniel Thomas/50 4.00 10.00
12 Delone Carter/50 3.00 8.00
13 DeMarco Murray/50 8.00 20.00
14 Greg Little/50 4.00 10.00
15 Jake Locker/50 10.00 25.00
16 Jamie Harper/50 4.00 10.00
17 Jerrel Jernigan/50 3.00 8.00
18 Jonathan Baldwin/50 4.00 10.00
19 Jordan Todman/50 2.50 6.00
20 Julio Jones/50 8.00 20.00
21 Kendall Hunter/50 4.00 10.00
23 Leonard Hankerson/50 4.00 10.00
24 Marcell Dareus/50 4.00 10.00
25 Mark Ingram/50 8.00 20.00
27 Randall Cobb/50 5.00 12.00
28 Ryan Mallett/50 8.00 20.00
29 Ryan Williams/50 5.00 12.00
30 Shane Vereen/50 4.00 10.00
31 Stevan Ridley/50 4.00 10.00
32 Taiwan Jones/50 4.00 10.00
33 Titus Young/50 5.00 12.00
34 Torrey Smith/50 5.00 12.00
35 Vincent Brown/50 4.00 10.00
36 Von Miller/50 5.00 12.00

2011 Panini Plates and Patches Rookie Prime Signatures Nameplate

*PLATE AU/25: .6X TO 1.5X BASE JSY AU/499
*PLATE AU/25: .5X TO 1.2X BASE JSY AU/299
STATED PRINT RUN 25 SER.#'d SETS
EXCH EXPIRATION: 8/1/2013
201 Cam Newton 125.00 250.00

2011 Panini Plates and Patches Signatures Gold

1-100 UNPRICED VET PRINT RUN 5-10
*GOLD/25: .6X TO 1.5X AU RC/273-405
*GOLD/25: .5X TO 1.2X AU RC/99-199
*GOLD/25: .4X TO 1X AU RC/49-50
101-200 ROOKIE PRINT RUN 25
195 Henry Hynoski/25 60.00 120.00
200 Patrick Peterson/25 50.00 100.00

2011 Panini Plates and Patches Signatures Silver

1-100 VETERAN PRINT RUN 10-25
*SILVER/50-100: .5X TO 1.2X AU RC/273-405
*SILVER/50-100: .4X TO 1X AU RC/99-199
*SILVER/50-100: .3X TO .8X AU RC/49-50
101-200 ROOKIE PRINT RUN 50-100
31 Montario Hardesty/25 5.00 12.00
85 Chad Ochocinco/25 6.00 15.00
93 Bo Scaife/25 4.00 10.00
195 Henry Hynoski/50 30.00 60.00
200 Patrick Peterson/50 30.00 60.00

2011 Panini Plates and Patches Team Supreme Materials

STATED PRINT RUN 4-50
1 Michael Turner/50 6.00 15.00
2 Roddy White/50 6.00 15.00
3 Terrell Suggs/50 5.00 12.00
4 Anquan Boldin/25 8.00 20.00
5 Ed Reed/35 8.00 20.00
6 Steve Johnson/15 10.00 25.00
7 Jon Beason/25 6.00 15.00
8 DeAngelo Williams/4
9 Brian Urlacher/50 8.00 20.00
10 Jermaine Gresham/20 8.00 20.00
11 Jordan Shipley/25 8.00 20.00
12 Felix Jones/50 6.00 15.00
13 Miles Austin/50 6.00 15.00
14 Brandon Lloyd/25 8.00 20.00
15 Calvin Johnson/50 8.00 20.00
16 Maurice Jones-Drew/50 6.00 15.00
17 Marcedes Lewis/6
18 Jamaal Charles/50 6.00 15.00
19 Tamba Hali/50 5.00 12.00
20 Dexter McCluster/50 5.00 12.00
21 Brandon Marshall/50 6.00 15.00
22 Bernard Berrian/50 5.00 12.00
23 Jared Allen/25 10.00 25.00
24 Wes Welker/50 8.00 20.00
25 Hakeem Nicks/25 8.00 20.00
26 Darrelle Revis/20 8.00 20.00
27 Santonio Holmes/25 8.00 20.00
28 Jason Campbell/25 8.00 20.00
29 Brent Celek/50 6.00 15.00
30 DeSean Jackson/50 6.00 15.00
31 Jeremy Maclin/50 6.00 15.00
32 James Harrison/25 10.00 25.00
33 Antonio Gates/50 6.00 15.00
34 Malcom Floyd/50 6.00 15.00
35 Patrick Willis/18 8.00 20.00
36 Earnest Graham/50 5.00 12.00
37 Chris Johnson/50 6.00 15.00
38 Cortland Finnegan/25 6.00 15.00
39 Kenny Britt/25 8.00 20.00
40 Chris Cooley/50 8.00 20.00
41 Ryan Torain/50 6.00 15.00
42 Santana Moss/50 6.00 15.00

2011 Panini Playbook

1-50 VETERAN AU PRINT RUN 5-99
51-100 ROOKIE AU PRINT RUN 199-299
101-136 ROOK.JSY AU PRINT RUN 99-399
EXCH EXPIRATION: 10/4/2013
1 Philip Rivers AU/10
2 Tom Brady AU/5 EXCH
3 Anquan Boldin AU/99 8.00 20.00
4 Antonio Gates AU/15
5 Braylon Edwards AU/99 8.00 20.00
6 C.J. Spiller AU/99 8.00 20.00
7 Chris Cooley AU/99 8.00 20.00
8 Donald Driver AU/99 15.00 30.00
9 Donovan McNabb AU/99 10.00 25.00
10 Eli Manning AU/34 50.00 80.00
11 Greg Jennings AU/53 15.00 30.00
12 Greg Olsen AU/99 6.00 15.00
13 Heath Miller AU/99 10.00 25.00
14 Hines Ward AU/35 30.00 60.00
15 Jay Cutler AU/71 15.00 30.00
16 Jimmy Graham AU/99 10.00 25.00
17 Josh Freeman AU/46 12.00 30.00
18 Kevin Walter AU/99 8.00 20.00
19 LaDainian Tomlinson AU/61 20.00 40.00
20 Larry Fitzgerald AU/38 15.00 40.00
21 Lee Evans AU/99 10.00 25.00
22 Malcom Floyd AU/99 8.00 20.00
23 Michael Crabtree AU/99 8.00 20.00
24 Mike Tolbert AU/99 8.00 20.00
25 Mike Wallace AU/48 12.00 30.00
26 Peyton Manning AU/18
27 Pierre Thomas AU/99 8.00 20.00
28 Santana Moss AU/50 10.00 25.00
29 Shonn Greene AU/35 12.00 30.00
30 Steve Johnson AU/94 10.00 25.00
31 Tony Moeaki AU/99 6.00 15.00
32 Troy Polamalu AU/25
33 Aaron Rodgers AU/12
34 Arian Foster AU/33
35 Ben Roethlisberger AU/30 40.00 80.00
36 Chad Ochocinco AU/99 8.00 20.00
37 Drew Brees AU/27 30.00 60.00
38 Jermaine Gresham AU/73 8.00 20.00
39 Jonathan Stewart AU/25 15.00 40.00
40 Sidney Rice AU/49 10.00 26.00
41 Tim Tebow AU/25 50.00 100.00
42 Dez Bryant AU/9
43 Jason Witten AU/38 15.00 40.00
44 LeSean McCoy AU/34 12.00 30.00
45 Matthew Stafford AU/20
46 Miles Austin AU/13
47 Reggie Wayne AU/25 15.00 40.00
48 Ryan Grant AU/72 10.00 25.00
49 Santonio Holmes AU/25 15.00 40.00
50 Vernon Davis AU/10
51 Aaron Williams AU/299 RC EXCH 4.00 10.00
52 Adrian Clayborn AU/299 RC EXCH 5.00 12.00
53 Akeem Ayers AU/299 RC EXCH 4.00 10.00
54 Aldon Smith AU/299 RC EXCH 12.00 30.00
55 Allen Bradford AU/299 RC 4.00 10.00
56 Brandon Harris AU/299 RC 3.00 8.00
57 Cameron Heyward AU/199 RC 5.00 12.00
58 Cameron Jordan AU/299 RC 4.00 10.00
59 Cecil Shorts AU/299 RC 4.00 10.00
60 Corey Liuget AU/299 RC 3.00 8.00
61 D.J. Williams AU/299 RC EXCH 5.00 12.00
62 Da'Quan Bowers AU/299 RC 5.00 12.00
63 Da'Rel Scott AU/299 RC 4.00 10.00
64 Denarius Moore AU/299 RC 8.00 20.00
65 Dion Lewis AU/299 RC 6.00 15.00
66 Greg Jones AU/299 RC 4.00 10.00
67 Greg Salas AU/299 RC 8.00 20.00
68 J.J. Watt AU/299 RC 6.00 15.00
69 Jacquizz Rodgers AU/299 RC 5.00 12.00
70 Jeremy Kerley AU/299 RC 5.00 12.00
71 Jimmy Smith AU/299 RC EXCH 5.00 12.00
72 Johnny White AU/299 RC 4.00 10.00
73 Julius Thomas AU/299 RC 4.00 10.00
74 Justin Houston AU/299 RC 6.00 15.00
75 Kris Durham AU/299 RC 4.00 10.00
76 Lance Kendricks AU/299 RC 4.00 10.00
77 Luke Stocker AU/299 RC 4.00 10.00
78 Nathan Enderle AU/299 RC EXCH 5.00 12.00
79 Niles Paul AU/299 RC 5.00 12.00
80 Phil Taylor AU/299 RC 4.00 10.00
81 Prince Amukamara AU/299 RC 5.00 12.00
82 Rahim Moore AU/299 RC 4.00 10.00
83 Ricky Stanzi AU/299 RC 6.00 15.00
84 Roy Helu AU/299 RC 10.00 25.00
85 Ryan Kerrigan AU/299 RC 6.00 15.00
86 T.J. Yates AU/299 RC 6.00 15.00
87 Tandon Doss AU/299 RC 4.00 10.00
88 Terrelle Pryor AU/299 RC 10.00 25.00
89 Tyrod Taylor AU/299 RC EXCH 6.00 15.00
90 Joe Lefeged AU/299 RC 4.00 10.00
91 Jacquian Williams AU/299 RC EXCH 5.00 12.00
92 K.J. Wright AU/299 RC 5.00 12.00
93 Mason Foster AU/299 RC 5.00 12.00
94 Casey Matthews AU/299 RC 5.00 12.00
95 Anthony Allen AU/299 RC 3.00 8.00
96 Armond Smith AU/299 RC 4.00 10.00
97 Dane Sanzenbacher AU/299 RC 6.00 15.00
98 Doug Baldwin AU/299 RC 8.00 20.00
99 LaQuan Williams AU/299 RC 4.00 10.00
100 Mark Herzlich AU/299 RC 4.00 10.00
101 A.J. Green JSY AU/299 RC 40.00 80.00
102 Alex Green JSY AU/399 RC 15.00 40.00
103 Andy Dalton JSY AU/399 RC 50.00 100.00
104 Austin Pettis JSY AU/399 RC 12.00 30.00
105 Bilal Powell JSY AU/99 RC 12.00 30.00
106 Blaine Gabbert JSY AU/299 RC 30.00 60.00
107 Cam Newton JSY AU/299 RC 150.00 300.00
108 Christian Ponder JSY AU/299 RC 50.00 100.00
109 Clyde Gates JSY AU/399 RC 12.00 30.00
110 Colin Kaepernick JSY AU/399 RC 20.00 50.00
111 Daniel Thomas JSY AU/399 RC 15.00 40.00
112 Delone Carter JSY AU/399 RC 12.00 30.00
113 DeMarco Murray JSY AU/99 RC 60.00 120.00
114 Greg Little JSY AU/399 RC 15.00 40.00
115 Jake Locker JSY AU/299 RC 50.00 100.00
116 Jamie Harper JSY AU/399 RC EXCH 15.00 40.00
117 Jerrel Jernigan JSY AU/399 RC 12.00 30.00
118 Jonathan Baldwin JSY AU/399 RC 15.00 40.00
119 Jordan Todman JSY AU/399 RC 10.00 25.00
120 Julio Jones JSY AU/399 RC EXCH 40.00 80.00
121 Kendall Hunter JSY AU/399 RC 12.00 30.00
122 Kyle Rudolph JSY AU/99 RC EXCH 20.00 50.00

123 Leonard Hankerson JSY AU/399 RC EXCH	15.00	40.00
124 Marcell Dareus JSY AU/399 RC	15.00	40.00
125 Mark Ingram JSY AU/299 RC	30.00	60.00
126 Mikel Leshoure JSY AU/399 RC	15.00	40.00
127 Randall Cobb JSY AU/99 RC	25.00	60.00
128 Ryan Mallett JSY AU/299 RC	40.00	80.00
129 Ryan Williams JSY AU/399 RC	20.00	50.00
130 Shane Vereen JSY AU/399 RC	15.00	40.00
131 Stevan Ridley JSY AU/399 RC	15.00	40.00
132 Taiwan Jones JSY AU/399 RC	15.00	40.00
133 Titus Young JSY AU/399 RC	20.00	50.00
134 Torrey Smith JSY AU/399 RC	20.00	50.00
135 Vincent Brown JSY AU/399 RC	15.00	40.00
136 Von Miller JSY AU/349 RC	30.00	60.00

2011 Panini Playbook Gold

*VETS/15-25: .5X TO 1.2X BASIC CARDS
1-50 VETERAN PRINT RUN 1-25
*51-100 ROOKIE AU/49: .6X TO 1.5X
*101-136 ROOK.JSY AU/49: .5X TO 1.2X
51-136 ROOKIE PRINT RUN 49
EXCH EXPIRATION: 10/4/2013

101 A.J. Green JSY AU/49	60.00	120.00
103 Andy Dalton JSY AU/49	125.00	200.00
107 Cam Newton JSY AU/49	200.00	350.00
115 Jake Locker JSY AU/49	75.00	150.00
120 Julio Jones JSY AU/49 EXCH	60.00	120.00
125 Mark Ingram JSY AU/49	40.00	100.00

2011 Panini Playbook Platinum

*51-100 ROOKIE AU/25: .6X TO 1.5X
*101-136 ROOK.JSY AU/25: .6X TO 1.5X
STATED PRINT RUN 25 SER.#'d SETS

101 A.J. Green JSY AU	75.00	150.00
103 Andy Dalton JSY AU	125.00	250.00
107 Cam Newton JSY AU	250.00	400.00
115 Jake Locker JSY AU	125.00	250.00

2011 Panini Playbook Accolades Signatures

STATED PRINT RUN 4-49

1 Charles Woodson/25	125.00	200.00
2 Arrelious Benn/49	6.00	15.00
3 Ronnie Brown/49	6.00	15.00
4 Danny White/49	12.00	30.00
5 Jim McMahon/49	12.00	30.00
6 Randall Cunningham/49	15.00	40.00
7 Paul Warfield/49	10.00	25.00
8 Andre Reed/49	10.00	25.00
9 Boomer Esiason/49	10.00	25.00
10 Junior Seau/49	30.00	60.00
11 Frank Gifford/49	15.00	40.00
12 Paul Hornung/49		
13 Jerome Bettis/49		
14 Priest Holmes/49	8.00	20.00
15 Doug Flutie/49		
16 Steve Largent/40	12.00	30.00
17 Keyshawn Johnson/49	8.00	20.00
18 Curtis Martin/49	20.00	40.00
19 Joe Montana/25	90.00	150.00
20 Cris Carter/49	15.00	40.00
21 Mark Duper/49		
22 Brett Favre/10		
23 Bernie Kosar/49	15.00	40.00
24 Marcus Allen/49	12.00	30.00
25 Mark Carrier/49		
26 Michael Irvin/45	20.00	40.00
27 Jim Plunkett/49		
28 Bo Jackson/49	30.00	60.00
29 Ed Too Tall Jones/49	10.00	25.00
30 Joe Greene/49	20.00	40.00
31 Phil Simms/49	12.00	30.00
32 Ronnie Lott/49		
33 Rod Woodson/49	25.00	50.00
34 Fran Tarkenton/49	12.00	30.00
35 Ben Tate/49		
36 Eric Dickerson/49	15.00	40.00
37 Thurman Thomas/49	12.00	30.00
38 John Elway/35	60.00	120.00
39 Sterling Sharpe/49	12.00	30.00
40 Harlon Hill/49	8.00	20.00
41 Archie Manning/49	25.00	50.00
42 Daryle Lamonica/49	10.00	25.00
43 Deion Sanders/49	30.00	60.00
44 Jim Otto/49	10.00	25.00
45 Rayfield Wright/49	10.00	25.00
46 Chad Henne/49		
47 Montario Hardesty/49	6.00	15.00
48 Dick Butkus/49	30.00	60.00
49 Jack Lambert/49	30.00	60.00
50 Lenny Moore/49	10.00	25.00
51 Richard Dent/49	10.00	25.00
52 Barry Sanders/25	75.00	135.00
53 Michael Strahan/40	10.00	25.00
54 Bob Griese/49	12.00	30.00
55 John Riggins/49		
56 Alan Page/45	10.00	25.00
57 James Lofton/49	12.00	30.00
58 Warren Sapp/30	10.00	25.00
59 Bo Scaife/49	6.00	15.00
60 Brian Hartline/49	6.00	15.00
61 Warren Moon/30	25.00	50.00
62 Matt Moore/49	6.00	15.00
63 Danny Amendola/49	6.00	15.00
64 Felix Jones/49	6.00	15.00
65 Clay Matthews/49	25.00	50.00
66 Deacon Jones/33	10.00	25.00
67 Bill Bates/49	15.00	40.00
68 Ed McCaffrey/49	12.00	30.00
69 Terrell Davis/30	25.00	50.00
70 Bernard Berrian/49	5.00	12.00
71 Brian Cushing/49	5.00	12.00
72 Jared Allen/49	15.00	40.00
73 Emmitt Smith/40	75.00	135.00
74 Jim Kelly/12		
75 Len Dawson/26	15.00	40.00
76 Knowshon Moreno/25	10.00	25.00
77 Matt Schaub/15	10.00	25.00
78 Peyton Hillis/10		
79 Raymond Berry/40	10.00	25.00
80 Jimmy Graham/49	8.00	20.00
81 Wayne Chrebet/15		
82 Eddie George/10		
83 Matt Ryan/15	15.00	40.00
84 Tony Romo/15		
85 Willie Brown/49	8.00	20.00
86 Mark Sanchez/10		
87 Sam Bradford/10		
88 Jamaal Charles/4		
89 Joe Namath/35	60.00	120.00
90 DeAngelo Williams/18	8.00	20.00
91 London Fletcher/34	12.00	30.00
92 Tiki Barber/10		
93 Bobby Bell/49	8.00	20.00
94 John Brodie/49	12.00	30.00
95 Floyd Little/25	12.00	30.00
96 Boyd Dowler/49	8.00	20.00
97 Alex Karras/49	10.00	25.00
98 Ace Parker/49	12.00	30.00
99 Leroy Kelly/49	12.00	30.00
100 Sonny Jurgensen/45	10.00	25.00

2011 Panini Playbook Chronicles Signatures

AUTO STATED PRINT RUN 1-15

25 Jimmy Orr/15	60.00	120.00
Lenny Moore		
Mike Curtis		
Raymond Berry		

2011 Panini Playbook Grass Roots Materials

STATED PRINT RUN 2-99
*PRIME/19-25: .8X TO 2X BASIC JSY/79-99
*PRIME/19-25: .6X TO 1.5X BASIC JSY/30-49
*PRIME/25: .5X TO 1.2X BASIC JSY/28

1 Doug Williams/49	4.00	10.00
2 Miles Austin/49	5.00	12.00
3 Nate Washington/49	4.00	10.00
4 Ray Rice/49	5.00	12.00
5 Mario Manningham/49	5.00	12.00
6 Robert Meachem/49	5.00	12.00
7 Shonn Greene/49	5.00	12.00
8 Tamba Hali/49	4.00	10.00
9 Tony Gonzalez/49	5.00	12.00
10 Junior Seau/49	6.00	15.00
11 Ryan Torain/49	4.00	10.00
12 Tony Romo/49	6.00	15.00
13 Matt Hasselbeck/49	5.00	12.00
14 Joe Flacco/49	6.00	15.00
15 Hakeem Nicks/49	5.00	12.00
16 Marques Colston/49	5.00	12.00
17 Mark Sanchez/99	5.00	12.00
18 Priest Holmes/49	4.00	10.00
20 Antonio Gates/49	5.00	12.00
21 London Fletcher/49	4.00	10.00
22 Dez Bryant/49	6.00	15.00
23 Eddie George/49	5.00	12.00
24 Ed Reed/49	5.00	12.00
25 Eli Manning/49	6.00	15.00
26 Drew Brees/49	6.00	15.00
27 Darrelle Revis/49	5.00	12.00
28 Matt Cassel/49	5.00	12.00
29 Matt Ryan/49	6.00	15.00
30 Vincent Jackson/49	5.00	12.00
31 John Riggins/99	6.00	15.00
32 Matthew Stafford/49	6.00	15.00
33 Marc Mariani/49	5.00	12.00
34 Anquan Boldin/49	5.00	12.00
35 Brandon Jacobs/49	5.00	12.00
36 Devery Henderson/99	3.00	8.00
37 Lee Roy Selmon/49	6.00	15.00
38 Steve Young/49	8.00	20.00
39 Mark Duper/49	4.00	10.00
40 Malcom Floyd/49	5.00	12.00
41 DeAngelo Hall/30	4.00	10.00
42 Felix Jones/49	5.00	12.00
43 Chris Johnson/49	5.00	12.00
44 Marshall Faulk/49	5.00	12.00
45 Ahmad Bradshaw/49	5.00	12.00
46 Devin Hester/49	6.00	15.00
47 Earnest Graham/49	4.00	10.00
48 Patrick Willis/49	5.00	12.00
49 Dan Marino/99	10.00	25.00
50 Ryan Mathews/28	6.00	15.00
51 Santana Moss/49	5.00	12.00
52 Don Meredith/49	6.00	15.00
53 Chad Greenway/49	5.00	12.00
54 Danny Amendola/49	5.00	12.00
55 Joe Greene/49	6.00	15.00
56 Brian Urlacher/49	6.00	15.00
57 Keyshawn Johnson/49	5.00	12.00
58 Frank Gore/99	4.00	10.00
59 Brandon Marshall/49	5.00	12.00
60 Art Monk/49	5.00	12.00
61 LaRon Landry/49	4.00	10.00
62 Bob Lilly/49	5.00	12.00
63 Visanthe Shiancoe/49	5.00	12.00
64 Wes Welker/49	6.00	15.00
65 Maurice Jones-Drew/49	5.00	12.00
66 Jim McMahon/49	6.00	15.00
67 Calvin Johnson/49	6.00	15.00
68 Jon Beason/49	4.00	10.00
69 Anthony Fasano/49	4.00	10.00
70 Raymond Berry/49	5.00	12.00
71 Deion Sanders/49	8.00	20.00
72 Darren McFadden/49	5.00	12.00
73 Cris Carter/49	8.00	20.00
74 Tom Brady/99	8.00	20.00
75 Andre Johnson/99	4.00	10.00
76 Dick Butkus/49	8.00	20.00
77 Jahvid Best/99	4.00	10.00
78 DeAngelo Williams/49	5.00	12.00
79 Aaron Rodgers/99	12.00	30.00
80 Brent Celek/99	4.00	10.00
81 Chris Cooley/49		
82 Terrell Davis/79	5.00	12.00
83 Alan Page/49	5.00	12.00
84 Cedric Benson/49	5.00	12.00
85 Jim Kelly/49	6.00	15.00
86 Boomer Esiason/49	5.00	12.00
87 Boomer Esiason/49	5.00	12.00
88 Tony Dorsett/49	6.00	15.00
89 Tony Dorsett/49	6.00	15.00
90 Brian Orakpo/49	5.00	12.00
91 Doug Flutie/99	4.00	10.00
92 Doug Flutie/49	5.00	12.00
93 Ronnie Lott/49	6.00	15.00
94 Ronnie Lott/49	6.00	15.00
96 Randy Moss/49	5.00	12.00
97 Curtis Martin/49	6.00	15.00
99 Randall Cunningham/49	6.00	15.00
100 Randall Cunningham/99	5.00	12.00

2011 Panini Playbook Limited Edition Materials

STATED PRINT RUN 49 SER.#'d SETS
*PRIME/15-25: .6X TO 1.5X BASIC JSY/49

1 Steve Bartkowski	5.00	12.00
2 Boomer Esiason	5.00	12.00
3 Bernie Kosar	5.00	12.00
4 Danny White	5.00	12.00
5 John Elway	10.00	25.00
6 Troy Aikman	8.00	20.00
7 Warren Moon	6.00	15.00
8 Bob Griese	6.00	15.00
9 Fran Tarkenton	6.00	15.00
10 Jim Plunkett	5.00	12.00
11 Philip Rivers	6.00	15.00
12 Sam Bradford	6.00	15.00
13 Jay Cutler	5.00	12.00
14 Bart Starr	10.00	25.00
15 Matt Schaub	5.00	12.00
16 Aaron Rodgers	12.00	30.00
17 Joe Namath	12.00	30.00
18 C.J. Spiller	5.00	12.00
19 Thurman Thomas	6.00	15.00
20 Gale Sayers	6.00	15.00
21 Jamaal Charles	5.00	12.00
22 Marcus Allen	6.00	15.00
23 Pierre Thomas	5.00	12.00
24 LaDainian Tomlinson	6.00	15.00
25 Franco Harris	8.00	20.00
26 Emmitt Smith	12.00	30.00
28 Steven Jackson	5.00	12.00
29 Lenny Moore	8.00	20.00
30 Johnny Knox	5.00	12.00
31 Larry Fitzgerald	5.00	12.00
32 Jacoby Ford	5.00	12.00
33 Steve Largent	6.00	15.00
34 Kenny Britt	5.00	12.00
35 Cris Collinsworth	5.00	12.00
36 Josh Cribbs	5.00	12.00
37 Paul Warfield	5.00	12.00
38 Eddie Royal	4.00	10.00
39 Brian Hartline	4.00	10.00
40 Plaxico Burress	5.00	12.00
41 Jason Witten	6.00	15.00
42 Dallas Clark	5.00	12.00
43 Terrell Suggs	4.00	10.00
44 Ray Lewis	6.00	15.00
45 Dick Lane	4.00	10.00
46 Michael Strahan	5.00	12.00
47 Howie Long	6.00	15.00
48 Haloti Ngata	4.00	10.00
49 Ndamukong Suh	8.00	20.00
50 John Randle	4.00	10.00

2011 Panini Playbook Mammoth Materials

STATED PRINT RUN 25-99
*PRIME/15-25: 1X TO 2.5X JSY/62-99
*PRIME/15-25: .8X TO 2X JSY/40-50
*PRIME/15-25: .6X TO 1.5X JSY/25

1 Calvin Johnson/42	8.00	20.00
2 Ed Reed/99	5.00	12.00
3 Robert Meachem/99	5.00	12.00
4 Jon Beason/49	5.00	12.00
5 Hakeem Nicks/99	5.00	12.00
6 Brian Urlacher/99	6.00	15.00
7 Plaxico Burress/99	5.00	12.00
8 Haloti Ngata/99	4.00	10.00
9 Miles Austin/99	5.00	12.00
10 Tamba Hali/99	6.00	15.00
11 Eddie Royal/99	4.00	10.00
12 Ray Lewis/99	6.00	15.00
13 Anthony Fasano/99	4.00	10.00
14 DeMarcus Ware/41	6.00	15.00
15 Devery Henderson/99	4.00	10.00
16 Visanthe Shiancoe/49	6.00	15.00
17 Anquan Boldin/99	5.00	12.00
18 Brian Orakpo/99	5.00	12.00
19 Ahmad Bradshaw/99	5.00	12.00
20 LaDainian Tomlinson/99	6.00	15.00
21 Drew Brees/99	6.00	15.00
22 Ryan Mathews/25	8.00	20.00
23 Joe Flacco/99	6.00	15.00
24 Devin Hester/99	6.00	15.00
25 Brandon Jacobs/99	5.00	12.00
26 Frank Gore/99	5.00	12.00
27 Marc Mariani/49	6.00	15.00
28 Marques Colston/99	5.00	12.00
29 Matt Hasselbeck/99	5.00	12.00
30 Ray Rice/99	5.00	12.00
31 Tim Tebow/50	15.00	40.00
32 DeAngelo Hall/40	5.00	12.00
33 Eli Manning/99	6.00	15.00
34 Mike Thomas/62	5.00	12.00
35 Tony Gonzalez/99	5.00	12.00
36 Chad Greenway/10		
37 Vincent Jackson/49	6.00	15.00
38 Pierre Thomas/99	5.00	12.00
39 Josh Cribbs/49	6.00	15.00
40 LaRon Landry/25	6.00	15.00
41 Dallas Clark/99	5.00	12.00
42 Shonn Greene/99	5.00	12.00
43 Steven Jackson/10		
44 Darren McFadden/73	5.00	12.00
45 Tom Brady/99	10.00	25.00
46 Matt Schaub/99	5.00	12.00
47 Ndamukong Suh/46	8.00	20.00
48 Jay Cutler/99	5.00	12.00
49 Santana Moss/25	8.00	20.00
50 Chris Johnson/99	5.00	12.00

2011 Panini Playbook Material Playbook

STATED PRINT RUN 5-49
*PRIME/14-25: .5X TO 1.2X BASIC INSERTS

2 DeMarcus Ware/49	15.00	30.00
Jared Allen		
James Harrison		
Tamba Hali		
3 Troy Polamalu/49	25.00	50.00
Darrelle Revis		
Deion Sanders		
Rod Woodson		
Ronnie Lott		
Ed Reed		
4 Adrian Peterson/49	30.00	60.00
LeSean McCoy		
Michael Turner		
Ray Rice		
Calvin Johnson		
Dwayne Bowe		
Santonio Holmes		
5 London Fletcher/49		
James Laurinaitis		
Patrick Willis		
Ray Lewis		
Clay Matthews		
Brian Urlacher		
Chad Greenway		
6 Brett Favre/49	75.00	150.00
Dan Marino		
Emmitt Smith		
Walter Payton		
Barry Sanders		
Jerry Rice		
Terrell Owens		
7 Drew Brees/49	50.00	100.00
Tom Brady		
Aaron Rodgers		
Eli Manning		
Matthew Stafford		
Philip Rivers		
8 LeSean McCoy/49	30.00	60.00
Adrian Peterson		
Ray Rice		
Arian Foster		
Rashard Mendenhall		
Michael Turner		
Frank Gore		
Maurice Jones-Drew		
9 Tony Gonzalez/47	15.00	30.00
Hines Ward		
Antonio Gates		
Larry Fitzgerald		
Reggie Wayne		
Chad Ochocinco		
10 Bruce Smith/34	20.00	40.00
Ed Too Tall Jones		
Michael Strahan		
Howie Long		
11 Alan Page/49		
Forrest Gregg		
Joe Greene		
Randy White		
Warren Sapp		
Merlin Olsen		
Alex Karras		
12 Bernie Kosar/49		
Bob Griese		
Boomer Esiason		
Doug Flutie		
Doug Williams		
Jim McMahon		
13 Don Meredith/49	50.00	100.00
Roger Staubach		
Danny White		
Troy Aikman		
14 Bob Griese/49	30.00	60.00
Ken Stabler		
Joe Montana		
Doug Williams		
Troy Aikman		
15 Jim Brown/49	20.00	40.00
Terrell Davis		
Marshall Faulk		
LaDainian Tomlinson		
16 Y.A. Tittle/49	20.00	50.00
Bart Starr		
John Brodie		
Ken Stabler		
17 Fran Tarkenton/49	25.00	50.00
Terry Bradshaw		
Ken Anderson		
Joe Theismann		
18 Dan Marino/49		
Marcus Allen		
Boomer Esiason		
Thurman Thomas		
19 Steve Young/49	40.00	80.00
Emmitt Smith		
Brett Favre		
Tom Brady		
20 Jay Cutler/49	30.00	60.00
Devin Hester		
Johnny Knox		
Marion Barber		
Matt Forte		
Lance Briggs		
Brian Urlacher		
21 Keyshawn Johnson/49	20.00	40.00
Lee Roy Selmon		
Warren Sapp		
Mike Alstott		
22 Buck Buchanan/49		
Len Dawson		
Priest Holmes		
Jamaal Charles		
Tamba Hali		
Dwayne Bowe		
23 Frank Gore/49	25.00	50.00
John Brodie		
Patrick Willis		
Steve Young		
Ronnie Lott		
24 Bernie Kosar/20		
Ernie Davis		
Jim Brown		
Lou Groza		
Otto Graham		
Ozzie Newsome		
25 Bart Starr/29		
Sterling Sharpe		
Clay Matthews		
Greg Jennings		
Ray Nitschke		
Keith Jackson		
Henry Jordan		
26 Curtis Martin/49		
Darrelle Revis		
Mark Sanchez		
Don Maynard		
Joe Klecko		
Joe Namath		
27 Cliff Branch/49	40.00	80.00
Daryle Lamonica		
Fred Biletnikoff		
Gene Upshaw		
George Blanda		
Howie Long		
28 Sam Bradford/49	15.00	30.00
Steven Jackson		
James Laurinaitis		
Danny Amendola		
29 Aaron Rodgers/49	40.00	80.00
AJ Hawk		
Clay Matthews		
Greg Jennings		
Charles Woodson		
30 Bo Jackson/49	40.00	80.00
Troy Aikman		
Keyshawn Johnson		
Michael Vick		
Eli Manning		
Sam Bradford		
31 Reggie Bush/18		
Vince Young		
AJ Hawk		
Jay Cutler		
Haloti Ngata		
Tamba Hali		
Santonio Holmes		
DeAngelo Williams		
32 Ronnie Brown/49	25.00	50.00
Braylon Edwards		
Cedric Benson		
Cadillac Williams		
DeMarcus Ware		
Aaron Rodgers		
Jason Campbell		
Roddy White		
33 Eli Manning/20		
Larry Fitzgerald		
Philip Rivers		
Kellen Winslow Jr.		
Steven Jackson		
Jonathan Vilma		
Lee Evans		
Will Smith		
34 Carson Palmer/49	20.00	40.00
Andre Johnson		
Terence Newman		
Terrell Suggs		
Troy Polamalu		
Willis McGahee		
Dallas Clark		
Nnamdi Asomugha		

2011 Panini Playbook Materials Prime

STATED PRINT RUN 1-49

1 Philip Rivers/25	10.00	25.00
3 Anquan Boldin/49	6.00	15.00
4 Antonio Gates/49	6.00	15.00
6 C.J. Spiller/42	6.00	15.00
7 Chris Cooley/49	6.00	15.00
10 Eli Manning/25	10.00	25.00
19 LaDainian Tomlinson/49	8.00	20.00
20 Larry Fitzgerald/25	8.00	20.00
22 Malcom Floyd/49	6.00	15.00
27 Pierre Thomas/49	6.00	15.00
28 Santana Moss/49	6.00	15.00
42 Dez Bryant/49	8.00	20.00
45 Matthew Stafford/14	10.00	25.00
46 Miles Austin/49	6.00	15.00

2010 Panini Player of the Day

This set was released by Panini to hobby shops participating in the Player of the Day contest in Fall 2010. The first four cards were produced using the basic 2010 Score football design and the fifth is a version of the 2010 Prestige Tim Tebow Rookie Card. Each card features the 2010 Player of the Day logo on the front. A parallel was created, and randomly inserted into 5-card sets, with each card serial numbered to 100 in gold foil. Other than the serial numbering, there are no noticeable differences between the two versions.

COMPLETE SET (5)	2.50	6.00
*SERIAL NUMBERED/100: .6X TO 1.5X		
PM1 Peyton Manning	.50	1.25
PM2 Peyton Manning	.50	1.25
PM3 Peyton Manning	.50	1.25
TT1 Tim Tebow (2010 Score design)	.75	2.00
TT2 Tim Tebow (2010 Prestige design)	.75	2.00

2011 Panini Player of the Day

COMPLETE SET (13)	6.00	15.00
POD1 Sam Bradford	.60	1.50
POD2 Joe Flacco	.60	1.50
POD3 A.J. Green	.75	2.00
POD4 Mark Ingram	.75	2.00
POD5 Calvin Johnson	.60	1.50
POD6 Julio Jones	.75	2.00
POD7 Eli Manning	.60	1.50
POD8 Darren McFadden	.50	1.25
POD9 Cam Newton	2.00	5.00
POD10 Adrian Peterson	.75	2.00
POD11 Matt Ryan	.60	1.50
POD12 Ndamukong Suh	.60	1.50
POD13 Tim Tebow	1.25	3.00

2011 Panini Preferred Player of the Day Autographs

DA Danny Amendola	10.00	25.00
JB Jahvid Best	10.00	25.00
JF Jermichael Finley	10.00	25.00
JM Jeremy Maclin	10.00	25.00
MF Matt Forte	10.00	25.00
MW Mike Williams	10.00	25.00
PH Percy Harvin	10.00	25.00
SG Shonn Greene	10.00	25.00
MJD Muarice Jones-Drew	10.00	25.00

2012 Panini Player of the Day National Convention

ISSUED AT 2012 NATIONAL CONVENTION

1 Cam Newton	1.50	4.00
2 Andrew Luck	6.00	15.00
3 Justin Blackmon	2.00	5.00
4 Kendall Wright	1.25	3.00
5 Michael Floyd	2.00	5.00
6 Peyton Manning	2.50	6.00
7 Robert Griffin III	5.00	12.00
8 Ryan Tannehill	2.50	6.00
9 Tim Tebow	2.00	5.00
10 Trent Richardson	3.00	8.00
BW Beanie Wells	1.25	3.00

2009 Panini Pop Warner

COMPLETE SET (6)	7.50	15.00
1 Brett Favre	3.00	8.00
2 Tom Brady	1.00	2.50
3 Adrian Peterson	1.00	2.50
4 Drew Brees	.60	1.50
5 Mark Sanchez	1.00	2.50
6 Michael Crabtree	.60	1.50

2011 Panini Team Colors National Convention

TC1 Jay Cutler	1.25	3.00
TC2 Brian Urlacher	1.25	3.00
TC3 Devin Hester	1.25	3.00
TC4 Matt Forte	1.25	3.00

1988 Panini Stickers

This set of 433 different stickers (457 different subjects including half stickers) was issued in 1988 by Panini. Panini had been producing stickers under Topps license but, beginning with this set, Panini established its own trade name in this country separate from Topps. The stickers measure approximately 2 1/8" by 2 3/4", are numbered on both the front and the back, and are in alphabetical order by team. The album for the set is easily obtainable. It is organized in team order like the sticker numbering. On the inside back cover of the sticker album the company offered (via direct mail-order) up to 30 different stickers of your choice for either ten cents each (only in Canada) or in trade one-for-one for your unwanted extra stickers (only in the United States) plus 1.00 for postage and handling; this is one reason why the values of the most popular players in these sticker sets are somewhat depressed compared to traditional card set prices. Each sticker pack included one foil sticker. Team name foils were produced in pairs; the other member of the pair is listed parenthetically. The team name foils contain a referee signal on the sticker back, the helmet foils have the team's stadium on the back, and the uniform foils include a team "Huddles" cartoon card on the back. The album for the set features John Elway on the cover. Bo Jackson appears in his Rookie Football Card year and Simon Fletcher appears one year prior to his Rookie Cards.

COMPLETE SET (447)	14.00	35.00
1 Super Bowl XXII Program Cover	.02	.10
2 Buffalo Bills Helmet FOIL	.02	.10
3 Buffalo Bills Action	.02	.10
4 Cornelius Bennett	.07	.20
5 Chris Burkett	.02	.10
6 Derrick Burroughs	.02	.10
7 Shane Conlan	.07	.20
8 Ronnie Harmon	.02	.10
9 Jim Kelly	.30	.75
10 Buffalo Bills FOIL (240)	.02	.10
11 Mark Kelso	.02	.10
12 Nate Odomes	.02	.10
13 Andre Reed	.07	.20
14 Fred Smerlas	.02	.10
15 Bruce Smith	.08	.25
16 Buffalo Bills Uniform FOIL	.02	.10
17 Cincinnati Bengals Helmet FOIL	.02	.10
18 Cincinnati Bengals Action	.02	.10
19 Jim Breech	.02	.10
20 James Brooks	.02	.10
21 Eddie Brown	.02	.10
22 Cris Collinsworth	.02	.10
23 Boomer Esiason	.07	.20
24 Rodney Holman	.02	.10
25 Cincinnati Bengals FOIL (255)	.02	.10
26 Larry Kinnebrew	.02	.10
27 Tim Krumrie	.02	.10
28 Anthony Munoz	.07	.20
29 Reggie Williams	.02	.10
30 Carl Zander	.02	.10
31 Cincinnati Bengals Uniform FOIL	.02	.10
32 Cleveland Browns Helmet FOIL	.02	.10
33 Browns Action (Bernie Kosar)	.02	.10
34 Earnest Byner	.07	.20
35 Hanford Dixon	.02	.10
36 Bob Golic	.02	.10
37 Mike Johnson	.02	.10
38 Bernie Kosar	.07	.20
39 Kevin Mack	.02	.10
40 Cleveland Browns FOIL (270)	.02	.10
41 Clay Matthews	.02	.10
42 Gerald McNeil	.02	.10
43 Frank Minnifield	.02	.10
44 Ozzie Newsome	.07	.20
45 Cody Risien	.02	.10
46 Cleveland Browns Uniform FOIL	.02	.10
47 Denver Broncos Helmet FOIL	.02	.10
48 Denver Broncos Action	.02	.10
49 Keith Bishop	.02	.10
50 Tony Dorsett	.07	.20
51 John Elway	1.50	4.00
52 Simon Fletcher	.02	.10
53 Mark Jackson	.02	.10
54 Vance Johnson	.02	.10
55 Denver Broncos FOIL (285)	.02	.10
56 Rulon Jones	.02	.10
57 Rich Karlis	.02	.10
58 Karl Mecklenburg	.02	.10
59 Ricky Nattiel	.02	.10
60 Sammy Winder	.02	.10
61 Denver Broncos Uniform FOIL	.02	.10
62 Houston Oilers Helmet FOIL	.02	.10
63 Oilers Action (Warren Moon)	.07	.20
64 Keith Bostic	.02	.10
65 Steve Brown	.02	.10
66 Ray Childress	.02	.10
67 Jeff Donaldson	.02	.10
68 John Grimsley	.02	.10
69 Robert Lyles	.02	.10
70 Houston Oilers FOIL (300)	.02	.10
71 Drew Hill	.02	.10
72 Warren Moon	.20	.50
73 Mike Munchak	.02	.10
74 Mike Rozier	.02	.10
75 Johnny Meads	.02	.10
76 Houston Oilers Uniform FOIL	.02	.10
77 Indianapolis Colts Helmet FOIL	.02	.10
78 Colts Action (Eric Dickerson)	.02	.10
79 Albert Bentley	.02	.10
80 Dean Biasucci	.02	.10
81 Duane Bickett	.02	.10
82 Bill Brooks	.02	.10
83 Johnie Cooks	.02	.10
84 Eric Dickerson	.07	.20
85 Indianapolis Colts FOIL (315)	.02	.10
86 Ray Donaldson	.02	.10
87 Chris Hinton	.02	.10
88 Cliff Odom	.02	.10
89 Barry Krauss	.02	.10
90 Jack Trudeau	.02	.10
91 Indianapolis Colts Uniform FOIL	.02	.10
92 Kansas City Chiefs Helmet FOIL	.02	.10
93 Kansas City Chiefs Action	.02	.10
94 Carlos Carson	.02	.10
95 Deron Cherry	.02	.10
96 Dino Hackett	.02	.10
97 Bill Kenney	.02	.10
98 Albert Lewis	.07	.20
99 Nick Lowery	.02	.10
100 Kansas City Chiefs FOIL (330)	.02	.10
101 Bill Maas	.02	.10
102 Christian Okoye	.07	.20
103 Stephone Paige	.02	.10
104 Paul Palmer	.02	.10
105 Kevin Ross	.02	.10
106 Kansas City Chiefs Uniform FOIL	.02	.10
107 Los Angeles Raiders Helmet FOIL	.02	.10
108 Raiders Action (Bo Jackson)	.07	.20
109 Marcus Allen	.10	.30
110 Todd Christensen	.02	.10
111 Mike Haynes	.02	.10
112 Bo Jackson	.07	.20
113 James Lofton	.07	.20
114 Howie Long	.07	.20
115 Los Angeles Raiders FOIL (345)	.02	.10
116 Rod Martin	.02	.10
117 Vann McElroy	.02	.10
118 Bill Pickel	.02	.10
119 Don Mosebar	.02	.10
120 Stacey Toran	.02	.10
121 Los Angeles Raiders Uniform FOIL	.02	.10
122 Miami Dolphins Helmet FOIL	.02	.10
123 Miami Dolphins Action	.02	.10
124 John Bosa	.02	.10
125 Mark Clayton	.02	.10
126 Mark Duper	.02	.10
127 Lorenzo Hampton	.02	.10
128 William Judson	.02	.10
129 Dan Marino	1.50	4.00
130 Miami Dolphins FOIL (360)	.02	.10
131 John Offerdahl	.02	.10
132 Reggie Roby	.02	.10
133 Jackie Shipp	.02	.10
134 Dwight Stephenson	.02	.10
135 Troy Stradford	.02	.10
136 Miami Dolphins Uniform FOIL	.02	.10
137 New England Patriots Helmet FOIL	.02	.10
138 New England Patriots Action	.02	.10
139 Bruce Armstrong	.02	.10
140 Raymond Clayborn	.02	.10
141 Reggie Dupard	.02	.10
142 Steve Grogan	.02	.10
143 Craig James	.02	.10
144 Ronnie Lippett	.02	.10
145 New England Patriots FOIL (375)	.02	.10
146 Fred Marion	.02	.10
147 Stanley Morgan	.02	.10
148 Mosi Tatupu	.02	.10
149 Andre Tippett	.02	.10
150 Garin Veris	.02	.10
151 New England Patriots Uniform FOIL	.02	.10
152 New York Jets Helmet FOIL	.02	.10
153 Jets Action (Ken O'Brien)	.02	.10
154 Bob Crable	.02	.10
155 Mark Gastineau	.02	.10
156 Pat Leahy	.02	.10
157 Johnny Hector	.02	.10
158 Marty Lyons	.02	.10
159 Freeman McNeil	.02	.10
160 New York Jets FOIL (390)	.02	.10
161 Ken O'Brien	.02	.10
162 Mickey Shuler	.02	.10
163 Al Toon	.02	.10
164 Roger Vick	.02	.10
165 Wesley Walker	.02	.10
166 New York Jets Uniform FOIL	.02	.10
167 Pittsburgh Steelers Helmet FOIL	.02	.10
168 Pittsburgh Steelers Action	.02	.10
169 Walter Abercrombie	.02	.10
170 Gary Anderson K	.02	.10
171 Todd Blackledge	.02	.10
172 Thomas Everett	.02	.10
173 Delton Hall	.02	.10
174 Bryan Hinkle	.02	.10
175 Pittsburgh Steelers FOIL (405)	.02	.10
176 Earnest Jackson	.02	.10
177 Louis Lipps	.02	.10
178 David Little	.02	.10
179 Mike Merriweather	.02	.10
180 Mike Webster	.02	.10
181 Pittsburgh Steelers Uniform FOIL	.02	.10
182 San Diego Chargers Helmet FOIL	.02	.10
183 San Diego Chargers Action	.02	.10
184 Gary Anderson RB	.02	.10
185 Chip Banks	.02	.10
186 Martin Bayless	.02	.10
187 Chuck Ehin	.02	.10
188 Vencie Glenn	.02	.10
189 Lionel James	.02	.10
190 San Diego Chargers FOIL (420)	.02	.10
191 Mark Malone	.02	.10
192 Ralf Mojsiejenko	.02	.10
193 Billy Ray Smith	.02	.10
194 Lee Williams	.02	.10
195 Kellen Winslow	.07	.20
196 San Diego Chargers Uniform FOIL	.02	.10
197 Seattle Seahawks Helmet FOIL	.02	.10
198 Seahawks Action (Dave Krieg)	.02	.10
199 Eugene Robinson	.02	.10
200 Jeff Bryant	.02	.10
201 Raymond Butler	.02	.10
202 Jacob Green	.02	.10
203 Norm Johnson	.02	.10
204 Dave Krieg	.02	.10
205 Seahawks FOIL (435)	.02	.10
206 Steve Largent	.20	.50
207 Joe Nash	.02	.10
208 Curt Warner	.02	.10
209 Bobby Joe Edmonds	.02	.10
210 Daryl Turner	.02	.10
211 Seattle Seahawks Uniform FOIL	.02	.10
212 AFC Logo	.02	.10
213 Bernie Kosar	.07	.20
214 Curt Warner	.02	.10
215 Jerry Rice and Steve Largent	.60	1.50
216 Mark Bavaro and Anthony Munoz	.02	.10
217 Gary Zimmerman and Bill Fralic	.07	.20
218 Dwight Stephenson and Mike Munchak	.02	.10
219 Joe Montana	2.00	5.00
220 Charles White and Eric Dickerson	.08	.25
221 Morten Andersen and Vai Sikahema	.02	.10
222 Bruce Smith and Reggie White	.10	.30
223 Michael Carter and Steve McMichael	.02	.10
224 Jim Arnold	.02	.10
225 Carl Banks and Andre Tippett	.02	.10
226 Barry Wilburn Singletary	.02	.10
227 Hanford Dixon and Frank Minnifield	.02	.10
228 Ronnie Lott and Joey Browner	.07	.20
229 NFC Logo	.02	.10
230 Gary Clark	.07	.20
231 Richard Dent	.07	.20
232 Atlanta Falcons Helmet FOIL	.02	.10
233 Atlanta Falcons Action	.02	.10
234 Rick Bryan	.02	.10
235 Bobby Butler	.02	.10
236 Tony Casillas	.02	.10
237 Floyd Dixon	.02	.10
238 Rick Donnelly	.02	.10
239 Bill Fralic	.02	.10
240 Atlanta Falcons FOIL (10)	.02	.10
241 Mike Gann	.02	.10
242 Chris Miller	.07	.20
243 Robert Moore	.02	.10
244 John Rade	.02	.10
245 Gerald Riggs	.02	.10
246 Atlanta Falcons Uniform FOIL	.02	.10
247 Chicago Bears Helmet FOIL	.02	.10
248 Bears Action (Jim McMahon)	.02	.10
249 Neal Anderson	.07	.20
250 Jim Covert	.02	.10
251 Richard Dent	.07	.20
252 Dave Duerson	.02	.10
253 Dennis Gentry	.02	.10
254 Jay Hilgenberg	.02	.10
255 Chicago Bears FOIL (25)	.02	.10
256 Jim McMahon	.07	.20
257 Steve McMichael	.02	.10
258 Matt Suhey	.02	.10
259 Mike Singletary	.07	.20
260 Otis Wilson	.02	.10
261 Chicago Bears Uniform FOIL	.02	.10

262 Dallas Cowboys Helmet FOIL .02 .10
263 Cowboys Action (Herschel Walker) .02 .10
264 Bill Bates .02 .10
265 Doug Cosbie .02 .10
266 Ron Francis .02 .10
267 Jim Jeffcoat .02 .10
268 Ed Too Tall Jones .07 .20
269 Eugene Lockhart .02 .10
270 Dallas Cowboys FOIL (40) .02 .10
271 Danny Noonan .02 .10
272 Steve Pelluer .02 .10
273 Herschel Walker .07 .20
274 Everson Walls .02 .10
275 Randy White .07 .20
276 Dallas Cowboys Uniform FOIL .02 .10
277 Detroit Lions Helmet FOIL .02 .10
278 Detroit Lions Action .02 .10
279 Jim Arnold .02 .10
280 Jerry Ball .02 .10
281 Michael Cofer .02 .10
282 Keith Ferguson .02 .10
283 Dennis Gibson .02 .10
284 James Griffin .02 .10
285 Detroit Lions FOIL (55) .02 .10
286 James Jones .02 .10
287 Chuck Long .02 .10
288 Pete Mandley .02 .10
289 Eddie Murray .02 .10
290 Garry James .02 .10
291 Detroit Lions Uniform FOIL .02 .10
292 Green Bay Packers Helmet FOIL .02 .10
293 Green Bay Packers Action .02 .10
294 John Anderson .02 .10
295 Dave Brown .02 .10
296 Alphonso Carreker .02 .10
297 Kenneth Davis .02 .10
298 Phillip Epps .02 .10
299 Brent Fullwood .02 .10
300 Green Bay Packers FOIL (70) .02 .10
301 Tim Harris .02 .10
302 Johnny Holland .02 .10
303 Mark Murphy .02 .10
304 Brian Noble .02 .10
305 Walter Stanley .02 .10
306 Green Bay Packers Uniform FOIL .02 .10
307 Los Angeles Rams Helmet FOIL .02 .10
308 Los Angeles Rams Action .02 .10
309 Jim Collins .02 .10
310 Henry Ellard .08 .25
311 Jim Everett .07 .20
312 Jerry Gray .02 .10
313 LeRoy Irvin .02 .10
314 Mike Lansford .02 .10
315 Los Angeles Rams FOIL (85) .02 .10
316 Mel Owens .02 .10
317 Jackie Slater .02 .10
318 Doug Smith .02 .10
319 Charles White .02 .10
320 Mike Wilcher .02 .10
321 Los Angeles Rams Uniform FOIL .02 .10
322 Minnesota Vikings Helmet FOIL .02 .10
323 Minnesota Vikings Action .02 .10
324 Joey Browner .02 .10
325 Anthony Carter .02 .10
326 Chris Doleman .07 .20
327 D.J. Dozier .02 .10
328 Steve Jordan .02 .10
329 Tommy Kramer .02 .10
330 Minnesota Vikings FOIL (100) .02 .10
331 Darrin Nelson .02 .10
332 Jesse Solomon .02 .10
333 Scott Studwell .02 .10
334 Wade Wilson .02 .10
335 Gary Zimmerman .07 .20
336 Minnesota Vikings Uniform FOIL .02 .10
337 New Orleans Saints Helmet FOIL .02 .10
338 Saints Action (Bobby Hebert) .02 .10
339 Morten Andersen .02 .10
340 Bruce Clark .02 .10
341 Brad Edelman .02 .10
342 Bobby Hebert .02 .10
343 Dalton Hilliard .02 .10
344 Rickey Jackson .02 .10
345 New Orleans Saints FOIL (115) .02 .10
346 Vaughan Johnson .02 .10
347 Rueben Mayes .02 .10
348 Sam Mills .07 .20
349 Pat Swilling .07 .20
350 Dave Waymer .02 .10
351 New Orleans Saints Uniform FOIL .02 .10
352 New York Giants Helmet FOIL .02 .10
353 New York Giants Action .02 .10
354 Carl Banks .02 .10
355 Mark Bavaro .02 .10
356 Jim Burt .02 .10
357 Harry Carson .02 .10
358 Terry Kinard .02 .10
359 Lionel Manuel .02 .10
360 New York Giants FOIL (130) .02 .10
361 Leonard Marshall .02 .10
362 George Martin .02 .10
363 Joe Morris .02 .10
364 Phil Simms .08 .25
365 George Adams .02 .10
366 New York Giants Uniform FOIL .02 .10
367 Philadelphia Eagles Helmet FOIL .02 .10
368 Eagles Action (Randall Cunningham) .07 .20
369 Jerome Brown .07 .20
370 Keith Byars .07 .20
371 Randall Cunningham .07 .20
372 Terry Hoage .02 .10
373 Seth Joyner .07 .20
374 Mike Quick .02 .10
375 Philadelphia Eagles FOIL (145) .02 .10
376 Clyde Simmons .02 .10
377 Anthony Toney .02 .10
378 Andre Waters .02 .10
379 Reggie White .20 .50
380 Roynell Young .02 .10
381 Philadelphia Eagles Uniform FOIL .02 .10
382 Phoenix Cardinals Helmet FOIL .02 .10
383 Phoenix Cardinals Action .02 .10
384 Robert Awalt .02 .10
385 Roy Green .02 .10
386 Neil Lomax .02 .10
387 Stump Mitchell .02 .10
388 Niko Noga .02 .10
389 Freddie Joe Nunn .02 .10
390 Phoenix Cardinals FOIL (160) .02 .10
391 Luis Sharpe .02 .10
392 Vai Sikahema .02 .10
393 J.T. Smith .02 .10
394 Leonard Smith .02 .10
395 Lonnie Young .02 .10
396 Phoenix Cardinals Uniform FOIL .02 .10
397 San Francisco 49ers Helmet FOIL .02 .10
398 49ers Action (Joe Montana) .40 1.00
399 Dwaine Board .02 .10
400 Michael Carter .02 .10
401 Roger Craig .02 .10
402 Jeff Fuller .02 .10
403 Don Griffin .02 .10
404 Ronnie Lott .07 .20
405 San Francisco 49ers FOIL (175) .02 .10
406 Joe Montana 2.00 5.00
407 Tom Rathman .07 .20
408 Jerry Rice 1.00 2.50
409 Keena Turner .02 .10
410 Michael Walter .02 .10
411 San Francisco 49ers Uniform FOIL .02 .10
412 Tampa Bay Bucs Helmet FOIL .02 .10
413 Tampa Bay Bucs Action .02 .10
414 Mark Carrier WR .07 .20
415 Gerald Carter .02 .10
416 Ron Holmes .02 .10
417 Rod Jones .02 .10
418 Calvin Magee .02 .10
419 Ervin Randle .02 .10
420 Tampa Bay Buccaneers FOIL (190) .02 .10
421 Donald Igwebuike .02 .10
422 Vinny Testaverde .07 .20
423 Jackie Walker .02 .10
424 Chris Washington .02 .10
425 James Wilder .02 .10
426 Tampa Bay Bucs Uniform FOIL .02 .10
427 Washington Redskins Helmet FOIL .02 .10
428 Redskins Action (Doug Williams) .02 .10
429 Gary Clark .07 .20
430 Monte Coleman .02 .10
431 Darrell Green .07 .20
432 Charles Mann .02 .10
433 Kelvin Bryant .02 .10
434 Art Monk .07 .20
435 Washington Redskins FOIL (205) .02 .10
436 Ricky Sanders .07 .20
437 Jay Schroeder .02 .10
438 Alvin Walton .02 .10
439 Barry Wilburn .02 .10
440 Doug Williams .07 .20
441 Washington Redskins Uniform FOIL .02 .10
442 Super Bowl action (Left half) .02 .10
443 Super Bowl action (Right half) .02 .10
444 Doug Williams (Super Bowl MVP) .02 .10
445 Super Bowl action .02 .10
446 Super Bowl action (Left half) .02 .10
447 Super Bowl action (Right half) .02 .10
NNO Panini Album (John Elway on cover) 1.00 2.50

1989 Panini Stickers

This set of 416 stickers was issued in 1989 by Panini. The stickers measure approximately 1 15/16" by 3" and are numbered on the front and on the back. The album for the set is easily obtainable. It is organized in team order like the sticker numbering. On the inside back cover of the sticker album the company offered (via direct mail-order) up to 30 different stickers of your choice for either ten cents each (only in Canada) or in trade one-for-one for your unwanted extra stickers (only in the United States) plus 1.00 for postage and handling; this is one reason why the values of the most popular players in these sticker sets are somewhat depressed compared to traditional card set prices. The album for the set features Joe Montana on the cover. Tim Brown, Cris Carter, Michael Irvin, Keith Jackson, Jay Novacek, Sterling Sharpe, Thurman Thomas, Rod Woodson appear in their Rookie Card year. The stickers were also issued in a UK version which is distinguished by the presence of stats printed on the sticker backs. The UK version album also features Joe Montana as well as the TV-4 logo.

COMPLETE SET (416) 8.00 20.00
COMP.UK SET (416) 100.00 250.00
*UK VERSION: 5X TO 10X
1 SB XXIII Program .02 .10
2 SB XXIII Program .02 .10
3 Floyd Dixon .02 .10
4 Tony Casillas .02 .10
5 Bill Fralic .02 .10
6 Aundray Bruce .02 .10
7 Scott Case .02 .10
8 Rick Donnelly .02 .10
9 Atlanta Falcons Logo FOIL .02 .10
10 Atlanta Falcons Helmet FOIL .02 .10
11 Marcus Cotton .02 .10
12 Chris Miller .02 .10
13 Robert Moore .02 .10
14 Bobby Butler .02 .10
15 Rick Bryan .02 .10
16 John Settle .02 .10
17 Jim McMahon .02 .10
18 Neal Anderson .02 .10
19 Dave Duerson .02 .10
20 Steve McMichael .02 .10
21 Jay Hilgenberg .02 .10
22 Dennis McKinnon .02 .10
23 Chicago Bears Logo FOIL .02 .10
24 Chicago Bears Helmet FOIL .02 .10
25 Richard Dent .02 .10
26 Dennis Gentry .02 .10
27 Mike Singletary .02 .10
28 Vestee Jackson .02 .10
29 Mike Tomczak .02 .10
30 Dan Hampton .02 .10
31 Michael Irvin .40 1.00
32 Eugene Lockhart .02 .10
33 Herschel Walker .02 .10
34 Kelvin Martin .02 .10
35 Jim Jeffcoat .02 .10
36 Everson Walls .02 .10
37 Dallas Cowboys Logo FOIL .02 .10
38 Dallas Cowboys Helmet FOIL .02 .10
39 Danny Noonan .02 .10
40 Ray Alexander .02 .10
41 Garry Cobb .02 .10
42 Ed Too Tall Jones .02 .10
43 Kevin Brooks .02 .10
44 Bill Bates .02 .10
45 Detroit Lions Logo FOIL .02 .10
46 Chuck Long .02 .10
47 Jim Arnold .02 .10
48 Michael Cofer .02 .10
49 Eddie Murray .02 .10
50 Keith Ferguson .02 .10
51 Pete Mandley .02 .10
52 Detroit Lions Helmet FOIL .02 .10
53 Jerry Ball .02 .10
54 Bennie Blades .02 .10
55 Dennis Gibson .02 .10
56 Chris Spielman .07 .20
57 Eric Williams .02 .10
58 Lomas Brown .02 .10
59 Johnny Holland .02 .10
60 Tim Harris .02 .10
61 Mark Murphy .02 .10
62 Walter Stanley .02 .10
63 Brent Fullwood .02 .10
64 Ken Ruettgers .02 .10
65 Green Bay Packers Logo FOIL .02 .10
66 Green Bay Packers Helmet FOIL .02 .10
67 John Anderson .02 .10
68 Brian Noble .02 .10
69 Sterling Sharpe .15 .40
70 Keith Woodside .02 .10
71 Mark Lee .02 .10
72 Don Majkowski .02 .10
73 Aaron Cox .02 .10
74 LeRoy Irvin .02 .10
75 Jim Everett .02 .10
76 Mike Lansford .02 .10
77 Mike Wilcher .02 .10
78 Henry Ellard .07 .20
79 Los Angeles Rams Helmet FOIL .02 .10
80 Jerry Gray .02 .10
81 Doug Smith .02 .10
82 Tom Newberry .02 .10
83 Jackie Slater .02 .10
84 Greg Bell .02 .10
85 Kevin Greene .07 .20
86 Chris Doleman .02 .10
87 Steve Jordan .02 .10
88 Jesse Solomon .02 .10
89 Randall McDaniel .20 .50
90 Hassan Jones .02 .10
91 Joey Browner .02 .10
92 Minnesota Vikings Logo FOIL .02 .10
93 Minnesota Vikings Helmet FOIL .02 .10
94 Anthony Carter .07 .20
95 Gary Zimmerman .07 .20
96 Wade Wilson .02 .10
97 Scott Studwell .02 .10
98 Keith Millard .02 .10
99 Carl Lee .02 .10
100 Morten Andersen .02 .10
101 Bobby Hebert .02 .10
102 Rueben Mayes .02 .10
103 Sam Mills .02 .10
104 Vaughan Johnson .02 .10
105 Pat Swilling .02 .10
106 New Orleans Saints Logo FOIL .02 .10
107 New Orleans Saints Helmet FOIL .02 .10
108 Brad Edelman .02 .10
109 Craig Heyward .02 .10
110 Eric Martin .02 .10
111 Dalton Hilliard .02 .10
112 Lonzell Hill .02 .10
113 Rickey Jackson .02 .10
114 Erik Howard .02 .10
115 Phil Simms .02 .10
116 Leonard Marshall .02 .10
117 Joe Morris .02 .10
118 Bart Oates .02 .10
119 Mark Bavaro .02 .10
120 New York Giants Logo FOIL .02 .10
121 New York Giants Helmet FOIL .02 .10
122 Terry Kinard .02 .10
123 Carl Banks .02 .10
124 Lionel Manuel .02 .10
125 Stephen Baker .02 .10
126 Pepper Johnson .02 .10
127 Jim Burt .02 .10
128 Cris Carter 1.00 2.50
129 Mike Quick .02 .10
130 Terry Hoage .02 .10
131 Keith Jackson .07 .20
132 Clyde Simmons .02 .10
133 Eric Allen .02 .10
134 Philadelphia Eagles Logo FOIL .02 .10
135 Philadelphia Eagles Helmet FOIL .02 .10
136 Randall Cunningham .20 .50
137 Mike Pitts .02 .10
138 Keith Byars .02 .10
139 Seth Joyner .02 .10
140 Jerome Brown .07 .20
141 Reggie White .07 .20
142 Jay Novacek .07 .20
143 Neil Lomax .02 .10
144 Ken Harvey .02 .10
145 Freddie Joe Nunn .02 .10
146 Robert Awalt .02 .10
147 Niko Noga .02 .10
148 Phoenix Cardinals Logo FOIL .02 .10
149 Phoenix Cardinals Helmet FOIL .02 .10
150 Tim McDonald .02 .10
151 Roy Green .02 .10
152 Stump Mitchell .02 .10
153 J.T. Smith .02 .10
154 Luis Sharpe .02 .10
155 Vai Sikahema .02 .10
156 Jeff Fuller .02 .10
157 Joe Montana 1.50 4.00
158 Harris Barton .02 .10
159 Michael Carter .02 .10
160 Jeff Fuller .02 .10
161 Jerry Rice .60 1.50
162 San Francisco 49ers Logo FOIL .02 .10
163 San Francisco 49ers Helmet FOIL .02 .10
164 Tom Rathman .02 .10
165 Roger Craig .07 .20
166 Ronnie Lott .07 .20
167 Charles Haley .07 .20
168 John Taylor .07 .20
169 Michael Walter .02 .10
170 Ron Hall .02 .10
171 Ervin Randle .02 .10
172 James Wilder .02 .10
173 Ron Holmes .02 .10
174 Mark Carrier WR .07 .20
175 William Howard .02 .10
176 Tampa Bay Bucs Logo FOIL .02 .10
177 Tampa Bay Bucs Helmet FOIL .02 .10
178 Lars Tate .02 .10
179 Vinny Testaverde .07 .20
180 Paul Gruber .02 .10
181 Bruce Hill .02 .10
182 Reuben Davis .02 .10
183 Ricky Reynolds .02 .10
184 Ricky Sanders .02 .10
185 Gary Clark .07 .20
186 Mark May .02 .10
187 Darrell Green .02 .10
188 Jim Lachey .02 .10
189 Doug Williams .02 .10
190 Washington Redskins Helmet FOIL .02 .10
191 Washington Redskins Logo FOIL .02 .10
192 Kelvin Bryant .02 .10
193 Charles Mann .02 .10
194 Alvin Walton .02 .10
195 Art Monk .07 .20
196 Barry Wilburn .02 .10
197 Mark Rypien .02 .10
198 NFC Logo .02 .10
199 Scott Case .02 .10
200 Herschel Walker .02 .10
201 Herschel Walker and Roger Craig .07 .20
202 Henry Ellard and Jerry Rice .20 .50
203 Bruce Matthews and Tom Newberry .02 .10
204 Gary Zimmerman and Anthony Munoz .07 .20
205 Boomer Esiason .02 .10
206 Jay Hilgenberg .02 .10
207 Keith Jackson .07 .20
208 Reggie White and Bruce Smith .07 .20
209 Keith Millard and Tim Krumrie .02 .10
210 Carl Lee and Frank Minnifield .02 .10
211 Joey Browner and Deron Cherry .02 .10
212 Shane Conlan .02 .10
213 Mike Singletary .02 .10
214 Cornelius Bennett .02 .10
215 AFC Logo .02 .10
216 Boomer Esiason .02 .10
217 Erik McMillan .02 .10
218 Jim Kelly .15 .40
219 Cornelius Bennett .02 .10
220 Fred Smerlas .02 .10
221 Shane Conlan .02 .10
222 Scott Norwood .02 .10
223 Mark Kelso .02 .10
224 Buffalo Bills Logo FOIL .02 .10
225 Buffalo Bills Helmet FOIL .02 .10
226 Thurman Thomas .30 .75
227 Pete Metzelaars .02 .10
228 Bruce Smith .07 .20
229 Art Still .02 .10
230 Kent Hull .02 .10
231 Andre Reed .07 .20
232 Tim Krumrie .02 .10
233 Boomer Esiason .02 .10
234 Ickey Woods .02 .10
235 Eric Thomas .02 .10
236 Rodney Holman .02 .10
237 Jim Skow .02 .10
238 Cincinnati Bengals Helmet FOIL .02 .10
239 James Brooks .02 .10
240 David Fulcher .02 .10
241 Carl Zander .02 .10
242 Eddie Brown .02 .10
243 Max Montoya .02 .10
244 Anthony Munoz .07 .20
245 Felix Wright .02 .10
246 Clay Matthews .02 .10
247 Hanford Dixon .02 .10
248 Ozzie Newsome .02 .10
249 Bernie Kosar .02 .10
250 Kevin Mack .02 .10
251 Cincinnati Bengals Helmet FOIL .02 .10
252 Brian Brennan .02 .10
253 Reggie Langhorne .02 .10
254 Cody Risien .02 .10
255 Webster Slaughter .02 .10
256 Mike Johnson .02 .10
257 Frank Minnifield .02 .10
258 Mike Horan .02 .10
259 Dennis Smith .02 .10
260 Ricky Nattiel .02 .10
261 Karl Mecklenburg .02 .10
262 Keith Bishop .02 .10
263 John Elway 1.25 3.00
264 Denver Broncos Helmet FOIL .02 .10
265 Denver Broncos Logo FOIL .02 .10
266 Simon Fletcher .02 .10
267 Vance Johnson .02 .10
268 Tony Dorsett .02 .10
269 Greg Kragen .02 .10
270 Mike Harden .02 .10
271 Mark Jackson .02 .10
272 Warren Moon .07 .20
273 Mike Rozier .02 .10
274 Houston Oilers Logo FOIL .02 .10
275 Allen Pinkett .02 .10
276 Tony Zendejas .02 .10
277 Alonzo Highsmith .02 .10
278 Johnny Meads .02 .10
279 Houston Oilers Helmet FOIL .02 .10
280 Mike Munchak .02 .10
281 John Grimsley .02 .10
282 Ernest Givins .02 .10
283 Drew Hill .02 .10
284 Bruce Matthews .02 .10
285 Ray Childress .02 .10
286 Indianapolis Colts Logo FOIL .02 .10
287 Chris Hinton .02 .10
288 Clarence Verdin .02 .10
289 Jon Hand .02 .10
290 Chris Chandler .40 1.00
291 Eugene Daniel .02 .10
292 Dean Biasucci .02 .10
293 Indianapolis Colts Helmet FOIL .02 .10
294 Duane Bickett .02 .10
295 Rohn Stark .02 .10
296 Albert Bentley .02 .10
297 Bill Brooks .02 .10
298 O'Brien Alston .02 .10
299 Ray Donaldson .02 .10
300 Carlos Carson .02 .10
301 Lloyd Burruss .02 .10
302 Steve DeBerg .02 .10
303 Irv Eatman .02 .10
304 Dino Hackett .02 .10
305 Albert Lewis .02 .10
306 Kansas City Chiefs Helmet FOIL .02 .10
307 Kansas City Chiefs Logo FOIL .02 .10
308 Deron Cherry .02 .10
309 Paul Palmer .02 .10
310 Neil Smith .10 .30
311 Christian Okoye .07 .20
312 Stephone Paige .02 .10
313 Bill Maas .02 .10
314 Marcus Allen .07 .20
315 Vann McElroy .02 .10
316 Mervyn Fernandez .02 .10
317 Bill Pickel .02 .10
318 Greg Townsend .02 .10
319 Tim Brown .50 1.25
320 Los Angeles Raiders Logo FOIL .02 .10
321 Los Angeles Raiders Helmet FOIL .02 .10
322 James Lofton .07 .20
323 Willie Gault .02 .10
324 Jay Schroeder .02 .10
325 Matt Millen .02 .10
326 Howie Long .07 .20
327 Bo Jackson .08 .25
328 Lorenzo Hampton .02 .10
329 Jarvis Williams .02 .10
330 Jim C. Jensen .02 .10
331 Dan Marino 1.25 3.00
332 John Offerdahl .02 .10
333 Brian Sochia .02 .10
334 Miami Dolphins Logo FOIL .02 .10
335 Miami Dolphins Helmet FOIL .02 .10
336 Ferrell Edmunds .02 .10
337 Mark Brown .02 .10
338 Mark Duper .02 .10
339 Troy Stradford .02 .10
340 T.J. Turner .02 .10
341 Mark Clayton .02 .10
342 New England Patriots Logo FOIL .02 .10
343 Johnny Rembert .02 .10
344 Garin Veris .02 .10
345 Stanley Morgan .02 .10
346 John Stephens .02 .10
347 Fred Marion .02 .10
348 Irving Fryar .07 .20
349 New England Patriots Helmet FOIL .02 .10
350 Andre Tippett .02 .10
351 Roland James .02 .10
352 Brent Williams .02 .10
353 Raymond Clayborn .02 .10
354 Tony Eason .02 .10
355 Bruce Armstrong .02 .10
356 New York Jets Logo FOIL .02 .10
357 Marty Lyons .02 .10
358 Bobby Humphery .02 .10
359 Pat Leahy .02 .10
360 Mickey Shuler .02 .10
361 James Hasty .02 .10
362 Ken O'Brien .02 .10
363 New York Jets Helmet FOIL .02 .10
364 Alex Gordon .02 .10
365 Al Toon .02 .10
366 Erik McMillan .02 .10
367 Johnny Hector .02 .10
368 Wesley Walker .02 .10
369 Freeman McNeil .02 .10
370 Pittsburgh Steelers Logo FOIL .02 .10
371 Gary Anderson K .02 .10
372 Rodney Carter .02 .10
373 Merril Hoge .02 .10
374 David Little .02 .10
375 Bubby Brister .10 .30
376 Thomas Everett .02 .10
377 Pittsburgh Steelers Helmet FOIL .02 .10
378 Rod Woodson .25 .60
379 Bryan Hinkle .02 .10
380 Tunch Ilkin .02 .10
381 Aaron Jones .02 .10
382 Louis Lipps .02 .10
383 Warren Williams .02 .10
384 Anthony Miller .07 .20
385 Gary Anderson RB .02 .10
386 Lee Williams .02 .10
387 Lionel James .02 .10
388 Gary Plummer .02 .10
389 Gill Byrd .02 .10
390 San Diego Chargers Helmet FOIL .02 .10
391 Ralf Mojsiejenko .02 .10
392 Rod Bernstine .02 .10
393 Keith Browner .02 .10
394 Billy Ray Smith .02 .10
395 Leslie O'Neal .02 .10
396 Jamie Holland .02 .10
397 Tony Woods .02 .10
398 Bruce Scholtz .02 .10
399 Joe Nash .02 .10
400 Curt Warner .02 .10
401 John L. Williams .02 .10
402 Bryan Millard .02 .10
403 Seattle Seahawks Logo FOIL .02 .10
404 Seattle Seahawks Helmet FOIL .02 .10
405 Steve Largent .10 .30
406 Norm Johnson .02 .10
407 Jacob Green .02 .10
408 Dave Krieg .02 .10
409 Paul Moyer .02 .10
410 Brian Blades .07 .20
411 SB XXIII .02 .10
412 Jerry Rice .60 1.50
413 SB XXIII .02 .10
414 SB XXIII .02 .10
415 SB XXIII .02 .10
416 SB XXIII .02 .10
NNO Panini Album (Joe Montana on cover) 1.25 3.00

1990 Panini Stickers

This set contains 396 colorful stickers. The stickers are numbered in team order. Each sticker measures approximately 1 7/8" by 2 15/16". The cover of the album contains pictures of Mike Singletary, Ronnie Lott, and Lawrence Taylor as the theme is "The Hitters." The stickers were also issued in a UK version which is distinguished by the presence of stats printed on the sticker backs.

COMPLETE SET (396) 8.00 20.00
COMP.UK SET (396) 100.00 250.00
*UK VERSION: 5X TO 10X
1 Super Bowl XXIV FOIL Program Cover (top) .01 .05
2 Super Bowl XXIV FOIL Program Cover (bottom) .01 .05
3 Buffalo Bills Crest FOIL .01 .05
4 Thurman Thomas .10 .30
5 Nate Odomes .01 .05
6 Jim Kelly .10 .30
7 Cornelius Bennett .02 .10
8 Scott Norwood .01 .05
9 Mark Kelso .01 .05
10 Kent Hull .01 .05
11 Jim Ritcher .01 .05
12 Darryl Talley .02 .10
13 Bruce Smith .07 .20
14 Shane Conlan .02 .10
15 Andre Reed .07 .20
16 Jason Buck .01 .05
17 David Fulcher .01 .05
18 Jim Skow .01 .05
19 Anthony Munoz .07 .20
20 Eric Thomas .01 .05
21 Eric Ball .01 .05
22 Tim Krumrie .02 .10
23 James Brooks .02 .10
24 Cincinnati Bengals Crest FOIL .01 .05
25 Rodney Holman .01 .05
26 Boomer Esiason .02 .10
27 Eddie Brown .02 .10
28 Tim McGee .01 .05
29 Cleveland Browns Crest FOIL .01 .05
30 Mike Johnson .01 .05
31 David Grayson .01 .05
32 Thane Gash .01 .05
33 Robert Banks DE .01 .05
34 Eric Metcalf .07 .20
35 Kevin Mack .01 .05
36 Reggie Langhorne .01 .05
37 Webster Slaughter .02 .10
38 Felix Wright .01 .05
39 Bernie Kosar .02 .10
40 Frank Minnifield .01 .05
41 Clay Matthews .02 .10
42 Vance Johnson .01 .05
43 Ron Holmes .01 .05
44 Melvin Bratton .01 .05
45 Greg Kragen .01 .05
46 Karl Mecklenburg .02 .10
47 Dennis Smith .01 .05
48 Bobby Humphrey .01 .05
49 Simon Fletcher .01 .05
50 Denver Broncos Crest FOIL .01 .05
51 Michael Brooks .01 .05
52 Steve Atwater .02 .10
53 John Elway 1.00 2.50
54 David Treadwell .01 .05
55 Houston Oilers Crest FOIL .01 .05
56 Bubba McDowell .02 .10
57 Ray Childress .02 .10
58 Bruce Matthews .02 .10
59 Allen Pinkett .01 .05
60 Warren Moon .07 .20
61 John Grimsley .01 .05
62 Alonzo Highsmith .01 .05
63 Mike Munchak .02 .10
64 Ernest Givins .02 .10
65 Johnny Meads .01 .05
66 Drew Hill .02 .10
67 William Fuller .02 .10
68 Duane Bickett .01 .05
69 Jack Trudeau .01 .05
70 Jon Hand .01 .05
71 Chris Hinton .02 .10
72 Bill Brooks .02 .10
73 Donnell Thompson .01 .05
74 Jeff Herrod .01 .05
75 Andre Rison .07 .20
76 Indianapolis Colts Crest FOIL .01 .05
77 Chris Chandler .10 .30
78 Ray Donaldson .01 .05
79 Albert Bentley .01 .05
80 Keith Taylor .01 .05
81 Kansas City Chiefs Crest FOIL .01 .05
82 Leonard Griffin .01 .05
83 Dino Hackett .01 .05
84 Christian Okoye .02 .10
85 Chris Martin .01 .05
86 John Alt .01 .05
87 Kevin Ross .01 .05
88 Steve DeBerg .02 .10
89 Albert Lewis .01 .05
90 Stephone Paige .01 .05
91 Derrick Thomas .07 .20
92 Neil Smith .07 .20
93 Pete Mandley .01 .05
94 Howie Long .07 .20
95 Greg Townsend .02 .10
96 Mervyn Fernandez .01 .05
97 Scott Davis .01 .05
98 Steve Beuerlein .02 .10
99 Mike Dyal .01 .05
100 Willie Gault .01 .05
101 Eddie Anderson .01 .05
102 Los Angeles Raiders Crest FOIL .01 .05
103 Terry McDaniel .02 .10
104 Bo Jackson .08 .25
105 Steve Wisniewski .02 .10
106 Steve Smith .01 .05
107 Miami Dolphins Crest FOIL .01 .05
108 Mark Clayton .02 .10
109 Louis Oliver .01 .05
110 Jarvis Williams .01 .05
111 Ferrell Edmunds .01 .05
112 Jeff Cross .01 .05
113 John Offerdahl .01 .05
114 Brian Sochia .01 .05
115 Dan Marino 1.00 2.50
116 Jim C. Jensen .01 .05
117 Sammie Smith .01 .05
118 Reggie Roby .01 .05
119 Roy Foster .01 .05
120 Bruce Armstrong .01 .05
121 Steve Grogan .02 .10
122 Hart Lee Dykes .01 .05
123 Andre Tippett .01 .05
124 Johnny Rembert .01 .05
125 Ed Reynolds .01 .05
126 Cedric Jones .01 .05
127 Vincent Brown .07 .20
128 New England Patriots Crest FOIL .01 .05
129 Brent Williams .01 .05
130 John Stephens .01 .05
131 Eric Sievers .01 .05
132 Maurice Hurst .01 .05
133 Jets Crest FOIL .01 .05
134 Johnny Hector .01 .05
135 Erik McMillan .01 .05
136 Jeff Lageman .02 .10
137 Al Toon .02 .10
138 James Hasty .01 .05
139 Kyle Clifton .01 .05
140 Ken O'Brien .02 .10
141 Jim Sweeney .01 .05
142 Jo Jo Townsell .01 .05
143 Dennis Byrd .02 .10
144 Mickey Shuler .01 .05
145 Alex Gordon .01 .05
146 Keith Willis .01 .05
147 Louis Lipps .02 .10
148 David Little .01 .05
149 Greg Lloyd .07 .20
150 Carnell Lake .02 .10
151 Tim Worley .01 .05
152 Dwayne Woodruff .01 .05
153 Gerald Williams .01 .05
154 Pittsburgh Steelers Crest FOIL .01 .05
155 Merril Hoge .01 .05
156 Bubby Brister .07 .20
157 Tunch Ilkin .01 .05
158 Rod Woodson .07 .20
159 San Diego Chargers Crest FOIL .01 .05
160 Leslie O'Neal .02 .10
161 Billy Ray Smith .01 .05
162 Marion Butts .02 .10
163 Lee Williams .01 .05
164 Gill Byrd .01 .05
165 Jim McMahon .02 .10
166 Courtney Hall .01 .05
167 Burt Grossman .01 .05
168 Gary Plummer .01 .05
169 Anthony Miller .07 .20
170 Billy Joe Tolliver .01 .05
171 Vencie Glenn .01 .05
172 Andy Heck .01 .05
173 Brian Blades .02 .10
174 Bryan Millard .01 .05
175 Tony Woods .01 .05
176 Rufus Porter .01 .05
177 David Wyman .01 .05
178 John L. Williams .01 .05
179 Jacob Green .01 .05
180 Seattle Seahawks Crest FOIL .01 .05
181 Eugene Robinson .01 .05
182 Jeff Bryant .01 .05
183 Dave Krieg .02 .10
184 Joe Nash .01 .05
185 Christian Okoye LL .01 .05
186 Felix Wright LL .01 .05
187 Rod Woodson LL .07 .20
188 Barry Sanders AP and .50 1.25
189 Jerry Rice AP and Sterling Sharpe AP .25 .60
190 Bruce Matthews AP .02 .10
191 Jay Hilgenberg AP .01 .05
192 Tom Newberry AP .01 .05
193 Anthony Munoz AP .07 .20
194 Jim Lachey AP .01 .05
195 Keith Jackson AP .01 .05
196 Joe Montana AP .80 2.00
197 David Fulcher AP and Ronnie Lott AP .01 .05
198 Albert Lewis AP and Eric Allen AP .01 .05
199 Reggie White AP .07 .20
200 Keith Millard AP .01 .05
201 Chris Doleman AP .01 .05
202 Mike Singletary AP .02 .10
203 Tim Harris AP .01 .05
204 Lawrence Taylor AP .07 .20
205 Rich Camarillo AP .01 .05
206 Sterling Sharpe LL .07 .20
207 Chris Doleman LL .01 .05
208 Barry Sanders LL .50 1.25
209 Atlanta Falcons Crest FOIL .01 .05
210 Michael Haynes .07 .20
211 Scott Case .01 .05
212 Marcus Cotton .01 .05
213 Chris Miller .07 .20
214 Keith Jones .01 .05
215 Tim Green .01 .05
216 Deion Sanders .30 .75
217 Shawn Collins .01 .05
218 John Settle .01 .05
219 Bill Fralic .01 .05
220 Aundray Bruce .01 .05
221 Jessie Tuggle .01 .05
222 James Thornton .01 .05
223 Dennis Gentry .01 .05
224 Richard Dent .02 .10
225 Jay Hilgenberg .01 .05
226 Steve McMichael .01 .05
227 Brad Muster .01 .05
228 Donnell Woolford .02 .10
229 Mike Singletary .02 .10
230 Chicago Bears Crest FOIL .01 .05
231 Mark Bortz .01 .05
232 Kevin Butler .01 .05
233 Neal Anderson .02 .10
234 Trace Armstrong .01 .05
235 Dallas Cowboys Crest FOIL .01 .05

236 Mark Tuinei .01 .05
237 Tony Tolbert .02 .10
238 Eugene Lockhart .01 .05
239 Daryl Johnston .07 .20
240 Troy Aikman .60 1.50
241 Jim Jeffcoat .01 .05
242 James Dixon .01 .05
243 Jesse Solomon .01 .05
244 Ken Norton Jr. .07 .20
245 Kelvin Martin .01 .05
246 Danny Noonan .01 .05
247 Michael Irvin .10 .30
248 Eric Williams .01 .05
249 Richard Johnson .01 .05
250 Michael Cofer .01 .05
251 Chris Spielman .07 .20
252 Rodney Peete .02 .10
253 Bennie Blades .01 .05
254 Jerry Ball .01 .05
255 Eddie Murray .01 .05
256 Detroit Lions Crest FOIL .01 .05
257 Barry Sanders 1.20 3.00
258 Jerry Holmes .01 .05
259 Dennis Gibson .01 .05
260 Lomas Brown .01 .05
261 Packers Crest FOIL .01 .05
262 Dave Brown .01 .05
263 Mark Murphy .01 .05
264 Perry Kemp .01 .05
265 Don Majkowski .02 .10
266 Chris Jacke .01 .05
267 Keith Woodside .01 .05
268 Tony Mandarich .01 .05
269 Robert Brown .01 .05
270 Sterling Sharpe .07 .20
271 Tim Harris .01 .05
272 Brent Fullwood .01 .05
273 Brian Noble .01 .05
274 Alvin Wright .01 .05
275 Flipper Anderson .02 .10
276 Jackie Slater .01 .05
277 Kevin Greene .02 .10
278 Pete Holohan .01 .05
279 Tom Newberry .01 .05
280 Jerry Gray .01 .05
281 Henry Ellard .02 .10
282 Rams Crest FOIL .01 .05
283 LeRoy Irvin .01 .05
284 Jim Everett .02 .10
285 Greg Bell .01 .05
286 Doug Smith .01 .05
287 Minnesota Vikings Crest FOIL .01 .05
288 Joey Browner .01 .05
289 Wade Wilson .02 .10
290 Chris Doleman .02 .10
291 Al Noga .01 .05
292 Herschel Walker .02 .10
293 Henry Thomas .02 .10
294 Steve Jordan .02 .10
295 Anthony Carter .02 .10
296 Keith Millard .01 .05
297 Carl Lee .01 .05
298 Randall McDaniel .05 .15
299 Gary Zimmerman .02 .10
300 Morten Andersen .01 .05
301 Rickey Jackson .02 .10
302 Sam Mills .02 .10
303 Hoby Brenner .01 .05
304 Dalton Hilliard .01 .05
305 Robert Massey .01 .05
306 John Fourcade .01 .05
307 Lonzell Hill .01 .05
308 Saints Crest FOIL .01 .05
309 Jim Dombrowski .01 .05
310 Pat Swilling .02 .10
311 Vaughan Johnson .02 .10
312 Eric Martin .01 .05
313 Giants Crest FOIL .01 .05
314 Ottis Anderson .02 .10
315 Myron Guyton .01 .05
316 Terry Kinard .01 .05
317 Mark Bavaro .01 .05
318 Phil Simms .02 .10
319 Lawrence Taylor .07 .20
320 Odessa Turner .01 .05
321 Erik Howard .01 .05
322 Mark Collins .01 .05
323 Dave Meggett .02 .10
324 Leonard Marshall .02 .10
325 Carl Banks .02 .10
326 Anthony Toney .01 .05
327 Seth Joyner .02 .10
328 Cris Carter .20 .50
329 Eric Allen .02 .10
330 Keith Jackson .02 .10
331 Clyde Simmons .02 .10
332 Byron Evans .01 .05
333 Keith Byars .02 .10
334 Philadelphia Eagles Crest FOIL .01 .05
335 Reggie White .07 .20
336 Izel Jenkins .01 .05
337 Jerome Brown .02 .10
338 David Alexander .01 .05
339 Phoenix Cardinals Crest FOIL .01 .05
340 Rich Camarillo .01 .05
341 Ken Harvey .02 .10
342 Luis Sharpe .01 .05
343 Timm Rosenbach .01 .05
344 Tim McDonald .01 .05
345 Vai Sikahema .01 .05
346 Freddie Joe Nunn .01 .05
347 Ernie Jones .01 .05
348 J.T. Smith .01 .05
349 Eric Hill .01 .05
350 Roy Green .02 .10
351 Anthony Bell .01 .05
352 Kevin Fagan .01 .05
353 Roger Craig .02 .10
354 Ronnie Lott .02 .10
355 Mike Cofer .01 .05
356 John Taylor .07 .20
357 Joe Montana 1.20 3.00
358 Charles Haley .07 .20
359 Guy McIntyre .01 .05
360 49ers Crest FOIL .01 .05
361 Pierce Holt .01 .05
362 Tom Rathman .02 .10
363 Jerry Rice .50 1.25
364 Michael Carter .01 .05
365 Buccaneers Crest FOIL .01 .05
366 Lars Tate .01 .05
367 Paul Gruber .01 .05
368 Winston Moss .01 .05
369 Reuben Davis .01 .05
370 Mark Robinson .01 .05
371 Bruce Hill .01 .05
372 Kevin Murphy .01 .05
373 Ricky Reynolds .01 .05
374 Harry Hamilton .01 .05
375 Vinny Testaverde .02 .10
376 Mark Carrier WR .02 .10
377 Ervin Randle .01 .05
378 Ricky Sanders .02 .10
379 Charles Mann .02 .10
380 Jim Lachey .01 .05
381 Wilber Marshall .01 .05
382 A.J. Johnson .01 .05
383 Darrell Green .02 .10
384 Mark Rypien .01 .05
385 Gerald Riggs .02 .10
386 Washington Redskins Crest FOIL .01 .05
387 Alvin Walton .01 .05
388 Art Monk .07 .20
389 Gary Clark .07 .20
390 Earnest Byner .02 .10
391 SB XXIV Action FOIL (Jerry Rice) .30 .75
392 SB XXIV Action FOIL (49er Offensive Line) .01 .05
393 SB XXIV Action FOIL (Tom Rathman) .01 .05
394 SB XXIV Action FOIL (Chet Brooks) .01 .05
395 SB XXIV Action FOIL (John Elway) .30 .75
396 Joe Montana FOIL SB XXIV MVP 1.60 4.00
NNO Panini Album .80 2.00

2010 Panini Stickers

COMPLETE SET (560) 25.00 50.00
1 NFL LOGO Foil .20 .50
2 NFLPA LOGO Foil .20 .50
3 AFC LOGO Foil .20 .50
4 NFC LOGO Foil .20 .50
5 AFC CHAMP LOGO Foil .20 .50
6 NFC CHAMP LOGO Foil .20 .50
7 PRO BOWL LOGO Foil .20 .50
8 Buffalo HEL Foil Miami HEL .20 .50
9 New England HEL Foil New York Jets HEL .20 .50
10 Baltimore HEL Foil Cincinnati HEL .20 .50
11 Cleveland HEL Foil Pittsburgh HEL .20 .50
12 Houston HEL Foil Indianapolis HEL .20 .50
13 Jacksonville HEL Foil Tennessee HEL .20 .50
14 Denver HEL Foil Kansas City HEL .20 .50
15 Oakland HEL Foil San Diego HEL .20 .50
16 Dallas HEL Foil New York Giants HEL .20 .50
17 Philadelphia HEL Foil Washington HEL .20 .50
18 Chicago HEL Foil Detroit HEL .20 .50
19 Green Bay HEL Foil Minnesota HEL .20 .50
20 Atlanta HEL Foil Carolina HEL .20 .50
21 New Orleans HEL Foil Tampa Bay HEL .20 .50
22 Arizona HEL Foil San Francisco HEL .20 .50
23 Seattle HEL Foil St. Louis HEL .20 .50
24 Buffalo Bills LOGO Foil .20 .50
25 Ryan Fitzpatrick .15 .40
26 C.J. Spiller .25 .60
27 Marshawn Lynch .12 .30
28 Fred Jackson .15 .40
29 Lee Evans .12 .30
30 Leodis McKelvin .10 .25
31 Marcus Easley .12 .30
32 Paul Posluszny .12 .30
33 Jairus Byrd .12 .30
34 Marcus Stroud .10 .25
35 Donte Whitner .10 .25
36 George Wilson .10 .25
37 Fred Jackson Foil .30 .75
38 Lee Evans Foil .25 .60
39 Paul Posluszny Foil .25 .60
40 Miami Dolphins LOGO Foil .20 .50
41 Chad Henne .12 .30
42 Ricky Williams .12 .30
43 Ronnie Brown .12 .30
44 Davone Bess .10 .25
45 Lex Hilliard .10 .25
46 Brian Hartline .12 .30
47 Anthony Fasano .10 .25
48 Brandon Marshall .12 .30
49 Yeremiah Bell .10 .25
50 Vontae Davis .10 .25
51 Channing Crowder .10 .25
52 Randy Starks .10 .25
53 Chad Henne Foil .25 .60
54 Ricky Williams Foil .25 .60
55 Ronnie Brown Foil .25 .60
56 New England Patriots LOGO Foil .20 .50
57 Tom Brady .25 .60
58 Laurence Maroney .12 .30
59 Wes Welker .15 .40
60 Randy Moss .15 .40
61 Julian Edelman .10 .25
62 Taylor Price .15 .40
63 Torry Holt .12 .30
64 Rob Gronkowski .40 1.00
65 Brandon Meriweather .10 .25
66 Leigh Bodden .10 .25
67 Tully Banta-Cain .10 .25
68 Jerod Mayo .12 .30
69 Tom Brady Foil .50 1.25
70 Wes Welker Foil .30 .75
71 Randy Moss Foil .30 .75
72 New York Jets LOGO Foil .20 .50
73 Mark Sanchez .15 .40
74 Shonn Greene .12 .30
75 LaDainian Tomlinson .15 .40
76 Joe McKnight .15 .40
77 Jerricho Cotchery .12 .30
78 Braylon Edwards .12 .30
79 Santonio Holmes .12 .30
80 Dustin Keller .12 .30
81 Darrelle Revis .12 .30
82 David Harris .10 .25
83 Calvin Pace .10 .25
84 Shaun Ellis .10 .25
85 Mark Sanchez Foil .30 .75
86 Braylon Edwards Foil .25 .60
87 Darrelle Revis Foil .25 .60
88 Baltimore Ravens LOGO Foil .20 .50
89 Joe Flacco .15 .40
90 Ray Rice .12 .30
91 Derrick Mason .12 .30
92 Willis McGahee .12 .30
93 Mark Clayton .10 .25
94 Anquan Boldin .12 .30
95 Todd Heap .10 .25
96 Michael Oher .12 .30
97 Ray Lewis .15 .40
98 Ed Reed .12 .30
99 Terrell Suggs .10 .25
100 Dawan Landry .10 .25
101 Joe Flacco Foil .30 .75
102 Ray Rice Foil .25 .60
103 Ray Lewis Foil .30 .75
104 Cincinnati Bengals LOGO Foil .20 .50
105 Carson Palmer .12 .30
106 Cedric Benson .12 .30
107 Bernard Scott .10 .25
108 Chad Ochocinco .12 .30
109 Andre Caldwell .10 .25
110 Jordan Shipley .15 .40
111 Jermaine Gresham .20 .50
112 Terrell Owens .15 .40
113 Johnathan Joseph .10 .25
114 Leon Hall .10 .25
115 Dhani Jones .10 .25
116 Matt Jones .10 .25
117 Carson Palmer Foil .25 .60
118 Cedric Benson Foil .25 .60
119 Chad Ochocinco Foil .25 .60
120 Cleveland Browns LOGO Foil .20 .50
121 Jake Delhomme .12 .30
122 Jerome Harrison .10 .25
123 Montario Hardesty .15 .40
124 Mohamed Massaquoi .12 .30
125 Colt McCoy .30 .75
126 Josh Cribbs .15 .40
127 Joe Thomas .10 .25
128 James Davis .10 .25
129 Eric Wright .10 .25
130 Abram Elam .15 .40
131 David Bowens .10 .25
132 Joe Haden .15 .40
133 Jerome Harrison Foil .20 .50
134 Mohamed Massaquoi Foil .25 .60
135 Josh Cribbs Foil .30 .75
136 Pittsburgh Steelers LOGO Foil .20 .50
137 Ben Roethlisberger .15 .40
138 Rashard Mendenhall .12 .30
139 Jonathan Dwyer .15 .40
140 Hines Ward .12 .30
141 Mike Wallace .12 .30
142 Emmanuel Sanders .15 .40
143 Heath Miller .12 .30
144 Troy Polamalu .15 .40
145 James Harrison .15 .40
146 LaMarr Woodley .10 .25
147 Lawrence Timmons .10 .25
148 James Farrior .10 .25
149 Ben Roethlisberger Foil .30 .75
150 Rashard Mendenhall Foil .25 .60
151 Troy Polamalu Foil .30 .75
152 Houston Texans LOGO Foil .20 .50
153 Matt Schaub .12 .30
154 Steve Slaton .10 .25
155 Ben Tate .20 .50
156 Andre Johnson .12 .30
157 Kevin Walter .12 .30
158 Owen Daniels .10 .25
159 Jacoby Jones .10 .25
160 Brian Cushing .10 .25
161 DeMeco Ryans .10 .25
162 Mario Williams .12 .30
163 Kareem Jackson .15 .40
164 Bernard Pollard .10 .25
165 Matt Schaub Foil .25 .60
166 Andre Johnson Foil .25 .60
167 Brian Cushing Foil .20 .50
168 Indianapolis Colts LOGO Foil .20 .50
169 Peyton Manning .25 .60
170 Robert Mathis .10 .25
171 Joseph Addai .12 .30
172 Donald Brown .12 .30
173 Reggie Wayne .12 .30
174 Austin Collie .12 .30
175 Pierre Garcon .12 .30
176 Dallas Clark .12 .30
177 Clint Session .10 .25
178 Dwight Freeney .12 .30
179 Bob Sanders .12 .30
180 Antoine Bethea .10 .25
181 Peyton Manning Foil .50 1.25
182 Joseph Addai Foil .25 .60
183 Dallas Clark Foil .25 .60
184 Jacksonville Jaguars LOGO Foil .20 .50
185 David Garrard .12 .30
186 Maurice Jones-Drew .12 .30
187 Rashad Jennings .10 .25
188 Mike Sims-Walker .12 .30
189 Aaron Kampman .12 .30
190 Marcedes Lewis .10 .25
191 Zach Miller .12 .30
192 Mike Thomas .12 .30
193 Daryl Smith .10 .25
194 Justin Durant .10 .25
195 Derrick Harvey .10 .25
196 Kirk Morrison .10 .25
197 David Garrard Foil .25 .60
198 Maurice Jones-Drew Foil .25 .60
199 Mike Sims-Walker Foil .25 .60
200 Tennessee Titans LOGO Foil .20 .50
201 Vince Young .10 .25
202 Chris Johnson .15 .40
203 Kenny Britt .12 .30
204 Nate Washington .10 .25
205 Bo Scaife .10 .25
206 Justin Gage .10 .25
207 Damian Williams .15 .40
208 Stephen Tulloch .10 .25
209 Rob Bironas .10 .25
210 Cortland Finnegan .10 .25
211 Michael Griffin .10 .25
212 Javon Ringer .10 .25
213 Vince Young Foil .20 .50
214 Chris Johnson Foil .30 .75
215 Cortland Finnegan Foil .20 .50
216 Denver Broncos LOGO Foil .20 .50
217 Kyle Orton .12 .30
218 Knowshon Moreno .12 .30
219 Jabar Gaffney .10 .25
220 Eddie Royal .10 .25
221 Correll Buckhalter .12 .30
222 Demaryius Thomas .20 .50
223 Eric Decker .20 .50
224 Tim Tebow .60 1.50
225 Brian Dawkins .12 .30
226 Champ Bailey .12 .30
227 Elvis Dumervil .10 .25
228 D.J. Williams .10 .25
229 Kyle Orton Foil .25 .60
230 Knowshon Moreno Foil .25 .60
231 Champ Bailey Foil .25 .60
232 Kansas City Chiefs LOGO Foil .20 .50
233 Matt Cassel .12 .30
234 Jamaal Charles .12 .30
235 Thomas Jones .12 .30
236 Dexter McCluster .15 .40
237 Chris Chambers .12 .30
238 Dwayne Bowe .12 .30
239 Leonard Pope .10 .25
240 Eric Berry .15 .40
241 Brandon Flowers .10 .25
242 Tamba Hali .10 .25
243 Derrick Johnson .10 .25
244 Demorrio Williams .10 .25
245 Matt Cassel Foil .25 .60
246 Jamaal Charles Foil .25 .60
247 Dwayne Bowe Foil .25 .60
248 Oakland Raiders LOGO Foil .20 .50
249 Jason Campbell .12 .30
250 Michael Bush .10 .25
251 Darren McFadden .12 .30
252 Louis Murphy .12 .30
253 Chaz Schilens .10 .25
254 Darrius Heyward-Bey .12 .30
255 Zach Miller .12 .30
256 Rolando McClain .15 .40
257 Shane Lechler .10 .25
258 Nnamdi Asomugha .12 .30
259 Tyvon Branch .10 .25
260 Trevor Scott .10 .25
261 Darren McFadden Foil .25 .60
262 Zach Miller Foil .25 .60
263 Nnamdi Asomugha Foil .25 .60
264 San Diego Chargers LOGO Foil .20 .50
265 Philip Rivers .15 .40
266 Ryan Mathews .30 .75
267 Darren Sproles .12 .30
268 Vincent Jackson .10 .25
269 Malcom Floyd .12 .30
270 Legedu Naanee .10 .25
271 Antonio Gates .12 .30
272 Stephen Cooper .10 .25
273 Eric Weddle .10 .25
274 Shawne Merriman .12 .30
275 Shaun Phillips .10 .25
276 Quentin Jammer .10 .25
277 Philip Rivers Foil .30 .75
278 Antonio Gates Foil .25 .60
279 Shaun Phillips Foil .20 .50
280 Dallas Cowboys LOGO Foil .20 .50
281 Tony Romo .20 .50
282 Felix Jones .12 .30
283 Marion Barber .12 .30
284 Tashard Choice .10 .25
285 Miles Austin .15 .40
286 Dez Bryant .50 1.25
287 Jason Witten .15 .40
288 Roy Williams WR .12 .30
289 Bradie James .10 .25
290 DeMarcus Ware .12 .30
291 Jay Ratliff .12 .30
292 Mike Jenkins .10 .25
293 Tony Romo Foil .40 1.00
294 Jason Witten Foil .30 .75
295 DeMarcus Ware Foil .25 .60
296 New York Giants LOGO Foil .20 .50
297 Eli Manning .15 .40
298 Brandon Jacobs .12 .30
299 Ahmad Bradshaw .12 .30
300 Mario Manningham .12 .30
301 Steve Smith USC .12 .30
302 Hakeem Nicks .12 .30
303 Kevin Boss .12 .30
304 Terrell Thomas .10 .25
305 Justin Tuck .12 .30
306 Kenny Phillips .10 .25
307 Osi Umenyiora .10 .25
308 Jason Pierre-Paul .25 .60
309 Eli Manning Foil .30 .75
310 Brandon Jacobs Foil .25 .60
311 Steve Smith USC Foil .25 .60
312 Philadelphia Eagles LOGO Foil .20 .50
313 Kevin Kolb .12 .30
314 Michael Vick .20 .50
315 LeSean McCoy .12 .30
316 Leonard Weaver .10 .25
317 DeSean Jackson .12 .30
318 Jeremy Maclin .12 .30
319 Brent Celek .12 .30
320 Quintin Mikell .10 .25
321 Trent Cole .10 .25
322 Asante Samuel .10 .25
323 Jason Avant .10 .25
324 Nate Allen .15 .40
325 LeSean McCoy Foil .25 .60
326 DeSean Jackson Foil .25 .60
327 Brent Celek Foil .25 .60
328 Washington Redskins LOGO Foil .20 .50
329 Donovan McNabb .15 .40
330 Clinton Portis .12 .30
331 Santana Moss .12 .30
332 Devin Thomas .10 .25
333 Chris Cooley .12 .30
334 Fred Davis .12 .30
335 London Fletcher .10 .25
336 Rocky McIntosh .10 .25
337 LaRon Landry .10 .25
338 Chris Horton .10 .25
339 Albert Haynesworth .10 .25
340 Trent Williams .15 .40
341 Clinton Portis Foil .25 .60
342 Santana Moss Foil .25 .60
343 Chris Cooley Foil .25 .60
344 Chicago Bears LOGO Foil .20 .50
345 Jay Cutler .15 .40
346 Matt Forte .12 .30
347 Chester Taylor .10 .25
348 Devin Hester .15 .40
349 Earl Bennett .12 .30
350 Johnny Knox .12 .30
351 Greg Olsen .10 .25
352 Lance Briggs .12 .30
353 Brian Urlacher .15 .40
354 Julius Peppers .12 .30
355 Zack Bowman .10 .25
356 Danieal Manning .10 .25
357 Jay Cutler Foil .30 .75
358 Matt Forte Foil .25 .60
359 Brian Urlacher Foil .30 .75
360 Detroit Lions LOGO Foil .20 .50
361 Matthew Stafford .15 .40
362 Kevin Smith .12 .30
363 Jahvid Best .25 .60
364 Calvin Johnson .15 .40
365 Bryant Johnson .10 .25
366 Brandon Pettigrew .10 .25
367 Dennis Northcutt .10 .25
368 Nate Burleson .10 .25
369 Louis Delmas .10 .25
370 Kyle Vanden Bosch .10 .25
371 Julian Peterson .10 .25
372 Ndamukong Suh .60 1.50
373 Matthew Stafford Foil .30 .75
374 Calvin Johnson Foil .30 .75
375 Brandon Pettigrew Foil .20 .50
376 Green Bay Packers LOGO Foil .20 .50
377 Aaron Rodgers .30 .75
378 Ryan Grant .12 .30
379 Brandon Jackson .10 .25
380 Greg Jennings .12 .30
381 Donald Driver .12 .30
382 Jermichael Finley .12 .30
383 James Jones .10 .25
384 Jordy Nelson .15 .40
385 Nick Barnett .10 .25
386 A.J. Hawk .12 .30
387 Charles Woodson .15 .40
388 Clay Matthews .15 .40
389 Aaron Rodgers Foil .60 1.50
390 Ryan Grant Foil .25 .60
391 Donald Driver Foil .25 .60
392 Minnesota Vikings LOGO Foil .20 .50
393 Brett Favre .40 1.00
394 Adrian Peterson .25 .60
395 Toby Gerhart .15 .40
396 Bernard Berrian .10 .25
397 Sidney Rice .12 .30
398 Percy Harvin .15 .40
399 Visanthe Shiancoe .12 .30
400 Jared Allen .15 .40
401 Chad Greenway .10 .25
402 Cedric Griffin .10 .25
403 Ray Edwards .10 .25
404 Kevin Williams .10 .25
405 Brett Favre Foil .75 2.00
406 Adrian Peterson Foil .50 1.25
407 Jared Allen Foil .30 .75
408 Atlanta Falcons LOGO Foil .20 .50
409 Matt Ryan .15 .40
410 Michael Turner .10 .25
411 Roddy White .12 .30
412 Michael Jenkins .10 .25
413 Jerious Norwood .10 .25
414 Tony Gonzalez .12 .30
415 Jason Snelling .12 .30
416 Curtis Lofton .10 .25
417 Jonathan Babineaux .10 .25
418 Brent Grimes .10 .25
419 Erik Coleman .10 .25
420 Mike Peterson .10 .25
421 Matt Ryan Foil .30 .75
422 Roddy White Foil .25 .60
423 Tony Gonzalez Foil .25 .60
424 Carolina Panthers LOGO Foil .20 .50
425 Matt Moore .12 .30
426 DeAngelo Williams .12 .30
427 Jonathan Stewart .12 .30
428 Steve Smith .12 .30
429 Jimmy Clausen .15 .40
430 Armanti Edwards .15 .40
431 Brandon LaFell .15 .40
432 Dante Rosario .10 .25
433 Dwayne Jarrett .10 .25
434 Jon Beason .10 .25
435 Richard Marshall .10 .25
436 Chris Gamble .10 .25
437 DeAngelo Williams Foil .25 .60
438 Jonathan Stewart Foil .25 .60
439 Steve Smith Foil .25 .60
440 New Orleans Saints LOGO Foil .20 .50
441 Drew Brees .15 .40
442 Pierre Thomas .12 .30
443 Reggie Bush .15 .40
444 Marques Colston .12 .30
445 Robert Meachem .12 .30
446 Jeremy Shockey .12 .30
447 Devery Henderson .10 .25
448 Garrett Hartley .10 .25
449 Jonathan Vilma .10 .25
450 Roman Harper .10 .25
451 Darren Sharper .12 .30
452 Will Smith .10 .25
453 Drew Brees Foil .30 .75
454 Marques Colston Foil .25 .60
455 Darren Sharper Foil .25 .60
456 Tampa Bay Buccaneers LOGO Foil .20 .50
457 Josh Freeman .15 .40
458 Cadillac Williams .12 .30
459 Derrick Ward .10 .25
460 Sammie Stroughter .10 .25
461 Mike Williams .25 .60
462 Kellen Winslow Jr. .12 .30
463 Arrelious Benn .15 .40
464 Maurice Stovall .10 .25
465 Gerald McCoy .15 .40
466 Barrett Ruud .10 .25
467 Tanard Jackson .10 .25
468 Ronde Barber .10 .25
469 Josh Freeman Foil .30 .75
470 Cadillac Williams Foil .25 .60
471 Kellen Winslow Jr. Foil .25 .60
472 Arizona Cardinals LOGO Foil .20 .50
473 Matt Leinart .12 .30
474 Larry Fitzgerald .15 .40
475 Chris Wells .12 .30
476 Steve Breaston .10 .25
477 Tim Hightower .10 .25
478 Early Doucet .10 .25
479 Andre Roberts .15 .40
480 LaRod Stephens-Howling .12 .30
481 Adrian Wilson .10 .25
482 Dominique Rodgers-Cromartie .10 .25
483 Joey Porter .10 .25
484 Calais Campbell .10 .25
485 Matt Leinart Foil .25 .60
486 Larry Fitzgerald Foil .30 .75
487 Chris Wells Foil .25 .60
488 San Francisco 49ers LOGO Foil .20 .50
489 Alex Smith QB .12 .30
490 Frank Gore .12 .30
491 Brian Westbrook .12 .30
492 Michael Crabtree .15 .40
493 Josh Morgan .12 .30
494 Vernon Davis .12 .30
495 Ted Ginn .12 .30
496 Patrick Willis .12 .30
497 Manny Lawson .10 .25
498 Justin Smith .10 .25
499 Dashon Goldson .10 .25
500 Takeo Spikes .10 .25
501 Frank Gore Foil .25 .60
502 Vernon Davis Foil .25 .60
503 Patrick Willis Foil .25 .60
504 Seattle Seahawks LOGO Foil .20 .50
505 Matt Hasselbeck .10 .25
506 Julius Jones .10 .25
507 Justin Forsett .12 .30
508 Leon Washington .12 .30
509 T.J. Houshmandzadeh .12 .30
510 Deion Branch .10 .25
511 John Carlson .10 .25
512 Golden Tate .15 .40
513 Aaron Curry .12 .30
514 Josh Wilson .10 .25
515 Lofa Tatupu .10 .25
516 Earl Thomas .15 .40
517 Matt Hasselbeck Foil .20 .50
518 Julius Jones Foil .20 .50
519 T.J. Houshmandzadeh Foil .25 .60
520 St. Louis Rams LOGO Foil .20 .50
521 Sam Bradford .60 1.50
522 Steven Jackson .12 .30
523 Donnie Avery .12 .30
524 Brandon Gibson .10 .25
525 Mardy Gilyard .15 .40
526 Donnie Jones .10 .25
527 Daniel Fells .15 .40
528 Danny Amendola .15 .40
529 James Laurinaitis .12 .30
530 C.J. Ah You .10 .25
531 Chris Long .10 .25
532 James Butler .10 .25
533 Steven Jackson .12 .30
534 Danny Amendola .15 .40
535 James Laurinaitis .12 .30
536 Matt Schaub LL .12 .30
537 Chris Johnson LL .15 .40
538 Andre Johnson LL .12 .30
539 Patrick Willis LL .12 .30
540 Elvis Dumervil LL .10 .25
541 Jairus Byrd LL .12 .30
542 Shane Lechler LL .10 .25
543 Danny Amendola LL .15 .40
544 Nate Kaeding LL .10 .25
545 Adrian Peterson LL .25 .60
546 Darrelle Revis LL .12 .30
547 Drew Brees LL .15 .40
548 Wes Welker LL .15 .40
549 David Akers LL .10 .25
550 New Orleans Saints LL .10 .25
551 New York Jets LL .10 .25
552 Super Bowl XLV Foil .20 .50
553 Super Bowl XLV Foil .20 .50
554 Super Bowl XLV Foil .20 .50
555 Super Bowl I Foil .20 .50
556 Super Bowl IX Foil .20 .50
557 Super Bowl XVIII Foil .20 .50
558 Super Bowl XXVII Foil .20 .50
559 Super Bowl XXXVI Foil .20 .50
560 Super Bowl XLIV Foil .20 .50

2011 Panini Stickers

1 NFL Logo .10 .25
2 TBD .10 .25
3 AFC Logo .10 .25
4 NFC Logo .10 .25
5 Buffalo Bills Foil .20 .50
6 Steve Johnson .12 .30
7 Paul Posluszny .10 .25
8 Ryan Fitzpatrick .12 .30
9 Lee Evans .12 .30
10 Roscoe Parrish .10 .25
11 C.J. Spiller .12 .30
12 Fred Jackson .15 .40
13 David Nelson .12 .30
14 Jairus Byrd .10 .25
15 Marcell Dareus .15 .40
16 Steve Johnson FOIL .25 .60
17 Paul Posluszny FOIL .20 .50
18 Ryan Fitzpatrick FOIL .25 .60
19 Miami Dolphins FOIL .20 .50
20 Brandon Marshall .12 .30
21 Jake Long .10 .25
22 Ronnie Brown .12 .30
23 Anthony Fasano .10 .25
24 Cameron Wake .10 .25
25 Chad Henne .12 .30
26 Davone Bess .10 .25
27 Ricky Williams .12 .30
28 Karlos Dansby .10 .25
29 Yeremiah Bell .10 .25
30 Brandon Marshall FOIL .25 .60
31 Jake Long FOIL .20 .50
32 Cameron Wake FOIL .20 .50
33 New England Patriots FOIL .20 .50
34 Tom Brady .25 .60
35 Wes Welker .15 .40
36 Devin McCourty .10 .25
37 Jerod Mayo .10 .25
38 Danny Woodhead .15 .40
39 Rob Gronkowski .15 .40
40 Deion Branch .10 .25
41 BenJarvus Green-Ellis .12 .30
42 Vince Wilfork .10 .25
43 Aaron Hernandez .12 .30
44 Tom Brady FOIL .50 1.25
45 Wes Welker FOIL .30 .75
46 Jerod Mayo FOIL .20 .50
47 New York Jets FOIL .20 .50
48 Darrelle Revis .12 .30
49 Mark Sanchez .15 .40
50 Brad Smith .10 .25
51 David Harris .10 .25
52 Braylon Edwards .12 .30
53 Dustin Keller .12 .30
54 Jerricho Cotchery .10 .25
55 LaDainian Tomlinson .15 .40
56 Santonio Holmes .12 .30
57 Shonn Greene .12 .30
58 Darrelle Revis FOIL .25 .60
59 Mark Sanchez FOIL .30 .75
60 LaDainian Tomlinson FOIL .30 .75
61 Baltimore Ravens FOIL .20 .50
62 Ray Lewis .15 .40
63 Joe Flacco .15 .40
64 Anquan Boldin .12 .30
65 Derrick Mason .10 .25
66 Ed Reed .12 .30
67 Michael Oher .10 .25
68 Ray Rice FOIL .12 .30
69 Terrell Suggs .10 .25
70 Todd Heap .10 .25
71 Haloti Ngata .10 .25
72 Ray Lewis FOIL .30 .75
73 Joe Flacco FOIL .30 .75
74 Ray Rice FOIL .25 .60
75 Cincinnati Bengals Foil .20 .50
76 Carson Palmer .12 .30
77 Chad Ochocinco .12 .30
78 Cedric Benson .12 .30
79 Terrell Owens .15 .40
80 Andy Dalton .40 1.00
81 Dhani Jones .10 .25
82 Jermaine Gresham .12 .30
83 A.J. Green .30 .75
84 Jordan Shipley .12 .30
85 Leon Hall .10 .25
86 Carson Palmer FOIL .25 .60
87 Chad Ochocinco FOIL .25 .60
88 Cedric Benson FOIL .25 .60
89 Cleveland Browns FOIL .20 .50
90 Peyton Hillis .12 .30
91 Colt McCoy .12 .30
92 Abram Elam .10 .25
93 Ben Watson .10 .25
94 Joe Haden .10 .25
95 T.J. Ward .10 .25
96 Joe Thomas .10 .25
97 Josh Cribbs .12 .30
98 Mohamed Massaquoi .12 .30
99 Scott Fujita .10 .25
100 Peyton Hillis FOIL .25 .60
101 Colt McCoy FOIL .25 .60
102 Josh Cribbs FOIL .25 .60
103 Pittsburgh Steelers FOIL .20 .50
104 Troy Polamalu .15 .40
105 Ben Roethlisberger .15 .40
106 Brett Keisel .12 .30
107 LaMarr Woodley .10 .25
108 Lawrence Timmons .10 .25
109 Heath Miller .12 .30
110 Hines Ward .12 .30
111 James Harrison .15 .40
112 Mike Wallace .15 .40
113 Rashard Mendenhall .12 .30
114 Troy Polamalu FOIL .30 .75
115 Ben Roethlisberger FOIL .30 .75
116 Hines Ward FOIL .25 .60
117 Houston Texans FOIL .20 .50
118 Andre Johnson .12 .30
119 Arian Foster .12 .30
120 Mario Williams .10 .25
121 Matt Schaub .12 .30
122 Brian Cushing .10 .25
123 DeMeco Ryans .10 .25
124 Jacoby Jones .10 .25
125 Kevin Walter .12 .30
126 Owen Daniels .10 .25
127 Bernard Pollard .10 .25
128 Andre Johnson FOIL .25 .60
129 Arian Foster FOIL .25 .60
130 Mario Williams FOIL .20 .50
131 Indianapolis Colts FOIL .20 .50
132 Peyton Manning .25 .60
133 Dwight Freeney .12 .30
134 Reggie Wayne .12 .30
135 Antoine Bethea .10 .25
136 Pierre Garcon .12 .30
137 Austin Collie .12 .30
138 Dallas Clark .12 .30
139 Donald Brown .10 .25
140 Joseph Addai .12 .30
141 Robert Mathis .10 .25
142 Peyton Manning FOIL .50 1.25
143 Dwight Freeney FOIL .25 .60
144 Reggie Wayne FOIL .25 .60
145 Jacksonville Jaguars FOIL .20 .50
146 Maurice Jones-Drew .12 .30
147 David Garrard .12 .30
148 Daryl Smith .10 .25
149 Kirk Morrison .10 .25
150 Marcedes Lewis .10 .25
151 Mike Sims-Walker .12 .30
152 Mike Thomas .12 .30
153 Rashad Jennings .10 .25
154 Rashean Mathis .10 .25
155 Blaine Gabbert .25 .60
156 Maurice Jones-Drew FOIL .25 .60
157 David Garrard FOIL .25 .60
158 Mike Thomas FOIL .25 .60
159 Tennessee Titans FOIL .20 .50
160 Chris Johnson .12 .30
161 Michael Griffin .10 .25
162 Bo Scaife .10 .25
163 Cortland Finnegan .10 .25
164 Jake Locker .40 1.00
165 Marc Mariani .12 .30
166 Kenny Britt .12 .30
167 Nate Washington .10 .25
168 Stephen Tulloch .10 .25
169 Vince Young .10 .25
170 Chris Johnson FOIL .25 .60
171 Michael Griffin FOIL .20 .50
172 Kenny Britt FOIL .25 .60
173 Denver Broncos FOIL .20 .50
174 Tim Tebow .30 .75
175 Champ Bailey .12 .30
176 Brandon Lloyd .12 .30
177 Brian Dawkins .12 .30
178 D.J. Williams .15 .40
179 Jabar Gaffney .10 .25
180 Von Miller .20 .50
181 Elvis Dumervil .10 .25
182 Knowshon Moreno .12 .30
183 Kyle Orton .12 .30
184 Tim Tebow FOIL .60 1.50
185 Champ Bailey FOIL .25 .60
186 Brandon Lloyd FOIL .25 .60
187 Kansas City Chiefs FOIL .20 .50
188 Jamaal Charles .12 .30
189 Dwayne Bowe .12 .30
190 Brandon Flowers .10 .25
191 Dexter McCluster .10 .25
192 Eric Berry .12 .30
193 Derrick Johnson .10 .25
194 Tony Moeaki .10 .25
195 Matt Cassel .12 .30
196 Jonathan Baldwin .15 .40
197 Thomas Jones .12 .30
198 Jamaal Charles FOIL .25 .60
199 Dwayne Bowe FOIL .25 .60
200 Matt Cassel FOIL .25 .60
201 Oakland Raiders FOIL .20 .50
202 Darren McFadden .12 .30
203 Nnamdi Asomugha .12 .30
204 Jacoby Ford .12 .30
205 Louis Murphy .12 .30
206 Jason Campbell .12 .30
207 Michael Bush .10 .25
208 Richard Seymour .10 .25
209 Rolando McClain .10 .25
210 Tyvon Branch .10 .25
211 Zach Miller .12 .30
212 Darren McFadden FOIL .25 .60
213 Richard Seymour FOIL .20 .50
214 Jason Campbell FOIL .25 .60
215 San Diego Chargers FOIL .20 .50
216 Philip Rivers .15 .40
217 Antonio Gates .12 .30
218 Darren Sproles .12 .30
219 Antoine Cason .10 .25
220 Eric Weddle .10 .25
221 Malcom Floyd .12 .30
222 Quentin Jammer .10 .25
223 Ryan Mathews .12 .30
224 Shaun Phillips .10 .25
225 Vincent Jackson .12 .30
226 Philip Rivers FOIL .30 .75
227 Antonio Gates FOIL .25 .60
228 Vincent Jackson FOIL .25 .60
229 Dallas Cowboys FOIL .20 .50
230 Tony Romo .15 .40
231 DeMarcus Ware .12 .30
232 Anthony Spencer .10 .25
233 Bradie James .10 .25
234 Dez Bryant .15 .40
235 Felix Jones .12 .30
236 Jason Witten .15 .40
237 Mike Jenkins .10 .25
238 Jay Ratliff .12 .30
239 Miles Austin .12 .30
240 Tony Romo FOIL .30 .75
241 DeMarcus Ware FOIL .25 .60
242 Jason Witten FOIL .30 .75
243 New York Giants FOIL .20 .50
244 Eli Manning .15 .40
245 Osi Umenyiora .10 .25
246 Ahmad Bradshaw .12 .30
247 Brandon Jacobs .12 .30
248 Hakeem Nicks .12 .30
249 Justin Tuck .12 .30
250 Kevin Boss .12 .30
251 Mario Manningham .12 .30
252 Steve Smith USC .12 .30
253 Terrell Thomas .10 .25
254 Eli Manning FOIL .30 .75
255 Osi Umenyiora FOIL .20 .50

256 Steve Smith USC FOIL .25 .60
257 Philadelphia Eagles FOIL .20 .50
258 Michael Vick .15 .40
259 DeSean Jackson .12 .30
260 Brent Celek .12 .30
261 Asante Samuel .10 .25
262 Nate Allen .10 .25
263 Jeremy Maclin .12 .30
264 Kevin Kolb .12 .30
265 LeSean McCoy .12 .30
266 Quintin Mikell .10 .25
267 Trent Cole .10 .25
268 Michael Vick FOIL .30 .75
269 DeSean Jackson FOIL .25 .60
270 LeSean McCoy FOIL .25 .60
271 Washington Redskins FOIL .20 .50
272 Chris Cooley .12 .30
273 London Fletcher .10 .25
274 Brian Orakpo .12 .30
275 DeAngelo Hall .10 .25
276 Keiland Williams .10 .25
277 Donovan McNabb .15 .40
278 LaRon Landry .10 .25
279 Ryan Torain .10 .25
280 Santana Moss .12 .30
281 Anthony Armstrong .12 .30
282 Chris Cooley FOIL .25 .60
283 London Fletcher FOIL .20 .50
284 DeAngelo Hall FOIL .20 .50
285 Chicago Bears FOIL .20 .50
286 Brian Urlacher .15 .40
287 Devin Hester .15 .40
288 Jay Cutler .12 .30
289 Julius Peppers .12 .30
290 Matt Forte .12 .30
291 Danieal Manning .10 .25
292 Earl Bennett .10 .25
293 Greg Olsen .10 .25
294 Johnny Knox .12 .30
295 Lance Briggs .12 .30
296 Brian Urlacher FOIL .30 .75
297 Devin Hester FOIL .30 .75
298 Jay Cutler FOIL .25 .60
299 Detroit Lions FOIL .20 .50
300 Ndamukong Suh .15 .40
301 Calvin Johnson .15 .40
302 Brandon Pettigrew .10 .25
303 Shaun Hill .10 .25
304 Jahvid Best .12 .30
305 Kyle Vanden Bosch .10 .25
306 Louis Delmas .10 .25
307 Nick Fairley .20 .50
308 Matthew Stafford .15 .40
309 Nate Burleson .10 .25
310 Ndamukong Suh FOIL .30 .75
311 Calvin Johnson FOIL .30 .75
312 Matthew Stafford FOIL .30 .75
313 Green Bay Packers FOIL .30 .75
314 Aaron Rodgers .25 .60
315 Clay Matthews .15 .40
316 Charles Woodson .15 .40
317 Donald Driver .12 .30
318 Greg Jennings .12 .30
319 Jermichael Finley .12 .30
320 Nick Collins .10 .25
321 A.J. Hawk .12 .30
322 Ryan Grant .12 .30
323 Tramon Williams .15 .40
324 Aaron Rodgers FOIL .50 1.25
325 Clay Matthews FOIL .30 .75
326 Charles Woodson FOIL .30 .75
327 Minnesota Vikings FOIL .20 .50
328 Adrian Peterson .20 .50
329 Jared Allen .12 .30
330 Sidney Rice .12 .30
331 Antoine Winfield .10 .25
332 Christian Ponder .30 .75
333 E.J. Henderson .10 .25
334 Percy Harvin .12 .30
335 Toby Gerhart .12 .30
336 Joe Webb .10 .25
337 Visanthe Shiancoe .12 .30
338 Adrian Peterson FOIL .40 1.00
339 Jared Allen FOIL .25 .60
340 Sidney Rice FOIL .25 .60
341 Atlanta Falcons FOIL .20 .50
342 Matt Ryan .15 .40
343 Michael Turner .12 .30
344 Roddy White .12 .30
345 Julio Jones .30 .75
346 Curtis Lofton .10 .25
347 Jason Snelling .12 .30
348 Eric Weems .15 .40
349 John Abraham .10 .25
350 Brent Grimes .15 .40
351 Tony Gonzalez .12 .30
352 Matt Ryan FOIL .30 .75
353 Michael Turner FOIL .25 .60
354 Roddy White FOIL .25 .60
355 Carolina Panthers FOIL .20 .50
356 Steve Smith .12 .30
357 DeAngelo Williams .12 .30
358 Charles Johnson .10 .25
359 Chris Gamble .10 .25
360 Cam Newton .75 2.00
361 Jimmy Clausen .10 .25
362 Jon Beason .10 .25
363 Jonathan Stewart .12 .30
364 James Anderson .10 .25
365 Mike Goodson .10 .25
366 Steve Smith FOIL .25 .60
367 DeAngelo Williams FOIL .25 .60
368 Jon Beason FOIL .20 .50
369 New Orleans Saints FOIL .20 .50
370 Drew Brees .15 .40
371 Jonathan Vilma .10 .25
372 Chris Ivory .12 .30
373 Robert Meachem .12 .30
374 Mark Ingram .30 .75
375 Marques Colston .12 .30
376 Pierre Thomas .12 .30
377 Reggie Bush .12 .30
378 Roman Harper .10 .25
379 Tracy Porter .10 .25
380 Drew Brees FOIL .30 .75
381 Jonathan Vilma FOIL .20 .50
382 Marques Colston FOIL .25 .60
383 Tampa Bay Buccaneers FOIL .20 .50
384 Josh Freeman .15 .40
385 Ronde Barber .10 .25
386 Aqib Talib .10 .25
387 Barrett Ruud .10 .25
388 Cadillac Williams .10 .25
389 Mike Williams .12 .30
390 Stylez White .10 .25
391 Gerald McCoy .10 .25
392 Kellen Winslow Jr. .12 .30
393 LeGarrette Blount .12 .30
394 Josh Freeman FOIL .30 .75
395 Ronde Barber FOIL .20 .50
396 Mike Williams FOIL .25 .60
397 Arizona Cardinals FOIL .20 .50
398 Adrian Wilson .10 .25
399 Larry Fitzgerald .12 .30
400 Paris Lenon .10 .25
401 Beanie Wells .12 .30
402 Darnell Dockett .10 .25
403 Dominique Rodgers-Cromartie .10 .25
404 Steve Breaston .10 .25
405 Tim Hightower .10 .25
406 John Skelton .10 .25
407 Patrick Peterson .25 .60
408 Adrian Wilson FOIL .20 .50
409 Larry Fitzgerald FOIL .25 .60
410 Dominique Rodgers-Cromartie FOIL .20 .50
411 St. Louis Rams FOIL .20 .50
412 Sam Bradford .15 .40
413 Steven Jackson .12 .30
414 Chris Long .10 .25
415 Daniel Fells .12 .30
416 Danny Amendola .12 .30
417 Donnie Avery .10 .25
418 James Laurinaitis .10 .25
419 Kenneth Darby .10 .25
420 Mark Clayton .10 .25
421 James Hall .10 .25
422 Sam Bradford FOIL .30 .75
423 Steven Jackson FOIL .25 .60
424 Danny Amendola FOIL .25 .60
425 San Francisco 49ers FOIL .20 .50
426 Patrick Willis .12 .30
427 Frank Gore .12 .30
428 Alex Smith QB .12 .30
429 Justin Smith .10 .25
430 Troy Smith .10 .25
431 Josh Morgan .12 .30
432 Colin Kaepernick .20 .50
433 Michael Crabtree .12 .30
434 Takeo Spikes .10 .25
435 Vernon Davis .12 .30
436 Patrick Willis FOIL .25 .60
437 Frank Gore FOIL .25 .60
438 Vernon Davis FOIL .25 .60
439 Seattle Seahawks FOIL .20 .50
440 Matt Hasselbeck .12 .30
441 Aaron Curry .10 .25
442 Chris Clemons .10 .25
443 Leon Washington .10 .25
444 Mike Williams USC .12 .30
445 John Carlson .10 .25
446 Earl Thomas .10 .25
447 Marshawn Lynch .12 .30
448 Justin Forsett .12 .30
449 Lofa Tatupu .10 .25
450 Matt Hasselbeck FOIL .25 .60
451 Aaron Curry FOIL .20 .50
452 Mike Williams USC FOIL .25 .60
453 Cam Newton FOIL 1.25 3.00
454 Von Miller FOIL .30 .75
455 Marcell Dareus FOIL .25 .60
456 A.J. Green FOIL .50 1.25
457 Patrick Peterson FOIL .40 1.00
458 Julio Jones FOIL .50 1.25
459 Jake Locker FOIL .60 1.50
460 Blaine Gabbert FOIL .40 1.00
461 Christian Ponder FOIL .50 1.25
462 Jonathan Baldwin FOIL .25 .60
463 Mark Ingram FOIL .50 1.25
464 Andy Dalton FOIL .60 1.50
465 Ben Roethlisberger AFC Champs .15 .40
466 Aaron Rodgers NFC Champs .25 .60
467 DeAngelo Hall PB .10 .25
468 AFC Divisional Playoff .10 .25
469 AFC Divisional Playoff .10 .25
470 Aaron Rodgers Div. Playoff .25 .60
471 NFC Divisional Playoff .10 .25
472 Super Bowl XLV .10 .25
473 Aaron Rodgers SB MVP .25 .60
474 Jordy Nelson SB .12 .30
475 Super Bowl XLV .15 .40
476 Super Bowl I .10 .25
Elijah Pitts
477 Super Bowl II .10 .25
478 Reggie White SB .15 .40
479 Super Bowl XLV .10 .25
480 Pop Warner Football .10 .25
481 Pop Warner Football .10 .25
482 Pop Warner Football .10 .25
483 Pop Warner Football .10 .25
484 Tim Tebow PW .30 .75
485 Pop Warner Football .10 .25
486 Adrenalyn Bowl Logo .10 .25
487 Marshall Faulk HOF .12 .30
488 Deion Sanders HOF .15 .40
489 Shannon Sharpe HOF .12 .30
490 Chris Hanburger HOF UER .10 .25
491 Les Richter HOF .10 .25
492 Richard Dent HOF .10 .25
493 Ed Sabol HOF .10 .25
494 Hall of Fame Logo .10 .25

1989 Panini Super Bowl Stickers

COMPLETE SET (23) 4.00 10.00
A Super Bowl I .20 .50
B Super Bowl II .20 .50
C Super Bowl III .20 .50
D Super Bowl IV .20 .50
E Super Bowl V .20 .50
F Super Bowl VI .20 .50
G Super Bowl VII .20 .50
H Super Bowl VIII .20 .50
I Super Bowl IX .20 .50
J Super Bowl X .20 .50
K Super Bowl XI .20 .50
L Super Bowl XII .20 .50
M Super Bowl XIII .20 .50
N Super Bowl XIV .20 .50
O Super Bowl XV .20 .50
P Super Bowl XVI .20 .50
Q Super Bowl XVII .20 .50
R Super Bowl XVIII .20 .60
S Super Bowl XIX .20 .50
T Super Bowl XX .20 .50
U Super Bowl XXI .20 .50
V Super Bowl XXII .20 .50
W Super Bowl XXIII .20 .50

2011 Panini Super Bowl XLV Promos

These three cards were released at the 2011 Super Bowl Card Show in Dallas as part of a wrapper redemption program at the Panini booth. The basic design was modeled after the 2010 Classics set.

COMPLETE SET (3) 5.00 12.00
SBRK1 Dez Bryant 2.50 6.00
SBMVP1 Troy Aikman 2.00 5.00
SBMVP2 Randy White 1.25 3.00

2010 Panini Threads

COMP.SET w/o RC's (150) 8.00 20.00
151-200 ROOKIE AUTO PRINT RUN 220-500
1 Chris Wells .25 .60
2 Larry Fitzgerald .30 .75
3 Matt Leinart .25 .60
4 Steve Breaston .20 .50
5 Matt Ryan .30 .75
6 Michael Turner .20 .50
7 Roddy White .25 .60
8 Tony Gonzalez .25 .60
9 Anquan Boldin .25 .60
10 Derrick Mason .25 .60
11 Joe Flacco .30 .75
12 Ray Rice .25 .60
13 Willis McGahee .25 .60
14 Fred Jackson .30 .75
15 Lee Evans .25 .60
16 Marshawn Lynch .25 .60
17 Ryan Fitzpatrick .30 .75
18 DeAngelo Williams .25 .60
19 Jonathan Stewart .25 .60
20 Matt Moore .25 .60
21 Steve Smith .25 .60
22 Brian Urlacher .30 .75
23 Devin Hester .30 .75
24 Greg Olsen .20 .50
25 Jay Cutler .30 .75
26 Matt Forte .25 .60
27 Andre Caldwell .20 .50
28 Antonio Bryant .20 .50
29 Carson Palmer .25 .60
30 Cedric Benson .25 .60
31 Chad Ochocinco .25 .60
32 Ben Watson .20 .50
33 Jake Delhomme .25 .60
34 Jerome Harrison .20 .50
35 Josh Cribbs .30 .75
36 Mohamed Massaquoi .25 .60
37 Felix Jones .25 .60
38 Jason Witten .30 .75
39 Marion Barber .25 .60
40 Miles Austin .30 .75
41 Tony Romo .40 1.00
42 Eddie Royal .20 .50
43 Jahar Gaffney .20 .50
44 Knowshon Moreno .25 .60
45 Kyle Orton .25 .60
46 Brandon Pettigrew .20 .50
47 Calvin Johnson .30 .75
48 Matthew Stafford .30 .75
49 Nate Burleson .20 .50
50 Aaron Rodgers .60 1.50
51 Donald Driver .25 .60
52 Greg Jennings .25 .60
53 Jermichael Finley .25 .60
54 Ryan Grant .25 .60
55 Andre Johnson .25 .60
56 Kevin Walter .25 .60
57 Matt Schaub .25 .60
58 Owen Daniels .20 .50
59 Steve Slaton .20 .50
60 Dallas Clark .25 .60
61 Joseph Addai .25 .60
62 Peyton Manning .50 1.25
63 Pierre Garcon .25 .60
64 Reggie Wayne .25 .60
65 David Garrard .25 .60
66 Maurice Jones-Drew .25 .60
67 Mike Sims-Walker .25 .60
68 Mike Thomas .25 .60
69 Chris Chambers .25 .60
70 Dwayne Bowe .25 .60
71 Jamaal Charles .25 .60
72 Matt Cassel .25 .60
73 Thomas Jones .25 .60
74 Brandon Marshall .25 .60
75 Brian Hartline .25 .60
76 Chad Henne .25 .60
77 Davone Bess .20 .50
78 Greg Camarillo .20 .50
79 Ronnie Brown .25 .60
80 Adrian Peterson .50 1.25
81 Brett Favre 1.25 3.00
82 Percy Harvin .30 .75
83 Sidney Rice .25 .60
84 Visanthe Shiancoe .25 .60
85 Laurence Maroney .25 .60
86 Randy Moss .30 .75
87 Tom Brady .50 1.25
88 Torry Holt .25 .60
89 Wes Welker .30 .75
90 Devery Henderson .20 .50
91 Drew Brees .30 .75
92 Jeremy Shockey .25 .60
93 Marques Colston .25 .60
94 Pierre Thomas .25 .60
95 Brandon Jacobs .25 .60
96 Eli Manning .30 .75
97 Hakeem Nicks .25 .60
98 Kevin Boss .25 .60
99 Steve Smith USC .25 .60
100 Braylon Edwards .25 .60
101 LaDainian Tomlinson .30 .75
102 Mark Sanchez .30 .75
103 Santonio Holmes .25 .60
104 Shonn Greene .25 .60
105 Chaz Schilens .20 .50
106 Darren McFadden .25 .60
107 Jason Campbell .25 .60
108 Louis Murphy .25 .60
109 Zach Miller .25 .60
110 Brent Celek .25 .60
111 DeSean Jackson .25 .60
112 Jeremy Maclin .25 .60
113 Kevin Kolb .25 .60
114 LeSean McCoy .25 .60
115 Ben Roethlisberger .30 .75
116 Heath Miller .25 .60
117 Hines Ward .25 .60
118 Rashard Mendenhall .25 .60
119 Troy Polamalu .30 .75
120 Antonio Gates .25 .60
121 Darren Sproles .25 .60
122 Philip Rivers .30 .75
123 Vincent Jackson .20 .50
124 Alex Smith QB .25 .60
125 Frank Gore .25 .60
126 Patrick Willis .25 .60
127 Michael Crabtree .30 .75
128 Vernon Davis .25 .60
129 Deion Branch .20 .50
130 John Carlson .20 .50
131 Julius Jones .20 .50
132 Matt Hasselbeck .20 .50
133 T.J. Houshmandzadeh .25 .60
134 Danny Amendola .30 .75
135 Donnie Avery .25 .60
136 James Laurinaitis .25 .60
137 Steven Jackson .25 .60
138 Cadillac Williams .25 .60
139 Josh Freeman .30 .75
140 Kellen Winslow Jr. .25 .60
141 Sammie Stroughter .20 .50
142 Bo Scaife .20 .50
143 Chris Johnson .30 .75
144 Kenny Britt .25 .60
145 Vince Young .20 .50
146 Chris Cooley .25 .60
147 Clinton Portis .25 .60
148 Donovan McNabb .30 .75
149 Larry Johnson .25 .60
150 Santana Moss .25 .60
151 Aaron Hernandez AU/441 RC 20.00 40.00
152 Andre Roberts AU/385 RC 8.00 20.00
153 Anthony McCoy AU/325 RC 6.00 15.00
154 Armanti Edwards AU/455 RC 8.00 20.00
155 Arrelious Benn AU/280 RC 8.00 20.00
156 Ben Tate AU/280 RC 10.00 25.00
157 Brandon LaFell AU/360 RC 8.00 20.00
158 Brandon Spikes AU/360 RC 8.00 20.00
159 C.J. Spiller AU/280 RC 25.00 60.00
160 Carlos Dunlap AU/360 RC 8.00 20.00
161 Carlton Mitchell AU/440 RC 6.00 15.00
162 Colt McCoy AU/250 RC 25.00 60.00
163 Damian Williams AU/440 RC 8.00 20.00
164 Dan LeFevour AU/440 RC 8.00 20.00
165 Demaryius Thomas AU/360 RC 10.00 25.00
166 Derrick Morgan AU/360 RC 6.00 15.00
167 Dexter McCluster AU/450 RC 8.00 20.00
168 Dez Bryant AU/270 RC 30.00 80.00
169 Dezmon Briscoe AU/385 RC 6.00 15.00
170 Earl Thomas AU/360 RC 8.00 20.00
171 Emmanuel Sanders AU/350 RC 8.00 20.00
172 Eric Berry AU/325 RC 20.00 50.00
173 Eric Decker AU/330 RC 10.00 25.00
174 Gerald McCoy AU/325 RC 8.00 20.00
175 Golden Tate AU/240 RC 8.00 20.00
176 Jacoby Ford AU/280 RC 20.00 40.00
177 Jahvid Best AU/220 RC 25.00 60.00
178 Jermaine Gresham AU/385 RC 10.00 25.00
179 Jimmy Clausen AU/280 RC 8.00 20.00
180 Joe Haden AU/325 RC 8.00 20.00
181 Joe McKnight AU/385 RC 8.00 20.00
182 John Skelton AU/280 RC 8.00 20.00
183 Jonathan Crompton AU/440 RC 6.00 15.00
184 Jonathan Dwyer AU/225 RC 8.00 20.00
185 Jordan Shipley AU/385 RC 10.00 25.00
186 Marcus Easley AU/330 RC 6.00 15.00
187 Mardy Gilyard AU/385 RC 8.00 20.00
188 Mike Kafka AU/375 RC 8.00 20.00
189 Mike Williams AU/440 RC 15.00 40.00
190 Montario Hardesty AU/440 RC 8.00 20.00
191 Ndamukong Suh AU/255 RC 40.00 80.00
192 Ricky Sapp AU/280 RC 6.00 15.00
193 Rob Gronkowski AU/500 RC 25.00 50.00
194 Rolando McClain AU/385 RC 8.00 20.00
195 Ryan Mathews AU/280 RC 40.00 80.00
196 Sam Bradford AU/280 RC 50.00 120.00
197 Taylor Mays AU/280 RC 8.00 20.00
198 Taylor Price AU/325 RC 8.00 20.00
199 Tim Tebow AU/250 RC 90.00 150.00
200 Toby Gerhart AU/385 RC 8.00 20.00
201 A.J. Edds RC 1.50 4.00
202 Alterraun Verner RC 1.50 4.00
203 Amari Spievey RC 1.50 4.00
204 Andre Anderson RC 1.25 3.00
205 Anthony Davis RC 1.25 3.00
206 Anthony Dixon RC 1.50 4.00
207 Antonio Brown RC 2.50 6.00
208 Blair White RC 1.50 4.00
209 Brandon Ghee RC 1.25 3.00
210 Brandon Graham RC 1.25 3.00
211 Brian Price RC 1.50 4.00
212 Bryan Bulaga RC 1.50 4.00
213 Chad Jones RC 1.50 4.00
214 Charles Scott RC 1.25 3.00
215 Chris Cook RC 1.50 4.00
216 Chris McGaha RC 1.00 2.50
217 Corey Wootton RC 1.25 3.00
218 Dan Williams RC 1.25 3.00
219 Darrell Stuckey RC 1.00 2.50
220 Darryl Sharpton RC 1.00 2.50
221 Daryl Washington RC 1.25 3.00
222 David Gettis RC 1.50 4.00
223 David Reed RC 1.25 3.00
224 Deji Karim RC 1.50 4.00
225 Dennis Pitta RC 1.50 4.00
226 Devin McCourty RC 1.50 4.00
227 Dominique Franks RC 1.00 2.50
228 Donald Butler RC 1.00 2.50
229 Ed Dickson RC 1.50 4.00
230 Ed Wang RC 1.50 4.00
231 Everson Griffen RC 1.50 4.00
232 Freddie Barnes RC 1.25 3.00
233 Garrett Graham RC 1.25 3.00
234 James Starks RC 2.50 6.00
235 Jared Odrick RC 1.50 4.00
236 Jarrett Brown RC 1.50 4.00
237 Jason Pierre-Paul RC 2.50 6.00
238 Jason Worilds RC 1.50 4.00
239 Javier Arenas RC 1.50 4.00
240 Jeremy Williams RC 1.00 2.50
241 Jermaine Cunningham RC 1.50 4.00
242 Jerome Murphy RC 1.25 3.00
243 Jerry Hughes RC 1.50 4.00
244 Jevan Snead RC 1.50 4.00
245 Jimmy Graham RC 3.00 8.00
246 Joe Webb RC 1.50 4.00
247 John Conner RC 1.50 4.00
248 Joique Bell RC 1.25 3.00
249 Kareem Jackson RC 1.50 4.00
250 Kerry Meier RC 1.25 3.00
251 Kevin Thomas RC 1.25 3.00
252 Koa Misi RC 1.50 4.00
253 Kyle Williams RC 1.50 4.00
254 Kyle Wilson RC 1.50 4.00
255 Lamarr Houston RC 1.50 4.00
256 LeGarrette Blount RC 2.50 6.00
257 Levi Brown RC 1.25 3.00
258 Linval Joseph RC 1.25 3.00
259 Lonyae Miller RC 1.25 3.00
260 Major Wright RC 1.50 4.00
261 Marc Mariani RC 1.50 4.00
262 Maurkice Pouncey RC 1.50 4.00
263 Mike Iupati RC 1.50 4.00
264 Mike Neal RC 1.50 4.00
265 Morgan Burnett RC 1.50 4.00
266 Myron Lewis RC 1.25 3.00
267 Nate Allen RC 1.50 4.00
268 NaVorro Bowman RC 1.50 4.00
269 Pat Angerer RC 1.50 4.00
270 Pat Paschall RC 1.25 3.00
271 Patrick Robinson RC 1.50 4.00
272 Perrish Cox RC 1.25 3.00
273 Perry Riley RC 1.50 4.00
274 Phillip Dillard RC 1.00 2.50
275 Rennie Curran RC 1.25 3.00
276 Riley Cooper RC 1.50 4.00
277 Rodger Saffold RC 1.00 2.50
278 Russell Okung RC 1.50 4.00
279 Rusty Smith RC 1.50 4.00
280 Sean Canfield RC 1.25 3.00
281 Sean Lee RC 1.50 4.00
282 Sean Weatherspoon RC 1.50 4.00
283 Sergio Kindle RC 1.50 4.00
284 Seyi Ajirotutu RC 1.50 4.00
285 Shay Hodge RC 1.25 3.00
286 T.J. Ward RC 1.50 4.00
287 Terrence Austin RC 1.25 3.00
288 Terrence Cody RC 1.25 3.00
289 Thaddeus Gibson RC 1.25 3.00
290 Timothy Toone RC 1.25 3.00
291 Tony Moeaki RC 1.50 4.00
292 Tony Pike RC 1.50 4.00
293 Torell Troup RC 1.25 3.00
294 Trent Williams RC 1.50 4.00
295 Trevard Lindley RC 1.00 2.50
296 Trindon Holliday RC 1.50 4.00
297 Tyson Alualu RC 1.25 3.00
298 Walter Thurmond RC 1.00 2.50
299 Zac Robinson RC 1.25 3.00
300 Zane Beadles RC 1.25 3.00

2010 Panini Threads Gold Holofoil

*VETS: 3X TO 8X BASIC CARDS
*ROOKIES: .8X TO 2X BASIC CARDS
STATED PRINT RUN 100 SER.#'d SETS

2010 Panini Threads Platinum Holofoil

*VETS: 5X TO 12X BASIC CARDS
*ROOKIES: 1.2X TO 3X BASIC CARDS
STATED PRINT RUN 25 SER.#'d SETS

2010 Panini Threads Silver Holofoil

*VETS 1-150: 2X TO 5X BASIC CARDS
*ROOKIES 201-300: .5X TO 1.2X BASIC CARDS
STATED PRINT RUN 250 SER.#'d SETS

2010 Panini Threads 2009 All Rookie Team

COMPLETE SET (5) 6.00 15.00
1 Mark Sanchez 1.50 4.00
2 Knowshon Moreno 1.25 3.00
3 Percy Harvin 1.50 4.00
4 Chris Wells 1.25 3.00
5 Brian Cushing 1.00 2.50

2010 Panini Threads 2009 All Rookie Team Threads

STATED PRINT RUN 299 SER.#'d SETS
*PRIME/50: .6X TO 1.5X BASIC JSY/299
1 Mark Sanchez 3.00 8.00
2 Knowshon Moreno 2.50 6.00
3 Percy Harvin 3.00 8.00
4 Chris Wells 2.50 6.00

2010 Panini Threads Autographs Silver

5-148 VETERAN PRINT RUN 1-100
204-299 ROOKIE PRINT RUN 399-499
EXCH EXPIRATION: 3/8/2012
30 Cedric Benson/15
31 Chad Ochocinco/15
62 Peyton Manning/18 75.00 150.00
66 Maurice Jones-Drew/15 10.00 25.00
95 Brandon Jacobs/15 10.00 25.00
103 Santonio Holmes/25 10.00 25.00
108 Louis Murphy/100 6.00 15.00
113 Kevin Kolb/25 10.00 25.00
119 Troy Polamalu/25 100.00 175.00
120 Antonio Gates/15 12.00 30.00
127 Michael Crabtree/35 12.00 30.00
144 Kenny Britt/25 10.00 25.00
204 Andre Anderson/499 4.00 10.00
206 Anthony Dixon/399 5.00 12.00
207 Antonio Brown/499 15.00 30.00
208 Blair White/499 5.00 12.00
210 Brandon Graham/499 4.00 10.00
212 Bryan Bulaga/499 5.00 12.00
213 Chad Jones/499 5.00 12.00
214 Charles Scott/499 4.00 10.00
216 Chris McGaha/499 3.00 8.00
217 Corey Wootton/499 4.00 10.00
222 David Gettis/499 5.00 12.00
226 Devin McCourty/499 6.00 15.00
229 Ed Dickson/499 5.00 12.00
231 Everson Griffen/499 5.00 12.00
232 Freddie Barnes/499 4.00 10.00
233 Garrett Graham/499 4.00 10.00
234 James Starks/499 12.00 30.00
236 Jarrett Brown/499 5.00 12.00
237 Jason Pierre-Paul/499 12.50 25.00
238 Jason Worilds/499 5.00 12.00
240 Jeremy Williams/499 3.00 8.00
243 Jerry Hughes/499 5.00 12.00
244 Jevan Snead/499 5.00 12.00
245 Jimmy Graham/499 12.50 25.00
248 Joique Bell/499 4.00 10.00
249 Kareem Jackson/399 5.00 12.00
256 LeGarrette Blount/499 10.00 25.00
259 Lonyae Miller/499 4.00 10.00
265 Morgan Burnett/499 5.00 12.00
271 Patrick Robinson/499 5.00 12.00
272 Perrish Cox/499 4.00 10.00
276 Riley Cooper/499 5.00 12.00
280 Sean Canfield/499 4.00 10.00
281 Sean Lee/499 5.00 12.00
282 Sean Weatherspoon/499 5.00 12.00
284 Seyi Ajirotutu/499 5.00 12.00
285 Shay Hodge/499 4.00 10.00
292 Tony Pike/499 5.00 12.00
299 Zac Robinson/399 4.00 10.00

2010 Panini Threads Century Legends

COMPLETE SET (14) 12.00 30.00
*HOLOFOIL/100: .6X TO 1.5X BASIC INSERTS
1 John Taylor 1.00 2.50
2 Art Monk 1.50 4.00
3 Len Dawson 1.50 4.00
4 Steve Young 2.00 5.00
5 Lenny Moore 1.25 3.00
6 Randall Cunningham 1.25 3.00
7 Frank Gifford 1.25 3.00
8 Joe Namath 2.00 5.00
10 Daryle Lamonica 1.00 2.50
11 Rod Woodson 1.50 4.00
12 Bo Jackson 2.00 5.00
13 Roger Craig 1.25 3.00
14 Terry Bradshaw 2.00 5.00
15 Dan Fouts 1.50 4.00

2010 Panini Threads Century Legends Materials

STATED PRINT RUN 50-175
*PRIME/15-25: .8X TO 2X BASIC JSY/160-175
*PRIME/15-25: .6X TO 1.5X BASIC JSY/100
*PRIME/15-25: .5X TO 1.2X BASIC JSY/50
1 John Taylor/175 3.00 8.00
2 Art Monk/160 6.00 15.00
3 Len Dawson/100 6.00 15.00
4 Steve Young/175 6.00 15.00
5 Lenny Moore/175 4.00 10.00
6 Randall Cunningham/175 4.00 10.00
7 Frank Gifford/100 5.00 12.00
8 Joe Namath/50 10.00 25.00
10 Daryle Lamonica/165 3.00 8.00
11 Rod Woodson/100 6.00 15.00
12 Bo Jackson/100 8.00 20.00
13 Roger Craig/50 6.00 15.00
14 Terry Bradshaw/175 6.00 15.00
15 Dan Fouts/175 5.00 12.00

2010 Panini Threads Century Stars

COMPLETE SET (25) 10.00 25.00
*HOLOFOIL/100: .6X TO 1.5X BASIC INSERTS
1 Antonio Gates 1.00 2.50
2 Carson Palmer 1.00 2.50
3 Brandon Jacobs 1.00 2.50
4 Philip Rivers 1.25 3.00
5 Clinton Portis 1.00 2.50
6 Donald Driver 1.00 2.50
7 Drew Brees 1.25 3.00
8 Eli Manning 1.25 3.00
9 Frank Gore 1.00 2.50
10 Darrelle Revis 1.00 2.50
11 Maurice Jones-Drew 1.00 2.50
12 Wes Welker 1.25 3.00
13 Ed Reed 1.00 2.50
14 Matt Hasselbeck .75 2.00
15 Dallas Clark 1.00 2.50
16 Chris Johnson 1.25 3.00
17 Troy Polamalu 1.25 3.00
18 Michael Turner .75 2.00
19 Jason Witten 1.25 3.00
20 Steven Jackson 1.00 2.50
21 Brian Urlacher 1.25 3.00
22 Reggie Wayne 1.00 2.50
23 Chad Ochocinco 1.00 2.50
24 Vernon Davis 1.00 2.50
25 Steve Smith 1.00 2.50

2010 Panini Threads Century Stars Materials Prime

STATED PRINT RUN 3-50
1 Antonio Gates/50 4.00 10.00
3 Brandon Jacobs/50 4.00 10.00
4 Philip Rivers/25 6.00 15.00
5 Clinton Portis/50 4.00 10.00
6 Donald Driver/50 4.00 10.00
8 Eli Manning/50 5.00 12.00
9 Frank Gore/50 4.00 10.00
10 Darrelle Revis/50 4.00 10.00
11 Maurice Jones-Drew/50 4.00 10.00
12 Wes Welker/50 5.00 12.00
14 Matt Hasselbeck/50 3.00 8.00
15 Dallas Clark/50 4.00 10.00
16 Chris Johnson/50 5.00 12.00
17 Troy Polamalu/50 5.00 12.00
18 Michael Turner/50 3.00 8.00
19 Jason Witten/50 5.00 12.00
20 Steven Jackson/50 4.00 10.00
21 Brian Urlacher/50 5.00 12.00
22 Reggie Wayne/50 4.00 10.00
23 Chad Ochocinco/50 4.00 10.00
24 Vernon Davis/50 4.00 10.00
25 Steve Smith/50 4.00 10.00

2010 Panini Threads Franchise Fabrics

STATED PRINT RUN 80-299
*PRIME/50: .6X TO 1.5X BASIC JSY/150-299
*PRIME/50: .5X TO 1.2X BASIC JSY/80-125
*PRIME/15-25: .8X TO 2X BASIC JSY/150-299
*PRIME/15-25: .6X TO 1.5X BASIC JSY/80-125
2 Calvin Johnson/299 3.00 8.00
3 Larry Fitzgerald/80 4.00 10.00
5 Vince Young/299 2.00 5.00
6 Chris Cooley/299 2.50 6.00
7 LeSean McCoy/190 2.50 6.00
8 Andre Johnson/299 2.50 6.00
9 Mark Sanchez/150 3.00 8.00
10 Darren Sproles/150 2.50 6.00
11 Matt Ryan/299 3.00 8.00
12 Ray Lewis/299 4.00 10.00
13 Matt Forte/299 2.50 6.00
14 Adrian Peterson/150 5.00 12.00
15 Joe Flacco/299 3.00 8.00
16 Sidney Rice/299 3.00 8.00
17 Peyton Manning/125 6.00 15.00
18 Tony Romo/100 5.00 12.00
19 DeAngelo Williams/299 2.50 6.00
20 Tom Brady/299 5.00 12.00

2010 Panini Threads Franchise Fabrics Autographs

EXCH EXPIRATION: 3/8/2012

2010 Panini Threads Game Day Jerseys

STATED PRINT RUN 115-299
*PRIME/50: .6X TO 1.5X BASIC JSY/150-299
*PRIME/50: .5X TO 1.2X BASIC JSY/115-140
2 Chris Wells/150 2.50 6.00
3 Braylon Edwards/299 2.50 6.00
5 Cadillac Williams/299 2.50 6.00
6 Devery Henderson/299 2.00 5.00
7 Dwayne Bowe/299 2.50 6.00
8 Knowshon Moreno/115 3.00 8.00
9 Ladell Betts/299 2.00 5.00
10 Louis Murphy/150 2.50 6.00
11 Reggie Bush/299 3.00 8.00
12 Tony Romo/299 4.00 10.00
14 Kevin Boss/299 3.00 8.00
15 Josh Cribbs/140 5.00 12.00
16 Ronnie Brown/299 2.50 6.00
17 Tony Gonzalez/175 2.50 6.00
19 Matthew Stafford/200 3.00 8.00
20 Dustin Keller/299 2.50 6.00
21 Darren McFadden/299 2.50 6.00
22 Bernard Berrian/299 2.00 5.00
23 Percy Harvin/299 3.00 8.00
24 Greg Olsen/299 2.00 5.00
25 Greg Jennings/250 2.50 6.00

2010 Panini Threads Game Day Jerseys Autographs

AUTO STATED PRINT RUN 1-15
3 Braylon Edwards/15 12.00 30.00
7 Dwayne Bowe/15 12.00 30.00
10 Louis Murphy/15 12.00 30.00
22 Bernard Berrian/15 10.00 25.00

2010 Panini Threads Generations

COMPLETE SET (15) 12.00 30.00
*HOLOFOIL/100: .6X TO 1.5X BASIC INSERTS
1 Brent Jones 1.00 2.50
Vernon Davis
2 Jim McMahon 1.25 3.00
Jay Cutler
3 Priest Holmes 1.00 2.50
Ray Rice
4 Cris Carter 1.25 3.00
Sidney Rice
5 Junior Seau 1.00 2.50
Shawne Merriman
6 Fran Tarkenton 3.00 8.00
Brett Favre
7 Rod Woodson 1.25 3.00
Troy Polamalu
8 Joe Namath 1.50 4.00
Mark Sanchez
9 Terry Bradshaw 1.50 4.00
Ben Roethlisberger
10 Bart Starr 2.50 6.00
Aaron Rodgers
11 Eddie George 1.25 3.00
Chris Johnson
12 Bo Jackson 1.50 4.00
Darren McFadden
13 Dan Fouts 1.25 3.00
Philip Rivers
14 Roger Craig 1.00 2.50
Frank Gore
15 Michael Irvin 1.25 3.00
Miles Austin

2010 Panini Threads Generations Materials

STATED PRINT RUN 50-200
*PRIME/30-50: .6X TO 1.5X BASIC JSY/200
*PRIME/25: .8X TO 2X BASIC JSY/200
*PRIME/25: .6X TO 1.5X BASIC JSY/100
1 Brent Jones 5.00 12.00
Vernon Davis
2 Jim McMahon 8.00 20.00
Jay Cutler
4 Cris Carter 6.00 15.00
Sidney Rice
5 Junior Seau 5.00 12.00
Shawne Merriman
7 Rod Woodson 10.00 25.00
Troy Polamalu
8 Joe Namath 10.00 25.00
Mark Sanchez
9 Terry Bradshaw 8.00 20.00
Ben Roethlisberger
11 Eddie George 6.00 15.00
Chris Johnson
12 Bo Jackson 8.00 20.00
Darren McFadden
13 Dan Fouts 6.00 15.00
Philip Rivers
14 Roger Craig 6.00 15.00
Frank Gore

2010 Panini Threads Gridiron Kings

*FRAMED BLACK/10: 1.5X TO 4X BASIC INS
*FRAMED BLUE/50: .8X TO 2X BASIC INS
*FRAMED GREEN/25: 1X TO 2.5X BASIC INS
*FRAMED RED/100: .6X TO 1.5X BASIC INSERTS
1 Bobby Bell 1.00 2.50
2 Jim McMahon 1.25 3.00
3 Johnny Morris 1.00 2.50
4 Art Monk 1.50 4.00
5 Jimmy Orr 1.00 2.50
6 Larry Little 1.00 2.50
7 Bart Starr 2.50 6.00
8 Paul Krause 1.00 2.50
9 Daryle Lamonica 1.00 2.50
10 Dan Fouts 1.50 4.00
11 Rick Casares 1.00 2.50
12 Priest Holmes 1.00 2.50
13 Fran Tarkenton 1.50 4.00
14 Eddie George 1.25 3.00
15 John Taylor 1.00 2.50
16 Steve Young 2.00 5.00
18 Willie Davis 1.00 2.50
19 Junior Seau 1.25 3.00
20 Mark Duper 1.00 2.50
21 Len Dawson 1.50 4.00
22 Boyd Dowler 1.00 2.50
23 Lenny Moore 1.25 3.00
24 Dante Lavelli 1.00 2.50
25 Frank Gifford 1.25 3.00
26 Lem Barney 1.00 2.50
27 Billy Howton 1.00 2.50
28 Cris Carter 1.50 4.00
29 Lydell Mitchell 1.00 2.50
30 Fred Williamson 1.00 2.50
31 Harlon Hill 1.00 2.50
32 Joe Namath 2.00 5.00
33 Brent Jones 1.00 2.50
34 Gary Collins 1.00 2.50
35 Mike Curtis 1.00 2.50
36 Phil Simms 1.25 3.00
37 Randall Cunningham 1.25 3.00
38 Charley Trippi 1.00 2.50
39 Jan Stenerud 1.00 2.50
40 Roger Craig 1.25 3.00
41 Rod Woodson 1.50 4.00
42 Terry Bradshaw 2.00 5.00
43 Cliff Harris 1.00 2.50
44 Lee Roy Selmon 1.00 2.50
45 Dub Jones 1.00 2.50
46 Hugh McElhenny 1.00 2.50
47 Leroy Kelly 1.25 3.00
48 Michael Irvin 1.25 3.00
49 Pete Retzlaff 1.00 2.50
50 Bo Jackson 2.00 5.00

2010 Panini Threads Gridiron Kings Autographs

STATED PRINT RUN 5-50
1 Bobby Bell/50 12.00 30.00
3 Johnny Morris/25 10.00 25.00
5 Jimmy Orr/50 8.00 20.00
6 Larry Little/50 8.00 20.00
8 Paul Krause/25 10.00 25.00
9 Daryle Lamonica/50 8.00 20.00
11 Rick Casares/50 8.00 20.00
18 Willie Davis/50 20.00 40.00
20 Mark Duper/50 8.00 20.00
21 Len Dawson/50 12.00 30.00
22 Boyd Dowler/50 8.00 20.00
23 Lenny Moore/50 10.00 25.00
24 Dante Lavelli/25 15.00 40.00
26 Lem Barney/50 8.00 20.00
27 Billy Howton/50 10.00 25.00
29 Lydell Mitchell/50 8.00 20.00
30 Fred Williamson/50 8.00 20.00
31 Harlon Hill/50 8.00 20.00
32 Joe Namath/25 60.00 120.00
34 Gary Collins/19 10.00 25.00
35 Mike Curtis/50 8.00 20.00
38 Charley Trippi/50 8.00 20.00
39 Jan Stenerud/50 8.00 20.00
40 Roger Craig/35 10.00 25.00
43 Cliff Harris/50 8.00 20.00
44 Lee Roy Selmon/50 8.00 20.00
45 Dub Jones/50 8.00 20.00
46 Hugh McElhenny/25 10.00 25.00
47 Leroy Kelly/50 12.00 30.00
49 Pete Retzlaff/50 8.00 20.00

2010 Panini Threads Gridiron Kings Materials
STATED PRINT RUN 15-299
2 Jim McMahon/200 4.00 10.00
4 Art Monk/200 6.00 15.00
7 Bart Starr/299 8.00 20.00
10 Dan Fouts/150 6.00 15.00
12 Priest Holmes/50 5.00 12.00
13 Fran Tarkenton/50 8.00 20.00
14 Eddie George/299 4.00 10.00
15 John Taylor/150 3.00 8.00
16 Steve Young/299 6.00 15.00
19 Junior Seau/299 4.00 10.00
23 Lenny Moore/100 5.00 12.00
25 Frank Gifford/50 6.00 15.00
26 Lem Barney/50 5.00 12.00
28 Cris Carter/299 5.00 12.00
32 Joe Namath/15 12.00 30.00
33 Brent Jones/50 5.00 12.00
36 Phil Simms/150 4.00 10.00
37 Randall Cunningham/65 5.00 12.00
42 Terry Bradshaw/150 6.00 15.00
43 Cliff Harris/50 5.00 12.00
44 Lee Roy Selmon/30 6.00 15.00
46 Hugh McElhenny/100 4.00 10.00
48 Michael Irvin/100 5.00 12.00
50 Bo Jackson/150 6.00 15.00

2010 Panini Threads Gridiron Kings Materials Prime
STATED PRINT RUN 1-50
4 Art Monk/50 12.00 30.00
12 Priest Holmes/50 6.00 15.00
14 Eddie George/50 8.00 20.00
15 John Taylor/25 8.00 20.00
16 Steve Young/15 15.00 40.00
19 Junior Seau/50 8.00 20.00
28 Cris Carter/50 10.00 25.00
33 Brent Jones/25 8.00 20.00
41 Rod Woodson/25 12.00 30.00
42 Terry Bradshaw/50 12.00 30.00
48 Michael Irvin/50 8.00 20.00

2010 Panini Threads Gridiron Kings Materials Autographs
STATED PRINT RUN 15-25
EXCH EXPIRATION: 3/8/2012
2 Jim McMahon/25 25.00 50.00
4 Art Monk/25 25.00 50.00
7 Bart Starr/15 100.00 175.00
8 Paul Krause/25 10.00 25.00
9 Daryle Lamonica/25 12.00 30.00
10 Dan Fouts/25 30.00 60.00
12 Priest Holmes/25 10.00 25.00
13 Fran Tarkenton/25 40.00 80.00
14 Eddie George/25 20.00 50.00
15 John Taylor/25 12.00 25.00
16 Steve Young/15 40.00 80.00
19 Junior Seau/25 40.00 80.00
20 Mark Duper/25 10.00 25.00
21 Len Dawson/25 20.00 40.00
23 Lenny Moore/25
25 Frank Gifford/25 20.00 40.00
26 Lem Barney/25 10.00 25.00
32 Joe Namath/25 100.00 175.00
33 Brent Jones/25
36 Phil Simms/25 15.00 40.00
37 Randall Cunningham/25 25.00 50.00
39 Jan Stenerud/25 10.00 25.00
40 Roger Craig/25 12.00 30.00
41 Rod Woodson/25 40.00 80.00
42 Terry Bradshaw/25 60.00 120.00
43 Cliff Harris/25 10.00 25.00
44 Lee Roy Selmon/25 15.00 40.00
46 Hugh McElhenny/25 10.00 25.00
47 Leroy Kelly/20 20.00 40.00
48 Michael Irvin/15 25.00 50.00
50 Bo Jackson/25 40.00 80.00

2010 Panini Threads Jerseys Prime
STATED PRINT RUN 10-50
1 Chris Wells/45 5.00 12.00
2 Larry Fitzgerald/25 8.00 20.00
5 Matt Ryan/50 6.00 15.00
6 Michael Turner/50 4.00 10.00
7 Roddy White/50 5.00 12.00
8 Tony Gonzalez/50 5.00 12.00
11 Joe Flacco/15 8.00 20.00
13 Willis McGahee/50 5.00 12.00
15 Lee Evans/15 6.00 15.00
16 Marshawn Lynch/50 5.00 12.00
18 DeAngelo Williams/50 5.00 12.00
19 Jonathan Stewart/50 5.00 12.00
21 Steve Smith/50 5.00 12.00
22 Brian Urlacher/30 8.00 20.00
23 Devin Hester/50 6.00 15.00
24 Greg Olsen/50 4.00 10.00
25 Jay Cutler/35 6.00 15.00
26 Matt Forte/50 5.00 12.00
30 Cedric Benson/50 5.00 12.00
31 Chad Ochocinco/50 5.00 12.00
35 Josh Cribbs/25 8.00 20.00
37 Felix Jones/50 5.00 12.00
38 Jason Witten/50 6.00 15.00
39 Marion Barber/50 5.00 12.00
41 Tony Romo/10
42 Eddie Royal/50 4.00 10.00
44 Knowshon Moreno/50 5.00 12.00
45 Kyle Orton/40 5.00 12.00
47 Calvin Johnson/50 6.00 15.00
51 Donald Driver/50 5.00 12.00
52 Greg Jennings/50 5.00 12.00
54 Ryan Grant/50 5.00 12.00
55 Andre Johnson/50 5.00 12.00
58 Owen Daniels/50 4.00 10.00
59 Steve Slaton/50 4.00 10.00
60 Dallas Clark/50 5.00 12.00
61 Joseph Addai/50 5.00 12.00
62 Peyton Manning/25 12.00 30.00
64 Reggie Wayne/50 5.00 12.00
65 David Garrard/50 5.00 12.00
66 Maurice Jones-Drew/50 5.00 12.00
70 Dwayne Bowe/50 5.00 12.00
71 Jamaal Charles/50 5.00 12.00
79 Ronnie Brown/50 5.00 12.00
80 Adrian Peterson/50 10.00 25.00
82 Percy Harvin/50 6.00 15.00
83 Sidney Rice/50 5.00 12.00
84 Visanthe Shiancoe/50 5.00 12.00
85 Laurence Maroney/50 5.00 12.00
86 Randy Moss/50 6.00 15.00
87 Tom Brady/50 10.00 25.00
89 Wes Welker/50 6.00 15.00
90 Devery Henderson/50 4.00 10.00
92 Jeremy Shockey/50 5.00 12.00
93 Marques Colston/50 5.00 12.00
95 Brandon Jacobs/50 5.00 12.00
96 Eli Manning/50 6.00 15.00
98 Kevin Boss/50 5.00 12.00
99 Steve Smith USC/50 5.00 12.00
100 Braylon Edwards/50 5.00 12.00
102 Mark Sanchez/25 8.00 20.00
104 Shonn Greene/50 5.00 12.00
106 Darren McFadden/50 5.00 12.00
108 Louis Murphy/50 5.00 12.00
112 Jeremy Maclin/50 5.00 12.00
114 LeSean McCoy/50 5.00 12.00
115 Ben Roethlisberger/10
116 Heath Miller/50 5.00 12.00
117 Hines Ward/50 5.00 12.00
118 Rashard Mendenhall/50 5.00 12.00
119 Troy Polamalu/50 6.00 15.00
120 Antonio Gates/50 5.00 12.00
121 Darren Sproles/50 5.00 12.00
122 Philip Rivers/25 8.00 20.00
123 Vincent Jackson/50 4.00 10.00
124 Alex Smith QB/50 5.00 12.00
125 Frank Gore/50 5.00 12.00
126 Patrick Willis/20 6.00 15.00
127 Michael Crabtree/50 6.00 15.00
128 Vernon Davis/50 5.00 12.00
129 Deion Branch/50 4.00 10.00
132 Matt Hasselbeck/50 4.00 10.00
137 Steven Jackson/50 5.00 12.00
138 Cadillac Williams/50 5.00 12.00
139 Josh Freeman/50 6.00 15.00
143 Chris Johnson/50 6.00 15.00
144 Kenny Britt/50 5.00 12.00
145 Vince Young/50 4.00 10.00
146 Chris Cooley/50 5.00 12.00
147 Clinton Portis/50 5.00 12.00
150 Santana Moss/50 5.00 12.00

2010 Panini Threads Rookie Autographs Combo
STATED PRINT RUN 25 SER.#'d SETS
EXCH EXPIRATION: 3/8/2012
1 Andre Roberts 12.00 30.00
John Skelton
2 Sean Weatherspoon 8.00 20.00
Dominique Franks
3 Sergio Kindle 12.00 30.00
Ed Dickson
4 Patrick Robinson
Jimmy Graham
5 Corey Wootton 10.00 25.00
Dan LeFevour
6 Jermaine Gresham
Carlos Dunlap
7 Joe Haden 15.00 40.00
Montario Hardesty
8 Dez Bryant 60.00 120.00
Sean Lee
9 Bryan Bulaga
Morgan Burnett
10 Kareem Jackson 15.00 40.00
Ben Tate

2010 Panini Threads Rookie Autographs Triple
STATED PRINT RUN 15 SER.#'d SETS
EXCH EXPIRATION: 3/8/2012
1 Jermaine Gresham
Carlos Dunlap
Jordan Shipley
2 Daryl Washington EXCH 15.00 40.00
Andre Roberts
John Skelton
3 Joe Haden 40.00 80.00
Montario Hardesty
Colt McCoy
4 Chris Cook
Toby Gerhart
Everson Griffen
5 Brandon Graham EXCH 12.00 30.00
Nate Allen
Mike Kafka
6 Taylor Mays EXCH
NaVorro Bowman
Anthony Dixon
7 Russell Okung 25.00 60.00
Earl Thomas
Golden Tate
8 Joe Haden
Earl Thomas
Kareem Jackson
9 Trent Williams EXCH
Russell Okung
Bryan Bulaga
10 Brandon Graham 15.00 40.00
Jason Pierre-Paul
Derrick Morgan

2010 Panini Threads Rookie Collection Materials
STATED PRINT RUN 299 SER.#'d SETS
*PRIME/50: .6X TO 1.5X BASIC JSY/299
1 Andre Roberts 3.00 8.00
2 Armanti Edwards 3.00 8.00
3 Arrelious Benn 3.00 8.00
4 Ben Tate 4.00 10.00
5 Brandon LaFell 3.00 8.00
6 C.J. Spiller 6.00 15.00
7 Colt McCoy 6.00 15.00
8 Damian Williams 3.00 8.00
9 Demaryius Thomas 4.00 10.00
10 Dexter McCluster 3.00 8.00
11 Dez Bryant 6.00 15.00
12 Emmanuel Sanders 3.00 8.00
13 Eric Berry 3.00 8.00
14 Eric Decker 4.00 10.00
15 Gerald McCoy 3.00 8.00
16 Golden Tate 3.00 8.00
17 Jahvid Best 6.00 15.00
18 Jermaine Gresham 4.00 10.00
19 Jimmy Clausen 3.00 8.00
20 Joe McKnight 3.00 8.00
21 Jonathan Dwyer 3.00 8.00
22 Jordan Shipley 3.00 8.00
23 Marcus Easley 2.50 6.00
24 Mardy Gilyard 3.00 8.00
25 Mike Kafka 3.00 8.00
26 Mike Williams 5.00 12.00
27 Montario Hardesty 3.00 8.00
28 Ndamukong Suh 6.00 15.00
29 Rob Gronkowski 8.00 20.00
30 Rolando McClain 3.00 8.00
31 Ryan Mathews 6.00 15.00
32 Sam Bradford 10.00 25.00
33 Taylor Price 3.00 8.00
34 Tim Tebow 12.00 30.00
35 Toby Gerhart 3.00 8.00

2010 Panini Threads Rookie Collection Materials Autographs
STATED PRINT RUN 25 SER.#'d SETS
*PRIME/15: .6X TO 1.5X BASIC JSY AU/25
EXCH EXPIRATION: 3/8/2012
1 Andre Roberts 10.00 25.00
2 Armanti Edwards 10.00 25.00
3 Arrelious Benn 10.00 25.00
4 Ben Tate 12.00 30.00
5 Brandon LaFell 10.00 25.00
6 C.J. Spiller 15.00 40.00
7 Colt McCoy 30.00 80.00
8 Damian Williams 10.00 25.00
9 Demaryius Thomas 12.00 30.00
10 Dexter McCluster 10.00 25.00
11 Dez Bryant 50.00 100.00
12 Emmanuel Sanders 10.00 25.00
13 Eric Berry 25.00 60.00
14 Eric Decker 12.00 30.00
15 Gerald McCoy 10.00 25.00
16 Golden Tate 10.00 25.00
17 Jahvid Best 15.00 40.00
18 Jermaine Gresham 12.00 30.00
19 Jimmy Clausen 10.00 25.00
20 Joe McKnight 10.00 25.00
21 Jonathan Dwyer 10.00 25.00
22 Jordan Shipley 10.00 25.00
23 Marcus Easley 8.00 20.00
24 Mardy Gilyard 10.00 25.00
25 Mike Kafka 10.00 25.00
26 Mike Williams 25.00 50.00
27 Montario Hardesty 10.00 25.00
28 Ndamukong Suh 20.00 50.00
29 Rob Gronkowski 30.00 60.00
30 Rolando McClain 10.00 25.00
31 Ryan Mathews 50.00 100.00
32 Sam Bradford 75.00 150.00
33 Taylor Price 10.00 25.00
34 Tim Tebow 125.00 200.00
35 Toby Gerhart 10.00 25.00

2010 Panini Threads Rookie Collection Materials Combo
STATED PRINT RUN 299 SER.#'d SETS
*PRIME/25: .8X TO 2X BASIC COMBO/299
1 C.J. Spiller 6.00 15.00
Marcus Easley
2 Tim Tebow 12.00 30.00
Demaryius Thomas
3 Jermaine Gresham 4.00 10.00
Jordan Shipley
4 Eric Berry 3.00 8.00
Dexter McCluster
5 Jimmy Clausen 3.00 8.00
Brandon LaFell
6 Emmanuel Sanders 4.00 10.00
Jonathan Dwyer
7 Gerald McCoy 4.00 10.00
Arrelious Benn
8 Colt McCoy 6.00 15.00
Montario Hardesty
9 Sam Bradford 8.00 20.00
Mardy Gilyard
10 Ndamukong Suh 6.00 15.00
Jahvid Best
11 Rob Gronkowski 8.00 20.00
Taylor Price
12 Ndamukong Suh 6.00 15.00
Gerald McCoy
13 Demaryius Thomas 8.00 20.00
Dez Bryant
14 C.J. Spiller 8.00 20.00
Ryan Mathews
15 Sam Bradford 12.00 30.00
Tim Tebow

2010 Panini Threads Rookie Collection Materials Quad
STATED PRINT RUN 299 SER.#'d SETS
*PRIME/25: .6X TO 1.5X BASIC QUAD/299
1 Sam Bradford 15.00 40.00
Ndamukong Suh
Gerald McCoy
Eric Berry
2 C.J. Spiller 8.00 20.00
Ryan Mathews
Jahvid Best
Toby Gerhart
3 Demaryius Thomas 12.00 30.00
Dez Bryant
Dexter McCluster
Arrelious Benn
4 Sam Bradford 15.00 40.00
Tim Tebow
Jimmy Clausen
Colt McCoy
5 Ndamukong Suh 8.00 20.00
Gerald McCoy
Eric Berry
Rolando McClain

2010 Panini Threads Triple Threat
COMPLETE SET (10) 10.00 25.00
*HOLOFOIL/100: .6X TO 1.5X BASIC INSERTS
1 Brett Favre 3.00 8.00
Adrian Peterson
Sidney Rice
2 Steve Smith 1.00 2.50
DeAngelo Williams
Jonathan Stewart
3 Drew Brees 1.25 3.00
Reggie Bush
Marques Colston
4 Mark Sanchez 1.25 3.00
Braylon Edwards
Jerricho Cotchery
5 Tony Romo 2.00 5.00
Felix Jones
Miles Austin
6 Vernon Davis 1.25 3.00
Frank Gore
Michael Crabtree
7 Donovan McNabb 1.25 3.00
Santana Moss
Clinton Portis
8 Joe Flacco 1.25 3.00
Ray Rice
Willis McGahee
9 Jay Cutler 1.25 3.00
Matt Forte
Johnny Knox
10 Carson Palmer 1.00 2.50
Chad Ochocinco
Cedric Benson

2010 Panini Threads Triple Threat Materials
STATED PRINT RUN 85-200
3 Drew Brees 6.00 15.00
Reggie Bush
Marques Colston
4 Mark Sanchez 5.00 12.00
Braylon Edwards
Jerricho Cotchery
6 Vernon Davis 5.00 12.00
Frank Gore
Michael Crabtree
7 Donovan McNabb 6.00 15.00
Santana Moss
Clinton Portis
9 Jay Cutler 6.00 15.00
Matt Forte
Johnny Knox
10 Carson Palmer 4.00 10.00
Chad Ochocinco
Cedric Benson

2010 Panini Threads Triple Threat Materials Prime
STATED PRINT RUN 7-25
2 Steve Smith 10.00 25.00
DeAngelo Williams
Jonathan Stewart
3 Drew Brees 12.00 30.00
Reggie Bush
Marques Colston
4 Mark Sanchez 12.00 30.00
Braylon Edwards
Jerricho Cotchery
6 Vernon Davis 12.00 30.00
Frank Gore
Michael Crabtree
9 Jay Cutler 15.00 40.00
Matt Forte
Johnny Knox
10 Carson Palmer
Chad Ochocinco
Cedric Benson

2011 Panini Threads

COMP.SET w/o AU's (250) 40.00 80.00
COMP.SET w/o RC's (150) 8.00 20.00
ROOKIE AUTO PRINT RUN 200-500
1 Beanie Wells .25 .60
2 Larry Fitzgerald .25 .60
3 Steve Breaston .20 .50
4 Tim Hightower .20 .50
5 Jason Snelling .25 .60
6 Matt Ryan .30 .75
7 Michael Turner .25 .60
8 Roddy White .25 .60
9 Tony Gonzalez .25 .60
10 Anquan Boldin .25 .60
11 Joe Flacco .30 .75
12 Ray Lewis .30 .75
13 Ray Rice .25 .60
14 Todd Heap .20 .50
15 C.J. Spiller .25 .60
16 Fred Jackson .30 .75
17 Lee Evans .25 .60
18 Ryan Fitzpatrick .25 .60
19 Steve Johnson .25 .60
20 DeAngelo Williams .25 .60
21 Jimmy Clausen .20 .50
22 Jonathan Stewart .25 .60
23 Steve Smith .25 .60
24 Brian Urlacher .30 .75
25 Devin Hester .30 .75
26 Jay Cutler .25 .60
27 Johnny Knox .25 .60
28 Matt Forte .25 .60
29 Carson Palmer .25 .60
30 Cedric Benson .25 .60
31 Chad Ochocinco .25 .60
32 Jordan Shipley .25 .60
33 Terrell Owens .30 .75
34 Ben Watson .20 .50
35 Colt McCoy .25 .60
36 Josh Cribbs .25 .60
37 Peyton Hillis .25 .60
38 Dez Bryant .30 .75
39 Felix Jones .25 .60
40 Jason Witten .30 .75
41 Miles Austin .25 .60
42 Tony Romo .30 .75
43 Brandon Lloyd .25 .60
44 Eddie Royal .20 .50
45 Jabar Gaffney .20 .50
46 Knowshon Moreno .25 .60
47 Tim Tebow .60 1.50
48 Brandon Pettigrew .20 .50
49 Calvin Johnson .30 .75
50 Jahvid Best .25 .60
51 Matthew Stafford .30 .75
52 Nate Burleson .20 .50
53 Aaron Rodgers .50 1.25
54 Clay Matthews .30 .75
55 Donald Driver .25 .60
56 Greg Jennings .25 .60
57 Jordy Nelson .25 .60
58 Andre Johnson .25 .60
59 Arian Foster .25 .60
60 Brian Cushing .20 .50
61 Kevin Walter .25 .60
62 Matt Schaub .25 .60
63 Austin Collie .25 .60
64 Dallas Clark .25 .60
65 Joseph Addai .25 .60
66 Peyton Manning .50 1.25
67 Reggie Wayne .25 .60
68 David Garrard .25 .60
69 Marcedes Lewis .20 .50
70 Maurice Jones-Drew .25 .60
71 Mike Sims-Walker .25 .60
72 Mike Thomas .25 .60
73 Dwayne Bowe .25 .60
74 Jamaal Charles .25 .60
75 Matt Cassel .25 .60
76 Tony Moeaki .20 .50
77 Brandon Marshall .25 .60
78 Brian Hartline .20 .50
79 Chad Henne .25 .60
80 Davone Bess .20 .50
81 Ronnie Brown .25 .60
82 Adrian Peterson .40 1.00
83 Percy Harvin .25 .60
84 Sidney Rice .25 .60
85 Joe Webb .20 .50
86 Visanthe Shiancoe .25 .60
87 BenJarvus Green-Ellis .25 .60
88 Danny Woodhead .30 .75
89 Deion Branch .20 .50
90 Tom Brady .50 1.25
91 Wes Welker .30 .75
92 Drew Brees .30 .75
93 Lance Moore .25 .60
94 Marques Colston .25 .60
95 Pierre Thomas .25 .60
96 Reggie Bush .25 .60
97 Ahmad Bradshaw .25 .60
98 Eli Manning .30 .75
99 Hakeem Nicks .25 .60
100 Mario Manningham .25 .60
101 Steve Smith USC .25 .60
102 Braylon Edwards .25 .60
103 LaDainian Tomlinson .30 .75
104 Mark Sanchez .30 .75
105 Santonio Holmes .25 .60
106 Shonn Greene .25 .60
107 Darren McFadden .25 .60
108 Jacoby Ford .25 .60
109 Louis Murphy .25 .60
110 Zach Miller .25 .60
111 DeSean Jackson .25 .60
112 Jeremy Maclin .25 .60
113 LeSean McCoy .25 .60
114 Michael Vick .30 .75
115 Ben Roethlisberger .30 .75
116 Hines Ward .25 .60
117 Mike Wallace .30 .75
118 Rashard Mendenhall .25 .60
119 Troy Polamalu .30 .75
120 Antonio Gates .25 .60
121 Malcom Floyd .25 .60
122 Mike Tolbert .25 .60
123 Philip Rivers .30 .75
124 Ryan Mathews .25 .60
125 Frank Gore .25 .60
126 Michael Crabtree .25 .60
127 Patrick Willis .25 .60
128 Vernon Davis .25 .60
129 John Carlson .20 .50
130 Marshawn Lynch .25 .60
131 Matt Hasselbeck .25 .60
132 Mike Williams USC .25 .60
133 Danny Amendola .25 .60
134 Donnie Avery .20 .50
135 Sam Bradford .30 .75
136 Steven Jackson .25 .60
137 Cadillac Williams .20 .50
138 Josh Freeman .30 .75
139 Kellen Winslow Jr. .25 .60
140 LeGarrette Blount .25 .60
141 Mike Williams .25 .60
142 Bo Scaife .20 .50
143 Chris Johnson .25 .60
144 Kenny Britt .25 .60
145 Nate Washington .20 .50
146 Randy Moss .25 .60
147 Chris Cooley .25 .60
148 Donovan McNabb .30 .75
149 Ryan Torain .20 .50
150 Santana Moss .25 .60
151 Aaron Williams RC .75 2.00
152 Adrian Clayborn RC 1.00 2.50
153 Ahmad Black RC .75 2.00
154 Akeem Ayers RC .75 2.00
155 Aldon Smith RC 1.50 4.00
156 Aldrick Robinson RC .60 1.50
157 Allen Bradford RC .75 2.00
158 Anthony Allen RC .60 1.50
159 Anthony Castonzo RC .60 1.50
160 Anthony Sherman RC .75 2.00
161 Baron Batch RC 1.00 2.50
162 Terrelle Pryor RC 2.00 5.00
163 Brandon Harris RC .60 1.50
164 Drandon Hogan RC .60 1.50
165 Brooks Reed RC 1.00 2.50
166 Bruce Carter RC 1.00 2.50
167 Cameron Heyward RC 1.00 2.50
168 Cameron Jordan RC .75 2.00
169 Casey Matthews RC 1.00 2.50
170 Chimdi Chekwa RC .75 2.00
171 Chris Conte RC .60 1.50
172 Chris Culliver RC .75 2.00
173 Corey Liuget RC .60 1.50
174 Curtis Brown RC 1.00 2.50
175 Curtis Marsh RC .75 2.00
176 Danny Watkins RC .75 2.00
177 Da'Rel Scott RC .75 2.00
178 David Ausberry RC .75 2.00
179 DeMarco Sampson RC .60 1.50
180 DeMarcus Van Dyke RC .75 2.00
181 Denarius Moore RC 1.25 3.00
182 Derek Sherrod RC 1.00 2.50
183 Dion Lewis RC 1.00 2.50
184 Dontay Moch RC .60 1.50
185 Dwayne Harris RC 1.00 2.50
186 Evan Royster RC 1.00 2.50
187 Gabe Carimi RC 1.00 2.50
188 Greg Jones RC .75 2.00
189 Greg McElroy RC 1.00 2.50
190 J.J. Watt RC 1.25 3.00
191 Jabaal Sheard RC 1.00 2.50
192 Jah Reid RC .60 1.50
193 Jaiquawn Jarrett RC .75 2.00
194 James Carpenter RC 1.00 2.50
195 Jarvis Jenkins RC .60 1.50
196 Jay Finley RC .75 2.00
197 Jimmy Smith RC 1.00 2.50
198 Johnny Patrick RC .75 2.00
199 Johnny White RC .75 2.00
200 Jonas Mouton RC .75 2.00
201 Jordan Cameron RC .75 2.00
202 Julius Thomas RC .75 2.00
203 Justin Houston RC 1.00 2.50
204 Kealoha Pilares RC 1.00 2.50
205 Kelvin Sheppard RC 1.00 2.50
206 Kris Durham RC .75 2.00
207 Lance Kendricks RC .75 2.00
208 Lee Smith RC .75 2.00
209 Luke Stocker RC .75 2.00
210 Malcolm Williams RC .60 1.50
211 Marcus Cannon RC .60 1.50
212 Marcus Gilbert RC 1.00 2.50
213 Marcus Gilchrist RC .60 1.50
214 Martez Wilson RC 1.00 2.50
215 Marvin Austin RC .75 2.00
216 Mason Foster RC 1.00 2.50
217 Matt Bosher RC .60 1.50
218 Mike Pouncey RC 1.00 2.50
219 Muhammad Wilkerson RC 1.00 2.50
220 Nate Irving RC .75 2.00
221 Nate Solder RC 1.00 2.50
222 Nathan Enderle RC 1.00 2.50
223 Orlando Franklin RC .75 2.00
224 Owen Marecic RC 1.00 2.50
225 Phil Taylor RC .75 2.00
226 Quan Sturdivant RC 1.00 2.50
227 Quinton Carter RC .60 1.50
228 Rahim Moore RC .75 2.00
229 Ras-I Dowling RC 1.00 2.50
230 Richard Gordon RC .75 2.00
231 Robert Housler RC .75 2.00
232 Robert Sands RC .75 2.00
233 Rodney Hudson RC .60 1.50
234 Ronald Johnson RC .75 2.00
235 Ross Homan RC 1.00 2.50
236 Ryan Kerrigan RC 1.00 2.50
237 Ryan Whalen RC .75 2.00
238 Scotty McKnight RC .75 2.00
239 Shane Bannon RC .60 1.50
240 Shareece Wright RC .75 2.00
241 Stanley Havili RC .60 1.50
242 Stefen Wisniewski RC 1.00 2.50
243 Stephen Burton RC .60 1.50
244 Stephen Paea RC 1.00 2.50
245 T.J. Yates RC 1.25 3.00
246 Terrell McClain RC .75 2.00
247 Tyler Sash RC 1.00 2.50
248 Tyrod Taylor RC 1.00 2.50
249 Tyron Smith RC 1.25 3.00
250 Virgil Green RC .75 2.00
251 Marcell Dareus AU RC/300 15.00 40.00
252 Von Miller AU RC/300 15.00 40.00
253 Andy Dalton AU RC/300 EXCH 30.00 60.00
254 Blaine Gabbert AU RC/350 25.00 50.00
255 Cam Newton AU RC/300 100.00 175.00
256 Christian Ponder AU RC/300 30.00 60.00
257 Colin Kaepernick AU RC/500 15.00 30.00
258 Jake Locker AU RC/300 50.00 100.00
259 Ryan Mallett AU RC/350 25.00 50.00
260 Bilal Powell AU RC/450 5.00 12.00
261 Daniel Thomas AU RC/300 10.00 25.00
262 Delone Carter AU RC/300 10.00 25.00
263 DeMarco Murray AU RC/300 30.00 60.00
264 Jamie Harper AU RC/300 8.00 20.00
265 Jordan Todman AU RC/300 5.00 12.00
266 Kendall Hunter AU RC/300 10.00 25.00
267 Mark Ingram AU RC/300 40.00 80.00
268 Mikel Leshoure AU RC/400 8.00 20.00
269 Ryan Williams AU RC/400 10.00 25.00
270 Shane Vereen AU RC/300 8.00 20.00
271 Stevan Ridley AU RC/360 8.00 20.00
272 Taiwan Jones AU RC/250 10.00 25.00
273 Kyle Rudolph AU RC/350 8.00 20.00
274 A.J. Green AU RC/250 25.00 50.00
275 Austin Pettis AU RC/450 6.00 15.00
276 Greg Little AU RC/450 10.00 25.00
277 Jerrel Jernigan AU RC/400 6.00 15.00
278 Jonathan Baldwin AU RC/350 10.00 25.00
279 Julio Jones AU RC/250 30.00 60.00
280 Leonard Hankerson AU RC/450 8.00 20.00
281 Randall Cobb AU RC/200 20.00 40.00
282 Titus Young AU RC/480 10.00 25.00
283 Torrey Smith AU RC/250 10.00 25.00
284 Vincent Brown AU RC/375 8.00 20.00
285 Clyde Gates AU RC/300 6.00 15.00
286 Alex Green AU RC/360 10.00 25.00
287 Da'Quan Bowers AU RC/300 8.00 20.00
288 Ricky Stanzi AU RC/300 20.00 40.00
289 Jacquizz Rodgers AU RC/350 8.00 20.00
290 Niles Paul AU RC/300 8.00 20.00
291 Tandon Doss AU RC/300 EXCH 6.00 15.00
292 Prince Amukamara AU RC/450 8.00 20.00
293 Roy Helu AU RC/280 15.00 40.00
294 D.J. Williams AU RC/400 10.00 25.00
295 Cecil Shorts AU RC/450 6.00 15.00
296 Jeremy Kerley AU RC/450 8.00 20.00
297 Greg Salas AU RC/375 8.00 20.00
298 Patrick Peterson/400 RC 10.00 25.00
299 Robert Quinn/250 RC 3.00 8.00
300 Nick Fairley/350 RC 4.00 10.00

2011 Panini Threads Gold
*1-150 VETS/100: 3X TO 8X BASIC CARDS
*151-250 ROOKIES/100: 1X TO 2.5X BASIC CARDS
STATED PRINT RUN 100 SER.#'d SETS

2011 Panini Threads Platinum
*1-150 VETS/25: 5X TO 12X BASIC CARDS
*151-250 ROOKIES/25: 1.5X TO 4X BASIC CARDS
STATED PRINT RUN 25 SER.#'d SETS

2011 Panini Threads Silver
*1-150 VETS/250: 2X TO 5X BASIC CARDS
*151-250 ROOKIES/250: .6X TO 1.5X BASIC CARDS
STATED PRINT RUN 250 SER.#'d SETS

2011 Panini Threads 2010 All Rookie Team
*HOLOFOIL/100: .5X TO 1.2X BASIC INSERTS
1 Colt McCoy 1.25 3.00
2 Dez Bryant 1.50 4.00
3 Jahvid Best 1.25 3.00
4 Jermaine Gresham 1.25 3.00
5 Mike Williams 1.25 3.00
6 Ndamukong Suh 1.50 4.00
7 Rob Gronkowski 1.50 4.00
8 Ryan Mathews 1.25 3.00
9 Sam Bradford 1.50 4.00
10 Tim Tebow 3.00 8.00

2011 Panini Threads 2010 All Rookie Team Autographs
STATED PRINT RUN 5-15
1 Colt McCoy/15
2 Dez Bryant/15
3 Jahvid Best/15 8.00 20.00
4 Jermaine Gresham/15 EXCH
5 Mike Williams/15 EXCH 8.00 20.00
10 Tim Tebow/15 60.00 120.00

2011 Panini Threads 2010 All Rookie Team Threads
STATED PRINT RUN 299 SER.#'d SETS
9 Sam Bradford 4.00 10.00
10 Tim Tebow 8.00 20.00

2011 Panini Threads 2010 All Rookie Team Threads Prime
STATED PRINT RUN 5-99
1 Colt McCoy/99 5.00 12.00
2 Dez Bryant/99 6.00 15.00
3 Jahvid Best/99 5.00 12.00
4 Jermaine Gresham/99 5.00 12.00
5 Mike Williams/99 5.00 12.00
6 Ndamukong Suh/99 6.00 15.00
7 Rob Gronkowski/99 6.00 15.00
8 Ryan Mathews/99 5.00 12.00
9 Sam Bradford/99 6.00 15.00

2011 Panini Threads Autographs Silver
VETERAN AU PRINT RUN 1-100
ROOKIE AU STATED PRINT RUN 299
11 Joe Flacco/15 12.00 30.00
21 Jimmy Clausen/35 10.00 25.00
31 Chad Ochocinco/20
37 Peyton Hillis/25 30.00 60.00
43 Brandon Lloyd/25 10.00 25.00
46 Knowshon Moreno/25 12.00 30.00
56 Greg Jennings/20
59 Arian Foster/20
61 Kevin Walter/30 8.00 20.00
78 Brian Hartline/25 8.00 20.00
87 BenJarvus Green-Ellis/25 30.00 60.00
107 Darren McFadden/25 12.00 30.00
113 LeSean McCoy/25 10.00 25.00
122 Mike Tolbert/100 5.00 12.00
123 Philip Rivers/25 20.00 40.00
151 Aaron Williams 5.00 12.00
152 Adrian Clayborn 6.00 15.00
153 Ahmad Black 5.00 12.00
154 Akeem Ayers 5.00 12.00
155 Aldon Smith 10.00 25.00
156 Aldrick Robinson 4.00 10.00
158 Anthony Allen 4.00 10.00
159 Anthony Castonzo 5.00 12.00
163 Brandon Harris 4.00 10.00
167 Cameron Heyward 6.00 15.00
168 Cameron Jordan 5.00 12.00
173 Corey Liuget 4.00 10.00
177 Da'Rel Scott 5.00 12.00
181 Denarius Moore 12.00 30.00
183 Dion Lewis 6.00 15.00
185 Dwayne Harris 6.00 15.00
186 Evan Royster 6.00 15.00
188 Greg Jones 5.00 12.00
190 J.J. Watt 8.00 20.00
197 Jimmy Smith 6.00 15.00
199 Johnny White 5.00 12.00
201 Jordan Cameron 5.00 12.00
202 Julius Thomas 5.00 12.00
203 Justin Houston 6.00 15.00
204 Kealoha Pilares 15.00 30.00
206 Kris Durham 5.00 12.00
207 Lance Kendricks 5.00 12.00
209 Luke Stocker 5.00 12.00
211 Marcus Cannon 4.00 10.00
214 Martez Wilson 6.00 15.00
225 Phil Taylor 5.00 12.00
227 Quinton Carter 4.00 10.00
228 Rahim Moore 5.00 12.00
234 Ronald Johnson 5.00 12.00
236 Ryan Kerrigan 6.00 15.00
238 Scotty McKnight 5.00 12.00
241 Stanley Havili 4.00 10.00
243 Stephen Burton 4.00 10.00
244 Stephen Paea 6.00 15.00
245 T.J. Yates 8.00 20.00
247 Tyler Sash 6.00 15.00
248 Tyrod Taylor 6.00 15.00
249 Tyron Smith 10.00 25.00

2011 Panini Threads Franchise Fabrics
STATED PRINT RUN 15-299
*PRIME/50: .8X TO 2X BASIC JSY/150-299
*PRIME/20-25: 1X TO 2.5X BASIC JSY/150-299
1 Aaron Rodgers/299 8.00 20.00
2 Andre Johnson/299 2.50 6.00
3 Antonio Gates/299 2.50 6.00
5 Calvin Johnson/299 3.00 8.00
6 Chris Cooley/299 3.00 8.00
7 Chris Johnson/299 2.50 6.00
8 Darrelle Revis/299 2.50 6.00
9 Hakeem Nicks/150 2.50 6.00
10 Joe Flacco/299 3.00 8.00
11 Larry Fitzgerald/220 2.50 6.00
12 Mark Sanchez/299 3.00 8.00
13 Marques Colston/299 2.50 6.00
15 Michael Vick/299 3.00 8.00
16 Miles Austin/299 3.00 8.00
17 Reggie Wayne/299 2.50 6.00
18 Steve Smith/170 2.50 6.00
19 Vernon Davis/299 2.50 6.00

2011 Panini Threads Game Day Jerseys
STATED PRINT RUN 290-299
1 Adrian Peterson/299 4.00 10.00
2 Ahmad Bradshaw/290 2.50 6.00
3 Brent Celek/299 2.50 6.00
4 Carson Palmer/299 2.50 6.00
5 Cedric Benson/299 2.50 6.00
6 Devin Hester/299 3.00 8.00
8 Donovan McNabb/299 3.00 8.00
9 Drew Brees/299 3.00 8.00
10 Eli Manning/299 3.00 8.00
11 Jason Witten/299 3.00 8.00
12 Jay Cutler/299 2.50 6.00
13 Jeremy Maclin/299 2.50 6.00
14 Jonathan Stewart/299 2.50 6.00
15 LaDainian Tomlinson/299 3.00 8.00
16 Matt Forte/299 2.50 6.00
17 Matt Schaub/299 2.50 6.00
18 Maurice Jones-Drew/299 2.50 6.00
19 Michael Turner/299 2.50 6.00
20 Peyton Manning/299 5.00 12.00
21 Reggie Bush/299 2.50 6.00
22 Roddy White/299 2.50 6.00
23 Steven Jackson/299 2.50 6.00
24 Tony Gonzalez/299 2.50 6.00
25 Tony Romo/299 3.00 8.00

2011 Panini Threads Game Day Jerseys Prime
*PRIME/30-50: .8X TO 2X BASIC JSY
*PRIME/25: 1X TO 2.5X BASIC JSY
STATED PRINT RUN 25-50
7 Donald Driver/50 5.00 12.00

2011 Panini Threads Game Day Jerseys Autographs
STATED PRINT RUN 15 SER.#'d SETS
EXCH EXPIRATION: 2/24/2013
1 Adrian Peterson 75.00 150.00
2 Ahmad Bradshaw EXCH 12.00 30.00
6 Devin Hester EXCH 15.00 40.00
8 Donovan McNabb
9 Drew Brees EXCH
10 Eli Manning 40.00 80.00
11 Jason Witten
12 Jay Cutler 12.00 30.00
13 Jeremy Maclin EXCH 12.00 30.00
14 Jonathan Stewart 12.00 30.00
15 LaDainian Tomlinson
16 Matt Forte
17 Matt Schaub
18 Maurice Jones-Drew 12.00 30.00
19 Michael Turner 12.00 30.00
20 Peyton Manning 75.00 150.00
21 Reggie Bush EXCH 12.00 30.00
22 Roddy White 12.00 30.00
23 Steven Jackson
25 Tony Romo 40.00 80.00

2011 Panini Threads Generations
*HOLOFOIL/100: .6X TO 1.5X BASIC INSERTS
1 Alan Page 1.00 2.50
Jared Allen
2 Jim Brown 1.50 4.00
Ernie Davis
3 Marshall Faulk 1.00 2.50
Steven Jackson
4 Joe Perry 1.00 2.50
Frank Gore
5 Richard Dent 1.00 2.50
Julius Peppers
6 Michael Irvin 1.25 3.00
Dez Bryant
7 John Elway 2.50 6.00
Tim Tebow
8 Peyton Manning 2.00 5.00
Sam Bradford
9 Ed Reed 1.00 2.50
Darrelle Revis
10 Steve Bartkowski 1.25 3.00
Matt Ryan

2011 Panini Threads Generations Materials
STATED PRINT RUN 200-299
1 Alan Page/299 5.00 12.00
Jared Allen
2 Jim Brown/299 15.00 30.00
Ernie Davis
3 Marshall Faulk/230 5.00 12.00
Steven Jackson
4 Joe Perry/200 5.00 12.00
Frank Gore

5 Richard Dent/299	6.00	15.00
Julius Peppers		
7 John Elway/299	12.00	30.00
Tim Tebow		
8 Peyton Manning/299	10.00	25.00
Sam Bradford		
9 Ed Reed/299	5.00	12.00
Darrelle Revis		
10 Steve Bartkowski/299	6.00	15.00
Matt Ryan		

2011 Panini Threads Generations Materials Prime

*PRIME/49-50: .6X TO 1.5X BASIC JSY/230-299
*PRIME/25: .8X TO 2X BASIC JSY/200
STATED PRINT RUN 25-50

6 Michael Irvin/50	12.00	30.00
Dez Bryant		

2011 Panini Threads Gridiron Kings

*FRMD BLACK/10: 1.5X TO 4X BASIC INSERTS
*FRAMED BLUE/50: .8X TO 2X BASIC INSERTS
*FRMD GREEN/25: 1X TO 2.5X BASIC INSERTS
*FRAMED RED/100: .6X TO 1.5X BASIC INSERTS

1 Vincent Jackson	1.25	3.00
2 Roy Williams WR	1.25	3.00
3 Bo Scaife	1.00	2.50
4 Anquan Boldin	1.25	3.00
5 Brian Urlacher	1.50	4.00
6 Chad Henne	1.25	3.00
7 DeAngelo Williams	1.25	3.00
8 Julius Peppers	1.25	3.00
9 Jared Allen	1.25	3.00
10 Ray Lewis	1.50	4.00
11 C.J. Spiller	1.25	3.00
12 Dwight Freeney	1.25	3.00
13 Asante Samuel	1.00	2.50
14 Dustin Keller	1.25	3.00
15 Darren Sproles	1.25	3.00
16 Shonn Greene	1.25	3.00
17 Pierre Thomas	1.25	3.00
18 Heath Miller	1.25	3.00
19 Dallas Clark	1.25	3.00
20 David Harris	1.00	2.50
21 Hines Ward	1.25	3.00
22 Cortland Finnegan	1.00	2.50
23 Patrick Willis	1.25	3.00
24 Steve Smith USC	1.25	3.00
25 London Fletcher	1.00	2.50
26 Ryan Grant	1.25	3.00
27 Sidney Rice	1.25	3.00
28 James Laurinaitis	1.00	2.50
29 Malcom Floyd	1.25	3.00
30 Michael Crabtree	1.25	3.00
31 Ryan Fitzpatrick	1.25	3.00
32 Lee Evans	1.25	3.00
33 Visanthe Shiancoe	1.25	3.00
34 Todd Heap	1.00	2.50
35 Matt Cassel	1.25	3.00
36 Ed Reed	1.25	3.00
37 Brian Cushing	1.00	2.50
38 David Garrard	1.25	3.00
39 Santonio Holmes	1.25	3.00
40 Ryan Mathews	1.25	3.00
41 Kevin Boss	1.25	3.00
42 Devery Henderson	1.00	2.50
43 Matthew Stafford	1.50	4.00
44 Ndamukong Suh	1.50	4.00
45 Troy Polamalu	1.50	4.00
46 Josh Cribbs	1.25	3.00
47 Eddie Royal	1.00	2.50
48 Brandon Jacobs	1.25	3.00
49 Rashard Mendenhall	1.25	3.00
50 Greg Olsen	1.00	2.50

2011 Panini Threads Gridiron Kings Autographs

STATED PRINT RUN 1-100

9 Jared Allen/25	20.00	40.00
17 Pierre Thomas/15		
20 David Harris/100	5.00	12.00
25 London Fletcher/35	6.00	15.00
26 Ryan Grant/25	12.00	30.00
28 James Laurinaitis/25		
37 Brian Cushing/35	6.00	15.00
50 Greg Olsen/25	10.00	25.00

2011 Panini Threads Gridiron Kings Materials

STATED PRINT RUN 98-299

1 Vincent Jackson/299	2.50	6.00
2 Roy Williams WR/299	2.50	6.00
3 Bo Scaife/299	2.00	5.00
4 Anquan Boldin/299	2.50	6.00
5 Brian Urlacher/299	3.00	8.00
6 Chad Henne/225	2.50	6.00
7 DeAngelo Williams/299	2.50	6.00
9 Jared Allen/299	3.00	8.00
10 Ray Lewis/299	3.00	8.00
11 C.J. Spiller/299	2.50	6.00
12 Dwight Freeney/299	2.50	6.00
13 Asante Samuel/190	2.00	5.00
14 Dustin Keller/299	2.50	6.00
15 Darren Sproles/299	2.50	6.00
16 Shonn Greene/299	2.50	6.00
18 Heath Miller/299	2.50	6.00
19 Dallas Clark/299	2.50	6.00
20 David Harris/299	2.00	5.00
21 Hines Ward/299	3.00	8.00
22 Cortland Finnegan/299	2.00	5.00
23 Patrick Willis/299	2.50	6.00
24 Steve Smith USC/299	2.50	6.00
25 London Fletcher/299	2.00	5.00
27 Sidney Rice/299	2.50	6.00
28 James Laurinaitis/98	2.50	6.00
29 Malcom Floyd/299	2.50	6.00
30 Michael Crabtree/299	2.50	6.00
31 Ryan Fitzpatrick/299	4.00	10.00
32 Lee Evans/299	2.50	6.00
33 Visanthe Shiancoe/299	2.50	6.00
34 Todd Heap/299	2.00	5.00
35 Matt Cassel/299	2.50	6.00
36 Ed Reed/299	3.00	8.00
38 David Garrard/299	2.50	6.00
39 Santonio Holmes/299	2.50	6.00
40 Ryan Mathews/299	2.50	6.00
41 Kevin Boss/299	2.50	6.00
42 Devery Henderson/299	2.00	5.00
43 Matthew Stafford/230	3.00	8.00
44 Ndamukong Suh/299	3.00	8.00
45 Troy Polamalu/299	5.00	12.00
46 Josh Cribbs/200	2.50	6.00
47 Eddie Royal/299	2.00	5.00
48 Brandon Jacobs/299	2.50	6.00
49 Rashard Mendenhall/299	2.50	6.00
50 Greg Olsen/299	2.00	5.00

2011 Panini Threads Gridiron Kings Materials Prime

*PRIME/90-99: .5X TO 1.2X BASIC JSY/190-299
*PRIME/99: .5X TO 1.2X BASIC JSY/98
*PRIME/50-60: .6X TO 1.5X BASIC JSY/190-299
*PRIME/25: .8X TO 2X BASIC JSY/225-299
PRIME STATED PRINT RUN 25-99

17 Pierre Thomas/99	4.00	10.00

2011 Panini Threads Gridiron Kings Materials Autographs

STATED PRINT RUN 9-25
EXCH EXPIRATION: 2/24/2013

3 Bo Scaife/20	10.00	25.00
4 Anquan Boldin/15		
6 Chad Henne/15	12.00	30.00
7 DeAngelo Williams/15	12.00	30.00
9 Jared Allen/15	30.00	60.00
11 C.J. Spiller/15		
16 Shonn Greene/15	12.00	30.00
18 Heath Miller/20		
19 Dallas Clark/15 EXCH		
20 David Harris/25		
21 Hines Ward/15	30.00	60.00
23 Patrick Willis/15	15.00	40.00
25 London Fletcher/15	25.00	50.00
27 Sidney Rice/15	12.00	30.00
28 James Laurinaitis/15		
29 Malcom Floyd/15 EXCH		
30 Michael Crabtree/15		
35 Matt Cassel/15		
38 David Garrard/15		
39 Santonio Holmes/15	12.00	30.00
42 Devery Henderson/15 EXCH		
43 Matthew Stafford/15		
45 Troy Polamalu/15	125.00	200.00
49 Rashard Mendenhall/15 EXCH	12.00	30.00
50 Greg Olsen/15	10.00	25.00

2011 Panini Threads Heritage Collection

*HOLOFOIL/100: .6X TO 1.5X BASIC INSERTS

1 Barry Sanders	2.50	6.00
2 Buck Buchanan	1.00	2.50
3 Knute Rockne	1.50	4.00
4 Bernie Kosar	1.25	3.00
5 John Brodie	1.00	2.50
6 Sam Huff	1.25	3.00
7 Bob Hayes	1.50	4.00
8 Franco Harris	1.50	4.00
9 Jay Novacek	1.25	3.00
10 Jim Parker	1.00	2.50
11 Lamar Lundy	1.00	2.50
12 Terrell Davis	1.50	4.00
13 Willie Brown	1.00	2.50
14 Y.A. Tittle	1.50	4.00
15 Mark Carrier	1.00	2.50

2011 Panini Threads Heritage Collection Materials

*PRIME/50: .6X TO 1.5X BASIC JSY
*PRIME/25: .8X TO 2X BASIC JSY

1 Barry Sanders	8.00	20.00
2 Buck Buchanan	3.00	8.00
3 Knute Rockne	10.00	25.00
4 Bernie Kosar	4.00	10.00
5 John Brodie	6.00	15.00
6 Sam Huff	4.00	10.00
7 Bob Hayes	6.00	15.00
8 Franco Harris	6.00	15.00
9 Jay Novacek	5.00	12.00
10 Jim Parker	3.00	8.00
12 Terrell Davis	5.00	12.00
13 Willie Brown	3.00	8.00
14 Y.A. Tittle	5.00	12.00
15 Mark Carrier	3.00	8.00

2011 Panini Threads Jerseys Prime

STATED PRINT RUN 10-99

1 Beanie Wells/99	4.00	10.00
2 Larry Fitzgerald/65	4.00	10.00
6 Matt Ryan/99	5.00	12.00
7 Michael Turner/99	4.00	10.00
8 Roddy White/99	4.00	10.00
9 Tony Gonzalez/99	4.00	10.00
10 Anquan Boldin/99	4.00	10.00
11 Joe Flacco/35	6.00	15.00
12 Ray Lewis/99	5.00	12.00
13 Ray Rice/99	4.00	10.00
14 Todd Heap/99	3.00	8.00
15 C.J. Spiller/99	4.00	10.00
16 Fred Jackson/99	6.00	15.00
17 Lee Evans/99	4.00	10.00
18 Ryan Fitzpatrick/99	6.00	15.00
20 DeAngelo Williams/99	4.00	10.00
21 Jimmy Clausen/25	5.00	12.00
22 Jonathan Stewart/99	4.00	10.00
23 Steve Smith/99	4.00	10.00
24 Brian Urlacher/99	5.00	12.00
25 Devin Hester/99	5.00	12.00
26 Jay Cutler/10	8.00	20.00
27 Johnny Knox/99	4.00	10.00
28 Matt Forte/99	4.00	10.00
29 Carson Palmer/99	4.00	10.00
30 Cedric Benson/99	4.00	10.00
31 Chad Ochocinco/99	4.00	10.00
32 Jordan Shipley/50	5.00	12.00
36 Josh Cribbs/60	4.00	10.00
37 Peyton Hillis/99	6.00	15.00
38 Dez Bryant/55	6.00	15.00
39 Felix Jones/99	4.00	10.00
40 Jason Witten/99	5.00	12.00
41 Miles Austin/99	5.00	12.00
42 Tony Romo/99	5.00	12.00
43 Brandon Lloyd/99	4.00	10.00
44 Eddie Royal/99	3.00	8.00
45 Jabar Gaffney/99	3.00	8.00
46 Knowshon Moreno/99	4.00	10.00
47 Tim Tebow/25	15.00	40.00
49 Calvin Johnson/99	5.00	12.00
50 Jahvid Best/99	4.00	10.00
51 Matthew Stafford/99	5.00	12.00
53 Aaron Rodgers/15	20.00	50.00
54 Clay Matthews/99	6.00	15.00
55 Donald Driver/99	5.00	12.00
58 Andre Johnson/99	4.00	10.00
59 Arian Foster/99	5.00	12.00
62 Matt Schaub/25	6.00	15.00
64 Dallas Clark/99	4.00	10.00
65 Joseph Addai/99	4.00	10.00
66 Peyton Manning/25	12.00	30.00
67 Reggie Wayne/99	4.00	10.00
68 David Garrard/85	4.00	10.00
69 Marcedes Lewis/99	3.00	8.00
70 Maurice Jones-Drew/99	4.00	10.00
72 Mike Thomas/99	4.00	10.00
73 Dwayne Bowe/99	4.00	10.00
74 Jamaal Charles/99	4.00	10.00
75 Matt Cassel/30	5.00	12.00
77 Brandon Marshall/99	4.00	10.00
79 Chad Henne/24	6.00	15.00
81 Ronnie Brown/99	4.00	10.00
82 Adrian Peterson/99	6.00	15.00
83 Percy Harvin/99	4.00	10.00
84 Sidney Rice/99	4.00	10.00
86 Visanthe Shiancoe/49	5.00	12.00
87 BenJarvus Green-Ellis/99	4.00	10.00
88 Danny Woodhead/99	10.00	25.00
90 Tom Brady/99	8.00	20.00
91 Wes Welker/99	5.00	12.00
92 Drew Brees/15	8.00	20.00
94 Marques Colston/99	4.00	10.00
95 Pierre Thomas/30	5.00	12.00
96 Reggie Bush/99	4.00	10.00
97 Ahmad Bradshaw/99	4.00	10.00
98 Eli Manning/99	5.00	12.00
99 Hakeem Nicks/99	4.00	10.00
101 Steve Smith USC/99	4.00	10.00
102 Braylon Edwards/99	4.00	10.00
103 LaDainian Tomlinson/55	6.00	15.00
104 Mark Sanchez/25	8.00	20.00
105 Santonio Holmes/99	4.00	10.00
106 Shonn Greene/20	6.00	15.00
107 Darren McFadden/99	4.00	10.00
108 Jacoby Ford/99	4.00	10.00
109 Louis Murphy/99	4.00	10.00
110 Zach Miller/99	4.00	10.00
111 DeSean Jackson/99	4.00	10.00
112 Jeremy Maclin/99	4.00	10.00
113 LeSean McCoy/65	4.00	10.00
114 Michael Vick/25	8.00	20.00
115 Ben Roethlisberger/99	8.00	20.00
116 Hines Ward/99	5.00	12.00
117 Mike Wallace/40	6.00	15.00
118 Rashard Mendenhall/99	4.00	10.00
119 Troy Polamalu/75	8.00	20.00
120 Antonio Gates/99	4.00	10.00
121 Malcom Floyd/45	5.00	12.00
123 Philip Rivers/99	5.00	12.00
124 Ryan Mathews/99	4.00	10.00
125 Frank Gore/99	4.00	10.00
126 Michael Crabtree/99	4.00	10.00
127 Patrick Willis/99	4.00	10.00
128 Vernon Davis/99	4.00	10.00
135 Sam Bradford/50	6.00	15.00
136 Steven Jackson/99	4.00	10.00
137 Cadillac Williams/70	3.00	8.00
138 Josh Freeman/70	5.00	12.00
139 Kellen Winslow Jr./99	4.00	10.00
142 Bo Scaife/99	3.00	8.00
143 Chris Johnson/99	4.00	10.00
144 Kenny Britt/99	4.00	10.00
145 Nate Washington/99	3.00	8.00
146 Randy Moss/99	4.00	10.00
147 Chris Cooley/99	5.00	12.00
148 Donovan McNabb/99	5.00	12.00
150 Santana Moss/99	4.00	10.00

2011 Panini Threads Rookie Autographs Combo

STATED PRINT RUN 15 SER.#'d SETS

1 Cam Newton	125.00	250.00
Kealoha Pilares		
2 A.J. Green	50.00	100.00
Andy Dalton		
3 Jake Locker	60.00	120.00
Akeem Ayers		
4 Blaine Gabbert	40.00	80.00
Cecil Shorts		
5 Julio Jones	50.00	100.00
Jacquizz Rodgers		
6 Von Miller	40.00	80.00
Rahim Moore		
7 Christian Ponder	40.00	80.00
Kyle Rudolph		
8 Marcell Dareus		
Aaron Williams		
9 Tyron Smith	40.00	80.00
DeMarco Murray		
10 Mark Ingram		
Martez Wilson		

2011 Panini Threads Rookie Collection Materials

STATED PRINT RUN 299 SER.#'d SETS
*PRIME/50: .8X TO 2X BASIC JSY/299

1 A.J. Green	5.00	12.00
2 Alex Green	4.00	10.00
3 Andy Dalton	6.00	15.00
4 Austin Pettis	2.00	5.00
5 Bilal Powell	1.50	4.00
6 Blaine Gabbert	4.00	10.00
7 Cam Newton	12.00	30.00
8 Christian Ponder	5.00	12.00
9 Colin Kaepernick	3.00	8.00
10 Daniel Thomas	2.50	6.00
11 Delone Carter	2.00	5.00
12 DeMarco Murray	5.00	12.00
13 Greg Little	2.50	6.00
14 Jake Locker	6.00	15.00
15 Jamie Harper	2.50	6.00
16 Jerrel Jernigan	2.00	5.00
17 Jonathan Baldwin	2.50	6.00
18 Jordan Todman	1.50	4.00
19 Julio Jones	5.00	12.00
20 Kendall Hunter	2.50	6.00
21 Kyle Rudolph	2.50	6.00
22 Leonard Hankerson	2.50	6.00
23 Marcell Dareus	2.50	6.00
24 Mark Ingram	8.00	20.00
25 Mikel Leshoure	2.50	6.00
26 Randall Cobb	3.00	8.00
27 Ryan Mallett	5.00	12.00
28 Ryan Williams	3.00	8.00
29 Shane Vereen	2.50	6.00
30 Stevan Ridley	2.50	6.00
31 Taiwan Jones	2.50	6.00
32 Titus Young	3.00	8.00
33 Torrey Smith	3.00	8.00
34 Vincent Brown	2.50	6.00
35 Von Miller	3.00	8.00
36 Clyde Gates	2.00	5.00

2011 Panini Threads Rookie Collection Materials Autographs

STATED PRINT RUN 25 SER.#'d SETS
*PRIME AU/15: .6X TO 1.5X BASIC AU/25

1 A.J. Green	30.00	60.00
2 Alex Green	15.00	40.00
3 Andy Dalton	40.00	80.00
4 Austin Pettis	8.00	20.00
5 Bilal Powell	6.00	15.00
6 Blaine Gabbert	40.00	80.00
7 Cam Newton	150.00	250.00
8 Christian Ponder	30.00	60.00
9 Colin Kaepernick	25.00	50.00
10 Daniel Thomas	10.00	25.00
11 Delone Carter	8.00	20.00
12 DeMarco Murray		
13 Greg Little	10.00	25.00
14 Jake Locker	60.00	120.00
15 Jamie Harper	10.00	25.00
16 Jerrel Jernigan	8.00	20.00
17 Jonathan Baldwin	10.00	25.00
18 Jordan Todman	6.00	15.00
19 Julio Jones	40.00	80.00
20 Kendall Hunter	10.00	25.00
21 Kyle Rudolph	10.00	25.00
22 Leonard Hankerson	10.00	25.00
23 Marcell Dareus	10.00	25.00
24 Mark Ingram	40.00	80.00
25 Mikel Leshoure	10.00	25.00
26 Randall Cobb	25.00	50.00
27 Ryan Mallett	30.00	60.00
28 Ryan Williams	12.00	30.00
29 Shane Vereen	10.00	25.00
30 Stevan Ridley	10.00	25.00
31 Taiwan Jones	10.00	25.00
32 Titus Young	12.00	30.00
33 Torrey Smith	12.00	30.00
34 Vincent Brown	10.00	25.00
35 Von Miller	12.00	30.00
36 Clyde Gates	8.00	20.00

2011 Panini Threads Rookie Collection Materials Combo

STATED PRINT RUN 299 SER.#'d SETS
*PRIME/50: .6X TO 1.5X BASIC JSY/299

1 Cam Newton	12.00	30.00
Mark Ingram		
2 Randall Cobb	5.00	12.00
Alex Green		
3 Jordan Todman	4.00	10.00
Vincent Brown		
4 Mikel Leshoure	5.00	12.00
Titus Young		
5 Ryan Mallett	6.00	15.00
Shane Vereen		
6 Christian Ponder	8.00	20.00
Kyle Rudolph		
7 Jake Locker	8.00	20.00
Jamie Harper		
8 A.J. Green	10.00	25.00
Andy Dalton		
9 Colin Kaepernick	5.00	12.00
Kendall Hunter		
10 Mark Ingram	8.00	20.00
Julio Jones		
11 Cam Newton	12.00	30.00
Jake Locker		
12 Mark Ingram	8.00	20.00
Ryan Williams		
13 A.J. Green	10.00	25.00
Julio Jones		
14 Christian Ponder	10.00	25.00
Andy Dalton		
15 Von Miller	5.00	12.00
Marcell Dareus		

2011 Panini Threads Rookie Collection Materials Quad

STATED PRINT RUN 299 SER.#'d SETS
*PRIME/50: .8X TO 2X BASIC QUAD/299

1 Cam Newton	20.00	50.00
Jake Locker		
Blaine Gabbert		
Christian Ponder		
2 Mark Ingram	8.00	20.00
Ryan Williams		
Shane Vereen		
Mikel Leshoure		
3 A.J. Green	8.00	20.00
Julio Jones		
Jonathan Baldwin		
Titus Young		
4 Cam Newton	20.00	50.00
Jake Locker		
A.J. Green		
Julio Jones		
5 Cam Newton	12.00	30.00
Von Miller		
Marcell Dareus		
A.J. Green		

2011 Panini Threads Star Factor

*HOLOFOIL/100: .6X TO 1.5X BASIC INSERTS

1 Arian Foster	1.00	2.50
2 Braylon Edwards	1.00	2.50
3 Chad Ochocinco	1.00	2.50
4 Clay Matthews	1.25	3.00
5 Danny Woodhead	1.25	3.00
6 Darren McFadden	1.00	2.50
7 DeSean Jackson	1.00	2.50
8 Dez Bryant	1.25	3.00
9 Dwayne Bowe	1.00	2.50
10 Felix Jones	1.00	2.50
11 Frank Gore	1.00	2.50
12 Greg Jennings	1.00	2.50
13 Jamaal Charles	1.00	2.50
14 Josh Freeman	1.25	3.00
15 Kenny Britt	1.00	2.50
16 Knowshon Moreno	1.00	2.50
17 LeSean McCoy	1.00	2.50
18 Michael Turner	1.00	2.50
19 Mike Wallace	1.25	3.00
20 Percy Harvin	1.00	2.50
21 Philip Rivers	1.25	3.00
22 Ray Rice	1.00	2.50
23 Sam Bradford	1.25	3.00
24 Tim Tebow	2.50	6.00
25 Tom Brady	2.00	5.00

2011 Panini Threads Star Factor Materials Prime

STATED PRINT RUN 25-99

1 Arian Foster/99	6.00	15.00
2 Braylon Edwards/99	5.00	12.00
3 Chad Ochocinco/99	5.00	12.00
4 Clay Matthews/90	8.00	20.00
5 Danny Woodhead/99	10.00	25.00
6 Darren McFadden/99	5.00	12.00
7 DeSean Jackson/99	5.00	12.00
8 Dez Bryant/90	6.00	15.00
9 Dwayne Bowe/99	5.00	12.00
10 Felix Jones/99	5.00	12.00
11 Frank Gore/99	5.00	12.00
13 Jamaal Charles/99	5.00	12.00
14 Josh Freeman/80	6.00	15.00
15 Kenny Britt/99	5.00	12.00
16 Knowshon Moreno/99	5.00	12.00
17 LeSean McCoy/99	5.00	12.00
18 Michael Turner/99	5.00	12.00
19 Mike Wallace/25	10.00	25.00
20 Percy Harvin/99	5.00	12.00
21 Philip Rivers/99	6.00	15.00
22 Ray Rice/99	5.00	12.00
23 Sam Bradford/99	6.00	15.00
24 Tim Tebow/25	20.00	50.00
25 Tom Brady/99	10.00	25.00

2011 Panini Threads Triple Threat

*HOLOFOIL/100: .6X TO 1.5X BASIC INSERTS

1 Ray Lewis	1.25	3.00
Ed Reed		
Terrell Suggs		
2 Matt Cassel	1.00	2.50
Dwayne Bowe		
Jamaal Charles		
3 Brian Orakpo	1.00	2.50
LaRon Landry		
London Fletcher		
4 Michael Vick	1.25	3.00
LeSean McCoy		
DeSean Jackson		
5 Philip Rivers	1.25	3.00
Antonio Gates		
Vincent Jackson		
6 Sam Bradford	1.25	3.00
Steven Jackson		
Danny Amendola		
7 Aaron Rodgers	2.50	6.00
Donald Driver		
Greg Jennings		
8 Matt Ryan	1.25	3.00
Michael Turner		
Roddy White		
9 David Garrard	1.00	2.50
Maurice Jones-Drew		
Mike Thomas		
10 Matt Schaub	1.00	2.50
Andre Johnson		
Arian Foster		

2011 Panini Threads Triple Threat Materials

*PRIME/25: 1X TO 2.5X BASIC JSY/125-200

1 Ray Lewis/200	6.00	15.00
Ed Reed		
Terrell Suggs		
2 Matt Cassel/200	5.00	12.00
Dwayne Bowe		
Jamaal Charles		
3 Brian Orakpo/125(LaRon Landry	6.00	15.00
London Fletcher		
4 Michael Vick/200	6.00	15.00
LeSean McCoy		
DeSean Jackson		
5 Philip Rivers/200	6.00	15.00
Antonio Gates		
Vincent Jackson		
7 Aaron Rodgers/75	25.00	50.00
Donald Driver		
Greg Jennings		
8 Matt Ryan/200	6.00	15.00
Michael Turner		
Roddy White		
9 David Garrard/200	5.00	12.00
Maurice Jones-Drew		
Mike Thomas		
10 Matt Schaub/200	5.00	12.00
Andre Johnson		
Arian Foster		

1995 Panthers SkyBox

This 21-card set of the Carolina Panthers features borderless color action player photos with the player's name and position in team color stripes at the bottom. The backs carry another color player picture along with player biographical information. The set includes 20 numbered player cards and one unnumbered cover/checklist card.

COMPLETE SET (21)	6.00	15.00
1 John Kasay	.40	1.00
2 Kerry Collins	2.00	5.00
3 Frank Reich	.40	1.00
4 Rod Smith	.60	1.50
5 Tim McKyer	.30	.75
6 Randy Baldwin	.30	.75
7 Bubba McDowell	.30	.75
8 Tyrone Poole	.60	1.50
9 Sam Mills	.50	1.25
10 Carlton Bailey	.30	.75
11 Darion Conner	.30	.75
12 Lamar Lathon	.40	1.00
13 Blake Brockermeyer	.40	1.00
14 Mike Fox	.30	.75
15 Don Beebe	.40	1.00
16 Mark Carrier	.60	1.50
17 Pete Metzelaars	.30	.75
18 Shawn King	.30	.75
19 Howard Griffith	.30	.75
20 Bob Christian	.40	1.00
NNO Cover Card	.30	.75
Checklist back		

1996 Panthers Fleer/SkyBox Impact Promo Sheet

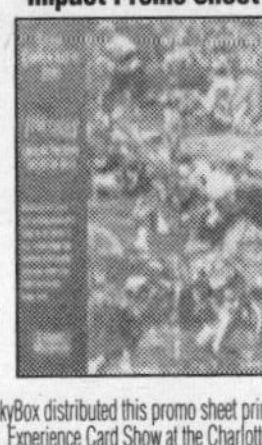

Fleer/SkyBox distributed this promo sheet primarily at the NFL Experience Card Show at the Charlotte Convention Center August 29-31, 1996. The sheet features six Panthers' players with individual card numbers CP1-CP6.

NNO Uncut Promo Sheet	2.00	5.00

1997 Panthers Collector's Choice

Upper Deck released several team sets in 1997 in a blister pack wrapper. Each of the 14-cards in this set are very similar to the base Collector's Choice cards except for the card numbering on the cardback. A cover/checklist card was added featuring the team helmet.

COMPLETE SET (14)	1.20	3.00
CA1 Wesley Walls	.05	.15
CA2 Mark Carrier WR	.08	.25
CA3 Muhsin Muhammad	.05	.15
CA4 John Kasay	.02	.10
CA5 Anthony Johnson	.02	.10
CA6 Kerry Collins	.40	1.00
CA7 Kevin Greene	.05	.15
CA8 Sam Mills	.02	.10
CA9 Rae Carruth	.02	.10
CA10 Micheal Barrow	.02	.10
CA11 Ernie Mills	.02	.10
CA12 Tim Biakabutuka	.05	.15
CA13 Winslow Oliver	.02	.10
CA14 Panthers Logo	.20	.50
Checklist		
(Kerry Collins on back		

1997 Panthers Score

This 15-card set of the Carolina Panthers was distributed in five-card packs with a suggested retail price of $1.99. The fronts feature color action player photos with white borders and the player's name and team logo printed in team color foil at the bottom. The backs carry player information and career statistics. Platinum Team parallel cards were randomly seeded in packs featuring all foil cardfronts.

COMPLETE SET (15)	2.40	6.00
*PLATINUM TEAMS: 1X TO 2X		
1 Kerry Collins	.60	1.50
2 Mark Carrier WR	.15	.40
3 Tim Biakabutuka	.30	.75
4 Anthony Johnson	.08	.25
5 Kevin Greene	.15	.40
6 Eric Davis	.08	.25
7 Muhsin Muhammad	.15	.40
8 Micheal Barrow	.08	.25
9 Wesley Walls	.15	.40
10 Winslow Oliver	.08	.25
11 Lamar Lathon	.08	.25
12 Sam Mills	.08	.25
13 Chad Cota	.08	.25
14 Michael Bates	.08	.25
15 John Kasay	.08	.25

2006 Panthers Topps

COMPLETE SET (12)	3.00	6.00
CAR1 Keary Colbert	.20	.50
CAR2 Jake Delhomme	.25	.60
CAR3 Dan Morgan	.20	.50
CAR4 Chris Gamble	.20	.50
CAR5 Julius Peppers	.25	.60
CAR6 Steve Smith	.30	.75
CAR7 DeShaun Foster	.25	.60
CAR8 Drew Carter	.20	.50
CAR9 Keyshawn Johnson	.25	.60
CAR10 Nick Goings	.20	.50
CAR11 Brad Hoover	.20	.50
CAR12 DeAngelo Williams	.40	1.00

2007 Panthers Topps

COMPLETE SET (12)	2.50	5.00
1 Julius Peppers	.25	.60
2 Jake Delhomme	.25	.60
3 DeAngelo Williams	.30	.75
4 Steve Smith	.30	.75
5 Dwayne Jarrett	.25	.60
6 DeShaun Foster	.25	.60
7 Drew Carter	.20	.50
8 Chris Gamble	.20	.50
9 David Carr	.25	.60
10 John Kasay	.20	.50
11 Dan Morgan	.20	.50
12 Jon Beason	.25	.60

2008 Panthers Topps

COMPLETE SET (12)	2.50	5.00
1 Steve Smith	.25	.60
2 DeAngelo Williams	.25	.60
3 Jeff King	.20	.50
4 Julius Peppers	.25	.60
5 Jon Beason	.20	.50
6 Matt Moore	.25	.60
7 Jake Delhomme	.25	.60
8 Richard Marshall	.20	.50
9 Chris Harris	.20	.50
10 Chris Gamble	.20	.50
11 Jonathan Stewart	.60	1.50
12 Dan Connor	.40	1.00

1998 Paramount

The 1998 Pacific Paramount set was issued in one series totalling 250 cards. The cards were issued in six card packs with 36 packs per box and 20 boxes per case. Each pack had a suggested retail of $1.49 per pack. The full border fronts feature an action photo on most of the cards with the "Pacific Paramount" logo on the upper left and the players name and position on the lower left. The teams logo is on the bottom right. The back has a color portait, biographical information, seasonal and career statistics as well as some personal information

COMPLETE SET (250)	30.00	60.00
1 Larry Centers	.07	.20
2 Chris Gedney	.07	.20
3 Rob Moore	.10	.30
4 Jake Plummer	.20	.50
5 Simeon Rice	.10	.30
6 Frank Sanders	.10	.30
7 Mark Smith DE	.07	.20
8 Eric Swann	.07	.20
9 Jamal Anderson	.20	.50
10 Chris Chandler	.10	.30
11 Bert Emanuel	.10	.30
12 Tony Graziani	.07	.20
13 Byron Hanspard	.07	.20
14 Terance Mathis	.10	.30
15 O.J. Santiago	.07	.20
16 Chuck Smith	.07	.20
17 Derrick Alexander WR	.10	.30
18 Peter Boulware	.07	.20
19 Jay Graham	.07	.20
20 Priest Holmes RC	10.00	20.00
21 Michael Jackson	.07	.20
22 Byron Bam Morris	.07	.20
23 Vinny Testaverde	.10	.30
24 Eric Zeier	.10	.30
25 Todd Collins	.07	.20
26 Quinn Early	.07	.20
27 Bryce Paup	.07	.20
28 Andre Reed	.10	.30
29 Jay Riemersma	.07	.20
30 Antowain Smith	.20	.50
31 Bruce Smith	.10	.30
32 Thurman Thomas	.20	.50
33 Michael Bates	.07	.20
34 Mark Carrier WR	.07	.20
35 Rae Carruth	.07	.20
36 Kerry Collins	.10	.30
37 Fred Lane	.07	.20
38 Lamar Lathon	.07	.20
39 Muhsin Muhammad	.10	.30
40 Wesley Walls	.10	.30
41 Darnell Autry	.07	.20
42 Curtis Conway	.10	.30
43 Raymont Harris	.07	.20
44 Tyrone Hughes	.07	.20
45 Chris Penn	.07	.20
46 Ricky Proehl	.07	.20
47 Steve Stenstrom	.07	.20
48 Ryan Wetnight RC	.07	.20
49 Jeff Blake	.10	.30
50 Ki-Jana Carter	.07	.20
51 Corey Dillon	.20	.50
52 David Dunn	.07	.20
53 Boomer Esiason	.07	.20
54 Brian Milne	.07	.20
55 Carl Pickens	.10	.30
56 Darnay Scott	.10	.30
57 Troy Aikman	.40	1.00
58 Eric Bjornson	.07	.20
59 Michael Irvin	.20	.50
60 Daryl Johnston	.10	.30
61 Anthony Miller	.07	.20
62 Deion Sanders	.20	.50
63 Emmitt Smith	.60	1.50
64 Omar Stoutmire RC	.07	.20
65 Sherman Williams	.07	.20
66 Terrell Davis	.20	.50
67 John Elway	.75	2.00
68 Darrien Gordon	.07	.20
69 Ed McCaffrey	.10	.30
70 Bill Romanowski	.07	.20
71 Shannon Sharpe	.10	.30
72 Neil Smith	.10	.30
73 Rod Smith WR	.10	.30
74 Maa Tanuvasa	.07	.20
75 Tommie Boyd	.07	.20
76 Glyn Milburn	.07	.20
77 Scott Mitchell	.10	.30
78 Herman Moore	.10	.30
79 Johnnie Morton	.10	.30
80 Robert Porcher	.07	.20
81 Barry Sanders	.60	1.50
82 Bryant Westbrook	.07	.20
83 Robert Brooks	.10	.30
84 LeRoy Butler	.07	.20
85 Mark Chmura	.10	.30
86 Brett Favre	.75	2.00
87 Antonio Freeman	.20	.50
88 Dorsey Levens	.20	.50
89 Eugene Robinson	.07	.20
90 Bill Schroeder RC	.60	1.50
91 Reggie White	.20	.50
92 Aaron Bailey	.07	.20
93 Quentin Coryatt	.07	.20
94 Zack Crockett	.07	.20
95 Sean Dawkins	.07	.20
96 Ken Dilger	.07	.20
97 Marshall Faulk	.25	.60
98 Jim Harbaugh	.10	.30
99 Marvin Harrison	.20	.50
100 Bryan Barker	.07	.20
101 Tony Boselli	.07	.20
102 Tony Brackens	.07	.20
103 Mark Brunell	.20	.50
104 Mike Hollis	.07	.20
105 Keenan McCardell	.10	.30
106 Natrone Means	.10	.30
107 Jimmy Smith	.10	.30
108 James Stewart	.10	.30
109 Marcus Allen	.20	.50
110 Kimble Anders	.10	.30
111 Dale Carter	.07	.20
112 Tony Gonzalez	.20	.50
113 Elvis Grbac	.10	.30
114 Greg Hill	.07	.20
115 Andre Rison	.10	.30
116 Will Shields	.07	.20
117 Derrick Thomas	.20	.50
118 Karim Abdul-Jabbar	.20	.50
119 Trace Armstrong	.07	.20
120 Damon Huard RC	.75	2.00
121 Charles Jordan	.07	.20
122 Dan Marino	.75	2.00
123 O.J. McDuffie	.10	.30
124 Irving Spikes	.07	.20
125 Zach Thomas	.20	.50
126 Cris Carter	.20	.50
127 Charles Woodson RC	.75	2.00
128 Brad Johnson	.20	.50
129 Randall McDaniel	.07	.20
130 John Randle	.10	.30
131 Jake Reed	.10	.30
132 Robert Smith	.20	.50
133 Todd Steussie	.07	.20
134 Bruce Armstrong	.07	.20
135 Drew Bledsoe	.30	.75
136 Ben Coates	.10	.30
137 Derrick Cullors RC	.07	.20
138 Terry Glenn	.20	.50
139 Shawn Jefferson	.07	.20
140 Curtis Martin	.20	.50
141 Chris Slade	.07	.20
142 Larry Whigham	.07	.20
143 Troy Davis	.07	.20
144 Andre Hastings	.07	.20
145 Randal Hill	.07	.20
146 Sammy Knight RC	.20	.50
147 William Roaf	.07	.20
148 Heath Shuler	.07	.20
149 Danny Wuerffel	.10	.30
150 Ray Zellars	.07	.20
151 Jessie Armstead	.07	.20
152 Tiki Barber	.20	.50
153 Chris Calloway	.07	.20
154 Danny Kanell	.10	.30
155 David Patten RC	.50	1.25
156 Michael Strahan	.10	.30
157 Charles Way	.07	.20
158 Tyrone Wheatley	.10	.30
159 Kyle Brady	.07	.20
160 Wayne Chrebet	.20	.50
161 Glenn Foley	.10	.30
162 Aaron Glenn	.07	.20
163 Leon Johnson	.07	.20
164 Adrian Murrell	.10	.30
165 Neil O'Donnell	.10	.30
166 Dedric Ward	.07	.20
167 Tim Brown	.20	.50
168 Rickey Dudley	.07	.20
169 Jeff George	.10	.30
170 Desmond Howard	.10	.30

171 James Jett .10 .30
172 Napoleon Kaufman .20 .50
173 Chester McGlockton .07 .20
174 Darrell Russell .07 .20
175 Ty Detmer .10 .30
176 Irving Fryar .10 .30
177 Charlie Garner .10 .30
178 Bobby Hoying .10 .30
179 Chad Lewis .10 .30
180 Duce Staley .25 .60
181 Kevin Turner .07 .20
182 Ricky Watters .10 .30
183 Jerome Bettis .20 .50
184 Will Blackwell .07 .20
185 Charles Johnson .07 .20
186 George Jones .07 .20
187 Levon Kirkland .07 .20
188 Carnell Lake .07 .20
189 Kordell Stewart .20 .50
190 Yancey Thigpen .07 .20
191 Tony Banks .10 .30
192 Isaac Bruce .20 .50
193 Ernie Conwell .07 .20
194 Craig Heyward .07 .20
195 Eddie Kennison .10 .30
196 Amp Lee .07 .20
197 Orlando Pace .07 .20
198 Torrance Small .07 .20
199 Gary Brown .07 .20
200 Kenny Bynum RC .07 .20
201 Freddie Jones .07 .20
202 Tony Martin .10 .30
203 Eric Metcalf .07 .20
204 Junior Seau .20 .50
205 Craig Whelihan RC .07 .20
206 William Floyd .07 .20
207 Merton Hanks .07 .20
208 Garrison Hearst .20 .50
209 Brent Jones .07 .20
210 Terrell Owens .20 .50
211 Jerry Rice .40 1.00
212 J.J. Stokes .10 .30
213 Rod Woodson .10 .30
214 Steve Young .20 .50
215 Steve Broussard .07 .20
216 Joey Galloway .10 .30
217 Cortez Kennedy .07 .20
218 Jon Kitna .20 .50
219 James McKnight .20 .50
220 Warren Moon .20 .50
221 Michael Sinclair .07 .20
222 Ryan Leaf RC .50 1.25
223 Darryl Williams .07 .20
224 Mike Alstott .20 .50
225 Reidel Anthony .10 .30
226 Derrick Brooks .20 .50
227 Horace Copeland .07 .20
228 Trent Dilfer .20 .50
229 Warrick Dunn .20 .50
230 Hardy Nickerson .07 .20
231 Warren Sapp .10 .30
232 Karl Williams .07 .20
233 Blaine Bishop .07 .20
234 Willie Davis .07 .20
235 Eddie George .20 .50
236 Derrick Mason .10 .30
237 Bruce Matthews .07 .20
238 Steve McNair .20 .50
239 Chris Sanders .07 .20
240 Rodney Thomas .07 .20
241 Frank Wycheck .07 .20
242 Terry Allen .20 .50
243 Jamie Asher .07 .20
244 Larry Bowie .07 .20
245 Albert Connell .07 .20
246 Stephen Davis .07 .20
247 Gus Frerotte .07 .20
248 Ken Harvey .07* .20
249 Leslie Shepherd .07 .20
250 Michael Westbrook .10 .30
S1 Mark Brunell Sample .40 1.00

1998 Paramount Copper

COMP.COPPER SET (250) 40.00 80.00
*COPPER STARS: 1.5X TO 3X BASIC CARDS
*COPPER RCs: .6X TO 1.5X
COPPER STATED ODDS 1:1 HOBBY

1998 Paramount Platinum Blue

*PLAT.BLUE STARS: 5X TO 12X
*PLAT.BLUE ROOKIES: 2X TO 5X
PLAT.BLUE STATED ODDS 1:73

1998 Paramount Red

COMP.RED SET (250) 60.00 120.00
*RED STARS: 1.5X TO 4X BASIC CARDS
*RED RCs: .8X TO 2X
ONE PER SPECIAL RETAIL

1998 Paramount Silver

COMP.SILVER SET (250) 40.00 80.00
*SILVER STARS: 1.5X TO 3X BASIC CARDS
*SILVER RCs: .6X TO 1.5X
ONE PER RETAIL PACK

1998 Paramount Kings of the NFL

COMPLETE SET (20) 50.00 120.00
STATED ODDS 1:73
*PROOF CARDS: 5X TO 12X BASIC INSERTS
PROOFS STATED PRINT RUN 20 SETS
1 Antowain Smith 2.00 5.00
2 Corey Dillon 2.00 5.00
3 Troy Aikman 4.00 10.00
4 Emmitt Smith 6.00 15.00
5 Terrell Davis 2.00 5.00
6 John Elway 8.00 20.00
7 Barry Sanders 6.00 15.00
8 Brett Favre 8.00 20.00
9 Dorsey Levens 2.00 5.00
10 Reggie White 2.00 5.00
11 Mark Brunell 2.00 5.00
12 Dan Marino 8.00 20.00
13 Curtis Martin 2.00 5.00
14 Drew Bledsoe 3.00 8.00
15 Jerome Bettis 2.00 5.00
16 Kordell Stewart 2.00 5.00
17 Jerry Rice 4.00 10.00
18 Steve Young 2.00 5.00
19 Warrick Dunn 2.00 5.00
20 Eddie George 2.00 5.00

1998 Paramount Personal Bests

COMPLETE SET (36) 25.00 60.00
STATED ODDS 4:37
1 Jake Plummer .60 1.50
2 Antowain Smith .40 1.00
3 Kerry Collins .40 1.00
4 Raymont Harris .25 .60
5 Corey Dillon .60 1.50
6 Troy Aikman 1.25 3.00
7 Deion Sanders .60 1.50
8 Emmitt Smith 2.00 5.00
9 Terrell Davis .60 1.50
10 John Elway 2.50 6.00
11 Shannon Sharpe .40 1.00
12 Herman Moore .25 .60
13 Barry Sanders 2.00 5.00
14 Brett Favre 2.50 6.00
15 Antonio Freeman .40 1.00
16 Dorsey Levens .40 1.00
17 Marshall Faulk .75 2.00
18 Mark Brunell .60 1.50
19 Dan Marino 2.50 6.00
20 Robert Smith .40 1.00
21 Curtis Martin .60 1.50
22 Drew Bledsoe 1.00 2.50
23 Danny Kanell .25 .60
24 Adrian Murrell .25 .60
25 Napoleon Kaufman .40 1.00
26 Jerome Bettis .60 1.50
27 Kordell Stewart .60 1.50
28 Terrell Owens .60 1.50
29 Jerry Rice 1.25 3.00
30 Steve Young .75 2.00
31 Warren Moon .60 1.50
32 Mike Alstott .60 1.50
33 Trent Dilfer .40 1.00
34 Warrick Dunn .60 1.50
35 Eddie George .60 1.50
36 Steve McNair .60 1.50

1998 Paramount Pro Bowl Die Cuts

COMPLETE SET (20) 40.00 100.00
STATED ODDS 1:37
1 Terrell Davis 2.50 6.00
2 John Elway 10.00 25.00
3 Shannon Sharpe 1.50 4.00
4 Herman Moore 1.50 4.00
5 Barry Sanders 8.00 20.00
6 Mark Chmura 1.50 4.00
7 Brett Favre 10.00 25.00
8 Dorsey Levens 2.50 6.00
9 Mark Brunell 2.50 6.00
10 Andre Rison 1.50 4.00
11 Cris Carter 2.50 6.00
12 Drew Bledsoe 4.00 10.00
13 Ben Coates 1.50 4.00
14 Jerome Bettis 2.50 6.00
15 Steve Young 2.50 6.00
16 Warren Moon 2.50 6.00
17 Mike Alstott 2.50 6.00
18 Trent Dilfer 2.50 6.00
19 Warrick Dunn 2.50 6.00
20 Eddie George 2.50 6.00

1998 Paramount Super Bowl XXXII

COMPLETE SET (10) 30.00 60.00
STATED ODDS 2:37
1 Terrell Davis 2.00 5.00
2 John Elway 8.00 20.00
3 John Elway 8.00 20.00
4 Brett Favre 8.00 20.00
5 Antonio Freeman 2.00 5.00
6 Dorsey Levens 2.00 5.00
7 Ed McCaffrey 1.25 3.00
8 Eugene Robinson .75 2.00
9 Bill Romanowski .75 2.00
10 Darren Sharper 1.25 3.00

1999 Paramount

This 250 card set was issued in six card packs and released in July, 1999. The set is sequenced in alphabetical order which is also in team order. Notable Rookie Cards in this set include Tim Couch, Edgerrin James and Ricky Williams.

COMPLETE SET (250) 20.00 50.00
1 David Boston RC .25 .60
2 Larry Centers .15 .40
3 Joel Makovicka RC .20 .50
4 Eric Metcalf .12 .30
5 Rob Moore .12 .30
6 Adrian Murrell .15 .40
7 Jake Plummer .15 .40
8 Frank Sanders .12 .30
9 Aeneas Williams .12 .30
10 Morten Andersen .12 .30
11 Jamal Anderson .15 .40
12 Chris Chandler .15 .40
13 Tim Dwight .15 .40
14 Terance Mathis .12 .30
15 Jeff Paulk RC .20 .50
16 O.J. Santiago .12 .30
17 Chuck Smith .12 .30
18 Peter Boulware .12 .30
19 Priest Holmes .20 .50
20 Michael Jackson .12 .30
21 Jermaine Lewis .12 .30
22 Ray Lewis .20 .50
23 Michael McCrary .12 .30
24 Bennie Thompson .12 .30
25 Rod Woodson .20 .50
26 Shawn Bryson RC .20 .50
27 Doug Flutie .20 .50
28 Eric Moulds .15 .40
29 Peerless Price RC .25 .60
30 Andre Reed .20 .50
31 Jay Riemersma .12 .30
32 Antowain Smith .12 .30
33 Bruce Smith .20 .50
34 Michael Bates .12 .30
35 Steve Beuerlein .15 .40
36 Tim Biakabutuka .15 .40
37 Kevin Greene .15 .40
38 Anthony Johnson .12 .30
39 Fred Lane .12 .30
40 Muhsin Muhammad .15 .40
41 Wesley Walls .15 .40
42 D'Wayne Bates RC .20 .50
43 Edgar Bennett .15 .40
44 Marty Booker RC .25 .60
45 Curtis Conway .15 .40
46 Bobby Engram .15 .40
47 Curtis Enis .12 .30
48 Erik Kramer .15 .40
49 Cade McNown RC .25 .60
50 Jeff Blake .15 .40
51 Scott Covington RC .20 .50
52 Corey Dillon .15 .40
53 Quincy Jackson RC .20 .50
54 Carl Pickens .15 .40
55 Darnay Scott .12 .30
56 Akili Smith RC .25 .60
57 Craig Yeast RC .20 .50
58 Jerry Ball .12 .30
59 Darrin Chiaverini RC .20 .50
60 Tim Couch RC .30 .75
61 Ty Detmer .15 .40
62 Kevin Johnson RC .25 .60
63 Terry Kirby .12 .30
64 Daylon McCutcheon RC .20 .50
65 Irv Smith .12 .30
66 Troy Aikman .30 .75
67 Ebenezer Ekuban RC .20 .50
68 Michael Irvin .20 .50
69 Daryl Johnston .20 .50
70 Wane McGarity RC .20 .50
71 Dat Nguyen RC .30 .75
72 Deion Sanders .20 .50
73 Emmitt Smith .50 1.25
74 Bubby Brister .12 .30
75 Terrell Davis .20 .50
76 Jason Elam .12 .30
77 Olandis Gary RC .30 .75
78 Brian Griese .15 .40
79 Ed McCaffrey .15 .40
80 Travis McGriff RC .20 .50
81 Shannon Sharpe .20 .50
82 Rod Smith .15 .40
83 Charlie Batch .15 .40
84 Chris Claiborne RC .20 .50
85 Germane Crowell .12 .30
86 Sedrick Irvin RC .20 .50
87 Herman Moore .15 .40
88 Johnnie Morton .15 .40
89 Barry Sanders .50 1.25
90 Robert Brooks .15 .40
91 Aaron Brooks RC .30 .75
92 Mark Chmura .12 .30
93 Brett Favre .60 1.50
94 Antonio Freeman .15 .40
95 Vonnie Holliday .12 .30
96 Dorsey Levens .15 .40
97 De'Mond Parker RC .20 .50
98 Ken Dilger .12 .30
99 Marvin Harrison .20 .50
100 Edgerrin James RC .40 1.00
101 Peyton Manning .60 1.50
102 Jerome Pathon .12 .30
103 Mike Peterson RC .25 .60
104 Marcus Pollard .12 .30
105 Tavian Banks .12 .30
106 Reggie Barlow .12 .30
107 Tony Boselli .15 .40
108 Mark Brunell .15 .40
109 Keenan McCardell .15 .40
110 Bryce Paup .12 .30
111 Jimmy Smith .15 .40
112 Fred Taylor .15 .40
113 Dave Thomas RC .25 .60
114 Kimble Anders .12 .30
115 Donnell Bennett .12 .30
116 Mike Cloud RC .20 .50
117 Tony Gonzalez .20 .50
118 Elvis Grbac .12 .30
119 Larry Parker RC .25 .60
120 Andre Rison .15 .40
121 Brian Shay RC .20 .50
122 Karim Abdul-Jabbar .15 .40
123 Oronde Gadsden .12 .30
124 James Johnson RC .20 .50
125 Rob Konrad RC .20 .50
126 Dan Marino .60 1.50
127 O.J. McDuffie .15 .40
128 Zach Thomas .20 .50
129 Cris Carter .20 .50
130 Daunte Culpepper RC .30 .75
131 Randall Cunningham .20 .50
132 Matthew Hatchette .15 .40
133 Leroy Hoard .12 .30
134 Randy Moss .20 .50
135 John Randle .15 .40
136 Jake Reed .15 .40
137 Robert Smith .15 .40
138 Michael Bishop RC .25 .60
139 Drew Bledsoe .20 .50
140 Ben Coates .15 .40
141 Kevin Faulk RC .30 .75
142 Terry Glenn .15 .40
143 Shawn Jefferson .12 .30
144 Andy Katzenmoyer RC .25 .60
145 Tony Simmons .12 .30
146 Cuncho Brown RC .20 .50
147 Cam Cleeland .12 .30
148 Mark Fields .12 .30
149 La'Roi Glover RC .30 .75
150 Andre Hastings .12 .30
151 Billy Joe Hobert .12 .30
152 William Roaf .15 .40
153 Billy Joe Tolliver .12 .30
154 Ricky Williams RC .50 1.25
155 Jessie Armstead .15 .40
156 Tiki Barber .20 .50
157 Gary Brown .12 .30
158 Kent Graham .12 .30
159 Ike Hilliard .15 .40
160 Joe Montgomery RC .20 .50
161 Amani Toomer .15 .40
162 Charles Way .12 .30
163 Wayne Chrebet .15 .40
164 Bryan Cox .15 .40
165 Aaron Glenn .12 .30
166 Keyshawn Johnson .15 .40
167 Leon Johnson .12 .30
168 Curtis Martin .20 .50
169 Vinny Testaverde .15 .40
170 Dedric Ward .12 .30
171 Tim Brown .20 .50
172 Dameane Douglas RC .20 .50
173 Rickey Dudley .12 .30
174 James Jett .12 .30
175 Napoleon Kaufman .12 .30
176 Darrell Russell .12 .30
177 Harvey Williams .12 .30
178 Charles Woodson .20 .50
179 Na Brown RC .20 .50
180 Hugh Douglas .15 .40
181 Cecil Martin RC .20 .50
182 Donovan McNabb RC 1.50 4.00
183 Duce Staley .15 .40
184 Kevin Turner .12 .30
185 Jerome Bettis .20 .50
186 Troy Edwards RC .25 .60
187 Jason Gildon .15 .40
188 Courtney Hawkins .12 .30
189 Malcolm Johnson RC .20 .50
190 Kordell Stewart .15 .40
191 Jerame Tuman RC .20 .50
192 Amos Zereoue RC .25 .60
193 Isaac Bruce .20 .50
194 Kevin Carter .12 .30
195 Jeremaine Copeland RC .25 .60
196 Joe Germaine RC .25 .60
197 Az-Zahir Hakim .12 .30
198 Torry Holt RC .50 1.25
199 Amp Lee .12 .30
200 Ricky Proehl .12 .30
201 Charlie Jones .12 .30
202 Freddie Jones .12 .30
203 Ryan Leaf .15 .40
204 Natrone Means .15 .40
205 Mikhael Ricks .12 .30
206 Junior Seau .20 .50
207 Bryan Still .12 .30
208 Garrison Hearst .15 .40
209 Terry Jackson RC .20 .50
210 R.W. McQuarters .12 .30
211 Ken Norton Jr. .12 .30
212 Terrell Owens .20 .50
213 Jerry Rice .40 1.00
214 J.J. Stokes .12 .30
215 Tai Streets RC .25 .60
216 Steve Young .25 .60
217 Karsten Bailey RC .20 .50
218 Chad Brown .12 .30
219 Joey Galloway .15 .40
220 Ahman Green .15 .40
221 Brock Huard RC .25 .60
222 Cortez Kennedy .12 .30
223 Jon Kitna .15 .40
224 Shawn Springs .12 .30
225 Ricky Watters .15 .40
226 Mike Alstott .20 .50
227 Reidel Anthony .12 .30
228 Trent Dilfer .15 .40
229 Warrick Dunn .15 .40
230 Bert Emanuel .15 .40
231 Martin Gramatica RC .20 .50
232 Jacquez Green .12 .30
233 Shaun King RC .25 .60
234 Anthony McFarland RC .25 .60
235 Warren Sapp .15 .40
236 Willie Davis .12 .30
237 Kevin Dyson .12 .30
238 Eddie George .15 .40
239 Darran Hall RC .20 .50
240 Jackie Harris .15 .40
241 Steve McNair .20 .50
242 Yancey Thigpen .12 .30
243 Frank Wycheck .15 .40
244 Stephen Alexander .12 .30
245 Champ Bailey RC .60 1.50
246 Stephen Davis .15 .40
247 Darrell Green .20 .50
248 Skip Hicks .12 .30
249 Brian Mitchell .15 .40
250 Michael Westbrook .12 .30

1999 Paramount Copper

COMPLETE SET (250) 60.00 120.00
*COPPER STARS: 1.2X TO 3X BASIC CARDS
*COPPER RCs: .5X TO 1.2X BASIC CARDS
ONE PER HOBBY PACK

1999 Paramount Premiere Date

*PREM.DATE STARS: 15X TO 40X BASIC CARDS
*PREMIERE DATE ROOKIES: 4X TO 10X
PREM.DATE STATED ODDS 1:37 HOB
PREMIERE DATE PRINT RUN 62 SER.#'d SETS

1999 Paramount Gold

COMPLETE SET (250) 60.00 120.00
*GOLD STARS: 1.25X TO 3X BASIC CARDS
*GOLD RCs: .5X TO 1.2X BASIC CARDS
GOLDS ONE PER RETAIL PACK

1999 Paramount HoloGold

*HOLO.GOLD STARS: 8X TO 20X BASIC CARDS
*HOLO.GOLD ROOKIES: 2.5X TO 6X
HOLO.GOLD PRINT RUN 199 SERIAL #'d SETS
HOLO.GOLDS INSERTED IN RETAIL PACKS

1999 Paramount HoloSilver

*HOLO.SILVER STARS: 12X TO 30X BASIC CARDS
*HOLO.SILVER ROOKIES: 4X TO 10X
HOLO.SILVER PRINT RUN 99 SERIAL #'d SETS
HOLO.SILVER INSERTED IN HOBBY PACKS

1999 Paramount Platinum Blue

*PLAT.BLUE STARS: 8X TO 20X BASIC CARDS
*PLATINUM BLUE ROOKIES: 2.5X TO 6X
PLATINUM BLUE STATED ODDS 1:73

1999 Paramount Canton Bound

COMPLETE SET (10) 60.00 150.00
STATED ODDS 1:361
*PROOFS: 1.2X TO 3X
PROOFS STATED PRINT RUN 20 SER.#'d SETS
1 Troy Aikman 8.00 20.00
2 Emmitt Smith 8.00 20.00
3 Terrell Davis 4.00 10.00
4 Barry Sanders 12.50 30.00
5 Brett Favre 12.50 30.00
6 Dan Marino 12.50 30.00
7 Randy Moss 10.00 25.00
8 Drew Bledsoe 5.00 12.00
9 Jerry Rice 8.00 20.00
10 Steve Young 5.00 12.00

1999 Paramount End Zone Net-Fusions

COMPLETE SET (20) 60.00 150.00
STATED ODDS 1:73
1 Jake Plummer 1.50 4.00
2 Jamal Anderson 2.50 6.00
3 Doug Flutie 2.50 6.00
4 Tim Couch 1.50 4.00
5 Troy Aikman 5.00 12.00
6 Emmitt Smith 5.00 12.00
7 Terrell Davis 2.50 6.00
8 Barry Sanders 8.00 20.00
9 Brett Favre 8.00 20.00
10 Peyton Manning 8.00 20.00
11 Mark Brunell 2.50 6.00
12 Fred Taylor 2.50 6.00
13 Dan Marino 8.00 20.00
14 Randy Moss 6.00 15.00
15 Drew Bledsoe 3.00 8.00
16 Ricky Williams 3.00 8.00
17 Jerry Rice 5.00 12.00
18 Steve Young 3.00 8.00
19 Jon Kitna 2.50 6.00
20 Eddie George 2.50 6.00

1999 Paramount Personal Bests

COMPLETE SET (36) 50.00 120.00
STATED ODDS 1:37
1 Jake Plummer .75 2.00
2 Jamal Anderson 1.25 3.00
3 Priest Holmes 2.00 5.00
4 Doug Flutie 1.25 3.00
5 Antowain Smith 1.25 3.00
6 Corey Dillon 1.25 3.00
7 Akili Smith .40 1.00
8 Tim Couch .60 1.50
9 Troy Aikman 2.50 6.00
10 Emmitt Smith 2.50 6.00
11 Terrell Davis 1.25 3.00
12 Barry Sanders 4.00 10.00
13 Brett Favre 4.00 10.00
14 Antonio Freeman 1.25 3.00
15 Edgerrin James 2.50 6.00
16 Peyton Manning 4.00 10.00
17 Mark Brunell 1.25 3.00
18 Fred Taylor 1.25 3.00
19 Dan Marino 4.00 10.00
20 Randall Cunningham 1.25 3.00
21 Randy Moss 3.00 8.00
22 Drew Bledsoe 1.50 4.00
23 Kevin Faulk .60 1.50
24 Ricky Williams 1.25 3.00
25 Curtis Martin 1.25 3.00
26 Napoleon Kaufman 1.25 3.00
27 Donovan McNabb 3.00 8.00
28 Jerome Bettis 1.25 3.00
29 Kordell Stewart .75 2.00
30 Terrell Owens 1.25 3.00
31 Jerry Rice 2.50 6.00
32 Steve Young 1.50 4.00
33 Jon Kitna 1.25 3.00
34 Warrick Dunn 1.25 3.00
35 Eddie George 1.25 3.00
36 Steve McNair 1.25 3.00

1999 Paramount Team Checklists

COMPLETE SET (31) 40.00 100.00
STATED ODDS 2:37
1 Jake Plummer 1.00 2.50
2 Jamal Anderson 1.50 4.00
3 Priest Holmes 2.50 6.00
4 Doug Flutie 1.50 4.00
5 Muhsin Muhammad 1.00 2.50
6 Cade McNown .50 1.25
7 Corey Dillon 1.50 4.00
8 Tim Couch .75 2.00
9 Troy Aikman 3.00 8.00
10 Terrell Davis 1.50 4.00
11 Barry Sanders 5.00 12.00
12 Brett Favre 5.00 12.00
13 Peyton Manning 5.00 12.00
14 Fred Taylor 1.50 4.00
15 Elvis Grbac 1.00 2.50
16 Dan Marino 5.00 12.00
17 Randy Moss 4.00 10.00
18 Drew Bledsoe 2.00 5.00
19 Ricky Williams 1.50 4.00
20 Ike Hilliard .60 1.50
21 Curtis Martin 1.50 4.00
22 Napoleon Kaufman 1.50 4.00
23 Donovan McNabb 4.00 10.00
24 Jerome Bettis 1.50 4.00
25 Torry Holt 2.00 5.00
26 Natrone Means 1.00 2.50
27 Jerry Rice 3.00 8.00
28 Jon Kitna 1.50 4.00
29 Warrick Dunn 1.50 4.00
30 Eddie George 1.50 4.00
31 Skip Hicks .60 1.50

2000 Paramount

Released as a 249-card base set, Paramount cards are numbered from 1-250. Shortly before release, card number 242 was intended to have been pulled from production, but apparently a very small number of cards packed out. Base cards feature a white border with full color player action photography and a background colored to match the featured player's team colors. Paramount was packaged in 36-pack boxes with packs containing six cards each.

COMPLETE SET (249) 15.00 40.00
1 David Boston .12 .30
2 Thomas Jones RC .40 1.00
3 Rob Moore .12 .30
4 Jake Plummer .15 .40
5 Simeon Rice .15 .40
6 Frank Sanders .12 .30
7 Raynoch Thompson RC .20 .50
8 Jamal Anderson .15 .40
9 Chris Chandler .15 .40
10 Bob Christian .12 .30
11 Tim Dwight .15 .40
12 Byron Hanspard .12 .30
13 Terance Mathis .12 .30
14 Mareno Philyaw RC .20 .50
15 Tony Banks .12 .30
16 Priest Holmes .20 .50
17 Qadry Ismail .15 .40
18 Pat Johnson .12 .30
19 Jamal Lewis RC .30 .75
20 Chris Redman RC .25 .60
21 Shannon Sharpe .20 .50
22 Travis Taylor RC .25 .60
23 Erik Flowers RC .20 .50
24 Doug Flutie .20 .50
25 Rob Johnson .15 .40
26 Jonathan Linton .12 .30
27 Corey Moore RC .20 .50
28 Eric Moulds .15 .40
29 Peerless Price .15 .40
30 Jay Riemersma .12 .30
31 Antowain Smith .15 .40
32 Rashard Anderson RC .20 .50
33 Steve Beuerlein .15 .40
34 Tim Biakabutuka .15 .40
35 Donald Hayes .12 .30
36 Patrick Jeffers .15 .40
37 Jeff Lewis .12 .30
38 Muhsin Muhammad .15 .40
39 Wesley Walls .12 .30
40 Bobby Engram .15 .40
41 Curtis Enis .12 .30
42 Cade McNown .12 .30
43 Jim Miller .12 .30
44 Marcus Robinson .15 .40
45 Brian Urlacher RC 1.25 3.00
46 Dez White RC .25 .60
47 Michael Basnight .12 .30
48 Corey Dillon .15 .40
49 Ron Dugans RC .20 .50
50 Willie Jackson .12 .30
51 Darnay Scott .15 .40
52 Akili Smith .12 .30
53 Peter Warrick RC .30 .75
54 Courtney Brown RC .25 .60
55 Darrin Chiaverini .12 .30
56 Tim Couch .15 .40
57 Kevin Johnson .12 .30
58 Terry Kirby .12 .30
59 Dennis Northcutt RC .25 .60
60 Travis Prentice RC .25 .60
61 Leslie Shepherd .12 .30
62 Troy Aikman .30 .75
63 Joey Galloway .15 .40
64 Rocket Ismail .15 .40
65 David LaFleur .12 .30
66 Emmitt Smith .50 1.25
67 Jason Tucker .12 .30
68 Chris Warren .12 .30
69 Michael Wiley RC .20 .50
70 Desmond Clark .12 .30
71 Chris Cole RC .25 .60
72 Terrell Davis .20 .50
73 Olandis Gary .15 .40
74 Brian Griese .15 .40
75 Jarious Jackson RC .25 .60
76 Ed McCaffrey .15 .40
77 Deltha O'Neal RC .25 .60
78 Rod Smith .15 .40
79 Charlie Batch .15 .40
80 Germane Crowell .12 .30
81 Reuben Droughns RC .30 .75
82 Terry Fair .12 .30
83 Herman Moore .15 .40
84 Johnnie Morton .15 .40
85 Barry Sanders .40 1.00
86 James Stewart .12 .30
87 Corey Bradford .12 .30
88 Tyrone Davis .12 .30
89 Brett Favre .60 1.50
90 Bubba Franks RC .30 .75
91 Antonio Freeman .15 .40
92 Matt Hasselbeck .20 .50
93 Dorsey Levens .15 .40
94 Anthony Lucas RC .20 .50
95 Bill Schroeder .15 .40
96 Ken Dilger .12 .30
97 E.G. Green .12 .30
98 Marvin Harrison .20 .50
99 Edgerrin James .20 .50
100 Peyton Manning .50 1.25
101 Jerome Pathon .12 .30
102 Marcus Washington RC .25 .60
103 Terrence Wilkins .12 .30
104 Kyle Brady .12 .30
105 Mark Brunell .15 .40
106 Kevin Hardy .12 .30
107 Keenan McCardell .15 .40
108 Jimmy Smith .15 .40
109 R.Jay Soward RC .20 .50
110 Shyrone Stith RC .20 .50
111 Fred Taylor .20 .50
112 Alvis Whitted .12 .30
113 Derrick Alexander .12 .30
114 Kimble Anders .12 .30
115 Donnell Bennett .12 .30
116 Tony Gonzalez .20 .50
117 Elvis Grbac .12 .30
118 Kevin Lockett .12 .30
119 Sylvester Morris RC .20 .50
120 Tony Richardson RC .25 .60
121 Deon Dyer RC .20 .50
122 Oronde Gadsden .15 .40
123 Damon Huard .15 .40
124 James Johnson .12 .30
125 Dan Marino .60 1.50
126 Tony Martin .15 .40
127 O.J. McDuffie .15 .40
128 Zach Thomas .20 .50
129 Cris Carter .20 .50
130 Daunte Culpepper .15 .40
131 Leroy Hoard .12 .30
132 Chris Hovan RC .25 .60
133 Randy Moss .20 .50
134 John Randle .15 .40
135 Robert Smith .15 .40
136 Troy Walters RC .20 .50
137 Drew Bledsoe .20 .50
138 Tom Brady RC 10.00 25.00
139 Troy Brown .15 .40
140 Kevin Faulk .15 .40
141 Terry Glenn .15 .40
142 J.R. Redmond RC .20 .50
143 Tony Simmons .12 .30
144 David Stachelski RC .20 .50
145 Jeff Blake .15 .40
146 Marc Bulger RC .30 .75
147 Cam Cleeland .12 .30
148 Sherrod Gideon RC .20 .50
149 Darren Howard RC .20 .50
150 Chad Morton RC .30 .75
151 Keith Poole .12 .30
152 Ricky Williams .20 .50
153 Tiki Barber .20 .50
154 Kerry Collins .15 .40
155 Ron Dayne RC .30 .75
156 Ike Hilliard .15 .40
157 Joe Jurevicius .12 .30
158 Pete Mitchell .12 .30
159 Joe Montgomery .12 .30
160 Amani Toomer .15 .40
161 John Abraham RC .30 .75
162 Anthony Becht RC .25 .60
163 Wayne Chrebet .15 .40
164 Laveranues Coles RC .30 .75
165 Ray Lucas .12 .30
166 Curtis Martin .20 .50
167 Chad Pennington RC .50 1.25
168 Vinny Testaverde .15 .40
169 Dedric Ward .12 .30
170 Tim Brown .20 .50
171 Rich Gannon .15 .40
172 Bobby Hoying .12 .30
173 James Jett .15 .40
174 Napoleon Kaufman .15 .40
175 Jerry Porter RC .30 .75
176 Tyrone Wheatley .12 .30
177 Charles Woodson .20 .50
178 Dameane Douglas .12 .30
179 Charles Johnson .12 .30
180 Donovan McNabb .20 .50
181 Todd Pinkston RC .20 .50
182 Gari Scott RC .20 .50
183 Torrance Small .12 .30
184 Duce Staley .15 .40
185 Jerome Bettis .20 .50
186 Plaxico Burress RC .30 .75
187 Troy Edwards .12 .30
188 Danny Farmer RC .20 .50
189 Richard Huntley .12 .30
190 Tee Martin RC .30 .75
191 Kordell Stewart .15 .40
192 Hines Ward .20 .50
193 Isaac Bruce .20 .50
194 Trung Canidate RC .25 .60
195 Marshall Faulk .20 .50
196 Az-Zahir Hakim .12 .30
197 Torry Holt .20 .50
198 Tony Horne .12 .30
199 Ricky Proehl .12 .30
200 Kurt Warner .30 .75
201 Jermaine Fazande .12 .30
202 Trevor Gaylor RC .20 .50
203 Jeff Graham .12 .30
204 Jim Harbaugh .15 .40
205 Freddie Jones .12 .30
206 Mikhael Ricks .12 .30
207 Junior Seau .20 .50
208 Fred Beasley .12 .30
209 Giovanni Carmazzi RC .20 .50
210 Jeff Garcia .15 .40
211 Charlie Garner .15 .40
212 Terrell Owens .20 .50
213 Tim Rattay RC .25 .60
214 Jerry Rice .40 1.00
215 J.J. Stokes .15 .40
216 Steve Young .25 .60
217 Shaun Alexander RC .40 1.00
218 Sean Dawkins .12 .30
219 Darrell Jackson RC .25 .60
220 Jon Kitna .15 .40
221 Derrick Mayes .12 .30
222 Charlie Rogers .12 .30
223 Shawn Springs .12 .30
224 Ricky Watters .15 .40
225 Mike Alstott .20 .50
226 Reidel Anthony .12 .30
227 Warrick Dunn .15 .40
228 Jacquez Green .12 .30
229 Joe Hamilton RC .20 .50
230 Keyshawn Johnson .15 .40
231 Shaun King .12 .30
232 Warren Sapp .15 .40
233 Keith Bulluck RC .25 .60
234 Kevin Dyson .15 .40
235 Eddie George .15 .40
236 Jevon Kearse .15 .40
237 Erron Kinney RC .20 .50
238 Steve McNair .20 .50
239 Neil O'Donnell .12 .30
240 Yancy Thigpen .12 .30
241 Frank Wycheck .15 .40
242 Julian Peterson SP RC 20.00 40.00
243 Champ Bailey .15 .40
244 Larry Centers .12 .30
245 Albert Connell .12 .30
246 Stephen Davis .15 .40
247 Todd Husak RC .20 .50
248 Brad Johnson .15 .40
249 Chris Samuels RC .25 .60
250 Michael Westbrook .12 .30

2000 Paramount Draft Picks 325

*ROOKIES/325: 2.5X TO 6X BASIC CARDS
STATED PRINT RUN 325 SERIAL #'d SETS
138 Tom Brady 100.00 175.00

2000 Paramount HoloGold

*VETS: 6X TO 15X BASIC CARDS
*ROOKIES: 4X TO 10X BASIC CARDS
RETAIL HOLOGOLD PRINT RUN 130
138 Tom Brady 150.00 250.00

2000 Paramount HoloSilver

*VETS: 10X TO 25X BASIC CARDS
*ROOKIES: 6X TO 15X BASIC CARDS
HOBBY HOLOSILVER PRINT RUN 85
138 Tom Brady 150.00 300.00

2000 Paramount Platinum Blue

*VETS: 10X TO 25X BASIC CARDS
*ROOKIES: 6X TO 15X BASIC CARDS
PLATINUM BLUE PRINT RUN 75
138 Tom Brady 175.00 300.00

2000 Paramount Premiere Date

*VETERANS: 10X TO 25X BASIC CARDS
*ROOKIES: 6X TO 15X BASIC CARDS
HOBBY PREM.DATE PRINT RUN 79
138 Tom Brady 175.00 300.00

2000 Paramount Draft Report

COMPLETE SET (31) 25.00 60.00
STATED ODDS 2:37
*NATIONAL LOGO/20: 8X TO 20X BASIC INSERT
1 Thomas Jones .75 2.00
2 Mareno Philyaw .40 1.00
3 Jamal Lewis .60 1.50
4 Erik Flowers .40 1.00
5 Rashard Anderson .40 1.00
6 Dez White .50 1.25
7 Peter Warrick .60 1.50
8 Dennis Northcutt .50 1.25
9 Michael Wiley .40 1.00
10 Deltha O'Neal .50 1.25
11 Reuben Droughns .60 1.50
12 Anthony Lucas .40 1.00
13 Marcus Washington UER .50 1.25
(listed as DE on front; LB on back)
14 R.Jay Soward .40 1.00
15 Sylvester Morris .40 1.00
16 Deon Dyer .40 1.00
17 Troy Walters .40 1.00
18 J.R. Redmond .40 1.00
19 Marc Bulger .60 1.50
20 Ron Dayne .60 1.50
21 Chad Pennington 1.00 2.50
22 Jerry Porter .60 1.50
23 Todd Pinkston .40 1.00
24 Plaxico Burress .60 1.50
25 Trung Canidate .50 1.25
26 Trevor Gaylor .40 1.00
27 Giovanni Carmazzi .40 1.00
28 Shaun Alexander .75 2.00
29 Joe Hamilton .40 1.00
30 Erron Kinney .40 1.00
31 Todd Husak .40 1.00

2000 Paramount End Zone Net-Fusions

COMPLETE SET (20) 30.00 80.00
STATED ODDS 1:73
1 Jake Plummer 1.25 3.00
2 Cade McNown 1.00 2.50
3 Tim Couch 1.25 3.00
4 Troy Aikman 3.00 8.00
5 Emmitt Smith 4.00 10.00
6 Terrell Davis 1.50 4.00
7 Brett Favre 5.00 12.00
8 Edgerrin James 1.50 4.00
9 Peyton Manning 4.00 10.00
10 Mark Brunell 1.25 3.00
11 Fred Taylor 1.50 4.00
12 Drew Bledsoe 1.50 4.00
13 Ricky Williams 1.50 4.00
14 Randy Moss 1.50 4.00
15 Marshall Faulk 1.50 4.00
16 Kurt Warner 2.50 6.00
17 Jerry Rice 3.00 8.00
18 Jon Kitna 1.25 3.00
19 Eddie George 1.25 3.00
20 Stephen Davis 1.25 3.00

2000 Paramount Game Used Footballs

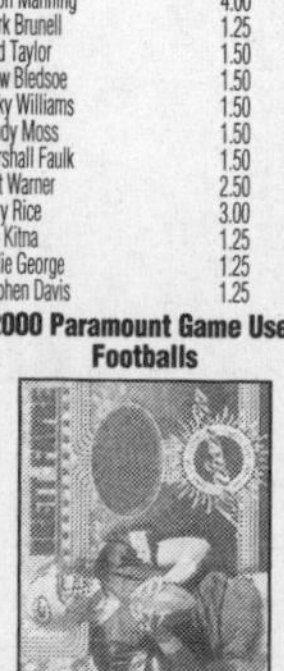

1 Troy Aikman	8.00	20.00
2 Emmitt Smith	12.00	30.00
3 Olandis Gary	4.00	10.00
4 Brett Favre	15.00	40.00
5 Edgerrin James	5.00	12.00
6 Peyton Manning	12.00	30.00
7 Randy Moss	5.00	12.00
8 Drew Bledsoe	5.00	12.00
9 Kurt Warner	8.00	20.00
10 Jerry Rice	10.00	25.00

2000 Paramount Sculptures

COMPLETE SET (10)	50.00	120.00
STATED ODDS 1:361		
*PROOF/20: 1.2X TO 3X BASIC INSERTS		
PROOF PRINT RUN 20 SER.#'d SETS		
UNPRICED CANVAS PRINT RUN 1		
1 Peter Warrick	4.00	10.00
2 Tim Couch	3.00	8.00
3 Emmitt Smith	10.00	25.00
4 Edgerrin James	4.00	10.00
5 Mark Brunell	3.00	8.00
6 Fred Taylor	4.00	10.00
7 Randy Moss	4.00	10.00
8 Kurt Warner	6.00	15.00
9 Eddie George	3.00	8.00
10 Stephen Davis	3.00	8.00

2000 Paramount Zoned In

COMPLETE SET (36)	60.00	120.00
STATED ODDS 1:37		
1 Thomas Jones	1.50	4.00
2 Jake Plummer	1.25	3.00
3 Jamal Lewis	1.25	3.00
4 Cade McNown	1.00	2.50
5 Marcus Robinson	1.25	3.00
6 Peter Warrick	1.25	3.00
7 Tim Couch	1.25	3.00
8 Troy Aikman	2.50	6.00
9 Emmitt Smith	4.00	10.00
10 Barry Sanders	3.00	8.00
11 Terrell Davis	1.50	4.00
12 Brian Griese	1.25	3.00
13 Brett Favre	5.00	12.00
14 Marvin Harrison	1.50	4.00
15 Edgerrin James	1.50	4.00
16 Peyton Manning	4.00	10.00
17 Mark Brunell	1.25	3.00
18 Fred Taylor	1.50	4.00
19 Drew Bledsoe	1.50	4.00
20 Ricky Williams	1.50	4.00
21 Ron Dayne	1.25	3.00
22 Chad Pennington	2.00	5.00
23 Randy Moss	1.50	4.00
24 Donovan McNabb	1.50	4.00
25 Plaxico Burress	1.25	3.00
26 Isaac Bruce	1.50	4.00
27 Marshall Faulk	1.50	4.00
28 Kurt Warner	2.50	6.00
29 Jerry Rice	3.00	8.00
30 Shaun Alexander	1.50	4.00
31 Jon Kitna	1.25	3.00
32 Shaun King	1.00	2.50
33 Eddie George	1.25	3.00
34 Steve McNair	1.50	4.00
35 Stephen Davis	1.25	3.00
36 Brad Johnson	1.25	3.00

1989 Parker Brothers Talking Football

Measuring approximately 2 5/8" by 3", this 34-card set was licensed only by the NFL Players Association. When players are shown together on a card, it relates to their respective position(s). The cards are unnumbered so they are listed below in alphabetical order according to the AFC (1-17) and the NFC (18-34). For cards with more than one subject, those players are in turn alphabetically listed so that they can be alphabetized consistently along with the single player cards.

COMPLETE SET (34)	150.00	300.00
1 AFC Team Roster	2.50	6.00
2 Marcus Allen	10.00	20.00
3 Cornelius Bennett	3.00	8.00
John Offerdahl		
4 Keith Bishop	2.50	6.00
Mike Munchak		
5 Keith Bostic	2.50	6.00
Deron Cherry		
Hanford Dixon		
6 Carlos Carson	2.50	6.00
Stanley Morgan		
7 Todd Christensen	2.50	6.00
Mickey Shuler		
8 Eric Dickerson	4.00	10.00
9 Ray Donaldson	2.50	6.00
Irving Fryar		
10 Jacob Green	2.50	6.00
Bruce Smith		
11 Mark Haynes	2.50	6.00
Frank Minnifield		
Dennis Smith		
12 Chris Hinton	2.50	6.00
Anthony Munoz		
13 Steve Largent	6.00	15.00
Al Toon		
14 Howie Long	5.00	12.00
Bill Maas		
15 Nick Lowery	2.50	6.00
Reggie Roby		
16 Dan Marino	40.00	80.00
17 Karl Mecklenburg	3.00	8.00
Andre Tippett		
18 NFC Team Roster	2.50	6.00
19 Morten Andersen	2.50	6.00
Jim Arnold		
20 Carl Banks	3.00	8.00
21 Mark Bavaro	2.50	6.00
Doug Cosbie		
22 Joey Browner	2.50	6.00
Darrell Green		
Leonard Smith		
23 Anthony Carter	12.00	30.00
Jerry Rice		
24 Gary Clark	3.00	8.00
Mike Quick		
25 Richard Dent	3.00	8.00
Chris Doleman		
26 Brad Edelman	2.50	6.00
Bill Fralic		
27 Carl Ekern	2.50	6.00
Rickey Jackson		
28 Jerry Gray	2.50	6.00
LeRoy Irvin		
Ronnie Lott		
29 Mel Gray	2.50	6.00
Jay Hilgenberg		
30 Dexter Manley	3.00	8.00
Reggie White		
31 Rueben Mayes	2.50	6.00
32 Joe Montana	40.00	80.00
33 Jackie Slater	2.50	6.00
Gary Zimmerman		
34 Herschel Walker	4.00	10.00

1968-70 Partridge Meats

This black and white (with a little bit of red trim) photo-like card set features players from all three Cincinnati major league sports teams of that time, Cincinnati Reds baseball (BB1-BB18), Cincinnati Bengals football (FB1-FB5), and Cincinnati Royals basketball (BK1-BK2). The cards measure approximately 4" by 5", although there are other sizes sometimes found which are attributable to other years of issue. The cards are blank backed. In addition to the cards listed below, a "Mr. Whopper" card was also issued in honor of an extremely large spokesperson. The Tom Rhoads football card was only recently verified, in 2012, adding to the prevailing thought that these cards were issued over a period of years since its format is slightly different than the other four more well-known football cards in the set.

COMPLETE SET (14)	400.00	800.00
FB1 Bob Johnson	10.00	20.00
FB2 Paul Robinson	20.00	40.00
FB3 John Stofa	20.00	40.00
FB4 Bob Trumpy	12.50	25.00
FB5 Tom Rhoads SP	75.00	150.00

1961 Patriots Team Issue

The Patriots issued these photos around 1961. Each measures roughly 8" by 10" and includes a black and white player image with the player's name and team name (Boston Patriots) to the left and the team logo and address to the right below the image. The backs are blank.

COMPLETE SET	50.00	100.00
1 Ron Burton	7.50	15.00
2 Gerry Delucca	6.00	12.00
3 Mike Holovak	7.50	15.00
4 Jim Hunt	6.00	12.00
5 Harry Jacobs	6.00	12.00
6 Dick Klein	6.00	12.00
7 Tommy Stephens	6.00	12.00
8 Clyde Washington	6.00	12.00

1967 Patriots Team Issue

The Patriots issued this set of photos and distributed them to fans through mail requests. Each measures roughly 8" by 10 1/8" and includes a black and white player photo. The cards are unnumbered and checklisted below in alphabetical order.

COMPLETE SET (8)	50.00	100.00
1 Houston Antwine	6.00	12.00
2 Gino Cappelletti	7.50	15.00
3 John Charles	6.00	12.00
4 Jim Hunt	6.00	12.00
5 Leroy Mitchell	6.00	12.00
6 Babe Parilli	7.50	15.00
7 Don Trull	6.00	12.00
8 Jim Whalen	6.00	12.00

1971 Patriots Team Sheets

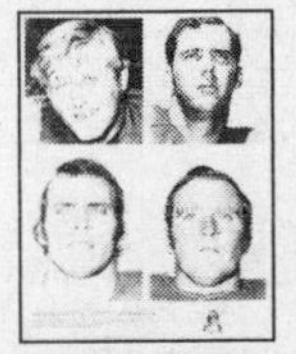

The New England Patriots issued these sheets of black-and-white player photos around 1971. Each measures roughly 8" by 10 1/8" and was printed on glossy stock with white borders. Each sheet includes photos of 4-players with the player's names, positions, team name and logo grouped below the photos. The coaches photo is a simple group shot with their names and positions listed below. The photo sheets are blankbacked.

COMPLETE SET (10)	50.00	100.00
1 Houston Antwine	5.00	10.00
Ike Lassiter		
Dennis Wirgowski		
Ron Berger		
2 Randall Edmunds	5.00	10.00
Jim Cheyunski		
Ed Philpott		
Ed Weisacosky		
3 Halvor Hagen	5.00	10.00
Mike Taliaferro		
Bill Lenkaitis		
Dave Rowe		
4 Jon Morris	5.00	10.00
Mike Montler		
Len St. Jean		
Tom Neville		
5 Jim Nance	6.00	12.00
Carl Garrett		
Jack Maitland		
Bob Gladieux		
6 John Outlaw	5.00	10.00
Larry Carwell		
Don Webb		
Clarence Scott		
7 Jim Plunkett	7.50	15.00
Randy Vataha		
Julius Adams		
Steve Kiner		
8 Perry Pruett	5.00	10.00
Ron Gardin		
Rickie Harris		
Tom Janik		
9 Sam Rutigliano CO	5.00	10.00
John Mazur CO		
Dick Evans CO		
Tom Fletcher CO		
John Meyer CO		
Bruce Beatty CO		
Jerry Stoltz CO		
10 Ron Sellers	5.00	10.00
Roland Moss		
Al Sykes		
Charlie Gogolak		

1974 Patriots Linnett

Noted sports Artist Charles Linnett drew these charcoal portraits of New England Patriots players. The 8 1/2" by 11" portraits were sold three per pack. Each is blankbacked and includes the player's name below the artwork.

COMPLETE SET (9)	35.00	60.00
1 Jim Plunkett	6.00	12.00
2 Jon Morris	3.00	6.00
3 Julius Adams	3.00	6.00
4 Randy Vataha	3.00	6.00
5 Sam Cunningham	4.00	8.00
6 Reggie Rucker	4.00	8.00
7 Tom Neville	3.00	6.00
8 Mack Herron	3.00	6.00
9 John Smith	3.00	6.00

1974 Patriots Team Issue

The Patriots issued this set of player photos for the purpose of media use only. The 4 7/8" by 7 1/8" black and white photos are blankbanked and unnumbered and checklisted below in alphabetical order.

COMPLETE SET (29)	75.00	150.00
1 Bob Adams	3.00	6.00
2 Julius Adams	3.00	6.00
3 Sam Adams	4.00	8.00
4 Josh Ashton	3.00	6.00
5 Bruce Barnes	3.00	6.00
6 Sam Cunningham	5.00	10.00
7 Sandy Durko	3.00	6.00
8 Allen Gallaher	3.00	6.00
9 Neil Graff	3.00	6.00
10 Leon Gray	4.00	8.00
11 John Hannah	7.50	15.00
12 Craig Hanneman	3.00	6.00
13 Andy Johnson	3.00	6.00
14 Steve King	3.00	6.00
15 Bill Lenkaitis	3.00	6.00
16 Prentice McCray	3.00	6.00
17 Jack Mildren	3.00	6.00
10 Arthur Moore	3.00	6.00
19 Jon Morris	3.00	6.00
20 Reggie Rucker	4.00	8.00
21 John Sanders	3.00	6.00
22 Steve Schubert	3.00	6.00
23 John Smith	3.00	6.00
24 John Tanner	3.00	6.00
25 John Tarver	3.00	6.00
26 Randy Vataha	3.00	6.00
27 George Webster	4.00	8.00
28 Joe Wilson	3.00	6.00
29 Bob Windsor	3.00	6.00

1976 Patriots Frito Lay

The New England Patriots issued this set sponsored by Frito Lay. The cards are blankbacked, measure approximately 5" by 7", and feature black and white player photos. The cards can be distinguished from other Patriots Frito Lay issues by the notation "Compliments of Frito Lay" contained at the bottom of the cardfront along with the "FL" logo. The left and right hand borders are much wider than the 1977-78 release. The player's are not identified on the photos and each appears in a kneeling (one hand on helmet) pose. Any additions to the list below are appreciated.

COMPLETE SET (44)		
1 Julius Adams	3.00	8.00
2 Sam Adams	4.00	10.00
3 Pete Barnes	3.00	8.00
4 Doug Beaudoin	3.00	8.00
5 Richard Bishop	3.00	8.00
6 Marlin Briscoe	3.00	8.00
7 Peter Brock	3.00	8.00
8 Steve Burks	3.00	8.00
9 Don Calhoun	3.00	8.00
10 Al Chandler	3.00	8.00
11 Dick Conn	3.00	8.00
12 Sam Cunningham	4.00	10.00
13 Ike Forte	3.00	8.00
14 Tim Fox	4.00	10.00
15 Russ Francis	5.00	12.00
16 Willie Germany	3.00	8.00
17 Leon Gray	3.00	8.00
18 Steve Grogan	6.00	15.00
(Kneeling pose)		
19 Ray Hamilton	3.00	8.00
20 John Hannah	8.00	20.00
21 Mike Haynes	5.00	12.00
22 Bob Howard	3.00	8.00
23 Sam Hunt	3.00	8.00
24 Andy Johnson	3.00	8.00
25 Steve King	3.00	8.00
26 Bill Lenkaitis	3.00	8.00
27 Prentice McCray	3.00	8.00
28 Tony McGee	4.00	10.00
29 Bob McKay	3.00	8.00
30 Arthur Moore	3.00	8.00
31 Steve Nelson	3.00	8.00
32 Tom Neville	3.00	8.00
33 Tom Owen	3.00	8.00
34 Mike Patrick	3.00	8.00
35 Jess Phillips	3.00	8.00
36 Jim Romaniszyn	3.00	8.00
37 John Smith	3.00	8.00
38 Darryl Stingley	4.00	10.00
39 Fred Sturt	3.00	8.00
40 Randy Vataha	3.00	8.00
41 George Webster	3.00	8.00
42 Steve Zabel	3.00	8.00
43 Coaches	3.00	8.00
Red Miller		
Ron Erhardt		
Ray Perkins		
Rollie Dotsch		
44 Team Photo	3.00	8.00

1977-78 Patriots Frito Lay

The New England Patriots issued this set sponsored by Frito Lay. The cards are blankbacked, measure approximately 5" by 7", and feature black and white player photos. The cards can be distinguished from other Patriots Frito Lay issues by the simple notation "Compliments of Frito Lay" contained at the bottom of the cardfront along with the "FL" logo. The left and right hand borders around the image are much thinner than the 1976 release, but otherwise the photos look the same. The player's are not identified on the photos and each appears in a kneeling (one hand on helmet) pose unless noted. Any additions to the list below are appreciated.

1 Richard Bishop	3.00	8.00
2 Sam Cunningham	4.00	10.00
3 Tim Fox	3.00	8.00
4 Leon Gray	3.00	8.00
5A Steve Grogan	6.00	15.00
(kneeling pose, same image as 1976)		
5B Steve Grogan	6.00	15.00
(action shot taking snap)		
5C Steve Grogan	6.00	15.00
(white jersey, ready to pass)		
6A Don Hasselbeck	3.00	8.00
(kneeling portrait)		
6B Don Hasselbeck	3.00	8.00
(game action image)		
7A Stanley Morgan	5.00	12.00
(kneeling portrait)		
7B Stanley Morgan	5.00	12.00
(game action image)		
8 Steve Nelson	3.00	8.00
9 Mike Patrick	3.00	8.00

1979 Patriots Frito Lay

The New England Patriots issued this set sponsored by Frito Lay. The cards are blankbacked, measure approximately 3 7/8" by 5 3/4", and contain black and white player photos. The cards can be distinguished from other Patriots Frito Lay issues by the notation "A WINNING TEAM" in all caps contained at the bottom of the cardfront. Each player's name is also printed below the photo with full first and last names. Any additions to the list below are appreciated.

COMPLETE SET (27)	100.00	200.00
1 Julius Adams	4.00	8.00
2 Sam Adams	4.00	8.00
3 Doug Beaudoin	4.00	8.00
4 Richard Bishop	4.00	8.00
5 Mark Buben	4.00	8.00
6 Matt Cavanaugh	5.00	10.00
7 Allan Clark	4.00	8.00
8 Ray Costict	4.00	8.00
9 Sam Cunningham	5.00	10.00
10 Russ Francis	5.00	10.00
11 Bob Golic	5.00	10.00
12 Ray Hamilton	4.00	8.00
13 John Hannah	6.00	12.00
14 Eddie Hare	4.00	8.00
15 Mike Hawkins	4.00	8.00
16 Horace Ivory	4.00	8.00
17 Harold Jackson	6.00	12.00
18 Andy Johnson	4.00	8.00
19 Shelby Jordan	4.00	8.00
20 Bill Lenkaitis	4.00	8.00
21 Bill Matthews	4.00	8.00
22 Stanley Morgan	4.00	8.00
23 Steve Nelson	4.00	8.00
24 Tom Owen	4.00	8.00
25 Carlos Pennywell	4.00	8.00
26 John Smith	4.00	8.00
27 Mosi Tatupu	4.00	8.00

1981 Patriots Frito Lay

The New England Patriots issued this set sponsored by Frito Lay. The cards are blankbacked, measure approximately 4" by 6", and contain black and white player photos. The cards can be distinguished from other Patriots Frito Lay issues by the title line "A Winning Team" contained at the top of the cardfront. Nearly all cards in this issue contain two player photos instead of one. The photos were issued before the season so they feature some players who never made the final roster.

COMPLETE SET (55)	200.00	400.00
1 Julius Adams	4.00	8.00
2 Richard Bishop	4.00	8.00
3 Don Blackmon	4.00	8.00
4 Pete Brock	4.00	8.00
5 Preston Brown	4.00	8.00
6 Mark Buben	4.00	8.00
7 Don Calhoun	4.00	8.00
8 Rich Camarillo	4.00	8.00
9 Matt Cavanaugh	5.00	10.00
10 Allan Clark	4.00	8.00
11 Steve Clark	4.00	8.00
(no second photo)		
12 Raymond Clayborn	5.00	10.00
13 Tony Collins	4.00	8.00
14 Charles Cook	4.00	8.00
(no second photo)		
15 Bob Cryder	4.00	8.00
16 Sam Cunningham	5.00	10.00
17 Lin Dawson	4.00	8.00
18 Ron Erhardt	4.00	8.00
19 Vagas Ferguson	4.00	8.00
20 Tim Fox	4.00	8.00
21 Bob Golic	5.00	10.00
22 Steve Grogan	7.50	15.00
23 Ray Hamilton	4.00	8.00
24 John Hannah	7.50	15.00
25 Don Hasselbeck	4.00	8.00
26 Mike Hawkins	4.00	8.00
27 Mike Haynes	7.50	15.00
28 Brian Holloway	4.00	8.00
29 Harold Jackson	5.00	10.00
30 Roland James	4.00	8.00
31 Andy Johnson	4.00	8.00
32 Shelby Jordan	4.00	8.00
33 Steve King	4.00	8.00
34 Keith Lee	4.00	8.00
35 Bill Lenkaitis UER	4.00	8.00
(photo reversed negative)		
36 Bill Matthews	4.00	8.00
37 Tony McGee	4.00	8.00
38 Larry McGrew	4.00	8.00
39 Stanley Morgan	6.00	12.00
40 Steve Nelson	4.00	8.00
41 Tom Owen	4.00	8.00
42 Carlos Pennywell	4.00	8.00
43 Garry Puetz	4.00	8.00
44 Rick Sanford	4.00	8.00
45 Rod Shoate	4.00	8.00
46 John Smith	4.00	8.00
47 Mosi Tatupu	4.00	8.00
48 John Tautolo	4.00	8.00
(no second photo)		
49 Ken Toler	4.00	8.00
(no second photo)		
50 Richard Villella	4.00	8.00
(no second photo)		
51 Don Westbrook	4.00	8.00
52 Dwight Wheeler	4.00	8.00
53 Ron Wooten	4.00	8.00
(no second photo)		
54 Gary Wright	4.00	8.00
(no second photo)		
55 John Zamberlin	4.00	8.00

1982 Patriots Frito Lay

The New England Patriots issued this set sponsored by Frito Lay. The cards are blankbacked, measure approximately 4" by 6", and contain black and white player photos. The cards can be distinguished from other Patriots Frito Lay issues by the title line "get up for it" contained at the top of the cardfront. Each player's name is printed with first initial and full last name below the photo. The photos were issued before the season so they feature some players who never made the final roster. Any additions to the list below are appreciated.

COMPLETE SET (35)	125.00	250.00
1 Julius Adams	4.00	8.00
2 Pete Brock	4.00	8.00
3 Preston Brown	4.00	8.00
4 Mark Buben	4.00	8.00
5 Don Calhoun	4.00	8.00
6 Matt Cavanaugh	5.00	10.00
7 Allan Clark	4.00	8.00
8 Raymond Clayborn	4.00	8.00
9 Bob Cryder	4.00	8.00
10 Bill Currier	4.00	8.00
11 Vagas Ferguson	4.00	8.00
12 Chuck Foreman	6.00	12.00
13 Tim Fox	4.00	8.00
14 Russ Francis	6.00	12.00
15 Steve Grogan	7.50	15.00
16 Ray Hamilton	4.00	8.00
17 John Hannah	7.50	15.00
18 Don Hasselbeck	4.00	8.00
19 Mike Haynes	7.50	15.00
20 Mike Hubach	4.00	8.00
21 Horace Ivory	4.00	8.00
22 Harold Jackson	5.00	10.00
23 Roland James	4.00	8.00
24 Andy Johnson	4.00	8.00
25 Steve King	4.00	8.00
26 Bill Matthews	4.00	8.00
27 Tony McGee	4.00	8.00
28 Stanley Morgan	7.50	15.00
29 Steve Nelson	4.00	8.00
30 Garry Puetz	4.00	8.00
31 Rick Sanford	4.00	8.00
32 Rod Shoate	4.00	8.00
33 John Smith	4.00	8.00
34 Mosi Tatupu	4.00	8.00
35 Dwight Wheeler	4.00	8.00

1985 Patriots Frito Lay

The New England Patriots issued this set sponsored by Frito Lay. The cards are blankbacked, measure approximately 4" by 6", and contain black and white player photos. The cards can be distinguished from other Patriots Frito Lay issues by the lack of any set title something commonly found on the other releases. Any additions to this list would be appreciated.

COMPLETE SET (16)	60.00	120.00
1 Tony Collins	5.00	10.00
2 Rich Camarillo	4.00	8.00
3 Paul Dombroski	4.00	8.00
4 Tim Golden	4.00	8.00
5 Darryl Haley	4.00	8.00
6 Brian Ingram	4.00	8.00
7 Cedric Jones WR	4.00	8.00
8 Ronnie Lippett	4.00	8.00
9 Larry McGrew	4.00	8.00
10 Steve Moore	4.00	8.00
11 Stanley Morgan	5.00	10.00
12 Steve Nelson	4.00	8.00
13 Tom Ramsey	4.00	8.00
15 Kenneth Sims	4.00	8.00
16 Stephen Starring	4.00	8.00
17 Clayton Weishuhn	4.00	8.00

1986 Patriots Frito Lay

The New England Patriots issued this set sponsored by Frito Lay. The cards are blankbacked, measure approximately 4" by 6", and contain black and white player photos. The cards can be distinguished from other Patriots Frito Lay issues by the title "Together We Win" printed at the bottom of the cardfront. The set is thought to be complete at 42-cards. Any additions to the list would be appreciated.

COMPLETE SET (42)	125.00	250.00
1 Greg Baty	4.00	8.00
2 Raymond Berry CO	6.00	12.00
3 Don Blackmon	4.00	8.00
4 Jim Bowman	4.00	8.00
5 Pete Brock	4.00	8.00
6 Raymond Clayborn	4.00	8.00
7 Tony Collins	5.00	10.00
8 Rich Camarillo	4.00	8.00
9 Steve Doig	4.00	8.00
10 Reggie Dupard	4.00	8.00
11 Tony Eason	5.00	10.00
12 Sean Farrell	4.00	8.00
13 Tony Franklin	4.00	8.00
14 Ernest Gibson	4.00	8.00
15 Steve Grogan	6.00	12.00
16 Greg Hawthorne	4.00	8.00
17 Brian Holloway	4.00	8.00
18 Craig James	6.00	12.00
19 Roland James	4.00	8.00
20 Eric Jordan	4.00	8.00
21 Ronnie Lippett	5.00	10.00
22 Fred Marion	4.00	8.00
23 Trevor Matich	4.00	8.00
24 Rod McSwain	4.00	8.00
25 Guy Morriss	4.00	8.00
26 Steve Nelson	4.00	8.00
27 Dennis Owens	4.00	8.00
28 Eugene Profit	4.00	8.00
29 Tom Ramsey	4.00	8.00
30 Johnny Rembert	4.00	8.00
31 Ed Reynolds	4.00	8.00
32 Mike Ruth	4.00	8.00
33 Stephen Starring	4.00	8.00
34 Willie Scott	4.00	8.00
35 Mosi Tatupu	4.00	8.00
36 Andre Tippett	6.00	12.00
37 Garin Veris	4.00	8.00
38 Robert Weathers	4.00	8.00
39 Brent Williams	4.00	8.00
40 Derwin Williams	4.00	8.00
41 Toby Williams	4.00	8.00
42 Ron Wooten	4.00	8.00

1987 Patriots Team Issue

Each photo in this series measures roughly 8" by 10" and features a group of two to four different black and white images of each player on the fronts. The player's name, the team name, and his position are included below the images in a variety of type styles. The backs are blank and the photos are listed below alphabetically.

COMPLETE SET (8)	20.00	40.00
1 Reggie Dupard	3.00	6.00
(2 photos)		
2 Cedric Jones	3.00	6.00
(4 photos)		
3 Ronnie Lippett	4.00	8.00
(3 photos)		
4 Trevor Matich	3.00	6.00
(2 photos)		
5 Kenneth Sims	3.00	6.00
(3 photos)		
6 Mosi Tatupu	4.00	8.00
(4 photos)		
7 Garin Veris	3.00	6.00
(3 photos)		
8 Ron Wooten	3.00	6.00
(4 photos)		

1988 Patriots Ace Fact Pack

Cards from this 33-card set measure approximately 2 1/4" by 3 5/8". This set consists of 22-player cards and 11-additional informational cards about the Patriots team. We've checklisted the cards alphabetically beginning with the 22-players. The cards have square corners (as opposed to rounded like the 1987 sets) and a playing card design on the back printed in blue. These cards were manufactured in West Germany (by Ace Fact Pack) and released primarily in Great Britain.

COMPLETE SET (33)	60.00	120.00
1 Bruce Armstrong	1.50	4.00
2 Raymond Clayborn	1.50	4.00
3 Reggie Dupard	1.50	4.00
4 Tony Eason	2.00	5.00
5 Sean Farrell	1.50	4.00
6 Tony Franklin	1.50	4.00
7 Irving Fryar	3.00	8.00
8 Steve Grogan	3.00	8.00
9 Craig James UER	2.00	5.00
(listed as James Craig)		
10 Ronnie Lippett	1.50	4.00
11 Fred Marion	1.50	4.00
12 Larry McGrew	1.50	4.00
13 Steve Moore	1.50	4.00
14 Stanley Morgan	3.00	8.00
15 Robert Perryman	1.50	4.00
16 Kenneth Sims	1.50	4.00
17 Stephen Starring	2.00	5.00
18 Mosi Tatupu	1.50	4.00
19 Andre Tippett	2.00	5.00
20 Garin Veris	1.50	4.00
21 Toby Williams	1.50	4.00
22 Ron Wooten	1.50	4.00
23 1987 Team Statistics	1.50	4.00
24 All-Time Greats	1.50	4.00
25 Career Record Holders	1.50	4.00
26 Coaching History	1.50	4.00
27 Game Record Holders	1.50	4.00
28 Patriots Helmet	1.50	4.00
(Cover Card)		
29 Patriots Helmet	1.50	4.00
(Informational Card)		
30 Patriots Uniform	1.50	4.00
31 Record 1968-87	1.50	4.00
32 Season Record Holders	1.50	4.00
33 Sullivan Stadium	1.50	4.00

1988 Patriots Holsum

This 12-card standard-size full-color set features players of the New England Patriots; cards were available only in Holsum Bread packages. The set was co-produced by Mike Schechter Associates on behalf of the NFL Players Association. Card fronts have a color photo within a green border and the backs are printed in black ink on white card stock.

COMPLETE SET (12)	25.00	60.00
1 Andre Tippett	2.50	6.00
2 Stanley Morgan	3.00	8.00
3 Steve Grogan	3.00	8.00
4 Ronnie Lippett	2.00	5.00
5 Kenneth Sims	2.00	5.00
6 Pete Brock	2.00	5.00
7 Sean Farrell	2.00	5.00
8 Garin Veris	2.00	5.00
9 Mosi Tatupu	2.00	5.00
10 Raymond Clayborn	2.50	6.00
11 Tony Franklin	2.00	5.00
12 Reggie Dupard	2.00	5.00

1990 Patriots Knudsen/Sealtest

This six-card set (of bookmarks) which measures approximately 2" by 8" was produced by Knudsen's and Sealtest to help promote readership by people under 15 years old in the New England area. Between the Knudsen or Sealtest company name, the front features a color action photo of the player superimposed on a football stadium. The field is green, the bleachers are yellow with gray print, and the scoreboard above the player reads "The Reading Team". The box below the player gives brief biographical information and player highlights. The back has logos of the sponsors and describes two books that are available at the public library. We have checklisted this set in alphabetical order because they are otherwise unnumbered except for the player's uniform number displayed on the card front.

COMPLETE SET (6)	12.00	30.00
1 Steve Grogan	2.40	6.00
2 Ronnie Lippett	2.00	5.00
3 Eric Sievers	2.00	5.00
4 Mosi Tatupu	2.00	5.00
5 Andre Tippett	2.40	6.00
6 Garin Veris	2.00	5.00

1997 Patriots Score

This 15-card set of the New England Patriots was distributed in five-card packs with a suggested retail price of $1.99. The fronts feature color action player photos with white borders and the player's name and team logo printed in team color foil at the bottom. The backs carry player information and career statistics. Platinum Team parallel cards were randomly seeded in packs featuring all foil cardfronts.

COMPLETE SET (15)	2.80	7.00
*PLATINUM TEAMS: 1X TO 2X		
1 Drew Bledsoe	.80	2.00
2 Curtis Martin	.80	2.00
3 Terry Glenn	.30	.75
4 Shawn Jefferson	.08	.25
5 Ben Coates	.15	.40
6 Willie McGinest	.08	.25
7 Keith Byars	.08	.25
8 Chris Slade	.08	.25
9 Tedy Bruschi	.30	.75
10 Ty Law	.15	.40
11 Devin Wyman	.08	.25
12 Sam Gash	.08	.25
13 Dave Meggett	.08	.25
14 Ferric Collons	.08	.25
15 Willie Clay	.08	.25

2005 Patriots Topps Super Bowl Champions

This set was issued by Topps in factory set form right after the Patriots victory in Super Bowl XXXIX. 38-different players are included in the set with 2-players appearing for the first time on cards. The set is rounded out by several Season Highlight cards and one jumbo card. Factory sets initially retailed for $19.95.

COMPLETE SET (56)	15.00	25.00
1 Corey Dillon	.40	1.00
2 Ty Warren	.20	.50
3 Adam Vinatieri	.40	1.00
4 Troy Brown	.40	1.00
5 Christian Fauria	.20	.50
6 Tom Brady	1.25	3.00
7 Willie McGinest	.30	.75
8 Deion Branch	.40	1.00
9 David Patten	.30	.75
10 Rodney Harrison	.30	.75
11 Kevin Faulk	.30	.75
12 Mike Vrabel	.40	1.00
13 Tedy Bruschi	.40	1.00
14 Josh Miller	.20	.50
15 Ty Law	.40	1.00
16 Roman Phifer	.20	.50
17 David Givens	.30	.75
18 Eugene Wilson	.20	.50
19 Patrick Pass	.20	.50
20 Bethel Johnson	.30	.75
21 Keith Traylor	.20	.50
22 Randall Gay	.20	.50
23 Rohan Davey	.30	.75
24 Richard Seymour	.30	.75
25 Ted Johnson	.30	.75
26 Asante Samuel	.20	.50
27 Steve Neal	.20	.50
28 Rosevelt Colvin	.20	.50
29 Larry Izzo	.20	.50
30 Daniel Graham	.30	.75
31 Tully Banta-Cain	.20	.50
32 Jarvis Green	.20	.50
33 Vince Wilfork	.40	1.00
34 Matt Light	.20	.50
35 Joe Andruzzi	.20	.50
36 Dan Koppen	.20	.50
37 Brandon Gorin	.20	.50
38 Rabih Abdullah	.20	.50
39 Tom Brady HL	.75	2.00
40 Pats 19th Win	.30	.75
41 Ty Law HL	.30	.75
42 Adam Vinatieri HL	.40	1.00
43 Corey Dillon HL	.40	1.00
44 Tedy Bruschi HL	.40	1.00
45 Corey Dillon HL	.40	1.00
46 Tom Brady HL	.75	2.00
47 Deion Branch HL	.40	1.00
48 Rodney Harrison HL	.30	.75
49 Tom Brady HL	.75	2.00
50 Mike Vrabel HL	.40	1.00
51 Deion Branch HL	.40	1.00
52 Rodney Harrison HL	.30	.75
53 Super Bowl XXXIX Champs	.40	1.00
54 Team Card	.20	.50
55 Deion Branch MVP	.40	1.00
NNO Jumbo Team Card	.30	.75

2005 Patriots Upper Deck Super Bowl Champions

This set was issued by Upper Deck in factory set form after the Patriots victory in Super Bowl XXXIX. Forty different players are included in the set with 2-players appearing for the first time on cards. The set is rounded out by several Season Highlight cards and one jumbo card. Factory sets initially retailed for $19.95.

COMPLETE SET (51)	15.00	25.00
1 Tom Ashworth	.20	.50
2 Tom Brady	1.25	3.00
3 Deion Branch	.40	1.00
4 Troy Brown	.40	1.00
5 Tedy Bruschi	.40	1.00
6 Je'Rod Cherry	.20	.50
7 Rohan Davey	.30	.75
8 Don Davis	.20	.50
9 Corey Dillon	.40	1.00
10 Kevin Faulk	.30	.75
11 Christian Fauria	.20	.50
12 Randall Gay	.20	.50
13 David Givens	.30	.75
14 Daniel Graham	.30	.75
15 Rodney Harrison	.30	.75
16 Russ Hochstein	.20	.50
17 Larry Izzo	.20	.50
18 Bethel Johnson	.30	.75
19 Ted Johnson	.30	.75
20 Dan Koppen	.20	.50
21 Ty Law	.40	1.00
22 Matt Light	.20	.50
23 Willie McGinest	.30	.75
24 Ben Watson	.50	1.25
25 Josh Miller	.20	.50
26 Steve Neal	.20	.50
27 Patrick Pass	.20	.50
28 David Patten	.30	.75
29 Lonie Paxton	.20	.50
30 Roman Phifer	.20	.50
31 Tyrone Poole	.30	.75
32 Asante Samuel	.20	.50
33 Richard Seymour	.30	.75
34 Keith Traylor	.20	.50
35 Adam Vinatieri	.40	1.00
36 Mike Vrabel	.40	1.00
37 Ty Warren	.20	.50
38 Jed Weaver	.20	.50
39 Vince Wilfork	.40	1.00
40 Eugene Wilson	.20	.50
41 Tom Brady HL	.75	2.00
42 Corey Dillon HL	.40	1.00
43 David Givens HL	.30	.75
44 Adam Vinatieri HL	.40	1.00
45 Deion Branch HL	.40	1.00
SH1 Tom Brady MM	.75	2.00
SH2 Corey Dillon MM	.40	1.00
SH3 David Givens MM	.30	.75
SH4 Rodney Harrison MM	.30	.75
MVP Deion Branch MVP	.40	1.00
SBC Jumbo Patriots Team	.30	.75

2006 Patriots Topps

COMPLETE SET (12)	4.00	8.00
NE1 Kevin Faulk	.25	.60
NE2 Corey Dillon	.25	.60
NE3 Ben Watson	.20	.50
NE4 Tom Brady	.50	1.25
NE5 Tedy Bruschi	.30	.75
NE6 Deion Branch	.25	.60
NE7 Mike Vrabel	.25	.60
NE8 Daniel Graham	.20	.50
NE9 Rodney Harrison	.20	.50
NE10 Richard Seymour	.20	.50
NE11 Laurence Maroney	1.00	2.50
NE12 Chad Jackson	.20	.50

2006 Patriots Upper Deck Boston Globe

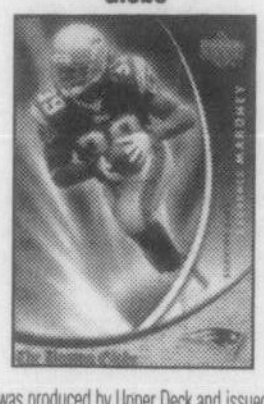

This set was produced by Upper Deck and issued by the Boston Glode in 12-card sheets over the course of three weeks in November 2006. Cards #1-12 released November 12, cards #13-24 on November 19, and cards #14-36 on November 26.

COMPLETE SET (36)	7.50	15.00
1 Tom Brady	1.00	2.50
2 Vince Wilfork	.30	.75
3 Dan Koppen	.25	.60
4 Ben Watson	.30	.75
5 Stephen Gostkowski	.40	1.00
6 Logan Mankins	.25	.60
7 Eugene Wilson	.30	.75
8 Chad Jackson	.75	2.00
9 Tully Banta-Cain	.25	.60
10 Junior Seau	.50	1.25
11 Artrell Hawkins	.25	.60
12 Heath Evans	.25	.60
13 Tedy Bruschi	.50	1.25
14 Matt Light	.25	.60
15 Mike Vrabel	.30	.75
16 Corey Dillon	.30	.75
17 Rodney Harrison	.30	.75
18 Ty Warren	.25	.60
19 Rosevelt Colvin	.30	.75
20 Steve Neal	.25	.60
21 Ryan O'Callaghan	.25	.60
22 Don Davis	.25	.60
23 David Thomas	.50	1.25
24 Matt Cassel	.75	2.00
25 Richard Seymour	.30	.75
26 Troy Brown	.30	.75
27 Asante Samuel	.30	.75
28 Daniel Graham	.25	.60
29 Laurence Maroney	1.25	3.00
30 Ellis Hobbs	.25	.60
31 Larry Izzo	.25	.60
32 Reche Caldwell	.30	.75
33 Kevin Faulk	.30	.75
34 Jarvis Green	.25	.60
35 Mike Wright	.25	.60
36 James Sanders	.25	.60

2007 Patriots Topps

COMPLETE SET (12)	3.00	6.00
1 Tom Brady	.50	1.25
2 Laurence Maroney	.25	.60
3 Kevin Faulk	.20	.50
4 Reche Caldwell	.20	.50
5 Ben Watson	.20	.50
6 Richard Seymour	.20	.50
7 Wes Welker	.30	.75
8 Donte' Stallworth	.25	.60
9 Tedy Bruschi	.30	.75
10 Adalius Thomas	.20	.50
11 Rodney Harrison	.20	.50
12 Randy Moss	.30	.75

2007 Patriots Upper Deck Boston Globe

This set was produced by Upper Deck and issued by the Boston Glode in 12-card sheets over the course of three weeks in the fall of 2007.

COMPLETE SET (36)	7.50	15.00
1 Larry Izzo	.25	.60
2 Ellis Hobbs	.25	.60
3 Matt Light	.25	.60
4 Donte Stallworth	.30	.75
5 Tom Brady	.60	1.50
6 Junior Seau	.40	1.00
7 Wes Welker	.40	1.00
8 Rosevelt Colvin	.25	.60
9 Stephen Gostkowski	.30	.75
10 Troy Brown	.30	.75
11 Mike Vrabel	.30	.75
12 Nick Kaczur	.25	.60
13 Dan Koppen	.25	.60
14 Kevin Faulk	.25	.60
15 Jabar Gaffney	.25	.60
16 Laurence Maroney	.30	.75
17 Richard Seymour	.25	.60
18 Adalius Thomas	.25	.60
19 Vince Wilfork	.25	.60
20 Steve Neal	.25	.60
21 Ben Watson	.25	.60
22 Ty Warren	.25	.60
23 Eugene Wilson	.25	.60
24 Rodney Harrison	.25	.60
25 Kyle Brady	.25	.60
26 Sammy Morris	.25	.60
27 Asante Samuel	.25	.60
28 Brandon Meriweather	.40	1.00
29 Randy Moss	.40	1.00
30 Tedy Bruschi	.40	1.00
31 James Sanders	.25	.60
32 Randall Gay	.25	.60
33 Jarvis Green	.25	.60
34 Mike Wright	.25	.60
35 Heath Evans	.25	.60
36 Logan Mankins	.25	.60

2008 Patriots Topps

COMPLETE SET (12)	2.50	5.00
1 Tom Brady	.50	1.25
2 Randy Moss	.30	.75
3 Laurence Maroney	.25	.60
4 Wes Welker	.30	.75
5 Mike Vrabel	.20	.50
6 Sammy Morris	.20	.50
7 Ben Watson	.20	.50
8 Vince Wilfork	.20	.50
9 Jabar Gaffney	.20	.50
10 Tedy Bruschi	.30	.75
11 Kevin O'Connell	.30	.75
12 Jerod Mayo	.40	1.00

2002 Peoria Pirates AF2

COMPLETE SET (24)	15.00	30.00
1 Brandon Campbell	.60	1.50
2 Ronnie Gordon	.60	1.50
3 Todd Kurz	.60	1.50
4 Jerome Hurd	.60	1.50
5 Geral Neasman	.60	1.50
6 Lincoln Dupree	.60	1.50
7 Walter Church	.60	1.50
8 Titcus Pettigrew	.75	2.00
9 Frank West	.60	1.50
10 Robert Meyer	.60	1.50
11 Tim Simpson	.60	1.50
12 Jon Verdegan	.60	1.50
13 Jason Hennigh	.60	1.50
14 Demond Gibson	.60	1.50
15 Cornell Craig	.60	1.50
16 Jermaine Sheffield	.60	1.50
17 Eric Johnson	.60	1.50
18 Terence Cook	.60	1.50
19 Rasche Hill	.75	2.00
20 Ken Bouie	.60	1.50
21 Bruce Cowdrey CO	.60	1.50
22 Tony Johnson Asst.CO	.60	1.50
23 Tony Johnson Asst.CO	.60	1.50
Treasure Life		
24 Cover Card	.60	1.50
Jermaine Sheffield		
Cornell Craig		

2003 Peoria Pirates AFL

This 30-card set was produced by Multi-Ad and distributed at a 2003 Pirates home game to attendees. Each includes a color photo of a Pirates player on the front with a bio and year of issue on the back.

COMPLETE SET (30)	15.00	30.00
1 Bryan Archibald	.50	1.25
2 Kraig Baker	.50	1.25
3 Anthony Chiaravalle	.50	1.25
4 Nick Cosentino	.50	1.25
5 Bruce Cowdrey	.50	1.25
6 Michael Cunningham	.50	1.25
7 Bryan Eakin	.50	1.25
8 Troy Edwards	.60	1.50
9 Steve Fickert	.50	1.25
10 Thomas Guynes	.50	1.25
11 Torrance Heggie	.50	1.25
12 Davaren Hightower	.50	1.25
13 Rasche Hill	.60	1.50
14 Eric Johnson	.50	1.25
15 Jay Johnson	.50	1.25
16 Tony Johnson	.50	1.25
17 David Knott	.50	1.25
18 Michael Leaks	.60	1.50
19 Chris Martin	.50	1.25
20 Eddie McKennie	.50	1.25
21 Gerald Neasman	.50	1.25
22 Charlie Peterson	.50	1.25
23 Matt Pike	.75	2.00
24 Ted Schmitz	.50	1.25
25 Jon Verdegan	.50	1.25
26 Frank West	.50	1.25
27 Tyshaun Whitson	.50	1.25
28 Jack Wilson	.50	1.25
29 Checklist	.50	1.25
30 Cover Card	.50	1.25

2004 Peoria Pirates AFL

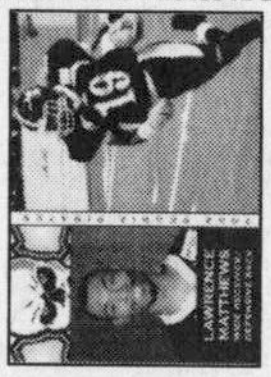

Cards in this set were produced by Multi-Ad and were given away four or five at a time to fans attending Pirates games in Peoria. We've catalogued those cards using a series number followed by a card number below. Also, at the last game of the year on July 31, 2004, a full 31-card set was issued with all of the cards being re-numbered (#1-31). We've cataloged those below with the prefix "T" to indicate team set. Two players were added to this "team set" version in place of two players dropped from the set. Cards in this version of the set are slightly different (in addition to the different card numbers) in that they have a different placement of the sponsor logo or the logo is printed in a different color. We've included the date of release for each card issued throughout the season when known. The cardfronts feature a larger action photo on the right side and a smaller head shot on the left. The backs include a short player bio. The cards in the weekly series are numbered 1 through 4 or 1 through 5 with each new series starting over. We've listed those below in alphabetical order for ease in cataloging.

COMP.TEAM T SET (31)	15.00	30.00
1-Jan Louie Aguiar 4/9	.75	2.00
2-Jan Lucas Brigman 4/9	.60	1.50
3-Jan Troy Edwards 4/9	.75	2.00
4-Jan Jerry Samuels 4/9	.60	1.50
5-Jan Enoch Smith 4/9	.60	1.50
1-Feb Brandon Campbell 5/15	.75	2.00
2-Feb Tony Pryor 5/15	.75	2.00
3-Feb Casey Urlacher 5/15	3.00	8.00
4-Feb Frank West 5/15	.60	1.50
1-Mar Kevin Brown 5/29	.60	1.50
2-Mar Lawrence Mathews 5/29	1.25	3.00
3-Mar Ben Sanderson 5/29	.60	1.50
4-Mar Paul Stefleck 5/29	.60	1.50
1-Apr Talmadge Hill 6/12	1.25	3.00
2-Apr Joe Laudano 6/12	.60	1.50
3-Apr Joe Peters 6/12	.60	1.50
4-Apr Chris Robinson 6/12	1.25	3.00
1-May Louie Aguiar RB 7/17	.75	2.00
2-May Ken Bouie RB 7/17	.60	1.50
3-May Bruce Cowdrey CO 7/17	.60	1.50
4-May Casey Urlacher RB 7/17	2.00	5.00
6-May Frank West RB 7/17	.60	1.50
7-May Team Mascot CL 7/17	.60	1.50
T1 Louie Aguiar	.75	2.00
T2 Ken Bouie	.60	1.50
T3 Milt Bowen	.60	1.50
T4 Lucas Brigman	.60	1.50
T5 Kevin Brown	.60	1.50
T6 Brandon Campbell	.75	2.00
T7 Mike Cunningham	.60	1.50
T8 Troy Edwards	.75	2.00
T9 Sameer Hamood	.60	1.50
T10 Talmadge Hill	1.25	3.00
T11 Colin Johnson	.60	1.50
T12 Eric Johnson	.60	1.50
T13 Joe Laudano	.60	1.50
T14 Lawrence Mathews	1.25	3.00
T15 Joe Peters	.60	1.50
T16 Tony Pryor	.75	2.00
T17 Andrew Webb	1.25	3.00
T18 Chris Robinson	1.25	3.00
T19 Jerald Burley	1.25	3.00
T20 Ben Sanderson	.60	1.50
T21 Enoch Smith	.60	1.50
T22 Mike Souza	.75	2.00
T23 Paul Stefleck	.60	1.50
T24 Casey Urlacher	3.00	8.00
T25 Frank West	.60	1.50
T26 Louie Aguiar RB	.75	2.00
T27 Casey Urlacher RB	2.00	5.00
T28 Frank West RB	.60	1.50
T29 Ken Bouie RB	.60	1.50
T30 Bruce Cowdrey CO	.60	1.50
T31 Team Mascot CL	.60	1.50

1976 Pepsi Discs

The 1976 Pepsi Discs set contains 40 numbered discs, each measuring approximately 3 1/2" in diameter. Each disc has a player photo, biographical information, and 1975 statistics. Disc numbers 1-20 are from many different teams and are known as "All-Stars." Numbers 21-40 feature Cincinnati Bengals, since this set was a regional issue produced in the Cincinnati area. Numbers 1, 5, 7, 8, and 14 are much scarcer than the other 35 and are marked SP in the checklist below. Ed Marinaro also exists as a New York Jet, which is very difficult to find. It has been reported that Ed Marinaro may be a sixth SP. The checklist for the set is printed on the tab; the checklist below values the discs with the tabs intact as that is the way they are most commonly found.

COMPLETE SET (40)	75.00	150.00
1 Steve Bartkowski SP	10.00	20.00
2 Lydell Mitchell	1.25	3.00
3 Wally Chambers	1.00	2.50
4 Doug Buffone	1.00	2.50
5 Jerry Sherk SP	7.50	15.00
6 Drew Pearson	1.50	4.00
7 Otis Armstrong SP	7.50	15.00
8 Charlie Sanders SP	7.50	15.00
9 John Brockington	1.25	3.00
10 Curley Culp	1.25	3.00
11 Jan Stenerud	1.25	3.00
12 Lawrence McCutchen	1.25	3.00
13 Chuck Foreman	1.25	3.00
14 Bob Pollard SP	7.50	15.00
15 Ed Marinaro	2.00	5.00
16 Jack Lambert	4.00	8.00
17 Terry Metcalf	1.25	3.00
18 Mel Gray	1.25	3.00
19 Russ Washington	1.00	2.50
20 Charley Taylor	1.50	4.00
21 Ken Anderson	2.00	5.00
22 Bob Brown DT	1.00	2.50
23 Ron Carpenter	1.00	2.50
24 Tommy Casanova	1.00	2.50
25 Boobie Clark	1.00	2.50
26 Isaac Curtis	1.25	3.00
27 Lenvil Elliott	1.00	2.50
28 Stan Fritts	1.00	2.50
29 Vern Holland	1.00	2.50
30 Bob Johnson	1.25	3.00
31 Ken Johnson	1.00	2.50
32 Bill Kollar	1.00	2.50
33 Jim LeClair	1.00	2.50
34 Chip Myers	1.00	2.50
35 Lemar Parrish	1.25	3.00
36 Ron Pritchard	1.00	2.50
37 Bob Trumpy	1.25	3.00
38 Sherman White	1.00	2.50
39 Archie Griffin	1.50	4.00
40 John Shinners	1.00	2.50

1964 Philadelphia

The 1964 Philadelphia Gum set of 198 standard-size cards, featuring National Football League players, is the first of four annual issues released by the company. The cards were issued in one-card penny packs, five-card nickel packs, as well as cello packs. Each card has a question about that player in a cartoon at the bottom of the reverse; the answer is given upside down in blue ink. Each team has a team picture card as well as a card diagramming one of the team's plays; this "play card" shows a small black and white picture of the team's coach on the front of the card. The card backs are printed in blue and black on a gray card stock. Within each team group the players are arranged alphabetically by last name. The two checklist cards erroneously say "Official 1963 Checklist" at the top. The key Rookie Cards in this set are Herb Adderley, Willie Davis, Jim Johnson, John Mackey and Merlin Olsen. Tatoo Transfers sheets were included as inserts in packs.

COMPLETE SET (198)	600.00	900.00
WRAPPER (1-CENT)	35.00	60.00
WRAPPER (5-CENT)	10.00	20.00
1 Raymond Berry	10.00	20.00
2 Tom Gilburg	1.25	2.50
3 John Mackey RC	20.00	40.00
4 Gino Marchetti	2.50	5.00
5 Jim Martin	1.25	2.50
6 Tom Matte RC	3.00	6.00
7 Jimmy Orr	1.50	3.00
8 Jim Parker	2.00	4.00
9 Bill Pellington	1.25	2.50
10 Alex Sandusky	1.25	2.50
11 Dick Szymanski	1.25	2.50
12 John Unitas	25.00	50.00
13 Baltimore Colts	1.50	3.00
Team Card		
14 Baltimore Colts	20.00	35.00
Play Card		
(Don Shula)		
15 Doug Atkins	2.50	5.00
16 Ronnie Bull	1.25	2.50
17 Mike Ditka	25.00	40.00
18 Joe Fortunato	1.25	2.50
19 Willie Galimore	1.50	3.00
20 Joe Marconi	1.25	2.50
21 Bennie McRae RC	1.25	2.50
22 Johnny Morris	1.25	2.50
23 Richie Petitbon	1.25	2.50
24 Mike Pyle RC	1.25	2.50
25 Roosevelt Taylor RC	2.00	4.00
26 Bill Wade	1.50	3.00
27 Chicago Bears	1.50	3.00
Team Card		
28 Chicago Bears	6.00	12.00
Play Card		
(George Halas)		
29 Johnny Brewer RC	1.25	2.50
30 Jim Brown	50.00	90.00
31 Gary Collins RC	4.00	8.00
32 Vince Costello	1.25	2.50
33 Galen Fiss	1.25	2.50
34 Bill Glass	1.25	2.50
35 Ernie Green RC	1.50	3.00
36 Rich Kreitling	1.25	2.50
37 John Morrow	1.25	2.50
38 Frank Ryan	1.50	3.00
39 Charlie Scales RC	1.25	2.50
40 Dick Schafrath RC	1.25	2.50
41 Cleveland Browns	1.50	3.00
Team Card		
42 Cleveland Browns	1.25	2.50
Play Card		
(Blanton Collier)		
43 Don Bishop	1.25	2.50
44 Frank Clarke RC	1.50	3.00
45 Mike Connelly	1.25	2.50
46 Lee Folkins RC	1.25	2.50
47 Cornell Green RC	4.00	8.00
48 Bob Lilly	25.00	40.00
49 Amos Marsh	1.25	2.50
50 Tommy McDonald	2.50	5.00
51 Don Meredith	20.00	35.00
52 Pettis Norman RC	1.50	3.00
53 Don Perkins	2.00	4.00
54 Guy Reese RC	1.25	2.50
55 Dallas Cowboys	2.00	4.00
Team Card		
56 Dallas Cowboys	12.00	20.00
Play Card		
(Tom Landry)		
57 Terry Barr	1.25	2.50
58 Roger Brown	1.50	3.00
59 Gail Cogdill	1.25	2.50
60 John Gordy RC	1.25	2.50
61 Dick Lane	2.00	4.00
62 Yale Lary	2.00	4.00
63 Dan Lewis	1.25	2.50
64 Darris McCord	1.25	2.50
65 Earl Morrall	1.50	3.00
66 Joe Schmidt	2.50	5.00
67 Pat Studstill RC	1.50	3.00
68 Wayne Walker RC	1.50	3.00
69 Detroit Lions	1.50	3.00
Team Card		
70 Detroit Lions	1.25	2.50
Play Card		
(George Wilson CO)		
71 Herb Adderley RC	20.00	35.00
72 Willie Davis RC	18.00	30.00
73 Forrest Gregg	2.50	5.00
74 Paul Hornung	20.00	35.00
75 Hank Jordan	2.50	5.00
76 Jerry Kramer	3.00	6.00
77 Tom Moore	1.50	3.00
78 Jim Ringo UER	2.50	5.00
(Green Bay on front&		
Philadelphia on back)		
79 Bart Starr	35.00	60.00
80 Jim Taylor	15.00	25.00
81 Jesse Whittenton RC	1.50	3.00
82 Willie Wood	4.00	8.00
83 Green Bay Packers	3.00	6.00
Team Card		
84 Green Bay Packers	20.00	35.00
Play Card		
(Vince Lombardi)		
85 Jon Arnett	1.25	2.50
86 Pervis Atkins RC	1.25	2.50
87 Dick Bass	1.50	3.00
88 Carroll Dale	2.00	4.00
89 Roman Gabriel	3.00	6.00
90 Ed Meador	1.25	2.50
91 Merlin Olsen RC	30.00	50.00
92 Jack Pardee RC	2.00	4.00
93 Jim Phillips	1.25	2.50
94 Carver Shannon RC	1.25	2.50
95 Frank Varrichione	1.25	2.50
96 Danny Villanueva	1.25	2.50
97 Los Angeles Rams	1.50	3.00
Team Card		
98 Los Angeles Rams	1.25	2.50
Play Card		
(Harland Svare)		
99 Grady Alderman RC	1.50	3.00
100 Larry Bowie RC	1.25	2.50
101 Bill Brown RC	3.00	6.00
102 Paul Flatley RC	1.25	2.50
103 Rip Hawkins	1.25	2.50
104 Jim Marshall	4.00	8.00
105 Tommy Mason	1.50	3.00
106 Jim Prestel	1.25	2.50
107 Jerry Reichow	1.25	2.50
108 Ed Sharockman	1.25	2.50
109 Fran Tarkenton	20.00	35.00
110 Mick Tingelhoff RC	3.00	6.00
111 Minnesota Vikings	1.50	3.00
Team Card		
112 Minnesota Vikings	2.00	4.00
Play Card		
(Norm Van Brocklin)		
113 Erich Barnes	1.25	2.50
114 Roosevelt Brown	2.00	4.00
115 Don Chandler	1.25	2.50
116 Darrell Dess	1.25	2.50
117 Frank Gifford	20.00	35.00
118 Dick James	1.25	2.50
119 Jim Katcavage	1.25	2.50
120 John Lovetere RC	1.25	2.50
121 Dick Lynch RC	1.50	3.00
122 Jim Patton	1.25	2.50
123 Del Shofner	1.25	2.50
124 Y.A. Tittle	10.00	20.00
125 New York Giants	1.50	3.00
Team Card		
126 New York Giants	1.25	2.50
Play Card		
(Allie Sherman)		
127 Sam Baker	1.25	2.50
128 Maxie Baughan	1.25	2.50
129 Timmy Brown	1.50	3.00
130 Mike Clark RC	1.25	2.50
131 Irv Cross RC	2.00	4.00
132 Ted Dean	1.25	2.50
133 Ron Goodwin RC	1.25	2.50
134 King Hill	1.25	2.50
135 Clarence Peaks	1.25	2.50
136 Pete Retzlaff	1.50	3.00
137 Jim Schrader	1.25	2.50
138 Norm Snead	1.50	3.00
139 Philadelphia Eagles	1.50	3.00
Team Card		
140 Philadelphia Eagles	1.25	2.50
Play Card		
(Nick Skorich)		
141 Gary Ballman RC	1.25	2.50
142 Charley Bradshaw RC	1.25	2.50
143 Ed Brown	1.50	3.00
144 John Henry Johnson	2.00	4.00
145 Joe Krupa	1.25	2.50
146 Bill Mack	1.25	2.50
147 Lou Michaels	1.25	2.50
148 Buzz Nutter	1.25	2.50
149 Myron Pottios	1.25	2.50
150 John Reger	1.25	2.50
151 Mike Sandusky	1.25	2.50
152 Clendon Thomas	1.25	2.50
153 Pittsburgh Steelers	1.50	3.00
Team Card		
154 Pittsburgh Steelers	1.25	2.50
Play Card		
(Buddy Parker)		
155 Kermit Alexander RC	1.50	3.00
156 Bernie Casey	1.50	3.00
157 Dan Colchico	1.25	2.50
158 Clyde Conner	1.25	2.50
159 Tommy Davis	1.25	2.50
160 Matt Hazeltine	1.25	2.50
161 Jim Johnson RC	15.00	25.00
162 Don Lisbon RC	1.25	2.50
163 Lamar McHan	1.25	2.50
164 Bob St. Clair	2.00	4.00
165 J.D. Smith	1.25	2.50
166 Abe Woodson	1.25	2.50
167 San Francisco 49ers	1.50	3.00
Team Card		
168 San Francisco 49ers	1.25	2.50
Play Card		
(Red Hickey)		
169 Garland Boyette UER RC	1.25	2.50
170 Bobby Joe Conrad	1.50	3.00
171 Bob DeMarco RC	1.25	2.50
172 Ken Gray RC	1.25	2.50
173 Jimmy Hill	1.25	2.50
174 Charley Johnson UER	1.50	3.00
(Misspelled Charley		
on both sides)		
175 Ernie McMillan	1.25	2.50
176 Dale Meinert RC	1.25	2.50
177 Luke Owens RC	1.25	2.50
178 Sonny Randle	1.25	2.50
179 Joe Robb RC	1.25	2.50
180 Bill Stacy	1.25	2.50
181 St. Louis Cardinals	1.50	3.00
Team Card		
182 St. Louis Cardinals	1.25	2.50
Play Card		
(Wally Lemm)		
183 Bill Barnes	1.25	2.50
184 Don Bosseler	1.25	2.50
185 Sam Huff	3.00	6.00
186 Sonny Jurgensen	10.00	20.00
187 Bob Khayat RC	1.25	2.50
188 Riley Mattson	1.25	2.50
189 Bobby Mitchell	3.00	6.00
190 John Nisby	1.25	2.50
191 Vince Promuto	1.25	2.50
192 Joe Rutgens RC	1.25	2.50
193 Lonnie Sanders RC	1.25	2.50
194 Jim Steffen RC	1.25	2.50
195 Washington Redskins	1.50	3.00
Team Card		
196 Washington Redskins	1.25	2.50
Play Card		
(Bill McPeak)		
197 Checklist 1 UER	18.00	30.00
(Dated 1963)		
198 Checklist 2 UER	30.00	55.00
(Dated 1963/174 Charley Johnson		
should be Charlie)		

1965 Philadelphia

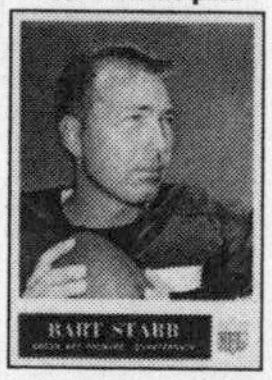

The 1965 Philadelphia Gum set of NFL players consists of 198 standard-size cards. The cards were issued in five-card nickel packs and cello packs. The card fronts have the player's name, team name and position in a black box beneath the photo. The NFL logo is at bottom right. The card backs feature statistics and a question and answer section that requires a coin to rub and reveal the answer. The card backs are printed in maroon on a gray card stock. Each team has a team picture card as well as a card featuring a diagram of one of the team's plays; this play card shows a small coach's picture in black and white on the front of the card. The card backs are printed in maroon on a gray card stock. The cards are numbered within team with the players arranged alphabetically by last name. The key Rookie Cards in this set are Carl Eller, Paul Krause, Mel Renfro, Charley Taylor, and Paul Warfield. Comic Transfers sheets were included as inserts into packs.

COMPLETE SET (198)	500.00	800.00
WRAPPER (5-CENT)	10.00	20.00
1 Baltimore Colts	7.50	15.00
Team Card		
2 Raymond Berry	5.00	10.00
3 Bob Boyd	1.00	2.00
4 Wendell Harris	1.00	2.00
5 Jerry Logan RC	1.00	2.00
6 Tony Lorick RC	1.00	2.00
7 Lou Michaels	1.00	2.00
8 Lenny Moore	4.00	8.00
9 Jimmy Orr	1.50	3.00
10 Jim Parker	2.00	4.00
11 Dick Szymanski	1.00	2.00
12 John Unitas	25.00	40.00
13 Bob Vogel RC	1.00	2.00
14 Baltimore Colts	12.00	20.00
Play Card		
(Don Shula)		
15 Chicago Bears	1.50	3.00
Team Card		
16 Jon Arnett	1.00	2.00
17 Doug Atkins	2.50	5.00
18 Rudy Bukich RC	1.50	3.00
19 Mike Ditka	25.00	40.00
20 Dick Evey RC	1.00	2.00
21 Joe Fortunato	1.00	2.00
22 Bobby Joe Green RC	1.00	2.00
23 Johnny Morris	1.00	2.00
24 Mike Pyle	1.00	2.00
25 Roosevelt Taylor	1.50	3.00
26 Bill Wade	1.50	3.00
27 Bob Wetoska RC	1.00	2.00
28 Chicago Bears	4.00	8.00
Play Card		
(George Halas)		
29 Cleveland Browns	1.50	3.00
Team Card		
30 Walter Beach RC	1.00	2.00
31 Jim Brown	50.00	80.00
32 Gary Collins	1.50	3.00
33 Bill Glass	1.00	2.00
34 Ernie Green	1.00	2.00
35 Jim Houston RC	1.00	2.00
36 Dick Modzelewski	1.00	2.00
37 Bernie Parrish	1.00	2.00
38 Walter Roberts RC	1.00	2.00
39 Frank Ryan	1.50	3.00
40 Dick Schafrath	1.00	2.00
41 Paul Warfield RC	50.00	90.00
42 Cleveland Browns	1.00	2.00
Play Card		
(Blanton Collier)		
43 Dallas Cowboys	1.50	3.00
Team Card UER		
(Cowboys Dallas on back)		
44 Frank Clarke	1.50	3.00
45 Mike Connelly	1.00	2.00
46 Buddy Dial	1.00	2.00
47 Bob Lilly	20.00	35.00
48 Tony Liscio RC	1.00	2.00
49 Tommy McDonald	2.50	5.00
50 Don Meredith	15.00	25.00
51 Pettis Norman	1.00	2.00
52 Don Perkins	2.00	4.00
53 Mel Renfro RC	25.00	40.00
54 Jim Ridlon	1.00	2.00
55 Jerry Tubbs	1.00	2.00
56 Dallas Cowboys	7.50	15.00
Play Card		
(Tom Landry)		
57 Detroit Lions	1.50	3.00
Team Card		
58 Terry Barr	1.00	2.00
59 Roger Brown	1.00	2.00
60 Gail Cogdill	1.00	2.00
61 Jim Gibbons	1.00	2.00
62 John Gordy	1.00	2.00
63 Yale Lary	2.00	4.00
64 Dick LeBeau RC	25.00	40.00
65 Earl Morrall	1.50	3.00
66 Nick Pietrosante	1.00	2.00
67 Pat Studstill	1.00	2.00
68 Wayne Walker	1.50	3.00
69 Tom Watkins RC	1.00	2.00
70 Detroit Lions	1.50	3.00
Play Card		
(Harry Gilmer CO)		
71 Green Bay Packers	4.00	8.00
Team Card		
72 Herb Adderley	4.00	8.00
73 Willie Davis	4.00	8.00
74 Boyd Dowler	2.00	4.00
75 Forrest Gregg	2.50	5.00
76 Paul Hornung	20.00	35.00
77 Hank Jordan	2.50	5.00
78 Tom Moore	1.50	3.00
79 Ray Nitschke	12.00	20.00
80 Elijah Pitts RC	4.00	8.00
81 Bart Starr	30.00	50.00
82 Jim Taylor	12.00	20.00
83 Willie Wood	3.00	6.00
84 Green Bay Packers	12.00	20.00
Play Card		
(Vince Lombardi)		
85 Los Angeles Rams	1.50	3.00
Team Card		
86 Dick Bass	1.50	3.00
87 Roman Gabriel	2.50	5.00
88 Roosevelt Grier	2.00	4.00
89 Deacon Jones	5.00	10.00
90 Lamar Lundy RC	2.00	4.00
91 Marlin McKeever	1.00	2.00
92 Ed Meador	1.00	2.00
93 Bill Munson RC	2.00	4.00
94 Merlin Olsen	7.50	15.00
95 Bobby Smith RC	1.00	2.00
96 Frank Varrichione	1.00	2.00
97 Ben Wilson RC	1.00	2.00
98 Los Angeles Rams	1.00	2.00
Play Card		
(Harland Svare)		
99 Minnesota Vikings	1.50	3.00
Team Card		
100 Grady Alderman	1.00	2.00
101 Hal Bedsole RC	1.00	2.00
102 Bill Brown	1.50	3.00
103 Bill Butler RC	1.00	2.00
104 Fred Cox RC	1.50	3.00
105 Carl Eller RC	18.00	30.00
106 Paul Flatley	1.00	2.00
107 Jim Marshall	3.00	6.00
108 Tommy Mason	1.00	2.00
109 George Rose RC	1.00	2.00
110 Fran Tarkenton	15.00	25.00
111 Mick Tingelhoff	1.50	3.00
112 Minnesota Vikings	2.00	4.00
Play Card		
(Norm Van Brocklin)		
113 New York Giants	1.50	3.00
Team Card		
114 Erich Barnes	1.00	2.00
115 Roosevelt Brown	2.00	4.00
116 Clarence Childs RC	1.00	2.00
117 Jerry Hillebrand	1.00	2.00
118 Greg Larson RC	1.00	2.00
119 Dick Lynch	1.00	2.00
120 Joe Morrison RC	2.00	4.00
121 Lou Slaby RC	1.00	2.00
122 Aaron Thomas RC	1.00	2.00
123 Steve Thurlow RC	1.00	2.00
124 Ernie Wheelwright RC	1.00	2.00
125 Gary Wood RC	1.50	3.00
126 New York Giants	1.00	2.00
Play Card		
(Allie Sherman)		
127 Philadelphia Eagles	1.50	3.00
Team Card		
128 Sam Baker	1.00	2.00
129 Maxie Baughan	1.00	2.00
130 Timmy Brown	1.50	3.00
131 Jack Concannon RC	1.00	2.00
132 Irv Cross	1.50	3.00
133 Earl Gros	1.00	2.00
134 Dave Lloyd RC	1.00	2.00

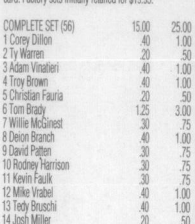

135 Floyd Peters RC	1.00	2.00
136 Nate Ramsey RC	1.00	2.00
137 Pete Retzlaff	1.50	3.00
138 Jim Ringo	2.00	4.00
139 Norm Snead	2.00	4.00
140 Philadelphia Eagles Play Card (Joe Kuharich)	1.00	2.00
141 Pittsburgh Steelers Team Card	1.50	3.00
142 John Baker	1.00	2.00
143 Gary Ballman	1.00	2.00
144 Charley Bradshaw	1.00	2.00
145 Ed Brown	1.00	2.00
146 Dick Haley	1.00	2.00
147 John Henry Johnson	2.00	4.00
148 Brady Keys RC	1.00	2.00
149 Ray Lemek	1.00	2.00
150 Ben McGee RC	1.00	2.00
151 Clarence Peaks UER (quiz reference on back incorrect)	1.00	2.00
152 Myron Pottios	1.00	2.00
153 Clendon Thomas	1.00	2.00
154 Pittsburgh Steelers Play Card (Buddy Parker)	1.00	2.00
155 St. Louis Cardinals Team Card	1.50	3.00
156 Jim Bakken RC	1.50	3.00
157 Joe Childress	1.00	2.00
158 Bobby Joe Conrad	1.50	3.00
159 Bob DeMarco	1.00	2.00
160 Pat Fischer RC	2.00	4.00
161 Irv Goode RC	1.00	2.00
162 Ken Gray	1.00	2.00
163 Charley Johnson UER (Misspelled Charley on both sides)	1.50	3.00
164 Bill Koman	1.00	2.00
165 Dale Meinert	1.00	2.00
166 Jerry Stovall RC	1.50	3.00
167 Abe Woodson	1.00	2.00
168 St. Louis Cardinals Play Card (Wally Lemm)	1.00	2.00
169 San Francisco 49ers Team Card	1.50	3.00
170 Kermit Alexander	1.00	2.00
171 John Brodie	5.00	10.00
172 Bernie Casey	1.50	3.00
173 John David Crow	1.50	3.00
174 Tommy Davis	1.00	2.00
175 Matt Hazeltine	1.00	2.00
176 Jim Johnson	2.00	4.00
177 Charlie Krueger RC	1.00	2.00
178 Roland Lakes RC	1.00	2.00
179 George Mira RC	1.50	3.00
180 Dave Parks RC	1.50	3.00
181 John Thomas RC	1.00	2.00
182 San Francisco 49ers Play Card (Jack Christiansen)	1.00	2.00
183 Washington Redskins Team Card	1.50	3.00
184 Pervis Atkins	1.00	2.00
185 Preston Carpenter	1.00	2.00
186 Angelo Cola	1.00	2.00
187 Sam Huff	3.00	6.00
188 Sonny Jurgensen	7.50	15.00
189 Paul Krause RC	20.00	40.00
190 Jim Martin	1.00	2.00
191 Bobby Mitchell	2.50	5.00
192 John Nisby	1.00	2.00
193 John Paluck	1.00	2.00
194 Vince Promuto	1.00	2.00
195 Charley Taylor RC	30.00	50.00
196 Washington Redskins Play Card (Bill McPeak)	1.00	2.00
197 Checklist 1	15.00	30.00
198 Checklist 2 UER (163 Charley Johnson should be Charlie)	25.00	50.00

1966 Philadelphia

The 1966 Philadelphia Gum football card set contains 198 standard-size cards featuring NFL players. The cards were issued in five-card nickel packs which came 24 packs to a box and cello packs. The card fronts feature the player's name, team name and position in a color bar above the photo. The NFL logo is at upper left. The card backs are printed in green and black on a white card stock. The backs contain the player's name, a card number, a short biography, and a "Guess Who" quiz. The quiz answer is found on another card. The last two cards in the set are checklist cards. Each team's "play card" shows a color photo of actual game action, described on the back. The cards are numbered within team with the players arranged alphabetically by last name. The set features the debut of Hall of Fame Chicago Bears' greats Dick Butkus and Gale Sayers. Other Rookie Cards include Cowboys Bob Hayes and Chuck Howley. Comic Transfers sheets were included as inserts into packs.

COMPLETE SET (198)	600.00	900.00
WRAPPER (5-CENT)	10.00	20.00
1 Atlanta Falcons Insignia	6.00	12.00
2 Larry Benz RC	1.00	2.00
3 Dennis Claridge RC	1.00	2.00
4 Perry Lee Dunn RC	1.00	2.00
5 Dan Grimm RC	1.00	2.00
6 Alex Hawkins	1.00	2.00
7 Ralph Heck RC	1.00	2.00
8 Frank Lasky RC	1.00	2.00
9 Guy Reese	1.00	2.00
10 Bob Richards RC	1.00	2.00
11 Ron Smith RC	1.00	2.00
12 Ernie Wheelwright	1.00	2.00
13 Atlanta Falcons Roster	1.50	3.00
14 Baltimore Colts Team Card	1.50	3.00
15 Raymond Berry	4.00	8.00
16 Bob Boyd	1.00	2.00
17 Jerry Logan	1.00	2.00
18 John Mackey	3.00	6.00
19 Tom Matte	2.00	4.00
20 Lou Michaels	1.00	2.00
21 Lenny Moore	4.00	8.00
22 Jimmy Orr	1.50	3.00
23 Jim Parker	2.00	4.00
24 John Unitas	30.00	50.00
25 Bob Vogel	1.00	2.00
26 Baltimore Colts Play Card (Lenny Moore Jim Parker)	2.00	4.00
27 Chicago Bears Team Card	1.50	3.00
28 Doug Atkins	2.00	4.00
29 Rudy Bukich	1.00	2.00
30 Ronnie Bull	1.00	2.00
31 Dick Butkus RC	150.00	250.00
32 Mike Ditka	20.00	35.00
33 Joe Fortunato	1.00	2.00
34 Bobby Joe Green	1.00	2.00
35 Roger LeClerc	1.00	2.00
36 Johnny Morris	1.00	2.00
37 Mike Pyle	1.00	2.00
38 Gale Sayers RC	125.00	225.00
39 Chicago Bears Play Card (Gale Sayers)	20.00	35.00
40 Cleveland Browns Team Card	1.50	3.00
41 Jim Brown	50.00	80.00
42 Gary Collins	1.50	3.00
43 Ross Fichtner RC	1.00	2.00
44 Ernie Green	1.00	2.00
45 Gene Hickerson RC	15.00	25.00
46 Jim Houston	1.00	2.00
47 John Morrow	1.00	2.00
48 Walter Roberts	1.00	2.00
49 Frank Ryan	1.50	3.00
50 Dick Schafrath	1.00	2.00
51 Paul Wiggin RC	1.00	2.00
52 Cleveland Browns Play Card (Ernie Green sweep)	1.00	2.00
53 Dallas Cowboys Team Card	1.50	3.00
54 George Andrie UER RC (Text says startling& should be starting)	2.00	4.00
55 Frank Clarke	1.50	3.00
56 Mike Connelly	1.00	2.00
57 Cornell Green	2.00	4.00
58 Bob Hayes RC	35.00	60.00
59 Chuck Howley RC	15.00	30.00
60 Bob Lilly	12.00	20.00
61 Don Meredith	15.00	25.00
62 Don Perkins	1.50	3.00
63 Mel Renfro	7.50	15.00
64 Danny Villanueva	1.00	2.00
65 Dallas Cowboys Play Card (Danny Villanueva)	1.00	2.00
66 Detroit Lions Team Card	1.50	3.00
67 Roger Brown	1.00	2.00
68 John Gordy	1.00	2.00
69 Alex Karras	5.00	10.00
70 Dick LeBeau	3.00	6.00
71 Amos Marsh	1.00	2.00
72 Milt Plum	1.50	3.00
73 Bobby Smith	1.00	2.00
74 Wayne Rasmussen RC	1.00	2.00
75 Pat Studstill	1.00	2.00
76 Wayne Walker	1.00	2.00
77 Tom Watkins	1.00	2.00
78 Detroit Lions Play Card (George Izo pass)	1.00	2.00
79 Green Bay Packers Team Card	3.00	6.00
80 Herb Adderley UER (Adderly on back)	3.00	6.00
81 Lee Roy Caffey RC	2.00	4.00
82 Don Chandler	1.50	3.00
83 Willie Davis	3.00	6.00
84 Boyd Dowler	2.00	4.00
85 Forrest Gregg	2.00	4.00
86 Tom Moore	1.50	3.00
87 Ray Nitschke	7.50	15.00
88 Bart Starr	30.00	50.00
89 Jim Taylor	12.00	20.00
90 Willie Wood	3.00	6.00
91 Green Bay Packers Play Card (Don Chandler FG)	1.00	2.00
92 Los Angeles Rams Team Card	1.50	3.00
93 Willie Brown RC	1.00	2.00
94 Dick Bass and Roman Gabriel	2.00	4.00
95 Bruce Gossett RC (Tom Landry small photo on back)	1.50	3.00
96 Deacon Jones	3.00	6.00
97 Tommy McDonald	2.50	5.00
98 Marlin McKeever	1.00	2.00
99 Aaron Martin RC	1.00	2.00
100 Ed Meador	1.00	2.00
101 Bill Munson	1.50	3.00
102 Merlin Olsen	4.00	8.00
103 Jim Stiger RC	1.00	2.00
104 Los Angeles Rams Play Card (Willie Brown run)	1.50	3.00
105 Minnesota Vikings Team Card	1.50	3.00
106 Grady Alderman	1.00	2.00
107 Bill Brown	1.50	3.00
108 Fred Cox	1.00	2.00
109 Paul Flatley	1.00	2.00
110 Rip Hawkins	1.00	2.00
111 Tommy Mason	1.00	2.00
112 Ed Sharockman	1.00	2.00
113 Gordon Smith RC	1.00	2.00
114 Fran Tarkenton	15.00	30.00
115 Mick Tingelhoff	1.50	3.00
116 Bobby Walden RC	1.00	2.00
117 Minnesota Vikings Play Card (Bill Brown run)	1.00	2.00
118 New York Giants Team Card	1.50	3.00
119 Roosevelt Brown	2.00	4.00
120 Henry Carr RC	1.50	3.00
121 Clarence Childs	1.00	2.00
122 Tucker Frederickson RC	1.50	3.00
123 Jerry Hillebrand	1.00	2.00
124 Greg Larson	1.00	2.00
125 Spider Lockhart RC	1.50	3.00
126 Dick Lynch	1.00	2.00
127 Earl Morrall and Bob Scholtz	1.50	3.00
128 Joe Morrison	1.00	2.00
129 Steve Thurlow	1.00	2.00
130 New York Giants Play Card (Chuck Mercein over)	1.00	2.00
131 Philadelphia Eagles Team Card	1.50	3.00
132 Sam Baker	1.00	2.00
133 Maxie Baughan	1.00	2.00
134 Bob Brown OT RC	7.50	15.00
135 Timmy Brown (Lou Groza small photo on back)	1.50	3.00
136 Irv Cross	1.50	3.00
137 Earl Gros	1.00	2.00
138 Ray Poage RC	1.00	2.00
139 Nate Ramsey	1.00	2.00
140 Pete Retzlaff	1.50	3.00
141 Jim Ringo (Joe Schmidt small photo on back)	2.00	4.00
142 Norm Snead (Norm Van Brocklin small photo on back)	2.00	4.00
143 Philadelphia Eagles Play Card (Earl Gros tackled)	1.00	2.00
144 Pittsburgh Steelers Team Card (Lee Roy Jordan small photo on back)	1.50	3.00
145 Gary Ballman	1.00	2.00
146 Charley Bradshaw	1.00	2.00
147 Jim Butler RC	1.00	2.00
148 Mike Clark	1.00	2.00
149 Dick Hoak RC	1.00	2.00
150 Roy Jefferson RC	1.50	3.00
151 Frank Lambert RC	1.00	2.00
152 Mike Lind RC	1.00	2.00
153 Bill Nelsen RC	2.00	4.00
154 Clarence Peaks	1.00	2.00
155 Clendon Thomas	1.00	2.00
156 Pittsburgh Steelers Play Card (Gary Ballman scores)	1.00	2.00
157 St. Louis Cardinals Team Card	1.50	3.00
158 Jim Bakken	1.00	2.00
159 Bobby Joe Conrad	1.50	3.00
160 Willis Crenshaw RC	1.00	2.00
161 Bob DeMarco	1.00	2.00
162 Pat Fischer	1.50	3.00
163 Charley Johnson UER (Misspelled Charley on both sides)	1.50	3.00
164 Dale Meinert	1.00	2.00
165 Sonny Randle	1.00	2.00
166 Sam Silas RC	1.00	2.00
167 Bill Triplett RC	1.00	2.00
168 Larry Wilson	2.00	4.00
169 St. Louis Cardinals Play Card (Bill Triplett tackled by Roosevelt Davis and Roger LaLonde)	1.00	2.00
170 San Francisco 49ers Team Card (Vince Lombardi small photo on back)	1.50	3.00
171 Kermit Alexander	1.00	2.00
172 Bruce Bosley	1.00	2.00
173 John Brodie	3.00	6.00
174 Bernie Casey	1.50	3.00
175 John David Crow	2.00	4.00
176 Tommy Davis	1.00	2.00
177 Jim Johnson	2.00	4.00
178 Gary Lewis RC	1.00	2.00
179 Dave Parks	1.00	2.00
180 Walter Rock (Paul Hornung small photo on back)	1.50	3.00
181 Ken Willard RC (George Halas small photo on back)	2.00	4.00
182 San Francisco 49ers Play Card (Tommy Davis FG)	1.00	2.00
183 Washington Redskins Team Card	1.50	3.00
184 Rickie Harris RC	1.00	2.00
185 Sonny Jurgensen	4.00	8.00
186 Paul Krause	3.00	6.00
187 Bobby Mitchell	3.00	6.00
188 Vince Promuto	1.00	2.00
189 Pat Richter RC (Craig Morton small photo on back)	1.00	2.00
190 Joe Rutgens	1.00	2.00
191 Johnny Sample	1.00	2.00
192 Lonnie Sanders	1.00	2.00
193 Jim Steffen	1.00	2.00
194 Charley Taylor UER (Called Charley and Charlie on card back	7.50	15.00
195 Washington Redskins Play Card (Dan Lewis tackled by Roger LaLonde)	1.00	2.00
196 Referee Signals	1.50	3.00
197 Checklist 1	12.50	25.00
198 Checklist 2 UER (163 Charley Johnson should be Charlie)	25.00	50.00

1967 Philadelphia

The 1967 Philadelphia Gum set of NFL players consists of 198 standard-size cards. It was the company's last issue. Cards were issued in five-card nickel packs and cello packs. This set is easily distinguished from the other Philadelphia football sets by its yellow border on the fronts of the cards. The player's name, team name and position are at the bottom in a color bar. The NFL logo is at the top right or left. Horizontally designed backs are printed in brown on a white card stock. The left side of the back contains a trivia question that requires a coin to scratch to reveal the answer. The right side has a brief write-up. The cards are numbered within team with players arranged alphabetically by last name. The key Rookie Cards in this set are Lee Roy Jordan, Leroy Kelly, Tommy Nobis, Dan Reeves and Jackie Smith.

COMPLETE SET (198)	400.00	650.00
WRAPPER (5-CENT)	10.00	20.00
1 Atlanta Falcons Team Card	5.00	10.00
2 Junior Coffey RC	1.50	3.00
3 Alex Hawkins	1.00	2.00
4 Randy Johnson RC	1.50	3.00
5 Lou Kirouac RC	1.00	2.00
6 Billy Martin RC	1.00	2.00
7 Tommy Nobis RC	10.00	20.00
8 Jerry Richardson RC	2.00	4.00
9 Marion Rushing RC	1.00	2.00
10 Ron Smith	1.00	2.00
11 Ernie Wheelwright UER (Misspelled Wheelright on both sides)	1.00	2.00
12 Atlanta Falcons Insignia	1.00	2.00
13 Baltimore Colts Team Card	1.50	3.00
14 Raymond Berry UER (Photo actually Bob Boyd	3.50	7.00
15 Bob Boyd	1.00	2.00
16 Ordell Braase RC	1.00	2.00
17 Alvin Haymond RC	1.00	2.00
18 Tony Lorick	1.00	2.00
19 Lenny Lyles RC	1.00	2.00
20 John Mackey	2.50	5.00
21 Tom Matte	1.50	3.00
22 Lou Michaels	1.00	2.00
23 John Unitas	25.00	40.00
24 Baltimore Colts Insignia	1.00	2.00
25 Chicago Bears Team Card	1.50	3.00
26 Rudy Bukich UER (Misspelled Buckich on card back)	1.00	2.00
27 Ronnie Bull	1.00	2.00
28 Dick Butkus	45.00	75.00
29 Mike Ditka	18.00	30.00
30 Dick Gordon RC	1.50	3.00
31 Roger LeClerc	1.00	2.00
32 Bennie McRae	1.00	2.00
33 Richie Petitbon	1.00	2.00
34 Mike Pyle	1.00	2.00
35 Gale Sayers	45.00	75.00
36 Chicago Bears Insignia	1.00	2.00
37 Cleveland Browns Team Card	1.50	3.00
38 Johnny Brewer	1.00	2.00
39 Gary Collins	1.50	3.00
40 Ross Fichtner	1.00	2.00
41 Ernie Green	1.00	2.00
42 Gene Hickerson	2.50	5.00
43 Leroy Kelly RC	25.00	50.00
44 Frank Ryan	1.50	3.00
45 Dick Schafrath	1.00	2.00
46 Paul Warfield	10.00	18.00
47 John Wooten RC	1.00	2.00
48 Cleveland Browns Insignia	1.00	2.00
49 Dallas Cowboys Team Card	1.50	3.00
50 George Andrie	1.00	2.00
51 Cornell Green	1.50	3.00
52 Bob Hayes	10.00	20.00
53 Chuck Howley	2.00	4.00
54 Lee Roy Jordan RC	12.00	20.00
55 Bob Lilly	7.50	15.00
56 Dave Manders RC	1.00	2.00
57 Don Meredith	15.00	25.00
58 Dan Reeves RC	18.00	30.00
59 Mel Renfro	3.00	6.00
60 Dallas Cowboys Insignia	1.50	3.00
61 Detroit Lions Team Card	1.50	3.00
62 Roger Brown	1.50	3.00
63 Gail Cogdill	1.00	2.00
64 John Gordy	1.00	2.00
65 Ron Kramer	1.00	2.00
66 Dick LeBeau	2.00	4.00
67 Mike Lucci RC	2.00	4.00
68 Amos Marsh	1.00	2.00
69 Tom Nowatzke RC	1.00	2.00
70 Pat Studstill	1.00	2.00
71 Karl Sweetan RC	1.00	2.00
72 Detroit Lions Insignia	1.00	2.00
73 Green Bay Packers Team Card	2.50	5.00
74 Herb Adderley UER (Adderly on back)	3.00	6.00
75 Lee Roy Caffey	1.50	3.00
76 Willie Davis	2.50	5.00
77 Forrest Gregg	2.00	4.00
78 Hank Jordan	2.00	4.00
79 Ray Nitschke	6.00	12.00
80 Dave Robinson RC	3.00	6.00
81 Bob Skoronski RC	1.50	3.00
82 Bart Starr	30.00	50.00
83 Willie Wood	2.50	5.00
84 Green Bay Packers Insignia	1.50	3.00
85 Los Angeles Rams Team Card	1.50	3.00
86 Dick Bass	1.50	3.00
87 Maxie Baughan	1.00	2.00
88 Roman Gabriel	2.00	4.00
89 Bruce Gossett	1.00	2.00
90 Deacon Jones	2.50	5.00
91 Tommy McDonald	2.50	5.00
92 Marlin McKeever	1.00	2.00
93 Tom Moore	1.00	2.00
94 Merlin Olsen	3.00	6.00
95 Clancy Williams RC	1.00	2.00
96 Los Angeles Rams Insignia	1.00	2.00
97 Minnesota Vikings Team Card	1.50	3.00
98 Grady Alderman	1.00	2.00
99 Bill Brown	1.50	3.00
100 Fred Cox	1.00	2.00
101 Paul Flatley	1.00	2.00
102 Dale Hackbart RC	1.00	2.00
103 Jim Marshall	2.00	4.00
104 Tommy Mason	1.00	2.00
105 Milt Sunde RC	1.00	2.00
106 Fran Tarkenton	10.00	20.00
107 Mick Tingelhoff	1.50	3.00
108 Minnesota Vikings Insignia	1.00	2.00
109 New York Giants Team Card	1.50	3.00
110 Henry Carr	1.00	2.00
111 Clarence Childs	1.00	2.00
112 Allen Jacobs RC	1.00	2.00
113 Homer Jones RC	1.50	3.00
114 Tom Kennedy RC	1.00	2.00
115 Spider Lockhart	1.00	2.00
116 Joe Morrison	1.00	2.00
117 Francis Peay RC	1.00	2.00
118 Jeff Smith LB RC	1.00	2.00
119 Aaron Thomas	1.00	2.00
120 New York Giants Insignia	1.00	2.00
121 New Orleans Saints Insignia (See also card 132)	1.50	3.00
122 Charley Bradshaw	1.00	2.00
123 Paul Hornung	12.50	25.00
124 Elbert Kimbrough RC	1.00	2.00
125 Earl Leggett RC	1.00	2.00
126 Obert Logan RC	1.00	2.00
127 Riley Mattson	1.00	2.00
128 John Morrow	1.00	2.00
129 Bob Scholtz RC	1.00	2.00
130 Dave Whitsell RC	1.00	2.00
131 Gary Wood	1.00	2.00
132 New Orleans Saints Roster UER (121 on back)	1.50	3.00
133 Philadelphia Eagles Team Card	1.50	3.00
134 Sam Baker	1.00	2.00
135 Bob Brown OT	2.00	5.00
136 Timmy Brown	1.50	3.00
137 Earl Gros	1.00	2.00
138 Dave Lloyd	1.00	2.00
139 Floyd Peters	1.00	2.00
140 Pete Retzlaff	1.50	3.00
141 Joe Scarpati RC	1.00	2.00
142 Norm Snead	1.50	3.00
143 Jim Skaggs RC	1.00	2.00
144 Philadelphia Eagles Insignia	1.00	2.00
145 Pittsburgh Steelers Team Card	1.50	3.00
146 Bill Asbury RC	1.00	2.00
147 John Baker	1.00	2.00
148 Gary Ballman	1.00	2.00
149 Mike Clark	1.00	2.00
150 Riley Gunnels	1.00	2.00
151 John Hilton RC	1.00	2.00
152 Roy Jefferson	1.50	3.00
153 Brady Keys	1.00	2.00
154 Ben McGee	1.00	2.00
155 Bill Nelsen	1.50	3.00
156 Pittsburgh Steelers Insignia	1.00	2.00
157 St. Louis Cardinals Team Card	1.50	3.00
158 Jim Bakken	1.00	2.00
159 Bobby Joe Conrad	1.50	3.00
160 Ken Gray	1.00	2.00
161 Charley Johnson UER (Misspelled Charley on both sides)	1.50	3.00
162 Joe Robb	1.00	2.00
163 Johnny Roland RC	1.50	3.00
164 Roy Shivers RC	1.00	2.00
165 Jackie Smith RC	10.00	20.00
166 Jerry Stovall	1.00	2.00
167 Larry Wilson	2.00	4.00
168 St. Louis Cardinals Insignia	1.00	2.00
169 San Francisco 49ers Team Card	1.50	3.00
170 Kermit Alexander	1.00	2.00
171 Bruce Bosley	1.00	2.00
172 John Brodie	3.00	6.00
173 Bernie Casey	1.50	3.00
174 Tommy Davis	1.00	2.00
175 Howard Mudd RC	2.00	4.00
176 Dave Parks	1.00	2.00
177 John Thomas	1.00	2.00
178 Dave Wilcox RC	12.50	25.00
179 Ken Willard	1.50	3.00
180 San Francisco 49ers Insignia	1.00	2.00
181 Washington Redskins Team Card	1.50	3.00
182 Charlie Gogolak RC	1.00	2.00
183 Chris Hanburger RC	7.50	15.00
184 Len Hauss RC	1.50	3.00
185 Sonny Jurgensen	3.50	7.00
186 Bobby Mitchell	2.50	5.00
187 Brig Owens RC	1.00	2.00
188 Jim Shorter RC	1.00	2.00
189 Jerry Smith RC	1.50	3.00
190 Charley Taylor	4.00	8.00
191 A.D. Whitfield RC	1.00	2.00
192 Washington Redskins Insignia	1.00	2.00
193 Cleveland Browns Play Card (Leroy Kelly)	3.00	6.00
194 New York Giants Play Card (Joe Morrison)	1.00	2.00
195 Atlanta Falcons Play Card (Ernie Wheelright)	1.00	2.00
196 Referee Signals	1.50	3.00
197 Checklist 1	12.00	20.00
198 Checklist 2 UER (161 Charley Johnson should be Charlie)	20.00	40.00

2009 Philadelphia

COMP.SET w/o SP's (200)	25.00	50.00
1 Kurt Warner	.30	.75
2 Matt Leinart	.25	.60
3 Edgerrin James	.25	.60
4 Tim Hightower	.20	.50
5 Larry Fitzgerald	.30	.75
6 Anquan Boldin	.25	.60
7 Karlos Dansby	.20	.50
8 Steve Breaston	.25	.60
9 Matt Ryan	.30	.75
10 Michael Turner	.25	.60
11 Jerious Norwood	.25	.60
12 Roddy White	.25	.60
13 John Abraham	.20	.50
14 Harry Douglas	.20	.50
15 Michael Jenkins	.20	.50
16 Joe Flacco	.30	.75
17 Willis McGahee	.25	.60
18 Ray Rice	.30	.75
19 Derrick Mason	.25	.60
20 Ray Lewis	.30	.75
21 Terrell Suggs	.20	.50
22 Trent Edwards	.20	.50
23 Marshawn Lynch	.25	.60
24 Lee Evans	.25	.60
25 Josh Reed	.20	.50
26 Paul Posluszny	.25	.60
27 Jake Delhomme	.25	.60
28 Jonathan Stewart	.25	.60
29 DeAngelo Williams	.30	.75
30 Steve Smith	.25	.60
31 Muhsin Muhammad	.25	.60
32 Jon Beason	.20	.50
33 Julius Peppers	.25	.60
34 Kyle Orton	.25	.60
35 Matt Forte	.30	.75
36 Devin Hester	.30	.75
37 Brian Urlacher	.30	.75
38 Lance Briggs	.25	.60
39 Charles Tillman	.20	.50
40 Greg Olsen	.20	.50
41 Carson Palmer	.30	.75
42 Chris Perry	.20	.50
43 T.J. Houshmandzadeh	.25	.60
44 Chad Ocho Cinco	.25	.60
45 Dhani Jones	.20	.50
46 Brady Quinn	.25	.60
47 Jamal Lewis	.25	.60
48 Braylon Edwards	.25	.60
49 Kellen Winslow	.25	.60
50 D'Qwell Jackson	.20	.50
51 Shaun Rogers	.20	.50
52 Tony Romo	.50	1.25
53 Marion Barber	.25	.60
54 Jason Witten	.30	.75
55 Terrell Owens	.30	.75
56 Felix Jones	.30	.75
57 Roy Williams WR	.25	.60
58 DeMarcus Ware	.25	.60
59 Zach Thomas	.25	.60
60 Jay Cutler	.30	.75
61 Tony Scheffler	.20	.50
62 Brandon Marshall	.25	.60
63 Eddie Royal	.25	.60
64 D.J. Williams	.20	.50
65 Ronald Curry	.20	.50
66 Kevin Smith	.25	.60
67 Rudi Johnson	.20	.50
68 Calvin Johnson	.30	.75
69 Ernie Sims	.20	.50
70 DeWayne White	.20	.50
71 Aaron Rodgers	.60	1.50
72 Ryan Grant	.25	.60
73 Greg Jennings	.30	.75
74 Donald Driver	.25	.60
75 A.J. Hawk	.25	.60
76 Aaron Kampman	.25	.60
77 Nick Collins	.20	.50
78 Matt Schaub	.25	.60
79 Steve Slaton	.25	.60
80 Andre Johnson	.25	.60
81 Owen Daniels	.20	.50
82 Kevin Walter	.25	.60
83 Mario Williams	.25	.60
84 Peyton Manning	.50	1.25
85 Joseph Addai	.30	.75
86 Reggie Wayne	.25	.60
87 Dwight Freeney	.25	.60
88 Anthony Gonzalez	.20	.50
89 Dallas Clark	.25	.60
90 Robert Mathis	.20	.50
91 David Garrard	.25	.60
92 Maurice Jones-Drew	.25	.60
93 Marcedes Lewis	.20	.50
94 Rashean Mathis	.20	.50
95 Mike Peterson	.20	.50
96 Matt Cassel	.25	.60
97 Larry Johnson	.25	.60
98 Jamaal Charles	.30	.75
99 Dwayne Bowe	.25	.60
100 Tony Gonzalez	.25	.60
101 Chad Pennington	.25	.60
102 Ronnie Brown	.25	.60
103 Ted Ginn	.25	.60
104 Greg Camarillo	.25	.60
105 Joey Porter	.25	.60
106 Adrian Peterson	.50	1.25
107 Bernard Berrian	.25	.60
108 Bobby Wade	.20	.50
109 Kevin Williams	.20	.50
110 Jared Allen	.30	.75
111 Gus Frerotte	.20	.50
112 Tom Brady	.50	1.25
113 Sammy Morris	.20	.50
114 Randy Moss	.30	.75
115 Wes Welker	.30	.75
116 Jerod Mayo	.25	.60
117 Brandon Meriweather	.20	.50
118 Drew Brees	.30	.75
119 Reggie Bush	.30	.75
120 Robert Meachem	.25	.60
121 Devery Henderson	.20	.50
122 Lance Moore	.25	.60
123 Jeremy Shockey	.20	.50
124 Jonathan Vilma	.20	.50
125 Marques Colston	.25	.60
126 Eli Manning	.30	.75
127 Brandon Jacobs	.25	.60
128 Osi Umenyiora	.25	.60
129 Steve Smith USC	.25	.60
130 Justin Tuck	.25	.60
131 Mathias Kiwanuka	.20	.50
132 Bart Scott	.20	.50
133 Thomas Jones	.25	.60
134 Laveranues Coles	.20	.50
135 Jerricho Cotchery	.25	.60
136 Chansi Stuckey	.20	.50
137 JaMarcus Russell	.20	.50
138 Darren McFadden	.30	.75
139 Zach Miller	.20	.50
140 Gibril Wilson	.20	.50
141 Justin Fargas	.20	.50
142 Donovan McNabb	.30	.75
143 Brian Westbrook	.25	.60
144 Correll Buckhalter	.20	.50
145 DeSean Jackson	.25	.60
146 Quintin Mikell RC	.30	.75
147 Asante Samuel	.20	.50
148 Hank Baskett	.20	.50
149 Ben Roethlisberger	.30	.75
150 Willie Parker	.20	.50
151 Santonio Holmes	.25	.60
152 Hines Ward	.25	.60
153 James Harrison	.30	.75
154 Troy Polamalu	.30	.75
155 LaMarr Woodley	.20	.50
156 Philip Rivers	.30	.75
157 LaDainian Tomlinson	.30	.75
158 Vincent Jackson	.25	.60
159 Antonio Gates	.25	.60
160 Chris Chambers	.25	.60
161 Antonio Cromartie	.20	.50
162 Shaun Hill	.20	.50
163 Frank Gore	.25	.60
164 Isaac Bruce	.25	.60
165 Patrick Willis	.25	.60
166 Takeo Spikes	.20	.50
167 Arnaz Battle	.20	.50
168 Matt Hasselbeck	.25	.60
169 Julius Jones	.20	.50
170 John Carlson	.25	.60
171 Lofa Tatupu	.25	.60
172 Julian Peterson	.20	.50
173 Patrick Kerney	.20	.50
174 Marc Bulger	.25	.60
175 Steven Jackson	.25	.60
176 Donnie Avery	.25	.60
177 Torry Holt	.25	.60
178 Chris Long	.25	.60
179 Oshiomogho Atogwe	.20	.50
180 Leonard Little	.20	.50
181 Jeff Garcia	.25	.60
182 Earnest Graham	.20	.50
183 Warrick Dunn	.25	.60
184 Antonio Bryant	.20	.50
185 Barrett Ruud	.20	.50
186 Ronde Barber	.20	.50
187 Vince Young	.25	.60
188 Kerry Collins	.25	.60
189 Chris Johnson	.30	.75
190 LenDale White	.25	.60
191 Bo Scaife	.20	.50
192 Albert Haynesworth	.20	.50
193 Cortland Finnegan	.20	.50
194 Jason Campbell	.20	.50
195 Clinton Portis	.25	.60
196 Santana Moss	.25	.60
197 Chris Cooley	.25	.60
198 Antwaan Randle El	.20	.50
199 London Fletcher	.20	.50
200 DeAngelo Hall	.25	.60
201 Matthew Stafford RC	8.00	20.00
202 Knowshon Moreno RC	1.50	4.00
203 Patrick Turner RC	1.25	3.00
204 Mike Goodson RC	1.50	4.00
205 Darrius Heyward-Bey RC	1.50	4.00
206 Javon Ringer RC	1.50	4.00
207 Aaron Curry RC	1.50	4.00
208 Brian Orakpo RC	1.50	4.00
209 Brandon Pettigrew RC	1.50	4.00
210 Michael Johnson RC	1.00	2.50
211 Rey Maualuga RC	1.50	4.00
212 William Moore RC	1.50	4.00
213 James Laurinaitis RC	1.50	4.00
214 Brian Cushing RC	1.50	4.00
215 Malcolm Jenkins RC	1.50	4.00
216 Alphonso Smith RC	1.25	3.00
217 Chase Coffman RC	1.25	3.00
218 Brian Robiskie RC	1.50	4.00
219 Marcus Freeman RC	1.50	4.00
220 Juaquin Iglesias RC	1.25	3.00
221 Vontae Davis RC	1.50	4.00
222 Michael Crabtree RC	3.00	8.00
223 Chris Wells RC	2.50	6.00
224 Mark Sanchez RC	5.00	12.00
225 Jeremy Maclin RC	2.50	6.00
226 Nathan Brown RC	1.25	3.00
227 LeSean McCoy RC	3.00	8.00
228 Percy Harvin RC	2.50	6.00
229 Jarett Dillard RC	1.25	3.00
230 Travis Beckum RC	1.25	3.00
231 Devin Moore RC	1.25	3.00
232 Graham Harrell RC	1.50	4.00
233 Demetrius Byrd RC	1.25	3.00
234 Aaron Kelly RC	1.25	3.00
235 Pat White RC	1.50	4.00
236 Shonn Greene RC	2.50	6.00
237 James Davis RC	1.50	4.00
238 P.J. Hill RC	1.25	3.00
239 Eben Britton RC	1.25	3.00
240 B.J. Raji RC	1.50	4.00
241 Ian Johnson RC	1.50	4.00
242 Quan Cosby RC	1.25	3.00
243 Darius Butler RC	1.50	4.00
244 Kenny Britt RC	2.00	5.00
245 Curtis Painter RC	1.50	4.00
246 Sen'Derrick Marks RC	1.00	2.50
247 Larry English RC	1.50	4.00
248 Sean Smith RC	1.50	4.00
249 Victor Harris RC	1.50	4.00
250 Everette Brown RC	1.25	3.00
251 Darry Beckwith RC	1.25	3.00
252 Mike Wallace RC	3.00	8.00
253 Derrick Williams RC	1.25	3.00
254 Clint Sintim RC	1.50	4.00
255 Mike Mickens RC	1.25	3.00
256 Patrick Chung RC	1.50	4.00
257 Aaron Maybin RC	1.25	3.00
258 Matt Shaughnessy RC	1.25	3.00
259 Fili Moala RC	1.25	3.00
260 Tyson Jackson RC	1.25	3.00
261 Peria Jerry RC	1.25	3.00
262 Rhett Bomar RC	1.25	3.00
263 Michael Oher RC	2.50	6.00
264 Eugene Monroe RC	1.00	2.50
265 Alex Mack RC	1.25	3.00
266 Duke Robinson RC	1.00	2.50
267 Josh Freeman RC	3.00	8.00
268 Jason Smith RC	1.25	3.00
269 Herman Johnson RC	1.25	3.00
270 Stephen McGee RC	1.50	4.00
271 Hakeem Nicks RC	2.50	6.00
272 Alex Boone RC	1.50	4.00
273 Rashad Jennings RC	1.50	4.00
274 Brandon Tate RC	1.50	4.00
275 Donald Brown RC	1.50	4.00
276 Alan Page	2.00	5.00
277 Lem Barney	1.50	4.00
278 Phil Simms	2.00	5.00
279 Jim Kelly	2.50	6.00
280 Jack Youngblood	1.50	4.00
281 Alex Karras	2.00	5.00
282 Fred Biletnikoff	2.50	6.00
283 Earl Campbell	2.50	6.00
284 Darrell Green	2.00	5.00
285 Steve Young	3.00	8.00
286 Ron Yary	1.50	4.00
287 Thurman Thomas	2.50	6.00
288 Lawrence Taylor	2.50	6.00
289 Steve Largent	2.50	6.00
290 Roger Staubach	3.00	8.00
291 Troy Aikman	3.00	8.00
292 John Elway	4.00	10.00
293 Tom Rathman	1.50	4.00
294 Fran Tarkenton	2.50	6.00
295 Terry Bradshaw	3.00	8.00
296 Barry Sanders	4.00	10.00
297 Merlin Olsen	2.00	5.00
298 Roger Craig	2.00	5.00
299 Ken Anderson	2.00	5.00
300 Jerry Rice	4.00	10.00
301 Barack Obama	1.50	4.00
302 Barack Obama	1.50	4.00
303 Barack Obama	1.50	4.00
304 Barack Obama	1.50	4.00
305 Barack Obama	1.50	4.00
306 Barack Obama	1.50	4.00
307 Barack Obama	1.50	4.00
308 Barack Obama	1.50	4.00
309 Barack Obama	1.50	4.00
310 Barack Obama	1.50	4.00
311 Barack Obama	1.50	4.00
312 Barack Obama	1.50	4.00
313 Barack Obama	1.50	4.00
314 Barack Obama	1.50	4.00
315 Barack Obama	1.50	4.00
316 Barack Obama	1.50	4.00
317 Barack Obama	1.50	4.00
318 Barack Obama	1.50	4.00
319 Barack Obama	1.50	4.00
320 Barack Obama	1.50	4.00
321 Barack Obama	1.50	4.00
322 Barack Obama	1.50	4.00
323 Barack Obama	1.50	4.00
324 Barack Obama	1.50	4.00
325 Barack Obama	1.50	4.00
326 Woodstock 40th Anniversary	1.25	3.00
327 Woodstock 40th Anniversary	1.25	3.00
328 Woodstock 40th Anniversary	1.25	3.00

329 Woodstock 40th Anniversary 1.25 3.00
330 Woodstock 40th Anniversary 1.25 3.00
331 The Vietnam War 1.25 3.00
332 The Vietnam War 1.25 3.00
333 The Vietnam War 1.25 3.00
334 The Vietnam War 1.25 3.00
335 The Vietnam War 1.25 3.00
336 The Vietnam War 1.25 3.00
337 The Vietnam War 1.25 3.00
338 The Vietnam War 1.25 3.00
339 The Vietnam War 1.25 3.00
340 The Vietnam War 1.25 3.00
341 Hubert Humphrey 1.25 3.00
Eugene McCarthy
342 Barry Goldwater 1.25 3.00
Nelson Rockefeller
343 Nelson Rockefeller 2.00 5.00
Ronald Reagan
344 Richard Nixon 1.50 4.00
Nelson Rockefeller
345 Lyndon Johnson 1.25 3.00
Henry Cabot Lodge
346 Spiro Agnew 1.25 3.00
Edmund Muskie
347 John F. Kennedy 2.00 5.00
Hubert Humphrey
348 Pat Brown 1.50 4.00
Richard Nixon
349 Ronald Reagan 2.00 5.00
Pat Brown
350 Hubert Humphrey 1.25 3.00
William Miller
351 John F. Kennedy 2.00 5.00
Richard Nixon
352 Anquan Boldin IA 1.25 3.00
353 Kurt Warner IA 1.50 4.00
354 Larry Fitzgerald IA 1.50 4.00
355 Roddy White IA 1.25 3.00
356 Matt Ryan IA 1.50 4.00
357 Michael Turner IA 1.25 3.00
358 Ray Lewis IA 1.50 4.00
359 Marshawn Lynch IA 1.25 3.00
360 DeAngelo Williams IA 1.50 4.00
361 Steve Smith IA 1.25 3.00
362 Julius Peppers IA 1.25 3.00
363 Brian Urlacher IA 1.50 4.00
364 T.J. Houshmandzadeh IA 1.25 3.00
365 DeMarcus Ware IA 1.25 3.00
366 Tony Romo IA 2.50 6.00
367 Marion Barber IA 1.25 3.00
368 Brandon Marshall IA 1.25 3.00
369 Jay Cutler IA 1.50 4.00
370 Calvin Johnson IA 1.50 4.00
371 Greg Jennings IA 1.50 4.00
372 Andre Johnson IA 1.25 3.00
373 Peyton Manning IA 2.50 6.00
374 Bob Sanders IA 1.25 3.00
375 Reggie Wayne IA 1.25 3.00
376 Maurice Jones-Drew IA 1.25 3.00
377 Dwayne Bowe IA 1.25 3.00
378 Ronnie Brown IA 1.25 3.00
379 Adrian Peterson IA 2.50 6.00
380 Randy Moss IA 1.50 4.00
381 Tom Brady IA 2.50 6.00
382 Drew Brees IA 1.50 4.00
383 Justin Tuck IA 1.25 3.00
384 Eli Manning IA 1.50 4.00
385 Brett Favre IA 4.00 10.00
386 Darren McFadden IA 1.50 4.00
387 Brian Dawkins IA 1.25 3.00
388 Donovan McNabb IA 1.50 4.00
389 Brian Westbrook IA 1.25 3.00
390 Troy Polamalu IA 1.50 4.00
391 Ben Roethlisberger IA 1.50 4.00
392 Philip Rivers IA 1.50 4.00
393 LaDainian Tomlinson IA 1.50 4.00
394 Frank Gore IA 1.25 3.00
395 Julian Peterson IA 1.00 2.50
396 Steven Jackson IA 1.25 3.00
397 Derrick Brooks IA 1.25 3.00
398 Darren Sproles IA 1.25 3.00
399 Chris Johnson IA 1.50 4.00
400 Clinton Portis IA 1.25 3.00

2009 Philadelphia Fabric

STATED ODDS 1:10 HOB, 1:24 RET
PFAG Antonio Gates 3.00 8.00
PFAJ Andre Johnson 3.00 8.00
PFAS Alex Smith 3.00 8.00
PFAV Adam Vinatieri 4.00 10.00
PFBA Ronde Barber 2.50 6.00
PFBE Braylon Edwards 3.00 8.00
PFBM Brandon Marshall 3.00 8.00
PFBQ Brady Quinn 3.00 8.00
PFBU Brian Urlacher 4.00 10.00
PFCA Jason Campbell 2.50 6.00
PFCB Champ Bailey 3.00 8.00
PFCP Carson Palmer 4.00 10.00
PFCT Chester Taylor 2.50 6.00
PFDB Drew Brees 4.00 10.00
PFDD Donald Driver 3.00 8.00
PFDE Deuce McAllister 3.00 8.00
PFDG David Garrard 3.00 8.00
PFDH Devin Hester 4.00 10.00
PFDM Donovan McNabb 4.00 10.00
PFDS Darren Sproles 3.00 8.00
PFDW DeAngelo Williams 4.00 10.00
PFEJ Edgerrin James 3.00 8.00
PFFG Frank Gore 3.00 8.00
PFHA Marvin Harrison 4.00 10.00
PFHO Torry Holt 3.00 8.00
PFJA Joseph Addai 4.00 10.00
PFJC Jay Cutler 4.00 10.00
PFJL Jamal Lewis 3.00 8.00
PFJP Julius Peppers 3.00 8.00
PFJT Jason Taylor 3.00 8.00
PFLE Lee Evans 3.00 8.00
PFLJ Larry Johnson 3.00 8.00
PFMC Marques Colston 3.00 8.00
PFMH Matt Hasselbeck 3.00 8.00
PFMJ Maurice Jones-Drew 3.00 8.00
PFML Marshawn Lynch 3.00 8.00
PFPB Plaxico Burress 3.00 8.00
PFRB Ronnie Brown 3.00 8.00
PFRC Ronald Curry 2.50 6.00
PFRG Ryan Grant 3.00 8.00
PFRL Ray Lewis 4.00 10.00
PFSH Santonio Holmes 3.00 8.00
PFSM Shawne Merriman 3.00 8.00
PFSS Steve Smith 3.00 8.00
PFTG Tony Gonzalez 3.00 8.00
PFTH T.J. Houshmandzadeh 3.00 8.00
PFTR Tony Romo
PFVJ Vincent Jackson 3.00 8.00
PFVY Vince Young 3.00 8.00
PFWP Willie Parker 2.50 6.00

2009 Philadelphia Jumbos

ONE JUMBO PER HOBBY BOX
RC1 Brandon Marshall 2.00 5.00
RC2 Brett Favre 6.00 15.00
RC3 Brian Westbrook 2.00 5.00
RC4 Calvin Johnson 2.50 6.00
RC5 Dallas Clark 2.00 5.00
RC6 Devin Hester 2.50 6.00
RC7 Drew Brees 2.50 6.00
RC8 Frank Gore 2.00 5.00
RC9 Hines Ward 2.00 5.00
RC10 Jay Cutler 2.50 6.00
RC11 A.J. Hawk 2.00 5.00
RC12 Chris Cooley 2.00 5.00
RC13 Greg Jennings 2.50 6.00
RC14 Patrick Willis 2.00 5.00
RC15 Anquan Boldin 2.00 5.00
RC16 Roman Gabriel 2.00 5.00
RC17 Joe Greene 2.50 6.00
RC18 Steve Young 3.00 8.00
RC19 Archie Manning 2.50 6.00
RC20 Paul Hornung 2.50 6.00
RC21 Jim Kelly 2.50 6.00
RC22 Don Maynard 2.00 5.00
RC23 Deion Sanders 2.50 6.00
RC24 Dick Butkus 3.00 8.00
RC25 Mike Singletary 2.50 6.00
RC26 Rey Maualuga 2.00 5.00
RC27 Malcolm Jenkins 2.00 5.00
RC28 LeSean McCoy 4.00 10.00
RC29 Michael Crabtree 4.00 10.00
RC30 Chris Wells 3.00 8.00
RC31 Brian Orakpo 2.00 5.00
RC32 William Moore 2.00 5.00
RC33 Knowshon Moreno 2.00 5.00
RC34 James Laurinaitis 2.00 5.00
RC35 Jeremy Maclin 3.00 8.00
RC36 Aaron Curry 2.00 5.00
RC37 Shonn Greene 3.00 8.00
RC38 Brandon Pettigrew 2.00 5.00
RC39 Darrius Heyward-Bey 2.00 5.00
RC40 Percy Harvin 3.00 8.00
RC41 Brian Cushing 2.00 5.00
RC42 Matthew Stafford 10.00 25.00
RC43 Darius Butler 2.00 5.00
RC44 D.J. Moore 1.50 4.00
RC45 Javon Ringer 2.00 5.00
RC46 Alphonso Smith 1.50 4.00
RC47 Mark Sanchez 6.00 15.00
RC48 Donald Brown 2.00 5.00
RC49 Josh Freeman 4.00 10.00
RC50 Nate Davis 1.50 4.00

2009 Philadelphia Jumbos Autographs

OVERALL AUTO STATED ODDS 1:20
RC1 Brandon Marshall
RC2 Brett Favre
RC3 Brian Westbrook
RC4 Calvin Johnson
RC5 Dallas Clark
RC6 Devin Hester
RC7 Drew Brees
RC8 Frank Gore
RC9 Hines Ward
RC10 Jay Cutler
RC11 A.J. Hawk
RC12 Chris Cooley
RC13 Greg Jennings
RC14 Patrick Willis 20.00 40.00
RC15 Anquan Boldin
RC16 Roman Gabriel
RC17 Joe Greene
RC18 Steve Young
RC19 Archie Manning
RC20 Paul Hornung 25.00 50.00
RC21 Jim Kelly
RC22 Don Maynard 20.00 40.00
RC23 Deion Sanders
RC24 Dick Butkus
RC25 Mike Singletary
RC26 Rey Maualuga 10.00 25.00
RC27 Malcolm Jenkins
RC28 LeSean McCoy 20.00 50.00
RC29 Michael Crabtree 40.00 80.00
RC30 Chris Wells 15.00 40.00
RC31 Brian Orakpo 10.00 25.00
RC32 William Moore EXCH 10.00 25.00
RC33 Knowshon Moreno 30.00 60.00
RC34 James Laurinaitis 10.00 25.00
RC35 Jeremy Maclin 15.00 40.00
RC36 Aaron Curry 10.00 25.00
RC37 Shonn Greene 15.00 40.00
RC38 Brandon Pettigrew 10.00 25.00
RC39 Darrius Heyward-Bey
RC40 Percy Harvin 40.00 80.00
RC41 Brian Cushing
RC42 Matthew Stafford 50.00 100.00
RC43 Darius Butler EXCH 10.00 25.00
RC44 D.J. Moore 8.00 20.00
RC45 Javon Ringer 10.00 25.00
RC46 Alphonso Smith 8.00 20.00
RC47 Mark Sanchez 50.00 100.00
RC48 Donald Brown 10.00 25.00
RC49 Josh Freeman 40.00 80.00
RC50 Nate Davis 8.00 20.00

2009 Philadelphia National Chicle

STATED ODDS 1:5
NC1 John F. Kennedy 2.50 10.00
NC2 Spiro Agnew 2.50 6.00
NC3 Pat Brown 2.50 6.00
NC4 Henry Cabot Lodge 2.50 6.00
NC5 Lyndon Johnson 2.50 6.00
NC6 Richard Nixon 2.50 8.00
NC7 Hubert Humphrey 2.50 6.00
NC8 Barry Goldwater 2.50 6.00
NC9 William Miller 2.50 6.00
NC10 Ronald Reagan 2.50 8.00
NC11 Eugene McCarthy 2.50 6.00
NC12 Edmund Muskie 2.50 6.00
NC13 Nelson Rockefeller 2.50 6.00
NC14 Robert Kennedy 2.50 8.00
NC15 Adlai Stevenson 2.50 6.00
NC16 William Scranton 2.50 6.00
NC17 George McGovern 2.50 6.00
NC18 Margaret Chase Smith 2.50 6.00
NC19 Ted Kennedy 2.50 6.00
NC20 Dodge Dart 2.50 6.00
NC21 Chevrolet Bel Air 2.50 6.00
NC22 Chevrolet El Camino 2.50 6.00
NC23 Dodge Charger 2.50 6.00
NC24 Chevrolet Corvette 2.50 6.00
NC25 Ford Mustang 2.50 6.00
NC26 Ford Thunderbird 2.50 6.00
NC27 Pontiac Bonneville 2.50 6.00
NC28 Pontiac GTO 2.50 6.00
NC29 Plymouth Barracuda 2.50 6.00
NC30 Martin B-26 Marauder 2.50 6.00
NC31 North American F-86 Sabre 2.50 6.00
NC32 Consolidated B-24 Liberator 2.50 6.00
NC33 FG-1D Corsair 2.50 6.00
NC34 Curtiss P-40 Warhawk 2.50 6.00
NC35 Northrop P-61 Black Widow 2.50 6.00
NC36 Boeing B-17 Flying Fortress 2.50 6.00
NC37 P51 Mustang 2.50 6.00
NC38 McDonnell FD-FH Phantom 2.50 6.00
NC39 Lockheed P-58 Chain Lightning 2.50 6.00
NC40 Golden Arrow Train 2.50 6.00
NC41 The 20th Century Ltd Train 2.50 6.00
NC42 Super Chief Train 2.50 6.00
NC43 Pioneer Zephyr Train 2.50 6.00
NC44 Flying Scotsman Train 2.50 6.00
NC45 Blue Train 2.50 6.00
NC46 TGV Train 2.50 6.00
NC47 Orient Express Train 2.50 6.00
NC48 Bullet Train 2.50 6.00
NC49 Indian Pacific Train 2.50 6.00
NC50 Brandon Marshall 1.50 4.00
NC51 Brett Favre 5.00 12.00
NC52 Brian Westbrook 1.50 4.00
NC53 Calvin Johnson 2.00 5.00
NC54 Dallas Clark 1.50 4.00
NC55 Devin Hester 2.00 5.00
NC56 Drew Brees 2.00 5.00
NC57 Frank Gore 1.50 4.00
NC58 Hines Ward 1.50 4.00
NC59 Jay Cutler 2.00 5.00
NC60 LaDainian Tomlinson 2.00 5.00
NC61 Marvin Harrison 2.00 5.00
NC62 Patrick Willis 1.50 4.00
NC63 Philip Rivers 2.00 5.00
NC64 Kurt Warner 2.00 5.00
NC65 T.J. Houshmandzadeh 1.50 4.00
NC66 Tony Romo 3.00 8.00
NC67 Brian Urlacher 2.00 5.00
NC68 Adrian Peterson 3.00 8.00
NC69 Anquan Boldin 1.50 4.00
NC70 Ben Roethlisberger 2.00 5.00
NC71 Clinton Portis 1.50 4.00
NC72 Eli Manning 2.00 5.00
NC73 Jason Witten 2.00 5.00
NC74 Larry Fitzgerald 2.00 5.00
NC75 Peyton Manning 3.00 8.00
NC76 Matthew Stafford 6.00 15.00
NC77 Nate Davis 1.00 2.50
NC78 Brian Orakpo 1.25 3.00
NC79 Michael Crabtree 2.50 6.00
NC80 Jeremy Maclin 2.00 5.00
NC81 Aaron Curry 1.25 3.00
NC82 Rey Maualuga 1.25 3.00
NC83 James Laurinaitis 1.25 3.00
NC84 Chris Wells 2.00 5.00
NC85 Brandon Pettigrew 1.25 3.00
NC86 Percy Harvin 2.00 5.00
NC87 LeSean McCoy 2.50 6.00
NC88 Darrius Heyward-Bey 1.25 3.00
NC89 Aaron Maybin 1.00 2.50
NC90 Brian Cushing 1.25 3.00
NC91 Everette Brown 1.00 2.50
NC92 Donald Brown 1.25 3.00
NC93 Knowshon Moreno 1.25 3.00
NC94 Chase Coffman 1.00 2.50
NC95 Malcolm Jenkins 1.25 3.00
NC96 Vontae Davis 1.25 3.00
NC97 Hakeem Nicks 2.00 5.00
NC98 Mark Sanchez 4.00 10.00
NC99 Andre Smith 1.00 2.50
NC100 Michael Oher 2.00 5.00

2009 Philadelphia National Chicle Autographs

NC51-NC75 VETS TOO SCARCE TO PRICE
OVERALL AUTO STATED ODDS 1:20
ROOKIE PRINT RUN 97-100
NC60 LaDainian Tomlinson/21
NC76 Matthew Stafford/100 60.00 120.00
NC77 Nate Davis/100 8.00 20.00
NC78 Brian Orakpo/100 10.00 25.00
NC79 Michael Crabtree/100 40.00 100.00
NC80 Jeremy Maclin/99 15.00 40.00
NC81 Aaron Curry/100 10.00 25.00
NC82 Rey Maualuga/100 10.00 25.00
NC83 James Laurinaitis/100 10.00 25.00
NC84 Chris Wells/100 25.00 60.00
NC85 Brandon Pettigrew/100 10.00 25.00
NC86 Percy Harvin/100 40.00 100.00
NC87 LeSean McCoy/98 20.00 50.00
NC88 Darrius Heyward-Bey/100 10.00 25.00
NC90 Brian Cushing/96 10.00 25.00
NC92 Donald Brown/100 10.00 25.00
NC93 Knowshon Moreno/100 30.00 80.00
NC94 Chase Coffman/100 8.00 20.00
NC95 Malcolm Jenkins/100 10.00 25.00
NC96 Vontae Davis/100 10.00 25.00
NC97 Hakeem Nicks/99 15.00 40.00
NC98 Mark Sanchez/100 60.00 120.00
NC99 Andre Smith/100 8.00 20.00
NC100 Michael Oher/100 40.00 80.00

2009 Philadelphia Signatures

OVERALL AUTO ODDS 1:20 H, 1:1500 R
PSAG Andre Gurode EXCH 6.00 15.00
PSAH Albert Haynesworth 5.00 12.00
PSAJ A.J. Hawk 8.00 20.00
PSAP Adrian Peterson 90.00 150.00
PSAW Adrian Wilson
PSBD Brian Dawkins
PSBF Brett Favre
PSBM Brandon Marshall
PSBO Dwayne Bowe 6.00 15.00
PSBR Ben Roethlisberger
PSBU Brian Urlacher
PSBW Brian Westbrook
PSCC Chris Cooley
PSCJ Calvin Johnson
PSCO Jerricho Cotchery 6.00 15.00
PSDB Drew Brees
PSDC Dallas Clark 8.00 20.00
PSDF Dwight Freeney
PSDH Devin Hester
PSDJ DeSean Jackson 8.00 20.00
PSDQ D'Qwell Jackson 5.00 12.00
PSDV Donovan McNabb
PSDW DeMarcus Ware 8.00 20.00
PSEM Eli Manning 60.00 100.00
PSER Ed Reed
PSFG Frank Gore 6.00 15.00
PSGC Greg Camarillo 8.00 20.00
PSJA Jared Allen 25.00 40.00
PSJF Joe Flacco
PSJH James Harrison
PSJM Jerod Mayo 6.00 15.00
PSJO Chris Johnson 15.00 30.00
PSJP Joey Porter 8.00 20.00
PSJS Jonathan Stewart 15.00 30.00
PSJW Jason Witten
PSLB Lance Briggs 10.00 25.00
PSLC Laveranues Coles
PSLE Lee Evans 6.00 15.00
PSLT LaDainian Tomlinson
PSMB Marion Barber
PSMC Matt Cassel 8.00 20.00
PSMF Matt Forte 10.00 25.00
PSMJ Maurice Jones-Drew 6.00 15.00
PSMR Matt Ryan
PSMT Michael Turner
PSMW Mario Williams 6.00 15.00
PSPM Peyton Manning 60.00 120.00
PSPW Patrick Willis 8.00 20.00
PSQJ Quentin Jammer 5.00 12.00
PSRL Ray Lewis
PSRW Roddy White
PSSS Steve Slaton 6.00 15.00
PSTB Tom Brady
PSTH T.J. Houshmandzadeh
PSTP Troy Polamalu
PSTR Tony Romo
PSWJ Walter Jones

1974 Philadelphia Bell WFL Team Issue

These photos were issued by the team for promotional purposes and fan mail requests. Each includes a black and white image printed above the subject's name and team logo. Each measures 5 1/2" by 7."

COMPLETE SET (8) 50.00 100.00
1 John Bosacco Pres. 6.00 12.00
2 Jim Corcoran 6.00 12.00
3 Richard Iannarella GM 6.00 12.00
4 J.J. Jennings 6.00 12.00
5 Ted Kwalick 6.00 12.00
6 Tim Rossovich 6.00 12.00
7 Claude Watts 6.00 12.00
8 Willie Wood 7.50 15.00

1992 Philadelphia Daily News

This nine-card set, which is aptly subtitled "Great Moments in Philadelphia Sports," was sponsored by the Philadelphia Daily News. The fronts of the standard-size cards have red borders and feature miniature reproductions of newspaper front pages with famous headlines and memorable photos. Each card captures a great moment in the history of Philadelphia sports. Sports represented are baseball, (cards 1 and 7-8) hockey, (2) basketball, (3-4) football, (5-6) and boxing (9). The backs are printed in gray, black and white and provide text relating to the event commemorated on the card.

COMPLETE SET (9) 1.40 3.50
5 Eagles Seek New CO, QB .10 .25
(Eagles win NFL Championship
6 Super .10 .25
Eagles win NFC Championship

1984 Philadelphia Stars USFL Team Issue

Each of these blankbacked photos was issued by the team, measures roughly 5" x 7" and features a black and white image of a player. The player's name, his position, and the team name are listed below the image to the left and the Stars' logo is oriented to the right below the image.

1 Jon Brooks 5.00 10.00
2 Kelvin Bryant 6.00 12.00
3 Frank Case 5.00 10.00
4 Willie Collier 5.00 10.00
5 Chuck Commiskey 5.00 10.00
6 George Cooper 5.00 10.00
7 Tom Donovan 5.00 10.00
8 Steve Folsom 5.00 10.00
9 Antonio Gibson 5.00 10.00
10 George Gilbert 5.00 10.00
11 Joe Happe 5.00 10.00
12 Allen Harvin 5.00 10.00
13 Glenn Howard 5.00 10.00
14 Sean Landeta 6.00 12.00
15 Sam Mills 6.00 12.00
16 Buddy Moor 5.00 10.00
17 Brad Oates 5.00 10.00
18 Dave Opfar 5.00 10.00
19 David Riley 5.00 10.00
20 Booker Russell 5.00 10.00
21 David Trout 5.00 10.00
22 Scott Woerner 5.00 10.00

1981-82 Philip Morris

This 18-card standard-size set was included in the Champions of American Sport program and features major stars from a variety of sports. The program was issued in conjunction with a traveling exhibition organized by the National Portrait Gallery and the Smithsonian Institution and sponsored by Philip Morris and Miller Brewing Company. The cards are either reproductions of works of art (paintings) or famous photographs of the time. The cards are frequently found with a perforated edge on at least one side. The cards were actually obtained from two perforated pages in the program. There is no notation anywhere on the cards indicating the manufacturer or sponsor.

COMPLETE SET (18) 40.00 100.00
11 Joe Namath 6.00 15.00
13 Knute Rockne 5.00 12.00
18 Johnny Unitas 6.00 15.00

1972 Phoenix Blazers Shamrock Dairy

The Shamrock Dairy issued these cards on the sides of milk cartons in 1972. Each features a member of the Phoenix Blazers minor league football team and was printed in green ink. The blankbacked cards when cut cleanly to the edges of the carton measure roughly 3 3/4" by 7 1/2" and include a brief player bio and Blazers home schedule. Any additions to this list are appreicated.

1 Darby Jones 10.00 20.00
2 Joe Spagnola 10.00 20.00

1999 Pinheads

These pins were produced by Pinheads Promotions and measure roughly 1" by 1 1/2" each. Each pin features an artist's rendering of the player with a typical pin style back along with the year and "Pinheads First Edition."

COMPLETE SET (12) 12.00 30.00
1 Troy Aikman 1.20 3.00
2 Drew Bledsoe 1.20 3.00
3 Terrell Davis 1.20 3.00
4 Brett Favre 1.20 3.00
5 Doug Flutie 1.00 2.50
6 Keyshawn Johnson 1.00 2.50
7 Peyton Manning 1.60 4.00
8 Dan Marino 1.60 4.00
9 Jerry Rice 1.20 3.00
10 Kordell Stewart 1.20 3.00
11 Ricky Williams 1.20 3.00
12 Steve Young 1.00 2.50

1991 Pinnacle Promo Panels

These (approximately) 5" by 7" promo panels each feature four cards to show the design of the 1991 Pinnacle series cards. They were introduced and initially distributed at the Super Bowl XXVI Card Show. The cards, which would measure the standard size if cut, display two color photos on a black panel with white borders. The backs carry a color cut-out action shot, biography, player profile, and statistics. The cards are numbered on the back as in the regular series; the panels themselves, however, are unnumbered. The panels are listed below alphabetically according to the player's name on the card featured at upper left corner of each panel.

1 John Alt 1.25 3.00
Eric Green
Don Mosebar
Greg Townsend
2 Morten Andersen 12.50 25.00
John Elway
Mike Merriweather
Ronnie Lott
3 Bruce Armstrong 15.00 30.00
Joe Montana
Jim Lachey
Bruce Matthews
4 Don Beebe 1.50 4.00
Irving Fryar
Ricky Proehl
Vinny Testaverde
5 Duane Bickett 1.25 3.00
Tony Bennett
John Friesz
Rob Burnett
6 Mark Bortz 1.50 4.00
Warren Moon
Jim Breech
Eric Metcalf
7 Roger Craig 1.25 3.00
Issiac Holt
Kevin Mack
Shane Conlan
8 Wendell Davis 1.25 3.00
Gaston Green
Tony Mandarich
Merril Hoge
9 Dermontti Dawson 1.25 3.00
Jerry Gray
Nick Lowery
Scott Case
10 Cris Dishman 1.25 3.00
Bill Fralic
John L. Williams
Simon Fletcher
11 Chris Doleman 10.00 20.00
Troy Aikman
Sterling Sharpe
Sean Landeta
12 Rodney Hampton 1.50 4.00
Bubby Brister
Johnny Bailey
Christian Okoye
13 Darryl Henley 1.50 4.00
Karl Mecklenburg
Sam Mills
Rod Woodson
14 Mark Higgs 1.50 4.00
Jay Schroeder
Mark Carrier DB
Jim Everett
15 Jay Hilgenburg 15.00 30.00
Dan Marino
Anthony Carter
Howie Long
16 Louis Lipps 1.50 4.00
John Offerdahl
Herschel Walker
Jeff George
17 Greg McMurtry 1.50 4.00
Henry Ellard
Brian Mitchell
Mark Clayton
18 Chris Miller 1.25 3.00
James Brooks
Eric Ball
Gerald Williams
19 Nate Odomes 1.25 3.00
Allen Pinkett
Don Majkowski
Dave Meggett
20 Andre Rison 1.50 4.00
Jeff Hostetler
Hugh Millen
Jack Del Rio
21 Emmitt Smith 15.00 30.00
Bill Brooks
Bobby Hebert
Dennis Smith
22 Rohn Stark 1.50 4.00
Neal Anderson
Barry Foster
Steve DeBerg
23 Reyna Thompson 1.50 4.00
Louis Oliver
Steve Broussard
Andre Reed
24 Lorenzo White 1.50 4.00
Jeff Herrod
Cornelius Bennett
Jessie Tuggle
25 Will Wolford 3.00 8.00
Tom Tupa
Derrick Thomas
Derrick Fenner

1991 Pinnacle

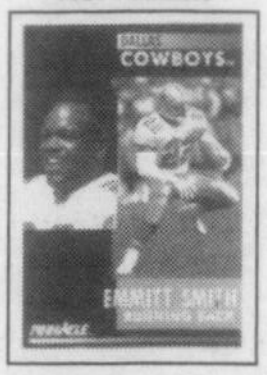

The premier edition of the 1991 Pinnacle set contains 415 standard-size cards. Cards were issued in 12-card packs. The front design of the veteran player cards features two color photos, an action photo and a head shot, on a black background with white borders. The card backs have a color action shot superimposed on a black background. The rookie cards have the same design, except with a green background on the front, and head shots rather than action shots on the back. The backs also include a biography, player profile, and statistics (where appropriate). The set includes 58 rookies (253, 281-336, 393) and four special cards. Special subsets featured are Head to Head (351-355), Technicians (356-362), Gamewinners (363-371), Idols (372-386), and Sideline (394-415). A patented anti-counterfeit device appears on the bottom border of each card back. Rookie Cards in this set include Bryan Cox, Lawrence Dawsey, Ricky Ervins, Jeff Graham, Randal Hill, Russell Maryland, Bryce Paup, Eric Pegram, Mike Pritchard, Leonard Russell, and Harvey Williams. An Emmitt Smith promo card was produced as well and listed below. It can be differentiated from the regular issue Smith card by the mention of his "holdout" on the cardback.

COMPLETE SET (415) 7.50 20.00
1 Warren Moon .15 .40
2 Morten Andersen .02 .10
3 Rohn Stark .02 .10
4 Mark Bortz .02 .10
5 Mark Higgs RC .02 .10
6 Troy Aikman .75 2.00
7 John Elway 1.25 3.00
8 Neal Anderson .07 .20
9 Chris Doleman .02 .10
10 Jay Schroeder .02 .10
11 Sterling Sharpe .15 .40
12 Steve DeBerg .02 .10
13 Ronnie Lott .07 .20
14 Sean Landeta .02 .10
15 Jim Everett .07 .20
16 Jim Breech .02 .10
17 Barry Foster .07 .20
18 Mike Merriweather .02 .10
19 Eric Metcalf .07 .20
20 Mark Carrier DB .07 .20
21 James Brooks .07 .20
22 Nate Odomes .02 .10
23 Rodney Hampton .15 .40
24 Chris Miller .07 .20
25 Roger Craig .07 .20
26 Louis Oliver .02 .10
27 Allen Pinkett .02 .10
28 Bubby Brister .02 .10
29 Reyna Thompson .02 .10
30 Issiac Holt .02 .10
31 Steve Broussard .02 .10
32 Christian Okoye .02 .10
33 Dave Meggett .07 .20
34 Andre Reed .07 .20
35 Shane Conlan .02 .10
36 Eric Ball .02 .10
37 Johnny Bailey .02 .10
38 Don Majkowski .02 .10
39 Gerald Williams .02 .10
40 Kevin Mack .02 .10
41 Jeff Herrod .02 .10
42 Emmitt Smith 2.50 6.00
43 Wendell Davis .02 .10
44 Lorenzo White .02 .10
45 Andre Rison .07 .20
46 Jerry Gray .02 .10
47 Dennis Smith .02 .10
48 Gaston Green .02 .10
49 Dermontti Dawson .02 .10
50 Jeff Hostetler .07 .20
51 Nick Lowery .02 .10
52 Merril Hoge .02 .10
53 Bobby Hebert .02 .10
54 Scott Case .02 .10
55 Jack Del Rio .07 .20
56 Cornelius Bennett .07 .20
57 Tony Mandarich .02 .10
58 Bill Brooks .02 .10
59 Jessie Tuggle .02 .10
60 Hugh Millen RC .02 .10
61 Tony Bennett .07 .20
62 Cris Dishman RC .02 .10
63 Darryl Henley RC .02 .10
64 Duane Bickett .02 .10
65 Jay Hilgenberg .02 .10
66 Joe Montana 1.25 3.00
67 Bill Fralic .02 .10
68 Sam Mills .02 .10
69 Bruce Armstrong .02 .10
70 Dan Marino 1.25 3.00
71 Jim Lachey .02 .10
72 Rod Woodson .15 .40
73 Simon Fletcher .02 .10
74 Bruce Matthews .07 .20
75 Howie Long .15 .40
76 John Friesz .15 .40
77 Karl Mecklenburg .02 .10
78 John L. Williams UER .02 .10
(Two photos show/42 Chris Warren)
79 Rob Burnett RC .07 .20
80 Anthony Carter .07 .20
81 Henry Ellard .07 .20
82 Don Beebe .02 .10
83 Louis Lipps .02 .10
84 Greg McMurtry .02 .10
85 Will Wolford .02 .10
86 Eric Green .02 .10
87 Irving Fryar .07 .20
88 John Offerdahl .02 .10
89 John Alt .02 .10
90 Tom Tupa .02 .10
91 Don Mosebar .02 .10
92 Jeff George .20 .50
93 Vinny Testaverde .07 .20
94 Greg Townsend .02 .10
95 Derrick Fenner .02 .10
96 Brian Mitchell .07 .20
97 Herschel Walker .07 .20
98 Ricky Proehl .02 .10
99 Mark Clayton .07 .20
100 Derrick Thomas .15 .40
101 Jim Harbaugh .15 .40
102 Barry Word .02 .10
103 Jerry Rice .75 2.00
104 Keith Byars .02 .10
105 Marion Butts .07 .20
106 Rich Moran .02 .10
107 Thurman Thomas .15 .40
108 Stephone Paige .02 .10
109 D.J. Johnson .02 .10
110 William Perry .07 .20
111 Haywood Jeffires .07 .20
112 Rodney Peete .07 .20
113 Andy Heck .02 .10
114 Kevin Ross .02 .10
115 Michael Carter .02 .10
116 Tim McKyer .02 .10
117 Kenneth Davis .02 .10
118 Richmond Webb .02 .10
119 Rich Camarillo .02 .10
120 James Francis .02 .10
121 Craig Heyward .07 .20
122 Hardy Nickerson .07 .20
123 Michael Brooks .02 .10
124 Fred Barnett .15 .40
125 Cris Carter .40 1.00
126 Brian Jordan .07 .20
127 Pat Leahy .02 .10
128 Kevin Greene .07 .20
129 Trace Armstrong .02 .10
130 Eugene Lockhart .02 .10
131 Albert Lewis .02 .10
132 Ernie Jones .02 .10
133 Eric Martin .02 .10
134 Anthony Thompson .02 .10
135 Tim Krumrie .02 .10
136 James Lofton .07 .20
137 John Taylor .07 .20
138 Jeff Cross .02 .10
139 Tommy Kane .02 .10
140 Robb Thomas .02 .10
141 Gary Anderson K .02 .10
142 Mark Murphy .02 .10
143 Rickey Jackson .02 .10
144 Ken O'Brien .02 .10
145 Ernest Givins .07 .20
146 Jessie Hester .02 .10
147 Deion Sanders .30 .75
148 Keith Henderson RC .02 .10
149 Chris Singleton .02 .10
150 Rod Bernstine .02 .10
151 Quinn Early .07 .20
152 Boomer Esiason .07 .20
153 Mike Gann .02 .10
154 Dino Hackett .02 .10
155 Perry Kemp .02 .10
156 Mark Ingram .07 .20
157 Daryl Johnston .30 .75
158 Eugene Daniel .02 .10
159 Dalton Hilliard .02 .10
160 Rufus Porter .02 .10
161 Tunch Ilkin .02 .10
162 James Hasty .02 .10
163 Keith McKeller .02 .10
164 Heath Sherman .02 .10
165 Vai Sikahema .02 .10
166 Pat Terrell .02 .10
167 Anthony Munoz .07 .20
168 Brad Edwards RC .02 .10
169 Tom Rathman .02 .10
170 Steve McMichael .07 .20
171 Vaughan Johnson .02 .10
172 Nate Lewis RC .02 .10
173 Mark Rypien .07 .20
174 Rob Moore .20 .50
175 Tim Green .02 .10
176 Tony Casillas .02 .10
177 Jon Hand .02 .10
178 Todd McNair .02 .10
179 Toi Cook RC .02 .10
180 Eddie Brown .02 .10
181 Mark Jackson .02 .10
182 Pete Stoyanovich .02 .10
183 Bryce Paup RC .15 .40
184 Anthony Miller .07 .20
185 Dan Saleaumua .02 .10
186 Guy McIntyre .02 .10
187 Broderick Thomas .02 .10
188 Frank Warren .02 .10
189 Drew Hill .02 .10
190 Reggie White .15 .40
191 Chris Hinton .02 .10
192 David Little .02 .10
193 David Fulcher .02 .10
194 Clarence Verdin .02 .10
195 Junior Seau .25 .60
196 Blair Thomas .02 .10
197 Stan Brock .02 .10
198 Gary Clark .15 .40
199 Michael Irvin .15 .40
200 Ronnie Harmon .02 .10
201 Steve Young .75 2.00
202 Brian Noble .02 .10
203 Dan Stryzinski .02 .10
204 Darryl Talley .02 .10
205 David Alexander .02 .10
206 Pat Swilling .07 .20
207 Gary Plummer .02 .10
208 Robert Delpino .02 .10
209 Norm Johnson .02 .10
210 Mike Singletary .07 .20
211 Anthony Johnson .15 .40
212 Eric Allen .02 .10
213 Gill Fenerty .02 .10
214 Neil Smith .15 .40
215 Joe Phillips .02 .10
216 Ottis Anderson .07 .20
217 LeRoy Butler .07 .20
218 Ray Childress .02 .10
219 Rodney Holman .02 .10
220 Kevin Fagan .02 .10
221 Bruce Smith .15 .40
222 Brad Muster .02 .10
223 Mike Horan .02 .10
224 Steve Atwater .02 .10
225 Rich Gannon .20 .50
226 Anthony Pleasant .02 .10
227 Steve Jordan .02 .10
228 Lomas Brown .02 .10
229 Jackie Slater .02 .10
230 Brad Baxter .02 .10
231 Joe Morris .02 .10
232 Marcus Allen .15 .40
233 Chris Warren .15 .40
234 Johnny Johnson .02 .10
235 Phil Simms .07 .20
236 Dave Krieg .07 .20
237 Jim McMahon .07 .20
238 Richard Dent .07 .20
239 John Washington RC .02 .10
240 Sammie Smith .02 .10
241 Brian Brennan .02 .10
242 Cortez Kennedy .15 .40
243 Tim McDonald .02 .10
244 Charles Haley .07 .20
245 Joey Browner .02 .10
246 Eddie Murray .02 .10

247 Bob Golic	.02	.10
248 Myron Guyton	.02	.10
249 Dennis Byrd	.02	.10
250 Barry Sanders	1.25	3.00
251 Clay Matthews	.07	.20
252 Pepper Johnson	.02	.10
253 Eric Swann RC	.15	.40
254 Lamar Lathon	.02	.10
255 Andre Tippett	.02	.10
256 Tom Newberry	.02	.10
257 Kyle Clifton	.02	.10
258 Leslie O'Neal	.07	.20
259 Bubba McDowell	.02	.10
260 Scott Davis	.02	.10
261 Wilber Marshall	.02	.10
262 Marv Cook	.02	.10
263 Jeff Lageman	.02	.10
264 Michael Young	.02	.10
265 Gary Zimmerman	.02	.10
266 Mike Munchak	.07	.20
267 David Treadwell	.02	.10
268 Steve Wisniewski	.02	.10
269 Mark Duper	.07	.20
270 Chris Spielman	.07	.20
271 Brett Perriman	.15	.40
272 Lionel Washington	.02	.10
273 Lawrence Taylor	.15	.40
274 Mark Collins	.02	.10
275 Mark Carrier WR	.15	.40
276 Paul Gruber	.02	.10
277 Earnest Byner	.02	.10
278 Andre Collins	.02	.10
279 Reggie Cobb	.02	.10
280 Art Monk	.07	.20
281 Henry Jones RC	.07	.20
282 Mike Pritchard RC	.15	.40
283 Moe Gardner RC	.02	.10
284 Chris Zorich RC	.15	.40
285 Keith Traylor RC	.02	.10
286 Mike Dumas RC	.02	.10
287 Ed King RC	.02	.10
288 Russell Maryland RC	.15	.40
289 Alfred Williams RC	.02	.10
290 Derek Russell RC	.02	.10
291 Vinnie Clark RC	.02	.10
292 Mike Croel RC	.02	.10
293 Todd Marinovich RC	.02	.10
294 Phil Hansen RC	.02	.10
295 Aaron Craver RC	.02	.10
296 Nick Bell RC	.02	.10
297 Kenny Walker RC	.02	.10
298 Roman Phifer RC	.02	.10
299 Kanavis McGhee RC	.02	.10
300 Ricky Ervins RC	.07	.20
301 Jim Price RC	.02	.10
302 John Johnson RC	.02	.10
303 George Thornton RC	.02	.10
304 Huey Richardson RC	.02	.10
305 Harry Colon RC	.02	.10
306 Antone Davis RC	.02	.10
307 Todd Lyght RC	.02	.10
308 Bryan Cox RC	.15	.40
309 Brad Goebel RC	.02	.10
310 Eric Moten RC	.02	.10
311 John Kasay RC	.07	.20
312 Esera Tuaolo RC	.02	.10
313 Bobby Wilson RC	.02	.10
314 Mo Lewis RC	.07	.20
315 Harvey Williams RC	.15	.40
316 Mike Stonebreaker	.02	.10
317 Charles McRae RC	.02	.10
318 John Flannery RC	.02	.10
319 Ted Washington RC	.02	.10
320 Stanley Richard RC	.02	.10
321 Browning Nagle RC	.02	.10
322 Ed McCaffrey RC	2.00	5.00
323 Jeff Graham RC	.15	.40
324 Stan Thomas	.02	.10
325 Lawrence Dawsey RC	.07	.20
326 Eric Bieniemy RC	.02	.10
327 Tim Barnett RC	.02	.10
328 Erric Pegram RC	.15	.40
329 Lamar Rogers RC	.02	.10
330 Ernie Mills RC	.07	.20
331 Pat Harlow RC	.02	.10
332 Greg Lewis RC	.02	.10
333 Jarrod Bunch RC	.02	.10
334 Dan McGwire RC	.02	.10
335 Randal Hill RC	.07	.20
336 Leonard Russell RC	.15	.40
337 Carnell Lake	.02	.10
338 Brian Blades	.07	.20
339 Darrell Green	.02	.10
340 Bobby Humphrey	.02	.10
341 Mervyn Fernandez	.02	.10
342 Ricky Sanders	.02	.10
343 Keith Jackson	.07	.20
344 Carl Banks	.02	.10
345 Gill Byrd	.02	.10
346 Al Toon	.07	.20
347 Stephen Baker	.02	.10
348 Randall Cunningham	.15	.40
349 Flipper Anderson	.02	.10
350 Jay Novacek	.15	.40
351 Steve Young HH	.15	.40
vs. Bruce Smith		
352 Barry Sanders	.30	.75
Browner HH		
353 Joe Montana HH	.30	.75
vs. Mark Carrier		
354 Thurman Thomas HH	.07	.20
vs. Lawrence Taylor		
355 Jerry Rice HH	.20	.50
vs. Darrell Green		
356 Warren Moon Tech	.07	.20
357 Anthony Munoz TECH	.02	.10
358 Barry Sanders Tech	.50	1.25
359 Jerry Rice Tech	.50	1.25
360 Joey Browner TECH	.02	.10
361 Morten Andersen TECH	.02	.10
362 Sean Landeta TECH	.02	.10
363 Thurman Thomas GW	.15	.40
364 Emmitt Smith GW	1.25	3.00
365 Gaston Green GW	.02	.10
366 Barry Sanders GW	.50	1.25
367 Christian Okoye GW	.02	.10
368 Earnest Byner GW	.02	.10
369 Neal Anderson GW	.02	.10
370 Herschel Walker GW	.07	.20
371 Rodney Hampton GW	.15	.40
372 Darryl Talley IDOL	.02	.10
Ted Hendricks		
373 Mark Carrier IDOL	.02	.10
Ronnie Lott		
374 Jim Breech IDOL	.02	.10
Jan Stenerud		
375 Rodney Hampton IDOL	.02	.10
Ottis Anderson		
376 Kevin Mack IDOL	.02	.10
Earnest Byner		
377 Steve Jordan IDOL	.02	.10
Oscar Robertson		
378 Boomer Esiason IDOL	.02	.10
Bert Jones		
379 Steve DeBerg IDOL	.07	.20
Roman Gabriel		
380 Al Toon IDOL	.02	.10
Wesley Walker		
381 Ronnie Lott IDOL	.07	.20
Charley Taylor		
382 Henry Ellard IDOL	.02	.10
Bob Hayes		
383 Troy Aikman IDOL	.50	1.25
Roger Staubach		
384 Thurman Thomas IDOL	.15	.40
Earl Campbell		
385 Dan Marino IDOL	.60	1.50
Terry Bradshaw		
386 Howie Long IDOL	.07	.20
Joe Greene		
387 Franco Harris	.07	.20
Immaculate Reception		
388 Esera Tuaolo	.02	.10
389 Super Bowl XXVI	.02	.10
(Super Bowl Records)		
390 Charles Mann	.02	.10
391 Kenny Walker	.02	.10
392 Reggie Roby	.02	.10
393 Bruce Pickens RC	.02	.10
394 Ray Childress SIDE	.02	.10
395 Karl Mecklenburg SIDE	.02	.10
396 Dean Biasucci SIDE	.02	.10
397 John Alt SIDE	.02	.10
398 Marcus Allen SIDE	.07	.20
399 John Offerdahl SIDE	.02	.10
400 Richard Tardits RC	.02	.10
401 Al Toon SIDE	.02	.10
402 Joey Browner SIDE	.02	.10
403 Spencer Tillman RC	.02	.10
404 Jay Novacek SIDE	.07	.20
405 Stephen Braggs SIDE	.02	.10
406 Mike Tice RC	.02	.10
407 Kevin Greene SIDE	.07	.20
408 Reggie White SIDE	.07	.20
409 Brian Noble SIDE	.02	.10
410 Bart Oates SIDE	.02	.10
411 Art Monk SIDE	.07	.20
412 Ron Wolfley SIDE	.02	.10
413 Louis Lipps SIDE	.02	.10
414 Dante Jones SIDE RC	.07	.20
415 Kenneth Davis SIDE	.02	.10
P1 Emmitt Smith Promo	12.50	25.00

1992 Pinnacle Samples

This six-card sample standard-size set features action color player photos on a black card face. The image of the player is partially cut out and extends beyond the photo background. A thin white line forms a frame near the card edge. The player's name appears at the bottom in a gradated bar that reflects the team's color. The horizontally oriented backs have white borders and black backgrounds. A gradated purple bar at the top contains the player's name, the word "sample," and the card number. A close-up player photo appears in the center. The back is rounded out with biography, statistics (1991 and career), player profile, and a picture of the team helmet in a circular format.

COMPLETE SET (6)	2.00	5.00
1 Reggie White	.80	2.00
5 Pepper Johnson	.30	.75
19 Chris Spielman	.30	.75
59 Mike Croel	.30	.75
100 Bobby Hebert	.30	.75
102 Rodney Hampton	.50	1.25

1992 Pinnacle

The 1992 Pinnacle set consists of 360 standard-size cards. Cards were issued in 16-card and 27-card super packs. The set closes with the following subsets: Rookies (314-330), Sidelines (331-334), Gamewinners (335-344), Hall of Famers (345-347), and Idols (348-357). Rookie Cards include Steve Bono, Edgar Bennett, Amp Lee and Tommy Vardell. An eight-card Promo Panel was produced and distributed at the Super Bowl XXVII Card Show in Pasadena.

COMPLETE SET (360)	12.50	25.00
1 Reggie White	.20	.50
2 Eric Green	.05	.15
3 Craig Heyward	.10	.30
4 Phil Simms	.10	.30
5 Pepper Johnson	.05	.15
6 Sean Landeta	.05	.15
7 Dino Hackett	.05	.15
8 Andre Ware	.05	.15
9 Ricky Nattiel	.05	.15
10 Jim Price	.05	.15
11 Jim Ritcher	.05	.15
12 Kelly Stouffer	.05	.15
13 Ray Crockett	.05	.15
14 Steve Tasker	.10	.30
15 Barry Sanders	1.25	3.00
16 Pat Swilling	.05	.15
17 Moe Gardner	.05	.15
18 Steve Young	.75	2.00
19 Chris Spielman	.10	.30
20 Richard Dent	.10	.30
21 Anthony Munoz	.10	.30
22 Thurman Thomas	.20	.50
23 Ricky Sanders	.05	.15
24 Steve Atwater	.05	.15
25 Tony Tolbert	.05	.15
26 Haywood Jeffires	.10	.30
27 Duane Bickett	.05	.15
28 Tim McDonald	.05	.15
29 Cris Carter	.30	.75
30 Derrick Thomas	.20	.50
31 Hugh Millen	.05	.15
32 Bart Oates	.05	.15
33 Darryl Talley	.05	.15
34 Marion Butts	.05	.15
35 Pete Stoyanovich	.05	.15
36 Ronnie Lott	.10	.30
37 Simon Fletcher	.05	.15
38 Morten Andersen	.05	.15
39 Clyde Simmons	.05	.15
40 Mark Rypien	.05	.15
41 Henry Ellard	.10	.30
42 Michael Irvin	.20	.50
43 Louis Lipps	.05	.15
44 John L. Williams	.05	.15
45 Broderick Thomas	.05	.15
46 Don Majkowski	.05	.15
47 William Perry	.10	.30
48 David Fulcher	.05	.15
49 Tony Bennett	.05	.15
50 Clay Matthews	.10	.30
51 Warren Moon	.20	.50
52 Bruce Armstrong	.05	.15
53 Bill Brooks	.05	.15
54 Greg Townsend	.05	.15
55 Steve Broussard	.05	.15
56 Mel Gray	.10	.30
57 Kevin Mack	.05	.15
58 Emmitt Smith	2.00	4.00
59 Mike Croel	.05	.15
60 Brian Mitchell	.10	.30
61 Bennie Blades	.05	.15
62 Carnell Lake	.05	.15
63 Cornelius Bennett	.10	.30
64 Darrell Thompson	.05	.15
65 Jessie Hester	.05	.15
66 Marv Cook	.05	.15
67 Tim Brown	.20	.50
68 Mark Duper	.05	.15
69 Robert Delpino	.05	.15
70 Eric Martin	.05	.15
71 Wendell Davis	.05	.15
72 Vaughan Johnson	.05	.15
73 Brian Blades	.10	.30
74 Ed King	.05	.15
75 Gaston Green	.05	.15
76 Christian Okoye	.05	.15
77 Rohn Stark	.05	.15
78 Kevin Greene	.10	.30
79 Jay Novacek	.10	.30
80 Chip Lohmiller	.05	.15
81 Cris Dishman	.05	.15
82 Ethan Horton	.05	.15
83 Pat Harlow	.05	.15
84 Mark Ingram	.05	.15
85 Mark Carrier DB	.05	.15
86 Sam Mills	.05	.15
87 Mark Higgs	.05	.15
88 Keith Jackson	.10	.30
89 Gary Anderson K	.05	.15
90 Ken Harvey	.05	.15
91 Anthony Carter	.10	.30
92 Randall McDaniel	.05	.15
93 Johnny Johnson	.05	.15
94 Shane Conlan	.05	.15
95 Sterling Sharpe	.20	.50
96 Guy McIntyre	.05	.15
97 Albert Lewis	.05	.15
98 Chris Doleman	.05	.15
99 Andre Rison	.10	.30
100 Bobby Hebert	.05	.15
101 Dan Owens	.05	.15
102 Rodney Hampton	.10	.30
103 Ernie Jones	.05	.15
104 Reggie Cobb	.05	.15
105 Wilber Marshall	.05	.15
106 Mike Munchak	.10	.30
107 Cortez Kennedy	.10	.30
108 Todd Lyght	.05	.15
109 Burt Grossman	.05	.15
110 Ferrell Edmunds	.05	.15
111 Jim Everett	.10	.30
112 Hardy Nickerson	.10	.30
113 Andre Tippett	.05	.15
114 Ronnie Harmon	.05	.15
115 Andre Waters	.05	.15
116 Ernest Givins	.10	.30
117 Eric Hill	.05	.15
118 Erric Pegram	.10	.30
119 Jarrod Bunch	.05	.15
120 Marcus Allen	.20	.50
121 Barry Foster	.10	.30
122 Kent Hull	.05	.15
123 Neal Anderson	.05	.15
124 Stephen Braggs	.05	.15
125 Nick Lowery	.05	.15
126 Jeff Hostetler	.10	.30
127 Michael Carter	.05	.15
128 Don Warren	.05	.15
129 Brad Baxter	.05	.15
130 John Taylor	.10	.30
131 Harold Green	.05	.15
132 Mike Merriweather	.05	.15
133 Gary Clark	.20	.50
134 Vince Buck	.05	.15
135 Dan Saleaumua	.05	.15
136 Gary Zimmerman	.05	.15
137 Richmond Webb	.05	.15
138 Art Monk	.10	.30
139 Mervyn Fernandez	.05	.15
140 Mark Jackson	.05	.15
141 Freddie Joe Nunn	.05	.15
142 Jeff Lageman	.05	.15
143 Kenny Walker	.05	.15
144 Mark Carrier WR	.10	.30
145 Jon Vaughn	.05	.15
146 Greg Davis	.05	.15
147 Bubby Brister	.05	.15
148 Mo Lewis	.05	.15
149 Howie Long	.20	.50
150 Rod Bernstine	.05	.15
151 Nick Bell	.05	.15
152 Terry Allen	.20	.50
153 William Fuller	.05	.15
154 Dexter Carter	.05	.15
155 Gene Atkins	.05	.15
156 Don Beebe	.05	.15
157 Mark Collins	.05	.15
158 Jerry Ball	.05	.15
159 Fred Barnett	.20	.50
160 Rodney Holman	.05	.15
161 Stephen Baker	.05	.15
162 Jeff Graham	.20	.50
163 Leonard Russell	.10	.30
164 Jeff Gossett	.05	.15
165 Vinny Testaverde	.10	.30
166 Maurice Hurst	.05	.15
167 Louis Oliver	.05	.15
168 Jim Morrissey	.05	.15
169 Greg Kragen	.05	.15
170 Andre Collins	.05	.15
171 Dave Meggett	.10	.30
172 Keith Henderson	.05	.15
173 Vince Newsome	.05	.15
174 Chris Hinton	.05	.15
175 James Hasty	.05	.15
176 John Offerdahl	.05	.15
177 Lomas Brown	.05	.15
178 Neil O'Donnell	.10	.30
179 Leonard Marshall	.05	.15
180 Bubba McDowell	.05	.15
181 Herman Moore	.20	.50
182 Rob Moore	.10	.30
183 Earnest Byner	.05	.15
184 Keith McCants	.05	.15
185 Floyd Turner	.05	.15
186 Steve Jordan	.05	.15
187 Nate Odomes	.05	.15
188 Jeff Herrod	.05	.15
189 Jim Harbaugh	.20	.50
190 Jessie Tuggle	.05	.15
191 Al Smith	.05	.15
192 Lawrence Dawsey	.10	.30
193 Steve Bono RC	.20	.50
194 Greg Lloyd	.10	.30
195 Steve Wisniewski	.05	.15
196 Larry Kelm	.05	.15
197 Tommy Kane	.05	.15
198 Mark Schlereth RC	.05	.15
199 Ray Childress	.05	.15
200 Vincent Brown	.05	.15
201 Rodney Peete	.10	.30
202 Dennis Smith	.05	.15
203 Bruce Matthews	.05	.15
204 Rickey Jackson	.05	.15
205 Eric Allen	.05	.15
206 Rich Camarillo	.05	.15
207 Jim Lachey	.05	.15
208 Kevin Ross	.05	.15
209 Irving Fryar	.10	.30
210 Mark Clayton	.10	.30
211 Keith Byars	.05	.15
212 John Elway	1.25	3.00
213 Harris Barton	.05	.15
214 Aeneas Williams	.10	.30
215 Rich Gannon	.20	.50
216 Toi Cook	.05	.15
217 Rod Woodson	.20	.50
218 Gary Anderson RB	.05	.15
219 Reggie Roby	.05	.15
220 Karl Mecklenburg	.05	.15
221 Rufus Porter	.05	.15
222 Jon Hand	.05	.15
223 Tim Barnett	.05	.15
224 Eric Swann	.10	.30
225 Eugene Robinson	.05	.15
226 Michael Young	.05	.15
227 Frank Warren	.05	.15
228 Mike Kenn	.05	.15
229 Tim Green	.05	.15
230 Barry Word	.05	.15
231 Mike Pritchard	.10	.30
232 John Kasay	.05	.15
233 Derek Russell	.05	.15
234 Jim Breech	.05	.15
235 Pierce Holt	.05	.15
236 Tim Krumrie	.05	.15
237 William Roberts	.05	.15
238 Erik Kramer	.10	.30
239 Brett Perriman	.20	.50
240 Reyna Thompson	.05	.15
241 Chris Miller	.10	.30
242 Drew Hill	.05	.15
243 Curtis Duncan	.05	.15
244 Seth Joyner	.05	.15
245 Ken Norton Jr.	.10	.30
246 Calvin Williams	.10	.30
247 James Joseph	.05	.15
248 Bennie Thompson RC	.05	.15
249 Tunch Ilkin	.05	.15
250 Brad Edwards	.05	.15
251 Jeff Jaeger	.05	.15
252 Gill Byrd	.05	.15
253 Jeff Feagles	.05	.15
254 Jamie Dukes RC	.05	.15
255 Greg McMurtry	.05	.15
256 Anthony Johnson	.10	.30
257 Lamar Lathon	.05	.15
258 John Roper	.05	.15
259 Lorenzo White	.05	.15
260 Brian Noble	.05	.15
261 Chris Singleton	.05	.15
262 Todd Marinovich	.05	.15
263 Jay Hilgenberg	.05	.15
264 Kyle Clifton	.05	.15
265 Tony Casillas	.05	.15
266 James Francis	.05	.15
267 Eddie Anderson	.05	.15
268 Tim Harris	.05	.15
269 James Lofton	.10	.30
270 Jay Schroeder	.05	.15
271 Ed West	.05	.15
272 Don Mosebar	.05	.15
273 Jackie Slater	.05	.15
274 Fred McAfee RC	.05	.15
275 Steve Sewell	.05	.15
276 Charles Mann	.05	.15
277 Ron Hall	.05	.15
278 Darrell Green	.05	.15
279 Jeff Cross	.05	.15
280 Jeff Wright	.05	.15
281 Issiac Holt	.05	.15
282 Dermontti Dawson	.05	.15
283 Michael Haynes	.10	.30
284 Tony Mandarich	.05	.15
285 Leroy Hoard	.10	.30
286 Darryl Henley	.05	.15
287 Tim McGee	.05	.15
288 Willie Gault	.10	.30
289 Dalton Hilliard	.05	.15
290 Tim McKyer	.05	.15
291 Tom Waddle	.05	.15
292 Eric Thomas	.05	.15
293 Herschel Walker	.10	.30
294 Donnell Woolford	.05	.15
295 James Brooks	.10	.30
296 Brad Muster	.05	.15
297 Brent Jones	.10	.30
298 Erik Howard	.05	.15
299 Alvin Harper UER	.10	.30
(Born in Frostproof&		
not Frostfree)		
300 Joey Browner	.05	.15
301 Jack Del Rio	.05	.15
302 Cleveland Gary	.05	.15
303 Brett Favre	3.00	6.00
304 Freeman McNeil	.05	.15
305 Willie Green	.05	.15
306 Percy Snow	.05	.15
307 Neil Smith	.20	.50
308 Eric Bieniemy	.05	.15
309 Keith Traylor	.05	.15
310 Ernie Mills	.05	.15
311 Will Wolford	.05	.15
312 Robert Young	.05	.15
313 Anthony Smith	.05	.15
314 Robert Porcher RC	.20	.50
315 Leon Searcy RC	.05	.15
316 Amp Lee RC	.05	.15
317 Siran Stacy RC	.05	.15
318 Patrick Rowe RC	.05	.15
319 Chris Mims RC	.05	.15
320 Matt Elliott RC	.05	.15
321 Ricardo McDonald RC	.05	.15
322 Keith Hamilton RC	.10	.30
323 Edgar Bennett RC	.20	.50
324 Chris Hakel RC	.05	.15
325 Dexter McNabb RC	.05	.15
326 Rod Milstead RC	.05	.15
327 Joe Bowden RC	.05	.15
328 Brian Bollinger RC	.05	.15
329 Darryl Williams RC	.05	.15
330 Tommy Vardell RC	.05	.15
331 Glenn Parker SIDE	.05	.15
Mitch Frerotte		
332 Herschel Walker SIDE	.05	.15
333 Mike Cofer SIDE	.05	.15
334 Mark Rypien SIDE	.05	.15
335 Andre Rison GW	.10	.30
336 Henry Ellard GW	.05	.15
337 Rob Moore GW	.05	.15
338 Fred Barnett GW	.05	.15
339 Mark Clayton GW	.05	.15
340 Eric Martin GW	.05	.15
341 Irving Fryar GW	.05	.15
342 Tim Brown GW	.10	.30
343 Sterling Sharpe GW	.10	.30
344 Gary Clark GW	.05	.15
345 John Mackey HOF	.05	.15
346 Lem Barney HOF	.05	.15
347 John Riggins HOF	.10	.30
348 Marion Butts IDOL	.05	.15
William Andrews		
349 Jeff Lageman IDOL	.05	.15
Jack Lambert		
350 Eric Green IDOL	.05	.15
Sam Rutigliano		
351 Reggie White IDOL	.10	.30
Bobby Jones		
352 Marv Cook IDOL	.05	.15
Dan Gable		
353 John Elway IDOL	.50	1.25
Roger Staubach		
354 Steve Tasker IDOL	.05	.15
Ed Podolak		
355 Nick Lowery IDOL	.05	.15
Jan Stenerud		
356 Mark Clayton IDOL	.05	.15
Paul Warfield		
357 Warren Moon IDOL	.10	.30
Roman Gabriel		
358 Eric Metcalf	.10	.30
359 Charles Haley	.10	.30
360 Terrell Buckley RC	.05	.15
P1 Promo Panel	2.00	5.00
Super Bowl XXVII promo		
John Elway		
Sterling Sharpe		
Warren Moon		
Tommy Vardell		
Derrick Thomas		
Pat Swilling		
Neil Smith		
Cortez Kennedy		

1992 Pinnacle Team Pinnacle

COMPLETE SET (13)	25.00	60.00
RANDOM INSERTS IN FOIL PACKS		
1 Mark Rypien	2.50	6.00
Ronnie Lott		
2 Barry Sanders	6.00	15.00
Derrick Thomas		
3 Thurman Thomas	3.00	8.00
Pat Swilling		
4 Eric Green	2.50	6.00
Steve Atwater		
5 Haywood Jeffires	2.50	6.00
Darrell Green		
6 Michael Irvin	3.00	8.00
Eric Allen		
7 Bruce Matthews	1.50	4.00
Jerry Ball		
8 Steve Wisniewski	1.50	4.00
Pepper Johnson		
9 William Roberts	1.50	4.00
Karl Mecklenburg		
10 Jim Lachey	1.50	4.00
William Fuller		
11 Anthony Munoz	3.00	8.00
Reggie White		
12 Mel Gray	2.50	6.00
Steve Tasker		
13 Jeff Jaeger	1.50	4.00
Jeff Gossett		

1992 Pinnacle Team 2000

COMPLETE SET (30)	7.50	15.00
TWO PER JUMBO PACK		
1 Todd Marinovich	.02	.10
2 Rodney Hampton	.08	.25
3 Mike Croel	.02	.10
4 Leonard Russell	.08	.25
5 Herman Moore	.15	.40
6 Rob Moore	.08	.25
7 Jon Vaughn	.02	.10
8 Lamar Lathon	.02	.10
9 Ed King	.02	.10
10 Moe Gardner	.02	.10
11 Barry Foster	.08	.25
12 Eric Green	.02	.10
13 Kenny Walker	.02	.10
14 Tim Barnett	.02	.10
15 Derrick Thomas	.15	.40
16 Steve Atwater	.02	.10
17 Nick Bell	.02	.10
18 John Friesz	.02	.10
19 Emmitt Smith	1.50	3.00
20 Eric Swann	.08	.25
21 Barry Sanders	1.25	2.50
22 Mark Carrier DB	.02	.10
23 Brett Favre	2.50	5.00
24 James Francis	.02	.10
25 Lawrence Dawsey	.08	.25
26 Keith McCants	.02	.10
27 Broderick Thomas	.02	.10
28 Mike Pritchard	.08	.25
29 Bruce Pickens	.02	.10
30 Todd Lyght	.02	.10

1993 Pinnacle Samples

This sample panel measures approximately 7 1/2" by 7" and features two rows of three cards each. If cut, the cards would measure the standard size. The fronts display color action player photos on a black card face accented by thin white picture frames. The team name and the player's name are printed above and below the picture respectively; the gold-foil stamped Pinnacle logo at the lower right corner rounds out the card face. On a black background, the horizontal backs carry a color close-up photo, biography, career summary, and 1992 season statistics. The cards are numbered at the upper left corner, and the word "Sample" is printed just below Score's anti-counterfeiting device.

COMPLETE SET (6)	3.20	8.00
1 Brett Favre	2.00	5.00
2 Tommy Vardell	.30	.75
3 Jarrod Bunch	.30	.75
4 Mike Croel	.30	.75
5 Morten Andersen	.30	.75
6 Barry Foster	.30	.75

1993 Pinnacle

The 1993 Pinnacle set consists of 360 standard-size cards that were issued in 15 and 27-card packs. The set closes with the Hall of Fame (353-356) and Hometown Hero (357-360) subsets. Rookie Cards include Dave Brown. For each order of 20 boxes, Pinnacle would send one of 3,000 autographed cards of its spokesman, Franco Harris.

COMPLETE SET (360)	7.50	20.00
1 Brett Favre	1.25	3.00
2 Tommy Vardell	.02	.10
3 Jarrod Bunch	.02	.10
4 Mike Croel	.02	.10
5 Morten Andersen	.02	.10
6 Barry Foster	.07	.20
7 Chris Spielman	.07	.20
8 Jim Jeffcoat	.02	.10
9 Ken Ruettgers	.02	.10
10 Cris Dishman	.02	.10
11 Ricky Watters	.15	.40
12 Alfred Williams	.02	.10
13 Mark Kelso	.02	.10
14 Moe Gardner	.02	.10
15 Terry Allen	.15	.40
16 Willie Gault	.02	.10
17 Bubba McDowell	.02	.10
18 Brian Mitchell	.07	.20
19 Karl Mecklenburg	.02	.10
20 Jim Everett	.07	.20
21 Bobby Humphrey	.02	.10
22 Tim Krumrie	.02	.10
23 Ken Norton Jr.	.07	.20
24 Wendell Davis	.02	.10
25 Brad Baxter	.02	.10
26 Mel Gray	.07	.20
27 Jon Vaughn	.02	.10
28 James Hasty	.02	.10
29 Chris Warren	.07	.20
30 Tim Harris	.02	.10
31 Eric Metcalf	.07	.20
32 Rob Moore	.07	.20
33 Charles Haley	.07	.20
34 Leonard Marshall	.02	.10
35 Jeff Graham	.07	.20
36 Eugene Robinson	.02	.10
37 Darryl Talley	.02	.10
38 Brent Jones	.07	.20
39 Reggie Roby	.02	.10
40 Bruce Armstrong	.02	.10
41 Audray McMillian	.02	.10
42 Bern Brostek	.02	.10
43 Tony Bennett	.02	.10
44 Albert Lewis	.02	.10
45 Derrick Thomas	.15	.40
46 Cris Carter	.15	.40
47 Richmond Webb	.02	.10
48 Sean Landeta	.02	.10
49 Cleveland Gary	.02	.10
50 Mark Carrier DB	.02	.10
51 Lawrence Dawsey	.02	.10
52 Lamar Lathon	.02	.10
53 Nick Bell	.02	.10
54 Curtis Duncan	.02	.10
55 Irving Fryar	.07	.20
56 Seth Joyner	.02	.10
57 Jay Novacek	.07	.20
58 John L. Williams	.02	.10
59 Amp Lee	.02	.10
60 Marion Butts	.02	.10
61 Clyde Simmons	.02	.10
62 Rich Gannon	.15	.40
63 Anthony Johnson	.07	.20
64 Dave Meggett	.02	.10
65 James Francis	.02	.10
66 Trace Armstrong	.02	.10
67 Mo Lewis	.02	.10
68 Cornelius Bennett	.07	.20
69 Mark Duper	.02	.10
70 Frank Reich	.07	.20
71 Eric Green	.02	.10
72 Bruce Matthews	.02	.10
73 Steve Broussard	.02	.10
74 Anthony Carter	.07	.20
75 Sterling Sharpe	.15	.40
76 Mike Kenn	.02	.10
77 Andre Rison	.07	.20
78 Todd Marinovich	.02	.10
79 Vincent Brown	.02	.10
80 Harold Green	.02	.10
81 Art Monk	.07	.20
82 Reggie Cobb	.02	.10
83 Johnny Johnson	.02	.10
84 Tommy Kane	.02	.10
85 Rohn Stark	.02	.10
86 Steve Tasker	.07	.20
87 Ronnie Harmon	.02	.10
88 Pepper Johnson	.02	.10
89 Hardy Nickerson	.07	.20
90 Alvin Harper	.07	.20
91 Louis Oliver	.02	.10
92 Rod Woodson	.15	.40
93 Sam Mills	.02	.10
94 Randall McDaniel	.05	.15
95 Johnny Holland	.02	.10
96 Jackie Slater	.02	.10
97 Don Mosebar	.02	.10
98 Andre Ware	.02	.10
99 Kelvin Martin	.02	.10
100 Emmitt Smith	1.00	2.50
101 Michael Brooks	.02	.10
102 Dan Saleaumua	.02	.10
103 John Elway	1.00	2.50
104 Henry Jones	.02	.10
105 William Perry	.07	.20
106 James Lofton	.07	.20
107 Carnell Lake	.02	.10
108 Chip Lohmiller	.02	.10
109 Andre Tippett	.02	.10
110 Barry Word	.02	.10
111 Haywood Jeffires	.07	.20
112 Kenny Walker	.02	.10
113 John Randle	.07	.20
114 Donnell Woolford	.02	.10
115 Johnny Bailey	.02	.10
116 Marcus Allen	.15	.40
117 Mark Jackson	.02	.10
118 Ray Agnew	.02	.10
119 Gill Byrd	.02	.10
120 Kyle Clifton	.02	.10
121 Marv Cook	.02	.10
122 Jerry Ball	.02	.10
123 Steve Jordan	.02	.10
124 Shannon Sharpe	.15	.40
125 Brian Blades	.07	.20
126 Rodney Hampton	.07	.20
127 Bobby Hebert	.02	.10
128 Jessie Tuggle	.02	.10
129 Tom Newberry	.02	.10
130 Keith McCants	.02	.10
131 Richard Dent	.07	.20
132 Herman Moore	.15	.40
133 Michael Irvin	.15	.40
134 Ernest Givins	.07	.20
135 Mark Rypien	.02	.10
136 Leonard Russell	.07	.20
137 Reggie White	.15	.40
138 Thurman Thomas	.15	.40
139 Nick Lowery	.02	.10
140 Al Smith	.02	.10
141 Jackie Harris	.02	.10
142 Duane Bickett	.02	.10
143 Lawyer Tillman	.02	.10
144 Steve Wisniewski	.02	.10
145 Derrick Fenner	.02	.10
146 Harris Barton	.02	.10
147 Rich Camarillo	.02	.10
148 John Offerdahl	.02	.10
149 Mike Johnson	.02	.10
150 Ricky Reynolds	.02	.10
151 Fred Barnett	.07	.20
152 Nate Newton	.07	.20
153 Chris Doleman	.02	.10
154 Todd Scott	.02	.10
155 Tim McKyer	.02	.10
156 Ken Harvey	.02	.10
157 Jeff Feagles	.02	.10
158 Vince Workman	.02	.10
159 Bart Oates	.02	.10
160 Chris Miller	.07	.20
161 Pete Stoyanovich	.02	.10
162 Steve Wallace	.02	.10
163 Dermontti Dawson	.02	.10
164 Kenneth Davis	.02	.10
165 Mike Munchak	.07	.20
166 George Jamison	.02	.10
167 Christian Okoye	.02	.10
168 Chris Hinton	.02	.10
169 Vaughan Johnson	.02	.10
170 Gaston Green	.02	.10
171 Kevin Greene	.07	.20
172 Rob Burnett	.02	.10
173 Norm Johnson	.02	.10
174 Eric Hill	.02	.10
175 Lomas Brown	.02	.10
176 Chip Banks	.02	.10
177 Greg Townsend	.02	.10
178 David Fulcher	.02	.10
179 Gary Anderson RB	.02	.10
180 Brian Washington	.02	.10
181 Brett Perriman	.15	.40
182 Chris Chandler	.07	.20
183 Phil Hansen	.02	.10
184 Mark Clayton	.02	.10
185 Frank Warren	.02	.10
186 Tim Brown	.15	.40
187 Mark Stepnoski	.02	.10
188 Bryan Cox	.02	.10
189 Gary Zimmerman	.02	.10
190 Neil O'Donnell	.15	.40
191 Anthony Smith	.02	.10
192 Craig Heyward	.07	.20
193 Keith Byars	.02	.10
194 Sean Salisbury	.02	.10
195 Todd Lyght	.02	.10
196 Jessie Hester	.02	.10
197 Rufus Porter	.02	.10
198 Steve Christie	.02	.10
199 Nate Lewis	.02	.10
200 Barry Sanders	.75	2.00
201 Michael Haynes	.07	.20
202 John Taylor	.07	.20
203 John Friesz	.07	.20
204 William Fuller	.02	.10
205 Dennis Smith	.02	.10
206 Adrian Cooper	.02	.10
207 Henry Thomas	.02	.10
208 Gerald Williams	.02	.10
209 Chris Burkett	.02	.10
210 Broderick Thomas	.02	.10
211 Marvin Washington	.02	.10
212 Bennie Blades	.02	.10
213 Tony Casillas	.02	.10
214 Bubby Brister	.02	.10
215 Don Griffin	.02	.10
216 Jeff Cross	.02	.10
217 Derrick Walker	.02	.10
218 Lorenzo White	.02	.10
219 Ricky Sanders	.02	.10
220 Rickey Jackson	.02	.10
221 Simon Fletcher	.02	.10
222 Troy Vincent	.02	.10
223 Gary Clark	.07	.20
224 Stanley Richard	.02	.10
225 Dave Krieg	.07	.20
226 Warren Moon	.15	.40
227 Reggie Langhorne	.02	.10
228 Kent Hull	.02	.10
229 Ferrell Edmunds	.02	.10
230 Cortez Kennedy	.07	.20
231 Hugh Millen	.02	.10
232 Eugene Chung	.02	.10
233 Rodney Peete	.02	.10
234 Tom Waddle	.02	.10
235 David Klingler	.02	.10
236 Mark Carrier WR	.07	.20
237 Jay Schroeder	.02	.10
238 James Jones	.02	.10
239 Phil Simms	.07	.20
240 Steve Atwater	.02	.10
241 Jeff Herrod	.02	.10
242 Dale Carter	.02	.10
243 Glenn Cadrez RC	.02	.10
244 Wayne Martin	.02	.10
245 Willie Davis	.15	.40
246 Lawrence Taylor	.15	.40
247 Stan Humphries	.07	.20
248 Byron Evans	.02	.10
249 Wilber Marshall	.02	.10
250 Michael Bankston RC	.02	.10
251 Steve McMichael	.07	.20
252 Brad Edwards	.02	.10
253 Will Wolford	.02	.10
254 Paul Gruber	.02	.10
255 Steve Young	.50	1.25
256 Chuck Cecil	.02	.10
257 Pierce Holt	.02	.10
258 Anthony Miller	.07	.20
259 Carl Banks	.02	.10
260 Brad Muster	.02	.10
261 Clay Matthews	.07	.20
262 Rod Bernstine	.02	.10
263 Tim Barnett	.02	.10

264 Greg Lloyd	.07	.20
265 Sean Jones	.02	.10
266 J.J. Birden	.02	.10
267 Tim McDonald	.02	.10
268 Charles Mann	.02	.10
269 Bruce Smith	.15	.40
270 Sean Gilbert	.07	.20
271 Ricardo McDonald	.02	.10
272 Jeff Hostetler	.07	.20
273 Russell Maryland	.02	.10
274 Dave Brown RC	.15	.40
275 Ronnie Lott	.07	.20
276 Jim Kelly	.15	.40
277 Joe Montana	1.00	2.50
278 Eric Allen	.02	.10
279 Browning Nagle	.02	.10
280 Neal Anderson	.02	.10
281 Troy Aikman	.50	1.25
282 Ed McCaffrey	.15	.40
283 Robert Jones	.02	.10
284 Dalton Hilliard	.02	.10
285 Johnny Mitchell	.02	.10
286 Jay Hilgenberg	.02	.10
287 Eric Martin	.02	.10
288 Steve Emtman	.02	.10
289 Vaughn Dunbar	.02	.10
290 Mark Wheeler	.02	.10
291 Leslie O'Neal	.07	.20
292 Jerry Rice	.60	1.50
293 Neil Smith	.15	.40
294 Kerry Cash	.02	.10
295 Dan McGwire	.02	.10
296 Carl Pickens	.07	.20
297 Terrell Buckley	.02	.10
298 Randall Cunningham	.15	.40
299 Santana Dotson	.07	.20
300 Keith Jackson	.07	.20
301 Jim Lachey	.02	.10
302 Dan Marino	1.00	2.50
303 Lee Williams	.02	.10
304 Burt Grossman	.02	.10
305 Kevin Mack	.02	.10
306 Pat Swilling	.02	.10
307 Arthur Marshall RC	.02	.10
308 Jim Harbaugh	.15	.40
309 Kurt Barber	.02	.10
310 Harvey Williams	.07	.20
311 Ricky Ervins	.02	.10
312 Flipper Anderson	.02	.10
313 Bernie Kosar	.07	.20
314 Boomer Esiason	.07	.20
315 Deion Sanders	.30	.75
316 Ray Childress	.02	.10
317 Howie Long	.15	.40
318 Henry Ellard	.07	.20
319 Marco Coleman	.02	.10
320 Chris Mims	.02	.10
321 Quentin Coryatt	.07	.20
322 Jason Hanson	.02	.10
323 Ricky Proehl	.02	.10
324 Randal Hill	.02	.10
325 Vinny Testaverde	.07	.20
326 Jeff George	.15	.40
327 Junior Seau	.15	.40
328 Earnest Byner	.02	.10
329 Andre Reed	.07	.20
330 Phillippi Sparks	.02	.10
331 Kevin Ross	.02	.10
332 Clarence Verdin	.02	.10
333 Darryl Henley	.02	.10
334 Dana Hall	.02	.10
335 Greg McMurtry	.02	.10
336 Ron Hall	.02	.10
337 Darrell Green	.02	.10
338 Carlton Bailey	.02	.10
339 Irv Eatman	.02	.10
340 Greg Kragen	.02	.10
341 Wade Wilson	.02	.10
342 Klaus Wilmsmeyer	.02	.10
343 Derek Brown TE	.02	.10
344 Erik Williams	.02	.10
345 Jim McMahon	.07	.20
346 Mike Sherrard	.02	.10
347 Mark Bavaro	.02	.10
348 Anthony Munoz	.07	.20
349 Eric Dickerson	.07	.20
350 Steve Beuerlein	.07	.20
351 Tim McGee	.02	.10
352 Terry McDaniel	.02	.10
353 Dan Fouts HOF	.02	.10
354 Chuck Noll HOF	.07	.20
355 Bill Walsh HOF RC	.07	.20
356 Larry Little HOF	.02	.10
357 Todd Marinovich HH	.02	.10
358 Jeff George HH	.15	.40
359 Bernie Kosar HH	.07	.20
360 Rob Moore HH	.07	.20
NNO Franco Harris	12.50	30.00
AUTO/3000		

1993 Pinnacle Men of Autumn

COMPLETE SET (55)	4.00	10.00
ONE PER SCORE FOIL AND JUMBO P		
1 Andre Rison	.05	.15
2 Thurman Thomas	.10	.30
3 Wendell Davis	.02	.10
4 Harold Green	.02	.10
5 Eric Metcalf	.05	.15
6 Michael Irvin	.10	.30
7 John Elway	1.00	2.00
8 Barry Sanders	.75	1.50
9 Sterling Sharpe	.10	.30
10 Warren Moon	.10	.30
11 Rohn Stark	.02	.10
12 Derrick Thomas	.10	.30
13 Terry McDaniel	.02	.10
14 Cleveland Gary	.02	.10
15 Dan Marino	1.00	2.00
16 Terry Allen	.10	.30
17 Marv Cook	.02	.10
18 Bobby Hebert	.02	.10
19 Rodney Hampton	.05	.15
20 Brad Baxter	.02	.10
21 Reggie White	.10	.30
22 Ricky Proehl	.02	.10
23 Barry Foster	.05	.15
24 Junior Seau	.10	.30
25 Steve Young	.40	1.00
26 Cortez Kennedy	.05	.15
27 Reggie Cobb	.02	.10
28 Mark Rypien	.02	.10
29 Deion Sanders	.25	.60
30 Bruce Smith	.10	.30
31 Richard Dent	.05	.15
32 Alfred Williams	.02	.10
33 Clay Matthews	.05	.15
34 Emmitt Smith	1.00	2.00
35 Simon Fletcher	.02	.10
36 Chris Spielman	.05	.15
37 Brett Favre	1.25	2.50
38 Bruce Matthews	.02	.10
39 Jeff Herrod	.02	.10
40 Nick Lowery	.02	.10
41 Steve Wisniewski	.02	.10
42 Jim Everett	.05	.15
43 Keith Jackson	.05	.15
44 Chris Doleman	.02	.10
45 Irving Fryar	.05	.15
46 Rickey Jackson	.02	.10
47 Pepper Johnson	.02	.10
48 Randall Cunningham	.10	.30
49 Rich Camarillo	.02	.10
50 Rod Woodson	.10	.30
51 Ronnie Harmon	.02	.10
52 Ricky Watters	.10	.30
53 Chris Warren	.05	.15
54 Lawrence Dawsey	.02	.10
55 Wilber Marshall	.02	.10

1993 Pinnacle Rookies

COMPLETE SET (25)	100.00	200.00
STATED ODDS 1:36 HOB/RET		
1 Drew Bledsoe	20.00	50.00
2 Garrison Hearst	6.00	15.00
3 John Copeland	2.50	6.00
4 Eric Curry	3.00	8.00
5 Curtis Conway	4.00	10.00
6 Lincoln Kennedy	2.50	6.00
7 Jerome Bettis	30.00	60.00
8 Dan Williams	2.50	6.00
9 Patrick Bates	2.50	6.00
10 Brad Hopkins	2.50	6.00
11 Wayne Simmons	2.50	6.00
12 Rick Mirer	4.00	10.00
13 Tom Carter	2.50	6.00
14 Irv Smith	3.00	8.00
15 Marvin Jones	2.50	6.00
16 Deon Figures	2.50	6.00
17 Leonard Renfro	2.50	6.00
18 O.J.McDuffie	4.00	10.00
19 Dana Stubblefield	4.00	10.00
20 Carlton Gray	2.50	6.00
21 Demetrius DuBose	2.50	6.00
22 Troy Drayton	2.50	6.00
23 Natrone Means	4.00	10.00
24 Reggie Brooks	3.00	8.00
25 Glyn Milburn	4.00	10.00

1993 Pinnacle Super Bowl XXVII

COMPLETE SET (10)	40.00	100.00
ONE PER SEALED HOBBY FOIL BOX		
1 Rose Bowl	1.50	4.00
2 Thomas Everett	1.50	4.00
3 Emmitt Smith	12.00	30.00
4 Ken Norton Jr.	2.00	5.00
5 Michael Irvin	5.00	12.00
6 Jay Novacek	2.50	6.00
7 Charles Haley	3.00	8.00
8 Leon Lett	2.00	5.00
9 Alvin Harper	2.50	6.00
10 Tony Casillas	2.00	5.00

1993 Pinnacle Team Pinnacle

COMPLETE SET (13)	60.00	150.00
STATED ODDS 1:90 HOB/RET		
1 Troy Aikman	20.00	50.00
Joe Montana		
2 Thurman Thomas	12.50	30.00
Emmitt Smith		
3 Rodney Hampton	5.00	12.00
Barry Foster		
4 Sterling Sharpe	5.00	12.00
Anthony Miller		
5 Haywood Jeffires	5.00	12.00
Michael Irvin		
6 Jay Novacek	5.00	12.00
Keith Jackson		
7 Richmond Webb	3.00	8.00
Steve Wallace		
8 Reggie White	5.00	12.00
Leslie O'Neal		
9 Cortez Kennedy	3.00	8.00
Sean Gilbert		
10 Derrick Thomas	5.00	12.00
Wilber Marshall		
11 Sam Mills	5.00	12.00
Junior Seau		
12 Rod Woodson	6.00	15.00
Deion Sanders		
13 Steve Atwater	3.00	8.00
Tim McDonald		

1993 Pinnacle Team 2001

COMPLETE SET (30)	7.50	15.00
ONE PER JUMBO PACK		
1 Junior Seau	.30	.75
2 Cortez Kennedy	.15	.40
3 Carl Pickens	.15	.40
4 David Klingler	.07	.20
5 Santana Dotson	.15	.40
6 Sean Gilbert	.15	.40
7 Brett Favre	3.00	6.00
8 Steve Emtman	.07	.20
9 Rodney Hampton	.15	.40
10 Browning Nagle	.07	.20
11 Amp Lee	.07	.20
12 Vaughn Dunbar	.07	.20
13 Quentin Coryatt	.15	.40
14 Marco Coleman	.07	.20
15 Johnny Mitchell	.07	.20
16 Arthur Marshall	.07	.20
17 Dale Carter	.07	.20
18 Henry Jones	.07	.20
19 Terrell Buckley	.07	.20
20 Tommy Vardell	.07	.20
21 Tommy Maddox	.07	.20
22 Barry Foster	.15	.40
23 Herman Moore	.30	.75
24 Ricky Watters	.30	.75
25 Mike Croel	.07	.20
26 Russell Maryland	.07	.20
27 Terry Allen	.30	.75
28 Jon Vaughn	.07	.20
29 Todd Marinovich	.07	.20
30 Jeff Graham	.15	.40

1993 Pinnacle Power

1 Alexandre Daigle	60.00	150.00
Franco Harris		
Eric Lindros		

1994 Pinnacle Samples

This ten-card standard-size set was issued to promote the 1994 Pinnacle football series. The cards are virtually identical to their counterparts in the regular series, with only a very slight difference when examined closely. We've noted the minor differences below. The sample cards also are punched in one corner to indicate that they are promotional samples not for sale.

COMPLETE SET (11)	3.20	8.00
1 Deion Sanders	.60	1.50
last line of text reads/'es for a 17.7-yard...'		
3 Barry Sanders	1.60	4.00
Trophy Collection		
name in brown ink on back		
24 Sean Gilbert	.20	.50
last line of text reads		
mage to earn...		
30 Alvin Harper	.20	.50
last line of text reads/'tions and scored...'		
32 Derrick Thomas	.30	.75
last line of text reads/'bles last season.'		
85 James Jett	.30	.75
hometown		
drafted line/1-3/16-inches long instead of 1-5/16-inches		
214 Chuck Levy	.20	.50
card number in white letters		
DP8 William Floyd	.30	.75
last line of text reads		
over would-be tacklers.		
NNO Ad Card Hobby	.20	.50
NNO Ad Card Retail	.20	.50
NNO Pick Pinnacle Redemp.Card	.20	.50
no player name on front		

1994 Pinnacle

The 1994 Pinnacle football set consists of 270 standard-size cards. The fronts feature full-bleed photos with the player's name and Pinnacle logo in gold foil at the bottom. Horizontal backs have a player photo, a brief write-up and statistics. Cards 190-221 comprise of a Rookies subset. Card 271, Jerry Rice, was issued only in jumbo packs. The set is considered complete without it. Odds of finding the Drew Bledsoe Pinnacle Passer were one in approximately 360 hobby packs. Key Rookie Cards in this set include Trent Dilfer and Marshall Faulk. The Franco Harris signed card was randomly seeded in cases of Pinnacle and Pinnacle Canton Bound.

COMPLETE SET (270)	8.00	20.00
1 Deion Sanders	.20	.50
2 Eric Metcalf	.07	.20
3 Barry Sanders	.75	2.00
4 Ernest Givins	.07	.20
5 Phil Simms	.07	.20
6 Rod Woodson	.07	.20
7 Michael Irvin	.15	.40
8 Cortez Kennedy	.07	.20
9 Eric Martin	.02	.10
10 Jeff Hostetler	.07	.20
11 Sterling Sharpe	.07	.20
12 John Elway	1.00	2.50
13 Neal Anderson	.02	.10
14 Terry Kirby	.15	.40
15 Jim Everett	.07	.20
16 Lawrence Dawsey	.02	.10
17 Kelvin Martin	.02	.10
18 Tim McGee	.02	.10
19 Cris Carter	.20	.50
20 Ronnie Harmon	.02	.10
21 Jim Kelly	.15	.40
22 Steve Young	.40	1.00
23 Johnny Johnson	.02	.10
24 Sean Gilbert	.02	.10
25 Brian Mitchell	.02	.10
26 Carl Pickens	.07	.20
27 Tim Brown	.15	.40
28 Reggie Langhorne	.02	.10
29 Webster Slaughter	.02	.10
30 Alvin Harper	.07	.20
31 Andre Rison	.07	.20
32 Derrick Thomas	.15	.40
33 Irving Fryar	.07	.20
34 Vinny Testaverde	.07	.20
35 Steve Beuerlein	.07	.20
36 Brett Favre	1.00	2.50
37 Barry Foster	.02	*.10
38 Vaughan Johnson	.02	.10
39 Carlton Bailey	.02	.10
40 Steve Emtman	.02	.10
41 Anthony Miller	.07	.20
42 Jeff Cross	.02	.10
43 Trace Armstrong	.02	.10
44 Derek Russell	.02	.10
45 Vincent Brisby	.07	.20
46 Mark Jackson	.02	.10
47 Eugene Robinson	.02	.10
48 John Friesz	.07	.20
49 Scott Mitchell	.07	.20
50 Steve Atwater	.02	.10
51 Ken Norton	.07	.20
52 Vincent Brown	.02	.10
53 Morten Andersen	.02	.10
54 Gary Anderson K	.02	.10
55 Eric Curry	.02	.10
56 Henry Jones	.02	.10
57 Flipper Anderson	.02	.10
58 Pat Swilling	.02	.10
59 Erric Pegram	.02	.10
60 Bruce Matthews	.02	.10
61 Willie Davis	.07	.20
62 O.J. McDuffie	.15	.40
63 Qadry Ismail	.15	.40
64 Anthony Smith	.02	.10
65 Eric Allen	.02	.10
66 Marion Butts	.02	.10
67 Chris Miller	.02	.10
68 Terrell Buckley	.02	.10
69 Thurman Thomas	.15	.40
70 Roosevelt Potts	.02	.10
71 Tony McGee	.02	.10
72 Jason Hanson	.02	.10
73 Victor Bailey	.02	.10
74 Albert Lewis	.02	.10
75 Nate Odomes	.02	.10
76 Ben Coates	.07	.20
77 Warren Moon	.15	.40
78 Derek Brown RBK	.02	.10
79 David Klingler	.02	.10
80 Cleveland Gary	.02	.10
81 Emmitt Smith	.75	2.00
82 Jay Novacek	.07	.20
83 Dana Stubblefield	.07	.20
84 Michael Brooks	.02	.10
85 James Jett	.02	.10
86 J.J. Birden	.02	.10
87 William Fuller	.02	.10
88 Glyn Milburn	.07	.20
89 Tim Worley	.02	.10
90 Brett Perriman	.07	.20
91 Randall Cunningham	.15	.40
92 Drew Bledsoe	.40	1.00
93 Jerome Bettis	.25	.60
94 Boomer Esiason	.07	.20
95 Garrison Hearst	.15	.40
96 Bruce Smith	.15	.40
97 Jackie Harris	.02	.10
98 Jeff George	.15	.40
99 Tom Waddle	.02	.10
100 John Copeland	.02	.10
101 Bobby Hebert	.02	.10
102 Joe Montana	1.00	2.50
103 Herman Moore	.15	.40
104 Rick Mirer	.15	.40
105 Ricky Watters	.07	.20
106 Neil O'Donnell	.15	.40
107 Herschel Walker	.07	.20
108 Rob Moore	.07	.20
109 Reggie Brooks	.07	.20
110 Tommy Vardell	.02	.10
111 Eric Green	.02	.10
112 Stan Humphries	.07	.20
113 Greg Robinson	.02	.10
114 Eric Swann	.07	.20
115 Courtney Hawkins	.02	.10
116 Andre Reed	.07	.20
117 Steve McMichael	.07	.20
118 Gary Brown	.02	.10
119 Terry Allen	.07	.20
120 Dan Marino	1.00	2.50
121 Gary Clark	.07	.20
122 Chris Warren	.07	.20
123 Pierce Holt	.02	.10
124 Anthony Carter	.07	.20
125 Quentin Coryatt	.02	.10
126 Harold Green	.02	.10
127 Leonard Russell	.02	.10
128 Tim McDonald	.02	.10
129 Chris Spielman	.07	.20
130 Cody Carlson	.02	.10
131 Ronald Moore	.02	.10
132 Renaldo Turnbull	.02	.10
133 Ronnie Lott	.07	.20
134 Natrone Means	.15	.40
135 Keith Byars	.02	.10
136 Henry Ellard	.07	.20
137 Steve Jordan	.02	.10
138 Calvin Williams	.07	.20
139 Brian Blades	.07	.20
140 Michael Jackson	.07	.20
141 Charles Haley	.07	.20
142 Curtis Conway	.15	.40
143 Nick Lowery	.02	.10
144 Bill Brooks	.02	.10
145 Michael Haynes	.07	.20
146 Willie Green	.02	.10
147 Duane Bickett	.02	.10
148 Shannon Sharpe	.07	.20
149 Ricky Proehl	.02	.10
150 Troy Aikman	.50	1.25
151 Mike Sherrard	.02	.10
152 Reggie Cobb	.02	.10
153 Norm Johnson	.02	.10
154 Neil Smith	.07	.20
155 James Francis	.02	.10
156 Greg McMurtry	.02	.10
157 Greg Townsend	.02	.10
158 Mel Gray	.02	.10
159 Rocket Ismail	.07	.20
160 Leslie O'Neal	.02	.10
161 Johnny Mitchell	.02	.10
162 Brent Jones	.07	.20
163 Chris Doleman	.02	.10
164 Seth Joyner	.02	.10
165 Marco Coleman	.02	.10
166 Mark Higgs	.02	.10
167 John L. Williams	.02	.10
168 Darrell Green	.02	.10
169 Mark Carrier WR	.07	.20
170 Reggie White	.15	.40
171 Darryl Talley	.02	.10
172 Russell Maryland	.02	.10
173 Mark Collins	.02	.10
174 Chris Jacke	.02	.10
175 Richard Dent	.07	.20
176 John Taylor	.07	.20
177 Rodney Hampton	.07	.20
178 Dwight Stone	.02	.10
179 Cornelius Bennett	.07	.20
180 Cris Dishman	.02	.10
181 Jerry Rice	.50	1.25
182 Rod Bernstine	.02	.10
183 Keith Hamilton	.02	.10
184 Keith Jackson	.02	.10
185 Craig Erickson	.02	.10
186 Marcus Allen	.15	.40
187 Marcus Robertson	.02	.10
188 Junior Seau	.15	.40
189 LeShon Johnson RC	.07	.20
190 Perry Klein RC	.02	.10
191 Bryant Young RC	.25	.60
192 Byron Bam Morris RC	.07	.20
193 Jeff Cothran RC	.02	.10
194 Lamar Smith RC	.60	1.50
195 Calvin Jones RC	.02	.10
196 James Bostic RC	.15	.40
197 Dan Wilkinson RC	.07	.20
198 Marshall Faulk RC	2.50	6.00
199 Heath Shuler RC	.15	.40
200 Willie McGinest RC	.15	.40
201 Trev Alberts RC	.07	.20
202 Trent Dilfer RC	.60	1.50
203 Sam Adams RC	.07	.20
204 Charles Johnson RC	.15	.40
205 Johnnie Morton RC	.60	1.50
206 Thomas Lewis RC	.07	.20
207 Greg Hill RC	.15	.40
208 William Floyd RC	.15	.40
209 Der.Alexander WR RC	.15	.40
210 Darnay Scott RC	.30	.75
211 Lake Dawson RC	.07	.20
212 Errict Rhett RC	.15	.40
213 Kevin Lee RC	.02	.10
214 Chuck Levy RC	.02	.10
215 David Palmer RC	.15	.40
216 Ryan Yarborough RC	.02	.10
217 Charlie Garner RC	.60	1.50
218 Mario Bates RC	.15	.40
219 Jamir Miller RC	.07	.20
220 Bucky Brooks RC	.02	.10
221 Donnell Bennett RC	.15	.40
222 Kevin Greene	.07	.20
223 LeRoy Butler	.02	.10
224 Anthony Pleasant	.02	.10
225 Steve Christie	.02	.10
226 Bill Romanowski	.02	.10
227 Darren Carrington	.02	.10
228 Chester McGlockton	.02	.10
229 Jack Del Rio	.02	.10
230 Kevin Smith	.02	.10
231 Chris Zorich	.02	.10
232 Donnell Woolford	.02	.10
233 Tony Casillas	.02	.10
234 Terry McDaniel	.02	.10
235 Ray Childress	.02	.10
236 John Randle	.07	.20
237 Clyde Simmons	.02	.10
238 Dante Jones	.02	.10
239 Karl Mecklenburg	.02	.10
240 Daryl Johnston	.07	.20
241 Hardy Nickerson	.07	.20
242 Jeff Lageman	.02	.10
243 Lewis Tillman	.02	.10
244 Jim McMahon	.07	.20
245 Mike Pritchard	.02	.10
246 Harvey Williams	.07	.20
247 Sean Jones	.02	.10
248 Stevon Moore	.02	.10
249 Pete Metzelaars	.02	.10
250 Mike Johnson	.02	.10
251 Chris Slade	.02	.10
252 Jessie Hester	.02	.10
253 Louis Oliver	.02	.10
254 Ken Harvey	.02	.10
255 Bryan Cox	.02	.10
256 Erik Kramer	.07	.20
257 Andy Harmon	.02	.10
258 Rickey Jackson	.02	.10
259 Mark Carrier DB	.02	.10
260 Greg Lloyd	.07	.20
261 Robert Brooks	.15	.40
262 Dave Brown	.07	.20
263 Dennis Smith	.02	.10
264 Michael Dean Perry	.07	.20
265 Dan Saleaumua	.02	.10
266 Mo Lewis	.02	.10
267 AFC Checklist	.02	.10
268 AFC Checklist	.02	.10
269 NFC Checklist	.02	.10
270 NFC Checklist	.02	.10
271SP Jerry Rice TD King	4.00	8.00
AU Franco Harris AU	12.00	30.00
NNO Drew Bledsoe	15.00	40.00
Pinnacle Passer		

1994 Pinnacle Trophy Collection

COMPLETE SET (270)	100.00	200.00
*STARS: 3X TO 8X BASIC CARDS		
*RCs: 2X TO 5X BASIC CARDS		

1994 Pinnacle Draft Pinnacle

COMPLETE SET (10)	15.00	40.00
STATED ODDS 1:24 HOBBY		
*DUFEX CARDS: SAME PRICE		
PRIZES FOR PICK PINNACLE WINNE		
PICK PINNACLE STATED ODDS 1:80		
DP1 Dan Wilkinson	.40	1.00
DP2 Marshall Faulk	15.00	30.00
DP3 Heath Shuler	1.00	2.00
DP4 Trent Dilfer	4.00	8.00
DP5 Charles Johnson	1.00	2.00
DP6 Johnnie Morton	4.00	8.00
DP7 Darnay Scott	2.00	4.00
DP8 William Floyd	1.00	2.00
DP9 Errict Rhett	1.00	2.00
DP10 Chuck Levy	.20	.50

1994 Pinnacle Performers

COMPLETE SET (18)	10.00	25.00
STATED ODDS 1:4 JUMBO		
PP1 Troy Aikman	1.50	3.00
PP2 Emmitt Smith	2.50	5.00
PP3 Sterling Sharpe	.20	.50
PP4 Barry Sanders	2.50	5.00
PP5 Jerry Rice	1.50	3.00
PP6 Steve Young	1.25	2.50
PP7 John Elway	3.00	6.00
PP8 Michael Irvin	.40	1.00
PP9 Jerome Bettis	.75	1.50
PP10 Tim Brown	.40	1.00
PP11 Joe Montana	3.00	6.00
PP12 Reggie Brooks	.20	.50
PP13 Brett Favre	3.00	6.00
PP14 Drew Bledsoe	1.25	2.50
PP15 Ricky Watters	.20	.50
PP16 Garrison Hearst	.40	1.00
PP17 Rodney Hampton	.20	.50
PP18 Dan Marino	3.00	6.00

1994 Pinnacle Team Pinnacle

COMPLETE SET (10)	25.00	60.00
*DUFEX BACK: .4X TO 1X BASIC CARDS		
STATED ODDS 1:90		
TP1 Troy Aikman	5.00	12.00
Joe Montana		
TP2 Brett Favre	5.00	12.00
Rick Mirer		
TP3 Emmitt Smith	4.00	10.00
Thurman Thomas		
TP4 Barry Sanders	4.00	10.00
Barry Foster		
TP5 Jerome Bettis	2.50	6.00
Natrone Means		
TP6 Sterling Sharpe	1.25	3.00
Tim Brown		
TP7 Jerry Rice	3.00	8.00
Anthony Miller		
TP8 Michael Irvin	2.00	5.00
James Jett		
TP9 Reggie White	2.00	5.00
Bruce Smith		
TP10 Sean Gilbert	.75	2.00
Cortez Kennedy		

1994 Pinnacle Canton Bound

These 25 standard-size cards feature Pinnacle's picks for future Hall of Fame inductees. Production was limited to 100,000 sets, and each set contained a numbered certificate of authenticity. The fronts feature color player action shots that are borderless, and carry the player's name in vertical gold-foil lettering near the right edge. On a borderless back composed of multiple player photos, the back carries the player's biography, career highlights, and statistics. A Ronnie Lott Sample card was produced as well and is listed below, but is not considered part of the set.

COMP.FACT SET (25)	4.00	10.00
1 Troy Aikman	.50	1.25
2 Emmitt Smith	1.00	2.50
3 Barry Sanders	1.00	2.50
4 Jerry Rice	.50	1.25
5 Sterling Sharpe	.10	.30
6 Ronnie Lott	.10	.30
7 John Elway	1.00	2.50
8 Joe Montana	1.00	2.50
9 Reggie White	.10	.30
10 Thurman Thomas	.20	.50
11 Bruce Smith	.05	.15
12 Cortez Kennedy	.05	.15
13 Dan Marino	1.00	2.50
14 Andre Rison	.10	.30
15 Art Monk	.10	.30
16 Warren Moon	.10	.30
17 Barry Foster	.05	.15
18 Steve Young	.40	1.00
19 Phil Simms	.10	.30
20 Richard Dent	.05	.15
21 Marcus Allen	.10	.30
22 Junior Seau	.10	.30
23 Michael Irvin	.20	.50
24 Deion Sanders	.30	.75
25 Jerome Bettis	.20	.50
S1 Ronnie Lott Sample	.40	1.00

1994 Pinnacle/Sportflics Super Bowl

This seven-card 1994 Magic Motion standard-size set was issued by Pinnacle Brands, Inc. (Score) at the 1994 Super Bowl Card Show in Atlanta. Cards were distributed individually by exchanging three Pinnacle Brands wrappers from foil packs. The cards were produced and distributed in the following quantities: 3,000 for Gary Brown and Emmitt Smith; 2,000 for Sterling Sharpe, Jerome Bettis/Reggie Brooks, and Drew Bledsoe/Rick Mirer; and 1,000 for Jerry Rice and Deion Sanders. The "Magic Motion" process is an improved version of the old Sportflics. An "S" prefix and a "B" suffix appear on either side of the card number printed on a yellow oval on the card back.

COMPLETE SET (7)	110.00	275.00
1 Gary Brown/3000	4.80	12.00
2 Emmitt Smith/3000	20.00	50.00
3 Sterling Sharpe/2000	8.00	20.00
4 Jerome Bettis/2000	12.00	30.00
Reggie Brooks		
5 Drew Bledsoe/2000	16.00	40.00
Rick Mirer		
6 Jerry Rice/1000	30.00	75.00
7 Deion Sanders/1000	20.00	50.00

1994 Pinnacle Team Histories

Cards from this set were issued in blister pack format along with a metal lapel pin featuring the team's logo. The card/pin combos were released to commemorate historic franchises for the NFL's 75th anniversary.

COMPLETE SET (12)	8.00	20.00
1 Dallas Cowboys	1.25	3.00
2 Miami Dolphins	1.00	2.50
3 Kansas City Chiefs	1.00	2.50
4 San Francisco 49ers	1.25	3.00
5 Los Angeles Raiders	1.00	2.50
6 New York Giants	1.00	2.50
7 Green Bay Packers	1.25	3.00
8 Philadelphia Eagles	1.00	2.50
9 Chicago Bears	1.00	2.50
10 Pittsburgh Steelers	1.25	3.00
11 Buffalo Bills	1.00	2.50
12 Washington Redskins	1.00	2.50

1995 Pinnacle Promos

These four cards were produced to promote the 1995 Pinnacle release. They include two base brand cards, one Showcase insert and an ad card.

COMPLETE SET (4)	3.20	8.00
1 Dan Marino	1.60	4.00
Showcase Card		
39 Barry Sanders	1.60	4.00
62 Steve Young	.50	1.25
NNO Ad Card	.20	.50

1995 Pinnacle

This 250 card set was issued by Pinnacle Brands and was available in 12 card packs for hobby and retail. Jumbo packs were also available. A special Deion Sanders card was issued only in jumbo packs and numbered 251SP. It features Sanders with his new team - the Dallas Cowboys. The set also contains a parallel called Trophy Collection, which features the same player shots with an all-foil dufex background. Trophy Collection cards were randomly inserted into packs at a rate of one in four. The Joe Montana Trophy Collection card (#193) is unique from the other cards because it does not have an Artist Proof parallel. Rookie Cards include Jeff Blake, Ki-Jana Carter, Kerry Collins, Joey Galloway, Steve McNair, Rashaan Salaam, Kordell Stewart, J.J. Stokes and Michael Westbrook

COMPLETE SET (250)	8.00	20.00
1 Reggie White	.15	.40
2 Troy Aikman	.40	1.00
3 Willie Davis	.07	.20
4 Jerry Rice	.40	1.00
5 Bruce Smith	.15	.40
6 Keith Byars	.02	.10
7 Chris Warren	.07	.20
8 Erik Kramer	.02	.10
9 Leon Lett	.02	.10
10 Greg Lloyd	.07	.20
11 Jackie Harris	.02	.10
12 Irving Fryar	.07	.20
13 Rodney Hampton	.07	.20
14 Michael Irvin	.15	.40
15 Michael Haynes	.07	.20
16 Irving Spikes	.07	.20
17 Calvin Williams	.07	.20
18 Ken Norton Jr.	.07	.20
19 Herman Moore	.15	.40
20 Lewis Tillman	.02	.10
21 Cortez Kennedy	.07	.20
22 Dan Marino	.75	2.00
23 Erric Pegram	.07	.20
24 Tim Brown	.15	.40
25 Jeff Blake RC	.30	.75
26 Brett Favre	.75	2.00
27 Garrison Hearst	.15	.40
28 Ronnie Harmon	.02	.10
29 Qadry Ismail	.07	.20
30 Ben Coates	.07	.20
31 Deion Sanders	.25	.60
32 John Elway	.75	2.00
33 Natrone Means	.07	.20
34 Derrick Alexander WR	.15	.40
35 Craig Heyward	.07	.20
36 Jake Reed	.07	.20
37 Steve Walsh	.02	.10
38 John Randle	.07	.20
39 Barry Sanders	.60	1.50
40 Tydus Winans	.02	.10
41 Thomas Lewis	.07	.20
42 Jim Kelly	.15	.40
43 Gus Frerotte	.07	.20
44 Cris Carter	.15	.40
45 Kevin Williams WR	.07	.20
46 Dave Meggett	.02	.10
47 Pat Swilling	.02	.10
48 Neil O'Donnell	.07	.20
49 Terance Mathis	.07	.20
50 Desmond Howard	.07	.20
51 Bryant Young	.07	.20
52 Stan Humphries	.07	.20
53 Alvin Harper	.02	.10
54 Henry Ellard	.07	.20
55 Jessie Hester	.02	.10
56 Lorenzo White	.02	.10
57 John Friesz	.07	.20
58 Anthony Smith	.02	.10
59 Bert Emanuel	.15	.40
60 Gary Clark	.02	.10
61 Bill Brooks	.02	.10
62 Steve Young	.30	.75
63 Jerome Bettis	.15	.40
64 John Taylor	.02	.10
65 Ricky Proehl	.02	.10
66 Junior Seau	.15	.40
67 Bubby Brister	.02	.10
68 Neil Smith	.07	.20
69 Dan McGwire	.02	.10
70 Brett Perriman	.07	.20
71 Chris Spielman	.07	.20
72 Jeff George	.07	.20
73 Emmitt Smith	.40	1.00
74 Chris Penn	.02	.10
75 Derrick Fenner	.02	.10
76 Reggie Brooks	.07	.20
77 Chris Chandler	.07	.20
78 Rod Woodson	.07	.20
79 Isaac Bruce	.25	.60
80 Reggie Cobb	.02	.10
81 Bryce Paup	.07	.20
82 Warren Moon	.07	.20
83 Bryan Reeves	.02	.10
84 Lake Dawson	.07	.20
85 Larry Centers	.07	.20
86 Marshall Faulk	.50	1.25
87 Jim Harbaugh	.07	.20
88 Ray Childress	.02	.10
89 Eric Metcalf	.07	.20
90 Ernie Mills	.02	.10
91 Lamar Lathon	.02	.10
92 Errict Rhett	.07	.20
93 David Klingler	.07	.20
94 Vincent Brown	.02	.10
95 Andre Rison	.07	.20
96 Brian Mitchell	.02	.10
97 Mark Rypien	.02	.10
98 Eugene Robinson	.02	.10
99 Eric Green	.02	.10
100 Rocket Ismail	.07	.20
101 Flipper Anderson	.02	.10
102 Randall Cunningham	.15	.40
103 Ricky Watters	.07	.20
104 Amp Lee	.02	.10
105 Ernest Givins	.02	.10
106 Daryl Johnston	.07	.20
107 Dave Krieg	.02	.10
108 Dana Stubblefield	.07	.20
109 Torrance Small	.02	.10
110 Yancey Thigpen RC	.07	.20
111 Chester McGlockton	.07	.20
112 Craig Erickson	.02	.10
113 Herschel Walker	.07	.20
114 Mlke Sherrard	.02	.10
115 Tony McGee	.02	.10
116 Adrian Murrell	.07	.20
117 Frank Reich	.02	.10
118 Hardy Nickerson	.02	.10
119 Andre Reed	.07	.20
120 Leonard Russell	.02	.10
121 Eric Allen	.02	.10
122 Jeff Hostetler	.07	.20
123 Barry Foster	.07	.20
124 Anthony Miller	.07	.20
125 Shawn Jefferson	.02	.10
126 Richie Anderson RC	.20	.50
127 Steve Bono	.07	.20
128 Seth Joyner	.02	.10
129 Darnay Scott	.07	.20
130 Johnny Mitchell	.02	.10
131 Eric Swann	.07	.20
132 Drew Bledsoe	.25	.60
133 Marcus Allen	.15	.40
134 Carl Pickens	.07	.20
135 Michael Brooks	.02	.10
136 John L. Williams	.02	.10
137 Steve Beuerlein	.07	.20
138 Robert Smith	.15	.40
139 O.J. McDuffie	.15	.40
140 Haywood Jeffires	.02	.10
141 Aeneas Williams	.02	.10
142 Rick Mirer	.07	.20
143 William Floyd	.07	.20
144 Fred Barnett	.07	.20
145 Leroy Hoard	.02	.10
146 Terry Kirby	.07	.20
147 Boomer Esiason	.07	.20
148 Ken Harvey	.02	.10
149 Cleveland Gary	.02	.10
150 Brian Blades	.07	.20
151 Eric Turner	.02	.10
152 Vinny Testaverde	.07	.20
153 Ronald Moore UER	.02	.10
card pictures Rob Moore		
154 Curtis Conway	.15	.40
155 Johnnie Morton	.07	.20
156 Kenneth Davis	.02	.10
157 Scott Mitchell	.07	.20
158 Sean Gilbert	.07	.20
159 Shannon Sharpe	.07	.20
160 Mark Seay	.07	.20
161 Cornelius Bennett	.07	.20
162 Heath Shuler	.07	.20
163 Byron Bam Morris	.02	.10
164 Robert Brooks	.15	.40
165 Glyn Milburn	.02	.10
166 Gary Brown	.02	.10
167 Jim Everett	.02	.10
168 Steve Atwater	.02	.10
169 Darren Woodson	.07	.20
170 Mark Ingram	.02	.10
171 Donnell Woolford	.02	.10
172 Trent Dilfer	.15	.40
173 Charlie Garner	.15	.40
174 Charles Johnson	.07	.20
175 Mike Pritchard	.02	.10
176 Derek Brown RBK	.02	.10
177 Chris Miller	.02	.10
178 Charles Haley	.07	.20
179 J.J. Birden	.02	.10
180 Jeff Graham	.02	.10
181 Bernie Parmalee	.07	.20
182 Mark Brunell	.25	.60

183 Greg Hill	.07	.20
184 Michael Timpson	.02	.10
185 Terry Allen	.07	.20
186 Ricky Ervins	.02	.10
187 Dave Brown	.07	.20
188 Dan Wilkinson	.07	.20
189 Jay Novacek	.07	.20
190 Harvey Williams	.02	.10
191 Mario Bates	.07	.20
192 Steve Young	.20	.50
193 Joe Montana	.75	2.00
194 Steve Young PP	.20	.50
195 Troy Aikman PP	.25	.60
196 Drew Bledsoe PP	.15	.40
197 Dan Marino PP	.40	1.00
198 John Elway PP	.40	1.00
199 Brett Favre PP	.40	1.00
200 Heath Shuler PP	.07	.20
201 Warren Moon PP	.02	.10
202 Jim Kelly PP	.15	.40
203 Jeff Hostetler PP	.07	.20
204 Rick Mirer PP	.07	.20
205 Dave Brown PP	.07	.20
206 Randall Cunningham PP	.07	.20
207 Neil O'Donnell PP	.07	.20
208 Jim Everett PP	.02	.10
209 Ki-Jana Carter RC	.15	.40
210 Steve McNair RC	1.25	3.00
211 Michael Westbrook RC	.15	.40
212 Kerry Collins RC	.75	2.00
213 Joey Galloway RC	.60	1.50
214 Kyle Brady RC	.15	.40
215 J.J. Stokes RC	.15	.40
216 Tyrone Wheatley RC	.50	1.25
217 Rashaan Salaam RC	.07	.20
218 Napoleon Kaufman RC	.50	1.25
219 Frank Sanders RC	.15	.40
220 Stoney Case RC	.02	.10
221 Todd Collins RC	.50	1.25
222 Warren Sapp RC	.60	1.50
223 Sherman Williams RC	.02	.10
224 Rob Johnson RC	.40	1.00
225 Mark Bruener RC	.07	.20
226 Derrick Brooks RC	.60	1.50
227 Chad May RC	.02	.10
228 James A.Stewart RC	.02	.10
229 Ray Zellars RC	.07	.20
230 Dave Barr RC	.02	.10
231 Kordell Stewart RC	.60	1.50
232 Jimmy Oliver RC	.02	.10
233 Tony Boselli RC	.15	.40
234 James O. Stewart RC	.50	1.25
235 Der. Alexander DE RC	.02	.10
236 Lovell Pinkney RC	.02	.10
237 John Walsh RC	.02	.10
238 Tyrone Davis RC	.02	.10
239 Joe Aska RC	.02	.10
240 Korey Stringer RC	.10	.30
241 Hugh Douglas RC	.15	.40
242 Christian Fauria RC	.07	.20
243 Terrell Fletcher RC	.02	.10
244 Dan Marino	.25	.60
245 Drew Bledsoe	.15	.40
246 John Elway	.15	.40
247 Emmitt Smith	.20	.50
248 Steve Young	.15	.40
249 Barry Sanders CL	.25	.60
250 Jerry Rice CL	.15	.40
Junior Seau CL		
251SP Deion Sanders SP	1.50	4.00

1995 Pinnacle Artist's Proofs

COMPLETE SET (249)	150.00	300.00
*AP STARS: 7.5X TO 20X BASIC CARDS		
*AP RCs: 4X TO 10X BASIC CARDS		
STATED ODDS 1:48		

1995 Pinnacle Trophy Collection

COMPLETE SET (250)	50.00	120.00
*TC STARS: 2X TO 5X BASIC CARDS		
*RCs: 1.25X TO 3X BASIC CARDS		
193 Joe Montana	25.00	50.00

1995 Pinnacle Black 'N Blue

COMPLETE SET (30)	30.00	60.00
STATED ODDS 1:18 JUMBO		
1 Junior Seau	1.00	2.50
2 Byron Bam Morris	.25	.60
3 Craig Heyward	.50	1.25
4 Drew Bledsoe	1.50	4.00
5 Barry Sanders	4.00	10.00
6 Jerome Bettis	1.00	2.50
7 William Floyd	.50	1.25
8 Greg Lloyd	.50	1.25
9 John Elway	5.00	12.00
10 Jerry Rice	2.50	6.00
11 Kevin Greene	.25	.60
12 Errict Rhett	.50	1.25
13 Steve Young	2.00	5.00
14 Bruce Smith	1.00	2.50
15 Steve Atwater	.25	.60
16 Natrone Means	.50	1.25
17 Ben Coates	.50	1.25
18 Reggie White	1.00	2.50
19 Ken Harvey	.25	.60
20 Dan Marino	5.00	12.00
21 Marshall Faulk	3.00	8.00
22 Seth Joyner	.25	.60
23 Rod Woodson	.50	1.25
24 Hardy Nickerson	.25	.60
25 Brett Favre	5.00	12.00
26 Bryan Cox	.25	.60
27 Rodney Hampton	.50	1.25
28 Jeff Hostetler	.50	1.25
29 Brent Jones	.25	.60
30 Emmitt Smith	2.50	6.00

1995 Pinnacle Clear Shots

COMPLETE SET (10)	25.00	60.00
STATED ODDS 1:60 HOB, 1:33 RETAIL		
1 Jerry Rice	2.50	6.00
2 Dan Marino	5.00	12.00
3 Steve Young	2.00	5.00
4 Drew Bledsoe	1.50	4.00
5 Emmitt Smith	2.50	6.00
6 Barry Sanders	4.00	10.00
7 Marshall Faulk	3.00	8.00
8 Troy Aikman	2.50	6.00
9 Ki-Jana Carter	.50	1.25
10 Steve McNair	4.00	10.00

1995 Pinnacle Gamebreakers

COMPLETE SET (15)	15.00	40.00
STATED ODDS 1:24 HOBBY		
1 Marshall Faulk	2.50	5.00
2 Emmitt Smith	2.00	4.00
3 Steve Young	1.50	3.00
4 Ki-Jana Carter	.30	.75
5 Drew Bledsoe	1.25	2.50
6 Troy Aikman	2.00	4.00
7 Rashaan Salaam	.15	.40
8 Tyrone Wheatley	1.25	2.50
9 Dan Marino	4.00	8.00
10 Natrone Means	.30	.75
11 Barry Sanders	3.00	6.00
12 Jerry Rice	2.00	4.00
13 Byron Bam Morris	.15	.40
14 Steve McNair	3.00	6.00
15 Kerry Collins	1.50	4.00

1995 Pinnacle Showcase

COMPLETE SET (21)	15.00	30.00
STATED ODDS 1:18 HOB, 1:14 JUM, 1:10 RET		
1 Drew Bledsoe	.75	1.50
2 Joey Galloway	.75	1.50
3 Steve Young	1.00	2.00
4 Joe Aska	.02	.10
5 Barry Sanders	2.00	4.00
6 Troy Aikman	1.25	2.50
7 Dan Marino	2.50	5.00
8 Randall Cunningham	.40	1.00
9 John Elway	2.50	5.00
10 Brett Favre	2.50	5.00
11 Jim Kelly	.40	1.00
12 Warren Moon	.20	.50
13 Dave Brown	.20	.50
14 Jeff Hostetler	.20	.50
15 Rick Mirer	.20	.50
16 Ki-Jana Carter	.15	.40
17 Kerry Collins	.75	2.00
18 J.J. Stokes	.15	.40
19 Kordell Stewart	2.00	4.00
20 Michael Westbrook	.15	.40
21 Todd Collins	.40	1.00

1995 Pinnacle Team Pinnacle

COMPLETE SET (10)	30.00	80.00
STATED ODDS 1:90 HOBBY, 1:49 RETAIL		
*DUFEX BACK: .4X TO 1X BASIC CARDS		
1 Steve Young	4.00	10.00
Drew Bledsoe		
2 Emmitt Smith	5.00	12.00
Marshall Faulk		
3 Barry Sanders	4.00	10.00
Natrone Means		
4 Dan Marino	5.00	12.00
Troy Aikman		
5 Jerry Rice	4.00	10.00
Tim Brown		
6 Errict Rhett	2.00	5.00
Byron Bam Morris		
7 Brett Favre	6.00	15.00
John Elway		
8 Rashaan Salaam	2.00	5.00
Ki-Jana Carter		
9 Kery Collins	3.00	8.00
Steve McNair		
10 Joey Galloway	2.00	5.00
Michael Westbrook		

1995 Pinnacle Dial Corporation

This 30-card standard-size set was sponsored by Dial and Purex and carries a Pinnacle '95 logo. It could be obtained by sending in UPC symbols from three Dial soap and Purex laundry products plus 2.50 to cover shipping and handling. The offer expired 1/31/96, or earlier if supplies became exhausted. The fronts feature full-bleed color action photos, with biography and statistical information on the backs. As part of a Dial Soap Super Bowl Contest, uncut sheets of the cards were issued as prizes. These sheets include 90-cards (3 complete sets) with one of the Bruce Smith cards autographed.

COMPLETE SET (30)	12.00	30.00
DC1 Troy Aikman	.80	2.00
DC2 Frank Reich	.08	.25
DC3 Drew Bledsoe	.80	2.00
DC4 Bubby Brister	.20	.50
DC5 Dave Brown	.08	.25
DC6 Randall Cunningham	.30	.75
DC7 John Elway	1.60	4.00
DC8 Boomer Esiason	.08	.25
DC9 Jim Everett	.08	.25
DC10 Bruce Smith	.20	.50
DC11 Brett Favre	1.60	4.00
DC12 Jim Harbaugh	.30	.75
DC13 Jeff Hostetler	.08	.25
DC14 Michael Irvin	.30	.75
DC15 Jim Kelly	.30	.75
DC16 David Klingler	.08	.25
DC17 Bernie Kosar	.08	.25
DC18 Dan Marino	1.60	4.00
DC19 Chris Miller	.08	.25
DC20 Rick Mirer	.20	.50
DC21 Warren Moon	.30	.75
DC22 Neil O'Donnell	.20	.50
DC23 Jerry Rice	.80	2.00
DC24 Mark Rypien	.08	.25
DC25 Barry Sanders	1.60	4.00
DC26 Junior Seau	.30	.75
DC27 Heath Shuler	.20	.50
DC28 Phil Simms	.08	.25
DC29 Emmitt Smith	1.20	3.00
DC30 Steve Young	.60	1.50
P1 Uncut Sheet Prize	15.00	40.00

1996 Pinnacle

The 1996 Pinnacle set was issued in one series totalling 200 cards with each base card printed with gold foil highlights. The 10-card packs retail for $2.49 each. The following subsets are included in the set: Rookies (153-182), Bid for 6 (183-194) and Checklists (195-199). A number of parallel sets were produced for this release with varying insertion ratios and packaging types.

COMPLETE SET (200)	8.00	20.00
1 Emmitt Smith	.60	1.50
2 Robert Brooks	.15	.40
3 Joey Galloway	.15	.40
4 Dan Marino	.75	2.00
5 Frank Sanders	.07	.20
6 Cris Carter	.15	.40
7 Jeff Blake	.15	.40
8 Steve McNair	.30	.75
9 Tamarick Vanover	.07	.20
10 Andre Reed	.07	.20
11 Junior Seau	.15	.40
12 Alvin Harper	.02	.10
13 Trent Dilfer	.15	.40
14 Kordell Stewart	.15	.40
15 Kyle Brady	.02	.10
16 Charles Haley	.07	.20
17 Greg Lloyd	.07	.20
18 Mario Bates	.07	.20
19 Shannon Sharpe	.07	.20
20 Scott Mitchell	.07	.20
21 Craig Heyward	.02	.10
22 Marcus Allen	.15	.40
23 Curtis Martin	.30	.75
24 Drew Bledsoe	.25	.60
25 Jerry Rice	.40	1.00
26 Charlie Garner	.07	.20
27 Michael Irvin	.15	.40
28 Curtis Conway	.15	.40
29 Terrell Davis	.30	.75
30 Jeff Hostetler	.02	.10
31 Neil O'Donnell	.07	.20
32 Errict Rhett	.07	.20
33 Stan Humphries	.07	.20
34 Jeff Graham	.02	.10
35 Floyd Turner	.02	.10
36 Vincent Brisby	.02	.10
37 Steve Young	.30	.75
38 Carl Pickens	.07	.20
39 Terance Mathis	.02	.10
40 Brett Favre	.75	2.00
41 Ki-Jana Carter	.07	.20
42 Jim Everett	.02	.10
43 Marshall Faulk	.20	.50
44 William Floyd	.07	.20
45 Deion Sanders	.25	.60
46 Garrison Hearst	.07	.20
47 Chris Sanders	.07	.20
48 Isaac Bruce	.15	.40
49 Natrone Means	.07	.20
50 Troy Aikman	.40	1.00
51 Ben Coates	.07	.20
52 Tony Martin	.07	.20
53 Rod Woodson	.07	.20
54 Edgar Bennett	.07	.20
55 Eric Zeier	.02	.10
56 Steve Bono	.02	.10
57 Tim Brown	.15	.40
58 Kevin Williams	.02	.10
59 Erik Kramer	.02	.10
60 Jim Kelly	.15	.40
61 Larry Centers	.07	.20
62 Terrell Fletcher	.02	.10
63 Michael Westbrook	.15	.40
64 Kerry Collins	.15	.40
65 Jay Novacek	.02	.10
66 J.J. Stokes	.15	.40
67 John Elway	.75	2.00
68 Jim Harbaugh	.07	.20
69 Aeneas Williams	.02	.10
70 Tyrone Wheatley	.07	.20
71 Chris Warren	.07	.20
72 Rodney Thomas	.02	.10
73 Jeff George	.07	.20
74 Rick Mirer	.07	.20
75 Yancey Thigpen	.07	.20
76 Herman Moore	.07	.20
77 Gus Frerotte	.07	.20
78 Anthony Miller	.07	.20
79 Ricky Watters	.07	.20
80 Sherman Williams	.02	.10
81 Hardy Nickerson	.02	.10
82 Henry Ellard	.02	.10
83 Aaron Craver	.02	.10
84 Rodney Peete	.02	.10
85 Eric Metcalf	.02	.10
86 Brian Blades	.02	.10
87 Rob Moore	.07	.20
88 Kimble Anders	.07	.20
89 Harvey Williams	.02	.10
90 Thurman Thomas	.15	.40
91 Dave Brown	.02	.10
92 Terry Allen	.07	.20
93 Ken Norton Jr.	.02	.10
94 Reggie White	.15	.40
95 Mark Chmura	.07	.20
96 Bert Emanuel	.07	.20
97 Brett Perriman	.02	.10
98 Antonio Freeman	.15	.40
99 Brian Mitchell	.02	.10
100 Orlando Thomas	.02	.10
101 Aaron Hayden	.02	.10
102 Quinn Early	.02	.10
103 Lovell Pinkney	.02	.10
104 Napoleon Kaufman	.15	.40
105 Daryl Johnston	.07	.20
106 Steve Tasker	.02	.10
107 Brent Jones	.02	.10
108 Mark Brunell	.25	.60
109 Leslie O'Neal	.02	.10
110 Irving Fryar	.07	.20
111 Jim Miller	.15	.40
112 Sean Dawkins	.02	.10
113 Boomer Esiason	.07	.20
114 Heath Shuler	.07	.20
115 Bruce Smith	.07	.20
116 Russell Maryland	.02	.10
117 Jake Reed	.07	.20
118 O.J. McDuffie	.07	.20
119 Erik Williams	.02	.10
120 Willie McGinest	.02	.10
121 Terry Kirby	.07	.20
122 Fred Barnett	.02	.10
123 Andre Hastings	.02	.10
124 Dale Hellestrae	.02	.10
125 Darren Woodson	.07	.20
126 Steve Atwater	.02	.10
127 Quentin Coryatt	.02	.10
128 Derrick Thomas	.15	.40
129 Nate Newton	.02	.10
130 Kevin Greene	.07	.20
131 Barry Sanders	.60	1.50
132 Warren Moon	.07	.20
133 Rashaan Salaam	.07	.20
134 Rodney Hampton	.07	.20
135 James O.Stewart	.07	.20
136 Erric Pegram	.02	.10
137 Bryan Cox	.02	.10
138 Adrian Murrell	.07	.20
139 Robert Smith	.07	.20
140 Bernie Parmalee	.02	.10
141 Bryce Paup	.02	.10
142 Darick Holmes	.02	.10
143 Hugh Douglas	.07	.20
144 Ken Dilger	.07	.20
145 Derek Loville	.02	.10
146 Horace Copeland	.02	.10
147 Wayne Chrebet	.25	.60
148 Andre Coleman	.02	.10
149 Greg Hill	.07	.20
150 Eric Swann	.02	.10
151 Tyrone Hughes	.02	.10
152 Ernie Mills	.02	.10
153 Terry Glenn RC	.50	1.25
154 Cedric Jones RC	.02	.10
155 Leeland McElroy RC	.07	.20
156 Bobby Engram RC	.15	.40
157 Willie Anderson RC	.02	.10
158 Mike Alstott RC	.50	1.25
159 Alex Van Dyke RC	.07	.20
160 Jeff Lewis RC	.07	.20
161 Keyshawn Johnson RC	.50	1.25
162 Regan Upshaw RC	.02	.10
163 Eric Moulds RC	.60	1.50
164 Tim Biakabutuka RC	.15	.40
165 Kevin Hardy RC	.15	.40
166 Marvin Harrison RC	1.25	3.00
167 Karim Abdul-Jabbar RC	.15	.40
168 Tony Brackens RC	.15	.40
169 Stepfret Williams RC	.07	.20
170 Eddie George RC	.60	1.50
171 Lawrence Phillips RC	.15	.40
172 Danny Kanell RC	.15	.40
173 Derrick Mayes RC	.15	.40
174 Daryl Gardener RC	.02	.10
175 Jonathan Ogden RC	.15	.40
176 Alex Molden RC	.02	.10
177 Chris Darkins RC	.02	.10
178 Stephen Davis RC	.75	2.00
179 Rickey Dudley RC	.15	.40
180 Eddie Kennison RC	.15	.40
181 Simeon Rice RC	.40	1.00
182 Bobby Hoying RC	.15	.40
183 Troy Aikman BF6	.20	.50
184 Emmitt Smith BF6	.40	1.00
185 Michael Irvin BF6	.07	.20
186 Deion Sanders BF6	.15	.40
187 Daryl Johnston BF6	.07	.20
188 Jay Novacek BF6	.02	.10
189 Steve Young BF6	.15	.40
190 Jerry Rice BF6	.20	.50
191 J.J. Stokes BF6	.15	.40
192 Ken Norton BF6	.02	.10
193 William Floyd BF6	.07	.20
194 Brent Jones BF6	.02	.10
195 Dan Marino CL	.15	.40
196 Brett Favre CL	.15	.40
197 Emmitt Smith CL	.15	.40
198 Barry Sanders CL	.15	.40
199 Dan Marino CL	.15	.40
Emmitt Smith CL		
Brett Favre CL		
Barry Sanders CL		
200 Brett Favre PackBack	.75	2.00

1996 Pinnacle Artist's Proofs

*AP STARS: 5X TO 12X BASIC CARDS		
*AP RCs: 2.5X TO 6X BASIC CARDS		
STATED ODDS 1:48 HOB, 1:12 PS, 1:67 JUM		

1996 Pinnacle Foil

COMP.FOIL SET (200)	8.00	20.00
*FOILS: SAME PRICE AS BASIC CARDS		
RANDOM INSERTS IN RETAIL JUMBOS		

1996 Pinnacle Premium Stock Silver

COMPLETE SET (200)	12.50	30.00
*PREMIUM STOCK: .6X TO 1.5X BASIC CARDS		

1996 Pinnacle Trophy Collection

COMPLETE SET (200)	60.00	150.00
*TC STARS: 2.5X TO 6X BASIC CARDS		
*TC RCs: 1.2X TO 3X BASIC CARDS		
STATED ODDS 1:5		

1996 Pinnacle Black 'N Blue

COMPLETE SET (25)	100.00	200.00
STATED ODDS 1:33 JUMBO		
1 Steve Young	5.00	12.00
2 Troy Aikman	6.00	15.00
3 Dan Marino	12.50	30.00
4 Michael Irvin	2.50	6.00
5 Jerry Rice	6.00	15.00
6 Emmitt Smith	10.00	25.00
7 Brett Favre	12.50	30.00
8 Drew Bledsoe	4.00	10.00
9 John Elway	12.50	30.00
10 Barry Sanders	10.00	25.00
11 Cris Carter	2.50	6.00
12 Jeff Blake	2.50	6.00
13 Chris Warren	1.25	3.00
14 Kerry Collins	2.50	6.00
15 Natrone Means	1.25	3.00
16 Herman Moore	1.25	3.00
17 Steve McNair	5.00	12.00
18 Ricky Watters	1.25	3.00
19 Tamarick Vanover	1.25	3.00
20 Deion Sanders	4.00	10.00
21 Terrell Davis	5.00	12.00
22 Rodney Thomas	.60	1.50
23 Rashaan Salaam	1.25	3.00
24 Darick Holmes	.60	1.50
25 Eric Zeier	.60	1.50

1996 Pinnacle Die Cut Jerseys

COMPLETE SET (20)	75.00	150.00
STATED ODDS 1:24 HOBBY		
*HOLOFOILS: .6X TO 1.5X BASIC INSERTS		
HOLOFOIL STATED ODDS 1:6 PREM.STOCK		
1 Errict Rhett	1.00	2.50
2 Marshall Faulk	2.50	6.00
3 Isaac Bruce	2.00	5.00
4 William Floyd	1.00	2.50
5 Heath Shuler	1.00	2.50
6 Kerry Collins	2.00	5.00
7 Kordell Stewart	2.00	5.00
8 Rashaan Salaam	1.00	2.50
9 Terrell Davis	4.00	10.00
10 Rodney Thomas	.75	2.00
11 Curtis Martin	4.00	10.00
12 Steve McNair	4.00	10.00
13 J.J. Stokes	2.00	5.00
14 Joey Galloway	2.00	5.00
15 Michael Westbrook	2.00	5.00
16 Keyshawn Johnson	3.00	6.00
17 Lawrence Phillips	.75	2.00
18 Terry Glenn	3.00	6.00
19 Tim Biakabutuka	.75	2.00
20 Eddie George	4.00	0.00

1996 Pinnacle Double Disguise

COMPLETE SET (20)	40.00	100.00
STATED ODDS 1:18 HOB, 1:5 PS, 1:25 JUM		
1 Emmitt Smith	3.00	8.00
Emmitt Smith		
2 Emmitt Smith	4.00	10.00
Dan Marino		
3 Emmitt Smith	4.00	10.00
Brett Favre		
4 Emmitt Smith	3.00	8.00
Steve Young		
5 Dan Marino	4.00	10.00
Dan Marino		
6 Dan Marino	4.00	10.00
Emmitt Smith		
7 Dan Marino	3.00	8.00
Kerry Collins		
8 Dan Marino	3.00	8.00
Steve Young		
9 Kerry Collins	2.50	6.00
Kerry Collins		
10 Kerry Collins	3.00	8.00
Dan Marino		
11 Kerry Collins	3.00	8.00
Brett Favre		
12 Kerry Collins	2.50	6.00
Steve Young		
13 Brett Favre	4.00	10.00
Brett Favre		
14 Brett Favre	3.00	8.00
Kerry Collins		
15 Brett Favre	4.00	10.00
Dan Marino		
16 Brett Favre	4.00	10.00
Emmitt Smith		
17 Steve Young	1.50	4.00
Steve Young		
18 Steve Young	3.00	8.00
Brett Favre		
19 Steve Young	3.00	8.00
Emmitt Smith		
20 Steve Young	2.50	6.00
Kerry Collins		

1996 Pinnacle On The Line

COMPLETE SET (15)	20.00	50.00
STATED ODDS 1:23 RETAIL		
1 Michael Irvin	3.00	8.00
2 Robert Brooks	3.00	8.00
3 Herman Moore	1.50	4.00
4 Cris Carter	3.00	8.00
5 Chris Sanders	1.50	4.00
6 Jerry Rice	8.00	20.00
7 Michael Westbrook	3.00	8.00
8 Carl Pickens	1.50	4.00
9 Bobby Engram	.60	1.50
10 Alex Van Dyke	.30	.75
11 Keyshawn Johnson	2.00	5.00
12 Terry Glenn	2.00	5.00
13 Eric Moulds	2.50	6.00
14 Marvin Harrison	5.00	12.00
15 Eddie Kennison	.60	1.50

1996 Pinnacle Team Pinnacle

COMPLETE SET (10)	40.00	100.00
STATED ODDS 1:90 H/R,1:20 PREM.STOCK		
1 Troy Aikman	5.00	12.00
Drew Bledsoe		
2 Steve Young	4.00	10.00
Jeff Blake		
3 Brett Favre	10.00	25.00
John Elway		
4 Kerry Collins	6.00	15.00
Dan Marino		
5 Emmitt Smith	6.00	15.00
Curtis Martin		
6 Barry Sanders	5.00	12.00
Chris Warren		
7 Errict Rhett	4.00	10.00
Marshall Faulk		
8 Jerry Rice	5.00	12.00
Carl Pickens		
9 Michael Irvin	3.00	8.00
Joey Galloway		
10 Isaac Bruce	3.00	8.00
Kordell Stewart		

1996 Pinnacle Bimbo Bread

These small (approximately 1 1/2" by 2 1/2") magic motion cards were distributed in Mexico through Bimbo Bakery snack products. The cardfronts feature a magic motion action photo of the player with the Bimbo logo. The backs are green with a player photo and player bio written in spanish.

COMPLETE SET (30)	60.00	120.00
1 Troy Aikman	4.00	10.00
2 Michael Irvin	2.00	5.00
3 Emmitt Smith	4.80	12.00
4 Jim Kelly	2.00	5.00
5 John Elway	6.00	15.00
6 Barry Sanders	6.00	15.00
7 Brett Favre	6.00	15.00
8 Jim Harbaugh	1.20	3.00
9 Dan Marino	6.00	15.00
10 Warren Moon	2.00	5.00
11 Drew Bledsoe	3.20	8.00
12 Jim Everett	.80	2.00
13 Jeff Hostetler	.80	2.00
14 Neil O'Donnell	.80	2.00
15 Junior Seau	1.20	3.00
16 Jerry Rice	4.00	10.00
17 Steve Young	3.20	8.00
18 Rick Mirer	1.20	3.00
19 Jeff Blake	1.20	3.00
20 David Klingler	.80	2.00
21 Boomer Esiason	1.20	3.00
22 Heath Shuler	.80	2.00
23 Dave Brown	.80	2.00
24 Bernie Kosar	.80	2.00
25 Kordell Stewart	2.40	6.00
26 Mark Brunell	3.20	8.00
27 Kerry Collins	2.00	5.00
28 Scott Mitchell	1.20	3.00
29 Erik Kramer	.80	2.00
30 Jeff George	1.20	3.00

1996 Pinnacle Super Bowl Card Show

This 15-card standard-size set features color action player photos on a metallic dufex background. The player's last name is printed in a metalic gold band with the Super Bowl XXX Card Show logo at the bottom. The horizontal backs carry the player's name, team, a career highlight, nickname, and sponsor logos on a dark blue marblized background. Pinnacle offered three-card packs to each Card Show attendee in exchange for two football card wrappers from 1995 Pinnacle football products. Although the cards carry a 1995 copyright date, the cards were released in January 1996 at the Tempe, Arizona Super Bowl Card Show.

COMPLETE SET (15)	6.00	15.00
1 Steve Young	.50	1.25
2 Dan Marino	1.20	3.00
3 Troy Aikman	.60	1.50
4 Drew Bledsoe	.50	1.25
5 John Elway	1.20	3.00
6 Brett Favre	1.20	3.00
7 Jim Harbaugh	.15	.40
8 Jeff Hostetler	.15	.40
9 Michael Irvin	.30	.75
10 Jim Kelly	.30	.75
11 Warren Moon	.30	.75
12 Jerry Rice	.60	1.50
13 Barry Sanders	1.20	3.00
14 Junior Seau	.30	.75
15 Emmitt Smith	1.00	2.50

1997 Pinnacle

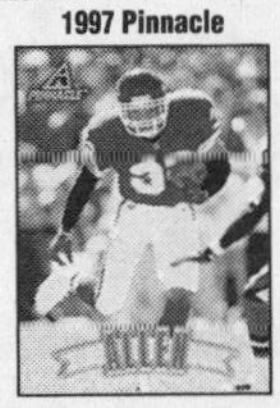

The 1997 Pinnacle set was issued in one series totalling 200 cards and was distributed in 10-card packs with a suggested retail price of $2.99. The fronts feature borderless color action player photos. The backs carry player information.

COMPLETE SET (200)	7.50	20.00
1 Brett Favre	.75	2.00
2 Dan Marino	.75	2.00
3 Emmitt Smith	.60	1.50
4 Steve Young	.25	.60
5 Drew Bledsoe	.25	.60
6 Eddie George	.20	.50
7 Barry Sanders	.60	1.50
8 Jerry Rice	.40	1.00
9 John Elway	.75	2.00
10 Troy Aikman	.40	1.00
11 Kerry Collins	.20	.50
12 Rick Mirer	.07	.20
13 Jim Harbaugh	.10	.30
14 Elvis Grbac	.10	.30
15 Gus Frerotte	.07	.20
16 Neil O'Donnell	.10	.30
17 Jeff George	.10	.30
18 Kordell Stewart	.20	.50
19 Junior Seau	.20	.50
20 Vinny Testaverde	.10	.30
21 Terry Glenn	.20	.50
22 Anthony Johnson	.07	.20
23 Boomer Esiason	.10	.30
24 Terrell Owens	.25	.60
25 Natrone Means	.10	.30
26 Marcus Allen	.20	.50
27 James Jett	.10	.30
28 Chris T. Jones	.07	.20
29 Stan Humphries	.10	.30
30 Keith Byars	.07	.20
31 John Friesz	.07	.20
32 Mike Alstott	.20	.50
33 Eddie Kennison	.10	.30
34 Eric Moulds	.20	.50
35 Frank Sanders	.10	.30
36 Daryl Johnston	.10	.30
37 Cris Carter	.20	.50
38 Errict Rhett	.07	.20
39 Ben Coates	.10	.30
40 Shannon Sharpe	.10	.30
41 Jamal Anderson	.20	.50
42 Tim Biakabutuka	.10	.30
43 Jeff Blake	.10	.30
44 Michael Irvin	.20	.50
45 Terrell Davis	.25	.60
46 Byron Bam Morris	.07	.20
47 Rashaan Salaam	.07	.20
48 Adrian Murrell	.10	.30
49 Ty Detmer	.10	.30
50 Terry Allen	.20	.50
51 Mark Brunell	.25	.60
52 O.J. McDuffie	.10	.30
53 Willie McGinest	.07	.20
54 Chris Warren	.10	.30
55 Trent Dilfer	.20	.50
56 Jerome Bettis	.20	.50
57 Tamarick Vanover	.10	.30
58 Ki-Jana Carter	.07	.20
59 Ray Zellars	.07	.20
60 J.J. Stokes	.10	.30
61 Cornelius Bennett	.07	.20
62 Scott Mitchell	.10	.30
63 Tyrone Wheatley	.10	.30
64 Steve McNair	.25	.60
65 Tony Banks	.10	.30
66 James O.Stewart	.10	.30
67 Robert Smith	.10	.30
68 Thurman Thomas	.20	.50
69 Mark Chmura	.10	.30
70 Napoleon Kaufman	.20	.50
71 Ken Norton	.07	.20
72 Herschel Walker	.10	.30
73 Joey Galloway	.10	.30
74 Neil Smith	.10	.30
75 Simeon Rice	.10	.30
76 Michael Jackson	.10	.30
77 Muhsin Muhammad	.10	.30
78 Kevin Hardy	.07	.20
79 Irving Fryar	.10	.30
80 Eric Swann	.07	.20
81 Yancey Thigpen	.07	.20
82 Jim Everett	.07	.20
83 Karim Abdul-Jabbar	.20	.50
84 Garrison Hearst	.10	.30
85 Lawrence Phillips	.07	.20
86 Bryan Cox	.07	.20
87 Larry Centers	.10	.30
88 Wesley Walls	.10	.30
89 Curtis Conway	.10	.30
90 Darnay Scott	.10	.30
91 Anthony Miller	.07	.20
92 Edgar Bennett	.10	.30
93 Willie Green	.07	.20
94 Kent Graham	.07	.20
95 Dave Brown	.07	.20
96 Wayne Chrebet	.20	.50
97 Ricky Watters	.10	.30
98 Tony Martin	.10	.30
99 Warren Moon	.20	.50
100 Curtis Martin	.25	.60
101 Dorsey Levens	.20	.50
102 Jim Pyne	.07	.20
103 Antonio Freeman	.20	.50
104 Leeland McElroy	.07	.20
105 Isaac Bruce	.20	.50
106 Chris Sanders	.07	.20
107 Tim Brown	.20	.50
108 Greg Lloyd	.07	.20
109 Terrell Buckley	.07	.20
110 Deion Sanders	.20	.50
111 Carl Pickens	.10	.30
112 Bobby Engram	.10	.30
113 Andre Reed	.10	.30
114 Terance Mathis	.10	.30
115 Herman Moore	.10	.30
116 Robert Brooks	.10	.30
117 Ken Dilger	.07	.20
118 Keenan McCardell	.10	.30
119 Andre Hastings	.07	.20
120 Willie Davis	.07	.20
121 Bruce Smith	.10	.30
122 Rob Moore	.10	.30
123 Johnnie Morton	.10	.30
124 Sean Dawkins	.07	.20
125 Mario Bates	.07	.20
126 Henry Ellard	.07	.20
127 Derrick Alexander WR	.10	.30
128 Kevin Greene	.10	.30
129 Derrick Thomas	.20	.50
130 Rod Woodson	.10	.30
131 Rodney Hampton	.10	.30
132 Marshall Faulk	.25	.60
133 Michael Westbrook	.10	.30
134 Erik Kramer	.07	.20
135 Todd Collins	.07	.20
136 Bill Romanowski	.07	.20
137 Jake Reed	.10	.30
138 Heath Shuler	.07	.20
139 Keyshawn Johnson	.20	.50
140 Marvin Harrison	.20	.50
141 Andre Rison	.10	.30
142 Zach Thomas	.20	.50
143 Eric Metcalf	.10	.30
144 Amani Toomer	.10	.30
145 Desmond Howard	.10	.30
146 Jimmy Smith	.10	.30
147 Brad Johnson	.20	.50
148 Troy Vincent	.07	.20
149 Bryce Paup	.07	.20
150 Reggie White	.20	.50
151 Jake Plummer RC	.75	2.00
152 Darnell Autry RC	.10	.30
153 Tiki Barber RC	1.25	3.00
154 Pat Barnes RC	.20	.50
155 Orlando Pace RC	.20	.50
156 Peter Boulware RC	.20	.50
157 Shawn Springs RC	.10	.30
158 Troy Davis RC	.10	.30
159 Ike Hilliard RC	.30	.75
160 Jim Druckenmiller RC	.10	.30
161 Warrick Dunn RC	.50	1.50
162 James Farrior RC	.20	.50
163 Tony Gonzalez RC	.75	2.00
164 Darrell Russell RC	.07	.20
165 Byron Hanspard RC	.10	.30
166 Corey Dillon RC	.75	2.00
167 Kenny Holmes RC	.20	.50
168 Walter Jones RC	.20	.50
169 Danny Wuerffel RC	.20	.50
170 Tom Knight RC	.07	.20
171 David LaFleur RC	.07	.20
172 Kevin Lockett RC	.10	.30
173 Will Blackwell RC	.10	.30
174 Reidel Anthony RC	.20	.50
175 Dwayne Rudd RC	.20	.50
176 Yatil Green RC	.10	.30
177 Antowain Smith RC	.50	1.25
178 Rae Carruth RC	.07	.20
179 Bryant Westbrook RC	.07	.20
180 Reinard Wilson RC	.10	.30
181 Joey Kent RC	.20	.50
182 Renaldo Wynn RC	.07	.20
183 Brett Favre I	.40	1.00
184 Emmitt Smith I	.30	.75
185 Dan Marino I	.40	1.00
186 Troy Aikman I	.20	.50
187 Jerry Rice I	.20	.50
188 Drew Bledsoe I	.10	.30
189 Eddie George I	.20	.50
190 Terry Glenn I	.10	.30
191 John Elway I	.40	1.00
192 Steve Young I	.10	.30
193 Mark Brunell I	.20	.50
194 Barry Sanders I	.30	.75
195 Kerry Collins I	.10	.30
196 Curtis Martin I	.20	.50
197 Terrell Davis I	.20	.50
198 Drew Bledsoe	.20	.50
Kerry Collins		
Dan Marino		
Checklist back		
199 Steve Young	.07	.20
Jeff George		
Mark Brunell		
Checklist back		
200 Troy Aikman	.07	.20
John Elway		
Rick Mirer CL		

1997 Pinnacle Artist's Proofs

*AP STARS: 8X TO 20X BASIC CARDS		
*AP RCs: 4X TO 10X BASIC CARDS		
STATED ODDS 1:39 HOBBY		

1997 Pinnacle Trophy Collection

COMPLETE SET (100)	125.00	250.00
*STARS: 3X TO 8X BASIC CARDS		
*RC'S: 1.5X TO 4X BASIC CARDS		
STATED ODDS 1:9 HOBBY		

1997 Pinnacle Power Pack Jumbos

COMPLETE SET (24)	20.00	50.00
1 Brett Favre	2.00	5.00
2 Dan Marino	2.00	5.00
3 Emmitt Smith	1.60	4.00
4 Steve Young	.80	2.00
5 Drew Bledsoe	1.00	2.50
6 Eddie George	.80	2.00
7 Barry Sanders	2.00	5.00
8 Jerry Rice	1.00	2.50
9 John Elway	2.00	5.00
10 Troy Aikman	1.00	2.50
11 Kerry Collins	.30	.75
12 Jim Harbaugh	.30	.75
13 Elvis Grbac	.15	.40
14 Gus Frerotte	.15	.40
15 Terrell Davis	1.60	4.00
16 Jeff George	.30	.75
17 Kordell Stewart	.80	2.00
18 Terry Glenn	.40	1.00
19 Jeff Blake	.30	.75
20 Michael Irvin	.40	1.00
21 Tony Banks	.30	.75
22 Curtis Martin	.80	2.00
23 Deion Sanders	.60	1.50
24 Herman Moore	.30	.75

1997 Pinnacle Scoring Core

COMPLETE SET (24)	200.00	400.00
STATED ODDS 1:89 HOBBY		
1 Emmitt Smith	12.50	30.00
2 Troy Aikman	8.00	20.00
3 Michael Irvin	4.00	10.00
4 Robert Brooks	2.50	6.00
5 Brett Favre	15.00	40.00

6 Antonio Freeman 4.00 10.00
7 Curtis Martin 5.00 12.00
8 Drew Bledsoe 5.00 12.00
9 Terry Glenn 4.00 10.00
10 Tim Biakabutuka 2.50 6.00
11 Kerry Collins 4.00 10.00
12 Muhsin Muhammad 2.50 6.00
13 Karim Abdul-Jabbar 4.00 10.00
14 Dan Marino 15.00 40.00
15 O.J. McDuffie 2.50 6.00
16 Terrell Davis 5.00 12.00
17 John Elway 15.00 40.00
18 Shannon Sharpe 2.50 6.00
19 Garrison Hearst 2.50 6.00
20 Steve Young 5.00 12.00
21 Jerry Rice 8.00 20.00
22 Natrone Means 2.50 6.00
23 Mark Brunell 5.00 12.00
24 Keenan McCardell 2.50 6.00
P1 Emmitt Smith Promo .75 2.00
P2 Troy Aikman Promo .50 1.25
P3 Michael Irvin Promo .20 .50
PV Mark Brunell Preview .40 1.00

1997 Pinnacle Team Pinnacle

COMPLETE SET (10) 100.00 200.00
*FOIL BACK: 4X TO 1X FOIL FRONT
STATED ODDS 1:240 HOBBY
*HOLO.MIRROR: .8X TO 2X BASIC INSERTS
HOLOGRAPHIC MIRROR RANDOM INSERTS IN PACKS
1 Dan Marino 12.50 30.00
Troy Aikman
2 Drew Bledsoe 12.50 30.00
Brett Favre
3 Mark Brunell 4.00 10.00
Kerry Collins
4 John Elway 12.50 30.00
Steve Young
5 Terrell Davis 12.50 30.00
Emmitt Smith
6 Curtis Martin 12.50 30.00
Barry Sanders
7 Eddie George 4.00 10.00
Tim Biakabutuka
8 Karim Abdul-Jabbar 4.00 10.00
Lawrence Phillips
9 Terry Glenn 7.50 20.00
Jerry Rice
10 Joey Galloway 4.00 10.00
Michael Irvin

1997 Pinnacle Tins

COMPLETE SET (6) 4.80 12.00
1 Troy Aikman .60 1.50
2 Drew Bledsoe .60 1.50
3 John Elway 1.20 3.00
4 Brett Favre 1.20 3.00
5 Dan Marino 1.20 3.00
6 Steve Young .50 1.25

1997 Pinnacle Epix

COMP.ORANGE SET (24) 75.00 150.00
*PURPLE CARDS: .6X TO 1.5X ORANGE
OVERALL STATED ODDS 1:19 HOBBY
*EMERALD CARDS: 1.2X TO 3X ORANGE
ONLY ORANGE CARDS PRICED BELOW
E1 Emmitt Smith GAME 5.00 12.00
E2 Troy Aikman GAME 3.00 8.00
E3 Terrell Davis GAME 2.50 6.00
E4 Drew Bledsoe GAME 2.00 5.00
E5 Jeff George GAME 1.00 2.50
E6 Kerry Collins GAME 1.00 2.50
E7 Antonio Freeman GAME 2.00 5.00
E8 Herman Moore GAME 1.00 2.50
E9 Barry Sanders MOMENT 6.00 15.00
E10 Brett Favre MOMENT 7.50 20.00
E11 Michael Irvin MOMENT 1.25 3.00
E12 Steve Young MOMENT 4.00 10.00
E13 Mark Brunell MOMENT 3.00 8.00
E14 Jerome Bettis MOMENT 1.25 3.00
E15 Deion Sanders MOMENT 3.00 8.00
E16 Jeff Blake MOMENT 1.25 3.00
E17 Dan Marino SEASON 6.00 15.00
E18 Eddie George SEASON 1.50 4.00
E19 Jerry Rice SEASON 4.00 10.00
E20 John Elway SEASON 6.00 15.00
E21 Curtis Martin SEASON 3.00 8.00
E22 Kordell Stewart SEASON 1.50 4.00
E23 Junior Seau SEASON 1.50 4.00
E24 Reggie White SEASON 1.50 4.00

1997 Pinnacle Magic Motion Puzzles

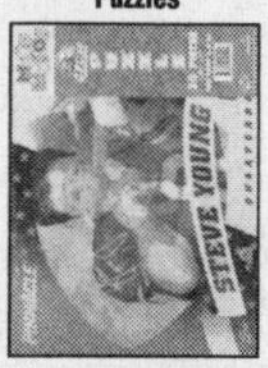

Pinnacle produced these large Magic Motion puzzles for traditional retailers in 1997. Each features a member of the Quarterback Club and was produced with 25-pieces mounted on a backer board. The overall size of each puzzle is 10 3/4" by 14." Any additions to the checklist below are appreciated.

1 Brett Favre 3.20 8.00
2 Steve Young 2.00 5.00

1997 Pinnacle Rembrandt

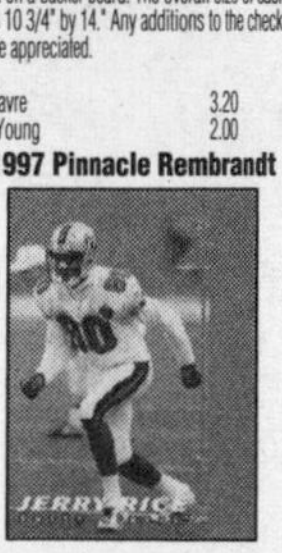

Pinnacle produced this set of nine-cards distributed by Rembrandt, Inc. with their line of Ultra-PRO plastic sheets. Each included a player photo with a bronze colored foil section to the right of the photo containing the Pinnacle and QB Club logos. One card was inserted into each box of sheets. There were also Silver and Gold parallel sets produced. As part of the promotion, collectors who assembled a complete Gold set could send the set to Rembrandt for $250 cash. A set of Silver cards could be redeemed for a gift box of Ultra-PRO products. A set of Bronze cards could be redeemed for a gold/silver/bronze set of one of the nine players. All sets sent in were returned with a cancelled stamp.

COMPLETE SET (9) 4.80 12.00
*GOLD CARDS: 5X TO 10X BASIC CARDS
*SILVER CARDS: 2.5X TO 5X BASIC CARDS
1 Brett Favre .80 2.00
2 Troy Aikman .40 1.00
3 John Elway .80 2.00
4 Dan Marino .80 2.00
5 Drew Bledsoe .40 1.00
6 Emmitt Smith .60 1.50
7 Jerry Rice .60 1.50
8 Barry Sanders .80 2.00
9 Mark Brunell .40 1.00

1998 Pinnacle Fanfest Elway

This one card set, issued at the All-Star FanFest in Denver in 1998 honored long time Denver Bronco hero, John Elway. The front of the card features him in an Oneonta Yankee uniform while the back has a brief biography; a ghosted photo of Elway as a Bronco and his career minor league stats. The card was available for a small charity donation at the Pinnacle Booth.

NNO John Elway 8.00 20.00

1998 Pinnacle Jerry Rice Jumbo

This card was released at the 1998 Super Bowl Card Show. It was sponsored by Breathe Right nasal strips and produced by Pinnacle Brands. It measures roughly 3 1/2" by 5."

NNO Jerry Rice 1.50 4.00

1998 Pinnacle Team Pinnacle Collector's Club Promos

This four-card set originally to have been issued to members of the Pinnacle Collector's Club. Ultimately the cards were released after the company's bankruptcy. Each card reads "Team Pinnacle" at the bottom of the cardfront with the player's name above the image on the front.

COMPLETE SET (4) 15.00 30.00
1 John Elway 3.00 8.00

1998 Pinnacle Team Pinnacle Collector's Club

COMPLETE SET
SEMISTARS
UNLISTED STARS
F1 Dan Marino 3.00 8.00
F2 Brett Favre 3.00 8.00
F3 Emmitt Smith 2.50 6.00
F4 Drew Bledsoe 1.00 2.50
F5 Eddie George .75 2.00
F6 Barry Sanders 2.00 5.00
F7 Terrell Davis 1.25 3.00
F8 Mark Brunell .75 2.00
F9 Jerry Rice 2.00 5.00
F10 Kordell Stewart .75 2.00

2010-11 Pinnacle Fans of the Game

COMPLETE SET (3) 4.00 10.00
2 Sam Bradford 2.50 6.00

2010-11 Pinnacle Fans of the Game Autographs

2 Sam Bradford 40.00 80.00

1997 Pinnacle Certified

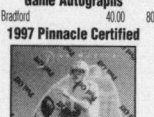

The 1997 Pinnacle Certified set was issued in one series totalling 150 cards and distributed in three-card hobby packs with a suggested price of $5.99. The cards feature color player photos printed on premium 24-point, silver foil card stock with bronze foil stamping.

COMPLETE SET (150) 15.00 40.00
1 Emmitt Smith 1.25 3.00
2 Dan Marino 1.50 4.00
3 Brett Favre 1.50 4.00
4 Steve Young .50 1.25
5 Kerry Collins .40 1.00
6 Troy Aikman .75 2.00
7 Drew Bledsoe .50 1.25
8 Eddie George .40 1.00
9 Jerry Rice .75 2.00
10 John Elway 1.50 4.00
11 Barry Sanders 1.25 3.00
12 Mark Brunell .50 1.25
13 Elvis Grbac .25 .60
14 Tony Banks .25 .60
15 Vinny Testaverde .25 .60
16 Rick Mirer .15 .40
17 Carl Pickens .25 .60
18 Deion Sanders .40 1.00
19 Terry Glenn .40 1.00
20 Heath Shuler .15 .40
21 Dave Brown .15 .40
22 Keyshawn Johnson .40 1.00
23 Jeff George .25 .60
24 Ricky Watters .25 .60
25 Kordell Stewart .40 1.00
26 Junior Seau .40 1.00
27 Terrell Owens .50 1.25
28 Warren Moon .40 1.00
29 Isaac Bruce .40 1.00
30 Steve McNair .50 1.25
31 Gus Frerotte .15 .40
32 Trent Dilfer .40 1.00
33 Shannon Sharpe .25 .60
34 Scott Mitchell .25 .60
35 Antonio Freeman .40 1.00
36 Jim Harbaugh .25 .60
37 Natrone Means .25 .60
38 Marcus Allen .40 1.00
39 Karim Abdul-Jabbar .25 .60
40 Tim Biakabutuka .25 .60
41 Jeff Blake .25 .60
42 Michael Irvin .40 1.00
43 Herschel Walker .25 .60
44 Curtis Martin .50 1.25
45 Eddie Kennison .25 .60
46 Napoleon Kaufman .40 1.00
47 Larry Centers .25 .60
48 Jamal Anderson .40 1.00
49 Derrick Alexander WR .25 .60
50 Bruce Smith .25 .60
51 Wesley Walls .25 .60
52 Rod Smith WR .40 1.00
53 Keenan McCardell .25 .60
54 Robert Brooks .25 .60
55 Willie Green .15 .40
56 Jake Reed .25 .60
57 Joey Galloway .25 .60
58 Eric Metcalf .25 .60
59 Chris Sanders .15 .40
60 Jeff Hostetler .15 .40
61 Kevin Greene .25 .60
62 Frank Sanders .25 .60
63 Dorsey Levens .40 1.00
64 Sean Dawkins .15 .40
65 Cris Carter .40 1.00
66 Andre Hastings .15 .40
67 Amani Toomer .25 .60
68 Adrian Murrell .25 .60
69 Ty Detmer .25 .60
70 Yancey Thigpen .25 .60
71 Jim Everett .15 .40
72 Todd Collins .15 .40
73 Curtis Conway .25 .60
74 Herman Moore .25 .60
75 Neil O'Donnell .25 .60
76 Rod Woodson .25 .60
77 Tony Martin .25 .60
78 Kent Graham .15 .40
79 Andre Reed .25 .60
80 Reggie White .40 1.00
81 Thurman Thomas .40 1.00
82 Garrison Hearst .25 .60
83 Chris Warren .25 .60
84 Wayne Chrebet .40 1.00
85 Chris T. Jones .15 .40
86 Anthony Miller .15 .40
87 Chris Chandler .25 .60
88 Terrell Davis .50 1.25
89 Mike Alstott .40 1.00
90 Terry Allen .40 1.00
91 Jerome Bettis .40 1.00
92 Stan Humphries .25 .60
93 Andre Rison .25 .60
94 Marshall Faulk .50 1.25
95 Erik Kramer .15 .40
96 O.J. McDuffie .25 .60
97 Robert Smith .25 .60
98 Keith Byars .15 .40
99 Rodney Hampton .25 .60
100 Desmond Howard .25 .60
101 Lawrence Phillips .15 .40
102 Michael Westbrook .25 .60
103 Johnnie Morton .25 .60
104 Ben Coates .25 .60
105 J.J. Stokes .25 .60
106 Terance Mathis .25 .60
107 Errict Rhett .15 .40
108 Tim Brown .40 1.00
109 Marvin Harrison .40 1.00
110 Muhsin Muhammad .25 .60
111 Byron Bam Morris .15 .40
112 Mario Bates .15 .40
113 Jimmy Smith .25 .60
114 Irving Fryar .25 .60
115 Tamarick Vanover .25 .60
116 Brad Johnson .40 1.00
117 Rashaan Salaam .15 .40
118 Ki-Jana Carter .15 .40
119 Tyrone Wheatley .25 .60
120 John Friesz .15 .40
121 Orlando Pace RC .50 1.25
122 Jim Druckenmiller RC .25 .60
123 Byron Hanspard RC .25 .60
124 David LaFleur RC .10 .30
125 Reidel Anthony RC .50 1.25
126 Antowain Smith RC 1.50 4.00
127 Bryant Westbrook RC .10 .30
128 Fred Lane RC .25 .60
129 Tiki Barber RC 3.00 8.00
130 Shawn Springs RC .25 .60
131 Ike Hilliard RC 1.00 2.50
132 James Farrior RC .50 1.25
133 Darrell Russell RC .10 .30
134 Walter Jones RC .50 1.25
135 Tom Knight RC .10 .30
136 Yatil Green RC .25 .60
137 Joey Kent RC .25 .60
138 Kevin Lockett RC .25 .60
139 Troy Davis RC .25 .60
140 Darnell Autry RC .25 .60
141 Pat Barnes RC .50 1.25
142 Rae Carruth RC .10 .30
143 Will Blackwell RC .25 .60
144 Warrick Dunn RC 1.50 4.00
145 Corey Dillon RC 2.00 5.00
146 Dwayne Rudd RC .50 1.25
147 Reinard Wilson RC .25 .60
148 Peter Boulware RC .50 1.25
149 Tony Gonzalez RC 2.00 5.00
150 Danny Wuerffel RC .25 .60

1997 Pinnacle Certified Mirror Blue

*STARS: 5X TO 12X BASE CARD HI
*ROOKIES: 3X TO 8X BASE CARD HI
STATED ODDS 1:199

1997 Pinnacle Certified Mirror Gold

*MIR.GOLD STARS: 12X TO 30X
*ROOKIES: 6X TO 15X
STATED ODDS 1:299

1997 Pinnacle Certified Mirror Red

COMPLETE SET (150) 400.00 800.00
*STARS: 4X TO 10X BASIC CARDS
*ROOKIES: 2.5X TO 6X
STATED ODDS 1:99

1997 Pinnacle Certified Red

COMPLETE SET (150) 75.00 150.00
*CERTIFIED RED STARS: 1.5X TO 4X BASIC CARDS
*CERTIFIED RED RCs: 1X TO 2X BASIC CARDS
STATED ODDS 1:5

1997 Pinnacle Certified Certified Team

COMPLETE SET (20) 25.00 60.00
SILVER STATED ODDS 1:19
*GOLDS: 1.5X TO 4X BASIC INSERTS
GOLD STATED ODDS 1:119
*MIRROR GOLDS: 12X TO 30X BASIC INSERTS
MIRROR GOLD STATED PRINT RUN 25 SETS
1 Brett Favre 4.00 10.00
2 Dan Marino 4.00 10.00
3 Emmitt Smith 3.00 8.00
4 Eddie George 1.00 2.50
5 Jerry Rice 2.00 5.00
6 Troy Aikman 2.00 5.00
7 Barry Sanders 3.00 8.00
8 Terrell Davis 1.25 3.00
9 Drew Bledsoe 1.25 3.00
10 Curtis Martin 1.25 3.00
11 Terry Glenn 1.00 2.50
12 Kerry Collins 1.00 2.50
13 John Elway 4.00 10.00
14 Kordell Stewart 1.00 2.50
15 Karim Abdul-Jabbar .60 1.50
16 Steve Young 1.25 3.00
17 Steve McNair 1.25 3.00
18 Terrell Owens 1.25 3.00
19 Keyshawn Johnson 1.00 2.50
20 Mark Brunell 1.25 3.00

1997 Pinnacle Certified Epix

COMP.ORANGE SET (24) 150.00 300.00
*PURPLE CARDS: .6X TO 1.5X ORANGE
OVERALL STATED ODDS 1:15
*EMERALD CARDS: 1.2X TO 3X ORANGE
ONLY ORANGE CARDS PRICED BELOW
E1 Emmitt Smith MOMENT 15.00 30.00
E2 Troy Aikman MOMENT 7.50 20.00
E3 Terrell Davis MOMENT 5.00 12.00
E4 Drew Bledsoe MOMENT 5.00 12.00
E5 Jeff George MOMENT 2.50 6.00
E6 Kerry Collins MOMENT 2.50 6.00
E7 A.Freeman MOMENT 5.00 10.00
E8 Herman Moore MOMENT 2.50 6.00
E9 Barry Sanders SEASON 7.50 20.00
E10 Brett Favre SEASON 10.00 25.00
E11 Michael Irvin SEASON 2.00 5.00
E12 Steve Young SEASON 5.00 12.00
E13 Mark Brunell SEASON 4.00 10.00
E14 Jerome Bettis SEASON 2.00 5.00
E15 Deion Sanders SEASON 4.00 10.00
E16 Jeff Blake SEASON 2.00 5.00
E17 Dan Marino GAME 7.50 20.00
E18 Eddie George GAME 1.50 4.00
E19 Jerry Rice GAME 5.00 12.00
E20 John Elway GAME 7.50 20.00
E21 Curtis Martin GAME 3.00 8.00
E22 Kordell Stewart GAME 1.50 4.00
E23 Junior Seau GAME 1.50 4.00
E24 Reggie White GAME 1.50 4.00

1995 Pinnacle Club Collection

This debut set contains 261-cards with members of the NFL Quarterback Club having nine cards each. Basic card fronts feature an all bleed photograph with the "Quarterback Club" logo and the player's name listed at the bottom against a gold foil background. Card backs are horizontal with the player's statistical information in yellow at the top and a statistical summary in yellow at the bottom. The cards are numbered against a blue marble background in the upper left corner of the card. The packs also included 20 Pin Redemption cards that were randomly inserted at a rate of one in 24. Collectors could receive a collectible pin of the Quarterback Club member pictured on the card by exchanging it with $1.95 before February 28, 1996. A John Elway signed card (75 autographed) was released as part of the prize list for Arms Race contest winners. The card is virtually identical to card #68 of the base set except for the gold foil being printed with a holographic foil pattern.

COMPLETE SET (261) 5.00 12.00
COMMON STEVE YOUNG .07 .20
COMMON DAN MARINO .20 .50
COMMON TROY AIKMAN .08 .25
COMMON DREW BLEDSOE .08 .25
COMMON BUDDY BRISTER .01 .05
COMMON DAVE BROWN .01 .05
COMMON RA.CUNNINGHAM .05 .15
COMMON JOHN ELWAY .20 .50
COMMON BOOMER ESIASON .02 .10
COMMON JIM EVERETT .01 .05
COMMON BRETT FAVRE .20 .50
COMMON JIM HARBAUGH .01 .05
COMMON JEFF HOSTETLER .01 .05
COMMON MICHAEL IRVIN .05 .15
COMMON JIM KELLY .05 .15
COMMON DAVID KLINGLER .01 .05
COMMON BERNIE KOSAR .01 .05
COMMON CHRIS MILLER .01 .05
COMMON RICK MIRER .01 .05
COMMON WARREN MOON .02 .10
COMMON NEIL O'DONNELL .01 .05
COMMON JERRY RICE .08 .25
COMMON MARK RYPIEN .01 .05
COMMON BARRY SANDERS .15 .40
COMMON JUNIOR SEAU .05 .15
COMMON EMMITT SMITH .10 .30
COMMON PHIL SIMMS .02 .10
COMMON HEATH SHULER .01 .05
COMMON FRANK REICH .01 .05
AU68 John Elway AUTO/75 100.00 175.00

1995 Pinnacle Club Collection Spotlight

COMPLETE SET (5) 10.00 25.00
STATED ODDS 1:90
1 Emmitt Smith 3.00 8.00
2 Barry Sanders 4.00 10.00
3 Jerry Rice 2.50 6.00
4 Michael Irvin 1.50 4.00
5 Junior Seau 1.50 4.00

1995 Pinnacle Club Collection Aerial Assault

COMPLETE SET (18) 20.00 50.00
STATED ODDS 1:36
AA1 Troy Aikman 2.50 6.00
AA2 Dave Brown .50 1.25
AA3 Drew Bledsoe 2.50 6.00
AA4 Randall Cunningham 1.50 4.00
AA5 Jim Everett .50 1.25
AA6 Jeff Hostetler .50 1.25
AA7 David Klingler .50 1.25
AA8 Dan Marino 5.00 12.00
AA9 Rick Mirer .50 1.25
AA10 Neil O'Donnell .50 1.25
AA11 Brett Favre 5.00 12.00
AA12 Boomer Esiason 1.00 2.50
AA13 Jim Harbaugh .50 1.25
AA14 John Elway 5.00 12.00
AA15 Steve Young 2.00 5.00
AA16 Warren Moon 1.00 2.50
AA17 Jim Kelly 1.50 4.00
AA18 Heath Shuler .50 1.25

1995 Pinnacle Club Collection Arms Race

COMPLETE SET (18) 8.00 20.00
STATED ODDS 1:18
1 Steve Young 1.00 2.50
2 Troy Aikman 1.25 3.00
3 John Elway 2.50 6.00
4 Dan Marino 2.50 6.00
5 Brett Favre WIN 2.50 6.00
6 Heath Shuler .25 .60
7 Jim Kelly .75 2.00
8 Randall Cunningham .75 2.00
9 Dave Brown .25 .60
10 Jim Everett .25 .60
11 Drew Bledsoe 1.25 3.00
12 Rick Mirer .25 .60
13 Jeff Hostetler .25 .60
14 Neil O'Donnell .25 .60
15 Warren Moon .50 1.25
16 Boomer Esiason .50 1.25
17 Chris Miller .25 .60
18 David Klingler .25 .60

1995 Pinnacle Club Collection Pin Redemption

1 Troy Aikman 2.50 6.00
2 Dave Brown 1.25 3.00
3 Jeff Hostetler 1.25 3.00
4 Michael Irvin 2.00 5.00
5 Chris Miller 1.25 3.00
6 Emmitt Smith 4.00 10.00
7 Steve Young 2.50 6.00

1995 Pinnacle Club Collection Promos

Issued in a cello pack, this 4-card standard-size set promoted the 1995 Pinnacle Club Collection series. The set features two regular issue cards, one "Arms Race" card, and an ad card. The backs of the player cards are clearly marked by the word "Promo" in white block lettering.

COMPLETE SET (4) 4.00 10.00
1 Steve Young .80 2.00
11 Dan Marino 2.00 5.00
AR11 Drew Bledsoe 1.20 3.00
Arm's Race
NNO Pinnacle Ad Card .20 .50

1997 Pinnacle Inscriptions Promos

2 Steve Young .50 1.25
13 Dan Marino 1.50 4.00
20 Barry Sanders 1.25 3.00

1997 Pinnacle Inscriptions

This 50-card standard-size set was issued by Pinnacle. The cards feature a metallic player photo against a solid background. The players name and position is located on the bottom left of the front. The backs feature a player photo along with some brief information and a smattering of statistics.

COMPLETE SET (50) 7.50 20.00
1 Mark Brunell .50 1.25
2 Steve Young .50 1.25
3 Rick Mirer .15 .40
4 Brett Favre 1.50 4.00
5 Tony Banks .25 .60
6 Elvis Grbac .25 .60
7 John Elway 1.50 4.00
8 Troy Aikman .75 2.00
9 Neil O'Donnell .25 .60
10 Kordell Stewart .40 1.00
11 Drew Bledsoe .50 1.25
12 Kerry Collins .40 1.00
13 Dan Marino 1.50 4.00
14 Jeff George .25 .60
15 Scott Mitchell .25 .60
16 Jim Harbaugh .25 .60
17 Dave Brown .15 .40
18 Jeff Blake .25 .60
19 Trent Dilfer .40 1.00
20 Barry Sanders 1.25 3.00
21 Jerry Rice .75 2.00
22 Emmitt Smith 1.25 3.00
23 Vinny Testaverde .25 .60
24 Warren Moon .40 1.00
25 Junior Seau .40 1.00
26 Gus Frerotte .15 .40
27 Heath Shuler .15 .40
28 Erik Kramer .15 .40
29 Boomer Esiason .25 .60
30 Jim Kelly .40 1.00
31 Mark Brunell TNL .40 1.00
32 Steve Young TNL .40 1.00
33 Brett Favre TNL 1.00 2.50
34 Tony Banks TNL .25 .60
35 John Elway TNL 1.00 2.50
36 Troy Aikman TNL .50 1.25
37 Kordell Stewart TNL .40 1.00
38 Drew Bledsoe TNL .40 1.00
39 Kerry Collins TNL .40 1.00
40 Dan Marino TNL 1.00 2.50
41 Jim Harbaugh TNL .25 .60
42 Jeff Blake TNL .25 .60
43 Barry Sanders TNL .75 2.00
44 Jerry Rice TNL .50 1.25
45 Emmitt Smith TNL .75 2.00
46 Rick Mirer TNL .15 .40
47 Jeff George TNL .25 .60
48 Neil O'Donnell TNL .15 .40
49 Elvis Grbac TNL .25 .60
50 Scott Mitchell TNL .15 .40

1997 Pinnacle Inscriptions Artist's Proofs

COMPLETE SET (50) 100.00 200.00
*AP STARS: 4X TO 10X BASIC CARDS
ARTIST PROOF STATED ODDS 1:35

1997 Pinnacle Inscriptions Challenge Collection

COMPLETE SET (50) 40.00 80.00
*CHALL.COLL.STARS: 2X TO 4X BASIC CARDS
STATED ODDS 1:7

1997 Pinnacle Inscriptions Autographs

STATED ODDS 1:23
1 Tony Banks/1925 6.00 15.00
2 Jeff Blake/1470 6.00 15.00
3 Drew Bledsoe/1970 10.00 25.00
4 Dave Brown/1970 5.00 12.00
5 Mark Brunell/2000 10.00 25.00
6 Kerry Collins/1300 8.00 20.00
7 Trent Dilfer/1950 8.00 20.00
8 John Elway/1975 40.00 75.00
9 Jim Everett/2000 6.00 15.00
10 Brett Favre/215 125.00 250.00
11 Gus Frerotte/1975 8.00 20.00
12 Jeff George/1935 8.00 20.00
13 Elvis Grbac/1985 6.00 15.00
14 Jim Harbaugh/1975 15.00 30.00
15 Jeff Hostetler/2000 6.00 15.00
16 Jim Kelly/1925 12.50 30.00
17 Bernie Kosar/1975 8.00 20.00
18 Erik Kramer/2000 5.00 12.00
19 Dan Marino/440 60.00 120.00
20 Rick Mirer/2000 6.00 15.00
21 Scott Mitchell/1995 6.00 15.00
22 Warren Moon/1975 8.00 20.00
23 Neil O'Donnell/1990 6.00 15.00
24 Jerry Rice/950 50.00 100.00
25 Barry Sanders/2053 40.00 75.00
26 Junior Seau/1900 25.00 50.00
27 Heath Shuler/1865 6.00 15.00
28 Emmitt Smith/220 100.00 200.00
29 Kordell Stewart/1495 8.00 20.00
30 Vinny Testaverde/1975 8.00 20.00
31 Steve Young/1900 20.00 40.00

1997 Pinnacle Inscriptions V2

COMPLETE SET (18) 25.00 60.00
STATED ODDS 1:11
V1 Mark Brunell 1.25 3.00
V2 Steve Young 1.25 3.00
V3 Brett Favre 4.00 10.00
V4 Tony Banks .60 1.50
V5 John Elway 4.00 10.00
V6 Troy Aikman 2.00 5.00
V7 Kordell Stewart 1.00 2.50
V8 Drew Bledsoe 1.25 3.00
V9 Kerry Collins 1.00 2.50
V10 Dan Marino 4.00 10.00
V11 Barry Sanders 3.00 8.00
V12 Jerry Rice 2.00 5.00
V13 Emmitt Smith 3.00 8.00
V14 Neil O'Donnell .60 1.50
V15 Scott Mitchell .60 1.50
V16 Jim Harbaugh .60 1.50
V17 Jeff Blake .60 1.50
V18 Trent Dilfer 1.00 2.50

1998 Pinnacle Inscriptions Promos

Pinnacle created several promo cards in 1998 for sets that were never officially released. We've listed all known cards below for the Inscriptions product. Any additions to the list below are appreciated.

33 John Elway 4.00 10.00
36 Steve Young 1.50 4.00
71 Barry Sanders 3.00 8.00

1998 Pinnacle Inscriptions Pen Pals

This set was originally scheduled to be released with the 1998 Pinnacle Inscriptions product. Due to the bankruptcy of Pinnacle Brands, the product was never released. However, these cards made their way onto the secondary market. Each card was signed by one, both or even none of the featured players and was printed on silver and gold foil stock. We've designed with an "AU" after the player's name each one that originally signed the card. The cards were also hand serial numbered of 50-cards each. Also please note that some of the signed and unsigned cards the serial number area on the card back is blank.

COMPLETE SET (11) 750.00 1,500.00
1 Troy Aikman AU 75.00 125.00
Kerry Collins AU
2 Troy Aikman AU 30.00 80.00
Michael Irvin
Emmitt Smith
3 Drew Bledsoe AU 50.00 100.00
Kordell Stewart AU
4 John Elway AU 75.00 150.00
Terrell Davis
5 John Elway AU 250.00 400.00
Brett Favre AU
6 John Elway AU 250.00 400.00
Dan Marino AU
7 Brett Favre AU 75.00 150.00
Barry Sanders No AU
8A Ryan Leaf AU 100.00 200.00
Peyton Manning AU
8B Ryan Leaf No Auto 2.00 5.00
Peyton Manning No Auto
9 Scott Mitchell AU 12.50 30.00
Barry Sanders
10 Jerry Rice AU 150.00 250.00
Steve Young AU
11 Barry Sanders 4.00 10.00
Emmitt Smith

1997 Pinnacle Inside

The 1997 Pinnacle Inside set was issued in one series totalling 150-cards and was distributed in 10-card packs inside 28 different collectible player cans. The cardfronts feature color player photos with a thin team colored player photo as the left border. The backs carry a small player head photo with a black-and-white player photo and player information.

COMPLETE SET (150) 7.50 20.00
1 Troy Aikman .40 1.00
2 Dan Marino .75 2.00
3 Barry Sanders .60 1.50
4 Drew Bledsoe .25 .60
5 Kerry Collins .20 .50
6 Emmitt Smith .60 1.50
7 Brett Favre .75 2.00
8 John Elway .75 2.00
9 Jerry Rice .40 1.00
10 Mark Brunell .25 .60
11 Elvis Grbac .10 .30
12 Junior Seau .20 .50
13 Eddie George .20 .50
14 Steve Young .25 .60
15 Terrell Davis .25 .60
16 Thurman Thomas .20 .50
17 Deion Sanders .20 .50
18 Terrell Owens .25 .60
19 Neil O'Donnell .10 .30
20 Carl Pickens .10 .30
21 Marcus Allen .20 .50
22 Ricky Watters .10 .30
23 Vinny Testaverde .10 .30
24 Kordell Stewart .20 .50
25 Tony Banks .10 .30
26 Terry Glenn .20 .50
27 Todd Collins .07 .20
28 Robert Brooks .10 .30
29 Heath Shuler .07 .20
30 Shannon Sharpe .10 .30
31 Michael Westbrook .10 .30
32 Reggie White .20 .50
33 Brad Johnson .20 .50
34 Tamarick Vanover .10 .30
35 Larry Centers .10 .30
36 Terance Mathis .10 .30
37 Hardy Nickerson .07 .20
38 Jamal Anderson .20 .50
39 Kevin Hardy .07 .20
40 Stan Humphries .10 .30
41 Chris Warren .10 .30
42 Tim Brown .20 .50
43 Joey Galloway .10 .30
44 Boomer Esiason .10 .30
45 Jake Reed .10 .30
46 Kent Graham .07 .20
47 Marshall Faulk .25 .60
48 Sean Dawkins .07 .20
49 Dave Brown .07 .20
50 Willie Green .07 .20
51 Andre Hastings .07 .20
52 Erik Kramer .07 .20
53 Michael Irvin .20 .50
54 Gus Frerotte .07 .20
55 Winslow Oliver .07 .20
56 Jimmy Smith .10 .30
57 Derrick Alexander WR .10 .30
58 Adrian Murrell .10 .30
59 Ki-Jana Carter .07 .20
60 Garrison Hearst .10 .30
61 Chris Sanders .07 .20
62 Johnnie Morton .10 .30
63 Lawrence Phillips .07 .20
64 Bobby Engram .10 .30
65 Tim Biakabutuka .10 .30
66 Anthony Johnson .07 .20
67 Keyshawn Johnson .20 .50
68 Jeff George .10 .30
69 Errict Rhett .07 .20
70 Cris Carter .20 .50
71 Chris T. Jones .07 .20
72 Eric Moulds .20 .50
73 Rick Mirer .07 .20
74 Keenan McCardell .10 .30
75 Simeon Rice .10 .30
76 Eddie Kennison .10 .30
77 Herman Moore .10 .30
78 Jim Harbaugh .10 .30
79 Robert Smith .10 .30
80 Bruce Smith .10 .30
81 John Friesz .07 .20
82 Irving Fryar .10 .30
83 Edgar Bennett .10 .30
84 Ty Detmer .10 .30
85 Curtis Conway .10 .30
86 Napoleon Kaufman .20 .50
87 Tony Martin .10 .30
88 Amani Toomer .10 .30
89 Willie McGinest .07 .20
90 Daryl Johnston .10 .30
91 Stanley Pritchett .07 .20
92 Chris Chandler .10 .30
93 Natrone Means .10 .30
94 Kimble Anders .10 .30
95 Steve McNair .25 .60
96 Curtis Martin .25 .60
97 O.J. McDuffie .10 .30
98 Ben Coates .10 .30
99 Jerome Bettis .20 .50
100 Andre Reed .10 .30
101 Jeff Blake .10 .30
102 Wesley Walls .10 .30
103 Warren Moon .20 .50
104 Isaac Bruce .20 .50
105 Terry Allen .20 .50
106 Rodney Hampton .10 .30
107 Karim Abdul-Jabbar .10 .30
108 Marvin Harrison .20 .50
109 Dorsey Levens .20 .50
110 Rashaan Salaam .07 .20
111 Scott Mitchell .10 .30
112 Darnay Scott .10 .30
113 Aeneas Williams .07 .20
114 Trent Dilfer .20 .50
115 Antonio Freeman .20 .50
116 Jim Everett .07 .20
117 Muhsin Muhammad .10 .30
118 Rickey Dudley .10 .30
119 Mike Alstott .20 .50
120 Jim Druckenmiller RC .10 .30
121 Tiki Barber RC 1.25 3.00
122 Ike Hilliard RC .30 .75
123 Orlando Pace RC .20 .50
124 Jake Plummer RC .75 2.00
125 Yatil Green RC .10 .30
126 Byron Hanspard RC .10 .30
127 James Farrior RC .10 .30
128 Corey Dillon RC .75 2.00
129 Pat Barnes RC .20 .50
130 Kenny Holmes RC .20 .50
131 Rae Carruth RC .07 .20
132 Danny Wuerffel RC .20 .50
133 Darnell Autry RC .10 .30
134 Reidel Anthony RC .20 .50
135 Darrell Russell RC .07 .20
136 Will Blackwell RC .10 .30
137 Peter Boulware RC .20 .50
138 Shawn Springs RC .20 .50
139 Joey Kent RC .20 .50
140 Troy Davis RC .10 .30

141 Antowain Smith RC	.50	1.25
142 Walter Jones RC	.20	.50
143 Tony Gonzalez RC	.75	2.00
144 David LaFleur RC	.07	.20
145 Warrick Dunn RC	.60	1.50
146 Bryant Westbrook RC	.07	.20
147 Dwayne Rudd RC	.20	.50
148 Tom Knight RC	.07	.20
149 Kevin Lockett RC	.10	.30
150 Checklist	.07	.20
P1 Troy Aikman Promo	.40	1.00
P2 Dan Marino Promo	.75	2.00
P7 Brett Favre Promo	.75	2.00

1997 Pinnacle Inside Gridiron Gold

COMPLETE SET (150) 500.00 1,000.00
*STARS: 15X TO 40X BASIC CARDS
*RCs: 6X TO 15X BASIC CARDS
STATED ODDS 1:63 HOB/RET

1997 Pinnacle Inside Silver Lining

COMPLETE SET (150) 125.00 250.00
*STARS: 5X TO 12X BASIC CARDS
*RCs: 2X TO 5X BASIC CARDS
STATED ODDS 1:7 HOB/RET

1997 Pinnacle Inside Autographs

STATED ODDS 1:251 HOB/RET

1 Tony Banks	10.00	25.00
2 Jeff Blake	10.00	25.00
3 Drew Bledsoe	20.00	40.00
4 Dave Brown	7.50	20.00
5 Mark Brunell	15.00	40.00
6 Kerry Collins	12.50	30.00
7 Trent Dilfer	12.50	30.00
8 John Elway	60.00	150.00
9 Jim Everett	7.50	20.00
10 Brett Favre	100.00	175.00
11 Gus Frerotte	7.50	20.00
12 Jeff George	10.00	25.00
13 Elvis Grbac	10.00	25.00
14 Jim Harbaugh	20.00	40.00
15 Jeff Hostetler	7.50	20.00
16 Jim Kelly	30.00	60.00
17 Bernie Kosar	7.50	20.00
18 Erik Kramer	7.50	20.00
19 Scott Mitchell	10.00	25.00
20 Rick Mirer	7.50	20.00
21 Warren Moon	12.50	30.00
23 Barry Sanders	75.00	150.00
22 Jerry Rice SP		
24 Junior Seau	25.00	50.00
25 Heath Shuler	7.50	20.00
26 Kordell Stewart	12.50	30.00
27 Vinny Testaverde	10.00	25.00
28 Steve Young	40.00	100.00

1997 Pinnacle Inside Cans

COMPLETE SET (28)	5.00	12.00
*OPENED GOLD CANS: 3X TO 6X		
GOLD CAN STATED ODDS 1:47		
1 Ice Bowl	.02	.10
2 Dan Marino RB	.60	1.25
3 Brett Favre MVP	.60	1.25
4 Jerome Bettis	.10	.30
5 Tony Banks	.10	.30
6 Deion Sanders	.10	.30
7 Drew Bledsoe	.15	.40
8 Jim Harbaugh	.07	.20
9 Keyshawn Johnson	.10	.30
10 Jeff George	.07	.20
11 Karim Abdul-Jabbar	.10	.30
12 Rick Mirer	.02	.10
13 Kordell Stewart	.10	.30
14 Jeff Blake	.07	.20
15 Eddie George	.10	.30
16 Terry Glenn	.10	.30
17 Curtis Martin	.15	.40
18 Terrell Davis	.15	.40
19 Jerry Rice	.25	.60
20 Steve Young	.15	.40
21 John Elway	.60	1.25
22 Mark Brunell	.15	.40
23 Kerry Collins	.10	.30
24 Barry Sanders	.40	1.00
25 Troy Aikman	.25	.60
26 Emmitt Smith	.40	1.00
27 Dan Marino	.60	1.25
28 Brett Favre	.60	1.25
P1 Cowboys vs. Packers Showdown in Titletown, numbered either 25 or 26 inside)	.02	.10

1997 Pinnacle Inside Fourth and Goal

COMPLETE SET (20)	125.00	250.00
STATED ODDS 1:23 HOB/RET		
1 Brett Favre	12.50	30.00
2 Drew Bledsoe	4.00	10.00
3 Troy Aikman	6.00	15.00
4 Mark Brunell	4.00	10.00
5 Steve Young	4.00	10.00
6 Vinny Testaverde	2.00	5.00
7 Dan Marino	12.50	30.00
8 Kerry Collins	3.00	8.00
9 John Elway	12.50	30.00
10 Emmitt Smith	10.00	25.00
11 Barry Sanders	10.00	25.00
12 Eddie George	3.00	8.00
13 Terrell Davis	4.00	10.00
14 Curtis Martin	4.00	10.00
15 Terry Glenn	3.00	8.00
16 Jerry Rice	6.00	15.00
17 Herman Moore	2.00	5.00
18 Jeff Blake	2.00	5.00
19 Warrick Dunn	5.00	12.00
20 Antowain Smith	4.00	10.00

1998 Pinnacle Inside Stand Up Guys Promos

These promos, for a product never issued, were released after Pinnacle ceased operations and old card inventory was liquidated. The Stand Up Guys cards include a cut out slot in which two cards featuring the same players were to be slid together to form a cross shaped pair.

1AB Dan Marino	6.00	15.00
John Elway		
Brett Favre		
Troy Aikman		
1CD Dan Marino	6.00	15.00
John Elway		
Brett Favre		
Troy Aikman		
2AB Steve Young	3.00	8.00
Kordell Stewart		
Mark Brunell		
Drew Bledsoe		
2CD Steve Young	3.00	8.00
Kordell Stewart		
Mark Brunell		
Drew Bledsoe		
3AB Steve McNair	2.50	6.00
Jake Plummer		
Brad Johnson		
Kerry Collins		
3CD Steve McNair	2.50	6.00
Jake Plummer		
Brad Johnson		
Kerry Collins		
4AB Barry Sanders	5.00	12.00
Emmitt Smith		
Terrell Davis		
Dorsey Levens		
4CD Barry Sanders	5.00	12.00
Emmitt Smith		
Terrell Davis		
Dorsey Levens		
5AB Jerome Bettis	3.00	8.00
Curtis Martin		
Karim Abdul-Jabbar		
Ricky Watters		
5CD Jerome Bettis	3.00	8.00
Curtis Martin		
Karim Abdul-Jabbar		
Ricky Watters		
9AB Tim Brown	4.00	10.00
Keenan McCardell		
Michael Jackson		
Andre Rison		
9CD Tim Brown	4.00	10.00
Keenan McCardell		
Michael Jackson		
Andre Rison		
10AB John Elway	6.00	15.00
Terrell Davis		
Shannon Sharpe		
Rod Smith		
10CD John Elway	6.00	15.00
Terrell Davis		
Shannon Sharpe		
Rod Smith		
14AB Ben Coates	2.50	6.00
Drew Bledsoe		
Willie McGinest		
Terry Glenn		
14CD Ben Coates	2.50	6.00
Drew Bledsoe		
Willie McGinest		
Terry Glenn		
15AB Scott Mitchell	2.00	5.00
Herman Moore		
Johnnie Morton		
15CD Scott Mitchell	2.00	5.00
Herman Moore		
Johnnie Morton		
16AB Trent Dilfer	2.00	5.00
Reidel Anthony		
Warrick Dunn		
Mike Alstott		
16CD Trent Dilfer	2.00	5.00
Reidel Anthony		
Warrick Dunn		
Mike Alstott		
17AB Karim Adbul-Jabbar	3.00	8.00
Yatil Green		
Troy Drayton		
17CD Karim Adbul-Jabbar	3.00	8.00
Yatil Green		
Troy Drayton		
21AB Cris Carter	4.00	10.00
Robert Smith		
Brad Johnson		
Jake Reed		
21CD Cris Carter	4.00	10.00
Robert Smith		
Brad Johnson		
Jake Reed		
22AB Peyton Manning	6.00	15.00
Brian Griese		
Ryan Leaf		
Thad Busby		
22CD Peyton Manning	6.00	15.00
Brian Griese		
Ryan Leaf		
Thad Busby		
23AB Curtis Enis	2.00	5.00
Fred Taylor		
Ahman Green		
Robert Edwards		
23CD Curtis Enis	2.00	5.00
Fred Taylor		
Ahman Green		
Robert Edwards		
24AB Randy Moss	3.00	8.00
Germane Crowell		
Jacquez Green		
Kevin Dyson		
24CD Randy Moss	3.00	8.00
Germane Crowell		
Jacquez Green		
Kevin Dyson		
25AB Dan Marino	6.00	15.00
Brett Favre		
Terrell Davis		
Barry Sanders		
25CD Dan Marino	6.00	15.00
Brett Favre		
Terrell Davis		
Barry Sanders		

1996 Pinnacle Mint

The 1996 Pinnacle Mint Collection set was issued in one series of 30-cards and 30-coins. The two-coin/three-card packs carried a suggested retail price of $3.99 each. The challenge was to fit the coins with the die-cut cards that pictured the same player. Two die-cut cards and two coins were inserted in each pack. Either one bronze, silver or gold card was also included in each pack. The fronts feature color action player photos with a cut-out area for the matching coin. Die cut cards are listed below.

COMP.DIE CUT SET (30)	4.00	10.00
1 Troy Aikman	.30	.75
2 John Elway	.60	1.50
3 Jim Kelly	.10	.30
4 Dan Marino	.60	1.50
5 Warren Moon	.05	.15
6 Steve Young	.25	.60
7 Boomer Esiason	.05	.15
8 Jim Everett	.02	.08
9 Brett Favre	.60	1.50
10 Jim Harbaugh	.05	.15
11 Jeff Hostetler	.02	.08
12 Neil O'Donnell	.05	.15
13 Drew Bledsoe	.20	.50
14 Rick Mirer	.05	.15
15 Emmitt Smith	.50	1.25
16 Jerry Rice	.30	.75
17 Barry Sanders	.50	1.25
18 Junior Seau	.10	.30
19 Dave Brown	.02	.08
20 Heath Shuler	.05	.15
21 Jeff Blake	.10	.30
22 Kerry Collins	.10	.30
23 Scott Mitchell	.05	.15
24 Kordell Stewart	.10	.30
25 Jeff George	.05	.15
26 Mark Brunell	.20	.50
27 Erik Kramer	.02	.08
28 Bernie Kosar	.02	.08
29 Frank Reich	.02	.08
30 Randall Cunningham	.10	.30
S2 John Elway Sample (die cut card)	.40	1.00
S13 Drew Bledsoe Sample (die cut card)	.20	.50
S14 Rick Mirer Sample (bronze card)	.08	.25

1996 Pinnacle Mint Bronze

COMP.BRONZE SET (30) 20.00 40.00
*BRONZE CARDS: .8X TO 2X DIE CUTS

1996 Pinnacle Mint Gold

COMP.GOLD SET (30) 150.00 300.00
*GOLD CARDS: 4X TO 10X DIE CUTS
STATED ODDS 1:48

1996 Pinnacle Mint Silver

COMP.SILVER SET (30) 75.00 150.00
*SILVER CARDS: 2.5X TO 6X DIE CUTS
STATED ODDS 1:20

1996 Pinnacle Mint Coins Brass

COMP.BRASS SET (30)	12.50	30.00
BRASS STATED ODDS 2:1		
*NICKEL COINS: 1.5X TO 4X BRASS		
NICKEL STATED ODDS 1:20		
*GOLD PLATED: 3X TO 8X BRASS		
GOLD STATED ODDS 1:48		
TWO COINS PER PACK		
1 Troy Aikman	.75	2.00
2 John Elway	1.50	4.00
3 Jim Kelly	.30	.75
4 Dan Marino	1.50	4.00
5 Warren Moon	.15	.40
6 Steve Young	.60	1.50
7 Boomer Esiason	.15	.40
8 Jim Everett	.07	.20
9 Brett Favre	1.50	4.00
10 Jim Harbaugh	.15	.40
11 Jeff Hostetler	.07	.20
12 Neil O'Donnell	.15	.40
13 Drew Bledsoe	.50	1.25
14 Rick Mirer	.15	.40
15 Emmitt Smith	1.25	3.00
16 Jerry Rice	.75	2.00
17 Barry Sanders	1.25	3.00
18 Junior Seau	.30	.75
19 Dave Brown	.07	.20
20 Heath Shuler	.15	.40
21 Jeff Blake	.30	.75
22 Kerry Collins	.30	.75
23 Scott Mitchell	.15	.40
24 Kordell Stewart	.30	.75
25 Jeff George	.15	.40
26 Mark Brunell	.50	1.25
27 Erik Kramer	.07	.20
28 Bernie Kosar	.07	.20
29 Frank Reich	.07	.20
30 David Klingler	.30	.75
SP1 Randall Cunningham	1.25	3.00

1997 Pinnacle Mint

The 1997 Pinnacle Mint set was issued in one series totalling 30-cards and 30-coins and was distributed in packs with one die-cut card, two random coins minted in brass, nickel-silver, solid silver or solid gold plated versions, and two foil stamped cards. The cards feature color action player photos with either a cut-out area for the matching coin or a replica foil coin. The set contains the topical subset: Minted Highlights (21-30). The bronze version of the cards is priced below.

COMPLETE SET (30)	6.00	15.00
1 Brett Favre	.75	2.00
2 Drew Bledsoe	.25	.60
3 Mark Brunell	.25	.60
4 Kerry Collins	.15	.40
5 Troy Aikman	.40	1.00
6 Steve Young	.25	.60
7 Dan Marino	.75	2.00
8 Barry Sanders	.60	1.50
9 John Elway	.75	2.00
10 Emmitt Smith	.60	1.50
11 Rick Mirer	.05	.15
12 Kordell Stewart	.15	.40
13 Tony Banks	.08	.25
14 Jeff George	.08	.25
15 Jerry Rice	.40	1.00
16 Jeff Blake	.08	.25
17 Jim Harbaugh	.08	.25
18 Heath Shuler	.05	.15
19 Scott Mitchell	.05	.15
20 Neil O'Donnell	.05	.15
21 Brett Favre MH	.40	1.00
22 Drew Bledsoe MH	.15	.40
23 Mark Brunell MH	.15	.40
24 Kerry Collins MH	.08	.25
25 Troy Aikman MH	.20	.50
26 Dan Marino MH	.40	1.00
27 Barry Sanders MH	.30	.75
28 Emmitt Smith MH	.30	.75
29 Tony Banks MH	.05	.15
30 John Elway MH	.40	1.00
P2 Drew Bledsoe Promo	.40	1.00
P6 Steve Young Promo (bronze card)	.40	1.00

1997 Pinnacle Mint Die Cuts

COMPLETE SET (30) 10.00 25.00
*DIE CUTS: .5X TO 1.2X BRONZE CARDS
STATED ODDS 2:1 HOB/RET

1997 Pinnacle Mint Gold Team Pinnacle

COMPLETE SET (30) 100.00 250.00
*GOLD TEAM PINN: 5X TO 12X BRONZES
STATED ODDS 1:47 HOB/1:71 RET

1997 Pinnacle Mint Silver Team Pinnacle

COMPLETE SET (30) 48.00 120.00
*SILVER TEAM PINN: 2X TO 5X BRONZE
STATED ODDS 1:1 HOB/RET

1997 Pinnacle Mint Coins Brass

COMP.BRASS SET (30)	12.50	30.00
BRASS COINS 2 PER HOBBY, 1 PER RETAIL		
*BRASS PROOFS: 3X TO 8X BRASS		
BRASS PROOF/500 ODDS 1.79H, 1.159R		
BRASS PROOF PRINT RUN 500 #'d SETS		
*GOLD PLATED: 2X TO 5X BRASS		
GOLD PLATED ODDS 1:47H, 1:95R		
*GOLD PROOFS: 12X TO 30X BRASS		
GOLD PROOF/100 ODDS 1:425H, 1:850R		
GOLD PROOF PRINT RUN 100 #'d SETS		
*NICKEL COINS: 1.2X TO 3X BRASS		
NICKEL ODDS 1:20H, 1:41R		
*SILVER PROOFS: 5X TO 12X BRASS		
SILVER PROOF ODDS 1:170H, 1:340R		
SILVER PROOF PRINT RUN 250 #'d SETS		
*SOLID SILVERS: 25X TO 50X BRASS		
SOLID SILVER ODDS 1:2880H, 1:4600R		
1 Brett Favre	2.00	5.00
2 Drew Bledsoe	.60	1.50
3 Mark Brunell	.60	1.50
4 Kerry Collins	.40	1.00
5 Troy Aikman	1.00	2.50
6 Steve Young	.60	1.50
7 Dan Marino	2.00	5.00
8 Barry Sanders	1.50	4.00
9 John Elway	2.00	5.00
10 Emmitt Smith	1.50	4.00
11 Rick Mirer	.15	.40
12 Kordell Stewart	.40	1.00
13 Tony Banks	.25	.60
14 Jeff George	.25	.60
15 Jerry Rice	1.00	2.50
16 Jeff Blake	.25	.60
17 Jim Harbaugh	.25	.60
18 Heath Shuler	.15	.40
19 Scott Mitchell	.15	.40
20 Neil O'Donnell	.15	.40
21 Brett Favre MH	1.00	2.50
22 Drew Bledsoe MH	.40	1.00
23 Mark Brunell MH	.40	1.00
24 Kerry Collins MH	.25	.60
25 Troy Aikman MH	.50	1.25
26 Dan Marino MH	1.00	2.50
27 Barry Sanders MH	.75	2.00
28 Emmitt Smith MH	.75	2.00
29 Tony Banks MH	.15	.40
30 John Elway MH	1.00	2.50

1997 Pinnacle Mint Commemorative Cards

COMPLETE SET (6)	20.00	50.00
STATED ODDS 1:31 HOB, 1:47 RET		
1 Barry Sanders	5.00	12.00
2 Brett Favre	6.00	15.00
3 Mark Brunell	2.00	5.00
4 Emmitt Smith	5.00	12.00
5 Dan Marino	6.00	15.00
6 Jerry Rice	3.00	8.00

1997 Pinnacle Mint Commemorative Coins

COMPLETE SET (6)	50.00	120.00
STATED ODDS 1:31 HOBBY		
1 Barry Sanders	10.00	25.00
2 Brett Favre	12.50	30.00
3 Mark Brunell	4.00	10.00
4 Emmitt Smith	10.00	25.00
5 Dan Marino	12.50	30.00
6 Jerry Rice	6.00	15.00

1998 Pinnacle Mint

Each of the 33 players in this set had three card versions within the set. The first 33-cards are die cut which could hold the coin, the next 33-cards are the base product, and the last 33-cards featured a portrait style photo on front and player profile information on back.

COMPLETE SET (100)	12.50	30.00
1 John Elway DC	.40	1.00
2 Barry Sanders DC	.30	.75
3 Brett Favre DC	.40	1.00
4 Drew Bledsoe DC	.20	.50
5 Steve Young DC	.10	.30
6 Kordell Stewart DC	.10	.30
7 Dan Marino DC	.40	1.00
8 Troy Aikman DC	.20	.50
9 Jake Plummer DC	.20	.50
10 Jerry Rice DC	.20	.50
11 Rick Mirer DC	.07	.20
12 Elvis Grbac DC	.07	.20
13 Trent Dilfer DC	.10	.30
14 Jeff George DC	.07	.20
15 Junior Seau DC	.10	.30
16 Warren Moon DC	.10	.30
17 Tony Banks DC	.07	.20
18 Scott Mitchell DC	.07	.20
19 Steve McNair DC	.10	.30
20 Gus Frerotte DC	.07	.20
21 Michael Irvin DC	.10	.30
22 Kerry Collins DC	.07	.20
23 Jim Harbaugh DC	.07	.20
24 Neil O'Donnell DC	.07	.20
25 Jeff Blake DC	.07	.20
26 Vinny Testaverde DC	.07	.20
27 Erik Kramer DC	.07	.20
28 Heath Shuler DC	.07	.20
29 Terrell Davis DC	.20	.50
30 Randall Cunningham DC	.10	.30
31 Ryan Leaf DC	.20	.50
32 Brad Johnson DC	.10	.30
33 Peyton Manning DC	1.50	4.00
34 John Elway	.75	2.00
35 Barry Sanders	.60	1.50
36 Brett Favre	.75	2.00
37 Drew Bledsoe	.30	.75
38 Steve Young	.20	.50
39 Kordell Stewart	.20	.50
40 Dan Marino	.75	2.00
41 Troy Aikman	.40	1.00
42 Jake Plummer	.20	.50
43 Jerry Rice	.40	1.00
44 Rick Mirer	.07	.20
45 Elvis Grbac	.10	.30
46 Trent Dilfer	.20	.50
47 Jeff George	.10	.30
48 Junior Seau	.20	.50
49 Warren Moon	.20	.50
50 Tony Banks	.20	.50
51 Scott Mitchell	.10	.30
52 Steve McNair	.20	.50
53 Gus Frerotte	.07	.20
54 Michael Irvin	.20	.50
55 Kerry Collins	.10	.30
56 Jim Harbaugh	.10	.30
57 Neil O'Donnell	.10	.30
58 Jeff Blake	.10	.30
59 Vinny Testaverde	.10	.30
60 Erik Kramer	.07	.20
61 Heath Shuler	.07	.20
62 Terrell Davis	.20	.50
63 Randall Cunningham	.20	.50
64 Ryan Leaf	.30	.75
65 Brad Johnson	.20	.50
66 Peyton Manning	3.00	8.00
67 John Elway PRO	.60	1.50
68 Barry Sanders PRO	.50	1.25
69 Brett Favre PRO	.60	1.50
70 Drew Bledsoe PRO	.20	.50
71 Steve Young PRO	.20	.50
72 Kordell Stewart PRO	.10	.30
73 Dan Marino PRO	.60	1.50
74 Troy Aikman PRO	.30	.75
75 Jake Plummer PRO	.20	.50
76 Jerry Rice PRO	.30	.75
77 Rick Mirer PRO	.07	.20
78 Elvis Grbac PRO	.07	.20
79 Trent Dilfer PRO	.10	.30
80 Jeff George PRO	.10	.30
81 Junior Seau PRO	.20	.50
82 Warren Moon PRO	.20	.50
83 Tony Banks PRO	.10	.30
84 Scott Mitchell PRO	.10	.30
85 Steve McNair PRO	.10	.30
86 Gus Frerotte PRO	.07	.20
87 Michael Irvin PRO	.10	.30
88 Kerry Collins PRO	.10	.30
89 Jim Harbaugh PRO	.10	.30
90 Neil O'Donnell PRO	.10	.30
91 Jeff Blake PRO	.10	.30
92 Vinny Testaverde PRO	.10	.30
93 Erik Kramer PRO	.07	.20
94 Heath Shuler PRO	.07	.20
95 Terrell Davis PRO	.20	.50
96 Randall Cunningham PRO	.10	.30
97 Ryan Leaf PRO	.20	.50
98 Brad Johnson PRO	.10	.30
99 Peyton Manning PRO	2.50	6.00
100 Checklist Card	.02	.10

1998 Pinnacle Mint Silver

COMPLETE SET (99) 50.00 120.00
*SILVER STARS: 1.2X TO 3X BASIC CARDS
*SILVER ROOKIES: .6X TO 1.5X BASE CARDS
STATED ODDS 1:7 HOB, 1:9 RET

1998 Pinnacle Mint Coins Brass

COMP.BRASS SET (33)	12.00	30.00
ONE COIN PER PACK		
*NICKEL: 3X TO 8X BRASS COINS		
NICKEL COIN ODDS 1:15H, 1:23R		
UNPRICED 24K GOLD COINS ISSUED		
1 John Elway	1.50	4.00
2 Barry Sanders	1.25	3.00
3 Brett Favre	1.50	4.00
4 Drew Bledsoe	.60	1.50
5 Steve Young	.50	1.25
6 Kordell Stewart	.40	1.00
7 Dan Marino	1.50	4.00
8 Troy Aikman	.75	2.00
9 Jake Plummer	.40	1.00
10 Jerry Rice	.75	2.00
11 Rick Mirer	.15	.40
12 Elvis Grbac	.25	.60
13 Trent Dilfer	.40	1.00
14 Jeff George	.25	.60
15 Junior Seau	.40	1.00
16 Warren Moon	.40	1.00
17 Tony Banks	.40	1.00
18 Scott Mitchell	.25	.60
19 Steve McNair	.40	1.00
20 Gus Frerotte	.15	.40
21 Michael Irvin	.40	1.00
22 Kerry Collins	.25	.60
23 Jim Harbaugh	.25	.60
24 Neil O'Donnell	.25	.60
25 Jeff Blake	.25	.60
26 Vinny Testaverde	.25	.60
27 Erik Kramer	.15	.40
28 Heath Shuler	.15	.40
29 Terrell Davis	.40	1.00
30 Randall Cunningham	.40	1.00
31 Ryan Leaf	.40	1.00
32 Brad Johnson	.40	1.00
33 Peyton Manning	6.00	15.00
NNO P.Manning R.Leaf (Nickel Redemption)	1.00	2.50

1998 Pinnacle Mint Gems

COMPLETE SET (15)	30.00	80.00
STATED ODDS 1:11H, 1:17R		
*PROMOS: .2X TO .5X BASIC INSERTS		
1 Brett Favre	5.00	12.00
2 Dan Marino	5.00	12.00
3 Kordell Stewart	.75	2.00
4 Peyton Manning	8.00	20.00
5 Ryan Leaf	.75	2.00
6 Drew Bledsoe	2.00	5.00
7 Troy Aikman	2.50	6.00
8 John Elway	5.00	12.00
9 Barry Sanders	4.00	10.00
10 Steve Young	1.50	4.00
11 Steve McNair	1.25	3.00
12 Trent Dilfer	.75	2.00
13 Terrell Davis	1.25	3.00
14 Jerry Rice	2.50	6.00
15 Jake Plummer	1.25	3.00

1998 Pinnacle Mint Impeccable

COMPLETE SET (10)	25.00	60.00
STATED ODDS 1:15H, 1:23R		
*PROMOS: .2X TO .5X BASIC INSERTS		
1 John Elway	5.00	12.00
2 Brett Favre	5.00	12.00
3 Troy Aikman	2.50	6.00
4 Kordell Stewart	.75	2.00
5 Jerry Rice	2.50	6.00
6 Barry Sanders	4.00	10.00
7 Dan Marino	5.00	12.00
8 Jake Plummer	1.25	3.00
9 Terrell Davis	1.25	3.00
10 Drew Bledsoe	1.25	3.00

1998 Pinnacle Mint Lasting Impressions

COMPLETE SET (10)	25.00	60.00
STATED ODDS 1:15H, 1:23R		
*PROMOS: .2X TO .5X BASIC INSERTS		
1 Brett Favre	5.00	12.00
2 John Elway	5.00	12.00
3 Barry Sanders	4.00	10.00
4 Dan Marino	5.00	12.00
5 Steve Young	1.50	4.00
6 Terrell Davis	1.25	3.00
7 Kordell Stewart	.75	2.00
8 Troy Aikman	2.50	6.00
9 Jake Plummer	1.25	3.00
10 Jerry Rice	2.50	6.00

1998 Pinnacle Mint Minted Moments

COMPLETE SET (15)	30.00	80.00
STATED ODDS 1:11H, 1:17R		
*PROMO CARDS: .2X TO .5X BASE INSERTS		
1 Peyton Manning	8.00	20.00
2 Ryan Leaf	.75	2.00
3 John Elway	5.00	12.00
4 Brett Favre	5.00	12.00
5 Drew Bledsoe	2.00	5.00
6 Kordell Stewart	.75	2.00
7 Dan Marino	5.00	12.00
8 Jerry Rice	2.50	6.00
9 Barry Sanders	4.00	10.00
10 Jake Plummer	1.25	3.00
11 Troy Aikman	2.50	6.00
12 Trent Dilfer	.75	2.00
13 Warren Moon	1.25	3.00
14 Steve Young	1.25	3.00
15 Terrell Davis	1.25	3.00

1998 Pinnacle Mint Team Pinnacle Points

COMPLETE SET (10)	2.00	5.00
*FIVE POINTS: .5X TO 1.2X		
*TEN POINTS: .6X TO 1.5X		
1 Troy Aikman	.30	.75
2 Drew Bledsoe	.15	.40
3 Warrick Dunn	.08	.25
4 John Elway	.50	1.25
5 Brett Favre	.60	1.50
6 Ryan Leaf	.08	.25
7 Dan Marino	.60	1.50
8 Jake Plummer	.08	.25
9 Kordell Stewart	.08	.25
10 Steve Young	.25	.60

1998 Pinnacle Performers Big Bang Promos

Pinnacle issued several promo cards in 1998 for sets that were never officially released. We've listed all known cards below for the Pinnacle Performers product. Any additions to the list below are appreciated.

10 John Elway	3.00	8.00
11 Steve Young	2.00	5.00
12 Drew Bledsoe	1.50	4.00

1998 Pinnacle Plus A Piece of the Game Promos

Pinnacle issued several promo cards in 1998 for sets that were never officially released. We've listed all known cards so any additions to the list below are appreciated.

1 Warrick Dunn	1.25	3.00
2 Dan Marino	5.00	12.00
3 Eddie George	1.25	3.00
6 Troy Aikman	2.50	6.00

1998 Pinnacle Plus Go To Guys Promos

Pinnacle issued several promo cards in 1998 for sets that were never officially released. We've listed all known cards so any additions to the list below are appreciated.

1 Emmitt Smith	5.00	12.00
3 Fred Lane	1.00	2.50
4 Curtis Conway	1.25	3.00
6 Barry Sanders	5.00	12.00
7 Brett Favre	6.00	15.00
8 Brad Johnson	1.00	2.50
9 Danny Wuerffel	1.25	3.00
10 Danny Kanell	1.25	3.00
17 Rob Johnson	1.25	3.00
18 Corey Dillon	2.00	4.00
20 Marshall Faulk	2.00	5.00
23 Dan Marino	6.00	15.00
26 Napoleon Kaufman	1.00	2.50
28 Natrone Means	1.25	3.00
30 Eddie George	1.25	3.00

1998 Pinnacle Plus Selected Promos

Pinnacle issued several promo cards in 1998 for sets that were never officially released. We've listed all known cards so any additions to the list below are appreciated.

1 Brett Favre	6.00	15.00
10 Steve Young	2.50	6.00

1998 Pinnacle Plus Sunday's Best Promos

Pinnacle issued several promo cards in 1998 for sets that were never officially released. We've listed all known cards so any additions to the list below are appreciated.

3 Emmitt Smith	5.00	12.00
8 Corey Dillon	1.50	4.00
10 Barry Sanders	5.00	12.00
11 Brett Favre	6.00	15.00
13 Eddie George	1.50	4.00
15 Terrell Davis	2.00	5.00

1997 Pinnacle Totally Certified Platinum Red

This 150 card set is parallel to regular base Certified set. However, it is the "base" set for the Totally Certified set. The totally certified set was issued only through Pinnacle hobby channels. It was issued in four box cases with three cards per pack. Each card in the three parallel version of this set (Platinum Blue, Red and Gold) are all individually serial numbered. The platinum red cards were issued two per pack and are sequentially numbered to 4,999.

COMPLETE SET (150)	60.00	150.00
*PROMOS: .3X TO .8X BASIC RED		
1 Emmitt Smith	5.00	12.00
2 Dan Marino	6.00	15.00
3 Brett Favre	6.00	15.00
4 Steve Young	2.00	5.00
5 Kerry Collins	1.50	4.00
6 Troy Aikman	3.00	8.00
7 Drew Bledsoe	2.00	5.00
8 Eddie George	1.50	4.00
9 Jerry Rice	3.00	8.00
10 John Elway	6.00	15.00
11 Barry Sanders	5.00	12.00
12 Mark Brunell	2.00	5.00
13 Elvis Grbac	1.00	2.50
14 Tony Banks	1.00	2.50
15 Vinny Testaverde	1.00	2.50
16 Rick Mirer	.60	1.50
17 Carl Pickens	1.00	2.50
18 Deion Sanders	1.50	4.00
19 Terry Glenn	1.50	4.00
20 Heath Shuler	.60	1.50
21 Dave Brown	.60	1.50
22 Keyshawn Johnson	1.50	4.00
23 Jeff George	1.00	2.50
24 Ricky Watters	1.00	2.50
25 Kordell Stewart	1.50	4.00
26 Junior Seau	1.50	4.00
27 Terrell Owens	2.00	5.00
28 Warren Moon	1.50	4.00
29 Isaac Bruce	1.50	4.00
30 Steve McNair	2.00	5.00
31 Gus Frerotte	.60	1.50
32 Trent Dilfer	1.50	4.00
33 Shannon Sharpe	1.50	4.00
34 Scott Mitchell	1.00	2.50
35 Antonio Freeman	1.50	4.00
36 Jim Harbaugh	1.00	2.50
37 Natrone Means	1.00	2.50
38 Marcus Allen	1.50	4.00
39 Karim Abdul-Jabbar	1.50	4.00
40 Tim Biakabutuka	1.00	2.50
41 Jeff Blake	1.00	2.50
42 Michael Irvin	1.50	4.00
43 Herschel Walker	1.00	2.50
44 Curtis Martin	2.00	5.00
45 Eddie Kennison	1.00	2.50
46 Napoleon Kaufman	1.50	4.00
47 Larry Centers	1.00	2.50
48 Jamal Anderson	1.50	4.00
49 Derrick Alexander WR	1.00	2.50
50 Bruce Smith	1.00	2.50
51 Wesley Walls	1.00	2.50
52 Rod Smith WR	1.50	4.00
53 Keenan McCardell	1.00	2.50
54 Robert Brooks	1.00	2.50
55 Willie Green	.60	1.50
56 Jake Reed	1.00	2.50
57 Joey Galloway	1.00	2.50
58 Eric Metcalf	1.00	2.50

59 Chris Sanders	.60	1.50
60 Jeff Hostetler	.60	1.50
61 Kevin Greene	1.00	2.50
62 Frank Sanders	1.00	2.50
63 Dorsey Levens	1.50	4.00
64 Sean Dawkins	.60	1.50
65 Cris Carter	1.50	4.00
66 Andre Hastings	.60	1.50
67 Amani Toomer	1.00	2.50
68 Adrian Murrell	1.00	2.50
69 Ty Detmer	1.00	2.50
70 Yancey Thigpen	.60	1.50
71 Jim Everett	.60	1.50
72 Todd Collins	.60	1.50
73 Curtis Conway	1.00	2.50
74 Herman Moore	1.00	2.50
75 Neil O'Donnell	1.00	2.50
76 Rod Woodson	1.00	2.50
77 Tony Martin	1.00	2.50
78 Kent Graham	.60	1.50
79 Andre Reed	1.00	2.50
80 Reggie White	1.50	4.00
81 Thurman Thomas	1.50	4.00
82 Garrison Hearst	1.00	2.50
83 Chris Warren	1.00	2.50
84 Wayne Chrebet	1.50	4.00
85 Chris T. Jones	.60	1.50
86 Anthony Miller	.60	1.50
87 Chris Chandler	1.00	2.50
88 Terrell Davis	2.00	5.00
89 Mike Alstott	1.50	4.00
90 Terry Allen	1.50	4.00
91 Jerome Bettis	1.50	4.00
92 Stan Humphries	1.00	2.50
93 Andre Rison	1.00	2.50
94 Marshall Faulk	2.00	5.00
95 Erik Kramer	.60	1.50
96 O.J. McDuffie	1.00	2.50
97 Robert Smith	1.00	2.50
98 Keith Byars	.60	1.50
99 Rodney Hampton	1.00	2.50
100 Desmond Howard	1.00	2.50
101 Lawrence Phillips	.60	1.50
102 Michael Westbrook	1.00	2.50
103 Johnnie Morton	1.00	2.50
104 Ben Coates	1.00	2.50
105 J.J. Stokes	1.00	2.50
106 Terance Mathis	1.00	2.50
107 Errict Rhett	.60	1.50
108 Tim Brown	1.50	4.00
109 Marvin Harrison	1.50	4.00
110 Muhsin Muhammad	1.00	2.50
111 Byron Bam Morris	.60	1.50
112 Mario Bates	.60	1.50
113 Jimmy Smith	1.00	2.50
114 Irving Fryar	1.00	2.50
115 Tamarick Vanover	1.00	2.50
116 Brad Johnson	1.50	4.00
117 Rashaan Salaam	.60	1.50
118 Ki-Jana Carter	.60	1.50
119 Tyrone Wheatley	1.00	2.50
120 John Friesz	.60	1.50
121 Orlando Pace RC	1.50	4.00
122 Jim Druckenmiller RC	.75	2.00
123 Byron Hanspard RC	1.00	2.50
124 David LaFleur RC	.40	1.00
125 Reidel Anthony RC	1.50	4.00
126 Antowain Smith RC	4.00	10.00
127 Bryant Westbrook RC	.40	1.00
128 Fred Lane RC	.75	2.00
129 Tiki Barber RC	10.00	25.00
130 Shawn Springs RC	.75	2.00
131 Ike Hilliard RC	3.00	6.00
132 James Farrior RC	1.50	4.00
133 Darrell Russell RC	.40	1.00
134 Walter Jones RC	1.50	4.00
135 Tom Knight RC	.40	1.00
136 Yatil Green RC	.75	2.00
137 Joey Kent RC	.75	2.00
138 Kevin Lockett RC	.75	2.00
139 Troy Davis RC	.75	2.00
140 Darnell Autry RC	.75	2.00
141 Pat Barnes RC	1.50	4.00
142 Rae Carruth RC	.40	1.00
143 Will Blackwell RC	.75	2.00
144 Warrick Dunn RC	5.00	12.00
145 Corey Dillon RC	6.00	15.00
146 Dwayne Rudd RC	1.50	4.00
147 Reinard Wilson RC	.75	2.00
148 Peter Boulware RC	1.50	4.00
149 Tony Gonzalez RC	6.00	15.00
150 Danny Wuerffel RC	1.50	4.00

1997 Pinnacle Totally Certified Platinum Blue

COMPLETE SET (150)	200.00	400.00
*BLUE VETS: .8X TO 2X BASIC CARDS		
*BLUE ROOKIES: .6X TO 1.5X		
STATED PRINT RUN 2499 SER.#'d SETS		
STATED ODDS ONE PER PACK		
*PROMOS: .2X TO .5X BASIC BLUE		

1997 Pinnacle Totally Certified Platinum Gold

*GOLD VETS/30: 6X TO 15X BASIC CARDS
*GOLD ROOKIE STARS/30: 3X TO 8X
GOLD PRINT RUN 30 SER.#'d SETS
STATED ODDS 1:79

1997 Pinnacle X-Press

The 1997 Pinnacle X-Press released was issued in one series totaling 150-cards and distributed in eight card packs plus one Pursuit of Paydirt card for a suggested retail price of $1.99. The fronts feature color player photos while the backs carry player information.

COMPLETE SET (150)	7.50	20.00
1 Drew Bledsoe	.25	.60
2 Steve Young	.25	.60
3 Brett Favre	.75	2.00
4 John Elway	.75	2.00
5 Dan Marino	.75	2.00
6 Jerry Rice	.40	1.00
7 Tony Banks	.10	.30
8 Kerry Collins	.20	.50
9 Mark Brunell	.25	.60
10 Troy Aikman	.40	1.00
11 Barry Sanders	.60	1.50
12 Elvis Grbac	.10	.30
13 Eddie George	.20	.50
14 Terry Glenn	.20	.50
15 Kordell Stewart	.20	.50
16 Junior Seau	.20	.50
17 Herman Moore	.10	.30
18 Gus Frerotte	.07	.20
19 Warren Moon	.20	.50
20 Emmitt Smith	.60	1.50
21 Henry Ellard	.07	.20
22 Rashaan Salaam	.07	.20
23 Sean Dawkins	.07	.20
24 Tyrone Wheatley	.10	.30
25 Lawrence Phillips	.07	.20
26 Ty Detmer	.10	.30
27 Vinny Testaverde	.10	.30
28 Dorsey Levens	.20	.50
29 Ricky Watters	.10	.30
30 Natrone Means	.10	.30
31 Curtis Conway	.10	.30
32 Larry Centers	.10	.30
33 Johnnie Morton	.10	.30
34 Desmond Howard	.10	.30
35 Marcus Allen	.20	.50
36 Cris Carter	.20	.50
37 James O.Stewart	.10	.30
38 Frank Sanders	.10	.30
39 Bruce Smith	.10	.30
40 Carl Pickens	.10	.30
41 Neil O'Donnell	.10	.30
42 Trent Dilfer	.20	.50
43 Rodney Peete	.07	.20
44 Terance Mathis	.10	.30
45 Muhsin Muhammad	.10	.30
46 Jake Reed	.10	.30
47 Jim Harbaugh	.10	.30
48 Todd Collins	.07	.20
49 Ki-Jana Carter	.07	.20
50 Scott Mitchell	.10	.30
51 Kevin Hardy	.07	.20
52 Stanley Pritchett	.07	.20
53 Dave Brown	.07	.20
54 Jeff George	.10	.30
55 Stan Humphries	.10	.30
56 Isaac Bruce	.20	.50
57 Eric Moulds	.20	.50
58 Robert Brooks	.10	.30
59 Steve McNair	.25	.60
60 Adrian Murrell	.10	.30
61 Rodney Hampton	.10	.30
62 Michael Jackson	.10	.30
63 Tamarick Vanover	.10	.30
64 Edgar Bennett	.10	.30
65 Andre Hastings	.07	.20
66 Robert Smith	.10	.30
67 Thurman Thomas	.20	.50
68 Tim Biakabutuka	.10	.30
69 Rick Mirer	.07	.20
70 Deion Sanders	.20	.50
71 Curtis Martin	.25	.60
72 Garrison Hearst	.10	.30
73 Kent Graham	.07	.20
74 Anthony Johnson	.07	.20
75 Antonio Freeman	.20	.50
76 Marshall Faulk	.25	.60
77 O.J. McDuffie	.10	.30
78 Heath Shuler	.07	.20
79 Napoleon Kaufman	.20	.50
80 Aeneas Williams	.07	.20
81 Hardy Nickerson	.07	.20
82 Keenan McCardell	.10	.30
83 Erik Kramer	.07	.20
84 Ben Coates	.10	.30
85 Shannon Sharpe	.10	.30
86 Tony Martin	.10	.30
87 Chris Sanders	.07	.20
88 Jamal Anderson	.20	.50
89 Karim Abdul-Jabbar	.20	.50
90 Keyshawn Johnson	.20	.50
91 Terrell Owens	.25	.60
92 Michael Irvin	.20	.50
93 John Friesz	.07	.20
94 Chris Warren	.10	.30
95 Errict Rhett	.07	.20
96 Terry Allen	.20	.50
97 Michael Westbrook	.10	.30
98 Simeon Rice	.10	.30
99 Willie Green	.07	.20
100 Jerome Bettis	.20	.50
101 Reggie White	.20	.50
102 Bert Emanuel	.10	.30
103 Zach Thomas	.20	.50
104 Tim Brown	.20	.50
105 Darnay Scott	.10	.30
106 Terrell Davis	.25	.60
107 Andre Reed	.10	.30
108 Amani Toomer	.10	.30
109 Irving Fryar	.10	.30
110 Joey Galloway	.10	.30
111 Marvin Harrison	.20	.50
112 Derrick Alexander WR	.10	.30
113 Jeff Blake	.10	.30
114 Brad Johnson	.20	.50
115 Eddie Kennison	.10	.30
116 Rae Carruth RC	.07	.20
117 Tony Gonzalez RC	.60	1.50
118 Joey Kent RC	.20	.50
119 Peter Boulware RC	.20	.50
120 Orlando Pace RC	.20	.50
121 David LaFleur RC	.07	.20
122 Darnell Autry RC	.10	.30
123 Tiki Barber RC	1.00	2.50
124 Troy Davis RC	.10	.30
125 Jim Druckenmiller RC	.10	.30
126 Corey Dillon RC	.60	1.50
127 Ike Hilliard RC	.25	.60
128 Reidel Anthony RC	.20	.50
129 Byron Hanspard RC	.10	.30
130 Antowain Smith RC	.40	1.00
131 Jake Plummer RC	.60	1.50
132 Warrick Dunn RC	.50	1.25
133 Bryant Westbrook RC	.07	.20
134 Darrell Russell RC	.07	.20
135 Yatil Green RC	.10	.30
136 Shawn Springs RC	.10	.30
137 Danny Wuerffel RC	.20	.50
138 Brett Favre PP	.40	1.00
139 Emmitt Smith PP	.30	.75
140 Barry Sanders PP	.30	.75
141 Troy Aikman PP	.20	.50
142 Drew Bledsoe PP	.20	.50
143 Jerry Rice PP	.20	.50
144 Dan Marino PP	.40	1.00
145 John Elway PP	.40	1.00
146 Kerry Collins PP	.10	.30
147 Mark Brunell PP	.20	.50
148 Brett Favre CL	.20	.50
149 Dan Marino CL	.20	.50
150 Troy Aikman CL	.20	.50

1997 Pinnacle X-Press Autumn Warriors

COMPLETE SET (150)	100.00	200.00
*STARS: 4X TO 10X BASIC CARDS		
*RCs: 2X TO 5X BASIC CARDS		
STATED ODDS 1:7 HOBBY		

1997 Pinnacle X-Press Bombs Away

COMPLETE SET (18)	50.00	100.00
STATED ODDS 1:19		
1 Brett Favre	8.00	20.00
2 Dan Marino	8.00	20.00
3 Troy Aikman	4.00	10.00
4 Drew Bledsoe	2.50	6.00
5 Kerry Collins	2.00	5.00
6 Mark Brunell	2.50	6.00
7 John Elway	8.00	20.00
8 Steve Young	2.50	6.00
9 Jeff Blake	1.25	3.00
10 Kordell Stewart	2.00	5.00
11 Jeff George	1.25	3.00
12 Rick Mirer	.75	2.00
13 Neil O'Donnell	1.25	3.00
14 Scott Mitchell	1.25	3.00
15 Jim Harbaugh	1.25	3.00
16 Warren Moon	2.00	5.00
17 Trent Dilfer	2.00	5.00
18 Jim Druckenmiller	1.00	2.00

1997 Pinnacle X-Press Divide and Conquer

COMPLETE SET (20)	150.00	400.00
STATED ODDS 1:299		
STATED PRINT RUN 500 SERIAL #'d SETS		
*PROMO CARDS: .1X TO .25X BASIC INSERTS		
1 Tim Biakabutuka	4.00	10.00
2 Karim Abdul-Jabbar	6.00	15.00
3 Jerome Bettis	6.00	15.00
4 Eddie George	6.00	15.00
5 Terrell Davis	8.00	20.00
6 Barry Sanders	20.00	50.00
7 Emmitt Smith	20.00	50.00
8 Brett Favre	25.00	60.00
9 Dan Marino	25.00	60.00
10 Troy Aikman	12.50	30.00
11 Jerry Rice	12.50	30.00
12 Drew Bledsoe	8.00	20.00
13 Kerry Collins	6.00	15.00
14 Mark Brunell	8.00	20.00
15 John Elway	25.00	60.00
16 Steve Young	8.00	20.00
17 Warrick Dunn	10.00	25.00
18 Byron Hanspard	2.50	6.00
19 Troy Davis	2.50	6.00
20 Jeff Blake	4.00	10.00

1997 Pinnacle X-Press Metal Works

COMP.BRONZE SET (20)	50.00	120.00
ONE BRONZE PER MASTER DECK		
*SILVER/400: 2.5X TO 6X BRONZE		
SILVER REDEMPTION/400 ODDS 1:470		
SILVER PRINT RUN 400 SERIAL #'d SETS		
*GOLD/200: 4X TO 10X BRONZE		
GOLD REDEMPTION/200 ODDS 1:950		
GOLD PRINT RUN 200 SERIAL #'d SETS		
1 Troy Aikman	4.00	10.00
2 Emmitt Smith	6.00	15.00
3 Dan Marino	8.00	20.00
4 Brett Favre	8.00	20.00
5 Barry Sanders	6.00	15.00
6 Drew Bledsoe	2.50	6.00
7 Kerry Collins	2.00	5.00
8 Mark Brunell	2.50	6.00
9 John Elway	8.00	20.00
10 Steve Young	2.50	6.00
11 Jerry Rice	4.00	10.00
12 Terrell Davis	2.50	6.00
13 Curtis Martin	2.50	6.00
14 Terry Glenn	2.00	5.00
15 Eddie George	2.00	5.00
16 Jerome Bettis	2.00	5.00
17 Jeff Blake	1.25	3.00
18 Kordell Stewart	2.00	5.00
19 Jeff George	1.25	3.00
20 Deion Sanders	2.00	5.00

1997 Pinnacle X-Press Pursuit of Paydirt

COMPLETE SET (60)	15.00	40.00
STATED ODDS 1:2		
1 Karim Abdul-Jabbar (RB Winner Card)	.75	2.00
2 Troy Aikman	.75	2.00
3 Marcus Allen	.40	1.00
4 Terry Allen	.40	1.00
5 Jamal Anderson	.40	1.00
6 Tony Banks	.25	.60
7 Tiki Barber	2.00	5.00
8 Jerome Bettis	.40	1.00
9 Tim Biakabutuka	.25	.60
10 Jeff Blake	.25	.60
11 Drew Bledsoe	.50	1.25
12 Dave Brown	.15	.40
13 Mark Brunell	.50	1.25
14 Ki-Jana Carter	.15	.40
15 Chris Chandler	.15	.40
16 Kerry Collins	.40	1.00
17 Todd Collins	.15	.40
18 Terrell Davis	.50	1.25
19 Troy Davis	.25	.60
20 Trent Dilfer	.40	1.00
21 Jim Druckenmiller	.25	.60
22 John Elway	1.50	4.00
23 Marshall Faulk	.50	1.25
24 Brett Favre WIN	2.50	5.00
25 Gus Frerotte	.15	.40
26A Eddie George	.40	1.00
26B Eddie George AUTO (signed prize card)	10.00	25.00
27 Jeff George	.25	.60
28 Elvis Grbac	.25	.60
29 Byron Hanspard	.25	.60
30 Jim Harbaugh	.25	.60
31 Garrison Hearst	.25	.60
32 Greg Hill	.15	.40
33 Stan Humphries	.25	.60
34 Brad Johnson	.40	1.00
35 Napoleon Kaufman	.40	1.00
36 Dorsey Levens	.40	1.00
37 Dan Marino	1.50	4.00
38 Curtis Martin	.50	1.25
39 Steve McNair	.50	1.25
40 Natrone Means	.25	.60
41 Rick Mirer	.15	.40
42 Scott Mitchell	.25	.60
43 Warren Moon	.40	1.00
44 Neil O'Donnell	.25	.60
45 Rodney Peete	.15	.40
46 Lawrence Phillips	.15	.40
47 Errict Rhett	.15	.40
48 Rashaan Salaam	.15	.40
49 Barry Sanders	1.25	3.00
50 Heath Shuler	.15	.40
51 Emmitt Smith	1.25	3.00
52 Robert Smith	.25	.60
53 James O.Stewart	.25	.60
54 Kordell Stewart	.40	1.00
55 Vinny Testaverde	.25	.60
56 Thurman Thomas	.40	1.00
57 Chris Warren	.25	.60
58 Ricky Watters	.25	.60
59 Tyrone Wheatley	.25	.60
60 Steve Young	.50	1.25

1992 Playoff Promos

These seven standard-size cards were issued to give collectors a preview of the forthcoming 1992 Playoff series. These cards are distinguished from other cards by the Tekchrome printing process, which enhances the action photography and gives the cards a three-dimensional appearance, and by their thicker (22 point) card stock. The fronts feature glossy full-bleed color player photos that exhibit a metallic-like sheen. The player's name appears in silver lettering in a black bar toward the bottom of the photo. The backs have a full-bleed color close-up photo with the player's name in a team color-coded vertical bar that descends from the top edge. The cards are numbered on the back "X of 6 Promo".

COMPLETE SET (7)	4.80	12.00
1 Calvin Williams	.20	.50
2 John Elway	2.00	5.00
3 Dalton Hilliard	.20	.50
4 Steve Young	1.00	2.50
5 Emmitt Smith	2.40	6.00
6 Mike Golic	.20	.50
NNO Header Intro Card	.20	.50

1992 Playoff

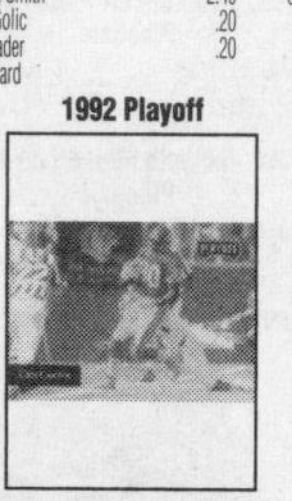

The 150 standard-size cards were issued in eight-card packs. The fronts display full-bleed, metallic player photos accented by the player's name in a black bar near the bottom. The backs have a full-bleed color close-up photo with the player's name in a team color-coded vertical bar that descends from the top edge. A black box centered at the bottom presents a detailed look at the player's performance during a key game in the 1992 season. Twelve different versions of the display box were produced, each featuring a different football player. Rookie Cards in this set include Steve Bono, Terrell Buckley, Willie Davis and Amp Lee.

COMPLETE SET (150)	10.00	25.00
1 Emmitt Smith	4.00	8.00
2 Steve Young	1.50	3.00
3 Jack Del Rio	.08	.25
4 Bobby Hebert	.08	.25
5 Shannon Sharpe	.30	.75
6 Gary Clark	.30	.75
7 Christian Okoye	.08	.25
8 Ernest Givins	.15	.40
9 Mike Horan	.08	.25
10 Dennis Gentry	.08	.25
11 Michael Irvin	.30	.75
12 Eric Floyd	.08	.25
13 Brent Jones	.15	.40
14 Anthony Carter	.15	.40
15 Tony Martin	.15	.40
16 Greg Lewis UER ('Returning' should be/'returned' on back)	.08	.25
17 Todd McNair	.08	.25
18 Earnest Byner	.08	.25
19 Steve Beuerlein	.15	.40
20 Roger Craig	.15	.40
21 Mark Higgs	.08	.25
22 Guy McIntyre	.08	.25
23 Don Warren	.08	.25
24 Alvin Harper	.15	.40
25 Mark Jackson	.08	.25
26 Chris Doleman	.08	.25
27 Jesse Sapolu	.08	.25
28 Tony Tolbert	.08	.25
29 Wendell Davis	.08	.25
30 Dan Saleaumua	.08	.25
31 Jeff Bostic	.08	.25
32 Jay Novacek	.15	.40
33 Cris Carter	.40	1.00
34 Tony Paige	.08	.25
35 Greg Kragen	.08	.25
36 Jeff Dellenbach	.08	.25
37 Keith DeLong	.08	.25
38 Todd Scott	.08	.25
39 Jeff Feagles	.08	.25
40 Mike Saxon	.08	.25
41 Martin Mayhew	.08	.25
42 Steve Bono RC	.30	.75
43 Willie Davis RC	.15	.40
44 Mark Stepnoski	.15	.40
45 Harry Newsome	.08	.25
46 Thane Gash	.08	.25
47 Gaston Green	.08	.25
48 James Washington	.08	.25
49 Kenny Walker	.08	.25
50 Jeff Davidson RC	.08	.25
51 Shane Conlan	.08	.25
52 Richard Dent	.15	.40
53 Haywood Jeffires	.15	.40
54 Harry Galbreath	.08	.25
55 Terry Allen	.30	.75
56 Tommy Barnhardt	.08	.25
57 Mike Golic	.08	.25
58 Dalton Hilliard	.08	.25
59 Danny Copeland	.08	.25
60 Jerry Fontenot RC	.08	.25
61 Kelvin Martin	.08	.25
62 Mark Kelso	.08	.25
63 Wymon Henderson	.08	.25
64 Mark Rypien	.08	.25
65 Bobby Humphrey	.08	.25
66 Rich Gannon UER (Tarkington misspelled; Minneapolis instead of Minnesota on back)	.30	.75
67 Darren Lewis	.08	.25
68 Barry Foster	.15	.40
69 Ken Norton Jr.	.15	.40
70 James Lofton	.15	.40
71 Trace Armstrong	.08	.25
72 Vestee Jackson	.08	.25
73 Clyde Simmons	.08	.25
74 Brad Muster	.08	.25
75 Cornelius Bennett	.15	.40
76 Mike Merriweather	.08	.25
77 John Elway	1.50	4.00
78 Herschel Walker	.15	.40
79 Hassan Jones UER (Minneapolis instead of Minnesota on back)	.08	.25
80 Jim Harbaugh	.30	.75
81 Issiac Holt	.08	.25
82 David Alexander	.08	.25
83 Brian Mitchell	.15	.40
84 Mark Tuinei	.08	.25
85 Tom Rathman	.08	.25
86 Reggie White	.30	.75
87 William Perry	.15	.40
88 Jeff Wright	.08	.25
89 Keith Kartz	.08	.25
90 Andre Waters	.08	.25
91 Darryl Talley	.08	.25
92 Morten Andersen	.08	.25
93 Tom Waddle	.08	.25
94 Felix Wright UER (Minneapolis instead of Minnesota on back)	.08	.25
95 Keith Jackson	.15	.40
96 Art Monk	.15	.40
97 Seth Joyner	.08	.25
98 Steve McMichael	.15	.40
99 Thurman Thomas	.30	.75
100 Warren Moon	.30	.75
101 Tony Casillas	.08	.25
102 Vance Johnson	.08	.25
103 Doug Dawson RC	.08	.25
104 Bill Maas	.08	.25
105 Mark Clayton	.15	.40
106 Hoby Brenner	.08	.25
107 Gary Anderson K	.08	.25
108 Marc Logan	.08	.25
109 Ricky Sanders	.08	.25
110 Vai Sikahema	.08	.25
111 Neil Smith	.30	.75
112 Cody Carlson	.08	.25
113 Jimmie Jones	.08	.25
114 Pat Swilling	.08	.25
115 Neil O'Donnell	.15	.40
116 Chip Lohmiller	.08	.25
117 Mike Croel	.08	.25
118 Pete Metzelaars	.08	.25
119 Ray Childress	.08	.25
120 Fred Banks	.08	.25
121 Derek Kennard	.08	.25
122 Daryl Johnston	.30	.75
123 Lorenzo White UER (Minneapolis instead of Minnesota on back)	.08	.25
124 Hardy Nickerson	.15	.40
125 Derrick Thomas	.30	.75
126 Steve Walsh	.08	.25
127 Doug Widell	.08	.25
128 Calvin Williams	.15	.40
129 Tim Harris	.08	.25
130 Rod Woodson	.30	.75
131 Craig Heyward	.15	.40
132 Barry Word	.08	.25
133 Mark Duper	.08	.25
134 Tim Johnson	.08	.25
135 John Gesek	.08	.25
136 Steve Jackson	.08	.25
137 Dave Krieg	.15	.40
138 Barry Sanders	1.50	4.00
139 Michael Haynes	.15	.40
140 Eric Metcalf	.15	.40
141 Stan Humphries	.30	.75
142 Sterling Sharpe	.30	.75
143 Todd Marinovich	.08	.25
144 Rodney Hampton	.15	.40
145 Rodney Peete	.15	.40
146 Darryl Williams RC	.08	.25
147 Darren Perry RC	.08	.25
148 Terrell Buckley RC	.08	.25
149 Amp Lee RC	.08	.25
150 Ricky Watters	.30	.75

1993 Playoff Promos

Measuring the standard-size, these six cards were issued to preview the design of the 1993 Playoff Collectors Editión football set. Printed on a thicker (22 point) card using the Tekchrome printing process, the action player photos on the fronts are full-bleed and have a metallic sheen to them. The cards are numbered "X of 6 Promo."

COMPLETE SET (6)	4.80	12.00
1 Emmitt Smith	2.40	6.00
2 Barry Foster	.30	.75
3 Quinn Early	.30	.75
4 Tim Brown	.50	1.25
5 Steve Young	1.20	3.00
6 Sterling Sharpe	.30	.75

1993 Playoff

The 1993 Playoff set consists of 315 standard-size cards that were issued in eight-card packs. Subsets featured include The Backs (277-282), Connections (283-292), and Rookies (293-315). Rookie Cards include Jerome Bettis, Drew Bledsoe, Reggie Brooks, Curtis Conway, Garrison Hearst, O.J. McDuffie, Rick Mirer, and Kevin Williams.

COMPLETE SET (315)	10.00	25.00
1 Troy Aikman	.60	1.50
2 Jerry Rice	.75	2.00
3 Keith Jackson	.07	.20
4 Sean Gilbert	.07	.20
5 Jim Kelly	.15	.40
6 Junior Seau	.15	.40
7 Deion Sanders	.40	1.00
8 Joe Montana	1.25	3.00
9 Terrell Buckley	.02	.10
10 Emmitt Smith	1.25	3.00
11 Pete Stoyanovich	.02	.10
12 Randall Cunningham	.15	.40
13 Boomer Esiason	.07	.20
14 Mike Saxon	.02	.10
15 Chuck Cecil	.02	.10
16 Vinny Testaverde	.07	.20
17 Jeff Hostetler	.07	.20
18 Mark Clayton	.02	.10
19 Nick Bell	.02	.10
20 Frank Reich	.07	.20
21 Henry Ellard	.07	.20
22 Andre Reed	.07	.20
23 Mark Ingram	.02	.10
24 Mike Brim	.02	.10
25A Bernie Kosar UER (Name spelled Kozar on both sides)	.07	.20
25B Bernie Kosar COR	.07	.20
26 Jeff George	.15	.40
27 Tommy Maddox	.15	.40
28 Kent Graham RC	.15	.40
29 David Klingler	.02	.10
30 Robert Delpino	.02	.10
31 Kevin Fagan	.02	.10
32 Mark Bavaro	.02	.10
33 Harold Green	.02	.10
34 Shawn McCarthy	.02	.10
35 Ricky Proehl	.02	.10
36 Eugene Robinson	.02	.10
37 Phil Simms	.07	.20
38 David Lang	.02	.10
39 Santana Dotson	.07	.20
40 Brett Perriman	.15	.40
41 Jim Harbaugh	.15	.40
42 Keith Byars	.02	.10
43 Quentin Coryatt	.07	.20
44 Louis Oliver	.02	.10
45 Howie Long	.15	.40
46 Mike Sherrard	.02	.10
47 Earnest Byner	.02	.10
48 Neil Smith	.15	.40
49 Audray McMillian	.02	.10
50 Vaughn Dunbar	.02	.10
51 Ronnie Lott	.07	.20
52 Clyde Simmons	.02	.10
53 Kevin Scott	.02	.10
54 Bubby Brister	.02	.10
55 Randal Hill	.02	.10
56 Pat Swilling	.02	.10
57 Steve Beuerlein	.07	.20
58 Gary Clark	.07	.20
59 Brian Noble	.02	.10
60 Leslie O'Neal	.07	.20
61 Vincent Brown	.02	.10
62 Edgar Bennett	.15	.40
63 Anthony Carter	.07	.20
64 Glenn Cadrez RC UER (Name misspelled Cadez on front)	.02	.10
65 Dalton Hilliard	.02	.10
66 James Lofton	.07	.20
67 Walter Stanley	.02	.10
68 Tim Harris	.02	.10
69 Carl Banks	.02	.10
70 Andre Ware	.02	.10
71 Karl Mecklenburg	.02	.10
72 Russell Maryland	.02	.10
73 Leroy Thompson	.02	.10
74 Tommy Kane	.02	.10
75 Dan Marino	1.25	3.00
76 Darrell Fullington	.02	.10
77 Jessie Tuggle	.02	.10
78 Bruce Smith	.15	.40
79 Neal Anderson	.02	.10
80 Kevin Mack	.02	.10
81 Shane Dronett	.02	.10
82 Nick Lowery	.02	.10
83 Sheldon White	.02	.10
84 Flipper Anderson	.02	.10
85 Jeff Herrod	.02	.10
86 Dwight Stone	.02	.10
87 Dave Krieg	.07	.20
88 Bryan Cox	.02	.10
89 Greg McMurtry	.02	.10
90 Rickey Jackson	.02	.10
91 Ernie Mills	.02	.10
92 Browning Nagle	.02	.10
93 John Taylor	.07	.20
94 Eric Dickerson	.07	.20
95 Johnny Holland	.02	.10
96 Anthony Miller	.07	.20
97 Fred Barnett	.07	.20
98 Ricky Ervins UER (Name misspelled Rickey on back)	.02	.10
99 Leonard Russell	.07	.20
100 Lawrence Taylor	.15	.40
101 Tony Casillas	.02	.10
102 John Elway	1.25	3.00
103 Bennie Blades	.02	.10
104 Harry Sydney	.02	.10
105 Bubba McDowell	.02	.10
106 Todd McNair	.02	.10
107 Steve Smith	.02	.10
108 Jim Everett	.07	.20
109 Bobby Humphrey	.02	.10
110 Rich Gannon	.15	.40
111 Marv Cook	.02	.10
112 Wayne Martin	.02	.10
113 Sean Landeta	.02	.10
114 Brad Baxter UER (Reversed negative on front)	.02	.10
115 Reggie White	.15	.40
116 Johnny Johnson	.02	.10
117 Jeff Graham	.07	.20
118 Darren Carrington RC	.02	.10
119 Ricky Watters	.15	.40
120 Art Monk UER (Reversed negative on back)	.07	.20
121 Cornelius Bennett	.07	.20
122 Wade Wilson	.02	.10
123 Daniel Stubbs	.02	.10
124 Brad Muster	.02	.10
125 Mike Tomczak	.02	.10
126 Jay Novacek	.07	.20
127 Shannon Sharpe	.15	.40
128 Rodney Peete	.02	.10
129 Daryl Johnston	.15	.40
130 Warren Moon	.15	.40
131 Willie Gault	.02	.10
132 Tony Martin	.15	.40
133 Terry Allen	.15	.40
134 Hugh Millen	.02	.10
135 Rob Moore	.07	.20
136 Andy Harmon RC	.07	.20
137 Kelvin Martin	.02	.10
138 Rod Woodson	.15	.40
139 Nate Lewis	.02	.10
140 Darryl Talley	.02	.10
141 Guy McIntyre	.02	.10
142 John L. Williams	.02	.10
143 Brad Edwards	.02	.10
144 Trace Armstrong	.02	.10
145 Kenneth Davis	.02	.10
146 Clay Matthews	.07	.20
147 Gaston Green	.02	.10
148 Chris Spielman	.07	.20
149 Cody Carlson	.02	.10
150 Derrick Thomas	.15	.40
151 Terry McDaniel	.02	.10
152 Kevin Greene	.07	.20
153 Roger Craig	.07	.20
154 Craig Heyward	.07	.20
155 Rodney Hampton	.07	.20
156 Heath Sherman	.02	.10
157 Mark Stepnoski	.02	.10
158 Chris Chandler	.07	.20
159 Rod Bernstine	.02	.10
160 Pierce Holt	.02	.10
161 Wilber Marshall	.02	.10
162 Reggie Cobb	.02	.10
163 Tom Rathman	.02	.10
164 Michael Haynes	.07	.20
165 Nate Odomes	.02	.10
166 Tom Waddle	.02	.10
167 Eric Ball	.02	.10
168 Brett Favre	1.50	4.00
169 Michael Jackson	.07	.20
170 Lorenzo White	.02	.10
171 Cleveland Gary	.02	.10
172 Jay Schroeder	.02	.10
173 Tony Paige	.02	.10
174 Jack Del Rio	.02	.10
175 Jon Vaughn	.02	.10
176 Morten Andersen UER (Misspelled Morton)	.02	.10
177 Chris Burkett	.02	.10
178 Vai Sikahema	.02	.10
179 Ronnie Harmon	.02	.10
180 Amp Lee	.02	.10
181 Chip Lohmiller	.02	.10
182 Steve Broussard	.02	.10
183 Don Beebe	.02	.10
184 Tommy Vardell	.02	.10
185 Keith Jennings	.02	.10
186 Simon Fletcher	.02	.10
187 Mel Gray	.07	.20
188 Vince Workman	.02	.10
189 Haywood Jeffires	.07	.20
190 Barry Word	.02	.10
191 Ethan Horton	.02	.10
192 Mark Higgs	.02	.10
193 Irving Fryar	.07	.20
194 Charles Haley	.07	.20
195 Steve Bono	.07	.20
196 Mike Golic	.02	.10
197 Gary Anderson K	.02	.10
198 Sterling Sharpe	.15	.40
199 Andre Tippett	.02	.10
200 Thurman Thomas	.15	.40
201 Chris Miller	.07	.20
202 Henry Jones	.02	.10
203 Mo Lewis	.02	.10
204 Marion Butts	.02	.10
205 Mike Johnson	.02	.10
206 Alvin Harper	.07	.20
207 Ray Childress	.02	.10
208 Anthony Johnson	.07	.20
209 Tony Bennett	.02	.10
210 Anthony Newman RC	.02	.10
211 Christian Okoye	.02	.10
212 Marcus Allen	.15	.40
213 Jackie Harris	.02	.10
214 Mark Duper	.02	.10
215 Cris Carter	.15	.40
216 John Stephens	.02	.10
217 Barry Sanders	1.00	2.50
218A Herman Moore ERR (First name misspelled Sherman)	.50	1.25
218B Herman Moore COR name spelled correctly	1.00	2.50
219 Marvin Washington	.02	.10
220 Calvin Williams	.07	.20
221 John Randle	.07	.20
222 Marco Coleman	.02	.10
223 Eric Martin	.02	.10
224 Dave Meggett	.02	.10
225 Brian Washington	.02	.10
226 Barry Foster	.07	.20
227 Michael Zordich	.02	.10
228 Stan Humphries	.07	.20
229 Mike Cofer	.02	.10
230 Chris Warren	.07	.20
231 Keith McCants	.02	.10
232 Mark Rypien	.02	.10
233 James Francis	.02	.10
234 Andre Rison	.07	.20
235 William Perry	.07	.20
236 Chip Banks	.02	.10
237 Willie Davis	.15	.40
238 Chris Doleman	.02	.10
239 Tim Brown	.15	.40
240 Darren Perry	.02	.10
241 Johnny Bailey	.02	.10
242 Ernest Givins UER (Spelled Givens on back)	.07	.20
243 John Carney	.02	.10
244 Cortez Kennedy	.07	.20
245 Lawrence Dawsey	.02	.10
246 Martin Mayhew	.02	.10
247 Shane Conlan	.02	.10
248 J.J. Birden	.02	.10
249 Quinn Early	.07	.20
250 Michael Irvin	.15	.40
251 Neil O'Donnell	.15	.40
252 Stan Gelbaugh	.02	.10
253 Drew Hill	.02	.10
254 Wendell Davis	.02	.10
255 Tim Johnson	.02	.10
256 Seth Joyner	.02	.10
257 Derrick Fenner	.02	.10
258 Steve Young	.60	1.50

259 Jackie Slater .02 .10
260 Eric Metcalf .07 .20
261 Rufus Porter .02 .10
262 Ken Norton Jr. .07 .20
263 Tim McDonald .02 .10
264 Mark Jackson .02 .10
265 Hardy Nickerson .07 .20
266 Anthony Munoz .07 .20
267 Mark Carrier WR .07 .20
268 Mike Pritchard .07 .20
269 Steve Emtman .02 .10
270 Ricky Sanders .02 .10
271 Robert Massey .02 .10
272 Pete Metzelaars .02 .10
273 Reggie Langhorne .02 .10
274 Tim McGee .02 .10
275 Reggie Rivers RC .02 .10
276 Jimmie Jones .02 .10
277 Lorenzo White TB .02 .10
278 Emmitt Smith TB .75 2.00
279 Thurman Thomas TB .15 .40
280 Barry Sanders TB .60 1.50
281 Rodney Hampton TB .07 .20
282 Barry Foster TB .07 .20
283 Troy Aikman PC .40 1.00
284 Michael Irvin PC .07 .20
285 Brett Favre PC 1.00 2.50
286 Sterling Sharpe PC .07 .20
287 Steve Young PC .40 1.00
288 Jerry Rice PC .50 1.25
289 Stan Humphries PC .07 .20
290 Anthony Miller PC .07 .20
291 Dan Marino PC .75 2.00
292 Keith Jackson PC .02 .10
293 Patrick Bates RC .02 .10
294 Jerome Bettis RC 4.00 10.00
295 Drew Bledsoe RC 2.50 6.00
296 Tom Carter RC .07 .20
297 Curtis Conway RC .40 1.00
298 John Copeland RC .07 .20
299 Eric Curry RC .02 .10
300 Reggie Brooks RC .07 .20
301 Steve Everitt RC .02 .10
302 Deon Figures RC .02 .10
303 Garrison Hearst RC .75 2.00
304 Qadry Ismail RC UER .15 .40
(Misspelled Quadry
on both sides)
305 Marvin Jones RC .02 .10
306 Lincoln Kennedy RC .02 .10
307 O.J. McDuffie RC .15 .40
308 Rick Mirer RC .15 .40
309 Wayne Simmons RC .02 .10
310 Irv Smith RC .02 .10
311 Robert Smith RC 1.25 3.00
312 Dana Stubblefield RC .15 .40
313 George Teague RC .07 .20
314 Dan Williams RC .02 .10
315 Kevin Williams RC .15 .40
NNO Santa Claus .75 2.00

1993 Playoff Checklists

COMPLETE SET (8) 2.50 6.00
1A Warren Moon UER .30 .75
(Kosar misspelled Kozar)
1B Warren Moon COR .30 .75
2 Barry Sanders 1.25 3.00
3 Deion Sanders .50 1.25
4 Rod Woodson .20 .50
5 Junior Seau .40 1.00
6 Mark Rypien .20 .50
7 Derrick Thomas .30 .75
8 Dallas Players UER .40 1.00
Daryl Johnston
Alvin Harper
Michael Irvin
(Stan Humphries listed as 299;
should be 289)

1993 Playoff Club

COMPLETE SET (7) 6.00 15.00
PC1 Joe Montana 5.00 12.00
PC2 Art Monk .30 .75
PC3 Lawrence Taylor .60 1.50
PC4 Ronnie Lott .30 .75
PC5 Reggie White .60 1.50
PC6 Anthony Munoz .30 .75
PC7 Jackie Slater .15 .40

1993 Playoff Brett Favre

COMPLETE SET (5) 12.50 30.00
COMMON FAVRE (1-5) 4.00 10.00
RANDOM INSERTS IN HOBBY PACKS

1993 Playoff Headliners Redemption

COMPLETE SET (6) 4.00 10.00
ONE SET PER REDEMPTION CARD BY
H1 Brett Favre 3.00 6.00
H2 Sterling Sharpe .25 .60
H3 Emmitt Smith 2.50 5.00
H4 Jerry Rice 1.50 3.00
H5 Thurman Thomas .25 .60
H6 David Klingler .05 .15
NNO Headliner Redemption .10 .30

1993 Playoff Promo Inserts

COMPLETE SET (6) 4.00 10.00
1 Michael Irvin .80 2.00
2 Barry Foster .60 1.50
3 Quinn Early .60 1.50
4 Tim Brown .80 2.00
5 Reggie White .80 2.00
6 Sterling Sharpe .60 1.50

1993 Playoff Rookie Roundup Redemption

COMPLETE SET (10) 7.50 20.00
ONE SET PER REDEMPTION CARD BY
R1 Jerome Bettis 8.00 20.00
R2 Drew Bledsoe 5.00 12.00
R3 Reggie Brooks .15 .40
R4 Derek Brown RBK .07 .20
R5 Garrison Hearst 1.50 4.00
R6 Terry Kirby .07 .20
R7 Glyn Milburn .07 .20
R8 Rick Mirer .30 .75
R9 Roosevelt Potts .07 .20
R10 Dana Stubblefield .30 .75
NNO Rookie Roundup .20 .50
Redemption Card

1993 Playoff Ricky Watters

COMPLETE SET (5) 4.00 10.00
COMMON WATTERS (1-5) 1.00 2.50
RANDOM INSERTS IN RETAIL PACKS

1994 Playoff Prototypes

These six standard-size prototypes feature on their fronts borderless metallic color player action shots. The player's name appears within an oval emblem in one corner. The borderless back carries a color closeup with the player's name, team helmet, and career highlights. Note that there is no mention of prototype on the cards themselves. Each is unnumbered and checklisted below in alphabetical order.

COMPLETE SET (6) 3.20 8.00
1 Marcus Allen .40 1.00
2 Rick Mirer .30 .75
3 Barry Sanders 1.20 3.00
4 Junior Seau .30 .75
5 Sterling Sharpe .30 .75
6 Emmitt Smith 1.00 2.50

1994 Playoff

These 336 standard-size feature borderless card fronts with metallic color player action shots. The cards were issued in eight-card hobby, retail and four-star packs. The player's name appears within an oval emblem in one corner. The borderless backs carry a color closeup with the player's name, team helmet, and career highlights. Topical subsets featured are Sack Pack (226-232), Ground Attack (233-262), Summerall's Best (263-290), and Rookies (291-336). Rookie Cards include Derrick Alexander, Isaac Bruce, Trent Dilfer, Marshall Faulk, William Floyd, Greg Hill, Charles Johnson, Errict Rhett, Darnay Scott and Heath Shuler.

COMPLETE SET (336) 12.50 30.00
1 Joe Montana 1.50 4.00
2 Derrick Thomas .20 .50
3 Dan Marino 1.50 4.00
4 Cris Carter .30 .75
5 Boomer Esiason .10 .30
6 Bruce Smith .20 .50
7 Andre Rison .10 .30
8 Curtis Conway .20 .50
9 Michael Irvin .20 .50
10 Shannon Sharpe .10 .30
11 Pat Swilling .05 .15
12 John Parrella .05 .15
13 Mel Gray .05 .15
14 Ray Childress .05 .15
15 Willie Davis .10 .30
16 Rocket Ismail .10 .30
17 Jim Everett .10 .30
18 Mark Higgs .05 .15
19 Trace Armstrong .05 .15
20 Jim Kelly .20 .50
21 Rob Burnett .05 .15
22 Jay Novacek .10 .30
23 Robert Delpino .05 .15
24 Brett Perriman .10 .30
25 Troy Aikman .75 2.00
26 Reggie White .20 .50
27 Lorenzo White .05 .15
28 Bubba McDowell .05 .15
29 Steve Emtman .05 .15
30 Brett Favre 1.50 4.00
31 Derek Russell .05 .15
32 Jeff Hostetler .10 .30
33 Henry Ellard .10 .30
34 Jack Del Rio .05 .15
35 Mike Saxon .05 .15
36 Rickey Jackson .05 .15
37 Phil Simms .10 .30
38 Quinn Early .10 .30
39 Russell Copeland .05 .15
40 Carl Pickens .10 .30
41 Lance Gunn .05 .15
42 Bernie Kosar .10 .30
43 John Elway 1.50 4.00
44 George Teague .05 .15
45 Nick Lowery .05 .15
46 Haywood Jeffires .10 .30
47 Will Shields .05 .15
48 Daryl Johnston .10 .30
49 Pete Metzelaars .05 .15
50 Warren Moon .20 .50
51 Cornelius Bennett .10 .30
52 Vinny Testaverde .10 .30
53 John Mangum RC .05 .15
54 Tommy Vardell .05 .15
55 Lincoln Coleman RC .05 .15
56 Karl Mecklenburg .05 .15
57 Jackie Harris .05 .15
58 Curtis Duncan .05 .15
59 Quentin Coryatt .05 .15
60 Tim Brown .20 .50
61 Irving Fryar .10 .30
62 Sean Gilbert .05 .15
63 Qadry Ismail .20 .50
64 Irv Smith .05 .15
65 Mark Jackson .05 .15
66 Ronnie Lott .10 .30
67 Henry Jones .05 .15
68 Horace Copeland .05 .15
69 John Copeland .05 .15
70 Mark Carrier WR .10 .30
71 Michael Jackson .10 .30
72 Jason Elam .10 .30
73 Rod Bernstine .05 .15
74 Wayne Simmons .05 .15
75 Cody Carlson .05 .15
76 Alexander Wright .05 .15
77 Shane Conlan .05 .15
78 Keith Jackson .05 .15
79 Sean Salisbury .05 .15
80 Vaughan Johnson .05 .15
81 Rob Moore .10 .30
82 Andre Reed .10 .30
83 David Klinger .05 .15
84 Jim Harbaugh .20 .50
85 John Jett RC .05 .15
86 Sterling Sharpe .10 .30
87 Webster Slaughter .05 .15
88 J.J. Birden .05 .15
89 O.J. McDuffie .20 .50
90 Andre Tippett .05 .15
91 Don Beebe .05 .15
92 Mark Stepnoski .05 .15
93 Neil Smith .10 .30
94 Terry Kirby .20 .50
95 Wade Wilson .05 .15
96 Darryl Talley .05 .15
97 Anthony Smith .05 .15
98 Willie Roaf .05 .15
99 Mo Lewis .05 .15
100 James Washington .05 .15
101 Nate Odomes .05 .15
102 Chris Gedney .05 .15
103 Joe Walter .05 .15
104 Alvin Harper .10 .30
105 Simon Fletcher .05 .15
106 Rodney Peete .05 .15
107 Terrell Buckley .05 .15
108 Jeff George .20 .50
109 James Jett .05 .15
110 Tony Casillas .05 .15
111 Marco Coleman .05 .15
112 Anthony Carter .10 .30
113 Lincoln Kennedy .05 .15
114 Chris Calloway .05 .15
115 Randall Cunningham .20 .50
116 Steve Beuerlein .10 .30
117 Neil O'Donnell .20 .50
118 Stan Humphries .10 .30
119 John Taylor .10 .30
120 Cortez Kennedy .10 .30
121 Santana Dotson .10 .30
122 Thomas Smith .05 .15
123 Kevin Williams .10 .30
124 Andre Ware .05 .15
125 Ethan Horton .05 .15
126 Mike Sherrard .05 .15
127 Fred Barnett .10 .30
128 Ricky Proehl .05 .15
129 Kevin Greene .10 .30
130 John Carney .05 .15
131 Tim McDonald .05 .15
132 Rick Mirer .20 .50
133 Blair Thomas .05 .15
134 Hardy Nickerson .10 .30
135 Heath Sherman .05 .15
136 Andre Hastings .10 .30
137 Randal Hill .05 .15
138 Mike Cofer .05 .15
139 Brian Blades .10 .30
140 Earnest Byner .05 .15
141 Bill Bates .10 .30
142 Junior Seau .20 .50
143 Johnny Bailey .05 .15
144 Dwight Stone .05 .15
145 Todd Kelly .05 .15
146 Tyrone Montgomery .05 .15
147 Herschel Walker .10 .30
148 Gary Clark .10 .30
149 Eric Green .05 .15
150 Steve Young .60 1.50
151 Anthony Miller .10 .30
152 Dana Stubblefield .10 .30
153 Dean Wells RC .05 .15
154 Vincent Brisby .10 .30
155 Chris Chandler .10 .30
156 Clyde Simmons .05 .15
157 Rod Woodson .10 .30
158 Nate Lewis .05 .15
159 Martin Harrison .05 .15
160 Kelvin Martin .05 .15
161 Craig Erickson .05 .15
162 Johnny Mitchell .05 .15
163 Calvin Williams .10 .30
164 Deon Figures .05 .15
165 Tom Rathman .05 .15
166 Rick Hamilton .05 .15
167 John L. Williams .05 .15
168 Demetrius DuBose .05 .15
169 Michael Brooks .05 .15
170 Marion Butts .05 .15
171 Brent Jones .10 .30
172 Bobby Hebert .05 .15
173 Brad Edwards .05 .15
174 David Wyman .05 .15
175 Herman Moore .20 .50
176 LeRoy Butler .05 .15
177 Reggie Langhorne .05 .15
178 Dave Krieg .10 .30
179 Patrick Bates .05 .15
180 Erik Kramer .10 .30
181 Troy Drayton .05 .15
182 Dave Meggett .05 .15
183 Eric Allen .05 .15
184 Mark Bavaro .05 .15
185 Leslie O'Neal .05 .15
186 Jerry Rice .75 2.00
187 Desmond Howard .10 .30
188 Deion Sanders .30 .75
189 Bill Maas .05 .15
190 Frank Wycheck RC .75 2.00
191 Ernest Givins .10 .30
192 Terry McDaniel .05 .15
193 Bryan Cox .05 .15
194 Guy McIntyre .05 .15
195 Pierce Holt .05 .15
196 Fred Stokes .05 .15
197 Mike Pritchard .05 .15
198 Terry Obee .05 .15
199 Mark Collins .05 .15
200 Drew Bledsoe .50 1.25
201 Barry Word .05 .15
202 Derrick Lassic .05 .15
203 Chris Spielman .10 .30
204 John Jurkovic RC .10 .30
205 Ken Norton Jr. .10 .30
206 Dale Carter .05 .15
207 Chris Doleman .05 .15
208 Keith Hamilton .05 .15
209 Andy Harmon .05 .15
210 John Friesz .10 .30
211 Steve Bono .10 .30
212 Mark Rypien .05 .15
213 Ricky Sanders .05 .15
214 Michael Haynes .10 .30
215 Todd McNair .05 .15
216 Leon Lett .05 .15
217 Scott Mitchell .10 .30
218 Mike Morris RC .05 .15
219 Darrin Smith .05 .15
220 Jim McMahon .10 .30
221 Garrison Hearst .20 .50
222 Leroy Thompson .05 .15
223 Darren Carrington .05 .15
224 Pete Stoyanovich .05 .15
225 Chris Miller .05 .15
226 Bruce Smith SP .10 .30
227 Simon Fletcher SP .05 .15
228 Reggie White SP .20 .50
229 Neil Smith SP .10 .30
230 Chris Doleman SP .05 .15
231 Keith Hamilton SP .05 .15
232 Dana Stubblefield SP .06 .16
233 Eric Pegram GA .05 .15
234 Thurman Thomas GA .20 .50
235 Lewis Tillman GA .05 .15
236 Harold Green GA .05 .15
237 Eric Metcalf GA .10 .30
238 Emmitt Smith GA 1.25 3.00
239 Glyn Milburn GA .10 .30
240 Barry Sanders GA 1.25 3.00
241 Edgar Bennett GA .10 .30
242 Gary Brown GA .05 .15
243 Roosevelt Potts GA .05 .15
244 Marcus Allen GA .20 .50
245 Greg Robinson GA .05 .15
246 Jerome Bettis GA .30 .75
247 Keith Byars GA .05 .15
248 Robert Smith GA .20 .50
249 Leonard Russell GA .05 .15
250 Derek Brown RBK GA .05 .15
251 Rodney Hampton GA .10 .30
252 Johnny Johnson GA .05 .15
253 Vaughn Hebron GA .05 .15
254 Ronald Moore GA .05 .15
255 Barry Foster GA .05 .15
256 Natrone Means GA .20 .50
257 Ricky Watters GA .10 .30
258 Chris Warren GA .20 .50
259 Vince Workman GA .05 .15
260 Reggie Brooks GA .05 .15
261 Carolina Panthers Logo .15 .40
262 Jacksonville Jaguars .15 .40
Logo
263 Troy Aikman SB .40 1.00
264 Barry Sanders SB .60 1.50
265 Emmitt Smith SB .60 1.50
266 Michael Irvin SB .20 .50
267 Jerry Rice SB .40 1.00
268 Shannon Sharpe SB .10 .30
269 Bob Kratch SB .05 .15
270 Howard Ballard SB .05 .15
271 Erik Williams SB .05 .15
272 Guy McIntyre SB .05 .15
273 Kelvin Williams SB .10 .30
274 Mel Gray SB .05 .15
275 Eddie Murray SB .05 .15
276 Mark Stepnoski SB .05 .15
277 Tommy Barnhardt SB .05 .15
278 Derrick Thomas SB .10 .30
279 Ken Norton Jr. SB .10 .30
280 Chris Spielman SB .05 .15
281 Deion Sanders SB .20 .50
282 Mark Collins SB .05 .15
283 Bruce Smith SB .10 .30
284 Reggie White SB .20 .50
285 Sean Gilbert SB .05 .15
286 Cortez Kennedy SB .10 .30
287 Steve Atwater SB .05 .15
288 Tim McDonald SB .05 .15
289 Jerome Bettis SB .30 .75
290 Dana Stubblefield SB .10 .30
291 Bert Emanuel RC .20 .50
292 Jeff Burris RC .10 .30
293 Bucky Brooks RC .05 .15
294 Dan Wilkinson RC .10 .30
295 Darnay Scott RC .40 1.00
296 Der.Alexander WR RC .20 .50
297 Antonio Langham RC .10 .30
298 Shante Carver RC .05 .15
299 Shelby Hill RC .05 .15
300 Larry Allen RC .20 .50
301 Johnnie Morton RC .75 2.00
302 Van Malone RC .05 .15
303 Aaron Taylor RC .05 .15
304 Marshall Faulk RC 2.50 6.00
305 Eric Mahlum RC .05 .15
306 Trev Alberts RC .10 .30
307 Greg Hill RC .20 .50
308 Donnell Bennett RC .20 .50
309 Rob Fredrickson RC .10 .30
310 James Folston RC .05 .15
311 Isaac Bruce RC 2.00 5.00
312 Tim Ruddy RC .05 .15
313 Aubrey Beavers RC .05 .15
314 David Palmer RC .20 .50
315 Dewayne Washington RC .10 .30
316 Willie McGinest RC .20 .50
317 Mario Bates RC .20 .50
318 Kevin Lee RC .05 .15
319 Jason Sehorn RC .30 .75
320 Thomas Randolph RC .05 .15
321 Ryan Yarborough RC .05 .15
322 Bernard Williams RC .05 .15
323 Chuck Levy RC .05 .15
324 Jamir Miller RC .10 .30
325 Charles Johnson RC .20 .50
326 Bryant Young RC .30 .75
327 William Floyd RC .20 .50
328 Kevin Mitchell RC .05 .15
329 Sam Adams RC .10 .30
330 Kevin Mawae RC .20 .50
331 Errict Rhett RC .20 .50
332 Trent Dilfer RC .60 1.50
333 Heath Shuler RC .20 .50
334 Aaron Glenn RC .20 .50
335 Todd Steussie RC .10 .30
336 Toby Wright RC .05 .15
NNO Gale Sayers 1.50 4.00
Player's Club
NNO Gale Sayers AUTO 25.00 60.00
signed Player's Club

1994 Playoff Jerome Bettis

COMPLETE SET (5) 15.00 40.00
COMMON BETTIS (1-5) 4.00 10.00
RANDOM INSERTS IN HOBBY PACKS

1994 Playoff Checklists

COMPLETE SET (10) 2.00 5.00
1 Keith Cash .20 .50
2 Kerry Cash .20 .50
3 Qadry Ismail .40 1.00
4 Rocket Ismail .40 1.00
5 Bruce Matthews .20 .50
6 Clay Matthews .20 .50
7 Shannon Sharpe .40 1.00
8 Sterling Sharpe .40 1.00
9 John Taylor .20 .50
10 Keith Taylor .20 .50

1994 Playoff Club

COMPLETE SET (6) 6.00 15.00
STATED ODDS 1:20
PC8 Jerry Rice 6.00 12.00
PC9 Marcus Allen 1.25 3.00
PC10 Howie Long 1.25 3.00
PC11 Clay Matthews .40 1.00
PC12 Richard Dent .75 2.00
PC13 Morten Andersen .40 1.00

1994 Playoff Headliners Redemption

COMPLETE SET (6) 3.00 6.00
ONE SET PER TRADE CARD BY MAIL
1 Tim Brown .75 1.50
2 Bernie Parmalee .20 .50
3 Sterling Sharpe .40 1.00
4 Natrone Means .75 1.50
5 Alvin Harper .40 1.00
6 Deion Sanders 1.25 2.50
NNO Headliners Redemption .20 .50

1994 Playoff Jerry Rice

COMPLETE SET (5) 25.00 60.00
COMMON RICE (1-5) 5.00 12.00
RANDOM INSERTS IN RETAIL PACKS

1994 Playoff Rookie Roundup Redemption

COMPLETE SET (9) 12.50 30.00
ONE SET PER TRADE CARD BY MAIL
1 Heath Shuler' 1.25 3.00
2 David Palmer 1.25 3.00
3 Dan Wilkinson 1.00 2.50
4 Marshall Faulk 5.00 12.00
5 Charlie Garner 2.00 5.00
6 Errict Rhett 1.25 3.00
7 Trent Dilfer 1.50 4.00
8 Antonio Langham 1.00 2.50
9 Gus Frerotte 2.50 6.00
NNO Redemption Card .20 .50

1994 Playoff Barry Sanders

COMPLETE SET (5) 40.00 80.00
COMMON B.SANDERS (1-5) 7.50 20.00
RANDOM INSERTS IN 4 STAR PACKS

1994 Playoff Super Bowl Redemption

COMPLETE SET (6) 8.00 20.00
ONE SET PER TRADE CARD BY MAIL
1 Troy Aikman - 3.00 8.00
2 Emmitt Smith 5.00 12.00
3 Leon Lett .25 .60
4 Michael Irvin .75 2.00
5 James Washington .25 .60
6 Darrin Smith .25 .60
NNO Super Bowl Redemp. .20 .50

1994 Playoff Julie Bell Art

This six-card standard-size set was available through mail redemption. Full-bleed, metallic card fronts contain Julie Bell's artwork of top players. The backs contain a quote from Bell that ties in with the theme on the front. A version marked "SAMPLE" on the back was also produced.

COMPLETE SET (6) 6.00 15.00
*SAMPLE: .4X TO 1X BASIC CARDS
1 Emmitt Smith 5.00 6.00
2 Marcus Allen .80 2.00
3 Junior Seau .50 1.25
4 Barry Sanders 3.00 6.00
5 Rick Mirer .50 1.25
6 Sterling Sharpe .50 1.25

1994 Playoff Super Bowl Promos

This six-card standard-size set was issued by Playoff to commemorate the 1994 Super Bowl. The fronts display borderless color action shots that have a metallic sheen. The player's name appears above and below the Playoff logo, both within a silver-colored oval in a lower corner. The white backs carry the 1994 Super Bowl logo in the center. The cards are numbered in the upper right corner with the word "Promo" printed below the number.

COMPLETE SET (6) 4.80 12.00
1 Jerry Rice 2.00 5.00
2 Daryl Johnston .50 1.25
3 Herschel Walker .50 1.25
4 Reggie White .80 2.00
5 Scott Mitchell .50 1.25
6 Thurman Thomas .80 2.00

1995 Playoff Night of the Stars

This six-card standard-size was given away during the Tuesday night Trade Show preceding the National Sports Collectors Convention in St. Louis. Collectors could also obtain the set by exchanging ten wrappers for one of the six cards at the Playoff Booth. The pro players are pictured in their pro uniforms, and the rookies in their collegiate uniforms. Though each back sports the same geometric design in a different color, all display on a black panel an advertisement for the National Sports Collectors Convention.

COMPLETE SET (6) 8.00 20.00
1 Jerome Bettis 1.20 3.00
2 Ben Coates .80 2.00
3 Deion Sanders 1.60 4.00
4 Ki-Jana Carter .80 2.00
5 Steve McNair 4.00 10.00
6 Errict Rhett .80 2.00

1995 Playoff Super Bowl Card Show

This eight-card standard-size set were given away during the Super Bowl XXIX Card Show. The fronts feature borderless metallic color action player cutouts superposed over a metallic red, silver and gold background. The player's name in silver-foil letters appears in the top left corner. On a black background, the backs carry the player's name, season highlights and the Super Bowl XXIX logo. Only 3,000 of each card was produced.

COMPLETE SET (8) 8.00 20.00
1 Marshall Faulk 3.20 8.00
2 Heath Shuler .80 2.00
3 David Palmer .50 1.25
4 Errict Rhett 1.20 3.00
5 Charlie Garner .80 2.00
6 Irving Spikes .50 1.25
7 Shante Carver .50 1.25
8 Greg Hill 1.00 2.50

1996 Playoff Felt

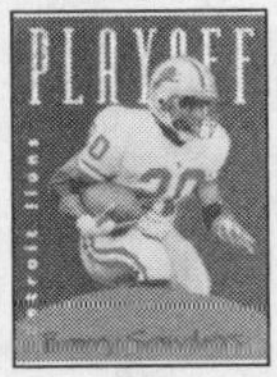

This set was produced for and sold exclusively for QVC television shopping network. Each features a top player produced with an all felt cardfront finish and a player bio on the back. Each player was produced with three different felt colors as listed below.

COMPLETE SET (9) 40.00 80.00
1A Barry Sanders Blue 6.00 15.00
1B Barry Sanders Gray 6.00 15.00
1C Barry Sanders Green 6.00 15.00
2A Deion Sanders Beige 3.00 8.00
2B Deion Sanders Blue 3.00 8.00
2C Deion Sanders Green 3.00 8.00
3A Drew Bledsoe Beige 3.00 8.00
3B Drew Bledsoe Orange 3.00 8.00
3C Drew Bledsoe Red 3.00 8.00

1996 Playoff Leatherbound

This set of leather cards was issued for QVC television shopping network. Each card was produced in both a silver and gold foil version and features a 1996 Leatherbound logo on the cardfront.

COMPLETE SET (6) 30.00 60.00
*GOLD CARDS: 1X TO 2X SILVERS
1 Eddie George 6.00 15.00
2 John Elway 15.00 30.00
3 Marshall Faulk 6.00 15.00
4 Reggie White 3.00 8.00
5 Kordell Stewart 3.00 8.00
6 Jerome Bettis 3.00 8.00

1996 Playoff National Promos

This seven-card set was distributed at the 1996 National Sports Collectors Convention in Anaheim as part of a wrapper redemption program. Collectors could redeem three wrappers from any Playoff product for one card, or a foil box worth of wrappers for a complete set. The Kordell Stewart card was only available as part of the complete set offer.

COMPLETE SET (7) 16.00 40.00
1 Kordell Stewart 3.20 8.00
2 Curtis Martin 3.20 8.00
3 Tyrone Wheatley 2.00 5.00
4 Joey Galloway 3.20 8.00
5 Steve McNair 3.20 8.00
6 Kerry Collins 1.20 3.00
7 Napoleon Kaufman 2.40 6.00

1996 Playoff Super Bowl Card Show

This six-card set features borderless color action player photos superimposed over an Arizona desert background. The player's name and Super Bowl Card Show logo rounds out the front design. The backs carry the card name, player's name, and a highlight from the 1995 season. Playoff offered one card to each Card Show attendee each day in exchange for one Playoff football card wrapper. Ten wrappers were good for a complete set any day of the show. Although the cards carry a 1995 copyright date, the cards were released in January 1996 at the Tempe, Arizona Super Bowl Card Show. Reportedly, 5500 sets were produced.

COMPLETE SET (6) 6.00 15.00
1 Deion Sanders 1.20 3.00
2 Rashaan Salaam .50 1.25
3 Garrison Hearst .50 1.25
4 Robert Brooks .50 1.25
5 Barry Sanders 3.20 8.00
6 Errict Rhett .50 1.25

1997 Playoff Sports Cards Picks

Playoff produced this set distributed by Sports Cards magazine as a subscription premium. It includes a short dream pick line-up of the staff's favorite players.

COMPLETE SET (6) 3.20 8.00
1 Brett Favre .80 2.00
2 Barry Sanders .80 2.00
3 Terrell Davis .80 2.00
4 Jerry Rice .40 1.00
5 Deion Sanders .30 .75
6 Kordell Stewart .40 1.00

1997 Playoff Super Bowl Card Show

Playoff produced this seven-card set released at the 1997 Super Bowl Card Show in New Orleans. All cards, except Terrell Davis, were available each day of the show in exchange for three Playoff card wrappers opened at the Playoff booth. Two different players were made available each day Thursday through Saturday with all six available on Sunday. Terrell Davis was only available by opening and redeeming a foil box worth of wrappers for a complete seven-card set. The cards are unnumbered and listed below alphabetically.

COMPLETE SET (7) 8.00 20.00
1 Terry Allen 1.00 2.50
2 Jerome Bettis 1.00 2.50
3 Terrell Davis 3.20 8.00
4 Marshall Faulk 1.50 4.00
5 Eddie George 1.50 4.00
6 Deion Sanders 1.25 3.00
7 Reggie White 1.00 2.50

1998 Playoff Super Bowl Card Show

Playoff produced this seven-card set for release at the 1998 Super Bowl Card Show in San Diego. The cards were available each day of the show in exchange for various Playoff card wrappers opened at the Playoff booth.

COMPLETE SET (7) 8.00 20.00
1 Trent Dilfer .50 1.25
2 Tony Martin .30 .75
3 Terrell Davis 3.20 8.00
4 Antonio Freeman 1.00 2.50
5 Herschel Walker .30 .75
6 Kordell Stewart 1.60 4.00
7 Drew Bledsoe 1.60 4.00

1998 Playoff Unsung Heroes Banquet

The 1998 Playoff Unsung Heroes Banquet set consisted of 31 player cards and a checklist card. These standard-sized cards are horizontal and have "Unsung" ghosted on the top of the card and "Hero" overprinted on the bottom, with the players name in script in the lower right hand corner. The back of the cards have the players name on the top and a short description why they were the unsung hero for 1997 on their team. This set was also sponsored by Sports Cards Magazine and EA Sports. There were reportedly only 1250 sets available, and those were distributed at the banquet. This set is noteworthy in that it contains an Eddie Robinson card, which is one of the few collector items that he has graced during his legendary career.

COMPLETE SET (32)	8.00	20.00
1 Frank Sanders	.75	2.00
2 Chuck Smith	.25	.60
3 Earnest Byner	.25	.60
4 Phil Hansen	.25	.60
5 Greg Kragen	.25	.60
6 Carl Reeves	.25	.60
7 Eric Bieniemy	.25	.60
8 Darren Woodson	.40	1.00
9 Howard Griffith	.25	.60
10 Kevin Glover	.25	.60
11 William Henderson	.25	.60
12 Jason Belser	.25	.60
13 Keenan McCardell	.40	1.00
14 Kimble Anders	.40	1.00
15 O.J. McDuffie	.40	1.00
16 Randall McDaniel	.25	.60
17 Troy Brown	.40	1.00
18 Richard Harvey	.25	.60
19 Charles Way	.40	1.00
20 Mo Lewis	.25	.60
21 Russell Maryland	.25	.60
22 Michael Zordich	.25	.60
23 Tim Lester	.25	.60
24 Ryan McNeil	.25	.60
25 Rodney Harrison	.40	1.00
26 Gary Plummer	.25	.60
27 Dean Wells	.25	.60
28 Brad Culpepper	.25	.60
29 Rodney Thomas	.25	.60
30 Marvcus Patton	.25	.60
NNO Checklist	.25	.60
NNO Eddie Robinson CO	.75	2.00

1999 Playoff Sanders/Williams/Davis Promo

Playoff Corporation issued this promo card featuring Barry Sanders, Ricky Williams, and Terrell Davis primarily to distributors in 1999. The card features the three players along with logos for the Donruss, Leaf, Playoff, and Score card brands. Each was serial numbered of 500-cards with just 50 being autographed by all three players.

1 Barry Sanders	7.50	15.00
Ricky Williams		
Terrell Davis		
1AU Barry Sanders AUTO/50*	200.00	400.00
Ricky Williams AUTO		
Terrell Davis AUTO		

2000 Playoff Hawaii Promo Autographs

This set of signed cards was produced by Playoff and released as Promos to attendees of the Kit Young Hawaii Trade Conference. Each card features an authentic signature from one or more star players along with Playoff's four brand logos across the top of the cardfront against a Green background. The cardbacks contain the four logos again with "Hawaii 2000" in large letters with serial numbering of 10-sets made. A brief bio on each player also is included. A Gold (serial numbered of 1) parallel set of each card was also produced.

1 John Elway	300.00	500.00
2 Brett Favre	250.00	400.00
3 Edgerrin James	175.00	300.00
4 Peyton Manning	250.00	400.00
5 Dan Marino	300.00	500.00
6 Randy Moss	250.00	400.00
7 Jerry Rice	250.00	400.00
8 Emmitt Smith	250.00	400.00
9 Kurt Warner	250.00	400.00
10 Ricky Williams	175.00	300.00
11 John Elway	240.00	600.00
Brett Favre		
12 John Elway	240.00	600.00
Dan Marino		
13 John Elway	300.00	600.00
Jerry Rice		
14 Brett Favre	300.00	600.00
Jerry Rice		
15 Brett Favre	240.00	600.00
Emmitt Smith		
16 Edgerrin James	240.00	600.00
Peyton Manning		
17 Edgerrin James	200.00	500.00
Emmitt Smith		
18 Edgerrin James	200.00	500.00
Ricky Williams		
19 Peyton Manning	240.00	600.00
Dan Marino		
20 Peyton Manning	240.00	600.00
Kurt Warner		
21 Dan Marino	240.00	600.00
Kurt Warner		
22 Randy Moss	200.00	500.00
Jerry Rice		
23 Randy Moss	240.00	600.00
Kurt Warner		
24 Randy Moss	200.00	500.00
Ricky Williams		
25 Emmitt Smith	200.00	500.00
Ricky Williams		
26 Dan Marino	400.00	700.00
Jerry Rice		
Emmitt Smith		
27 Randy Moss	280.00	700.00
Kurt Warner		
Ricky Williams		
28 Edgerrin James	300.00	750.00
Peyton Manning		
Randy Moss		
29 John Elway	300.00	750.00
Brett Favre		
Dan Marino		
30 John Elway	280.00	700.00
Peyton Manning		
Kurt Warner		
31 Edgerrin James	240.00	600.00
Emmitt Smith		
Ricky Williams		
32 Brett Favre	400.00	700.00
Randy Moss		
Jerry Rice		
33 John Elway	300.00	750.00
Peyton Manning		
Dan Marino		
34 John Elway	320.00	800.00
Dan Marino		
Jerry Rice		
Emmitt Smith		
35 Edgerrin James	280.00	700.00
Randy Moss		
Kurt Warner		
Ricky Williams		
36 Brett Favre	300.00	750.00
Randy Moss		
Jerry Rice		
Kurt Warner		
37 Edgerrin James	300.00	750.00
Peyton Manning		
Emmitt Smith		
Ricky Williams		

2000 Playoff Super Bowl Card Show

Playoff produced this seven-card set for release at the 2000 Super Bowl Card Show. The cards were available each day of the show in exchange for wrappers from various 2000 Playoff products opened at the Playoff booth.

COMPLETE SET (7)	6.00	12.00
SB1 Dan Marino	1.00	2.50
SB2 Peyton Manning	.75	2.00
SB3 Kurt Warner	1.50	4.00
SB4 Emmitt Smith	.60	1.50
SB5 Fred Taylor	.40	1.00
SB6 Steve McNair	.40	1.00
SB7 Ricky Williams	.60	1.50

2000 Playoff Unsung Heroes Banquet

The 2000 Playoff Unsung Heroes Banquet set consists of 31-player cards. They were released at the April 7, 2000 Unsung Heroes Banquet.

COMPLETE SET (31)	25.00	50.00
UH1 Ronald McKinnon	.75	2.00
UH2 Tim Dwight	1.25	3.00
UH3 Bennie Thompson	.75	2.00
UH4 Phil Hansen	.75	2.00
UH5 Patrick Jeffers	1.25	3.00
UH6 Marcus Robinson	1.25	3.00
UH7 Oliver Gibson	.75	2.00
UH8 Lomas Brown	.75	2.00
UH9 Dexter Coakley	.75	2.00
UH10 Olandis Gary	1.50	4.00
UH11 James Jones	.75	2.00
UH12 Corey Bradford	1.25	3.00
UH13 Ken Dilger	.75	2.00
UH14 Lonnie Marts	.75	2.00
UH15 Tony Gonzalez	1.50	4.00
UH16 Damon Huard	1.25	3.00
UH17 Robert Griffith	.75	2.00
UH18 Troy Brown	1.25	3.00
UH19 La'Roi Glover	.75	2.00
UH20 Sam Garnes	.75	2.00
UH21 Kevin Mawae	.75	2.00
UH22 Lincoln Kennedy	.75	2.00
UH23 Eric Bieniemy	.75	2.00
UH24 Josh Miller	.75	2.00
UH25 John Parrella	.75	2.00
UH26 Charlie Garner	1.25	3.00
UH27 Walter Jones	.75	2.00
UH28 Kurt Warner	4.00	8.00
UH29 Shaun King	.75	2.00
UH30 Jason Fisk	.75	2.00
UH31 Sam Shade	.75	2.00

2001 Playoff Unsung Heroes Banquet

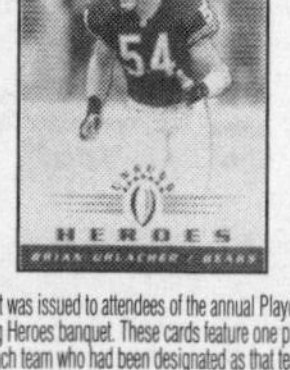

This set was issued to attendees of the annual Playoff Unsung Heroes banquet. These cards feature one player from each team who had been designated as that team's unsung hero. These cards were issued to a stated print run of 2000 serial numbered sets.

COMPLETE SET (31)	25.00	50.00
UH1 Bob Christian	.75	2.00
UH2 Ronald McKinnon	.75	2.00
UH3 Trent Dilfer	1.25	3.00
UH4 Shawn Price	.75	2.00
UH5 Mike Minter	1.25	3.00
UH6 Brian Urlacher	5.00	10.00
UH7 Takeo Spikes	.75	2.00
UH8 Wali Rainer	.75	2.00
UH9 Larry Allen	.75	2.00
UH10 Howard Griffith	.75	2.00
UH11 James Jones	.75	2.00
UH12 Russell Maryland	.75	2.00
UH13 Tarik Glenn	.75	2.00
UH14 Daimon Shelton	.75	2.00
UH15 Mike Maslowski	.75	2.00
UH16 Brian Walker	.75	2.00
UH17 Chris Walsh	.75	2.00
UH18 Tedy Bruschi	2.00	5.00
UH19 La'Roi Glover	.75	2.00
UH20 Greg Comella	.75	2.00
UH21 Richie Anderson	.75	2.00
UH22 Greg Biekert	.75	2.00
UH23 Cecil Martin	.75	2.00
UH24 John Fiala	.75	2.00
UH25 John Parrella	.75	2.00
UH26 Bryant Young	.75	2.00
UH27 Fabien Bownes	.75	2.00
UH28 Ray Agnew	.75	2.00
UH29 John Lynch	1.25	3.00
UH30 Lorenzo Neal	.75	2.00
UH31 James Thrash	1.25	3.00

2004 Playoff Super Bowl XXXVIII Jerseys

These three cards were released by Donruss Playoff at the 2004 Super Bowl XXXVIII Card Show in Houston. Each features a swatch(s) from an actual game used jersey(s) for the featured two players.

COMPLETE SET (3)	30.00	60.00
*PRIME: .6X TO 1.5X BASIC JSY		
SB1 David Carr	12.00	20.00
SB2 Warren Moon	12.00	20.00
SB3 David Carr	18.00	30.00
Warren Moon		

2007 Playoff Pop Warner Super Bowl Promos

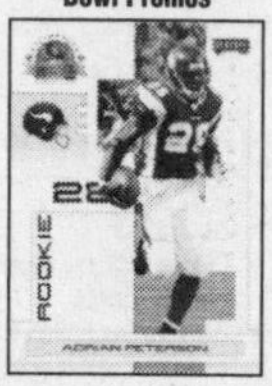

1 Tony Romo	1.25	3.00
2 Brett Favre	2.00	5.00
3 Vince Young	.75	2.00
4 Adrian Peterson	3.00	8.00
5 Randy Moss	1.00	2.50
6 Calvin Johnson	3.00	8.00

2008 Playoff Super Bowl XLII Card Show

1 Vince Young	.75	2.00
2 Brett Favre	2.50	6.00
3 Tony Romo	1.25	3.00
4 Peyton Manning	1.50	4.00
5 Randy Moss	1.00	2.50
6 Ben Roethlisberger	1.00	2.50
8 Brian Urlacher	1.00	2.50
9 Brady Quinn	.75	2.00
10 Calvin Johnson	1.00	2.50
11 Adrian Peterson	1.50	4.00
12 Reggie Bush	1.00	2.50

1993 Playoff Contenders Promos

This six-card standard-size set was issued to herald the release of the 150-card 1993 Playoff Contenders set. The fronts display borderless color action shots that have a metallic sheen. The player's name appears below the Playoff logo, both within a silver-colored box in a lower corner. The horizontal back carries a color player close-up on the left, and a broad team color-coded stripe on the right, in which appears the player's name, his team's helmet, and season highlights. The cards are numbered on the back by Roman numerals.

COMPLETE SET (6)	4.00	10.00
1 Drew Bledsoe	1.00	2.50
2 Neil Smith	.20	.50
3 Rick Mirer	.30	.75
4 Rodney Hampton	.20	.50
5 Barry Sanders	1.20	3.00
6 Emmitt Smith	1.20	3.00

1993 Playoff Contenders

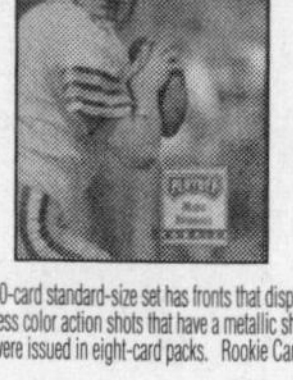

This 150-card standard-size set has fronts that display borderless color action shots that have a metallic sheen. Cards were issued in eight-card packs. Rookie Cards include Jerome Bettis, Drew Bledsoe, Vincent Brisby, Reggie Brooks, Curtis Conway, Garrison Hearst, Terry Kirby, Natrone Means, O.J. McDuffie, Rick Mirer, Ron Moore, Robert Smith and Kevin Williams.

COMPLETE SET (150)	7.50	20.00
1 Brett Favre	1.50*	3.00
2 Thurman Thomas	.15	.40
3 Barry Word	.02	.10
4 Herman Moore	.15	.40
5 Reggie Langhorne	.02	.10
6 Wilber Marshall	.02	.10
7 Ricky Watters	.15	.40
8 Marcus Allen	.15	.40
9 Jeff Hostetler	.07	.20
10 Steve Young	.40	1.00
11 Bobby Hebert	.02	.10
12 David Klingler	.02	.10
13 Craig Heyward	.07	.20
14 Andre Reed	.07	.20
15 Tommy Vardell	.02	.10
16 Anthony Carter	.07	.20
17 Mel Gray	.07	.20
18 Dan Marino	1.00	2.50
19 Haywood Jeffires	.07	.20
20 Joe Montana	1.00	2.50
21 Tim Brown	.15	.40
22 Jim McMahon	.07	.20
23 Scott Mitchell	.15	.40
24 Rickey Jackson	.02	.10
25 Troy Aikman	.60	1.50
26 Rodney Hampton	.07	.20
27 Fred Barnett	.07	.20
28 Gary Clark	.07	.20
29 Barry Foster	.07	.20
30 Brian Blades	.07	.20
31 Tim McDonald	.02	.10
32 Kelvin Martin	.02	.10
33 Henry Jones	.02	.10
34 Erric Pegram	.07	.20
35 Don Beebe	.02	.10
36 Eric Metcalf	.07	.20
37 Charles Haley	.07	.20
38 Robert Delpino	.02	.10
39 Leonard Russell UER	.07	.20
(Detroit Lions logo on back)		
40 Jackie Harris	.02	.10
41 Ernest Givins	.07	.20
42 Willie Davis	.15	.40
43 Alexander Wright	.02	.10
44 Keith Byars	.02	.10
45 Dave Meggett	.02	.10
46 Johnny Johnson	.02	.10
47 Mark Bavaro	.02	.10
48 Seth Joyner	.02	.10
49 Junior Seau	.15	.40
50 Emmitt Smith	1.25	2.50
51 Shannon Sharpe	.15	.40
52 Rodney Peete	.02	.10
53 Andre Rison	.07	.20
54 Cornelius Bennett	.07	.20
55 Mark Carrier WR	.07	.20
56 Mark Clayton	.02	.10
57 Warren Moon	.15	.40
58 J.J. Birden	.02	.10
59 Howie Long	.15	.40
60 Irving Fryar	.07	.20
61 Mark Jackson	.02	.10
62 Eric Martin	.02	.10
63 Herschel Walker	.07	.20
64 Cortez Kennedy	.07	.20
65 Steve Beuerlein	.07	.20
66 Jim Kelly	.15	.40
67 Bernie Kosar	.07	.20
68 Pat Swilling	.02	.10
69 Michael Irvin	.15	.40
70 Harvey Williams	.07	.20
71 Steve Smith	.02	.10
72 Wade Wilson	.02	.10
73 Phil Simms	.07	.20
74 Vinny Testaverde	.07	.20
75 Barry Sanders	1.00	2.50
76 Ken Norton Jr.	.07	.20
77 Rod Woodson	.15	.40
78 Webster Slaughter	.02	.10
79 Derrick Thomas	.15	.40
80 Mike Sherrard	.02	.10
81 Calvin Williams	.07	.20
82 Jay Novacek	.07	.20
83 Michael Brooks	.02	.10
84 Randall Cunningham	.15	.40
85 Chris Warren	.07	.20
86 Johnny Mitchell	.02	.10
87 Jim Harbaugh	.15	.40
88 Rod Bernstine	.02	.10
89 John Elway	1.00	2.50
90 Jerry Rice	.60	1.50
91 Brent Jones	.07	.20
92 Cris Carter	.15	.40
93 Alvin Harper	.07	.20
94 Horace Copeland RC	.07	.20
95 Rocket Ismail	.07	.20
96 Darrin Smith RC	.07	.20
97 Reggie Brooks RC	.07	.20
98 Demetrius DuBose RC	.02	.10
99 Eric Curry RC	.02	.10
100 Rick Mirer RC	.15	.40
101 Carlton Gray RC UER	.02	.10
(Name spelled Grey on front)		
102 Dana Stubblefield RC	.15	.40
103 Todd Kelly RC	.02	.10
104 Natrone Means RC	.15	.40
105 Darrien Gordon RC	.02	.10
106 Deon Figures RC	.02	.10
107 Garrison Hearst RC	.50	1.25
108 Ronald Moore RC	.07	.20
109 Leonard Renfro RC	.02	.10
110 Lester Holmes	.02	.10
111 Vaughn Hebron RC	.02	.10
112 Marvin Jones RC	.02	.10
113 Irv Smith RC	.02	.10
114 Willie Roaf RC	.07	.20
115 Derek Brown RBK RC	.07	.20
116 Vincent Brisby RC	.15	.40
117 Drew Bledsoe RC	1.50	4.00
118 Gino Torretta RC	.07	.20
119 Robert Smith RC	.75	2.00
120 Qadry Ismail RC	.15	.40
121 O.J. McDuffie RC	.15	.40
122 Terry Kirby RC	.15	.40
123 Troy Drayton RC	.07	.20
124 Jerome Bettis RC	2.50	6.00
125 Patrick Bates RC	.02	.10
126 Roosevelt Potts RC	.02	.10
127 Tom Carter RC	.07	.20
128 Patrick Robinson RC	.02	.10
129 Brad Hopkins RC	.02	.10
130 George Teague RC	.07	.20
131 Wayne Simmons RC	.02	.10
132 Mark Brunell RC	1.00	2.50
133 Ryan McNeil RC	.15	.40
134 Dan Williams RC	.02	.10
135 Glyn Milburn RC	.15	.40
136 Kevin Williams RC	.15	.40
137 Derrick Lassic RC	.02	.10
138 Steve Everitt RC	.02	.10
139 Lance Gunn RC	.02	.10
140 John Copeland RC	.07	.20
141 Curtis Conway RC	.40	1.00
142 Thomas Smith RC	.07	.20
143 Russell Copeland RC	.07	.20
144 Lincoln Kennedy RC	.02	.10
145 Boomer Esiason CL	.02	.10
146 Neil Smith CL	.02	.10
147 Jack Del Rio CL	.02	.10
148 Morten Andersen CL	.02	.10
149 Sterling Sharpe CL	.07	.20
150 Reggie White CL	.07	.20

1993 Playoff Contenders Rick Mirer

COMPLETE SET (5)	6.00	15.00
COMMON MIRER (1-5)	1.50	4.00

1993 Playoff Contenders Rookie Contenders

COMPLETE SET (10)	20.00	50.00
STATED ODDS 1:40		
1 Jerome Bettis	15.00	40.00
2 Drew Bledsoe UER	10.00	25.00
(Text states he played for Washington; he played for Washington St.)		
3 Reggie Brooks	.50	1.25
4 Derek Brown RBK	.50	1.25
5 Garrison Hearst	3.00	8.00
6 Vaughn Hebron	.25	.60
7 Qadry Ismail	1.00	2.50
8 Derrick Lassic	.25	.60
9 Glyn Milburn	1.00	2.50
10 Dana Stubblefield	1.00	2.50

1994 Playoff Contenders Promos

This seven-card standard-size set was issued to herald the release of the 120-card 1994 Playoff Contenders series. The fronts display borderless color action shots that have a metallic sheen. The player's name in silver foil appears in a grass border on the bottom. The team name is printed in the upper portion of the photo. The backs carry a color player close-up with season highlights. The cards are unnumbered and checklisted below in alphabetical order.

COMPLETE SET (7)	2.00	5.00
1 Qadry Ismail	.40	1.00
2 Daryl Johnston	.40	1.00
3 John Jurkovic	.20	.50
4 Eric Metcalf	.40	1.00
5 Andre Reed	.40	1.00
6 Calvin Williams	.20	.50
7 Title Card	.20	.50

1994 Playoff Contenders

Distributed through hobby stores in the U.S. and Canada only, this 120-card set measures the standard size. A subset "Draft Picks" (94-120) is featured in this set. Rookie Cards include Derrick Alexander, Lake Dawson, Trent Dilfer, Bert Emanuel, Marshall Faulk, William Floyd, Gus Frerotte, Greg Hill, Charles Johnson, Byron Bam Morris, Errict Rhett and Heath Shuler.

COMPLETE SET (120)	7.50	20.00
1 Drew Bledsoe	.40	1.00
2 Barry Sanders	1.00	2.50
3 Jerry Rice	.60	1.50
4 Rod Woodson	.07	.20
5 Irving Fryar	.07	.20
6 Charles Haley	.07	.20
7 Chris Warren	.07	.20
8 Craig Erickson	.02	.10
9 Eric Metcalf	.07	.20
10 Marcus Allen	.15	.40
11 Chris Miller	.02	.10
12 Andre Rison	.07	.20
13 Art Monk	.07	.20
14 Calvin Williams	.07	.20
15 Shannon Sharpe	.07	.20
16 Rodney Hampton	.07	.20
17 Marion Butts	.02	.10
18 John Jurkovic RC	.07	.20
19 Jim Kelly	.15	.40
20 Emmitt Smith	1.00	2.50
21 Jeff Hostetler	.07	.20
22 Barry Foster	.02	.10
23 Boomer Esiason	.07	.20
24 Jim Harbaugh	.15	.40
25 Joe Montana	1.25	3.00
26 Jeff George	.15	.40
27 Warren Moon	.15	.40
28 Steve Young	.50	1.25
29 Randall Cunningham	.15	.40
30 Shawn Jefferson	.02	.10
31 Cortez Kennedy	.07	.20
32 Reggie Brooks	.07	.20
33 Alvin Harper	.07	.20
34 Brent Jones	.07	.20
35 O.J. McDuffie	.15	.40
36 Jerome Bettis	.25	.60
37 Daryl Johnston	.07	.20
38 Herman Moore	.15	.40
39 Dave Meggett	.02	.10
40 Reggie White	.15	.40
41 Junior Seau	.15	.40
42 Dan Marino	1.25	3.00
43 Scott Mitchell	.07	.20
44 John Elway	1.25	3.00
45 Troy Aikman	.60	1.50
46 Terry Allen	.07	.20
47 David Klingler	.02	.10
48 Stan Humphries	.07	.20
49 Rick Mirer	.15	.40
50 Neil O'Donnell	.15	.40
51 Keith Jackson	.02	.10
52 Ricky Watters	.07	.20
53 Dave Brown	.07	.20
54 Neil Smith	.07	.20
55 Johnny Mitchell	.02	.10
56 Jackie Harris	.02	.10
57 Terry Kirby	.15	.40
58 Willie Davis	.07	.20
59 Rob Moore	.07	.20
60 Nate Newton	.02	.10
61 Deion Sanders	.30	.75
62 John Taylor	.07	.20
63 Sterling Sharpe	.07	.20
64 Natrone Means	.15	.40
65 Steve Beuerlein	.07	.20
66 Erik Kramer	.07	.20
67 Qadry Ismail	.15	.40
68 Johnny Johnson	.02	.10
69 Herschel Walker	.07	.20
70 Mark Stepnoski	.02	.10
71 Brett Favre	1.25	3.00
72 Dana Stubblefield	.07	.20
73 Bruce Smith	.15	.40
74 Leroy Hoard	.02	.10
75 Steve Walsh	.02	.10
76 Jay Novacek	.07	.20
77 Derrick Thomas	.15	.40
78 Keith Byars	.02	.10
79 Ben Coates	.07	.20
80 Lorenzo Neal	.02	.10
81 Ronnie Lott	.07	.20
82 Tim Brown	.15	.40
83 Michael Irvin	.15	.40
84 Ronald Moore	.02	.10
85 Andre Reed	.07	.20
86 James Jett	.02	.10
87 Curtis Conway	.15	.40
88 Bernie Parmalee RC	.15	.40
89 Keith Cash	.02	.10
90 Russell Copeland	.02	.10
91 Kevin Williams	.07	.20
92 Gary Brown	.02	.10
93 Thurman Thomas	.15	.40
94 Jamir Miller RC	.07	.20
95 Bert Emanuel RC	.15	.40
96 Bucky Brooks RC	.02	.10
97 Jeff Burris RC	.07	.20
98 Antonio Langham RC	.07	.20
99 Derrick Alexander WR RC	.15	.40
100 Dan Wilkinson RC	.07	.20
101 Shante Carver RC	.02	.10
102 Johnnie Morton RC	.75	2.00
103 LeShon Johnson RC	.07	.20
104 Marshall Faulk RC	2.50	6.00
105 Greg Hill RC	.15	.40
106 Lake Dawson RC	.07	.20
107 Irving Spikes RC	.07	.20
108 David Palmer RC	.15	.40
109 Willie McGinest RC	.15	.40
110 Joe Johnson RC	.02	.10
111 Aaron Glenn RC	.15	.40
112 Charlie Garner RC	.60	1.50
113 Charles Johnson RC	.15	.40
114 Byron Bam Morris RC	.07	.20
115 Bryant Young RC	.25	.60
116 William Floyd RC	.15	.40
117 Trent Dilfer RC	.60	1.50
118 Errict Rhett RC	.15	.40
119 Heath Shuler RC	.15	.40
120 Gus Frerotte RC	.75	2.00

1994 Playoff Contenders Back-to-Back

COMPLETE SET (60)	400.00	800.00
STATED ODDS 1:24		
1 Joe Montana	40.00	100.00
Dan Marino		
2 Drew Bledsoe	25.00	60.00
John Elway		
3 Jerry Rice	15.00	40.00
Sterling Sharpe		
4 Barry Sanders	50.00	100.00
Emmitt Smith		
5 Troy Aikman	25.00	60.00
Steve Young		
6 Erik Kramer	3.00	8.00
Steve Walsh		
7 Nate Newton	4.00	10.00
Bruce Smith		
8 Johnny Mitchell	6.00	15.00
Tim Brown		
9 Neil O'Donnell	3.00	8.00
Jay Novacek		
10 Herman Moore	6.00	15.00
Calvin Williams		
11 Alvin Harper	6.00	15.00
Michael Irvin		
12 Jim Harbaugh	4.00	10.00
Curtis Conway		
13 Brett Favre	25.00	60.00
LeShon Johnson		
14 Eric Metcalf	10.00	20.00
Marshall Faulk		
15 Qadry Ismail	4.00	10.00
David Palmer		
16 Deion Sanders	7.50	20.00
Andre Rison		
17 Jackie Harris	4.00	10.00
Errict Rhett		
18 Keith Jackson	3.00	8.00
Irving Spikes		
19 Dave Meggett	3.00	8.00
Jeff Burris		
20 Dana Stubblefield	4.00	10.00
William Floyd		
21 Randall Cunningham	6.00	15.00
Reggie White		
22 Shannon Sharpe	3.00	8.00
Keith Cash		
23 Marcus Allen	6.00	15.00
Derrick Thomas		
24 Irving Fryar	3.00	8.00
Russell Copeland		
25 Johnny Johnson	3.00	8.00
Ben Coates		
26 John Taylor	4.00	10.00
Brent Jones		
27 Terry Kirby	4.00	10.00
Bernie Parmalee		
28 Ricky Watters	6.00	15.00
Ronnie Lott		
29 Scott Mitchell	3.00	8.00
James Jett		
30 O.J. McDuffie	4.00	10.00
Keith Byars		
31 Shawn Jefferson	4.00	10.00
Andre Reed		
32 Rodney Hampton	4.00	10.00
Lorenzo Neal		
33 Chris Miller	3.00	8.00
Ronald Moore		
34 Charles Haley	6.00	15.00
Thurman Thomas		
35 Herschel Walker	3.00	8.00
Leroy Hoard		
36 Natrone Means	4.00	10.00
Stan Humphries		
37 Willie Davis	4.00	10.00
Kevin Williams WR		
38 Dave Brown	3.00	8.00
Gary Brown		
39 Jerome Bettis	7.50	20.00
Terry Allen		
40 Cortez Kennedy	6.00	15.00
Junior Seau		
41 David Klingler	4.00	10.00
Derrick Alexander WR		
42 Chris Warren	4.00	10.00
Bucky Brooks		
43 Mark Stepnoski	4.00	10.00
Greg Hill		
44 Steve Beuerlein	6.00	15.00
Johnnie Morton		
45 Rob Moore	4.00	10.00
James Jett		
46 Neil Smith	4.00	10.00
Lake Dawson		
47 Rick Mirer	4.00	10.00
Bryant Young		
48 Daryl Johnston	6.00	15.00
Charlie Garner		
49 Reggie Brooks	5.00	12.00
Gus Frerotte		
50 Barry Foster	4.00	10.00
Byron Bam Morris		
51 Art Monk	6.00	15.00
Heath Shuler		
52 Craig Erickson	6.00	15.00
Trent Dilfer		
53 Jeff George	4.00	10.00
Bert Emanuel		
54 Rod Woodson	4.00	10.00
Antonio Langham		
55 Marion Butts	6.00	15.00
Willie McGinest		
56 John Jurkovic	3.00	8.00
Dan Wilkinson		
57 Jim Kelly	6.00	15.00
Shante Carver		
58 Jeff Hostetler	3.00	8.00
Charles Johnson		
59 Boomer Esiason	3.00	8.00
Jamir Miller		
60 Warren Moon	4.00	10.00
Joe Johnson		

1994 Playoff Contenders Rookie Contenders

COMPLETE SET (6)	20.00	40.00
STATED ODDS 1:48		
1 Heath Shuler	1.50	4.00
2 Trent Dilfer	2.50	6.00
3 David Palmer	1.00	2.50
4 Marshall Faulk	10.00	25.00
5 Charlie Garner	2.50	6.00
6 Dan Wilkinson	1.00	2.50

1994 Playoff Contenders Sophomore Contenders

COMPLETE SET (6)	12.50	30.00
STATED ODDS 1:48		
1 Drew Bledsoe	6.00	15.00
2 Jerome Bettis	4.00	10.00
3 Reggie Brooks	1.25	3.00
4 Rick Mirer	2.50	6.00
5 Natrone Means	2.50	6.00
6 O.J.McDuffie	2.50	6.00

1994 Playoff Contenders Throwbacks

COMPLETE SET (30)	40.00	100.00
STATED ODDS 1:12		
1 Larry Centers	.40	1.00
2 Andre Rison	.40	1.00
3 Jim Kelly	.75	2.00
4 Curtis Conway	.75	2.00
5 David Klingler	.20	.50
6 Vinny Testaverde	.75	2.00
7 Troy Aikman	3.00	8.00
8 Emmitt Smith	5.00	12.00
9 John Elway	6.00	15.00
10 Barry Sanders	5.00	12.00
11 Sterling Sharpe	.40	1.00
12 Gary Brown	.20	.50
13 Jim Harbaugh	.75	2.00
14 Joe Montana	6.00	15.00
15 Tim Brown	.75	2.00
16 Chris Miller	.20	.50
17 Dan Marino	6.00	15.00
18 Terry Allen	.40	1.00
19 Marion Butts	.20	.50
20 Jim Everett	.20	.50
21 Dave Brown	.40	1.00
22 Johnny Johnson	.20	.50
23 Randall Cunningham	.75	2.00
24 Barry Foster	.20	.50
25 Stan Humphries	.40	1.00
26 Jerry Rice	3.00	8.00
27 Steve Young	2.50	6.00
28 Chris Warren	.40	1.00
29 Errict Rhett	.75	2.00
30 John Friesz	.20	.50

1995 Playoff Contenders

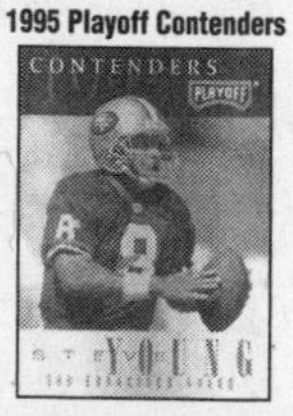

The 1995 Playoff Contenders was issued in one series totalling 150 cards. The six-card pack retailed for $3.75. The set features the topical subset: Rookies (121-150). Rookie Cards include Kerry Collins, Terrell Davis, Joey Galloway, Curtis Martin, Steve McNair, Rashaan Salaam, Kordell Stewart, J.J. Stokes, Yancey Thigpen, Tamarick Vanover and Michael Westbrook.

COMPLETE SET (150)	10.00	25.00
1 Steve Young	.40	1.00
2 Jeff Blake RC	.30	.75
3 Rick Mirer	.07	.20
4 Brett Favre	1.25	2.50
5 Heath Shuler	.07	.20
6 Steve Bono	.07	.20
7 John Elway	1.00	2.50
8 Troy Aikman	.50	1.25
9 Rodney Peete	.02	.10
10 Gus Frerotte	.07	.20
11 Drew Bledsoe	.30	.75
12 Jim Kelly	.15	.40
13 Dan Marino	1.00	2.50

14 Errict Rhett .07 .20
15 Jeff Hostetler .07 .20
16 Erik Kramer .02 .10
17 Jim Everett .02 .10
18 Elvis Grbac .15 .40
19 Scott Mitchell .07 .20
20 Barry Sanders .75 2.00
21 Deion Sanders .30 .75
22 Emmitt Smith .75 2.00
23 Garrison Hearst .15 .40
24 Mario Bates .07 .20
25 Mark Brunell .30 .75
26 Robert Smith .15 .40
27 Rodney Hampton .07 .20
28 Marshall Faulk .60 1.50
29 Greg Hill .07 .20
30 Bernie Parmalee .07 .20
31 Natrone Means .07 .20
32 Marcus Allen .15 .40
33 Byron Bam Morris .02 .10
34 Edgar Bennett .07 .20
35 Vincent Brisby .02 .10
36 Jerome Bettis .15 .40
37 Craig Heyward .07 .20
38 Anthony Miller .07 .20
39 Curtis Conway .15 .40
40 William Floyd .07 .20
41 Chris Warren .07 .20
42 Terry Kirby .07 .20
43 Herschel Walker .07 .20
44 Eric Metcalf .07 .20
45 Darnay Scott .07 .20
46 Jackie Harris .02 .10
47 Dana Stubblefield .07 .20
48 Daryl Johnston .07 .20
49 Dave Meggett .02 .10
50 Ricky Watters .07 .20
51 Ken Norton .07 .20
52 Boomer Esiason .07 .20
53 Lake Dawson .07 .20
54 Eric Green .02 .10
55 Junior Seau .15 .40
56 Yancey Thigpen RC .15 .40
57 James Jett .07 .20
58 Leonard Russell .02 .10
59 Brent Jones .02 .10
60 Trent Dilfer .15 .40
61 Terance Mathis .07 .20
62 Jeff George .07 .20
63 Alvin Harper .02 .10
64 Terry Allen .07 .20
65 Stan Humphries .07 .20
66 Robert Green .02 .10
67 Bryce Paup .07 .20
68 Tamarick Vanover RC .15 .40
69 Desmond Howard .07 .20
70 Derek Loville .02 .10
71 Dave Brown .07 .20
72 Carl Pickens .07 .20
73 Gary Clark .02 .10
74 Gary Brown .02 .10
75 Brett Perriman .07 .20
76 Charlie Garner .15 .40
77 Ben Coates .07 .20
78 Bruce Smith .15 .40
79 Eric Pegram .07 .20
80 Jerry Rice .50 1.25
81 Tim Brown .15 .40
82 John Taylor .02 .10
83 Will Moore .02 .10
84 Jay Novacek .07 .20
85 Kevin Williams .07 .20
86 Rocket Ismail .07 .20
87 Robert Brooks .15 .40
88 Michael Irvin .15 .40
89 Mark Chmura .15 .40
90 Shannon Sharpe .07 .20
91 Henry Ellard .07 .20
92 Reggie White .15 .40
93 Isaac Bruce .30 .75
94 Charles Haley .07 .20
95 Jake Reed .07 .20
96 Pete Metzelaars .02 .10
97 Dave Krieg .02 .10
98 Tony Martin .07 .20
99 Charles Jordan RC .07 .20
100 Bert Emanuel .15 .40
101 Andre Rison .07 .20
102 Jeff Graham .02 .10
103 O.J. McDuffie .15 .40
104 Randall Cunningham .15 .40
105 Harvey Williams .02 .10
106 Cris Carter .15 .40
107 Irving Fryar .07 .20
108 Jim Harbaugh .07 .20
109 Bernie Kosar .02 .10
110 Charles Johnson .07 .20
111 Warren Moon .07 .20
112 Neil O'Donnell .07 .20
113 Fred Barnett .07 .20
114 Herman Moore .15 .40
115 Chris Miller .02 .10
116 Vinny Testaverde .07 .20
117 Craig Erickson .02 .10
118 Qadry Ismail .07 .20
119 Willie Davis .07 .20
120 Michael Jackson .07 .20
121 Stoney Case RC .15 .40
122 Frank Sanders RC .15 .40
123 Todd Collins RC 1.00 2.50
124 Kerry Collins RC .75 2.00
125 Sherman Williams RC .02 .10
126 Terrell Davis RC 1.00 2.50
127 Luther Elliss RC .02 .10
128 Steve McNair RC 1.25 3.00
129 Chris Sanders RC .15 .40
130 Ki-Jana Carter RC .15 .40
131 Rodney Thomas RC .15 .40
132 Tony Boselli RC .15 .40
133 Rob Johnson RC .40 1.00
134 James O. Stewart RC .50 1.25
135 Chad May RC .02 .10
136 Eric Bjornson RC .07 .20
137 Tyrone Wheatley RC .50 1.25
138 Kyle Brady RC .15 .40
139 Curtis Martin RC 1.25 3.00
140 Eric Zeier RC .15 .40
141 Ray Zellars RC .07 .20
142 Napoleon Kaufman RC .50 1.25
143 Mike Mamula RC .07 .20
144 Mark Bruener RC .07 .20
145 Kordell Stewart RC .60 1.50
146 J.J. Stokes RC .15 .40
147 Joey Galloway RC .60 1.50
148 Warren Sapp RC .60 1.50
149 Michael Westbrook RC .15 .40
150 Rashaan Salaam RC .15 .40

1995 Playoff Contenders Back-to-Back

COMPLETE SET (75) 150.00 400.00
STATED ODDS 1:19
1 Dan Marino 10.00 25.00
Troy Aikman
2 Marshall Faulk 10.00 25.00
Emmitt Smith
3 John Elway 12.50 30.00
Brett Favre
4 Drew Bledsoe 6.00 15.00
Steve Young
5 Errict Rhett 7.50 20.00
Barry Sanders
6 Jerry Rice 6.00 15.00
Deion Sanders
7 Rick Mirer 3.00 8.00
Jeff Blake
8 Tim Brown 3.00 8.00
Michael Irvin
9 Ricky Watters 2.00 5.00
Chris Warren
10 Vincent Brisby 3.00 8.00
Herman Moore
11 Eric Metcalf 2.00 5.00
James Jett
12 Terance Mathis 2.00 5.00
Henry Ellard
13 Isaac Bruce 5.00 12.00
Curtis Conway
14 Jeff Hostetler 2.00 5.00
Steve Bono
15 Harvey Williams 2.00 5.00
Greg Hill
16 Jerome Bettis 4.00 10.00
Garrison Hearst
17 Brent Jones 2.00 5.00
Jay Novacek
18 Bruce Smith 3.00 8.00
Reggie White
19 Shannon Sharpe 2.00 5.00
Eric Green
20 Jeff George 2.00 5.00
Gus Frerotte
21 Scott Mitchell 1.25 3.00
Erik Kramer
22 Jim Kelly 3.00 8.00
Warren Moon
23 Ben Coates 2.00 5.00
Mark Chmura
24 Heath Shuler 3.00 8.00
Trent Dilfer
25 Edgar Bennett 2.00 5.00
Craig Heyward
26 Dave Brown 1.25 3.00
Jim Everett
27 Andre Rison 1.25 3.00
Bert Emanuel
28 Alvin Harper 1.25 3.00
Robert Brooks
29 Tony Martin 2.00 5.00
Desmond Howard
30 Fred Barnett 1.25 3.00
Rodney Peete
31 William Floyd 2.00 5.00
Natrone Means
32 Rocket Ismail 1.25 3.00
Brett Perriman
33 Irving Fryar 2.00 5.00
Cris Carter
34 Darnay Scott 2.00 5.00
Tamarick Vanover
35 Dana Stubblefield 2.00 5.00
Charles Haley
36 Ken Norton 1.25 3.00
Bryce Paup
37 Herschel Walker 3.00 8.00
Marcus Allen
38 Terry Allen 1.25 3.00
Leonard Russell
39 Derek Loville 3.00 8.00
Junior Seau
40 Charles Johnson 2.00 5.00
Lake Dawson
41 Charles Jordan 1.25 3.00
Kevin Williams
42 Carl Pickens 2.00 5.00
Jeff Graham
43 O.J.McDuffie 2.00 5.00
Anthony Miller
44 Jim Harbaugh 2.00 5.00
Elvis Grbac
45 Terry Kirby 2.00 5.00
Dave Meggett
46 Stan Humphries 1.25 3.00
Dave Krieg
47 Boomer Esiason 4.00 10.00
Mark Brunell
48 Vinny Testaverde 1.25 3.00
Craig Erickson
49 Bernie Kosar 1.25 3.00
Randall Cunningham
50 Charlie Garner 1.25 3.00
Eric Pegram
51 Gary Clark 1.25 3.00
Will Moore
52 Willie Davis 2.00 5.00
Qadry Ismail
53 Chris Miller 1.25 3.00
Neil O'Donnell
54 Robert Smith 2.00 5.00
Mario Bates
55 Bernie Parmalee 2.00 5.00
Rodney Hampton
56 Daryl Johnston 2.00 5.00
Byron Bam Morris
57 Jake Reed 2.00 5.00
Jackie Harris
58 Pete Metzelaars 1.25 3.00
John Taylor
59 Michael Jackson 3.00 8.00
Yancey Thigpen
60 Robert Green 1.25 3.00
Gary Brown
61 N.Kaufman 3.00 8.00
Rashaan Salaam
62 Kyle Brady 1.25 3.00
Mark Bruener
63 Rodney Thomas 3.00 8.00
Ki-Jana Carter
64 Steve McNair 7.50 20.00
Chad May
65 J.J.Stokes 3.00 8.00
Frank Sanders
66 Warren Sapp 1.25 3.00
Mike Mamula
67 Stoney Case 3.00 8.00
Kordell Stewart
68 Curtis Martin 10.00 25.00
Terrell Davis
69 Chris Sanders 3.00 8.00
Sherman Williams
70 Eric Bjornson 2.00 5.00
James O. Stewart
71 Ray Zellars 3.00 8.00
Tyrone Wheatley
72 Luther Elliss 3.00 8.00
Tony Boselli
73 Todd Collins 6.00 15.00
Rob Johnson
74 Eric Zeier 2.00 5.00
Kerry Collins
75 Michael Westbrook 3.00 8.00
Joey Galloway

1995 Playoff Contenders Hog Heaven

COMPLETE SET (30) 100.00 250.00
STATED ODDS 1:48
HH1 Troy Aikman 8.00 20.00
HH2 Marcus Allen 2.50 6.00
HH3 Jeff Blake 5.00 12.00
HH4 Drew Bledsoe 5.00 12.00
HH5 Steve Bono 1.25 3.00
HH6 Isaac Bruce 5.00 12.00
HH7 Trent Dilfer 2.50 6.00
HH8 John Elway 15.00 40.00
HH9 Marshall Faulk 10.00 25.00
HH10 Brett Favre 15.00 40.00
HH11 Gus Frerotte 1.25 3.00
HH12 Irving Fryar 1.25 3.00
HH13 Jeff George 1.25 3.00
HH14 Rodney Hampton 1.25 3.00
HH15 Garrison Hearst 2.50 6.00
HH16 Michael Irvin 2.50 6.00
HH17 Erik Kramer .60 1.50
HH18 Dan Marino 15.00 40.00
HH19 Natrone Means 1.25 3.00
HH20 Errict Rhett 1.25 3.00
HH21 Jerry Rice 8.00 20.00
HH22 Barry Sanders 12.50 30.00
HH23 Deion Sanders 5.00 12.00
HH24 Shannon Sharpe 1.25 3.00
HH25 Emmitt Smith 12.50 30.00
HH26 Robert Smith 2.50 6.00
HH27 Chris Warren 1.25 3.00
HH28 Reggie White 2.50 6.00
HH29 Harvey Williams .60 1.50
HH30 Steve Young 6.00 15.00

1995 Playoff Contenders Rookie Kickoff

COMPLETE SET (30) 50.00 120.00
STATED ODDS 1:24
RK01 Eric Bjornson .25 .60
RK02 Tony Boselli .50 1.25
RK03 Kyle Brady .50 1.25
RK04 Mark Bruener .25 .60
RK05 Ki-Jana Carter .50 1.25
RK06 Stoney Case .50 1.25
RK07 Kerry Collins 2.50 6.00
RK08 Todd Collins 1.50 4.00
RK09 Terrell Davis 3.00 8.00
RK010 Luther Elliss .10 .30
RK011 Joey Galloway 2.00 5.00
RK012 Rob Johnson 1.25 3.00
RK013 Napoleon Kaufman 1.50 4.00
RK014 Mike Mamula .25 .60
RK015 Curtis Martin 4.00 10.00
RK016 Chad May .10 .30
RK017 Steve McNair 4.00 10.00
RK018 Rashaan Salaam .50 1.25
RK019 Chris Sanders .50 1.25
RK020 Frank Sanders .50 1.25
RK021 Warren Sapp 2.00 5.00
RK022 James O. Stewart 1.50 4.00
RK023 Kordell Stewart 2.00 5.00
RK024 J.J. Stokes .50 1.25
RK025 Rodney Thomas .50 1.25
RK026 Michael Westbrook .50 1.25
RK027 Tyrone Wheatley 1.50 4.00
RK028 Sherman Williams .10 .30
RK029 Eric Zeier .50 1.25
RK030 Ray Zellars .25 .60

1996 Playoff Contenders Leather

The 1996 Playoff Contenders Leather set was issued in one series totalling 100 cards. The three-card packs retail for $6.99 each, and contained one Leather, one parallel Pennant, and one parallel Open Field card. The fronts of the Leather cards feature a player image on a genuine leather background with a borderless player portrait on the backs. The set is divided into three color-coded insertion ratios: 50 "Scarce" greens which are the most common, 25 "Rare" purples with a ration of 1:11, and 25 "Ultra Rare" reds with a 1:22 ratio.

COMPLETE SET (100) 100.00 250.00
1 Brett Favre R 12.50 30.00
2 Steve Young P 4.00 10.00
3 Herman Moore P 1.00 2.50
4 Jim Harbaugh P 1.00 2.50
5 Curtis Martin R 5.00 12.00
6 Junior Seau G 1.00 2.50
7 John Elway R 12.50 30.00
8 Troy Aikman R 6.00 15.00
9 Terry Allen G .60 1.50
10 Kordell Stewart R 2.50 6.00
11 Drew Bledsoe R 4.00 10.00
12 Jim Kelly R 2.50 6.00
13 Dan Marino R 12.50 30.00
14 Andre Rison G .60 1.50
15 Jeff Hostetler G .30 .75
16 Scott Mitchell G .60 1.50
17 Carl Pickens G .60 1.50
18 Larry Centers R 1.25 3.00
19 Craig Heyward G .30 .75
20 Barry Sanders R 10.00 25.00
21 Deion Sanders P 3.00 8.00
22 Emmitt Smith R 10.00 25.00
23 Rashaan Salaam P 1.00 2.50
24 Mario Bates G .60 1.50
25 Lawrence Phillips R 1.25 3.00
26 Napoleon Kaufman P 1.50 4.00
27 Rodney Hampton G .60 1.50
28 Marshall Faulk R 3.00 8.00
29 Trent Dilfer G 1.00 2.50
30 Leeland McElroy G .60 1.50
31 Marcus Allen G 1.00 2.50
32 Ricky Watters R 1.25 3.00
33 Karim Abdul-Jabbar R 2.50 6.00
34 Herschel Walker G .60 1.50
35 Thurman Thomas G 1.00 2.50
36 Jerome Bettis G 1.00 2.50
37 Gus Frerotte P 1.00 2.50
38 Neil O'Donnell P 1.00 2.50
39 Rick Mirer G .60 1.50
40 Mike Alstott P 2.50 6.00
41 Vinny Testaverde P 1.00 2.50
42 Derek Loville G .30 .75
43 Ben Coates G .60 1.50
44 Steve McNair G 2.00 5.00
45 Bobby Engram G 1.00 2.50
46 Yancey Thigpen G .60 1.50
47 Lake Dawson G .30 .75
48 Terrell Davis G 2.00 5.00
49 Kerry Collins P 1.50 4.00
50 Eric Metcalf G .30 .75
51 Stanley Pritchett P .50 1.25
52 Robert Brooks G 1.00 2.50
53 Isaac Bruce R 2.50 6.00
54 Tim Brown G 1.00 2.50
55 Edgar Bennett G .60 1.50
56 Warren Moon G .60 1.50
57 Jerry Rice R 6.00 15.00
58 Michael Westbrook G 1.00 2.50
59 Keyshawn Johnson R 2.50 6.00
60 Steve Bono G .30 .75
61 Derrick Mayes G .60 1.50
62 Erik Kramer G .30 .75
63 Rodney Peete G .30 .75
64 Eddie Kennison P 1.50 4.00
65 Derrick Thomas G 1.00 2.50
66 Joey Galloway P 1.50 4.00
67 Amani Toomer G 1.00 2.50
68 Reggie White P 1.50 4.00
69 Heath Shuler R 1.25 3.00
70 Dave Brown R .75 2.00
71 Tony Banks G 1.00 2.50
72 Chris Warren R 1.25 3.00
73 J.J. Stokes R 2.50 6.00
74 Rickey Dudley G 1.00 2.50
75 Stan Humphries G .60 1.50
76 Jason Dunn G .30 .75
77 Tyrone Wheatley P 1.50 4.00
78 Jim Everett R .75 2.00
79 Cris Carter P 1.50 4.00
80 Alex Van Dyke G .60 1.50
81 O.J. McDuffie G .60 1.50
82 Mark Chmura G .60 1.50
83 Terry Glenn G 1.00 2.50
84 Boomer Esiason G .60 1.50
85 Bruce Smith G .60 1.50
86 Curtis Conway P 1.50 4.00
87 Ki-Jana Carter G .60 1.50
88 Tamarick Vanover G .60 1.50
89 Michael Jackson G .60 1.50
90 Mark Brunell P 4.00 10.00
91 Tim Biakabutuka P 1.50 4.00
92 Anthony Miller P .50 1.25
93 Marvin Harrison P 5.00 12.00
94 Jeff George R 1.25 3.00
95 Jeff Blake P 1.50 4.00
96 Eddie George R 4.00 10.00
97 Eric Moulds G 1.00 2.50
98 Mike Tomczak P .50 1.25
99 Chris Sanders P 1.00 2.50
100 Chris Chandler G .60 1.50

1996 Playoff Contenders Leather Accents

COMMON CARD (1-100) 3.00 8.00
SEMISTARS 6.00 15.00
UNLISTED STARS 10.00 25.00
STATED ODDS 1:216
1 Brett Favre 40.00 100.00
2 Steve Young 15.00 40.00
5 Curtis Martin 12.50 30.00
7 John Elway 40.00 100.00
8 Troy Aikman 20.00 50.00
11 Drew Bledsoe 12.50 30.00
13 Dan Marino 40.00 100.00
20 Barry Sanders 30.00 80.00
21 Deion Sanders 12.50 30.00
22 Emmitt Smith 30.00 80.00
28 Marshall Faulk 12.50 30.00
44 Steve McNair 12.50 30.00
48 Terrell Davis 12.50 30.00
57 Jerry Rice 20.00 50.00
93 Marvin Harrison 12.50 30.00

1996 Playoff Contenders Open Field Foil

The 1996 Playoff Contenders Open Field Foil set was issued in one series totalling 100 cards. The three-card packs retail for $6.99 each, and contained one Open Field Foil, one parallel Pennant, and one parallel Leather card. This holographic mini card set features a color player image on a football field background. The set is divided into three color-coded insertion ratios: 50 "Scarce" greens which are the most common, 25 "Rare" purples with a ration of 1:11, and 25 "Ultra Rare" reds with a 1:22 ratio.

COMPLETE SET (100) 50.00 120.00
1 Brett Favre P 5.00 12.00
2 Steve Young R 4.00 10.00
3 Herman Moore P .60 1.50
4 Jim Harbaugh G .50 1.25
5 Curtis Martin P 2.00 5.00
6 Junior Seau P 1.25 3.00
7 John Elway P 5.00 12.00
8 Troy Aikman R 5.00 12.00
9 Terry Allen G .50 1.25
10 Kordell Stewart P 1.25 3.00
11 Drew Bledsoe G 1.25 3.00
12 Jim Kelly G .75 2.00
13 Dan Marino R 10.00 25.00
14 Andre Rison P .60 1.50
15 Jeff Hostetler G .30 .75
16 Scott Mitchell R 1.25 3.00
17 Carl Pickens G .50 1.25
18 Larry Centers G .50 1.25
19 Craig Heyward R .60 1.50
20 Barry Sanders R 7.50 20.00
21 Deion Sanders P 1.50 4.00
22 Emmitt Smith P 4.00 10.00
23 Rashaan Salaam R 1.25 3.00
24 Mario Bates P .40 1.00
25 Lawrence Phillips P .60 1.50
26 Napoleon Kaufman G .75 2.00
27 Rodney Hampton G .50 1.25
28 Marshall Faulk R 2.00 5.00
29 Trent Dilfer G .75 2.00
30 Leeland McElroy R 1.25 3.00
31 Marcus Allen G .75 2.00
32 Ricky Watters P .60 1.50
33 Karim Abdul-Jabbar P 1.25 3.00
34 Herschel Walker R 1.25 3.00
35 Thurman Thomas G .75 2.00
36 Jerome Bettis G .75 2.00
37 Gus Frerotte R 1.25 3.00
38 Neil O'Donnell G .50 1.25
39 Rick Mirer G .50 1.25
40 Mike Alstott G 1.00 2.50
41 Vinny Testaverde G .50 1.25
42 Derek Loville G .30 .75
43 Ben Coates G .50 1.25
44 Steve McNair G 1.25 3.00
45 Bobby Engram R 2.00 5.00
46 Yancey Thigpen G .50 1.25
47 Lake Dawson P .40 1.00
48 Terrell Davis G 1.25 3.00
49 Kerry Collins P 1.25 3.00
50 Eric Metcalf G .30 .75
51 Stanley Pritchett G .30 .75
52 Robert Brooks P .60 1.50
53 Isaac Bruce P 1.25 3.00
54 Tim Brown P 1.25 3.00
55 Edgar Bennett G .50 1.25
56 Warren Moon P 1.25 3.00
57 Jerry Rice P 2.50 6.00
58 Michael Westbrook G .75 2.00
59 Keyshawn Johnson P 1.25 3.00
60 Steve Bono G .30 .75
61 Derrick Mayes R 2.00 5.00
62 Erik Kramer G .30 .75
63 Rodney Peete G .30 .75
64 Eddie Kennison G .75 2.00
65 Derrick Thomas G .75 2.00
66 Joey Galloway R 1.25 3.00
67 Amani Toomer R 2.50 6.00
68 Reggie White R 2.00 5.00
69 Heath Shuler P .60 1.50
70 Dave Brown G .30 .75
71 Tony Banks R 2.00 5.00
72 Chris Warren G .50 1.25
73 J.J. Stokes G .75 2.00
74 Rickey Dudley R 2.00 5.00
75 Stan Humphries G .50 1.25
76 Jason Dunn R .60 1.50
77 Tyrone Wheatley G .50 1.25
78 Jim Everett G .30 .75
79 Cris Carter G .75 2.00
80 Alex Van Dyke R 1.25 3.00
81 O.J. McDuffie P 1.25 3.00
82 Mark Chmura G .50 1.25
83 Terry Glenn R 2.00 5.00
84 Boomer Esiason G .50 1.25
85 Bruce Smith G .50 1.25
86 Curtis Conway G .50 1.25
87 Ki-Jana Carter R 1.25 3.00
88 Tamarick Vanover P .60 1.50
89 Michael Jackson R 1.25 3.00
90 Mark Brunell G 1.25 3.00
91 Tim Biakabutuka G .75 2.00
92 Anthony Miller G .50 1.25
93 Marvin Harrison G 2.50 6.00
94 Jeff George G .50 1.25
95 Jeff Blake G .75 2.00
96 Eddie George P 1.50 4.00
97 Eric Moulds R 2.50 6.00
98 Mike Tomczak R .60 1.50
99 Chris Sanders G .50 1.25
100 Chris Chandler G .50 1.25

1996 Playoff Contenders Pennants

The 1996 Playoff Contenders Pennants set was issued in one series totalling 100 cards. The three-card packs retail for $6.99 each, and contained one Pennant, one parallel Open Field Foil, and one parallel Leather card. The fronts of this Pennant set feature a color player image on a felt-like pennant shaped card with the player's name and team name on the back. The set is divided into three color-coded insertion ratios: 50 "Scarce" greens which are the most common, 25 "Rare" purples with a ratio of 1:11, and 25 "Ultra Rare" reds with a 1:22 ratio. These three colors refer to the Playoff logo on the cardfront that reads "1996 Pennants" and not the color of the actual felt on the front. The felt color can vary for the same player (but generally is a team color) as a number of different colors were used to produce the cards.

COMPLETE SET (100) 50.00 120.00
1 Brett Favre R 12.50 30.00
2 Steve Young R 5.00 12.00
3 Herman Moore R 1.50 4.00
4 Jim Harbaugh R 1.50 4.00
5 Curtis Martin R 5.00 12.00
6 Junior Seau G 1.00 2.50
7 John Elway R 12.50 30.00
8 Troy Aikman P 3.00 8.00
9 Terry Allen G .60 1.50
10 Kordell Stewart R 2.50 6.00
11 Drew Bledsoe G 2.00 5.00
12 Jim Kelly P 1.25 3.00
13 Dan Marino P 6.00 15.00
14 Andre Rison G .60 1.50
15 Jeff Hostetler G .30 .75
16 Scott Mitchell G .60 1.50
17 Carl Pickens R 1.50 4.00
18 Larry Centers P .40 1.00
19 Craig Heyward G .30 .75
20 Barry Sanders P 5.00 12.00
21 Deion Sanders R 4.00 10.00
22 Emmitt Smith R 10.00 25.00
23 Rashaan Salaam R 1.50 4.00
24 Mario Bates G .60 1.50
25 Lawrence Phillips G 1.00 2.50
26 Napoleon Kaufman G 1.00 2.50
27 Rodney Hampton G .60 1.50
28 Marshall Faulk P 1.50 4.00
29 Trent Dilfer G 1.00 2.50
30 Leeland McElroy P .75 2.00
31 Marcus Allen P 1.25 3.00
32 Ricky Watters G .60 1.50
33 Karim Abdul-Jabbar G 1.00 2.50
34 Herschel Walker P .75 2.00
35 Thurman Thomas R 2.50 6.00
36 Jerome Bettis P 1.25 3.00
37 Gus Frerotte G .60 1.50
38 Neil O'Donnell G .60 1.50
39 Rick Mirer G .60 1.50
40 Mike Alstott R 2.50 6.00
41 Vinny Testaverde R 1.50 4.00
42 Derek Loville G .30 .75
43 Ben Coates G .60 1.50
44 Steve McNair R 5.00 12.00
45 Bobby Engram P 1.25 3.00
46 Yancey Thigpen G .60 1.50
47 Lake Dawson G .30 .75
48 Terrell Davis P 3.00 8.00
49 Kerry Collins R 2.50 6.00
50 Eric Metcalf G .30 .75
51 Stanley Pritchett R .75 2.00
52 Robert Brooks R 1.50 4.00
53 Isaac Bruce G 1.00 2.50
54 Tim Brown G 1.00 2.50
55 Edgar Bennett P .40 1.00
56 Warren Moon G .60 1.50
57 Jerry Rice R 6.00 15.00
58 Michael Westbrook G 1.00 2.50
59 Keyshawn Johnson G 1.00 2.50
60 Steve Bono R .30 .75
61 Derrick Mayes P 1.25 3.00
62 Erik Kramer P .40 1.00
63 Rodney Peete G .30 .75
64 Eddie Kennison G 1.00 2.50
65 Derrick Thomas G 1.00 2.50
66 Joey Galloway R 2.50 6.00
67 Amani Toomer P 1.25 3.00
68 Reggie White G 1.00 2.50
69 Heath Shuler G .60 1.50
70 Dave Brown G .30 .75
71 Tony Banks P 1.25 3.00
72 Chris Warren G .60 1.50
73 J.J. Stokes G 1.00 2.50
74 Rickey Dudley P 1.25 3.00
75 Stan Humphries G .60 1.50
76 Jason Dunn P .40 1.00
77 Tyrone Wheatley G .60 1.50
78 Jim Everett G .30 .75
79 Cris Carter P 1.25 3.00
80 Alex Van Dyke P .40 1.00
81 O.J. McDuffie G .60 1.50
82 Mark Chmura P .40 1.00
83 Terry Glenn P 1.25 3.00
84 Boomer Esiason R 1.50 4.00
85 Bruce Smith G .60 1.50
86 Curtis Conway G .60 1.50
87 Ki-Jana Carter G .60 1.50
88 Tamarick Vanover G .60 1.50
89 Michael Jackson G .60 1.50
90 Mark Brunell G 2.00 5.00
91 Tim Biakabutuka R 2.50 6.00
92 Anthony Miller G .60 1.50
93 Marvin Harrison R 6.00 15.00
94 Jeff George P .75 2.00
95 Jeff Blake R 2.50 6.00
96 Eddie George G 1.50 4.00
97 Eric Moulds P 1.50 4.00
98 Mike Tomczak G .30 .75
99 Chris Sanders G .60 1.50
100 Chris Chandler G .60 1.50

1996 Playoff Contenders Air Command

COMPLETE SET (8) 50.00 100.00
STATED ODDS 1:96
AC1 Dan Marino 8.00 20.00
AC2 Brett Favre 15.00 40.00
AC3 Troy Aikman 4.00 10.00
AC4 Mike Tomczak .40 1.00
AC5 John Elway 15.00 40.00
AC6 Jeff George 1.00 2.50
AC7 Chris Chandler .75 2.00
AC8 Steve Bono .40 1.00

1996 Playoff Contenders Ground Hogs

COMPLETE SET (8) 60.00 120.00
RANDOM INSERTS IN HOBBY PACKS
GH1 Emmitt Smith 12.50 30.00
GH2 Barry Sanders 12.50 30.00
GH3 Marshall Faulk 12.50 25.00
GH4 Curtis Martin 7.50 20.00
GH5 Chris Warren 6.00 15.00
GH6 Ricky Watters 6.00 15.00
GH7 Thurman Thomas 7.50 20.00
GH8 Terrell Davis 7.50 20.00

1996 Playoff Contenders Honors

COMPLETE SET (3) 50.00 120.00
RANDOM INSERTS IN HOBBY PACKS
PH4 Dan Marino 30.00 80.00
PH5 Deion Sanders 15.00 40.00
PH6 Marcus Allen 15.00 40.00

1996 Playoff Contenders Pennant Flyers

COMPLETE SET (8) 60.00 120.00
RANDOM INSERTS IN HOBBY PACKS
PF1 Jerry Rice 20.00 40.00
PF2 Joey Galloway 7.50 15.00
PF3 Isaac Bruce 7.50 15.00
PF4 Herman Moore 7.50 15.00
PF5 Carl Pickens 5.00 10.00
PF6 Yancey Thigpen 5.00 10.00
PF7 Deion Sanders 10.00 20.00
PF8 Robert Brooks 7.50 15.00

1997 Playoff Contenders

Distributed in four-card packs, this 150-card set features color player photos printed on super-premium 30 pt. card stock with two-sided action foil etching. The fronts display a double-etched pattern with a silver holographic starburst behind the player. The backs carry the player's name stamped in silver across the card with the etch adding movement and light.

COMPLETE SET (150) 15.00 40.00
UNPRICED GOLD PRINT RUN 1
1 Kent Graham .15 .40
2 Leeland McElroy .15 .40
3 Rob Moore .25 .60
4 Frank Sanders .25 .60
5 Jake Plummer RC 1.50 4.00
6 Chris Chandler .25 .60
7 Bert Emanuel .25 .60
8 O.J. Santiago RC .25 .60
9 Byron Hanspard RC .25 .60
10 Vinny Testaverde .25 .60
11 Michael Jackson .25 .60
12 Earnest Byner .15 .40
13 Jermaine Lewis .40 1.00
14 Derrick Alexander WR .25 .60
15 Jay Graham RC .25 .60
16 Todd Collins .15 .40
17 Thurman Thomas .40 1.00
18 Bruce Smith .25 .60
19 Andre Reed .25 .60
20 Quinn Early .15 .40
21 Antowain Smith RC 1.00 2.50
22 Kerry Collins .40 1.00
23 Tim Biakabutuka .25 .60
24 Anthony Johnson .15 .40
25 Wesley Walls .25 .60
26 Fred Lane RC .25 .60
27 Rae Carruth RC .15 .40
28 Raymont Harris .15 .40
29 Rick Mirer .15 .40
30 Darnell Autry RC .25 .60
31 Jeff Blake .25 .60
32 Ki-Jana Carter .15 .40
33 Carl Pickens .25 .60
34 Darnay Scott .25 .60
35 Corey Dillon RC 1.50 4.00
36 Troy Aikman .75 2.00
37 Emmitt Smith 1.25 3.00
38 Michael Irvin .40 1.00
39 Deion Sanders .40 1.00
40 Anthony Miller .15 .40
41 Eric Bjornson .15 .40
42 David LaFleur RC .15 .40
43 John Elway 1.50 4.00
44 Terrell Davis .40 1.00
45 Shannon Sharpe .25 .60
46 Ed McCaffrey .25 .60
47 Rod Smith WR .40 1.00
48 Scott Mitchell .25 .60
49 Barry Sanders 1.25 3.00
50 Herman Moore .25 .60
51 Brett Favre 1.50 4.00
52 Dorsey Levens .40 1.00
53 William Henderson .25 .60
54 Derrick Mayes .25 .60
55 Antonio Freeman .40 1.00
56 Robert Brooks .25 .60
57 Mark Chmura .25 .60
58 Reggie White .40 1.00
59 Darren Sharper RC 8.00 20.00
60 Jim Harbaugh .25 .60
61 Marshall Faulk .40 1.00
62 Marvin Harrison .40 1.00
63 Mark Brunell .40 1.00
64 Natrone Means .25 .60
65 Jimmy Smith .25 .60
66 Keenan McCardell .25 .60
67 Elvis Grbac .25 .60
68 Greg Hill .15 .40
69 Marcus Allen .40 1.00
70 Andre Rison .25 .60
71 Kimble Anders .25 .60
72 Tony Gonzalez RC 1.50 4.00
73 Pat Barnes RC .40 1.00
74 Dan Marino 1.50 4.00
75 Karim Abdul-Jabbar .25 .60
76 Zach Thomas .40 1.00
77 O.J. McDuffie .25 .60
78 Brian Manning RC .15 .40
79 Brad Johnson .40 1.00
80 Cris Carter .40 1.00
81 Jake Reed .25 .60
82 Robert Smith .25 .60
83 Drew Bledsoe .40 1.00
84 Curtis Martin .40 1.00
85 Ben Coates .25 .60
86 Terry Glenn .40 1.00
87 Shawn Jefferson .15 .40
88 Heath Shuler .15 .40
89 Mario Bates .15 .40
90 Andre Hastings .15 .40
91 Troy Davis RC .25 .60
92 Danny Wuerffel RC .40 1.00
93 Dave Brown .15 .40
94 Chris Calloway .15 .40
95 Tiki Barber RC 2.50 6.00
96 Mike Cherry RC .15 .40
97 Neil O'Donnell .25 .60
98 Keyshawn Johnson .40 1.00
99 Adrian Murrell .25 .60
100 Wayne Chrebet .40 1.00
101 Dedric Ward RC .25 .60
102 Leon Johnson RC .25 .60
103 Jeff George .25 .60
104 Napoleon Kaufman .40 1.00
105 Tim Brown .40 1.00
106 James Jett .25 .60
107 Ty Detmer .25 .60
108 Ricky Watters .25 .60
109 Irving Fryar .25 .60
110 Michael Timpson .15 .40
111 Chad Lewis RC .40 1.00
112 Kordell Stewart .40 1.00
113 Jerome Bettis .40 1.00
114 Charles Johnson .25 .60
115 George Jones RC .25 .60
116 Will Blackwell RC .25 .60
117 Stan Humphries .25 .60
118 Junior Seau .40 1.00
119 Freddie Jones RC .25 .60
120 Steve Young .60 1.50
121 Jerry Rice .75 2.00
122 Garrison Hearst .25 .60
123 William Floyd .25 .60
124 Terrell Owens .40 1.00
125 J.J. Stokes .25 .60
126 Marc Edwards RC .15 .40
127 Jim Druckenmiller RC .25 .60
128 Warren Moon .40 1.00
129 Chris Warren .25 .60
130 Joey Galloway .25 .60
131 Shawn Springs RC .25 .60
132 Tony Banks .25 .60
133 Lawrence Phillips .15 .40
134 Isaac Bruce .40 1.00
135 Eddie Kennison .25 .60
136 Orlando Pace RC .40 1.00
137 Trent Dilfer .40 1.00
138 Mike Alstott .40 1.00
139 Horace Copeland .15 .40
140 Jackie Harris .15 .40
141 Warrick Dunn RC 1.25 3.00
142 Reidel Anthony RC .40 1.00
143 Steve McNair .40 1.00
144 Eddie George .40 1.00
145 Chris Sanders .15 .40
146 Gus Frerotte .15 .40
147 Terry Allen .40 1.00
148 Henry Ellard .15 .40
149 Leslie Shepherd .15 .40
150 Michael Westbrook .25 .60
S1 Terrell Davis Sample .75 2.00

1997 Playoff Contenders Blue

COMPLETE SET (150) 150.00 300.00
*BLUE VETS: 1.2X TO 3X BASIC CARDS
*BLUE ROOKIES: .6X TO 1.5X
BLUE STATED ODDS 1:4

1997 Playoff Contenders Red

*RED VETS: 15X TO 40X BASIC CARDS
*RED ROOKIES: 8X TO 20X
RED PRINT RUN 25 SER.#'d SETS
59 Darren Sharper 50.00 120.00

1997 Playoff Contenders Clash

COMPLETE SET (12) 50.00 120.00
SILVER STATED ODDS 1:48
*BLUES: .8X TO 2X SILVERS
BLUE STATED ODDS 1:192
1 Brett Favre 12.50 30.00
Troy Aikman
2 Barry Sanders 10.00 25.00
Brad Johnson
3 Curtis Martin 5.00 12.00
Warrick Dunn
4 Steve Young 12.50 30.00
John Elway
5 Jerry Rice 7.50 20.00
Marcus Allen
6 Dan Marino 12.50 30.00
Drew Bledsoe
7 Terrell Davis 5.00 12.00
Napoleon Kaufman
8 Eddie George 12.50 30.00
Emmitt Smith
9 Mark Brunell 5.00 12.00
Tim Brown
10 Kerry Collins 4.00 10.00
Reggie White
11 Deion Sanders 4.00 10.00
Carl Pickens
12 Mike Alstott 4.00 10.00
Keyshawn Johnson

1997 Playoff Contenders Leather Helmet Die Cuts

COMPLETE SET (18) 100.00 200.00
SILVER STATED ODDS 1:24
*BLUES: 2.5X TO 3X BASIC INSERTS
BLUE STATED ODDS 1:216
*REDS: 4X TO 10X BASIC INSERTS
RED STATED PRINT RUN 25 SERIAL #'d SETS
1 Dan Marino 12.50 30.00
2 Troy Aikman 6.00 15.00
3 Brett Favre 12.50 30.00
4 Barry Sanders 10.00 25.00
5 Drew Bledsoe 4.00 10.00
6 Deion Sanders 3.00 8.00
7 Curtis Martin 4.00 10.00
8 Warrick Dunn 3.00 8.00
9 Napoleon Kaufman 3.00 8.00
10 Eddie George 3.00 8.00
11 Antowain Smith 2.50 6.00
12 Emmitt Smith 10.00 25.00
13 John Elway 12.50 30.00
14 Steve Young 4.00 10.00
15 Mark Brunell 4.00 10.00
16 Terrell Davis 4.00 10.00
17 Terry Glenn 3.00 8.00
18 Terrell Owens 4.00 10.00

1997 Playoff Contenders Pennants Black Felt

COMPLETE SET (36) 125.00 250.00
SILVER STATED ODDS 1:12
*BLUES: .8X TO 2X BASIC INSERTS
BLUE STATED ODDS 1:72
1 Dan Marino 8.00 20.00
2 Kordell Stewart 2.00 5.00
3 Drew Bledsoe 2.50 6.00
4 Kerry Collins 2.00 5.00
5 John Elway 8.00 20.00
6 Trent Dilfer 2.00 5.00
7 Jerry Rice 4.00 10.00
8 Emmitt Smith 6.00 15.00
9 Jeff George 1.25 3.00
10 Eddie George 2.00 5.00
11 Terrell Davis 2.50 6.00
12 Mike Alstott 2.00 5.00
13 Jim Druckenmiller .75 2.00
14 Antowain Smith 2.00 5.00
15 Marcus Allen 2.00 5.00
16 Jerome Bettis 2.00 5.00
17 Terrell Owens 2.50 6.00
18 Gus Frerotte .75 2.00
19 Troy Aikman 4.00 10.00
20 Andre Rison 1.25 3.00
21 Mark Brunell 2.00 5.00
22 Antonio Freeman 2.00 5.00
23 Brett Favre 8.00 20.00
24 Steve McNair 2.50 6.00
25 Barry Sanders 6.00 15.00
26 Steve Young 2.50 6.00
27 Curtis Martin 2.50 6.00
28 Napoleon Kaufman 2.00 5.00
29 Deion Sanders 2.00 5.00
30 Terry Glenn 2.00 5.00
31 Warrick Dunn 2.50 6.00
32 Danny Wuerffel .75 2.00
33 Elvis Grbac 1.25 3.00
34 Cris Carter 2.00 5.00
35 Joey Galloway 1.25 3.00
36 Corey Dillon 5.00 12.00

1997 Playoff Contenders Performer Plaques

COMPLETE SET (45) 125.00 250.00
SILVER STATED ODDS 1:12
*BLUES: .8X TO 2X BASIC INSERTS
BLUE STATED ODDS 1:36
1 Jim Druckenmiller .75 2.00
2 Danny Wuerffel .75 2.00
3 Antowain Smith 2.00 5.00
4 Warrick Dunn 2.50 6.00
5 Terrell Owens 2.50 6.00
6 Elvis Grbac 1.25 3.00
7 Andre Rison 1.25 3.00
8 Tim Brown 2.00 5.00
9 Trent Dilfer 2.00 5.00
10 Brad Johnson 2.00 5.00
11 Deion Sanders 2.00 5.00
12 Dan Marino 8.00 20.00
13 Kerry Collins 2.00 5.00
14 Steve McNair 2.50 6.00
15 Eddie George 2.00 5.00
16 Ricky Watters 1.25 3.00
17 Jerome Bettis 2.00 5.00
18 Robert Brooks 1.25 3.00
19 Keyshawn Johnson 2.00 5.00
20 Antonio Freeman 2.00 5.00
21 Eddie Kennison 1.25 3.00
22 Mike Alstott 2.00 5.00
23 Brett Favre 8.00 20.00
24 Troy Aikman 4.00 10.00
25 Emmitt Smith 6.00 15.00
26 Terrell Davis 2.50 6.00
27 John Elway 8.00 20.00
28 Barry Sanders 6.00 15.00
29 Steve Young 2.50 6.00
30 Curtis Martin 2.50 6.00
31 Cris Carter 2.00 5.00
32 Drew Bledsoe 2.50 6.00
33 Mark Brunell 2.50 6.00
34 Kordell Stewart 2.00 5.00
35 Tony Banks 1.25 3.00
36 Napoleon Kaufman 2.00 5.00
37 Marcus Allen 2.00 5.00
38 Terry Glenn 2.00 5.00
39 Herman Moore 1.25 3.00
40 Michael Irvin 2.00 5.00
41 Joey Galloway 1.25 3.00
42 Karim Abdul-Jabbar 1.25 3.00
43 Reggie White 2.00 5.00
44 Jerry Rice 4.00 10.00
45 Gus Frerotte .75 2.00

1997 Playoff Contenders Rookie Wave Pennants Black Felt

COMPLETE SET (27) 40.00 80.00
*BLUE: .4X TO 1X BLACK FELT
*GREEN: .4X TO 1X BLACK FELT
*ORANGE: .4X TO 1X BLACK FELT
OVERALL STATED ODDS 1:6
1 Jim Druckenmiller 1.00 2.50
2 Antowain Smith 2.00 5.00
3 Will Blackwell 1.00 2.50
4 Tiki Barber 5.00 12.00
5 Rae Carruth .75 2.00
6 Jay Graham 1.00 2.50
7 Darnell Autry 1.00 2.50
8 David LaFleur .75 2.00
9 Tony Gonzalez 4.00 10.00
10 Chad Lewis 1.25 3.00
11 Freddie Jones 1.00 2.50
12 Shawn Springs 1.00 2.50
13 Danny Wuerffel 1.25 3.00
14 Warrick Dunn 2.50 6.00
15 Troy Davis 1.00 2.50
16 Reidel Anthony 1.25 3.00
17 Jake Plummer 3.00 8.00
18 Byron Hanspard 1.00 2.50
19 Fred Lane 1.00 2.50
20 Corey Dillon 3.00 8.00
21 Darren Sharper 4.00 10.00
22 Pat Barnes 1.25 3.00
23 Mike Cherry .75 2.00
24 Leon Johnson 1.00 2.50
25 George Jones 1.00 2.50
26 Marc Edwards .75 2.00
27 Orlando Pace 1.25 3.00

1998 Playoff Contenders Leather

This 100-card set features color action player images silhouetted on a die-cut football background and printed on actual leather. The backs carry player information.

COMPLETE SET (100) 100.00 200.00
1 Adrian Murrell .60 1.50
2 Michael Pittman 1.00 2.50
3 Jake Plummer 1.00 2.50
4 Andre Wadsworth .60 1.50
5 Jamal Anderson 1.00 2.50
6 Chris Chandler .60 1.50
7 Tim Dwight 1.00 2.50
8 Pat Johnson .60 1.50
9 Jermaine Lewis .60 1.50
10 Doug Flutie 1.00 2.50
11 Antowain Smith 1.00 2.50
12 Muhsin Muhammad .60 1.50
13 Bobby Engram .60 1.50
14 Curtis Enis .30 .75
15 Alonzo Mayes .30 .75
16 Corey Dillon 1.00 2.50
17 Carl Pickens .60 1.50
18 Troy Aikman 2.00 5.00
19 Michael Irvin 1.00 2.50
20 Deion Sanders 1.00 2.50
21 Emmitt Smith 3.00 8.00
22 Terrell Davis 1.00 2.50
23 John Elway 4.00 10.00
24 Brian Griese 2.00 5.00
25 Rod Smith WR .60 1.50
26 Charlie Batch 1.00 2.50
27 Germane Crowell .30 .75
28 Terry Fair .30 .75
29 Herman Moore .60 1.50
30 Barry Sanders 3.00 8.00
31 Brett Favre 4.00 10.00
32 Antonio Freeman 1.00 2.50
33 Vonnie Holliday .60 1.50
UER front and back Holiday
34 Reggie White 1.00 2.50
35 Marshall Faulk 1.25 3.00
36 Marvin Harrison 1.00 2.50
37 Peyton Manning 12.50 25.00
38 Jerome Pathon 1.00 2.50
39 Tavian Banks .60 1.50
40 Mark Brunell 1.00 2.50
41 Keenan McCardell .60 1.50
42 Fred Taylor 1.50 4.00
43 Elvis Grbac .60 1.50
44 Andre Rison .60 1.50
45 Rashaan Shehee .30 .75
46 Karim Abdul-Jabbar 1.00 2.50
47 John Avery .30 .75
48 Dan Marino 4.00 10.00
49 O.J. McDuffie .60 1.50
50 Cris Carter 1.00 2.50
51 Brad Johnson 1.00 2.50
52 Randy Moss 6.00 15.00
53 Robert Smith 1.00 2.50
54 Drew Bledsoe 1.50 4.00
55 Ben Coates .60 1.50
56 Robert Edwards .60 1.50
57 Chris Floyd .30 .75
58 Terry Glenn 1.00 2.50
59 Cameron Cleeland .30 .75
60 Kerry Collins .60 1.50
61 Danny Kanell .60 1.50
62 Charles Way .40 1.00
63 Glenn Foley .40 1.00
64 Keyshawn Johnson 1.00 2.50
65 Curtis Martin 1.00 2.50
66 Tim Brown 1.00 2.50
67 Jeff George .60 1.50
68 Napoleon Kaufman 1.00 2.50
69 Charles Woodson 1.25 3.00
70 Irving Fryar .60 1.50
71 Bobby Hoying .60 1.50
72 Jerome Bettis 1.00 2.50
73 Kordell Stewart 1.00 2.50
74 Hines Ward 5.00 10.00
75 Ryan Leaf 1.00 2.50
76 Natrone Means .60 1.50
77 Mikhael Ricks .30 .75
78 Junior Seau 1.00 2.50
79 Garrison Hearst 1.00 2.50
80 Terrell Owens 1.00 2.50
81 Jerry Rice 2.00 5.00
82 Steve Young 1.25 3.00
83 Joey Galloway .60 1.50
84 Ahman Green 2.50 6.00
85 Warren Moon 1.00 2.50
86 Ricky Watters .60 1.50
87 Tony Banks .60 1.50
88 Isaac Bruce 1.00 2.50
89 Robert Holcombe .60 1.50
90 Mike Alstott 1.00 2.50
91 Trent Dilfer 1.00 2.50
92 Warrick Dunn 1.00 2.50
93 Jacquez Green .60 1.50
94 Kevin Dyson 1.00 2.50
95 Eddie George 1.00 2.50
96 Steve McNair 1.00 2.50
97 Yancey Thigpen .40 1.00
98 Terry Allen 1.00 2.50
99 Skip Hicks .60 1.50
100 Michael Westbrook .60 1.50

1998 Playoff Contenders Leather Gold

*STARS/70-94: 6X TO 15X BASIC CARDS
*STARS/45-69: 8X TO 20X BASIC CARDS
*RCs/45-69: 4X TO 10X BASIC CARDS
*STARS/30-44: 10X TO 25X BASIC CARDS
*RCs/30-44: 5X TO 12X BASIC CARDS
*STARS/20-29: 12X TO 30X BASIC CARDS
*RCs/20-29: 6X TO 15X BASIC CARDS
*STARS/16-19: 20X TO 50X BASIC CARDS
37 Peyton Manning/36 150.00 300.00
52 Randy Moss/25 75.00 150.00

1998 Playoff Contenders Leather Red

COMP.RED SET (100) 200.00 400.00
*RED STARS: 1X TO 2.5X BASIC LEATHER
*RED ROOKIES: .6X TO 1.5X BASIC LEATHER
STATED ODDS 1:9 HOBBY

1998 Playoff Contenders Leather Registered Exchange

COMPLETE SET (100) 400.00 800.00
*REGISTERED STARS: 2X TO 5X BASIC CARDS
*REGISTERED ROOKIES: 1X TO 2.5X BASIC CARDS
ANNOUNCED PRINT RUN 51 SETS

1998 Playoff Contenders Pennants Blue Felt

COMPLETE SET (100) 60.00 150.00
ONE PENNANT PER PACK
EACH CARD ISSUED IN 6-FELT COLORS
6-FELT COLOR VARIATIONS SAME PRICE
1 Jake Plummer 1.00 2.50
2 Frank Sanders .40 1.00
3 Jamal Anderson 1.00 2.50
4 Tim Dwight 1.00 2.50
5 Jammi German .30 .75
6 Tony Martin .60 1.50
7 Jim Harbaugh .60 1.50
8 Rod Woodson .60 1.50
9 Rob Johnson .60 1.50
10 Eric Moulds 1.00 2.50
11 Antowain Smith 1.00 2.50
12 Steve Beuerlein .60 1.50
13 Fred Lane .40 1.00
14 Curtis Enis .30 .75
15 Corey Dillon 1.00 2.50
16 Neil O'Donnell .60 1.50
17 Carl Pickens .60 1.50
18 Darnay Scott .60 1.50
19 Takeo Spikes 1.00 2.50
20 Troy Aikman 2.00 5.00
21 Michael Irvin 1.00 2.50
22 Deion Sanders 1.00 2.50
23 Emmitt Smith 3.00 8.00
24 Chris Warren .60 1.50
25 Terrell Davis 1.00 2.50
26 John Elway 4.00 10.00
27 Brian Griese 2.00 5.00
28 Ed McCaffrey 1.00 2.50
29 Marcus Nash .30 .75
30 Shannon Sharpe .60 1.50
31 Rod Smith WR .60 1.50
32 Charlie Batch 1.00 2.50
33 Germane Crowell .30 .75
34 Herman Moore .60 1.50
35 Barry Sanders 3.00 8.00
36 Mark Chmura .40 1.00
37 Brett Favre 4.00 10.00
38 Antonio Freeman 1.00 2.50
39 Reggie White 1.00 2.50
40 Marshall Faulk 1.25 3.00
41 E.G. Green .30 .75
42 Peyton Manning 20.00 40.00
43 Jerome Pathon 1.00 2.50
44 Mark Brunell 1.00 2.50
45 Jonathan Quinn .60 1.50
46 Fred Taylor 1.50 4.00
47 Tony Gonzalez 1.00 2.50
48 Andre Rison .60 1.50
49 Karim Abdul-Jabbar 1.00 2.50
50 John Avery .30 .75
51 Dan Marino 4.00 10.00
52 Cris Carter 1.00 2.50
53 Randall Cunningham 1.00 2.50
54 Brad Johnson 1.00 2.50
55 Randy Moss 8.00 20.00
56 Robert Smith 1.00 2.50
57 Drew Bledsoe 1.50 4.00
58 Robert Edwards .60 1.50
59 Terry Glenn 1.00 2.50
60 Tony Simmons .60 1.50
61 Tiki Barber 1.00 2.50
62 Joe Jurevicius 1.00 2.50
63 Danny Kanell .60 1.50
64 Keyshawn Johnson 1.00 2.50
65 Curtis Martin 1.00 2.50
66 Vinny Testaverde .60 1.50
67 Tim Brown 1.00 2.50
68 Jeff George .60 1.50
69 Napoleon Kaufman 1.00 2.50
70 Jon Ritchie .60 1.50
71 Charles Woodson 1.25 3.00
72 Irving Fryar .60 1.50
73 Duce Staley 1.00 2.50
74 Jerome Bettis 1.00 2.50
75 Chris Fuamatu-Ma'afala .60 1.50
76 Kordell Stewart 1.00 2.50
77 Hines Ward 5.00 12.00
78 Ryan Leaf 1.00 2.50
79 Natrone Means .60 1.50
80 Mikhael Ricks .30 .75
81 Garrison Hearst 1.00 2.50
82 R.W. McQuarters .30 .75
83 Jerry Rice 2.00 5.00
84 J.J. Stokes .60 1.50
85 Steve Young 1.25 3.00
86 Joey Galloway .60 1.50
87 Ahman Green 3.00 8.00
88 Warren Moon 1.00 2.50
89 Ricky Watters .60 1.50
90 Isaac Bruce 1.00 2.50
91 Robert Holcombe .60 1.50
92 Mike Alstott 1.00 2.50
93 Trent Dilfer 1.00 2.50
94 Warrick Dunn 1.00 2.50
95 Jacquez Green .60 1.50
96 Kevin Dyson 1.00 2.50
97 Eddie George 1.00 2.50
98 Steve McNair 1.00 2.50
99 Terry Allen 1.00 2.50
100 Skip Hicks .60 1.50

1998 Playoff Contenders Pennants Gold Foil

*GOLD STARS: 4X TO 10X BASIC PENNANTS
*GOLD ROOKIES: 3X TO 7X BASIC PENNANTS
STATED PRINT RUN 98 SERIAL #'d SETS

1998 Playoff Contenders Pennants Red Foil

COMP.RED SET (100) 200.00 400.00
*RED STARS: 1X TO 2.5X BASIC PENNANT
*RED ROOKIES: .6X TO 1.5X BASIC PENNANT
STATED ODDS 1:9 HOBBY

1998 Playoff Contenders Pennants Registered Exchange

COMPLETE SET (100) 400.00 800.00
*REGISTERED STARS: 2X TO 5X BASIC CARDS
*REGISTERED ROOKIES: 1X TO 2.5X BASIC CARDS
ANNOUNCED PRINT RUN 51 SETS

1998 Playoff Contenders Ticket

This 99-card skip-numbered set features color action player photos printed on conventional card stock with foil stamping in a ticket design. The draft picks subset featured authentic player autographs on the cards. Playoff later anounced the print runs for each of those cards. A red foil parallel version of this set was produced and seeded in packs at 1:9. A gold foil parallel version was issued and sequentially numbered to just 25. Please note the following card numbers were never released: 84, 91, 101, and 102.

COMP.SET w/o SPs (80) 25.00 60.00
1 Rob Moore .50 1.25
2 Jake Plummer .75 2.00
3 Jamal Anderson .75 2.00
4 Terance Mathis .50 1.25
5 Priest Holmes RC 10.00 25.00
6 Michael Jackson .30 .75
7 Eric Zeier .50 1.25
8 Andre Reed .50 1.25
9 Antowain Smith .75 2.00
10 Bruce Smith .50 1.25
11 Thurman Thomas .75 2.00
12 Rocket Ismail .30 .75
13 Wesley Walls .50 1.25
14 Curtis Conway .50 1.25
15 Jeff Blake .50 1.25
16 Corey Dillon .75 2.00
17 Carl Pickens .50 1.25
18 Troy Aikman 1.50 4.00
19 Michael Irvin .75 2.00
20 Ernie Mills .30 .75
21 Deion Sanders .75 2.00
22 Emmitt Smith 2.50 6.00
23 Terrell Davis .75 2.00
24 John Elway 3.00 8.00
25 Neil Smith .50 1.25
26 Rod Smith WR .50 1.25
27 Herman Moore .50 1.25
28 Johnnie Morton .50 1.25
29 Barry Sanders 2.50 6.00
30 Robert Brooks .50 1.25
31 Brett Favre 3.00 8.00
32 Antonio Freeman .75 2.00
33 Dorsey Levens .75 2.00
34 Reggie White .75 2.00
35 Marshall Faulk .75 2.00
36 Mark Brunell .75 2.00
37 Jimmy Smith .50 1.25
38 James Stewart .50 1.25
39 Donnell Bennett .30 .75
40 Andre Rison .50 1.25
41 Derrick Thomas .75 2.00
42 Karim Abdul-Jabbar .75 2.00
43 Dan Marino 3.00 8.00
44 Cris Carter .75 2.00
45 Brad Johnson .75 2.00
46 Robert Smith .75 2.00
47 Drew Bledsoe .75 2.00
48 Terry Glenn .75 2.00
49 Lamar Smith .50 1.25
50 Ike Hilliard .50 1.25
51 Danny Kanell .50 1.25
52 Wayne Chrebet .75 2.00
53 Keyshawn Johnson .75 2.00
54 Curtis Martin .75 2.00
55 Tim Brown .75 2.00
56 Rickey Dudley .30 .75
57 Jeff George .50 1.25
58 Napoleon Kaufman .75 2.00
59 Irving Fryar .50 1.25
60 Jerome Bettis .75 2.00
61 Charles Johnson .30 .75
62 Kordell Stewart .75 2.00
63 Natrone Means .50 1.25
64 Bryan Still .30 .75
65 Garrison Hearst .75 2.00
66 Jerry Rice 1.50 4.00
67 Steve Young 1.00 2.50
68 Joey Galloway .50 1.25
69 Warren Moon .75 2.00
70 Ricky Watters .50 1.25
71 Isaac Bruce .75 2.00
72 Mike Alstott .75 2.00
73 Reidel Anthony .50 1.25
74 Trent Dilfer .75 2.00
75 Warrick Dunn .75 2.00
76 Warren Sapp .50 1.25
77 Eddie George .75 2.00
78 Steve McNair .75 2.00
79 Terry Allen .75 2.00
80 Gus Frerotte .30 .75
81 Andre Wadsworth AU/500* 10.00 25.00
82 Tim Dwight AU/500* 12.00 30.00
83 Curtis Enis AU/400* 15.00 40.00
85 Charlie Batch AU/500* 15.00 40.00
86 Germane Crowell AU/500* 10.00 25.00
87 Peyton Manning AUTO/200* 2,000.00 3,500.00
88 Jerome Pathon AU/500* 10.00 25.00
89 Fred Taylor AU/500* 40.00 80.00
90 Tavian Banks AU/500* 10.00 25.00
92 Randy Moss AU/300* 200.00 350.00
93 Robert Edwards AU/500* 10.00 25.00
94 Hines Ward AU/500* 150.00 250.00
95 Ryan Leaf AU/200* 25.00 50.00
96 Mikhael Ricks AU/500* 10.00 25.00
97 Ahman Green AU/500* 20.00 50.00
98 Jacquez Green AU/500* 10.00 25.00
99 Kevin Dyson AU/500* 12.00 30.00
100 Skip Hicks AU/500* 10.00 25.00
103 Chris Fuamatu-Ma'afala AUTO/500* 10.00 25.00

1998 Playoff Contenders Ticket Gold

*VETS: 12X TO 30X BASIC CARDS
5 Priest Holmes 60.00 150.00
81 Andre Wadsworth 12.50 30.00
82 Tim Dwight 25.00 60.00
83 Curtis Enis 15.00 40.00
85 Charlie Batch 25.00 60.00
86 Germane Crowell 12.50 30.00
87 Peyton Manning 500.00 800.00
88 Jerome Pathon 15.00 40.00
89 Fred Taylor 40.00 100.00
90 Tavian Banks 12.50 30.00
92 Randy Moss 200.00 400.00
93 Robert Edwards 15.00 40.00
94 Hines Ward 150.00 250.00
95 Ryan Leaf 25.00 60.00
96 Mikhael Ricks 12.50 30.00
97 Ahman Green 60.00 150.00
98 Jacquez Green 15.00 40.00
99 Kevin Dyson 15.00 40.00
100 Skip Hicks 12.50 30.00
103 Chris Fuamatu-Ma'afala 15.00 40.00

1998 Playoff Contenders Ticket Red

*RED STARS: 1X TO 2.5X BASIC CARDS
RED TICKET STATED ODDS 1:9 HOB
5 Priest Holmes 20.00 50.00
81 Andre Wadsworth 2.50 6.00
82 Tim Dwight 3.00 8.00
83 Curtis Enis 2.00 5.00
85 Charlie Batch 3.00 8.00
86 Germane Crowell 2.50 6.00
87 Peyton Manning 75.00 135.00
88 Jerome Pathon 3.00 8.00
89 Fred Taylor 6.00 15.00
90 Tavian Banks 2.50 6.00
92 Randy Moss 25.00 60.00
93 Robert Edwards 2.50 6.00
94 Hines Ward 25.00 50.00
95 Ryan Leaf 3.00 8.00
96 Mikhael Ricks 2.50 6.00
97 Ahman Green 10.00 25.00
98 Jacquez Green 2.50 6.00
99 Kevin Dyson 3.00 8.00
100 Skip Hicks 2.50 6.00
103 Chris Fuamatu-Ma'afala 2.50 6.00

1998 Playoff Contenders Checklist Jumbos

COMPLETE SET (30) 75.00 150.00
ONE PER HOBBY BOX
1 Jake Plummer 2.00 5.00
2 Jamal Anderson 2.00 5.00
3 Jermaine Lewis 1.25 3.00
4 Antowain Smith 2.00 5.00
5 Muhsin Muhammad 1.25 3.00
6 Curtis Enis .75 2.00
7 Corey Dillon 2.00 5.00
8 Deion Sanders 2.00 5.00
9 Terrell Davis 2.00 5.00
10 Barry Sanders 6.00 15.00
11 Brett Favre 8.00 20.00
12 Peyton Manning 12.50 25.00
13 Mark Brunell 2.00 5.00
14 Andre Rison 1.25 3.00
15 Dan Marino 8.00 20.00
16 Randy Moss 6.00 15.00
17 Drew Bledsoe 3.00 8.00
18 Kerry Collins 1.25 3.00
19 Danny Kanell 1.25 3.00
20 Curtis Martin 2.00 5.00
21 Tim Brown 2.00 5.00
22 Irving Fryar 1.25 3.00
23 Kordell Stewart 2.00 5.00
24 Natrone Means 1.25 3.00
25 Steve Young 2.50 6.00
26 Isaac Bruce 2.00 5.00
27 Warren Moon 2.00 5.00
28 Warrick Dunn 2.00 5.00
29 Eddie George 2.00 5.00
30 Terry Allen 2.00 5.00

1998 Playoff Contenders Honors

COMPLETE SET (3) 50.00 100.00
STATED ODDS 1:3241 HOBBY
19 Dan Marino 30.00 80.00
20 Jerry Rice 15.00 40.00
21 Mark Brunell 10.00 25.00

1998 Playoff Contenders MVP Contenders

COMPLETE SET (36) 75.00 150.00
STATED ODDS 1:19 HOBBY
1 Terrell Davis 2.00 5.00
2 Jerry Rice 4.00 10.00
3 Jerome Bettis 2.00 5.00
4 Brett Favre 8.00 20.00
5 Natrone Means 1.25 3.00
6 Steve Young 2.50 6.00
7 John Elway 8.00 20.00
8 Troy Aikman 4.00 10.00
9 Steve McNair 2.00 5.00
10 Kordell Stewart 2.00 5.00
11 Drew Bledsoe 3.00 8.00
12 Tim Brown 2.00 5.00
13 Dan Marino 8.00 20.00
14 Mark Brunell 2.00 5.00
15 Marshall Faulk 2.50 6.00
16 Jake Plummer 2.00 5.00
17 Corey Dillon 2.00 5.00
18 Carl Pickens 1.25 3.00
19 Keyshawn Johnson 2.00 5.00
20 Barry Sanders 6.00 15.00
21 Deion Sanders 2.00 5.00
22 Emmitt Smith 6.00 15.00
23 Antowain Smith 2.00 5.00
24 Curtis Martin 2.00 5.00
25 Cris Carter 2.00 5.00
26 Napoleon Kaufman 2.00 5.00
27 Eddie George 2.00 5.00
28 Warrick Dunn 2.00 5.00
29 Antonio Freeman 2.00 5.00
30 Joey Galloway 1.25 3.00
31 Herman Moore 1.25 3.00
32 Jamal Anderson 2.00 5.00
33 Terry Glenn 2.00 5.00
34 Garrison Hearst 2.00 5.00
35 Robert Smith 2.00 5.00
36 Mike Alstott 2.00 5.00

1998 Playoff Contenders Rookie of the Year

COMPLETE SET (12) 50.00 120.00
STATED ODDS 1:55 HOBBY
1 Tim Dwight 2.50 6.00
2 Curtis Enis 1.50 4.00
3 Charlie Batch 2.50 6.00
4 Peyton Manning 25.00 50.00
5 Fred Taylor 4.00 10.00
6 John Avery 1.50 4.00
7 Randy Moss 12.00 30.00
8 Robert Edwards 1.50 4.00
9 Charles Woodson 3.00 8.00
10 Ryan Leaf 2.50 6.00
11 Jacquez Green 1.50 4.00
12 Kevin Dyson 2.50 6.00

1998 Playoff Contenders Rookie Stallions

COMPLETE SET (18) 40.00 100.00
STATED ODDS 1:19 HOBBY
1 Tim Dwight 1.25 3.00
2 Curtis Enis .75 2.00
3 Brian Griese 2.50 6.00
4 Charlie Batch 1.25 3.00
5 Germane Crowell .75 2.00
6 Peyton Manning 15.00 30.00
7 Tavian Banks .75 2.00
8 Fred Taylor 2.00 5.00
9 Rashaan Shehee .75 2.00
10 John Avery .75 2.00
11 Randy Moss 8.00 20.00
12 Robert Edwards .75 2.00
13 Charles Woodson 1.50 4.00
14 Ryan Leaf 1.25 3.00
15 Ahman Green 3.00 8.00
16 Jacquez Green .75 2.00
17 Kevin Dyson 1.25 3.00
18 Skip Hicks .75 2.00

1998 Playoff Contenders Super Bowl Leather

STATED ODDS 1:2401 HOBBY
1 Robert Brooks 12.50 30.00
2 Terrell Davis 25.00 60.00
3 John Elway 75.00 200.00
4 Brett Favre 60.00 150.00
5 Antonio Freeman 25.00 60.00
6 Rod Smith 20.00 50.00

1998 Playoff Contenders Touchdown Tandems

COMPLETE SET (24) 75.00 150.00
STATED ODDS 1:19 HOBBY
1 Brett Favre 7.50 20.00
Antonio Freeman
2 Dan Marino 7.50 20.00
Karim Abdul-Jabbar
3 Emmitt Smith 6.00 15.00
Troy Aikman
4 Barry Sanders 6.00 15.00
Herman Moore
5 Eddie George 3.00 8.00
Steve McNair
6 Robert Edwards 3.00 8.00
Drew Bledsoe
7 Terrell Davis 3.00 8.00
Rod Smith
8 Mark Brunell 3.00 8.00
Fred Taylor
9 Jerry Rice 4.00 10.00
Steve Young
10 Jerome Bettis 3.00 8.00
Kordell Stewart
11 Curtis Martin 3.00 8.00
Keyshawn Johnson
12 Mike Alstott 3.00 8.00
Warrick Dunn
13 Isaac Bruce 3.00 8.00
Tony Banks
14 Adrian Murrell 3.00 8.00
Jake Plummer
15 Tim Brown 3.00 8.00
Napoleon Kaufman
16 Cris Carter 6.00 15.00
Randy Moss
17 Joey Galloway 2.00 5.00
Ricky Watters
18 Peyton Manning 10.00 20.00
Marshall Faulk
19 Ryan Leaf 3.00 8.00
Natrone Means
20 Carl Pickens 3.00 8.00
Corey Dillon
21 Dooug Flutie 3.00 8.00
Antowain Smith
22 Randall Cunningham 2.00 5.00
Robert Smith
23 Chris Chandler 3.00 8.00
Jamal Anderson
24 John Elway 7.50 20.00
Ed McCaffrey

1999 Playoff Contenders SSD

Released as a 200-card base set, the 1999 Playoff Contenders SSD contains 145 veteran cards, 44 rookie tickets featuring authentic player autographs, and 15 Quarterback Club Playoff tickets seeded at one in seven packs. The cards were printed on thick 30-point card stock with a rainbow holofoil effect. Many of the autographed rookies were issued via mail redemption cards that carried an expiration date of 12/31/2000. While most of those were issued as planned, 3-players did not sign any cards for the set -- Chris McAlister, Shaun King, and James Johnson. Playoff issued these three cards with "No Autograph" printed on the fronts along with another card of the same number signed by a replacement player.

COMPLETE SET (205) 750.00 1,500.00
COMP.SET w/o SP's (141) 25.00 60.00
1 Randy Moss .60 1.50
2 Randall Cunningham .60 1.50
3 Cris Carter .60 1.50
4 Robert Smith .50 1.25
5 Jake Reed .50 1.25
6 Albert Connell .40 1.00
7 Jeff George .40 1.00
8 Brett Favre 2.00 5.00
9 Antonio Freeman .50 1.25
10 Dorsey Levens .50 1.25
11 Mark Chmura .40 1.00
12 Mike Alstott .60 1.50
13 Warrick Dunn .50 1.25
14 Trent Dilfer .50 1.25
15 Jacquez Green .40 1.00
16 Reidel Anthony .40 1.00
17 Warren Sapp .50 1.25
18 Amani Toomer .50 1.25
19 Curtis Enis .40 1.00
20 Curtis Conway .50 1.25
21 Bobby Engram .50 1.25
22 Barry Sanders 1.50 4.00
23 Charlie Batch .50 1.25
24 Herman Moore .50 1.25
25 Johnnie Morton .50 1.25
26 Greg Hill .40 1.00
27 Germane Crowell .40 1.00
28 Kerry Collins .50 1.25
29 Ike Hilliard .50 1.25
30 Joe Jurevicius .40 1.00
31 Stephen Davis .50 1.25
32 Brad Johnson .50 1.25
33 Skip Hicks .40 1.00
34 Michael Westbrook .40 1.00
35 Jake Plummer .50 1.25
36 Adrian Murrell .50 1.25
37 Frank Sanders .40 1.00
38 Rob Moore .40 1.00
39 Gary Brown .40 1.00
40 Duce Staley .50 1.25
41 Charles Johnson .40 1.00
42 Emmitt Smith 1.50 4.00
43 Troy Aikman 1.00 2.50
44 Michael Irvin .60 1.50
45 Deion Sanders .60 1.50
46 Rocket Ismail .50 1.25
47 Jerry Rice 1.25 3.00
48 Terrell Owens .60 1.50
49 Steve Young .75 2.00
50 Garrison Hearst .50 1.25
51 J.J. Stokes .40 1.00
52 Lawrence Phillips .50 1.25
53 Jamal Anderson .50 1.25
54 Chris Chandler .50 1.25
55 Terance Mathis .40 1.00
56 Tim Dwight .50 1.25
57 Charlie Garner .50 1.25
58 Chris Calloway .40 1.00
59 Eddie Kennison .50 1.25
60 Billy Joe Hobert .40 1.00
61 Tim Biakabutuka .50 1.25
62 Muhsin Muhammad .50 1.25
63 Olandis Gary AU/1825* RC 5.00 12.00
64 Wesley Walls .50 1.25
65 Isaac Bruce .60 1.50
66 Marshall Faulk .60 1.50
67 Kordell Stewart .50 1.25
68 Jerome Bettis .60 1.50
69 Hines Ward .60 1.50
70 Corey Dillon .50 1.25
71 Carl Pickens .50 1.25
72 Darnay Scott .40 1.00
73 Steve McNair .60 1.50
74 Eddie George .50 1.25
75 Yancey Thigpen .40 1.00
76 Kevin Dyson .40 1.00
77 Fred Taylor .50 1.25
78 Mark Brunell .50 1.25
79 Jimmy Smith .50 1.25
80 Keenan McCardell .50 1.25
81 James Stewart .40 1.00
82 Jermaine Lewis .40 1.00
83 Priest Holmes .60 1.50
84 Stoney Case .40 1.00
85 Errict Rhett .40 1.00
86 Bill Schroeder .50 1.25
87 Terry Kirby .40 1.00
88 Leslie Shepherd .40 1.00
89 Terrence Wilkins AU/825* RC 4.00 10.00
90 Dan Marino 2.00 5.00
91 O.J. McDuffie .50 1.25
92 Karim Abdul-Jabbar .50 1.25
93 Zach Thomas .60 1.50
94 Terry Allen .50 1.25
95 Tony Martin .50 1.25
96 Drew Bledsoe .60 1.50
97 Terry Glenn .50 1.25
98 Ben Coates .50 1.25
99 Tony Simmons .40 1.00
100 Curtis Martin .60 1.50
101 Keyshawn Johnson .50 1.25

102 Vinny Testaverde .50 1.25
103 Wayne Chrebet .50 1.25
104 Peyton Manning 2.00 5.00
105 Marvin Harrison .60 1.50
106 E.G. Green .40 1.00
107 Doug Flutie .60 1.50
108 Thurman Thomas .60 1.50
109 Andre Reed .60 1.50
110 Eric Moulds .50 1.25
111 Antowain Smith .40 1.00
112 Bruce Smith .60 1.50
113 Terrell Davis .60 1.50
114 John Elway 2.00 5.00
115 Ed McCaffrey .50 1.25
116 Rod Smith .50 1.25
117 Shannon Sharpe .60 1.50
118 Jeff Garcia AU/325* RC 25.00 60.00
119 Brian Griese .50 1.25
120 Justin Watson AU/325* RC 6.00 15.00
121 Bubby Brister .40 1.00
122 Ryan Leaf .50 1.25
123 Natrone Means .50 1.25
124 Mikhael Ricks .40 1.00
125 Junior Seau .60 1.50
126 Jim Harbaugh .50 1.25
127 Andre Rison .50 1.25
128 Elvis Grbac .40 1.00
129 Bam Morris .40 1.00
130 Rashaan Shehee .40 1.00
131 Warren Moon .60 1.50
132 Tony Gonzalez .60 1.50
133 Derrick Alexander .40 1.00
134 Jon Kitna .50 1.25
135 Ricky Watters .50 1.25
136 Joey Galloway .50 1.25
137 Ahman Green .50 1.25
138 Derrick Mayes .40 1.00
139 Tyrone Wheatley .50 1.25
140 Napoleon Kaufman .40 1.00
141 Tim Brown .60 1.50
142 Charles Woodson .60 1.50
143 Rich Gannon .50 1.25
144 Rickey Dudley .40 1.00
145 Az-Zahir Hakim .40 1.00
146 Kurt Warner AU/1825* RC 75.00 150.00
147 Sean Bennett AU/1325* RC 3.00 8.00
148 Brandon Stokley AU/1325* RC 6.00 15.00
149 Amos Zereoue AU/1325* RC 4.00 10.00
150 Brock Huard AU/1325* RC 4.00 10.00
151 Tim Couch AU/1025* RC 8.00 20.00
152 Ricky Williams AU/725* RC 25.00 50.00
153 Donovan McNabb AU/525* RC 25.00 60.00
154 Edgerrin James AU/525* RC 20.00 50.00
155 Torry Holt AU/1025* RC 15.00 40.00
156 Daunte Culpepper AU/1025* RC 15.00 30.00
157 Akili Smith AU/1025* RC 4.00 10.00
158 Champ Bailey AU/1725* RC 20.00 40.00
159 Chris Claiborne AU/1825* RC 3.00 8.00
160A Chris McAlister No AU/1825* RC 4.00 10.00
160B Jason Tucker AU/1825* 4.00 10.00
161 Troy Edwards AU/1225* RC 4.00 10.00
162 Jevon Kearse AU/325* RC 20.00 50.00
163 Darnell McDonald AU/1825* RC 3.00 8.00
164 David Boston AU/1025* RC 4.00 10.00
165 Peerless Price AU/1325* RC 4.00 10.00
166 Cecil Collins AU/1025* RC 3.00 8.00
167 Rob Konrad AU/1325* RC 3.00 8.00
168 Cade McNown AU/1025* RC 4.00 10.00
169 Shawn Bryson AU/1825* RC 3.00 8.00
170 Kevin Faulk AU/1325* RC 10.00 25.00
171 Corby Jones AU/1825* RC 3.00 8.00
172A James Johnson No AU/1325* RC 3.00 8.00
172B Patrick Jeffers AU/1325* 5.00 12.00
173 Autry Denson AU/1825* RC 3.00 8.00
174 Sedrick Irvin AU/1825* RC 3.00 8.00
175 Michael Bishop AU/1825* RC 4.00 10.00
176 Joe Germaine AU/825* RC 4.00 10.00
177 De'Mond Parker AU/1325* RC 3.00 8.00
178A Shaun King No AU/1825* RC 4.00 10.00
178B Ray Lucas AU/1825* 4.00 10.00
179 D'Wayne Bates AU/1825* RC 3.00 8.00
180 Tai Streets AU/1825* RC 4.00 10.00
181 Na Brown AU/1825* RC 3.00 8.00
182 Desmond Clark AU/1825* RC 4.00 10.00
183 Jim Kleinsasser AU/1825* RC 5.00 12.00
184 Kevin Johnson AU/1325* RC 4.00 10.00
185 Joe Montgomery AU/1325* RC 3.00 8.00
186 John Elway PT 3.00 8.00
187 Dan Marino PT 3.00 8.00
188 Jerry Rice PT 2.00 5.00
189 Barry Sanders PT 2.50 6.00
190 Steve Young PT 1.25 3.00
191 Doug Flutie PT 1.00 2.50
192 Troy Aikman PT 1.50 4.00
193 Drew Bledsoe PT 1.00 2.50
194 Brett Favre PT 3.00 8.00
195 Randall Cunningham PT 1.00 2.50
196 Terrell Davis PT 1.00 2.50
197 Kordell Stewart PT .75 2.00
198 Keyshawn Johnson PT .75 2.00
199 Jake Plummer PT .75 2.00
200 Peyton Manning PT 3.00 8.00
201 Jay Fiedler AU/1825* 5.00 12.00
202 Kevin Daft AU/325* 6.00 15.00

1999 Playoff Contenders SSD Finesse Gold

*VETS: 10X TO 25X BASIC CARDS
*ROOKIE AUTO: 1.2X TO 3X
*PT VETS: 5X TO 12X BASIC CARDS
STATED PRINT RUN 25 SER.#'d SETS
118 Jeff Garcia 100.00 200.00
146 Kurt Warner 150.00 300.00
153 Donovan McNabb 150.00 300.00

1999 Playoff Contenders SSD Power Blue

*VETS: 5X TO 12X BASIC CARDS
*ROOKIE AUTOS: .8X TO 2X
*PT VETS: 4X TO 10X BASIC CARDS
STATED PRINT RUN 50 SER.#'d SETS
63 Olandis Gary 20.00 50.00
89 Terrence Wilkins 12.00 30.00
118 Jeff Garcia 40.00 100.00
146 Kurt Warner 125.00 225.00
153 Donovan McNabb 75.00 150.00
166 Cecil Collins No AU 3.00 8.00
171 Corby Jones 6.00 15.00

1999 Playoff Contenders SSD Speed Red

*VETS: 3X TO 8X BASIC CARDS
*ROOKIE AUTOS: .6X TO 1.5X
*PT VETS: 2X TO 5X BASIC CARDS
STATED PRINT RUN 100 SER.#'d SETS
118 Jeff Garcia 40.00 80.00
146 Kurt Warner 100.00 175.00
153 Donovan McNabb 60.00 150.00
166 Cecil Collins No AU 2.00 5.00

1999 Playoff Contenders SSD Game Day Souvenirs

STATED ODDS 1:308
GS1 Terrell Owens 15.00 40.00
GS2 Jerry Rice 25.00 60.00
GS3 Steve Young 20.00 50.00
GS4 Akili Smith 10.00 25.00
GS5 Tim Couch 12.00 30.00
GS6 Mark Brunell 12.00 30.00
GS7 Eddie George 12.00 30.00
GS8 Dorsey Levens 12.00 30.00
GS9 Brett Favre 25.00 60.00
GS10 Antonio Freeman 12.00 30.00
GS11 Ricky Williams 15.00 40.00
GS12 Steve McNair 15.00 40.00
GS13 Kurt Warner 25.00 60.00
GS14 John Elway 40.00 100.00
GS15 Terrell Davis 15.00 40.00

1999 Playoff Contenders SSD MVP Contenders

COMPLETE SET (20) 75.00 150.00
STATED ODDS 1:43
MC1 Jamal Anderson 3.00 8.00
MC2 Eddie George 3.00 8.00
MC3 Emmitt Smith 6.00 15.00
MC4 Jerry Rice 6.00 15.00
MC5 Barry Sanders 10.00 25.00
MC6 Keyshawn Johnson 3.00 8.00
MC7 Brett Favre 10.00 25.00
MC8 Randy Moss 8.00 20.00
MC9 Mark Brunell 3.00 8.00
MC10 Fred Taylor 3.00 8.00
MC11 Dan Marino 10.00 25.00
MC12 Peyton Manning 10.00 25.00
MC13 Drew Bledsoe 4.00 10.00
MC14 Antonio Freeman 3.00 8.00
MC15 Steve Young 4.00 10.00
MC16 Terrell Davis 3.00 8.00
MC17 Terrell Owens 3.00 8.00
MC18 Troy Aikman 6.00 15.00
MC19 Steve McNair 3.00 8.00
MC20 Jake Plummer 2.00 5.00

1999 Playoff Contenders SSD Quads

COMPLETE SET (12) 100.00 200.00
STATED ODDS 1:57
CQ1 Jake Plummer 5.00 12.00
David Boston
Emmitt Smith
Troy Aikman
CQ2 Jerry Rice 7.50 20.00
Steve Young
Jamal Anderson
Chris Chandler
CQ3 Randy Moss 12.50 30.00
Cris Carter
Brett Favre
Antonio Freeman
CQ4 Warrick Dunn 5.00 12.00
Mike Alstott
Stephen Davis
Brad Johnson
CQ5 Cade McNown 12.50 30.00
Curtis Enis
Barry Sanders
Charlie Batch
CQ6 Ricky Williams 7.50 20.00
Eddie Kennison
Marshall Faulk
Torry Holt
CQ7 Kordell Stewart 5.00 12.00
Jerome Bettis
Eddie George
Steve McNair
CQ8 Doug Flutie 5.00 12.00
Eric Moulds
Drew Bledsoe
Terry Glenn
CQ9 Dan Marino 12.50 30.00
Cecil Collins
Keyshawn Johnson
Curtis Martin
CQ10 Terrell Davis 5.00 12.00
Brian Griese
Mark Brunell
Fred Taylor
CQ11 Jon Kitna 5.00 12.00
Joey Galloway
Napolean Kaufman
Tim Brown
CQ12 Peyton Manning 25.00 50.00
Edgerrin James
Tim Couch
Kevin Johnson

1999 Playoff Contenders SSD Round Numbers Autographs

STATED ODDS 1:109
RN1 Kevin Johnson 10.00 25.00
Peerless Price
RN2 Ricky Williams 25.00 60.00
Edgerrin James
RN3 Donovan McNabb 30.00 80.00
Akili Smith
RN4 Sean Bennett 10.00 25.00
Brandon Stokley
RN5 Tim Couch 12.00 30.00
Cade McNown
RN6 David Boston 10.00 25.00
Troy Edwards
RN7 Daunte Culpepper 20.00 50.00
Torry Holt
RN8 Kevin Faulk 10.00 25.00
Jermaine Fazande
RN9 Joe Montgomery 8.00 20.00
Rob Konrad
RN10 Cecil Collins 8.00 20.00
De'Mond Parker

1999 Playoff Contenders SSD ROY Contenders

COMPLETE SET (12) 50.00 100.00
STATED ODDS 1:29
1 Tim Couch 2.00 5.00
2 Donovan McNabb 6.00 15.00
3 Akili Smith 2.00 5.00
4 Daunte Culpepper 5.00 12.00
5 Cade McNown 2.00 5.00
6 Edgerrin James 5.00 12.00
7 Ricky Williams 2.50 6.00
8 Cecil Collins 2.00 5.00
9 Torry Holt 3.00 8.00
10 David Boston 2.00 5.00
11 Troy Edwards 2.00 5.00
12 Champ Bailey 2.50 6.00

1999 Playoff Contenders SSD ROY Contenders Autographs

STATED PRINT RUN 100 SER.#'d SETS
1 Tim Couch 10.00 25.00
2 Donovan McNabb 40.00 80.00
3 Akili Smith 8.00 20.00
4 Daunte Culpepper 10.00 25.00
5 Cade McNown 8.00 20.00
6 Edgerrin James 12.00 30.00
7 Ricky Williams 15.00 40.00
8 Cecil Collins 6.00 15.00
9 Torry Holt 15.00 40.00
10 David Boston 8.00 20.00
11 Troy Edwards 8.00 20.00
12 Champ Bailey 20.00 50.00

1999 Playoff Contenders SSD Touchdown Tandems

COMPLETE SET (24) 50.00 100.00
STATED ODDS 1:15
T1 Keyshawn Johnson 1.25 3.00
Curtis Martin
T2 Dan Marino 5.00 12.00
Tony Martin
T3 Drew Bledsoe 2.00 5.00
Terry Glenn
T4 Peyton Manning 4.00 10.00
Marvin Harrison
T5 Doug Flutie 1.50 4.00
Thurman Thomas
T6 Steve McNair 1.50 4.00
Eddie George
T7 Kordell Stewart 1.25 3.00
Jerome Bettis
T8 Akili Smith 1.25 3.00
Carl Pickens
T9 Mark Brunell 1.50 4.00
Jimmy Smith
T10 Jon Kitna 1.25 3.00
Joey Galloway
T11 John Elway 4.00 10.00
Terrell Davis
T12 Napoleon Kaufman 1.25 3.00
Tim Brown
T13 Troy Aikman 3.00 8.00
Emmitt Smith
T14 Jake Plummer 1.25 3.00
Rob Moore
T15 Donovan McNabb 3.00 8.00
Charles Johnson
T16 Brad Johnson 1.25 3.00
Michael Westbrook
T17 Brett Favre 4.00 10.00
Antonio Freeman
T18 Randall Cunningham 3.00 8.00
Randy Moss
T19 Mike Alstott 1.25 3.00
Warrick Dunn
T20 Cade McNown 1.25 3.00
Curtis Enis
T21 Barry Sanders 4.00 10.00
Herman Moore
T22 Steve Young 3.00 8.00
Jerry Rice
T23 Chris Chandler 1.25 3.00
Jamal Anderson
T24 Marshall Faulk 2.50 6.00
Isaac Bruce

1999 Playoff Contenders SSD Touchdown Tandems Die Cuts

T1 Keyshawn Johnson 20.00 40.00
Curtis Martin
T2 Dan Marino 50.00 100.00
Tony Martin
T3 Drew Bledsoe 25.00 50.00
Terry Glenn
T4 Peyton Manning 40.00 100.00
Marvin Harrison
T5 Doug Flutie 20.00 40.00
Thurman Thomas
T6 Steve McNair 20.00 40.00
Eddie George
T7 Kordell Stewart 20.00 50.00
Jerome Bettis
T8 Akili Smith 6.00 15.00
Carl Pickens
T9 Mark Brunell 25.00 50.00
Jimmy Smith
T10 Jon Kitna 15.00 40.00
Joey Galloway
T11 John Elway 20.00 50.00
Terrell Davis
T12 Napoleon Kaufman 30.00 60.00
Tim Brown
T13 Troy Aikman 40.00 80.00
Emmitt Smith
T14 Jake Plummer 12.50 30.00
Rob Moore
T15 Donovan McNabb 12.50 30.00
Charles Johnson
T16 Brad Johnson 20.00 50.00
Michael Westbrook
T17 Brett Favre 20.00 50.00
Antonio Freeman
T18 Randall Cunningham 15.00 40.00
Randy Moss
T19 Mike Alstott 30.00 60.00
Warrick Dunn
T20 Cade McNown 10.00 25.00
Curtis Enis
T21 Barry Sanders 150.00 250.00
Herman Moore
T22 Steve Young 12.50 30.00
Jerry Rice
T23 Chris Chandler 6.00 15.00
Jamal Anderson
T24 Marshall Faulk 50.00 100.00
Isaac Bruce

1999 Playoff Contenders SSD Triple Threat

COMPLETE SET (20) 30.00 60.00
STATED ODDS 1:15
TT1 Jake Plummer 1.00 2.50
David Boston
Frank Sanders
TT2 Deion Sanders 2.50 6.00
Troy Aikman
Emmitt Smith
TT3 Terrell Owens 2.00 5.00
Jerry Rice
Steve Young
TT4 Dan Marino 3.00 8.00
O.J. McDuffie
Cecil Collins
TT5 Keyshawn Johnson 1.00 2.50
Wayne Chrebet
Curtis Martin
TT6 Jamal Anderson 1.00 2.50
Chris Chandler
Terance Mathis
TT7 Brian Griese 1.00 2.50
Terrell Davis
Shannon Sharpe
TT8 Fred Taylor 1.00 2.50
Mark Brunell
Keenan McCardell
TT9 Randy Moss 3.00 8.00
Cris Carter
Randall Cunningham
TT10 Antonio Freeman 3.00 8.00
Brett Favre
Dorsey Levens
TT11 Brad Johnson 1.25 3.00
Skip Hicks
Champ Bailey
TT12 Barry Sanders 3.00 8.00
Herman Moore
Charlie Batch
TT13 Eddie George 1.00 2.50
Steve McNair
Yancey Thigpen
TT14 Kordell Stewart 1.00 2.50
Jerome Bettis
Troy Edwards
TT15 Antowain Smith 1.00 2.50
Eric Moulds
Doug Flutie
TT16 Terry Glenn 1.50 4.00
Kevin Faulk
Drew Bledsoe
TT17 Mike Alstott 1.00 2.50
Warrick Dunn
Shaun King
TT18 Peyton Manning 6.00 15.00
Marvin Harrison
Edgerrin James
TT19 Corey Dillon 1.00 2.50
Akili Smith
Carl Pickens
TT20 Isaac Bruce 3.00 8.00
Torry Holt
Marshall Faulk

1999 Playoff Contenders SSD Triple Threat Red

TT4 Dan Marino/23 75.00 200.00
TT7 Brian Griese/33 25.00 60.00
TT11 Brad Johnson/48 7.50 20.00
TT12 Barry Sanders/73 25.00 60.00
TT13 Eddie George/37 12.50 30.00
TT16 Terry Glenn/86 5.00 12.00
TT18 Peyton Manning/26 75.00 200.00
TT19 Corey Dillon/66 6.00 15.00
TT20 Isaac Bruce/80 5.00 12.00
TT23 Jerry Rice/75 15.00 40.00
TT24 O.J. McDuffie/90 2.50 6.00
TT25 Wayne Chrebet/63 6.00 15.00
TT26 Chris Chandler/25 15.00 40.00
TT27 Terrell Davis/21 30.00 60.00
TT28 Mark Brunell/20 35.00 80.00
TT30 Brett Favre/31 60.00 150.00
TT32 Herman Moore/82 5.00 12.00
TT35 Eric Moulds/84 5.00 12.00
TT37 Warrick Dunn/50 7.50 20.00
TT38 Marvin Harrison/61 6.00 15.00
TT39 Akili Smith/32 15.00 40.00
TT41 Frank Sanders/89 2.50 6.00
TT43 Steve Young/36 35.00 80.00
TT44 Cecil Collins/28 15.00 40.00
TT45 Curtis Martin/60 6.00 15.00
TT48 Keenan McCardell/67 3.00 8.00
TT49 Randall Cunningham/34 12.50 30.00
TT50 Dorsey Levens/50 7.50 20.00
TT51 Champ Bailey/22 20.00 50.00
TT52 Charlie Batch/98 3.00 8.00
TT54 Troy Edwards/27 15.00 40.00
TT55 Doug Flutie/20 35.00 80.00
TT56 Drew Bledsoe/20 35.00 80.00
TT57 Shaun King/36 15.00 40.00
TT59 Carl Pickens/67 3.00 8.00
TT60 Marshall Faulk/78 7.50 20.00

2000 Playoff Contenders

Released in mid January 2001, The 200-card contenders set is divided into 100-base cards, 50-autographed Rookie Tickets, 40-autographed NFL Europe prospect cards and 10-autographed Playoff Tickets. Base cards feature player action photography set against a colored background designed to match team colors. A silver foil enhanced "ticket" on the right side containing the player's name. All autographed cards feature an embossed Playoff Authentic Signature stamp on the card front and a color shift to gold on the ticket part of the card. Some RCs were issued in packs as redemption cards which carried an expiration date of 12/31/2002. Four of those players, Thomas Jones, Derrick Ham, Ronnie Powell, and Fred Taylor PT, never signed for the set but unsigned Thomas Jones cards were released at a later date. The NFL Europe cards have player photos on the right and tickets on the left. Contenders was packaged in 12-pack boxes with each pack containing five cards and carried a suggested retail price of $9.99.

COMP.SET w/o SP's (100) 7.50 20.00
1 David Boston .20 .50
2 Jake Plummer .25 .60
3 Chris Chandler .25 .60
4 Jamal Anderson .25 .60
5 Tim Dwight .25 .60
6 Qadry Ismail .25 .60
7 Tony Banks .20 .50
8 Lamar Smith .20 .50
9 Doug Flutie .30 .75
10 Eric Moulds .25 .60
11 Peerless Price .25 .60
12 Rob Johnson .25 .60
13 Muhsin Muhammad .25 .60
14 Reggie White .30 .75
15 Steve Beuerlein .25 .60
16 Cade McNown .20 .50
17 Derrick Alexander .20 .50
18 Marcus Robinson .25 .60
19 Akili Smith .20 .50
20 Corey Dillon .25 .60
21 Kevin Johnson .20 .50
22 Tim Couch .25 .60
23 Emmitt Smith .75 2.00
24 Joey Galloway .25 .60
25 Rocket Ismail .25 .60
26 Troy Aikman .50 1.25
27 Brian Griese .25 .60
28 Ed McCaffrey .25 .60
29 John Elway .75 2.00
30 Olandis Gary .25 .60
31 Rod Smith .25 .60
32 Terrell Davis .30 .75
33 Charlie Batch .25 .60
34 Germane Crowell .20 .50
35 James Stewart .20 .50
36 Barry Sanders .60 1.50
37 Antonio Freeman .25 .60
38 Brett Favre 1.00 2.50
39 Dorsey Levens .25 .60
40 Edgerrin James .30 .75
41 Marvin Harrison .30 .75
42 Peyton Manning .75 2.00
43 Fred Taylor .30 .75
44 Jimmy Smith .25 .60
45 Mark Brunell .25 .60
46 Elvis Grbac .20 .50
47 Tony Gonzalez .30 .75
48 Dan Marino 1.00 2.50
49 Joe Horn .25 .60
50 Jay Fiedler .25 .60
51 Thurman Thomas .30 .75
52 Cris Carter .30 .75
53 Daunte Culpepper .25 .60
54 Randy Moss .30 .75
55 Robert Smith .25 .60
56 Drew Bledsoe .30 .75
57 Terry Glenn .25 .60
58 Ricky Williams .30 .75
59 Amani Toomer .25 .60
60 Kerry Collins .25 .60
61 Curtis Martin .30 .75
62 Vinny Testaverde .25 .60
63 Wayne Chrebet .25 .60
64 Rich Gannon .25 .60
65 Tim Brown .30 .75
66 Tyrone Wheatley .20 .50
67 Donovan McNabb .30 .75
68 Duce Staley .25 .60
69 Jerome Bettis .30 .75
70 Jermaine Fazande .20 .50
71 Junior Seau .30 .75
72 Donald Hayes .20 .50
73 Charlie Garner .25 .60
74 Jeff Garcia .25 .60
75 Jerry Rice .60 1.50
76 Steve Young .40 1.00
77 Terrell Owens .30 .75
78 Tiki Barber .30 .75
79 Tim Riakabutuka .25 .60
80 Ricky Watters .25 .60
81 Isaac Bruce .30 .75
82 Kurt Warner .50 1.25
83 Marshall Faulk .30 .75
84 Torry Holt .30 .75
85 Keyshawn Johnson .25 .60
86 Mike Alstott .30 .75
87 Shaun King .20 .50
88 Warren Sapp .25 .60
89 Warrick Dunn .25 .60
90 Eddie George .25 .60
91 Jevon Kearse .25 .60
92 Steve McNair .30 .75
93 Carl Pickens .25 .60
94 Albert Connell .20 .50
95 Brad Johnson .25 .60
96 Bruce Smith .30 .75
97 Deion Sanders .30 .75
98 Jeff George .25 .60
99 Michael Westbrook UER .20 .50
(photo is Stephen Davis)
100 Stephen Davis UER .25 .60
(photo is Michael Westbrook)
101 Courtney Brown AU RC 4.00 10.00
102 Corey Simon AU RC 4.00 10.00
103 Brian Urlacher AU RC 40.00 80.00
104 Deon Grant AU RC 3.00 8.00
105 Peter Warrick AU RC 5.00 12.00
106 Jamal Lewis AU RC 8.00 20.00
107 Thomas Jones No AU RC 6.00 15.00
108 Plaxico Burress AU RC 15.00 30.00
109 Travis Taylor AU RC 4.00 10.00
110 Ron Dayne AU RC 5.00 12.00
111 Bubba Franks AU RC 5.00 12.00
112 Chad Pennington AU RC 12.00 30.00
113 Shaun Alexander AU RC 10.00 25.00
114 Sylvester Morris AU RC 3.00 8.00
115 Mike Anderson AU RC 5.00 12.00
116 R.Jay Soward AU RC 3.00 8.00
117 Trung Canidate AU RC 4.00 10.00
118 Dennis Northcutt AU RC 4.00 10.00
119 Todd Pinkston AU RC 3.00 8.00
120 Jerry Porter AU RC 5.00 12.00
121 Travis Prentice AU RC 4.00 10.00
122 Giovanni Carmazzi AU RC 3.00 8.00
123 Ron Dugans AU RC 3.00 8.00
124 Dez White AU RC 4.00 10.00
125 Chris Cole AU RC 4.00 10.00
126 Ron Dixon AU RC 3.00 8.00
127 Chris Redman AU RC 4.00 10.00
128 J.R. Redmond AU RC 3.00 8.00
129 Laveranues Coles AU RC 5.00 12.00
130 JaJuan Dawson AU RC 3.00 8.00
131 Darrell Jackson AU RC 4.00 10.00
132 Reuben Droughns AU RC 5.00 12.00
133 Doug Chapman AU RC 3.00 8.00
134 Curtis Keaton AU RC 3.00 8.00
135 Gari Scott AU RC 3.00 8.00
136 Danny Farmer AU RC 3.00 8.00
137 Trevor Gaylor AU RC 3.00 8.00
138 Avion Black AU RC 3.00 8.00
139 Michael Wiley AU RC 3.00 8.00
140 Sammy Morris AU RC 4.00 10.00
141 Tee Martin AU RC 5.00 12.00
142 Troy Walters AU RC 3.00 8.00
143 Marc Bulger AU RC 10.00 25.00
144 Tom Brady AU RC 600.00 1,000.00
145 Todd Husak AU RC 3.00 8.00
146 Tim Rattay AU RC 4.00 10.00
147 Jarious Jackson AU RC 4.00 10.00
148 Joe Hamilton AU RC 3.00 8.00
149 Shyrone Stith AU RC 3.00 8.00
150 Kwame Cavil AU RC 3.00 8.00
151 Antonio Banks ET AU RC 2.00 5.00
152 Jonathan Brown ET AU RC 2.00 5.00
153 Ontiwaun Carter ET AU RC 2.00 5.00
154 Jeremaine Copeland ET 2.00 5.00
155 Ralph Dawkins ET AU RC 2.00 5.00
156 Marques Douglas ET AU RC 2.00 5.00
157 Kevin Drake ET AU RC 2.00 5.00
158 Damon Dunn ET AU RC 2.00 5.00
159 Todd Floyd ET AU RC 2.00 5.00
160 Tony Graziani ET AU 2.50 6.00
162 Duane Hawthorne 2.00 5.00
ET AU RC
163 Alonzo Johnson ET AU RC 2.00 5.00
164 Mark Kacmarynski 2.00 5.00
ET AU RC
165 Eric Kresser ET AU 2.00 5.00
166 Jim Kubiak ET AU RC 2.00 5.00
167 Blaine McElmurry ET AU RC 2.00 5.00
168 Scott Milanovich ET AU 2.00 5.00
169 Norman Miller ET AU RC 2.00 5.00
170 Sean Morey ET AU RC 2.00 5.00
171 Jeff Ogden ET AU 2.00 5.00
172 Pepe Pearson ET AU RC 2.00 5.00
173 Ron Powlus ET AU RC 3.00 8.00
174 Jason Shelley ET AU RC 2.00 5.00
175 Ben Snell ET AU RC 2.00 5.00
176 Aaron Stecker ET AU RC 2.50 6.00
177 L.C. Stevens ET AU 2.00 5.00
178 Mike Sutton ET AU RC 2.00 5.00
179 Damian Vaughn ET AU RC 2.00 5.00
180 Ted White ET AU 2.00 5.00
181 Marcus Crandell ET AU RC 2.00 5.00
182 Darryl Daniel ET AU RC 2.00 5.00
183 Jesse Haynes ET AU
184 Matt Lytle ET AU RC 2.00 5.00
185 Deon Mitchell ET AU RC 2.50 6.00
186 Kendrick Nord ET AU RC 2.00 5.00
188 Selucio Sanford ET AU RC 2.00 5.00
189 Corey Thomas ET AU 2.00 5.00
190 Vershan Jackson ET AU RC 2.00 5.00
191 Jake Plummer PT AU 8.00 20.00
192 Jim Kelly PT AU 20.00 40.00
193 Bernie Kosar PT AU 10.00 25.00
194 Marvin Harrison PT AU 15.00 40.00
196 Kerry Collins PT AU 8.00 20.00
197 Kurt Warner PT AU 30.00 60.00
198 Jevon Kearse PT AU 8.00 20.00
199 Brad Johnson PT AU 8.00 20.00
200 Jeff George PT AU 8.00 20.00

2000 Playoff Contenders Championship Ticket

*VETS 1-100: 4X TO 10X BASIC CARDS
*ROOKIE AU 101-150: 1X TO 2.5X BASIC CARDS
*ET AU 151-190: .6X TO 1.5X BASIC CARDS
*PT AU 191-200: .5X TO 1.2X BASIC CARDS
CHAMP.TICKET PRINT RUN 100 SER.#'d SETS
144 Tom Brady AU 1,500.00 3,000.00

2000 Playoff Contenders Championship Fabric

STATED PRINT RUN 25-300
CF1 Az Zahir Hakim P/300 5.00 12.00
CF2 Grant Wistrom P/300 5.00 12.00
CF3 Isaac Bruce P/300 8.00 20.00
CF4 Kevin Carter P/300 5.00 12.00
CF5 Kurt Warner P/75* 20.00 50.00
CF5A Kurt Warner P AU/25* 100.00 200.00
CF6 Marshall Faulk P/300 8.00 20.00
CF7 Tony Horne P/300 5.00 12.00
CF8 Robert Holcombe P/300 5.00 12.00
CF9 Todd Collins P/300 5.00 12.00
CF10 Torry Holt P/300 8.00 20.00
CF11 Az-Zahir Hakim J/300 5.00 12.00
CF12 Grant Wistrom J/300 5.00 12.00
CF13 Isaac Bruce J/300 8.00 20.00
CF14 Kevin Carter J/300 5.00 12.00
CF15 Kurt Warner J/250* 12.00 30.00
CF15A Kurt Warner J AU/50* 75.00 150.00
CF16 Marshall Faulk J/300 8.00 20.00
CF17 Tony Horne J/300 5.00 12.00
CF18 Robert Holcombe J/300 5.00 12.00
CF19 Todd Collins J/300 5.00 12.00
CF20 Torry Holt J/300 8.00 20.00
CF21 Az-Zahir Hakim P 8.00 20.00
J/100
CF22 Grant Wistrom P 8.00 20.00
J/100
CF23 Isaac Bruce P 12.00 30.00
J/100
CF24 Kevin Carter P 8.00 20.00
J/100
CF25 Kurt Warner P 20.00 50.00
J/75*
CF25A Kurt Warner P 100.00 200.00
J AU/25*
CF26 Marshall Faulk P 12.00 30.00
J/100
CF27 Tony Horne P 8.00 20.00
J/100
CF28 Robert Holcombe P 8.00 20.00
J/100
CF29 Todd Collins P 8.00 20.00
J/100
CF30 Torry Holt P 12.00 30.00
J/100
CF31 Kurt Warner P/25 30.00 80.00
Torry Holt
CF32 Marshall Faulk P/25 20.00 50.00
Isaac Bruce
CF33 Tony Horne P/25 12.00 30.00
Az-Zahir Hakim
CF34 Grant Wistrom P/25 12.00 30.00
Robert Holcombe
CF35 Todd Collins P/25 12.00 30.00
Kevin Carter
CF36 Kurt Warner J/25 30.00 80.00
Marshall Faulk
CF37 Isaac Bruce J/25 20.00 50.00
Torry Holt
CF38 Kevin Carter J/25 12.00 30.00
Az-Zahir Hakim
CF39 Grant Wistrom J/25 12.00 30.00
Robert Holcombe
CF40 Todd Collins J/25 12.00 30.00
Tony Horne
CF41 Isaac Bruce P 30.00 80.00
J/25
Kurt Warner
CF42 Torry Holt P 20.00 50.00
J/25
Marshall Faulk
CF43 Az-Zahir Hakim P 12.00 30.00
J/25
Robert Holcombe
CF44 Kevin Carter P 12.00 30.00
J/25
Tony Horne
CF45 Grant Wistrom P 12.00 30.00
J/25
Todd Collins

2000 Playoff Contenders Hawaii 5-0

COMPLETE SET (50) 30.00 80.00
STATED ODDS 1:11
1 Steve Beuerlein .75 2.00
2 Muhsin Muhammad .75 2.00
3 Jim Kelly 1.25 3.00
4 Doug Flutie 1.00 2.50
5 Reggie White 1.00 2.50
6 Corey Dillon .75 2.00
7 Emmitt Smith 2.50 6.00
8 Troy Aikman 1.50 4.00
9 Randall Cunningham 1.00 2.50
10 John Elway 2.50 6.00
11 Terrell Davis 1.00 2.50
12 Barry Sanders 2.00 5.00
13 Herman Moore .75 2.00
14 Brett Favre 3.00 8.00
15 Dorsey Levens .75 2.00
16 Antonio Freeman .75 2.00
17 Peyton Manning 2.50 6.00
18 Edgerrin James 1.00 2.50
19 Marvin Harrison 1.00 2.50
20 Mark Brunell .75 2.00
21 Jimmy Smith .75 2.00
22 Warren Moon 1.00 2.50
23 Dan Marino 3.00 8.00
24 Randy Moss 1.00 2.50
25 Cris Carter 1.00 2.50
26 Robert Smith .75 2.00
27 Drew Bledsoe 1.00 2.50
28 Tony Gonzalez 1.00 2.50
29 Rich Gannon .75 2.00
30 Curtis Martin 1.00 2.50
31 Vinny Testaverde .75 2.00
32 Frank Wycheck .75 2.00
33 Jerome Bettis 1.00 2.50
34 Junior Seau 1.00 2.50
35 Jerry Rice 2.00 5.00
36 Steve Young 1.25 3.00
37 Ricky Watters .75 2.00
38 Kurt Warner 1.50 4.00
39 Marshall Faulk 1.00 2.50
40 Isaac Bruce 1.00 2.50
41 Keyshawn Johnson .75 2.00
42 Mike Alstott 1.00 2.50
43 Warren Sapp .75 2.00
44 Eddie George .75 2.00
45 Jevon Kearse .75 2.00
46 Carl Pickens .75 2.00
47 Terry Glenn .75 2.00
48 Brad Johnson .75 2.00
49 Bruce Smith 1.00 2.50
50 Deion Sanders 1.00 2.50

2000 Playoff Contenders MVP Contenders

COMPLETE SET (30) 40.00 100.00
STATED ODDS 1:35
MVP1 Cade McNown .75 2.00
MVP2 Tim Couch 1.00 2.50
MVP3 Troy Aikman 2.00 5.00
MVP4 Terrell Davis 1.25 3.00
MVP5 Drew Bledsoe 1.25 3.00
MVP6 Ricky Williams 1.25 3.00
MVP7 Jerry Rice 2.50 6.00
MVP8 Jamal Anderson 1.00 2.50
MVP9 Dorsey Levens 1.00 2.50
MVP10 Cris Carter 1.25 3.00
MVP11 Emmitt Smith 3.00 8.00
MVP12 Brett Favre 4.00 10.00
MVP13 Peyton Manning 3.00 8.00
MVP14 Edgerrin James 1.25 3.00
MVP15 Fred Taylor 1.25 3.00
MVP16 Randy Moss 1.25 3.00
MVP17 Curtis Martin 1.25 3.00
MVP18 Marshall Faulk 1.25 3.00
MVP19 Steve McNair 1.25 3.00
MVP20 Stephen Davis 1.00 2.50
MVP21 Mark Brunell 1.00 2.50
MVP22 Daunte Culpepper 1.00 2.50
MVP23 Kurt Warner 2.00 5.00
MVP24 Eddie George 1.00 2.50
MVP25 Marvin Harrison 1.25 3.00
MVP26 Isaac Bruce 1.25 3.00
MVP27 Shaun King .75 2.00
MVP28 Keyshawn Johnson 1.00 2.50
MVP29 Brad Johnson 1.00 2.50
MVP30 Jimmy Smith 1.00 2.50

2000 Playoff Contenders Quads

COMPLETE SET (15) 30.00 80.00
STATED ODDS 1:59
*ULTIMATE/80-159: .8X TO 2X BASIC INSERTS
*ULTIMATE/44-60: 1X TO 2.5X BASIC INSERTS
*ULTIMATE/25: 1.5X TO 4X BASIC INSERTS
ULTIMATE QUAD PRINT RUN 8-159
CQ1 Plaxico Burress 1.50 4.00
Jerome Bettis
Travis Prentice
Tim Couch
CQ2 Troy Aikman 5.00 12.00
Emmitt Smith
Brad Johnson
Stephen Davis
CQ3 Curtis Martin 3.00 8.00
Chad Pennington
Edgerrin James
Peyton Manning
CQ4 Shaun King 2.00 5.00
Keyshawn Johnson
Daunte Culpepper
Randy Moss
CQ5 Fred Taylor 2.00 5.00
Eddie George
Mark Brunell
Steve McNair
CQ6 Ricky Watters 1.50 4.00
Jerry Porter
Tim Brown
Shaun Alexander
CQ7 Antonio Freeman 6.00 15.00
Brett Favre
Marcus Robinson
Cade McNown
CQ8 Donovan McNabb 2.00 5.00
Duce Staley
Kerry Collins
Ron Dayne
CQ9 Jamal Lewis 1.50 4.00
Akili Smith
Peter Warrick
Travis Taylor
CQ10 Jeff Blake 2.00 5.00
Ricky Williams

Thomas Jones		
Jake Plummer		
CQ11 Jerry Rice	4.00	10.00
Terrell Owens		
Marshall Faulk		
Kurt Warner		
CQ12 Drew Bledsoe	2.00	5.00
Peerless Price		
Terry Glenn		
Eric Moulds		
CQ13 Terrell Davis	1.25	3.00
Brian Griese		
Sylvester Morris		
Elvis Grbac		
CQ14 Steve Beuerlein	1.50	4.00
Muhsin Muhammad		
Jamal Anderson		
Chris Chandler		
CQ15 Ryan Leaf	1.50	4.00
Jermaine Fazande		
Jay Fiedler		
Damon Huard		

2000 Playoff Contenders Round Numbers Autographs

STATED ODDS 1:173		
1 Jamal Lewis	15.00	40.00
Travis Taylor		
2 Thomas Jones	20.00	50.00
Shaun Alexander		
4 Sylvester Morris AUTO	6.00	15.00
R.Jay Soward No Auto		
5 Todd Pinkston	10.00	25.00
Jerry Porter		
7 Giovanni Carmazzi	8.00	20.00
Chris Redman		
8 Travis Prentice	8.00	20.00
JaJuan Dawson		
9 Ron Dugans	10.00	25.00
Laveranues Coles		
10 Corey Simon	25.00	60.00
Brian Urlacher		
11 Marc Bulger	200.00	400.00
Tom Brady		
12 Tim Rattay	8.00	20.00
Joe Hamilton		
13 Trevor Gaylor	6.00	15.00
Avion Black		
15 Curtis Keaton	6.00	15.00
Gari Scott		

2000 Playoff Contenders Round Numbers Autographs Gold

STATED PRINT RUN 10-70		
5 Todd Pinkston/20	25.00	60.00
Jerry Porter		
6 J.R.Redmond/30	12.00	30.00
Doug Chapman		
7 Giovanni Carmazzi/30	15.00	40.00
Chris Redman		
8 Travis Prentice/30	15.00	40.00
JaJuan Dawson		
9 Ron Dugans/30	20.00	50.00
Laveranues Coles		
11 Marc Bulger/60	350.00	500.00
Tom Brady		
12 Tim Rattay/70	12.00	30.00
Joe Hamilton		
13 Trevor Gaylor/40	12.00	30.00
Avion Black		
15 Curtis Keaton/40	12.00	30.00
Gari Scott		

2000 Playoff Contenders ROY Contenders

COMPLETE SET (20)	20.00	50.00
STATED ODDS 1:23		
ROY1 Thomas Jones	1.00	2.50
ROY2 Jamal Lewis	.75	2.00
ROY3 Travis Taylor	.60	1.50
ROY4 Brian Urlacher	3.00	8.00
ROY5 Peter Warrick	.75	2.00
ROY6 Travis Prentice	.60	1.50
ROY7 Courtney Brown	.60	1.50
ROY8 Bubba Franks	.75	2.00
ROY9 R.Jay Soward	.50	1.25
ROY10 Sylvester Morris	.50	1.25
ROY11 J.R. Redmond	.50	1.25
ROY12 Ron Dayne	.75	2.00
ROY13 Chad Pennington	1.25	3.00
ROY14 Laveranues Coles	.75	2.00
ROY15 Jerry Porter	.75	2.00
ROY16 Todd Pinkston	.50	1.25
ROY17 Corey Simon	.60	1.50
ROY18 Plaxico Burress	.75	2.00
ROY19 Shaun Alexander	1.00	2.50
ROY20 Darrell Jackson	.60	1.50

2000 Playoff Contenders ROY Contenders Autographs

STATED PRINT RUN 100 SER.#'d SETS		
ROY1 Thomas Jones	12.00	30.00
ROY2 Jamal Lewis	10.00	25.00
ROY3 Travis Taylor	8.00	20.00
ROY4 Brian Urlacher	40.00	100.00
ROY5 Peter Warrick	10.00	25.00
ROY6 Travis Prentice	8.00	20.00
ROY7 Courtney Brown	8.00	20.00
ROY8 Bubba Franks	10.00	25.00
ROY10 Sylvester Morris	6.00	15.00
ROY13 Chad Pennington	15.00	40.00
ROY14 Laveranues Coles	10.00	25.00
ROY15 Jerry Porter	10.00	25.00
ROY16 Todd Pinkston	6.00	15.00
ROY17 Corey Simon	8.00	20.00
ROY19 Shaun Alexander	12.00	30.00
ROY20 Darrell Jackson	8.00	20.00

2000 Playoff Contenders Touchdown Tandems

COMPLETE SET (30)	25.00	60.00
STATED ODDS 1:11		
*TOTALS/67: 2X TO 5X BASIC INSERTS		
*TOTALS/30-39: 3X TO 8X BASIC INSERTS		
*TOTALS/20-28: 4X TO 10X BASIC INSERTS		
*TOTALS/10-19: 5X TO 12X BASIC INSERTS		
TOTALS STATED PRINT RUN 7-67		
TD1 Randy Moss	.75	2.00
Marvin Harrison		
TD2 Kurt Warner	2.00	5.00
Peyton Manning		
TD3 Marshall Faulk	.75	2.00
Edgerrin James		
TD4 Eddie George	.75	2.00
Fred Taylor		
TD5 Emmitt Smith	2.00	5.00
Stephen Davis		
TD6 Isaac Bruce	1.50	4.00
Jerry Rice		
TD7 Antonio Freeman	.75	2.00
Cris Carter		
TD8 Drew Bledsoe	.75	2.00
Mark Brunell		
TD9 Jake Plummer	.75	2.00
Steve McNair		
TD10 Curtis Martin	.75	2.00
Duce Staley		
TD11 Keyshawn Johnson	.60	1.50
Marcus Robinson		
TD12 Dan Marino	2.50	6.00
Steve Young		
TD13 Brett Favre	2.50	6.00
Troy Aikman		
TD14 Tim Brown	.75	2.00
Eric Moulds		
TD15 Jerome Bettis	.75	2.00
Mike Alstott		
TD16 Dorsey Levens	.60	1.50
James Stewart		
TD17 Olandis Gary	.60	1.50
Ricky Watters		
TD18 Brian Griese	.60	1.50
Charlie Batch		
TD19 Terrell Owens	.75	2.00
Torry Holt		
TD20 Jimmy Smith	.60	1.50
Joey Galloway		
TD21 Kevin Johnson	.50	1.25
Michael Westbrook		
TD22 Corey Dillon	.75	2.00
Ricky Williams		
TD23 Donovan McNabb	.75	2.00
Akili Smith		
TD24 Tim Couch	.60	1.50
Cade McNown		
TD25 Shaun King	.60	1.50
Jon Kitna		
TD26 Peter Warrick	.75	2.00
Plaxico Burress		
TD27 Jamal Lewis	.75	2.00
Shaun Alexander		
TD28 Ron Dayne	.75	2.00
Thomas Jones		
TD29 Sylvester Morris	.50	1.25
Travis Taylor		
TD30 Chad Pennington	.60	1.50
Chris Redman		

2001 Playoff Contenders Samples

*VETS 1-100: .8X TO 2X BASIC CARDS		
COMMON ROOKIE (101-200)	.75	2.00
ROOKIE SEMISTARS	1.00	2.50
ROOKIE UNL.STARS	1.25	3.00
*GOLD VETS: 1X TO 2.5X SILVER		
*GOLD ROOKIES: 1.2X TO 3X SILVER		
GOLD ANNOUNCED PRINT RUN 30		
113 Chad Johnson	2.00	5.00
114 Chris Chambers	1.25	3.00
123 Deuce McAllister	1.25	3.00
124 Drew Brees	8.00	20.00
150 LaDainian Tomlinson	4.00	10.00
157 Michael Vick	5.00	12.00
166 Reggie Wayne	2.50	6.00
175 Santana Moss	1.50	4.00
177 T.J. Houshmandzadeh	1.50	4.00
190 Steve Smith	2.50	6.00

2001 Playoff Contenders

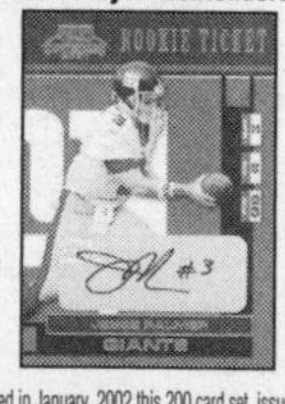

Released in January, 2002 this 200 card set, issued in five-card packs, featured a mix of 100 leading veterans and 100 rookies who had (or were expected to later have) an impact in the NFL. In addition, nearly all of the Rookie Cards were autographed. However, a few players did not return their cards in time for inclusion in packs. Those cards were issued via mail redemptions that could be redeemed until April 2, 2003. Playoff announced some print run totals on the signed RCs as noted below.

COMP.SET w/o RC's (100)	10.00	25.00
1 David Boston	.20	.50
2 Jake Plummer	.25	.60
3 Jamal Anderson	.25	.60
4 Chris Chandler	.25	.60
5 Elvis Grbac	.25	.60
6 Brandon Stokley	.25	.60
7 Travis Taylor	.20	.50
8 Ray Lewis	.30	.75
9 Rob Johnson	.25	.60
10 Eric Moulds	.25	.60
11 Tim Biakabutuka	.20	.50
12 Muhsin Muhammad	.25	.60
13 James Allen	.20	.50
14 Brian Urlacher	.40	1.00
15 Peter Warrick	.25	.60
16 Corey Dillon	.25	.60
17 Tim Couch	.20	.50
18 Kevin Johnson	.20	.50
19 Rickey Dudley	.20	.50
20 Emmitt Smith	.75	2.00
21 Joey Galloway	.25	.60
22 Brian Griese	.25	.60
23 Terrell Davis	.30	.75
24 Mike Anderson	.25	.60
25 Ed McCaffrey	.25	.60
26 Rod Smith	.25	.60
27 Charlie Batch	.25	.60
28 James Stewart	.20	.50
29 Germane Crowell	.20	.50
30 Johnnie Morton	.25	.60
31 Brett Favre	1.00	2.50
32 Ahman Green	.30	.75
33 Antonio Freeman	.30	.75
34 Peyton Manning	.75	2.00
35 Edgerrin James	.30	.75
36 Marvin Harrison	.30	.75
37 Jerome Pathon	.20	.50
38 Mark Brunell	.25	.60
39 Fred Taylor	.30	.75
40 Keenan McCardell	.25	.60
41 Jimmy Smith	.25	.60
42 Trent Green	.30	.75
43 Priest Holmes	.30	.75
44 Tony Gonzalez	.30	.75
45 Derrick Alexander	.20	.50
46 Jay Fiedler	.25	.60
47 Lamar Smith	.25	.60
48 Zach Thomas	.30	.75
49 Oronde Gadsden	.20	.50
50 Daunte Culpepper	.25	.60
51 Randy Moss	.30	.75
52 Cris Carter	.30	.75
53 Drew Bledsoe	.30	.75
54 J.R. Redmond	.20	.50
55 Troy Brown	.25	.60
56 Aaron Brooks	.25	.60
57 Ricky Williams	.30	.75
58 Joe Horn	.25	.60
59 Kerry Collins	.25	.60
60 Tiki Barber	.30	.75
61 Ron Dayne	.25	.60
62 Ike Hilliard	.25	.60
63 Vinny Testaverde	.25	.60
64 Curtis Martin	.30	.75
65 Wayne Chrebet	.25	.60
66 Laveranues Coles	.25	.60
67 Rich Gannon	.25	.60
68 Tyrone Wheatley	.25	.60
69 Tim Brown	.30	.75
70 Jerry Rice	.60	1.50
71 Donovan McNabb	.30	.75
72 Duce Staley	.25	.60
73 Todd Pinkston	.20	.50
74 Kordell Stewart	.25	.60
75 Jerome Bettis	.30	.75
76 Plaxico Burress	.25	.60
77 Doug Flutie	.30	.75
78 Junior Seau	.30	.75
79 Jeff Garcia	.25	.60
80 Garrison Hearst	.25	.60
81 Terrell Owens	.30	.75
82 Matt Hasselbeck	.30	.75
83 Ricky Watters	.25	.60
84 Shaun Alexander	.30	.75
85 Darrell Jackson	.25	.60
86 Kurt Warner	.50	1.25
87 Marshall Faulk	.30	.75
88 Isaac Bruce	.30	.75
89 Torry Holt	.25	.60
90 Brad Johnson	.25	.60
91 Keyshawn Johnson	.25	.60
92 Warrick Dunn	.30	.75
93 Warren Sapp	.25	.60
94 Steve McNair	.30	.75
95 Eddie George	.30	.75
96 Derrick Mason	.25	.60
97 Jevon Kearse	.25	.60
98 Stephen Davis	.25	.60
99 Bruce Smith	.30	.75
100 Michael Westbrook	.20	.50
101 Adam Archuleta/50* RC	30.00	80.00
102 Alex Bannister AU RC	3.00	8.00
103 Alge Crumpler AU RC	6.00	15.00
104 Andre Carter AU/100* RC	15.00	40.00
105 Anthony Thomas AU/600* RC	5.00	12.00
106 Ben Leard AU RC	3.00	8.00
107 Bobby Newcombe AU RC	4.00	10.00
108 Brian Allen AU RC	3.00	8.00
109 Carlos Polk AU RC	3.00	8.00
110 Casey Hampton No Auto RC	5.00	12.00
111 Cedric Scott AU RC	3.00	8.00
112 Cedrick Wilson AU RC	4.00	10.00
113 Chad Johnson AU RC	30.00	80.00
114 Chris Chambers AU/170* RC	30.00	80.00
115 Chris Weinke AU/350* RC	5.00	12.00
116 Correll Buckhalter AU/590* RC	10.00	25.00
117 Damione Lewis AU RC	4.00	10.00
118 Dan Morgan AU RC	4.00	10.00
119 Daniel Guy AU RC	3.00	8.00
120 David Allen AU RC	3.00	8.00
121 David Terrell AU/500* RC	4.00	10.00
122 Ken Lucas AU/276* RC	4.00	10.00
123 Deuce McAllister AU/500* RC	20.00	50.00
124 Drew Brees AU/500* RC	500.00	750.00
125 Eddie Berlin AU RC	3.00	8.00
126 Boo Williams AU/50* RC	25.00	60.00
127 Ennis Davis AU RC	3.00	8.00
128 Freddie Mitchell AU RC	3.00	8.00
129 Gary Baxter AU RC	3.00	8.00
130 Gerard Warren AU/200* RC	6.00	15.00
131 Hakim Akbar AU RC	3.00	8.00
132 Heath Evans AU RC	4.00	10.00
133 Jabari Holloway AU RC	3.00	8.00
134 Jamal Reynolds AU/500* RC	3.00	8.00
135 James Jackson AU RC	3.00	8.00
136 Jamie Winborn AU RC	4.00	10.00
137 Javon Green AU RC	3.00	8.00
138 Jesse Palmer AU RC	4.00	10.00
139 Dominic Rhodes AU/300* RC	8.00	20.00
140 Josh Heupel AU/150* RC	15.00	40.00
141 Justin Smith AU RC	5.00	12.00
142 Karon Riley AU RC	3.00	8.00
143 Keith Adams/50* RC	25.00	60.00
144 Kendrell Bell AU RC	5.00	12.00
145 Kenny Smith AU RC	3.00	8.00
146 Kenyatta Walker AU/50* RC	25.00	60.00
147 Ken-Yon Rambo AU RC	3.00	8.00
148 Kevan Barlow AU RC	4.00	10.00
149 Koren Robinson AU/400* RC	4.00	10.00
150 LaDainian Tomlinson AU/600* RC	150.00	300.00
151 LaMont Jordan AU/50* RC	30.00	80.00
152 Leonard Davis/50* RC	40.00	100.00
153 Marcus Stroud AU RC	4.00	10.00
154 Marques Tuiasosopo AU RC	4.00	10.00
155 Snoop Minnis AU/295* RC	3.00	8.00
156 Michael Bennett AU/600* RC	6.00	15.00
157 Michael Vick AU/327* RC	250.00	450.00
158 Mike McMahon AU/529* RC	4.00	10.00
159 Moran Norris AU RC	3.00	8.00
160 Morlon Greenwood AU RC	3.00	8.00
161 Nate Clements/50* RC	30.00	80.00
162 Quincy Carter AU SP RC	15.00	40.00
163 Quincy Morgan AU RC	4.00	10.00
164 Jamar Fletcher/50* RC	25.00	60.00
165 Reggie Germany AU RC	3.00	8.00
166 Reggie Wayne AU/400* RC	75.00	150.00
167 Reggie White AU RC	3.00	8.00
168 Richard Seymour/50* RC	40.00	100.00
169 Robert Carswell/50* RC	25.00	60.00
170 Robert Ferguson AU RC	5.00	12.00
171 Rod Gardner AU/75* RC	30.00	80.00
172 Ronney Daniels AU RC	3.00	8.00
173 Rudi Johnson AU RC	15.00	40.00
174 Sage Rosenfels AU/400* RC	12.50	25.00
175 Santana Moss AU/500* RC	15.00	40.00
176 Shaun Rogers AU RC	5.00	12.00
177 T.J. Houshmandzadeh AU RC	15.00	40.00
178 Tim Hasselbeck AU RC	4.00	10.00
179 Todd Heap AU/169* RC	40.00	80.00
180 Tony Stewart AU RC	4.00	10.00
181 Torrance Marshall AU RC	3.00	8.00
182 Travis Henry AU/369* RC	10.00	25.00
183 Travis Minor AU RC	4.00	10.00
184 Vinny Sutherland AU RC	3.00	8.00
185 Will Allen AU RC	5.00	12.00
186 Willie Howard AU RC	3.00	8.00
187 Willie Middlebrooks/50* RC	30.00	80.00
188 Derrick Blaylock AU/200* RC	6.00	15.00
189 A.J. Feeley AU/200* RC	6.00	15.00
190 Steve Smith AU/300* RC	60.00	120.00
191 Onome Ojo AU/200* RC	5.00	12.00
192 Dee Brown AU/300* RC	3.00	8.00
193 Kevin Kasper AU/200* RC	5.00	12.00
194 Dave Dickenson AU/300* RC	4.00	10.00
195 Chris Barnes AU/200* RC	5.00	12.00
196 Scotty Anderson AU/300* RC	3.00	8.00
197 Chris Taylor AU/300* RC	3.00	8.00
198 Cedric James AU/300* RC	3.00	8.00
199 Justin McCareins AU/200* RC	6.00	15.00
200 Tommy Polley AU/200* RC	5.00	12.00

2001 Playoff Contenders Championship Ticket

*VETS 1-100: 3X TO 8X BASIC CARDS		
COMMON ROOKIE (101-200)	3.00	8.00
ROOKIE SEMISTARS	4.00	10.00
ROOKIE UNL.STARS	5.00	12.00
STATED PRINT RUN 100 SER.#'d SETS		
113 Chad Johnson	8.00	20.00
114 Chris Chambers	5.00	12.00
123 Deuce McAllister	5.00	12.00
124 Drew Brees	100.00	200.00
150 LaDainian Tomlinson	50.00	100.00
157 Michael Vick	50.00	100.00
166 Reggie Wayne	10.00	25.00
175 Santana Moss	6.00	15.00
177 T.J. Houshmandzadeh	6.00	15.00
190 Steve Smith	10.00	25.00

2001 Playoff Contenders Legendary Contenders Autographs

PRINT RUNS ANNC'd BY PLAYOFF		
1 Archie Griffin	15.00	40.00
2 Archie Manning/50*	15.00	40.00
3 Art Monk/25*	50.00	100.00
4 Bart Starr/25*	150.00	300.00
5 Billy Sims	12.00	30.00
6 Bob Griese/25*	40.00	80.00
7 Charlie Joiner/50*	15.00	40.00
8 Charley Taylor/50*	15.00	40.00
9 Cris Collinsworth/50*	15.00	40.00
10 Craig Morton	12.00	30.00
11 Dan Fouts/25*	50.00	100.00
12 Deacon Jones/25*	50.00	100.00
13 Dick Butkus/225*	30.00	60.00
14 Don Maynard/25*	30.00	80.00
15 Drew Pearson/25*	15.00	40.00
16 Dwight Clark/50*	15.00	40.00
17 Earl Campbell/225*	30.00	60.00
18 Eric Dickerson/25*	30.00	80.00
19 Fran Tarkenton/25*	50.00	100.00
20 Franco Harris/50*	50.00	80.00
21 Frank Gifford/25*	50.00	100.00
22 Fred Biletnikoff/125*	15.00	40.00
23 John Fuqua	15.00	40.00
24 Gale Sayers/125*	40.00	80.00
25 George Blanda/125*	25.00	50.00
26 Harvey Martin No Auto	3.00	8.00
27 Henry Ellard	10.00	25.00
28 Irving Fryar	12.00	30.00
29 James Lofton/25*	30.00	80.00
30 Jim Brown/150*	50.00	100.00
31 Jim Plunkett/125*	15.00	40.00
32 Joe Greene/125*	50.00	80.00
33 Joe Montana/50*	100.00	175.00
34 Joe Namath/100*	50.00	120.00
35 Joe Theismann/125*	15.00	40.00
36 John Hadl	10.00	25.00
37 John Stallworth/50*	50.00	80.00
38 Johnny Unitas/25*	200.00	350.00
39 Kellen Winslow	12.00	30.00
40 Ken Anderson/50*	15.00	40.00
41 Ken Stabler/100*	40.00	80.00
42 Lance Alworth/125*	25.00	50.00
43 Warren Moon/72*	20.00	50.00
44 Mike Singletary/125*	25.00	50.00
45 Otto Graham/125*	25.00	50.00
46 Ozzie Newsome/25*	30.00	60.00
47 Paul Hornung/125*	30.00	60.00
48 Paul Warfield/125*	15.00	40.00
49 Raymond Berry/125*	12.00	30.00
50 Rocky Bleier	25.00	50.00
51 Roger Craig/25*	30.00	80.00
52 Roger Staubach/25*	100.00	175.00
53 Ronnie Lott/50*	30.00	60.00
54 Sammy Baugh/125*	75.00	150.00
55 Sonny Jurgensen/25*	60.00	100.00
56 Steve Largent/25*	50.00	100.00
57 Terry Bradshaw/25*	100.00	175.00
58 Todd Christensen	10.00	25.00
59 Tony Dorsett/25*	60.00	120.00
60 Y.A. Tittle/125*	30.00	60.00
61 Larry Csonka/225*	25.00	50.00
62 Lawrence Taylor/52*	40.00	80.00
63 Marcus Allen/50*	60.00	100.00
64 Barry Sanders/50*	100.00	175.00
65 Boomer Esiason/159*	12.00	30.00
66 Dan Marino/59*	100.00	200.00
67 Jim Kelly/58*	40.00	80.00
68 John Elway/53*	100.00	175.00
69 Michael Irvin	15.00	40.00
70 Phil Simms/57*	30.00	60.00
71 Steve Young/54*	40.00	80.00

2001 Playoff Contenders MVP Contenders

COMPLETE SET (20)	15.00	40.00
STATED ODDS 1:16		
1 Brett Favre	2.50	6.00
2 Brian Griese	.60	1.50
3 Corey Dillon	.60	1.50
4 Cris Carter	.75	2.00
5 Daunte Culpepper	.60	1.50
6 Drew Bledsoe	.75	2.00
7 Eddie George	.75	2.00
8 Edgerrin James	.75	2.00
9 Emmitt Smith	2.00	5.00
10 Isaac Bruce	.75	2.00
11 Aaron Brooks	.60	1.50
12 Jerry Rice	1.50	4.00
13 Kurt Warner	1.25	3.00
14 Mark Brunell	.60	1.50
15 Marshall Faulk	.75	2.00
16 Peyton Manning	2.00	5.00
17 Randy Moss	.75	2.00
18 Ray Lewis	.75	2.00
19 Ricky Williams	.75	2.00
20 Stephen Davis	.60	1.50

2001 Playoff Contenders MVP Contenders Autographs

STATED PRINT RUN 25 SER.#'d SETS		
1 Brett Favre	250.00	400.00
2 Brian Griese	25.00	60.00
3 Corey Dillon	30.00	80.00
4 Cris Carter	40.00	100.00
5 Daunte Culpepper	30.00	80.00
6 Drew Bledsoe	40.00	100.00
7 Eddie George	40.00	100.00
8 Edgerrin James	40.00	100.00
9 Emmitt Smith	150.00	300.00
10 Isaac Bruce	40.00	100.00
11 Aaron Brooks	25.00	60.00
12 Jerry Rice	175.00	300.00
13 Kurt Warner	60.00	150.00
14 Mark Brunell	30.00	80.00
15 Marshall Faulk	40.00	100.00
16 Peyton Manning	125.00	250.00
17 Randy Moss	60.00	120.00
18 Ray Lewis	60.00	120.00
19 Ricky Williams	40.00	100.00
20 Stephen Davis	25.00	60.00

2001 Playoff Contenders Round Numbers Autographs

*GOLD/20: .8X TO 2X BASIC AU		
*GOLD/30: .6X TO 1.5X BASIC AU		
GOLD PRINT RUN 10-30		
1 Michael Vick	100.00	200.00
LaDainian Tomlinson		
2 Deuce McAllister	15.00	40.00
Michael Bennett		
3 David Terrell	10.00	25.00
Koren Robinson		
4 Nate Clements	7.50	20.00
Will Allen No Auto		
5 Todd Heap	30.00	60.00
Reggie Wayne		
6 Richard Seymour No Auto	7.50	20.00
Justin Smith Auto		
7 Drew Brees	75.00	150.00
Quincy Carter		
8 Anthony Thomas	12.00	30.00
Travis Henry		
9 Chad Johnson	25.00	60.00
Quincy Morgan		
10 Robert Ferguson	15.00	40.00
Chris Chambers		
11 Shaun Rogers	10.00	25.00
Kendrell Bell		
12 Kevan Barlow	10.00	25.00
Travis Minor		
13 James Jackson	7.50	20.00
Snoop Minnis		
14 Rudi Johnson	15.00	40.00
Correll Buckhalter		
15 Chris Weinke	10.00	25.00
Jesse Palmer		

2001 Playoff Contenders ROY Contenders

COMPLETE SET (20)	20.00	50.00
STATED ODDS 1:32		
1 Anthony Thomas	.75	2.00
2 Chad Johnson	1.25	3.00
3 Chris Chambers	.75	2.00
4 Chris Weinke	.60	1.50
5 David Terrell	.60	1.50
6 Deuce McAllister	.75	2.00
7 Drew Brees	5.00	12.00
8 Freddie Mitchell	.50	1.25
9 James Jackson	.50	1.25
10 Kevan Barlow	.60	1.50
11 Koren Robinson	.60	1.50
12 LaDainian Tomlinson	2.50	6.00
13 Snoop Minnis	.50	1.25
14 Michael Bennett	.60	1.50
15 Michael Vick	3.00	8.00
16 Quincy Carter	.60	1.50
17 Quincy Morgan	.75	2.00
18 Reggie Wayne	1.50	4.00
19 Travis Henry	.60	1.50
20 Travis Minor	.60	1.50

2001 Playoff Contenders ROY Contenders Autographs

STATED PRINT RUN 50 SER.#'d SETS		
1 Anthony Thomas	12.00	30.00
2 Chad Johnson	20.00	50.00
3 Chris Chambers	12.00	30.00
4 Chris Weinke	10.00	25.00
5 David Terrell	10.00	25.00
6 Deuce McAllister	12.00	30.00
7 Drew Brees	150.00	250.00
8 Freddie Mitchell	8.00	20.00
9 James Jackson	8.00	20.00
10 Kevan Barlow	10.00	25.00
11 Koren Robinson	10.00	25.00
12 LaDainian Tomlinson	100.00	200.00
13 Snoop Minnis	8.00	20.00
14 Michael Bennett	10.00	25.00
15 Michael Vick	100.00	200.00
16 Quincy Morgan	10.00	25.00
17 Quincy Carter	10.00	25.00
18 Reggie Wayne	50.00	80.00
19 Travis Henry	10.00	25.00
20 Travis Minor	10.00	25.00

2001 Playoff Contenders Chicago Collection

NOT PRICED DUE TO SCARCITY

2002 Playoff Contenders Samples

*1-100 VETS: .8X TO 2X BASIC CARDS		
*1-100 GOLD VETS: 1X TO 2.5X SILVER		
*101-186 ROOKIES : .8X TO 2X SILVER		
UNPRICED EMERALD ANNC'D PRINT RUN 1		
101 Adrian Peterson	1.25	3.00
102 Albert Haynesworth	1.25	3.00
103 Alex Brown	1.25	3.00
104 Andra Davis	.75	2.00
105 Andre Davis	1.00	2.50
106 Andre Lott	.75	2.00
107 Anthony Weaver	.75	2.00
108 Antonio Bryant	1.25	3.00
109 Antwaan Randle El	1.25	3.00
110 Ashley Lelie	1.00	2.50
111 Brian Poli-Dixon	.75	2.00
112 Brian Westbrook	2.00	5.00
113 Bryant McKinnie	.75	2.00
114 Chad Hutchinson	.75	2.00
115 Charles Grant	1.25	3.00
116 Chester Taylor	1.25	3.00
117 Cliff Russell	.75	2.00
118 Clinton Portis	1.50	4.00
119 Randy McMichael	1.25	3.00
120 Damien Anderson	.75	2.00
121 Daniel Graham	1.00	2.50
122 David Carr	1.25	3.00
123 David Garrard	1.50	4.00
124 Deion Branch	1.25	3.00
125 John Simon	.75	2.00
126 DeShaun Foster	1.25	3.00
127 Donte Stallworth	1.25	3.00
128 Dwight Freeney	1.50	4.00
129 Ed Reed	5.00	12.00
130 Eric Crouch	1.25	3.00
131 Freddie Milons	.75	2.00
132 Jabar Gaffney	1.25	3.00
133 Javon Walker	1.25	3.00
134 Jeremy Shockey	2.00	5.00
135 Jerramy Stevens	1.25	3.00
136 Joey Harrington	1.25	3.00
137 John Henderson	1.00	2.50
138 Jonathan Wells	1.25	3.00
139 Josh McCown	1.25	3.00
140 Josh Reed	1.00	2.50
141 Josh Scobey	1.00	2.50
142 Julius Peppers	2.50	6.00
143 Kalimba Edwards	1.00	2.50
144 Kelly Campbell	1.00	2.50
145 Ken Simonton	.75	2.00
146 Keyuo Craver	.75	2.00
147 Kahlil Hill	.75	2.00
148 Kurt Kittner	.75	2.00
149 Ladell Betts	1.25	3.00
150 Lamar Gordon	1.00	2.50
151 Levar Fisher	.75	2.00
152 Lito Sheppard	1.25	3.00
153 Luke Staley	.75	2.00
154 Marquise Walker	.75	2.00
155 Maurice Morris	1.00	2.50
156 Mike Rumph	.75	2.00
157 Mike Williams	.75	2.00
158 Najeh Davenport	1.25	3.00
159 Napoleon Harris	1.00	2.50
160 Patrick Ramsey	1.25	3.00
161 Phillip Buchanon	1.25	3.00
162 Quentin Jammer	1.25	3.00
163 Randy Fasani	1.00	2.50
164 Reche Caldwell	1.25	3.00
165 Robert Thomas	.75	2.00
166 Rocky Calmus	1.00	2.50
167 Rohan Davey	1.25	3.00
168 Ron Johnson	1.00	2.50
169 Roy Williams	1.25	3.00
170 Ryan Sims	1.25	3.00
171 Tavon Mason	.75	2.00
172 Terry Charles	.75	2.00
173 T.J. Duckett	1.25	3.00
174 Tim Carter	1.00	2.50
175 Travis Stephens	.75	2.00
176 Trev Faulk	.75	2.00
177 Wendell Bryant	.75	2.00
178 William Green	1.00	2.50
179 Woody Dantzler	1.00	2.50
180 Tony Fisher	1.00	2.50
181 Javin Hunter	.75	2.00
182 Daryl Jones	.75	2.00
183 Jesse Chatman	.75	2.00
184 J.T. O'Sullivan	1.00	2.50
185 Josh Norman	.75	2.00
186 James Mungro	1.25	3.00

2002 Playoff Contenders

Issued in late December 2002, this 186 card set is composed of 100 veteran and 86 rookie ticket seqentially numbered autograph cards. Some of the autographed tickets were issued via redemption card only. Cards were packaged in a larger box with 2 sealed mini boxes inside containing 10 packs per mini box with 5 cards per pack. Each mini box contained one rookie ticket autograph card on average. Exchange deadline for rookie ticket cards was 6/23/2004.

COMP.SET w/o SP's (100)	10.00	25.00
ROOKIE AUTO PRINT RUN 40-900		
1 Drew Bledsoe	.30	.75
2 Travis Henry	.20	.50
3 Eric Moulds	.25	.60
4 Chris Chambers	.25	.60
5 Ricky Williams	.25	.60
6 Zach Thomas	.30	.75
7 Tom Brady	.75	2.00
8 Antowain Smith	.25	.60
9 Troy Brown	.25	.60
10 Curtis Martin	.30	.75
11 Vinny Testaverde	.25	.60
12 Chad Pennington	.30	.75
13 Jeff Blake	.25	.60
14 Jamal Lewis	.25	.60
15 Ray Lewis	.30	.75
16 Michael Westbrook	.20	.50
17 Corey Dillon	.25	.60
18 Peter Warrick	.25	.60
19 Tim Couch	.20	.50
20 Quincy Morgan	.20	.50
21 Kevin Johnson	.20	.50
22 Kordell Stewart	.25	.60
23 Plaxico Burress	.25	.60
24 Jerome Bettis	.30	.75
25 James Allen	.20	.50
26 Corey Bradford	.20	.50
27 Mark Brunell	.25	.60
28 Fred Taylor	.25	.60
29 Jimmy Smith	.25	.60
30 Peyton Manning	.60	1.50
31 Reggie Wayne	.30	.75
32 Marvin Harrison	.30	.75
33 Edgerrin James	.25	.60
34 Steve McNair	.30	.75
35 Eddie George	.25	.60
36 Jevon Kearse	.25	.60
37 Derrick Mason	.25	.60
38 Brian Griese	.25	.60
39 Terrell Davis	.30	.75
40 Ed McCaffrey	.25	.60
41 Rod Smith	.25	.60
42 Trent Green	.25	.60
43 Priest Holmes	.30	.75
44 Johnnie Morton	.25	.60
45 Tony Gonzalez	.30	.75
46 Rich Gannon	.25	.60
47 Tim Brown	.30	.75
48 Jerry Rice	.60	1.50
49 Charlie Garner	.25	.60
50 Drew Brees	.50	1.25
51 LaDainian Tomlinson	.40	1.00
52 Junior Seau	.30	.75
53 Quincy Carter	.20	.50
54 Emmitt Smith	.75	2.00
55 Joey Galloway	.25	.60
56 Kerry Collins	.25	.60
57 Tiki Barber	.30	.75
58 Michael Strahan	.30	.75
59 Donovan McNabb	.30	.75
60 Duce Staley	.25	.60
61 Antonio Freeman	.30	.75
62 Derrius Thompson	.20	.50
63 Stephen Davis	.25	.60
64 Rod Gardner	.20	.50
65 Anthony Thomas	.25	.60
66 Marty Booker	.25	.60
67 Brian Urlacher	.30	.75
68 James Stewart	.20	.50
69 Az-Zahir Hakim	.20	.50
70 Brett Favre	.75	2.00
71 Ahman Green	.25	.60
72 Donald Driver	.30	.75
73 Daunte Culpepper	.25	.60
74 Michael Bennett	.25	.60
75 Randy Moss	.30	.75
76 Michael Vick	.50	1.25
77 Warrick Dunn	.25	.60
78 Chris Weinke	.20	.50
79 Lamar Smith	.25	.60
80 Steve Smith	.30	.75
81 Aaron Brooks	.25	.60
82 Deuce McAllister	.25	.60
83 Joe Horn	.25	.60
84 Brad Johnson	.25	.60
85 Keyshawn Johnson	.25	.60
86 Mike Alstott	.25	.60
87 Warren Sapp	.25	.60
88 Jake Plummer	.25	.60
89 Thomas Jones	.30	.75
90 David Boston	.20	.50
91 Kurt Warner	.30	.75
92 Marshall Faulk	.30	.75
93 Isaac Bruce	.30	.75
94 Torry Holt	.30	.75
95 Jeff Garcia	.25	.60
96 Garrison Hearst	.25	.60
97 Kevan Barlow	.20	.50
98 Terrell Owens	.30	.75
99 Trent Dilfer	.25	.60
100 Shaun Alexander	.25	.60
101 Adrian Peterson AU/360 RC	6.00	15.00
102 Albert Haynesworth	8.00	20.00
No Auto RC		
103 Alex Brown AU/410 RC	6.00	15.00
104 Andra Davis AU/510 RC	3.00	8.00
105 Andre Davis AU/360 RC	5.00	12.00
106 Andre Lott AU/750 RC	3.00	8.00
107 Anthony Weaver AU/450 RC	3.00	8.00
108 Antonio Bryant AU/165 RC	15.00	40.00
109 Antwaan Randle El AU/135 RC	25.00	60.00
110 Ashley Lelie AU/360 RC	5.00	12.00
111 Brian Poli-Dixon AU/460 RC	3.00	8.00
112 Brian Westbrook AU/600 RC	12.00	30.00
113 Bryant McKinnie AU/600 RC	3.00	8.00
114 C Hutchinson AU/450 RC	3.00	8.00
115 Charles Grant AU/450 RC	5.00	12.00

116 Chester Taylor AU/315 RC 12.00 30.00
117 Cliff Russell AU/545 RC 3.00 8.00
118 Clinton Portis AU/360 RC 25.00 60.00
119 Randy McMichael AU/400 RC 6.00 15.00
120 Damien Anderson AU/460 RC 3.00 8.00
121 Daniel Graham AU/185 RC 6.00 15.00
122 David Carr AU/250 RC 10.00 25.00
123 David Garrard AU/310 RC 12.00 30.00
124 Deion Branch AU/650 RC 10.00 20.00
125 John Simon AU/400 RC 4.00 10.00
126 DeShaun Foster AU/310 RC 8.00 20.00
127 Donte Stallworth AU/302 RC 6.00 15.00
128 Dwight Freeney AU/410 RC 30.00 60.00
129 Ed Reed AU/550 RC 60.00 100.00
130 Eric Crouch AU/280 RC 8.00 20.00
131 Freddie Milons AU/380 RC 4.00 10.00
132 Jabar Gaffney AU/315 RC 6.00 15.00
133 Javon Walker AU/435 RC 6.00 15.00
134 Jeremy Shockey AU/160 RC 25.00 60.00
135 Jerramy Stevens AU/250 RC 8.00 20.00
136 Joey Harrington AU/250 RC 8.00 20.00
137 John Henderson AU/560 RC 4.00 10.00
138 Jonathan Wells AU/485 RC 5.00 12.00
139 Josh McCown AU/595 RC 5.00 12.00
140 Josh Reed AU/290 RC 6.00 15.00
141 Josh Scobey AU/615 RC 4.00 10.00
142 Julius Peppers AU/40 RC 350.00 600.00
143 Kalimba Edwards AU/510 RC 4.00 10.00
144 Kelly Campbell AU/360 RC 5.00 12.00
145 Ken Simonton AU/650 RC 3.00 8.00
146 Keyuo Craver AU/850 RC 3.00 8.00
147 Kahlil Hill AU/850 RC 3.00 8.00
148 Kurt Kittner AU/235 RC 5.00 12.00
149 Ladell Betts AU/600 RC 8.00 20.00
150 Lamar Gordon AU/600 RC 4.00 10.00
151 Levar Fisher AU/760 RC 3.00 8.00
152 Lito Sheppard AU/410 RC 10.00 25.00
153 Luke Staley AU/360 RC 4.00 10.00
154 Marquise Walker AU/330 RC 4.00 10.00
155 Maurice Morris AU/153 RC 15.00 40.00
156 Mike Rumph AU/510 RC 3.00 8.00
157 Mike Williams AU/500 RC 3.00 8.00
158 Najeh Davenport AU/460 RC 5.00 12.00
159 Napoleon Harris AU/900 RC 4.00 10.00
160 Patrick Ramsey AU/575 RC 5.00 12.00
161 Buchanon No AU/310 RC 10.00 25.00
162 Quentin Jammer AU/300 RC 8.00 20.00
163 Randy Fasani AU/500 RC 4.00 10.00
164 Reche Caldwell AU/340 RC 6.00 15.00
165 Robert Thomas AU/460 RC 3.00 8.00
166 Rocky Calmus AU/385 RC 5.00 12.00
167 Rohan Davey AU/295 RC 8.00 20.00
168 Ron Johnson AU/385 RC 5.00 12.00
169 Roy Williams AU/250 RC 20.00 40.00
170 Ryan Sims No Auto/360 RC 6.00 15.00
171 Tavon Mason AU/690 RC 3.00 8.00
172 Terry Charles AU/750 RC 3.00 8.00
173 T.J. Duckett AU/335 RC 8.00 20.00
174 Tim Carter AU/600 RC 4.00 10.00
175 Travis Stephens AU/170 RC 5.00 12.00
176 Trev Faulk AU/600 RC 3.00 8.00
177 Wendell Bryant AU/560 RC 3.00 8.00
178 William Green AU/317 RC 5.00 12.00
179 Woody Dantzler AU/185 RC 6.00 15.00
180 Tony Fisher AU/340 RC 5.00 12.00
181 Javin Hunter AU/400 RC 4.00 10.00
182 Daryl Jones AU/400 RC 4.00 10.00
183 Jesse Chatman AU/400 RC 4.00 10.00
184 J.T. O'Sullivan AU/340 RC 5.00 12.00
185 Josh Norman AU/340 RC 4.00 10.00
186 James Mungro AU/100 RC 25.00 50.00

2002 Playoff Contenders 10th Anniversary

UNPRICED 10th ANNIV PRINT RUN 10

2002 Playoff Contenders Championship Ticket

*VETS 1-100: 2.5X TO 6X BASIC CARDS
1-100 VETERAN PRINT RUN 250
COMMON ROOKIE (101-186) 5.00 12.00
ROOKIE SEMISTARS 6.00 15.00
ROOKIE UNL.STARS 7.50 20.00
101-186 ROOKIE PRINT RUN 50
108 Antonio Bryant 8.00 20.00
112 Brian Westbrook 12.00 30.00
116 Chester Taylor 8.00 20.00
118 Clinton Portis 10.00 25.00
123 David Garrard 10.00 25.00
128 Dwight Freeney 10.00 25.00
129 Ed Reed 30.00 80.00
134 Jeremy Shockey 12.00 30.00
142 Julius Peppers 15.00 40.00
169 Roy Williams 8.00 20.00

2002 Playoff Contenders Hawaii 2003

*VETS 1-100 : 15X TO 40X BASIC CARDS
1-100 VETERAN PRINT RUN 15
UNPRICED 101-150 ROOKIE AU PRINT RUN 5

2002 Playoff Contenders All-Time Contenders

STATED ODDS 1:12
AT1 Corey Dillon 1.25 3.00
AT2 Ray Lewis 1.50 4.00
AT3 Mark Brunell 1.25 3.00
AT4 Eric Moulds 1.25 3.00
AT5 Tony Gonzalez 1.50 4.00
AT6 Marcus Robinson 1.25 3.00
AT7 Tim Brown 1.50 4.00
AT8 Brian Griese 1.25 3.00
AT9 Cris Carter 1.50 4.00
AT10 Tony Banks 1.00 2.50
AT11 Jamal Lewis 1.25 3.00
AT12 Jimmy Smith 1.25 3.00
AT13 Michael Strahan 1.50 4.00
AT14 David Boston 1.00 2.50
AT15 Marvin Harrison 1.50 4.00
AT16 Emmitt Smith 4.00 10.00
AT17 Robert Ferguson 1.25 3.00
AT18 Boo Williams 1.00 2.50
AT19 Mike Anderson 1.25 3.00
AT20 Isaac Bruce 1.50 4.00
AT21 Shaun Rogers 1.00 2.50
AT22 Jamal Anderson 1.25 3.00
AT23 Torry Holt 1.50 4.00
AT24 Aaron Brooks 1.25 3.00
AT25 Drew Bledsoe 1.50 4.00
AT26 Jake Plummer 1.25 3.00
AT27 Jevon Kearse 1.25 3.00
AT28 Kerry Collins 1.25 3.00
AT29 Terrell Davis 1.50 4.00
AT30 Jeff Blake 1.25 3.00
AT31 Randall Cunningham 1.50 4.00
AT32 Ricky Williams 1.25 3.00
AT33 Brett Favre 4.00 10.00

2002 Playoff Contenders All-Time Contenders Autographs

STATED PRINT RUN 8-140
SERIAL #'d UNDER 15 NOT PRICED
AT1 Corey Dillon/15 15.00 40.00
AT3 Mark Brunell/25 15.00 40.00
AT4 Eric Moulds/20 15.00 40.00
AT5 Tony Gonzalez/25 20.00 50.00
AT6 Marcus Robinson/135 10.00 25.00
AT7 Tim Brown/28 30.00 80.00
AT8 Brian Griese/25 15.00 40.00
AT9 Cris Carter/25 30.00 80.00
AT10 Tony Banks/100 8.00 20.00
AT11 Jamal Lewis/20 15.00 40.00
AT12 Jimmy Smith/50 10.00 25.00
AT13 Michael Strahan/25 20.00 50.00
AT14 David Boston/19 12.00 30.00
AT15 Marvin Harrison/25 30.00 80.00
AT18 Boo Williams/50 8.00 20.00
AT19 Mike Anderson/32 15.00 40.00
AT20 Isaac Bruce/57 12.00 30.00
AT21 Shaun Rogers/20 12.00 30.00
AT23 Torry Holt/25 20.00 50.00
AT24 Aaron Brooks/15 15.00 40.00
AT26 Jake Plummer/15 15.00 40.00
AT28 Kerry Collins/18 15.00 40.00
AT30 Jeff Blake/140 10.00 25.00
AT31 Randall Cunningham/140 12.00 30.00
AT32 Ricky Williams/46 30.00 80.00
AT33 Brett Favre/15 150.00 300.00

2002 Playoff Contenders Legendary Contenders

STATED ODDS 1:12
LC1 Boomer Esiason 1.25 3.00
LC2 Dan Marino 4.00 10.00
LC3 Jim Kelly 2.00 5.00
LC4 John Elway 3.00 8.00
LC5 Phil Simms 1.25 3.00
LC6 Steve Young 2.00 5.00
LC7 Troy Aikman 2.50 6.00
LC8 Warren Moon 1.50 4.00
LC9 Barry Sanders 2.50 6.00
LC10 Joe Montana 4.00 10.00
LC11 John Riggins 1.50 4.00
LC12 Ronnie Lott 1.50 4.00
LC13 Thurman Thomas 1.50 4.00
LC14 Ozzie Newsome 1.25 3.00
LC15 Jack Lambert 1.50 4.00

2002 Playoff Contenders Legendary Contenders Autographs

STATED PRINT RUN 10-143
SERIAL #'d UNDER 15 NOT PRICED
LC1 Boomer Esiason/17 25.00 50.00
LC2 Dan Marino/15 100.00 200.00
LC3 Jim Kelly/15 50.00 100.00
LC4 John Elway/15 100.00 200.00
LC5 Phil Simms/75 25.00 60.00
LC6 Steve Young/50 50.00 100.00
LC7 Troy Aikman/25 60.00 120.00
LC9 Barry Sanders/19 75.00 150.00
LC10 Joe Montana/63 100.00 200.00
LC11 John Riggins/141 20.00 50.00
LC13 Thurman Thomas/25 15.00 40.00
LC14 Ozzie Newsome/125 15.00 30.00
LC15 Jack Lambert/125 40.00 80.00

2002 Playoff Contenders MVP Contenders

COMPLETE SET (10) 15.00 40.00
STATED ODDS 1:12
MVP1 Brett Favre 3.00 8.00
MVP2 Jerry Rice 2.50 6.00
MVP3 Ricky Williams 1.00 2.50
MVP4 Edgerrin James 1.00 2.50
MVP5 Emmitt Smith 3.00 8.00
MVP6 Kurt Warner 1.25 3.00
MVP7 Marshall Faulk 1.25 3.00
MVP8 Randy Moss 1.25 3.00
MVP9 Jeff Garcia 1.00 2.50
MVP10 Ahman Green 1.00 2.50

2002 Playoff Contenders MVP Contenders Autographs

STATED PRINT RUN 25 SER.#'d SETS
MVP1 Brett Favre 200.00 350.00
MVP2 Jerry Rice 125.00 250.00
MVP3 Ricky Williams 20.00 50.00
MVP4 Edgerrin James 20.00 50.00
MVP5 Emmitt Smith 200.00 350.00
MVP6 Kurt Warner 30.00 80.00
MVP7 Marshall Faulk 25.00 60.00
MVP8 Randy Moss 50.00 100.00
MVP9 Jeff Garcia 20.00 50.00
MVP10 Ahman Green 20.00 50.00

2002 Playoff Contenders Rookie Idols

COMPLETE SET (10) 15.00 40.00
STATED ODDS 1:12
RI1 Ladell Betts 1.00 2.50
Thurman Thomas
RI2 Antonio Bryant 1.00 2.50
Michael Irvin
RI3 David Garrard 1.25 3.00
Phil Simms
RI4 Eric Crouch 2.00 5.00
John Elway
RI5 William Green 1.50 4.00
Barry Sanders
RI6 Josh McCown 2.50 6.00
Brett Favre
RI7 Joey Harrington 2.50 6.00
Dan Marino
RI8 Donte Stallworth 2.00 5.00
Jerry Rice
RI9 Jabar Gaffney 1.00 2.50
Tim Brown
RI10 Rohan Davey 1.00 2.50
Daunte Culpepper

2002 Playoff Contenders Rookie Idols Autographs

STATED PRINT RUN 25 SER.#'d SETS
RI1 Ladell Betts 25.00 60.00
Thurman Thomas
RI2 Antonio Bryant 25.00 60.00
Michael Irvin
RI3 David Garrard 30.00 80.00
Phil Simms
RI4 Eric Crouch 100.00 200.00
John Elway
RI5 William Green 75.00 150.00
Barry Sanders
RI6 Josh McCown 125.00 250.00
Brett Favre
RI7 Joey Harrington 100.00 200.00
Dan Marino
RI8 Donte Stallworth 75.00 150.00
Jerry Rice
RI9 Jabar Gaffney 25.00 60.00
Tim Brown
RI10 Rohan Davey 25.00 60.00
Daunte Culpepper

2002 Playoff Contenders Round Numbers Autographs

STATED PRINT RUN 75 SER.#'d SETS
*GOLD/20-30: .5X TO 1.2X BASIC AU
*GOLD/40-60: .4X TO 1X BASIC AU
GOLD STATED PRINT RUN 10-40
RN1 David Carr 15.00 40.00
Joey Harrington
RN2 Quentin Jammer 15.00 40.00
Roy Williams
RN3 Jabar Gaffney 15.00 40.00
Rocho Caldwell
RN4 Antonio Bryant 15.00 40.00
Josh Reed
RN5 Josh McCown 15.00 40.00
Eric Crouch
RN6 Marquise Walker 10.00 25.00
Cliff Russell
RN7 Jonathan Wells 15.00 40.00
Travis Stephens
RN8 David Garrard 20.00 50.00
Rohan Davey
RN9 Randy Fasani 12.00 30.00
Kurt Kittner
RN10 Josh Scobey 15.00 40.00
Chester Taylor

2002 Playoff Contenders ROY Contenders

COMPLETE SET (10) 8.00 20.00
STATED ODDS 1:12
ROY1 Antonio Bryant 1.00 2.50
ROY2 Ashley Lelie .75 2.00
ROY3 David Carr 1.00 2.50
ROY4 DeShaun Foster 1.00 2.50
ROY5 Donte Stallworth 1.00 2.50
ROY6 Joey Harrington 1.00 2.50
ROY7 Quentin Jammer 1.00 2.50
ROY8 Patrick Ramsey 1.00 2.50
ROY9 T.J. Duckett 1.00 2.50
ROY10 William Green .75 2.00

2002 Playoff Contenders ROY Contenders Autographs

STATED PRINT RUN 25 SER.#'d SETS
ROY1 Antonio Bryant 15.00 40.00
ROY2 Ashley Lelie 12.00 30.00
ROY3 David Carr 15.00 40.00
ROY4 DeShaun Foster 15.00 40.00
ROY5 Donte Stallworth 15.00 40.00
ROY6 Joey Harrington 15.00 40.00
ROY7 Quentin Jammer 15.00 40.00
ROY8 Patrick Ramsey 15.00 40.00
ROY9 T.J. Duckett 15.00 40.00
ROY10 William Green 12.00 30.00

2002 Playoff Contenders Sophomore Contenders

STATED ODDS 1:12
SC1 Chad Johnson .75 2.00
SC2 Chris Chambers .60 1.50
SC3 David Terrell .50 1.25
SC4 Jesse Palmer .50 1.25
SC5 Kevan Barlow .50 1.25
SC6 Koren Robinson .50 1.25
SC7 LaMont Jordan .60 1.50
SC8 Michael Bennett .60 1.50
SC9 Quincy Carter .50 1.25
SC10 Santana Moss .60 1.50
SC11 Mike McMahon .50 1.25
SC12 Ken-Yon Rambo .50 1.25
SC13 Will Allen .50 1.25
SC14 Todd Heap .60 1.50
SC15 T.J. Houshmandzadeh .75 2.00
SC16 Travis Henry .50 1.25
SC17 Sage Rosenfels .60 1.50
SC18 Torrance Marshall .50 1.25
SC19 Rudi Johnson .75 2.00
SC20 Travis Minor .50 1.25

2002 Playoff Contenders Sophomore Contenders Autographs

STATED PRINT RUN 16-400
SC1 Chad Johnson/26 15.00 40.00
SC2 Chris Chambers/28 12.00 30.00
SC3 David Terrell/188 6.00 15.00
SC4 Jesse Palmer/300 6.00 15.00
SC5 Kevan Barlow/200 6.00 15.00
SC6 Koren Robinson/40 8.00 20.00
SC7 LaMont Jordan/250 8.00 20.00
SC8 Michael Bennett/34 12.00 30.00
SC9 Quincy Carter/300 6.00 15.00
SC10 Santana Moss/400 8.00 20.00
SC11 Mike McMahon/16 12.00 30.00
SC12 Ken-Yon Rambo/300 6.00 15.00
SC13 Will Allen/130 6.00 15.00
SC14 Todd Heap/61 10.00 25.00
SC15 T.J. Houshmandzadeh/220 10.00 25.00
SC16 Damione Lewis/400 6.00 15.00
SC17 Sage Rosenfels/70 10.00 25.00
SC18 Torrance Marshall/50 8.00 20.00
SC19 Rudi Johnson/350 10.00 25.00
SC20 Travis Minor/35 10.00 25.00

2003 Playoff Contenders

Released in January of 2004, this set consists of 200 cards including 100 veterans and 100 rookie ticket autographs. Within the rookie ticket autographs subset are 95 players and 5 coaches. Each rookie ticket is serial numbered to various quantities as noted below. Many players signed a number of cards in both black and blue ink. Playoff announced the print runs of many of those color variations in April 2004. We've noted below just those variations for key players with a significant print run difference. Several rookies were only issued in packs as exchange cards with an expiration date of 7/1/2005. Boxes contained 24 packs of 5 cards. SRP was $6 per pack.

COMP.SET w/o SP's (100) 7.50 20.00
1 Roy Williams .25 .60
2 Antonio Bryant .20 .50
3 Jeremy Shockey .30 .75
4 Kerry Collins .25 .60
5 Tiki Barber .30 .75
6 Michael Strahan .30 .75
7 Donovan McNabb .30 .75
8 Duce Staley .25 .60
9 Todd Pinkston .20 .50
10 Patrick Ramsey .25 .60
11 Laveranues Coles .20 .50
12 Rod Gardner .20 .50
13 Drew Bledsoe .30 .75
14 Travis Henry .20 .50
15 Eric Moulds .25 .60
16 Josh Reed .20 .50
17 Ricky Williams .25 .60
18 Jay Fiedler .20 .50
19 Chris Chambers .25 .60
20 Zach Thomas .30 .75
21 Junior Seau .30 .75
22 Tom Brady .75 2.00
23 Troy Brown .25 .60
24 Chad Pennington .30 .75
25 Curtis Martin .30 .75
26 Santana Moss .25 .60
27 Emmitt Smith .75 2.00
28 Jeff Garcia .25 .60
29 Terrell Owens .30 .75
30 Kevan Barlow .20 .50
31 Shaun Alexander .25 .60
32 Matt Hasselbeck .25 .60
33 Koren Robinson .25 .60
34 Kurt Warner .30 .75
35 Marshall Faulk .30 .75
36 Torry Holt .30 .75
37 Isaac Bruce .30 .75
38 Clinton Portis .25 .60
39 Jake Plummer .25 .60
40 Rod Smith .25 .60
41 Ed McCaffrey .25 .60
42 Ashley Lelie .20 .50
43 Priest Holmes .30 .75
44 Trent Green .25 .60
45 Tony Gonzalez .30 .75
46 Jerry Rice .60 1.50
47 Rich Gannon .25 .60
48 Tim Brown .30 .75
49 Jerry Porter .20 .50
50 Charles Woodson .30 .75
51 LaDainian Tomlinson .30 .75
52 Drew Brees .30 .75
53 David Boston .20 .50
54 Brian Urlacher .30 .75
55 Kordell Stewart .25 .60
56 Marty Booker .25 .60
57 Joey Harrington .20 .50
58 Brett Favre .75 2.00
59 Ahman Green .25 .60
60 Donald Driver .30 .75
61 Javon Walker .25 .60
62 Randy Moss .30 .75
63 Daunte Culpepper .25 .60
64 Michael Bennett .25 .60
65 Jamal Lewis .25 .60
66 Ray Lewis .30 .75
67 Corey Dillon .25 .60
68 Chad Johnson .30 .75
69 William Green .20 .50
70 Tim Couch .20 .50
71 Quincy Morgan .20 .50
72 Plaxico Burress .25 .60
73 Tommy Maddox .25 .60
74 Hines Ward .30 .75
75 Antwaan Randle El .25 .60
76 Michael Vick .40 1.00
77 Peerless Price .20 .50
78 Warrick Dunn .25 .60
79 T.J. Duckett .25 .60
80 Julius Peppers .30 .75
81 Stephen Davis .25 .60
82 Deuce McAllister .25 .60
83 Aaron Brooks .25 .60
84 Joe Horn .25 .60
85 Donte Stallworth .20 .50
86 Mike Alstott .30 .75
87 Brad Johnson .25 .60
88 Keyshawn Johnson .30 .75
89 Warren Sapp .25 .60
90 David Carr .25 .60
91 Jabar Gaffney .20 .50
92 Peyton Manning .60 1.50
93 Edgerrin James .30 .75
94 Marvin Harrison .30 .75
95 Mark Brunell .25 .60
96 Fred Taylor .25 .60
97 Jimmy Smith .25 .60
98 Steve McNair .30 .75
99 Eddie George .25 .60
100 Jevon Kearse .25 .60
101 Lee Suggs AU/499 RC 5.00 12.00
102 Charles Rogers AU/204 RC 15.00 40.00
103 Brandon Lloyd AU/589 RC 15.00 30.00
104 Terrence Edwards AU/399 RC 4.00 10.00
105 Mike Pinkard AU/849 RC 4.00 10.00
106 DeWayne White AU/524 RC 4.00 10.00
107 Jerome McDougle AU/339 RC 4.00 10.00
108 Jimmy Kennedy AU/514 RC 5.00 12.00
109 William Joseph AU/764 RC 4.00 10.00
110 E.J. Henderson AU/774 RC 5.00 12.00
111 Mike Doss AU/574 RC 6.00 15.00
112A Chris Simms Blu AU/310* RC 15.00 40.00
112B Chris Simms Blk AU/79* RC 40.00 80.00
113 Cecil Sapp AU/474 RC 4.00 10.00
114 Justin Gage AU/579 RC 5.00 12.00
115 Sam Aiken AU/664 RC 5.00 12.00
116 Doug Gabriel AU/389 RC 5.00 12.00
117 Jason Witten AU/599 RC 60.00 100.00
118 Bennie Joppru AU/449 RC 4.00 10.00
119 Chris Kelsay AU/864 RC 5.00 12.00
120 Johnathan Sullivan/924 RC 2.50 6.00
121 Kevin Williams AU/764 RC 10.00 20.00
122 Rien Long AU/849 RC 4.00 10.00
123 Kenny Peterson/674 RC 3.00 8.00
124 Boss Bailey AU/564 RC 5.00 12.00
125 Dennis Weathersby AU/774 RC 4.00 10.00
126A Carson Palmer Blk AU/36* RC 200.00 400.00
126B Carson Palmer Blue AU/158* RC 125.00 250.00
127 Byron Leftwich AU/169 RC 20.00 50.00
128 Kyle Boller AU/439 RC 7.50 20.00
129 Rex Grossman AU/494 RC 20.00 40.00
130 Dave Ragone AU/344 RC 4.00 10.00
131 Brian St.Pierre AU/554 RC 5.00 12.00
132 Kliff Kingsbury AU/879 RC 5.00 12.00
133 Seneca Wallace AU/864 RC 10.00 25.00
134 Larry Johnson AU/344 RC 12.00 30.00
135 Will McGahee AU/369 RC 15.00 40.00
136 Justin Fargas AU/354 RC 10.00 25.00
137 Onterrio Smith AU/414 RC 4.00 10.00
138 Chris Brown AU/279 RC 7.50 20.00
139 Musa Smith AU/379 RC 4.00 10.00
140 Artose Pinner AU/364 RC 4.00 10.00
141 Andre Johnson AU/199 RC 150.00 250.00
142 Kelley Washington AU/472 RC 4.00 10.00
143 Taylor Jacobs AU/349 RC 4.00 10.00
144 Bryant Johnson AU/389 RC 6.00 15.00
145 Tyrone Calico AU/499 RC 5.00 12.00
146 Anquan Boldin AU/524 RC 25.00 60.00
147 Bethel Johnson AU/484 RC 4.00 10.00
148 Nate Burleson AU/549 RC 5.00 12.00
149 Kevin Curtis AU/455 RC 10.00 25.00
150 Dallas Clark AU/539 RC 40.00 80.00
151 Teyo Johnson AU/309 RC 5.00 12.00
152 Terrell Suggs AU/564 RC 20.00 40.00
153 DeWayne Robertson/689 RC 3.00 8.00
154 Terence Newman AU/364 RC 10.00 25.00
155 Marcus Trufant AU/739 RC 5.00 12.00
156 Tony Romo AU/999 RC 150.00 300.00
157 Brooks Bollinger AU/974 RC 5.00 12.00
158 Ken Dorsey AU/774 RC 5.00 12.00
159 Kirk Farmer AU/999 RC 5.00 12.00
160 Jason Gesser AU/999 RC 5.00 12.00
161 Brock Forsey AU/999 RC 5.00 12.00
162 Quentin Griffin AU/999 RC 5.00 12.00
163 Avon Cobourne AU/974 RC 4.00 10.00
164 Domanick Davis AU/999 RC 5.00 12.00
165 Tony Hollings AU/974 RC 5.00 12.00
166 LaBrandon Toefield AU/799 RC 5.00 12.00
167 Arlen Harris AU/974 RC 4.00 10.00
168 Sultan McCullough AU/989 RC 4.00 10.00
169 Visanthe Shiancoe AU/999 RC 10.00 20.00
170 L.J. Smith AU/974 RC 6.00 15.00
171 LaTarence Dunbar AU/999 RC 4.00 10.00
172 Walter Young AU/889 RC 4.00 10.00
173 Bobby Wade AU/989 RC 5.00 12.00
174 Zuriel Smith AU/989 RC 4.00 10.00
175 Adrian Madise AU/999 RC 4.00 10.00
176 Ken Hamlin AU/989 RC 6.00 15.00
177 Carl Ford AU/999 RC 4.00 10.00
178 Cortez Hankton AU/989 RC 5.00 12.00
179 J.R. Tolver AU/889 RC 5.00 12.00
180 Keenan Howry AU/999 RC 4.00 10.00
181 Billy McMullen AU/899 RC 4.00 10.00
182 Arnaz Battle AU/989 RC 7.50 20.00
183 Shaun McDonald AU/899 RC 5.00 12.00
184 Andre Woolfolk AU/989 RC 5.00 12.00
185 Sammy Davis AU/999 RC 5.00 12.00
186 Calvin Pace AU/999 RC 5.00 12.00
187 Michael Haynes AU/999 RC 4.00 10.00
188 Ty Warren AU/999 RC 5.00 12.00
189 Nick Barnett AU/999 RC 12.50 25.00
190 Troy Polamalu AU/989 RC 250.00 400.00
191 Eric Parker AU/589 RC 6.00 15.00
192 Justin Griffith AU/589 RC 5.00 12.00
193 David Tyree AU/599 RC 10.00 25.00
194 Pisa Tinoisamoa/599 RC 4.00 10.00
195 Rashean Mathis AU/589 RC 5.00 12.00
196 Mike Sherman AU/574 RC 10.00 25.00
197 Dave Wannstedt AU/574 RC 7.50 20.00
198 Dick Vermeil AU/574 RC 15.00 30.00
199 Tony Dungy AU/574 RC 30.00 60.00
200 Mike Martz AU/574 RC 7.50 20.00

2003 Playoff Contenders Championship Ticket

PRINT RUN 1 SERIAL #'d SET
NOT PRICED DUE TO SCARCITY

2003 Playoff Contenders Hawaii 2004

*VETS 1-100: 8X TO 20X BASIC CARDS
UNPRICED ROOKIE AU PRINT RUN 5-10

2003 Playoff Contenders Orange County

UNPRICED ORANGE COUNTY PRINT RUN 5

2003 Playoff Contenders Playoff Ticket

*VETS: 4X TO 10X BASIC CARDS
1-100 VET STATED PRINT RUN 150
101-200 ROOKIE PRINT RUN 30
101 Lee Suggs 10.00 25.00
102 Charles Rogers 10.00 25.00
103 Brandon Lloyd 20.00 50.00
104 Terrence Edwards 8.00 20.00
105 Mike Pinkard 8.00 20.00
106 DeWayne White 8.00 20.00
107 Jerome McDougle 8.00 20.00
108 Jimmy Kennedy 10.00 25.00
109 William Joseph 8.00 20.00
110 E.J. Henderson 10.00 25.00
111 Mike Doss 12.00 30.00
112 Chris Simms 12.00 30.00
113 Cecil Sapp 8.00 20.00
114 Justin Gage 10.00 25.00
115 Sam Aiken 10.00 25.00
116 Doug Gabriel 10.00 25.00
117 Jason Witten 30.00 80.00
118 Bennie Joppru 8.00 20.00
119 Chris Kelsay 10.00 25.00
120 Johnathan Sullivan 8.00 20.00
121 Kevin Williams 12.00 30.00
122 Rien Long 8.00 20.00
123 Kenny Peterson 10.00 25.00
124 Boss Bailey 10.00 25.00
125 Dennis Weathersby 8.00 20.00
126 Carson Palmer 25.00 60.00
127 Byron Leftwich 12.00 30.00
128 Kyle Boller 12.00 30.00
129 Rex Grossman 12.00 30.00
130 Dave Ragone 8.00 20.00
131 Brian St.Pierre 10.00 25.00
132 Kliff Kingsbury 10.00 25.00
133 Seneca Wallace 12.00 30.00
134 Larry Johnson 12.00 30.00
135 Willis McGahee 15.00 40.00
136 Justin Fargas 12.00 30.00
137 Onterrio Smith 8.00 20.00
138 Chris Brown 8.00 20.00
139 Musa Smith 8.00 20.00
140 Artose Pinner 8.00 20.00
141 Andre Johnson 30.00 80.00
142 Kelley Washington 8.00 20.00
143 Taylor Jacobs 8.00 20.00
144 Bryant Johnson 12.00 30.00
145 Tyrone Calico 10.00 25.00
146 Anquan Boldin 20.00 50.00
147 Bethel Johnson 10.00 25.00
148 Nate Burleson 10.00 25.00
149 Kevin Curtis 12.00 30.00
150 Dallas Clark 20.00 50.00
151 Teyo Johnson 10.00 25.00
152 Terrell Suggs 12.00 30.00
153 DeWayne Robertson 10.00 25.00
154 Terence Newman 10.00 25.00
155 Marcus Trufant 10.00 25.00
156 Tony Romo 125.00 250.00
157 Brooks Bollinger 10.00 25.00
158 Ken Dorsey 10.00 25.00
159 Kirk Farmer 10.00 25.00
160 Jason Gesser 10.00 25.00
161 Brock Forsey 10.00 25.00
162 Quentin Griffin 10.00 25.00
163 Avon Cobourne 8.00 20.00
164 Domanick Davis 10.00 25.00
165 Tony Hollings 10.00 25.00
166 LaBrandon Toefield 10.00 25.00
167 Arlen Harris 8.00 20.00
168 Sultan McCullough 8.00 20.00
169 Visanthe Shiancoe 12.00 30.00
170 L.J. Smith 12.00 30.00
171 LaTarence Dunbar 8.00 20.00
172 Walter Young 10.00 25.00
173 Bobby Wade 10.00 25.00
174 Zuriel Smith 8.00 20.00
175 Adrian Madise 8.00 20.00
176 Ken Hamlin 12.00 30.00
177 Carl Ford 8.00 20.00
178 Cortez Hankton 10.00 25.00
179 J.R. Tolver 10.00 25.00
180 Keenan Howry 8.00 20.00
181 Billy McMullen 8.00 20.00
182 Arnaz Battle 12.00 30.00
183 Shaun McDonald 10.00 25.00
184 Andre Woolfolk 10.00 25.00
185 Sammy Davis 10.00 25.00
186 Calvin Pace 10.00 25.00
187 Michael Haynes 8.00 20.00
188 Ty Warren 10.00 25.00
189 Nick Barnett 12.00 30.00
190 Troy Polamalu 150.00 250.00
191 Eric Parker 12.00 30.00
192 Justin Griffith 10.00 25.00
193 David Tyree 12.00 30.00
194 Pisa Tinoisamoa 10.00 25.00
195 Rashean Mathis 10.00 25.00
196 Mike Sherman 12.00 30.00
197 Dave Wannstedt 12.00 30.00
198 Dick Vermeil 12.00 30.00
199 Tony Dungy
200 Mike Martz 10.00 25.00

2003 Playoff Contenders Legendary Contenders

COMPLETE SET (10) 15.00 30.00
STATED ODDS 1:24
LC1 Barry Sanders 3.00 8.00
LC2 Franco Harris 2.00 5.00
LC3 Jim Brown 2.50 6.00
LC4 Jim Kelly 2.00 5.00
LC5 Joe Greene 1.50 4.00
LC6 Larry Csonka 1.50 4.00
LC7 Reggie White 1.50 4.00
LC8 Roger Staubach 2.50 6.00
LC9 Steve Largent 1.50 4.00
LC10 Cris Carter 1.50 4.00

2003 Playoff Contenders Legendary Contenders Autographs

STATED PRINT RUN 25 SERIAL #'d SETS
LC1 Barry Sanders 100.00 175.00
LC2 Franco Harris 40.00 80.00
LC3 Jim Brown 60.00 120.00
LC4 Jim Kelly 40.00 80.00
LC5 Joe Greene 35.00 60.00
LC6 Larry Csonka 40.00 80.00
LC7 Reggie White 125.00 225.00
LC8 Roger Staubach 50.00 100.00
LC9 Steve Largent 50.00 100.00
LC10 Cris Carter 30.00 60.00

2003 Playoff Contenders MVP Contenders

COMPLETE SET (15) 15.00 40.00
STATED ODDS 1:24
MVP1 Brett Favre 3.00 8.00
MVP2 Brian Urlacher 1.25 3.00
MVP3 Chad Pennington 1.25 3.00
MVP4 Clinton Portis 1.00 2.50
MVP5 Drew Bledsoe 1.25 3.00
MVP6 Jeff Garcia 1.00 2.50
MVP7 Jerry Rice 2.50 6.00
MVP8 Joey Harrington .75 2.00
MVP9 Kurt Warner 1.25 3.00
MVP10 LaDainian Tomlinson 1.25 3.00
MVP11 Marvin Harrison 1.25 3.00
MVP12 Michael Vick 1.50 4.00
MVP13 Randy Moss 1.25 3.00
MVP14 Ricky Williams 1.00 2.50
MVP15 Tom Brady 3.00 8.00

2003 Playoff Contenders MVP Contenders Autographs

STATED PRINT RUN 25 SER.#'d SETS
MVP1 Brett Favre 175.00 300.00
MVP2 Brian Urlacher 25.00 60.00
MVP3 Chad Pennington 25.00 60.00
MVP4 Clinton Portis 20.00 50.00
MVP5 Drew Bledsoe 25.00 60.00
MVP6 Jeff Garcia 20.00 50.00
MVP7 Jerry Rice 150.00 250.00
MVP8 Joey Harrington 15.00 40.00
MVP9 Kurt Warner 25.00 60.00
MVP10 LaDainian Tomlinson 75.00 135.00
MVP11 Marvin Harrison 25.00 60.00
MVP12 Michael Vick 60.00 100.00
MVP13 Randy Moss 75.00 150.00
MVP14 Ricky Williams 20.00 50.00
MVP15 Tom Brady 175.00 300.00

2003 Playoff Contenders Rookie Round Up

PRINT RUN 375 SERIAL #'d SETS
RR1 Anquan Boldin 2.50 6.00
RR2 Bryant Johnson 1.50 4.00
RR3 Kyle Boller 1.50 4.00
RR4 Musa Smith 1.00 2.50
RR5 Terrell Suggs 1.50 4.00
RR6 Sam Aiken 1.25 3.00
RR7 Willis McGahee 2.00 5.00
RR8 Walter Young 1.00 2.50
RR9 Rex Grossman 1.50 4.00
RR10 Carson Palmer 3.00 8.00
RR11 Kelley Washington 1.00 2.50
RR12 Ken Hamlin 1.50 4.00
RR13 Terence Newman 1.25 3.00
RR14 Adrian Madise 1.00 2.50
RR15 Artose Pinner 1.00 2.50
RR16 Boss Bailey 1.25 3.00
RR17 Charles Rogers 1.25 3.00
RR18 Eugene Wilson 1.50 4.00
RR19 Nick Barnett 1.50 4.00
RR20 Andre Johnson 4.00 10.00
RR21 Dave Ragone 1.00 2.50
RR22 Domanick Davis 1.25 3.00
RR23 Tony Hollings 1.25 3.00
RR24 Dallas Clark 2.50 6.00
RR25 Mike Doss 1.50 4.00
RR26 Byron Leftwich 1.50 4.00
RR27 LaBrandon Toefield 1.25 3.00
RR28 Larry Johnson 1.50 4.00
RR29 J.R. Tolver 1.25 3.00
RR30 Nate Burleson 1.25 3.00
RR31 Onterrio Smith 1.00 2.50
RR32 Bethel Johnson 1.00 2.50
RR33 Cortez Hankton 1.25 3.00
RR34 B.J. Askew 1.25 3.00
RR35 DeWayne Robertson 1.25 3.00
RR36 Justin Fargas 1.50 4.00
RR37 Teyo Johnson 1.25 3.00
RR38 Billy McMullen 1.00 2.50
RR39 Jerome McDougle 1.00 2.50
RR40 Troy Polamalu 15.00 30.00
RR41 Sammy Davis 1.25 3.00
RR42 Arnaz Battle 1.50 4.00
RR43 Brandon Lloyd 2.50 6.00
RR44 Marcus Trufant 1.25 3.00
RR45 Seneca Wallace 1.50 4.00
RR46 Kevin Curtis 1.50 4.00
RR47 Shaun McDonald 1.25 3.00
RR48 Chris Simms 1.50 4.00
RR49 Tyrone Calico 1.25 3.00
RR50 Taylor Jacobs 1.00 2.50

2003 Playoff Contenders Round Numbers Autographs

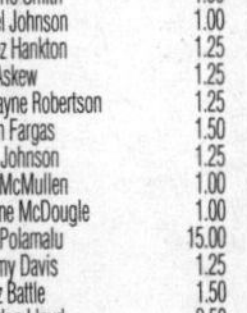

RN1-RN10 DUAL AU PRINT RUN 100
RN11-RN15 QUAD AU PRINT RUN 50
*RN1-RN10 GOLD/20-30: .8X TO 2X
*RN11-RN15 GOLD/20-30: .5X TO 1.2X
GOLD STATED PRINT RUN 10-30
RN1 Carson Palmer 40.00 100.00
Byron Leftwich
RN2 Charles Rogers 15.00 40.00
Bryant Johnson
RN3 Kyle Boller 25.00 60.00
Rex Grossman

RN4 Willis McGahee 20.00 50.00
Larry Johnson
RN5 Tyler Jacobs 25.00 60.00
Anquan Boldin
RN6 Bethel Johnson 10.00 25.00
Tyrone Calico
RN7 Dave Ragone 15.00 40.00
Chris Simms
RN8 Musa Smith 10.00 25.00
Chris Brown
RN9 Justin Fargas 15.00 40.00
Kevin Curtis
RN10 Kelley Washington 12.00 30.00
Nate Burleson
RN11 Carson Palmer 75.00 200.00
Byron Leftwich
Charles Rogers
Andre Johnson
RN12 Kyle Boller 30.00 80.00
Rex Grossman
Willis McGahee
Larry Johnson
RN13 Tyler Jacobs 60.00 120.00
Anquan Boldin
Bethel Johnson
Tyrone Calico
RN14 Dave Ragone 25.00 60.00
Chriss Simms
Musa Smith
Chris Brown
RN15 Justin Fargas 12.00 30.00
Kevin Curtis
Kelley Washington
Nate Burleson

2003 Playoff Contenders ROY Contenders

COMPLETE SET (10) 12.00 30.00
STATED ODDS 1:24
ROY1 Carson Palmer 2.00 5.00
ROY2 Byron Leftwich 1.00 2.50
ROY3 Charles Rogers .75 2.00
ROY4 Andre Johnson 2.50 6.00
ROY5 DeWayne Robertson .75 2.00
ROY6 Terence Newman .75 2.00
ROY7 Terrell Suggs 1.00 2.50
ROY8 Kyle Boller 1.00 2.50
ROY9 Rex Grossman 1.00 2.50
ROY10 Larry Johnson 1.00 2.50

2003 Playoff Contenders ROY Contenders Autographs

STATED PRINT RUN 25 SER.#'d SETS
ROY1 Carson Palmer 100.00 175.00
ROY2 Byron Leftwich 15.00 40.00
ROY3 Charles Rogers 12.00 30.00
ROY4 Andre Johnson 125.00 200.00
ROY5 DeWayne Robertson No Auto 6.00 15.00
ROY6 Terence Newman 12.00 30.00
ROY7 Terrell Suggs 30.00 60.00
ROY8 Kyle Boller 15.00 40.00
ROY9 Rex Grossman 15.00 40.00
ROY10 Larry Johnson 15.00 40.00

2004 Playoff Contenders

Playoff Contenders initially released in mid-January 2005 and was once-again one of the most popular releases of the 2004 season. The base set consists of 200-cards including 100-autographed rookie cards. While the signed cards are not serial numbered this year, Playoff did publicly announce print runs on many of the cards as noted below. Hobby boxes contained 24-packs of 4-cards and carried an S.R.P. of $6 per pack. Two parallel sets and a variety of inserts can be found seeded in packs highlighted by the Legendary Contenders Autographs, the MVP Contenders Autographs, and the ROY Contenders Autograph inserts.

COMP.SET w/o SP's (100) 7.50 20.00
1 Anquan Boldin .30 .75
2 Emmitt Smith .75 2.00
3 Josh McCown .25 .60
4 Michael Vick .40 1.00
5 Peerless Price .20 .50
6 T.J. Duckett .25 .60
7 Warrick Dunn .25 .60
8 Jamal Lewis .25 .60
9 Kyle Boller .25 .60
10 Ray Lewis .30 .75
11 Drew Bledsoe .30 .75
12 Eric Moulds .25 .60
13 Travis Henry .20 .50
14 Willis McGahee .30 .75
15 DeShaun Foster .25 .60
16 Jake Delhomme .25 .60
17 Stephen Davis .25 .60
18 Steve Smith .30 .75
19 Brian Urlacher .30 .75
20 Rex Grossman .25 .60
21 Thomas Jones .30 .75
22 Carson Palmer .30 .75
23 Chad Johnson .30 .75
24 Rudi Johnson .25 .60
25 Jeff Garcia .25 .60
26 Lee Suggs .25 .60
27 William Green .20 .50
28 Keyshawn Johnson .25 .60
29 Roy Williams S .25 .60
30 Eddie George .25 .60
31 Ashley Lelie .20 .50
32 Jake Plummer .25 .60
33 Quentin Griffin .20 .50
34 Rod Smith .25 .60
35 Charles Rogers .20 .50
36 Joey Harrington .25 .60
37 Ahman Green .25 .60
38 Brett Favre .75 2.00
39 Javon Walker .20 .50
40 Andre Johnson .30 .75
41 David Carr .20 .50
42 Domanick Davis .20 .50
43 Edgerrin James .25 .60
44 Marvin Harrison .30 .75
45 Peyton Manning .60 1.50
46 Byron Leftwich .25 .60
47 Fred Taylor .25 .60
48 Jimmy Smith .25 .60
49 Priest Holmes .30 .75
50 Tony Gonzalez .30 .75
51 Trent Green .25 .60
52 A.J. Feeley .20 .50
53 Chris Chambers .25 .60
54 Deion Sanders .30 .75
55 Daunte Culpepper .25 .60
56 Michael Bennett .25 .60
57 Randy Moss .30 .75
58 Corey Dillon .25 .60
59 Deion Branch .25 .60
60 Tom Brady .60 1.50
61 Aaron Brooks .25 .60
62 Deuce McAllister .25 .60
63 Donte Stallworth .20 .50
64 Joe Horn .25 .60
65 Amani Toomer .25 .60
66 Jeremy Shockey .25 .60
67 Michael Strahan .30 .75
68 Tiki Barber .30 .75
69 Chad Pennington .30 .75
70 Curtis Martin .30 .75
71 Santana Moss .25 .60
72 Jerry Porter .20 .50
73 Jerry Rice .60 1.50
74 Warren Sapp .25 .60
75 Brian Westbrook .30 .75
76 Donovan McNabb .30 .75
77 Jevon Kearse .25 .60
78 Terrell Owens .30 .75
79 Antwaan Randle El .25 .60
80 Hines Ward .30 .75
81 Jerome Bettis .30 .75
82 LaDainian Tomlinson .30 .75
83 Kevan Barlow .20 .50
84 Tim Rattay .20 .50
85 Koren Robinson .20 .50
86 Matt Hasselbeck .25 .60
87 Shaun Alexander .25 .60
88 Isaac Bruce .25 .60
89 Marc Bulger .25 .60
90 Marshall Faulk .30 .75
91 Torry Holt .25 .60
92 Brad Johnson .25 .60
93 Mike Alstott .25 .60
94 Chris Brown .20 .50
95 Derrick Mason .25 .60
96 Steve McNair .30 .75
97 Clinton Portis .30 .75
98 LaVar Arrington .25 .60
99 Laveranues Coles .20 .50
100 Mark Brunell .25 .60
101 Adimchinobe Echemandu AU RC 5.00 12.00
102 Ahmad Carroll AU/574* RC 4.00 10.00
103 Andy Hall AU RC 4.00 10.00
104 B.J. Johnson AU RC 4.00 10.00
105 B.J. Symons AU RC 4.00 10.00
106 Ben Roethlisberger AU/541* RC 200.00 350.00
107 Ben Troupe AU/540* RC 5.00 12.00
108 Ben Watson AU/660* RC 6.00 15.00
109 Bernard Berrian AU/653* RC 10.00 25.00
110 Brandon Miree AU RC 4.00 10.00
111 Bruce Perry AU RC 4.00 10.00
112 Carlos Francis AU RC 4.00 10.00
113 Casey Bramlet AU RC 4.00 10.00
114 Cedric Cobbs AU/630* RC 4.00 10.00
115 Chris Gamble AU/490* RC 5.00 12.00
116 Chris Perry AU/478* RC 6.00 15.00
117 Clarence Moore AU RC 4.00 10.00
118 Cody Pickett AU RC 5.00 12.00
119 Craig Krenzel AU RC 5.00 12.00
120 D.J. Hackett AU/325* RC 8.00 20.00
121 D.J. Williams AU/490* RC 6.00 15.00
122 Darius Watts AU RC 4.00 10.00
123 DeAngelo Hall AU RC 10.00 25.00
124 Derrick Hamilton AU/373* RC 5.00 12.00
125 Derrick Ward AU RC 6.00 15.00
126 Devard Darling AU/325* RC 5.00 12.00
127 Devery Henderson AU/475* RC 10.00 25.00
128 Drew Carter AU RC 5.00 12.00
129 Drew Henson AU/415* RC 4.00 10.00
130 Dunta Robinson AU/660* RC 4.00 10.00
131 Eli Manning AU/372* RC 300.00 500.00
132 Ernest Wilford AU/365* RC 6.00 15.00
133 Greg Jones AU/553* RC 6.00 15.00
134 J.P. Losman AU/358* RC 8.00 20.00
135 Jamaar Taylor AU RC 4.00 10.00
136 Jared Lorenzen AU RC 5.00 12.00
137 Jarrett Payton AU RC 5.00 12.00
138 Jason Babin AU RC 6.00 15.00
139 Jeff Smoker AU RC 5.00 12.00
140 Jerricho Cotchery AU/325* RC 8.00 20.00
141 Jim Sorgi AU RC 5.00 12.00
142 John Navarre AU RC 4.00 10.00
143 Johnnie Morant AU/325* RC 5.00 12.00
144 Jonathan Vilma AU SP RC 6.00 15.00
145 Josh Harris AU/555* RC 4.00 10.00
146 Julius Jones AU/252* RC 10.00 25.00
147 Keary Colbert AU/495* RC 4.00 10.00
148 Kellen Winslow AU/135* RC 40.00 80.00
149 Kenechi Udeze AU/475* RC 5.00 12.00
150 Kevin Jones AU/327* RC 8.00 20.00
151 Larry Fitzgerald AU/50* RC 500.00 800.00
152 Lee Evans AU/375* RC 10.00 25.00
153 Luke McCown AU/543* RC 5.00 12.00
154 Matt Mauck AU RC 4.00 10.00
155 Matt Schaub AU/367* RC 60.00 100.00
156 Maurice Mann AU RC 4.00 10.00
157 Mewelde Moore AU/435* RC 8.00 20.00
158 Michael Clayton AU/325* RC 8.00 20.00
159 Michael Jenkins AU/412* RC 8.00 20.00
160 Michael Turner AU/535* RC 25.00 60.00
161 P.K. Sam AU/300* RC 5.00 12.00
162 Philip Rivers AU/556* RC 125.00 200.00
163 Quincy Wilson AU/350* RC 6.00 15.00
164 Ran Carthon AU RC 4.00 10.00
165 Rashaun Woods AU RC 4.00 10.00
166 Reggie Williams AU/336* RC 8.00 20.00
167 Ricardo Colclough AU/640* RC 5.00 12.00
168 Robert Gallery AU/310* RC 10.00 25.00
169 Roy Williams AU/564* RC 10.00 25.00
170 Samie Parker AU/356* RC 5.00 12.00
171 Sean Jones AU RC 5.00 12.00
172 Sean Taylor/575* RC No Auto 8.00 20.00
173 Sloan Thomas AU RC 5.00 12.00
174 Steven Jackson AU/333* RC 30.00 60.00
175 Tatum Bell AU/539* RC 6.00 15.00
176 Tommie Harris AU/365* RC 6.00 15.00
177 Triandos Luke AU RC 4.00 10.00
178 Troy Fleming AU RC 4.00 10.00
179 Vince Wilfork AU/315* RC 15.00 40.00
180 Will Smith AU/565* RC 5.00 12.00
181 Marcus Tubbs AU RC 4.00 10.00
182 Michael Boulware AU RC 6.00 15.00
183 Kris Wilson AU RC 5.00 12.00
184 Richard Smith AU RC 4.00 10.00
185 Teddy Lehman AU RC 4.00 10.00
186 Chris Cooley AU RC 15.00 40.00
187 Thomas Tapeh AU RC 5.00 12.00
188A Willie Parker Blk AU RC 10.00 25.00
188B Willie Parker Blu AU RC 15.00 40.00
189 Patrick Crayton AU RC 8.00 20.00
190 Kendrick Starling AU RC 4.00 10.00
191 B.J. Sams AU RC 4.00 10.00
192 Derick Armstrong AU RC 4.00 10.00
193 Wes Welker AU RC 75.00 135.00
194 Erik Coleman AU RC 5.00 12.00
195 Gibril Wilson AU RC 6.00 15.00
196 Andy Reid AU/335* RC 15.00 30.00
197 Brian Billick AU/585* RC 6.00 15.00
198 Jeff Fisher AU/585* RC 8.00 20.00
199 Jon Gruden AU/585* RC 6.00 15.00
200 Marvin Lewis AU/585* RC 6.00 15.00

2004 Playoff Contenders Playoff Ticket

1-100 PRINT RUN 150 SER.#'d SETS
COMMON ROOKIE 101-200 3.00 8.00
ROOKIE SEMISTARS 4.00 10.00
ROOKIE UNL.STARS 5.00 12.00
101-200 PRINT RUN 50 SER.#'d SETS
106 Ben Roethlisberger 40.00 100.00
116 Chris Perry 4.00 10.00
123 DeAngelo Hall 5.00 12.00
131 Eli Manning 40.00 100.00
134 J.P. Losman 4.00 10.00
146 Julius Jones 4.00 10.00
148 Kellen Winslow Jr. 5.00 12.00
151 Larry Fitzgerald 12.00 30.00
152 Lee Evans 5.00 12.00
155 Matt Schaub 10.00 25.00
160 Michael Turner 6.00 15.00
162 Philip Rivers 20.00 50.00
169 Roy Williams WR 5.00 12.00
174 Steven Jackson 8.00 20.00
188 Willie Parker 6.00 15.00
189 Patrick Crayton 5.00 12.00
193 Wes Welker 20.00 50.00
196 Andy Reid 5.00 12.00
197 Brian Billick 5.00 12.00
198 Jeff Fisher 5.00 12.00
199 Jon Gruden 5.00 12.00
200 Marvin Lewis 5.00 12.00

2004 Playoff Contenders Hawaii 2005

*SINGLES: 6X TO 15X BASIC CARDS
STATED PRINT RUN 25 SER.#'d SETS

2004 Playoff Contenders Legendary Contenders Orange

ORANGE PRINT RUN 2000 SER.#'d SETS
*BLUE/250: .6X TO 1.5X ORNG/2000
BLUE PRINT RUN 250 SER.#'d SETS
*GREEN/100: 1X TO 2.5X ORNG/2000
GREEN PRINT RUN 100 SER.#'d SETS
*RED/750: .5X TO 1.2X ORNG/2000
RED PRINT RUN 750 SER.#'d SETS
LC1 Barry Sanders 2.50 6.00
LC2 Don Shula 1.25 3.00
LC3 Gale Sayers 1.50 4.00
LC4 Herman Edwards 1.00 2.50
LC5 Joe Montana 3.00 8.00
LC6 Joe Namath 2.00 5.00
LC7 Larry Csonka 1.25 3.00
LC8 Mark Bavaro .75 2.00
LC9 Michael Irvin 1.25 3.00
LC10 Roger Staubach 2.00 5.00

2004 Playoff Contenders Legendary Contenders Autographs

AUTOS PRINT RUN 25 SER.#'d SETS
LC1 Barry Sanders 100.00 175.00
LC2 Don Shula 30.00 60.00
LC3 Gale Sayers 40.00 80.00
LC4 Herman Edwards 25.00 50.00
LC5 Joe Montana 125.00 250.00
LC6 Joe Namath 75.00 150.00
LC7 Larry Csonka 30.00 60.00
LC8 Mark Bavaro 25.00 50.00
LC9 Michael Irvin 40.00 80.00
LC10 Roger Staubach 60.00 120.00

2004 Playoff Contenders MVP Contenders Red

RED PRINT RUN 1250 SER.#'d SETS
*BLUE/100: 1X TO 2.5X RED/1250
BLUE PRINT RUN 100 SER.#'d SETS
*GREEN/250: .6X TO 1.5X RED/1250
GREEN PRINT RUN 250 SER.#'d SETS
*ORANGE/500: .5X TO 1.2X RED/1250
ORANGE PRINT RUN 500 SER.#'d SETS
MC1 Ahman Green 1.00 2.50
MC2 Brett Favre 3.00 8.00
MC3 Clinton Portis 1.25 3.00
MC4 Deuce McAllister 1.00 2.50
MC5 Donovan McNabb 1.25 3.00
MC6 LaDainian Tomlinson 1.25 3.00
MC7 Matt Hasselbeck 1.00 2.50
MC8 Priest Holmes 1.25 3.00
MC9 Brian Urlacher 1.25 3.00
MC10 Jake Delhomme 1.00 2.50
MC11 Shaun Alexander 1.00 2.50
MC12 Stephen Davis 1.00 2.50
MC13 Steve McNair 1.25 3.00
MC14 Tom Brady 2.50 6.00
MC15 Torry Holt 1.00 2.50

2004 Playoff Contenders MVP Contenders Autographs

AUTOS PRINT RUN 25 SER.#'d SETS
MC1 Ahman Green 12.00 30.00
MC2 Brett Favre 150.00 250.00
MC3 Clinton Portis 15.00 40.00
MC4 Deuce McAllister 12.00 30.00
MC5 Donovan McNabb 25.00 60.00
MC6 LaDainian Tomlinson 40.00 80.00
MC7 Matt Hasselbeck 12.00 30.00
MC8 Priest Holmes 15.00 40.00
MC9 Brian Urlacher 30.00 80.00
MC10 Jake Delhomme 12.00 30.00
MC11 Shaun Alexander 12.00 30.00
MC12 Stephen Davis 12.00 30.00
MC13 Steve McNair 30.00 60.00
MC14 Tom Brady 150.00 250.00
MC15 Torry Holt 12.00 30.00

2004 Playoff Contenders Rookie Round Up

STATED PRINT RUN 375 SER.#'d SETS
RU1 Eli Manning 6.00 15.00
RU2 Robert Gallery 1.00 2.50
RU3 Larry Fitzgerald 2.50 6.00
RU4 Philip Rivers 4.00 10.00
RU5 Sean Taylor 2.00 5.00
RU6 Kellen Winslow Jr. 1.00 2.50
RU7 Roy Williams WR 1.00 2.50
RU8 DeAngelo Hall 1.00 2.50
RU9 Reggie Williams .75 2.00
RU10 Dunta Robinson .60 1.50
RU11 Ben Roethlisberger 6.00 15.00
RU12 Jonathan Vilma 1.00 2.50
RU13 Lee Evans 1.00 2.50
RU14 Tommie Harris 1.00 2.50
RU15 Michael Clayton .75 2.00
RU16 D.J. Williams 1.00 2.50
RU17 Will Smith .75 2.00
RU18 Kenechi Udeze .75 2.00
RU19 Vince Wilfork 1.00 2.50
RU20 J.P. Losman .75 2.00
RU21 Marcus Tubbs .60 1.50
RU22 Steven Jackson 1.50 4.00
RU23 Ahmad Carroll .60 1.50
RU24 Chris Perry .75 2.00
RU25 Jason Babin 1.00 2.50
RU26 Chris Gamble .75 2.00
RU27 Michael Jenkins 1.00 2.50
RU28 Kevin Jones .75 2.00
RU29 Rashaun Woods .60 1.50
RU30 Ben Watson 1.00 2.50
RU31 Karlos Dansby 1.00 2.50
RU32 Teddy Lehman .60 1.50
RU33 Ricardo Colclough .75 2.00
RU34 Daryl Smith .60 1.50
RU35 Ben Troupe .75 2.00
RU36 Tatum Bell .75 2.00
RU37 Julius Jones .75 2.00
RU38 Erik Coleman .75 2.00
RU39 Dontarrious Thomas .75 2.00
RU40 Keiwan Ratliff .60 1.50
RU41 Devery Henderson 1.00 2.50
RU42 Michael Boulware 1.00 2.50
RU43 Darius Watts .60 1.50
RU44 Greg Jones .60 1.50
RU45 Madieu Williams .60 1.50
RU46 Shawntae Spencer .60 1.50
RU47 Courtney Watson .60 1.50
RU48 Keary Colbert .60 1.50
RU49 Cedric Cobbs .60 1.50
RU50 Drew Henson .60 1.50

2004 Playoff Contenders Round Numbers Blue

RN1-RN10 BLUE PRINT RUN 1500 SETS
RN11-RN15 BLUE PRINT RUN 1000 SETS
*GREEN: .5X TO 1.2X BLUE
RN1-RN10 GREEN PRINT RUN 750 SETS
RN11-RN15 GREEN PRINT RUN 500 SETS
*ORANGE: .6X TO 1.5X BLUE
RN1-RN10 ORANGE PRINT RUN 500 SETS
RN11-RN15 ORANGE PRINT RUN 250 SETS
*RED: .8X TO 2X BLUE
RN1-RN10 RED PRINT RUN 250 SETS
RN11-RN15 RED PRINT RUN 100 SETS
RN1 Eli Manning 5.00 12.00
Philip Rivers
RN2 Ben Roethlisberger 5.00 12.00
J.P. Losman
RN3 Roy Williams WR .75 2.00
Reggie Williams
RN4 Michael Clayton .75 2.00
Michael Jenkins
RN5 Steven Jackson 1.25 3.00
Kevin Jones
RN6 Ben Troupe .60 1.50
Greg Jones
RN7 Tatum Bell .60 1.50
Julius Jones
RN8 Darius Watts .50 1.25
Keary Colbert
RN9 Derrick Hamilton 1.50 4.00
Matt Schaub
RN10 Bernard Berrian .75 2.00
Devard Darling
RN11 Eli Manning 6.00 15.00
Philip Rivers
Ben Roethlisberger
J.P. Losman
RN12 Reggie Williams 1.50 4.00
Chris Perry
Steven Jackson
Kevin Jones
RN13 Roy Williams WR 1.00 2.50
Lee Evans
Michael Clayton
Michael Jenkins
RN14 Tatum Bell .75 2.00
Julius Jones
Greg Jones
Keary Colbert
RN15 Derrick Hamilton 2.00 5.00
Matt Schaub
Bernard Berrian
Devard Darling

2004 Playoff Contenders Round Numbers Autographs

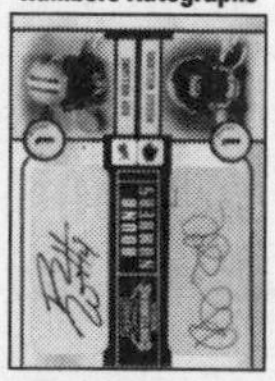

RN1-RN10 PRINT RUN 100 SER.#'d SETS
RN11-RN15 PRINT RUN 50 SER.#'d SETS
*GOLD/30: .5X TO 1.2X BASIC INSERTS
*GOLD/20: .6X TO 1.5X BASIC INSERTS
GOLD/10 TOO SCARCE TO PRICE
RN1 Eli Manning 75.00 150.00
Philip Rivers
RN2 Ben Roethlisberger 60.00 150.00
J.P. Losman
RN3 Roy Williams WR 12.00 30.00
Reggie Williams
RN4 Michael Clayton 12.00 30.00
Michael Jenkins
RN5 Steven Jackson 30.00 80.00
Kevin Jones
RN6 Ben Troupe 10.00 25.00
Greg Jones
RN7 Tatum Bell 10.00 25.00
Julius Jones
RN8 Darius Watts 8.00 20.00
Keary Colbert
RN9 Derrick Hamilton 25.00 60.00
Matt Schaub
RN10 Bernard Berrian 12.00 30.00
Devard Darling
RN11 Eli Manning 200.00 400.00
Philip Rivers
Ben Roethlisberger
J.P. Losman
RN12 Reggie Williams 100.00 175.00
Chris Perry
Steven Jackson
Kevin Jones
RN13 Roy Williams WR 30.00 80.00
Lee Evans
Michael Clayton
Michael Jenkins
RN14 Tatum Bell 20.00 50.00
Julius Jones
Greg Jones
Keary Colbert
RN15 Derrick Hamilton 40.00 100.00
Matt Schaub
Bernard Berrian
Devard Darling

2004 Playoff Contenders ROY Contenders Green

GREEN PRINT RUN 2000 SER.#'d SETS
*BLUE/750: .6X TO 1.5X GREEN/2000
BLUE PRINT RUN 750 SER.#'d SETS
*ORANGE/100: 1.2X TO 3X GRN/2000
ORANGE PRINT RUN 100 SER.#'d SETS
*RED/250: .8X TO 2X GREEN/2000
RED PRINT RUN 250 SER.#'d SETS
ROY1 Ben Roethlisberger 4.00 10.00
ROY2 DeAngelo Hall .60 1.50
ROY3 Drew Henson .40 1.00
ROY4 Eli Manning 4.00 10.00
ROY5 Kellen Winslow Jr. .60 1.50
ROY6 Kevin Jones .50 1.25
ROY7 Philip Rivers 2.50 6.00
ROY8 Reggie Williams .50 1.25
ROY9 Roy Williams WR .60 1.50
ROY10 Steven Jackson 1.00 2.50

2004 Playoff Contenders ROY Contenders Autographs

AUTO PRINT RUN 25 SER.#'d SETS
ROY1 Ben Roethlisberger 100.00 175.00
ROY2 DeAngelo Hall 20.00 50.00
ROY3 Drew Henson 12.00 30.00
ROY4 Eli Manning 100.00 175.00
ROY5 Kellen Winslow Jr. 20.00 50.00
ROY6 Kevin Jones 15.00 40.00
ROY7 Philip Rivers 60.00 120.00
ROY8 Reggie Williams 15.00 40.00
ROY9 Roy Williams WR 20.00 50.00
ROY10 Steven Jackson 40.00 100.00

2004 Playoff Contenders Toe 2 Toe

STATED PRINT RUN 375 SER.#'d SETS
TT1 Anquan Boldin 1.50 4.00
Torry Holt
TT2 Marc Bulger 1.25 3.00
Matt Hasselbeck
TT3 Shaun Alexander 1.25 3.00
Kevan Barlow
TT4 Emmitt Smith 4.00 10.00
Marshall Faulk
TT5 Brett Favre 4.00 10.00
Rex Grossman
TT6 Isaac Bruce 1.25 3.00
Koren Robinson
TT7 Joey Harrington 1.25 3.00
Daunte Culpepper
TT8 Michael Bennett 1.25 3.00
Ahman Green
TT9 Randy Moss .75 2.00
Roy Williams WR
TT10 Kevin Jones .75 2.00
Brian Urlacher
TT11 Aaron Brooks 2.00 5.00
Michael Vick
TT12 Deuce McAllister 1.25 3.00
Stephen Davis
TT13 Brad Johnson 1.25 3.00
Jake Delhomme
TT14 Joe Horn 1.50 4.00
Steve Smith
TT15 Michael Clayton .75 2.00
Michael Jenkins
TT16 Julius Jones .75 2.00
Tiki Barber
TT17 Eli Manning 5.00 12.00
Mark Brunell
TT18 Laveranues Coles 1.25 3.00
Amani Toomer
TT19 Terrell Owens 1.50 4.00
Keyshawn Johnson
TT20 Roy Williams S 3.00 8.00
Sean Taylor
TT21 Brian Westbrook 1.50 4.00
Clinton Portis
TT22 Donovan McNabb 1.50 4.00
Eddie George
TT23 Jevon Kearse 1.50 4.00
Michael Strahan
TT24 Jeremy Shockey 1.25 3.00
Lavar Arrington
TT25 LaDainian Tomlinson 1.50 4.00
Priest Holmes
TT26 Philip Rivers 3.00 8.00
Trent Green
TT27 Rod Smith 3.00 8.00
Jerry Rice
TT28 Antonio Gates 1.50 4.00
Tony Gonzalez
TT29 Charles Woodson 1.50 4.00
Champ Bailey
TT30 Jamal Lewis 1.25 3.00
Rudi Johnson
TT31 Jeff Garcia 1.50 4.00
Carson Palmer
TT32 Kyle Boller 5.00 12.00
Ben Roethlisberger
TT33 Kendrell Bell 1.50 4.00
Ray Lewis
TT34 Todd Heap .75 2.00
Kellen Winslow Jr.
TT35 Hines Ward 1.50 4.00
Chad Johnson
TT36 Peter Warrick 1.25 3.00
Antwaan Randle El
TT37 Andre Johnson 1.50 4.00
Marvin Harrison
TT38 David Carr 1.25 3.00
Byron Leftwich
TT39 Peyton Manning 3.00 8.00
Steve McNair
TT40 Edgerrin James 1.25 3.00
Fred Taylor
TT41 Domanick Davis 1.00 2.50
Chris Brown
TT42 Tyrone Calico 1.25 3.00
Reggie Williams
TT43 Tom Brady 3.00 8.00
Drew Bledsoe
TT44 Chad Pennington 1.50 4.00
A.J. Feeley
TT45 Willis McGahee 1.50 4.00
Curtis Martin
TT46 Corey Dillon 1.25 3.00
Travis Henry
TT47 Santana Moss 1.25 3.00
Chris Chambers
TT48 Zach Thomas 1.50 4.00
Tedy Bruschi
TT49 Deion Branch .75 2.00
Lee Evans
TT50 Justin McCareins 1.25 3.00
Eric Moulds

2005 Playoff Contenders

This 200-card set was released in January, 2006. The set was issued through the hobby in five-card packs which came 24 packs to a box. Cards numbered 1-100 feature veterans mainly in alphabetical order by team while cards numbered 101-200 feature signed rookies. A few players signed less cards for this product and playoff announced the print runs for those players signatures. A few players did not return their signatures in time for pack out and those cards could be redeemed until August 1, 2007.

COMP.SET w/o RC's (100) 7.50 20.00
AU PRINT RUNS ANNOUNCED BY PLAYOFF
UNPRICED CHAMPION.PRINT RUN 1 SET
1 Anquan Boldin .25 .60
2 Kurt Warner .30 .75
3 Larry Fitzgerald .30 .75
4 Michael Vick .30 .75
5 T.J. Duckett .20 .50
6 Warrick Dunn .25 .60
7 Derrick Mason .25 .60
8 Jamal Lewis .25 .60
9 Kyle Boller .25 .60
10 Ray Lewis .30 .75
11 J.P. Losman .20 .50
12 Lee Evans .25 .60
13 Willis McGahee .30 .75
14 DeShaun Foster .25 .60
15 Jake Delhomme .25 .60
16 Steve Smith .30 .75
17 Brian Urlacher .30 .75
18 Muhsin Muhammad .25 .60
19 Rex Grossman .25 .60
20 Carson Palmer .30 .75
21 Chad Johnson .25 .60
22 Rudi Johnson .25 .60
23 Lee Suggs .20 .50
24 Trent Dilfer .25 .60
25 Drew Bledsoe .30 .75
26 Jason Witten .30 .75
27 Julius Jones .20 .50
28 Keyshawn Johnson .25 .60
29 Ashley Lelie .20 .50
30 Jake Plummer .25 .60
31 Rod Smith .25 .60
32 Tatum Bell .20 .50
33 Joey Harrington .25 .60
34 Kevin Jones .20 .50
35 Roy Williams WR .25 .60
36 Ahman Green .25 .60
37 Brett Favre .75 2.00
38 Javon Walker .20 .50
39 Andre Johnson .30 .75
40 David Carr .20 .50
41 Domanick Davis .20 .50
42 Edgerrin James .25 .60
43 Marvin Harrison .30 .75
44 Peyton Manning .60 1.50
45 Reggie Wayne .30 .75
46 Byron Leftwich .25 .60
47 Fred Taylor .25 .60
48 Jimmy Smith .25 .60
49 Priest Holmes .25 .60
50 Tony Gonzalez .25 .60
51 Trent Green .25 .60
52 Chris Chambers .25 .60
53 Ricky Williams .25 .60
54 Daunte Culpepper .25 .60
55 Michael Bennett .25 .60
56 Nate Burleson .20 .50
57 Corey Dillon .25 .60
58 Deion Branch .20 .50
59 Tom Brady .60 1.50
60 Aaron Brooks .20 .50
61 Deuce McAllister .25 .60
62 Joe Horn .25 .60
63 Eli Manning .50 1.25
64 Jeremy Shockey .30 .75
65 Plaxico Burress .25 .60
66 Tiki Barber .30 .75
67 Chad Pennington .30 .75
68 Curtis Martin .30 .75
69 Laveranues Coles .20 .50
70 Kerry Collins .25 .60
71 LaMont Jordan .25 .60
72 Randy Moss .30 .75
73 Brian Westbrook .25 .60
74 Donovan McNabb .30 .75
75 Terrell Owens .30 .75
76 Ben Roethlisberger .50 1.25
77 Duce Staley .25 .60
78 Hines Ward .30 .75
79 Jerome Bettis .30 .75
80 Antonio Gates .30 .75
81 Drew Brees .30 .75
82 LaDainian Tomlinson .30 .75
83 Brandon Lloyd .20 .50
84 Kevan Barlow .20 .50
85 Darrell Jackson .20 .50
86 Matt Hasselbeck .25 .60
87 Shaun Alexander .25 .60
88 Isaac Bruce .25 .60
89 Marc Bulger .25 .60
90 Steven Jackson .30 .75
91 Torry Holt .25 .60
92 Brian Griese .25 .60
93 Derrick Brooks .25 .60
94 Chris Brown .20 .50
95 Drew Bennett .25 .60
96 Steve McNair .30 .75
97 Travis Henry .20 .50
98 Clinton Portis .25 .60
99 LaVar Arrington .25 .60
100 Santana Moss .25 .60
101 Aaron Rodgers AU/530* RC 600.00 1,000.00
102 Adam Jones AU RC 4.00 10.00
103 Adrian McPherson AU/365* RC 12.00 40.00
104 Alvin Pearman AU RC 4.00 10.00
105 Airese Currie AU RC 4.00 10.00
106 Alex Smith QB AU/401* RC 60.00 100.00
107 Andrew Walter AU/99* RC 50.00 100.00
108 Anthony Davis AU/366* RC 5.00 12.00
109 Antrel Rolle AU RC 6.00 15.00
110 Brandon Jacobs AU RC 12.00 30.00
111 Brandon Jones AU RC 5.00 12.00
112 Braylon Edwards AU RC 12.00 30.00
113 Bryant McFadden AU/315* RC 6.00 15.00
114 Carlos Rogers AU RC 10.00 25.00
115 Cadillac Williams AU/380* RC 12.00 30.00
116 Cedric Benson AU/289* RC 12.00 30.00
117 Cedric Houston AU/116* RC 40.00 100.00
118 Chad Owens AU RC 5.00 12.00
119 Charlie Frye AU RC 6.00 15.00
120 Chris Henry AU RC 6.00 15.00
121 Ciatrick Fason AU RC 4.00 10.00
122 Courtney Roby AU RC 5.00 12.00
123 Craig Bragg AU/425* RC 5.00 12.00
124 C.Thorpe AU/416* RC 5.00 12.00
125 Damien Nash AU RC 5.00 12.00
126 Dan Cody AU/315* RC 6.00 15.00
127 Dan Orlovsky AU RC 6.00 15.00
128 Dante Ridgeway AU/373* RC 5.00 12.00
129 Darren Sproles AU/454* RC 25.00 50.00
130 David Greene AU RC 4.00 10.00
131 David Pollack AU RC 5.00 12.00
132 Deandra Cobb AU/440* RC 5.00 12.00
133 DeMarcus Ware AU RC 25.00 50.00
134 Derek Anderson AU/450* RC 6.00 15.00
135 Derrick Johnson AU RC 10.00 25.00
136 Erasmus James AU RC 5.00 12.00
137 Eric Shelton AU RC 4.00 10.00
138 Fabian Washington AU RC 5.00 12.00
139 Frank Gore AU RC 25.00 50.00
140 Fred Gibson AU/476* RC 6.00 15.00
141 Heath Miller AU/510* RC 20.00 50.00
142 J.J. Arrington AU/465* RC 6.00 15.00
143 J.R. Russell AU/489* RC 5.00 12.00
144 Jason Campbell AU RC 15.00 40.00
145 Jason White AU RC 6.00 15.00
146 Jerome Mathis AU/416* RC 8.00 20.00
147 Josh Davis AU RC 4.00 10.00
148 Kay-Jay Harris AU RC 4.00 10.00
149 Kyle Orton AU RC 10.00 25.00
150 Larry Brackins AU RC 4.00 10.00
151 Lionel Gates AU/241* RC 8.00 20.00
152 Marion Barber AU RC 8.00 20.00
153 Mark Bradley AU RC 4.00 10.00
154 Mark Clayton AU/494* RC 6.00 15.00
155 Marlin Jackson AU RC 4.00 10.00
156 Matt Jones AU/165* RC 20.00 40.00
157 Matt Roth AU RC 5.00 12.00
158 Maurice Clarett AU/89* 25.00 60.00
159 Mike Williams AU/73* 60.00 100.00
160 Paris Warren AU/241* RC 10.00 25.00
161 Rasheed Marshall AU RC 5.00 12.00
162 Reggie Brown AU/528* RC 5.00 12.00
163 Roddy White AU RC 15.00 30.00
164 Ronnie Brown AU/550* RC 20.00 50.00
165 Roscoe Parrish AU RC 4.00 10.00
166 Roydell Williams AU/491* RC 6.00 15.00
167 Ryan Fitzpatrick AU/284* RC 60.00 120.00
168 Ryan Moats AU RC 4.00 10.00
169 Shaun Cody AU RC 5.00 12.00
170 Shawne Merriman AU RC 12.00 30.00
171 Stefan LeFors AU RC 4.00 10.00
172 Steve Savoy AU RC 4.00 10.00
173 T.A. McLendon AU RC 4.00 10.00
174 Tab Perry AU RC 4.00 10.00
175 Taylor Stubblefield AU RC 4.00 10.00
176 Terrence Murphy AU RC 4.00 10.00
177 Thomas Davis AU RC 4.00 10.00
178 Travis Johnson AU RC 4.00 10.00
179 T.Williamson AU/402* RC 10.00 25.00
180 Vernand Morency AU RC 4.00 10.00
181 Vincent Jackson AU RC 12.00 30.00
182 Alex Smith TE AU RC 4.00 10.00
183 Channing Crowder AU RC 5.00 12.00
184 Darrent Williams AU RC 15.00 40.00
185 Derrick Wimbush AU RC 5.00 12.00
186 James Kilian AU RC 4.00 10.00
187 Josh Cribbs AU RC 25.00 50.00
188 LeRon McCoy AU RC 4.00 10.00
189 Luis Castillo AU RC 5.00 12.00
190 Matt Cassel AU RC 15.00 40.00
191 Mike Patterson AU RC 4.00 10.00
192 Nate Washington AU RC 6.00 15.00
193 Noah Herron AU RC 4.00 10.00
194 Fred Amey AU RC 4.00 10.00
195 Tyson Thompson AU RC 4.00 10.00
196 Mike Nugent AU RC 5.00 12.00
197 Odell Thurman AU RC 6.00 15.00
198 Chris Carr AU RC 4.00 10.00
199 Bo Scaife AU RC 5.00 12.00
200 Billy Bajema AU RC 4.00 10.00

2005 Playoff Contenders Playoff Ticket

*VETERANS 1-100: 2.5X TO 6X BASIC CARDS
1-100 PRINT RUN 199 SER.#'d SETS
COMMON ROOKIE (101-200) 4.00 10.00
ROOKIE SEMISTARS 5.00 12.00
ROOKIE UNL.STARS 6.00 15.00
101-200 ROOK.PRINT RUN 25 SER.#'d SETS
101 Aaron Rodgers 75.00 135.00
106 Alex Smith QB 10.00 25.00
110 Brandon Jacobs 8.00 20.00
112 Braylon Edwards 8.00 20.00
115 Cadillac Williams 6.00 15.00
133 DeMarcus Ware 12.00 30.00
134 Derek Anderson 5.00 12.00
139 Frank Gore 10.00 25.00
141 Heath Miller 8.00 20.00
144 Jason Campbell 8.00 20.00
152 Marion Barber 6.00 15.00
156 Matt Jones 6.00 15.00
164 Ronnie Brown 8.00 20.00
170 Shawne Merriman 6.00 15.00
181 Vincent Jackson 8.00 20.00
187 Josh Cribbs 40.00 80.00
190 Matt Cassel 12.00 30.00
195 Tyson Thompson 6.00 15.00
198 Chris Carr 4.00 10.00

2005 Playoff Contenders Autographs

ANNOUNCED PRINT RUN 2-50
15 Jake Delhomme/250* 12.00 30.00
16 Steve Smith/41* 15.00 40.00
25 Drew Bledsoe/46* 40.00 80.00
28 Keyshawn Johnson/40* 15.00 40.00

39 Andre Johnson/250*	15.00	40.00
41 Domanick Davis/250*	10.00	25.00
69 Laveranues Coles/25*	15.00	40.00
93 Derrick Brooks/250*	12.00	30.00
95 Drew Bennett/250*	12.00	30.00

2005 Playoff Contenders Legendary Contenders Blue

BLUE PRINT RUN 2000 SER.#'d SETS
*GOLD: .8X TO 2X BASIC BLUE
GOLD PRINT RUN 250 SER.#'d SETS
*GREEN: .5X TO 1.2X BASIC BLUE
GREEN PRINT RUN 750 SER.#'d SETS
*RED: 1X TO 2.5X BASIC BLUE
RED PRINT RUN 100 SER.#'d SETS

1 Bo Jackson	2.00	5.00
2 Bob Griese	1.50	4.00
3 Deacon Jones	1.25	3.00
4 Don Meredith	1.50	4.00
5 Don Shula	1.25	3.00
6 Earl Campbell	1.50	4.00
7 Fran Tarkenton	1.50	4.00
8 Franco Harris	1.50	4.00
9 Jack Lambert	1.50	4.00
10 Jim Brown	2.00	5.00
11 Jim Kelly	2.00	5.00
12 Joe Namath	2.50	6.00
13 Len Dawson	1.50	4.00
14 Sonny Jurgensen	1.25	3.00
15 Tony Dorsett	1.25	3.00

2005 Playoff Contenders Legendary Contenders Autographs

STATED PRINT RUN 25-150

1 Bo Jackson/25	50.00	100.00
2 Bob Griese/95	15.00	40.00
3 Deacon Jones/25	15.00	40.00
4 Don Meredith/25	50.00	100.00
5 Don Shula/103	25.00	50.00
6 Earl Campbell/25	25.00	50.00
7 Fran Tarkenton/25	30.00	60.00
8 Franco Harris/65	30.00	60.00
9 Jack Lambert/25	50.00	100.00
10 Jim Brown/150	40.00	80.00
11 Jim Kelly/26	40.00	80.00
12 Joe Namath/175	40.00	80.00
13 Len Dawson/150	25.00	50.00
14 Sonny Jurgensen/25	30.00	60.00
15 Tony Dorsett/25	30.00	60.00

2005 Playoff Contenders MVP Contenders Gold

GOLD PRINT RUN 1250 SER.#'d SETS
*BLUE: .6X TO 1.5X BASIC GOLD
BLUE PRINT RUN 250 SER.#'d SETS
*GREEN: 1X TO 2.5X BASIC GOLD
GREEN PRINT RUN 100 SER.#'d SETS
*RED: .5X TO 1.2X BASIC GOLD
RED PRINT RUN 500 SER.#'d SETS

1 Ben Roethlisberger	2.00	5.00
2 Brett Favre	3.00	8.00
3 Byron Leftwich	1.00	2.50
4 Chad Pennington	1.25	3.00
5 Donovan McNabb	1.25	3.00
6 Eli Manning	2.00	5.00
7 Julius Jones	.75	2.00
8 Michael Vick	1.25	3.00
9 Priest Holmes	1.00	2.50
10 Willis McGahee	1.25	3.00

2005 Playoff Contenders MVP Contenders Autographs

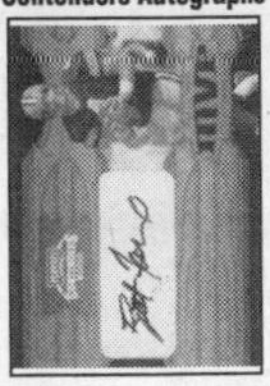

STATED PRINT RUN 25 SER.#'d SETS

1 Ben Roethlisberger	100.00	200.00
2 Brett Favre	125.00	250.00
3 Byron Leftwich	10.00	25.00
4 Chad Pennington	12.00	30.00
5 Donovan McNabb	25.00	60.00
6 Eli Manning	100.00	175.00
7 Julius Jones	8.00	20.00
8 Michael Vick	30.00	80.00
9 Priest Holmes	10.00	25.00
10 Willis McGahee	12.00	30.00

2005 Playoff Contenders Rookie Round Up

STATED PRINT RUN 450 SER.#'d SETS

1 Alex Smith QB	1.50	4.00
2 Ronnie Brown	1.25	3.00
3 Braylon Edwards	1.25	3.00
4 Cedric Benson	1.00	2.50
5 Cadillac Williams	1.00	2.50
6 Adam Jones	.75	2.00
7 Troy Williamson	.75	2.00
8 Antrel Rolle	1.00	2.50
9 Carlos Rogers	1.00	2.50
10 Mike Williams	1.00	2.50
11 DeMarcus Ware	2.00	5.00
12 Shawne Merriman	1.00	2.50
13 Thomas Davis	.60	1.50
14 Derrick Johnson	.75	2.00
15 Travis Johnson	.60	1.50
16 David Pollack	.75	2.00
17 Erasmus James	.75	2.00
18 Marcus Spears	.75	2.00
19 Matt Jones	1.00	2.50
20 Mark Clayton	1.00	2.50
21 Aaron Rodgers	20.00	40.00
22 Jason Campbell	1.25	3.00
23 Roddy White	1.25	3.00
24 Heath Miller	1.25	3.00
25 Reggie Brown	.60	1.50
26 Mark Bradley	.60	1.50
27 J.J. Arrington	.75	2.00
28 Eric Shelton	.60	1.50
29 Roscoe Parrish	.60	1.50
30 Terrence Murphy	.60	1.50
31 Vincent Jackson	1.25	3.00
32 Frank Gore	1.50	4.00
33 Charlie Frye	1.00	2.50
34 Courtney Roby	.75	2.00
35 Andrew Walter	.75	2.00
36 Vernand Morency	.75	2.00
37 Ryan Moats	.75	2.00
38 Chris Henry	1.00	2.50
39 David Greene	.60	1.50
40 Brandon Jones	.75	2.00
41 Luis Castillo	.75	2.00
42 Kyle Orton	1.00	2.50
43 Marion Barber	1.00	2.50
44 Brandon Jacobs	1.25	3.00
45 Ciatrick Fason	.60	1.50
46 Jerome Mathis	1.00	2.50
47 Stefan LeFors	.60	1.50
48 Alvin Pearman	.60	1.50
49 Darren Sproles	1.00	2.50
50 Mike Patterson	.60	1.50

2005 Playoff Contenders Round Numbers Green

RN1-RN10 PRINT RUN 1500 SER.#'d SETS
RN11-RN15 PRINT RUN 1000 SER.#'d SETS
*BLUE: .5X TO 1.2X BASIC GREEN
BLUE RN1-RN10 PRINT RUN 750 SER.#'d SETS
BLUE RN11-RN15 PRINT RUN 500 SETS
*GOLD: .8X TO 2X BASIC GREEN
GOLD RN1-RN10 PRINT RUN 250 SER.#'d SETS
GOLD RN11-RN15 PRINT RUN 100 SETS
*RED: .6X TO 1.5X BASIC GREEN
RED RN1-RN10 PRINT RUN 500 SER.#'d SETS
RED RN11-RN15 PRINT RUN 250 SER.#'d SETS

RN1 Alex Smith QB	6.00	15.00
Aaron Rodgers		
RN2 Jason Campbell	1.00	2.50
Carlos Rogers		
RN3 Ronnie Brown	1.00	2.50
Cadillac Williams		
RN4 Braylon Edwards	1.00	2.50
Troy Williamson		
RN5 Cedric Benson	1.00	2.50
Heath Miller		
RN6 Mark Clayton	1.00	2.50
Roddy White		
RN7 J.J. Arrington	.60	1.50
Eric Shelton		
RN8 Reggie Brown	1.00	2.50
Vincent Jackson		
RN9 Charlie Frye	.75	2.00
David Greene		
RN10 Kyle Orton	.75	2.00
Stefan LeFors		
RN11 Alex Smith QB	8.00	20.00
Aaron Rodgers		
Cedric Benson		
Mark Clayton		
RN12 Ronnie Brown	1.25	3.00
Cadillac Williams		
Jason Campbell		
Carlos Rogers		
RN13 Braylon Edwards	1.25	3.00
Troy Williamson		
Mike Williams		
Matt Jones		
RN14 J.J. Arrington	1.25	3.00
Eric Shelton		
Reggie Brown		
Vincent Jackson		
RN15 Charlie Frye	1.50	4.00
David Greene		
Frank Gore		
Ryan Moats		

2005 Playoff Contenders Round Numbers Autographs

RN1-RN10 PRINT RUN 50 SER.#'d SETS
RN11-RN15 PRINT RUN 25 SER.#'d SETS
UNPRICED GOLD PRINT RUN 5-20 CARDS

RN1 Alex Smith QB	175.00	300.00
Aaron Rodgers		
RN2 Jason Campbell	20.00	50.00
Carlos Rogers		
RN3 Ronnie Brown	60.00	150.00
Cadillac Williams		
RN4 Braylon Edwards	25.00	60.00
Troy Williamson		
RN5 Cedric Benson	20.00	50.00
Heath Miller		
RN6 Mark Clayton	25.00	50.00
Roddy White		
RN7 J.J. Arrington	12.00	30.00
Eric Shelton		
RN8 Reggie Brown	12.00	30.00
Vincent Jackson		
RN9 Charlie Frye	12.00	30.00
David Greene		
RN10 Kyle Orton	20.00	40.00
Stefan LeFors		
RN11 Alex Smith QB	200.00	350.00
Aaron Rodgers		
Cedric Benson		
Mark Clayton		
RN12 Ronnie Brown	125.00	250.00
Cadillac Williams		
Jason Campbell		
Carlos Rogers		
RN13 Braylon Edwards	125.00	200.00
Mike Williams WR		
Troy Williamson		
Matt Jones		
RN14 J.J. Arrington	30.00	80.00
Eric Shelton		
Reggie Brown		
Vincent Jackson		
RN15 Charlie Frye	40.00	100.00
David Greene		
Frank Gore		
Ryan Moats		

2005 Playoff Contenders ROY Contenders Red

RED PRINT RUN 2000 SER.#'d SETS
*BLUE: 1X TO 2.5X BASIC REDS
BLUE PRINT RUN 100 SER.#'d SETS
*GOLD: .5X TO 1.2X BASIC REDS
GOLD PRINT RUN 750 SER.#'d SETS
*GREEN: .6X TO 1.5X BASIC REDS
GREEN PRINT RUN 250 SER.#'d SETS

1 Alex Smith QB	1.25	3.00
2 Braylon Edwards	1.00	2.50
3 Cadillac Williams	.75	2.00
4 Cedric Benson	.75	2.00
5 J.J. Arrington	.60	1.50
6 Mark Clayton	.75	2.00
7 Matt Jones	.75	2.00
8 Mike Williams	.75	2.00
9 Ronnie Brown	1.00	2.50
10 Troy Williamson	.60	1.50

2005 Playoff Contenders ROY Contenders Autographs

STATED PRINT RUN 25 SER.#'d SETS

1 Alex Smith QB	50.00	100.00
2 Braylon Edwards	30.00	80.00
3 Cadillac Williams	30.00	80.00
4 Cedric Benson	25.00	50.00
5 J.J. Arrington	25.00	50.00
6 Mark Clayton	25.00	50.00
7 Matt Jones	25.00	50.00
8 Mike Williams	25.00	50.00
9 Ronnie Brown	60.00	120.00
10 Troy Williamson	25.00	50.00

2005 Playoff Contenders Toe to Toe

STATED PRINT RUN 450 SER.#'d SETS

1 Edgerrin James	1.50	4.00
Jamal Lewis		
2 Ashley Lelie	1.00	2.50
Chris Chambers		
3 Michael Vick	2.50	6.00
Donovan McNabb		
4 Kevin Jones	1.50	4.00
Cedric Benson		
5 Deion Branch	1.00	2.50
Steve Smith		
6 Clinton Portis	2.00	5.00
Julius Jones		
7 Chad Pennington	1.50	4.00
Byron Leftwich		
8 Randy Moss	1.50	4.00
Terrell Owens		
9 Aaron Brooks	1.50	4.00
Daunte Culpepper		
10 Chad Johnson	1.50	4.00
Andre Johnson		
11 Peyton Manning	4.00	10.00
Steve McNair		
12 Brett Favre	4.00	10.00
Jake Delhomme		
13 Ahman Green	1.50	4.00
Deuce McAllister		
14 Ben Roethlisberger	4.00	10.00
Drew Brees		
15 Muhsin Muhammad	1.50	4.00
Troy Williamson		
16 Ronnie Brown	4.00	10.00
Cadillac Williams		
17 Shaun Alexander	2.00	5.00
Domanick Davis		
18 Marvin Harrison	1.50	4.00
Torry Holt		
19 Javon Walker	1.00	2.50
Nate Burleson		
20 Ray Lewis	1.50	4.00
Brian Urlacher		
21 LaMont Jordan	1.00	2.50
Willis McGahee		
22 Priest Holmes	1.50	4.00
LaDainian Tomlinson		
23 Fred Taylor	1.50	4.00
Steven Jackson		
24 Derrick Mason	1.50	4.00
Hines Ward		
25 Trent Green	1.00	2.50
Kerry Collins		
26 Darrell Jackson	1.00	2.50
Anquan Boldin		
27 Alex Smith QB	4.00	10.00
Eli Manning		
28 LaVar Arrington	1.50	4.00
Derrick Brooks		
29 Roy Williams WR	1.50	4.00
Larry Fitzgerald		
30 Marc Bulger	1.50	4.00
Matt Hasselbeck		
31 Brian Westbrook	1.50	4.00
Tiki Barber		
32 Keyshawn Johnson	1.50	4.00
Mike Williams		
33 Jerry Porter	1.00	2.50
Santana Moss		
34 Drew Bledsoe	1.50	4.00
Jake Plummer		
35 Joe Horn	1.00	2.50
Laveranues Coles		
36 Michael Bennett	1.00	2.50
Lee Suggs		
37 Jeremy Shockey	1.50	4.00
Jason Witten		
38 Rudi Johnson	1.00	2.50
Duce Staley		
39 Kyle Boller	1.00	2.50
David Carr		
40 Reggie Wayne	1.00	2.50
Jimmy Smith		
41 Tom Brady	4.00	10.00
J.P. Losman		
42 Kurt Warner	1.50	4.00
Patrick Ramsey		
43 Eddie Kennison	1.00	2.50
Plaxico Burress		
44 Rod Smith	1.00	2.50
Lee Evans		
45 Carson Palmer	1.50	4.00
Joey Harrington		
46 Antonio Gates	1.50	4.00
Tony Gonzalez		
47 Michael Clayton	1.00	2.50
Roddy White		
48 Corey Dillon	1.50	4.00
Curtis Martin		
49 Drew Bennett	1.50	4.00
Matt Jones		
50 Mark Clayton	2.50	6.00
Braylon Edwards		

2006 Playoff Contenders

This 242-card set was released in January, 2007. The set was issued into the hobby in five-card packs, with a $6 SRP, which came 24 packs to a box. Cards numbered 1-100 feature veterans in team alphabetical order while cards numbered 101-242. A few players signed less cards then other players in the set and we have notated the announced print runs of those players in our checklist.

COMP.SET w/o RC's (100)	8.00	20.00
1 Anquan Boldin	.25	.60
2 Edgerrin James	.25	.60
3 Larry Fitzgerald	.30	.75
4 Alge Crumpler	.25	.60
5 Michael Vick	.30	.75
6 Warrick Dunn	.25	.60
7 Steve McNair	.25	.60
8 Mark Clayton	.25	.60
9 Derrick Mason	.25	.60
10 Lee Evans	.25	.60
11 Willis McGahee	.25	.60
12 Jake Delhomme	.25	.60
13 Keyshawn Johnson	.25	.60
14 Steve Smith	.30	.75
15 Cedric Benson	.25	.60
16 Brian Urlacher	.30	.75
17 Thomas Jones	.25	.60
18 Carson Palmer	.30	.75
19 Chad Johnson	.25	.60
20 Rudi Johnson	.25	.60
21 T.J. Houshmandzadeh	.25	.60
22 Charlie Frye	.25	.60
23 Braylon Edwards	.25	.60
24 Reuben Droughns	.25	.60
25 Tony Romo	.75	2.00
26 Julius Jones	.20	.50
27 Roy Williams S	.25	.60
28 Terrell Owens	.30	.75
29 Javon Walker	.25	.60
30 Rod Smith	.25	.60
31 Tatum Bell	.20	.50
32 Roy Williams WR	.25	.60
33 Kevin Jones	.20	.50
34 Brett Favre	.60	1.50
35 Robert Ferguson	.20	.50
36 Samkon Gado	.25	.60
37 Andre Johnson	.30	.75
38 David Carr	.20	.50
39 Domanick Davis	.20	.50
40 Eric Moulds	.20	.50
41 Dallas Clark	.25	.60
42 Marvin Harrison	.30	.75
43 Peyton Manning	.50	1.25
44 Reggie Wayne	.25	.60
45 Matt Jones	.20	.50
46 Byron Leftwich	.25	.60
47 Fred Taylor	.25	.60
48 Larry Johnson	.25	.60
49 Priest Holmes	.25	.60
50 Tony Gonzalez	.25	.60
51 Trent Green	.25	.60
52 Chris Chambers	.25	.60
53 Daunte Culpepper	.25	.60
54 Ronnie Brown	.30	.75
55 Chester Taylor	.25	.60
56 Brad Johnson	.25	.60
57 Corey Dillon	.25	.60
58 Deion Branch	.25	.60
59 Tom Brady	.50	1.25
60 Tedy Bruschi	.30	.75
61 Deuce McAllister	.25	.60
62 Donte Stallworth	.20	.50
63 Drew Brees	.30	.75
64 Eli Manning	.40	1.00
65 Jeremy Shockey	.30	.75
66 Tiki Barber	.30	.75
67 Chad Pennington	.25	.60
68 Curtis Martin	.30	.75
69 Laveranues Coles	.20	.50
70 Randy Moss	.30	.75
71 LaMont Jordan	.25	.60
72 Jerry Porter	.20	.50
73 Donovan McNabb	.30	.75
74 Reggie Brown	.20	.50
75 Ben Roethlisberger	.40	1.00
76 Hines Ward	.30	.75
77 Willie Parker	.25	.60
78 Antonio Gates	.30	.75
79 Philip Rivers	.30	.75
80 LaDainian Tomlinson	.30	.75
81 Alex Smith QB	.30	.75
82 Antonio Bryant	.20	.50
83 Kevan Barlow	.20	.50
84 Darrell Jackson	.25	.60
85 Matt Hasselbeck	.25	.60
86 Nate Burleson	.20	.50
87 Shaun Alexander	.25	.60
88 Marc Bulger	.25	.60
89 Steven Jackson	.30	.75
90 Isaac Bruce	.25	.60
91 Torry Holt	.25	.60
92 Cadillac Williams	.25	.60
93 Chris Simms	.25	.60
94 Joey Galloway	.25	.60
95 Chris Brown	.20	.50
96 David Givens	.25	.60
97 Drew Bennett	.25	.60
98 Clinton Portis	.30	.75
99 Santana Moss	.25	.60
100 Mark Brunell	.25	.60
101 Malcom Floyd AU RC	25.00	40.00
102 Bart Scott AU RC	8.00	25.00
103 Reggie McNeal AU/457* RC	5.00	12.00
104 Domenik Hixon AU/586* RC	8.00	20.00
105 Vince Young AU/487* RC	20.00	50.00
UER (college listed as Texas A&M)		
106 Marcedes Lewis AU RC	6.00	15.00
107 Wali Lundy AU400* RC	6.00	15.00
108 Tarvaris Jackson AU RC	10.00	25.00
109 Ko Simpson AU RC	5.00	12.00
110 Jason Allen AU RC	5.00	12.00
111 Anthony Fasano AU RC	6.00	15.00
112 Joe Klopfenstein AU RC	4.00	10.00
113 Marques Hagans AU RC	4.00	10.00
114 Jason Avant AU RC	4.00	10.00
115 Santonio Holmes AU RC	15.00	30.00
116 Marcus Vick AU/149* RC	20.00	50.00
117 Antonio Cromartie AU/322* RC	10.00	25.00
118 DeAngelo Williams AU RC	12.00	30.00
119 Laurence Maroney AU RC	8.00	20.00
120 Daniel Bullocks AU RC	6.00	15.00
121 Jonathan Orr AU RC	5.00	12.00
122 Mike Bell AU RC	6.00	15.00
123 Kellen Clemens AU RC	5.00	12.00
124 Tim Jennings AU RC	5.00	12.00
125 Cory Rodgers AU RC	5.00	12.00
126 Jerome Harrison AU RC	6.00	15.00
127 Brad Smith AU/570* RC	8.00	20.00
128 Jeff Webb AU/250* RC	5.00	12.00
129 Will Blackmon AU RC	5.00	12.00
130 Quinton Ganther AU RC	4.00	10.00
131 Drew Olson AU RC	4.00	10.00
132 Omar Jacobs AU RC	4.00	10.00
133 Adam Jennings AU RC	5.00	12.00
134 Cedric Humes AU RC	4.00	10.00
135 Derrick Ross AU/250* RC	40.00	80.00
136 Charlie Whitehurst AU RC	10.00	25.00
137 Bobby Carpenter AU RC	4.00	10.00
138 Darryl Tapp AU RC	5.00	12.00
139 A.J. Hawk AU/399* RC	15.00	40.00
140 Bruce Gradkowski AU RC	6.00	15.00
141 Chad Greenway AU RC	6.00	15.00
142 John David Washington AU RC	5.00	12.00
143 Kamerion Wimbley AU RC	6.00	15.00
144 LenDale White AU/549* RC	6.00	15.00
145 Johnathan Joseph AU/549* RC	5.00	12.00
146 Maurice Drew AU RC	20.00	50.00
147 Brandon Marshall AU/608* RC	20.00	40.00
148 Vernon Davis AU/537* RC	20.00	40.00
149 Joseph Addai AU RC	10.00	25.00
150 Bennie Brazell AU RC	5.00	12.00
151 D.J. Shockley AU RC	5.00	12.00
152 Jay Cutler AU/501* RC	50.00	100.00
153 Wendell Mathis AU RC	5.00	12.00
154 Demetrius Williams AU RC	5.00	12.00
155 Dusty Dvoracek AU RC	6.00	15.00
156 DeMario Minter AU RC	5.00	12.00
157 Marcus Maxey AU RC	5.00	12.00
158 Brodie Croyle AU RC	6.00	15.00
159 Jeremy Bloom AU/473* RC	6.00	15.00
160 Todd Watkins AU RC	4.00	10.00
161 Cory Ross AU RC	6.00	15.00
162 Tamba Hali AU/500* RC	10.00	25.00
163 P.J. Daniels AU/555* RC	4.00	10.00
164 Brandon Williams AU RC	4.00	10.00
165 Devin Hester AU RC	25.00	50.00
166 Kelly Jennings AU/393* RC	5.00	12.00
167 Dawan Landry AU RC	6.00	15.00
168 Greg Jennings AU RC	20.00	40.00
169 Mathias Kiwanuka AU RC	8.00	20.00
170 Leon Washington AU RC	8.00	25.00
171 Richard Marshall AU RC	5.00	12.00
172 Haloti Ngata AU RC	8.00	20.00
173 Sinorice Moss AU RC	6.00	15.00
174 Greg Blue AU RC	5.00	12.00
175 Chris Barclay AU RC	5.00	12.00
176 D'Qwell Jackson AU RC	5.00	12.00
177 Eric Smith AU RC	5.00	12.00
178 Ethan Kilmer AU RC	5.00	12.00
179 Mike Hass AU RC	5.00	12.00
180 Derek Hagan AU RC	5.00	12.00
181 Travis Wilson AU RC	4.00	10.00
182 Reggie Bush AU/645* RC	30.00	60.00
183 Maurice Stovall AU/579* RC	5.00	12.00
184 Skyler Green AU RC	4.00	10.00
185 Calvin Lowry AU RC	6.00	15.00
186 Jerious Norwood AU RC	5.00	12.00
187 Brodrick Bunkley AU/518* RC	5.00	12.00
188 Ernie Sims AU/611* RC	5.00	12.00
189 Ingle Martin AU RC	5.00	12.00
190 Anthony Mix AU RC	5.00	12.00
191 Patrick Cobbs AU RC	5.00	12.00
192 Delanie Walker AU/212* RC	40.00	80.00
193 Gabe Watson AU RC	4.00	10.00
194 Willie Reid AU/515* RC	5.00	12.00
195 Michael Huff AU RC	8.00	25.00
196 Mario Williams AU/395* RC	15.00	30.00
197 Chad Jackson AU RC	4.00	10.00
198 David Kirtman AU RC	5.00	12.00
199 Brian Calhoun AU/407* RC	5.00	12.00
200 Michael Robinson AU/512* RC	8.00	20.00
201 D'Brickashaw Ferguson AU/386* RC	8.00	20.00
202 Donte Whitner AU/518* RC	6.00	15.00
203 Roman Harper AU RC	5.00	12.00
204 Manny Lawson AU RC	5.00	12.00
205 DeMeco Ryans AU RC	10.00	25.00
206 Anthony Smith AU RC	8.00	20.00
207 Thomas Howard AU RC	5.00	12.00
208 John McCargo AU RC	4.00	10.00
209 David Pittman AU RC	5.00	12.00
210 Danieal Manning AU RC	6.00	15.00
211 Nate Salley AU RC	5.00	12.00
212 Jimmy Williams AU/524* RC	6.00	15.00
213 Rocky McIntosh AU RC	5.00	12.00
214 Montell Owens AU RC	5.00	12.00
215 Devin Aromashodu AU RC	10.00	25.00
216 Ben Obomanu AU RC	6.00	15.00
217 David Anderson AU RC	5.00	12.00
218 Marques Colston AU RC	15.00	40.00
219 Miles Austin AU RC	30.00	60.00
220 Tony Scheffler AU/526* RC	12.00	30.00
221 Leonard Pope AU/495* RC	6.00	15.00
222 David Thomas AU RC	5.00	12.00
223 Dominique Byrd AU RC	5.00	12.00
224 Owen Daniels AU RC	6.00	15.00
225 Garrett Mills AU RC	6.00	15.00
226 Hank Baskett AU RC	6.00	15.00
227 Jason Carter AU RC	5.00	12.00
228 Sam Hurd AU RC	4.00	10.00
229 Charles Sharon AU/250* RC	40.00	80.00
230 Chris Hannon AU RC	5.00	12.00
231 John Madsen AU RC	6.00	15.00
232 Shaun Bodiford AU RC	5.00	12.00
233 Mike Espy AU RC	6.00	15.00
234 Abdul Hodge AU RC	4.00	10.00
235 Anthony Montgomery AU RC	5.00	12.00
236 Matt Leinart AU/567* RC	12.00	30.00
237 Bernard Pollard AU/307* RC	10.00	25.00
238 Pat Watkins AU/343* RC	6.00	15.00
239 Cedric Griffin AU/357* RC	8.00	20.00
240 A.J. Nicholson AU RC	4.00	10.00
241 Claude Wroten AU/306* RC	12.00	30.00
242 Tye Hill AU/368* RC	8.00	20.00

2006 Playoff Contenders Championship Ticket

UNPRICED CHAMP.TICKET PRINT RUN 1

2006 Playoff Contenders Playoff Ticket

*VETS/199: 2.5X TO 6X BASIC CARDS

COMMON ROOKIE (101-242)	4.00	10.00
ROOKIE SEMISTARS	6.00	15.00
ROOKIE UNL.STARS	8.00	20.00

1-100 PRINT RUN 199 SER.#'d SETS
101-242 AU PRINT RUN 25 SER.#'d SETS

25 Tony Romo	6.00	15.00
102 Bart Scott	15.00	40.00
104 Domenik Hixon	8.00	20.00
105 Vince Young	10.00	25.00
115 Santonio Holmes	10.00	25.00
118 DeAngelo Williams	10.00	25.00
119 Laurence Maroney	6.00	15.00
123 Kellen Clemens	6.00	15.00
139 A.J. Hawk	8.00	20.00
140 Bruce Gradkowski	8.00	20.00
144 LenDale White	6.00	15.00
146 Maurice Drew	12.00	30.00
149 Joseph Addai	8.00	20.00
152 Jay Cutler	15.00	40.00
158 Brodie Croyle	8.00	20.00
165 Devin Hester	12.00	30.00
168 Greg Jennings	12.00	30.00
169 Mathias Kiwanuka	8.00	20.00
170 Leon Washington	6.00	15.00
182 Reggie Bush	15.00	40.00
186 Jerious Norwood	6.00	15.00
188 Ernie Sims	6.00	15.00
196 Mario Williams	8.00	20.00
205 DeMeco Ryans	8.00	20.00
218 Marques Colston	25.00	60.00
219 Miles Austin	20.00	50.00
228 Sam Hurd	5.00	12.00
236 Matt Leinart	8.00	20.00

2006 Playoff Contenders Award Winners

STATED PRINT RUN 1000 SER.#'d SETS
*GOLD/250: .5X TO 1.2X BASIC INSERTS
GOLD PRINT RUN 250 SER.#'d SETS
*HOLOFOIL/100: .8X TO 2X BASIC INSERTS
HOLOFOIL PRINT RUN 100 SER.#'d SETS

18 Marcus Allen	2.00	5.00
19 Terry Baker	1.50	4.00
20 Joe Bellino	1.50	4.00
21 Billy Cannon	1.50	4.00
22 John Cappelletti	1.50	4.00
23 Howard Cassady	2.00	5.00
24 Eric Crouch	2.00	5.00
25 John David Crow	1.50	4.00
26 Tony Dorsett	2.50	6.00
27 Paul Hornung	2.00	5.00
28 John Huarte	1.50	4.00
29 Dick Kazmaier	1.50	4.00
30 John Lattner	1.50	4.00
31 John Lujack	2.00	5.00
32 Steve Owens	2.00	5.00
33 Johnny Rodgers	2.00	5.00
34 Billy Sims	2.00	5.00
35 Jason White	2.00	5.00
36 Eddie George	2.00	5.00
37 Doc Blanchard	2.00	5.00
38 Pete Dawkins	2.00	5.00
Doc Blanchard		
39 Roger Staubach	4.00	10.00
Joe Bellino		
40 Mike Rozier	2.50	6.00
Eric Crouch		
Johnny Rodgers		
41 John Huarte	2.00	5.00
Paul Hornung		
John Lattner		
John Lujack		
42 Steve Owens	2.50	6.00
Billy Sims		
Jason White		
43 Archie Griffin	2.00	5.00
Howard Cassady		
Eddie George		
44 Mike Garrett	2.50	6.00
Charles White		
Marcus Allen		
45 Matt Leinart	4.00	10.00
Reggie Bush		

2006 Playoff Contenders Award Winners Autographs

STATED PRINT RUN 50-200

18 Marcus Allen	20.00	50.00
19 Terry Baker	15.00	40.00
20 Joe Bellino	10.00	25.00
21 Billy Cannon	12.00	30.00
22 John Cappelletti	10.00	25.00
23 Howard Cassady	10.00	25.00
24 Eric Crouch	12.00	30.00
25 John David Crow	25.00	60.00
26 Tony Dorsett	20.00	50.00
27 Paul Hornung	15.00	40.00
28 John Huarte	25.00	50.00
29 Richard Kazmaier	12.00	30.00
30 John Lattner	12.00	30.00
31 John Lujack	15.00	40.00
32 Steve Owens	12.00	30.00
33 Johnny Rodgers	12.00	30.00
34 Billy Sims	12.00	30.00
35 Jason White	10.00	25.00
36 Eddie George	15.00	40.00
39 Roger Staubach	90.00	150.00
Joe Bellino/50		
40 Mike Rozier	40.00	80.00
Eric Crouch		
Johnny Rodgers/50		
41 John Huarte/50	60.00	120.00
Paul Hornung		
John Lattner		
John Lujack		
42 Steve Owens	50.00	100.00
Billy Sims		
Jason White/50		
43 Archie Griffin/50	50.00	100.00
Howard Cassady		
Eddie George		
44 Mike Garrett/50	50.00	100.00
Charles White		
Marcus Allen		

2006 Playoff Contenders Draft Class

STATED PRINT RUN 1000 SER.#'d SETS
*HOLOFOIL/100: .8X TO 2X BASIC INSERTS
HOLOFOIL PRINT RUN 100 SER.#'d SETS
*GOLD/250: .5X TO 1.2X BASIC INSERTS
GOLD PRINT RUN 250 SER.#'d SETS
UNPRICED AUTO PRINT RUN 10

1 Mario Williams	2.00	5.00
Wali Lundy		
2 Reggie Bush	3.00	8.00
Marques Colston		
3 Vince Young	2.00	5.00
LenDale White		
4 D'Brickashaw Ferguson	1.25	3.00
Brad Smith		
5 A.J. Hawk	4.00	10.00
Greg Jennings		
6 Vernon Davis	2.00	5.00
Michael Robinson		
7 Michael Huff	1.50	4.00
Darnell Bing		
8 Donte Whitner	1.25	3.00
John McCargo		
9 Ernie Sims	1.50	4.00
Brian Calhoun		
10 Matt Leinart	1.50	4.00
Leonard Pope		
11 Jay Cutler	3.00	8.00
Tony Scheffler		
12 Haloti Ngata	1.50	4.00
Demetrius Williams		
13 Travis Wilson	1.25	3.00
Jerome Harrison		
14 Brodrick Bunkley	1.25	3.00
Jason Avant		
15 Tye Hill	1.25	3.00
Dominique Byrd		
16 Jason Allen	1.25	3.00
Derek Hagan		
17 Chad Greenway	1.50	4.00
Tarvaris Jackson		
18 Bobby Carpenter	1.50	4.00
Anthony Fasano		
19 Antonio Cromartie	1.25	3.00
Charlie Whitehurst		
20 Tamba Hali	2.00	5.00
Brodie Croyle		
21 Laurence Maroney	1.25	3.00
Chad Jackson		
22 Brandon Williams	1.25	3.00
Manny Lawson		
23 Maurice Stovall	1.50	4.00
Bruce Gradkowski		
24 Johnathan Joseph	1.00	2.50
A.J. Nicholson		
25 Omar Jacobs	2.50	6.00
Santonio Holmes		
26 Danieal Manning	2.50	6.00
Devin Hester		
27 DeAngelo Williams	2.00	5.00
Richard Marshall		
28 Marcedes Lewis	3.00	8.00
Maurice Drew		
29 Rocky McIntosh	1.25	3.00
Anthony Montgomery		
30 Joseph Addai	1.50	4.00
Tim Jennings		
31 Kelly Jennings	1.25	3.00
David Kirtman		
32 Mathias Kiwanuka	1.50	4.00
Sinorice Moss		

2006 Playoff Contenders Legendary Contenders

STATED PRINT RUN 1000 SER.#'d SETS
*HOLOFOIL/100: .8X TO 2X BASIC INSERTS
HOLOFOIL PRINT RUN 100 SER.#'d SETS
*GOLD/250: .5X TO 1.2X BASIC INSERTS
GOLD PRINT RUN 250 SER.#'d SETS

1 Troy Aikman	2.00	5.00
2 Dan Marino	3.00	8.00
3 John Elway	2.50	6.00
4 Don Meredith	1.50	4.00
5 Bob Griese	1.50	4.00
6 Dave Casper	1.00	2.50
7 Fran Tarkenton	2.00	5.00
8 Ickey Woods	1.00	2.50
9 Jim Otto	1.00	2.50
10 Jim Plunkett	1.25	3.00
11 Phil Simms	1.25	3.00
12 Lee Roy Selmon	1.25	3.00
13 Ozzie Newsome	1.25	3.00
14 Paul Krause	1.00	2.50
15 Paul Lowe	1.00	2.50
16 Len Dawson	1.50	4.00
17 Steve Largent	1.50	4.00
18 Jim Kelly	2.00	5.00
19 Tony Dorsett	1.50	4.00
20 Jerry Rice	2.50	6.00
21 Steve Young	2.00	5.00
22 Thurman Thomas	1.25	3.00
23 Y.A. Tittle	1.50	4.00
24 Terrell Davis	1.50	4.00
25 Sonny Jurgensen	1.25	3.00
26 Willie Brown	1.00	2.50

2006 Playoff Contenders Legendary Contenders Autographs

STATED PRINT RUN 10-100
SERIAL #'d UNDER 25 NOT PRICED

1 Troy Aikman/25	60.00	120.00
2 Dan Marino/30	100.00	200.00
3 John Elway/25	75.00	150.00
4 Don Meredith/100	50.00	80.00
5 Bob Griese/75	20.00	40.00
6 Dave Casper/50	20.00	40.00
7 Fran Tarkenton/50	25.00	50.00
8 Ickey Woods/100	12.50	25.00
9 Jim Otto/35	20.00	40.00
10 Jim Plunkett/25	20.00	40.00
11 Phil Simms/50	20.00	40.00
12 Lee Roy Selmon/75	30.00	60.00
13 Ozzie Newsome/50	12.50	25.00
14 Paul Krause/40	12.50	25.00
15 Paul Lowe/100	10.00	20.00
16 Len Dawson/50	20.00	40.00
17 Steve Largent/75	20.00	40.00
18 Jim Kelly/50	35.00	60.00
19 Tony Dorsett/25		
20 Jerry Rice/25	90.00	175.00
25 Sonny Jurgensen/25	20.00	40.00
26 Willie Brown/100	15.00	30.00

2006 Playoff Contenders MVP Contenders

STATED PRINT RUN 1000 SER.#'d SETS
*HOLOFOIL/100: .8X TO 2X BASIC INSERTS
HOLOFOIL PRINT RUN 100 SER.#'d SETS
*GOLD/250: .5X TO 1.2X BASIC INSERTS
GOLD PRINT RUN 250 SER.#'d SETS

1 Larry Johnson	1.50	4.00
2 Shaun Alexander	1.50	4.00
3 Peyton Manning	2.50	6.00
4 LaDainian Tomlinson	1.50	4.00
5 Eli Manning	2.00	5.00
6 Tiki Barber	1.50	4.00
7 Edgerrin James	1.50	4.00
8 Steve Smith	1.50	4.00
9 Donovan McNabb	1.50	4.00
10 Carson Palmer	1.50	4.00
11 Steven Jackson	1.50	4.00
12 Brett Favre	3.00	8.00
13 Chad Johnson	1.00	2.50
14 Larry Fitzgerald	1.50	4.00
15 Cadillac Williams	1.25	3.00

2006 Playoff Contenders MVP Contenders Autographs

STATED PRINT RUN 4-25
SERIAL #'d UNDER 25 NOT PRICED
2 Shaun Alexander/25 20.00 50.00
3 Peyton Manning/25 100.00 200.00
4 LaDainian Tomlinson/25 40.00 80.00
5 Eli Manning/25 60.00 100.00
7 Edgerrin James/25 20.00 50.00
9 Donovan McNabb/25 30.00 60.00
10 Carson Palmer/25 30.00 60.00
11 Steven Jackson/25 20.00 50.00
12 Brett Favre/25 125.00 250.00
13 Chad Johnson/25 20.00 50.00
14 Larry Fitzgerald/25 20.00 50.00
15 Cadillac Williams/25 20.00 50.00

2006 Playoff Contenders Round Numbers

STATED PRINT RUN 1000 SER.#'d SETS
*HOLOFOIL/100: .8X TO 2X BASIC INSERTS
HOLOFOIL PRINT RUN 100 SER.#'d SETS
*GOLD/250: .5X TO 1.2X BASIC INSERTS
GOLD PRINT RUN 250 SER.#'d SETS
UNPRICED AU PRINT RUN 5-10
1 Reggie Bush / Vince Young 2.00 5.00
2 Matt Leinart / Jay Cutler 2.00 5.00
3 A.J. Hawk / Bobby Carpenter 1.00 2.50
4 Mario Williams / D'Brickashaw Ferguson 1.00 2.50
5 Joseph Addai / Laurence Maroney 1.00 2.50
6 Vernon Davis / Marcedes Lewis 1.25 3.00
7 Kellen Clemens / Tarvaris Jackson 1.00 2.50
8 Chad Jackson / Sinorice Moss 1.00 2.50
9 LenDale White / Maurice Drew 1.50 4.00
10 Anthony Fasano / Joe Klopfenstein 1.00 2.50
11 DeMeco Ryans / Rocky McIntosh 1.00 2.50
12 Brandon Williams / Maurice Stovall .60 1.50
13 Charlie Whitehurst / Brodie Croyle 1.00 2.50
14 David Thomas / Dominique Byrd .75 2.00
15 Brian Calhoun / Jerious Norwood .75 2.00
16 Reggie Bush / Vince Young / Matt Leinart / Jay Cutler 2.00 5.00
17 Haloti Ngata / Kamerion Wimbley / Brodrick Bunkley / Tamba Hali 1.00 2.50
18 Michael Huff / Donte Whitner / Tye Hill / Jason Allen 1.00 2.50
19 Vernon Davis / Santonio Holmes / DeAngelo Williams / A.J. Hawk 1.25 3.00
20 Devin Hester / Greg Jennings / Tony Scheffler / Anthony Fasano 2.00 5.00
21 Travis Wilson / Charlie Whitehurst / Derek Hagan / Brodie Croyle 1.00 2.50
22 Michael Robinson / Brad Smith / Cory Rodgers / Demetrius Williams 1.00 2.50
23 Leon Washington / Brandon Marshall / Skyler Green / Jason Avant .75 2.00
24 Jerome Harrison / Jeremy Bloom / Ingle Martin / Omar Jacobs 1.00 2.50
25 Wali Lundy / Mike Hass / Reggie McNeal / Bruce Gradkowski 1.00 2.50

2006 Playoff Contenders ROY Contenders

STATED PRINT RUN 1000 SER.#'d SETS
*HOLOFOIL/100: .8X TO 2X BASIC INSERTS
HOLOFOIL PRINT RUN 100 SER.#'d SETS
*GOLD/250: .5X TO 1.2X BASIC INSERTS
GOLD PRINT RUN 250 SER.#'d SETS
1 Reggie Bush 2.00 5.00
2 Joseph Addai 1.00 2.50
3 LenDale White .75 2.00
4 Santonio Holmes 1.25 3.00
5 Laurence Maroney .75 2.00
6 Jay Cutler 2.00 5.00
7 Jerious Norwood .75 2.00
8 Vince Young 1.25 3.00
9 Vernon Davis 1.25 3.00
10 Mario Williams 1.00 2.50
11 Leon Washington .75 2.00
12 DeAngelo Williams 1.25 3.00
13 Matt Leinart 1.00 2.50
14 Jason Avant .60 1.50
15 A.J. Hawk 1.00 2.50
16 Mike Bell 1.50 4.00
17 Marques Colston 2.00 5.00
18 Michael Robinson .75 2.00
19 Chad Jackson .60 1.50
20 Greg Jennings 1.50 4.00
21 D'Qwell Jackson .75 2.00
22 Manny Lawson .75 2.00
23 Kamerion Wimbley 1.00 2.50
24 Wali Lundy .75 2.00
25 Maurice Drew 1.50 4.00
26 Jerome Harrison 1.00 2.50
27 Demetrius Williams .75 2.00
28 Tamba Hali 1.00 2.50
29 Haloti Ngata 1.00 2.50
30 Dawan Landry 1.00 2.50
31 Ernie Sims .75 2.00
32 Devin Hester 1.50 4.00

2006 Playoff Contenders ROY Contenders Autographs

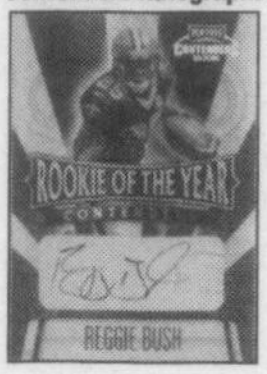

STATED PRINT RUN 25 SER.#'d SETS
1 Reggie Bush 75.00 150.00
2 Joseph Addai 30.00 80.00
3 LenDale White 10.00 25.00
4 Santonio Holmes 15.00 40.00
5 Laurence Maroney 10.00 25.00
6 Jay Cutler 75.00 150.00
7 Jerious Norwood 15.00 40.00
8 Vince Young 40.00 100.00
9 Vernon Davis 15.00 40.00
10 Mario Williams 12.00 30.00
11 Leon Washington 30.00 60.00
12 DeAngelo Williams 30.00 80.00
13 Matt Leinart 30.00 80.00
14 Jason Avant 8.00 20.00
15 A.J. Hawk 12.00 30.00
16 Mike Bell 12.00 30.00
17 Marques Colston 50.00 100.00
18 Michael Robinson 10.00 25.00
19 Chad Jackson 8.00 20.00
20 Greg Jennings 35.00 60.00
21 D'Qwell Jackson 10.00 25.00
22 Manny Lawson 10.00 25.00
23 Kamerion Wimbley 12.00 30.00
24 Wali Lundy 10.00 25.00
25 Maurice Drew 20.00 50.00
26 Jerome Harrison 12.00 30.00
27 Demetrius Williams 10.00 25.00
28 Tamba Hali 12.00 30.00
29 Haloti Ngata 12.00 30.00
30 Dawan Landry 12.00 30.00
31 Ernie Sims 10.00 25.00
32 Devin Hester 60.00 100.00

2007 Playoff Contenders

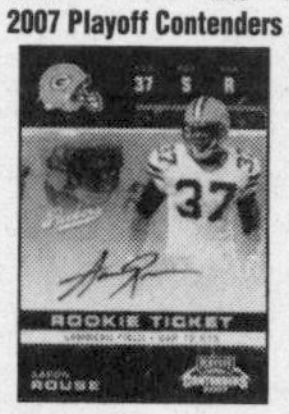

COMP.SET w/o RC's (100) 8.00 20.00
1 Edgerrin James .25 .60
2 Larry Fitzgerald .30 .75
3 Anquan Boldin .25 .60
4 Matt Leinart .25 .60
5 Joey Harrington .25 .60
6 Warrick Dunn .25 .60
7 Joe Horn .25 .60
8 Steve McNair .25 .60
9 Willis McGahee .25 .60
10 Derrick Mason .25 .60
11 J.P. Losman .20 .50
12 Lee Evans .25 .60
13 Josh Reed .20 .50
14 Jake Delhomme .25 .60
15 DeShaun Foster .25 .60
16 Steve Smith .25 .60
17 Rex Grossman .25 .60
18 Bernard Berrian .20 .50
19 Cedric Benson .25 .60
20 Carson Palmer .25 .60
21 Chad Johnson .25 .60
22 T.J. Houshmandzadeh .25 .60
23 Rudi Johnson .25 .60
24 Braylon Edwards .25 .60
25 Kellen Winslow .25 .60
26 Jamal Lewis .25 .60
27 Tony Romo .40 1.00
28 Terrell Owens .30 .75
29 Jason Witten .30 .75
30 Julius Jones .20 .50
31 Jay Cutler .30 .75
32 Javon Walker .25 .60
33 Travis Henry .25 .60
34 Jon Kitna .20 .50
35 Roy Williams WR .25 .60
36 Tatum Bell .20 .50
37 Brett Favre .60 1.50
38 Donald Driver .30 .75
39 Greg Jennings .30 .75
40 Matt Schaub .25 .60
41 Ahman Green .25 .60
42 Andre Johnson .25 .60
43 Peyton Manning .50 1.25
44 Joseph Addai .25 .60
45 Marvin Harrison .30 .75
46 Reggie Wayne .25 .60
47 David Garrard .25 .60
48 Fred Taylor .25 .60
49 Maurice Jones-Drew .30 .75
50 Larry Johnson .20 .50
51 Damon Huard .25 .60
52 Tony Gonzalez .25 .60
53 Trent Green .25 .60
54 Ronnie Brown .25 .60
55 Chris Chambers .25 .60
56 Troy Williamson .20 .50
57 Tarvaris Jackson .20 .50
58 Chester Taylor .20 .50
59 Tom Brady .50 1.25
60 Randy Moss .30 .75
61 Laurence Maroney .25 .60
62 Drew Brees .30 .75
63 Deuce McAllister .25 .60
64 Reggie Bush .30 .75
65 Eli Manning .30 .75
66 Brandon Jacobs .25 .60
67 Plaxico Burress .25 .60
68 Chad Pennington .25 .60
69 Laveranues Coles .20 .50
70 Thomas Jones .25 .60
71 Ronald Curry .25 .60
72 LaMont Jordan .25 .60
73 Jerry Porter .25 .60
74 Donovan McNabb .30 .75
75 Brian Westbrook .25 .60
76 Ben Roethlisberger .30 .75
77 Willie Parker .25 .60
78 Hines Ward .30 .75
79 LaDainian Tomlinson .30 .75
80 Philip Rivers .30 .75
81 Antonio Gates .30 .75
82 Alex Smith QB .30 .75
83 Frank Gore .30 .75
84 Darrell Jackson .20 .50
85 Vernon Davis .25 .60
86 Deion Branch .25 .60
87 Matt Hasselbeck .25 .60
88 Shaun Alexander .25 .60
89 Marc Bulger .25 .60
90 Steven Jackson .30 .75
91 Torry Holt .25 .60
92 Jeff Garcia .25 .60
93 Cadillac Williams .25 .60
94 Joey Galloway .25 .60
95 Vince Young .25 .60
96 Chris Brown .20 .50
97 Brandon Jones .20 .50
98 Jason Campbell .25 .60
99 Clinton Portis .25 .60
100 Santana Moss .25 .60
101 Aaron Ross AU RC 10.00 25.00
102 Aaron Rouse AU RC 6.00 15.00
103 Adam Carriker AU/333* RC 15.00 40.00
104 Adrian Peterson AU/355* RC 150.00 300.00
105 Ahmad Bradshaw No AU RC 3.00 8.00
106 Alan Branch No AU RC 1.25 3.00
107 Amobi Okoye AU RC 8.00 20.00
108 Anthony Gonzalez AU RC 8.00 20.00
109 Anthony Spencer AU RC 8.00 20.00
110 Antonio Pittman AU RC 5.00 12.00
111 Aundrae Allison AU RC 5.00 12.00
112 Ben Patrick AU RC 6.00 15.00
113 Biren Ealy AU RC 6.00 15.00
114 Bobby Sippio AU RC 6.00 15.00
115 Brady Quinn AU/534* RC 15.00 30.00
116 Brandon Jackson AU RC 12.50 25.00
117 Brandon Mebane AU RC 6.00 15.00
118 Brandon Meriweather AU RC 8.00 20.00
119 Brandon Siler AU RC 5.00 12.00
120 Brian Leonard AU RC 6.00 15.00
121 Brian Robison AU RC 8.00 20.00
122 Buster Davis AU/246* RC 15.00 40.00
123 Calvin Johnson AU/525* RC 125.00 200.00
124 Chansi Stuckey AU/502* RC 8.00 20.00
125 Charles Johnson No AU RC 2.00 5.00
126 Chris Davis AU RC 5.00 12.00
127 Chris Henry RB AU RC 5.00 12.00
128 Chris Houston AU RC 6.00 15.00
129 Clifton Ryan AU RC 6.00 15.00
130 Clifton Dawson AU RC 8.00 20.00
131 Courtney Taylor AU RC 6.00 15.00
132 Craig Buster Davis No AU RC 1.25 3.00
133 Dallas Baker AU RC 5.00 12.00
134 Dan Bazuin AU/198* RC 25.00 50.00
135 Daymeion Hughes AU/383* RC 10.00 25.00
136 Dante Rosario AU RC 8.00 20.00
137 David Irons AU/198* RC 15.00 40.00
138 Darrelle Revis AU/533* RC 15.00 30.00
139 David Clowney AU/410* RC 6.00 15.00
140 David Harris AU RC 6.00 15.00
141 DeShawn Wynn AU/429* RC 6.00 15.00
142 Drew Stanton AU RC 5.00 12.00
143 Dwayne Bowe AU RC 15.00 30.00
144 Dwayne Jarrett AU/484* RC 6.00 15.00
145 Dwayne Wright AU/410* RC 6.00 15.00
146 Ed Johnson AU RC 6.00 15.00
147 Eric Frampton AU/452* RC 6.00 15.00
148 Eric Weddle AU RC 8.00 20.00
149 Eric Wright No AU RC 1.50 4.00
150 Fred Bennett AU RC 5.00 12.00
151 Gaines Adams AU RC 8.00 20.00
152 Garrett Wolfe AU RC 10.00 25.00
153 Glenn Holt AU RC 6.00 15.00
154 Glenn Martinez AU RC 8.00 20.00
155 Greg Olsen AU RC 10.00 25.00
156 Greg Peterson AU RC 6.00 15.00
157 H.B. Blades AU/383* RC 5.00 12.00
158 Ikaika Alama-Francis AU/222* RC 15.00 40.00
159 Isaiah Stanback AU/510* RC 5.00 12.00
160 Jacoby Jones AU/435* RC 12.50 25.00
161 Jamaal Anderson AU/123* RC 25.00 60.00
162 JaMarcus Russell AU RC 8.00 20.00
163 James Jones AU RC 10.00 25.00
164 Jared Zabransky AU/347* RC 15.00 40.00
165 Jarvis Moss AU/227* RC 15.00 40.00
166 Jason Hill AU RC SP 8.00 20.00
167 Jeff Rowe AU/362* RC 10.00 25.00
168 Joe Thomas AU/129* RC 40.00 80.00
169 Joel Filani AU/483* RC 6.00 15.00
170 John Beck AU RC 10.00 25.00
171 John Broussard AU RC 6.00 15.00
172 Johnnie Lee Higgins AU RC 6.00 15.00
173 Jon Beason AU RC 6.00 15.00
174 Jonathan Wade No AU RC 1.50 4.00
175 Jordan Kent AU RC 6.00 15.00
176 Josh Wilson AU/501* RC 6.00 15.00
177 Justin Durant AU RC 6.00 15.00
178 Kenneth Darby AU RC 6.00 15.00
179 Kenny Irons No AU/50* RC 100.00 200.00
180 Kenton Keith AU RC 8.00 20.00
181 Kevin Kolb AU RC 12.00 30.00
182 Keyunta Dawson AU RC 6.00 15.00
183 Kolby Smith AU/444* RC 6.00 15.00
184 LaMarr Woodley AU RC 10.00 25.00
185 LaRon Landry AU RC 12.00 30.00
186 Laurent Robinson AU RC 10.00 25.00
187 Lawrence Timmons AU RC 8.00 20.00
188 Legedu Naanee AU RC 12.50 25.00
189 Leon Hall AU RC 6.00 15.00
190 Levi Brown AU/369* RC 8.00 20.00
191 Lorenzo Booker AU RC 6.00 15.00
192 Marcus McCauley AU/386* RC 15.00 40.00
193 Marcus Thomas AU RC 6.00 15.00
194 Marshawn Lynch AU/533* RC 15.00 30.00
195 Martrez Milner AU RC 5.00 12.00
196 Mason Crosby AU RC 6.00 15.00
197 Matt Gutierrez AU RC 8.00 20.00
198 Matt Moore AU RC 8.00 20.00
199 Matt Spaeth AU/237* RC 15.00 40.00
200 Michael Bush AU RC 8.00 20.00
201 Michael Griffin AU RC 8.00 20.00
202 Michael Okwo AU/261* RC 10.00 25.00
203 Mike Walker AU/248* RC 15.00 40.00
204 Nick Folk AU RC 8.00 20.00
205 Patrick Willis AU/239* RC 40.00 80.00
206 Paul Posluszny AU RC 12.00 30.00
207 Paul Williams AU RC 5.00 12.00
208 Pierre Thomas AU RC 12.00 30.00
209 Quentin Moses AU/498* RC 6.00 15.00
210 Ray McDonald AU/519* RC 6.00 15.00
211 Reggie Ball AU RC 6.00 15.00
212 Reggie Nelson AU RC 6.00 15.00
213 Robert Meachem AU RC 8.00 20.00
214 Roy Hall AU RC 8.00 20.00
215 Rufus Alexander AU RC 6.00 15.00
216 Ryne Robinson AU/430* RC 6.00 15.00
217 Sabby Piscitelli AU/337* RC 10.00 25.00
218 Scott Chandler AU RC 8.00 20.00
219 Selvin Young No AU RC 2.00 5.00
220 Sidney Rice AU/529* RC 15.00 40.00
221 Stephen Nicholas AU RC 6.00 15.00
222 Steve Breaston AU/274* RC 15.00 40.00
223 Steve Smith AU/541 RC 10.00 25.00
224 Stewart Bradley AU RC 6.00 15.00
225 Syndric Steptoe AU/149* RC 25.00 60.00
226 Tanard Jackson No AU RC 1.00 2.50
227 Ted Ginn AU/519 RC 10.00 25.00
228 Thomas Clayton AU RC 6.00 15.00
229 Tim Crowder AU/454* RC 8.00 20.00
230 Tim Shaw AU/408* RC 6.00 15.00
231 Tony Hunt AU RC 5.00 12.00
232 Trent Edwards AU RC 8.00 20.00
233 Troy Smith AU RC 10.00 25.00
234 Turk McBride AU RC 6.00 15.00
235 Tyler Palko AU RC 10.00 25.00
236 Tyler Thigpen AU RC 8.00 20.00
237 Victor Abiamiri AU/449* RC 8.00 20.00
238 Yamon Figurs AU RC 5.00 12.00
239 Zak DeOssie AU RC 6.00 15.00
240 Zach Miller AU RC 8.00 20.00

2007 Playoff Contenders Championship Ticket

UNPRICED CHAMP.TICKET PRINT RUN 1

2007 Playoff Contenders Playoff Ticket

*VETS 1-100: 2.5X TO 6X BASIC CARDS
COMMON ROOKIE (101-240) 2.50 6.00
ROOKIE SEMISTARS 3.00 8.00
ROOKIE UNL.STARS 4.00 10.00
STATED PRINT RUN 99-199 SER.#'d SETS
104 Adrian Peterson 15.00 40.00
105 Ahmad Bradshaw 6.00 15.00
108 Anthony Gonzalez 4.00 10.00
115 Brady Quinn 4.00 10.00
123 Calvin Johnson 12.00 30.00
138 Darrelle Revis 6.00 15.00
143 Dwayne Bowe 5.00 12.00
155 Greg Olsen 3.00 8.00
181 Kevin Kolb 6.00 15.00
194 Marshawn Lynch 4.00 10.00
198 Matt Moore 4.00 10.00
205 Patrick Willis 8.00 20.00
208 Pierre Thomas 10.00 25.00
220 Sidney Rice 5.00 12.00
223 Steve Smith USC 4.00 10.00
227 Ted Ginn Jr. 3.00 8.00
232 Trent Edwards 4.00 10.00
233 Troy Smith 4.00 10.00

2007 Playoff Contenders Draft Class

STATED PRINT RUN 1000 SER.#'d SETS
*GOLD HOLO/250: .5X TO 1.2X BASIC INSERTS
GOLD HOLOFOIL PRINT RUN 250 SER.#'d SETS
*BLACK/100: .8X TO 2X BASIC INSERTS
BLACK PRINT RUN 100 SER.#'d SETS
1 Alan Branch / Levi Brown 1.25 3.00
2 Laurent Robinson / Jamaal Anderson 1.25 3.00
3 Troy Smith / Yamon Figurs 1.25 3.00
4 Paul Posluszny / Trent Edwards 1.25 3.00
5 Dwayne Wright / Marshawn Lynch 1.25 3.00
6 Jon Beason / Dwayne Jarrett 1.00 2.50
7 Garrett Wolfe / Greg Olsen 1.00 2.50
8 Leon Hall / Jeff Rowe 1.00 2.50
9 Brady Quinn / Eric Wright 1.25 3.00
10 Isaiah Stanback / Anthony Spencer 1.25 3.00
11 Selvin Young / Tim Crowder 1.25 3.00
12 Calvin Johnson / Ikaika Alama-Francis 3.00 8.00
13 Brandon Jackson / James Jones 1.25 3.00
14 Jacoby Jones / Amobi Okoye 1.25 3.00
15 Anthony Gonzalez / Daymeion Hughes 1.25 3.00
16 Dwayne Bowe / Kolby Smith 1.50 4.00
17 Ted Ginn Jr. / Lorenzo Booker 1.00 2.50
18 Adrian Peterson / Sidney Rice 5.00 12.00
19 Steve Smith USC / Aaron Ross 1.25 3.00
20 Robert Meachem / Tyler Palko 1.25 3.00
21 Darrelle Revis / David Harris 2.00 5.00
22 JaMarcus Russell / Johnnie Lee Higgins 1.00 2.50
23 Kevin Kolb / Tony Hunt 2.00 5.00
24 Matt Spaeth / LaMarr Woodley 1.25 3.00
25 Craig Buster Davis / Scott Chandler 1.25 3.00
26 Patrick Willis / Jason Hill 2.50 6.00
27 Courtney Taylor / Josh Wilson 1.00 2.50
28 Brian Leonard / Adam Carriker 1.00 2.50
29 Gaines Adams / Sabby Piscitelli 1.25 3.00
30 Chris Henry RB / Michael Griffin 1.25 3.00
31 Paul Williams / Chris Davis .75 2.00
32 LaRon Landry / H.B. Blades 1.25 3.00

2007 Playoff Contenders Draft Class Autographs

STATED PRINT RUN 25 SER.#'d SETS
2 Laurent Robinson / Jamaal Anderson 12.00 25.00
4 Paul Posluszny / Trent Edwards 12.00 30.00
5 Dwayne Wright / Marshawn Lynch 12.00 30.00
6 Jon Beason / Dwayne Jarrett 10.00 25.00
7 Garrett Wolfe / Greg Olsen 10.00 25.00
8 Leon Hall / Jeff Rowe 10.00 25.00
10 Isaiah Stanback / Anthony Spencer 12.00 30.00
12 Calvin Johnson / Ikaika Alama-Francis 40.00 100.00
14 Jacoby Jones / Amobi Okoye 12.00 30.00
15 Anthony Gonzalez / Daymeion Hughes 12.00 30.00
16 Dwayne Bowe / Kolby Smith 25.00 60.00
17 Ted Ginn Jr. / Lorenzo Booker 10.00 25.00
18 Adrian Peterson / Sidney Rice 125.00 250.00
19 Steve Smith USC / Aaron Ross 12.00 30.00
20 Robert Meachem / Tyler Palko 12.00 30.00
21 Darrelle Revis / David Harris 10.00 25.00
22 JaMarcus Russell / Johnnie Lee Higgins 10.00 25.00
23 Kevin Kolb / Tony Hunt 25.00 60.00
24 Matt Spaeth / LaMarr Woodley 25.00 60.00
26 Patrick Willis / Jason Hill 40.00 80.00
27 Courtney Taylor / Josh Wilson 10.00 25.00
28 Brian Leonard / Adam Carriker 10.00 25.00
29 Gaines Adams / Sabby Piscitelli 12.00 30.00
30 Chris Henry RB / Michael Griffin 12.00 30.00
31 Paul Williams / Chris Davis 8.00 20.00
32 LaRon Landry / H.B. Blades 12.00 30.00

2007 Playoff Contenders Legendary Contenders

STATED PRINT RUN 1000 SER.#'d SETS
*GOLD HOLO/250: .5X TO 1.2X BASIC INSERTS
GOLD HOLOFOIL PRINT RUN 250 SER.#'d SETS
*BLACK/100: .8X TO 2X BASIC INSERTS
BLACK PRINT RUN 100 SER.#'d SETS
1 Barry Sanders 2.50 6.00
2 Bill Bates 1.25 3.00
3 Charlie Joiner 1.25 3.00
4 Cris Collinsworth 1.25 3.00
5 Dan Fouts 1.50 4.00
6 Dan Marino 3.00 8.00
7 Dave Casper 1.25 3.00
8 Don Perkins 1.00 2.50
9 Eric Dickerson 1.25 3.00
10 Gene Upshaw 1.00 2.50
11 Jim Brown 2.00 5.00
12 Joe Montana 3.00 8.00
13 Lenny Moore 1.25 3.00
14 Paul Warfield 1.25 3.00
15 Steve Young 2.00 5.00
16 Thurman Thomas 1.25 3.00
17 Tim Brown 1.50 4.00

2007 Playoff Contenders Legendary Contenders Autographs

STATED PRINT RUN 10-100
SERIAL #'d UNDER 25 NOT PRICED
2 Bill Bates/50 12.50 25.00
3 Charlie Joiner/75 12.50 25.00
4 Cris Collinsworth/75 12.50 25.00
5 Dan Fouts/100 20.00 40.00
7 Dave Casper/75 12.50 25.00
8 Don Perkins/100 20.00 40.00
9 Eric Dickerson/25 25.00 50.00
10 Gene Upshaw/100 12.50 25.00
11 Jim Brown/25 60.00 120.00
13 Lenny Moore/50 12.50 25.00
14 Paul Warfield/75 15.00 30.00
16 Thurman Thomas/75 15.00 30.00
17 Tim Brown/75 15.00 30.00

2007 Playoff Contenders MVP Contenders

STATED PRINT RUN 1000 SER.#'d SETS
*GOLD HOLO/250: .5X TO 1.2X BASIC INSERTS
GOLD HOLOFOIL PRINT RUN 250 SER.#'d SETS
*BLACK/100: .8X TO 2X BASIC INSERTS
BLACK PRINT RUN 100 SER.#'d SETS
1 Frank Gore 1.50 4.00
2 Peyton Manning 2.50 6.00
3 LaDainian Tomlinson 1.50 4.00
4 Drew Brees 1.50 4.00
5 Vince Young 1.25 3.00
6 Chad Johnson 1.25 3.00
7 Reggie Bush 1.50 4.00
8 Larry Johnson 1.00 2.50
9 Steve Smith 1.25 3.00
10 Carson Palmer 1.25 3.00
11 Tony Romo 2.00 5.00
12 Brett Favre 3.00 8.00
13 Tom Brady 2.50 6.00
14 Steven Jackson 1.50 4.00
15 Joseph Addai 1.25 3.00

2007 Playoff Contenders MVP Contenders Autographs

STATED PRINT RUN 10-25
SERIAL #'d UNDER 25 NOT PRICED
1 Frank Gore/25 12.00 30.00
4 Drew Brees/25 40.00 80.00
6 Chad Johnson/25 10.00 25.00
8 Larry Johnson/25 8.00 20.00
9 Steve Smith/25 10.00 25.00
14 Steven Jackson/25 12.00 30.00
15 Joseph Addai/25

2007 Playoff Contenders Rookie Roll Call

STATED PRINT RUN 1000 SER.#'d SETS
*GOLD HOLO/250: .5X TO 1.2X BASIC INSERTS
GOLD HOLOFOIL PRINT RUN 250 SER.#'d SETS
*BLACK/100: .8X TO 2X BASIC INSERTS
BLACK PRINT RUN 100 SER.#'d SETS
1 Calvin Johnson 3.00 8.00
2 LaRon Landry 1.00 2.50
3 Adrian Peterson 4.00 10.00
4 Ted Ginn Jr. .75 2.00
5 Patrick Willis 2.00 5.00
6 Marshawn Lynch 1.00 2.50
7 Brady Quinn 1.00 2.50
8 Dwayne Bowe 1.25 3.00
9 Robert Meachem 1.00 2.50
10 Craig Buster Davis .75 2.00
11 Greg Olsen .75 2.00
12 Anthony Gonzalez 1.00 2.50
13 Sidney Rice 1.25 3.00
14 Steve Smith USC 1.00 2.50
15 Brian Leonard .75 2.00
16 Brandon Jackson .75 2.00
17 Lorenzo Booker .75 2.00
18 Jacoby Jones 1.00 2.50
19 Yamon Figurs .60 1.50
20 JaMarcus Russell .60 1.50
21 Jason Hill 1.00 2.50
22 Matt Spaeth 1.00 2.50
23 James Jones 1.00 2.50
24 Paul Williams .60 1.50
25 Trent Edwards 1.00 2.50
26 Garrett Wolfe .60 1.50
27 Johnnie Lee Higgins .75 2.00
28 DeShawn Wynn .75 2.00
29 Kevin Kolb 1.50 4.00
30 Dwayne Jarrett .75 2.00
31 Chris Henry RB .60 1.50
32 Chris Davis .60 1.50

2007 Playoff Contenders Rookie Roll Call Autographs

STATED PRINT RUN 25 SER.#'d SETS
1 Calvin Johnson 75.00 150.00
2 LaRon Landry 12.00 30.00
3 Adrian Peterson 150.00 300.00
4 Ted Ginn Jr. 10.00 25.00
5 Patrick Willis 40.00 100.00
6 Marshawn Lynch 20.00 40.00
7 Brady Quinn 12.00 30.00
8 Dwayne Bowe 15.00 40.00
9 Robert Meachem 12.00 30.00
11 Greg Olsen 10.00 25.00
12 Anthony Gonzalez 12.00 30.00
13 Sidney Rice 15.00 40.00
14 Steve Smith USC 12.00 30.00
15 Brian Leonard 10.00 25.00
16 Brandon Jackson 10.00 25.00
17 Lorenzo Booker 10.00 25.00
18 Jacoby Jones 12.00 30.00
19 Yamon Figurs 8.00 20.00
20 JaMarcus Russell 8.00 20.00
21 Jason Hill 12.00 30.00
22 Matt Spaeth 12.00 30.00
23 James Jones 12.00 30.00
24 Paul Williams 8.00 20.00
25 Trent Edwards 12.00 30.00
26 Garrett Wolfe 8.00 20.00
27 Johnnie Lee Higgins 10.00 25.00
28 DeShawn Wynn 10.00 25.00
29 Kevin Kolb 20.00 50.00
30 Dwayne Jarrett 10.00 25.00
31 Chris Henry RB 8.00 20.00
32 Chris Davis 8.00 20.00

2007 Playoff Contenders Round Numbers

STATED PRINT RUN 1000 SER.#'d SETS
*GOLD HOLO/250: .5X TO 1.2X BASIC INSERTS
GOLD HOLOFOIL PRINT RUN 250 SER.#'d SETS
*BLACK/100: .8X TO 2X BASIC INSERTS
BLACK PRINT RUN 100 SER.#'d SETS
1 Calvin Johnson / Adrian Peterson 6.00 15.00
2 JaMarcus Russell / Brady Quinn 1.00 2.50
3 Gaines Adams / Anthony Spencer 1.00 2.50
4 Ted Ginn Jr. / Marshawn Lynch 1.00 2.50
5 LaRon Landry / Darrelle Revis 1.00 2.50
6 Michael Griffin / Aaron Ross 1.00 2.50
7 Dwayne Bowe / Robert Meachem 1.00 2.50
8 Craig Buster Davis / Anthony Gonzalez 1.00 2.50
9 Brandon Meriweather / Greg Olsen 1.00 2.50
10 Joe Thomas / Levi Brown 1.00 2.50
11 Patrick Willis / Jon Beason 2.00 5.00
12 Leon Hall / Reggie Nelson .75 2.00
13 Jamaal Anderson / Adam Carriker .75 2.00
14 Kevin Kolb / John Beck 1.50 4.00
15 Chris Henry RB / Brandon Jackson .75 2.00
16 Paul Posluszny / David Harris .75 2.00
17 Sidney Rice / Dwayne Jarrett 1.25 3.00
18 Steve Smith USC / Brian Leonard 1.00 2.50
19 Zach Miller / Sabby Piscitelli 1.00 2.50
20 Lorenzo Booker / Tony Hunt .75 2.00
21 James Jones / Paul Williams 1.00 2.50
22 Matt Spaeth / Johnnie Lee Higgins 1.00 2.50
23 Jacoby Jones / Yamon Figurs 1.00 2.50
24 Laurent Robinson / Jason Hill 1.00 2.50
25 Trent Edwards / Garrett Wolfe 1.00 2.50
26 Jonathan Wade / Aaron Rouse .75 2.00
27 Antonio Pittman / Dwayne Wright .60 1.50
28 Chris Davis / Scott Chandler 1.00 2.50
29 Aundrae Allison / Kolby Smith .75 2.00
30 Tim Shaw / Troy Smith 1.00 2.50
31 H.B. Blades / Courtney Taylor .75 2.00
32 DeShawn Wynn / Ahmad Bradshaw 1.50 4.00

2007 Playoff Contenders Round Numbers Autographs

STATED PRINT RUN 25 SER.#'d SETS
1 Calvin Johnson / Adrian Peterson 175.00 350.00
2 JaMarcus Russell / Brady Quinn 25.00 60.00
3 Gaines Adams / Anthony Spencer 12.00 30.00
4 Ted Ginn Jr. / Marshawn Lynch 25.00 50.00
5 LaRon Landry / Darrelle Revis 20.00 50.00
6 Michael Griffin / Aaron Ross 12.00 30.00
7 Dwayne Bowe / Robert Meachem 25.00 60.00
9 Brandon Meriweather / Greg Olsen 12.00 30.00
10 Joe Thomas / Levi Brown 12.00 30.00
11 Patrick Willis / Jon Beason 40.00 80.00
12 Leon Hall / Reggie Nelson 10.00 25.00
13 Jamaal Anderson / Adam Carriker 10.00 25.00
14 Kevin Kolb / John Beck 25.00 60.00
15 Chris Henry RB / Brandon Jackson 20.00 40.00
16 Paul Posluszny / David Harris 12.00 30.00
17 Sidney Rice / Dwayne Jarrett 15.00 40.00
18 Steve Smith USC / Brian Leonard 15.00 40.00
19 Zach Miller / Sabby Piscitelli 12.00 30.00
20 Lorenzo Booker / Tony Hunt 10.00 25.00
21 James Jones / Paul Williams 15.00 40.00
22 Matt Spaeth / Johnnie Lee Higgins 12.00 30.00
23 Jacoby Jones / Yamon Figurs 15.00 40.00
24 Laurent Robinson / Jason Hill 12.00 30.00
25 Trent Edwards / Garrett Wolfe 12.00 30.00
26 Jonathan Wade / Aaron Rouse 10.00 25.00
27 Antonio Pittman / Dwayne Wright 10.00 25.00
28 Chris Davis / Scott Chandler 12.00 30.00
30 Tim Shaw / Troy Smith 12.00 30.00
31 H.B. Blades / Courtney Taylor 10.00 25.00
32 DeShawn Wynn / Ahmad Bradshaw 15.00 40.00

2007 Playoff Contenders ROY Contenders

STATED PRINT RUN 1000 SER.#'d SETS
*GOLD HOLO/250: .5X TO 1.2X BASIC INSERTS
GOLD HOLOFOIL PRINT RUN 250 SER.#'d SETS
*BLACK/100: .8X TO 2X BASIC INSERTS
BLACK PRINT RUN 100 SER.#'d SETS
1 Aaron Rouse .75 2.00
2 Adrian Peterson 4.00 10.00
3 Anthony Gonzalez 1.00 2.50
4 Anthony Spencer 1.00 2.50
5 Brady Quinn 1.00 2.50
6 Brandon Jackson .75 2.00
7 Brandon Meriweather 1.00 2.50
8 Calvin Johnson 3.00 8.00
9 Chris Henry RB .60 1.50
10 Darrelle Revis 1.50 4.00
11 Dwayne Bowe 1.25 3.00
12 Dwayne Jarrett .75 2.00
13 Gaines Adams 1.00 2.50
14 Greg Olsen .75 2.00
15 Jacoby Jones 1.00 2.50
16 JaMarcus Russell .60 1.50
17 James Jones 1.00 2.50
18 Jason Hill 1.00 2.50
19 John Beck 1.00 2.50
20 LaMarr Woodley 1.00 2.50
21 LaRon Landry 1.00 2.50
22 Lorenzo Booker .75 2.00
23 Marshawn Lynch 1.00 2.50
24 Matt Spaeth 1.00 2.50
25 Michael Griffin 1.00 2.50
26 Patrick Willis 2.00 5.00
27 Paul Posluszny 1.00 2.50
28 Paul Williams .60 1.50
29 Reggie Nelson .75 2.00
30 Steve Smith USC 1.00 2.50
31 Ted Ginn Jr. .75 2.00
32 Trent Edwards 1.00 2.50

2007 Playoff Contenders ROY Contenders Autographs

STATED PRINT RUN 50 SER.#'d SETS
1 Aaron Rouse 8.00 20.00
2 Adrian Peterson 125.00 250.00
3 Anthony Gonzalez 10.00 25.00
4 Anthony Spencer 10.00 25.00
5 Brady Quinn 20.00 50.00
6 Brandon Jackson 8.00 20.00
7 Brandon Meriweather 10.00 25.00
8 Calvin Johnson 75.00 135.00
9 Chris Henry RB 6.00 15.00
10 Darrelle Revis 15.00 40.00
11 Dwayne Bowe 25.00 60.00
12 Dwayne Jarrett 8.00 20.00
13 Gaines Adams 10.00 25.00
14 Greg Olsen 8.00 20.00
15 Jacoby Jones 10.00 25.00
16 JaMarcus Russell 6.00 15.00
17 James Jones 10.00 25.00
18 Jason Hill 10.00 25.00
19 John Beck 10.00 25.00
20 LaMarr Woodley 12.00 30.00
21 LaRon Landry 10.00 25.00

22 Lorenzo Booker	8.00	20.00
23 Marshawn Lynch	12.00	30.00
24 Matt Spaeth	10.00	25.00
25 Michael Griffin	10.00	25.00
26 Patrick Willis	25.00	60.00
27 Paul Posluszny	10.00	25.00
28 Paul Williams	6.00	15.00
29 Reggie Nelson	8.00	20.00
30 Steve Smith USC	10.00	25.00
31 Ted Ginn Jr.	8.00	20.00
32 Trent Edwards	10.00	25.00

2008 Playoff Contenders

This set was released on January 7, 2009. The base set consists of 225 cards. Cards 1-100 feature veterans, and cards 101-225 are autographed rookies. Some rookies were issued via mail redemption cards. Playoff also announced actual print runs on the short-printed signed RCs with a production run of 250 or less.

COMP.SET w/o RC's (100)	8.00	20.00
PLAYOFF ANNOUNCED SOME PRINT RUNS		
1 Kurt Warner	.30	.75
2 Larry Fitzgerald	.30	.75
3 Anquan Boldin	.25	.60
4 Edgerrin James	.25	.60
5 Jerious Norwood	.25	.60
6 Roddy White	.25	.60
7 Michael Turner	.30	.75
8 Willis McGahee	.25	.60
9 Derrick Mason	.25	.60
10 Le'Ron McClain	.30	.75
11 Trent Edwards	.20	.50
12 Marshawn Lynch	.25	.60
13 Lee Evans	.25	.60
14 Steve Smith	.25	.60
15 DeAngelo Williams	.25	.60
16 Jake Delhomme	.25	.60
17 Greg Olsen	.25	.60
18 Devin Hester	.30	.75
19 Kyle Orton	.25	.60
20 Carson Palmer	.30	.75
21 Chad Johnson	.25	.60
22 T.J. Houshmandzadeh	.25	.60
23 Chris Perry	.20	.50
24 Derek Anderson	.20	.50
25 Jamal Lewis	.25	.60
26 Braylon Edwards	.25	.60
27 Tony Romo	.40	1.00
28 Terrell Owens	.30	.75
29 Marion Barber	.25	.60
30 Jason Witten	.30	.75
31 Jay Cutler	.30	.75
32 Selvin Young	.20	.50
33 Brandon Marshall	.25	.60
34 Jon Kitna	.25	.60
35 Roy Williams WR	.25	.60
36 Calvin Johnson	.30	.75
37 Aaron Rodgers	.60	1.50
38 Ryan Grant	.30	.75
39 Greg Jennings	.30	.75
40 Matt Schaub	.25	.60
41 Ahman Green	.25	.60
42 Andre Johnson	.25	.60
43 Peyton Manning	.50	1.25
44 Joseph Addai	.25	.60
45 Reggie Wayne	.25	.60
46 David Garrard	.25	.60
47 Fred Taylor	.25	.60
48 Maurice Jones-Drew	.25	.60
49 Brodie Croyle	.25	.60
50 Larry Johnson	.25	.60
51 Tony Gonzalez	.25	.60
52 Chad Pennington	.25	.60
53 Ronnie Brown	.25	.60
54 Ted Ginn Jr.	.25	.60
55 Tarvaris Jackson	.25	.60
56 Adrian Peterson	.50	1.25
57 Chester Taylor	.20	.50
58 Tom Brady	.50	1.25
59 Randy Moss	.30	.75
60 Laurence Maroney	.25	.60
61 Drew Brees	.30	.75
62 Reggie Bush	.30	.75
63 Marques Colston	.25	.60
64 Eli Manning	.30	.75
65 Plaxico Burress	.25	.60
66 Brandon Jacobs	.25	.60
67 Brett Favre	1.50	4.00
68 Leon Washington	.25	.60
69 Laveranues Coles	.20	.50
70 Javon Walker	.25	.60
71 JaMarcus Russell	.25	.60
72 Justin Fargas	.20	.50
73 Donovan McNabb	.30	.75
74 Brian Westbrook	.25	.60
75 Kevin Curtis	.20	.50
76 Ben Roethlisberger	.30	.75
77 Willie Parker	.25	.60
78 Santonio Holmes	.25	.60
79 Philip Rivers	.30	.75
80 LaDainian Tomlinson	.30	.75
81 Vincent Jackson	.20	.50
82 Antonio Gates	.30	.75
83 J.T. O'Sullivan	.20	.50
84 Frank Gore	.25	.60
85 Isaac Bruce	.25	.60
86 Matt Hasselbeck	.25	.60
87 Deion Branch	.25	.60
88 Julius Jones	.20	.50
89 Marc Bulger	.25	.60
90 Steven Jackson	.30	.75
91 Torry Holt	.25	.60
92 Warrick Dunn	.25	.60
93 Jeff Garcia	.25	.60
94 Joey Galloway	.25	.60
95 Vince Young	.25	.60
96 LenDale White	.25	.60
97 Justin Gage	.20	.50
98 Jason Campbell	.25	.60
99 Clinton Portis	.25	.60
100 Chris Cooley	.25	.60
101 Adrian Arrington AU RC	6.00	15.00
102 Ali Highsmith AU/214* RC	25.00	40.00
103 Allen Patrick AU RC	6.00	15.00
104 Andre Caldwell AU RC	6.00	15.00
105 Andre Woodson AU/250* RC	12.00	30.00
106 Antoine Cason AU RC	8.00	20.00
107 Aqib Talib AU RC	8.00	20.00
108 Brad Cottam AU/132* RC	30.00	60.00
109 Brandon Flowers AU/192* RC	25.00	50.00
110 Brian Brohm AU RC	10.00	25.00
111 Calais Campbell AU RC	6.00	15.00
112 Chad Henne AU RC	15.00	40.00
113 Chauncey Washington AU/114* RC	25.00	60.00
114 Chevis Jackson AU RC	5.00	12.00
115 Chris Johnson AU RC	75.00	150.00
116 Chris Long AU RC	8.00	20.00
117 Colt Brennan AU RC	10.00	25.00
118 Craig Steltz AU RC	6.00	15.00
119 Curtis Lofton AU RC	6.00	15.00
120 Dan Connor AU RC	8.00	20.00
121 Dantrell Savage AU/76* RC	20.00	50.00
122 Darius Reynaud AU RC	5.00	12.00
123 Darren McFadden AU RC	30.00	80.00
124 Davone Bess AU RC	8.00	20.00
125 Dennis Dixon AU RC	20.00	40.00
126 Derrick Harvey AU RC	5.00	12.00
127 DeSean Jackson AU RC	25.00	50.00
128 Devin Thomas AU RC	10.00	25.00
129 Dexter Jackson AU RC	6.00	15.00
130 Dominique Rodgers-Cromartie AU RC	8.00	20.00
131 Donnie Avery AU RC	6.00	15.00
132 Dustin Keller AU RC	12.00	30.00
133 Earl Bennett AU RC	10.00	25.00
134 Early Doucet AU/113* RC	20.00	50.00
135 Eddie Royal AU RC	10.00	25.00
136 Erik Ainge AU/107* RC	20.00	50.00
137 Erin Henderson AU/158* RC	15.00	40.00
138 Felix Jones AU RC	20.00	50.00
139 Fred Davis AU RC	8.00	20.00
140 Glenn Dorsey AU RC	8.00	20.00
141 Harry Douglas AU RC	6.00	15.00
142 Jacob Hester AU RC	8.00	20.00
143 Jacob Tamme AU RC	10.00	25.00
144 Jake Long AU/163* RC	15.00	40.00
145 Jamaal Charles AU RC	25.00	50.00
146 James Hardy AU RC	6.00	15.00
147 Jed Collins AU/30* RC	150.00	300.00
148 Jermichael Finley AU/231* RC	40.00	80.00
149 Jerod Mayo AU RC	10.00	25.00
150 Jerome Simpson AU RC	8.00	20.00
151 Joe Flacco AU/220* RC	100.00	200.00
152 John Carlson AU RC	8.00	20.00
153 John David Booty AU RC	10.00	25.00
154A Jonathan Stewart AU Blk RC	20.00	50.00
154B Jonathan Stewart AU Blu RC	30.00	60.00
155 Jordon Dizon AU/188* RC	20.00	40.00
156 Jordy Nelson AU RC	20.00	40.00
157 Josh Johnson AU RC	8.00	20.00
158 Josh Morgan AU RC	10.00	25.00
159 Justin Forsett AU RC	15.00	30.00
160 Keenan Burton AU RC	5.00	12.00
161 Keith Rivers AU RC	10.00	25.00
162 Kellen Davis AU RC	5.00	12.00
163 Kenny Phillips AU RC	8.00	20.00
164 Kentwan Balmer AU RC	6.00	15.00
165 Kevin O'Connell AU RC	6.00	15.00
166 Kevin Smith AU RC	8.00	20.00
167 Lavelle Hawkins AU RC	5.00	12.00
168 Lawrence Jackson AU RC	6.00	15.00
169 Leodis McKelvin AU RC	6.00	15.00
170 Limas Sweed AU RC	8.00	20.00
171 Malcolm Kelly AU/141* RC	15.00	40.00
173 Marcus Thomas AU/165* RC	12.00	30.00
174 Mario Manningham AU RC	12.50	25.00
175 Martellus Bennett AU RC	6.00	15.00
176 Martin Rucker AU RC	6.00	15.00
177 Matt Flynn AU RC	75.00	150.00
178 Matt Forte AU RC	15.00	40.00
179 Matt Ryan AU/246* RC	125.00	250.00
180 Mike Hart AU RC	8.00	20.00
181 Mike Jenkins AU RC	8.00	20.00
182 Owen Schmitt AU RC	8.00	20.00
183 Pat Sims AU RC	6.00	15.00
184 Peyton Hillis AU/113* RC	100.00	200.00
185 Phillip Merling AU/100* RC	20.00	50.00
186 Quentin Groves AU RC	6.00	15.00
187 Rashard Mendenhall AU RC	30.00	60.00
188 Ray Rice AU RC	30.00	60.00
189 Reggie Smith AU/196* RC	20.00	40.00
190 Ryan Torain AU/70* RC	60.00	100.00
191 Sedrick Ellis AU RC	8.00	20.00
192 Steve Slaton AU RC	8.00	20.00
193 Tashard Choice AU RC	6.00	15.00
194 Terrell Thomas AU RC	6.00	15.00
195 Thomas Brown AU/151* RC	20.00	40.00
196 Tim Hightower AU RC	12.00	30.00
197 Vernon Gholston AU RC	6.00	15.00
198 Will Franklin AU RC	6.00	15.00
199 Xavier Adibi AU RC	5.00	12.00
200 Brian Witherspoon AU/150* RC	25.00	60.00
201 Caleb Hanie AU RC	20.00	50.00
202 Charles Godfrey AU RC	8.00	20.00
203 Chaz Schilens AU RC	12.00	30.00
204 Chris Horton AU RC	8.00	20.00
205 Derek Fine AU RC	6.00	15.00
206 Zackary Bowman AU RC	6.00	15.00
207 Dwight Lowery AU RC	8.00	20.00
208 Jalen Parmele AU RC	6.00	15.00
209 Jerome Felton AU RC	5.00	12.00
210 Kendall Langford AU RC	8.00	20.00
211 Kregg Lumpkin AU RC	8.00	20.00
212 Marcus Henry AU RC	6.00	15.00
213 Matt Slater AU RC	8.00	20.00
214 Mike Cox AU RC	6.00	15.00
215 Mike Tolbert AU/199* RC	25.00	50.00
216 Pierre Garcon AU RC	20.00	50.00
217 Quintin Demps AU RC	8.00	20.00
218 Sam Baker AU RC	5.00	12.00
219 Steve Johnson AU RC	30.00	50.00
220 Tavares Gooden AU RC	6.00	15.00
221 Terrence Wheatley AU RC	5.00	12.00
222 Tom Santi AU RC	6.00	15.00
223 Tom Zbikowski AU/149* RC	25.00	60.00
224 Tyvon Branch AU RC	6.00	15.00
225 Xavier Omon AU/124* RC	20.00	50.00

2008 Playoff Contenders Championship Ticket

UNPRICED CHAMPIONSHIP PRINT RUN 1

2008 Playoff Contenders Playoff Ticket

*VETS 1-100: 3X TO 8X BASIC CARDS		
COMMON ROOKIE (101-225)	2.00	5.00
ROOKIE SEMISTARS	2.50	6.00
ROOKIE UNL.STARS	3.00	8.00
STATED PRINT RUN 99 SER.#'d SETS		
67 Brett Favre	6.00	15.00
110 Brian Brohm	3.00	8.00
112 Chad Henne	3.00	8.00
115 Chris Johnson	8.00	20.00
116 Chris Long	3.00	8.00
117 Colt Brennan	3.00	8.00
123 Darren McFadden	8.00	20.00
124 Davone Bess	3.00	8.00
127 DeSean Jackson	6.00	15.00
131 Donnie Avery	2.50	6.00
135 Eddie Royal	3.00	8.00
138 Felix Jones	5.00	12.00
140 Glenn Dorsey	3.00	8.00
144 Jake Long	3.00	8.00
145 Jamaal Charles	5.00	12.00
149 Jerod Mayo	3.00	8.00
151 Joe Flacco	10.00	25.00
154 Jonathan Stewart	5.00	12.00
156 Jordy Nelson	4.00	10.00
165 Kevin O'Connell	2.50	6.00
166 Kevin Smith	3.00	8.00
170 Limas Sweed	3.00	8.00
177 Matt Flynn	8.00	20.00
178 Matt Forte	5.00	12.00
179 Matt Ryan	12.00	30.00
180 Mike Hart	3.00	8.00
184 Peyton Hillis	6.00	15.00
187 Rashard Mendenhall	6.00	15.00
188 Ray Rice	6.00	15.00
192 Steve Slaton	3.00	8.00
196 Tim Hightower	3.00	8.00
201 Caleb Hanie	15.00	40.00
204 Chris Horton	3.00	8.00
216 Pierre Garcon	4.00	10.00
223 Tom Zbikowski	3.00	8.00

2008 Playoff Contenders College Rookie Ticket Playoff Ticket

*ROOK/99: .4X TO 1X BASE PLAY.TICKET		
STATED PRINT RUN 99 SER.#'d SETS		
1 Brian Brohm	3.00	8.00
2 Brandon Flowers	3.00	8.00
3 Chad Henne	3.00	8.00
4 Chris Long	3.00	8.00
5 Chris Johnson	8.00	20.00
6 Dan Connor	3.00	8.00
7 Darren McFadden	8.00	20.00
8 DeSean Jackson	6.00	15.00
9 Devin Thomas	2.50	6.00
10 Donnie Avery	2.50	6.00
11 Dustin Keller	3.00	8.00
12 Early Doucet	2.50	6.00
13 Felix Jones	5.00	12.00
14 Glenn Dorsey	3.00	8.00
15 Jake Long	3.00	8.00
16 Jamaal Charles	5.00	12.00
17 James Hardy	2.50	6.00
18 Jerod Mayo	3.00	8.00
19 Joe Flacco	10.00	25.00
20 John David Booty	2.50	6.00
21 John Carlson	3.00	8.00
22 Jonathan Stewart	5.00	12.00
23 Jordon Dizon	3.00	8.00
24 Jordy Nelson	4.00	10.00
25 Kenny Phillips	3.00	8.00
26 Kevin Smith	3.00	8.00
27 Limas Sweed	3.00	8.00
28 Malcolm Kelly	2.50	6.00
29 Matt Ryan	12.00	30.00
30 Matt Forte	5.00	12.00
31 Phillip Merling	2.50	6.00
32 Rashard Mendenhall	6.00	15.00
33 Ray Rice	6.00	15.00
34 Steve Slaton	3.00	8.00
35 Vernon Gholston	2.50	6.00

2008 Playoff Contenders College Rookie Ticket Autographs

UNPRICED CHAMPIONSHIP PRINT RUN 1		
1 Brian Brohm	20.00	50.00
2 Brandon Flowers	20.00	50.00
3 Chad Henne	60.00	120.00
4 Chris Long	20.00	50.00
5 Chris Johnson	150.00	250.00
6 Dan Connor	20.00	50.00
7 Darren McFadden	100.00	200.00
8 DeSean Jackson	40.00	100.00
9 Devin Thomas EXCH	15.00	40.00
10 Donnie Avery	15.00	40.00
11 Dustin Keller	20.00	60.00
12 Early Doucet	15.00	40.00
13 Felix Jones	75.00	150.00
14 Glenn Dorsey	20.00	50.00
15 Jake Long	20.00	50.00
16 Jamaal Charles	40.00	80.00
17 James Hardy	15.00	40.00
18 Jerod Mayo	20.00	50.00
19 Joe Flacco	200.00	350.00
20 John David Booty	20.00	50.00
21 John Carlson	20.00	50.00
22 Jonathan Stewart	60.00	120.00
23 Jordon Dizon	20.00	50.00
24 Jordy Nelson	40.00	80.00
25 Kenny Phillips	20.00	50.00
26 Kevin Smith	20.00	50.00
27 Limas Sweed	20.00	50.00
28 Malcolm Kelly	15.00	40.00
29 Matt Ryan	250.00	400.00
30 Matt Forte	75.00	150.00
31 Phillip Merling	15.00	40.00
32 Rashard Mendenhall	60.00	120.00
33 Ray Rice	50.00	100.00
34 Steve Slaton	30.00	80.00
35 Vernon Gholston	15.00	40.00

2008 Playoff Contenders Draft Class

STATED PRINT RUN 500 SER.#'d SETS		
*GOLD/100: .5X TO 1.2X BASIC INSERTS		
GOLD PRINT RUN 100 SER.#'d SETS		
*BLACK/50: .6X TO 1.5X BASIC INSERTS		
BLACK PRINT RUN 50 SER.#'d SETS		
UNPRICED AUTO PRINT RUN 10		
1 Early Doucet	1.50	4.00
Dominique Rodgers-Cromartie		
2 Matt Ryan	5.00	12.00
Curtis Lofton		
3 Chevis Jackson	1.25	3.00
Harry Douglas		
4 Joe Flacco	3.00	8.00
Ray Rice		
5 Leodis McKelvin	1.25	3.00
James Hardy		
6 Jonathan Stewart	3.00	8.00
Dan Connor		
7 Matt Forte	3.00	8.00
Earl Bennett		
8 Keith Rivers	1.50	4.00
Jerome Simpson		
9 Andre Caldwell	1.25	3.00
Pat Sims		
10 Martin Rucker	1.25	3.00
Paul Hubbard		
11 Felix Jones	3.00	8.00
Mike Jenkins		
12 Martellus Bennett	1.25	3.00
Tashard Choice		
13 Eddie Royal	1.50	4.00
Ryan Torain		
14 Jordon Dizon	1.50	4.00
Kevin Smith		
15 Jordy Nelson	2.00	5.00
Brian Brohm		
16 Steve Slaton	1.50	4.00
Xavier Adibi		
17 Jacob Tamme	1.50	4.00
Mike Hart		
18 Derrick Harvey	1.25	3.00
Quentin Groves		
19 Glenn Dorsey	2.50	6.00
Jamaal Charles		
20 Vernon Gholston	1.50	4.00
Dustin Keller		
21 Jake Long	1.50	4.00
Chad Henne		
22 Jerod Mayo	1.50	4.00
Kevin O'Connell		
23 Sedrick Ellis	1.50	4.00
Tracy Porter		
24 Kenny Phillips	1.50	4.00
Mario Manningham		
25 Darren McFadden	3.00	8.00
Tyvon Branch		
26 DeSean Jackson	3.00	8.00
Jed Collins		
27 Rashard Mendenhall	3.00	8.00
Limas Sweed		
28 Antoine Cason	1.50	4.00
Jacob Hester		
29 Kentwan Balmer	1.25	3.00
Reggie Smith		
30 Lawrence Jackson	1.50	4.00
John Carlson		
31 Chris Long	1.50	4.00
Donnie Avery		
32 Aqib Talib	1.50	4.00
Dexter Jackson		
33 Chris Johnson	3.00	8.00
Lavelle Hawkins		
34 Devin Thomas	1.50	4.00
Fred Davis		
35 Malcolm Kelly	1.50	4.00
Colt Brennan		

2008 Playoff Contenders ROY Contenders

STATED PRINT RUN 500 SER.#'d SETS		
*GOLD/100: .5X TO 1.2X BASIC INSERTS		
GOLD PRINT RUN 100 SER.#'d SETS		
*BLACK/50: .6X TO 1.5X BASIC INSERTS		
BLACK PRINT RUN 50 SER.#'d SETS		
1 Chris Long	1.25	3.00
2 Matt Ryan	5.00	12.00
3 Darren McFadden	3.00	8.00
4 Glenn Dorsey	1.25	3.00
5 Vernon Gholston	1.00	2.50
6 Sedrick Ellis	1.25	3.00
7 Derrick Harvey	.75	2.00
8 Keith Rivers	1.25	3.00
9 Jerod Mayo	1.25	3.00
10 Jonathan Stewart	2.00	5.00
11 Joe Flacco	4.00	10.00
12 Felix Jones	2.00	5.00
13 Rashard Mendenhall	2.50	6.00
14 Chris Johnson	3.00	8.00
15 Dustin Keller	1.25	3.00
16 Kenny Phillips	1.25	3.00
17 Donnie Avery	1.00	2.50
18 Devin Thomas	1.00	2.50
19 John Carlson	1.25	3.00
20 Fred Davis	1.25	3.00
21 Eddie Royal	1.25	3.00
22 Jordy Nelson	1.50	4.00
23 Matt Forte	2.00	5.00
24 Chad Henne	1.25	3.00
25 Jerome Simpson	1.25	3.00
26 James Hardy	1.00	2.50
27 Ray Rice	2.50	6.00
28 Limas Sweed	1.25	3.00
29 DeSean Jackson	2.50	6.00
30 Malcolm Kelly	1.00	2.50
31 Leodis McKelvin	1.00	2.50
32 Kevin Smith	1.25	3.00
33 Dominique Rodgers-Cromartie	1.25	3.00
34 Aqib Talib	1.25	3.00
35 Antoine Cason	1.25	3.00

2008 Playoff Contenders ROY Contenders Autographs

STATED PRINT RUN 25 SER.#'d SETS		
1 Chris Long	12.00	30.00
2 Matt Ryan	100.00	200.00
3 Darren McFadden	30.00	80.00
4 Glenn Dorsey	12.00	30.00
5 Vernon Gholston	10.00	25.00
6 Sedrick Ellis	12.00	30.00
7 Derrick Harvey	8.00	20.00
8 Keith Rivers	12.00	30.00
9 Jerod Mayo	12.00	30.00
10 Jonathan Stewart	30.00	80.00
11 Joe Flacco	75.00	150.00
12 Felix Jones	30.00	60.00
13 Rashard Mendenhall	30.00	60.00
14 Chris Johnson	60.00	120.00
15 Dustin Keller	12.00	30.00
16 Kenny Phillips	12.00	30.00
17 Donnie Avery	10.00	25.00
18 Devin Thomas EXCH	10.00	25.00
19 John Carlson	12.00	30.00
20 Fred Davis	12.00	30.00
21 Eddie Royal	12.00	30.00
22 Jordy Nelson	30.00	60.00
23 Matt Forte	20.00	50.00
24 Chad Henne	30.00	60.00
25 Jerome Simpson	12.00	30.00
26 James Hardy	10.00	25.00
27 Ray Rice	25.00	60.00
28 Limas Sweed	12.00	30.00
29 DeSean Jackson	25.00	60.00
30 Malcolm Kelly	10.00	25.00
31 Leodis McKelvin	10.00	25.00
32 Kevin Smith	12.00	30.00
33 Dominique Rodgers-Cromartie	12.00	30.00
34 Aqib Talib	12.00	30.00
35 Antoine Cason	12.00	30.00

2008 Playoff Contenders Rookie Roll Call

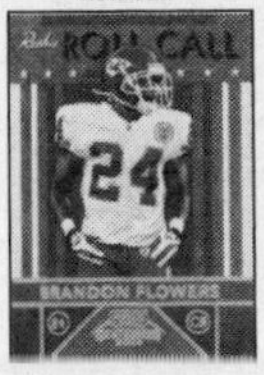

STATED PRINT RUN 500 SER.#'d SETS		
*GOLD/100: .5X TO 1.2X BASIC INSERTS		
GOLD PRINT RUN 100 SER.#'d SETS		
*BLACK/50: .6X TO 1.5X BASIC INSERTS		
BLACK PRINT RUN 50 SER.#'d SETS		
1 Vernon Gholston	1.00	2.50
2 Donnie Avery	1.00	2.50
3 Chris Johnson	3.00	8.00
4 Devin Thomas	1.00	2.50
5 Rashard Mendenhall	2.50	6.00
6 Kenny Phillips	1.25	3.00
7 Brandon Flowers	1.25	3.00
8 Jordy Nelson	1.50	4.00
9 Felix Jones	2.00	5.00
10 Jonathan Stewart	2.00	5.00
11 Joe Flacco	4.00	10.00
12 James Hardy	1.00	2.50
13 Jerome Simpson	1.25	3.00
14 Matt Forte	2.00	5.00
15 Eddie Royal	1.25	3.00
16 Limas Sweed	1.25	3.00
17 DeSean Jackson	2.50	6.00
18 Fred Davis	1.25	3.00
19 Malcolm Kelly	1.00	2.50
20 Matt Ryan	5.00	12.00
21 Leodis McKelvin	1.00	2.50
22 Keith Rivers	1.25	3.00
23 Glenn Dorsey	1.25	3.00
24 Jake Long	1.25	3.00
25 Jerod Mayo	1.25	3.00
26 Darren McFadden	3.00	8.00
27 Chris Long	1.25	3.00
28 Colt Brennan	1.25	3.00
29 Jordon Dizon	1.25	3.00
30 Martellus Bennett	1.00	2.50
31 Brian Brohm	1.25	3.00
32 Jamaal Charles	2.00	5.00
33 Ray Rice	2.50	6.00
34 Chad Henne	1.25	3.00
35 Dan Connor	1.25	3.00

2008 Playoff Contenders Rookie Roll Call Autographs

STATED PRINT RUN 25 SER.#'d SETS		
1 Vernon Gholston	10.00	25.00
2 Donnie Avery	10.00	25.00
3 Chris Johnson	60.00	120.00
4 Devin Thomas EXCH	10.00	25.00
5 Rashard Mendenhall	25.00	60.00
6 Kenny Phillips	12.00	30.00
7 Brandon Flowers	12.00	30.00
8 Jordy Nelson	30.00	60.00
9 Felix Jones	30.00	80.00
10 Jonathan Stewart	20.00	50.00
11 Joe Flacco	75.00	150.00
12 James Hardy	10.00	25.00
13 Jerome Simpson	12.00	30.00
14 Matt Forte	20.00	50.00
15 Eddie Royal	12.00	30.00
16 Limas Sweed	12.00	30.00
17 DeSean Jackson	25.00	60.00
18 Fred Davis	12.00	30.00
19 Malcolm Kelly	10.00	25.00
20 Matt Ryan	75.00	150.00
21 Leodis McKelvin	10.00	25.00
22 Keith Rivers	12.00	30.00
23 Glenn Dorsey	12.00	30.00
24 Jake Long	12.00	30.00
25 Jerod Mayo	12.00	30.00
26 Darren McFadden	30.00	80.00
27 Chris Long	12.00	30.00
28 Colt Brennan	12.00	30.00
29 Jordon Dizon	12.00	30.00
30 Martellus Bennett	10.00	25.00
31 Brian Brohm	12.00	30.00
32 Jamaal Charles	20.00	50.00
33 Ray Rice	25.00	60.00
34 Chad Henne	20.00	50.00
35 Dan Connor	12.00	30.00

2008 Playoff Contenders Round Numbers

STATED PRINT RUN 500 SER.#'d SETS		
*GOLD/100: .5X TO 1.2X BASIC INSERTS		
GOLD PRINT RUN 100 SER.#'d SETS		
*BLACK/50: .6X TO 1.5X BASIC INSERTS		
BLACK PRINT RUN 50 SER.#'d SETS		
UNPRICED AUTO PRINT RUN 10		
1 Jake Long	1.25	3.00
Chris Long		
2 Matt Ryan	4.00	10.00
Darren McFadden		
3 Glenn Dorsey	1.25	3.00
Vernon Gholston		
4 Jonathan Stewart	3.00	8.00
Joe Flacco		
5 Keith Rivers	1.25	3.00
Jerod Mayo		
6 Leodis McKelvin	1.25	3.00
Dominique Rodgers-Cromartie		
7 Felix Jones	2.50	6.00
Rashard Mendenhall		
8 Dustin Keller	1.25	3.00
Kenny Phillips		
9 Sedrick Ellis	1.25	3.00
Derrick Harvey		
10 Mike Jenkins	1.25	3.00
Antoine Cason		
11 Donnie Avery	1.00	2.50
Devin Thomas		
12 Eddie Royal	1.50	4.00
Jordy Nelson		
13 Jerome Simpson	1.25	3.00
James Hardy		
14 Matt Forte	2.00	5.00
Chad Henne		
15 John Carlson	1.25	3.00
Fred Davis		
16 DeSean Jackson	2.50	6.00
Malcolm Kelly		
17 Limas Sweed	2.50	6.00
Ray Rice		
18 Dan Connor	1.25	3.00
Shawn Crable		
19 Kevin O'Connell	1.25	3.00
Kevin Smith		
20 Jamaal Charles	2.00	5.00
Steve Slaton		
21 Brad Cottam	1.25	3.00
Jermichael Finley		
22 Earl Bennett	1.25	3.00
Early Doucet		
23 Harry Douglas	1.25	3.00
Mario Manningham		
24 Will Franklin	1.00	2.50
Marcus Smith		
25 Martin Rucker	1.25	3.00
Jacob Tamme		
26 Lavelle Hawkins	.75	2.00
Keenan Burton		
27 John David Booty	1.00	2.50
Dennis Dixon		
28 Josh Johnson	1.25	3.00
Erik Ainge		
29 Tim Hightower	1.25	3.00
Ryan Torain		
30 Colt Brennan	1.25	3.00
Andre Woodson		
31 Thomas Brown	1.25	3.00
Mike Hart		
32 Josh Morgan	1.25	3.00
Kevin Robinson		
33 Matt Flynn	2.50	6.00
Chauncey Washington		
34 Cory Boyd	1.00	2.50
Allen Patrick		
35 Adrian Arrington	1.50	4.00
Peyton Hillis		

2009 Playoff Contenders

COMP.SET w/o RC's (100)	10.00	25.00
OVERALL AUTOGRAPH ODDS 1:6		
PANINI ANNOUNCED SOME PRINT RUNS		
1 Kurt Warner	.30	.75
2 Larry Fitzgerald	.30	.75
3 Tim Hightower	.20	.50
4 Matt Ryan	.30	.75
5 Michael Turner	.25	.60
6 Roddy White	.25	.60
7 Tony Gonzalez	.25	.60
8 Joe Flacco	.30	.75
9 Mark Clayton	.20	.50
10 Willis McGahee	.25	.60
11 Lee Evans	.25	.60
12 Marshawn Lynch	.25	.60
13 Terrell Owens	.30	.75
14 DeAngelo Williams	.30	.75
15 Jake Delhomme	.25	.60
16 Steve Smith	.25	.60
17 Devin Hester	.30	.75
18 Greg Olsen	.20	.50
19 Jay Cutler	.30	.75
20 Matt Forte	.30	.75
21 Carson Palmer	.30	.75
22 Chad Ochocinco	.25	.60
23 Cedric Benson	.25	.60
24 Josh Cribbs	.30	.75
25 Braylon Edwards	.25	.60
26 Jamal Lewis	.25	.60
27 Roy Williams WR	.25	.60
28 Marion Barber	.25	.60
29 Tony Romo	.50	1.25
30 Brandon Marshall	.25	.60
31 Eddie Royal	.25	.60
32 Kyle Orton	.25	.60
33 Calvin Johnson	.30	.75
34 Bryant Johnson	.20	.50
35 Kevin Smith	.25	.60
36 Aaron Rodgers	.60	1.50
37 Greg Jennings	.30	.75
38 Ryan Grant	.25	.60
39 Andre Johnson	.25	.60
40 Matt Schaub	.25	.60
41 Steve Slaton	.25	.60
42 Anthony Gonzalez	.20	.50
43 Joseph Addai	.30	.75
44 Peyton Manning	.50	1.25
45 Reggie Wayne	.25	.60
46 David Garrard	.25	.60
47 Maurice Jones-Drew	.25	.60
48 Torry Holt	.25	.60
49 Dwayne Bowe	.25	.60
50 Jamaal Charles	.30	.75
51 Matt Cassel	.25	.60
52 Chad Henne	.25	.60
53 Ted Ginn	.25	.60
54 Ronnie Brown	.25	.60
55 Adrian Peterson	.50	1.25
56 Bernard Berrian	.25	.60
57 Brett Favre	4.00	10.00
58 Randy Moss	.30	.75
59 Tom Brady	.50	1.25
60 Laurence Maroney	.25	.60
61 Drew Brees	.30	.75
62 Marques Colston	.25	.60
63 Reggie Bush	.30	.75
64 Brandon Jacobs	.25	.60
65 Eli Manning	.30	.75
66 Steve Smith USC	.25	.60
67 Jerricho Cotchery	.25	.60
68 Leon Washington	.25	.60
69 Thomas Jones	.25	.60
70 Darren McFadden	.30	.75
71 JaMarcus Russell	.20	.50
72 Zach Miller	.20	.50
73 Brian Westbrook	.25	.60
74 DeSean Jackson	.25	.60
75 Donovan McNabb	.30	.75
76 Ben Roethlisberger	.30	.75
77 Santonio Holmes	.25	.60
78 Willie Parker	.20	.50
79 Antonio Gates	.25	.60
80 LaDainian Tomlinson	.30	.75
81 Philip Rivers	.30	.75
82 Vincent Jackson	.25	.60
83 Frank Gore	.25	.60
84 Josh Morgan	.20	.50
85 Vernon Davis	.25	.60
86 Julius Jones	.20	.50
87 Matt Hasselbeck	.25	.60
88 T.J. Houshmandzadeh	.25	.60
89 Donnie Avery	.25	.60
90 Marc Bulger	.25	.60
91 Steven Jackson	.25	.60
92 Antonio Bryant	.20	.50
93 Derrick Ward	.20	.50
94 Kellen Winslow Jr.	.25	.60
95 Bo Scaife	.20	.50
96 Chris Johnson	.30	.75
97 Kerry Collins	.25	.60
98 Chris Cooley	.25	.60
99 Clinton Portis	.25	.60
100 Santana Moss	.25	.60
101 Matthew Stafford AU/540* RC	200.00	300.00
102 Jason Smith AU/237* RC	15.00	40.00
103 Tyson Jackson AU/443* RC	5.00	12.00
104 Aaron Curry AU RC	10.00	25.00
105 Mark Sanchez AU RC	40.00	100.00
106 Darrius Heyward-Bey AU/540* RC	12.00	30.00
107 Michael Crabtree AU/539* RC	20.00	50.00
108 Knowshon Moreno AU/445* RC	15.00	40.00
109 Josh Freeman AU RC	25.00	60.00
110 Jeremy Maclin AU/278* RC	12.00	30.00
111 Brandon Pettigrew AU RC	6.00	15.00
112 Percy Harvin AU/497* RC	20.00	50.00
113 Donald Brown AU/465* RC	10.00	25.00
114 Hakeem Nicks AU/318* RC	30.00	60.00
115 Kenny Britt AU RC EXCH	20.00	40.00
116 Chris Wells AU/531* RC	12.00	30.00
117 Brian Robiskie AU RC	10.00	25.00
118 Pat White AU RC	10.00	25.00
119 Mohamed Massaquoi AU RC	10.00	25.00
120 LeSean McCoy AU RC	30.00	60.00
121 Shonn Greene AU RC	12.00	30.00
122 Glen Coffee AU RC	12.50	25.00
123 Derrick Williams AU RC	10.00	25.00
124 Mike Wallace AU RC	20.00	40.00
125 Ramses Barden AU RC	4.00	10.00
126 Patrick Turner AU RC	5.00	12.00
127 Deon Butler AU RC	5.00	12.00
128 Juaquin Iglesias AU/467* RC	5.00	12.00
129 Stephen McGee AU RC	12.50	25.00
130 Mike Thomas AU RC	8.00	20.00
131 Andre Brown AU/363* RC	10.00	25.00
132 Rhett Bomar AU RC	5.00	12.00
133 Nate Davis AU RC	10.00	25.00
134 Javon Ringer AU RC	6.00	15.00
135 Aaron Brown AU RC	6.00	15.00
136 Aaron Kelly AU/21* RC	150.00	300.00
137 Aaron Maybin AU/99* RC	30.00	80.00
138 Alphonso Smith AU/99* RC	20.00	50.00
139 Anthony Hill AU RC	4.00	10.00
140 Vontae Davis AU RC	6.00	15.00
141 Austin Collie AU RC	8.00	20.00
142 B.J. Raji AU RC	12.00	30.00
143 Bernard Scott AU RC	6.00	15.00
144 Brandon Gibson AU RC	6.00	15.00
145 Brandon Myers AU/99* RC	25.00	60.00
146 Brandon Tate AU RC	10.00	25.00
147 Brian Cushing AU/151* RC	20.00	50.00
148 Brian Hartline AU RC	6.00	15.00
149 Brian Hoyer AU RC	15.00	30.00
150 Brian Orakpo AU/199* RC	20.00	40.00
151 Brooks Foster AU RC	4.00	10.00
152 Cameron Morrah AU RC	4.00	10.00
153 Captain Munnerlyn AU RC	5.00	12.00
154 Chase Coffman AU RC	5.00	12.00
155 Chase Daniel AU RC	15.00	30.00
156 Clay Matthews AU RC	50.00	100.00
157 Clint Sintim AU/247* RC	6.00	15.00
158 Cornelius Ingram AU RC	4.00	10.00
159 Curtis Painter AU RC	8.00	20.00
160 David Johnson AU RC	5.00	12.00
161 Demetrius Byrd AU/505* RC	5.00	12.00
162 Dominique Edison AU RC	4.00	10.00
163 Everette Brown AU RC	5.00	12.00
164 Frank Summers AU RC	6.00	15.00
165 Gartrell Johnson AU RC	5.00	12.00
166 Hunter Cantwell AU/281* RC	6.00	15.00
167 Jake O'Connell AU RC	4.00	10.00
168 James Casey AU RC	5.00	12.00
169 James Laurinaitis AU RC	6.00	15.00
170 Jared Cook AU RC	6.00	15.00
171 Jarett Dillard AU RC	6.00	15.00
172 Zach Miller AU RC	5.00	12.00
173 John Nalbone AU RC	4.00	10.00
174 John Phillips AU RC	6.00	15.00
175 Johnny Knox AU RC	8.00	20.00
176 Julian Edelman AU RC	6.00	15.00
177 Keith Null AU RC	5.00	12.00
178 Kenny McKinley AU RC	6.00	15.00
179 Kevin Ogletree AU/493* RC	8.00	20.00
180 Kory Sheets AU/449* RC	5.00	12.00
181 Lardarius Webb AU RC	6.00	15.00
182 LaRod Stephens-Howling AU RC	12.00	30.00
183 Larry English AU/510* RC	6.00	15.00
184 Louis Delmas AU RC	10.00	25.00
185 Louis Murphy AU/99* RC	60.00	100.00
186 Malcolm Jenkins AU/393* RC	6.00	15.00
187 Manuel Johnson AU RC	5.00	12.00
188 Marko Mitchell AU RC	5.00	12.00
189 Mike Teel AU RC	6.00	15.00
190 Mike Goodson No AU/99* RC	20.00	50.00
191 Nick Miller AU RC	4.00	10.00
192 P.J. Hill AU RC	5.00	12.00
193 Quan Cosby AU/311* RC	12.00	30.00
194 Quinn Johnson AU RC	5.00	12.00
195 Rashad Jennings AU RC	6.00	15.00
196 Rey Maualuga AU/157* RC	25.00	60.00
197 Richard Quinn AU RC	5.00	12.00
198 Ryan Mouton AU/99* RC EXCH	50.00	100.00
199 Sammie Stroughter AU RC	6.00	15.00
200 Sean Smith AU RC	6.00	15.00
201 Shawn Nelson AU/99* RC EXCH	30.00	80.00
202 Sherrod Martin AU RC	5.00	12.00
203 Stefan Logan AU RC	10.00	25.00
204 Tom Brandstater AU/63* RC	60.00	120.00
205 Tony Fiammetta AU RC	5.00	12.00
206 Travis Beckum AU RC	5.00	12.00
207 Tyrell Sutton AU/440* RC	10.00	25.00
208 James Davis AU/99* RC	30.00	80.00
209 Michael Oher AU/99* RC	50.00	100.00

2009 Playoff Contenders Playoff Ticket

*VETS 1-100: 3X TO 8X BASIC CARDS		
COMMON ROOKIE (101-209)	1.50	4.00
ROOKIE SEMISTARS	2.00	5.00
ROOKIE UNL.STARS	2.50	6.00
STATED PRINT RUN 99 SER.#'d SETS		
57 Brett Favre	10.00	25.00
101 Matthew Stafford	6.00	15.00
104 Aaron Curry	2.50	6.00
105 Mark Sanchez	8.00	20.00
106 Darrius Heyward-Bey	2.50	6.00
107 Michael Crabtree	5.00	12.00
108 Knowshon Moreno	2.50	6.00
109 Josh Freeman	5.00	12.00
110 Jeremy Maclin	4.00	10.00
111 Brandon Pettigrew	2.50	6.00
112 Percy Harvin	4.00	10.00
113 Donald Brown	2.50	6.00
114 Hakeem Nicks	4.00	10.00
115 Kenny Britt	3.00	8.00
116 Chris Wells	4.00	10.00
118 Pat White	2.50	6.00
120 LeSean McCoy	5.00	12.00
121 Shonn Greene	4.00	10.00
122 Glen Coffee	2.00	5.00
124 Mike Wallace	5.00	12.00
141 Austin Collie	2.50	6.00
142 B.J. Raji	2.50	6.00

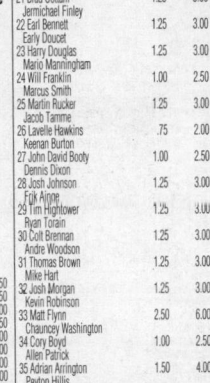

147 Brian Cushing 2.50 6.00
150 Brian Orakpo 2.50 6.00
155 Chase Daniel 2.50 6.00
156 Clay Matthews 8.00 20.00
169 James Laurinaitis* 2.50 6.00
175 Johnny Knox 4.00 10.00
176 Julian Edelman 2.50* 6.00
182 LaRod Stephens-Howling 3.00 8.00
196 Rey Maualuga 2.50 6.00
209 Michael Oher 8.00 20.00

2009 Playoff Contenders College Rookie Ticket Autographs

OVERALL AUTOGRAPH ODDS 1:6
PANINI ANNOUNCED SOME PRINT RUNS
1 Mark Sanchez/64* 150.00 300.00
2 Knowshon Moreno/65* 40.00 100.00
3 Brandon Pettigrew/50* 20.00 50.00
4 Kenny Britt/55* 30.00 60.00
5 Matthew Stafford/61* 175.00 300.00
6 Derrick Williams/55* 15.00 40.00
7 Deon Butler/51* 15.00 40.00
8 Andre Brown/64* 12.00 30.00
9 Javon Ringer/65* 20.00 50.00
10 Stephen McGee/60* 30.00 60.00
11 Mike Wallace/80* 50.00 100.00
12 LeSean McCoy/55* 75.00 150.00
13 Brian Robiskie/55* 20.00 50.00
14 Mohamed Massaquoi/59* 15.00 40.00
15 Michael Crabtree/55* 60.00 120.00
16 Jeremy Maclin/65* 30.00 80.00
17 Percy Harvin/55* 60.00 120.00
18 Hakeem Nicks/55* 30.00 80.00
19 Shonn Greene/68* 25.00 60.00
20 Patrick Turner/64* 15.00 40.00
21 Rhett Bomar/65* 15.00 40.00
22 Aaron Curry/64* 20.00 50.00
23 Donald Brown/65* 15.00 40.00
24 Glen Coffee/55* 15.00 40.00
25 Juaquin Iglesias/66* 15.00 40.00
26 Nate Davis/68* 15.00 40.00
27 Ramses Barden/63* 12.00 30.00
28 Chris Wells/63* 40.00 100.00
29 Pat White/65* 25.00 60.00
30 Josh Freeman/65* 75.00 150.00
31 Darrius Heyward-Bey/65* 25.00 60.00
32 Mike Thomas/64* 20.00 50.00

2009 Playoff Contenders College Rookie Ticket Playoff Ticket

STATED PRINT RUN 99 SER.#'d SETS
1 Mark Sanchez 8.00 20.00
2 Knowshon Moreno 2.50 6.00
3 Brandon Pettigrew 2.50 6.00
4 Kenny Britt 3.00 8.00
5 Matthew Stafford 6.00 15.00
6 Derrick Williams 2.00 5.00
7 Deon Butler 2.00 5.00
8 Andre Brown 1.50 4.00
9 Javon Ringer 2.50 6.00
10 Stephen McGee 2.50 6.00
11 Mike Wallace 5.00 12.00
12 LeSean McCoy 5.00 12.00
13 Brian Robiskie 2.50 6.00
14 Mohamed Massaquoi 2.00 5.00
15 Michael Crabtree 5.00 12.00
16 Jeremy Maclin 4.00 10.00
17 Percy Harvin 4.00 10.00
18 Hakeem Nicks 4.00 10.00
19 Shonn Greene 4.00 10.00
20 Patrick Turner 2.00 5.00
21 Rhett Bomar 2.00 5.00
22 Aaron Curry 2.50 6.00
23 Donald Brown 2.50 6.00
24 Glen Coffee 2.00 5.00
25 Juaquin Iglesias 2.00 5.00
26 Nate Davis 2.00 5.00
27 Ramses Barden 1.50 4.00
28 Chris Wells 4.00 10.00
29 Pat White 2.50 6.00
30 Josh Freeman 5.00 12.00
31 Darrius Heyward-Bey 2.50 6.00
32 Mike Thomas 2.50 6.00

2009 Playoff Contenders Draft Class

*BLACK/50: .6X TO 1.5X BASIC INSERTS
*GOLD/100: .5X TO 1.2X BASIC INSERTS
1 Aaron Maybin .75 2.00
Shawn Nelson
2 Everette Brown 1.00 2.50
Mike Goodson
3 Juaquin Iglesias 1.50 4.00
Johnny Knox
4 Rey Maualuga 1.00 2.50
Chase Coffman
5 Brian Robiskie 1.00 2.50
Mohamed Massaquoi
6 Stephen McGee 1.00 2.50
Kevin Ogletree
7 Knowshon Moreno 1.00 2.50
Kenny McKinley
8 Matthew Stafford 5.00 12.00
Brandon Pettigrew
9 B.J. Raji 1.25 3.00
Clay Matthews
10 Brian Cushing 1.00 2.50
James Casey
11 Donald Brown 1.00 2.50
Austin Collie
12 Mike Thomas 1.00 2.50
Jarett Dillard
13 Vontae Davis 1.00 2.50
Pat White
14 Malcolm Jenkins 1.00 2.50
P.J. Hill
15 Hakeem Nicks 1.50 4.00
Clint Sintim
16 Mark Sanchez 3.00 8.00
Shonn Greene
17 Darrius Heyward-Bey 1.00 2.50
Louis Murphy
18 Jeremy Maclin 1.50 4.00
LeSean McCoy
19 Larry English 1.00 2.50
Demetrius Byrd
20 Michael Crabtree 2.00 5.00
Glen Coffee
21 Aaron Curry 1.00 2.50
Deon Butler
22 Jason Smith 1.00 2.50
James Laurinaitis
23 Kenny Britt 1.25 3.00
Jared Cook
24 Andre Brown .75 2.00
Rhett Bomar
25 Cornelius Ingram 1.00 2.50
Brandon Gibson

2009 Playoff Contenders Legendary Contenders

*GOLD/100: .5X TO 1.2X BASIC INSERTS
1 Alan Page 1.25 3.00
2 Andre Reed 1.25 3.00
3 Archie Manning 1.50 4.00
4 Bart Starr 2.50 6.00
5 Bert Jones 1.00 2.50
6 Billy Sims 1.25 3.00
7 Bob Lilly 1.25 3.00
8 Bobby Bell 1.00 2.50
9 Boyd Dowler 1.00 2.50
10 Brett Favre 4.00 10.00
11 Carl Eller 1.00 2.50
12 Charley Trippi 1.00 2.50
13 Charlie Joiner 1.00 2.50
14 Chuck Bednarik 1.25 3.00
15 Chuck Foreman 1.00 2.50
16 Ace Parker 1.00 2.50
17 Cris Collinsworth 1.25 3.00
18 Dan Fouts 1.50 4.00
19 Dan Hampton 1.00 2.50
20 Dan Marino 3.00 8.00
21 Danny White 1.25 3.00
22 Daryl Johnston 1.50 4.00
23 Dave Casper 1.00 2.50
24 Deion Sanders 1.50 4.00
25 Del Shofner 1.00 2.50
26 Dick Butkus 2.00 5.00
27 Dub Jones 1.00 2.50
28 Earl Campbell 1.50 4.00
29 Emmitt Smith 2.50 6.00
30 Forrest Gregg 1.00 2.50
31 Franco Harris 1.50 4.00
32 Frank Gifford 1.50 4.00
33 Fred Dryer 1.00 2.50
34 Gale Sayers 2.00 5.00
35 Garo Yepremian 1.00 2.50
36 George Blanda 1.25 3.00
37 Harlon Hill 1.00 2.50
38 Howie Long 1.50 4.00
39 Hugh McElhenny 1.00 2.50
40 Jack Youngblood 1.00 2.50
41 James Lofton 1.00 2.50
42 Jan Stenerud 1.00 2.50
43 Jay Novacek 1.25 3.00
44 Jethro Pugh 1.00 2.50
45 Jim Brown 2.00 5.00
46 Jim McMahon 1.25 3.00
47 Jimmy Orr 1.00 2.50
48 Joe Greene 1.50 4.00
49 Joe Klecko 1.00 2.50
50 Joe Namath 2.00 5.00
51 John Elway 2.50 6.00
52 John Mackey 1.25 3.00
53 John Riggins 1.25 3.00
54 John Stallworth 1.25 3.00
55 Johnny Morris 1.00 2.50
56 Ken Stabler 1.50 4.00
57 Lance Alworth 1.25 3.00
58 Lee Roy Selmon 1.00 2.50
59 Lem Barney 1.00 2.50
60 Lenny Moore 1.25 3.00
61 Lydell Mitchell 1.00 2.50
62 Marcus Allen 1.50 4.00
63 Michael Irvin 1.25 3.00
64 Mike Curtis 1.00 2.50
65 Mike Singletary 1.50 4.00
66 Ozzie Newsome 1.25 3.00
67 Paul Hornung 1.50 4.00
68 Paul Warfield 1.25 3.00
69 Randall Cunningham 1.50 4.00
70 Randy White 1.50 4.00
71 Raymond Berry 1.25 3.00
72 Rick Casares 1.00 2.50
73 Roger Craig 1.25 3.00
74 Roger Staubach 2.00 5.00
75 Ronnie Lott 1.50 4.00
76 Sterling Sharpe 1.25 3.00
77 Ted Hendricks 1.00 2.50
78 Tiki Barber 1.25 3.00
79 Tim Brown 1.50 4.00
80 Tommy McDonald 1.00 2.50
81 Troy Aikman 2.00 5.00
82 Warren Moon 1.50 4.00
83 Yale Lary 1.00 2.50
84 Y.A. Tittle 1.50 4.00

2009 Playoff Contenders Legendary Contenders Autographs

OVERALL AUTOGRAPH ODDS 1:6
PANINI ANNC'D SOME PRINT RUNS
1 Alan Page 12.00 30.00
2 Andre Reed 10.00 25.00
3 Archie Manning/35* 25.00 50.00
4 Bart Starr/62* 90.00 150.00
5 Bert Jones/33* 12.00 30.00
6 Billy Sims 10.00 25.00
7 Bob Lilly 12.00 30.00
8 Bobby Bell/24* 20.00 40.00
9 Boyd Dowler/77* 12.00 30.00
10 Brett Favre/4*
11 Carl Eller 10.00 25.00
12 Charley Trippi/29* 12.00 30.00
13 Charlie Joiner 8.00 20.00
14 Chuck Bednarik 10.00 25.00
15 Chuck Foreman 8.00 20.00
16 Ace Parker 12.00 30.00
17 Cris Collinsworth/99* 10.00 25.00
18 Dan Fouts/60* 35.00 60.00
19 Dan Hampton 20.00 40.00
20 Dan Marino/2*
21 Danny White/85* 20.00 40.00
22 Daryl Johnston/94* 20.00 40.00
23 Dave Casper 8.00 20.00
24 Deion Sanders/58* 50.00 80.00
25 Del Shofner/5*
26 Dick Butkus 35.00 60.00
27 Dub Jones 8.00 20.00
28 Earl Campbell/47* 12.00 30.00
29 Emmitt Smith/11*
30 Forrest Gregg 25.00 50.00
31 Franco Harris 25.00 50.00
32 Frank Gifford/66* 25.00 50.00
33 Fred Dryer/45* 12.00 30.00
34 Gale Sayers/84* 30.00 60.00
35 Garo Yepremian/14*
36 George Blanda/55* 20.00 40.00
37 Harlon Hill 10.00 25.00
38 Howie Long 25.00 50.00
39 Hugh McElhenny/25* 12.00 30.00
40 Jack Youngblood 8.00 20.00
41 James Lofton 8.00 20.00
42 Jan Stenerud/65* 10.00 25.00
43 Jay Novacek 10.00 25.00
44 Jethro Pugh 8.00 20.00
45 Jim Brown/60* 40.00 80.00
46 Jim McMahon/62* 20.00 40.00
47 Jimmy Orr/67* 10.00 25.00
48 Joe Greene/27* 30.00 50.00
49 Joe Klecko 8.00 20.00
50 Joe Namath/30* 50.00 100.00
51 John Elway/4*
52 John Mackey 12.00 30.00
53 John Riggins/57* 20.00 40.00
54 John Stallworth/86* 20.00 40.00
55 Johnny Morris 8.00 20.00
56 Ken Stabler/25* 30.00 60.00
57 Lance Alworth/41* 35.00 60.00
58 Lee Roy Selmon/31* 25.00 50.00
59 Lem Barney/6*
60 Lenny Moore 10.00 25.00
61 Lydell Mitchell/57* 12.00 30.00
62 Marcus Allen/6*
63 Michael Irvin/33* 35.00 60.00
64 Mike Curtis/44* 20.00 40.00
65 Mike Singletary/91* 20.00 40.00
66 Ozzie Newsome 10.00 25.00
67 Paul Hornung 20.00 40.00
68 Paul Warfield/38* 12.00 30.00
69 Randall Cunningham/54* 20.00 40.00
70 Randy White 12.00 30.00
71 Raymond Berry 12.00 30.00
72 Rick Casares/18* 25.00 50.00
73 Roger Craig 10.00 25.00
74 Roger Staubach/66* 50.00 100.00
75 Ronnie Lott/26* 40.00 80.00
76 Sterling Sharpe/82* 20.00 40.00
77 Ted Hendricks 10.00 25.00
78 Tiki Barber 10.00 25.00
79 Tim Brown/46* 35.00 60.00
80 Tommy McDonald 10.00 25.00
81 Troy Aikman/39* 40.00 80.00
82 Warren Moon 20.00 40.00
83 Yale Lary/6*
84 Y.A. Tittle/25* 20.00 40.00

2009 Playoff Contenders Rookie Roll Call

*BLACK/50: .6X TO 1.5X BASIC INSERTS
*GOLD/100: .5X TO 1.2X BASIC INSERTS
1 Ramses Barden .60 1.50
2 Brian Robiskie 1.00 2.50
3 Jeremy Maclin 1.50 4.00
4 Matthew Stafford 5.00 12.00
5 Chris Wells 1.50 4.00
6 Malcolm Jenkins 1.00 2.50
7 Rey Maualuga 1.00 2.50
8 Shonn Greene 1.50 4.00
9 Aaron Curry 1.00 2.50
10 Donald Brown 1.00 2.50
11 Brian Cushing 1.00 2.50
12 LeSean McCoy 2.00 5.00
13 Darrius Heyward-Bey 1.00 2.50
14 Percy Harvin 1.50 4.00
15 Kenny Britt 1.25 3.00
16 Mark Sanchez 3.00 8.00
17 Vontae Davis 1.00 2.50
18 Derrick Williams .75 2.00
19 Brian Orakpo 1.00 2.50
20 Mohamed Massaquoi .75 2.00
21 Michael Crabtree 2.00 5.00
22 Josh Freeman 2.00 5.00
23 Hakeem Nicks 1.50 4.00
24 Knowshon Moreno 1.00 2.50
25 James Laurinaitis 1.00 2.50

2009 Playoff Contenders Round Numbers

*BLACK/50: .6X TO 1.5X BASIC INSERTS
*GOLD/100: .5X TO 1.2X BASIC INSERTS
1 Matthew Stafford 5.00 12.00
Jason Smith
2 Tyson Jackson 1.00 2.50
Aaron Curry
3 Mark Sanchez 3.00 8.00
Darrius Heyward-Bey
4 B.J. Raji 2.00 5.00
Michael Crabtree
5 Aaron Maybin 1.00 2.50
Knowshon Moreno
6 Brian Orakpo 1.00 2.50
Malcolm Jenkins
7 Brian Cushing 1.00 2.50
Larry English
8 Josh Freeman 1.50 4.00
Jeremy Maclin
9 Brandon Pettigrew 1.50 4.00
Percy Harvin
10 Vontae Davis 2.50 6.00
Clay Matthews
11 Donald Brown 1.50 4.00
Hakeem Nicks
12 Kenny Britt 1.50 4.00
Chris Wells
13 James Laurinaitis 1.00 2.50
Brian Robiskie
14 Rey Maualuga 1.00 2.50
Everette Brown
15 Mohamed Massaquoi 2.00 5.00
LeSean McCoy
16 Shonn Greene 1.50 4.00
Glen Coffee
17 Derrick Williams 1.00 2.50
Brandon Tate
18 Mike Wallace 2.00 5.00
Ramses Barden
19 Patrick Turner 1.00 2.50
Jared Cook
20 Deon Butler .75 2.00
Chase Coffman
21 Juaquin Iglesias .75 2.00
Travis Beckum
22 Stephen McGee 1.00 2.50
Mike Thomas
23 Shawn Nelson 1.00 2.50
Louis Murphy
24 Tony Fiammetta .75 2.00
Andre Brown
25 Kenny McKinley 1.00 2.50
Jarett Dillard

2009 Playoff Contenders ROY Contenders

*BLACK/50: .6X TO 1.5X BASIC INSERTS
*GOLD/100: .5X TO 1.2X BASIC INSERTS
1 Percy Harvin 1.50 4.00
2 Ramses Barden .60 1.50
3 B.J. Raji 1.00 2.50
4 Matthew Stafford 5.00 12.00
5 Johnny Knox 1.50 4.00
6 Brian Robiskie 1.00 2.50
7 James Laurinaitis 1.00 2.50
8 Kenny Britt 1.25 3.00
9 Mark Sanchez 3.00 8.00
10 Aaron Curry 1.00 2.50
11 Brandon Pettigrew 1.00 2.50
12 Hakeem Nicks 1.50 4.00
13 Derrick Williams .75 2.00
14 Mohamed Massaquoi .75 2.00
15 Shonn Greene 1.50 4.00
16 Brian Orakpo 1.00 2.50
17 Chris Wells 1.50 4.00
18 Darrius Heyward-Bey 1.00 2.50
19 Jeremy Maclin 1.50 4.00
20 Tyson Jackson .75 2.00
21 Josh Freeman 2.00 5.00
22 Brian Cushing 1.00 2.50
23 LeSean McCoy 2.00 5.00
24 Knowshon Moreno 1.00 2.50
25 Donald Brown 1.00 2.50

2010 Playoff Contenders

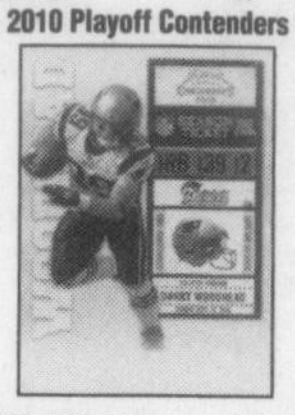

COMP.SET w/o RC's (100) 8.00 20.00
EXCH EXPIRATION: 8/16/2012
1 Larry Fitzgerald .30 .75
2 Steve Breaston .20 .50
3 Tim Hightower .20 .50
4 Matt Ryan .30 .75
5 Michael Turner .20 .50
6 Roddy White .25 .60
7 Anquan Boldin .25 .60
8 Joe Flacco .30 .75
9 Ray Rice .25 .60
10 Lee Evans .25 .60
11 Fred Jackson .30 .75
12 Ryan Fitzpatrick .30 .75
13 DeAngelo Williams .25 .60
14 Jonathan Stewart .25 .60
15 Steve Smith .25 .60
16 Jay Cutler .30 .75
17 Johnny Knox .25 .60
18 Matt Forte .25 .60
19 Carson Palmer .25 .60
20 Cedric Benson .25 .60
21 Chad Ochocinco .25 .60
22 Ben Watson .20 .50
23 Josh Cribbs .30 .75
24 Peyton Hillis .30 .75
25 Jason Witten .30 .75
26 Miles Austin .30 .75
27 Tony Romo .40 1.00
28 Brandon Lloyd .25 .60
29 Knowshon Moreno .25 .60
30 Kyle Orton .25 .60
31 Calvin Johnson .30 .75
32 Matthew Stafford .30 .75
33 Brandon Pettigrew .20 .50
34 Aaron Rodgers .40 1.00
35 Clay Matthews .30 .75
36 Donald Driver .25 .60
37 Andre Johnson .25 .60
38 Arian Foster .25 .60
39 Matt Schaub .25 .60
40 Dallas Clark .25 .60
41 Peyton Manning .50 1.25
42 Reggie Wayne .25 .60
43 David Garrard .25 .60
44 Maurice Jones-Drew .25 .60
45 Mike Sims-Walker .25 .60
46 Dwayne Bowe .25 .60
47 Jamaal Charles .25 .60
48 Matt Cassel .25 .60
49 Brandon Marshall .25 .60
50 Chad Henne .25 .60
51 Ronnie Brown .25 .60
52 Adrian Peterson .50 1.25
53 Brett Favre .75 2.00
54 Percy Harvin .30 .75
55 Randy Moss .30 .75
56 Danny Woodhead RC 2.50 6.00
57 BenJarvus Green-Ellis .30 .75
58 Tom Brady .50 1.25
59 Wes Welker .30 .75
60 Drew Brees .30 .75
61 Marques Colston .25 .60
62 Reggie Bush .30 .75
63 Ahmad Bradshaw .25 .60
64 Eli Manning .30 .75
65 Hakeem Nicks .25 .60
66 Braylon Edwards .25 .60
67 Mark Sanchez .30 .75
68 Shonn Greene .25 .60
69 Bruce Gradkowski .20 .50
70 Darren McFadden .25 .60
71 Darrius Heyward-Bey .25 .60
72 DeSean Jackson .25 .60
73 Jeremy Maclin .25 .60
74 LeSean McCoy .25 .60
75 Michael Vick .40 1.00
76 Ben Roethlisberger .30 .75
77 Mike Wallace .25 .60
78 Rashard Mendenhall .25 .60
79 Troy Polamalu .30 .75
80 Antonio Gates .25 .60
81 Malcom Floyd .25 .60
82 Philip Rivers .30 .75
83 Frank Gore .25 .60
84 Michael Crabtree .30 .75
85 Vernon Davis .25 .60
86 Mike Williams USC .25 .60
87 Marshawn Lynch .25 .60
88 Matt Hasselbeck .20 .50
89 Danny Amendola .30 .75
90 Mark Clayton .20 .50
91 Steven Jackson .25 .60
92 Cadillac Williams .25 .60
93 Josh Freeman .30 .75
94 Kellen Winslow Jr. .25 .60
95 Chris Johnson .30 .75
96 Kenny Britt .25 .60
97 Vince Young .20 .50
98 Chris Cooley .25 .60
99 Donovan McNabb .30 .75
100 Anthony Armstrong RC 1.50 4.00
101 Aaron Hernandez AU RC 12.50 25.00
102 Andrew Quarless AU RC 8.00 20.00
103 Anthony Dixon AU/360* RC 15.00 40.00
104 Anthony McCoy AU RC 5.00 12.00
105 Antonio Brown AU RC 20.00 40.00
106 Blair White AU/75* RC 75.00 150.00
107 Brandon Banks AU/500* RC 8.00 20.00
108 Brandon Graham AU/306* RC 6.00 15.00
109 Brandon Spikes AU/500* RC 8.00 20.00
110 Brody Eldridge AU RC 8.00 20.00
111 Bryan Bulaga AU RC 6.00 15.00
112 Carlos Dunlap AU RC 10.00 25.00
113 Carlton Mitchell AU/496* RC 10.00 25.00
114 Chris Cook AU RC 6.00 15.00
115 Chris Ivory AU/500* RC 8.00 20.00
116 Chris McGaha AU/441* RC 6.00 15.00
117 Clay Harbor AU RC 6.00 15.00
118 Corey Wootton AU RC 5.00 12.00
119 Dan LeFevour AU/455* RC 8.00 20.00
120 Dan Williams AU RC 5.00 12.00
121 Danario Alexander AU/300* RC 10.00 25.00
122 David Gettis AU RC 5.00 12.00
123 David Nelson AU/500* RC 10.00 20.00
124 David Reed AU RC 6.00 15.00
125 Deji Karim AU RC 6.00 15.00
126 Dennis Pitta AU/500* RC 8.00 20.00
127 Derrick Morgan AU RC 5.00 12.00
128 Devin McCourty AU RC 6.00 15.00
129 Dezmon Briscoe AU/495* RC EXCH 10.00 25.00
130 Dominique Curry AU/190* RC 30.00 80.00
131 Dominique Franks AU RC 4.00 10.00
132 Donald Jones AU RC 8.00 20.00
133 Dorin Dickerson AU RC 8.00 20.00
134 Duke Calhoun AU RC 6.00 15.00
135 Earl Thomas AU RC 6.00 15.00
136 Ed Dickson AU RC 6.00 15.00
137 Ed Wang AU/500* RC 8.00 20.00
138 Everson Griffen AU RC 5.00 12.00
139 Fendi Onobun AU RC 6.00 15.00
140 Garrett Graham AU RC 6.00 15.00
141 Jacoby Ford AU RC 8.00 20.00
142 James Starks AU RC 8.00 20.00
143 Jared Odrick AU RC 8.00 20.00
144 Jason Pierre-Paul AU RC 15.00 30.00
145 Jason Worilds AU RC 6.00 15.00
146 Javier Arenas AU RC 6.00 15.00
147 Jeremy Horne AU/500* RC 10.00 25.00
148 Jeremy Williams AU/194* RC 20.00 50.00
149A Jerry Hughes AU RC 6.00 15.00
149B Joique Bell AU SP RC UER 30.00 80.00
(card was intended to be #156)
150 Jim Dray AU RC 5.00 12.00
151 Jimmy Graham AU/358* RC 75.00 125.00
152 Joe Haden AU RC 8.00 20.00
153 Joe Webb AU RC 8.00 20.00
154 John Conner AU RC 6.00 15.00
155 John Skelton AU RC 8.00 20.00
157 Kareem Jackson AU/500* RC 12.00 30.00
158 Keiland Williams AU/500* RC 8.00 20.00
159 Keith Toston AU RC 6.00 15.00
160 Kerry Meier AU RC 5.00 12.00
161 Koa Misi AU/190* RC 12.00 30.00
162 Kyle Williams AU/436* RC 10.00 25.00
163 Sergio Kindle AU RC 6.00 15.00
164 Lamarr Houston AU/500* RC 6.00 15.00
165 LeGarrette Blount AU/287* RC 25.00 50.00
166 Lonyae Miller AU/412* RC 10.00 25.00
167 Marc Mariani AU RC 8.00 20.00
168 Marlon Moore AU/500* RC 6.00 15.00
169 Max Hall AU/401* RC 6.00 15.00
170 Max Komar AU/500* RC EXCH 10.00 25.00
171 Michael Hoomanawanui AU RC 8.00 20.00
172 Mickey Shuler AU RC 6.00 15.00
173 Morgan Burnett AU RC 6.00 15.00
174 Nate Allen AU RC 8.00 20.00
175 Nate Byham AU RC 5.00 12.00
176 NaVorro Bowman AU RC 6.00 15.00
177 Patrick Robinson AU RC 6.00 15.00
178 Perrish Cox AU RC 5.00 12.00
179 Preston Parker AU/190* RC 12.00 30.00
180 Ricky Sapp AU RC 5.00 12.00
181 Riley Cooper AU RC 6.00 15.00
182 Roberto Wallace AU RC 6.00 15.00
183 Russell Okung AU/174* RC 30.00 60.00
184 Rusty Smith AU/190* RC 30.00 60.00
185 Michael Palmer AU RC 8.00 20.00
186 Sean Lee AU RC 10.00 20.00
187 Sean Weatherspoon AU RC 5.00 12.00
188 Chris Gronkowski AU/500* RC 10.00 25.00
189 Seyi Ajirotutu AU/384* RC 6.00 15.00
190 Shay Hodge AU RC 5.00 12.00
191 Stephen Williams AU RC 5.00 12.00
192 T.J. Ward AU/500* RC 6.00 15.00
193 Taylor Mays AU RC 6.00 15.00
194 Thaddeus Lewis AU/190* RC 25.00 60.00
195 Tony Moeaki AU RC 8.00 20.00
196 Tony Pike AU RC 8.00 20.00
197 Trent Williams AU/500* RC EXCH 12.00 30.00
198 Tyson Alualu AU/190* RC 25.00 60.00
199 Victor Cruz AU RC 60.00 100.00
200 Zac Robinson AU/340* RC 20.00 50.00
201A Andre Roberts RJ AU/498* RC 5.00 12.00
(red jersey)
201B Andre Roberts WJ AU/498* RC 5.00 12.00
(white jersey)
202A Armanti Edwards BJ AU RC 5.00 12.00
(black jersey)
202B Armanti Edwards WJ AU RC 5.00 12.00
(white jersey)
203A Arrelious Benn RJ AU/285* RC 10.00 25.00
(red jersey)
203B Arrelious Benn WJ AU/285* RC 10.00 25.00
(white jersey)
204A Ben Tate Cut AU RC 10.00 25.00
(cutting pose)
204B Ben Tate Stnd AU RC 10.00 25.00
(standing facing forward)
205A Brandon LaFell BJ AU/312* RC 6.00 15.00
(black jersey)
205B Brandon LaFell WJ AU/312* RC 6.00 15.00
(white jersey)
206A C.J. Spiller BJ AU/372* RC 15.00 40.00
(blue jersey)
206B C.J. Spiller WJ AU/372* RC 15.00 40.00
(white jersey)
207A Colt McCoy BJ AU/394* RC 20.00 50.00
(brown jersey)
207B Colt McCoy WJ AU/394* RC 20.00 50.00
(white jersey)
208A Damian Williams BJ AU/412* RC 5.00 12.00
(blue jersey)
208B Damian Williams WJ AU/412* RC 5.00 12.00
(white jersey)
209A Demaryius Thomas Cut AU RC 25.00 40.00
(cutting to his left)
209B Demaryius Thomas Fwd AU RC 25.00 40.00
(running forward)
210A Dexter McCluster RJ AU RC 6.00 15.00
(red jersey)
210B Dexter McCluster WJ AU RC 6.00 15.00
(white jersey)
211A Dez Bryant BJ AU/360* RC 50.00 100.00
(blue jersey)
211B Dez Bryant WJ AU/360* RC 50.00 100.00
(white jersey)
212A Emmanuel Sanders BJ AU RC 8.00 20.00
(black jersey)
212B Emmanuel Sanders WJ AU RC 8.00 20.00
(white jerey)
213A Eric Berry Stnd AU/97* RC 30.00 60.00
(standing, feet planted)
213B Eric Berry Run AU/97* RC 30.00 60.00
(running pose)
214A Eric Decker BJ AU/492* RC 15.00 30.00
(blue jersey)
214B Eric Decker OJ AU/492* RC 15.00 30.00
(orange jersey)
215A Gerald McCoy RJ AU/82* RC 30.00 80.00
(red jersey)
215B Gerald McCoy WJ AU/82* RC 30.00 80.00
(white jersey)
216A Golden Tate Cut AU RC 6.00 15.00
(cutting pose)
216B Golden Tate Run AU RC 6.00 15.00
(running pose)
217A Jahvid Best BJ AU RC 15.00 30.00
(blue jersey)
217B Jahvid Best WJ AU RC 15.00 30.00
(white jersey)
218A Jermaine Gresham BJ AU/500* RC 6.00 15.00
(black jersey)
218B Jermaine Gresham WJ AU/500* RC 6.00 15.00
(white jersey)
219A Jimmy Clausen BJ AU/403* RC 8.00 20.00
(black jersey)
219B Jimmy Clausen WJ AU/403* RC 8.00 20.00
(white jersey)
220A Joe McKnight GJ AU/392* RC 8.00 20.00
(green jersey)
220B Joe McKnight WJ AU/392* RC 8.00 20.00
(white jersey)
221A Jonathan Dwyer AU/439* RC 6.00 15.00
221B Jonathan Dwyer AU/439* RC 6.00 15.00
222A Jordan Shipley BJ AU/499* RC 8.00 20.00
(black jersey)
222B Jordan Shipley WJ AU/499* RC 8.00 20.00
(white jersey)
223A Marcus Easley Cut AU RC 5.00 12.00
(cutting to his left)
223B Marcus Easley Fwd AU RC 5.00 12.00
(running slightly forward)
224A Mardy Gilyard Cut AU RC 6.00 15.00
(cutting to his right)
224B Mardy Gilyard Fwd AU RC 6.00 15.00
(running forward)
225A Mike Kafka GJ AU RC 8.00 20.00
(green jersey)
225B Mike Kafka WJ AU RC 8.00 20.00
(white jersey)
226A Mike Williams AU/391* RC 15.00 40.00
(red jersey)
226B Mike Williams AU/391* RC 15.00 40.00
(white jersey)
227A Montario Hardesty Jsy # AU RC 8.00 20.00
(jersey number visible)
227B Montario Hardesty No # AU RC 8.00 20.00
(jersey number obscured)
228A Ndamukong Suh BJ AU/326* RC 30.00 60.00
(blue jersey)
228B Ndamukong Suh WJ AU/326* RC 30.00 60.00
(white jersey)
229A Rob Gronkowski BJ AU/499* RC 40.00 80.00
(blue jersey)
229B Rob Gronkowski WJ AU/499* RC 40.00 80.00
(white jersey)
230A Rolando McClain Run AU/378* RC 6.00 15.00
(running pose)
230B Rolando McClain Set AU/378* RC 6.00 15.00
(feet set)
231A Ryan Mathews Shld AU/300* RC 30.00 60.00
(sun shield on facemask)
231B Ryan Mathews No Shld AU/300* RC 30.00 60.00
(no shield on facemask)
232A Sam Bradford Fwd AU/377* RC 75.00 150.00
(facing forward. throwing)
232B Sam Bradford Lft AU/377* RC 75.00 150.00
(facing to his left)
233A Taylor Price Fwd AU RC 6.00 15.00
(facing forward)
233B Taylor Price Rgt AU RC 6.00 15.00
(facing right)
234A Tim Tebow BJ AU/400* RC 90.00 175.00
(blue jersey)
234B Tim Tebow WJ AU/400* RC 90.00 175.00
(white jersey)
235A Toby Gerhart Jsy # AU/495* RC 10.00 25.00
(jersey number visible)
235B Toby Gerhart No Jsy # AU/495* RC 10.00 25.00
(jersey number obscured)

2010 Playoff Contenders Playoff Ticket

*1-99 VETS: 3X TO 8X BASIC CARDS
COMMON ROOKIE (100-200) 2.50 6.00
ROOKIE SEMISTAR 100-200 3.00 8.00
ROOKIE UNL.STAR 100-200 4.00 10.00
COMMON ROOKIE (201-235) 2.50 6.00
ROOKIE UNL.STAR 201-235 3.00 8.00
201-235 HAVE TWO CARDS OF EQUAL VALUE
STATED PRINT RUN 99 SER.#'d SETS
56 Danny Woodhead 12.00 30.00
100 Anthony Armstrong 5.00 12.00
101 Aaron Hernandez 6.00 15.00
102 Andrew Quarless 4.00 10.00
107 Brandon Banks 5.00 12.00
109 Brandon Spikes 4.00 10.00
115 Chris Ivory 5.00 12.00
117 Clay Harbor 4.00 10.00
123 David Nelson 4.00 10.00
128 Devin McCourty 4.00 10.00
142 James Starks 6.00 15.00
153 Joe Webb 4.00 10.00
158 Keiland Williams 4.00 10.00
165 LeGarrette Blount 6.00 15.00
167 Marc Mariani 4.00 10.00
169 Max Hall 4.00 10.00
172 Mickey Shuler 4.00 10.00
188 Chris Gronkowski 4.00 10.00
195 Tony Moeaki 4.00 10.00
197 Trent Williams 4.00 10.00
206A C.J. Spiller 5.00 12.00
207A Colt McCoy 6.00 15.00
209A Demaryius Thomas 4.00 10.00
210A Dexter McCluster 3.00 8.00
211A Dez Bryant 10.00 25.00
212A Emmanuel Sanders 3.00 8.00
213A Eric Berry 3.00 8.00
215A Gerald McCoy 3.00 8.00
216A Golden Tate 3.00 8.00
217A Jahvid Best 5.00 12.00
218A Jermaine Gresham 4.00 10.00
219A Jimmy Clausen 3.00 8.00
222A Jordan Shipley 3.00 8.00
226A Mike Williams 5.00 12.00
228A Ndamukong Suh 8.00 20.00
229A Rob Gronkowski 8.00 20.00
230A Rolando McClain 3.00 8.00
231A Ryan Mathews 6.00 15.00
232A Sam Bradford 25.00 50.00
234A Tim Tebow 15.00 40.00
235A Toby Gerhart 3.00 8.00

2010 Playoff Contenders Draft Class

*BLACK/50: .8X TO 2X BASIC INSERTS
*GOLD/100: .6X TO 1.5X BASIC INSERTS
1 Sam Bradford 3.00 8.00
Tim Tebow
2 C.J. Spiller 1.50 4.00
Ryan Mathews
3 Demaryius Thomas 2.00 5.00
Dez Bryant
4 Jermaine Gresham 2.00 5.00
Rob Gronkowski
5 Mardy Gilyard 2.50 6.00
Sam Bradford
6 Jahvid Best 1.50 4.00
Ndamukong Suh
7 Jermaine Gresham 1.00 2.50
Jordan Shipley
8 Brandon LaFell .75 2.00
Jimmy Clausen
9 Golden Tate .75 2.00
Jimmy Clausen
10 Jermaine Gresham 2.50 6.00
Sam Bradford
11 Colt McCoy 1.50 4.00
Jordan Shipley
12 Demaryius Thomas 2.50 6.00
Tim Tebow
13 Dexter McCluster .75 2.00
Tony Moeaki
14 Arrelious Benn 1.25 3.00
Mike Williams
15 Aaron Hernandez 2.00 5.00
Rob Gronkowski
16 Gerald McCoy 1.50 4.00
Ndamukong Suh
17 Russell Okung .75 2.00
Trent Williams
18 Eric Berry .75 2.00
Joe Haden
19 Brandon Graham .75 2.00
Rolando McClain
20 Derrick Morgan 1.25 3.00
Jason Pierre-Paul
21 Colt McCoy 1.50 4.00
Jimmy Clausen
22 Dexter McCluster 1.25 3.00
Jahvid Best
23 Arrelious Benn .75 2.00
Golden Tate
24 Aaron Hernandez 1.25 3.00
Tony Moeaki
25 Dez Bryant 2.00 5.00
Sean Lee

2010 Playoff Contenders Golden Ticket

EXCH EXPIRATION: 8/16/2012

2010 Playoff Contenders Legendary Contenders

*BLACK/50: .8X TO 2X BASIC INSERTS
*GOLD/100: .6X TO 1.5X BASIC INSERTS
1 Joe Namath 1.50 4.00
2 Lydell Mitchell .75 2.00
3 Jim Brown 1.50 4.00
4 Charley Taylor .75 2.00
5 Steve Largent 1.25 3.00
6 Pete Retzlaff .75 2.00
7 Barry Sanders 2.00 5.00
8 Todd Christensen .75 2.00
9 Joe Montana 2.50 6.00
10 Rick Casares .75 2.00
11 John Elway 2.00 5.00
12 Randall Cunningham 1.00 2.50
13 Bart Starr 2.00 5.00
14 Fred Biletnikoff 1.25 3.00
15 Art Monk 1.25 3.00
16 Dave Casper .75 2.00
17 Floyd Little .75 2.00
18 Jim Kelly 1.25 3.00
19 Michael Irvin 1.00 2.50
20 Daryle Lamonica .75 2.00
21 Leroy Kelly 1.00 2.50
22 Jim Plunkett 1.00 2.50
23 Jim Taylor 1.25 3.00
24 Fran Tarkenton 1.25 3.00
25 Don Maynard 1.00 2.50

2010 Playoff Contenders Legendary Contenders Autographs

PANINI ANNOUNCED PRINT RUNS 15-250
1 Joe Namath/25* 50.00 100.00
2 Lydell Mitchell/250* 8.00 20.00
3 Jim Brown/25* 40.00 80.00
4 Charley Taylor/200* 8.00 20.00
5 Steve Largent/65* 12.00 30.00
6 Pete Retzlaff/250* 8.00 20.00
7 Barry Sanders/25* 75.00 150.00
8 Todd Christensen/100* 8.00 20.00
9 Joe Montana/20* 75.00 150.00
10 Rick Casares/250* 8.00 20.00
11 John Elway/20* 100.00 175.00
12 Randall Cunningham/45* 20.00 50.00
13 Bart Starr/40 75.00 150.00
14 Fred Biletnikoff/55* 20.00 40.00
15 Art Monk/35* 30.00 60.00
16 Dave Casper/40* 12.00 30.00
17 Floyd Little/50* 10.00 25.00
18 Jim Kelly/25* 30.00 60.00
19 Michael Irvin/15* 50.00 100.00
20 Daryle Lamonica/55* 12.00 30.00
21 Leroy Kelly/75* 10.00 25.00
22 Jim Plunkett/100* 10.00 25.00
23 Jim Taylor/60* 30.00 60.00
24 Fran Tarkenton/45* 25.00 50.00
25 Don Maynard/40* 10.00 25.00

2010 Playoff Contenders Rookie Ink

ANNOUNCED PRINT RUN 50
EXCH EXPIRATION: 8/16/2012
1 Colt McCoy 40.00 80.00
2 Jahvid Best 25.00 50.00
3 Taylor Price 10.00 25.00
4 Toby Gerhart 12.00 30.00
5 Andre Roberts 10.00 25.00
6 Emmanuel Sanders 10.00 25.00
7 Rob Gronkowski 30.00 60.00
8 Brandon LaFell 10.00 25.00
9 Rolando McClain 10.00 25.00
10 Jordan Shipley 10.00 25.00
11 Dexter McCluster 10.00 25.00
12 Armanti Edwards 10.00 25.00
13 Jermaine Gresham 12.00 30.00
14 Eric Berry 25.00 60.00
15 Sam Bradford 100.00 200.00
16 Ndamukong Suh 30.00 60.00
17 Demaryius Thomas 12.00 30.00
18 Arrelious Benn 10.00 25.00
19 Tim Tebow 100.00 200.00
20 Ryan Mathews 25.00 60.00
21 Mardy Gilyard 10.00 25.00
22 Eric Decker 12.00 30.00
23 Golden Tate 10.00 25.00
24 C.J. Spiller 15.00 40.00
25 Dez Bryant 50.00 100.00
26 Damian Williams 10.00 25.00
27 Gerald McCoy 20.00 40.00
28 Jonathan Dwyer EXCH 10.00 25.00
29 Jimmy Clausen 10.00 25.00
30 Mike Williams 20.00 50.00

2010 Playoff Contenders Rookie Roll Call

*BLACK/50: .8X TO 2X BASIC INSERTS
*GOLD/100: .6X TO 1.5X BASIC INSERTS
1 Sam Bradford 3.00 8.00
2 Tim Tebow 3.00 8.00
3 Jimmy Clausen .75 2.00
4 Colt McCoy 1.50 4.00
5 C.J. Spiller 1.25 3.00
6 Ryan Mathews 1.50 4.00
7 Jahvid Best 1.25 3.00
8 Ndamukong Suh 1.50 4.00
9 Demaryius Thomas 1.00 2.50
10 Dez Bryant 2.50 6.00
11 Golden Tate .75 2.00
12 Dexter McCluster .75 2.00
13 Jermaine Gresham 1.00 2.50
14 Rob Gronkowski 2.00 5.00
15 Arrelious Benn .75 2.00
16 Marc Mariani .75 2.00
17 Mardy Gilyard .75 2.00
18 Eric Decker 1.00 2.50
19 Toby Gerhart .75 2.00
20 Tony Moeaki .75 2.00
21 Jordan Shipley .75 2.00
22 Mike Williams 1.25 3.00
23 Aaron Hernandez 1.25 3.00
24 Max Hall .75 2.00
25 Rolando McClain .75 2.00

2010 Playoff Contenders ROY Contenders

*BLACK/50: .8X TO 2X BASIC INSERTS
*GOLD/100: .6X TO 1.5X BASIC INSERTS
1 Sam Bradford 3.00 8.00
2 Aaron Hernandez 1.25 3.00
3 Jahvid Best 1.25 3.00
4 Jimmy Clausen .75 2.00
5 Ryan Mathews 1.50 4.00
6 C.J. Spiller 1.25 3.00
7 Mike Williams 1.25 3.00
8 Dexter McCluster .75 2.00
9 Jordan Shipley .75 2.00
10 Golden Tate .75 2.00
11 Rob Gronkowski 2.00 5.00
12 Dez Bryant 2.50 6.00
13 Demaryius Thomas 1.00 2.50
14 Marc Mariani .75 2.00
15 Brandon LaFell .75 2.00
16 T.J. Ward .75 2.00
17 Mardy Gilyard .75 2.00
18 Tony Moeaki .75 2.00
19 Arrelious Benn .75 2.00
20 Max Hall .75 2.00
21 Nate Allen .75 2.00
22 Ndamukong Suh 1.50 4.00
23 Rolando McClain .75 2.00
24 Brandon Graham .60 1.50
25 Sean Weatherspoon .75 2.00

2010 Playoff Contenders Super Bowl Ticket

*BLACK/50: .8X TO 2X BASIC INSERTS
*GOLD/100: .6X TO 1.5X BASIC INSERTS
1 Bart Starr 2.50 6.00
2 Jim Taylor 1.50 4.00
3 Willie Wood 1.25 3.00
4 Bart Starr 2.50 6.00
5 Willie Davis 1.25 3.00
6 Boyd Dowler 1.25 3.00
7 Joe Namath 2.00 5.00
8 Don Maynard 1.25 3.00
9 Len Dawson 1.50 4.00
10 Willie Lanier 1.00 2.50
11 Bobby Bell 1.00 2.50
12 Jan Stenerud 1.00 2.50
13 Chuck Howley 1.00 2.50
14 Roger Staubach 2.00 5.00
15 Cliff Harris 1.00 2.50
16 John Niland 1.00 2.50
17 Bob Lilly 1.25 3.00
18 Lee Roy Jordan 1.25 3.00
19 Mel Renfro 1.00 2.50
20 Larry Little 1.00 2.50
21 Paul Warfield 1.25 3.00
22 Jack Lambert 1.50 4.00
23 L.C. Greenwood 1.25 3.00
24 Fred Biletnikoff 1.50 4.00
25 Willie Brown 1.00 2.50
26 Dave Casper 1.00 2.50
27 Ken Stabler 1.50 4.00
28 Randy White 1.25 3.00
29 Tony Dorsett 1.50 4.00
30 Ed Too Tall Jones 1.25 3.00
31 D.D. Lewis 1.00 2.50
32 Terry Bradshaw 2.00 5.00
33 Terry Bradshaw 2.00 5.00
34 Jim Plunkett 1.25 3.00
35 Joe Montana 3.00 8.00
36 Russ Grimm 1.00 2.50
37 Jim Plunkett 1.25 3.00
38 Joe Montana 3.00 8.00
39 William Perry 1.00 2.50
40 Jim McMahon 1.25 3.00
41 Phil Simms 1.25 3.00
42 Doug Williams 1.25 3.00
43 Jerry Rice 2.50 6.00
44 Joe Montana 3.00 8.00
45 Tom Rathman 1.00 2.50
46 Ottis Anderson 1.00 2.50
47 Art Monk 1.50 4.00
48 Troy Aikman 2.00 5.00
49 Mark Stepnoski 1.00 2.50
50 Emmitt Smith 2.50 6.00
51 Michael Irvin 1.25 3.00
52 Darren Woodson 1.25 3.00
53 Steve Young 2.00 5.00
54 Brent Jones 1.00 2.50
55 John Taylor 1.00 2.50
56 Deion Sanders 1.50 4.00
57 Rod Woodson 1.50 4.00
58 Brett Favre 4.00 10.00
59 Terrell Davis 1.50 4.00
60 Ed McCaffrey 1.00 2.50
61 John Elway 2.50 6.00
62 Marshall Faulk 1.25 3.00
63 Tom Brady 2.50 6.00
64 Tom Brady 2.50 6.00
65 Tom Brady 2.50 6.00
66 Ben Roethlisberger 1.50 4.00
67 Peyton Manning 2.50 6.00
68 Reggie Wayne 1.25 3.00
69 Eli Manning 1.50 4.00
70 Brandon Jacobs 1.25 3.00
71 Ben Roethlisberger 1.50 4.00
72 Santonio Holmes 1.25 3.00
73 Drew Brees 1.50 4.00
74 Keyshawn Johnson 1.00 2.50
75 Marques Colston 1.25 3.00

2010 Playoff Contenders Super Bowl Ticket Autographs

PANINI ANNOUNCED PRINT RUNS 1-250
5 Willie Davis/250* 15.00 40.00
6 Boyd Dowler/250* 10.00 25.00
7 Joe Namath/25* 50.00 100.00
8 Don Maynard/15* 15.00 40.00
9 Len Dawson/15* 25.00 50.00
10 Willie Lanier/65* 12.00 30.00
11 Bobby Bell/35* 12.00 30.00
12 Jan Stenerud/75* 10.00 25.00
15 Cliff Harris/75* 12.00 30.00
16 John Niland/65* 10.00 25.00
17 Bob Lilly/100* 12.00 30.00
18 Lee Roy Jordan/35* 12.00 30.00
19 Mel Renfro/25* 15.00 40.00
20 Larry Little/50* 10.00 25.00
21 Paul Warfield/15* 15.00 40.00
22 Jack Lambert/76* 40.00 80.00
23 L.C. Greenwood/45* 15.00 40.00
24 Fred Biletnikoff/50* 20.00 50.00
25 Willie Brown/75* 10.00 25.00
26 Dave Casper/20* 12.00 30.00
27 Ken Stabler/25* 20.00 50.00
28 Randy White/30* 15.00 40.00
29 Tony Dorsett/33* 30.00 60.00
30 Ed Too Tall Jones/15* 20.00 50.00
31 D.D. Lewis/20* 12.00 30.00
34 Jim Plunkett/35* 12.00 30.00
35 Joe Montana/20* 125.00 200.00
36 Russ Grimm/65* 12.00 30.00
39 William Perry/45* 12.00 30.00
40 Jim McMahon/25* 30.00 60.00
42 Doug Williams/25* 25.00 50.00
45 Tom Rathman/35* 15.00 40.00
46 Ottis Anderson/50* 12.00 30.00
47 Art Monk/15* 90.00 150.00
49 Mark Stepnoski/25* 15.00 40.00
52 Darren Woodson/15* 20.00 50.00
53 Steve Young/15* 75.00 150.00
60 Ed McCaffrey/25* 25.00 50.00
61 John Elway/20* 125.00 200.00
62 Marshall Faulk/25* 40.00 80.00
70 Brandon Jacobs/15* 12.00 30.00
72 Santonio Holmes/50* 25.00 50.00
74 Keyshawn Johnson/25* 15.00 40.00

2011 Playoff Contenders

COMP.SET w/o RC's (100) 8.00 20.00
OVERALL AUTO ODDS 4 PER HOBBY BOX
EXCH EXPIRATION: 8/8/2013
1 Fred Jackson .30 .75
2 Ryan Fitzpatrick .25 .60
3 Steve Johnson .25 .60
4 Brandon Marshall .25 .60
5 Chad Henne .25 .60
6 Reggie Bush .25 .60
7 Chad Ochocinco .25 .60
8 Deion Branch .20 .50
9 Tom Brady .50 1.25
10 Wes Welker .30 .75
11 Mark Sanchez .30 .75
12 Santonio Holmes .25 .60
13 Shonn Greene .25 .60
14 Anquan Boldin .25 .60
15 Joe Flacco .30 .75
16 Lee Evans .25 .60
17 Ray Rice .25 .60
18 Andre Caldwell .20 .50
19 Cedric Benson .25 .60
20 Rey Maualuga .20 .50
21 Ben Watson .20 .50
22 Colt McCoy .25 .60
23 Peyton Hillis .25 .60
24 Ben Roethlisberger .30 .75
25 Mike Wallace .30 .75
26 Rashard Mendenhall .25 .60
27 Andre Johnson .25 .60
28 Arian Foster .25 .60
29 Matt Schaub .25 .60
30 Dallas Clark .25 .60
31 Peyton Manning .50 1.25
32 Reggie Wayne .25 .60
33 Marcedes Lewis .20 .50
34 Maurice Jones-Drew .25 .60
35 Mike Thomas .25 .60
36 Chris Johnson .25 .60
37 Kenny Britt .25 .60
38 Matt Hasselbeck .25 .60
39 Knowshon Moreno .25 .60
40 Kyle Orton .25 .60
41 Willis McGahee .20 .50
42 Dwayne Bowe .25 .60
43 Jamaal Charles .25 .60
44 Matt Cassel .25 .60
45 Darren McFadden .25 .60
46 Carson Palmer .25 .60
47 Michael Bush .20 .50
48 Malcom Floyd .25 .60
49 Philip Rivers .30 .75
50 Vincent Jackson .25 .60
51 Dez Bryant .30 .75
52 Felix Jones .25 .60
53 Miles Austin .25 .60
54 Tony Romo .30 .75
55 Eli Manning .30 .75
56 Hakeem Nicks .25 .60
57 Mario Manningham .25 .60
58 DeSean Jackson .25 .60
59 LeSean McCoy .25 .60
60 Michael Vick .30 .75
61 DeAngelo Hall .20 .50
62 Santana Moss .25 .60
63 Tim Hightower .20 .50
64 Jay Cutler .25 .60
65 Marion Barber .25 .60
66 Matt Forte .25 .60
67 Calvin Johnson .30 .75
68 Jahvid Best .25 .60
69 Matthew Stafford .30 .75
70 Ndamukong Suh .30 .75
71 Aaron Rodgers .50 1.25
72 Greg Jennings .25 .60
73 Jermichael Finley .25 .60
74 Adrian Peterson .40 1.00
75 Michael Jenkins .20 .50
76 Percy Harvin .25 .60
77 Matt Ryan .30 .75
78 Michael Turner .25 .60
79 Roddy White .25 .60
80 DeAngelo Williams .25 .60
81 Jon Beason .20 .50
82 Steve Smith .25 .60
83 Drew Brees .30 .75
84 Marques Colston .25 .60
85 Pierre Thomas .25 .60
86 Josh Freeman .30 .75
87 LeGarrette Blount .25 .60
88 Mike Williams .25 .60
89 Beanie Wells .25 .60
90 Kevin Kolb .25 .60
91 Larry Fitzgerald .25 .60
92 Alex Smith QB .25 .60
93 Frank Gore .25 .60
94 Vernon Davis .25 .60
95 Marshawn Lynch .25 .60
96 Sidney Rice .25 .60
97 Tarvaris Jackson .20 .50
98 Danny Amendola .25 .60
99 Sam Bradford .30 .75
100 Steven Jackson .25 .60
101 Terrelle Pryor AU RC 12.00 30.00
102 Aaron Williams AU/99* RC EXCH 75.00 150.00
103 Adrian Clayborn AU/114* SP RC 40.00 80.00
104 Ahmad Black AU RC 5.00 12.00
105 Akeem Ayers AU/100* RC 20.00 40.00
106 Aldon Smith AU/102* SP RC 100.00 175.00
107 Aldrick Robinson AU RC 4.00 10.00
108 Alex Henery AU RC 6.00 15.00
109 Allen Bradford AU RC 4.00 10.00
110 Anthony Allen AU RC 4.00 10.00
111 Anthony Castonzo AU RC 4.00 10.00
112 Anthony Sherman AU RC 5.00 12.00
113 Armond Smith AU RC 5.00 12.00
114 Brandon Harris AU RC 4.00 10.00
115 Cameron Heyward AU/99* RC 75.00 125.00
116 Cameron Jordan AU/99* RC 90.00 150.00
117 Casey Matthews AU RC 6.00 15.00
118 Cecil Shorts AU/99* RC 50.00 100.00
119 Charles Clay AU/99* RC 75.00 125.00
120 Colin Cochart AU RC 4.00 10.00
121 Corey Liuget AU RC 4.00 10.00
122 D.J. Williams AU/171* RC 30.00 60.00
123 Da'Quan Bowers AU RC 15.00 30.00
124 Da'Rel Scott AU RC 10.00 25.00
125 Dane Sanzenbacher AU RC 8.00 20.00
126 Darren Evans AU RC 5.00 12.00
127 David Ausberry AU RC 8.00 20.00
128 DeMarco Sampson AU/99* RC EXCH 60.00 120.00
129 Denarius Moore AU RC 15.00 30.00
130 Dion Lewis AU/224* RC 15.00 40.00
131 Doug Baldwin AU RC 10.00 25.00
132 Mark Herzlich AU RC 5.00 12.00
133 Evan Royster AU RC 6.00 15.00
134 Greg Jones AU RC 5.00 12.00
135 Greg McElroy AU/204* RC 25.00 50.00
136 Greg Salas AU RC 5.00 12.00
137 J.J. Watt AU RC 10.00 25.00
138 Jacquizz Rodgers AU RC 6.00 15.00
139 Jamar Newsome AU RC 4.00 10.00
140 Jeremy Kerley AU/82* RC 75.00 150.00
141 Jimmy Smith AU/173* RC 25.00 60.00
142 Joe Lefeged AU RC 5.00 12.00
143 Johnny White AU RC 5.00 12.00
144 Jordan Cameron AU RC 5.00 12.00
145 Josh Portis AU RC 6.00 15.00
146 Julius Thomas AU/99* RC
147 Justin Houston AU RC 6.00 15.00
148 Kealoha Pilares AU/128* RC 30.00 60.00
149 Kris Durham AU RC 5.00 12.00
150 Kyle Adams AU RC 4.00 10.00
151 Lance Kendricks/298* AU RC 12.00 30.00
152 LaQuan Williams AU RC 5.00 12.00
153 Lee Smith AU RC 5.00 12.00
154 Luke Stocker AU RC 5.00 12.00
155 Jake Ballard AU/99* RC EXCH 90.00 150.00
156 Marcus Gilchrist AU RC 4.00 10.00
157 Martez Wilson AU/134* RC 40.00 80.00
158 Mason Foster AU RC 6.00 15.00
159 Bruce Miller AU RC 5.00 12.00
160 Nathan Enderle AU/99* RC EXCH 60.00 120.00
161 Niles Paul AU/152* RC 25.00 50.00
162 Owen Marecic AU/99* RC EXCH 60.00 120.00
163 Phil Taylor AU/371* RC 12.00 30.00
164 Phillip Tanner AU RC 8.00 20.00
165 Prince Amukamara AU/213* RC 25.00 50.00
166 Quinton Carter AU RC 4.00 10.00
167 Rahim Moore AU/316* RC 15.00 30.00
168 Richard Gordon AU RC 5.00 12.00
169 Ricky Stanzi AU RC 15.00 30.00
170 Robert Housler AU RC 5.00 12.00
171 Ronald Johnson AU/192* RC 20.00 50.00
172 Roy Helu AU RC 12.00 30.00
173 Ryan Kerrigan AU RC 6.00 15.00
174 Ryan Taylor AU RC 5.00 12.00
175 Ryan Whalen AU RC 5.00 12.00
176 Jackie Battle AU RC 6.00 15.00
177 Shane Bannon AU RC 4.00 10.00
178 Stanley Havili AU RC 4.00 10.00
179 Stephen Burton AU/140* RC 15.00 40.00
180 Stephen Paea AU RC 8.00 20.00
181 T.J. Yates AU RC 8.00 20.00
182 Tandon Doss AU RC 5.00 12.00
183 Tyler Sash AU/193* RC 25.00 50.00
184 Tyrod Taylor AU RC 8.00 20.00
185 Tyron Smith AU/23* RC 500.00 800.00
186 Virgil Green AU RC 5.00 12.00
187 Weslye Saunders AU/99* RC EXCH 100.00 175.00
188 Curtis Brinkley AU RC 6.00 15.00
189 Zack Pianalto AU RC 5.00 12.00
190 Buster Skrine AU RC 5.00 12.00
191 Chimdi Chekwa AU RC 5.00 12.00
192 Chris Harris AU RC 5.00 12.00
193 Chris White AU RC 5.00 12.00
194 Dan Bailey AU RC 6.00 15.00
195 Henry Hynoski AU RC 8.00 20.00
196 Jacquian Williams AU/99* RC EXCH 75.00 150.00
197 K.J. Wright AU RC 6.00 15.00
199 Patrick Peterson AU/343* RC 40.00 80.00
200 Robert Quinn AU RC 8.00 20.00
201A Marcell Dareus AU RC EXCH 6.00 15.00
202A Randall Cobb AU RC 12.00 30.00
202B Randall Cobb no logo AU/250* 15.00 40.00
203A Ryan Mallett AU RC 40.00 80.00
203B Ryan Mallett no logo AU/25* 150.00 250.00
204A Greg Little AU RC 8.00 20.00
205A Christian Ponder AU RC 25.00 60.00
205B Christian Ponder no logo AU/50* 90.00 150.00
206A Jamie Harper AU RC 6.00 15.00
206B Jamie Harper no logo AU/250* 8.00 20.00
207A Alex Green AU RC 6.00 15.00
208A Austin Pettis AU RC 5.00 12.00
208B Austin Pettis no logo AU/50* 12.00 30.00
209A Ryan Williams AU RC 8.00 20.00
209B Ryan Williams no logo AU/250* 12.00 30.00
210A Taiwan Jones AU RC 6.00 15.00
210B Taiwan Jones no logo AU/25* 90.00 150.00
211A Jake Locker AU RC 50.00 100.00
211B Jake Locker no shldr # AU/50* 125.00 200.00
212A Blaine Gabbert AU RC 20.00 50.00
212B Blaine Gabbert no logo AU/25*
213A Mark Ingram AU RC 20.00 50.00
213B Mark Ingram no logo AU/100* 60.00 120.00
214A Stevan Ridley AU RC EXCH 8.00 20.00
215A Daniel Thomas AU RC 8.00 20.00
216A Jordan Todman AU RC 4.00 10.00
216B Jordan Todman no logo AU/250* 6.00 15.00
217A Shane Vereen AU RC 6.00 15.00
217B Shane Vereen no logo AU/250* 10.00 25.00
218A Titus Young AU RC 8.00 20.00
219A Jonathan Baldwin AU RC 8.00 20.00
219B Jonathan Baldwin no logo AU/250* 12.00 30.00
220A Von Miller AU RC 12.00 30.00
220B Von Miller no logo AU/100* 25.00 50.00
221A Julio Jones AU RC EXCH 20.00 50.00
222A A.J. Green AU RC 40.00 80.00
222B A.J. Green no logo AU/25* 100.00 200.00
223A Bilal Powell AU RC 10.00 25.00
223B Bilal Powell no logo AU/25* 25.00 50.00
224A Kyle Rudolph AU RC 8.00 20.00
224B Kyle Rudolph no watch AU/100* 12.00 30.00
225A Andy Dalton AU RC 50.00 100.00
225B Andy Dalton no logo AU/100* 75.00 150.00
226A Clyde Gates AU RC 5.00 12.00
226B Clyde Gates no logo AU/50* 12.00 30.00
227A Colin Kaepernick AU RC 12.00 30.00
227B Colin Kaepernick no logo AU/250* 15.00 40.00
228A Cam Newton AU RC 175.00 300.00
228B Cam Newton no logo AU/25* 400.00 600.00
229A Mikel Leshoure AU RC 10.00 25.00
229B Mikel Leshoure no logo AU/250* 12.00 30.00
230A Torrey Smith AU RC 10.00 25.00
230B Torrey Smith no logo AU/250* 15.00 40.00
231A DeMarco Murray AU RC 40.00 80.00
231B DeMarco Murray no logo AU/250* 60.00 120.00
(no Riddell logo on helmet)
232A Kendall Hunter AU RC 8.00 20.00
232B Kendall Hunter no logo AU/100* 12.00 30.00
233A Vincent Brown AU RC 6.00 15.00
233B Vincent Brown no logo AU/250* 10.00 25.00
234A Leonard Hankerson AU RC 6.00 15.00
234B Leonard Hankerson no logo AU/100* 12.00 30.00
235A Jerrel Jernigan AU RC 5.00 12.00
235B Jerrel Jernigan no logo AU/50* 12.00 30.00
236A Delone Carter AU RC 6.00 15.00
236B Delone Carter no logo AU/100* 12.00 30.00

2011 Playoff Contenders Playoff Ticket

*1-100 VETS/99: 3X TO 8X BASIC CARDS
COMMON ROOKIE (101-236) 2.50 6.00
ROOKIE SEMISTARS 3.00 8.00
ROOKIE UNL.STARS 4.00 10.00
STATED PRINT RUN 99 SER.#'d SETS
101 Terrelle Pryor 5.00 12.00
106 Aldon Smith 6.00 15.00
129 Denarius Moore 5.00 12.00
131 Doug Baldwin 6.00 15.00
137 J.J. Watt 5.00 12.00
155 Jake Ballard 8.00 20.00
169 Ricky Stanzi 5.00 12.00
172 Roy Helu 8.00 20.00
174 Ryan Taylor 3.00 8.00
176 Jackie Battle 5.00 12.00
181 T.J. Yates 5.00 12.00
185 Tyron Smith 15.00 30.00
187 Weslye Saunders 12.00 30.00
195 Henry Hynoski 10.00 25.00
196 Jacquian Williams 4.00 10.00
198 Nick Fairley 5.00 12.00
199 Patrick Peterson 6.00 15.00
202 Randall Cobb 5.00 12.00
203 Ryan Mallett 8.00 20.00
205 Christian Ponder 8.00 20.00
209 Ryan Williams 5.00 12.00
211 Jake Locker 10.00 25.00
212 Blaine Gabbert 6.00 15.00
213 Mark Ingram 8.00 20.00
215 Daniel Thomas 4.00 10.00
218 Titus Young 5.00 12.00
220 Von Miller 5.00 12.00
221 Julio Jones 8.00 20.00
222 A.J. Green 8.00 20.00
225 Andy Dalton 10.00 25.00
227 Colin Kaepernick 5.00 12.00
228 Cam Newton 25.00 60.00
230 Torrey Smith 5.00 12.00
231 DeMarco Murray 8.00 20.00

2011 Playoff Contenders Draft Class

*BLACK/50: .8X TO 2X BASIC INSERTS
*GOLD/100: .6X TO 1.5X BASIC INSERTS
1 Colin Kaepernick 1.00 2.50
Kendall Hunter
2 A.J. Green 2.00 5.00
Andy Dalton
3 Marcell Dareus .75 2.00
Aaron Williams
4 Von Miller 1.00 2.50
Rahim Moore
5 Greg Little .75 2.00
Jordan Cameron
6 Adrian Clayborn .75 2.00
Da'Quan Bowers
7 Vincent Brown .75 2.00
Jordan Todman
8 Jonathan Baldwin 1.00 2.50
Ricky Stanzi
9 Daniel Thomas .75 2.00
Clyde Gates
10 Julio Jones 1.50 4.00
Jacquizz Rodgers
11 Jerrel Jernigan .60 1.50
Da'Rel Scott
12 Blaine Gabbert 1.25 3.00
Cecil Shorts
13 Jeremy Kerley .75 2.00
Scotty McKnight
14 Bilal Powell .75 2.00
Greg McElroy
15 Randall Cobb 1.00 2.50
Alex Green
16 Christian Ponder 1.50 4.00
Kyle Rudolph
17 Shane Vereen .75 2.00
Stevan Ridley
18 Taiwan Jones 1.00 2.50
Denarius Moore
19 Austin Pettis .75 2.00
Greg Salas
20 Torrey Smith 1.00 2.50
Tandon Doss
21 Leonard Hankerson 1.00 2.50
Niles Paul
22 Roy Helu 1.25 3.00
Evan Royster
23 Cameron Jordan 1.50 4.00
Mark Ingram
24 J.J. Watt 1.00 2.50
Brandon Harris
25 Jake Locker 2.00 5.00
Jamie Harper

2011 Playoff Contenders Legendary Contenders

*BLACK/50: .8X TO 2X BASIC INSERTS
*GOLD/100: .6X TO 1.5X BASIC INSERTS
1 Art Monk 1.00 2.50
2 Earl Campbell 1.25 3.00
3 Bill Bates 1.00 2.50
4 Cris Collinsworth 1.00 2.50
5 Emmitt Smith 2.00 5.00
6 Bruce Smith 1.00 2.50
7 Steve Largent 1.25 3.00
8 Gale Sayers 1.25 3.00
9 Darrell Green 1.00 2.50
10 Don Maynard 1.00 2.50
11 Larry Csonka 1.00 2.50
12 Dick Lane .75 2.00
13 Fred Biletnikoff 1.00 2.50
14 Barry Sanders 2.00 5.00
15 Alan Page 1.00 2.50
16 Henry Ellard .75 2.00
17 Bo Jackson 1.50 4.00
18 John Randle .75 2.00
19 Brent Jones .75 2.00
20 Curtis Martin 1.25 3.00
21 Deacon Jones 1.00 2.50
22 Tom Rathman .75 2.00
23 Danny White 1.00 2.50
24 Junior Seau 1.25 3.00
25 Irving Fryar .75 2.00

2011 Playoff Contenders Legendary Contenders Autographs

ANNOUNCED PRINT RUN 5-25
3 Bill Bates/25* 25.00 50.00
7 Steve Largent/25* 15.00 40.00
15 Alan Page/25* 15.00 40.00
16 Henry Ellard/25* 10.00 25.00
17 Bo Jackson/25* 50.00 100.00
18 John Randle/25* 15.00 40.00
19 Brent Jones/25* 10.00 25.00
20 Curtis Martin/25* 30.00 60.00
21 Deacon Jones/25* 15.00 40.00
22 Tom Rathman/25* 15.00 40.00
23 Danny White/25* 25.00 50.00
25 Irving Fryar/25* 15.00 40.00

2011 Playoff Contenders Rookie Ink

ANNOUNCED AU PRINT RUN 25-100
EXCH EXPIRATION: 8/8/2013
1 Jamie Harper/100* 10.00 25.00
2 Ryan Williams/100* 12.00 30.00
3 Julio Jones/100* EXCH 25.00 60.00
4 Delone Carter/100* 8.00 20.00
5 Colin Kaepernick/100* 20.00 50.00
6 Bilal Powell/25* 15.00 40.00
7 Marcell Dareus/50* EXCH 10.00 25.00
8 Blaine Gabbert/25* 30.00 60.00
9 Jonathan Baldwin/100* 12.00 30.00
10 Kendall Hunter/100* 15.00 40.00
11 Clyde Gates/50* 8.00 20.00
12 Ryan Mallett/25* 50.00 100.00
13 Taiwan Jones/25* 15.00 40.00
14 Kyle Rudolph/100* 10.00 25.00
15 Vincent Brown/100* 10.00 25.00
16 Andy Dalton/100* 40.00 80.00
17 Randall Cobb/100* 20.00 50.00
18 Austin Pettis/50* 8.00 20.00
19 Chano Voroon/100* 10.00 25.00
20 Mark Ingram/100* 25.00 60.00
21 Mikel Leshoure/100* 12.00 30.00
22 Cam Newton/25* 150.00 300.00
23 Leonard Hankerson/100* 10.00 25.00
24 Greg Little/50* 10.00 25.00
25 Jake Locker/50* 60.00 120.00
26 Torrey Smith/100* 12.00 30.00
27 Jerrel Jernigan/50* 8.00 20.00
28 DeMarco Murray/100* 40.00 80.00
29 Christian Ponder/50* 40.00 80.00
30 A.J. Green/25* 75.00 150.00
31 Von Miller/100* 15.00 40.00
32 Alex Green/100* EXCH 10.00 25.00
33 Titus Young/100* EXCH 12.00 30.00
34 Daniel Thomas/100* 12.00 30.00
35 Jordan Todman/100* 6.00 15.00
36 Stevan Ridley/50* EXCH 10.00 25.00

2011 Playoff Contenders Rookie Roll Call

COMPLETE SET (25) 15.00 40.00
*GOLD/100: 1X TO 2.5X BASIC INSERTS
1 Alex Green .75 2.00
2 Bilal Powell .50 1.25
3 Cam Newton 4.00 10.00
4 Christian Ponder 1.50 4.00
5 Delone Carter .60 1.50
6 DeMarco Murray 1.50 4.00
7 Jake Locker 2.00 5.00
8 Jamie Harper .75 2.00
9 Jordan Todman .50 1.25
10 Mikel Leshoure .75 2.00
11 Randall Cobb 1.00 2.50
12 Ryan Mallett 1.50 4.00
13 Ryan Williams 1.00 2.50
14 Shane Vereen .75 2.00
15 Stevan Ridley .75 2.00
16 Taiwan Jones .75 2.00
17 Titus Young 1.00 2.50
18 Aaron Williams .60 1.50
19 Aldon Smith 1.25 3.00
20 Corey Liuget .50 1.25
21 Jimmy Smith .75 2.00
22 Lance Kendricks .60 1.50
23 Prince Amukamara .75 2.00
24 Ryan Kerrigan .75 2.00
25 Terrelle Pryor 1.00 2.50

2011 Playoff Contenders ROY Contenders

COMPLETE SET (25) 15.00 40.00
*GOLD/100: 1X TO 2.5X BASIC INSERTS
1 A.J. Green 1.50 4.00
2 Andy Dalton 2.00 5.00
3 Austin Pettis .60 1.50
4 Blaine Gabbert 1.25 3.00
5 Cam Newton 4.00 10.00
6 Daniel Thomas .75 2.00
7 Greg Little .75 2.00
8 Julio Jones 1.50 4.00
9 Kyle Rudolph .75 2.00
10 Marcell Dareus .75 2.00
11 Mark Ingram 1.50 4.00
12 Torrey Smith 1.00 2.50
13 Dane Sanzenbacher .75 2.00
14 Von Miller 1.00 2.50
15 Roy Helu 1.50 4.00
16 Denarius Moore 1.00 2.50
17 Mason Foster .75 2.00
18 Stevan Ridley .75 2.00
19 Clyde Gates .60 1.50
20 Ryan Kerrigan .75 2.00
21 Delone Carter .60 1.50
22 Kendall Hunter .75 2.00
23 Adrian Clayborn .75 2.00
24 Aldon Smith 1.25 3.00
25 J.J. Watt 1.00 2.50

2011 Playoff Contenders ROY Contenders Black

*BLACK/50: 1.2X TO 3X BASIC INSERTS
BLACK PRINT RUN 50 SER.#'d SETS
5 Cam Newton 20.00 50.00

2011 Playoff Contenders Signs of Greatness

ANNOUNCED PRINT RUN 5-25
EXCH EXPIRATION: 8/8/2013
5 Hakeem Nicks/25* 12.00 30.00
6 Jahvid Best/25* 12.00 30.00
15 Shonn Greene/25* 10.00 25.00
16 Sidney Rice/25* 12.00 30.00
18 Tony Moeaki/25* 10.00 25.00
19 BenJarvus Green-Ellis/25* 15.00 40.00
30 Matt Forte/25* 15.00 40.00
32 Ryan Torain/25* 12.00 30.00
35 Danny Amendola/25* 12.00 30.00
36 Ron Mix/25* 10.00 25.00
37 Harlon Hill/25* 15.00 40.00
38 Boyd Dowler/25* 15.00 40.00
39 Mike Curtis/25* 10.00 25.00
40 Willie Brown/25* 10.00 25.00
42 Rick Casares/25* 12.00 30.00
44 Paul Krause/25* 10.00 25.00
46 Lydell Mitchell/25* 10.00 25.00
49 Leroy Kelly/25* 12.00 30.00
50 Rosey Grier/25* 12.00 30.00

2011 Playoff Contenders Super Bowl Tickets

*BLACK/50: .8X TO 2X BASIC INSERTS
*GOLD/100: .6X TO 1.5X BASIC INSERTS
UNPRICED AUTO ANNC'D PRINT RUN 10
1 Aaron Rodgers 2.50 6.00
2 Greg Jennings 1.25 3.00
3 Donald Driver 1.25 3.00
4 Pierre Thomas 1.25 3.00
5 Larry Fitzgerald 1.25 3.00
6 Ahmad Bradshaw 1.25 3.00
7 Dallas Clark 1.25 3.00
8 Hines Ward 1.25 3.00
9 Troy Polamalu 1.50 4.00
10 Donovan McNabb 1.50 4.00
11 Steve Smith 1.25 3.00
12 Mike Alstott 1.00 2.50
13 Charles Woodson 1.50 4.00
14 Eddie George 1.25 3.00
15 Rod Smith 1.00 2.50
16 Shannon Sharpe 1.25 3.00
17 Ronnie Lott 1.25 3.00
18 Mike Singletary 1.50 4.00
19 Marcus Allen 1.50 4.00
20 John Riggins 1.25 3.00
21 Franco Harris 1.50 4.00
22 John Stallworth 1.25 3.00
23 Joe Greene 1.50 4.00
24 Bob Griese 1.50 4.00
25 John Mackey 1.25 3.00

1997 Playoff First and Ten Prototypes

This set was issued to promote the 1997 Playoff First and Ten brand. The cards appear very similar to their regular issue counterparts and can be distinguished primarily by the different card numbering.

COMPLETE SET (6) 1.60 4.00
1 Antonio Freeman .20 .50
2 Terry Allen .20 .50
3 Terrell Davis .80 2.00
4 Eddie George .50 1.25
5 Karim Abdul-Jabbar .20 .50
6 Curtis Martin .30 .75

1997 Playoff First and Ten

The 1997 Playoff First and Ten set was issued in one series totalling 250-cards and was distributed in nine-card packs plus one "Chip Shot" or plastic token with a suggested retail price of $1.99. The cards feature player photos printed in full-color on high-gloss coated card stock.

COMPLETE SET (250) 7.50 20.00
1 Marcus Allen .20 .50
2 Eric Bieniemy .07 .20
3 Jason Dunn .07 .20
4 Jim Harbaugh .10 .30
5 Michael Westbrook .10 .30
6 Tiki Barber RC 1.25 3.00
7 Frank Reich .07 .20
8 Irving Fryar .10 .30
9 Courtney Hawkins .07 .20
10 Eric Zeier .10 .30
11 Kent Graham .07 .20
12 Trent Dilfer .20 .50
13 Neil O'Donnell .10 .30
14 Reidel Anthony RC .20 .50
15 Jeff Hostetler .07 .20
16 Lawrence Phillips .07 .20
17 Dave Brown .07 .20
18 Mike Tomczak .07 .20
19 Jake Reed .10 .30
20 Anthony Miller .07 .20
21 Eric Metcalf .10 .30
22 Sedrick Shaw RC .10 .30
23 Anthony Johnson .07 .20
24 Mario Bates .07 .20
25 Dorsey Levens .20 .50
26 Stan Humphries .10 .30
27 Ben Coates .10 .30
28 Tyrone Wheatley .10 .30
29 Adrian Murrell .10 .30
30 William Henderson .10 .30
31 Warrick Dunn RC .60 1.50
32 LeShon Johnson .07 .20
33 James O.Stewart .10 .30
34 Edgar Bennett .10 .30
35 Raymont Harris .07 .20
36 LeRoy Butler .07 .20
37 Darren Woodson .07 .20
38 Darnell Autry RC .10 .30
39 Johnnie Morton .10 .30
40 William Floyd .10 .30
41 Terrell Fletcher .07 .20
42 Leonard Russell .07 .20
43 Henry Ellard .07 .20
44 Terrell Owens .25 .60
45 John Friesz .07 .20
46 Antowain Smith RC .50 1.25
47 Charles Johnson .10 .30
48 Rickey Dudley .10 .30
49 Lake Dawson .07 .20
50 Bert Emanuel .10 .30
51 Zach Thomas .20 .50
52 Earnest Byner .07 .20
53 Yatil Green RC .10 .30
54 Chris Spielman .07 .20
55 Muhsin Muhammad .10 .30
56 Bobby Engram .10 .30
57 Eric Bjornson .07 .20
58 Willie Green .07 .20
59 Derrick Mayes .10 .30
60 Chris Sanders .07 .20
61 Jimmy Smith .10 .30
62 Tony Gonzalez RC .75 2.00
63 Rich Gannon .20 .50
64 Stanley Pritchett .07 .20
65 Brad Johnson .20 .50
66 Rodney Peete .07 .20
67 Sam Gash .07 .20
68 Chris Calloway .07 .20
69 Chris T. Jones .07 .20
70 Will Blackwell RC .10 .30
71 Mark Bruener .07 .20
72 Terry Kirby .10 .30
73 Brian Blades .07 .20
74 Craig Hayward .07 .20
75 Jamie Asher .07 .20
76 Terance Mathis .10 .30
77 Troy Davis RC .10 .30
78 Bruce Smith .10 .30
79 Simeon Rice .10 .30
80 Fred Barnett .07 .20
81 Tim Brown .20 .50
82 James Jett .10 .30
83 Mark Carrier WR .07 .20
84 Shawn Jefferson .07 .20
85 Ken Dilger .07 .20
86 Rae Carruth RC .07 .20
87 Keenan McCardell .10 .30
88 Michael Irvin .20 .50
89 Mark Chmura .10 .30
90 Derrick Alexander WR .10 .30
91 Andre Reed .10 .30
92 Ed McCaffrey .10 .30
93 Erik Kramer .07 .20
94 Albert Connell RC .20 .50
95 Frank Wycheck .07 .20
96 Zack Crockett .07 .20
97 Jim Everett .07 .20
98 Michael Haynes .07 .20
99 Jeff Graham .07 .20
100 Brent Jones .10 .30
101 Troy Aikman .40 1.00
102 Byron Hanspard RC .10 .30
103 Robert Brooks .10 .30
104 Karim Abdul-Jabbar .20 .50
105 Drew Bledsoe .25 .60
106 Napoleon Kaufman .20 .50
107 Steve Young .25 .60
108 Leeland McElroy .07 .20
109 Jamal Anderson .20 .50
110 David LaFleur RC .07 .20
111 Vinny Testaverde .10 .30
112 Eric Moulds .20 .50
113 Tim Blakabutuka .10 .30
114 Rick Mirer .07 .20
115 Jeff Blake .10 .30
116 Jim Schwantz RC .07 .20
117 Herman Moore .10 .30
118 Ike Hilliard RC .30 .75
119 Reggie White .20 .50
120 Steve McNair .25 .60
121 Marshall Faulk .25 .60
122 Natrone Means .10 .30
123 Greg Hill .07 .20
124 O.J. McDuffie .10 .30
125 Robert Smith .10 .30
126 Bryant Westbrook RC .07 .20
127 Ray Zellars 07 .20
128 Rodney Hampton .10 .30
129 Wayne Chrebet .20 .50
130 Desmond Howard .10 .30
131 Ty Detmer .10 .30
132 Erric Pegram .07 .20
133 Yancey Thigpen .10 .30
134 Danny Wuerffel RC .20 .50
135 Charlie Jones .10 .30
136 Chris Warren .10 .30
137 Isaac Bruce .20 .50
138 Errict Rhett .07 .20
139 Gus Frerotte .07 .20
140 Frank Sanders .10 .30
141 Todd Collins .07 .20
142 Jake Plummer RC .75 2.00
143 Darnay Scott .10 .30
144 Rashaan Salaam .07 .20
145 Terrell Davis .25 .60
146 Scott Mitchell .10 .30
147 Junior Seau .20 .50
148 Warren Moon .20 .50
149 Wesley Walls .10 .30
150 Daryl Johnston .10 .30
151 Brett Favre .75 2.00
152 Emmitt Smith .60 1.50
153 Dan Marino .75 2.00
154 Larry Centers .10 .30
155 Michael Jackson .10 .30
156 Kerry Collins .20 .50
157 Curtis Conway .10 .30
158 Peter Boulware RC .20 .50
159 Carl Pickens .10 .30
160 Shannon Sharpe .10 .30
161 Brett Perriman .07 .20
162 Eddie George .20 .50
163 Mark Brunell .25 .60
164 Tamarick Vanover .10 .30
165 Cris Carter .20 .50
166 Corey Dillon RC .75 2.00
167 Curtis Martin .25 .60
168 Amani Toomer .10 .30
169 Jeff George .10 .30
170 Kordell Stewart .20 .50
171 Garrison Hearst .10 .30
172 Tony Banks .10 .30
173 Mike Alstott .20 .50
174 Jim Druckenmiller RC .10 .30
175 Chris Chandler .10 .30
176 Byron Bam Morris .07 .20
177 Billy Joe Hobert .10 .30
178 Ernie Mills .07 .20
179 Ki-Jana Carter .07 .20
180 Deion Sanders .20 .50
181 Ricky Watters .10 .30
182 Shawn Springs RC .10 .30
183 Barry Sanders .60 1.50
184 Antonio Freeman .20 .50
185 Marvin Harrison .20 .50
186 Elvis Grbac .10 .30
187 Terry Glenn .20 .50
188 Willie Roaf .07 .20
189 Keyshawn Johnson .20 .50
190 Orlando Pace RC .20 .50
191 Jerome Bettis .20 .50
192 Tony Martin .10 .30
193 Jerry Rice .40 1.00
194 Joey Galloway .10 .30
195 Terry Allen .20 .50

196 Eddie Kennison .10 .30
197 Thurman Thomas .20 .50
198 Darrell Russell RC .07 .20
199 Rob Moore .10 .30
200 John Elway .75 2.00
201 Quinn Early .07 .20
202 Kevin Greene .10 .30
203 Robert Green .07 .20
204 Tony Carter .07 .20
205 Michael Timpson .07 .20
206 Kevin Smith .07 .20
207 Herschel Walker .10 .30
208 Steve Atwater .07 .20
209 Tyrone Braxton .07 .20
210 Willie Davis .07 .20
211 Lamont Warren .07 .20
212 Sean Dawkins .07 .20
213 Dale Carter .07 .20
214 Kimble Anders .10 .30
215 Derrick Thomas .20 .50
216 Chris Penn .07 .20
217 Irving Spikes .07 .20
218 Amp Lee .07 .20
219 Qadry Ismail .10 .30
220 Dave Meggett .07 .20
221 Tyrone Hughes .07 .20
222 Haywood Jeffires .07 .20
223 Torrance Small .07 .20
224 Danny Kanell .10 .30
225 Thomas Lewis .07 .20
226 Kyle Brady .07 .20
227 Harvey Williams .07 .20
228 Bobby Hoying .10 .30
229 Charlie Garner .10 .30
230 Andre Hastings .07 .20
231 Heath Shuler .07 .20
232 J.J. Stokes .10 .30
233 Ken Norton .07 .20
234 Steve Walsh .07 .20
235 Harold Green .07 .20
236 Reggie Brooks .07 .20
237 Robb Thomas .07 .20
238 Brian Mitchell .07 .20
239 Bill Brooks .07 .20
240 Leslie Shepherd .07 .20
241 Jay Graham RC .10 .30
242 Kevin Lockett RC .10 .30
243 Derrick Mason RC .50 1.25
244 Marc Edwards RC .07 .20
245 Joey Kent RC .20 .50
246 Pat Barnes RC .20 .50
247 Sherman Williams .07 .20
248 Ray Brown G .07 .20
249 Stephen Davis .20 .50
250 Lamar Smith .20 .50

1997 Playoff First and Ten Kickoff

COMPLETE SET (250) 100.00 200.00
*KICKOFF STARS: 4X TO 10X BASIC CARDS
*KICKOFF RCs: 2X TO 5X BASIC CARDS
STATED ODDS 1:9

1997 Playoff First and Ten Chip Shots Green

COMPLETE SET (250) 125.00 250.00
*1-200: .4X TO 1X ABSOLUTE CHIP SHOTS
1-200: ONE PER PACK
201-250: ONE PER SPECIAL RETAIL PACK
WITH WHITE STRIPES ON COIN'S EDGE
EACH PRINTED IN GREEN, YELLOW, AND RED
201 Quinn Early .25 .60
202 Kevin Greene .25 .60
203 Robert Green .25 .60
204 Tony Carter .25 .60
205 Michael Timpson .25 .60
206 Kevin Smith .25 .60
207 Herschel Walker .40 1.00
208 Steve Atwater .25 .60
209 Tyrone Braxton .25 .60
210 Willie Davis .25 .60
211 Lamont Warren .25 .60
212 Sean Dawkins .25 .60
213 Dale Carter .25 .60
214 Kimble Anders .25 .60
215 Derrick Thomas .75 2.00
216 Chris Penn .25 .60
217 Irving Spikes .25 .60
218 Amp Lee .25 .60
219 Qadry Ismail .40 1.00
220 Dave Meggett .25 .60
221 Tyrone Hughes .25 .60
222 Haywood Jeffires .25 .60
223 Torrance Small .25 .60
224 Danny Kanell .25 .60
225 Thomas Lewis .25 .60
226 Kyle Brady .75 2.00
227 Harvey Williams .25 .60
228 Bobby Hoying .75 2.00
229 Charlie Garner .40 1.00
230 Andre Hastings .25 .60
231 Heath Shuler .25 .60
232 J.J. Stokes .40 1.00
233 Ken Norton .25 .60
234 Steve Walsh .25 .60
235 Harold Green .25 .60
236 Reggie Brooks .25 .60
237 Robb Thomas .25 .60
238 Brian Mitchell .25 .60
239 Bill Brooks .25 .60
240 Leslie Shepherd .25 .60
241 Jay Graham .25 .60
242 Kevin Lockett .25 .60
243 Derrick Mason .75 2.00
244 Marc Edwards .25 .60
245 Joey Kent .25 .60
246 Pat Barnes .25 .60
247 Sherman Williams .25 .60
248 Ray Brown .25 .60
249 Stephen Davis .75 2.00
250 Lamar Smith .75 2.00

1997 Playoff First and Ten Hot Pursuit

COMPLETE SET (100) 350.00 700.00
STATED ODDS 1:180
1 Brett Favre 20.00 50.00
2 Dorsey Levens 5.00 12.00
3 Antonio Freeman 5.00 12.00
4 Robert Brooks 3.00 8.00
5 Mark Chmura 3.00 8.00
6 Reggie White 5.00 12.00
7 Drew Bledsoe 6.00 15.00
8 Curtis Martin 6.00 15.00
9 Ben Coates 3.00 8.00
10 Terry Glenn 5.00 12.00
11 Kerry Collins 5.00 12.00
12 Tim Biakabutuka 3.00 8.00
13 Anthony Johnson 2.00 5.00
14 Wesley Walls 3.00 8.00
15 Muhsin Muhammad 3.00 8.00
16 Mark Brunell 6.00 15.00
17 Natrone Means 3.00 8.00
18 Jimmy Smith 3.00 8.00
19 John Elway 20.00 50.00
20 Terrell Davis 6.00 15.00
21 Anthony Miller 2.00 5.00
22 Shannon Sharpe 3.00 8.00
23 Steve Young 6.00 15.00
24 Garrison Hearst 3.00 8.00
25 Jerry Rice 10.00 25.00
26 Troy Aikman 10.00 25.00
27 Deion Sanders 5.00 12.00
28 Emmitt Smith 15.00 40.00
29 Michael Irvin 5.00 12.00
30 Kordell Stewart 5.00 12.00
31 Jerome Bettis 5.00 12.00
32 Charles Johnson 3.00 8.00
33 Ty Detmer 3.00 8.00
34 Ricky Watters 3.00 8.00
35 Irving Fryar 3.00 8.00
36 Todd Collins 2.00 5.00
37 Thurman Thomas 5.00 12.00
38 Bruce Smith 3.00 8.00
39 Eric Moulds 5.00 12.00
40 Brad Johnson 5.00 12.00
41 Robert Smith 3.00 8.00
42 Cris Carter 5.00 12.00
43 Elvis Grbac 3.00 8.00
44 Greg Hill 2.00 5.00
45 Marcus Allen 5.00 12.00
46 Gus Frerotte 2.00 5.00
47 Terry Allen 5.00 12.00
48 Michael Westbrook 3.00 8.00
49 Jim Harbaugh 3.00 8.00
50 Marshall Faulk 6.00 15.00
51 Marvin Harrison 5.00 12.00
52 Jeff Blake 3.00 8.00
53 Ki-Jana Carter 2.00 5.00
54 Carl Pickens 3.00 8.00
55 Junior Seau 5.00 12.00
56 Tony Martin 3.00 8.00
57 Dan Marino 20.00 50.00
58 Karim Abdul-Jabbar 5.00 12.00
59 Stanley Pritchett 2.00 5.00
60 Zach Thomas 5.00 12.00
61 Steve McNair 6.00 15.00
62 Eddie George 5.00 12.00
63 Chris Sanders 2.00 5.00
64 Rick Mirer 2.00 5.00
65 Rashaan Salaam 2.00 5.00
66 Curtis Conway 3.00 8.00
67 Bobby Engram 3.00 8.00
68 Kent Graham 2.00 5.00
69 Leeland McElroy 2.00 5.00
70 Larry Centers 3.00 8.00
71 Frank Sanders 3.00 8.00
72 Jeff George 3.00 8.00
73 Napoleon Kaufman 5.00 12.00
74 Desmond Howard 3.00 8.00
75 Tim Brown 5.00 12.00
76 John Friesz 2.00 5.00
77 Chris Warren 3.00 8.00
78 Joey Galloway 3.00 8.00
79 Tony Banks 3.00 8.00
80 Lawrence Phillips 2.00 5.00
81 Isaac Bruce 5.00 12.00
82 Eddie Kennison 3.00 8.00
83 Errict Rhett 2.00 5.00
84 Mike Alstott 5.00 12.00
85 Rodney Hampton 3.00 8.00
86 Amani Toomer 3.00 8.00
87 Scott Mitchell 3.00 8.00
88 Barry Sanders 15.00 40.00
89 Herman Moore 3.00 8.00
90 Vinny Testaverde 3.00 8.00
91 Byron Bam Morris 2.00 5.00
92 Michael Jackson 3.00 8.00
93 Chris Chandler 3.00 8.00
94 Eric Metcalf 3.00 8.00
95 Jamal Anderson 5.00 12.00
96 Jim Everett 2.00 5.00
97 Mario Bates 2.00 5.00
98 Wayne Chrebet 5.00 12.00
99 Adrian Murrell 3.00 8.00
100 Keyshawn Johnson 5.00 12.00

1997 Playoff First and Ten Xtra Point

COMPLETE SET (10) 125.00 250.00
STATED ODDS 1:432
AUTOGRAPHS STATED ODDS 1:4454
XP1 Kordell Stewart 5.00 12.00
XP2 Dan Marino 20.00 50.00
XP3 Brett Favre 20.00 50.00
XP4 Emmitt Smith 15.00 40.00
XP5 John Elway 20.00 50.00
XP6 Eddie George 5.00 12.00
XP7 Karim Abdul-Jabbar 5.00 12.00
XP8 Terry Glenn 5.00 12.00
XP9 Curtis Martin 6.00 15.00
XP10 Joey Galloway 3.00 8.00
XPA1 Tony Banks AUTO 10.00 25.00
XPA2 Terrell Davis AUTO 30.00 80.00

2003 Playoff Hogg Heaven

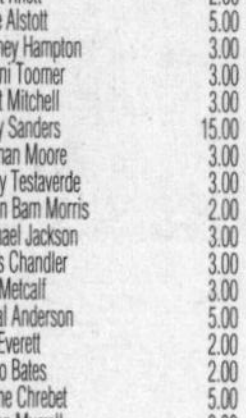

Released in October of 2003, this set consists of 230 cards including 150 veterans and 80 rookies. Rookies 151-200 are serial numbered to 1000. Rookies 201-250 feature event worn jersey swatches and are serial numbered to 750. Boxes contained 20 packs of 5 cards. SRP was $6.00.

COMP.SET w/o SP's (150) 12.50 30.00
151-200 ROOKIE PRINT RUN 1000
201-230 ROOKIE JSY PRINT RUN 750
1 Emmitt Smith 1.00 2.50
2 Marcel Shipp .25 .60
3 Michael Vick .50 1.25
4 Warrick Dunn .30 .75
5 T.J. Duckett .30 .75
6 Peerless Price .25 .60
7 Brian Finneran .25 .60
8 Chris Redman .25 .60
9 Jamal Lewis .30 .75
10 Todd Heap .30 .75
11 Travis Taylor .25 .60
12 Ray Lewis .40 1.00
13 Peter Boulware .30 .75
14 Ed Reed .40 1.00
15 Drew Bledsoe .40 1.00
16 Travis Henry .25 .60
17 Eric Moulds .30 .75
18 Josh Reed .25 .60
19 Takeo Spikes .25 .60
20 Julius Peppers .40 1.00
21 Stephen Davis .30 .75
22 Muhsin Muhammad .30 .75
23 Wesley Walls .30 .75
24 Anthony Thomas .30 .75
25 Brian Urlacher .40 1.00
26 Marty Booker .30 .75
27 Mike Brown .30 .75
28 Kordell Stewart .30 .75
29 Dez White .25 .60
30 Corey Dillon .30 .75
31 Chad Johnson .40 1.00
32 Peter Warrick .30 .75
33 Tim Couch .25 .60
34 William Green .25 .60
35 Andre Davis .25 .60
36 Quincy Morgan .25 .60
37 Kevin Johnson .25 .60
38 Dennis Northcutt .25 .60
39 Antonio Bryant .25 .60
40 Terry Glenn .30 .75
41 Joey Galloway .30 .75
42 Roy Williams .30 .75
43 Darren Woodson .30 .75
44 Jake Plummer .30 .75
45 Clinton Portis .30 .75
46 Mike Anderson .30 .75
47 Rod Smith .30 .75
48 Ed McCaffrey .30 .75
49 Ashley Lelie .25 .60
50 Shannon Sharpe .40 1.00
51 Al Wilson .25 .60
52 Joey Harrington .25 .60
53 James Stewart .25 .60
54 Brett Favre 1.00 2.50
55 Ahman Green .30 .75
56 Darren Sharper .30 .75
57 Donald Driver .40 1.00
58 Javon Walker .30 .75
59 Robert Ferguson .25 .60
60 David Carr .30 .75
61 Jabar Gaffney .25 .60
62 Stacey Mack .25 .60
63 Marvin Harrison .40 1.00
64 Peyton Manning .75 2.00
65 Edgerrin James .40 1.00
66 Reggie Wayne .40 1.00
67 Fred Taylor .30 .75
68 Mark Brunell .30 .75
69 Jimmy Smith .30 .75
70 Hugh Douglas .25 .60
71 Priest Holmes .40 1.00
72 Trent Green .30 .75
73 Tony Gonzalez .40 1.00
74 Marc Boerigter .25 .60
75 Ricky Williams .30 .75
76 Jay Fiedler .25 .60
77 Chris Chambers .30 .75
78 Zach Thomas .40 1.00
79 Jason Taylor .30 .75
80 Junior Seau .40 1.00
81 Randy McMichael .25 .60
82 Patrick Surtain .25 .60
83 Randy Moss .40 1.00
84 Michael Bennett .30 .75
85 Daunte Culpepper .30 .75
86 Tom Brady 1.00 2.50
87 Troy Brown .30 .75
88 Ty Law .30 .75
89 Aaron Brooks .30 .75
90 Deuce McAllister .30 .75
91 Donte Stallworth .25 .60
92 Joe Horn .30 .75
93 Michael Strahan .40 1.00
94 Kerry Collins .30 .75
95 Tiki Barber .40 1.00
96 Amani Toomer .30 .75
97 Jeremy Shockey .40 1.00
98 Chad Pennington .40 1.00
99 Curtis Martin .40 1.00
100 Santana Moss .30 .75
101 Rich Gannon .30 .75
102 Jerry Rice .75 2.00
103 Tim Brown .40 1.00
104 Jerry Porter .25 .60
105 Charlie Garner .30 .75
106 Charles Woodson .40 1.00
107 Donovan McNabb .40 1.00
108 Duce Staley .30 .75
109 James Thrash .25 .60
110 Chad Lewis .30 .75
111 Troy Vincent .30 .75
112 Tommy Maddox .30 .75
113 Plaxico Burress .30 .75
114 Hines Ward .40 1.00
115 Antwaan Randle El .30 .75
116 Jerome Bettis .40 1.00
117 Kendrell Bell .25 .60
118 LaDainian Tomlinson .40 1.00
119 Drew Brees .40 1.00
120 David Boston .25 .60
121 Jeff Garcia .30 .75
122 Terrell Owens .40 1.00
123 Tai Streets .25 .60
124 Kevan Barlow .25 .60
125 Matt Hasselbeck .30 .75
126 Koren Robinson .30 .75
127 Shaun Alexander .30 .75
128 Kurt Warner .40 1.00
129 Marc Bulger .40 1.00
130 Marshall Faulk .40 1.00
131 Torry Holt .40 1.00
132 Isaac Bruce .40 1.00
133 Brad Johnson .30 .75
134 Keyshawn Johnson .40 1.00
135 Warren Sapp .30 .75
136 Derrick Brooks .30 .75
137 John Lynch .30 .75
138 Michael Pittman .25 .60
139 Mike Alstott .40 1.00
140 Steve McNair .40 1.00
141 Eddie George .30 .75
142 Jevon Kearse .30 .75
143 Keith Bulluck .25 .60
144 Derrick Mason .30 .75
145 Patrick Ramsey .30 .75
146 Ladell Betts .25 .60
147 Laveranues Coles .25 .60
148 Rod Gardner .25 .60
149 Champ Bailey .40 1.00
150 Bruce Smith .30 .75
151 Ken Dorsey RC 2.00 5.00
152 Lee Suggs RC 2.00 5.00
153 Domanick Davis RC 2.00 5.00
154 Quentin Griffin RC 2.00 5.00
155 LaBrandon Toefield RC 2.00 5.00
156 B.J. Askew RC 2.00 5.00
157 Jason Witten RC 6.00 15.00
158 Bennie Joppru RC 1.50 4.00
159 L.J. Smith RC 2.50 6.00
160 Billy McMullen RC 1.50 4.00
161 Shaun McDonald RC 2.00 5.00
162 Brandon Lloyd RC 4.00 10.00
163 Sam Aiken RC 2.00 5.00
164 Bobby Wade RC 2.00 5.00
165 Justin Gage RC 2.00 5.00
166 Doug Gabriel RC 2.00 5.00
167 David Kircus RC 2.50 6.00
168 Arnaz Battle RC 2.50 6.00
169 Kareem Kelly RC 1.50 4.00
170 Talman Gardner RC 1.50 4.00
171 Ryan Hoag RC 1.50 4.00
172 LaTarence Dunbar RC 1.50 4.00
173 Johnathan Sullivan RC 1.50 4.00
174 Kevin Williams RC 2.50 6.00
175 Jimmy Kennedy RC 2.00 5.00
176 Ty Warren RC 2.00 5.00
177 William Joseph RC 1.50 4.00
178 Michael Haynes RC 1.50 4.00
179 Jerome McDougle RC 1.50 4.00
180 Calvin Pace RC 2.00 5.00
181 Tyler Brayton RC 2.00 5.00
182 Chris Kelsay RC 2.00 5.00
183 DeWayne White RC 1.50 4.00
184 E.J. Henderson RC 2.00 5.00
185 Charles Rogers RC 2.00 5.00
186 Terry Pierce RC 1.50 4.00
187 Nick Barnett RC 2.50 6.00
188 Boss Bailey RC 2.00 5.00
189 Pisa Tinoisamoa RC 2.50 6.00
190 Chaun Thompson RC 1.50 4.00
191 Andre Woolfolk RC 2.00 5.00
192 Sammy Davis RC 2.00 5.00
193 Eugene Wilson RC 2.50 6.00
194 Drayton Florence RC 2.50 6.00
195 Ricky Manning RC 2.00 5.00
196 Donald Strickland RC 1.50 4.00
197 Dennis Weathersby RC 1.50 4.00
198 Troy Polamalu RC 12.50 25.00
199 Ken Hamlin RC 2.50 6.00
200 Mike Doss RC 2.50 6.00
201 Carson Palmer JSY RC 6.00 15.00
202 Byron Leftwich JSY RC 3.00 8.00
203 Kyle Boller JSY RC 3.00 8.00
204 Rex Grossman JSY RC 3.00 8.00
205 Andre Johnson JSY RC 8.00 20.00
206 Bryant Johnson JSY RC 3.00 8.00
207 Larry Johnson JSY RC 3.00 8.00
208 Taylor Jacobs JSY RC 2.00 5.00
209 Bethel Johnson JSY RC 2.00 5.00
210 Anquan Boldin JSY RC 5.00 12.00
211 Tyrone Calico JSY RC 2.50 6.00
212 Teyo Johnson JSY RC 2.50 6.00
213 Kelley Washington JSY RC 2.00 5.00
214 Musa Smith JSY RC 2.00 5.00
215 Chris Brown JSY RC 2.00 5.00
216 Justin Fargas JSY RC 3.00 8.00
217 Artose Pinner JSY RC 2.00 5.00
218 Onterrio Smith JSY RC 2.00 5.00
219 Brian St.Pierre JSY RC 2.50 6.00
220 Dave Ragone JSY RC 2.00 5.00
221 Dallas Clark JSY RC 5.00 12.00
222 Seneca Wallace JSY RC 3.00 8.00
223 Terrell Suggs JSY RC 3.00 8.00
224 Terence Newman JSY RC 2.50 6.00
225 DeWayne Robertson JSY RC 2.50 6.00
226 Marcus Trufant JSY RC 2.50 6.00
227 Kliff Kingsbury JSY RC 2.50 6.00
228 Kevin Curtis JSY RC 3.00 8.00
229 Willis McGahee JSY RC 4.00 10.00
230 Nate Burleson JSY RC 2.50 6.00

2003 Playoff Hogg Heaven Hogg Wild

*VETS: 3X TO 8X BASIC CARDS
1-150 VETERAN PRINT RUN 150
*ROOKIES 151-200: .8X TO 2X
151-200 ROOKIE PRINT RUN 100
*ROOKIE JSY 201-230: 1.2X TO 3X
201-230 ROOKIE JSY PRINT RUN 25

2003 Playoff Hogg Heaven Accent

STATED PRINT RUN 25 SER.#'d SETS
A1 Michael Vick 12.00 30.00
A2 Donovan McNabb 10.00 25.00
A3 Peyton Manning 20.00 50.00
A4 Brett Favre 25.00 60.00
A5 Rich Gannon 8.00 20.00
A6 Jeff Garcia 8.00 20.00
A7 LaDainian Tomlinson 10.00 25.00
A8 Marshall Faulk 10.00 25.00
A9 Emmitt Smith 25.00 60.00
A10 Edgerrin James 10.00 25.00
A11 Ricky Williams 8.00 20.00
A12 Deuce McAllister 8.00 20.00
A13 Priest Holmes 10.00 25.00
A14 Ahman Green 8.00 20.00
A15 Marvin Harrison 10.00 25.00
A16 Terrell Owens 10.00 25.00
A17 Randy Moss 10.00 25.00
A18 Jerry Rice 20.00 50.00
A19 Tim Brown 10.00 25.00
A20 Jeremy Shockey 10.00 25.00

2003 Playoff Hogg Heaven Branded

STATED ODDS 1:19
B1 Michael Vick 2.50 6.00
B2 Donovan McNabb 2.00 5.00
B3 Peyton Manning 4.00 10.00
B4 Brett Favre 5.00 12.00
B5 Drew Bledsoe 2.00 5.00
B6 Tom Brady 5.00 12.00
B7 LaDainian Tomlinson 2.00 5.00
B8 Edgerrin James 2.00 5.00
B9 Ricky Williams 1.50 4.00
B10 Deuce McAllister 1.50 4.00
B11 Ahman Green 1.50 4.00
B12 Marshall Faulk 2.00 5.00
B13 Priest Holmes 2.00 5.00
B14 Marvin Harrison 2.00 5.00
B15 Terrell Owens 2.00 5.00
B16 Randy Moss 2.00 5.00
B17 Jerry Rice 4.00 10.00
B18 David Boston 1.25 3.00
B19 Tony Gonzalez 2.00 5.00
B20 Jeremy Shockey 2.00 5.00
B21 Warren Sapp 1.50 4.00
B22 Brian Urlacher 2.00 5.00
B23 Zach Thomas 2.00 5.00
B24 Ray Lewis 2.00 5.00
B25 Charles Woodson 2.00 5.00

2003 Playoff Hogg Heaven Hogg of Fame

PRINT RUN 500 SERIAL #'d SETS
HF1 Dan Marino 4.00 10.00
HF2 John Riggins 1.50 4.00
HF3 Steve Young 2.00 5.00
HF4 Brett Favre 4.00 10.00
HF5 Jerry Rice 3.00 8.00
HF6 Emmitt Smith 4.00 10.00
HF7 Tim Brown 1.50 4.00
HF8 Cris Carter 1.50 4.00
HF9 Peyton Manning 3.00 8.00
HF10 Marvin Harrison 1.50 4.00
HF11 Edgerrin James 1.50 4.00
HF12 Randy Moss 1.50 4.00
HF13 Terrell Owens 1.50 4.00
HF14 Ricky Williams 1.25 3.00
HF15 Michael Vick 2.00 5.00
HF16 Donovan McNabb 1.50 4.00
HF17 Clinton Portis 1.25 3.00
HF18 Priest Holmes 1.50 4.00
HF19 Marshall Faulk 1.50 4.00
HF20 Brian Urlacher 1.50 4.00
HF21 Ray Lewis 1.50 4.00
HF22 Jeremy Shockey 1.50 4.00
HF23 LaDainian Tomlinson 1.50 4.00
HF24 Deuce McAllister 1.25 3.00
HF25 Kurt Warner 1.50 4.00
HF26 Tom Brady 4.00 10.00
HF27 Drew Bledsoe 1.50 4.00
HF28 Drew Brees 1.50 4.00

2003 Playoff Hogg Heaven Hogg of Fame Materials Bronze

BRONZE PRINT RUN 125 SER.#'d SETS
*SILVER/75: .5X TO 1.2X BRONZE/125
SILVER PRINT RUN 75 SER.#'d SETS
*GOLD/25: .8X TO 2X BRONZE/125
GOLD PRINT RUN 25 SER.#'d SETS
HF1 Dan Marino 20.00 50.00
HF2 John Riggins 10.00 25.00
HF3 Steve Young 10.00 25.00
HF4 Brett Favre 12.00 30.00
HF5 Jerry Rice 10.00 25.00
HF6 Emmitt Smith 12.00 30.00
HF7 Tim Brown 5.00 12.00
HF8 Cris Carter 5.00 12.00
HF9 Peyton Manning 10.00 25.00
HF10 Marvin Harrison 5.00 12.00
HF11 Edgerrin James 5.00 12.00
HF12 Randy Moss 5.00 12.00
HF13 Terrell Owens 5.00 12.00
HF14 Ricky Williams 4.00 10.00
HF15 Michael Vick 6.00 15.00
HF16 Donovan McNabb 5.00 12.00
HF17 Clinton Portis 4.00 10.00
HF18 Priest Holmes 5.00 12.00
HF19 Marshall Faulk 5.00 12.00
HF20 Brian Urlacher 5.00 12.00
HF21 Ray Lewis 5.00 12.00
HF22 Jeremy Shockey 5.00 12.00
HF23 LaDainian Tomlinson 5.00 12.00
HF24 Deuce McAllister 4.00 10.00
HF25 Kurt Warner 5.00 12.00
HF26 Tom Brady 12.00 30.00
HF27 Drew Bledsoe 5.00 12.00
HF28 Drew Brees 5.00 12.00

2003 Playoff Hogg Heaven Leather in Leather

STATED PRINT RUN 250 SER.#'d SETS
*LACES/25: .8X TO 2X LEATHER/250
LACES PRINT RUN 25 SERIAL #'d SETS
LL1 Emmitt Smith 12.00 30.00
LL2 Donovan McNabb 5.00 12.00
LL3 Steve McNair 5.00 12.00
LL4 Drew Bledsoe 5.00 12.00
LL5 Kurt Warner 5.00 12.00
LL6 Aaron Brooks 4.00 10.00
LL7 Tom Brady 12.00 30.00
LL8 Marvin Harrison 5.00 12.00
LL9 Chad Pennington 5.00 12.00
LL10 Randy Moss 5.00 12.00
LL11 Carson Palmer 6.00 15.00
LL12 Byron Leftwich 3.00 8.00
LL13 Kyle Boller 3.00 8.00
LL14 Rex Grossman 3.00 8.00
LL15 Andre Johnson 8.00 20.00
LL16 Bryant Johnson 3.00 8.00
LL17 Larry Johnson 3.00 8.00
LL18 Taylor Jacobs 2.00 5.00
LL19 Bethel Johnson 2.00 5.00
LL20 Anquan Boldin 5.00 12.00
LL21 Tyrone Calico 2.50 6.00
LL22 Teyo Johnson 2.50 6.00
LL23 Kelley Washington 2.00 5.00
LL24 Musa Smith 2.00 5.00
LL25 Chris Brown 2.00 5.00
LL26 Justin Fargas 3.00 8.00
LL27 Artose Pinner 2.00 5.00
LL28 Onterrio Smith 2.00 5.00
LL29 Brian St.Pierre 2.50 6.00
LL30 Dave Ragone 2.00 5.00
LL31 Dallas Clark 5.00 12.00
LL32 Seneca Wallace 3.00 8.00
LL33 Terrell Suggs 3.00 8.00
LL34 Terence Newman 2.50 6.00
LL35 DeWayne Robertson 2.50 6.00
LL36 Marcus Trufant 2.50 6.00
LL37 Kliff Kingsbury 2.50 6.00
LL38 Kevin Curtis 3.00 8.00
LL39 Willis McGahee 4.00 10.00
LL40 Nate Burleson 2.50 6.00

2003 Playoff Hogg Heaven Material Hoggs Bronze

BRONZE PRINT RUN 200 SER.#'d SETS
*SILVER/125: .5X TO 1.2X BRONZE/200
SILVER PRINT RUN 125 SER.#'d SETS
*GOLD/25: 1X TO 2.5X BRONZE/200
GOLD PRINT RUN 25 SER.#'d SETS
MH1 Emmitt Smith 12.00 30.00
MH2 Jerry Rice 10.00 25.00
MH3 Donovan McNabb 5.00 12.00
MH4 Peyton Manning 10.00 25.00
MH5 Brett Favre 12.00 30.00
MH6 Michael Vick 6.00 15.00
MH7 Aaron Brooks 4.00 10.00
MH8 Ahman Green 4.00 10.00
MH9 Antwaan Randle El 4.00 10.00
MH10 Brian Urlacher 5.00 12.00
MH11 Chad Pennington 5.00 12.00
MH12 Chris Chambers 4.00 10.00
MH13 Clinton Portis 4.00 10.00
MH14 Corey Dillon 4.00 10.00
MH15 Curtis Martin 5.00 12.00
MH16 Daunte Culpepper 4.00 10.00
MH17 David Boston 3.00 8.00
MH18 David Carr 4.00 10.00
MH19 Deuce McAllister 4.00 10.00
MH20 Donald Driver 5.00 12.00
MH21 Donte Stallworth 3.00 8.00
MH22 Drew Bledsoe 5.00 12.00
MH23 Drew Brees 5.00 12.00
MH24 Ed McCaffrey 4.00 10.00
MH25 Eddie George 4.00 10.00
MH26 Edgerrin James 5.00 12.00
MH27 Eric Moulds 4.00 10.00
MH28 Fred Taylor 4.00 10.00
MH29 Garrison Hearst 4.00 10.00
MH30 Hines Ward 5.00 12.00
MH31 Isaac Bruce 5.00 12.00
MH32 Jake Plummer 4.00 10.00
MH33 Chris Redman 3.00 8.00
MH34 Jeff Garcia 4.00 10.00
MH35 Jeremy Shockey 5.00 12.00
MH36 Jerome Bettis 5.00 12.00
MH37 Jevon Kearse 4.00 10.00
MH38 Jimmy Smith 4.00 10.00
MH39 Joey Harrington 3.00 8.00
MH40 Julius Peppers 5.00 12.00
MH41 Kurt Warner 5.00 12.00
MH42 Laveranues Coles 3.00 8.00
MH43 Mark Brunell 4.00 10.00
MH44 Marshall Faulk 5.00 12.00
MH45 Marvin Harrison 5.00 12.00
MH46 Jamal Lewis 4.00 10.00
MH47 Plaxico Burress 4.00 10.00
MH48 Ricky Williams 4.00 10.00
MH49 Santana Moss 4.00 10.00
MH50 Terrell Davis 5.00 12.00

2003 Playoff Hogg Heaven Pig Pens Autographs

STATED PRINT RUN 25-250
PP1 Kurt Warner/200 15.00 40.00
PP2 Michael Vick/25 50.00 80.00
PP3 Dan Marino/50 90.00 150.00
PP4 John Riggins/100 20.00 50.00
PP5 Carson Palmer/50 40.00 100.00
PP6 Byron Leftwich/75 25.00 60.00
PP7 Kendrell Bell/25 12.00 30.00
PP8 Deuce McAllister/25 15.00 40.00
PP9 David Carr/25 15.00 40.00
PP10 Patrick Ramsey/25 15.00 40.00
PP11 Roy Williams/50 10.00 25.00
PP12 Joey Harrington/25 12.00 30.00
PP13 Anthony Thomas/50 10.00 25.00
PP14 Derrick Mason/70 10.00 25.00
PP15 Donald Driver/35 30.00 60.00
PP16 Marty Booker/30 15.00 40.00
PP17 Bethel Johnson/35 12.00 30.00
PP18 Antowain Smith/50 10.00 25.00
PP19 Garrison Hearst/75 10.00 25.00
PP20 Hines Ward/50 25.00 50.00
PP21 Jerome Bettis/50 50.00 80.00
PP22 Joe Horn/100 8.00 20.00
PP23 Deion Branch/75 10.00 25.00
PP24 Laveranues Coles/45 8.00 20.00
PP25 Marvin Harrison/50 15.00 40.00
PP26 Mike Alstott/50 12.00 30.00
PP27 Priest Holmes/25 20.00 50.00
PP28 Randy Moss/35 50.00 100.00
PP29 Rod Gardner/50 8.00 20.00
PP30 Sonny Jurgensen/141 15.00 40.00
PP31 Terrell Owens/25 20.00 50.00
PP32 Tommy Maddox/75 10.00 25.00
PP33 Zach Thomas/75 15.00 40.00
PP34 Charley Taylor/208 8.00 20.00
PP35 Jimmy Smith/75 10.00 25.00
PP36 E.J. Henderson/250 6.00 15.00
PP37 Musa Smith/250 5.00 12.00
PP38 Chris Brown/250 5.00 12.00
PP39 Dennis Weathersby/250 5.00 12.00
PP40 Kyle Boller/155 8.00 20.00
PP41 Marc Boerigter/250 5.00 12.00
PP42 Taylor Jacobs/200 5.00 12.00
PP43 Terrence Edwards/250 5.00 12.00
PP44 DeWayne White/250 5.00 12.00
PP45 Jerome McDougle/250 5.00 12.00
PP46 Kevin Curtis/250 8.00 20.00
PP47 Sam Aiken/250 6.00 15.00
PP48 Doug Gabriel/250 6.00 15.00
PP49 Chris Kelsay/250 6.00 15.00
PP50 Kevin Williams/250 8.00 20.00

2003 Playoff Hogg Heaven Rival Hoggs

PRINT RUN 500 SERIAL #'d SETS
RH1 Brett Favre / Randy Moss 3.00 8.00
RH2 Joey Harrington / Brian Urlacher 1.25 3.00
RH3 Drew Bledsoe / Tom Brady 3.00 8.00
RH4 Ricky Williams / Deuce McAllister 1.00 2.50
RH5 Plaxico Burress / Ray Lewis 1.25 3.00
RH6 Michael Strahan / Warren Sapp 1.25 3.00
RH7 Emmitt Smith / Terrell Owens 3.00 8.00
RH8 LaDainian Tomlinson / Clinton Portis 1.25 3.00
RH9 Priest Holmes / Marshall Faulk 1.25 3.00
RH10 Peyton Manning / Steve McNair 2.50 6.00
RH11 William Green / Jerome Bettis 1.25 3.00
RH12 Travis Henry / Zach Thomas 1.25 3.00
RH13 Shaun Alexander / Ahman Green 1.00 2.50
RH14 Jevon Kearse / Julius Peppers 1.25 3.00
RH15 Michael Vick / Donovan McNabb 1.50 4.00
RH16 Antonio Bryant / Rod Gardner .75 2.00
RH17 Jamal Lewis / Kendrell Bell 1.00 2.50
RH18 Marvin Harrison / Jerry Rice 2.50 6.00
RH19 Jeremy Shockey / Tony Gonzalez 1.25 3.00
RH20 Kurt Warner / Jeff Garcia 1.25 3.00
RH21 Tim Brown / David Boston 1.25 3.00
RH22 Drew Brees / Rich Gannon 1.25 3.00
RH23 Daunte Culpepper / Kordell Stewart 1.00 2.50
RH24 Edgerrin James / Eddie George 1.25 3.00
RH25 David Carr / Mark Brunell 1.00 2.50
RH26 Walter Payton / Emmitt Smith 4.00 10.00
RH27 T.J. Duckett / Mike Alstott 1.25 3.00
RH28 Aaron Brooks / Brad Johnson 1.00 2.50
RH29 Hines Ward / Keyshawn Johnson 1.25 3.00
RH30 Michael Bennett / Anthony Thomas 1.00 2.50

2003 Playoff Hogg Heaven Rival Hoggs Materials

PRINT RUN 125 SERIAL #'d SETS
RH1 Brett Favre / Randy Moss 15.00 40.00
RH2 Joey Harrington / Brian Urlacher 6.00 15.00
RH3 Drew Bledsoe / Tom Brady 15.00 40.00
RH4 Ricky Williams / Deuce McAllister 5.00 12.00
RH5 Plaxico Burress / Ray Lewis 6.00 15.00
RH6 Michael Strahan / Warren Sapp 6.00 15.00
RH7 Emmitt Smith / Terrell Owens 15.00 40.00
RH8 LaDainian Tomlinson / Clinton Portis 6.00 15.00
RH9 Priest Holmes / Marshall Faulk 6.00 15.00
RH10 Peyton Manning / Steve McNair 12.00 30.00
RH11 William Green / Jerome Bettis 6.00 15.00
RH12 Travis Henry / Zach Thomas 6.00 15.00
RH13 Shaun Alexander / Ahman Green 5.00 12.00
RH14 Jevon Kearse / Julius Peppers 6.00 15.00
RH15 Michael Vick / Donovan McNabb 8.00 20.00
RH16 Antonio Bryant / Rod Gardner 4.00 10.00
RH17 Jamal Lewis / Kendrell Bell 5.00 12.00
RH18 Marvin Harrison / Jerry Rice 12.00 30.00
RH19 Jeremy Shockey / Tony Gonzalez 6.00 15.00
RH20 Kurt Warner / Jeff Garcia 6.00 15.00
RH21 Tim Brown / David Boston 6.00 15.00
RH22 Drew Brees / Rich Gannon 6.00 15.00
RH23 Daunte Culpepper / Kordell Stewart 5.00 12.00
RH24 Edgerrin James / Eddie George 6.00 15.00
RH25 David Carr / Mark Brunell 5.00 12.00
RH26 Walter Payton / Emmitt Smith 30.00 80.00
RH27 T.J. Duckett / Mike Alstott 6.00 15.00
RH28 Aaron Brooks / Brad Johnson 5.00 12.00
RH29 Hines Ward / Keyshawn Johnson 6.00 15.00
RH30 Michael Bennett / Anthony Thomas 5.00 12.00

2003 Playoff Hogg Heaven Rookie Hoggs

STATED ODDS 1:19
RCH1 Carson Palmer 3.00 8.00
RCH2 Byron Leftwich 1.50 4.00
RCH3 Kyle Boller 1.50 4.00
RCH4 Chris Simms 1.50 4.00
RCH5 Rex Grossman 1.50 4.00
RCH6 Willis McGahee 2.00 5.00
RCH7 Larry Johnson 1.50 4.00
RCH8 Lee Suggs 1.25 3.00
RCH9 Musa Smith 1.00 2.50
RCH10 Chris Brown 1.00 2.50
RCH11 Charles Rogers 1.25 3.00
RCH12 Andre Johnson 4.00 10.00
RCH13 Taylor Jacobs 1.00 2.50
RCH14 Kelley Washington 1.00 2.50
RCH15 Bryant Johnson 1.50 4.00
RCH16 Brandon Lloyd 2.50 6.00
RCH17 Tyrone Calico 1.25 3.00
RCH18 Jason Witten 4.00 10.00
RCH19 Dallas Clark 2.50 6.00
RCH20 Terrell Suggs 1.50 4.00
RCH21 DeWayne Robertson 1.25 3.00
RCH22 Jimmy Kennedy 1.25 3.00
RCH23 Boss Bailey 1.25 3.00
RCH24 Terence Newman 1.25 3.00
RCH25 Marcus Trufant 1.25 3.00

2003 Playoff Hogg Heaven National Previews

Distributed by Playoff at the 2003 National Convention in Atlantic City, this set consists of 6 NFL superstars. Sets were randomly distributed to collectors visiting the Donruss/Playoff booth.

COMPLETE SET (6) 2.50 6.00
1 Brett Favre 1.00 2.50
2 Jeff Garcia .30 .75
3 Clinton Portis .30 .75
4 Jeremy Shockey .40 1.00
5 Michael Vick .50 1.25
6 Ricky Williams .30 .75

2004 Playoff Hogg Heaven

Playoff Hogg Heaven initially released in early September 2004. The base set consists of 180-cards including 50-rookies serial numbered to 750 and 30-rookie jersey cards numbered of 750. Hobby boxes contained 12-packs of 5-cards and carried an S.R.P. of $6 per pack. One parallel set and a variety of inserts can be found seeded in packs highlighted by a large number of jersey card inserts and the Rookie Hoggs and Pig Pens Autograph inserts.

COMP.SET w/o SP's (100) 12.50 30.00
101-150 RC PRINT RUN 750 SER.#'d SETS
151-180 RPH RC PRINT RUN 750 SER.#'d SETS
1 Anquan Boldin .40 1.00
2 Emmitt Smith 1.00 2.50
3 Josh McCown .30 .75
4 Michael Vick .50 1.25
5 Peerless Price .25 .60
6 T.J. Duckett .30 .75
7 Jamal Lewis .30 .75
8 Kyle Boller .30 .75
9 Ray Lewis .40 1.00
10 Terrell Owens .40 1.00
11 Drew Bledsoe .40 1.00
12 Eric Moulds .30 .75
13 Travis Henry .25 .60
14 Jake Delhomme .30 .75
15 Stephen Davis .30 .75
16 Steve Smith .40 1.00
17 Anthony Thomas .30 .75
18 Brian Urlacher .40 1.00
19 Rex Grossman .30 .75
20 Carson Palmer .40 1.00
21 Chad Johnson .40 1.00
22 Peter Warrick .30 .75
23 Rudi Johnson .30 .75
24 Andre Davis .25 .60
25 Lee Suggs .30 .75
26 Keyshawn Johnson .30 .75
27 Quincy Carter .25 .60
28 Roy Williams S .30 .75
29 Ashley Lelie .25 .60
30 Jake Plummer .30 .75
31 Rod Smith .30 .75
32 Charles Rogers .25 .60
33 Joey Harrington .30 .75
34 Ahman Green .30 .75
35 Brett Favre 1.00 2.50
36 Javon Walker .25 .60
37 Andre Johnson .40 1.00
38 David Carr .25 .60
39 Domanick Davis .25 .60
40 Edgerrin James .30 .75
41 Marvin Harrison .40 1.00
42 Peyton Manning .75 2.00
43 Reggie Wayne .40 1.00
44 Byron Leftwich .30 .75
45 Fred Taylor .30 .75
46 Jimmy Smith .30 .75
47 Priest Holmes .40 1.00
48 Tony Gonzalez .40 1.00
49 Trent Green .30 .75
50 A.J. Feeley .25 .60
51 Chris Chambers .30 .75
52 Ricky Williams .30 .75
53 Zach Thomas .40 1.00
54 Daunte Culpepper .30 .75
55 Michael Bennett .30 .75
56 Randy Moss .40 1.00
57 Deion Branch .30 .75
58 Tom Brady .75 2.00
59 Ty Law .30 .75
60 Aaron Brooks .30 .75
61 Deuce McAllister .30 .75
62 Joe Horn .30 .75
63 Jeremy Shockey .30 .75
64 Kerry Collins .30 .75
65 Michael Strahan .40 1.00
66 Tiki Barber .40 1.00
67 Chad Pennington .40 1.00
68 Curtis Martin .40 1.00
69 Santana Moss .30 .75
70 Jerry Rice .75 2.00
71 Rich Gannon .30 .75
72 Tim Brown .40 1.00
73 Brian Westbrook .40 1.00
74 Donovan McNabb .40 1.00
75 Jevon Kearse .30 .75
76 Hines Ward .40 1.00
77 Jerome Bettis .40 1.00
78 Kendrell Bell .25 .60
79 David Boston .25 .60
80 Drew Brees .40 1.00
81 LaDainian Tomlinson .40 1.00
82 Jeff Garcia .30 .75
83 Kevan Barlow .25 .60
84 Tim Rattay .25 .60
85 Koren Robinson .25 .60
86 Matt Hasselbeck .30 .75
87 Shaun Alexander .30 .75
88 Isaac Bruce .30 .75
89 Marc Bulger .30 .75
90 Marshall Faulk .40 1.00
91 Torry Holt .30 .75
92 Brad Johnson .30 .75
93 Keenan McCardell .25 .60
94 Warren Sapp .30 .75
95 Derrick Mason .30 .75
96 Steve McNair .40 1.00
97 Eddie George .30 .75
98 Clinton Portis .40 1.00
99 Laveranues Coles .25 .60
100 Mark Brunell .30 .75
101 Adimchinobe Echemandu RC 1.25 3.00
102 Ahmad Carroll RC 1.00 2.50
103 Andy Hall RC 1.00 2.50
104 B.J. Symons RC 1.00 2.50
105 Bradlee Van Pelt RC 1.25 3.00
106 Brandon Miree RC 1.00 2.50
107 Bruce Perry RC 1.00 2.50
108 Carlos Francis RC 1.00 2.50
109 Casey Bramlet RC 1.00 2.50
110 Chris Gamble RC 1.25 3.00
111 Clarence Moore RC 1.00 2.50
112 Cody Pickett RC 1.25 3.00
113 Craig Krenzel RC 1.25 3.00
114 D.J. Hackett RC 1.25 3.00
115 D.J. Williams RC 1.50 4.00
116 Derrick Ward RC 1.50 4.00
117 Drew Carter RC 1.25 3.00
118 Ernest Wilford RC 1.25 3.00
119 Drew Henson RC 1.00 2.50
120 Jamaar Taylor RC 1.00 2.50
121 Jared Lorenzen RC 1.25 3.00
122 Jarrett Payton RC 1.25 3.00
123 Jason Babin RC 1.50 4.00
124 Jeff Smoker RC 1.25 3.00
125 Jeris McIntyre RC 1.00 2.50
126 Jerricho Cotchery RC 1.25 3.00
127 Jim Sorgi RC 1.25 3.00
128 John Navarre RC 1.00 2.50
129 Johnnie Morant RC 1.00 2.50
130 Sean Taylor RC 3.00 8.00
131 Jonathan Vilma RC 1.50 4.00
132 Josh Harris RC 1.00 2.50
133 Kenechi Udeze RC 1.25 3.00
134 Marcus Tubbs RC 1.00 2.50
135 Mark Jones RC 1.00 2.50
136 Matt Mauck RC 1.00 2.50
137 Maurice Mann RC 1.00 2.50
138 Michael Turner RC 2.00 5.00
139 P.K. Sam RC 1.00 2.50
140 Patrick Crayton RC 1.50 4.00
141 Quincy Wilson RC 1.25 3.00
142 Ran Carthon RC 1.00 2.50
143 Ryan Krause RC 1.00 2.50
144 Samie Parker RC 1.00 2.50
145 Sloan Thomas RC 1.25 3.00
146 Tommie Harris RC 1.50 4.00
147 Triandos Luke RC 1.00 2.50
148 Troy Fleming RC 1.00 2.50
149 Vince Wilfork RC 1.50 4.00
150 Will Smith RC 1.25 3.00
151 Larry Fitzgerald RPH RC 6.00 15.00
152 DeAngelo Hall RPH RC 2.50 6.00
153 Matt Schaub RPH RC 5.00 12.00
154 Michael Jenkins RPH RC 2.50 6.00
155 Devard Darling RPH RC 1.50 4.00
156 J.P. Losman RPH RC 2.00 5.00
157 Lee Evans RPH RC 2.50 6.00
158 Keary Colbert RPH RC 1.50 4.00
159 Bernard Berrian RPH RC 2.50 6.00
160 Chris Perry RPH RC 2.00 5.00
161 Kellen Winslow RPH RC 2.50 6.00
162 Luke McCown RPH RC 2.00 5.00
163 Julius Jones RPH RC 2.00 5.00
164 Darius Watts RPH RC 1.50 4.00
165 Tatum Bell RPH RC 2.00 5.00
166 Kevin Jones RPH RC 2.00 5.00
167 Roy Williams RPH RC 2.50 6.00
168 Greg Jones RPH RC 1.50 4.00
169 Reggie Williams RPH RC 2.00 5.00
170 Ben Watson RPH RC 2.50 6.00
171 Cedric Cobbs RPH RC 1.50 4.00
172 Devery Henderson RPH RC 2.50 6.00
173 Eli Manning RPH RC 15.00 40.00
174 Ben Roethlisberger RPH RC 15.00 40.00
175 Philip Rivers RPH RC 10.00 25.00
176 Derrick Hamilton RPH RC 1.50 4.00
177 Rashaun Woods RPH RC 1.50 4.00
178 Steven Jackson RPH RC 4.00 10.00
179 Michael Clayton RPH RC 2.00 5.00
180 Ben Troupe RPH RC 2.00 5.00

2004 Playoff Hogg Heaven Hogg Wild

*VETS 1-100: 3X TO 8X BASIC CARDS
*ROOKIES 101-150: .8X TO 2X
101-150 PRINT RUN 125 SER.#'d SETS
*ROOKIES 151-180: 1.2X TO 3X
151-180 PRINT RUN 25 SER.#'d SETS

2004 Playoff Hogg Heaven Accent

ACCENT PRINT RUN 25 SETS
A1 Andre Johnson 6.00 15.00
A2 Brian Urlacher 6.00 15.00
A3 Byron Leftwich 5.00 12.00
A4 Carson Palmer 6.00 15.00
A5 Clinton Portis 6.00 15.00
A6 Daunte Culpepper 5.00 12.00
A7 David Carr 4.00 10.00
A8 Deuce McAllister 5.00 12.00
A9 Edgerrin James 5.00 12.00
A10 Emmitt Smith 15.00 40.00
A11 Jake Delhomme 5.00 12.00
A12 Jeremy Shockey 5.00 12.00
A13 Jerry Rice 12.00 30.00
A14 Joey Harrington 5.00 12.00
A15 LaDainian Tomlinson 6.00 15.00
A16 Marvin Harrison 6.00 15.00
A17 Matt Hasselbeck 5.00 12.00
A18 Michael Vick 8.00 20.00
A19 Peyton Manning 12.00 30.00
A20 Priest Holmes 6.00 15.00
A21 Randy Moss 6.00 15.00
A22 Roy Williams S 5.00 12.00
A23 Santana Moss 5.00 12.00
A24 Stephen Davis 5.00 12.00
A25 Tom Brady 12.00 30.00

2004 Playoff Hogg Heaven Branded

COMPLETE SET (25) 20.00 50.00
STATED PRINT RUN 1250 SER.#'d SETS
B1 Ahman Green 1.00 2.50
B2 Andre Johnson 1.25 3.00
B3 Anquan Boldin 1.25 3.00
B4 Brian Urlacher 1.25 3.00
B5 Byron Leftwich 1.00 2.50
B6 Carson Palmer 1.25 3.00
B7 Clinton Portis 1.25 3.00
B8 Daunte Culpepper 1.00 2.50
B9 David Carr .75 2.00
B10 Deuce McAllister 1.00 2.50
B11 Edgerrin James 1.00 2.50
B12 Jake Delhomme 1.00 2.50
B13 Jeremy Shockey 1.00 2.50
B14 Joey Harrington 1.00 2.50
B15 LaDainian Tomlinson 1.25 3.00
B16 Marvin Harrison 1.25 3.00
B17 Matt Hasselbeck 1.00 2.50
B18 Priest Holmes 1.25 3.00
B19 Randy Moss 1.25 3.00
B20 Roy Williams S 1.00 2.50
B21 Santana Moss 1.00 2.50
B22 Shaun Alexander 1.00 2.50
B23 Stephen Davis 1.00 2.50
B24 Tom Brady 2.50 6.00
B25 Torry Holt 1.00 2.50

2004 Playoff Hogg Heaven Hogg of Fame

COMPLETE SET (25) 20.00 50.00
STATED ODDS 1:12
HF1 Brett Favre 2.50 6.00
HF2 Chad Pennington 1.00 2.50
HF3 Clinton Portis 1.00 2.50
HF4 David Carr .60 1.50
HF5 Deion Sanders 1.00 2.50
HF6 Donovan McNabb 1.00 2.50
HF7 Drew Bledsoe 1.00 2.50
HF8 Emmitt Smith 2.50 6.00
HF9 Jamal Lewis .75 2.00
HF10 Jerry Rice 2.00 5.00
HF11 Jim Kelly 1.00 2.50
HF12 Joe Montana 2.50 6.00
HF13 Joey Harrington .75 2.00
HF14 Marshall Faulk 1.00 2.50
HF15 Marvin Harrison 1.00 2.50
HF16 Michael Irvin 1.00 2.50
HF17 Michael Vick 1.25 3.00
HF18 Mike Singletary 1.00 2.50
HF19 Peyton Manning 2.00 5.00
HF20 Ricky Williams .75 2.00
HF21 Steve McNair 1.00 2.50
HF22 Terrell Davis 1.00 2.50
HF23 Terrell Owens 1.00 2.50
HF24 Tom Brady 2.00 5.00
HF25 Warren Moon .75 2.00

2004 Playoff Hogg Heaven Hogg of Fame Jerseys Bronze

BRONZE PRINT RUN 150 SER.#'d SETS
*GOLD/25: 1X TO 2.5X BRONZE
GOLD PRINT RUN 25 SER.#'d SETS
UNPRICED PLATINUM PRINT RUN 1 SET
*SILVER/75: .5X TO 1.2X BRONZE
SILVER PRINT RUN 75 SER.#'d SETS
HF1 Brett Favre 10.00 25.00
HF2 Chad Pennington 4.00 10.00
HF3 Clinton Portis 4.00 10.00
HF4 David Carr 2.50 6.00
HF5 Deion Sanders 4.00 10.00
HF6 Donovan McNabb 4.00 10.00
HF7 Drew Bledsoe 4.00 10.00
HF8 Emmitt Smith 10.00 25.00
HF9 Jamal Lewis 3.00 8.00
HF10 Jerry Rice 8.00 20.00
HF11 Jim Kelly 4.00 10.00
HF12 Joe Montana 10.00 25.00
HF13 Joey Harrington 3.00 8.00
HF14 Marshall Faulk 4.00 10.00
HF15 Marvin Harrison 4.00 10.00
HF16 Michael Irvin 4.00 10.00
HF17 Michael Vick 5.00 12.00
HF18 Mike Singletary 4.00 10.00
HF19 Peyton Manning 8.00 20.00
HF20 Ricky Williams 3.00 8.00
HF21 Steve McNair 4.00 10.00
HF22 Terrell Davis 4.00 10.00
HF23 Terrell Owens 4.00 10.00
HF24 Tom Brady 8.00 20.00
HF25 Warren Moon 3.00 8.00

2004 Playoff Hogg Heaven Leather in Leather

LEATHER PRINT RUN 250 SER.#'d SETS
*LACE VETS/25: 1.2X TO 3X LEATHER
*LACE ROOKIE/25: 1X TO 2.5X LEATHER
LACES PRINT RUN 25 SER.#'d SETS
LL1 Ahman Green 3.00 8.00
LL2 Anquan Boldin 4.00 10.00
LL3 Chad Johnson 4.00 10.00
LL4 Donovan McNabb 4.00 10.00
LL5 Emmitt Smith 10.00 25.00
LL6 Jamal Lewis 3.00 8.00
LL7 Jeff Garcia 3.00 8.00
LL8 Kevan Barlow 2.50 6.00
LL9 Koren Robinson 2.50 6.00
LL10 Marc Bulger 3.00 8.00
LL11 Matt Hasselbeck 3.00 8.00
LL12 Randy Moss 4.00 10.00
LL13 Ray Lewis 4.00 10.00
LL14 Ricky Williams 3.00 8.00
LL15 Rudi Johnson 3.00 8.00
LL16 Shaun Alexander 3.00 8.00
LL17 Steve McNair 4.00 10.00
LL18 Steve Smith 4.00 10.00
LL19 Terrell Owens 4.00 10.00
LL20 Terrell Suggs 3.00 8.00
LL21 Eli Manning 12.00 30.00
LL22 Philip Rivers 8.00 20.00
LL23 Ben Roethlisberger 12.00 30.00
LL24 J.P. Losman 2.50 6.00
LL25 Larry Fitzgerald 6.00 15.00
LL26 Roy Williams WR 3.00 8.00
LL27 Reggie Williams 2.50 6.00
LL28 Lee Evans 3.00 8.00
LL29 Steven Jackson 5.00 12.00
LL30 Chris Perry 2.50 6.00
LL31 Kevin Jones 2.50 6.00
LL32 Tatum Bell 2.50 6.00
LL33 Michael Clayton 2.50 6.00
LL34 Kellen Winslow Jr. 3.00 8.00
LL35 Michael Jenkins 3.00 8.00
LL36 Julius Jones 2.50 6.00
LL37 Matt Schaub 6.00 15.00
LL38 Luke McCown 2.50 6.00
LL39 Rashaun Woods 2.50 6.00
LL40 Greg Jones 2.00 5.00

2004 Playoff Hogg Heaven Leather Quads

STATED PRINT RUN 1250 SER.#'d SETS
LQ1 Josh McCown 1.25 3.00
Anquan Boldin
Bryant Johnson
Marcel Shipp
LQ2 Michael Vick 1.50 4.00
Peerless Price
T.J. Duckett
Warrick Dunn
LQ3 Kyle Boller 1.25 3.00
Jamal Lewis
Ray Lewis
Todd Heap
LQ4 Drew Bledsoe 1.25 3.00
Travis Henry
Eric Moulds
Josh Reed
LQ5 Rex Grossman 1.25 3.00
Anthony Thomas
Brian Urlacher
David Terrell
LQ6 Tim Couch 1.00 2.50
William Green
Kelly Holcomb
Dennis Northcutt
LQ7 Brett Favre 3.00 8.00
Ahman Green
Donald Driver
Javon Walker
LQ8 Peyton Manning 2.50 6.00
Edgerrin James
Marvin Harrison
Reggie Wayne
LQ9 Trent Green 1.25 3.00
Priest Holmes
Dante Hall
Tony Gonzalez
LQ10 Jay Fiedler 1.25 3.00
Ricky Williams
Chris Chambers
Zach Thomas
LQ11 Aaron Brooks 1.00 2.50
Deuce McAllister
Donte Stallworth
Joe Horn
LQ12 Kerry Collins 1.25 3.00
Tiki Barber
Amani Toomer
Jeremy Shockey
LQ13 Chad Pennington 1.25 3.00
Curtis Martin
John Abraham
Shaun Ellis
LQ14 Rich Gannon 2.50 6.00
Jerry Rice
Tim Brown
Charles Woodson
LQ15 Donovan McNabb 1.25 3.00
Correll Buckhalter
Freddie Mitchell
Todd Pinkston
LQ16 Jerome Bettis 1.25 3.00
Hines Ward
Kendrell Bell
Plaxico Burress
LQ17 Doug Flutie 1.25 3.00
LaDainian Tomlinson
Drew Brees
David Doston
LQ18 Kurt Warner 1.25 3.00
Marshall Faulk
Isaac Bruce
Torry Holt
LQ19 Brad Johnson 1.00 2.50
Mike Alstott
Keyshawn Johnson
Warren Sapp
LQ20 Steve McNair 1.25 3.00
Eddie George
Jevon Kearse
Derrick Mason
LQ21 Patrick Ramsey 1.00 2.50
Laveranues Coles
Rod Gardner
LaVar Arrington
LQ22 Eli Manning 5.00 12.00
Philip Rivers
Ben Roethlisberger
J.P. Losman
LQ23 Larry Fitzgerald 2.00 5.00
Roy Williams
Reggie Williams
Lee Evans
LQ24 Steven Jackson 1.25 3.00
Chris Perry
Kevin Jones
Tatum Bell
LQ25 Michael Clayton 1.00 2.50
Kellen Winslow Jr..
Michael Jenkins
Julius Jones

2004 Playoff Hogg Heaven Leather Quads Jerseys Single

SINGLE PRINT RUN 150 SER.#'d SETS
*DOUBLE/100: .5X TO 1.2X SINGLE
DOUBLE PRINT RUN 100 SER.#'d SETS
*TRIPLE/50: .8X TO 2X SINGLE
TRIPLE PRINT RUN 50 SER.#'d SETS
*QUADS/25: 1X TO 2.5X SINGLE
QUAD PRINT RUN 25 SER.#'d SETS
LQ1 Josh McCown 4.00 10.00
Anquan Boldin
Bryant Johnson
Marcel Shipp
LQ2 Michael Vick 5.00 12.00
Peerless Price
T.J. Duckett
Warrick Dunn
LQ3 Kyle Boller 4.00 10.00
Jamal Lewis
Ray Lewis
Todd Heap
LQ4 Drew Bledsoe 4.00 10.00
Travis Henry
Eric Moulds
Josh Reed
LQ5 Rex Grossman 4.00 10.00
Anthony Thomas
Brian Urlacher
David Terrell
LQ6 Tim Couch 3.00 8.00
William Green
Kelly Holcomb
Dennis Northcutt
LQ7 Brett Favre 10.00 25.00
Ahman Green
Donald Driver
Javon Walker
LQ8 Peyton Manning 8.00 20.00
Edgerrin James
Marvin Harrison
Reggie Wayne
LQ9 Trent Green 4.00 10.00
Priest Holmes
Dante Hall
Tony Gonzalez
LQ10 Jay Fiedler 4.00 10.00
Ricky Williams
Chris Chambers
Zach Thomas
LQ11 Aaron Brooks 3.00 8.00
Deuce McAllister
Donte Stallworth
Joe Horn
LQ12 Kerry Collins 4.00 10.00
Tiki Barber
Amani Toomer
Jeremy Shockey
LQ13 Chad Pennington 4.00 10.00
Curtis Martin
John Abraham
Shaun Ellis
LQ14 Rich Gannon 6.00 15.00
Jerry Rice
Tim Brown
Charles Woodson
LQ15 Donovan McNabb 4.00 10.00
Correll Buckhalter
Freddie Mitchell
Todd Pinkston
LQ16 Jerome Bettis 4.00 10.00
Hines Ward
Kendrell Bell
Plaxico Burress
LQ17 Doug Flutie 4.00 10.00
LaDainian Tomlinson
Drew Brees
David Boston
LQ18 Kurt Warner 4.00 10.00
Marshall Faulk
Isaac Bruce
Torry Holt
LQ19 Brad Johnson 3.00 8.00
Mike Alstott
Keyshawn Johnson
Warren Sapp
LQ20 Steve McNair 4.00 10.00
Eddie George
Jevon Kearse
Derrick Mason
LQ21 Patrick Ramsey 3.00 8.00
Laveranues Coles
Rod Gardner
LaVar Arrington
LQ22 Eli Manning 15.00 40.00
Philip Rivers
Ben Roethlisberger
J.P. Losman
LQ23 Larry Fitzgerald 6.00 15.00
Roy Williams
Reggie Williams
Lee Evans
LQ24 Steven Jackson 4.00 10.00
Chris Perry
Kevin Jones
Tatum Bell
LQ25 Michael Clayton 4.00 10.00
Kellen Winslow Jr.
Michael Jenkins
Julius Jones

2004 Playoff Hogg Heaven Material Hoggs Bronze

BRONZE PRINT RUN 150 SER.#'d SETS
*GOLD/25: 1X TO 2.5X BRONZE/150
GOLD PRINT RUN 25 SER.#'d SETS
UNPRICED PLATINUM PRINT RUN 1
*SILVER/75: .5X TO 1.2X BRONZE/150
SILVER PRINT RUN 75 SER.#'d SETS
MH1 Aaron Brooks 3.00 8.00
MH2 Anquan Boldin 4.00 10.00
MH3 Brett Favre 10.00 25.00
MH4 Brian Urlacher 4.00 10.00
MH5 Bruce Smith 4.00 10.00
MH6 Byron Leftwich 3.00 8.00
MH7 Chad Johnson 4.00 10.00
MH8 Chad Pennington 4.00 10.00
MH9 Charles Rogers 2.50 6.00
MH10 Clinton Portis 4.00 10.00
MH11 Curtis Martin 4.00 10.00
MH12 Daunte Culpepper 3.00 8.00
MH13 David Carr 2.50 6.00
MH14 Deuce McAllister 3.00 8.00
MH15 Donovan McNabb 4.00 10.00
MH16 Eddie George 3.00 8.00
MH17 Edgerrin James 3.00 8.00
MH18 Emmitt Smith 10.00 25.00
MH19 Fred Taylor 3.00 8.00
MH20 Jamal Lewis 3.00 8.00
MH21 Jeff Garcia 3.00 8.00
MH22 Jeremy Shockey 3.00 8.00
MH23 Jerome Bettis 4.00 10.00
MH24 Jerry Rice 8.00 20.00
MH25 Jevon Kearse 3.00 8.00
MH26 Joey Harrington 3.00 8.00
MH27 Josh McCown 3.00 8.00
MH28 Kendrell Bell 2.50 6.00
MH29 Keyshawn Johnson 3.00 8.00
MH30 Kurt Warner 4.00 10.00
MH31 LaDainian Tomlinson 4.00 10.00
MH32 Mark Brunell 3.00 8.00
MH33 Marshall Faulk 4.00 10.00
MH34 Marvin Harrison 4.00 10.00
MH35 Michael Bennett 3.00 8.00
MH36 Michael Vick 5.00 12.00
MH37 Patrick Ramsey 3.00 8.00
MH38 Peyton Manning 8.00 20.00
MH39 Priest Holmes 4.00 10.00
MH40 Randy Moss 4.00 10.00
MH41 Ricky Williams 3.00 8.00
MH42 Roy Williams S 3.00 8.00
MH43 Santana Moss 3.00 8.00
MH44 Shaun Alexander 3.00 8.00
MH45 Steve McNair 4.00 10.00
MH46 Terrell Owens 4.00 10.00
MH47 Terrell Davis 4.00 10.00
MH48 Tiki Barber 4.00 10.00
MH49 Tim Brown 4.00 10.00
MH50 Torry Holt 3.00 8.00

2004 Playoff Hogg Heaven Pig Pals

STATED PRINT RUN 1050 SER.#'d SETS
PP1 Anquan Boldin 4.00 10.00
Emmitt Smith
PP2 Michael Vick 2.00 5.00
Peerless Price
PP3 Jamal Lewis 1.50 4.00
Ray Lewis
PP4 Drew Bledsoe 1.50 4.00
Eric Moulds
PP5 Stephen Davis 1.25 3.00
Julius Peppers
PP6 Brian Urlacher 1.50 4.00
Rex Grossman
PP7 Chad Johnson 1.50 4.00
Peter Warrick
PP8 Roy Williams S 1.25 3.00
Terence Newman
PP9 Jake Plummer 1.50 4.00
Clinton Portis
PP10 Joey Harrington 1.25 3.00
Charles Rogers
PP11 Brett Favre 4.00 10.00
Ahman Green
PP12 David Carr 1.50 4.00
Andre Johnson
PP13 Peyton Manning 3.00 8.00
Edgerrin James
PP14 Byron Leftwich 1.25 3.00
Jimmy Smith
PP15 Priest Holmes 1.50 4.00
Tony Gonzalez
PP16 Ricky Williams 1.50 4.00
Zach Thomas
PP17 Randy Moss 1.50 4.00
Michael Bennett
PP18 Tom Brady 3.00 8.00
Ty Law
PP19 Aaron Brooks 1.25 3.00
Deuce McAllister
PP20 Kerry Collins 1.50 4.00
Michael Strahan
PP21 Chad Pennington 1.50 4.00
Curtis Martin
PP22 Jerry Rice 3.00 8.00
Tim Brown
PP23 Donovan McNabb 1.50 4.00
Correll Buckhalter
PP24 Jerome Bettis 1.50 4.00
Hines Ward
PP25 Drew Brees 1.50 4.00
LaDainian Tomlinson
PP26 Matt Hasselbeck 1.25 3.00
Koren Robinson
PP27 Marc Bulger 1.25 3.00
Isaac Bruce
PP28 Brad Johnson 1.25 3.00
Warren Sapp
PP29 Steve McNair 1.50 4.00
Eddie George
PP30 Patrick Ramsey 1.25 3.00
Laveranues Coles

2004 Playoff Hogg Heaven Pig Pals Jerseys

STATED PRINT RUN 100 SER.#'d SETS
UNPRICED PRIME PRINT RUN 1 SET
PP1 Anquan Boldin 15.00 40.00
Emmitt Smith
PP2 Michael Vick 8.00 20.00
Peerless Price
PP3 Jamal Lewis 6.00 15.00
Ray Lewis
PP4 Drew Bledsoe 6.00 15.00
Eric Moulds
PP5 Stephen Davis 5.00 12.00
Julius Peppers
PP6 Brian Urlacher 6.00 15.00
Rex Grossman
PP7 Chad Johnson 6.00 15.00
Peter Warrick
PP8 Roy Williams S 5.00 12.00
Terence Newman
PP9 Jake Plummer 6.00 15.00
Clinton Portis
PP10 Joey Harrington 5.00 12.00
Charles Rogers
PP11 Brett Favre 15.00 40.00
Ahman Green
PP12 David Carr 6.00 15.00
Andre Johnson
PP13 Peyton Manning 12.00 30.00
Edgerrin James
PP14 Byron Leftwich 5.00 12.00
Jimmy Smith
PP15 Priest Holmes 6.00 15.00
Tony Gonzalez
PP16 Ricky Williams 6.00 15.00
Zach Thomas
PP17 Randy Moss 6.00 15.00
Michael Bennett
PP18 Tom Brady 12.00 30.00
Ty Law
PP19 Aaron Brooks 5.00 12.00
Deuce McAllister
PP20 Kerry Collins 6.00 15.00
Michael Strahan
PP21 Chad Pennington 6.00 15.00
Curtis Martin
PP22 Jerry Rice 12.00 30.00
Tim Brown
PP23 Donovan McNabb 6.00 15.00
Correll Buckhalter
PP24 Jerome Bettis 6.00 15.00
Hines Ward
PP25 Drew Brees 6.00 15.00
LaDainian Tomlinson
PP26 Matt Hasselbeck 5.00 12.00
Koren Robinson
PP27 Marc Bulger 5.00 12.00
Isaac Bruce
PP28 Brad Johnson 5.00 12.00
Warren Sapp
PP29 Steve McNair 6.00 15.00
Eddie George
PP30 Patrick Ramsey 5.00 12.00
Laveranues Coles

2004 Playoff Hogg Heaven Pig Pens Autographs

STATED PRINT RUN 50-250
PP51 ISSUED AS EXCH REPLACEMENT
PP1 Aaron Brooks/50 10.00 25.00
PP2 Ahman Green/50 10.00 25.00
PP3 Anquan Boldin/100 10.00 25.00
PP4 Dante Hall/50 10.00 25.00
PP5 Deuce McAllister/50 10.00 25.00
PP6 Domanick Davis/250 6.00 15.00
PP7 George Blanda/100 25.00 50.00
PP8 Ickey Woods/150 10.00 25.00
PP9 James Lofton/170 10.00 25.00
PP10 Jim Brown/50 50.00 100.00
PP11 Jim Plunkett/50 12.00 30.00
PP12 Joe Greene/50 25.00 50.00
PP13 Joe Namath/100 40.00 80.00
PP14 John Riggins/100 20.00 50.00
PP16 Kyle Boller/150 8.00 20.00
PP17 Matt Hasselbeck/75 10.00 25.00
PP18 Mel Blount/53 12.00 30.00
PP19 Ozzie Newsome/187 12.00 30.00
PP20 Patrick Ramsey/50 10.00 25.00
PP21 Priest Holmes/50 12.00 30.00
PP23 Roy Williams S/50 10.00 25.00
PP24 Rudi Johnson/100 8.00 20.00
PP25 Sammy Baugh/150 No Auto 10.00 25.00
PP26 Shaun Alexander/50 10.00 25.00
PP27 Steve Smith/150 10.00 25.00
PP28 Terence Newman/150 8.00 20.00
PP29 Todd Heap/89 10.00 25.00
PP30 Warren Moon/75 12.00 30.00
PP31 Ahmad Carroll/141 6.00 15.00
PP32 Bernard Berrian/125 15.00 40.00
PP33 Cedric Cobbs/150 6.00 15.00
PP34 D.J. Hackett/150 8.00 20.00
PP35 D.J. Williams/150 10.00 25.00
PP36 Devard Darling/150 6.00 15.00
PP37 Dunta Robinson/150 6.00 15.00
PP38 Ernest Wilford/75 10.00 25.00
PP39 Jerricho Cotchery/150 8.00 20.00
PP40 Johnnie Morant/100 6.00 15.00
PP41 Jonathan Vilma/150 10.00 25.00
PP42 Josh Harris/150 6.00 15.00
PP43 Julius Jones/100 8.00 20.00
PP44 Luke McCown/150 8.00 20.00
PP45 Mewelde Moore/150 8.00 20.00
PP46 Michael Jenkins/125 10.00 25.00
PP47 Philip Rivers/150 50.00 80.00
PP48 Ricardo Colclough/150 8.00 20.00
PP49 Tatum Bell/61 10.00 25.00
PP51 T.J. Houshmandzadeh/150 10.00 25.00

2004 Playoff Hogg Heaven Rookie Hoggs

STATED PRINT RUN 750 SER.#'d SETS
RH1 Eli Manning 8.00 20.00
RH2 Robert Gallery 1.25 3.00
RH3 Larry Fitzgerald 3.00 8.00
RH4 Philip Rivers 5.00 12.00
RH5 Sean Taylor 2.50 6.00
RH6 Kellen Winslow Jr. 1.25 3.00
RH7 Roy Williams WR 1.25 3.00
RH8 DeAngelo Hall 1.25 3.00
RH9 Reggie Williams 1.00 2.50
RH10 Dunta Robinson .75 2.00
RH11 Ben Roethlisberger 8.00 20.00
RH12 Jonathan Vilma 1.25 3.00
RH13 Lee Evans 1.25 3.00
RH14 Tommie Harris 1.25 3.00
RH15 Michael Clayton 1.00 2.50
RH16 D.J. Williams 1.25 3.00
RH17 Will Smith 1.00 2.50
RH18 Kenechi Udeze 1.00 2.50
RH19 Vince Wilfork 1.25 3.00
RH20 J.P. Losman 1.00 2.50
RH21 Marcus Tubbs .75 2.00
RH22 Steven Jackson 2.00 5.00
RH23 Ahmad Carroll .75 2.00
RH24 Chris Perry 1.00 2.50
RH25 Jason Babin 1.25 3.00
RH26 Chris Gamble 1.00 2.50
RH27 Michael Jenkins 1.25 3.00
RH28 Kevin Jones 1.00 2.50
RH29 Rashaun Woods .75 2.00
RH30 Ben Watson 1.25 3.00
RH31 Ben Troupe 1.00 2.50
RH32 Tatum Bell 1.00 2.50
RH33 Julius Jones 1.00 2.50
RH34 Ernest Wilford 1.00 2.50
RH35 Devery Henderson 1.25 3.00
RH36 Darius Watts .75 2.00
RH37 Greg Jones .75 2.00
RH38 Sean Jones 1.00 2.50
RH39 Keary Colbert .75 2.00
RH40 Derrick Hamilton .75 2.00
RH41 Bernard Berrian 1.25 3.00
RH42 Devard Darling .75 2.00
RH43 Matt Schaub 2.50 6.00
RH44 Carlos Francis .75 2.00
RH45 Samie Parker .75 2.00
RH46 Luke McCown 1.00 2.50
RH47 Jerricho Cotchery 1.00 2.50
RH48 Mewelde Moore 1.00 2.50
RH49 Cedric Cobbs .75 2.00
RH50 Drew Henson .75 2.00

2004 Playoff Hogg Heaven Rookie Hoggs Autographs

STATED PRINT RUN 150 SER.#'d SETS
RH2 Robert Gallery 8.00 20.00
RH4 Philip Rivers 30.00 80.00
RH7 Roy Williams WR 8.00 20.00
RH8 DeAngelo Hall 8.00 20.00
RH10 Dunta Robinson 5.00 12.00
RH13 Lee Evans 8.00 20.00
RH15 Michael Clayton 6.00 15.00
RH20 J.P. Losman 6.00 15.00
RH24 Chris Perry 6.00 15.00
RH27 Michael Jenkins 8.00 20.00
RH30 Ben Watson 8.00 20.00
RH31 Ben Troupe 6.00 15.00
RH32 Tatum Bell 6.00 15.00
RH33 Julius Jones 6.00 15.00
RH35 Devery Henderson 8.00 20.00
RH36 Darius Watts 5.00 12.00
RH37 Greg Jones 5.00 12.00
RH39 Keary Colbert 5.00 12.00
RH40 Derrick Hamilton 5.00 12.00
RH41 Bernard Berrian 8.00 20.00
RH42 Devard Darling 5.00 12.00
RH46 Luke McCown 6.00 15.00
RH48 Mewelde Moore 6.00 15.00
RH49 Cedric Cobbs 5.00 12.00

2004 Playoff Hogg Heaven Unsung Hoggs

COMPLETE SET (25) 20.00 50.00
STATED PRINT RUN 1250 SER.#'d SETS
UH1 Keith Brooking 1.25 3.00
UH2 Ed Reed 1.50 4.00
UH3 Takeo Spikes 1.25 3.00
UH4 Kris Jenkins 1.50 4.00
UH5 Marty Booker 1.50 4.00
UH6 Quincy Morgan 1.25 3.00
UH7 Dat Nguyen 1.25 3.00
UH8 Al Wilson 1.25 3.00
UH9 Kabeer Gbaja-Biamila 1.50 4.00
UH10 Dwight Freeney 1.50 4.00
UH11 Marcus Stroud 1.25 3.00

UH12 Tony Richardson 1.25 3.00
UH13 Patrick Surtain 1.25 3.00
UH14 Jim Kleinsasser 1.25 3.00
UH15 Tedy Bruschi 2.00 5.00
UH16 Michael Lewis 1.50 4.00
UH17 Tyrone Wheatley 1.50 4.00
UH18 Brian Dawkins 1.50 4.00
UH19 Joey Porter 1.50 4.00
UH20 Julian Peterson 1.50 4.00
UH21 Darrell Jackson 1.50 4.00
UH22 Keenan McCardell 1.25 3.00
UH23 Joe Jurevicius 1.25 3.00
UH24 Keith Bulluck 1.25 3.00
UH25 Damerien McCants 1.25 3.00

2001 Playoff Honors

Released as a 232-card set, this product was issued 16 packs per box with 6 cards per pack.This set includes 100 veterans and 132 rookies. The first 100 rookies (101-200) are serial numbered to 250, and the remaining rookies are numbered to 725. Cards numbered 201 through 235 contained swatches of game used memorabilia. Cards number 209, 211 and 221 were not produced.

COMP.SET w/o RC's (100) 10.00 25.00
201-235 ROOKIE JSY PRINT RUN 725
1 Rob Johnson .30 .75
2 Eric Moulds .30 .75
3 Marvin Harrison .40 1.00
4 Edgerrin James .40 1.00
5 Peyton Manning 1.00 2.50
6 Jay Fiedler .30 .75
7 Lamar Smith .30 .75
8 Zach Thomas .40 1.00
9 Dan Marino 1.00 2.50
10 Drew Bledsoe .40 1.00
11 Terry Glenn .30 .75
12 Wayne Chrebet .30 .75
13 Curtis Martin .40 1.00
14 Chad Pennington .40 1.00
15 Vinny Testaverde .30 .75
16 Corey Dillon .30 .75
17 Jon Kitna .30 .75
18 Akili Smith .25 .60
19 Peter Warrick .30 .75
20 Kevin Johnson .25 .60
21 Tim Couch .25 .60
22 Eddie George .40 1.00
23 Steve McNair .40 1.00
24 Jevon Kearse .30 .75
25 Jerome Bettis .40 1.00
26 Kordell Stewart .30 .75
27 Plaxico Burress .30 .75
28 Mark Brunell .30 .75
29 Keenan McCardell .30 .75
30 Jimmy Smith .30 .75
31 Fred Taylor .40 1.00
32 Elvis Grbac .30 .75
33 Jamal Lewis .40 1.00
34 Ray Lewis .40 1.00
35 Mike Anderson .30 .75
36 Terrell Davis .40 1.00
37 John Elway 1.00 2.50
38 Brian Griese .30 .75
39 Ed McCaffrey .30 .75
40 Tony Gonzalez .40 1.00
41 Trent Green .40 1.00
42 Sylvester Morris .25 .60
43 Tim Brown .40 1.00
44 Rich Gannon .30 .75
45 Charlie Garner .30 .75
46 Tyrone Wheatley .30 .75
47 Charles Woodson .40 1.00
48 Tim Dwight .30 .75
49 Doug Flutie .40 1.00
50 Junior Seau .40 1.00
51 Shaun Alexander .40 1.00
52 Matt Hasselbeck .40 1.00
53 Ricky Watters .30 .75
54 Tony Banks .25 .60
55 Joey Galloway .30 .75
56 Emmitt Smith 1.00 2.50
57 Troy Aikman .60 1.50
58 Kerry Collins .30 .75
59 Ron Dayne .30 .75
60 Donovan McNabb .40 1.00
61 Duce Staley .30 .75
62 David Boston .25 .60
63 Thomas Jones .30 .75
64 Jake Plummer .30 .75
65 Stephen Davis .30 .75
66 Jeff George .30 .75
67 Michael Westbrook .25 .60
68 Deion Sanders .40 1.00
69 James Allen .25 .60
70 Cade McNown .30 .75
71 Marcus Robinson .30 .75
72 Brian Urlacher .50 1.25
73 Germane Crowell .25 .60
74 Charlie Batch .30 .75
75 James Stewart .25 .60
76 Brett Favre 1.25 3.00
77 Antonio Freeman .40 1.00
78 Ahman Green .40 1.00
79 Cris Carter .40 1.00
80 Daunte Culpepper .30 .75
81 Randy Moss .40 1.00
82 Mike Alstott .30 .75
83 Warrick Dunn .40 1.00
84 Brad Johnson .30 .75
85 Keyshawn Johnson .30 .75
86 Warren Sapp .30 .75
87 Jamal Anderson .30 .75
88 Chris Chandler .30 .75
89 Isaac Bruce .40 1.00
90 Marshall Faulk .40 1.00
91 Torry Holt .30 .75
92 Kurt Warner .60 1.50
93 Aaron Brooks .30 .75
94 Albert Connell .25 .60
95 Ricky Williams .40 1.00
96 Jeff Garcia .30 .75
97 Terrell Owens .40 1.00
98 Steve Young .50 1.25
99 Jerry Rice .75 2.00
100 Jeff Lewis .25 .60
101 Rashard Casey RC 2.00 5.00
102 A.J. Feeley RC 2.50 6.00
103 Josh Booty RC 2.50 6.00
104 LaMont Jordan RC 3.00 8.00
105 Ben Leard RC 2.00 5.00
106 David Rivers RC 2.00 5.00
107 Tim Hasselbeck RC 2.50 6.00
108 Jason McKinley RC 2.00 5.00
109 Correll Buckhalter RC 3.00 8.00
110 Dan Alexander RC 2.50 6.00
111 Derrick Blaylock RC 2.50 6.00
112 Chris Barnes RC 2.00 5.00
113 Dee Brown RC 2.00 5.00
114 Derek Combs RC 2.00 5.00
115 David Allen RC 2.00 5.00
116 DeAngelo Evans RC 2.50 6.00
117 Reggie White RC 2.00 5.00
118 Heath Evans RC 2.50 6.00
119 George Layne RC 2.00 5.00
120 Moran Norris RC 2.00 5.00
121 Bhawoh Jue RC 2.50 6.00
122 Dustin McClintock RC 2.50 6.00
123 Ja'Mar Toombs RC 2.00 5.00
124 Steve Smith RC 6.00 15.00
125 Milton Wynn RC 2.00 5.00
126 Justin McCareins RC 2.50 6.00
127 Jarrod Cooper RC 2.50 6.00
128 Vinny Sutherland RC 2.00 5.00
129 Alex Bannister RC 2.00 5.00
130 Scotty Anderson RC 2.00 5.00
131 Onome Ojo RC 2.00 5.00
132 Damerien McCants RC 2.50 6.00
133 Eddie Berlin RC 2.00 5.00
134 Jonathan Carter RC 2.00 5.00
135 Bobby Newcombe RC 2.50 6.00
136 Cedrick Wilson RC 2.50 6.00
137 Kevin Kasper RC 2.00 5.00
138 Francis St. Paul RC 2.00 5.00
139 David Martin RC 2.00 5.00
140 T.J. Houshmandzadeh RC 4.00 10.00
141 John Capel RC 2.00 5.00
142 Reggie Germany RC 2.00 5.00
143 Chris Taylor RC 2.00 5.00
144 Ken-Yon Rambo RC 2.00 5.00
145 Richmond Flowers RC 2.00 5.00
146 Quentin McCord RC 2.50 6.00
147 Andre King RC 2.00 5.00
148 Boo Williams RC 2.00 5.00
149 Daniel Guy RC 2.00 5.00
150 Javon Green RC 2.00 5.00
151 Ronney Daniels RC 2.00 5.00
152 Alge Crumpler RC 3.00 8.00
153 Tony Driver RC 2.50 6.00
154 Shad Meier RC 2.00 5.00
155 Jabari Holloway RC 2.00 5.00
156 Ryan Pickett RC 2.00 5.00
157 Cedric James RC 2.00 5.00
158 Tony Stewart RC 2.50 6.00
159 Sean Brewer RC 2.00 5.00
160 Orlando Huff RC 2.00 5.00
161 Nate Clements RC 2.50 6.00
162 Will Allen RC 3.00 8.00
163 Willie Middlebrooks RC 2.50 6.00
164 Jamar Fletcher RC 2.00 5.00
165 Ken Lucas RC 2.50 6.00
166 Fred Smoot RC 3.00 8.00
167 Michael Stone RC 2.00 5.00
168 Tony Dixon RC 2.00 5.00
169 Andre Dyson RC 2.00 5.00
170 Gary Baxter RC 2.00 5.00
171 Adam Archuleta RC 2.50 6.00
172 Derrick Gibson RC 2.00 5.00
173 Edgerton Hartwell RC 2.00 5.00
174 Jamal Reynolds RC 2.00 5.00
175 Richard Seymour RC 3.00 8.00
176 Brandon Manumaleuna RC 2.50 6.00
177 Idrees Bashir RC 2.00 5.00
178 DeLawrence Grant RC 2.00 5.00
179 Karon Riley RC 2.00 5.00
180 Cedric Scott RC 2.00 5.00
181 Damione Lewis RC 2.50 6.00
182 Marcus Stroud RC 2.50 6.00
183 Casey Hampton RC 3.00 8.00
184 Willie Howard RC 2.00 5.00
185 Shaun Rogers RC 3.00 8.00
186 Kenny Smith RC 2.00 5.00
187 Marcus Bell DT RC 2.00 5.00
188 Mario Fatafehi RC 2.00 5.00
189 Kendrell Bell RC 3.00 8.00
190 Tommy Polley RC 2.00 5.00
191 Jamie Winborn RC 2.50 6.00
192 Sedrick Hodge RC 2.00 5.00
193 Torrance Marshall RC 2.00 5.00
194 Eric Westmoreland RC 2.00 5.00
195 Brian Allen RC 2.00 5.00
196 Morlon Greenwood RC 2.00 5.00
197 Brandon Spoon RC 2.50 6.00
198 Carlos Polk RC 2.00 5.00
199 Alex Lincoln RC 2.00 5.00
200 Keith Adams RC 2.00 5.00
201 Kevan Barlow JSY RC 2.50 6.00
202 Michael Bennett JSY RC 2.50 6.00
203 Drew Brees JSY RC 25.00 50.00
204 Quincy Carter JSY RC 2.50 6.00
205 Andre Carter JSY RC 2.50 6.00
206 Chris Chambers JSY RC 3.00 8.00
207 Robert Ferguson JSY RC 3.00 8.00
208 Rod Gardner JSY RC 2.50 6.00
210 Travis Henry JSY RC 2.50 6.00
212 Chad Johnson JSY RC 5.00 12.00
213 Rudi Johnson JSY RC 3.00 8.00
214 Sage Rosenfels JSY RC 3.00 8.00
215 Deuce McAllister JSY RC 3.00 8.00
216 Mike McMahon JSY RC 2.50 6.00
217 Snoop Minnis JSY RC 2.00 5.00
218 Travis Minor JSY RC 2.50 6.00
219 Freddie Mitchell JSY RC 2.00 5.00
220 Quincy Morgan JSY RC 2.50 6.00
222 Santana Moss JSY RC 4.00 10.00
223 Jesse Palmer JSY RC 2.50 6.00
224 Koren Robinson JSY RC 2.50 6.00
225 Josh Heupel JSY RC 3.00 8.00
226 Justin Smith JSY RC 3.00 8.00
227 David Terrell JSY RC 2.50 6.00
228 Anthony Thomas JSY RC 3.00 8.00
229 LaDainian Tomlinson JSY RC 10.00 25.00
230 Marques Tuiasosopo JSY RC 2.50 6.00
231 Michael Vick JSY RC 12.00 30.00
232 Gerard Warren JSY RC 2.50 6.00
233 Reggie Wayne JSY RC 6.00 15.00
234 Chris Weinke JSY RC 2.50 6.00
235 Leonard Davis JSY RC 3.00 8.00

2001 Playoff Honors Chicago Collection

NOT PRICED DUE TO SCARCITY

2001 Playoff Honors X's and O's

*VETS/200-300: 3X TO 8X BASIC CARDS
*VETS/140-199: 4X TO 10X BASIC CARDS
*VETS/100-139: 5X TO 12X BASIC CARDS
*VETS/70-99: 6X TO 15X BASIC CARDS
*ROOKIES/70-80: .4X TO 1X
*VETS/50-69: 8X TO 20X BASIC CARDS
*ROOKIES/50-60: .5X TO 1.2X
*ROOKIES JSY/50-60: .8X TO 2X
*VETS/30-45: 10X TO 25X BASIC CARDS
*ROOKIES/30-40: .6X TO 1.5X
*ROOKIES JSY/30-40: 1X TO 2.5X
*VETS/21-29: 12X TO 30X BASIC CARDS
*ROOKIES/20: 1X TO 2.5X
*ROOKIES JSY/20: 1.5X TO 4X
*VETS/10-19: 15X TO 40X BASIC CARDS
*ROOKIES/10: 1.2X TO 3X
*ROOKIES JSY/10: 2X TO 5X
203 Drew Brees JSY/20 100.00 250.00

2001 Playoff Honors Alma Mater Materials

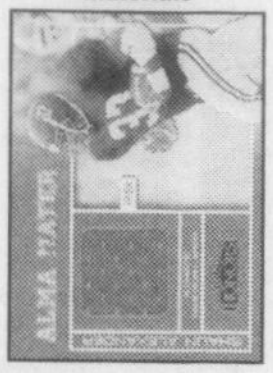

STATED ODDS 1:32
*VARSITY PATCH/50: .8X TO 2X BASIC JSY
VARSITY PATCH PRINT RUN 50
AM1 Shaun Alexander 10.00 25.00
AM2 Drew Bledsoe 15.00 30.00
AM3 Earl Campbell 12.50 25.00
AM4 Sam Cowart 5.00 12.00
AM5 Terrell Davis 8.00 20.00
AM6 Tony Dorsett 12.50 30.00
AM7 John Elway SP 35.00 80.00
AM8 Eddie George SP 20.00 40.00
AM9 Edgerrin James 8.00 20.00
AM10 Keyshawn Johnson 6.00 15.00
AM11 Jevon Kearse 6.00 15.00
AM12 Fred Taylor SP 8.00 20.00
AM13 Ricky Williams SP 8.00 20.00
AM14 Olandis Gary 5.00 12.00
AM15 E.G. Green 5.00 12.00

2001 Playoff Honors Alma Mater Materials Varsity Patch Autographs

STATED PRINT RUN 25 SER.#'d SETS
AM3 Earl Campbell 75.00 125.00
AM6 Tony Dorsett 90.00 150.00
AM9 Edgerrin James 60.00 100.00

2001 Playoff Honors Game Day Jerseys

STATED ODDS 1:16
*SOUVENIRS/25: 1X TO 2.5X JERSEY
SOUVENIRS PRINT RUN 25 SER.#'d SETS
GD1 Troy Aikman 10.00 25.00
GD2 Mike Alstott 5.00 12.00
GD3 Jerome Bettis 6.00 15.00
GD4 Drew Bledsoe 6.00 15.00
GD5 Jamal Anderson 5.00 12.00
GD6 Isaac Bruce 6.00 15.00
GD7 Tim Brown 6.00 15.00
GD8 Mark Brunell 5.00 12.00
GD9 Cris Carter 6.00 15.00
GD10 Kerry Collins 5.00 12.00
GD11 Tim Couch 4.00 10.00
GD12 Daunte Culpepper 5.00 12.00
GD13 Stephen Davis 5.00 12.00
GD14 Terrell Davis 6.00 15.00
GD15 Ron Dayne 5.00 12.00
GD16 Corey Dillon 5.00 12.00
GD17 Warrick Dunn 6.00 15.00
GD18 Johnnie Morton 5.00 12.00
GD19 Marshall Faulk 6.00 15.00
GD20 Brett Favre 20.00 50.00
GD21 Eddie George 6.00 15.00
GD22 Brian Griese 5.00 12.00
GD23 Marvin Harrison 6.00 15.00
GD24 Torry Holt 5.00 12.00
GD25 Edgerrin James 6.00 15.00
GD26 Keyshawn Johnson 5.00 12.00
GD27 Jevon Kearse 5.00 12.00
GD28 Charlie Batch 5.00 12.00
GD29 Peyton Manning 15.00 40.00
GD30 Dan Marino 15.00 40.00
GD31 Curtis Martin 6.00 15.00
GD32 Donovan McNabb 6.00 15.00
GD33 Steve McNair 6.00 15.00
GD34 Joe Montana 15.00 40.00
GD35 Randy Moss 6.00 15.00
GD36 Eric Moulds 5.00 12.00
GD37 Jake Plummer 5.00 12.00
GD38 Jerry Rice 12.00 30.00
GD39 Charles Woodson 8.00 15.00
GD40 Deion Sanders 6.00 15.00
GD41 Warren Sapp 5.00 12.00
GD42 Junior Seau 6.00 15.00
GD43 Emmitt Smith 15.00 40.00
GD44 Fred Taylor 6.00 15.00
GD45 Frank Sanders 4.00 10.00
GD46 Lamar Smith 5.00 12.00
GD47 Kurt Warner 10.00 25.00
GD48 Peter Warrick 5.00 12.00
GD49 Ricky Williams 6.00 15.00
GD50 Steve Young 8.00 20.00

2001 Playoff Honors Game Day Jerseys Autographs

ANNOUNCED PRINT RUN 25 SETS
GD5 Jamal Anderson 25.00 60.00
GD7 Tim Brown 30.00 80.00
GD22 Brian Griese 25.00 60.00
GD23 Marvin Harrison 30.00 80.00
GD24 Torry Holt
GD28 Charlie Batch 25.00 60.00
GD30 Dan Marino 200.00 350.00
GD36 Eric Moulds 25.00 60.00
GD42 Junior Seau 50.00 100.00
GD43 Emmitt Smith 200.00 350.00
GD47 Kurt Warner 40.00 100.00
GD48 Peter Warrick 25.00 60.00
GD49 Ricky Williams 30.00 80.00
GD50 Steve Young 75.00 150.00

2001 Playoff Honors Honor Roll Autographs

STATED ODDS 1:48
20 Jerome Bettis 99PreCL/60 40.00 80.00
40 Fabien Bownes 01PlaUH/31 7.50 20.00
41 Tim Brown 99PreCL/61 12.50 30.00
42 Isaac Bruce 98Mom/30 20.00 40.00
45 Tedy Bruschi 01PlaUH/37 100.00 175.00
48 Bob Christian 01PlaUH/32 7.50 20.00
51 Greg Comella 01PlaUH/20 7.50 20.00
53 Germane Crowell 98Con/165 7.50 20.00
70 Randall Cunningham 99Mom/70 10.00 25.00
71 Randall Cunningham 00Abs/92 10.00 25.00
72 Randall Cunningham 00AbsCA/25 12.50 30.00
73 Randall Cunningham 00ConHFO/34 12.50 30.00
74 Randall Cunningham 00Pre/56 10.00 25.00
76 Terrell Davis 99AbsTS/28 20.00 50.00
77 Terrell Davis 99AbsTS/50 20.00 50.00
78 Terrell Davis 99AbsTS/41 20.00 50.00
79 Terrell Davis 99AbsTS/33 20.00 50.00
92 Corey Dillon 99PreCL/29 15.00 30.00
99 Kevin Faulk 99PreCL/25 20.00 40.00
108 John Fiala 01PlaUH/30 7.50 20.00
111 Chris Fuamatu-Ma'afala 98ConTic/20 12.50 30.00
113 Joey Galloway 99PreCL/49 12.50 30.00
115 Olandis Gary 99Con/55 12.50 30.00
119 Tarik Glenn 01PlaUH/35 10.00 25.00
123 Jacquez Green 98ConTic/196 10.00 25.00
130 Brock Huard 99Con/25 12.50 30.00
140 Kevin Johnson 99PreCL/25 12.50 30.00
150 John Lynch 01PlaUH/35 12.50 30.00
151 Peyton Manning 98Abs/43 75.00 150.00
157 Peyton Manning 98PreHob/33 75.00 150.00
158 Peyton Manning 98PreRet/26 75.00 150.00
165 Dan Marino 99MomSG/125 40.00 80.00
172 Cecil Martin 01PlaUH/32 7.50 20.00
173 Russell Maryland 01PlaUH/37 7.50 20.00
176 Ronald McKinnon 01PlaUH/37 7.50 20.00
177 Donovan McNabb 99Con/25 100.00 200.00
184 Cade McNown 99PreCL/97 7.50 20.00
185 Cade McNown 99PreEXP/32 12.50 30.00
190 Cade McNown 00Pre/24 12.50 30.00
216 Warren Moon 99Con/61 12.50 30.00
220 Warren Moon 00Abs/47 15.00 40.00
222 Warren Moon 00ConHFO/34 15.00 40.00
223 Warren Moon 00Pre/32 15.00 40.00
230 Jake Plummer 97Abs/29 12.50 30.00
239 Jake Plummer PT 99Con/22 15.00 40.00
244 Jake Plummer 99PreCL/26 12.50 30.00
245 Jake Plummer 00Abs/45 12.50 30.00
246 Jake Plummer 00Con/43 12.50 30.00
247 Jake Plummer 00Mom/70 10.00 25.00
248 Jake Plummer 00Pre/35 12.50 30.00
259 Barry Sanders 99Mom/26 60.00 120.00
260 Barry Sanders 99PreCL/21 60.00 120.00
262 Barry Sanders 00Abs/49 40.00 80.00
263 Barry Sanders 00Mom/72 30.00 60.00
264 Barry Sanders 00Pre/30 50.00 100.00
268 Akili Smith 99ConROY/20 10.00 25.00
271 Takeo Spikes 01PlaUH/37 7.50 20.00
273 Kordell Stewart 99MomSG/20 12.50 30.00
279 Fred Taylor 99MomSG/50 20.00 40.00
280 Fred Taylor 99PreCL/28 20.00 50.00
289 Vinny Testaverde 97Abs/44 12.50 30.00
296 Vinny Testaverde 99Con/68 10.00 25.00
299 Vinny Testaverde 00Con/41 12.50 30.00
300 Vinny Testaverde 00ConHFO/32 12.50 30.00
301 Vinny Testaverde 00Mom/66 10.00 25.00
302 Vinny Testaverde 00Pre/27 12.50 30.00
303 James Thrash 01PlaUH/24 12.50 30.00
305 Brian Urlacher 01PlaUH/31 40.00 80.00
307 Chris Walsh 01PlaUH/34 7.50 20.00
310 Ricky Williams 99AbsEXP/34 30.00 80.00
313 Ricky Williams 99PreCL/34 30.00 80.00
315 Ricky Williams 99PreEXP/37 30.00 80.00
317 Bryant Young 01PlaUH/24 12.50 30.00

2001 Playoff Honors Rookie Hidden Gems Autographs

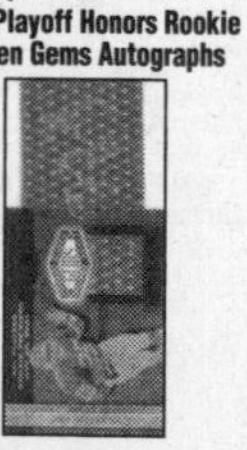

STATED PRINT RUN 50 SER.#'d SETS
201 Kevan Barlow 12.00 30.00
202 Michael Bennett 12.00 30.00
203 Drew Brees 125.00 200.00
204 Quincy Carter 12.00 30.00
205 Andre Carter 12.00 30.00
206 Chris Chambers 15.00 40.00
207 Robert Ferguson 15.00 40.00
208 Rod Gardner 12.00 30.00
210 Travis Henry 12.00 30.00
212 Chad Johnson 25.00 60.00
213 Rudi Johnson 15.00 40.00
214 Sage Rosenfels 15.00 40.00
215 Deuce McAllister 15.00 40.00
216 Mike McMahon 12.00 30.00
217 Snoop Minnis 10.00 25.00
218 Travis Minor 12.00 30.00
219 Freddie Mitchell 10.00 25.00
220 Quincy Morgan 12.00 30.00
222 Santana Moss 20.00 50.00
223 Jesse Palmer 12.00 30.00
224 Koren Robinson 12.00 30.00
225 Josh Heupel 15.00 40.00
226 Justin Smith 15.00 40.00
227 David Terrell 12.00 30.00
228 Anthony Thomas 15.00 40.00
229 LaDainian Tomlinson 100.00 200.00
230 Marques Tuiasosopo 12.00 30.00
231 Michael Vick 60.00 150.00
232 Gerard Warren 12.00 30.00
233 Reggie Wayne 30.00 80.00
234 Chris Weinke 12.00 30.00
235 Leonard Davis 15.00 40.00

2001 Playoff Honors Rookie Quad Footballs

OVERALL QUAD/TANDEM ODDS 1:16
*JERSEY QUAD: .5X TO 1.2X FB QUAD
*JSY/FB QUAD/25: .8X TO 2X FB QUAD
JERSEY/BALL COMBOS SER.#'d OF 25
RQ1 Michael Vick 25.00 60.00
Quincy Carter
Chris Weinke
Mike McMahon
RQ2 Drew Brees 40.00 100.00
LaDainian Tomlinson
Anthony Thomas
David Terrell
RQ3 Sage Rosenfels 10.00 25.00
Rod Gardner
Rudi Johnson
Chad Johnson
RQ4 Josh Heupel 6.00 15.00
Travis Minor
James Jackson
Quincy Morgan
RQ5 Koren Robinson 12.00 30.00
Reggie Wayne
Freddie Mitchell
Santana Moss
RQ6 Michael Bennett 6.00 15.00
Deuce McAllister
Travis Henry
Kevan Barlow
RQ7 Chris Chambers 6.00 15.00
Snoop Minnis
Robert Ferguson
Todd Heap
RQ8 Marques Tuiasosopo 6.00 15.00
Jesse Palmer
Justin Smith
Gerard Warren

2001 Playoff Honors Rookie Tandem Footballs

OVERALL QUAD/TANDEM ODDS 1:16
*JERSEYS: .5X TO 1.2X BALLS
*JSY/FB/100: .8X TO 2X FOOTBALL
JERSEY/FB COMBOS #'d OF 100
RT1 Michael Vick 20.00 50.00
Quincy Carter
RT2 Chris Weinke 4.00 10.00
Mike McMahon
RT3 Drew Brees 20.00 50.00
LaDainian Tomlinson
RT4 Anthony Thomas 5.00 12.00
David Terrell
RT5 Sage Rosenfels 5.00 12.00
Rod Gardner
RT6 Rudi Johnson 8.00 20.00
Chad Johnson
RT7 Josh Heupel 5.00 12.00
Travis Minor
RT8 James Jackson 4.00 10.00
Quincy Morgan
RT9 Koren Robinson 10.00 25.00
Reggie Wayne
RT10 Freddie Mitchell 6.00 15.00
Santana Moss
RT11 Michael Bennett 5.00 12.00
Deuce McAllister
RT12 Travis Henry 4.00 10.00
Kevan Barlow
RT13 Chris Chambers 5.00 12.00
Snoop Minnis
RT14 Robert Ferguson 5.00 12.00
Todd Heap
RT15 Marques Tuiasosopo 4.00 10.00
Jesse Palmer
RT16 Justin Smith 5.00 12.00
Gerard Warren
RT17 Andre Carter 4.00 10.00
Dan Morgan

2001 Playoff Honors Souvenirs

STATED ODDS 1:108
PB1 Jerry Rice 15.00 40.00
PB2 Mark Brunell 6.00 15.00
PB3 John Elway 25.00 60.00
PB4 Jimmy Smith 6.00 15.00
PB5 Peyton Manning 20.00 50.00
PB6 Eddie George 8.00 20.00
PB7 Roger Staubach FB 15.00 40.00
PB8 Bob Griese FB 10.00 25.00
PB9 Drew Bledsoe 8.00 20.00
PB10 Jamal Lewis Pylon 8.00 20.00

2001 Playoff Honors Souvenirs Signs of Greatness

STATED PRINT RUN 25 SER.#'d SETS
PB1 Jerry Rice 175.00 300.00
PB2 Mark Brunell 25.00 60.00
PB3 John Elway 200.00 350.00
PB4 Jimmy Smith 25.00 60.00
PB5 Peyton Manning No Auto 10.00 25.00
PB6 Eddie George 30.00 80.00
PB7 Roger Staubach 125.00 200.00
PB8 Bob Griese 30.00 80.00
PB9 Drew Bledsoe 50.00 120.00
PB10 Jamal Lewis 30.00 80.00

2002 Playoff Honors Samples

*SAMPLE SILVER: .8X TO 2X BASE CARDS
*SAMPLE GOLD: 1.2X TO 3X BASE CARDS

2002 Playoff Honors

Released in late November as a 232-card set, this product was issued with two mini boxes containing 12 packs each with 6 cards per pack. SRP per pack was 5.99.This set includes 100 veterans and 132 rookies. The first 100 rookies (101-200) are serial numbered to 1000, and the remaining rookies are numbered to 725. Cards numbered 201 through 232 contained swatches of game used memorabilia.

COMP.SET w/o SP's (100) 10.00 25.00
201-232 ROOKIE JSY PRINT RUN 650
1 David Boston .25 .60
2 Jake Plummer .30 .75
3 Warrick Dunn .30 .75
4 Michael Vick .60 1.50
5 Jamal Lewis .30 .75
6 Chris Redman .25 .60
7 Ray Lewis .40 1.00
8 Drew Bledsoe .40 1.00
9 Travis Henry .25 .60
10 Eric Moulds .30 .75
11 Lamar Smith .30 .75
12 Steve Smith .40 1.00
13 Chris Weinke .25 .60
14 Chris Chandler .30 .75
15 David Terrell .25 .60
16 Anthony Thomas .30 .75
17 Brian Urlacher .40 1.00
18 Corey Dillon .30 .75
19 Peter Warrick .30 .75
20 Tim Couch .25 .60
21 James Jackson .25 .60
22 Kevin Johnson .25 .60
23 Quincy Carter .25 .60
24 Joey Galloway .30 .75
25 Emmitt Smith 1.00 2.50
26 Terrell Davis .40 1.00
27 Brian Griese .30 .75
28 Rod Smith .30 .75
29 Germane Crowell .25 .60
30 Az-Zahir Hakim .25 .60
31 Mike McMahon .25 .60
32 Brett Favre 1.00 2.50
33 Terry Glenn .30 .75
34 Ahman Green .30 .75
35 James Allen .25 .60
36 Corey Bradford .25 .60
37 Marvin Harrison .40 1.00
38 Peyton Manning .75 2.00
39 Edgerrin James .30 .75
40 Reggie Wayne .40 1.00
41 Mark Brunell .30 .75
42 Fred Taylor .30 .75
43 Jimmy Smith .30 .75
44 Tony Gonzalez .40 1.00
45 Trent Green .30 .75
46 Priest Holmes .40 1.00
47 Snoop Minnis .25 .60
48 Chris Chambers .30 .75
49 Jay Fiedler .30 .75
50 Ricky Williams .30 .75
51 Zach Thomas .40 1.00
52 Randy Moss .40 1.00
53 Daunte Culpepper .30 .75
54 Michael Bennett .30 .75
55 Tom Brady 1.00 2.50
56 Troy Brown .30 .75
57 Antowain Smith .30 .75
58 Aaron Brooks .30 .75
59 Deuce McAllister .30 .75
60 Tiki Barber .40 1.00
61 Kerry Collins .30 .75
62 Amani Toomer .30 .75
63 Michael Strahan .40 1.00
64 Curtis Martin .40 1.00
65 Vinny Testaverde .30 .75
66 Chad Pennington .40 1.00
67 Laveranues Coles .30 .75
68 Tim Brown .40 1.00
69 Rich Gannon .30 .75
70 Jerry Rice .75 2.00
71 Donovan McNabb .40 1.00
72 Freddie Mitchell .25 .60
73 Duce Staley .30 .75
74 Jerome Bettis .40 1.00
75 Plaxico Burress .30 .75
76 Kordell Stewart .30 .75
77 Drew Brees .60 1.50
78 Doug Flutie .40 1.00
79 LaDainian Tomlinson .50 1.25
80 Jeff Garcia .30 .75
81 Garrison Hearst .30 .75
82 Terrell Owens .40 1.00
83 Shaun Alexander .30 .75
84 Trent Dilfer .30 .75
85 Koren Robinson .25 .60
86 Isaac Bruce .40 1.00
87 Marshall Faulk .40 1.00
88 Torry Holt .40 1.00
89 Kurt Warner .40 1.00
90 Mike Alstott .30 .75
91 Brad Johnson .30 .75
92 Keyshawn Johnson .30 .75
93 Keenan McCardell .30 .75
94 Steve McNair .40 1.00
95 Eddie George .30 .75
96 Jevon Kearse .30 .75
97 Derrick Mason .30 .75
98 Stephen Davis .30 .75
99 Sage Rosenfels .30 .75
100 Rod Gardner .25 .60
101 Randy Fasani RC 1.25 3.00
102 Kurt Kittner RC 1.00 2.50
103 Brandon Doman RC 1.00 2.50
104 Craig Nall RC 1.25 3.00
105 J.T. O'Sullivan RC 1.25 3.00
106 Seth Burford RC 1.00 2.50
107 Jeff Kelly RC 1.00 2.50
108 Ronald Curry RC 1.25 3.00
109 Wes Pate RC 1.00 2.50
110 Chad Hutchinson RC 1.00 2.50
111 Major Applewhite RC 1.50 4.00
112 Preston Parsons RC 1.00 2.50
113 David Priestley RC 1.00 2.50
114 Lamar Gordon RC 1.25 3.00
115 Brian Westbrook RC 2.50 6.00
116 Jonathan Wells RC 1.50 4.00
117 Omar Easy RC 1.25 3.00
118 Verron Haynes RC 1.00 2.50
119 Josh Scobey RC 1.25 3.00
120 Larry Ned RC 1.00 2.50
121 Adrian Peterson RC 1.50 4.00
122 Brian Allen RC 1.00 2.50
123 Chester Taylor RC 1.50 4.00
124 Luke Staley RC 1.00 2.50
125 Antwoine Womack RC 1.00 2.50
126 Leonard Henry RC 1.00 2.50
127 Jesse Chatman RC 1.00 2.50
128 Damien Anderson RC 1.00 2.50
129 Eric McCoo RC 1.00 2.50
130 Tellis Redmon RC 1.00 2.50
131 Joe Burns RC 1.00 2.50
132 Delvon Flowers RC 1.00 2.50
133 Ken Simonton RC 1.00 2.50
134 Ricky Williams RC 1.25 3.00
135 Dicenzo Miller RC 1.00 2.50
136 James Mungro RC 1.50 4.00
137 Randy McMichael RC 1.50 4.00
138 Deion Branch RC 1.50 4.00
139 Terry Charles RC 1.00 2.50
140 Herb Haygood RC 1.00 2.50
141 Jason McAddley RC 1.25 3.00
142 Jake Schifino RC 1.00 2.50
143 Freddie Milons RC 1.00 2.50
144 Kahlil Hill RC 1.00 2.50
145 Lamont Brightful RC 1.00 2.50
146 Chris Luzar RC 1.00 2.50
147 Daryl Jones RC 1.00 2.50
148 Woody Dantzler RC 1.25 3.00
149 Kelly Campbell RC 1.25 3.00
150 Brian Poli-Dixon RC 1.00 2.50
151 Atrews Bell RC 1.00 2.50
152 Jarrod Baxter RC 1.00 2.50
153 Eddie Drummond RC 1.00 2.50
154 Jerramy Stevens RC 1.50 4.00
155 Doug Jolley RC 1.00 2.50
156 Jamar Martin RC 1.25 3.00
157 Najeh Davenport RC 1.50 4.00
158 Dwight Freeney RC 2.00 5.00
159 Bryan Thomas RC 1.00 2.50
160 Charles Grant RC 1.50 4.00
161 Kalimba Edwards RC 1.25 3.00
162 Ryan Denney RC 1.00 2.50
163 Will Overstreet RC 1.00 2.50
164 Dennis Johnson RC 1.00 2.50
165 Alex Brown RC 1.50 4.00
166 Kenyon Coleman RC 1.00 2.50
167 Ryan Sims RC 1.50 4.00
168 John Henderson RC 1.25 3.00
169 Wendell Bryant RC 1.00 2.50
170 Albert Haynesworth RC 1.50 4.00
171 Larry Tripplett RC 1.00 2.50
172 Eddie Freeman RC 1.00 2.50
173 Anthony Weaver RC 1.00 2.50
174 Quentin Jammer RC 1.50 4.00
175 Phillip Buchanon RC 1.50 4.00
176 Lito Sheppard RC 1.50 4.00
177 Mike Rumph RC 1.00 2.50
178 Roosevelt Williams RC 1.00 2.50
179 Derek Ross RC 1.25 3.00
180 Mike Echols RC 1.00 2.50
181 Keyou Craver RC 1.00 2.50
182 Ed Reed RC 7.50 15.00
183 Lamont Thompson RC 1.25 3.00
184 Tank Williams RC 1.25 3.00
185 Michael Lewis RC 1.50 4.00
186 Napoleon Harris RC 1.25 3.00
187 Robert Thomas RC 1.00 2.50
188 Raonall Smith RC 1.00 2.50
189 Levar Fisher RC 1.00 2.50
190 Rocky Calmus RC 1.25 3.00
191 Andra Davis RC 1.00 2.50
192 Nick Rolovich RC 1.00 2.50
193 Zak Kustok RC 1.00 2.50
194 Dusty Bonner RC 1.00 2.50
195 Tony Fisher RC 1.25 3.00
196 Sam Simmons RC 1.00 2.50
197 Lee Mays RC 1.00 2.50
198 Jamin Elliott RC 1.00 2.50
199 Javin Hunter RC 1.00 2.50
200 Kendall Newson RC 1.00 2.50
201 Ladell Betts JSY RC 3.00 8.00
202 Antonio Bryant JSY RC 3.00 8.00
203 Reche Caldwell JSY RC 3.00 8.00
204 David Carr JSY RC 3.00 8.00
205 Tim Carter JSY RC 2.50 6.00
206 Eric Crouch JSY RC 3.00 8.00
207 Rohan Davey JSY RC 3.00 8.00
208 Andre Davis JSY RC 2.50 6.00
209 T.J. Duckett JSY RC 3.00 8.00
210 DeShaun Foster JSY RC 3.00 8.00
211 Jabar Gaffney JSY RC 3.00 8.00
212 David Garrard JSY RC 4.00 10.00
213 Daniel Graham JSY RC 2.50 6.00
214 William Green JSY RC 2.50 6.00
215 Joey Harrington JSY RC 3.00 8.00
216 Ron Johnson JSY RC 2.50 6.00
217 Ashley Lelie JSY RC 2.50 6.00
218 Josh McCown JSY RC 3.00 8.00
219 Maurice Morris JSY RC 2.50 6.00
220 Julius Peppers JSY RC 6.00 15.00
221 Clinton Portis JSY RC 4.00 10.00
222 Patrick Ramsey JSY RC 3.00 8.00
223 Antwaan Randle El JSY RC 3.00 8.00
224 Josh Reed JSY RC 2.50 6.00
225 Cliff Russell JSY RC 2.00 5.00
226 Jeremy Shockey JSY RC 5.00 12.00
227 Donte Stallworth JSY RC 3.00 8.00
228 Travis Stephens JSY RC 2.00 5.00
229 Javon Walker JSY RC 3.00 8.00
230 Marquise Walker JSY RC 2.00 5.00
231 Roy Williams JSY RC 3.00 8.00
232 Mike Williams JSY RC 2.00 5.00
RWH1 Walter Payton 40.00 100.00
Emmitt Smith JSY/250
RWH1A Walter Payton 200.00 400.00
Emmitt Smith AUTO/22

2002 Playoff Honors 10th Anniversary

STATED PRINT RUN 10 SER.#'d SETS

2002 Playoff Honors O's

*1-100 VETS: 4X TO 10X BASIC CARDS
1-100 VETERAN PRINT RUN 100
*101-200 ROOKIES: 1X TO 2.5X
101-200 ROOKIE PRINT RUN 50
*201-232 ROOKIE JSY: 1.5X TO 4X
201-232 ROOKIE JSY PRINT RUN 25
RANDOM INSERTS IN RETAIL PACKS

2002 Playoff Honors X's

*1-100 VETS: 4X TO 10X BASIC CARDS
1-100 VETERAN PRINT RUN 100
*101-200 ROOKIES: 1X TO 2.5X
101-200 ROOKIE PRINT RUN 50
*201-232 ROOKIE JSY: 1.5X TO 4X
201-232 ROOKIE JSY PRINT RUN 25

2002 Playoff Honors Rookie Hidden Gems Autographs

STATED PRINT RUN 50 SER.#'d SETS
201 Ladell Betts 20.00 50.00
202 Antonio Bryant 20.00 50.00
203 Reche Caldwell 20.00 50.00
204 David Carr 20.00 50.00
205 Tim Carter 15.00 40.00
206 Eric Crouch 20.00 50.00
207 Rohan Davey 20.00 50.00
208 Andre Davis 15.00 40.00
209 T.J. Duckett 20.00 50.00
210 DeShaun Foster 20.00 50.00
211 Jabar Gaffney 20.00 50.00
212 David Garrard 25.00 60.00
213 Daniel Graham 15.00 40.00
214 William Green 15.00 40.00
215 Joey Harrington 20.00 50.00
216 Ron Johnson 15.00 40.00
217 Ashley Lelie 15.00 40.00
218 Josh McCown 20.00 50.00
219 Maurice Morris 15.00 40.00
220 Julius Peppers 75.00 125.00
221 Clinton Portis 25.00 60.00
222 Patrick Ramsey 20.00 50.00

223 Antwaan Randle El	20.00	50.00
224 Josh Reed	15.00	40.00
225 Cliff Russell	12.00	30.00
226 Jeremy Shockey	30.00	80.00
227 Donte Stallworth	20.00	50.00
228 Travis Stephens	12.00	30.00
229 Javon Walker	20.00	50.00
230 Marquise Walker	12.00	30.00
231 Roy Williams	20.00	50.00
232 Mike Williams	12.00	30.00

2002 Playoff Honors Alma Mater Materials

STATED PRINT RUN 25-400

AM1 Doug Flutie JSY/150	10.00	25.00
AM2 Ahman Green JSY/150	8.00	20.00
AM3 Travis Minor Shoes/100	6.00	15.00
AM4 Laverneus Coles JSY/250	5.00	12.00
AM5 Drew Brees Shoes/100	15.00	40.00
AM6 Terrell Davis HEL/75	12.00	30.00
AM7 Javon Walker Shoes/100	10.00	25.00
AM8 James Jackson JSY/250	4.00	10.00
AM9 Reggie Wayne JSY/400	6.00	15.00
AM10 Champ Bailey HEL/75	12.00	30.00
AM11 Snoop Minnis GLV/25	10.00	25.00
AM12 Dan Morgan JSY/25	10.00	25.00
AM13 Peyton Manning HEL/75	25.00	60.00
AM14 Santana Moss JSY/250	5.00	12.00
AM15 Peter Warrick GLV/25	12.00	30.00

2002 Playoff Honors Alma Mater Materials Varsity Patches

STATED PRINT RUN 25 SER.#'d SETS

AM1 Doug Flutie JSY	12.00	30.00
AM2 Ahman Green JSY AU	20.00	50.00
AM3 Travis Minor Shoes AU	15.00	40.00
AM4 Laverneus Coles JSY	10.00	25.00
AM5 Drew Brees Shoes AU	60.00	120.00
AM6 Terrell Davis HEL AU	25.00	60.00
AM7 Javon Walker Shoes	12.00	30.00
AM8 James Jackson JSY AU		
AM9 Reggie Wayne JSY AU	25.00	60.00
AM10 Champ Bailey HEL	12.00	30.00
AM11 Snoop Minnis GLV	8.00	20.00
AM12 Dan Morgan JSY AU	15.00	40.00
AM13 Peyton Manning HEL	25.00	60.00
AM14 Santana Moss JSY AU	20.00	50.00
AM15 Peter Warrick GLV AU	20.00	50.00

2002 Playoff Honors Award Winning Materials

STATED PRINT RUN 150 SER.#'d SETS
UNPRICED AUTO PRINT RUN 10

AW1 Anthony Thomas	5.00	12.00
AW2 Edgerrin James	5.00	12.00
AW3 Randy Moss	6.00	15.00
AW4 Curtis Martin	6.00	15.00
AW5 Eddie George	5.00	12.00
AW6 Marshall Faulk	6.00	15.00
AW7 Kurt Warner	6.00	15.00
AW8 Terrell Davis	6.00	15.00
AW9 Barry Sanders	10.00	25.00
AW10 Brett Favre	15.00	40.00
AW11 Emmitt Smith	15.00	40.00
AW12 Steve Young	8.00	20.00

2002 Playoff Honors Game Day Souvenirs

STATED PRINT RUN 250 SER.#'d SETS

GD1 Donovan McNabb	6.00	15.00
GD2 Emmitt Smith	15.00	40.00
GD3 Jerry Rice	12.00	30.00
GD4 Jeff Garcia	5.00	12.00
GD5 Brian Urlacher	6.00	15.00
GD6 Brett Favre	15.00	40.00

2002 Playoff Honors Honorable Signatures

ANNOUNCED PRINT RUNS BELOW

HS1 Barry Sanders/50*	75.00	150.00
HS2 Joe Montana	60.00	120.00
HS3 Joe Namath	45.00	80.00
HS4 Jeff Blake	6.00	15.00
HS5 Kerry Collins	8.00	20.00
HS6 Randall Cunningham	8.00	20.00
HS7 Anthony Thomas	6.00	15.00
HS8 Damione Lewis	5.00	12.00
HS9 Dan Morgan	5.00	12.00
HS10 LaMont Jordan	6.00	15.00
HS11 Jesse Palmer	5.00	12.00
HS12 Boo Williams	5.00	12.00
HS13 Isaac Bruce	8.00	20.00
HS14 Jimmy Smith	6.00	15.00
HS15 Santana Moss	6.00	15.00
HS16 Quincy Carter	5.00	12.00
HS17 Sage Rosenfels	6.00	15.00
HS18 T.J. Houshmandzadeh	8.00	20.00
HS19 Robert Ferguson	6.00	15.00
HS20 Aaron Brooks/100*	10.00	25.00
HS21 Brett Favre/50*	150.00	250.00
HS22 Cade McNown	6.00	15.00
HS23 Drew Bledsoe/100*	15.00	40.00
HS24 Jerry Rice/49*	100.00	200.00
HS25 Junior Seau/75*	30.00	60.00
HS26 Kordell Stewart/75*	10.00	25.00
HS27 Tony Banks	5.00	12.00
HS28 Chris Chambers/50*	10.00	25.00
HS29 David Terrell	5.00	12.00
HS30 Edgerrin James/51*	10.00	25.00
HS31 Gerard Warren	5.00	12.00
HS32 Jamal Anderson/45*	10.00	25.00
HS33 Jamal Lewis/100*	10.00	25.00
HS34 Justin Smith	5.00	12.00
HS35 Ken-Yon Rambo	5.00	12.00
HS36 Kurt Warner/100*	20.00	50.00
HS37 Marcus Robinson	6.00	15.00
HS38 Mark Brunell/100*	10.00	25.00
HS39 Marshall Faulk/50*	15.00	40.00
HS40 Mike McMahon/75*	8.00	20.00
HS41 Peter Warrick/100*	10.00	25.00
HS42 Quincy Morgan	5.00	12.00
HS43 Rudi Johnson	8.00	20.00
HS44 Shaun Rogers/100*	8.00	20.00
HS45 Stephen Davis/41*	10.00	25.00
HS46 Tim Brown/50*	12.00	30.00
HS47 Travis Minor/100*	8.00	20.00
HS48 Warren Moon/25*	25.00	50.00
HS49 Dan Marino/25*	100.00	200.00
HS50 John Elway /25*	100.00	200.00

2002 Playoff Honors Rookie Class Jerseys

STATED PRINT RUN 50 SER.#'d SETS

RC1 Emmitt Smith	30.00	80.00
Junior Seau		
Eddie George		
RC2 Curtis Conway	12.00	30.00
Drew Bledsoe		
Mark Brunell		
RC3 Jerome Bettis	12.00	30.00
Michael Strahan		
O.J. McDuffie		
RC4 Trent Dilfer	12.00	30.00
Charlie Garner		
Isaac Bruce		
RC5 Kerry Collins	12.00	30.00
Curtis Martin		
Terrell Davis		
RC6 Keyshawn Johnson	12.00	30.00
Terrell Owens		
Terry Glenn		
RC7 Peyton Manning	25.00	60.00
Kevin Dyson		
Ryan Leaf		
RC8 Brian Griese	12.00	30.00
Randy Moss		
Fred Taylor		
RC9 Edgerrin James	12.00	30.00
Donovan McNabb		
Jeff Garcia		
RC10 Kurt Warner	12.00	30.00
Ricky Williams		
Daunte Culpepper		
RC11 Tom Brady	30.00	80.00
Brian Urlacher		
Shaun Alexander		
RC12 Michael Vick	20.00	50.00
LaDainian Tomlinson		
Anthony Thomas		

2002 Playoff Honors Rookie Stallion Autographs

STATED PRINT RUN 100 SER.#'d SETS

RS2 Alex Brown	8.00	20.00
RS3 Andra Davis	5.00	12.00
RS4 Andre Lott	5.00	12.00
RS5 Antwaan Randle El	8.00	20.00
RS6 Ashley Lolie	6.00	15.00
RS7 Brian Westbrook	40.00	80.00
RS8 Bryant McKinnie	5.00	12.00
RS9 Chad Hutchinson	5.00	12.00
RS10 Cliff Russell	5.00	12.00
RS11 Cortlen Johnson	5.00	12.00
RS12 Damien Anderson	5.00	12.00
RS13 David Garrard	20.00	50.00
RS14 Deion Branch	10.00	25.00
RS15 Mike Williams	5.00	12.00
RS16 Donte Stallworth	8.00	20.00
RS17 Ed Reed	50.00	100.00
RS18 Eric Crouch	8.00	20.00
RS19 Freddie Milons	5.00	12.00
RS20 Jabar Gaffney	8.00	20.00
RS21 Javon Walker	8.00	20.00
RS22 Jerramy Stevens	8.00	20.00
RS23 John Henderson	6.00	15.00
RS25 Josh McCown	8.00	20.00
RS26 Josh Scobey	6.00	15.00
RS27 Levar Fisher	5.00	12.00
RS28 Kalimba Edwards	6.00	15.00
RS29 Ken Simonton	5.00	12.00
RS30 Keyuo Craver	5.00	12.00
RS31 Kurt Kittner	5.00	12.00
RS32 Lito Sheppard	8.00	20.00
RS33 Marquise Walker	5.00	12.00
RS34 Mike Rumph	5.00	12.00
RS35 Najeh Davenport	8.00	20.00
RS36 Patrick Ramsey	8.00	20.00
RS37 Randy Fasani	6.00	15.00
RS38 Robert Thomas	5.00	12.00
RS39 Rocky Calmus	6.00	15.00
RS40 Tavon Mason	5.00	12.00
RS41 Terry Charles	5.00	12.00
RS42 T.J. Duckett	8.00	20.00
RS43 Tim Carter	6.00	15.00
RS44 Trev Faulk	5.00	12.00
RS45 Wendall Bryant	5.00	12.00
RS46 William Green	6.00	15.00
RS47 Kahlil Hill	5.00	12.00
RS48 Ladell Betts	8.00	20.00
RS49 Lamar Gordon	6.00	15.00
RS50 Napoleon Harris	6.00	15.00

2002 Playoff Honors Rookie Stallions

COMPLETE SET (50)	25.00	60.00
STATED ODDS 1:12		
RS1 Albert Haynesworth	.75	2.00
RS2 Alex Brown	.75	2.00
RS3 Andra Davis	.50	1.25
RS4 Andre Lott	.50	1.25
RS5 Antwaan Randle El	.75	2.00
RS6 Ashley Lelie	.60	1.50
RS7 Brian Westbrook	1.25	3.00
RS8 Bryant McKinnie	.50	1.25
RS9 Chad Hutchinson	.50	1.25
RS10 Cliff Russell	.50	1.25
RS11 Cortlen Johnson	.50	1.25
RS12 Damien Anderson	.50	1.25
RS13 David Garrard	1.00	2.50
RS14 Deion Branch	.75	2.00
RS15 Mike Williams	.50	1.25
RS16 Donte Stallworth	.75	2.00
RS17 Ed Reed	3.00	8.00
RS18 Eric Crouch	.75	2.00
RS19 Freddie Milons	.50	1.25
RS20 Jabar Gaffney	.75	2.00
RS21 Javon Walker	.75	2.00
RS22 Jerramy Stevens	.75	2.00
RS23 John Henderson	.60	1.50
RS24 Jonathan Wells	.75	2.00
RS25 Josh McCown	.75	2.00
RS26 Josh Scobey	.60	1.50
RS27 Levar Fisher	.50	1.25
RS28 Kalimba Edwards	.60	1.50
RS29 Ken Simonton	.50	1.25
RS30 Keyuo Craver	.50	1.25
RS31 Kurt Kittner	.50	1.25
RS32 Lito Sheppard	.75	2.00
RS33 Marquise Walker	.50	1.25
RS34 Mike Rumph	.50	1.25
RS35 Najeh Davenport	.75	2.00
RS36 Patrick Ramsey	.75	2.00
RS37 Randy Fasani	.60	1.50
RS38 Robert Thomas	.50	1.25
RS39 Rocky Calmus	.60	1.50
RS40 Tavon Mason	.50	1.25
RS41 Terry Charles	.50	1.25
RS42 T.J. Duckett	.75	2.00
RS43 Tim Carter	.60	1.50
RS44 Trev Faulk	.50	1.25
RS45 Wendall Bryant	.50	1.25
RS46 William Green	.60	1.50
RS47 Kahlil Hill	.50	1.25
RS48 Ladell Betts	.75	2.00
RS49 Lamar Gordon	.60	1.50
RS50 Napoleon Harris	.60	1.50

2002 Playoff Honors Rookie Tandems/Quads

RQ16-RQ22 STATED PRINT RUN 500
*RT1-RT15 GOLD: .6X TO 1.5X BASIC DUAL
RT1-RT15 TANDEM GOLD PRINT RUN 250
RQ16-RQ22 QUAD GOLD PRINT RUN 25

RT1 David Carr	4.00	10.00
Jabar Gaffney		
RT2 Travis Stephens	2.50	6.00
Marquise Walker		
RT3 Patrick Ramsey	4.00	10.00
Cliff Russell		
RT4 Antonio Bryant	4.00	10.00
Roy Williams		
RT5 Clinton Portis	5.00	12.00
Ashley Lelie		
RT6 Maurice Morris	3.00	8.00
Andre Davis		
RT7 DeShaun Foster	8.00	20.00
Julius Peppers		
RT8 Eric Crouch	4.00	10.00
Antwaan Randle El		
RT9 Joey Harrington	5.00	12.00
David Garrard		
RT10 Josh McCown	4.00	10.00
Rohan Davey		
RT11 Donte Stallworth	4.00	10.00
Reche Caldwell		
RT12 Javon Walker	4.00	10.00
Ron Johnson		
RT13 Josh Reed	3.00	8.00
Tim Carter		
RT14 T.J.Duckett	4.00	10.00
Ladell Betts		
RT15 Jermy Shockey	6.00	15.00
Daniel Graham		
RQ16 David Carr	5.00	12.00
Jabar Gaffney		
Travis Stephens		
Marquise Walker		
RQ17 Patrick Ramsey	5.00	12.00
Cliff Russel		
Antonio Bryant		
Roy Williams		
RQ18 Clinton Portis	4.00	10.00
Ashley Lelie		
Maurice Morris		
Andre Davis		
RQ19 DeShaun Foster	10.00	25.00
Julius Peppers		
Eric Crouch		
Antwaan Randle El		
RQ20 Joey Harrington	6.00	15.00
David Garrard		
Josh McCown		
Rohan Davey		
RQ21 Donte Stallworth	5.00	12.00
Reche Caldwell		
Javon Walker		
Ron Johnson		
RQ22 Josh Reed	5.00	12.00
Tim Carter		
T.J. Duckett		
Ladell Betts		

2002 Playoff Honors Player of the Week

ANNOUNCED PRINT RUN 100 SETS
*PANELIST/10: .8X TO 2X

1 Priest Holmes	3.00	8.00
2 Drew Bledsoe	3.00	8.00
3 Tom Brady	8.00	20.00
4 Shaun Alexander	2.50	6.00
5 Rich Gannon	2.50	6.00
6 Drew Brees	5.00	12.00
7 Marshall Faulk	3.00	8.00
8 Michael Vick	5.00	12.00
9 Brad Johnson	2.50	6.00
10 Rich Gannon	2.50	6.00
11 Donovan McNabb	3.00	8.00
12 Priest Holmes	3.00	8.00
13 LaDainian Tomlinson	4.00	10.00
14 Ricky Williams	2.50	6.00
15 Clinton Portis	4.00	10.00
16 Amani Toomer	2.50	6.00
17 Clinton Portis	4.00	10.00
18 Jeff Garcia	2.50	6.00
19 Steve McNair	3.00	8.00
20 Rich Gannon	2.50	6.00
21 Dexter Jackson	3.00	8.00

2003 Playoff Honors

Released in November of 2003, this set consists of 230 cards, including 100 veterans and 130 rookies. Rookies 101-150, found only in hobby packs, are serial numbered to 550. Rookies 151-200, found only in retail packs, are serial numbered to 200. Rookies 201-230 feature event worn jerseys and are serial numbered to 700. Each box contained two 10-pack mini-boxes. SRP was $6 per 6 card in pack.

COMP.SET w/o SP's (100)	7.50	20.00
1 Aaron Brooks	.25	.60
2 Ahman Green	.25	.60
3 Amani Toomer	.25	.60
4 Anthony Thomas	.25	.60
5 Antonio Bryant	.20	.50
6 Antwaan Randle El	.25	.60
7 Ashley Lelie	.20	.50
8 Brad Johnson	.25	.60
9 Brett Favre	.75	2.00
10 Brian Urlacher	.30	.75
11 Bruce Smith	.25	.60
12 Chad Johnson	.30	.75
13 Chad Pennington	.30	.75
14 Charlie Garner	.25	.60
15 Chris Chambers	.25	.60
16 Clinton Portis	.25	.60
17 Corey Dillon	.25	.60
18 Curtis Martin	.30	.75
19 Daunte Culpepper	.25	.60
20 David Boston	.20	.50
21 David Carr	.25	.60
22 Deuce McAllister	.25	.60
23 Donald Driver	.30	.75
24 Donovan McNabb	.30	.75
25 Donte Stallworth	.20	.50
26 Drew Bledsoe	.30	.75
27 Drew Brees	.30	.75
28 Duce Staley	.25	.60
29 Ed McCaffrey	.25	.60
30 Eddie George	.25	.60
31 Edgerrin James	.30	.75
32 Emmitt Smith	.75	2.00
33 Eric Moulds	.25	.60
34 Fred Taylor	.25	.60
35 Garrison Hearst	.25	.60
36 Hines Ward	.30	.75
37 Isaac Bruce	.30	.75
38 Jabar Gaffney	.20	.50
39 Jake Plummer	.25	.60
40 Jamal Lewis	.25	.60
41 Jay Fiedler	.20	.50
42 Jeff Garcia	.25	.60
43 Jeremy Shockey	.30	.75
44 Jerome Bettis	.30	.75
45 Jerry Porter	.20	.50
46 Jerry Rice	.60	1.50
47 Jevon Kearse	.25	.60
48 Jimmy Smith	.25	.60
49 Joe Horn	.25	.60
50 Joey Harrington	.20	.50
51 Josh Reed	.20	.50
52 Julius Peppers	.30	.75
53 Kendrell Bell	.20	.50
54 Kerry Collins	.25	.60
55 Keyshawn Johnson	.30	.75
56 Kordell Stewart	.25	.60
57 Koren Robinson	.25	.60
58 Kurt Warner	.30	.75
59 LaDainian Tomlinson	.30	.75
60 Laveranues Coles	.20	.50
61 Mark Brunell	.25	.60
62 Marshall Faulk	.30	.75
63 Marvin Harrison	.30	.75
64 Matt Hasselbeck	.25	.60
65 Michael Bennett	.25	.60
66 Michael Strahan	.30	.75
67 Michael Vick	.40	1.00
68 Mike Alstott	.30	.75
69 Patrick Ramsey	.25	.60
70 Peerless Price	.20	.50
71 Peyton Manning	.60	1.50
72 Plaxico Burress	.25	.60
73 Priest Holmes	.30	.75
74 Randy Moss	.30	.75
75 Ray Lewis	.30	.75
76 Rich Gannon	.25	.60
77 Ricky Williams	.25	.60
78 Rod Gardner	.20	.50
79 Rod Smith	.25	.60
80 Roy Williams	.25	.60
81 Shaun Alexander	.25	.60
82 Stephen Davis	.25	.60
83 Steve McNair	.30	.75
84 T.J. Duckett	.25	.60
85 Terrell Owens	.30	.75
86 Tiki Barber	.30	.75
87 Tim Brown	.30	.75
88 Tim Couch	.20	.50
89 Todd Heap	.25	.60
90 Tom Brady	.75	2.00
91 Tommy Maddox	.25	.60
92 Tony Gonzalez	.30	.75
93 Torry Holt	.30	.75
94 Travis Henry	.20	.50
95 Trent Green	.25	.60
96 Troy Brown	.25	.60
97 Warren Sapp	.25	.60
98 Warrick Dunn	.25	.60
99 William Green	.20	.50
100 Zach Thomas	.30	.75
101 Chris Simms RC	2.00	5.00
102 Brooks Bollinger RC	1.50	4.00
103 Gibran Hamdan RC	1.25	3.00
104 Ken Dorsey RC	1.50	4.00
105 Jason Gesser RC	1.50	4.00
106 Brad Banks RC	1.50	4.00
107 Tony Romo RC	20.00	50.00
108 B.J. Askew RC	1.50	4.00
109 Domanick Davis RC	1.50	4.00
110 Lee Suggs RC	1.50	4.00
111 LaBrandon Toefield RC	1.50	4.00
112 Brock Forsey RC	1.50	4.00
113 Malaefou MacKenzie RC	1.25	3.00
114 Andrew Pinnock RC	1.50	4.00
115 Ahmaad Galloway RC	1.50	4.00
116 Tony Hollings RC	1.50	4.00
117 Charles Rogers RC	1.50	4.00
118 Billy McMullen RC	1.25	3.00
119 Shaun McDonald RC	1.50	4.00
120 Brandon Lloyd RC	3.00	8.00
121 Sam Aiken RC	1.50	4.00
122 Bobby Wade RC	1.50	4.00
123 Justin Gage RC	1.50	4.00
124 Adrian Madise RC	1.25	3.00
125 Jon Olinger RC	1.25	3.00
126 Doug Gabriel RC	1.50	4.00
127 J.R. Tolver RC	1.50	4.00
128 David Kircus RC	2.00	5.00
129 Zuriel Smith RC	1.25	3.00
130 LaTarence Dunbar RC	1.25	3.00
131 Arnaz Battle RC	2.00	5.00
132 Willie Ponder RC	1.25	3.00
133 Kareem Kelly RC	1.25	3.00
134 David Tyree RC	2.00	5.00
135 Keenan Howry RC	1.25	3.00
136 Taco Wallace RC	1.25	3.00
137 Walter Young RC	1.25	3.00
138 Talman Gardner RC	1.25	3.00
139 DeAndrew Rubin RC	1.25	3.00
140 Kevin Walter RC	3.00	8.00
141 Carl Ford RC	1.25	3.00
142 Travis Anglin RC	1.25	3.00
143 Ryan Hoag RC	1.25	3.00
144 Terrence Edwards RC	1.25	3.00
145 Bennie Joppru RC	1.25	3.00
146 L.J. Smith RC	2.00	5.00
147 Jason Witten RC	5.00	12.00
148 Andre Woolfolk RC	1.50	4.00
149 Nnamdi Asomugha RC	6.00	12.00
150 Troy Polamalu RC	15.00	30.00
151 Nate Hybl RC	3.00	8.00
152 Curt Anes RC	2.50	6.00
153 Avon Cobourne RC	2.50	6.00
154 Cecil Sapp RC	2.50	6.00
155 Casey Urlacher RC	4.00	10.00
156 Dwone Hicks RC	2.50	6.00
157 Jeremi Johnson RC	2.50	6.00
158 Kirk Farmer RC	3.00	8.00
159 James MacPherson RC	3.00	8.00
160 Chris Davis RC	3.00	8.00
161 Brandon Drumm RC	2.50	6.00
162 J.T. Wall RC	2.50	6.00
163 Casey Moore RC	2.50	6.00
164 Mike Seidman RC	2.50	6.00
165 Visanthe Shiancoe RC	4.00	10.00
166 George Wrighster RC	2.50	6.00
167 Dan Curley RC	2.50	6.00
168 Donald Lee RC	3.00	8.00
169 Aaron Walker RC	3.00	8.00
170 Trent Smith RC	3.00	8.00
171 Spencer Nead RC	2.50	6.00
172 Richard Angulo RC	2.50	6.00
173 Mike Pinkard RC	2.50	6.00
174 Johnathan Sullivan RC	2.50	6.00
175 Kevin Williams RC	4.00	10.00
176 Jimmy Kennedy RC	3.00	8.00
177 Ty Warren RC	3.00	8.00
178 William Joseph RC	2.50	6.00
179 Michael Haynes RC	2.50	6.00
180 Jerome McDougle RC	2.50	6.00
181 Calvin Pace RC	3.00	8.00
182 Tyler Brayton RC	3.00	8.00
183 Chris Kelsay RC	3.00	8.00
184 Osi Umenyiora RC	5.00	12.00
185 Alonzo Jackson RC	2.50	6.00
186 DeWayne White RC	2.50	6.00
187 Kenny Peterson RC	3.00	8.00
188 Nick Barnett RC	4.00	10.00
189 Boss Bailey RC	3.00	8.00
190 E.J. Henderson RC	3.00	8.00
191 Pisa Tinoisamoa RC	4.00	10.00
192 Sammy Davis RC	3.00	8.00
193 Charles Tillman RC	5.00	12.00
194 Eugene Wilson RC	4.00	10.00
195 Drayton Florence RC	4.00	10.00
196 Ricky Manning RC	3.00	8.00
197 Rashean Mathis RC	3.00	8.00
198 Ken Hamlin RC	4.00	10.00
199 Mike Doss RC	4.00	10.00
200 Julian Battle RC	3.00	8.00
201 Andre Johnson JSY RC	8.00	20.00
202 Anquan Boldin JSY RC	5.00	12.00
203 Artose Pinner JSY RC	2.00	5.00
204 Bethel Johnson JSY RC	2.00	5.00
205 Brian St.Pierre JSY RC	2.50	6.00
206 Bryant Johnson JSY RC	3.00	8.00
207 Byron Leftwich JSY RC	3.00	8.00
208 Carson Palmer JSY RC	6.00	15.00
209 Chris Brown JSY RC	2.00	5.00
210 Dallas Clark JSY RC	5.00	12.00
211 Dave Ragone JSY RC	2.00	5.00
212 DeWayne Robertson JSY RC	2.50	6.00
213 Justin Fargas JSY RC	3.00	8.00
214 Kelley Washington JSY RC	2.00	5.00
215 Kevin Curtis JSY RC	3.00	8.00
216 Kliff Kingsbury JSY RC	2.50	6.00
217 Kyle Boller JSY RC	3.00	8.00
218 Larry Johnson JSY RC	3.00	8.00
219 Marcus Trufant JSY RC	2.50	6.00
220 Musa Smith JSY RC	2.00	5.00
221 Nate Burleson JSY RC	2.50	6.00
222 Onterrio Smith JSY RC	2.00	5.00
223 Rex Grossman JSY RC	3.00	8.00
224 Seneca Wallace JSY RC	3.00	8.00
225 Taylor Jacobs JSY RC	2.00	5.00
226 Terrell Suggs JSY RC	3.00	8.00
227 Terence Newman JSY RC	2.50	6.00
228 Teyo Johnson JSY RC	2.50	6.00
229 Tyrone Calico JSY RC	2.50	6.00
230 Willis McGahee JSY RC	4.00	10.00

2003 Playoff Honors O's

*VETS 1-100: 4X TO 10X BASIC CARDS
1-100 VETERAN PRINT RUN 100
*ROOKIES 151-200: .6X TO 1.5X
151-200 ROOKIE PRINT RUN 50
*ROOKIE JSY 201-230: 1.2X TO 3X
201-230 JSY PRINT RUN 25
O's FOUND ONLY IN RETAIL PACKS

2003 Playoff Honors X's

*VETS 1-100: 2X TO 5X BASIC CARDS
1-100 VETERAN PRINT RUN 250
*ROOKIES 101-150: 1X TO 2.5X
101-150 ROOKIE PRINT RUN 100
*ROOKIE JSY 201-230: 1.2X TO 3X
201-230 JSY PRINT RUN 25
X's FOUND ONLY IN HOBBY PACKS

107 Tony Romo	40.00	100.00
150 Troy Polamalu	60.00	100.00

2003 Playoff Honors Rookie Hidden Gems Autographs

FIRST 50 BASE CARDS SIGNED

201 Andre Johnson JSY	40.00	100.00
202 Anquan Boldin JSY	25.00	60.00
203 Artose Pinner JSY	10.00	25.00
204 Bethel Johnson JSY	10.00	25.00
205 Brian St.Pierre JSY	12.00	30.00
206 Bryant Johnson JSY	15.00	40.00
207 Byron Leftwich JSY	15.00	40.00
208 Carson Palmer JSY	30.00	80.00
209 Chris Brown JSY	10.00	25.00
210 Dallas Clark JSY	25.00	60.00
211 Dave Ragone JSY	10.00	25.00
212 DeWayne Robertson JSY	12.00	30.00
213 Justin Fargas JSY	15.00	40.00
214 Kelley Washington JSY	10.00	25.00
215 Kevin Curtis JSY	15.00	40.00
216 Kliff Kingsbury JSY	12.00	30.00
217 Kyle Boller JSY	15.00	40.00
218 Larry Johnson JSY	15.00	40.00
219 Marcus Trufant JSY	12.00	30.00
220 Musa Smith JSY	10.00	25.00
221 Nate Burleson JSY	12.00	30.00
222 Onterrio Smith JSY	10.00	25.00
223 Rex Grossman JSY	15.00	40.00
224 Seneca Wallace JSY	15.00	40.00
225 Taylor Jacobs JSY	10.00	25.00
226 Terrell Suggs JSY	25.00	50.00
227 Terence Newman JSY	12.00	30.00
228 Teyo Johnson JSY	12.00	30.00
229 Tyrone Calico JSY	12.00	30.00
230 Willis McGahee JSY	20.00	50.00

2003 Playoff Honors Alma Mater Materials

STATED PRINT RUN 25-400

AM1 Fred Taylor/400	5.00	12.00
AM2 Jevon Kearse/150	6.00	15.00
AM3 Michael Pittman/400	4.00	10.00
AM4 Ahman Green/250	5.00	12.00
AM5 Eddie George/150	6.00	15.00
AM6 Shaun Alexander/200	5.00	12.00
AM7 Terrell Davis/150	8.00	20.00
AM8 Frank Wycheck/400	4.00	10.00
AM9 Laveranues Coles/250	4.00	10.00
AM10 Edgerrin James/300	6.00	15.00
AM11 Reggie Wayne/400	6.00	15.00
AM12 Dan Morgan/400	5.00	12.00
AM13 Santana Moss/300	5.00	12.00
AM14 Jeremy Shockey/150	8.00	20.00
AM15 Clinton Portis/50	8.00	20.00
AM16 Tony Dorsett/25	20.00	50.00
AM16AU Tony Dorsett/25 AU	50.00	100.00
AM17 Earl Campbell/125	10.00	25.00
AM17AU Earl Campbell/125 AU	40.00	80.00
AM18 Ricky Williams/150	6.00	15.00
AM19 Drew Bledsoe/150	8.00	20.00
AM20 Doug Flutie/250	6.00	15.00
AM21 Curtis Martin/200	6.00	15.00
AM22 Anquan Boldin/350	6.00	15.00
AM23 Keyshawn Johnson/200	6.00	15.00
AM24 Tyrone Calico/400	5.00	12.00
AM25 Kyle Boller/200	6.00	15.00
AM26 Fred Taylor	6.00	15.00
Jevon Kearse/100		
AM27 Ahman Green	6.00	15.00
Eddie George/100		
AM28 Shaun Alexander	8.00	20.00
Terrell Davis/100		
AM29 Edgerrin James	8.00	20.00
Clinton Portis/100		
AM30 Santana Moss	8.00	20.00
Jeremy Shockey/100		
AM31 Laveranues Coles	8.00	20.00
Reggie Wayne/100		
AM32 Earl Campbell	10.00	25.00
Ricky Williams/100		
AM33 Drew Bledsoe	8.00	20.00
Doug Flutie/100		
AM34 Curtis Martin	8.00	20.00
Anquan Boldin/100		
AM35 Keyshawn Johnson	8.00	20.00
Tyrone Calico/100		
AM36 Fred Taylor	20.00	50.00
Shaun Alexander		
Terrell Davis/25		
AM37 Ahman Green	25.00	60.00
Earl Campbell		
Ricky Williams/25		
AM38 Edgerrin James	20.00	50.00
Clinton Portis		
Jeremy Shockey/25		
AM39 Drew Bledsoe	20.00	50.00
Doug Flutie		
Kyle Boller/25		
AM40 Tony Dorsett	25.00	60.00
Curtis Martin		
Eddie George/25		

2003 Playoff Honors Class Reunion Tandems

PRINT RUN 150 SERIAL #'d SETS

CRT1 Emmitt Smith	15.00	40.00
Junior Seau		
CRT2 Brett Favre	15.00	40.00
Ed McCaffrey		
CRT3 Rod Smith	5.00	12.00
Jimmy Smith		
CRT4 Drew Bledsoe	6.00	15.00
Jerome Bettis		
CRT5 Marshall Faulk	6.00	15.00
Isaac Bruce		
CRT6 Terrell Davis	6.00	15.00
Curtis Martin		
CRT7 Steve McNair	6.00	15.00
Warren Sapp		
CRT8 Keyshawn Johnson	6.00	15.00
Eric Moulds		
CRT9 Terrell Owens	6.00	15.00
Marvin Harrison		
CRT10 Ray Lewis	6.00	15.00
Zach Thomas		
CRT11 Tony Gonzalez	6.00	15.00
Tiki Barber		
CRT12 Peyton Manning	6.00	15.00
Priest Holmes		
CRT13 Randy Moss	6.00	15.00
Hines Ward		
CRT14 Ahman Green	5.00	12.00
Fred Taylor		
CRT15 Edgerrin James	6.00	15.00
Ricky Williams		
CRT16 Donovan McNabb	6.00	15.00
Daunte Culpepper		
CRT17 Torry Holt	6.00	15.00
David Boston		
CRT18 Tim Brown	6.00	15.00
Sterling Sharpe		
CRT19 Aaron Brooks	5.00	12.00
Donald Driver		
CRT20 Laveranues Coles	6.00	15.00
Chad Pennington		
CRT21 Jamal Lewis	5.00	12.00
Shaun Alexander		
CRT22 Plaxico Burress	6.00	15.00
Brian Urlacher		
CRT23 Michael Vick	8.00	20.00
Drew Brees		
CRT24 LaDainian Tomlinson	6.00	15.00
Deuce McAllister		
CRT25 Koren Robinson	5.00	12.00
Rod Gardner		
CRT26 Michael Bennett	5.00	12.00
Travis Henry		
CRT27 Chris Chambers	5.00	12.00
Kendrell Bell		
CRT28 David Carr	5.00	12.00
Joey Harrington		
CRT29 Jeremy Shockey	6.00	15.00
Clinton Portis		
CRT30 Donte Stallworth	5.00	12.00
Antwaan Randle El		

2003 Playoff Honors Game Day Souvenirs Bronze

BRONZE PRINT RUN 150
*SILVER/75: .5X TO 1.2X BRONZE/150
SILVER PRINT RUN 75 SER.#'d SETS
*GOLD/25: 1X TO 2.5X BRONZE/150
GOLD PRINT RUN 25 SER.#'d SETS

GDS1 Emmitt Smith	15.00	40.00
GDS2 Donovan McNabb	6.00	15.00
GDS3 Steve McNair	6.00	15.00
GDS4 Curtis Martin	6.00	15.00
GDS5 Edgerrin James	6.00	15.00
GDS6 Rich Gannon	5.00	12.00
GDS7 Kurt Warner	6.00	15.00
GDS8 Aaron Brooks	5.00	12.00
GDS9 LaDainian Tomlinson	6.00	15.00
GDS10 Peyton Manning	12.00	30.00
GDS11 David Boston	4.00	10.00
GDS12 Michael Vick	8.00	20.00

2003 Playoff Honors Jersey Quads

JSY PRINT RUN 250 SER.#'d SETS
*TD/50: .5X TO 1.2X JSY QUAD/250
FOOTBALL STATED PRINT RUN 50
*JSY-FB/25: .8X TO 2X JSY QUAD/250
JSY-FOOTBALL STATED PRINT RUN 25

JQ1 Carson Palmer	8.00	20.00
Kelley Washington		
Byron Leftwich		
Dallas Clark		
JQ2 Larry Johnson	2.50	6.00
Artose Pinner		
Nate Burleson		
Onterrio Smith		
JQ3 Andre Johnson	10.00	25.00
Dave Ragone		
Chris Brown		
Tyrone Calico		
JQ4 Brian St.Pierre	2.50	6.00
Seneca Wallace		
Rex Grossman		
Taylor Jacobs		
JQ5 Bethel Johnson	6.00	15.00
Anquan Boldin		
Willis McGahee		
Kevin Curtis		
JQ6 Justin Fargas	4.00	10.00
Teyo Johnson		
Kyle Boller		
Musa Smith		
JQ7 Kliff Kingsbury	4.00	10.00
Bethel Johnson		
Terrell Suggs		
Terence Newman		

2003 Playoff Honors Jersey Tandems

*FB/100: .5X TO 1.2X JSY TANDEM
FOOTBALL STATED PRINT RUN 100
*JSY-FB/75: .6X TO 1.5X JSY TANDEM
JSY-FOOTBALL STATED PRINT RUN 75

JT1 Carson Palmer	6.00	15.00
Kelley Washington		
JT2 Byron Leftwich	5.00	12.00
Dallas Clark		
JT3 Larry Johnson	3.00	8.00
Artose Pinner		
JT4 Nate Burleson	2.00	5.00
Onterrio Smith		
JT5 Andre Johnson	8.00	20.00
Dave Ragone		
JT6 Chris Brown	2.50	6.00
Tyrone Calico		
JT7 Brian St.Pierre	3.00	8.00
Seneca Wallace		
JT8 Rex Grossman	2.00	5.00
Taylor Jacobs		
JT9 Bryant Johnson	5.00	12.00
Anquan Boldin		
JT10 Willis McGahee	4.00	10.00
Kevin Curtis		
JT11 Justin Fargas	3.00	8.00
Teyo Johnson		
JT12 Kyle Boller	3.00	8.00
Musa Smith		
JT13 Kliff Kingsbury	2.00	5.00
Bethel Johnson		
JT14 DeWayne Robertson	3.00	8.00
Terrell Suggs		
JT15 Terence Newman	2.50	6.00
Marcus Trufant		

2003 Playoff Honors Patches

PATCH PRINT RUN 75 SER.#'d SETS
*PLATE/40-65: .5X TO 1.2X PATCH/75
*PLATE/30-38: .6X TO 1.5X PATCH/75
*PLATE/20-29: .8X TO 2X PATCH/75
PLATES PRINT RUN 1-65
*PLATE-PATCH/45: .6X TO 1.5X PATCH/75
*PLATE-PATCH/31-34: .8X TO 2X PATCH/75
*PLATE-PATCH/20-28: 1X TO 2.5X PATCH/75
PLATE-PATCH PRINT RUN 3-45
SERIAL #'d UNDER 20 NOT PRICED

PP1 Michael Vick	10.00	25.00
PP2 Brett Favre	20.00	50.00
PP3 Peyton Manning	15.00	40.00
PP4 Donovan McNabb	8.00	20.00
PP5 Daunte Culpepper	6.00	15.00
PP6 Jeff Garcia	6.00	15.00
PP7 David Carr	6.00	15.00
PP8 Joey Harrington	5.00	12.00
PP9 Kurt Warner	8.00	20.00
PP10 Drew Brees	8.00	20.00
PP11 Drew Bledsoe	8.00	20.00
PP12 Tom Brady	20.00	50.00
PP13 LaDainian Tomlinson	8.00	20.00
PP14 Deuce McAllister	6.00	15.00
PP15 Ricky Williams	6.00	15.00
PP16 Marshall Faulk	8.00	20.00
PP17 Edgerrin James	8.00	20.00
PP18 Travis Henry	5.00	12.00
PP19 Michael Bennett	6.00	15.00
PP20 Emmitt Smith	20.00	50.00
PP21 Priest Holmes	8.00	20.00
PP22 Clinton Portis	6.00	15.00
PP23 William Green	5.00	12.00
PP24 T.J. Duckett	6.00	15.00
PP25 Randy Moss	8.00	20.00
PP26 Jerry Rice	15.00	40.00
PP27 Terrell Owens	8.00	20.00
PP28 David Boston	5.00	12.00
PP29 Marvin Harrison	8.00	20.00
PP30 Tim Brown	8.00	20.00
PP31 Donte Stallworth	5.00	12.00
PP32 Ashley Lelie	5.00	12.00
PP33 Antwaan Randle El	6.00	15.00
PP34 Tony Gonzalez	8.00	20.00
PP35 Jeremy Shockey	8.00	20.00
PP36 Brian Urlacher	8.00	20.00
PP37 Kendrell Bell	5.00	12.00
PP38 Zach Thomas	8.00	20.00
PP39 Warren Sapp	6.00	15.00
PP40 Julius Peppers	8.00	20.00

2003 Playoff Honors Prime Signatures

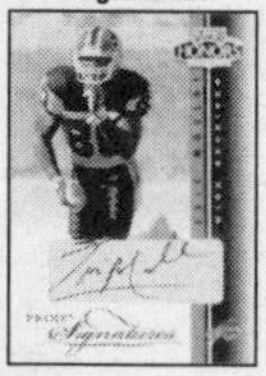

STATED PRINT RUN 1-300
SERIAL #'d UNDER 20 NOT PRICED
UNPRICED PRIME CUT PRINT RUN 5

PS1 Kurt Warner/300	15.00	40.00
PS2 Eric Moulds/81	10.00	25.00
PS3 Marc Boerigter/95	8.00	20.00
PS4 Tim Brown/88	12.00	30.00
PS5 Ahman Green/75	12.00	30.00
PS7 Jimmy Smith/95	10.00	25.00
PS8 Michael Vick/70	30.00	60.00
PS9 Charlie Garner/75	12.00	30.00
PS11 Jamal Lewis/50	12.00	30.00
PS12 Jerry Rice/40	100.00	175.00
PS14 Shaun Alexander/70	12.00	30.00
PS15 Steve McNair/59	15.00	40.00
PS16 Tommy Maddox/70	12.00	30.00
PS17 Chris Chambers/60	12.00	30.00
PS18 Tom Jackson/55	12.00	30.00
PS19 David Carr/50	12.00	30.00
PS20 Deuce McAllister/50	12.00	30.00
PS21 Jeff Garcia/50	12.00	30.00
PS22 Torry Holt/50	15.00	40.00
PS23 Zach Thomas/95	12.00	30.00
PS24 Anthony Thomas/70	12.00	30.00
PS25 Eddie George/45	12.00	30.00
PS26 Marty Booker/45	12.00	30.00
PS27 Priest Holmes/45	15.00	40.00
PS29 Ricky Williams/25	15.00	40.00
PS30 Brett Favre/21	125.00	250.00
PS31 Drew Bledsoe/20	20.00	50.00
PS33 Jerome Bettis/45	40.00	80.00
PS35 Kendrell Bell/20	10.00	25.00
PS36 LaDainian Tomlinson/20	40.00	80.00
PS37 Laveranues Coles/45	10.00	25.00
PS38 Dan Marino/32	100.00	200.00
PS39 Mike Alstott/45	15.00	40.00
PS40 Rod Gardner/45	10.00	25.00
PS41 Carson Palmer/20	30.00	80.00
PS42 Byron Leftwich/20	15.00	40.00
PS43 Kliff Kingsbury/300	8.00	20.00
PS45 Anquan Boldin/300	8.00	20.00
PS46 Bethel Johnson/300	6.00	15.00
PS47 Nate Burleson/300	8.00	20.00
PS48 Onterrio Smith/300	6.00	15.00
PS49 Bryant Johnson/290	10.00	25.00
PS50 Terrence Edwards/300	6.00	15.00
PS51 Teyo Johnson/300	8.00	20.00
PS52 DeWayne White/300	6.00	15.00
PS53 Jerome McDougle/300	6.00	15.00
PS54 Terrell Suggs/300	12.00	30.00
PS55 Terence Newman/300	8.00	20.00
PS56 Brian St.Pierre/300	8.00	20.00
PS57 Artose Pinner/250	6.00	15.00
PS58 Cecil Sapp/300	6.00	15.00
PS59 Doug Gabriel/300	8.00	20.00

2003 Playoff Honors Rookie Year Jerseys

STATED PRINT RUN 100 SER.#'d SETS

RYJ1 Curtis Martin	6.00	15.00
RYJ2 Isaac Bruce	6.00	15.00
RYJ3 Keyshawn Johnson	6.00	15.00
RYJ4 Mark Brunell	5.00	12.00
RYJ5 Peyton Manning	12.00	30.00
RYJ6 Randy Moss	6.00	15.00
RYJ7 Ricky Williams	5.00	12.00
RYJ8 Tim Couch	4.00	10.00
RYJ9 LaDainian Tomlinson	6.00	15.00
RYJ10 Chris Chambers	5.00	12.00
RYJ11 Koren Robinson	5.00	12.00
RYJ12 Michael Vick	8.00	20.00
RYJ13 Anthony Thomas	5.00	12.00
RYJ14 David Terrell	4.00	10.00
RYJ15 Joey Harrington	4.00	10.00
RYJ16 Clinton Portis	5.00	12.00
RYJ17 Jeremy Shockey	6.00	15.00
RYJ18 David Carr	5.00	12.00
RYJ19 Antwaan Randle El	5.00	12.00
RYJ20 Donte Stallworth	4.00	10.00

2004 Playoff Honors

Playoff Honors initially released in mid-October 2004. The base set consists of 233-cards including 50-rookies inserted in hobby packs, 50-rookies inserted in retail packs and 33-rookie jersey cards serial numbered of 750. Hobby boxes contained 12-packs of 6-cards and carried an S.R.P. of $6 per pack. Two parallel sets and a variety of inserts can be found seeded in packs highlighted by the Rookie Hidden Gems Autographs inserts.

COMP.SET w/o SP's (100)	7.50	20.00
1 Anquan Boldin	.40	1.00
2 Emmitt Smith	1.00	2.50
3 Josh McCown	.30	.75
4 Michael Vick	.50	1.25
5 Peerless Price	.25	.60
6 T.J. Duckett	.30	.75
7 Warrick Dunn	.30	.75
8 Jamal Lewis	.30	.75
9 Kyle Boller	.30	.75
10 Ray Lewis	.40	1.00
11 Drew Bledsoe	.40	1.00
12 Eric Moulds	.30	.75
13 Travis Henry	.25	.60
14 DeShaun Foster	.30	.75
15 Jake Delhomme	.30	.75
16 Steve Smith	.40	1.00
17 Stephen Davis	.30	.75
18 Brian Urlacher	.40	1.00
19 Rex Grossman	.30	.75
20 Thomas Jones	.40	1.00
21 Carson Palmer	.40	1.00
22 Chad Johnson	.40	1.00
23 Rudi Johnson	.30	.75
24 Jeff Garcia	.30	.75
25 Lee Suggs	.30	.75
26 Keyshawn Johnson	.30	.75
27 Quincy Carter	.25	.60
28 Roy Williams S	.30	.75
29 Jake Plummer	.30	.75
30 Quentin Griffin	.25	.60
31 Rod Smith	.30	.75
32 Charles Rogers	.25	.60
33 Joey Harrington	.30	.75
34 Ahman Green	.30	.75
35 Brett Favre	1.00	2.50
36 Javon Walker	.25	.60
37 Andre Johnson	.40	1.00
38 David Carr	.25	.60
39 Domanick Davis	.25	.60
40 Edgerrin James	.30	.75
41 Marvin Harrison	.40	1.00
42 Peyton Manning	.75	2.00
43 Byron Leftwich	.30	.75
44 Fred Taylor	.30	.75
45 Jimmy Smith	.30	.75
46 Priest Holmes	.40	1.00
47 Tony Gonzalez	.40	1.00
48 Trent Green	.30	.75
49 A.J. Feeley	.25	.60
50 Chris Chambers	.30	.75
51 Ricky Williams	.30	.75
52 Daunte Culpepper	.30	.75
53 Michael Bennett	.30	.75
54 Randy Moss	.40	1.00
55 Corey Dillon	.30	.75
56 Deion Branch	.30	.75
57 Tom Brady	.75	2.00
58 Aaron Brooks	.30	.75
59 Deuce McAllister	.30	.75
60 Joe Horn	.30	.75
61 Jeremy Shockey	.30	.75
62 Michael Strahan	.40	1.00
63 Tiki Barber	.40	1.00
64 Chad Pennington	.40	1.00
65 Curtis Martin	.40	1.00
66 Santana Moss	.30	.75
67 Jerry Rice	.75	2.00
68 Justin Fargas	.30	.75
69 Kerry Collins	.30	.75
70 Tim Brown	.40	1.00
71 Brian Westbrook	.40	1.00
72 Donovan McNabb	.40	1.00
73 Jevon Kearse	.30	.75
74 Terrell Owens	.40	1.00
75 Duce Staley	.30	.75
76 Hines Ward	.40	1.00
77 Jerome Bettis	.40	1.00
78 Tommy Maddox	.30	.75
79 Drew Brees	.40	1.00
80 LaDainian Tomlinson	.40	1.00
81 Kevan Barlow	.25	.60
82 Tim Rattay	.25	.60
83 Koren Robinson	.25	.60
84 Matt Hasselbeck	.30	.75
85 Shaun Alexander	.30	.75
86 Isaac Bruce	.30	.75
87 Marc Bulger	.30	.75
88 Marshall Faulk	.40	1.00
89 Torry Holt	.30	.75
90 Brad Johnson	.30	.75
91 Charlie Garner	.30	.75
92 Keenan McCardell	.25	.60
93 Chris Brown	.25	.60
94 Derrick Mason	.30	.75
95 Eddie George	.30	.75
96 Steve McNair	.40	1.00
97 Clinton Portis	.40	1.00
98 LaVar Arrington	.30	.75
99 Laveranues Coles	.25	.60
100 Mark Brunell	.30	.75
101 Drew Henson RC	1.25	3.00
102 Craig Krenzel RC	1.50	4.00
103 Andy Hall RC	1.25	3.00
104 Josh Harris RC	1.25	3.00
105 Jim Sorgi RC	1.50	4.00
106 Jeff Smoker RC	1.50	4.00
107 John Navarre RC	1.25	3.00
108 Cody Pickett RC	1.50	4.00
109 Casey Bramlet RC	1.25	3.00
110 Matt Mauck RC	1.25	3.00
111 B.J. Symons RC	1.25	3.00
112 Bradlee Van Pelt RC	1.50	4.00
113 Michael Turner RC	2.50	6.00
114 Troy Fleming RC	1.25	3.00
115 Adimchinobe Echemandu RC	1.50	4.00
116 Quincy Wilson RC	1.50	4.00
117 Derrick Ward RC	2.00	5.00
118 Bruce Perry RC	1.25	3.00
119 Brandon Miree RC	1.25	3.00
120 Carlos Francis RC	1.25	3.00
121 Samie Parker RC	1.25	3.00
122 Jerricho Cotchery RC	1.50	4.00
123 Ernest Wilford RC	1.50	4.00
124 Johnnie Morant RC	1.25	3.00
125 Maurice Mann RC	1.25	3.00
126 D.J. Hackett RC	1.50	4.00
127 Drew Carter RC	1.50	4.00
128 P.K. Sam RC	1.25	3.00
129 Jamaar Taylor RC	1.25	3.00
130 Ryan Krause RC	1.25	3.00
131 Triandos Luke RC	1.25	3.00
132 Jeris McIntyre RC	1.25	3.00
133 Clarence Moore RC	1.25	3.00
134 Mark Jones RC	1.25	3.00
135 Sloan Thomas RC	1.50	4.00
136 Jonathan Smith RC	1.25	3.00
137 Patrick Crayton RC	2.00	5.00
138 Derek Abney RC	1.25	3.00
139 Kris Wilson RC	1.50	4.00
140 Sean Taylor RC	4.00	10.00
141 Jonathan Vilma RC	2.00	5.00
142 Tommie Harris RC	2.00	5.00
143 D.J. Williams RC	2.00	5.00
144 Will Smith RC	1.50	4.00
145 Kenechi Udeze RC	1.50	4.00
146 Vince Wilfork RC	2.00	5.00
147 Marcus Tubbs RC	1.25	3.00
148 Ahmad Carroll RC	1.25	3.00
149 Jason Babin RC	2.00	5.00
150 Chris Gamble RC	1.50	4.00
151 Willie Parker RC	6.00	15.00
152 Darnell Dockett RC	2.00	5.00
153 Nate Poole RC	2.00	5.00
154 Matt Kegel RC	3.00	8.00
155 Kendrick Starling RC	2.00	5.00
156 Tramon Douglas RC	2.00	5.00
157 Ryan Dinwiddie RC	2.00	5.00
158 Brian Gaither RC	2.00	5.00
159 Ran Carthon RC	2.00	5.00
160 Derick Armstrong	2.00	5.00
161 Chris Cooley RC	3.00	8.00
162 Casey Clausen RC	2.50	6.00
163 Omar Jenkins RC	2.00	5.00
164 Justin Jenkins RC	2.00	5.00
165 Wes Welker RC	10.00	25.00
166 Terrance Copper RC	4.00	10.00
167 Jarrett Payton RC	2.50	6.00
168 Zamir Cobb RC	2.00	5.00
169 Derrick Knight RC	2.00	5.00
170 Romby Bryant RC	2.00	5.00
171 Larry Croom RC	2.00	5.00
172 Thomas Tapeh RC	2.50	6.00
173 Brock Lesnar RC	15.00	30.00
174 Richard Smith RC	2.00	5.00
175 Ricky Ray RC	3.00	8.00
176 John Booth RC	2.00	5.00
177 Huey Whittaker RC	2.00	5.00
178 Fred Russell RC	2.50	6.00
179 Ben Hartsock RC	2.00	5.00
180 Tim Euhus RC	2.00	5.00
181 Ricardo Colclough RC	2.50	6.00
182 Keiwan Ratliff RC	2.00	5.00
183 Shawntae Spencer RC	2.00	5.00
184 Joey Thomas RC	2.00	5.00
185 Keith Smith RC	2.00	5.00
186 Derrick Strait RC	2.00	5.00
187 Jeremy LeSueur RC	2.00	5.00
188 Matt Ware RC	3.00	8.00
189 Rich Gardner RC	2.50	6.00
190 Daryl Smith RC	2.00	5.00
191 Dontarrious Thomas RC	2.50	6.00
192 Courtney Watson RC	2.00	5.00
193 Karlos Dansby RC	3.00	8.00
194 Teddy Lehman RC	2.00	5.00
195 Michael Boulware RC	3.00	8.00
196 Bob Sanders RC	8.00	20.00
197 Travis LaBoy RC	2.50	6.00
198 Antwan Odom RC	2.50	6.00
199 Marquise Hill RC	2.00	5.00
200 Terry Johnson RC	2.00	5.00
201 Larry Fitzgerald JSY RC	5.00	12.00
202 DeAngelo Hall JSY RC	2.00	5.00
203 Matt Schaub JSY RC	4.00	10.00
204 Michael Jenkins JSY RC	2.00	5.00
205 Devard Darling JSY RC	1.25	3.00
206 J.P. Losman JSY RC	1.50	4.00
207 Lee Evans JSY RC	2.00	5.00
208 Keary Colbert JSY RC	1.25	3.00
209 Bernard Berrian JSY RC	2.00	5.00
210 Chris Perry JSY RC	1.50	4.00
211 Kellen Winslow JSY RC	2.00	5.00
212 Luke McCown JSY RC	1.50	4.00
213 Julius Jones JSY RC	1.50	4.00
214 Darius Watts JSY RC	1.25	3.00
215 Tatum Bell JSY RC	1.50	4.00
216 Kevin Jones JSY RC	1.50	4.00
217 Roy Williams JSY RC	2.00	5.00
218 Dunta Robinson JSY RC	1.25	3.00
219 Greg Jones JSY RC	1.25	3.00
220 Reggie Williams JSY RC	1.50	4.00
221 Mewelde Moore JSY RC	1.50	4.00
222 Ben Watson JSY RC	2.00	5.00
223 Cedric Cobbs JSY RC	1.25	3.00
224 Devery Henderson JSY RC	2.00	5.00
225 Eli Manning JSY RC	12.00	30.00
226 Robert Gallery JSY RC	2.00	5.00
227 Ben Roethlisberger JSY RC	12.00	30.00
228 Philip Rivers JSY RC	8.00	20.00
229 Derrick Hamilton JSY RC	1.50	4.00
230 Rashaun Woods JSY RC	1.50	4.00
231 Steven Jackson JSY RC	3.00	8.00
232 Michael Clayton JSY RC	1.50	4.00
233 Ben Troupe JSY RC	1.50	4.00

2004 Playoff Honors O's

*VETS 1-100: 2.5X TO 6X BASIC CARDS
1-100 VETERAN PRINT RUN 175
*ROOKIES 151-200: .6X TO 1.5X BASE CARDS
151-200 ROOKIE PRINT RUN 100
*ROOKIE JSY 201-233: 1.5X TO 4X
201-233 ROOKIE JSY PRINT RUN 25
INSERTS IN RETAIL PACKS ONLY

2004 Playoff Honors X's

*VETS 1-100: 2X TO 5X BASE CARD HI
1-100 VETERAN PRINT RUN 199
*ROOKIES 101-150: .6X TO 1.5X
101-150 ROOKIE PRINT RUN 99
*ROOK.JSY 201-233: 1.5X TO 4X
201-233 ROOKIE JSY PRINT RUN 25
INSERTS IN HOBBY PACKS ONLY

2004 Playoff Honors Accolades

STATED PRINT RUN 1000 SER.#'d SETS
UNPRICED DIE CUT PRINT RUN 5

A1 Aaron Brooks	1.50	4.00
A2 Ahman Green	1.50	4.00
A3 Andre Johnson	2.00	5.00
A4 Anquan Boldin	2.00	5.00
A5 Barry Sanders	4.00	10.00
A6 Brett Favre	5.00	12.00
A7 Brian Urlacher	2.00	5.00
A8 Byron Leftwich	1.50	4.00
A9 Carson Palmer	2.00	5.00
A10 Chad Johnson	2.00	5.00
A11 Chad Pennington	2.00	5.00
A12 Chris Chambers	1.50	4.00
A13 Clinton Portis	2.00	5.00
A14 Daunte Culpepper	1.50	4.00
A15 David Carr	1.25	3.00
A16 Deuce McAllister	1.50	4.00
A17 Domanick Davis	1.25	3.00
A18 Donovan McNabb	2.00	5.00
A19 Drew Bledsoe	2.00	5.00
A20 Edgerrin James	1.50	4.00
A21 Emmitt Smith	5.00	12.00
A22 Fred Taylor	1.50	4.00
A23 Jack Lambert	2.50	6.00
A24 Jake Delhomme	1.50	4.00
A25 Jake Plummer	1.50	4.00
A26 Jamal Lewis	1.50	4.00
A27 Jeremy Shockey	1.50	4.00
A28 Jerry Rice	4.00	10.00
A29 Jim Brown	3.00	8.00
A30 Joe Namath	3.00	8.00
A31 Joey Harrington	1.50	4.00
A32 John Riggins	2.00	5.00
A33 LaDainian Tomlinson	2.00	5.00
A34 Marc Bulger	1.50	4.00
A35 Marshall Faulk	2.00	5.00
A36 Marvin Harrison	2.00	5.00
A37 Matt Hasselbeck	1.50	4.00
A38 Michael Vick	2.50	6.00
A39 Peyton Manning	4.00	10.00
A40 Priest Holmes	2.00	5.00
A41 Randy Moss	2.00	5.00
A42 Ray Lewis	2.00	5.00
A43 Rex Grossman	1.50	4.00
A44 Ricky Williams	1.50	4.00
A45 Shaun Alexander	1.50	4.00
A46 Steve McNair	2.00	5.00
A47 Terrell Owens	2.00	5.00
A48 Tom Brady	4.00	10.00
A49 Torry Holt	1.50	4.00
A50 Travis Henry	1.25	3.00

2004 Playoff Honors Alma Mater Materials

AM1-AM25 STATED ODDS 1:50
AM26-AM35 PRINT RUN 100 SER.#'d SETS
AM36-AM40 PRINT RUN 25 SER.#'d SETS

AM1 Aaron Brooks	4.00	10.00
AM2 Anquan Boldin	5.00	12.00
AM3 Laveranues Coles	3.00	8.00
AM4 Ahman Green	4.00	10.00
AM5 Barry Sanders	20.00	40.00
AM6 Ricky Williams	4.00	10.00
AM7 Drew Bledsoe	5.00	12.00
AM8 Reggie Williams	4.00	10.00
AM9 Marshall Faulk	5.00	12.00
AM10 Steven Jackson	8.00	20.00
AM11 DeShaun Foster	4.00	10.00
AM12 Keyshawn Johnson	4.00	10.00
AM13 Carson Palmer	5.00	12.00
AM14 Kyle Boller	4.00	10.00
AM15 Doug Flutie	5.00	12.00
AM16 Edgerrin James	4.00	10.00
AM17 Clinton Portis	5.00	12.00
AM18 Jeremy Shockey	4.00	10.00
AM19 Santana Moss	4.00	10.00
AM20 Curtis Martin	5.00	12.00
AM21 Andre Johnson	5.00	12.00
AM22 Herschel Walker	10.00	25.00
AM23 Shaun Alexander	4.00	10.00
AM24 Fred Taylor	4.00	10.00
AM25 Eddie George	6.00	15.00
AM26 Anquan Boldin	6.00	15.00
Aaron Brooks		
AM27 Barry Sanders	30.00	60.00
Ahman Green		
AM28 Drew Bledsoe	6.00	15.00
Reggie Williams		
AM29 Marshall Faulk	10.00	25.00
Steven Jackson		
AM30 Dan Morgan	5.00	12.00
DeShaun Foster		
AM31 Carson Palmer	6.00	15.00
Kyle Boller		
AM32 Edgerrin James	6.00	15.00
Andre Johnson		
AM33 Laveranues Coles	6.00	15.00
Clinton Portis		
AM34 Jeremy Shockey	6.00	15.00
Santana Moss		
AM35 Herschel Walker	12.50	30.00
Shaun Alexander		
AM36 Aaron Brooks	6.00	15.00
Anquan Boldin		
Laveranues Coles		
AM37 Barry Sanders	30.00	80.00
Ahman Green		
Ricky Williams		
AM38 Drew Bledsoe	15.00	40.00
Reggie Williams		
Steven Jackson		
AM39 Carson Palmer	12.50	30.00
Kyle Boller		
Doug Flutie		
AM40 Edgerrin James	12.50	30.00
Jeremy Shockey		
Clinton Portis		

2004 Playoff Honors Class Reunion

STATED PRINT RUN 1500 SER.#'d SETS

CR1 Emmitt Smith	3.00	8.00
Shannon Sharpe		
CR2 Brett Favre	3.00	8.00
Keenan McCardell		
CR3 Jerome Bettis	1.25	3.00
Mark Brunell		
CR4 Marshall Faulk	1.25	3.00
Charlie Garner		
CR5 Steve McNair	1.25	3.00
Ty Law		
CR6 Terrell Owens	1.25	3.00
Ray Lewis		
CR7 Marvin Harrison	1.25	3.00
Eric Moulds		
CR8 Eddie George	1.00	2.50
Stephen Davis		
CR9 Ahman Green	1.00	2.50
Matt Hasselbeck		
CR10 Priest Holmes	1.25	3.00
Charles Woodson		
CR11 Peyton Manning	2.50	6.00
Fred Taylor		
CR12 Randy Moss	1.25	3.00
Hines Ward		
CR13 Ricky Williams	1.00	2.50
David Boston		
CR14 Donovan McNabb	1.25	3.00
Jevon Kearse		
CR15 Daunte Culpepper	1.00	2.50
Aaron Brooks		
CR16 Edgerrin James	1.00	2.50
Torry Holt		
CR17 Tom Brady	2.50	6.00
Chad Pennington		
CR18 Marc Bulger	1.00	2.50
Shaun Alexander		
CR19 LaVar Arrington	1.00	2.50
Laveranues Coles		
CR20 Jamal Lewis	1.00	2.50
Keith Bulluck		
CR21 Brian Urlacher	1.25	3.00
Thomas Jones		
CR22 Michael Vick	1.50	4.00
Deuce McAllister		
CR23 LaDainian Tomlinson	1.25	3.00
Travis Henry		
CR24 Clinton Portis	1.25	3.00
Jeremy Shockey		
CR25 Joey Harrington	1.00	2.50
Javon Walker		
CR26 David Carr	1.00	2.50
Josh McCown		
CR27 Andre Johnson	1.25	3.00
Charles Rogers		
CR28 Anquan Boldin	1.25	3.00
Terrell Suggs		
CR29 Byron Leftwich	1.00	2.50
Tyrone Calico		
CR30 Kyle Boller	1.00	2.50
Rex Grossman		

2004 Playoff Honors Class Reunion Jerseys

STATED PRINT RUN 150 SER.#'d SETS

CR1 Emmitt Smith	12.00	30.00
Shannon Sharpe		
CR2 Brett Favre	12.00	30.00
Keenan McCardell		
CR3 Jerome Bettis	5.00	12.00
Mark Brunell		
CR4 Marshall Faulk	5.00	12.00
Charlie Garner		
CR5 Steve McNair	5.00	12.00
Ty Law		
CR6 Terrell Owens	5.00	12.00
Ray Lewis		
CR7 Marvin Harrison	5.00	12.00
Eric Moulds		
CR8 Eddie George	4.00	10.00
Stephen Davis		
CR9 Ahman Green	4.00	10.00
Matt Hasselbeck		
CR10 Priest Holmes	5.00	12.00
Charles Woodson		
CR11 Peyotn Manning	10.00	25.00
Fred Taylor		
CR12 Randy Moss	5.00	12.00
Hines Ward		
CR13 Ricky Williams	4.00	10.00
David Boston		
CR14 Donovan McNabb	5.00	12.00
Jevon Kearse		
CR15 Daunte Culpepper	4.00	10.00
Aaron Brooks		
CR16 Edgerrin James	4.00	10.00
Torry Holt		
CR17 Tom Brady	10.00	25.00
Chad Pennington		
CR18 Marc Bulger	4.00	10.00
Shaun Alexander		
CR19 LaVar Arrington	4.00	10.00
Laveranues Coles		
CR20 Jamal Lewis	4.00	10.00
Keith Bulluck		
CR21 Brian Urlacher	5.00	12.00
Thomas Jones		
CR22 Michael Vick	8.00	20.00
Deuce McAllister		
CR23 LaDainian Tomlinson	5.00	12.00
Travis Henry		
CR24 Clinton Portis	5.00	12.00
Jeremy Shockey		
CR25 Joey Harrington	4.00	10.00
Javon Walker		
CR26 David Carr	4.00	10.00
Josh McCown		
CR27 Andre Johnson	5.00	12.00
Charles Rogers		
CR28 Anquan Boldin	5.00	12.00
Terrell Suggs		
CR29 Byron Leftwich	4.00	10.00
Tyrone Calico		
CR30 Kyle Boller	4.00	10.00
Rex Grossman		

.2004 Playoff Honors Fans of the Game Silver

COMPLETE SET (6)	4.00	10.00
*HOLOGOLD: .5X TO 1.2X SILVER		
234 Ray Romano Giants	1.00	2.50
234 Ray Romano Jets	1.00	2.50
235 Darius Rucker	.75	2.00
236 Mel Kiper	.75	2.00
237 Chris Mortensen	.75	2.00
238 John O'Hurley	.75	2.00

2004 Playoff Honors Fans of the Game Autographs

234 Ray Romano Giants SP	100.00	200.00
234 Ray Romano Jets SP	100.00	200.00
235 Darius Rucker	20.00	50.00
236A Mel Kiper	12.50	30.00
236B Mel Kiper The Viper	15.00	40.00
237 Chris Mortensen	12.50	30.00
238 John O'Hurley	12.50	30.00

2004 Playoff Honors Game Day

STATED PRINT RUN 1750 SER.#'d SETS

GS1 Ahman Green	.75	2.00
GS2 Anquan Boldin	1.00	2.50
GS3 Brett Favre	2.50	6.00
GS4 Chad Johnson	1.00	2.50
GS5 Daunte Culpepper	.75	2.00
GS6 Donovan McNabb	1.00	2.50
GS7 Eddie George	.75	2.00
GS8 Emmitt Smith	2.50	6.00
GS9 Jamal Lewis	.75	2.00
GS10 Jerry Rice	2.00	5.00
GS11 Koren Robinson	.60	1.50
GS12 LaDainian Tomlinson	1.00	2.50
GS13 LaVar Arrington	.75	2.00
GS14 Marc Bulger	.75	2.00
GS15 Marshall Faulk	1.00	2.50
GS16 Matt Hasselbeck	.75	2.00
GS17 Michael Vick	1.25	3.00
GS18 Randy Moss	1.00	2.50
GS19 Ray Lewis	1.00	2.50
GS20 Ricky Williams	.75	2.00
GS21 Shaun Alexander	.75	2.00
GS22 Stephen Davis	.75	2.00
GS23 Steve McNair	1.00	2.50
GS24 Terrell Suggs	.75	2.00
GS25 Torry Holt	.75	2.00

2004 Playoff Honors Game Day Souvenirs

STATED PRINT RUN 250 SER.#'d SETS
*PRIME/25: 1X TO 2.5X DUAL/250
PRIME PRINT RUN 25 SER.#'d SETS

GS1 Ahman Green	4.00	10.00
GS2 Anquan Boldin	5.00	12.00
GS3 Brett Favre	12.00	30.00
GS4 Chad Johnson	5.00	12.00
GS5 Daunte Culpepper	4.00	10.00
GS6 Donovan McNabb	5.00	12.00
GS7 Eddie George	4.00	10.00
GS8 Emmitt Smith	12.00	30.00
GS9 Jamal Lewis	4.00	10.00
GS10 Jerry Rice	10.00	25.00
GS11 Koren Robinson	3.00	8.00
GS12 LaDainian Tomlinson	5.00	12.00
GS13 LaVar Arrington	4.00	10.00
GS14 Marc Bulger	4.00	10.00
GS15 Marshall Faulk	5.00	12.00
GS16 Matt Hasselbeck	4.00	10.00
GS17 Michael Vick	8.00	20.00
GS18 Randy Moss	5.00	12.00
GS19 Ray Lewis	5.00	12.00
GS20 Ricky Williams	4.00	10.00
GS21 Shaun Alexander	4.00	10.00
GS22 Stephen Davis	4.00	10.00
GS23 Steve McNair	5.00	12.00
GS24 Terrell Suggs	4.00	10.00
GS25 Torry Holt	4.00	10.00

2004 Playoff Honors Patches

PATCHES PRINT RUN 75 SER.#'d SETS
*PLATES/41-50: .5X TO 1.2X PATCHES
*PLATES/31-39: .6X TO 1.5X PATCHES
*PLATES/20-25: .8X TO 2X PATCHES
*PLATES/10-19: 1X TO 2.5X PATCHES
*PLATE&PATCH/10: 1.2X TO 3X PATCHES
PLATES AND PATCHES PRINT RUN 10

PP1 Anquan Boldin	6.00	15.00
PP2 Brett Favre	15.00	40.00
PP3 Brian Urlacher	6.00	15.00
PP4 Chad Johnson	6.00	15.00
PP5 Chad Pennington	6.00	15.00
PP6 Clinton Portis	6.00	15.00
PP7 Daunte Culpepper	5.00	12.00
PP8 Deuce McAllister	5.00	12.00
PP9 Donovan McNabb	6.00	15.00
PP10 Drew Bledsoe	6.00	15.00
PP11 Edgerrin James	5.00	12.00
PP12 Emmitt Smith	15.00	40.00
PP13 Jerry Rice	12.00	30.00
PP14 LaDainian Tomlinson	6.00	15.00
PP15 LaVar Arrington	5.00	12.00
PP16 Marc Bulger	5.00	12.00
PP17 Marshall Faulk	6.00	15.00
PP18 Matt Hasselbeck	5.00	12.00
PP19 Peyton Manning	12.00	30.00
PP20 Priest Holmes	6.00	15.00
PP21 Randy Moss	6.00	15.00
PP22 Ricky Williams	5.00	12.00
PP23 Shaun Alexander	5.00	12.00
PP24 Steve McNair	6.00	15.00
PP25 Tom Brady	12.00	30.00

2004 Playoff Honors Prime Signature Previews

STATED PRINT RUN 999 SER.#'d SETS

PS1 Aaron Brooks	1.00	2.50
PS2 Adam Vinatieri	1.25	3.00
PS3 Deacon Jones	1.25	3.00
PS4 Domanick Davis	.75	2.00
PS5 Don Maynard	1.25	3.00
PS6 George Blanda	1.50	4.00
PS7 Herschel Walker	1.25	3.00
PS8 Jack Lambert	2.00	5.00
PS9 Jim Brown	2.50	6.00
PS10 Jim Plunkett	1.25	3.00
PS11 Joe Greene	1.50	4.00
PS12 Joe Namath	2.50	6.00
PS13 L.C. Greenwood	1.25	3.00
PS14 Laveranues Coles	.75	2.00
PS15 Leroy Kelly	1.25	3.00
PS16 Mel Blount	1.25	3.00
PS17 Michael Strahan	1.25	3.00
PS18 Paul Warfield	1.25	3.00
PS19 Richard Dent	1.00	2.50
PS20 Sonny Jurgensen	1.25	3.00
PS21 Steve Smith	1.25	3.00
PS22 Tom Brady	2.50	6.00
PS23 Ernest Wilford	1.00	2.50
PS24 Philip Rivers	3.00	8.00
PS25 Samie Parker	.75	2.00

2004 Playoff Honors Prime Signature Previews Autographs

STATED PRINT RUN 25-300

PS1 Aaron Brooks/25	12.00	30.00
PS2 Adam Vinatieri/200	30.00	60.00
PS3 Deacon Jones/125	12.00	30.00
PS4 Domanick Davis/300	6.00	15.00
PS5 Don Maynard/100	12.00	30.00
PS7 Herschel Walker/25	15.00	40.00
PS8 Jack Lambert/25	75.00	125.00
PS9 Jim Brown/34	40.00	80.00
PS10 Jim Plunkett/25	15.00	40.00
PS11 Joe Greene/25	40.00	80.00
PS12 Joe Namath/70	50.00	100.00
PS14 Laveranues Coles/100	8.00	20.00
PS15 Leroy Kelly/206	15.00	40.00
PS17 Michael Strahan/25	15.00	40.00
PS18 Paul Warfield/25	15.00	40.00
PS20 Sonny Jurgensen/25	15.00	40.00
PS21 Steve Smith/300	10.00	25.00
PS22 Tom Brady/25	150.00	250.00
PS23 Ernest Wilford/300	8.00	20.00
PS24 Philip Rivers/300	40.00	80.00
PS25 Samie Parker/300	6.00	15.00

2004 Playoff Honors Rookie Hidden Gems Autographs

STATED PRINT RUN 50 SER.#'d SETS

201 Larry Fitzgerald JSY	75.00	150.00
202 DeAngelo Hall JSY	25.00	60.00
203 Matt Schaub JSY	50.00	125.00
204 Michael Jenkins JSY	25.00	60.00
205 Devard Darling JSY	15.00	40.00
206 J.P. Losman JSY	20.00	50.00
207 Lee Evans JSY	25.00	60.00
208 Keary Colbert JSY	15.00	40.00
209 Bernard Berrian JSY	25.00	60.00
210 Chris Perry JSY	20.00	50.00
211 Kellen Winslow Jr. JSY	25.00	60.00
212 Luke McCown JSY	20.00	50.00
213 Julius Jones JSY	20.00	50.00
214 Darius Watts JSY	15.00	40.00
215 Tatum Bell JSY	20.00	50.00
216 Kevin Jones JSY	20.00	50.00
217 Roy Williams WR JSY	25.00	60.00
218 Dunta Robinson JSY	15.00	40.00
219 Greg Jones JSY	15.00	40.00
220 Reggie Williams JSY	20.00	50.00
221 Mewelde Moore JSY	20.00	50.00
222 Ben Watson JSY	25.00	60.00
223 Cedric Cobbs JSY	15.00	40.00
224 Devery Henderson JSY	25.00	60.00
225 Eli Manning JSY	175.00	300.00
226 Robert Gallery JSY	25.00	60.00
227 Ben Roethlisberger JSY	150.00	300.00
228 Philip Rivers JSY	75.00	150.00
229 Derrick Hamilton JSY	15.00	40.00
230 Rashaun Woods JSY	15.00	40.00
231 Steven Jackson JSY	50.00	120.00
232 Michael Clayton JSY	20.00	50.00
233 Ben Troupe JSY	20.00	50.00

2004 Playoff Honors Rookie Quad

STATED PRINT RUN 1250 SER.#'d SETS

RQ1 Eli Manning	10.00	25.00
Julius Jones		
Michael Clayton		
Keary Colbert		
RQ2 Larry Fitzgerald	5.00	12.00
DeAngelo Hall		
Michael Jenkins		
Matt Schaub		
RQ3 Philip Rivers	6.00	15.00
Devery Henderson		
Tatum Bell		
Darius Watts		
RQ4 Ben Roethlisberger	10.00	25.00
Devard Darling		
Kellen Winslow		
Luke McCown		
RQ5 Kevin Jones	2.00	5.00
Roy Williams WR		
Bernard Berrian		
Mewelde Moore		
RQ6 Greg Jones	1.50	4.00
Reggie Williams		
Dunta Robinson		
Ben Troupe		
RQ7 J.P. Losman	2.00	5.00
Lee Evans		
Cedric Cobbs		
Ben Watson		
RQ8 Steven Jackson	3.00	8.00
Chris Perry		
Rashaun Woods		
Derrick Hamilton		

2004 Playoff Honors Rookie Quad Jerseys

JERSEY PRINT RUN 250 SER.#'d SETS
*FOOTBALL/75: .6X TO 1.5X JSY/250
FOOTBALLS PRINT RUN 75 SER.#'d SETS
*JSY-FB/25: 1X TO 2.5X QUAD JSY/250
JSY/FB PRINT RUN 25 SER.#'d SETS

RQ1 Eli Manning	20.00	50.00

Julius Jones
Michael Clayton
Keary Colbert
RQ2 Larry Fitzgerald 10.00 25.00
DeAngelo Hall
Michael Jenkins
Matt Schaub
RQ3 Philip Rivers 12.00 30.00
Devery Henderson
Tatum Bell
Darius Watts
RQ4 Ben Roethlisberger 20.00 50.00
Devard Darling
Kellen Winslow
Luke McCown
RQ5 Kevin Jones 4.00 10.00
Roy Williams WR
Bernard Berrian
Mewelde Moore
RQ6 Greg Jones 3.00 8.00
Reggie Williams
Dunta Robinson
Ben Troupe
RQ7 J.P. Losman 4.00 10.00
Lee Evans
Cedric Cobbs
Ben Watson
RQ8 Steven Jackson 6.00 15.00
Chris Perry
Rashaun Woods
Derrick Hamilton

2004 Playoff Honors Rookie Tandem

STATED ODDS 1:13
RT1 Eli Manning 5.00 12.00
Julius Jones
RT2 Michael Clayton .60 1.50
Keary Colbert
RT3 Larry Fitzgerald 2.00 5.00
DeAngelo Hall
RT4 Michael Jenkins 1.50 4.00
Matt Schaub
RT5 Philip Rivers 3.00 8.00
Devery Henderson
RT6 Tatum Bell .60 1.50
Darius Watts
RT7 Ben Roethlisberger 5.00 12.00
Devard Darling
RT8 Kellen Winslow Jr. .75 2.00
Luke McCown
RT9 Kevin Jones .75 2.00
Roy Williams
RT10 Bernard Berrian .75 2.00
Mewelde Moore
RT11 Greg Jones .60 1.50
Reggie Williams
RT12 Dunta Robinson .75 2.00
Ben Troupe
RT13 J.P. Losman .75 2.00
Lee Evans
RT14 Cedric Cobbs .75 2.00
Ben Watson
RT15 Steven Jackson 1.25 3.00
Chris Perry
RT16 Rashaun Woods .50 1.25
Derrick Hamilton

2004 Playoff Honors Rookie Tandem Jerseys

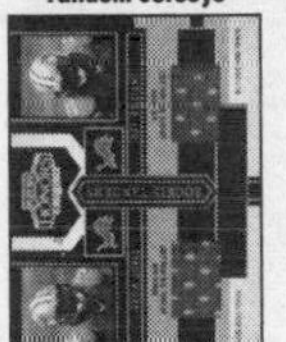

STATED ODDS 1:68
*FOOTBALL/125: .6X TO 1.5X TANDEM JSY
FOOTBALLS PRINT RUN 125 SER.#'d SETS
*JSY-FB/50: .8X TO 2X TANDEM JSY
JERSEY AND FOOTBALL PRINT RUN 50
RT1 Eli Manning 20.00 50.00
Julius Jones
RT2 Michael Clayton 2.50 6.00
Keary Colbert
RT3 Larry Fitzgerald 8.00 20.00
DeAngelo Hall
RT4 Michael Jenkins 6.00 15.00
Matt Schaub
RT5 Philip Rivers 12.00 30.00
Devery Henderson
RT6 Tatum Bell 2.50 6.00
Darius Watts
RT7 Ben Roethlisberger 20.00 50.00
Devard Darling
RT8 Kellen Winslow Jr. 3.00 8.00
Luke McCown
RT9 Kevin Jones 3.00 8.00
Roy Williams WR
RT10 Bernard Berrian 3.00 8.00
Mewelde Moore
RT11 Greg Jones 2.50 6.00
Reggie Williams
RT12 Dunta Robinson 2.50 6.00
Ben Troupe
RT13 J.P. Losman 3.00 8.00
Lee Evans
RT14 Cedric Cobbs 3.00 8.00
Ben Watson
RT15 Steven Jackson 5.00 12.00
Chris Perry
RT16 Rashaun Woods 2.00 5.00
Derrick Hamilton

2004 Playoff Honors Rookie Year

STATED ODDS 1:12
RY1 Curtis Martin 1.25 3.00
RY2 David Carr .75 2.00
RY3 Jeremy Shockey 1.00 2.50
RY4 Joey Harrington 1.00 2.50
RY5 John Riggins 1.25 3.00
RY6 Koren Robinson .75 2.00
RY7 LaDainian Tomlinson 1.25 3.00
RY8 Mark Brunell 1.00 2.50
RY9 Keyshawn Johnson 1.00 2.50
RY10 Peyton Manning 2.50 6.00
RY11 Randy Moss 1.25 3.00
RY12 Ricky Williams 1.00 2.50
RY13 Roy Williams S 1.00 2.50
RY14 Quincy Carter .75 2.00
RY15 Andre Johnson 1.25 3.00
RY16 Anquan Boldin 1.25 3.00
RY17 Byron Leftwich 1.00 2.50
RY18 Kyle Boller 1.00 2.50
RY19 Rex Grossman 1.00 2.50
RY20 Terrell Suggs 1.00 2.50

2004 Playoff Honors Rookie Year Jerseys

STATED PRINT RUN 150 SER.#'d SETS
RY1 Curtis Martin 4.00 10.00
RY2 David Carr 2.50 6.00
RY3 Jeremy Shockey 3.00 8.00
RY4 Joey Harrington 3.00 8.00
RY5 John Riggins 8.00 20.00
RY6 Koren Robinson 2.50 6.00
RY7 LaDainian Tomlinson 4.00 10.00
RY8 Mark Brunell 3.00 8.00
RY9 Keyshawn Johnson 3.00 8.00
RY10 Peyton Manning 8.00 20.00
RY11 Randy Moss 4.00 10.00
RY12 Ricky Williams 3.00 8.00
RY13 Roy Williams S 3.00 8.00
RY14 Quincy Carter 2.50 6.00
RY15 Andre Johnson 4.00 10.00
RY16 Anquan Boldin 4.00 10.00
RY17 Byron Leftwich 3.00 8.00
RY18 Kyle Boller 3.00 8.00
RY19 Rex Grossman 3.00 8.00
RY20 Terrell Suggs 3.00 8.00

2005 Playoff Honors

This 229-card set was released in October, 2005. The set was issued through the hobby in six-card packs with an $5 SRP which came 12 packs to a box. Cards numbered 1-99 feature veterans sequenced in alphabetical order by team while cards numbered 101-229 all feature rookies. In that rookie grouping, cards numbered 201-229 all have a player-worn swatch. The rookies are split up thusly: Cards numbered 101-150 were issued to a stated print run of 699 serial numbered packs; cards numbered 151-200 were issued to a stated print run of 399 serial numbered sets and cards numbered 201-229 were issued to a stated print run of 750 serial numbered sets.

COMP.SET w/o SP's (100) 7.50 20.00
101-150 INSERTED IN HOBBY PACKS
101-150 PRINT RUN 699 SER.#'d SETS
151-200 INSERTED IN RETAIL PACKS
151-200 PRINT RUN 399 SER.#'d SETS
ROOKIE JSY PRINT RUN 750 SER.#'d SETS
1 Anquan Boldin .30 .75
2 Larry Fitzgerald .40 1.00
3 Kurt Warner .40 1.00
4 Michael Vick .40 1.00
5 Alge Crumpler .30 .75
6 Warrick Dunn .30 .75
7 Jamal Lewis .30 .75
8 Kyle Boller .30 .75
9 Ray Lewis .40 1.00
10 Derrick Mason .30 .75
11 Eric Moulds .25 .60
12 J.P. Losman .25 .60
13 Willis McGahee .40 1.00
14 Jake Delhomme .30 .75
15 Steve Smith .40 1.00
16 DeShaun Foster .30 .75
17 Rex Grossman .30 .75
18 Brian Urlacher .40 1.00
19 Muhsin Muhammad .30 .75
20 Carson Palmer .40 1.00
21 Chad Johnson .30 .75
22 Rudi Johnson .30 .75
23 Lee Suggs .25 .60
24 Trent Dilfer .30 .75
25 Reuben Droughns .25 .60
26 Drew Bledsoe .40 1.00
27 Julius Jones .25 .60
28 Keyshawn Johnson .30 .75
29 Roy Williams S .25 .60
30 Ashley Lelie .25 .60
31 Jake Plummer .30 .75
32 Rod Smith .30 .75
33 Tatum Bell .25 .60
34 Joey Harrington .30 .75
35 Kevin Jones .25 .60
36 Roy Williams WR .30 .75
37 Ahman Green .30 .75
38 Brett Favre 1.00 2.50
39 Javon Walker .25 .60
40 Andre Johnson .40 1.00
41 David Carr .25 .60
42 Domanick Davis .25 .60
43 Marvin Harrison .40 1.00
44 Edgerrin James .30 .75
45 Peyton Manning .75 2.00
46 Reggie Wayne .40 1.00
47 Fred Taylor .30 .75
48 Byron Leftwich .30 .75
49 Jimmy Smith .30 .75
50 Priest Holmes .30 .75
51 Tony Gonzalez .30 .75
52 Trent Green .30 .75
53 A.J. Feeley .25 .60
54 Chris Chambers .30 .75
55 Daunte Culpepper .30 .75
56 Nate Burleson .25 .60
57 Michael Bennett .30 .75
58 Corey Dillon .30 .75
59 Deion Branch .25 .60
60 Tedy Bruschi .40 1.00
61 Tom Brady .75 2.00
62 Aaron Brooks .25 .60
63 Deuce McAllister .30 .75
64 Joe Horn .30 .75
65 Eli Manning .60 1.50
66 Tiki Barber .40 1.00
67 Plaxico Burress .30 .75
68 Jeremy Shockey .40 1.00
69 Chad Pennington .40 1.00
70 Curtis Martin .40 1.00
71 Laveranues Coles .25 .60
72 Kerry Collins .30 .75
73 Randy Moss .40 1.00
74 LaMont Jordan .30 .75
75 Brian Westbrook .30 .75
76 Donovan McNabb .40 1.00
77 Terrell Owens .40 1.00
78 Ben Roethlisberger .60 1.50
79 Hines Ward .40 1.00
80 Duce Staley .30 .75
81 Jerome Bettis .40 1.00
82 Drew Brees .40 1.00
83 LaDainian Tomlinson .40 1.00
84 Antonio Gates .40 1.00
85 Kevan Barlow .25 .60
86 Brandon Lloyd .25 .60
87 Darrell Jackson .25 .60
88 Matt Hasselbeck .30 .75
89 Shaun Alexander .30 .75
90 Marc Bulger .30 .75
91 Torry Holt .30 .75
92 Steven Jackson .40 1.00
93 Brian Griese .30 .75
94 Michael Clayton .25 .60
95 Drew Bennett .30 .75
96 Steve McNair .40 1.00
97 Chris Brown .25 .60
98 Clinton Portis .30 .75
99 LaVar Arrington .30 .75
100 Santana Moss .30 .75
101 Cedric Benson RC 2.00 5.00
102 Mike Williams 2.00 5.00
103 DeMarcus Ware RC 4.00 10.00
104 Shawne Merriman RC 2.00 5.00
105 Thomas Davis RC 1.25 3.00
106 Derrick Johnson RC 1.50 4.00
107 David Pollack RC 1.50 4.00
108 Erasmus James RC 1.50 4.00
109 Marcus Spears RC 1.50 4.00
110 Fabian Washington RC 1.50 4.00
111 Aaron Rodgers RC 25.00 50.00
112 Marlin Jackson RC 1.25 3.00
113 Heath Miller RC 2.50 6.00
114 Alex Smith TE RC 1.25 3.00
115 Chris Henry RC 2.00 5.00
116 David Greene RC 1.25 3.00
117 Brandon Jones RC 1.50 4.00
118 Marion Barber RC 2.00 5.00
119 Brandon Jacobs RC 2.50 6.00
120 Jerome Mathis RC 2.00 5.00
121 Craphonso Thorpe RC 1.25 3.00
122 Manuel White RC 1.50 4.00
123 Alvin Pearman RC 1.25 3.00
124 Darren Sproles RC 2.00 5.00
125 Fred Gibson RC 1.50 4.00
126 Roydell Williams RC 1.50 4.00
127 Airese Currie RC 1.25 3.00
128 Damien Nash RC 1.50 4.00
129 Dan Orlovsky RC 2.00 5.00
130 Adrian McPherson RC 1.25 3.00
131 Larry Brookins RC 1.25 3.00
132 Rasheed Marshall RC 1.50 4.00
133 Cedric Houston RC 2.00 5.00
134 Chad Owens RC 1.50 4.00
135 Tab Perry RC 1.25 3.00
136 Dante Ridgeway RC UER 1.25 3.00
137 Craig Bragg RC 1.25 3.00
138 Deandra Cobb RC 1.25 3.00
139 Derek Anderson RC 1.50 4.00
140 Travis Johnson RC 1.25 3.00
141 Paris Warren RC 1.50 4.00
142 LeRon McCoy RC 1.25 3.00
143 James Kilian RC 1.25 3.00
144 Matt Cassel RC 4.00 10.00
145 Lionel Gates RC 1.25 3.00
146 Harry Williams RC 1.50 4.00
147 Anthony Davis RC 1.25 3.00
148 Noah Herron RC 1.25 3.00
149 Ryan Fitzpatrick RC 3.00 8.00
150 J.R. Russell RC 1.25 3.00
151 Cole Magner RC 1.50 4.00
152 Luis Castillo RC 2.00 5.00
153 Mike Patterson RC 1.50 4.00
154 Brodney Pool RC 2.50 6.00
155 Barrett Ruud RC 2.50 6.00
156 Shaun Cody RC 2.00 5.00
157 Stanford Routt RC 2.00 5.00
158 Josh Bullocks RC 2.00 5.00
159 Kevin Burnett RC 2.00 5.00
160 Corey Webster RC 2.00 5.00
161 Lofa Tatupu RC 2.50 6.00
162 Matt Roth RC 2.00 5.00
163 Mike Nugent RC 2.00 5.00
164 Odell Thurman RC 2.50 6.00
165 Ronald Bartell RC 2.00 5.00
166 Nick Collins RC 2.50 6.00
167 Dan Cody RC 2.00 5.00
168 Darrent Williams RC 2.50 6.00
169 Justin Miller RC 2.00 5.00
170 Jerome Collins RC 2.00 5.00
171 Justin Green RC 2.50 6.00
172 Eric Green RC 1.50 4.00
173 Joel Dreessen RC 2.00 5.00
174 Bo Scaife RC 2.00 5.00
175 Antonio Perkins RC 2.00 5.00
176 Nehemiah Broughton RC 2.00 5.00
177 Patrick Estes RC 1.50 4.00
178 Billy Bajema RC 1.50 4.00
179 Madison Hedgecock RC 2.50 6.00
180 Roscoe Crosby RC 1.50 4.00
181 Kendrick Mosley RC 1.50 4.00
182 Tyson Thompson RC 2.50 6.00
183 Fred Amey RC 2.00 5.00
184 Brock Berlin RC 2.00 5.00
185 Gino Guidugli RC 1.50 4.00
186 Walter Reyes RC 1.50 4.00
187 Lydell Ross RC 2.00 5.00
188 Carlyle Holiday RC 2.00 5.00
189 Bryan Randall RC 2.00 5.00
190 Derrick Tinsley RC 2.00 5.00
191 Ryan Grant RC 40.00 100.00
192 Bobby Purify RC 2.00 5.00
193 Leonard Weaver RC 1.50 4.00
194 Vincent Fuller RC 2.00 5.00
195 Tony Brown RC 2.00 5.00
196 Zach Tuiasosopo RC 1.50 4.00
197 Craig Ochs RC 2.00 5.00
198 Ruvell Martin RC 3.00 8.00
199 Manuel Wright RC 2.00 5.00
200 Travis Daniels RC 2.00 5.00
201 Adam Jones JSY RC 2.50 6.00
202 Alex Smith QB JSY RC 10.00 25.00
203 Andrew Walter JSY RC 2.50 6.00
204 Antrel Rolle JSY RC 3.00 8.00
205 Braylon Edwards JSY RC 6.00 15.00
206 Cadillac Williams JSY RC 3.00 8.00
207 Carlos Rogers JSY RC 3.00 8.00
208 Charlie Frye JSY RC 3.00 8.00
209 Ciatrick Fason JSY RC 2.00 5.00
210 Courtney Roby JSY RC 2.50 6.00
211 Eric Shelton JSY RC 2.00 5.00
212 Frank Gore JSY RC 6.00 15.00
213 J.J. Arrington JSY RC 2.50 6.00
214 Jason Campbell JSY RC 4.00 10.00
215 Kyle Orton JSY RC 3.00 8.00
216 Mark Bradley JSY RC 2.00 5.00
217 Mark Clayton JSY RC 3.00 8.00
218 Matt Jones JSY RC 3.00 8.00
219 Maurice Clarett JSY 2.50 6.00
220 Reggie Brown JSY RC 2.00 5.00
221 Ronnie Brown JSY RC 10.00 25.00
222 Roddy White JSY RC 4.00 10.00
223 Ryan Moats JSY RC 2.50 6.00
224 Roscoe Parrish JSY RC 2.00 5.00
225 Stefan LeFors JSY RC 2.00 5.00
226 Terrence Murphy JSY RC 2.00 5.00
227 Troy Williamson JSY RC 2.50 6.00
228 Vernand Morency JSY RC 2.50 6.00
229 Vincent Jackson JSY RC 4.00 10.00

2005 Playoff Honors O's

*VETERANS: 2X TO 5X BASIC CARDS
1-100 PRINT RUN 150 SER.#'d SETS
*ROOKIES 151-200: .8X TO 2X BASIC CARDS
151-200 PRINT RUN 99 SER.#'d SETS
*JSY 201-229: 1.5X TO 4X BASIC JSYs
201-229 JSY PRINT RUN 25 SER.#'d SETS
O's INSERTED IN RETAIL PACKS ONLY
191 Ryan Grant 40.00 100.00

2005 Playoff Honors Vanguard

*VETERANS 1-100: 2.5X TO 6X BASIC CARDS
1-100 PRINT RUN 99 SER.#'d SETS
*ROOKIES 151-200: 1X TO 2.5X BASIC CARDS
151-200 PRINT RUN 50 SER.#'d SETS
VANGUARD INSERTED IN BLASTER PACKS
191 Ryan Grant 50.00 120.00

2005 Playoff Honors X's

*VETERANS 1-100: 1.5X TO 4X BASIC CARDS
1-100 PRINT RUN 299 SER.#'d SETS
*ROOKIES 101-150: .8X TO 2X BASIC CARDS
101-150 PRINT RUN 99 SER.#'d SETS
*JSY 201-229: 1.5X TO 4X BASIC JSYs
201-229 JSY PRINT RUN 25 SER.#'d SETS
X's INSERTED IN HOBBY PACKS ONLY

2005 Playoff Honors Accolades

STATED PRINT RUN 699 SER.#'d SETS
UNPRICED DIE CUT PRINT RUN 10 SETS
A1 Alex Smith QB 3.00 8.00
A2 Antonio Gates 1.00 2.50
A3 Ben Roethlisberger 2.50 6.00
A4 Braylon Edwards 2.50 6.00
A5 Brett Favre 2.50 6.00
A6 Brian Urlacher 1.00 2.50
A7 Byron Leftwich 1.00 2.50
A8 Cadillac Williams 2.00 5.00
A9 Carson Palmer 1.00 2.50
A10 Cedric Benson 1.50 4.00
A11 Chad Pennington 1.00 2.50
A12 Clinton Portis 1.00 2.50
A13 Corey Dillon .60 1.50
A14 Curtis Martin 1.00 2.50
A15 Daunte Culpepper 1.00 2.50
A16 David Carr 1.00 2.50
A17 Deion Sanders 1.00 2.50
A18 Deuce McAllister 1.00 2.50
A19 Domanick Davis .60 1.50
A20 Donovan McNabb 1.25 3.00
A21 Edgerrin James 1.00 2.50
A22 Eli Manning 2.00 5.00
A23 J.P. Losman 1.00 2.50
A24 Jake Delhomme 1.00 2.50
A25 Jake Plummer .60 1.50
A26 Jamal Lewis 1.00 2.50
A27 Javon Walker .60 1.50
A28 Jerome Bettis 1.00 2.50
A29 Jerry Rice 2.00 5.00
A30 Jim Brown 2.00 5.00
A31 Joe Montana 3.00 8.00
A32 Joe Namath 2.00 5.00
A33 Julius Jones 1.25 3.00
A34 Kevin Jones 1.00 2.50
A35 LaDainian Tomlinson 1.00 2.50
A36 Larry Fitzgerald 1.00 2.50
A37 LaVar Arrington 1.00 2.50
A38 Marc Bulger 1.00 2.50
A39 Matt Hasselbeck .60 1.50
A40 Michael Vick 1.50 4.00
A41 Peyton Manning 1.50 4.00
A42 Priest Holmes 1.00 2.50
A43 Randy Moss 1.00 2.50
A44 Ronnie Brown 3.00 8.00
A45 Rudi Johnson .60 1.50
A46 Roy Williams WR 1.00 2.50
A47 Steven Jackson 1.00 2.50
A48 Terrell Owens 1.00 2.50
A49 Tom Brady 2.50 6.00
A50 Willis McGahee 1.00 2.50

2005 Playoff Honors Alma Mater Materials

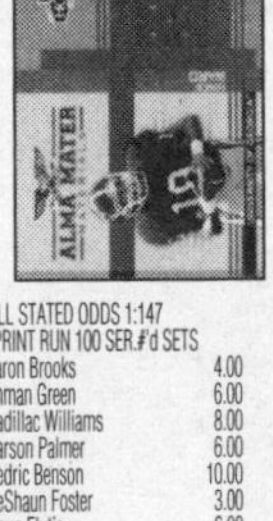

OVERALL STATED ODDS 1:147
DUAL PRINT RUN 100 SER.#'d SETS
AM1 Aaron Brooks 4.00 10.00
AM2 Ahman Green 6.00 15.00
AM3 Cadillac Williams 8.00 20.00
AM4 Carson Palmer 6.00 15.00
AM5 Cedric Benson 10.00 25.00
AM6 DeShaun Foster 3.00 8.00
AM7 Doug Flutie 6.00 15.00
AM8 Drew Bledsoe 6.00 15.00
AM9 Hines Ward SP 7.50 20.00
AM10 Jevon Kearse 4.00 10.00
AM11 John Elway 15.00 40.00
AM12 Julius Jones 7.50 20.00
AM13 Kyle Boller 4.00 10.00
AM14 Lee Suggs 3.00 8.00
AM15 Marshall Faulk 6.00 15.00
AM16 Michael Clayton 4.00 10.00
AM17 Michael Vick 7.50 20.00
AM18 Mike Singletary 6.00 15.00
AM19 Reggie Williams 3.00 8.00
AM20 Roy Williams S 6.00 15.00
AM21 Santana Moss 4.00 10.00
AM22 Steven Jackson 6.00 15.00
AM23 Tony Dorsett 7.50 20.00
AM24 Tyrone Calico 3.00 8.00
AM25 Willis McGahee 6.00 15.00
AM26 Clinton Portis 7.50 20.00
Santana Moss /100
AM27 Michael Vick 12.50 30.00
Lee Suggs/100
AM28 John Elway 20.00 50.00
Drew Bledsoe /100
AM29 Andre Johnson 6.00 15.00
Reggie Wayne /100
AM30 Carson Palmer 10.00 25.00
Steven Jackson /100
AM31 Willis McGahee 7.50 20.00
Anquan Boldin /100
AM32 Doug Flutie 7.50 20.00
Marshall Faulk /100
AM33 Hines Ward 15.00 40.00
Cadillac Williams/100
AM34 Tony Dorsett 12.50 30.00
Julius Jones /100
AM35 Cedric Benson 20.00 50.00
Barry Sanders /100
AM36 Reggie Wayne 20.00 40.00
Jeremy Shockey
Willis McGahee /25
AM37 John Elway 40.00 75.00
Drew Bledsoe
Carson Palmer /25
AM38 Tony Dorsett 20.00 50.00
Julius Jones
Roy Williams /25
AM39 Michael Vick 20.00 50.00
Doug Flutie
Aaron Brooks/25
AM40 Cedric Benson 40.00 75.00
Barry Sanders
Ahman Green /25

2005 Playoff Honors Award Winners

STATED ODDS 1:12 HOB, 1:24 RET
*FOIL: .5X TO 1.2X BASIC INSERTS
FOIL PRINT RUN 250 SER.#'d SETS
*HOLOFOIL: .8X TO 2X BASIC INSERTS
HOLOFOIL PRINT RUN 100 SER.#'d SETS
AW1 Andre Ware .75 2.00
AW2 Archie Griffin 1.25 3.00
AW3 Charles White .75 2.00
AW4 Danny Wuerffel .75 2.00
AW5 Chris Weinke .75 2.00
AW6 Doug Flutie 1.25 3.00
AW7 Gary Beban .75 2.00
AW8 George Rogers 1.50 4.00
AW9 Gino Torretta .75 2.00
AW10 Glenn Davis .75 2.00
AW11 Mike Garrett .75 2.00
AW12 Mike Rozier 1.25 3.00
AW13 Pat Sullivan .75 2.00
AW14 Pete Dawkins 1.25 3.00
AW15 Roger Staubach 2.50 6.00
AW16 Rashaan Salaam .75 2.00
AW17 Ty Detmer .75 2.00

2005 Playoff Honors Award Winners Autographs

STATED PRINT RUN 300 SER.#'d SETS
AW1 Andre Ware 7.50 20.00
AW2 Archie Griffin 15.00 40.00
AW3 Charles White 7.50 20.00
AW4 Danny Wuerffel 10.00 25.00
AW5 Chris Weinke 7.50 20.00
AW6 Doug Flutie 15.00 30.00
AW7 Gary Beban 7.50 20.00
AW8 George Rogers 12.50 30.00
AW9 Gino Torretta 10.00 25.00
AW10 Glenn Davis 20.00 50.00
AW11 Mike Garrett 10.00 25.00
AW12 Mike Rozier 12.50 30.00
AW13 Pat Sullivan 10.00 25.00
AW14 Pete Dawkins 12.50 30.00
AW15 Roger Staubach 30.00 60.00
AW16 Rashaan Salaam 6.00 15.00
AW17 Ty Detmer 6.00 15.00

2005 Playoff Honors Class Reunion

STATED ODDS 1:9 HOB, 1:24 RET
*FOIL: .5X TO 1.2X BASIC INSERTS
FOIL PRINT RUN 250 SER.#'d SETS
*HOLOFOIL: .6X TO 1.5X BASIC INSERTS
HOLOFOIL PRINT RUN 100 SER.#'d SETS
CR1 Keyshawn Johnson .50 1.25
Eddie George
CR2 Terrell Owens .75 2.00
Marvin Harrison
CR3 Peyton Manning 1.25 3.00
Brian Griese
CR4 Ahman Green .75 2.00
Fred Taylor
CR5 Randy Moss .75 2.00
Charles Woodson
CR6 Donovan McNabb 1.00 2.50
Daunte Culpepper
CR7 Edgerrin James .75 2.00
Aaron Brooks
CR8 Torry Holt .75 2.00
Peerless Price
CR9 Brian Urlacher .75 2.00
Thomas Jones
CR10 Shaun Alexander 1.00 2.50
LaVar Arrington
CR11 Laveranues Coles .75 2.00
Chad Pennington
CR12 Plaxico Burress .75 2.00
Jamal Lewis
CR13 Marc Bulger 2.00 5.00
Tom Brady
CR14 Michael Vick 1.00 2.50
LaDainianTomlinson
CR15 Santana Moss .50 1.25
Reggie Wayne
CR16 Todd Heap .75 2.00
Deuce McAllister
CR17 Chris Chambers .75 2.00
Chad Johnson
CR18 Rudi Johnson .75 2.00
Drew Brees
CR19 David Carr .75 2.00
Joey Harrington
CR20 Clinton Portis .75 2.00
Javon Walker
CR21 Patrick Ramsey .50 1.25
Ashley Lelie
CR22 Carson Palmer .75 2.00
Byron Leftwich
CR23 Kyle Boller .50 1.25
Rex Grossman
CR24 Willis McGahee .75 2.00
Chris Brown
CR25 Andre Johnson .50 1.25
Anquan Boldin
CR26 Larry Fitzgerald .75 2.00
Michael Clayton
CR27 Roy Williams WR .75 2.00
Kevin Jones
CR28 Eli Manning 2.00 5.00
Ben Roethlisberger
CR29 Steven Jackson .75 2.00
Julius Jones
CR30 Lee Evans .75 2.00
J.P. Losman

2005 Playoff Honors Class Reunion Materials

STATED PRINT RUN 160 SER.#'d SETS
*PRIME: .8X TO 2X BASIC JERSEYS
PRIME PRINT RUN 25 SER.#'d SETS
CR1 Keyshawn Johnson 4.00 10.00
Eddie George
CR2 Terrell Owens 5.00 12.00
Marvin Harrison
CR3 Peyton Manning 7.50 20.00
Brian Griese
CR4 Ahman Green 5.00 12.00
Fred Taylor
CR5 Randy Moss 5.00 12.00
Charles Woodson
CR6 Donovan McNabb 6.00 15.00
Daunte Culpepper
CR7 Edgerrin James 5.00 12.00
Aaron Brooks
CR8 Torry Holt 4.00 10.00
Peerless Price
CR9 Brian Urlacher 5.00 12.00
Thomas Jones
CR10 Shaun Alexander 6.00 15.00
LaVar Arrington
CR11 Laveranues Coles 5.00 12.00
Chad Pennington
CR12 Plaxico Burress 5.00 12.00
Jamal Lewis
CR13 Marc Bulger 7.50 20.00
Tom Brady
CR14 Michael Vick 7.50 20.00
LaDainianTomlinson
CR15 Santana Moss 4.00 10.00
Reggie Wayne
CR16 Todd Heap 4.00 10.00
Deuce McAllister
CR17 Chris Chambers 4.00 10.00
Chad Johnson
CR18 Rudi Johnson 5.00 12.00
Drew Brees
CR19 David Carr 5.00 12.00
Joey Harrington
CR20 Clinton Portis 5.00 12.00
Javon Walker
CR21 Patrick Ramsey 4.00 10.00
Ashley Lelie
CR22 Carson Palmer 5.00 12.00
Byron Leftwich
CR23 Kyle Boller 4.00 10.00
Rex Grossman
CR24 Willis McGahee 5.00 12.00
Chris Brown
CR25 Andre Johnson 4.00 10.00
Anquan Boldin
CR26 Larry Fitzgerald 4.00 10.00
Michael Clayton
CR27 Roy Williams WR 5.00 12.00
Kevin Jones
CR28 Eli Manning 12.50 30.00
Ben Roethlisberger
CR29 Steven Jackson 6.00 15.00
Julius Jones
CR30 Lee Evans 5.00 12.00
J.P. Losman

2005 Playoff Honors Game Day

STATED ODDS 1:9 HOB, 1:24 RET
*FOIL: .5X TO 1.2X BASIC INSERTS
FOIL PRINT RUN 250 SER.#'d SETS
*HOLOFOIL: .6X TO 1.5X BASIC INSERTS
HOLOFOIL PRINT RUN 100 SER.#'d SETS
GD1 Anquan Boldin .50 1.25
GD2 Larry Fitzgerald .75 2.00
GD3 Chad Pennington .75 2.00
GD4 Tom Brady 2.00 5.00
GD5 Corey Dillon .50 1.25
GD6 Curtis Martin .75 2.00
GD7 Matt Hasselbeck .50 1.25
GD8 Shaun Alexander 1.00 2.50
GD9 Koren Robinson .50 1.25
GD10 Michael Clayton .75 2.00
GD11 Tiki Barber .75 2.00
GD12 Jeremy Shockey .75 2.00
GD13 Aaron Brooks .50 1.25
GD14 Deuce McAllister .75 2.00
GD15 Marc Bulger .75 2.00
GD16 Torry Holt .75 2.00
GD17 Steven Jackson .75 2.00
GD18 Donovan McNabb 1.00 2.50
GD19 Chris Chambers .50 1.25
GD20 Brian Urlacher .75 2.00
GD21 Steve McNair .75 2.00
GD22 Peyton Manning 1.25 3.00
GD23 Jamal Lewis .75 2.00
GD24 Todd Heap .50 1.25
GD25 Michael Strahan .50 1.25

2005 Playoff Honors Game Day Souvenirs

STATED PRINT RUN 250 SER.#'d SETS
*PRIME: 1X TO 2.5X BASIC INSERTS
PRIME PRINT RUN 25 SER.#'d SETS
GD1 Anquan Boldin 4.00 10.00
GD2 Larry Fitzgerald 4.00 10.00
GD3 Chad Pennington 5.00 12.00
GD4 Tom Brady 12.50 30.00
GD5 Corey Dillon 4.00 10.00
GD6 Curtis Martin 5.00 12.00
GD7 Matt Hasselbeck 4.00 10.00
GD8 Shaun Alexander 6.00 15.00
GD9 Koren Robinson 4.00 10.00
GD10 Michael Clayton 4.00 10.00
GD11 Tiki Barber 5.00 12.00
GD12 Jeremy Shockey 5.00 12.00
GD13 Aaron Brooks 4.00 10.00
GD14 Deuce McAllister 5.00 12.00
GD15 Marc Bulger 4.00 10.00
GD16 Torry Holt 5.00 12.00
GD17 Steven Jackson 5.00 12.00
GD18 Donovan McNabb 6.00 15.00
GD19 Chris Chambers 4.00 10.00
GD20 Brian Urlacher 5.00 12.00
GD21 Steve McNair 5.00 12.00
GD22 Peyton Manning 7.50 20.00
GD23 Jamal Lewis 5.00 12.00
GD24 Todd Heap 4.00 10.00
GD25 Michael Strahan 4.00 10.00

2005 Playoff Honors Honorable Signatures

HS1 Aaron Brooks/100 6.00 15.00
HS2 Andre Johnson/75 10.00 25.00
HS3 Antonio Gates/100 12.50 30.00
HS4 Ben Roethlisberger/25 100.00 175.00
HS6 Domanick Davis/25 10.00 25.00
HS7 Donnie Edwards/100 10.00 25.00
HS8 Michael Vick/25 40.00 80.00
HS9 Rex Grossman/25 25.00 50.00
HS10 Rudi Johnson/25 12.00 30.00
HS11 Tatum Bell/25 10.00 25.00
HS12 Terence Newman/100 10.00 25.00
HS13 Todd Heap/100 6.00 15.00
HS14 Christian Okoye/150 6.00 15.00
HS15 Ickey Woods/150 10.00 25.00
HS16 John Taylor/100 7.50 20.00
HS17 Richard Dent/150 6.00 15.00
HS18 Alex Smith QB/50 50.00 100.00
HS19 Adrian McPherson/150 7.50 20.00
HS20 Cadillac Williams/50 20.00 50.00
HS21 Fred Gibson/150 6.00 15.00
HS22 J.J. Arrington/100 7.50 20.00
HS23 Jason Campbell/50 20.00 40.00
HS24 Ronnie Brown/100 30.00 80.00
HS25 Troy Williamson/50 20.00 40.00

2005 Playoff Honors Patches

PATCHES PRINT RUN 50-95 SER.#'d SETS
*PLATES/35-45: .5X TO 1.2X PATCHES
*PLATES/20-30: .6X TO 1.5X PATCHES
PLATES PRINT RUN 15-45 SER.#'d SETS
PLATES #'d UNDER 20 NOT PRICED
UNPRICED PLATES/PATCHES #'d TO 10
PP1 Anquan Boldin/75 5.00 12.00
PP2 Ben Roethlisberger/50 20.00 50.00
PP3 Brett Favre/75 15.00 40.00
PP4 Carson Palmer/75 6.00 15.00
PP5 Chad Johnson/75 5.00 12.00
PP6 Chad Pennington/50 6.00 15.00
PP7 Daunte Culpepper/99 6.00 15.00
PP8 Deuce McAllister/99 5.00 12.00
PP9 Donovan McNabb/75 7.50 20.00
PP10 Edgerrin James/99 6.00 15.00
PP11 Eli Manning/65 12.50 30.00
PP12 Joey Harrington/75 6.00 15.00
PP13 Julius Jones/75 7.50 20.00
PP14 LaDainian Tomlinson/75 6.00 15.00
PP15 Kevin Jones/50 7.50 20.00
PP16 Larry Fitzgerald/75 5.00 12.00
PP17 LaVar Arrington/75 6.00 15.00
PP18 Marvin Harrison/99 6.00 15.00
PP19 Michael Clayton/75 5.00 12.00
PP20 Peyton Manning/89 10.00 25.00
PP21 Randy Moss/75 6.00 15.00
PP22 Steven Jackson/75 6.00 15.00
PP23 Terrell Owens/75 6.00 15.00
PP24 Trent Green/75 5.00 12.00
PP25 Tom Brady/50 15.00 40.00

2005 Playoff Honors Rookie Hidden Gems Autographs

STATED PRINT RUN 50 SER.#'d SETS
201 Adam Jones JSY 15.00 40.00
202 Alex Smith QB JSY 60.00 120.00
203 Andrew Walter JSY 15.00 40.00
204 Antrel Rolle JSY 20.00 50.00
205 Braylon Edwards JSY 60.00 120.00
206 Cadillac Williams JSY 30.00 80.00
207 Carlos Rogers JSY 20.00 50.00
208 Charlie Frye JSY 20.00 50.00
209 Ciatrick Fason JSY 12.00 30.00
210 Courtney Roby JSY 15.00 40.00
211 Eric Shelton JSY 12.00 30.00
212 Frank Gore JSY 40.00 80.00
213 J.J. Arrington JSY 15.00 40.00
214 Jason Campbell JSY 25.00 60.00
215 Kyle Orton JSY 30.00 60.00
216 Mark Bradley JSY 12.00 30.00
217 Mark Clayton JSY 20.00 50.00
218 Matt Jones JSY 20.00 50.00
219 Maurice Clarett JSY 15.00 40.00
220 Reggie Brown JSY 12.00 30.00
221 Ronnie Brown JSY 75.00 150.00
222 Roddy White JSY 30.00 60.00
223 Ryan Moats JSY 15.00 40.00
224 Roscoe Parrish JSY 12.00 30.00
225 Stefan LeFors JSY 12.00 30.00
226 Terrence Murphy JSY 12.00 30.00
227 Troy Williamson JSY 15.00 40.00
228 Vernand Morency JSY 15.00 40.00
229 Vincent Jackson JSY 25.00 60.00

2005 Playoff Honors Rookie Tandem

STATED ODDS 1:12 HOB, 1:24 RET
*FOIL: .5X TO 1.2X BASIC INSERTS
FOIL PRINT RUN 250 SER.#'d SETS
*HOLOFOIL: .6X TO 1.5X BASIC INSERTS
HOLOFOIL PRINT RUN 100 SER.#'d SETS
RT1 Alex Smith QB 1.25 3.00
Frank Gore
RT2 Ronnie Brown 1.00 2.50
Cadillac Williams
RT3 Braylon Edwards 1.00 2.50
Charlie Frye

RT4 Adam Jones	.60	1.50
Courtney Roby		
RT5 Troy Williamson	.60	1.50
Ciatrick Fason		
RT6 Antrel Rolle	.75	2.00
J.J. Arrington		
RT7 Matt Jones	.60	1.50
Mark Clayton		
RT8 Roddy White	1.00	2.50
Terrence Murphy		
RT9 Charles Rogers	1.00	2.50
Jason Campbell		
RT10 Roscoe Parrish	1.00	2.50
Vincent Jackson		
RT11 Reggie Brown	.50	1.25
Ryan Moats		
RT12 Mark Bradley	.75	2.00
Kyle Orton		
RT13 Eric Shelton	.50	1.25
Stefan LeFors		
RT14 Vernand Morency	.50	1.25
Maurice Clarett		
RT15 Alex Smith QB	1.25	3.00
Andrew Walter		

2005 Playoff Honors Rookie Tandem Jerseys

*FOOTBALLS: .5X TO 1.2X JERSEYS
FOOTBALLS PRINT RUN 125 SER.#'d SETS
*COMBOS: .8X TO 2X JERSEYS
COMBOS PRINT RUN 50 SER.#'d SETS

RT1 Alex Smith QB	10.00	25.00
Frank Gore		
RT2 Ronnie Brown	10.00	25.00
Cadillac Williams		
RT3 Braylon Edwards	6.00	15.00
Charlie Frye		
RT4 Adam Jones	3.00	8.00
Courtney Roby		
RT5 Troy Williamson	3.00	8.00
Ciatrick Fason		
RT6 Antrel Rolle	3.00	8.00
J.J. Arrington		
RT7 Matt Jones	3.00	8.00
Mark Clayton		
RT8 Roddy White	3.00	8.00
Terrence Murphy		
RT9 Charles Rogers	6.00	15.00
Jason Campbell		
RT10 Roscoe Parrish	4.00	10.00
Vincent Jackson		
RT11 Reggie Brown	3.00	8.00
Ryan Moats		
RT12 Mark Bradley	3.00	8.00
Kyle Orton		
RT13 Eric Shelton	3.00	8.00
Stefan LeFors		
RT14 Vernand Morency	3.00	8.00
Maurice Clarett		
RT15 Alex Smith QB	10.00	25.00
Andrew Walter		

2005 Playoff Honors Rookie Quad

STATED PRINT RUN 250 SER.#'d SETS
*FOIL: .5X TO 1.2X BASIC INSERTS
FOIL PRINT RUN 100 SER.#'d SETS
*HOLOFOIL: .8X TO 2X BASIC INSERTS
HOLOFOIL PRINT RUN 25 SER.#'d SETS

RQ1 Alex Smith QB	3.00	8.00
Frank Gore		
Antrell Rolle		
J.J. Arrington		
RQ2 Carlos Rogers	2.50	6.00
Jason Campbell		
Ronnie Brown		
Cadillac Williams		
RQ3 Braylon Edwards	4.00	10.00
Charlie Frye		
Troy Williamson		
Ciatrick Fason		
RQ4 Adam Jones	1.50	4.00
Courtney Roby		
Matt Jones		
Mark Clayton		
RQ5 Andrew Walter	2.50	6.00
Maurice Clarett		
Roscoe Parrish		
Vincent Jackson		
RQ6 Reggie Brown	2.00	5.00
Ryan Moats		
Mark Bradley		
Kyle Orton		
RQ7 Roddy White	2.50	6.00
Terrence Murphy		
Eric Shelton		
Stefan LeFors		

2005 Playoff Honors Rookie Quad Jerseys

JERSEY PRINT RUN 250 SER.#'d SETS
*FOOTBALLS: .6X TO 1.5X JERSEYS
FOOTBALLS PRINT RUN 75 SER.#'d SETS
*COMBOS: .8X TO 2X JERSEYS
COMBOS PRINT RUN 25 SER.#'d SETS

RQ1 Alex Smith QB	15.00	40.00
Frank Gore		
Antell Rolle		
J.J. Arrington		
RQ2 Carlos Rogers	20.00	50.00
Jason Campbell		
Ronnie Brown		
Cadillac Williams		
RQ3 Braylon Edwards	10.00	25.00
Charlie Frye		
Troy Williamson		
Ciatrick Fason		
RQ4 Adam Jones	7.50	20.00
Courtney Roby		
Matt Jones		
Mark Clayton		
RQ5 Andrew Walter	6.00	15.00
Maurice Clarett		
Roscoe Parrish		
Vincent Jackson		
RQ6 Reggie Brown	6.00	15.00
Ryan Moats		
Mark Bradley		
Kyle Orton		
RQ7 Roddy White	6.00	15.00
Terrence Murphy		
Eric Shelton		
Stefan LeFors		

2005 Playoff Honors Touchdown Tandems

STATED ODDS 1:12 RET, 1:24 RET
*FOIL: .5X TO 1.2X BASIC INSERTS
FOIL PRINT RUN 250 SER.#'d SETS
*HOLOFOIL: .6X TO 1.5X BASIC INSERTS
HOLOFOIL PRINT RUN 100 SER.#'d SETS

TT1 Michael Vick	1.00	2.50
Alge Crumpler		
TT2 J.P. Losman	.75	2.00
Lee Evans		
TT3 Jake Delhomme	1.00	2.50
Steve Smith		
TT4 Carson Palmer	1.00	2.50
Chad Johnson		
TT5 Michael Irvin	1.50	4.00
Troy Aikman		
TT6 Jake Plummer	.75	2.00
Ashley Lelie		
TT7 Joey Harrington	.75	2.00
Roy Williams WR		
TT8 Brett Favre	2.50	6.00
Javon Walker		
TT9 David Carr	1.00	2.50
Andre Johnson		
TT10 Peyton Manning	2.00	5.00
Marvin Harrison		
TT11 Byron Leftwich	.75	2.00
Jimmy Smith		
TT12 Trent Green	.75	2.00
Tony Gonzalez		
TT13 Daunte Culpepper	.75	2.00
Nate Burleson		
TT14 Tom Brady	2.00	5.00
Deion Branch		
TT15 Eli Manning	1.50	4.00
Jeremy Shockey		
TT16 Chad Pennington	1.00	2.50
Laveranues Coles		
TT17 Kerry Collins	.75	2.00
Jerry Porter		
TT18 Donovan McNabb	1.00	2.50
Terrell Owens		
TT19 Ben Roethlisberger	1.50	4.00
Hines Ward		
TT20 Drew Brees	1.00	2.50
Antonio Gates		
TT21 Joe Montana	3.00	8.00
Jerry Rice		
TT22 Marc Bulger	.75	2.00
Torry Holt		
TT23 Matt Hasselbeck	.75	2.00
Darrell Jackson		
TT24 Steve McNair	1.00	2.50
Drew Bennett		
TT25 Aaron Brooks	.75	2.00
Joe Horn		

2005 Playoff Honors Touchdown Tandems Materials

MATERIAL PRINT RUN 125 SER.#'d SETS
*PRIME/25: 1X TO 2.5X BASIC DUAL/125
PRIME PRINT RUN 25 SER.#'d SETS

TT1 Michael Vick	6.00	15.00
Alge Crumpler		
TT2 J.P. Losman	5.00	12.00
Lee Evans		
TT3 Jake Delhomme	4.00	10.00
Steve Smith		
TT4 Carson Palmer	5.00	12.00
Chad Johnson		
TT5 Michael Irvin	10.00	25.00
Troy Aikman		
TT6 Jake Plummer	4.00	10.00
Ashley Lelie		
TT7 Joey Harrington	5.00	12.00
Roy Williams WR		
TT8 Brett Favre	12.50	30.00
Javon Walker		
TT9 David Carr	5.00	12.00
Andre Johnson		
TT10 Peyton Manning	7.50	20.00
Marvin Harrison		
TT11 Byron Leftwich	5.00	12.00
Jimmy Smith		
TT12 Trent Green	4.00	10.00
Tony Gonzalez		
TT13 Daunte Culpepper	5.00	12.00
Nate Burleson		
TT14 Tom Brady	12.50	30.00
Deion Branch		
TT15 Eli Manning	10.00	25.00
Jeremy Shockey		
TT16 Chad Pennington	5.00	12.00
Laveranues Coles		
TT17 Kerry Collins	4.00	10.00
Jerry Porter		
TT18 Donovan McNabb	6.00	15.00
Terrell Owens		
TT19 Ben Roethlisberger	12.50	30.00
Hines Ward		
TT20 Drew Brees	5.00	12.00
Antonio Gates		
TT21 Joe Montana	20.00	50.00
Jerry Rice		
TT22 Marc Bulger	5.00	12.00
Torry Holt		
TT23 Matt Hasselbeck	4.00	10.00
Darrell Jackson		
TT24 Steve McNair	5.00	12.00
Drew Bennett		
TT25 Aaron Brooks	4.00	10.00
Joe Horn		

1996 Playoff Illusions

This 120-card 1996 Playoff Illusions set was distributed in five-card packs with a suggested retail price of $4.39. The set features six different designs representing the six NFL divisions. Cards 1-63 appear four cards per pack and cards 64-120 appear one per pack. The fonts display color player photos with tie-dyed color graphics.

COMPLETE SET (120)	20.00	50.00
COMP.SERIES 1 (63)	4.00	10.00
COMP.SERIES 2 (57)	15.00	40.00
1 Troy Aikman	.60	1.50
2 Larry Centers	.10	.30
3 Terance Mathis	.05	.15
4 Michael Irvin	.25	.60
5 Jim Kelly	.25	.60
6 Tim Biakabutuka RC	.25	.60
7 Rashaan Salaam	.10	.30
8 Ki-Jana Carter	.10	.30
9 Anthony Miller	.10	.30
10 Deion Sanders	.30	.75
11 Scott Mitchell	.10	.30
12 Robert Brooks	.25	.60
13 Willie Davis	.05	.15
14 Zack Crockett	.05	.15
15 James O.Stewart	.10	.30
16 Tamarick Vanover	.10	.30
17 Stanley Pritchett	.05	.15
18 Warren Moon	.10	.30
19 Shawn Jefferson	.05	.15
20 Shannon Sharpe	.10	.30
21 Jim Everett	.05	.15
22 Dave Brown	.05	.15
23 Adrian Murrell	.10	.30
24 Rickey Dudley RC	.25	.60
25 Chris T. Jones	.10	.30
26 Andre Hastings	.05	.15
27 Stan Humphries	.10	.30
28 Steve Young	.50	1.25
29 Joey Galloway	.25	.60
30 Jim Harbaugh	.10	.30
31 Eddie Kennison RC	.25	.60
32 Mike Alstott RC	.75	2.00
33 Michael Westbrook	.25	.60
34 Leeland McElroy RC	.10	.30
35 Erik Kramer	.05	.15
36 Mark Chmura	.10	.30
37 Cris Carter	.25	.60
38 Ben Coates	.10	.30
39 Wayne Chrebet	.40	1.00
40 Jerome Bettis	.25	.60
41 Tim Brown	.25	.60
42 Jason Dunn RC	.10	.30
43 William Henderson	.25	.60
44 Rick Mirer	.10	.30
45 J.J. Stokes	.25	.60
46 Rodney Peete	.05	.15
47 Neil O'Donnell	.10	.30
48 Tyrone Wheatley	.10	.30
49 Terry Glenn RC	.75	2.00
50 Junior Seau	.25	.60
51 Jake Reed	.10	.30
52 O.J. McDuffie	.10	.30
53 Steve Bono	.05	.15
54 Steve McNair	.50	1.25
55 Antonio Freeman	.25	.60
56 Johnnie Morton	.10	.30
57 Eric Metcalf	.05	.15
58 Andre Reed	.10	.30
59 Bobby Engram RC	.25	.60
60 Gus Frerotte	.10	.30
61 Jeff Blake	.25	.60
62 Erric Pegram	.05	.15
63 Jeff Hostetler	.05	.15
64 Edgar Bennett	.25	.60
65 Eddie George RC	1.50	4.00
66 Marvin Harrison RC	3.00	8.00
67 LeShon Johnson	.10	.30
68 Jamal Anderson RC	.60	1.50
69 Thurman Thomas	.50	1.25
70 Barry Sanders	2.00	5.00
71 Muhsin Muhammad RC	1.25	3.00
72 Robert Green	.10	.30
73 Garrison Hearst	.25	.60
74 John Elway	2.50	6.00
75 Herman Moore	.25	.60
76 Chris Chandler	.10	.30
77 Marshall Faulk	.60	1.50
78 Mark Brunell	.75	2.00
79 Tony Banks RC	.50	1.25
80 Terrell Davis	1.00	2.50
81 Marcus Allen	.50	1.25
82 Dan Marino	2.50	6.00
83 Robert Smith	.25	.60
84 Curtis Martin	1.00	2.50
85 Amani Toomer RC	1.50	4.00
86 Napoleon Kaufman	.25	.60
87 Ricky Watters	.25	.60
88 Kordell Stewart	.50	1.25
89 Keyshawn Johnson RC	1.25	3.00
90 Emmitt Smith	2.00	5.00
91 Chris Warren	.25	.60
92 Isaac Bruce	.50	1.25
93 Terry Allen	.25	.60
94 Trent Dilfer	.25	.60
95 Vinny Testaverde	.25	.60
96 Bruce Smith	.50	1.25
97 Kerry Collins	.50	1.25
98 Curtis Conway	.50	1.25
99 Karim Abdul-Jabbar RC	.50	1.25
100 Brett Favre	2.50	6.00
101 Carl Pickens	.25	.60
102 Brett Perriman	.10	.30
103 Keith Jackson	.10	.30
104 Drew Bledsoe	.75	2.00
105 Rodney Hampton	.10	.30
106 Ray Zellars	.10	.30
107 Jeff Graham	.10	.30
108 Irving Fryar	.25	.60
109 Lawrence Phillips RC	.50	1.25
110 Jerry Rice	1.25	3.00
111 Mike Tomczak	.10	.30
112 Tony Martin	.25	.60
113 Brian Blades	.25	.60
114 Bill Brooks	.10	.30
115 Rob Moore	.25	.60
116 Quinn Early	.10	.30
117 Darnay Scott	.25	.60
118 Ken Dilger	.10	.30
119 Derek Loville	.10	.30
120 Reggie White	.50	1.25
P1 Robert Brooks Promo	.30	.75

1996 Playoff Illusions Spectralusion Dominion

*SINGLES: 1.5X TO 4X ELITES
STATED ODDS 1:192

1996 Playoff Illusions Spectralusion Elite

COMP.SPECT.ELITE SET (120)	175.00	300.00
COMMON SPECT.ELITE (1-120)	.40	1.00
SEMISTARS	.75	2.00
UNLISTED STARS	1.50	4.00
STATED ODDS 1:5		
1 Troy Aikman	5.00	10.00
10 Deion Sanders	3.00	6.00
28 Steve Young	4.00	8.00
32 Mike Alstott	2.00	5.00
39 Wayne Chrebet	2.50	6.00
54 Steve McNair	4.00	10.00
65 Eddie George	2.50	6.00
66 Marvin Harrison	5.00	12.00
70 Barry Sanders	6.00	15.00
74 John Elway	7.50	20.00
77 Marshall Faulk	2.00	5.00
78 Mark Brunell	2.50	6.00
80 Terrell Davis	4.00	10.00
82 Dan Marino	7.50	20.00
84 Curtis Martin	4.00	10.00
89 Keyshawn Johnson	2.00	5.00
90 Emmitt Smith	7.50	15.00
100 Brett Favre	7.50	20.00
104 Drew Bledsoe	2.50	6.00
110 Jerry Rice	5.00	10.00

1996 Playoff Illusions XXXI

STATED ODDS 1:12

1996 Playoff Illusions XXXI Spectralusion

*SINGLES: 2X TO 5X ELITES
STATED ODDS 1:96

1996 Playoff Illusions Optical Illusions

COMPLETE SET (18)	125.00	300.00
STATED ODDS 1:96		
1 Brett Favre	20.00	50.00
Jerry Rice		
2 Troy Aikman	20.00	50.00
Barry Sanders		
3 Dan Marino	20.00	50.00
Emmitt Smith		
4 Warren Moon	3.00	8.00
Carl Pickens		
5 John Elway	15.00	40.00
Herman Moore		
6 Steve Young	10.00	25.00
Anthony Miller		
7 Jim Harbaugh	6.00	15.00
Terrell Davis		
8 Kordell Stewart	3.00	8.00
Kordell Stewart		
9 Deion Sanders	7.50	20.00
Deion Sanders		
10 Kerry Collins	6.00	15.00
Curtis Martin		
11 Scott Mitchell	3.00	8.00
Robert Brooks		
12 Jeff Blake	3.00	8.00
Tony Martin		
13 Mark Brunell	7.50	20.00
Marshall Faulk		
14 Drew Bledsoe	10.00	25.00
Jerome Bettis		
15 Gus Frerotte	6.00	15.00
Karim Abdul-Jabbar		
16 Steve Bono	3.00	8.00
Ricky Watters		
17 Chris Chandler	3.00	8.00
Terry Allen		
18 Tony Banks	3.00	8.00
Keyshawn Johnson		

1998 Playoff Momentum Hobby

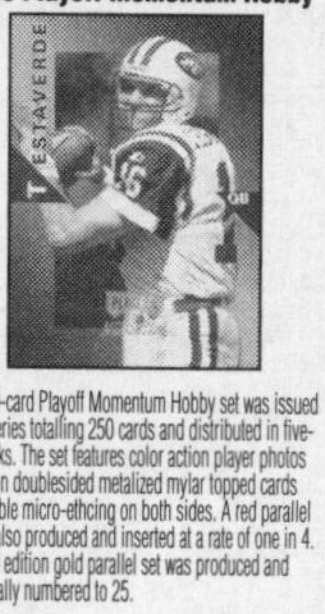

This 250-card Playoff Momentum Hobby set was issued in one series totalling 250 cards and distributed in five-card packs. The set features color action player photos printed on doublesided metalized mylar topped cards with double micro-ethcing on both sides. A red parallel set was also produced and inserted at a rate of one in 4. A limited edition gold parallel set was produced and sequentially numbered to 25.

COMPLETE SET (250)	100.00	250.00
1 Jake Plummer	1.00	2.50
2 Eric Metcalf	.40	1.00
3 Adrian Murrell	.60	1.50
4 Larry Centers	.40	1.00
5 Frank Sanders	.60	1.50
6 Rob Moore	.60	1.50
7 Andre Wadsworth RC	1.50	4.00
8 Chris Chandler	.60	1.50
9 Jamal Anderson	1.00	2.50
10 Tony Martin	.60	1.50
11 Terance Mathis	.60	1.50
12 Tim Dwight RC	2.00	5.00
13 Jammi German RC	1.00	2.50
14 O.J. Santiago	.40	1.00
15 Jim Harbaugh	.60	1.50
16 Eric Zeier	.60	1.50
17 Duane Starks RC	1.00	2.50
18 Rod Woodson	.60	1.50
19 Errict Rhett	.60	1.50
20 Jay Graham	.40	1.00
21 Ray Lewis	1.00	2.50
22 Michael Jackson	.40	1.00
23 Jermaine Lewis	.60	1.50
24 Pat Johnson RC	1.50	4.00
25 Eric Green	.40	1.00
26 Doug Flutie	1.00	2.50
27 Rob Johnson	.60	1.50
28 Antowain Smith	1.00	2.50
29 Thurman Thomas	1.00	2.50
30 Jonathan Linton RC	1.50	4.00
31 Bruce Smith	.60	1.50
32 Eric Moulds	1.00	2.50
33 Kevin Williams	.40	1.00
34 Andre Reed	.60	1.50
35 Steve Beuerlein	.60	1.50
36 Kerry Collins	.60	1.50
37 Anthony Johnson	.40	1.00
38 Fred Lane	.40	1.00
39 William Floyd	.40	1.00
40 Rocket Ismail	.40	1.00
41 Wesley Walls	.60	1.50
42 Muhsin Muhammad	.60	1.50
43 Rae Carruth	.40	1.00
44 Kevin Greene	.60	1.50
45 Greg Lloyd	.40	1.00
46 Moses Moreno RC	1.00	2.50
47 Erik Kramer	.40	1.00
48 Edgar Bennett	.40	1.00
49 Curtis Enis RC	1.00	2.50
50 Curtis Conway	.60	1.50
51 Bobby Engram	.60	1.50
52 Alonzo Mayes RC	1.00	2.50
53 Jeff Blake	.60	1.50
54 Neil O'Donnell	.60	1.50
55 Corey Dillon	1.00	2.50
56 Takeo Spikes RC	2.00	5.00
57 Carl Pickens	.60	1.50
58 Tony McGee	.40	1.00
59 Darnay Scott	.60	1.50
60 Troy Aikman	2.00	5.00
61 Deion Sanders	1.00	2.50
62 Emmitt Smith	3.00	8.00
63 Darren Woodson	.40	1.00
64 Chris Warren	.60	1.50
65 Daryl Johnston	.60	1.50
66 Ernie Mills	.40	1.00
67 Billy Davis	.40	1.00
68 Michael Irvin	1.00	2.50
69 David LaFleur	.40	1.00
70 John Elway	4.00	10.00
71 Brian Griese RC	4.00	10.00
72 Steve Atwater	.40	1.00
73 Terrell Davis	1.00	2.50
74 Rod Smith	.60	1.50
75 Marcus Nash RC	1.00	2.50
76 Shannon Sharpe	.60	1.50
77 Ed McCaffrey	.60	1.50
78 Neil Smith	.60	1.50
79 Charlie Batch RC	2.00	5.00
80 Germane Crowell RC	1.50	4.00
81 Scott Mitchell	.60	1.50
82 Barry Sanders	3.00	8.00
83 Terry Fair RC	1.50	4.00
84 Herman Moore	.60	1.50
85 Johnnie Morton	.60	1.50
86 Brett Favre	4.00	10.00
87 Rick Mirer	.40	1.00
88 Dorsey Levens	1.00	2.50
89 William Henderson	.60	1.50
90 Derrick Mayes	.60	1.50
91 Antonio Freeman	1.00	2.50
92 Robert Brooks	.60	1.50
93 Mark Chmura	.60	1.50
94 Vonnie Holliday RC	1.50	4.00
95 Reggie White	1.00	2.50
96 E.G. Green RC	1.50	4.00
97 Jerome Pathon RC	2.00	5.00
98 Peyton Manning RC	25.00	50.00
99 Marshall Faulk	1.25	3.00
100 Zack Crockett	.40	1.00
101 Ken Dilger	.40	1.00
102 Marvin Harrison	1.00	2.50
103 Mark Brunell	1.00	2.50
104 Jonathan Quinn RC	2.00	5.00
105 Tavian Banks RC	1.50	4.00
106 Fred Taylor RC	3.00	8.00
107 James Stewart	.60	1.50
108 Jimmy Smith	.60	1.50
109 Keenan McCardell	.60	1.50
110 Elvis Grbac	.60	1.50
111 Rich Gannon	1.00	2.50
112 Rashaan Shehee RC	1.50	4.00
113 Donnell Bennett	.40	1.00
114 Kimble Anders	.60	1.50
115 Derrick Thomas	1.00	2.50
116 Kevin Lockett	.40	1.00
117 Derrick Alexander WR	.60	1.50
118 Tony Gonzalez	1.00	2.50
119 Andre Rison	.60	1.50
120 Craig Erickson	.40	1.00
121 Dan Marino	4.00	10.00
122 John Avery RC	1.50	4.00
123 Karim Abdul-Jabbar	1.00	2.50
124 Zach Thomas	1.00	2.50
125 O.J. McDuffie	.60	1.50
126 Troy Drayton	.40	1.00
127 Randall Cunningham	1.00	2.50
128 Brad Johnson	1.00	2.50
129 Robert Smith	1.00	2.50
130 Cris Carter	1.00	2.50
131 Randy Moss RC	12.00	30.00
132 Jake Reed	.60	1.50
133 John Randle	.60	1.50
134 Drew Bledsoe	1.50	4.00
135 Tony Simmons RC	1.50	4.00
136 Sedrick Shaw	.40	1.00
137 Chris Floyd RC	1.00	2.50
138 Robert Edwards RC	1.50	4.00
139 Rod Rutledge RC	1.00	2.50
140 Shawn Jefferson	.40	1.00
141 Ben Coates	.60	1.50
142 Terry Glenn	1.00	2.50
143 Heath Shuler	.40	1.00
144 Danny Wuerffel	.60	1.50
145 Troy Davis	.40	1.00
146 Qadry Ismail	.60	1.50
147 Ray Zellars	.40	1.00
148 Lamar Smith	.60	1.50
149 Cameron Cleeland RC	1.00	2.50
150 Sean Dawkins	.40	1.00
151 Andre Hastings	.40	1.00
152 Danny Kanell	.60	1.50
153 Tiki Barber	1.00	2.50
154 Tyrone Wheatley	.60	1.50
155 Charles Way	.40	1.00
156 Gary Brown	.40	1.00
157 Shaun Williams RC	1.50	4.00
158 Chris Calloway	.40	1.00
159 Amani Toomer	.60	1.50
160 Brian Alford RC	1.00	2.50
161 Joe Jurevicius RC	2.00	5.00
162 Ike Hilliard	.60	1.50
163 Michael Strahan	.60	1.50
164 Glenn Foley	.60	1.50
165 Vinny Testaverde	.60	1.50
166 Keyshawn Johnson	1.00	2.50
167 Curtis Martin	1.00	2.50
168 Leon Johnson	.40	1.00
169 Keith Byars	.40	1.00
170 Wayne Chrebet	1.00	2.50
171 Kyle Brady	.40	1.00
172 Dedric Ward	.40	1.00
173 Jeff George	.60	1.50
174 Charles Woodson RC	4.00	10.00
175 Napoleon Kaufman	1.00	2.50
176 Jon Ritchie RC	1.50	4.00
177 Tim Brown	1.00	2.50
178 James Jett	.60	1.50
179 Rickey Dudley	.40	1.00
180 Bobby Hoying	.60	1.50
181 Duce Staley	1.25	3.00
182 Charlie Garner	.60	1.50
183 Irving Fryar	.60	1.50
184 Jeff Graham	.40	1.00
185 Jason Dunn	.40	1.00
186 Kordell Stewart	1.00	2.50
187 Jerome Bettis	1.00	2.50
188 Andre Coleman	.40	1.00
189 C.Fuamatu-Ma'afala RC	1.50	4.00
190 Charles Johnson	.40	1.00
191 Hines Ward RC	10.00	20.00
192 Mark Bruener	.40	1.00
193 Courtney Hawkins	.40	1.00
194 Will Blackwell	.40	1.00
195 Levon Kirkland	.40	1.00
196 Mikhael Ricks RC	1.50	4.00
197 Ryan Leaf RC	2.00	5.00
198 Natrone Means	.60	1.50
199 Junior Seau	1.00	2.50
200 Bryan Still	.40	1.00
201 Freddie Jones	.40	1.00
202 Steve Young	1.25	3.00
203 Jim Druckenmiller	.40	1.00
204 Garrison Hearst	1.00	2.50
205 R.W. McQuarters RC	1.50	4.00
206 Merton Hanks	.40	1.00
207 Marc Edwards	.40	1.00
208 Jerry Rice	2.00	5.00
209 Terrell Owens	1.00	2.50
210 J.J. Stokes	.60	1.50
211 Tony Banks	.60	1.50
212 Robert Holcombe RC	1.50	4.00
213 Greg Hill	.40	1.00
214 Amp Lee	.40	1.00
215 Jerald Moore	.40	1.00
216 Isaac Bruce	1.00	2.50
217 Az-Zahir Hakim RC	2.00	5.00
218 Eddie Kennison	.60	1.50
219 Grant Wistrom RC	1.50	4.00
220 Warren Moon	1.00	2.50
221 Ahman Green RC	5.00	12.00
222 Steve Broussard	.40	1.00
223 Ricky Watters	.60	1.50
224 James McKnight	1.00	2.50
225 Joey Galloway	.60	1.50
226 Mike Pritchard	.40	1.00
227 Trent Dilfer	1.00	2.50
228 Warrick Dunn	1.00	2.50
229 Mike Alstott	1.00	2.50
230 John Lynch	.60	1.50
231 Jacquez Green RC	1.50	4.00
232 Reidel Anthony	.60	1.50
233 Bert Emanuel	.60	1.50
234 Warren Sapp	.60	1.50
235 Steve McNair	1.00	2.50
236 Eddie George	1.00	2.50
237 Chris Sanders	.40	1.00
238 Yancey Thigpen	.40	1.00
239 Willie Davis	.40	1.00
240 Kevin Dyson RC	2.00	5.00
241 Frank Wycheck	.40	1.00
242 Trent Green	1.00	2.50
243 Gus Frerotte	.40	1.00
244 Skip Hicks RC	1.50	4.00
245 Terry Allen	1.00	2.50
246 Stephen Davis	.40	1.00
247 Stephen Alexander RC	1.50	4.00
248 Michael Westbrook	.60	1.50
249 Dana Stubblefield SP	1.00	2.50
250 Dan Wilkinson SP	1.00	2.50

1998 Playoff Momentum Hobby Gold

*GOL VETS: 12X TO 30X BASIC CARDS
*GOLD ROOKIES: 2.5X TO 6X
STATED PRINT RUN 25 SERIAL #'d SETS

98 Peyton Manning	200.00	350.00

1998 Playoff Momentum Hobby Red

COMPLETE SET (250)	400.00	800.00

*RED VETS: 1.5X TO 3X BASIC CARDS
*RED ROOKIES: .6X TO 1.2X BASIC CARDS
STATED ODDS 1:4 HOB/RET

1998 Playoff Momentum Retail

The 1998 Playoff Momentum Retail set was issued in one series totalling 250 card and was distributed in 4 card packs with a suggested retail price of $2.99. The set features color action player photos printed on embossed football leather-like card stock with black foil stamping. The set includes a shortprinted Rookie subset. A red foil parallel version of the set was also produced.

COMPLETE SET (250)	75.00	150.00
ROOKIE SUBSET ODDS 1:3 RETAIL		
1 Karim Abdul-Jabbar	.30	.75
2 Troy Aikman	.60	1.50
3 Derrick Alexander	.20	.50
4 Stephen Alexander	.50	1.25
5 Brian Alford RC	.50	1.25
6 Terry Allen	.30	.75
7 Mike Alstott	.30	.75
8 Kimble Anders	.20	.50
9 Jamal Anderson	.30	.75
10 Reidel Anthony	.20	.50
11 Steve Atwater	.10	.30
12 John Avery RC	.75	2.00
13 Tavian Banks RC	.75	2.00
14 Tony Banks	.20	.50
15 Tiki Barber	.30	.75
16 Charlie Batch RC	1.00	2.50
17 Donnell Bennett	.10	.30
18 Edgar Bennett	.10	.30
19 Jerome Bettis	.30	.75
20 Steve Beuerlein	.20	.50
21 Will Blackwell	.10	.30
22 Jeff Blake	.20	.50
23 Drew Bledsoe	.50	1.25
24 Kyle Brady	.10	.30
25 Robert Brooks	.20	.50
26 Steve Broussard	.10	.30
27 Gary Brown	.10	.30
28 Tim Brown	.30	.75
29 Isaac Bruce	.30	.75
30 Mark Bruener	.10	.30
31 Mark Brunell	.30	.75
32 Keith Byars	.10	.30
33 Chris Calloway	.10	.30
34 Rae Carruth	.10	.30
35 Cris Carter	.30	.75
36 Larry Centers	.10	.30
37 Chris Chandler	.20	.50
38 Mark Chmura	.20	.50
39 Wayne Chrebet	.30	.75
40 Cameron Cleeland RC	.50	1.25
41 Ben Coates	.20	.50
42 Kerry Collins	.20	.50
43 Andre Coleman	.10	.30
44 Curtis Conway	.20	.50
45 Zack Crockett	.10	.30
46 Germane Crowell RC	.75	2.00
47 Randall Cunningham	.30	.75
48 Billy Davis	.10	.30
49 Stephen Davis	.10	.30
50 Terrell Davis	.30	.75
51 Troy Davis	.10	.30
52 Willie Davis	.10	.30
53 Sean Dawkins	.10	.30
54 Trent Dilfer	.30	.75
55 Ken Dilger	.10	.30
56 Corey Dillon	.30	.75
57 Troy Drayton	.10	.30
58 Jim Druckenmiller	.10	.30
59 Rickey Dudley	.10	.30
60 Jason Dunn	.10	.30
61 Warrick Dunn	.30	.75
62 Tim Dwight RC	1.00	2.50
63 Kevin Dyson RC	1.00	2.50
64 Marc Edwards	.10	.30
65 Robert Edwards RC	.75	2.00
66 John Elway	1.25	3.00
67 Bert Emanuel	.20	.50
68 Bobby Engram	.20	.50
69 Curtis Enis RC	.50	1.25
70 Craig Erickson	.10	.30
71 Terry Fair RC	.75	2.00
72 Marshall Faulk	.40	1.00
73 Brett Favre	1.25	3.00
74 Chris Floyd	.30	.75
75 William Floyd	.10	.30
76 Doug Flutie	.30	.75
77 Glenn Foley	.20	.50
78 Antonio Freeman	.30	.75
79 Gus Frerotte	.10	.30
80 Irving Fryar	.20	.50
81 C.Fuamatu-Ma'afala RC	.75	2.00
82 Joey Galloway	.20	.50
83 Rich Gannon	.30	.75
84 Charlie Garner	.20	.50
85 Eddie George	.30	.75
86 Jeff George	.20	.50
87 Jammi German RC	.50	1.25
88 Terry Glenn	.30	.75
89 Tony Gonzalez	.30	.75
90 Jay Graham	.10	.30
91 Jeff Graham	.10	.30
92 Elvis Grbac	.20	.50
93 Ahman Green RC	2.50	6.00
94 E.G. Green RC	.75	2.00
95 Eric Green	.10	.30
96 Jacquez Green RC	.75	2.00
97 Trent Green	.30	.75
98 Kevin Greene	.20	.50
99 Brian Griese RC	2.00	5.00
100 Az-Zahir Hakim RC	1.00	2.50
101 Merton Hanks	.10	.30
102 Jim Harbaugh	.20	.50
103 Marvin Harrison	.30	.75
104 Andre Hastings	.10	.30
105 Courtney Hawkins	.10	.30
106 Garrison Hearst	.30	.75
107 William Henderson	.20	.50
108 Skip Hicks RC	.75	2.00
109 Greg Hill	.10	.30
110 Ike Hilliard	.20	.50
111 Robert Holcombe RC	.75	2.00
112 Vonnie Holliday RC	.75	2.00
113 Bobby Hoying	.20	.50
114 Michael Irvin	.30	.75
115 Qadry Ismail	.20	.50
116 Rocket Ismail	.10	.30
117 Michael Jackson	.10	.30
118 Shawn Jefferson	.10	.30
119 James Jett	.20	.50
120 Anthony Johnson	.10	.30
121 Brad Johnson	.30	.75
122 Charles Johnson	.10	.30
123 Keyshawn Johnson	.30	.75
124 Leon Johnson	.10	.30
125 Pat Johnson RC	.75	2.00
126 Rob Johnson	.20	.50
127 Daryl Johnston	.20	.50
128 Freddie Jones	.10	.30
129 Joe Jurevicius RC	1.00	2.50
130 Danny Kanell	.20	.50
131 Napoleon Kaufman	.30	.75
132 Eddie Kennison	.20	.50
133 Levon Kirkland	.10	.30
134 Erik Kramer	.10	.30
135 David LaFleur	.10	.30
136 Fred Lane	.10	.30
137 Ryan Leaf RC	1.00	2.50
138 Amp Lee	.10	.30
139 Dorsey Levens	.30	.75
140 Jermaine Lewis	.20	.50
141 Ray Lewis	.30	.75
142 Jonathan Linton RC	.75	2.00
143 Greg Lloyd	.10	.30
144 Kevin Lockett	.10	.30
145 John Lynch	.20	.50
146 Peyton Manning RC	8.00	20.00
147 Dan Marino	1.25	3.00
148 Curtis Martin	.30	.75
149 Tony Martin	.20	.50
150 Terance Mathis	.20	.50
151 Alonzo Mayes RC	.50	1.25
152 Derrick Mayes	.20	.50
153 Ed McCaffrey	.20	.50
154 Keenan McCardell	.20	.50
155 O.J. McDuffie	.20	.50
156 Tony McGee	.10	.30
157 James McKnight	.30	.75
158 Steve McNair	.30	.75
159 R.W. McQuarters RC	.75	2.00
160 Natrone Means	.20	.50
161 Eric Metcalf	.10	.30
162 Ernie Mills	.10	.30
163 Rick Mirer	.10	.30
164 Scott Mitchell	.20	.50
165 Warren Moon	.30	.75
166 Herman Moore	.20	.50
167 Jerald Moore	.10	.30
168 Rob Moore	.20	.50
169 Moses Moreno RC	.50	1.25
170 Johnnie Morton	.20	.50
171 Randy Moss RC	6.00	15.00
172 Eric Moulds	.30	.75
173 Muhsin Muhammad	.20	.50
174 Adrian Murrell	.20	.50
175 Marcus Nash RC	.50	1.25
176 Neil O'Donnell	.20	.50
177 Terrell Owens	.30	.75
178 Jerome Pathon RC	1.00	2.50
179 Carl Pickens	.20	.50
180 Jake Plummer	.30	.75
181 Mike Pritchard	.10	.30
182 Jonathan Quinn RC	1.00	2.50
183 John Randle	.20	.50
184 Andre Reed	.20	.50
185 Jake Reed	.20	.50
186 Errict Rhett	.20	.50
187 Jerry Rice	.60	1.50
188 Mikhael Ricks RC	.75	2.00
189 Andre Rison	.20	.50
190 Jon Ritchie RC	.75	2.00
191 Rod Rutledge	.30	.75
192 Barry Sanders	1.00	2.50
193 Chris Sanders	.10	.30
194 Deion Sanders	.30	.75
195 Frank Sanders	.20	.50
196 O.J. Santiago	.10	.30
197 Warren Sapp	.20	.50
198 Darnay Scott	.20	.50
199 Junior Seau	.30	.75
200 Shannon Sharpe	.20	.50
201 Sedrick Shaw	.10	.30
202 Rashaan Shehee RC	.75	2.00
203 Heath Shuler	.10	.30
204 Tony Simmons RC	.75	2.00
205 Antowain Smith	.30	.75
206 Bruce Smith	.20	.50
207 Emmitt Smith	1.00	2.50
208 Jimmy Smith	.20	.50
209 Lamar Smith	.20	.50

210 Neil Smith .20 .50
211 Robert Smith .30 .75
212 Rod Smith .20 .50
213 Takeo Spikes RC 1.00 2.50
214 Duce Staley .40 1.00
215 Duane Starks RC .50 1.25
216 James Stewart .20 .50
217 Kordell Stewart .30 .75
218 Bryan Still .10 .30
219 J.J. Stokes .20 .50
220 Michael Strahan .20 .50
221 Dana Stubblefield .10 .30
222 Fred Taylor RC 1.50 4.00
223 Vinny Testaverde .20 .50
224 Yancey Thigpen .10 .30
225 Derrick Thomas .30 .75
226 Thurman Thomas .30 .75
227 Zach Thomas .30 .75
228 Amani Toomer .20 .50
229 Andre Wadsworth RC .75 2.00
230 Wesley Walls .20 .50
231 Dedric Ward .10 .30
232 Hines Ward RC 4.00 10.00
233 Chris Warren .20 .50
234 Ricky Watters .20 .50
235 Charles Way .10 .30
236 Michael Westbrook .20 .50
237 Tyrone Wheatley .20 .50
238 Reggie White .30 .75
239 Dan Wilkinson .10 .30
240 Kevin Williams .10 .30
241 Shaun Williams RC .75 2.00
242 Grant Wistrom RC .75 2.00
243 Charles Woodson RC 2.00 5.00
244 Darren Woodson .10 .30
245 Rod Woodson .20 .50
246 Danny Wuerffel .20 .50
247 Frank Wycheck .10 .30
248 Steve Young .40 1.00
249 Eric Zeier .20 .50
250 Ray Zellars .10 .30

1998 Playoff Momentum Retail Red

COMPLETE SET (250) 125.00 250.00
*RED VETS: 1.5X TO 3X BASIC CARDS
*RED ROOKIES: .6X TO 1.2X BASIC CARDS
STATED ODDS 1:4 RETAIL
146 Peyton Manning 12.00 30.00

1998 Playoff Momentum 7-11

This 100-card set is a special version of the Playoff Momentum Retail set made specifically for 7-11 stores. This cards are essentially a back-to-back parallel set of the basic issue Momentum Retail with no additional distinguishing features. The unnumbered cards have been arranged below alphabetically according to which player on each card is alphabetized first.

COMPLETE SET (100) 24.00 60.00
1 Karim Abdul-Jabbar .80 2.00
Mark Brunell
2 Troy Aikman 1.20 3.00
Irving Fryar
3 Derrick Alexander .25 .60
Edgar Bennett
4 Terry Allen .25 .60
James Jett
5 Mike Alstott 1.60 4.00
Brett Favre
6 Kimble Anders .10 .30
Greg Hill
7 Jamal Anderson .50 1.25
Gary Brown
8 Reidel Anthony .10 .30
Merton Hanks
9 Steve Atwater .50 1.25
Jeff Blake
10 Tony Banks .50 1.25
Ben Coates
11 Tiki Barber .50 1.25
Kerry Collins
12 Donnell Bennett .50 1.25
Corey Dillon
13 Jerome Bettis .50 1.25
Chris Calloway
14 Steve Beuerlein .50 1.25
Rich Gannon
15 Will Blackwell .50 1.25
Keyshawn Johnson
16 Drew Bledsoe .60 1.50
Wayne Chrebet
17 Kyle Brady .10 .30
Eric Green
18 Robert Brooks .50 1.25
Randall Cunningham
19 Steve Broussard .10 .30
Jason Dunn
20 Tim Brown .50 1.25
Chris Chandler
21 Isaac Bruce .50 1.25
Terry Glenn
22 Mark Bruener .25 .60
Trent Dilfer
23 Keith Byars .50 1.25
Joey Galloway
24 Rae Carruth .10 .30
Anthony Johnson
25 Cris Carter .50 1.25
William Floyd
26 Larry Centers .10 .30
Ike Hilliard
27 Mark Chmura .25 .60
Jim Harbaugh
28 Andre Coleman .10 .30
Michael Jackson
29 Curtis Conway .25 .60
Craig Erickson
30 Zack Crockett .25 .60
Garrison Hearst
31 Billy Davis .50 1.25
Trent Green
32 Stephen Davis .50 1.25
Bert Emanuel
33 Terrell Davis .80 2.00
Andre Hastings
34 Troy Davis .10 .30
Charles Johnson
35 Willie Davis .10 .30
Glenn Foley
36 Sean Dawkins .25 .60
Michael Irvin
37 Ken Dilger .25 .60
Gus Frerotte
38 Troy Drayton .10 .30
Shawn Jefferson
39 Jim Druckenmiller .50 1.25
Marshall Faulk
40 Rickey Dudley .25 .60
William Henderson
41 Warrick Dunn .50 1.25
Keith Green
42 Marc Edwards .50 1.25
Antonio Freeman
43 John Elway 1.60 4.00
Qadry Ismail
44 Bobby Engram .25 .60
Jeff Graham
45 Doug Flutie .60 1.50
Eddie George
46 Charlie Garner .50 1.25
Brad Johnson
47 Jeff George .25 .60
Bobby Hoying
48 Tony Gonzalez .50 1.25
Marvin Harrison
49 Jay Graham .25 .60
Rocket Ismail
50 Elvis Grbac .25 .60
Courtney Hawkins
51 Leon Johnson .25 .60
Ed McCaffrey
52 Rob Johnson .50 1.25
Dorsey Levens
53 Daryl Johnston .25 .60
Adrian Murrell
54 Freddie Jones .10 .30
Ray Zellars
55 Danny Kanell .50 1.25
Robert Smith
56 Napoleon Kaufman .50 1.25
Deion Sanders
57 Eddie Kennison .25 .60
Herman Moore
58 Levon Kirkland .10 .30
Frank Wycheck
59 Erik Kramer .10 .30
Greg Lloyd
60 David LaFleur .25 .60
Carl Pickens
61 Fred Lane .10 .30
Derrick Mayes
62 Amp Lee .25 .60
Keenan McCardell
63 Jermaine Lewis .25 .60
Derrick Thomas
64 Ray Lewis .50 1.25
Ernie Mills
65 Kevin Lockett .25 .60
Ricky Watters
66 John Lynch .50 1.25
Terrell Owens
67 Dan Marino 1.60 4.00
Kevin Williams
68 Curtis Martin .50 1.25
Duce Staley
69 Tony Martin .25 .60
O.J.Santiago
70 Terance Mathis .25 .60
Rob Moore
71 O.J. McDuffie .25 .60
Muhsin Muhammad
72 Tony McGee .25 .60
Tyrone Wheatley
73 James McKnight .50 1.25
Neil Smith
74 Steve McNair .50 1.25
Chris Sanders
75 Natrone Means .50 1.25
Warren Moon
76 Eric Metcalf .10 .30
Danny Wuerffel
77 Rick Mirer .25 .60
Heath Shuler
78 Scott Mitchell .25 .60
Vinny Testaverde
79 Jerald Moore .10 .30
Dedric Ward
80 Johnny Morton .25 .60
Errict Rhett
81 Eric Moulds .25 .60
Bryan Still
82 Neil O'Donnell .25 .60
Thurman Thomas
83 Jake Plummer 1.20 3.00
Emmitt Smith
84 Mike Pritchard .80 2.00
Jerry Rice
85 John Randle .25 .60
Darren Woodson
86 Andre Reed .50 1.25
James Stewart
87 Jake Reed .25 .60
Warren Sapp
88 Andre Rison .25 .60
Sedrick Shaw
89 Barry Sanders 1.60 4.00
Eric Zeier
90 Frank Sanders .25 .60
Wesley Walls
91 Junior Seau .25 .60
Charles Way
92 Darnay Scott .25 .60
Bruce Smith
93 Shannon Sharpe .25 .60
Jimmy Smith
94 Antowain Smith .50 1.25
Kordell Stewart
95 Lamar Smith .25 .60
Michael Strahan
96 Rod Smith WR .25 .60
Amani Toomer
97 J.J.Stokes .25 .60
Michael Westbrook
98 Yancey Thigpen .25 .60
Rod Woodson
99 Zach Thomas .50 1.25
Reggie White
100 Chris Warren .60 1.50
Steve Young

1998 Playoff Momentum Class Reunion Quads

COMPLETE SET (16) 125.00 300.00
STATED ODDS 1:81 HOBBY
*JUMBOS: .1X TO .25X
JUMBOS: ONE PER HOBBY BOX
1 Dan Marino 20.00 50.00
John Elway
Bruce Matthews
Darrell Green
2 Steve Young 7.50 20.00
Irving Fryar
Reggie White
Jeff Hostetler
3 Jerry Rice 10.00 25.00
Bruce Smith
Andre Reed
Doug Flutie
4 Keith Byars 4.00 10.00
Leslie O'Neal
Seth Joyner
Ray Brown
5 Cris Carter 5.00 12.00
Vinny Testaverde
Jim Harbaugh
Rod Woodson
6 Tim Brown 5.00 12.00
Chris Chandler
Michael Irvin
Neil Smith
7 Troy Aikman 20.00 50.00
Barry Sanders
Deion Sanders
Andre Rison
8 Emmitt Smith 12.50 30.00
Jeff George
Neil O'Donnell
Shannon Sharpe
9 Brett Favre 15.00 40.00
Herman Moore
Yancey Thigpen
Ricky Watters
10 Mark Chmura 5.00 12.00
Brad Johnson
Carl Pickens
Robert Brooks
11 Drew Bledsoe 12.50 30.00
Jerome Bettis
Mark Brunell
Garrison Hearst
12 Trent Dilfer 10.00 25.00
Dorsey Levens
Marshall Faulk
Isaac Bruce
13 Terrell Davis 7.50 20.00
Kordell Stewart
Napoleon Kaufman
Curtis Martin
14 Eddie George 6.00 15.00
Keyshawn Johnson
Karim Abdul-Jabbar
Terry Glenn
15 Warrick Dunn 6.00 15.00
Corey Dillon
Jake Plummer
Antowain Smith
16 Peyton Manning 20.00 40.00
Ryan Leaf
Curtis Enis
Randy Moss

1998 Playoff Momentum Class Reunion Tandems

COMPLETE SET (16) 250.00 500.00
STATED ODDS 1:121 RETAIL
1 Dan Marino 30.00 80.00
John Elway
2 Steve Young 12.50 30.00
Reggie White
3 Jerry Rice 15.00 40.00
Bruce Smith
4 Keith Byars 6.00 15.00
Leslie O'Neil
5 Cris Carter 10.00 25.00
Vinny Testaverde
6 Tim Brown 10.00 25.00
Michael Irvin
7 Troy Aikman 30.00 80.00
Barry Sanders
8 Emmitt Smith 20.00 50.00
Jeff George
9 Brett Favre 25.00 60.00
Herman Moore
10 Brad Johnson 10.00 25.00
Carl Pickens
11 Drew Bledsoe 20.00 50.00
Mark Brunell
12 Dorsey Levens 12.50 30.00
Isaac Bruce
13 Terrell Davis 10.00 25.00
Kordell Stewart
14 Eddie George 10.00 25.00
Keyshawn Johnson
15 Warrick Dunn 10.00 25.00
Jake Plummer
16 Peyton Manning 20.00 40.00
Ryan Leaf

1998 Playoff Momentum Endzone X-press

COMPLETE DIE CUT SET (29) 60.00 120.00
DIE CUT STATED ODDS 1:9 HOBBY
*NON-DIE CUTS: .4X TO .8X DIE CUTS
NON-DIE CUT STATED ODDS 1:13 RETAIL
1 Jake Plummer 1.50 4.00
2 Herman Moore 1.00 2.50
3 Terrell Davis 1.50 4.00
4 Antowain Smith 1.50 4.00
5 Curtis Enis .30 .75
6 Corey Dillon 1.50 4.00
7 Troy Aikman 3.00 8.00
8 John Elway 6.00 15.00
9 Barry Sanders 5.00 12.00
10 Brett Favre 6.00 15.00
11 Peyton Manning 12.00 30.00
12 Mark Brunell 1.50 4.00
13 Andre Rison 1.00 2.50
14 Dan Marino 6.00 15.00
15 Randy Moss 4.00 10.00
16 Drew Bledsoe 2.50 6.00
17 Jerome Bettis 1.50 4.00
18 Tim Brown 1.50 4.00
19 Antonio Freeman 1.50 4.00
20 Napoleon Kaufman 1.50 4.00
21 Emmitt Smith 5.00 12.00
22 Kordell Stewart 1.50 4.00
23 Curtis Martin 1.50 4.00
24 Ryan Leaf .50 1.50
25 Jerry Rice 3.00 8.00
26 Joey Galloway 1.00 2.50
27 Warrick Dunn 1.50 4.00
28 Eddie George 1.50 4.00
29 Steve McNair 1.50 4.00

1998 Playoff Momentum Headliners

COMPLETE SET (23) 100.00 200.00
BLUE STATED ODDS 1:49 HOBBY
*RED CARDS: .4X TO .8X BLUES
RED STATED ODDS 1:73 RETAIL
1 Brett Favre 10.00 25.00
2 Jerry Rice 5.00 12.00
3 Barry Sanders 8.00 20.00
4 Troy Aikman 5.00 12.00
5 Warrick Dunn 2.50 6.00
6 Dan Marino 10.00 25.00
7 John Elway 10.00 25.00
8 Drew Bledsoe 4.00 10.00
9 Kordell Stewart 2.50 6.00
10 Mark Brunell 2.50 6.00
11 Eddie George 2.50 6.00
12 Terrell Davis 2.50 6.00
13 Emmitt Smith 8.00 20.00
14 Steve McNair 2.50 6.00
15 Mike Alstott 2.50 6.00
16 Peyton Manning 10.00 20.00
17 Antonio Freeman 2.50 6.00
18 Curtis Martin 2.50 6.00
19 Terry Glenn 2.50 6.00
20 Brad Johnson 2.50 6.00
21 Karim Abdul-Jabbar 2.50 6.00
22 Ryan Leaf .75 2.00
23 Jerome Bettis 2.50 6.00

1998 Playoff Momentum Headliners Gold

2 Jerry Rice/166 20.00 50.00
5 Warrick Dunn/49 15.00 40.00
6 Dan Marino/24 150.00 300.00
7 John Elway/138 40.00 100.00
8 Drew Bledsoe/44 30.00 80.00
11 Eddie George/32 20.00 50.00
13 Emmitt Smith/112 25.00 60.00
15 Mike Alstott/65 15.00 40.00
16 Peyton Manning/33 150.00 250.00
19 Terry Glenn/90 10.00 25.00
22 Ryan Leaf/33 12.00 30.00

1998 Playoff Momentum Honors

COMPLETE SET (3) 50.00 120.00
STATED ODDS 1:3841 HOBBY
PH16 Brett Favre 30.00 80.00
PH17 Kordell Stewart 10.00 25.00
PH18 Troy Aikman 25.00 50.00

1998 Playoff Momentum NFL Rivals

COMP.HOBBY SET (22) 100.00 200.00
STATED ODDS 1:49 HOBBY
*RETAIL SILVER: .3X TO .8X HOBBY
SILVER STATED ODDS 1:73 RETAIL
1 Mark Brunell 7.50 20.00
John Elway
2 Jerome Bettis 3.00 8.00
Eddie George
3 Barry Sanders 10.00 25.00
Emmitt Smith
4 Dan Marino 7.50 20.00
Drew Bledsoe
5 Troy Aikman 3.00 8.00
Jake Plummer
6 Terrell Davis 3.00 8.00
Napoleon Kaufman
7 Cris Carter 2.00 5.00
Herman Moore
8 Warrick Dunn 3.00 8.00
Dorsey Levens
9 Kordell Stewart 3.00 8.00
Steve McNair
10 Curtis Martin 3.00 8.00
Antowain Smith
11 Jerry Rice 5.00 12.00
Michael Irvin
12 Steve Young 10.00 25.00
Brett Favre
13 Corey Dillon 3.00 8.00
Fred Taylor
14 Tim Brown 3.00 8.00
Andre Rison
15 Mike Alstott 2.00 5.00
Robert Smith
16 Brad Johnson 2.00 5.00
Scott Mitchell
17 Robert Edwards 3.00 8.00
John Avery
18 Deion Sanders 3.00 8.00
Rob Moore
19 Antonio Freeman 10.00 25.00
Randy Moss
20 Peyton Manning 15.00 30.00
Ryan Leaf
21 Curtis Enis 2.00 5.00
Jacquez Green
22 Keyshawn Johnson 2.00 5.00
Terry Glenn

1998 Playoff Momentum Rookie Double Feature Hobby

COMPLETE SET (20) 60.00 120.00
STATED ODDS 1:17 HOBBY
1 Peyton Manning 20.00 40.00
Brian Griese
2 Ryan Leaf 2.00 5.00
Charlie Batch
3 Charles Woodson 2.50 6.00
Terry Fair
4 Curtis Enis 1.00 2.50
Tavian Banks
5 Fred Taylor 2.50 6.00
John Avery
6 Kevin Dyson 2.00 5.00
E.G. Green
7 Robert Edwards 1.50 4.00
Chris Fuamatu-Ma'afala
8 Randy Moss 10.00 25.00
Tim Dwight
9 Marcus Nash 2.00 5.00
Joe Jurevicius
10 Jerome Pathon 2.00 5.00
Az Hakim
11 Jacquez Green 1.50 4.00
Tony Simmons
12 Robert Holcombe 1.50 4.00
Jon Ritchie
13 Cameron Cleeland 1.00 2.50
Alonzo Mayes
14 Patrick Johnson 1.50 4.00
Mikhael Ricks
15 Germaine Crowell 6.00 12.00
Hines Ward
16 Skip Hicks 1.50 4.00
Chris Floyd
17 Brian Alford 1.00 2.50
Jammi German
18 Ahman Green 5.00 12.00
Rashan Shehee
19 Jonathan Quinn 1.50 4.00
Moses Moreno
20 R.W. McQuarters 1.00 2.50
Duane Starks

1998 Playoff Momentum Rookie Double Feature Retail

COMPLETE SET (40) 75.00 150.00
STATED ODDS 1:25 RETAIL
R1 Peyton Manning 12.50 25.00
R2 Ryan Leaf .60 1.50
R3 Charles Woodson 2.00 5.00
R4 Curtis Enis .60 1.50
R5 Fred Taylor 1.50 4.00
R6 Kevin Dyson 1.00 2.50
R7 Robert Edwards .60 1.50
R8 Randy Moss 6.00 15.00
R9 Marcus Nash .30 .75
R10 Jerome Pathon .60 1.50
R11 Jacquez Green .60 1.50
R12 Robert Holcombe .30 .75
R13 Cameron Cleeland .30 .75
R14 Pat Johnson .30 .75
R15 Germane Crowell .60 1.50
R16 Skip Hicks .30 .75
R17 Brian Alford .30 .75
R18 Ahman Green 2.50 6.00
R19 Jonathan Quinn .30 .75
R20 R.W. McQuarters .30 .75
R21 Brian Griese 2.00 5.00
R22 Charlie Batch 1.00 2.50
R23 Terry Fair .30 .75
R24 Tavian Banks .30 .75
R25 John Avery .30 .75
R26 E.G. Green .30 .75
R27 Chris Fuamatu-Ma'afala .30 .75
R28 Tim Dwight 1.00 2.50
R29 Joe Jurevicius 1.00 2.50
R30 Az-Zahir Hakim .60 1.50
R31 Tony Simmons .30 .75
R32 Jon Ritchie .30 .75
R33 Alonzo Mayes .30 .75
R34 Mikhael Ricks .30 .75
R35 Hines Ward 4.00 10.00
R36 Chris Floyd .30 .75
R37 Jammi German .30 .75
R38 Rashaan Shehee .30 .75
R39 Moses Moreno .30 .75
R40 Duane Starks .30 .75

1998 Playoff Momentum Team Threads Home

COMP.HOBBY SET (20) 100.00 250.00
HOME STATED ODDS 1:33 HOBBY
*AWAY CARDS: .6X TO 1.5X
AWAY CARD STATED ODDS 1:65 HOBBY
*RETAIL HOME: .4X TO .8X HOBBY HOME
RETAIL HOME STATED ODDS 1:49
*RETAIL AWAY: .4X TO .8X HOBBY AWAY
RETAIL AWAY STATED ODDS 1:97
1 Jerry Rice 7.50 20.00
2 Terrell Davis 4.00 10.00
3 Warrick Dunn 4.00 10.00
4 Brett Favre 12.50 30.00
5 Napoleon Kaufman 4.00 10.00
6 Corey Dillon 4.00 10.00
7 John Elway 12.50 30.00
8 Troy Aikman 7.50 20.00
9 Mark Brunell 4.00 10.00
10 Kordell Stewart 4.00 10.00
11 Drew Bledsoe 6.00 15.00
12 Curtis Martin 4.00 10.00
13 Dan Marino 12.50 30.00
14 Jerome Bettis 4.00 10.00
15 Eddie George 4.00 10.00
16 Ryan Leaf 4.00 10.00
17 Jake Plummer 4.00 10.00
18 Peyton Manning 20.00 40.00
19 Steve Young 5.00 12.00
20 Barry Sanders 12.50 30.00

1999 Playoff Momentum SSD

The 1999 Playoff Momentum set was issued as a 200 card set done a plastic card stock with color action photos. Cards numbered one through 100 were issued at a rate of four in every pack. Cards numbered 101 through 150 were available one per pack and cards numbered 151 through 200 were the short printed rookie cards and were available at a rate of one in five packs. Also inserted were game used Barry Sanders cards featuring pieces of Game worn Jerseys and Helmets. Also inserted were the Star Gazing Red Certified hand signed cards.

COMPLETE SET (200) 150.00 300.00
COMP.SHORT SET (150) 50.00 100.00
1 Rob Moore .20 .50
2 Adrian Murrell .25 .60
3 Frank Sanders .20 .50
4 Andre Wadsworth .20 .50
5 Tim Dwight .25 .60
6 Terance Mathis .20 .50
7 Priest Holmes .30 .75
8 Jermaine Lewis .20 .50
9 Scott Mitchell .20 .50
10 Patrick Johnson .20 .50
11 Tony Banks .25 .60
12 Thurman Thomas .30 .75
13 Andre Reed .30 .75
14 Bruce Smith .30 .75
15 Tim Biakabutuka .25 .60
16 Muhsin Muhammad .25 .60
17 Wesley Walls .25 .60
18 Rae Carruth .20 .50
19 Curtis Conway .25 .60
20 Bobby Engram .25 .60
21 Jeff Blake .25 .60
22 Darnay Scott .20 .50
23 Ty Detmer .25 .60
24 Leslie Shepherd .20 .50
25 Sedrick Shaw .20 .50
26 Michael Irvin .30 .75
27 Rocket Ismail .25 .60
28 Ed McCaffrey .25 .60
29 Marcus Nash .20 .50
30 Shannon Sharpe .30 .75
31 Neil Smith .20 .50
32 Rod Smith .25 .60
33 Bubby Brister .20 .50
34 Germane Crowell .20 .50
35 Johnnie Morton .25 .60
36 Bill Schroeder .25 .60
37 Mark Chmura .20 .50
38 Marvin Harrison .30 .75
39 E.G. Green .20 .50
40 Jerome Pathon .20 .50
41 Keenan McCardell .25 .60
42 Jimmy Smith .25 .60
43 Kyle Brady .20 .50
44 Tavian Banks .20 .50
45 Warren Moon .30 .75
46 Derrick Alexander WR .20 .50
47 Elvis Grbac .20 .50
48 Andre Rison .25 .60
49 Byron Bam Morris .20 .50
50 Rashaan Shehee .20 .50
51 Karim Abdul-Jabbar .25 .60
52 John Avery .20 .50
53 Tony Martin .25 .60
54 O.J. McDuffie .25 .60
55 Oronde Gadsden .20 .50
56 Robert Smith .25 .60
57 Jeff George .20 .50
58 Jake Reed .25 .60
59 Leroy Hoard .20 .50
60 Terry Allen .25 .60
61 Terry Glenn .25 .60
62 Ben Coates .25 .60
63 Tony Simmons .20 .50
64 Cameron Cleeland .20 .50
65 Eddie Kennison .25 .60
66 Billy Joe Hobert .20 .50
67 Amani Toomer .25 .60
68 Kerry Collins .25 .60
69 Ike Hilliard .25 .60
70 Gary Brown .20 .50
71 Joe Jurevicius .20 .50
72 Wayne Chrebet .25 .60
73 Vinny Testaverde .25 .60
74 Charles Woodson .30 .75
75 James Jett .20 .50
76 Charles Johnson .20 .50
77 Duce Staley .25 .60
78 Hines Ward .30 .75
79 Jim Harbaugh .25 .60
80 Ryan Leaf .25 .60
81 Junior Seau .30 .75
82 Mikhael Ricks .20 .50
83 Garrison Hearst .25 .60
84 J.J. Stokes .20 .50
85 Lawrence Phillips .25 .60
86 Derrick Mayes .20 .50
87 Mike Pritchard .20 .50
88 Ahman Green .25 .60
89 Ricky Watters .25 .60
90 Robert Holcombe .20 .50
91 Isaac Bruce .30 .75
92 Trent Dilfer .25 .60
93 Reidel Anthony .20 .50
94 Jacquez Green .20 .50
95 Warren Sapp .25 .60
96 Kevin Dyson .20 .50
97 Yancey Thigpen .20 .50
98 Stephen Davis .25 .60
99 Irving Fryar .25 .60
100 Michael Westbrook .20 .50
101 Jake Plummer .40 1.00
102 Jamal Anderson .40 1.00
103 Chris Chandler .40 1.00
104 Doug Flutie .50 1.25
105 Eric Moulds .40 1.00
106 Antowain Smith .30 .75
107 Jonathan Linton .30 .75
108 Curtis Enis .30 .75
109 Corey Dillon .40 1.00
110 Carl Pickens .40 1.00
111 Emmitt Smith 1.25 3.00
112 Troy Aikman .75 2.00
113 Deion Sanders .50 1.25
114 John Elway 1.50 4.00
115 Terrell Davis .50 1.25
116 Brian Griese .40 1.00
117 Barry Sanders 1.25 3.00
118 Charlie Batch .40 1.00
119 Herman Moore .40 1.00
120 Brett Favre 1.50 4.00
121 Antonio Freeman .40 1.00
122 Dorsey Levens .40 1.00
123 Peyton Manning 1.50 4.00
124 Fred Taylor .40 1.00
125 Mark Brunell .40 1.00
126 Dan Marino 1.50 4.00
127 Randy Moss .50 1.25
128 Cris Carter .50 1.25
129 Randall Cunningham .50 1.25
130 Drew Bledsoe .50 1.25
131 Keyshawn Johnson .40 1.00
132 Curtis Martin .50 1.25
133 Tim Brown .50 1.25
134 Napoleon Kaufman .30 .75
135 Kordell Stewart .40 1.00
136 Jerome Bettis .50 1.25
137 Natrone Means .40 1.00
138 Jerry Rice 1.00 2.50
139 Steve Young .60 1.50
140 Terrell Owens .50 1.25
141 Joey Galloway .40 1.00
142 Jon Kitna .40 1.00
143 Marshall Faulk .50 1.25
144 Kurt Warner RC 5.00 12.00
145 Warrick Dunn .40 1.00
146 Mike Alstott .50 1.25
147 Eddie George .40 1.00
148 Steve McNair .50 1.25
149 Brad Johnson .40 1.00
150 Skip Hicks .30 .75
151 Tim Couch RC 2.00 5.00
152 Donovan McNabb RC 5.00 12.00
153 Akili Smith RC 1.50 4.00
154 Edgerrin James RC 2.50 6.00
155 Ricky Williams RC 3.00 8.00
156 Torry Holt RC 3.00 8.00
157 Champ Bailey RC 4.00 10.00
158 David Boston RC 1.50 4.00
159 Chris Claiborne RC 1.25 3.00
160 Chris McAlister RC 1.50 4.00
161 Daunte Culpepper RC 2.00 5.00
162 Cade McNown RC 1.50 4.00
163 Troy Edwards RC 1.50 4.00
164 Jevon Kearse RC 2.00 5.00
165 Kevin Johnson RC 1.50 4.00
166 James Johnson RC 1.25 3.00
167 Reginald Kelly RC 1.25 3.00
168 Rob Konrad RC 1.25 3.00
169 Jim Kleinsasser RC 2.00 5.00
170 Kevin Faulk RC 2.00 5.00
171 Joe Montgomery RC 1.25 3.00
172 Shaun King RC 1.50 4.00
173 Peerless Price RC 1.50 4.00
174 Mike Cloud RC 1.25 3.00
175 Jermaine Fazande RC 1.25 3.00
176 D'Wayne Bates RC 1.25 3.00
177 Brock Huard RC 1.50 4.00
178 Marty Booker RC 1.50 4.00
179 Karsten Bailey RC 1.25 3.00
180 Shawn Bryson RC 1.25 3.00
181 Jeff Paulk RC 1.25 3.00
182 Travis McGriff RC 1.25 3.00
183 Amos Zereoue RC 1.50 4.00
184 Craig Yeast RC 1.25 3.00
185 Joe Germaine RC 1.50 4.00
186 Dameane Douglas RC 1.25 3.00
187 Sedrick Irvin RC 1.25 3.00
188 Brandon Stokley RC 2.00 5.00
189 Larry Parker RC 1.50 4.00
190 Sean Bennett RC 1.25 3.00
191 Wane McGarity RC 1.25 3.00
192 Olandis Gary RC 2.00 5.00
193 Na Brown RC 1.25 3.00
194 Aaron Brooks RC 2.00 5.00
195 Cecil Collins RC 1.25 3.00
196 Darrin Chiaverini RC 1.25 3.00
197 Kevin Daft RC 1.25 3.00
198 Darnell McDonald RC 1.25 3.00
199 Joel Makovicka RC 1.25 3.00
200 Michael Bishop RC 1.50 4.00

1999 Playoff Momentum SSD O's

*1-100 STARS: 30X TO 80X BASIC CARDS
*101-150 STARS: 20X TO 50X BASIC CARDS
*144/151-200 RCs: 2X TO 5X
STATED PRINT RUN 25 SERIAL #'d SETS

1999 Playoff Momentum SSD X's

*1-100 STARS: 4X TO 10X BASIC CARDS
*101-150 STARS: 2.5X TO 6X BASIC CARDS
*144/151-200 RCs: .8X TO 2X
STATED PRINT RUN 300 SERIAL #'d SETS

1999 Playoff Momentum SSD Chart Toppers

COMPLETE SET (24) 75.00 150.00
STATED ODDS 1:33
CT1 Donovan McNabb 5.00 12.00
CT2 Randy Moss 5.00 12.00
CT3 Cade McNown .75 2.00
CT4 Brett Favre 6.00 15.00
CT5 Edgerrin James 4.00 10.00
CT6 Dan Marino 6.00 15.00
CT7 Jamal Anderson 2.00 5.00
CT8 Barry Sanders 6.00 15.00
CT9 Kordell Stewart 1.25 3.00
CT10 John Elway 6.00 15.00
CT11 Eddie George 1.25 3.00
CT12 Terrell Davis 2.00 5.00
CT13 Ricky Williams 3.00 8.00
CT14 Peyton Manning 6.00 15.00
CT15 Tim Couch 1.25 3.00
CT16 Emmitt Smith 4.00 10.00
CT17 Doug Flutie 1.25 3.00
CT18 Troy Aikman 4.00 10.00
CT19 Steve Young 2.50 6.00
CT20 Jerry Rice 4.00 10.00
CT21 Mark Brunell 1.25 3.00
CT22 Fred Taylor 2.00 5.00
CT23 Jake Plummer 1.25 3.00
CT24 Drew Bledsoe 2.50 6.00

1999 Playoff Momentum SSD Terrell Davis Salute

COMPLETE SET (5) 20.00 50.00
COMMON CARD (TD11-TD15) 4.00 10.00
STATED ODDS 1:255
COMMON AUTO (TD11-TD15) 12.00 30.00
AUTO STATED PRINT RUN 150

1999 Playoff Momentum SSD Gridiron Force

COMPLETE SET (24) 40.00 80.00
STATED ODDS 1:17
GF1 Cris Carter 1.25 3.00
GF2 Brett Favre 4.00 10.00
GF3 Jamal Anderson 1.25 3.00
GF4 Dan Marino 4.00 10.00
GF5 Deion Sanders 1.25 3.00
GF6 Barry Sanders 4.00 10.00
GF7 Jerome Bettis 1.25 3.00
GF8 John Elway 4.00 10.00
GF9 Eddie George .75 2.00
GF10 Peyton Manning 4.00 10.00
GF11 Warrick Dunn 1.25 3.00
GF12 Troy Aikman 2.50 6.00
GF13 Keyshawn Johnson 1.25 3.00
GF14 Jerry Rice 2.50 6.00
GF15 Terrell Owens 1.25 3.00
GF16 Randy Moss 3.00 8.00
GF17 Fred Taylor 1.25 3.00
GF18 Mark Brunell .75 2.00
GF19 Steve Young 1.50 4.00
GF20 Drew Bledsoe 1.50 4.00
GF21 Kordell Stewart .75 2.00
GF22 Emmitt Smith 2.50 6.00
GF23 Terrell Davis 1.25 3.00
GF24 Jake Plummer .75 2.00

1999 Playoff Momentum SSD Hog Heaven

COMPLETE SET (12) 100.00 200.00
STATED ODDS 1:81
HH1 Ricky Williams 5.00 12.00
HH2 Terrell Davis 4.00 10.00
HH3 Emmitt Smith 7.50 20.00
HH4 Brett Favre 12.50 30.00
HH5 Fred Taylor 4.00 10.00
HH6 Tim Couch 4.00 10.00
HH7 John Elway 12.50 30.00
HH8 Dan Marino 12.50 30.00
HH9 Randy Moss 7.50 20.00
HH10 Barry Sanders 12.50 30.00
HH11 Jerry Rice 7.50 20.00
HH12 Jake Plummer 4.00 10.00

1999 Playoff Momentum SSD Rookie Quads

COMPLETE SET (12) 100.00 200.00
STATED ODDS 1:97
*GOLDS: 1X TO 2.5X BASIC INSERTS
GOLDS STATED PRINT RUN 50 SER.#'d SETS
1 Tim Couch 5.00 12.00
Aaron Brooks
Shaun King
Michael Bishop
2 Edgerrin James 12.50 30.00
Mike Cloud
Jeff Paulk
Joel Makovicka
3 Torry Holt 7.50 20.00
Reggie Kelly
Marty Booker
Dameane Douglas
4 Champ Bailey 4.00 10.00
Chris Claiborne
Chris McAlister
Anthony McFarland
5 David Boston 4.00 10.00
Jim Kleinsasser
Karsten Bailey
Brandon Stokley
6 Ricky Williams 6.00 15.00
Amos Zereoue
Cecil Collins
Jerry Azumah
7 Donovan McNabb 12.50 30.00
Brock Huard
Daunte Culpepper
Scott Covington
8 James Johnson 4.00 10.00
Jerame Fazande
Sedrick Irvin
Sean Bennett
9 Troy Edwards 4.00 10.00
Peerless Price
Travis McGriff
Larry Parker
10 Rob Konrad 4.00 10.00
Kevin Faulk

Joe Montgomery
Shawn Bryson
11 Cade McNown 4.00 10.00
Joe Germaine
Akili Smith
Chris Greisen
12 Kevin Johnson 7.50 20.00
D'Wayne Bates
Craig Yeast
Wane McGarity

1999 Playoff Momentum SSD Rookie Recall

COMPLETE SET (30) 100.00 200.00
STATED ODDS 1:49
1 Jerome Bettis 2.50 6.00
2 Tim Brown 2.50 6.00
3 Cris Carter 2.50 6.00
4 Marshall Faulk 3.00 8.00
5 Doug Flutie 1.50 4.00
6 Randall Cunningham 1.50 4.00
7 Brett Favre 8.00 20.00
8 Dan Marino 8.00 20.00
9 Barry Sanders 8.00 20.00
10 John Elway 8.00 20.00
11 Emmitt Smith 5.00 12.00
12 Troy Aikman 5.00 12.00
13 Jerry Rice 5.00 12.00
14 Steve Young 3.00 8.00
15 Randy Moss 5.00 12.00
16 Peyton Manning 6.00 15.00
17 Fred Taylor 2.50 6.00
18 Jake Plummer 1.50 4.00
19 Drew Bledsoe 3.00 8.00
20 Mark Brunell 1.50 4.00
21 Charlie Batch 1.00 2.50
22 Antonio Freeman 1.50 4.00
23 Curtis Martin 2.50 6.00
24 Eddie George 1.50 4.00
25 Kordell Stewart 1.50 4.00
26 Jamal Anderson 1.50 4.00
27 Curtis Enis 1.00 2.50
28 Terrell Davis 2.50 6.00
29 Eric Moulds 1.50 4.00
30 Terrell Owens 2.50 6.00

1999 Playoff Momentum SSD Barry Sanders Commemorative

COMPLETE SET (5) 20.00 50.00
COMMON CARD (RR7-RR11) 5.00 12.00
STATED ODDS 1:275

1999 Playoff Momentum SSD Barry Sanders Memorabilia

JERSEY PRINT RUN 300 SERIAL #'d CARDS
HELMET PRINT RUN 125 SERIAL #'d CARDS
RR1 Barry Sanders Jsy/300 20.00 50.00
RR5 Barry Sanders Hel/125 40.00 100.00

1999 Playoff Momentum SSD Star Gazing

COMPLETE SET (45) 200.00 400.00
SG1-SG8 RED AUTO STATED ODDS 1:185
SG9-SG30 BLUE STATED ODDS 1:17
SG31-SG45 GREEN STATED ODDS 1:65
GOLD STATED PRINT RUN 50 SER.#'d SETS
SG1 Terrell Davis AU 10.00 25.00
SG2 Dan Marino AU 40.00 80.00
SG3 Joey Galloway AU 7.50 20.00
SG4 Steve McNair AU 10.00 25.00
SG5 Doug Flutie AU 12.50 30.00
SG6 Kordell Stewart AU 7.50 20.00
SG7 Fred Taylor AU 10.00 25.00
SG8 Jamal Anderson AU 7.50 20.00
SG9 Karim Abdul-Jabbar .50 1.25
SG10 Mike Alstott .50 1.25
SG11 Jerome Bettis .50 1.25
SG12 Carl Pickens .50 1.25
SG13 Cris Carter .50 1.25
SG14 Randall Cunningham .50 1.25
SG15 Corey Dillon .50 1.25
SG16 Tim Dwight .50 1.25
SG17 Cade McNown .50 1.25
SG18 Marshall Faulk 1.25 3.00
SG19 Napoleon Kaufman .50 1.25
SG20 Antonio Freeman .50 1.25
SG21 Edgerrin James 1.50 4.00
SG22 Terrell Owens .75 2.00
SG23 Garrison Hearst .50 1.25
SG24 Keyshawn Johnson .50 1.25
SG25 Akili Smith .50 1.25
SG26 Curtis Martin .50 1.25
SG27 Dorsey Levens .50 1.25
SG28 Deion Sanders .50 1.25
SG29 Herman Moore .50 1.25
SG30 Eric Moulds .50 1.25
SG31 Randy Moss 3.00 8.00
SG32 Eddie George 1.50 4.00
SG33 Barry Sanders 5.00 12.00
SG34 John Elway 5.00 12.00
SG35 Peyton Manning 4.00 10.00
SG36 Emmitt Smith 3.00 8.00
SG37 Troy Aikman 3.00 8.00
SG38 Jerry Rice 3.00 8.00
SG39 Mark Brunell 2.00 5.00
SG40 Steve Young 2.00 5.00
SG41 Tim Couch 2.00 5.00
SG42 Ricky Williams 3.00 8.00
SG43 Donovan McNabb 5.00 12.00
SG44 Drew Bledsoe 2.00 5.00
SG45 Brett Favre 5.00 12.00

1999 Playoff Momentum SSD Star Gazing Gold

*SG9-SG30 STARS: 3X TO 8X BASIC INSERTS
*SG9-SG30 ROOKIES: 1.5X TO 4X BASIC INS.
*SG31-SG45 STARS: 2X TO 5X BASIC INSERTS
*SG31-SG45 ROOKIES: 1.2X TO 3X BASIC INS.
SG1 Terrell Davis 10.00 25.00
SG2 Dan Marino 40.00 80.00
SG3 Joey Galloway 7.50 20.00
SG4 Steve McNair 10.00 25.00
SG5 Doug Flutie 12.50 25.00
SG6 Kordell Stewart 7.50 20.00
SG7 Fred Taylor 10.00 25.00
SG8 Jamal Anderson 7.50 20.00

1999 Playoff Momentum SSD Team Thread Checklists

COMPLETE SET (31) 100.00 250.00
STATED ODDS 1:17
TTC1 Dan Marino 10.00 25.00
TTC2 Drew Bledsoe 4.00 10.00
TTC3 Keyshawn Johnson 3.00 8.00
TTC4 Eric Moulds 3.00 8.00
TTC5 Peyton Manning 8.00 20.00
TTC6 Natrone Means 2.00 5.00
TTC7 Jon Kitna 2.00 5.00
TTC8 Byron Bam Morris .75 2.00
TTC9 Tim Brown 3.00 8.00
TTC10 Terrell Davis 3.00 8.00
TTC11 Kordell Stewart 2.00 5.00
TTC12 Fred Taylor 2.50 6.00
TTC13 Tim Couch 2.00 5.00
TTC14 Eddie George 2.00 5.00
TTC15 Priest Holmes 2.50 6.00
TTC16 Akili Smith .30 .75
TTC17 Emmitt Smith 6.00 15.00
TTC18 Skip Hicks 1.00 2.50
TTC19 Jake Plummer 2.00 5.00
TTC20 Donovan McNabb 8.00 20.00
TTC21 Ike Hilliard .75 2.00
TTC22 Barry Sanders 10.00 25.00
TTC23 Cade McNown 1.50 4.00
TTC24 Randy Moss 6.00 15.00
TTC25 Brett Favre 10.00 25.00
TTC26 Mike Alstott 3.00 8.00
TTC27 Marshall Faulk 4.00 10.00
TTC28 Ricky Williams 3.00 8.00
TTC29 Jamal Anderson 3.00 8.00
TTC30 Jerry Rice 6.00 15.00
TTC31 Tim Biakabutuka 1.25 3.00

2000 Playoff Momentum

Released as a 200-card set, Momentum is comprised of 100 base veteran cards and 100 short printed rookie cards sequentially numbered to 750. Base cards were etched silver foil with a border along the left side of the card and an oval nameplate centered along the bottom. One or two Beckett Grading Services cards were included as a box topper, where 210 of each veteran were graded and 175 of each rookie were graded. Momentum was packaged in 16-pack boxes with each pack containing six cards.

COMP.SET w/o RC's (100) 6.00 15.00
1 David Boston .15 .40
2 Jake Plummer .20 .50
3 Chris Chandler .20 .50
4 Jamal Anderson .20 .50
5 Tim Dwight .20 .50
6 Qadry Ismail .20 .50
7 Peerless Price .20 .50
8 Antowain Smith .20 .50
9 Eric Moulds .20 .50
10 Rob Johnson .20 .50
11 Natrone Means .20 .50
12 Muhsin Muhammad .20 .50
13 Steve Beuerlein .20 .50
14 Patrick Jeffers .20 .50
15 Curtis Enis .15 .40
16 Cade McNown .15 .40
17 Marcus Robinson .20 .50
18 Corey Dillon .20 .50
19 Akili Smith .15 .40
20 Carl Pickens .20 .50
21 Tim Couch .20 .50
22 Kevin Johnson .15 .40
23 Troy Aikman .40 1.00
24 Emmitt Smith .60 1.50
25 Joey Galloway .20 .50
26 Rocket Ismail .20 .50
27 Olandis Gary .20 .50
28 John Elway .60 1.50
29 Brian Griese .20 .50
30 Ed McCaffrey .20 .50
31 Terrell Davis .25 .60
32 Charlie Batch .20 .50
33 James Stewart .15 .40
34 Germane Crowell .15 .40
35 Barry Sanders .50 1.25
36 Herman Moore .20 .50
37 Antonio Freeman .20 .50
38 Dorsey Levens .20 .50
39 Brett Favre * .75 2.00
40 Edgerrin James .25 .60
41 Marvin Harrison .25 .60
42 Peyton Manning .60 1.50
43 Fred Taylor .25 .60
44 Keenan McCardell .20 .50
45 Mark Brunell .20 .50
46 Jimmy Smith .20 .50
47 Elvis Grbac .15 .40
48 Tony Gonzalez .25 .60
49 James Johnson .15 .40
50 Dan Marino .75 2.00
51 Thurman Thomas .25 .60
52 Cris Carter .25 .60
53 Robert Smith .20 .50
54 Randy Moss .25 .60
55 Daunte Culpepper .20 .50
56 Terry Glenn .20 .50
57 Kevin Faulk .20 .50
58 Drew Bledsoe .25 .60
59 Ricky Williams .25 .60
60 Amani Toomer .20 .50
61 Kerry Collins .20 .50
62 Vinny Testaverde .20 .50
63 Curtis Martin .25 .60
64 Rich Gannon .20 .50
65 Tyrone Wheatley .15 .40
66 Napoleon Kaufman .20 .50
67 Tim Brown .25 .60
68 Duce Staley .20 .50
69 Donovan McNabb .25 .60
70 Kordell Stewart .20 .50
71 Troy Edwards .15 .40
72 Jerome Bettis .25 .60
73 Jim Harbaugh .20 .50
74 Jermaine Fazande .15 .40
75 Steve Young .30 .75
76 Charlie Garner .20 .50
77 Terrell Owens .25 .60
78 Jerry Rice .50 1.25
79 Jeff Garcia .20 .50
80 Ricky Watters .20 .50
81 Jon Kitna .20 .50
82 Marshall Faulk .25 .60
83 Isaac Bruce .25 .60
84 Torry Holt .25 .60
85 Kurt Warner .40 1.00
86 Keyshawn Johnson .20 .50
87 Warrick Dunn .20 .50
88 Mike Alstott .25 .60
89 Warren Sapp .20 .50
90 Shaun King .15 .40
91 Eddie George .20 .50
92 Steve McNair .25 .60
93 Jevon Kearse .20 .50
94 Bruce Smith .25 .60
95 Deion Sanders .25 .60
96 Albert Connell .15 .40
97 Michael Westbrook .15 .40
98 Brad Johnson .20 .50
99 Jeff George .20 .50
100 Stephen Davis .20 .50
101 Peter Warrick RC 3.00 8.00
102 Jamal Lewis RC 3.00 8.00
103 Thomas Jones RC 4.00 10.00
104 Plaxico Burress RC 3.00 8.00
105 Travis Taylor RC 2.50 6.00
106 Ron Dayne RC 3.00 8.00
107 Bubba Franks RC 3.00 8.00
108 Sebastian Janikowski RC 3.00 8.00
109 Chad Pennington RC 5.00 12.00
110 Shaun Alexander RC 4.00 10.00
111 Sylvester Morris RC 2.00 5.00
112 Anthony Becht RC 2.50 6.00
113 R.Jay Soward RC 2.00 5.00
114 Trung Canidate RC 2.50 6.00
115 Dennis Northcutt RC 2.50 6.00
116 Todd Pinkston RC 2.00 5.00
117 Jerry Porter RC 3.00 8.00
118 Travis Prentice RC 2.50 6.00
119 Giovanni Carmazzi RC 2.00 5.00
120 Ron Dugans RC 2.00 5.00
121 Erron Kinney RC 2.00 5.00
122 Dez White RC 2.50 6.00
123 Chris Cole RC 2.50 6.00
124 Ron Dixon RC 2.00 5.00
125 Chris Redman RC 2.50 6.00
126 J.R. Redmond RC 2.00 5.00
127 Laveranues Coles RC 3.00 8.00
128 JaJuan Dawson RC 2.00 5.00
129 Darrell Jackson RC 2.50 6.00
130 Reuben Droughns RC 3.00 8.00
131 Doug Chapman RC 2.00 5.00
132 Terrelle Smith RC 2.00 5.00
133 Curtis Keaton RC 2.00 5.00
134 Gari Scott RC 2.00 5.00
135 Courtney Brown RC 2.50 6.00
136 Corey Simon RC 2.50 6.00
137 Brian Urlacher RC 12.00 30.00
138 Shaun Ellis RC 3.00 8.00
139 John Abraham RC 3.00 8.00
140 Deltha O'Neal RC 2.50 6.00
141 Rashard Anderson RC 2.00 5.00
142 Ahmed Plummer RC 2.00 5.00
143 Chris Hovan RC 2.50 6.00
144 Erik Flowers RC 2.00 5.00
145 Rob Morris RC 2.50 6.00
146 Keith Bulluck RC 2.50 6.00
147 Darren Howard RC 2.00 5.00
148 John Engelberger RC 2.00 5.00
149 Ian Gold RC 2.00 5.00
150 Raynoch Thompson RC 2.00 5.00
151 Cornelius Griffin RC 2.00 5.00
152 Rogers Beckett RC 2.00 5.00
153 Dwayne Goodrich RC 2.00 5.00
154 Barrett Green RC 2.00 5.00
155 Kevin Thompson RC 2.00 5.00
156 Ben Kelly RC 2.00 5.00
157 Danny Farmer RC 2.00 5.00
158 Aaron Shea RC 2.50 6.00
159 Trevor Gaylor RC 2.00 5.00
160 Mike Brown RC 3.00 8.00
161 Frank Moreau RC 2.00 5.00
162 Deon Dyer RC 2.00 5.00
163 Avion Black RC 2.00 5.00
164 Spergon Wynn RC 2.50 6.00
165 Billy Volek RC 3.00 8.00
166 Michael Wiley RC 2.00 5.00
167 Dante Hall RC 3.00 8.00
168 Ronney Jenkins RC 2.00 5.00
169 Sammy Morris RC 2.50 6.00
170 Kevin McDougal RC 2.00 5.00
171 Tee Martin RC 3.00 8.00
172 Troy Walters RC 2.00 5.00
173 Chad Morton RC 3.00 8.00
174 Jamel White RC 2.00 5.00
175 Shockmain Davis RC 2.00 5.00
176 Mario Edwards RC 2.00 5.00
177 Brandon Short RC 2.00 5.00
178 James Williams RC 2.00 5.00
179 Mike Anderson RC 3.00 8.00
180 Tom Brady RC 250.00 400.00
181 Na'il Diggs RC 2.00 5.00
182 Todd Husak RC 2.00 5.00
183 JaJuan Seider RC 2.00 5.00
184 Tim Rattay RC 2.50 6.00
185 Jarious Jackson RC 2.50 6.00
186 Joe Hamilton RC 2.00 5.00
187 Shyrone Stith RC 2.00 5.00
188 Mondriel Fulcher RC 2.00 5.00
189 Bashir Yamini RC 2.00 5.00
190 Herbert Goodman RC 2.00 5.00
191 Mike Green RC 3.00 8.00
192 Demario Brown RC 2.00 5.00
193 Charles Lee RC 2.00 5.00
194 Doug Johnson RC 2.50 6.00
195 Windrell Hayes RC 2.00 5.00
196 Julian Peterson RC 3.00 8.00
197 Kwame Cavil RC 2.00 5.00
198 Hank Poteat RC 2.00 5.00
199 Clint Stoerner RC 3.00 8.00
200 Mark Simoneau RC 2.00 5.00

2000 Playoff Momentum O's

*VETS/120: 6X TO 15X BASIC CARD
*VETS/60-90: 8X TO 20X BASIC CARD
*ROOKIES/60-90: .6X TO 1.5X
*VETS/40-50: 10X TO 25X BASIC CARD
*ROOKIES/40-50: .8X TO 2X
*VETS/30: 12X TO 30X BASIC CARD
*ROOKIES/30: 1X TO 2.5X
*VETS/20: 15X TO 40X BASIC CARD
*ROOKIES/20: 1.2X TO 3X
*VETS/10: 20X TO 50X BASIC CARD
*ROOKIES/10: 1.5X TO 4X
STATED PRINT RUN 10-120
180 Tom Brady/60 300.00 500.00

2000 Playoff Momentum X's

*VETS/201-326: 5X TO 12X BASIC CARD
*ROOKIES/200-326: .4X TO 1X
*VETS/100-199: 6X TO 15X BASIC CARD
*ROOKIES/100-199: .5X TO 1.2X
*VETS/60-99: 8X TO 20X BASIC CARD
*ROOKIES/60-99: .6X TO 1.5X
*VETS/40-53: 10X TO 25X BASIC CARD
*ROOKIES/40-53: .8X TO 2X
*VETS/30-39: 12X TO 30X BASIC CARD
*ROOKIES/30-39: 1X TO 2.5X
*VETS/21-29: 15X TO 40X BASIC CARD
*ROOKIES/21-29: 1.2X TO 3X
*VETS/10-19: 20X TO 50X BASIC CARD
*ROOKIES/10: 1.5X TO 4X
STATED PRINT RUN 10-326
180 Tom Brady/199 250.00 400.00

2000 Playoff Momentum Game Day Jerseys

GDS1-GDS30 SINGLE JSY PRINT RUN 50-75
FIRST 25 LOTT AND LONG CARDS SIGNED
GDS31-GDS45 DUAL JSY PRINT RUN 25
GDS1 Joe Montana 30.00 80.00
GDS2 Dan Marino 30.00 80.00
GDS3 Joe Montana 30.00 80.00
GDS4 John Elway 25.00 60.00
GDS5 Terry Bradshaw 25.00 60.00
GDS6 Roger Staubach 20.00 50.00
GDS7 Bob Griese 10.00 25.00
GDS8 Fran Tarkenton 12.00 30.00
GDS9 Phil Simms 10.00 25.00
GDS10 Lawrence Taylor 10.00 25.00
GDS11 Ronnie Lott 10.00 25.00
GDS11A Ronnie Lott AU/25 60.00 120.00
GDS12 Boomer Esiason 10.00 25.00
GDS13 Joe Namath 20.00 50.00
GDS14 Don Maynard 8.00 20.00
GDS15 Howie Long 10.00 25.00
GDS15A Howie Long AU/25 90.00 150.00
GDS16 Marcus Allen 10.00 25.00
GDS17 Jim Kelly 12.00 30.00
GDS18 Thurman Thomas 10.00 25.00
GDS19 Fred Taylor 8.00 20.00
GDS20 Mark Brunell 6.00 15.00
GDS21 Randy Moss 8.00 20.00
GDS22 Antonio Freeman 6.00 15.00
GDS23 Ricky Williams 8.00 20.00
GDS24 Tim Couch 6.00 15.00
GDS25 Kurt Warner 12.00 30.00
GDS26 Eddie George 6.00 15.00
GDS27 Troy Aikman 12.00 30.00
GDS28 Steve Young 15.00 40.00
GDS29 Dorsey Levens 6.00 15.00
GDS30 Barry Sanders 15.00 40.00
GDS31 Joe Montana 150.00 300.00
Dan Marino
GDS32 Joe Montana 150.00 300.00
John Elway
GDS33 Terry Bradshaw 30.00 80.00
Roger Staubach
GDS34 Bob Griese 25.00 60.00
Fran Tarkenton
GDS35 Phil Simms 20.00 50.00
Lawrence Taylor
GDS36 Ronnie Lott 20.00 50.00
Boomer Esiason
GDS37 Joe Namath 40.00 100.00
Don Maynard
GDS38 Howie Long 20.00 50.00
Marcus Allen
GDS39 Jim Kelly 25.00 60.00
Thurman Thomas
GDS41 Randy Moss 15.00 40.00
Antonio Freeman
GDS42 Ricky Williams 12.00 30.00
Tim Couch
GDS43 Kurt Warner 25.00 60.00
Eddie George
GDS44 Troy Aikman 30.00 80.00
Steve Young
GDS45 Dorsey Levens 30.00 80.00
Barry Sanders

2000 Playoff Momentum Game Day Signatures

GDS1-GDS30 PRINT RUN 75
GDS31-GDS45 PRINT RUN 25
GDS1 Joe Montana 60.00 120.00
GDS2 Dan Marino 60.00 120.00
GDS3 Joe Montana 60.00 120.00
GDS4 John Elway 60.00 120.00
GDS5 Terry Bradshaw 40.00 100.00
GDS6 Roger Staubach 40.00 100.00
GDS7 Bob Griese 15.00 40.00
GDS8 Fran Tarkenton 25.00 50.00
GDS9 Phil Simms 15.00 40.00
GDS10 Lawrence Taylor 25.00 50.00
GDS11 Ronnie Lott 30.00 60.00
GDS12 Boomer Esiason 15.00 40.00
GDS13 Joe Namath 50.00 120.00
GDS14 Don Maynard 12.00 30.00
GDS15 Howie Long 50.00 100.00
GDS17 Jim Kelly 30.00 60.00
GDS18 Thurman Thomas 15.00 40.00
GDS19 Fred Taylor 12.00 30.00
GDS20 Mark Brunell 10.00 25.00
GDS22 Antonio Freeman 10.00 25.00
GDS23 Ricky Williams 12.00 30.00
GDS24 Tim Couch 10.00 25.00
GDS25 Kurt Warner 25.00 50.00
GDS26 Eddie George 10.00 25.00
GDS27 Troy Aikman 35.00 80.00
GDS28 Steve Young 40.00 80.00
GDS29 Dorsey Levens 10.00 25.00
GDS30 Barry Sanders 60.00 120.00
GDS31 Joe Montana 200.00 400.00
Dan Marino
GDS32 Joe Montana 200.00 400.00
John Elway
GDS33 Terry Bradshaw 150.00 300.00
Roger Staubach
GDS34 Bob Griese 60.00 120.00
Fran Tarkenton
GDS35 Phil Simms 60.00 120.00
Lawrence Taylor
GDS36 Ronnie Lott 40.00 80.00
Boomer Esiason
GDS37 Joe Namath 75.00 150.00
Don Maynard
GDS38 Howie Long
Marcus Allen
GDS39 Jim Kelly 125.00 250.00
Thurman Thomas
GDS40 Fred Taylor 25.00 60.00
Mark Brunell
GDS42 Ricky Williams EXCH
Tim Couch
GDS43 Kurt Warner 40.00 80.00
Eddie George
GDS44 Troy Aikman 75.00 150.00
Steve Young
GDS45 Dorsey Levens 60.00 150.00
Barry Sanders

2000 Playoff Momentum Game Day Souvenirs

COMPLETE SET (45) 60.00 120.00
GDS1-GDS30 STATED ODDS 1:15
GDS31-GDS45 STATED ODDS 1:47
GDS1 Joe Montana 3.00 8.00
GDS2 Dan Marino 3.00 8.00
GDS3 Joe Montana 3.00 8.00
GDS4 John Elway 2.50 6.00
GDS5 Terry Bradshaw 2.50 6.00
GDS6 Roger Staubach 2.00 5.00
GDS7 Bob Griese 1.00 2.50
GDS8 Fran Tarkenton 1.25 3.00
GDS9 Phil Simms 1.00 2.50
GDS10 Lawrence Taylor 1.00 2.50
GDS11 Ronnie Lott 1.00 2.50
GDS12 Boomer Esiason 1.00 2.50
GDS13 Joe Namath 2.00 5.00
GDS14 Don Maynard .75 2.00
GDS15 Howie Long 1.00 2.50
GDS16 Marcus Allen 1.00 2.50
GDS17 Jim Kelly 1.25 3.00
GDS18 Thurman Thomas 1.00 2.50
GDS19 Fred Taylor 1.00 2.50
GDS20 Mark Brunell .75 2.00
GDS21 Randy Moss 1.00 2.50
GDS22 Antonio Freeman .75 2.00
GDS23 Ricky Williams 1.00 2.50
GDS24 Tim Couch .75 2.00
GDS25 Kurt Warner 1.50 4.00
GDS26 Eddie George .75 2.00
GDS27 Troy Aikman 1.50 4.00
GDS28 Steve Young 1.25 3.00
GDS29 Dorsey Levens .75 2.00
GDS30 Barry Sanders 2.00 5.00
GDS31 Joe Montana 4.00 10.00
Dan Marino
GDS32 Joe Montana 4.00 10.00
John Elway
GDS33 Terry Bradshaw 3.00 8.00
Roger Staubach
GDS34 Bob Griese 1.50 4.00
Fran Tarkenton
GDS35 Phil Simms 1.25 3.00
Lawrence Taylor
GDS36 Ronnie Lott 1.25 3.00
Boomer Esiason
GDS37 Joe Namath 2.50 6.00
Don Maynard
GDS38 Howie Long 1.25 3.00
Marcus Allen
GDS39 Jim Kelly 1.50 4.00
Thurman Thomas
GDS40 Fred Taylor 1.25 3.00
Mark Brunell
GDS41 Randy Moss 1.25 3.00
Antonio Freeman
GDS42 Ricky Williams 1.00 2.50
Tim Couch
GDS43 Kurt Warner 2.00 5.00
Eddie George
GDS44 Troy Aikman 2.00 5.00
Steve Young
GDS45 Dorsey Levens 2.50 6.00
Barry Sanders

2000 Playoff Momentum Generations

COMPLETE SET (50) 30.00 80.00
STATED ODDS 1:8
*GOLD/50: 3X TO 8X BASIC INSERTS
GOLD PRINT RUN 50 SER.#'d SETS
GN1 Jake Plummer .50 1.25
GN2 Tim Couch .50 1.25
GN3 Emmitt Smith 1.50 4.00
GN4 Troy Aikman 1.00 2.50
GN5 John Elway 1.50 4.00
GN6 Terrell Davis .60 1.50
GN7 Barry Sanders 1.25 3.00
GN8 Brett Favre 2.00 5.00
GN9 Peyton Manning 1.50 4.00
GN10 Edgerrin James .60 1.50
GN11 Mark Brunell .50 1.25
GN12 Fred Taylor .60 1.50
GN13 Dan Marino 2.00 5.00
GN14 Randy Moss .60 1.50
GN15 Drew Bledsoe .60 1.50
GN16 Ricky Williams .60 1.50
GN17 Jerry Rice 1.25 3.00
GN18 Steve Young .75 2.00
GN19 Kurt Warner 1.00 2.50
GN20 Eddie George .50 1.25
GN21 Eric Moulds .50 1.25
GN22 Cade McNown .40 1.00
GN23 Corey Dillon .50 1.25
GN24 Kevin Johnson .40 1.00
GN25 Joey Galloway .50 1.25
GN26 Dorsey Levens .50 1.25
GN27 Antonio Freeman .50 1.25
GN28 Marvin Harrison .60 1.50
GN29 Daunte Culpepper .50 1.25
GN30 Cris Carter .60 1.50
GN31 Curtis Martin .60 1.50
GN32 Tim Brown .60 1.50
GN33 Donovan McNabb .60 1.50
GN34 Terrell Owens .60 1.50
GN35 Peter Warrick .60 1.50
GN36 Jamal Lewis .60 1.50
GN37 Thomas Jones .75 2.00
GN38 Plaxico Burress .60 1.50
GN39 Travis Taylor .50 1.25
GN40 Ron Dayne .60 1.50
GN41 Chad Pennington 1.00 2.50
GN42 Shaun Alexander .75 2.00
GN43 Marshall Faulk .60 1.50
GN44 Keyshawn Johnson .50 1.25
GN45 Steve McNair .60 1.50
GN46 Stephen Davis .50 1.25
GN47 Brad Johnson .50 1.25
GN48 Akili Smith .40 1.00
GN49 Brian Griese .50 1.25
GN50 Isaac Bruce .60 1.50

2000 Playoff Momentum Rookie Quads

COMPLETE SET (12) 40.00 80.00
STATED ODDS 1:159
RQ1 Peter Warrick 2.50 6.00
Avion Black
Ron Dugans
Charles Lee
RQ2 Plaxico Burress 2.00 5.00
Trevor Gaylor
JaJuan Dawson
Dez White
RQ3 Travis Taylor 2.50 6.00
Danny Farmer
Jerry Porter
Laveranues Coles
RQ4 Gari Scott 1.50 4.00
Sylvester Morris
Todd Pinkston
Ron Dixon
RQ5 Darrell Jackson 1.50 4.00
R.Jay Soward
Dennis Northcutt
Chris Cole
RQ6 Jamal Lewis 2.50 6.00
Ronney Jenkins
Doug Chapman
Reuben Droughns
RQ7 Thomas Jones 1.50 4.00
Chad Morton
J.R. Redmond
Curtis Keaton
RQ8 Ron Dayne 2.00 5.00
Sammy Morris
Travis Prentice
Frank Moreau
RQ9 Shaun Alexander 1.50 4.00
Dante Hall
Trung Canidate
Michael Wiley
RQ10 Chad Pennington 1.50 4.00
Todd Husak
Tee Martin
Billy Volek
RQ11 Giovanni Carmazzi 50.00 100.00
Tim Rattay
Chris Redman
Tom Brady
RQ12 Courtney Brown 10.00 25.00
Shaun Ellis
Corey Simon
Brian Urlacher

2000 Playoff Momentum Rookie Tandems

COMPLETE SET (24) 40.00 80.00
STATED ODDS 1:95 RETAIL
RT1 Peter Warrick 1.25 3.00
Avion Black
RT2 Ron Dugans .75 2.00
Charles Lee
RT3 Plaxico Burress 1.25 3.00
Trevor Gaylor
RT4 Dez White 1.00 2.50
JaJuan Dawson
RT5 Travis Taylor .75 2.00
Danny Farmer
RT6 Jerry Porter 1.25 3.00
Laveranues Coles
RT7 Sylvester Morris .75 2.00
Gari Scott
RT8 Todd Pinkston .75 2.00
Ron Dixon
RT9 R.Jay Soward .75 2.00
Darrell Jackson
RT10 Dennis Northcutt 1.00 2.50
Chris Cole
RT11 Jamal Lewis 1.25 3.00
Ronney Jenkins
RT12 Reuben Droughns 1.25 3.00
Doug Chapman
RT13 Thomas Jones 1.50 4.00
Chad Morton
RT14 J.R. Redmond .75 2.00
Curtis Keaton
RT15 Ron Dayne 1.00 2.50
Sammy Morris
RT16 Travis Prentice 1.00 2.50
Frank Moreau
RT17 Shaun Alexander 1.50 4.00
Dante Hall
RT18 Trung Canidate .75 2.00
Michael Wiley
RT19 Chad Pennington .75 2.00
Todd Husak
RT20 Tee Martin 1.25 3.00
Billy Volek
RT21 Giovanni Carmazzi 1.00 2.50
Tim Rattay
RT22 Chris Redman 1.00 2.50
Tom Brady
RT23 Courtney Brown 1.25 3.00
Shaun Ellis
RT24 Corey Simon 5.00 12.00
Brian Urlacher

2000 Playoff Momentum Signing Bonus Quads

STATED ODDS 1:684
RQ1 Peter Warrick 25.00 60.00
R.Jay Soward
Plaxico Burress
Sylvester Morris
RQ2 Jamal Lewis 25.00 60.00
Dez White
Shaun Alexander
Travis Taylor
RQ3 Ron Dayne 25.00 60.00
Chad Pennington
Chris Redman
Thomas Jones No Auto

2000 Playoff Momentum Signing Bonus Tandems

STATED ODDS 1:675 RETAIL
RT3 Jamal Lewis 10.00 25.00
Dez White
RT4 Travis Taylor 15.00 40.00
Shaun Alexander
RT5 Thomas Jones 10.00 25.00
Chris Redman
RT6 Ron Dayne 12.00 30.00
Chad Pennington

2000 Playoff Momentum Star Gazing Green

GREEN STATED ODDS 1:15
*GREEN DIE CUT/25: 3X TO 8X GREEN
GREEN DIE CUT PRINT RUN 25
*BLUE: .6X TO 1.5X GREEN
BLUE STATED ODDS 1:47
*BLUE DIE CUT/50: 2X TO 5X GREEN
BLUE DIE CUT PRINT RUN 50 SER.#'d SETS
*RED: 1X TO 2.5X GREEN
RED STATED ODDS 1:95
*RED DIE CUT/75: 1.5X TO 4X GREEN
RED DIE CUT PRINT RUN 75 SER.#'d SETS
SG1 Jake Plummer .75 2.00
SG2 Tim Couch .75 2.00
SG3 Emmitt Smith 2.50 6.00
SG4 Troy Aikman 1.50 4.00
SG5 John Elway 2.50 6.00
SG6 Terrell Davis 1.00 2.50
SG7 Charlie Batch .75 2.00
SG8 Barry Sanders 2.00 5.00
SG9 Brett Favre 3.00 8.00
SG10 Peyton Manning 2.50 6.00
SG11 Edgerrin James 1.00 2.50
SG12 Mark Brunell .75 2.00
SG13 Fred Taylor 1.00 2.50
SG14 Dan Marino 3.00 8.00
SG15 Randy Moss 1.00 2.50
SG16 Drew Bledsoe 1.00 2.50
SG17 Ricky Williams 1.00 2.50
SG18 Jerry Rice 2.00 5.00
SG19 Steve Young 1.25 3.00
SG20 Kurt Warner 1.50 4.00
SG21 Eddie George .75 2.00
SG22 Jamal Anderson .75 2.00
SG23 Eric Moulds .75 2.00
SG24 Antowain Smith .75 2.00
SG25 Curtis Enis .60 1.50
SG26 Cade McNown .60 1.50
SG27 Deion Sanders 1.00 2.50
SG28 Joey Galloway .75 2.00
SG29 Olandis Gary .75 2.00
SG30 Dorsey Levens .75 2.00
SG31 Antonio Freeman .75 2.00
SG32 Marvin Harrison 1.00 2.50
SG33 Daunte Culpepper .75 2.00
SG34 Cris Carter 1.00 2.50
SG35 Robert Smith .75 2.00
SG36 Terry Glenn .75 2.00
SG37 Curtis Martin 1.00 2.50
SG38 Napoleon Kaufman .75 2.00
SG39 Tim Brown 1.00 2.50
SG40 Duce Staley .75 2.00
SG41 Donovan McNabb 1.00 2.50
SG42 Kordell Stewart .75 2.00
SG43 Jerome Bettis 1.00 2.50
SG44 Terrell Owens 1.00 2.50
SG45 Jon Kitna .75 2.00
SG46 Marshall Faulk 1.00 2.50
SG47 Torry Holt 1.00 2.50
SG48 Mike Alstott 1.00 2.50
SG49 Shaun King .60 1.50
SG50 Keyshawn Johnson .75 2.00
SG51 Steve McNair 1.00 2.50
SG52 Stephen Davis .75 2.00
SG53 Brad Johnson .75 2.00
SG54 David Boston .60 1.50
SG55 Chris Chandler .75 2.00
SG56 Qadry Ismail .75 2.00
SG57 Peerless Price .75 2.00
SG58 Rob Johnson .75 2.00
SG59 Muhsin Muhammad .75 2.00
SG60 Steve Beuerlein .75 2.00
SG61 Patrick Jeffers .75 2.00
SG62 Marcus Robinson .75 2.00
SG63 Akili Smith .60 1.50
SG64 Rocket Ismail .75 2.00
SG65 Ed McCaffrey .75 2.00
SG66 Brian Griese .75 2.00
SG67 Germane Crowell .60 1.50
SG68 James Stewart .60 1.50
SG69 Keenan McCardell .75 2.00
SG70 Jimmy Smith .75 2.00
SG71 Elvis Grbac .60 1.50
SG72 Thurman Thomas 1.00 2.50
SG73 Amani Toomer .75 2.00
SG74 Vinny Testaverde .75 2.00
SG75 Tyrone Wheatley .60 1.50
SG76 Rich Gannon .75 2.00
SG77 Troy Edwards .60 1.50
SG78 Jim Harbaugh .75 2.00
SG79 Jermaine Fazande .60 1.50
SG80 Natrone Means .75 2.00
SG81 Charlie Garner .75 2.00
SG82 Jeff Garcia .75 2.00
SG83 Ricky Watters .75 2.00
SG84 Isaac Bruce 1.00 2.50
SG85 Warren Sapp .75 2.00
SG86 Jevon Kearse .75 2.00
SG87 Bruce Smith 1.00 2.50
SG88 Michael Westbrook .60 1.50
SG89 Albert Connell .60 1.50
SG90 Jeff George .75 2.00
SG91 Peter Warrick 1.00 2.50
SG92 Jamal Lewis 1.00 2.50
SG93 Thomas Jones 1.25 3.00
SG94 Plaxico Burress 1.00 2.50
SG95 Travis Taylor .75 2.00
SG96 Ron Dayne 1.00 2.50
SG97 Chad Pennington 1.50 4.00
SG98 Shaun Alexander 1.25 3.00
SG99 Corey Dillon .75 2.00
SG100 Kevin Johnson .60 1.50

2000 Playoff Momentum Super Bowl Souvenirs

SB1-SB24 PRINT RUN 100 SER.#'d SETS
SB25-SB36 PRINT RUN 50 SER.#'d SETS
SB37-SB40 PRINT RUN 25 SER.#'d SETS
SB1 Bob Griese 12.00 30.00
SB2 Roger Staubach 25.00 60.00
SB3 Larry Csonka 12.00 30.00
SB4 Fran Tarkenton 15.00 40.00
SB5 Terry Bradshaw 30.00 80.00
SB6 Franco Harris 20.00 50.00
SB7 Terry Bradshaw 30.00 80.00
SB8 Roger Staubach 25.00 60.00
SB9 Ken Stabler 15.00 40.00
SB10 Fran Tarkenton 15.00 40.00
SB11 Franco Harris 20.00 50.00
SB12 Joe Greene 12.00 30.00
SB13 Walter Payton 50.00 125.00
SB14 Jim McMahon 15.00 40.00
SB15 John Elway 30.00 80.00
SB16 Darrell Green 10.00 25.00
SB17 Joe Montana 40.00 100.00
SB18 John Elway 30.00 80.00
SB19 Steve Young 15.00 40.00
SB20 Jerry Rice 25.00 60.00
SB21 Kurt Warner 20.00 50.00
SB22 Steve McNair 12.00 30.00
SB23 Marshall Faulk 12.00 30.00
SB24 Eddie George 10.00 25.00
SB25 Bob Griese 30.00 80.00
Roger Staubach
SB26 Larry Csonka 20.00 50.00
Fran Tarkenton
SB27 Terry Bradshaw 40.00 100.00
Franco Harris

SB28 Terry Bradshaw 40.00 100.00
Roger Staubach
SB29 Ken Stabler 20.00 50.00
Fran Tarkenton
SB30 Franco Harris 15.00 40.00
Joe Greene
SB31 Walter Payton 60.00 150.00
Jim McMahon
SB32 John Elway 40.00 100.00
Darrell Green
SB33 Joe Montana 125.00 250.00
John Elway
SB34 Steve Young 30.00 80.00
Jerry Rice
SB35 Kurt Warner 25.00 60.00
Steve McNair
SB36 Marshall Faulk 15.00 40.00
Eddie George
SB37 Roger Staubach 100.00 200.00
Fran Tarkenton
Terry Bradshaw
SB38 Kurt Warner 100.00 200.00
John Elway
Joe Montana
SB39 Ken Stabler 75.00 150.00
Bob Griese
Steve Young
SB40 Franco Harris 100.00 200.00
Walter Payton
Eddie George

2000 Playoff Momentum Super Bowl Souvenirs Signs of Greatness

STATED PRINT RUN 25 SER.#'d SETS
SB1 Bob Griese 40.00 80.00
SB2 Roger Staubach 100.00 200.00
SB3 Larry Csonka 50.00 100.00
SB4 Fran Tarkenton 60.00 120.00
SB5 Terry Bradshaw 125.00 200.00
SB6 Franco Harris 60.00 120.00
SB7 Terry Bradshaw 125.00 200.00
SB8 Roger Staubach 100.00 200.00
SB9 Ken Stabler 100.00 200.00
SB10 Fran Tarkenton 60.00 120.00
SB11 Franco Harris 60.00 120.00
SB12 Joe Greene 40.00 80.00
SB13 Walter Payton No AU 60.00 150.00
SB14 Jim McMahon 60.00 120.00
SB15 John Elway 125.00 250.00
SB17 Joe Montana 200.00 325.00
SB18 John Elway 125.00 250.00
SB19 Steve Young 75.00 150.00
SB20 Jerry Rice 125.00 200.00
SB21 Kurt Warner 75.00 150.00
SB22 Steve McNair 40.00 80.00
SB23 Marshall Faulk 40.00 80.00
SB24 Eddie George 30.00 60.00

2006 Playoff National Treasures

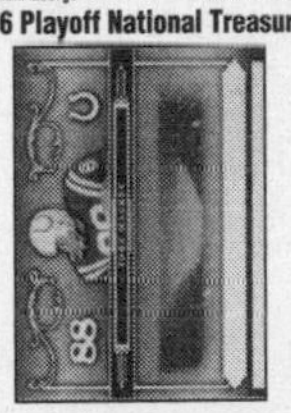

This 200-card set was released in January, 2007. The set was issued into the hobby in seven-card packs (boxes) with a $500 SRP. Cards numbered 1-100 feature a mix of active and retired NFL greats while cards numbered 101-200 feature 2006 rookies. Cards numbered 1-100 were issued to a stated print run of 125 serial numbered sets. The rookies have the following subsets: 101-146 have both player-worn swatches as well as an autograph and those cards were issued to a stated print run of 99 serial numbered sets, cards 147-188 were signed by the player and had a stated print run of 200 serial numbered sets and cards numbered 189-200 were signed by the player and also had a stated print run of 99 serial numbered sets. Some players did not return their signatures in time for pack out and those cards could be redeemed until August 1, 2008.

1-100 PRINT RUN 125 SER.#'d SETS
101-146 JSY AU PRINT RUN 99
147-188 AU RC PRINT RUN 200
189-200 AU RC PRINT RUN 99
UNPRICED PLATINUM PRINT RUN 1
1 Barry Sanders 8.00 20.00
2 Bo Jackson 6.00 15.00
3 Cadillac Williams 4.00 10.00
4 Cedric Benson 4.00 10.00
5 Charley Taylor 4.00 10.00
6 Clinton Portis 5.00 12.00
7 Curtis Martin 5.00 12.00
8 Dutch Clark 4.00 10.00
9 Earl Campbell 5.00 12.00
10 Edgerrin James 4.00 10.00
11 Ernie Nevers 4.00 10.00
12 Frank Gifford 4.00 10.00
13 Jim Thorpe 12.00 30.00
14 Hugh McElhenny 4.00 10.00
15 Jim Brown 6.00 15.00
16 Jim Taylor 5.00 12.00
17 John Henry Johnson 4.00 10.00
18 John Riggins 5.00 12.00
19 Julius Jones 3.00 8.00
20 Kevin Jones 3.00 8.00
21 LaDainian Tomlinson 5.00 12.00
22 Larry Johnson 4.00 10.00
23 Lenny Moore 4.00 10.00
24 Leroy Kelly 4.00 10.00
25 Ollie Matson 4.00 10.00
26 Paul Hornung 5.00 12.00
27 Red Grange 6.00 15.00
28 Ronnie Brown 5.00 12.00
29 Shaun Alexander 4.00 10.00
30 Steve Van Buren 4.00 10.00
31 Steven Jackson 5.00 12.00
32 Terrell Davis 5.00 12.00
33 Tiki Barber 5.00 12.00
34 Tony Dorsett 5.00 12.00
35 Willie Parker 4.00 10.00
36 Willis McGahee 4.00 10.00
37 Deion Sanders 6.00 15.00
38 Lawrence Taylor 5.00 12.00
39 Anquan Boldin 4.00 10.00
40 Bobby Mitchell 4.00 10.00
41 Braylon Edwards 4.00 10.00
42 Chad Johnson 4.00 10.00
43 Charlie Joiner 4.00 10.00
44 Cliff Branch 4.00 10.00
45 Dante Lavelli 4.00 10.00
46 Don Maynard 4.00 10.00
47 Hines Ward 5.00 12.00
48 James Lofton 4.00 10.00
49 Jerry Rice 8.00 20.00
50 Jimmy Johnson 3.00 8.00
51 Lance Alworth 4.00 10.00
52 Larry Fitzgerald 5.00 12.00
53 Marvin Harrison 5.00 12.00
54 Matt Jones 3.00 8.00
55 Paul Warfield 4.00 10.00
56 Randy Moss 5.00 12.00
57 Raymond Berry 4.00 10.00
58 Roy Williams WR 4.00 10.00
59 Steve Largent 5.00 12.00
60 Steve Smith 5.00 12.00
61 Terrell Owens 5.00 12.00
62 Tommy McDonald 3.00 8.00
63 Torry Holt 4.00 10.00
64 Antonio Gates 5.00 12.00
65 Dave Casper 3.00 8.00
66 John Mackey 4.00 10.00
67 Ozzie Newsome 4.00 10.00
68 Aaron Rodgers 10.00 25.00
69 Alex Smith QB 5.00 12.00
70 Ben Roethlisberger 6.00 15.00
71 Bill Dudley 4.00 10.00
72 Bob Griese 5.00 12.00
73 Brett Favre 10.00 25.00
74 Carson Palmer 5.00 12.00
75 Charley Trippi 3.00 8.00
76 Johnny Unitas 8.00 20.00
77 Dan Marino 10.00 25.00
78 Daunte Culpepper 4.00 10.00
79 Don Meredith 5.00 12.00
80 Donovan McNabb 5.00 12.00
81 Drew Bledsoe 5.00 12.00
82 Eli Manning 6.00 15.00
83 Fran Tarkenton 6.00 15.00
84 George Blanda 4.00 10.00
85 Jim Kelly 6.00 15.00
86 Joe Montana 10.00 25.00
87 Len Dawson 5.00 12.00
88 Michael Vick 5.00 12.00
89 Otto Graham 5.00 12.00
90 Peyton Manning 8.00 20.00
91 Philip Rivers 5.00 12.00
92 Roger Staubach 8.00 20.00
93 Sonny Jurgensen 4.00 10.00
94 Steve McNair 4.00 10.00
95 Steve Young 6.00 15.00
96 Terry Bradshaw 8.00 20.00
97 Tom Brady 8.00 20.00
98 Troy Aikman 6.00 15.00
99 Warren Moon 5.00 12.00
100 Y.A. Tittle 5.00 12.00
101 Anthony Fasano JSY AU RC 15.00 40.00
102 Bobby Carpenter JSY AU RC 10.00 25.00
103 D'Brickashaw Ferguson JSY AU RC 15.00 40.00
104 Jay Cutler JSY AU RC 40.00 100.00
105 Joe Klopfenstein JSY AU RC 10.00 25.00
106 John David Washington JSY AU RC 12.00 30.00
107 Joseph Addai JSY AU RC 15.00 40.00
108 Laurence Maroney JSY AU RC 12.00 30.00
109 Mario Williams JSY AU RC 15.00 40.00
110 Mathias Kiwanuka JSY AU RC 15.00 40.00
111 Matt Leinart JSY AU RC 15.00 40.00
112 Santonio Holmes JSY AU RC 20.00 50.00
113 Sinorice Moss JSY AU RC 15.00 40.00
114 Tye Hill JSY AU RC 10.00 25.00
115 Vince Young JSY AU RC 20.00 50.00
116 Brandon Marshall JSY AU RC 15.00 40.00
117 Brandon Williams JSY AU RC 10.00 25.00
118 Brian Calhoun JSY AU RC 10.00 25.00
119 Omar Jacobs JSY AU RC 10.00 25.00
120 A.J. Hawk JSY AU RC 15.00 40.00
121 Chad Jackson JSY AU RC 10.00 25.00
122 DeAngelo Williams JSY AU RC 20.00 50.00
123 Demetrius Williams JSY AU RC 12.00 30.00
124 Derek Hagan JSY AU RC 12.00 30.00
125 Jason Avant JSY AU RC 10.00 25.00
126 Jerious Norwood JSY AU RC 12.00 30.00
127 Kellen Clemens JSY AU RC 12.00 30.00
128 LenDale White JSY AU RC 12.00 30.00
129 Leon Washington JSY AU RC 12.00 30.00
130 Marcedes Lewis JSY AU RC 15.00 40.00
131 Maurice Drew JSY AU RC 30.00 60.00
132 Maurice Stovall JSY AU RC 10.00 25.00
133 Michael Huff JSY AU RC 12.00 30.00
134 Michael Robinson JSY AU RC 12.00 30.00
135 Tarvaris Jackson JSY AU RC 20.00 40.00
136 Travis Wilson JSY AU RC 10.00 25.00
137 Vernon Davis JSY AU RC 30.00 60.00
138 Charlie Whitehurst JSY AU RC 15.00 40.00
139 Brad Smith JSY AU RC 15.00 40.00
140 Bruce Gradkowski JSY AU RC 15.00 40.00
141 Hank Baskett JSY AU RC 15.00 40.00
142 Mike Bell JSY AU RC 15.00 40.00
143 Reggie Bush JSY AU RC 30.00 80.00
144 Devin Hester JSY AU RC 50.00 100.00
145 Jerome Harrison JSY AU RC 15.00 40.00
146 Brodie Croyle JSY AU RC 15.00 40.00
147 Greg Jennings AU RC 20.00 50.00
148 Marques Colston AU RC 30.00 80.00
149 Sam Hurd AU RC 5.00 12.00
150 Wali Lundy AU RC 6.00 15.00
151 Skyler Green AU RC 5.00 12.00
152 Ingle Martin AU RC 6.00 15.00
153 Adam Jennings AU RC 6.00 15.00
154 Antonio Cromartie AU RC 8.00 20.00
155 Brodrick Bunkley AU RC 6.00 15.00
156 Cedric Humes AU RC 5.00 12.00
157 Chad Greenway AU RC 8.00 20.00
158 Marcus Vick AU RC 5.00 12.00
159 David Thomas AU RC 6.00 15.00
160 Delanie Walker AU RC 8.00 20.00
161 Derrick Ross AU RC 6.00 15.00
162 Domenik Hixon AU RC 8.00 20.00
163 Ethan Kilmer AU RC 6.00 15.00
164 Haloti Ngata AU RC 8.00 20.00
165 Jason Allen AU RC 6.00 15.00
166 Jeff Webb AU RC 6.00 15.00
167 Jeremy Bloom AU RC 6.00 15.00
168 John McCargo AU RC 5.00 12.00
169 Johnathan Joseph AU RC 6.00 15.00
170 Jonathan Orr AU RC 6.00 15.00
171 Kelly Jennings AU RC 6.00 15.00
172 Leonard Pope AU RC 8.00 20.00
173 Manny Lawson AU RC 6.00 15.00
174 Mike Hass AU RC 6.00 15.00
175 Miles Austin AU RC 40.00 80.00
176 P.J. Daniels AU RC 5.00 12.00
177 Patrick Cobbs AU RC 6.00 15.00
178 Quinton Ganther AU RC 5.00 12.00
179 Tamba Hali AU RC 8.00 20.00
180 Tony Scheffler AU RC 8.00 20.00
181 Will Blackmon AU RC 6.00 15.00
182 D.J. Shockley AU RC 6.00 15.00
183 Dominique Byrd AU RC 6.00 15.00
184 Donte Whitner AU RC 8.00 20.00
185 Ernie Sims AU RC 6.00 15.00
186 Kamerion Wimbley AU RC 8.00 20.00
187 Marques Hagans AU RC 5.00 12.00
188 Willie Reid AU RC 6.00 15.00
189 Reggie McNeal AU/99 RC 10.00 25.00
190 Drew Olson AU/99 RC 8.00 20.00
191 Owen Daniels AU/99 RC 12.00 30.00
192 Garrett Mills AU/99 RC 12.00 30.00
193 D'Qwell Jackson AU/99 RC 10.00 25.00
194 DeMeco Ryans AU/99 RC 12.00 30.00
195 Rocky McIntosh AU/99 RC 10.00 25.00
196 Thomas Howard AU/99 RC 10.00 25.00
197 Roman Harper AU/99 RC 10.00 25.00
198 Abdul Hodge AU/99 RC 8.00 20.00
199 Richard Marshall AU/99 RC 8.00 20.00
200 Dawan Landry AU/99 RC 12.00 30.00

2006 Playoff National Treasures Gold

*VETS/25: .8X TO 2X BASIC CARDS
VETERANS PRINT RUN 25 SER.#'d SETS
*ROOKIE JSY AU/30: .5X TO 1.2X
*ROOKIE AU/52: .6X TO 1.5X BASIC CARDS
*ROOKIE AU/25: .5X TO 1.2X BASIC CARDS
ROOKIES PRINT RUN 25-52 SER.#'d SETS
175 Miles Austin AU/52 75.00 150.00

2006 Playoff National Treasures Rookie Signature Gold

*SIG GOLD/15: .4X TO 1X BASE JSY AU RCs

2006 Playoff National Treasures Rookie Signature Silver

*SIG SILVER: .25X TO .6X BASE JSY AU RCs
STATED PRINT RUN 30 SER.#'d SETS
UNPRICED GOLD PRINT RUN 5-15
UNPRICED PLATINUM PRINT RUN 1
101 Anthony Fasano 10.00 25.00
102 Bobby Carpenter 6.00 15.00
103 D'Brickashaw Ferguson 10.00 25.00
104 Jay Cutler 20.00 50.00
105 Joe Klopfenstein 6.00 15.00
106 John David Washington 8.00 20.00
107 Joseph Addai 10.00 25.00
108 Laurence Maroney 8.00 20.00
109 Mario Williams 10.00 25.00
110 Mathias Kiwanuka 10.00 25.00
111 Matt Leinart 10.00 25.00
112 Santonio Holmes 12.00 30.00
113 Sinorice Moss 10.00 25.00
114 Tye Hill 6.00 15.00
115 Vince Young 12.00 30.00
116 Brandon Marshall 10.00 25.00
117 Brandon Williams 6.00 15.00
118 Omar Jacobs 6.00 15.00
120 A.J. Hawk 10.00 25.00
121 Chad Jackson 6.00 15.00
122 DeAngelo Williams 12.00 30.00
123 Demetrius Williams 8.00 20.00
124 Derek Hagan 8.00 20.00
125 Jason Avant 6.00 15.00
126 Jerious Norwood 8.00 20.00
127 Kellen Clemens 8.00 20.00
128 LenDale White 8.00 20.00
129 Leon Washington 8.00 20.00
130 Marcedes Lewis 10.00 25.00
131 Maurice Drew 15.00 40.00
132 Maurice Stovall 6.00 15.00
133 Michael Huff 8.00 20.00
134 Michael Robinson 8.00 20.00
135 Tarvaris Jackson 10.00 25.00
136 Travis Wilson 6.00 15.00
137 Vernon Davis 12.00 30.00
138 Charlie Whitehurst 10.00 25.00
139 Brad Smith 10.00 25.00
140 Bruce Gradkowski 10.00 25.00
141 Hank Baskett 10.00 25.00
142 Mike Bell 10.00 25.00
143 Reggie Bush 20.00 50.00
144 Devin Hester 25.00 60.00
145 Jerome Harrison 10.00 25.00
146 Brodie Croyle 10.00 25.00

2006 Playoff National Treasures Rookie Signature Material Gold

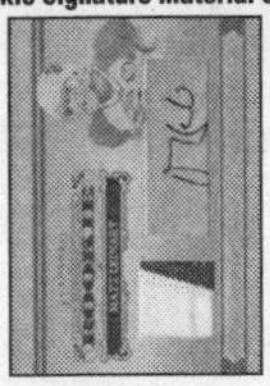

*GOLD/25: .6X TO 1.5X BASE JSY AU RCs
GOLD PRINT RUN 25 SER.#'d SETS

2006 Playoff National Treasures Rookie Signature Material Silver

*SILVER/49: .5X TO 1.2X BASE JSY AU RCs
SILVER PRINT RUN 49 SER.#'d SETS
UNPRICED PLATINUM PRINT RUN 1
101 Anthony Fasano 20.00 50.00
102 Bobby Carpenter 12.00 30.00
103 D'Brickashaw Ferguson 20.00 50.00
104 Jay Cutler 40.00 100.00
105 Joe Klopfenstein 12.00 30.00
106 John David Washington 15.00 40.00
107 Joseph Addai 20.00 50.00
108 Laurence Maroney 15.00 40.00
109 Mario Williams 20.00 50.00
110 Mathias Kiwanuka 20.00 50.00
111 Matt Leinart 20.00 50.00
112 Santonio Holmes 25.00 60.00
113 Sinorice Moss 20.00 50.00
114 Tye Hill 12.00 30.00
115 Vince Young 25.00 60.00
116 Brandon Marshall 20.00 50.00
117 Brandon Williams 12.00 30.00
118 Brian Calhoun 12.00 30.00
119 Omar Jacobs 12.00 30.00
120 A.J. Hawk 20.00 50.00
121 Chad Jackson 12.00 30.00
122 DeAngelo Williams 25.00 60.00
123 Demetrius Williams 15.00 40.00
124 Derek Hagan 15.00 40.00
125 Jason Avant 12.00 30.00
126 Jerious Norwood 15.00 40.00
127 Kellen Clemens 15.00 40.00
128 LenDale White 15.00 40.00
129 Leon Washington 15.00 40.00
130 Marcedes Lewis 20.00 50.00
131 Maurice Drew 30.00 80.00
132 Maurice Stovall 12.00 30.00
133 Michael Huff 15.00 40.00
134 Michael Robinson 15.00 40.00
135 Tarvaris Jackson 20.00 50.00
136 Travis Wilson 12.00 30.00
137 Vernon Davis 40.00 80.00
138 Charlie Whitehurst 20.00 50.00
139 Brad Smith 20.00 50.00
140 Bruce Gradkowski 20.00 50.00
141 Hank Baskett 20.00 50.00
142 Mike Bell 20.00 50.00
143 Reggie Bush 40.00 100.00
144 Devin Hester 50.00 120.00
145 Jerome Harrison 20.00 50.00
146 Brodie Croyle 20.00 50.00

2006 Playoff National Treasures 50th Anniversary Team Materials

STATED PRINT RUN 49 SER.#'d SETS
*PRIME/25: .5X TO 1.2X BASIC INSERTS
PRIME PRINT RUN 25 SER.#'d SETS
GS Gale Sayers 15.00 40.00
JB Jim Brown 15.00 40.00
JT Jim Thorpe/25 150.00 250.00
RN Ray Nitschke 12.00 30.00

2006 Playoff National Treasures 50th Anniversary Team Materials Signature

UNPRICED SIGNATURE PRINT RUN 15
*PRIME/25: .6X TO 1.2X BASIC INSERTS
PRIME PRINT RUN 20-25
GS Gale Sayers 40.00 80.00
JB Jim Brown 60.00 120.00

2006 Playoff National Treasures 50th Anniversary Team Signature

STATED PRINT RUN 10-25 SER.#'d SETS
JM John Mackey/25 25.00 50.00

2006 Playoff National Treasures 75th Anniversary Team Materials

STATED PRINT RUN 49 SER.#'d SETS
*PRIME/25: .5X TO 1.2X BASIC INSERTS
PRIME PRINT RUN 3-25
GS Gale Sayers 15.00 40.00
JB Jim Brown 15.00 40.00
JM Joe Montana 25.00 60.00
JR Jerry Rice 20.00 50.00
JU Johnny Unitas 20.00 50.00
OG Otto Graham 25.00 50.00
RB Raymond Berry 10.00 25.00
WP Walter Payton 25.00 60.00

2006 Playoff National Treasures 75th Anniversary Team Materials Signature

STATED PRINT RUN 5-25
UNPRICED PRIME PRINT RUN 1-16
JB Jim Brown/25 60.00 120.00

2006 Playoff National Treasures 75th Anniversary Team Signature

STATED PRINT RUN 1-25
JB Jim Brown/25 50.00 100.00
SB Sammy Baugh/22

2006 Playoff National Treasures Canton Classics Materials

STATED PRINT RUN 1-99
*PRIME/25: .6X TO 1.5X BASIC INSERTS
PRIME PRINT RUN 1-25
*JUMBO JERSEY/25: .6X TO 1.5X
JUMBO JERSEY PRINT RUN 1-25
*JUMBO JSY PRIME/25: .8X TO 2X
JUMBO JERSEY PRIME PRINT RUN 1-25
SERIAL #'d UNDER 25 NOT PRICED
BG Bob Griese 10.00 25.00
CJ Charlie Joiner 8.00 20.00
CT Charley Taylor 8.00 20.00
DJ Deacon Jones 8.00 20.00
DM Dan Marino 20.00 50.00
EC Earl Campbell 10.00 25.00
FG Forrest Gregg 6.00 15.00
FT Fran Tarkenton 12.00 30.00
GB George Blanda 8.00 20.00
GS Gale Sayers 12.00 30.00
HM Hugh McElhenny 8.00 20.00
JB Jim Brown/32 15.00 40.00
JE John Elway 15.00 40.00
JG Joe Greene 10.00 25.00
JK Jim Kelly 12.00 30.00
JM Joe Montana 20.00 50.00
JO Jim Otto 6.00 15.00
JR John Riggins 10.00 25.00
JU Johnny Unitas/50 20.00 50.00
JY Jack Youngblood 8.00 20.00
LB Lem Barney 8.00 20.00
LD Len Dawson 10.00 25.00
LK Leroy Kelly/50 10.00 25.00
LM Lenny Moore 8.00 20.00
LS Lee Roy Selmon 8.00 20.00
LT Lawrence Taylor 10.00 25.00
OG Otto Graham 15.00 40.00
ON Ozzie Newsome 8.00 20.00
PH Paul Hornung 10.00 25.00
PK Paul Krause 6.00 15.00
RB Raymond Berry 8.00 20.00
RS Roger Staubach 15.00 40.00
SJ Sonny Jurgensen/50 10.00 25.00
SL Steve Largent 10.00 25.00
SY Steve Young 12.00 30.00
TA Troy Aikman 12.00 30.00
TB Terry Bradshaw/90 15.00 40.00
TD Tony Dorsett 10.00 25.00
TH Ted Hendricks 8.00 20.00
WB Willie Brown 8.00 20.00
WM Warren Moon 10.00 25.00
WP Walter Payton 20.00 50.00
YT Y.A. Tittle 10.00 25.00
BSA Barry Sanders 15.00 40.00
BST Bart Starr 15.00 40.00
DCA Dave Casper 6.00 15.00
DOM Don Maynard 8.00 20.00
JLA Jack Lambert 10.00 25.00
JLO James Lofton/22

2006 Playoff National Treasures Canton Classics Materials Signature

STATED PRINT RUN 25 SER.#'d SETS
*PRIME/15-25: .6X TO 1.2X BASIC INSERTS
PRIME PRINT RUN 1-25
CJ Charlie Joiner 15.00 40.00
CT Charley Taylor 15.00 40.00
DC Dave Casper 15.00 40.00
DJ Deacon Jones 15.00 40.00
DM Dan Marino 125.00 250.00
DOM Don Maynard 15.00 40.00
GB George Blanda 40.00 80.00
GS Gale Sayers 40.00 80.00
HM Hugh McElhenny 15.00 40.00
JB Jim Brown 60.00 120.00
JE John Elway 75.00 150.00
JG Joe Greene 40.00 80.00
JLA Jack Lambert/20
JLO James Lofton 20.00 50.00
JM Joe Montana 100.00 200.00
JR John Riggins 20.00 50.00
JY Jack Youngblood 20.00 50.00
LB Lem Barney 15.00 40.00
LD Len Dawson 30.00 60.00
LK Leroy Kelly 15.00 40.00
LM Lenny Moore 20.00 50.00
LT Lawrence Taylor 40.00 80.00
ON Ozzie Newsome 20.00 50.00
PH Paul Hornung 40.00 100.00
PK Paul Krause 15.00 40.00
PW Paul Warfield/15
RB Raymond Berry 20.00 50.00
RS Roger Staubach 50.00 120.00
SJ Sonny Jurgensen 40.00 80.00
SL Steve Largent 40.00 80.00
SY Steve Young 75.00 150.00
TB Terry Bradshaw 60.00 120.00
TD Tony Dorsett 30.00 60.00
TH Ted Hendricks 30.00 60.00
WB Willie Brown 15.00 40.00
WM Warren Moon 20.00 50.00
YT Y.A. Tittle 20.00 50.00

2006 Playoff National Treasures Canton Classics Materials Signature Jersey Number

STATED PRINT RUN 1-87
CT Charley Taylor/42 15.00 40.00
DC Dave Casper/87 20.00 50.00
DJ Deacon Jones/75 12.00 30.00
HM Hugh McElhenny/39 20.00 50.00
JB Jim Brown/32 50.00 120.00
JG Joe Greene/75 30.00 60.00
JL James Lofton/80 20.00 50.00
JR John Riggins/44 20.00 50.00
JY Jack Youngblood/85 15.00 40.00
LB Lem Barney/20 15.00 40.00
LM Lenny Moore/24 20.00 50.00
LT Lawrence Taylor/56 30.00 60.00
ON Ozzie Newsome/82 15.00 40.00
PK Paul Krause/22
RB Raymond Berry/82 15.00 40.00
SL Steve Largent/80 30.00 60.00
TD Tony Dorsett/33 30.00 60.00
TH Ted Hendricks/83 20.00 50.00
WB Willie Brown/24 15.00 40.00
YL Yale Lary/28 20.00 40.00

2006 Playoff National Treasures Canton Classics Materials Signature Jersey Number Prime

*PRIME/24-85: .6X TO 1.2X BASIC INSERTS
PRIME PRINT RUN 1-85 SER.#'d SETS
EC Earl Campbell/34 40.00 80.00
GS Gale Sayers/40 50.00 100.00
JL Jack Lambert/58 50.00 100.00
LK Leroy Kelly/44 20.00 40.00

2006 Playoff National Treasures Canton Classics Materials Signature Position

POSITION PRINT RUN 5-25
*PRIME/25: .75X TO 1.5X MATERIAL SIG
POSITION PRIME PRINT RUN 1-25
CJ Charlie Joiner 25.00 50.00
CT Charley Taylor 25.00 50.00
DC Dave Casper 25.00 50.00
DJ Deacon Jones 25.00 50.00
DM Dan Marino 125.00 250.00
FT Fran Tarkenton 30.00 60.00
GB George Blanda 40.00 80.00
GS Gale Sayers 50.00 100.00
HM Hugh McElhenny 25.00 50.00
JB Jim Brown 75.00 150.00
JE John Elway 100.00 200.00
JG Joe Greene 50.00 100.00
JM Joe Montana 100.00 200.00
JR John Riggins 30.00 60.00
JY Jack Youngblood 30.00 60.00
LB Lem Barney 25.00 50.00
LD Len Dawson 40.00 80.00
LK Leroy Kelly 25.00 50.00
LM Lenny Moore 30.00 60.00
LT Lawrence Taylor 50.00 100.00
ON Ozzie Newsome 30.00 60.00
PH Paul Hornung 60.00 120.00
PK Paul Krause 25.00 50.00
RB Raymond Berry 30.00 60.00
RS Roger Staubach 60.00 120.00
SJ Sonny Jurgensen 50.00 100.00
SL Steve Largent 50.00 100.00
SY Steve Young 75.00 150.00
TB Terry Bradshaw 75.00 150.00
TD Tony Dorsett 40.00 80.00
TH Ted Hendricks 40.00 80.00
WB Willie Brown 25.00 50.00
WM Warren Moon 30.00 60.00
YL Yale Lary 20.00 40.00
YT Y.A. Tittle 30.00 60.00
BSA Barry Sanders 75.00 150.00
DME Don Meredith/24 60.00 120.00
DOM Don Maynard 25.00 50.00
FGI Frank Gifford 25.00 50.00
FGR Forrest Gregg 30.00 60.00
JLO James Lofton 30.00 60.00

2006 Playoff National Treasures Canton Classics Signature

STATED PRINT RUN 1-99
BD Bill Dudley/50 25.00 60.00
DC Dave Casper/25 15.00 40.00
HM Hugh McElhenny/99 15.00 40.00
JB Jim Brown/32 50.00 100.00
JG Joe Greene/89 25.00 50.00
JJ Jimmy Johnson/99 12.00 30.00
JL James Lofton/80 10.00 25.00
JO Jim Otto/77 12.00 30.00
JP Joe Perry/99 20.00 40.00
JR John Riggins/99 15.00 40.00
JT Jim Taylor/50 25.00 60.00
JY Jack Youngblood/70 12.00 30.00
LB Lem Barney/96 10.00 25.00
LK Leroy Kelly/44 12.00 30.00
LM Lenny Moore/24 20.00 40.00
PH Paul Hornung/86 25.00 60.00
PK Paul Krause/39 12.00 30.00
TH Ted Hendricks/54 20.00 50.00
TM Tommy McDonald/99 12.00 30.00
WB Willie Brown/99 12.00 30.00
WM Warren Moon/99 15.00 40.00
YL Yale Lary/99 12.00 30.00
CTT Charley Trippi/65 15.00 40.00
DME Don Meredith/99 50.00 80.00
DOM Don Maynard/99 10.00 25.00
JHJ John Henry Johnson/99 No AU 10.00 25.00
JMA John Mackey/99 15.00 40.00
JMO Joe Montana/16 75.00 150.00

2006 Playoff National Treasures Canton Classics Signature Cuts

STATED PRINT RUN 1-99
RBR Roosevelt Brown/99 25.00 50.00

2006 Playoff National Treasures Charter Class Signature Cuts

STATED PRINT RUN 1-102
BB Bert Bell/35 300.00 450.00
BN Bronko Nagurski/102 250.00 400.00
SB Sammy Baugh/100 125.00 250.00

2006 Playoff National Treasures Charter Class Materials

STATED PRINT RUN 10-50
UNPRICED CUT AUTO PRINT RUN 1-4
JT Jim Thorpe/50 90.00 150.00

2006 Playoff National Treasures Face Masks

STATED PRINT RUN 25 SER.#'d SETS
1 Barry Sanders 20.00 50.00
6 Clinton Portis 12.00 30.00
7 Curtis Martin 12.00 30.00
9 Earl Campbell 12.00 30.00
21 LaDainian Tomlinson 12.00 30.00
29 Shaun Alexander 12.00 30.00
32 Terrell Davis 12.00 30.00
34 Tony Dorsett 12.00 30.00
36 Willis McGahee 12.00 30.00
38 Lawrence Taylor 12.00 30.00
47 Hines Ward 12.00 30.00
49 Jerry Rice 20.00 50.00
53 Marvin Harrison 12.00 30.00
56 Randy Moss 12.00 30.00
60 Steve Smith 12.00 30.00
63 Torry Holt 10.00 25.00
73 Brett Favre 25.00 60.00
74 Carson Palmer 12.00 30.00
77 Dan Marino 25.00 60.00
80 Donovan McNabb 12.00 30.00
82 Eli Manning 15.00 40.00
85 Jim Kelly 15.00 40.00
86 Joe Montana 25.00 60.00
87 Len Dawson 12.00 30.00
88 Michael Vick 12.00 30.00
90 Peyton Manning 20.00 50.00
92 Roger Staubach 20.00 50.00
95 Steve Young 15.00 40.00
97 Tom Brady 20.00 50.00
98 Troy Aikman 15.00 40.00

2006 Playoff National Treasures Face Masks Signature

STATED PRINT RUN 5-25
9 Earl Campbell/25 30.00 60.00
32 Terrell Davis/25 25.00 50.00

2006 Playoff National Treasures Helmets

*HELMET/25: .4X TO 1X FACE MASK
HELMET PRINT RUN 1-25
7 Curtis Martin/25 12.00 30.00
32 Terrell Davis/25 12.00 30.00
53 Marvin Harrison/25 12.00 30.00
85 Jim Kelly/25 15.00 40.00
87 Len Dawson/25 12.00 30.00
88 Michael Vick/25 12.00 30.00

2006 Playoff National Treasures Helmets Signature

STATED PRINT RUN 1-25
32 Terrell Davis/25 30.00 60.00

2006 Playoff National Treasures Historical Cuts

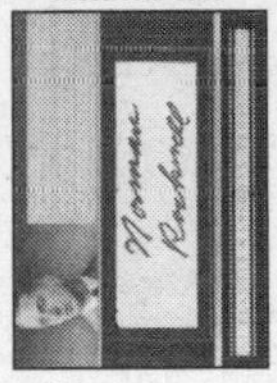

STATED PRINT RUN 1-60
SERIAL #'d UNDER 25 NOT PRICED
DW1 DeAngelo Williams/50 15.00 40.00
DW2 DeAngelo Williams/55 15.00 40.00
LM1 Laurence Maroney/60 10.00 25.00
LM2 Laurence Maroney/60 10.00 25.00
RB1 Reggie Bush/50 40.00 80.00
RB2 Reggie Bush/54 40.00 80.00

2006 Playoff National Treasures HOF Greatness Material Jumbo Jersey

*JUMBO/25: .5X TO 1.2X TRIPLE MATERIAL
STATED PRINT RUN 25 SER.#'d SETS
UNPRICED PRIME PRINT RUN 10
BS Barry Sanders 30.00 80.00
JK Jim Kelly 25.00 60.00
SL Steve Largent 20.00 50.00

2006 Playoff National Treasures HOF Greatness Material Triple

STATED PRINT RUN 49 SER.#'d SETS
*PRIME/25: .5X TO 1.2X BASIC INSERTS
PRIME PRINT RUN 1-25
*FIVE MATER/40: .5X TO 1.2X BASIC INSERTS
*FIVE MAT PRIME/25: .6X TO 1.5X
UNPRICED SIX MATERIAL PRINT RUN 1-5
*QUAD MAT/25-49: .5X TO 1.2X
*QUAD MAT.PRIME/25: .6X TO 1.5X
DM Dan Marino 30.00 80.00
EC Earl Campbell 15.00 40.00
ED Eric Dickerson 12.00 30.00
JE John Elway/24 25.00 60.00
JM Joe Montana 30.00 80.00
MA Marcus Allen 15.00 40.00
RL Ronnie Lott 12.00 30.00
RS Roger Staubach 25.00 60.00
SY Steve Young 20.00 50.00
TB Terry Bradshaw 25.00 60.00
TD Tony Dorsett 15.00 40.00

2006 Playoff National Treasures HOF Greatness Material Signature Quad

STATED PRINT RUN 7-49
*PRIME/25: .6X TO 1.2X BASIC INSERTS
PRIME PRINT RUN 1-25
SL Steve Largent/49 50.00 100.00

2006 Playoff National Treasures HOF Greatness Material Signature Triple

STATED PRINT RUN 2-49
*PRIME/25: .6X TO 1.2X BASIC INSERTS
PRIME PRINT RUN 1-25
EC Earl Campbell/49 40.00 80.00
JM Joe Montana/49 100.00 200.00
MA Marcus Allen/49 40.00 80.00
RL Ronnie Lott/49 40.00 80.00
RS Roger Staubach/30 75.00 150.00
SL Steve Largent/49 40.00 80.00
SY Steve Young/49 75.00 150.00
TB Terry Bradshaw/49 75.00 150.00

2006 Playoff National Treasures Material Jersey Numbers

STATED PRINT RUN 1-89
*PRIME/24-89: .5X TO 1.2X BASIC INSERTS
PRIME PRINT RUN 1-89 SER.#'d SETS
2 Bo Jackson/34 15.00 40.00
3 Cadillac Williams/24
4 Cedric Benson/32 12.00 30.00
5 Charley Taylor/42 10.00 25.00
6 Clinton Portis/26 12.00 30.00
7 Curtis Martin/28 12.00 30.00
9 Earl Campbell/34 12.00 30.00
14 Hugh McElhenny/39 10.00 25.00
15 Jim Brown/32 15.00 40.00
18 John Riggins/44 12.00 30.00
19 Julius Jones/21
20 Kevin Jones/34 12.00 30.00
21 LaDainian Tomlinson/21
22 Larry Johnson/27 12.00 30.00
23 Lenny Moore/24
24 Leroy Kelly/44 10.00 25.00
28 Ronnie Brown/23
29 Shaun Alexander/37 12.00 30.00
31 Steven Jackson/39 12.00 30.00
32 Terrell Davis/30 12.00 30.00
33 Tiki Barber/21
34 Tony Dorsett/33 12.00 30.00
35 Willie Parker/39 10.00 25.00
36 Willis McGahee/21
37 Deion Sanders/21
38 Lawrence Taylor/56 10.00 25.00
39 Anquan Boldin/81 6.00 15.00
42 Chad Johnson/85 6.00 15.00
44 Cliff Branch/21
49 Jerry Rice/80 15.00 40.00
53 Marvin Harrison/88 10.00 25.00
55 Paul Warfield/42 10.00 25.00
57 Raymond Berry/82 8.00 20.00
59 Steve Largent/80 10.00 25.00
60 Steve Smith/89 10.00 25.00
63 Torry Holt/81 6.00 15.00
64 Antonio Gates/85 10.00 25.00
65 Dave Casper/87 6.00 15.00
67 Ozzie Newsome/82 8.00 20.00

2006 Playoff National Treasures Material Prime

STATED PRINT RUN 25 SER.#'d SETS
UNPRICED BRAND LOGO PRINT RUN 1-10
UNPRICED BUTTON PRINT RUN 4
UNPRICED LAUNDRY TAG PRINT RUN 1-10
UNPRICED NFL LOGO PRINT RUN 1
1 Barry Sanders 25.00 60.00
2 Bo Jackson 20.00 50.00
3 Cadillac Williams 12.00 30.00
5 Charley Taylor 12.00 30.00
6 Clinton Portis 15.00 40.00
7 Curtis Martin 15.00 40.00
9 Earl Campbell 15.00 40.00
15 Jim Brown 20.00 50.00
18 John Riggins 15.00 40.00
19 Julius Jones 15.00 40.00
20 Kevin Jones 15.00 40.00
21 LaDainian Tomlinson 15.00 40.00
22 Larry Johnson 15.00 40.00
23 Lenny Moore 12.00 30.00
28 Ronnie Brown 15.00 40.00
29 Shaun Alexander 15.00 40.00
31 Steven Jackson 15.00 40.00
32 Terrell Davis 15.00 40.00
33 Tiki Barber 15.00 40.00
34 Tony Dorsett 15.00 40.00
35 Willie Parker 12.00 30.00
36 Willis McGahee 15.00 40.00
37 Deion Sanders 20.00 50.00
38 Lawrence Taylor 15.00 40.00
41 Braylon Edwards/24 15.00 40.00
42 Chad Johnson 12.00 30.00
43 Charlie Joiner 12.00 30.00
47 Hines Ward 15.00 40.00
49 Jerry Rice 25.00 60.00
52 Larry Fitzgerald 15.00 40.00
53 Marvin Harrison 15.00 40.00
54 Matt Jones 15.00 40.00
56 Randy Moss 15.00 40.00
58 Roy Williams WR 15.00 40.00
59 Steve Largent 15.00 40.00
60 Steve Smith 15.00 40.00
63 Torry Holt 12.00 30.00
64 Antonio Gates 15.00 40.00
68 Aaron Rodgers 30.00 80.00
69 Alex Smith QB 15.00 40.00
70 Ben Roethlisberger 25.00 60.00
72 Bob Griese 15.00 40.00
73 Brett Favre 30.00 80.00
74 Carson Palmer 15.00 40.00
76 Johnny Unitas 25.00 60.00
77 Dan Marino 30.00 80.00
80 Donovan McNabb 15.00 40.00
82 Eli Manning 20.00 50.00
83 Fran Tarkenton 20.00 50.00
85 Jim Kelly 20.00 50.00
86 Joe Montana 30.00 80.00
88 Michael Vick 15.00 40.00
90 Peyton Manning 25.00 60.00
91 Philip Rivers 15.00 40.00
92 Roger Staubach 25.00 60.00
95 Steve Young 20.00 50.00
97 Tom Brady 25.00 60.00
98 Troy Aikman 20.00 50.00

2006 Playoff National Treasures Material Signature Jersey Numbers

STATED PRINT RUN 1-82
2 Bo Jackson/34 60.00 120.00
3 Cadillac Williams/24 20.00 50.00
4 Cedric Benson/32 15.00 40.00
14 Hugh McElhenny/39 20.00 50.00
15 Jim Brown/32 60.00 120.00
18 John Riggins/44 20.00 50.00
19 Julius Jones/21
20 Kevin Jones/34 15.00 40.00
23 Lenny Moore/24 30.00 60.00
29 Shaun Alexander/37 20.00 50.00
31 Steven Jackson/39 20.00 50.00
35 Willie Parker/39 20.00 50.00
37 Deion Sanders/21 40.00 80.00
44 Cliff Branch/21

57 Raymond Berry/82 15.00 40.00
90 Peyton Manning/18 90.00 150.00

2006 Playoff National Treasures Material Signature Jersey Numbers Prime

*PRIME/24-88: .6X TO 1.2X BASIC INSERTS
PRIME PRINT RUN 1-88
5 Charley Taylor/42 15.00 40.00
9 Earl Campbell/34 30.00 60.00
24 Leroy Kelly/44 15.00 40.00
32 Terrell Davis/30 20.00 50.00
34 Tony Dorsett/33 30.00 60.00
38 Lawrence Taylor/56 30.00 60.00
53 Marvin Harrison/88 30.00 60.00
55 Paul Warfield/42 20.00 50.00
59 Steve Largent/80 30.00 60.00
65 Dave Casper/87 20.00 50.00
67 Ozzie Newsome/82 15.00 40.00

2006 Playoff National Treasures Material Signature Prime

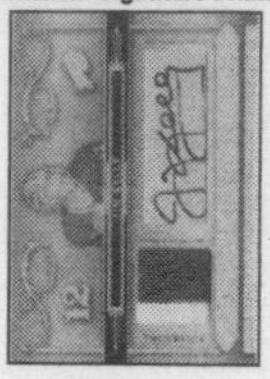

STATED PRINT RUN 1-25
UNPRICED BRAND LOGO PRINT RUN 1
UNPRICED BUTTON PRINT RUN 1
UNPRICED LAUNDRY TAG PRINT RUN 1
UNPRICED NFL LOGO PRINT RUN 1
5 Charley Taylor/25 20.00 50.00
15 Jim Brown/25 75.00 150.00
23 Lenny Moore/25 25.00 60.00
26 Paul Hornung/25 40.00 100.00
31 Steven Jackson/25 25.00 60.00
35 Willie Parker/25 25.00 60.00
36 Willis McGahee/25 20.00 50.00
37 Deion Sanders/25 40.00 80.00
59 Steve Largent/25 50.00 100.00
67 Ozzie Newsome/25 25.00 60.00
81 Drew Bledsoe/25 25.00 60.00
83 Fran Tarkenton/25 40.00 80.00
85 Jim Kelly/25 50.00 100.00
86 Joe Montana/25 125.00 250.00
87 Len Dawson/25 40.00 80.00
92 Roger Staubach/25 75.00 150.00
95 Steve Young/25 50.00 100.00
96 Terry Bradshaw/25 75.00 150.00

2006 Playoff National Treasures Material Quads

STATED PRINT RUN 25 SER.#'d SETS
*PRIME/25: .5X TO 1.2X BASIC INSERTS
PRIME PRINT RUN 2-25
BGMM Raymond Berry 30.00 60.00
Frank Gifford
Hugh McElhenny
Lenny Moore
BJOG Drew Bledsoe 30.00 60.00
Julius Jones
Terrell Owens
Terry Glenn
BKGN Jim Brown 50.00 100.00
Leroy Kelly
Otto Graham
Ozzie Newsome
CBBO Dave Casper 40.00 80.00
Fred Biletnikoff
George Blanda
Jim Otto
CBSS Earl Campbell
Terry Bradshaw
Ken Stabler
Roger Staubach
DJYE Eric Dickerson 30.00 60.00
Deacon Jones
Jack Youngblood
Henry Ellard
GJBU Rex Grossman 30.00 60.00
Thomas Jones
Cedric Benson
Brian Urlacher
HKSB Paul Hornung 50.00 100.00
Leroy Kelly
Gale Sayers
Jim Brown
MBSB Eli Manning 30.00 60.00
Tiki Barber
Jeremy Shockey
Plaxico Burress
MHWC Peyton Manning 60.00 120.00
Marvin Harrison
Reggie Wayne
Dallas Clark
MMYT Hugh McElhenny 60.00 120.00
Joe Montana
Steve Young
Y.A. Tittle
MWBB Donovan McNabb 30.00 60.00
Brian Westbrook
Reggie Brown
Correll Buckhalter
PJJH Carson Palmer 30.00 60.00
Rudi Johnson
Chad Johnson
T.J. Houshmandzadeh
RPWP Ben Roethlisberger 50.00 100.00
Willie Parker
Hines Ward
Troy Polamalu
SDLS Roger Staubach 30.00 80.00
Tony Dorsett
Bob Lilly
Jackie Smith
SGHN Bart Starr 60.00 120.00
Forrest Gregg
Paul Hornung
Ray Nitschke
SLGG John Stallworth 60.00 120.00
Jack Lambert
Joe Greene
L.C. Greenwood
SLWC Barry Sanders 60.00 120.00
Bobby Layne
Doak Walker
Dutch Clark
STHL Mike Singletary 30.00 60.00
Lawrence Taylor
Ted Hendricks
Jack Lambert

2006 Playoff National Treasures Material Trios

STATED PRINT RUN 25 SER.#'d SETS
*PRIME/25: .6X TO 1.2X BASIC INSERTS
PRIME PRINT RUN 1-25
*HOF/25: .5X TO 1X BASIC INSERTS
*HOF PRIME/25: .6X TO 1.2X BASIC INSERTS
*NFL/25: .5X TO 1X BASIC INSERTS
*NFL PRIME/25: .6X TO 1.2X BASIC INSERTS
CKS Dave Casper 20.00 40.00
Jim Kelly
John Stallworth
DNT Eric Dickerson 20.00 40.00
Ozzie Newsome
Lawrence Taylor
EFS John Elway 40.00 80.00
Brett Favre
Barry Sanders
GCM Bob Griese 40.00 80.00
Larry Csonka
Dan Marino
HBS Franco Harris 30.00 80.00
Terry Bradshaw
John Stallworth
JSU Sonny Jurgensen 40.00 80.00
Bart Starr
Johnny Unitas
SDA Roger Staubach 30.00 60.00
Tony Dorsett
Troy Aikman
SDT Barry Sanders 25.00 50.00
Terrell Davis
Thurman Thomas/20
SSB Barry Sanders 30.00 60.00
Billy Sims
Lem Barney
TBS Bulldog Turner 25.00 50.00
Dick Butkus
Mike Singletary
TJS Charley Taylor 30.00 60.00
Sonny Jurgensen
Bart Starr
TRJ Charley Taylor 20.00 40.00
John Riggins
Sonny Jurgensen
UMB Johnny Unitas 40.00 80.00
Lenny Moore
Raymond Berry

2006 Playoff National Treasures Rookie Autographed Letters

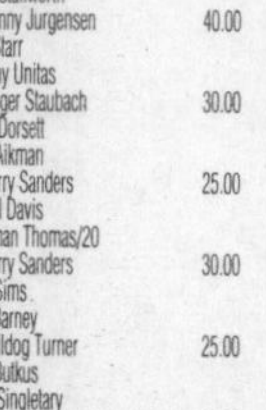

STATED PRINT RUN 70-80
AH A.J. Hawk/80 12.00 30.00
CJ Chad Jackson/70 8.00 20.00
DW DeAngelo Williams/80 15.00 40.00
JA Joseph Addai/80 12.00 30.00
JC Jay Cutler/80 25.00 60.00
LM Laurence Maroney/80 10.00 25.00
LW LenDale White/80 10.00 25.00
MB Mike Bell/80 12.00 30.00
MC Marques Colston/80 25.00 60.00
ML Matt Leinart/80 12.00 30.00
RB Reggie Bush/80 25.00 60.00
SH Santonio Holmes/80 15.00 40.00
SM Sinorice Moss/80 12.00 30.00
VD Vernon Davis/80 15.00 40.00
VY Vince Young/80 15.00 40.00

2006 Playoff National Treasures Rookie Jumbo Material Silver

STATED PRINT RUN 25 SER.#'d SETS
UNPRICED GOLD PRINT RUN 10
UNPRICED PLATINUM PRINT RUN 1
101 Anthony Fasano 6.00 15.00
102 Bobby Carpenter 4.00 10.00
103 D'Brickashaw Ferguson 6.00 15.00
104 Jay Cutler 12.00 30.00
105 Joe Klopfenstein 4.00 10.00
106 John David Washington 5.00 12.00
107 Joseph Addai 6.00 15.00
108 Laurence Maroney 5.00 12.00
109 Mario Williams 6.00 15.00
110 Mathias Kiwanuka 6.00 15.00
111 Matt Leinart 6.00 15.00
112 Santonio Holmes 8.00 20.00
113 Sinorice Moss 6.00 15.00
114 Tye Hill 4.00 10.00
115 Vince Young 8.00 20.00
116 Brandon Marshall 6.00 15.00
117 Brandon Williams 4.00 10.00
118 Brian Calhoun 4.00 10.00
119 Omar Jacobs 4.00 10.00
120 A.J. Hawk 6.00 15.00
121 Chad Jackson 4.00 10.00
122 DeAngelo Williams 8.00 20.00
123 Demetrius Williams 5.00 12.00
124 Derek Hagan 5.00 12.00
125 Jason Avant 4.00 10.00
126 Jerious Norwood 5.00 12.00
127 Kellen Clemens 5.00 12.00
128 LenDale White 5.00 12.00
129 Leon Washington 5.00 12.00
130 Marcedes Lewis 6.00 15.00
131 Maurice Drew 10.00 25.00
132 Maurice Stovall 4.00 10.00
133 Michael Huff 5.00 12.00
134 Michael Robinson 5.00 12.00
135 Tarvaris Jackson 6.00 15.00
136 Travis Wilson 4.00 10.00
137 Vernon Davis 8.00 20.00
138 Charlie Whitehurst 6.00 15.00
139 Brad Smith 6.00 15.00
140 Bruce Gradkowski 6.00 15.00
141 Hank Baskett 6.00 15.00
142 Mike Bell 6.00 15.00
143 Reggie Bush 12.00 30.00
144 Devin Hester 10.00 25.00
145 Jerome Harrison 6.00 15.00
146 Brodie Croyle 6.00 15.00

2006 Playoff National Treasures Signature Gold

*GOLD: .5X TO 1.2X SILVER SIG
GOLD PRINT RUN 1-62
SERIAL #'d UNDER 24 NOT PRICED
15 Jim Brown/32 50.00 100.00
35 Willie Parker/39 20.00 50.00
75 Charley Trippi/62 15.00 40.00
84 George Blanda/49 30.00 60.00
93 Sonny Jurgensen/49 15.00 40.00

2006 Playoff National Treasures Signature Silver

SILVER PRINT RUN 7-99
UNPRICED PLATINUM PRINT RUN 1
SERIAL #'d UNDER 25 NOT PRICED
10 Edgerrin James/61 12.00 30.00
16 Jim Taylor/59 25.00 60.00
18 John Riggins/99 15.00 40.00
23 Lenny Moore/71 12.00 30.00
26 Paul Hornung/69 20.00 50.00
31 Steven Jackson/99 15.00 40.00
40 Bobby Mitchell/99 10.00 25.00
41 Braylon Edwards/55 12.00 30.00
44 Cliff Branch/59 12.00 30.00
45 Dante Lavelli/65 20.00 50.00
46 Don Maynard/99 10.00 25.00
48 James Lofton/80 10.00 25.00
50 Jimmy Johnson/81 12.00 30.00
53 Marvin Harrison/43 25.00 50.00
62 Tommy McDonald/91 12.00 30.00
66 John Mackey/74 15.00 40.00
71 Bill Dudley/66 25.00 60.00
74 Carson Palmer/23
79 Don Meredith/99 50.00 80.00
80 Donovan McNabb/34 40.00 80.00
86 Joe Montana/68 60.00 120.00
88 Michael Vick/32 40.00 80.00
93 Sonny Jurgensen/32 20.00 50.00
95 Steve Young/57 50.00 100.00
99 Warren Moon/75 15.00 40.00

2006 Playoff National Treasures Signature Combos

STATED PRINT RUN 5-25
SERIAL #'d UNDER 25 NOT PRICED
1 Jim Brown 75.00 150.00
Y.A. Tittle
2 Dante Lavelli 30.00 60.00
Lenny Moore
3 Lem Barney 40.00 80.00
John Riggins
4 Steve Largent 50.00 100.00
Lee Roy Selmon
5 Joe Montana 150.00 250.00
Ronnie Lott
6 Marcus Allen 40.00 80.00
James Lofton
7 John Elway 125.00 250.00
Barry Sanders
8 Dan Marino 150.00 250.00
Steve Young
9 Troy Aikman 50.00 100.00
Warren Moon
10 Jim Kelly 50.00 100.00
John Stallworth/24
11 Eric Dickerson 40.00 80.00
Lawrence Taylor
12 Mike Singletary 30.00 60.00
Paul Krause
13 Leroy Kelly 20.00 40.00
Jackie Smith
14 Gale Sayers 50.00 100.00
Forrest Gregg
15 Deacon Jones 30.00 60.00
Bob Lilly

2006 Playoff National Treasures Signature Trios

STATED PRINT RUN 1-25
SERIAL #'d UNDER 25 NOT PRICED
CBA Dave Casper 60.00 120.00
Fred Biletnikoff
Marcus Allen/25
DJB Bill Dudley 60.00 120.00
John Henry Johnson No AU
Terry Bradshaw/25
JMW Sonny Jurgensen 30.00 80.00
Bobby Mitchell
Paul Warfield/25
KLD Ken Kavanaugh 30.00 80.00
Dante Lavelli
Bill Dudley/25
LBK Dante Lavelli 60.00 120.00
Jim Brown
Leroy Kelly/25
MMB John Mackey 60.00 120.00
Lenny Moore
Raymond Berry/25
MTJ Bobby Mitchell 30.00 80.00
Charley Taylor
Sonny Jurgensen/25
MYT Joe Montana 150.00 300.00
Steve Young
Y.A. Tittle/25
SBS Barry Sanders 125.00 200.00
Lem Barney
Billy Sims/25
SBT Gale Sayers 125.00 200.00
Jim Brown
Jim Taylor/25

2006 Playoff National Treasures Timeline Material AFC/NFC

STATED PRINT RUN 2-25
*PRIME/15-25: .5X TO 1.2X AFC/NFC/20-25
PRIME PRINT RUN 1-25
BE Boomer Esiason/25 12.00 30.00
BF Brett Favre/25 30.00 80.00
BJ Bo Jackson/25 20.00 50.00
BLI Bob Lilly/25 12.00 30.00
BS Barry Sanders/20 25.00 60.00
BT Bulldog Turner/25 15.00 40.00
CJ Charlie Joiner/25 12.00 30.00
CT Charley Taylor/25 12.00 30.00
DB Dick Butkus/25 20.00 50.00
DC Dave Casper/25 10.00 25.00
DJ Deacon Jones/25 12.00 30.00
DL Daryle Lamonica/25 10.00 25.00
DM Dan Marino/25 30.00 80.00
DS Deion Sanders/25 20.00 50.00
DW Doak Walker/25 15.00 40.00
EC Earl Campbell/25 15.00 40.00
ED Eric Dickerson/25 12.00 30.00
FGR Forrest Gregg/25 10.00 25.00
FT Fran Tarkenton/25 20.00 50.00
GB George Blanda/25 12.00 30.00
GS Gale Sayers/25 20.00 50.00
HM Hugh McElhenny/25 12.00 30.00
HW Hines Ward/25 15.00 40.00
JB Jerome Bettis/25 25.00 60.00
JE John Elway/25 25.00 60.00
JER Jerry Rice/25 25.00 60.00
JK Jim Kelly/25 20.00 50.00
JM Joe Montana/25 30.00 80.00
JO Jim Otto/25 10.00 25.00
JP Jim Plunkett/25 12.00 30.00
JSM Jackie Smith/25 10.00 25.00
JST John Stallworth/25 12.00 30.00
JT Joe Theismann/25 15.00 40.00
JU Johnny Unitas/25 25.00 60.00
LB Lem Barney/25 12.00 30.00
LD Len Dawson/25 15.00 40.00
LM Lenny Moore/25 12.00 30.00
LS Lee Roy Selmon/25 12.00 30.00
LT Lawrence Taylor/25 15.00 40.00
MA Marcus Allen/25 15.00 40.00
MS Mike Singletary/25 15.00 40.00
OG Otto Graham/25 20.00 50.00
ON Ozzie Newsome/25 12.00 30.00
PK Paul Krause/25 10.00 25.00
PM Peyton Manning/25 25.00 60.00
PS Phil Simms/25 12.00 30.00
RB Raymond Berry/25 12.00 30.00
RN Ray Nitschke/25 25.00 50.00
RS Roger Staubach/25 25.00 60.00
RW Reggie White/25 20.00 50.00
SA Shaun Alexander/25 12.00 30.00
SL Steve Largent/25 15.00 40.00
SY Steve Young/25 20.00 50.00
TA Troy Aikman/25 20.00 50.00
TDA Terrell Davis/20 15.00 40.00
TDO Tony Dorsett/25 15.00 40.00
WB Willie Brown/25 12.00 30.00
WM Warren Moon/25 15.00 40.00
WP Walter Payton/25 30.00 80.00

2006 Playoff National Treasures Timeline Material HOF

HOF JERSEY PRINT RUN 2-25
*PRIME/15-25: .5X TO 1.2X HOF JSY/20-25
BLI Bob Lilly/25 12.00 30.00
BS Barry Sanders/20 25.00 60.00
BST Bart Starr/25 25.00 60.00
BT Bulldog Turner/25 15.00 40.00
CT Charley Taylor/25 12.00 30.00
DB Dick Butkus/25 20.00 50.00
DJ Deacon Jones/25 12.00 30.00
DM Dan Marino/25 30.00 80.00
DW Doak Walker/25 15.00 40.00
EC Earl Campbell/25 15.00 40.00
ED Eric Dickerson/25 12.00 30.00
FGR Forrest Gregg/25 10.00 25.00
FT Fran Tarkenton/25 20.00 50.00
GB George Blanda/25 12.00 30.00
GS Gale Sayers/25 20.00 50.00
HM Hugh McElhenny/25 12.00 30.00
JB Jim Brown/25 20.00 50.00
JE John Elway/25 25.00 60.00
JK Jim Kelly/25 20.00 50.00
JM Joe Montana/25 30.00 80.00
JO Jim Otto/25 10.00 25.00
JSM Jackie Smith/25 10.00 25.00
JST John Stallworth/25 12.00 30.00
JU Johnny Unitas/25 25.00 60.00
LB Lem Barney/25 12.00 30.00
LD Len Dawson/25 15.00 40.00
LM Lenny Moore/25 12.00 30.00
LS Lee Roy Selmon/25 12.00 30.00
LT Lawrence Taylor/25 15.00 40.00
MA Marcus Allen/25 15.00 40.00
MS Mike Singletary/25 15.00 40.00
OG Otto Graham/25 20.00 50.00
ON Ozzie Newsome/25 12.00 30.00
PH Paul Hornung/25 15.00 40.00
PK Paul Krause/25 10.00 25.00
RB Raymond Berry/25 12.00 30.00
RN Ray Nitschke/25 25.00 50.00
RS Roger Staubach/25 25.00 60.00
RW Reggie White/25 20.00 50.00
SL Steve Largent/25 15.00 40.00
SY Steve Young/25 20.00 50.00
TA Troy Aikman/25 20.00 50.00
TDO Tony Dorsett/25 15.00 40.00
WB Willie Brown/25 12.00 30.00
WM Warren Moon/25 15.00 40.00
WP Walter Payton/25 30.00 80.00

2006 Playoff National Treasures Timeline Material Jumbo Jersey

JUMBO JERSEY PRINT RUN 1-25
*PRIME/15-25: .5X TO 1.2X JUMBO/15-25
PRIME PRINT RUN 1-25
BE Boomer Esiason/25 12.00 30.00
BF Brett Favre/25 30.00 80.00
BJ Bo Jackson/25 20.00 50.00
BLA Bobby Layne/20 20.00 50.00
BLI Bob Lilly/25 12.00 30.00
BS Barry Sanders/25 25.00 60.00
BST Bart Starr/25 25.00 60.00
BT Bulldog Turner/25 15.00 40.00
CJ Charlie Joiner/25 12.00 30.00
CT Charley Taylor/25 12.00 30.00
DB Dick Butkus/25 20.00 50.00
DC Dave Casper/25 10.00 25.00
DM Dan Marino/25 30.00 80.00
DS Deion Sanders/25 20.00 50.00
EC Earl Campbell/25 15.00 40.00
ED Eric Dickerson/25 12.00 30.00
FGR Forrest Gregg/25 10.00 25.00
FT Fran Tarkenton/25 20.00 50.00
GS Gale Sayers/15 20.00 50.00
HM Hugh McElhenny/25 12.00 30.00
JB Jim Brown/25 20.00 50.00
JB Jerome Bettis/25 25.00 60.00
JE John Elway/25 25.00 60.00
JER Jerry Rice/17 25.00 60.00
JK Jim Kelly/25 20.00 50.00
JM Joe Montana/25 30.00 80.00
JO Jim Otto/25 10.00 25.00
JP Jim Plunkett/25 12.00 30.00
JSM Jackie Smith/25 10.00 25.00
JST John Stallworth/25 12.00 30.00
JT Joe Theismann/25 15.00 40.00
LB Lem Barney/25 12.00 30.00
LM Lenny Moore/25 12.00 30.00
LS Lee Roy Selmon/25 12.00 30.00
LT Lawrence Taylor/25 15.00 40.00
MA Marcus Allen/25 15.00 40.00
MS Mike Singletary/25 15.00 40.00
OG Otto Graham/25 20.00 50.00
PM Peyton Manning/25 25.00 60.00
PS Phil Simms/25 12.00 30.00
RB Raymond Berry/25 12.00 30.00
RN Ray Nitschke/25 25.00 50.00
RS Roger Staubach/25 25.00 60.00
RW Reggie White/25 20.00 50.00
SA Shaun Alexander/25 12.00 30.00
SL Steve Largent/25 15.00 40.00
SY Steve Young/25 20.00 50.00
TA Troy Aikman/25 20.00 50.00
TDO Tony Dorsett/25 15.00 40.00
WB Willie Brown/25 12.00 30.00
WM Warren Moon/25 15.00 40.00
WP Walter Payton/25 30.00 80.00

2006 Playoff National Treasures Timeline Material MVP

STATED PRINT RUN 2-25
*PRIME/15-25: .5X TO 1.2X MVP/20-25
BE Boomer Esiason/25 12.00 30.00
BF Brett Favre/25 30.00 80.00
BS Barry Sanders/20 25.00 60.00
BST Bart Starr/25 25.00 60.00
DM Dan Marino/25 30.00 80.00
EC Earl Campbell/25 15.00 40.00
FT Fran Tarkenton/25 20.00 50.00
HW Hines Ward/25 15.00 40.00
JB Jim Brown/25 20.00 50.00
JE John Elway/25 25.00 60.00
JM Joe Montana/25 30.00 80.00
JP Jim Plunkett/25 12.00 30.00
JT Joe Theismann/25 15.00 40.00
JU Johnny Unitas/25 25.00 60.00
LD Len Dawson/25 15.00 40.00
LT Lawrence Taylor/25 15.00 40.00
MA Marcus Allen/25 15.00 40.00
PH Paul Hornung/25 15.00 40.00
PM Peyton Manning/25 25.00 60.00
PS Phil Simms/25 12.00 30.00
RS Roger Staubach/25 25.00 60.00
SA Shaun Alexander/25 12.00 30.00
SY Steve Young/25 20.00 50.00
TA Troy Aikman/25 20.00 50.00
TD Terrell Davis/20 15.00 40.00
WP Walter Payton/25 30.00 80.00
JER Jerry Rice/25 25.00 60.00

2006 Playoff National Treasures Timeline Material NFL

COMMON CARD/60-99 6.00 15.00
SEMISTARS/60-99 8.00 20.00
UNL.STARS/60-99 10.00 25.00
COMMON CARD/30-50 10.00 25.00
UNL.STARS/30-50 12.00 30.00
COMMON CARD/16-29 10.00 25.00
SEMISTARS/16-29 12.00 30.00
UNL.STARS/16-29 15.00 40.00
STATED PRINT RUN 4-99
*PRIME/15-25: .5X TO 1.2X AFC/NFC
BE Boomer Esiason/30 10.00 25.00
BF Brett Favre/99 20.00 50.00
BJ Bo Jackson/99 12.00 30.00
BT Bulldog Turner/99 10.00 25.00
CJ Charlie Joiner/99 8.00 20.00
CT Charley Taylor/99 8.00 20.00
DB Dick Butkus/99 12.00 30.00
DC Dave Casper/99 6.00 15.00
DL Daryle Lamonica/75 6.00 15.00
DM Dan Marino/99 20.00 50.00
DS Deion Sanders/99 12.00 30.00
DW Doak Walker/37 12.00 30.00
EC Earl Campbell/99 10.00 25.00
ED Eric Dickerson/29 12.00 30.00
FT Fran Tarkenton/99 12.00 30.00
GB George Blanda/16 12.00 30.00
GS Gale Sayers/40 15.00 40.00
HM Hugh McElhenny/99 8.00 20.00
HW Hines Ward/60 10.00 25.00
JE John Elway/50 20.00 50.00
JK Jim Kelly/49 15.00 40.00
JM Joe Montana/50 25.00 60.00
JO Jim Otto/99 6.00 15.00
JP Jim Plunkett/99 8.00 20.00
JU Johnny Unitas/19 25.00 60.00
LB Lem Barney/99 8.00 20.00
LD Len Dawson/45 12.00 30.00
LM Lenny Moore/99 8.00 20.00
LS Lee Roy Selmon/50 10.00 25.00
LT Lawrence Taylor/99 10.00 25.00
MA Marcus Allen/99 10.00 25.00
MS Mike Singletary/50 12.00 30.00
OG Otto Graham/99 12.00 30.00
ON Ozzie Newsome/50 10.00 25.00
PK Paul Krause/22 10.00 25.00
PM Peyton Manning/99 15.00 40.00
PS Phil Simms/99 8.00 20.00
RB Raymond Berry/99 8.00 20.00
RN Ray Nitschke/66 12.00 30.00
RS Roger Staubach/99 15.00 40.00
RW Reggie White/92 12.00 30.00
SA Shaun Alexander/99 8.00 20.00
SL Steve Largent/99 10.00 25.00
SY Steve Young/99 12.00 30.00
TA Troy Aikman/99 12.00 30.00
WB Willie Brown/99 8.00 20.00
WM Warren Moon/99 10.00 25.00
WP Walter Payton/50 25.00 60.00
BLI Bob Lilly/99 8.00 20.00
BS Barry Sanders/50 20.00 50.00
BST Bart Starr/50 20.00 50.00
FGR Forrest Gregg/99 6.00 15.00
JBE Jerome Bettis/99 15.00 40.00
JBR Jim Brown/32 15.00 40.00
JER Jerry Rice/99 15.00 40.00
JOT Joe Theismann/99 10.00 25.00
JSM Jackie Smith/99 6.00 15.00
JST John Stallworth/99 8.00 20.00
TDA Terrell Davis/20 15.00 40.00
TDO Tony Dorsett/99 10.00 25.00

2006 Playoff National Treasures Timeline Material Signature AFC/NFC

STATED PRINT RUN 1-25
*PRIME/15-25: .6X TO 1.2X AFC/NFC SIG
PRIME PRINT RUN 1-25
SERIAL #'d UNDER 20 NOT PRICED
BE Boomer Esiason/15 20.00 50.00
BJ Bo Jackson/20 40.00 80.00
BL Bob Lilly/20 20.00 50.00
BS Barry Sanders/15 75.00 150.00
CJ Charlie Joiner/25 15.00 40.00
DB Dick Butkus/25 60.00 120.00
DC Dave Casper/20 20.00 50.00
DJ Deacon Jones/25 15.00 40.00
DL Daryle Lamonica/25 15.00 40.00
DS Deion Sanders/25 30.00 60.00
ED Eric Dickerson/25 40.00 80.00
FB Fred Biletnikoff/15 30.00 60.00
HM Hugh McElhenny/25 15.00 40.00
JB Jerome Bettis/25 75.00 150.00
JE John Elway/15 75.00 150.00
JM Joe Montana/16 75.00 150.00
JO Jim Otto/15 20.00 50.00
JP Jim Plunkett/16 20.00 50.00
JT Joe Theismann/25 40.00 80.00
LB Lem Barney/25 15.00 40.00
LM Lenny Moore/25 20.00 50.00
LS Lee Roy Selmon/15 20.00 50.00
LT Lawrence Taylor/25 40.00 80.00
MA Marcus Allen/25 30.00 60.00
MS Mike Singletary/20 25.00 60.00
ON Ozzie Newsome/15 20.00 50.00
PK Paul Krause/25 15.00 40.00
PS Phil Simms/25 30.00 60.00
RB Raymond Berry/25 20.00 50.00
RL Ronnie Lott/15 30.00 80.00
RS Roger Staubach/25 60.00 120.00
SJ Sonny Jurgensen/20 40.00 80.00
SL Steve Largent/25 40.00 80.00
SY Steve Young/15 40.00 80.00
TD Terrell Davis/15 20.00 50.00
WB Willie Brown/25 15.00 40.00
WM Warren Moon/15 40.00 80.00
JLO James Lofton/15 20.00 50.00
JOR John Riggins/25 20.00 50.00
JSM Jackie Smith/25 15.00 40.00
JST John Stallworth/25 40.00 80.00
TDO Tony Dorsett/25 30.00 60.00

2006 Playoff National Treasures Timeline Material Signature HOF

STATED PRINT RUN 1-25
*PRIME/15-25: .6X TO 1.2X AFC/NFC SIG
PRIME PRINT RUN 1-25
SERIAL #'d UNDER 15 NOT PRICED
DB Dick Butkus/25 60.00 120.00
DJ Deacon Jones/25 15.00 40.00
ED Eric Dickerson/25 40.00 80.00
HM Hugh McElhenny/25 15.00 40.00
JB Jim Brown/23 60.00 120.00
JR John Riggins/25 20.00 50.00
LB Lem Barney/25 15.00 40.00
LM Lenny Moore/25 20.00 50.00
LT Lawrence Taylor/25 40.00 80.00
MA Marcus Allen/25 30.00 60.00
MS Mike Singletary/20 25.00 60.00
PH Paul Hornung/25 50.00 100.00
PK Paul Krause/25 15.00 40.00
RB Raymond Berry/25 20.00 50.00
RS Roger Staubach/25 60.00 120.00
SL Steve Largent/25 40.00 80.00
TD Tony Dorsett/25 30.00 60.00
WB Willie Brown/25 15.00 40.00
BLI Bob Lilly/20 20.00 50.00
JSM Jackie Smith/25 15.00 40.00
JST John Stallworth/25 40.00 80.00

2006 Playoff National Treasures Timeline Material Signature MVP

*MVP/15-25: .4X TO 1X AFC/NFC SIG
MVP PRINT RUN 2-25
*PRIME/15-25: .6X TO 1.2X AFC/NFC SIG
PRIME PRINT RUN 1-25
SERIAL #'d UNDER 15 NOT PRICED
BE Boomer Esiason/15 20.00 50.00
FB Fred Biletnikoff/15 25.00 60.00
JB Jim Brown/25 60.00 120.00
JE John Elway/15 75.00 150.00
JM Joe Montana/16 75.00 150.00
JP Jim Plunkett/16 20.00 50.00
JT Joe Theismann/25 40.00 80.00
LT Lawrence Taylor/25 40.00 80.00
MA Marcus Allen/25 30.00 60.00
PH Paul Hornung/25 50.00 100.00
PM Peyton Manning/18
PS Phil Simms/25 30.00 60.00
RS Roger Staubach/25 60.00 120.00
SY Steve Young/15 40.00 80.00
TD Terrell Davis/15 20.00 50.00
BSA Barry Sanders/15 75.00 150.00
JOR John Riggins/25 20.00 50.00

2006 Playoff National Treasures Timeline Material Signature NFL

*NFL/15-25: .4X TO 1X AFC/NFC SIG
NFL PRINT RUN 1-25
*PRIME/15-25: .6X TO 1.2X AFC/NFC SIG
PRIME PRINT RUN 1-25
SERIAL #'d UNDER 15 NOT PRICED
PH Paul Hornung/25 50.00 100.00

2006 Playoff National Treasures Timeline Signature

STATED PRINT RUN 1-99
SERIAL #'d UNDER 24 NOT PRICED
UNPRICED SIG CUT PRINT RUN 1-10
DB Dick Butkus/60 40.00 100.00
DL Daryle Lamonica/76 15.00 40.00
FB Fred Biletnikoff/30 25.00 60.00
HM Hugh McElhenny/29 20.00 50.00
JBE Jerome Bettis/87 50.00 100.00
JBR Jim Brown/32 50.00 100.00
JL James Lofton/80 10.00 25.00
JOR John Riggins/99 15.00 40.00
JS Jackie Smith/64 12.00 30.00
JT Joe Theismann/99 20.00 50.00
LB Lem Barney/99 10.00 25.00
LK Leroy Kelly/25 15.00 40.00
LM Lenny Moore/24 15.00 40.00
MA Marcus Allen/99 20.00 50.00
PS Phil Simms/44 20.00 50.00
RB Raymond Berry/30 15.00 40.00
RL Ronnie Lott/49 20.00 50.00
SJ Sonny Jurgensen/95 15.00 40.00
TDA Terrell Davis/26 20.00 50.00
WB Willie Brown/99 12.00 30.00
YL Yale Lary/54 15.00 40.00
YT Y.A. Tittle/22

2007 Playoff National Treasures

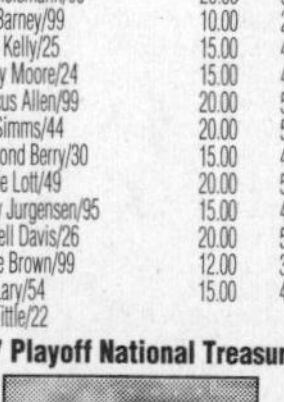

This 200-card set was released in January, 2008. The set was issued in seven-card pack (boxes) with an $500 SRP. Cards numbered 1-54 feature veterans while cards numbered 55-100 feature retired greats. All cards numbered 1-100 were issued to a stated print run of 100 serial numbered sets. Cards numbered 101-134 are 2007 NFL rookies and feature both player-worn jersey swatches and a signature and those cards were issued to a stated print run of 99 serial numbered sets. Cards numbered 135-200 are also NFL rookies and those were signed and issued to a stated print run of 99 serial numbered sets. A few players did not return their cards in time for pack out and those cards could be redeemed until August 1, 2009.

1-100 PRINT RUN 100 SER.#'d SETS
101-134 JSY AU RC PRINT RUN 99
135-200 AU RC PRINT RUN 99-299
UNPRICED GOLD PRINT RUN 5
UNPRICED PLATINUM PRINT RUN 1
1 Tom Brady 6.00 15.00
2 Brett Favre 8.00 20.00
3 Tony Romo 5.00 12.00
4 Carson Palmer 3.00 8.00
5 Eli Manning 4.00 10.00
6 Peyton Manning 6.00 15.00
7 Philip Rivers 4.00 10.00
8 Donovan McNabb 4.00 10.00
9 Vince Young 3.00 8.00
10 Drew Brees 4.00 10.00
11 Ben Roethlisberger 4.00 10.00
12 Jay Cutler 4.00 10.00
13 Brian Westbrook 3.00 8.00
14 Willie Parker 3.00 8.00
15 LaDainian Tomlinson 4.00 10.00
16 Ronnie Brown 3.00 8.00
17 Willis McGahee 3.00 8.00
18 Steven Jackson 4.00 10.00
19 Larry Johnson 2.50 6.00
20 Laurence Maroney 3.00 8.00
21 Clinton Portis 3.00 8.00
22 Shaun Alexander 3.00 8.00
23 Maurice Jones-Drew 4.00 10.00
24 Frank Gore 4.00 10.00
25 Cadillac Williams 3.00 8.00
26 Edgerrin James 3.00 8.00
27 Brandon Jacobs 3.00 8.00
28 Marion Barber 3.00 8.00
29 Cedric Benson 3.00 8.00
30 Fred Taylor 3.00 8.00
31 Randy Moss 4.00 10.00
32 Chad Johnson 3.00 8.00
33 Antonio Gates 4.00 10.00
34 Larry Fitzgerald 4.00 10.00
35 Plaxico Burress 3.00 8.00
36 Kellen Winslow 3.00 8.00
37 T.J. Houshmandzadeh 3.00 8.00
38 Steve Smith 3.00 8.00
39 Terrell Owens 4.00 10.00
40 Tony Gonzalez 3.00 8.00
41 Roy Williams WR 3.00 8.00
42 Donald Driver 4.00 10.00
43 Torry Holt 3.00 8.00
44 Hines Ward 4.00 10.00
45 Reggie Wayne 3.00 8.00
46 Marvin Harrison 4.00 10.00
47 Laveranues Coles 2.50 6.00
48 Jeremy Shockey 3.00 8.00
49 Anquan Boldin 3.00 8.00
50 Dallas Clark 2.50 6.00
51 Devin Hester 4.00 10.00
52 Joey Galloway 3.00 8.00
53 Andre Johnson 3.00 8.00
54 Reggie Bush 4.00 10.00
55 Joe Montana 8.00 20.00
56 Joe Namath 5.00 12.00
57 John Elway 6.00 15.00
58 Johnny Morris 2.50 6.00
59 Ken Strong 2.50 6.00
60 Larry Csonka 4.00 10.00
61 Lawrence Taylor 4.00 10.00
62 Mel Hein 2.50 6.00
63 Michael Irvin 3.00 8.00
64 Paul Krause 2.50 6.00
65 Randall Cunningham 3.00 8.00
66 Rick Casares 2.50 6.00
67 Emmitt Smith 8.00 20.00
68 Lydell Mitchell 2.50 6.00
69 Roger Craig 3.00 8.00
70 Sam Huff 3.00 8.00
71 Sammy Baugh 4.00 10.00
72 Sid Luckman 4.00 10.00
73 Sonny Jurgensen 3.00 8.00
74 Walter Payton 8.00 20.00
75 Steve Largent 4.00 10.00
76 Thurman Thomas 3.00 8.00
77 Tommy McDonald 2.50 6.00
78 Bob Waterfield 2.50 6.00
79 Tom Fears 2.50 6.00
80 Dick Lane 2.50 6.00
81 Jim Parker 2.50 6.00
82 Norm Van Brocklin 3.00 8.00
83 Ollie Matson 3.00 8.00
84 Tom Landry 5.00 12.00
85 Barry Sanders 6.00 15.00
86 Bo Jackson 5.00 12.00
87 Bob Griese 4.00 10.00
88 Red Grange 5.00 12.00
89 Yale Lary 2.50 6.00
90 Cris Collinsworth 3.00 8.00
91 Daryle Lamonica 2.50 6.00
92 Doak Walker 3.00 8.00
93 Fred Biletnikoff 4.00 10.00
94 George Blanda 3.00 8.00
95 Harlon Hill 2.50 6.00
96 Marion Motley 2.50 6.00
97 Jimmy Orr 2.50 6.00
98 Jim Thorpe 5.00 12.00
99 Ernie Nevers 3.00 8.00
100 Otto Graham 4.00 10.00
101 Adrian Peterson JSY AU RC 250.00 500.00
102 Anthony Gonzalez JSY AU RC 20.00 50.00
103 Antonio Pittman JSY AU RC 12.00 30.00
104 Brady Quinn JSY AU RC 20.00 50.00
105 Brandon Jackson JSY AU RC 15.00 40.00
106 Brian Leonard JSY AU RC 15.00 40.00
107 Calvin Johnson JSY AU RC 175.00 300.00
108 Chris Henry RB JSY AU RC 12.00 30.00
109 Drew Stanton JSY AU RC 12.00 30.00
110 Dwayne Jarrett JSY AU RC 15.00 40.00
111 Dwayne Bowe JSY AU RC 40.00 80.00
112 Gaines Adams JSY AU RC 20.00 50.00
113 Garrett Wolfe JSY AU RC 12.00 30.00
114 Greg Olsen JSY AU RC 15.00 40.00
115 JaMarcus Russell JSY AU RC 12.00 30.00
116 Jason Hill JSY AU RC 20.00 50.00
117 Joe Thomas JSY AU RC 20.00 50.00
118 John Beck JSY AU RC 20.00 50.00
119 Johnnie Lee Higgins JSY AU RC 15.00 40.00
120 Kenny Irons JSY No AU RC 5.00 12.00
121 Kevin Kolb JSY AU RC 50.00 100.00
122 Lorenzo Booker JSY AU RC 15.00 40.00
123 Marshawn Lynch JSY AU RC 40.00 80.00
124 Michael Bush JSY AU RC 20.00 50.00
125 Patrick Willis JSY AU RC 50.00 100.00
126 Paul Williams JSY AU RC 12.00 30.00
127 Robert Meachem JSY AU RC 20.00 50.00
128 Sidney Rice JSY AU RC 25.00 60.00
129 Steve Smith JSY AU RC 20.00 50.00
130 Ted Ginn JSY AU RC 15.00 40.00
131 Tony Hunt JSY AU RC 12.00 30.00
132 Trent Edwards JSY AU RC 20.00 50.00
133 Troy Smith JSY AU RC 20.00 50.00
134 Yamon Figurs JSY AU RC 12.00 30.00
135 Darrelle Revis AU RC 20.00 40.00
137 LaRon Landry AU RC 8.00 20.00
138 James Jones AU RC 8.00 20.00
139 Michael Griffin AU RC 8.00 20.00
140 Aundrae Allison AU RC 5.00 12.00
141 Craig Buster Davis No AU RC 2.50 6.00
142 David Harris AU RC 6.00 15.00

143 DeShawn Wynn AU RC 6.00 15.00
144 Dwayne Wright AU RC 6.00 15.00
145 Jacoby Jones AU/299 RC 10.00 20.00
146 John Broussard AU/299 RC 5.00 12.00
147 Jon Beason AU/299 RC 5.00 12.00
148 Kenton Keith AU RC 8.00 20.00
149 Kolby Smith AU RC 6.00 15.00
150 Leon Hall AU RC 6.00 15.00
151 Reggie Nelson AU RC 6.00 15.00
152 Roy Hall AU/299 RC 6.00 15.00
153 Ryne Robinson AU/299 RC 5.00 12.00
154 Selvin Young AU RC 6.00 15.00
155 Steve Breaston AU/243 RC 6.00 15.00
156 Chris Davis AU RC 5.00 12.00
157 Glenn Holt AU RC 6.00 15.00
158 Kenneth Darby AU RC 6.00 15.00
159 Mike Walker AU/299 RC 10.00 20.00
160 Chris Houston AU RC 6.00 15.00
161 David Clowney AU RC 6.00 15.00
162 Mason Crosby AU/299 RC 10.00 25.00
163 Bobby Sippio AU/299 RC 5.00 12.00
164 Biren Ealy AU RC 6.00 15.00
166 Laurent Robinson AU RC 10.00 25.00
167 Lawrence Timmons AU RC 10.00 25.00
168 Legedu Naanee AU RC 10.00 25.00
169 Brandon Meriweather AU RC 8.00 20.00
170 Brian Robison AU RC 8.00 20.00
171 Greg Peterson AU RC 6.00 15.00
172 Ikaika Alama-Francis AU/190 RC 6.00 15.00
173 Isaiah Stanback AU RC 5.00 12.00
174 Ed Johnson AU RC 6.00 15.00
175 Eric Frampton AU/299 RC 5.00 12.00
176 Eric Weddle AU/299 RC 6.00 15.00
177 Fred Bennett AU/299 RC 4.00 10.00
178 Dante Rosario AU RC 8.00 20.00
179 Clifton Dawson AU/299 RC 6.00 15.00
180 Jeff Rowe AU/299 RC 4.00 10.00
181 Justin Durant AU RC 6.00 15.00
182 Charles Johnson No AU RC 2.00 5.00
183 Paul Posluszny AU RC 8.00 20.00
184 Pierre Thomas AU RC 15.00 40.00
185 Quentin Moses AU/299 RC 5.00 12.00
186 Ray McDonald AU RC 6.00 15.00
187 Sabby Piscitelli AU/299 RC 6.00 15.00
188 Scott Chandler AU RC 8.00 20.00
189 Matt Gutierrez AU RC 8.00 20.00
190 Matt Moore AU RC 8.00 20.00
191 Martrez Milner AU RC 5.00 12.00
192 Amobi Okoye AU RC 8.00 20.00
193 Adam Carriker AU RC 6.00 15.00
194 Alan Branch No AU RC 2.50 6.00
195 Anthony Spencer AU/299 RC 6.00 15.00
196 Tyler Thigpen AU RC 8.00 20.00
197 Victor Abiamiri AU/299 RC 6.00 15.00
198 Zach Miller AU RC 8.00 20.00
199 Jarvis Moss AU/199 RC 5.00 12.00
200 LaMarr Woodley AU RC 12.50 25.00

2007 Playoff National Treasures Silver

*VETS: 1X TO 2.5X BASIC CARDS
SILVER PRINT RUN 25 SER.#'d SETS

2007 Playoff National Treasures All Decade Material Jumbo

JUMBO PRINT RUN 1-25
*BASE MAT/15-25: .3X TO .8X JUMBO/15-25
BASE MATERIAL PRINT RUN 1-25
*JUMBO PRIME/15-25: .6X TO 1.5X JUMBO/15-25
JUMBO PRIME PRINT RUN 1-25
SER.#'d UNDER 20 NOT PRICED
AP Alan Page 15.00 40.00
BF Brett Favre 30.00 80.00
BST Bart Starr 25.00 60.00
BS Barry Sanders 25.00 60.00
BT Bulldog Turner 15.00 40.00
CB Chuck Bednarik 12.00 30.00
CH Cliff Harris 12.00 30.00
CT Charley Taylor 12.00 30.00
DB Dick Butkus 20.00 50.00
DC Dave Casper 10.00 25.00
DG Darrell Green 15.00 40.00
DH Dan Hampton 12.00 30.00
DJ Deacon Jones 12.00 30.00
EC Earl Campbell 15.00 40.00
ED Eric Dickerson 12.00 30.00
ES Emmitt Smith/22 30.00 80.00
FG Forrest Gregg 10.00 25.00
GS Gale Sayers 20.00 50.00
HM Hugh McElhenny 12.00 30.00
JE John Elway 25.00 60.00
JL Jack Lambert 15.00 40.00
JLO James Lofton 10.00 25.00
JMO Joe Montana 30.00 80.00
JM John Mackey 12.00 30.00
JP Jim Parker 10.00 25.00
JR John Riggins 12.00 30.00
JU Johnny Unitas 25.00 60.00
JY Jack Youngblood 12.00 30.00
KSG Ken Strong 15.00 40.00
KS Ken Stabler 20.00 50.00
LB Lem Barney 12.00 30.00
LM Lenny Moore 12.00 30.00
LS Lee Roy Selmon/20 12.00 30.00
LT Lawrence Taylor 15.00 40.00
MH Mel Hein 15.00 40.00
MM Marion Motley 15.00 40.00
MS Mike Singletary 15.00 40.00
NV Norm Van Brocklin 25.00 60.00
OG Otto Graham 12.00 30.00
ON Ozzie Newsome 12.00 30.00
PW Paul Warfield 12.00 30.00
RB Roosevelt Brown 10.00 25.00
RL Ronnie Lott 12.00 30.00
RN Ray Nitschke 15.00 40.00
SB Sammy Baugh 20.00 50.00
SJ Sonny Jurgensen 12.00 30.00
SLA Steve Largent 15.00 40.00
SL Sid Luckman 20.00 50.00
TB Tim Brown 15.00 40.00
TH Ted Hendricks 12.00 30.00
TT Thurman Thomas 12.00 30.00
WP Walter Payton 30.00 80.00

2007 Playoff National Treasures All Decade Material Quads

BASE QUAD PRINT RUN 1-25
*PRIME/22-25: .5X TO 1.2X BASIC QUAD/25
PRIME PRINT RUN 1-25
BIGL Tim Brown 25.00 60.00
Michael Irvin
Darrell Green
Ronnie Lott
BLWT Sammy Baugh 40.00 100.00
Sid Luckman
Bob Waterfield
Clyde Turner
EFSS John Elway 50.00 120.00
Brett Favre
Barry Sanders
Emmitt Smith
FHVM Tom Fears 40.00 80.00
Elroy Hirsch
Norm Van Brocklin
Ollie Matson
GLMB Otto Graham 30.00 60.00
Bobby Layne
Hugh McElhenny
Raymond Berry
JBON Deacon Jones 30.00 60.00
Dick Butkus
Merlin Olsen
Ray Nitschke
JSMT Sonny Jurgensen 40.00 100.00
Bart Starr
John Mackey
Charley Taylor
LHLH Larry Little 30.00 60.00
Ted Hendricks
Jack Lambert
Cliff Harris
MFDR Joe Montana 25.00 60.00
Dan Fouts
Eric Dickerson
John Riggins
SCHP Roger Staubach 30.00 80.00
Earl Campbell
Franco Harris
Walter Payton
SHST Lee Roy Selmon 20.00 50.00
Dan Hampton
Mike Singletary
Lawrence Taylor
YGLP Jack Youngblood 20.00 50.00
Joe Greene
Bob Lilly
Alan Page

2007 Playoff National Treasures All Decade Material Signature

MATERIAL SIG PRINT RUN 1-25
*POSITION/25: .4X TO 1X BASE MATERIAL SIG
POSITION MAT.SIG PRINT RUN 1-25
SER.#'d UNDER 25 NOT PRICED
AP Alan Page/25 25.00 60.00
DH Dan Hampton/25 20.00 50.00
JE John Elway/25 75.00 150.00
JM Joe Montana/25 75.00 150.00
LM Lenny Moore/25 20.00 50.00
LT Lawrence Taylor/25 30.00 80.00
MI Michael Irvin/25 40.00 80.00
RS Roger Staubach/25 50.00 100.00
SL Steve Largent/25 25.00 60.00
TB Tim Brown/25 25.00 60.00

2007 Playoff National Treasures All Decade Material Signature Jersey Numbers

STATED PRINT RUN 4-99
SER.#'d UNDER 22 NOT PRICED
LM Lenny Moore/24 20.00 50.00
CH Cliff Harris/43 20.00 50.00
DH Dan Hampton/99 15.00 40.00
ED Eric Dickerson/29 25.00 60.00
ES Emmitt Smith/22 150.00 250.00
LT Lawrence Taylor/56 25.00 60.00
ON Ozzie Newsome/82 15.00 40.00
PW Paul Warfield/42 20.00 50.00
RL Ronnie Lott/42 20.00 50.00
SL Steve Largent/80 20.00 50.00

2007 Playoff National Treasures All Decade Material Trios

BASE TRIO JSY PRINT RUN 2-25
*PRIME/25: .6X TO 1.5X BASE JSY/25
PRIME PRINT RUN 1-25
*HOF/25: .4X TO 1X BASE JSY/25
HOF TRIO PRINT RUN 2-25
*HOF PRIME/25: .6X TO 1.5X BASE JSY/25
HOF TRIO PRIME PRINT RUN 1-25
*NFL TRIO/25: .4X TO 1X BASE JSY/25
NFL TRIO PRINT RUN 2-25
*NFL PRIME/25: .6X TO 1.5X BASE JSY/25
NFL TRIO PRIME PRINT RUN 1-25
SER.#'d UNDER 25 NOT PRICED
BLW Sammy Baugh 30.00 80.00
Sid Luckman
Bob Waterfield
BFH Raymond Berry 15.00 40.00
Tom Fears
Elroy Hirsch
BNB Dick Butkus 25.00 50.00
Ray Nitschke
Lem Barney
BPB Rosey Brown 15.00 40.00
Jim Parker
Chuck Bednarik
CHP Earl Campbell 30.00 80.00
Franco Harris
Walter Payton
EFI John Elway 30.00 80.00
Brett Favre
Michael Irvin
FRN Dan Fouts 15.00 40.00
John Riggins
Ozzie Newsome
GJO Forrest Gregg 15.00 40.00
Deacon Jones
Merlin Olsen
GLV Otto Graham 12.00 30.00
Bobby Layne
Norm Van Brocklin
JSM Sonny Jurgensen 25.00 60.00
Bart Starr
John Mackey
MMM Ollie Matson 15.00 40.00
Hugh McElhenny
Lenny Moore
PHL Alan Page 15.00 40.00
Ted Hendricks
Jack Lambert
RLL Jerry Rice 25.00 60.00
Steve Largent
James Lofton
SST Barry Sanders 30.00 80.00
Emmitt Smith
Thurman Thomas
STL Mike Singletary 15.00 40.00
Lawrence Taylor
Ronnie Lott
TMK Charley Taylor 15.00 40.00
John Mackey
Leroy Kelly
YGL Jack Youngblood 15.00 40.00
Joe Greene
Bob Lilly

2007 Playoff National Treasures All Decade Signature

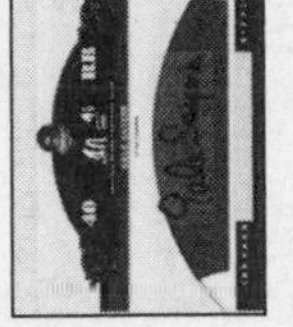

STATED PRINT RUN 1-99
SERIAL #'d UNDER 20 NOT PRICED
DL Dante Lavelli 12.00 30.00
AP Alan Page 15.00 40.00
BD Boyd Dowler 12.00 30.00
BL Bob Lilly/21 20.00 50.00
BS Bart Starr/35 90.00 150.00
CB Chuck Bednarik/50 15.00 40.00
CT Charley Trippi 12.00 30.00
CT Charley Taylor 12.00 30.00
DC Dave Casper 10.00 25.00
DF Dan Fouts/50 15.00 40.00
DH Dan Hampton/42 12.00 30.00
DJ Deacon Jones 12.00 30.00
FG Forrest Gregg/24 25.00 60.00
GS Gale Sayers 25.00 60.00
GU Gene Upshaw 15.00 40.00
HM Hugh McElhenny 12.00 30.00
JB Jim Brown 40.00 80.00
JL James Lofton/23 15.00 40.00
JR John Riggins 15.00 40.00
KW Kellen Winslow Sr./75 12.00 30.00
LB Lem Barney 10.00 25.00
LL Larry Little 10.00 25.00
LM Lenny Moore 12.00 30.00
LS Lee Roy Selmon 12.00 30.00
LT Lawrence Taylor 20.00 50.00
PH Paul Hornung 20.00 50.00
PW Paul Warfield/66 12.00 30.00
RB Raymond Berry 12.00 30.00
RC Roger Craig 10.00 25.00
SH Sam Huff/83 15.00 40.00
SJ Sonny Jurgensen/75 15.00 40.00
SL Steve Largent/82 15.00 40.00
WB Willie Brown 12.00 30.00
YL Yale Lary 10.00 25.00

2007 Playoff National Treasures All Decade Signature Cuts

STATED PRINT RUN 1-100 SER.#'d SETS
AP Alan Page/25 25.00 60.00
AW Alex Wojciechowicz/36 75.00 150.00
BF Brett Favre/21 150.00 250.00
BS Barry Sanders/25 100.00 200.00
BST Bart Starr/29 125.00 200.00
BT Bulldog Turner/100 40.00 100.00
BW Bob Waterfield/39 60.00 120.00
CBE Chuck Bednarik/25 40.00 80.00
CB Cliff Battles/41 125.00 225.00
CT Charley Trippi/50 25.00 60.00
DC Dutch Clark/30 175.00 300.00
DF Dan Fortmann/21 175.00 300.00
DFO Dan Fouts/25 25.00 60.00
DJ Deacon Jones/50 20.00 50.00
DLV Dante Lavelli/25 40.00 80.00
DL Dick Lane/32 125.00 250.00
FC Earl Campbell/50 25.00 60.00
ED Eric Dickerson/60 25.00 60.00
EH Ed Healey/22 150.00 300.00
EN Ernie Nevers/21 250.00 400.00
ES Ernie Stautner/100 40.00 80.00
FH Franco Harris/50 50.00 100.00
GC George Connor/70 30.00 80.00
GM George McAfee/56 60.00 120.00
GS Gale Sayers/59 40.00 80.00
CT George Trafton/67 125.00 250.00
HM Hugh McElhenny/50 20.00 50.00
JB Jim Brown/25 60.00 120.00
JE John Elway/25 75.00 150.00
JLO James Lofton/30 15.00 40.00
JL Jack Lambert/25 90.00 150.00
JM Joe Montana/25 90.00 175.00
JR John Riggins/25 30.00 80.00
KST Ken Strong/40 50.00 100.00
LM Lenny Moore/59 20.00 50.00
MH Mel Hein/61 60.00 120.00
MS Mike Singletary/50 25.00 60.00
OG Otto Graham/100 40.00 100.00
OM Ollie Matson/21 40.00 80.00
ON Ozzie Newsome/50 15.00 40.00
PH Paul Hornung/50 40.00 80.00
PP Pete Pihos/32 50.00 100.00
RB Roosevelt Brown/50 25.00 60.00
RBE Raymond Berry/50 25.00 60.00
RG Red Grange/40 250.00 500.00
SB Sammy Baugh/50 100.00 200.00
SJ Sonny Jurgensen/25 25.00 60.00
SLU Sid Luckman/42 125.00 250.00
SL Steve Largent/50 40.00 80.00
SV Steve Van Buren/32 125.00 200.00
TC Tony Canadeo/100 60.00 120.00
WP Walter Payton/34 200.00 400.00

2007 Playoff National Treasures Fearsome Foursome

STATED PRINT RUN 100
*PRIME/25: .6X TO 1.5X BASE JSY/100
PRIME PRINT RUN 25
1 Lamar Lundy 15.00 40.00
Rosey Grier
Merlin Olsen
Deacon Jones

2007 Playoff National Treasures Material Face Mask

STATED PRINT RUN 3-25
SERIAL #'d UNDER 25 NOT PRICED
1 Tom Brady 20.00 50.00
2 Brett Favre 25.00 60.00
4 Carson Palmer 10.00 25.00
5 Eli Manning 12.00 30.00
6 Peyton Manning 20.00 50.00
8 Donovan McNabb 12.00 30.00
10 Drew Brees 12.00 30.00
15 LaDainian Tomlinson 12.00 30.00
21 Clinton Portis 10.00 25.00
22 Shaun Alexander 10.00 25.00
26 Edgerrin James 10.00 25.00
38 Steve Smith 10.00 25.00
44 Hines Ward 12.00 30.00
46 Marvin Harrison 12.00 30.00
48 Jeremy Shockey/39 10.00 25.00
53 Andre Johnson 10.00 25.00
55 Joe Montana 25.00 60.00
57 John Elway 20.00 50.00
65 Randall Cunningham 10.00 25.00
69 Roger Craig 10.00 25.00
76 Thurman Thomas 10.00 25.00

2007 Playoff National Treasures Material Helmet

STATED PRINT RUN 1-25
SERIAL #'d UNDER 25 NOT PRICED
46 Marvin Harrison/25 10.00 25.00
92 Doak Walker/25 60.00 100.00

2007 Playoff National Treasures Material Jersey Numbers

STATED PRINT RUN 4-89
SERIAL #'d UNDER 20 NOT PRICED
13 Brian Westbrook/36 6.00 15.00
14 Willie Parker/39 6.00 15.00
15 LaDainian Tomlinson/21 10.00 25.00
16 Ronnie Brown/23 8.00 20.00
18 Steven Jackson/39 8.00 20.00
19 Larry Johnson/27 6.00 15.00
20 Laurence Maroney/39 6.00 15.00
21 Clinton Portis/26 8.00 20.00
22 Shaun Alexander/37 6.00 15.00
23 Maurice Jones-Drew/32 8.00 20.00
24 Frank Gore/21 10.00 25.00
25 Cadillac Williams/24 8.00 20.00
27 Brandon Jacobs/27 8.00 20.00
28 Marion Barber/24 8.00 20.00
29 Cedric Benson/32 6.00 15.00
30 Fred Taylor/28 8.00 20.00
31 Randy Moss/81 6.00 15.00
32 Chad Johnson/85 5.00 12.00
33 Antonio Gates/85 6.00 15.00
37 T.J. Houshmandzadeh/84 5.00 12.00
38 Steve Smith/89 5.00 12.00
39 Terrell Owens/81 6.00 15.00
40 Tony Gonzalez/88 5.00 12.00
42 Donald Driver/80 6.00 15.00
43 Torry Holt/81 5.00 12.00
44 Hines Ward/86 6.00 15.00
45 Reggie Wayne/87 5.00 12.00
46 Marvin Harrison/88 6.00 15.00
47 Laveranues Coles/87 4.00 10.00
48 Jeremy Shockey/80 5.00 12.00
49 Anquan Boldin/81 5.00 12.00
50 Dallas Clark/44 5.00 12.00
51 Devin Hester/23 10.00 25.00
52 Joey Galloway/84 5.00 12.00
53 Andre Johnson/80 5.00 12.00
54 Reggie Bush/25 10.00 25.00
59 Ken Strong/50 12.00 30.00
60 Larry Csonka/39 10.00 25.00
61 Lawrence Taylor/56 8.00 20.00
63 Michael Irvin/88 6.00 15.00
67 Emmitt Smith/22 25.00 60.00
71 Sammy Baugh/33 10.00 25.00
74 Walter Payton/34 20.00 50.00
75 Steve Largent/80 8.00 20.00
76 Thurman Thomas/34 8.00 20.00
77 Tommy McDonald/25 8.00 20.00
79 Tom Fears/55 5.00 12.00
83 Ollie Matson/33 8.00 20.00
84 Tom Landry/49 12.00 30.00
85 Barry Sanders/20 20.00 50.00
86 Bo Jackson/34 12.00 30.00
90 Cris Collinsworth/80 6.00 15.00
93 Fred Biletnikoff/25 12.00 30.00
96 Marion Motley/36 10.00 25.00

2007 Playoff National Treasures Material Prime

STATED PRINT RUN 4-25
SERIAL #'d UNDER 25 NOT PRICED
UNPRICED BRAND LOGO PRINT RUN 1-10
UNPRICED BUTTON PRINT RUN 3-5
UNPRICED LAUN.TAG PRINT RUN 1-10
UNPRICED NFL LOGO PRINT RUN 1
1 Tom Brady 20.00 50.00
2 Brett Favre 25.00 60.00
3 Tony Romo 15.00 40.00
4 Carson Palmer 10.00 25.00
5 Eli Manning 12.00 30.00
6 Peyton Manning 20.00 50.00
7 Philip Rivers 12.00 30.00
8 Donovan McNabb 12.00 30.00
9 Vince Young 10.00 25.00
11 Ben Roethlisberger 12.00 30.00
12 Jay Cutler 12.00 30.00
13 Brian Westbrook 10.00 25.00
14 Willie Parker 10.00 25.00
15 LaDainian Tomlinson 12.00 30.00
16 Ronnie Brown 10.00 25.00
18 Steven Jackson 12.00 30.00
19 Larry Johnson 8.00 20.00
20 Laurence Maroney 10.00 25.00
21 Clinton Portis 10.00 25.00
22 Shaun Alexander 10.00 25.00
23 Maurice Jones-Drew 12.00 30.00
24 Frank Gore 12.00 30.00
25 Cadillac Williams 10.00 25.00
27 Brandon Jacobs 10.00 25.00
28 Marion Barber 12.00 30.00
29 Cedric Benson 10.00 25.00
30 Fred Taylor 10.00 25.00
31 Randy Moss 12.00 30.00
32 Chad Johnson 10.00 25.00
33 Antonio Gates 12.00 30.00
35 Plaxico Burress 10.00 25.00
36 Kellen Winslow 10.00 25.00
37 T.J. Houshmandzadeh 10.00 25.00
38 Steve Smith 10.00 25.00
39 Terrell Owens 12.00 30.00
40 Tony Gonzalez 10.00 25.00
41 Roy Williams WR 10.00 25.00
42 Donald Driver 12.00 30.00
43 Torry Holt 10.00 25.00
44 Hines Ward 12.00 30.00
45 Reggie Wayne 10.00 25.00
46 Marvin Harrison 12.00 30.00
47 Laveranues Coles 8.00 20.00
48 Jeremy Shockey 10.00 25.00
49 Anquan Boldin 10.00 25.00
50 Dallas Clark 8.00 20.00
51 Devin Hester 12.00 30.00
52 Joey Galloway 10.00 25.00
53 Andre Johnson 10.00 25.00
54 Reggie Bush 12.00 30.00
55 Joe Montana 30.00 80.00
57 John Elway 25.00 60.00
59 Ken Strong 15.00 40.00
61 Lawrence Taylor 15.00 40.00
62 Mel Hein 15.00 40.00
63 Michael Irvin 12.00 30.00
67 Emmitt Smith 30.00 80.00
75 Steve Largent 15.00 40.00
85 Barry Sanders 25.00 60.00
86 Bo Jackson 20.00 50.00
90 Cris Collinsworth 12.00 30.00
93 Fred Biletnikoff 15.00 40.00
96 Marion Motley 15.00 40.00
100 Otto Graham 12.00 30.00

2007 Playoff National Treasures Material Quads

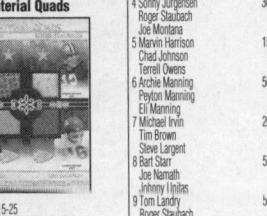

STATED PRINT RUN 5-25
*PRIME/25: .5X TO 1.2X BASE QUAD JSY
PRIME PRINT RUN 25 SER.#'d SETS
SERIAL #'d UNDER 25 NOT PRICED
1 Emmitt Smith 75.00 150.00
Walter Payton
Barry Sanders
Jim Brown
2 Emmitt Smith 60.00 120.00
Marcus Allen
Walter Payton
LaDainian Tomlinson
3 Jerry Rice 30.00 80.00
Tim Brown
James Lofton
Marvin Harrison
4 Brett Favre 100.00 200.00
Dan Marino
John Elway
Warren Moon
5 Bob Lilly 25.00 60.00
Cliff Harris
Jack Lambert
Joe Greene
6 Troy Aikman 40.00 100.00
Michael Irvin
Joe Montana
Jerry Rice
8 Fran Tarkenton 25.00 60.00
Alan Page
Len Dawson
Jan Stenerud
9 Tom Landry CO 50.00 120.00
Roger Staubach
Hank Stram
Len Dawson
10 Roger Staubach 50.00 120.00
Joe Montana
Troy Aikman
Steve Young
11 Troy Aikman 30.00 80.00
Emmitt Smith
Jim Kelly
Thurman Thomas
12 Joe Greene 20.00 50.00
Alan Page
Merlin Olsen
Bob Lilly
14 Jim Otto 20.00 50.00
Jim Parker
Ron Mix
Chuck Bednarik
15 Norm Van Brocklin 40.00 100.00
Bob Waterfield
Bobby Layne
Otto Graham

2007 Playoff National Treasures Material Signature Face Mask

STATED PRINT RUN 1-25
UNPRICED HELMET PRINT RUN 1-18
SERIAL #'d UNDER 20 NOT PRICED
5 Eli Manning/25 60.00 120.00
6 Peyton Manning/25 75.00 150.00
10 Drew Brees/25 40.00 80.00
38 Steve Smith/25 20.00 50.00
61 Lawrence Taylor/25 30.00 80.00
65 Randall Cunningham/25 25.00 60.00
67 Emmitt Smith/22 125.00 250.00
69 Roger Craig/25 15.00 40.00

2007 Playoff National Treasures Material Signature Jersey Numbers

STATED PRINT RUN 4-87
UNPRICED BRAND LOGO PRINT RUN 1
UNPRICED BUTTON PRINT RUN 1
UNPRICED LAUN.TAG PRINT RUN 1
UNPRICED NFL LOGO PRINT RUN 1
SERIAL #'d UNDER 20 NOT PRICED
13 Brian Westbrook/36 20.00 50.00
15 LaDainian Tomlinson/21 60.00 120.00
16 Ronnie Brown/23 20.00 50.00
18 Steven Jackson/39 20.00 50.00
19 Larry Johnson/27
20 Laurence Maroney/39 20.00 50.00
23 Maurice Jones-Drew/32 20.00 50.00
24 Frank Gore/21 20.00 50.00
25 Cadillac Williams/24
27 Brandon Jacobs/27 30.00 60.00
28 Marion Barber/24 25.00 60.00
29 Cedric Benson/32 15.00 40.00
30 Fred Taylor/28 20.00 50.00
37 T.J. Houshmandzadeh/84 15.00 40.00
43 Torry Holt/81 15.00 40.00
45 Reggie Wayne/87 20.00 50.00
51 Devin Hester/23 50.00 100.00
54 Reggie Bush/25 40.00 100.00
61 Lawrence Taylor/56 30.00 60.00
67 Emmitt Smith/22 125.00 250.00
75 Steve Largent/80 20.00 50.00
76 Thurman Thomas/34 20.00 50.00
77 Tommy McDonald/25 15.00 40.00
86 Bo Jackson/34 40.00 80.00
90 Cris Collinsworth/80 12.00 30.00
93 Fred Biletnikoff/20 40.00 80.00

2007 Playoff National Treasures Material Trios

STATED PRINT RUN 25 SER.#'d SETS
*HOF/25: .4X TO 1X BASE TRIO
HOF PRINT RUN 25
*HOF PRIME/25: .6X TO 1.5X BASE TRIO
HOF PRIME PRINT RUN 25
*NFL/25: .4X TO 1X BASE TRIO
NFL PRINT RUN 25
*NFL PRIME/25: .6X TO 1.5X BASE TRIO
NFL PRIME PRINT RUN 25
*PRIME/25: .6X TO 1.5X BASE TRIO
PRIME PRINT RUN 25
1 Peyton Manning 50.00 120.00
Tom Brady
Brett Favre
2 Emmitt Smith 40.00 100.00
Walter Payton
Barry Sanders
3 Brett Favre 50.00 120.00
Dan Marino
John Elway
4 Sonny Jurgensen 30.00 80.00
Roger Staubach
Joe Montana
5 Marvin Harrison 15.00 40.00
Chad Johnson
Terrell Owens
6 Archie Manning 50.00 100.00
Peyton Manning
Eli Manning
7 Michael Irvin 20.00 50.00
Tim Brown
Steve Largent
8 Bart Starr 50.00 120.00
Joe Namath
Johnny Unitas
9 Tom Landry 50.00 100.00
Roger Staubach
Tony Dorsett
10 Hank Stram 15.00 40.00
Len Dawson
Jan Stenerud
11 Tom Fears 15.00 40.00
Jim Parker
Dick Lane
12 Earl Campbell 30.00 80.00
Franco Harris
Walter Payton
13 Jim Brown 30.00 80.00
Earl Campbell
Barry Sanders
14 Sterling Sharpe 25.00 60.00
Michael Irvin
Jerry Rice/15
15 Joe Namath 25.00 60.00
Fran Tarkenton
Archie Manning

2007 Playoff National Treasures Notable Nicknames Signature

STATED PRINT RUN 25-126
10 Joe Greene/54 30.00 60.00
AP Adrian Peterson/28 300.00 600.00
BD Bill Dudley/54 20.00 50.00
FB Fred Biletnikoff/52 25.00 50.00
JN Joe Namath/55 90.00 150.00
LM Lenny Moore/126 20.00 50.00
MD Mark Duper/74 15.00 40.00
SM Shawne Merriman/25 30.00 60.00
WL Willie Lanier/38 25.00 60.00
WL Willie Lanier/85 20.00 50.00

2007 Playoff National Treasures Pen Pals

STATED PRINT RUN 12-30
GG Ted Ginn Jr.
Anthony Gonzalez
JM Calvin Johnson 40.00 80.00
Robert Meachem/29
JO Calvin Johnson 60.00 120.00
Greg Olsen
JS Dwayne Jarrett 15.00 40.00
Steve Smith USC
PL Adrian Peterson 200.00 400.00
Marshawn Lynch
RQ JaMarcus Russell 20.00 50.00
Brady Quinn
SP Troy Smith 20.00 50.00
Antonio Pittman

2007 Playoff National Treasures Rookie Jumbo Material

STATED PRINT RUN 49 SER.#'d SETS
UNPRICED BRAND LOGO PRINT RUN 10
UNPRICED PRIME PRINT RUN 1
UNPRICED LAUNDRY TAG PRINT RUN 10
UNPRICED NFL SHIELD PRINT RUN 1
101 Adrian Peterson 15.00 40.00
102 Anthony Gonzalez 4.00 10.00
103 Antonio Pittman 2.50 6.00
104 Brady Quinn 4.00 10.00
105 Brandon Jackson 3.00 8.00
106 Brian Leonard 3.00 8.00
107 Calvin Johnson 12.00 30.00
108 Chris Henry RB 2.50 6.00
109 Drew Stanton 2.50 6.00
110 Dwayne Jarrett 3.00 8.00
111 Dwayne Bowe 5.00 12.00
112 Gaines Adams 4.00 10.00
113 Garrett Wolfe 2.50 6.00
114 Greg Olsen 3.00 8.00
115 JaMarcus Russell 2.50 6.00
116 Jason Hill 4.00 10.00
117 Joe Thomas 4.00 10.00
118 John Beck 4.00 10.00
119 Johnnie Lee Higgins 3.00 8.00
120 Kenny Irons 2.50 6.00
121 Kevin Kolb 6.00 15.00
122 Lorenzo Booker 3.00 8.00
123 Marshawn Lynch 4.00 10.00
124 Michael Bush 4.00 10.00
125 Patrick Willis 8.00 20.00
126 Paul Williams 2.50 6.00
127 Robert Meachem 4.00 10.00
128 Sidney Rice 5.00 12.00
129 Steve Smith USC 4.00 10.00
130 Ted Ginn Jr. 3.00 8.00
131 Tony Hunt 2.50 6.00
132 Trent Edwards 4.00 10.00
133 Troy Smith 4.00 10.00
134 Yamon Figurs 2.50 6.00

2007 Playoff National Treasures Rookie Signature Combo Material Silver

*SILV.COMBO/25: .3X TO .8X BASE JSY AU/99
SILVER COMBO PRINT RUN 25
UNPRICED GOLD PRINT RUN 10
UNPRICED PLATINUM PRINT RUN 1
101 Adrian Peterson 200.00 400.00
107 Calvin Johnson 125.00 250.00
121 Kevin Kolb 50.00 120.00

2007 Playoff National Treasures Rookie Signature Jumbo Material Gold

GOLD JUMBO PRINT RUN 25
*GOLD JUMBO/25: .4X TO 1X BASE JSY AU/99
UNPRICED PLATINUM PRINT RUN 5
UNPRICED BLACK PRINT RUN 1
101 Adrian Peterson 250.00 500.00
107 Calvin Johnson 100.00 200.00
121 Kevin Kolb 50.00 120.00

2007 Playoff National Treasures Rookie Signature Material Gold

*GOLD: .3X TO .8X BASE JSY AU/99
GOLD PRINT RUN 25 SER.#'d SETS
101 Adrian Peterson 200.00 400.00
107 Calvin Johnson 125.00 250.00

2007 Playoff National Treasures Rookie Signature Material Silver

*SILVER/49: .25X TO .6X BASE JSY AU/99
SILVER PRINT RUN 49 SER.#'d SETS
UNPRICED PLATINUM PRINT RUN 1
101 Adrian Peterson 150.00 300.00
107 Calvin Johnson 75.00 150.00

2007 Playoff National Treasures Signature Combos

STATED PRINT RUN 20 SER.#'d SETS
UNPRICED SIG TRIOS PRINT RUN 15
2 Roger Craig
Frank Gore
3 Jim Kelly 60.00 100.00
Thurman Thomas
4 Phil Simms 75.00 125.00
Eli Manning
5 Fred Taylor
Maurice Jones-Drew
6 Joe Namath 60.00 120.00
Don Maynard
7 Warren Moon 50.00 100.00
Earl Campbell
8 Donald Driver 50.00 100.00
Greg Jennings
9 Steve Smith 15.00 40.00
DeAngelo Williams
10 Marcus Allen 50.00 100.00
Tim Brown
11 Eric Dickerson 50.00 100.00
Steven Jackson
12 Steve McNair
Willis McGahee
13 John Stallworth 60.00 120.00
Hines Ward
14 Fran Tarkenton 40.00 100.00
Paul Krause
15 Cliff Harris 25.00 50.00
Bill Bates

2007 Playoff National Treasures Signature Gold

GOLD PRINT RUN 4-49
SER.#'d UNDER 25 NOT PRICED
5 Eli Manning 50.00 100.00
10 Drew Brees 50.00 100.00
13 Brian Westbrook 20.00 50.00
16 Ronnie Brown 15.00 40.00
17 Willis McGahee 15.00 40.00
18 Steven Jackson 20.00 50.00
19 Larry Johnson 12.00 30.00
20 Laurence Maroney 15.00 40.00
23 Maurice Jones-Drew 20.00 50.00
24 Frank Gore 20.00 50.00
25 Cadillac Williams 15.00 40.00
27 Brandon Jacobs 15.00 40.00
28 Marion Barber 20.00 50.00
29 Cedric Benson 15.00 40.00
34 Larry Fitzgerald 20.00 50.00
37 T.J. Houshmandzadeh 15.00 40.00
38 Steve Smith 15.00 40.00
41 Roy Williams WR 15.00 40.00
43 Torry Holt 15.00 40.00
58 Johnny Morris 12.00 30.00
61 Lawrence Taylor 25.00 60.00
63 Michael Irvin 30.00 60.00
64 Paul Krause 15.00 40.00
65 Randall Cunningham 20.00 50.00
66 Rick Casares 20.00 50.00
68 Lydell Mitchell 12.00 30.00
69 Roger Craig 15.00 40.00
70 Sam Huff 15.00 40.00
73 Sonny Jurgensen 20.00 50.00
75 Steve Largent 20.00 50.00
77 Tommy McDonald 12.00 30.00
86 Bo Jackson 40.00 80.00
89 Yale Lary 12.00 30.00
90 Cris Collinsworth 15.00 40.00
91 Daryle Lamonica 20.00 50.00
94 George Blanda 30.00 80.00
95 Harlon Hill 12.00 30.00
97 Jimmy Orr 12.00 30.00
101 Adrian Peterson 150.00 300.00
102 Anthony Gonzalez 20.00 50.00
103 Antonio Pittman 6.00 15.00
104 Brady Quinn 25.00 60.00
105 Brandon Jackson 8.00 20.00
106 Brian Leonard 8.00 20.00
107 Calvin Johnson 60.00 150.00
108 Chris Henry RB 6.00 15.00
109 Drew Stanton 6.00 15.00
110 Dwayne Jarrett 8.00 20.00
111 Dwayne Bowe 20.00 50.00
112 Gaines Adams 10.00 25.00
113 Garrett Wolfe 6.00 15.00
114 Greg Olsen 8.00 20.00
115 JaMarcus Russell 20.00 50.00
116 Jason Hill 10.00 25.00
117 Joe Thomas 12.00 30.00
118 John Beck 10.00 25.00
119 Johnnie Lee Higgins 8.00 20.00
121 Kevin Kolb 30.00 80.00
122 Lorenzo Booker 8.00 20.00
123 Marshawn Lynch 5.00 50.00
124 Michael Bush 10.00 25.00
125 Patrick Willis 25.00 60.00
126 Paul Williams 6.00 15.00
127 Robert Meachem 15.00 40.00
128 Sidney Rice 12.00 30.00
129 Steve Smith USC 10.00 25.00
130 Ted Ginn Jr. 20.00 50.00
131 Tony Hunt 6.00 15.00
132 Trent Edwards 10.00 25.00
133 Troy Smith 10.00 25.00
134 Yamon Figurs 6.00 15.00
135 Darrelle Revis 25.00 50.00
137 LaRon Landry 8.00 20.00
138 James Jones 8.00 20.00
139 Michael Griffin 8.00 20.00
140 Aundrae Allison 5.00 12.00

143 DeShawn Wynn 6.00 15.00
144 Dwayne Wright 6.00 15.00
145 Jacoby Jones 8.00 20.00
146 John Broussard 6.00 15.00
147 Jon Beason 6.00 15.00
148 Kenton Keith 8.00 20.00
149 Kolby Smith 6.00 15.00
150 Leon Hall 6.00 15.00
151 Reggie Nelson 6.00 15.00
152 Roy Hall 8.00 20.00
153 Ryne Robinson 6.00 15.00
154 Selvin Young 6.00 15.00
155 Steve Breaston 8.00 20.00
156 Chris Davis 5.00 12.00
157 Glenn Holt 6.00 15.00
158 Kenneth Darby 6.00 15.00
159 Mike Walker 8.00 20.00
160 Chris Houston 6.00 15.00
161 David Clowney 6.00 15.00
162 Mason Crosby 12.00 30.00
163 Bobby Sippio 6.00 15.00
164 Biren Ealy 6.00 15.00
166 Laurent Robinson 10.00 25.00
167 Lawrence Timmons 8.00 20.00
168 Legedu Naanee 8.00 20.00
169 Brandon Meriweather 8.00 20.00
170 Brian Robison 8.00 20.00
171 Greg Peterson 6.00 15.00
172 Ikaika Alama-Francis 8.00 20.00
173 Isaiah Stanback 5.00 12.00
174 Ed Johnson 6.00 15.00
175 Eric Frampton 6.00 15.00
176 Eric Weddle 8.00 20.00
177 Fred Bennett 5.00 12.00
178 Dante Rosario 8.00 20.00
179 Clifton Dawson 8.00 20.00
180 Jeff Rowe 5.00 12.00
181 Justin Durant 6.00 15.00
183 Paul Posluszny 8.00 20.00
184 Pierre Thomas 50.00 100.00
185 Quentin Moses 6.00 15.00
186 Ray McDonald 6.00 15.00
187 Sabby Piscitelli 8.00 20.00
188 Scott Chandler 8.00 20.00
189 Matt Gutierrez 8.00 20.00
190 Matt Moore 8.00 20.00
191 Martrez Milner 5.00 12.00
192 Amobi Okoye 8.00 20.00
193 Adam Carriker 6.00 15.00
195 Anthony Spencer 8.00 20.00
196 Tyler Thigpen 8.00 20.00
197 Victor Abiamiri 8.00 20.00
198 Zach Miller 8.00 20.00
199 Jarvis Moss 6.00 15.00
200 LaMarr Woodley 12.00 30.00

2007 Playoff National Treasures Signature Silver

SILVER PRINT RUN 12-50
UNPRICED PLATINUM PRINT RUN 1
SER.#'d UNDER 20 NOT PRICED
5 Eli Manning 40.00 80.00
6 Peyton Manning/25 60.00 120.00
10 Drew Brees 40.00 80.00
12 Jay Cutler/20 25.00 60.00
13 Brian Westbrook 15.00 40.00
16 Ronnie Brown 12.00 30.00
17 Willis McGahee 12.00 30.00
18 Steven Jackson 15.00 40.00
19 Larry Johnson 10.00 25.00
20 Laurence Maroney 12.00 30.00
23 Maurice Jones-Drew 15.00 40.00
24 Frank Gore 15.00 40.00
25 Cadillac Williams 12.00 30.00
27 Brandon Jacobs 12.00 30.00
28 Marion Barber 15.00 40.00
29 Cedric Benson 12.00 30.00
30 Fred Taylor/31 12.00 30.00
34 Larry Fitzgerald/49 20.00 40.00
37 T.J. Houshmandzadeh 12.00 30.00
41 Roy Williams WR 12.00 30.00
42 Donald Driver/35 25.00 50.00
55 Joe Montana/20 75.00 150.00
56 Joe Namath/25 60.00 120.00
58 Johnny Morris 10.00 25.00
61 Lawrence Taylor 20.00 50.00
63 Michael Irvin 20.00 50.00
64 Paul Krause 12.00 30.00
65 Randall Cunningham 15.00 40.00
66 Rick Casares 15.00 40.00
68 Lydell Mitchell 10.00 25.00
69 Roger Craig 12.00 30.00
70 Sam Huff 12.00 30.00
73 Sonny Jurgensen 15.00 40.00
75 Steve Largent 15.00 40.00
77 Tommy McDonald 10.00 25.00
86 Bo Jackson 30.00 60.00
87 Bob Griese/38 15.00 30.00
89 Yale Lary 10.00 25.00
90 Cris Collinsworth 12.00 30.00
91 Daryle Lamonica 15.00 40.00
94 George Blanda 25.00 60.00
95 Harlon Hill 10.00 25.00
97 Jimmy Orr 10.00 25.00
101 Adrian Peterson 125.00 250.00
102 Anthony Gonzalez 8.00 20.00
103 Antonio Pittman 5.00 12.00
104 Brady Quinn 20.00 50.00
105 Brandon Jackson 6.00 15.00
106 Brian Leonard 6.00 15.00
107 Calvin Johnson 60.00 120.00
108 Chris Henry RB 5.00 12.00
109 Drew Stanton 5.00 12.00
110 Dwayne Jarrett 6.00 15.00
111 Dwayne Bowe 15.00 40.00
112 Gaines Adams 8.00 20.00
113 Garrett Wolfe 5.00 12.00
114 Greg Olsen 6.00 15.00
115 JaMarcus Russell 5.00 12.00
116 Jason Hill 8.00 20.00
117 Joe Thomas 8.00 20.00
118 John Beck 8.00 20.00
119 Johnnie Lee Higgins 6.00 15.00
121 Kevin Kolb 20.00 50.00
122 Lorenzo Booker 6.00 15.00
123 Marshawn Lynch 15.00 40.00
124 Michael Bush 8.00 20.00
125 Patrick Willis 20.00 50.00
126 Paul Williams 5.00 12.00
127 Robert Meachem 10.00 25.00
128 Sidney Rice 20.00 40.00
129 Steve Smith USC 8.00 20.00
130 Ted Ginn Jr. 6.00 15.00
131 Tony Hunt 5.00 12.00
132 Trent Edwards/34 8.00 20.00
133 Troy Smith 8.00 20.00
134 Yamon Figurs 5.00 12.00

2007 Playoff National Treasures Signature Trios

SIGNATURE TRIOS PRINT RUN 15
2 LaDainian Tomlinson 50.00 100.00
  Michael Turner
  Shawne Merriman
3 Bernard Berrian 25.00 50.00
  Cedric Benson
  Devin Hester
5 Len Dawson 30.00 60.00
  Willie Lanier
  Jan Stenerud
6 Peyton Manning 75.00 150.00
  Marvin Harrison
  Joseph Addai
7 Bob Griese 75.00 150.00
  Larry Csonka
  Paul Warfield
8 Brett Favre 150.00 250.00
  Greg Jennings
  A.J. Hawk
10 Reggie Bush 40.00 80.00
  Deuce McAllister
  Marques Colston

2007 Playoff National Treasures Super Bowl Signatures Cuts

STATED PRINT RUN 1-50
DM Dan Marino/25 125.00 200.00
FT Fran Tarkenton/25 40.00 80.00
JE John Elway/15 75.00 200.00
JE John Elway/15 75.00 200.00
JK Jim Kelly/25 50.00 100.00
JL Jack Lambert/25 90.00 150.00
JN Joe Namath/25 60.00 120.00
JR John Riggins/25 30.00 80.00
LD Len Dawson/50 30.00 60.00
MA Marcus Allen/25 20.00 50.00
MI Michael Irvin/34 40.00 80.00
RS Roger Staubach/29 50.00 100.00
SY Steve Young/50 50.00 100.00
TD Tony Dorsett/50 40.00 80.00
WP Walter Payton/34 200.00 400.00

2007 Playoff National Treasures Super Bowl Material

STATED PRINT RUN 10-49
*PRIME/25: .5X TO 1.2X BASE JSY/40-49
*PRIME/25: .4X TO 1X BASE JSY/20-30
PRIME PRINT RUN 1-25
SERIAL #'d UNDER 19 NOT PRICED
BF Brett Favre 40.00 100.00
BG Bob Griese 20.00 50.00
BS Bart Starr 30.00 80.00
CT Charley Taylor 15.00 40.00
DB Deion Branch 15.00 40.00
DG Darrell Green 20.00 50.00
DH Devin Hester 20.00 50.00
DL Daryle Lamonica 15.00 40.00
DM Dan Marino 40.00 100.00
ES1 Emmitt Smith 40.00 100.00
ES2 Emmitt Smith 40.00 100.00
FB Fred Biletnikoff 20.00 50.00
FT Fran Tarkenton 25.00 60.00
HW Hines Ward 20.00 50.00
JE1 John Elway/25 40.00 100.00
JE2 John Elway/25 40.00 100.00
JK Jim Kelly/25 30.00 80.00
JL Jack Lambert 20.00 50.00
JM2 Joe Montana/19 50.00 125.00
JM3 Joe Montana/24 50.00 125.00
JMA John Mackey 15.00 40.00
JMC Jim McMahon/25 30.00 80.00
JN Joe Namath/25 30.00 80.00
JP Jim Plunkett 15.00 40.00
JR1 Jerry Rice/30 40.00 100.00
JR2 Jerry Rice/30 40.00 100.00
JRI John Riggins/44 15.00 40.00
KW Kurt Warner 15.00 40.00
LC Larry Csonka/25 25.00 60.00
LD Len Dawson 20.00 50.00
MA Mike Alstott/48 15.00 40.00
MI Michael Irvin 15.00 40.00
PM Peyton Manning 30.00 80.00
PS Phil Simms 15.00 40.00
RL Ray Lewis 20.00 50.00
RS Roger Staubach/25 40.00 100.00
SS Steve Smith 15.00 40.00
SY Steve Young 25.00 60.00
TA Troy Aikman 25.00 60.00
TD Tony Dorsett 20.00 50.00
TO Terrell Owens 20.00 50.00
TT Thurman Thomas 15.00 40.00
WP Walter Payton/40 40.00 100.00
MAL Marcus Allen 20.00 50.00
TB1 Tom Brady/20 40.00 100.00
TB2 Tom Brady/20 40.00 100.00
WPA Willie Parker 15.00 40.00

2007 Playoff National Treasures Super Bowl Material Signatures

STATED PRINT RUN 1-25
SER.#'d UNDER 20 NOT PRICED
DM Dan Marino/25 125.00 250.00
FB Fred Biletnikoff/20 40.00 80.00
FT Fran Tarkenton/25 40.00 80.00
JM Joe Montana/24 125.00 200.00
MI Michael Irvin/25 40.00 100.00
PM Peyton Manning/25 125.00 200.00
PS Phil Simms/25 40.00 80.00
RS Roger Staubach/25 60.00 120.00
SS Steve Smith/25 25.00 60.00
SY Steve Young/25 50.00 100.00
TD Tony Dorsett/25 40.00 80.00

2007 Playoff National Treasures Super Bowl Signatures

STATED PRINT RUN 5-25
SER.#'d UNDER 24 NOT PRICED
UNPRICED DUAL SIG PRINT RUN 10
CT Charley Taylor/25 15.00 40.00
DL Daryle Lamonica/25 20.00 50.00
DM Dan Marino/25 100.00 200.00
FT Fran Tarkenton/25 25.00 60.00
JM Joe Montana/24 100.00 175.00
JM John Mackey/25 20.00 50.00
JN Joe Namath/25 60.00 120.00
JR John Riggins/25 25.00 60.00
LD Len Dawson/25 20.00 50.00
SY Steve Young/29 50.00 100.00
TD Tony Dorsett/33 30.00 60.00

2007 Playoff National Treasures Timeline Material NFL

STATED PRINT RUN 10-99
*AFC/NFC/25: .6X TO 1.5X BASE NFL JSY/50-99
*AFC/NFC/25: .4X TO 1X BASE NFL JSY/15-25
AFC/NFC PRINT RUN 10-25
*AFC/NFC PRIME/25: .8X TO 2X BASE NFL JSY/50-99
AFC/NFC PRIME PRINT RUN 1-25
*HOF/25: .6X TO 1.5X NFL JSY/50-99
*HOF/25: .5X TO 1X NFL JSY/15-25
HOF PRINT RUN 10-25
*HOF PRIME/25: .8X TO 2X NFL JSY/50-99
HOF PRIME PRINT RUN 1-25
*JUMBO/21-25: .6X TO 1.5X NFL JSY/50-99
*JUMBO/21-25: .4X TO 1X NFL JSY/15-25
JUMBO PRINT RUN 1-25
*JUMBO PRIME/25: 1X TO 2.5X NFL JSY/50-99
*JUMBO PRIME/25: .6X TO 1.5X NFL JSY/15-25
JUMBO PRIME PRINT RUN 1-25
*NFL PRIME/25: .8X TO 2X BASE NFL JSY/50-99
NFL PRIME PRINT RUN 1-25
*MVP/25: .6X TO 1.5X BASE NFL JSY/50-99
*MVP/25: .4X TO 1X BASE NFL JSY/25
MVP PRINT RUN 25
*MVP PRIME/20-25: .8X TO 2X BASE NFL JSY/50-99
*MVP PRIME/25: .5X TO 1.2X BASE NFL JSY/25
MVP PRIME PRINT RUN 3-25
AM Archie Manning 10.00 25.00
AP Alan Page 10.00 25.00
BB Bill Bates 8.00 20.00
BF Brett Favre 20.00 50.00
BL Bob Lilly/15 12.00 30.00
BR Ben Roethlisberger 10.00 25.00
BS Barry Sanders 15.00 40.00
BW Bob Waterfield/25 12.00 30.00
CB Chuck Bednarik 8.00 20.00
CH Cliff Harris 8.00 20.00
CJ Chad Johnson/20 12.00 30.00
DF Dan Fouts/25 15.00 40.00
DG Darrell Green 10.00 25.00
DL Dick Lane/25 10.00 25.00
DM Don Maynard/25 12.00 30.00
EH Elroy Hirsch/25 12.00 30.00
ES Emmitt Smith 20.00 50.00
GU Gene Upshaw 6.00 15.00
HS Hank Stram 15.00 30.00
JB Jim Brown/25 20.00 50.00
JG Joe Greene/50 10.00 25.00
JH John Hannah 6.00 15.00
JK Jim Kelly/25 20.00 50.00
JL James Lofton 6.00 15.00
JM Jim McMahon/50 12.00 30.00
JN Joe Namath/25 20.00 50.00
JO Jim Otto/50 6.00 15.00
JP Jim Parker/50 6.00 15.00
JR Jerry Rice/25 25.00 60.00
JS Jan Stenerud/20 10.00 25.00
JT Jim Thorpe/25 125.00 200.00
JY Jack Youngblood 8.00 20.00
KS Ken Stabler 12.00 30.00
LA Lance Alworth/25 12.00 30.00
LC Larry Csonka/25 15.00 40.00
LG Lou Groza 8.00 20.00
LL Larry Little/10 8.00 20.00
LT LaDainian Tomlinson/50 10.00 25.00
MD Mark Duper/50 6.00 15.00
MI Michael Irvin 8.00 20.00
MO Merlin Olsen/50 8.00 20.00
NV Norm Van Brocklin 15.00 40.00
OM Ollie Matson 8.00 20.00
PM Peyton Manning 15.00 40.00
PS Phil Simms 8.00 20.00
RB Reggie Bush 10.00 25.00
RC Randall Cunningham 8.00 20.00
RG Rosey Grier 6.00 15.00
RM Randy Moss 10.00 25.00
RS Roger Staubach 15.00 40.00
SA Shaun Alexander 8.00 20.00
SB Sammy Baugh 12.00 30.00
SJ Sonny Jurgensen 8.00 20.00
SL Sid Luckman 12.00 30.00
TB Tom Brady/50 15.00 40.00
TF Tom Fears 8.00 20.00
TL Tom Landry 25.00 50.00
TM Tommy McDonald 10.00 25.00
TR Tony Romo 12.00 30.00
TT Thurman Thomas 8.00 20.00
VY Vince Young 10.00 25.00
WL Willie Lanier 8.00 20.00
WP Walter Payton/50 20.00 50.00
BLA Bobby Layne/25 15.00 40.00
JTH Joe Theismann 10.00 25.00
KST Ken Strong 10.00 25.00
RMI Ron Mix/50 6.00 15.00
TBA Tiki Barber 10.00 25.00
TBR Tim Brown 10.00 25.00

2007 Playoff National Treasures Timeline Material Signature AFC/NFC Prime

AFC/NFC PRIME PRINT RUN 1-25
*NFL PRM/15-25: .4X TO 1X AFC/NFC PRM/15-25
NFL PRIME PRINT RUN 1-25
JT Joe Theismann/25 50.00 100.00
AM Archie Manning/25 30.00 80.00
BB Bill Bates/25 30.00 80.00
CH Cliff Harris/15 20.00 50.00
JO Jim Otto/25 25.00 60.00
MD Mark Duper/25 20.00 50.00
MI Michael Irvin/25 50.00 100.00
PM Peyton Manning/25 125.00 250.00
PS Phil Simms/15 25.00 60.00
RB Reggie Bush/15 30.00 80.00
RS Roger Staubach/25 60.00 120.00
SS Sterling Sharpe/25 25.00 60.00
TB Tim Brown/25 30.00 80.00
TB Tiki Barber/25 25.00 60.00

2007 Playoff National Treasures Timeline Material Signature HOF

STATED PRINT RUN 1-25
*PRIME/25: .5X TO 1.2X BASE HOF SIG
PRIME PRINT RUN 1-25
AP Alan Page 25.00 60.00
BL Bob Lilly 25.00 60.00
CB Chuck Bednarik 40.00 80.00
DF Dan Fouts 25.00 60.00
DM Don Maynard 20.00 50.00
GU Gene Upshaw 15.00 40.00
JL James Lofton 20.00 50.00
JN Joe Namath 75.00 150.00
JO Jim Otto 25.00 60.00
JS Jan Stenerud/20 15.00 40.00
JY Jack Youngblood 25.00 50.00
LA Lance Alworth 40.00 80.00
LL Larry Little 15.00 40.00
MI Michael Irvin 40.00 100.00
RM Ron Mix 15.00 40.00
RS Roger Staubach 50.00 100.00
SJ Sonny Jurgensen 40.00 80.00
TM Tommy McDonald 15.00 40.00
WL Willie Lanier 20.00 50.00

2007 Playoff National Treasures Timeline Material Signature MVP

MVP PRINT RUN 3-25
*PRIME/15-25: .5X TO 1.2X BASE MVP SIG
MVP PRIME PRINT RUN 1-25
AP Alan Page/25 25.00 60.00
DF Dan Fouts/25 25.00 60.00
JB Jim Brown/25 60.00 120.00
JN Joe Namath/25 75.00 150.00
JR Jerry Rice/15 125.00 200.00
JT Joe Theismann/25 25.00 60.00
LT LaDainian Tomlinson/15 30.00 80.00
PM Peyton Manning/25 100.00 200.00
RC Randall Cunningham/25 30.00 60.00
RS Roger Staubach/25 50.00 100.00
TT Thurman Thomas/15 30.00 80.00

2007 Playoff National Treasures Timeline Signature

STATED PRINT RUN 1-99
SER.#'d UNDER 25 NOT PRICED
AM Archie Manning/99 20.00 50.00
AP Alan Page/85 15.00 40.00
BD Bill Dudley/99 20.00 50.00
BD Boyd Dowler/99 12.00 30.00
BH Billy Howton/99 12.00 30.00
CB Chuck Bednarik/75 15.00 40.00
DF Dan Fouts/50 15.00 40.00
DM Don Maynard/99 10.00 25.00
GU Gene Upshaw/99 10.00 25.00
JB Jim Brown/56 40.00 80.00
JN Joe Namath/25 60.00 120.00
JO Jim Otto/99 15.00 40.00
JS Jan Stenerud/99 10.00 25.00
KW Kellen Winslow Sr./58 12.00 30.00
LA Lance Alworth/30 20.00 50.00
LL Larry Little/47 12.00 30.00
MD Mark Duper/99 10.00 25.00
MO Merlin Olsen/30 15.00 40.00
RC Randall Cunningham/99 15.00 40.00
RG Rosey Grier/92 15.00 40.00
RM Ron Mix/99 10.00 25.00
SJ Sonny Jurgensen/75 15.00 40.00
SS Sterling Sharpe/99 12.00 30.00
TB Tiki Barber/32 20.00 50.00
TB Tim Brown/33 20.00 50.00
WL Willie Lanier/45 12.00 30.00
YL Yale Lary/99 10.00 25.00

2007 Playoff National Treasures Timeline Signature Cuts

STATED PRINT RUN 1-100
SER.#'d UNDER 20 NOT PRICED
AP Alan Page/25 25.00 60.00
BF Brett Favre/25 150.00 250.00
BH Billy Howton/50 15.00 40.00
BS Barry Sanders/34 100.00 175.00
BW Bob Waterfield/100 75.00 150.00
CB Chuck Bednarik/25 25.00 60.00
DF Dan Fouts/25 25.00 60.00
DL Dick Lane/40 100.00 200.00
DM Don Maynard/50 15.00 40.00
JB Jim Brown/25 60.00 120.00
JK Jim Kelly/25 50.00 100.00
JL James Lofton/30 15.00 40.00
JN Joe Namath/25 60.00 120.00
JO Jim Otto/50 20.00 50.00
LA Lance Alworth/25 30.00 60.00
OM Ollie Matson/20 25.00 50.00
RB Reggie Bush/50 25.00 60.00
SB Sammy Baugh/50 100.00 200.00
SJ Sonny Jurgensen/25 40.00 80.00
SL Sid Luckman/35 125.00 250.00
TT Thurman Thomas/20 25.00 50.00
WP Walter Payton/34 200.00 400.00

2008 Playoff National Treasures

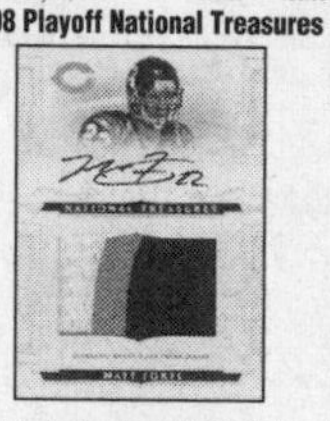

This set was released on January 28, 2009. The base set consists of 200 cards. Cards 1-100 feature veterans serial numbered of 99, and cards 101-200 are autographed rookies serial numbered of 99. This product was released with 7 cards per pack and 1 pack per hobby box.

1-100 STATED PRINT RUN 99
101-134 JSY AU RC PRINT RUN 99
135-200 AU RC PRINT RUN 49-99
UNPRICED GOLD 1-100 PRINT RUN 5
UNPRICED PLATINUM 1-100 PRINT RUN 1
UNPRICED ROOKIE SIG PLAT.PRINT RUN 1
UNPRICED SIG.PLATINUM PRINT RUN 1
1 LaDainian Tomlinson 3.00 8.00
2 Adrian Peterson 5.00 12.00
3 Brian Westbrook 2.50 6.00
4 Willie Parker 2.50 6.00
5 Clinton Portis 2.50 6.00
6 Fred Taylor 2.50 6.00
7 Marshawn Lynch 2.50 6.00
8 Frank Gore 2.50 6.00
9 Joseph Addai 2.50 6.00
10 Steven Jackson 3.00 8.00
11 Brandon Jacobs 2.50 6.00
12 Marion Barber 2.50 6.00
13 Ryan Grant 3.00 8.00
14 Selvin Young 2.00 5.00
15 Larry Johnson 2.50 6.00
16 Tom Brady 5.00 12.00
17 Drew Brees 3.00 8.00
18 Tony Romo 4.00 10.00
19 Brett Favre 8.00 20.00
20 Peyton Manning 5.00 12.00
21 Jay Cutler 3.00 8.00
22 Eli Manning 3.00 8.00
23 Donovan McNabb 3.00 8.00
24 Ben Roethlisberger 3.00 8.00
25 Philip Rivers 3.00 8.00
26 Trent Edwards 2.00 5.00
27 Carson Palmer 3.00 8.00
28 Reggie Wayne 2.50 6.00
29 Randy Moss 3.00 8.00
30 Chad Johnson 2.50 6.00
31 Larry Fitzgerald 3.00 8.00
32 Terrell Owens 3.00 8.00
33 Brandon Marshall 2.50 6.00
34 Braylon Edwards 2.50 6.00
35 Marques Colston 2.50 6.00
36 Roddy White 2.50 6.00
37 Torry Holt 2.50 6.00
38 Wes Welker 3.00 8.00
39 Tony Gonzalez 2.50 6.00
40 T.J. Houshmandzadeh 2.50 6.00
41 Jerricho Cotchery 2.50 6.00
42 Laveranues Coles 2.00 5.00
43 Kellen Winslow 2.50 6.00
44 Jason Witten 3.00 8.00
45 Donald Driver 2.50 6.00
46 Greg Jennings 3.00 8.00
47 Plaxico Burress 2.50 6.00
48 Steve Smith 2.50 6.00
49 Jake Delhomme 2.50 6.00
50 Hines Ward 2.50 6.00
51 Anquan Boldin 2.50 6.00
52 Dwayne Bowe 2.50 6.00
53 Antonio Gates 3.00 8.00
54 Lee Evans 2.50 6.00
55 Santana Moss 2.00 5.00
56 Chris Cooley 2.50 6.00
57 Calvin Johnson 3.00 8.00
58 Reggie Bush 3.00 8.00
59 Anthony Gonzalez 2.00 5.00
60 Michael Turner 3.00 8.00
61 Earnest Graham 2.00 5.00
62 Kevin Curtis 2.00 5.00
63 Dallas Clark 2.50 6.00
64 Laurence Maroney 2.50 6.00
65 Santonio Holmes 2.50 6.00
66 Sidney Rice 3.00 8.00
67 Vincent Jackson 2.00 5.00
68 Barry Sanders 5.00 12.00
69 Bert Jones 2.00 5.00
70 Bill Dudley 2.00 5.00
71 Billy Howton 2.00 5.00
72 Dan Marino 6.00 15.00
73 Dave Casper 2.50 6.00
74 Earl Campbell 3.00 8.00
75 Franco Harris 3.00 8.00
76 Gale Sayers 4.00 10.00
77 Jack Lambert 3.00 8.00
78 James Lofton 2.00 5.00
79 Jim Brown 4.00 10.00
80 Joe Montana 6.00 15.00
81 John Elway 5.00 12.00
82 Bobby Bell 2.00 5.00
83 Charley Trippi 2.00 5.00
84 Ace Clarence Parker 2.00 5.00
85 Dante Lavelli 2.00 5.00
86 Del Shofner 2.00 5.00
87 Dub Jones 2.00 5.00
88 Fred Williamson 2.00 5.00
89 Gary Collins 2.00 5.00
90 Hugh McElhenny 2.00 5.00
91 Jim Taylor 3.00 8.00
92 Lydell Mitchell 2.00 5.00
93 Mike Curtis 2.00 5.00
94 Paul Krause 2.00 5.00
95 Pete Retzlaff 2.00 5.00
96 William Perry 2.00 5.00
97 Willie Davis 2.00 5.00
98 Don Perkins 2.00 5.00
99 Willie Wood 2.00 5.00
100 Yale Lary 2.00 5.00
101 Darren McFadden JSY AU RC 75.00 150.00
102 Jonathan Stewart JSY AU RC 25.00 60.00
103 Felix Jones JSY AU RC 30.00 80.00
104 Rashard Mendenhall JSY AU RC 75.00 125.00
105 Chris Johnson JSY AU RC 100.00 200.00
106 Matt Forte JSY AU RC 50.00 120.00
107 Ray Rice JSY AU RC 75.00 125.00
108 Kevin Smith JSY AU RC 15.00 40.00
109 Jamaal Charles JSY AU RC 50.00 100.00
110 Steve Slaton JSY AU RC 15.00 40.00
111 Matt Ryan JSY AU RC 200.00 350.00
112 Joe Flacco JSY AU RC 150.00 300.00
113 Brian Brohm JSY AU RC 15.00 40.00
114 Chad Henne JSY AU RC 30.00 80.00
115 Kevin O'Connell JSY AU RC 12.00 30.00
116 John David Booty JSY AU RC 12.00 30.00
117 Andre Caldwell JSY AU RC 12.00 30.00
118 Donnie Avery JSY AU RC 12.00 30.00
119 Devin Thomas JSY AU RC 12.00 30.00
120 Jordy Nelson JSY AU RC 40.00 80.00
121 James Hardy JSY AU RC 12.00 30.00
122 Eddie Royal JSY AU RC 15.00 40.00
123 Jerome Simpson JSY AU RC 15.00 40.00
124 DeSean Jackson JSY AU RC 50.00 120.00
125 Malcolm Kelly JSY AU RC 12.00 30.00
126 Limas Sweed JSY AU RC EXCH 15.00 40.00
127 Dexter Jackson JSY AU RC 12.00 30.00
128 Earl Bennett JSY AU RC 15.00 40.00
129 Early Doucet JSY AU RC 12.00 30.00
130 Harry Douglas JSY AU RC 12.00 30.00
131 Mario Manningham JSY AU RC 30.00 60.00
132 Dustin Keller JSY AU RC 15.00 40.00
133 Glenn Dorsey JSY AU RC 15.00 40.00
134 Jake Long JSY AU RC 15.00 40.00
135 Adrian Arrington AU RC 6.00 15.00
136 Ali Highsmith AU RC 5.00 12.00
137 Antoine Cason AU RC 8.00 20.00
138 Aqib Talib AU RC 8.00 20.00
139 Brad Cottam AU RC 6.00 15.00
140 Brandon Flowers AU RC 8.00 20.00
141 Brian Witherspoon AU/49 RC 6.00 15.00
142 Calais Campbell AU RC 6.00 15.00
143 Chauncey Washington AU/49 RC 6.00 15.00
144 Chaz Schilens AU RC 12.50 25.00
145 Chevis Jackson AU RC 5.00 12.00
146 Chris Long AU RC 8.00 20.00
147 Colt Brennan AU RC 20.00 50.00
148 Curtis Lofton AU RC 8.00 20.00
149 Dan Connor AU RC 8.00 20.00
150 Dantrell Savage AU/49 RC 6.00 15.00
151 Davone Bess AU RC 8.00 20.00
152 Dennis Dixon AU RC 25.00 50.00
153 Derrick Harvey AU RC 5.00 12.00
154 Dominique Rodgers-Cromartie AU RC 10.00 25.00
155 Erik Ainge AU RC 8.00 20.00
156 Erin Henderson AU RC 8.00 20.00
157 Fred Davis AU RC 8.00 20.00
158 Jacob Hester AU RC 8.00 20.00
159 Jacob Tamme AU RC 8.00 20.00
160 Jermichael Finley AU RC 30.00 60.00
161 Jerod Mayo AU RC 12.00 30.00
162 John Carlson AU RC 8.00 20.00
163 Jordon Dizon AU RC 8.00 20.00
164 Josh Johnson AU RC 12.00 30.00
165 Josh Morgan AU RC 8.00 20.00
166 Justin Forsett AU RC 12.50 25.00
167 Keenan Burton AU RC 5.00 12.00
168 Keith Rivers AU RC 8.00 20.00
169 Kellen Davis AU RC 5.00 12.00
170 Kenny Phillips AU RC 8.00 20.00
171 Kentwan Balmer AU RC 6.00 15.00
172 Kregg Lumpkin AU RC 8.00 20.00
173 Lavelle Hawkins AU RC 5.00 12.00
174 Lawrence Jackson AU RC 6.00 15.00
175 Leodis McKelvin AU RC 6.00 15.00
176 Marcus Henry AU RC 6.00 15.00
177 Marcus Smith AU/49 RC EXCH 6.00 15.00
178 Marcus Thomas AU RC 6.00 15.00
179 Martellus Bennett AU RC 6.00 15.00
180 Martin Rucker AU RC 6.00 15.00
181 Matt Flynn AU RC 200.00 300.00
182 Matt Slater AU/49 RC 8.00 20.00
183 Mike Hart AU RC 8.00 20.00
184 Mike Jenkins AU RC 8.00 20.00
185 Owen Schmitt AU RC 10.00 25.00
186 Pat Sims AU RC 6.00 15.00
187 Phillip Merling AU RC 6.00 15.00
188 Pierre Garcon AU/49 RC 75.00 150.00
189 Quentin Groves AU RC 6.00 15.00
190 Reggie Smith AU RC 6.00 15.00
191 Ryan Torain AU/49 RC 25.00 60.00
192 Sedrick Ellis AU RC 8.00 20.00
193 Steve Johnson AU RC 35.00 60.00
194 Tashard Choice AU RC 6.00 15.00
195 Terrell Thomas AU RC 6.00 15.00
196 Tim Hightower AU RC 12.00 30.00
197 Vernon Gholston AU RC 6.00 15.00
198 Will Franklin AU RC 6.00 15.00
199 Xavier Adibi AU RC 5.00 12.00
200 Xavier Omon AU/49 RC 8.00 20.00

2008 Playoff National Treasures 50th Anniversary Material

STATED PRINT RUN 25 SER.#'d SETS
*PRIME/14-25: .6X TO 1.5X MATERIAL/25
PRIME PRINT RUN 3-25
UNPRICED SIGN PRINT RUN 10
1 Jim Brown 12.00 30.00
2 Gale Sayers 12.00 30.00
3 Hugh McElhenny 10.00 25.00
4 John Mackey 10.00 25.00
5 Chuck Bednarik 10.00 25.00
6 Ray Nitschke 15.00 40.00
7 Raymond Berry 10.00 25.00
8 Norm Van Brocklin 12.00 30.00
9 Mel Hein 10.00 25.00
10 Lenny Moore 10.00 25.00

2008 Playoff National Treasures 75th Anniversary Material

STATED PRINT RUN 4-25
UNPRICED SIG PRINT RUN 1-10
3 Joe Montana 20.00 50.00
5 Marion Motley 12.00 30.00
6 Walter Payton 25.00 60.00
7 Gale Sayers 15.00 40.00
8 Lance Alworth 20.00 50.00
9 Raymond Berry 10.00 25.00
10 Jerry Rice 20.00 50.00
11 Mike Ditka 20.00 50.00
14 Gene Upshaw 8.00 20.00
17 Reggie White 15.00 40.00
18 Joe Greene 15.00 40.00
19 Bob Lilly 10.00 25.00
20 Merlin Olsen 10.00 25.00
21 Dick Butkus/20 20.00 50.00
23 Jack Lambert/15 20.00 50.00
28 Ronnie Lott 15.00 40.00
29 Jan Stenerud 10.00 25.00

2008 Playoff National Treasures All Pros Material NFL

BASIC MATERIAL PRINT RUN 1-25
*JUMBO MAT/13-25: .4X TO 1X MATERIAL/25
JUMBO MATERIAL PRINT RUN 1-25
*HOF MAT/25: .4X TO 1X MATERIAL/25
HOF MATERIAL PRINT RUN 1-25
*MVP MAT/25: .4X TO 1X MATERIAL/25
MVP MATERIAL PRINT RUN 1-25
SERIAL #'d UNDER 13 NOT PRICED
3 Andre Reed/25 12.00 30.00
9 Carl Eller/25 10.00 25.00
11 Charlie Joiner/25 10.00 25.00
21 Jim Kelly/25 15.00 40.00
24 Joe Klecko/25 10.00 25.00
27 Emmitt Smith/25 30.00 80.00
33 Ollie Matson/22 12.00 30.00
36 Randall Cunningham/25 15.00 40.00
39 Sterling Sharpe/25 12.00 30.00
41 Tiki Barber/25 12.00 30.00

2008 Playoff National Treasures All Pros Material Quads

STATED PRINT RUN 25 SER.#'d SETS
*PRIME/15-25: .5X TO 1.2X BASIC QUAD/25
PRIME PRINT RUN 15-25
1 Barry Sanders 50.00 100.00
  Emmitt Smith
  Isaac Bruce
  Jerry Rice
2 John Elway 50.00 100.00
  Steve Young
  Jerry Rice
  Tim Brown
4 Junior Seau 15.00 40.00
  Tony Gonzalez
  Randy Moss
  Terrell Owens
5 Deuce McAllister 25.00 60.00
  Jeremy Shockey
  Jerry Rice
  Terrell Owens
6 Peyton Manning 20.00 50.00
  Alge Crumpler
  Hines Ward
  Marvin Harrison
7 LaDainian Tomlinson 15.00 40.00
  Tony Gonzalez
  Chad Johnson
  Terrell Owens
8 Tom Brady 20.00 50.00
  Shaun Alexander
  Chris Cooley
  Steve Smith
9 Devin Hester 12.00 30.00
  Antonio Gates
  Andre Johnson
  Torry Holt
10 Brian Westbrook 15.00 40.00
  Fred Taylor
  LaDainian Tomlinson
  Willie Parker

2008 Playoff National Treasures All Pros Material Signature NFL

STATED PRINT RUN 1-25
*HOF/25: .4X TO 1X MATER.SIG/25
HOF MAT.SIG PRINT RUN 1-25
*MVP/25: .4X TO 1X MATER.SIG/25
MVP MAT.SIG PRINT RUN 1-25
SERIAL #'d UNDER 15 NOT PRICED
2 Alex Karras/25 50.00 100.00
3 Andre Reed/25 25.00 50.00
9 Carl Eller/25 30.00 60.00
11 Charlie Joiner/25 30.00 60.00
17 Fred Dryer/15 30.00 60.00
19 Howie Long/25 75.00 135.00
21 Jim Kelly/25 60.00 100.00
24 Joe Klecko/25 20.00 40.00
27 Emmitt Smith/22 125.00 200.00
32 Mark Gastineau/18 20.00 40.00
36 Randall Cunningham/25 30.00 60.00
39 Sterling Sharpe/25 25.00 50.00
41 Tiki Barber/25 25.00 50.00

2008 Playoff National Treasures All Pros Material Trios

STATED PRINT RUN 25 SER.#'d SETS
*PRIME/25: .5X TO 1.2X BASIC TRIO/25
PRIME PRINT RUN 25 SER.#'d SETS
*NFL/25: .4X TO 1X BASIC TRIO/25
NFL TRIO PRINT RUN 22-25
*NFL PRIME/25: .5X TO 1.2X BASIC TRIO/25
NFL PRIME PRINT RUN 25
1 John Elway 25.00 60.00
  Marcus Allen
  Michael Irvin
2 Dan Marino 50.00 100.00
  Emmitt Smith
  Jerry Rice
3 Dan Marino 30.00 80.00
  Troy Aikman
  Steve Young
4 Barry Sanders 30.00 80.00
  Emmitt Smith
  Jerry Rice
5 Brett Favre 30.00 80.00
  John Elway
  Steve Young
6 Barry Sanders 20.00 50.00
  Steve Young
  Randy Moss
7 Isaac Bruce 10.00 25.00
  Marvin Harrison
  Junior Seau
9 Kurt Warner 12.00 30.00
  Ahman Green
  Terrell Owens
10 Ricky Williams 10.00 25.00
  Tony Gonzalez
  Randy Moss
11 Brett Favre 20.00 50.00
  Brian Westbrook
  Torry Holt
12 Peyton Manning 15.00 40.00
  Hines Ward
  Jason Witten
13 Matt Hasselbeck 10.00 25.00
  Larry Johnson
  Marvin Harrison
14 Peyton Manning 15.00 40.00
  LaDainian Tomlinson
  Chad Johnson
15 Tom Brady 20.00 50.00
  Adrian Peterson
  Terrell Owens

2008 Playoff National Treasures All Pros Signature Cuts

STATED PRINT RUN 1-50
SERIAL #'d UNDER 15 NOT PRICED
6 Bob Waterfield/35 60.00 120.00
8 Bulldog Turner/58 50.00 100.00
15 Doak Walker/29 150.00 225.00
25 Johnny Unitas/25 200.00 350.00
31 Lou Groza/15 30.00 60.00
45 Y.A. Tittle/50 30.00 60.00

2008 Playoff National Treasures Champions Cuts

UNPRICED CUT AU PRINT RUN 1-22
6 Dan Marino/22

2008 Playoff National Treasures Champions Material Jumbo

MATERIAL JUMBO PRINT RUN 25
*JUM.PRIME/15-25: .5X TO 1.2X MAT.JUMB/25
JUMBO PRIME PRINT RUN 10-25
*MATER/14-25: .3X TO .8X MAT.JUMBO/25
BASIC MATERIAL PRINT RUN 1-25
1 Barry Sanders 20.00 50.00
2 Bo Jackson 20.00 50.00
3 Cliff Harris 10.00 25.00
4 Cris Collinsworth 10.00 25.00
5 Dan Fouts 15.00 40.00
6 Dan Marino 30.00 80.00
7 Danny White 15.00 40.00
11 Don Maynard 10.00 25.00
12 Earl Campbell 12.00 30.00
13 Eric Dickerson 12.00 30.00
15 Garo Yepremian 10.00 25.00
16 Jack Youngblood 10.00 25.00
17 Jay Novacek 12.00 30.00
18 John Matuszak 12.00 30.00
19 Knute Rockne Jkt 40.00 80.00
22 Paul Hornung 15.00 40.00
24 Tom Landry 20.00 50.00
25 Willie Brown 10.00 25.00

2008 Playoff National Treasures Champions Signature Material

STATED PRINT RUN 1-25
SERIAL #'d UNDER 23 NOT PRICED
1 Barry Sanders 75.00 150.00
2 Bo Jackson 60.00 120.00
3 Cliff Harris 25.00 50.00
4 Cris Collinsworth 20.00 40.00
5 Dan Fouts 40.00 80.00
6 Dan Marino 125.00 250.00
7 Danny White 40.00 80.00
12 Earl Campbell 40.00 80.00
13 Eric Dickerson 40.00 80.00
15 Garo Yepremian 15.00 40.00
17 Jay Novacek 30.00 60.00
21 Mark Duper 15.00 40.00
22 Paul Hornung/23 30.00 60.00
25 Willie Brown 15.00 40.00

2008 Playoff National Treasures Championships Material VS

MATERIAL VS PRINT RUN 10-50
UNPRICED MAT.VS PRIME PRINT RUN 2-10
UNPRICED MAT.SCORE PRINT RUN 1-5
UNPRICED MAT.YR PRINT RUN 1-10
1 Bulldog Turner 15.00 40.00
  Mel Hein/50
2 Sammy Baugh 15.00 40.00
  Sid Luckman/50
3 Lou Groza 10.00 25.00
  Bob Waterfield/50
4 Otto Graham 12.00 30.00
  Tom Fears/50
5 Bobby Layne 12.00 30.00
  Otto Graham/50
6 Doak Walker 15.00 40.00
  Otto Graham/50
7 Norm Van Brocklin 12.00 30.00
  Otto Graham/50
8 Bobby Layne 15.00 40.00
  Jim Brown/50

2008 Playoff National Treasures College Material

STATED PRINT RUN 25-99
1 Lee Evans 8.00 20.00
2 Edgerrin James 8.00 20.00
3 Darren McFadden/99 15.00 40.00
4 Larry Fitzgerald 10.00 25.00
5 Dwayne Bowe 8.00 20.00
6 Brady Quinn 8.00 20.00
7 Jay Cutler 10.00 25.00
8 Felix Jones 12.00 30.00
9 Adrian Peterson/99 8.00 20.00
10 Braylon Edwards 12.00 30.00

2008 Playoff National Treasures College Material Signature

STATED PRINT RUN 2-25
SERIAL #'d UNDER 22 NOT PRICED
7 Jay Cutler/22 40.00 80.00

8 Felix Jones	30.00	60.00
9 Adrian Peterson	90.00	150.00
10 Braylon Edwards	25.00	50.00

2008 Playoff National Treasures Heisman Cuts

STATED PRINT RUN 1-63

2 Larry Kelley/26	40.00	100.00
6 Angelo Bertelli/47	40.00	100.00
8 Glenn Davis/51	40.00	100.00
10 Leon Hart/35	40.00	100.00
11 Vic Janowicz/63	40.00	100.00

2008 Playoff National Treasures Notable Nicknames Signature

STATED PRINT RUN 25-50

1 Lenny Moore/25	25.00	50.00
2 Dante Lavelli/25	20.00	40.00
3 Joe Montana/50	100.00	175.00
4 Chuck Bednarik/25	25.00	50.00
5 Del Shofner/27	30.00	60.00
6 Paul Hornung/25	50.00	100.00
7 Lance Alworth/25	60.00	120.00
8 Tommy McDonald/36	25.00	50.00
9 Randy White/50	30.00	60.00
10 Mike Singletary/50	30.00	60.00
11 Pete Retzlaff/26	20.00	40.00

2008 Playoff National Treasures Pen Pals

1 Felix Jones	50.00	120.00
Darren McFadden		
2 Jamaal Charles	15.00	40.00
Limas Sweed		
3 Jerome Simpson	12.00	30.00
Andre Caldwell		
4 Harry Douglas	15.00	40.00
Brian Brohm		
5 Matt Forte	30.00	60.00
Earl Bennett		
6 Chad Henne	25.00	50.00
Jake Long		
7 Jordy Nelson	25.00	50.00
Brian Brohm		
8 Joe Flacco	75.00	125.00
Ray Rice		
9 Devin Thomas	15.00	40.00
Malcolm Kelly		
10 Donnie Avery		
Chris Long		
11 Rashard Mendenhall	30.00	60.00
Limas Sweed		
12 Chris Long		
Glenn Dorsey		
Jake Long EXCH		
13 Mario Manningham	40.00	80.00
Chad Henne		
Jake Long		
14 Eddie Royal	40.00	80.00
Jerome Simpson		
DeSean Jackson		
Malcolm Kelly		
15 Donnie Avery		
Devin Thomas		
Jordy Nelson		
James Hardy		
16 Darren McFadden	100.00	200.00
Jonathan Stewart		
Felix Jones		
Rashard Mendenhall		
17 Matt Ryan	150.00	300.00
Joe Flacco		
Brian Brohm		
Chad Henne		
18 Limas Sweed	30.00	60.00
Dexter Jackson		
Earl Bennett		
Early Doucet		

2008 Playoff National Treasures Rookie Combo Material

STATED PRINT RUN 25 SER.#'d SETS
UNPRICED BRAND LOGO PRINT RUN 1-10
UNPRICED LAUNDRY TAG PRINT RUN 1-10
UNPRICED NFL SHIELDS PRINT RUN 1-9

1 Harry Douglas	6.00	15.00
Brian Brohm		
2 Rashard Mendenhall	12.00	30.00
Jonathan Stewart		
3 Glenn Dorsey	6.00	15.00
Early Doucet		
4 Chad Henne	6.00	15.00
Mario Manningham		
5 Matt Ryan	30.00	80.00
Joe Flacco		
6 Jamaal Charles	10.00	25.00
Limas Sweed		
7 Matt Ryan	25.00	60.00
Darren McFadden		
8 Brian Brohm	6.00	15.00
Chad Henne		
9 Darren McFadden	15.00	40.00
Felix Jones		
10 Eddie Royal	6.00	15.00
James Hardy		
11 Jamaal Charles	10.00	25.00
Steve Slaton		
12 Jonathan Stewart	10.00	25.00
Felix Jones		
13 Jake Long	6.00	15.00
Glenn Dorsey		
14 Matt Forte	12.00	30.00
Ray Rice		
15 Donnie Avery	5.00	12.00
Devin Thomas		
16 Rashard Mendenhall	15.00	40.00
Chris Johnson		
17 Devin Thomas	8.00	20.00
Jordy Nelson		
18 Devin Thomas	6.00	15.00
Mario Manningham		
19 Donnie Avery	6.00	15.00
Kevin Smith		
20 Dustin Keller	6.00	15.00
Donnie Avery		
21 DeSean Jackson	12.00	30.00
Malcolm Kelly		
22 Ray Rice	12.00	30.00
Steve Slaton		
23 Matt Ryan	25.00	60.00
Eddie Royal		
24 Chris Johnson	15.00	40.00
Matt Forte		
25 DeSean Jackson	12.00	30.00
Kevin O'Connell		
26 Jamaal Charles	10.00	25.00
Glenn Dorsey		
27 Brian Brohm	12.00	30.00
Jordy Nelson		
28 Chad Henne	6.00	15.00
Jake Long		
29 Devin Thomas	5.00	12.00
Malcolm Kelly		
30 Matt Forte	10.00	25.00
Earl Bennett		
31 Matt Ryan	25.00	60.00
Harry Douglas		
32 Rashard Mendenhall	12.00	30.00
Limas Sweed		
33 Andre Caldwell	6.00	15.00
Jerome Simpson		
34 Ray Rice	30.00	80.00
Joe Flacco		

2008 Playoff National Treasures Rookie Signature Jumbo Material Gold

*GLD JMBO/25: .5X TO 1.2X BASE JSY AU RC
STATED PRINT RUN 25 SER.#'d SETS
UNPRICED BLACK JUMBO PRINT RUN 1
UNPRICED PLATINUM JUMBO PRINT RUN 5

101 Darren McFadden	125.00	250.00
105 Chris Johnson	175.00	350.00
111 Matt Ryan	200.00	400.00
112 Joe Flacco	175.00	350.00

2008 Playoff National Treasures Rookie Signature Material Gold

*MAT.GOLD/25: .4X TO 1X BASE JSY AU RC
GOLD PRINT RUN 25 SER.#'d SETS
UNPRICED PLATINUM PRINT RUN 1
UNPRICED SIG. BRAND LOGO PRINT RUN 1
UNPRICED SIG.COMBO MAT. PRINT RUN 10
UNPRICED SIG.COMBO PLAT. PRINT RUN 1
UNPRICED SIG.LAUN.TAG PRINT RUN 1

101 Darren McFadden	125.00	200.00
102 Jonathan Stewart	25.00	60.00
103 Felix Jones	50.00	120.00
104 Rashard Mendenhall	60.00	150.00
105 Chris Johnson	125.00	250.00
106 Matt Forte	50.00	120.00
107 Ray Rice	60.00	150.00
108 Kevin Smith	15.00	40.00
109 Jamaal Charles	50.00	120.00
110 Steve Slaton	15.00	40.00
111 Matt Ryan	200.00	400.00
112 Joe Flacco	125.00	250.00
113 Brian Brohm	15.00	40.00
114 Chad Henne	60.00	150.00
115 Kevin O'Connell	12.00	30.00
116 John David Booty	12.00	30.00
117 Andre Caldwell	12.00	30.00
118 Donnie Avery	12.00	30.00
119 Devin Thomas	12.00	30.00
120 Jordy Nelson	50.00	100.00
121 James Hardy	12.00	30.00
122 Eddie Royal	15.00	40.00
123 Jerome Simpson	15.00	40.00
124 DeSean Jackson	50.00	120.00
125 Malcolm Kelly	12.00	30.00
126 Limas Sweed	15.00	40.00
127 Dexter Jackson	12.00	30.00
128 Earl Bennett	15.00	40.00
129 Early Doucet	12.00	30.00
130 Harry Douglas	12.00	30.00
131 Mario Manningham	30.00	60.00
132 Dustin Keller	15.00	40.00
133 Glenn Dorsey	15.00	40.00
134 Jake Long	15.00	40.00

2008 Playoff National Treasures Signature Patches College

STATED PRINT RUN 24-52

1 Troy Aikman/25	50.00	100.00
2 Ace Clarence Parker/25	25.00	60.00
3 Lee Roy Selmon/26	20.00	50.00
4 Charley Trippi/26	15.00	40.00
5 Warren Moon/26	25.00	60.00
6 Lenny Moore/26	20.00	50.00
7 Jack Youngblood/26	15.00	40.00
8 Earl Campbell/50	40.00	80.00
17 Gary Collins/24	15.00	40.00
18 Dan Fouts/25	25.00	60.00
19 Dante Lavelli/25	15.00	40.00
20 John Mackey/25	15.00	40.00
21 Dan Hampton/25	15.00	40.00
22 Len Dawson/25	25.00	60.00
23 Alan Page/25	20.00	50.00
24 Charley Taylor/25	15.00	40.00
25 Dave Casper/25	20.00	50.00
26 Joe Montana/25	125.00	200.00
27 Rosey Grier/25	15.00	40.00
28 Lawrence Taylor/26	40.00	80.00
29 Bob Griese/26	25.00	60.00
46 Paul Hornung/24	25.00	60.00
47 Daryle Lamonica/25	20.00	50.00
48 Paul Warfield/25	20.00	50.00
49 Danny White/26	25.00	60.00
50 Fran Tarkenton/26	25.00	60.00
51 Fred Biletnikoff/26	40.00	80.00
52 George Blanda/26	25.00	60.00
53 Jim Otto/26	25.00	60.00
54 Jim Taylor/26	25.00	60.00
55 Lance Alworth/28	40.00	80.00
56 Michael Irvin/26	25.00	60.00
57 Roger Staubach/26	40.00	80.00
58 Steve Largent/26	25.00	60.00
59 Tommy McDonald/26	20.00	50.00
60 Dick Butkus/26	50.00	100.00
61 Franco Harris/26	25.00	60.00
62 Gale Sayers/26	40.00	80.00
63 Hugh McElhenny/26	15.00	40.00
64 Jim Brown/26	50.00	100.00
65 Randy White/26	20.00	50.00
66 Roger Craig/26	20.00	50.00
67 Thurman Thomas/27	20.00	50.00
69 Ken Stabler/26	25.00	60.00
70 Lydell Mitchell/26	15.00	40.00
71 John Elway/27	75.00	150.00
73 John Riggins/50	20.00	50.00
74 Billy Sims/51	15.00	40.00
75 Bert Jones/52	15.00	40.00
80 Ozzie Newsome/52	15.00	40.00
83 Y.A. Tittle/26	25.00	60.00
84 Daryl Johnston/25	25.00	60.00
85 James Lofton/26	15.00	40.00
93 Emmitt Smith/26	100.00	200.00
95 Barry Sanders/25	75.00	150.00
97 Dan Marino/26	100.00	200.00
99 Howie Long/26	40.00	100.00
100 Marcus Allen/26	25.00	60.00
101 Mark Gastineau/26	15.00	40.00
102 Ronnie Lott/26	25.00	60.00
103 Tim Brown/26	40.00	80.00
104 Tony Dorsett/26	25.00	60.00
105 Mike Curtis/26	15.00	40.00
106 Archie Manning/26	25.00	60.00
107 Bo Jackson/25	100.00	200.00
110 Willie Wood/25	20.00	50.00
112 Frank Gifford/50	25.00	60.00
135 Jim Kelly/25	40.00	80.00

2008 Playoff National Treasures Signature Patches NFL

STATED PRINT RUN 25-53

1 Troy Aikman/25	60.00	100.00
9 John Stallworth/25	20.00	50.00
10 Willie Brown/26	15.00	40.00
11 Bobby Bell/25	15.00	40.00
12 Forrest Gregg/25	20.00	50.00
13 Joe Klecko/25	15.00	40.00
14 Randall Cunningham/25	25.00	60.00
15 Raymond Berry/25	20.00	50.00
16 Merlin Olsen/25	20.00	50.00
17 Gary Collins/25	15.00	40.00
18 Dan Fouts/25	25.00	60.00
19 Dante Lavelli/25	15.00	40.00
20 John Mackey/25	15.00	40.00
21 Dan Hampton/25	20.00	50.00
22 Len Dawson/25	25.00	60.00
23 Alan Page/25	20.00	50.00
24 Charley Taylor/25	15.00	40.00
25 Dave Casper/25	20.00	50.00
26 Joe Montana/25	100.00	175.00
27 Rosey Grier/25	20.00	50.00
28 Lawrence Taylor/25	40.00	80.00
29 Bob Griese/25	25.00	60.00
30 Bob Lilly/26	20.00	50.00
31 Carl Eller/26	15.00	40.00
32 Chuck Bednarik/26	20.00	50.00
33 Don Maynard/26	15.00	40.00
34 Joe Greene/26	25.00	60.00
35 Larry Little/26	15.00	40.00
36 Leroy Kelly/26	20.00	50.00
37 Paul Krause/26	15.00	40.00
38 Steve Young/26	60.00	100.00
39 Willie Davis/26	15.00	40.00
40 Alex Karras/26	20.00	50.00
41 Charlie Joiner/26	20.00	50.00
42 Lem Barney/26	15.00	40.00
43 Del Shofner NY/26	15.00	40.00
44 Del Shofner Rams/26	15.00	40.00
45 Jan Stenerud/26	15.00	40.00
46 Paul Hornung/26	25.00	60.00
47 Daryle Lamonica/26	20.00	50.00
48 Paul Warfield/26	20.00	50.00
49 Danny White/26	40.00	80.00
50 Fran Tarkenton/26	25.00	60.00
51 Fred Biletnikoff/26	40.00	80.00
52 George Blanda/26	25.00	60.00
53 Jim Otto/26	25.00	60.00
54 Jim Taylor/26	25.00	60.00
55 Lance Alworth/26	50.00	100.00
56 Michael Irvin/26	40.00	80.00
57 Roger Staubach/26	60.00	100.00
58 Steve Largent/26	25.00	60.00
59 Tommy McDonald/26	15.00	40.00
60 Dick Butkus/26	50.00	100.00
61 Franco Harris/26	40.00	80.00
62 Gale Sayers/26	40.00	80.00
63 Hugh McElhenny/26	15.00	40.00
64 Jim Brown/26	50.00	100.00
65 Randy White/26	40.00	80.00
66 Roger Craig/26	20.00	50.00
67 Thurman Thomas/26	20.00	50.00
68 Jim McMahon/27	25.00	60.00
69 Ken Stabler/25	25.00	60.00
70 Lydell Mitchell/27	15.00	40.00
71 John Elway/27	75.00	150.00
72 Fred Williamson/50	15.00	40.00
73 John Riggins/50	25.00	60.00
74 Billy Sims/51	15.00	40.00
75 Bert Jones/51	20.00	40.00
76 Dub Jones/52	15.00	40.00
77 Jerry Rice/52	75.00	150.00
78 Willie Lanier/52	15.00	40.00
79 Billy Howton/52	15.00	40.00
80 Ozzie Newsome/52	15.00	40.00
81 Mike Singletary/53	25.00	60.00
82 Mark Duper/53	15.00	40.00
83 Y.A. Tittle/26	25.00	60.00
84 Daryl Johnston/26	25.00	60.00
85 James Lofton/53	15.00	40.00
86 Jay Novacek/26	25.00	60.00
88 William Perry/25	25.00	60.00
92 Darrell Green/26	50.00	80.00
93 Emmitt Smith/26	125.00	200.00
95 Barry Sanders/26	75.00	150.00
97 Dan Marino/26	150.00	250.00
98 Fred Dryer/26	15.00	40.00
99 Howie Long/26	60.00	120.00
100 Marcus Allen/26	25.00	60.00
101 Mark Gastineau/26	15.00	40.00
102 Ronnie Lott/26	25.00	60.00
103 Tim Brown/26	40.00	80.00
104 Tony Dorsett/26	25.00	60.00
105 Mike Curtis/26	15.00	40.00
106 Archie Manning/26	25.00	60.00
107 Bo Jackson/25	60.00	120.00
110 Willie Wood/25	20.00	50.00
112 Frank Gifford/50	25.00	60.00
114 Tony Romo/25	60.00	120.00
133 Jermichael Finley/25	25.00	60.00
135 Jim Kelly/25	40.00	80.00
136 Mike Ditka Bears/26	50.00	100.00
137 Mike Ditka Cowboys/26	50.00	100.00

2008 Playoff National Treasures Signature Patches NFL Logo

STATED PRINT RUN 2-25
SERIAL #'d UNDER 25 NOT PRICED

2 Ace Clarence Parker/25	30.00	60.00
132 Adrian Peterson/25	100.00	200.00

2008 Playoff National Treasures Super Bowl Material Final Score

MATERIAL FINAL SCORE PRINT RUN 14-25
UNPRICED FNL SCR PRME PRINT RUN 1-10
*SB MATERIAL/15-25: .4X TO 1X FINAL SCORE
SUPER BOWL MATERIAL PRINT RUN 1-25
UNPRICED MATERIAL YR PRINT RUN 1-10
UNPRICED MATERIAL MVP PRINT RUN 2-10
UNPRICED MATERIAL PRIME PRINT RUN 2-10

1 Bart Starr	40.00	80.00
2 Len Dawson	15.00	40.00
3 Franco Harris	15.00	40.00
4 Roger Staubach	20.00	50.00
5 Fred Biletnikoff	15.00	40.00
6 Randy White	12.00	30.00
7 John Riggins/14	12.00	30.00
8 Joe Montana	30.00	80.00
9 Jerry Rice	25.00	60.00
10 Marcus Allen	15.00	40.00
11 Phil Simms	12.00	30.00
12 Steve Young	20.00	50.00
13 Troy Aikman	20.00	50.00
14 Emmitt Smith	30.00	80.00
15 John Elway	25.00	60.00
16 Bob Griese	15.00	40.00
17 Tony Dorsett	15.00	40.00
18 John Stallworth	15.00	40.00
19 Roger Craig	12.00	30.00
20 Jim McMahon	15.00	40.00
21 Mike Singletary/15	15.00	40.00
22 Thurman Thomas	12.00	30.00
23 Michael Irvin	15.00	40.00
24 Joe Greene	15.00	40.00
25 Lawrence Taylor	15.00	40.00
26 Tom Landry	30.00	60.00
27 Kurt Warner	15.00	40.00
28 Tom Brady	25.00	60.00
29 Peyton Manning	25.00	60.00
30 Eli Manning	15.00	40.00

2008 Playoff National Treasures Super Bowl Signature Cuts

STATED PRINT RUN 1-27
SERIAL #'d UNDER 27 NOT PRICED

4 Roger Staubach/27	60.00	100.00
15 John Elway/27	75.00	150.00
23 Michael Irvin/27	30.00	60.00

2008 Playoff National Treasures Promos

CJ Chris Johnson	2.50	6.00
DJ DeSean Jackson	2.00	5.00
DM Darren McFadden	2.50	6.00
ER Eddie Royal	1.00	2.50
FJ Felix Jones	1.50	4.00
JF Joe Flacco	3.00	8.00
JS Jonathan Stewart	1.50	4.00
MF Matt Forte	1.50	4.00
MR Matt Ryan	4.00	10.00
SS Steve Slaton	1.00	2.50

2009 Playoff National Treasures

STATED PRINT RUN 99 SER.#'d SETS
EXCH EXPIRATION: 8/3/2011

1 Kurt Warner	3.00	8.00
2 Larry Fitzgerald	3.00	8.00
3 Tim Hightower	2.00	5.00
4 Matt Ryan	3.00	8.00
5 Michael Turner	2.50	6.00
6 Roddy White	2.50	6.00
7 Tony Gonzalez	2.50	6.00
8 Joe Flacco	3.00	8.00
9 Derrick Mason	2.50	6.00
10 Ray Rice	3.00	8.00
11 Trent Edwards	2.00	5.00
12 Lee Evans	2.50	6.00
13 Terrell Owens	3.00	8.00
14 DeAngelo Williams	3.00	8.00
15 Jonathan Stewart	2.50	6.00
16 Muhsin Muhammad	2.50	6.00
17 Devin Hester	3.00	8.00
18 Greg Olsen	2.00	5.00
19 Jay Cutler	3.00	8.00
20 Matt Forte	3.00	8.00
21 Carson Palmer	3.00	8.00
22 Chad Ochocinco	2.50	6.00
23 Cedric Benson	2.50	6.00
24 Derek Anderson	2.00	5.00
25 Braylon Edwards	2.50	6.00
26 Jamal Lewis	2.50	6.00
27 Jason Witten	3.00	8.00
28 Marion Barber	2.50	6.00
29 Tony Romo	5.00	12.00
30 Brandon Marshall	2.50	6.00
31 Brandon Stokley	2.50	6.00
32 Correll Buckhalter	2.00	5.00
33 Calvin Johnson	3.00	8.00
34 Bryant Johnson	2.00	5.00
35 Kevin Smith	2.50	6.00
36 Aaron Rodgers	6.00	15.00
37 Greg Jennings	3.00	8.00
38 Ryan Grant	2.50	6.00
39 Andre Johnson	2.50	6.00
40 Owen Daniels	2.00	5.00
41 Steve Slaton	2.50	6.00
42 Anthony Gonzalez	2.00	5.00
43 Joseph Addai	3.00	8.00
44 Peyton Manning	6.00	15.00
45 Reggie Wayne	2.50	6.00
46 David Garrard	2.50	6.00
47 Maurice Jones-Drew	2.50	6.00
48 Torry Holt	2.50	6.00
49 Dwayne Bowe	2.50	6.00
50 Jamaal Charles	3.00	8.00
51 Matt Cassel	2.50	6.00
52 Chad Henne	2.50	6.00
53 Ronnie Brown	2.50	6.00
54 Ricky Williams	2.50	6.00
55 Adrian Peterson	12.50	25.00
56 Bernard Berrian	2.50	6.00
57 Brett Favre	25.00	40.00
58 Laurence Maroney	2.50	6.00
59 Randy Moss	3.00	8.00
60 Tom Brady	6.00	15.00
61 Wes Welker	3.00	8.00
62 Drew Brees	3.00	8.00
63 Marques Colston	2.50	6.00
64 Devery Henderson	2.00	5.00
65 Brandon Jacobs	2.50	6.00
66 Eli Manning	3.00	8.00
67 Steve Smith	2.50	6.00
68 Jerricho Cotchery	2.50	6.00
69 Thomas Jones	2.50	6.00
70 Darren McFadden	3.00	8.00
71 JaMarcus Russell	2.00	5.00
72 Zach Miller	2.00	5.00
73 Brian Westbrook	2.50	6.00
74 Michael Vick	4.00	10.00
75 Donovan McNabb	3.00	8.00
76 Ben Roethlisberger	3.00	8.00
77 Santonio Holmes	2.50	6.00
78 Willie Parker	2.00	5.00
79 Antonio Gates	2.50	6.00
80 LaDainian Tomlinson	3.00	8.00
81 Philip Rivers	3.00	8.00
82 Vincent Jackson	2.50	6.00
83 Frank Gore	2.50	6.00
84 Isaac Bruce	2.50	6.00
85 Vernon Davis	2.50	6.00
86 Julius Jones	2.00	5.00
87 Matt Hasselbeck	2.50	6.00
88 T.J. Houshmandzadeh	2.50	6.00
89 Donnie Avery	2.50	6.00
90 Marc Bulger	2.50	6.00
91 Steven Jackson	2.50	6.00
92 Antonio Bryant	2.00	5.00
93 Cadillac Williams	2.50	6.00
94 Kellen Winslow Jr.	2.50	6.00
95 Chris Johnson	3.00	8.00
96 Justin Gage	2.00	5.00
97 Vince Young	2.50	6.00
98 Chris Cooley	2.50	6.00
99 Clinton Portis	2.50	6.00
100 Jason Campbell	2.00	5.00
101 Aaron Curry JSY AU RC	15.00	40.00
102 Andre Brown JSY AU RC	10.00	25.00
103 Brandon Pettigrew JSY AU RC	15.00	40.00
104 Brian Robiskie JSY AU RC	15.00	40.00
105 Chris Wells JSY AU RC	30.00	80.00
106 Darrius Heyward-Bey JSY AU RC	15.00	40.00
107 Deon Butler JSY AU RC	12.00	30.00
108 Derrick Williams JSY AU RC	12.00	30.00
109 Donald Brown JSY AU RC	15.00	40.00
110 Glen Coffee JSY AU RC	12.00	30.00
111 Hakeem Nicks JSY AU RC	30.00	60.00
112 Jason Smith JSY AU RC	12.00	30.00
113 Javon Ringer JSY AU RC	15.00	40.00
114 Jeremy Maclin JSY AU RC	30.00	80.00
115 Josh Freeman JSY AU RC	75.00	150.00
116 Juaquin Iglesias JSY AU RC	12.00	30.00
117 Kenny Britt JSY AU RC	20.00	50.00
118 Knowshon Moreno JSY AU RC	25.00	60.00
119 LeSean McCoy JSY AU RC	100.00	175.00
120 Mark Sanchez JSY AU RC	100.00	200.00
121 Matthew Stafford JSY AU RC	250.00	400.00
122 Michael Crabtree JSY AU RC	40.00	100.00
123 Mike Thomas JSY AU RC	16.00	40.00
124 Mike Wallace JSY AU RC	50.00	100.00
125 Mohamed Massaquoi JSY AU RC	12.00	30.00
126 Nate Davis JSY AU RC	12.00	30.00
127 Pat White JSY AU RC	15.00	40.00
128 Patrick Turner JSY AU RC	12.00	30.00
129 Percy Harvin JSY AU RC	60.00	120.00
130 Ramses Barden JSY AU RC	10.00	25.00
131 Rhett Bomar JSY AU RC	12.00	30.00
132 Shonn Greene JSY AU RC	30.00	80.00
133 Stephen McGee JSY AU RC	20.00	50.00
134 Tyson Jackson JSY AU RC	12.00	30.00
135 Aaron Brown AU RC	8.00	20.00
136 Aaron Maybin AU RC	6.00	15.00
137 Alphonso Smith AU RC	6.00	15.00
138 Austin Collie AU RC	12.00	30.00
139 B.J. Raji AU RC	10.00	25.00
140 Bernard Scott AU RC	10.00	25.00
141 Brandon Gibson AU RC	8.00	20.00
142 Brandon Tate AU RC	8.00	20.00
143 Brian Cushing AU RC	8.00	20.00
144 Brian Hartline AU RC	8.00	20.00
145 Brian Hoyer AU RC	20.00	40.00
146 Brian Orakpo AU RC	8.00	20.00
147 Brooks Foster AU RC	5.00	12.00
148 Chase Coffman AU RC	6.00	15.00
149 Chase Daniel AU RC	15.00	40.00
150 Clay Matthews AU RC	60.00	100.00
151 Clint Sintim AU RC	8.00	20.00
152 Everette Brown AU RC	6.00	15.00
153 Frank Summers AU RC	8.00	20.00
154 Gartrell Johnson AU RC	5.00	12.00
155 James Casey AU RC	6.00	15.00
156 James Davis AU RC	10.00	25.00
157 James Laurinaitis AU RC	8.00	20.00
158 Jared Cook AU RC	8.00	20.00
159 Jarett Dillard AU RC	8.00	20.00
160 Johnny Knox AU RC	20.00	40.00
161 Julian Edelman AU RC	8.00	20.00
162 Keith Null AU RC	6.00	15.00
163 Kenny McKinley AU RC	8.00	20.00
164 Kory Sheets AU RC	6.00	15.00
165 Lardarius Webb AU RC	8.00	20.00
166 LaRod Stephens-Howling AU RC	10.00	25.00
167 Larry English AU RC	8.00	20.00
168 Louis Delmas AU RC	8.00	20.00
169 Louis Murphy AU RC	15.00	30.00
170 Malcolm Jenkins AU RC	8.00	20.00
171 Mike Teel AU RC	8.00	20.00
172 Mike Goodson No AU RC	3.00	8.00
173 Quinn Johnson AU RC	6.00	15.00
174 Rashad Jennings AU RC	8.00	20.00
175 Rey Maualuga AU RC	8.00	20.00
176 Richard Quinn AU RC	6.00	15.00
177 Sammie Stroughter AU RC	8.00	20.00
178 Sean Smith AU RC	8.00	20.00
179 Shawn Nelson No AU RC	2.50	6.00
180 Stefan Logan AU RC	8.00	20.00
181 Tom Brandstater AU RC	8.00	20.00
182 Tony Fiammetta AU RC	6.00	15.00
183 Travis Beckum AU RC	6.00	15.00
184 Vontae Davis AU RC	8.00	20.00
185 Alex Karras	2.50	6.00
186 Andre Reed	2.50	6.00
187 Archie Manning	3.00	8.00
188 Billy Howton	2.00	5.00
189 Bob Lilly	2.50	6.00
190 Boyd Dowler	2.00	5.00
191 Charley Taylor	2.00	5.00
192 Cliff Harris	2.50	6.00
193 Danny White	2.50	6.00
194 Dante Lavelli	2.00	5.00
195 Dave Casper	2.00	5.00
196 Del Shofner	2.00	5.00
197 Don Perkins	2.00	5.00
198 Dub Jones	2.00	5.00
199 Gary Collins	2.00	5.00
200 Harlon Hill	2.00	5.00
201 Jim Taylor	3.00	8.00
202 Joe Klecko	2.00	5.00
203 Johnny Morris	2.00	5.00
204 Johnny Unitas	5.00	12.00
205 Kellen Winslow Sr.	2.50	6.00
206 Lee Roy Selmon	2.00	5.00
207 Leroy Kelly	2.50	6.00
208 Mark Gastineau	2.00	5.00
209 Mike Curtis	2.00	5.00
210 Ozzie Newsome	2.50	6.00
211 Roger Craig	2.50	6.00
212 Rosey Grier	2.00	5.00
213 Sonny Jurgensen	2.50	6.00
214 Sterling Sharpe	3.00	8.00
215 Tiki Barber	2.50	6.00
216 William Perry	2.50	6.00
217 Willie Wood	2.50	6.00
218 Jim Thorpe	8.00	20.00
219 Deion Sanders	3.00	8.00
220 Jim Brown	4.00	10.00
221 Jim McMahon	2.50	6.00
222 Joe Namath	4.00	10.00
223 Sammy Baugh	3.00	8.00
224 Tony Dorsett	3.00	8.00
225 Lawrence Taylor	3.00	8.00
226 John Elway	5.00	12.00
227 Thurman Thomas	3.00	8.00
228 Bo Jackson	4.00	10.00
229 Walter Payton	6.00	15.00
230 Barry Sanders	6.00	15.00
231 Joe Greene	3.00	8.00
232 Len Dawson	3.00	8.00
233 Paul Warfield	2.50	6.00
234 Steve Young	4.00	10.00

2009 Playoff National Treasures AFL 50th Anniversary Materials

STATED PRINT RUN 30-99
*PRIME/15-35: .8X TO 2X BASIC JSY
PRIME PRINT RUN 1-35

1 George Blanda/99	8.00	20.00
3 Don Maynard/99	6.00	15.00
4 Joe Namath/30	15.00	30.00
5 Jim Otto/99	5.00	12.00
6 Willie Brown/99	5.00	12.00
7 Lance Alworth/99	8.00	20.00
9 Len Dawson/99	8.00	20.00
10 Daryle Lamonica/99	5.00	12.00
11 Bob Griese/90	8.00	20.00
12 Charlie Joiner/99	5.00	12.00
13 Fred Biletnikoff/99	8.00	20.00
14 Gene Upshaw/99	5.00	12.00
15 Jan Stenerud/35	6.00	15.00
16 Larry Csonka/99	8.00	20.00
17 Larry Little/90	5.00	12.00
18 Ron Mix/50	5.00	12.00
19 Willie Lanier/99	5.00	12.00

2009 Playoff National Treasures AFL 50th Anniversary Signature Materials

STATED PRINT RUN 12-50
*PRIME/17-25: X TO X BASIC JSY AU
SERIAL #'d UNDER 17 NOT PRICED

1 George Blanda/50	25.00	50.00
3 Don Maynard/35	15.00	40.00
4 Joe Namath/15	50.00	100.00
5 Jim Otto/50	15.00	40.00
6 Willie Brown/35	12.00	30.00
7 Lance Alworth/50	40.00	80.00
9 Len Dawson/25	30.00	60.00
10 Daryle Lamonica/50	15.00	40.00
11 Bob Griese/25	20.00	50.00
12 Charlie Joiner/50	12.00	30.00
13 Fred Biletnikoff/50	30.00	60.00
15 Jan Stenerud/50	12.00	30.00
18 Ron Mix/50	12.00	30.00
19 Willie Lanier/50	12.00	30.00
20 Ken Stabler/40	40.00	80.00

2009 Playoff National Treasures Biography Materials

STATED PRINT RUN 20-50
*PRIME/25: .8X TO 2X BASIC JSY
PRIME PRINT RUN 1-25

1 Alex Karras	6.00	15.00
2 Bill Bates	6.00	15.00
3 Cris Collinsworth	6.00	15.00
4 Darrell Green	8.00	20.00
5 Deacon Jones	6.00	15.00
6 Dick Lane	8.00	20.00
7 Doak Walker	10.00	25.00
8 Elroy Hirsch	10.00	25.00
9 Fred Dryer	5.00	12.00
10 Howie Long	8.00	20.00
11 James Lofton	5.00	12.00
12 Joe Theismann	8.00	20.00
13 John Mackey	6.00	15.00
14 Ken Strong	8.00	20.00
15 Lem Barney	6.00	15.00
16 Marion Motley	10.00	25.00
17 Ollie Matson	6.00	15.00
18 Paul Krause/20	6.00	15.00
19 Tommy McDonald	5.00	12.00
20 Reggie White	10.00	25.00
21 Walter Payton	15.00	40.00
22 Randall Cunningham	8.00	20.00

2009 Playoff National Treasures Biography Materials Signature

STATED PRINT RUN 4-50
*PRIME/25: .5X TO 1.2X BASIC JSY
PRIME PRINT RUN 1-25
SERIAL #'d UNDER 15 NOT PRICED

1 Alex Karras/15	15.00	40.00
2 Bill Bates/40	12.00	30.00
3 Cris Collinsworth/50	12.00	30.00
4 Darrell Green/17	30.00	60.00
9 Fred Dryer/50	12.00	30.00
10 Howie Long/50	25.00	60.00
11 James Lofton/50	10.00	25.00
12 Joe Theismann/41	15.00	40.00
13 John Mackey/50	12.00	30.00
15 Lem Barney/50	10.00	25.00
19 Tommy McDonald/50	12.00	30.00
22 Randall Cunningham/50	15.00	40.00

2009 Playoff National Treasures Century Material Prime

STATED PRINT RUN 1-50
SERIAL #'d UNDER 15 NOT PRICED

2 Larry Fitzgerald/50	6.00	15.00
5 Michael Turner/30	5.00	12.00
6 Roddy White/40	5.00	12.00
11 Trent Edwards/50	4.00	10.00
12 Lee Evans/50	5.00	12.00
14 DeAngelo Williams/50	6.00	15.00
16 Muhsin Muhammad/50	5.00	12.00
17 Devin Hester/15	8.00	20.00
18 Greg Olsen/30	4.00	10.00
21 Carson Palmer/30	6.00	15.00
22 Chad Ochocinco/50	5.00	12.00
24 Derek Anderson/50	4.00	10.00
26 Jamal Lewis/50	5.00	12.00
27 Jason Witten/40	6.00	15.00
28 Marion Barber/50	5.00	12.00
29 Tony Romo/50	10.00	25.00
31 Brandon Stokley/23	6.00	15.00
33 Calvin Johnson/30	6.00	15.00
36 Aaron Rodgers/50	12.00	30.00
37 Greg Jennings/50	6.00	15.00
38 Ryan Grant/50	5.00	12.00
39 Andre Johnson/50	5.00	12.00
43 Joseph Addai/50	6.00	15.00
44 Peyton Manning/15	15.00	40.00
45 Reggie Wayne/50	5.00	12.00
46 David Garrard/30	5.00	12.00
47 Maurice Jones-Drew/50	5.00	12.00
49 Dwayne Bowe/30	5.00	12.00
53 Ronnie Brown/50	5.00	12.00
54 Ricky Williams/50	5.00	12.00
55 Adrian Peterson/50	10.00	25.00
58 Laurence Maroney/50	5.00	12.00
59 Randy Moss/50	6.00	15.00
60 Tom Brady/50	10.00	25.00
61 Wes Welker/50	6.00	15.00
62 Drew Brees/50	8.00	20.00
65 Brandon Jacobs/50	5.00	12.00
67 Steve Smith/50	5.00	12.00
68 Jerricho Cotchery/30	5.00	12.00
69 Thomas Jones/50	5.00	12.00
70 Darren McFadden/30	6.00	15.00
71 JaMarcus Russell/50	4.00	10.00
72 Zach Miller/30	5.00	12.00
73 Brian Westbrook/40	5.00	12.00
77 Santonio Holmes/50	5.00	12.00
78 Willie Parker/50	4.00	10.00
79 Antonio Gates/50	5.00	12.00
80 LaDainian Tomlinson/50	6.00	15.00
81 Philip Rivers/15	8.00	20.00
82 Vincent Jackson/50	5.00	12.00
83 Frank Gore/50	5.00	12.00
85 Vernon Davis/35	5.00	12.00
87 Matt Hasselbeck/30	5.00	12.00
90 Marc Bulger/40	5.00	12.00
91 Steven Jackson/50	5.00	12.00
93 Cadillac Williams/50	5.00	12.00
95 Chris Johnson/50	6.00	15.00
96 Justin Gage /50	4.00	10.00
98 Chris Cooley/50	5.00	12.00
99 Clinton Portis/50	5.00	12.00
100 Jason Campbell/35	4.00	10.00
186 Andre Reed/25	8.00	20.00
204 Johnny Unitas/25	40.00	80.00
214 Sterling Sharpe/25	8.00	20.00
215 Tiki Barber/25	8.00	20.00
216 William Perry/25	8.00	20.00
219 Deion Sanders/25	12.00	30.00
222 Joe Namath/25	12.00	30.00
225 Lawrence Taylor/25	10.00	25.00
226 John Elway/25	15.00	40.00
229 Walter Payton/25	20.00	50.00
230 Barry Sanders/25	15.00	40.00
234 Steve Young/25	12.00	30.00

2009 Playoff National Treasures Century Material Signature Prime

PRIME PRINT RUN 1-25
SERIAL #'d UNDER 15 NOT PRICED

12 Lee Evans/16	12.00	30.00
63 Marques Colston/25	12.00	30.00
186 Andre Reed/25	15.00	40.00
191 Charley Taylor/25	12.00	30.00
214 Sterling Sharpe/25	20.00	50.00
215 Tiki Barber/25	15.00	40.00
216 William Perry/15	20.00	50.00
219 Deion Sanders/25	50.00	100.00
225 Lawrence Taylor/25	30.00	60.00
227 Thurman Thomas/15	20.00	50.00
228 Bo Jackson/22	40.00	80.00
234 Steve Young/25	50.00	100.00

2009 Playoff National Treasures Champions Materials Combo

STATED PRINT RUN 50-99
*PRIME/25: .6X TO 1.5X BASIC DUAL
PRIME PRINT RUN 2-25

1 Sid Luckman	15.00	30.00
Clyde Turner		
2 Frank Gifford	8.00	20.00
Roosevelt Brown		
3 Raymond Berry	8.00	20.00
Lenny Moore		
4 Daryle Lamonica	10.00	25.00
Fred Biletnikoff		
5 Joe Namath	12.00	30.00
Don Maynard		
6 Len Dawson	10.00	25.00
Willie Lanier		
7 Gene Upshaw	8.00	20.00
Ted Hendricks		
8 Joe Montana	20.00	50.00
Ronnie Lott		
9 Phil Simms	10.00	25.00
Lawrence Taylor		
10 Troy Aikman	15.00	40.00
Emmitt Smith		

2009 Playoff National Treasures Champions Materials Quads

STATED PRINT RUN 50-99
*PRIME/25: .6X TO 1.5X BASIC QUAD
PRIME PRINT RUN 1-25

1 George Blanda	12.00	30.00
Fred Biletnikoff		
Daryle Lamonica		
Jim Otto		
2 Bob Griese/50	12.00	30.00
Larry Csonka		
Paul Warfield		
Larry Little		
3 Franco Harris	20.00	50.00
John Stallworth		
Joe Greene		
Jack Lambert		
4 Jim McMahon	25.00	60.00
Walter Payton		
Mike Singletary		
Dan Hampton		
5 Joe Montana	25.00	60.00
Jerry Rice		
Ronnie Lott		
Steve Young		
6 Troy Aikman	20.00	50.00
Emmitt Smith		
Michael Irvin		
Jay Novacek		
7 Tom Landry	20.00	50.00
Roger Staubach		
Tony Dorsett		
Randy White		
8 Ben Roethlisberger	10.00	25.00
Hines Ward		
Willie Parker		
Antwaan Randle El		
9 Peyton Manning	15.00	40.00
Reggie Wayne		
Dallas Clark		
Bob Sanders		
10 Eli Manning	10.00	25.00
Brandon Jacobs		
Aaron Ross		
Amani Toomer		

2009 Playoff National Treasures Champions Materials Trios

STATED PRINT RUN 30-99
*PRIME/25: .6X TO 1.5X BASIC TRIO
PRIME TRIO PRINT RUN 10-25

1 Joe Montana	25.00	60.00
Jerry Rice		
Ronnie Lott		
2 Franco Harris	12.00	30.00
John Stallworth		
Joe Greene		
3 Fred Biletnikoff	12.00	30.00
Willie Brown		
Ted Hendricks		
4 Bart Starr/30	25.00	60.00
Paul Hornung		
Forrest Gregg		
5 Jim Parker	10.00	25.00
Raymond Berry		
Lenny Moore		

2009 Playoff National Treasures Champions Signatures

STATED PRINT RUN 5-99

1 Dante Lavelli/99	15.00	40.00
2 Charley Trippi/50	10.00	25.00
3 Yale Lary/30	10.00	25.00
4 Rick Casares/99	10.00	25.00
5 Daryle Lamonica/99	12.00	30.00
7 Lawrence Taylor/99	15.00	40.00
8 Ronnie Lott/99	15.00	40.00
9 Frank Gifford/50	15.00	40.00

2009 Playoff National Treasures Champions Signature Combo

COMBO AUTO PRINT RUN 5-50

1 Dub Jones	20.00	50.00
Dante Lavelli		
3 Raymond Berry	20.00	50.00
Lenny Moore		

2009 Playoff National Treasures College Material

STATED PRINT RUN 10-99

2 Larry Csonka/99	8.00	20.00
3 Roger Staubach/99	10.00	25.00
4 Lawrence Taylor/99	8.00	20.00
5 Thurman Thomas/99	8.00	20.00

7 Dan Marino/45	20.00	50.00
9 Joe Greene/99	8.00	20.00
10 Steve Largent/99	8.00	20.00
11 Eric Dickerson/99	8.00	20.00
12 John Elway/15	40.00	80.00
13 Peyton Manning/55	20.00	50.00
14 Marcus Allen/99	10.00	25.00
15 Adrian Peterson/99	8.00	20.00
22 Knute Rockne/99	15.00	40.00
30 Hugh McElhenny/99	5.00	12.00

2009 Playoff National Treasures College Material Prime

PRIME PRINT RUN 50 SER.#'d SETS

2 Larry Csonka	12.00	30.00
4 Lawrence Taylor	12.00	30.00
5 Thurman Thomas	12.00	30.00
6 Barry Sanders	20.00	50.00
7 Dan Marino	25.00	60.00
10 Steve Largent	12.00	30.00
11 Eric Dickerson	10.00	25.00
14 Marcus Allen	10.00	25.00
15 Adrian Peterson	10.00	25.00
22 Knute Rockne	25.00	50.00

2009 Playoff National Treasures College Material Signature

STATED PRINT RUN 1-99
*PRIME/15: .8X TO 2X BASIC JSY AU/25-35
PRIME PRINT RUN 1-15
SERIAL #'d UNDER 25 NOT PRICED

3 Roger Staubach/25	40.00	80.00
4 Lawrence Taylor/25	30.00	60.00
5 Thurman Thomas/25	20.00	40.00
8 Tony Dorsett/30	30.00	60.00
9 Joe Greene/35	25.00	50.00
30 Hugh McElhenny/99	12.00	30.00

2009 Playoff National Treasures College Materials Quad

STATED PRINT RUN 25-99
*PRIME/15-25: .5X TO 1.2X BASIC QUAD
QUAD PRIME PRINT RUN 1-25

1 Earl Campbell	20.00	50.00
Ricky Williams		
Cedric Benson		
Jamaal Charles		
2 Eric Dickerson	20.00	50.00
Barry Sanders		
Tony Dorsett		
Marcus Allen		
3 Roger Staubach	25.00	60.00
Dan Marino		
John Elway		
Peyton Manning		
4 Clinton Portis	10.00	25.00
Reggie Wayne		
Willis McGahee		
Santana Moss		
5 Marcus Allen	12.00	30.00
Carson Palmer		
Reggie Bush		
Matt Leinart		

2009 Playoff National Treasures College Signature

STATED PRINT RUN 1-99

1 Mike Singletary/15	25.00	50.00
4 Lawrence Taylor/15	30.00	60.00
8 Tony Dorsett/20	25.00	50.00
9 Joe Greene/25	20.00	50.00
16 Ace Parker/25	20.00	50.00
17 Billy Sims/99	10.00	25.00
19 Bo Jackson/18	40.00	80.00
20 Deion Sanders/25	40.00	80.00
21 Joe Namath/25	50.00	100.00
23 Lydell Mitchell/99	8.00	20.00
24 Tim Brown/50	25.00	50.00
25 Carl Eller/99	8.00	20.00
26 Troy Aikman/20	40.00	80.00
28 Rick Casares/99	10.00	25.00
30 Hugh McElhenny/99	8.00	20.00

2009 Playoff National Treasures Colossal Materials

STATED PRINT RUN 2-99

1 Adrian Peterson/99	8.00	20.00
2 Andre Johnson/99	4.00	10.00
3 LaDainian Tomlinson/25	6.00	15.00
4 Ben Roethlisberger/25	6.00	15.00
5 Brian Westbrook/25	5.00	12.00
7 Dallas Clark/15	5.00	12.00
8 DeAngelo Williams/25	6.00	15.00
9 Drew Brees/50	8.00	20.00
10 Peyton Manning/15	15.00	40.00
11 Tony Romo/99	8.00	20.00
12 Frank Gore/45	4.00	10.00
14 Lee Evans/25	5.00	12.00
15 Matt Ryan/50	5.00	12.00
17 Michael Turner/65	4.00	10.00

2009 Playoff National Treasures Colossal Materials Jersey Numbers

STATED PRINT RUN 2-80

1 Adrian Peterson/28	10.00	25.00
2 Andre Johnson/80	4.00	10.00
3 LaDainian Tomlinson/21	6.00	15.00
5 Brian Westbrook/36	5.00	12.00
6 Chad Ochocinco/65	4.00	10.00
7 Dallas Clark/44	4.00	10.00
8 DeAngelo Williams/34	6.00	15.00
10 Peyton Manning/18	10.00	25.00
12 Frank Gore/21	5.00	12.00
14 Lee Evans/25	5.00	12.00
16 Maurice Jones-Drew/32	5.00	12.00
17 Michael Turner/33	5.00	12.00
20 Willie Parker/39	3.00	8.00

2009 Playoff National Treasures Colossal Materials Position

STATED PRINT RUN 5-99

2 Andre Johnson/99	4.00	10.00
3 LaDainian Tomlinson/25	6.00	15.00
4 Ben Roethlisberger/25	6.00	15.00
5 Brian Westbrook/25	5.00	12.00
7 Dallas Clark/15	5.00	12.00
8 DeAngelo Williams/25	6.00	15.00
9 Drew Brees/50	5.00	12.00
10 Peyton Manning/25	10.00	25.00
11 Tony Romo/99	8.00	20.00
12 Frank Gore/50	4.00	10.00
14 Lee Evans/25	5.00	12.00
15 Matt Ryan/50	5.00	12.00
16 Maurice Jones-Drew/34	5.00	12.00

2009 Playoff National Treasures Colossal Materials Position Prime

POSITION PRIME PRINT RUN 1-20

6 Chad Ochocinco/20	8.00	20.00
8 DeAngelo Williams/20	10.00	25.00
14 Lee Evans/20	8.00	20.00
20 Willie Parker/20	6.00	15.00

2009 Playoff National Treasures Colossal Materials Signature

UNPRICED SIG JSY NUM PRIME 1-10
UNPRICED SIG POSITION PRIME 1-10

2009 Playoff National Treasures Combo Material

STATED PRINT RUN 80-95
*PRIME/25: .8X TO 2X BASIC COMBO

1 Barry Sanders	12.00	30.00
Eric Dickerson		
2 Marcus Allen	8.00	20.00
Reggie Bush		
3 Larry Fitzgerald	8.00	20.00
Roy Williams WR		

2009 Playoff National Treasures League Leaders Materials

STATED PRINT RUN 50-99
*PRIME/17-25: .8X TO 2X BASIC JSY/50-99
PRIME PRINT RUN 5-25

1 Emmitt Smith/99	12.00	30.00
2 Eric Dickerson/99	6.00	15.00
3 Jerry Rice/75	12.00	30.00
4 Jim Brown/50	10.00	25.00
5 Michael Irvin/99	6.00	15.00
6 Norm Van Brocklin/99	6.00	15.00
7 Otto Graham/99	8.00	20.00
8 Sammy Baugh/99	10.00	25.00
9 Tom Brady/50	10.00	25.00
10 Walter Payton/99	15.00	40.00

2009 Playoff National Treasures League Leaders Materials Combo

STATED PRINT RUN 80-99
*PRIME/20-25: .8X TO 2X BASIC INSERTS
PRIME PRINT RUN 3-25

1 Sid Luckman	10.00	25.00
Bob Waterfield		
2 Bobby Layne	10.00	25.00
Tom Fears		
3 Jim Brown	12.00	30.00
Gale Sayers		
4 Bert Jones	8.00	20.00
Fran Tarkenton		
5 Earl Campbell	15.00	40.00
Walter Payton		
6 Steve Largent	10.00	25.00
John Stallworth		
7 Dan Fouts	15.00	40.00
Joe Montana		
8 Dan Marino	15.00	40.00
Eric Dickerson		
9 Eric Dickerson	15.00	40.00
Walter Payton		
10 Dan Marino	15.00	40.00
John Elway		
11 Barry Sanders	12.00	30.00
Thurman Thomas		
12 Dan Marino	15.00	40.00
Emmitt Smith		
13 Jerry Rice	12.00	30.00
Michael Irvin		
14 Emmitt Smith	12.00	30.00
Barry Sanders		
15 Drew Brees	12.00	30.00
Peyton Manning		

2009 Playoff National Treasures League Leaders Materials Quads

STATED PRINT RUN 10-99
*PRIME/25: .6X TO 1.5X BASIC QUAD

1 Warren Moon	15.00	40.00
Jim Kelly		
Emmitt Smith		
Barry Sanders		
2 Dan Marino	20.00	50.00
Steve Young		
Jim Kelly		
Troy Aikman		
3 Torry Holt	8.00	20.00
Randy Moss		
Anquan Boldin		
Chad Ochocinco		
4 Randy Moss/35	10.00	25.00
Torry Holt		
Chris Chambers		
Tony Gonzalez		
5 Tom Brady	20.00	50.00
Drew Brees		
Tony Romo		
Brett Favre		
6 LaDainian Tomlinson	12.00	30.00
Adrian Peterson		
Brian Westbrook		
Willie Parker		
7 Reggie Wayne	8.00	20.00
Randy Moss		
Chad Ochocinco		
Larry Fitzgerald		
9 Adrian Peterson	12.00	30.00
Michael Turner		
DeAngelo Williams		
Clinton Portis		
10 Andre Johnson	8.00	20.00
Larry Fitzgerald		
Steve Smith		
Roddy White		

2009 Playoff National Treasures League Leaders Materials Trios

STATED PRINT RUN 70-99
*PRIME/25: .6X TO 1.5X BASIC TRIO

1 Franco Harris	20.00	50.00
Chuck Foreman		
Walter Payton		
2 Walter Payton	20.00	50.00
Tony Dorsett		
Franco Harris		
3 Dan Fouts	10.00	25.00
Earl Campbell		
Steve Largent		
4 Eric Dickerson	10.00	25.00
John Riggins		
Marcus Allen		
5 Dan Marino	20.00	50.00
Eric Dickerson		
Jerry Rice		
6 Warren Moon	15.00	40.00
Barry Sanders		
Jerry Rice		
7 Emmitt Smith	15.00	40.00
Barry Sanders		
Thurman Thomas		
8 John Elway	12.00	30.00
Steve Young		
Warren Moon		
9 Steve Young	20.00	50.00
Brett Favre		
Dan Marino		
10 Brett Favre	20.00	50.00
Emmitt Smith		
Jerry Rice		
11 Brett Favre	20.00	50.00
Steve Young		
Peyton Manning		
12 Peyton Manning	10.00	25.00
Edgerrin James		
Torry Holt		
13 Kurt Warner	20.00	50.00
Peyton Manning		
Brett Favre		
14 LaDainian Tomlinson	8.00	20.00
Larry Johnson		
Frank Gore		
15 Chad Ochocinco/70	8.00	20.00
Marvin Harrison		
Reggie Wayne		

2009 Playoff National Treasures League Leaders Signatures

STATED PRINT RUN 3-99
SERIAL #'d UNDER 25 NOT PRICED

1 Ace Parker/50	12.50	30.00
8 Johnny Morris/99	8.00	20.00
10 Michael Irvin/25	25.00	50.00

2009 Playoff National Treasures League Leaders Signature Combo

STATED PRINT RUN 5-15

3 Jim Brown	50.00	100.00
Del Shofner		
4 Jim Brown	50.00	100.00
Lenny Moore		
5 Sonny Jurgensen	25.00	50.00
Tommy McDonald		
6 Tommy McDonald	20.00	40.00
Del Shofner		
7 Jim Brown	50.00	100.00
Don Perkins		
8 Sonny Jurgensen	40.00	80.00
Gale Sayers		
9 Gale Sayers	40.00	80.00
Leroy Kelly		
10 Sonny Jurgensen	40.00	80.00
Fran Tarkenton		
11 Bert Jones	40.00	80.00
Fran Tarkenton		
14 Dan Marino	150.00	250.00
John Elway		
15 Jerry Rice	100.00	200.00
Michael Irvin		

2009 Playoff National Treasures League Leaders Signature Materials

STATED PRINT RUN 15-50

1 Emmitt Smith/22	100.00	175.00
2 Eric Dickerson/15	30.00	60.00
3 Jerry Rice/15	125.00	200.00
4 Jim Brown/32	50.00	100.00
5 Michael Irvin/50	25.00	50.00

2009 Playoff National Treasures Pen Pals

1 Michael Crabtree	20.00	50.00
Brandon Pettigrew		
2 Matthew Stafford	50.00	100.00
Brandon Pettigrew		
3 Matthew Stafford	75.00	150.00
Mark Sanchez		
4 Knowshon Moreno	30.00	60.00
Chris Wells		
5 Michael Crabtree	30.00	60.00
Jeremy Maclin		
6 Donald Brown	25.00	50.00
LeSean McCoy		
7 Darrius Heyward-Bey	30.00	60.00
Percy Harvin		
8 Brian Robiskie	12.00	30.00
Mohamed Massaquoi		
9 Pat White	12.00	30.00
Patrick Turner		
10 Mark Sanchez	50.00	100.00
Shonn Greene		
11 LeSean McCoy	25.00	50.00
Jeremy Maclin		
12 Glen Coffee	30.00	60.00
Michael Crabtree		
13 Aaron Curry	12.00	30.00
Deon Butler		
14 Hakeem Nicks	20.00	40.00
Brandon Tate		
15 Stephen McGee	10.00	25.00
Rhett Bomar		
16 Chris Wells	20.00	50.00
Brian Robiskie		
17 Kenny Britt	12.00	30.00
Javon Ringer		
18 Matthew Stafford	100.00	200.00
Mark Sanchez		
Josh Freeman		
19 Knowshon Moreno	40.00	80.00
Chris Wells		
Donald Brown		
20 Darrius Heyward-Bey	40.00	100.00
Michael Crabtree		
Jeremy Maclin		
21 Knowshon Moreno	50.00	120.00
Mohamed Massaquoi		
Matthew Stafford		
22 Mike Thomas		
Derrick Williams		
Deon Butler		
23 Patrick Turner	20.00	50.00
Deon Butler		
Juaquin Iglesias		
24 Matthew Stafford	50.00	120.00
Brandon Pettigrew		
Derrick Williams		
25 Nate Davis	30.00	80.00
Michael Crabtree		
Glen Coffee		
26 Matthew Stafford	125.00	250.00
Mark Sanchez		
Josh Freeman		
Pat White		
27 Knowshon Moreno	60.00	120.00
Chris Wells		
Donald Brown		
LeSean McCoy		
28 Michael Crabtree	60.00	120.00
Jeremy Maclin		
Darrius Heyward-Bey		
Percy Harvin		
29 Matthew Stafford	100.00	175.00
Mark Sanchez		
Michael Crabtree		
Jeremy Maclin		
30 Matthew Stafford	60.00	120.00
Knowshon Moreno		
Michael Crabtree		
Brandon Pettigrew		
31 Knowshon Moreno	60.00	120.00
Chris Wells		
Michael Crabtree		
Jeremy Maclin		
32 Derrick Williams	40.00	80.00
Brandon Tate		
Mike Wallace		
Ramses Barden		
33 Hakeem Nicks	40.00	80.00
Ramses Barden		
Rhett Bomar		
Andre Brown		

2009 Playoff National Treasures Retired Materials Jersey Numbers Prime

PRIME PRINT RUN 1-25

1 Jim Kelly/25	15.00	40.00
2 Otto Graham/25	15.00	40.00
5 Jim Parker/25	10.00	25.00
6 Raymond Berry/25	12.00	30.00
11 Dan Marino/20	20.00	50.00
14 Don Maynard/15	12.00	30.00
15 Dan Fouts/25	15.00	40.00
16 Earl Campbell/25	12.00	30.00
17 Walter Payton/25	25.00	60.00
24 Mel Hein/25	25.00	50.00
26 Y.A. Tittle/25	15.00	40.00
29 Lawrence Taylor/25	15.00	40.00
31 Bob Waterfield/25	12.00	30.00
32 Merlin Olsen/25	12.00	30.00
35 Joe Montana/25	20.00	50.00
36 Steve Largent/25	15.00	40.00

2009 Playoff National Treasures Retired Materials Signature Jersey Numbers Prime

SIGNATURE PRIME PRINT RUN 2-25

1 Jim Kelly/25	50.00	100.00
6 Raymond Berry/25	30.00	60.00
9 Willie Lanier/25	25.00	50.00
15 Dan Fouts/25	50.00	100.00
16 Earl Campbell/25	40.00	80.00
22 Fran Tarkenton/15	50.00	100.00
26 Y.A. Tittle/25	40.00	80.00
27 Frank Gifford/16	25.00	50.00
29 Lawrence Taylor/20	40.00	80.00
32 Merlin Olsen/25	30.00	60.00

2009 Playoff National Treasures Rookie Colossal Materials

STATED PRINT RUN 50 SER.#'d SETS
*PRIME/25: .6X TO 1.5X BASIC JSY/50
*BRAND LOGO/14-15: 1X TO 2.5X BASIC INSERTS
*JSY NMBR/25: .6X TO 1.5X BASIC JSY/50
*POSITION/25: .6X TO 1.5X BASIC JSY/50
*PRIME TAG/50: .6X TO 1.5X BASIC JSY/50

1 Mark Sanchez	10.00	25.00
2 Matthew Stafford	15.00	40.00
3 LeSean McCoy	6.00	15.00
4 Knowshon Moreno	3.00	8.00
5 Kenny Britt	4.00	10.00
6 Juaquin Iglesias	2.50	6.00
7 Josh Freeman	6.00	15.00
8 Jeremy Maclin	5.00	12.00
9 Javon Ringer	3.00	8.00
10 Jason Smith	2.50	6.00
11 Hakeem Nicks	5.00	12.00
12 Glen Coffee	2.50	6.00
13 Michael Crabtree	6.00	15.00
14 Aaron Curry	3.00	8.00
15 Andre Brown	2.00	5.00
16 Brandon Pettigrew	3.00	8.00
17 Brian Robiskie	3.00	8.00
18 Chris Wells	5.00	12.00
19 Darrius Heyward-Bey	3.00	8.00
20 Deon Butler	2.50	6.00
21 Derrick Williams	2.50	6.00
22 Donald Brown	3.00	8.00
23 Tyson Jackson	2.50	6.00
24 Stephen McGee	3.00	8.00
25 Shonn Greene	5.00	12.00
26 Rhett Bomar	2.50	6.00
27 Ramses Barden	2.00	5.00
28 Percy Harvin	5.00	12.00
29 Patrick Turner	2.50	6.00
30 Pat White	3.00	8.00
31 Nate Davis	2.50	6.00
32 Mohamed Massaquoi	2.50	6.00
33 Mike Wallace	6.00	15.00
34 Mike Thomas	3.00	8.00

2009 Playoff National Treasures Rookie Colossal Materials Signatures Jersey Numbers

JERSEY NUMBERS PRINT RUN 26-50
*BASE MAT SIG/50: .4X TO 1X JSY NUM
MATERIAL SIGN PRINT RUN 11-50
*POSITION/50: .4X TO 1X JSY NUM

1 Mark Sanchez/50	50.00	100.00
2 Matthew Stafford/50	60.00	120.00
3 LeSean McCoy/50	40.00	80.00
4 Knowshon Moreno/50	10.00	25.00
5 Kenny Britt/50	12.00	30.00
6 Juaquin Iglesias/50	8.00	20.00
7 Josh Freeman/50	20.00	50.00
8 Jeremy Maclin/50	15.00	40.00
9 Javon Ringer/50	10.00	25.00
10 Jason Smith/50	8.00	20.00
11 Hakeem Nicks/50	15.00	40.00
12 Glen Coffee/50	8.00	20.00
13 Michael Crabtree/50	35.00	60.00
14 Aaron Curry/50	10.00	25.00
15 Andre Brown/50	6.00	15.00
16 Brandon Pettigrew/50	10.00	25.00
17 Brian Robiskie/50	10.00	25.00
18 Chris Wells/50	15.00	40.00
19 Darrius Heyward-Bey/26	10.00	25.00
20 Deon Butler/50	8.00	20.00
21 Derrick Williams/50	8.00	20.00
22 Donald Brown/50	10.00	25.00
23 Tyson Jackson/32	8.00	20.00
24 Stephen McGee/50	10.00	25.00
25 Shonn Greene/50	15.00	40.00
26 Rhett Bomar/50	8.00	20.00
27 Ramses Barden/50	6.00	15.00
28 Percy Harvin/50	40.00	80.00
29 Patrick Turner/50	8.00	20.00
30 Pat White/50	10.00	25.00
31 Nate Davis/50	8.00	20.00
32 Mohamed Massaquoi/50	8.00	20.00
33 Mike Wallace/50	20.00	50.00
34 Mike Thomas/50	10.00	25.00

2009 Playoff National Treasures Rookie Signature Material Gold

*ROOKIE JSY AU: .5X TO 1.2X BASIC JSY AU
STATED PRINT RUN 25 SER.#'d SETS
EXCH EXPIRATION: 8/3/2011

115 Josh Freeman	150.00	300.00
119 LeSean McCoy	175.00	300.00
120 Mark Sanchez	200.00	400.00
121 Matthew Stafford	350.00	600.00

2009 Playoff National Treasures Signature Patches College

STATED PRINT RUN 2-86

1 Anthony Gonzalez/26	12.00	30.00
2 Bart Starr/27	90.00	150.00
4 Braylon Edwards/26	15.00	40.00
6 Brian Cushing/50	12.00	30.00
8 Chad Ochocinco/26	15.00	40.00
9 Cris Collinsworth/28	20.00	50.00
11 Drew Brees/26	60.00	120.00
12 Frank Gore/27	15.00	40.00
13 Fred Taylor/26	20.00	50.00
14 James Casey/35	12.00	30.00
15 Jason Witten/27	40.00	80.00
16 Jermichael Finley/26	30.00	60.00
17 Joe Theismann/25	20.00	50.00
18 Joseph Addai/26	20.00	50.00
20 Justin Fargas/31	12.00	30.00
22 Malcolm Jenkins/51	12.00	30.00
24 Marshawn Lynch/24	15.00	40.00
25 Paul Hornung/50	20.00	50.00
28 Reggie Wayne/25	25.00	50.00
29 Ronnie Brown/26	30.00	60.00
30 Shonn Greene/86	20.00	50.00
31 Troy Aikman/25	40.00	80.00
32 Wes Welker/26	30.00	60.00
33 Willie Parker/26	12.00	30.00
34 Yale Lary/26	15.00	40.00
36 Joe Montana/16	125.00	200.00
38 Joe Namath/26	60.00	120.00
39 Emmitt Smith/22	100.00	175.00

2009 Playoff National Treasures Signature Patches NFL

STATED PRINT RUN 22-106

1 Anthony Gonzalez/26	12.00	30.00
2 Bart Starr/27	125.00	200.00
3 Ben Roethlisberger/26	50.00	100.00
5 Brett Favre/25	125.00	250.00
8 Chad Ochocinco/27	15.00	40.00
9 Cris Collinsworth/54	12.00	30.00
10 Donald Driver/26	20.00	50.00
11 Drew Brees/27	60.00	100.00
12 Frank Gore/27	15.00	40.00
15 Jason Witten/27	30.00	60.00
18 Joseph Addai/26	15.00	40.00
20 Justin Fargas/26	12.00	30.00
23 Marion Barber/51	15.00	40.00
24 Marshawn Lynch/25	12.00	30.00
25 Paul Hornung/50	20.00	50.00
28 Reggie Wayne/26	20.00	50.00
29 Ronnie Brown/26	20.00	50.00
31 Troy Aikman/25	40.00	80.00
32 Wes Welker/26	30.00	60.00
33 Willie Parker/26	12.00	30.00
34 Yale Lary/26	15.00	40.00
35 Cliff Harris/106	15.00	40.00
36 Joe Montana/26	75.00	150.00
37 Joe Montana/26	75.00	150.00
38 Joe Namath/26	75.00	150.00
39 Emmitt Smith/22	100.00	200.00

2009 Playoff National Treasures Signature Patches NFL Logo

STATED PRINT RUN 1-45

6 Brian Cushing/35	15.00	40.00
21 LeSean McCoy/25	50.00	100.00
22 Malcolm Jenkins/35	15.00	30.00
30 Shonn Greene/45	30.00	60.00

2009 Playoff National Treasures Timeline Materials Player Name

STATED PRINT RUN 1-99

1 Dan Marino/25	25.00	60.00
2 Brett Favre/99	15.00	40.00
3 John Elway/99	12.00	30.00
5 Jim Brown/32	12.00	30.00
8 Peyton Manning/18	15.00	40.00
9 LaDainian Tomlinson/15	'8.00	20.00
10 Troy Aikman/99	10.00	25.00
11 Joe Montana/99	15.00	40.00
12 Jerry Rice/25	15.00	40.00
14 Walter Payton/50	15.00	40.00
15 Reggie White/99	10.00	25.00
16 Adrian Peterson/28	12.00	30.00
17 Clinton Portis/99	5.00	12.00
19 Andre Johnson/20	6.00	15.00
20 Brian Westbrook/25	6.00	15.00

2009 Playoff National Treasures Timeline Materials Player Name Prime

NAME PRIME PRINT RUN 1-50
*TEAM PRIME/21-50: .4X TO 1X NAMES PRIME

2 Brett Favre/15	25.00	60.00
4 Barry Sanders/50	15.00	40.00
7 Tom Brady/50	15.00	40.00
9 LaDainian Tomlinson/20	12.00	30.00
10 Troy Aikman/20	15.00	40.00
17 Clinton Portis/50	8.00	20.00
20 Brian Westbrook/50	8.00	20.00

2009 Playoff National Treasures Timeline Materials Team Name

*TEAM NAME/15-99: .4X TO 1X NAMES
TEAM NICKNAME PRINT RUN 1-99

1 Dan Marino/15	20.00	50.00
2 Brett Favre/99	15.00	40.00
3 John Elway/99	12.00	30.00
4 Barry Sanders/25	15.00	40.00
5 Jim Brown/32	12.00	30.00
8 Peyton Manning/25	12.00	30.00
10 Troy Aikman/99	10.00	25.00
11 Joe Montana/99	15.00	40.00
12 Jerry Rice/25	15.00	40.00
14 Walter Payton/50	15.00	40.00
15 Reggie White/99	10.00	25.00
16 Adrian Peterson/28	12.00	30.00
17 Clinton Portis/50	5.00	12.00
19 Andre Johnson/25	6.00	15.00
20 Brian Westbrook/25	6.00	15.00

2009 Playoff National Treasures Timeline Materials Signature Player Name

PLAYER NAME AU PRINT RUN 2-25
*TEAM NAME/15-25: .4X TO 1X SIG/15-25
*PLYR NAME PRIME/15: .5X TO 1.2X SIG/15
*TEAM NAME PRIME/25: .5X TO 1.2X SIG/25

1 Dan Marino/15	125.00	250.00
5 Jim Brown/25	50.00	100.00
10 Troy Aikman/25	50.00	100.00
12 Jerry Rice/15	100.00	200.00
13 Tim Brown/25	30.00	60.00

2010 Playoff National Treasures

STATED PRINT RUN 99 SER.#'d SETS
EXCH EXPIRATION: 9/2/2012

1 Chris Wells	2.50	6.00
2 Larry Fitzgerald	3.00	8.00
3 Steve Breaston	2.00	5.00
4 Tim Hightower	2.00	5.00
5 Curtis Lofton	2.00	5.00
6 Matt Ryan	3.00	8.00
7 Michael Turner	2.00	5.00
8 Roddy White	2.50	6.00
9 Anquan Boldin	2.50	6.00
10 Joe Flacco	3.00	8.00
11 Ray Lewis	3.00	8.00
12 Ray Rice	2.50	6.00
13 Todd Heap	2.00	5.00
14 Willis McGahee	2.50	6.00
15 Fred Jackson	3.00	8.00
16 Lee Evans	2.50	6.00
17 Roscoe Parrish	2.00	5.00
18 Ryan Fitzpatrick	3.00	8.00
19 Steve Johnson	2.50	6.00
20 DeAngelo Williams	2.50	6.00
21 Dwayne Jarrett	2.00	5.00
22 Jonathan Stewart	2.50	6.00
23 Steve Smith	2.50	6.00
24 Brian Urlacher	3.00	8.00
26 Jay Cutler	3.00	8.00
26 Devin Hester	3.00	8.00
27 Johnny Knox	2.50	6.00
28 Matt Forte	2.50	6.00
29 Carson Palmer	2.50	6.00
30 Cedric Benson	2.50	6.00
31 Chad Ochocinco	2.50	6.00
32 Terrell Owens	3.00	8.00
33 Ben Watson	2.00	5.00
34 Josh Cribbs	3.00	8.00
35 Mohamed Massaquoi	2.50	6.00
36 Peyton Hillis	3.00	8.00
37 DeMarcus Ware	2.50	6.00
38 Felix Jones	2.50	6.00
39 Jason Witten	3.00	8.00
40 Miles Austin	3.00	8.00
41 Tony Romo	4.00	10.00
42 Brandon Lloyd	2.50	6.00
43 Eddie Royal	2.00	5.00
44 Knowshon Moreno	2.50	6.00
45 Kyle Orton	2.50	6.00
46 Brandon Pettigrew	2.00	5.00
47 Calvin Johnson	3.00	8.00
48 Matthew Stafford	3.00	8.00
49 Nate Burleson	2.00	5.00
50 Aaron Rodgers	8.00	20.00
51 Charles Woodson	3.00	8.00
52 Clay Matthews	3.00	8.00
53 Donald Driver	2.50	6.00
54 Greg Jennings	2.50	6.00
55 Andre Johnson	2.50	6.00
56 Arian Foster	2.50	6.00
57 Kevin Walter	2.50	6.00
58 Matt Schaub	2.50	6.00
59 Owen Daniels	2.00	5.00
60 Austin Collie	2.50	6.00
61 Dallas Clark	2.50	6.00
62 Joseph Addai	2.50	6.00
63 Peyton Manning	8.00	20.00
64 Reggie Wayne	2.50	6.00
65 David Garrard	2.50	6.00
66 Marcedes Lewis	2.00	5.00
67 Maurice Jones-Drew	2.50	6.00
68 Mike Sims-Walker	2.50	6.00
69 Chris Chambers	2.50	6.00
70 Dwayne Bowe	2.50	6.00
71 Jamaal Charles	2.50	6.00
72 Matt Cassel	2.50	6.00
73 Thomas Jones	2.50	6.00
74 Anthony Fasano	2.00	5.00
75 Brandon Marshall	2.50	6.00
76 Brian Hartline	2.50	6.00
77 Chad Henne	2.50	6.00
78 Ronnie Brown	2.50	6.00
79 Adrian Peterson	8.00	20.00
80 Bernard Berrian	2.00	5.00
81 Brett Favre	12.50	25.00
82 Percy Harvin	3.00	8.00
83 Randy Moss	3.00	8.00
84 Visanthe Shiancoe	2.50	6.00
85 BenJarvus Green-Ellis	3.00	8.00
86 Brandon Meriweather	2.00	5.00
87 Deion Branch	2.00	5.00
88 Tom Brady	6.00	15.00
89 Wes Welker	3.00	8.00
90 Devery Henderson	2.00	5.00
91 Drew Brees	3.00	8.00
92 Marques Colston	2.50	6.00
93 Pierre Thomas	2.50	6.00
94 Reggie Bush	3.00	8.00
95 Robert Meachem	2.50	6.00
96 Ahmad Bradshaw	2.50	6.00
97 Brandon Jacobs	2.50	6.00
98 Eli Manning	3.00	8.00
99 Hakeem Nicks	2.50	6.00
100 Steve Smith USC	2.50	6.00
101 Braylon Edwards	2.50	6.00
102 Darrelle Revis	2.50	6.00
103 LaDainian Tomlinson	3.00	8.00
104 Mark Sanchez	3.00	8.00
105 Shonn Greene	2.50	6.00
106 Darren McFadden	2.50	6.00
107 Darrius Heyward-Bey	2.50	6.00
108 Jason Campbell	2.50	6.00
109 Louis Murphy	2.50	6.00
110 Zach Miller	2.50	6.00
111 DeSean Jackson	2.50	6.00
112 Jeremy Maclin	2.50	6.00
113 Kevin Kolb	2.50	6.00
114 LeSean McCoy	2.50	6.00
115 Michael Vick	4.00	10.00
116 Ben Roethlisberger	3.00	8.00
117 Heath Miller	2.50	6.00
118 Hines Ward	2.50	6.00
119 Mike Wallace	2.50	6.00
120 Rashard Mendenhall	2.50	6.00
121 Troy Polamalu	4.00	10.00
122 Antonio Gates	2.50	6.00
123 Darren Sproles	2.50	6.00
124 Malcom Floyd	2.50	6.00
125 Philip Rivers	3.00	8.00
126 Frank Gore	2.50	6.00
127 Michael Crabtree	3.00	8.00
128 Patrick Willis	2.50	6.00
129 Vernon Davis	2.50	6.00
130 John Carlson	2.00	5.00
131 Marshawn Lynch	2.50	6.00
132 Matt Hasselbeck	2.00	5.00
133 Mike Williams USC	2.50	6.00
134 Danny Amendola	3.00	8.00
135 James Laurinaitis	2.50	6.00
136 Brandon Gibson	2.00	5.00
137 Steven Jackson	2.50	6.00
138 Cadillac Williams	2.50	6.00
139 Josh Freeman	3.00	8.00
140 Kellen Winslow Jr.	2.50	6.00
141 Ronde Barber	2.00	5.00
142 Bo Scaife	2.00	5.00
143 Chris Johnson	3.00	8.00
144 Kenny Britt	2.50	6.00
145 Nate Washington	2.00	5.00
146 Vince Young	2.00	5.00
147 Chris Cooley	2.50	6.00
148 Clinton Portis	2.50	6.00
149 Donovan McNabb	3.00	8.00
150 Santana Moss	2.50	6.00
151 Deion Sanders	4.00	10.00
152 Thurman Thomas	4.00	10.00
153 Tom Landry	5.00	12.00
154 Walter Payton	6.00	15.00
155 Andre Reed	3.00	8.00
156 Frank Gifford	3.00	8.00
157 Jack Lambert	4.00	10.00
158 Jan Stenerud	2.50	6.00
159 Joe Greene	4.00	10.00
160 Joe Klecko	2.50	6.00
161 Kellen Winslow	3.00	8.00
162 Lem Barney	2.50	6.00
163 Leroy Kelly	3.00	8.00
164 Mark Duper	2.50	6.00
165 Paul Krause	2.50	6.00
166 Chuck Bednarik	3.00	8.00
167 Billy Howton	2.50	6.00
168 Bobby Bell	2.50	6.00
169 Boyd Dowler	2.50	6.00
170 Marshall Faulk	3.00	8.00
171 Dante Lavelli	2.50	6.00
172 Ottis Anderson	2.50	6.00
173 Don Perkins	2.50	6.00
174 Doug Williams	3.00	8.00
175 Dub Jones	2.50	6.00
176 Everson Walls	2.50	6.00
177 Floyd Little	2.50	6.00
178 Fred Williamson	2.50	6.00
179 Gary Collins	2.50	6.00
180 Harlon Hill	2.50	6.00
181 Jim Taylor	4.00	10.00
182 Jimmy Orr	2.50	6.00
183 Johnny Morris	2.50	6.00
184 Lee Roy Jordan	3.00	8.00
185 Lydell Mitchell	2.50	6.00
186 Mel Renfro	2.50	6.00
187 Mike Curtis	2.50	6.00
188 Pete Retzlaff	2.50	6.00
189 Rayfield Wright	2.50	6.00
190 Rick Casares	2.50	6.00
191 Russ Grimm	2.50	6.00
192 Willie Davis	2.50	6.00
193 Cliff Harris	2.50	6.00
194 Joe Namath	5.00	12.00
195 Ed McCaffrey	2.50	6.00
196 Archie Manning	4.00	10.00
197 Art Monk	4.00	10.00
198 Jack Youngblood	2.50	6.00
199 Roosevelt Grier	2.50	6.00
200 Vince Lombardi	6.00	15.00
201 Aaron Hernandez AU RC	15.00	40.00
202 Andrew Quarless AU RC	8.00	20.00
203 Anthony Dixon AU RC	10.00	25.00
204 Anthony McCoy AU RC	6.00	15.00
205 Antonio Brown AU RC	50.00	80.00
206 Blair White AU RC	8.00	20.00
207 Brandon Banks AU RC	10.00	25.00
208 Brandon Graham AU RC	6.00	15.00
209 Brandon Spikes AU RC	10.00	25.00
210 Brody Eldridge AU RC	8.00	20.00
211 Bryan Bulaga AU RC	8.00	20.00
212 Carlos Dunlap AU RC	8.00	20.00
213 Carlton Mitchell AU RC	6.00	15.00
214 Chris Cook AU RC	8.00	20.00
215 Chris Ivory AU RC	10.00	25.00
216 Chris McGaha AU RC	5.00	12.00
217 Clay Harbor AU RC	6.00	15.00
218 Corey Wootton AU RC	6.00	15.00
219 Dan LeFevour AU RC	10.00	25.00
220 Dan Williams AU RC	6.00	15.00
221 Danario Alexander AU RC	12.00	30.00
222 David Gettis AU RC	8.00	20.00
223 David Nelson AU RC	10.00	25.00
224 David Reed AU RC	8.00	20.00
225 Deji Karim AU RC	8.00	20.00
226 Dennis Pitta AU RC	8.00	20.00
227 Derrick Morgan AU RC	6.00	15.00
228 Devin McCourty AU RC	12.00	30.00
229 Dezmon Briscoe AU RC	6.00	15.00
230 Dominique Curry AU RC	6.00	15.00
231 Dominique Franks AU RC	5.00	12.00
232 Donald Jones AU RC	10.00	25.00
233 Dorin Dickerson AU RC	5.00	12.00
234 Duke Calhoun AU RC	6.00	15.00
235 Earl Thomas AU RC	10.00	25.00
236 Ed Dickson AU RC	8.00	20.00
237 Ed Wang AU RC	8.00	20.00
238 Everson Griffen AU RC	8.00	20.00
239 Fendi Onobun AU RC	6.00	15.00
240 Garrett Graham AU RC	6.00	15.00
241 Jacoby Ford AU RC	10.00	25.00
242 James Starks AU RC	15.00	40.00
243 Jared Odrick AU RC	8.00	20.00
244 Jason Pierre-Paul AU RC	30.00	60.00
245 Jason Worilds AU RC	8.00	20.00
246 Javier Arenas AU RC	10.00	25.00
247 Jeremy Horne AU RC	6.00	15.00
248 Jeremy Williams AU RC	5.00	12.00
249 Jerry Hughes AU RC	8.00	20.00
250 Jim Dray AU RC	6.00	15.00
251 Jimmy Graham AU RC	50.00	80.00
252 Joe Haden AU RC	12.00	30.00
253 Joe Webb AU RC	15.00	30.00
254 John Conner AU RC	8.00	20.00
255 John Skelton AU RC	12.00	30.00
256 Joique Bell AU RC	6.00	15.00
257 Kareem Jackson AU RC	8.00	20.00
258 Keiland Williams AU RC	8.00	20.00
259 Keith Toston AU RC	8.00	20.00
260 Kerry Meier AU RC	6.00	15.00
261 Koa Misi AU RC	8.00	20.00
262 Kyle Williams AU RC	8.00	20.00
263 Sergio Kindle AU RC	8.00	20.00
264 Lamarr Houston AU RC	8.00	20.00
265 LeGarrette Blount AU RC	40.00	80.00
266 Lonyae Miller AU RC	6.00	15.00
267 Marc Mariani AU RC	8.00	20.00
268 Marlon Moore AU RC	8.00	20.00
269 Max Hall AU RC	8.00	20.00
270 Max Komar AU RC EXCH	8.00	20.00

271 Michael Hoomanawanui AU RC 8.00 20.00
272 Mickey Shuler AU RC 8.00 20.00
273 Morgan Burnett AU RC 8.00 20.00
274 Nate Allen AU RC 8.00 20.00
275 Nate Byham AU RC 6.00 15.00
276 NaVorro Bowman AU RC 12.00 30.00
277 Patrick Robinson AU RC 8.00 20.00
278 Perrish Cox AU RC 6.00 15.00
279 Preston Parker AU RC 6.00 15.00
280 Ricky Sapp AU RC 6.00 15.00
281 Riley Cooper AU RC 8.00 20.00
282 Roberto Wallace AU RC 6.00 15.00
283 Russell Okung AU RC 10.00 25.00
284 Rusty Smith AU RC 8.00 20.00
285 Michael Palmer AU RC 6.00 15.00
286 Sean Lee AU RC 12.00 30.00
287 Sean Weatherspoon AU RC 8.00 20.00
288 Chris Gronkowski AU RC 8.00 20.00
289 Seyi Ajirotutu AU RC 8.00 20.00
290 Shay Hodge AU RC 8.00 20.00
291 Stephen Williams AU RC 6.00 15.00
292 T.J. Ward AU RC 8.00 20.00
293 Taylor Mays AU RC 8.00 20.00
294 Thaddeus Lewis AU RC 6.00 15.00
295 Tony Moeaki AU RC 12.00 30.00
296 Tony Pike AU RC 8.00 20.00
297 Trent Williams AU RC EXCH 8.00 20.00
298 Tyson Alualu AU RC 6.00 15.00
299 Victor Cruz AU RC 100.00 175.00
300 Zac Robinson AU RC 6.00 15.00
301 Andre Roberts JSY AU RC 20.00 50.00
302 Armanti Edwards JSY AU RC 20.00 50.00
303 Arrelious Benn JSY AU RC 30.00 80.00
304 Ben Tate JSY AU RC 30.00 80.00
305 Brandon LaFell JSY AU RC 30.00 60.00
306 C.J. Spiller JSY AU RC 60.00 120.00
307 Colt McCoy JSY AU RC 50.00 120.00
308 Damian Williams JSY AU RC 30.00 60.00
309 Demaryius Thomas JSY AU RC 90.00 150.00
310 Dexter McCluster JSY AU RC EXCH 20.00 50.00
311 Dez Bryant JSY AU RC 150.00 300.00
312 Emmanuel Sanders JSY AU RC 40.00 80.00
313 Eric Berry JSY AU RC 50.00 100.00
314 Eric Decker JSY AU RC 50.00 80.00
315 Gerald McCoy JSY AU RC 30.00 80.00
316 Golden Tate JSY AU RC 20.00 50.00
317 Jahvid Best JSY AU RC 75.00 150.00
318 Jermaine Gresham JSY AU RC 25.00 60.00
319 Jimmy Clausen JSY AU RC 25.00 60.00
320 Joe McKnight JSY AU RC 20.00 50.00
321 Jonathan Dwyer JSY AU RC 30.00 60.00
322 Jordan Shipley JSY AU RC 30.00 60.00
323 Marcus Easley JSY AU RC 15.00 40.00
324 Mardy Gilyard JSY AU RC 20.00 50.00
325 Mike Kafka JSY AU RC 40.00 80.00
326 Mike Williams JSY AU RC 60.00 120.00
327 Montario Hardesty JSY AU RC 40.00 80.00
328 Ndamukong Suh JSY AU RC 125.00 250.00
329 Rob Gronkowski JSY AU RC 150.00 250.00
330 Rolando McClain JSY AU RC 20.00 50.00
331 Ryan Mathews JSY AU RC 125.00 250.00
332 Sam Bradford JSY AU RC 400.00 700.00
333 Taylor Price JSY AU RC EXCH 20.00 50.00
334 Tim Tebow JSY AU RC 450.00 700.00
335 Toby Gerhart JSY AU RC 40.00 80.00

2010 Playoff National Treasures Century Silver

*1-150 VETS: .8X TO 2X BASIC CARDS
*151-200 LEGENDS: .6X TO 1.5X BASIC CARDS
STATED PRINT RUN 25 SER.#'d SETS

2010 Playoff National Treasures Rookie Signature Material Gold

*GOLD/25: .6X TO 1.5X BASE JSY AU/99
GOLD JSY AU PRINT RUN 25
306 C.J. Spiller 100.00 200.00
307 Colt McCoy 150.00 300.00
309 Demaryius Thomas 150.00 250.00
311 Dez Bryant 300.00 600.00
313 Eric Berry 100.00 200.00
317 Jahvid Best 125.00 250.00
319 Jimmy Clausen 50.00 120.00
326 Mike Williams 100.00 200.00
328 Ndamukong Suh 200.00 400.00
329 Rob Gronkowski 250.00 400.00
331 Ryan Mathews 200.00 400.00
332 Sam Bradford 500.00 800.00
334 Tim Tebow 700.00 1,000.00

2010 Playoff National Treasures Century Gold Signature

*1-200 GOLD AU PRINT RUN 5-25
*201-300 ROOK/25: .6X TO 1.5X BASE RC AU/99
201-300 ROOKIE GOLD AU PRINT RUN 25
22 Jonathan Stewart/25 12.00 30.00
34 Josh Cribbs/25 12.00 30.00
50 Aaron Rodgers/21 175.00 300.00
60 Austin Collie/25 15.00 40.00
63 Peyton Manning/18 125.00 200.00
64 Reggie Wayne/17 15.00 40.00
78 Ronnie Brown/25 10.00 25.00
109 Louis Murphy/25 10.00 25.00
116 Ben Roethlisberger/18 60.00 120.00
117 Heath Miller/25 12.00 30.00
120 Rashard Mendenhall/25 12.00 30.00
127 Michael Crabtree/25 15.00 40.00
138 Cadillac Williams/25 10.00 25.00
155 Andre Reed/25 10.00 25.00
158 Jan Stenerud/25 10.00 25.00
160 Joe Klecko/25 10.00 25.00
161 Kellen Winslow/25 10.00 25.00
162 Lem Barney/25 12.00 30.00
163 Leroy Kelly/25 12.00 30.00
164 Mark Duper/25 10.00 25.00
166 Chuck Bednarik/25 12.00 30.00
167 Billy Howton/25 12.00 30.00
168 Bobby Bell/25 15.00 40.00
169 Boyd Dowler/25 12.00 30.00
172 Ottis Anderson/25 12.00 30.00
173 Don Perkins/25 12.00 30.00
175 Dub Jones/25 10.00 25.00
176 Everson Walls/25 10.00 25.00
179 Gary Collins/25 10.00 25.00
180 Harlon Hill/25 10.00 25.00
182 Jimmy Orr/25 10.00 25.00
183 Johnny Morris/25 12.00 30.00
185 Lydell Mitchell/25 12.00 30.00
186 Mel Renfro/25 12.00 30.00
187 Mike Curtis/25 10.00 25.00
188 Pete Retzlaff/25 10.00 25.00
190 Rick Casares/25 12.00 30.00
192 Willie Davis/25 12.00 30.00
196 Archie Manning/25 15.00 40.00
198 Jack Youngblood/25 10.00 25.00
251 Jimmy Graham/25 100.00 175.00
265 LeGarrette Blount/25 75.00 150.00
299 Victor Cruz/25 175.00 300.00

2010 Playoff National Treasures Century Material

STATED PRINT RUN 1-99
1 Chris Wells/99 3.00 8.00
6 Matt Ryan/99 4.00 10.00
7 Michael Turner/99 2.50 6.00
8 Roddy White/25 5.00 12.00
11 Ray Lewis/25 6.00 15.00
12 Ray Rice/25 5.00 12.00
16 Lee Evans/99 3.00 8.00
20 DeAngelo Williams/25 5.00 12.00
23 Steve Smith/30 4.00 10.00
24 Brian Urlacher/25 6.00 15.00
26 Jay Cutler/25 6.00 15.00
26 Devin Hester/99 4.00 10.00
28 Matt Forte/25 5.00 12.00
29 Carson Palmer/25 5.00 12.00
31 Chad Ochocinco/99 3.00 8.00
37 DeMarcus Ware/99 3.00 8.00
38 Felix Jones/25 5.00 12.00
39 Jason Witten/99 4.00 10.00
40 Miles Austin/25 6.00 15.00
41 Tony Romo/25 8.00 20.00
45 Kyle Orton/99 3.00 8.00
47 Calvin Johnson/99 4.00 10.00
48 Matthew Stafford/99 4.00 10.00
50 Aaron Rodgers/25 12.00 30.00
53 Donald Driver/35 4.00 10.00
54 Greg Jennings/25 5.00 12.00
55 Andre Johnson/99 3.00 8.00
58 Matt Schaub/99 3.00 8.00
61 Dallas Clark/99 3.00 8.00
63 Peyton Manning/25 10.00 25.00
64 Reggie Wayne/99 3.00 8.00
65 David Garrard/99 3.00 8.00
70 Dwayne Bowe/99 3.00 8.00
72 Matt Cassel/99 3.00 8.00
78 Ronnie Brown/29 5.00 12.00
79 Adrian Peterson/28 10.00 25.00
81 Brett Favre/25 15.00 40.00
82 Percy Harvin/99 4.00 10.00
88 Tom Brady/49 8.00 20.00
90 Devery Henderson/99 2.50 6.00
91 Drew Brees/99 4.00 10.00
94 Reggie Bush/25 6.00 15.00
96 Ahmad Bradshaw/99 3.00 8.00
97 Brandon Jacobs/49 4.00 10.00
98 Eli Manning/99 4.00 10.00
100 Steve Smith USC/99 3.00 8.00
101 Braylon Edwards/99 3.00 8.00
103 LaDainian Tomlinson/99 4.00 10.00
104 Mark Sanchez/99 4.00 10.00
105 Shonn Greene/99 3.00 8.00
106 Darren McFadden/99 3.00 8.00
115 Michael Vick/99 8.00 20.00
120 Rashard Mendenhall/99 3.00 8.00
121 Troy Polamalu/83 6.00 15.00
122 Antonio Gates/99 3.00 8.00
125 Philip Rivers/49 5.00 12.00
126 Frank Gore/99 3.00 8.00
127 Michael Crabtree/89 4.00 10.00
132 Matt Hasselbeck/99 2.50 6.00
137 Steven Jackson/99 3.00 8.00
138 Cadillac Williams/99 3.00 8.00
142 Bo Scaife/99 2.50 6.00
147 Chris Cooley/99 3.00 8.00
148 Clinton Portis/99 3.00 8.00
149 Donovan McNabb/99 5.00 12.00
150 Santana Moss/50 3.00 8.00
151 Deion Sanders/99 6.00 15.00
152 Thurman Thomas/99 5.00 12.00
153 Tom Landry/99 12.00 30.00
154 Walter Payton/99 12.00 30.00
155 Andre Reed/99 4.00 10.00
157 Jack Lambert/25 8.00 20.00
170 Marshall Faulk/99 4.00 10.00
194 Joe Namath/25 10.00 25.00
195 Ed McCaffrey/70 3.00 8.00
196 Archie Manning/99 5.00 12.00
198 Jack Youngblood/25 5.00 12.00
199 Roosevelt Grier/15 5.00 12.00

2010 Playoff National Treasures Century Material Prime

STATED PRINT RUN 1-50
6 Matt Ryan/50 6.00 15.00
7 Michael Turner/50 4.00 10.00
8 Roddy White/50 4.00 10.00
10 Joe Flacco/40 6.00 15.00
11 Ray Lewis/50 6.00 15.00
12 Ray Rice/25 8.00 20.00
13 Todd Heap/50 4.00 10.00
16 Lee Evans/50 5.00 12.00
20 DeAngelo Williams/25 6.00 15.00
24 Brian Urlacher/25 6.00 15.00
26 Devin Hester/50 5.00 12.00
26 Jay Cutler/50 6.00 15.00
28 Matt Forte/50 5.00 12.00
29 Carson Palmer/50 5.00 12.00
30 Cedric Benson/50 5.00 12.00
31 Chad Ochocinco/50 5.00 12.00
37 DeMarcus Ware/50 5.00 12.00
38 Felix Jones/50 5.00 12.00
39 Jason Witten/50 5.00 12.00
40 Miles Austin/50 6.00 15.00
41 Tony Romo/50 8.00 20.00
44 Knowshon Moreno/50 5.00 12.00
45 Kyle Orton/50 5.00 12.00
47 Calvin Johnson/50 6.00 15.00
50 Aaron Rodgers/50 20.00 50.00
51 Charles Woodson/15 8.00 20.00
53 Donald Driver/35 5.00 12.00
58 Matt Schaub/50 5.00 12.00
61 Dallas Clark/50 5.00 12.00
62 Joseph Addai/50 5.00 12.00
64 Reggie Wayne/50 5.00 12.00
65 David Garrard/50 5.00 12.00
67 Maurice Jones-Drew/50 6.00 15.00
70 Dwayne Bowe/50 5.00 12.00
71 Jamaal Charles/50 6.00 15.00
78 Ronnie Brown/23 6.00 15.00
79 Adrian Peterson/50 10.00 25.00
80 Bernard Berrian/50 4.00 10.00
82 Percy Harvin/50 6.00 15.00
83 Randy Moss/50 6.00 15.00
84 Visanthe Shiancoe/50 5.00 12.00
88 Tom Brady/50 10.00 25.00
89 Wes Welker/35 6.00 15.00
90 Devery Henderson/50 4.00 10.00
91 Drew Brees/50 6.00 15.00
92 Marques Colston/50 5.00 12.00
94 Reggie Bush/30 6.00 15.00
96 Ahmad Bradshaw/50 5.00 12.00
97 Brandon Jacobs/50 5.00 12.00
98 Eli Manning/50 6.00 15.00
100 Steve Smith USC/30 5.00 12.00
101 Braylon Edwards/50 5.00 12.00
102 Darrelle Revis/50 5.00 12.00
103 LaDainian Tomlinson/50 6.00 15.00
104 Mark Sanchez/50 6.00 15.00
105 Shonn Greene/50 5.00 12.00
106 Darren McFadden/50 5.00 12.00
111 DeSean Jackson/50 5.00 12.00
112 Jeremy Maclin/50 5.00 12.00
113 Kevin Kolb/50 5.00 12.00
114 LeSean McCoy/50 6.00 15.00
118 Hines Ward/50 8.00 20.00
120 Rashard Mendenhall/30 5.00 12.00
121 Troy Polamalu/50 12.00 30.00
122 Antonio Gates/50 5.00 12.00
123 Darren Sproles/50 5.00 12.00
125 Philip Rivers/50 6.00 15.00
128 Patrick Willis/50 5.00 12.00
129 Vernon Davis/50 5.00 12.00
132 Matt Hasselbeck/50 4.00 10.00
137 Steven Jackson/50 5.00 12.00
138 Cadillac Williams/50 6.00 15.00
143 Chris Johnson/50 6.00 15.00
144 Kenny Britt/50 5.00 12.00
147 Chris Cooley/50 5.00 12.00
148 Clinton Portis/50 5.00 12.00
149 Donovan McNabb/15 8.00 20.00
150 Santana Moss/50 4.00 10.00
151 Deion Sanders/50 10.00 25.00
152 Thurman Thomas/50 8.00 20.00
154 Walter Payton/50 20.00 50.00
157 Jack Lambert/50 8.00 20.00
158 Jan Stenerud/50 6.00 15.00
159 Joe Greene/50 8.00 20.00
164 Mark Duper/50 5.00 12.00
170 Marshall Faulk/50 6.00 15.00
194 Joe Namath/50 12.00 30.00
195 Ed McCaffrey/50 5.00 12.00

2010 Playoff National Treasures Century Material Signature Prime

PRIME JSY AU PRINT RUN 1-25
1 Chris Wells/20 12.00 30.00
7 Michael Turner/20 12.00 30.00
20 DeAngelo Williams/20 12.00 30.00
26 Jay Cutler/20 12.00 30.00
37 DeMarcus Ware/20 15.00 40.00
53 Donald Driver/20 30.00 60.00
56 Arian Foster/20 40.00 80.00
64 Reggie Wayne/20 15.00 40.00
67 Maurice Jones-Drew/20 15.00 40.00
80 Bernard Berrian/20 15.00 40.00
84 Visanthe Shiancoe/20 EXCH
97 Brandon Jacobs/20 12.00 30.00
98 Eli Manning/20 40.00 80.00
101 Braylon Edwards/20 12.00 30.00
104 Mark Sanchez/20 40.00 80.00
105 Shonn Greene/20 15.00 40.00
112 Jeremy Maclin/20 15.00 40.00
113 Kevin Kolb/20 15.00 40.00
114 LeSean McCoy/20 20.00 50.00
120 Rashard Mendenhall/20 20.00 50.00
123 Darren Sproles/20 12.00 30.00
144 Kenny Britt/20 15.00 40.00
151 Deion Sanders/20 50.00 100.00
152 Thurman Thomas/20 20.00 50.00
157 Jack Lambert/20 50.00 100.00
158 Jan Stenerud/20 15.00 40.00
159 Joe Greene/20 30.00 60.00
164 Mark Duper/20 15.00 40.00
170 Marshall Faulk/25 50.00 100.00
194 Joe Namath/20 150.00 250.00
195 Ed McCaffrey/20 20.00 50.00

2010 Playoff National Treasures Colossal Materials

STATED PRINT RUN 8-50
1 Aaron Rodgers/15 25.00 50.00
2 Adrian Peterson/50 10.00 25.00
3 Andre Johnson/50 5.00 12.00
4 Antonio Gates/50 5.00 12.00
5 Arian Foster/50 8.00 20.00
7 Brandon Jacobs/50 5.00 12.00
8 Braylon Edwards/50 5.00 12.00
9 Brent Celek/50 5.00 12.00
10 Brett Favre/50 15.00 40.00
11 Brian Urlacher/50 6.00 15.00
12 Calvin Johnson/50 6.00 15.00
14 Carson Palmer/50 5.00 12.00
15 Cedric Benson/50 5.00 12.00
17 Chris Cooley/50 5.00 12.00
18 Chris Johnson/50 6.00 15.00
19 Clinton Portis/50 5.00 12.00
20 Dallas Clark/50 5.00 12.00
21 Darrelle Revis/40 5.00 12.00
22 Darren Sproles/50 5.00 12.00
23 Darren McFadden/50 5.00 12.00
24 DeAngelo Williams/50 5.00 12.00
25 DeSean Jackson/50 5.00 12.00
27 Donovan McNabb/50 6.00 15.00
28 Eli Manning/50 6.00 15.00
29 Felix Jones/50 5.00 12.00
30 Frank Gore/50 5.00 12.00
31 Devin Hester/50 6.00 15.00
32 Jamaal Charles/50 6.00 15.00
33 Heath Miller/15 6.00 15.00
34 Jason Witten/50 5.00 12.00
35 Joe Flacco/25 8.00 20.00
36 Knowshon Moreno/50 5.00 12.00
37 LaDainian Tomlinson/50 6.00 15.00
38 Lee Evans/50 5.00 12.00
39 Mark Sanchez/50 6.00 15.00
40 Matt Forte/50 5.00 12.00
41 Matt Ryan/50 6.00 15.00
42 Matt Schaub/50 5.00 12.00
43 Percy Harvin/50 6.00 15.00
44 Peyton Manning/50 12.00 30.00
45 Philip Rivers/50 6.00 15.00
46 Randy Moss/50 6.00 15.00
48 Ray Lewis/50 8.00 20.00
49 Ray Rice/50 6.00 15.00
50 Reggie Bush/50 6.00 15.00
51 Reggie Wayne/50 5.00 12.00
52 Roddy White/50 5.00 12.00
54 Shonn Greene/50 5.00 12.00
55 Steven Jackson/50 5.00 12.00
56 Tom Brady/50 12.00 30.00
57 Tony Romo/50 8.00 20.00
60 Wes Welker/50 6.00 15.00

2010 Playoff National Treasures Colossal Materials Jersey Numbers Prime

*JSY # PRIME/15-25: .4X TO 1X PRIME/15-25
STATED PRINT RUN 4-25
5 Arian Foster/25 12.00 30.00

2010 Playoff National Treasures Colossal Materials Position Prime

*POS.PRIME/15-25: .4X TO 1X PRIME/15-25
STATED PRINT RUN 5-25
5 Arian Foster/25 12.00 30.00

2010 Playoff National Treasures Colossal Materials Prime

STATED PRINT RUN 2-25
2 Adrian Peterson/25 15.00 40.00
4 Antonio Gates/25 8.00 20.00
7 Brandon Jacobs/25 8.00 20.00
8 Braylon Edwards/15 8.00 20.00
9 Brent Celek/24 8.00 20.00
11 Brian Urlacher/25 10.00 25.00
12 Calvin Johnson/25 10.00 25.00
14 Carson Palmer/25 8.00 20.00
15 Cedric Benson/15 8.00 20.00
16 Chad Ochocinco/25 8.00 20.00
17 Chris Cooley/25 8.00 20.00
18 Chris Johnson/25 10.00 25.00
19 Clinton Portis/25 8.00 20.00
21 Darrelle Revis/25 8.00 20.00
22 Darren Sproles/25 8.00 20.00
24 DeAngelo Williams/25 8.00 20.00
25 DeSean Jackson/25 8.00 20.00
26 Devery Henderson/25 6.00 15.00
28 Eli Manning/25 10.00 25.00
29 Felix Jones/25 8.00 20.00
30 Frank Gore/25 8.00 20.00
31 Devin Hester/25 10.00 25.00
32 Jamaal Charles/25 10.00 25.00
34 Jason Witten/25 10.00 25.00
36 Knowshon Moreno/15 8.00 20.00
37 LaDainian Tomlinson/25 10.00 25.00
38 Lee Evans/25 8.00 20.00
39 Mark Sanchez/15 10.00 25.00
40 Matt Forte/25 8.00 20.00
42 Matt Schaub/25 8.00 20.00
46 Randy Moss/15 10.00 25.00
48 Ray Lewis/25 15.00 40.00
49 Ray Rice/15 8.00 20.00
50 Reggie Bush/25 10.00 25.00
54 Shonn Greene/15 8.00 20.00
55 Steven Jackson/25 8.00 20.00
56 Tom Brady/25 20.00 50.00
57 Tony Romo/25 12.00 30.00
59 Vernon Davis/25 8.00 20.00
60 Wes Welker/25 10.00 25.00

2010 Playoff National Treasures Colossal Materials Signature

STATED PRINT RUN 1-25
9 Brent Celek/25 15.00 40.00

2010 Playoff National Treasures Emblems of the Hall

STATED PRINT RUN 99 SER.#'d SETS
1 Terry Bradshaw 5.00 12.00
2 Johnny Unitas 6.00 15.00
3 Bob Hayes 4.00 10.00
4 Mike Singletary 4.00 10.00
5 Michael Irvin 3.00 8.00
6 Earl Campbell 4.00 10.00
7 Bruce Smith 3.00 8.00
8 Barry Sanders 6.00 15.00
9 Bart Starr 6.00 15.00
10 Dan Fouts 4.00 10.00
12 Emmitt Smith 8.00 20.00
14 Jerry Rice 6.00 15.00
15 Jim Brown 6.00 15.00
16 Joe Montana 8.00 20.00
17 Joe Namath 5.00 12.00
18 Joe Perry 3.00 8.00
19 John Elway 6.00 15.00
20 Rickey Jackson 2.50 6.00

2010 Playoff National Treasures Emblems of the Hall Materials

STATED PRINT RUN 47-99
*PRIME/23-25: .8X TO 2X BASE JSY/55-99
1 Terry Bradshaw/99 8.00 20.00
2 Johnny Unitas/99 10.00 25.00
3 Bob Hayes/99 8.00 20.00
4 Mike Singletary/99 6.00 15.00
5 Michael Irvin/99 6.00 15.00
6 Earl Campbell/47 8.00 20.00
7 Bruce Smith/55 5.00 12.00
8 Barry Sanders/99 10.00 25.00
9 Bart Starr/99 10.00 25.00
10 Dan Fouts/99 6.00 15.00
12 Emmitt Smith/99 12.00 30.00
14 Jerry Rice/99 10.00 25.00
15 Jim Brown/99 8.00 20.00
16 Joe Montana/99 15.00 40.00
17 Joe Namath/99 10.00 25.00
18 Joe Perry/99 5.00 12.00
19 John Elway/99 10.00 25.00
20 Rickey Jackson/99 6.00 15.00

2010 Playoff National Treasures Emblems of the Hall Signature Materials

STATED PRINT RUN 10-25
4 Mike Singletary/20 20.00 50.00
5 Michael Irvin/25 40.00 80.00
6 Earl Campbell/25 40.00 80.00
7 Bruce Smith/25 20.00 50.00
8 Barry Sanders/25 100.00 200.00
9 Bart Starr/25 100.00 200.00
10 Dan Fouts/25 50.00 100.00
12 Emmitt Smith/10
14 Jerry Rice/12
15 Jim Brown/25 50.00 100.00
16 Joe Montana/25 125.00 200.00
17 Joe Namath/25 75.00 150.00
18 Joe Perry/25 EXCH 15.00 40.00
19 John Elway/25 100.00 200.00
20 Rickey Jackson/25 20.00 50.00

2010 Playoff National Treasures Emblems of the Hall Signature Materials Prime

*PRIME/15: .5X TO 1.2X BASIC JSY/20-25
PRIME STATED PRINT RUN 2-15
12 Emmitt Smith/15 150.00 250.00

2010 Playoff National Treasures Emblems of the Hall Signatures

STATED PRINT RUN 5-50
5 Michael Irvin/18 30.00 60.00
6 Earl Campbell/50 30.00 60.00
7 Bruce Smith/50 15.00 40.00
8 Barry Sanders/50 75.00 135.00
9 Bart Starr/50 75.00 150.00
10 Dan Fouts/50 20.00 50.00
15 Jim Brown/50 40.00 80.00
16 Joe Montana/16 100.00 175.00
18 Joe Perry/50 EXCH 12.00 30.00
20 Rickey Jackson/50 15.00 40.00

2010 Playoff National Treasures NFL Gear Prime

PRIME PRINT RUN 49 SER.#'d SETS
*BASE NFL GEAR/25: .4X TO 1X PRIME/49
*LAUNDRY TAG/15: .6X TO 1.5X PRIME/49
*TRIPLE NFL GEAR/25: .4X TO 1X PRIME/49
*TRIPLE GEAR PRIME/49: .4X TO 1X PRIME/49
1 Tim Tebow 20.00 50.00
2 Sam Bradford 20.00 50.00
3 C.J. Spiller 8.00 20.00
4 Dez Bryant 15.00 40.00
5 Eric Berry 8.00 20.00
6 Jahvid Best 8.00 20.00
7 Jordan Shipley 8.00 20.00
8 Jimmy Clausen 8.00 20.00
9 Joe McKnight 8.00 20.00
10 Andre Roberts 8.00 20.00
11 Arrelious Benn 8.00 20.00
12 Brandon LaFell 8.00 20.00
13 Ryan Mathews 10.00 25.00
14 Rolando McClain 8.00 20.00
15 Mike Williams 8.00 20.00
16 Montario Hardesty 8.00 20.00
17 Jonathan Dwyer 6.00 15.00
18 Mardy Gilyard 6.00 15.00
19 Eric Decker 6.00 15.00
20 Armanti Edwards 6.00 15.00
21 Demaryius Thomas 6.00 15.00
22 Emmanuel Sanders 5.00 12.00
23 Jermaine Gresham 6.00 15.00
24 Toby Gerhart 5.00 12.00
25 Ben Tate 6.00 15.00
26 Mike Kafka 6.00 15.00
27 Rob Gronkowski 12.00 30.00
28 Taylor Price 5.00 12.00
29 Marcus Easley 4.00 10.00
30 Ndamukong Suh 12.00 30.00
31 Gerald McCoy 8.00 20.00
32 Golden Tate 5.00 12.00
33 Colt McCoy 10.00 25.00
34 Dexter McCluster 5.00 12.00
35 Damian Williams 5.00 12.00

2010 Playoff National Treasures NFL Gear Signatures Prime

DUAL PRIME AU PRINT RUN 25 SER.#'d SETS
20.00
*TRIPLE PRIME/19-25: .5X TO 1.2X PRIME DUAL/25
1 Tim Tebow 150.00 250.00
2 Sam Bradford 100.00 200.00
3 C.J. Spiller 30.00 60.00
4 Dez Bryant 75.00 135.00
5 Eric Berry 30.00 60.00
6 Jahvid Best 40.00 80.00
7 Jordan Shipley 8.00 20.00
8 Jimmy Clausen 8.00 20.00
9 Joe McKnight 8.00 20.00
10 Andre Roberts 8.00 20.00
11 Arrelious Benn 8.00 20.00
12 Brandon LaFell 8.00 20.00
13 Ryan Mathews 40.00 80.00
14 Rolando McClain 8.00 20.00
15 Mike Williams 15.00 40.00
16 Montario Hardesty 20.00 50.00
17 Jonathan Dwyer EXCH 8.00 20.00
18 Mardy Gilyard 8.00 20.00
19 Eric Decker 15.00 30.00
20 Armanti Edwards 8.00 20.00
21 Demaryius Thomas 15.00 40.00
22 Emmanuel Sanders 8.00 20.00
23 Jermaine Gresham 8.00 20.00
24 Toby Gerhart 15.00 40.00
25 Ben Tate 12.00 30.00
26 Mike Kafka 12.00 30.00
27 Rob Gronkowski 60.00 120.00
28 Taylor Price 8.00 20.00
29 Marcus Easley 8.00 20.00
31 Gerald McCoy 8.00 20.00
32 Golden Tate 8.00 20.00
33 Colt McCoy 20.00 50.00
34 Dexter McCluster EXCH 12.00 30.00
35 Damian Williams 8.00 20.00

2010 Playoff National Treasures NFL Greatest

STATED PRINT RUN 99 SER.#'d SETS
1 Deacon Jones 3.00 8.00
2 Charlie Joiner 2.50 6.00
3 Sonny Jurgensen 3.00 8.00
4 Hugh McElhenny 2.50 6.00
5 Jim Kelly 4.00 10.00
6 George Blanda 3.00 8.00
7 James Lofton 2.50 6.00
8 Charley Taylor 2.50 6.00
9 Larry Little 2.50 6.00
10 Dave Casper 2.50 6.00
11 Willie Lanier 2.50 6.00
12 Merlin Olsen 3.00 8.00
13 Gale Sayers 5.00 12.00
14 Paul Hornung 4.00 10.00
15 Roger Staubach 5.00 12.00
16 Raymond Berry 3.00 8.00
17 Forrest Gregg 2.50 6.00
18 Sammy Baugh 4.00 10.00
19 Bob Griese 4.00 10.00
20 Junior Seau 4.00 10.00
21 Ron Mix 2.50 6.00
22 Alan Page 3.00 8.00
23 Bob Lilly 3.00 8.00
24 Dan Marino 8.00 20.00
25 Dick Butkus 5.00 12.00
26 Don Maynard 3.00 8.00
27 Fran Tarkenton 4.00 10.00
28 Franco Harris 4.00 10.00
29 Fred Biletnikoff 4.00 10.00
30 Howie Long 4.00 10.00
31 Jim Otto 2.50 6.00
32 John Randle 2.50 6.00
33 Lee Roy Selmon 2.50 6.00
34 Len Dawson 4.00 10.00
35 Lenny Moore 3.00 8.00

2010 Playoff National Treasures NFL Greatest Materials

STATED PRINT RUN 20-99
*PRIME/35-49: .6X TO 1.5X BASIC JSY
*PRIME/49: .5X TO 1.2X BASIC JSY/49
*PRIME/15-29: .8X TO 2X BASIC JSY
1 Deacon Jones/90 4.00 10.00
2 Charlie Joiner/99 3.00 8.00
3 Sonny Jurgensen/99 5.00 12.00
4 Hugh McElhenny/99 6.00 15.00
5 Jim Kelly/99 6.00 15.00
6 George Blanda/99 5.00 12.00
7 James Lofton/99 5.00 12.00
8 Charley Taylor/99 5.00 12.00
9 Larry Little/99 3.00 8.00
11 Willie Lanier/20 6.00 15.00
12 Merlin Olsen/99 4.00 10.00
13 Gale Sayers/99 6.00 15.00
14 Paul Hornung/99 6.00 15.00
15 Roger Staubach/99 10.00 25.00
16 Raymond Berry/99 5.00 12.00
17 Forrest Gregg/99 4.00 10.00
18 Sammy Baugh/99 8.00 20.00
19 Bob Griese/99 5.00 12.00
20 Junior Seau/49 4.00 10.00
22 Alan Page/99 4.00 10.00
23 Bob Lilly/99 4.00 10.00
24 Dan Marino/99 10.00 25.00
25 Dick Butkus/99 6.00 15.00
26 Don Maynard/99 4.00 10.00
27 Fran Tarkenton/99 6.00 15.00
28 Franco Harris/99 6.00 15.00
29 Fred Biletnikoff/99 5.00 12.00
30 Howie Long/99 5.00 12.00
31 Jim Otto/99 4.00 10.00
32 John Randle/99 3.00 8.00
33 Lee Roy Selmon/99 3.00 8.00
34 Len Dawson/99 5.00 12.00
35 Lenny Moore/99 5.00 12.00

2010 Playoff National Treasures NFL Greatest Signature Materials

STATED PRINT RUN 8-25
1 Deacon Jones/25 15.00 40.00
2 Charlie Joiner/25 20.00 50.00
3 Sonny Jurgensen/25 15.00 40.00
4 Hugh McElhenny/25 15.00 40.00
5 Jim Kelly/25 30.00 60.00
6 George Blanda/25 25.00 50.00
7 James Lofton/25 15.00 40.00
8 Charley Taylor/25 12.00 30.00
9 Larry Little/25 15.00 40.00
11 Willie Lanier/25 12.00 30.00
13 Gale Sayers/25 40.00 80.00
14 Paul Hornung/25 30.00 60.00
15 Roger Staubach/15 40.00 80.00
16 Raymond Berry/25 20.00 50.00
17 Forrest Gregg/25 20.00 50.00
19 Bob Griese/25 EXCH 20.00 50.00
20 Junior Seau/25 40.00 80.00
22 Alan Page/25 15.00 40.00
23 Bob Lilly/25 15.00 40.00
24 Dan Marino/8
25 Dick Butkus/10
26 Don Maynard/25 15.00 40.00
27 Fran Tarkenton/25 30.00 60.00
28 Franco Harris/25 30.00 60.00
29 Fred Biletnikoff/25 30.00 60.00
30 Howie Long/25 20.00 50.00
31 Jim Otto/25 15.00 40.00
32 John Randle/25 15.00 40.00
33 Lee Roy Selmon/25 15.00 40.00
34 Len Dawson/25 25.00 50.00
35 Lenny Moore/25 15.00 40.00

2010 Playoff National Treasures NFL Greatest Signature Materials Prime

*PRIME AU/14-15: .5X TO 1.2X JSY AU/15-25
PRIME JSY AU PRINT RUN 3-15
21 Ron Mix/15 15.00 40.00
25 Dick Butkus/15 50.00 100.00

2010 Playoff National Treasures NFL Greatest Signatures

STATED PRINT RUN 1-15
2 Charlie Joiner/15 20.00 50.00
17 Forrest Gregg/15 15.00 40.00

2010 Playoff National Treasures Notable Numbers

STATED PRINT RUN 99 SER.#'d SETS
1 Bo Jackson 5.00 12.00
2 Bernie Kosar 4.00 10.00
3 Brent Jones 2.50 6.00
4 Eddie George 3.00 8.00
5 William Perry 2.50 6.00
6 L.C. Greenwood 2.50 6.00
7 Rod Smith 2.50 6.00
8 Irving Fryar 2.50 6.00
9 Boomer Esiason 2.50 6.00
10 John Taylor 3.00 8.00
11 Buck Buchanan 2.50 6.00
12 Chuck Howley 2.50 6.00
13 Cris Carter 4.00 10.00
14 Curtis Martin 3.00 8.00
15 Daryle Lamonica 3.00 8.00
16 Ernie Davis 5.00 12.00
17 Walter Payton 8.00 20.00
18 Michael Strahan 3.00 8.00
19 Ed Too Tall Jones 3.00 8.00
20 Mike Alstott 2.50 6.00
21 Phil Simms 3.00 8.00
22 Priest Holmes 2.50 6.00
23 Randall Cunningham 3.00 8.00
24 Roger Craig 3.00 8.00
25 Ozzie Newsome 3.00 8.00
26 Paul Warfield 3.00 8.00
27 Randy White 3.00 8.00
28 Rod Woodson 4.00 10.00
29 Steve Largent 4.00 10.00
30 Steve Young 5.00 12.00
31 Tony Dorsett 4.00 10.00
32 Troy Aikman 5.00 12.00
33 Craig James 2.50 6.00
34 Willie Brown 2.50 6.00
35 Ronnie Lott 4.00 10.00

2010 Playoff National Treasures Notable Numbers Materials

STATED PRINT RUN 9-99
1 Bo Jackson/99 8.00 20.00
3 Brent Jones/99 4.00 10.00
4 Eddie George/99 4.00 10.00
7 Rod Smith/99 3.00 8.00
8 Irving Fryar/99 4.00 10.00
9 Boomer Esiason/99 4.00 10.00
11 Buck Buchanan/99 4.00 10.00
12 Chuck Howley/99 3.00 8.00
13 Cris Carter/99 5.00 12.00
14 Curtis Martin/99 4.00 10.00
15 Daryle Lamonica/99 4.00 10.00
16 Ernie Davis/99 15.00 30.00
17 Walter Payton/99 10.00 25.00
18 Michael Strahan/99 4.00 10.00
19 Ed Too Tall Jones/99 4.00 10.00
20 Mike Alstott/99 4.00 10.00
21 Phil Simms/99 3.00 8.00
22 Priest Holmes/99 3.00 8.00
23 Randall Cunningham/99 5.00 12.00
24 Roger Craig/99 4.00 10.00
25 Ozzie Newsome/99 4.00 10.00
26 Paul Warfield/99 4.00 10.00
27 Randy White/99 5.00 12.00
28 Rod Woodson/99 5.00 12.00
29 Steve Largent/99 5.00 12.00
30 Steve Young/99 6.00 15.00
31 Tony Dorsett/99 6.00 15.00
32 Troy Aikman/99 6.00 15.00
33 Craig James/99 3.00 8.00
34 Willie Brown/99 3.00 8.00
35 Ronnie Lott/99 5.00 12.00

2010 Playoff National Treasures Notable Numbers Materials Prime

*PRIME/30-50: .5X TO 1.2X BASIC JSY/99
*PRIME/25: .6X TO 1.5X BASIC JSY/99
PRIME STATED PRINT RUN 11-50
5 William Perry/50 5.00 12.00

2010 Playoff National Treasures Notable Numbers Signature Materials

STATED PRINT RUN 5-25
1 Bo Jackson/25 40.00 80.00
2 Bernie Kosar/25 20.00 50.00
3 Brent Jones/25 12.00 30.00
4 Eddie George/25 30.00 60.00
6 William Perry/25 20.00 50.00
6 L.C. Greenwood/25 30.00 60.00
7 Rod Smith/25 12.00 30.00
8 Irving Fryar/25 12.00 30.00
9 Boomer Esiason/25 15.00 40.00
12 Chuck Howley/25 15.00 40.00
14 Curtis Martin/25 25.00 60.00
15 Daryle Lamonica/25 15.00 40.00
18 Michael Strahan/25 15.00 40.00
20 Mike Alstott/25 30.00 60.00
21 Phil Simms/25 15.00 40.00
22 Priest Holmes/25 15.00 40.00
23 Randall Cunningham/25 25.00 50.00
24 Roger Craig/25 15.00 40.00
25 Ozzie Newsome/25 15.00 40.00
26 Paul Warfield/25 15.00 40.00
27 Randy White/25 15.00 40.00
28 Rod Woodson/25 40.00 80.00
29 Steve Largent/25 20.00 50.00
30 Steve Young/25 50.00 100.00
31 Tony Dorsett/25 30.00 60.00
33 Craig James/25 15.00 40.00
34 Willie Brown/25 15.00 40.00
35 Ronnie Lott/25 20.00 50.00

2010 Playoff National Treasures Notable Numbers Signature Materials Prime

*PRIME AU/15-25: .5X TO 1.2X JSY AU/25
PRIME JSY AU PRINT RUN 1-15
10 John Taylor/15 30.00 60.00
32 Troy Aikman/15 60.00 120.00

2010 Playoff National Treasures Pen Pals

1 Colt McCoy 100.00 200.00
Jordan Shipley
Sam Bradford
Jermaine Gresham
2 Jimmy Clausen 25.00 60.00
Golden Tate
Joe McKnight
Damian Williams
3 C.J. Spiller 25.00 50.00
Marcus Easley
4 Jimmy Clausen 20.00 50.00
Brandon LaFell
Armanti Edwards
5 Jermaine Gresham 20.00 40.00
Jordan Shipley
6 Colt McCoy 40.00 80.00
Montario Hardesty
7 Tim Tebow 90.00 150.00
Demaryius Thomas
Eric Decker
8 Ndamukong Suh 75.00 135.00
Jahvid Best
9 Rob Gronkowski 25.00 50.00
Taylor Price
10 Sam Bradford 75.00 150.00
Mardy Gilyard
11 Sam Bradford 200.00 400.00
Tim Tebow
Jimmy Clausen
Colt McCoy
12 Demaryius Thomas 50.00 120.00
Dez Bryant
Dexter McCluster
Arrelious Benn
13 C.J. Spiller 60.00 120.00
Ryan Mathews
Jahvid Best
Toby Gerhart
14 Sam Bradford
Tim Tebow
Demaryius Thomas
Dez Bryant
C.J. Spiller
Ryan Mathews
Jermaine Gresham
Rob Gronkowski
15 Tim Tebow 125.00 200.00
Jahvid Best
Dexter McCluster
Arrelious Benn
Rob Gronkowski
Jimmy Clausen
Toby Gerhart
Ben Tate
16 Montario Hardesty 40.00 100.00
Golden Tate
Damian Williams
Brandon LaFell
Emmanuel Sanders
Jordan Shipley
Colt McCoy
Eric Decker
17 Sam Bradford
Ndamukong Suh
Gerald McCoy
Eric Berry
Rolando McClain
C.J. Spiller
Ryan Mathews
Jermaine Gresham
18 Sam Bradford
Tim Tebow
Jimmy Clausen
Colt McCoy
C.J. Spiller
Ryan Mathews
Jahvid Best
Toby Gerhart

2010 Playoff National Treasures Ring of Honor

STATED PRINT RUN 99 SER.#'d SETS
1 Bart Starr 8.00 20.00
2 Jim Taylor 5.00 12.00
3 Willie Davis 3.00 8.00
4 Joe Namath 6.00 15.00
5 Len Dawson 5.00 12.00
6 Chuck Howley 3.00 8.00
7 Roger Staubach 6.00 15.00
8 Larry Little 3.00 8.00
9 Paul Warfield 4.00 10.00
10 Jack Lambert 5.00 12.00
11 L.C. Greenwood 4.00 10.00
12 Fred Biletnikoff 5.00 12.00
13 Randy White 3.00 8.00
14 Ed Too Tall Jones 4.00 10.00
15 Terry Bradshaw 6.00 15.00
16 Terry Bradshaw 6.00 15.00
17 Jim Plunkett 4.00 10.00
18 Joe Montana 10.00 25.00
19 Russ Grimm 3.00 8.00
20 Jim Plunkett 4.00 10.00
21 Joe Montana 10.00 25.00
22 William Perry 3.00 8.00
23 Phil Simms 4.00 10.00
24 Doug Williams 4.00 10.00
25 Jerry Rice 8.00 20.00
26 Joe Montana 10.00 25.00
27 Ottis Anderson 3.00 8.00
28 Art Monk 5.00 12.00
29 Troy Aikman 6.00 15.00
30 Emmitt Smith 8.00 20.00
31 Steve Young 5.00 12.00
32 John Taylor 3.00 8.00
33 Deion Sanders 5.00 12.00
34 Brett Favre 12.00 30.00
35 Terrell Davis 5.00 12.00
36 John Elway 8.00 20.00
37 Rod Smith 3.00 8.00
38 Marshall Faulk 4.00 10.00
39 Rod Woodson 5.00 12.00
40 Tom Brady 6.00 15.00
41 Mike Alstott 4.00 10.00
42 Keyshawn Johnson 3.00 8.00
43 Tom Brady 6.00 15.00
44 Tom Brady 6.00 15.00
45 Ben Roethlisberger 5.00 12.00

46 Peyton Manning 8.00 20.00
47 Reggie Wayne 4.00 10.00
48 Eli Manning 5.00 12.00
49 Santonio Holmes 4.00 10.00
50 Drew Brees 5.00 12.00

2010 Playoff National Treasures Ring of Honor Signatures

STATED PRINT RUN 4-50
1 Bart Starr/50 75.00 150.00
2 Jim Taylor/35 25.00 50.00
3 Willie Davis/50 15.00 40.00
5 Len Dawson/25 25.00 50.00
8 Larry Little/25 12.00 30.00
9 Paul Warfield/50 12.00 30.00
10 Jack Lambert/50 40.00 80.00
11 L.C. Greenwood/50 25.00 50.00
12 Fred Biletnikoff/50 25.00 50.00
13 Randy White/45 12.00 30.00
17 Jim Plunkett/15 25.00 50.00
18 Joe Montana/16 100.00 175.00
19 Russ Grimm/50 15.00 40.00
20 Jim Plunkett/15 25.00 50.00
21 Joe Montana/19 100.00 175.00
22 William Perry/50 15.00 40.00
23 Phil Simms/21 15.00 40.00
24 Doug Williams/50 15.00 40.00
26 Joe Montana/24 100.00 175.00
27 Ottis Anderson/50 12.00 30.00
28 Art Monk/50 30.00 60.00
30 Emmitt Smith/22 125.00 250.00
32 John Taylor/50 12.00 30.00
33 Deion Sanders/27 40.00 80.00
36 John Elway/25 100.00 175.00
37 Rod Smith/33 12.00 30.00
38 Marshall Faulk/50 40.00 80.00
39 Rod Woodson/35 40.00 80.00
41 Mike Alstott/50 25.00 50.00
42 Keyshawn Johnson/50 15.00 40.00
45 Ben Roethlisberger/25 75.00 150.00
46 Peyton Manning/18 100.00 200.00
49 Santonio Holmes/50 15.00 40.00

2010 Playoff National Treasures Souvenir Cuts

CUT AU STATED PRINT RUN 1-88
2 Bill Dudley/35 20.00 50.00
7 Hank Stram/16
9 Johnny Unitas/40 200.00 350.00
11 Kyle Rote/88 20.00 50.00
14 Paul Brown/62 40.00 80.00
17 Walter Payton/61 175.00 300.00
18 Weeb Ewbank/74 20.00 50.00

2010 Playoff National Treasures Timeline Materials Player Name

STATED PRINT RUN 5-99
1 Alex Karras/99 5.00 12.00
3 Danny White/99 5.00 12.00
4 Warren Moon/99 6.00 15.00
5 D.D. Lewis/99 5.00 12.00
6 Doug Flutie/99 5.00 12.00
7 Henry Ellard/55 4.00 10.00
8 Paul Hornung/99 6.00 15.00
9 Jim McMahon/99 6.00 15.00
10 Y.A. Tittle/99 6.00 15.00
12 Ken Stabler/99 8.00 20.00
14 Steve McNair/99 5.00 12.00
15 Terrell Davis/99 6.00 15.00
16 Tiki Barber/30 6.00 15.00
17 Todd Christensen/99 4.00 10.00
18 Tom Rathman/99 4.00 10.00
20 Derrick Thomas/99 20.00 50.00

2010 Playoff National Treasures Timeline Materials Player Name Prime

*PRIME/20-25: .6X TO 1.5X BASIC JSY/99
PRIME STATED PRINT RUN 1-50
13 Keyshawn Johnson/50 5.00 12.00

2010 Playoff National Treasures Timeline Materials Team Name

*TEAM/85-99: .4X TO 1X PLAYER/55-99
STATED PRINT RUN 5-99
2 Jim Plunkett/89 5.00 12.00
16 Tiki Barber/21 8.00 20.00
18 Tom Rathman/20 6.00 15.00

2010 Playoff National Treasures Timeline Materials Signature Team Name

TEAM NAME AU PRINT RUN 4-25
*TN PRIME/15: .5X TO 1.2X TN JSY AU/15-25
*PLY.NME/15-25: .4X TO 1X TEAM JSY AU/15-25
*PN PRIME/15: .5X TO 1.2X TN JSY AU/19-25
1 Alex Karras/25 15.00 40.00
2 Jim Plunkett/20 15.00 40.00
3 Danny White/25 15.00 40.00
4 Warren Moon/25 30.00 80.00
5 D.D. Lewis/15 12.00 30.00
6 Doug Flutie/25 15.00 40.00
7 Henry Ellard/25 15.00 40.00
8 Paul Hornung/25 15.00 40.00
9 Jim McMahon/25 30.00 60.00
10 Y.A. Tittle/25 20.00 50.00
12 Ken Stabler/20 30.00 60.00
13 Keyshawn Johnson/19 20.00 50.00
15 Terrell Davis/15 40.00 80.00
16 Tiki Barber/25 15.00 40.00
17 Todd Christensen/25 15.00 40.00
18 Tom Rathman/25 15.00 40.00
19 Wayne Chrebet/25 15.00 40.00

2010 Playoff National Treasures Timeline Materials Team Name Prime

*PRIME/24-25: .6X TO 1.5X TEAM NAME JSY/99
PRIME STATED PRINT RUN 1-25
13 Keyshawn Johnson/50 5.00 12.00

2011 Playoff National Treasures

STATED PRINT RUN 99 SER.#'d SETS
EACH EXPIRATION: 10/4/2013
1 Beanie Wells 2.50 6.00
2 Early Doucet 2.00 5.00
3 Kevin Kolb 2.50 6.00
4 Larry Fitzgerald 2.50 6.00
5 Curtis Lofton 2.00 5.00
6 Matt Ryan 3.00 8.00
7 Michael Turner 2.50 6.00
8 Roddy White 2.50 6.00
9 Tony Gonzalez 2.50 6.00
10 Anquan Boldin 2.50 6.00
11 Joe Flacco 3.00 8.00
12 Lee Evans 2.50 6.00
13 Ray Rice 2.50 6.00
14 Ricky Williams 2.50 6.00
15 C.J. Spiller 2.50 6.00
16 David Nelson 2.50 6.00
17 Fred Jackson 3.00 8.00
18 Ryan Fitzpatrick 2.50 6.00
19 Steve Johnson 2.50 6.00
20 Brandon LaFell 2.00 5.00
21 DeAngelo Williams 2.50 6.00
22 Greg Olsen 2.00 5.00
23 Jonathan Stewart 2.50 6.00
24 Steve Smith 2.50 6.00
25 Brian Urlacher 3.00 8.00
26 Devin Hester 3.00 8.00
27 Jay Cutler 2.50 6.00
28 Johnny Knox 2.50 6.00
29 Matt Forte 2.50 6.00
30 Cedric Benson 2.50 6.00
31 Jermaine Gresham 2.50 6.00
32 Jerome Simpson 2.00 5.00
33 Jordan Shipley 2.50 6.00
34 Colt McCoy 2.50 6.00
35 Josh Cribbs 2.50 6.00
36 Mohamed Massaquoi 2.50 6.00
37 Peyton Hillis 2.50 6.00
38 Dez Bryant 3.00 8.00
39 Felix Jones 2.50 6.00
40 Jason Witten 3.00 8.00
41 Miles Austin 2.50 6.00
42 Tony Romo 3.00 8.00
43 Brandon Lloyd 2.50 6.00
44 Eric Decker 2.50 6.00
45 Knowshon Moreno 2.50 6.00
46 Kyle Orton 2.50 6.00
47 Willis McGahee 2.00 5.00
48 Calvin Johnson 3.00 8.00
49 Jahvid Best 2.50 6.00
50 Matthew Stafford 3.00 8.00
51 Nate Burleson 2.00 5.00
52 Ndamukong Suh 3.00 8.00
53 Aaron Rodgers 6.00 15.00
54 Greg Jennings 2.50 6.00
55 James Starks 2.50 6.00
56 Jermichael Finley 2.50 6.00
57 Jordy Nelson 2.50 6.00
58 Andre Johnson 2.50 6.00
59 Arian Foster 2.50 6.00
60 Ben Tate 2.50 6.00
61 Matt Schaub 2.50 6.00
62 Owen Daniels 2.00 5.00
63 Dallas Clark 2.50 6.00
64 Joseph Addai 2.50 6.00
65 Peyton Manning 5.00 12.00
66 Pierre Garcon 2.50 6.00
67 Reggie Wayne 2.50 6.00
68 Marcedes Lewis 2.00 5.00
69 Maurice Jones-Drew 2.50 6.00
70 Mike Thomas 2.50 6.00
71 Paul Posluszny 2.00 5.00
72 Dexter McCluster 2.00 5.00
73 Dwayne Bowe 2.50 6.00
74 Jamaal Charles 2.50 6.00
75 Matt Cassel 2.50 6.00
76 Thomas Jones 2.50 6.00
77 Anthony Fasano 2.00 5.00
78 Brandon Marshall 2.50 6.00
79 Chad Henne 2.50 6.00
80 Davone Bess 2.00 5.00
81 Reggie Bush 2.50 6.00
82 Adrian Peterson 4.00 10.00
83 Toby Gerhart 2.50 6.00
84 Jared Allen 2.50 6.00
85 Percy Harvin 2.50 6.00
86 Visanthe Shiancoe 2.50 6.00
87 Aaron Hernandez 2.50 6.00
88 BenJarvus Green-Ellis 2.50 6.00
89 Chad Ochocinco 2.50 6.00
90 Rob Gronkowski 3.00 8.00
91 Tom Brady 5.00 12.00
92 Wes Welker 3.00 8.00
93 Darren Sproles 2.50 6.00
94 Drew Brees 3.00 8.00
95 Jimmy Graham 3.00 8.00
96 Marques Colston 2.50 6.00
97 Pierre Thomas 2.50 6.00
98 Ahmad Bradshaw 2.50 6.00
99 Brandon Jacobs 2.50 6.00
100 Eli Manning 3.00 8.00
101 Hakeem Nicks 2.50 6.00
102 Mario Manningham 2.50 6.00
103 Dustin Keller 2.50 6.00
104 Mark Sanchez 3.00 8.00
105 Plaxico Burress 2.50 6.00
106 Santonio Holmes 2.50 6.00
107 Shonn Greene 2.50 6.00
108 Darren McFadden 2.50 6.00
109 Jacoby Ford 2.50 6.00
110 Carson Palmer 2.50 6.00
111 Michael Bush 2.00 5.00
112 DeSean Jackson 2.50 6.00
113 Jeremy Maclin 2.50 6.00
114 LeSean McCoy 2.50 6.00
115 Michael Vick 3.00 8.00
116 Nnamdi Asomugha 2.50 6.00
117 Antonio Brown 3.00 8.00
118 Ben Roethlisberger 3.00 8.00
119 Mike Wallace 3.00 8.00
120 Rashard Mendenhall 2.50 6.00
121 Troy Polamalu 3.00 8.00
122 Antonio Gates 2.50 6.00
123 Mike Tolbert 2.50 6.00
124 Philip Rivers 3.00 8.00
125 Ryan Mathews 2.50 6.00
126 Vincent Jackson 2.50 6.00
127 Alex Smith QB 2.50 6.00
128 Braylon Edwards 2.50 6.00
129 Frank Gore 2.50 6.00
130 Vernon Davis 2.50 6.00
131 Marshawn Lynch 2.50 6.00
132 Sidney Rice 2.50 6.00
133 Tarvaris Jackson 2.00 5.00
134 Zach Miller 2.50 6.00
135 Brandon Gibson 2.00 5.00
136 Cadillac Williams 2.00 5.00
137 Sam Bradford 3.00 8.00
138 Steven Jackson 2.50 6.00
139 Josh Freeman 3.00 8.00
140 Kellen Winslow Jr. 2.50 6.00
141 LeGarrette Blount 2.50 6.00
142 Mike Williams 2.50 6.00
143 Chris Johnson 2.50 6.00
144 Kenny Britt 2.50 6.00
145 Matt Hasselbeck 2.50 6.00
146 Nate Washington 2.00 5.00
147 Fred Davis 2.50 6.00
148 Rex Grossman 2.50 6.00
149 Santana Moss 2.50 6.00
150 Tim Hightower 2.00 5.00
151 Art Monk 2.50 6.00
152 Bernie Kosar 2.50 6.00
153 Boomer Esiason 2.50 6.00
154 Chuck Howley 2.00 5.00
155 Ernie Davis 3.00 8.00
156 Floyd Little 2.00 5.00
157 Forrest Gregg 2.00 5.00
158 Fred Biletnikoff 2.50 6.00
159 Fred Williamson 2.00 5.00
160 Garo Yepremian 2.00 5.00
161 Gene Upshaw 2.00 5.00
162 Hugh McElhenny 2.00 5.00
163 Irving Fryar 2.00 5.00
164 Jay Novacek 2.50 6.00
165 Jerome Bettis 3.00 8.00
166 Jim Plunkett 2.50 6.00
167 John Brodie 2.00 5.00
168 John Fuqua 2.00 5.00
169 John Hadl 2.00 5.00
170 John Hannah 2.00 5.00
171 John Matuszak 2.00 5.00
172 Junior Seau 3.00 8.00
173 Keith Jackson 2.00 5.00
174 Ken Anderson 2.50 6.00
175 Knute Rockne 3.00 8.00
176 Larry Csonka 2.50 6.00
177 Mark Carrier 2.00 5.00
178 Merlin Olsen 2.50 6.00
179 Mike Alstott 2.00 5.00
180 Ozzie Newsome 2.50 6.00
181 Paul Krause 2.00 5.00
182 Paul Warfield 2.50 6.00
183 Pete Retzlaff 2.00 5.00
184 Randall Cunningham 2.50 6.00
185 Randy White 2.50 6.00
186 Richard Dent 2.00 5.00
187 Rickey Jackson 2.00 5.00
188 Rod Woodson 2.50 6.00
189 Roger Craig 2.50 6.00
190 Ron Mix 2.00 5.00
191 Ronnie Lott 2.50 6.00
192 Sterling Sharpe 2.50 6.00
193 Bo Jackson 4.00 10.00
194 Steve Bartkowski 2.50 6.00
195 Ted Hendricks 2.00 5.00
196 Tony Dorsett 3.00 8.00
197 Eddie George 2.50 6.00
198 Warren Sapp 2.50 6.00
199 Willie Brown 2.00 5.00
200 Y.A. Tittle 3.00 8.00
201 Aaron Williams AU RC EXCH 6.00 15.00
202 Adrian Clayborn AU RC EXCH 8.00 20.00
203 Ahmad Black AU RC 6.00 15.00
204 Akeem Ayers AU RC EXCH 6.00 15.00
205 Aldon Smith AU RC EXCH 20.00 40.00
206 Aldrick Robinson AU RC 5.00 12.00
207 Alex Henery AU RC 6.00 15.00
208 Allen Bradford AU RC 6.00 15.00
209 Anthony Allen AU RC 5.00 12.00
210 Anthony Castonzo AU RC 5.00 12.00
211 Anthony Sherman AU RC 6.00 15.00
212 Armond Smith AU RC 6.00 15.00
213 Brandon Harris AU RC 5.00 12.00
214 Bruce Miller AU RC 6.00 15.00
215 Buster Skrine AU RC 6.00 15.00
216 Cameron Heyward AU RC 8.00 20.00
217 Cameron Jordan AU RC 6.00 15.00
218 Casey Matthews AU RC 8.00 20.00
219 Cecil Shorts AU RC 6.00 15.00
220 Charles Clay AU RC 6.00 15.00
221 Chimdi Chekwa AU RC 6.00 15.00
222 Chris Harris AU RC 6.00 15.00
223 Chris White AU RC 6.00 15.00
224 Colin Cochart AU RC 5.00 12.00
225 Corey Liuget AU RC 5.00 12.00
226 D.J. Williams AU RC EXCH 8.00 20.00
227 Da'Quan Bowers AU RC 8.00 20.00
228 Da'Rel Scott AU RC 6.00 15.00
229 Dan Bailey AU RC 8.00 20.00
230 Dane Sanzenbacher AU RC 8.00 20.00
231 Darren Evans AU RC 6.00 15.00
232 David Ausberry AU RC 6.00 15.00
233 DeMarco Sampson AU RC EXCH 5.00 12.00
234 Denarius Moore AU RC EXCH 20.00 40.00
235 Dion Lewis AU RC 8.00 20.00
236 Doug Baldwin AU RC 12.00 30.00
237 Mark Herzlich AU RC 6.00 15.00
238 Evan Royster AU RC 8.00 20.00
239 Greg Jones AU RC 6.00 15.00
240 Greg McElroy AU RC EXCH 8.00 20.00
241 Greg Salas AU RC 8.00 20.00
242 Henry Hynoski AU RC 8.00 20.00
243 J.J. Watt AU RC 12.00 30.00
244 Jacquian Williams AU RC EXCH 8.00 20.00
245 Jacquizz Rodgers AU RC 10.00 25.00
246 Jamar Newsome AU RC 5.00 12.00
247 Jeremy Kerley AU RC 8.00 20.00
248 Jimmy Smith AU RC EXCH 8.00 20.00
249 Joe Lefeged AU RC 6.00 15.00
250 Johnny White AU RC 6.00 15.00
251 Jordan Cameron AU RC 6.00 15.00
252 Josh Portis AU RC 8.00 20.00
253 Julius Thomas AU RC 6.00 15.00
254 Justin Houston AU RC 8.00 20.00
255 K.J. Wright AU RC 8.00 20.00
256 Kealoha Pilares AU RC 8.00 20.00
257 Kris Durham AU RC 6.00 15.00
258 Kyle Adams AU RC 5.00 12.00
259 Lance Kendricks AU RC 6.00 15.00
260 LaQuan Williams AU RC 6.00 15.00
261 Lee Smith AU RC 6.00 15.00
262 Luke Stocker AU RC 6.00 15.00
263 Marcus Cannon AU RC 5.00 12.00
264 Marcus Gilchrist AU RC 5.00 12.00
266 Mason Foster AU RC 8.00 20.00
267 Nathan Enderle AU RC EXCH 8.00 20.00
268 Niles Paul AU RC 8.00 20.00
269 Owen Marecic AU RC EXCH 8.00 20.00
270 Phil Taylor AU RC 6.00 15.00
271 Phillip Tanner AU RC 8.00 20.00
272 Prince Amukamara AU RC 8.00 20.00
273 Quinton Carter AU RC 5.00 12.00
274 Rahim Moore AU RC 6.00 15.00
275 Richard Gordon AU RC 6.00 15.00
276 Ricky Stanzi AU RC 12.00 30.00
277 Robert Housler AU RC 6.00 15.00
279 Roy Helu AU RC 30.00 60.00
280 Ryan Kerrigan AU RC 8.00 20.00
281 Ryan Taylor AU RC 6.00 15.00
282 Ryan Whalen AU RC 6.00 15.00
283 Scott Tolzien AU RC EXCH 8.00 20.00
284 Shane Bannon AU RC 5.00 12.00
285 Stanley Havili AU RC 5.00 12.00
286 Stephen Burton AU RC 5.00 12.00
287 Stephen Paea AU RC 8.00 20.00
288 T.J. Yates AU RC 15.00 30.00
289 Tandon Doss AU RC 6.00 15.00
290 Terrelle Pryor AU RC 20.00 40.00
291 Tyler Sash AU RC 8.00 20.00
292 Tyrod Taylor AU RC 8.00 20.00
293 Tyron Smith AU RC 12.00 30.00
294 Virgil Green AU RC 6.00 15.00
295 Weslye Saunders AU RC EXCH 8.00 20.00
296 Will Yeatman AU RC EXCH 6.00 15.00
297 Zack Pianalto AU RC 6.00 15.00
299 Patrick Peterson AU RC 30.00 60.00
300 Robert Quinn AU RC 8.00 20.00
301 Christian Ponder JSY AU RC 100.00 200.00
302 Clyde Gates JSY AU RC 15.00 40.00
303 Jamie Harper JSY AU RC 20.00 50.00
304 Blaine Gabbert JSY AU RC 75.00 150.00
305 Mikel Leshoure JSY AU RC EXCH 30.00 80.00
306 Stevan Ridley JSY AU RC 50.00 100.00
307 Von Miller JSY AU RC 30.00 80.00
308 Leonard Hankerson JSY AU RC 20.00 50.00
309 Delone Carter JSY AU RC 15.00 40.00
310 Kyle Rudolph JSY AU RC 20.00 50.00
311 Austin Pettis JSY AU RC
312 Daniel Thomas JSY AU RC 30.00 80.00
313 Torrey Smith JSY AU RC 50.00 120.00
314 Marcell Dareus JSY AU RC 20.00 50.00
315 Ryan Mallett JSY AU RC 100.00 200.00
316 Alex Green JSY AU RC 20.00 50.00
317 Jerrel Jernigan JSY AU RC 15.00 40.00
318 Mark Ingram JSY AU RC 75.00 150.00
319 Vincent Brown JSY AU RC 25.00 60.00
320 Titus Young JSY AU RC 40.00 80.00
321 Bilal Powell JSY AU RC 12.00 30.00
322 Kendall Hunter JSY AU RC 30.00 80.00
323 Julio Jones JSY AU RC EXCH 150.00 250.00
324 Jordan Todman JSY AU RC 12.00 30.00
325 Jake Locker JSY AU RC 200.00 400.00
326 Andy Dalton JSY AU RC 200.00 400.00
327 Colin Kaepernick JSY AU RC 60.00 120.00
328 Cam Newton JSY AU RC 800.00 1,500.00
329 A.J. Green JSY AU RC 150.00 300.00
330 Randall Cobb JSY AU RC 40.00 80.00
331 DeMarco Murray JSY AU RC 150.00 300.00
332 Taiwan Jones JSY AU RC 20.00 50.00
333 Greg Little JSY AU RC 20.00 50.00
334 Ryan Williams JSY AU RC 25.00 60.00
335 Jonathan Baldwin JSY AU RC 25.00 60.00
336 Shane Vereen JSY AU RC 25.00 60.00

2011 Playoff National Treasures Century Silver

*SLVER/25: .8X TO 2X BASIC CARDS
STATED PRINT RUN 25 SER.#'d SETS

2011 Playoff National Treasures 1958 Goal Post

1 Johnny Unitas/58 40.00 80.00

2011 Playoff National Treasures Century Black Signature

1-199 UNPRICED PRINT RUN 1-10
*201-300 ROOKIE AU/25: .6X TO 1.5X BASIC AU/99
201-300 ROOKIE AU PRINT RUN 25
205 Aldon Smith/25 EXCH 40.00 100.00
276 Ricky Stanzi/25 30.00 60.00

2011 Playoff National Treasures Century Gold Signature

1-200 VETERAN PRINT RUN 1-25
*201-300 GOLD AU/49: .5X TO 1.2X AU RC/99
201-300 ROOKIE AU PRINT RUN 49
95 Jimmy Graham/25 25.00 50.00
205 Aldon Smith/49 EXCH 30.00 80.00

2011 Playoff National Treasures Century Material Prime

STATED PRINT RUN 1-49
8 Roddy White/49 5.00 12.00
9 Tony Gonzalez/49 5.00 12.00
10 Anquan Boldin/49 5.00 12.00
11 Joe Flacco/49 6.00 15.00
13 Ray Rice/49 5.00 12.00
15 C.J. Spiller/25 6.00 15.00
18 Ryan Fitzpatrick/49 5.00 12.00
25 Brian Urlacher/49 6.00 15.00
26 Devin Hester/49 6.00 15.00
29 Matt Forte/49 5.00 12.00
30 Cedric Benson/49 5.00 12.00
35 Josh Cribbs/49 5.00 12.00
38 Dez Bryant/49 6.00 15.00
39 Felix Jones/49 5.00 12.00
41 Miles Austin/49 5.00 12.00
42 Tony Romo/49 6.00 15.00
48 Calvin Johnson/15 8.00 20.00
52 Ndamukong Suh/24 8.00 20.00
66 Pierre Garcon/26 6.00 15.00
69 Maurice Jones-Drew/49 5.00 12.00
70 Mike Thomas/39 5.00 12.00
72 Dexter McCluster/49 4.00 10.00
73 Dwayne Bowe/15 6.00 15.00
74 Jamaal Charles/49 5.00 12.00
75 Matt Cassel/23 6.00 15.00
77 Anthony Fasano/49 4.00 10.00
78 Brandon Marshall/25 6.00 15.00
88 BenJarvus Green-Ellis/25 6.00 15.00
92 Wes Welker/49 8.00 20.00
94 Drew Brees/49 8.00 20.00
96 Marques Colston/49 5.00 12.00
97 Pierre Thomas/49 5.00 12.00
98 Ahmad Bradshaw/49 5.00 12.00
99 Brandon Jacobs/49 5.00 12.00
101 Hakeem Nicks/49 5.00 12.00
102 Mario Manningham/49 5.00 12.00
105 Plaxico Burress/49 5.00 12.00
107 Shonn Greene/49 5.00 12.00
108 Darren McFadden/25 6.00 15.00
116 Nnamdi Asomugha/49 5.00 12.00
122 Antonio Gates/49 5.00 12.00
125 Ryan Mathews/49 5.00 12.00
126 Vincent Jackson/49 5.00 12.00
129 Frank Gore/49 5.00 12.00
134 Zach Miller/49 5.00 12.00
138 Steven Jackson/49 5.00 12.00
143 Chris Johnson/49 5.00 12.00
145 Matt Hasselbeck/24 6.00 15.00
149 Santana Moss/49 5.00 12.00
152 Bernie Kosar/49 6.00 15.00
164 Jay Novacek/49 8.00 20.00
165 Jerome Bettis/22 15.00 40.00
166 Jim Plunkett/49 6.00 15.00
167 John Brodie/49 8.00 20.00
168 John Fuqua/49 6.00 15.00
169 John Hadl/49 5.00 12.00
171 John Matuszak/18 6.00 15.00
173 Keith Jackson/49 8.00 20.00
174 Ken Anderson/49 6.00 15.00
175 Knute Rockne/49 25.00 50.00
177 Mark Carrier/49 5.00 12.00
179 Mike Alstott/49 5.00 12.00
180 Ozzie Newsome/49 6.00 15.00
182 Paul Warfield/25 8.00 20.00
184 Randall Cunningham/49 6.00 15.00
185 Randy White/49 8.00 20.00
186 Richard Dent/49 8.00 20.00
187 Rickey Jackson/49 5.00 12.00
188 Rod Woodson/48 8.00 20.00
191 Ronnie Lott/49 8.00 20.00
194 Steve Bartkowski/49 6.00 15.00
195 Ted Hendricks/49 5.00 12.00
196 Tony Dorsett/49 8.00 20.00
197 Eddie George/49 8.00 20.00

2011 Playoff National Treasures Century Material Signature Prime

PRIME STATED PRINT RUN 1-15
10 Anquan Boldin/15 15.00 40.00
15 C.J. Spiller/15 15.00 40.00
29 Matt Forte/15 15.00 40.00
41 Miles Austin/15 20.00 50.00
42 Tony Romo/15 40.00 80.00
69 Maurice Jones-Drew/15 20.00 50.00
75 Matt Cassel/15 15.00 40.00
96 Marques Colston/15 15.00 40.00
97 Pierre Thomas/15 20.00 50.00
104 Mark Sanchez/15 20.00 50.00
107 Shonn Greene/15 15.00 40.00
116 Nnamdi Asomugha/15 15.00 40.00
122 Antonio Gates/15 15.00 40.00
126 Vincent Jackson/15 15.00 40.00
149 Santana Moss/15 12.00 30.00
152 Bernie Kosar/15 20.00 50.00
165 Jerome Bettis/15 125.00 200.00
166 Jim Plunkett/15 25.00 60.00
167 John Brodie/15 30.00 60.00
177 Mark Carrier/15 15.00 40.00
179 Mike Alstott/15 20.00 50.00
182 Paul Warfield/15 20.00 50.00
184 Randall Cunningham/15 30.00 60.00
186 Richard Dent/15 30.00 60.00
187 Rickey Jackson/15 20.00 50.00
188 Rod Woodson/15 90.00 150.00
191 Ronnie Lott/15 30.00 60.00

2011 Playoff National Treasures Colossal Materials

STATED PRINT RUN 14-99
1 Adrian Peterson/18 8.00 20.00
2 Antonio Gates/50 4.00 10.00
4 Cedric Benson/5 5.00 12.00
5 Chris Johnson/99 4.00 10.00
6 Danny Amendola/99 4.00 10.00
7 DeAngelo Williams/99 4.00 10.00
8 Eli Manning/99 5.00 12.00
9 Felix Jones/99 4.00 10.00
10 Frank Gore/85 4.00 10.00
11 Jason Witten/14 6.00 15.00
12 Jermaine Gresham/85 4.00 10.00
13 Knowshon Moreno/99 4.00 10.00
14 LaDainian Tomlinson/15 6.00 15.00
15 LeSean McCoy/71 4.00 10.00
16 Mark Sanchez/99 5.00 12.00
17 Matt Cassel/99 4.00 10.00
19 Maurice Jones-Drew/15 5.00 12.00
20 Michael Turner/15 5.00 12.00
21 Miles Austin/99 4.00 10.00
23 Roddy White/5 5.00 12.00
24 Santana Moss/99 4.00 10.00
26 Jason Campbell/99 4.00 10.00
29 Troy Polamalu/99 8.00 20.00
30 Vernon Davis/30 5.00 12.00
31 Jerod Mayo/99 3.00 8.00
32 Montell Owens/99 3.00 8.00
33 Roman Harper/99 3.00 8.00
34 David Akers/99 3.00 8.00
35 Ray Lewis/99 6.00 15.00
36 Matt Light/99 4.00 10.00
37 Jeff Saturday/99 4.00 10.00
38 Terrell Suggs/99 3.00 8.00
39 Reggie Wayne/99 4.00 10.00
40 John Abraham/99 3.00 8.00
41 Antrel Rolle/90 3.00 8.00
42 Ryan Kalil/99 3.00 8.00
43 Alex Mack/99 3.00 8.00
44 London Fletcher/99 3.00 8.00
45 Jamaal Charles/99 4.00 10.00
46 Eric Weems/99 5.00 12.00
47 Billy Cundiff/99 3.00 8.00
48 Dwayne Bowe/99 4.00 10.00
49 Darrelle Revis/99 4.00 10.00
50 Zach Miller/99 4.00 10.00
51 Tony Gonzalez/99 4.00 10.00
52 John Denney/99 3.00 8.00
53 Michael Griffin/99 3.00 8.00
54 Drew Brees/99 5.00 12.00
55 Arian Foster/99 5.00 12.00
56 Joe Thomas/99 4.00 10.00
57 Brian Waters/99 3.00 8.00
58 Jay Ratliff/99 4.00 10.00
59 Larry Fitzgerald/99 4.00 10.00
60 Adrian Wilson/99 3.00 8.00
61 Ovie Mughelli/99 3.00 8.00
62 Vonta Leach/99 3.00 8.00
63 Marc Mariani/99 5.00 12.00
64 Carl Nicks/99 3.00 8.00
65 Michael Vick/99 5.00 12.00
66 Steven Jackson/99 4.00 10.00
67 Jonathan Vilma/99 3.00 8.00
68 Mat McBriar/99 3.00 8.00
69 Devin McCourty/99 3.00 8.00
70 Jahri Evans/99 3.00 8.00

2011 Playoff National Treasures Colossal Materials Prime

PRIME STATED PRINT RUN 6-49
1 Adrian Peterson/35 10.00 25.00
2 Antonio Gates/49 6.00 15.00
3 DeAngelo Hall/25 6.00 15.00
4 Cedric Benson/44 6.00 15.00
5 Chris Johnson/49 6.00 15.00
6 Danny Amendola/40 6.00 15.00
7 DeAngelo Williams/49 6.00 15.00
8 Eli Manning/15 10.00 25.00
9 Felix Jones/49 6.00 15.00
10 Frank Gore/20 8.00 20.00
12 Jermaine Gresham/37 6.00 15.00
14 LaDainian Tomlinson/17 10.00 25.00
18 Matt Forte/18 8.00 20.00
19 Maurice Jones-Drew/49 8.00 20.00
20 Michael Turner/40 6.00 15.00
21 Miles Austin/49 8.00 20.00
22 Philip Rivers/40 8.00 20.00
23 Roddy White/39 6.00 15.00
24 Santana Moss/49 6.00 15.00
25 Santonio Holmes/20 8.00 20.00
27 Dexter McCluster/25 6.00 15.00
28 Brian Hartline/49 6.00 15.00
31 Jerod Mayo/49 5.00 12.00
32 Montell Owens/49 5.00 12.00
33 Roman Harper/49 5.00 12.00
34 David Akers/49 5.00 12.00
35 Ray Lewis/49 10.00 25.00
36 Matt Light/49 6.00 15.00
37 Jeff Saturday/49 6.00 15.00
38 Terrell Suggs/49 5.00 12.00
39 Reggie Wayne/49 6.00 15.00
40 John Abraham/49 5.00 12.00
41 Antrel Rolle/49 5.00 12.00
42 Ryan Kalil/49 5.00 12.00
43 Alex Mack/49 5.00 12.00
44 London Fletcher/49 5.00 12.00
45 Jamaal Charles/49 6.00 15.00
46 Eric Weems/49 8.00 20.00
47 Billy Cundiff/49 5.00 12.00
48 Dwayne Bowe/49 6.00 15.00
49 Darrelle Revis/49 6.00 15.00
50 Zach Miller/49 6.00 15.00
51 Tony Gonzalez/49 6.00 15.00
52 John Denney/49 5.00 12.00
53 Michael Griffin/49 5.00 12.00
54 Drew Brees/25 12.00 30.00
55 Arian Foster/49 8.00 20.00
56 Joe Thomas/49 6.00 15.00
57 Brian Waters/49 5.00 12.00
58 Jay Ratliff/49 6.00 15.00
59 Larry Fitzgerald/35 6.00 15.00
60 Adrian Wilson/49 5.00 12.00
61 Ovie Mughelli/49 5.00 12.00
62 Vonta Leach/49 5.00 12.00
63 Marc Mariani/49 8.00 20.00
64 Carl Nicks/49 5.00 12.00
65 Michael Vick/13 10.00 25.00
66 Steven Jackson/49 6.00 15.00
67 Jonathan Vilma/49 5.00 12.00
68 Mat McBriar/43 5.00 12.00
69 Devin McCourty/49 5.00 12.00
70 Jahri Evans/49 5.00 12.00

2011 Playoff National Treasures Colossal Materials Signature

STATED PRINT RUN 2-49
6 Danny Amendola/49 8.00 20.00
7 DeAngelo Williams/20 12.00 30.00
12 Jermaine Gresham/49 8.00 20.00
17 Matt Cassel/15 12.00 30.00
28 Brian Hartline/35 8.00 20.00
31 Jerod Mayo/49 6.00 15.00

2011 Playoff National Treasures Colossal Materials Signature Prime

PRIME STATED PRINT RUN 1-25
3 DeAngelo Hall/25 12.00 30.00
6 Danny Amendola/25 15.00 40.00
12 Jermaine Gresham/25 15.00 40.00
18 Matt Forte/20 20.00 50.00
28 Brian Hartline/25 12.00 30.00

2011 Playoff National Treasures Emblems of the Hall

STATED PRINT RUN 99 SER.#'d SETS
1 Deion Sanders 3.00 8.00
2 Fran Tarkenton 3.00 8.00
3 Jim Parker 2.00 5.00
4 Shannon Sharpe 2.50 6.00
5 Chris Hanburger 2.00 5.00
6 Les Richter 2.00 5.00
7 Ozzie Newsome 2.50 6.00
8 Bobby Layne 2.50 6.00
9 Carl Eller 2.00 5.00
10 Buck Buchanan 2.00 5.00
11 Dan Hampton 2.00 5.00
12 Deacon Jones 2.50 6.00
13 Eric Dickerson 2.50 6.00
14 Darrell Green 3.00 8.00
15 Derrick Thomas 15.00 30.00
16 Lou Groza 2.50 6.00
17 Richard Dent 2.00 5.00
18 Sam Huff 2.50 6.00
19 Steve Largent 3.00 8.00
20 Jan Stenerud 2.00 5.00
21 Jack Youngblood 2.00 5.00
22 Jack Lambert 3.00 8.00
23 Joe Greene 3.00 8.00
24 Don Maynard 2.50 6.00
25 Gale Sayers 3.00 8.00
26 Bob Griese 3.00 8.00
27 Chuck Bednarik 2.50 6.00
28 Frank Gifford 2.50 6.00
29 Jim Kelly 3.00 8.00
30 John Mackey 2.50 6.00

2011 Playoff National Treasures Emblems of the Hall Materials

STATED PRINT RUN 1-99
1 Deion Sanders/99 8.00 20.00
2 Fran Tarkenton/99 6.00 15.00
3 Jim Parker/99 4.00 10.00
4 Shannon Sharpe/57 5.00 12.00
7 Ozzie Newsome/99 5.00 12.00
9 Carl Eller/99 4.00 10.00
10 Buck Buchanan/99 4.00 10.00
11 Dan Hampton/49 5.00 12.00
14 Darrell Green/99 6.00 15.00
18 Sam Huff/47 5.00 12.00
19 Steve Largent/99 6.00 15.00
20 Jan Stenerud/99 4.00 10.00
23 Joe Greene/99 6.00 15.00
24 Don Maynard/99 5.00 12.00
25 Gale Sayers/49 6.00 15.00
26 Bob Griese/99 6.00 15.00
29 Jim Kelly/99 6.00 15.00

2011 Playoff National Treasures Emblems of the Hall Materials Prime

*PRIME/25: .8X TO 2X BASIC JSY/47-99
PIRME STATED PRINT RUN 1-25
15 Derrick Thomas/25 90.00 150.00

2011 Playoff National Treasures Emblems of the Hall Signature Materials

STATED PRINT RUN 2-25
*PRIME/15: .6X TO 1.5X BASIC JSY/15-25
2 Fran Tarkenton/25 20.00 50.00
4 Shannon Sharpe/25 20.00 50.00
9 Carl Eller/15 12.00 30.00
18 Sam Huff/25 15.00 40.00
19 Steve Largent/25 15.00 40.00
20 Jan Stenerud/25 12.00 30.00
23 Joe Greene/25 20.00 50.00
26 Bob Griese/25 20.00 50.00
29 Jim Kelly/25 20.00 50.00

2011 Playoff National Treasures Emblems of the Hall Signatures

STATED PRINT RUN 5-99
2 Fran Tarkenton/25 25.00 50.00
4 Shannon Sharpe/99 20.00 40.00
12 Deacon Jones/49 15.00 40.00
13 Eric Dickerson/25 25.00 50.00
18 Sam Huff/99 10.00 25.00
19 Steve Largent/49 12.00 30.00
21 Jack Youngblood/38 12.00 30.00
22 Jack Lambert/49 30.00 60.00
23 Joe Greene/25 25.00 50.00
25 Gale Sayers/25 30.00 60.00
26 Bob Griese/15 15.00 40.00
27 Chuck Bednarik/25 12.00 30.00
28 Frank Gifford/25 20.00 40.00

2011 Playoff National Treasures Fans of the Game

EXCH EXPIRATION: 10/4/2013
1 Alyssa Milano 1.50 4.00
1AU Alyssa Milano AU 75.00 125.00

2011 Playoff National Treasures Hall of Fame Leather Autographs

STATED PRINT RUN 5-53
1 Barry Sanders/20 90.00 150.00
2 Bart Starr/50 60.00 120.00
3 Bob Griese/27 25.00 50.00
5 Deion Sanders/25 40.00 80.00
7 Eric Dickerson/27 30.00 60.00
8 Forrest Gregg/27 20.00 40.00
9 Franco Harris/18 30.00 60.00
10 Jim Kelly/25 25.00 50.00
11 Joe Greene/26 30.00 60.00
12 Joe Namath/49 60.00 120.00
14 Michael Irvin/25 30.00 60.00
15 Paul Hornung/26 20.00 40.00
16 Paul Warfield/26 15.00 30.00
17 Raymond Berry/27 20.00 40.00
18 Bobby Bell/37 15.00 30.00
19 Chuck Bednarik/35 20.00 40.00
20 Frank Gifford/17 25.00 50.00
21 Hugh McElhenny/38 15.00 30.00
22 Kellen Winslow/37 20.00 40.00
23 Larry Little/35 15.00 30.00
24 Lenny Moore/37 15.00 30.00
25 Marcus Allen/53 20.00 40.00

2011 Playoff National Treasures HOF Patch Autographs

STATED PRINT RUN 20-45
1 Dick Butkus/21 40.00 80.00
2 Frank Gifford/20 25.00 50.00
3 Howie Long/21 30.00 60.00
4 John Riggins/21 25.00 50.00
5 Ronnie Lott/21 30.00 60.00
6 Steve Largent/26 20.00 40.00
7 Alan Page/36 20.00 40.00
8 Barry Sanders/32 90.00 150.00
9 Bart Starr/45 60.00 120.00
10 Bob Griese/40 25.00 50.00
11 Dan Marino/45 100.00 200.00
12 Deion Sanders/30 50.00 100.00
13 Emmitt Smith/37 125.00 200.00
14 Eric Dickerson/40 30.00 60.00
15 Forrest Gregg/30 20.00 40.00
16 Franco Harris/40 25.00 50.00
17 Jim Kelly/40 25.00 50.00
18 Joe Greene/35 30.00 60.00
19 Joe Montana/26 100.00 175.00
20 Joe Namath/45 60.00 120.00
21 John Elway/30 90.00 150.00
22 Lenny Moore/30 20.00 40.00
23 Marcus Allen/30 25.00 50.00
24 Michael Irvin/40 25.00 50.00
25 Paul Hornung/40 20.00 40.00
26 Paul Warfield/40 15.00 30.00
27 Raymond Berry/25 20.00 40.00

2011 Playoff National Treasures NFL Gear Combos

STATED PRINT RUN 99 SER.#'d SETS
*TRIPLE/99: .5X TO 1.2X COMBO/99
2 Alex Green 3.00 8.00
3 Andy Dalton 8.00 20.00
4 Austin Pettis 2.50 6.00
5 Bilal Powell 2.00 5.00
6 Blaine Gabbert 5.00 12.00
7 Cam Newton 15.00 40.00
9 Clyde Gates 2.50 6.00
10 Colin Kaepernick 4.00 10.00
11 Daniel Thomas 3.00 8.00
12 Delone Carter 2.50 6.00
13 DeMarco Murray 6.00 15.00
14 Greg Little 3.00 8.00
15 Jake Locker 8.00 20.00
16 Jamie Harper 3.00 8.00
17 Jerrel Jernigan 2.50 6.00
18 Jonathan Baldwin 3.00 8.00
19 Jordan Todman 2.00 5.00
20 Julio Jones 6.00 15.00
21 Kendall Hunter 3.00 8.00
23 Leonard Hankerson 3.00 8.00
24 Marcell Dareus 3.00 8.00
25 Mark Ingram 6.00 15.00
26 Mikel Leshoure 3.00 8.00
27 Randall Cobb 4.00 10.00
28 Ryan Mallett 6.00 15.00
29 Ryan Williams 4.00 10.00
30 Shane Vereen 3.00 8.00
31 Stevan Ridley 3.00 8.00
32 Taiwan Jones 3.00 8.00
33 Titus Young 4.00 10.00
34 Torrey Smith 4.00 10.00
35 Vincent Brown 3.00 8.00
36 Von Miller 4.00 10.00

2011 Playoff National Treasures NFL Gear Combos Prime

*PRIME/49: .6X TO 1.5X BASIC JSY/99
PRIME STATED PRINT RUN 49
*TRIPLE PRIME/49: .5X TO 1.2X PRIME/49
1 A.J. Green 10.00 25.00
8 Christian Ponder 10.00 25.00

2011 Playoff National Treasures NFL Gear Combos ID Tag Signatures

STATED PRINT RUN 1-25
3 Andy Dalton/25 90.00 150.00
5 Bilal Powell/20 15.00 40.00
8 Christian Ponder/15 50.00 120.00
9 Clyde Gates/15 20.00 50.00
15 Jake Locker/25 100.00 200.00
34 Torrey Smith/20 30.00 80.00
35 Vincent Brown/25 25.00 60.00
36 Von Miller/25 30.00 80.00

2011 Playoff National Treasures NFL Gear Combos Laundry Tag Signatures

STATED PRINT RUN 3-25
3 Andy Dalton/15 90.00 150.00
5 Bilal Powell/25 15.00 40.00
9 Clyde Gates/15 20.00 50.00
10 Colin Kaepernick/25 30.00 80.00
15 Jake Locker/25 100.00 200.00
16 Jamie Harper/20 25.00 60.00
18 Jonathan Baldwin/25 25.00 60.00
25 Mark Ingram/15 75.00 150.00
26 Mikel Leshoure/25 25.00 60.00
28 Ryan Mallett/25 50.00 120.00
30 Shane Vereen/25 25.00 60.00
31 Stevan Ridley/25 25.00 60.00
33 Titus Young/25 30.00 80.00
34 Torrey Smith/25 30.00 80.00
36 Von Miller/25 30.00 80.00

2011 Playoff National Treasures NFL Gear Combos Signatures

STATED PRINT RUN 25-49
*TRIPLE/25-49: .5X TO 1.2X COMBO/25-49
2 Alex Green/49 8.00 20.00
3 Andy Dalton/49 30.00 80.00
4 Austin Pettis/49 6.00 15.00
5 Bilal Powell/49 5.00 12.00
6 Blaine Gabbert/49 12.00 30.00
7 Cam Newton/25 150.00 250.00
9 Clyde Gates/49 6.00 15.00
10 Colin Kaepernick/49 15.00 40.00
15 Jake Locker/49 40.00 100.00
17 Jerrel Jernigan/49 6.00 15.00
18 Jonathan Baldwin/49 8.00 20.00
19 Jordan Todman/49 5.00 12.00
21 Kendall Hunter/49 8.00 20.00
23 Leonard Hankerson/49 8.00 20.00
25 Mark Ingram/25 20.00 50.00
26 Mikel Leshoure/49 8.00 20.00
27 Randall Cobb/49 12.00 30.00
28 Ryan Mallett/49 15.00 40.00
29 Ryan Williams/49 10.00 25.00
30 Shane Vereen/49 8.00 20.00
31 Stevan Ridley/49 10.00 25.00
32 Taiwan Jones/49 8.00 20.00
34 Torrey Smith/49 12.00 30.00
35 Vincent Brown/49 8.00 20.00

2011 Playoff National Treasures NFL Gear Combos Signatures Prime

*PRIME/25: .8X TO 2X COMBO AU/25-49
PRIME STATED PRINT RUN 10-25
*TRIP.PRIME/25: .4X TO 1X CMBO PRIME/25
1 A.J. Green/25 50.00 100.00

2011 Playoff National Treasures NFL Greatest
STATED PRINT RUN 99 SER.#'d SETS
1 Walter Payton 6.00 15.00
2 Randy Moss 2.00 5.00
3 Brett Favre 5.00 12.00
4 Joe Montana 6.00 15.00
5 Roger Staubach 4.00 10.00
6 Warren Moon 2.50 6.00
7 Barry Sanders 5.00 12.00
8 Bruce Smith 2.50 6.00
9 Doak Walker 3.00 8.00
10 Franco Harris 3.00 8.00
11 Jerry Rice 5.00 12.00
12 Jim Brown 4.00 10.00
13 Jim Thorpe 4.00 10.00
14 Johnny Unitas 5.00 12.00
15 Reggie White 3.00 8.00
16 Terry Bradshaw 4.00 10.00
17 Troy Aikman 4.00 10.00
18 Dan Fouts 3.00 8.00
19 Dan Marino 6.00 15.00
20 Emmitt Smith 5.00 12.00
21 Steve Young 4.00 10.00
22 John Elway 5.00 12.00
23 Dick Butkus 4.00 10.00
24 Tom Brady 4.00 10.00
25 Peyton Manning 4.00 10.00
26 Sammy Baugh 3.00 8.00
27 Dick Lane 2.00 5.00
28 Mike Singletary 3.00 8.00
29 Lee Roy Selmon 2.00 5.00
30 Jim Otto 2.00 5.00
31 Ray Nitschke 2.50 6.00
32 Otto Graham 3.00 8.00

2011 Playoff National Treasures NFL Greatest Materials
STATED PRINT RUN 25-99
3 Brett Favre/99 10.00 25.00
4 Joe Montana/99 10.00 25.00
5 Roger Staubach/99 8.00 20.00
6 Warren Moon/99 4.00 10.00
9 Doak Walker/99 8.00 20.00
10 Franco Harris/99 5.00 12.00
11 Jerry Rice/99 8.00 20.00
12 Jim Brown/99 6.00 15.00
15 Reggie White/77 8.00 20.00
16 Terry Bradshaw/99 6.00 15.00
17 Troy Aikman/99 6.00 15.00
18 Dan Fouts/99 5.00 12.00
19 Dan Marino/25 15.00 40.00
20 Emmitt Smith/99 8.00 20.00
21 Steve Young/99 6.00 15.00
22 John Elway/99 8.00 20.00
23 Dick Butkus/99 6.00 15.00
24 Tom Brady/99 8.00 20.00
26 Sammy Baugh/57 10.00 25.00
27 Dick Lane/99 5.00 12.00
29 Lee Roy Selmon/99 3.00 8.00
30 Jim Otto/99 3.00 8.00
31 Ray Nitschke/99 8.00 20.00
32 Otto Graham/99 8.00 20.00

2011 Playoff National Treasures NFL Greatest Materials Prime
STATED PRINT RUN 4-49
1 Walter Payton/49 15.00 40.00
2 Randy Moss/49 6.00 15.00
4 Joe Montana/20 20.00 50.00
5 Roger Staubach/49 12.00 30.00
7 Barry Sanders/25 15.00 40.00
8 Bruce Smith/49 6.00 15.00
11 Jerry Rice/49 15.00 40.00
17 Troy Aikman/49 10.00 25.00
18 Dan Fouts/49 8.00 20.00
19 Dan Marino/25 20.00 50.00
20 Emmitt Smith/49 12.00 30.00
21 Steve Young/49 10.00 25.00
28 Mike Singletary/45 8.00 20.00
29 Lee Roy Selmon/49 6.00 15.00
30 Jim Otto/25 6.00 15.00

2011 Playoff National Treasures NFL Greatest Signature Materials
STATED PRINT RUN 5-25
3 Brett Favre/25 125.00 200.00
4 Joe Montana/25 90.00 150.00
6 Warren Moon/25 25.00 50.00
22 John Elway/25 90.00 150.00
30 Jim Otto/25 15.00 30.00

2011 Playoff National Treasures NFL Greatest Signature Materials Prime
*PRIME/15: .6X TO 1.5X BASIC JSY AU/25
PRIME STATED PRINT RUN 5-15
21 Steve Young/15 50.00 100.00

2011 Playoff National Treasures NFL Greatest Signatures
STATED PRINT RUN 5-25
3 Brett Favre/15 100.00 200.00
4 Joe Montana/25 75.00 125.00
6 Warren Moon/24 20.00 40.00
7 Barry Sanders/25 75.00 135.00
30 Jim Otto/25 12.50 25.00

2011 Playoff National Treasures NFL Leather Autographs
STATED PRINT RUN 6-103
1 Archie Manning/50 25.00 50.00
2 Bo Jackson/25 50.00 100.00
3 Brandon Lloyd/27 10.00 25.00
4 Danny White/27 20.00 40.00
5 Don Perkins/53 12.00 30.00
6 Doug Flutie/50 20.00 40.00
7 Ed Too Tall Jones/27 12.00 30.00
8 Henry Ellard/35 12.00 30.00
10 Jim McMahon/27 25.00 50.00
11 Keyshawn Johnson/27 10.00 25.00
12 Larry Fitzgerald/27 40.00 80.00
13 Lydell Mitchell/103 8.00 20.00
14 Mark Sanchez/25 25.00 50.00
15 Matt Ryan/27 25.00 50.00
17 Miles Austin/25 25.00 50.00
19 Priest Holmes/27 20.00 40.00
20 Randall Cunningham/26 25.00 50.00
21 Sam Bradford/22 30.00 60.00
23 Tony Romo/27 40.00 80.00
24 Troy Polamalu/27 100.00 175.00

2011 Playoff National Treasures NFL MVPs Leather Autographs
STATED PRINT RUN 7-38
2 Bart Starr/23 90.00 150.00
3 Dan Marino/14 150.00 250.00
4 Emmitt Smith/17 125.00 200.00
6 Adrian Peterson/27 75.00 125.00
7 Alan Page/38 20.00 40.00
8 Ben Roethlisberger/27 50.00 100.00
9 Boomer Esiason/26 25.00 50.00
10 Curtis Martin/26 25.00 50.00
11 Frank Gifford/20 20.00 40.00
12 LaDainian Tomlinson/26 25.00 50.00

2011 Playoff National Treasures Pen Pals
STATED PRINT RUN 15-25
1 Colin Kaepernick/25 25.00 50.00
Kendall Hunter
2 Andy Dalton/25 90.00 150.00
A.J. Green
3 Jordan Todman/25 12.00 30.00
Vincent Brown
4 Mikel Leshoure/25 20.00 40.00
Titus Young
5 Alex Green/25 20.00 40.00
Randall Cobb
6 Ryan Mallett/25 30.00 60.00
Chono Voroon
Stevan Ridley
7 Christian Ponder/25 40.00 80.00
Kyle Rudolph
8 Marcell Dareus/25 20.00 40.00
Von Miller
9 Jake Locker/15 150.00 300.00
Blaine Gabbert
Christian Ponder
Andy Dalton
Colin Kaepernick
Ryan Mallett
10 Ryan Williams/15 75.00 150.00
Shane Vereen
Mikel Leshoure
Daniel Thomas
DeMarco Murray
Stevan Ridley
11 Alex Green/15 40.00 80.00
Kendall Hunter
Delone Carter
Taiwan Jones
Bilal Powell
Jamie Harper
12 A.J. Green/15 60.00 120.00
Julio Jones
Jonathan Baldwin
Titus Young
Torrey Smith
Greg Little
13 Von Miller/15 125.00 250.00
Marcell Dareus
A.J. Green
Julio Jones
Jake Locker
Blaine Gabbert
Christian Ponder
Jonathan Baldwin
14 Andy Dalton/15 75.00 150.00
Colin Kaepernick
Ryan Williams
Kyle Rudolph
Titus Young
Shane Vereen
Mikel Leshoure
Torrey Smith
15 Greg Little/15 75.00 150.00
Daniel Thomas
Randall Cobb
DeMarco Murray
Stevan Ridley
Ryan Mallett
Austin Pettis
Leonard Hankerson
16 Vincent Brown/15 40.00 80.00
Jerrel Jernigan
Alex Green
Kendall Hunter
Delone Carter
Taiwan Jones
Bilal Powell
Jamie Harper
17 Ryan Williams/15 100.00 200.00
Shane Vereen
Mikel Leshoure
Daniel Thomas
A.J. Green
Julio Jones
Jonathan Baldwin
Titus Young
18 Jake Locker/15 150.00 300.00
Blaine Gabbert
Christian Ponder
Andy Dalton
A.J. Green
Julio Jones
Jonathan Baldwin
Titus Young
19 A.J. Green/15 100.00 200.00
Julio Jones
Jonathan Baldwin
Titus Young
Torrey Smith
Greg Little
Randall Cobb
Austin Pettis
20 Ryan Williams/15 100.00 200.00
Shane Vereen
Mikel Leshoure
Daniel Thomas
DeMarco Murray
Stevan Ridley
Alex Green
Kendall Hunter

2011 Playoff National Treasures Pro Bowl Materials
STATED PRINT RUN 99 SER.#'d SETS
*PRIME/49: .6X TO 1.5X BASIC JSY/99
1 John Abraham 3.00 8.00
2 Ray Lewis 5.00 12.00
3 Darrelle Revis 4.00 10.00
4 Larry Fitzgerald 4.00 10.00
5 Steven Jackson 4.00 10.00
6 Dwayne Bowe 4.00 10.00
7 Tony Gonzalez 4.00 10.00
8 Drew Brees 5.00 12.00
9 Jerod Mayo 3.00 8.00
10 Reggie Wayne 4.00 10.00
11 Vonta Leach 3.00 8.00
12 Devin McCourty 3.00 8.00
13 Terrell Suggs 3.00 8.00
14 Jamaal Charles 4.00 10.00
15 Michael Vick 5.00 12.00
16 Michael Griffin 3.00 8.00
17 Zach Miller 4.00 10.00
18 London Fletcher 3.00 8.00
19 Arian Foster 4.00 10.00
20 Adrian Wilson 3.00 8.00

2011 Playoff National Treasures Pro Bowl Signature Materials
STATED PRINT RUN 10-25
9 Jerod Mayo/25 10.00 25.00
18 London Fletcher/25 15.00 40.00

2011 Playoff National Treasures Ring of Honor
STATED PRINT RUN 99 SER.#'d SETS
1 Bart Starr 5.00 12.00
2 Bob Lilly 2.50 6.00
3 John Stallworth 2.50 6.00
4 Russ Grimm 2.00 5.00
5 Terrell Davis 3.00 8.00
6 Jim McMahon 2.50 6.00
7 Ken Stabler 3.00 8.00
8 Cliff Branch 2.00 5.00
9 Raymond Berry 2.50 6.00
10 Doug Williams 2.00 5.00
11 Joe Namath 4.00 10.00
12 Larry Little 2.00 5.00
13 Len Dawson 3.00 8.00
14 Howie Long 3.00 8.00
15 Jim Taylor 2.50 6.00
16 Michael Strahan 2.00 5.00

2011 Playoff National Treasures Ring of Honor Signatures
STATED PRINT RUN 5-49
1 Bart Starr/15 75.00 150.00
4 Russ Grimm/49 12.00 30.00
5 Terrell Davis/38 25.00 50.00
6 Jim McMahon/49 25.00 50.00
9 Raymond Berry/49 15.00 40.00
10 Doug Williams/17 25.00 50.00
12 Larry Little/49 12.00 30.00
13 Len Dawson/15 25.00 50.00
14 Howie Long/49 25.00 50.00
15 Jim Taylor/49 25.00 50.00
16 Michael Strahan/49 20.00 40.00

2011 Playoff National Treasures Rookie Signature Material Black
*BLACK/25: .6X TO 1.5X BASIC JSY AU/99
STATED PRINT RUN 25 SER.#'d SETS
301 Christian Ponder 300.00 600.00
304 Blaine Gabbert 250.00 400.00
313 Torrey Smith 150.00 300.00
318 Mark Ingram 200.00 400.00
325 Jake Locker 500.00 800.00
326 Andy Dalton 500.00 800.00
328 Cam Newton 2,000.00 3,000.00
331 DeMarco Murray 300.00 600.00
333 Greg Little 75.00 150.00
335 Jonathan Baldwin 60.00 120.00

2011 Playoff National Treasures Rookie Signature Material Gold
*GOLD/49: .5X TO 1.2X BASIC JSY AU/99
STATED PRINT RUN 49 SER.#'d SETS
301 Christian Ponder 150.00 250.00
313 Torrey Smith 125.00 250.00
318 Mark Ingram 125.00 250.00
319 Vincent Brown 60.00 120.00
325 Jake Locker 300.00 500.00
326 Andy Dalton 300.00 500.00
328 Cam Newton 1,000.00 1,800.00
331 DeMarco Murray 200.00 400.00

2011 Playoff National Treasures Souvenir Cuts
STATED PRINT RUN 1-49
1 Bob Waterfield/26 60.00 120.00
3 Joe Perry/49 20.00 40.00
5 Dante Lavelli/14 30.00 60.00
6 Frank Gatski/20 20.00 40.00

2011 Playoff National Treasures Stamp Jumbo Material
2 Knute Rockne/19 60.00 120.00

2011 Playoff National Treasures Super Bowl MVPs Leather Autographs
STATED PRINT RUN 2-52
5 John Elway/33 100.00 175.00
6 Aaron Rodgers/27 200.00 300.00
7 Drew Brees/27 90.00 150.00
9 Jim Plunkett/27 15.00 40.00
10 Peyton Manning/52 125.00 200.00
11 Ottis Anderson/35 15.00 40.00
12 Terrell Davis/27 30.00 60.00

2011 Playoff National Treasures Timeline Materials Custom Names
STATED PRINT RUN 50-99
*PRIME/15: .8X TO 2X BASIC JSY/99
*TEAM/50-99: .4X TO 1X CUSTOM/50-99
1 Dan Fouts/99 6.00 15.00
2 Dan Marino/99 12.00 30.00
3 Emmitt Smith/50 10.00 25.00
4 George Blanda/99 5.00 12.00
5 Keyshawn Johnson/50 5.00 12.00
6 Marshall Faulk/99 5.00 12.00
7 Phil Simms/99 5.00 12.00
8 Steve Young/99 8.00 20.00
9 John Elway/99 10.00 25.00
10 Dick Butkus/50 8.00 20.00

2011 Playoff National Treasures Timeline Materials Signature Custom Names
STATED PRINT RUN 22-25
*TEAM/25: .4X TO 1X CUSTOM/25
2 Dan Marino/25 125.00 200.00
3 Emmitt Smith/22 125.00 200.00
5 Keyshawn Johnson/25 10.00 25.00
7 Phil Simms/25 15.00 40.00
8 Steve Young/25 50.00 100.00
9 John Elway/25 90.00 150.00
10 Dick Butkus/25 40.00 80.00

2006 Playoff NFL Playoffs

This 150-card set was released in factory set form in December, 2006. The set was issued with an $100 SRP price tag. Cards numbered 1-70 feature veterans, most of whom were sequenced in first name alphabetical order while cards numbered 71-150 feature 2006 rookies.

COMP.FACT SET (155) 60.00 100.00
COMPLETE SET (150) 20.00 50.00
1 Alex Smith QB .30 .75
2 Alge Crumpler .25 .60
3 Andre Johnson .30 .75
4 Anquan Boldin .25 .60
5 Antonio Gates .30 .75
6 Ben Roethlisberger .40 1.00
7 Braylon Edwards .25 .60
8 Brian Urlacher .30 .75
9 Brett Favre .60 1.50
10 Byron Leftwich .25 .60
11 Cadillac Williams .25 .60
12 Carson Palmer .30 .75
13 Cedric Benson .25 .60
14 Chad Johnson .25 .60
15 Charlie Frye .25 .60
16 Chris Brown .20 .50
17 Chris Chambers .25 .60
18 Clinton Portis .30 .75
19 Dallas Clark .25 .60
20 Darrell Jackson .25 .60
21 Deion Branch .25 .60
22 Domanick Davis .20 .50
23 Donovan McNabb .30 .75
24 Drew Bennett .25 .60
25 Drew Bledsoe .30 .75
26 Edgerrin James .25 .60
27 Eli Manning .40 1.00
28 Hines Ward .30 .75
29 Jake Delhomme .25 .60
30 Jerry Porter .20 .50
31 Julius Jones .20 .50
32 Kevin Jones .20 .50
33 LaDainian Tomlinson .30 .75
34 LaMont Jordan .25 .60
35 Larry Fitzgerald .30 .75
36 Larry Johnson .25 .60
37 Lee Evans .25 .60
38 Marc Bulger .25 .60
39 Mark Clayton .25 .60
40 Matt Hasselbeck .25 .60
41 Marvin Harrison .30 .75
42 Matt Jones .20 .50
43 Michael Vick .30 .75
44 Nate Burleson .20 .50
45 Peyton Manning .50 1.25
46 Philip Rivers .30 .75
47 Priest Holmes .25 .60
48 Reggie Brown .20 .50
49 Reggie Wayne .25 .60
50 Robert Ferguson .20 .50
51 Ronnie Brown .30 .75
52 Roy Williams S .25 .60
53 Roy Williams WR .25 .60
54 Rudi Johnson .25 .60
55 Samkon Gado .25 .60
56 Santana Moss .25 .60
57 Shaun Alexander .25 .60
58 Steven Jackson .30 .75
59 Steve Smith .30 .75
60 T.J. Houshmandzadeh .25 .60
61 Tatum Bell .20 .50
62 Thomas Jones .25 .60
63 Tiki Barber .30 .75
64 Torry Holt .25 .60
65 Tedy Bruschi .30 .75
66 Willie Parker .25 .60
67 Willis McGahee .25 .60
68 Drew Brees .30 .75
69 Dominic Rhodes .25 .60
70 Brian Westbrook .25 .60
71 Reggie Bush RC 2.00 5.00
72 Matt Leinart RC 1.00 2.50
73 Vince Young RC 1.25 3.00
74 Jay Cutler RC 2.00 5.00
75 DeAngelo Williams RC 1.25 3.00
76 LenDale White RC .75 2.00
77 Laurence Maroney RC .75 2.00
78 Santonio Holmes RC 1.25 3.00
79 Brodie Croyle RC 1.00 2.50
80 Sinorice Moss RC 1.00 2.50
81 Jeremy Bloom RC .75 2.00
82 A.J. Hawk RC 1.00 2.50
83 Joseph Addai RC 1.00 2.50
84 Vernon Davis RC 1.25 3.00
85 Michael Huff RC .75 2.00
86 Mario Williams RC 1.00 2.50
87 Demetrius Williams RC .75 2.00
88 Donte Whitner RC 1.00 2.50
89 Haloti Ngata RC 1.00 2.50
90 Tamba Hali RC 1.00 2.50
91 Omar Jacobs RC .60 1.50
92 Leonard Pope RC 1.00 2.50
93 Chad Jackson RC .60 1.50
94 Maurice Stovall RC .60 1.50
95 D'Brickashaw Ferguson RC 1.00 2.50
96 Charlie Whitehurst RC 1.00 2.50
97 Ingle Martin RC .75 2.00
98 Brian Calhoun RC .60 1.50
99 Leon Washington RC .75 2.00
100 Marcedes Lewis RC 1.00 2.50
101 Anthony Fasano RC 1.00 2.50
102 Derek Hagan RC .75 2.00
103 Devin Hester RC 1.50 4.00
104 Bobby Carpenter RC .60 1.50
105 Brodrick Bunkley RC .75 2.00
106 Maurice Drew RC 1.50 4.00
107 P.J. Daniels RC .60 1.50
108 Marques Hagans RC .60 1.50
109 Joe Klopfenstein RC .60 1.50
110 Tony Scheffler RC 1.00 2.50
111 Cory Rodgers RC .75 2.00
112 Tye Hill RC .60 1.50
113 Johnathan Joseph RC .75 2.00
114 John McCargo RC .60 1.50
115 Kamerion Wimbley RC 1.00 2.50
116 Jerious Norwood RC .75 2.00
117 Michael Robinson RC .75 2.00
118 Jason Avant RC .60 1.50
119 Manny Lawson RC .75 2.00
120 Mathias Kiwanuka RC 1.00 2.50
121 Kellen Clemens RC .75 2.00
122 Jerome Harrison RC 1.00 2.50
123 Dominique Byrd RC .75 2.00
124 Travis Wilson RC .60 1.50
125 Brandon Williams RC .60 1.50
126 Brandon Marshall RC 1.00 2.50
127 Greg Jennings RC 1.50 4.00
128 Brad Smith RC 1.00 2.50
129 Domenik Hixon RC 1.00 2.50
130 Kelly Jennings RC .75 2.00
131 Ernie Sims RC .75 2.00
132 Jason Allen RC .75 2.00
133 Tarvaris Jackson RC 1.00 2.50
134 David Thomas RC .75 2.00
135 Willie Reid RC .75 2.00
136 Skyler Green RC .60 1.50
137 Antonio Cromartie RC 1.00 2.50
138 Chad Greenway RC 1.00 2.50
139 Owen Daniels RC 1.00 2.50
140 Garrett Mills RC 1.00 2.50
141 Will Blackmon RC .75 2.00
142 David Kirtman RC .75 2.00
143 DeMeco Ryans RC 1.00 2.50
144 D'Qwell Jackson RC .75 2.00
145 Rocky McIntosh RC .75 2.00
146 Wali Lundy RC .75 2.00
147 Mike Bell RC 1.00 2.50
148 Daniel Bullocks RC 1.00 2.50
149 Marques Colston RC 2.00 5.00
150 Roman Harper RC .75 2.00

2006 Playoff NFL Playoffs Gold Proof
*VETERANS: 5X TO 12X BASIC CARDS
*ROOKIES: 1.2X TO 3X BASIC CARDS
STATED PRINT RUN 100 SER.#'d SETS

2006 Playoff NFL Playoffs Red
*VETERANS: 2X TO 5X BASIC CARDS
*ROOKIES: .5X TO 1.2X BASIC CARDS

2006 Playoff NFL Playoffs Platinum
UNPRICED PLATINUM PRINT RUN 1

2006 Playoff NFL Playoffs Silver Proof
*VETERANS: 3X TO 8X BASIC CARDS
*ROOKIES: .8X TO 2X BASIC CARDS
STATED PRINT RUN 250 SER.#'d SETS

2006 Playoff NFL Playoffs Jersey Signature Proofs Silver
SILVER PRINT RUN 10-100
*GOLD: .5X TO 1.2X SLVR JSY AU
GOLD PRINT RUN 4-50
UNPRICED PLATINUM PRINT RUN 1
SERIAL #'d UNDER 24 NOT PRICED
2 Alge Crumpler/25
5 Antonio Gates/25
6 Ben Roethlisberger/25 60.00 120.00
7 Braylon Edwards/25
8 Brian Urlacher/50 20.00 50.00
9 Brett Favre/25 125.00 250.00
14 Chad Johnson/25 15.00 40.00
15 Charlie Frye/25
16 Chris Brown/25 7.50 20.00
19 Dallas Clark/25
20 Darrell Jackson/25
21 Deion Branch/25
22 Domanick Davis/100 7.50 20.00
24 Drew Bennett/100 7.50 20.00
30 Jerry Porter/24
35 Larry Fitzgerald/25 25.00 50.00
37 Lee Evans/25
39 Mark Clayton/25
40 Matt Hasselbeck/25
45 Peyton Manning/25 75.00 150.00
49 Reggie Wayne/25 15.00 40.00
51 Ronnie Brown/25
52 Roy Williams S/25
54 Rudi Johnson/25
55 Samkon Gado/100 7.50 20.00
58 Steven Jackson/25
60 T.J. Houshmandzadeh/25
61 Tatum Bell/25
62 Thomas Jones/25
63 Tiki Barber/25
65 Tedy Bruschi/25 50.00 100.00
66 Willie Parker/25
71 Reggie Bush/25 50.00 120.00
72 Matt Leinart/25
73 Vince Young/25 40.00 100.00
75 DeAngelo Williams/50 25.00 60.00
76 LenDale White/25
77 Laurence Maroney/25 20.00 50.00
78 Santonio Holmes/25 15.00 40.00
80 Sinorice Moss/25
82 A.J. Hawk/25
84 Vernon Davis/25
85 Michael Huff/75 12.00 30.00
86 Mario Williams/75 15.00 40.00
87 Demetrius Williams/25
91 Omar Jacobs/60 12.50 30.00
93 Chad Jackson/25
94 Maurice Stovall/25
96 Charlie Whitehurst/25 12.50 30.00
98 Brian Calhoun/25
99 Leon Washington/49 12.00 30.00
100 Marcedes Lewis/100 7.50 20.00
102 Derek Hagan/100 7.50 20.00
106 Maurice Drew/25 40.00 80.00
109 Joe Klopfenstein/100 6.00 15.00
116 Jerious Norwood/100 10.00 25.00
117 Michael Robinson/25
118 Jason Avant/25 12.50 30.00
121 Kellen Clemens/25
124 Travis Wilson/50 12.00 30.00
125 Brandon Williams/25
126 Brandon Marshall/50 12.00 30.00
133 Tarvaris Jackson/25

2008 Playoff NFL Playoffs Signature Proofs Silver

1-70 SILVER PRINT RUN 7-150
71-150 SILVER PRINT RUN 148-150
*GOLD VETS: .5X TO 1.2X SILVER AU
*GOLD ROOKIES: .6X TO 1.5X SILVER AU
GOLD PRINT RUN 4-50
UNPRICED PLATINUM PRINT RUN 1
SERIAL #'d UNDER 24 NOT PRICED
2 Alge Crumpler/86 10.00 20.00
3 Andre Johnson/150 8.00 20.00
4 Anquan Boldin/25 10.00 25.00
5 Antonio Gates/50 10.00 25.00
6 Ben Roethlisberger/25 60.00 120.00
7 Braylon Edwards/25 15.00 40.00
8 Brian Urlacher/150 15.00 40.00
9 Brett Favre/25 125.00 250.00
10 Byron Leftwich/75 8.00 20.00
11 Cadillac Williams/25 15.00 40.00
13 Cedric Benson/25 10.00 25.00
14 Chad Johnson/25 12.00 30.00
15 Charlie Frye/148 10.00 25.00
16 Chris Brown/47 8.00 20.00
17 Chris Chambers/100 8.00 20.00
19 Dallas Clark/150 8.00 20.00
20 Darrell Jackson/50 6.00 15.00
21 Deion Branch/86 8.00 20.00
22 Domanick Davis/150 6.00 15.00
24 Drew Bennett/150 6.00 15.00
29 Jake Delhomme/25 12.00 30.00
35 Larry Fitzgerald/25 15.00 40.00
36 Larry Johnson/25 15.00 40.00
37 Lee Evans/140 6.00 15.00
38 Marc Bulger/62 8.00 20.00
39 Mark Clayton/50 10.00 25.00
40 Matt Hasselbeck/25 15.00 40.00
44 Nate Burleson/75 10.00 25.00
45 Peyton Manning/25 75.00 150.00
46 Philip Rivers/25 20.00 50.00
49 Reggie Wayne/50 12.50 30.00
53 Roy Williams WR/25 10.00 25.00
54 Rudi Johnson/50 10.00 25.00
55 Samkon Gado/150 8.00 20.00
56 Santana Moss/98 10.00 25.00
58 Steven Jackson/25 15.00 40.00
59 Steve Smith/25 15.00 40.00
60 T.J. Houshmandzadeh/150 8.00 20.00
61 Tatum Bell/50 8.00 20.00
62 Thomas Jones/50 8.00 20.00
63 Tiki Barber/25 10.00 25.00
65 Tedy Bruschi/50 30.00 60.00
66 Willie Parker/50 12.00 30.00
67 Willis McGahee/25 10.00 25.00
68 Drew Brees/40 30.00 60.00
69 Dominic Rhodes/24 15.00 40.00
71 Reggie Bush 25.00 60.00
72 Matt Leinart 10.00 25.00
73 Vince Young 15.00 40.00
74 Jay Cutler 30.00 80.00
75 DeAngelo Williams 15.00 40.00
76 LenDale White 5.00 12.00
77 Laurence Maroney 5.00 12.00
78 Santonio Holmes 8.00 20.00
79 Brodie Croyle 6.00 15.00
80 Sinorice Moss 6.00 15.00
81 Jeremy Bloom 5.00 12.00
82 A.J. Hawk 20.00 40.00
83 Joseph Addai 10.00 25.00
84 Vernon Davis 8.00 20.00
85 Michael Huff 5.00 12.00
86 Mario Williams 6.00 15.00
87 Demetrius Williams 5.00 12.00
88 Donte Whitner 6.00 15.00
89 Haloti Ngata 6.00 15.00
90 Tamba Hali 6.00 15.00
91 Omar Jacobs 4.00 10.00
92 Leonard Pope 6.00 15.00
93 Chad Jackson 4.00 10.00
94 Maurice Stovall 4.00 10.00
95 D'Brickashaw Ferguson 6.00 15.00
96 Charlie Whitehurst 6.00 15.00
97 Ingle Martin 5.00 12.00
98 Brian Calhoun 4.00 10.00
99 Leon Washington 5.00 12.00
100 Marcedes Lewis 6.00 15.00
101 Anthony Fasano 6.00 15.00
102 Derek Hagan 5.00 12.00
103 Devin Hester 15.00 40.00
104 Bobby Carpenter 4.00 10.00
105 Brodrick Bunkley 5.00 12.00
106 Maurice Drew 20.00 50.00
107 P.J. Daniels 4.00 10.00
108 Marques Hagans 4.00 10.00
109 Joe Klopfenstein 4.00 10.00
110 Tony Scheffler 6.00 15.00
111 Cory Rodgers 5.00 12.00
112 Tye Hill 4.00 10.00
113 Johnathan Joseph 5.00 12.00
114 John McCargo 4.00 10.00
115 Kamerion Wimbley 6.00 15.00
116 Jerious Norwood 5.00 12.00
117 Michael Robinson 5.00 12.00
118 Jason Avant 4.00 10.00
119 Manny Lawson 5.00 12.00
120 Mathias Kiwanuka 6.00 15.00
121 Kellen Clemens 5.00 12.00
122 Jerome Harrison 6.00 15.00
123 Dominique Byrd 5.00 12.00
124 Travis Wilson 4.00 10.00
125 Brandon Williams 4.00 10.00
126 Brandon Marshall 10.00 25.00
127 Greg Jennings 12.00 30.00
128 Brad Smith 6.00 15.00
129 Domenik Hixon 6.00 15.00
130 Kelly Jennings 5.00 12.00
131 Ernie Sims 5.00 12.00
132 Jason Allen 5.00 12.00
133 Tarvaris Jackson 6.00 15.00
134 David Thomas 5.00 12.00
135 Willie Reid 5.00 12.00
136 Skyler Green 4.00 10.00
137 Antonio Cromartie 6.00 15.00
138 Chad Greenway 6.00 15.00
139 Owen Daniels 6.00 15.00
140 Garrett Mills 6.00 15.00
141 Will Blackmon 5.00 12.00
142 David Kirtman 5.00 12.00
143 DeMeco Ryans/148 6.00 15.00
144 D'Qwell Jackson 5.00 12.00
145 Rocky McIntosh 5.00 12.00
146 Wali Lundy 5.00 12.00
147 Mike Bell 6.00 15.00
148 Daniel Bullocks 6.00 15.00
149 Marques Colston 20.00 50.00
150 Roman Harper 5.00 12.00

2007 Playoffs NFL Playoffs Preview
This set was issued in a foil wrapper through the Shop at Home Network to preview the 2007 Playoff NFL Playoffs product.

COMPLETE SET (6) 15.00 30.00
P1 JaMarcus Russell .50 1.25
P2 Adrian Peterson 3.00 8.00
P3 Calvin Johnson 2.50 6.00
P4 Brady Quinn .75 2.00
P5 Marshawn Lynch .75 2.00
P6 Ted Ginn Jr. .60 1.50

2007 Playoffs NFL Playoffs Preview Bonus
This set was issued in a foil wrapper through the Shop at Home Network. Each card was produced in the style of the 2006 NFL Playoffs product with an udated player photo and a 2007 copyright line on the back. Red foil highlights appear at the top of the basic cards with a series of parallels issued in different foil colors. One Jersey card and one parallel card was issued in each foil pack along with the basic 10-card red foil set.

COMPLETE SET (10) 6.00 12.00
*GOLD/300: 1X TO 2.5X RED FOIL
*GREEN/125: 1.5X TO 4X RED FOIL
*BLUE/600: .8X TO 2X RED FOIL
UNPRICED BLACK PRINT RUN 1
B1 Reggie Bush .60 1.50
B2 Vince Young .50 1.25
B3 Maurice Jones-Drew .60 1.50
B4 Matt Leinart .50 1.25
B5 Laurence Maroney .50 1.25
B6 Vernon Davis .50 1.25
B7 DeAngelo Williams .00 1.50
B8 Joseph Addai .50 1.25
B9 Leon Washington .50 1.25
B10 Santonio Holmes .50 1.25

2007 Playoffs NFL Playoffs Preview Bonus Jerseys Red
COMPLETE SET (10) 50.00 100.00
*BLUE/500: .5X TO 1.2X RED FOIL
*GOLD/250: .8X TO 2X RED FOIL
*GREEN/50: 1.5X TO 4X RED FOIL
UNPRICED BLACK PRINT RUN 1
B1 Reggie Bush 4.00 10.00
B2 Vince Young 3.00 8.00
B3 Maurice Jones-Drew 4.00 10.00
B4 Matt Leinart 3.00 8.00
B5 Laurence Maroney 3.00 8.00
B6 Vernon Davis 3.00 8.00
B7 DeAngelo Williams 4.00 10.00
B8 Joseph Addai 3.00 8.00
B9 Leon Washington 3.00 8.00
B10 Santonio Holmes 3.00 8.00

2007 Playoff NFL Playoffs

This 180-card set was released in December, 2007. The set was issued as part of a factory set with an $100 SRP. The first 100 cards in this set are in alphabetical team order while the final 80 cards in the set feature 2007 NFL rookies.

COMP.FACT.SET (180) 60.00 100.00
COMPLETE SET (184) 15.00 40.00
UNPRICED BLACK PROOF PRINT RUN 5
UNPRICED BLACK HOLOFOIL PRINT RUN 10
UNPRICED GOLD PROOF PRINT RUN 10
UNPRICED PLATINUM PRINT RUN 1
UNPRICED PLATINUM HOLOFOIL PRINT RUN 1
UNPRICED PLATINUM METAL PRINT RUN 1
UNPRICED PLATINUM PROOF PRINT RUN 1
1 Anquan Boldin .25 .60
2 Larry Fitzgerald .30 .75
3 Edgerrin James .25 .60
4 Matt Leinart .25 .60
5 Alge Crumpler .25 .60
6 Jerious Norwood .25 .60
7 Warrick Dunn .25 .60
8 Steve McNair .25 .60
9 Demetrius Williams .20 .50
10 Willis McGahee .25 .60
11 J.P. Losman .20 .50
12 Lee Evans .25 .60
13 Steve Smith .25 .60
14 DeAngelo Williams .30 .75
15 Jake Delhomme .25 .60
16 Bernard Berrian .20 .50
17 Cedric Benson .25 .60
18 Rex Grossman .25 .60
19 Chad Johnson .25 .60
20 Rudi Johnson .25 .60
21 T.J. Houshmandzadeh .25 .60
22 Carson Palmer .25 .60
23 Braylon Edwards .25 .60
24 Kellen Winslow .25 .60
25 Terrell Owens .30 .75
26 Julius Jones .20 .50
27 Marion Barber .25 .60
28 Tony Romo .40 1.00
29 Jay Cutler .30 .75
30 Mike Bell .25 .60
31 Brandon Marshall .25 .60
32 Jon Kitna .20 .50
33 Roy Williams WR .25 .60
34 Mike Furrey .25 .60
35 Brett Favre .60 1.50
36 Donald Driver .30 .75
37 Greg Jennings .30 .75
38 A.J. Hawk .25 .00
39 Andre Johnson .25 .60
40 Matt Schaub .25 .60
41 Ahman Green .25 .60
42 Peyton Manning .50 1.25
43 Joseph Addai .25 .60
44 Marvin Harrison .30 .75
45 Reggie Wayne .25 .60
46 Fred Taylor .25 .60
47 David Garrard .25 .60
48 Maurice Jones-Drew .30 .75
49 Larry Johnson .20 .50
50 Tony Gonzalez .25 .60
51 Trent Green .25 .00
52 Chris Chambers .25 .60
53 Ronnie Brown .25 .60
54 Chester Taylor .20 .50
55 Tarvaris Jackson .20 .50
56 Tom Brady .50 1.25
57 Randy Moss .30 .75
58 Laurence Maroney .25 .60
59 Deuce McAllister .25 .60
60 Drew Brees .30 .75
61 Marques Colston .30 .75
62 Reggie Bush .30 .75
63 Jeremy Shockey .25 .60
64 Plaxico Burress .25 .60
65 Brandon Jacobs .25 .60
66 Eli Manning .30 .75
67 Chad Pennington .25 .60
68 Jerricho Cotchery .25 .60
69 Leon Washington .25 .60
70 Thomas Jones .25 .60
71 LaMont Jordan .25 .60
72 Daunte Culpepper .25 .60
73 Brian Westbrook .25 .60
74 Donovan McNabb .30 .75
75 Hank Baskett .25 .60
76 Hines Ward .30 .75
77 Willie Parker .25 .60
78 Santonio Holmes .25 .60
79 Ben Roethlisberger .30 .75
80 Antonio Gates .30 .75
81 LaDainian Tomlinson .30 .75
82 Philip Rivers .30 .75
83 Shawne Merriman .25 .60
84 Vincent Jackson .25 .60
85 Alex Smith QB .30 .75
86 Frank Gore .30 .75
87 Vernon Davis .25 .60
88 Deion Branch .25 .60
89 Matt Hasselbeck .25 .60
90 Shaun Alexander .25 .60
91 Marc Bulger .25 .60
92 Torry Holt .25 .60
93 Steven Jackson .30 .75
94 Joey Galloway .25 .60
95 Cadillac Williams .25 .60
96 LenDale White .25 .60
97 Vince Young .25 .60
98 Clinton Portis .25 .60
99 Jason Campbell .25 .60
100 Ladell Betts .20 .50
101 Adrian Peterson RC 3.00 8.00
102 Anthony Gonzalez RC .75 2.00
103 Yamon Figurs RC .50 1.25
104 Brady Quinn RC .75 2.00
105 Brandon Jackson RC .60 1.50
106 Brian Leonard RC .60 1.50
107 Calvin Johnson RC 2.50 6.00
108 Chris Henry RB RC .50 1.25
109 Drew Stanton RC .50 1.25

110 Dwayne Bowe RC 1.00 2.50
111 Dwayne Jarrett RC .60 1.50
112 Gaines Adams RC .75 2.00
113 Garrett Wolfe RC .50 1.25
114 Greg Olsen RC .60 1.50
115 JaMarcus Russell RC .50 1.25
116 Jason Hill RC .75 2.00
117 Joe Thomas RC .75 2.00
118 John Beck RC .75 2.00
119 Johnnie Lee Higgins RC .60 1.50
120 Kenny Irons RC .50 1.25
121 Kevin Kolb RC 1.25 3.00
122 Lorenzo Booker RC .60 1.50
123 Marshawn Lynch RC .75 2.00
124 Michael Bush RC .75 2.00
125 Patrick Willis RC 1.50 4.00
126 Paul Williams RC .50 1.25
127 Robert Meachem RC .75 2.00
128 Sidney Rice RC 1.00 2.50
129 Steve Smith RC .75 2.00
130 Ted Ginn Jr. RC .60 1.50
131 Tony Hunt RC .50 1.25
132 Trent Edwards RC .75 2.00
133 Troy Smith RC .75 2.00
134 Antonio Pittman RC .50 1.25
135 Levi Brown RC .75 2.00
136 LaRon Landry RC .75 2.00
137 Jamaal Anderson RC .60 1.50
138 Amobi Okoye RC .75 2.00
139 Adam Carriker RC .60 1.50
140 Darrelle Revis RC 1.25 3.00
141 Lawrence Timmons RC .75 2.00
142 Leon Hall RC .60 1.50
143 Michael Griffin RC .75 2.00
144 Aaron Ross RC .75 2.00
145 Reggie Nelson RC .60 1.50
146 Brandon Meriweather RC .75 2.00
147 Jon Beason RC .60 1.50
148 Chris Davis RC .50 1.25
149 Jeff Rowe RC .50 1.25
150 Courtney Taylor RC .60 1.50
151 Dallas Baker RC .50 1.25
152 Roy Hall RC .75 2.00
153 Jordan Kent RC .60 1.50
154 David Clowney RC .60 1.50
155 Scott Chandler RC .75 2.00
156 Anthony Spencer RC .75 2.00
157 Paul Posluszny RC .75 2.00
158 Craig Buster Davis RC .60 1.50
159 Zach Miller RC .75 2.00
160 Alan Branch RC .60 1.50
161 Chris Houston RC .60 1.50
162 Laurent Robinson RC .75 2.00
163 LaMarr Woodley RC .75 2.00
164 James Jones RC .75 2.00
165 David Harris RC .60 1.50
166 Mike Walker RC .75 2.00
167 Eric Wright RC .75 2.00
168 Isaiah Stanback RC .50 1.25
169 Josh Wilson RC .60 1.50
170 Dwayne Wright RC .60 1.50
171 Tim Crowder RC .75 2.00
172 Ryne Robinson RC .60 1.50
173 Jacoby Jones RC .75 2.00
174 Steve Breaston RC .75 2.00
175 Dan Bazuin RC .60 1.50
176 Aundrae Allison RC .50 1.25
177 Sabby Piscitelli RC .75 2.00
178 Kolby Smith RC .60 1.50
179 Matt Spaeth RC .75 2.00
180 DeShawn Wynn RC .60 1.50

2007 Playoff NFL Playoffs Black

*VETS/199: 2.5X TO 6X BASIC CARDS
*ROOKIES/199: 1X TO 2.5X BASIC CARDS
STATED PRINT RUN 199 SER.#'d SETS

2007 Playoff NFL Playoffs Black Metalized

*VETS/49: 4X TO 10X BASIC CARDS
*ROOKIES/49: 1.5X TO 4X BASIC CARDS
STATED PRINT RUN 49 SER.#'d SETS

2007 Playoff NFL Playoffs Gold

*VETS/299: 2X TO 5X BASIC CARDS
*ROOKIES/299: .8X TO 2X BASIC CARDS
STATED PRINT RUN 299 SER.#'d SETS

2007 Playoff NFL Playoffs Gold Holofoil

*VETS/25: 8X TO 12X BASIC CARDS
*ROOKIES/25: 2X TO 5X BASIC CARDS
STATED PRINT RUN 25 SER.#'d SETS

2007 Playoff NFL Playoffs Gold Metalized

*VETS/ 149: 2.5X TO 6X BASIC CARDS
*ROOKIES/149: 1X TO 2.5X BASIC CARDS
STATED PRINT RUN 149 SER.#'d SETS

2007 Playoff NFL Playoffs Red Holofoil

*VETS/125: 3X TO 8X BASIC CARDS
*ROOKIES/125: 1.2X TO 3X BASIC CARDS
STATED PRINT RUN 125 SER.#'d SETS

2007 Playoff NFL Playoffs Red Metalized

*VETS/399: 1.5X TO 4X BASIC CARDS
*ROOKIES/399: .6X TO 1.5X BASIC CARDS
STATED PRINT RUN 399 SER.#'d SETS

2007 Playoff NFL Playoffs Red Proof

*VETERANS: 1.5X TO 4X BASIC CARDS
*ROOKIES: .6X TO 1.5X BASIC CARDS

2007 Playoff NFL Playoffs Silver Holofoil

*VETS/99: 3X TO 8X BASIC CARDS
*ROOKIES/99: 1.2X TO 3X BASIC CARDS
STATED PRINT RUN 99 SER.#'d SETS

2007 Playoff NFL Playoffs Silver Metalized

*VETS/249: 2X TO 5X BASIC CARDS
*ROOKIES/249: .8X TO 2X BASIC CARDS
STATED PRINT RUN 249 SER.#'d SETS

2007 Playoff NFL Playoffs Silver Proof

*VETS/50: 4X TO 10X BASIC CARDS
*ROOKIES/50: 1.5X TO 4X BASIC CARDS
STATED PRINT RUN 50 SER.#'d SETS

2007 Playoff NFL Playoffs Material Signatures Red

RED PRINT RUN 50 SER.#'d SETS
*RED PRIME/50: .5X TO 1.2X RED/50
RED PRIME PRINT RUN 50 SER.#'d SETS
*SILVER/25: .5X TO 1.2X RED/50
SILVER PRINT RUN 25 SER.#'d SETS
*SILVER PRIME/20-25: .6X TO 1.5X RED/50
SILVER PRIME PRINT RUN 20-25
UNPRICED GOLD PRINT RUN 10
UNPRICED GOLD PRIME PRINT RUN 10
UNPRICED BLACK PRINT RUN 5
UNPRICED BLACK PRIME PRINT RUN 5
UNPRICED PLATINUM PRINT RUN 1
UNPRICED PLATINUM PRIME PRINT RUN 1
101 Adrian Peterson 60.00 120.00
102 Anthony Gonzalez 12.00 30.00
103 Yamon Figurs 8.00 20.00
104 Brady Quinn 12.00 30.00
105 Brandon Jackson 10.00 25.00
106 Brian Leonard 10.00 25.00
107 Calvin Johnson 40.00 100.00
108 Chris Henry RB 8.00 20.00
109 Drew Stanton 8.00 20.00
110 Dwayne Bowe 15.00 40.00
111 Dwayne Jarrett 10.00 25.00
112 Gaines Adams 12.00 30.00
113 Garrett Wolfe 8.00 20.00
114 Greg Olsen 10.00 25.00
115 JaMarcus Russell 8.00 20.00
116 Jason Hill 12.00 30.00
117 Joe Thomas 12.00 30.00
118 John Beck 12.00 30.00
119 Johnnie Lee Higgins 10.00 25.00
120 Kenny Irons No AU 5.00 12.00
121 Kevin Kolb 20.00 50.00
122 Lorenzo Booker 10.00 25.00
123 Marshawn Lynch 12.00 30.00
124 Michael Bush 12.00 30.00
125 Patrick Willis 25.00 60.00
126 Paul Williams 8.00 20.00
127 Robert Meachem 12.00 30.00
128 Sidney Rice 15.00 40.00
129 Steve Smith USC 12.00 30.00
130 Ted Ginn Jr. 10.00 25.00
131 Tony Hunt 8.00 20.00
132 Trent Edwards 12.00 30.00
133 Troy Smith 12.00 30.00

2007 Playoff NFL Playoffs Materials Gold

GOLD PRINT RUN 25 SER.#'d SETS
*RED/100: .25X TO .6X GOLD/25
RED PRINT RUN 100 SER.#'d SETS
*SILVER/50: .3X TO .8X GOLD/25
SILVER PRINT RUN 50 SER.#'d SETS
UNPRICED RED PRIME PRINT RUN 10-20
UNPRICED SILVER PRIME PRINT RUN 13-15
UNPRICED GOLD PRIME PRINT RUN 10
UNPRICED BLACK PRINT RUN 5-10
UNPRICED BLACK PRIME PRINT RUN 5
UNPRICED PLATINUM PRINT RUN 1
UNPRICED PLATINUM PRIME PRINT RUN 1
1 Anquan Boldin 5.00 12.00
2 Larry Fitzgerald 6.00 15.00
3 Edgerrin James 5.00 12.00
4 Matt Leinart 5.00 12.00
5 Alge Crumpler 5.00 12.00
6 Jerious Norwood 5.00 12.00
7 Warrick Dunn 5.00 12.00
8 Steve McNair 5.00 12.00
9 Demetrius Williams 4.00 10.00
11 J.P. Losman 4.00 10.00
12 Lee Evans 5.00 12.00
13 Steve Smith 5.00 12.00
14 DeAngelo Williams 6.00 15.00
15 Jake Delhomme 5.00 12.00
16 Bernard Berrian 4.00 10.00
17 Cedric Benson 5.00 12.00
18 Rex Grossman 5.00 12.00
19 Chad Johnson 5.00 12.00
20 Rudi Johnson 5.00 12.00
21 T.J. Houshmandzadeh 5.00 12.00
22 Carson Palmer 5.00 12.00
23 Braylon Edwards 5.00 12.00
24 Kellen Winslow 5.00 12.00
25 Terrell Owens 6.00 15.00
26 Julius Jones 4.00 10.00
27 Marion Barber 6.00 15.00
28 Tony Romo 8.00 20.00
29 Jay Cutler 6.00 15.00
30 Mike Bell 5.00 12.00
31 Brandon Marshall 5.00 12.00
32 Jon Kitna 4.00 10.00
33 Roy Williams WR 5.00 12.00
34 Mike Furrey 5.00 12.00
35 Brett Favre 12.00 30.00
36 Donald Driver 6.00 15.00
37 Greg Jennings 6.00 15.00
38 A.J. Hawk 5.00 12.00
39 Andre Johnson 5.00 12.00
41 Ahman Green/10 5.00 12.00
42 Peyton Manning 10.00 25.00
43 Joseph Addai 5.00 12.00
44 Marvin Harrison 6.00 15.00
45 Reggie Wayne 5.00 12.00
46 Fred Taylor 5.00 12.00
48 Maurice Jones-Drew 6.00 15.00
49 Larry Johnson 4.00 10.00
50 Tony Gonzalez 5.00 12.00
52 Chris Chambers 5.00 12.00
53 Ronnie Brown 5.00 12.00
54 Chester Taylor 4.00 10.00
55 Tarvaris Jackson 4.00 10.00
56 Tom Brady 10.00 25.00
57 Randy Moss 6.00 15.00
58 Laurence Maroney 5.00 12.00
59 Deuce McAllister 5.00 12.00
60 Drew Brees 6.00 15.00
61 Marques Colston 6.00 15.00
62 Reggie Bush 6.00 15.00
63 Jeremy Shockey 5.00 12.00
64 Plaxico Burress 5.00 12.00
65 Brandon Jacobs 5.00 12.00
66 Eli Manning 6.00 15.00
67 Chad Pennington 5.00 12.00
68 Jerricho Cotchery 5.00 12.00
69 Leon Washington 5.00 12.00
71 LaMont Jordan 5.00 12.00
73 Brian Westbrook 5.00 12.00
74 Donovan McNabb 6.00 15.00
75 Hank Baskett 5.00 12.00
76 Hines Ward 6.00 15.00
77 Willie Parker 5.00 12.00
78 Santonio Holmes 5.00 12.00
79 Ben Roethlisberger 6.00 15.00
80 Antonio Gates 6.00 15.00
81 LaDainian Tomlinson 6.00 15.00
82 Philip Rivers 6.00 15.00
83 Shawne Merriman 5.00 12.00
84 Vincent Jackson 5.00 12.00
85 Alex Smith QB 6.00 15.00
86 Frank Gore 6.00 15.00
87 Vernon Davis 5.00 12.00
88 Deion Branch 5.00 12.00
89 Matt Hasselbeck 5.00 12.00
90 Shaun Alexander 5.00 12.00
91 Marc Bulger 5.00 12.00
92 Torry Holt 5.00 12.00
93 Steven Jackson 6.00 15.00
94 Joey Galloway 5.00 12.00
95 Cadillac Williams 5.00 12.00
96 LenDale White 5.00 12.00
97 Vince Young 5.00 12.00
98 Clinton Portis 5.00 12.00
99 Jason Campbell 5.00 12.00
100 Ladell Betts 4.00 10.00
101 Adrian Peterson 25.00 60.00
102 Anthony Gonzalez 4.00 10.00
103 Yamon Figurs 2.50 6.00
104 Brady Quinn 4.00 10.00
105 Brandon Jackson 3.00 8.00
106 Brian Leonard 3.00 8.00
107 Calvin Johnson 12.00 30.00
108 Chris Henry RB 2.50 6.00
109 Drew Stanton 2.50 6.00
110 Dwayne Bowe 5.00 12.00
111 Dwayne Jarrett 3.00 8.00
112 Gaines Adams 4.00 10.00
113 Garrett Wolfe 2.50 6.00
114 Greg Olsen 3.00 8.00
115 JaMarcus Russell 2.50 6.00
116 Jason Hill 4.00 10.00
117 Joe Thomas 4.00 10.00
118 John Beck 4.00 10.00
119 Johnnie Lee Higgins 3.00 8.00
120 Kenny Irons 2.50 6.00
121 Kevin Kolb 6.00 15.00
122 Lorenzo Booker 3.00 8.00
123 Marshawn Lynch 4.00 10.00
124 Michael Bush 4.00 10.00
125 Patrick Willis 8.00 20.00
126 Paul Williams 2.50 6.00
127 Robert Meachem 4.00 10.00
128 Sidney Rice 5.00 12.00
129 Steve Smith USC 4.00 10.00
130 Ted Ginn Jr. 3.00 8.00
131 Tony Hunt 2.50 6.00
132 Trent Edwards 4.00 10.00
133 Troy Smith 4.00 10.00

2007 Playoff NFL Playoffs Signatures Red

STATED PRINT RUN 15-100 SER.#'d SETS
*SILVER/25: .6X TO 1.5X RED AUTO/91-100
*SILVER/25: .5X TO 1.2X RED AUTO/34-52
*SILVER/25: .4X TO 1X RED AUTO/25
SILVER PRINT RUN 10-25
UNPRICED GOLD PRINT RUN 10
UNPRICED BLACK PRINT RUN 5
UNPRICED PLATINUM PRINT RUN 1
101 Adrian Peterson/25 125.00 250.00
102 Anthony Gonzalez/25 12.00 30.00
103 Yamon Figurs/15 8.00 20.00
104 Brady Quinn/25 12.00 30.00
105 Brandon Jackson/25 10.00 25.00
106 Brian Leonard/100 6.00 15.00
107 Calvin Johnson/25 40.00 100.00
108 Chris Henry RB/25 8.00 20.00
109 Drew Stanton/25 8.00 20.00
110 Dwayne Bowe/25 15.00 40.00
111 Dwayne Jarrett/25 10.00 25.00
112 Gaines Adams/50 10.00 25.00
113 Garrett Wolfe/100 5.00 12.00
114 Greg Olsen/25 10.00 25.00
115 JaMarcus Russell/25 8.00 20.00
116 Jason Hill/100 8.00 20.00
117 Joe Thomas/100
118 John Beck/100 8.00 20.00
119 Johnnie Lee Higgins/100 6.00 15.00
121 Kevin Kolb/25 20.00 50.00
122 Lorenzo Booker/50 8.00 20.00
123 Marshawn Lynch/25 12.00 30.00
124 Michael Bush/25 12.00 30.00
125 Patrick Willis/41 20.00 50.00
126 Paul Williams/100 5.00 12.00
127 Robert Meachem/25 12.00 30.00
128 Sidney Rice/25 15.00 40.00
129 Steve Smith USC/50 10.00 25.00
130 Ted Ginn Jr./25 10.00 25.00
131 Tony Hunt/50 6.00 15.00
132 Trent Edwards/50 10.00 25.00
133 Troy Smith/25 12.00 30.00
134 Antonio Pittman/100 5.00 12.00
135 Levi Brown/100 8.00 20.00
136 LaRon Landry/100 8.00 20.00
137 Jamaal Anderson/52 8.00 20.00
138 Amobi Okoye/100 8.00 20.00
139 Adam Carriker/100 6.00 15.00
140 Darrelle Revis/100 12.00 30.00
141 Lawrence Timmons/100 8.00 20.00
142 Leon Hall/100 6.00 15.00
143 Michael Griffin/34 10.00 25.00
144 Aaron Ross/91 8.00 20.00
145 Reggie Nelson/100 6.00 15.00
146 Brandon Meriweather/100 8.00 20.00
147 Jon Beason/100 6.00 15.00
148 Chris Davis/100 5.00 12.00
149 Jeff Rowe/100 5.00 12.00
150 Courtney Taylor/100 6.00 15.00
151 Dallas Baker/100 5.00 12.00
152 Roy Hall/100 8.00 20.00
153 Jordan Kent/100 6.00 15.00
154 David Clowney/100 6.00 15.00
155 Scott Chandler/100 8.00 20.00
156 Anthony Spencer/100 8.00 20.00
157 Paul Posluszny/100 8.00 20.00
159 Zach Miller/100 8.00 20.00
161 Chris Houston/100 6.00 15.00
162 Laurent Robinson/100 8.00 20.00
163 LaMarr Woodley/100 8.00 20.00
164 James Jones/100 8.00 20.00
165 David Harris/100 6.00 15.00
166 Mike Walker/100 8.00 20.00
168 Isaiah Stanback/100 5.00 12.00
169 Josh Wilson/100 6.00 15.00
170 Dwayne Wright/100 6.00 15.00
171 Tim Crowder/100 8.00 20.00
172 Ryne Robinson/100 6.00 15.00
173 Jacoby Jones/100 8.00 20.00
174 Steve Breaston/100 8.00 20.00
175 Dan Bazuin/100 6.00 15.00
176 Aundrae Allison/100 5.00 12.00
177 Sabby Piscitelli/100 8.00 20.00
178 Kolby Smith/100 6.00 15.00
179 Matt Spaeth/100 8.00 20.00
180 DeShawn Wynn/100 6.00 15.00

2002 Playoff Piece of the Game

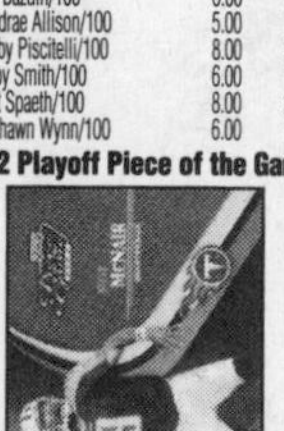

Released in October 2002, this set contains 75 veterans, 25 rookies #'d to 500, and 32 rookies #'d to 500 that feature a jersey swatch. Boxes contained 6 packs of 5 cards, with each pack containing 4 base cards and one memorabilia card.

COMP.SET w/o SP's (75) 30.00 50.00
76-132 ROOKIE PRINT RUN 500
1 Daunte Culpepper .40 1.00
2 Tim Couch .30 .75
3 Michael Vick .75 2.00
4 Brett Favre 1.25 3.00
5 Drew Bledsoe .50 1.25
6 Mark Brunell .40 1.00
7 Jake Plummer .40 1.00
8 Mike McMahon .30 .75
9 Brian Griese .40 1.00
10 Aaron Brooks .40 1.00
11 Chris Weinke .30 .75
12 Peyton Manning 1.00 2.50
13 Trent Green .40 1.00
14 Quincy Carter .30 .75
15 Tom Brady 1.25 3.00
16 Vinny Testaverde .40 1.00
17 Drew Brees .75 2.00
18 Kordell Stewart .40 1.00
19 Kerry Collins .40 1.00
20 Kurt Warner .50 1.25
21 Rich Gannon .40 1.00
22 Jeff Garcia .40 1.00
23 Shaun Alexander .40 1.00
24 Doug Flutie .50 1.25
25 Donovan McNabb .50 1.25
26 Steve McNair .50 1.25
27 Michael Bennett .40 1.00
28 Jamal Lewis .40 1.00
29 Marshall Faulk .50 1.25
30 Curtis Martin .50 1.25
31 James Jackson .30 .75
32 Terrell Davis .50 1.25
33 Travis Henry .30 .75
34 Corey Dillon .40 1.00
35 Deuce McAllister .40 1.00
36 Priest Holmes .50 1.25
37 Antowain Smith .40 1.00
38 Anthony Thomas .40 1.00
39 Ricky Williams .40 1.00
40 Charlie Garner .40 1.00
41 Jerome Bettis .50 1.25
42 Ahman Green .40 1.00
43 Emmitt Smith 1.25 3.00
44 Edgerrin James .40 1.00
45 Warrick Dunn .40 1.00
46 LaDainian Tomlinson .60 1.50
47 Fred Taylor .40 1.00
48 Eddie George .40 1.00
49 Garrison Hearst .40 1.00
50 Stephen Davis .40 1.00
51 Snoop Minnis .30 .75
52 Troy Brown .40 1.00
53 Cris Carter .50 1.25
54 Jerry Rice 1.00 2.50
55 Terry Glenn .40 1.00
56 Plaxico Burress .40 1.00
57 David Boston .30 .75
58 Marvin Harrison .50 1.25
59 Randy Moss .50 1.25
60 Eric Moulds .40 1.00
61 Rod Smith .40 1.00
62 Freddie Mitchell .30 .75
63 Chris Chambers .40 1.00
64 Keyshawn Johnson .40 1.00
65 Terrell Owens .50 1.25
66 Isaac Bruce .50 1.25
67 Tim Brown .50 1.25
68 Tony Gonzalez .50 1.25
69 Jevon Kearse .40 1.00
70 Warren Sapp .40 1.00
71 Junior Seau .50 1.25
72 Michael Strahan .50 1.25
73 Ray Lewis .50 1.25
74 Zach Thomas .50 1.25
75 Brian Urlacher .50 1.25
76 Quentin Jammer RC 2.00 5.00
77 Kurt Kittner RC 1.25 3.00
78 Chad Hutchinson RC 1.25 3.00
79 Randy Fasani RC 1.50 4.00
80 Lamar Gordon RC 1.50 4.00
81 Brian Westbrook RC 3.00 8.00
82 Josh Scobey RC 1.50 4.00
83 Chester Taylor RC 2.00 5.00
84 Luke Staley RC 1.25 3.00
85 Deion Branch RC 2.00 5.00
86 Terry Charles RC 1.25 3.00
87 Kahlil Hill RC 1.25 3.00
88 Freddie Milons RC 1.25 3.00
89 Woody Dantzler RC 1.50 4.00
90 Kelly Campbell RC 1.50 4.00
91 Dwight Freeney RC 2.50 6.00
92 Bryan Thomas RC 1.25 3.00
93 Ryan Sims RC 2.00 5.00
94 John Henderson RC 1.50 4.00
95 Wendell Bryant RC 1.25 3.00
96 Albert Haynesworth RC 2.00 5.00
97 Phillip Buchanon RC 2.00 5.00
98 Lito Sheppard RC 2.00 5.00
99 Ed Reed RC 7.50 15.00
100 Napoleon Harris RC 1.50 4.00
101 David Carr JSY RC 4.00 10.00
102 Rohan Davey JSY RC 4.00 10.00
103 Joey Harrington JSY RC 4.00 10.00
104 Josh McCown JSY RC 4.00 10.00
105 Patrick Ramsey JSY RC 4.00 10.00
106 Ladell Betts JSY RC 4.00 10.00
107 T.J. Duckett JSY RC 4.00 10.00
108 DeShaun Foster JSY RC 4.00 10.00
109 William Green JSY RC 3.00 8.00
110 Maurice Morris JSY RC 3.00 8.00
111 Clinton Portis JSY RC 5.00 12.00
112 Travis Stephens JSY RC 2.50 6.00
113 Antonio Bryant JSY RC 4.00 10.00
114 Reche Caldwell JSY RC 4.00 10.00
115 Tim Carter JSY RC 3.00 8.00
116 Eric Crouch JSY RC 4.00 10.00
117 Andre Davis JSY RC 3.00 8.00
118 Jabar Gaffney JSY RC 4.00 10.00
119 Ron Johnson JSY RC 3.00 8.00
120 Ashley Lelie JSY RC 3.00 8.00
121 Antwaan Randle El JSY RC 4.00 10.00
122 Josh Reed JSY RC 3.00 8.00
123 Cliff Russell JSY RC 2.50 6.00
124 Donte Stallworth JSY RC 4.00 10.00
125 Javon Walker JSY RC 4.00 10.00
126 Marquise Walker JSY RC 2.50 6.00
127 Jeremy Shockey JSY RC 6.00 15.00
128 Daniel Graham JSY RC 3.00 8.00
129 David Garrard JSY RC 5.00 12.00
130 Roy Williams JSY RC 4.00 10.00
131 Julius Peppers JSY RC 8.00 20.00
132 Mike Williams JSY RC 2.50 6.00

2002 Playoff Piece of the Game Materials

59-63 DUAL PLAYER PRINT RUN 500
64-68 DUAL SWATCH PRINT RUN 250
*1-58 1st DOWN/250: .5X TO 1.2X
*59-63 1st DOWN/100: .5X TO 1.2X
*64-68 1st DOWN/50: .6X TO 1.5X
FIRST DOWN PRINT RUN 50-250
*1-58 2nd DOWN/150: .6X TO 1.5X
*59-63 2nd DOWN/50: .6X TO 1.5X
*64-68 2nd DOWN/25 : 1X TO 2.5X
SECOND DOWN PRINT RUN 25-150
*1-58 3rd DOWN/50: .8X TO 2X
*59-63 3rd DOWN/25 : 1X TO 2.5X
64-68 3rd DOWN/10 NOT PRICED
THIRD DOWN PRINT RUN 10-50
*1-58 4th DOWN/25 : 1.2X TO 3X
64-68 4th DOWN/5 NOT PRICED
OVERALL MATERIAL ODDS ONE PER PACK
1F Ahman Green FB 3.00 8.00
1J Ahman Green JSY SP 4.00 10.00
2F Antonio Freeman FB 4.00 10.00
2J Antonio Freeman JSY 4.00 10.00
3J Barry Sanders JSY 8.00 20.00
4F Brett Favre FB 10.00 25.00
4J Brett Favre JSY 10.00 25.00
5F Brian Griese FB 3.00 8.00
5J Brian Griese JSY 3.00 8.00
6J Charles Woodson JSY 4.00 10.00
7F Chris Chambers FB 3.00 8.00
7J Chris Chambers JSY 3.00 8.00
8F Corey Dillon FB 3.00 8.00
8J Corey Dillon JSY 3.00 8.00
9J Cory Schlesinger JSY 2.50 6.00
10F Cris Carter FB 4.00 10.00
10J Cris Carter JSY 4.00 10.00
11F Curtis Martin FB SP 5.00 12.00
11J Curtis Martin JSY 4.00 10.00
11P Curtis Martin Pants 4.00 10.00
12J Dan Marino JSY 12.00 30.00
13J Darren Woodson JSY 3.00 8.00
14F Daunte Culpepper FB 3.00 8.00
14J Daunte Culpepper JSY 3.00 8.00
15F David Boston FB SP 3.00 8.00
15J David Boston JSY 2.50 6.00
15P David Boston Pants 2.50 6.00
16F Donovan McNabb FB SP 5.00 12.00
16J Donovan McNabb JSY 4.00 10.00
17J Ed McCaffrey JSY 3.00 8.00
18F Eddie George FB 3.00 8.00
18J Eddie George JSY 3.00 8.00
19F Edgerrin James FB 3.00 8.00
19J Edgerrin James JSY 3.00 8.00
20F Emmitt Smith FB SP 12.00 30.00
20J Emmitt Smith JSY 10.00 25.00
21P Frank Wycheck Pants SP 3.00 8.00
22J Fred Taylor JSY 3.00 8.00
23J Isaac Bruce JSY 4.00 10.00
24J Jake Plummer JSY 3.00 8.00
24P Jake Plummer Pants 3.00 8.00
25F Jeff Garcia FB SP 4.00 10.00
25J Jeff Garcia JSY 3.00 8.00
26J Jerome Bettis JSY SP 5.00 12.00
27J Jerry Rice JSY 8.00 20.00
28J Jevon Kearse JSY 3.00 8.00
29J Jim Kelly JSY 6.00 15.00
30J Jimmy Smith JSY SP 4.00 10.00
31J John Elway JSY 10.00 25.00
32J Junior Seau JSY 4.00 10.00
33J Kevin Johnson JSY 2.50 6.00
33P Kevin Johnson Pants 2.50 6.00
34J Kordell Stewart JSY 3.00 8.00
35F Kurt Warner FB SP 5.00 12.00
35J Kurt Warner JSY 4.00 10.00
35P Kurt Warner Pants 4.00 10.00
36F LaDainian Tomlinson FB 5.00 12.00
36J LaDainian Tomlinson JSY 5.00 12.00
37J Mark Brunell JSY 3.00 8.00
38J Marshall Faulk JSY 4.00 10.00
39F Marvin Harrison FB 4.00 10.00
39J Marvin Harrison JSY 4.00 10.00
40J Michael Irvin JSY 5.00 12.00
41J Mike Alstott JSY 3.00 8.00
42J Peyton Manning JSY SP 10.00 25.00
43F Randy Moss FB 4.00 10.00
43J Randy Moss JSY 4.00 10.00
44F Rich Gannon FB 3.00 8.00
44J Rich Gannon JSY 3.00 8.00
45F Ron Dayne FB SP 4.00 10.00
45J Ron Dayne JSY 3.00 8.00
46F Stephen Davis FB 3.00 8.00
46J Stephen Davis JSY 3.00 8.00
47F Steve McNair FB 4.00 10.00
47J Steve McNair JSY 4.00 10.00
48J Steve Young JSY 6.00 15.00
49F Terrell Davis FB 4.00 10.00
49J Terrell Davis JSY 4.00 10.00
50F Terrell Owens FB 4.00 10.00
50J Terrell Owens JSY 4.00 10.00
51J Thurman Thomas JSY 4.00 10.00
52F Tim Brown FB 4.00 10.00
52J Tim Brown JSY 4.00 10.00
53F Tim Couch FB SP 3.00 8.00
53J Tim Couch JSY 2.50 6.00
54F Tony Gonzalez FB 4.00 10.00
54J Tony Gonzalez JSY 4.00 10.00
55J Troy Aikman JSY 8.00 20.00
56F Vinny Testaverde FB 3.00 8.00
56J Vinny Testaverde JSY 3.00 8.00
57J Warren Sapp JSY 3.00 8.00
58J Zach Thomas JSY 4.00 10.00
59J Steve McNair JSY 6.00 15.00
Eddie George JSY/500
60J Brian Griese JSY 6.00 15.00
Terrell Davis JSY/500
61J Peyton Manning JSY 12.00 30.00
Edgerrin James JSY/500
62J Kurt Warner JSY 6.00 15.00
Marshall Faulk JSY/500
63J Troy Aikman JSY 15.00 40.00
Emmitt Smith JSY/500
64J Cris Carter JSY/250 6.00 15.00
65J Jeff Garcia JSY/250 5.00 12.00
66J Emmitt Smith JSY/250 15.00 40.00
67J Kurt Warner JSY/250 6.00 15.00
68J Randy Moss JSY/250 6.00 15.00

2001 Playoff Preferred Samples

*SILVERS: .5X TO 1.2X BASE CARDS
*GOLD: 1X TO 2.5X SILVER

2001 Playoff Preferred

Released as a 225-card set, this product was issued 12 packs per box, with three cards per pack. This set includes 100 veterans and 125 rookies. The first 100 rookies are serial numbered to 1100, and the remaining rookies have stated print runs numbered to 400, 600, or 750. Those shorter printed cards have swatches of game used jerseys or footballs on the card front.

COMP.SET w/o RC's (100) 30.00 60.00
1 Elvis Grbac .40 1.00
2 Ray Lewis .50 1.25
3 Travis Taylor .30 .75
4 Rob Johnson .40 1.00
5 Eric Moulds .40 1.00
6 Corey Dillon .40 1.00
7 Peter Warrick .40 1.00
8 Tim Couch .30 .75
9 Kevin Johnson .30 .75
10 Brian Griese .40 1.00
11 Mike Anderson .40 1.00
12 Rod Smith .40 1.00
13 Terrell Davis .50 1.25
14 Olandis Gary .30 .75
15 Peyton Manning 1.25 3.00
16 Edgerrin James .50 1.25
17 Marvin Harrison .50 1.25
18 Terrence Wilkins .30 .75
19 Mark Brunell .40 1.00
20 Fred Taylor .50 1.25
21 Keenan McCardell .40 1.00
22 Jimmy Smith .40 1.00
23 Stacey Mack .30 .75
24 Trent Green .50 1.25
25 Priest Holmes .50 1.25
26 Tony Gonzalez .50 1.25
27 Jay Fiedler .40 1.00
28 Lamar Smith .40 1.00
29 Zach Thomas .50 1.25
30 Drew Bledsoe .50 1.25
31 Antowain Smith .40 1.00
32 Troy Brown .40 1.00
33 Tom Brady 4.00 10.00
34 Vinny Testaverde .40 1.00
35 Wayne Chrebet .40 1.00
36 Curtis Martin .50 1.25
37 Rich Gannon .40 1.00
38 Tyrone Wheatley .40 1.00
39 Jerry Rice 1.00 2.50
40 Tim Brown .50 1.25
41 Charles Woodson .50 1.25
42 Charlie Garner .40 1.00
43 Kordell Stewart .40 1.00
44 Jerome Bettis .50 1.25
45 Doug Flutie .50 1.25
46 Junior Seau .50 1.25
47 Matt Hasselbeck .50 1.25
48 Trent Dilfer .40 1.00
49 Shaun Alexander .50 1.25
50 Ricky Watters .40 1.00
51 Eddie George .50 1.25
52 Steve McNair .50 1.25
53 Jevon Kearse .40 1.00
54 David Boston .30 .75
55 Jake Plummer .40 1.00
56 Chris Chandler .40 1.00
57 Maurice Smith .30 .75
58 Muhsin Muhammad .40 1.00
59 Wesley Walls .30 .75
60 James Allen .30 .75
61 Marcus Robinson .40 1.00
62 Brian Urlacher .60 1.50
63 Clint Stoerner .40 1.00
64 Ryan Leaf .30 .75
65 Emmitt Smith 1.25 3.00
66 Joey Galloway .40 1.00
67 Charlie Batch .40 1.00
68 James Stewart .30 .75
69 Brett Favre 1.50 4.00
70 Ahman Green .50 1.25
71 Bill Schroeder .40 1.00
72 Bubba Franks .40 1.00
73 Daunte Culpepper .40 1.00
74 Randy Moss .50 1.25
75 Cris Carter .50 1.25
76 Aaron Brooks .40 1.00
77 Ricky Williams .50 1.25
78 Albert Connell .30 .75
79 Kerry Collins .40 1.00
80 Ron Dayne .40 1.00
81 Jason Sehorn .40 1.00
82 Amani Toomer .40 1.00
83 Donovan McNabb .50 1.25
84 James Thrash .40 1.00
85 Duce Staley .40 1.00
86 Jeff Garcia .40 1.00
87 Garrison Hearst .40 1.00
88 Terrell Owens .50 1.25
89 Kurt Warner .75 2.00
90 Marshall Faulk .50 1.25
91 Torry Holt .40 1.00
92 Isaac Bruce .50 1.25
93 Brad Johnson .40 1.00
94 Warrick Dunn .50 1.25
95 Mike Alstott .40 1.00
96 Keyshawn Johnson .40 1.00
97 Warren Sapp .40 1.00
98 Tony Banks .30 .75
99 Stephen Davis .40 1.00
100 Champ Bailey .50 1.25
101 Michael Vick RC 8.00 20.00
102 Drew Brees RC 10.00 25.00
103 Marques Tuiasosopo RC 1.25 3.00
104 Sage Rosenfels RC 1.50 4.00
105 Jesse Palmer RC 1.25 3.00
106 Mike McMahon RC 1.25 3.00
107 A.J. Feeley RC 1.25 3.00
108 Josh Booty RC 1.25 3.00
109 Josh Heupel RC 1.50 4.00
110 Henry Burris RC 1.50 4.00
111 Roderick Robinson RC 1.00 2.50
112 Tory Woodbury RC 1.00 2.50
113 Dave Dickenson RC 1.25 3.00
114 Deuce McAllister RC 1.50 4.00
115 Michael Bennett RC 1.25 3.00
116 Rudi Johnson RC 1.50 4.00
117 Derrick Blaylock RC 1.25 3.00
118 Dee Brown RC 1.00 2.50
119 Eric Kelly RC 1.00 2.50
120 Dominic Rhodes RC 1.50 4.00
121 Jason Brookins RC 1.50 4.00
122 Nick Goings RC 1.50 4.00
123 Markus Steele RC 1.00 2.50
124 Benjamin Gay RC 1.25 3.00
125 Tony Taylor RC 1.00 2.50
126 Elvis Joseph RC 1.00 2.50
127 Tay Cody RC 1.00 2.50
128 Heath Evans RC 1.25 3.00
129 George Layne RC 1.00 2.50
130 Moran Norris RC 1.00 2.50
131 Jameel Cook RC 1.25 3.00
132 Patrick Washington RC 1.00 2.50
133 Chad Johnson RC 2.50 6.00
134 Santana Moss RC 2.00 5.00
135 Reggie Wayne RC 3.00 8.00
136 Robert Ferguson RC 1.50 4.00
137 Steve Smith RC 3.00 8.00
138 Justin McCareins RC 1.25 3.00
139 Vinny Sutherland RC 1.00 2.50
140 Alex Bannister RC 1.00 2.50
141 Scotty Anderson RC 1.00 2.50
142 Onome Ojo RC 1.00 2.50
143 Darnerien McCants RC 1.25 3.00
144 Eddie Berlin RC 1.00 2.50
145 Cedrick Wilson RC 1.25 3.00
146 Kevin Kasper RC 1.00 2.50
147 T.J. Houshmandzadeh RC 2.00 5.00
148 Reggie Germany RC 1.00 2.50
149 Chris Taylor RC 1.00 2.50
150 Ken-Yon Rambo RC 1.00 2.50
151 Quentin McCord RC 1.25 3.00
152 Andre King RC 1.00 2.50
153 Arnold Jackson RC 1.00 2.50
154 Tim Baker RC 1.00 2.50
155 Drew Bennett RC 1.50 4.00
156 Cedric James RC 1.00 2.50
157 Todd Heap RC 1.50 4.00
158 Alge Crumpler RC 1.50 4.00
159 Sean Brewer RC 1.00 2.50
160 Shad Meier RC 1.00 2.50
161 Brandon Manumaleuna RC 1.25 3.00
162 Tony Stewart RC 1.25 3.00
163 David Martin RC 1.00 2.50
164 Matt Dominguez RC 1.00 2.50
165 Boo Williams RC 1.00 2.50
166 Justin Smith RC 1.50 4.00
167 Andre Carter RC 1.25 3.00
168 Jamal Reynolds RC 1.00 2.50
169 Ryan Pickett RC 1.00 2.50
170 Aaron Schobel RC 1.50 4.00
171 Derrick Burgess RC 1.50 4.00
172 DeLawrence Grant RC 1.00 2.50
173 Karon Riley RC 1.00 2.50
174 Richard Seymour RC 1.50 4.00
175 Marcus Stroud RC 1.25 3.00
176 Casey Hampton RC 1.50 4.00
177 Shaun Rogers RC 1.50 4.00
178 Kris Jenkins RC 1.50 4.00
179 Eric Downing RC 1.00 2.50
180 Kenny Smith RC 1.00 2.50
181 Marcus Bell RC 1.00 2.50
182 Dan Morgan RC 1.25 3.00
183 Kendrell Bell RC 1.50 4.00
184 Tommy Polley RC 1.00 2.50
185 Jamie Winborn RC 1.25 3.00
186 Quinton Caver RC 1.00 2.50
187 Sedrick Hodge RC 1.00 2.50
188 Brian Allen RC 1.00 2.50
189 Torrance Marshall RC 1.00 2.50
190 Willie Middlebrooks RC 1.25 3.00
191 Jamar Fletcher RC 1.00 2.50
192 Ken Lucas RC 1.25 3.00
193 Fred Smoot RC 1.50 4.00
194 Andre Dyson RC 1.00 2.50
195 Anthony Henry RC 1.50 4.00
196 Adam Archuleta RC 1.25 3.00
197 Idrees Bashir RC 1.00 2.50
198 Adrian Wilson RC 4.00 10.00
199 Cory Bird RC 1.25 3.00
200 Jarrod Cooper RC 1.25 3.00
201 LaDainian Tomlinson JSY/400 RC 20.00 50.00
202 Chris Weinke JSY/400 RC 3.00 8.00
203 Anthony Thomas FB/400 RC 4.00 10.00
204 Koren Robinson JSY/400 RC 3.00 8.00
205 James Jackson JSY/400 RC 2.50 6.00
206 Kevan Barlow FB/400 RC 3.00 8.00
207 Quincy Morgan JSY/400 RC 3.00 8.00
208 Nate Clements JSY/400 RC 3.00 8.00
209 Travis Henry JSY/400 RC 3.00 8.00
210 Damione Lewis FB/400 RC 3.00 8.00
211 Snoop Minnis FB/400 RC 2.50 6.00
212 David Terrell FB/600 RC 2.50 6.00
213 Gerard Warren JSY/600 RC 2.50 6.00
214 Chris Chambers JSY/600 RC 3.00 8.00
215 Will Allen FB/750 RC 3.00 8.00
216 Leonard Davis JSY/750 RC 3.00 8.00
217 Travis Minor JSY/750 RC 2.50 6.00
218 Will Peterson FB/750 RC 2.50 6.00
219 Rod Gardner FB/750 RC 2.50 6.00
220 Freddie Mitchell FB/750 RC 2.00 5.00
221 Derrick Gibson FB/750 RC 2.00 5.00
222 Kyle Vanden Bosch JSY/750 RC 3.00 8.00
223 LaMont Jordan FB/750 RC 3.00 8.00
224 Quincy Carter FB/750 RC 2.50 6.00
225 Correll Buckhalter FB/750 RC 3.00 8.00

2001 Playoff Preferred National Treasures Gold

*VETS 1-100: 3X TO 8X BASIC CARDS
1-100 VETERAN PRINT RUN 100
*ROOKIES 101-200: 1.5X TO 4X
101-200 ROOKIE PRINT RUN 50
*ROOKIE JSY: 1.5X TO 4X JSY/FB/400
*ROOKIE JSY: 2X TO 5X JSY/FB/600-750
201-225 ROOKIE JSY PRINT RUN 10

2001 Playoff Preferred National Treasures Silver

*VETS 1-100: 1.2X TO 3X BASIC CARDS
1-100 VETERAN PRINT RUN 400
*ROOKIES 101-200: .8X TO 2X
101-200 ROOKIE PRINT RUN 275
*ROOKIE JSY: 1X TO 2.5X BASE JSY/400
*ROOK.JSY: 1.2X TO 3X BASE JSY/600-750
201-225 ROOKIE JSY PRINT RUN 25

2001 Playoff Preferred Materials

STATED PRINT RUN 100-600
1 Barry Sanders/100 15.00 40.00
2 Dan Marino/100 15.00 40.00
3 Warren Moon/100 10.00 25.00
4 Walter Payton/100 40.00 100.00
5 Brett Favre/100 20.00 50.00
6 Daunte Culpepper/100 5.00 12.00
7 Eddie George/100 6.00 15.00
8 Edgerrin James/100 6.00 15.00
9 Steve McNair/100 6.00 15.00
10 Terrell Owens/100 6.00 15.00
11 Troy Aikman/100 10.00 25.00
12 Randy Moss/100 6.00 15.00
13 Peyton Manning/100 15.00 40.00
14 Emmitt Smith/100 15.00 40.00
15 Marshall Faulk/100 6.00 15.00
16 Jevon Kearse/100 5.00 12.00
17 Jake Plummer/100 5.00 12.00
18 Jim Kelly/100 12.00 30.00
19 Boomer Esiason/250 6.00 15.00
20 John Elway/250 20.00 50.00
21 Brian Griese/250 4.00 10.00
22 Cris Carter/250 5.00 12.00
23 Isaac Bruce/250 5.00 12.00
24 Ricky Williams/250 5.00 12.00
25 Kurt Warner/250 8.00 20.00
26 Corey Dillon/250 4.00 10.00
27 Tyrone Wheatley/250 4.00 10.00

28 Rod Smith/250	4.00	10.00
29 Earl Campbell/400	6.00	15.00
30 Curtis Martin/400	4.00	10.00
31 Donovan McNabb/400	4.00	10.00
32 Lamar Smith/400	3.00	8.00
33 Tim Couch/400	2.50	6.00
34 Mark Brunell/400	3.00	8.00
35 Stephen Davis/400	3.00	8.00
36 Charles Woodson/400	5.00	12.00
37 Eric Moulds/400	3.00	8.00
38 Jay Fiedler/400	3.00	8.00
39 Jason Sehorn/400	3.00	8.00
40 Steve Young/500	8.00	20.00
41 Drew Bledsoe/500	4.00	10.00
42 Mike Alstott/500	3.00	8.00
43 Ron Dayne/500	3.00	8.00
44 Jeff Garcia/500	3.00	8.00
45 Torry Holt/500	3.00	8.00
46 Warren Sapp/500	3.00	8.00
47 Junior Seau/500	4.00	10.00
48 Wayne Chrebet/600	3.00	8.00
49 Jimmy Smith/600	3.00	8.00
50 David Boston/600	2.50	6.00

2001 Playoff Preferred Signatures Bronze

1 A.J. Feeley	5.00	12.00
2 Alan Page	15.00	30.00
3 Andre Carter/75*	6.00	15.00
10 Cedric James	4.00	10.00
11 Charlie Batch	5.00	12.00
12 Chris Barnes	4.00	10.00
13 Chris Chambers	12.50	30.00
16 Corey Dillon/50*	6.00	15.00
17 Damione Lewis	5.00	12.00
18 Dan Alexander	5.00	12.00
19 Dan Fouts/45*	20.00	40.00
21 Dave Dickenson	5.00	12.00
23 Dee Brown	4.00	10.00
24 Derrick Blaylock/45*	6.00	15.00
27 Earl Campbell/30*	20.00	50.00
32 Frank Gifford/37*	20.00	40.00
35 George Blanda/50*	30.00	60.00
39 Joe Montana/25*	75.00	150.00
40 Joe Namath/25*	40.00	80.00
43 Jonathan Carter	4.00	10.00
44 Josh Booty	5.00	12.00
46 Kellen Winslow/50*	8.00	20.00
47 Kevin Kasper/45*	5.00	12.00
50 Larry Csonka/60*	30.00	60.00
51 Lawrence Taylor/52*	35.00	60.00
53 Marshall Faulk25*	20.00	50.00
54 Marvin Harrison/25*	20.00	50.00
56 Onome Ojo/45*	5.00	12.00
58 Ozzie Newsome/25*	10.00	25.00
59 Paul Hornung/25*	20.00	50.00
61 Ray Lewis/25*	40.00	80.00
64 Roger Craig/25*	20.00	50.00
66 Ronnie Lott/25*	15.00	40.00
71 Steve Smith	25.00	60.00
72 Terry Bradshaw/29*	40.00	80.00
73 Tim Brown/50*	15.00	30.00
74 Tommy Polley	4.00	10.00
75 Tony Dorsett/54*	25.00	50.00
76 Tony Gonzalez/25*	12.00	30.00
77 Torry Holt	5.00	12.00
79 Chad Pennington	15.00	40.00
80 Cris Carter/25*	15.00	40.00
81 Laveranues Coles	5.00	12.00
82 Correll Buckhalter	6.00	15.00
83 Jamal Anderson/32*	10.00	25.00
85 Marcus Robinson	5.00	12.00
87 Wesley Walls	4.00	10.00
88 Terrell Owens/25*	25.00	60.00
89 Thurman Thomas/25*	20.00	50.00
90 Doug Johnson	4.00	10.00
91 Ron Dugans	4.00	10.00
93 Kenyatta Walker	4.00	10.00
94 Reggie Germany	4.00	10.00
96 Justin Smith	6.00	15.00
97 Heath Evans	5.00	12.00
100 Alge Crumpler	10.00	25.00
101 Shaun Rogers	6.00	15.00
102 Will Allen	6.00	15.00
103 Moran Norris	4.00	10.00
104 Travis Minor	5.00	12.00
105 Brian Allen/75*	5.00	12.00
109 Anthony Thomas/50*	8.00	20.00
110 James Jackson	4.00	10.00

2001 Playoff Preferred Signatures Silver

STATED PRINT RUN 100 SER.#'d SETS

1 A.J. Feeley	8.00	20.00
2 Alan Page	12.00	30.00
3 Andre Carter	8.00	20.00
5 Archie Manning	20.00	40.00
6 Art Monk	20.00	40.00
11 Charlie Batch	8.00	20.00
13 Chris Chambers	10.00	25.00
14 Chris Taylor	6.00	15.00
16 Corey Dillon	8.00	20.00
17 Damione Lewis	8.00	20.00
18 Dan Alexander	8.00	20.00
19 Dan Fouts	15.00	40.00
21 Dave Dickenson	8.00	20.00
23 Dee Brown	6.00	15.00
28 Boo Williams	6.00	15.00
30 Eric Dickerson	20.00	40.00
31 Fran Tarkenton	20.00	40.00
35 George Blanda	25.00	50.00
43 Jonathan Carter	6.00	15.00
44 Josh Booty	8.00	20.00
50 Larry Csonka	30.00	60.00
52 Marcus Allen	20.00	50.00
58 Ozzie Newsome	10.00	25.00
65 Roger Staubach	50.00	100.00
68 Scotty Anderson	6.00	15.00
69 Sonny Jurgensen	20.00	40.00
70 Steve Largent	20.00	40.00
71 Steve Smith	30.00	80.00
74 Tommy Polley	6.00	15.00
76 Tony Gonzalez	10.00	25.00
77 Torry Holt	8.00	20.00
79 Chad Pennington	10.00	25.00
80 Cris Carter	20.00	40.00
82 Correll Buckhalter	10.00	25.00
85 Marcus Robinson	8.00	20.00
87 Wesley Walls	6.00	15.00
88 Terrell Owens	15.00	40.00
90 Doug Johnson	6.00	15.00
91 Ron Dugans	6.00	15.00
94 Reggie Germany	6.00	15.00
95 Mike McMahon	8.00	20.00
96 Justin Smith	10.00	25.00
97 Heath Evans	8.00	20.00
98 Eddie Berlin	6.00	15.00
100 Alge Crumpler	10.00	25.00
101 Shaun Rogers	10.00	25.00
102 Will Allen	10.00	25.00
103 Moran Norris	6.00	15.00
104 Travis Minor	8.00	20.00
105 Brian Allen	6.00	15.00
108 Alex Bannister	6.00	15.00
100 Anthony Thomas	10.00	25.00
110 James Jackson	6.00	15.00

2001 Playoff Preferred Signatures Gold

STATED PRINT RUN 25 SER.#'d SETS

1 A.J. Feeley	15.00	40.00
2 Alan Page	20.00	50.00
3 Andre Carter	15.00	40.00
4 Archie Griffin	15.00	40.00
6 Art Monk	40.00	100.00
7 Bart Starr	125.00	250.00
8 Bob Griese	40.00	80.00
9 Brian Griese	15.00	40.00
10 Cedric James	12.00	30.00
11 Charlie Batch	15.00	40.00
13 Chris Chambers	25.00	60.00
14 Chris Taylor	12.00	30.00
15 Chris Weinke	15.00	40.00
16 Corey Dillon	15.00	40.00
17 Damione Lewis	15.00	40.00
18 Dan Alexander	15.00	40.00
19 Dan Fouts	25.00	60.00
21 Dave Dickenson	15.00	40.00
22 Deacon Jones	20.00	50.00
25 Don Maynard	20.00	50.00
26 Drew Pearson	20.00	50.00
27 Earl Campbell	40.00	80.00
29 Edgerrin James	20.00	50.00
30 Eric Dickerson	40.00	80.00
31 Fran Tarkenton	50.00	100.00
33 Fred Biletnikoff	20.00	50.00
35 George Blanda	40.00	80.00
36 James Lofton	15.00	40.00
38 Jim Plunkett	20.00	50.00
39 Joe Montana	100.00	200.00
40 Joe Namath	100.00	200.00
41 Joe Theismann	25.00	60.00
42 Johnny Unitas	200.00	350.00
43 Jonathan Carter	12.00	30.00
44 Josh Booty	15.00	40.00
45 Justin McCareins	15.00	40.00
49 Lance Alworth	40.00	80.00
50 Larry Csonka	40.00	80.00
51 Lawrence Taylor	25.00	60.00
54 Marvin Harrison	20.00	50.00
55 Mike Singletary	50.00	100.00
57 Otto Graham	50.00	100.00
60 Paul Warfield	20.00	50.00
61 Ray Lewis	50.00	100.00
63 Rod Gardner	15.00	40.00
64 Roger Craig	20.00	50.00
65 Roger Staubach	75.00	150.00
66 Ronnie Lott	40.00	80.00
67 Sammy Baugh	75.00	150.00
68 Scotty Anderson	12.00	30.00
69 Sonny Jurgensen	25.00	60.00
70 Steve Largent	40.00	80.00
71 Steve Smith	40.00	100.00
72 Terry Bradshaw	75.00	150.00
74 Tommy Polley	12.00	30.00
75 Tony Dorsett	60.00	120.00
76 Tony Gonzalez	20.00	50.00
77 Torry Holt	15.00	40.00
78 Y.A. Tittle	20.00	50.00
79 Chad Pennington	20.00	50.00
80 Cris Carter	20.00	50.00
81 Laveranues Coles	15.00	40.00
82 Correll Buckhalter	20.00	50.00
83 Jamal Anderson	15.00	40.00
85 Marcus Robinson	15.00	40.00
86 Mark Brunell	15.00	40.00
87 Wesley Walls	12.00	30.00
88 Terrell Owens	20.00	50.00
89 Thurman Thomas	30.00	80.00
90 Doug Johnson	12.00	30.00
91 Ron Dugans	12.00	30.00
92 Eddie George	20.00	50.00
93 Kenyatta Walker	12.00	30.00
94 Reggie Germany	12.00	30.00
97 Heath Evans	15.00	40.00
98 Eddie Berlin	12.00	30.00
99 Jerome Bettis	40.00	80.00
100 Alge Crumpler	20.00	50.00
101 Shaun Rogers	20.00	50.00
102 Will Allen	20.00	50.00
103 Moran Norris	12.00	30.00
105 Brian Allen	12.00	30.00
106 Emmitt Smith	125.00	250.00
107 Kurt Warner	40.00	80.00
108 Alex Bannister	12.00	30.00
109 Anthony Thomas	20.00	50.00
110 James Jackson	12.00	30.00

1998 Playoff Prestige Samples

Playoff produced this six-card set to promote the upcoming Prestige football cards. Each card was produced with a textured foil cardfront and resembles the base card of the same player.

COMPLETE SET (6)	3.20	8.00
1 Eddie George	.80	2.00
2 Napoleon Kaufman	.40	1.00
3 Dorsey Levens	.40	1.00
4 Jerome Bettis	.40	1.00
5 Corey Dillon	.80	2.00
6 Terrell Davis	1.20	3.00

1998 Playoff Prestige Hobby

The 1998 Playoff Prestige SSD (signed, sealed, and delivered) set was issued in one series totalling 200-cards and was distributed in five-card packs to the hobby market. The fronts feature borderless color action player photos printed on 30-point etched silver foil stock. A retail version of the product was released at a later date printed on thinner stock with different foil highlights than the hobby version.

COMP.HOBBY SET (200)	40.00	100.00
1 John Elway	3.00	8.00
2 Steve Atwater	.30	.75
3 Terrell Davis	.75	2.00
4 Bill Romanowski	.30	.75
5 Rod Smith	.50	1.25
6 Shannon Sharpe	.50	1.25
7 Ed McCaffrey	.50	1.25
8 Neil Smith	.50	1.25
9 Brett Favre	3.00	8.00
10 Dorsey Levens	.75	2.00
11 LeRoy Butler	.30	.75
12 Antonio Freeman	.75	2.00
13 Robert Brooks	.50	1.25
14 Mark Chmura	.50	1.25
15 Gilbert Brown	.30	.75
16 Kordell Stewart	.75	2.00
17 Jerome Bettis	.75	2.00
18 Carnell Lake	.30	.75
19 Dermontti Dawson	.30	.75
20 Charles Johnson	.30	.75
21 Greg Lloyd	.30	.75
22 Levon Kirkland	.30	.75
23 Steve Young	1.00	2.50
24 Jim Druckenmiller	.30	.75
25 Garrison Hearst	.75	2.00
26 Merton Hanks	.30	.75
27 Ken Norton	.30	.75
28 Jerry Rice	1.50	4.00
29 Terrell Owens	.75	2.00
30 J.J. Stokes	.50	1.25
31 Trent Dilfer	.75	2.00
32 Warrick Dunn	.75	2.00
33 Mike Alstott	.75	2.00
34 Reidel Anthony	.50	1.25
35 Warren Sapp	.50	1.25
36 Elvis Grbac	.50	1.25
37 Kimble Anders	.50	1.25
38 Ted Popson	.30	.75
39 Derrick Thomas	.75	2.00
40 Tony Gonzalez	.75	2.00
41 Andre Rison	.50	1.25
42 Derrick Alexander	.50	1.25
43 Brad Johnson	.75	2.00
44 Robert Smith	.75	2.00
45 Randall McDaniel	.30	.75
46 Cris Carter	.75	2.00
47 Jake Reed	.50	1.25
48 John Randle	.50	1.25
49 Drew Bledsoe	1.25	3.00
50 Willie Clay	.30	.75
51 Chris Slade	.30	.75
52 Willie McGinest	.30	.75
53 Shawn Jefferson	.30	.75
54 Ben Coates	.50	1.25
55 Terry Glenn	.75	2.00
56 Jason Hanson	.30	.75
57 Scott Mitchell	.50	1.25
58 Barry Sanders	2.50	6.00
59 Herman Moore	.50	1.25
60 Johnnie Morton	.50	1.25
61 Mark Brunell	.75	2.00
62 James Stewart	.50	1.25
63 Tony Boselli	.30	.75
64 Jimmy Smith	.50	1.25
65 Keenan McCardell	.50	1.25
66 Dan Marino	3.00	8.00
67 Troy Drayton	.30	.75
68 Bernie Parmalee	.30	.75
69 Karim Abdul-Jabbar	.75	2.00
70 Zach Thomas	.75	2.00
71 O.J. McDuffie	.50	1.25
72 Tim Bowens	.30	.75
73 Danny Kanell	.50	1.25
74 Tiki Barber	.75	2.00
75 Tyrone Wheatley	.50	1.25
76 Charles Way	.30	.75
77 Jason Sehorn	.50	1.25
78 Ike Hilliard	.50	1.25
79 Michael Strahan	.50	1.25
80 Troy Aikman	1.50	4.00
81 Deion Sanders	.75	2.00
82 Emmitt Smith	2.50	6.00
83 Darren Woodson	.30	.75
84 Daryl Johnston	.50	1.25
85 Michael Irvin	.75	2.00
86 David LaFleur	.30	.75
87 Glenn Foley	.50	1.25
88 Neil O'Donnell	.50	1.25
89 Keyshawn Johnson	.75	2.00
90 Aaron Glenn	.30	.75
91 Wayne Chrebet	.75	2.00
92 Curtis Martin	.75	2.00
93 Steve McNair	.75	2.00
94 Eddie George	.75	2.00
95 Bruce Matthews	.30	.75
96 Frank Wycheck	.30	.75
97 Yancey Thigpen UER back Yancy	.30	.75
98 Gus Frerotte	.30	.75
99 Terry Allen	.75	2.00
100 Michael Westbrook	.50	1.25
101 Jamie Asher	.30	.75
102 Marshall Faulk	1.00	2.50
103 Zack Crockett	.30	.75
104 Ken Dilger	.30	.75
105 Marvin Harrison	.75	2.00
106 Chris Chandler	.50	1.25
107 Byron Hanspard	.30	.75
108 Jamal Anderson	.75	2.00
109 Terance Mathis	.50	1.25
110 Peter Boulware	.30	.75
111 Michael Jackson	.30	.75
112 Jim Harbaugh	.50	1.25
113 Errict Rhett	.50	1.25
114 Antowain Smith	.75	2.00
115 Thurman Thomas	.75	2.00
116 Bruce Smith	.50	1.25
117 Doug Flutie	.75	2.00
118 Rob Johnson	.50	1.25
119 Kerry Collins	.50	1.25
120 Fred Lane	.30	.75
121 Wesley Walls	.50	1.25
122 William Floyd	.30	.75
123 Kevin Greene	.50	1.25
124 Erik Kramer	.30	.75
125 Darnell Autry	.30	.75
126 Curtis Conway	.50	1.25
127 Edgar Bennett	.30	.75
128 Jeff Blake	.50	1.25
129 Corey Dillon	.75	2.00
130 Carl Pickens	.50	1.25
131 Darnay Scott	.50	1.25
132 Jake Plummer	.75	2.00
133 Larry Centers	.30	.75
134 Frank Sanders	.50	1.25
135 Rob Moore	.50	1.25
136 Adrian Murrell	.50	1.25
137 Troy Davis	.30	.75
138 Ray Zellars	.30	.75
139 Willie Roaf	.30	.75
140 Andre Hastings	.30	.75
141 Jeff George	.50	1.25
142 Napoleon Kaufman	.75	2.00
143 Desmond Howard	.50	1.25
144 Tim Brown	.75	2.00
145 James Jett	.50	1.25
146 Rickey Dudley	.30	.75
147 Bobby Hoying	.50	1.25
148 Duce Staley	1.00	2.50
149 Charlie Garner	.50	1.25
150 Irving Fryar	.50	1.25
151 Chris T. Jones	.30	.75
152 Tony Banks	.50	1.25
153 Craig Heyward	.30	.75
154 Isaac Bruce	.75	2.00
155 Eddie Kennison	.50	1.25
156 Junior Seau	.75	2.00
157 Tony Martin	.50	1.25
168 Freddie Jones	.30	.75
159 Natrone Means	.50	1.25
160 Warren Moon	.75	2.00
161 Steve Broussard	.30	.75
162 Joey Galloway	.50	1.25
163 Brian Blades	.30	.75
164 Ricky Watters	.50	1.25
165 Peyton Manning RC	10.00	25.00
166 Ryan Leaf RC	1.25	3.00
167 Andre Wadsworth RC	1.00	2.50
168 Charles Woodson RC	1.50	4.00
169 Curtis Enis RC	.60	1.50
170 Fred Taylor RC	2.00	5.00
171 Kevin Dyson RC	1.25	3.00
172 Robert Edwards RC	1.00	2.50
173 Randy Moss RC	6.00	15.00
174 R.W. McQuarters RC	1.00	2.50
175 John Avery RC	1.00	2.50
176 Marcus Nash RC	.60	1.50
177 Jerome Pathon RC	1.25	3.00
178 Jacquez Green RC	1.00	2.50
179 Robert Holcombe RC	1.00	2.50
180 Pat Johnson RC	1.00	2.50
181 Germane Crowell RC	1.00	2.50
182 Tony Simmons RC	1.00	2.50
183 Joe Jurevicius RC	1.25	3.00
184 Mikhael Ricks RC	1.00	2.50
185 Charlie Batch RC	1.25	3.00
186 Jon Ritchie RC	1.00	2.50
187 Scott Frost RC	.60	1.50
188 Skip Hicks RC	1.00	2.50
189 Brian Alford RC	.60	1.50
190 E.G. Green RC	1.00	2.50
191 Jammi German RC	.60	1.50
192 Ahman Green RC	2.50	6.00
193 Chris Floyd RC	.60	1.50
194 Larry Shannon RC	.60	1.50
195 Jonathan Quinn RC	1.25	3.00
196 Rashaan Shehee RC	1.00	2.50
197 Brian Griese RC	2.50	6.00
198 Hines Ward RC	5.00	10.00
199 Michael Pittman RC	2.00	4.00
200 Az-Zahir Hakim RC	1.25	3.00

1998 Playoff Prestige Hobby Gold

*GOLD STARS: 12X TO 30X		
*GOLD RCs: 4X TO 10X		
GOLDS PRINT RUN 25 SERIAL #'d SETS		
165 Peyton Manning	200.00	350.00

1998 Playoff Prestige Hobby Red

COMP.RED SET (200)	300.00	600.00
*RED STARS: 1X TO 2.5X BASIC CARDS		
*RED RCs: .6X TO 1.5X		
RED STATED ODDS 1:3 HOBBY		

1998 Playoff Prestige Retail

COMPLETE SET (200)	40.00	80.00
*RETAIL: .25X TO .5X HOBBY		

1998 Playoff Prestige Retail Green

COMPLETE SET (200)	150.00	300.00
*GREEN VETS: 1.5X TO 3X BASIC RETAIL		
*GREEN ROOKIES: .8X TO 2X BASIC CARDS		

1998 Playoff Prestige Retail Red

COMP.RED SET (200)	150.00	300.00
*RED STARS: 1.5X TO 3X BASIC CARDS		
*RED RCs: .8X TO 2X		
RED STATED ODDS 1:3 RETAIL		

1998 Playoff Prestige 7-Eleven

*STARS: .6X TO 1.5X BASIC RETAIL

1998 Playoff Prestige Alma Maters

COMP.SILVER SET (28)	175.00	350.00
SILVER STATED ODDS 1:17 HOBBY		
*BLUE CARDS: .3X TO .6X SILVERS		
BLUE STATED ODDS 1:25 RETAIL		
1 Brett Favre	15.00	40.00
Michael Jackson		
Pat Carter		
2 Michael Irvin	3.00	8.00
Russell Maryland		
Vinny Testaverde		
3 Warrick Dunn	5.00	12.00
Andre Wadsworth		
Peter Boulware		
4 Deion Sanders	5.00	12.00
Edgar Bennett		
Brad Johnson		
5 Emmitt Smith	12.50	25.00
Fred Taylor		
Reidel Anthony		
6 Antowain Smith	4.00	10.00
Kimble Anders		
Lamar Lathon		
7 Barry Sanders	15.00	40.00
Thurman Thomas		
R.W. McQuarters		
8 Ryan Leaf	7.50	20.00
Drew Bledsoe		
Brian Hansen		
9 Mark Brunell	5.00	12.00
Warren Moon		
Rashaan Shehee		
10 Napoleon Kaufman	5.00	12.00
Corey Dillon		
Jerome Pathon		
11 Peyton Manning	15.00	30.00
Carl Pickens		
Reggie White		
12 Kordell Stewart	3.00	8.00
Rae Carruth		
Michael Westbrook		
13 Curtis Enis	5.00	12.00
Kerry Collins		
O.J. McDuffie		
14 Eddie George	5.00	12.00
Bobby Hoying		
Ricky Dudley		
15 Cris Carter	3.00	8.00
Terry Glenn		
Joey Galloway		
16 Elvis Grbac	3.00	8.00
Jim Harbaugh		
Charles Woodson		
17 John Elway	15.00	40.00
Ed McCaffrey		
Glyn Milburn		
18 Terrell Davis	5.00	12.00
Garrison Hearst		
Robert Edwards		
19 Herschel Walker	10.00	20.00
Andre Hastings		
Hines Ward		
20 Dan Marino	15.00	40.00
Curtis Martin		
Craig Heyward		
21 Troy Aikman	10.00	20.00
J.J. Stokes		
Skip Hicks		
22 Junior Seau	5.00	12.00
Keyshawn Johnson		
Johnnie Morton		
23 Jerome Bettis	3.00	8.00
Tim Brown		
Ricky Watters		
24 Marshall Faulk	7.50	20.00
Darnay Scott		
Az-Zahir Hakim		
25 Bruce Smith	4.00	10.00
Jim Druckenmiller		
Antonio Freeman		
26 Jake Plummer	5.00	12.00
Darren Woodson		
Mario Bates		
27 Herman Moore	5.00	12.00
Tiki Barber		
Charles Way		
28 John Avery	3.00	8.00
Wesley Walls		
Tim Bowens		

1998 Playoff Prestige Award Winning Performers

COMP.SILVER SET (22)	125.00	300.00
SILVER STATED ODDS 1:65 HOBBY		
*BLUE: .25X TO .6X SILVER		
BLUE STATED ODDS 1:97 RETAIL		
1 Terrell Davis	5.00	12.00
2 Troy Aikman	10.00	25.00
3 Brett Favre	20.00	50.00
4 Barry Sanders	15.00	40.00
5 Warrick Dunn	5.00	12.00
6 John Elway	20.00	50.00
7 Jerome Bettis	5.00	12.00
8 Jake Plummer	5.00	12.00
9 Corey Dillon	5.00	12.00
10 Jerry Rice	10.00	25.00
11 Steve Young	6.00	15.00
12 Mark Brunell	5.00	12.00
13 Drew Bledsoe	7.50	20.00
14 Dan Marino	20.00	50.00
15 Kordell Stewart	5.00	12.00
16 Emmitt Smith	15.00	40.00
17 Deion Sanders	5.00	12.00
18 Mike Alstott	5.00	12.00
19 Herman Moore	5.00	12.00
20 Cris Carter	5.00	12.00
21 Eddie George	5.00	12.00
22 Dorsey Levens	5.00	12.00

1998 Playoff Prestige Best of the NFL

COMP.DIE CUT SET (24)	125.00	250.00
DIE CUT STATED ODDS 1:33 HOBBY		
*NON-DIE CUTS: .3X TO .6X DIE CUTS		
NON-DIE CUT STATED ODDS 1:49 RETAIL		
1 Terrell Davis	3.00	8.00
2 Troy Aikman	6.00	15.00
3 Brett Favre	12.50	30.00
4 Barry Sanders	10.00	25.00
5 Warrick Dunn	3.00	8.00
6 John Elway	12.50	30.00
7 Jerome Bettis	3.00	8.00
8 Jake Plummer	3.00	8.00
9 Corey Dillon	3.00	8.00
10 Jerry Rice	6.00	15.00
11 Steve Young	4.00	10.00
12 Mark Brunell	3.00	8.00
13 Drew Bledsoe	5.00	12.00
14 Dan Marino	12.50	30.00
15 Kordell Stewart	3.00	8.00
16 Emmitt Smith	10.00	25.00
17 Deion Sanders	3.00	8.00
18 Mike Alstott	3.00	8.00
19 Herman Moore	2.00	5.00
20 Cris Carter	3.00	8.00
21 Eddie George	3.00	8.00
22 Dorsey Levens	3.00	8.00
23 Peyton Manning	20.00	40.00
24 Ryan Leaf	2.00	5.00

1998 Playoff Prestige Checklists

COMPLETE SET (30)	125.00	250.00
SILVER STATED ODDS 1:17 HOBBY		
*GOLD CARDS: .2X TO .5X SILVERS		
GOLD STATED ODDS 1:17 RETAIL		
1 Troy Aikman	6.00	15.00
2 Drew Bledsoe	5.00	12.00
3 Isaac Bruce	3.00	8.00
4 Mark Brunell	3.00	8.00
5 Cris Carter	3.00	8.00
6 Troy Davis	1.25	3.00
7 Corey Dillon	3.00	8.00
8 Warrick Dunn	3.00	8.00
9 John Elway	12.50	30.00
10 Brett Favre	12.50	30.00
11 Glenn Foley	2.00	5.00
12 Gus Frerotte	1.25	3.00
13 Joey Galloway	2.00	5.00
14 Eddie George	3.00	8.00
15 Byron Hanspard	1.25	3.00
16 Bobby Hoying	2.00	5.00
17 Michael Jackson	1.25	3.00
18 Danny Kanell	2.00	5.00
19 Napoleon Kaufman	3.00	8.00
20 Erik Kramer	1.25	3.00
21 Ryan Leaf	1.50	4.00
22 Peyton Manning	15.00	30.00
23 Dan Marino	12.50	30.00
24 Jake Plummer	3.00	8.00
25 Jerry Rice	6.00	15.00
26 Andre Rison	2.00	5.00
27 Barry Sanders	10.00	25.00
28 Antowain Smith	3.00	8.00
29 Kordell Stewart	3.00	8.00
30 Wesley Walls	2.00	5.00

1998 Playoff Prestige Draft Picks

COMPLETE SILVER SET (33)	50.00	120.00
SILVER STATED ODDS 1:9 HOBBY		
*JUMBOS: .5X TO 1.2X		
SILVER JUMBOS ONE PER HOBBY BOX		
*BRONZE CARDS: .2X TO .5X SILVERS		
BRONZE STATED ODDS 1:9 RETAIL		
*BRONZE JUMBOS: .5X TO 1.2X SILVERS		
BRONZE JUMBOS ONE PER RETAIL BOX		
*BRON.JUMBOS LIM.EDITION: 2X TO 5X SILV.		
BRON.JUMBO LIM.EDITION 50 SER.#'d SETS		
*GREEN CARDS: .4X TO .8X SILVERS		
GREEN ODDS 1 PER SPECIAL RETAIL BOX		
*GREEN JUMBOS: .4X TO .8X BASIC INSERTS		
GREEN JUMBOS ONE PER SPECIAL RET.BOX		
*GREEN LIMIT.EDITION: 4X TO 10X SILVERS		
GREEN LIMIT.EDITION PRINT RUN 25 SETS		
1 Peyton Manning	12.50	25.00
2 Ryan Leaf	1.25	3.00
3 Andre Wadsworth	1.00	2.50
4 Charles Woodson	1.50	4.00
5 Curtis Enis	.60	1.50
6 Fred Taylor	2.00	5.00
7 Kevin Dyson	1.25	3.00
8 Robert Edwards	1.00	2.50
9 Randy Moss	6.00	15.00
10 R.W. McQuarters	1.00	2.50
11 John Avery	1.00	2.50
12 Marcus Nash	.60	1.50
13 Jerome Pathon	1.25	3.00
14 Jacquez Green	1.00	2.50
15 Robert Holcombe	1.00	2.50
16 Pat Johnson	1.00	2.50
17 Germane Crowell	1.00	2.50
18 Tony Simmons	1.00	2.50
19 Joe Jurevicius	1.25	3.00
20 Mikhael Ricks	1.00	2.50
21 Charlie Batch	1.25	3.00
22 Jon Ritchie	1.00	2.50
23 Scott Frost	.60	1.50
24 Skip Hicks	1.00	2.50
25 Brian Alford	.60	1.50
26 E.G. Green	1.00	2.50
27 Jammi German	.60	1.50
28 Ahman Green	2.50	6.00
29 Chris Floyd	.60	1.50
30 Larry Shannon	.60	1.50
31 Jonathan Quinn	1.25	3.00
32 Rashaan Shehee	1.00	2.50
33 Brian Griese	2.50	6.00

1998 Playoff Prestige Honors

COMPLETE SET (3)	40.00	100.00
STATED ODDS 1:3200 HOBBY		
1 Terrell Davis	12.50	30.00
2 Warrick Dunn	10.00	25.00
3 Barry Sanders	25.00	60.00

1998 Playoff Prestige Inside the Numbers

COMP.DIE CUT (18)	150.00	300.00
DIE CUT STATED ODDS 1:49 HOBBY		
*NON-DIE CUTS: .3X TO .6X DIE CUTS		
NON-DIE CUT STATED ODDS 1:72 RETAIL		
1 Barry Sanders	15.00	40.00
2 Terrell Davis	6.00	15.00
3 Jerry Rice	10.00	25.00
4 Kordell Stewart	4.00	10.00
5 Dan Marino	20.00	50.00
6 Warrick Dunn	6.00	15.00
7 Corey Dillon UER (Dillion on front)	6.00	15.00
8 Drew Bledsoe	7.50	20.00
9 Herman Moore	4.00	10.00
10 Troy Aikman	10.00	25.00
11 Brett Favre	20.00	50.00
12 Mark Brunell	6.00	15.00
13 Tim Brown	6.00	15.00
14 Jerome Bettis	6.00	15.00
15 Eddie George	6.00	15.00
16 Dorsey Levens	6.00	15.00
17 Napoleon Kaufman	6.00	15.00
18 John Elway	20.00	50.00

1998 Playoff Prestige Dan Marino Milestone Autographs

COMMON CARD (1-5)	40.00	100.00
STATED ODDS 1:321		
P1 Dan Marino (15-photo Promo sheet)	2.00	5.00

1999 Playoff Prestige EXP

This 200 card retail only set was issued in August, 1999. The set has a rookie subset for the first 40 cards. There is also a special Barry Sanders commemorative card at the end of these listings, that card honors Sanders' chase for the all-time rushing record and was inserted one every 289 packs. Notable Rookie Cards inlcude Tim Couch, Edgerrin James and Ricky Williams.

COMPLETE SET (200)	25.00	50.00
1 Anthony McFarland RC	.40	1.00
2 Al Wilson RC	.50	1.25
3 Jevon Kearse RC	.50	1.25
4 Aaron Brooks RC	.50	1.25
5 Travis McGriff RC	.30	.75
6 Jeff Paulk RC	.30	.75
7 Shawn Bryson RC	.30	.75
8 Karsten Bailey RC	.30	.75
9 Mike Cloud RC	.30	.75
10 James Johnson RC	.30	.75
11 Tai Streets RC	.40	1.00
12 Jermaine Fazande RC	.30	.75
13 Ebenezer Ekuban RC	.30	.75
14 Joe Montgomery RC	.30	.75
15 Craig Yeast RC	.30	.75
16 Joe Germaine RC	.40	1.00
17 Andy Katzenmoyer RC	.40	1.00
18 Kevin Faulk RC	.50	1.25
19 Chris McAlister RC	.40	1.00
20 Sedrick Irvin RC	.30	.75
21 Brock Huard RC	.40	1.00
22 Cade McNown RC	.40	1.00
23 Shaun King RC	.40	1.00
24 Amos Zereoue RC	.40	1.00
25 Dameane Douglas RC	.30	.75
26 D'Wayne Bates RC	.30	.75
27 Kevin Johnson RC	.40	1.00
28 Rob Konrad RC	.30	.75
29 Troy Edwards RC	.40	1.00
30 Peerless Price RC	.40	1.00
31 Daunte Culpepper RC	.50	1.25
32 Akili Smith RC	.40	1.00
33 David Boston RC	.40	1.00
34 Chris Claiborne RC	.30	.75
35 Torry Holt RC	.75	2.00
36 Champ Bailey RC	1.00	2.50
37 Edgerrin James RC	.60	1.50
38 Donovan McNabb RC	1.25	3.00
39 Ricky Williams RC	.75	2.00
40 Tim Couch RC	.50	1.25
41 Charles Woodson RP	.30	.75
42 Skip Hicks RP	.20	.50
43 Brian Griese RP	.25	.60
44 Tim Dwight RP	.25	.60
45 Ryan Leaf RP	.25	.60
46 Curtis Enis RP	.20	.50
47 Charlie Batch RP	.25	.60
48 Fred Taylor RP	.25	.60
49 Peyton Manning RP	1.00	2.50
50 Randy Moss RP	.30	.75
51 Jim Harbaugh	.25	.60
52 Warren Moon	.30	.75
53 Jeff George	.20	.50
54 Rich Gannon	.25	.60
55 Scott Mitchell	.20	.50
56 Kerry Collins	.25	.60
57 Brad Johnson	.25	.60
58 Charles Johnson	.20	.50
59 Chris Calloway	.20	.50
60 Tyrone Wheatley	.25	.60
61 Michael Westbrook	.20	.50
62 Skip Hicks	.20	.50
63 Terry Allen	.25	.60
64 Albert Connell	.20	.50
65 Kevin Dyson	.20	.50
66 Frank Wycheck	.25	.60
67 Yancey Thigpen	.20	.50
68 Steve McNair	.30	.75
69 Eddie George	.25	.60
70 Eric Zeier	.20	.50
71 Jacquez Green	.20	.50
72 Reidel Anthony	.20	.50
73 Warren Sapp	.25	.60
74 Mike Alstott	.30	.75
75 Warrick Dunn	.25	.60
76 Trent Dilfer	.25	.60
77 Ahman Green	.25	.60
78 Joey Galloway	.25	.60
79 Ricky Watters	.25	.60
80 Jon Kitna	.25	.60
81 Amp Lee	.20	.50
82 Isaac Bruce	.30	.75
83 Robert Holcombe	.20	.50
84 Greg Hill	.20	.50
85 Marshall Faulk	.30	.75
86 Trent Green	.25	.60
87 J.J. Stokes	.20	.50
88 Terrell Owens	.30	.75
89 Jerry Rice	.60	1.50
90 Garrison Hearst	.25	.60
91 Steve Young	.40	1.00
92 Junior Seau	.30	.75
93 Mikhael Ricks	.20	.50
94 Natrone Means	.25	.60
95 Ryan Leaf	.25	.60
96 Courtney Hawkins	.20	.50
97 C.Fuamatu-Ma'afala UER	.20	.50
98 Jerome Bettis	.30	.75
99 Kordell Stewart	.25	.60
100 Bobby Hoying	.20	.50
101 Charlie Garner	.25	.60
102 Duce Staley	.25	.60
103 Charles Woodson	.30	.75
104 James Jett	.20	.50
105 Rickey Dudley	.20	.50
106 Tim Brown	.30	.75
107 Napoleon Kaufman	.20	.50
108 Wayne Chrebet	.25	.60
109 Keyshawn Johnson	.25	.60
110 Vinny Testaverde	.25	.60
111 Curtis Martin	.30	.75
112 Joe Jurevicius	.20	.50
113 Tiki Barber	.30	.75
114 Ike Hilliard	.25	.60
115 Kent Graham	.20	.50
116 Gary Brown	.20	.50
117 Lamar Smith	.20	.50
118 Eddie Kennison	.25	.60
119 Cam Cleeland	.20	.50
120 Tony Simmons	.20	.50
121 Ben Coates	.25	.60
122 Darick Holmes	.20	.50
123 Terry Glenn	.25	.60
124 Drew Bledsoe	.30	.75
125 Leroy Hoard	.20	.50
126 Jake Reed	.25	.60
127 Randy Moss	.30	.75
128 Cris Carter	.30	.75
129 Robert Smith	.25	.60
130 Randall Cunningham	.30	.75
131 Lamar Thomas	.20	.50
132 John Avery	.20	.50
133 O.J. McDuffie	.25	.60
134 Dan Marino	1.00	2.50
135 Karim Abdul-Jabbar	.25	.60
136 Rashaan Shehee	.20	.50
137 Derrick Alexander WR	.20	.50
138 Byron Bam Morris	.20	.50
139 Andre Rison	.25	.60
140 Elvis Grbac	.20	.50
141 Tavian Banks	.20	.50
142 Keenan McCardell	.25	.60
143 Jimmy Smith	.25	.60
144 Fred Taylor	.25	.60
145 Mark Brunell	.25	.60
146 Jerome Pathon	.20	.50
147 Marvin Harrison	.30	.75
148 Peyton Manning	1.00	2.50
149 Robert Brooks	.25	.60
150 Mark Chmura	.20	.50
151 Antonio Freeman	.25	.60
152 Dorsey Levens	.25	.60
153 Brett Favre	1.00	2.50
154 Johnnie Morton	.25	.60
155 Germane Crowell	.20	.50
156 Barry Sanders	.75	2.00
157 Herman Moore	.25	.60
158 Charlie Batch	.25	.60
159 Marcus Nash	.20	.50
160 Shannon Sharpe	.30	.75

161 Rod Smith	.25	.60
162 Ed McCaffrey	.25	.60
163 Terrell Davis	.30	.75
164 John Elway	1.00	2.50
165 Ernie Mills	.20	.50
166 Michael Irvin	.30	.75
167 Deion Sanders	.30	.75
168 Emmitt Smith	.75	2.00
169 Troy Aikman	.50	1.25
170 Chris Spielman	.25	.60
171 Terry Kirby	.20	.50
172 Ty Detmer	.25	.60
173 Leslie Shepherd	.20	.50
174 Darnay Scott	.20	.50
175 Jeff Blake	.25	.60
176 Carl Pickens	.25	.60
177 Corey Dillon	.25	.60
178 Bobby Engram	.25	.60
179 Curtis Conway	.25	.60
180 Curtis Enis	.20	.50
181 Muhsin Muhammad	.25	.60
182 Steve Beuerlein	.25	.60
183 Tim Biakabutuka	.25	.60
184 Bruce Smith	.30	.75
185 Andre Reed	.30	.75
186 Thurman Thomas	.30	.75
187 Eric Moulds	.25	.60
188 Antowain Smith	.20	.50
189 Doug Flutie	.30	.75
190 Jermaine Lewis	.20	.50
191 Priest Holmes	.30	.75
192 O.J. Santiago	.20	.50
193 Tim Dwight	.25	.60
194 Terance Mathis	.20	.50
195 Chris Chandler	.25	.60
196 Jamal Anderson	.25	.60
197 Rob Moore	.20	.50
198 Frank Sanders	.20	.50
199 Adrian Murrell	.25	.60
200 Jake Plummer	.25	.60
RR1 Barry Sanders RFR	7.50	20.00

1999 Playoff Prestige EXP Reflections Gold

COMPLETE SET (200)	125.00	250.00
*GOLD STARS: 2X TO 5X BASIC CARDS		
*GOLD RCs: 1.2X TO 3X		
GOLD STATED PRINT RUN 1000 SER.#'d SETS		

1999 Playoff Prestige EXP Reflections Silver

COMPLETE SET (200)	60.00	120.00
*SILVER STARS: 1X TO 2.5X BASIC CARDS		
*SILVER RCs: .6X TO 1.5X		
SILVER PRINT RUN 3250 SERIAL #'d SETS		

1999 Playoff Prestige EXP Alma Maters

COMPLETE SET (30)	50.00	100.00
STATED ODDS 1:25		
AM1 Priest Holmes	1.00	2.50
Ricky Williams		
AM2 Tim Couch	.50	1.25
Dermontti Dawson		
AM3 Terrell Davis	1.00	2.50
Garrison Hearst		
AM4 Troy Brown	2.50	6.00
Randy Moss		
AM5 Barry Sanders	3.00	8.00
Thurman Thomas		
AM6 Emmitt Smith	2.00	5.00
Fred Taylor		
AM7 Doug Flutie	1.00	2.50
Bill Romanowski		
AM8 Brett Favre	3.00	8.00
Michael Jackson		
AM9 Charlie Batch	1.00	2.50
Ron Rice		
AM10 Mark Brunell	1.00	2.50
Chris Chandler		
AM11 Warrick Dunn	1.00	2.50
Deion Sanders		
AM12 Cris Carter	1.00	2.50
Eddie George		
AM13 Drew Bledsoe	1.25	3.00
Ryan Leaf		
AM14 Corey Dillon	1.00	2.50
Napoleon Kaufman		
AM15 Jerome Bettis	1.00	2.50
Tim Brown		
AM16 Marshall Faulk	1.25	3.00
Darnay Scott		
AM17 Tiki Barber	1.00	2.50
Herman Moore		
AM18 Jamal Anderson	1.00	2.50
Chris Fuamatu-Maafala		
AM19 Troy Aikman	2.00	5.00
Cade McNown		
AM20 Brian Griese	1.00	2.50
Charles Woodson		
AM21 Charles Johnson	.60	1.50
Kordell Stewart		
AM22 Kevin Faulk	.50	1.25
Eddie Kennison		
AM23 Donovan McNabb	2.50	6.00
Rob Moore		
AM24 Steve McNair	1.00	2.50
John Thierry		
AM25 Michael Irvin	.60	1.50
Vinny Testaverde		
AM26 Randall Cunningham	1.00	2.50
Keenan McCardell		
AM27 Keyshawn Johnson	1.00	2.50
Junior Seau		
AM28 Karim Abdul-Jabbar	.60	1.50
Skip Hicks		
AM29 Curtis Enis	.60	1.50
O.J. McDuffie		
AM30 Joey Galloway	.60	1.50
Robert Smith		

1999 Playoff Prestige EXP Checklists

COMPLETE SET (31)	50.00	100.00
STATED ODDS 1:25		
CL1 Jake Plummer	.75	2.00
CL2 Chris Chandler	.75	2.00
CL3 Priest Holmes	2.00	5.00
CL4 Doug Flutie	1.25	3.00
CL5 Wesley Walls	.75	2.00
CL6 Curtis Enis	.50	1.25
CL7 Corey Dillon	1.25	3.00
CL8 Kevin Johnson	.60	1.50
CL9 Troy Aikman	2.50	6.00
CL10 Terrell Davis	1.25	3.00
CL11 Barry Sanders	4.00	10.00
CL12 Antonio Freeman	1.25	3.00
CL13 Peyton Manning	4.00	10.00
CL14 Fred Taylor	1.25	3.00
CL15 Andre Rison	.75	2.00
CL16 Dan Marino	4.00	10.00
CL17 Randy Moss	3.00	8.00
CL18 Kevin Faulk	.60	1.50
CL19 Ricky Williams	1.25	3.00
CL20 Joe Montgomery	.40	1.00
CL21 Vinny Testaverde	.75	2.00
CL22 Tim Brown	1.25	3.00
CL23 Duce Staley	1.25	3.00
CL24 Jerome Bettis	1.25	3.00
CL25 Natrone Means	.75	2.00
CL26 Terrell Owens	1.25	3.00
CL27 Joey Galloway	.75	2.00
CL28 Isaac Bruce	1.25	3.00
CL29 Mike Alstott	1.25	3.00
CL30 Eddie George	1.25	3.00
CL31 Skip Hicks	.50	1.25

1999 Playoff Prestige EXP Crowd Pleasers

COMPLETE SET (30)	100.00	200.00
STATED ODDS 1:49		
CP1 Terrell Davis	2.00	5.00
CP2 Fred Taylor	2.00	5.00
CP3 Corey Dillon	2.00	5.00
CP4 Eddie George	2.00	5.00
CP5 Napoleon Kaufman	2.00	5.00
CP6 Jamal Anderson	2.00	5.00
CP7 Tim Couch	.75	2.00
CP8 Emmitt Smith	4.00	10.00
CP9 Deion Sanders	2.00	5.00
CP10 Garrison Hearst	1.25	3.00
CP11 Peyton Manning	6.00	15.00
CP12 Ricky Williams	1.50	4.00
CP13 Barry Sanders	6.00	15.00
CP14 Jerry Rice	4.00	10.00
CP15 Jake Plummer	1.25	3.00
CP16 Tim Brown	2.00	5.00
CP17 Terrell Owens	2.00	5.00
CP18 Dan Marino	6.00	15.00
CP19 Chris Chandler	1.25	3.00
CP20 Drew Bledsoe	2.50	6.00
CP21 Charlie Batch	2.00	5.00
CP22 Mark Brunell	2.00	5.00
CP23 Troy Aikman	4.00	10.00
CP24 John Elway	6.00	15.00
CP25 Jon Kitna	2.00	5.00
CP26 Jerome Bettis	2.00	5.00
CP27 Brett Favre	6.00	15.00
CP28 Steve Young	2.50	6.00
CP29 Randy Moss	5.00	12.00
CP30 Antonio Freeman	2.00	5.00

1999 Playoff Prestige EXP Draft Picks

COMPLETE SET (30)	35.00	70.00
STATED ODDS 1:13		
DP1 Tim Couch	.50	1.25
DP2 Ricky Williams	1.00	2.50
DP3 Donovan McNabb	2.50	6.00
DP4 Edgerrin James	2.00	5.00
DP5 Champ Bailey	.60	1.50
DP6 Torry Holt	1.25	3.00
DP7 Chris Claiborne	.20	.50
DP8 David Boston	.50	1.25
DP9 Akili Smith	.30	.75
DP10 Daunte Culpepper	2.00	5.00
DP11 Peerless Price	.50	1.25
DP12 Troy Edwards	.30	.75
DP13 Rob Konrad	.50	1.25
DP14 Kevin Johnson	.50	1.25
DP15 D'Wayne Bates	.30	.75
DP16 Cecil Collins	.20	.50
DP17 Amos Zereoue	.50	1.25
DP18 Shaun King	.30	.75
DP19 Cade McNown	.30	.75
DP20 Brock Huard	.50	1.25
DP21 Sedrick Irvin	.20	.50
DP22 Chris McAlister	.30	.75
DP23 Kevin Faulk	.50	1.25
DP24 Jevon Kearse	.75	2.00
DP25 Joe Germaine	.30	.75
DP26 Andy Katzenmoyer	.30	.75
DP27 Joe Montgomery	.30	.75
DP28 Al Wilson	.20	.50
DP29 Jermaine Fazande	.30	.75
DP30 Ebenezer Ekuban	.20	.50

1999 Playoff Prestige EXP Performers

COMPLETE SET (24)	100.00	200.00
STATED ODDS 1:97		
PP1 Marshall Faulk	4.00	10.00
PP2 Jake Plummer	2.00	5.00
PP3 Antonio Freeman	3.00	8.00
PP4 Brett Favre	10.00	25.00
PP5 Troy Aikman	6.00	15.00
PP6 Randy Moss	8.00	20.00
PP7 John Elway	10.00	25.00
PP8 Mark Brunell	3.00	8.00
PP9 Jamal Anderson	3.00	8.00
PP10 Doug Flutie	3.00	8.00
PP11 Drew Bledsoe	4.00	10.00
PP12 Barry Sanders	10.00	25.00
PP13 Dan Marino	10.00	25.00
PP14 Randall Cunningham	3.00	8.00
PP15 Steve Young	4.00	10.00
PP16 Carl Pickens	2.00	5.00
PP17 Peyton Manning	10.00	25.00
PP18 Herman Moore	2.00	5.00
PP19 Eddie George	3.00	8.00
PP20 Fred Taylor	3.00	8.00
PP21 Garrison Hearst	2.00	5.00
PP22 Emmitt Smith	6.00	15.00
PP23 Jerry Rice	6.00	15.00
PP24 Terrell Davis	3.00	8.00

1999 Playoff Prestige EXP Stars of the NFL

COMPLETE SET (20)	75.00	150.00
STATED ODDS 1:73		
ST1 Jerry Rice	5.00	12.00
ST2 Steve Young	3.00	8.00
ST3 Drew Bledsoe	3.00	8.00
ST4 Jamal Anderson	2.50	6.00
ST5 Eddie George	2.50	6.00
ST6 Keyshawn Johnson	2.50	6.00
ST7 Kordell Stewart	1.50	4.00
ST8 Barry Sanders	8.00	20.00
ST9 Tim Brown	2.50	6.00
ST10 Mark Brunell	2.50	6.00
ST11 Fred Taylor	2.50	6.00
ST12 Randy Moss	6.00	15.00
ST13 Peyton Manning	8.00	20.00
ST14 Emmitt Smith	5.00	12.00
ST15 Deion Sanders	2.00	5.00
ST16 Troy Aikman	5.00	12.00
ST17 Brett Favre	8.00	20.00
ST18 Dan Marino	8.00	20.00
ST19 Terrell Davis	2.50	6.00
ST20 John Elway	8.00	20.00

1999 Playoff Prestige EXP Terrell Davis Salute

COMPLETE SET (5)	20.00	40.00
COMMON CARD (TD1-TD5)	4.00	10.00
STATED ODDS 1:289		
COMMON AUTO (TD1-TD5)	15.00	40.00
FIRST 150-CARDS WERE AUTOGRAPHED		

1999 Playoff Prestige SSD

This 200 card set was issued in five card packs. The last 50 cards, which feature either the best 1998 rookies (151-160) or 40 key rookies entering the 1999 season (161-200) were inserted at a rate of one every two packs. Notable Rookie Cards include Tim Couch, Edgerrin James and Ricky Williams.

COMPLETE SET (200)	75.00	150.00
COMP.SET w/o SP's (150)	25.00	50.00
1 Jake Plummer	.30	.75
2 Adrian Murrell	.30	.75
3 Frank Sanders	.25	.60
4 Rob Moore	.25	.60
5 Jamal Anderson	.30	.75
6 Chris Chandler	.30	.75
7 Terance Mathis	.25	.60
8 Tim Dwight	.30	.75
9 O.J. Santiago	.25	.60
10 Priest Holmes	.40	1.00
11 Jermaine Lewis	.25	.60
12 Doug Flutie	.40	1.00
13 Antowain Smith	.25	.60
14 Eric Moulds	.30	.75
15 Thurman Thomas	.40	1.00
16 Andre Reed	.40	1.00
17 Bruce Smith	.40	1.00
18 Tim Biakabutuka	.30	.75
19 Steve Beuerlein	.30	.75
20 Muhsin Muhammad	.30	.75
21 Curtis Enis	.25	.60
22 Curtis Conway	.30	.75
23 Bobby Engram	.30	.75
24 Corey Dillon	.30	.75
25 Carl Pickens	.30	.75
26 Jeff Blake	.30	.75
27 Darnay Scott	.25	.60
28 Leslie Shepherd	.25	.60
29 Ty Detmer	.30	.75
30 Terry Kirby	.25	.60
31 Chris Spielman	.30	.75
32 Troy Aikman	.60	1.50
33 Emmitt Smith	1.00	2.50
34 Deion Sanders	.40	1.00
35 Michael Irvin	.40	1.00
36 Ernie Mills	.25	.60
37 John Elway	1.25	3.00
38 Terrell Davis	.40	1.00
39 Ed McCaffrey	.30	.75
40 Rod Smith	.30	.75
41 Shannon Sharpe	.40	1.00
42 Marcus Nash	.25	.60
43 Charlie Batch	.30	.75
44 Herman Moore	.30	.75
45 Barry Sanders	1.00	2.50
46 Germane Crowell	.25	.60
47 Johnnie Morton	.30	.75
48 Brett Favre	1.25	3.00
49 Dorsey Levens	.30	.75
50 Antonio Freeman	.30	.75
51 Mark Chmura	.25	.60
52 Robert Brooks	.30	.75
53 Peyton Manning	1.25	3.00
54 Marvin Harrison	.40	1.00
55 Jerome Pathon	.25	.60
56 Mark Brunell	.30	.75
57 Fred Taylor	.30	.75
58 Jimmy Smith	.30	.75
59 Keenan McCardell	.30	.75
60 Tavian Banks	.25	.60
61 Elvis Grbac	.25	.60
62 Andre Rison	.30	.75
63 Byron Bam Morris	.25	.60
64 Derrick Alexander WR	.25	.60
65 Rashaan Shehee	.25	.60
66 Karim Abdul-Jabbar	.30	.75
67 Dan Marino	1.25	3.00
68 O.J. McDuffie	.30	.75
69 John Avery	.25	.60
70 Lamar Thomas	.25	.60
71 Randall Cunningham	.40	1.00
72 Robert Smith	.30	.75
73 Cris Carter	.40	1.00
74 Randy Moss	.40	1.00
75 Jake Reed	.30	.75
76 Leroy Hoard	.25	.60
77 Drew Bledsoe	.40	1.00
78 Terry Glenn	.30	.75
79 Darick Holmes	.25	.60
80 Ben Coates	.30	.75
81 Tony Simmons	.25	.60
82 Cam Cleeland	.25	.60
83 Eddie Kennison	.30	.75
84 Lamar Smith	.25	.60
85 Gary Brown	.25	.60
86 Kent Graham	.25	.60
87 Ike Hilliard	.30	.75
88 Tiki Barber	.40	1.00
89 Joe Jurevicius	.25	.60
90 Curtis Martin	.40	1.00
91 Vinny Testaverde	.30	.75
92 Keyshawn Johnson	.30	.75
93 Wayne Chrebet	.30	.75
94 Napoleon Kaufman	.25	.60
95 Tim Brown	.40	1.00
96 Rickey Dudley	.25	.60
97 James Jett	.25	.60
98 Charles Woodson	.40	1.00
99 Duce Staley	.30	.75
100 Charlie Garner	.30	.75
101 Bobby Hoying	.25	.60
102 Kordell Stewart	.30	.75
103 Jerome Bettis	.40	1.00
104 Chris Fuamatu-Ma'afala	.25	.60
105 Courtney Hawkins	.25	.60
106 Ryan Leaf	.30	.75
107 Natrone Means	.30	.75
108 Mikhael Ricks	.25	.60
109 Junior Seau	.40	1.00
110 Steve Young	.50	1.25
111 Garrison Hearst	.30	.75
112 Jerry Rice	.75	2.00
113 Terrell Owens	.40	1.00
114 J.J. Stokes	.25	.60
115 Trent Green	.30	.75
116 Marshall Faulk	.40	1.00
117 Greg Hill	.25	.60
118 Robert Holcombe	.25	.60
119 Isaac Bruce	.40	1.00
120 Amp Lee	.25	.60
121 Jon Kitna	.30	.75
122 Ricky Watters	.30	.75
123 Joey Galloway	.30	.75
124 Ahman Green	.30	.75
125 Trent Dilfer	.30	.75
126 Warrick Dunn	.30	.75
127 Mike Alstott	.40	1.00
128 Warren Sapp	.30	.75
129 Reidel Anthony	.25	.60
130 Jacquez Green	.25	.60
131 Eric Zeier	.25	.60
132 Eddie George	.30	.75
133 Steve McNair	.40	1.00
134 Yancey Thigpen	.25	.60
135 Frank Wycheck	.30	.75
136 Kevin Dyson	.25	.60
137 Albert Connell	.25	.60
138 Terry Allen	.30	.75
139 Skip Hicks	.25	.60
140 Michael Westbrook	.25	.60
141 Tyrone Wheatley	.30	.75
142 Chris Calloway	.25	.60
143 Charles Johnson	.25	.60
144 Brad Johnson	.30	.75
145 Kerry Collins	.30	.75
146 Scott Mitchell	.25	.60
147 Rich Gannon	.30	.75
148 Jeff George	.25	.60
149 Warren Moon	.40	1.00
150 Jim Harbaugh	.30	.75
151 Randy Moss RP	.75	2.00
152 Peyton Manning RP	2.50	6.00
153 Fred Taylor RP	.60	1.50
154 Charlie Batch RP	.60	1.50
155 Curtis Enis RP	.50	1.25
156 Ryan Leaf RP	.60	1.50
157 Tim Dwight RP	.60	1.50
158 Brian Griese RP	.60	1.50
159 Skip Hicks RP	.50	1.25
160 Charles Woodson RP	.75	2.00
161 Tim Couch RC	1.50	4.00
162 Ricky Williams RC	2.50	6.00
163 Donovan McNabb RC	4.00	10.00
164 Edgerrin James RC	2.00	5.00
165 Champ Bailey RC	3.00	8.00
166 Torry Holt RC	2.50	6.00
167 Chris Claiborne RC	1.00	2.50
168 David Boston RC	1.25	3.00
169 Akili Smith RC	1.25	3.00
170 Daunte Culpepper RC	1.50	4.00
171 Peerless Price RC	1.25	3.00
172 Troy Edwards RC	1.25	3.00
173 Rob Konrad RC	1.00	2.50
174 Kevin Johnson RC	1.25	3.00
175 D'Wayne Bates RC	1.00	2.50
176 Dameane Douglas RC	1.00	2.50
177 Amos Zereoue RC	1.25	3.00
178 Shaun King RC	1.25	3.00
179 Cade McNown RC	1.25	3.00
180 Brock Huard RC	1.25	3.00
181 Sedrick Irvin RC	1.00	2.50
182 Chris McAlister RC	1.25	3.00
183 Kevin Faulk RC	1.50	4.00
184 Andy Katzenmoyer RC	1.25	3.00
185 Joe Germaine RC	1.25	3.00
186 Craig Yeast RC	1.00	2.50
187 Joe Montgomery RC	1.00	2.50
188 Ebenezer Ekuban RC	1.00	2.50
189 Jermaine Fazande RC	1.00	2.50
190 Tai Streets RC	1.25	3.00
191 James Johnson RC	1.00	2.50
192 Mike Cloud RC	1.00	2.50
193 Karsten Bailey RC	1.00	2.50
194 Shawn Bryson RC	1.00	2.50
195 Jeff Paulk RC	1.00	2.50
196 Travis McGriff RC	1.00	2.50
197 Aaron Brooks RC	1.50	4.00
198 Jevon Kearse RC	1.50	4.00
199 Al Wilson RC	1.50	4.00
200 Anthony McFarland RC	1.25	3.00

1999 Playoff Prestige SSD Spectrum Blue

*STARS: 1.2X TO 3X BASIC CARDS
*RCs: .6X TO 1.5X BASIC CARDS
STATED PRINT RUN 500 SETS

1999 Playoff Prestige SSD Spectrum Gold

*GOLDS: .4X TO 1X SPECTRUM BLUES
STATED PRINT RUN 500 SETS

1999 Playoff Prestige SSD Spectrum Green

*GREENS: .4X TO 1X SPECTRUM BLUES
STATED PRINT RUN 500 SETS

1999 Playoff Prestige SSD Spectrum Purple

*PURPLES: .4X TO 1X SPECTRUM BLUES
STATED PRINT RUN 500 SETS

1999 Playoff Prestige SSD Spectrum Red

*REDS: .4X TO 1X SPECTRUM BLUES
STATED PRINT RUN 500 SETS

1999 Playoff Prestige SSD Alma Maters

COMPLETE SET (30)	100.00	200.00
STATED ODDS 1:17		
*JUMBOS: .3X TO .8X BASIC INSERTS		
JUMBOS ONE PER SSD HOBBY BOX		
AM1 Ricky Williams	2.00	5.00
Priest Holmes		
AM2 Tim Couch	1.00	2.50
Dermontti Dawson		
AM3 Terrell Davis	3.00	8.00
Garrison Hearst		
AM4 Randy Moss	8.00	20.00
Troy Brown		
AM5 Barry Sanders	10.00	25.00
Thurman Thomas		
AM6 Fred Taylor	6.00	15.00
Emmitt Smith		
AM7 Doug Flutie	3.00	8.00
Bill Romanowski		
AM8 Brett Favre	10.00	25.00
Michael Jackson		
AM9 Charlie Batch	3.00	8.00
Ron Rice		
AM10 Mark Brunell	3.00	8.00
Chris Chandler		
AM11 Warrick Dunn	3.00	8.00
Deion Sanders		
AM12 Eddie George	3.00	8.00
Cris Carter		
AM13 Drew Bledsoe	4.00	10.00
Ryan Leaf		
AM14 Corey Dillon	3.00	8.00
Napoloen Kaufman		
AM15 Jerome Bettis	3.00	8.00
Tim Brown		
AM16 Marshall Faulk	4.00	10.00
Darnay Scott		
AM17 Herman Moore	2.00	5.00
Tiki Barber		
AM18 Jamal Anderson	3.00	8.00
Chris Fuamatu-Ma'afala		
AM19 Troy Aikman	6.00	15.00
Cade McNown		
AM20 Brian Griese	3.00	8.00
Charles Woodson		
AM21 Kordell Stewart	2.00	5.00
Charles Johnson		
AM22 Kevin Faulk	1.00	2.50
Eddie Kennison		
AM23 Donovan McNabb	5.00	12.00
Rob Moore		
AM24 Steve McNair	3.00	8.00
John Thierry		
AM25 Vinny Testaverde	2.00	5.00
Michael Irvin		
AM26 Randall Cunningham	3.00	8.00
Keenan McCardell		
AM27 Keyshawn Johnson	3.00	8.00
Junior Seau		
AM28 Skip Hicks	2.00	5.00
Karim Abdul-Jabbar		
AM29 Curtis Enis	2.00	5.00
O.J. McDuffie		
AM30 Joey Galloway	2.00	5.00
Robert Smith		

1999 Playoff Prestige SSD Checklists

COMPLETE SET (31)	100.00	200.00
STATED ODDS 1:17		
CL1 Jake Plummer	1.25	3.00
CL2 Chris Chandler	1.25	3.00
CL3 Priest Holmes	3.00	8.00
CL4 Doug Flutie	2.00	5.00
CL5 Wesley Walls	1.25	3.00
CL6 Curtis Enis	.75	2.00
CL7 Corey Dillon	2.00	5.00
CL8 Kevin Johnson	1.50	4.00
CL9 Troy Aikman	5.00	12.00
CL10 Terrell Davis	2.00	5.00
CL11 Barry Sanders	8.00	20.00
CL12 Antonio Freeman	2.00	5.00
CL13 Peyton Manning	8.00	20.00
CL14 Fred Taylor	2.00	5.00
CL15 Byron Bam Morris	.75	2.00
CL16 Dan Marino	8.00	20.00
CL17 Randy Moss	6.00	15.00
CL18 Kevin Faulk	1.50	4.00
CL19 Ricky Williams	2.50	6.00
CL20 Joe Montgomery	1.25	3.00
CL21 Vinny Testaverde	1.25	3.00
CL22 Tim Brown	2.00	5.00
CL23 Duce Staley	2.00	5.00
CL24 Jerome Bettis	2.00	5.00
CL25 Natrone Means	1.25	3.00
CL26 Terrell Owens	2.00	5.00
CL27 Joey Galloway	1.25	3.00
CL28 Isaac Bruce	2.00	5.00
CL29 Mike Alstott	2.00	5.00
CL30 Eddie George	2.00	5.00
CL31 Skip Hicks	.75	2.00

1999 Playoff Prestige SSD Checklists Autographs

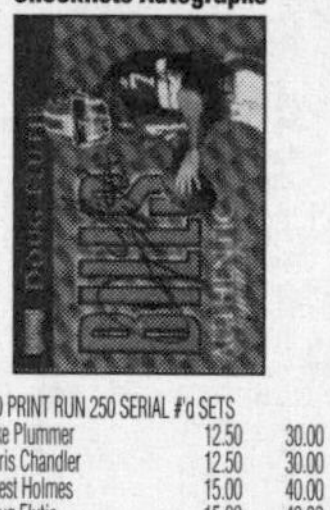

STATED PRINT RUN 250 SERIAL #'d SETS		
CL1 Jake Plummer	12.50	30.00
CL2 Chris Chandler	12.50	30.00
CL3 Priest Holmes	15.00	40.00
CL4 Doug Flutie	15.00	40.00
CL5 Wesley Walls	7.50	20.00
CL6 Cade McNown	7.50	20.00
CL7 Corey Dillon	15.00	40.00
CL8 Kevin Johnson	7.50	20.00
CL9 Troy Aikman	40.00	80.00
CL10 Terrell Davis	15.00	40.00
CL11 Barry Sanders	50.00	100.00
CL12 Antonio Freeman	12.50	30.00
CL13 Peyton Manning	60.00	120.00
CL14 Fred Taylor	15.00	40.00
CL15 Byron Bam Morris SP	7.50	20.00
CL16 Dan Marino	60.00	120.00
CL17 Randy Moss	40.00	80.00
CL18 Kevin Faulk	12.50	30.00
CL19 Ricky Williams	15.00	40.00
CL20 Joe Montgomery	7.50	20.00
CL21 Vinny Testaverde	12.50	30.00
CL22 Tim Brown	15.00	40.00
CL23 Duce Staley	15.00	40.00
CL24 Jerome Bettis	40.00	80.00
CL25 Natrone Means	12.50	30.00
CL26 Terrell Owens	15.00	40.00
CL27 Joey Galloway	12.50	30.00
CL28 Isaac Bruce	15.00	40.00
CL29 Mike Alstott	15.00	40.00
CL30 Eddie George	15.00	40.00

1999 Playoff Prestige SSD Draft Picks

COMPLETE SET (30)	75.00	150.00
STATED ODDS 1:9		
DP1 Tim Couch	1.50	4.00
DP2 Ricky Williams	2.50	6.00
DP3 Donovan McNabb	6.00	15.00
DP4 Edgerrin James	5.00	12.00
DP5 Champ Bailey	2.00	5.00
DP6 Torry Holt	3.00	8.00
DP7 Chris Claiborne	.75	2.00
DP8 David Boston	1.50	4.00
DP9 Akili Smith	.60	1.50
DP10 Daunte Culpepper	5.00	12.00
DP11 Peerless Price	1.50	4.00
DP12 Troy Edwards	1.25	3.00
DP13 Rob Konrad	1.50	4.00
DP14 Kevin Johnson	1.50	4.00
DP15 D'Wayne Bates	1.25	3.00
DP16 Cecil Collins	.75	2.00
DP17 Amos Zereoue	1.50	4.00
DP18 Shaun King	1.25	3.00
DP19 Cade McNown	1.25	3.00
DP20 Brock Huard	1.50	4.00
DP21 Sedrick Irvin	.75	2.00
DP22 Chris McAlister	1.25	3.00
DP23 Kevin Faulk	1.50	4.00
DP24 Jevon Kearse	2.00	5.00
DP25 Joe Germaine	1.25	3.00
DP26 Andy Katzenmoyer	1.25	3.00
DP27 Joe Montgomery	1.25	3.00
DP28 Al Wilson	1.25	3.00
DP29 Jermaine Fazande	1.25	3.00
DP30 Ebenezer Ekuban	1.25	3.00

1999 Playoff Prestige SSD For the Record

COMPLETE SET (30)	300.00	600.00
STATED ODDS 1:161		
FR1 Mark Brunell	6.00	15.00
FR2 Jerry Rice	15.00	40.00
FR3 Peyton Manning	25.00	60.00
FR4 Barry Sanders	25.00	60.00
FR5 Deion Sanders	6.00	15.00
FR6 Eddie George	6.00	15.00
FR7 Corey Dillon	6.00	15.00
FR8 Jerome Bettis	6.00	15.00
FR9 Curtis Martin	6.00	15.00
FR10 Ricky Williams	8.00	20.00
FR11 Jake Plummer	4.00	10.00
FR12 Emmitt Smith	15.00	40.00
FR13 Dan Marino	25.00	60.00
FR14 Terrell Davis	6.00	15.00
FR15 Fred Taylor	6.00	15.00
FR16 Warrick Dunn	6.00	15.00
FR17 Steve McNair	6.00	15.00
FR18 Cris Carter	6.00	15.00
FR19 Mike Alstott	6.00	15.00
FR20 Steve Young	10.00	25.00
FR21 Charlie Batch	6.00	15.00
FR22 Tim Couch	5.00	12.00
FR23 Jamal Anderson	6.00	15.00
FR24 Randy Moss	20.00	50.00
FR25 Brett Favre	25.00	60.00
FR26 Drew Bledsoe	10.00	25.00
FR27 Troy Aikman	15.00	40.00
FR28 John Elway	25.00	60.00
FR29 Kordell Stewart	4.00	10.00
FR30 Keyshawn Johnson	6.00	15.00

1999 Playoff Prestige SSD Gridiron Heritage

COMPLETE SET (24)	125.00	300.00
STATED ODDS 1:33		
GH1 Randy Moss	10.00	25.00
GH2 Terrell Davis	3.00	8.00
GH3 Brett Favre	12.50	30.00
GH4 Barry Sanders	12.50	30.00
GH5 Peyton Manning	12.50	30.00
GH6 John Elway	12.50	30.00
GH7 Fred Taylor	3.00	8.00
GH8 Cris Carter	3.00	8.00
GH9 Jamal Anderson	3.00	8.00
GH10 Jake Plummer	2.00	5.00
GH11 Steve Young	5.00	12.00
GH12 Mark Brunell	3.00	8.00
GH13 Dan Marino	12.50	30.00
GH14 Emmitt Smith	8.00	20.00
GH15 Deion Sanders	3.00	8.00
GH16 Troy Aikman	8.00	20.00
GH17 Drew Bledsoe	5.00	12.00
GH18 Jerry Rice	8.00	20.00
GH19 Ricky Williams	5.00	12.00
GH20 Tim Couch	3.00	8.00
GH21 Jerome Bettis	3.00	8.00
GH22 Eddie George	3.00	8.00
GH23 Marshall Faulk	4.00	10.00
GH24 Terrell Owens	3.00	8.00

1999 Playoff Prestige SSD Inside the Numbers

COMPLETE SET (20)	100.00	250.00
OVERALL STATED ODDS 1:49		
IN1 Tim Brown/1012	3.00	8.00
IN2 Charlie Batch/2178	4.00	10.00
IN3 Deion Sanders/226	5.00	12.00
IN4 Eddie George/1294	4.00	10.00
IN5 Keyshawn Johnson/1131	4.00	10.00
IN6 Jamal Anderson/1846	4.00	10.00
IN7 Steve Young/4170	4.00	10.00
IN8 Tim Couch/4275	4.00	10.00
IN9 Ricky Williams/6279	4.00	10.00
IN10 Jerry Rice/1157	10.00	25.00
IN11 Randy Moss/1313	10.00	25.00
IN12 Edgerrin James/1416	15.00	40.00
IN13 Peyton Manning/3739	7.50	20.00
IN14 John Elway/2803	12.50	30.00
IN15 Terrell Davis/2008	4.00	10.00
IN16 Fred Taylor/1213	4.00	10.00
IN17 Brett Favre/4212	10.00	25.00
IN18 Jake Plummer/3737	4.00	10.00
IN19 Mark Brunell/2601	4.00	10.00
IN20 Barry Sanders/1491	15.00	40.00

1999 Playoff Prestige SSD Barry Sanders

COMPLETE SET (10)	350.00	700.00
OVERALL STATED ODDS 1:161		
1 Barry Sanders/89	30.00	80.00
2 Barry Sanders/90	30.00	80.00
3 Barry Sanders/91	30.00	80.00
4 Barry Sanders/92	30.00	80.00
5 Barry Sanders/93	30.00	80.00
6 Barry Sanders/94	30.00	80.00
7 Barry Sanders/95	30.00	80.00
8 Barry Sanders/96	30.00	80.00
9 Barry Sanders/97	30.00	80.00
10 Barry Sanders/98	30.00	80.00

2000 Playoff Prestige

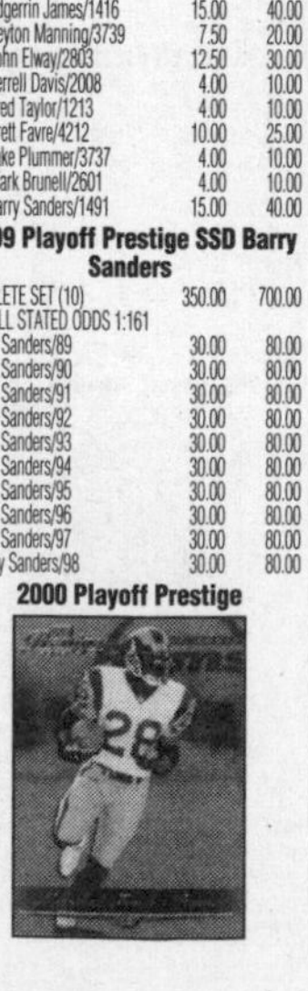

Released in late July of 2000, Prestige features a 300-card base set comprised of 200 base veteran cards, 50 Performer cards sequentially numbered to 2500, and 50 Rookie cards sequentially numbered to 2500. Base cards are on foil board card stock. Prestige was packaged in 16-pack boxes with packs containing six cards.

COMPLETE SET (300)	175.00	350.00
COMP.SET w/o SP's (200)	10.00	25.00
251-300 ROOKIE PRINT RUN 2500		
1 Frank Sanders	.15	.40
2 Rob Moore	.15	.40
3 Michael Pittman	.15	.40
4 Jake Plummer	.20	.50
5 David Boston	.15	.40
6 Chris Chandler	.20	.50
7 Tim Dwight	.20	.50
8 Shawn Jefferson	.15	.40
9 Terance Mathis	.15	.40
10 Jamal Anderson	.20	.50
11 Byron Hanspard	.15	.40
12 Ken Oxendine	.15	.40
13 Priest Holmes	.25	.60
14 Tony Banks	.15	.40
15 Shannon Sharpe	.25	.60
16 Rod Woodson	.25	.60
17 Jermaine Lewis	.15	.40
18 Qadry Ismail	.20	.50
19 Eric Moulds	.20	.50
20 Doug Flutie	.25	.60
21 Jay Riemersma	.15	.40
22 Antowain Smith	.20	.50
23 Jonathan Linton	.15	.40
24 Peerless Price	.20	.50
25 Rob Johnson	.20	.50
26 Muhsin Muhammad	.20	.50
27 Wesley Walls	.15	.40
28 Tim Biakabutuka	.20	.50
29 Steve Beuerlein	.20	.50
30 Patrick Jeffers	.20	.50
31 Natrone Means	.20	.50
32 Curtis Enis	.15	.40
33 Bobby Engram	.20	.50
34 Marcus Robinson	.20	.50
35 Marty Booker	.20	.50
36 Cade McNown	.15	.40
37 Darnay Scott	.20	.50
38 Carl Pickens	.20	.50
39 Corey Dillon	.20	.50
40 Akili Smith	.15	.40
41 Michael Basnight	.15	.40
42 Karim Abdul-Jabbar	.15	.40
43 Tim Couch	.20	.50
44 Kevin Johnson	.15	.40
45 Darrin Chiaverini	.15	.40
46 Errict Rhett	.20	.50
47 Emmitt Smith	.60	1.50
48 Deion Sanders	.25	.60
49 Michael Irvin	.25	.60
50 Rocket Ismail	.20	.50
51 Troy Aikman	.40	1.00
52 Jason Tucker	.15	.40
53 Joey Galloway	.20	.50
54 David LaFleur	.15	.40
55 Wane McGarity	.15	.40
56 Ed McCaffrey	.20	.50
57 Rod Smith	.20	.50
58 Brian Griese	.20	.50
59 John Elway	.60	1.50
60 Gus Frerotte	.20	.50
61 Neil Smith	.15	.40
62 Terrell Davis	.25	.60
63 Olandis Gary	.20	.50
64 Johnnie Morton	.20	.50
65 Charlie Batch	.20	.50
66 Barry Sanders	.50	1.25
67 James Stewart	.15	.40
68 Germane Crowell	.15	.40
69 Sedrick Irvin	.15	.40
70 Herman Moore	.20	.50
71 Corey Bradford	.15	.40
72 Dorsey Levens	.20	.50
73 Antonio Freeman	.20	.50
74 Brett Favre	.75	2.00
75 De'Mond Parker	.15	.40
76 Bill Schroeder	.20	.50
77 Donald Driver	.40	1.00
78 E.G. Green	.15	.40
79 Marvin Harrison	.25	.60
80 Peyton Manning	.60	1.50
81 Terrence Wilkins	.15	.40
82 Edgerrin James	.25	.60
83 Keenan McCardell	.20	.50
84 Mark Brunell	.20	.50
85 Fred Taylor	.25	.60
86 Jimmy Smith	.20	.50
87 Derrick Alexander	.15	.40
88 Andre Rison	.20	.50
89 Elvis Grbac	.15	.40
90 Tony Gonzalez	.25	.60
91 Donnell Bennett	.15	.40
92 Warren Moon	.25	.60
93 Kimble Anders	.15	.40
94 Tony Richardson RC	.20	.50
95 Jay Fiedler	.20	.50
96 Zach Thomas	.25	.60
97 Oronde Gadsden	.20	.50
98 Dan Marino	.75	2.00
99 O.J. McDuffie	.20	.50
100 Tony Martin	.20	.50
101 James Johnson	.15	.40
102 Rob Konrad	.15	.40
103 Damon Huard	.20	.50
104 Thurman Thomas	.25	.60
105 Randy Moss	.25	.60
106 Cris Carter	.25	.60
107 Robert Smith	.20	.50
108 Randall Cunningham	.25	.60
109 John Randle	.20	.50
110 Leroy Hoard	.15	.40
111 Daunte Culpepper	.20	.50
112 Matthew Hatchette	.15	.40
113 Troy Brown	.20	.50
114 Tony Simmons	.15	.40
115 Terry Glenn	.20	.50
116 Ben Coates	.15	.40
117 Drew Bledsoe	.25	.60
118 Terry Allen	.20	.50
119 Kevin Faulk	.20	.50
120 Ricky Williams	.25	.60
121 Jake Delhomme RC	.60	1.50
122 Jake Reed	.20	.50
123 Jeff Blake	.20	.50
124 Amani Toomer	.20	.50
125 Kerry Collins	.20	.50
126 Tiki Barber	.25	.60
127 Ike Hilliard	.20	.50
128 Joe Montgomery	.15	.40
129 Sean Bennett	.15	.40
130 Curtis Martin	.25	.60
131 Vinny Testaverde	.20	.50
132 Wayne Chrebet	.20	.50
133 Ray Lucas	.15	.40
134 Tyrone Wheatley	.15	.40

135 Napoleon Kaufman .20 .50
136 Tim Brown .25 .60
137 Rickey Dudley .15 .40
138 James Jett .20 .50
139 Rich Gannon .20 .50
140 Charles Woodson .25 .60
141 Duce Staley .20 .50
142 Donovan McNabb .25 .60
143 Na Brown .15 .40
144 Kordell Stewart .20 .50
145 Jerome Bettis .25 .60
146 Hines Ward .25 .60
147 Troy Edwards .15 .40
148 Curtis Conway .20 .50
149 Junior Seau .25 .60
150 Jim Harbaugh .20 .50
151 Jermaine Fazande .15 .40
152 Terrell Owens .25 .60
153 J.J. Stokes .20 .50
154 Charlie Garner .20 .50
155 Jerry Rice .50 1.25
156 Garrison Hearst .15 .40
157 Steve Young .30 .75
158 Jeff Garcia .20 .50
159 Derrick Mayes .15 .40
160 Ahman Green .20 .50
161 Ricky Watters .20 .50
162 Jon Kitna .20 .50
163 Karsten Bailey .15 .40
164 Sean Dawkins .15 .40
165 Az-Zahir Hakim .15 .40
166 Isaac Bruce .25 .60
167 Marshall Faulk .25 .60
168 Trent Green .20 .50
169 Kurt Warner .40 1.00
170 Torry Holt .25 .60
171 Robert Holcombe .15 .40
172 Kevin Carter .15 .40
173 Keyshawn Johnson .20 .50
174 Jacquez Green .15 .40
175 Reidel Anthony .15 .40
176 Warren Sapp .20 .50
177 Mike Alstott .25 .60
178 Warrick Dunn .20 .50
179 Trent Dilfer .20 .50
180 Shaun King .15 .40
181 Neil O'Donnell .15 .40
182 Eddie George .20 .50
183 Yancey Thigpen .15 .40
184 Steve McNair .25 .60
185 Kevin Dyson .20 .50
186 Frank Wycheck .20 .50
187 Jevon Kearse .20 .50
188 Adrian Murrell .15 .40
189 Jeff George .20 .50
190 Stephen Davis .20 .50
191 Stephen Alexander .15 .40
192 Darrell Green .20 .50
193 Skip Hicks .15 .40
194 Brad Johnson .20 .50
195 Michael Westbrook .15 .40
196 Albert Connell .15 .40
197 Irving Fryar .20 .50
198 Bruce Smith .25 .60
199 Champ Bailey .20 .50
200 Larry Centers .15 .40
201 Jake Plummer PP .40 1.00
202 Doug Flutie PP .50 1.25
203 Eric Moulds PP .40 1.00
204 Muhsin Muhammad PP .40 1.00
205 Marcus Robinson PP .40 1.00
206 Cade McNown PP .30 .75
207 Corey Dillon PP .40 1.00
208 Tim Couch PP .40 1.00
209 Kevin Johnson PP .30 .75
210 Emmitt Smith PP 1.25 3.00
211 Troy Aikman PP .75 2.00
212 Brian Griese PP .40 1.00
213 Olandis Gary PP .40 1.00
214 Germane Crowell PP .30 .75
215 Brett Favre PP 1.50 4.00
216 Charlie Batch PP .40 1.00
217 Antonio Freeman PP .40 1.00
218 Dorsey Levens PP .40 1.00
219 Peyton Manning PP 1.25 3.00
220 Edgerrin James PP .50 1.25
221 Marvin Harrison PP .50 1.25
222 Fred Taylor PP .50 1.25
223 Mark Brunell PP .40 1.00
224 Jimmy Smith PP .40 1.00
225 Dan Marino PP 1.50 4.00
226 Randy Moss PP .50 1.25
227 Cris Carter PP .50 1.25
228 Robert Smith PP .40 1.00
229 Drew Bledsoe PP .50 1.25
230 Terry Glenn PP .40 1.00
231 Ricky Williams PP .50 1.25
232 Amani Toomer PP .40 1.00
233 Keyshawn Johnson PP .40 1.00
234 Curtis Martin PP .50 1.25
235 Ray Lucas PP .30 .75
236 Tim Brown PP .50 1.25
237 Duce Staley PP .40 1.00
238 Donovan McNabb PP .50 1.25
239 Jerry Rice PP 1.00 2.50
240 Jon Kitna PP .40 1.00
241 Isaac Bruce PP .50 1.25
242 Kurt Warner PP .75 2.00
243 Torry Holt PP .50 1.25
244 Mike Alstott PP .50 1.25
245 Marshall Faulk PP .50 1.25
246 Shaun King PP .30 .75
247 Eddie George PP .40 1.00
248 Steve McNair PP .50 1.25
249 Stephen Davis PP .40 1.00
250 Brad Johnson PP .40 1.00
251 Rondell Mealey RC 1.00 2.50
252 Peter Warrick RC 1.50 4.00
253 Courtney Brown RC 1.25 3.00
254 Plaxico Burress RC 1.50 4.00
255 Corey Simon RC 1.25 3.00
256 Thomas Jones RC 2.00 5.00
257 Travis Taylor RC 1.25 3.00
258 Shaun Alexander RC 2.00 5.00
259 Chris Hedman RC 1.25 3.00
260 Chad Pennington RC 2.50 6.00
261 Jamal Lewis RC 1.50 4.00
262 Bubba Franks RC 1.50 4.00
263 Dez White RC 1.25 3.00
264 Ron Dayne RC 1.50 4.00
265 Sylvester Morris RC 1.00 2.50
266 R.Jay Soward RC 1.00 2.50
267 Sherrod Gideon RC 1.00 2.50
268 Travis Prentice RC 1.25 3.00
269 Darrell Jackson RC 1.25 3.00
270 Giovanni Carmazzi RC 1.00 2.50
271 Anthony Lucas RC 1.00 2.50
272 Danny Farmer RC 1.00 2.50
273 Dennis Northcutt RC 1.25 3.00
274 Troy Walters RC 1.00 2.50
275 Laveranues Coles RC 1.50 4.00
276 Tee Martin RC 1.50 4.00
277 J.R. Redmond RC 1.00 2.50
278 Jerry Porter RC 1.50 4.00
279 Sebastian Janikowski RC 1.50 4.00
280 Michael Wiley RC 1.00 2.50
281 Reuben Droughns RC 1.50 4.00
282 Trung Canidate RC 1.25 3.00
283 Shyrone Stith RC 1.00 2.50
284 Trevor Gaylor RC 1.00 2.50
285 Marc Bulger RC 1.50 4.00
286 Tom Brady RC 40.00 80.00
287 Todd Husak RC 1.00 2.50
288 Jarious Jackson RC 1.25 3.00
289 Terrelle Smith RC 1.00 2.50
290 Chad Morton RC 1.50 4.00
291 Chris Cole RC 1.25 3.00
292 Kwame Cavil RC 1.00 2.50
293 JaJuan Dawson RC 1.00 2.50
294 Curtis Keaton RC 1.00 2.50
295 Tim Rattay RC 1.25 3.00
296 Joe Hamilton RC 1.00 2.50
297 Gari Scott RC 1.00 2.50
298 Mike Anderson RC 1.50 4.00
299 Ron Dugans RC 1.00 2.50
300 Todd Pinkston RC 1.00 2.50

2000 Playoff Prestige Spectrum Green

*VETS 1-200: 20X TO 50X BASIC CARDS
*VET PP 201-250: 10X TO 25X
*ROOKIES 251-300: 3X TO 8X
GREEN PRINT RUN 25 SER.#'d SETS
GREEN/RED OVERALL ODDS 1:28
286 Tom Brady 500.00 800.00

2000 Playoff Prestige Spectrum Red

*VETS 1-200: 8X TO 20X BASIC CARDS
*VET PP 201-250: 4X TO 10X
*ROOKIES 251-300: 1.2X TO 3X
RED PRINT RUN 100 SER.#'d SETS
GREEN/RED OVERALL ODDS 1:28
286 Tom Brady 250.00 400.00

2000 Playoff Prestige Alma Mater Materials

STATED ODDS 1:335
*PATCHES: .6X TO 1.5X BASIC JSY
PATCH STATED ODDS 1:2005
AM1 John Elway 30.00 80.00
AM2 Drew Bledsoe 20.00 50.00
AM3 Ricky Williams 20.00 50.00
AM4 Edgerrin James 20.00 50.00
AM5 Fred Taylor 20.00 50.00
AM6 J.J. Stokes 15.00 40.00
AM7 Eddie George 15.00 40.00
AM8 Frank Wycheck 15.00 40.00
AM9 Tim Biakabutuka 15.00 40.00
AM10 Ryan Leaf 15.00 40.00

2000 Playoff Prestige Award Winning Materials

SINGLE JERSEY PRINT RUN 75
TRIPLE JERSEY PRINT RUN 25
OVERALL STATED ODDS 1:429
AW1 Brett Favre 30.00 80.00
AW2 Barry Sanders 20.00 50.00
AW3 Thurman Thomas 10.00 25.00
AW4 Thurman Thomas 50.00 120.00
Barry Sanders
Brett Favre
AW5 Dan Marino 30.00 80.00
AW6 Steve Young 12.00 30.00
AW7 Kurt Warner 15.00 40.00
AW8 Dan Marino 50.00 120.00
Steve Young
Kurt Warner
AW9 John Elway 25.00 60.00
AW10 Terrell Davis 10.00 25.00
AW11 Phil Simms 10.00 25.00
AW12 John Elway 40.00 100.00
Terrell Davis
Phil Simms
AW13 Troy Aikman 15.00 40.00
AW14 Emmitt Smith 25.00 60.00
AW15 Jerry Rice 20.00 50.00
AW16 Troy Aikman 40.00 100.00
Emmitt Smith
Jerry Rice
AW17 Randy Moss 10.00 25.00
AW18 Eddie George 8.00 20.00
AW19 Jerome Bettis 10.00 25.00
AW20 Randy Moss 15.00 40.00
Eddie George
Jerome Bettis
AW21 Edgerrin James 10.00 25.00
AW22 Curtis Martin 10.00 25.00
AW23 Marshall Faulk 10.00 25.00
AW24 Edgerrin James 15.00 40.00
Curtis Martin
Marshall Faulk

2000 Playoff Prestige Award Winning Performers

COMPLETE SET (24) 25.00 60.00
STATED ODDS 1:31 HOBBY
AW1 Brett Favre 2.50 6.00
AW2 Barry Sanders 1.50 4.00
AW3 Thurman Thomas .75 2.00
AW4 Thurman Thomas 2.50 6.00
Barry Sanders
Brett Favre
AW5 Dan Marino 2.50 6.00
AW6 Steve Young 1.00 2.50
AW7 Kurt Warner 1.25 3.00
AW8 Dan Marino 2.50 6.00
Steve Young
Kurt Warner
AW9 John Elway 2.00 5.00
AW10 Terrell Davis .75 2.00
AW11 Phil Simms .75 2.00
AW12 John Elway 2.00 5.00
Terrell Davis
Phil Simms
AW13 Troy Aikman 1.25 3.00
AW14 Emmitt Smith 2.00 5.00
AW15 Jerry Rice 1.50 4.00
AW16 Troy Aikman 2.00 5.00
Emmitt Smith
Jerry Rice
AW17 Randy Moss .75 2.00
AW18 Eddie George .60 1.50
AW19 Jerome Bettis .75 2.00
AW20 Randy Moss .75 2.00
Eddie George
Jerome Bettis
AW21 Edgerrin James .75 2.00
AW22 Curtis Martin .75 2.00
AW23 Marshall Faulk .75 2.00
AW24 Edgerrin James .75 2.00
Curtis Martin
Marshall Faulk

2000 Playoff Prestige Award Winning Signatures

SINGLE AUTO PRINT RUN 100
TRIPLE AUTO PRINT RUN 25
OVERALL STATED ODDS 1:330
AW1 Brett Favre 125.00 200.00
AW2 Barry Sanders 60.00 120.00
AW3 Thurman Thomas 15.00 40.00
AW4 Thurman Thomas 250.00 400.00
Barry Sanders
Brett Favre
AW5 Dan Marino 100.00 200.00
AW6 Steve Young 30.00 60.00
AW7 Kurt Warner 40.00 80.00
AW8 Dan Marino 250.00 400.00
Steve Young
Kurt Warner
AW9 John Elway 75.00 150.00
AW10 Terrell Davis 15.00 40.00
AW11 Phil Simms 15.00 40.00
AW12 John Elway 150.00 300.00
Terrell Davis
Phil Simms
AW13 Troy Aikman 40.00 100.00
AW14 Emmitt Smith 125.00 250.00
AW15 Jerry Rice 60.00 120.00
AW16 Troy Aikman 300.00 450.00
Emmitt Smith
Jerry Rice
AW17 Randy Moss 40.00 80.00
AW18 Eddie George 12.00 30.00
AW19 Jerome Bettis 50.00 80.00
AW20 Randy Moss 125.00 250.00
Eddie George
Jerome Bettis
AW21 Edgerrin James 15.00 40.00
AW23 Marshall Faulk 15.00 40.00
AW24 Edgerrin James 125.00 250.00
Curtis Martin
Marshall Faulk

2000 Playoff Prestige Draft Picks

COMPLETE SET (10) 15.00 40.00
STATED ODDS 1:8 HOBBY
DP1 Joe Hamilton .40 1.00
DP2 Peter Warrick .60 1.50
DP3 Courtney Brown .50 1.25
DP4 Plaxico Burress .60 1.50
DP5 Thomas Jones .75 2.00
DP6 Travis Taylor .50 1.25
DP7 Shaun Alexander .75 2.00
DP8 Chris Redman .50 1.25
DP9 Chad Pennington 1.00 2.50
DP10 Jamal Lewis .60 1.50
DP11 Bubba Franks .60 1.50
DP12 Dez White .50 1.25
DP13 Ron Dayne .60 1.50
DP14 Sylvester Morris .40 1.00
DP15 R.Jay Soward .40 1.00
DP16 Travis Prentice .50 1.25
DP17 Darrell Jackson .50 1.25
DP18 Giovanni Carmazzi .40 1.00
DP19 Danny Farmer .40 1.00
DP20 Dennis Northcutt .50 1.25
DP21 Laveranues Coles .60 1.50
DP22 J.R. Redmond .40 1.00
DP23 Jerry Porter .60 1.50
DP24 Reuben Droughns .60 1.50
DP25 Trung Canidate .50 1.25
DP26 Trevor Gaylor .40 1.00
DP27 Chris Cole .50 1.25
DP28 Tim Rattay .50 1.25
DP29 Ron Dugans .40 1.00
DP30 Todd Pinkston .40 1.00

2000 Playoff Prestige Human Highlight Film

COMPLETE SET (70) 75.00 150.00
STATED ODDS 1:15H, 1:30R
*GOLD/50: 2X TO 5X BASIC INSERTS
GOLD PRINT RUN 50 SER.#'d SETS
HH1 Randy Moss 1.25 3.00
HH2 Brett Favre 4.00 10.00
HH3 Dan Marino 4.00 10.00
HH4 Barry Sanders 2.50 6.00
HH5 John Elway 3.00 8.00
HH6 Peyton Manning 3.00 8.00
HH7 Terrell Davis 1.25 3.00
HH8 Emmitt Smith 3.00 8.00
HH9 Troy Aikman 2.00 5.00
HH10 Jerry Rice 2.50 6.00
HH11 Fred Taylor 1.25 3.00
HH12 Jake Plummer 1.00 2.50
HH13 Charlie Batch 1.00 2.50
HH14 Drew Bledsoe 1.25 3.00
HH15 Mark Brunell 1.00 2.50
HH16 Steve Young 1.50 4.00
HH17 Eddie George 1.00 2.50
HH18 Mike Alstott 1.25 3.00
HH19 Jamal Anderson 1.00 2.50
HH20 Jerome Bettis 1.25 3.00
HH21 Tim Brown 1.25 3.00
HH22 Cris Carter 1.25 3.00
HH23 Stephen Davis 1.00 2.50
HH24 Corey Dillon 1.00 2.50
HH25 Warrick Dunn 1.00 2.50
HH26 Curtis Enis .75 2.00
HH27 Marshall Faulk 1.25 3.00
HH28 Doug Flutie 1.25 3.00
HH29 Antonio Freeman 1.00 2.50
HH30 Joey Galloway 1.00 2.50
HH31 Terry Glenn 1.00 2.50
HH32 Marvin Harrison 1.25 3.00
HH33 Brad Johnson 1.00 2.50
HH34 Keyshawn Johnson 1.00 2.50
HH35 Jon Kitna 1.00 2.50
HH36 Dorsey Levens 1.00 2.50
HH37 Curtis Martin 1.25 3.00
HH38 Steve McNair 1.25 3.00
HH39 Eric Moulds 1.00 2.50
HH40 Terrell Owens 1.25 3.00
HH41 Deion Sanders 1.25 3.00
HH42 Antowain Smith 1.00 2.50
HH43 Robert Smith 1.00 2.50
HH44 Duce Staley 1.00 2.50
HH45 Kordell Stewart 1.00 2.50
HH46 Isaac Bruce 1.25 3.00
HH47 Germane Crowell .75 2.00
HH48 Michael Irvin 1.25 3.00
HH49 Ed McCaffrey 1.00 2.50
HH50 Muhsin Muhammad 1.00 2.50
HH51 Jimmy Smith 1.00 2.50
HH52 James Stewart .75 2.00
HH53 Amani Toomer 1.00 2.50
HH54 Ricky Watters 1.00 2.50
HH55 Michael Westbrook .75 2.00
HH56 Brian Griese 1.00 2.50
HH57 Marcus Robinson 1.00 2.50
HH58 Kurt Warner 2.00 5.00
HH59 Edgerrin James 1.25 3.00
HH60 Tim Couch 1.00 2.50
HH61 Ricky Williams 1.25 3.00
HH62 Donovan McNabb 1.25 3.00
HH63 Cade McNown .75 2.00
HH64 Daunte Culpepper 1.00 2.50
HH65 Akili Smith .75 2.00
HH66 Torry Holt 1.25 3.00
HH67 Peerless Price 1.00 2.50
HH68 Kevin Johnson .75 2.00
HH69 Shaun King .75 2.00
HH70 Olandis Gary 1.00 2.50

2000 Playoff Prestige Inside the Numbers

COMPLETE SET (100) 125.00 250.00
STATED ODDS 1:15 HOB, 1:30 RET
IN1 Ricky Williams 1.50 4.00
IN2 Edgerrin James 1.50 4.00
IN3 Brett Favre 5.00 12.00
IN4 Donovan McNabb 1.50 4.00
IN5 James Stewart 1.00 2.50
IN6 Corey Dillon 1.25 3.00
IN7 Tim Couch 1.25 3.00
IN8 Doug Flutie 1.50 4.00
IN9 Jake Plummer 1.25 3.00
IN10 Akili Smith 1.00 2.50
IN11 Jerry Rice 3.00 8.00
IN12 Brian Griese 1.25 3.00
IN13 Peyton Manning 4.00 10.00
IN14 Fred Taylor 1.50 4.00
IN15 Brad Johnson 1.25 3.00
IN16 Courtney Brown 1.25 3.00
IN17 Randy Moss 1.50 4.00
IN18 Deion Sanders 1.50 4.00
IN19 Bruce Smith 1.50 4.00
IN20 Natrone Means 1.25 3.00
IN21 Dez White 1.25 3.00
IN22 Robert Smith 1.25 3.00
IN23 Jon Kitna 1.25 3.00
IN24 Duce Staley 1.25 3.00
IN25 Emmitt Smith 4.00 10.00
IN26 Dennis Northcutt 1.25 3.00
IN27 Antowain Smith 1.25 3.00
IN28 Mike Alstott 1.50 4.00
IN29 Ike Hilliard 1.25 3.00
IN30 Ed McCaffrey 1.25 3.00
IN31 Cade McNown 1.00 2.50
IN32 Jamal Lewis 1.50 4.00
IN33 Ron Dayne 1.50 4.00
IN34 Isaac Bruce 1.50 4.00
IN35 Tim Brown 1.50 4.00
IN36 Steve Beuerlein 1.25 3.00
IN37 Olandis Gary 1.25 3.00
IN38 Shyrone Stith 1.00 2.50
IN39 Jerome Bettis 1.50 4.00
IN40 Todd Pinkston 1.00 2.50
IN41 Kurt Warner 2.50 6.00
IN42 Peter Warrick 1.50 4.00
IN43 Steve Young 2.00 5.00
IN44 Corey Simon 1.25 3.00
IN45 Drew Bledsoe 1.50 4.00
IN46 Ron Dugans 1.00 2.50
IN47 Germane Crowell 1.00 2.50
IN48 Dan Marino 5.00 12.00
IN49 Eric Moulds 1.25 3.00
IN50 Peerless Price 1.25 3.00
IN51 Travis Taylor 1.25 3.00
IN52 Torry Holt 1.50 4.00
IN53 Charlie Batch 1.25 3.00
IN54 Shaun Alexander 2.00 5.00
IN55 John Elway 4.00 10.00
IN56 Amani Toomer 1.25 3.00
IN57 Thomas Jones 2.00 5.00
IN58 David Boston 1.00 2.50
IN59 Terrell Davis 1.50 4.00
IN60 Marvin Harrison 1.50 4.00
IN61 Priest Holmes 1.50 4.00
IN62 Troy Aikman 2.50 6.00
IN63 Chris Redman 1.25 3.00
IN64 Eddie George 1.25 3.00
IN65 Plaxico Burress 1.50 4.00
IN66 Kevin Johnson 1.00 2.50
IN67 Chad Pennington 2.50 6.00
IN68 Marshall Faulk 1.50 4.00
IN69 Sylvester Morris 1.00 2.50
IN70 Jimmy Smith 1.25 3.00
IN71 Dorsey Levens 1.25 3.00
IN72 Joey Galloway 1.25 3.00
IN73 Daunte Culpepper 1.25 3.00
IN74 Curtis Martin 1.50 4.00
IN75 Shaun King 1.00 2.50
IN76 Stephen Davis 1.25 3.00
IN77 Danny Farmer 1.00 2.50
IN78 Travis Prentice 1.25 3.00
IN79 Terrell Owens 1.50 4.00
IN80 Jamal Anderson 1.25 3.00
IN81 Antonio Freeman 1.25 3.00
IN82 Mark Brunell 1.25 3.00
IN83 Steve McNair 1.50 4.00
IN84 Marcus Robinson 1.25 3.00
IN85 Keenan McCardell 1.25 3.00
IN86 Jevon Kearse 1.25 3.00
IN87 Thurman Thomas 1.50 4.00
IN88 Patrick Jeffers 1.25 3.00
IN89 Keyshawn Johnson 1.25 3.00
IN90 Terry Glenn 1.25 3.00
IN91 Jerry Porter 1.50 4.00
IN92 J.R. Redmond 1.00 2.50
IN93 Yancey Thigpen 1.00 2.50
IN94 Troy Edwards 1.00 2.50
IN95 Cris Carter 1.50 4.00
IN96 Muhsin Muhammad 1.25 3.00
IN97 Ricky Watters 1.25 3.00
IN98 R.Jay Soward 1.00 2.50
IN99 Barry Sanders 3.00 8.00
IN100 James Johnson 1.00 2.50

2000 Playoff Prestige League Leader Quads

COMPLETE SET (12) 50.00 100.00
STATED ODDS 1:159 HOBBY
1 Peyton Manning 10.00 25.00
Rich Gannon
Ray Lucas
Mark Brunell
2 Elvis Grbac 4.00 10.00
Tony Banks
Steve McNair
Jon Kitna
3 Kurt Warner 6.00 15.00
Steve Beuerlein
Jeff George
Brad Johnson
4 Charlie Batch 6.00 15.00
Gus Frerotte
Chris Chandler
Troy Aikman
5 Edgerrin James 4.00 10.00
Curtis Martin
Eddie George
Ricky Watters
6 Corey Dillon 4.00 10.00
Olandis Gary
Jerome Bettis
Tyrone Wheatley
7 Stephen Davis 10.00 25.00
Emmitt Smith
Marshall Faulk
Duce Staley
8 Charlie Garner 4.00 10.00
Dorsey Levens
Robert Smith
Mike Alstott
9 Marvin Harrison 4.00 10.00
Jimmy Smith
Tim Brown
Kevin Johnson
10 Terry Glenn 3.00 8.00
Rocket Ismail
Tony Martin
Darnay Scott
11 Randy Moss 4.00 10.00
Marcus Robinson
Germane Crowell
Muhsin Muhammad
12 Armani Toomer 4.00 10.00
Cris Carter
Michael Westbrook
Isaac Bruce

2000 Playoff Prestige League Leader Tandems

COMPLETE SET (24) 30.00 60.00
STATED ODDS 1:95 RETAIL
1 Peyton Manning 3.00 8.00
Rich Gannon
2 Ray Lucas 1.00 2.50
Mark Brunell
3 Elvis Grbac .75 2.00
Tony Banks
4 Steve McNair 1.25 3.00
Jon Kitna
5 Kurt Warner 2.00 5.00
Steve Beuerlein
6 Jeff George 1.00 2.50
Brad Johnson
7 Charlie Batch 1.00 2.50
Gus Frerotte
8 Chris Chandler 2.00 5.00
Troy Aikman
9 Edgerrin James 1.25 3.00
Curtis Martin
10 Eddie George 1.00 2.50
Ricky Watters
11 Corey Dillon 1.00 2.50
Olandis Gary
12 Jerome Bettis 1.25 3.00
{Tyrone Wheatley
13 Stephen Davis 3.00 8.00
Emmitt Smith
14 Marshall Faulk 1.25 3.00
Duce Staley
15 Charlie Garner 1.00 2.50
Dorsey Levens
16 Robert Smith 1.25 3.00
Mike Alstott
17 Marvin Harrison 1.25 3.00
Jimmy Smith
18 Tim Brown 1.25 3.00
Kevin Johnson
19 Terry Glenn 1.00 2.50
Qadry Ismail
20 Tony Martin 1.00 2.50
Darnay Scott
21 Randy Moss 1.25 3.00
Marcus Robinson
22 Germane Crowell 1.00 2.50
Muhsin Muhammad
23 Cris Carter 1.25 3.00
Amani Toomer
24 Isaac Bruce 1.25 3.00
Michael Westbrook

2000 Playoff Prestige Stars of the NFL

COMPLETE SET (30) 40.00 100.00
STATED ODDS 1:47 RETAIL
STATED PRINT RUN 500 SER.#'d SETS
1 Randy Moss 1.50 4.00
2 Brett Favre 5.00 12.00
3 Dan Marino 5.00 12.00
4 Barry Sanders 3.00 8.00
5 John Elway 4.00 10.00
6 Peyton Manning 4.00 10.00
7 Terrell Davis 1.50 4.00
8 Emmitt Smith 4.00 10.00
9 Troy Aikman 2.50 6.00
10 Jerry Rice 3.00 8.00
11 Fred Taylor 1.50 4.00
12 Jake Plummer 1.25 3.00
13 Drew Bledsoe 1.50 4.00
14 Mark Brunell 1.25 3.00
15 Steve Young 2.00 5.00
16 Eddie George 1.25 3.00
17 Cris Carter 1.50 4.00
18 Marshall Faulk 1.50 4.00
19 Marvin Harrison 1.50 4.00
20 Brad Johnson 1.25 3.00
21 Keyshawn Johnson 1.25 3.00
22 Jon Kitna 1.25 3.00
23 Dorsey Levens 1.25 3.00
24 Steve McNair 1.50 4.00
25 Eric Moulds 1.25 3.00
26 Brian Griese 1.25 3.00
27 Kurt Warner 2.50 6.00
28 Edgerrin James 1.50 4.00
29 Tim Couch 1.25 3.00
30 Ricky Williams 1.50 4.00

2000 Playoff Prestige Team Checklist

CL1-CL31 ODDS 1:15H, 1:18R
CL32-CL62 ODDS 1:31H, 1:62R
CL63-CL93 ODDS 1:63H, 1:126R
CL1 Jake Plummer .50 1.25
CL2 Jamal Anderson .50 1.25
CL3 Jamal Lewis .60 1.50
CL4 Rob Johnson .50 1.25
CL5 Muhsin Muhammad .50 1.25
CL6 Marcus Robinson .50 1.25
CL7 Peter Warrick .60 1.50
CL8 Tim Couch .50 1.25
CL9 Emmitt Smith 1.50 4.00
CL10 Terrell Davis .60 1.50
CL11 Charlie Batch .50 1.25
CL12 Brett Favre 2.00 5.00
CL13 Peyton Manning 1.50 4.00
CL14 Mark Brunell .50 1.25
CL15 Sylvester Morris .40 1.00
CL16 Elvis Grbac .40 1.00
CL17 Randy Moss .60 1.50
CL18 Drew Bledsoe .60 1.50
CL19 Jeff Blake .50 1.25
CL20 Kerry Collins .50 1.25
CL21 Chad Pennington 1.00 2.50
CL22 Tim Brown .60 1.50
CL23 Duce Staley .50 1.25
CL24 Jerome Bettis .60 1.50
CL25 Jim Harbaugh .50 1.25
CL26 Jerry Rice 1.25 3.00
CL27 Jon Kitna .50 1.25
CL28 Kurt Warner 1.00 2.50
CL29 Keyshawn Johnson .50 1.25
CL30 Eddie George .50 1.25
CL31 Stephen Davis .50 1.25
CL32 Thomas Jones 1.00 2.50
CL33 Chris Chandler .60 1.50
CL34 Tony Banks .50 1.25
CL35 Eric Moulds .60 1.50
CL36 Tim Biakabutuka .60 1.50
CL37 Curtis Enis .50 1.25
CL38 Corey Dillon .60 1.50
CL39 Courtney Brown .60 1.50
CL40 Troy Aikman 1.25 3.00
CL41 Brian Griese .60 1.50
CL42 Herman Moore .60 1.50
CL43 Antonio Freeman .60 1.50
CL44 Edgerrin James .75 2.00
CL45 Fred Taylor .75 2.00
CL46 Derrick Alexander .50 1.25
CL47 James Johnson .50 1.25
CL48 Cris Carter .75 2.00
CL49 Terry Glenn .60 1.50
CL50 Sherrod Gideon .50 1.25
CL51 Ron Dayne .75 2.00
CL52 Curtis Martin .75 2.00
CL53 Rich Gannon .60 1.50
CL54 Todd Pinkston .50 1.25
CL55 Kordell Stewart .60 1.50
CL56 Junior Seau .75 2.00
CL57 Steve Young 1.00 2.50
CL58 Shaun Alexander 1.00 2.50
CL59 Marshall Faulk .75 2.00
CL60 Shaun King .50 1.25
CL61 Jevon Kearse .60 1.50
CL62 Brad Johnson .60 1.50
CL63 Frank Sanders AU 6.00 15.00
CL64 Tim Dwight AU 8.00 20.00
CL65 Qadry Ismail AU 8.00 20.00
CL66 Antowain Smith AU 8.00 20.00
CL67 Patrick Jeffers AU 8.00 20.00
CL68 Cade McNown AU 6.00 15.00
CL69 Akili Smith AU 6.00 15.00
CL70 Kevin Johnson AU 6.00 15.00
CL71 Joey Galloway AU 8.00 20.00
CL72 Olandis Gary AU 8.00 20.00
CL73 Germane Crowell AU 6.00 15.00
CL74 Dorsey Levens AU 8.00 20.00
CL75 Marvin Harrison AU 10.00 25.00
CL76 Jimmy Smith AU 8.00 20.00
CL77 Elvis Grbac AU 6.00 15.00
CL78 Tony Martin AU 8.00 20.00
CL79 Daunte Culpepper AU 20.00 40.00
CL80 Kevin Faulk AU 8.00 20.00
CL81 Ricky Williams AU 10.00 25.00
CL82 Amani Toomer AU 8.00 20.00
CL83 Ray Lucas AU 6.00 15.00
CL84 Tyrone Wheatley AU 6.00 15.00
CL85 Donovan McNabb AU 20.00 40.00
CL86 Troy Edwards AU 6.00 15.00
CL87 Jermaine Fazande AU 6.00 15.00
CL88 Charlie Garner AU 8.00 20.00
CL89 Derrick Mayes AU 6.00 15.00
CL90 Isaac Bruce AU 10.00 25.00
CL91 Mike Alstott AU 10.00 25.00
CL92 Steve McNair AU 12.00 30.00
CL93 Albert Connell AU 6.00 15.00

2000 Playoff Prestige Team Checklist Inaugural Years

OVERALL STATED ODDS 1:216
STATED PRINT RUN 20-99
CL1 Jake Plummer/20 6.00 15.00
CL2 Jamal Anderson/66 4.00 10.00
CL3 Jamal Lewis/50 5.00 12.00
CL4 Rob Johnson/60 4.00 10.00
CL5 Muhsin Muhammad/95 3.00 8.00
CL6 Marcus Robinson/20 6.00 15.00
CL7 Peter Warrick/68 5.00 12.00
CL8 Tim Couch/99 3.00 8.00
CL9 Emmitt Smith/60 12.00 30.00
CL10 Terrell Davis/60 5.00 12.00
CL11 Charlie Batch/30 5.00 12.00
CL12 Brett Favre/21 60.00 150.00
CL13 Peyton Manning/53 12.00 30.00
CL14 Mark Brunell/95 3.00 8.00
CL15 Sylvester Morris/60 3.00 8.00
CL16 Dan Marino/66 15.00 40.00
CL17 Randy Moss/61 5.00 12.00
CL18 Drew Bledsoe/60 5.00 12.00
CL19 Jeff Blake/67 4.00 10.00
CL20 Kerry Collins/25 6.00 15.00
CL21 Chad Pennington/60 8.00 20.00
CL22 Tim Brown/60 5.00 12.00
CL23 Duce Staley/33 5.00 12.00
CL24 Jerome Bettis/33 6.00 15.00
CL25 Jim Harbaugh/60 4.00 10.00
CL26 Jerry Rice/50 10.00 25.00
CL27 Jon Kitna/76 4.00 10.00
CL28 Kurt Warner/37 10.00 25.00
CL29 Keyshawn Johnson/76 4.00 10.00
CL30 Eddie George/60 4.00 10.00
CL31 Stephen Davis/32 5.00 12.00
CL32 Thomas Jones/20 10.00 25.00
CL33 Chris Chandler/66 4.00 10.00
CL34 Tony Banks/50 3.00 8.00
CL35 Eric Moulds/60 4.00 10.00
CL36 Tim Biakabutuka/95 3.00 8.00
CL37 Curtis Enis/20 5.00 12.00
CL38 Corey Dillon/68 4.00 10.00
CL39 Courtney Brown/99 3.00 8.00
CL40 Troy Aikman/60 8.00 20.00
CL41 Brian Griese/60 4.00 10.00
CL42 Herman Moore/30 5.00 12.00
CL43 Antonio Freeman/21 6.00 15.00
CL44 Edgerrin James/53 5.00 12.00
CL45 Fred Taylor/95 4.00 10.00
CL46 Derrick Alexander/60 3.00 8.00
CL47 James Johnson/66 3.00 8.00
CL48 Cris Carter/61 5.00 12.00
CL49 Terry Glenn/60 4.00 10.00
CL50 Sherrod Gideon/67 3.00 8.00
CL51 Ron Dayne/25 8.00 20.00
CL52 Curtis Martin/60 5.00 12.00
CL53 Rich Gannon/60 4.00 10.00
CL54 Todd Pinkston/33 4.00 10.00
CL55 Kordell Stewart/33 5.00 12.00
CL56 Junior Seau/60 5.00 12.00
CL57 Steve Young/50 6.00 15.00
CL58 Shaun Alexander/76 6.00 15.00
CL59 Marshall Faulk/37 6.00 15.00
CL60 Shaun King/76 3.00 8.00
CL61 Jevon Kearse/60 4.00 10.00
CL62 Brad Johnson/32 5.00 12.00
CL63 Frank Sanders/20* 5.00 12.00
CL64 Tim Dwight/66* 4.00 10.00
CL65 Qadry Ismail/50* 4.00 10.00
CL66 Antowain Smith/60* 4.00 10.00
CL67 Patrick Jeffers/95* 3.00 8.00
CL68 Cade McNown/20* 5.00 12.00
CL69 Akili Smith/68* 3.00 8.00
CL70 Kevin Johnson/99* 2.50 6.00
CL71 Joey Galloway/60* 4.00 10.00
CL72 Olandis Gary/60* 4.00 10.00
CL73 Germane Crowell/30* 4.00 10.00
CL74 Dorsey Levens/21* 6.00 15.00
CL75 Marvin Harrison/53* 5.00 12.00
CL76 Jimmy Smith/95* 4.00 10.00
CL77 Elvis Grbac/60* 3.00 8.00
CL78 Tony Martin/66* 4.00 10.00
CL79 Daunte Culpepper/61* 4.00 10.00
CL80 Kevin Faulk/60* 4.00 10.00
CL81 Ricky Williams/67* 5.00 12.00
CL82 Amani Toomer/25* 6.00 15.00
CL83 Ray Lucas/60* 3.00 8.00
CL84 Tyrone Wheatley/60* 3.00 8.00
CL85 Donovan McNabb/33* 6.00 15.00
CL86 Troy Edwards/33* 4.00 10.00
CL87 Jermaine Fazande/60* 3.00 8.00
CL88 Charlie Garner/50* 4.00 10.00
CL89 Derrick Mayes/76* 3.00 8.00
CL90 Isaac Bruce/37* 6.00 15.00
CL91 Mike Alstott/76* 5.00 12.00
CL92 Steve McNair/60* 5.00 12.00
CL93 Albert Connell/32* 4.00 10.00

2000 Playoff Prestige Xtra Points

COMPLETE SET (40) 60.00 120.00
STATED ODDS 1:47 HOBBY
XP1 Randy Moss 1.50 4.00
XP2 Brett Favre 5.00 12.00
XP3 Dan Marino 5.00 12.00
XP4 Peyton Manning 4.00 10.00
XP5 Emmitt Smith 4.00 10.00
XP6 Troy Aikman 2.50 6.00
XP7 Jerry Rice 3.00 8.00
XP8 Fred Taylor 1.50 4.00
XP9 Jake Plummer 1.25 3.00
XP10 Drew Bledsoe 1.50 4.00
XP11 Mark Brunell 1.25 3.00
XP12 Eddie George 1.25 3.00
XP13 Cris Carter 1.50 4.00
XP14 Stephen Davis 1.25 3.00
XP15 Corey Dillon 1.25 3.00
XP16 Marshall Faulk 1.50 4.00
XP17 Doug Flutie 1.50 4.00
XP18 Antonio Freeman 1.25 3.00
XP19 Terry Glenn 1.25 3.00
XP20 Marvin Harrison 1.50 4.00
XP21 Brad Johnson 1.25 3.00
XP22 Keyshawn Johnson 1.25 3.00
XP23 Jon Kitna 1.25 3.00
XP24 Dorsey Levens 1.25 3.00
XP25 Curtis Martin 1.50 4.00
XP26 Steve McNair 1.50 4.00
XP27 Isaac Bruce 1.50 4.00
XP28 Germane Crowell 1.00 2.50
XP29 Muhsin Muhammad 1.25 3.00
XP30 Jimmy Smith 1.25 3.00
XP31 Brian Griese 1.25 3.00
XP32 Marcus Robinson 1.25 3.00
XP33 Kurt Warner 2.50 6.00
XP34 Edgerrin James 1.50 4.00
XP35 Tim Couch 1.25 3.00
XP36 Ricky Williams 1.50 4.00
XP37 Torry Holt 1.50 4.00
XP38 Kevin Johnson 1.00 2.50
XP39 Shaun King 1.00 2.50
XP40 Olandis Gary 1.25 3.00

2002 Playoff Prestige Samples

*SAMPLE SILVER: .6X TO 1.5X BASE CARDS
*SAMPLE GOLD: 1.2X TO 2.5X BASE CARDS

2002 Playoff Prestige

This 216-card set includes 150-veterans and 66-short printed rookies. The product was released in early May 2002 with boxes containing 20-packs of 5 cards each. The SRP was $4 per pack.

COMP.SET w/o SP's (150) 15.00 40.00
1 David Boston .25 .60
2 MarTay Jenkins .25 .60
3 Jake Plummer .30 .75
4 Chris Chandler .30 .75
5 Jamal Anderson .30 .75
6 Michael Vick .60 1.50
7 Maurice Smith .25 .60
8 Elvis Grbac .25 .60
9 Jamal Lewis .30 .75
10 Todd Heap .30 .75
11 Qadry Ismail .30 .75
12 Shannon Sharpe .40 1.00
13 Ray Lewis .40 1.00
14 Rod Woodson .40 1.00
15 Travis Henry .25 .60
16 Rob Johnson .30 .75
17 Eric Moulds .30 .75
18 Nate Clements .25 .60
19 Donald Hayes .25 .60
20 Muhsin Muhammad .30 .75
21 Steve Smith .40 1.00
22 Wesley Walls .30 .75
23 Chris Weinke .25 .60
24 James Allen .25 .60
25 David Terrell .25 .60
26 Anthony Thomas .30 .75
27 Dez White .25 .60
28 Brian Urlacher .40 1.00
29 Mike Brown .30 .75
30 Corey Dillon .30 .75
31 Chad Johnson .40 1.00
32 Peter Warrick .30 .75
33 Justin Smith .25 .60
34 Tim Couch .25 .60

35 James Jackson .25 .60
36 Quincy Morgan .25 .60
37 Kevin Johnson .25 .60
38 Gerard Warren .25 .60
39 Anthony Henry .25 .60
40 Quincy Carter .25 .60
41 Joey Galloway .30 .75
42 Rocket Ismail .30 .75
43 Ryan Leaf .25 .60
44 Emmitt Smith 1.00 2.50
45 Troy Hambrick .25 .60
46 Mike Anderson .30 .75
47 Terrell Davis .40 1.00
48 Brian Griese .30 .75
49 Rod Smith .30 .75
50 Ed McCaffrey .30 .75
51 Charlie Batch .25 .60
52 Johnnie Morton .30 .75
53 Germane Crowell .25 .60
54 James Stewart .25 .60
55 Shaun Rogers .25 .60
56 Brett Favre 1.00 2.50
57 Antonio Freeman .40 1.00
58 Ahman Green .30 .75
59 Bill Schroeder .25 .60
60 Kabeer Gbaja-Biamila .30 .75
61 Marvin Harrison .40 1.00
62 Terrence Wilkins .25 .60
63 Dominic Rhodes .30 .75
64 Reggie Wayne .40 1.00
65 Edgerrin James .30 .75
66 Mark Brunell .30 .75
67 Keenan McCardell .30 .75
68 Jimmy Smith .30 .75
69 Fred Taylor .30 .75
70 Derrick Alexander .25 .60
71 Tony Gonzalez .40 1.00
72 Trent Green .30 .75
73 Priest Holmes .40 1.00
74 Snoop Minnis .25 .60
75 Chris Chambers .30 .75
76 Jay Fiedler .30 .75
77 Travis Minor .25 .60
78 Lamar Smith .30 .75
79 Zach Thomas .40 1.00
80 Michael Bennett .30 .75
81 Cris Carter .40 1.00
82 Daunte Culpepper .30 .75
83 Randy Moss .40 1.00
84 Drew Bledsoe .40 1.00
85 Tom Brady 1.00 2.50
86 Troy Brown .30 .75
87 Antowain Smith .30 .75
88 Aaron Brooks .30 .75
89 Joe Horn .30 .75
90 Deuce McAllister .30 .75
91 Ricky Williams .30 .75
92 Kerry Collins .30 .75
93 Ron Dayne .30 .75
94 Michael Strahan .40 1.00
95 Jason Sehorn .30 .75
96 Wayne Chrebet .30 .75
97 Laveranues Coles .30 .75
98 LaMont Jordan .30 .75
99 Curtis Martin .40 1.00
100 Santana Moss .30 .75
101 Vinny Testaverde .30 .75
102 Tim Brown .40 1.00
103 Jerry Porter .25 .60
104 Jerry Rice .75 2.00
105 Charlie Garner .30 .75
106 Tyrone Wheatley .30 .75
107 Charles Woodson .40 1.00
108 Correll Buckhalter .30 .75
109 Todd Pinkston .25 .60
110 Freddie Mitchell .25 .60
111 James Thrash .30 .75
112 Duce Staley .30 .75
113 Jerome Bettis .40 1.00
114 Plaxico Burress .30 .75
115 Kordell Stewart .30 .75
116 Hines Ward .40 1.00
117 Kendrell Bell .25 .60
118 Drew Brees .60 1.50
119 Curtis Conway .30 .75
120 Doug Flutie .40 1.00
121 LaDainian Tomlinson .50 1.25
122 Junior Seau .40 1.00
123 Kevan Barlow .25 .60
124 Jeff Garcia .30 .75
125 Garrison Hearst .30 .75
126 Terrell Owens .40 1.00
127 Andre Carter .25 .60
128 Shaun Alexander .30 .75
129 Matt Hasselbeck .40 1.00
130 Koren Robinson .25 .60
131 Ricky Watters .30 .75
132 Isaac Bruce .40 1.00
133 Trung Canidate .25 .60
134 Marshall Faulk .40 1.00
135 Torry Holt .40 1.00
136 Kurt Warner .40 1.00
137 Mike Alstott .30 .75
138 Warrick Dunn .30 .75
139 Brad Johnson .30 .75
140 Keyshawn Johnson .30 .75
141 Warren Sapp .30 .75
142 Eddie George .30 .75
143 Derrick Mason .30 .75
144 Steve McNair .40 1.00
145 Jevon Kearse .30 .75
146 Stephen Davis .30 .75
147 Rod Gardner .25 .60
148 Champ Bailey .40 1.00
149 Bruce Smith .40 1.00
150 Houston Texans .40 1.00
151 David Carr RC 1.25 3.00
152 Julius Peppers RC 2.50 6.00
153 Joey Harrington RC 1.25 3.00
154 Quentin Jammer RC 1.25 3.00
155 Ryan Sims RC 1.25 3.00
156 Bryant McKinnie RC .75 2.00
157 Roy Williams RC 1.25 3.00
158 John Henderson RC 1.00 2.50
159 Dwight Freeney RC 1.50 4.00
160 Wendell Bryant RC .75 2.00
161 Donte Stallworth RC 1.25 3.00
162 Jeremy Shockey RC 2.00 5.00
163 Albert Haynesworth RC 1.25 3.00
164 William Green RC 1.00 2.50
165 Phillip Buchanon RC 1.25 3.00
166 T.J. Duckett RC 1.25 3.00
167 Ashley Lelie RC 1.00 2.50
168 Javon Walker RC 1.25 3.00
169 Daniel Graham RC 1.00 2.50
170 Napoleon Harris RC 1.00 2.50
171 Lito Sheppard RC 1.25 3.00
172 Robert Thomas RC .75 2.00
173 Patrick Ramsey RC 1.25 3.00
174 Jabar Gaffney RC 1.25 3.00
175 DeShaun Foster RC 1.25 3.00
176 Kalimba Edwards RC 1.00 2.50
177 Josh Reed RC 1.00 2.50
178 Larry Tripplett RC .75 2.00
179 Andre Davis RC 1.00 2.50
180 Reche Caldwell RC 1.25 3.00
181 Levar Fisher RC .75 2.00
182 Clinton Portis RC 1.50 4.00
183 Anthony Weaver RC .75 2.00
184 Maurice Morris RC 1.00 2.50
185 Ladell Betts RC 1.25 3.00
186 Antwaan Randle El RC 1.25 3.00
187 Antonio Bryant RC 1.25 3.00
188 Rocky Calmus RC 1.00 2.50
189 Josh McCown RC 1.25 3.00
190 Lamar Gordon RC 1.00 2.50
191 Marquise Walker RC .75 2.00
192 Cliff Russell RC .75 2.00
193 Eric Crouch RC 1.25 3.00
194 Dennis Johnson RC .75 2.00
195 Alex Brown RC 1.25 3.00
196 David Garrard RC 1.50 4.00
197 Rohan Davey RC 1.25 3.00
198 Alan Harper RC .75 2.00
199 Ron Johnson RC 1.00 2.50
200 Andra Davis RC .75 2.00
201 Kurt Kittner RC .75 2.00
202 Freddie Milons RC .75 2.00
203 Adrian Peterson RC 1.25 3.00
204 Luke Staley RC .75 2.00
205 Tracey Wistrom RC 1.00 2.50
206 Woody Dantzler RC 1.00 2.50
207 Chad Hutchinson RC .75 2.00
208 Zak Kustok RC .75 2.00
209 Damien Anderson RC .75 2.00
210 James Mungro RC 1.25 3.00
211 Cortlen Johnson RC .75 2.00
212 Demontray Carter RC .75 2.00
213 Kelly Campbell RC 1.00 2.50
214 Brian Poli-Dixon RC .75 2.00
215 Mike Rumph RC .75 2.00
216 Najeh Davenport RC 1.25 3.00

2002 Playoff Prestige Xtra Points Green

*1-150 VETS: 2.5X TO 6X BASIC CARDS
1-150 VETERAN PRINT RUN 150
*151-216 ROOKIES: 3X TO 8X
151-216 ROOKIE PRINT RUN 25

2002 Playoff Prestige Xtra Points Purple

*1-150 VETS: 2.5X TO 6X BASIC CARDS
1-150 VETERAN PRINT RUN 150
*151-216 ROOKIES: 3X TO 8X
151-216 ROOKIE PRINT RUN 25

2002 Playoff Prestige Banner Season

STATED PRINT RUN 1947-1991
BS1 Archie Griffin/1979 1.00 2.50
BS2 Archie Manning/1980 1.50 4.00
BS3 Art Monk/1984 1.25 3.00
BS4 Charley Taylor/1966 1.25 3.00
BS5 Cris Collinsworth/1986 1.25 3.00
BS6 Craig Morton/1981 1.25 3.00
BS7 Dick Butkus/1965 2.50 6.00
BS8 Don Maynard/1967 1.25 3.00
BS9 Drew Pearson/1979 1.25 3.00
BS10 Dwight Clark/1981 1.25 3.00
BS11 Eric Dickerson/1984 1.25 3.00
BS12 Fran Tarkenton/1975 1.50 4.00
BS13 Franco Harris/1975 1.50 4.00
BS14 Frank Gifford/1956 1.50 4.00
BS15 Fred Biletnikoff/1969 1.50 4.00
BS16 John Fuqua/1970 1.00 2.50
BS17 Gale Sayers/1966 2.00 5.00
BS18 Henry Ellard/1988 1.00 2.50
BS19 James Lofton/1991 1.00 2.50
BS20 Jim Plunkett/1983 1.25 3.00
BS21 Joe Greene/1972 1.50 4.00
BS22 Joe Theismann/1983 1.50 4.00
BS23 John Hadl/1968 1.00 2.50
BS24 John Stallworth/1984 1.25 3.00
BS25 Kellen Winslow/1980 1.25 3.00
BS26 Ken Anderson/1981 1.25 3.00
BS27 Lance Alworth/1965 1.50 4.00
BS28 Mike Singletary/1985 1.50 4.00
BS29 Otto Graham/1953 1.25 3.00
BS30 Paul Hornung/1960 1.50 4.00
BS31 Paul Warfield/1971 1.25 3.00
BS32 Raymond Berry/1960 1.25 3.00
BS33 Rocky Bleier/1976 1.25 3.00
BS34 Ronnie Lott/1986 1.50 4.00
BS35 Sammy Baugh/1947 1.50 4.00
BS36 Sonny Jurgensen/1967 1.50 4.00
BS37 Steve Largent/1979 1.50 4.00
BS38 Terry Bradshaw/1978 2.50 6.00
BS39 Todd Christensen/1983 1.00 2.50
BS40 Y.A. Tittle/1963 1.25 3.00

2002 Playoff Prestige Banner Season Ink Autographs

STATED PRINT RUN 25 SER.#'d SETS
BS1 Archie Griffin 12.00 30.00
BS2 Archie Manning 20.00 50.00
BS3 Art Monk
BS4 Charley Taylor 15.00 40.00
BS5 Cris Collinsworth 15.00 40.00
BS6 Craig Morton 15.00 40.00
BS7 Dick Butkus 60.00 100.00
BS8 Don Maynard 15.00 40.00
BS9 Drew Pearson 15.00 40.00
BS10 Dwight Clark 15.00 40.00
BS11 Eric Dickerson 15.00 40.00
BS12 Fran Tarkenton 30.00 60.00
BS13 Franco Harris 60.00 100.00
BS14 Frank Gifford 20.00 50.00
BS15 Fred Biletnikoff
BS16 John Fuqua 20.00 50.00
BS17 Gale Sayers 25.00 60.00
BS18 Henry Ellard
BS19 James Lofton 12.00 30.00
BS20 Jim Plunkett 15.00 40.00
BS21 Joe Greene 25.00 60.00
BS22 Joe Theismann 20.00 50.00
BS23 John Hadl
BS24 John Stallworth 30.00 60.00
BS25 Kellen Winslow 15.00 40.00
BS26 Ken Anderson 15.00 40.00
BS27 Lance Alworth 25.00 60.00
BS28 Mike Singletary 25.00 60.00
BS29 Otto Graham 40.00 80.00
BS30 Paul Hornung 20.00 50.00
BS31 Paul Warfield 20.00 50.00
BS32 Raymond Berry
BS33 Rocky Bleier 20.00 50.00
BS34 Ronnie Lott 40.00 80.00
BS35 Sammy Baugh 75.00 150.00
BS36 Sonny Jurgensen 20.00 50.00
BS37 Steve Largent 20.00 50.00
BS38 Terry Bradshaw 75.00 150.00
BS39 Todd Christensen 12.00 30.00
BS40 Y.A. Tittle 15.00 40.00

2002 Playoff Prestige Connections Jerseys

STATED PRINT RUN 500 SER.#'d SETS
C1 Kurt Warner 5.00 12.00
Isaac Bruce
C2 Daunte Culpepper 5.00 12.00
Cris Carter
C3 Jay Fiedler 4.00 10.00
Chris Chambers
C4 Tom Brady 12.00 30.00
Troy Brown
C5 Brian Griese 4.00 10.00
Ed McCaffrey
C6 Jeff Garcia 5.00 12.00
Terrell Owens
C7 Chris Weinke 4.00 10.00
Muhsin Muhammed
C8 Jake Plummer 4.00 10.00
David Boston
C9 Vinny Testaverde 4.00 10.00
Lavernues Coles
C10 Brett Favre 12.00 30.00
Antonio Freeman
C11 Mark Brunell 4.00 10.00
Jimmy Smith
C12 Rob Johnson 4.00 10.00
Eric Moulds
C13 Tim Couch 4.00 10.00
Quincy Morgan
C14 Kerry Collins 4.00 10.00
Amani Toomer
C15 Rich Gannon 5.00 12.00
Tim Brown
C16 Donovan McNabb 5.00 12.00
Todd Pinkston
C17 Charlie Batch 3.00 8.00
Germane Crowell
C18 Kurt Warner 5.00 12.00
Az-Zahir Hakim
C19 Brad Johnson 4.00 10.00
Keyshawn Johnson
C20 Mark Brunell 4.00 10.00
Keenan McCardell
C21 Peyton Manning 10.00 25.00
Marvin Harrison
C22 Brian Griese 4.00 10.00
Rod Smith
C23 Steve McNair 5.00 12.00
Kevin Dyson
C24 Kurt Warner 5.00 12.00
Torry Holt
C25 Tim Couch 3.00 8.00
Kevin Johnson
C26 Jake Plummer 4.00 10.00
Frank Sanders
C27 Kordell Stewart 4.00 10.00
Plaxico Burress
C28 Daunte Culpepper 5.00 12.00
Randy Moss
C29 Vinny Testaverde 4.00 10.00
Wayne Chrebet
C30 Rich Gannon 10.00 25.00
Jerry Rice

2002 Playoff Prestige Draft Picks

STATED PRINT RUN 2002 SER.#'d SETS
DP1 David Carr 1.25 3.00
DP2 Joey Harrington 1.25 3.00
DP3 Kurt Kittner .75 2.00
DP4 Rohan Davey 1.25 3.00
DP5 Eric Crouch 1.25 3.00
DP6 William Green 1.00 2.50
DP7 T.J. Duckett 1.25 3.00
DP8 DeShaun Foster 1.25 3.00
DP9 Travis Stephens .75 2.00
DP10 Luke Staley .75 2.00
DP11 Clinton Portis 1.50 4.00
DP12 Antonio Bryant 1.25 3.00
DP13 Josh Reed 1.00 2.50
DP14 Marquise Walker .75 2.00
DP15 Andre Davis 1.00 2.50
DP16 Ashley Lelie 1.00 2.50
DP17 Jabar Gaffney 1.25 3.00
DP18 Reche Caldwell 1.25 3.00
DP19 Daniel Graham 1.00 2.50
DP20 Jeremy Shockey 2.00 5.00
DP21 Julius Peppers 2.50 6.00
DP22 John Henderson 1.00 2.50
DP23 Ed Reed 5.00 12.00
DP24 Roy Williams 1.25 3.00
DP25 Bryant McKinnie .75 2.00

2002 Playoff Prestige Draft Picks Autographs

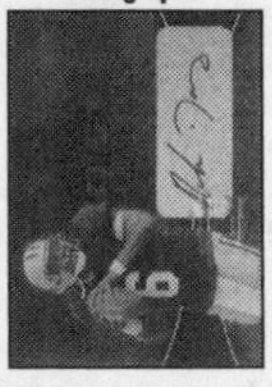

STATED PRINT RUN 50 SER.#'d SETS
1 David Carr 12.00 30.00
2 Joey Harrington 12.00 30.00
3 Kurt Kittner 8.00 20.00
4 Rohan Davey 12.00 30.00
5 Eric Crouch 12.00 30.00
6 William Green 10.00 25.00
7 T.J. Duckett 12.00 30.00
8 DeShaun Foster 12.00 30.00
10 Luke Staley 8.00 20.00
11 Clinton Portis 15.00 40.00
12 Antonio Bryant 12.00 30.00
13 Josh Reed 10.00 25.00
14 Marquise Walker 8.00 20.00
15 Andre Davis 10.00 25.00
16 Ashley Lelie 10.00 25.00
17 Jabar Gaffney 12.00 30.00
19 Daniel Graham 10.00 25.00
20 Jeremy Shockey 20.00 50.00
21 Julius Peppers 75.00 150.00
22 John Henderson 10.00 25.00
23 Ed Reed 50.00 100.00
24 Roy Williams 12.00 30.00
25 Bryant McKinnie 8.00 20.00

2002 Playoff Prestige Gridiron Heritage Helmets

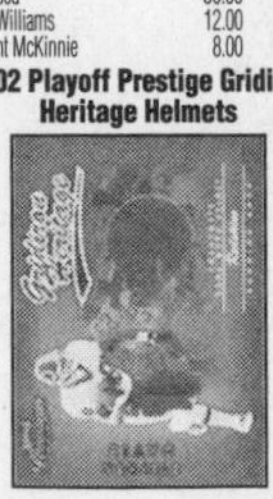

STATED PRINT RUN 100 SER.#'d SETS
GH1 Mike Anderson 8.00 20.00
GH2 Stephen Davis 8.00 20.00
GH3 Mark Brunell 8.00 20.00
GH4 Rich Gannon 8.00 20.00
GH5 Kordell Stewart 8.00 20.00
GH6 Curtis Martin 10.00 25.00
GH7 Michael Vick 15.00 40.00
GH8 Duce Staley 8.00 20.00
GH9 Troy Aikman 20.00 50.00
GH10 Warren Moon 10.00 25.00
GH11 Daunte Culpepper 8.00 20.00
GH12 Jerome Bettis 10.00 25.00
GH13 Junior Seau 10.00 25.00
GH14 Cris Carter 10.00 25.00
GH15 John Elway 25.00 60.00
GH16 Lamar Smith 8.00 20.00
GH17 Doug Flutie 10.00 25.00
GH18 Keyshawn Johnson 8.00 20.00
GH19 LaDainian Tomlinson 12.00 30.00
GH20 Aaron Brooks 8.00 20.00

2002 Playoff Prestige Inside the Numbers

STATED ODDS 1:18
*GOLD/52-89: 1.2X TO 3X BASIC INSERTS
*GOLD/32-37: 2X TO 5X BASIC INSERTS
*GOLD/21-28: 2.5X TO 6X BASIC INSERTS
GOLD STATED PRINT RUN 2-89
SERIAL #'d UNDER 20 NOT PRICED
IN1 Aaron Brooks .75 2.00
IN2 Mark Brunell .75 2.00
IN3 Daunte Culpepper .75 2.00
IN4 Brad Johnson .75 2.00
IN5 Steve McNair 1.00 2.50
IN6 Kurt Warner 1.00 2.50
IN7 Donovan McNabb 1.00 2.50
IN8 Brian Griese .75 2.00
IN9 Tom Brady 2.50 6.00
IN10 Marshall Faulk 1.00 2.50
IN11 Edgerrin James .75 2.00
IN12 LaDainian Tomlinson 1.25 3.00
IN13 Eddie George .75 2.00
IN14 Curtis Martin 1.00 2.50
IN15 Jerome Bettis 1.00 2.50
IN16 Shaun Alexander .75 2.00
IN17 Ricky Williams .75 2.00
IN18 Emmitt Smith 2.50 6.00
IN19 Randy Moss 1.00 2.50
IN20 Jimmy Smith .75 2.00
IN21 Troy Brown .75 2.00
IN22 Rod Smith .75 2.00
IN23 Chris Chambers .75 2.00
IN24 Terrell Owens 1.00 2.50
IN25 Marvin Harrison 1.00 2.50
IN26 Tim Brown 1.00 2.50
IN27 David Boston .60 1.50
IN28 Ray Lewis 1.00 2.50
IN29 Brian Urlacher 1.00 2.50
IN30 Zach Thomas 1.00 2.50

2002 Playoff Prestige League Leader Tandems

STATED ODDS 1:18
LL1 Brian Griese 1.25 3.00
Kurt Warner
LL2 Peyton Manning 3.00 8.00
Brett Favre
LL3 Rich Gannon 1.00 2.50
Daunte Culpepper
LL4 Doug Flutie 1.25 3.00
Kerry Collins
LL5 Jay Fiedler 1.00 2.50
Jake Plummer
LL6 Mark Brunell 1.00 2.50
Jeff Garcia
LL7 Kordell Stewart 1.00 2.50
Brad Johnson
LL8 Jerome Bettis 1.25 3.00
Ricky Williams
LL9 Shaun Alexander 1.00 2.50
Ahman Green
LL10 Curtis Martin 1.25 3.00
Marshall Faulk
LL11 LaDainian Tomlinson 1.50 4.00
Stephen Davis
LL12 Corey Dillon 1.25 3.00
Tiki Barber
LL13 Lamar Smith 3.00 8.00
Emmitt Smith
LL14 Rod Smith 1.00 2.50
David Boston
LL15 Marvin Harrison 1.25 3.00
Terrell Owens
LL16 Troy Brown 1.00 2.50
Keyshawn Johnson
LL17 Tim Brown 1.25 3.00
Isaac Bruce
LL18 Jimmy Smith 1.00 2.50
Johnnie Morton
LL19 Kevin Johnson 1.25 3.00
Torry Holt
LL20 Jevon Kearse 1.25 3.00
Michael Strahan

2002 Playoff Prestige League Leader Tandems Materials

STATED PRINT RUN 250 SER.#'d SETS
LL1 Brian Griese 6.00 15.00
Kurt Warner
LL2 Peyton Manning 15.00 40.00
Brett Favre
LL3 Rich Gannon 5.00 12.00
Daunte Culpepper
LL4 Doug Flutie 6.00 15.00
Kerry Collins
LL5 Jay Fiedler 5.00 12.00
Jake Plummer
LL6 Mark Brunell 5.00 12.00
Jeff Garcia
LL7 Kordell Stewart 5.00 12.00
Brad Johnson
LL8 Jerome Bettis 6.00 15.00
Ricky Williams
LL9 Shaun Alexander 5.00 12.00
Ahman Green
LL10 Curtis Martin 6.00 15.00
Marshall Faulk
LL11 LaDainian Tomlinson 8.00 20.00
Stephen Davis
LL12 Corey Dillon 6.00 15.00
Tiki Barber
LL13 Lamar Smith 15.00 40.00
Emmitt Smith
LL14 Rod Smith 5.00 12.00
David Boston
LL15 Marvin Harrison 6.00 15.00
Terrell Owens
LL16 Troy Brown 5.00 12.00
Keyshawn Johnson
LL17 Tim Brown 6.00 15.00
Isaac Bruce
LL18 Jimmy Smith 5.00 12.00
Johnnie Morton
LL19 Kevin Johnson 6.00 15.00
Torry Holt
LL20 Jevon Kearse 6.00 15.00
Michael Strahan

2002 Playoff Prestige Sophomore Signatures

SS1 Mike McMahon SP 5.00 12.00
SS2 Alge Crumpler SP 6.00 15.00
SS3 Anthony Thomas 5.00 12.00
SS4 Carlos Polk 4.00 10.00
SS5 Cedric Scott 4.00 10.00
SS6 Cedrick Wilson 5.00 12.00
SS7 Chad Johnson 6.00 15.00
SS8 Chris Weinke 4.00 10.00
SS9 David Terrell 4.00 10.00
SS10 Deuce McAllister 5.00 12.00
SS11 Drew Brees 40.00 80.00
SS12 Ennis Davis 4.00 10.00
SS13 Hakim Akbar 4.00 10.00
SS14 Heath Evans 5.00 12.00
SS15 Jamal Reynolds 4.00 10.00
SS16 Jesse Palmer 4.00 10.00
SS17 Justin Smith 4.00 10.00
SS18 Karon Riley 4.00 10.00
SS19 Kendrell Bell SP 5.00 12.00
SS20 Kenny Smith 4.00 10.00
SS21 Kenyatta Walker 4.00 10.00
SS22 Ken-Yon Rambo 4.00 10.00
SS23 Kevan Barlow 4.00 10.00
SS24 Koren Robinson 4.00 10.00
SS25 Marcus Stroud 4.00 10.00
SS26 Snoop Minnis No Auto/100 4.00 10.00
SS27 Michael Bennett 5.00 12.00
SS28 Moran Norris SP 5.00 12.00
SS29 Morlon Greenwood SP 5.00 12.00
SS30 Nate Clements No Auto/100 4.00 10.00
SS31 Quincy Carter 4.00 10.00
SS32 Quincy Morgan 4.00 10.00
SS33 Reggie Germany 4.00 10.00
SS34 Robert Ferguson 5.00 12.00
SS35 Rudi Johnson 6.00 15.00
SS36 Santana Moss 5.00 12.00
SS37 T.J. Houshmandzadeh 6.00 15.00
SS38 Todd Heap 5.00 12.00
SS39 Travis Henry No Auto/100 4.00 10.00
SS40 Travis Minor 4.00 10.00

2002 Playoff Prestige Stars of the NFL Jerseys

STATED PRINT RUN 300 SER.#'d SETS
SN1 Edgerrin James 4.00 10.00
SN2 Jerome Bettis 5.00 12.00
SN3 Shaun Alexander 4.00 10.00
SN4 Brett Favre 12.00 30.00
SN5 Donovan McNabb 5.00 12.00
SN6 Marshall Faulk 5.00 12.00
SN7 John Elway 12.00 30.00
SN8 Troy Aikman 10.00 25.00
SN9 Jeff Garcia 4.00 10.00
SN10 Randy Moss 5.00 12.00
SN11 Stephen Davis 4.00 10.00
SN12 Emmitt Smith 12.00 30.00
SN13 Dan Marino 15.00 40.00
SN14 Brian Urlacher 5.00 12.00
SN15 Mike Anderson 4.00 10.00
SN16 Jevon Kearse 4.00 10.00
SN17 Terrell Owens 5.00 12.00
SN18 Peyton Manning 10.00 25.00
SN19 Ricky Williams 4.00 10.00
SN20 Warren Sapp 4.00 10.00

2002 Playoff Prestige Stars of the NFL Autographs

STATED PRINT RUN 4-90
SERIAL #'d UNDER 34 NOT PRICED
SN11 Stephen Davis/48 15.00 40.00
SN14 Brian Urlacher/54 40.00 100.00
SN15 Mike Anderson/38 15.00 40.00
SN16 Jevon Kearse/90 15.00 40.00
SN17 Terrell Owens/81 25.00 60.00
SN19 Ricky Williams/34 25.00 50.00

2003 Playoff Prestige Atlantic City National Promos

UNPRICED PROMO PRINT RUN 5

2003 Playoff Prestige Samples

*VETS 1-150: .8X TO 2X BASE CARDS

2003 Playoff Prestige Samples Gold

*VETS 1-150: 2.5X TO 6X BASE CARDS

2003 Playoff Prestige

This 229-card set was released in May, 2003. The set was issued in six-card packs with a $3 SRP which came 24 to a box. Cards numbered 1-150 feature veterans while cards numbered 151-230 featured rookies. The rookies were issued at a stated rate of one in two packs. Please note that card number 169 was never released.

COMP.SET w/o RC's (150) 12.50 30.00
151-230 ROOKIE STATED ODDS 1:2
1 David Boston .25 .60
2 Thomas Jones .40 1.00
3 Jake Plummer .30 .75
4 Marcel Shipp .25 .60
5 T.J. Duckett .30 .75
6 Warrick Dunn .30 .75
7 Michael Vick .50 1.25
8 Jeff Blake .30 .75
9 Todd Heap .30 .75
10 Jamal Lewis .30 .75
11 Ray Lewis .40 1.00
12 Drew Bledsoe .40 1.00
13 Travis Henry .25 .60
14 Eric Moulds .30 .75
15 Peerless Price .25 .60
16 Josh Reed .25 .60
17 DeShaun Foster .30 .75
18 Muhsin Muhammad .30 .75
19 Steve Smith .40 1.00
20 Julius Peppers .40 1.00
21 Marty Booker .30 .75
22 David Terrell .25 .60
23 Anthony Thomas .30 .75
24 Brian Urlacher .40 1.00
25 Corey Dillon .30 .75
26 Chad Johnson .40 1.00
27 Jon Kitna .30 .75
28 Peter Warrick .30 .75
29 Tim Couch .25 .60
30 Andre Davis .25 .60
31 William Green .25 .60
32 Quincy Morgan .25 .60
33 Dennis Northcutt .25 .60
34 Antonio Bryant .25 .60
35 Quincy Carter .25 .60
36 Troy Hambrick .25 .60
37 Chad Hutchinson .25 .60
38 Emmitt Smith 1.00 2.50
39 Roy Williams .30 .75
40 Brian Griese .30 .75
41 Ashley Lelie .25 .60
42 Ed McCaffrey .30 .75
43 Clinton Portis .30 .75
44 Rod Smith .30 .75
45 Germane Crowell .25 .60
46 Az-Zahir Hakim .25 .60
47 Joey Harrington .25 .60
48 James Stewart .25 .60
49 Donald Driver .40 1.00
50 Brett Favre 1.00 2.50
51 Terry Glenn .30 .75
52 Ahman Green .30 .75
53 Javon Walker .30 .75
54 Corey Bradford .25 .60
55 David Carr .30 .75
56 Jabar Gaffney .25 .60
57 Jonathan Wells .25 .60
58 Marvin Harrison .40 1.00
59 Edgerrin James .40 1.00
60 Peyton Manning .75 2.00
61 James Mungro .25 .60
62 Reggie Wayne .40 1.00
63 Mark Brunell .30 .75
64 David Garrard .40 1.00
65 Stacey Mack .25 .60
66 Jimmy Smith .30 .75
67 Fred Taylor .30 .75
68 Marc Boerigter .25 .60
69 Tony Gonzalez .40 1.00
70 Trent Green .30 .75
71 Priest Holmes .40 1.00
72 Eddie Kennison .25 .60
73 Cris Carter .40 1.00
74 Chris Chambers .30 .75
75 Jay Fiedler .25 .60
76 Randy McMichael .25 .60
77 Zach Thomas .40 1.00
78 Ricky Williams .30 .75
79 Michael Bennett .30 .75
80 Todd Bouman .25 .60
81 Daunte Culpepper .30 .75
82 Randy Moss .40 1.00
83 Tom Brady 1.00 2.50
84 Deion Branch .30 .75
85 Troy Brown .30 .75
86 Kevin Faulk .30 .75
87 Antowain Smith .30 .75
88 Aaron Brooks .30 .75
89 Joe Horn .30 .75
90 Deuce McAllister .30 .75
91 Donte Stallworth .25 .60
92 Tiki Barber .40 1.00
93 Kerry Collins .30 .75
94 Jeremy Shockey .40 1.00
95 Michael Strahan .40 1.00
96 Amani Toomer .30 .75
97 Laveranues Coles .25 .60
98 LaMont Jordan .30 .75
99 Curtis Martin .40 1.00
100 Santana Moss .30 .75
101 Chad Pennington .40 1.00
102 Tim Brown .40 1.00
103 Rich Gannon .30 .75
104 Charlie Garner .30 .75
105 Jerry Rice .75 2.00
106 Charles Woodson .40 1.00
107 Antonio Freeman .30 .75
108 Dorsey Levens .30 .75
109 Donovan McNabb .40 1.00
110 Duce Staley .30 .75
111 James Thrash .25 .60
112 Jerome Bettis .40 1.00
113 Plaxico Burress .30 .75
114 Tommy Maddox .30 .75
115 Antwaan Randle El .30 .75
116 Kordell Stewart .30 .75
117 Hines Ward .40 1.00
118 Drew Brees .40 1.00
119 Curtis Conway .25 .60
120 Junior Seau .40 1.00
121 LaDainian Tomlinson .40 1.00
122 Kevan Barlow .25 .60
123 Jeff Garcia .30 .75
124 Garrison Hearst .30 .75
125 Terrell Owens .40 1.00
126 Shaun Alexander .30 .75
127 Trent Dilfer .30 .75
128 Darrell Jackson .30 .75
129 Maurice Morris .25 .60
130 Koren Robinson .30 .75
131 Isaac Bruce .40 1.00
132 Marc Bulger .40 1.00
133 Marshall Faulk .40 1.00
134 Torry Holt .40 1.00
135 Kurt Warner .40 1.00
136 Mike Alstott .40 1.00
137 Brad Johnson .30 .75
138 Keyshawn Johnson .40 1.00
139 Dexter Jackson RC .40 1.00
140 Warren Sapp .30 .75
141 Kevin Dyson .25 .60
142 Eddie George .30 .75
143 Jevon Kearse .30 .75
144 Derrick Mason .30 .75
145 Steve McNair .40 1.00
146 Stephen Davis .30 .75
147 Rod Gardner .25 .60
148 Shane Matthews .25 .60
149 Patrick Ramsey .30 .75
150 Derrius Thompson .25 .60
151 Byron Leftwich RC 1.25 3.00
152 Carson Palmer RC 2.50 6.00
153 Chris Simms RC 1.25 3.00
154 Kliff Kingsbury RC 1.00 2.50
155 Dave Ragone RC .75 2.00
156 Jason Gesser RC 1.00 2.50
157 Ken Dorsey RC 1.00 2.50
158 Kyle Boller RC 1.25 3.00
159 Brad Banks RC 1.00 2.50
160 Rex Grossman RC 1.25 3.00
161 Seneca Wallace RC 1.25 3.00
162 Brian St.Pierre RC 1.00 2.50
163 Larry Johnson RC 1.25 3.00
164 Earnest Graham RC 1.25 3.00
165 Musa Smith RC .75 2.00
166 Lee Suggs RC 1.00 2.50
167 Willis McGahee RC 1.50 4.00
168 Onterrio Smith RC .75 2.00
170 Sultan McCullough RC .75 2.00
171 Chris Brown RC .75 2.00
172 Justin Fargas RC 1.25 3.00
173 Avon Cobourne RC .75 2.00
174 Dahrran Diedrick RC .75 2.00
175 LaBrandon Toefield RC 1.00 2.50
176 Artose Pinner RC .75 2.00
177 Quentin Griffin RC 1.00 2.50
178 ReShard Lee RC 1.25 3.00
179 Andrew Pinnock RC 1.00 2.50
180 B.J. Askew RC 1.00 2.50
181 Andre Johnson RC 3.00 8.00
182 Brandon Lloyd RC 2.00 5.00
183 Bryant Johnson RC 1.25 3.00
184 Charles Rogers RC 1.00 2.50
185 Doug Gabriel RC 1.00 2.50
186 Justin Gage RC 1.00 2.50
187 Kareem Kelly RC .75 2.00
188 Kelley Washington RC .75 2.00
189 Taylor Jacobs RC .75 2.00
190 Terrence Edwards RC .75 2.00
191 Anquan Boldin RC 2.00 5.00
192 Billy McMullen RC .75 2.00
193 Talman Gardner RC .75 2.00
194 Arnaz Battle RC 1.25 3.00
195 Sam Aiken RC 1.00 2.50
196 Bobby Wade RC 1.00 2.50
197 Mike Bush RC .75 2.00
198 Keenan Howry RC .75 2.00
199 Jerel Myers RC .75 2.00
200 Dallas Clark RC 2.00 5.00
201 Mike Pinkard RC .75 2.00
202 Teyo Johnson RC 1.00 2.50
203 Trent Smith RC 1.00 2.50
204 George Wrighster RC .75 2.00
205 Jason Witten RC 3.00 8.00
206 Cory Redding RC 1.00 2.50
207 DeWayne White RC .75 2.00
208 Jerome McDougle RC .75 2.00
209 Michael Haynes RC .75 2.00
210 Chris Kelsay RC 1.00 2.50
211 Calvin Pace RC 1.00 2.50
212 Kenny King RC 1.00 2.50
213 Jimmy Kennedy RC 1.00 2.50
214 William Joseph RC .75 2.00
215 DeWayne Robertson RC 1.00 2.50
216 Jarret Johnson RC 1.00 2.50
217 Rien Long RC .75 2.00
218 Boss Bailey RC 1.00 2.50
219 Terrell Suggs RC 1.25 3.00
220 Terry Pierce RC .75 2.00
221 Bradie James RC 1.25 3.00
222 Angelo Crowell RC 1.00 2.50
223 Andre Woolfolk RC 1.00 2.50
224 Dennis Weathersby RC .75 2.00
225 Marcus Trufant RC 1.00 2.50
226 Terence Newman RC 1.00 2.50
227 Ricky Manning RC 1.00 2.50
228 Mike Doss RC 1.25 3.00
229 Julian Battle RC 1.00 2.50
230 Rashean Mathis RC 1.00 2.50
LH1 Lester Hayes Promo 1.50 4.00

2003 Playoff Prestige Xtra Points Green

*VETS 1-150: 3X TO 8X BASIC CARDS
1-250 VETERAN PRINT RUN 100
*ROOKIES 151-230: 2.5X TO 6X
151-230 ROOKIE PRINT RUN 25
ISSUED ONLY IN RETAIL PACKS

2003 Playoff Prestige Xtra Points Purple

*VETS 1-150: 3X TO 8X BASIC CARDS
1-150 VETERAN PRINT RUN 100
*ROOKIES 151-230: 2.5X TO 6X
151-230 ROOKIE PRINT RUN 25

2003 Playoff Prestige 2002 Reunion

COMPLETE SET (30) 20.00 50.00
STATED PRINT RUN 2002 SER.#'d SETS
R1 David Carr .75 2.00
R2 Joey Harrington .60 1.50
R3 Patrick Ramsey .75 2.00
R4 William Green .60 1.50
R5 T.J. Duckett .75 2.00
R6 DeShaun Foster .75 2.00
R7 Jonathan Wells .60 1.50
R8 Clinton Portis .75 2.00
R9 Brian Westbrook 1.00 2.50
R10 Donte Stallworth .60 1.50
R11 Ashley Lelie .60 1.50
R12 Javon Walker .75 2.00
R13 Jabar Gaffney .60 1.50
R14 Josh Reed .60 1.50
R15 Andre Davis .60 1.50
R16 Antwaan Randle El .75 2.00
R17 Antonio Bryant .60 1.50
R18 Deion Branch .75 2.00
R19 Jeremy Shockey 1.00 2.50
R20 Daniel Graham .60 1.50
R21 Randy McMichael .60 1.50
R22 Julius Peppers 1.00 2.50
R23 Dwight Freeney .75 2.00
R24 John Henderson .75 2.00
R25 Quentin Jammer .60 1.50
R26 Phillip Buchanon .60 1.50
R27 Roy Williams .75 2.00
R28 Ed Reed 1.00 2.50
R29 Coy Wire .60 1.50
R30 Napoleon Harris .60 1.50

2003 Playoff Prestige 2002 Reunion Materials

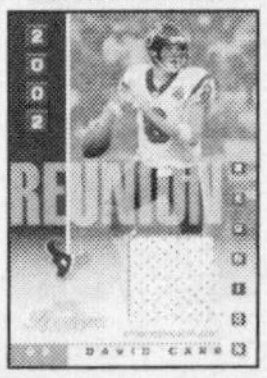

STATED PRINT RUN 150 SER.#'d SETS
R1 David Carr 5.00 12.00
R2 Joey Harrington 4.00 10.00
R4 William Green 4.00 10.00
R5 T.J. Duckett 5.00 12.00
R8 Clinton Portis 5.00 12.00
R10 Donte Stallworth 4.00 10.00
R14 Josh Reed 4.00 10.00
R19 Jeremy Shockey 6.00 15.00
R22 Julius Peppers 6.00 15.00
R27 Roy Williams 5.00 12.00

2003 Playoff Prestige Backfield Tandems

STATED PRINT RUN 400 SER.#'d SETS
BT1 Jake Plummer 4.00 10.00
Marcel Shipp
BT2 Drew Bledsoe 5.00 12.00
Travis Henry
BT3 Tim Couch 3.00 8.00
William Green
BT4 Brian Griese 4.00 10.00
Clinton Portis
BT5 Brett Favre 12.00 30.00
Ahman Green
BT6 James Stewart 4.00 10.00
Joey Harrington
BT7 Peyton Manning 10.00 25.00
Edgerrin James
BT8 Mark Brunell 4.00 10.00
Fred Taylor
BT9 Trent Green 5.00 12.00
Priest Holmes
BT10 Jay Fiedler 4.00 10.00
Ricky Williams
BT11 Daunte Culpepper 4.00 10.00
Michael Bennett
BT12 Tom Brady 12.00 30.00
Antowain Smith
BT13 Aaron Brooks 4.00 10.00
Deuce McAllister
BT14 Chad Pennington 5.00 12.00
Curtis Martin
BT15 Donovan McNabb 5.00 12.00
Duce Staley
BT16 Kordell Stewart 5.00 12.00
Jerome Bettis
BT17 Drew Brees 5.00 12.00
LaDainian Tomlinson
BT18 Jeff Garcia 4.00 10.00
Garrison Hearst
BT19 Kurt Warner 5.00 12.00
Marshall Faulk
BT20 Steve McNair 5.00 12.00
Eddie George

2003 Playoff Prestige Game Day Jerseys

1-20 STATED ODDS 1:34 HOBBY
21-40 STATED ODDS 1:28 RETAIL
GDJ1 Aaron Brooks 3.00 8.00
GDJ2 Brett Favre 10.00 25.00
GDJ3 Brian Griese 3.00 8.00
GDJ4 Daunte Culpepper 3.00 8.00
GDJ5 Emmitt Smith 10.00 25.00
GDJ6 Isaac Bruce 4.00 10.00
GDJ7 Jevon Kearse 3.00 8.00
GDJ8 Joe Horn 3.00 8.00
GDJ9 Kordell Stewart 3.00 8.00
GDJ10 Kurt Warner 4.00 10.00
GDJ11 Marshall Faulk 4.00 10.00
GDJ12 Marvin Harrison 4.00 10.00
GDJ13 Mike Alstott 4.00 10.00
GDJ14 Peyton Manning 8.00 20.00
GDJ15 Randy Moss 4.00 10.00
GDJ16 Rod Smith 3.00 8.00
GDJ17 Terry Glenn 3.00 8.00
GDJ18 Tiki Barber 4.00 10.00
GDJ19 Tim Brown 4.00 10.00
GDJ20 Torry Holt 4.00 10.00
GDJ21 Akili Smith 3.00 8.00
GDJ22 Amani Toomer 3.00 8.00
GDJ23 Corey Simon 3.00 8.00
GDJ24 Curtis Martin 4.00 10.00
GDJ25 Dennis Northcutt 2.50 6.00
GDJ26 Duce Staley 3.00 8.00
GDJ27 Frank Sanders 2.50 6.00
GDJ28 Freddie Mitchell 3.00 8.00
GDJ29 Ike Hilliard 2.50 6.00
GDJ30 Jamel White 2.50 6.00
GDJ31 Jason Sehorn 3.00 8.00
GDJ32 Jimmy Smith 3.00 8.00
GDJ33 J.J. Stokes 2.50 6.00
GDJ34 Junior Seau 4.00 10.00
GDJ35 Kevin Johnson 2.50 6.00
GDJ36 Marcel Shipp 2.50 6.00
GDJ37 Mark Brunell 3.00 8.00
GDJ38 Samari Rolle 3.00 8.00
GDJ39 Shaun King 2.50 6.00
GDJ40 Stephen Davis 3.00 8.00

2003 Playoff Prestige Game Day Jerseys Autographs

STATED PRINT RUN 25 SER.#'d SETS
GDJ8 Joe Horn 20.00 50.00
GDJ10 Kurt Warner 40.00 80.00
GDJ15 Randy Moss 50.00 100.00
GDJ16 Rod Smith 20.00 50.00

2003 Playoff Prestige Gridiron Heritage

COMPLETE SET (25) 15.00 40.00
STATED ODDS 1:17
GH1 Randy Moss .75 2.00
GH2 Ray Lewis .75 2.00
GH3 Cris Carter .75 2.00
GH4 Corey Dillon .60 1.50
GH5 Marvin Harrison 1.00 2.50
GH6 Jake Plummer .60 1.50
GH7 Tim Couch .50 1.25
GH8 Hines Ward .75 2.00
GH9 Edgerrin James .75 2.00
GH10 Jevon Kearse .60 1.50
GH11 Garrison Hearst .60 1.50
GH12 Anthony Thomas .60 1.50
GH13 Brett Favre 2.00 5.00
GH14 Junior Seau .75 2.00
GH15 Emmitt Smith 2.00 5.00
GH16 Kurt Warner .75 2.00
GH17 Donovan McNabb .75 2.00
GH18 Terrell Owens .75 2.00
GH19 Chad Pennington .75 2.00
GH20 Eric Moulds .60 1.50
GH21 Jeff Garcia .60 1.50
GH22 David Boston .50 1.25
GH23 Derrick Mason .60 1.50
GH24 Fred Taylor .60 1.50
GH25 Thomas Jones .75 2.00

2003 Playoff Prestige Gridiron Heritage Jerseys

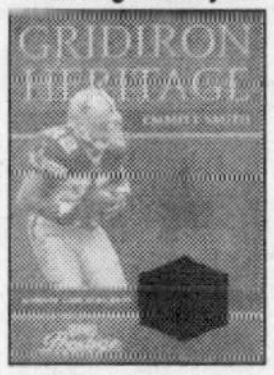

1-10 HELMET SWATCH PRINT RUN 100
11-25 JSY SWATCH PRINT RUN 250
GH1 Randy Moss HEL 8.00 20.00
GH2 Ray Lewis HEL 8.00 20.00
GH3 Cris Carter HEL 8.00 20.00
GH4 Corey Dillon HEL 6.00 15.00
GH5 Marvin Harrison HEL 8.00 20.00
GH6 Jake Plummer HEL 6.00 15.00
GH7 Tim Couch HEL 5.00 12.00
GH8 Hines Ward HEL 8.00 20.00
GH9 Edgerrin James HEL 8.00 20.00
GH10 Jevon Kearse HEL 6.00 15.00
GH11 Garrison Hearst JSY 4.00 10.00
GH12 Anthony Thomas JSY 4.00 10.00
GH13 Brett Favre JSY 12.00 30.00
GH14 Junior Seau JSY 5.00 12.00
GH15 Emmitt Smith JSY 12.00 30.00
GH16 Kurt Warner JSY 5.00 12.00
GH17 Donovan McNabb JSY 5.00 12.00
GH18 Terrell Owens JSY 5.00 12.00
GH19 Chad Pennington JSY 5.00 12.00
GH20 Eric Moulds JSY 4.00 10.00
GH21 Jeff Garcia JSY 4.00 10.00
GH22 David Boston JSY 3.00 8.00
GH23 Derrick Mason JSY 4.00 10.00
GH24 Fred Taylor JSY 4.00 10.00
GH25 Thomas Jones JSY 5.00 12.00

2003 Playoff Prestige Inside the Numbers

COMPLETE SET (25) 15.00 40.00
STATED PRINT RUN 2002 SER.#'d SETS
*DIE CUT/80-96: 2X TO 5X BASE INSERT
*DIE CUT/31-34: 3X TO 8X BASE INSERT
*DIE CUT/20-28: 4X TO 10X BASE INSERT
DIE CUT PRINT RUN 2-96
IN1 Brett Favre 2.50 6.00
IN2 Rich Gannon .75 2.00
IN3 Tommy Maddox .75 2.00
IN4 Drew Bledsoe 1.00 2.50
IN5 Chad Pennington 1.00 2.50
IN6 Jeff Garcia .75 2.00
IN7 Aaron Brooks .75 2.00
IN8 Michael Vick 1.25 3.00
IN9 LaDainian Tomlinson 1.00 2.50
IN10 Priest Holmes 1.00 2.50
IN11 Deuce McAllister .75 2.00
IN12 Marshall Faulk .75 2.00
IN13 Ricky Williams .75 2.00
IN14 Jamal Lewis .75 2.00
IN15 Travis Henry .60 1.50
IN16 Michael Bennett .75 2.00
IN17 Marvin Harrison 1.00 2.50
IN18 Eric Moulds .75 2.00
IN19 Peerless Price .60 1.50
IN20 Jerry Rice 2.00 5.00
IN21 Donald Driver 1.00 2.50
IN22 Plaxico Burress 1.00 2.50
IN23 Terrell Owens 1.00 2.50
IN24 Julius Peppers 1.00 2.50
IN25 Andre Carter .60 1.50

2003 Playoff Prestige Signature Impressions

STATED PRINT RUN 50 SER.#'d SETS
SI1 Antowain Smith 15.00 40.00
SI2 Brian Urlacher 40.00 100.00
SI3 Deion Branch 15.00 40.00
SI5 Donald Driver 30.00 60.00
SI6 Drew Bledsoe 20.00 50.00
SI7 Eddie George 15.00 40.00
SI8 Garrison Hearst 15.00 40.00
SI9 Jeff Garcia 15.00 40.00
SI10 Jerome Bettis 35.00 60.00
SI11 LaDainian Tomlinson 40.00 80.00
SI12 Mike Alstott 20.00 50.00
SI13 Priest Holmes 20.00 50.00
SI16 Hines Ward 35.00 60.00
SI19 Ed McCaffrey 15.00 40.00
SI22 Terrell Owens 20.00 50.00
SI24 Kurt Warner 20.00 50.00
SI25 Michael Vick 40.00 80.00

2003 Playoff Prestige Stars of the NFL Jerseys

STATED PRINT RUN 250 SER.#'d SETS
*PATCH/50: 1X TO 2.5X JSY/250
PATCHES PRINT RUN 50 SER.#'d SETS
SN1 Anthony Thomas 4.00 10.00
SN2 Chris Chambers 4.00 10.00
SN3 Donte Stallworth 3.00 8.00
SN4 Eddie George 4.00 10.00
SN5 Eric Moulds 4.00 10.00
SN6 Isaac Bruce 5.00 12.00
SN7 Jeff Garcia 4.00 10.00
SN8 Jerome Bettis 5.00 12.00
SN9 Jerry Rice 10.00 25.00
SN10 Joey Harrington 3.00 8.00
SN11 Koren Robinson 4.00 10.00
SN12 Kurt Warner 5.00 12.00
SN13 Mark Brunell 4.00 10.00
SN14 Michael Bennett 4.00 10.00
SN15 Michael Strahan 5.00 12.00
SN16 Plaxico Burress 4.00 10.00
SN17 Rich Gannon 4.00 10.00
SN18 Rod Smith 4.00 10.00
SN19 Steve McNair 5.00 12.00
SN20 Terrell Owens 5.00 12.00

2003 Playoff Prestige Stars of the NFL Patches Autographs

STATED PRINT RUN 25 SETS
5 Eric Moulds 25.00 60.00
12 Kurt Warner 30.00 80.00
17 Rich Gannon 25.00 60.00
19 Steve McNair 30.00 80.00

2003 Playoff Prestige Turning Pro Jerseys

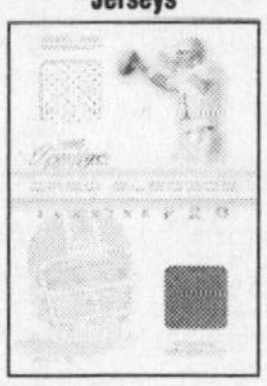

STATED PRINT RUN 250 SER.#'d SETS
TP1 Drew Bledsoe 8.00 20.00
TP2 Curtis Martin 8.00 20.00
TP3 Fred Taylor 6.00 15.00
TP4 Jevon Kearse 6.00 15.00
TP5 Ahman Green 6.00 15.00
TP6 Eddie George 6.00 15.00
TP7 Shaun Alexander 6.00 15.00
TP8 Edgerrin James 8.00 20.00
TP9 Keyshawn Johnson 8.00 20.00
TP10 Ricky Williams 6.00 15.00

2003 Playoff Prestige Draft Picks

COMPLETE SET (24) 25.00 60.00
STATED PRINT RUN 2003 SER.#'d SETS
DP1 Byron Leftwich 1.00 2.50
DP2 Carson Palmer 2.00 5.00
DP3 Dave Ragone .60 1.50
DP4 Larry Johnson 1.00 2.50
DP5 Musa Smith .60 1.50
DP6 Lee Suggs .75 2.00
DP7 Onterrio Smith .60 1.50
DP8 Chris Brown .60 1.50
DP9 Andre Johnson 2.50 6.00
DP10 Brandon Lloyd 1.50 4.00
DP11 Bryant Johnson 1.00 2.50
DP12 Charles Rogers .75 2.00
DP13 Kelley Washington .60 1.50
DP14 Taylor Jacobs .60 1.50
DP15 Terrence Edwards .60 1.50
DP16 Mike Pinkard .60 1.50
DP17 Teyo Johnson .75 2.00
DP18 DeWayne White .60 1.50
DP19 Jerome McDougal .60 1.50
DP20 Jimmy Kennedy .75 2.00
DP21 William Joseph .60 1.50
DP22 Terrell Suggs 1.00 2.50
DP24 Terence Newman .75 2.00
DP25 Mike Doss 1.00 2.50

2003 Playoff Prestige Draft Picks Autographs

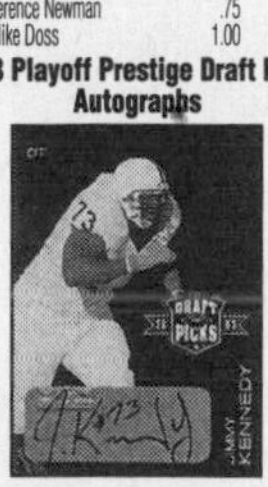

STATED PRINT RUN 50 SER.#'d SETS
DP1 Byron Leftwich 15.00 40.00
DP2 Carson Palmer 30.00 80.00
DP4 Larry Johnson 20.00 50.00
DP5 Musa Smith
DP6 Lee Suggs 12.00 30.00
DP7 Onterrio Smith 10.00 25.00
DP8 Chris Brown 10.00 25.00
DP9 Andre Johnson 50.00 100.00
DP12 Charles Rogers 12.00 30.00
DP13 Kelley Washington 10.00 25.00
DP15 Terrence Edwards 10.00 25.00
DP18 DeWayne White
DP19 Jerome McDougal 10.00 25.00
DP20 Jimmy Kennedy 12.00 30.00
DP21 William Joseph 10.00 25.00
DP23 Terrell Suggs 25.00 50.00
DP24 Terence Newman 12.00 30.00

2003 Playoff Prestige League Leader Quads

COMPLETE SET (10) 30.00 80.00
STATED PRINT RUN 500 SER.#'d SETS
LLQ1 Jeff Garcia 2.50 6.00
Rich Gannon
Brett Favre
Chad Pennington
LLQ2 Steve McNair 2.00 5.00
Brad Johnson
Drew Bledsoe
Aaron Brooks
LLQ3 Peyton Manning 3.00 8.00
Michael Vick
Tom Brady
Kerry Collins
LLQ4 LaDainian Tomlinson 2.50 6.00
Marshall Faulk
Priest Holmes
Deuce McAllister
LLQ5 Ricky Williams 2.00 5.00
Ahman Green
Corey Dillon
Michael Bennett
LLQ6 Clinton Portis 6.00 15.00
James Stewart
Fred Taylor
Emmitt Smith
LLQ7 Marvin Harrison 2.50 6.00
Joe Horn
Eric Moulds
Keyshawn Johnson
LLQ8 Peerless Price 5.00 12.00
Torry Holt
Jerry Rice
Terrell Owens
LLQ9 Plaxico Burress 2.50 6.00
Donald Driver
Hines Ward
Randy Moss
LLQ10 Julius Peppers 2.50 6.00
Zach Thomas
Warren Sapp
Keith Bulluck

2003 Playoff Prestige League Leader Quads Materials

STATED PRINT RUN 25 SER.#'d SETS
LLQ1 Jeff Garcia 15.00 40.00
Rich Gannon
Brett Favre
Chad Pennington
LLQ2 Steve McNair 12.00 30.00
Brad Johnson
Drew Bledsoe
Aaron Brooks
LLQ3 Peyton Manning 20.00 50.00
Michael Vick
Tom Brady
Kerry Collins
LLQ4 LaDainian Tomlinson 15.00 40.00
Marshall Faulk
Priest Holmes
Deuce McAllister
LLQ5 Ricky Williams 12.00 30.00
Ahman Green
Corey Dillon
Michael Bennett
LLQ6 Clinton Portis 40.00 100.00
James Stewart
Fred Taylor
Emmitt Smith
LLQ7 Marvin Harrison 15.00 40.00
Joe Horn
Eric Moulds
Keyshawn Johnson
LLQ8 Peerless Price 30.00 80.00
Torry Holt
Jerry Rice
Terrell Owens
LLQ9 Plaxico Burress 15.00 40.00
Donald Driver
Hines Ward
Randy Moss
LLQ10 Julius Peppers 15.00 40.00
Zach Thomas
Warren Sapp
Keith Bulluck

2003 Playoff Prestige League Leader Tandems

COMPLETE SET (20) 20.00 50.00
STATED PRINT RUN 2002 SER.#'d SETS
LLT1 Jeff Garcia .75 2.00
Rich Gannon
LLT2 Brett Favre 1.00 2.50
Chad Pennington
LLT3 Steve McNair 1.00 2.50
Brad Johnson
LLT4 Drew Bledsoe .75 2.00
Aaron Brooks
LLT5 Peyton Manning 1.25 3.00
Michael Vick
LLT6 Tom Brady 2.50 6.00
Kerry Collins
LLT7 LaDainian Tomlinson 1.00 2.50
Marshall Faulk
LLT8 Priest Holmes 1.00 2.50
Deuce McAllister
LLT9 Ricky Williams .75 2.00
Ahman Green
LLT10 Corey Dillon .75 2.00
Michael Bennett
LLT11 Clinton Portis .75 2.00
James Stewart
LLT12 Fred Taylor 2.50 6.00
Emmitt Smith
LLT13 Marvin Harrison 1.00 2.50
Joe Horn
LLT14 Eric Moulds 1.00 2.50
Keyshawn Johnson
LLT15 Peerless Price 1.00 2.50
Torry Holt
LLT16 Jerry Rice 2.00 5.00
Terrell Owens
LLT17 Plaxico Burress 1.00 2.50
Donald Driver
LLT18 Hines Ward 1.00 2.50
Randy Moss
LLT19 Julius Peppers 1.00 2.50
Zach Thomas
LLT20 Warren Sapp .75 2.00
Keith Bulluck

2003 Playoff Prestige League Leader Tandems Materials

STATED PRINT RUN 250 SER.#'d SETS
LLT1 Jeff Garcia 5.00 12.00
Rich Gannon
LLT2 Brett Favre 6.00 15.00
Chad Pennington
LLT3 Steve McNair 6.00 15.00
Brad Johnson
LLT4 Drew Bledsoe 5.00 12.00
Aaron Brooks
LLT5 Peyton Manning 8.00 20.00
Michael Vick
LLT6 Tom Brady 15.00 40.00
Kerry Collins
LLT7 LaDainian Tomlinson 6.00 15.00
Marshall Faulk
LLT8 Priest Holmes 6.00 15.00
Deuce McAllister
LLT9 Ricky Williams 5.00 12.00
Ahman Green
LLT10 Corey Dillon 5.00 12.00
Michael Bennett
LLT11 Clinton Portis 5.00 12.00
James Stewart
LLT12 Fred Taylor 15.00 40.00
Emmitt Smith
LLT13 Marvin Harrison 6.00 15.00
Joe Horn
LLT14 Eric Mould 6.00 15.00
Keyshawn Johnson
LLT15 Peerless Price 6.00 15.00
Torry Holt
LLT16 Jerry Rice 12.00 30.00
Terrell Owens
LLT17 Plaxico Burress 6.00 15.00
Donald Driver
LLT18 Hines Ward 6.00 15.00
Randy Moss
LLT19 Julius Peppers 6.00 15.00
Zach Thomas
LLT20 Warren Sapp 5.00 12.00
Keith Bulluck

2004 Playoff Prestige

Playoff Prestige released in May of 2004 and was the first full NFL product of the year. The base set consists of 227 cards including 150 veterans and 77 rookies. Within the rookie subset, ten cards were short-printed and seeded at a ratio of 1:6 boxes. Note that Mike Williams and Maurice Clarett both made an appearance in this product although they were declared ineligible for the NFL Draft. Hobby boxes contained 24-packs of 6-cards along with an extensive selection of insert and game-used sets highlighted by the Draft Picks Rights Autograph set and the very first LaVar Arrington game-used memorabilia card.

COMP.SET w/o RC's (150) 10.00 25.00
SP RC ANNOUNCED ODDS 1:6 BOXES
1 Anquan Boldin .40 1.00
2 Emmitt Smith 1.00 2.50
3 Jeff Blake .30 .75
4 Marcel Shipp .25 .60
5 Michael Vick .50 1.25
6 Peerless Price .25 .60
7 T.J. Duckett .30 .75
8 Warrick Dunn .30 .75
9 Ed Reed .30 .75
10 Jamal Lewis .30 .75
11 Kyle Boller .30 .75
12 Ray Lewis .40 1.00
13 Todd Heap .30 .75
14 Drew Bledsoe .40 1.00
15 Eric Moulds .30 .75
16 Josh Reed .25 .60
17 Travis Henry .25 .60
18 DeShaun Foster .30 .75
19 Stephen Davis .30 .75
20 Jake Delhomme .30 .75
21 Julius Peppers .30 .75
22 Steve Smith .40 1.00
23 Anthony Thomas .30 .75
24 Brian Urlacher .40 1.00
25 Marty Booker .30 .75
26 Rex Grossman .30 .75
27 Chad Johnson .40 1.00
28 Corey Dillon .30 .75
29 Carson Palmer .40 1.00
30 Peter Warrick .30 .75
31 Rudi Johnson .30 .75
32 Andre Davis .25 .60
33 Quincy Morgan .25 .60
34 William Green .25 .60
35 Kelly Holcomb .25 .60
36 Antonio Bryant .30 .75
37 Quincy Carter .25 .60
38 Roy Williams S .30 .75
39 Terence Newman .30 .75
40 Terry Glenn .30 .75
41 Troy Hambrick .30 .75
42 Ashley Lelie .30 .75
43 Clinton Portis .40 1.00
44 Rod Smith .30 .75
45 Shannon Sharpe .40 1.00
46 Mike Anderson .30 .75
47 Jake Plummer .30 .75
48 Charles Rogers .25 .60
49 Joey Harrington .25 .60
50 Ahman Green .30 .75
51 Brett Favre 1.00 2.50
52 Donald Driver .25 .60
53 Javon Walker .25 .60
54 Robert Ferguson .25 .60
55 Andre Johnson .40 1.00
56 David Carr .25 .60
57 Domanick Davis .25 .60
58 Jabar Gaffney .25 .60
59 Dwight Freeney .30 .75
60 Dallas Clark .40 1.00
61 Edgerrin James .30 .75
62 Marvin Harrison .40 1.00
63 Peyton Manning .75 2.00
64 Reggie Wayne .40 1.00
65 Byron Leftwich .30 .75
66 Fred Taylor .30 .75
67 Jimmy Smith .30 .75
68 Johnnie Morton .30 .75
69 Priest Holmes .40 1.00
70 Tony Gonzalez .40 1.00
71 Trent Green .30 .75
72 Chris Chambers .30 .75
73 Jay Fiedler .25 .60
74 Randy McMichael .25 .60
75 Ricky Williams .30 .75
76 Zach Thomas .40 1.00
77 Daunte Culpepper .30 .75
78 Kelly Campbell .25 .60
79 Michael Bennett .30 .75
80 Moe Williams .25 .60
81 Nate Burleson .30 .75
82 Randy Moss .40 1.00
83 Deion Branch .30 .75
84 Kevin Faulk .30 .75
85 Tom Brady .75 2.00
86 Troy Brown .30 .75
87 Tedy Bruschi .40 1.00
88 Aaron Brooks .30 .75
89 Deuce McAllister .30 .75
90 Donte Stallworth .25 .60
91 Joe Horn .30 .75
92 Amani Toomer .30 .75
93 Ike Hilliard .30 .75
94 Jeremy Shockey .30 .75
95 Kerry Collins .30 .75
96 Michael Strahan .30 .75
97 Tiki Barber .40 1.00
98 Chad Pennington .40 1.00
99 Curtis Martin .40 1.00
100 LaMont Jordan .30 .75
101 Santana Moss .30 .75
102 Charlie Garner .30 .75
103 Jerry Porter .25 .60
104 Jerry Rice .75 2.00
105 Justin Fargas .30 .75
106 Rich Gannon .30 .75
107 Rod Woodson .30 .75
108 Tim Brown .40 1.00
109 Brian Westbrook .40 1.00
110 Correll Buckhalter .30 .75
111 Donovan McNabb .40 1.00
112 Freddie Mitchell .25 .60
113 James Thrash .25 .60
114 Amos Zereoue .25 .60
115 Antwaan Randle El .30 .75
116 Hines Ward .40 1.00
117 Joey Porter .30 .75
118 Kendrell Bell .25 .60
119 Plaxico Burress .30 .75
120 David Boston .25 .60
121 Drew Brees .40 1.00
122 LaDainian Tomlinson .40 1.00
123 Jeff Garcia .30 .75
124 Kevan Barlow .25 .60
125 Tai Streets .25 .60
126 Terrell Owens .40 1.00
127 Tim Rattay .25 .60
128 Darrell Jackson .30 .75
129 Koren Robinson .30 .75
130 Matt Hasselbeck .30 .75
131 Shaun Alexander .30 .75
132 Isaac Bruce .30 .75
133 Marc Bulger .30 .75
134 Marshall Faulk .40 1.00
135 Torry Holt .30 .75
136 Brad Johnson .30 .75
137 Derrick Brooks .30 .75
138 Keenan McCardell .25 .60
139 Keyshawn Johnson .30 .75
140 Mike Alstott .30 .75
141 Derrick Mason .30 .75
142 Drew Bennett .30 .75
143 Jevon Kearse .30 .75
144 Justin McCareins .25 .60
145 Steve McNair .40 1.00
146 Tyrone Calico .30 .75
147 Bruce Smith .40 1.00
148 Laveranues Coles .25 .60
149 Patrick Ramsey .30 .75
150 LaVar Arrington .30 .75
151 Eli Manning RC 6.00 15.00
152 Larry Fitzgerald RC 2.50 6.00
153 Philip Rivers RC 4.00 10.00
154 Sean Taylor RC 1.00 2.50
155 Kellen Winslow RC 1.00 2.50
156 Roy Williams RC 1.00 2.50
157 DeAngelo Hall RC 1.00 2.50
158 Reggie Williams RC .75 2.00
159 Ben Roethlisberger RC 6.00 15.00
160 Jonathan Vilma RC 1.00 2.50
161 Lee Evans RC 1.00 2.50
162 Tommie Harris RC 1.00 2.50
163 Michael Clayton RC .75 2.00
164 D.J. Williams SP RC 10.00 25.00
165 Will Smith RC .75 2.00
166 Kenechi Udeze RC .75 2.00
167 Vince Wilfork SP RC 10.00 25.00
168 J.P. Losman RC .75 2.00
169 Steven Jackson SP RC 20.00 50.00
170 Ahmad Carroll RC .60 1.50
171 Chris Perry RC .75 2.00
172 Jason Babin SP RC 10.00 25.00
173 Chris Gamble RC .75 2.00
174 Michael Jenkins RC 1.00 2.50
175 Kevin Jones RC .75 2.00
176 Rashaun Woods RC .60 1.50
177 Ben Watson RC 1.00 2.50
178 Karlos Dansby RC 1.00 2.50
179 Teddy Lehman RC .60 1.50
180 Ricardo Colclough SP RC 8.00 20.00
181 Daryl Smith RC .60 1.50
182 Ben Troupe RC .75 2.00
183 Tatum Bell RC .75 2.00
184 Julius Jones RC .75 2.00
185 Bob Sanders RC 2.50 6.00
186 Devery Henderson RC 1.00 2.50
187 Dwan Edwards RC .60 1.50
188 Michael Boulware RC 1.00 2.50
189 Darius Watts RC .60 1.50
190 Greg Jones RC .60 1.50
191 Antwan Odom RC .75 2.00
192 Sean Jones SP RC 8.00 20.00
193 Courtney Watson RC .60 1.50
194 Keary Colbert RC .60 1.50
195 Keith Smith RC .60 1.50
196 Derrick Strait RC .60 1.50
197 Bernard Berrian RC 1.00 2.50
198 Devard Darling RC .60 1.50
199 Matt Schaub RC 2.00 5.00
200 Will Poole RC 1.00 2.50
201 Samie Parker RC .60 1.50
202 Luke McCown SP RC 8.00 20.00
203 Jericho Cotchery RC .75 2.00
204 Meweldé Moore RC .75 2.00
205 Ernest Wilford RC .75 2.00
206 Cedric Cobbs SP RC 6.00 15.00
207 Johnnie Morant RC .60 1.50
208 Craig Krenzel RC .75 2.00
209 Michael Turner RC 1.25 3.00
210 D.J. Hackett RC .75 2.00
211 P.K. Sam RC .60 1.50
212 Josh Harris RC .60 1.50
213 Drew Henson RC .60 1.50
214 Jeff Smoker RC .75 2.00
215 John Navarre RC .60 1.50
216 Cody Pickett RC .75 2.00
217 Quincy Wilson RC .75 2.00
218 Derek Abney RC .60 1.50
219 Maurice Clarett SP RC 8.00 20.00
220 Mike Williams SP RC 8.00 20.00
221 B.J. Johnson RC .60 1.50
222 Brandon Everage RC .60 1.50
223 Derek McCoy RC .60 1.50
224 Jared Lorenzen RC .75 2.00
225 Jarrett Payton RC .75 2.00
226 Jason Fife RC .60 1.50
227 Robert Kent RC .60 1.50

2004 Playoff Prestige Xtra Points Black

*VETS: 10X TO 25X BASIC CARDS
*ROOKIES: 5X TO 12X BASIC RC
*ROOKIES: .5X TO 1.2X BASIC SP RC
HOBBY INSERT PRINT RUN 25
19 Stephen Davis AU 15.00 40.00
38 Roy Williams S AU 15.00 40.00
57 Domanick Davis AU 12.00 30.00
67 Jimmy Smith AU 15.00 40.00
72 Chris Chambers AU 15.00 40.00
88 Aaron Brooks AU 15.00 40.00
91 Joe Horn AU 15.00 40.00
97 Tiki Barber AU 20.00 50.00
116 Hines Ward AU 50.00 100.00
141 Derrick Mason AU 15.00 40.00
213 Drew Henson AU 12.00 30.00

2004 Playoff Prestige Xtra Points Green

*VETS: 10X TO 25X BASIC CARDS
*ROOKIES: 5X TO 12X BASIC RC
*ROOKIES: .5X TO 1.2X BASIC SP RC
PRINT RUN 25 SER.#'d SETS RETAIL ONLY

2004 Playoff Prestige Xtra Points Purple

*VETS: 4X TO 10X BASIC CARDS
*ROOKIES: 1.5X TO 4X BASIC RC
*ROOKIES: .15X TO .4X BASIC SP RC
HOBBY INSERT PRINT RUN 75

2004 Playoff Prestige Xtra Points Red

*VETS: 3X TO 8X BASE CARD HI
*ROOKIES: 1.5X TO 4X BASIC RC
*ROOKIES: .15X TO .4X BASIC SP RC
RETAIL INSERT PRINT RUN 100

2004 Playoff Prestige Achievements

COMPLETE SET (15) 12.50 30.00
A1 Brian Urlacher 1.00 2.50
A2 Emmitt Smith 2.50 6.00
A3 Clinton Portis 1.00 2.50
A4 Brett Favre 2.50 6.00
A5 Peyton Manning 2.00 5.00
A6 Ricky Williams .75 2.00
A7 Randy Moss 1.00 2.50
A8 Tom Brady 2.00 5.00
A9 LaDainian Tomlinson 1.00 2.50
A10 Marshall Faulk 1.00 2.50
A11 Jamal Lewis .75 2.00
A12 Steve McNair 1.00 2.50
A13 Rich Gannon .75 2.00
A14 Kurt Warner 1.00 2.50
A15 Torry Holt .75 2.00

2004 Playoff Prestige Achievements Materials

STATED PRINT RUN 93-103
A1 Brian Urlacher/100 5.00 12.00
A2 Emmitt Smith/93 12.00 30.00
A3 Clinton Portis/102 5.00 12.00
A4 Brett Favre/97 12.00 30.00
A5 Peyton Manning/103 10.00 25.00
A6 Ricky Williams/102 4.00 10.00
A7 Randy Moss/98 5.00 12.00
A8 Tom Brady/101 10.00 25.00
A9 LaDainian Tomlinson/102 5.00 12.00
A10 Marshall Faulk/100 5.00 12.00
A11 Jamal Lewis/103 4.00 10.00
A12 Steve McNair/103 5.00 12.00
A13 Rich Gannon/102 4.00 10.00
A14 Kurt Warner/99 5.00 12.00
A15 Torry Holt/103 4.00 10.00

2004 Playoff Prestige Changing Stripes

STATED PRINT RUN 225 SER.#'d SETS
*PRIME/25: 1X TO 2.5X BASIC DUAL/225
PRIME PRINT RUN 25 SER.#'d SETS
CS1 David Boston 3.00 8.00
CS2 Priest Holmes 5.00 12.00
CS3 Trent Green 4.00 10.00
CS4 Jerry Rice 10.00 25.00
CS5 Jake Plummer 4.00 10.00
CS6 Emmitt Smith 12.00 30.00
CS7 Laveranues Coles 3.00 8.00
CS8 Brad Johnson 4.00 10.00
CS9 Junior Seau 5.00 12.00
CS10 Stephen Davis 4.00 10.00

2004 Playoff Prestige Draft Picks

COMPLETE SET (25) 30.00 80.00
DP1 Ben Roethlisberger 6.00 15.00
DP2 Eli Manning 6.00 15.00
DP3 J.P. Losman .75 2.00
DP4 Philip Rivers 4.00 10.00
DP5 Steven Jackson 1.50 4.00
DP6 Kevin Jones .75 2.00
DP7 Chris Perry .75 2.00
DP8 Greg Jones .60 1.50
DP9 Michael Turner 1.25 3.00
DP10 Roy Williams WR 1.00 2.50
DP11 Rashaun Woods .60 1.50
DP12 Reggie Williams .75 2.00
DP13 Michael Clayton .75 2.00
DP14 Lee Evans 1.00 2.50
DP15 Kellen Winslow Jr. 1.00 2.50
DP16 Matt Schaub 2.00 5.00
DP17 Quincy Wilson .60 1.50
DP18 Julius Jones .75 2.00
DP19 Larry Fitzgerald 2.50 6.00
DP20 Ernest Wilford .75 2.00
DP21 Keary Colbert .60 1.50
DP22 Tommie Harris 1.00 2.50

DP23 Jonathan Vilma	1.00	2.50
DP24 Chris Gamble	.75	2.00
DP25 Sean Taylor	2.00	5.00

2004 Playoff Prestige Draft Picks Autographs

STATED PRINT RUN 50 SER.#'d SETS		
DP1 Ben Roethlisberger	75.00	150.00
DP2 Eli Manning	90.00	150.00
DP3 J.P. Losman	12.00	30.00
DP4 Philip Rivers	60.00	120.00
DP5 Steven Jackson	40.00	100.00
DP6 Kevin Jones	12.00	30.00
DP7 Chris Perry	12.00	30.00
DP8 Greg Jones	10.00	25.00
DP9 Michael Turner	20.00	50.00
DP10 Roy Williams WR	15.00	40.00
DP12 Reggie Williams	12.00	30.00
DP13 Michael Clayton	12.00	30.00
DP14 Lee Evans	15.00	40.00
DP15 Kellen Winslow Jr.	15.00	40.00
DP16 Matt Schaub	50.00	100.00
DP17 Quincy Wilson	12.00	30.00
DP18 Julius Jones	12.00	30.00
DP19 Larry Fitzgerald	75.00	125.00
DP20 Ernest Wilford	12.00	30.00
DP21 Keary Colbert	10.00	25.00
DP23 Jonathan Vilma	15.00	40.00
DP24 Chris Gamble	12.00	30.00

2004 Playoff Prestige Game Day Jerseys

GJ1-GJ20 INSERTED IN HOBBY PACKS		
GJ21-GJ40 INSERTED IN RETAIL PACKS		
GJ1 Anquan Boldin	4.00	10.00
GJ2 Marcel Shipp	2.50	6.00
GJ3 Peerless Price	2.50	6.00
GJ4 Travis Henry	2.50	6.00
GJ5 Jimmy Smith	3.00	8.00
GJ6 Amani Toomer	3.00	8.00
GJ7 Tim Brown	4.00	10.00
GJ8 Correll Buckhalter	3.00	8.00
GJ9 Donovan McNabb	4.00	10.00
GJ10 Jerome Bettis	4.00	10.00
GJ11 Jeff Garcia	3.00	8.00
GJ12 Isaac Bruce	3.00	8.00
GJ13 Warren Sapp	3.00	8.00
GJ14 Steve McNair	4.00	10.00
GJ15 Jamal Lewis	3.00	8.00
GJ16 Roy Williams S	3.00	8.00
GJ17 David Carr	2.50	6.00
GJ18 Peyton Manning	8.00	20.00
GJ19 Chris Chambers	3.00	8.00
GJ20 Michael Bennett	3.00	8.00
GJ21 Jason McAddley	2.50	6.00
GJ22 Muhsin Muhammad	3.00	8.00
GJ23 David Terrell	2.50	6.00
GJ24 Dennis Northcutt	2.50	6.00
GJ25 William Green	2.50	6.00
GJ26 Tim Couch	3.00	8.00
GJ27 Rod Smith	3.00	8.00
GJ28 Scotty Anderson	2.50	6.00
GJ29 Antonio Freeman	3.00	8.00
GJ30 Fred Taylor	3.00	8.00
GJ31 Mark Brunell	3.00	8.00
GJ32 Byron Chamberlain	2.50	6.00
GJ33 Antowain Smith	3.00	8.00
GJ34 Tedy Bruschi	8.00	10.00
GJ35 Ike Hilliard	3.00	8.00
GJ36 Ron Dayne	3.00	8.00
GJ37 Wayne Chrebet	3.00	8.00
GJ38 Josh McCown	3.00	8.00
GJ39 Duce Staley	3.00	8.00
GJ40 Jeremy Shockey	3.00	8.00

2004 Playoff Prestige Gamers

STATED PRINT RUN 750 SER.#'d SETS		
G1 Michael Vick	2.00	5.00
G2 Jamal Lewis	1.25	3.00
G3 Ray Lewis	1.50	4.00
G4 Travis Henry	1.00	2.50
G5 Brian Urlacher	1.50	4.00
G6 Clinton Portis	1.50	4.00
G7 Brett Favre	4.00	10.00
G8 Ahman Green	1.25	3.00
G9 David Carr	1.00	2.50
G10 Marvin Harrison	1.50	4.00
G11 Peyton Manning	3.00	8.00
G12 Priest Holmes	1.50	4.00
G13 Ricky Williams	1.25	3.00
G14 Daunte Culpepper	1.25	3.00
G15 Randy Moss	1.50	4.00
G16 Tom Brady	3.00	8.00
G17 Deuce McAllister	1.25	3.00
G18 Jeremy Shockey	1.25	3.00
G19 Chad Pennington	1.50	4.00
G20 Jerry Rice	3.00	8.00
G21 Donovan McNabb	1.50	4.00
G22 LaDainian Tomlinson	1.50	4.00
G23 Terrell Owens	1.50	4.00
G24 Torry Holt	1.25	3.00
G25 Steve McNair	1.50	4.00

2004 Playoff Prestige Gamers Jerseys

STATED PRINT RUN 100 SER.#'d SETS		
G1 Michael Vick	6.00	15.00
G2 Jamal Lewis	4.00	10.00
G3 Ray Lewis	5.00	12.00
G4 Travis Henry	3.00	8.00
G5 Brian Urlacher	5.00	12.00
G6 Clinton Portis	5.00	12.00
G7 Brett Favre	12.00	30.00
G8 Ahman Green	4.00	10.00
G9 David Carr	3.00	8.00
G10 Marvin Harrison	5.00	12.00
G11 Peyton Manning	10.00	25.00
G12 Priest Holmes	5.00	12.00
G13 Ricky Williams	4.00	10.00
G14 Daunte Culpepper	4.00	10.00
G15 Randy Moss	5.00	12.00
G16 Tom Brady	10.00	25.00
G17 Deuce McAllister	4.00	10.00
G18 Jeremy Shockey	4.00	10.00
G19 Chad Pennington	5.00	12.00
G20 Jerry Rice	10.00	25.00
G21 Donovan McNabb	5.00	12.00
G22 LaDainian Tomlinson	5.00	12.00
G23 Terrell Owens	5.00	12.00
G24 Torry Holt	4.00	10.00
G25 Steve McNair	5.00	12.00

2004 Playoff Prestige Gridiron Heritage

COMPLETE SET (20)	15.00	40.00
GH1 Marcel Shipp	.75	2.00
GH2 Eric Moulds	1.00	2.50
GH3 Anthony Thomas	1.00	2.50
GH4 Corey Dillon	1.00	2.50
GH5 Kelly Holcomb	.75	2.00
GH6 Rod Smith	1.00	2.50
GH7 Joey Harrington	1.00	2.50
GH8 Brett Favre	3.00	8.00
GH9 Edgerrin James	1.00	2.50
GH10 Fred Taylor	1.00	2.50
GH11 Zach Thomas	1.25	3.00
GH12 Aaron Brooks	1.00	2.50
GH13 Tiki Barber	1.25	3.00
GH14 Curtis Martin	1.25	3.00
GH15 Tim Brown	1.25	3.00
GH16 Correll Buckhalter	1.00	2.50
GH17 Hines Ward	1.25	3.00
GH18 Jeff Garcia	1.00	2.50
GH19 Mike Alstott	1.00	2.50
GH20 Eddie George	1.00	2.50

2004 Playoff Prestige Gridiron Heritage Jerseys

GH1 Marcel Shipp	2.50	6.00
GH2 Eric Moulds	3.00	8.00
GH3 Anthony Thomas	3.00	8.00
GH4 Corey Dillon	3.00	8.00
GH5 Kelly Holcomb	2.50	6.00
GH6 Rod Smith	3.00	8.00
GH7 Joey Harrington	3.00	8.00
GH8 Brett Favre	10.00	25.00
GH9 Edgerrin James	3.00	8.00
GH10 Fred Taylor	3.00	8.00
GH11 Zach Thomas	4.00	10.00
GH12 Aaron Brooks	3.00	8.00
GH13 Tiki Barber	4.00	10.00
GH14 Curtis Martin	4.00	10.00
GH15 Tim Brown	4.00	10.00
GH16 Correll Buckhalter	3.00	8.00
GH17 Hines Ward	4.00	10.00
GH18 Jeff Garcia	3.00	8.00
GH19 Mike Alstott	3.00	8.00
GH20 Eddie George	3.00	8.00

2004 Playoff Prestige League Leaders

COMPLETE SET (20)	20.00	50.00
LL1 Peyton Manning	2.50	6.00
Trent Green		
LL2 Aaron Brooks	1.00	2.50
Daunte Culpepper		
LL3 Brett Favre	3.00	8.00
Quincy Carter		
LL4 Donovan McNabb	1.25	3.00
Kerry Collins		
LL5 Brad Johnson	1.00	2.50
Marc Bulger		
LL6 Steve McNair	2.50	6.00
Tom Brady		
LL7 Jamal Lewis	1.00	2.50
Ricky Williams		
LL8 Deuce McAllister	1.00	2.50
Stephen Davis		
LL9 Clinton Portis	1.25	3.00
Curtis Martin		
LL10 Fred Taylor	1.25	3.00
Priest Holmes		
LL11 Ahman Green	1.00	2.50
Shaun Alexander		
LL12 LaDainian Tomlinson	1.25	3.00
Travis Henry		
LL13 Eddie George	1.00	2.50
Edgerrin James		
LL14 Anthony Thomas	1.25	3.00
Tiki Barber		
LL15 Laveranues Coles	1.00	2.50
Torry Holt		
LL16 Anquan Boldin	1.25	3.00
Randy Moss		
LL17 Chad Johnson	1.25	3.00
Derrick Mason		
LL18 Hines Ward	1.25	3.00
Marvin Harrison		
LL19 Andre Johnson	1.25	3.00
Santana Moss		
LL20 Amani Toomer	1.25	3.00
Terrell Owens		

2004 Playoff Prestige League Leaders Jerseys

LL1 Peyton Manning	10.00	25.00
Trent Green		
LL2 Aaron Brooks	4.00	10.00
Daunte Culpepper		
LL3 Brett Favre	12.00	30.00
Quincy Carter		
LL4 Donovan McNabb	5.00	12.00
Kerry Collins		
LL5 Brad Johnson	4.00	10.00
Marc Bulger		
LL6 Steve McNair	10.00	25.00
Tom Brady		
LL7 Jamal Lewis	4.00	10.00
Ricky Williams		
LL8 Deuce McAllister	4.00	10.00
Stephen Davis		
LL9 Clinton Portis	5.00	12.00
Curtis Martin		
LL10 Fred Taylor	5.00	12.00
Priest Holmes		
LL11 Ahman Green	4.00	10.00
Shaun Alexander		
LL12 LaDainian Tomlinson	5.00	12.00
Travis Henry		
LL13 Eddie George	4.00	10.00
Edgerrin James		
LL14 Anthony Thomas	5.00	12.00
Tiki Barber		
LL15 Laveranues Coles	4.00	10.00
Torry Holt		
LL16 Anquan Boldin	5.00	12.00
Randy Moss		
LL17 Chad Johnson	5.00	12.00
Derrick Mason		
LL18 Hines Ward	5.00	12.00
Marvin Harrison		
LL19 Andre Johnson	5.00	12.00
Santana Moss		
LL20 Amani Toomer	5.00	12.00
Terrell Owens		

2004 Playoff Prestige Stars of the NFL Jerseys

STATED PRINT RUN 150 SER.#'d SETS		
*PATCH/25: 1X TO 2.5X BASIC JSY/150		
PATCH STATED PRINT RUN 25		
NFL1 Michael Vick	8.00	20.00
NFL2 Jamal Lewis	4.00	10.00
NFL3 Drew Bledsoe	5.00	12.00
NFL4 Brian Urlacher	5.00	12.00
NFL5 Clinton Portis	5.00	12.00
NFL6 Emmitt Smith	12.00	30.00
NFL7 Ahman Green	4.00	10.00
NFL8 Brett Favre	12.00	30.00
NFL9 David Carr	3.00	8.00
NFL10 Edgerrin James	4.00	10.00
NFL11 Peyton Manning	10.00	25.00
NFL12 Priest Holmes	5.00	12.00
NFL13 Ricky Williams	4.00	10.00
NFL14 Randy Moss	5.00	12.00
NFL15 Tom Brady	10.00	25.00
NFL16 Deuce McAllister	4.00	10.00
NFL17 Jeremy Shockey	4.00	10.00
NFL18 Chad Pennington	5.00	12.00
NFL19 Jerry Rice	10.00	25.00
NFL20 Donovan McNabb	5.00	12.00
NFL21 LaDainian Tomlinson	5.00	12.00
NFL22 Jeff Garcia	4.00	10.00
NFL23 LaVar Arrington	5.00	12.00
NFL24 Marshall Faulk	5.00	12.00
NFL25 Steve McNair	5.00	12.00

2004 Playoff Prestige Stars of the NFL Patches Autographs

STATED PRINT RUN 25 SER.#'d SETS		
NFL7 Ahman Green	40.00	80.00
NFL15 Tom Brady	200.00	350.00
NFL16 Deuce McAllister	40.00	80.00

2004 Playoff Prestige Super Bowl Heroes

COMPLETE SET (10)	12.50	30.00
SB1 Tom Brady	4.00	10.00
SB2 Deion Branch	1.50	4.00
SB3 Adam Vinatieri	2.00	5.00
SB4 Mike Vrabel	2.00	5.00
SB5 Antowain Smith	1.50	4.00
SB6 David Givens	1.25	3.00
SB7 Troy Brown	1.50	4.00
SB8 Kevin Faulk	1.50	4.00
SB9 Jake Delhomme	1.50	4.00
SB10 Muhsin Muhammad	1.50	4.00

2004 Playoff Prestige Turning Pro Jerseys

STATED PRINT RUN 225 SER.#'d SETS		
*PRIME/25: .8X TO 2X DUAL JSY/225		
PRIME PRINT RUN 25 SER.#'d SETS		
TP1 Anquan Boldin	8.00	20.00
TP2 Doug Flutie	8.00	20.00
TP3 Clinton Portis	8.00	20.00
TP4 Ahman Green	6.00	15.00
TP5 Edgerrin James	6.00	15.00
TP6 Reggie Wayne	8.00	20.00
TP7 Jeremy Shockey	6.00	15.00
TP8 Marshall Faulk	8.00	20.00
TP9 Tyrone Calico	6.00	15.00
TP10 Andre Johnson	8.00	20.00

2005 Playoff Prestige

Playoff Prestige was initially released in mid-May 2005. The base set consists of 244-cards including 94-rookies issued one per pack. Ten of those rookie cards were short-printed. Hobby boxes contained 24-packs of 8-cards and carried an S.R.P. of $3 per pack. Four parallel sets and a variety of inserts can be found seeded in packs highlighted by the Draft Picks Right Autograph inserts.

COMP.SET w/o SP's (234)	50.00	100.00
COMP.SET w/o RC's (150)	10.00	25.00
ONE 151-244 DRAFT PICK PER PACK		
1 Anquan Boldin	.30	.75
2 Emmitt Smith	.75	2.00
3 Josh McCown	.30	.75
4 Larry Fitzgerald	.40	1.00
5 Michael Vick	.40	1.00
6 Peerless Price	.25	.60
7 Alge Crumpler	.30	.75
8 T.J. Duckett	.25	.60
9 Warrick Dunn	.30	.75
10 Ed Reed	.30	.75
11 Jamal Lewis	.30	.75
12 Kyle Boller	.30	.75
13 Ray Lewis	.40	1.00
14 Todd Heap	.30	.75
15 Drew Bledsoe	.40	1.00
16 Eric Moulds	.25	.60
17 Lee Evans	.30	.75
18 Travis Henry	.25	.60
19 Willis McGahee	.40	1.00
20 Anthony Thomas	.25	.60
21 Brian Urlacher	.40	1.00
22 Rex Grossman	.30	.75
23 David Terrell	.25	.60
24 Thomas Jones	.40	1.00
25 Carson Palmer	.40	1.00
26 Chad Johnson	.30	.75
27 Peter Warrick	.25	.60
28 Rudi Johnson	.30	.75
29 Antonio Bryant	.25	.60
30 William Green	.25	.60
31 Jeff Garcia	.30	.75
32 Kellen Winslow	.30	.75
33 Lee Suggs	.25	.60
34 Drew Henson	.25	.60
35 Julius Jones	.25	.60
36 Jason Witten	.40	1.00
37 Keyshawn Johnson	.30	.75
38 Roy Williams S	.25	.60
39 Ashley Lelie	.25	.60
40 Champ Bailey	.30	.75
41 Jake Plummer	.30	.75
42 Reuben Droughns	.25	.60
43 Rod Smith	.30	.75
44 Charles Rogers	.25	.60
45 Joey Harrington	.30	.75
46 Kevin Jones	.25	.60
47 Roy Williams WR	.30	.75
48 Ahman Green	.30	.75
49 Donald Driver	.40	1.00
50 Javon Walker	.25	.60
51 Brett Favre	1.00	2.50
52 Andre Johnson	.40	1.00
53 David Carr	.25	.60
54 Domanick Davis	.25	.60
55 Jabar Gaffney	.25	.60
56 Edgerrin James	.30	.75
57 Marvin Harrison	.40	1.00
58 Brandon Stokley	.25	.60
59 Peyton Manning	.75	2.00
60 Reggie Wayne	.40	1.00
61 Byron Leftwich	.30	.75
62 Fred Taylor	.30	.75
63 Jimmy Smith	.30	.75
64 Priest Holmes	.30	.75
65 Tony Gonzalez	.30	.75
66 Johnnie Morton	.30	.75
67 Trent Green	.30	.75
68 Chris Chambers	.30	.75
69 Randy McMichael	.25	.60
70 A.J. Feeley	.25	.60
71 Zach Thomas	.40	1.00
72 Daunte Culpepper	.30	.75
73 Marcus Robinson	.25	.60
74 Mewelde Moore	.25	.60
75 Nate Burleson	.25	.60
76 Onterrio Smith	.25	.60
77 Randy Moss	.40	1.00
78 Corey Dillon	.30	.75
79 Tom Brady	.75	2.00
80 Deion Branch	.25	.60
81 Tedy Bruschi	.40	1.00
82 David Givens	.25	.60
83 David Patten	.25	.60
84 Aaron Brooks	.25	.60
85 Deuce McAllister	.30	.75
86 Donte Stallworth	.25	.60
87 Joe Horn	.30	.75
88 Eli Manning	.60	1.50
89 Jeremy Shockey	.40	1.00
90 Kurt Warner	.40	1.00
91 Michael Strahan	.40	1.00
92 Tiki Barber	.40	1.00
93 Amani Toomer	.30	.75
94 Chad Pennington	.40	1.00
95 Curtis Martin	.40	1.00
96 Santana Moss	.30	.75
97 Justin McCareins	.25	.60
98 Charles Woodson	.40	1.00
99 Kerry Collins	.30	.75
100 Warren Sapp	.30	.75
101 Jerry Porter	.25	.60
102 Donovan McNabb	.40	1.00
103 Jevon Kearse	.30	.75
104 Terrell Owens	.40	1.00
105 Brian Westbrook	.30	.75
106 Todd Pinkston	.25	.60
107 Duce Staley	.30	.75
108 Hines Ward	.40	1.00
109 Jerome Bettis	.40	1.00
110 Joey Porter	.25	.60
111 Plaxico Burress	.30	.75
112 Ben Roethlisberger	.60	1.50
113 Drew Brees	.40	1.00
114 LaDainian Tomlinson	.40	1.00
115 Keenan McCardell	.30	.75
116 Philip Rivers	.40	1.00
117 Antonio Gates	.40	1.00
118 Eric Johnson	.25	.60
119 Kevan Barlow	.25	.60
120 Brandon Lloyd	.25	.60
121 Tim Rattay	.25	.60
122 Darrell Jackson	.25	.60
123 Koren Robinson	.25	.60
124 Jerry Rice	.75	2.00
125 Matt Hasselbeck	.30	.75
126 Shaun Alexander	.30	.75
127 Isaac Bruce	.30	.75
128 Marc Bulger	.30	.75
129 Marshall Faulk	.40	1.00
130 Steven Jackson	.40	1.00
131 Torry Holt	.30	.75
132 Derrick Brooks	.30	.75
133 Michael Clayton	.25	.60
134 Michael Pittman	.25	.60
135 Chris Simms	.30	.75
136 Chris Brown	.25	.60
137 Derrick Mason	.30	.75
138 Drew Bennett	.30	.75
139 Steve McNair	.40	1.00
140 Clinton Portis	.30	.75
141 LaVar Arrington	.30	.75
142 Laveranues Coles	.25	.60
143 Patrick Ramsey	.30	.75
144 Rod Gardner	.25	.60
145 DeShaun Foster	.30	.75
146 Stephen Davis	.30	.75
147 Jake Delhomme	.30	.75
148 Muhsin Muhammad	.30	.75
149 Steve Smith	.40	1.00
150 Keary Colbert	.25	.60
151 Aaron Rodgers SP RC	25.00	50.00
152 Adrian McPherson SP RC	6.00	15.00
153 Alex Smith QB RC	1.50	4.00
154 Andrew Walter RC	.75	2.00
155 Brock Berlin RC	.75	2.00
156 Charlie Frye SP RC	10.00	25.00
157 Chris Rix RC	.75	2.00
158 Dan Orlovsky RC	1.00	2.50
159 Darian Durant RC	.60	1.50
160 David Greene RC	.60	1.50
161 Derek Anderson RC	.75	2.00
162 Gino Guidugli RC	.60	1.50
163 Jason Campbell RC	1.25	3.00
164 Jason White RC	1.00	2.50
165 Kyle Orton RC	1.00	2.50
166 Matt Jones SP RC	10.00	25.00
167 Ryan Fitzpatrick RC	1.50	4.00
168 Stefan LeFors RC	.60	1.50
169 Timmy Chang RC	.75	2.00
170 Alvin Pearman RC	.60	1.50
171 Anthony Davis RC	.60	1.50
172 Brandon Jacobs RC	1.25	3.00
173 Cadillac Williams RC	1.00	2.50
174 Cedric Benson RC	1.00	2.50
175 Cedric Houston RC	1.00	2.50
176 Ciatrick Fason RC	.60	1.50
177 Damien Nash RC	.75	2.00
178 Darren Sproles RC	1.00	2.50
179 Eric Shelton SP RC	6.00	15.00
180 Frank Gore SP RC	15.00	40.00
181 J.J. Arrington SP RC	8.00	20.00
182 Kay-Jay Harris RC	.60	1.50
183 Marion Barber RC	1.00	2.50
184 Ronnie Brown RC	1.25	3.00
185 Ryan Moats RC	.75	2.00
186 T.A. McLendon RC	.60	1.50
187 Vernand Morency RC	.75	2.00
188 Walter Reyes RC	.60	1.50
189 Braylon Edwards RC	1.25	3.00
190 Charles Frederick RC	.60	1.50
191 Chris Henry RC	1.00	2.50
192 Courtney Roby RC	.75	2.00
193 Craig Bragg RC	.60	1.50
194 Craphonso Thorpe SP RC	6.00	15.00
195 Dante Ridgeway RC	.60	1.50
196 Fred Amey RC	.75	2.00
197 Fred Gibson RC	.75	2.00
198 J.R. Russell RC	.60	1.50
199 Jerome Mathis SP RC	10.00	25.00
200 Josh Davis RC	.60	1.50
201 Larry Brackins RC	.60	1.50
202 Mark Bradley RC	.60	1.50
203 Mark Clayton SP RC	10.00	25.00
204 Mike Williams	1.00	2.50
205 Reggie Brown RC	.60	1.50
206 Roddy White RC	1.25	3.00
207 Roscoe Parrish RC	.60	1.50
208 Roydell Williams RC	.75	2.00
209 Steve Savoy RC	.60	1.50
210 Tab Perry RC	.60	1.50
211 Taylor Stubblefield RC	.60	1.50
212 Terrence Murphy RC	.60	1.50
213 Troy Williamson RC	.75	2.00
214 Vincent Jackson RC	1.25	3.00
215 Alex Smith TE RC	.60	1.50
216 Heath Miller RC	1.25	3.00
217 Dan Cody RC	.75	2.00
218 David Pollack RC	.75	2.00
219 Erasmus James RC	.75	2.00
220 Justin Tuck RC	1.25	3.00
221 Marcus Spears RC	.75	2.00
222 Matt Roth RC	.75	2.00
223 Anttaj Hawthorne RC	.60	1.50
224 Mike Patterson RC	.60	1.50
225 Shaun Cody RC	.75	2.00
226 Travis Johnson RC	.60	1.50
227 Channing Crowder RC	.75	2.00
228 Darryl Blackstock RC	.60	1.50
229 DeMarcus Ware RC	2.00	5.00
230 Derrick Johnson RC	.75	2.00
231 Kevin Burnett RC	.75	2.00
232 Shawne Merriman RC	1.00	2.50
233 Adam Jones RC	.75	2.00
234 Antrel Rolle RC	1.00	2.50
235 Brandon Browner RC	1.00	2.50
236 Bryant McFadden RC	.75	2.00
237 Carlos Rogers RC	1.00	2.50
238 Corey Webster RC	.75	2.00
239 Fabian Washington RC	.75	2.00
240 Justin Miller RC	.75	2.00
241 Marlin Jackson RC	.60	1.50
242 Ernest Shazor RC	.75	2.00
243 Josh Bullocks RC	.75	2.00
244 Thomas Davis RC	.60	1.50

2005 Playoff Prestige Xtra Points Black

*VETERANS: 8X TO 20X BASIC CARDS		
*ROOKIES: 4X TO 10X BASIC CARDS		
*ROOKIES: .5X TO 1.2X BASIC SP RC		
STATED PRINT RUN 25 SER.#'d SETS		
151 Aaron Rodgers	150.00	250.00

2005 Playoff Prestige Xtra Points Green

*VETERANS: 5X TO 12X BASIC CARDS		
*ROOKIES: 2.5X TO 6X BASIC CARDS		
*ROOKIES: .3X TO .8X BASIC RC SP		
STATED PRINT RUN 50 SER.#'d SETS		
151 Aaron Rodgers	90.00	150.00

2005 Playoff Prestige Xtra Points Purple

*VETERANS: 3X TO 8X BASIC CARDS		
*ROOKIES: 1.5X TO 4X BASIC CARDS		
*ROOKIES: .25X TO .6X BASIC SP RC		
STATED PRINT RUN 100 SER.#'d SETS		
151 Aaron Rodgers	75.00	125.00

2005 Playoff Prestige Xtra Points Red

*VETERANS: 3X TO 8X BASIC CARDS		
*ROOKIES: 1.5X TO 4X BASIC CARDS		
*ROOKIES: .25X TO .6X BASIC SP RC		
VETERAN PRINT RUN 125 SER.#'d SETS		
ROOKIE PRINT RUN 150 SER.#'d SETS		
151 Aaron Rodgers	60.00	100.00

2005 Playoff Prestige Changing Stripes

STATED PRINT RUN 250 SER.#'d SETS		
*PRIME: 1X TO 2.5X BASIC INSERTS		
PRIME PRINT RUN 25 SER.#'d SETS		
CS1 Ahman Green	6.00	15.00
CS2 Clinton Portis	6.00	15.00
CS3 Duce Staley	6.00	15.00
CS4 Jevon Kearse	6.00	15.00
CS5 Terrell Owens	8.00	20.00
CS6 Jeff Garcia	6.00	15.00
CS7 Keyshawn Johnson	6.00	15.00
CS8 Drew Bledsoe	8.00	20.00
CS9 Jake Plummer	6.00	15.00
CS10 Marshall Faulk	8.00	20.00

2005 Playoff Prestige Draft Picks

COMPLETE SET (10)	15.00	40.00
STATED ODDS 1:24		
*FOIL: 1X TO 2.5X BASIC INSERTS		
FOIL PRINT RUN 100 SER.#'d SETS		
*HOLOFOIL: 2.5X TO 6X BASIC INSERTS		
HOLOFOIL PRINT RUN 25 SER.#'d SETS		
DP1 Alex Smith QB	1.50	4.00
DP2 Aaron Rodgers	8.00	20.00
DP3 Charlie Frye	1.00	2.50
DP4 Cedric Benson	1.00	2.50
DP5 Ronnie Brown	1.25	3.00
DP6 Cadillac Williams	1.00	2.50
DP7 Vernand Morency	.75	2.00
DP8 Braylon Edwards	1.25	3.00
DP9 Troy Williamson	.75	2.00
DP10 Roddy White	1.25	3.00

2005 Playoff Prestige Draft Picks Rights Autographs

STATED PRINT RUN 50 SER.#'d SETS		
DP1 Alex Smith QB	30.00	60.00
DP2 Aaron Rodgers	250.00	400.00
DP3 Charlie Frye	15.00	40.00
DP4 Cedric Benson	20.00	50.00
DP5 Ronnie Brown	30.00	80.00
DP6 Cadillac Williams	15.00	40.00
DP7 Vernand Morency	10.00	25.00
DP8 Braylon Edwards	25.00	60.00
DP9 Troy Williamson	12.00	30.00
DP10 Roddy White	20.00	50.00

2005 Playoff Prestige Fans of the Game

COMPLETE SET (4)	4.00	10.00
STATED ODDS 1:24		
FG1 Rick Reilly	1.00	2.50
FG2 Heather Mitts	1.25	3.00
FG3 Rulon Gardner	.75	2.00
FG4 Sue Bird	1.25	3.00

2005 Playoff Prestige Fans of the Game Autographs

STATED ODDS 1:625		
FG1 Rick Reilly	12.00	30.00
FG2 Heather Mitts	20.00	50.00
FG3 Rulon Gardner	12.00	30.00
FG4 Sue Bird	20.00	50.00

2005 Playoff Prestige Game Day Jerseys

STATED ODDS 1:49		
GJ1 David Carr	3.00	8.00
GJ2 Peyton Manning	10.00	25.00
GJ3 Randy Moss	5.00	12.00
GJ4 Donovan McNabb	5.00	12.00
GJ5 Tom Brady	10.00	25.00
GJ6 Larry Fitzgerald	5.00	12.00
GJ7 Shaun Alexander	4.00	10.00
GJ8 Anquan Boldin	4.00	10.00
GJ9 Daunte Culpepper	4.00	10.00
GJ10 Chris Brown	3.00	8.00
GJ11 Isaac Bruce	4.00	10.00
GJ12 Rod Smith	4.00	10.00
GJ13 Roy Williams S	3.00	8.00
GJ14 Tony Gonzalez	4.00	10.00
GJ15 Torry Holt	4.00	10.00
GJ16 John Abraham	3.00	8.00
GJ17 Ike Hilliard	3.00	8.00
GJ18 Jimmy Smith	4.00	10.00
GJ19 Byron Leftwich	4.00	10.00
GJ20 Stephen Davis	4.00	10.00
GJ21 T.J. Duckett	3.00	8.00
GJ22 Travis Henry	3.00	8.00
GJ23 Julius Peppers	4.00	10.00
GJ24 Charles Rogers	3.00	8.00
GJ25 Eric Moulds	3.00	8.00
GJ26 Freddie Mitchell	3.00	8.00
GJ27 Anthony Thomas	3.00	8.00
GJ28 Steve McNair	5.00	12.00
GJ29 Brian Urlacher	5.00	12.00
GJ30 Donte Stallworth	3.00	8.00

2005 Playoff Prestige Gridiron Heritage

STATED ODDS 1:24		
*FOIL: .6X TO 1.5X BASIC INSERTS		
FOIL PRINT RUN 100 SER.#'d SETS		
*HOLOFOIL: 2X TO 5X BASIC INSERTS		
HOLOFOIL PRINT RUN 25 SER.#'d SETS		
GH1 Brett Favre	3.00	8.00
GH2 Edgerrin James	1.00	2.50
GH3 Byron Leftwich	1.00	2.50
GH4 Peyton Manning	2.50	6.00
GH5 Larry Fitzgerald	1.25	3.00
GH6 Shaun Alexander	1.00	2.50
GH7 Daunte Culpepper	1.00	2.50
GH8 Marshall Faulk	1.25	3.00
GH9 Steve McNair	1.25	3.00
GH10 Zach Thomas	1.25	3.00
GH11 Mike Alstott	1.00	2.50
GH12 Jeremiah Trotter	.75	2.00
GH13 Drew Brees	1.25	3.00
GH14 Isaac Bruce	1.00	2.50
GH15 Chris Chambers	1.00	2.50
GH16 Santana Moss	1.00	2.50
GH17 Peerless Price	.75	2.00
GH18 Donald Driver	1.25	3.00
GH19 Amani Toomer	1.00	2.50
GH20 Todd Pinkston	.75	2.00
GH21 Derrick Mason	1.00	2.50
GH22 Jimmy Smith	1.00	2.50
GH23 Michael Vick	1.25	3.00
GH24 Andre Johnson	1.25	3.00
GH25 Josh McCown	1.00	2.50

2005 Playoff Prestige Gridiron Heritage Jerseys

STATED ODDS 1:60		
GH1 Brett Favre	10.00	25.00
GH2 Edgerrin James	3.00	8.00
GH3 Byron Leftwich	3.00	8.00
GH4 Peyton Manning	8.00	20.00
GH5 Larry Fitzgerald	4.00	10.00
GH6 Shaun Alexander	3.00	8.00
GH7 Daunte Culpepper	3.00	8.00
GH8 Marshall Faulk	4.00	10.00
GH9 Steve McNair	4.00	10.00
GH10 Zach Thomas	4.00	10.00
GH11 Mike Alstott	3.00	8.00
GH12 Jeremiah Trotter	2.50	6.00
GH13 Drew Brees	4.00	10.00
GH14 Isaac Bruce	3.00	8.00
GH15 Chris Chambers	3.00	8.00
GH16 Santana Moss	3.00	8.00
GH17 Peerless Price	2.50	6.00
GH18 Donald Driver	4.00	10.00
GH19 Amani Toomer	3.00	8.00
GH20 Todd Pinkston	2.50	6.00
GH21 Derrick Mason	3.00	8.00
GH22 Jimmy Smith	3.00	8.00
GH23 Michael Vick	4.00	10.00
GH24 Andre Johnson	4.00	10.00
GH25 Josh McCown	3.00	8.00

2005 Playoff Prestige League Leaders

STATED ODDS 1:24		
*FOIL: .6X TO 1.5X BASIC INSERTS		
FOIL PRINT RUN 100 SER.#'d SETS		
*HOLOFOIL: 2X TO 5X BASIC INSERTS		
HOLOFOIL PRINT RUN 25 SER.#'d SETS		
LL1 Peyton Manning	2.50	6.00
Trent Green		
LL2 Daunte Culpepper	3.00	8.00
Brett Favre		
LL3 Donovan McNabb	1.25	3.00
Aaron Brooks		
LL4 Jake Plummer	1.25	3.00
Drew Bledsoe		
LL5 Tom Brady	2.50	6.00
David Carr		
LL6 Marc Bulger	1.00	2.50
Matt Hasselbeck		
LL7 Carson Palmer	1.25	3.00
Byron Leftwich		
LL8 Shaun Alexander	1.00	2.50
Clinton Portis		
LL9 Edgerrin James	1.00	2.50
Corey Dillon		
LL10 Curtis Martin	1.25	3.00
LaDainian Tomlinson		
LL11 Tiki Barber	1.25	3.00
Ahman Green		
LL12 Rudi Johnson	1.00	2.50
Fred Taylor		
LL13 Willis McGahee	1.25	3.00
Domanick Davis		
LL14 Kevin Jones	1.00	2.50
Deuce McAllister		
LL15 Keyshawn Johnson	1.00	2.50
Laveranues Coles		
LL16 Javon Walker	1.00	2.50
Torry Holt		
LL17 Chad Johnson	1.00	2.50
Drew Bennett		
LL18 Isaac Bruce	1.25	3.00
Terrell Owens		
LL19 Rod Smith	1.00	2.50
Plaxico Burress		
LL20 Michael Clayton	.75	2.00
Darrell Jackson		
LL21 Curtis Martin	1.25	3.00
Corey Dillon		
Shaun Alexander		
Tiki Barber		
LL22 Edgerrin James	1.50	4.00
LaDainian Tomlinson		
Clinton Portis		
Ahman Green		
LL23 Rudi Johnson	1.25	3.00
Fred Taylor		
Kevin Jones		
Deuce McAllister		
LL24 Trent Green	4.00	10.00
Peyton Manning		
Brett Favre		
Daunte Culpepper		
LL25 Jake Plummer	3.00	8.00
Tom Brady		
Jake Delhomme		
Donovan McNabb		
LL26 David Carr	1.50	4.00
Carson Palmer		
Marc Bulger		
Aaron Brooks		
LL27 Chad Johnson	1.25	3.00
Drew Bennett		
Keyshawn Johnson		
Laveranues Coles		
LL28 Tony Gonzalez	1.25	3.00
Plaxico Burress		
Javon Walker		
Torry Holt		
LL29 Jimmy Smith	1.50	4.00
Rod Smith		
Isaac Bruce		
Donald Driver		
LL30 Derrick Mason	1.50	4.00
Andre Johnson		
Terrell Owens		
Michael Clayton		

2005 Playoff Prestige League Leaders Jerseys

STATED PRINT RUN 250 SER.#'d SETS
*PRIME: 1X TO 2.5X BASIC JERSEYS
PRIME PRINT RUN 25 SER.#'d SETS
LL1 Peyton Manning 10.00 25.00
Trent Green
LL2 Daunte Culpepper 12.00 30.00
Brett Favre
LL3 Donovan McNabb 5.00 12.00
Aaron Brooks
LL4 Jake Plummer 5.00 12.00
Drew Bledsoe
LL5 Tom Brady 10.00 25.00
David Carr
LL6 Marc Bulger 4.00 10.00
Matt Hasselbeck
LL7 Carson Palmer 5.00 12.00
Byron Leftwich
LL8 Shaun Alexander 4.00 10.00
Clinton Portis
LL9 Edgerrin James 4.00 10.00
Corey Dillon
LL10 Curtis Martin 5.00 12.00
LaDainian Tomlinson
LL11 Tiki Barber 5.00 12.00
Ahman Green
LL12 Rudi Johnson 4.00 10.00
Fred Taylor
LL13 Willis McGahee 5.00 12.00
Domanick Davis
LL14 Kevin Jones 4.00 10.00
Deuce McAllister
LL15 Keyshawn Johnson 4.00 10.00
Laveranues Coles
LL16 Javon Walker 4.00 10.00
Torry Holt
LL17 Chad Johnson 4.00 10.00
Drew Bennett
LL18 Isaac Bruce 5.00 12.00
Terrell Owens
LL19 Rod Smith 4.00 10.00
Plaxico Burress
LL20 Michael Clayton 3.00 8.00
Darrell Jackson
LL21 Curtis Martin 8.00 20.00
Corey Dillon
Shaun Alexander
Tiki Barber
LL22 Edgerrin James 8.00 20.00
LaDainian Tomlinson
Clinton Portis
Ahman Green
LL23 Rudi Johnson 6.00 15.00
Fred Taylor
Kevin Jones
Deuce McAllister
LL24 Trent Green 20.00 50.00
Peyton Manning
Brett Favre
Daunte Culpepper
LL25 Jake Plummer 15.00 40.00
Tom Brady
Jake Delhomme
Donovan McNabb
LL26 David Carr 8.00 20.00
Carson Palmer
Marc Bulger
Aaron Brooks
LL27 Chad Johnson 6.00 15.00
Drew Bennett
Keyshawn Johnson
Laveranues Coles
LL28 Tony Gonzalez 6.00 15.00
Plaxico Burress
Javon Walker
Torry Holt
LL29 Jimmy Smith 8.00 20.00
Rod Smith
Isaac Bruce
Donald Driver
LL30 Derrick Mason 0.00 20.00
Andre Johnson
Terrell Owens
Michael Clayton

2005 Playoff Prestige Prestigious Pros Orange

ORANGE PRINT RUN 500 SER.#'d SETS
*BLUE/250: .6X TO 1.5X ORANGE
BLUE PRINT RUN 250 SER.#'d SETS
*GOLD/25: 2X TO 5X BASIC INSERTS
GOLD PRINT RUN 25 SER.#'d SETS
*GREEN/75: 1X TO 2.5X BASIC INSERTS
GREEN PRINT RUN 75 SER.#'d SETS
*PLATINUM/10: 3X TO 8X ORANGE
UNPRICED PLATINUM PRINT RUN 10 SETS
*PURPLE/100: 1X TO 2.5X BASIC INSERTS
PURPLE PRINT RUN 100 SER.#'d SETS
*RED/150: .8X TO 2X BASIC INSERTS
RED PRINT RUN 150 SER.#'d SETS
*SILVER/50: 1.2X TO 3X BASIC INSERTS
SILVER PRINT RUN 50 SER.#'d SETS
PP1 Aaron Brooks .60 1.50
PP2 Andre Johnson 1.00 2.50
PP3 Ben Roethlisberger 1.50 4.00
PP4 Brett Favre 2.50 6.00
PP5 Brian Urlacher 1.00 2.50
PP6 Byron Leftwich .75 2.00
PP7 Carson Palmer 1.00 2.50
PP8 Chad Pennington 1.00 2.50
PP9 Corey Dillon .75 2.00
PP10 Daunte Culpepper .75 2.00
PP11 David Carr .60 1.50
PP12 Deuce McAllister .75 2.00
PP13 Donovan McNabb 1.00 2.50
PP14 Drew Bledsoe 1.00 2.50
PP15 Drew Brees 1.00 2.50
PP16 Duce Staley .75 2.00
PP17 Edgerrin James .75 2.00
PP18 Hines Ward 1.00 2.50
PP19 Isaac Bruce .75 2.00
PP20 Jake Plummer .75 2.00
PP21 Jamal Lewis .75 2.00
PP22 Javon Walker .60 1.50
PP23 Jeff Garcia .75 2.00
PP24 Jeremy Shockey 1.00 2.50
PP25 Jevon Kearse .75 2.00
PP26 Joey Harrington .75 2.00
PP27 Keyshawn Johnson .75 2.00
PP28 LaDainian Tomlinson 1.00 2.50
PP29 LaVar Arrington .75 2.00
PP30 Lee Suggs .60 1.50
PP31 Marc Bulger .75 2.00
PP32 Marshall Faulk 1.00 2.50
PP33 Marvin Harrison 1.00 2.50
PP34 Matt Hasselbeck .75 2.00
PP35 Michael Vick 1.00 2.50
PP36 Peyton Manning 2.00 5.00
PP37 Plaxico Burress .75 2.00
PP38 Priest Holmes .75 2.00
PP39 Randy Moss 1.00 2.50
PP40 Ray Lewis 1.00 2.50
PP41 Rex Grossman .75 2.00
PP42 Rudi Johnson .75 2.00
PP43 Shaun Alexander .75 2.00
PP44 Steve McNair 1.00 2.50
PP45 Terrell Owens 1.00 2.50
PP46 Tiki Barber 1.00 2.50
PP47 Tom Brady 2.00 5.00
PP48 Tony Gonzalez .75 2.00
PP49 Torry Holt .75 2.00
PP50 Trent Green .75 2.00

2005 Playoff Prestige Prestigious Pros Jerseys Gold

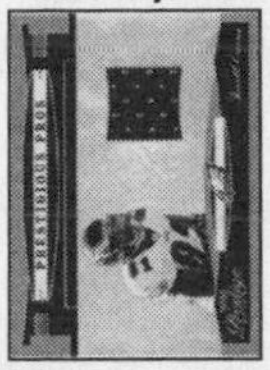

GOLD PRINT RUN 100 SER.#'d SETS
UNPRICED PLAT.PATCH PRINT RUN 10
PP1 Aaron Brooks 3.00 8.00
PP2 Andre Johnson 5.00 12.00
PP3 Ben Roethlisberger 8.00 20.00
PP4 Brett Favre 12.00 30.00
PP5 Brian Urlacher 5.00 12.00
PP6 Byron Leftwich 4.00 10.00
PP7 Carson Palmer 5.00 12.00
PP8 Chad Pennington 5.00 12.00
PP9 Corey Dillon 4.00 10.00
PP10 Daunte Culpepper 4.00 10.00
PP11 David Carr 3.00 8.00
PP12 Deuce McAllister 4.00 10.00
PP13 Donovan McNabb 5.00 12.00
PP14 Drew Bledsoe 5.00 12.00
PP15 Drew Brees 5.00 12.00
PP16 Duce Staley 4.00 10.00
PP17 Edgerrin James 4.00 10.00
PP18 Hines Ward 5.00 12.00
PP19 Isaac Bruce 4.00 10.00
PP20 Jake Plummer 4.00 10.00
PP21 Jamal Lewis 4.00 10.00
PP22 Javon Walker 3.00 8.00
PP23 Jeff Garcia 4.00 10.00
PP24 Jeremy Shockey 5.00 12.00
PP25 Jevon Kearse 4.00 10.00
PP26 Joey Harrington 4.00 10.00
PP27 Keyshawn Johnson 4.00 10.00
PP28 LaDainian Tomlinson 5.00 12.00
PP29 LaVar Arrington 4.00 10.00
PP30 Lee Suggs 3.00 8.00
PP31 Marc Bulger 4.00 10.00
PP32 Marshall Faulk 5.00 12.00
PP33 Marvin Harrison 5.00 12.00
PP34 Matt Hasselbeck 4.00 10.00
PP35 Michael Vick 5.00 12.00
PP36 Peyton Manning 10.00 25.00
PP37 Plaxico Burress 4.00 10.00
PP38 Priest Holmes 4.00 10.00
PP39 Randy Moss 5.00 12.00
PP40 Ray Lewis 5.00 12.00
PP41 Rex Grossman 4.00 10.00
PP42 Rudi Johnson 4.00 10.00
PP43 Shaun Alexander 4.00 10.00
PP44 Steve McNair 5.00 12.00
PP45 Terrell Owens 5.00 12.00
PP46 Tiki Barber 5.00 12.00
PP47 Tom Brady 10.00 25.00
PP48 Tony Gonzalez 4.00 10.00
PP49 Torry Holt 4.00 10.00
PP50 Trent Green 4.00 10.00

2005 Playoff Prestige Stars of the NFL

STATED ODDS 1:24
*FOIL: .8X TO 2X BASIC INSERTS
FOIL PRINT RUN 100 SER.#'d SETS
*HOLOFOIL: 2X TO 5X BASIC INSERTS
HOLOFOIL PRINT RUN 25 SER.#'d SETS
1 Aaron Brooks .75 2.00
2 Andre Johnson 1.25 3.00
3 Brett Favre 3.00 8.00
4 Brian Urlacher 1.25 3.00
5 Byron Leftwich 1.00 2.50
6 Chad Johnson 1.00 2.50
7 Chad Pennington 1.25 3.00
8 Chris Brown .75 2.00
9 Daunte Culpepper 1.00 2.50
10 David Carr .75 2.00
11 Donovan McNabb 1.25 3.00
12 Drew Bledsoe 1.25 3.00
13 Edgerrin James 1.00 2.50
14 Isaac Bruce 1.00 2.50
15 Jake Delhomme 1.00 2.50
16 Javon Walker .75 2.00
17 Jeremy Shockey 1.25 3.00
18 LaDainian Tomlinson 1.25 3.00
19 Marvin Harrison 1.25 3.00
20 Matt Hasselbeck 1.00 2.50
21 Michael Vick 1.25 3.00
22 Peyton Manning 2.50 6.00
23 Randy Moss 1.25 3.00
24 Priest Holmes 1.00 2.50
25 Tom Brady 2.50 6.00

2005 Playoff Prestige Stars of the NFL Jersey

STATED ODDS 1:104
*PRIME: 1X TO 2.5X BASIC INSERTS
PRIME PRINT RUN 25 SER.#'d SETS
1 Aaron Brooks 2.50 6.00
2 Andre Johnson 4.00 10.00
3 Brett Favre 10.00 25.00
4 Brian Urlacher 4.00 10.00
5 Byron Leftwich 3.00 8.00
6 Chad Johnson 3.00 8.00
7 Chad Pennington 4.00 10.00
8 Chris Brown 2.50 6.00
9 Daunte Culpepper 3.00 8.00
10 David Carr 2.50 6.00
11 Donovan McNabb 4.00 10.00
12 Drew Bledsoe 4.00 10.00
13 Edgerrin James 3.00 8.00
14 Isaac Bruce 3.00 8.00
15 Jake Delhomme 3.00 8.00
16 Javon Walker 2.50 6.00
17 Jeremy Shockey 4.00 10.00
18 LaDainian Tomlinson 4.00 10.00
19 Marvin Harrison 4.00 10.00
20 Matt Hasselbeck 3.00 8.00
21 Michael Vick 4.00 10.00
22 Peyton Manning 8.00 20.00
23 Randy Moss 4.00 10.00
24 Priest Holmes 3.00 8.00
25 Tom Brady 8.00 20.00

2005 Playoff Prestige Super Bowl Heroes

COMPLETE SET (10) 7.50 20.00
STATED ODDS 1:24
*FOIL: .8X TO 2X BASIC INSERTS
FOIL PRINT RUN 100 SER.#'d SETS
SH1 Tom Brady 2.50 6.00
SH2 Deion Branch .75 2.00
SH3 Corey Dillon 1.00 2.50
SH4 David Givens .75 2.00
SH5 Mike Vrabel 1.25 3.00
SH6 Tedy Bruschi 1.25 3.00
SH7 Rodney Harrison 1.00 2.50
SH8 Adam Vinatieri 1.25 3.00
SH9 Donovan McNabb 1.25 3.00
SH10 Terrell Owens 1.25 3.00

2005 Playoff Prestige Super Bowl Heroes Holofoil

HOLOFOIL PRINT RUN 25 SER.#'d SETS
SH1 Tom Brady SP 40.00 100.00
SH1AU Tom Brady AU 175.00 300.00
SH2 Deion Branch 4.00 10.00
SH3 Corey Dillon AU 40.00 80.00
SH4 David Givens 4.00 10.00
SH5 Mike Vrabel 6.00 15.00
SH6 Tedy Bruschi SP 10.00 25.00
SH6AU Tedy Bruschi AU SP 90.00 150.00
SH7 Rodney Harrison 5.00 12.00
SH8 Adam Vinatieri SP 15.00 40.00
SH8AU Adam Vinatieri AU SP 60.00 100.00
SH9 Donovan McNabb AU 50.00 100.00
SH10 Terrell Owens

2005 Playoff Prestige Turning Pro Jerseys

STATED PRINT RUN 250 SER.#'d SETS
*PRIME: 1X TO 2.5X BASIC INSERTS
PRIME PRINT RUN 25 SER.#'d SETS
TP1 Lee Suggs 4.00 10.00
TP2 Barry Sanders 12.00 30.00
TP3 Andre Johnson 6.00 15.00
TP4 Kyle Boller 5.00 12.00
TP5 Carson Palmer 6.00 15.00
TP6 Michael Vick 6.00 15.00
TP7 Laveranues Coles 4.00 10.00
TP8 Clinton Portis 5.00 12.00
TP9 Edgerrin James 5.00 12.00
TP10 Marshall Faulk 6.00 15.00

2006 Playoff Prestige

This 250-card set was released in May, 2006. The set was issued in both hobby and retail form. The hobby packs had five-cards in them with an $3 SRP and those packs came 24 to a box while the retail packs had eight cards, with a $2.99 SRP, and those packs also came 24 to a box. Cards numbered 1-150 featured players in first name alphabetical order sequenced in alphabetical team order while cards numbered 151-250 featured 2006 rookies in first name alphabetical order. The rookies were inserted into the packs at a stated rate of oner per. A few rookies were printed in shorter quantity and we have notated those cards in our checklist.

COMP.SET w/o SP's (239) 50.00 100.00
COMP.SET w/o RC's (150) 10.00 25.00
ONE ROOKIE PER HOBBY PACK
1 Anquan Boldin .30 .75
2 J.J. Arrington .25 .60
3 Josh McCown .25 .60
4 Larry Fitzgerald .40 1.00
5 Marcel Shipp .25 .60
6 Alge Crumpler .30 .75
7 Michael Vick .40 1.00
8 T.J. Duckett .25 .60
9 Warrick Dunn .30 .75
10 Michael Jenkins .30 .75
11 Derrick Mason .30 .75
12 Jamal Lewis .30 .75
13 Kyle Boller .30 .75
14 Mark Clayton .30 .75
15 Ray Lewis .40 1.00
16 Eric Moulds .25 .60
17 J.P. Losman .30 .75
18 Lee Evans .30 .75
19 Willis McGahee .30 .75
20 Jake Delhomme .30 .75
21 Julius Peppers .30 .75
22 Keary Colbert .25 .60
23 Stephen Davis .30 .75
24 Steve Smith .40 1.00
25 Brian Urlacher .40 1.00
26 Cedric Benson .30 .75
27 Kyle Orton .40 1.00
28 Mark Bradley .25 .60
29 Muhsin Muhammad .30 .75
30 Thomas Jones .30 .75
31 Carson Palmer .40 1.00
32 Chad Johnson .30 .75
33 Rudi Johnson .30 .75
34 T.J. Houshmandzadeh .30 .75
35 Braylon Edwards .30 .75
36 Dennis Northcutt .25 .60
37 Antonio Bryant .25 .60
38 Reuben Droughns .30 .75
39 Trent Dilfer .30 .75
40 Drew Bledsoe .40 1.00
41 Jason Witten .40 1.00
42 Julius Jones .25 .60
43 Keyshawn Johnson .30 .75
44 Roy Williams S .30 .75
45 Terry Glenn .30 .75
46 Ashley Lelie .25 .60
47 Jake Plummer .30 .75
48 Mike Anderson .30 .75
49 Rod Smith .30 .75
50 Tatum Bell .25 .60
51 Joey Harrington .25 .60
52 Kevin Jones .25 .60
53 Mike Williams .25 .60
54 Roy Williams WR .30 .75
55 Aaron Rodgers .75 2.00
56 Brett Favre .75 2.00
57 Donald Driver .40 1.00
58 Javon Walker .30 .75
59 Ahman Green .30 .75
60 Andre Johnson .40 1.00
61 Corey Bradford .25 .60
62 David Carr .25 .60
63 Domanick Davis .25 .60
64 Jabar Gaffney .25 .60
65 Brandon Stokley .30 .75
66 Dallas Clark .30 .75
67 Edgerrin James .30 .75
68 Marvin Harrison .40 1.00
69 Peyton Manning .60 1.50
70 Reggie Wayne .30 .75
71 Byron Leftwich .30 .75
72 Fred Taylor .30 .75
73 Jimmy Smith .30 .75
74 Matt Jones .25 .60
75 Reggie Williams .30 .75
76 Eddie Kennison .25 .60
77 Larry Johnson .30 .75
78 Priest Holmes .30 .75
79 Tony Gonzalez .30 .75
80 Trent Green .30 .75
81 Chris Chambers .30 .75
82 Marty Booker .25 .60
83 Randy McMichael .25 .60
84 Ricky Williams .25 .60
85 Ronnie Brown .40 1.00
86 Zach Thomas .40 1.00
87 Daunte Culpepper .30 .75
88 Mewelde Moore .25 .60
89 Nate Burleson .25 .60
90 Jim Kleinsasser .25 .60
91 Corey Dillon .30 .75
92 David Givens .30 .75
93 Deion Branch .30 .75
94 Tedy Bruschi .40 1.00
95 Tom Brady .60 1.50
96 Aaron Brooks .30 .75
97 Deuce McAllister .30 .75
98 Donte Stallworth .25 .60
99 Joe Horn .30 .75
100 Amani Toomer .30 .75
101 Eli Manning .50 1.25
102 Jeremy Shockey .40 1.00
103 Plaxico Burress .30 .75
104 Tiki Barber .40 1.00
105 Chad Pennington .30 .75
106 Curtis Martin .40 1.00
107 Justin McCareins .25 .60
108 Laveranues Coles .25 .60
109 Jerry Porter .25 .60
110 Kerry Collins .30 .75
111 LaMont Jordan .30 .75
112 Randy Moss .40 1.00
113 Brian Westbrook .30 .75
114 Donovan McNabb .40 1.00
115 Terrell Owens .40 1.00
116 L.J. Smith .25 .60
117 Ben Roethlisberger .50 1.25
118 Hines Ward .40 1.00
119 Heath Miller .30 .75
120 Willie Parker .30 .75
121 Jerome Bettis .40 1.00
122 Antonio Gates .40 1.00
123 Drew Brees .40 1.00
124 Keenan McCardell .30 .75
125 LaDainian Tomlinson .40 1.00
126 Alex Smith QB .40 1.00
127 Brandon Lloyd .25 .60
128 Frank Gore .40 1.00
129 Kevan Barlow .25 .60
130 Darrell Jackson .30 .75
131 Joe Jurevicius .25 .60
132 Matt Hasselbeck .30 .75
133 Shaun Alexander .30 .75
134 Isaac Bruce .30 .75
135 Marc Bulger .30 .75
136 Marshall Faulk .30 .75
137 Steven Jackson .40 1.00
138 Torry Holt .30 .75
139 Cadillac Williams .30 .75
140 Derrick Brooks .30 .75
141 Joey Galloway .30 .75
142 Michael Clayton .25 .60
143 Brandon Jones .25 .60
144 Chris Brown .25 .60
145 Steve McNair .30 .75
146 Tyrone Calico .25 .60
147 Clinton Portis .40 1.00
148 Mark Brunell .30 .75
149 Santana Moss .30 .75
150 David Patten .25 .60
151 A.J. Hawk SP RC 15.00 40.00
152 Abdul Hodge RC .75 2.00
153 Alan Zemaitis RC 1.25 3.00
154 Andre Hall RC 1.00 2.50
155 Anthony Fasano RC 1.25 3.00
156 Ashton Youboty RC .75 2.00
157 Erik Meyer RC 1.00 2.50
158 Bobby Carpenter RC .75 2.00
159 Brad Smith RC 1.25 3.00
160 Brandon Kirsch RC 1.00 2.50
161 Brandon Marshall SP RC 8.00 20.00
162 Brandon Williams RC .75 2.00
163 Brian Calhoun SP RC 6.00 15.00
164 Brodie Croyle SP RC 10.00 25.00
165 Brodrick Bunkley RC 1.00 2.50
166 Bruce Gradkowski RC 1.25 3.00
167 Cedric Griffin RC 1.00 2.50
168 Cedric Humes RC .75 2.00
169 Chad Greenway RC 1.25 3.00
170 Chad Jackson RC .75 2.00
171 Charlie Whitehurst RC 1.25 3.00
172 Cory Rodgers RC 1.00 2.50
173 D.J. Shockley RC 1.00 2.50
174 Darnell Bing RC 1.00 2.50
175 Darrell Hackney RC 1.00 2.50
176 David Thomas SP RC 6.00 15.00
177 D'Brickashaw Ferguson RC 1.25 3.00
178 DeAngelo Williams RC 1.50 4.00
179 Dee Webb RC 1.00 2.50
180 Delanie Walker RC 1.25 3.00
181 DeMeco Ryans RC 1.25 3.00
182 Demetrius Williams RC 1.00 2.50
183 Derek Hagan RC 1.00 2.50
184 Devin Aromashodu RC 1.25 3.00
185 Dominique Byrd RC 1.00 2.50
186 DonTrell Moore RC 1.00 2.50
187 D'Qwell Jackson RC 1.00 2.50
188 Drew Olson RC .75 2.00
189 Eric Winston RC .75 2.00
190 Ernie Sims RC 1.00 2.50
191 Gerald Riggs RC 1.00 2.50
192 Greg Jennings RC 2.00 5.00
193 Greg Lee RC .75 2.00
194 Haloti Ngata RC 1.25 3.00
195 Hank Baskett RC 1.25 3.00
196 Jason Avant RC .75 2.00
197 Jason Carter RC 1.00 2.50
198 Jay Cutler RC 2.50 6.00
199 Jeff Webb RC 1.00 2.50
200 Jeremy Bloom RC 1.00 2.50
201 Jerious Norwood RC 1.00 2.50
202 Jerome Harrison RC 1.25 3.00
203 Jimmy Williams RC 1.25 3.00
204 Joe Klopfenstein RC .75 2.00
205 Johnathan Joseph RC 1.00 2.50
206 Jonathan Orr RC 1.00 2.50
207 Joseph Addai RC 1.25 3.00
208 Kai Parham RC 1.25 3.00
209 Kamerion Wimbley RC 1.25 3.00
210 Kellen Clemens RC 1.00 2.50
211 Kelly Jennings RC 1.00 2.50
212 Ko Simpson RC 1.00 2.50
213 Laurence Maroney RC 1.00 2.50
214 Lawrence Vickers RC 1.00 2.50
215 LenDale White RC 1.00 2.50
216 Leon Washington RC 1.00 2.50
217 Leonard Pope RC 1.25 3.00
218 Marcedes Lewis RC 1.25 3.00
219 Marcus Vick SP RC 8.00 20.00
220 Mario Williams RC 1.25 3.00
221 Martin Nance RC 1.00 2.50
222 Mathias Kiwanuka RC 1.25 3.00
223 Matt Leinart RC 1.25 3.00
224 Maurice Drew SP RC 15.00 30.00
225 Maurice Stovall SP RC 6.00 15.00
226 Michael Huff RC 1.00 2.50
227 Michael Robinson SP RC 6.00 15.00
228 Mike Hass RC 1.00 2.50
229 Omar Jacobs RC .75 2.00
230 Paul Pinegar RC .75 2.00
231 Reggie Bush RC 2.50 6.00
232 Reggie McNeal RC 1.00 2.50
233 Rodrique Wright RC .75 2.00
234 Santonio Holmes RC 1.50 4.00
235 Sinorice Moss RC 1.25 3.00
236 Skyler Green RC .75 2.00
237 Tamba Hali RC 1.25 3.00
238 Tarvaris Jackson RC 1.25 3.00
239 Taurean Henderson RC 1.25 3.00
240 Terrence Whitehead RC 1.00 2.50
241 Tim Day SP RC 6.00 15.00
242 Todd Watkins RC .75 2.00
243 Travis Wilson RC .75 2.00
244 Tye Hill RC .75 2.00
245 Vernon Davis RC 1.50 4.00
246 Vince Young RC 1.50 4.00
247 Wali Lundy RC 1.00 2.50
248 Wendell Mathis RC 1.00 2.50
249 Willie Reid SP RC 6.00 15.00
250 Winston Justice RC 1.00 2.50

2006 Playoff Prestige Xtra Points Black

*VETERANS: 8X TO 20X BASIC CARDS
*ROOKIES: 3X TO 8X BASIC CARDS
*ROOKIE SPs: .5X TO 1.2X BASIC CARDS
STATED PRINT RUN 25 SER.#'d SETS

2006 Playoff Prestige Xtra Points Blue

*VETERANS: 1.5X TO 4X BASIC CARDS
*ROOKIES: .8X TO 2X BASIC CARDS
*ROOKIE SPs: .1X TO .25X BASIC CARDS
RANDOM INSERTS IN RETAIL PACKS

2006 Playoff Prestige Xtra Points Brown Retail

*VETS: 2X TO 5X BASIC CARDS
*ROOKIES: 1X TO 2.5X BASIC CARDS
*ROOKIE SPs: .25X TO .6X BASIC CARDS
RANDOM INSERTS IN RETAIL PACKS

2006 Playoff Prestige Xtra Points Gold

*VETS: 2X TO 5X BASIC CARDS
*ROOKIES: 1X TO 2.5X BASIC CARDS
*ROOKIE SPs: .25X TO .6X BASIC CARDS

2006 Playoff Prestige Xtra Points Green

*VETERANS: 5X TO 12X BASIC CARDS
*ROOKIES: 2X TO 5X BASIC CARDS
*ROOKIE SPs: .4X TO 1X BASIC CARDS
STATED PRINT RUN 50 SER.#'d SETS

2006 Playoff Prestige Xtra Points Purple

*VETERANS: 4X TO 10X BASIC CARDS
*ROOKIES: 1.5X TO 4X BASIC CARDS
*ROOKIE SPs: .3X TO .8X BASIC CARDS
STATED PRINT RUN 75 SER.#'d SETS

2006 Playoff Prestige Xtra Points Red

*VETERANS: 3X TO 8X BASIC CARDS
*ROOKIES: 1.2X TO 3X BASIC CARDS
*ROOKIE SPs: .3X TO .8X BASIC CARDS
STATED PRINT RUN 100 SER.#'d SETS

2006 Playoff Prestige Changing Stripes

STATED PRINT RUN 250 SER.#'d SETS
*PRIME/25: 1X TO 2.5X BASIC JSYs
1 Randy Moss 8.00 20.00
2 Drew Bledsoe 8.00 20.00
3 Laveranues Coles 6.00 15.00
4 Corey Dillon 6.00 15.00
5 Curtis Martin 8.00 20.00
6 Justin McCareins 5.00 12.00
7 Ricky Williams 6.00 15.00
8 Thomas Jones 6.00 15.00
9 Trent Green 6.00 15.00
10 Warrick Dunn 6.00 15.00

2006 Playoff Prestige Draft Picks

STATED ODDS 1:14
*FOIL: 1X TO 2.5X BASIC INSERTS
FOIL PRINT RUN 100 SER.#'d SETS
*HOLOFOIL: 2X TO 5X BASIC INSERTS
HOLOFOIL PRINT RUN 25 SER.#'d SETS
1 Reggie Bush 2.00 5.00
2 Matt Leinart 1.00 2.50
3 Vince Young 1.25 3.00
4 Jay Cutler 2.00 5.00
5 DeAngelo Williams 1.25 3.00
6 Joseph Addai 1.00 2.50
7 Santonio Holmes 1.25 3.00
8 Demetrius Williams .75 2.00
9 Jason Avant .60 1.50
10 D'Brickashaw Ferguson 1.00 2.50
11 Mario Williams 1.00 2.50
12 A.J. Hawk 1.00 2.50
13 Tye Hill .60 1.50
14 Michael Huff .75 2.00
15 Joe Klopfenstein .60 1.50
16 Sinorice Moss 1.00 2.50
17 Maurice Stovall .60 1.50
18 Michael Robinson .75 2.00
19 Travis Wilson .60 1.50
20 LenDale White .75 2.00

2006 Playoff Prestige Draft Picks Rights Autographs

STATED PRINT RUN 50 SER.#'d SETS
DP1 Reggie Bush 60.00 150.00
DP2 Matt Leinart 15.00 40.00
DP3 Vince Young 20.00 50.00
DP4 Jay Cutler 75.00 150.00
DP5 DeAngelo Williams 20.00 50.00
DP6 Joseph Addai 15.00 40.00
DP7 Santonio Holmes 20.00 50.00
DP8 Demetrius Williams 12.00 30.00
DP9 Jason Avant 10.00 25.00
DP10 D'Brickashaw Ferguson 15.00 40.00
DP11 Mario Williams 15.00 40.00
DP12 A.J. Hawk 15.00 40.00
DP13 Tye Hill 10.00 25.00
DP14 Michael Huff 12.00 30.00
DP15 Joe Klopfenstein 10.00 25.00
DP16 Sinorice Moss 15.00 40.00
DP17 Maurice Stovall 10.00 25.00
DP18 Michael Robinson 12.00 30.00
DP19 Travis Wilson 10.00 25.00
DP20 LenDale White 12.00 30.00

2006 Playoff Prestige Gridiron Heritage

STATED ODDS 1:17 HOB, 1:10 RET
*FOIL: .8X TO 2X BASIC INSERTS
FOIL PRINT RUN 100 SER.#'d SETS
*HOLOFOIL: 2X TO 5X BASIC INSERTS
HOLOFOIL PRINT RUN 25 SER.#'d SETS
1 Aaron Brooks 1.00 2.50
2 Ahman Green 1.00 2.50
3 Alge Crumpler 1.00 2.50
4 Antonio Gates 1.25 3.00
5 Byron Leftwich 1.00 2.50
6 Jonathan Vilma 1.00 2.50
7 Julius Peppers 1.00 2.50
8 Darrell Jackson 1.00 2.50
9 Daunte Culpepper 1.00 2.50
10 David Carr .75 2.00
11 David Givens 1.00 2.50
12 Brett Favre 2.50 6.00
13 Chad Pennington 1.00 2.50
14 Deuce McAllister 1.00 2.50
15 Domanick Davis .75 2.00
16 Terrell Suggs 1.00 2.50
17 Drew Brees 1.25 3.00
18 Eric Moulds .75 2.00
19 Jerome Bettis 1.25 3.00
20 Kyle Brady .75 2.00
21 Kevin Jones .75 2.00
22 Keyshawn Johnson 1.00 2.50
23 Marc Bulger 1.00 2.50
24 Marcel Shipp .75 2.00
25 Marvin Harrison 1.25 3.00
26 Matt Hasselbeck 1.00 2.50
27 Michael Vick 1.25 3.00
28 Richard Seymour .75 2.00
29 Peyton Manning 2.00 5.00
30 Randy Moss 1.25 3.00
31 Ricky Williams .75 2.00
32 Shaun Alexander 1.00 2.50
33 Michael Bennett .75 2.00
34 Tony Gonzalez 1.00 2.50
35 Trent Green 1.00 2.50

2006 Playoff Prestige Gridiron Heritage Jerseys

*PRIME/50: .6X TO 1.5X BASIC INSERTS
*PRIME/20: 1X TO 2.5X BASIC INSERTS
PRIME PRINT RUN 20-50 SER.#'d SETS
1 Aaron Brooks 3.00 8.00
2 Ahman Green 4.00 10.00
3 Alge Crumpler 3.00 8.00
4 Antonio Gates 4.00 10.00
5 Byron Leftwich 3.00 8.00
6 Jonathan Vilma 3.00 8.00
7 Julius Peppers 3.00 8.00
8 Darrell Jackson 3.00 8.00
9 Daunte Culpepper 4.00 10.00
10 David Carr 3.00 8.00
11 David Givens 2.50 6.00
12 Brett Favre 10.00 25.00
13 Chad Pennington 3.00 8.00
14 Deuce McAllister 3.00 8.00
15 Domanick Davis 3.00 8.00
16 Terrell Suggs 3.00 8.00
17 Drew Brees 4.00 10.00
18 Eric Moulds 3.00 8.00
19 Jerome Bettis 4.00 10.00
20 Kyle Brady 2.50 6.00
21 Kevin Jones 4.00 10.00
22 Keyshawn Johnson 3.00 8.00
23 Marc Bulger 3.00 8.00
24 Marcel Shipp 2.50 6.00
25 Marvin Harrison 4.00 10.00
26 Matt Hasselbeck 4.00 10.00
27 Michael Vick 4.00 10.00
28 Richard Seymour 2.50 6.00
29 Peyton Manning 6.00 15.00
30 Randy Moss 4.00 10.00
31 Ricky Williams 3.00 8.00
32 Shaun Alexander 5.00 12.00
33 Michael Bennett 2.50 6.00
34 Tony Gonzalez 3.00 8.00
35 Trent Green 3.00 8.00

2006 Playoff Prestige League Leaders

STATED ODDS 1:11
*FOIL: 1X TO 2.5X BASIC INSERTS
FOIL PRINT RUN 100 SER.#'d SETS
*HOLOFOIL: 2.5X TO 6X BASIC INSERTS
HOLOFOIL PRINT RUN 25 SER.#'d SETS
1 Brett Favre 2.00 5.00
Eli Manning
2 Tom Brady 1.50 4.00
Trent Green
3 Drew Bledsoe 1.00 2.50
Carson Palmer
4 Matt Hasselbeck .75 2.00
Kerry Collins
5 Shaun Alexander 1.00 2.50
Tiki Barber
6 Larry Johnson .75 2.00
Edgerrin James
7 Clinton Portis 1.00 2.50
LaDainian Tomlinson
8 Warrick Dunn .75 2.00
Rudi Johnson
9 Steve Smith 1.00 2.50
Santana Moss
10 Chad Johnson 1.00 2.50
Marvin Harrison
11 Larry Fitzgerald 1.00 2.50
Chris Chambers
12 Anquan Boldin .75 2.00
Rod Smith
13 Shaun Alexander 1.00 2.50
Steve Smith
14 Larry Johnson 1.00 2.50
LaDainian Tomlinson
15 Stephen Davis .75 2.00
Edgerrin James
16 Tiki Barber 1.00 2.50
Corey Dillon
17 Steve Smith 1.00 2.50
Larry Fitzgerald
18 Marvin Harrison 1.00 2.50
Chris Chambers
19 Shaun Alexander .75 2.00
Stephen Davis
20 Larry Johnson 1.00 2.50
LaDainian Tomlinson
21 Brett Favre 2.50 6.00
Tom Brady
Eli Manning
Trent Green
22 Drew Bledsoe 1.25 3.00
Carson Palmer
Matt Hasselbeck
Kerry Collins
23 Shaun Alexander 1.25 3.00
Larry Johnson
Tiki Barber
Edgerrin James
24 Clinton Portis 1.25 3.00
LaDainian Tomlinson
Warrick Dunn
Rudi Johnson
25 Steve Smith 1.25 3.00
Chad Johnson
Santana Moss
Marvin Harrison
26 Larry Fitzgerald 1.25 3.00
Chris Chambers
Anquan Boldin
Rod Smith
27 Shaun Alexander 1.25 3.00
Larry Johnson
Steve Smith
LaDainian Tomlinson
28 Stephen Davis 1.25 3.00
Edgerrin James
Tiki Barber
Corey Dillon
29 Steve Smith 1.25 3.00
Marvin Harrison
Larry Fitzgerald
Chris Chambers
30 Shaun Alexander 1.25 3.00
Larry Johnson
Stephen Davis
LaDainian Tomlinson

2006 Playoff Prestige League Leaders Jerseys

STATED PRINT RUN 250 SER.#'d SETS
*PRIME/25: 1X TO 2.5X BASIC JSYs
1 Brett Favre 12.50 30.00
Eli Manning
2 Tom Brady 8.00 20.00
Trent Green
3 Drew Bledsoe 6.00 15.00
Carson Palmer
4 Matt Hasselbeck 5.00 12.00
Kerry Collins
5 Shaun Alexander 6.00 15.00
Tiki Barber
6 Larry Johnson 6.00 15.00
Edgerrin James
7 Clinton Portis 6.00 15.00
LaDainian Tomlinson
8 Warrick Dunn 4.00 10.00
Rudi Johnson
9 Steve Smith 4.00 10.00
Santana Moss
10 Chad Johnson 5.00 12.00
Marvin Harrison
11 Larry Fitzgerald 4.00 10.00
Chris Chambers
12 Anquan Boldin 4.00 10.00
Rod Smith
13 Shaun Alexander 6.00 15.00
Steve Smith
14 Larry Johnson 6.00 15.00
LaDainian Tomlinson
15 Stephen Davis 5.00 12.00
Edgerrin James
16 Tiki Barber 5.00 12.00
Corey Dillon
17 Steve Smith 4.00 10.00
Larry Fitzgerald
18 Marvin Harrison 5.00 12.00
Chris Chambers
19 Shaun Alexander 6.00 15.00
Stephen Davis
20 Larry Johnson 6.00 15.00
LaDainian Tomlinson
21 Brett Favre 15.00 40.00
Tom Brady
Eli Manning
Trent Green
22 Drew Bledsoe 8.00 20.00
Carson Palmer
Matt Hasselbeck
Kerry Collins
23 Shaun Alexander 8.00 20.00
Larry Johnson
Tiki Barber
Edgerrin James
24 Clinton Portis 6.00 15.00
LaDainian Tomlinson
Warrick Dunn
Rudi Johnson
25 Steve Smith 6.00 15.00
Chad Johnson
Santana Moss
Marvin Harrison

26 Larry Fitzgerald 5.00 12.00
Chris Chambers
Anquan Boldin
Rod Smith
27 Shaun Alexander 6.00 15.00
Larry Johnson
Steve Smith
LaDainian Tomlinson
28 Stephen Davis 6.00 15.00
Edgerrin James
Tiki Barber
Corey Dillon
29 Steve Smith 5.00 12.00
Marvin Harrison
Larry Fitzgerald
Chris Chambers
30 Shaun Alexander 6.00 15.00
Larry Johnson
Stephen Davis
LaDainian Tomlinson

2006 Playoff Prestige Prestigious Pros Bronze

*BLACK: 1X TO 2.5X BRONZE
BLACK PRINT RUN 125 SER.#'d SETS
*BLUE: .8X TO 2X BRONZE
BLUE PRINT RUN 250 SER.#'d SETS
*GOLD: 2.5X TO 6X BRONZE
GOLD PRINT RUN 25 SER.#'d SETS
*GREEN: 1.2X TO 3X BRONZE
GREEN PRINT RUN 75 SER.#'d SETS
*ORANGE: .5X TO 1.2X BRONZE
ORANGE PRINT RUN 500 SER.#'d SETS
UNPRICED PLATINUM SER.#'d TO 10
*PURPLE: 1.2X TO 3X BRONZE
PURPLE PRINT RUN 100 SER.#'d SETS
*RED: 1X TO 2.5X BRONZE
RED PRINT RUN 150 SER.#'d SETS
*SILVER: 1.5X TO 4X BRONZE
SILVER PRINT RUN 50 SER.#'d SETS
UNPRICED AUTO PRINT RUN 1-10 SETS

1 Amani Toomer .75 2.00
2 Andre Johnson 1.00 2.50
3 Antwaan Randle El .75 2.00
4 Ashley Lelie .60 1.50
5 Anquan Boldin .75 2.00
6 Ben Roethlisberger 1.25 3.00
7 Bethel Johnson .60 1.50
8 Brandon Lloyd .60 1.50
9 Brian Urlacher 1.00 2.50
10 Bryant Johnson .60 1.50
11 Chad Johnson .75 2.00
12 Carson Palmer 1.00 2.50
13 Darrell Jackson .75 2.00
14 Domanick Davis .60 1.50
15 Donovan McNabb 1.00 2.50
16 Isaac Bruce .75 2.00
17 J.P. Losman .75 2.00
18 Jake Delhomme .75 2.00
19 Jevon Kearse .75 2.00
20 Jeff Garcia .75 2.00
21 Jimmy Smith .75 2.00
22 Corey Dillon .75 2.00
23 Josh McCown .60 1.50
24 Josh Reed .60 1.50
25 Curtis Martin 1.00 2.50
26 Julius Jones .60 1.50
27 Randy McMichael .60 1.50
28 Keary Colbert .60 1.50
29 Joey Harrington .60 1.50
30 LaMont Jordan .75 2.00
31 Marshall Faulk .75 2.00
32 Tom Brady 1.50 4.00
33 Michael Strahan .75 2.00
34 Nate Clements .60 1.50
35 Mike Anderson .75 2.00
36 Nick Barnett .75 2.00
37 Randy Moss 1.00 2.50
38 Reggie Wayne .75 2.00
39 Rex Grossman .75 2.00
40 Priest Holmes .75 2.00
41 Ricky Williams .60 1.50
42 Rudi Johnson .75 2.00
43 T.J. Duckett .60 1.50
44 Steve Smith 1.00 2.50
45 Tatum Bell .60 1.50
46 Donte Stallworth .60 1.50
47 Thomas Jones .75 2.00
48 Torry Holt .75 2.00
49 Wayne Chrebet .60 1.50
50 Robert Ferguson .60 1.50

2006 Playoff Prestige Prestigious Pros Jerseys Green

GREEN PRINT RUN 100 SER.#'d SETS
*BLACK/15: .8X TO 2X GREEN JSYs
*BRONZE/122-250: .3X TO .8X GREEN JSYs
*BRONZE/35-50: .5X TO 1.2X GREEN JSYs
*GOLD/25: .6X TO 1.5X GREEN JSYs
*PLATINUM/25: .8X TO 2X GREEN JSYs
*ORANGE: .3X TO .8X GREEN JSYs

1 Amani Toomer 5.00 12.00
2 Andre Johnson 6.00 15.00
3 Antwaan Randle El 5.00 12.00
4 Ashley Lelie 4.00 10.00
5 Anquan Boldin 5.00 12.00
6 Ben Roethlisberger 10.00 25.00
7 Bethel Johnson 4.00 10.00
8 Brandon Lloyd 4.00 10.00
9 Brian Urlacher 6.00 15.00
10 Bryant Johnson 4.00 10.00
11 Chad Johnson 5.00 12.00
12 Carson Palmer 6.00 15.00
13 Darrell Jackson 5.00 12.00
14 Domanick Davis 4.00 10.00
15 Donovan McNabb 6.00 15.00
16 Isaac Bruce 5.00 12.00
17 J.P. Losman 5.00 12.00
18 Jake Delhomme 5.00 12.00
19 Jevon Kearse 5.00 12.00
20 Jeff Garcia 5.00 12.00
21 Jimmy Smith 5.00 12.00
22 Corey Dillon 5.00 12.00
23 Josh McCown 4.00 10.00
24 Josh Reed 4.00 10.00
25 Curtis Martin 6.00 15.00
26 Julius Jones 4.00 10.00
27 Randy McMichael 4.00 10.00
28 Keary Colbert 4.00 10.00
29 Joey Harrington 4.00 10.00
30 LaMont Jordan 5.00 12.00
31 Marshall Faulk 5.00 12.00
32 Tom Brady 12.50 30.00
33 Michael Strahan 5.00 12.00
34 Nate Clements 4.00 10.00
35 Mike Anderson 5.00 12.00
36 Nick Barnett 5.00 12.00
37 Randy Moss 6.00 15.00
38 Reggie Wayne 5.00 12.00
39 Rex Grossman 5.00 12.00
40 Priest Holmes 5.00 12.00
41 Ricky Williams 4.00 10.00
42 Rudi Johnson 5.00 12.00
43 T.J. Duckett 4.00 10.00
44 Steve Smith 6.00 15.00
45 Tatum Bell 4.00 10.00
46 Donte Stallworth 4.00 10.00
47 Thomas Jones 5.00 12.00
48 Torry Holt 5.00 12.00
49 Wayne Chrebet 4.00 10.00
50 Robert Ferguson 4.00 10.00

2006 Playoff Prestige Prestigious Pros Autographs

UNPRICED AUTO PRINT RUN 1-10 SETS

2006 Playoff Prestige Stars of the NFL

STATED ODDS 1:17 HOB, 1:10 RET
*FOIL: .8X TO 2X BASIC INSERTS
FOIL PRINT RUN 100 SER.#'d SETS
*HOLOFOIL: 2X TO 5X BASIC INSERTS
HOLOFOIL PRINT RUN 25 SER.#'d SETS

1 LaDainian Tomlinson 1.25 3.00
2 Michael Vick 1.25 3.00
3 Peyton Manning 2.00 5.00
4 Tom Brady 2.00 5.00
5 Steven Jackson 1.25 3.00
6 Shaun Alexander 1.00 2.50
7 Julius Jones .75 2.00
8 Priest Holmes 1.00 2.50
9 Randy Moss 1.25 3.00
10 Steve Smith 1.25 3.00
11 Terrell Owens 1.25 3.00
12 Donovan McNabb 1.25 3.00
13 Brett Favre 2.50 6.00
14 Clinton Portis 1.25 3.00
15 Carson Palmer 1.25 3.00
16 Chad Johnson 1.00 2.50
17 Drew Bledsoe 1.25 3.00
18 Edgerrin James 1.00 2.50
19 Eli Manning 1.50 4.00
20 Larry Fitzgerald 1.25 3.00
21 Ben Roethlisberger 1.50 4.00
22 Thomas Jones 1.00 2.50
23 Willis McGahee 1.00 2.50
24 Ronnie Brown 1.25 3.00
25 Cadillac Williams 1.00 2.50
26 Laveranues Coles .75 2.00
27 Matt Hasselbeck 1.00 2.50
28 Torry Holt 1.00 2.50
29 Trent Green 1.00 2.50
30 Tiki Barber 1.25 3.00
31 Jake Delhomme 1.00 2.50
32 Jake Plummer 1.00 2.50
33 Warrick Dunn 1.00 2.50
34 Steve McNair 1.00 2.50
35 Keyshawn Johnson 1.00 2.50

2006 Playoff Prestige Stars of the NFL Jerseys

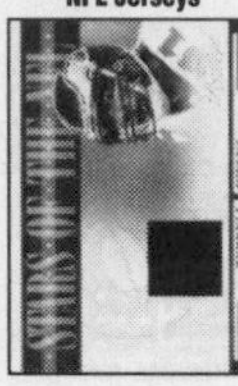

*PRIME/25: 1.2X TO 3X BASIC JSYs

1 LaDainian Tomlinson 4.00 10.00
2 Michael Vick 4.00 10.00
3 Peyton Manning 6.00 15.00
4 Tom Brady 6.00 15.00
5 Steven Jackson 4.00 10.00
6 Shaun Alexander 5.00 12.00
7 Julius Jones 4.00 10.00
8 Priest Holmes 3.00 8.00
9 Randy Moss 4.00 10.00
10 Steve Smith 3.00 8.00
11 Terrell Owens 4.00 10.00
12 Donovan McNabb 4.00 10.00
13 Brett Favre 10.00 25.00
14 Clinton Portis 4.00 10.00
15 Carson Palmer 4.00 10.00
16 Chad Johnson 3.00 8.00
17 Drew Bledsoe 4.00 10.00
18 Edgerrin James 4.00 10.00
19 Eli Manning 5.00 12.00
20 Larry Fitzgerald 3.00 8.00
21 Ben Roethlisberger 6.00 15.00
22 Thomas Jones 3.00 8.00
23 Willis McGahee 3.00 8.00
24 Ronnie Brown 5.00 10.00
25 Cadillac Williams 4.00 10.00
26 Laveranues Coles 3.00 8.00
27 Matt Hasselbeck 4.00 10.00
28 Torry Holt 3.00 8.00
29 Trent Green 3.00 8.00
30 Tiki Barber 4.00 10.00
31 Jake Delhomme 4.00 10.00
32 Jake Plummer 3.00 8.00
33 Warrick Dunn 3.00 8.00
34 Steve McNair 4.00 10.00
35 Keyshawn Johnson 3.00 8.00

2006 Playoff Prestige Super Bowl Heroes

STATED ODDS 1:29 HOB, 1:152 RET
*FOIL: .8X TO 2X BASIC INSERTS
FOIL PRINT RUN 100 SER.#'d SETS
*HOLOFOIL: 2X TO 5X BASIC INSERTS
HOLOFOIL PRINT RUN 25 SER.#'d SETS
UNPRICED AUTO PRINT RUN 10 SETS

1 Hines Ward 1.25 3.00
2 Willie Parker 1.00 2.50
3 Ben Roethlisberger 1.50 4.00
4 Antwaan Randle El 1.00 2.50
5 Jerome Bettis 1.25 3.00
6 Troy Polamalu 1.50 4.00
7 Matt Hasselbeck 1.00 2.50
8 Shaun Alexander 1.00 2.50
9 Jerramy Stevens 1.00 2.50
10 Darrell Jackson 1.00 2.50

2006 Playoff Prestige Super Bowl Heroes Holofoil Autographs

UNPRICED AUTO PRINT RUN 10 SETS

2006 Playoff Prestige Turning Pro

STATED ODDS 1:29 HOB, 1:152 RET
*FOIL: .6X TO 1.5X BASIC INSERTS
FOIL PRINT RUN 100 SER.#'d SETS
*HOLOFOIL: 1.5X TO 4X BASIC INSERTS
HOLOFOIL PRINT RUN 25 SER.#'d SETS

1 Cadillac Williams 1.25 3.00
2 Cedric Benson 1.25 3.00
3 Julius Jones 1.00 2.50
4 Michael Clayton 1.00 2.50
5 Roy Williams S 1.25 3.00
6 Steven Jackson 1.50 4.00
7 Hines Ward 1.50 4.00
8 Ronnie Brown 1.50 4.00
9 Willis McGahee 1.25 3.00
10 Braylon Edwards 1.25 3.00

2006 Playoff Prestige Turning Pro Jerseys

STATED PRINT RUN 250 SER.#'d SETS

1 Cadillac Williams 6.00 15.00
2 Cedric Benson 6.00 15.00
3 Julius Jones 6.00 15.00
4 Michael Clayton 5.00 12.00
5 Roy Williams S 5.00 12.00
6 Steven Jackson 6.00 15.00
7 Hines Ward 6.00 15.00
8 Ronnie Brown 6.00 15.00
9 Willis McGahee 5.00 12.00
10 Braylon Edwards 6.00 15.00

2007 Playoff Prestige

This 252-card set was released in May, 2007. The set was issued into the hobby in eight-card packs, with a $3 SRP, which came 24 packs to a box. Cards numbered 1-150 feature veterans in their 2006 team alphabetical order while cards numbered 151-252 feature 2007 NFL rookies. A few rookies were printed in lesser quantities and we have notated that information in our checklist and cards numbered 251 and 252 were issued to a stated print run of 100 copies.

COMP.SET w/o SP's (240) 75.00 150.00
COMP.SET w/o RC's (150) 10.00 25.00
1 Anquan Boldin .30 .75
2 Edgerrin James .30 .75
3 Larry Fitzgerald .40 1.00
4 Matt Leinart .30 .75
5 Alge Crumpler .30 .75
6 Michael Vick .40 1.00
7 Jerious Norwood .30 .75
8 Michael Jenkins .30 .75
9 Warrick Dunn .30 .75
10 Todd Heap .25 .60
11 Jamal Lewis .30 .75
12 Mark Clayton .30 .75
13 Demetrius Williams .25 .60
14 Steve McNair .30 .75
15 Ray Lewis .40 1.00
16 J.P. Losman .25 .60
17 Josh Reed .25 .60
18 Lee Evans .30 .75
19 Willis McGahee .30 .75
20 DeAngelo Williams .40 1.00
21 DeShaun Foster .30 .75
22 Jake Delhomme .30 .75
23 Keyshawn Johnson .30 .75
24 Steve Smith .30 .75
25 Bernard Berrian .25 .60
26 Brian Urlacher .40 1.00
27 Cedric Benson .30 .75
28 Muhsin Muhammad .30 .75
29 Rex Grossman .30 .75
30 Thomas Jones .30 .75
31 Carson Palmer .30 .75
32 Chad Johnson .30 .75
33 Rudi Johnson .30 .75
34 T.J. Houshmandzadeh .30 .75
35 Braylon Edwards .30 .75
36 Kellen Winslow .30 .75
37 Charlie Frye .30 .75
38 Reuben Droughns .30 .75
39 Terry Glenn .30 .75
40 Julius Jones .25 .60
41 Roy Williams S .30 .75
42 Marion Barber .40 1.00
43 Terrell Owens .40 1.00
44 Tony Romo .50 1.25
45 Javon Walker .30 .75
46 Jay Cutler .40 1.00
47 Mike Bell .30 .75
48 Brandon Marshall .30 .75
49 Tatum Bell .25 .60
50 Jon Kitna .25 .60
51 Kevin Jones .25 .60
52 Roy Williams WR .30 .75
53 Mike Furrey .30 .75
54 A.J. Hawk .30 .75
55 Brett Favre .75 2.00
56 Donald Driver .40 1.00
57 Greg Jennings .40 1.00
58 Ahman Green .30 .75
59 Andre Johnson .30 .75
60 David Carr .30 .75
61 Eric Moulds .30 .75
62 Owen Daniels .25 .60
63 Wali Lundy .25 .60
64 Joseph Addai .30 .75
65 Marvin Harrison .40 1.00
66 Peyton Manning .60 1.50
67 Reggie Wayne .30 .75
68 Dallas Clark .25 .60
69 Byron Leftwich .30 .75
70 Fred Taylor .30 .75
71 Marcedes Lewis .25 .60
72 Maurice Jones-Drew .40 1.00
73 Reggie Williams .30 .75
74 Eddie Kennison .25 .60
75 Larry Johnson .25 .60
76 Tony Gonzalez .30 .75
77 Trent Green .30 .75
78 Chris Chambers .30 .75
79 Daunte Culpepper .30 .75
80 Marty Booker .25 .60
81 Ronnie Brown .30 .75
82 Chester Taylor .25 .60
83 Tarvaris Jackson .25 .60
84 Troy Williamson .25 .60
85 Travis Taylor .25 .60
86 Ben Watson .25 .60
87 Tom Brady .60 1.50
88 Corey Dillon .30 .75
89 Laurence Maroney .30 .75
90 Deuce McAllister .30 .75
91 Drew Brees .40 1.00
92 Marques Colston .40 1.00
93 Reggie Bush .40 1.00
94 Joe Horn .30 .75
95 Brandon Jacobs .30 .75
96 Eli Manning .40 1.00
97 Jeremy Shockey .30 .75
98 Plaxico Burress .30 .75
99 Chad Pennington .30 .75
100 Jerricho Cotchery .30 .75
101 Laveranues Coles .25 .60
102 Leon Washington .30 .75
103 Kevan Barlow .30 .75
104 Ronald Curry .30 .75
105 LaMont Jordan .30 .75
106 John Madsen .25 .60
107 Michael Huff .30 .75
108 Randy Moss .40 1.00
109 Brian Westbrook .30 .75
110 Donovan McNabb .40 1.00
111 Hank Baskett .30 .75
112 Donte Stallworth .30 .75
113 Reggie Brown .25 .60
114 Ben Roethlisberger .40 1.00
115 Hines Ward .40 1.00
116 Troy Polamalu .40 1.00
117 Willie Parker .30 .75
118 Santonio Holmes .30 .75
119 Antonio Gates .40 1.00
120 LaDainian Tomlinson .40 1.00
121 Vincent Jackson .30 .75
122 Philip Rivers .40 1.00
123 Shawne Merriman .30 .75
124 Alex Smith QB .40 1.00
125 Antonio Bryant .25 .60
126 Frank Gore .40 1.00
127 Vernon Davis .30 .75
128 Darrell Jackson .25 .60
129 Deion Branch .30 .75
130 Matt Hasselbeck .30 .75
131 Shaun Alexander .30 .75
132 Isaac Bruce .30 .75
133 Marc Bulger .30 .75
134 Steven Jackson .40 1.00
135 Joe Klopfenstein .25 .60
136 Torry Holt .30 .75
137 Bruce Gradkowski .25 .60
138 Cadillac Williams .30 .75
139 Joey Galloway .30 .75
140 Mike Alstott .30 .75
141 Adam Jones .25 .60
142 Drew Bennett .25 .60
143 LenDale White .30 .75
144 Vince Young .30 .75
145 Travis Henry .30 .75
146 Clinton Portis .30 .75
147 Jason Campbell .30 .75
148 Ladell Betts .25 .60
149 Santana Moss .30 .75
150 Chris Cooley .25 .60
151 Brady Quinn RC 1.25 3.00
152 JaMarcus Russell RC .75 2.00
153 Troy Smith RC 1.25 3.00
154 Drew Stanton RC .75 2.00
155 Adrian Peterson RC 5.00 12.00
156 Marshawn Lynch RC 1.25 3.00
157 Michael Bush RC 1.25 3.00
158 Kenny Irons SP RC 8.00 20.00
159 Antonio Pittman RC .75 2.00
160 Tony Hunt RC .75 2.00
161 Darius Walker SP RC 8.00 20.00
162 DeShawn Wynn RC 1.00 2.50
163 Calvin Johnson RC 4.00 10.00
164 Ted Ginn Jr. RC 1.00 2.50
165 Dwayne Jarrett RC 1.00 2.50
166 Sidney Rice RC 1.50 4.00
167 Dwayne Bowe RC 1.50 4.00
168 Robert Meachem RC 1.25 3.00
169 Anthony Gonzalez SP RC 12.00 30.00
170 Craig Buster Davis RC 1.00 2.50
171 Johnnie Lee Higgins RC 1.00 2.50
172 Steve Smith USC RC 1.25 3.00
173 Chansi Stuckey RC 1.25 3.00
174 David Clowney RC 1.00 2.50
175 Aundrae Allison RC .75 2.00
176 Jason Hill SP RC 12.00 30.00
177 Zach Miller RC 1.25 3.00
178 Greg Olsen RC 1.00 2.50
179 Gaines Adams RC 1.25 3.00
180 Jamaal Anderson RC 1.00 2.50
181 Victor Abiamiri RC 1.25 3.00
182 Adam Carriker RC 1.00 2.50
183 LaMarr Woodley RC 1.25 3.00
184 Quentin Moses RC 1.00 2.50
185 Charles Johnson RC .75 2.00
186 Alan Branch RC 1.00 2.50
187 Amobi Okoye RC 1.25 3.00
188 DeMarcus Tank Tyler RC .75 2.00
189 Patrick Willis SP RC 25.00 60.00
190 Paul Posluszny RC 1.25 3.00
191 Lawrence Timmons RC 1.25 3.00
192 Darrelle Revis RC 2.00 5.00
193 Leon Hall RC 1.00 2.50
194 Daymeion Hughes RC 1.00 2.50
195 Chris Houston RC 1.00 2.50
196 A.J. Davis RC .75 2.00
197 Aaron Ross RC 1.25 3.00
198 LaRon Landry RC 1.25 3.00
199 Reggie Nelson RC 1.00 2.50
200 Michael Griffin RC 1.25 3.00
201 Trent Edwards RC 1.25 3.00
202 Kevin Kolb RC 2.00 5.00
203 John Beck RC 1.25 3.00
204 Kenneth Darby RC 1.00 2.50
205 Lorenzo Booker RC 1.00 2.50
206 Jason Snelling RC 1.25 3.00
207 Selvin Young RC 1.00 2.50
208 Ahmad Bradshaw RC 2.00 5.00
209 Brandon Jackson RC 1.00 2.50
210 Courtney Taylor RC 1.00 2.50
211 Paul Williams SP RC 8.00 20.00
212 Rhema McKnight RC .75 2.00
213 David Ball RC 1.00 2.50
214 Syvelle Newton RC 1.00 2.50
215 Joel Filani RC 1.00 2.50
216 Chris Davis RC .75 2.00
217 Laurent Robinson RC 1.25 3.00
218 Jarrett Hicks RC 1.00 2.50
219 Dallas Baker RC .75 2.00
220 Matt Trannon RC .75 2.00
221 Mike Walker RC 1.25 3.00
222 Anthony Spencer RC 1.25 3.00
223 Jarvis Moss RC 1.00 2.50
224 Tim Crowder RC 1.25 3.00
225 Brandon Siler RC .75 2.00
226 David Harris RC 1.00 2.50
227 Buster Davis RC 1.00 2.50
228 Jon Abbate RC .75 2.00
229 Rufus Alexander RC 1.00 2.50
230 Jon Beason RC 1.00 2.50
231 Jonathan Wade RC 1.00 2.50
232 Marcus McCauley RC 1.00 2.50
233 Tanard Jackson RC .75 2.00
234 Kenny Scott RC .75 2.00
235 Brandon Meriweather RC 1.25 3.00
236 Aaron Rouse RC 1.00 2.50
237 Eric Weddle RC 1.25 3.00
238 Brian Leonard RC 1.00 2.50
239 Jared Zabransky SP RC 10.00 25.00
240 Chris Leak SP RC 10.00 25.00
241 Jordan Palmer SP RC 10.00 25.00
242 Garrett Wolfe SP RC 8.00 20.00
243 Gary Russell RC 1.00 2.50
244 Isaiah Stanback RC .75 2.00
245 Tyler Palko RC 1.00 2.50
246 Jeff Rowe RC .75 2.00
247 Kolby Smith RC 1.00 2.50
248 Dwayne Wright RC 1.00 2.50
249 Nate Ilaoa RC 1.00 2.50
250 Steve Breaston RC 1.25 3.00
251 Chris Henry RC/100*
(released for the player at the/2007 Rookie Premiere event))
252 Joe Thomas RC/100*
(released for the player at the/2007 Rookie Premiere event))

2007 Playoff Prestige Draft Picks Light Blue

*ROOKIES: .8X TO 2X BASIC CARDS
*ROOKIES: .08X TO .2X BASIC SPs
STATED PRINT RUN 999 SER.#'d SETS

2007 Playoff Prestige Xtra Points Black

UNPRICED BLACK PRINT RUN 10

2007 Playoff Prestige Xtra Points Gold

*VETS 1-150: 2X TO 5X BASIC CARDS
*ROOKIES 151-250: .8X TO 2X BASIC CARDS
*ROOKIE SPs: .08X TO .2X BASIC CARDS
STATED ODDS 1:14

2007 Playoff Prestige Xtra Points Green

*VETS 1-150: 6X TO 15X BASIC CARDS
*ROOKIES 151-250: 3X TO 8X BASIC CARDS
*ROOKIE SPs: .3X TO .8X BASIC CARDS
GREEN PRINT RUN 25 SER.#'d SETS

2007 Playoff Prestige Xtra Points Purple

*VETS 1-150: 5X TO 1X BASIC CARDS
*ROOKIES 151-250: 2X TO 5X BASIC CARDS
*ROOKIE SPs: .2X TO .5X BASIC CARDS
PURPLE PRINT RUN 50 SER.#'d SETS

2007 Playoff Prestige Xtra Points Red

*VET 1-150: 3X TO 8X BASIC CARDS
*ROOKIES 151-250: 1.2X TO 3X BASIC CARDS
*ROOKIE SPs: .1X TO .3X BASIC CARDS
RED PRINT RUN 100 SER.#'d SETS

2007 Playoff Prestige Changing Stripes Materials

STATED PRINT RUN 250 SER.#'d SETS
*PRIME/25: 1X TO 2.5X BASIC JSYs
PRIME PRINT RUN 25 SER.#'d SETS

1 Drew Brees 6.00 15.00
2 Terrell Owens 6.00 15.00
3 Edgerrin James 5.00 12.00
4 Donte Stallworth 5.00 12.00
5 Deion Branch 5.00 12.00
6 Javon Walker 5.00 12.00
7 Steve McNair 5.00 12.00
8 Daunte Culpepper 5.00 12.00
9 Keyshawn Johnson 5.00 12.00
10 Chester Taylor 4.00 10.00

2007 Playoff Prestige Draft Picks Rights Autographs

STATED PRINT RUN 5-150
SERIAL #'d UNDER 25 NOT PRICED

151 Brady Quinn/25 25.00 60.00
152 JaMarcus Russell/25 20.00 50.00
154 Drew Stanton/50 10.00 25.00
155 Adrian Peterson/25 150.00 300.00
156 Marshawn Lynch/50 20.00 50.00
161 Darius Walker/50 10.00 25.00
163 Calvin Johnson/25 100.00 200.00
164 Ted Ginn Jr./50 12.00 30.00
165 Dwayne Jarrett/50 12.00 30.00
166 Sidney Rice/50 20.00 50.00
167 Dwayne Bowe/50 30.00 60.00
168 Robert Meachem/50 15.00 40.00
172 Steve Smith USC/50 15.00 40.00
173 Chansi Stuckey/50 15.00 40.00
174 David Clowney/50 12.00 30.00
176 Jason Hill/50 15.00 40.00
178 Greg Olsen/50 12.00 30.00
179 Gaines Adams/50 15.00 40.00
181 Victor Abiamiri/150 8.00 20.00
182 Adam Carriker/50 12.00 30.00
183 LaMarr Woodley/150 12.00 30.00
184 Quentin Moses/150 6.00 15.00
191 Lawrence Timmons/25 20.00 50.00
193 Leon Hall/100 8.00 20.00
196 A.J. Davis/150 5.00 12.00
198 LaRon Landry/50 15.00 40.00
199 Reggie Nelson/25 15.00 40.00
204 Kenneth Darby/25 15.00 40.00
205 Lorenzo Booker/25 15.00 40.00
208 Ahmad Bradshaw/100 15.00 40.00
211 Paul Williams/50 10.00 25.00
213 David Ball/150 6.00 15.00
215 Joel Filani/100 8.00 20.00
219 Dallas Baker/100 6.00 15.00
221 Mike Walker/100 10.00 25.00
225 Brandon Siler/150 5.00 12.00
226 David Harris/150 6.00 15.00
229 Rufus Alexander/150 6.00 15.00
230 Jon Beason/150 6.00 15.00
232 Marcus McCauley/150 6.00 15.00
234 Kenny Scott/150 5.00 12.00
236 Aaron Rouse/150 6.00 15.00
239 Jared Zabransky/50 12.00 30.00
245 Tyler Palko/150 6.00 15.00
246 Jeff Rowe/150 5.00 12.00
247 Kolby Smith/25 15.00 40.00

2007 Playoff Prestige Gridiron Heritage

STATED ODDS 1:35 HOB, 1:19 RET
*FOIL/100: .5X TO 1.2X BASIC INSERTS
FOIL PRINT RUN 100 SER.#'d SETS
*HOLOFOIL/25: 1.2X TO 3X BASIC INSERTS
HOLOFOIL PRINT RUN 25 SER.#'d SETS

1 Tony Gonzalez 1.25 3.00
2 Trent Green 1.25 3.00
3 Larry Johnson 1.00 2.50
4 Aaron Rodgers 4.00 10.00
5 Ahman Green 1.25 3.00
6 Alge Crumpler 1.25 3.00
7 Andre Johnson 1.25 3.00
8 Anquan Boldin 1.25 3.00
9 Bernard Berrian 1.00 2.50
10 Braylon Edwards 1.25 3.00
11 Brian Westbrook 1.25 3.00
12 Brian Urlacher 1.50 4.00
13 Cadillac Williams 1.25 3.00
14 Chris Chambers 1.25 3.00
15 Clinton Portis 1.25 3.00
16 Curtis Martin 1.50 4.00
17 Darrell Jackson 1.00 2.50
18 Deuce McAllister 1.25 3.00
19 Donald Driver 1.50 4.00
20 Fred Taylor 1.25 3.00
21 Hines Ward 1.50 4.00
22 Isaac Bruce 1.25 3.00
23 J.P. Losman 1.00 2.50
24 Jake Delhomme 1.25 3.00
25 Jamal Lewis 1.25 3.00
26 Jason Campbell 1.25 3.00
27 Jason Witten 1.50 4.00
28 Jeremy Shockey 1.25 3.00
29 Joe Horn 1.25 3.00
30 Joey Galloway 1.25 3.00
31 Julius Jones 1.00 2.50
32 Kevin Jones 1.00 2.50
33 LaMont Jordan 1.25 3.00
34 Larry Fitzgerald 1.50 4.00
35 Laveranues Coles 1.00 2.50
36 Lee Evans 1.25 3.00
37 Mark Clayton 1.25 3.00
38 Matt Hasselbeck 1.25 3.00
39 Matt Jones 1.25 3.00
40 Michael Strahan 1.25 3.00
41 Muhsin Muhammad 1.25 3.00
42 Randy McMichael .75 2.00
43 Randy Moss 1.50 4.00
44 Reggie Brown 1.00 2.50
45 Reggie Wayne 1.25 3.00
46 Rudi Johnson 1.25 3.00
47 T.J. Houshmandzadeh 1.25 3.00
48 Thomas Jones 1.25 3.00
49 Todd Heap 1.00 2.50
50 Willis McGahee 1.25 3.00

2007 Playoff Prestige Gridiron Heritage Materials

STATED ODDS 1:46 HOB, 1:88 RET
*PRIME/50: .8X TO 2X BASIC INSERTS
PRIME PRINT RUN 50 SER.#'d SETS

1 Tony Gonzalez 3.00 8.00
2 Trent Green 3.00 8.00
3 Larry Johnson 2.50 6.00
4 Aaron Rodgers 12.00 30.00
5 Ahman Green 3.00 8.00
6 Alge Crumpler 3.00 8.00
7 Andre Johnson 3.00 8.00
8 Anquan Boldin 3.00 8.00
9 Bernard Berrian 2.50 6.00
10 Braylon Edwards 3.00 8.00
11 Brian Westbrook 3.00 8.00
12 Brian Urlacher 4.00 10.00
13 Cadillac Williams 3.00 8.00
14 Chris Chambers 3.00 8.00
15 Clinton Portis 3.00 8.00
16 Curtis Martin 4.00 10.00
17 Darrell Jackson 2.50 6.00
18 Deuce McAllister 3.00 8.00
19 Donald Driver 4.00 10.00
20 Fred Taylor 3.00 8.00
21 Hines Ward 4.00 10.00
22 Isaac Bruce 3.00 8.00
23 J.P. Losman 2.50 6.00
24 Jake Delhomme 3.00 8.00
25 Jamal Lewis 3.00 8.00
26 Jason Campbell 3.00 8.00
27 Jason Witten 4.00 10.00
28 Jeremy Shockey 3.00 8.00
29 Joe Horn 3.00 8.00
30 Joey Galloway 3.00 8.00
31 Julius Jones 2.50 6.00
32 Kevin Jones 2.50 6.00
33 LaMont Jordan 3.00 8.00
34 Larry Fitzgerald 4.00 10.00
35 Laveranues Coles 2.50 6.00
36 Lee Evans 3.00 8.00
37 Mark Clayton 3.00 8.00
38 Matt Hasselbeck 3.00 8.00
39 Matt Jones 3.00 8.00
40 Michael Strahan 3.00 8.00
41 Muhsin Muhammad 3.00 8.00
42 Randy McMichael 2.00 5.00
43 Randy Moss 4.00 10.00
44 Reggie Brown 2.50 6.00
45 Reggie Wayne 3.00 8.00
46 Rudi Johnson 3.00 8.00
47 T.J. Houshmandzadeh 3.00 8.00
48 Thomas Jones 3.00 8.00
49 Todd Heap 2.50 6.00
50 Willis McGahee 3.00 8.00

2007 Playoff Prestige League Leaders

STATED ODDS 1:35 HOB, 1:19 RET
*FOIL/100: .8X TO 2X BASIC INSERTS
FOIL PRINT RUN 100 SER.#'d SETS
*HOLOFOIL/25: 2X TO 5X BASIC INSERTS
HOLOFOIL PRINT RUN 25 SER.#'d SETS

1 Drew Brees 1.50 4.00
Peyton Manning
2 Marc Bulger .75 2.00
Jon Kitna
3 Carson Palmer 2.00 5.00
Brett Favre
4 Tom Brady 1.50 4.00
Ben Roethlisberger
5 Philip Rivers 1.00 2.50
Chad Pennington
6 Eli Manning 1.00 2.50
Rex Grossman
7 LaDainian Tomlinson 1.00 2.50
Larry Johnson
8 Frank Gore 1.00 2.50
Tiki Barber
9 Steven Jackson 1.00 2.50
Willie Parker
10 Rudi Johnson .75 2.00
Brian Westbrook
11 Chad Johnson 1.00 2.50
Marvin Harrison
12 Reggie Wayne .75 2.00
Roy Williams WR
13 Donald Driver 1.00 2.50
Lee Evans
14 Anquan Boldin .75 2.00
Torry Holt
15 Terrell Owens 1.00 2.50
Steve Smith WR
16 Matt Leinart .75 2.00
Vince Young
17 Joseph Addai 1.00 2.50
Maurice Jones-Drew
18 Terrell Owens 1.00 2.50
Marvin Harrison
19 Darrell Jackson .75 2.00
Plaxico Burress
20 LaDainian Tomlinson 1.00 2.50
Larry Johnson
21 Drew Brees 2.00 5.00
LaDainian Tomlinson
Peyton Manning
Larry Johnson
22 Marc Bulger 1.25 3.00
Frank Gore
Jon Kitna
Tiki Barber
23 Chad Johnson 1.25 3.00
Marvin Harrison
Reggie Wayne
Roy Williams WR
24 LaDainian Tomlinson 1.25 3.00
Terrell Owens
Larry Johnson
Marvin Harrison
25 Matt Leinart 1.25 3.00
Joseph Addai
Vince Young
Maurice Jones-Drew

2007 Playoff Prestige League Leaders Materials

LEAGUE LDR JERSEY PRINT RUN 50-250
*PRIME/25: 1X TO 2.5X BASIC JSY/250
*PRIME/25: .8X TO 2X BASIC JSY/100
PRIME PRINT RUN 10-25

1 Drew Brees 12.00 30.00
Peyton Manning/100
2 Marc Bulger 5.00 12.00
Jon Kitna/250
3 Carson Palmer 12.00 30.00
Brett Favre/250
4 Tom Brady 12.00 30.00
Ben Roethlisberger/100
5 Philip Rivers 6.00 15.00
Chad Pennington/250
6 Eli Manning 6.00 15.00
Rex Grossman/250
7 LaDainian Tomlinson 8.00 20.00
Larry Johnson/100
8 Frank Gore 6.00 15.00
Tiki Barber/250
9 Steven Jackson 6.00 15.00
Willie Parker/250
10 Rudi Johnson 5.00 12.00
Brian Westbrook/250
11 Chad Johnson 6.00 15.00
Marvin Harrison/250
12 Reggie Wayne 5.00 12.00
Roy Williams WR/250
13 Donald Driver 6.00 15.00
Lee Evans/250
14 Anquan Boldin 5.00 12.00
Torry Holt/250
15 Terrell Owens 8.00 20.00
Steve Smith WR/100
16 Matt Leinart 10.00 25.00
Vince Young/50
17 Joseph Addai 6.00 15.00
Maurice Jones-Drew/250
18 Terrell Owens 6.00 15.00
Marvin Harrison/250
19 Darrell Jackson 5.00 12.00
Plaxico Burress/250
20 LaDainian Tomlinson 8.00 20.00
Larry Johnson/100
21 Drew Brees 25.00 60.00
LaDainian Tomlinson
Peyton Manning
Larry Johnson/50
22 Marc Bulger 15.00 40.00
Frank Gore
Jon Kitna
Tiki Barber/50
23 Chad Johnson 15.00 40.00
Marvin Harrison
Reggie Wayne
Roy Williams WR/50
24 LaDainian Tomlinson 15.00 40.00
Terrell Owens
Larry Johnson
Marvin Harrison/50
25 Matt Leinart 15.00 40.00
Joseph Addai
Vince Young
Maurice Jones-Drew/50

2007 Playoff Prestige NFL Draft

STATED ODDS 1:20 HOB, 1:12 RET
*RED: .4X TO 1X BASIC INSERTS
RED INSERTS IN SPECIAL RETAIL BOXES
*FOIL/100: .8X TO 2X BASIC INSERTS
FOIL PRINT RUN 100 SER.#'d SETS
*HOLOFOIL/25: 2X TO 5X BASIC INSERTS
HOLOFOIL PRINT RUN 25 SER.#'d SETS

1 Brady Quinn 1.25 3.00
2 JaMarcus Russell .75 2.00
3 Troy Smith 1.25 3.00
4 Drew Stanton .75 2.00
5 Adrian Peterson 5.00 12.00
6 Marshawn Lynch 1.25 3.00
7 Michael Bush 1.25 3.00
8 Kenny Irons .75 2.00
9 Antonio Pittman .75 2.00
10 Tony Hunt .75 2.00
11 Darius Walker .75 2.00
12 DeShawn Wynn 1.00 2.50
13 Calvin Johnson 4.00 10.00
14 Ted Ginn Jr. 1.00 2.50
15 Dwayne Jarrett 1.00 2.50
16 Sidney Rice 1.50 4.00
17 Dwayne Bowe 1.50 4.00
18 Robert Meachem 1.25 3.00
19 Anthony Gonzalez 1.25 3.00
20 Craig Buster Davis 1.00 2.50
21 Johnnie Lee Higgins 1.00 2.50
22 Steve Smith USC 1.25 3.00
23 Chansi Stuckey 1.25 3.00
24 David Clowney 1.00 2.50
25 Aundrae Allison .75 2.00
26 Jason Hill 1.25 3.00
27 Zach Miller 1.25 3.00
28 Greg Olsen 1.00 2.50
29 Gaines Adams 1.25 3.00
30 Jamaal Anderson 1.00 2.50
31 Alan Branch 1.00 2.50
32 Amobi Okoye 1.25 3.00
33 DeMarcus Tank Tyler .75 2.00
34 Patrick Willis 2.50 6.00
35 Paul Posluszny 1.25 3.00
36 Darrelle Revis 2.00 5.00
37 Aaron Ross 1.25 3.00
38 LaRon Landry 1.25 3.00
39 Paul Williams .75 2.00
40 Jordan Palmer 1.00 2.50

2007 Playoff Prestige NFL Draft Autographs

STATED PRINT RUN 5-50
SERIAL #'d UNDER 25 NOT PRICED
1 Brady Quinn/25 30.00 80.00
2 JaMarcus Russell/25 12.00 30.00
4 Drew Stanton/50 10.00 25.00
5 Adrian Peterson/25 150.00 300.00
6 Marshawn Lynch/50 20.00 50.00
11 Darius Walker/50 10.00 25.00
13 Calvin Johnson/25 100.00 200.00
14 Ted Ginn Jr./50 12.00 30.00
15 Dwayne Jarrett/50 12.00 30.00
16 Sidney Rice/50 20.00 50.00
17 Dwayne Bowe/50 20.00 50.00
18 Robert Meachem/50 15.00 40.00
22 Steve Smith USC/50 15.00 40.00
23 Chansi Stuckey/50 15.00 40.00
24 David Clowney/50 12.00 30.00
26 Jason Hill/50 15.00 40.00
28 Greg Olsen/50 12.00 30.00
29 Gaines Adams/50 15.00 40.00
38 LaRon Landry/50 15.00 40.00
39 Paul Williams/50 10.00 25.00

2007 Playoff Prestige Prestigious Picks Blue

BLUE PRINT RUN 1000 SER.#'d SETS
*RED/750: .4X TO 1X BLUE/1000
RED PRINT RUN 750 SER.#'d SETS
*BLACK/500: .5X TO 1.2X BLUE/1000
BLACK PRINT RUN 500 SER.#'d SETS
*PURPLE/250: .6X TO 1.5X BLUE/1000
PURPLE PRINT RUN 250 SER.#'d SETS
*GREEN/100: .8X TO 2X BLUE/1000
GREEN PRINT RUN 100 SER.#'d SETS
*SILVER/50: 1.2X TO 3X BLUE/1000
SILVER PRINT RUN 50 SER.#'d SETS
*GOLD/25: 2X TO 5X BLUE/1000
GOLD PRINT RUN 25 SER.#'d SETS
*PLATINUM/10: 3X TO 8X BLUE/1000
PLATINUM PRINT RUN 10 SER.#'d SETS
1 Kenny Irons .75 2.00
2 JaMarcus Russell .75 2.00
3 Robert Meachem 1.25 3.00
4 Dwayne Bowe 1.50 4.00
5 Craig Buster Davis 1.00 2.50
6 Adrian Peterson 5.00 12.00
7 Dwayne Jarrett 1.00 2.50
8 Steve Smith USC 1.25 3.00
9 Brady Quinn 1.25 3.00
10 Zach Miller 1.25 3.00

2007 Playoff Prestige Prestigious Picks Materials Gold

GOLD PRINT RUN 50 SER.#'d SETS
*BLACK/25: .8X TO 2X GOLD/50
BLACK PRINT RUN 25 SER.#'d SETS
UNPRICED PLATINUM PATCH PRINT RUN 10
1 Kenny Irons 3.00 8.00
2 JaMarcus Russell 3.00 8.00
3 Robert Meachem 5.00 12.00
4 Dwayne Bowe 6.00 15.00
5 Craig Buster Davis 4.00 10.00
6 Adrian Peterson 20.00 50.00
7 Dwayne Jarrett 4.00 10.00
8 Steve Smith USC 5.00 12.00
9 Brady Quinn 5.00 12.00
10 Zach Miller 5.00 12.00

2007 Playoff Prestige Prestigious Pros Blue

BLUE PRINT RUN 1000 SER.#'d SETS
*RED/750: .4X TO 1X BLUE/1000
RED PRINT RUN 750 SER.#'d SETS
*BLACK/500: .5X TO 1.2X BLUE/1000
BLACK PRINT RUN 500 SER.#'d SETS
*PURPLE/250: .6X TO 1.5X BLUE/1000
PURPLE PRINT RUN 250 SER.#'d SETS
*GREEN/100: .8X TO 2X BLUE/1000
GREEN PRINT RUN 100 SER.#'d SETS
*SILVER/50: 1X TO 2.5X BLUE/1000
SILVER PRINT RUN 50 SER.#'d SETS
*GOLD/25: 1.5X TO 4X BLUE/1000
GOLD PRINT RUN 25 SER.#'d SETS
*PLATINUM/10: 3X TO 8X BLUE/1000
PLATINUM PRINT RUN 10 SER.#'d SETS
1 Ahman Green 1.00 2.50
2 Brian Westbrook 1.00 2.50
3 Clinton Portis 1.00 2.50
4 Jake Delhomme 1.00 2.50
5 Kevin Jones .75 2.00
6 Reggie Brown .75 2.00
7 Rudi Johnson 1.00 2.50
8 Tony Gonzalez 1.00 2.50
9 Alex Smith QB 1.25 3.00
10 Ben Roethlisberger 1.25 3.00
11 Tom Brady 2.00 5.00
12 Willie Parker 1.00 2.50
13 Frank Gore 1.25 3.00
14 Ronnie Brown 1.00 2.50
15 LaDainian Tomlinson 1.25 3.00
16 Tiki Barber 1.25 3.00
17 Roy Williams WR 1.00 2.50
18 Brett Favre 2.50 6.00
19 Steven Jackson 1.25 3.00
20 Torry Holt 1.00 2.50
21 Larry Johnson .75 2.00
22 Anquan Boldin 1.00 2.50
23 Cadillac Williams 1.00 2.50
24 Hines Ward 1.25 3.00
25 Julius Jones .75 2.00
26 Matt Hasselbeck 1.00 2.50
27 Reggie Wayne 1.00 2.50
28 Thomas Jones 1.00 2.50
29 Willis McGahee 1.00 2.50
30 Antonio Gates 1.25 3.00
31 Tony Romo 1.50 4.00
32 Peyton Manning 2.00 5.00
33 Shaun Alexander 1.00 2.50
34 Carson Palmer 1.00 2.50
35 Michael Vick 1.25 3.00
36 Philip Rivers 1.25 3.00
37 Chad Johnson 1.00 2.50
38 Drew Brees 1.25 3.00
39 Eli Manning 1.25 3.00
40 Steve Smith 1.00 2.50

2007 Playoff Prestige Prestigious Pros Autographs

STATED PRINT RUN 1-25
SERIAL #'d UNDER 20 NOT PRICED
6 Reggie Brown/20 20.00 40.00
7 Rudi Johnson/25 10.00 25.00
13 Frank Gore/25 12.00 30.00
26 Matt Hasselbeck/25 20.00 50.00
28 Thomas Jones/25 10.00 25.00

2007 Playoff Prestige Prestigious Pros Materials Red

RED STATED ODDS 1:68 RETAIL
*PURPLE/250: .4X TO 1X RED JSYs
PURPLE PRINT RUN 250 SER.#'d SETS
*GREEN/100: .5X TO 1.2X RED JSYs
GREEN PRINT RUN 100 SER.#'d SETS
*GOLD/50: .6X TO 1.5X RED JSYs
GOLD PRINT RUN 50 SER.#'d SETS
*BLACK/25: 1X TO 2.5X RED JSYs
BLACK PRINT RUN 25 SER.#'d SETS
UNPRICED PLATINUM PATCH PRINT RUN 10
1 Ahman Green 3.00 8.00
2 Brian Westbrook 3.00 8.00
3 Clinton Portis 3.00 8.00
4 Jake Delhomme 3.00 8.00
5 Kevin Jones 2.50 6.00
6 Reggie Brown 2.50 6.00
7 Rudi Johnson 3.00 8.00
8 Tony Gonzalez 3.00 8.00
9 Alex Smith QB 4.00 10.00
10 Ben Roethlisberger 4.00 10.00
11 Tom Brady 6.00 15.00
12 Willie Parker 3.00 8.00
13 Frank Gore 4.00 10.00
14 Ronnie Brown 3.00 8.00
15 LaDainian Tomlinson 4.00 10.00
16 Tiki Barber 4.00 10.00
17 Roy Williams WR 3.00 8.00
18 Brett Favre 8.00 20.00
19 Steven Jackson 4.00 10.00
20 Torry Holt 3.00 8.00
21 Larry Johnson 2.50 6.00
22 Anquan Boldin 3.00 8.00
23 Cadillac Williams 3.00 8.00
24 Hines Ward 4.00 10.00
25 Julius Jones 2.50 6.00
26 Matt Hasselbeck 3.00 8.00
27 Reggie Wayne 3.00 8.00
28 Thomas Jones 3.00 8.00
29 Willis McGahee 3.00 8.00
30 Antonio Gates 4.00 10.00
31 Tony Romo 5.00 12.00
32 Peyton Manning 6.00 15.00
33 Shaun Alexander 3.00 8.00
34 Carson Palmer 3.00 8.00
35 Michael Vick 4.00 10.00
36 Philip Rivers 4.00 10.00
37 Chad Johnson 3.00 8.00
38 Drew Brees 4.00 10.00
39 Eli Manning 4.00 10.00
40 Steve Smith 3.00 8.00

2007 Playoff Prestige Stars of the NFL

STATED ODDS 1:35 HOB, 1:19 RET
*FOIL/100: .8X TO 2X BASIC INSERTS
FOIL PRINT RUN 100 SER.#'d SETS
*HOLOFOIL/25: 2X TO 5X BASIC INSERTS
HOLOFOIL PRINT RUN 25 SER.#'d SETS
1 Alex Smith QB 1.00 2.50
2 Antonio Gates 1.00 2.50
3 Ben Roethlisberger 1.00 2.50
4 Tony Romo 1.25 3.00
5 Tom Brady 1.50 4.00
6 Peyton Manning 1.50 4.00
7 Willie Parker .75 2.00
8 Shaun Alexander .75 2.00
9 Frank Gore 1.00 2.50
10 Carson Palmer .75 2.00
11 Ronnie Brown .75 2.00
12 Michael Vick 1.00 2.50
13 LaDainian Tomlinson 1.00 2.50
14 Philip Rivers 1.00 2.50
15 Marvin Harrison 1.00 2.50
16 Larry Johnson .60 1.50
17 Tiki Barber 1.00 2.50
18 Chad Johnson .75 2.00
19 Roy Williams WR .75 2.00
20 Drew Brees 1.00 2.50
21 Brett Favre 2.00 5.00
22 Eli Manning 1.00 2.50
23 Steven Jackson 1.00 2.50
24 Steve Smith .75 2.00
25 Torry Holt .75 2.00

2007 Playoff Prestige Stars of the NFL Materials

STATED ODDS 1:46 HOB, 1:90 RET
*PRIME/25: 1X TO 2.5X BASIC INSERTS
PRIME PRINT RUN 25
UNPRICED AUTOs SER.#'d TO 10
1 Alex Smith QB 4.00 10.00
2 Antonio Gates 4.00 10.00
3 Ben Roethlisberger 4.00 10.00
4 Tony Romo 5.00 12.00
5 Tom Brady 6.00 15.00
6 Peyton Manning 6.00 15.00
7 Willie Parker 3.00 8.00
8 Shaun Alexander 3.00 8.00
9 Frank Gore 4.00 10.00
10 Carson Palmer 3.00 8.00
11 Ronnie Brown 3.00 8.00
12 Michael Vick 4.00 10.00
13 LaDainian Tomlinson 4.00 10.00
14 Philip Rivers 4.00 10.00
15 Marvin Harrison 4.00 10.00
16 Larry Johnson 2.50 6.00
17 Tiki Barber 4.00 10.00
18 Chad Johnson 3.00 8.00
19 Roy Williams WR 3.00 8.00
20 Drew Brees 4.00 10.00
21 Brett Favre 8.00 20.00
22 Eli Manning 4.00 10.00
23 Steven Jackson 4.00 10.00
24 Steve Smith 3.00 8.00
25 Torry Holt 3.00 8.00

2007 Playoff Prestige Stars of the NFL Materials Prime Autographs

STATED PRINT RUN 10 SER.#'d SETS

2007 Playoff Prestige Super Bowl Heroes

STATED ODDS 1:46 HOB, 1:80 RET
*FOIL/100: 1X TO 2.5X BASIC INSERTS
FOIL PRINT RUN 100 SER.#'d SETS
*HOLOFOIL/25: 2.5X TO 6X BASIC INSERTS
HOLOFOIL PRINT RUN 25 SER.#'d SETS
1 Peyton Manning 3.00 8.00
2 Reggie Wayne 1.50 4.00
3 Dominic Rhodes 1.50 4.00
4 Joseph Addai 1.50 4.00
5 Marvin Harrison 2.00 5.00
6 Adam Vinatieri 1.50 4.00
7 Kelvin Hayden 1.25 3.00
8 Devin Hester 2.00 5.00
9 Thomas Jones* 1.50 4.00
10 Brian Urlacher 2.00 5.00

2007 Playoff Prestige Super Bowl Heroes Holofoil Autographs

STATED PRINT RUN 1-25
SERIAL #'d UNDER 25 NOT PRICED
9 Thomas Jones/25 15.00 30.00

2007 Playoff Prestige Turning Pro

STATED ODDS 1:46 HOBBY
STATED ODDS 1:80 RETAIL
*FOIL/100: .8X TO 2X BASIC INSERTS
FOIL PRINT RUN 100 SER.#'d SETS
*HOLOFOIL/25: 1.5X TO 4X BASIC INSERTS
HOLOFOIL PRINT RUN 25 SER.#'d SETS
1 Jay Cutler 1.50 4.00
2 Matt Leinart 1.25 3.00
3 Joseph Addai 1.25 3.00
4 Maurice Jones-Drew 1.50 4.00
5 Reggie Bush 1.50 4.00
6 Laurence Maroney 1.25 3.00
7 Mario Williams 1.25 3.00
8 Sinorice Moss 1.25 3.00
9 LenDale White 1.25 3.00
10 Demetrius Williams 1.00 2.50

2007 Playoff Prestige Turning Pro Materials

STATED PRINT RUN 250 SER.#'d SETS
*PRIME/25: .8X TO 2X BASIC JSYs
PRIME PRINT RUN 25 SER.#'d SETS
1 Jay Cutler 6.00 15.00
2 Matt Leinart 5.00 12.00
3 Joseph Addai 5.00 12.00
4 Maurice Jones-Drew 6.00 15.00
5 Reggie Bush 6.00 15.00
6 Laurence Maroney 5.00 12.00
7 Mario Williams 5.00 12.00
8 Sinorice Moss 5.00 12.00
9 LenDale White 5.00 12.00
10 Demetrius Williams 4.00 10.00

2008 Playoff Prestige

This set was released on May 14, 2008. The base set consists of 200 cards. Cards 1-100 feature veterans, and cards 101-200 are rookies. Card #201 Jake Long was issued only in Target and Wal-Mart retail blaster boxes.

COMP.SET w/o SP's (190) 40.00 80.00
COMP.SET w/o RC's (100) 8.00 20.00
ONE ROOKIE CARD PER PACK
1 Anquan Boldin .25 .60
2 Larry Fitzgerald .30 .75
3 Edgerrin James .25 .60
4 Matt Leinart .30 .75
5 Warrick Dunn .25 .60
6 Roddy White .25 .60
7 Derrick Mason .25 .60
8 Todd Heap .20 .50
9 Willis McGahee .25 .60
10 J.P. Losman .20 .50
11 Lee Evans .25 .60
12 Marshawn Lynch .25 .60
13 Steve Smith .25 .60
14 Keary Colbert .20 .50
15 DeShaun Foster .25 .60
16 Bernard Berrian .25 .60
17 Cedric Benson .25 .60
18 Devin Hester .30 .75
19 Carson Palmer .30 .75
20 Rudi Johnson .25 .60
21 T.J. Houshmandzadeh .25 .60
22 Chad Johnson .25 .60
23 Derek Anderson .20 .50
24 Kellen Winslow .25 .60
25 Braylon Edwards .25 .60
26 Tony Romo .40 1.00
27 Terrell Owens .30 .75
28 Marion Barber .25 .60
29 Jay Cutler .30 .75
30 Javon Walker .25 .60
31 Brandon Marshall .25 .60
32 Jon Kitna .25 .60
33 Calvin Johnson .30 .75
34 Roy Williams WR .25 .60
35 Brett Favre .75 2.00
36 Donald Driver .25 .60
37 Greg Jennings .30 .75
38 Matt Schaub .25 .60
39 Andre Johnson .25 .60
40 Ahman Green .25 .60
41 Peyton Manning .50 1.25
42 Joseph Addai .25 .60
43 Reggie Wayne .25 .60
44 Marvin Harrison .30 .75
45 David Garrard .25 .60
46 Fred Taylor .25 .60
47 Maurice Jones-Drew .25 .60
48 Tony Gonzalez .25 .60
49 Dwayne Bowe .25 .60
50 Larry Johnson .25 .60
51 Ted Ginn Jr. .25 .60
52 Ronnie Brown .25 .60
53 Tarvaris Jackson .25 .60
54 Adrian Peterson .50 1.25
55 Chester Taylor .20 .50
56 Tom Brady .50 1.25
57 Randy Moss .30 .75
58 Wes Welker .30 .75
59 Laurence Maroney .25 .60
60 Drew Brees .30 .75
61 Reggie Bush .30 .75
62 Deuce McAllister .25 .60
63 Marques Colston .25 .60
64 Eli Manning .30 .75
65 Brandon Jacobs .25 .60
66 Plaxico Burress .25 .60
67 Jeremy Shockey .25 .60
68 Jerricho Cotchery .25 .60
69 Laveranues Coles .20 .50
70 Thomas Jones .25 .60
71 JaMarcus Russell .25 .60
72 Jerry Porter .20 .50
73 Ronald Curry .25 .60
74 Donovan McNabb .30 .75
75 Brian Westbrook .25 .60
76 Kevin Curtis .20 .50
77 Ben Roethlisberger .30 .75
78 Willie Parker .25 .60
79 Hines Ward .25 .60
80 Philip Rivers .30 .75
81 Antonio Gates .30 .75
82 LaDainian Tomlinson .30 .75
83 Alex Smith QB .30 .75
84 Frank Gore .25 .60
85 Vernon Davis .25 .60
86 Matt Hasselbeck .25 .60
87 Shaun Alexander .25 .60
88 Deion Branch .25 .60
89 Marc Bulger .25 .60
90 Steven Jackson .30 .75
91 Torry Holt .25 .60
92 Jeff Garcia .25 .60
93 Joey Galloway .25 .60
94 Cadillac Williams .25 .60
95 Vince Young .25 .60
96 LenDale White .25 .60
97 Brandon Jones .20 .50
98 Jason Campbell .25 .60
99 Clinton Portis .25 .60
100 Chris Cooley .25 .60
101 Adarius Bowman RC .75 2.00
102 Adrian Arrington RC .75 2.00
103 Ali Highsmith RC .60 1.50
104 Allen Patrick RC .75 2.00
105 Andre Caldwell RC .75 2.00
106 Andre Woodson RC 1.00 2.50
107 Anthony Alridge RC .75 2.00
108 Antoine Cason RC 1.00 2.50
109 Aqib Talib RC 1.00 2.50
110 Chauncey Washington SP RC 10.00 25.00
111 Bernard Morris RC .75 2.00
112 Brad Cottam RC .75 2.00
113 Brian Brohm RC 1.00 2.50
114 Chad Henne RC 1.00 2.50
115 Chris Johnson RC 2.50 6.00
116 Chris Long SP RC 10.00 25.00
117 Colt Brennan RC 1.00 2.50
118 Cory Boyd RC .60 1.50
119 Curtis Lofton RC .75 2.00
120 DJ Hall RC .75 2.00
121 Dan Connor SP RC 12.00 30.00
122 Dantrell Savage RC .75 2.00
123 Darius Reynaud RC .60 1.50
124A Darren McFadden Red RC 2.50 6.00
124B Darren McFadden Wht RC 5.00 12.00
white jersey in photo
(inserted in retail packs)
125 Davone Bess RC 1.00 2.50
126 Dennis Dixon RC 1.00 2.50
127 Derrick Harvey RC .60 1.50
128 DeSean Jackson RC 2.00 5.00
129 Devin Thomas RC .75 2.00
130 Dexter Jackson RC .75 2.00
131 Dominique Rodgers-Cromartie RC 1.00 2.50
132 Donnie Avery RC .75 2.00
133 Dorien Bryant RC .75 2.00
134 Earl Bennett RC 1.00 2.50
135 Early Doucet RC .75 2.00
136 Eddie Royal RC 1.00 2.50
137 Erik Ainge RC 1.00 2.50
138 Erin Henderson RC 1.00 2.50
139 Felix Jones SP RC 15.00 40.00
140 Fred Davis RC 1.00 2.50
141 Glenn Dorsey RC 1.00 2.50
142 Harry Douglas SP RC 8.00 20.00
143 Jacob Hester RC 1.00 2.50
144 Jacob Tamme RC 1.00 2.50
145 Jamaal Charles RC 1.50 4.00
146 James Hardy RC .75 2.00
147 Jason Rivers RC .75 2.00
148 Jed Collins SP RC 8.00 20.00
149 Jermichael Finley RC 1.00 2.50
150 Jerome Simpson RC 1.00 2.50
151 Joe Flacco RC 3.00 8.00
152 John Carlson RC 1.00 2.50
153 John David Booty RC .75 2.00
154 Jonathan Stewart RC 1.50 4.00
155 Jordy Nelson SP RC 12.00 30.00
156 Josh Johnson RC 1.00 2.50
157 Josh Morgan RC 1.00 2.50
158 Justin Forsett RC 1.00 2.50
159 Kalvin McRae RC .60 1.50
160 Keenan Burton RC .60 1.50
161 Keith Rivers RC 1.00 2.50
162 Kellen Davis RC .60 1.50
163 Kenny Phillips RC 1.00 2.50
164 Kevin O'Connell RC .75 2.00
165 Kevin Robinson RC .60 1.50
166 Kevin Smith SP RC 10.00 25.00
167 Lavelle Hawkins RC .60 1.50
168 Leodis McKelvin RC .75 2.00
169 Limas Sweed RC 1.00 2.50
170 Malcolm Kelly RC .75 2.00
171 Marcus Monk RC .75 2.00
172 Marcus Smith RC .75 2.00
173 Mario Manningham RC 1.00 2.50
174 Mark Bradford RC .60 1.50
175 Martellus Bennett RC .75 2.00
176 Martin Rucker RC .75 2.00
177 Matt Flynn SP RC 15.00 30.00
178 Matt Forte RC 1.50 4.00
179 Matt Ryan RC 4.00 10.00
180 Mike Hart RC 1.00 2.50
181 Mike Jenkins RC 1.00 2.50
182 Owen Schmitt RC 1.00 2.50
183 Paul Hubbard RC .75 2.00
184 Paul Smith RC 1.00 2.50
185 Peyton Hillis RC 2.00 5.00
186 Quentin Groves RC .75 2.00
187 Rashard Mendenhall RC 2.00 5.00
188 Ray Rice RC 2.00 5.00
189 Reggie Smith SP RC 8.00 20.00
190 Ryan Grice-Mullen RC .60 1.50
191 Sam Keller RC .75 2.00
192 Sedrick Ellis RC 1.00 2.50
193 Steve Slaton RC 1.00 2.50
194 Tashard Choice RC .75 2.00
195 Terrell Thomas RC .75 2.00
196 Thomas Brown RC .75 2.00
197 Tracy Porter RC 1.00 2.50
198 Vernon Gholston RC .75 2.00
199 Will Franklin RC .75 2.00
200 Xavier Adibi RC .60 1.50
201 Jake Long RC 75.00 150.00
(issued in Target & Wal-Mart/ retail packs only)

2008 Playoff Prestige 10th Anniversary

*VETS 1-100: 12X TO 30X BASIC CARDS
*ROOKIES: 5X TO 12X BASIC RC
*ROOKIES: .6X TO 1.5X BASIC RC SP
10TH ANNIVERSARY PRINT RUN 10

2008 Playoff Prestige Draft Picks Light Blue

*ROOKIES: .8X TO 1.5X BASIC RC
*ROOKIES: .1X TO .25X BASIC SP RC
STATED PRINT RUN 999 SER.#'d SETS

2008 Playoff Prestige Xtra Points

*VETS 1-100: 2X TO 5X BASIC CARDS
*ROOKIES 101-200: .8X TO 2X BASIC RC
*ROOKIES: .1X TO .3X BASIC SP RC
STATED PRINT RUN 300 SER.#'d SETS

2008 Playoff Prestige Xtra Points Black

*VETS 1-100: 12X TO 30X BASIC CARDS
*ROOKIES: 5X TO 12X BASIC RC
*ROOKIES: .6X TO 1.5X BASIC SP RC
XTRA POINTS BLACK PRINT RUN 10
124 Darren McFadden 30.00 80.00

2008 Playoff Prestige Xtra Points Gold

*VETS 1-100: 2X TO 5X BASIC CARDS
*ROOKIES: .8X TO 2X BASIC RC
*ROOKIES: .1X TO .3X BASIC SP RC
STATED PRINT RUN 250 SER.#'d SETS

2008 Playoff Prestige Xtra Points Green

*VETS 1-100: 6X TO 15X BASIC CARDS
*ROOKIES: 2.5X TO 6X BASIC RC
*ROOKIES: .4X TO 1X BASIC SP RC
STATED PRINT RUN 25 SER.#'d SETS

2008 Playoff Prestige Xtra Points Purple

*VETS 1-100: 4X TO 10X BASIC CARDS
*ROOKIES: 1.5X TO 4X BASIC RC
*ROOKIES: .25X TO .6X BASIC SP RC
STATED PRINT RUN 50 SER.#'d SETS

2008 Playoff Prestige Xtra Points Red

*VETS 1-100: 2.5X TO 6X BASIC CARDS
*ROOKIES: 1X TO 2.5X BASIC RC
*ROOKIES: .15X TO .4X BASIC SP RC
STATED PRINT RUN 100 SER.#'d SETS

2008 Playoff Prestige Award Winners

*FOIL/100: .5X TO 1.2X BASIC INSERTS
FOIL PRINT RUN 100 SER.#'d SETS
*HOLOFOIL/25: 1.2X TO 3X BASIC INSERTS
HOLOFOIL PRINT RUN 25 SER.#'d SETS
UNPRICED AUTO PRINT RUN 4-10
1 Adrian Peterson 2.50 6.00
2 Patrick Willis 1.25 3.00
3 Bob Sanders 1.25 3.00
4 Tom Brady 2.50 6.00
5 Greg Ellis 1.00 2.50
6 Tom Brady 2.50 6.00
7 Brett Favre 4.00 10.00
8 Brett Favre 4.00 10.00
9 Eli Manning 1.50 4.00
10 Adrian Peterson 2.50 6.00

2008 Playoff Prestige Award Winners Autographs

UNPRICED AUTO PRINT RUN 4-10

2008 Playoff Prestige Award Winners Materials

STATED PRINT RUN 100 SER.#'d SETS
*PRIME/25: .8X TO 2X BASIC JSY
PRIME PRINT RUN 25 SER.#'d SETS
1 Adrian Peterson 8.00 20.00
2 Patrick Willis 4.00 10.00
4 Tom Brady 8.00 20.00
6 Tom Brady 8.00 20.00
7 Brett Favre 12.00 30.00
8 Brett Favre 12.00 30.00
9 Eli Manning 5.00 12.00
10 Adrian Peterson 8.00 20.00

2008 Playoff Prestige Connections

*FOIL/100: .6X TO 1.5X BASIC INSERTS
FOIL PRINT RUN 100 SER.#'d SETS
*HOLOFOIL/25: 1.2X TO 3X BASIC INSERTS
HOLOFOIL PRINT RUN 25 SER.#'d SETS
1 Tony Romo 2.00 5.00
Terrell Owens
2 Tom Brady 2.50 6.00
Randy Moss
3 Ben Roethlisberger 1.50 4.00
Santonio Holmes
4 Carson Palmer 1.50 4.00
Chad Johnson
5 Derek Anderson 1.25 3.00
Braylon Edwards
6 Carson Palmer 1.50 4.00
T.J. Houshmandzadeh
7 Peyton Manning 2.50 6.00
Dallas Clark
8 Philip Rivers 1.50 4.00
Antonio Gates
9 Drew Brees 1.50 4.00
Marques Colston
10 Eli Manning 1.50 4.00
Plaxico Burress
11 Peyton Manning 2.50 6.00
Reggie Wayne
12 Jon Kitna 1.25 3.00
Roy Williams WR
13 Brett Favre 4.00 10.00
Greg Jennings
14 Jeff Garcia 1.25 3.00
Joey Galloway
15 Kurt Warner 1.50 4.00
Larry Fitzgerald
16 Matt Schaub 1.25 3.00
Andre Johnson
17 Tom Brady 2.50 6.00
Wes Welker
18 Jay Cutler 1.50 4.00
Brandon Marshall
19 Marc Bulger 1.25 3.00
Torry Holt
20 Jason Campbell 1.25 3.00
Chris Cooley

2008 Playoff Prestige Connections Materials

STATED PRINT RUN 250 SER.#'d SETS
*PRIME/25: 1X TO 2.5X BASIC JSYs
PRIME PRINT RUN 25 SER.#'d SETS
1 Tony Romo 8.00 20.00
Terrell Owens
2 Tom Brady 20.00 50.00
Randy Moss
3 Ben Roethlisberger 6.00 15.00
Santonio Holmes
4 Carson Palmer 6.00 15.00
Chad Johnson
5 Derek Anderson 5.00 12.00
Braylon Edwards
6 Carson Palmer 6.00 15.00
T.J. Houshmandzadeh
7 Peyton Manning 8.00 20.00
Dallas Clark
8 Philip Rivers 6.00 15.00
Antonio Gates
9 Drew Brees 6.00 15.00
Marques Colston
10 Eli Manning 6.00 15.00
Plaxico Burress
11 Peyton Manning 8.00 20.00
Reggie Wayne
12 Jon Kitna 5.00 12.00
Roy Williams WR
13 Brett Favre 15.00 40.00
Greg Jennings
14 Jeff Garcia 5.00 12.00
Joey Galloway
15 Kurt Warner 6.00 15.00
Larry Fitzgerald
16 Matt Schaub 5.00 12.00
Andre Johnson
17 Tom Brady 12.00 30.00
Wes Welker
18 Jay Cutler 6.00 15.00
Brandon Marshall
19 Marc Bulger 5.00 12.00
Torry Holt
20 Jason Campbell 5.00 12.00
Chris Cooley

2008 Playoff Prestige Draft Picks Rights Autographs

AUTO PRINT RUN 50-250
101 Adarius Bowman/250 5.00 12.00
104 Allen Patrick/250 5.00 12.00
105 Andre Caldwell/250 5.00 12.00
106 Andre Woodson/100 8.00 20.00
107 Anthony Alridge/250 5.00 12.00
108 Antoine Cason/250 6.00 15.00
110 Chauncey Washington/250 5.00 12.00
111 Bernard Morris/250 5.00 12.00
112 Brad Cottam/250 5.00 12.00
113 Brian Brohm/50 10.00 25.00
114 Chad Henne/100 8.00 20.00
115 Chris Johnson/250 35.00 60.00
116 Chris Long/100 8.00 20.00
117 Colt Brennan/100 15.00 40.00
118 Cory Boyd/250 4.00 10.00
119 Curtis Lofton/250 5.00 12.00
120 DJ Hall/250 5.00 12.00
121 Dan Connor/250 6.00 15.00
122 Dantrell Savage/250 5.00 12.00
123 Darius Reynaud/250 4.00 10.00
124 Darren McFadden/100 30.00 60.00
125 Davone Bess/250 6.00 15.00
126 Dennis Dixon/100 10.00 25.00
128 DeSean Jackson/50 25.00 50.00
129 Devin Thomas/100 6.00 15.00
130 Dexter Jackson/250 5.00 12.00
131 Dominique Rodgers-Cromartie 6.00 15.00
-250
132 Donnie Avery/100 6.00 15.00
133 Dorien Bryant/250 5.00 12.00
134 Earl Bennett/100 10.00 25.00
137 Erik Ainge/100 8.00 20.00
138 Erin Henderson/250 6.00 15.00
139 Felix Jones/100 30.00 60.00
143 Jacob Hester/250 6.00 15.00
144 Jacob Tamme/250 6.00 15.00
145 Jamaal Charles/250 10.00 25.00
146 James Hardy/100 6.00 15.00
148 Jed Collins/250 5.00 12.00
151 Joe Flacco/200 40.00 80.00
152 John Carlson/250 6.00 15.00
153 John David Booty/100 6.00 15.00
154 Jonathan Stewart/100 25.00 50.00
156 Josh Johnson/250 6.00 15.00
157 Josh Morgan/250 6.00 15.00
158 Justin Forsett/250 6.00 15.00
159 Kalvin McRae/250 4.00 10.00
161 Keith Rivers/250 6.00 15.00
162 Kellen Davis/250 4.00 10.00
164 Kevin O'Connell/100 6.00 15.00
167 Lavelle Hawkins/250 4.00 10.00
168 Leodis McKelvin/250 5.00 12.00
169 Limas Sweed/100 8.00 20.00
170 Malcolm Kelly/100 6.00 15.00
171 Marcus Monk/250 8.00 20.00
173 Mario Manningham/250 10.00 20.00
174 Mark Bradford/250 4.00 10.00
175 Martellus Bennett/250 8.00 20.00
177 Matt Flynn/250 15.00 30.00
178 Matt Forte/250 25.00 50.00
179 Matt Ryan/100 50.00 120.00
180 Mike Hart/250 6.00 15.00
182 Owen Schmitt/250 6.00 15.00
183 Paul Hubbard/250 5.00 12.00
184 Paul Smith/250 6.00 15.00
185 Peyton Hillis/250 15.00 30.00
186 Quentin Groves/250 5.00 12.00
187 Rashard Mendenhall/100 40.00 80.00
188 Ray Rice/250 20.00 40.00
191 Sam Keller/250 5.00 12.00
194 Tashard Choice/100 6.00 15.00
195 Terrell Thomas/250 5.00 12.00
197 Tracy Porter/250 8.00 20.00
198 Vernon Gholston/250 5.00 12.00
199 Will Franklin/250 5.00 12.00

2008 Playoff Prestige League Leaders

*FOIL/100: .8X TO 2X BASIC INSERTS
FOIL PRINT RUN 100 SER.#'d SETS
*HOLOFOIL/25: 1.5X TO 4X BASIC INSERTS
HOLOFOIL PRINT RUN 25 SER.#'d SETS
1 Tom Brady 2.00 5.00
Drew Brees
2 Tony Romo 3.00 8.00
Brett Favre
3 Carson Palmer 1.25 3.00
Jon Kitna
4 Peyton Manning 2.00 5.00
Matt Hasselbeck
5 Derek Anderson 1.25 3.00
Jay Cutler
6 LaDainian Tomlinson 2.00 5.00
Adrian Peterson
7 Brian Westbrook 1.00 2.50
Willie Parker
8 Jamal Lewis 1.00 2.50
Clinton Portis
9 Edgerrin James 1.00 2.50
Willis McGahee
10 Fred Taylor 1.00 2.50
Thomas Jones
11 Reggie Wayne 1.25 3.00
Randy Moss
12 Chad Johnson 1.25 3.00
Larry Fitzgerald
13 Terrell Owens 1.25 3.00
Brandon Marshall
14 Braylon Edwards 1.00 2.50
Marques Colston
15 Roddy White 1.00 2.50
Torry Holt
16 Tom Brady 4.00 10.00
Drew Brees
Tony Romo
Brett Favre
17 LaDainian Tomlinson 2.50 6.00
Adrian Peterson
Brian Westbrook
Willie Parker
18 Reggie Wayne 1.50 4.00
Randy Moss
Chad Johnson
Larry Fitzgerald
19 Carson Palmer 2.50 6.00
Jon Kitna
Peyton Manning
Matt Hasselbeck
20 Jamal Lewis 1.25 3.00
Clinton Portis
Edgerrin James
Willis McGahee
21 Terrell Owens 1.50 4.00
Brandon Marshall
Braylon Edwards
Marques Colston
22 Randy Moss 1.50 4.00
Braylon Edwards
Terrell Owens
Plaxico Burress
23 LaDainian Tomlinson 2.50 6.00
Joseph Addai
Adrian Peterson
Clinton Portis
24 Tom Brady 2.50 6.00
Tony Romo
Ben Roethlisberger
Peyton Manning
25 Randy Moss 1.50 4.00
LaDainian Tomlinson
Braylon Edwards
Joseph Addai

2008 Playoff Prestige League Leaders Materials

STATED PRINT RUN 250 SER.#'d SETS
*PRIME: .8X TO 2X BASIC INSERTS
PRIME PRINT RUN 25 SER.#'d SETS
1 Tom Brady 8.00 20.00
Drew Brees
2 Tony Romo 15.00 40.00
Brett Favre
3 Carson Palmer 6.00 15.00
Jon Kitna
4 Peyton Manning 8.00 20.00
Matt Hasselbeck
5 Derek Anderson 6.00 15.00
Jay Cutler
6 LaDainian Tomlinson 10.00 25.00
Adrian Peterson
7 Brian Westbrook 5.00 12.00
Willie Parker
8 Jamal Lewis 5.00 12.00
Clinton Portis
9 Edgerrin James 5.00 12.00
Willis McGahee
10 Fred Taylor 5.00 12.00
Thomas Jones
11 Reggie Wayne 6.00 15.00
Randy Moss
12 Chad Johnson 6.00 15.00
Larry Fitzgerald
13 Terrell Owens 6.00 15.00
Brandon Marshall
14 Braylon Edwards 5.00 12.00
Marques Colston
15 Roddy White 5.00 12.00
Torry Holt
16 Tom Brady 20.00 40.00
Drew Brees
Tony Romo
Brett Favre
17 LaDainian Tomlinson 12.00 30.00
Adrian Peterson
Brian Westbrook
Willie Parker
18 Reggie Wayne 8.00 20.00
Randy Moss
Chad Johnson
Larry Fitzgerald
19 Carson Palmer 12.00 30.00
Jon Kitna
Peyton Manning
Matt Hasselbeck
20 Jamal Lewis 6.00 15.00
Clinton Portis
Edgerrin James
Willis McGahee
21 Terrell Owens 8.00 20.00
Brandon Marshall
Braylon Edwards
Marques Colston
22 Randy Moss 8.00 20.00
Braylon Edwards
Terrell Owens
Plaxico Burress

23 LaDainian Tomlinson 12.00 30.00
Joseph Addai
Adrian Peterson
Clinton Portis
24 Tom Brady 20.00 40.00
Tony Romo
Ben Roethlisberger
Peyton Manning
25 Randy Moss 8.00 20.00
LaDainian Tomlinson
Braylon Edwards
Joseph Addai

2008 Playoff Prestige NFL Draft

26-35 ISSUED IN RETAIL PACKS
*FOIL/100: .6X TO 1.5X BASIC INSERTS
FOIL PRINT RUN 100 SER.#'d SETS
*HOLOFOIL/25: 1.2X TO 3X BASIC INSERTS
HOLOFOIL PRINT RUN 25 SER.#'d SETS
1 Darren McFadden 2.50 6.00
2 Matt Ryan 4.00 10.00
3 Keith Rivers 1.00 2.50
4 Mike Jenkins 1.00 2.50
5 DeSean Jackson 2.00 5.00
6 Kenny Phillips 1.00 2.50
7 Jonathan Stewart 1.50 4.00
8 Brian Brohm 1.00 2.50
9 Leodis McKelvin .75 2.00
10 Rashard Mendenhall 2.00 5.00
11 Dan Connor 1.00 2.50
12 Fred Davis 1.00 2.50
13 Felix Jones 1.50 4.00
14 James Hardy .75 2.00
15 Dominique Rodgers-Cromartie 1.00 2.50
16 Antoine Cason 1.00 2.50
17 Malcolm Kelly .75 2.00
18 Early Doucet .75 2.00
19 Mario Manningham 1.00 2.50
20 Chad Henne 1.00 2.50
21 Jamaal Charles 1.50 4.00
22 Chris Johnson 2.50 6.00
23 Andre Woodson 1.00 2.50
24 Martellus Bennett .75 2.00
25 Andre Caldwell .75 2.00
26 Chris Long 2.00 5.00
27 John David Booty 1.50 4.00
28 Mike Hart 2.00 5.00
29 Colt Brennan 2.00 5.00
30 Ray Rice 4.00 10.00
31 Limas Sweed 2.00 5.00
32 Devin Thomas 1.50 4.00
33 Kevin Smith 2.00 5.00
34 Steve Slaton 2.00 5.00
35 Joe Flacco 6.00 15.00

2008 Playoff Prestige NFL Draft Autographs

STATED PRINT RUN 25-100
1 Darren McFadden/50 25.00 60.00
2 Matt Ryan/50 60.00 120.00
3 Keith Rivers/25 12.00 30.00
5 DeSean Jackson/25 30.00 80.00
7 Jonathan Stewart/50 15.00 40.00
8 Brian Brohm/25
9 Leodis McKelvin/100 6.00 15.00
10 Rashard Mendenhall/25 40.00 100.00
11 Dan Connor/25 15.00 40.00
13 Felix Jones/25 25.00 60.00
14 James Hardy/50 15.00 40.00
15 Dominique Rodgers-Cromartie/100 8.00 20.00
16 Antoine Cason/100 8.00 20.00
17 Malcolm Kelly/25 30.00 60.00
19 Mario Manningham/50 15.00 30.00
20 Chad Henne/25 15.00 40.00
21 Jamaal Charles/25 25.00 60.00
22 Chris Johnson/25 40.00 100.00
23 Andre Woodson/50 10.00 25.00
24 Martellus Bennett/100 6.00 15.00
25 Andre Caldwell/50 8.00 20.00

2008 Playoff Prestige NFL Draft Autographed Patch College Logo

STATED PRINT RUN 50-100
1 Matt Ryan/50 60.00 120.00
2 Chad Henne/50 40.00 80.00
3 Erik Ainge/100 30.00 50.00
4 Darren McFadden/50 25.00 60.00
5 Jonathan Stewart/50 40.00 80.00
6 Rashard Mendenhall/50 40.00 80.00
7 Tashard Choice/100 6.00 15.00
8 Malcolm Kelly/50 30.00 60.00
9 Limas Sweed/50 10.00 25.00
10 Devin Thomas/100 20.00 40.00

2008 Playoff Prestige NFL Draft Autographed Patch Draft Logo

STATED PRINT RUN 100-250
1 Matt Ryan/100 50.00 120.00
2 Chad Henne/100 30.00 60.00
3 Erik Ainge/250 15.00 30.00
4 Darren McFadden/100 20.00 50.00
5 Jonathan Stewart/100 30.00 60.00
6 Rashard Mendenhall/100 40.00 80.00
7 Tashard Choice/250 5.00 12.00
8 Malcolm Kelly/100 20.00 50.00
9 Limas Sweed/100 8.00 20.00
10 Devin Thomas/250 12.00 30.00

2008 Playoff Prestige NFL Draft Autographed Patch NFL Logo

STATED PRINT RUN 25 SER.#'d SETS
1 Matt Ryan 75.00 150.00
2 Chad Henne 50.00 120.00
3 Erik Ainge 30.00 60.00
4 Darren McFadden 30.00 80.00
5 Jonathan Stewart 50.00 100.00
6 Rashard Mendenhall 60.00 120.00
7 Tashard Choice 12.00 30.00
8 Malcolm Kelly 50.00 100.00
9 Limas Sweed 15.00 40.00

2008 Playoff Prestige Preferred Materials

STATED PRINT RUN 100 SER.#'d SETS
*PRIME/25: .8X TO 2X BASIC JSYs
PRIME PRINT RUN 25 SER.#'d SETS
UNPRICED AUTO PRINT RUN 7-24
1 Peyton Manning 10.00 25.00
2 Marion Barber 5.00 12.00
3 T.J. Houshmandzadeh 5.00 12.00
4 Joseph Addai 5.00 12.00
5 Tony Romo 8.00 20.00
6 Adrian Peterson 10.00 25.00
7 Willie Parker 5.00 12.00
8 LaDainian Tomlinson 6.00 15.00
9 Eli Manning 6.00 15.00
10 Willis McGahee 5.00 12.00

2008 Playoff Prestige Preferred Materials Signatures Prime

PATCH AUTO PRINT RUN 5-25
SERIAL #'d UNDER 25 NOT PRICED
2 Marion Barber/25 30.00 60.00
10 Willis McGahee/25 25.00 50.00

2008 Playoff Prestige Preferred Materials Signatures

UNPRICED AUTO PRINT RUN 7-24
SERIAL #'d UNDER 24 NOT PRICED
2 Marion Barber/24 25.00 50.00

2008 Playoff Prestige Preferred Signatures

STATED PRINT RUN 10-25
SERIAL #'d UNDER 25 NOT PRICED
2 Marion Barber/25 20.00 40.00
10 Willis McGahee/25 15.00 30.00

2008 Playoff Prestige Prestigious Picks Blue

BLUE PRINT RUN 1000 SER.#'d SETS
*RED/750: .4X TO 1X BLUE/1000
RED PRINT RUN 750 SER.#'d SETS
*BLACK/500: .4X TO 1X BLUE/1000
BLACK PRINT RUN 500 SER.#'d SETS
*PURPLE/250: .5X TO 1.2X BLUE/1000
PURPLE PRINT RUN 250 SER.#'d SETS
*GREEN/100: .6X TO 1.5X BLUE/1000
GREEN PRINT RUN 100 SER.#'d SETS
*SILVER/50: .8X TO 2X BLUE/1000
SILVER PRINT RUN 50 SER.#'d SETS
*GOLD/25: 1X TO 2.5X BLUE/1000
GOLD PRINT RUN 25 SER.#'d SETS
*PLATINUM/10: 2X TO 5X BLUE/1000
PLATINUM PRINT RUN 10 SER.#'d SETS
1 Simeon Castille .75 2.00
2 Shawn Crable .60 1.50
3 Chris Long 1.00 2.50
4 DJ Hall .75 2.00
5 Antoine Cason 1.00 2.50
6 Felix Jones 1.50 4.00
7 Darren McFadden 2.50 6.00
8 Marcus Monk .75 2.00
9 Quentin Groves .75 2.00
10 Matt Ryan 4.00 10.00
11 DeSean Jackson 2.00 5.00
12 Colt Brennan 1.00 2.50
13 Rashard Mendenhall 2.00 5.00
14 Aqib Talib 1.00 2.50
15 Harry Douglas .75 2.00
16 Brian Brohm 1.00 2.50
17 Glenn Dorsey 1.00 2.50
18 Early Doucet .75 2.00
19 Ali Highsmith .60 1.50
20 Chevis Jackson .60 1.50
21 Matt Flynn 2.00 5.00
22 Craig Steltz .75 2.00
23 Kenny Phillips 1.00 2.50
24 Calais Campbell .75 2.00
25 Mike Hart 1.00 2.50
26 Chad Henne 1.00 2.50
27 Jamar Adams .75 2.00
28 Mario Manningham 1.00 2.50
29 Adrian Arrington .75 2.00
30 Ernie Wheelwright .75 2.00
31 Vernon Gholston .75 2.00
32 Malcolm Kelly .75 2.00
33 Allen Patrick .75 2.00
34 Jonathan Stewart 1.50 4.00
35 Dennis Dixon 1.00 2.50
36 Dan Connor 1.00 2.50
37 Erik Ainge 1.00 2.50
38 Jonathan Hefney .75 2.00
39 Jamaal Charles 1.50 4.00
40 Limas Sweed 1.00 2.50
41 Robert Killebrew .75 2.00
42 Sedrick Ellis 1.00 2.50
43 Keith Rivers 1.00 2.50
44 Fred Davis 1.00 2.50
45 John David Booty .75 2.00
46 Terrell Thomas .75 2.00
47 Xavier Adibi .60 1.50
48 Brandon Flowers 1.00 2.50
49 Eddie Royal 1.00 2.50
50 Steve Slaton 1.00 2.50

2008 Playoff Prestige Prestigious Picks Autographs

STATED PRINT RUN 25-100
1 Simeon Castille/25 12.00 30.00
2 Shawn Crable/100 5.00 12.00
3 Chris Long/50 10.00 25.00
4 DJ Hall/25 12.00 30.00
5 Antoine Cason/100 8.00 20.00
6 Felix Jones/25 25.00 60.00
7 Darren McFadden/25 40.00 100.00
8 Marcus Monk/100 6.00 15.00
9 Quentin Groves/25 12.00 30.00
10 Matt Ryan/25 60.00 120.00
11 DeSean Jackson/25 30.00 80.00
12 Colt Brennan/25 25.00 60.00
13 Rashard Mendenhall/25 30.00 80.00
16 Brian Brohm/25
20 Chevis Jackson/100 5.00 12.00
21 Matt Flynn/25 40.00 80.00
22 Craig Steltz/25 12.00 30.00
24 Calais Campbell/25 12.00 30.00
25 Mike Hart/25 15.00 40.00
26 Chad Henne/25 30.00 80.00
27 Jamar Adams/100 6.00 15.00
28 Mario Manningham/50 12.00 30.00
30 Ernie Wheelwright/100 6.00 15.00
31 Vernon Gholston/100 6.00 15.00
32 Malcolm Kelly/25 12.00 30.00
33 Allen Patrick/25 12.00 30.00
34 Jonathan Stewart/25 30.00 80.00
35 Dennis Dixon/50 10.00 25.00
36 Dan Connor/25 15.00 40.00
37 Erik Ainge /25 15.00 40.00
39 Jamaal Charles/25 25.00 60.00
40 Limas Sweed/25 15.00 40.00
43 Keith Rivers/25 15.00 40.00
45 John David Booty/25 12.00 30.00
46 Terrell Thomas/100 6.00 15.00
48 Brandon Flowers/100 8.00 20.00

2008 Playoff Prestige Prestigious Picks Materials Red

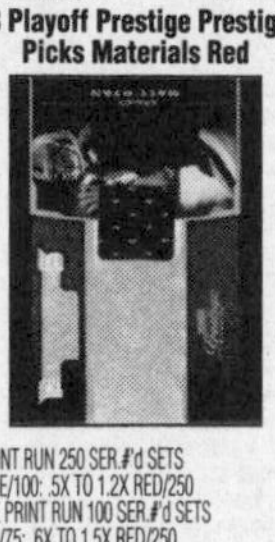

RED PRINT RUN 250 SER.#'d SETS
*PURPLE/100: .5X TO 1.2X RED/250
PURPLE PRINT RUN 100 SER.#'d SETS
*GREEN/75: .6X TO 1.5X RED/250
GREEN PRINT RUN 75 SER.#'d SETS
*GOLD/50: .6X TO 1.5X RED/250
GOLD PRINT RUN 50 SER.#'d SETS
*BLACK/25: .8X TO 2X RED/250
BLACK PRINT RUN 25 SER.#'d SETS
*PLAT.PATCH/25: 1X TO 2.5X RED/250
PLATINUM PATCHES PRINT RUN 25 SER.#'d SETS
1 Simeon Castille 2.00 5.00
2 Shawn Crable 1.50 4.00
3 Chris Long 2.50 6.00
4 DJ Hall 2.00 5.00
5 Antoine Cason 2.50 6.00
6 Felix Jones 4.00 10.00
7 Darren McFadden 6.00 15.00
8 Marcus Monk 2.00 5.00
9 Quentin Groves 2.00 5.00
10 Matt Ryan 10.00 25.00
11 DeSean Jackson 5.00 12.00
12 Colt Brennan 2.50 6.00
13 Rashard Mendenhall 5.00 12.00
14 Aqib Talib 2.50 6.00
15 Harry Douglas 2.50 6.00
16 Brian Brohm 2.50 6.00
17 Glenn Dorsey 2.50 6.00
18 Early Doucet 2.00 5.00
19 Ali Highsmith 2.50 6.00
20 Chevis Jackson 1.50 4.00
21 Matt Flynn 5.00 12.00
22 Craig Steltz 2.00 5.00
23 Kenny Phillips 2.50 6.00
24 Calais Campbell 2.50 6.00
25 Mike Hart 2.50 6.00
26 Chad Henne 2.50 6.00
27 Jamar Adams 2.50 6.00
28 Mario Manningham 2.50 6.00
29 Adrian Arrington 2.00 5.00
30 Ernie Wheelwright 2.50 6.00
31 Vernon Gholston 2.00 5.00
32 Malcolm Kelly 2.00 5.00
33 Allen Patrick 2.00 5.00
34 Jonathan Stewart 4.00 10.00
35 Dennis Dixon 2.50 6.00
36 Dan Connor 2.50 6.00
37 Erik Ainge 4.00 10.00
38 Jonathan Hefney 2.50 6.00
39 Jamaal Charles 4.00 10.00
40 Limas Sweed 2.50 6.00
41 Robert Killebrew 2.50 6.00
42 Sedrick Ellis 2.50 6.00
43 Keith Rivers 2.50 6.00
44 Fred Davis 2.50 6.00
45 John David Booty 2.00 5.00
46 Terrell Thomas 2.50 6.00
47 Xavier Adibi 2.50 6.00
48 Brandon Flowers 2.50 6.00
49 Eddie Royal 2.50 6.00
50 Steve Slaton 2.50 6.00

2008 Playoff Prestige Prestigious Pros Blue

BLUE PRINT RUN 1000 SER.#'d SETS
*RED/750: .4X TO 1X BLUE/1000
RED PRINT RUN 750 SER.#'d SETS
*BLACK/500: .5X TO 1.2X BLUE/1000
BLACK PRINT RUN 500 SER.#'d SETS
*PURPLE/250: .6X TO 1.5X BLUE/1000
PURPLE PRINT RUN 250 SER.#'d SETS
*GREEN/100: .8X TO 2X BLUE/1000
GREEN PRINT RUN 100 SER.#'d SETS
*SILVER/50: 1X TO 2.5X BLUE/1000
SILVER PRINT RUN 50 SER.#'d SETS
*GOLD/25: 1.2X TO 3X BLUE/1000
GOLD PRINT RUN 25 SER.#'d SETS
*PLATINUM/10: 2.5X TO 6X BLUE/1000
PLATINUM PRINT RUN 10 SER.#'d SETS
1 Matt Hasselbeck 1.00 2.50
2 Derek Anderson .75 2.00
3 Jeff Garcia 1.00 2.50
4 Philip Rivers 1.25 3.00
5 Alex Smith QB 1.25 3.00
6 Thomas Jones 1.00 2.50
7 Ronnie Brown 1.00 2.50
8 DeShaun Foster 1.00 2.50
9 Larry Johnson 1.00 2.50
10 Brandon Jacobs 1.00 2.50
11 Cedric Benson 1.00 2.50
12 Frank Gore 1.00 2.50
13 Shaun Alexander 1.00 2.50
14 Warrick Dunn 1.00 2.50
15 Laurence Maroney 1.00 2.50
16 Steven Jackson 1.25 3.00
17 Rudi Johnson 1.00 2.50
18 Anquan Boldin 1.00 2.50
19 Torry Holt 1.00 2.50
20 Brandon Marshall 1.00 2.50
21 Antonio Gates 1.25 3.00
22 Roy Williams WR 1.00 2.50
23 Donald Driver 1.00 2.50
24 Dwayne Bowe 1.00 2.50
25 Steve Smith 1.00 2.50
26 Marvin Harrison 1.25 3.00
27 Andre Johnson 1.00 2.50
28 Marion Barber 1.00 2.50
29 Tony Gonzalez 1.00 2.50
30 Jerricho Cotchery 1.00 2.50
31 Peyton Manning 2.00 5.00
32 Tom Brady 2.00 5.00
33 Tony Romo 1.50 4.00
34 Brett Favre 3.00 8.00
35 Adrian Peterson 2.00 5.00
36 Willie Parker 1.00 2.50
37 Marshawn Lynch 1.00 2.50
38 LaDainian Tomlinson 1.25 3.00
39 Brian Westbrook 1.00 2.50
40 Randy Moss 1.25 3.00
41 Reggie Wayne 1.00 2.50
42 Terrell Owens 1.25 3.00
43 Larry Fitzgerald 1.25 3.00
44 Marques Colston 1.00 2.50
45 Reggie Bush 1.25 3.00
46 Maurice Jones-Drew 1.00 2.50
47 Ben Roethlisberger 1.25 3.00
48 Jay Cutler 1.25 3.00
49 Plaxico Burress 1.00 2.50
50 Edgerrin James 1.00 2.50

2008 Playoff Prestige Prestigious Pros Autographs

STATED PRINT RUN 1-100
SERIAL #'d UNDER 25 NOT PRICED
7 Ronnie Brown/35 10.00 25.00
9 Larry Johnson/50 10.00 25.00
10 Brandon Jacobs/30 10.00 25.00
11 Cedric Benson/50 6.00 15.00
12 Frank Gore/35 8.00 20.00
16 Steven Jackson/25 12.00 30.00
17 Rudi Johnson/50 6.00 15.00
18 Anquan Boldin/25 10.00 25.00
20 Brandon Marshall/100 6.00 15.00
23 Donald Driver/25 10.00 25.00
30 Jerricho Cotchery/75 6.00 15.00
44 Marques Colston/100 6.00 15.00
46 Maurice Jones-Drew/25 10.00 25.00

2008 Playoff Prestige Prestigious Pros Materials Green

GREEN PRINT RUN 50-100
*GOLD/50: .5X TO 1.2X GREEN
GOLD PRINT RUN 50 SER.#'d SETS
*BLACK/25: .8X TO 2X GREEN
BLACK PRINT RUN 25 SER.#'d SETS
*PLAT.PATCH/25: 1X TO 2.5X GREEN
PLATINUM PATCH PRINT RUN 25
1 Matt Hasselbeck 4.00 10.00
2 Derek Anderson 3.00 8.00
3 Jeff Garcia 4.00 10.00
4 Philip Rivers 5.00 12.00
5 Alex Smith QB 5.00 12.00
6 Thomas Jones 4.00 10.00
7 Ronnie Brown 4.00 10.00
9 Larry Johnson 4.00 10.00
10 Brandon Jacobs 4.00 10.00
11 Cedric Benson 4.00 10.00
12 Frank Gore 4.00 10.00
13 Shaun Alexander 4.00 10.00
14 Warrick Dunn 4.00 10.00
15 Laurence Maroney 4.00 10.00
16 Steven Jackson 5.00 12.00
17 Rudi Johnson 4.00 10.00
18 Anquan Boldin 4.00 10.00
19 Torry Holt 4.00 10.00
20 Brandon Marshall 4.00 10.00
21 Antonio Gates 5.00 12.00
22 Roy Williams WR 4.00 10.00
23 Donald Driver 4.00 10.00
24 Dwayne Bowe 4.00 10.00
25 Steve Smith 4.00 10.00
26 Marvin Harrison 5.00 12.00
27 Andre Johnson 4.00 10.00
28 Marion Barber 4.00 10.00
29 Tony Gonzalez 4.00 10.00
30 Jerricho Cotchery 4.00 10.00
31 Peyton Manning/75 8.00 20.00
32 Tom Brady/50 8.00 20.00
33 Tony Romo 6.00 15.00
34 Brett Favre 12.00 30.00
35 Adrian Peterson 8.00 20.00
36 Willie Parker 4.00 10.00
37 Marshawn Lynch 4.00 10.00
38 LaDainian Tomlinson 5.00 12.00
39 Brian Westbrook 4.00 10.00
40 Randy Moss 5.00 12.00
41 Reggie Wayne 4.00 10.00
42 Terrell Owens 5.00 12.00
43 Larry Fitzgerald 5.00 12.00
44 Marques Colston 4.00 10.00
45 Reggie Bush 5.00 12.00
46 Maurice Jones-Drew 4.00 10.00
47 Ben Roethlisberger 5.00 12.00
48 Jay Cutler 5.00 12.00
49 Plaxico Burress 4.00 10.00
50 Edgerrin James 4.00 10.00

2008 Playoff Prestige Rookie Review

151A A.J. Hawk 1.25 3.00
151B Brady Quinn 1.25 3.00
152 JaMarcus Russell 1.25 3.00
153 Troy Smith 1.25 3.00
155 Adrian Peterson 5.00 12.00
156 Marshawn Lynch 1.25 3.00
157 Michael Bush 1.25 3.00
158 Kenny Irons 1.00 2.50
161 Brandon Marshall 1.25 3.00
162 Brandon Williams 1.00 2.50
163 Calvin Johnson 1.50 4.00
164 Ted Ginn Jr. 1.25 3.00
165 Dwayne Jarrett 1.25 3.00
166 Sidney Rice 1.50 4.00
167 Dwayne Bowe 1.25 3.00
168 Robert Meachem 1.25 3.00
169 Anthony Gonzalez 1.00 2.50
170 Chad Jackson 1.25 3.00
172 Steve Smith USC 1.25 3.00
176 Jason Hill 1.00 2.50
178A Greg Olsen 1.25 3.00
178B DeAngelo Williams 1.25 3.00
183 Derek Hagan 1.00 2.50
189 Patrick Willis 1.25 3.00
196 Jason Avant 1.00 2.50
201B Trent Edwards 1.00 2.50
201A Jerious Norwood 1.25 3.00
202 Kevin Kolb 1.25 3.00
203 John Beck 1.00 2.50
209 Brandon Jackson 1.25 3.00
210 Kellen Clemens 1.25 3.00
211 Paul Williams 1.00 2.50
213 Laurence Maroney 1.25 3.00
215 LenDale White 1.25 3.00
216 Leon Washington 1.25 3.00
223 Matt Leinart 1.50 4.00
224 Maurice Jones-Drew 1.25 3.00
227 Michael Robinson 1.00 2.50
231 Reggie Bush 1.50 4.00
234 Santonio Holmes 1.25 3.00
235 Sinorice Moss 1.25 3.00
238B Brian Leonard 1.00 2.50
238A Tarvaris Jackson 1.25 3.00
242 Garrett Wolfe 1.25 3.00
245 Vernon Davis 1.25 3.00
246 Vince Young 1.25 3.00
251 Chris Henry RB 1.25 3.00
252 Joe Thomas 1.25 3.00
253 Yamon Figurs 1.00 2.50
254 Marques Colston 1.25 3.00

2008 Playoff Prestige Rookie Review Autographs

STATED PRINT RUN 1-50
SERIAL #'d UNDER 25 NOT PRICED
151 A.J. Hawk/50 12.00 30.00
161 Brandon Marshall/25 12.00 30.00
178 DeAngelo Williams/25 12.00 30.00
201 Jerious Norwood/35 8.00 20.00
215 LenDale White/25 10.00 25.00
224 Maurice Jones-Drew/32 12.00 30.00
242 Garrett Wolfe/25 10.00 25.00
252 Joe Thomas/42 8.00 20.00
254 Marques Colston/50 8.00 20.00

2008 Playoff Prestige Rookie Review Materials

*PRIME/50-100: .8X TO 2X BASIC JSYs
PRIME PRINT RUN 1-100
151 Brady Quinn 4.00 10.00
151 A.J. Hawk 4.00 10.00
152 JaMarcus Russell 4.00 10.00
153 Troy Smith 4.00 10.00
155 Adrian Peterson 8.00 20.00
156 Marshawn Lynch 4.00 10.00
157 Michael Bush 4.00 10.00
158 Kenny Irons 3.00 8.00
161 Brandon Marshall 4.00 10.00
162 Brandon Williams 3.00 8.00
163 Calvin Johnson 5.00 12.00
164 Ted Ginn Jr. 4.00 10.00
165 Dwayne Jarrett 4.00 10.00
166 Sidney Rice 5.00 12.00
167 Dwayne Bowe 4.00 10.00
168 Robert Meachem 4.00 10.00
169 Anthony Gonzalez 3.00 8.00
170 Chad Jackson 4.00 10.00
172 Steve Smith USC 4.00 10.00
176 Jason Hill 3.00 8.00
178 DeAngelo Williams 4.00 10.00
178 Greg Olsen 4.00 10.00
183 Derek Hagan 3.00 8.00
189 Patrick Willis 4.00 10.00
196 Jason Avant 3.00 8.00
201 Jerious Norwood 4.00 10.00
201 Trent Edwards 3.00 8.00
202 Kevin Kolb 4.00 10.00
203 John Beck 3.00 8.00
209 Brandon Jackson 4.00 10.00
210 Kellen Clemens 4.00 10.00
211 Paul Williams 3.00 8.00
213 Laurence Maroney 4.00 10.00
215 LenDale White 4.00 10.00
216 Leon Washington 4.00 10.00
223 Matt Leinart 5.00 12.00
224 Maurice Jones-Drew 4.00 10.00
227 Michael Robinson 3.00 8.00
231 Reggie Bush 5.00 12.00
234 Santonio Holmes 4.00 10.00
235 Sinorice Moss 4.00 10.00
238 Tarvaris Jackson 4.00 10.00
238 Brian Leonard 3.00 8.00
242 Garrett Wolfe 4.00 10.00
245 Vernon Davis 4.00 10.00
246 Vince Young 4.00 10.00
251 Chris Henry RB 4.00 10.00
252 Joe Thomas 4.00 10.00
253 Yamon Figurs 3.00 8.00

2008 Playoff Prestige Stars of the NFL

*FOIL/100: .8X TO 2X BASIC INSERTS
FOIL PRINT RUN 100 SER.#'d SETS
*HOLOFOIL/25: 1.5X TO 4X BASIC INSERTS
HOLOFOIL PRINT RUN 25 SER.#'d SETS
1 Tom Brady 2.00 5.00
2 Tony Romo 1.50 4.00
3 Ben Roethlisberger 1.25 3.00
4 Peyton Manning 2.00 5.00
5 Chad Johnson 1.00 2.50
6 Terrell Owens 1.25 3.00
7 Randy Moss 1.25 3.00
8 LaDainian Tomlinson 1.25 3.00
9 Reggie Bush 1.25 3.00
10 Vince Young 1.00 2.50
11 Willie Parker 1.00 2.50
12 Reggie Wayne 1.00 2.50
13 Marshawn Lynch 1.00 2.50
14 Calvin Johnson 1.25 3.00
15 Adrian Peterson 2.00 5.00
16 Brett Favre 3.00 8.00
17 Steve Smith 1.00 2.50
18 Joseph Addai 1.00 2.50
19 Eli Manning 1.25 3.00
20 Brian Westbrook 1.00 2.50

2008 Playoff Prestige Stars of the NFL Materials

STATED PRINT RUN 100 SER.#'d SETS
*PRIME/25: .8X TO 2X BASIC JSYs
PRIME PRINT RUN 25 SER.#'d SETS
1 Tom Brady 8.00 20.00
2 Tony Romo 6.00 15.00
3 Ben Roethlisberger 5.00 12.00
4 Peyton Manning 8.00 20.00
5 Chad Johnson 4.00 10.00
6 Terrell Owens 5.00 12.00
7 Randy Moss 5.00 12.00
8 LaDainian Tomlinson 5.00 12.00
9 Reggie Bush 5.00 12.00
10 Vince Young 4.00 10.00
11 Willie Parker 4.00 10.00
12 Reggie Wayne 4.00 10.00
13 Marshawn Lynch 4.00 10.00
14 Calvin Johnson 5.00 12.00
15 Adrian Peterson 8.00 20.00
16 Brett Favre 12.00 30.00
17 Steve Smith 4.00 10.00
18 Joseph Addai 4.00 10.00
19 Eli Manning 5.00 12.00
20 Brian Westbrook 4.00 10.00

2008 Playoff Prestige TD Sensations

*FOIL/100: .6X TO 1.5X BASIC INSERTS
FOIL PRINT RUN 100 SER.#'d SETS
*HOLOFOIL/25: 1.2X TO 3X BASIC INSERTS
HOLOFOIL PRINT RUN 25 SER.#'d SETS
1 Randy Moss 1.50 4.00
2 Braylon Edwards 1.25 3.00
3 T.J. Houshmandzadeh 1.25 3.00
4 Plaxico Burress 1.25 3.00
5 Terrell Owens 1.50 4.00
6 Wes Welker 1.50 4.00
7 Dallas Clark 1.25 3.00
8 Laveranues Coles 1.00 2.50
9 Santonio Holmes 1.25 3.00
10 Greg Jennings 1.50 4.00
11 Adrian Peterson 2.50 6.00
12 LaDainian Tomlinson 1.50 4.00
13 Joseph Addai 1.25 3.00
14 Marion Barber 1.25 3.00
15 Marshawn Lynch 1.25 3.00
16 Clinton Portis 1.25 3.00
17 Edgerrin James 1.25 3.00
18 Maurice Jones-Drew 1.25 3.00
19 Brian Westbrook 1.25 3.00
20 Devin Hester 1.50 4.00

2008 Playoff Prestige TD Sensations Materials

STATED PRINT RUN 100 SER.#'d SETS
*PRIME/25: .8X TO 2X BASIC JSYs
PRIME PRINT RUN 25 SER.#'d SETS
1 Randy Moss 5.00 12.00
2 Braylon Edwards 4.00 10.00
3 T.J. Houshmandzadeh 4.00 10.00
4 Plaxico Burress 4.00 10.00
5 Terrell Owens 5.00 12.00
6 Wes Welker 6.00 15.00
7 Dallas Clark 4.00 10.00
8 Laveranues Coles 3.00 8.00
9 Santonio Holmes 4.00 10.00
10 Greg Jennings 5.00 12.00
11 Adrian Peterson 8.00 20.00
12 LaDainian Tomlinson 5.00 12.00
13 Joseph Addai 4.00 10.00
14 Marion Barber 4.00 10.00
15 Marshawn Lynch 4.00 10.00
16 Clinton Portis 4.00 10.00
17 Edgerrin James 4.00 10.00
18 Maurice Jones-Drew 4.00 10.00
19 Brian Westbrook 4.00 10.00
20 Devin Hester 6.00 15.00

2008 Playoff Prestige True Colors

*FOIL/100: .6X TO 1.5X BASIC INSERTS
FOIL PRINT RUN 100 SER.#'d SETS
*HOLOFOIL/25: 1.2X TO 3X BASIC INSERTS
HOLOFOIL PRINT RUN 25 SER.#'d SETS
UNPRICED AUTO PRINT RUN 4-10
1 Carson Palmer 1.50 4.00
2 Tom Brady 2.50 6.00
3 Terrell Owens 1.50 4.00
4 Clinton Portis 1.25 3.00
5 Vince Young 1.25 3.00
6 Jay Cutler 1.50 4.00
7 Brett Favre 4.00 10.00
8 Reggie Bush 1.50 4.00
9 Ben Roethlisberger 1.50 4.00
10 LaDainian Tomlinson 1.50 4.00

2008 Playoff Prestige True Colors Autographs

UNPRICED AUTO PRINT RUN 4-10

2008 Playoff Prestige True Colors Materials

STATED PRINT RUN 100 SER.#'d SETS
*PRIME/25: .8X TO 2X BASIC JSYs
PRIME PRINT RUN 25 SER.#'d SETS
1 Carson Palmer 5.00 12.00
2 Tom Brady 8.00 20.00
3 Terrell Owens 5.00 12.00
4 Clinton Portis 4.00 10.00
5 Vince Young 4.00 10.00
6 Jay Cutler 5.00 12.00
7 Brett Favre 12.00 30.00
8 Reggie Bush 5.00 12.00
9 Ben Roethlisberger 5.00 12.00
10 LaDainian Tomlinson 5.00 12.00

2008 Playoff Prestige Hawaii Trade Conference

COMPLETE SET (6) 6.00 12.00
1 Adrian Peterson .75 2.00
2 Tom Brady .75 2.00
3 Eli Manning .50 1.25
Award Winners
4 Darren McFadden 1.00 2.50
NFL Draft
5 Matt Ryan 1.50 4.00
NFL Draft
6 Devin Hester .50 1.25
TD Sensations

2009 Playoff Prestige

COMP.SET w/o RC's (100) 8.00 20.00
ONE ROOKIE PER PACK
1 Kurt Warner .30 .75
2 Larry Fitzgerald .30 .75
3 Anquan Boldin .25 .60
4 Tim Hightower .20 .50
5 Roddy White .25 .60
6 Michael Turner .25 .60
7 Matt Ryan .30 .75
8 Willis McGahee .25 .60
9 Joe Flacco .30 .75
10 Trent Edwards .20 .50
11 Marshawn Lynch .25 .60
12 Lee Evans .25 .60
13 Steve Smith .25 .60
14 DeAngelo Williams .30 .75
15 Jake Delhomme .25 .60
16 Jonathan Stewart .25 .60
17 Greg Olsen .20 .50
18 Kyle Orton .25 .60
19 Matt Forte .30 .75
20 Carson Palmer .30 .75
21 Chad Ocho Cinco .25 .60
22 T.J. Houshmandzadeh .25 .60
23 Brady Quinn .25 .60
24 Jamal Lewis .25 .60
25 Kellen Winslow .25 .60
26 Braylon Edwards .25 .60
27 Tony Romo .50 1.25
28 Terrell Owens .30 .75
29 Marion Barber .25 .60
30 Roy Williams WR .25 .60
31 Jay Cutler .30 .75
32 Brandon Marshall .25 .60
33 Eddie Royal .25 .60
34 Calvin Johnson .30 .75
35 Kevin Smith .25 .60
36 Aaron Rodgers .60 1.50
37 Ryan Grant .25 .60
38 Greg Jennings .30 .75
39 Matt Schaub .25 .60
40 Andre Johnson .25 .60
41 Steve Slaton .25 .60
42 Peyton Manning .50 1.25
43 Joseph Addai .30 .75
44 Reggie Wayne .25 .60
45 Anthony Gonzalez .20 .50
46 David Garrard .25 .60
47 Matt Jones .25 .60
48 Maurice Jones-Drew .25 .60
49 Larry Johnson .25 .60
50 Dwayne Bowe .25 .60
51 Chad Pennington .25 .60
52 Ronnie Brown .25 .60
53 Ted Ginn .25 .60
54 Bernard Berrian .25 .60
55 Adrian Peterson .50 1.25
56 Chester Taylor .20 .50
57 Tom Brady .50 1.25
58 Randy Moss .30 .75
59 Wes Welker .30 .75
60 Drew Brees .30 .75
61 Reggie Bush .30 .75
62 Marques Colston .25 .60
63 Eli Manning .30 .75
64 Steve Smith USC .25 .60
65 Brandon Jacobs .25 .60
66 Kellen Clemens .20 .50
67 Jerricho Cotchery .25 .60
68 Leon Washington .25 .60
69 Thomas Jones .25 .60
70 JaMarcus Russell .20 .50
71 Justin Fargas .20 .50
72 Darren McFadden .30 .75
73 Donovan McNabb .30 .75
74 Brian Westbrook .25 .60
75 DeSean Jackson .25 .60
76 Ben Roethlisberger .30 .75
77 Willie Parker .20 .50
78 Hines Ward .25 .60
79 Santonio Holmes .25 .60
80 Philip Rivers .30 .75
81 LaDainian Tomlinson .30 .75
82 Antonio Gates .25 .60
83 Frank Gore .25 .60
84 Vernon Davis .25 .60
85 Matt Hasselbeck .25 .60
86 Deion Branch .25 .60
87 Julius Jones .20 .50
88 Marc Bulger .25 .60
89 Steven Jackson .25 .60
90 Torry Holt .25 .60
91 Antonio Bryant .20 .50
92 Earnest Graham .20 .50
93 Michael Clayton .20 .50
94 Kerry Collins .25 .60
95 LenDale White .25 .60
96 Chris Johnson .30 .75
97 Jason Campbell .20 .50
98 Clinton Portis .25 .60
99 Santana Moss .25 .60
100 Chris Cooley .25 .60
101A Aaron Curry RC 1.00 2.50
(College photo)
101B Aaron Curry SP 6.00 15.00
(Draft day photo)
102 Aaron Kelly RC .75 2.00
103 Aaron Maybin RC .75 2.00
104 Alphonso Smith RC .75 2.00
105 Andre Brown RC .60 1.50
106 Andre Smith RC .75 2.00
107 Arian Foster RC 2.00 5.00
108 Asher Allen RC .75 2.00
109 Austin Collie RC 1.00 2.50
110 B.J. Raji SP RC 15.00 30.00
111 Brandon Gibson RC 1.00 2.50
112A Brandon Pettigrew RC 1.00 2.50
(White pants)
112B Brandon Pettigrew SP 4.00 10.00
(Orange pants)
113 Brandon Tate RC 1.00 2.50
114A Brian Cushing SP RC 10.00 25.00
(College photo)
114B Brian Cushing SP 10.00 25.00
(Draft day photo)
115A Brian Orakpo RC 1.00 2.50
(College photo)
115B Brian Orakpo SP 8.00 20.00
(Draft day photo)
116A Brian Robiskie RC 1.00 2.50
(White jersey)
116B Brian Robiskie SP 6.00 15.00
(Red jersey)
117 Brooks Foster RC .60 1.50
118 Cedric Peerman RC .75 2.00
119A Chase Coffman RC .75 2.00
(White jersey)
119B Chase Coffman SP 4.00 10.00
(Yellow jersey)
120 Chase Daniel SP RC 10.00 25.00
121 Chip Vaughn RC .60 1.50
122A Chris Wells RC 1.50 4.00
(Red jersey)
122B Chris Wells SP 10.00 20.00
(White jersey)
123 Clay Matthews RC 2.50 6.00
124A Clint Sintim RC 1.00 2.50
(Blue jersey)
124B Clint Sintim SP 4.00 10.00
(White jersey)
125 Cornelius Ingram RC .60 1.50
126 Tony Fiammetta RC .75 2.00
127A D.J. Moore RC .75 2.00
(White jersey)
127B D.J. Moore SP 3.00 8.00
(Gold jersey)
128 Darius Butler RC 1.00 2.50
129 Darius Passmore RC .75 2.00
130A Darrius Heyward-Bey RC 1.00 2.50
(Red jersey)
130B Darrius Heyward-Bey SP 8.00 20.00
(White jersey)
131 Travis Beckum RC .75 2.00
132 Deon Butler RC .75 2.00
133 Victor Harris RC 1.00 2.50
134A Derrick Williams RC .75 2.00
(White jersey)
134B Derrick Williams SP 4.00 10.00
(Blue jersey)
135A Donald Brown RC 1.00 2.50
(White jersey)
135B Donald Brown SP 10.00 25.00
(Blue jersey)
136 Eugene Monroe RC .60 1.50
137 Everette Brown RC .75 2.00
138 Duke Robinson RC .60 1.50
139 Glen Coffee RC .75 2.00
140A Graham Harrell SP RC 10.00 25.00
(white jersey)
140B Graham Harrell SP 10.00 25.00
(Red jersey)
141 Demetrius Byrd RC .75 2.00
142A Hakeem Nicks SP RC 6.00 15.00
(Football in both hands)
142B Hakeem Nicks SP 12.50 30.00
(Football in left arm)
143 Hunter Cantwell RC 1.00 2.50
144 Ian Johnson SP RC 10.00 25.00
145 Jairus Byrd RC 1.00 2.50
146A James Casey RC .75 2.00
(Blue jersey)
146B James Casey SP 3.00 8.00
(White jersey)
147 James Davis RC 1.00 2.50
148A James Laurinaitis RC 1.00 2.50
(White jersey)
148B James Laurinaitis SP 4.00 10.00
(Red jersey)
149 Jared Cook SP RC 6.00 15.00
150 Jarett Dillard RC 1.00 2.50
151 Jason Smith RC .75 2.00
152A Javon Ringer RC 1.00 2.50
(Football in right arm)
152B Javon Ringer SP 4.00 10.00
(Football in left arm)
153A Jeremiah Johnson RC 1.00 2.50
(Green jersey)
153B Jeremiah Johnson SP 4.00 10.00
(Yellow jersey)
154 Vontae Davis RC 1.00 2.50
155A Jeremy Maclin RC 1.50 4.00
(Black jersey)
155B Jeremy Maclin SP 6.00 15.00
(Yellow jersey)
156 John Parker Wilson RC 1.00 2.50
157 John Phillips RC 1.00 2.50
158A Josh Freeman RC 2.00 5.00
(College photo)
158B Josh Freeman SP 10.00 25.00
(Draft day photo)
159A Juaquin Iglesias SP RC 12.00 30.00
(Red jersey)
159B Juaquin Iglesias SP 10.00 25.00
(White jersey)
160 Keenan Lewis RC 1.00 2.50
161A Kenny Britt RC 1.25 3.00
(White jersey)
161B Kenny Britt SP 5.00 12.00
(Red jersey)
162 Kenny McKinley RC 1.00 2.50
163 Kevin Ogletree RC 1.00 2.50

164A Knowshon Moreno RC 1.00 2.50
(Red jersey)
164B Knowshon Moreno SP 8.00 20.00
(White jersey)
165 Larry English RC 1.00 2.50
166A LeSean McCoy RC 2.00 5.00
(white jersey)
166B LeSean McCoy SP 8.00 20.00
(Blue jersey)
167 William Moore RC 1.00 2.50
168 Louis Delmas RC 1.00 2.50
169A Louis Murphy RC 1.00 2.50
(Blue jersey)
169B Louis Murphy SP 4.00 10.00
(White jersey)
170A Malcolm Jenkins RC 1.00 2.50
(White jersey)
170B Malcolm Jenkins SP 4.00 10.00
(Red jersey)
171A Mark Sanchez RC 3.00 8.00
(Red jersey)
171B Mark Sanchez SP 15.00 30.00
(White jersey)
172A Matthew Stafford RC 5.00 12.00
(College photo)
172B Matthew Stafford SP 15.00 30.00
(Draft day photo)
173 Tom Brandstater RC 1.00 2.50
174A Michael Crabtree RC 2.00 5.00
(College photo)
174B Michael Crabtree SP 12.50 25.00
(Draft day photo)
175 Michael Hamlin RC .75 2.00
176 Michael Johnson RC .60 1.50
177 Michael Oher RC 1.50 4.00
178 Mike Mickens RC .75 2.00
179 Mike Thomas RC 1.00 2.50
180 Mohamed Massaquoi SP RC 6.00 15.00
181A Nate Davis RC .75 2.00
(Red jersey)
181B Nate Davis SP 3.00 8.00
(White jersey)
182 Nic Harris RC .75 2.00
183 P.J. Hill RC .75 2.00
184A Pat White RC 1.00 2.50
(Blue jersey)
184B Pat White SP 10.00 25.00
(White jersey)
185 Patrick Chung RC 1.00 2.50
186 Patrick Turner RC .75 2.00
187A Percy Harvin RC 1.50 4.00
(Blue jersey)
187B Percy Harvin SP 10.00 25.00
(White jersey)
188 Peria Jerry RC .75 2.00
189 Quan Cosby RC .75 2.00
190 Quinn Johnson RC .75 2.00
191A Ramses Barden RC .60 1.50
(Holding a football)
191B Ramses Barden SP 4.00 10.00
(Without football in photo)
192A Rashad Jennings RC 1.00 2.50
(Senior Bowl visible in photo)
192B Rashad Jennings SP 4.00 10.00
(only Bowl visible in photo)
193 Rashad Johnson RC .75 2.00
194A Rey Maualuga RC 1.00 2.50
(Maroon jersey)
194B Rey Maualuga SP 8.00 20.00
(White jersey)
195 Rhett Bomar RC .75 2.00
196 Sean Smith RC 1.00 2.50
197 Shawn Nelson RC .75 2.00
198 Sherrod Martin RC .75 2.00
199A Shonn Greene SP RC 10.00 25.00
(Black jersey)
199B Shonn Greene SP 12.50 25.00
(White jersey)
200 Stephen McGee RC 1.00 2.50

2009 Playoff Prestige Draft Picks Light Blue

*LIGHT BLUE/999: .6X TO 1.5X BASIC RC
*LIGHT BLUE/999: .1X TO .25X BASIC SP RC
STATED PRINT RUN 999 SER.#'d SETS

2009 Playoff Prestige Xtra Points Black

*VETS: 10X TO 25X BASIC CARDS
*ROOKIES: 4X TO 10X BASIC RC
*ROOKIES: .5X TO 1.2X BASIC SP RC
STATED PRINT RUN 10 SER.#'d SETS

2009 Playoff Prestige Xtra Points Gold

*VETS: 2X TO 5X BASIC CARDS
*ROOKIES: .8X TO 2X BASIC RC
*ROOKIES: .1X TO .3X BASIC SP RC
STATED PRINT RUN 250 SER.#'d SETS

2009 Playoff Prestige Xtra Points Green

*VETS: 6X TO 15X BASIC CARDS
*ROOKIES: 2.5X TO 6X BASIC RC
*ROOKIES: .4X TO 1X BASIC SP RC
STATED PRINT RUN 25 SER.#'d SETS

2009 Playoff Prestige Xtra Points Orange

*VETS: 2X TO 5X BASIC CARDS
*ROOKIES: .8X TO 2X BASIC RC
*ROOKIES: .1X TO .3X BASIC SP RC
STATED PRINT RUN 300 SER.#'d SETS

2009 Playoff Prestige Xtra Points Purple

*VETS: 4X TO 10X BASIC CARDS
*ROOKIES: 1.5X TO 4X BASIC SP RC
*ROOKIES: .25X TO .6X BASIC SP RC
STATED PRINT RUN 50 SER.#'d SETS

2009 Playoff Prestige Xtra Points Red

*VETS: 3X TO 8X BASIC CARDS
*ROOKIES: 1.2X TO 3X BASIC RC
*ROOKIES: .2X TO .5X BASIC SP RC
STATED PRINT RUN 100 SER.#'d SETS

2009 Playoff Prestige Connections

1 Kurt Warner 1.50 4.00
Anquan Boldin
2 Aaron Rodgers 3.00 8.00
Greg Jennings
3 Kellen Clemens 1.00 2.50
Laveranues Coles
4 Ben Roethlisberger 1.50 4.00
Hines Ward
5 Matt Ryan 1.50 4.00
Roddy White
6 Philip Rivers 1.50 4.00
Vincent Jackson
7 Jay Cutler 1.50 4.00
Eddie Royal
8 Jake Delhomme 1.25 3.00
Muhsin Muhammad
9 Peyton Manning 2.50 6.00
Marvin Harrison
10 Jake Delhomme 1.25 3.00
Steve Smith
11 Kurt Warner 1.50 4.00
Larry Fitzgerald
12 Tony Romo 2.50 6.00
Terrell Owens
13 Jason Campbell 1.25 3.00
Santana Moss
14 Donovan McNabb 1.50 4.00
Brian Westbrook
15 Peyton Manning 2.50 6.00
Reggie Wayne
16 Philip Rivers 1.50 4.00
Antonio Gates
17 Aaron Rodgers 3.00 8.00
Donald Driver
18 Kellen Clemens 1.25 3.00
Jerricho Cotchery
19 Jeff Garcia 1.25 3.00
Ike Hilliard
20 Eli Manning 1.50 4.00
Amani Toomer

2009 Playoff Prestige Connections Materials

STATED PRINT RUN 29-250
*PRIME/25: .8X TO 2X BASIC JSY/250
*PRIME/25: .6X TO 1.5X BASIC JSY/59
*PRIME/25: .6X TO 1.5X BASIC JSY/29
PRIME PRINT RUN 9-25
3 Kellen Clemens 4.00 10.00
Laveranues Coles/250
4 Ben Roethlisberger 6.00 15.00
Hines Ward/250
5 Matt Ryan 6.00 15.00
Roddy White/250
6 Philip Rivers 6.00 15.00
Vincent Jackson/250
7 Jay Cutler 6.00 15.00
Eddie Royal/250
9 Peyton Manning 12.00 30.00
Marvin Harrison/29
10 Jake Delhomme 6.00 15.00
Steve Smith/95
12 Tony Romo 10.00 25.00
Terrell Owens/250
13 Jason Campbell 5.00 12.00
Santana Moss/250
14 Donovan McNabb 6.00 15.00
Brian Westbrook/250
15 Peyton Manning 8.00 20.00
Reggie Wayne/250
16 Philip Rivers 6.00 15.00
Antonio Gates/250
17 Aaron Rodgers 15.00 40.00
Donald Driver/59
18 Kellen Clemens 5.00 12.00
Jerricho Cotchery/250
19 Jeff Garcia 5.00 12.00
Ike Hilliard/250
20 Eli Manning 6.00 15.00
Amani Toomer/250

2009 Playoff Prestige Draft Picks Autographs

STATED PRINT RUN 99-499
102 Aaron Kelly/499 5.00 12.00
109 Austin Collie/499 8.00 20.00
110 B.J. Raji/499 6.00 15.00
111 Brandon Gibson/399 6.00 15.00
113 Brandon Tate/299 12.50 25.00
114 Brian Cushing/399 6.00 15.00
115 Brian Orakpo/399 8.00 20.00
117 Brooks Foster/499 4.00 10.00
118 Cedric Peerman/299 5.00 12.00
119 Chase Coffman/499 5.00 12.00
122 Chris Wells/199 10.00 25.00
123 Clay Matthews/399 30.00 60.00
124 Clint Sintim/499 6.00 15.00
125 Cornelius Ingram/499 4.00 10.00
130 Darrius Heyward-Bey/199 6.00 15.00
132 Deon Butler/499 5.00 12.00
135 Donald Brown/199 6.00 15.00
140 Graham Harrell/499 10.00 25.00
142 Hakeem Nicks/399 10.00 25.00
146 James Casey/299 5.00 12.00
149 Jared Cook/399 6.00 15.00
155 Jeremy Maclin/199 10.00 25.00
156 John Parker Wilson/299 6.00 15.00
158 Josh Freeman/199 12.00 30.00
159 Juaquin Iglesias/199 5.00 12.00
162 Kenny McKinley/499 6.00 15.00
163 Kevin Ogletree/499 6.00 15.00
164 Knowshon Moreno/199 15.00 40.00
165 Larry English/499 6.00 15.00
166 LeSean McCoy/99 25.00 50.00
170 Malcolm Jenkins/199 6.00 15.00
171 Mark Sanchez/299 30.00 80.00
172 Matthew Stafford/199 50.00 100.00
173 Tom Brandstater/299 6.00 15.00
174 Michael Crabtree/299 15.00 40.00
179 Mike Thomas/299 6.00 15.00
180 Mohamed Massaquoi/299 5.00 12.00
183 P.J. Hill/499 5.00 12.00
184 Pat White/199 6.00 15.00
186 Patrick Turner/499 5.00 12.00
187 Percy Harvin/99 30.00 60.00
189 Quan Cosby/499 5.00 12.00
190 Quinn Johnson/499 5.00 12.00
191 Ramses Barden/299 4.00 10.00
192 Rashad Jennings/399 6.00 15.00
194 Rey Maualuga/399 6.00 15.00
197 Shawn Nelson/499 5.00 12.00

2009 Playoff Prestige Inside the Numbers

1 Michael Turner 1.25 3.00
2 Brandon Jacobs 1.25 3.00
3 Thomas Jones 1.25 3.00
4 Larry Fitzgerald 1.50 4.00
5 Roddy White 1.25 3.00
6 Calvin Johnson 1.50 4.00
7 Adrian Peterson 2.50 6.00
8 Clinton Portis 1.25 3.00
9 Andre Johnson 1.25 3.00
10 Marion Barber 1.25 3.00

2009 Playoff Prestige Inside the Numbers Autographs

STATED PRINT RUN 15-25
1 Michael Turner/25 10.00 25.00
2 Brandon Jacobs/25 10.00 25.00
5 Roddy White/25 10.00 25.00
6 Calvin Johnson/15 12.00 30.00
7 Adrian Peterson/15 50.00 100.00
10 Marion Barber/15 15.00 40.00

2009 Playoff Prestige Inside the Numbers Materials

STATED PRINT RUN 43-100
*PRIME/50: .6X TO 1.5X BASIC JSY/100
*PRIME/50: .8X TO 2X BASIC JSY/100
PRIME PRINT RUN 25-50
1 Michael Turner/43 5.00 12.00
2 Brandon Jacobs/100 4.00 10.00
3 Thomas Jones/100 4.00 10.00
4 Larry Fitzgerald/100 5.00 12.00
5 Roddy White/100 4.00 10.00
6 Calvin Johnson/100 5.00 12.00
7 Adrian Peterson/100 8.00 20.00
8 Clinton Portis/100 4.00 10.00
9 Andre Johnson/100 4.00 10.00
10 Marion Barber/100 4.00 10.00

2009 Playoff Prestige League Leaders

1 Drew Brees 1.25 3.00
Kurt Warner
2 Jay Cutler 2.50 6.00
Aaron Rodgers
3 Philip Rivers 2.00 5.00
Peyton Manning
4 Adrian Peterson 2.00 5.00
Michael Turner
5 DeAngelo Williams 1.25 3.00
Clinton Portis
6 Thomas Jones 1.00 2.50
Steve Slaton
7 Matt Forte 1.25 3.00
Chris Johnson
8 Ryan Grant 1.25 3.00
LaDainian Tomlinson
9 Brandon Jacobs 1.00 2.50
Steven Jackson
10 Andre Johnson 1.25 3.00
Larry Fitzgerald
11 Steve Smith 1.00 2.50
Roddy White
12 Calvin Johnson 1.25 3.00
Greg Jennings
13 Brandon Marshall 1.25 3.00
Wes Welker
14 Reggie Wayne 1.00 2.50
Vincent Jackson
15 Tony Gonzalez 1.25 3.00
Terrell Owens
16 Santana Moss 1.00 2.50
Hines Ward
17 Matt Ryan 1.25 3.00
Joe Flacco
18 Steve Slaton 1.25 3.00
Matt Forte
Chris Johnson
Jonathan Stewart
19 Adrian Peterson 2.00 5.00
Michael Turner
Andre Johnson
Larry Fitzgerald
20 DeAngelo Williams 1.25 3.00
Michael Turner
Brandon Jacobs
Thomas Jones
21 Larry Fitzgerald 1.25 3.00
Calvin Johnson
Anquan Boldin
Randy Moss
22 DeAngelo Williams 1.25 3.00
Michael Turner
Brandon Jacobs
LenDale White
23 Adrian Peterson 2.00 5.00
Michael Turner
DeAngelo Williams
Clinton Portis
24 Andre Johnson 1.25 3.00
Larry Fitzgerald
Steve Smith
Roddy White
25 Matt Ryan 1.25 3.00
Steve Slaton
Eddie Royal
Matt Forte

2009 Playoff Prestige League Leaders Materials

3-17 DUAL PRINT RUN 250
18-25 QUAD PRINT RUN 150
*PRIME/25: .8X TO 2X BASIC DUAL
*PRIME/25: .6X TO 1.5X BASIC QUAD
PRIME PRINT RUN 25 SER.#'d SETS
3 Philip Rivers 8.00 20.00
Peyton Manning
4 Adrian Peterson 8.00 20.00
Michael Turner
5 DeAngelo Williams 5.00 12.00
Clinton Portis
6 Thomas Jones 4.00 10.00
Steve Slaton
7 Matt Forte 5.00 12.00
Chris Johnson
8 Ryan Grant 5.00 12.00
LaDainian Tomlinson
9 Brandon Jacobs 4.00 10.00
Steven Jackson
10 Andre Johnson 5.00 12.00
Larry Fitzgerald
11 Steve Smith 4.00 10.00
Roddy White
12 Calvin Johnson 5.00 12.00
Greg Jennings
13 Brandon Marshall 5.00 12.00
Wes Welker
14 Reggie Wayne 4.00 10.00
Vincent Jackson
15 Tony Gonzalez 5.00 12.00
Terrell Owens
16 Santana Moss 4.00 10.00
Hines Ward
17 Matt Ryan 5.00 12.00
Joe Flacco
18 Steve Slaton 8.00 20.00
Matt Forte
Chris Johnson
Jonathan Stewart
19 Adrian Peterson 12.00 30.00
Michael Turner
Andre Johnson
Larry Fitzgerald
20 DeAngelo Williams 8.00 20.00
Michael Turner
Brandon Jacobs
Thomas Jones
21 Larry Fitzgerald 8.00 20.00
Calvin Johnson
Anquan Boldin
Randy Moss
22 DeAngelo Williams 8.00 20.00
Michael Turner
Brandon Jacobs
LenDale White
23 Adrian Peterson 12.00 30.00
Michael Turner
DeAngelo Williams
Clinton Portis
24 Andre Johnson 8.00 20.00
Larry Fitzgerald
Steve Smith
Roddy White
25 Matt Ryan 8.00 20.00
Steve Slaton
Eddie Royal
Matt Forte

2009 Playoff Prestige NFL Draft

1 Aaron Curry 1.00 2.50
2 Andre Brown .60 1.50
3 Brandon Pettigrew 1.00 2.50
4 Brian Robiskie 1.00 2.50
5 Chris Wells 1.50 4.00
6 Darrius Heyward-Bey 1.00 2.50
7 Donald Brown 1.00 2.50
8 Graham Harrell 1.00 2.50
9 Hakeem Nicks 1.50 4.00
10 James Casey .75 2.00
11 Jared Cook 1.00 2.50
12 Jeremy Maclin 1.50 4.00
13 Josh Freeman 2.00 5.00
14 Knowshon Moreno 1.00 2.50
15 LeSean McCoy 2.00 5.00
16 Malcolm Jenkins 1.00 2.50
17 Mark Sanchez 3.00 8.00
18 Matthew Stafford 5.00 12.00
19 Michael Crabtree 2.00 5.00
20 Nate Davis .75 2.00
21 Pat White 1.00 2.50
22 Percy Harvin 1.50 4.00
23 Rashad Jennings 1.00 2.50
24 Rey Maualuga 1.00 2.50
25 Shonn Greene 1.50 4.00
26 Brian Cushing 1.00 2.50
27 Brian Orakpo 1.00 2.50
28 Cedric Peerman .75 2.00
29 D.J. Moore .75 2.00
30 James Laurinaitis 1.00 2.50
31 Javon Ringer 1.00 2.50
32 Juaquin Iglesias .75 2.00
33 Kenny Britt 1.25 3.00
34 Rhett Bomar .75 2.00
35 Vontae Davis 1.00 2.50

2009 Playoff Prestige NFL Draft Autographed Patch College Logo

STATED PRINT RUN 35-50
6 Darrius Heyward-Bey/50 12.00 30.00
7 Donald Brown/50 12.00 30.00
8 Graham Harrell/50 20.00 50.00
9 Hakeem Nicks/50 20.00 50.00
10 James Casey/50 10.00 25.00
11 Jared Cook/50 12.00 30.00
12 Jeremy Maclin/50 20.00 50.00
14 Knowshon Moreno/50 50.00 100.00
17 Mark Sanchez/35 75.00 150.00
18 Matthew Stafford/50 75.00 150.00
19 Michael Crabtree/50 50.00 100.00
21 Pat White/35 40.00 80.00
27 Brian Orakpo/50 12.00 30.00
28 Cedric Peerman/50 10.00 25.00
32 Juaquin Iglesias/50 10.00 25.00

2009 Playoff Prestige NFL Draft Autographed Patch Draft Logo

DRAFT LOGO PATCH PRINT RUN 100
*NFL EQUIP/25: .6X TO 1.5X DRAFT/100
NFL EQUIPMENT PRINT RUN 25
6 Darrius Heyward-Bey 10.00 25.00
7 Donald Brown 10.00 25.00
8 Graham Harrell 15.00 40.00
9 Hakeem Nicks 15.00 40.00
10 James Casey 8.00 20.00
11 Jared Cook 10.00 25.00
12 Jeremy Maclin 15.00 40.00
14 Knowshon Moreno 10.00 25.00
18 Matthew Stafford 60.00 120.00
19 Michael Crabtree 20.00 50.00
23 Rashad Jennings 10.00 25.00
27 Brian Orakpo 10.00 25.00
28 Cedric Peerman 8.00 20.00
32 Juaquin Iglesias 8.00 20.00

2009 Playoff Prestige NFL Draft Autographs

STATED PRINT RUN 50-100
5 Chris Wells/100 25.00 50.00
6 Darrius Heyward-Bey/100 8.00 20.00
7 Donald Brown/50 10.00 25.00
8 Graham Harrell/100 12.00 30.00
9 Hakeem Nicks/50 15.00 40.00
10 James Casey/100 6.00 15.00
11 Jared Cook/50 10.00 25.00
12 Jeremy Maclin/100 12.00 30.00
13 Josh Freeman/100 15.00 40.00
14 Knowshon Moreno/50 40.00 80.00
15 LeSean McCoy/100 15.00 40.00
16 Malcolm Jenkins/100 8.00 20.00
17 Mark Sanchez/100 40.00 80.00
18 Matthew Stafford/50 50.00 100.00
19 Michael Crabtree/50 40.00 80.00
21 Pat White/100 20.00 50.00
22 Percy Harvin/100 40.00 80.00
23 Rashad Jennings/50 10.00 25.00
24 Rey Maualuga/100 8.00 20.00
26 Brian Cushing/100 8.00 20.00
27 Brian Orakpo/50 10.00 25.00
28 Cedric Peerman/50 8.00 20.00
32 Juaquin Iglesias/50 8.00 20.00

2009 Playoff Prestige Preferred Materials

STATED PRINT RUN 100 SER.#'d SETS
*PATCH/25: .8X TO 2X BASIC JSY
PATCH PRINT RUN 25 SER.#'d SETS
1 Frank Gore 5.00 12.00
2 Joseph Addai 6.00 15.00
3 DeAngelo Williams 6.00 15.00
4 Drew Brees 6.00 15.00
5 Jason Witten 6.00 15.00
6 Matt Forte 6.00 15.00
7 Steve Slaton 5.00 12.00
8 Chris Johnson 6.00 15.00
9 Eddie Royal 5.00 12.00
10 Wes Welker 6.00 15.00

2009 Playoff Prestige Preferred Signatures

STATED PRINT RUN 25-50
1 Frank Gore/25 10.00 25.00
2 Joseph Addai/50 10.00 25.00
3 DeAngelo Williams/50 10.00 25.00
4 Drew Brees/50 30.00 60.00
5 Jason Witten/50 12.00 30.00
6 Matt Forte/25 15.00 40.00
7 Steve Slaton/50 8.00 20.00
9 Eddie Royal/50 8.00 20.00
10 Wes Welker/25 25.00 50.00

2009 Playoff Prestige Prestigious Picks Blue

BLUE PRINT RUN 1000 SER.#'d SETS
*BLACK/25: 1X TO 2.5X BLUE/1000
BLACK PRINT RUN 25 SER.#'d SETS
*GOLD/100: .6X TO 1.5X BLUE/1000
GOLD PRINT RUN 100 SER.#'d SETS
*GREEN/500: .5X TO 1.2X BLUE/1000
GREEN PRINT RUN 500 SER.#'d SETS
*PLATINUM/10: 2X TO 5X BLUE/1000
PLATINUM PRINT RUN 10 SER.#'d SETS
1 Aaron Curry 1.00 2.50
2 Andre Smith .75 2.00
3 B.J. Raji 1.00 2.50
4 Brandon Pettigrew 1.00 2.50
5 Brandon Tate 1.00 2.50
6 Brandon Gibson 1.00 2.50
7 Brian Orakpo 1.00 2.50
8 Brian Cushing 1.00 2.50
9 Brian Robiskie 1.00 2.50
10 Brooks Foster .60 1.50
11 Chase Coffman .75 2.00
12 Chris Wells 1.50 4.00
13 Clint Sintim 1.00 2.50
14 Cornelius Ingram .60 1.50
15 D.J. Moore .75 2.00
16 Darrius Heyward-Bey 1.00 2.50
17 Derrick Williams .75 2.00
18 Donald Brown 1.00 2.50
19 Eugene Monroe .60 1.50
20 Everette Brown .75 2.00
21 Graham Harrell 1.00 2.50
22 Hakeem Nicks 1.50 4.00
23 James Laurinaitis 1.00 2.50
24 James Casey .75 2.00
25 Jared Cook 1.00 2.50
26 Jarett Dillard 1.00 2.50
27 Javon Ringer 1.00 2.50
28 Jeremiah Johnson 1.00 2.50
29 Jeremy Maclin 1.50 4.00
30 Josh Freeman 2.00 5.00
31 Juaquin Iglesias .75 2.00
32 Kenny Britt 1.25 3.00
33 Knowshon Moreno 1.00 2.50
34 Larry English 1.00 2.50
35 LeSean McCoy 2.00 5.00
36 Louis Murphy 1.00 2.50
37 Malcolm Jenkins 1.00 2.50
38 Mark Sanchez 3.00 8.00
39 Matthew Stafford 5.00 12.00
40 Michael Crabtree 2.00 5.00
41 Michael Johnson .60 1.50
42 Mohamed Massaquoi .75 2.00
43 Nate Davis .75 2.00
44 Pat White 1.00 2.50
45 Percy Harvin 1.50 4.00
46 Quan Cosby .75 2.00
47 Ramses Barden .60 1.50
48 Rashad Jennings 1.00 2.50
49 Rey Maualuga 1.00 2.50
50 Shonn Greene 1.50 4.00

2009 Playoff Prestige Prestigious Picks Autographs

STATED PRINT RUN 100 SER.#'d SETS
3 B.J. Raji 6.00 15.00
5 Brandon Tate 6.00 15.00
6 Brandon Gibson 6.00 15.00
7 Brian Orakpo 6.00 15.00
8 Brian Cushing 6.00 15.00
10 Brooks Foster 4.00 10.00
11 Chase Coffman 5.00 12.00
12 Chris Wells 25.00 50.00
13 Clint Sintim 6.00 15.00
14 Cornelius Ingram 4.00 10.00
16 Darrius Heyward-Bey 6.00 15.00
18 Donald Brown 6.00 15.00
21 Graham Harrell 10.00 25.00
22 Hakeem Nicks 10.00 25.00
24 James Casey 5.00 12.00
25 Jared Cook 6.00 15.00
29 Jeremy Maclin 10.00 25.00
30 Josh Freeman 12.00 30.00
31 Juaquin Iglesias 5.00 12.00
33 Knowshon Moreno 25.00 60.00
34 Larry English 6.00 15.00
35 LeSean McCoy 12.00 30.00
37 Malcolm Jenkins 6.00 15.00
38 Mark Sanchez 50.00 100.00
39 Matthew Stafford 50.00 100.00
40 Michael Crabtree 25.00 60.00
42 Mohamed Massaquoi 5.00 12.00
44 Pat White 20.00 40.00
45 Percy Harvin 30.00 60.00
46 Quan Cosby 5.00 12.00
47 Ramses Barden 4.00 10.00
48 Rashad Jennings 6.00 15.00
49 Rey Maualuga 6.00 15.00

2009 Playoff Prestige Prestigious Picks Materials Blue

BLUE PRINT RUN 250 SER.#'d SETS
*BLACK/25: .8X TO 2X BLUE/250
BLACK PRINT RUN 25 SER.#'d SETS
*GOLD/50: .6X TO 1.5X BLUE/250
GOLD PRINT RUN 50 SER.#'d SETS
*GREEN/100: .5X TO 1.2X BLUE/250
GREEN PRINT RUN 100 SER.#'d SETS
*PLAT.PATCH/25: 1X TO 2.5X BLUE/250
PLATINUM PATCH PRINT RUN 25
5 Brandon Tate 2.50 6.00
6 Brandon Gibson 3.00 8.00
7 Brian Orakpo 3.00 8.00
8 Brian Cushing 2.50 6.00
17 Derrick Williams 3.00 8.00
18 Donald Brown 2.50 6.00
21 Graham Harrell 3.00 8.00
23 James Laurinaitis 5.00 12.00
28 Jeremiah Johnson 4.00 10.00
30 Josh Freeman 5.00 12.00
31 Juaquin Iglesias 2.00 5.00
35 LeSean McCoy 5.00 12.00
38 Mark Sanchez 8.00 20.00
39 Matthew Stafford 8.00 20.00
42 Mohamed Massaquoi 3.00 8.00
46 Quan Cosby 3.00 8.00
47 Ramses Barden 3.00 8.00
49 Rey Maualuga 2.50 6.00

2009 Playoff Prestige Prestigious Pros Blue

BLUE PRINT RUN 1000 SER.#'d SETS
*BLACK/25: 1.2X TO 3X BLUE/1000
BLACK PRINT RUN 25 SER.#'d SETS
*GOLD/100: .6X TO 1.5X BLUE/1000
GOLD PRINT RUN 100 SER.#'d SETS
*GREEN/500: .5X TO 1.2X BLUE/1000
GREEN PRINT RUN 500 SER.#'d SETS
*PLATINUM/10: 2.5X TO 6X BLUE/1000
PLATINUM PRINT RUN 10 SER.#'d SETS
1 Aaron Rodgers 2.50 6.00
2 Adrian Peterson 2.00 5.00
3 Andre Johnson 1.00 2.50
4 Anthony Gonzalez .75 2.00
5 Ben Roethlisberger 1.25 3.00
6 Brandon Jacobs 1.00 2.50
7 Brandon Marshall 1.00 2.50
8 Braylon Edwards 1.00 2.50
9 Brian Westbrook 1.00 2.50
10 Chad Ocho Cinco 1.00 2.50
11 Chris Cooley 1.00 2.50
12 Clinton Portis 1.00 2.50
13 Selvin Young .75 2.00
14 DeAngelo Williams 1.25 3.00
15 Donovan McNabb 1.25 3.00
16 Drew Brees 1.25 3.00
17 Eli Manning 1.25 3.00
18 Frank Gore 1.00 2.50
19 Jake Delhomme 1.00 2.50
20 Jason Campbell .75 2.00
21 Jason Witten 1.25 3.00
22 Jay Cutler 1.25 3.00
23 Jerricho Cotchery 1.00 2.50
24 Kellen Winslow 1.00 2.50
25 Kevin Curtis .75 2.00
26 Kurt Warner 1.25 3.00
27 LaDainian Tomlinson 1.25 3.00
28 Larry Fitzgerald 1.25 3.00
29 Larry Johnson 1.00 2.50
30 Lee Evans 1.00 2.50
31 Marion Barber 1.00 2.50
32 Marques Colston 1.00 2.50
33 Marshawn Lynch 1.00 2.50
34 Michael Turner 1.00 2.50
35 Peyton Manning 2.00 5.00
36 Philip Rivers 1.25 3.00
37 Reggie Bush 1.25 3.00
38 Reggie Wayne 1.00 2.50
39 Roddy White 1.00 2.50
40 Ronnie Brown 1.00 2.50
41 Ryan Grant 1.00 2.50
42 Steven Jackson 1.00 2.50
43 Terrell Owens 1.25 3.00
44 Thomas Jones 1.00 2.50
45 T.J. Houshmandzadeh 1.00 2.50
46 Tom Brady 2.00 5.00
47 Tony Romo 2.00 5.00
48 Trent Edwards .75 2.00
49 Willie Parker .75 2.00
50 Willis McGahee 1.00 2.50

2009 Playoff Prestige Prestigious Pros Autographs

STATED PRINT RUN 5-100
SERIAL #'d UNDER 15 NOT PRICED
2 Adrian Peterson/15 50.00 100.00
4 Anthony Gonzalez/100 6.00 15.00
6 Brandon Jacobs/25 10.00 25.00
7 Brandon Marshall/25 10.00 25.00
8 Braylon Edwards/25 10.00 25.00
10 Chad Ocho Cinco/50 8.00 20.00
13 Selvin Young/50 6.00 15.00
14 DeAngelo Williams/50 10.00 25.00
16 Drew Brees/50 30.00 60.00
18 Frank Gore/25 10.00 25.00
21 Jason Witten/25 15.00 30.00
25 Kevin Curtis/100 6.00 15.00
29 Larry Johnson/50 8.00 20.00
32 Marques Colston/100 8.00 20.00
38 Reggie Wayne/25 10.00 25.00
39 Roddy White/25 10.00 25.00
40 Ronnie Brown/50 8.00 20.00
45 T.J. Houshmandzadeh/25 10.00 25.00
47 Tony Romo/25 30.00 60.00
48 Trent Edwards/100 6.00 16.00
49 Willie Parker/25 15.00 30.00

2009 Playoff Prestige Prestigious Pros Materials Blue

BLUE PRINT RUN 250 SER.#'d SETS
*BLACK/25: .8X TO 2X BLUE/250
BLACK PRINT RUN 25 SER.#'d SETS
*GOLD/50: .6X TO 1.5X BLUE/250
GOLD PRINT RUN 50 SER.#'d SETS
*GREEN/100: .5X TO 1.2X BLUE/250
GREEN PRINT RUN 100 SER.#'d SETS
*PLAT.PATCH/25: 1X TO 2.5X BLUE/250
PLATINUM PATCH PRINT RUN 25
2 Adrian Peterson 6.00 15.00
3 Andre Johnson 3.00 8.00
4 Anthony Gonzalez 2.50 6.00
5 Ben Roethlisberger 4.00 10.00
6 Brandon Jacobs 3.00 8.00
7 Brandon Marshall 3.00 8.00
8 Braylon Edwards 3.00 8.00
9 Brian Westbrook 3.00 8.00
10 Chad Ocho Cinco 3.00 8.00
11 Chris Cooley 3.00 8.00
12 Clinton Portis 3.00 8.00
13 Selvin Young 2.50 6.00
14 DeAngelo Williams 4.00 10.00
15 Donovan McNabb 4.00 10.00
16 Drew Brees 4.00 10.00
17 Eli Manning 4.00 10.00
18 Frank Gore 3.00 8.00
20 Jason Campbell 2.50 6.00
21 Jason Witten 4.00 10.00
22 Jay Cutler 4.00 10.00
23 Jerricho Cotchery 3.00 8.00
24 Kellen Winslow 3.00 8.00
25 Kevin Curtis 2.50 6.00
27 LaDainian Tomlinson 4.00 10.00
28 Larry Fitzgerald 4.00 10.00
29 Larry Johnson 3.00 8.00
30 Lee Evans 3.00 8.00
31 Marion Barber 3.00 8.00
32 Marques Colston 3.00 8.00
33 Marshawn Lynch 3.00 8.00
34 Michael Turner 3.00 8.00
35 Peyton Manning 6.00 15.00
36 Philip Rivers 4.00 10.00
37 Reggie Bush 4.00 10.00
38 Reggie Wayne 3.00 8.00
39 Roddy White 3.00 8.00
40 Ronnie Brown 3.00 8.00
41 Ryan Grant 3.00 8.00
42 Steven Jackson 3.00 8.00
43 Terrell Owens 4.00 10.00
44 Thomas Jones 3.00 8.00
45 T.J. Houshmandzadeh 3.00 8.00
46 Tom Brady 6.00 15.00
47 Tony Romo 6.00 15.00
48 Trent Edwards 2.50 6.00
49 Willie Parker 2.50 6.00
50 Willis McGahee 3.00 8.00

2009 Playoff Prestige Rookie Review

1 Andre Caldwell 1.00 2.50
2 Aqib Talib 1.00 2.50
3 Brandon Flowers 1.00 2.50
4 Brian Brohm 1.00 2.50
5 Chad Henne 1.25 3.00
6 Chris Horton 1.25 3.00
7 Chris Johnson 1.50 4.00
8 Chris Long 1.25 3.00
9 Curtis Lofton 1.00 2.50
10 Darren McFadden 1.50 4.00
11 Davone Bess 1.00 2.50
12 DeSean Jackson 1.25 3.00
13 Devin Thomas 1.00 2.50
14 Dexter Jackson 1.00 2.50
15 Donnie Avery 1.25 3.00
16 Dustin Keller 1.00 2.50
17 Earl Bennett 1.25 3.00
18 Early Doucet 1.25 3.00
19 Eddie Royal 1.25 3.00
20 Felix Jones 1.50 4.00
21 Glenn Dorsey 1.00 2.50
22 Harry Douglas 1.00 2.50
23 Jake Long 1.00 2.50
24 Jamaal Charles 1.50 4.00
25 James Hardy 1.25 3.00
26 Jerod Mayo 1.25 3.00
27 Jerome Simpson 1.00 2.50
28 Joe Flacco 1.50 4.00
29 John Carlson 1.25 3.00
30 John David Booty 1.25 3.00
31 Jonathan Stewart 1.25 3.00
32 Jordy Nelson 1.50 4.00
33 Josh Morgan 1.00 2.50
34 Kenny Phillips 1.00 2.50
35 Kevin O'Connell 1.00 2.50
36 Kevin Smith 1.25 3.00
37 Leodis McKelvin 1.00 2.50
38 Limas Sweed 1.25 3.00
39 Malcolm Kelly 1.00 2.50
40 Mario Manningham 1.25 3.00
41 Martellus Bennett 1.00 2.50
42 Matt Forte 1.50 4.00
43 Matt Ryan 1.50 4.00
44 Peyton Hillis 1.50 4.00
45 Quintin Demps 1.00 2.50
46 Rashard Mendenhall 1.25 3.00
47 Ray Rice 1.50 4.00
48 Steve Slaton 1.25 3.00
49 Tashard Choice 1.00 2.50
50 Tim Hightower 1.00 2.50

2009 Playoff Prestige Rookie Review Autographs

STATED PRINT RUN 13-250
SERIAL #'d UNDER 20 NOT PRICED
1 Andre Caldwell/250 5.00 12.00
2 Aqib Talib/250 5.00 12.00
3 Brandon Flowers/100 6.00 15.00
4 Brian Brohm/100 6.00 15.00
5 Chad Henne/100 8.00 20.00
6 Chris Horton/250 6.00 15.00
8 Chris Long/250 6.00 15.00
9 Curtis Lofton/250 5.00 12.00
11 Davone Bess/250 5.00 12.00
12 DeSean Jackson/100 8.00 20.00
13 Devin Thomas/250 5.00 12.00
14 Dexter Jackson/250 5.00 12.00
15 Donnie Avery/250 6.00 15.00
16 Dustin Keller/100 6.00 15.00
17 Earl Bennett/250 6.00 15.00
18 Early Doucet/50 8.00 20.00
19 Eddie Royal/100 8.00 20.00
20 Felix Jones/50 20.00 40.00
22 Harry Douglas/250 5.00 12.00
23 Jake Long/250 5.00 12.00
24 Jamaal Charles/250 8.00 20.00
25 James Hardy/250 6.00 15.00
26 Jerod Mayo/50 10.00 25.00
27 Jerome Simpson/250 5.00 12.00
28 Joe Flacco/50 20.00 40.00
29 John Carlson/100 8.00 20.00
30 John David Booty/250 6.00 15.00
31 Jonathan Stewart/50 8.00 20.00
32 Jordy Nelson/50 10.00 25.00
33 Josh Morgan/250 5.00 12.00
34 Kenny Phillips/250 5.00 12.00
35 Kevin O'Connell/250 5.00 12.00
36 Kevin Smith/250 6.00 15.00
37 Leodis McKelvin/250 5.00 12.00
38 Limas Sweed/250 6.00 15.00
40 Mario Manningham/100 8.00 20.00
41 Martellus Bennett/100 6.00 15.00
42 Matt Forte/50 20.00 40.00
43 Matt Ryan/50 30.00 60.00
44 Peyton Hillis/250 20.00 40.00
45 Quintin Demps/250 5.00 12.00
46 Rashard Mendenhall/100 8.00 20.00
47 Ray Rice/250 8.00 20.00
48 Steve Slaton/250 6.00 15.00
49 Tashard Choice/50 6.00 15.00
50 Tim Hightower/50 6.00 15.00

2009 Playoff Prestige Rookie Review Materials

*PRIME/50: .8X TO 2X BASIC JSY
*PRIME/25-35: 1X TO 2.5X BASIC JSY
PRIME PRINT RUN 25-50
1 Andre Caldwell 2.50 6.00
4 Brian Brohm 2.50 6.00
5 Chad Henne 3.00 8.00
7 Chris Johnson 4.00 10.00
10 Darren McFadden 4.00 10.00
12 DeSean Jackson 3.00 8.00
13 Devin Thomas 2.50 6.00
14 Dexter Jackson 2.50 6.00
15 Donnie Avery 3.00 8.00
16 Dustin Keller 2.50 6.00
17 Earl Bennett 3.00 8.00
18 Early Doucet 3.00 8.00
19 Eddie Royal 3.00 8.00
20 Felix Jones 4.00 10.00
21 Glenn Dorsey 2.50 6.00
22 Harry Douglas 2.50 6.00
23 Jake Long 2.50 6.00
24 Jamaal Charles 4.00 10.00
25 James Hardy 3.00 8.00
27 Jerome Simpson 2.50 6.00
28 Joe Flacco 4.00 10.00
30 John David Booty 3.00 8.00
31 Jonathan Stewart 3.00 8.00
32 Jordy Nelson 4.00 10.00
35 Kevin O'Connell 2.50 6.00
36 Kevin Smith 3.00 8.00
38 Limas Sweed 3.00 8.00
39 Malcolm Kelly 2.50 6.00
40 Mario Manningham 3.00 8.00
42 Matt Forte 4.00 10.00
43 Matt Ryan 4.00 10.00
46 Rashard Mendenhall 3.00 8.00
47 Ray Rice 4.00 10.00
48 Steve Slaton 3.00 8.00

2009 Playoff Prestige Stars of the NFL

1 Tom Brady 2.00 5.00
2 Matt Ryan 1.25 3.00
3 Tony Romo 2.00 5.00
4 Eli Manning 1.25 3.00
5 Eddie Royal 1.00 2.50
6 Matt Forte 1.25 3.00
7 Andre Johnson 1.00 2.50
8 Torry Holt 1.00 2.50
9 Maurice Jones-Drew 1.00 2.50
10 Adrian Peterson 2.00 5.00
11 Brian Westbrook 1.00 2.50
12 Philip Rivers 1.25 3.00
13 Clinton Portis 1.00 2.50
14 Randy Moss 1.25 3.00
15 Hines Ward 1.00 2.50
16 Anquan Boldin 1.00 2.50
17 Reggie Wayne 1.00 2.50
18 Fred Taylor 1.00 2.50
19 Antonio Gates 1.00 2.50
20 Chris Johnson 1.25 3.00

2009 Playoff Prestige Stars of the NFL Materials

STATED PRINT RUN 100 SER.#'d SETS
*PRIME/50: .6X TO 1.5X BASIC JSY/100
*PRIME/25: .8X TO 2X BASIC JSY/100
PRIME PRINT RUN 25-50
1 Tom Brady 8.00 20.00
2 Matt Ryan 5.00 12.00
3 Tony Romo 8.00 20.00
4 Eli Manning 5.00 12.00
5 Eddie Royal 4.00 10.00
6 Matt Forte 5.00 12.00
7 Andre Johnson 4.00 10.00
8 Torry Holt 4.00 10.00
9 Maurice Jones-Drew 4.00 10.00
10 Adrian Peterson 8.00 20.00
11 Brian Westbrook 4.00 10.00
12 Philip Rivers 5.00 12.00
13 Clinton Portis 4.00 10.00
14 Randy Moss 5.00 12.00
15 Hines Ward 4.00 10.00
16 Anquan Boldin 4.00 10.00
17 Reggie Wayne 4.00 10.00
18 Fred Taylor 4.00 10.00
19 Antonio Gates 4.00 10.00
20 Chris Johnson 5.00 12.00

2009 Playoff Prestige TD Sensations

1 Thomas Jones 1.25 3.00
2 Michael Turner 1.25 3.00
3 LenDale White 1.25 3.00
4 DeAngelo Williams 1.50 4.00
5 Brandon Jacobs 1.25 3.00
6 Brian Westbrook 1.25 3.00
7 Anquan Boldin 1.25 3.00
8 Maurice Jones-Drew 1.25 3.00
9 Ronnie Brown 1.25 3.00
10 Matt Forte 1.50 4.00
11 Marion Barber 1.25 3.00
12 Adrian Peterson 2.50 6.00
13 Steve Slaton 1.25 3.00
14 Reggie Bush 1.50 4.00
15 Calvin Johnson 1.50 4.00
16 Marshawn Lynch 1.25 3.00
17 Randy Moss 1.50 4.00
18 Terrell Owens 1.50 4.00
19 Frank Gore 1.25 3.00
20 Greg Jennings 1.50 4.00

2009 Playoff Prestige TD Sensations Materials

STATED PRINT RUN 100 SER.#'d SETS
*PRIME/45-50: .6X TO 1.5X BASIC JSY/100
*PRIME/25: .8X TO 2X BASIC JSY/100
PRIME PRINT RUN 25-50
1 Thomas Jones 4.00 10.00
2 Michael Turner 4.00 10.00
3 LenDale White 4.00 10.00
4 DeAngelo Williams 5.00 12.00
5 Brandon Jacobs 4.00 10.00
6 Brian Westbrook 4.00 10.00
7 Anquan Boldin 4.00 10.00
8 Maurice Jones-Drew 4.00 10.00
9 Ronnie Brown 4.00 10.00
10 Matt Forte 5.00 12.00
11 Marion Barber 4.00 10.00
12 Adrian Peterson 8.00 20.00
13 Steve Slaton 4.00 10.00
14 Reggie Bush 5.00 12.00
15 Calvin Johnson 5.00 12.00
16 Marshawn Lynch 4.00 10.00
17 Randy Moss 5.00 12.00
18 Terrell Owens 5.00 12.00
19 Frank Gore 4.00 10.00
20 Greg Jennings 5.00 12.00

2009 Playoff Prestige True Colors

1 Greg Jennings 1.50 4.00
2 Vincent Jackson 1.25 3.00
3 Dallas Clark 1.25 3.00
4 Randy Moss 1.50 4.00
5 T.J. Houshmandzadeh 1.25 3.00
6 Santonio Holmes 1.25 3.00
7 Derrick Ward 1.00 2.50
8 Dwayne Bowe 1.25 3.00
9 Brian Westbrook 1.25 3.00
10 Brandon Marshall 1.25 3.00

2009 Playoff Prestige True Colors Autographs

STATED PRINT RUN 15-50
1 Greg Jennings/50 10.00 25.00
2 Vincent Jackson/50 8.00 20.00
3 Dallas Clark/50 8.00 20.00
5 T.J. Houshmandzadeh/25 10.00 25.00
6 Santonio Holmes/25 10.00 25.00
7 Derrick Ward/25 8.00 20.00
10 Brandon Marshall/25 10.00 25.00

2009 Playoff Prestige True Colors Materials

STATED PRINT RUN 100 SER.#'d SETS
*PRIMARY COLOR/50: .6X TO 1.5X BASIC JSY
PRIMARY COLORS PRINT RUN 50
1 Greg Jennings 5.00 12.00
2 Vincent Jackson 4.00 10.00
3 Dallas Clark 4.00 10.00
4 Randy Moss 5.00 12.00
5 T.J. Houshmandzadeh 4.00 10.00
6 Santonio Holmes 4.00 10.00
7 Derrick Ward 3.00 8.00
8 Dwayne Bowe 4.00 10.00
9 Brian Westbrook 4.00 10.00
10 Brandon Marshall 4.00 10.00

2009 Playoff Prestige Xtra Points Black Autographs

STATED PRINT RUN 5-100
SERIAL #'d UNDER 23 NOT PRICED
4 Tim Hightower/50 6.00 15.00
5 Roddy White/50 8.00 20.00
6 Michael Turner/50 8.00 20.00
7 Matt Ryan/50 30.00 60.00
8 Willis McGahee/25 10.00 25.00
9 Joe Flacco/50 20.00 40.00
10 Trent Edwards/100 6.00 15.00
11 Marshawn Lynch/25 10.00 25.00
14 DeAngelo Williams/100 6.00 15.00
16 Jonathan Stewart/50 8.00 20.00
19 Matt Forte/25 20.00 40.00
21 Chad Ocho Cinco/25 10.00 25.00
22 T.J. Houshmandzadeh/25 10.00 25.00
26 Braylon Edwards/25 10.00 25.00
27 Tony Romo/25 30.00 60.00
29 Marion Barber/25 20.00 40.00
30 Roy Williams WR/44 8.00 20.00
32 Brandon Marshall/25 10.00 25.00
33 Eddie Royal/100 8.00 20.00
34 Calvin Johnson/25 20.00 40.00
35 Kevin Smith/100 8.00 20.00
38 Greg Jennings/100 10.00 25.00
41 Steve Slaton/100 8.00 20.00
43 Joseph Addai/25 12.00 30.00
44 Reggie Wayne/25 12.00 30.00
45 Anthony Gonzalez/100 6.00 15.00
48 Maurice Jones-Drew/25 10.00 25.00
49 Larry Johnson/50 8.00 20.00
52 Ronnie Brown/50 8.00 20.00
54 Bernard Berrian/50 8.00 20.00
55 Adrian Peterson/25 60.00 120.00
56 Chester Taylor/50 6.00 15.00
60 Drew Brees/25 40.00 80.00
62 Marques Colston/100 8.00 20.00
65 Brandon Jacobs/25 10.00 25.00
67 Jerricho Cotchery/23 10.00 25.00
71 Justin Fargas/100 6.00 15.00
77 Willie Parker/25 12.00 30.00
79 Santonio Holmes/100 10.00 25.00
83 Frank Gore/25 10.00 25.00
84 Vernon Davis/100 8.00 20.00
89 Steven Jackson/25 10.00 25.00
95 LenDale White/50 8.00 20.00

2009 Playoff Prestige Promos

Cards from this promo set were issued at either the 2009 Hawaii Trade Conference Mainland Edition or the actual NFL Draft in April 2009.

MC Michael Crabtree/500* 5.00 12.00
(issued at 2009 NFL Draft)
MS Matthew Stafford/1000* 5.00 12.00
(issued at 2009 Trade Show and NFL Draft)

1995 Playoff Prime

COMPLETE SET (200) 5.00 12.00
*PRIME CARDS: .3X TO .8X ABSOLUTE

1995 Playoff Prime Fantasy Team

COMPLETE SET (20) 20.00 50.00
STATED ODDS 1:25 PRIME
FT1 Jerome Bettis 1.00 2.50
FT2 Shannon Sharpe .50 1.25
FT3 Fuad Reveiz .25 .60
FT4 John Carney .25 .60
FT5 Steve Young 2.00 5.00
FT6 Brett Favre 5.00 12.00
FT7 Tim Brown 1.00 2.50
FT8 Ben Coates .50 1.25
FT9 Marshall Faulk 3.00 8.00
FT10 Stan Humphries .50 1.25
FT11 Dan Marino 5.00 12.00
FT12 Jerry Rice 2.50 6.00
FT13 Errict Rhett .50 1.25
FT14 Chris Warren .50 1.25
FT15 Barry Sanders 4.00 10.00
FT16 Cris Carter 1.00 2.50
FT17 Michael Irvin 1.00 2.50
FT18 Emmitt Smith 4.00 10.00
FT19 Terance Mathis .50 1.25
FT20 Herman Moore 1.00 2.50

1995 Playoff Prime Minis

COMPLETE SET (200) 60.00 150.00
*STARS: 3X TO 8X BASIC ABSOLUTES
*ROOKIES: 1.2X TO 3X BASIC ABSOLUTES
STATED ODDS 1:7 PRIME

1996 Playoff Prime Samples

These promo cards were issued to preview the 1996 Playoff Prime release. Each is very similar to its base brand card in design, except for the word "sample" where the card number otherwise would be.

COMPLETE SET (3) 2.50 6.00
1 Zack Crockett .30 .75
2 Terrell Davis 1.20 3.00
3 Antonio Freeman .50 1.25
4 Rashaan Salaam .40 1.00
5 J.J. Stokes .30 .75
6 Tamarick Vanover .30 .75

1996 Playoff Prime

The 1996 Playoff Prime set was issued in one series totalling 200 cards. The five-card packs retail for $3.75 each and were distributed in three color-coded pack types: bronze (#1-100), silver (#101-150), and gold (#151-200). The fronts feature color player photos with player statistics on the backs.

COMPLETE SET (200) 40.00 100.00
COMP. BRONZE SET (100) 6.00 15.00
1 Brett Favre 1.25 3.00
2 Jerry Rice .60 1.50
3 Troy Aikman .60 1.50
4 Bruce Smith .08 .25
5 Marshall Faulk .25 .60
6 Erik Kramer .02 .10
7 Carl Pickens .08 .25
8 Anthony Miller .08 .25
9 Cris Carter .20 .50
10 Todd Kinchen .02 .10
11 Stoney Case .02 .10
12 Chris Calloway .02 .10
13 Andre Rison .08 .25
14 Bill Brooks .02 .10
15 Shawn Jefferson .02 .10
16 Eric Zeier .02 .10
17 Yancey Thigpen .08 .25
18 Edgar Bennett .08 .25
19 Garrison Hearst .08 .25
20 Daryl Johnston .08 .25
21 Tyrone Wheatley .08 .25
22 Darick Holmes .02 .10
23 Dave Brown .02 .10
24 Leeland McElroy RC .08 .25
25 Craig Heyward .02 .10
26 Kevin Hardy RC .20 .50
27 Scott Mitchell .08 .25
28 Willie Green .02 .10
29 Vincent Brisby .02 .10
30 Mike Tomczak .02 .10
31 Luther Elliss .02 .10
32 Mike Pritchard .02 .10
33 Robert Green .02 .10
34 Jeff Graham .02 .10
35 Tamarick Vanover .08 .25
36 William Floyd .08 .25
37 Alvin Harper .02 .10
38 Stan Humphries .08 .25
39 Herman Moore .08 .25
40 Tony Martin .08 .25
41 Jonathan Ogden RC .20 .50
42 Randall Cunningham .20 .50
43 Chris Warren .08 .25
44 Bobby Hebert .02 .10
45 Jerome Bettis .20 .50
46 Joey Galloway .20 .50
47 Ernie Mills .02 .10
48 Steve McNair .40 1.00
49 Karim Abdul-Jabbar RC .20 .50
50 Chad May .02 .10
51 Jim Everett .02 .10
52 Robert Smith .08 .25
53 Tony Boselli .02 .10
54 William Henderson .20 .50
55 Terry Glenn RC UER .60 1.50
(Joey Galloway biography on back of card)
56 Neil O'Donnell .08 .25
57 Chris Chandler .08 .25
58 Michael Jackson .08 .25
59 Jason Dunn RC .08 .25
60 James O. Stewart .08 .25
61 Greg Hill .08 .25
62 Mark Carrier WR .02 .10
63 Bernie Parmalee .02 .10
64 Chris Sanders .08 .25
65 Jeff Hostetler .02 .10
66 Eric Moulds RC .75 2.00
67 James Jett .08 .25
68 Henry Ellard .02 .10
69 Mario Bates .08 .25
70 Natrone Means .08 .25
71 Bobby Engram RC .20 .50
72 Christian Fauria .02 .10
73 Gus Frerotte .08 .25
74 Aaron Hayden .02 .10
75 Reggie White .20 .50
76 Dave Meggett .02 .10
77 Harvey Williams .02 .10
78 Terance Mathis .02 .10
79 Byron Bam Morris .02 .10
80 Trent Dilfer .20 .50
81 Irving Fryar .08 .25
82 Quinn Early .02 .10
83 Lake Dawson .02 .10
84 Todd Collins .08 .25
85 Eric Metcalf .02 .10
86 Tim Biakabutuka RC .20 .50
87 Rob Johnson .20 .50
88 Charlie Garner .08 .25
89 Mike Mamula .02 .10
90 Steve Walsh .02 .10
91 Charles Haley .08 .25
92 Mike Alstott RC .60 1.50
93 Wayne Chrebet .30 .75
94 Vinny Testaverde .08 .25
95 Fred Barnett .02 .10
96 Boomer Esiason .08 .25
97 Zack Crockett .02 .10
98 Kevin Williams .02 .10
99 Eric Bieniemy .02 .10
100 Bryan Cox .02 .10
101 Larry Centers .40 1.00
102 Jeff George .40 1.00
103 Bryce Paup .40 1.00
104 Kerry Collins .75 2.00
105 Derrick Moore .20 .50
106 Adrian Murrell .40 1.00
107 Harold Green .20 .50
108 Ki-Jana Carter .40 1.00
109 Sherman Williams .20 .50
110 Deion Sanders 2.00 4.00
111 Emmitt Smith 3.00 8.00
112 Shannon Sharpe .40 1.00
113 Johnnie Morton .40 1.00
114 Eddie Kennison RC .40 1.00
115 Marvin Harrison RC 4.00 10.00
116 Amani Toomer RC .75 2.00
117 Rickey Dudley RC .75 2.00
118 Alex Van Dyke RC .40 1.00
119 Dorsey Levens .75 2.00
120 Antonio Freeman .75 2.00
121 Willie Davis .40 1.00
122 Lamont Warren .20 .50
123 Sean Dawkins .20 .50
124 Willie Jackson .40 1.00
125 Kimble Anders .20 .50
126 Dan Marino 4.00 10.00
127 Terry Kirby .40 1.00
128 Amp Lee .20 .50
129 Jake Reed .40 1.00
130 Curtis Martin 1.50 4.00
131 Ray Zellars .20 .50
132 Herschel Walker .40 1.00
133 Mike Sherrard .20 .50
134 Kyle Brady .40 1.00
135 Rocket Ismail .40 1.00
136 Ricky Watters .40 1.00
137 Kordell Stewart .75 2.00
138 Andre Hastings .02 .10
139 Ronnie Harmon .02 .10
140 Terrell Fletcher .20 .50
141 J.J. Stokes .75 2.00
142 Brent Jones .20 .50
143 Tony McGee .20 .50
144 Brian Blades .40 1.00
145 Isaac Bruce .75 2.00
146 Errict Rhett .40 1.00
147 Warren Sapp .20 .50
148 Horace Copeland .20 .50
149 Heath Shuler .40 1.00
150 Michael Westbrook .75 2.00
151 Frank Sanders .60 1.50
152 Rob Moore .60 1.50
153 Bert Emanuel .60 1.50
154 J.J. Birden .30 .75
155 Thurman Thomas 1.00 2.50
156 Jim Kelly 1.00 2.50
157 Curtis Conway .60 1.50
158 Darnay Scott .60 1.50
159 Jeff Blake 1.00 2.50
160 Jay Novacek .60 1.50
161 Michael Irvin 1.00 2.50
162 John Elway 5.00 12.00
163 Terrell Davis 2.50 6.00
164 Barry Sanders 3.00 8.00
165 Brett Perriman .30 .75
166 Keyshawn Johnson RC 2.00 5.00
167 Eddie George RC 2.50 6.00
168 Derrick Mayes RC 1.00 2.50
169 Simeon Rice RC 2.50 6.00
170 Lawrence Phillips RC .60 1.50
171 Robert Brooks .60 1.50
172 Mark Chmura .60 1.50
173 Rodney Thomas .30 .75
174 Jim Harbaugh .60 1.50
175 Ken Dilger .60 1.50
176 Mark Brunell 2.00 5.00
177 Steve Bono .60 1.50
178 Marcus Allen 1.00 2.50
179 O.J. McDuffie .60 1.50
180 Eric Green .30 .75
181 Warren Moon 1.00 2.50
182 Drew Bledsoe 2.00 5.00
183 Ben Coates .60 1.50
184 Michael Haynes .60 1.50
185 Rodney Hampton .60 1.50
186 Rashaan Salaam .60 1.50
187 Napoleon Kaufman 1.00 2.50
188 Tim Brown 1.00 2.50
189 Rodney Peete .30 .75
190 Calvin Williams .30 .75
191 Eric Pegram .60 1.50
192 Mark Bruener .30 .75
193 Junior Seau 1.00 2.50
194 Steve Young 2.50 6.00
195 Derek Loville .30 .75
196 Rick Mirer .60 1.50
197 Mark Rypien .30 .75
198 Jackie Harris .30 .75
199 Terry Allen .60 1.50
200 Brian Mitchell .30 .75

1996 Playoff Prime X's and O's

*1-100 STARS: 4X TO 10X BASE CARD
*1-100 ROOKIES: 1.5X TO 4X BASE CARD
*101-150 STARS: 1.2X TO 3X BASE CARD
*101-150 ROOKIES: .6X TO 1.5X BASE CARD
*151-200 STARS: .8X TO 2X BASE CARD
*151-200 ROOKIES: .5X TO 1.2X BASE CARDS
STATED ODDS 1:7.2

1996 Playoff Prime Boss Hogs

COMPLETE SET (18) 40.00 80.00
STATED ODDS 1:96
1 Curtis Martin 3.00 8.00
2 Chris Warren 1.25 3.00
3 Emmitt Smith 6.00 15.00
4 Barry Sanders 6.00 15.00
5 Rashaan Salaam 2.00 5.00
6 Marshall Faulk 2.50 6.00
7 Errict Rhett 1.25 3.00
8 Thurman Thomas 2.00 5.00
9 Kerry Collins 2.00 5.00
10 Dan Marino 7.50 20.00
11 Jerry Rice 4.00 10.00
12 Troy Aikman 4.00 10.00
13 Jeff George 1.25 3.00
14 Brett Favre 7.50 20.00
15 Robert Brooks 2.00 5.00
16 John Elway 7.50 20.00
17 Deion Sanders 2.50 6.00
18 Kordell Stewart 2.00 5.00

1996 Playoff Prime Honors

COMPLETE SET (3) 30.00 80.00
STATED ODDS 1:7200
PH1 Emmitt Smith 15.00 40.00
PH2 Curtis Martin 7.50 20.00
PH3 Brett Favre 20.00 50.00

1996 Playoff Prime Surprise

COMPLETE SET (14) 25.00 60.00
STATED ODDS 1:288
1 Dan Marino 5.00 12.00
2 Brett Favre 5.00 12.00
3 Emmitt Smith 5.00 12.00
4 Kordell Stewart .75 2.00
5 Jerry Rice 2.50 6.00
6 Troy Aikman 2.50 6.00
7 Barry Sanders 4.00 10.00
8 Curtis Martin 1.00 2.50
9 Marshall Faulk 1.00 2.50
10 Joey Galloway .50 1.25
11 Robert Brooks .50 1.25
12 Deion Sanders 1.00 2.50
13 Reggie White .75 2.00
14 Marcus Allen .75 2.00

2002 Playoff Prime Signatures Samples

*1-64 SILVER VETS: .4X TO 1X BASE CARDS
*65-110 SLVR ROOKIES: .1X TO .25X
*1-64 GOLD VETS: .8X TO 2X BASE CARDS
*65-110 GOLD ROOKIES: .2X TO .5X

2002 Playoff Prime Signatures

Released in early January 2003, this set consists of 64 veterans, and 46 rookies. The rookies were serial #'d to 250. SRP for each tin was $40. Each tin contained one autograph, one rookie, and two base cards. Each tin was also serial numbered, and limited to 10,000 produced.

ROOKIE PRINT RUN 250 SER.#'d SETS
1 Aaron Brooks 1.00 2.50
2 Brett Favre 3.00 8.00
3 Drew Bledsoe 1.25 3.00
4 Jake Plummer 1.00 2.50
5 Jeff Blake 1.00 2.50
6 Jevon Kearse 1.00 2.50
7 Ricky Williams 1.00 2.50
8 Terrell Davis 1.00 2.50
9 Chris Chambers 1.00 2.50
10 Cris Carter 1.25 3.00
11 Emmitt Smith 3.00 8.00
12 Randall Cunningham 1.25 3.00
13 Corey Dillon 1.00 2.50
14 Brian Griese 1.00 2.50
15 Isaac Bruce 1.25 3.00
16 Koren Robinson .75 2.00
17 David Terrell .75 2.00
18 Mark Brunell 1.00 2.50
19 Eric Moulds 1.00 2.50
20 Kevan Barlow .75 2.00
21 David Boston .75 2.00
22 LaMont Jordan 1.00 2.50
23 Jimmy Smith 1.00 2.50
24 Marvin Harrison 1.25 3.00
25 Marcus Robinson 1.00 2.50
26 Ray Lewis 1.25 3.00
27 Mike Anderson 1.00 2.50
28 Randy Moss 1.25 3.00
29 Michael Bennett 1.00 2.50
30 Quincy Carter .75 2.00
31 Tim Brown 1.25 3.00
32 Michael Strahan 1.25 3.00
33 Tony Gonzalez 1.25 3.00
34 Santana Moss 1.00 2.50
35 Torry Holt 1.25 3.00
36 Anthony Thomas 1.00 2.50
37 Chris Weinke .75 2.00
38 Deuce McAllister 1.00 2.50
39 Drew Brees 2.00 5.00
40 Edgerrin James 1.00 2.50
41 Freddie Mitchell .75 2.00
42 James Jackson .75 2.00
43 Kendrell Bell .75 2.00
44 LaDainian Tomlinson 1.50 4.00
45 Mike McMahon .75 2.00
46 Quincy Morgan .75 2.00
47 Robert Ferguson 1.00 2.50
48 Steve Smith 1.25 3.00
49 Terrell Owens 1.25 3.00
50 Eddie George 1.00 2.50
51 Kurt Warner 1.25 3.00
52 Chad Johnson 1.25 3.00
53 Dan Marino 5.00 12.00
54 Jim Kelly 2.50 6.00
55 John Elway 4.00 10.00
56 Michael Irvin 2.00 5.00
57 Phil Simms 1.50 4.00
58 Steve Young 2.50 6.00
59 Troy Aikman 3.00 8.00
60 Warren Moon 2.00 5.00
61 Barry Sanders 3.00 8.00
62 Joe Montana 5.00 12.00
63 Joe Namath 3.00 8.00
64 Thurman Thomas 2.00 5.00
65 T.J. Duckett RC 3.00 8.00
66 William Green RC 2.50 6.00
67 Travis Stephens RC 2.00 5.00
68 Tim Carter RC 2.50 6.00
69 Terry Charles RC 2.00 5.00
70 Roy Williams RC 3.00 8.00
71 Marquise Walker RC 2.00 5.00
72 Rohan Davey RC 3.00 8.00
73 Quentin Jammer RC 3.00 8.00
74 Reche Caldwell RC 3.00 8.00
75 Maurice Morris RC 2.50 6.00
76 Woody Dantzler RC 2.50 6.00
77 Patrick Ramsey RC 3.00 8.00
78 Tavon Mason RC 2.00 5.00
79 Ladell Betts RC 3.00 8.00
80 Kahlil Hill RC 2.00 5.00
81 Josh Scobey RC 2.50 6.00
82 Brian Westbrook RC 5.00 12.00
83 Javon Walker RC 3.00 8.00
84 DeShaun Foster RC 3.00 8.00
85 Kelly Campbell RC 2.50 6.00
86 Ashley Lelie RC 2.50 6.00
87 Donte Stallworth RC 3.00 8.00
88 David Carr RC 3.00 8.00
89 Kurt Kittner RC 2.00 5.00
90 Clinton Portis RC 4.00 10.00
91 Josh Reed RC 2.50 6.00
92 Joey Harrington RC 3.00 8.00
93 Antwaan Randle El RC 3.00 8.00
94 Randy Fasani RC 2.50 6.00
95 Cliff Russell RC 2.00 5.00
96 John Henderson RC 3.00 8.00
97 Luke Staley RC 2.00 5.00
98 Antonio Bryant RC 3.00 8.00
99 Jonathan Wells RC 3.00 8.00
100 Chester Taylor RC 3.00 8.00
101 Lamar Gordon RC 2.50 6.00
102 Deion Branch RC 3.00 8.00
103 Josh McCown RC 3.00 8.00
104 Andre Davis RC 2.00 5.00
105 Freddie Milons RC 2.00 5.00
106 David Garrard RC 4.00 10.00
107 Chad Hutchinson RC 2.00 5.00
108 Jabar Gaffney RC 3.00 8.00
109 Eric Crouch RC 3.00 8.00
110 Albert Haynesworth RC 3.00 8.00
NNO Jeff Garcia TIN 1.25 3.00

2002 Playoff Prime Signatures Proofs

*1-52 VETS: 1.5X TO 4X BASIC CARDS
*53-64 RETIRED: 1.2X TO 3X BASIC CARDS
1-64 STATED PRINT RUN 50
*ROOKIES: 1X TO 2.5X BASIC CARDS
65-110 ROOKIE PRINT RUN 25

2002 Playoff Prime Signatures Honor Roll Autographs

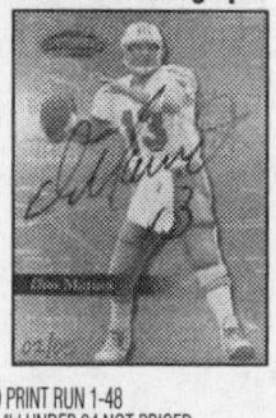

STATED PRINT RUN 1-48
SERIAL #'d UNDER 24 NOT PRICED
50 Doug Flutie 00ConHaw/33 12.00 30.00
51 Doug Flutie 00Pre/36 12.00 30.00
59 Doug Flutie 99Con/48 12.00 30.00
62 Doug Flutie 99ConPlayoffTix/24 15.00 40.00
65 Doug Flutie 99Mom/25 15.00 40.00
114 Ricky Williams 99AbsGreen/20

2002 Playoff Prime Signatures Autographs

AUTO/5-250 ODDS ONE PER PACK
SERIAL #'d UNDER 20 NOT PRICED
UNPRICED PRIME CUTS SER.#'d OF 5
1 Aaron Brooks/58 12.00 30.00
2 Brett Favre/62 125.00 250.00
4 Jake Plummer/20 20.00 50.00
7 Ricky Williams/116 10.00 25.00
8 Terrell Davis/21 25.00 60.00
9 Chris Chambers/223 10.00 25.00
10 Cris Carter/38 20.00 50.00
11 Emmitt Smith/40 150.00 300.00
13 Corey Dillon/102 10.00 25.00
14 Brian Griese/81 10.00 25.00
15 Isaac Bruce/53 15.00 40.00
16 Koren Robinson/147 8.00 20.00
17 David Terrell/233 8.00 20.00
19 Eric Moulds/30 15.00 40.00
20 Kevan Barlow/210 8.00 20.00
22 LaMont Jordan/115 10.00 25.00
23 Jimmy Smith/30 15.00 40.00
24 Marvin Harrison/94 12.00 30.00
25 Marcus Robinson/20 20.00 50.00
28 Randy Moss/195 30.00 60.00
29 Michael Bennett/250 10.00 25.00
30 Quincy Carter/95 8.00 20.00
31 Tim Brown/57 30.00 60.00
32 Michael Strahan/20 25.00 60.00
33 Tony Gonzalez/87 12.00 30.00
34 Santana Moss/115 10.00 25.00
35 Torry Holt/174 12.00 30.00
36 Anthony Thomas/131 10.00 25.00
37 Chris Weinke/99 8.00 20.00
38 Deuce McAllister/113 10.00 25.00
39 Drew Brees/57 40.00 80.00
40 Edgerrin James/28 20.00 50.00
41 Freddie Mitchell/126 8.00 20.00
42 James Jackson/126 8.00 20.00
43 Kendrell Bell/145 8.00 20.00
44 LaDainian Tomlinson/59 60.00 120.00
45 Mike McMahon/192 8.00 20.00
46 Quincy Morgan/160 8.00 20.00
47 Robert Ferguson/225 10.00 25.00
48 Steve Smith/209 12.00 30.00
49 Terrell Owens/98 20.00 50.00
50 Eddie George/22 20.00 50.00
51 Kurt Warner/176 15.00 40.00
52 Chad Johnson/216 12.00 30.00
53 Dan Marino/40 100.00 200.00
54 Jim Kelly/39 40.00 80.00
55 John Elway/68 75.00 150.00
56 Michael Irvin/143 20.00 50.00
57 Phil Simms/62 20.00 50.00
58 Steve Young/101 30.00 80.00
59 Troy Aikman/64 50.00 100.00
61 Barry Sanders/38 75.00 150.00
62 Joe Montana/98 75.00 150.00
63 Joe Namath/216 40.00 80.00
64 Thurman Thomas/40 15.00 40.00
67 Travis Stephens/20 15.00 40.00
68 Tim Carter/120 10.00 25.00
69 Terry Charles/145 8.00 20.00
70 Roy Williams/70 15.00 40.00
71 Marquise Walker/95 8.00 20.00
72 Rohan Davey/20 25.00 60.00
73 Quentin Jammer/95 12.00 30.00
74 Reche Caldwell/45 15.00 40.00
75 Maurice Morris/20 20.00 50.00
76 Woody Dantzler/20 20.00 50.00
77 Patrick Ramsey/120 12.00 30.00
78 Tavon Mason/95 8.00 20.00
79 Ladell Betts/95 10.00 25.00
80 Kahlil Hill/45 10.00 25.00
81 Josh Scobey/145 10.00 25.00
82 Brian Westbrook/145 50.00 80.00
84 DeShaun Foster/70 15.00 40.00
85 Kelly Campbell/45 10.00 25.00
86 Ashley Lelie/120 10.00 25.00
87 Donte Stallworth/95 12.00 30.00
88 David Carr/70 15.00 40.00
89 Kurt Kittner/45 10.00 25.00
90 Clinton Portis/95 30.00 80.00
91 Josh Reed/120 10.00 25.00
92 Joey Harrington/95 12.00 30.00
93 Antwaan Randle El/45 15.00 40.00
94 Randy Fasani/120 10.00 25.00
95 Cliff Russell/95 8.00 20.00
96 John Henderson/95 10.00 25.00
97 Luke Staley/95 8.00 20.00
98 Antonio Bryant/45 15.00 40.00
100 Chester Taylor/95 12.00 30.00
101 Lamar Gordon/45 10.00 25.00
102 Deion Branch/95 15.00 40.00
103 Josh McCown/95 10.00 25.00
104 Andre Davis/95 10.00 25.00
105 Freddie Milons/75 10.00 25.00
106 David Garrard/120 15.00 40.00
107 Chad Hutchinson/145 8.00 20.00
108 Jabar Gaffney/95 12.00 30.00
109 Eric Crouch/95 12.00 30.00

2004 Playoff Prime Signatures

Playoff Prime Signatures initially released in mid-December 2004. The base set consists of 158-cards including 100-veteran or retired player cards serial numbered of 999, 25-dual rookie autographed cards numbered of 199 and 33-autographed rookie cards numbered of 99 signed on replica jersey material. Hobby boxes contained 1-pack of 4-cards and carried an S.R.P. of $60 per pack. Four parallel sets and a variety of autograph inserts can be found seeded in packs making it a hot product for autographed card collectors.

126-158 ROOKIE AU PRINT RUN 99
UNPRICED PLATINUM PRINT RUN 1
UNPRICED PRIME CUT PRINT RUN 1
1 Anquan Boldin 1.50 4.00
2 Josh McCown 1.25 3.00
3 Alge Crumpler 1.25 3.00
4 Michael Vick 2.00 5.00
5 Jamal Lewis 1.25 3.00
6 Todd Heap 1.25 3.00
7 Jim Kelly 2.00 5.00
8 Thurman Thomas 1.50 4.00
9 Travis Henry 1.00 2.50
10 Jake Delhomme 1.25 3.00
11 Stephen Davis 1.25 3.00
12 Steve Smith 1.50 4.00
13 Brian Urlacher 1.50 4.00
14 Dick Butkus 3.00 8.00
15 Gale Sayers 2.50 6.00
16 Mike Ditka 2.00 5.00
17 Mike Singletary 2.00 5.00
18 Rex Grossman 1.25 3.00
19 Richard Dent 1.25 3.00
20 Chad Johnson 1.50 4.00
21 Rudi Johnson 1.25 3.00
22 Jim Brown 3.00 8.00
23 Lee Suggs 1.25 3.00
24 Ozzie Newsome 1.50 4.00
25 Paul Warfield 1.50 4.00
26 Quincy Morgan 1.00 2.50
27 William Green 1.00 2.50
28 Antonio Bryant 1.25 3.00
29 Herschel Walker 1.50 4.00
30 Jimmy Johnson 1.50 4.00
31 Keyshawn Johnson 1.25 3.00
32 Roger Staubach 3.00 8.00
33 Terence Newman 1.25 3.00
34 Tony Dorsett 2.00 5.00
35 Terrell Davis 2.00 5.00
36 Joey Harrington 1.25 3.00
37 Ahman Green 1.25 3.00
38 Javon Walker 1.00 2.50
39 Paul Hornung 2.00 5.00
40 Reggie White 2.00 5.00
41 Robert Ferguson 1.00 2.50
42 Sterling Sharpe 1.50 4.00
43 David Carr 1.00 2.50
44 Domanick Davis 1.00 2.50
45 Earl Campbell 2.00 5.00
46 Peyton Manning 3.00 8.00
47 Reggie Wayne 1.50 4.00
48 Dante Hall 1.25 3.00
49 Priest Holmes 1.50 4.00
50 Trent Green 1.25 3.00
51 A.J. Feeley 1.00 2.50
52 Don Shula 2.00 5.00
53 Chris Chambers 1.25 3.00
54 Travis Minor 1.00 2.50
55 Fran Tarkenton 2.00 5.00
56 Bill Belichick 2.00 5.00
57 Tom Brady 3.00 8.00
58 Aaron Brooks 1.25 3.00
59 Deuce McAllister 1.25 3.00
60 Boo Williams 1.00 2.50
61 Joe Horn 1.25 3.00
62 Lawrence Taylor 2.00 5.00
63 Mark Bavaro 1.25 3.00
64 Michael Strahan 1.50 4.00
65 Tiki Barber 1.50 4.00
66 Herman Edwards 1.25 3.00
67 Joe Namath 3.00 8.00
68 Justin McCareins 1.00 2.50
69 LaMont Jordan 1.25 3.00
70 Santana Moss 1.25 3.00
71 Bo Jackson 3.00 8.00
72 Fred Biletnikoff 2.00 5.00
73 George Blanda 2.00 5.00
74 Jim Plunkett 1.50 4.00
75 Marcus Allen 2.00 5.00
76 Barry Switzer 2.50 6.00
77 Correll Buckhalter 1.25 3.00
78 Donovan McNabb 1.50 4.00
79 Antwaan Randle El 1.25 3.00
80 Bill Cowher 1.50 4.00
81 Franco Harris 2.50 6.00
82 Jack Lambert 2.50 6.00
83 Joe Greene 2.00 5.00
84 Kendrell Bell 1.00 2.50
85 L.C. Greenwood 1.50 4.00
86 Mel Blount 1.50 4.00
87 Terry Bradshaw 3.00 8.00
88 LaDainian Tomlinson 1.50 4.00
89 Andre Carter 1.00 2.50
90 Bill Walsh 2.00 5.00
91 Shaun Alexander 1.25 3.00
92 Steve Largent 2.00 5.00
93 Matt Hasselbeck 1.25 3.00
94 Torry Holt 1.25 3.00
95 Clinton Portis 1.50 4.00
96 Laveranues Coles 1.00 2.50
97 Mark Brunell 1.25 3.00
98 Patrick Ramsey 1.25 3.00
99 Reuben Droughns 1.25 3.00
100 Sonny Jurgensen 1.50 4.00
101 Matt Mauck AU RC 6.00 15.00
Triandos Luke Staley RC
102 D.J. Williams AU RC 10.00 25.00
Brandon Miree AU RC
103 Carlos Francis AU RC 6.00 15.00
Johnnie Morant AU RC
104 Jonathan Vilma AU RC 10.00 25.00
Derrick Ward AU RC
105 Vince Wilfork AU RC 10.00 25.00
P.K. Sam AU RC
106 Jim Sorgi AU RC 8.00 20.00
Ran Carthon AU RC
107 Troy Fleming AU RC 8.00 20.00
Jarrett Payton AU RC
108 Jason Babin AU RC 10.00 25.00
B.J. Symons AU RC
109 Josh Harris AU RC 6.00 15.00
Clarence Moore AU RC
110 Maurice Mann AU RC 6.00 15.00
Casey Bramlet AU RC
111 Sean Jones AU RC 8.00 20.00
Adimchinobe Echemandu AU RC
112 Andy Hall AU RC 6.00 15.00
Bruce Perry AU RC
113 Jamaar Taylor AU RC 8.00 20.00
Jared Lorenzen AU RC
114 Chris Gamble AU RC 8.00 20.00
Drew Carter AU RC
115 Drew Henson AU RC 8.00 20.00
Craig Krenzel AU RC
116 Tommie Harris AU RC 10.00 25.00
Ahmad Carroll AU RC
117 Jeff Smoker AU RC 8.00 20.00
D.J. Hackett AU RC
118 Ernest Wilford AU RC 8.00 20.00
Jerricho Cotchery AU RC
119 Will Smith AU RC 8.00 20.00
Kenechi Udeze AU RC
120 Samie Parker AU RC 12.00 30.00
Michael Turner AU RC
121 Sloan Thomas AU RC 8.00 20.00
B.J. Johnson AU RC
122 John Navarre AU RC 8.00 20.00
Cody Pickett AU RC
123 Ricardo Colclough AU RC 8.00 20.00
Quincy Wilson AU RC
124 Sean Taylor RC 20.00 40.00
Chris Cooley AU RC
125 Michael Boulware AU RC 10.00 25.00
Teddy Lehman RC
126 J.P. Losman AU RC 10.00 25.00
127 Lee Evans AU RC 12.00 30.00
128 Ben Watson AU RC 12.00 30.00
129 Cedric Cobbs AU RC 8.00 20.00
130 Devard Darling AU RC 8.00 20.00
131 Chris Perry AU RC 10.00 25.00
132 Kellen Winslow AU RC 12.00 30.00
133 Luke McCown AU RC 10.00 25.00
134 Ben Roethlisberger AU RC 100.00 200.00
135 Dunta Robinson AU RC 8.00 20.00
136 Greg Jones AU RC 8.00 20.00
137 Reggie Williams AU RC 10.00 25.00
138 Ben Troupe AU RC 10.00 25.00
139 Tatum Bell AU RC 10.00 25.00
140 Darius Watts AU RC 8.00 20.00
141 Robert Gallery AU RC 12.00 30.00
142 Philip Rivers AU RC 40.00 100.00
143 Julius Jones AU RC 10.00 25.00
144 Eli Manning AU RC 125.00 200.00
145 Bernard Berrian AU RC 15.00 40.00
146 Roy Williams AU RC 15.00 40.00
147 Kevin Jones AU RC 10.00 25.00
148 Mewelde Moore AU RC 10.00 25.00

149 DeAngelo Hall AU RC 12.00 30.00
150 Michael Jenkins AU RC 12.00 30.00
151 Matt Schaub AU RC 25.00 60.00
152 Keary Colbert AU RC 8.00 20.00
153 Devery Henderson AU RC 12.00 30.00
154 Michael Clayton AU RC 10.00 25.00
155 Larry Fitzgerald AU RC 50.00 100.00
156 Rashaun Woods AU RC 8.00 20.00
157 Derrick Hamilton AU RC 8.00 20.00
158 Steven Jackson AU RC 20.00 50.00

2004 Playoff Prime Signatures Bronze Proofs

*VETS: 1.2X TO 3X BASIC CARDS
*RETIRED: 1X TO 2.5X BASIC CARDS
STATED PRINT RUN 50 SER.#'d SETS

2004 Playoff Prime Signatures Gold Proofs

UNPRICED 1-100 PRINT RUN 5
*GOLD DUAL AUTO/50: .5X TO 1.2X
101-125 AU PRINT RUN 50
UNPRICED 126-158 AU PRINT RUN 5

2004 Playoff Prime Signatures Silver Proofs

*VETS: 2X TO 5X BASIC CARDS
*RETIRED: 1.5X TO 4X BASIC CARDS
SILVER PRINT RUN 25 SER.#'d SETS

2004 Playoff Prime Signatures Prime Cuts Autographs

UNPRICED PRIME CUT PRINT RUN 1

2004 Playoff Prime Signatures Prime Pairings Autographs

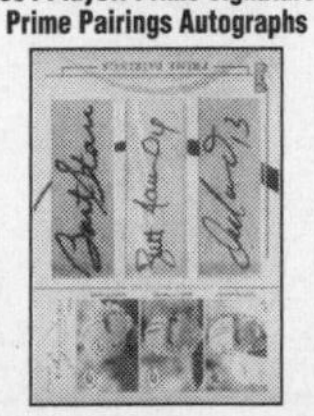

STATED PRINT RUN 1-50
CARDS SER.#'d UNDER 20 NOT PRICED
PP1 Brett Favre 125.00 250.00
Daunte Culpepper
Kyle Boller/42
PP2 Byron Leftwich 25.00 60.00
Chad Pennington
Jake Delhomme/50
PP4 Joe Montana 175.00 300.00
Ken Stabler
Carson Palmer
Jeff Garcia/28
PP5 Barry Sanders 125.00 250.00
Chris Perry
Marshall Faulk
Kevan Barlow/31
PP6 Jerry Rice 125.00 250.00
Michael Clayton
Marvin Harrison
Andre Johnson/31
PP7 Ray Lewis 75.00 125.00
Kendrell Bell
Dan Morgan
Jonathan Vilma/24
PP8 Tony Gonzalez 25.00 60.00
Dallas Clark
Alge Crumpler
Todd Heap/26
PP9 Troy Aikman 150.00 250.00
Michael Irvin
Drew Henson
Julius Jones/26
PP10 J.P. Losman 40.00 100.00
Willis McGahee
James Lofton
Lee Evans/39
PP11 Dan Marino 175.00 300.00
Bob Griese
Larry Csonka
Ricky Williams/28
PP13 Deuce McAllister 25.00 60.00
T.J. Duckett
Eddie George
Domanick Davis/50
PP17 Bart Starr 200.00 400.00
Sammy Baugh
Archie Manning
Troy Aikman
Randall Cunningham
Drew Bledsoe/33
PP18 John Riggins 50.00 100.00
Steven Jackson
Ickey Woods
Quentin Griffin
Tatum Bell
Onterrio Smith/49
PP20 Deacon Jones 125.00 200.00
Deion Sanders
Ed Reed
Julius Peppers
Adam Vinatieri
Dan Morgan/33
PP21 Reggie Williams 40.00 100.00
Steve Smith
Jimmy Smith
Reggie Wayne
Kelley Washington
Brandon Lloyd/50
PP22 Edgerrin James 30.00 80.00
Corey Dillon
Travis Henry
Julius Jones
Brian Westbrook
Michael Bennett/20
PP23 Deion Branch 30.00 80.00
Peter Warrick
Bethel Johnson
Keary Colbert
Rod Gardner
Bernard Berrian/41
PP25 Michael Irvin 50.00 120.00
Charles Rogers
Laveranues Coles
Don Maynard
Ashley Lelie
Derrick Mason/24

2004 Playoff Prime Signatures Signature Proofs Bronze

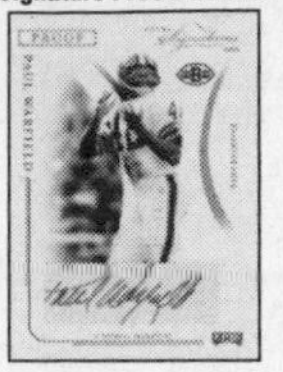

BRONZE STATED PRINT RUN 3-150
BRONZE SER.#'d UNDER 20 NOT PRICED
1 Anquan Boldin/125 10.00 25.00
2 Josh McCown/65 10.00 25.00
3 Alge Crumpler/150 8.00 20.00
4 Michael Vick/85 25.00 50.00
5 Jamal Lewis/31 15.00 40.00
6 Todd Heap/150 8.00 20.00
7 Jim Kelly/44 25.00 50.00
8 Thurman Thomas/46 15.00 40.00
9 Travis Henry/81 8.00 20.00
10 Jake Delhomme/150 8.00 20.00
11 Stephen Davis/125 8.00 20.00
12 Steve Smith/150 10.00 25.00
14 Dick Butkus/51 40.00 80.00
15 Gale Sayers/51 30.00 60.00
16 Mike Ditka/89 20.00 40.00
17 Mike Singletary/110 12.00 30.00
18 Rex Grossman/150 8.00 20.00
19 Richard Dent/50 10.00 25.00
20 Chad Johnson/85 12.00 30.00
21 Rudi Johnson/150 8.00 20.00
22 Jim Brown/150 30.00 60.00
23 Lee Suggs/20 12.00 30.00
24 Ozzie Newsome/82 10.00 25.00
25 Paul Warfield/125 10.00 25.00
26 Quincy Morgan/109 6.00 15.00
27 William Green/87 8.00 20.00
28 Antonio Bryant/59 10.00 25.00
29 Herschel Walker/134 10.00 25.00
30 Jimmy Johnson/45 15.00 40.00
31 Keyshawn Johnson/64 10.00 25.00
32 Roger Staubach/75 40.00 80.00
33 Terence Newman/83 10.00 25.00
34 Tony Dorsett/75 15.00 40.00
35 Terrell Davis/68 12.00 30.00
36 Joey Harrington/83 10.00 25.00
38 Javon Walker/133 6.00 15.00
39 Paul Hornung/99 15.00 40.00
40 Reggie White/92 150.00 250.00
41 Robert Ferguson/112 6.00 15.00
42 Sterling Sharpe/125 8.00 20.00
43 David Carr/65 8.00 20.00
44 Domanick Davis/150 6.00 15.00
45 Earl Campbell/65 15.00 40.00
46 Peyton Manning/75 60.00 100.00
47 Reggie Wayne/87 12.00 30.00
48 Dante Hall/82 10.00 25.00
49 Priest Holmes/57 12.00 30.00
50 Trent Green/89 10.00 25.00
51 A.J. Feeley/94 8.00 20.00
52 Don Shula/40 20.00 50.00
53 Chris Chambers/63 10.00 25.00
55 Fran Tarkenton/86 15.00 40.00
56 Bill Belichick/125 60.00 120.00
57 Tom Brady/86 125.00 250.00
58 Aaron Brooks/99 10.00 25.00
59 Deuce McAllister/125 8.00 20.00
61 Joe Horn/49 10.00 25.00
62 Lawrence Taylor/65 20.00 40.00
64 Michael Strahan/125 10.00 25.00
65 Tiki Barber/139 10.00 25.00
66 Herman Edwards/65 12.00 30.00
67 Joe Namath/99 40.00 80.00
68 Justin McCareins/49 8.00 20.00
69 LaMont Jordan/96 10.00 25.00
70 Santana Moss/81 10.00 25.00
71 Bo Jackson/49 30.00 80.00
72 Fred Biletnikoff/75 12.00 30.00
73 George Blanda/150 20.00 40.00
74 Jim Plunkett/143 10.00 25.00
75 Marcus Allen/150 12.00 30.00
76 Barry Switzer/125 30.00 60.00
78 Donovan McNabb/50 40.00 80.00
79 Antwaan Randle El/82 10.00 25.00
80 Bill Cowher/125 50.00 100.00
81 Franco Harris/60 30.00 50.00
82 Jack Lambert/58 40.00 80.00
83 Joe Greene/75 15.00 40.00
84 Kendrell Bell/150 6.00 15.00
85 L.C. Greenwood/96 12.00 30.00
86 Mel Blount/87 15.00 40.00
87 Terry Bradshaw/94 40.00 80.00
88 LaDainian Tomlinson/68 25.00 60.00
90 Bill Walsh/125 75.00 125.00
91 Shaun Alexander/99 10.00 25.00
92 Steve Largent/150 12.00 30.00
93 Matt Hasselbeck/108 8.00 20.00
94 Torry Holt/69 10.00 25.00
95 Clinton Portis/65 12.00 30.00
96 Laveranues Coles/150 6.00 15.00
97 Mark Brunell/49 12.00 30.00
98 Patrick Ramsey/99 10.00 25.00
99 Reuben Droughns/150 8.00 20.00
100 Sonny Jurgensen/150 10.00 25.00

2004 Playoff Prime Signatures Signature Proofs Gold

*GOLD/21-50: .8X TO 2X BRONZE
GOLD SER.#'d UNDER 20 NOT PRICED
40 Reggie White/25 175.00 300.00
54 Travis Minor/50 12.00 30.00
56 Bill Belichick/45 125.00 200.00
60 Boo Williams/23 15.00 40.00
69 LaMont Jordan/34 20.00 50.00
77 Correll Buckhalter/50 15.00 40.00
89 Andre Carter/21 15.00 40.00
90 Bill Walsh/49 75.00 150.00

2004 Playoff Prime Signatures Signature Proofs Silver

*SILVER: .5X TO 1.2X BRONZE
SILVER SER.#'d UNDER 20 NOT PRICED
40 Reggie White/38 175.00 300.00
54 Travis Minor/100 8.00 20.00
56 Bill Belichick/99 100.00 175.00
57 Tom Brady/55 150.00 300.00
77 Correll Buckhalter/100 10.00 25.00
90 Bill Walsh/83 75.00 125.00

1996 Playoff Trophy Contenders Samples

These "sample" cards were issued before the rest of the product to promote the release of the 1996 Playoff Trophy Contenders set. Each card is nearly identical to the corresponding base set issue except for very slight differences in print style as noted below. There are likely more cards that belong to this listing, therefore any additions are welcomed.

40 Sherman Williams .40 1.00
(Six lines of type on card-back instead of seven)
79 Zack Crockett .40 1.00
(printed in USA does not cross into player photo on cardback)
118 Mark Chmura .40 1.00
(on cardback tight end spelled out instead of abbreviated TE)

1996 Playoff Trophy Contenders

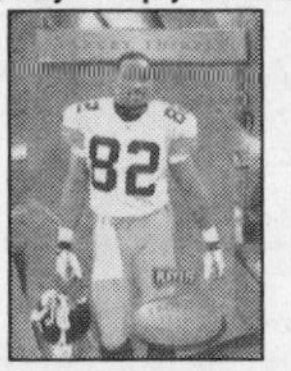

The 1996 Playoff Trophy Contenders set was issued in one series totalling 120 cards. The six-card packs retail for $3.75 each. The only Rookie Card of note in this set is Aaron Hayden.

COMPLETE SET (120) 7.50 20.00
1 Brett Favre .75 2.00
2 Troy Aikman .40 1.00
3 Dan Marino .75 2.00
4 Emmitt Smith .60 1.50
5 Marshall Faulk .20 .50
6 Jeff Blake .15 .40
7 John Elway .75 2.00
8 Steve Young .30 .75
9 Curtis Martin .30 .75
10 Kordell Stewart .15 .40
11 Drew Bledsoe .25 .60
12 Jim Kelly .15 .40
13 Steve Bono .02 .10
14 Neil O'Donnell .07 .20
15 Jeff Hostetler .02 .10
16 Jim Harbaugh .07 .20
17 Jim Everett .02 .10
18 Erric Pegram .02 .10
19 Tyrone Wheatley .07 .20
20 Barry Sanders .60 1.50
21 Deion Sanders .25 .60
22 Harvey Williams .02 .10
23 Garrison Hearst .07 .20
24 Aaron Hayden RC .02 .10
25 Dorsey Levens .15 .40
26 Napoleon Kaufman .15 .40
27 Rodney Hampton .07 .20
28 Scott Mitchell .07 .20
29 Greg Hill .07 .20
30 Charlie Garner .07 .20
31 Rashaan Salaam .07 .20
32 Errict Rhett .07 .20
33 Byron Bam Morris .02 .10
34 Edgar Bennett .07 .20
35 Jeff George .07 .20
36 Rodney Peete .02 .10
37 Stan Humphries .07 .20
38 Kimble Anders .07 .20
39 Natrone Means .07 .20
40 Sherman Williams .02 .10
41 Eric Metcalf .02 .10
42 Chris Warren .07 .20
43 Marcus Allen .15 .40
44 Bill Brooks .02 .10
45 Wayne Chrebet .25 .60
46 Irving Fryar .07 .20
47 Tony Martin .07 .20
48 Daryl Johnston .07 .20
49 O.J. McDuffie .07 .20
50 Frank Sanders .07 .20
51 Ken Norton .02 .10
52 Jake Reed .07 .20
53 Bert Emanuel .07 .20
54 Floyd Turner .02 .10
55 Junior Seau .15 .40
56 Ernie Mills .02 .10
57 Mark Pike .02 .10
58 Warren Moon .07 .20
59 Mike Mamula .02 .10
60 Kerry Collins .15 .40
61 Nate Newton .02 .10
62 Terry Allen .07 .20
63 Bernie Parmalee .02 .10
64 James O.Stewart .07 .20
65 Isaac Bruce .15 .40
66 Lake Dawson .02 .10
67 Terance Mathis .02 .10
68 Chris Sanders .07 .20
69 Anthony Miller .07 .20
70 Jay Novacek .02 .10
71 Sean Dawkins .02 .10
72 J.J. Birden .02 .10
73 Calvin Williams .02 .10
74 Rick Mirer .07 .20
75 Steve McNair .30 .75
76 Lamont Warren .02 .10
77 Rod Woodson .07 .20
78 Larry Brown .02 .10
79 Zack Crockett .02 .10
80 Jerry Rice .40 1.00
81 Tim Brown .15 .40
82 Yancey Thigpen .07 .20
83 J.J. Stokes .15 .40
84 Herman Moore .07 .20
85 Kevin Williams .02 .10
86 Gus Frerotte .07 .20
87 Robert Brooks .15 .40
88 Michael Irvin .15 .40
89 Steve Tasker .02 .10
90 Joey Galloway .15 .40
91 Kevin Greene .07 .20
92 Reggie White .15 .40
93 Cris Carter .15 .40
94 Charles Haley .07 .20
95 Bryce Paup .02 .10
96 Heath Shuler .07 .20
97 Eric Zeier .02 .10
98 Antonio Freeman .15 .40
99 Erik Kramer .02 .10
100 Derek Loville .02 .10
101 Rodney Thomas .02 .10
102 Terrell Davis .30 .75
103 Ricky Watters .07 .20
104 Craig Heyward .02 .10
105 Terry Kirby .07 .20
106 Bruce Smith .07 .20
107 Curtis Conway .15 .40
108 Charles Johnson .02 .10
109 Brett Perriman .02 .10
110 Carl Pickens .07 .20
111 Michael Westbrook .15 .40
112 Brent Jones .02 .10
113 Ken Dilger .07 .20
114 Fred Barnett .02 .10
115 Mark Bruener .02 .10
116 Tamarick Vanover .07 .20
117 Quinn Early .02 .10
118 Mark Chmura .07 .20
119 Andre Hastings .02 .10
120 Craig Newsome .02 .10

1996 Playoff Trophy Contenders Mini Back-To-Backs

COMPLETE SET (60) 200.00 400.00
STATED ODDS 1:17
1 Troy Aikman 7.50 20.00
Neil O'Donnell
2 Kordell Stewart 5.00 12.00
Sherman Williams
3 Deion Sanders 6.00 15.00
Andre Hastings
4 Emmitt Smith 10.00 25.00
Byron Bam Morris
5 Daryl Johnston 2.00 5.00
Erric Pegram
6 Nate Newton 2.00 5.00
Kevin Greene
7 Larry Brown 2.00 5.00
Charles Johnson
8 Jay Novacek 3.00 8.00
Mark Bruener
9 Yancey Thigpen 3.00 8.00
Kevin Williams
10 Michael Irvin 5.00 12.00
Ernie Mills
11 Charles Haley 3.00 8.00
Rod Woodson
12 Brett Favre 15.00 40.00
Steve Young
13 Edgar Bennett 3.00 8.00
Derek Loville
14 Reggie White 5.00 12.00
Ken Norton
15 Jerry Rice 7.50 20.00
Robert Brooks
16 J.J. Stokes 5.00 12.00
Dorsey Levens
17 Mark Chmura 3.00 8.00
Brent Jones
18 Craig Newsome 5.00 12.00
Antonio Freeman
19 Dan Marino 12.50 30.00
Jim Kelly
20 Bernie Parmalee 3.00 8.00
Bruce Smith
21 Irving Fryar 2.00 5.00
Bill Brooks
22 O.J. McDuffie 3.00 8.00
Steve Tasker
23 Terry Kirby 3.00 8.00
Bryce Paup
24 Jim Harbaugh 3.00 8.00
Steve Bono
25 Marshall Faulk 6.00 15.00
Greg Hill
26 Lamont Warren 5.00 12.00
Marcus Allen
27 Floyd Turner 2.00 5.00
Kimble Anders
28 Sean Dawkins 3.00 8.00
Lake Dawson
29 Tamarick Vanover 5.00 12.00
Zack Crockett
30 Scott Mitchell 2.00 5.00
Rodney Peete
31 Barry Sanders 12.50 30.00
Ricky Watters
32 Brett Perriman 3.00 8.00
Calvin Williams
33 Herman Moore 3.00 8.00
Fred Barnett
34 Stan Humphries 3.00 8.00
Jeff George
35 Natrone Means 3.00 8.00
Craig Heyward
36 Aaron Hayden 2.00 5.00
Terance Mathis
37 Junior Seau 5.00 12.00
Bert Emanuel
38 Tony Martin 2.00 5.00
J.J. Birden
39 Jeff Blake 3.00 8.00
Carl Pickens
40 Erik Kramer 3.00 8.00
Curtis Conway
41 Frank Sanders 5.00 12.00
Garrison Hearst
42 John Elway 12.50 30.00
Anthony Miller
43 Steve McNair 6.00 15.00
Chris Sanders
44 Warren Moon 3.00 8.00
Cris Carter
45 Curtis Martin 6.00 15.00
Drew Bledsoe
46 Jim Everett 3.00 8.00
Quinn Early
47 Rodney Hampton 3.00 8.00
Tyrone Wheatley
48 Jeff Hostetler 5.00 12.00
Tim Brown
49 Joey Galloway 5.00 12.00
Rick Mirer
50 Michael Westbrook 3.00 8.00
Gus Frerotte
51 Heath Shuler 3.00 8.00
Terry Allen
52 Charlie Garner 3.00 8.00
Mike Mamula
53 Napoleon Kaufman 3.00 8.00
Harvey Williams
54 Errict Rhett 3.00 8.00
Rashaan Salaam
55 Kerry Collins 5.00 12.00
Mark Pike
56 Ken Dilger 3.00 8.00
Eric Zeier
57 Terrell Davis 6.00 15.00
Chris Warren
58 Isaac Bruce 5.00 12.00
Jake Reed
59 Eric Metcalf 6.00 15.00
Wayne Chrebet
60 James O.Stewart 3.00 8.00
Rodney Thomas

1996 Playoff Trophy Contenders Playoff Zone

COMPLETE SET (36) 100.00 200.00
STATED ODDS 1:24
1 Troy Aikman 5.00 12.00
2 Jeff Blake 2.00 5.00
3 John Elway 10.00 25.00
4 Brett Favre 10.00 25.00
5 Jeff George 1.00 2.50
6 Jim Harbaugh 1.00 2.50
7 Erik Kramer .50 1.25
8 Dan Marino 10.00 25.00
9 Scott Mitchell 1.00 2.50
10 Warren Moon 1.00 2.50
11 Neil O'Donnell 1.00 2.50
12 Steve Young 4.00 10.00
13 Marcus Allen 2.00 5.00
14 Terry Allen 1.00 2.50
15 Edgar Bennett 1.00 2.50
16 Marshall Faulk 2.50 6.00
17 Rodney Hampton 1.00 2.50
18 Craig Heyward .50 1.25
19 Errict Rhett 1.00 2.50
20 Barry Sanders 8.00 20.00
21 Emmitt Smith 8.00 20.00
22 Chris Warren 1.00 2.50
23 Ricky Watters 1.00 2.50
24 Harvey Williams .50 1.25
25 Robert Brooks 2.00 5.00
26 Isaac Bruce 2.00 5.00
27 Cris Carter 2.00 5.00
28 Curtis Conway 2.00 5.00
29 Michael Irvin 2.00 5.00
30 Anthony Miller 1.00 2.50
31 Herman Moore 1.00 2.50
32 Brett Perriman .50 1.25
33 Carl Pickens 1.00 2.50
34 Jerry Rice 5.00 12.00
35 Deion Sanders 3.00 8.00
36 Yancey Thigpen 1.00 2.50

1996 Playoff Trophy Contenders Rookie Stallions

COMPLETE SET (20) 40.00 100.00
STATED ODDS 1:24
1 Mark Bruener .50 1.25
2 Wayne Chrebet 3.00 8.00
3 Kerry Collins 2.00 5.00
4 Zack Crockett .50 1.25
5 Terrell Davis 4.00 10.00
6 Antonio Freeman 2.00 5.00
7 Joey Galloway 2.00 5.00
8 Napoleon Kaufman 2.00 5.00
9 Curtis Martin 4.00 10.00
10 Steve McNair 4.00 10.00
11 Rashaan Salaam 1.00 2.50
12 Chris Sanders 1.00 2.50
13 Frank Sanders 1.00 2.50
14 Kordell Stewart 2.00 5.00
15 J.J. Stokes 2.00 5.00
16 Rodney Thomas .50 1.25
17 Tamarick Vanover 1.00 2.50
18 Michael Westbrook 2.00 5.00
19 Tyrone Wheatley 1.00 2.50
20 Eric Zeier .50 1.25

1997 Playoff Zone

The 1997 Playoff Zone set was issued in one series totalling 150 cards and was distributed in five-card packs with a suggested retail price of $2.99. The fronts feature color action player photos printed on 24 pt. Tekchrome card stock. The backs carry player information and complete career stats. Gold foil parallel cards of the base set as well as every insert set were produced and numbered of 5-sets made.

COMPLETE SET (150) 10.00 25.00
1 Brett Favre .75 2.00
2 Dorsey Levens .20 .50
3 William Henderson .10 .30
4 Derrick Mayes .10 .30
5 Antonio Freeman .20 .50
6 Robert Brooks .10 .30
7 Mark Chmura .10 .30
8 Reggie White .20 .50
9 Randall Cunningham .20 .50
10 Brad Johnson .20 .50
11 Robert Smith .10 .30
12 Cris Carter .20 .50
13 Jake Reed .10 .30
14 Trent Dilfer .20 .50
15 Errict Rhett .07 .20
16 Mike Alstott .20 .50
17 Scott Mitchell .10 .30
18 Barry Sanders .60 1.50
19 Herman Moore .10 .30
20 Erik Kramer .07 .20
21 Rick Mirer .07 .20
22 Rashaan Salaam .07 .20
23 Troy Aikman .40 1.00
24 Deion Sanders .20 .50
25 Emmitt Smith .60 1.50
26 Daryl Johnston .10 .30
27 Anthony Miller .07 .20
28 Eric Bjornson .07 .20
29 Michael Irvin .20 .50
30 Chris T. Jones .07 .20
31 Ty Detmer .10 .30
32 Ricky Watters .10 .30
33 Irving Fryar .10 .30
34 Rodney Peete .07 .20
35 Jeff Hostetler .07 .20
36 Terry Allen .20 .50
37 Michael Westbrook .10 .30
38 Gus Frerotte .07 .20
39 Frank Sanders .10 .30
40 Larry Centers .10 .30
41 Kent Graham .07 .20
42 Dave Brown .07 .20
43 Rodney Hampton .10 .30
44 Tyrone Wheatley .10 .30
45 Chris Calloway .07 .20
46 Ernie Mills .07 .20
47 Tim Biakabutuka .10 .30
48 Anthony Johnson .07 .20
49 Wesley Walls .10 .30
50 Muhsin Muhammad .10 .30
51 Kerry Collins .20 .50
52 Terrell Owens .25 .60
53 Garrison Hearst .10 .30
54 Jerry Rice .40 1.00
55 Steve Young .25 .60
56 Lawrence Phillips .07 .20
57 Isaac Bruce .20 .50
58 Eddie Kennison .10 .30
59 Tony Banks .10 .30
60 Heath Shuler .07 .20
61 Andre Hastings .07 .20
62 Mario Bates .07 .20
63 Chris Chandler .10 .30
64 Jamal Anderson .20 .50
65 Bert Emanuel .10 .30
66 Drew Bledsoe .25 .60
67 Curtis Martin .25 .60
68 Ben Coates .10 .30
69 Terry Glenn .20 .50
70 Dan Marino .75 2.00
71 Karim Abdul-Jabbar .20 .50
72 Fred Barnett .07 .20
73 O.J. McDuffie .10 .30
74 Jim Harbaugh .10 .30
75 Marshall Faulk .25 .60
76 Zack Crockett .07 .20
77 Ken Dilger .07 .20
78 Marvin Harrison .20 .50
79 Keyshawn Johnson .20 .50
80 Neil O'Donnell .10 .30
81 Adrian Murrell .10 .30
82 Wayne Chrebet .20 .50
83 Todd Collins .07 .20
84 Thurman Thomas .20 .50
85 Bruce Smith .10 .30
86 Eric Moulds .20 .50
87 Rob Johnson .20 .50
88 Mark Brunell .25 .60
89 Natrone Means .10 .30
90 Jimmy Smith .10 .30
91 Keenan McCardell .10 .30
92 Kordell Stewart .20 .50
93 Jerome Bettis .20 .50
94 Charles Johnson .10 .30
95 Courtney Hawkins .07 .20
96 Greg Lloyd .07 .20
97 Ki-Jana Carter .07 .20
98 Carl Pickens .10 .30
99 Jeff Blake .10 .30
100 Steve McNair .25 .60
101 Chris Sanders .07 .20
102 Eddie George .20 .50
103 Vinny Testaverde .10 .30
104 Michael Jackson .10 .30
105 Derrick Alexander WR .10 .30
106 Willie Green .07 .20
107 Shannon Sharpe .10 .30
108 Rod Smith WR .20 .50
109 Terrell Davis .25 .60
110 John Elway .75 2.00
111 Elvis Grbac .10 .30
112 Greg Hill .07 .20
113 Marcus Allen .20 .50
114 Derrick Thomas .20 .50
115 Brett Perriman .07 .20
116 Andre Rison .10 .30
117 Rickey Dudley .10 .30
118 Tim Brown .20 .50
119 Desmond Howard .10 .30
120 Napoleon Kaufman .20 .50
121 Jeff George .10 .30
122 Warren Moon .20 .50
123 John Friesz .07 .20
124 Chris Warren .10 .30
125 Joey Galloway .10 .30
126 Stan Humphries .10 .30
127 Tony Martin .10 .30
128 Eric Metcalf .10 .30
129 Jim Everett .07 .20
130 Warrick Dunn RC .60 1.50
131 Reidel Anthony RC .20 .50
132 Derrick Mason RC .40 1.00
133 Joey Kent RC .20 .50
134 Will Blackwell RC UER .10 .30
(wrong college listed on back)
135 Jim Druckenmiller RC UER .10 .30
(wrong college listed on back)
136 Byron Hanspard RC .10 .30
137 John Allred RC .07 .20
138 David LaFleur RC .07 .20
139 Danny Wuerffel RC .20 .50
140 Tiki Barber RC 1.25 3.00
141 Ike Hilliard RC UER .30 .75
(Name mispelled Hillard on back; stats are incorrect on back)
142 Troy Davis RC .10 .30
143 Leon Johnson RC .10 .30
144 Tony Gonzalez RC .75 2.00
145 Jake Plummer RC .75 2.00
146 Antowain Smith RC .50 1.25
147 Rae Carruth RC .07 .20
148 Darnell Autry RC .10 .30
149 Corey Dillon RC .75 2.00
150 Orlando Pace RC .20 .50

1997 Playoff Zone Close-Ups

COMPLETE SET (32) 50.00 100.00
STATED ODDS 1:6
1 Brett Favre 4.00 10.00
2 Mark Brunell 1.25 3.00
3 Dan Marino 4.00 10.00
4 Kerry Collins 1.00 2.50
5 Troy Aikman 2.00 5.00
6 Drew Bledsoe 1.25 3.00
7 John Elway 4.00 10.00
8 Kordell Stewart 1.00 2.50
9 Steve Young 1.25 3.00
10 Steve McNair 1.25 3.00
11 Tony Banks .60 1.50
12 Emmitt Smith 3.00 8.00
13 Barry Sanders 3.00 8.00
14 Jerry Rice 2.00 5.00
15 Deion Sanders 1.00 2.50
16 Terrell Davis 1.25 3.00
17 Curtis Martin 1.25 3.00
18 Karim Abdul-Jabbar 1.00 2.50
19 Terry Glenn 1.00 2.50
20 Eddie George 1.00 2.50
21 Keyshawn Johnson 1.00 2.50
22 Marvin Harrison 1.00 2.50
23 Muhsin Muhammad .60 1.50
24 Joey Galloway .60 1.50
25 Terrell Owens 1.25 3.00
26 Antonio Freeman 1.00 2.50
27 Ricky Watters .60 1.50
28 Jeff Blake .60 1.50
29 Reggie White 1.00 2.50
30 Michael Irvin 1.00 2.50
31 Eddie Kennison .60 1.50
32 Robert Brooks .60 1.50

1997 Playoff Zone Frenzy

COMPLETE SET (26) 75.00 150.00
STATED ODDS 1:12
1 Brett Favre 8.00 20.00
2 Dan Marino 8.00 20.00
3 Troy Aikman 4.00 10.00
4 Drew Bledsoe 2.50 6.00
5 John Elway 8.00 20.00
6 Kordell Stewart 2.00 5.00
7 Steve Young 2.50 6.00
8 Steve McNair 2.50 6.00
9 Tony Banks 1.25 3.00
10 Emmitt Smith 6.00 15.00
11 Barry Sanders 6.00 15.00
12 Deion Sanders 2.00 5.00
13 Terrell Davis 2.50 6.00
14 Curtis Martin 2.50 6.00
15 Karim Abdul-Jabbar 2.00 5.00
16 Terry Glenn 2.00 5.00
17 Eddie George 2.00 5.00
18 Keyshawn Johnson 2.00 5.00
19 Marvin Harrison 2.00 5.00
20 Joey Galloway 1.25 3.00
21 Antonio Freeman 2.00 5.00
22 Jeff Blake 1.25 3.00
23 Michael Irvin 2.00 5.00
24 Eddie Kennison 1.25 3.00
25 Reggie White 2.00 5.00
26 Robert Brooks 1.25 3.00

1997 Playoff Zone Prime Target

COMPLETE SET (20) 60.00 120.00
STATED ODDS 1:24
*RED: .8X TO 2X BASIC INSERTS
RED STATED ODDS 1:96
*PURPLE: .4X TO 1X BASIC INSERTS
PURPLES INSERTED IN SPECIAL RETAIL
1 Emmitt Smith 10.00 25.00
2 Barry Sanders 10.00 25.00
3 Jerry Rice 6.00 15.00
4 Terrell Davis 4.00 10.00
5 Curtis Martin 4.00 10.00
6 Karim Abdul-Jabbar 3.00 8.00
7 Terry Glenn 3.00 8.00
8 Eddie George 3.00 8.00
9 Keyshawn Johnson 3.00 8.00
10 Joey Galloway 2.00 5.00
11 Antonio Freeman 3.00 8.00
12 Herman Moore 2.00 5.00
13 Tim Brown 3.00 8.00
14 Michael Irvin 3.00 8.00
15 Isaac Bruce 3.00 8.00
16 Eddie Kennison 2.00 5.00
17 Shannon Sharpe 2.00 5.00
18 Cris Carter 3.00 8.00
19 Napoleon Kaufman 3.00 8.00
20 Carl Pickens 2.00 5.00

1997 Playoff Zone Rookies

COMPLETE SET (24) 15.00 40.00
STATED ODDS 1:8
1 Jake Plummer 2.50 6.00
2 George Jones .25 .60
3 Pat Barnes .40 1.00
4 Brian Manning .25 .60
5 O.J. Santiago .40 1.00
6 Byron Hanspard .40 1.00
7 Antowain Smith 1.50 4.00
8 Rae Carruth .25 .60
9 Darnell Autry .40 1.00
10 Corey Dillon 2.50 6.00
11 David LaFleur .25 .60
12 Tony Gonzalez 2.50 6.00
13 Leon Johnson .40 1.00
14 Danny Wuerffel .60 1.50
15 Troy Davis .40 1.00
16 Jay Graham .25 .60
17 Tiki Barber 4.00 10.00
18 Will Blackwell .40 1.00
19 Jim Druckenmiller .40 1.00
20 Orlando Pace .60 1.50
21 Warrick Dunn 2.00 5.00
22 Reidel Anthony .60 1.50
23 Derrick Mason 1.25 3.00
24 Joey Kent .60 1.50

1997 Playoff Zone Sharpshooters

COMPLETE SET (18) 60.00 150.00
STATED ODDS 1:24
*REDS: .6X TO 1.5X BASIC INSERTS
RED STATED ODDS 1:72
1 Brett Favre 8.00 20.00
2 Dan Marino 8.00 20.00
3 John Elway 8.00 20.00
4 Troy Aikman 4.00 10.00
5 Drew Bledsoe 2.50 6.00
6 Todd Collins .75 2.00
7 Brad Johnson 2.00 5.00
8 Stan Humphries 1.25 3.00
9 John Friesz .75 2.00
10 Tony Banks 1.25 3.00
11 Ty Detmer 1.25 3.00
12 Steve McNair 2.50 6.00
13 Rob Johnson 2.00 5.00
14 Kordell Stewart 2.00 5.00
15 Danny Wuerffel 2.00 5.00
16 Jim Druckenmiller 1.25 3.00
17 Jake Plummer 10.00 25.00
18 Kerry Collins 2.00 5.00

1997 Playoff Zone Treasures

COMPLETE SET (12) 75.00 200.00
STATED ODDS 1:196
1 Brett Favre 15.00 40.00
2 Dan Marino 15.00 40.00
3 Troy Aikman 8.00 20.00
4 Drew Bledsoe 5.00 12.00
5 Emmitt Smith 12.50 30.00
6 Barry Sanders 12.50 30.00
7 Warrick Dunn 6.00 15.00
8 Deion Sanders 4.00 10.00
9 Terrell Davis 5.00 12.00
10 Curtis Martin 5.00 12.00
11 Tiki Barber 12.50 30.00
12 Eddie George 4.00 10.00

1985 Police Raiders/Rams

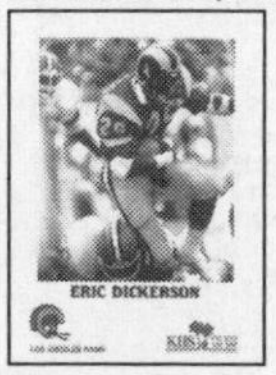

This 30-card set is actually two subsets, 15 cards featuring Los Angeles Rams and 15 cards featuring Los Angeles Raiders. The set was actually sponsored by the Sheriff's Department of Los Angeles County, KIIS Radio, and the Rams/Raiders, so technically it is a safety set but not a "police" set. The cards are unnumbered except for the uniform number listed on the card back. The list below is organized alphabetically within each team. Card backs are printed in black ink on white card stock. Cards measure approximately 2 13/16" by 4 1/8".

COMPLETE SET (30) 10.00 25.00
1 Marcus Allen 3.00 8.00
2 Lyle Alzado .50 1.25
3 Todd Christensen .50 1.25
4 Dave Dalby .40 1.00
5 Mike Davis .40 1.00
6 Ray Guy .50 1.25
7 Frank Hawkins .40 1.00
8 Lester Hayes .50 1.25
9 Mike Haynes .50 1.25
10 Howie Long .75 2.00
11 Rod Martin .40 1.00

12 Mickey Marvin	.40	1.00
13 Jim Plunkett	.50	1.25
14 Brad Van Pelt	.40	1.00
15 Dokie Williams	.40	1.00
16 Bill Bain	.30	.75
17 Mike Barber	.30	.75
18 Dieter Brock	.40	1.00
19 Nolan Cromwell	.40	1.00
20 Eric Dickerson	.75	2.00
21 Reggie Doss	.30	.75
22 Carl Ekern	.30	.75
23 Kent Hill	.30	.75
24 LeRoy Irvin	.40	1.00
25 Johnnie Johnson	.30	.75
26 Jeff Kemp	.40	1.00
27 Mike Lansford	.30	.75
28 Mel Owens	.30	.75
29 Barry Redden	.30	.75
30 Mike Wilcher	.30	.75

1986 Police Bears/Patriots

This set was supposedly not an authorized police issue as it is unclear which police department(s) truly sponsored the set. The 17 cards feature members of the Chicago Bears and New England Patriots who were in the Super Bowl in early 1986. The cards measure approximately 2 5/8" by 4 1/4". The card fronts give the player's name and uniform number under his red/blue bordered color photo. The card backs are printed in black ink on white card stock. Cards are numbered on the back in the lower right corner: the Bears (2-9) and the Patriots (10-17).

COMPLETE SET (17)	.75	2.00
1 Title Card (Checklist on back of card)	.02	.10
2 Richard Dent	.10	.30
3 Walter Payton	.40	1.00
4 William Perry	.07	.20
5 Jim McMahon	.07	.20
6 Dave Duerson	.02	.10
7 Gary Fencik	.02	.10
8 Otis Wilson	.02	.10
9 Willie Gault	.02	.10
10 Craig James	.07	.20
11 Fred Marion	.02	.10
12 Ronnie Lippett	.02	.10
13 Stanley Morgan	.07	.20
14 John Hannah	.07	.20
15 Andre Tippett	.02	.10
16 Tony Franklin	.02	.10
17 Tony Eason	.02	.10

1976 Popsicle Teams

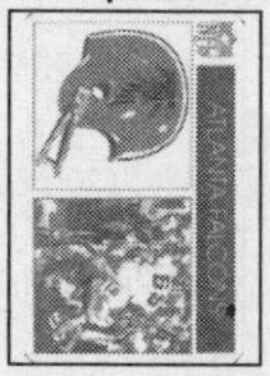

This set of 28 teams is printed on plastic material similar to that found on thin credit cards. There is a variation on the New York Giants card; one version shows the helmet logo as Giants and the other shows it as New York. The title card appears to be short-printed and reads, "Pro Quarterback, Pro Football's Leading Magazine". The cards measure approximately 3 3/8" by 2 1/8", have rounded corners, and are slightly thinner than a credit card. Below the NFL logo and the team, the front features a color helmet shot and a color action photo. We've noted below prominent players that can be identified in the photos. The backs contais a brief team history. Some consider the new expansion teams, Tampa Bay and Seattle, to be somewhat tougher to find. The cards are unnumbered and are ordered below alphabetically by team location name. The set is considered complete with just the 28 team cards.

COMPLETE SET (28)	40.00	80.00
1 Atlanta Falcons	1.50	3.00
2 Baltimore Colts	1.50	3.00
3 Buffalo Bills	1.50	3.00
4 Chicago Bears	1.50	3.00
5 Cincinnati Bengals	1.50	3.00
6 Cleveland Browns	1.50	3.00
7 Dallas Cowboys (Bob Lilly, Lee Roy Jordan)	2.00	4.00
8 Denver Broncos	1.50	3.00
9 Detroit Lions	1.50	3.00
10 Green Bay Packers	1.50	3.00
11 Houston Oilers	1.50	3.00
12 Kansas City Chiefs	1.50	3.00
13 Los Angeles Rams	1.50	3.00
14 Miami Dolphins (Bob Griese)	2.00	4.00
15 Minnesota Vikings	1.50	3.00
16 New England Patriots	1.50	3.00
17 New Orleans Saints (Archie Manning)	1.50	3.00
18A New York Giants (Giants on helmet)	1.50	3.00
18B New York Giants (New York on helmet)	1.50	3.00
19 New York Jets	1.50	3.00
20 Oakland Raiders (Ken Stabler)	2.00	4.00
21 Philadelphia Eagles	1.50	3.00
22 Pittsburgh Steelers (Franco Harris)	2.00	4.00
23 St. Louis Cardinals	1.50	3.00
24 San Diego Chargers	1.50	3.00
25 San Francisco 49ers	2.00	4.00
26 Seattle Seahawks	1.50	3.00
27 Tampa Bay Buccaneers	1.50	3.00
28 Washington Redskins	2.00	4.00
NNO Title Card SP Pro Quarterback, Pro Football's Leading Magazine	15.00	30.00

1974 Portland Storm WFL Team Issue 5X7

The photos measure roughly 5" x 7 1/2" and feature black and white images with the player's name in the lower left below the photo, his position (initials) centered, and the team name on the right side below the photo. The backs are blank.

1 Dick Coury CO	6.00	12.00
2 Marv Kendricks	6.00	12.00
3 Mike Taylor	6.00	12.00
4 Tony Terry	6.00	12.00

1960 Post Cereal

These large cards measure approximately 7" by 8 3/4". The 1960 Post Cereal Sports Stars set contains nine cards depicting current baseball, football and basketball players. Each card comprised the entire back of a Grape Nuts Flakes Box and is blank backed. The color player photos are set on a colored background surrounded by a wooden frame design, and they are unnumbered (assigned numbers below for reference according to sport). The catalog designation is F278-26.

COMPLETE SET (9)	3,000.00	5,000.00
FB1 Frank Gifford (football)	200.00	400.00
FB2 John Unitas (football)	350.00	600.00

1962 Post Cereal

The 1962 Post Cereal set of 200 cards is Post's only American football issue. The cards were distributed on the back panels of various flavors of Post Cereals. As is typical of the Post package-back issues, the cards are blank-backed and are typically found poorly cut from the cereal box. The cards (when properly trimmed) measure 2 1/2" by 3 1/2". The cards are grouped in order of the team's 1961 season finish. The players within each team are also grouped in alphabetical order with the exception of 135 Frank Clarke of the Cowboys. Certain cards printed only on unpopular types of cereal are relatively difficult to obtain. Thirty-one such cards are known and are indicated by an SP (short printed) in the checklist. Some players who had been traded had asterisks after their positions. Jim Ninowski (57) and Sam Baker (74) can be found with either a red or black (traded) asterisk. The set price below does not include both variations. The cards of Jim Johnson, Bob Lilly, and Larry Wilson predate their Rookie Cards. Also noteworthy is the card of Fran Tarkenton, whose rookie year for cards is 1962.

COMPLETE SET (200)	2,700.00	4,500.00
1 Dan Currie	3.50	7.00
2 Boyd Dowler	3.50	7.00
3 Bill Forester	2.50	5.00
4 Forrest Gregg	4.00	8.00
5 Dave Hanner	2.50	5.00
6 Paul Hornung	10.00	20.00
7 Hank Jordan	4.00	8.00
8 Jerry Kramer SP	25.00	40.00
9 Max McGee SP	15.00	25.00
10 Tom Moore SP	125.00	200.00
11 Jim Ringo	4.00	8.00
12 Bart Starr	15.00	25.00
13 Jim Taylor	7.50	15.00
14 Fuzzy Thurston	3.50	7.00
15 Jesse Whittenton	2.00	4.00
16 Erich Barnes	2.50	5.00
17 Roosevelt Brown	3.50	7.00
18 Bob Gaiters	2.00	4.00
19 Roosevelt Grier	3.50	7.00
20 Sam Huff	5.00	10.00
21 Jim Katcavage	2.50	5.00
22 Cliff Livingston	2.00	4.00
23 Dick Lynch	2.00	4.00
24 Joe Morrison SP	35.00	60.00
25 Dick Nolan SP	30.00	50.00
26 Andy Robustelli	4.00	8.00
27 Kyle Rote	3.50	7.00
28 Del Shofner SP	60.00	100.00
29 Y.A. Tittle SP (Only player in set shown with helmet on)	75.00	125.00
30 Alex Webster	2.50	5.00
31 Bill Barnes	2.00	4.00
32 Maxie Baughan	2.50	5.00
33 Chuck Bednarik	5.00	10.00
34 Tom Brookshier	3.50	7.00
35 Jimmy Carr	2.00	4.00
36 Ted Dean SP	30.00	50.00
37 Sonny Jurgensen	7.50	15.00
38 Tommy McDonald	3.50	7.00
39 Clarence Peaks	2.00	4.00
40 Pete Retzlaff	2.50	5.00
41 Jesse Richardson SP	50.00	100.00
42 Leo Sugar	2.00	4.00
43 Bobby Walston SP	35.00	70.00
44 Chuck Weber	5.00	10.00
45 Ed Khayat	2.00	4.00
46 Howard Cassady	2.50	5.00
47 Gail Cogdill	2.00	4.00
48 Jim Gibbons SP	25.00	50.00
49 Bill Glass	2.00	4.00
50 Alex Karras	5.00	10.00
51 Dick Lane	3.50	7.00
52 Yale Lary	3.50	7.00
53 Dan Lewis	2.00	4.00
54 Darris McCord SP	40.00	80.00
55 Jim Martin	2.00	4.00
56 Earl Morrall	2.50	5.00
57A Jim Ninowski (red asterisk)	2.50	5.00
57B Jim Ninowski (black asterisk)	2.50	5.00
58 Nick Pietrosante	2.50	5.00
59 Joe Schmidt SP	60.00	100.00
60 Harley Sewell	2.00	4.00
61 Jim Brown	40.00	75.00
62 Galen Fiss SP	35.00	60.00
63 Bob Gain	2.00	4.00
64 Jim Houston	2.00	4.00
65 Mike McCormack	3.50	7.00
66 Gene Hickerson	5.00	10.00
67 Bobby Mitchell	4.00	8.00
68 John Morrow	2.00	4.00
69 Bernie Parrish	2.00	4.00
70 Milt Plum	2.50	5.00
71 Ray Renfro	2.50	5.00
72 Dick Schafrath	2.50	5.00
73 Jim Ray Smith	2.00	4.00
74A Sam Baker SP (red asterisk)	200.00	350.00
74B Sam Baker SP (black asterisk)	175.00	300.00
75 Paul Wiggin SP	15.00	30.00
76 Raymond Berry	5.00	10.00
77 Bob Boyd	2.00	4.00
78 Ordell Braase	2.00	4.00
79 Art Donovan	5.00	10.00
80 Dee Mackey	2.00	4.00
81 Gino Marchetti	4.00	8.00
82 Lenny Moore	5.00	10.00
83 Jim Mutscheller	2.00	4.00
84 Steve Myhra	2.00	4.00
85 Jimmy Orr	2.50	5.00
86 Jim Parker	4.00	8.00
87 Bill Pellington	2.00	4.00
88 Alex Sandusky	2.00	4.00
89 Dick Szymanski	2.00	4.00
90 Johnny Unitas	15.00	30.00
91 Bruce Bosley	2.00	4.00
92 John Brodie	6.00	12.00
93 Dave Baker SP	250.00	400.00
94 Tommy Davis	2.00	4.00
95 Bob Harrison	2.00	4.00
96 Matt Hazeltine	2.00	4.00
97 Jim Johnson SP	35.00	70.00
98 Billy Kilmer	3.50	7.00
99 Jerry Mertens	2.00	4.00
100 Frank Morze	2.00	4.00
101 R.C. Owens	2.50	5.00
102 J.D. Smith	2.00	4.00
103 Bob St. Clair SP	45.00	80.00
104 Monty Stickles	2.00	4.00
105 Abe Woodson	2.00	4.00
106 Doug Atkins	4.00	8.00
107 Ed Brown	2.50	5.00
108 J.C. Caroline	2.00	4.00
109 Rick Casares	2.50	5.00
110 Angelo Coia SP	150.00	250.00
111 Mike Ditka SP	75.00	125.00
112 Joe Fortunato	2.00	4.00
113 Willie Galimore	2.50	5.00
114 Bill George	3.50	7.00
115 Stan Jones	3.50	7.00
116 Johnny Morris	2.50	5.00
117 Larry Morris SP	35.00	60.00
118 Richie Petitbon	2.50	5.00
119 Bill Wade	2.50	5.00
120 Maury Youmans	2.00	4.00
121 Preston Carpenter	2.00	4.00
122 Buddy Dial	2.50	5.00
123 Bobby Joe Green	2.00	4.00
124 Mike Henry	2.00	4.00
125 John Henry Johnson	4.00	8.00
126 Bobby Layne	10.00	20.00
127 Gene Lipscomb	3.50	7.00
128 Lou Michaels	2.50	5.00
129 John Nisby	2.00	4.00
130 John Reger	2.00	4.00
131 Mike Sandusky	2.00	4.00
132 George Tarasovic	2.00	4.00
133 Tom Tracy SP	70.00	110.00
134 Glynn Gregory	2.00	4.00
135 Frank Clarke SP	45.00	80.00
136 Mike Connelly SP	35.00	70.00
137 L.G. Dupre	2.00	4.00
138 Bob Fry	2.00	4.00
139 Allen Green SP	75.00	125.00
140 Billy Howton	2.50	5.00
141 Bob Lilly	25.00	40.00
142 Don Meredith	20.00	35.00
143 Dick Moegle	2.00	4.00
144 Don Perkins	3.50	7.00
145 Jerry Tubbs SP	75.00	125.00
146 J.W. Lockett	2.00	4.00
147 Ed Cook	2.00	4.00
148 John David Crow	2.50	5.00
149 Sam Etcheverry	2.00	4.00
150 Frank Fuller	2.00	4.00
151 Prentice Gautt	2.00	4.00
152 Jimmy Hill	2.00	4.00
153 Bill Koman SP	30.00	50.00
154 Larry Wilson	7.50	15.00
155 Dale Meinert	2.00	4.00
156 Ed Henke	2.00	4.00
157 Sonny Randle	2.00	4.00
158 Ralph Guglielmi SP	30.00	50.00
159 Joe Childress	2.00	4.00
160 Jon Arnett	2.50	5.00
161 Dick Bass	2.00	4.00
162 Zeke Bratkowski	2.50	5.00
163 Carroll Dale SP	25.00	40.00
164 Art Hunter	2.00	4.00
165 John Lovetere	2.00	4.00
166 Lamar Lundy	2.50	5.00
167 Ollie Matson	5.00	10.00
168 Ed Meador	2.00	4.00
169 Jack Pardee SP	45.00	80.00
170 Jim Phillips	2.00	4.00
171 Les Richter	2.50	5.00
172 Frank Ryan	2.50	5.00
173 Frank Varrichione	2.00	4.00
174 Grady Alderman	2.50	5.00
175 Rip Hawkins	2.00	4.00
176 Don Joyce SP	75.00	125.00
177 Bill Lapham	2.00	4.00
178 Tommy Mason	2.50	5.00
179 Hugh McElhenny	5.00	10.00
180 Dave Middleton	2.00	4.00
181 Dick Pesonen SP	20.00	35.00
182 Karl Rubke	2.00	4.00
183 George Shaw	2.00	4.00
184 Fran Tarkenton	30.00	50.00
185 Mel Triplett	2.00	4.00
186 Frank Youso SP	60.00	100.00
187 Bill Bishop	2.50	5.00
188 Bill Anderson SP	40.00	75.00
189 Don Bosseler	2.00	4.00
190 Fred Hageman	2.00	4.00
191 Sam Horner	2.00	4.00
192 Jim Kerr	2.00	4.00
193 Joe Krakoski SP	150.00	250.00
194 Fred Dugan	2.00	4.00
195 John Paluck	2.00	4.00
196 Vince Promuto	2.00	4.00
197 Joe Rutgens	2.00	4.00
198 Norm Snead	3.50	7.00
199 Andy Stynchula	2.00	4.00
200 Bob Toneff	2.00	4.00

1962 Post Booklets

Each of these booklets measures approximately 5" by 3" and contained fifteen pages. The front cover carries the title of each booklet and a color cartoon headshot of the player inside a circle. While the first page presents biography and career summary, the remainder of each booklet consists of various tips, diagrams of basic formations and plays, officials' signals, football lingo, statistics, or team standings. The booklets are illustrated throughout by crude color drawings. These booklets are numbered on the front page in the upper right corner.

COMPLETE SET (4)	75.00	150.00
1 Jon Arnett Football Formations To Watch (Important Rules of the Game)	15.00	30.00
2 Paul Hornung Fundamentals of Football	25.00	50.00
3 Sonny Jurgensen How To Play On Offense (How To Call Signals And Key Plays)	20.00	40.00
4 Sam Huff How To Play Defense	20.00	40.00

2002 Post Cereal

These cards were issued in specially marked boxes of Post Brand cereals in 2002. Each measures 2 5/8" by 3 3/4" and was produced with lenticular (magic motion) technology and rounded corners. Two players per card are included and the helmet logos have been removed since the cards were only licensed through Players Inc.

1 Mark Clayton Dan Marino	3.00	8.00
2 Joe Montana Jerry Rice	3.00	8.00
4 Johnny Unitas Raymond Berry	2.50	6.00

1977 Pottsville Maroons 1925

Reportedly issued in 1977, this standard-size 17-card set features helmetless player photos of the disputed 1925 NFL champion Pottsville Maroons on the card fronts. The pictures are white-bordered and red-screened, with the player's name, card number, and team name in red beneath each photo. The player's name, team, and card number appear again at the top of the card back, along with the name of the college (if any) attended previous to playing for the Maroons and brief biographical information, all in red. The set producer's name, Joseph C. Zacko Sr., appears at the bottom, along with the copyright date, 1977.

COMPLETE SET (17)	10.00	20.00
1 Team History	.75	2.00
2 The Symbolic Shoe	.75	1.50
3 Jack Ernst	.75	2.00
4 Tony Latone	.75	1.50
5 Duke Osborn	.75	1.50
6 Frank Bucher	.75	1.50
7 Frankie Racis	.75	1.50
8 Russ Hathaway	.75	1.50
9 W.H.(Hoot) Flanagan	.75	1.50
10 Charlie Berry	1.00	2.00
11 Russ Stein Herb Stein	.75	1.50
12 Howard Lebengood	.75	1.50
13 Denny Hughes	.75	1.50
14 Barney Wentz	.75	1.50
15 Eddie Doyle UER (Bio says American troops landed in Africa/1943; should be 1942)	.75	1.50
16 Walter French	.75	1.50
17 Dick Rauch	.75	2.00

1992 Power

The 1992 Power set produced by Pro Set consists of 330 standard-size cards that were issued in 12-card packs. Rookie Cards include Edgar Bennett, Steve Bono, Quentin Coryatt, Steve Emtman, Amp Lee, Johnny Mitchell, Carl Pickens and Tommy Vardell.

COMPLETE SET (330)	5.00	12.00
1 Warren Moon	.08	.25
2 Mike Horan	.01	.05
3 Bobby Hebert	.01	.05
4 Jim Harbaugh	.08	.25
5 Sean Landeta	.01	.05
6 Bubby Brister	.02	.10
7 John Elway	.50	1.25
8 Troy Aikman	.30	.75
9 Rodney Peete	.02	.10
10 Dan McGwire	.01	.05
11 Mark Rypien	.01	.05
12 Randall Cunningham	.08	.25
13 Dan Marino	.50	1.25
14 Vinny Testaverde	.02	.10
15 Jeff Hostetler	.02	.10
16 Joe Montana	.50	1.25
17 Dave Krieg	.02	.10
18 Jeff Jaeger	.01	.05
19 Bernie Kosar	.02	.10
20 Barry Sanders	.50	1.25
21 Deion Sanders	.20	.50
22 Emmitt Smith	.60	1.50
23 Mel Gray	.02	.10
24 Stanley Richard	.01	.05
25 Brad Muster	.01	.05
26 Rod Woodson	.08	.25
27 Rodney Hampton	.02	.10
28 Darrell Green	.01	.05
29 Barry Foster	.02	.10
30 Dave Meggett	.02	.10
31 Lonnie Young	.01	.05
32 Marcus Allen	.08	.25
33 Merril Hoge	.01	.05
34 Thurman Thomas	.08	.25
35 Neal Anderson	.01	.05
36 Bennie Blades	.01	.05
37 Pat Terrell	.01	.05
38 Nick Bell	.01	.05
39 Johnny Johnson	.01	.05
40 Bill Bates	.01	.05
41 Keith Byars	.01	.05
42 Ronnie Lott	.02	.10
43 Elvis Patterson	.01	.05
44 Lorenzo White	.01	.05
45 Tony Stargell	.01	.05
46 Tim McDonald	.01	.05
47 Kirby Jackson	.01	.05
48 Lionel Washington	.01	.05
49 Dennis Smith	.01	.05
50 Mike Singletary	.02	.10
51 Mike Croel	.01	.05
52 Pepper Johnson	.01	.05
53 Vaughan Johnson	.01	.05
54 Chris Spielman	.02	.10
55 Junior Seau	.08	.25
56 Lawrence Taylor	.08	.25
57 Clay Matthews	.02	.10
58 Derrick Thomas	.08	.25
59 Seth Joyner	.01	.05
60 Stan Thomas	.01	.05
61 Nate Newton	.01	.05
62 Matt Brock	.01	.05
63 Gene Chilton RC	.01	.05
64 Randall McDaniel	.02	.10
65 Max Montoya	.01	.05
66 Joe Jacoby	.01	.05
67 Russell Maryland	.01	.05
68 Ed King	.01	.05
69 Mark Schlereth RC	.01	.05
70 Charles McRae	.01	.05
71 Charles Mann	.01	.05
72 William Perry	.02	.10
73 Simon Fletcher	.01	.05
74 Paul Gruber	.01	.05
75 Howie Long	.08	.25
76 Steve McMichael	.02	.10
77 Karl Mecklenburg	.01	.05
78 Anthony Munoz	.02	.10
79 Ray Childress	.01	.05
80 Jerry Rice	.30	.75
81 Art Monk	.02	.10
82 John Taylor	.02	.10
83 Andre Reed	.02	.10
84 Haywood Jeffires	.02	.10
85 Mark Duper	.01	.05
86 Fred Barnett	.02	.10
87 Tom Waddle	.01	.05
88 Michael Irvin	.08	.25
89 Brian Blades	.02	.10
90 Neil Smith	.08	.25
91 Kevin Greene	.02	.10
92 Reggie White	.08	.25
93 Jerry Ball	.01	.05
94 Charles Haley	.02	.10
95 Richard Dent	.02	.10
96 Clyde Simmons	.01	.05
97 Cornelius Bennett	.02	.10
98 Eric Swann	.02	.10
99 Doug Smith	.01	.05
100 Jim Kelly	.08	.25
101 Michael Jackson	.02	.10
102 Steve Christie	.01	.05
103 Timm Rosenbach	.01	.05
104 Brett Favre	1.00	2.50
105 Jeff Feagles	.01	.05
106 Kevin Butler	.01	.05
107 Boomer Esiason	.02	.10
108 Steve Young	.25	.60
109 Norm Johnson	.01	.05
110 Jay Schroeder	.01	.05
111 Jeff George	.08	.25
112 Chris Miller	.02	.10
113 Steve Bono RC	.08	.25
114 Neil O'Donnell	.02	.10
115 David Klingler RC	.01	.05
116 Rich Gannon	.08	.25
117 Chris Chandler	.08	.25
118 Stan Gelbaugh	.01	.05
119 Scott Mitchell	.02	.10
120 Mark Carrier DB	.01	.05
121 Terry Allen	.08	.25
122 Tim McKyer	.01	.05
123 Barry Word	.01	.05
124 Freeman McNeil	.02	.10
125 Louis Oliver	.01	.05
126 Jarvis Williams	.01	.05
127 Steve Atwater	.01	.05
128 Cris Dishman	.01	.05
129 Eric Dickerson	.02	.10
130 Brad Baxter	.01	.05
131 Frank Minnifield	.01	.05
132 Ricky Watters	.08	.25
133 David Fulcher	.01	.05
134 Herschel Walker	.02	.10
135 Christian Okoye	.01	.05
136 Jerome Henderson	.01	.05
137 Nate Odomes	.01	.05
138 Todd Scott	.01	.05
139 Robert Delpino	.01	.05
140 Gary Anderson RB	.01	.05
141 Todd Lyght	.01	.05
142 Chris Warren	.02	.10
143 Mike Brim RC	.01	.05
144 Tom Rathman	.01	.05
145 Dexter McNabb RC	.01	.05
146 Vince Workman	.01	.05
147 Anthony Johnson	.02	.10
148 Brian Washington	.01	.05
149 David Tate	.01	.05
150 Johnny Holland	.01	.05
151 Monte Coleman	.01	.05
152 Keith McCants	.01	.05
153 Eugene Seale RC	.01	.05
154 Al Smith	.01	.05
155 Andre Collins	.01	.05
156 Pat Swilling	.01	.05
157 Rickey Jackson	.01	.05
158 Wilber Marshall	.01	.05
159 Kyle Clifton	.01	.05
160 Fred Stokes	.01	.05
161 Lance Smith	.01	.05
162 Guy McIntyre	.01	.05
163 Bill Maas	.01	.05
164 Gerald Perry	.01	.05
165 Bart Oates	.01	.05
166 Tony Jones	.01	.05
167 Moe Gardner	.01	.05
168 Joe Wolf	.01	.05
169 Tim Krumrie	.01	.05
170 Leonard Marshall	.01	.05
171 Kevin Call	.01	.05
172 Keith Kartz	.01	.05
173 Ron Heller	.01	.05
174 Steve Wallace	.01	.05
175 Tony Casillas	.01	.05
176 Tim Irwin	.01	.05
177 Pat Harlow	.01	.05
178 Bruce Smith	.08	.25
179 Jim Lachey	.01	.05
180 Andre Rison	.02	.10
181 Michael Haynes	.02	.10
182 Rod Bernstine	.01	.05
183 Mark Clayton	.02	.10
184 Jay Novacek	.02	.10
185 Rob Moore	.02	.10
186 Willie Green	.01	.05
187 Ricky Proehl	.01	.05
188 Al Toon	.02	.10
189 Webster Slaughter	.01	.05
190 Tony Bennett	.01	.05
191 Jeff Cross	.01	.05
192 Michael Dean Perry	.02	.10
193 Greg Townsend	.01	.05
194 Alfred Williams	.01	.05
195 William Fuller	.01	.05
196 Cortez Kennedy	.02	.10
197 Henry Thomas	.01	.05
198 Esera Tuaolo	.01	.05
199 Tim Green	.01	.05
200 Keith Jackson	.02	.10
201 Don Majkowski	.01	.05
202 Steve Beuerlein	.02	.10
203 Hugh Millen	.01	.05
204 Browning Nagle	.01	.05
205 Chip Lohmiller	.01	.05
206 Phil Simms	.02	.10
207 Jim Everett	.02	.10
208 Erik Kramer	.02	.10
209 Todd Marinovich	.01	.05
210 Henry Jones	.01	.05
211 Dwight Stone	.01	.05
212 Andre Waters	.01	.05
213 Darryl Henley	.01	.05
214 Mark Higgs	.01	.05
215 Dalton Hilliard	.01	.05
216 Earnest Byner	.01	.05
217 Eric Metcalf	.02	.10
218 Gill Byrd	.01	.05
219 Robert Williams RC	.01	.05
220 Kenneth Davis	.01	.05
221 Larry Brown DB	.01	.05
222 Mark Collins	.01	.05
223 Vinnie Clark	.01	.05
224 Patrick Hunter	.01	.05
225 Gaston Green	.01	.05
226 Everson Walls	.01	.05
227 Harold Green	.01	.05
228 Albert Lewis	.01	.05
229 Don Griffin	.01	.05
230 Lorenzo Lynch	.01	.05
231 Brian Mitchell	.02	.10
232 Thomas Everett	.01	.05
233 Leonard Russell	.02	.10
234 Eric Bieniemy	.01	.05
235 John L. Williams	.01	.05
236 Leroy Hoard	.02	.10
237 Darren Lewis	.01	.05
238 Reggie Cobb	.01	.05
239 Steve Broussard	.01	.05
240 Marion Butts	.01	.05
241 Mike Pritchard	.02	.10
242 Dexter Carter	.01	.05
243 Aeneas Williams	.02	.10
244 Bruce Pickens	.01	.05
245 Harvey Williams	.02	.10
246 Bobby Humphrey	.01	.05
247 Duane Bickett	.01	.05
248 James Francis	.01	.05
249 Broderick Thomas	.01	.05
250 Chip Banks	.01	.05
251 Bryan Cox	.02	.10
252 Sam Mills	.01	.05
253 Ken Norton Jr.	.02	.10
254 Jeff Herrod	.01	.05
255 John Roper	.01	.05
256 Darryl Talley	.01	.05
257 Andre Tippett	.01	.05
258 Jeff Lageman	.01	.05
259 Chris Doleman	.01	.05
260 Shane Conlan	.01	.05
261 Jessie Tuggle	.01	.05
262 Eric Hill	.01	.05
263 Bruce Armstrong	.01	.05
264 Bill Fralic	.01	.05
265 Alvin Harper	.02	.10
266 Bill Brooks	.01	.05
267 Henry Ellard	.02	.10
268 Cris Carter	.20	.50
269 Irving Fryar	.02	.10
270 Lawrence Dawsey	.02	.10
271 James Lofton	.02	.10
272 Ernest Givins	.02	.10
273 Terance Mathis	.02	.10
274 Randal Hill	.01	.05
275 Eddie Brown	.01	.05
276 Tim Brown	.08	.25
277 Anthony Carter	.02	.10
278 Wendell Davis	.01	.05
279 Mark Ingram	.01	.05
280 Anthony Miller	.02	.10
281 Clarence Verdin	.01	.05
282 Flipper Anderson	.01	.05
283 Ricky Sanders	.01	.05
284 Steve Jordan	.01	.05
285 Gary Clark	.02	.10
286 Sterling Sharpe	.08	.25
287 Herman Moore	.08	.25
288 Stephen Baker	.01	.05
289 Marv Cook	.01	.05
290 Ernie Jones	.01	.05
291 Eric Green	.01	.05
292 Mervyn Fernandez	.01	.05
293 Greg McMurtry	.01	.05
294 Quinn Early	.02	.10
295 Tim Harris	.01	.05
296 Will Furrer RC	.01	.05
297 Jason Hanson RC	.02	.10
298 Chris Hakel RC	.01	.05
299 Ty Detmer	.08	.25
300 David Klingler	.01	.05
301 Amp Lee RC	.01	.05
302 Troy Vincent RC	.01	.05
303 Kevin Smith RC	.01	.05
304 Terrell Buckley RC	.01	.05
305 Dana Hall RC	.01	.05
306 Tony Smith RC	.01	.05
307 Steve Israel RC	.01	.05
308 Vaughn Dunbar RC	.01	.05
309 Ashley Ambrose RC	.08	.25
310 Edgar Bennett RC	.08	.25
311 Dale Carter RC	.02	.10
312 Rodney Culver RC	.01	.05
313 Matt Darby RC	.01	.05
314 Tommy Vardell RC	.01	.05
315 Quentin Coryatt RC	.01	.05
316 Robert Jones RC	.01	.05
317 Joe Bowden RC	.01	.05
318 Eugene Chung RC	.01	.05
319 Troy Auzenne RC	.01	.05
320 Santana Dotson RC	.02	.10
321 Greg Skrepenak RC	.01	.05
322 Steve Emtman RC	.01	.05
323 Carl Pickens RC	.08	.25
324 Johnny Mitchell RC	.01	.05
325 Patrick Rowe RC	.01	.05
326 Alonzo Spellman RC	.02	.10
327 Robert Porcher RC	.08	.25
328 Chris Mims RC	.01	.05
329 Marc Boutte RC	.01	.05
330 Shane Dronett RC	.01	.05

1992 Power Combos

COMPLETE SET (10)	10.00	25.00
RANDOM INSERTS IN FOIL PACKS		
1 Steve Emtman Quentin Coryatt	1.25	3.00
2 Barry Word Christian Okoye	.75	2.00
3 Sam Mills Vaughan Johnson	.75	2.00
4 Broderick Thomas Keith McCants	.75	2.00
5 Michael Irvin Emmitt Smith	5.00	12.00
6 Jerry Ball Chris Spielman	.75	2.00
7 Ricky Sanders Gary Clark Art Monk	1.50	4.00
8 D.J. Johnson Rod Woodson	1.25	3.00
9 Bill Fralic Chris Hinton	.75	2.00
10 Irving Fryar Marv Cook	1.25	3.00

1992-93 Power Emmitt Smith

This ten-card standard size set features Emmitt Smith's career highlights. The production run was 25,000 sets. The offer for this set was found on the back of a Pro Set Emmitt Smith special card, which was randomly inserted in second series foil packs. To order the ten-card set, the collector had to mail in ten 1992 NFL Pro Set (first or second series) wrappers and ten 1992 Pro Set Power wrappers along with 7.50 for each set ordered (limit four sets per person). For an additional 20.00, the first 7500 orders received a personally autographed uncut sheet hand numbered. The signed sheet had a limit of one per person. The cards are numbered on the back and have a "PS" prefix.

COMPLETE SET (10)	10.00	25.00
COMMON CARD (1-10)	1.20	3.00
S1 Emmitt Smith Sheet AU/7500	75.00	125.00

1993 Power Prototypes

This nine-card standard-size set was issued to preview the style of the 1993 Pro Set Power football series. Pro Set sent one of these prototype cards to each dealer or wholesaler. The cards were also packaged in a cello pack with an ad card and given away at the 1993 National Sports Collectors Convention. The full-bleed color action photos on the fronts have a shadow-border effect that gives the appearance of depth to the pictures. The player's name and team name are printed in a red, gray, and blue-striped box at the lower left corner. The Pro Set Power logo is silver foil stamped on the fronts. The horizontal backs carry a color close-up photo, career summary, and a rating of players (from 1 to 10).

COMPLETE SET (10)	4.00	10.00
20 Barry Sanders	.80	2.00
22 Emmitt Smith	.80	2.00
26 Rod Woodson	.10	.30
32 Ricky Watters	.10	.30
37 Larry Centers	.10	.30
71 Santana Dotson	.10	.30
80 Jerry Rice	.40	1.00
138 Reggie Rivers	.10	.30
193 Trace Armstrong	.10	.30
NNO Title Ad Card	.10	.30

1993 Power

The 1993 Power set produced by Pro Set consists of 200 standard-size cards. Including foil and jumbo cases, a total of 8,000 cases were produced. Cards were issued in 12 and 25-card packs. Randomly inserted in 1993 Power foil packs were two redemption cards entitling the collector to receive an Emmitt Smith hologram (HOLO) card through a mail-in offer. Randomly inserted in jumbo packs were seven update cards depicting traded players in their new uniforms. Except for the new player photos and "UD" suffixes on the back, the design is identical to the regular Power cards. Also one parallel gold Power card was inserted in every pack. These are distinguished by gold within the Power logo on front. Larry Centers is the only Rookie Card of note in this set.

COMPLETE SET (200)	4.00	10.00
1 Warren Moon	.08	.25
2 Steve Christie	.01	.05
3 Jim Breech	.01	.05
4 Brett Favre	.75	2.00
5 Sean Landeta	.01	.05
6 Jim Arnold	.01	.05
7 John Elway	.60	1.50
8 Troy Aikman	.30	.75
9 Rodney Peete	.01	.05
10 Pete Stoyanovich	.01	.05
11 Mark Rypien	.01	.05
12 Jim Kelly	.08	.25
13 Dan Marino	.60	1.50
14 Neil O'Donnell	.08	.25
15 David Klingler	.01	.05
16 Rich Gannon	.08	.25
16UD Rich Gannon	.08	.25
17 Dave Krieg	.02	.10
18 Jeff Jaeger	.01	.05

19 Bernie Kosar .02 .10
20 Barry Sanders .50 1.25
21 Deion Sanders .20 .50
22 Emmitt Smith .60 1.50
23 Barry Word .01 .05
23UD Barry Word .02 .10
24 Stanley Richard .01 .05
25 Louis Oliver .01 .05
26 Rod Woodson .08 .25
27 Rodney Hampton .02 .10
28 Cris Dishman .01 .05
29 Barry Foster .02 .10
30 Dave Meggett .01 .05
31 Kevin Ross .01 .05
32 Ricky Watters .08 .25
33 Darren Lewis .01 .05
34 Thurman Thomas .08 .25
35 Rodney Culver .01 .05
36 Bennie Blades .01 .05
37 Larry Centers RC .08 .25
38 Todd Scott .01 .05
39 Darren Perry .01 .05
40 Robert Massey .01 .05
41 Keith Byars .01 .05
41UD Keith Byars UER .02 .10
(Misspelled Mimai
on back)
42 Chris Warren .02 .10
43 Cleveland Gary .01 .05
44 Lorenzo White .01 .05
45 Tony Stargell .01 .05
46 Bennie Thompson .01 .05
47 A.J. Johnson .01 .05
48 Daryl Johnston .08 .25
49 Dennis Smith .01 .05
50 Johnny Holland .01 .05
51 Ken Norton Jr. .02 .10
52 Pepper Johnson .01 .05
52UD Pepper Johnson .02 .10
53 Vaughan Johnson .01 .05
54 Chris Spielman .02 .10
55 Junior Seau .08 .25
56 Chris Doleman .01 .05
57 Rickey Jackson .01 .05
58 Derrick Thomas .08 .25
59 Seth Joyner .01 .05
60 Stan Thomas .01 .05
61 Nate Newton .02 .10
62 Matt Brock .01 .05
63 Mike Munchak .02 .10
64 Randall McDaniel .02 .10
65 Ron Hallstrom .01 .05
66 Andy Heck .01 .05
67 Russell Maryland .01 .05
68 Bruce Wilkerson .01 .05
69 Mark Schlereth .01 .05
70 John Fina .01 .05
71 Santana Dotson .02 .10
72 Don Mosebar UER .01 .05
(Listed as tackle;
should be center)
73 Simon Fletcher .01 .05
74 Paul Gruber .01 .05
75 Howard Ballard .01 .05
76 John Alt .01 .05
77 Carlton Haselrig .01 .05
78 Bruce Smith .08 .25
79 Ray Childress .01 .05
80 Jerry Rice .40 1.00
81 Art Monk .02 .10
82 John Taylor .02 .10
83 Andre Reed .02 .10
84 Sterling Sharpe .08 .25
85 Sam Graddy .01 .05
86 Fred Barnett .02 .10
87 Ricky Proehl .01 .05
88 Michael Irvin .08 .25
89 Webster Slaughter .01 .05
90 Tony Bennett .01 .05
91 Leslie O'Neal .02 .10
92 Michael Dean Perry .02 .10
93 Greg Townsend .01 .05
94 Anthony Smith .01 .05
95 Richard Dent .02 .10
96 Clyde Simmons .01 .05
97 Cornelius Bennett .02 .10
98 Eric Swann .01 .05
99 Cortez Kennedy .02 .10
100 Emmitt Smith .40 1.00
101 Michael Jackson .02 .10
102 Lin Elliott .01 .05
103 Rohn Stark .01 .05
104 Jim Harbaugh .08 .25
105 Greg Davis .01 .05
106 Mike Cofer .01 .05
107 Morten Andersen .01 .05
108 Steve Young .30 .75
109 Norm Johnson .01 .05
110 Dan McGwire .01 .05
111 Jim Everett .02 .10
112 Randall Cunningham .08 .25
113 Steve Bono .02 .10
114 Cody Carlson .01 .05
115 Jeff Hostetler .02 .10
116 Rich Camarillo .01 .05
117 Chris Chandler .02 .10
118 Stan Gelbaugh .01 .05
119 Tony Sacca .01 .05
120 Henry Jones .01 .05
121 Terry Allen .08 .25
122 Amp Lee .01 .05
123 Mel Gray .02 .10
124 Jon Vaughn .01 .05
124UD Jon Vaughn UER .02 .10
(Misspelled Saehawks
on front)
125 Bubba McDowell .01 .05
126 Audray McMillian .01 .05
127 Terrell Buckley .01 .05
128 Dana Hall .01 .05
129 Eric Dickerson .02 .10
130 Martin Bayless .01 .05
131 Steve Israel .01 .05
132 Vaughn Dunbar .01 .05
133 Ronnie Harmon .01 .05
134 Dale Carter .01 .05
135 Neal Anderson .01 .05
136 Merton Hanks .01 .05
137 James Washington .01 .05
138 Reggie Rivers RC .01 .05
139 Bruce Pickens .01 .05
140 Gary Anderson RB .01 .05
141 Eugene Robinson .01 .05
142 Charles Mincy RC UER .01 .05
(Listed as running back;
he is a defensive back)
143 Matt Darby .01 .05
144 Tom Rathman .01 .05
145 Mike Prior .01 .05
146 Sean Lumpkin .01 .05
147 Greg Jackson .01 .05
148 Wes Hopkins .01 .05
149 David Tate UER .01 .05
(Listed as linebacker;
should be safety)
150 James Francis .01 .05
151 Bryan Cox .01 .05
152 Keith McCants .01 .05
152UD Keith McCants .02 .10
153 Mark Stepnoski .01 .05
154 Al Smith .01 .05
155 Robert Jones .01 .05
156 Lawrence Taylor .08 .25
157 Clay Matthews .02 .10
158 Wilber Marshall .01 .05
158UD Wilber Marshall UER .02 .10
(Misspelled Marshal
on front)
159 Mike Johnson .01 .05
160 Adam Schreiber RC .01 .05
161 Tim Grunhard .01 .05
162 Mark Bortz .01 .05
163 Gene Chilton .01 .05
164 Jamie Dukes .01 .05
165 Bart Oates .01 .05
166 Kevin Gogan .01 .05
167 Kent Hull .01 .05
168 Ed King .01 .05
169 Eugene Chung .01 .05
170 Troy Auzenne .01 .05
171 Charles Mann .01 .05
172 William Perry .02 .10
173 Mike Lodish .01 .05
174 Bruce Matthews .01 .05
175 Tony Casillas .01 .05
176 Steve Wisniewski .01 .05
177 Karl Mecklenburg .01 .05
178 Richmond Webb .01 .05
179 Erik Williams .01 .05
180 Andre Rison .02 .10
181 Michael Haynes .02 .10
182 Don Beebe .01 .05
183 Anthony Miller .02 .10
184 Jay Novacek .02 .10
185 Rob Moore .02 .10
186 Willie Green .01 .05
187 Tom Waddle .01 .05
188 Keith Jackson .02 .10
189 Steve Tasker .02 .10
190 Marco Coleman .01 .05
191 Jeff Wright .01 .05
192 Burt Grossman .01 .05
193 Trace Armstrong .01 .05
194 Charles Haley .02 .10
195 Greg Lloyd .02 .10
196 Marc Boutte .01 .05
197 Rufus Porter .01 .05
198 Dennis Gibson .01 .05
199 Shane Dronett .01 .05
200 Joe Montana .60 1.50
H1 Emmitt Smith 7.50 20.00
Hologram Redemption
Back to Back
H2 Emmitt Smith 7.50 20.00
Hologram Redemption
Super Day

1993 Power Gold

COMPLETE SET (200) 15.00 40.00
*GOLD CARDS: .8X TO 2X BASIC CARDS
ONE GOLD PER PACK

1993 Power All-Power Defense

COMPLETE SET (25) 2.00 5.00
*GOLDS: .8X to 2X BASIC INSERTS
TWO PER JUMBO PACK
1 Clyde Simmons .05 .15
2 Anthony Smith .05 .15
3 Ray Childress .05 .15
4 Michael Dean Perry .10 .30
5 Bruce Smith .30 .75
6 Cortez Kennedy .10 .30
7 Charles Haley .10 .30
8 Marco Coleman .05 .15
9 Alonzo Spellman .05 .15
10 Junior Seau .30 .75
11 Ken Norton Jr. .10 .30
12 Derrick Thomas .30 .75
13 Wilber Marshall .05 .15
14 Chris Doleman .05 .15
15 Seth Joyner .05 .15
16 Al Smith .05 .15
17 Deion Sanders .60 1.50
18 Rod Woodson .30 .75
19 Audray McMillian .05 .15
20 Dale Carter .05 .15
21 Terrell Buckley .05 .15
22 Bennie Thompson .05 .15
23 Chris Spielman .10 .30
24 Lawrence Taylor .30 .75
25 Tony Bennett .05 .15

1993 Power Combos

COMPLETE SET (10) 2.00 5.00
RANDOM INSERTS IN FOIL PACKS
*GOLDS: .8X to 2X BASIC INSERTS
ONE GOLD PER PACK
TWO GOLDS PER JUMBO PACK
*PRISMS: 1.2X to 3X BASIC INSERTS
RANDOM INSERTS IN UPDATE JUMBO
1 Emmitt Smith 1.25 3.00
Barry Sanders
2 Terrell Buckley .20 .50
Sterling Sharpe
3 Junior Seau .30 .75
Gary Plummer
4 Deion Sanders .40 1.00
Tim McKyer
5 Bruce Smith .30 .75
Darryl Talley
6 Warren Moon .30 .75
Webster Slaughter
7 Chris Doleman .10 .30
Henry Thomas
8 Karl Mecklenburg .10 .30
Michael Brooks
9 Ken Norton Jr. .20 .50
Robert Jones
10 Marco Coleman .20 .50
Bryan Cox

1993 Power Draft Picks

COMPLETE SET (30) 2.50 6.00
*GOLDS: .8X TO 2X BASIC INSERTS
ONE GOLD PER PACK
TWO GOLDS PER JUMBO PACK
1 Lincoln Kennedy UER .05 .15
(Misnumbered 10)
2 Thomas Smith UER .05 .15
(Misnumbered 20)
3 Robert Smith UER .50 1.25
(Misnumbered 30)
4 John Copeland UER .05 .15
(Misnumbered 40)
5 Dan Footman UER .05 .15
(Misnumbered 50)
6 Darrin Smith UER .05 .15
(Misnumbered 60)
7 Qadry Ismail UER .20 .50
(Misnumbered 70)
8 Ryan McNeil UER .20 .50
(Misnumbered 80)
9 George Teague UER .05 .15
(Misnumbered 90)
10 Brad Hopkins .05 .15
11 Ernest Dye .05 .15
12 Jaime Fields .05 .15
13 Patrick Bates .05 .15
14 Jerome Bettis 2.00 5.00
15 O.J. McDuffie .20 .50
16 Gino Torretta .08 .25
17 Drew Bledsoe 1.25 3.00
18 Irv Smith .05 .15
19 Marcus Buckley .05 .15
20 Coleman Rudolph .05 .15
21 Leonard Renfro .05 .15
22 Garrison Hearst .30 .75
23 Deon Figures .05 .15
24 Natrone Means .20 .50
25 Todd Kelly .05 .15
26 Carlton Gray .05 .15
27 Eric Curry .05 .15
28 Tom Carter .05 .15
29 AFC Logo CL .05 .15
30 NFC Logo CL .05 .15

1993 Power Moves

COMPLETE SET (40) 2.00 5.00
COMP.SERIES 1 (30) 1.25 3.00
COMP.SERIES 2 (10) .75 2.00
PM1-PM30 RANDOM INS.IN FOIL PA
PM31-PM40 RANDOM INS.IN JUMBO
*GOLDS: .8X TO 2X BASIC INSERTS
ONE GOLD PER PACK
TWO GOLDS PER JUMBO PACK
PM1 Bobby Hebert .05 .15
PM2 Bill Brooks .08 .25
PM3 Vinny Testaverde .08 .25
PM4 Hugh Millen .05 .15
PM5 Rod Bernstine .05 .15
PM6 Robert Delpino .05 .15
PM7 Pat Swilling .08 .25
PM8 Reggie White .20 .50
PM9 Aaron Cox .05 .15
PM10 Joe Montana 1.00 2.50
PM11 Gaston Green .05 .15
PM12 Jeff Hostetler .08 .25
PM13 Shane Conlan .05 .15
PM14 Irv Eatman .05 .15
PM15 Mark Ingram .05 .15
PM16 Irving Fryar .08 .25
PM17 Don Majkowski .05 .15
PM18 Will Wolford .05 .15
PM19 Boomer Esiason .08 .25
PM20 Ronnie Lott .08 .25
PM21 Johnny Johnson .05 .15
PM22 Steve Beuerlein .08 .25
PM23 Chuck Cecil .05 .15
PM24 Gary Clark .08 .25
PM25 Kevin Greene .08 .25
PM26 Jerrol Williams .05 .15
PM27 Tim McDonald .05 .15
PM28 Ferrell Edmunds .05 .15
PM29 Kelvin Martin .05 .15
PM30 Hardy Nickerson .05 .15
PM31 Jerry Ball .05 .15
PM32 Jim McMahon .08 .25
PM33 Marcus Allen .20 .50
PM34 John Stephens .05 .15
PM35 John Booty .05 .15
PM36 Wade Wilson .05 .15
PM37 Mark Bavaro .05 .15
PM38 Bill Fralic .05 .15
PM39 Mark Clayton .05 .15
PM40 Mike Sherrard .05 .15

1993 Power Update Moves

COMPLETE SET (50) 2.00 5.00
PMUD PREFIX ON CARD NUMBERS
*GOLDS: .8X to 2X BASIC INSERTS
1 Bobby Hebert .02 .10
2 Bill Brooks .05 .15
3 Vinny Testaverde .05 .15
4 Hugh Millen .02 .10
5 Rod Bernstine .02 .10
6 Robert Delpino .02 .10
7 Pat Swilling .05 .15
8 Reggie White .08 .25
9 Aaron Cox .02 .10
10 Joe Montana 1.00 2.50
11 Vinnie Clark UER .02 .10
(Name misspelled
Vinny on card)
12 Jeff Hostetler .05 .15
13 Shane Conlan .02 .10
14 Irv Eatman .02 .10
15 Mark Ingram .05 .15
16 Irving Fryar .05 .15
17 Don Majkowski .02 .10
18 Will Wolford .02 .10
19 Boomer Esiason .05 .15
20 Ronnie Lott .05 .15
21 Johnny Johnson .02 .10
22 Steve Beuerlein .05 .15
23 Chuck Cecil .02 .10
24 Gary Clark .05 .15
25 Kevin Greene .05 .15
26 Jerrol Williams .02 .10
27 Tim McDonald .02 .10
28 Ferrell Edmunds .02 .10
29 Kelvin Martin .02 .10
30 Hardy Nickerson .02 .10
31 Jumpy Geathers .02 .10
32 Craig Heyward .05 .15
33 Tim McKyer .02 .10
34 Mark Carrier WR .08 .25
35 Gary Zimmerman .02 .10
36 Jay Schroeder .02 .10
37 Keith Millard UER .02 .10
(incorrect college listed on back)
38 Vince Workman .02 .10
39 Kirk Lowdermilk .02 .10
40 Fred Stokes .02 .10
41 Ernie Jones UER .02 .10
(photo is actually Mitchell Price)
42 Keith Byars .02 .10
43 Carlton Bailey .02 .10
44 Michael Brooks .02 .10
45 Tim McGee .02 .10
46 Leonard Marshall .02 .10
47 Bubby Brister .02 .10
48 Mike Tomczak .05 .15
49 Mark Jackson .02 .10
50 Wade Wilson .02 .10

1993 Power Update Prospects

These 60 standard-size cards were issued in nine-card retail packs with the Power Update Moves cards. The cards are numbered on the back with a "PP" prefix. Rookie Cards include Jerome Bettis, Drew Bledsoe, Reggie Brooks , Curtis Conway, Garrison Hearst, Rick Mirer, Ronald Moore and Kevin Williams. Gold Parallel cards were also inserted in packs.

COMPLETE SET (60) 7.50 15.00
1 Drew Bledsoe RC 1.00 2.50
2 Rick Mirer RC .08 .25
3 Trent Green RC 4.00 10.00
4 Mark Brunell RC .60 1.50
5 Billy Joe Hobert RC UER .08 .25
Name spelled Hebert on back
6 Ronald Moore RC .02 .10
7 Elvis Grbac RC UER .60 1.50
(Spelled Grback on both sides)
8 Garrison Hearst RC .30 .75
9 Jerome Bettis RC 1.50 4.00
10 Reggie Brooks RC .02 .10
11 Robert Smith RC .50 1.25
12 Vaughn Hebron RC .01 .05
13 Derek Brown RBK RC .02 .10
14 Roosevelt Potts RC .02 .10
15 Terry Kirby RC UER .02 .10
(Card says wide receiver;
he is a running back)
16 Glyn Milburn RC .02 .10
17 Greg Robinson RC .01 .05
18 Natrone Means RC .08 .25
19 Curtis Conway RC .15 .40
20 James Jett RC .08 .25
21 O.J. McDuffie RC .08 .25
22 Rocket Ismail .08 .25
23 Qadry Ismail RC .08 .25
24 Kevin Williams RC .02 .10
25 Victor Bailey RC UER .01 .05
(Name spelled Baily on front)
26 Vincent Brisby RC .08 .25
27 Irv Smith RC .01 .05
28 Troy Drayton RC .01 .05
29 Wayne Simmons RC .01 .05
30 Marvin Jones RC .01 .05
31 Demetrius DuBose RC .01 .05
32 Chad Brown RC .02 .10
33 Micheal Barrow RC .08 .25
34 Darrin Smith RC .01 .05
35 Deon Figures RC .01 .05
36 Darrien Gordon RC .01 .05
37 Patrick Bates RC .01 .05
38 George Teague RC .01 .05
39 Lance Gunn RC .01 .05
40 Tom Carter RC .01 .05
41 Carlton Gray RC .01 .05
42 John Copeland RC .01 .05
43 Eric Curry RC .01 .05
44 Dana Stubblefield RC .08 .25
45 Leonard Renfro RC .01 .05
46 Dan Williams RC .01 .05
47 Todd Kelly RC .01 .05
48 Chris Slade RC .01 .05
49 Carl Simpson RC UER .01 .05
(Defensive Back spelled
Dfensive on back)
50 Coleman Rudolph RC .01 .05
51 Michael Strahan RC .60 1.50
52 Dan Footman RC .01 .05
53 Steve Everitt RC .01 .05
54 Will Shields RC .08 .25
55 Ben Coleman RC .01 .05
56 Willie Roaf RC .02 .10
57 Lincoln Kennedy RC .01 .05
58 Brad Hopkins RC .01 .05
59 Ernest Dye RC .01 .05
60 Jason Elam RC .08 .25

1993 Power Update Prospects Gold

COMPLETE SET (60) 12.50 25.00
*GOLDS: .8X TO 2X BASIC CARDS
ONE GOLD PER UPDATE PACK
TWO GOLDS PER UPDATE JUMBO PACK

1993 Power Update Combos

COMPLETE SET (10) 3.00 8.00
RANDOM INS.IN POWER UPDATE PAC
*GOLDS: .6X to 1.5X BASIC INSERTS
RANDOM INS.IN POWER UPDATE PAC
*PRISMS: 1X to 2.5X BASIC INSERTS
RANDOM INS.IN UPDATE JUMBOS
PC1 Andre Rison .30 .75
Michael Haynes
Mike Pritchard
Drew Hill
PC2 Steve Young UER 1.50 3.00
Jerry Rice
(Young's uniform number
on back is 7)
PC3 Jim Kelly .40 1.00
Frank Reich
PC4 Alvin Harper .40 1.00
Michael Irvin
PC5 Rod Woodson .20 .50
Deon Figures
PC6 Bruce Smith .30 .75
Cornelius Bennett
PC7 Bryan Cox .20 .50
Marco Coleman
PC8 Troy Aikman 2.50 3.00
Emmitt Smith
PC9 Tim Brown .40 1.00
Rocket Ismail
PC10 Art Monk UER .30 .75
Desmond Howard
Ricky Sanders
(Atlanta Falcons on back)

1993 Power Update Impact Rookies

COMPLETE SET (15) 3.00 8.00
RANDOM INS.IN POWER UPDATE PAC
*GOLDS: .8X TO 2X BASIC INSERTS
RANDOM INS.IN POWER UPDATE PACKS
IR1 Rick Mirer .30 .75
IR2 Drew Bledsoe 1.50 4.00
IR3 Jerome Bettis 2.50 6.00
IR4 Derek Brown RBK .10 .30
IR5 Roosevelt Potts .10 .30
IR6 Glyn Milburn .20 .50
IR7 Adrian Murrell .30 .75
IR8 Victor Bailey .10 .30
IR9 Vincent Brisby .20 .50
IR10 O.J. McDuffie .30 .75
IR11 James Jett .10 .30
IR12 Eric Curry .10 .30
IR13 Dana Stubblefield .20 .50
IR14 Willie Roaf .20 .50
IR15 Patrick Bates .10 .30

1997-98 Premier Replays

This set of cards was produced by Premier Replays and initially released in 1997. The cards were released throughout 1998 as well with the addition of Randy Moss to the list. Each card is a lenticular designed motion card mounted on a black plastic backing. The player's name and NFL logos are also included on the cardfronts and the cardbacks are blank. The Randy Moss card was issued, after the initial 8-cards, primarily to dealers and features two photos of Moss' first touchdown reception.

COMPLETE SET (9) 12.00 30.00
1 Troy Aikman 1.20 3.00
2 Drew Bledsoe 1.20 3.00
3 Kerry Collins .80 2.00
4 Terrell Davis 2.40 6.00
5 Brett Favre 2.40 6.00
6 Curtis Martin 1.20 3.00
7 Emmitt Smith 2.00 5.00
8 Reggie White 1.00 2.50
9 Randy Moss 4.80 12.00

1994 Press Pass SB Photo Board

Press Pass shipped 50,000 individually numbered (approximately) 10" by 14" Photo Boards to hobby and retail outlets Jan. 24, the day after both Buffalo and Dallas earned their Super Bowl berths. The front describes each team's road to the Super Bowl with color photos from NFL playoff action. The back carries color action photos of AFC and NFC statistical leaders and an outstanding 1993 rookie from each conference as well as accompanying statistics. The sheet is unnumbered, and the AFC and NFC statistical leaders honored on its back are listed below.

1 John Elway 3.20 8.00
Rick Mirer
Reggie Langhorne
Neil Smith
Nate Odomes
Thurman Thomas
Steve Young
Jerome Bettis
Sterling Sharpe
Reggie White
Deion Sanders
Emmitt Smith

2010 Prestige

COMP.SET w/o RC's (200) 10.00 25.00
ONE ROOKIE PER HOBBY PACK
1 Anquan Boldin .25 .60
2 Chris Wells .25 .60
3 Dominique Rodgers-Cromartie .20 .50
4 Matt Leinart .25 .60
5 Larry Fitzgerald .30 .75
6 Adrian Wilson .50 1.25
7 Tim Hightower .20 .50
8 Jason Snelling .25 .60
9 Matt Ryan .30 .75
10 Michael Jenkins .20 .50
11 Michael Turner .20 .50
12 Roddy White .25 .60
13 Tony Gonzalez .25 .60
14 Derrick Mason .25 .60
15 Joe Flacco .30 .75
16 Mark Clayton .20 .50
17 Ray Lewis .30 .75
18 Ray Rice .25 .60
19 Todd Heap .20 .50
20 Willis McGahee .25 .60
21 Fred Jackson .30 .75
22 Jairus Byrd .25 .60
23 Lee Evans .25 .60
24 Marshawn Lynch .25 .60
25 Ryan Fitzpatrick .30 .75
26 Aaron Schobel .20 .50
27 DeAngelo Williams .25 .60
28 Jon Beason .20 .50
29 Jonathan Stewart .25 .60
30 Julius Peppers .25 .60
31 Muhsin Muhammad .25 .60
32 Steve Smith .25 .60
33 Brian Urlacher .30 .75
34 Devin Hester .30 .75
35 Earl Bennett .25 .60
36 Greg Olsen .20 .50
37 Jay Cutler .30 .75
38 Johnny Knox .25 .60
39 Matt Forte .25 .60
40 Andre Caldwell .20 .50
41 Carson Palmer .25 .60
42 Cedric Benson .25 .60
43 Chad Ochocinco .25 .60
44 Dhani Jones .20 .50
45 Johnathan Joseph .20 .50
46 Abram Elam RC .30 .75
47 Jake Delhomme .25 .60
48 Jerome Harrison .20 .50
49 Josh Cribbs .30 .75
50 Kamerion Wimbley .20 .50
51 Mohamed Massaquoi .25 .60
52 DeMarcus Ware .25 .60
53 Felix Jones .25 .60
54 Jason Witten .30 .75
55 Jay Ratliff .25 .60
56 Marion Barber .25 .60
57 Miles Austin .30 .75
58 Tony Romo .40 1.00
59 Brandon Marshall .25 .60
60 Elvis Dumervil .20 .50
61 Jabar Gaffney .20 .50
62 Knowshon Moreno .25 .60
63 Kyle Orton .25 .60
64 Tony Scheffler .20 .50
65 Brandon Pettigrew .20 .50
66 Bryant Johnson .20 .50
67 Calvin Johnson .30 .75
68 Kevin Smith .25 .60
69 Matthew Stafford .30 .75
70 Aaron Rodgers .60 1.50
71 Charles Woodson .30 .75
72 Donald Driver .25 .60
73 Greg Jennings .25 .60
74 Jermichael Finley .25 .60
75 Ryan Grant .25 .60
76 Andre Johnson .25 .60
77 Brian Cushing .20 .50
78 Kevin Walter .25 .60
79 Matt Schaub .25 .60
80 Owen Daniels .20 .50
81 Steve Slaton .20 .50
82 Anthony Gonzalez .20 .50
83 Dallas Clark .25 .60
84 Dwight Freeney .25 .60
85 Joseph Addai .25 .60
86 Peyton Manning .50 1.25
87 Pierre Garcon .25 .60
88 Reggie Wayne .25 .60
89 David Garrard .25 .60
90 Marcedes Lewis .20 .50
91 Maurice Jones-Drew .25 .60
92 Mike Sims-Walker .25 .60
93 Mike Thomas .25 .60
94 Torry Holt .25 .60
95 Brandon Flowers .20 .50
96 Chris Chambers .25 .60
97 Dwayne Bowe .25 .60
98 Jamaal Charles .25 .60
99 Matt Cassel .25 .60
100 Brian Hartline .25 .60
101 Chad Henne .25 .60
102 Davone Bess .20 .50
103 Greg Camarillo .20 .50
104 Ricky Williams .25 .60
105 Ronnie Brown .25 .60
106 Ted Ginn .25 .60
107 Adrian Peterson .50 1.25
108 Bernard Berrian .20 .50
109 Brett Favre .75 2.00
110 Jared Allen .30 .75
111 Percy Harvin .30 .75
112 Sidney Rice .25 .60
113 Visanthe Shiancoe .25 .60
114 Ben Watson .20 .50
115 Julian Edelman .20 .50
116 Laurence Maroney .25 .60
117 Randy Moss .30 .75
118 Tom Brady .50 1.25
119 Wes Welker .30 .75
120 Devery Henderson .20 .50
121 Drew Brees .30 .75
122 Jeremy Shockey .25 .60
123 Marques Colston .25 .60
124 Pierre Thomas .25 .60
125 Reggie Bush .30 .75
126 Robert Meachem .25 .60
127 Ahmad Bradshaw .25 .60
128 Brandon Jacobs .25 .60
129 Eli Manning .30 .75
130 Hakeem Nicks .25 .60
131 Kevin Boss .25 .60
132 Mario Manningham .25 .60
133 Steve Smith USC .25 .60
134 Braylon Edwards .25 .60
135 Darrelle Revis .25 .60
136 Jerricho Cotchery .25 .60
137 Leon Washington .25 .60
138 Mark Sanchez .30 .75
139 Shonn Greene .25 .60
140 Thomas Jones .25 .60
141 Chaz Schilens .20 .50
142 Darren McFadden .25 .60
143 Louis Murphy .25 .60
144 Michael Bush .20 .50
145 Nnamdi Asomugha .25 .60
146 Zach Miller .25 .60
147 Asante Samuel .20 .50
148 Brent Celek .25 .60
149 Brian Westbrook .25 .60
150 DeSean Jackson .25 .60
151 Donovan McNabb .30 .75
152 Jeremy Maclin .25 .60
153 LeSean McCoy .25 .60
154 Ben Roethlisberger .30 .75
155 Heath Miller .25 .60
156 Hines Ward .25 .60
157 Mike Wallace .25 .60
158 Rashard Mendenhall .25 .60
159 Santonio Holmes .25 .60
160 Troy Polamalu .30 .75
161 Antonio Gates .25 .60
162 Darren Sproles .25 .60
163 LaDainian Tomlinson .30 .75
164 Malcom Floyd .25 .60
165 Philip Rivers .30 .75
166 Vincent Jackson .20 .50
167 Shawne Merriman .25 .60
168 Alex Smith QB .25 .60
169 Frank Gore .25 .60
170 Josh Morgan .25 .60
171 Michael Crabtree .30 .75
172 Patrick Willis .25 .60
173 Vernon Davis .25 .60
174 John Carlson .20 .50
175 Julius Jones .20 .50
176 Justin Forsett .25 .60
177 Matt Hasselbeck .20 .50
178 Nate Burleson .20 .50
179 T.J. Houshmandzadeh .25 .60
180 Brandon Gibson .20 .50
181 Donnie Avery .25 .60
182 James Laurinaitis .25 .60
183 Kyle Boller .20 .50
184 Steven Jackson .25 .60
185 Antonio Bryant .20 .50
186 Aqib Talib .20 .50
187 Cadillac Williams .25 .60
188 Derrick Ward .20 .50
189 Josh Freeman .30 .75
190 Kellen Winslow .25 .60
191 Bo Scaife .20 .50
192 Chris Johnson .30 .75
193 Kenny Britt .25 .60
194 Nate Washington .20 .50
195 Vince Young .20 .50
196 Antwaan Randle El .50 1.25
197 Chris Cooley .25 .60
198 Clinton Portis .25 .60
199 Devin Thomas .20 .50
200 Santana Moss .25 .60
201 Aaron Hernandez SP RC 12.00 30.00
202 Andre Anderson RC .60 1.50
203 Andre Dixon RC .75 2.00
204 Andre Roberts RC .75 2.00
205 Anthony Dixon RC .75 2.00
206 Anthony McCoy RC .60 1.50
207 Antonio Brown RC 1.25 3.00
208 Arrelious Benn SP RC 8.00 20.00
209 Ben Tate RC 1.00 2.50
210 Blair White RC .75 2.00
211 Brandon Graham RC .60 1.50
212 Brandon LaFell RC .75 2.00
213 Brandon Spikes RC .75 2.00
214A Bryan Bulaga RC .75 2.00
214B Bryan Bulaga Draft SP 8.00 20.00
215A C.J. Spiller RC 1.25 3.00
215B C.J. Spiller Draft SP 12.00 30.00
216 Carlos Dunlap RC .75 2.00
217 Carlton Mitchell RC .60 1.50
218 Chad Jones RC .75 2.00
219 Charles Scott RC .60 1.50
220 Chris Brown RC .75 2.00
221 Chris Cook RC .75 2.00
222 Chris McGaha RC .50 1.25
223 Colt McCoy RC 1.50 4.00
224 Corey Wootton RC .60 1.50
225 Damian Williams RC .75 2.00
226 Dan LeFevour SP RC 10.00 25.00
227 Danario Alexander RC .75 2.00
228 Daryl Washington RC .60 1.50
229 David Gettis RC .75 2.00
230A Demaryius Thomas RC 1.00 2.50
230B Demaryius Thomas Draft SP 8.00 20.00
231A Derrick Morgan RC .60 1.50
231B Derrick Morgan Draft SP 8.00 20.00
232 Devin McCourty RC .75 2.00
233 Dexter McCluster SP RC 8.00 20.00
234 Dez Bryant RC 2.50 6.00
235 Dezmon Briscoe RC .60 1.50
236 Dominique Franks RC .50 1.25
237 Earl Thomas RC .75 2.00
238 Ed Dickson RC .75 2.00
239A Eric Berry RC .75 2.00
239B Eric Berry Draft SP 12.00 30.00
240 Eric Decker RC 1.00 2.50
241 Everson Griffen RC .75 2.00
242 Freddie Barnes RC .60 1.50
243 Garrett Graham RC .60 1.50
244A Gerald McCoy SP RC 8.00 20.00
244B Gerald McCoy Draft SP 8.00 20.00
245 Golden Tate RC .75 2.00
246 Jacoby Ford RC .75 2.00
247A Jahvid Best RC 1.25 3.00
247B Jahvid Best Draft SP 15.00 30.00
248 James Starks RC 1.25 3.00
249 Jarrett Brown RC .75 2.00
250 Jason Pierre-Paul RC 1.25 3.00
251 Jason Worilds RC .75 2.00
252 Jeremy Williams RC .50 1.25
253 Jermaine Gresham RC 1.00 2.50
254 Jerry Hughes RC .75 2.00
255 Jevan Snead RC .75 2.00
256 Jimmy Clausen RC .75 2.00
257 Jimmy Graham RC 1.50 4.00
258A Joe Haden RC .75 2.00
258B Joe Haden Draft SP 8.00 20.00
259 Joe McKnight RC .75 2.00
260 John Skelton RC .75 2.00
261 Joique Bell RC .60 1.50
262 Jonathan Crompton RC .60 1.50
263 Jonathan Dwyer RC .75 2.00
264 Jordan Shipley SP RC 8.00 20.00
265 Kareem Jackson RC .75 2.00
266 Kyle Wilson RC .75 2.00
267 LeGarrette Blount RC 1.25 3.00
268 Lonyae Miller RC .60 1.50
269 Marcus Easley RC .60 1.50
270 Mardy Gilyard RC .75 2.00
271 Mike Kafka RC .75 2.00
272 Mike Williams SP RC 10.00 25.00
273 Montario Hardesty RC .75 2.00
274 Morgan Burnett RC .75 2.00
275 Nate Allen RC .75 2.00
276 NaVorro Bowman RC .75 2.00
277A Ndamukong Suh RC 1.50 4.00
277B Ndamukong Suh Draft SP 20.00 40.00
278 Pat Paschall RC .60 1.50
279 Patrick Robinson RC .75 2.00
280 Perrish Cox RC .60 1.50
281 Ricky Sapp RC .60 1.50
282 Riley Cooper RC .75 2.00
283A Rob Gronkowski RC 2.00 5.00
283B Rob Gronkowski Draft SP 15.00 40.00
284 Rolando McClain SP RC 6.00 15.00
285A Russell Okung SP RC 10.00 25.00
285B Russell Okung Draft SP 10.00 25.00
286 Ryan Mathews RC 1.50 4.00
287A Sam Bradford RC 3.00 8.00
287B Sam Bradford Draft SP 20.00 40.00
288 Sean Canfield SP RC 6.00 15.00
289 Sean Lee RC .75 2.00
290 Sean Weatherspoon RC .75 2.00
291 Sergio Kindle RC .75 2.00
292 Seyi Ajirotutu RC .75 2.00
293 Shay Hodge RC .60 1.50
294 Taylor Mays RC .75 2.00
295 Taylor Price RC .75 2.00
296A Tim Tebow RC 5.00 12.00
296B Tim Tebow Draft SP 25.00 50.00
297 Toby Gerhart RC .75 2.00
298 Tony Pike RC .75 2.00
299A Trent Williams RC .75 2.00
299B Trent Williams Draft SP 6.00 15.00
300 Zac Robinson RC .60 1.50
301 Ed Wang SP RC 30.00 60.00
302 Lamarr Houston Draft SP RC 20.00 40.00
303 Jared Odrick Draft SP RC 25.00 50.00
304 Dan Williams Draft SP RC 20.00 40.00

2010 Prestige Draft Picks Light Blue

*ROOKIES: .5X TO 1.2X BASIC RC
*ROOKIES: .05X TO .15X BASIC SP RC
STATED PRINT RUN 999 SER.#'d SETS

2010 Prestige Xtra Points Black

*1-200 VETS: 10X TO 25X BASIC CARDS
*201-300 ROOKIES: 4X TO 10X BASIC RC
*201-300 ROOKIES: .5X TO 1.2X BASIC SP RC
STATED PRINT RUN 10 SER.#'d SETS

2010 Prestige Xtra Points Gold
*1-200 VETS: 2X TO 5X BASIC CARDS
*201-300 ROOKIES: .8X TO 2X BASIC RC
*201-300 ROOKIES: .1X TO .25X BASIC SP RC
STATED PRINT RUN 250 SER.#'d SETS

2010 Prestige Xtra Points Green
*VETS: 8X TO 20X BASIC CARDS
*ROOKIES: 3X TO 8X BASIC RC
*ROOKIES: .4X TO 1X BASIC SP RC
STATED PRINT RUN 25 SER.#'d SETS

2010 Prestige Xtra Points Orange
*1-200 VETS: 3X TO 8X BASIC CARDS
*201-300 ROOKIES: 1.2X TO 3X BASIC RC
*201-300 ROOKIES: .15X TO .4X BASIC SP RC
RANDOM INSERTS IN RETAIL PACKS

2010 Prestige Xtra Points Purple
*1-200 VETS: 4X TO 10X BASIC CARDS
*201-300 ROOKIES: 1.5X TO 4X BASIC RC
*201-300 ROOKIES: .2X TO .5X BASIC SP RC
STATED PRINT RUN 50 SER.#'d SETS

2010 Prestige Xtra Points Red
*1-200 VETS: 3X TO 8X BASIC CARDS
*201-300 ROOKIES: 1.2X TO 3X BASIC RC
*201-300 ROOKIES: 1.5X TO .4X BASIC SP RC
STATED PRINT RUN 100 SER.#'d SETS

2010 Prestige Collegiate Lettermen Autographs
1 Jimmy Clausen 12.00 30.00
2 Sam Bradford 60.00 120.00
3 Colt McCoy 50.00 100.00
4 Tim Tebow 100.00 200.00
5 C.J. Spiller 25.00 60.00
6 Toby Gerhart 30.00 60.00
7 Dez Bryant 40.00 80.00
8 Golden Tate 12.00 30.00
10 Jordan Shipley 20.00 50.00
11 Jermaine Gresham 15.00 40.00

2010 Prestige Connections
1 Brett Favre 4.00 10.00
Sidney Rice
2 Tom Brady 2.50 6.00
Wes Welker
3 Matt Schaub 1.25 3.00
Andre Johnson
4 Peyton Manning 2.50 6.00
Reggie Wayne
5 Ben Roethlisberger 1.50 4.00
Santonio Holmes
6 Eli Manning 1.50 4.00
Steve Smith USC
7 Philip Rivers 1.50 4.00
Antonio Gates
8 Donovan McNabb 1.50 4.00
DeSean Jackson
9 Drew Brees 1.50 4.00
Marques Colston
10 Matt Hasselbeck 1.00 2.50
Nate Burleson
11 Kyle Orton 1.25 3.00
Brandon Marshall
12 Tony Romo 2.00 5.00
Miles Austin
13 Kurt Warner 1.50 4.00
Larry Fitzgerald
14 Carson Palmer 1.25 3.00
Chad Ochocinco
15 Matt Ryan 1.50 4.00
Roddy White
16 Joe Flacco 1.50 4.00
Derrick Mason
17 Aaron Rodgers 3.00 8.00
Donald Driver
18 Jay Cutler 1.50 4.00
Greg Olsen
19 David Garrard 1.25 3.00
Mike Sims-Walker
20 Alex Smith QB 1.25 3.00
Vernon Davis

2010 Prestige Connections Materials
STATED PRINT RUN 250 SER.#'d SETS
1 Brett Favre 12.00 30.00
Sidney Rice
3 Matt Schaub 4.00 10.00
Andre Johnson
4 Peyton Manning 6.00 15.00
Reggie Wayne
5 Ben Roethlisberger 5.00 12.00
Santonio Holmes
7 Philip Rivers 5.00 12.00
Antonio Gates
9 Drew Brees 5.00 12.00
Marques Colston
10 Matt Hasselbeck 3.00 8.00
Nate Burleson
12 Tony Romo 12.00 30.00
Miles Austin
14 Carson Palmer 4.00 10.00
Chad Ochocinco
15 Matt Ryan 6.00 15.00
Roddy White
16 Joe Flacco 5.00 12.00
Derrick Mason
17 Aaron Rodgers 6.00 15.00
Donald Driver
18 Jay Cutler 5.00 12.00
Greg Olsen
20 Alex Smith QB 4.00 10.00
Vernon Davis

2010 Prestige Connections Materials Prime
*PRIME/50: .6X TO 1.5X BASIC DUAL JSY
PRIME PRINT RUN 5-50
2 Tom Brady 12.00 30.00
Wes Welker

2010 Prestige Draft Picks Rights Autographs
STATED PRINT RUN 99-999
201 Aaron Hernandez/399 10.00 25.00
202 Andre Anderson/999 4.00 10.00
204 Andre Roberts/399 5.00 12.00
206 Anthony McCoy/999 4.00 10.00
207 Antonio Brown/999 8.00 20.00
208 Arrelious Benn/299 6.00 15.00
209 Ben Tate/399 8.00 20.00
210 Blair White/999 5.00 12.00
211 Brandon Graham/399 5.00 12.00
212 Brandon LaFell/299 6.00 15.00
214 Bryan Bulaga/399 6.00 15.00
215 C.J. Spiller/199 12.00 30.00
218 Chad Jones/399 6.00 15.00
221 Chris Cook/399 6.00 15.00
222 Chris McGaha/999
223 Colt McCoy/199 15.00 40.00
224 Corey Wootton/799 4.00 10.00
225 Damian Williams/299 6.00 15.00
226 Dan LeFevour/599 5.00 12.00
227 Danario Alexander/999
229 David Gettis/999 5.00 12.00
230 Demaryius Thomas/299 8.00 20.00
231 Derrick Morgan/399 5.00 12.00
232 Devin McCourty/399 6.00 15.00
233 Dexter McCluster/199 8.00 20.00
234 Dez Bryant/199 35.00 60.00
235 Dezmon Briscoe/599 4.00 10.00
236 Dominique Franks/799 3.00 8.00
237 Earl Thomas/399 6.00 15.00
238 Ed Dickson/399 6.00 15.00
240 Eric Decker/199 10.00 25.00
242 Freddie Barnes/999 4.00 10.00
243 Garrett Graham/799 4.00 10.00
245 Golden Tate/99 12.00 30.00
246 Jacoby Ford/399 8.00 20.00
247 Jahvid Best/199 12.00 30.00
248 James Starks/599 10.00 25.00
249 Jarrett Brown/999 5.00 12.00
250 Jason Pierre-Paul/399 10.00 25.00
251 Jason Worilds/399 6.00 15.00
252 Jeremy Williams/999 3.00 8.00
253 Jermaine Gresham/399 8.00 20.00
254 Jerry Hughes/399 6.00 15.00
255 Jevan Snead/999 5.00 12.00
256 Jimmy Clausen/99 12.00 30.00
261 Joique Bell/999 4.00 10.00
262 Jonathan Crompton/399 5.00 12.00
263 Jonathan Dwyer/399 6.00 15.00
264 Jordan Shipley/399 6.00 15.00
267 LeGarrette Blount/999 8.00 20.00
268 Lonyae Miller/999 4.00 10.00
271 Mike Kafka/599 5.00 12.00
273 Montario Hardesty/399 6.00 15.00
274 Morgan Burnett/399 6.00 15.00
275 Nate Allen/399 6.00 15.00
278 Pat Paschall/999
279 Patrick Robinson/399 6.00 15.00
283 Rob Gronkowski/399 15.00 40.00
284 Rolando McClain/399 6.00 15.00
286 Ryan Mathews/199 25.00 50.00
287 Sam Bradford/199 50.00 100.00
288 Sean Canfield/999 4.00 10.00
289 Sean Lee/399 8.00 20.00
290 Sean Weatherspoon/399 6.00 15.00
292 Seyi Ajirotutu/999 5.00 12.00
293 Shay Hodge/999 4.00 10.00
295 Taylor Price/399 6.00 15.00
296 Tim Tebow/99 75.00 150.00
297 Toby Gerhart/299 6.00 15.00
298 Tony Pike/499 6.00 15.00
300 Zac Robinson/799 4.00 10.00

2010 Prestige Inside The Numbers
1 Chris Johnson 1.50 4.00
2 Miles Austin 1.50 4.00
3 Percy Harvin 1.50 4.00
4 Reggie Wayne 1.25 3.00
5 Josh Cribbs 1.50 4.00
6 Drew Brees 1.50 4.00
7 Adrian Peterson 2.50 6.00
8 Andre Johnson 1.25 3.00
9 Wes Welker 1.50 4.00
10 Maurice Jones-Drew 1.25 3.00

2010 Prestige Inside The Numbers Autographs
STATED PRINT RUN 5-25
1 Chris Johnson/10
5 Josh Cribbs/25 25.00 50.00
6 Drew Brees/5

2010 Prestige Inside The Numbers Materials
STATED PRINT RUN 220-250
*PRIME/50: .8X TO 2X BASIC JSY
*PRIME/20: 1X TO 2.5X BASIC JSY
PRIME PRINT RUN 20-50
1 Chris Johnson/250 4.00 10.00
2 Miles Austin/220 6.00 15.00
3 Percy Harvin/250 4.00 10.00
4 Reggie Wayne/250 3.00 8.00
5 Josh Cribbs/250 4.00 10.00
6 Drew Brees/250 4.00 10.00
7 Adrian Peterson/250 6.00 15.00
8 Andre Johnson/250 3.00 8.00
9 Wes Welker/250 4.00 10.00
10 Maurice Jones-Drew/250 3.00 8.00

2010 Prestige League Leaders
1 Matt Schaub 2.00 5.00
Peyton Manning
2 Tony Romo 2.50 6.00
Aaron Rodgers
3 Tom Brady 2.00 5.00
Drew Brees
4 Ben Roethlisberger 1.25 3.00
Philip Rivers
5 Brett Favre 3.00 8.00
Eli Manning
6 Chris Johnson 1.25 3.00
Steven Jackson
7 Thomas Jones 1.00 2.50
Maurice Jones-Drew
8 Adrian Peterson 2.00 5.00
Ray Rice
9 Ryan Grant 1.00 2.50
Cedric Benson
10 Jonathan Stewart 1.00 2.50
Ricky Williams
11 Andre Johnson 1.25 3.00
Wes Welker
12 Miles Austin 1.25 3.00
Sidney Rice
13 Randy Moss 1.25 3.00
Reggie Wayne
14 Santonio Holmes 1.00 2.50
Steve Smith USC
15 Vincent Jackson 1.00 2.50
DeSean Jackson
16 Drew Brees 4.00 10.00
Brett Favre
Peyton Manning
Aaron Rodgers
17 Adrian Peterson 2.50 6.00
Maurice Jones-Drew
Chris Johnson
Thomas Jones
18 Vernon Davis 1.50 4.00
Larry Fitzgerald
Randy Moss
Miles Austin
19 Matt Schaub 3.00 8.00
Peyton Manning
Tony Romo
Aaron Rodgers
20 Chris Johnson 1.50 4.00
Steven Jackson
Thomas Jones
Maurice Jones-Drew
21 Andre Johnson 1.50 4.00
Wes Welker
Miles Austin
Sidney Rice
22 Drew Brees 2.50 6.00
Adrian Peterson
Vernon Davis
Josh Cribbs
23 Adrian Peterson 2.50 6.00
Maurice Jones-Drew
Vernon Davis
Larry Fitzgerald
24 Elvis Dumervil 1.50 4.00
Jared Allen
Dwight Freeney
LaMarr Woodley
25 Jairus Byrd 1.50 4.00
Asante Samuel
Darren Sharper
Charles Woodson

2010 Prestige League Leaders Materials
1-13 DUAL JSY PRINT RUN 145-250
16-23 QUAD JSY PRINT RUN 100
*PRIME DUAL/50: .6X TO 1.5X BASIC DUAL
*PRIME QUAD/25: .6X TO 1.5X BASIC QUAD
STATED PRINT RUN 1-50
1 Matt Schaub 8.00 20.00
Peyton Manning
2 Tony Romo 10.00 25.00
Aaron Rodgers
3 Tom Brady 8.00 20.00
Drew Brees
4 Ben Roethlisberger 5.00 12.00
Philip Rivers
5 Brett Favre 12.00 30.00
Eli Manning
6 Chris Johnson 5.00 12.00
Steven Jackson
7 Thomas Jones 4.00 10.00
Maurice Jones-Drew
9 Ryan Grant/145 4.00 10.00
Cedric Benson
10 Jonathan Stewart 4.00 10.00
Ricky Williams
11 Andre Johnson 5.00 12.00
Wes Welker
12 Miles Austin 8.00 20.00
Sidney Rice
13 Randy Moss 5.00 12.00
Reggie Wayne
16 Drew Brees 20.00 50.00
Brett Favre
Peyton Manning
Aaron Rodgers
17 Adrian Peterson 12.00 30.00
Maurice Jones-Drew
Chris Johnson
Thomas Jones
18 Vernon Davis 8.00 20.00
Larry Fitzgerald
Randy Moss
Miles Austin
19 Matt Schaub 15.00 40.00
Peyton Manning
Tony Romo
Aaron Rodgers
20 Chris Johnson 8.00 20.00
Steven Jackson
Thomas Jones
Maurice Jones-Drew
21 Andre Johnson 12.00 30.00
Wes Welker
Miles Austin
Sidney Rice
22 Drew Brees 12.00 30.00
Adrian Peterson
Vernon Davis
Josh Cribbs
23 Adrian Peterson 12.00 30.00
Maurice Jones-Drew
Vernon Davis
Larry Fitzgerald

2010 Prestige NFL Draft
1 Ndamukong Suh 2.00 5.00
2 Eric Berry 1.00 2.50
3 Gerald McCoy 1.00 2.50
4 Russell Okung 1.00 2.50
5 Joe Haden 1.00 2.50
6 C.J. Spiller 1.50 4.00
7 Jimmy Clausen 1.00 2.50
8 Derrick Morgan .75 2.00
9 Sam Bradford 4.00 10.00
10 Rolando McClain 1.00 2.50
11 Dez Bryant 3.00 8.00
12 Taylor Mays 1.00 2.50
13 Carlos Dunlap 1.00 2.50
14 Trent Williams 1.00 2.50
15 Golden Tate 1.00 2.50
16 Ricky Sapp .75 2.00
17 Jonathan Dwyer 1.00 2.50
18 Earl Thomas 1.00 2.50
19 Sergio Kindle 1.00 2.50
20 Colt McCoy 2.00 5.00
21 Tim Tebow 4.00 10.00
22 Jahvid Best 1.50 4.00
23 Ryan Mathews 2.00 5.00
24 Brandon LaFell 1.00 2.50
25 Jermaine Gresham 1.25 3.00
26 Damian Williams 1.00 2.50
27 Brandon Spikes 1.00 2.50
28 Jordan Shipley 1.00 2.50
29 Demaryius Thomas 1.25 3.00
30 Arrelious Benn 1.00 2.50
31 Anthony Dixon 1.00 2.50
32 Carlton Mitchell .75 2.00
33 Dezmon Briscoe .75 2.00
34 Joe McKnight 1.00 2.50
35 Toby Gerhart 1.00 2.50

2010 Prestige NFL Draft Autographed Patch Draft Logo
3 Gerald McCoy 12.00 30.00
5 Joe Haden 12.00 30.00
6 C.J. Spiller 30.00 60.00
7 Jimmy Clausen 12.00 30.00
8 Derrick Morgan 10.00 25.00
9 Sam Bradford 50.00 120.00
10 Rolando McClain 12.00 30.00
11 Dez Bryant 40.00 100.00
15 Golden Tate 12.00 30.00
17 Jonathan Dwyer 12.00 30.00
18 Earl Thomas 12.00 30.00
20 Colt McCoy 30.00 80.00
21 Tim Tebow 90.00 150.00
22 Jahvid Best 25.00 50.00
23 Ryan Mathews 40.00 80.00
24 Brandon LaFell 12.00 30.00
25 Jermaine Gresham 15.00 40.00
26 Damian Williams 12.00 30.00
28 Jordan Shipley 12.00 30.00
29 Demaryius Thomas 15.00 40.00
30 Arrelious Benn 12.00 30.00
33 Dezmon Briscoe 10.00 25.00
35 Toby Gerhart 12.00 30.00

2010 Prestige NFL Draft Autographed Patch NFL Equipment Logo
*NFL EQUIP LOGO: .5X TO 1.2X DRAFT LOGO
9 Sam Bradford 100.00 200.00
21 Tim Tebow 125.00 250.00

2010 Prestige NFL Draft Autographed Patch NFL Shield Logo
*NFL SHIELD LOGO: .6X TO 1.5X DRAFT LOGO
9 Sam Bradford 100.00 200.00
21 Tim Tebow 100.00 200.00

2010 Prestige NFL Draft Autographs
3 Gerald McCoy 6.00 15.00
5 Joe Haden 6.00 15.00
6 C.J. Spiller 25.00 50.00
7 Jimmy Clausen 12.00 30.00
8 Derrick Morgan 5.00 12.00
9 Sam Bradford 50.00 100.00
10 Rolando McClain 6.00 15.00
11 Dez Bryant 30.00 80.00
15 Golden Tate 6.00 15.00
17 Jonathan Dwyer 6.00 15.00
18 Earl Thomas 6.00 15.00
20 Colt McCoy 30.00 60.00
21 Tim Tebow 60.00 120.00
22 Jahvid Best 30.00 60.00
23 Ryan Mathews 30.00 60.00
24 Brandon LaFell 6.00 15.00
25 Jermaine Gresham 8.00 20.00
26 Damian Williams 6.00 15.00
28 Jordan Shipley 6.00 15.00
29 Demaryius Thomas 8.00 20.00
30 Arrelious Benn 6.00 15.00
33 Dezmon Briscoe 5.00 12.00
35 Toby Gerhart 12.00 30.00

2010 Prestige Preferred Materials
STATED PRINT RUN 250 SER.#'d SETS
1 Brandon Marshall 3.00 8.00
3 Drew Brees 4.00 10.00
4 Jamaal Charles 3.00 8.00
7 Sidney Rice 4.00 10.00
8 Brett Favre 15.00 40.00
9 Roddy White 3.00 8.00

2010 Prestige Preferred Materials Patch
*PATCH/25: 1X TO 2.5X BASIC JSY/250
PATCH PRINT RUN 25 SER.#'d SETS
10 Ryan Grant 8.00 20.00

2010 Prestige Preferred Materials Signatures
STATED PRINT RUN 10-25
1 Brandon Marshall/15 12.00 30.00
3 Drew Brees/10
4 Jamaal Charles/15 12.00 30.00
7 Sidney Rice/20 20.00 40.00
8 Brett Favre/10
9 Roddy White/10
10 Ryan Grant/25 12.00 30.00

2010 Prestige Preferred Signatures
STATED PRINT RUN 4-30
1 Brandon Marshall/5
2 DeSean Jackson/5
3 Drew Brees/5
4 Jamaal Charles/8
5 Rashard Mendenhall/13
6 Ray Rice/30 10.00 25.00
8 Brett Favre/4

2010 Prestige Prestigious Pros Blue
*BLACK/25: 1.2X TO 3X BLUE
*GOLD/100: .6X TO 1.5X BLUE
*GREEN/250: .5X TO 1.2X BLUE
*PLATINUM/10: 2.5X TO 6X BLUE
1 Anquan Boldin 1.00 2.50
2 Bernard Berrian .75 2.00
3 Brandon Jacobs 1.00 2.50
4 Brian Westbrook 1.00 2.50
5 Cadillac Williams 1.00 2.50
6 Chester Taylor .75 2.00
7 Chris Cooley 1.00 2.50
8 Dallas Clark 1.00 2.50
9 Jerricho Cotchery 1.00 2.50
10 Darren McFadden 1.00 2.50
11 Darren Sproles 1.00 2.50
12 David Garrard 1.00 2.50
13 Davone Bess .75 2.00
14 Devery Henderson .75 2.00
15 Devin Hester 1.25 3.00
16 Donald Driver 1.00 2.50
17 Dustin Keller 1.00 2.50
18 Eddie Royal .75 2.00
19 Felix Jones 1.00 2.50
20 Greg Jennings 1.00 2.50
21 Greg Olsen .75 2.00
22 Heath Miller 1.00 2.50
23 James Jones .75 2.00
24 Jeremy Maclin 1.00 2.50
25 Jermichael Finley 1.00 2.50
26 Jonathan Stewart 1.00 2.50
27 Joseph Addai 1.00 2.50
28 Ladell Betts .75 2.00
29 Laurence Maroney 1.00 2.50
30 Lee Evans 1.00 2.50
31 Mario Manningham 1.00 2.50
32 Marion Barber 1.00 2.50
33 Marques Colston 1.00 2.50
34 Matt Forte 1.00 2.50
35 Matt Ryan 1.25 3.00
36 Matthew Stafford 1.25 3.00
37 Michael Crabtree 1.25 3.00
38 Michael Turner .75 2.00
39 Steven Jackson 1.00 2.50
40 Patrick Crayton .75 2.00
41 Pierre Garcon 1.00 2.50
42 Rashard Mendenhall 1.00 2.50
43 Ray Rice 1.00 2.50
44 Ronnie Brown 1.00 2.50
45 Santana Moss 1.00 2.50
46 Steve Smith 1.00 2.50
47 Tony Romo 1.50 4.00
48 Vince Young .75 2.00
49 Visanthe Shiancoe 1.00 2.50
50 Zach Miller 1.00 2.50

2010 Prestige Prestigious Pros Autographs
STATED PRINT RUN 7-100
2 Bernard Berrian/7
6 Chester Taylor/25 10.00 25.00
13 Davone Bess/50 6.00 15.00
14 Devery Henderson/100 6.00 15.00
17 Dustin Keller/75 8.00 20.00
18 Eddie Royal/75 6.00 15.00
23 James Jones/75
24 Jeremy Maclin/14
25 Jermichael Finley/100 10.00 25.00
26 Jonathan Stewart/20 12.00 30.00
28 Ladell Betts/53 6.00 15.00
31 Mario Manningham/100 8.00 20.00
33 Marques Colston/23 12.00 30.00
34 Matt Forte/50 8.00 20.00
36 Matthew Stafford/15 30.00 60.00
37 Michael Crabtree/15 25.00 50.00
40 Patrick Crayton/87 6.00 15.00
41 Pierre Garcon/100 10.00 25.00
42 Rashard Mendenhall/10
43 Ray Rice/34 10.00 25.00

2010 Prestige Prestigious Pros Materials Gold
GOLD PRINT RUN 50 SER.#'d SETS
*BLACK/10: .8X TO 2X GOLD/50
BLACK PRINT RUN 10 SER.#'d SETS
*BLUE/240-250: .25X TO .6X GOLD/50
*BLUE/35: .4X TO 1X GOLD/50
BLUE PRINT RUN 35-250
*GREEN/100: .3X TO .8X GOLD/50
*GREEN/25: .5X TO 1.2X GOLD/50
GREEN PRINT RUN 25-100
*PLAT.PATCH/25: .6X TO 1.5X GOLD/50
PLATINUM PATCH PRINT RUN 25
1 Anquan Boldin 5.00 12.00
2 Bernard Berrian 4.00 10.00
3 Brandon Jacobs 5.00 12.00
4 Brian Westbrook 5.00 12.00
5 Cadillac Williams 5.00 12.00
6 Chester Taylor 4.00 10.00
7 Chris Cooley 5.00 12.00
8 Dallas Clark 5.00 12.00
9 Jerricho Cotchery 5.00 12.00
10 Darren McFadden 5.00 12.00
11 Darren Sproles 5.00 12.00
12 David Garrard 5.00 12.00
14 Devery Henderson 4.00 10.00
15 Devin Hester 6.00 15.00
16 Donald Driver 5.00 12.00
17 Dustin Keller 5.00 12.00
18 Eddie Royal 4.00 10.00
19 Felix Jones 5.00 12.00
20 Greg Jennings 5.00 12.00
21 Greg Olsen 4.00 10.00
22 Heath Miller 5.00 12.00
23 James Jones 4.00 10.00
24 Jeremy Maclin 5.00 12.00
26 Jonathan Stewart 5.00 12.00
27 Joseph Addai 5.00 12.00
28 Ladell Betts 4.00 10.00
29 Laurence Maroney 5.00 12.00
30 Lee Evans 5.00 12.00
32 Marion Barber 5.00 12.00
33 Marques Colston 5.00 12.00
34 Matt Forte 5.00 12.00
35 Matt Ryan 6.00 15.00
36 Matthew Stafford 6.00 15.00
37 Michael Crabtree 6.00 15.00
38 Michael Turner 4.00 10.00
39 Steven Jackson 5.00 12.00
40 Patrick Crayton 4.00 10.00
44 Ronnie Brown 5.00 12.00
45 Santana Moss 5.00 12.00
46 Steve Smith 5.00 12.00
47 Tony Romo 8.00 20.00
48 Vince Young 4.00 10.00
49 Visanthe Shiancoe 5.00 12.00
50 Zach Miller 5.00 12.00

2010 Prestige Pro Helmets Autographs
AB Arrelious Benn 12.00 30.00
AH Aaron Hernandez 20.00 50.00
AM Anthony McCoy 10.00 25.00
BL Brandon LaFell 12.00 30.00
CM Colt McCoy 25.00 60.00
CS C.J. Spiller 20.00 50.00
DB Dez Bryant 50.00 100.00
DBR Dezmon Briscoe 10.00 25.00
DM Derrick Morgan 10.00 25.00
DMC Dexter McCluster 12.00 30.00
DT Demaryius Thomas 15.00 40.00
DW Damian Williams 12.00 30.00
ED Eric Decker 15.00 40.00
ET Earl Thomas 12.00 30.00
GM Gerald McCoy 12.00 30.00
GT Golden Tate 12.00 30.00
JB Jahvid Best 20.00 50.00
JBR Jarrett Brown 12.00 30.00
JC Jimmy Clausen 12.00 30.00
JD Jonathan Dwyer 12.00 30.00
JG Jermaine Gresham 15.00 40.00
JH Joe Haden 12.00 30.00
JS Jevan Snead 12.00 30.00
JSH Jordan Shipley 12.00 30.00
JW Jeremy Williams 8.00 20.00
RG Rob Gronkowski 30.00 60.00
RM Ryan Mathews 30.00 80.00
RMC Rolando McClain 12.00 30.00
SB Sam Bradford 60.00 150.00
SC Sean Canfield 10.00 25.00
TG Toby Gerhart 12.00 30.00
TP Tony Pike 12.00 30.00
TT Tim Tebow 75.00 150.00

2010 Prestige Rookie Review
1 Mark Sanchez 1.25 3.00
2 Matthew Stafford 1.25 3.00
3 Josh Freeman 1.25 3.00
4 Chris Wells 1.00 2.50
5 Knowshon Moreno 1.00 2.50
6 LeSean McCoy 1.00 2.50
7 Shonn Greene 1.00 2.50
8 Percy Harvin 1.25 3.00
9 Jeremy Maclin 1.00 2.50
10 Kenny Britt 1.00 2.50
11 Hakeem Nicks 1.00 2.50
12 Michael Crabtree 1.25 3.00
13 Mike Thomas 1.00 2.50
14 Mike Wallace 1.00 2.50
15 Mohamed Massaquoi 1.00 2.50
16 Brandon Pettigrew .75 2.00
17 Darrius Heyward-Bey 1.00 2.50
18 Aaron Curry 1.00 2.50
19 Glen Coffee 1.00 2.50
20 Donald Brown 1.00 2.50
21 Tyson Jackson .75 2.00
22 Jason Smith .75 2.00
23 Brandon Gibson .75 2.00
24 Sammie Stroughter .75 2.00
25 Julian Edelman .75 2.00
26 Louis Murphy 1.00 2.50
27 Brian Hartline 1.00 2.50
28 James Laurinaitis 1.00 2.50
29 Brian Cushing .75 2.00
30 Jairus Byrd 1.00 2.50
31 Brian Orakpo .75 2.00
32 Clay Matthews 1.25 3.00
33 LaRod Stephens-Howling 1.00 2.50
34 Johnny Knox 1.00 2.50
35 Austin Collie 1.00 2.50

2010 Prestige Rookie Review Autographs
2 Matthew Stafford 25.00 50.00
3 Josh Freeman 12.00 30.00
4 Chris Wells 10.00 25.00
5 Knowshon Moreno 12.00 30.00
7 Shonn Greene
9 Jeremy Maclin 10.00 25.00
12 Michael Crabtree 12.00 30.00
14 Mike Wallace 10.00 25.00
16 Brandon Pettigrew 8.00 20.00
22 Jason Smith 8.00 20.00
26 Louis Murphy 10.00 25.00

2010 Prestige Rookie Review Materials
1 Mark Sanchez DP 6.00 15.00
2 Matthew Stafford DP 5.00 12.00
3 Josh Freeman 5.00 12.00
4 Chris Wells 4.00 10.00
5 Knowshon Moreno 4.00 10.00
6 LeSean McCoy 6.00 15.00
7 Shonn Greene 4.00 10.00
8 Percy Harvin DP 5.00 12.00
9 Jeremy Maclin 4.00 10.00
10 Kenny Britt 4.00 10.00
11 Hakeem Nicks 4.00 10.00
13 Mike Thomas 4.00 10.00
14 Mike Wallace 4.00 10.00
15 Mohamed Massaquoi 4.00 10.00
16 Brandon Pettigrew 3.00 8.00
17 Darrius Heyward-Bey 4.00 10.00
18 Aaron Curry 4.00 10.00
19 Glen Coffee 4.00 10.00
20 Donald Brown 4.00 10.00
21 Tyson Jackson 3.00 8.00
22 Jason Smith 3.00 8.00

2010 Prestige Rookie Review Materials Prime
*PRIME/50: .8X TO 2X BASIC JSY
PRIME PRINT RUN 50 SER.#'d SETS
12 Michael Crabtree 10.00 25.00

2010 Prestige Stars of the NFL
1 Aaron Rodgers 2.50 6.00
2 Adrian Peterson 2.00 5.00
3 Andre Johnson 1.00 2.50
4 Calvin Johnson 1.25 3.00
5 Chris Johnson 1.25 3.00
6 Donovan McNabb 1.25 3.00
7 Maurice Jones-Drew 1.00 2.50
8 Peyton Manning 2.00 5.00
9 Santonio Holmes 1.00 2.50
10 Tom Brady 2.00 5.00
11 Tony Romo 1.50 4.00
12 Vincent Jackson .75 2.00
13 Chad Ochocinco 1.00 2.50
14 Drew Brees 1.25 3.00
15 Frank Gore 1.00 2.50
16 Wes Welker 1.25 3.00
17 Philip Rivers 1.25 3.00
18 DeAngelo Williams 1.00 2.50
19 Eli Manning 1.25 3.00
20 Thomas Jones 1.00 2.50

2010 Prestige Stars of the NFL Materials
STATED PRINT RUN 100-250
1 Aaron Rodgers/180 6.00 15.00
2 Adrian Peterson/250 6.00 15.00
3 Andre Johnson/250 3.00 8.00
4 Calvin Johnson/250 4.00 10.00
5 Chris Johnson/250 4.00 10.00
6 Donovan McNabb/250 4.00 10.00
7 Maurice Jones-Drew/250 3.00 8.00
8 Peyton Manning/250 6.00 15.00
9 Santonio Holmes/250 3.00 8.00
10 Tom Brady/170 6.00 15.00
11 Tony Romo/250 5.00 12.00
12 Vincent Jackson/250 2.50 6.00
13 Chad Ochocinco/250 3.00 8.00
14 Drew Brees/250 4.00 10.00
15 Frank Gore/250 3.00 8.00
17 Philip Rivers/250 4.00 10.00
18 DeAngelo Williams/250 3.00 8.00
19 Eli Manning/250 4.00 10.00
20 Thomas Jones/100 4.00 10.00

2010 Prestige Stars of the NFL Materials Prime
*PRIME/40-50: .8X TO 2X BASIC JSY/170-250
*PRIME/24: 1X TO 2.5X BASIC JSY/250
*PRIME/20: .8X TO 2X BASIC JSY/100
PRIME PRINT RUN 20-50
16 Wes Welker/50 8.00 20.00

2010 Prestige Touchdown Sensations
1 Adrian Peterson 2.00 5.00
2 Brandon Marshall 1.00 2.50
3 Chris Johnson 1.25 3.00
4 DeSean Jackson 1.00 2.50
5 Frank Gore 1.00 2.50
6 Joseph Addai 1.00 2.50
7 LaDainian Tomlinson 1.25 3.00
8 Larry Fitzgerald 1.25 3.00
9 Marques Colston 1.00 2.50
10 Maurice Jones-Drew 1.00 2.50
11 Michael Turner .75 2.00
12 Miles Austin 1.25 3.00
13 Percy Harvin 1.25 3.00
14 Randy Moss 1.25 3.00
15 Reggie Wayne 1.00 2.50
16 Ricky Williams 1.00 2.50
17 Thomas Jones 1.00 2.50
18 Vernon Davis 1.00 2.50
19 Visanthe Shiancoe 1.00 2.50
20 Willis McGahee 1.00 2.50

2010 Prestige Touchdown Sensations Materials
STATED PRINT RUN 50-250
*PRIME/50: .8X TO 2X BASIC JSY/250
*PRIME/25: .6X TO 1.5X BASIC JSY/50
PRIME PRINT RUN 25-50
1 Adrian Peterson/250 6.00 15.00
2 Brandon Marshall/250 3.00 8.00
3 Chris Johnson/250 4.00 10.00
5 Frank Gore/250 3.00 8.00
6 Joseph Addai/250 3.00 8.00
7 LaDainian Tomlinson/250 4.00 10.00
8 Larry Fitzgerald/250 4.00 10.00
9 Marques Colston/250 3.00 8.00
10 Maurice Jones-Drew/250 3.00 8.00
11 Michael Turner/250 2.50 6.00
12 Miles Austin/250 6.00 15.00
13 Percy Harvin/250 4.00 10.00
14 Randy Moss/250 4.00 10.00
15 Reggie Wayne/250 3.00 8.00
16 Ricky Williams/250 3.00 8.00
17 Thomas Jones/50 5.00 12.00
18 Vernon Davis/250 3.00 8.00
19 Visanthe Shiancoe/250 3.00 8.00
20 Willis McGahee/250 3.00 8.00

2010 Prestige True Colors
1 Jason Witten 1.25 3.00
2 Larry Fitzgerald 1.25 3.00
3 Brett Favre 3.00 8.00
4 LaDainian Tomlinson 1.25 3.00
5 Marshawn Lynch 1.00 2.50
6 Chad Ochocinco 1.00 2.50
7 Frank Gore 1.00 2.50
8 Drew Brees 1.25 3.00
9 Andre Johnson 1.00 2.50
10 Ryan Grant 1.00 2.50

2010 Prestige True Colors Autographs
3 Brett Favre/4
8 Drew Brees/5

2010 Prestige True Colors Materials
STATED PRINT RUN 200-250
*PRIMARY CLR/50: .8X TO 2X BASIC JSY/250
*PRIMARY CLR/15-25: 1X TO 2.5X BASIC JSY/200-250

PRIMARY COLOR PRINT RUN 15-50
1 Jason Witten 4.00 10.00
2 Larry Fitzgerald 4.00 10.00
3 Brett Favre 15.00 40.00
4 LaDainian Tomlinson 4.00 10.00
5 Marshawn Lynch 3.00 8.00
6 Chad Ochocinco 3.00 8.00
7 Frank Gore 3.00 8.00
8 Drew Brees 4.00 10.00
9 Andre Johnson 3.00 8.00
10 Ryan Grant 3.00 8.00

2010 Prestige Xtra Points Black Autographs
STATED PRINT RUN 4-250
2 Chris Wells/12
3 Dominique Rodgers-Cromartie/134
8 Jason Snelling/44 10.00 25.00
9 Matt Ryan/26 25.00 50.00
15 Joe Flacco/25 25.00 50.00
27 DeAngelo Williams/10
29 Jonathan Stewart/19 12.00 30.00
35 Earl Bennett/50 8.00 20.00
39 Matt Forte/97 8.00 20.00
49 Josh Cribbs/15 25.00 50.00
59 Brandon Marshall/25 12.00 30.00
68 Kevin Smith/41 10.00 25.00
69 Matthew Stafford/42 30.00 60.00
74 Jermichael Finley/97 10.00 25.00
81 Steve Slaton/12
87 Pierre Garcon/125 10.00 25.00
92 Mike Sims-Walker/5
95 Brandon Flowers/96 6.00 15.00
102 Davone Bess/63 6.00 15.00
109 Brett Favre/10
120 Devery Henderson/250 5.00 12.00
121 Drew Brees/4
132 Mario Manningham/113 8.00 20.00
135 Darrelle Revis/100 10.00 25.00
141 Chaz Schilens/250 5.00 12.00
150 DeSean Jackson/30 10.00 25.00
157 Mike Wallace/150 8.00 20.00
167 Shawne Merriman/5
171 Michael Crabtree/50 15.00 40.00
172 Patrick Willis/17 15.00 40.00
176 Justin Forsett/250 6.00 15.00

2011 Prestige

COMP.SET w/o RCs (200) 10.00 25.00
ONE ROOKIE PER PACK
1 Chris Wells .25 .60
2 Early Doucet .20 .50
3 Larry Fitzgerald .25 .60
4 Steve Breaston .20 .50
5 Tim Hightower .20 .50
6 Curtis Lofton .20 .50
7 Jason Snelling .25 .60
8 Matt Ryan .30 .75
9 Michael Turner .25 .60
10 Roddy White .25 .60
11 Tony Gonzalez .25 .60
12 Anquan Boldin .25 .60
13 Ed Reed .25 .60
14 Haloti Ngata .20 .50
15 Joe Flacco .30 .75
16 Ray Lewis .30 .75
17 Ray Rice .25 .60
18 T.J. Houshmandzadeh .25 .60
19 Todd Heap .20 .50
20 C.J. Spiller .25 .60
21 Fred Jackson .30 .75
22 Lee Evans .25 .60
23 Roscoe Parrish .20 .50
24 Ryan Fitzpatrick .25 .60
25 Steve Johnson .25 .60
26 DeAngelo Williams .25 .60
27 Mike Goodson .20 .50
28 Jimmy Clausen .20 .50
29 Jon Beason .20 .50
30 Jonathan Stewart .25 .60
31 Steve Smith .25 .60
32 Brian Urlacher .30 .75
33 Devin Hester .30 .75
34 Earl Bennett .20 .50
35 Greg Olsen .20 .50
36 Jay Cutler .25 .60
37 Johnny Knox .25 .60
38 Julius Peppers .25 .60
39 Matt Forte .25 .60
40 Carson Palmer .25 .60
41 Cedric Benson .25 .60
42 Chad Johnson .25 .60
43 Jermaine Gresham .25 .60
44 Jordan Shipley .25 .60
45 Terrell Owens .30 .75
46 Ben Watson .20 .50
47 Colt McCoy .25 .60
48 Josh Cribbs .25 .60
49 Mohamed Massaquoi .25 .60
50 Peyton Hillis .25 .60
51 DeMarcus Ware .25 .60
52 Dez Bryant .30 .75
53 Felix Jones .25 .60
54 Jason Witten .30 .75
55 Miles Austin .25 .60
56 Roy Williams WR .25 .60
57 Tony Romo .30 .75
58 Brandon Lloyd .25 .60

59 Eddie Royal .20 .50
60 Jabar Gaffney .20 .50
61 Knowshon Moreno .25 .60
62 Champ Bailey .25 .60
63 Tim Tebow .60 1.50
64 Brandon Pettigrew .20 .50
65 Calvin Johnson .30 .75
66 Jahvid Best .25 .60
67 Matthew Stafford .30 .75
68 Nate Burleson .20 .50
69 Ndamukong Suh .30 .75
70 Aaron Rodgers .50 1.25
71 Charles Woodson .30 .75
72 Clay Matthews .30 .75
73 Donald Driver .25 .60
74 Greg Jennings .25 .60
75 Jordy Nelson .25 .60
76 Ryan Grant .25 .60
77 Andre Johnson .25 .60
78 Arian Foster .25 .60
79 Brian Cushing .20 .50
80 Jacoby Jones .20 .50
81 Kevin Walter .25 .60
82 Matt Schaub .25 .60
83 Austin Collie .25 .60
84 Dallas Clark .25 .60
85 Dwight Freeney .25 .60
86 Jacob Tamme .25 .60
87 Joseph Addai .25 .60
88 Peyton Manning .50 1.25
89 Reggie Wayne .25 .60
90 David Garrard .25 .60
91 Marcedes Lewis .20 .50
92 Maurice Jones-Drew .25 .60
93 Mike Sims-Walker .25 .60
94 Mike Thomas .25 .60
95 Brandon Flowers .20 .50
96 Dexter McCluster .20 .50
97 Dwayne Bowe .25 .60
98 Jamaal Charles .25 .60
99 Matt Cassel .25 .60
100 Thomas Jones .25 .60
101 Tony Moeaki .20 .50
102 Anthony Fasano .20 .50
103 Brandon Marshall .25 .60
104 Brian Hartline .20 .50
105 Chad Henne .25 .60
106 Davone Bess .20 .50
107 Ronnie Brown .25 .60
108 Adrian Peterson .40 1.00
109 Jared Allen .25 .60
110 Percy Harvin .25 .60
111 Sidney Rice .25 .60
112 Tarvaris Jackson .20 .50
113 Visanthe Shiancoe .25 .60
114 Aaron Hernandez .25 .60
115 BenJarvus Green-Ellis .25 .00
116 Brandon Meriweather .20 .50
117 Danny Woodhead .30 .75
118 Deion Branch .20 .50
119 Rob Gronkowski .30 .75
120 Tom Brady .50 1.25
121 Wes Welker .30 .75
122 Drew Brees .30 .75
123 Lance Moore .25 .60
124 Marques Colston .25 .60
125 Pierre Thomas .25 .60
126 Reggie Bush .25 .60
127 Robert Meachem .25 .60
128 Ahmad Bradshaw .25 .60
129 Brandon Jacobs .25 .60
130 Eli Manning .30 .75
131 Hakeem Nicks .25 .00
132 Kevin Boss .25 .60
133 Mario Manningham .25 .60
134 Steve Smith USC .25 .60
135 Braylon Edwards .25 .60
136 Darrelle Revis .25 .60
137 Dustin Keller .25 .60
138 LaDainian Tomlinson .30 .75
139 Mark Sanchez .30 .75
140 Santonio Holmes .25 .60
141 Shonn Greene .25 .60
142 Darren McFadden .25 .60
143 Darrius Heyward-Bey .20 .50
144 Louis Murphy .25 .60
145 Jacoby Ford .25 .60
146 Michael Huff .20 .50
147 Zach Miller .25 .60
148 Asante Samuel .20 .50
149 Brent Celek .25 .60
150 DeSean Jackson .25 .60
151 Jeremy Maclin .25 .60
152 LeSean McCoy .25 .60
153 Michael Vick .30 .75
154 Ben Roethlisberger .30 .75
155 Heath Miller .25 .60
156 Hines Ward .25 .60
157 James Harrison .30 .75
158 Mike Wallace .30 .75
159 Rashard Mendenhall .25 .60
160 Troy Polamalu .30 .75
161 Antonio Gates .25 .60
162 Darren Sproles .25 .60
163 Malcom Floyd .25 .60
164 Mike Tolbert .25 .60
165 Philip Rivers .30 .75
166 Ryan Mathews .25 .60
167 Frank Gore .25 .60
168 Josh Morgan .25 .60
169 Michael Crabtree .25 .60
170 Patrick Willis .25 .60
171 Alex Smith .25 .60
172 Vernon Davis .25 .60
173 John Carlson .20 .50
174 Justin Forsett .25 .60
175 Marshawn Lynch .25 .60
176 Matt Hasselbeck .25 .60
177 Mike Williams USC .25 .60
178 Brandon Gibson .20 .50
179 Danny Amendola .25 .60
180 Donnie Avery .20 .50
181 James Laurinaitis .20 .50
182 Sam Bradford .30 .75
183 Steven Jackson .25 .60
184 Barrett Ruud .20 .50
185 Cadillac Williams .20 .50
186 Josh Freeman .30 .75
187 Kellen Winslow Jr. .25 .60
188 LeGarrette Blount .25 .60
189 Mike Williams .25 .60
190 Bo Scaife .20 .50
191 Chris Johnson .25 .60
192 Kenny Britt .25 .60
193 Nate Washington .20 .50
194 Randy Moss .25 .60
195 Vince Young .20 .50
196 Chris Cooley .25 .60
197 Ryan Torain .20 .50
198 Donovan McNabb .30 .75
199 LaRon Landry .20 .50
200 Santana Moss .25 .60
201A A.J. Green RC 1.50 4.00
201B A.J. Green Draft SP 6.00 15.00
202 Aaron Williams RC .60 1.50
203A Adrian Clayborn SP RC 12.00 30.00
203B Adrian Clayborn Draft SP 6.00 15.00
204 Ahmad Black SP RC 6.00 15.00
205 Akeem Ayers RC .60 1.50
206A Aldon Smith RC 1.25 3.00
206B Aldon Smith Draft SP 5.00 12.00
207 Andy Dalton RC 2.00 5.00
208 Austin Pettis RC .60 1.50
209 Bilal Powell RC .50 1.25
210A Blaine Gabbert RC 1.25 3.00
210B Blaine Gabbert Draft SP 5.00 12.00
211 Brandon Harris RC .50 1.25
212 Brooks Reed RC .75 2.00
213 Bruce Carter SP RC 8.00 20.00
214A Cam Newton RC 4.00 10.00
(light blue ghosted team name on front)
214B Cam Newton SP Draft 8.00 20.00
(NFL Draft photo on front)
214C Cam Newton SP Blu Name 6.00 15.00
(blue team name on front)
215 Cameron Heyward RC .75 2.00
216A Cameron Jordan RC .60 1.50
216B Cameron Jordan Draft SP 2.50 6.00
217 Cecil Shorts RC .60 1.50
218 Christian Ballard RC .60 1.50
219 Christian Ponder RC 1.50 4.00
220 Colin Kaepernick RC 1.00 2.50
221 Colin McCarthy RC .60 1.50
222 Corey Liuget RC .50 1.25
223 Courtney Smith RC .60 1.50
224 Curtis Brown SP RC 10.00 25.00
225 D.J. Williams RC .75 2.00
226 Daniel Thomas RC .75 2.00
227 Da'Quan Bowers RC .75 2.00
228 Darvin Adams RC .60 1.50
229 Davon House RC .60 1.50
230 DeAndre Brown RC .75 2.00
231 DeAndre McDaniel RC .60 1.50
232 Delone Carter RC .60 1.50
233 DeMarco Murray RC 1.50 4.00
234 Denarius Moore RC 1.00 2.50
235 Derrick Locke RC .60 1.50
236 Dion Lewis RC .75 2.00
237 Drake Nevis RC .75 2.00
238 Dwayne Harris RC .75 2.00
239 Edmond Gates SP RC 10.00 25.00
240 Evan Royster RC .75 2.00
241 Greg Jones RC .60 1.50
242 Greg Little RC .75 2.00
243 Greg Salas RC .75 2.00
244A J.J. Watt RC 1.00 2.50
244B J.J. Watt Draft SP 4.00 10.00
245 Jabaal Sheard RC .75 2.00
246 Jacquizz Rodgers RC .75 2.00
247 Jake Locker RC 2.00 5.00
248 Jamie Harper RC .75 2.00
249 Jeremy Kerley RC .75 2.00
250 Jerrel Jernigan RC .60 1.50
251 Jimmy Smith RC .75 2.00
252 John Clay RC .75 2.00
253 Jonathan Baldwin RC .75 2.00
254 Jordan Todman RC .50 1.25
255 Tyron Smith SP RC 12.00 30.00
256A Julio Jones RC 1.50 4.00
256B Julio Jones Draft SP 6.00 15.00
257 Justin Houston RC .75 2.00
258 Kendall Hunter RC .75 2.00
259 Kyle Rudolph RC .75 2.00
260 Lance Kendricks RC .60 1.50
261 Leonard Hankerson RC .75 2.00
262 Luke Stocker RC .60 1.50
263A Marcell Dareus RC .75 2.00
263B Marcell Dareus Draft SP 3.00 8.00
264 Mark Herzlich RC .60 1.50
265A Mark Ingram SP RC 15.00 40.00
265B Mark Ingram Draft SP 6.00 15.00
266 Martez Wilson RC .75 2.00
267 Mike McNeill SP RC 12.00 30.00
268 Mikel Leshoure RC .75 2.00
269A Nick Fairley SP RC 15.00 30.00
269B Nick Fairley Draft SP 6.00 15.00
270 Niles Paul RC .75 2.00
271 Noel Devine RC .75 2.00
272 Owen Marecic RC .75 2.00
273 Pat Devlin RC .75 2.00
274A Patrick Peterson RC 1.25 3.00
274B Patrick Peterson Draft SP 5.00 12.00
275A Phil Taylor RC .60 1.50
275B Phil Taylor Draft SP 3.00 8.00
276A Prince Amukamara RC .75 2.00
276B Prince Amukamara Draft SP 3.00 8.00
277 Quan Sturdivant RC .75 2.00
278 Quinton Carter RC .50 1.25
279 Rahim Moore RC .60 1.50
280 Randall Cobb RC 1.00 2.50
281 Ricky Stanzi SP RC 15.00 40.00
282 Rob Housler RC .60 1.50
283 Robert Quinn RC .75 2.00
284 Ronald Johnson RC .60 1.50
285A Ryan Kerrigan RC .75 2.00
285B Ryan Kerrigan Draft SP 4.00 10.00
286 Ryan Mallett RC 1.50 4.00
287 Ryan Whalen RC .60 1.50
288 Ryan Williams RC 1.00 2.50
289 Shane Vereen RC .75 2.00
290 Stanley Havili RC .50 1.25
291 Stephen Paea RC .75 2.00
292 Stevan Ridley RC .75 2.00
293 Taiwan Jones RC .75 2.00
294 Tandon Doss RC .60 1.50
295 Terrence Toliver RC .60 1.50
296 Titus Young RC 1.00 2.50
297 Torrey Smith RC 1.00 2.50
298 Tyler Sash RC .75 2.00
299 Vincent Brown RC .75 2.00
300A Von Miller RC 1.00 2.50
300B Von Miller Draft SP 5.00 12.00
301 Mike Pouncey Drft SP RC 4.00 10.00

2011 Prestige Draft Picks Light Blue

*ROOKIES/999: .5X TO 1.2X BASIC RC
*ROOKIES/999: .05X TO .15X BASIC SP RC
STATED PRINT RUN 999 SER.#'d SETS

2011 Prestige Xtra Points Black

*1-200 VETS: 10X TO 25X BASIC CARDS
*201-300 ROOKIES: .4X TO 10X BASIC RC
*201-300 ROOKIES: .5X TO 1.2X BASIC SP RC
STATED PRINT RUN 10 SER.#'d SETS

2011 Prestige Xtra Points Gold

*1-200 VETS: 2X TO 5X BASIC CARDS
*201-300 ROOKIES: .8X TO 2X BASIC RC
*201-300 ROOKIES: .1X TO .25X BASIC SP RC
STATED PRINT RUN 250 SER.#'d SETS

2011 Prestige Xtra Points Green

*1-200 VETS: 8X TO 20X BASIC CARDS
*201-300 ROOKIES: 3X TO 8X BASIC RC
*201-300 ROOKIES: .4X TO 1X BASIC SP RC
STATED PRINT RUN 25 SER.#'d SETS

2011 Prestige Xtra Points Orange

*1-200 VETS: 3X TO 8X BASIC CARDS
*201-300 ROOKIES: 1.2X TO 3X BASIC RC
*201-300 ROOKIES: .15X TO .4X BASIC SP RC
RANDOM INSERTS IN RETAIL PACKS

2011 Prestige Xtra Points Purple

*1-200 VETS: 4X TO 10X BASIC CARDS
*201-300 ROOKIES: 1.5X TO 4X BASIC RC
*201-300 ROOKIES: .2X TO .5X BASIC SP RC
STATED PRINT RUN 50 SER.#'d SETS

2011 Prestige Xtra Points Red

*1-200 VETS: 3X TO 8X BASIC CARDS
*201-300 ROOKIES: 1.2X TO 3X BASIC RC
*201-300 ROOKIES: .15X TO .4X BASIC SP RC
STATED PRINT RUN 100 SER.#'d SETS

2011 Prestige Collegiate Lettermen Autographs

RANDOM INSERTS IN PACKS
1 A.J. Green 20.00 50.00
2 Blaine Gabbert 15.00 40.00
4 D.J. Williams 10.00 25.00
5 Daniel Thomas 10.00 25.00
6 DeMarco Murray 30.00 60.00
7 Jake Locker 40.00 80.00
8 Jerrel Jernigan 8.00 20.00
9 Jonathan Baldwin 10.00 25.00
10 Jordan Todman 8.00 20.00
11 Julio Jones 25.00 50.00
12 Kyle Rudolph 10.00 25.00
13 Leonard Hankerson 10.00 25.00
15 Mikel Leshoure 10.00 25.00
16 Randall Cobb 12.00 30.00
17 Ronald Johnson 8.00 20.00
18 Ryan Mallett 25.00 60.00
19 Ryan Williams 12.00 30.00
20 Torrey Smith 12.00 30.00

2011 Prestige Connections

RANDOM INSERTS IN PACKS
1 Matt Cassel 1.00 2.50
Dwayne Bowe
2 Calvin Johnson 1.25 3.00
Jahvid Best
3 Aaron Rodgers 2.00 5.00
Greg Jennings
4 Philip Rivers 1.25 3.00
Antonio Gates
5 Eli Manning 1.25 3.00
Hakeem Nicks
6 Michael Vick 1.25 3.00
Jeremy Maclin
7 Dez Bryant 1.25 3.00
Miles Austin
8 Ben Roethlisberger 1.25 3.00
Mike Wallace
9 Matt Ryan 1.25 3.00
Roddy White
10 Drew Brees 1.25 3.00
Marques Colston
11 Michael Crabtree 1.00 2.50
Vernon Davis
12 Matt Schaub 1.00 2.50
Andre Johnson
13 Mark Sanchez 1.25 3.00
Braylon Edwards
14 Joe Flacco 1.25 3.00
Anquan Boldin
15 Peyton Manning 2.00 5.00
Reggie Wayne
16 Jay Cutler 1.00 2.50
Greg Olsen
17 Jonathan Stewart 1.00 2.50
Steve Smith
18 Brandon Jacobs 1.00 2.50
Steve Smith USC
19 Donovan McNabb 1.25 3.00
Santana Moss
20 Adrian Peterson 1.50 4.00
Percy Harvin
21 Chad Henne 1.00 2.50
Brandon Marshall
22 Shonn Greene 1.00 2.50
Santonio Holmes
23 Tom Brady 2.00 5.00
Wes Welker
24 Jason Campbell 1.00 2.50
Darren McFadden
25 David Garrard 1.00 2.50
Maurice Jones-Drew

2011 Prestige Connections Materials

STATED PRINT RUN 249-250
*PRIME/50: .6X TO 1.5X BASIC DUAL
*PRIME/25: .8X TO 2X BASIC DUAL
1 Matt Cassel/250 4.00 10.00
Dwayne Bowe
3 Aaron Rodgers/250 8.00 20.00
Greg Jennings
4 Philip Rivers/250 5.00 12.00
Antonio Gates
5 Eli Manning/250 5.00 12.00
Hakeem Nicks
6 Michael Vick/250 5.00 12.00
Jeremy Maclin
7 Dez Bryant/250 5.00 12.00
Miles Austin
8 Ben Roethlisberger/249 8.00 20.00
Mike Wallace
9 Matt Ryan/250 5.00 12.00
Roddy White
10 Drew Brees/250 5.00 12.00
Marques Colston
11 Michael Crabtree/250 4.00 10.00
Vernon Davis
12 Matt Schaub/250 4.00 10.00
Andre Johnson
13 Mark Sanchez/250 5.00 12.00
Braylon Edwards
14 Joe Flacco/250 5.00 12.00
Anquan Boldin
15 Peyton Manning/250 8.00 20.00
Reggie Wayne
16 Jay Cutler/250 4.00 10.00
Greg Olsen
17 Jonathan Stewart/250 4.00 10.00
Steve Smith
18 Brandon Jacobs/250 4.00 10.00
Steve Smith USC
19 Donovan McNabb/250 5.00 12.00
Santana Moss
20 Adrian Peterson/250 6.00 15.00
Percy Harvin
22 Shonn Greene/250 4.00 10.00
Santonio Holmes
23 Tom Brady/250 8.00 20.00
Wes Welker
24 Jason Campbell/250 4.00 10.00
Darren McFadden
25 David Garrard/250 4.00 10.00
Maurice Jones-Drew

2011 Prestige Draft Picks Rights Autographs

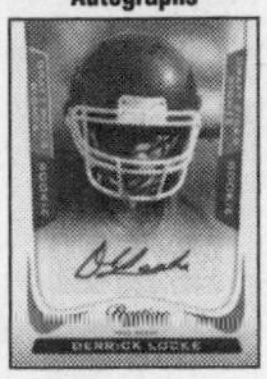

STATED PRINT RUN 50-1499
EXCH EXPIRATION: 11/25/2012
201 A.J. Green/99 20.00 40.00
202 Aaron Williams/599 4.00 10.00
203 Adrian Clayborn/599 8.00 20.00
204 Ahmad Black/699 4.00 10.00
205 Akeem Ayers/99 6.00 15.00
206 Aldon Smith/99 12.00 30.00
207 Andy Dalton/499 20.00 40.00
208 Austin Pettis/199 5.00 12.00
209 Bilal Powell/599 3.00 8.00
210 Blaine Gabbert/99 25.00 50.00
211 Brandon Harris/599 3.00 8.00
215 Cameron Heyward/599 5.00 12.00
216 Cameron Jordan/599 4.00 10.00
217 Cecil Shorts/699 4.00 10.00
219 Christian Ponder/199 20.00 40.00
220 Colin Kaepernick/299 15.00 40.00
222 Corey Liuget/599 3.00 8.00
223 Courtney Smith/1499 3.00 8.00
225 D.J. Williams/299 6.00 15.00
226 Daniel Thomas/99 10.00 25.00
227 Da'Quan Bowers/99 8.00 20.00
228 Darvin Adams/99 EXCH 6.00 15.00
231 DeAndre McDaniel/1499 3.00 8.00
232 Delone Carter/599 4.00 10.00
233 DeMarco Murray/99 25.00 60.00
234 Denarius Moore/99 20.00 40.00
235 Derrick Locke/1499 3.00 8.00
236 Dion Lewis/599 5.00 12.00
238 Dwayne Harris/99 8.00 20.00
239 Edmond Gates/599 4.00 10.00
240 Evan Royster/599 5.00 12.00
241 Greg Jones/99 6.00 15.00
242 Greg Little/499 5.00 12.00
243 Greg Salas/499 5.00 12.00
244 J.J. Watt/699 8.00 20.00
246 Jacquizz Rodgers/99 8.00 20.00
247 Jake Locker/99 40.00 80.00
248 Jamie Harper/199 6.00 15.00
249 Jeremy Kerley/799 5.00 12.00
250 Jerrel Jernigan/499 4.00 10.00
251 Jimmy Smith/599 6.00 15.00
252 John Clay/1499 4.00 10.00
253 Jonathan Baldwin/99 8.00 20.00
254 Jordan Todman/50 10.00 25.00
256 Julio Jones/99 25.00 50.00
257 Justin Houston/99 8.00 20.00
258 Kendall Hunter/499 5.00 12.00
259 Kyle Rudolph/99 8.00 20.00
260 Lance Kendricks/99 6.00 15.00
261 Leonard Hankerson/99 8.00 20.00
262 Luke Stocker/599 4.00 10.00
263 Marcell Dareus/299 6.00 15.00
266 Martez Wilson/99 8.00 20.00
268 Mikel Leshoure/99 8.00 20.00
270 Niles Paul/499 5.00 12.00
271 Noel Devine/99 EXCH 8.00 20.00
273 Pat Devlin/1499 4.00 10.00
276 Prince Amukamara/299 6.00 15.00
278 Quinton Carter/99 8.00 20.00
279 Rahim Moore/99 6.00 15.00
280 Randall Cobb/99 20.00 40.00
281 Ricky Stanzi/99 25.00 50.00
284 Ronald Johnson/99 6.00 15.00
285 Ryan Kerrigan/599 5.00 12.00
286 Ryan Mallett/299 20.00 40.00
287 Ryan Whalen/99 6.00 15.00
288 Ryan Williams/99 10.00 25.00
289 Shane Vereen/199 6.00 15.00
290 Stanley Havili/699 3.00 8.00
291 Stephen Paea/99 8.00 20.00
292 Stevan Ridley/599 5.00 12.00
293 Taiwan Jones/699 5.00 12.00
294 Tandon Doss/99 6.00 15.00
295 Terrence Toliver/1499 3.00 8.00
296 Titus Young/99 10.00 25.00
297 Torrey Smith/99 10.00 25.00
298 Tyler Sash/699 5.00 12.00
299 Vincent Brown/99 8.00 20.00
300 Von Miller/499 10.00 25.00

2011 Prestige Inside The Numbers

RANDOM INSERTS IN PACKS
1 Aaron Rodgers 2.00 5.00
2 Adrian Peterson 1.50 4.00
3 Andre Johnson 1.00 2.50
4 Arian Foster 1.00 2.50
5 Drew Brees 1.25 3.00
6 Jamaal Charles 1.00 2.50
7 Maurice Jones-Drew 1.00 2.50
8 Philip Rivers 1.25 3.00
9 Reggie Wayne 1.00 2.50
10 Roddy White 1.00 2.50

2011 Prestige Inside The Numbers Autographs

STATED PRINT RUN 25 SER.#'d SETS
8 Philip Rivers 25.00 50.00

2011 Prestige Inside The Numbers Materials

STATED PRINT RUN 100-250
*PRIME/35-50: .8X TO 2X BASIC JSY/250
*PRIME/35-50: .6X TO 1.5X BASIC JSY/100
1 Aaron Rodgers/250 6.00 15.00
2 Adrian Peterson/250 5.00 12.00
3 Andre Johnson/250 3.00 8.00
4 Arian Foster/250 5.00 12.00
5 Drew Brees/250 4.00 10.00
6 Jamaal Charles/200 3.00 8.00
7 Maurice Jones-Drew/100 4.00 10.00
8 Philip Rivers/250 4.00 10.00
9 Reggie Wayne/250 3.00 8.00
10 Roddy White/250 3.00 8.00

2011 Prestige League Leaders

RANDOM INSERTS IN PACKS
1 Philip Rivers 1.50 4.00
Peyton Manning
2 Drew Brees 1.00 2.50
Matt Schaub
3 Eli Manning 1.00 2.50
Carson Palmer
4 Aaron Rodgers 1.50 4.00
Tom Brady
5 Arian Foster .75 2.00
Jamaal Charles
6 Michael Turner .75 2.00
Chris Johnson
7 Maurice Jones-Drew 1.25 3.00
Adrian Peterson
8 Rashard Mendenhall .75 2.00
Steven Jackson
9 Brandon Lloyd .75 2.00
Roddy White
10 Reggie Wayne .75 2.00
Greg Jennings
11 Mike Wallace 1.00 2.50
Andre Johnson
12 Dwayne Bowe .75 2.00
Larry Fitzgerald
13 Arian Foster .75 2.00
Dwayne Bowe
14 Tom Brady 1.50 4.00
Drew Brees
15 Ed Reed .75 2.00
Devin McCourty
16 Philip Rivers 2.00 5.00
Peyton Manning
Drew Brees
Matt Schaub
17 Eli Manning 2.00 5.00
Carson Palmer
Aaron Rodgers
Tom Brady
18 Arian Foster 1.00 2.50
Jamaal Charles
Michael Turner
Chris Johnson
19 Maurice Jones-Drew 1.50 4.00
Adrian Peterson
Rashard Mendenhall
Steven Jackson
20 Brandon Lloyd 1.00 2.50
Roddy White
Reggie Wayne
Greg Jennings
21 Mike Wallace 1.25 3.00
Andre Johnson
Dwayne Bowe
Larry Fitzgerald
22 Dwayne Bowe 1.00 2.50
Greg Jennings
Arian Foster
BenJarvus Green-Ellis
23 Tom Brady 2.00 5.00
Drew Brees
Peyton Manning
Eli Manning
24 Ed Reed 1.50 4.00
Devin McCourty
Troy Polamalu
Asante Samuel
25 DeMarcus Ware 1.25 3.00
Tamba Hali
Cameron Wake
Clay Matthews

2011 Prestige League Leaders Materials

1-14 STATED PRINT RUN 130-200
16-23 STATED PRINT RUN 100
*1-14 PRIME/50: .6X TO 1.5X DUAL/130-200
*16-23 PRIME/50: .5X TO 1.2X TRPL/100
1 Philip Rivers/200 8.00 20.00
Peyton Manning
2 Drew Brees/200 5.00 12.00
Matt Schaub
3 Eli Manning/200 5.00 12.00
Carson Palmer
4 Aaron Rodgers/200 8.00 20.00
Tom Brady
5 Arian Foster/200 6.00 15.00
Jamaal Charles
6 Michael Turner/200 4.00 10.00
Chris Johnson
7 Maurice Jones-Drew/200 6.00 15.00
Adrian Peterson
8 Rashard Mendenhall/200 4.00 10.00
Steven Jackson
9 Brandon Lloyd/200 4.00 10.00
Roddy White
10 Reggie Wayne/130 4.00 10.00
Greg Jennings
11 Mike Wallace/200 5.00 12.00
Andre Johnson
12 Dwayne Bowe/200 4.00 10.00
Larry Fitzgerald
13 Arian Foster/200 4.00 10.00
Dwayne Bowe
14 Tom Brady/200 8.00 20.00
Drew Brees
16 Philip Rivers/100 12.00 30.00
Peyton Manning
Drew Brees
Matt Schaub
17 Eli Manning/100 12.00 30.00
Carson Palmer
Aaron Rodgers
Tom Brady
18 Arian Foster/100 6.00 15.00
Jamaal Charles
Michael Turner
Chris Johnson
19 Maurice Jones-Drew/100 10.00 25.00
Adrian Peterson
Rashard Mendenhall
Steven Jackson
20 Brandon Lloyd/100 6.00 15.00
Roddy White
Reggie Wayne
Greg Jennings
21 Mike Wallace/100 8.00 20.00
Andre Johnson
Dwayne Bowe
Larry Fitzgerald
23 Tom Brady/100 12.00 30.00
Drew Brees
Peyton Manning
Eli Manning

2011 Prestige NFL Draft

RANDOM INSERTS IN PACKS
1 A.J. Green 1.25 3.00
2 Aldon Smith 1.00 2.50
3 Austin Pettis .50 1.25
4 Blaine Gabbert 1.00 2.50
5 Cam Newton 3.00 8.00
6 Christian Ponder 1.25 3.00
7 D.J. Williams .60 1.50
8 Daniel Thomas .60 1.50
9 Da'Quan Bowers .60 1.50
10 DeAndre McDaniel .50 1.25
11 Delone Carter .50 1.25
12 DeMarco Murray 1.25 3.00
13 Jacquizz Rodgers .60 1.50
14 Jake Locker 1.50 4.00
15 Jamie Harper .60 1.50
16 Jerrel Jernigan .50 1.25
17 Jonathan Baldwin .60 1.50
18 Jordan Todman .40 1.00
19 Julio Jones 1.25 3.00
20 Kendall Hunter .60 1.50
21 Kyle Rudolph .60 1.50
22 Leonard Hankerson .60 1.50
23 Mark Ingram 1.25 3.00
24 Martez Wilson .60 1.50
25 Mikel Leshoure .60 1.50
26 Nick Fairley .75 2.00
27 Niles Paul .60 1.50
28 Pat Devlin .60 1.50
29 Patrick Peterson 1.00 2.50
30 Prince Amukamara .60 1.50
31 Quinton Carter .40 1.00
32 Randall Cobb .75 2.00
33 Ronald Johnson .50 1.25
34 Ryan Mallett 1.25 3.00
35 Ryan Williams .75 2.00
36 Shane Vereen .60 1.50
37 Tandon Doss .50 1.25
38 Titus Young .75 2.00
39 Torrey Smith .75 2.00
40 Von Miller .75 2.00
BF1 Mark Ingram BF 1.00 2.50
(inserted in Black Friday packs; updated photo)
BF2 Cam Newton BF 2.50 6.00
(inserted in Black Friday packs; updated photo)
BF3 Terrelle Pryor BF .60 1.50
(inserted in Black Friday packs)

2011 Prestige NFL Draft Autographed Patch Draft Logo

RANDOM INSERTS IN PACKS
EXCH EXPIRATION: 11/25/2012
*NFL EQUIP: .5X TO 1.2X DRFT PATCH AU
*NFL SHIELD: .6X TO 1.5X DRFT PTCH AU
1 A.J. Green 25.00 50.00
2 Aldon Smith 15.00 40.00
3 Austin Pettis 8.00 20.00
4 Blaine Gabbert 15.00 40.00
6 Christian Ponder 20.00 50.00
7 D.J. Williams 10.00 25.00
8 Daniel Thomas 10.00 25.00
9 Da'Quan Bowers 10.00 25.00
10 DeAndre McDaniel 8.00 20.00
11 Delone Carter 8.00 20.00
12 DeMarco Murray 20.00 50.00
13 Jacquizz Rodgers 10.00 25.00
14 Jake Locker 40.00 80.00
15 Jamie Harper 10.00 25.00
16 Jerrel Jernigan 8.00 20.00
17 Jonathan Baldwin 10.00 25.00
18 Jordan Todman 6.00 15.00
19 Julio Jones 25.00 50.00
20 Kendall Hunter 10.00 25.00
21 Kyle Rudolph 10.00 25.00
22 Leonard Hankerson 10.00 25.00
24 Martez Wilson 10.00 25.00
25 Mikel Leshoure 10.00 25.00
27 Niles Paul 10.00 25.00
28 Pat Devlin 10.00 25.00
30 Prince Amukamara 10.00 25.00
31 Quinton Carter 6.00 15.00
32 Randall Cobb 20.00 40.00
33 Ronald Johnson 8.00 20.00
34 Ryan Mallett 25.00 50.00
35 Ryan Williams 20.00 40.00
36 Shane Vereen 10.00 25.00
37 Tandon Doss 8.00 20.00
38 Titus Young 12.00 30.00
39 Torrey Smith 12.00 30.00
40 Von Miller 12.00 30.00

2011 Prestige NFL Draft Autographs

RANDOM INSERTS IN PACKS
EXCH EXPIRATION: 11/25/2012
1 A.J. Green 12.00 30.00
2 Aldon Smith 10.00 25.00
3 Austin Pettis 5.00 12.00
4 Blaine Gabbert 10.00 25.00
6 Christian Ponder 12.00 30.00
7 D.J. Williams 6.00 15.00
8 Daniel Thomas 6.00 15.00
9 Da'Quan Bowers 6.00 15.00
10 DeAndre McDaniel 5.00 12.00
11 Delone Carter 5.00 12.00
12 DeMarco Murray 12.00 30.00
13 Jacquizz Rodgers 6.00 15.00
14 Jake Locker 15.00 40.00
15 Jamie Harper 6.00 15.00
16 Jerrel Jernigan 5.00 12.00
17 Jonathan Baldwin 6.00 15.00
18 Jordan Todman 4.00 10.00
19 Julio Jones 12.00 30.00
20 Kendall Hunter 6.00 15.00
21 Kyle Rudolph 6.00 15.00
22 Leonard Hankerson 6.00 15.00
24 Martez Wilson 8.00 20.00
25 Mikel Leshoure 6.00 15.00
27 Niles Paul 6.00 15.00
28 Pat Devlin 5.00 12.00
30 Prince Amukamara 6.00 15.00
31 Quinton Carter 8.00 20.00
32 Randall Cobb 8.00 20.00
33 Ronald Johnson 5.00 12.00
34 Ryan Mallett 12.00 30.00
35 Ryan Williams
36 Shane Vereen 6.00 15.00
37 Tandon Doss 5.00 12.00
38 Titus Young 8.00 20.00
39 Torrey Smith 8.00 20.00
40 Von Miller 8.00 20.00
BFAU Terrelle Pryor AU/22 BF 30.00 60.00
(inserted in Black Friday packs)

2011 Prestige NFL Passport

RAMDOM INSERTS IN PACKS
*HOLOKOTE/100: .6X TO 1.5X BASIC INSERTS
1 A.J. Green 2.00 5.00
2 Aaron Williams .75 2.00
3 Adrian Clayborn 1.00 2.50
4 Ahmad Black .75 2.00
5 Aldon Smith 1.50 4.00
6 Blaine Gabbert 1.50 4.00
7 Brandon Harris .60 1.50
8 Cam Newton 5.00 12.00
9 Christian Ponder 2.00 5.00
10 D.J. Williams 1.00 2.50
11 Daniel Thomas 1.00 2.50
12 Da'Quan Bowers 1.00 2.50
13 DeAndre McDaniel .75 2.00
14 Delone Carter .75 2.00
15 DeMarco Murray 2.00 5.00
16 Jake Locker 2.50 6.00
17 Jerrel Jernigan .75 2.00
18 Jonathan Baldwin 1.00 2.50
19 Jordan Todman .60 1.50
20 Julio Jones 2.00 5.00
21 Kyle Rudolph 1.00 2.50
22 Leonard Hankerson 1.00 2.50
23 Marcell Dareus 1.00 2.50
24 Mark Ingram 2.00 5.00
25 Martez Wilson 1.00 2.50
26 Mikel Leshoure 1.00 2.50
27 Nick Fairley 1.25 3.00
28 Owen Marecic 1.00 2.50
29 Patrick Peterson 1.50 4.00
30 Prince Amukamara 1.00 2.50
31 Quinton Carter .60 1.50
32 Rahim Moore .75 2.00
33 Randall Cobb 1.25 3.00
34 Robert Quinn 1.00 2.50
35 Ronald Johnson .75 2.00
36 Ryan Mallett 2.00 5.00
37 Ryan Williams 1.25 3.00
38 Stephen Paea 1.00 2.50
39 Torrey Smith 1.25 3.00
40 Von Miller 1.25 3.00

2011 Prestige NFL Passport Autographs

STATED PRINT RUN 25 SER.#'d SETS
EXCH EXPIRATION: 11/25/2012
1 A.J. Green 30.00 60.00
2 Aaron Williams 8.00 20.00
3 Adrian Clayborn 20.00 50.00
4 Ahmad Black 15.00 40.00
5 Aldon Smith
6 Blaine Gabbert 30.00 60.00
7 Brandon Harris 6.00 15.00
9 Christian Ponder 30.00 60.00
10 D.J. Williams 10.00 25.00
11 Daniel Thomas 20.00 40.00
12 Da'Quan Bowers 10.00 25.00
13 DeAndre McDaniel 8.00 20.00
14 Delone Carter 8.00 20.00
15 DeMarco Murray 30.00 60.00
16 Jake Locker 40.00 80.00
17 Jerrel Jernigan 8.00 20.00
18 Jonathan Baldwin 12.00 30.00
19 Jordan Todman 12.00 30.00
20 Julio Jones 20.00 50.00
21 Kyle Rudolph 10.00 25.00
22 Leonard Hankerson 10.00 25.00
23 Marcell Dareus 10.00 25.00
25 Martez Wilson 12.00 30.00
26 Mikel Leshoure 10.00 25.00
30 Prince Amukamara 10.00 25.00
31 Quinton Carter 12.00 30.00
32 Rahim Moore 8.00 20.00
33 Randall Cobb 25.00 50.00
35 Ronald Johnson 8.00 20.00
36 Ryan Mallett 30.00 60.00
37 Ryan Williams 20.00 40.00
38 Stephen Paea 10.00 25.00
39 Torrey Smith 12.00 30.00
40 Von Miller 15.00 40.00

2011 Prestige Platinum Patches

RANDOM INSERTS IN PACKS
8 Matt Ryan 8.00 20.00
9 Michael Turner 5.00 12.00
10 Roddy White 5.00 12.00
11 Tony Gonzalez 5.00 12.00
12 Anquan Boldin 5.00 12.00
16 Ray Lewis 8.00 20.00
19 Todd Heap 4.00 10.00
20 C.J. Spiller 5.00 12.00
22 Lee Evans 5.00 12.00
24 Ryan Fitzpatrick 8.00 20.00
26 DeAngelo Williams 5.00 12.00
31 Steve Smith 5.00 12.00
32 Brian Urlacher 6.00 15.00
33 Devin Hester 6.00 15.00
35 Greg Olsen 4.00 10.00
36 Jay Cutler 5.00 12.00
39 Matt Forte 5.00 12.00
40 Carson Palmer 5.00 12.00
41 Cedric Benson 5.00 12.00
42 Chad Johnson 5.00 12.00
49 Mohamed Massaquoi 5.00 12.00
51 DeMarcus Ware 5.00 12.00
52 Dez Bryant 6.00 15.00
53 Felix Jones 5.00 12.00
54 Jason Witten 6.00 15.00
55 Miles Austin 5.00 12.00
56 Roy Williams WR 5.00 12.00
57 Tony Romo 6.00 15.00
59 Eddie Royal 4.00 10.00
63 Tim Tebow 12.00 30.00
65 Calvin Johnson 6.00 15.00
77 Andre Johnson 5.00 12.00
84 Dallas Clark 5.00 12.00
87 Joseph Addai 5.00 12.00
92 Maurice Jones-Drew 5.00 12.00
93 Mike Sims-Walker 5.00 12.00
97 Dwayne Bowe 5.00 12.00
98 Jamaal Charles 5.00 12.00
99 Matt Cassel 5.00 12.00
108 Adrian Peterson 8.00 20.00
109 Jared Allen 6.00 15.00
110 Percy Harvin 5.00 12.00
111 Sidney Rice 5.00 12.00
112 Tarvaris Jackson 4.00 10.00
113 Visanthe Shiancoe 5.00 12.00
120 Tom Brady 10.00 25.00
121 Wes Welker 6.00 15.00
122 Drew Brees 6.00 15.00
124 Marques Colston 5.00 12.00
125 Pierre Thomas 5.00 12.00
126 Reggie Bush 5.00 12.00
127 Robert Meachem 5.00 12.00
128 Ahmad Bradshaw 5.00 12.00
129 Brandon Jacobs 5.00 12.00
130 Eli Manning 6.00 15.00
131 Hakeem Nicks 5.00 12.00
132 Kevin Boss 5.00 12.00
134 Steve Smith USC 5.00 12.00
136 Darrelle Revis 5.00 12.00
141 Shonn Greene 5.00 12.00
144 Louis Murphy 5.00 12.00
150 DeSean Jackson 5.00 12.00
151 Jeremy Maclin 5.00 12.00
152 LeSean McCoy 5.00 12.00
153 Michael Vick 6.00 15.00
155 Heath Miller 5.00 12.00
156 Hines Ward 5.00 12.00
158 Mike Wallace 6.00 15.00
160 Troy Polamalu 8.00 20.00
161 Antonio Gates 5.00 12.00
162 Darren Sproles 5.00 12.00
163 Malcom Floyd 5.00 12.00
165 Philip Rivers 6.00 15.00
166 Ryan Mathews 5.00 12.00
169 Michael Crabtree 5.00 12.00
170 Patrick Willis 5.00 12.00
171 Alex Smith 5.00 12.00
172 Vernon Davis 5.00 12.00
176 Matt Hasselbeck 5.00 12.00
183 Steven Jackson 5.00 12.00
190 Bo Scaife 4.00 10.00
191 Chris Johnson 5.00 12.00
192 Kenny Britt 5.00 12.00
194 Randy Moss 5.00 12.00
195 Vince Young 4.00 10.00

196 Chris Cooley 5.00 12.00
199 LaRon Landry 4.00 10.00
200 Santana Moss 5.00 12.00

2011 Prestige Preferred Materials

RANDOM INSERTS IN PACKS
*PATCH/50: .6X TO 1.5X BASIC JSY/250
UNPRICED JSY AU PRINT RUN 10
UNPRICED PATCH AU PRINT RUN 5
1 Calvin Johnson 4.00 10.00
2 Dwayne Bowe 3.00 8.00
3 LeSean McCoy 3.00 8.00
4 Mark Sanchez 4.00 10.00
5 Matt Ryan 4.00 10.00
6 Michael Turner 3.00 8.00
7 Peyton Manning 6.00 15.00
8 Rashard Mendenhall 3.00 8.00
9 Sam Bradford 4.00 10.00
10 Tom Brady 6.00 15.00

2011 Prestige Preferred Signatures

STATED PRINT RUN 5-15
3 LeSean McCoy/15
4 Mark Sanchez/15 40.00 80.00
6 Michael Turner/15
8 Rashard Mendenhall/15 12.00 30.00
9 Sam Bradford/15 60.00 100.00

2011 Prestige Prestigious Pros Autographs

STATED PRINT RUN 5-25
3 Chris Wells 10.00 25.00
5 Brent Celek 12.00 30.00
7 C.J. Spiller 12.00 30.00
14 Darren Sproles 12.00 30.00
18 DeMarcus Ware 12.00 30.00
22 Donald Driver 15.00 40.00
24 Frank Gore 12.00 30.00
30 Jeremy Maclin 12.00 30.00
40 Rashard Mendenhall 12.00 30.00
42 Ronnie Brown 12.00 30.00
43 Ryan Grant 12.00 30.00
44 Ryan Mathews 12.00 30.00
45 Santonio Holmes 12.00 30.00
46 Sidney Rice 12.00 30.00

2011 Prestige Prestigious Pros Red

RANDOM INSERTS IN PACKS
*BLACK/25: 1.2X TO 3X BASIC RED
*GREEN/250: .5X TO 1.2X BASIC RED
*GOLD/100: .6X TO 1.5X BASIC RED
*PLATINUM/10: 2.5X TO 6X BASIC RED
1 Adrian Peterson 1.50 4.00
2 Anquan Boldin 1.00 2.50
3 Chris Wells 1.00 2.50
4 Brandon Marshall 1.00 2.50
5 Brent Celek 1.00 2.50
6 Braylon Edwards 1.00 2.50
7 C.J. Spiller 1.00 2.50
8 Cadillac Williams .75 2.00
9 Cedric Benson 1.00 2.50
10 Chad Greenway 1.00 2.50
11 Chad Henne 1.00 2.50
12 Clinton Portis 1.00 2.50
13 Dallas Clark 1.00 2.50
14 Darren Sproles 1.00 2.50
15 David Garrard 1.00 2.50
16 DeAngelo Hall .75 2.00
17 DeAngelo Williams 1.00 2.50
18 DeMarcus Ware 1.00 2.50
19 Devery Henderson .75 2.00
20 Devin Hester 1.25 3.00
21 Dez Bryant 1.25 3.00
22 Donald Driver 1.00 2.50
23 Dustin Keller 1.00 2.50
24 Frank Gore 1.00 2.50
25 Greg Olsen .75 2.00
26 Hakeem Nicks 1.00 2.50
27 Heath Miller 1.00 2.50
28 Jamaal Charles 1.00 2.50
29 Jared Allen 1.00 2.50
30 Jeremy Maclin 1.00 2.50
31 Johnny Knox 1.00 2.50
32 Josh Freeman 1.25 3.00
33 Julius Peppers 1.00 2.50
34 Kenny Britt 1.00 2.50
35 LaDainian Tomlinson 1.25 3.00
36 Lee Evans 1.00 2.50
37 Marques Colston 1.00 2.50
38 Nate Washington .75 2.00
39 Randy Moss 1.00 2.50
40 Rashard Mendenhall 1.00 2.50
41 Reggie Bush 1.00 2.50
42 Ronnie Brown 1.00 2.50
43 Ryan Grant 1.00 2.50
44 Ryan Mathews 1.00 2.50
45 Santonio Holmes 1.00 2.50
46 Sidney Rice 1.00 2.50
47 Terrell Suggs .75 2.00
48 Tim Tebow 2.50 6.00
49 Tony Romo 1.25 3.00
50 Visanthe Shiancoe 1.00 2.50

2011 Prestige Prestigious Pros Materials Green

GREEN STATED PRINT RUN 90-100
*BLACK/10: 1X TO 2.5X GREEN/90-100
*GOLD/50: .5X TO 1.2X GREEN/90-100
*PLATINUM/45-50: .6X TO 1.5X GRN/90-100
*RED/170-250: .3X TO .8X GREEN/90-100
1 Adrian Peterson/100 6.00 15.00
2 Anquan Boldin/100 4.00 10.00
3 Chris Wells/100 4.00 10.00
5 Brent Celek/100 4.00 10.00
6 Braylon Edwards/100 4.00 10.00
7 C.J. Spiller/100 4.00 10.00
8 Cadillac Williams/100 3.00 8.00
9 Cedric Benson/100 4.00 10.00
10 Chad Greenway/100 5.00 12.00
12 Clinton Portis/100 4.00 10.00
13 Dallas Clark/100 4.00 10.00
14 Darren Sproles/100 4.00 10.00
15 David Garrard/100 4.00 10.00
16 DeAngelo Hall/100 3.00 8.00
17 DeAngelo Williams/100 4.00 10.00
18 DeMarcus Ware/100 4.00 10.00
19 Devery Henderson/100 3.00 8.00
20 Devin Hester/100 5.00 12.00
21 Dez Bryant/90 5.00 12.00
22 Donald Driver/100 4.00 10.00
23 Dustin Keller/100 4.00 10.00
24 Frank Gore/100 4.00 10.00
25 Greg Olsen/100 3.00 8.00
26 Hakeem Nicks/100 4.00 10.00
27 Heath Miller/100 4.00 10.00
28 Jamaal Charles/100 4.00 10.00
29 Jared Allen/100 4.00 10.00
30 Jeremy Maclin/100 4.00 10.00
31 Johnny Knox/100 4.00 10.00
32 Josh Freeman/100 5.00 12.00
34 Kenny Britt/100 4.00 10.00
35 LaDainian Tomlinson/100 5.00 12.00
36 Lee Evans/100 4.00 10.00
37 Marques Colston/100 4.00 10.00
38 Nate Washington/100 3.00 8.00
39 Randy Moss/100 4.00 10.00
40 Rashard Mendenhall/100 4.00 10.00
41 Reggie Bush/100 4.00 10.00
42 Ronnie Brown/100 4.00 10.00
43 Ryan Grant/100 4.00 10.00
44 Ryan Mathews/100 4.00 10.00
45 Santonio Holmes/100 4.00 10.00
46 Sidney Rice/100 4.00 10.00
47 Terrell Suggs/100 3.00 8.00
48 Tim Tebow/100 8.00 20.00
49 Tony Romo/100 5.00 12.00
50 Visanthe Shiancoe/100 4.00 10.00

2011 Prestige Pro Helmets Autographs

RANDOM INSERTS IN PACKS
2 Da'Quan Bowers 12.00 30.00
3 Jake Locker 60.00 120.00
4 Ryan Williams 25.00 50.00
5 Von Miller 25.00 50.00
6 Aldon Smith 20.00 50.00
7 Delone Carter 10.00 25.00
8 Leonard Hankerson 12.00 30.00
9 Tandon Doss 10.00 25.00
11 D.J. Williams 12.00 30.00
12 A.J. Green 30.00 60.00
13 Mikel Leshoure 12.00 30.00
14 Julio Jones 30.00 60.00
15 Ronald Johnson 10.00 25.00
17 Titus Young 15.00 40.00
18 Prince Amukamara 12.00 30.00
19 DeMarco Murray 40.00 80.00
20 Jonathan Baldwin 12.00 30.00
21 Blaine Gabbert 30.00 60.00
22 Kyle Rudolph 12.00 30.00
23 Niles Paul 12.00 30.00
24 Ryan Mallett 25.00 50.00
26 Jacquizz Rodgers 12.00 30.00
27 Austin Pettis 10.00 25.00
28 Shane Vereen 12.00 30.00
29 Quinton Carter 8.00 20.00
30 Kendall Hunter 12.00 30.00
31 Jamie Harper 10.00 25.00
32 Daniel Thomas 12.00 30.00
33 Torrey Smith 15.00 40.00
34 Christian Ponder 30.00 80.00
35 Jerrel Jernigan 10.00 25.00
36 Randall Cobb 25.00 50.00
37 Jordan Todman 10.00 25.00
38 Martez Wilson 12.00 30.00

2011 Prestige Rookie Debut Autographed Patch

RANDOM INSERTS IN PACKS
1 Prince Amukamara 12.00 30.00
2 Randall Cobb 15.00 40.00
3 Blaine Gabbert 20.00 50.00
4 Mark Ingram 25.00 60.00
5 Julio Jones 25.00 60.00
6 Von Miller 15.00 40.00
7 Patrick Peterson 20.00 50.00
8 Aldon Smith 20.00 50.00

2011 Prestige Rookie Review

RANDOM INSERTS IN PACKS
1 Aaron Hernandez 1.00 2.50
2 Arrelious Benn 1.00 2.50
3 Blair White .75 2.00
4 Brandon LaFell .75 2.00
5 C.J. Spiller 1.00 2.50
6 Chris Ivory 1.00 2.50
7 Colt McCoy 1.00 2.50
8 Damian Williams .75 2.00
9 Danario Alexander .75 2.00
10 David Gettis .75 2.00
11 Demaryius Thomas 1.00 2.50
12 Devin McCourty .75 2.00
13 Dexter McCluster .75 2.00
14 Dez Bryant 1.25 3.00
15 Eric Berry 1.00 2.50
16 Eric Decker 1.00 2.50
17 Gerald McCoy .75 2.00
18 Golden Tate .75 2.00
19 Jacoby Ford 1.00 2.50
20 Jahvid Best 1.00 2.50
21 Jason Pierre-Paul 1.25 3.00
22 Jermaine Gresham 1.00 2.50
23 Jimmy Clausen .75 2.00
24 Jimmy Graham 1.25 3.00
25 Joe Haden .75 2.00
26 Jordan Shipley 1.00 2.50
27 Keiland Williams .75 2.00
28 LeGarrette Blount 1.00 2.50
29 Mardy Gilyard .75 2.00
30 Mike Williams 1.00 2.50
31 Ndamukong Suh 1.25 3.00
32 Marc Mariani 1.00 2.50
33 Rob Gronkowski 1.25 3.00
34 Rolando McClain .75 2.00
35 Ryan Mathews 1.00 2.50
36 Sam Bradford 1.25 3.00
37 Seyi Ajirotutu .75 2.00
38 Tim Tebow 2.50 6.00
39 T.J. Ward .75 2.00
40 Toby Gerhart 1.00 2.50

2011 Prestige Rookie Review Autographs

RANDOM INSERTS IN PACKS
2 Arrelious Benn 6.00 15.00
4 Brandon LaFell 5.00 12.00
5 C.J. Spiller 6.00 15.00
7 Colt McCoy 20.00 40.00
8 Damian Williams 5.00 12.00
16 Eric Decker 8.00 20.00
18 Golden Tate 5.00 12.00
23 Jimmy Clausen 5.00 12.00
34 Rolando McClain 5.00 12.00
35 Ryan Mathews 15.00 30.00
36 Sam Bradford 40.00 80.00
38 Tim Tebow 40.00 80.00
40 Toby Gerhart

2011 Prestige Rookie Review Materials Prime

*BASE JSY: .25X TO .6X PRIME JSY
RANDOM INSERTS IN PACKS
2 Arrelious Benn 5.00 12.00
4 Brandon LaFell 4.00 10.00
5 C.J. Spiller 5.00 12.00
7 Colt McCoy 5.00 12.00
8 Damian Williams 4.00 10.00
11 Demaryius Thomas 5.00 12.00
13 Dexter McCluster 4.00 10.00
14 Dez Bryant 6.00 15.00
15 Eric Berry 5.00 12.00
16 Eric Decker 5.00 12.00
17 Gerald McCoy 4.00 10.00
18 Golden Tate 4.00 10.00
20 Jahvid Best 5.00 12.00
22 Jermaine Gresham 5.00 12.00
23 Jimmy Clausen 4.00 10.00
26 Jordan Shipley 5.00 12.00
29 Mardy Gilyard 4.00 10.00
30 Mike Williams 5.00 12.00
31 Ndamukong Suh 8.00 20.00
33 Rob Gronkowski 6.00 15.00
34 Rolando McClain 4.00 10.00
35 Ryan Mathews 5.00 12.00
36 Sam Bradford 6.00 15.00
38 Tim Tebow 12.00 30.00
40 Toby Gerhart 5.00 12.00

2011 Prestige Stars of the NFL

RANDOM INSERTS IN PACKS
1 Aaron Rodgers 1.50 4.00
2 Ahmad Bradshaw .75 2.00
3 Andre Johnson .75 2.00
4 Antonio Gates .75 2.00
5 Arian Foster .75 2.00
6 Ben Roethlisberger 1.00 2.50
7 Brian Urlacher 1.00 2.50
8 Calvin Johnson 1.00 2.50
9 Carson Palmer .75 2.00
10 Chad Johnson .75 2.00
11 Chris Cooley .75 2.00
12 Chris Johnson .75 2.00
13 Clay Matthews 1.00 2.50
14 Darrelle Revis .75 2.00
15 Darren McFadden .75 2.00
16 DeSean Jackson .75 2.00
17 Donovan McNabb 1.00 2.50
18 Drew Brees 1.00 2.50
19 Dwayne Bowe .75 2.00
20 Ed Reed .75 2.00
21 Eli Manning 1.00 2.50
22 Felix Jones .75 2.00
23 Greg Jennings .75 2.00
24 James Harrison 1.00 2.50
25 Jason Witten 1.00 2.50
26 Jay Cutler .75 2.00
27 Joe Flacco 1.00 2.50
28 Knowshon Moreno .75 2.00
29 Larry Fitzgerald .75 2.00
30 LeSean McCoy .75 2.00
31 Mark Sanchez 1.00 2.50
32 Matt Forte .75 2.00
33 Matt Ryan 1.00 2.50
34 Matt Schaub .75 2.00
35 Maurice Jones-Drew .75 2.00
36 Michael Turner .75 2.00
37 Miles Austin .75 2.00
38 Percy Harvin .75 2.00
39 Peyton Manning 1.50 4.00
40 Philip Rivers 1.00 2.50
41 Ray Lewis 1.00 2.50
42 Ray Rice .75 2.00
43 Reggie Wayne .75 2.00
44 Roddy White .75 2.00
45 Sam Bradford 1.00 2.50
46 Steve Smith .75 2.00
47 Steven Jackson .75 2.00
48 Tom Brady 1.50 4.00
49 Vernon Davis .75 2.00
50 Wes Welker 1.00 2.50

2011 Prestige Stars of the NFL Materials

STATED PRINT RUN 100-250
*PRIME/30-50: .8X TO 2X JSY/145-250
*PRIME/50: .6X TO 1.5X JSY/100
*PRIME/20: 1X TO 2.5X JSY/250
1 Aaron Rodgers/250 6.00 15.00
2 Ahmad Bradshaw/250 3.00 8.00
3 Andre Johnson/250 3.00 8.00
4 Antonio Gates/250 3.00 8.00
5 Arian Foster/250 3.00 8.00
7 Brian Urlacher/250 4.00 10.00
8 Calvin Johnson/250 4.00 10.00
9 Carson Palmer/250 3.00 8.00
10 Chad Johnson/250 3.00 8.00
11 Chris Cooley/250 3.00 8.00
12 Chris Johnson/250 3.00 8.00
13 Clay Matthews/250 5.00 12.00
14 Darrelle Revis/250 3.00 8.00
15 Darren McFadden/250 3.00 8.00
16 DeSean Jackson/250 3.00 8.00
17 Donovan McNabb/250 4.00 10.00
18 Drew Brees/250 4.00 10.00
19 Dwayne Bowe/250 3.00 8.00
20 Ed Reed/145 3.00 8.00
21 Eli Manning/250 4.00 10.00
22 Felix Jones/250 3.00 8.00
23 Greg Jennings/250 3.00 8.00
24 James Harrison/250 4.00 10.00
25 Jason Witten/250 4.00 10.00
26 Jay Cutler/250 3.00 8.00
27 Joe Flacco/250 4.00 10.00
28 Knowshon Moreno/250 3.00 8.00
29 Larry Fitzgerald/250 3.00 8.00
30 LeSean McCoy/250 3.00 8.00
31 Mark Sanchez/250 4.00 10.00
32 Matt Forte/250 3.00 8.00
33 Matt Ryan/250 4.00 10.00
34 Matt Schaub/250 3.00 8.00
35 Maurice Jones-Drew/100 4.00 10.00
36 Michael Turner/250 3.00 8.00
37 Miles Austin/250 3.00 8.00
38 Percy Harvin/250 3.00 8.00
39 Peyton Manning/250 6.00 15.00
40 Philip Rivers/250 4.00 10.00
41 Ray Lewis/250 4.00 10.00
42 Ray Rice/250 3.00 8.00
43 Reggie Wayne/250 3.00 8.00
44 Roddy White/190 3.00 8.00
45 Sam Bradford/250 4.00 10.00
46 Steve Smith/250 3.00 8.00
47 Steven Jackson/250 3.00 8.00
48 Tom Brady/250 6.00 15.00
49 Vernon Davis/250 3.00 8.00
50 Wes Welker/250 4.00 10.00

2011 Prestige Xtra Points Black Autographs

STATED PRINT RUN 1-25
9 Michael Turner/25 12.00 30.00
11 Tony Gonzalez/25 12.00 30.00
15 Joe Flacco/25 20.00 50.00
17 Ray Rice/25 12.00 30.00
30 Jonathan Stewart/25 12.00 30.00
31 Steve Smith/25 10.00 25.00
36 Jay Cutler/15 12.00 30.00
48 Josh Cribbs/25 12.00 30.00
51 DeMarcus Ware/25 15.00 40.00
64 Brandon Pettigrew/25 10.00 25.00
76 Ryan Grant/25 12.00 30.00
83 Austin Collie/25 12.00 30.00
84 Dallas Clark/15 12.00 30.00
86 Jacob Tamme/25 12.00 30.00
111 Sidney Rice/20 12.00 30.00
112 Tarvaris Jackson/16 10.00 25.00
129 Brandon Jacobs/16 12.00 30.00
132 Kevin Boss/25 12.00 30.00
136 Darrelle Revis/25 12.00 30.00
139 Mark Sanchez/15 40.00 80.00
140 Santonio Holmes/25 12.00 30.00
144 Louis Murphy/25 12.00 30.00
149 Brent Celek/17 12.00 30.00
150 DeSean Jackson/15 12.00 30.00
151 Jeremy Maclin/25 12.00 30.00
153 Michael Vick/25 40.00 80.00
159 Rashard Mendenhall/15 12.00 30.00
164 Mike Tolbert/25 12.00 30.00
165 Philip Rivers/15 25.00 50.00
166 Ryan Mathews/25 15.00 40.00
169 Michael Crabtree/25 12.00 30.00

2011 Prestige National Convention

These cards were issued randomly at the 2011 National Convention through the Panini wrapper redemption program. The numbered versions have an announced print run, i.e. XX/25, and are not serial numbered.

TP Terrelle Pryor 3.00 8.00
TPR Terrelle Pryor Red/25 6.00 15.00

2012 Prestige

COMP.SET w/o RC's (200) 10.00 25.00
DRAFT SP STATED ODDS 1:24 HOB
1 Larry Fitzgerald .25 .60
2 Beanie Wells .25 .60
3 Kevin Kolb .25 .60
4 Patrick Peterson .25 .60
5 Early Doucet III .20 .50
6 Andre Roberts .20 .50
7 Michael Turner .25 .60
8 Julio Jones .25 .60
9 Roddy White .25 .60
10 Tony Gonzalez .25 .60
11 Matt Ryan .25 .60
12 John Abraham .20 .50
13 Ray Lewis .30 .75
14 Ray Rice .25 .60
15 Anquan Boldin .25 .60
16 Ed Reed .25 .60
17 Haloti Ngata .20 .50
18 Joe Flacco .25 .60
19 Ryan Fitzpatrick .25 .60
20 Fred Jackson .25 .60
21 Steve Johnson .25 .60
22 Marcell Dareus .20 .50
23 David Nelson .20 .50
24 Scott Chandler .20 .50
25 Cam Newton .50 1.25
26 DeAngelo Williams .25 .60
27 Steve Smith WR .25 .60
28 Greg Olsen .20 .50
29 Jon Beason .20 .50
30 Jonathan Stewart .25 .60
31 Brian Urlacher .30 .75
32 Jay Cutler .25 .60
33 Devin Hester .30 .75
34 Julius Peppers .25 .60
35 Matt Forte .25 .60
36 Johnny Knox .25 .60
37 Andy Dalton .30 .75
38 Randy Moss .25 .60
39 A.J. Green .25 .60
40 Jermaine Gresham .25 .60
41 Jerome Simpson .20 .50
42 Andre Caldwell .20 .50
43 Colt McCoy .25 .60
44 Peyton Hillis .20 .50
45 D'Qwell Jackson .20 .50
46 Greg Little .20 .50
47 DeMarcus Ware .25 .60
48 Tony Romo .30 .75
49 DeMarco Murray .25 .60
50 Jason Witten .30 .75
51 Dez Bryant .30 .75
52 Laurent Robinson .20 .50
53 Miles Austin .25 .60
54 Sean Lee .20 .50
55 Von Miller .25 .60
56 Tim Tebow .50 1.25
57 Willis McGahee .20 .50
58 Champ Bailey .25 .60
59 D.J. Williams .20 .50
60 Eric Decker .25 .60
61 Jahvid Best .25 .60
62 Brandon Pettigrew .20 .50
63 Nate Burleson .20 .50
64 Ndamukong Suh .30 .75
65 Matthew Stafford .30 .75
66 Calvin Johnson .30 .75
67 Charles Woodson .30 .75
68 Clay Matthews .30 .75
69 Aaron Rodgers .50 1.25
70 Greg Jennings .25 .60
71 Jordy Nelson .25 .60
72 Jermichael Finley .25 .60
73 Ryan Grant .25 .60
74 A.J. Hawk .25 .60
75 Andre Johnson .25 .60
76 Arian Foster .25 .60
77 Jacoby Jones .20 .50
78 Matt Schaub .25 .60
79 Brian Cushing .20 .50
80 Owen Daniels .20 .50
81 Reggie Wayne .25 .60
82 Peyton Manning .75 2.00
83 Austin Collie .25 .60
84 Donald Brown .25 .60
85 Pierre Garcon .25 .60
86 Maurice Jones-Drew .25 .60
87 Blaine Gabbert .25 .60
88 Paul Posluszny .25 .60
89 Marcedes Lewis .20 .50
90 Mike Thomas .25 .60
91 Jamaal Charles .25 .60
92 Eric Berry .25 .60
93 Dwayne Bowe .25 .60
94 Matt Cassel .25 .60
95 Tamba Hali .20 .50
96 Dexter McCluster .20 .50
97 Reggie Bush .25 .60
98 Brandon Marshall .20 .50
99 Matt Moore .20 .50
100 Cameron Wake .20 .50
101 Brian Hartline .20 .50
102 Jared Allen .25 .60
103 Adrian Peterson .30 .75
104 Michael Jenkins .20 .50
105 Percy Harvin .25 .60
106 Christian Ponder .25 .60
107 Tom Brady .50 1.25
108 BenJarvus Green-Ellis .25 .60
109 Rob Gronkowski .25 .60
110 Wes Welker .30 .75
111 Aaron Hernandez .25 .60
112 Jerod Mayo .25 .60
113 Sterling Moore RC .30 .75
114 Drew Brees .30 .75
115 Mark Ingram .25 .60
116 Jimmy Graham .25 .60
117 Marques Colston .25 .60
118 Darren Sproles .25 .60
119 Robert Meachem .25 .60
120 Jonathan Vilma .20 .50
121 Lance Moore .25 .60
122 Eli Manning .30 .75
123 Brandon Jacobs .25 .60
124 Victor Cruz .30 .75
125 Antrel Rolle .20 .50
126 Hakeem Nicks .25 .60
127 Ahmad Bradshaw .25 .60
128 Darrelle Revis .25 .60
129 Mark Sanchez .25 .60
130 Plaxico Burress .25 .60
131 Santonio Holmes .25 .60
132 Shonn Greene .25 .60
133 Dustin Keller .20 .50
134 LaDainian Tomlinson .30 .75
135 David Harris .20 .50
136 Darren McFadden .25 .60
137 Terrelle Pryor .25 .60
138 Richard Seymour .20 .50
139 Carson Palmer .25 .60
140 Jacoby Ford .20 .50
141 Darrius Heyward-Bey .20 .50
142 Nnamdi Asomugha .20 .50
143 Michael Vick .30 .75
144 LeSean McCoy .25 .60
145 DeSean Jackson .25 .60
146 Jeremy Maclin .25 .60
147 Asante Samuel .25 .60
148 Brent Celek .25 .60
149 Jason Babin .20 .50
150 Ben Roethlisberger .30 .75
151 Rashard Mendenhall .25 .60
152 Troy Polamalu .30 .75
153 Heath Miller .25 .60
154 Mike Wallace .25 .60
155 Antonio Brown .25 .60
156 James Harrison .30 .75
157 Brett Keisel .20 .50
158 Philip Rivers .25 .60
159 Ryan Mathews .25 .60
160 Antonio Gates .25 .60
161 Vincent Jackson .25 .60
162 Eric Weddle .20 .50
163 Takeo Spikes .20 .50
164 Mike Tolbert .25 .60
165 Malcom Floyd .20 .50
166 Patrick Willis .25 .60
167 Alex Smith QB .25 .60
168 Frank Gore .25 .60
169 Ted Ginn Jr. .20 .50
170 Aldon Smith .25 .60
171 Michael Crabtree .25 .60
172 NaVorro Bowman .20 .50
173 Vernon Davis .25 .60
174 Tarvaris Jackson .20 .50
175 Marshawn Lynch .25 .60
176 Sidney Rice .25 .60
177 Doug Baldwin .25 .60
178 Earl Thomas .20 .50
179 Golden Tate .25 .60
180 Steven Jackson .25 .60
181 James Laurinaitis .20 .50
182 Sam Bradford .30 .75
183 Brandon Gibson .20 .50
184 Brandon Lloyd .25 .60
185 Chris Long .20 .50
186 LeGarrette Blount .20 .50
187 Josh Freeman .25 .60
188 Mike Williams .25 .60
189 Kellen Winslow Jr. .25 .60
190 Ronde Barber .20 .50
191 Matt Hasselbeck .25 .60
192 Chris Johnson .25 .60
193 Nate Washington .20 .50
194 Kenny Britt .25 .60
195 Jason McCourty RC .30 .75
196 Brian Orakpo .20 .50
197 Roy Helu Jr. .25 .60
198 London Fletcher .20 .50
199 Santana Moss .25 .60
200 DeAngelo Hall .20 .50
201 Morris Claiborne RC 1.50 4.00
202A Dre Kirkpatrick RC 1.25 3.00
202B Dre Kirkpatrick Draft SP 2.50 6.00
203 Vinny Curry SP RC 6.00 15.00
204 Janoris Jenkins SP RC 6.00 15.00
205A Quinton Coples RC .75 2.00
205B Quinton Coples Draft SP 2.00 5.00
206 Nick Perry RC .75 2.00
207 Whitney Mercilus RC .75 2.00
208 Andre Branch RC .60 1.50
209 Jared Crick RC .75 2.00
210 Fletcher Cox RC .75 2.00
211 Chandler Jones RC .75 2.00
212 Devon Still RC .75 2.00
213A Michael Brockers SP RC 5.00 12.00
213B Michael Brockers Draft SP 1.50 4.00
214 Luke Kuechly RC 1.00 2.50
215A Dont'a Hightower RC 1.25 3.00
215B Dont'a Hightower Draft SP 2.50 6.00
216 Alfred Morris RC .60 1.50
217 David DeCastro RC 1.00 2.50
218A Melvin Ingram RC 1.00 2.50
218B Melvin Ingram Draft SP 2.00 5.00
219A Courtney Upshaw RC 1.00 2.50
219B Courtney Upshaw Draft SP 2.00 5.00
220 Zach Brown RC .60 1.50
221 Lavonte David RC 1.00 2.50
222 Bobby Wagner RC .75 2.00
223 Ronnell Lewis RC .75 2.00
224 Dontari Poe SP RC 6.00 15.00
225 George Iloka RC .60 1.50
226A Matt Kalil RC 1.00 2.50
226B Matt Kalil Draft SP 2.50 6.00
227 Riley Reiff RC .75 2.00
228 Jonathan Martin RC .60 1.50
229A Andrew Luck RC 6.00 15.00
229B Andrew Luck Draft SP 10.00 25.00
230A Robert Griffin III RC 6.00 15.00
230B Robert Griffin III Draft SP 10.00 25.00
231A Ryan Tannehill RC 2.00 5.00
231B Ryan Tannehill Draft SP 4.00 10.00
232 Nick Foles RC 1.25 3.00
233 Brock Osweiler RC 1.00 2.50
234 Ryan Lindley RC .75 2.00
235 Kirk Cousins RC 1.25 3.00
236 Brandon Weeden RC 1.50 4.00
237 B.J. Coleman RC 1.00 2.50
238 Russell Wilson RC 1.25 3.00
239 Chandler Harnish SP RC 6.00 15.00
240 Kellen Moore RC 1.25 3.00
241 Case Keenum RC 1.00 2.50
242A Trent Richardson RC 2.50 6.00
242B Trent Richardson Draft SP 5.00 12.00
243 Lamar Miller RC 1.00 2.50
244 David Wilson RC 1.50 4.00
245 Doug Martin RC 1.25 3.00
246 B.J. Cunningham RC .60 1.50
247 Isaiah Pead RC .75 2.00
248 Bernard Pierce RC .75 2.00
249 LaMichael James RC 1.50 4.00
250 Cyrus Gray RC .75 2.00
251 Ronnie Hillman RC 1.00 2.50
252 Chris Rainey RC .75 2.00
253 Bruce Irvin RC 1.00 2.50
254 Dan Herron RC .75 2.00
255 Robert Turbin SP RC 6.00 15.00
256 Vick Ballard RC .60 1.50
257 Terrance Ganaway RC .60 1.50
258 Bryce Brown RC .75 2.00
259 Greg Childs RC .75 2.00
260 Harrison Smith RC .75 2.00
261 Marc Tyler RC .75 2.00
262A Mark Barron RC 1.25 3.00
262B Mark Barron Draft SP 2.50 6.00
263 Dwayne Allen RC .75 2.00
264A Coby Fleener RC 1.00 2.50
264B Coby Fleener Draft SP 2.00 5.00
265 Orson Charles SP RC 6.00 15.00
266 Michael Egnew RC .60 1.50
267 Ladarius Green SP RC 6.00 15.00
268 Mychal Kendricks RC .75 2.00
269 Shea McClellin SP RC 8.00 20.00
270A Justin Blackmon RC 1.50 4.00
270B Justin Blackmon Draft SP 3.00 8.00
271A Kendall Wright RC 1.00 2.50
271B Kendall Wright Draft SP 2.00 5.00
272A Michael Floyd RC 1.50 4.00
272B Michael Floyd Draft SP 3.00 8.00
273 Mohamed Sanu RC .75 2.00
274 Alshon Jeffery RC 1.25 3.00
275A Rueben Randle RC .75 2.00
275B Rueben Randle Draft SP 2.00 5.00
276A Stephen Hill RC .75 2.00
276B Stephen Hill Draft SP 1.50 4.00
277 Nick Toon RC 1.00 2.50
278 Juron Criner RC .60 1.50
279 Keshawn Martin RC .75 2.00
280 Brian Quick RC 1.00 2.50
281 Tommy Streeter SP RC 6.00 15.00
282 Joe Adams RC .75 2.00
283 Chris Givens RC .60 1.50
284 T.Y. Hilton RC .75 2.00
285 DeVier Posey RC .75 2.00
286 Marvin Jones RC .60 1.50
287 Kevin Zeitler RC .60 1.50
288 Jarius Wright RC .75 2.00
289 Marvin McNutt RC .75 2.00
290 Jeff Fuller RC 1.00 2.50
291 Rishard Matthews RC .75 2.00
292 Ryan Broyles RC .75 2.00
293 LaVon Brazill RC .60 1.50
294 Michael Smith RC .60 1.50
295 A.J. Jenkins RC 1.00 2.50
296 Stephon Gilmore RC .75 2.00
297 T.J. Graham RC .75 2.00
298 Danny Coale RC 1.25 3.00
299 Devon Wylie RC .75 2.00
300 Travis Benjamin RC .75 2.00
301 Eric LeGrand SP RC 12.00 30.00

2012 Prestige Extra Points Blue

*ROOKIE/999: .5X TO 1.2X BASIC RC
*ROOKIE/999: .05X TO .15X SP RC
STATED PRINT RUN 999 SER.#'d SETS

2012 Prestige Extra Points Black

*1-200 VETS/10: 8X TO 20X BASIC CARDS
*201-300 ROOKIE/10: 3X TO 8X BASIC RC
*201-300 ROOKIE/10: .4X TO 1X SP RC
BLACK STATED PRINT RUN 10

2012 Prestige Extra Points Gold

*1-200 VETS: 1.5X TO 4X BASIC CARDS
*201-300 ROOKIES: .6X TO 1.5X BASIC RC
*201-300 ROOKIES: .08X TO .2X SP RC

2012 Prestige Extra Points Green

*1-200 VETS/25: 5X TO 12X BASIC CARDS
*201-300 ROOKIE/25: 2X TO 5X BASIC RC
*201-300 ROOKIE/25: .25X TO .6X SP RC
STATED PRINT RUN 25 SER.#'d SETS

2012 Prestige Connections

1 Tom Brady / Wes Welker 2.00 5.00
2 Matthew Stafford / Calvin Johnson 1.25 3.00
3 Aaron Rodgers / Jordy Nelson 2.00 5.00
4 Drew Brees / Jimmy Graham 1.25 3.00
5 Dez Bryant / DeMarco Murray 1.25 3.00
6 Eli Manning / Victor Cruz 1.25 3.00
7 Philip Rivers / Antonio Gates 1.00 2.50
8 Greg Jennings / Jermichael Finley 1.00 2.50
9 Tony Romo / Jason Witten 1.25 3.00
10 Andy Dalton / A.J. Green 1.25 3.00
11 Rob Gronkowski / Aaron Hernandez 1.00 2.50
12 Mark Sanchez / Plaxico Burress 1.00 2.50
13 Matt Ryan / Julio Jones 1.00 2.50
14 Michael Turner / Roddy White 1.00 2.50
15 Blaine Gabbert / Maurice Jones-Drew 1.00 2.50
16 Joe Flacco / Ray Rice 1.00 2.50
17 Michael Vick / LeSean McCoy 1.25 3.00
18 Arian Foster / Andre Johnson 1.00 2.50
19 Alex Smith QB / Frank Gore 1.00 2.50
20 Knowshon Moreno / Willis McGahee 1.00 2.50
21 Tarvaris Jackson / Marshawn Lynch 1.00 2.50
22 Ryan Mathews / Antonio Gates 1.00 2.50
23 Christian Ponder / Adrian Peterson 1.25 3.00
24 Jay Cutler / Matt Forte 1.00 2.50
25 Ryan Fitzpatrick / Fred Jackson 1.00 2.50

2012 Prestige Connections Materials

STATED PRINT RUN 5-249
*PRIME/49: .6X TO 1.5X BASIC JSY/249
1 Tom Brady/30 / Wes Welker 15.00 30.00
5 Dez Bryant/249 / DeMarco Murray 5.00 12.00
9 Tony Romo/15 / Jason Witten 15.00 30.00
10 Andy Dalton/249 / A.J. Green 5.00 12.00
12 Mark Sanchez/249 / Plaxico Burress 4.00 10.00
16 Joe Flacco/249 / Ray Rice 4.00 10.00
18 Arian Foster/5 / Andre Johnson
20 Knowshon Moreno/100 / Willis McGahee 5.00 12.00

2012 Prestige Draft City Destination

*HOLOKOTE/100: 1X TO 2.5X BASIC INSERTS
1 A.J. Jenkins .75 2.00
2 Andrew Luck 4.00 10.00
3 Brandon Weeden 1.25 3.00
4 David Wilson 1.25 3.00
5 Doug Martin 1.00 2.50
6 Justin Blackmon 1.25 3.00
7 Kendall Wright .75 2.00
8 Michael Floyd 1.25 3.00
9 Robert Griffin III 3.00 8.00
10 Ryan Tannehill 1.50 4.00
11 Trent Richardson 2.00 5.00
12 Alshon Jeffery 1.00 2.50
13 Bernard Pierce .60 1.50
14 Brian Quick .75 2.00
15 Brock Osweiler .75 2.00
16 Coby Fleener .75 2.00
17 DeVier Posey .60 1.50
18 Isaiah Pead .60 1.50
19 Chris Givens .50 1.25
20 Joe Adams .60 1.50
21 LaMichael James 1.25 3.00
22 Mohamed Sanu .60 1.50
23 Nick Foles 1.00 2.50
24 Nick Toon .75 2.00
25 Ronnie Hillman .75 2.00
26 Rueben Randle .60 1.50
27 Russell Wilson 1.00 2.50
28 Ryan Broyles .60 1.50
29 Stephen Hill .60 1.50
30 T.J. Graham .60 1.50

2012 Prestige Draft City Destination Autographs

1 A.J. Jenkins 8.00 20.00
2 Andrew Luck 125.00 200.00
3 Brandon Weeden 20.00 50.00
4 David Wilson 12.00 30.00
5 Doug Martin 10.00 25.00
6 Justin Blackmon 25.00 50.00
7 Kendall Wright 8.00 20.00
8 Michael Floyd 12.00 30.00
9 Robert Griffin III 100.00 175.00
10 Ryan Tannehill 30.00 60.00
11 Trent Richardson 40.00 80.00
12 Alshon Jeffery 12.00 30.00
13 Bernard Pierce 6.00 15.00
14 Brian Quick 8.00 20.00
15 Brock Osweiler 10.00 25.00
16 Coby Fleener 8.00 20.00
17 DeVier Posey 6.00 15.00
18 Isaiah Pead 6.00 15.00
19 Chris Givens 5.00 12.00
20 Joe Adams 6.00 15.00
21 LaMichael James 12.00 30.00
22 Mohamed Sanu 6.00 15.00
23 Nick Foles 10.00 25.00
24 Nick Toon 8.00 20.00
25 Ronnie Hillman 8.00 20.00
26 Rueben Randle 8.00 20.00
27 Russell Wilson 10.00 25.00
28 Ryan Broyles 6.00 15.00
29 Stephen Hill 6.00 15.00
30 T.J. Graham 5.00 12.00

2012 Prestige Extra Points Black Autographs

STATED PRINT RUN 1-25
5 Early Doucet/25 10.00 25.00
6 Andre Roberts/25 10.00 25.00
8 Julio Jones/16 12.00 30.00
23 David Nelson/25 10.00 25.00
27 Steve Smith WR/25 12.00 30.00
28 Greg Olsen/25 10.00 25.00
30 Jonathan Stewart/25 12.00 30.00
33 Devin Hester/15
37 Andy Dalton/25 20.00 40.00
39 A.J. Green/25 20.00 40.00
44 Peyton Hillis/23 10.00 25.00
70 Greg Jennings/25 12.00 30.00
99 Matt Moore/25
101 Brian Hartline/25 10.00 25.00
106 Christian Ponder/25 20.00 40.00
112 Jerod Mayo/25 12.00 30.00
116 Jimmy Graham/25 12.00 30.00
117 Marques Colston/25 12.00 30.00
132 Shonn Greene/21 12.00 30.00
135 David Harris/25
144 LeSean McCoy/25 12.00 30.00
147 Asante Samuel/25 15.00 40.00
153 Heath Miller/25 12.00 30.00
154 Mike Wallace/25 12.00 30.00
164 Mike Tolbert/25 12.00 30.00
172 NaVorro Bowman/25
176 Sidney Rice/22 12.00 30.00
178 Earl Thomas/25 10.00 25.00
179 Golden Tate/25 12.00 30.00
181 James Laurinaitis/16 12.00 30.00
188 Mike Williams/25 12.00 30.00
197 Roy Helu Jr./25 12.00 30.00
199 Santana Moss/25 12.00 30.00
200 DeAngelo Hall/25 10.00 25.00

2012 Prestige Gamers Materials

*PRIME: .8X TO 2X BASIC JSY
1 Sam Bradford 4.00 10.00
2 Robert Meachem 3.00 8.00
3 Owen Daniels 2.50 6.00
4 Malcom Floyd 2.50 6.00
5 Mark Ingram 3.00 8.00
6 Colt McCoy 3.00 8.00
7 Kenny Britt 3.00 8.00
8 Larry Fitzgerald 3.00 8.00
9 James Harrison 4.00 10.00
10 Santana Moss 3.00 8.00
11 Joseph Addai 2.50 6.00
12 Johnny Knox 3.00 8.00
13 Ray Lewis 4.00 10.00
14 Von Miller 3.00 8.00
15 Eli Manning 4.00 10.00
16 Carson Palmer 3.00 8.00
17 Braylon Edwards 3.00 8.00
18 Hakeem Nicks 3.00 8.00
19 Beanie Wells 3.00 8.00
20 Joe Flacco 3.00 8.00
21 Jahvid Best 3.00 8.00
22 Tony Romo 4.00 10.00
23 Santonio Holmes 3.00 8.00
24 Steven Jackson 3.00 8.00
25 Dez Bryant 4.00 10.00
26 Cam Newton 6.00 15.00
27 Tony Gonzalez 3.00 8.00
28 Clay Matthews 4.00 10.00
29 Percy Harvin 3.00 8.00
30 Shonn Greene 3.00 8.00
31 Mike Thomas 3.00 8.00
32 John Abraham 2.50 6.00
33 Kevin Kolb 3.00 8.00

34 Willis McGahee 2.50 6.00
35 Frank Gore 3.00 8.00
36 Jon Beason 2.50 6.00
37 LaDainian Tomlinson 4.00 10.00
38 Mark Sanchez 3.00 8.00
39 Plaxico Burress 3.00 8.00
40 Anquan Boldin 3.00 8.00
41 Haloti Ngata 2.50 6.00
42 Jerod Mayo 3.00 8.00
43 Jay Cutler 3.00 8.00
44 Arian Foster 3.00 8.00
45 Marques Colston 3.00 8.00
46 London Fletcher 2.50 6.00
47 Ed Reed 3.00 8.00
48 Miles Austin 3.00 8.00
49 Tamba Hali 2.50 6.00
50 Tarvaris Jackson 2.50 6.00
51 Reggie Wayne 3.00 8.00
52 Jonathan Vilma 2.50 6.00
53 Marcell Dareus 2.50 6.00
54 Darren Sproles 3.00 8.00
55 A.J. Green 3.00 8.00
56 Patrick Willis 3.00 8.00
57 Chris Johnson 3.00 8.00
58 Julius Peppers 3.00 8.00
59 Dallas Clark 3.00 8.00
60 A.J. Hawk 3.00 8.00
61 Dustin Keller 2.50 6.00
62 Brent Celek 3.00 8.00
63 DeMarco Murray 3.00 8.00
64 Darrelle Revis 3.00 8.00
65 Matt Hasselbeck 3.00 8.00
66 Matt Schaub 3.00 8.00
67 Hines Ward 4.00 10.00
68 Matt Cassel 3.00 8.00
69 Brian Urlacher 4.00 10.00
70 Dwayne Bowe 3.00 8.00
71 Nnamdi Asomugha 2.50 6.00
72 Jamaal Charles 3.00 8.00
73 Drew Brees 4.00 10.00
74 Andy Dalton 4.00 10.00
75 Jacoby Ford 2.50 6.00
76 David Harris 2.50 6.00
77 Brian Hartline 2.50 6.00
78 Adrian Wilson 2.50 6.00
79 Ahmad Bradshaw 3.00 8.00
80 Andre Johnson 3.00 8.00
82 Bernard Berrian 2.50 6.00
83 Brandon Jacobs 3.00 8.00
84 Brandon Lloyd 3.00 8.00
85 Brian Orakpo 2.50 6.00
86 C.J. Spiller 3.00 8.00
87 Cadillac Williams 2.50 6.00
88 Carson Palmer 3.00 8.00
89 Chad Greenway 3.00 8.00
90 Chad Ochocinco 3.00 8.00
91 Danny Amendola 3.00 8.00
92 Darren Sproles 3.00 8.00
93 LaDainian Tomlinson 4.00 10.00
94 Vincent Jackson 3.00 8.00
95 Vernon Davis 3.00 8.00
96 Tony Gonzalez 3.00 8.00
97 Felix Jones 3.00 8.00
98 Jeremy Maclin 3.00 8.00
99 Reggie Bush 3.00 8.00
100 Ray Rice 3.00 8.00

2012 Prestige League Leaders

1 Drew Brees 1.50 4.00
Tom Brady
2 Matthew Stafford 1.00 2.50
Eli Manning
3 Aaron Rodgers 1.50 4.00
Philip Rivers
4 Tony Romo 1.00 2.50
Matt Ryan
5 Maurice Jones-Drew .75 2.00
Ray Rice
6 Michael Turner .75 2.00
LeSean McCoy
7 Arian Foster .75 2.00
Frank Gore
8 Marshawn Lynch .75 2.00
Willis McGahee
9 Calvin Johnson 1.00 2.50
Wes Welker
10 Victor Cruz 1.00 2.50
Larry Fitzgerald
11 Steve Smith WR .75 2.00
Rob Gronkowski
12 Jimmy Graham .75 2.00
Roddy White
13 LeSean McCoy .75 2.00
Rob Gronkowski
14 Drew Brees 1.50 4.00
Aaron Rodgers
15 Charles Woodson 1.00 2.50
Kyle Arrington
16 Drew Brees 2.00 5.00
Tom Brady
Matthew Stafford
Eli Manning
17 Aaron Rodgers 2.00 5.00
Philip Rivers
Tony Romo
Matt Ryan
18 Maurice Jones-Drew 1.00 2.50
Ray Rice
Michael Turner
LeSean McCoy
19 Arian Foster 1.00 2.50
Frank Gore
Marshawn Lynch
Willis McGahee
20 Calvin Johnson 1.25 3.00
Wes Welker
Victor Cruz
Larry Fitzgerald
21 Steve Smith WR 1.00 2.50
Rob Gronkowski
Jimmy Graham
Roddy White
22 Rob Gronkowski 2.00 5.00
Calvin Johnson
LeSean McCoy
Cam Newton
23 Drew Brees 2.00 5.00
Aaron Rodgers
Matthew Stafford
Tom Brady
24 Eric Weddle 1.25 3.00
Charles Woodson
Kyle Arrington
Corey Webster
25 Jared Allen 1.00 2.50
DeMarcus Ware
Jason Babin
Jason Pierre-Paul

2012 Prestige League Leaders Materials

STATED PRINT RUN 249 SER.#'d SETS
1 Drew Brees 8.00 20.00
Tom Brady
4 Tony Romo 5.00 12.00
Matt Ryan
7 Arian Foster 4.00 10.00
Frank Gore
16 Drew Brees 12.00 30.00
Tom Brady
Matthew Stafford
Eli Manning

2012 Prestige League Leaders Materials Prime

STATED PRINT RUN 49 SER.#'d SETS
5 Maurice Jones-Drew 6.00 15.00
Ray Rice
7 Arian Foster 6.00 15.00
Frank Gore
9 Calvin Johnson 8.00 20.00
Wes Welker

2012 Prestige NFL Draft Combo Materials

1 Andrew Luck 40.00 80.00
Robert Griffin III
2 Justin Blackmon 8.00 20.00
Michael Floyd
3 Trent Richardson 12.00 30.00
Ryan Tannehill
4 Robert Griffin III 20.00 50.00
Kendall Wright
5 Morris Claiborne 12.00 30.00
Mark Barron

2012 Prestige NFL Draft Materials

STATED PRINT RUN 99-249
*PRIME/15-25: 1X TO 2.5X BASIC JSY/199-249
1 Andrew Luck/99 25.00 50.00
2 Robert Griffin III/99 15.00 40.00
3 Trent Richardson/99 10.00 25.00
4 Matt Kalil/249 4.00 10.00
5 Justin Blackmon/99 6.00 15.00
6 Morris Claiborne/199 8.00 20.00
7 Mark Barron/199 4.00 10.00
8 Ryan Tannehill/99 8.00 20.00
9 Stephon Gilmore/249 2.50 6.00
10 Dontari Poe/249 2.50 6.00
11 Fletcher Cox/249 2.50 6.00
12 Michael Floyd/99 6.00 15.00
13 Michael Brockers/249 2.50 6.00
14 Quinton Coples/249 2.50 6.00
15 Dre Kirkpatrick/199 4.00 10.00
16 Melvin Ingram/249 3.00 8.00
17 Shea McClellin/249 3.00 8.00
18 Kendall Wright/99 4.00 10.00
19 Dont'a Hightower/249 4.00 10.00
20 Nick Perry/249 4.00 10.00

2012 Prestige NFL Draft Tickets

*HOLOKOTE/100: .8X TO 2X BASIC INSERTS
1 Andrew Luck 5.00 12.00
2 Robert Griffin III 4.00 10.00
3 Trent Richardson 2.50 6.00
4 Justin Blackmon 1.50 4.00
5 Ryan Tannehill 2.00 5.00
6 Michael Floyd 1.50 4.00
7 Kendall Wright 1.00 2.50
8 Brandon Weeden 1.50 4.00
9 A.J. Jenkins 1.00 2.50
10 Doug Martin 1.25 3.00
11 David Wilson 1.50 4.00
12 Alshon Jeffery 1.25 3.00
13 Bernard Pierce .75 2.00
14 Brian Quick 1.00 2.50
15 Brock Osweiler 1.00 2.50
16 Coby Fleener 1.00 2.50
17 DeVier Posey .75 2.00
18 Dwayne Allen .75 2.00
19 Isaiah Pead .75 2.00
20 Chris Givens .60 1.50
21 Joe Adams .75 2.00
22 Lamar Miller 1.00 2.50
23 LaMichael James 1.50 4.00
24 Michael Egnew .60 1.50
25 Mohamed Sanu .75 2.00
26 Nick Foles 1.25 3.00
27 Nick Toon 1.00 2.50
28 Robert Turbin .75 2.00
29 Ronnie Hillman 1.00 2.50
30 Rueben Randle .75 2.00
31 Russell Wilson 1.25 3.00
32 Ryan Broyles .75 2.00
33 Stephen Hill .75 2.00
34 T.J. Graham .75 2.00
35 T.Y. Hilton .75 2.00

2012 Prestige NFL Draft Tickets Autographs

1 Andrew Luck 125.00 200.00
2 Robert Griffin III 100.00 175.00
3 Trent Richardson 40.00 80.00
4 Justin Blackmon 25.00 50.00
5 Ryan Tannehill 30.00 60.00
6 Michael Floyd 15.00 40.00
7 Kendall Wright 8.00 20.00
8 Brandon Weeden 20.00 50.00
9 A.J. Jenkins 8.00 20.00
10 Doug Martin 10.00 25.00
11 David Wilson 15.00 40.00
12 Alshon Jeffery 10.00 25.00
13 Bernard Pierce 6.00 15.00
14 Brian Quick 8.00 20.00
15 Brock Osweiler 8.00 20.00
16 Coby Fleener 8.00 20.00
17 DeVier Posey 5.00 12.00
18 Dwayne Allen 6.00 15.00
19 Isaiah Pead 6.00 15.00
20 Chris Givens 5.00 12.00
21 Joe Adams 5.00 12.00
22 Lamar Miller 8.00 20.00
23 LaMichael James 12.00 30.00
24 Michael Egnew 5.00 12.00
25 Mohamed Sanu 6.00 15.00
26 Nick Foles 6.00 15.00
27 Nick Toon 8.00 20.00
28 Robert Turbin 6.00 15.00
29 Ronnie Hillman 6.00 15.00
30 Rueben Randle 6.00 15.00
31 Russell Wilson 10.00 25.00
32 Ryan Broyles 6.00 15.00
33 Stephen Hill 6.00 15.00
34 T.J. Graham 6.00 15.00

2012 Prestige NFL Passport

*HOLOKOTE/100: .8X TO 2X BASIC INSERTS
1 A.J. Jenkins 1.00 2.50
2 Andrew Luck 5.00 12.00
3 Brandon Weeden 1.50 4.00
4 David Wilson 1.50 4.00
5 Doug Martin 1.25 3.00
6 Justin Blackmon 1.50 4.00
7 Kendall Wright 1.00 2.50
8 Michael Floyd 1.50 4.00
9 Robert Griffin III 4.00 10.00
10 Ryan Tannehill 2.00 5.00
11 Trent Richardson 2.50 6.00
12 Alshon Jeffery 1.25 3.00
13 Bernard Pierce .75 2.00
14 Brian Quick 1.00 2.50
15 Brock Osweiler 1.00 2.50
16 Coby Fleener 1.00 2.50
17 DeVier Posey .75 2.00
18 Dwayne Allen .75 2.00
19 Isaiah Pead .75 2.00
20 Chris Givens .60 1.50
21 Joe Adams .75 2.00
22 Lamar Miller 1.00 2.50
23 LaMichael James 1.50 4.00
24 Michael Egnew .60 1.50
25 Mohamed Sanu .75 2.00
26 Nick Foles 1.25 3.00
27 Nick Toon 1.00 2.50
28 Robert Turbin .75 2.00
29 Ronnie Hillman 1.00 2.50
30 Rueben Randle .75 2.00
31 Russell Wilson 1.25 3.00
32 Ryan Broyles .75 2.00
33 Stephen Hill .75 2.00
34 T.J. Graham .75 2.00
35 T.Y. Hilton .75 2.00

2012 Prestige NFL Passport Autographs

1 A.J. Jenkins 8.00 20.00
2 Andrew Luck 125.00 200.00
3 Brandon Weeden 20.00 50.00
4 David Wilson 15.00 40.00
5 Doug Martin 10.00 25.00
6 Justin Blackmon 25.00 50.00
7 Kendall Wright 8.00 20.00
8 Michael Floyd 15.00 40.00
9 Robert Griffin III 100.00 175.00
10 Ryan Tannehill 30.00 60.00
11 Trent Richardson 40.00 80.00
12 Alshon Jeffery 10.00 25.00
13 Bernard Pierce 6.00 15.00
14 Brian Quick 8.00 20.00
15 Brock Osweiler 8.00 20.00
16 Coby Fleener 8.00 20.00
17 DeVier Posey 5.00 12.00
18 Dwayne Allen 6.00 15.00
19 Isaiah Pead 6.00 15.00
20 Chris Givens 5.00 12.00
21 Joe Adams 5.00 12.00
22 Lamar Miller 8.00 20.00
23 LaMichael James 12.00 30.00
24 Michael Egnew 5.00 12.00
25 Mohamed Sanu 6.00 15.00
26 Nick Foles 10.00 25.00
27 Nick Toon 8.00 20.00
28 Robert Turbin 6.00 15.00
29 Ronnie Hillman 6.00 15.00
30 Rueben Randle 6.00 15.00
31 Russell Wilson 10.00 25.00
32 Ryan Broyles 6.00 15.00
33 Stephen Hill 6.00 15.00
34 T.J. Graham 6.00 15.00

2012 Prestige Prestigious Picks

*BLACK/25: 1.2X TO 3X BASIC INSERTS
*PLATINUM/10: 2X TO 5X BASIC INSERTS
1 Andrew Luck 5.00 12.00
2 Robert Griffin III 4.00 10.00
3 Trent Richardson 2.50 6.00
4 Justin Blackmon 1.50 4.00
5 Ryan Tannehill 2.00 5.00
6 Michael Floyd 1.50 4.00
7 Kendall Wright 1.00 2.50
8 Brandon Weeden 1.50 4.00
9 A.J. Jenkins 1.00 2.50
10 Doug Martin 1.25 3.00
11 David Wilson 1.50 4.00
12 Alshon Jeffery 1.25 3.00
13 Bernard Pierce .75 2.00
14 Brian Quick 1.00 2.50
15 Brock Osweiler 1.00 2.50
16 Coby Fleener 1.00 2.50
17 DeVier Posey .75 2.00
18 Dwayne Allen .75 2.00
19 Isaiah Pead .75 2.00
20 Chris Givens .60 1.50
21 Joe Adams .75 2.00
22 Lamar Miller 1.00 2.50
23 LaMichael James 1.50 4.00
24 Michael Egnew .60 1.50
25 Mohamed Sanu .75 2.00
26 Nick Foles 1.25 3.00
27 Nick Toon 1.00 2.50
28 Robert Turbin .75 2.00
29 Ronnie Hillman 1.00 2.50
30 Rueben Randle .75 2.00
31 Russell Wilson 1.25 3.00
32 Ryan Broyles .75 2.00
33 Stephen Hill .75 2.00
34 T.J. Graham .75 2.00
35 T.Y. Hilton .75 2.00
36 Bruce Irvin 1.00 2.50
37 Chandler Jones .75 2.00
38 Dont'a Hightower 1.25 3.00
39 Dontari Poe .75 2.00
40 Dre Kirkpatrick 1.25 3.00
41 Fletcher Cox .75 2.00
42 Harrison Smith .75 2.00
43 Luke Kuechly 1.00 2.50
44 Mark Barron 1.25 3.00
45 Melvin Ingram 1.00 2.50
46 Michael Brockers .75 2.00
47 Morris Claiborne 1.50 4.00
48 Quinton Coples .75 2.00
49 Shea McClellin 1.00 2.50
50 Stephon Gilmore .75 2.00

2012 Prestige Prestigious Picks Materials

STATED PRINT RUN 299 SER.#'d SETS
*BLACK/149: .4X TO 1X BASIC JSY/299
1 Andrew Luck 15.00 40.00
2 Robert Griffin III 15.00 40.00
3 Trent Richardson 8.00 20.00
4 Justin Blackmon 5.00 12.00
5 Ryan Tannehill 6.00 15.00
6 Michael Floyd 5.00 12.00
7 Kendall Wright 3.00 8.00
8 Brandon Weeden 5.00 12.00
9 A.J. Jenkins 3.00 8.00
10 Doug Martin 4.00 10.00
11 David Wilson 5.00 12.00
12 Alshon Jeffery 4.00 10.00
13 Bernard Pierce 2.50 6.00
14 Brian Quick 3.00 8.00
15 Brock Osweiler 3.00 8.00
16 Coby Fleener 3.00 8.00
17 DeVier Posey 2.50 6.00
18 Dwayne Allen 2.50 6.00
19 Isaiah Pead 2.50 6.00
20 Chris Givens 2.00 5.00
21 Joe Adams 2.50 6.00
22 Lamar Miller 3.00 8.00
23 LaMichael James 5.00 12.00
24 Michael Egnew 2.00 5.00
25 Mohamed Sanu 2.50 6.00
26 Nick Foles 4.00 10.00
27 Nick Toon 3.00 8.00
28 Robert Turbin 2.50 6.00
29 Ronnie Hillman 3.00 8.00
30 Rueben Randle 2.50 6.00
31 Russell Wilson 4.00 10.00
32 Ryan Broyles 2.50 6.00
33 Stephen Hill 2.50 6.00
34 T.J. Graham 2.50 6.00

2012 Prestige Prestigious Picks Materials Prime Autographs

STATED PRINT RUN 40-99
1 Andrew Luck/99 200.00 350.00
2 Robert Griffin III/99 125.00 250.00
3 Trent Richardson/99 50.00 100.00
4 Justin Blackmon/99 40.00 80.00
5 Ryan Tannehill/99 40.00 80.00
6 Michael Floyd/99 30.00 60.00
7 Kendall Wright/99 12.00 30.00
8 Brandon Weeden/99 30.00 60.00
9 A.J. Jenkins/99 12.00 30.00
10 Doug Martin/99 30.00 60.00
11 David Wilson/99 20.00 50.00
12 Alshon Jeffery/99 25.00 50.00
13 Bernard Pierce/99 10.00 25.00
14 Brian Quick/99 12.00 30.00
15 Brock Osweiler/99 25.00 50.00
16 Coby Fleener/99 20.00 40.00
17 DeVier Posey/99 10.00 25.00
18 Dwayne Allen/99 10.00 25.00
19 Isaiah Pead/99 10.00 25.00
20 Chris Givens/99 8.00 20.00
21 Joe Adams/99 10.00 25.00
22 Lamar Miller/99 12.00 30.00
23 LaMichael James/99 25.00 50.00
24 Michael Egnew/99 8.00 20.00
25 Mohamed Sanu/99 12.00 30.00
26 Nick Foles/99 15.00 40.00
27 Nick Toon/99 15.00 40.00
28 Robert Turbin/99 10.00 25.00
29 Ronnie Hillman/99 12.00 30.00
30 Rueben Randle/99 15.00 40.00
31 Russell Wilson/99 15.00 40.00
32 Ryan Broyles/99 10.00 25.00
33 Stephen Hill/99 10.00 25.00
34 T.J. Graham/40 10.00 25.00

2012 Prestige Rookie Autographs

STATED PRINT RUN 183-999
EXCH EXPIRATION: 12/27/2013
201 Morris Claiborne/249 12.00 30.00
202 Dre Kirkpatrick/499 EXCH 8.00 20.00
205A Quinton Coples/799 5.00 12.00
205B Quinton Coples Draft 8.00 20.00
206 Nick Perry/499 12.00 30.00
207 Whitney Mercilus/899 5.00 12.00
208 Andre Branch/899 4.00 10.00
209 Jared Crick/899 5.00 12.00
210 Fletcher Cox/799 5.00 12.00
212 Devon Still/899 5.00 12.00
213A Michael Brockers/899 5.00 12.00
213B Michael Brockers Draft 8.00 20.00
214 Luke Kuechly/799 6.00 15.00
215A Dont'a Hightower/499 10.00 25.00
215B Dont'a Hightower Draft 15.00 40.00
216 Alfred Morris/899 4.00 10.00
217 David DeCastro/899 8.00 20.00
218 Melvin Ingram/499 EXCH 6.00 15.00
219A Courtney Upshaw/599 6.00 15.00
219B Courtney Upshaw Draft 10.00 25.00
222 Bobby Wagner/799 5.00 12.00
224 Dontari Poe/899 5.00 12.00
225 George Iloka/899 4.00 10.00
226A Matt Kalil/899 6.00 15.00
226B Matt Kalil Draft 10.00 25.00
227 Riley Reiff/899 6.00 15.00
228 Jonathan Martin/899 4.00 10.00
229A Andrew Luck/299 150.00 250.00
229B Andrew Luck Draft 250.00 400.00
230A Robert Griffin III/299 125.00 200.00
230B Robert Griffin III Draft 250.00 400.00
231A Ryan Tannehill/299 40.00 80.00
231B Ryan Tannehill Draft 50.00 100.00
232 Nick Foles/499 8.00 20.00
233 Brock Osweiler/299 15.00 30.00
235 Kirk Cousins/299 10.00 25.00
236 Brandon Weeden/299 25.00 50.00
238 Russell Wilson/499 10.00 25.00
240 Kellen Moore/499 8.00 20.00
242A Trent Richardson/299 50.00 100.00
242B Trent Richardson Draft 60.00 120.00
243 Lamar Miller/499 6.00 15.00
244 David Wilson/499 15.00 40.00
245 Doug Martin/499 15.00 40.00
247 Isaiah Pead/499 5.00 12.00
248 Bernard Pierce/286 6.00 15.00
249 LaMichael James/499 15.00 40.00
250 Cyrus Gray/499 5.00 12.00
254 Dan Herron/799 5.00 12.00
255 Robert Turbin/349 6.00 15.00
256 Vick Ballard/699 4.00 10.00
257 Terrance Ganaway/645 4.00 10.00
260 Harrison Smith/999 6.00 15.00
261 Marc Tyler/899 5.00 12.00
262 Mark Barron/499 EXCH 8.00 20.00
263 Dwayne Allen/899 5.00 12.00
264A Coby Fleener/899 6.00 15.00
264B Coby Fleener Draft 10.00 25.00
265 Orson Charles/840 5.00 12.00
266 Michael Egnew/899 4.00 10.00
267 Ladarius Green/899 5.00 12.00
268 Mychal Kendricks/899 5.00 12.00
270A Justin Blackmon/299 20.00 50.00
270B Justin Blackmon Draft 40.00 80.00
271A Kendall Wright/499 6.00 15.00
271B Kendall Wright Draft 10.00 25.00
272A Michael Floyd/499 15.00 40.00
272B Michael Floyd Draft 30.00 60.00
273 Mohamed Sanu/499 5.00 12.00
274 Alshon Jeffery/299 15.00 40.00
275 Rueben Randle/499 6.00 15.00
276A Stephen Hill/183 8.00 20.00
276B Stephen Hill Draft 12.00 30.00
277 Nick Toon/799 6.00 15.00
278 Juron Criner/799 4.00 10.00
280 Brian Quick/799 6.00 15.00
282 Joe Adams/799 5.00 12.00
283 Chris Givens/799 4.00 10.00
284 T.Y. Hilton/799 5.00 12.00
285 DeVier Posey/499 5.00 12.00
286 Marvin Jones/799 4.00 10.00
288 Jarius Wright/499 5.00 12.00
289 Marvin McNutt/899 5.00 12.00
290 Jeff Fuller/799 6.00 15.00
291 Rishard Matthews/799 5.00 12.00
292 Ryan Broyles/799 5.00 12.00
295 A.J. Jenkins/499 8.00 20.00
296 Stephon Gilmore/499 EXCH 6.00 15.00
298 Danny Coale/599 15.00 30.00

2012 Prestige Stars of the NFL

1 Larry Fitzgerald .60 1.50
2 Michael Turner .60 1.50
3 Ray Lewis .75 2.00
4 Fred Jackson .60 1.50
5 Cam Newton 1.25 3.00
6 Brian Urlacher .75 2.00
7 Cedric Benson .60 1.50
8 Peyton Hillis .50 1.25
9 DeMarcus Ware .60 1.50
10 Tim Tebow 1.25 3.00
11 Ndamukong Suh .75 2.00
12 Calvin Johnson .75 2.00
13 Aaron Rodgers 1.25 3.00
14 Clay Matthews .75 2.00
15 Andre Johnson .60 1.50
16 Peyton Manning 2.00 5.00
17 Maurice Jones-Drew .60 1.50
18 Jamaal Charles .60 1.50
19 Reggie Bush .60 1.50
20 Adrian Peterson .75 2.00
21 Tom Brady 1.25 3.00
22 Drew Brees .75 2.00
23 Ahmad Bradshaw .60 1.50
24 Mark Sanchez .60 1.50
25 Darren McFadden .60 1.50
26 Michael Vick .75 2.00
27 Ben Roethlisberger .75 2.00
28 Antonio Gates .60 1.50
29 Philip Rivers .60 1.50
30 Frank Gore .60 1.50
31 Marshawn Lynch .60 1.50
32 James Laurinaitis .50 1.25
33 LeGarrette Blount .50 1.25
34 Chris Johnson .60 1.50
35 Brian Orakpo .50 1.25
36 Jason Witten .75 2.00
37 Jared Allen .60 1.50
38 Rob Gronkowski .60 1.50
39 Eric Berry .60 1.50
40 LeSean McCoy .60 1.50
41 DeSean Jackson .60 1.50
42 Tony Romo .75 2.00
43 Darrelle Revis .60 1.50
44 Devin Hester .75 2.00
45 Ray Rice .60 1.50
46 Marques Colston .60 1.50
47 Greg Jennings .60 1.50
48 Reggie Wayne .60 1.50
49 Ryan Mathews .60 1.50
50 Dez Bryant .75 2.00

2012 Prestige Stars of the NFL Materials

STATED PRINT RUN 2-249
1 Larry Fitzgerald/249 3.00 8.00
2 Michael Turner/249 3.00 8.00
3 Ray Lewis/249 4.00 10.00
5 Cam Newton/249 6.00 15.00
6 Brian Urlacher/249 4.00 10.00
7 Cedric Benson/115 3.00 8.00
8 Peyton Hillis/5
9 DeMarcus Ware/249 4.00 10.00
10 Tim Tebow/55 8.00 20.00
12 Calvin Johnson/2
13 Aaron Rodgers/185 10.00 25.00
14 Clay Matthews/249 4.00 10.00
15 Andre Johnson/175 3.00 8.00
16 Peyton Manning/40 12.00 30.00
17 Maurice Jones-Drew/185 3.00 8.00
18 Jamaal Charles/240 3.00 8.00
19 Reggie Bush/185 3.00 8.00
20 Adrian Peterson/35 6.00 15.00
21 Tom Brady/249 6.00 15.00
22 Drew Brees/249 4.00 10.00
23 Ahmad Bradshaw/120 3.00 8.00
24 Mark Sanchez/249 3.00 8.00
25 Darren McFadden/95 4.00 10.00
26 Michael Vick/249 4.00 10.00
28 Antonio Gates/120 3.00 8.00
30 Frank Gore/249 3.00 8.00
32 James Laurinaitis/125 2.50 6.00
34 Chris Johnson/249 3.00 8.00
35 Brian Orakpo/140 2.50 6.00
37 Jared Allen/220 3.00 8.00
42 Tony Romo/249 4.00 10.00
43 Darrelle Revis/249 3.00 8.00
44 Devin Hester/50 5.00 12.00
45 Ray Rice/249 3.00 8.00
46 Marques Colston/249 3.00 8.00
48 Reggie Wayne/249 3.00 8.00
50 Dez Bryant/249 4.00 10.00

2012 Prestige Stars of the NFL Materials Prime

PRIME STATED PRINT RUN 5-49
3 Ray Lewis/20 8.00 20.00
5 Cam Newton/49 10.00 25.00
6 Brian Urlacher/49 6.00 15.00
7 Cedric Benson/49 5.00 12.00
9 DeMarcus Ware/49 6.00 15.00
10 Tim Tebow/49 10.00 25.00
14 Clay Matthews/15 8.00 20.00
17 Maurice Jones-Drew/49 5.00 12.00
18 Jamaal Charles/49 5.00 12.00
22 Drew Brees/35 6.00 15.00
23 Ahmad Bradshaw/49 5.00 12.00
25 Darren McFadden/30 5.00 12.00
28 Antonio Gates/49 5.00 12.00
30 Frank Gore/49 5.00 12.00
34 Chris Johnson/49 5.00 12.00
35 Brian Orakpo/49 4.00 10.00
42 Tony Romo/49 6.00 15.00
43 Darrelle Revis/49 5.00 12.00
44 Devin Hester/49 6.00 15.00
45 Ray Rice/49 5.00 12.00
46 Marques Colston/49 5.00 12.00
49 Ryan Mathews/49 5.00 12.00
50 Dez Bryant/49 6.00 15.00

2012 Prestige Team Foundations Combo Materials

STATED PRINT RUN 249 SER.#'d SETS
*PRIME/49: .8X TO 2X BASIC COMBO/249
1 Jeremy Maclin 4.00 10.00
LeSean McCoy
2 Frank Gore 4.00 10.00
Vernon Davis
3 Roddy White 4.00 10.00
Matt Ryan
4 Calvin Johnson 6.00 15.00
Matthew Stafford
5 Ben Roethlisberger 5.00 12.00
Rashard Mendenhall

2012 Prestige Team Foundations Materials

STATED PRINT RUN 1-249
*PRIME/49: .8X TO 2X BASIC JSY/249
1 Adrian Peterson/249 4.00 10.00
2 Beanie Wells/249 3.00 8.00
3 Ben Roethlisberger/249 4.00 10.00
4 Calvin Johnson/249 4.00 10.00
5 Cam Newton/249 6.00 15.00
6 Chris Johnson/249 3.00 8.00
7 Darren McFadden/249 3.00 8.00
8 Darrius Heyward-Bey/249 2.50 6.00
9 Dez Bryant/249 4.00 10.00
10 Dwayne Bowe/249 3.00 8.00
11 Eli Manning/249 4.00 10.00
12 Felix Jones/249 3.00 8.00
13 Frank Gore/249 3.00 8.00
14 Hakeem Nicks/249 3.00 8.00
15 Jeremy Maclin/249 3.00 8.00
16 Joe Flacco/249 3.00 8.00
17 Kenny Britt/249 3.00 8.00
18 Knowshon Moreno/249 3.00 8.00
19 Larry Fitzgerald/249 3.00 8.00
20 LeSean McCoy/249 3.00 8.00
22 Matthew Stafford/249 4.00 10.00
23 Maurice Jones-Drew/249 3.00 8.00
24 Michael Crabtree/249 3.00 8.00
25 Mike Williams/249 3.00 8.00
26 Ndamukong Suh/249 4.00 10.00
27 Philip Rivers/249 3.00 8.00
28 Rashard Mendenhall/249 3.00 8.00
29 Ray Rice/249 3.00 8.00
30 Roddy White/249 3.00 8.00
31 Rob Gronkowski/249 3.00 8.00
32 Sam Bradford/249 4.00 10.00
33 Von Miller/249 3.00 8.00
34 Vernon Davis/249 3.00 8.00
35 A.J. Green/1

2012 Prestige Team Foundations Quad Materials

STATED PRINT RUN 149-249
*PRIME/49: 1X TO 2.5X BASIC QUAD/249
1 Frank Gore/249 10.00 25.00
Vernon Davis
Patrick Willis
Michael Crabtree
2 Jermaine Gresham/249 6.00 15.00
Jordan Shipley
Andy Dalton
A.J. Green
3 Ed Reed/149 10.00 25.00
Joe Flacco
Anquan Boldin
Ray Lewis
4 Larry Fitzgerald/249 5.00 12.00
Early Doucet III
Beanie Wells
Andre Roberts
5 Calvin Johnson/249 12.00 30.00
Matthew Stafford
Jahvid Best
Ndamukong Suh

2012 Prestige Team Foundations Trios Materials

STATED PRINT RUN 99-249
*PRIME/49: .8X TO 2X BASIC TRIO/249
1 Ed Reed/99 6.00 15.00
Joe Flacco
Anquan Boldin
2 Frank Gore/249 5.00 12.00
Vernon Davis
Patrick Willis
3 Dwayne Bowe/249 5.00 12.00
Dexter McCluster
Jonathan Baldwin
4 Felix Jones/249 10.00 25.00
Dez Bryant
DeMarco Murray
5 Roddy White/249 5.00 12.00
Matt Ryan
Julio Jones

2012 Prestige Tim Tebow

COMMON TEBOW (1-14) 1.25 3.00
15 Tim Tebow AU/15 EXCH

2012 Prestige National Wrapper Redemption

ISSUED AT 2012 NATIONAL CONVENTION
CRACKED ICE/25 2.5X TO 6X
56 Tim Tebow 1.50 4.00
(Jets photo)
82 Peyton Manning 2.00 5.00
(Broncos photo)

2012 Prestige Father's Day NFL Equipment Autographs

1 Robert Griffin III 500.00 800.00
2 Andrew Luck 500.00 800.00

1960 Prest-o-Lite Postcards

These postcards were issued to promote the "Prest-O-Lite" batteries. The front contains an action photo of the star while the back has a promotion for those batteries. There might be more photos so any additions are appreiciated.

1 Leon Hart 12.50 25.00

2011 Prime Signatures

ROOKIE AUTO PRINT RUN 99-249
EXCH EXPIRATION: 9/28/2013
1 Aaron Rodgers 3.00 8.00
2 Adrian Peterson 2.00 5.00
3 Alex Karras 1.25 3.00
4 Andre Reed 1.25 3.00
5 Anquan Boldin 1.25 3.00
6 Antonio Gates 1.25 3.00
7 Arian Foster 1.25 3.00
8 Arrelious Benn 1.25 3.00
9 Austin Collie 1.25 3.00
10 Barry Sanders 2.50 6.00
11 Bart Starr 2.50 6.00
12 Beanie Wells 1.25 3.00
13 Ben Roethlisberger 1.50 4.00
14 Ben Tate 1.25 3.00
15 BenJarvus Green-Ellis 1.25 3.00
16 Billy Howton 1.00 2.50
17 Bo Jackson 2.00 5.00
18 Bo Scaife 1.00 2.50
19 Brandon Lloyd 1.25 3.00
20 Brandon Meriweather 1.00 2.50
21 Brandon Spikes 1.00 2.50
22 Brett Favre 3.00 8.00
23 Brian Cushing 1.00 2.50
24 Brian Hartline 1.00 2.50
25 C.J. Spiller 1.25 3.00
26 Chad Greenway 1.25 3.00
27 Chad Henne 1.25 3.00
28 Chad Ochocinco 1.25 3.00
29 Charley Taylor 1.00 2.50
30 Charley Trippi 1.00 2.50
31 Charlie Joiner 1.25 3.00
32 Chris Cooley 1.25 3.00
33 Clay Matthews 1.50 4.00
34 Colt McCoy 1.25 3.00
35 Craig James 1.00 2.50
36 Cris Carter 1.50 4.00
37 Curtis Martin 1.50 4.00
38 Dallas Clark 1.25 3.00
39 Dan Marino 3.00 8.00
40 Danny Amendola 1.25 3.00
41 Darrelle Revis 1.25 3.00
42 Darren McFadden 1.25 3.00
43 Darren Woodson 1.00 2.50
44 Daryle Lamonica 1.00 2.50
45 Dave Casper 1.00 2.50
46 David Harris 1.00 2.50
47 DeAngelo Hall 1.00 2.50
48 DeAngelo Williams 1.25 3.00
49 Deion Sanders 1.50 4.00
50 Demaryius Thomas 1.25 3.00
51 DeSean Jackson 1.25 3.00
52 Dez Bryant 1.50 4.00
53 Don Perkins 1.00 2.50
54 Donald Driver 1.25 3.00
55 Drew Brees 1.50 4.00
56 Dub Jones 1.00 2.50
57 Dwayne Bowe 1.25 3.00
58 Ed Too Tall Jones 1.00 2.50
59 Eddie George 1.25 3.00
60 Eli Manning 1.50 4.00
61 Emmanuel Sanders 1.00 2.50
62 Emmitt Smith 2.50 6.00
63 Eric Dickerson 1.25 3.00
64 Everson Walls 1.00 2.50
65 Felix Jones 1.25 3.00
66 Franco Harris 1.50 4.00
67 Frank Gore 1.25 3.00
68 Gale Sayers 1.50 4.00
69 Gary Collins 1.00 2.50
70 Greg Jennings 1.25 3.00
71 Greg Olsen 1.00 2.50
72 Hakeem Nicks 1.25 3.00
73 Harlon Hill 1.00 2.50
74 Heath Miller 1.25 3.00
75 Hines Ward 1.25 3.00
76 Irving Fryar 1.00 2.50
77 Jack Youngblood 1.00 2.50
78 Jacoby Ford 1.25 3.00
79 Jahvid Best 1.25 3.00
80 Jamaal Charles 1.25 3.00
81 James Laurinaitis 1.00 2.50
82 Jan Stenerud 1.00 2.50
83 Jared Allen 1.25 3.00
84 Jason Witten 1.50 4.00
85 Jay Cutler 1.25 3.00
86 Jermaine Gresham 1.25 3.00
87 Jerod Mayo 1.00 2.50
88 Jerome Bettis 1.50 4.00
89 Jerome Simpson 1.00 2.50
90 Jerry Rice 2.50 6.00
91 Jim Kelly 1.50 4.00
92 Jim Plunkett 1.25 3.00
93 Jimmy Graham 1.50 4.00
94 Jimmy Orr 1.00 2.50
95 Joe Flacco 1.50 4.00
96 Joe Greene 1.50 4.00
97 Joe Klecko 1.00 2.50
98 Joe Montana 4.00 10.00
99 Joe Namath 2.00 5.00
100 John Brodie 1.00 2.50
101 John Elway 2.50 6.00
102 Jonathan Stewart 1.25 3.00
103 Josh Freeman 1.50 4.00
104 Kevin Walter 1.25 3.00
105 Knowshon Moreno 1.25 3.00
106 LaDainian Tomlinson 1.50 4.00
107 Larry Fitzgerald 1.25 3.00
108 Laurent Robinson 1.25 3.00
109 Lem Barney 1.00 2.50
110 Lenny Moore 1.25 3.00
111 Leroy Kelly 1.25 3.00
112 LeSean McCoy 1.25 3.00
113 Lydell Mitchell 1.00 2.50
114 Malcom Floyd 1.25 3.00
115 Mark Carrier 1.00 2.50
116 Mark Duper 1.00 2.50
117 Mark Sanchez 1.50 4.00
118 Matt Cassel 1.25 3.00
119 Matt Forte 1.25 3.00
120 Matt Ryan 1.50 4.00
121 Matt Schaub 1.25 3.00
122 Matthew Stafford 1.50 4.00
123 Maurice Jones-Drew 1.25 3.00
124 Michael Crabtree 1.25 3.00
125 Michael Turner 1.25 3.00
126 Michael Vick 1.50 4.00
127 Mike Tolbert 1.25 3.00
128 Mike Wallace 1.50 4.00
129 Mike Williams 1.25 3.00
130 Miles Austin 1.25 3.00
131 Nnamdi Asomugha 1.25 3.00
132 Ottis Anderson 1.00 2.50
133 Ozzie Newsome 1.25 3.00
134 Percy Harvin 1.25 3.00
135 Pete Retzlaff 1.00 2.50
136 Peyton Hillis 1.25 3.00
137 Peyton Manning 2.50 6.00
138 Philip Rivers 1.50 4.00
139 Pierre Thomas 1.25 3.00
140 Randy Moss 1.25 3.00
141 Rashard Mendenhall 1.25 3.00
142 Ray Rice 1.25 3.00
143 Reggie Bush 1.25 3.00
144 Reggie Wayne 1.25 3.00
145 Rick Casares 1.00 2.50
146 Rod Woodson 1.25 3.00
147 Roddy White 1.25 3.00
148 Roger Craig 1.25 3.00
149 Ron Mix 1.00 2.50
150 Rosey Grier 1.25 3.00
151 Russ Grimm 1.00 2.50
152 Ryan Mathews 1.25 3.00
153 Ryan Torain 1.00 2.50
154 Sam Bradford 1.50 4.00
155 Santana Moss 1.25 3.00
156 Santonio Holmes 1.25 3.00
157 Sidney Rice 1.25 3.00
158 Steve Bartkowski 1.25 3.00
159 Steve Johnson 1.25 3.00
160 Steve Smith 1.25 3.00
161 Steve Young 2.00 5.00
162 Terrell Davis 1.50 4.00
163 Thurman Thomas 1.50 4.00
164 Tim Tebow 3.00 8.00
165 Todd Christensen 1.00 2.50
166 Tom Brady 2.50 6.00
167 Tony Moeaki 1.00 2.50
168 Tony Romo 1.50 4.00
169 Troy Aikman 2.00 5.00
170 Troy Polamalu 1.50 4.00
171 Vernon Davis 1.25 3.00
172 Warren Moon 1.25 3.00
173 Warren Sapp 1.25 3.00
174 William Perry 1.25 3.00
175 Willie Davis 1.00 2.50
176 Aaron Williams AU/199 RC EXCH 5.00 12.00
177 Adrian Clayborn AU/199 RC EXCH 6.00 15.00
178 Akeem Ayers AU/199 RC EXCH 5.00 12.00
179 Aldon Smith AU/199 RC EXCH 15.00 30.00
180 Allen Bradford AU/199 RC 5.00 12.00
181 Brandon Harris AU/199 RC 4.00 10.00
182 Cameron Heyward AU/199 RC 6.00 15.00
183 Cameron Jordan AU/199 RC 5.00 12.00
184 Cecil Shorts AU/199 RC 5.00 12.00
185 Corey Liuget AU/199 RC 4.00 10.00
186 D.J. Williams AU/199 RC EXCH 6.00 15.00
187 Da'Quan Bowers AU/199 RC 6.00 15.00
188 Da'Rel Scott AU/199 RC 5.00 12.00
189 Denarius Moore AU/199 RC EXCH 8.00 20.00
190 Dion Lewis AU/199 RC 6.00 15.00
191 Greg Jones AU/199 RC 5.00 12.00
192 Greg Salas AU/199 RC 6.00 15.00

193 J.J. Watt AU/199 RC	8.00	20.00
194 Jacquizz Rodgers AU/199 RC	6.00	15.00
195 Jeremy Kerley AU/199 RC	6.00	15.00
196 Jimmy Smith AU/199 RC EXCH	6.00	15.00
197 Johnny White AU/199 RC	5.00	12.00
198 Julius Thomas AU/199 RC	5.00	12.00
199 Justin Houston AU/199 RC	6.00	15.00
200 Kris Durham AU/199 RC	5.00	12.00
201 Lance Kendricks AU/199 RC	5.00	12.00
202 Luke Stocker AU/199 RC	5.00	12.00
203 Nathan Enderle AU/199 RC EXCH	6.00	15.00
204 Niles Paul AU/199 RC	6.00	15.00
205 Phil Taylor AU/199 RC	5.00	12.00
206 Prince Amukamara AU/199 RC	6.00	15.00
207 Rahim Moore AU/199 RC	5.00	12.00
208 Ricky Stanzi AU/199 RC	8.00	20.00
209 Roy Helu AU/199 RC EXCH	12.00	30.00
210 Ryan Kerrigan AU/199 RC	6.00	15.00
211 T.J. Yates AU/199 RC	8.00	20.00
212 Tandon Doss AU/199 RC	5.00	12.00
213 Terrelle Pryor AU/199 RC	12.00	30.00
214 Tyrod Taylor AU/199 RC	6.00	15.00
215 Joe Lefeged AU/199 RC	5.00	12.00
216 Jacquian Williams AU/199 RC EXCH	6.00	15.00
217 K.J. Wright AU/199 RC	6.00	15.00
218 Mason Foster AU/199 RC	6.00	15.00
219 Casey Matthews AU/199 RC	6.00	15.00
220 Anthony Allen AU/199 RC	4.00	10.00
221 Armond Smith AU/199 RC	5.00	12.00
222 Dane Sanzenbacher AU/199 RC	6.00	15.00
223 Doug Baldwin AU/199 RC	10.00	25.00
224 LaQuan Williams AU/199 RC	5.00	12.00
225 Mark Herzlich AU/199 RC	5.00	12.00
226 A.J. Green AU/199 RC	20.00	40.00
227 Alex Green AU/249 RC	6.00	15.00
228 Andy Dalton AU/249 RC	30.00	60.00
229 Austin Pettis AU/249 RC EXCH	5.00	12.00
230 Bilal Powell AU/99 RC EXCH	5.00	12.00
231 Blaine Gabbert AU/199 RC	10.00	25.00
232 Cam Newton AU/199 RC	125.00	200.00
233 Christian Ponder AU/199 RC	15.00	40.00
234 Clyde Gates AU/249 RC	5.00	12.00
235 Colin Kaepernick AU/249 RC	8.00	20.00
236 Daniel Thomas AU/249 RC EXCH	6.00	15.00
237 Delone Carter AU/249 RC	5.00	12.00
238 DeMarco Murray AU/99 RC	30.00	60.00
239 Greg Little AU/249 RC	6.00	15.00
240 Jake Locker AU/199 RC	30.00	60.00
241 Jamie Harper AU/249 RC	6.00	15.00
242 Jerrel Jernigan AU/249 RC EXCH	5.00	12.00
243 Jonathan Baldwin AU/249 RC	6.00	15.00
244 Jordan Todman AU/249 RC	4.00	10.00
245 Julio Jones AU/249 RC EXCH	20.00	40.00
246 Kendall Hunter AU/249 RC	6.00	15.00
247 Kyle Rudolph AU/249 RC	8.00	20.00
248 Leonard Hankerson AU/249 RC	6.00	15.00
249 Marcell Dareus AU/249 RC EXCH	6.00	15.00
250 Mark Ingram AU/199 RC	15.00	40.00
251 Mikel Leshoure AU/249 RC EXCH	6.00	15.00
252 Randall Cobb AU/99 RC	15.00	30.00
253 Ryan Mallett AU/199 RC	15.00	40.00
254 Ryan Williams AU/249 RC EXCH	8.00	20.00
255 Shane Vereen AU/249 RC EXCH	6.00	15.00
256 Stevan Ridley AU/249 RC	6.00	15.00
257 Taiwan Jones AU/249 RC	6.00	15.00
258 Titus Young AU/249 RC	8.00	20.00
259 Torrey Smith AU/249 RC	8.00	20.00
260 Vincent Brown AU/249 RC	6.00	15.00
261 Von Miller AU/249 RC	8.00	20.00

2011 Prime Signatures Prime Proof Blue

*BLUE/49: 1.2X TO 3X BASIC CARDS
BLUE STATED PRINT RUN 49

2011 Prime Signatures Prime Proof Green

*GREEN/25: 2X TO 5X BASIC CARDS
GREEN STATED PRINT RUN 25

2011 Prime Signatures Prime Proof Red

*RED/99: .8X TO 2X BASIC CARDS
RED STATED PRINT RUN 99

2011 Prime Signatures Autographs Bronze

*BRONZE/59-75: .25X TO .6X GOLD/20-25
*BRONZE/39-49: .3X TO .8X GOLD/20-25
*BRONZE/33-50: .25X TO .6X GOLD/10-15
BRONZE PRINT RUN 33-75

2011 Prime Signatures Autographs Gold

1-175 VETS/RET PRINT RUN 10-25
*ROOKIES/49: .5X TO 1.2X BASIC AU RC
176-261 ROOKIE AU PRINT RUN 49
EXCH EXPIRATION: 9/28/2013

1 Aaron Rodgers/20	125.00	200.00
3 Alex Karras/25	12.00	30.00
4 Andre Reed/25	12.00	30.00
5 Anquan Boldin/25	10.00	25.00
6 Antonio Gates/25	10.00	25.00
7 Arian Foster/25	25.00	50.00
8 Arrelious Benn/25	10.00	25.00
9 Austin Collie/15		
10 Barry Sanders/20	60.00	120.00
11 Bart Starr/20	75.00	135.00
12 Beanie Wells/10	12.00	30.00
13 Ben Roethlisberger/20	50.00	100.00
14 Ben Tate/25	10.00	25.00
15 BenJarvus Green-Ellis/25	10.00	25.00
16 Billy Howton/25	10.00	25.00
17 Bo Jackson/25	30.00	60.00
18 Bo Scaife/25	8.00	20.00
19 Brandon Lloyd/25	10.00	25.00
20 Brandon Meriweather/25	8.00	20.00
21 Brandon Spikes/25	10.00	25.00
22 Brett Favre/20	100.00	175.00
23 Brian Cushing/25	8.00	20.00
24 Brian Hartline/25	8.00	20.00
25 C.J. Spiller/25	10.00	25.00
26 Chad Greenway/25	10.00	25.00
27 Chad Henne/25	10.00	25.00
28 Chad Ochocinco/25	10.00	25.00
29 Charley Taylor/25	12.00	30.00
30 Charley Trippi/20		
31 Charlie Joiner/10		
32 Chris Cooley/25		
33 Clay Matthews/25	40.00	80.00
34 Colt McCoy/25	10.00	25.00
35 Craig James/25		
36 Cris Carter/25	40.00	80.00
37 Curtis Martin/25	30.00	60.00
38 Dallas Clark/25 EXCH	20.00	40.00
39 Dan Marino/10		
40 Danny Amendola/25	10.00	25.00
42 Darren McFadden/10		
43 Darren Woodson/25	25.00	50.00
44 Daryle Lamonica/25	10.00	25.00
45 Dave Casper/25		
46 David Harris/25	8.00	20.00
47 DeAngelo Hall/15		
48 DeAngelo Williams/25	10.00	25.00
49 Deion Sanders/20	40.00	80.00
50 Demaryius Thomas/25	10.00	25.00
51 DeSean Jackson/10		
52 Dez Bryant/25	12.00	30.00
53 Don Perkins/25	12.00	30.00
54 Donald Driver/25	15.00	40.00
55 Drew Brees/20		
56 Dub Jones/25	10.00	25.00
57 Dwayne Bowe/15 EXCH	12.00	30.00
58 Ed Too Tall Jones/25	15.00	40.00
59 Eddie George/25	25.00	50.00
60 Eli Manning/25	50.00	100.00
61 Emmanuel Sanders/25	8.00	20.00
62 Emmitt Smith/20	100.00	175.00
63 Eric Dickerson/25	20.00	40.00
64 Everson Walls/10	25.00	50.00
65 Felix Jones/25		
66 Franco Harris/25		
67 Frank Gore/25 EXCH	10.00	25.00
68 Gale Sayers/25	30.00	60.00
69 Gary Collins/15		
70 Greg Jennings/25	15.00	40.00
71 Greg Olsen/20	8.00	20.00
72 Hakeem Nicks/25	10.00	25.00
73 Harlon Hill/25	12.00	30.00
74 Heath Miller/25	10.00	25.00
75 Hines Ward/25	40.00	80.00
76 Irving Fryar/20	12.00	30.00
77 Jack Youngblood/15		
78 Jacoby Ford/25	10.00	25.00
79 Jahvid Best/25	10.00	25.00
80 Jamaal Charles/25	12.00	30.00
81 James Laurinaitis/15	10.00	25.00
82 Jan Stenerud/10	12.00	30.00
83 Jared Allen/25	20.00	40.00
84 Jason Witten/25	20.00	40.00
85 Jay Cutler/25	30.00	60.00
86 Jermaine Gresham/25	10.00	25.00
87 Jerod Mayo/20	8.00	20.00
88 Jerome Bettis/25		
89 Jerome Simpson/15	10.00	25.00
90 Jerry Rice/20	100.00	175.00
91 Jim Kelly/15		
92 Jim Plunkett/25	12.00	30.00
93 Jimmy Graham/25	12.00	30.00
94 Jimmy Orr/25	10.00	25.00
96 Joe Greene/25	30.00	60.00
97 Joe Klecko/25	12.00	30.00
98 Joe Montana/20	90.00	150.00
99 Joe Namath/20		
100 John Brodie/25	15.00	40.00
101 John Elway/20	75.00	135.00
102 Jonathan Stewart/25	10.00	25.00
103 Josh Freeman/25	12.00	30.00
104 Kevin Walter/25	10.00	25.00
105 Knowshon Moreno/25	10.00	25.00
106 LaDainian Tomlinson/25	15.00	40.00
107 Larry Fitzgerald/15		
108 Laurent Robinson/20		
109 Lem Barney/25	10.00	25.00
110 Lenny Moore/25	15.00	40.00
111 Leroy Kelly/25	12.00	30.00
112 LeSean McCoy/25	10.00	25.00
113 Lydell Mitchell/25	10.00	25.00
114 Malcom Floyd/25	10.00	25.00
115 Mark Carrier/25	12.00	30.00
116 Mark Duper/25	10.00	25.00
117 Mark Sanchez/25	25.00	50.00
118 Matt Cassel/20	10.00	25.00
119 Matt Forte/10	12.00	30.00
120 Matt Ryan/15	25.00	50.00
121 Matt Schaub/25	10.00	25.00
122 Matthew Stafford/25	25.00	50.00
123 Maurice Jones-Drew/20		
124 Michael Crabtree/20	10.00	25.00
125 Michael Turner/20	10.00	25.00
127 Mike Tolbert/25	10.00	25.00
128 Mike Wallace/20	12.00	30.00
129 Mike Williams/25		
130 Miles Austin/25	15.00	40.00
131 Nnamdi Asomugha/10	15.00	40.00
132 Ottis Anderson/15	12.00	30.00
133 Ozzie Newsome/25	12.00	30.00
134 Percy Harvin/25	10.00	25.00
135 Pete Retzlaff/25	10.00	25.00
136 Peyton Hillis/25	12.00	30.00
137 Peyton Manning/18		
138 Philip Rivers/25	15.00	40.00
139 Pierre Thomas/25	10.00	25.00
140 Randy Moss/25 EXCH	12.00	30.00
141 Rashard Mendenhall/25 EXCH	10.00	25.00
142 Ray Rice/25 EXCH	15.00	40.00
143 Reggie Bush/25 EXCH		
144 Reggie Wayne/25	10.00	25.00
145 Rick Casares/25	12.00	30.00
146 Rod Woodson/15		
148 Roger Craig/15		
149 Ron Mix/25	10.00	25.00
150 Rosey Grier/15	15.00	40.00
151 Russ Grimm/25	12.00	30.00
152 Ryan Mathews/25 EXCH	10.00	25.00
153 Ryan Torain/25	8.00	20.00
154 Sam Bradford/25	20.00	40.00
155 Santana Moss/25	10.00	25.00
156 Santonio Holmes/25	10.00	25.00
157 Sidney Rice/15	12.00	30.00
158 Steve Bartkowski/25		
159 Steve Johnson/25	10.00	25.00
160 Steve Smith/25	10.00	25.00
161 Steve Young/20		
162 Terrell Davis/25		
163 Thurman Thomas/25	15.00	40.00
164 Tim Tebow/20	50.00	100.00
165 Todd Christensen/15	12.00	30.00
166 Tom Brady/10 EXCH		
167 Tony Moeaki/25	8.00	20.00
168 Tony Romo/20	60.00	120.00
169 Troy Aikman/20 EXCH		
170 Troy Polamalu/25	60.00	120.00
171 Vernon Davis/15	12.00	30.00
172 Warren Moon/25	25.00	50.00
173 Warren Sapp/25	12.00	30.00
174 William Perry/10		
175 Willie Davis/15	15.00	40.00
228 Andy Dalton/49	50.00	100.00
232 Cam Newton/49	125.00	250.00
240 Jake Locker/49	40.00	80.00

2011 Prime Signatures Autographs Platinum

*ROOKIES/25: .6X TO 1.5X BASIC AU RC
1-175 UNPRICED PLATINUM PRINT RUN 5
EXCH EXPIRATION: 9/28/2013

226 A.J. Green	40.00	80.00
228 Andy Dalton	60.00	120.00
232 Cam Newton	150.00	300.00
240 Jake Locker	50.00	100.00

2011 Prime Signatures Autographs Silver

*SILVER/30-49: .3X TO .8X GOLD/20-25
*SILVER/31-49: .25X TO .6X GOLD/15
*SILVER/20-29: .3X TO .8X GOLD/10-15
*SILVER/30-39: .25X TO .6X GOLD/10
*SILVER/15-19: .4X TO 1X GOLD/10
SILVER PRINT RUN 15-49

2000 Private Stock

Released as a 150-card base set, Private Stock is comprised of 100 veteran cards and 50 rookie cards which are sequentially numbered to 278. Base cards feature a player image that appears to have been sketched on the card which is printed to look like canvas. Cards are enhanced with gold foil highlights. Private Stock packs contained five cards.

COMP.SET w/o SP's (100)	10.00	25.00
1 Rob Moore	.25	.60
2 Jake Plummer	.30	.75
3 Frank Sanders	.25	.60
4 Jamal Anderson	.30	.75
5 Chris Chandler	.30	.75
6 Tim Dwight	.30	.75
7 Tony Banks	.25	.60
8 Priest Holmes	.40	1.00
9 Doug Flutie	.40	1.00
10 Rob Johnson	.30	.75
11 Eric Moulds	.30	.75
12 Antowain Smith	.30	.75
13 Steve Beuerlein	.30	.75
14 Tim Biakabutuka	.30	.75
15 Patrick Jeffers	.30	.75
16 Muhsin Muhammad	.30	.75
17 Curtis Enis	.25	.60
18 Cade McNown	.25	.60
19 Marcus Robinson	.30	.75
20 Corey Dillon	.30	.75
21 Akili Smith	.25	.60
22 Tim Couch	.30	.75
23 Kevin Johnson	.25	.60
24 Troy Aikman	.60	1.50
25 Rocket Ismail	.30	.75
26 Emmitt Smith	1.00	2.50
27 Terrell Davis	.40	1.00
28 Olandis Gary	.30	.75
29 Brian Griese	.30	.75
30 Ed McCaffrey	.30	.75
31 Charlie Batch	.30	.75
32 Germane Crowell	.25	.60
33 Herman Moore	.30	.75
34 Barry Sanders	.75	2.00
35 Brett Favre	1.25	3.00
36 Antonio Freeman	.30	.75
37 Dorsey Levens	.30	.75
38 Marvin Harrison	.40	1.00
39 Edgerrin James	.40	1.00
40 Peyton Manning	1.00	2.50
41 Terrence Wilkins	.25	.60
42 Mark Brunell	.30	.75
43 Keenan McCardell	.30	.75
44 Jimmy Smith	.30	.75
45 Fred Taylor	.40	1.00
46 Derrick Alexander	.25	.60
47 Donnell Bennett	.25	.60
48 Tony Gonzalez	.40	1.00
49 Elvis Grbac	.25	.60
50 Damon Huard	.30	.75
51 James Johnson	.25	.60
52 Dan Marino	1.25	3.00
53 O.J. McDuffie	.30	.75
54 Cris Carter	.40	1.00
55 Daunte Culpepper	.30	.75
56 Randy Moss	.40	1.00
57 Robert Smith	.30	.75
58 Drew Bledsoe	.40	1.00
59 Kevin Faulk	.30	.75
60 Terry Glenn	.30	.75
61 Keith Poole	.25	.60
62 Ricky Williams	.40	1.00
63 Kerry Collins	.30	.75
64 Ike Hilliard	.30	.75
65 Amani Toomer	.30	.75
66 Wayne Chrebet	.30	.75
67 Ray Lucas	.25	.60
68 Curtis Martin	.40	1.00
69 Tim Brown	.40	1.00
70 Rich Gannon	.30	.75
71 Napoleon Kaufman	.30	.75
72 Donovan McNabb	.40	1.00
73 Duce Staley	.30	.75
74 Jerome Bettis	.40	1.00
75 Troy Edwards	.25	.60
76 Kordell Stewart	.30	.75
77 Isaac Bruce	.40	1.00
78 Marshall Faulk	.40	1.00
79 Torry Holt	.40	1.00
80 Kurt Warner	.60	1.50
81 Jermaine Fazande	.25	.60
82 Jim Harbaugh	.30	.75
83 Junior Seau	.40	1.00
84 Charlie Garner	.30	.75
85 Terrell Owens	.40	1.00
86 Jerry Rice	.75	2.00
87 Jon Kitna	.30	.75
88 Derrick Mayes	.25	.60
89 Ricky Watters	.30	.75
90 Mike Alstott	.40	1.00
91 Warrick Dunn	.30	.75
92 Jacquez Green	.25	.60
93 Shaun King	.25	.60
94 Eddie George	.30	.75
95 Jevon Kearse	.30	.75
96 Steve McNair	.40	1.00
97 Yancey Thigpen	.25	.60
98 Stephen Davis	.30	.75
99 Brad Johnson	.30	.75
100 Michael Westbrook	.25	.60
101 Thomas Jones RC	8.00	20.00
102 Doug Johnson RC	5.00	12.00
103 Mareno Philyaw RC	4.00	10.00
104 Jamal Lewis RC	6.00	15.00
105 Chris Redman RC	5.00	12.00
106 Travis Taylor RC	5.00	12.00
107 Frank Murphy RC	4.00	10.00
108 Dez White RC	5.00	12.00
109 Ron Dugans RC	4.00	10.00
110 Curtis Keaton RC	4.00	10.00
111 Peter Warrick RC	6.00	15.00
112 Courtney Brown RC	5.00	12.00
113 JaJuan Dawson RC	4.00	10.00
114 Dennis Northcutt RC	5.00	12.00
115 Travis Prentice RC	5.00	12.00
116 Michael Wiley RC	4.00	10.00
117 Chris Cole RC	5.00	12.00
118 Jarious Jackson RC	5.00	12.00
119 Reuben Droughns RC	6.00	15.00
120 Bubba Franks RC	6.00	15.00
121 Anthony Lucas RC	4.00	10.00
122 Rondell Mealey RC	4.00	10.00
123 R.Jay Soward RC	4.00	10.00
124 Shyrone Stith RC	4.00	10.00
125 Sylvester Morris RC	4.00	10.00
126 Quinton Spotwood RC	4.00	10.00
127 Troy Walters RC	4.00	10.00
128 Tom Brady RC	100.00	200.00
129 J.R. Redmond RC	4.00	10.00
130 Marc Bulger RC	6.00	15.00
131 Sherrod Gideon RC	4.00	10.00
132 Ron Dayne RC	6.00	15.00
133 Anthony Becht RC	5.00	12.00
134 Laveranues Coles RC	6.00	15.00
135 Chad Pennington RC	10.00	25.00
136 Sebastian Janikowski RC	6.00	15.00
137 Jerry Porter RC	6.00	15.00
138 Todd Pinkston RC	4.00	10.00
139 Gari Scott RC	4.00	10.00
140 Plaxico Burress RC	6.00	15.00
141 Danny Farmer RC	4.00	10.00
142 Tee Martin RC	6.00	15.00
143 Trung Canidate RC	5.00	12.00
144 Trevor Gaylor RC	4.00	10.00
145 Giovanni Carmazzi RC	4.00	10.00
146 Tim Rattay RC	5.00	12.00
147 Shaun Alexander RC	8.00	20.00
148 Darrell Jackson RC	5.00	12.00
149 Joe Hamilton RC	4.00	10.00
150 Todd Husak RC	4.00	10.00
S1 Jon Kitna Sample	.40	1.00

2000 Private Stock Retail

COMP.SET w/o RCs (100)	10.00	25.00

*VETS 1-100: .4X TO 1X HOBBY
*ROOKIES 101-150: .2X TO .5X HOBBY
101-150 ROOKIE PRINT RUN 650

128 Tom Brady RC	75.00	150.00

2000 Private Stock Gold

*VETS 1-100: 3X TO 8X BASIC CARDS
*ROOKIES 101-150: .2X TO .5X
GOLD PRINT RUN 181 SER.#'d SETS

128 Tom Brady	100.00	200.00

2000 Private Stock Premiere Date

*VETS 1-100: 5X TO 12X BASIC CARDS
*ROOKIES 101-150: .3X TO .8X
PREM.DATE PRINT RUN 95 SER.#'d SETS

128 Tom Brady	250.00	400.00

2000 Private Stock Silver

*VETS 1-100: 2.5X TO 6X BASIC CARDS
*ROOKIES 101-150: .15X TO .4X
SILVER/330 STATED ODDS 3:25
SILVER STAT.PRINT RUN 330 SER.#'d SETS

128 Tom Brady	75.00	150.00

2000 Private Stock Artist's Canvas

COMPLETE SET (20)	30.00	80.00

STATED ODDS 1:45
UNPRICED PROOF PRINT RUN 1

1 Jamal Lewis	1.50	4.00
2 Peter Warrick	1.50	4.00
3 Tim Couch	1.50	4.00
4 Emmitt Smith	5.00	12.00
5 Olandis Gary	1.50	4.00
6 Marvin Harrison	2.00	5.00
7 Edgerrin James	2.00	5.00
8 Mark Brunell	1.50	4.00
9 Fred Taylor	2.00	5.00
10 Randy Moss	2.00	5.00
11 Ron Dayne	1.50	4.00
12 Chad Pennington	2.50	6.00
13 Jerome Bettis	2.00	5.00
14 Plaxico Burress	1.50	4.00
15 Marshall Faulk	2.00	5.00
16 Kurt Warner	3.00	8.00
17 Jon Kitna	1.50	4.00
18 Shaun King	1.25	3.00
19 Eddie George	1.50	4.00
20 Stephen Davis	1.50	4.00

2000 Private Stock Extreme Action

COMPLETE SET (20)	15.00	40.00

STATED ODDS 2:23

1 Jake Plummer	1.00	2.50
2 Tim Couch	1.00	2.50
3 Emmitt Smith	3.00	8.00
4 Olandis Gary	1.00	2.50
5 Marvin Harrison	1.25	3.00
6 Edgerrin James	1.25	3.00
7 Mark Brunell	1.00	2.50
8 Fred Taylor	1.25	3.00
9 Randy Moss	1.25	3.00
10 Drew Bledsoe	1.25	3.00
11 Ricky Williams	1.25	3.00
12 Ron Dayne	1.25	3.00
13 Donovan McNabb	1.25	3.00
14 Isaac Bruce	1.25	3.00
15 Marshall Faulk	1.25	3.00
16 Kurt Warner	2.00	5.00
17 Jon Kitna	1.00	2.50
18 Shaun King	.75	2.00
19 Steve McNair	1.25	3.00
20 Stephen Davis	1.00	2.50

2000 Private Stock Private Signings

TWO PER HOBBY BOX

1 Thomas Jones	10.00	25.00
2 Jamal Lewis	8.00	20.00
3 Chris Redman	6.00	15.00
4 Travis Taylor	6.00	15.00
5 Dez White	6.00	15.00
6 Peter Warrick	8.00	20.00
8 JaJuan Dawson	5.00	12.00
9 Dennis Northcutt	6.00	15.00
11 Michael Wiley	5.00	12.00
12 Chris Cole	6.00	15.00
13 Reuben Droughns	8.00	20.00
14 Anthony Lucas	5.00	12.00
15 Rondell Mealey	5.00	12.00
16 R.Jay Soward	5.00	12.00
17 Shyrone Stith	5.00	12.00
18 Sylvester Morris	5.00	12.00
19 Quinton Spotwood	5.00	12.00
20 Troy Walters	5.00	12.00
21 J.R. Redmond	5.00	12.00
22 Marc Bulger	8.00	20.00
23 Ron Dayne	8.00	20.00
24 Laveranues Coles	8.00	20.00
25 Chad Pennington	12.00	30.00
28 Plaxico Burress	15.00	30.00
29 Danny Farmer	5.00	12.00
30 Tee Martin	8.00	20.00
31 Chafie Fields	5.00	12.00
32 Tim Rattay	6.00	15.00
33 Shaun Alexander	10.00	25.00
36 Todd Husak	5.00	12.00

2000 Private Stock PS2000 Action

COMPLETE SET (60)	10.00	25.00

STATED ODDS 2:1

1 Thomas Jones	.30	.75
2 Jake Plummer	.20	.50
3 Jamal Lewis	.25	.60
4 Chris Redman	.20	.50
5 Travis Taylor	.20	.50
6 Doug Flutie	.25	.60
7 Cade McNown	.15	.40
8 Marcus Robinson	.20	.50
9 Dez White	.20	.50
10 Akili Smith	.15	.40
11 Peter Warrick	.25	.60
12 Tim Couch	.20	.50
13 Dennis Northcutt	.20	.50
14 Travis Prentice	.20	.50
15 Troy Aikman	.40	1.00
16 Emmitt Smith	.60	1.50
17 Terrell Davis	.25	.60
18 Olandis Gary	.20	.50
19 Brian Griese	.20	.50
20 Reuben Droughns	.25	.60
21 Barry Sanders	.50	1.25
22 Brett Favre	.75	2.00
23 Antonio Freeman	.20	.50
24 Marvin Harrison	.25	.60
25 Edgerrin James	.25	.60
26 Peyton Manning	.60	1.50
27 Mark Brunell	.20	.50
28 R.Jay Soward	.15	.40
29 Fred Taylor	.25	.60
30 Sylvester Morris	.15	.40
31 Dan Marino	.75	2.00
32 Cris Carter	.25	.60
33 Randy Moss	.25	.60
34 Drew Bledsoe	.25	.60
35 J.R. Redmond	.15	.40
36 Ricky Williams	.25	.60
37 Ron Dayne	.25	.60
38 Laveranues Coles	.25	.60
39 Curtis Martin	.25	.60
40 Chad Pennington	.40	1.00
41 Napoleon Kaufman	.20	.50
42 Donovan McNabb	.25	.60
43 Jerome Bettis	.25	.60
44 Plaxico Burress	.25	.60
45 Tee Martin	.25	.60
46 Isaac Bruce	.25	.60
47 Marshall Faulk	.25	.60
48 Kurt Warner	.40	1.00
49 Giovanni Carmazzi	.15	.40
50 Terrell Owens	.25	.60
51 Jerry Rice	.50	1.25
52 Shaun Alexander	.30	.75
53 Jon Kitna	.20	.50
54 Warrick Dunn	.20	.50
55 Joe Hamilton	.15	.40
56 Shaun King	.15	.40
57 Eddie George	.20	.50
58 Steve McNair	.25	.60
59 Stephen Davis	.20	.50
60 Brad Johnson	.20	.50

2000 Private Stock PS2000 New Wave

COMPLETE SET (25)	30.00	80.00

STATED PRINT RUN 202 SER.#'d SETS

1 Jake Plummer	1.25	3.00
2 Eric Moulds	1.25	3.00
3 Cade McNown	1.00	2.50
4 Marcus Robinson	1.25	3.00
5 Akili Smith	1.00	2.50
6 Tim Couch	1.25	3.00
7 Kevin Johnson	1.00	2.50
8 Olandis Gary	1.25	3.00
9 Brian Griese	1.25	3.00
10 Marvin Harrison	1.50	4.00
11 Edgerrin James	1.50	4.00
12 Peyton Manning	4.00	10.00
13 Fred Taylor	1.50	4.00
14 Tony Gonzalez	1.50	4.00
15 Damon Huard	1.25	3.00
16 Randy Moss	1.50	4.00
17 Ricky Williams	1.50	4.00
18 Donovan McNabb	1.50	4.00
19 Duce Staley	1.25	3.00
20 Kurt Warner	2.50	6.00
21 Terrell Owens	1.50	4.00
22 Jon Kitna	1.25	3.00
23 Shaun King	1.00	2.50
24 Steve McNair	1.50	4.00
25 Stephen Davis	1.25	3.00

2000 Private Stock PS2000 Rookies

COMPLETE SET (25)	60.00	150.00

STATED PRINT RUN 106 SER.#'d SETS

1 Thomas Jones	2.00	5.00
2 Jamal Lewis	1.50	4.00
3 Chris Redman	1.25	3.00
4 Travis Taylor	1.25	3.00
5 Dez White	1.25	3.00
6 Ron Dugans	1.00	2.50
7 Peter Warrick	1.50	4.00
8 Dennis Northcutt	1.25	3.00
9 Travis Prentice	1.25	3.00
10 Reuben Droughns	1.50	4.00
11 R.Jay Soward	1.00	2.50
12 Sylvester Morris	1.00	2.50
13 Troy Walters	1.00	2.50
14 J.R. Redmond	1.00	2.50
15 Ron Dayne	1.50	4.00
16 Laveranues Coles	1.50	4.00
17 Chad Pennington	2.50	6.00
18 Jerry Porter	1.50	4.00
19 Todd Pinkston	1.00	2.50
20 Plaxico Burress	1.50	4.00
21 Tee Martin	1.50	4.00
22 Giovanni Carmazzi	1.00	2.50
23 Shaun Alexander	2.00	5.00
24 Joe Hamilton	1.00	2.50
25 Todd Husak	1.00	2.50

2000 Private Stock PS2000 Stars

COMPLETE SET (25)	25.00	60.00

STATED PRINT RUN 298 SER.#'d SETS

1 Jamal Anderson	1.25	3.00
2 Doug Flutie	1.50	4.00
3 Troy Aikman	2.50	6.00
4 Emmitt Smith	4.00	10.00
5 Terrell Davis	1.50	4.00
6 Herman Moore	1.25	3.00
7 Barry Sanders	3.00	8.00
8 Brett Favre	5.00	12.00
9 Antonio Freeman	1.25	3.00
10 Dorsey Levens	1.25	3.00
11 Mark Brunell	1.25	3.00
12 Dan Marino	5.00	12.00
13 Cris Carter	1.50	4.00
14 Robert Smith	1.25	3.00
15 Drew Bledsoe	1.50	4.00
16 Curtis Martin	1.50	4.00
17 Tim Brown	1.50	4.00
18 Napoleon Kaufman	1.25	3.00
19 Jerome Bettis	1.50	4.00
20 Isaac Bruce	1.50	4.00
21 Marshall Faulk	1.50	4.00
22 Jerry Rice	3.00	8.00
23 Warrick Dunn	1.25	3.00
24 Eddie George	1.25	3.00
25 Brad Johnson	1.25	3.00

2000 Private Stock Reserve

COMPLETE SET (20)	30.00	80.00

STATED ODDS 1:23 HOBBY

1 Cade McNown	1.00	2.50
2 Peter Warrick	1.50	4.00
3 Tim Couch	1.25	3.00
4 Troy Aikman	2.50	6.00
5 Emmitt Smith	4.00	10.00
6 Terrell Davis	1.50	4.00
7 Barry Sanders	3.00	8.00
8 Brett Favre	5.00	12.00
9 Edgerrin James	1.50	4.00
10 Peyton Manning	4.00	10.00
11 Mark Brunell	1.25	3.00
12 Fred Taylor	1.50	4.00
13 Randy Moss	1.50	4.00
14 Ron Dayne	1.50	4.00
15 Chad Pennington	2.50	6.00
16 Marshall Faulk	1.50	4.00
17 Kurt Warner	2.50	6.00
18 Jerry Rice	3.00	8.00
19 Shaun Alexander	2.00	5.00
20 Eddie George	1.25	3.00

2001 Private Stock

Pacific released its Private Stock set in August of 2001. The set was made up of 175 cards, 75 of those were short printed rookies (serial numbered of 200). The hobby packs carried an SRP of $14.99, due to the jersey card in every pack. The cards were highlighted with gold-foil lettering and a gold-foil Private Stock logo.

COMP.SET w/o RC's (100)	30.00	60.00
1 David Boston	.25	.60
2 Thomas Jones	.30	.75
3 Jake Plummer	.30	.75
4 Jamal Anderson	.30	.75
5 Chris Chandler	.30	.75
6 Eric Zeier	.25	.60
7 Elvis Grbac	.30	.75
8 Jamal Lewis	.40	1.00
9 Shannon Sharpe	.40	1.00
10 Rob Johnson	.30	.75
11 Eric Moulds	.30	.75
12 Peerless Price	.25	.60
13 Tim Biakabutuka	.25	.60
14 Jeff Lewis	.25	.60
15 Muhsin Muhammad	.30	.75
16 James Allen	.25	.60
17 Cade McNown	.30	.75
18 Marcus Robinson	.30	.75
19 Brian Urlacher	.50	1.25
20 Corey Dillon	.30	.75
21 Jon Kitna	.30	.75
22 Akili Smith	.25	.60
23 Peter Warrick	.30	.75
24 Tim Couch	.25	.60
25 Kevin Johnson	.25	.60
26 Travis Prentice	.25	.60
27 Rocket Ismail	.30	.75
28 Emmitt Smith	1.00	2.50
29 Mike Anderson	.30	.75
30 Terrell Davis	.40	1.00
31 Brian Griese	.30	.75
32 Ed McCaffrey	.30	.75
33 Charlie Batch	.30	.75
34 Germane Crowell	.25	.60
35 James Stewart	.25	.60
36 Brett Favre	1.25	3.00
37 Antonio Freeman	.40	1.00
38 Ahman Green	.40	1.00
39 Marvin Harrison	.40	1.00
40 Edgerrin James	.40	1.00
41 Peyton Manning	1.00	2.50
42 Mark Brunell	.30	.75
43 Jimmy Smith	.30	.75
44 Fred Taylor	.40	1.00
45 Derrick Alexander	.25	.60
46 Tony Gonzalez	.40	1.00
47 Trent Green	.40	1.00
48 Priest Holmes	.40	1.00
49 Jay Fiedler	.30	.75
50 Oronde Gadsden	.25	.60
51 Lamar Smith	.30	.75
52 Cris Carter	.40	1.00
53 Daunte Culpepper	.30	.75
54 Randy Moss	.40	1.00
55 Drew Bledsoe	.40	1.00
56 Kevin Faulk	.30	.75
57 Terry Glenn	.30	.75
58 Jeff Blake	.30	.75
59 Aaron Brooks	.30	.75
60 Joe Horn	.30	.75
61 Ricky Williams	.40	1.00
62 Tiki Barber	.40	1.00
63 Kerry Collins	.30	.75
64 Ron Dayne	.30	.75
65 Amani Toomer	.30	.75
66 Wayne Chrebet	.30	.75
67 Curtis Martin	.40	1.00
68 Vinny Testaverde	.30	.75
69 Tim Brown	.40	1.00
70 Rich Gannon	.30	.75
71 Charlie Garner	.30	.75
72 Jerry Rice	.75	2.00
73 Tyrone Wheatley	.30	.75
74 Donovan McNabb	.40	1.00
75 Duce Staley	.30	.75
76 Jerome Bettis	.40	1.00
77 Kordell Stewart	.30	.75
78 Hines Ward	.40	1.00
79 Isaac Bruce	.40	1.00
80 Marshall Faulk	.40	1.00
81 Torry Holt	.30	.75
82 Kurt Warner	.60	1.50
83 Curtis Conway	.30	.75
84 Doug Flutie	.40	1.00
85 Jeff Garcia	.30	.75
86 Terrell Owens	.40	1.00
87 Shaun Alexander	.40	1.00
88 Matt Hasselbeck	.40	1.00
89 Darrell Jackson	.30	.75
90 Ricky Watters	.30	.75
91 Mike Alstott	.30	.75
92 Warrick Dunn	.40	1.00
93 Keyshawn Johnson	.30	.75
94 Brad Johnson	.30	.75
95 Eddie George	.40	1.00
96 Derrick Mason	.30	.75
97 Steve McNair	.40	1.00
98 Stephen Davis	.30	.75
99 Jeff George	.30	.75
100 Michael Westbrook	.25	.60
101 Bobby Newcombe RC	2.50	6.00
102 Corey Brown RC	2.00	5.00
103 Alge Crumpler RC	3.00	8.00
104 Vinny Sutherland RC	2.00	5.00
105 Michael Vick RC	12.00	30.00
106 Chris Barnes RC	2.00	5.00
107 Todd Heap RC	3.00	8.00
108 Nate Clements RC	2.50	6.00
109 Tim Hasselbeck RC	2.50	6.00
110 Travis Henry RC	2.50	6.00
111 Dee Brown RC	2.00	5.00
112 Dan Morgan RC	2.50	6.00
113 Steve Smith RC	6.00	15.00
114 Chris Weinke RC	2.50	6.00
115 John Capel RC	2.00	5.00
116 David Terrell RC	2.50	6.00
117 Anthony Thomas RC	3.00	8.00
118 T.J. Houshmandzadeh RC	4.00	10.00
119 Chad Johnson RC	5.00	12.00
120 Rudi Johnson RC	3.00	8.00
121 James Jackson RC	2.00	5.00
122 Quincy Morgan RC	2.50	6.00
123 Quincy Carter RC	2.50	6.00
124 Kevin Kasper RC	2.00	5.00
125 Scotty Anderson RC	2.00	5.00
126 Mike McMahon RC	2.50	6.00
127 Robert Ferguson RC	3.00	8.00
128 David Martin RC	2.00	5.00
129 Jamal Reynolds RC	2.00	5.00
130 Reggie Wayne RC	6.00	15.00
131 Richmond Flowers RC	2.00	5.00
132 Marcus Stroud RC	2.50	6.00
133 Derrick Blaylock RC	2.50	6.00
134 Snoop Minnis RC	2.00	5.00
135 Chris Chambers RC	3.00	8.00
136 Jamar Fletcher RC	2.00	5.00
137 Josh Heupel RC	3.00	8.00
138 Travis Minor RC	2.50	6.00
139 Michael Bennett RC	2.50	6.00
140 Deuce McAllister RC	3.00	8.00
141 Moran Norris RC	2.00	5.00
142 Onomo Ojo RC	2.00	5.00
143 Will Allen RC	3.00	8.00
144 Jonathan Carter RC	2.00	5.00
145 Jesse Palmer RC	2.50	6.00
146 LaMont Jordan RC	3.00	8.00
147 Santana Moss RC	4.00	10.00
148 Derek Combs RC	2.00	5.00
149 Derrick Gibson RC	2.00	5.00
150 Javon Green RC	2.00	5.00
151 Ken-Yon Rambo RC	2.00	5.00
152 Marques Tuiasosopo RC	2.50	6.00
153 Correll Buckhalter RC	3.00	8.00
154 Freddie Mitchell RC	2.00	5.00
155 Joey Getherall RC	2.00	5.00
156 Chris Taylor RC	2.00	5.00
157 Adam Archuleta RC	2.50	6.00
158 David Rivers RC	2.00	5.00
159 Francis St. Paul RC	2.00	5.00
160 Drew Brees RC	20.00	50.00
161 LaDainian Tomlinson RC	10.00	25.00
162 David Allen RC	2.00	5.00
163 Kevan Barlow RC	2.50	6.00
164 Andre Carter RC	2.50	6.00
165 Cedrick Wilson RC	2.50	6.00
166 Alex Bannister RC	2.00	5.00
167 Josh Booty RC	2.50	6.00
168 Heath Evans RC	2.50	6.00
169 Koren Robinson RC	2.50	6.00
170 Margin Hooks RC	2.00	5.00
171 Dan Alexander RC	2.50	6.00
172 Eddie Berlin RC	2.00	5.00
173 Rod Gardner RC	2.50	6.00
174 Damerien McCants RC	2.50	6.00
175 Sage Rosenfels RC	3.00	8.00

2001 Private Stock Blue Framed

*VETS 1-100: 5X TO 12X BASIC CARDS
*ROOKIES 101-175: .5X TO 1.2X
STATED PRINT RUN 75 SER. #'d SETS

2001 Private Stock Gold Framed

*VETS 1-100: 6X TO 15X BASIC CARDS
*ROOKIES 101-175: .6X TO 1.5X
STATED PRINT RUN 49 SER. #'d SETS

2001 Private Stock Premiere Date

*VETS 1-100: 3X TO 8X BASIC CARDS
*ROOKIES 101-175: .3X TO .8X
STATED PRINT RUN 95 SER. #'d SETS

2001 Private Stock Retail

Pacific released its Private Stock set in August of 2001. The set was made up of 175-cards. The retail cards were highlighted with silver-foil lettering and a silver-foil Private Stock logo instead of gold. Each retail Rookie Card was serial numbered fo 500.

COMP.SET w/o RCs (100)	30.00	60.00

*VETS 1-100: .4X TO 1X HOBBY
*ROOKIES 101-175: .25X TO .6X HOBBY
101-175 ROOKIES PRINT RUN 500

2001 Private Stock Silver Framed

*VETS 1-100: 3X TO 8X BASIC CARDS
*ROOKIES 101-175: .3X TO .8X
STATED PRINT RUN 99 SER. #'d SETS

2001 Private Stock Artists Reserve

COMPLETE SET (10)	50.00	120.00

STATED PRINT RUN 99 SER.#'d SETS

1 Michael Vick	12.00	30.00
2 Chris Weinke	2.50	6.00
3 David Terrell	2.50	6.00
4 Quincy Carter	2.50	6.00
5 Michael Bennett	2.50	6.00
6 Deuce McAllister	3.00	8.00
7 Marques Tuiasosopo	2.50	6.00
8 Drew Brees	20.00	50.00
9 LaDainian Tomlinson	10.00	25.00
10 Koren Robinson	2.50	6.00

2001 Private Stock Game Worn Gear

STATED ODDS 1:1 HOB, 1:49 RET		
*PATCH/175-375: .6X TO 1.5X BASIC JSY		
*PATCH/75-150: .8X TO 2X BASIC JSY		
*PATCH/50: 1X TO 2.5X BASIC JSY		
*PATCH/25: 1.5X TO 4X BASIC JSY		
PATCH PRINT RUN 25-375		
1 Thomas Jones JSY	4.00	10.00
2 Rob Moore	3.00	8.00
3 Jake Plummer JSY	4.00	10.00
4 Frank Sanders	3.00	8.00
5 Chris Chandler	4.00	10.00
6 Doug Johnson	3.00	8.00
7 Terance Mathis	3.00	8.00
8 Randall Cunningham	5.00	12.00
9 Elvis Grbac	4.00	10.00
10 Jamal Lewis	5.00	12.00
12 Shawn Bryson	3.00	8.00
13 Kwame Cavil	3.00	8.00
14 Jonathan Linton	3.00	8.00
15 Jeremy McDaniel	3.00	8.00
16 Eric Moulds	4.00	10.00
17 Thurman Thomas	5.00	12.00
18 Michael Bates	3.00	8.00
19 Dameyune Craig	3.00	8.00
20 William Floyd	3.00	8.00
21 Patrick Jeffers	3.00	8.00
22 Wesley Walls	3.00	8.00
23 Chris Weinke	4.00	10.00
24 Marlon Barnes	3.00	8.00
25 D'Wayne Bates	3.00	8.00
26 Marty Booker	4.00	10.00
27 Cade McNown	4.00	10.00
28 Anthony Thomas	5.00	12.00
29 Brian Urlacher	6.00	15.00
30 Brandon Bennett	3.00	8.00
31 Curtis Keaton	3.00	8.00
32 Jon Kitna	4.00	10.00
33 Peter Warrick JSY	4.00	10.00
34 Darrin Chiaverini	3.00	8.00
35 Tim Couch	3.00	8.00
36 Rickey Dudley	3.00	8.00
37 Curtis Enis	3.00	8.00
38 Kevin Johnson	3.00	8.00
39 Dennis Northcutt	3.00	8.00
40 Troy Aikman	8.00	20.00
41 Wane McGarity	3.00	8.00
42 Carl Pickens	4.00	10.00
43 Emmitt Smith	12.00	30.00
44 Michael Wiley	3.00	8.00
45 Anthony Wright	3.00	8.00
46 Mike Anderson	4.00	10.00
47 Steve Beuerlein	4.00	10.00
48 Terrell Davis	5.00	12.00
49 Olandis Gary	3.00	8.00
50 Brian Griese	4.00	10.00
51 Eddie Kennison	4.00	10.00
52 Deltha O'Neal	3.00	8.00
53 Keith Poole	3.00	8.00
54 Bill Romanowski	4.00	10.00
55 Charlie Batch	4.00	10.00
56 Desmond Howard	4.00	10.00
57 Sedrick Irvin	3.00	8.00
58 Tyrone Davis	3.00	8.00
59 Donald Driver	5.00	12.00
60 Brett Favre	15.00	40.00
61 Ahman Green	5.00	12.00
62 Charles Lee	3.00	8.00
63 Bill Schroeder	4.00	10.00
64 E.G. Green	3.00	8.00
65 Edgerrin James	5.00	12.00
66 Peyton Manning	12.00	30.00
67 Jerome Pathon	3.00	8.00
68 Marcus Pollard	3.00	8.00
69 Kyle Brady	3.00	8.00
70 Mark Brunell	4.00	10.00
71 Jamie Martin	3.00	8.00
72 Keenan McCardell	4.00	10.00
73 Shyrone Stith	3.00	8.00
74 Fred Taylor	5.00	12.00
75 Alvis Whitted	3.00	8.00
76 Derrick Alexander	3.00	8.00
77 Kimble Anders	3.00	8.00
78 Mike Cloud	3.00	8.00
79 Trent Green	5.00	12.00
80 Tony Horne	3.00	8.00
81 Warren Moon	5.00	12.00
82 Rob Konrad	3.00	8.00
83 Ray Lucas	3.00	8.00
84 Tony Martin	4.00	10.00
85 O.J. McDuffie	3.00	8.00
86 James McKnight	3.00	8.00
87 Leslie Shepherd	3.00	8.00
88 Dedric Ward	3.00	8.00
89 Cris Carter	5.00	12.00
90 Daunte Culpepper	4.00	10.00
91 Randy Moss	5.00	12.00
92 Jake Reed	4.00	10.00
93 Robert Smith	4.00	10.00
94 Moe Williams	3.00	8.00
95 Michael Bishop	4.00	10.00
96 Drew Bledsoe	5.00	12.00
97 Troy Brown	4.00	10.00
98 Bert Emanuel	3.00	8.00
99 David Patten	3.00	8.00
100 J.R. Redmond	3.00	8.00
101 Albert Connell	3.00	8.00
102 Willie Jackson	3.00	8.00
103 Chad Morton	3.00	8.00
104 Ricky Williams	5.00	12.00
105 Ron Dayne	4.00	10.00
106 Ron Dixon	3.00	8.00
107 Joe Jurevicius	3.00	8.00
108 Richie Anderson	3.00	8.00
109 Matthew Hatchette	3.00	8.00
110 Chad Pennington	5.00	12.00
111 Reggie Barlow	3.00	8.00
112 Napoleon Kaufman	3.00	8.00
113 Jerry Rice	10.00	25.00
114 Andre Rison	4.00	10.00
115 Marques Tuiasosopo	4.00	10.00
116 Charles Woodson	5.00	12.00
118 Freddie Mitchell	3.00	8.00
119 Trung Canidate	3.00	8.00
120 Marshall Faulk JSY	5.00	12.00
121 Kurt Warner JSY	8.00	20.00
122 Drew Brees	20.00	50.00
124 Jermaine Fazande	3.00	8.00
125 Doug Flutie	5.00	12.00
126 LaDainian Tomlinson	10.00	25.00
127 Jeff Garcia	4.00	10.00
128 Tai Streets	3.00	8.00
129 Shaun Alexander	5.00	12.00
130 Matt Hasselbeck	5.00	12.00
131 Warrick Dunn	5.00	12.00
132 Shaun King	3.00	8.00
133 Ryan Leaf	3.00	8.00
134 Eddie George	5.00	12.00
135 Jevon Kearse	4.00	10.00
136 Steve McNair	5.00	12.00
137 Chris Sanders	3.00	8.00
138 Donnell Bennett	3.00	8.00
139 Kevin Lockett	3.00	8.00
140 David Boston Pants	3.00	8.00
141 Thomas Jones Pants	4.00	10.00
142 Jake Plummer Pants	4.00	10.00
143 Corey Dillon Pants	4.00	10.00
144 Akili Smith Pants	3.00	8.00
145 Peter Warrick Pants	4.00	10.00
146 Isaac Bruce Pants	5.00	12.00
147 Marshall Faulk Pants	5.00	12.00
148 Az-Zahir Hakim Pants	3.00	8.00
149 Torry Holt Pants	4.00	10.00
150 Kurt Warner Pants	8.00	20.00

2001 Private Stock Moments In Time

COMPLETE SET (15)	25.00	60.00
STATED PRINT RUN 499 SER.#'d SETS		
1 Michael Vick	3.00	8.00
2 Travis Henry	.60	1.50
3 Chris Weinke	.60	1.50
4 David Terrell	.60	1.50
5 Anthony Thomas	.75	2.00
6 Quincy Carter	.60	1.50
7 Michael Bennett	.60	1.50
8 Deuce McAllister	.75	2.00
9 Santana Moss	1.00	2.50
10 Marques Tuiasosopo	.60	1.50
11 Freddie Mitchell	.50	1.25
12 Drew Brees	5.00	12.00
13 LaDainian Tomlinson	2.50	6.00
14 Koren Robinson	.60	1.50
15 Rod Gardner	.60	1.50

2001 Private Stock PS-2001

COMP.SET w/o SP's (152)	40.00	80.00
OVERALL STATED ODDS TWO PER PACK		
*SMALL CARD #: .4X TO 1X BASIC CARD		
1 David Boston	.30	.75
2 Thomas Jones	.40	1.00
3 Jake Plummer	.40	1.00
4 Jamal Anderson	.40	1.00
5 Terance Mathis	.30	.75
6 Elvis Grbac	.40	1.00
7 Jamal Lewis	.50	1.25
8 Chris Redman	.50	1.25
9 Shannon Sharpe	.50	1.25
10 Travis Taylor	.30	.75
11 Rob Johnson	.40	1.00
12 Eric Moulds	.40	1.00
13 Peerless Price	.30	.75
14 Tim Biakabutuka	.30	.75
15 Patrick Jeffers	.30	.75
16 Muhsin Muhammad	.40	1.00
17 James Allen	.30	.75
18 Cade McNown	.40	1.00
19 Marcus Robinson	.40	1.00
20 Brian Urlacher	.60	1.50
21 Corey Dillon	.40	1.00
22 Peter Warrick	.40	1.00
23 Tim Couch	.30	.75
24 Kevin Johnson	.30	.75
25 Dennis Northcutt	.30	.75
26 Travis Prentice	.30	.75
27 Rocket Ismail	.40	1.00
28 Emmitt Smith	1.25	3.00
29 Mike Anderson	.40	1.00
30 Terrell Davis	.50	1.25
31 Brian Griese	.40	1.00
32 Ed McCaffrey	.40	1.00
33 Charlie Batch	.40	1.00
34 Johnnie Morton	.40	1.00
35 James Stewart	.30	.75
36 Brett Favre	1.50	4.00
37 Antonio Freeman	.50	1.25
38 Ahman Green	.50	1.25
39 Marvin Harrison	.50	1.25
40 Jerome Pathon	.30	.75
41 Terrence Wilkins	.30	.75
42 Mark Brunell	.40	1.00
43 Keenan McCardell	.40	1.00
44 Jimmy Smith	.40	1.00
45 Fred Taylor	.50	1.25
46 Derrick Alexander	.30	.75
47 Tony Gonzalez	.50	1.25
48 Trent Green	.50	1.25
49 Sylvester Morris	.30	.75
50 Jay Fiedler	.40	1.00
51 Oronde Gadsden	.30	.75
52 Lamar Smith	.40	1.00
53 Cris Carter	.50	1.25
54 Doug Chapman	.30	.75
55 Daunte Culpepper	.40	1.00
56 Drew Bledsoe	.50	1.25
57 Kevin Faulk	.40	1.00
58 Terry Glenn	.40	1.00
59 J.R. Redmond	.30	.75
60 Jeff Blake	.40	1.00
61 Aaron Brooks	.40	1.00
62 Joe Horn	.40	1.00
63 Ricky Williams	.50	1.25
64 Tiki Barber	.50	1.25
65 Kerry Collins	.40	1.00
66 Ron Dayne	.40	1.00
67 Amani Toomer	.40	1.00
68 Curtis Martin	.50	1.25
69 Chad Pennington	.50	1.25
70 Vinny Testaverde	.40	1.00
71 Tim Brown	.50	1.25
72 Rich Gannon	.40	1.00
73 Jerry Rice	1.00	2.50
74 Tyrone Wheatley	.40	1.00
75 Donovan McNabb	.50	1.25
76 Duce Staley	.40	1.00
77 Jerome Bettis	.50	1.25
78 Kordell Stewart	.40	1.00
79 Isaac Bruce	.50	1.25
80 Marshall Faulk	.50	1.25
81 Az-Zahir Hakim	.30	.75
82 Torry Holt	.40	1.00
83 Tim Dwight	.40	1.00
84 Doug Flutie	.50	1.25
85 Jeff Garcia	.40	1.00
86 Terrell Owens	.50	1.25
87 Shaun Alexander	.50	1.25
88 Matt Hasselbeck	.50	1.25
89 Darrell Jackson	.40	1.00
90 Ricky Watters	.40	1.00
91 Mike Alstott	.40	1.00
92 Warrick Dunn	.50	1.25
93 Brad Johnson	.40	1.00
94 Keyshawn Johnson	.40	1.00
95 Eddie George	.50	1.25
96 Derrick Mason	.40	1.00
97 Steve McNair	.50	1.25
98 Stephen Davis	.40	1.00
99 Jeff George	.40	1.00
100 Michael Westbrook	.30	.75
101 Bobby Newcombe	.40	1.00
102 Alge Crumpler	.50	1.25
103 Vinny Sutherland	.30	.75
104 Todd Heap	.50	1.25
105 Tim Hasselbeck	.40	1.00
106 Travis Henry	.40	1.00
107 Dee Brown	.30	.75
108 Dan Morgan	.40	1.00
109 Steve Smith	1.00	2.50
110 Chris Weinke	.40	1.00
111 Anthony Thomas	.50	1.25
112 T.J. Houshmandzadeh	.60	1.50
113 Chad Johnson	.75	2.00
114 Rudi Johnson	.50	1.25
115 James Jackson	.30	.75
116 Quincy Morgan	.40	1.00
117 Quincy Carter	.40	1.00
118 Kevin Kasper	.30	.75
119 Scotty Anderson	.30	.75
120 Mike McMahon	.40	1.00
121 Robert Ferguson	.50	1.25
122 Reggie Wayne	1.00	2.50
123 Derrick Blaylock	.40	1.00
124 Snoop Minnis	.30	.75
125 Chris Chambers	.50	1.25
126 Jamar Fletcher	.30	.75
127 Josh Heupel	.50	1.25
128 Travis Minor	.40	1.00
129 Michael Bennett	.40	1.00
130 Deuce McAllister	.50	1.25
131 Moran Norris	.30	.75
132 Will Allen	.50	1.25
133 Jonathan Carter	.30	.75
134 Jesse Palmer	.40	1.00
135 LaMont Jordan	.50	1.25
136 Ken-Yon Rambo	.30	.75
137 Marques Tuiasosopo	.40	1.00
138 Correll Buckhalter	.50	1.25
139 Freddie Mitchell	.30	.75
140 Chris Taylor	.30	.75
141 Adam Archuleta	.40	1.00
142 Francis St. Paul	.30	.75
143 Kevan Barlow	.40	1.00
144 Cedrick Wilson	.40	1.00
145 Alex Bannister	.30	.75
146 Josh Booty	.40	1.00
147 Heath Evans	.40	1.00
148 Dan Alexander	.40	1.00
149 Eddie Berlin	.30	.75
150 Rod Gardner	.40	1.00
151 Damerien McCants	.40	1.00
152 Sage Rosenfels	.50	1.25
153 Michael Vick SP		
154 David Terrell SP		
155 Edgerrin James SP		
156 Peyton Manning SP		
157 Randy Moss SP		
158 Santana Moss SP		
159 Kurt Warner SP		
160 Drew Brees SP		
161 LaDainian Tomlinson SP		
162 Koren Robinson SP		

2001 Private Stock Reserve

COMPLETE SET (20)	40.00	80.00
STATED ODDS 1:21 HOBBY		
1 Jamal Lewis	2.00	5.00
2 Peter Warrick	1.25	3.00
3 Emmitt Smith	3.00	8.00
4 Mike Anderson	1.25	3.00
5 Terrell Davis	1.50	4.00
6 Brian Griese	1.50	4.00
7 Brett Favre	5.00	12.00
8 Edgerrin James	2.00	5.00
9 Peyton Manning	4.00	10.00
10 Mark Brunell	1.50	4.00
11 Daunte Culpepper	1.50	4.00
12 Randy Moss	3.00	8.00
13 Drew Bledsoe	2.00	5.00
14 Ricky Williams	1.50	4.00
15 Ron Dayne	1.25	3.00
16 Donovan McNabb	2.00	5.00
17 Marshall Faulk	2.00	5.00
18 Kurt Warner	3.00	8.00
19 Eddie George	1.50	4.00
20 Steve McNair	1.50	4.00

2002 Private Stock

This 150-card set includes 100 veterans and 50 rookie year players. The rookie year player cards were serial numbered to their jersey number and feature a swatch of a game-used football on the front.

COMP.SET w/o SP's (100)	15.00	40.00
1 David Boston	.30	.75
2 Thomas Jones	.50	1.25
3 Jake Plummer	.40	1.00
4 Jamal Anderson	.40	1.00
5 Warrick Dunn	.40	1.00
6 Shawn Jefferson	.30	.75
7 Michael Vick	.75	2.00
8 Jamal Lewis	.40	1.00
9 Chris Redman	.30	.75
10 Travis Taylor	.30	.75
11 Travis Henry	.30	.75
12 Eric Moulds	.40	1.00
13 Peerless Price	.30	.75
14 Muhsin Muhammad	.40	1.00
15 Lamar Smith	.40	1.00
16 Chris Weinke	.30	.75
17 Marty Booker	.40	1.00
18 Jim Miller	.30	.75
19 Anthony Thomas	.40	1.00
20 Corey Dillon	.40	1.00
21 Darnay Scott	.40	1.00
22 Peter Warrick	.40	1.00
23 Tim Couch	.30	.75
24 James Jackson	.30	.75
25 Kevin Johnson	.30	.75
26 Quincy Carter	.30	.75
27 Rocket Ismail	.40	1.00
28 Emmitt Smith	1.25	3.00
29 Mike Anderson	.40	1.00
30 Terrell Davis	.50	1.25
31 Brian Griese	.40	1.00
32 Rod Smith	.40	1.00
33 Mike McMahon	.30	.75
34 Johnnie Morton	.40	1.00
35 Brett Favre	1.25	3.00
36 Antonio Freeman	.50	1.25
37 Ahman Green	.40	1.00
38 Corey Bradford	.30	.75
39 Jermaine Lewis	.30	.75
40 Jamie Sharper	.40	1.00
41 Marvin Harrison	.50	1.25
42 Edgerrin James	.40	1.00
43 Mark Brunell	.40	1.00
44 Jimmy Smith	.40	1.00
45 Fred Taylor	.40	1.00
46 Tony Gonzalez	.50	1.25
47 Trent Green	.40	1.00
48 Priest Holmes	.50	1.25
49 Chris Chambers	.40	1.00
50 Jay Fiedler	.40	1.00
51 James McKnight	.30	.75
52 Ricky Williams	.40	1.00
53 Michael Bennett	.40	1.00
54 Cris Carter	.50	1.25
55 Daunte Culpepper	.40	1.00
56 Randy Moss	.50	1.25
57 Drew Bledsoe	.50	1.25
58 Tom Brady	1.25	3.00
59 Troy Brown	.40	1.00
60 Antowain Smith	.40	1.00
61 Aaron Brooks	.40	1.00
62 Joe Horn	.40	1.00
63 Deuce McAllister	.40	1.00
64 Tiki Barber	.50	1.25
65 Kerry Collins	.40	1.00
66 Ron Dayne	.40	1.00
67 Laveranues Coles	.40	1.00
68 Curtis Martin	.50	1.25
69 Vinny Testaverde	.40	1.00
70 Tim Brown	.50	1.25
71 Rich Gannon	.40	1.00
72 Jerry Rice	1.00	2.50
73 Correll Buckhalter	.40	1.00
74 Duce Staley	.40	1.00
75 James Thrash	.40	1.00
76 Jerome Bettis	.50	1.25
77 Plaxico Burress	.40	1.00
78 Kordell Stewart	.40	1.00
79 Hines Ward	.50	1.25
80 Isaac Bruce	.50	1.25
81 Marshall Faulk	.50	1.25
82 Torry Holt	.50	1.25
83 Kurt Warner	.50	1.25
84 Drew Brees	.75	2.00
85 Doug Flutie	.50	1.25
86 LaDainian Tomlinson	.60	1.50
87 Jeff Garcia	.40	1.00
88 Garrison Hearst	.40	1.00
89 Terrell Owens	.50	1.25
90 Shaun Alexander	.40	1.00
91 Trent Dilfer	.40	1.00
92 Darrell Jackson	.40	1.00
93 Ricky Watters	.40	1.00
94 Brad Johnson	.40	1.00
95 Keyshawn Johnson	.40	1.00
96 Eddie George	.40	1.00
97 Derrick Mason	.40	1.00
98 Steve McNair	.50	1.25
99 Stephen Davis	.40	1.00
100 Rod Gardner	.30	.75
101 Damien Anderson FB/20	10.00	25.00
102 Ladell Betts FB/46	15.00	40.00
103 Antonio Bryant FB/80	12.00	30.00
104 Wendell Bryant FB/77	8.00	20.00
111 Andre Davis FB/80	10.00	25.00
113 DeShaun Foster FB/26	15.00	40.00
116 Lamar Gordon FB/28	12.00	30.00
117 Daniel Graham FB/89	10.00	25.00
121 Verron Haynes FB/35	10.00	25.00
122 John Henderson FB/98	10.00	25.00
132 James Mungro FB/23	15.00	40.00
135 Brian Poli-Dixon FB/82	8.00	20.00
136 Clinton Portis FB/28	20.00	50.00
139 Josh Reed FB/25	12.00	30.00
143 Jeremy Shockey FB/88	20.00	50.00
147 Javon Walker FB/80	12.00	30.00
149 Brian Westbrook FB/20	25.00	60.00
150 Roy Williams FB/38	15.00	40.00

2002 Private Stock Retail

*RETAIL VETS 1-100: .25X TO .6X HOBBY		
101 Damien Anderson RC	.60	1.50
102 Ladell Betts RC	1.00	2.50
103 Antonio Bryant RC	1.00	2.50
104 Wendell Bryant RC	.60	1.50
105 Reche Caldwell RC	1.00	2.50
106 Kelly Campbell RC	.75	2.00
107 David Carr RC	1.00	2.50
108 Eric Crouch RC	1.00	2.50
109 Ronald Curry RC	.75	2.00
110 Rohan Davey RC	1.00	2.50
111 Andre Davis RC	.75	2.00
112 T.J. Duckett RC	1.00	2.50
113 DeShaun Foster RC	1.00	2.50
114 Jabar Gaffney RC	1.00	2.50
115 David Garrard RC	1.25	3.00
116 Lamar Gordon RC	.75	2.00
117 Daniel Graham RC	.75	2.00
118 William Green RC	.75	2.00
119 Joey Harrington RC	1.00	2.50
120 Napoleon Harris RC	.75	2.00
121 Verron Haynes RC	.60	1.50
122 John Henderson RC	.75	2.00
123 Kahlil Hill RC	.60	1.50
124 Quentin Jammer RC	1.00	2.50
125 Ron Johnson RC	.75	2.00
126 Kurt Kittner RC	.60	1.50
127 Zak Kustok RC	.60	1.50
128 Ashley Lelie RC	.75	2.00
129 Josh McCown RC	1.00	2.50
130 Freddie Milons RC	.60	1.50
131 Maurice Morris RC	.75	2.00
132 James Mungro RC	1.00	2.50
133 David Neill RC	.60	1.50
134 Adrian Peterson RC	1.00	2.50
135 Brian Poli-Dixon RC	.60	1.50
136 Clinton Portis RC	1.25	3.00
137 Patrick Ramsey RC	1.00	2.50
138 Antwaan Randle El RC	1.00	2.50
139 Josh Reed RC	.75	2.00
140 Cliff Russell RC	.60	1.50
141 Josh Scobey RC	.75	2.00
142 Lito Sheppard RC	1.00	2.50
143 Jeremy Shockey RC	1.50	4.00
144 Luke Staley RC	.60	1.50
145 Donte Stallworth RC	1.00	2.50
146 Lamont Thompson RC	.75	2.00
147 Javon Walker RC	1.00	2.50
148 Marquise Walker RC	.60	1.50
149 Brian Westbrook RC	1.50	4.00
150 Roy Williams RC	1.00	2.50

2002 Private Stock Atomic Previews

STATED ODDS 1:9		
101 Damien Anderson	1.00	2.50
102 Ladell Betts	1.50	4.00
103 Antonio Bryant	1.50	4.00
104 Reche Caldwell	1.50	4.00
105 Kelly Campbell	1.25	3.00
106 David Carr	1.50	4.00
107 Rohan Davey	1.50	4.00
108 Andre Davis	1.25	3.00
109 T.J. Duckett	1.50	4.00
110 DeShaun Foster	1.50	4.00
111 David Garrard	2.00	5.00
112 Lamar Gordon	1.25	3.00
113 William Green	1.25	3.00
114 Joey Harrington	1.50	4.00
115 Kurt Kittner	1.00	2.50
116 Ashley Lelie	1.25	3.00
117 Josh McCown	1.50	4.00
118 Clinton Portis	2.00	5.00
119 Patrick Ramsey	1.50	4.00
120 Antwaan Randle El	1.50	4.00
121 Josh Reed	1.25	3.00
122 Luke Staley	1.00	2.50
123 Donte Stallworth	1.50	4.00
124 Marquise Walker	1.00	2.50
125 Brian Westbrook	2.50	6.00

2002 Private Stock Banner Year

COMPLETE SET (10)	15.00	40.00
STATED ODDS 1:17		
1 Michael Vick	2.00	5.00
2 Anthony Thomas	1.00	2.50
3 Emmitt Smith	3.00	8.00
4 Brett Favre	3.00	8.00
5 Randy Moss	1.25	3.00
6 Tom Brady	3.00	8.00
7 Jerry Rice	2.50	6.00
8 Marshall Faulk	1.25	3.00
9 Kurt Warner	1.25	3.00
10 LaDainian Tomlinson	1.50	4.00

2002 Private Stock Class Act

COMPLETE SET (20)	12.00	30.00
STATED ODDS 2:9		
1 Antonio Bryant	.75	2.00
2 Reche Caldwell	.75	2.00
3 David Carr	.75	2.00
4 Eric Crouch	.75	2.00
5 Rohan Davey	.75	2.00
6 Andre Davis	.60	1.50
7 T.J. Duckett	.75	2.00
8 DeShaun Foster	.75	2.00
9 Lamar Gordon	.60	1.50
10 William Green	.60	1.50
11 Joey Harrington	.75	2.00
12 Kurt Kittner	.50	1.25
13 Ashley Lelie	.60	1.50
14 Josh McCown	.75	2.00
15 Clinton Portis	1.00	2.50
16 Patrick Ramsey	.75	2.00
17 Antwaan Randle El	.75	2.00
18 Josh Reed	.60	1.50
19 Luke Staley	.50	1.25
20 Donte Stallworth	.75	2.00

2002 Private Stock Divisional Realignment

STATED ODDS 1:9		
1 David Boston	.75	2.00
2 Michael Vick	2.00	5.00
3 Jamal Lewis	1.00	2.50
4 Travis Henry	.75	2.00
5 Chris Weinke	.75	2.00
6 Anthony Thomas	1.00	2.50
7 Corey Dillon	1.00	2.50
8 Tim Couch	.75	2.00
9 Emmitt Smith	3.00	8.00
10 Terrell Davis	1.25	3.00
11 Mike McMahon	.75	2.00
12 Brett Favre	3.00	8.00
13 Jermaine Lewis	.75	2.00
14 Edgerrin James	1.00	2.50
15 Mark Brunell	1.00	2.50
16 Priest Holmes	1.25	3.00
17 Chris Chambers	1.00	2.50
18 Randy Moss	1.25	3.00
19 Tom Brady	3.00	8.00
20 Aaron Brooks	1.00	2.50
21 Ron Dayne	1.00	2.50
22 Curtis Martin	1.25	3.00
23 Jerry Rice	2.50	6.00
24 Duce Staley	1.00	2.50
25 Jerome Bettis	1.25	3.00
26 Kurt Warner	1.25	3.00
27 LaDainian Tomlinson	1.50	4.00
28 Jeff Garcia	1.00	2.50
29 Shaun Alexander	1.00	2.50
30 Mike Alstott	1.00	2.50
31 Eddie George	1.00	2.50
32 Rod Gardner	.75	2.00

2002 Private Stock Game Worn Jerseys

OVERALL ODDS ONE PER PACK		
ANNOUNCED PRINT RUNS 56-1000		
1 David Boston	2.50	6.00
2 Steve Bush	2.50	6.00
3 Arnold Jackson	2.50	6.00
4 Thomas Jones/398*	4.00	10.00
5 Rob Moore/400*	2.50	6.00
6 Jake Plummer	3.00	8.00
7 Jamal Anderson/395*	3.00	8.00
8 Maurice Smith	2.50	6.00
9 Michael Vick/510*	6.00	15.00
10 Todd Heap	3.00	8.00
11 Travis Taylor/511*	2.50	6.00
12 Randall Cunningham/250*	4.00	10.00
13 Elvis Grbac	2.50	6.00
14 Jamal Lewis/100*	4.00	10.00
15 Ray Lewis	4.00	10.00
16 Shannon Sharpe/560*	4.00	10.00
17 Moe Williams	2.50	6.00
18 Larry Centers	3.00	8.00
19 Travis Henry/387*	2.50	6.00
20 Isaac Byrd/112*	3.00	8.00
21 Jim Harbaugh	3.00	8.00
22 Richard Huntley	2.50	6.00
23 Chris Weinke/110*	2.50	6.00
24 Autry Denson	2.50	6.00
25 David Terrell/259*	2.50	6.00
26 Anthony Thomas/111*	4.00	10.00
27 Brian Urlacher/512*	4.00	10.00
28 Corey Dillon/500*	3.00	8.00
29 T.J. Houshmandzadeh/313*	4.00	10.00
30 Chad Johnson/264*	4.00	10.00
31 Rudi Johnson	4.00	10.00
32 Jon Kitna	3.00	8.00
33 Peter Warrick/276*	3.00	8.00
34 Tim Couch/510*	2.50	6.00
35 Darrin Chiaverini/111*	3.00	8.00
36 Richmond Flowers	2.50	6.00
37 Joey Galloway	3.00	8.00
38 La'Roi Glover/506*	2.50	6.00
39 Troy Hambrick/260*	2.50	6.00
40 Emmitt Smith	12.00	30.00
41 Mike Anderson/197*	3.00	8.00
42 Tony Carter	2.50	6.00
43 Terrell Davis	4.00	10.00
44 Brian Griese	3.00	8.00
45 Todd Husak	3.00	8.00
46 Kevin Kasper/313*	2.50	6.00
47 Scotty Anderson/260*	2.50	6.00
48 Karsten Bailey/302*	2.50	6.00
49 Reggie Brown	3.00	8.00
50 Brett Favre	12.00	30.00
51 Robert Ferguson/262*	3.00	8.00
52 Antonio Freeman	4.00	10.00
53 Ahman Green/490*	3.00	8.00
54 David Martin/508*	2.50	6.00
55 Jermaine Lewis	2.50	6.00
56 Frank Moreau	2.50	6.00
57 Marvin Harrison	4.00	10.00
58 Edgerrin James/411*	3.00	8.00
59 Tony Simmons	2.50	6.00
60 Mark Brunell	3.00	8.00
61 Sean Dawkins	3.00	8.00
62 Jimmy Smith	3.00	8.00
63 Fred Taylor	3.00	8.00
64 Tony Gonzalez	4.00	10.00
65 Trent Green	3.00	8.00
66 Mikhael Ricks	2.50	6.00
67 Cade McNown/259*	3.00	8.00
68 Ricky Williams	3.00	8.00
69 Michael Bennett/159*	3.00	8.00
70 Cris Carter	4.00	10.00
71 Corey Chavous	2.50	6.00
72 Daunte Culpepper/510*	3.00	8.00
73 Randy Moss/509*	6.00	15.00
74 Travis Prentice	2.50	6.00
75 Drew Bledsoe	4.00	10.00
76 Tom Brady/505*	12.00	30.00
77 Marc Edwards	2.50	6.00
78 Kevin Faulk	3.00	8.00
79 Antowain Smith	3.00	8.00
80 Aaron Brooks/261*	3.00	8.00
81 Albert Connell/503*	2.50	6.00
82 Deuce McAllister/162*	3.00	8.00
83 Wane McGarity/170*	2.50	6.00
84 Jake Reed	3.00	8.00
85 Ron Dayne/504*	3.00	8.00
86 Curtis Martin/442*	4.00	10.00
87 Chad Morton	2.50	6.00
88 Craig Yeast/67*	3.00	8.00
89 Tim Brown	4.00	10.00
90 Rich Gannon	3.00	8.00
91 Charlie Garner	3.00	8.00
92 Jerry Rice	8.00	20.00
93 Freddie Mitchell/309*	2.50	6.00
94 Todd Pinkston	2.50	6.00
95 James Thrash	3.00	8.00
96 Jerome Bettis	4.00	10.00
97 Kordell Stewart	3.00	8.00
98 Hines Ward	4.00	10.00
99 Isaac Bruce/511*	4.00	10.00
100 Marshall Faulk	4.00	10.00
101 Damon Griffin	2.50	6.00
102 Kurt Warner/509*	4.00	10.00
103 Drew Brees/497*	6.00	15.00
104 Doug Flutie	4.00	10.00
105 LaDainian Tomlinson/405*	5.00	12.00
106 Jeff Garcia/435*	3.00	8.00
107 Terrell Owens	4.00	10.00
108 Tim Rattay	3.00	8.00
109 Shockmain Davis	2.50	6.00
110 Bobby Engram/56*	4.00	10.00
111 Matt Hasselbeck	4.00	10.00
112 Koren Robinson/314*	2.50	6.00
113 Ricky Watters/403*	3.00	8.00
114 Mike Alstott/500*	3.00	8.00
115 Marco Battaglia	2.50	6.00
116 Rob Johnson	3.00	8.00
117 Brad Johnson	3.00	8.00
118 Michael Pittman	3.00	8.00
119 Dan Alexander	2.50	6.00
120 Eddie Berlin	2.50	6.00
121 Eddie George	3.00	8.00
122 Skip Hicks	2.50	6.00
123 Derrick Mason	3.00	8.00
124 Steve McNair	4.00	10.00
125 Rod Gardner/260*	2.50	6.00

2002 Private Stock Game Worn Jerseys Logos

COMMON CARD/104-194	3.00	8.00
SEMISTARS/104-194	4.00	10.00
UNL.STARS/104-194	5.00	12.00
COMMON CARD/60-92	4.00	10.00
SEMISTARS/60-92	5.00	12.00
UNL.STARS/60-92	6.00	15.00
COMMON CARD/30-56	5.00	12.00
SEMISTARS/30-56	6.00	15.00
UNL.STARS/30-56	8.00	20.00
COMMON CARD/20-28	8.00	20.00
UNL.STARS/20-28	10.00	25.00
STATED PRINT RUN 2-194		
SERIAL #'d UNDER 20 NOT PRICED		
27 Brian Urlacher/108	5.00	12.00
40 Emmitt Smith/44	20.00	50.00
76 Tom Brady/24	25.00	60.00
92 Jerry Rice/160	10.00	25.00
105 LaDainian Tomlinson/42	10.00	25.00

2002 Private Stock Game Worn Jerseys Numbers

COMMON CARD/80-97	4.00	10.00
SEMISTARS/80-97	5.00	12.00
UNL.STARS/80-97	6.00	15.00
COMMON CARD/30-54	5.00	12.00
SEMISTARS/30-54	6.00	15.00
UNL.STARS/30-54	8.00	20.00
COMMON CARD/20-29	6.00	15.00
SEMISTARS/20-29	8.00	20.00
UNL.STARS/20-29	10.00	25.00
STATED PRINT RUN 1-97		
SERIAL #'d UNDER 20 NOT PRICED		
27 Brian Urlacher/54	8.00	20.00
40 Emmitt Smith/22	25.00	60.00
73 Randy Moss/84	8.00	20.00
92 Jerry Rice/80	12.00	30.00
105 LaDainian Tomlinson/21	12.00	30.00

2002 Private Stock Game Worn Jerseys Patches

COMMON CARD (1-122)	3.00	8.00
SEMISTARS	4.00	10.00
UNLISTED STARS	5.00	12.00
COMMON CARD/76-102	4.00	10.00
SEMISTARS/76-102	5.00	12.00
COMMON CARD/31-55	5.00	12.00
SEMISTARS/31-55	6.00	15.00
COMMON CARD/20-25	6.00	15.00
SEMISTARS/20-25	8.00	20.00
STATED PRINT RUN 4-252		
27 Brian Urlacher/126	5.00	12.00
40 Emmitt Smith/199	12.00	30.00
50 Brett Favre/50	20.00	50.00
73 Randy Moss/201	6.00	15.00
76 Tom Brady/101	15.00	40.00
92 Jerry Rice/201	10.00	25.00

2002 Private Stock Moments in Time

STATED ODDS 1:193		
STATED PRINT RUN 90 SER.#'d SETS		
1 Antonio Bryant	3.00	8.00
2 David Carr	3.00	8.00
3 T.J. Duckett	3.00	8.00
4 DeShaun Foster	3.00	8.00
5 William Green	2.50	6.00
6 Joey Harrington	3.00	8.00
7 Kurt Kittner	2.00	5.00
8 Clinton Portis	4.00	10.00
9 Patrick Ramsey	3.00	8.00
10 Donte Stallworth	3.00	8.00

1990-94 Pro Athletes Outreach

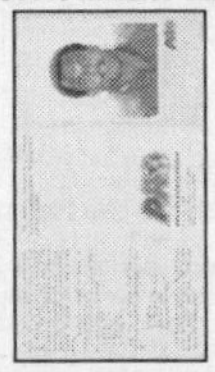

This 12-card set was issued by Pro Athletes Outreach, a Christian leadership training ministry for pro athletes and their families. The tri-fold cards measure approximately 7 1/8" by 4 1/8". The right portion of the tri-fold carries a color player photo bordered in white on a light gray background. Below the picture are the player's name, position, and the PAO logo. The remainder of the card front and back contains the player's personal Christian testimony followed by an invitation to write them in care of the PAO address, for more information. With the exception of the Gill Byrd card, a second black-and-white player photo appears on the left portion of the tri-fold card. A brief career summary rounds out the card. The cards are unnumbered and checklisted below in alphabetical order.

COMPLETE SET (13)	4.00	10.00
1 Mark Boyer	.20	.50
2 Gill Byrd	.30	.75
3 Darren Carrington	.20	.50
4 Ron Coder	.20	.50
5 Paul Coffman	.20	.50
6 Burnell Dent	.20	.50
7 Johnny Holland	.20	.50
8 Jeff Kemp	.30	.75
9 Steve Largent	1.60	4.00
10 John Offerdahl	.20	.50
11 Stephone Paige	.20	.50
12 Doug Smith	.20	.50
13 Rob Taylor	.20	.50

1993 Pro Bowl POGs

These POGs measure approximately 1 5/8" in diameter and feature members selected to the 1993 Pro Bowl team.

COMPLETE SET (24)	6.00	15.00
1 Gill Byrd	.20	.50
2 Barry Foster	.30	.75
3 Mel Gray	.20	.50
4 Harold Green	.20	.50
5 Rodney Hampton	.30	.75
6 Joel Hilgenberg	.20	.50
7 Pierce Holt	.20	.50
8 Haywood Jeffires	.30	.75
9 Brent Jones	.30	.75
10 Nick Lowery	.20	.50
11 Tim McDonald	.20	.50
12 Guy McIntyre	.20	.50
13 Jay Novacek	.40	1.00
14 Richmond Webb	.30	.75
15 Todd Scott	.20	.50
16 Elbert Shelley	.20	.50
17 Clyde Simmons	.30	.75
18 Emmitt Smith	2.00	5.00
19 Mark Stepnoski	.20	.50
20 Jessie Tuggle	.20	.50
21 Will Wolford	.20	.50
22 NFL Players	.20	.50
23 1993 Pro Bowlers Show Blaisdell Arena	.20	.50
24 1993 Pro Bowlers Show	.20	.50

1996 Pro Cube

Pro Cubes feature one player and measure roughly 3 1/8" square. Each includes numerous photos of the player and can be folded and twisted to form the different pictures. They were distributed primarily through major retail outlets with one cube per package.

COMPLETE SET (10)	14.00	35.00
1 Troy Aikman	1.60	4.00
2 Terrell Davis	1.60	4.00
3 John Elway	2.00	5.00
4 Brett Favre	2.00	5.00
5 Dan Marino	2.00	5.00
6 Jerry Rice	1.60	4.00
7 Barry Sanders	2.00	5.00
8 Emmitt Smith	2.00	5.00
9 Kordell Stewart	1.20	3.00
10 Steve Young	1.20	3.00

1990-91 Pro Line Samples

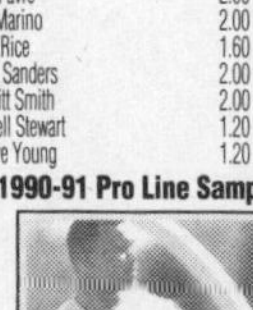

Unlike the borderless regular set, the fronts of these standard-size cards have silver borders. Many photos (both front and back) are different or are cropped differently than the corresponding regular-issue cards, and many of the quotes on the back also are different from the regular issue cards. The word "SAMPLE" is printed in small type next to the mugshots on the backs.

The cards are skipnumbered on the back by odd numbers except that sample card number 15 was apparently not issued.

COMPLETE SET (18)	48.00	120.00
1 Charles Mann	2.00	5.00
3 Troy Aikman	6.00	15.00
5 Boomer Esiason	2.80	7.00
7 Warren Moon	4.00	10.00
9 Bill Fralic	2.00	5.00
11 Lawrence Taylor	4.00	10.00
13 George Seifert CO	2.00	5.00
17 Dan Marino	12.00	30.00
19 Jim Everett	2.80	7.00
21 John Elway	12.00	30.00
23 Jeff George	2.80	7.00
25 Lindy Infante CO	2.00	5.00
27 Dan Reeves CO	2.80	7.00
29 Steve Largent	4.00	10.00
31 Roger Craig	2.80	7.00
33 Marty Schottenheimer CO	2.00	5.00
35 Mike Ditka CO	4.00	10.00
37 Sam Wyche CO	2.00	5.00

1991 Pro Line Portraits

This 300-card standard-size set features some of the NFL's most popular players in non-game shots. The players and coaches are posed wearing their team's colors. The fronts are full-color borderless shots of the players, while the backs feature a quote from the player and a portrait pose of the player. The cards were available in wax packs. Essentially the whole set was available individually autographed; these certified autographed cards were randomly seeded into packs and feature no card numbers. An Emmitt Smith card was printed for inclusion in the Autographs set, but was never released in packs. A very small number of signed copies of the card were released at the 1992 Super Bowl Card Show with the majority of the Smith cards remaining unsigned. However, all of the Emmitt cards produced carried the certified stamp or crimp on the lower right hand corner of the card. The Santa Claus card could be obtained through a mail-in offer in exchange for ten 1991 ProLine Portraits foil pack wrappers. Complete sets featuring "National 1991" embossed logos were produced and distributed to guests of an event at The National Sports Collector's Convention in Anaheim. Reportedly, 250-complete sets were produced with the special logo.

COMPLETE SET (300)	3.00	6.00
1 Jim Kelly	.07	.20
2 Carl Banks	.01	.05
3 Neal Anderson	.02	.10
4 James Brooks	.01	.05
5 Reggie Langhorne	.01	.05
6 Robert Awalt	.01	.05
7 Greg Kragen	.01	.05
8 Steve Young	.25	.60
9 Nick Bell RC	.01	.05
10 Ray Childress	.02	.10
11 Albert Bentley	.01	.05
12 Albert Lewis	.01	.05
13 Howie Long	.02	.10
14 Flipper Anderson	.01	.05
15 Mark Clayton	.02	.10
16 Jarrod Bunch RC	.01	.05
17 Bruce Armstrong	.01	.05
18 Vinnie Clark RC	.01	.05
19 Rob Moore	.02	.10
20 Eric Allen	.01	.05
21 Timm Rosenbach	.01	.05
22 Gary Anderson K	.01	.05
23 Martin Bayless	.01	.05
24 Kevin Fagan	.01	.05
25 Brian Blades	.02	.10
26 Gary Anderson RB	.01	.05
27 Earnest Byner	.02	.10
28 O.J. Simpson RET	.07	.20
29 Dan Henning CO	.01	.05
30 Sean Landeta	.01	.05
31 James Lofton	.02	.10
32 Mike Singletary	.02	.10
33 David Fulcher	.01	.05
34 Mark Murphy	.01	.05
35 Issiac Holt	.01	.05
36 Dennis Smith	.01	.05
37 Lomas Brown	.01	.05
38 Ernest Givins	.02	.10
39 Duane Bickett	.01	.05
40 Barry Word	.01	.05
41 Tony Mandarich	.01	.05
42 Cleveland Gary	.01	.05
43 Ferrell Edmunds	.01	.05
44 Randal Hill RC	.02	.10
45 Irving Fryar	.02	.10
46 Henry Jones RC	.02	.10
47 Blair Thomas	.01	.05
48 Andre Waters	.01	.05
49 J.T. Smith	.01	.05
50 Thomas Everett	.01	.05
51 Marion Butts	.02	.10
52 Tom Rathman	.01	.05
53 Vann McElroy	.01	.05
54 Mark Carrier WR	.02	.10
55 Jim Lachey	.01	.05
56 Joe Theismann RET	.02	.10
57 Jerry Glanville CO	.01	.05
58 Doug Riesenberg	.01	.05
59 Cornelius Bennett	.02	.10
60 Mark Carrier DB	.02	.10
61 Rodney Holman	.01	.05
62 Leroy Hoard	.02	.10
63 Michael Irvin	.07	.20
64 Bobby Humphrey	.01	.05
65 Mel Gray	.02	.10
66 Brian Noble	.01	.05
67 Al Smith	.01	.05
68 Eric Dickerson	.02	.10
69 Steve DeBerg	.02	.10
70 Jay Schroeder	.01	.05
71 Irv Pankey	.01	.05
72 Reggie Roby	.01	.05
73 Wade Wilson	.01	.05
74 Johnny Rembert	.01	.05
75 Russell Maryland RC	.02	.10
76 Al Toon	.02	.10
77 Randall Cunningham	.07	.20
78 Lonnie Young	.01	.05
79 Carnell Lake	.01	.05
80 Burt Grossman	.01	.05
81 Jim Mora CO	.01	.05
82 Dave Krieg	.01	.05
83 Bruce Hill	.01	.05
84 Ricky Sanders	.01	.05
85 Roger Staubach RET	.07	.20
86 Richard Williamson CO	.01	.05
87 Everson Walls	.01	.05
88 Shane Conlan	.01	.05
89 Mike Ditka CO	.07	.20
90 Mark Bortz	.01	.05
91 Tim McGee	.01	.05
92 Michael Dean Perry	.02	.10
93 Danny Noonan	.01	.05
94 Mark Jackson	.01	.05
95 Chris Miller	.02	.10
96 Ed McCaffrey RC	.30	.75
97 Lorenzo White	.02	.10
98 Ray Donaldson	.01	.05
99 Nick Lowery	.01	.05
100 Steve Smith	.01	.05
101 Jackie Slater	.01	.05
102 Louis Oliver	.01	.05
103 Kanavis McGhee RC	.01	.05
104 Ray Agnew	.01	.05
105 Sam Mills	.02	.10
106 Bill Pickel	.01	.05
107 Keith Byars	.02	.10
108 Ricky Proehl	.01	.05
109 Merril Hoge	.01	.05
110 Rod Bernstine	.01	.05
111 Andy Heck	.01	.05
112 Broderick Thomas	.01	.05
113 Andre Collins	.01	.05
114 Paul Warfield RET	.02	.10
115 Bill Belichick CO RC	.60	1.50
116 Ottis Anderson	.02	.10
117 Andre Reed	.02	.10
118 Andre Rison	.02	.10
119 Dexter Carter	.01	.05
120 Anthony Munoz	.02	.10
121 Bernie Kosar	.02	.10
122 Alonzo Highsmith	.01	.05
123 David Treadwell	.01	.05
124 Rodney Peete	.02	.10
125 Haywood Jeffires	.02	.10
126 Clarence Verdin	.01	.05
127 Christian Okoye	.01	.05
128 Greg Townsend	.01	.05
129 Tom Newberry	.01	.05
130 Keith Sims	.01	.05
131 Myron Guyton	.01	.05
132 Andre Tippett	.01	.05
133 Steve Walsh	.01	.05
134 Erik McMillan	.01	.05
135 Jim McMahon	.02	.10
136 Derek Hill	.01	.05
137 D.J. Johnson	.01	.05
138 Leslie O'Neal	.02	.10
139 Pierce Holt	.01	.05
140 Cortez Kennedy	.02	.10
141 Danny Peebles	.01	.05
142 Alvin Walton	.01	.05
143 Drew Pearson RET	.01	.05
144 Dick MacPherson CO	.01	.05
145 Erik Howard	.01	.05
146 Steve Tasker	.02	.10
147 Bill Fralic	.01	.05
148 Don Warren	.01	.05
149 Eric Thomas	.01	.05
150 Jack Pardee CO	.01	.05
151 Gary Zimmerman	.02	.10
152 Leonard Marshall	.01	.05
153 Chris Spielman	.02	.10
154 Sam Wyche CO	.01	.05
155 Rohn Stark	.01	.05
156 Stephone Paige	.01	.05
157 Lionel Washington	.01	.05
158 Henry Ellard	.02	.10
159 Dan Marino	.60	1.50
160 Lindy Infante CO	.01	.05
161 Dan McGwire RC	.01	.05
162 Ken O'Brien	.01	.05
163 Tim McDonald	.01	.05
164 Louis Lipps	.01	.05
165 Billy Joe Tolliver	.01	.05
166 Harris Barton	.01	.05
167 Tony Woods	.01	.05
168 Matt Millen	.02	.10
169 Gale Sayers RET	.07	.20
170 Ron Meyer CO	.01	.05
171 William Roberts	.01	.05
172 Thurman Thomas	.07	.20
173 Steve McMichael	.01	.05
174 Ickey Woods	.01	.05
175 Eugene Lockhart	.01	.05
176 George Seifert CO	.02	.10
177 Keith Jones	.01	.05
178 Jack Trudeau	.01	.05
179 Kevin Porter	.01	.05
180 Ronnie Lott	.02	.10
181 M. Schottenheimer CO	.01	.05
182 Morten Andersen	.01	.05
183 Anthony Thompson	.01	.05
184 Tim Worley	.01	.05
185 Billy Ray Smith	.01	.05
186 David Whitmore RC	.01	.05
187 Jacob Green	.01	.05
188 Browning Nagle RC	.01	.05
189 Franco Harris RET	.02	.10
190 Art Shell CO	.02	.10
191 Bart Oates	.01	.05
192 William Perry	.02	.10
193 Chuck Noll CO	.02	.10
194 Troy Aikman	.30	.75
195 Jeff George	.02	.10
196 Derrick Thomas	.07	.20
197 Roger Craig	.02	.10
198 John Fourcade	.01	.05
199 Rod Woodson	.07	.20
200 Anthony Miller	.02	.10
201 Jerry Rice	.30	.75
202 Eugene Robinson	.01	.05
203 Charles Mann	.01	.05
204 Mel Blount RET	.02	.10
205 Don Shula CO	.02	.10
206 Jumbo Elliott	.01	.05
207 Jay Hilgenberg	.01	.05
208 Deron Cherry	.01	.05
209 Dan Reeves CO	.02	.10
210 Roman Phifer RC	.01	.05
211 David Little	.01	.05
212 Lee Williams	.01	.05
213 John Taylor	.02	.10
214 Monte Coleman	.01	.05
215 Walter Payton RET	.20	.50
216 John Robinson CO	.01	.05
217 Pepper Johnson	.01	.05
218 Tom Thayer	.01	.05
219 Dan Saleaumua	.01	.05
220 Ernest Spears RC	.01	.05
221 Bubby Brister	.01	.05
222 Junior Seau	.07	.20
223 Brent Jones	.02	.10
224 Rufus Porter	.01	.05
225 Jack Kemp RET	.07	.20
226 Wayne Fontes CO	.01	.05
227 Phil Simms	.02	.10
228 Shaun Gayle	.01	.05
229 Bill Maas	.01	.05
230 Renaldo Turnbull	.01	.05
231 Bryan Hinkle	.01	.05
232 Gary Plummer	.01	.05
233 Jerry Burns CO	.01	.05
234 Lawrence Taylor	.02	.10
235 Joe Gibbs CO	.02	.10
236 Neil Smith	.07	.20
237 Rich Kotite CO	.01	.05
238 Jim Covert	.01	.05
239 Tim Grunhard	.01	.05
240 Joe Bugel CO	.01	.05
241 David Wyman	.01	.05
242 Maury Buford	.01	.05
243 Kevin Ross	.01	.05
244 Jimmy Johnson CO	.02	.10
245 Jim Morrissey RC	.01	.05
246 Jeff Hostetler	.02	.10
247 Andre Ware	.02	.10
248 Steve Largent RET	.07	.20
249 Chuck Knox CO	.01	.05
250 Boomer Esiason	.02	.10
251 Kevin Butler	.01	.05
252 Bruce Smith	.07	.20
253 Webster Slaughter	.02	.10
254 Mike Sherrard	.01	.05
255 Steve Broussard	.01	.05
256 Warren Moon	.07	.20
257 John Elway	.60	1.50
258 Bob Golic	.01	.05
259 Jim Everett	.02	.10
260 Bruce Coslet CO	.01	.05
261 James Francis	.01	.05
262 Eric Dorsey	.01	.05
263 Marcus Dupree	.08	.25
264 Hart Lee Dykes	.01	.05
265 Vinny Testaverde	.02	.10
266 Chip Lohmiller	.01	.05
267 John Riggins RET	.02	.10
268 Mike Schad	.01	.05
269 Kevin Greene	.02	.10
270 Dean Biasucci	.01	.05
271 Mike Pritchard RC	.02	.10
272 Ted Washington RC	.01	.05
273 Alfred Williams RC	.01	.05
274 Chris Zorich RC	.02	.10
275 Reggie Barrett	.01	.05
276 Chris Hinton	.01	.05
277 Tracy Johnson RC	.01	.05
278 Jim Harbaugh	.02	.10
279 John Roper	.01	.05
280 Mike Dumas RC	.01	.05
281 Herman Moore RC	.07	.20
282 Eric Turner RC	.02	.10
283 Steve Atwater	.01	.05
284 Michael Cofer	.01	.05
285 Darion Conner	.01	.05
286 Darryl Talley	.01	.05
287 Donnell Woolford	.01	.05
288 Keith McCants	.01	.05
289 Ray Handley CO	.01	.05
290 Ahmad Rashad RET	.02	.10
291 Eric Swann RC	.02	.10
292 Dalton Hilliard	.01	.05
293 Rickey Jackson	.02	.10
294 Vaughan Johnson	.01	.05
295 Eric Martin	.01	.05
296 Pat Swilling	.02	.10
297 Anthony Carter	.02	.10
298 Guy McIntyre	.01	.05
299 Bennie Blades	.01	.05
300 Paul Farren	.01	.05
P1 Derrick Thomas Promo	.20	.50
(The National July 1991)		
PLC1 Rashad Family	.30	.75
PLC2 Payne Stewart	.30	.75
NNO Emmitt Smith	6.00	15.00
NNO Santa Claus 1991	.30	.75

1991 Pro Line Portraits Autographs

1 Ray Agnew	6.00	15.00
2 Troy Aikman	30.00	80.00
3 Eric Allen	6.00	15.00
4 Morten Andersen	6.00	15.00
5 Flipper Anderson	6.00	15.00
6 Gary Anderson K	12.50	25.00
7 Gary Anderson RB	6.00	15.00
8 Neal Anderson	8.00	20.00
9 Ottis Anderson	8.00	20.00
10 Bruce Armstrong	8.00	20.00
11 Steve Atwater	10.00	25.00
12 Robert Awalt	5.00	12.00
13 Carl Banks	8.00	20.00
14 Reggie Barrett	5.00	12.00
15 Harris Barton	5.00	12.00
16 Martin Bayless	5.00	12.00
17 Bill Belichick CO	50.00	80.00
18 Nick Bell	5.00	12.00
19 Cornelius Bennett	8.00	20.00
20 Albert Bentley	5.00	12.00
21 Rod Bernstine	5.00	12.00
22 Dean Biasucci	5.00	12.00
23 Duane Bickett	6.00	15.00
24 Bennie Blades	5.00	12.00
25 Brian Blades	8.00	20.00
26 Mel Blount RET	10.00	25.00
27 Mark Bortz	5.00	12.00
28 Bubby Brister	6.00	15.00
29 James Brooks	6.00	15.00
30 Steve Broussard	5.00	12.00
31 Lomas Brown	5.00	12.00
32 Maury Buford	5.00	12.00
33 Joe Bugel CO	5.00	12.00
34 Jarrod Bunch	5.00	12.00
35 Jerry Burns CO	5.00	12.00
36 Kevin Butler	8.00	20.00
37 Marion Butts	6.00	15.00
38 Keith Byars	6.00	15.00
39 Earnest Byner	6.00	15.00
40 Mark Carrier DB SP	50.00	100.00
(released in 1992 Pro Line)		
41 Mark Carrier WR	6.00	15.00
42 Anthony Carter	8.00	20.00
43 Dexter Carter	5.00	12.00
44 Deron Cherry	5.00	12.00
45 Ray Childress	6.00	15.00
46 Vinnie Clark	5.00	12.00
47 Mark Clayton	8.00	20.00
48 Michael Cofer	5.00	12.00
49 Monte Coleman	6.00	15.00
50 Andre Collins	5.00	12.00
51 Shane Conlan	5.00	12.00
52 Darion Conner	5.00	12.00
53 Bruce Coslet CO	5.00	12.00
54 Jim Covert	5.00	12.00
55 Roger Craig	10.00	25.00
56 Randall Cunningham	12.50	25.00
57 Steve DeBerg	6.00	15.00
58 Eric Dickerson	15.00	40.00
59 Mike Ditka CO	15.00	30.00
60 Ray Donaldson	8.00	20.00
61 Eric Dorsey	5.00	12.00
62 Mike Dumas	5.00	12.00
63 Marcus Dupree	20.00	40.00
64 Hart Lee Dykes	5.00	12.00
65 Ferrell Edmunds	5.00	12.00
66 Henry Ellard	6.00	15.00
67 Jumbo Elliott	5.00	12.00
68 John Elway	40.00	100.00
69 Boomer Esiason	10.00	25.00
70 Jim Everett	6.00	15.00
71 Thomas Everett	5.00	12.00
72 Kevin Fagan	5.00	12.00
73 Paul Farren	5.00	12.00
74 Wayne Fontes CO	5.00	12.00
75 John Fourcade	5.00	12.00
76 Bill Fralic	5.00	12.00
77 James Francis SP	175.00	300.00
78 Irving Fryar	8.00	20.00
79 David Fulcher	5.00	12.00
80 Cleveland Gary	6.00	20.00
81 Shaun Gayle	5.00	12.00
82 Jeff George	8.00	20.00
83 Joe Gibbs CO	15.00	30.00
84 Ernest Givins	6.00	15.00
85 Jerry Glanville CO	6.00	15.00
86 Bob Golic	6.00	15.00
87 Mel Gray	6.00	15.00
88 Jacob Green	5.00	12.00
89 Kevin Greene	8.00	20.00
90 Burt Grossman	5.00	12.00
91 Tim Grunhard	5.00	12.00
92 Myron Guyton	5.00	12.00
93 Ray Handley CO	8.00	20.00
94 Jim Harbaugh	15.00	30.00
95 Franco Harris RET	25.00	50.00
96 Andy Heck	5.00	12.00
97 Dan Henning CO	5.00	12.00
98 Alonzo Highsmith SP	90.00	150.00
(released in 1992 Pro Line)		
99 Jay Hilgenberg	5.00	12.00
(issued through Impel promotion)		
100 Bruce Hill	5.00	12.00
101 Derek Hill	5.00	12.00
102 Randal Hill	6.00	15.00
103 Dalton Hilliard	6.00	15.00
104 Bryan Hinkle	5.00	12.00
105 Chris Hinton	5.00	12.00
106 Leroy Hoard	8.00	20.00
107 Merril Hoge	8.00	20.00
108 Rodney Holman SP	150.00	300.00
109 Issiac Holt	5.00	12.00
110 Pierce Holt	5.00	12.00
111 Jeff Hostetler	6.00	15.00
112 Erik Howard	5.00	12.00
113 Bobby Humphrey	5.00	12.00
(issued through Impel promotion)		
114 Lindy Infante CO	5.00	12.00
115 Michael Irvin	20.00	35.00
116 Mark Jackson	6.00	15.00
117 Rickey Jackson	25.00	50.00
118 Haywood Jeffires	6.00	15.00
119 D.J. Johnson	5.00	12.00
120 Jimmy Johnson CO	15.00	40.00
121 Pepper Johnson	6.00	15.00
(issued through Impel promotion)		
122 Tracy Johnson	5.00	12.00
123 Vaughan Johnson	5.00	12.00
124 Brent Jones	6.00	15.00
125 Henry Jones	5.00	12.00
126 Keith Jones	5.00	12.00
127A Jim Kelly Autopen	8.00	20.00
127B Jim Kelly Real	125.00	250.00
128 Jack Kemp Autopen	12.50	30.00
129 Cortez Kennedy	20.00	40.00
130 Chuck Knox CO	6.00	15.00
131 Bernie Kosar	10.00	25.00
132 Rich Kotite CO	5.00	12.00
133 Greg Kragen	6.00	15.00
134 Dave Krieg	6.00	15.00
135 Jim Lachey	6.00	15.00
136 Carnell Lake	6.00	15.00
137 Sean Landeta	5.00	12.00
138 Reggie Langhorne SP	125.00	250.00
(released in 1992 Pro Line)		
139 Steve Largent RET	12.50	30.00
140 Albert Lewis SP	40.00	80.00
141 Louis Lipps	6.00	15.00
142 David Little	8.00	20.00
143 Eugene Lockhart	5.00	12.00
144 James Lofton	8.00	20.00
145 Chip Lohmiller	5.00	12.00
146 Howie Long	20.00	40.00
147 Ronnie Lott	10.00	25.00
148 Nick Lowery	5.00	12.00
149 Dick MacPherson CO	5.00	12.00
150 Ed McCaffrey	8.00	20.00
151 Keith McCants	5.00	12.00
152 Vann McElroy	5.00	12.00
153 Tim McGee	5.00	12.00
154 Kanavis McGhee	5.00	12.00
155 Dan McGwire	5.00	12.00
156 Guy McIntyre SP	30.00	80.00
(released at Super Bowl Card Show)		
157 Jim McMahon SP	150.00	300.00
158 Steve McMichael	6.00	15.00
159 Erik McMillan	5.00	12.00
160 Bill Maas	5.00	12.00
161 Tony Mandarich	6.00	15.00
162 Charles Mann	6.00	15.00
163 Dan Marino	50.00	120.00
164 Leonard Marshall	8.00	20.00
165 Eric Martin	6.00	15.00
166 Russell Maryland	6.00	15.00
167 Tim McDonald SP		
168 Ron Meyer CO	5.00	12.00
169 Matt Millen	6.00	15.00
170 Anthony Miller	6.00	15.00
171 Chris Miller	6.00	15.00
172 Sam Mills	15.00	30.00
173 Warren Moon	15.00	30.00
174 Herman Moore	10.00	25.00
175 Rob Moore	8.00	20.00
176 Jim Mora CO	5.00	12.00
177 Jim Morrissey	5.00	12.00
178 Anthony Munoz	8.00	20.00
179 Mark Murphy	5.00	12.00
180 Browning Nagle	5.00	12.00
181 Tom Newberry	5.00	12.00
182 Brian Noble	5.00	12.00
183 Chuck Noll CO	25.00	50.00
184 Danny Noonan	5.00	12.00
185 Ken O'Brien	6.00	15.00
186 Leslie O'Neal	6.00	15.00
187 Bart Oates	5.00	12.00
188 Christian Okoye	6.00	15.00
189 Louis Oliver	5.00	12.00
190 Stephone Paige	5.00	12.00
191 Irv Pankey	5.00	12.00
192 Jack Pardee CO	5.00	12.00
193 Walter Payton RET	125.00	250.00
194 Drew Pearson RET	8.00	20.00
195 Danny Peebles	5.00	12.00
196 Rodney Peete	6.00	15.00
197 Michael Dean Perry	6.00	15.00
(issued through Impel promotion)		
198 William Perry	15.00	30.00
199 Roman Phifer	5.00	12.00
200 Bill Pickel	5.00	12.00
201 Gary Plummer	5.00	12.00
202 Kevin Porter	5.00	12.00
203 Rufus Porter	5.00	12.00
204 Mike Pritchard	5.00	12.00
205 Ricky Proehl	6.00	15.00
206 Ahmad Rashad RET SP	125.00	200.00
(released in 1992 Pro Line)		
207 Tom Rathman	8.00	20.00
208 Andre Reed	8.00	20.00
209 Dan Reeves CO	8.00	20.00
210 Johnny Rembert	5.00	12.00
211 Jerry Rice	40.00	100.00
(released at Super Bowl Card Show)		
212 Doug Riesenberg	5.00	12.00
213 John Riggins RET	20.00	50.00
214 Andre Rison Pen	6.00	15.00
(released at Super Bowl Card Show)		
215 Andre Rison Sharpie	15.00	30.00
(released at Super Bowl Card Show)		
216 William Roberts	5.00	12.00
(issued through Impel promotion)		
217 Eugene Robinson	6.00	15.00
218 John Robinson CO	6.00	15.00
219 Reggie Roby	15.00	30.00
220 John Roper	5.00	12.00
221 Timm Rosenbach	5.00	12.00
222 Kevin Ross	5.00	12.00
223 Ricky Sanders	5.00	12.00
224 Dan Saleaumua	5.00	12.00
225 Gale Sayers RET	15.00	30.00
226 Mike Schad	5.00	12.00
227 M. Schottenheimer CO	8.00	20.00
228 Jay Schroeder	5.00	12.00
229 Junior Seau	20.00	40.00
230 George Seifert CO	8.00	20.00
231 Art Shell CO	12.50	30.00
232 Mike Sherrard	5.00	12.00
233 Don Shula CO !	15.00	40.00
234 O.J. Simpson RET	75.00	150.00
(released in 1992 Pro Line)		
235 Phil Simms	12.50	30.00
(issued through Impel promotion)		
236 Keith Sims	5.00	12.00
237 Mike Singletary	40.00	80.00
(released at Super Bowl Card Show)		
238 Jackie Slater	8.00	20.00
239 Webster Slaughter	6.00	15.00
240 Al Smith	5.00	12.00
241 Billy Ray Smith	5.00	12.00
242 Bruce Smith	15.00	30.00
(issued through Impel promotion)		
243 Dennis Smith	8.00	20.00
244 J.T. Smith	5.00	12.00
245 Emmitt Smith SP	75.00	150.00
(released at Super Bowl Card Show)		
246 Neil Smith	35.00	60.00
247 Steve Smith	5.00	12.00
248 Ernest Spears	5.00	12.00
249 Chris Spielman	8.00	20.00
250 Rohn Stark	5.00	12.00
251 Roger Staubach RET	60.00	120.00
(released at Super Bowl Card Show)		
252 Eric Swann	6.00	15.00
253 Pat Swilling	6.00	15.00
254 Darryl Talley	6.00	15.00
255 Steve Tasker	8.00	20.00
256 John Taylor	8.00	20.00
257 Lawrence Taylor	12.50	30.00
258 Vinny Testaverde	6.00	15.00
259 Tom Thayer	5.00	12.00
260 Joe Theismann RET	15.00	30.00
261 Blair Thomas	5.00	12.00
262 Broderick Thomas	5.00	12.00
263 Derrick Thomas	30.00	50.00
264 Eric Thomas	5.00	12.00
265 Thurman Thomas	12.50	30.00
266 Anthony Thompson	5.00	12.00
267 Andre Tippett	5.00	12.00
268 Billy Joe Tolliver	5.00	12.00
269 Al Toon	6.00	15.00
270 Greg Townsend SP	90.00	175.00
(released in 1992 Pro Line)		
271 David Treadwell	5.00	12.00
272 Jack Trudeau	5.00	12.00
273 Renaldo Turnbull	6.00	15.00
274 Eric Turner	8.00	20.00
275 Clarence Verdin	5.00	12.00
276 Everson Walls	6.00	15.00
277 Steve Walsh	5.00	12.00
278 Alvin Walton	5.00	12.00
279 Andre Ware	8.00	20.00
280 Paul Warfield RET	8.00	20.00
281 Don Warren	8.00	20.00
282 Lionel Washington SP	75.00	150.00
283 Ted Washington	6.00	15.00
284 Andre Waters	5.00	12.00
285 Lorenzo White	5.00	12.00
286 David Whitmore	5.00	12.00
287 Alfred Williams	5.00	12.00
288 Lee Williams	5.00	12.00
289 Richard Williamson CO	5.00	12.00
290 Wade Wilson	5.00	12.00
291 Ickey Woods	6.00	15.00
292 Tony Woods	5.00	12.00
293 Rod Woodson	30.00	60.00
294 Donnell Woolford	5.00	12.00
295 Barry Word	5.00	12.00
296 Tim Worley	6.00	15.00
297 Sam Wyche CO	6.00	.15.00
298 David Wyman	5.00	12.00
299 Lonnie Young	5.00	12.00
300 Steve Young	20.00	50.00
301 Gary Zimmerman	15.00	40.00
302 Chris Zorich	6.00	15.00
PLC2 Payne Stewart	100.00	200.00
NNO Santa Claus Unnumbered	12.50	30.00
NNO Santa Claus/200	25.00	60.00

1991 Pro Line Portraits Wives

COMPLETE SET (7)	.30	.75
SC1 Jennifer Montana	.10	.30
SC2 Babette Kosar	.02	.10
SC3 Janet Elway	.02	.10
SC4 Michelle Oates	.02	.10
SC5 Toni Lipps	.02	.10
SC6 Stacey O'Brien	.02	.10
SC7 Phylicia Rashad	.05	.15

1991 Pro Line Portraits Wives Autographs

1 Janet Elway	20.00	50.00
2 Babette Kosar	6.00	15.00
3 Toni Lipps	6.00	15.00
4 Jennifer Montana	50.00	100.00
(issued through Impel promotion)		
5 Michelle Oates	6.00	15.00
6 Stacey O'Brien	6.00	15.00
7 Phylicia Rashad	350.00	600.00

1991 Pro Line Portraits National Convention

COMP.FACTORY SET (309)	150.00	300.00

*PLAYER NATIONAL CARDS: 15X TO 40X
*WIVES NATIONAL CARDS: 8X TO 20X

1991 Pro Line Punt, Pass and Kick

This 12-card standard-size set was issued to honor 1991 NFL quarterbacks in conjunction with the long-standing Punt, Pass, and Kick program. Cards 1-11 show each quarterback in various still-life poses. Card fronts also feature an embossed Punt, Pass, and Kick logo in the lower right corner and the NFL Pro Line Portraits logo at the bottom center.

COMPLETE SET (12)	40.00	100.00
PPK1 Troy Aikman	8.00	20.00
PPK2 Bubby Brister	1.60	4.00
PPK3 Randall Cunningham	2.40	6.00
PPK4 John Elway	12.00	30.00
PPK5 Boomer Esiason	1.60	4.00
PPK6 Jim Everett	1.60	4.00
PPK7 Jim Kelly	2.40	6.00
PPK8 Bernie Kosar	1.20	3.00
PPK9 Dan Marino	12.00	30.00
PPK10 Warren Moon	2.40	6.00
PPK11 Phil Simms	1.60	4.00
SC3 Punt Pass and Kick Checklist Card	1.20	3.00

1991-92 Pro Line Profiles Anthony Munoz

This nine-card standard-size set was inserted into the Super Bowl XXVI game program. The slick four-color cards depict different phases of the career of Munoz, and the Pro Line Profile logo is centered at the bottom of each perforated card.

COMPLETE SET (9)	1.60	4.00
COMMON CARD (1-9)	.20	.50

1992 Pro Line Draft Day

Each of these draft day collectible cards measures the standard size. The fronts feature full-bleed color photos, while the horizontally oriented backs have an head shot surrounded by an extended quote. Emtman is pictured sitting on a boat holding a fishing rod, with a "stringer" of NFL helmets dangling from the bow. The other card features a group picture of NFL coaches on the front, while the head shot and extended quote on the back are by Chris Berman, an ESPN commentator.

1 Steve Emtman	1.00	2.50
2 Coaches Photo	1.00	2.50

1992 Pro Line Mobil

Produced by NFL Properties, this 72-card regionally distributed standard-size set consists of 1991 Portraits (1-9) and 1992 Profiles (10-72) cards. The set was part of an eight-week promotion in Southern California. Each week a nine-card pack could be obtained by purchasing at least eight gallons of Mobil Super Unleaded Plus. The nine cards available the first week were a title card, a checklist, and seven Portrait cards which have printed on their fronts the dates that nine-card packs of that player would be available. During the following seven weeks, one player was featured per week in the packs. The cards carry full-bleed posed and action color player/family photos. The Pro Line logo is at the bottom. The backs feature player information with the Mobil logo at the bottom. Card number 9 picturing Eric Dickerson in a Raiders' uniform is exclusive to the set. The cards are numbered on the back "X of 9" and arranged below chronologically according to the eight-week promotion. The week the cards were available is listed under the first card of the nine-card subsets. Each nine-card cello pack included an unperforated sheet with four coupon offers.

COMPLETE SET (72)	3.20	8.00
1 Title Card	.02	.10
(October 3-9)		
2 Checklist	.02	.10
3 Ronnie Lott	.05	.15
4 Junior Seau	.08	.25
5 Jim Everett	.02	.10
6 Howie Long	.05	.15
7 Jerry Rice	.30	.75
8 Art Shell CO	.05	.15
9 Eric Dickerson	.05	.15
10 Ronnie Lott	.05	.15
(October 10-16)/(Making Hit)		
11 Ronnie Lott	.05	.15
(Little Leaguer)		
12 Ronnie Lott	.05	.15
(Playing for USC)		
13 Ronnie Lott	.05	.15
(Exultation)		
14 Ronnie Lott	.05	.15
(Portrait)		
15 Ronnie Lott	.05	.15
(Behind Bar)		
16 Ronnie Lott	.05	.15
(With Family)		
17 Ronnie Lott	.05	.15
(Catching Ball)		
18 Ronnie Lott	.05	.15
(Tuxedo)		
19 Junior Seau	.08	.25
(October 17-23)/(With Ball)		
20 Junior Seau	.08	.25
(Young Junior)		
21 Junior Seau	.08	.25
(Pointing)		
22 Junior Seau	.08	.25
(Over Fallen Opponent)		
23 Junior Seau	.08	.25
(Portrait)		
24 Junior Seau	.08	.25
(With Wife)		
25 Junior Seau	.08	.25
(Running in Surf)		
26 Junior Seau	.08	.25
(Weightlifting)		
27 Junior Seau	.08	.25
(Seaweed Boa)		
28 Jim Everett	.02	.10
(October 24-30)/(Looking for Receiver)		
29 Jim Everett	.02	.10
(Young Jim)		
30 Jim Everett	.02	.10
(Playing for Purdue)		
31 Jim Everett	.02	.10
(With Parents& Sister)		
32 Jim Everett	.02	.10
(Portrait)		
33 Jim Everett	.02	.10
(Eluding Rush)		
34 Jim Everett	.02	.10
(Fishing)		
35 Jim Everett	.02	.10
(Handing Off)		
36 Jim Everett	.02	.10
(Studio Photo)		
37 Howie Long	.05	.15
(October 31-November 6)/(Hand Up to Block Pass)		
38 Howie Long	.05	.15
(High School Footballer)		
39 Howie Long	.05	.15
(Closing in for Sack)		
40 Howie Long	.05	.15
(With Family)		
41 Howie Long	.05	.15
(Portrait)		
42 Howie Long	.05	.15
(Fundraising for Kids)		
43 Howie Long	.05	.15
(Hitting the Heavy Bag)		
44 Howie Long	.05	.15
(Taking Swipe at Ball)		
45 Howie Long	.05	.15
(Studio Photo)		
46 Jerry Rice	.30	.75
(November 7-13)/(With Trophy)		
47 Jerry Rice	.30	.75
(Avoiding Block)		
48 Jerry Rice	.30	.75
(Eluding Steeler)		
49 Jerry Rice	.30	.75
(With Family)		
50 Jerry Rice	.30	.75
(Portrait)		
51 Jerry Rice	.30	.75
(With Toddler)		
52 Jerry Rice	.30	.75
(Playing Tennis)		
53 Jerry Rice	.30	.75
(Scoring TD)		
54 Jerry Rice	.30	.75
(Studio Photo)		
55 Art Shell CO	.05	.15
(November 14-20)/(In Front of His Team)		
56 Art Shell CO	.05	.15
(At Maryland State)		
57 Art Shell CO	.05	.15
(Blocking Viking)		
58 Art Shell CO	.05	.15
(Playing Basketball)		
59 Art Shell CO	.05	.15
(Portrait)		
60 Art Shell CO	.05	.15
(Talking to Player)		
61 Art Shell CO	.05	.15
(In Front of TV)		
62 Art Shell CO	.05	.15
(Blocking for Raiders)		
63 Art Shell CO	.05	.15
(With Teddy Bear)		
64 Eric Dickerson	.05	.15
(November 21-30)/(Studio Suit Up)		
65 Eric Dickerson	.05	.15
(Running for SMU)		
66 Eric Dickerson	.05	.15
(With Mom)		
67 Eric Dickerson	.05	.15
(49ers in Pursuit)		

68 Eric Dickerson (Portrait)	.05	.15
69 Eric Dickerson (Running for Colts)	.05	.15
70 Eric Dickerson (On Training Ramp)	.05	.15
71 Eric Dickerson (Running Against Rams)	.05	.15
72 Eric Dickerson (Posed With Football)	.05	.15

1992 Pro Line Prototypes

This 13-card sample standard-size set was distributed by Pro Line to show the design of their 1992 Pro Line football card series. The cards were distributed as a complete set in a cello pack. The fronts feature full-bleed color photos, while the backs carry a color close-up photo, extended quote, or statistics. The set includes samples of the following Pro Line series: Profiles (28-36), Spirit (12), and Portraits (379, 386). The cards are numbered on the back, and their numbering is the same as in the regular series. These cards were also distributed by Classic at major card and trade shows. These prototypes can be distinguished from the regular issue cards in that they are vertically marked "prototype" in the lower left corner of the Profiles reverse and or "sample" next to the picture on the Portraits reverse.

COMPLETE SET (13)	3.20	8.00
12 Kathie Lee Gifford	.30	.75
28 Thurman Thomas (Bills' uniform, action shot)	.30	.75
29 Thurman Thomas (With his mother)	.30	.75
30 Thurman Thomas (OSU Cowboy uniform action shot)	.30	.75
31 Thurman Thomas (With family)	.30	.75
32 Thurman Thomas (Color portrait)	.30	.75
33 Thurman Thomas (Action shot, Super Bowl XXV)	.30	.75
34 Thurman Thomas (Fishing)	.30	.75
35 Thurman Thomas (Stretching on track)	.30	.75
36 Thurman Thomas (Close-up photo)	.30	.75
379 Jessie Tuggle	.20	.50
386 Neil O'Donnell	.30	.75
NNO Advertisement Card	.20	.50

1992 Pro Line Portraits

This 167-card standard-size set is numbered in continuation of the 1991 ProLine Portraits set. Each Pro Line Collection pack contained nine Profiles and three Portraits cards. Pro Line's goal was to have an autographed card in each box and, as a bonus, some 1991 ProLine Portrait autographed cards were included. Also autograph cards could be obtained through a mail-in offer in exchange for 12 1991 ProLine Portraits wrappers (black) and 12 1992 ProLine wrappers (white). The fronts display full-bleed color photos in non-game shots while the backs carry personal information. A special boxed set, with the cards displayed in two notebooks, was distributed at the National. The promo cards differ from the regular series in two respects: the cards are unnumbered and are stamped with a "The National, 1992" seal. The key Rookie Cards in this set are Edgar Bennett, Terrell Buckley, Dale Carter, Marco Coleman, Quentin Coryatt, Steve Emtman, Johnny Mitchell and Tommy Vardell. The 1992 ProLine Santa Claus card could be obtained through a mail-in offer in exchange for ten 1991 Pro Line Portraits wrappers (black) and ten 1992 Pro Line Collection wrappers (white). The first 10,000 to respond to the offer received Mrs. Claus card.through a mail-in offer in exchange for ten 1991 Pro Line Portraits wrappers (black) and ten 1992 Pro Line Collection wrappers (white). The first 10,000 to respond to the offer received a Mrs. Claus card.

COMPLETE SET (167)	2.50	6.00
301 Steve Emtman RC	.01	.05
302 Al Edwards	.01	.05
303 Wendell Davis	.01	.05
304 Lewis Billups	.01	.05
305 Brian Brennan	.01	.05
306 John Gesek	.01	.05
307 Terrell Buckley RC	.01	.05
308 Johnny Mitchell RC	.01	.05
309 LeRoy Butler	.01	.05
310 William Fuller	.01	.05
311 Bill Brooks	.02	.10
312 Dino Hackett	.01	.05
313 Willie Gault	.02	.10
314 Aaron Cox	.01	.05
315 Jeff Cross	.01	.05
316 Emmitt Smith	.75	2.00
317 Marv Cook	.01	.05
318 Gill Fenerty	.01	.05
319 Jeff Carlson RC	.01	.05
320 Brad Baxter	.01	.05
321 Fred Barnett	.02	.10
322 Kurt Barber RC	.01	.05
323 Eric Green	.02	.10
324 Greg Clark RC	.01	.05
325 Keith DeLong	.01	.05
326 Patrick Hunter	.01	.05
327 Troy Vincent RC	.01	.05
328 Gary Clark	.02	.10
329 Joe Montana	1.00	2.50
330 Michael Haynes	.02	.10
331 Edgar Bennett RC	.07	.20
332 Darren Lewis	.01	.05
333 Derrick Fenner	.01	.05
334 Rob Burnett	.01	.05
335 Alvin Harper	.02	.10
336 Vance Johnson	.01	.05
337 William White	.01	.05
338 Sterling Sharpe	.07	.20
339 Sean Jones	.01	.05
340 Jeff Herrod	.01	.05
341 Chris Martin	.01	.05
342 Ethan Horton	.01	.05
343 Robert Delpino	.01	.05
344 Mark Higgs	.01	.05
345 Chris Doleman	.02	.10
346 Tommy Hodson	.01	.05
347 Craig Heyward	.02	.10
348 Cary Conklin	.01	.05
349 James Hasty	.01	.05
350 Antone Davis	.01	.05
351 Ernie Jones	.01	.05
352 Greg Lloyd	.02	.10
353 John Friesz	.02	.10
354 Charles Haley	.02	.10
355 Tracy Scroggins RC	.01	.05
356 Paul Gruber	.01	.05
357 Ricky Ervins	.01	.05
358 Brad Muster	.01	.05
359 Deion Sanders	.20	.50
360 Mitch Frerotte RC	.01	.05
361 Stan Thomas	.01	.05
362 Harold Green	.02	.10
363 Eric Metcalf	.07	.20
364 Ken Norton Jr.	.02	.10
365 Dave Widell	.01	.05
366 Mike Tomczak	.01	.05
367 Bubba McDowell	.01	.05
368 Jessie Hester	.01	.05
369 Ervin Randle	.01	.05
370 Anthony Smith DT	.01	.05
371 Pat Terrell	.01	.05
372 Jim C. Jensen	.01	.05
373 Mike Merriweather	.01	.05
374 Chris Singleton	.01	.05
375 Floyd Turner	.01	.05
376 Jim Sweeney	.01	.05
377 Keith Jackson	.02	.10
378 Walter Reeves	.01	.05
379 Neil O'Donnell	.02	.10
380 Nate Lewis	.01	.05
381 Keith Henderson	.01	.05
382 Kelly Stouffer	.01	.05
383 Ricky Reynolds	.01	.05
384 Joe Jacoby	.01	.05
385 Fred Biletnikoff RET	.02	.10
386 Jessie Tuggle	.01	.05
387 Tom Waddle	.01	.05
388 David Shula CO RC	.01	.05
389 Van Waiters RC	.01	.05
390 Jay Novacek	.02	.10
391 Michael Young	.01	.05
392 Mike Holmgren CO RC	.07	.20
393 Doug Smith	.01	.05
394 Mike Prior	.01	.05
395 Harvey Williams	.02	.10
396 Aaron Wallace	.01	.05
397 Tony Zendejas	.01	.05
398 Sammie Smith	.01	.05
399 Henry Thomas	.01	.05
400 Jon Vaughn	.01	.05
401 Brian Washington	.01	.05
402 Leon Searcy RC	.01	.05
403 Lance Smith	.01	.05
404 Warren Williams	.01	.05
405 Bobby Ross CO RC	.01	.05
406 Harry Sydney	.01	.05
407 John L. Williams	.01	.05
408 Ken Willis	.01	.05
409 Brian Mitchell	.02	.10
410 Dick Butkus RET	.02	.10
411 Chuck Knox CO	.01	.05
412 Robert Porcher RC	.07	.20
413 Calvin Williams	.02	.10
414 Bill Cowher CO RC	.30	.75
415 Eric Moore	.01	.05
416 Derek Brown TE RC	.01	.05
417 Dennis Green CO RC	.02	.10
418 Tom Flores CO	.01	.05
419 Dale Carter RC	.02	.10
420 Tony Dorsett RET	.02	.10
421 Marco Coleman RC	.01	.05
422 Sam Wyche CO	.01	.05
423 Ray Crockett	.01	.05
424 Dan Fouts RET	.02	.10
425 Hugh Millen	.01	.05
426 Quentin Coryatt RC	.01	.05
427 Brian Jordan	.02	.10
428 Frank Gifford RET	.02	.10
429 Toby Caston RC	.01	.05
430 Ted Marchibroda CO	.01	.05
431 Cris Carter	.07	.20
432 Tim Krumrie	.01	.05
433 Otto Graham RET	.02	.10
434 Vaughn Dunbar RC	.01	.05
435 John Fina RC	.01	.05
436 Sonny Jurgensen RET	.02	.10
437 Robert Jones RC	.01	.05
438 Steve DeOssie	.01	.05
439 Eddie LeBaron RET	.01	.05
440 Chester McGlockton RC	.02	.10
441 Ken Stabler RET	.02	.10
442 Joe DeLamielleure RET	.02	.10
443 Charley Taylor RET	.01	.05
444 Greg Skrepenak RC	.01	.05
445 Y.A. Tittle RET	.02	.10
446 Chuck Smith RC	.01	.05
447 Kellen Winslow RET	.01	.05
448 Kevin Smith RC	.01	.05
449 Phillippi Sparks RC	.01	.05
450 Alonzo Spellman RC	.02	.10
451 Mark Rypien	.01	.05
452 Darryl Williams RC	.01	.05
453 Tommy Vardell RC	.01	.05
454 Tommy Maddox RC	.60	1.50
455 Steve Israel RC	.01	.05
456 Marquez Pope RC	.01	.05
457 Eugene Chung RC	.01	.05
458 Lynn Swann RET	.02	.10
459 Sean Gilbert RC	.02	.10
460 Chris Mims RC	.01	.05
461 Al Davis OWN	.02	.10
462 Richard Todd RET	.01	.05
463 Mike Fox	.01	.05
464 David Klingler RC	.01	.05
465 Darren Woodson RC	.07	.20
466 Jason Hanson RC	.02	.10
467 Lem Barney RET	.01	.05
NNO Santa Claus Sendaway	.40	1.00
NNO Mrs.Claus Sendaway	.40	1.00

1992 Pro Line Portraits Autographs

1 Kurt Barber	4.00	10.00
2 Fred Barnett	5.00	12.00
3 Lem Barney RET	5.00	12.00
4 Brad Baxter	4.00	10.00
5 Edgar Bennett	6.00	15.00
6 Fred Biletnikoff RET	25.00	60.00
7 Lewis Billups	4.00	10.00
8 Brian Brennan	4.00	10.00
9 Bill Brooks	5.00	12.00
10 Derek Brown TE	4.00	10.00
11 Terrell Buckley	5.00	12.00
12 Rob Burnett	4.00	10.00
13 Dick Butkus RET	15.00	30.00
14 LeRoy Butler	8.00	20.00
15 Jeff Carlson	4.00	10.00
16 Cris Carter	10.00	25.00
17 Dale Carter	5.00	12.00
18 Toby Caston	4.00	10.00
19 Eugene Chung	4.00	10.00
20 Gary Clark	5.00	12.00
21 Greg Clark	4.00	10.00
22 Marco Coleman	5.00	12.00
23 Cary Conklin	4.00	10.00
24 Marv Cook	4.00	10.00
25 Quentin Coryatt	5.00	12.00
26 Bill Cowher CO	30.00	50.00
27 Aaron Cox	4.00	10.00
28 Ray Crockett	4.00	10.00
29 Jeff Cross	4.00	10.00
30 Joe DeLamielleure RET	5.00	12.00
31 Keith DeLong	4.00	10.00
32 Steve DeOssie	4.00	10.00
33 Al Davis OWN	250.00	350.00
34 Antone Davis	4.00	10.00
35 Wendell Davis	4.00	10.00
36 Robert Delpino	4.00	10.00
37 Chris Doleman	6.00	15.00
38 Tony Dorsett RET	15.00	30.00
39 Vaughn Dunbar	4.00	10.00
40 Al Edwards	4.00	10.00
41 Steve Emtman	4.00	10.00
42 Ricky Ervins	4.00	10.00
43 Gill Fenerty	4.00	10.00
44 Derrick Fenner	4.00	10.00
45 John Fina	4.00	10.00
46 Tom Flores CO	5.00	12.00
47 Dan Fouts RET	8.00	20.00
48 Mike Fox	4.00	10.00
49 Mitch Frerotte	4.00	10.00
50 John Friesz	4.00	10.00
51 William Fuller	5.00	12.00
52 Willie Gault	6.00	15.00
53 John Gesek	4.00	10.00
54 Sean Gilbert	4.00	10.00
55 Otto Graham RET	15.00	30.00
56 Eric Green	4.00	10.00
57 Harold Green	4.00	10.00
58 Paul Gruber	4.00	10.00
59 Dino Hackett	4.00	10.00
60 Charles Haley	6.00	15.00
61 Jason Hanson	8.00	20.00
62 Alvin Harper	5.00	12.00
63 Michael Haynes	5.00	12.00
64 Keith Henderson	4.00	10.00
65 Jeff Herrod	4.00	10.00
66 Jessie Hester	4.00	10.00
67 Craig Heyward	15.00	30.00
68 Mark Higgs	4.00	10.00
69 Tommy Hodson	4.00	10.00
70 Mike Holmgren CO	15.00	30.00
71 Ethan Horton	4.00	10.00
72 Patrick Hunter	4.00	10.00
73 Steve Israel	4.00	10.00
74 Keith Jackson	5.00	12.00
75 Joe Jacoby	6.00	15.00
76 Jim C. Jensen	4.00	10.00
77 Vance Johnson	4.00	10.00
78 Ernie Jones	4.00	10.00
79 Robert Jones	4.00	10.00
80 Sean Jones	5.00	12.00
81 Brian Jordan	6.00	15.00
82 Sonny Jurgensen RET	12.00	30.00
83 David Klingler	4.00	10.00
84 Chuck Knox CO	4.00	10.00
85 Tim Krumrie	4.00	10.00
86 Eddie LeBaron RET	6.00	15.00
87 Darren Lewis	4.00	10.00
88 Nate Lewis	4.00	10.00
89 Greg Lloyd	15.00	30.00
90 Bubba McDowell	4.00	10.00
91 Chester McGlockton	5.00	12.00
92 Tommy Maddox	10.00	25.00
93 Ted Marchibroda CO	6.00	15.00
94 Chris Martin	4.00	10.00
95 Mike Merriweather	4.00	10.00
96 Eric Metcalf	5.00	12.00
97 Chris Mims	4.00	10.00
98 Hugh Millen	4.00	10.00
99 Brian Mitchell	6.00	15.00
100 Johnny Mitchell	4.00	10.00
101 Joe Montana	40.00	100.00
102 Eric Moore	4.00	10.00
103 Brad Muster	4.00	10.00
104 Ken Norton Jr.	5.00	12.00
105 Jay Novacek	8.00	20.00
106 Neil O'Donnell	6.00	15.00
107 Marquez Pope	4.00	10.00
108 Robert Porcher	5.00	12.00
109 Mike Prior	4.00	10.00
110 Ervin Randle	4.00	10.00
111 Walter Reeves	4.00	10.00
112 Ricky Reynolds	4.00	10.00
113 Bobby Ross CO	5.00	12.00
114 Mark Rypien	40.00	75.00
115 Deion Sanders	25.00	60.00
116 Tracy Scroggins	4.00	10.00
117 Leon Searcy	4.00	10.00
118 Sterling Sharpe	6.00	15.00
119 David Shula CO	4.00	10.00
120 Chris Singleton	4.00	10.00
121 Greg Skrepenak	4.00	10.00
122 Chuck Smith	4.00	10.00
123 Doug Smith	4.00	10.00
124 Emmitt Smith	50.00	100.00
125 Kevin Smith	4.00	10.00
126 Lance Smith	4.00	10.00
127 Sammie Smith	4.00	10.00
128 Phillippi Sparks	4.00	10.00
129 Alonzo Spellman	4.00	10.00
130 Ken Stabler RET	15.00	30.00
131 Kelly Stouffer	4.00	10.00
132 Lynn Swann RET	50.00	80.00
133 Jim Sweeney	4.00	10.00
134 Harry Sydney	4.00	10.00
135 Charley Taylor RET	6.00	15.00
136 Pat Terrell	4.00	10.00
137 Henry Thomas	4.00	10.00
138 Stan Thomas	4.00	10.00
139 Y.A. Tittle RET	12.50	25.00
140 Mike Tomczak	4.00	10.00
141 Jessie Tuggle	4.00	10.00
142 Floyd Turner	4.00	10.00
143 Tommy Vardell	5.00	12.00
144 Jon Vaughn	4.00	10.00
145 Troy Vincent	6.00	15.00
146 Tom Waddle	4.00	10.00
147 Van Waiters	4.00	10.00
148 Aaron Wallace	4.00	10.00
149 Brian Washington	4.00	10.00
150 William White	4.00	10.00
151 Dave Widell	4.00	10.00
152 Calvin Williams	5.00	12.00
153 Darryl Williams	4.00	10.00
154 Harvey Williams	4.00	10.00
155 John L. Williams	5.00	12.00
156 Warren Williams	4.00	10.00
157 Ken Willis	4.00	10.00
158 Kellen Winslow RET	8.00	20.00
159 Darren Woodson	8.00	20.00
160 Sam Wyche CO	5.00	12.00
161 Michael Young	4.00	10.00
162 Tony Zendejas	4.00	10.00
NNO Santa Claus	6.00	15.00
NNO Mrs. Santa	10.00	25.00
NNO Santa Mrs. Claus Dual	8.00	20.00

1992 Pro Line Portraits Collectibles

COMPLETE SET (6)	1.50	4.00
PLC3 Coaches Photo Chris Berman	.20	.50
PLC4 Joe Gibbs CO (Racing)	.20	.50
PLC5 Gifford Family Frank Gifford Kathie Lee Gifford Cody Gifford	.20	.50
PLC6 Dale Jarrett (NASCAR driver)	.40	1.00
PLC7 Paul Tagliabue COM	.20	.50
PLC8 Don Shula CO and David Shula CO	.40	1.00

1992 Pro Line Portraits Collectibles Autographs

1 Coaches Photo Chris Berman	15.00	30.00
2 Dale Jarrett (NASCAR driver)	20.00	50.00
3 Don Shula CO David Shula CO	25.00	50.00
4 Paul Tagliabue COM	15.00	30.00

1992 Pro Line Portraits QB Gold

COMPLETE SET (18)	3.00	8.00
RANDOM INSERTS IN FOIL PACKS		
ONE PER SPECIAL RETAIL PACK		
ONE SET PER HOBBY CASE		
1 Troy Aikman	.40	1.00
2 Bubby Brister	.10	.30
3 Randall Cunningham	.20	.50
4 John Elway	.75	2.00
5 Boomer Esiason	.10	.30
6 Jim Everett	.07	.20
7 Jeff George	.10	.30
8 Jim Harbaugh	.10	.30
9 Jeff Hostetler	.10	.30
10 Jim Kelly	.20	.50
11 Bernie Kosar	.07	.20
12 Dan Marino	.75	2.00
13 Chris Miller UER (Birthdate incorrectly listed as 8-91-65)	.07	.20
14 Joe Montana	.75	2.00
15 Warren Moon	.20	.50
16 Mark Rypien	.07	.20
17 Phil Simms	.10	.30
18 Steve Young	.30	.75
3AU Boomer Esiason/1992 (issued with Score Board COA)	5.00	12.00

1992 Pro Line Portraits Rookie Gold

COMPLETE SET (28)	2.50	6.00
ONE PER JUMBO PACK		
1 Tony Smith	.08	.25
2 John Fina	.08	.25
3 Alonzo Spellman	.08	.25
4 David Klinger	.15	.40
5 Tommy Vardell	.15	.40
6 Kevin Smith	.08	.25
7 Tommy Maddox	.50	1.25
8 Robert Porcher	.08	.25
9 Terrell Buckley	.15	.40
10 Eddie Robinson	.08	.25
11 Steve Emtman	.15	.40
12 Quentin Coryatt	.15	.40
13 Dale Carter	.15	.40
14 Chester McGlockton	.15	.40
15 Sean Gilbert	.15	.40
16 Troy Vincent	.08	.25
17 Robert Harris	.08	.25
18 Eugene Chung	.08	.25
19 Vaughn Dunbar	.08	.25
20 Derek Brown TE	.08	.25
21 Johnny Mitchell	.15	.40
22 Siran Stacy	.08	.25
23 Tony Sacca	.08	.25
24 Leon Searcy	.08	.25
25 Chris Mims	.08	.25
26 Dana Hall	.08	.25
27 Courtney Hawkins	.15	.40
28 Shane Collins	.08	.25

1992 Pro Line Portraits Team NFL

COMPLETE SET (5)	2.50	6.00
TNC1 Muhammad Ali	1.25	3.00
TNC2 Milton Berle	.40	1.00
TNC3 Don Mattingly	.60	1.50
TNC4 Martin Mull	.40	1.00
TNC5 Isiah Thomas	.40	1.00

1992 Pro Line Portraits Team NFL Autographs

1A Muhammad Ali (signed on the card back)	250.00	500.00
1B Cassius Clay (signed on back)	500.00	800.00
2 Milton Berle	20.00	50.00
3 Don Mattingly	20.00	50.00
4 Martin Mull	6.00	15.00
5 Isiah Thomas (Card is signed Isiah)	10.00	25.00

1992 Pro Line Portraits Wives

COMPLETE SET (16)	.40	1.00
SC8 Ortancis Carter	.02	.10
SC9 Faith Cherry	.02	.10
SC10 Kaye Cowher	.02	.10
SC11 Dainnese Gault	.02	.10
SC12 Kathie Lee Gifford	.07	.20
SC13 Carole Hinton	.02	.10
SC14 Diane Long	.02	.10
SC15 Karen Lott	.02	.10
SC16 Felicia Moon	.02	.10
SC17 Cindy Noble	.02	.10
SC18 Linda Seifert	.02	.10
SC19 Mitzi Testaverde	.02	.10
SC20 Robin Swilling	.02	.10
SC21 Lesley Visser ANN	.07	.20
SC22 Toni Doleman	.02	.10
SC23 Diana Ditka (With Mike Ditka)	.15	.40

1992 Pro Line Portraits Wives Autographs

COMPLETE SET (16)	75.00	125.00
1 Ortancis Carter	4.00	10.00
2 Faith Cherry	4.00	10.00
3 Kaye Cowher	8.00	20.00
4 Diana Ditka (With Mike Ditka)	6.00	15.00
5 Toni Doleman	4.00	10.00
6 Dainnese Gault	4.00	10.00
7 Carole Hinton	4.00	10.00
8 Diane Long	8.00	20.00
9 Karen Lott	8.00	20.00
10 Felicia Moon	4.00	10.00
11 Cindy Noble	4.00	10.00
12 Linda Seifert	4.00	10.00
13 Mitzi Testaverde	4.00	10.00
14 Robin Swilling	4.00	10.00
15 Lesley Visser ANN	5.00	12.00

1992 Pro Line Portraits National Convention

COMP.FACT.SET (194)	300.00	600.00
*PLAYER NATIONAL CARDS: 15X TO 40X		
*WIVES NATIONAL CARDS: 10X TO 25X		
*PLC NATIONAL CARDS: 6X TO 15X		
*TEAM NFL NATIONAL CARDS: 3X TO 8X		

1992 Pro Line Profiles

Together with the 1992 Pro Line Portraits, this 495-card standard-size set constitutes the bulk of the 1992 ProLine issue. This Profiles set consists of nine-card mini-biographies on 55 of the NFL's most well-known personalities. Each set chronicles the player's career from his days in college to the present day, including his life off of the football field. Each Pro Line pack contained nine Profiles and three Portraits cards, and Quarterback Gold cards were randomly inserted throughout the packs. The fronts display full-bleed color photos, and the fifth card in each subset features a color portrait by a noted sports artist. The text on the backs captures moments from the player's career or life, including quotes from the player himself. The set concludes with a ten-card Art Monk bonus set, which was available through a mail-in offer in exchange for ten 1991 ProLine Portraits wrappers (black) and ten 1992 ProLine wrappers (white). The cards in each subset are numbered "X of 9." A special boxed set, with the cards displayed in two notebooks, was distributed at the National. These cards differ from the regular series in two respects, the cards are unnumbered (except within nine-card subsets) and are stamped with a "The National, 1992" seal.

COMPLETE SET (495)	4.00	10.00
COMMON RONNIE LOTT	.02	.10
COMMON RODNEY PEETE	.01	.05
COMMON CARL BANKS	.01	.05
COMMON THURMAN THOMAS	.07	.20
COMMON ROGER STAUBACH	.07	.20
COMMON JERRY RICE	.20	.50
COMMON VINNY TESTAVERDE	.02	.10
COMMON ANTHONY CARTER	.02	.10
COMMON STERLING SHARPE	.02	.10
COMMON ANTHONY MUNOZ	.01	.05
COMMON BUDDY BRISTER	.01	.05
COMMON BERNIE KOSAR	.01	.05
COMMON ART SHELL	.02	.10
COMMON DON SHULA	.02	.10
COMMON JOE GIBBS	.02	.10
COMMON JUNIOR SEAU	.07	.20
COMMON AL TOON	.01	.05
COMMON JACK KEMP	.07	.20
COMMON JIM HARBAUGH	.02	.10
COMMON DAN MCGWIRE	.01	.05
COMMON TROY AIKMAN	.20	.50
COMMON KEITH BYARS	.01	.05
COMMON TIMM ROSENBACH	.01	.05
COMMON GARY CLARK	.02	.10
COMMON CHRIS DOLEMAN	.01	.05
COMMON JOHN ELWAY	.40	1.00
COMMON BOOMER ESIASON	.02	.10
COMMON JIM EVERETT	.02	.10
COMMON ERIC GREEN	.01	.05
COMMON JERRY GLANVILLE	.01	.05
COMMON JEFF HOSTLETER	.01	.05
COMMON HAYWOOD JEFFIRES	.02	.10
COMMON MICHAEL IRVIN	.07	.20
COMMON STEVE LARGENT	.07	.20
COMMON KEN O'BRIEN	.01	.05
COMMON CHRISTIAN OKOYE	.01	.05
COMMON MICHAEL DEAN PERRY	.02	.10
COMMON CHRIS MILLER	.01	.05
COMMON PHIL SIMMS	.07	.20
COMMON BRUCE SMITH	.02	.10
COMMON DERRICK THOMAS	.07	.20
COMMON PAT SWILLING	.01	.05
COMMON ERIC DICKERSON	.02	.10
COMMON HOWIE LONG	.02	.10
COMMON MIKE SINGLETARY	.02	.10
COMMON JOHN TAYLOR	.01	.05
COMMON ANDRE TIPPETT	.01	.05
COMMON JIM KELLY	.07	.20
COMMON MARK RYPIEN	.01	.05
COMMON WARREN MOON	.02	.10
COMMON DEION SANDERS	.07	.20
COMMON LAWRENCE TAYLOR	.07	.20
COMMON RANDALL CUNNINGHAM	.02	.10
COMMON EARNEST BYNER	.01	.05
COMMON MIKE DITKA	.02	.10
MONK SENDAWAY (496-504)	.15	.40

1992 Pro Line Profiles Autographs

TROY AIKMAN (181-189)	20.00	50.00
CARL BANKS (19-27)	3.00	8.00
BUBBY BRISTER (91-99)	3.00	8.00
KEITH BYARS (190-198)	3.00	8.00
EARNEST BYNER (478-486)	5.00	12.00
ANTHONY CARTER (64-72)	3.00	8.00
GARY CLARK (208-216)	3.00	8.00
RAND.CUNNINGHAM (469-477)	10.00	25.00
ERIC DICKERSON (379-387)	15.00	40.00
MIKE DITKA (487-495)	12.50	25.00
CHRIS DOLEMAN (217-225)	2.50	6.00
JOHN ELWAY (226-234)	40.00	80.00
BOOMER ESIASON (235-243)	6.00	15.00
JIM EVERETT (244-252)	5.00	12.00
JOE GIBBS (127-135)	20.00	40.00
JERRY GLANVILLE (262-270)	2.50	6.00
ERIC GREEN (253-261)	2.50	6.00
JIM HARBAUGH (163-171)	6.00	15.00
JEFF HOSTETLER (271-279)	3.00	8.00
MICHAEL IRVIN (289-297)	15.00	30.00
HAYWOOD JEFFIRES (280-288)	3.00	8.00
JIM KELLY (424-432)	20.00	35.00
JACK KEMP (154-162)	15.00	30.00
BERNIE KOSAR (100-108)	10.00	25.00
STEVE LARGENT (298-306)	12.50	30.00
HOWIE LONG (388-396)	15.00	40.00
RONNIE LOTT (1-9)	8.00	20.00
DAN MCGWIRE (172-180)	2.50	6.00
ART MONK (496-504)	20.00	40.00
WARREN MOON (442-450)	10.00	25.00
ANTHONY MUNOZ (82-90)	5.00	12.00
KEN O'BRIEN (307-315)	2.50	6.00
CHRISTIAN OKOYE (316-324)	6.00	15.00
RODNEY PEETE (10-18)	2.50	6.00
MICHAEL D. PERRY (325-333)	2.50	6.00
JERRY RICE (46-54)	40.00	100.00
TIMM ROSENBACH (199-207)	3.00	8.00
DEION SANDERS (451-459)	20.00	40.00
JUNIOR SEAU (136-144)	20.00	50.00
STERLING SHARPE (73-81)	10.00	25.00
ART SHELL (109-117)	10.00	25.00
DON SHULA (118-126)	12.50	30.00
PHIL SIMMS (343-351)	8.00	20.00
MIKE SINGLETARY (397-405)	6.00	15.00
BRUCE SMITH (352-360)	15.00	40.00
ROGER STAUBACH (37-45)	20.00	50.00
PAT SWILLING (370-378)	3.00	8.00
JOHN TAYLOR (406-414)	5.00	12.00
LAWRENCE TAYLOR (460-468)	15.00	30.00
VINNY TESTAVERDE (55-63)	5.00	12.00
DERRICK THOMAS (361-369)	30.00	50.00
THURMAN THOMAS (28-36)	8.00	20.00
ANDRE TIPPETT (415-423)	6.00	15.00
AL TOON (145-153)	3.00	8.00
46 Jerry Rice SP	75.00	135.00
47 Jerry Rice SP	75.00	135.00
48 Jerry Rice SP	75.00	135.00
49 Jerry Rice SP	75.00	135.00
102 Bernie Kosar SP	25.00	50.00
111 Art Shell CO SP	25.00	50.00
426 Jim Kelly SP	75.00	135.00

1992 Pro Line Profiles National Convention

COMPLETE SET (495)	150.00	300.00
*NATIONAL CARDS: 15X TO 40X		

1992-93 Pro Line SB Program

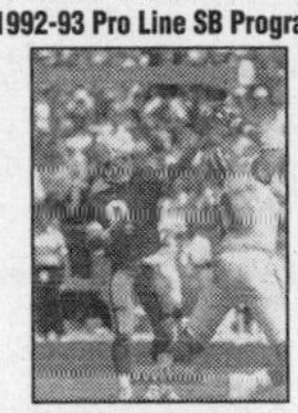

This nine-card standard-size set features Steve Young. One Steve Young promo card was inserted in each copy of the 1993 Super Bowl program. The fronts display full-bleed glossy color photos that capture Young both on and off the field. In text printed around a small color picture, the backs discuss chapters in Young's career and life and carry Young's comments as well. The cards are numbered on the back "X of 9."

COMPLETE SET (9)	3.20	8.00
COMMON CARD (1-9)	.40	1.00

1993 Pro Line Live Draft Day NYC

Packaged in a cello pack, this set of ten standard-size cards was passed out at the NFL Draft held April 25th in New York. The cards were created in anticipation of the draft, thus portraying the featured players with several possible teams, and to preview the 1993 Classic NFL Pro Line card design. The full-bleed color player photos on the fronts are accented on the right by a team color-coded stripe that carries the player's name and team name. The "Classic ProLine Live" and "NFL Draft 1993" logos at the lower corners round out the card face. Above a team color-coded panel presenting biography, statistics, and career highlights, the backs display a full-bleed color close-up photo. All the cards are numbered "1" on the back and are checklisted below alphabetically according to player's last name. Suffixes have been added in order to differentiate specific cards. Reportedly about 1,000 sets were distributed at the NFL Draft in New York City.

COMPLETE SET (10)	12.00	30.00
COMMON DREW BLEDSOE	3.00	8.00
COMMON ERIC CURRY	.40	1.00
COMMON MARVIN JONES	.40	1.00
COMMON RICK MIRER	.75	2.00

1993 Pro Line Live Draft Day QVC

Packaged in a cello pack, this set of ten standard-size cards has the same fronts as the set passed out at the NFL Draft held April 25th in New York. The cards were created in anticipation of the draft, thus portraying the featured players with several possible teams, and to preview the 1993 Classic NFL Pro Line card design. The full-bleed color player photos on the fronts are accented on the right by a team color-coded stripe that carries the player's name and team name. The "Classic ProLine Live" and "NFL Draft 1993" logos at the lower corners round out the card face. On a white, screened back with "1993 Draft Day" in gray lettering, the QVC-version's back has an oversized version of the Classic ProLine Live logo with black lettering immediately below. Reportedly only 9,300 sets with this special back were produced for sale through QVC.

COMPLETE SET (10)	6.00	15.00
COMMON DREW BLEDSOE	2.00	5.00
COMMON ERIC CURRY	.20	.50
COMMON MARVIN JONES	.20	.50
COMMON RICK MIRER	.40	1.00

1993 Pro Line Previews

Featuring the last five number one NFL Draft Picks, these five standard-size cards were randomly inserted in 1993 Classic Football Draft Pick foil packs. Twelve Thousand of each card were produced. The fronts from the Classic Pro Line Live, Profiles and Portraits sets appear in this preview of Pro Line's main sets. The backs, however, are more or less the same, featuring the set logo, year and player who was selected the number one draft pick, all printed on a gray background of diagonal Team NFL logos. The NFL and Classic logos appear in the bottom corners. The production number is shown at the bottom.

COMPLETE SET (5)	25.00	35.00
PL1 Troy Aikman Live	10.00	12.00
PL2 Jeff George Profile	3.00	6.00
PL3 Russell Maryland Live	2.00	3.00
PL4 Steve Emtman	2.00	3.00
PL5 Drew Bledsoe Portrait	10.00	15.00

1993 Pro Line Live

The 1993 edition of Pro Line consists of 285 Pro Line Live cards, 48 Portraits and thirteen nine-card (117) Profiles. All three sets were distributed by Classic through 12 and 23-card packs. The fronts feature full-bleed color action photos that are bordered on the right by a team color-coded stripe that carries the player's name and team name. The top portion of the back has a second color action photo, while the bottom portion consists of a team color-coded panel overprinted with player information. A collector could also have ordered a 100-card uncut sheet - featuring better players - from Classic for $39.95 plus shipping and handling. The cards are numbered on the back and checklisted below alphabetically according to teams. Rookie Cards include Jerome Bettis, Drew Bledsoe, Reggie Brooks, Curtis Conway, Garrison Hearst, Billy Joe Hobert, Terry Kirby, O.J. McDuffie, Natrone Means, Glyn Milburn, Rick Mirer, Robert Smith and Kevin Williams. Troy Aikman promo cards were produced and are listed below.

COMPLETE SET (285)	7.00	15.00
1 Michael Haynes	.02	.10
2 Chris Hinton	.01	.05
3 Pierce Holt	.01	.05
4 Chris Miller	.02	.10
5 Mike Pritchard	.02	.10
6 Andre Rison	.02	.10
7 Deion Sanders	.20	.50
8 Jessie Tuggle	.01	.05
9 Lincoln Kennedy RC	.01	.05
10 Roger Harper RC	.01	.05
11 Cornelius Bennett	.02	.10
12 Henry Jones	.01	.05
13 Jim Kelly	.08	.25
14 Bill Brooks	.01	.05
15 Nate Odomes	.01	.05
16 Andre Reed	.02	.10
17 Frank Reich	.02	.10
18 Bruce Smith	.08	.25
19 Steve Tasker	.02	.10
20 Thurman Thomas	.08	.25
21 Thomas Smith RC	.02	.10
22 John Parrella RC	.01	.05
23 Neal Anderson	.01	.05
24 Mark Carrier DB	.01	.05
25 Jim Harbaugh	.08	.25
26 Darren Lewis	.01	.05
27 Steve McMichael	.02	.10
28 Alonzo Spellman	.01	.05
29 Tom Waddle	.01	.05
30 Curtis Conway RC	.15	.40
31 Carl Simpson RC	.01	.05
32 David Fulcher	.01	.05
33 Harold Green	.01	.05
34 David Klingler	.01	.05
35 Tim Krumrie	.01	.05
36 Carl Pickens	.02	.10
37 Alfred Williams	.01	.05
38 Darryl Williams	.01	.05
39 John Copeland RC	.02	.10
40 Tony McGee RC	.02	.10
41 Bernie Kosar	.02	.10
42 Kevin Mack	.01	.05
43 Clay Matthews	.02	.10
44 Eric Metcalf	.02	.10
45 Michael Dean Perry	.02	.10
46 Vinny Testaverde	.02	.10
47 Jerry Ball	.01	.05
48 Tommy Vardell	.01	.05
49 Steve Everitt RC	.01	.05
50 Dan Footman RC	.01	.05
51 Troy Aikman	.30	.75
52 Daryl Johnston	.08	.25
53 Tony Casillas	.01	.05
54 Charles Haley	.02	.10
55 Alvin Harper	.02	.10
56 Michael Irvin	.08	.25
57 Robert Jones	.01	.05
58 Russell Maryland	.01	.05
59 Nate Newton	.02	.10
60 Ken Norton Jr.	.02	.10
61 Jay Novacek	.02	.10
62 Emmitt Smith	.60	1.50
63 Kevin Smith	.02	.10
64 Kevin Williams RC	.01	.05
65 Darrin Smith RC	.02	.10
66 Steve Atwater	.01	.05
67 Rod Bernstine	.01	.05
68 Mike Croel	.01	.05
69 John Elway	.60	1.50
70 Tommy Maddox	.08	.25
71 Karl Mecklenburg	.01	.05
72 Shannon Sharpe	.08	.25
73 Dennis Smith	.01	.05
74 Dan Williams RC	.01	.05
75 Glyn Milburn RC	.08	.25
76 Pat Swilling	.01	.05
77 Bennie Blades	.01	.05
78 Herman Moore	.08	.25
79 Rodney Peete	.01	.05
80 Brett Perriman	.08	.25
81 Barry Sanders	.50	1.25
82 Chris Spielman	.02	.10
83 Andre Ware	.01	.05
84 Ryan McNeil RC	.08	.25
85 Antonio London RC	.01	.05
86 Tony Bennett	.01	.05
87 Terrell Buckley	.01	.05
88 Brett Favre	.75	2.00

89 Brian Noble	.01	.05
90 Ken O'Brien	.01	.05
91 Sterling Sharpe	.08	.25
92 Reggie White	.08	.25
93 John Stephens	.01	.05
94 Wayne Simmons RC	.01	.05
95 George Teague RC	.02	.10
96 Ray Childress	.01	.05
97 Curtis Duncan	.01	.05
98 Ernest Givins	.02	.10
99 Haywood Jeffires	.02	.10
100 Bubba McDowell	.01	.05
101 Warren Moon	.08	.25
102 Al Smith	.01	.05
103 Lorenzo White	.01	.05
104 Brad Hopkins RC	.01	.05
105 Micheal Barrow RC UER (Name misspelled Michael)	.08	.25
106 Duane Bickett	.01	.05
107 Quentin Coryatt	.02	.10
108 Steve Emtman	.01	.05
109 Jeff George	.08	.25
110 Anthony Johnson	.02	.10
111 Reggie Langhorne	.01	.05
112 Jack Trudeau	.01	.05
113 Clarence Verdin	.01	.05
114 Jessie Hester	.01	.05
115 Roosevelt Potts RC	.01	.05
116 Dale Carter	.01	.05
117 Dave Krieg	.02	.10
118 Nick Lowery	.01	.05
119 Christian Okoye	.01	.05
120 Neil Smith	.08	.25
121 Derrick Thomas	.08	.25
122 Harvey Williams	.02	.10
123 Barry Word	.01	.05
124 Joe Montana	.60	1.50
125 Marcus Allen	.08	.25
126 James Lofton	.02	.10
127 Nick Bell	.01	.05
128 Tim Brown	.08	.25
129 Eric Dickerson	.02	.10
130 Jeff Hostetler	.02	.10
131 Howie Long	.08	.25
132 Todd Marinovich	.01	.05
133 Greg Townsend	.01	.05
134 Patrick Bates RC	.01	.05
135 Billy Joe Hobert RC	.08	.25
136 Flipper Anderson	.01	.05
137 Shane Conlan	.01	.05
138 Henry Ellard	.02	.10
139 Jim Everett	.02	.10
140 Cleveland Gary	.01	.05
141 Sean Gilbert	.02	.10
142 Todd Lyght	.01	.05
143 Jerome Bettis RC	1.50	4.00
144 Troy Drayton RC	.02	.10
145 Louis Oliver	.01	.05
146 Marco Coleman	.01	.05
147 Bryan Cox	.01	.05
148 Mark Duper	.01	.05
149 Irving Fryar	.02	.10
150 Mark Higgs	.01	.05
151 Keith Jackson	.02	.10
152 Dan Marino	.60	1.50
153 Troy Vincent	.01	.05
154 Richmond Webb	.01	.05
155 O.J. McDuffie RC	.08	.25
156 Terry Kirby RC	.08	.25
157 Terry Allen	.08	.25
158 Anthony Carter	.02	.10
159 Cris Carter	.08	.25
160 Chris Doleman	.01	.05
161 Randall McDaniel	.02	.10
162 Audray McMillian	.01	.05
163 Henry Thomas	.01	.05
164 Gary Zimmerman	.01	.05
165 Robert Smith RC	.50	1.25
166 Qadry Ismail RC	.08	.25
167 Vincent Brown	.01	.05
168 Marv Cook	.01	.05
169 Greg McMurtry	.01	.05
170 Jon Vaughn	.01	.05
171 Leonard Russell	.02	.10
172 Andre Tippett	.01	.05
173 Scott Zolak	.01	.05
174 Drew Bledsoe RC	1.00	2.50
175 Chris Slade RC	.02	.10
176 Morten Andersen	.01	.05
177 Vaughn Dunbar	.01	.05
178 Rickey Jackson	.01	.05
179 Vaughan Johnson	.01	.05
180 Eric Martin	.01	.05
181 Sam Mills	.01	.05
182 Brad Muster	.01	.05
183 Willie Roaf RC	.02	.10
184 Irv Smith RC UER (Birthdate is 7/31/61; should be 9/13/71)	.01	.05
185 Reggie Freeman RC	.01	.05
186 Michael Brooks	.01	.05
187 Dave Brown RC	.08	.25
188 Rodney Hampton	.02	.10
189 Pepper Johnson	.01	.05
190 Ed McCaffrey	.08	.25
191 Dave Meggett	.01	.05
192 Bart Oates	.01	.05
193 Phil Simms	.02	.10
194 Lawrence Taylor	.08	.25
195 Michael Strahan RC	.60	1.50
196 Brad Baxter	.01	.05
197 Johnny Johnson	.01	.05
198 Boomer Esiason	.02	.10
199 Ronnie Lott	.02	.10
200 Johnny Mitchell	.01	.05
201 Rob Moore	.02	.10
202 Browning Nagle	.01	.05
203 Blair Thomas	.01	.05
204 Marvin Jones RC	.01	.05
205 Coleman Rudolph RC	.01	.05
206 Eric Allen	.01	.05
207 Fred Barnett	.02	.10
208 Tim Harris	.01	.05
209 Randall Cunningham	.08	.25
210 Seth Joyner	.01	.05
211 Clyde Simmons	.01	.05
212 Herschel Walker	.02	.10
213 Calvin Williams	.02	.10
214 Lester Holmes RC	.01	.05
215 Leonard Renfro RC	.01	.05
216 Chris Chandler	.02	.10
217 Gary Clark	.02	.10
218 Ken Harvey	.01	.05
219 Randal Hill	.01	.05
220 Steve Beuerlein	.02	.10
221 Ricky Proehl	.01	.05
222 Timm Rosenbach	.01	.05
223 Garrison Hearst RC	.30	.75
224 Ernest Dye RC	.01	.05
225 Bubby Brister	.01	.05
226 Dermontti Dawson	.01	.05
227 Barry Foster	.02	.10
228 Kevin Greene	.02	.10
229 Merril Hoge	.01	.05
230 Greg Lloyd	.02	.10
231 Neil O'Donnell	.08	.25
232 Rod Woodson	.08	.25
233 Deon Figures RC	.01	.05
234 Chad Brown RC	.02	.10
235 Marion Butts	.01	.05
236 Gill Byrd	.01	.05
237 Ronnie Harmon	.01	.05
238 Stan Humphries	.02	.10
239 Anthony Miller	.02	.10
240 Leslie O'Neal	.02	.10
241 Stanley Richard	.01	.05
242 Junior Seau	.08	.25
243 Darrien Gordon RC	.01	.05
244 Natrone Means RC	.08	.25
245 Dana Hall	.01	.05
246 Brent Jones	.02	.10
247 Tim McDonald	.01	.05
248 Steve Bono	.02	.10
249 Jerry Rice	.40	1.00
250 John Taylor	.02	.10
251 Ricky Watters	.08	.25
252 Steve Young	.30	.75
253 Dana Stubblefield RC	.08	.25
254 Todd Kelly RC	.01	.05
255 Brian Blades	.02	.10
256 Ferrell Edmunds	.01	.05
257 Stan Gelbaugh	.01	.05
258 Cortez Kennedy	.02	.10
259 Dan McGwire	.01	.05
260 Chris Warren	.02	.10
261 John L. Williams	.01	.05
262 David Wyman	.01	.05
263 Rick Mirer RC	.08	.25
264 Carlton Gray RC	.01	.05
265 Marty Carter	.01	.05
266 Reggie Cobb	.01	.05
267 Lawrence Dawsey	.01	.05
268 Santana Dotson	.02	.10
269 Craig Erickson	.02	.10
270 Paul Gruber	.01	.05
271 Keith McCants	.01	.05
272 Broderick Thomas	.01	.05
273 Eric Curry RC	.01	.05
274 Demetrius DuBose RC	.01	.05
275 Earnest Byner UER (name misspelled Ernest)	.01	.05
276 Ricky Ervins	.01	.05
277 Brad Edwards	.01	.05
278 Jim Lachey	.01	.05
279 Charles Mann	.01	.05
280 Carl Banks	.01	.05
281 Art Monk	.02	.10
282 Mark Rypien	.01	.05
283 Ricky Sanders	.01	.05
284 Tom Carter RC	.02	.10
285 Reggie Brooks RC	.02	.10
P1 Troy Aikman Promo Numbered 51	.50	1.25
P2 Troy Aikman Promo Tri-Star Prod. Back	.40	1.00

1993 Pro Line Live Autographs

STATED PRINT RUN 400-1200		
1 Troy Aikman/700	25.00	50.00
2 Neal Anderson/1050	6.00	15.00
3 Rod Bernstine/1000	5.00	12.00
4 Terrell Buckley/1050	5.00	12.00
5 Earnest Byner/750 UER (name misspelled Ernest)	6.00	15.00
6 Anthony Carter/950	6.00	15.00
7 Ray Childress/950	6.00	15.00
8 Gary Clark/1050	6.00	15.00
9 Marco Coleman/1000	5.00	12.00
10 Quentin Coryatt/900	6.00	15.00
11 Eric Dickerson/900	12.50	30.00
12 Chris Doleman/1000	5.00	12.00
13 Steve Emtman/800	6.00	15.00
14 Brett Favre/650	75.00	150.00
15 Barry Foster/750	6.00	15.00
16 Jeff George/1050	6.00	15.00
17 Rodney Hampton/650	6.00	15.00
18 Keith Jackson/650	8.00	20.00
19 Haywood Jeffires/950	6.00	15.00
20 David Klingler/1200	5.00	12.00
21 Howie Long/950	20.00	40.00
22 Ronnie Lott/1050	10.00	25.00
23 Tommy Maddox/1050	6.00	15.00
24 Art Monk/750	15.00	30.00
25 Joe Montana/600	40.00	100.00
26 Rob Moore/900	6.00	15.00
27 Neil O'Donnell/1050	6.00	15.00
28 Christian Okoye/900	6.00	15.00
29 Rodney Peete/1000	6.00	15.00
30 Andre Reed/1050	8.00	20.00
31 Deion Sanders/900	20.00	40.00
32 Junior Seau/900	30.00	60.00
33 Sterling Sharpe/1050	8.00	20.00
34 Emmitt Smith/700	75.00	150.00
35 Neil Smith/1050	8.00	20.00
36 Pat Swilling/950	12.00	30.00
37 Vinny Testaverde/900	6.00	15.00
38 Derrick Thomas/550	50.00	100.00
39 Herschel Walker/400	8.00	20.00

1993 Pro Line Live Future Stars

COMPLETE SET (28)	5.00	12.00
ONE PER JUMBO PACK		
1 Patrick Bates	.05	.15
2 Jerome Bettis	4.00	10.00
3 Drew Bledsoe	2.50	6.00
4 Tom Carter	.08	.25
5 Curtis Conway	.40	1.00
6 Steve Everitt	.05	.15
7 Deon Figures	.05	.15
8 Darrien Gordon	.05	.15
9 Lester Holmes	.05	.15
10 Brad Hopkins	.05	.15
11 Marvin Jones	.05	.15
12 Lincoln Kennedy	.05	.15
13 O.J. McDuffie	.25	.60
14 Rick Mirer	.25	.60
15 Willie Roaf	.08	.25
16 Will Shields	.05	.15
17 Wayne Simmons	.05	.15
18 Robert Smith	1.25	3.00
19 Thomas Smith	.08	.25
20 Michael Strahan	1.50	4.00
21 Dana Stubblefield	.25	.60
22 Dan Williams	.05	.15
23 Kevin Williams WR	.05	.15
24 Garrison Hearst	.75	2.00
25 John Copeland	.08	.25
26 Ryan McNeil	.25	.60
27 Eric Curry	.05	.15
28 Roosevelt Potts	.05	.15

1993 Pro Line Live Illustrated

COMPLETE SET (6)	6.00	15.00
SP1 Troy Aikman	2.00	5.00
SP2 Jerry Rice	2.50	6.00
SP3 Michael Irvin	.60	1.50
SP4 Thurman Thomas	.60	1.50
SP5 Lawrence Taylor	.60	1.50
SP6 Deion Sanders	1.25	3.00

1993 Pro Line Live LPs

COMPLETE SET (20)	6.00	15.00
LP1 Chris Webber (Dunking football)	.75	2.00
LP2 Shaquille O'Neal (Wearing street clothes)	1.50	4.00
LP3 Jamal Mashburn (Wearing ProLine apparel)	.10	.30
LP4 Marcus Allen	.30	.75
LP5 Neal Anderson	.05	.15
LP6 Reggie Cobb	.05	.15
LP7 Rod Bernstine	.05	.15
LP8 Barry Word	.05	.15
LP9 Troy Aikman	1.00	2.50
LP10 Brett Favre	2.50	6.00
LP11 Ricky Watters	.30	.75
LP12 Terry Allen	.30	.75
LP13 Rodney Hampton	.10	.30
LP14 Garrison Hearst	1.00	2.50
LP15 Jerome Bettis	5.00	12.00
LP16 Barry Foster	.10	.30
LP17 Harold Green	.05	.15
LP18 Tommy Vardell	.05	.15
LP19 Lorenzo White	.05	.15
LP20 Marion Butts	.05	.15

1993 Pro Line Live Tonx

COMPLETE SET (6)	1.60	4.00
1 Troy Aikman	.60	1.50
2 Michael Irvin	.15	.40
3 Jerry Rice	.60	1.50
4 Deion Sanders	.25	.60
5 Lawrence Taylor	.08	.25
6 Thurman Thomas	.15	.40

1993 Pro Line Portraits

As part of the 1993 Classic Pro Line issue, this 44-card standard-size set features full-bleed non-game photos on the front. The bottom center of the back has a color head shot, and a player quote on a silver panel wraps around the picture. The set closes with a Throwbacks (507-511) subset. The cards are numbered on the back in continuation of the 1992 Pro Line Portraits set. This set was the last of the Portraits series ('91-'93). Rookie Cards include Jerome Bettis, Drew Bledsoe, Garrison Hearst and Rick Mirer.

COMPLETE SET (44)	2.50	6.00
468 Willie Roaf RC	.02	.10
469 Terry Allen	.07	.20
470 Jerry Ball	.01	.05
471 Patrick Bates RC	.01	.05
472 Ray Bentley	.01	.05
473 Jerome Bettis RC	1.50	4.00
474 Steve Beuerlein	.02	.10
475 Drew Bledsoe RC	1.00	2.50
476 Dave Brown RC	.07	.20
477 Gill Byrd	.01	.05
478 Tony Casillas	.01	.05
479 Chuck Cecil	.01	.05
480 Reggie Cobb	.01	.05
481 Pat Harlow	.01	.05
482 John Copeland RC	.02	.10
483 Bryan Cox	.01	.05
484 Eric Curry RC	.01	.05
485 Jeff Lageman	.01	.05
486 Brett Favre UER	.75	2.00
487 Barry Foster	.02	.10
488 Gaston Green	.01	.05
489 Rodney Hampton	.02	.10
490 Tim Harris	.01	.05
491 Garrison Hearst RC	.30	.75
492 Tony Smith	.01	.05
493 Marvin Jones RC	.01	.05
494 Lincoln Kennedy RC	.01	.05
495 Wilber Marshall	.01	.05
496 Terry McDaniel	.01	.05
497 Rick Mirer RC	.07	.20
498 Art Monk	.02	.10
499 Mike Munchak	.02	.10
500 Frank Reich	.02	.10
501 Barry Sanders	.60	1.50
502 Shannon Sharpe	.07	.20
503 Gino Torretta RC	.01	.05
504 Ricky Watters	.07	.20
505 Richmond Webb	.01	.05
506 Reggie White	.07	.20
507 Bert Jones TB	.01	.05
508 Billy Kilmer TB	.01	.05
509 John Mackey TB	.01	.05
510 Archie Manning TB	.02	.10
511 Harvey Martin TB	.01	.05

1993 Pro Line Portraits Autographs

COMPLETE SET (27)	400.00	750.00
1 Patrick Bates	7.50	20.00
2 Jerome Bettis	60.00	120.00
3 Steve Beuerlein	10.00	25.00
4 Drew Bledsoe	50.00	80.00
5 Tony Casillas	7.50	20.00
6 Chuck Cecil	7.50	20.00
7 Reggie Cobb	7.50	20.00
8 John Copeland	7.50	20.00
9 Eric Curry	7.50	20.00
10 Brett Favre	175.00	300.00
11 Gaston Green	7.50	20.00
12 Rodney Hampton	10.00	25.00
13 Pat Harlow	7.50	20.00
14 Bert Jones TB	10.00	25.00
15 Marvin Jones	7.50	20.00
16 Lincoln Kennedy	7.50	20.00
17 Billy Kilmer TB	10.00	25.00
18 Jeff Lageman	7.50	20.00
19 Archie Manning TB	12.50	30.00
20 Harvey Martin TB	25.00	50.00
21 Terry McDaniel	7.50	20.00
22 Mike Munchak	20.00	40.00
23 Frank Reich	7.50	20.00
24 Willie Roaf	7.50	20.00
25 Shannon Sharpe	25.00	50.00
26 Tony Smith	7.50	20.00
27 Gino Torretta	12.50	30.00

1993 Pro Line Portraits Wives

COMPLETE SET (4)	.20	.50
SC25 Annette Rypien	.05	.15
SC26 Ann Stark	.05	.15
SC27 Cindy Walker	.05	.15
SC28 Cindy Reed	.05	.15

1993 Pro Line Portraits Wives Autographs

COMPLETE SET (3)	20.00	50.00
1 Cindy Reed	7.50	20.00
2 Annette Rypien	6.00	15.00
3 Ann Stark	7.50	20.00

1993 Pro Line Profiles

As part of the 1993 Classic Pro Line issue, this 117-card standard-size set features thirteen nine-card subsets devoted to outstanding NFL players. The fronts display full-bleed color action player photos. The lettering and the stripe carrying the player's name are team color-coded. The backs have a second color action shot, career highlights in the form of an expanded caption, and a player quote. The cards are individually numbered on the back as an extension of the 1992 Profiles issue. Each subset ("X of 9") is also numbered.

COMPLETE SET (117)	2.50	6.00
COMMON RAY CHILDRESS	.01	.04
COMMON JEFF GEORGE	.01	.04
COMMON FRANCO HARRIS	.02	.08
COMMON KEITH JACKSON	.01	.04
COMMON JIMMY JOHNSON	.03	.15
COMMON JAMES LOFTON	.02	.08
COMMON DAN MARINO	.25	.60
COMMON JOE MONTANA	.30	.75
COMMON JAY NOVACEK	.01	.04
COMMON GALE SAYERS	.02	.08
COMMON EMMITT SMITH	.25	.60
COMMON HERSCHEL WALKER	.02	.08
COMMON STEVE YOUNG	.10	.30

1993 Pro Line Profiles Autographs

RAY CHILDRESS (496-504)	4.00	10.00
JEFF GEORGE (505-513)	6.00	15.00
FRANCO HARRIS (514-521)	12.50	30.00
KEITH JACKSON (523-531)	4.00	10.00
J.JOHNSON (533/535/538-540)	8.00	20.00
J.JOHNSON (532/534/536/537)	25.00	50.00
JAY NOVACEK (568-576)	10.00	25.00
GALE SAYERS (577-585)	15.00	40.00
EMMITT SMITH (586-594)	60.00	150.00

1994 Pro Line Live Draft Day NYC

This 13-card standard-size set previews the 1994 NFL Draft by portraying the featured players with several possible teams (with the exception of Troy Aikman) and were distributed in part at the NFL Draft in New York. The fronts feature full-bleed color action player photos. At the bottom the player's name is printed in team color-coded letters, which in turn are underscored by a team color-coded stripe. The backs have a full-bleed ghosted photo except for a square at the player's head. The set name, draft date (April 24, 1994), and production figures (1 of 19,940) are stenciled over the ghosted photo. Note that the cards follow the 1994 Pro Line Live card design, but contain the Classic logo on the cardfronts not the Pro Line Live logo.

COMPLETE SET (13)	10.00	25.00
FD1 Dan Wilkinson Bengals	.40	1.00
FD2 Dan Wilkinson Patriots	.40	1.00
FD3 Marshall Faulk Bengals	2.40	6.00
FD4 Marshall Faulk Colts	2.40	6.00
FD5 Marshall Faulk Buccaneers	2.40	6.00
FD6 Troy Aikman/1989 First Pick	1.60	4.00
FD7 Trent Dilfer Redskins	1.00	2.50
FD8 Trent Dilfer Colts	1.00	2.50
FD9 Heath Shuler Redskins	.50	1.25
FD10 Heath Shuler Colts	.50	1.25
FD11 Aaron Glenn Buccaneers	.40	1.00
FD12 Aaron Glenn Rams	.40	1.00
FD13 Dan Wilkinson Cardinals	.40	1.00

1994 Pro Line Live Previews

Randomly inserted in 1994 Classic NFL Draft Picks packs, the five standard-size cards comprising this set feature borderless color player action shots on their fronts. The player's name in upper case lettering, along with his team's name in a colored stripe, appears at the bottom. The back carries a color player action shot with colored borders above and on one side. The player's name and position appear in the margin above the photo; career highlights and a brief biography appear in the margin alongside. Player statistics appear within a ghosted band near the bottom of the photo. A message in black lettering states that production was limited to 12,000 of each card. The cards are numbered on the back with a "PL" prefix.

COMPLETE SET (5)	25.00	50.00
PL1 Troy Aikman	6.00	12.00
PL2 Jerry Rice	6.00	12.00
PL3 Steve Young	5.00	10.00
PL4 Rick Mirer	4.00	8.00
PL5 Drew Bledsoe	4.00	10.00

1994 Pro Line Live

Produced by Classic, these 405 standard-size cards were issued in 10 and 16-card packs. Cards feature borderless fronts and color action shots. The player's name appears in uppercase lettering at the bottom along with his team name within a team color-coded stripe. The backs carry another color player action shot with statistics appearing within a ghosted stripe near the bottom of the photo. Career highlights and biography appear within a team color-coded band down the left side. Rookie Cards include Derrick Alexander, Isaac Bruce, Lake Dawson, Marshall Faulk, William Floyd, Greg Hill, Charles Johnson, Bam Morris, Errict Rhett, Darnay Scott and Heath Shuler.

COMPLETE SET (405)	7.50	20.00
1 Emmitt Smith	.50	1.25
2 Andre Rison	.02	.10
3 Deion Sanders	.15	.40
4 Jeff George	.08	.25
5 Cornelius Bennett	.02	.10
6 Jim Kelly	.08	.25
7 Andre Reed	.02	.10
8 Bruce Smith	.08	.25
9 Thurman Thomas	.08	.25
10 Mark Carrier DB	.01	.05
11 Curtis Conway	.08	.25
12 Donnell Woolford	.01	.05
13 Chris Zorich	.01	.05
14 Erik Kramer	.02	.10
15 John Copeland	.01	.05
16 Harold Green	.01	.05
17 David Klingler	.01	.05
18 Tony McGee	.01	.05
19 Carl Pickens	.02	.10
20 Michael Jackson	.02	.10
21 Eric Metcalf	.02	.10
22 Michael Dean Perry	.02	.10
23 Vinny Testaverde	.02	.10
24 Eric Turner	.01	.05
25 Tommy Vardell	.01	.05
26 Troy Aikman	.30	.75
27 Charles Haley	.02	.10
28 Michael Irvin	.08	.25
29 Pierce Holt	.01	.05
30 Russell Maryland	.01	.05
31 Erik Williams	.01	.05
32 Thomas Everett	.01	.05
33 Steve Atwater	.01	.05
34 John Elway	.60	1.50
35 Glyn Milburn	.02	.10
36 Shannon Sharpe	.02	.10
37 Anthony Miller	.02	.10
38 Barry Sanders	.50	1.25
39 Chris Spielman	.02	.10
40 Pat Swilling	.01	.05
41 Brett Perriman	.02	.10
42 Herman Moore	.08	.25
43 Scott Mitchell	.02	.10
44 Edgar Bennett	.08	.25
45 Terrell Buckley	.01	.05
46 LeRoy Butler	.01	.05
47 Brett Favre	.60	1.50
48 Jackie Harris	.01	.05
49 Sterling Sharpe	.02	.10
50 Reggie White	.08	.25
51 Gary Brown	.01	.05
52 Cody Carlson	.01	.05
53 Ray Childress	.01	.05
54 Ernest Givins	.02	.10
55 Bruce Matthews	.01	.05
56 Quentin Coryatt	.01	.05
57 Steve Emtman	.01	.05
58 Roosevelt Potts	.01	.05
59 Tony Bennett	.01	.05
60 Marcus Allen	.08	.25
61 Joe Montana	.60	1.50
62 Neil Smith	.02	.10
63 Derrick Thomas	.08	.25
64 Dale Carter	.01	.05
65 Tim Brown	.08	.25
66 Jeff Hostetler	.02	.10
67 Terry McDaniel	.01	.05
68 Chester McGlockton	.01	.05
69 Anthony Smith	.01	.05
70 Albert Lewis	.01	.05
71 Jerome Bettis	.20	.50
72 Shane Conlan	.01	.05
73 Troy Drayton	.01	.05
74 Sean Gilbert	.01	.05
75 Chris Miller	.01	.05
76 Bryan Cox	.01	.05
77 Irving Fryar	.02	.10
78 Keith Jackson	.01	.05
79 Terry Kirby	.08	.25
80 Dan Marino	.60	1.50
81 O.J. McDuffie	.08	.25
82 Terry Allen	.02	.10
83 Cris Carter	.15	.40
84 Chris Doleman	.01	.05
85 Randall McDaniel	.02	.10
86 John Randle	.02	.10
87 Robert Smith	.08	.25
88 Jason Belser	.01	.05
89 Jack Del Rio	.01	.05
90 Vincent Brown	.01	.05
91 Ben Coates	.02	.10
92 Chris Slade	.01	.05
93 Derek Brown RBK	.01	.05
94 Morten Andersen	.01	.05
95 Willie Roaf	.01	.05
96 Irv Smith	.01	.05
97 Tyrone Hughes	.02	.10
98 Michael Haynes	.02	.10
99 Jim Everett	.02	.10
100 Michael Brooks	.01	.05
101 Leroy Thompson	.01	.05
102 Rodney Hampton	.02	.10
103 Dave Meggett	.01	.05
104 Phil Simms	.02	.10
105 Boomer Esiason	.02	.10
106 Johnny Johnson	.01	.05
107 Gary Anderson K	.01	.05
108 Mo Lewis	.01	.05
109 Ronnie Lott	.02	.10
110 Johnny Mitchell	.01	.05
111 Howard Cross	.01	.05
112 Victor Bailey	.01	.05
113 Fred Barnett	.02	.10
114 Randall Cunningham	.08	.25
115 Calvin Williams	.02	.10
116 Steve Beuerlein	.02	.10
117 Gary Clark	.02	.10
118 Ronald Moore	.01	.05
119 Ricky Proehl	.01	.05
120 Eric Swann	.02	.10
121 Barry Foster	.01	.05
122 Kevin Greene	.02	.10
123 Greg Lloyd	.02	.10
124 Neil O'Donnell	.08	.25
125 Rod Woodson	.02	.10
126 Ronnie Harmon	.01	.05
127 Mark Higgs	.01	.05
128 Stan Humphries	.02	.10
129 Leslie O'Neal	.01	.05
130 Chris Mims	.01	.05
131 Stanley Richard	.01	.05
132 Junior Seau	.08	.25
133 Brent Jones	.02	.10
134 Tim McDonald	.01	.05
135 Jerry Rice	.30	.75
136 Dana Stubblefield	.02	.10
137 Ricky Watters	.02	.10
138 Steve Young	.25	.60
139 Cortez Kennedy	.02	.10
140 Rick Mirer	.08	.25
141 Eugene Robinson	.01	.05
142 Chris Warren	.02	.10
143 Nate Odomes	.01	.05
144 Howard Ballard	.01	.05
145 Flipper Anderson	.01	.05
146 Chris Jacke	.01	.05
147 Santana Dotson	.02	.10
148 Craig Erickson	.01	.05
149 Hardy Nickerson	.02	.10
150 Lawrence Dawsey	.01	.05
151 Terry Wooden	.01	.05
152 Ethan Horton	.01	.05
153 John Kasay	.01	.05
154 Desmond Howard	.02	.10
155 Ken Harvey	.01	.05
156 William Fuller	.01	.05
157 Clyde Simmons	.01	.05
158 Randal Hill	.01	.05
159 Garrison Hearst	.08	.25
160 Mike Pritchard	.01	.05
161 Jessie Tuggle	.01	.05
162 Erric Pegram	.01	.05
163 Kevin Ross	.01	.05
164 Bill Brooks	.01	.05
165 Darryl Talley	.01	.05
166 Steve Tasker	.02	.10
167 Pete Stoyanovich	.01	.05
168 Dante Jones	.01	.05
169 Vencie Glenn	.01	.05
170 Tom Waddle	.01	.05
171 Harlon Barnett	.01	.05
172 Trace Armstrong	.01	.05
173 Tim Worley	.01	.05
174 Alfred Williams	.01	.05
175 Louis Oliver	.01	.05
176 Darryl Williams	.01	.05
177 Clay Matthews	.01	.05
178 Kyle Clifton	.01	.05
179 Alvin Harper	.02	.10
180 Jay Novacek	.02	.10
181 Ken Norton Jr.	.02	.10
182 Kevin Williams	.02	.10
183 Daryl Johnston	.02	.10
184 Rod Bernstine	.01	.05
185 Karl Mecklenburg	.01	.05
186 Dennis Smith	.01	.05
187 Robert Delpino	.01	.05
188 Bennie Blades	.01	.05
189 Jason Hanson	.01	.05
190 Derrick Moore	.01	.05
191 Mark Clayton	.01	.05
192 Webster Slaughter	.01	.05
193 Haywood Jeffires	.02	.10
194 Bubba McDowell	.01	.05
195 Warren Moon	.08	.25
196 Al Smith	.01	.05
197 Bill Romanowski	.01	.05
198 John Carney	.01	.05
199 Kerry Cash	.01	.05
200 Darren Carrington	.01	.05
201 Jeff Lageman	.01	.05
202 Tracy Simien	.01	.05
203 Willie Davis	.02	.10
204 Dan Saleaumua	.01	.05
205 Rocket Ismail	.02	.10
206 James Jett	.01	.05
207 Todd Lyght	.01	.05
208 Roman Phifer	.01	.05
209 Jimmie Jones	.01	.05
210 Jeff Cross	.01	.05
211 Eric Davis	.01	.05
212 Keith Byars	.01	.05
213 Richmond Webb	.01	.05
214 Anthony Carter	.02	.10
215 Henry Thomas	.01	.05
216 Andre Tippett	.01	.05
217 Rickey Jackson	.01	.05
218 Vaughan Johnson	.01	.05
219 Eric Martin	.01	.05
220 Sam Mills	.01	.05
221 Renaldo Turnbull	.01	.05
222 Mark Collins	.01	.05
223 Mike Johnson	.01	.05
224 Rob Moore	.02	.10
225 Seth Joyner	.01	.05
226 Herschel Walker	.02	.10
227 Eric Green	.01	.05
228 Marion Butts	.01	.05
229 John Friesz	.02	.10
230 John Taylor	.02	.10
231 Dexter Carter	.01	.05
232 Brian Blades	.02	.10
233 Reggie Cobb	.01	.05
234 Paul Gruber	.01	.05
235 Ricky Reynolds	.01	.05
236 Vince Workman	.01	.05
237 Darrell Green	.01	.05
238 Jim Lachey	.01	.05
239 James Hasty	.01	.05
240 Howie Long	.08	.25
241 Aeneas Williams	.01	.05
242 Mike Kenn	.01	.05
243 Henry Jones	.01	.05
244 Kenneth Davis	.01	.05
245 Tim Krumrie	.01	.05
246 Derrick Fenner	.01	.05
247 Mark Carrier WR	.02	.10
248 Robert Porcher	.01	.05
249 Darren Woodson	.02	.10
250 Kevin Smith	.01	.05
251 Mark Stepnoski	.01	.05
252 Simon Fletcher	.01	.05
253 Derek Russell	.01	.05
254 Mike Croel	.01	.05
255 Johnny Holland	.01	.05
256 Bryce Paup	.02	.10
257 Cris Dishman	.01	.05
258 Sean Jones	.01	.05
259 Marcus Robertson	.01	.05
260 Steve Jackson	.01	.05
261 Jeff Herrod	.01	.05
262 John Alt	.01	.05
263 Nick Lowery	.01	.05
264 Greg Robinson	.01	.05
265 Alexander Wright	.01	.05
266 Steve Wisniewski	.01	.05
267 Henry Ellard	.02	.10
268 Tracy Scroggins	.01	.05
269 Jackie Slater	.01	.05
270 Troy Vincent	.01	.05
271 Qadry Ismail	.08	.25
272 Steve Jordan	.01	.05
273 Leonard Russell	.01	.05
274 Maurice Hurst	.01	.05
275 Scottie Graham RC	.02	.10
276 Carlton Bailey	.01	.05
277 John Elliott	.01	.05
278 Corey Miller	.01	.05
279 Brad Baxter	.01	.05
280 Brian Washington	.01	.05
281 Tim Harris	.01	.05
282 Byron Evans	.01	.05
283 Dermontti Dawson	.01	.05
284 Carnell Lake	.01	.05
285 Jeff Graham	.01	.05
286 Merton Hanks	.02	.10
287 Harris Barton	.01	.05
288 Guy McIntyre	.01	.05
289 Kelvin Martin	.01	.05
290 John L. Williams	.01	.05
291 Courtney Hawkins	.01	.05
292 Vaughn Hebron	.01	.05
293 Brian Mitchell	.01	.05
294 Andre Collins	.01	.05
295 Art Monk	.02	.10
296 Mark Rypien	.01	.05
297 Ricky Sanders	.01	.05
298 Eric Hill	.01	.05
299 Larry Centers	.08	.25
300 Norm Johnson	.01	.05
301 Pete Metzelaars	.01	.05
302 Ricardo McDonald	.01	.05
303 Stevon Moore	.01	.05
304 Mike Sherrard	.01	.05
305 Andy Harmon	.01	.05
306 Anthony Johnson	.02	.10
307 J.J. Birden	.01	.05
308 Neal Anderson	.01	.05
309 Lewis Tillman	.01	.05
310 Richard Dent	.02	.10
311 Nate Newton	.01	.05
312 Sean Dawkins RC	.08	.25
313 Lawrence Taylor	.08	.25
314 Wilber Marshall	.01	.05
315 Tom Carter	.01	.05
316 Reggie Brooks	.02	.10
317 Eric Curry	.01	.05
318 Horace Copeland	.01	.05
319 Natrone Means	.08	.25
320 Eric Allen	.01	.05
321 Marvin Jones	.01	.05
322 Keith Hamilton	.01	.05
323 Vincent Brisby	.02	.10
324 Drew Bledsoe	.30	.75
325 Tom Rathman	.01	.05
326 Ed McCaffrey	.08	.25
327 Steve Israel	.01	.05
328 Dan Wilkinson RC	.02	.10
329 Marshall Faulk RC	2.00	5.00
330 Heath Shuler RC	.08	.25
331 Willie McGinest RC	.08	.25
332 Trev Alberts RC	.02	.10
333 Trent Dilfer RC	.50	1.25
334 Bryant Young RC	.15	.40
335 Sam Adams RC	.02	.10
336 Antonio Langham RC	.02	.10
337 Jamir Miller RC	.02	.10
338 John Thierry RC	.01	.05
339 Aaron Glenn RC	.08	.25
340 Joe Johnson RC	.01	.05
341 Bernard Williams RC	.01	.05
342 Wayne Gandy RC	.01	.05
343 Aaron Taylor RC	.01	.05
344 Charles Johnson RC	.08	.25
345 Dewayne Washington RC	.02	.10
346 Todd Steussie RC	.02	.10
347 Tim Bowens RC	.02	.10
348 Johnnie Morton RC	.20	.50
349 Rob Fredrickson RC	.02	.10
350 Shante Carver RC	.01	.05
351 Thomas Lewis RC	.02	.10
352 Greg Hill RC	.08	.25
353 Henry Ford RC	.01	.05
354 Jeff Burris RC	.02	.10
355 William Floyd RC	.08	.25
356 Derrick Alexander WR RC	.08	.25
357 Darnay Scott RC	.20	.50
358 Isaac Bruce RC	2.00	4.00
359 Errict Rhett RC	.08	.25
360 Kevin Lee RC	.01	.05
361 Chuck Levy RC	.01	.05
362 David Palmer RC	.08	.25
363 Ryan Yarborough RC	.01	.05
364 Charlie Garner RC	.50	1.25

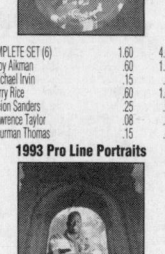

365 Isaac Davis RC .01 .05
366 Mario Bates RC .08 .25
367 Bert Emanuel RC .08 .25
368 Thomas Randolph RC .01 .05
369 Bucky Brooks RC .01 .05
370 Allen Aldridge RC .01 .05
371 Charlie Ward RC .08 .25
1993 Heisman Trophy Winner
372 Aubrey Beavers RC .01 .05
373 Donnell Bennett RC .08 .25
374 Jason Gchorn RC .15 .40
375 Lonnie Johnson RC .01 .05
376 Tyronne Drakeford RC .01 .05
377 Andre Coleman RC .01 .05
378 Lamar Smith RC .50 1.25
379 Calvin Jones RC .01 .05
380 LeShon Johnson RC .02 .10
381 Byron Bam Morris RC .02 .10
382 Lake Dawson RC .02 .10
383 Corey Sawyer RC .02 .10
384 Willie Jackson RC .08 .25
385 Perry Klein RC .01 .05
386 Ronnie Woolfork RC .01 .05
387 Doug Nussmeier RC .01 .05
388 Rob Waldrop RC .01 .05
389 Glenn Foley RC .08 .25
390 Troy Aikman CC .15 .40
Michael Irvin
391 Steve Young CC .15 .40
Jerry Rice
392 Brett Favre CC .30 .75
Sterling Sharpe
393 Jim Kelly CC .08 .25
Andre Reed
394 John Elway CC .30 .75
Shannon Sharpe
395 Carolina Panthers .05 .15
396 Jacksonville Jaguars .05 .15
397 Checklist 1 .01 .05
398 Checklist 2 .01 .05
399 Checklist 3 .01 .05
400 Checklist 4 .01 .05
401 Sterling Sharpe ILL .02 .10
402 Derrick Thomas ILL .02 .10
403 Joe Montana ILL .25 .60
404 Emmitt Smith ILL .20 .50
405 Barry Sanders ILL .25 .60
ES1 Emmitt Smith/15000 6.00 15.00
Super Bowl MVP
JB1 Jerome Bettis ROY 5.00 12.00
P1 Troy Aikman Promo .50 1.25
International Sportscard
Expo back
PR1 Emmitt Smith Promo .75 2.00
numbered PR1

1994 Pro Line Live Autographs

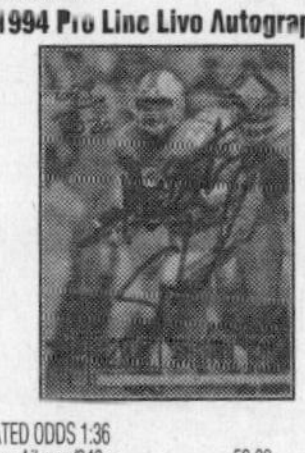

STATED ODDS 1:36
1 Troy Aikman/340 50.00 100.00
2 Derrick Alexander WR/950 5.00 12.00
3 Eric Allen/1980 5.00 12.00
4 Steve Atwater/1040 5.00 12.00
5 Victor Bailey/450 4.00 10.00
6 Harris Barton/2120 6.00 15.00
7 Mario Bates/1145 4.00 10.00
8 Brad Baxter/1070 4.00 10.00
9 Aubrey Beavers/1150 4.00 10.00
10 Donnell Bennett/1130 4.00 10.00
11 Rod Bernstine/1010 20.00 50.00
(rumored to be short-printed)
12 Steve Beuerlein/970 5.00 12.00
13 Drew Bledsoe/1150 12.00 30.00
14 Bill Brooks/1030 4.00 10.00
15 Bucky Brooks/1090 4.00 10.00
16 Reggie Brooks/460 5.00 12.00
17 Derek Brown RBK/449 4.00 10.00
18 Gary Brown/950 4.00 10.00
19 Tim Brown/1920 12.50 30.00
20 Jeff Burris/1140 4.00 10.00
21 Marion Butts/2040 4.00 10.00
22 Keith Byars/1020 5.00 12.00
23 Anthony Carter/1020 5.00 12.00
24 Dale Carter/1031 5.00 12.00
25 Tom Carter/460 4.00 10.00
26 Shante Carver/1160 4.00 10.00
27 Ray Childress/2240 5.00 12.00
28 Andre Coleman/1000 4.00 10.00
29 Andre Collins/1100 4.00 10.00
30 Shane Conlan/1110 4.00 10.00
31 Horace Copeland/450 4.00 10.00
32 Quentin Coryatt/970 5.00 12.00
33 Isaac Davis/1150 4.00 10.00
34 Kenneth Davis/1170 5.00 12.00
35 Lake Dawson/1100 5.00 12.00
36 Robert Delpino/1030 4.00 10.00
37 Trent Dilfer/2680 6.00 15.00
38 Troy Drayton/450 4.00 10.00
39 John Elliott/2150 4.00 10.00
40 John Elway/1000 50.00 100.00
41 Steve Emtman/1900 4.00 10.00
42 Boomer Esiason/920 6.00 15.00
43 Jim Everett/1265 5.00 12.00
44 Marshall Faulk/2230 25.00 50.00
45 Brett Favre/1130 60.00 120.00
46 William Floyd/950 5.00 12.00
47 Glenn Foley/890 4.00 10.00
48 Henry Ford/1110 4.00 10.00
49 Barry Foster/1080 5.00 12.00
50 Rob Fredrickson/1160 4.00 10.00
51 John Friesz/2150 4.00 10.00
52 Irving Fryar/1040 6.00 15.00
53 Wayne Gandy/1040 4.00 10.00
54 Charlie Garner/1130 5.00 12.00
55 Jeff George/2140 5.00 12.00
56 Aaron Glenn/1140 5.00 12.00
57 Rodney Hampton/1090 5.00 12.00
58 Garrison Hearst/1435 5.00 12.00
59 Mark Higgs/980 4.00 10.00
60 Greg Hill/1145 5.00 12.00
61 Pierce Holt/2020 4.00 10.00
62 Jeff Hostetler/955 5.00 12.00
63 Tyrone Hughes/470 15.00 30.00
64 Michael Irvin/450 15.00 30.00
65 Qadry Ismail/450 5.00 12.00
66 Steve Israel/2020 4.00 10.00
67 Keith Jackson/1020 5.00 12.00
68 Michael Jackson/1490 5.00 12.00
69 Willie Jackson/1140 5.00 12.00
70 Charles Johnson/950 5.00 12.00
71 Brent Jones/1880 5.00 12.00
72 Calvin Jones/960 12.00 30.00
73 Perry Klein/1000 4.00 10.00
74 David Klingler/2140 4.00 10.00
75 Erik Kramer/1020 5.00 12.00
76 Jim Lachey/1850 4.00 10.00
77 Carnell Lake/1985 4.00 10.00
78 Antonio Langham/1240 5.00 12.00
79 Kevin Lee/1190 4.00 10.00
80 Chuck Levy/950 5.00 12.00
81 Thomas Lewis/1140 4.00 10.00
82 Ronnie Lott/910 12.00 30.00
83 Ed McCaffrey/2030 6.00 15.00
84 Terry McDaniel/1980 4.00 10.00
85 Tim McDonald/2040 4.00 10.00
86 Willie McGinest/3520 5.00 12.00
87 Russell Maryland/1945 5.00 12.00
88 Clay Matthews/2000 6.00 15.00
89 Natrone Means/445 6.00 15.00
90 Glyn Milburn/440 4.00 10.00
91 Anthony Miller/2070 5.00 12.00
92 Sam Mills/1115 15.00 30.00
93 Joe Montana/920 50.00 100.00
94 Rob Moore/1025 5.00 12.00
95 Byron Bam Morris/1130 4.00 10.00
96 Johnnie Morton/2945 6.00 15.00
97 Hardy Nickerson/1175 4.00 10.00
98 Doug Nussmeier/1150 4.00 10.00
99 Leslie O'Neal/2050 4.00 10.00
100 David Palmer/950 4.00 10.00
101 Erric Pegram/1020 4.00 10.00
102 Roman Phifer/2140 4.00 10.00
103 Ricky Proehl/1020 5.00 12.00
104 Thomas Randolph/1100 4.00 10.00
105 Tom Rathman/2230 12.50 30.00
106 Errict Rhett/1120 5.00 12.00
107 Darnay Scott/1400 5.00 12.00
108 Jason Sehorn/950 5.00 12.00
109 Shannon Sharpe/1020 10.00 25.00
110 Sterling Sharpe/450 12.50 30.00
111 Heath Shuler/2020 5.00 12.00
112 Jackie Slater/1110 6.00 15.00
113 Emmitt Smith/925 60.00 120.00
114 Irv Smith/470 4.00 10.00
115 Lamar Smith/1130 5.00 12.00
116 Neil Smith/1000 6.00 15.00
117 Todd Steussie/2100 5.00 12.00
118 Aaron Taylor/950 4.00 10.00
119 John Taylor/1030 6.00 15.00
120 John Thierry/1150 4.00 10.00
121 Derrick Thomas/1087 50.00 80.00
122 Andre Tippett/1090 20.00 40.00
123 Renaldo Turnbull/945 4.00 10.00
124 Eric Turner/1030 6.00 15.00
125 Tommy Vardell/1000 4.00 10.00
126 D.Washington/1040 5.00 12.00
127 Richmond Webb/1020 5.00 12.00
128 Dan Wilkinson/1900 6.00 12.00
129 Steve Wisniewski/2150 4.00 10.00
130 Donnell Woolford/1000 4.00 10.00
131 Ronnie Woolfork/360 4.00 10.00
132 Steve Young/925 15.00 40.00
133 Troy Aikman Combo/345 50.00 120.00
Michael Irvin
134 Steve Young Combo/450 60.00 150.00
Jerry Rice

1994 Pro Line Live MVP Sweepstakes

COMPLETE SET (45) 50.00 120.00
STATED ODDS 1:72
1 Jeff George 1.00 2.50
2 Andre Rison .40 1.00
3 Jim Kelly 1.00 2.50
4 Thurman Thomas 1.00 2.50
5 Troy Aikman 3.00 8.00
6 Emmitt Smith 5.00 12.00
7 Michael Irvin 1.00 2.50
8 John Elway 6.00 15.00
9 Brett Favre 6.00 15.00
10 Sterling Sharpe .40 1.00
11 Barry Sanders 5.00 12.00
12 Scott Mitchell .40 1.00
13 Gary Brown .20 .50
14 Warren Moon 1.00 2.50
15 Marcus Allen 1.00 2.50
16 Joe Montana 6.00 15.00
17 Tim Brown 1.00 2.50
18 Jeff Hostetler .40 1.00
19 Dan Marino 6.00 15.00
20 Terry Kirby 1.00 2.50
21 Terry Allen .40 1.00
22 Drew Bledsoe 3.00 8.00
23 Chris Miller .20 .50
24 Jerome Bettis 2.00 5.00
25 Derek Brown RBK .20 .50
26 Rodney Hampton .40 1.00
27 Phil Simms .40 1.00
28 Randall Cunningham 1.00 2.50
29 Barry Foster .20 .50
30 Neil O'Donnell 1.00 2.50
31 Boomer Esiason .40 1.00
32 Johnny Johnson .20 .50
33 Garrison Hearst 1.00 2.50
34 Ronald Moore .20 .50
35 Natrone Means 1.00 2.50
36 Steve Young 2.50 6.00
37 Ricky Watters .40 1.00
38 Jerry Rice 3.00 8.00
39 Rick Mirer 1.00 2.50
40 Chris Warren .40 1.00
41 Reggie Brooks .40 1.00
42 Marshall Faulk 6.00 15.00
43 Heath Shuler .40 1.00
44 Trent Dilfer 1.50 4.00
45 Field Card .20 .50

1994 Pro Line Live Spotlight

COMPLETE SET (25) 6.00 15.00
ONE PER 16-CARD PACK
PB1 Trent Dilfer .25 .60
PB2 Heath Shuler .07 .20
PB3 Marshall Faulk 1.00 2.50
PB4 Troy Aikman .50 1.25
PB5 Emmitt Smith .75 2.00
PB6 Thurman Thomas .15 .40
PB7 Andre Rison .07 .20
PB8 Jerry Rice .50 1.25
PB9 Sterling Sharpe .07 .20
PB10 Brett Favre 1.00 2.50
PB11 Steve Young .40 1.00
PB12 Drew Bledsoe .50 1.25
PB13 Rick Mirer .15 .40
PB14 Barry Sanders .75 2.00
PB15 Joe Montana 1.00 2.50
PB16 Jerome Bettis .30 .75
PB17 Ricky Watters .07 .20
PB18 Rodney Hampton .07 .20
PB19 Tim Brown .15 .40
PB20 Reggie Brooks .07 .20
PB21 Natrone Means .15 .40
PB22 Marcus Allen .15 .40
PB23 Gary Brown .02 .10
PB24 Barry Foster .02 .10
PB25 Dan Marino 1.00 2.50

1995 Pro Line GameBreakers Previews

COMPLETE SET (5) 10.00 25.00
STATED ODDS 1:36 CLASSIC NFL ROOKIES
GP1 Dan Marino 4.00 10.00
GP2 Natrone Means .25 .60
GP3 Joe Montana 4.00 10.00
GP4 Barry Sanders 3.00 8.00
GP5 Deion Sanders 1.00 2.50

1995 Pro Line Previews Phone Cards $2

COMPLETE $2 SET (5) 2.50 6.00
RANDOM INS.IN CLASSIC BK ROOKIES
*$5 PHONE CARDS: .8X TO 2X $2 CARDS
1 Troy Aikman .75 2.00
2 Drew Bledsoe .50 1.25
3 Ki-Jana Carter .25 .60
4 Marshall Faulk 1.00 2.50
5 Steve Young .60 1.50

1995 Pro Line

The set was produced by Classic. This 400-card standard-size set was issued in 10-card packs. These packs are in 36 count boxes with 12 boxes per case. Each box was guaranteed by the manufacturer to contain a signed card. Hot boxes (containing mostly insert cards) are inserted one in ten cases for retail and one in five for hobby. The hobby "Hot Boxes" are identified while the retail "Hot Boxes" are not explicitly identified. The full-bleed fronts feature color action photos. The player's name, position and team name are printed in white lettering near the bottom. The backs feature another color photo, biographical information, player information as well as recent and career statistics. Rookie Cards in this set include Jeff Blake, Ki-Jana Carter, Kerry Collins, Joey Galloway, Steve McNair, Kordell Stewart, J.J. Stokes, Yancey Thigpen, Tamarick Vanover and Michael Westbrook. The basic set includes three parallels: a Silver set inserted one per hobby and retail pack, a Printer's Proof set inserted two per hobby box and a Printer's Proof Silver set inserted one per hobby box. A Marshall Faulk GameBreakers Promo card was produced for distribution at the 1995 St.Louis National Card Collectors Convention. It carries the card number NA1.

COMPLETE SET (400) 8.00 20.00
1 Garrison Hearst .08 .25
2 Anthony Miller .02 .10
3 Brett Favre .60 1.50
4 Jessie Hester .01 .05
5 Mike Fox .01 .05
6 Jeff Blake RC .25 .60
7 J.J. Birden .01 .05
8 Greg Jackson .01 .05
9 Leon Lett .01 .05
10 Bruce Matthews .01 .05
11 Andre Reed .02 .10
12 Joe Montana .60 1.50
13 Craig Heyward .02 .10
14 Henry Ellard UER .02 .10
15 Chris Spielman .02 .10
16 Tony Woods .01 .05
17 Carl Banks .01 .05
18 Eric Zeier RC .08 .25
19 Michael Brooks .01 .05
20 Kevin Ross .01 .05
21 Qadry Ismail .02 .10
22 Mel Gray .01 .05
23 Ty Law RC .50 1.25
24 Mark Collins .01 .05
25 Neil O'Donnell .02 .10
26 Ellis Johnson RC .01 .05
27 Rick Mirer .02 .10
28 Fred Barnett .02 .10
29 Mike Mamula RC .01 .05
30 Jim Jeffcoat .01 .05
31 Reggie Cobb .01 .05
32 Mark Carrier WR UER .02 .10
Mark Carrier of the Bears
is on front of card
33 Darnay Scott .02 .10
34 Michael Jackson .02 .10
35 Terrell Buckley .01 .05
36 Nolan Harrison .01 .05
37 Thurman Thomas .08 .25
38 Anthony Smith .01 .05
39 Phillippi Sparks .01 .05
40 Cornelius Bennett .02 .10
41 Robert Young .01 .05
42 Pierce Holt .01 .05
43 Greg Lloyd .02 .10
44 Chad May RC .01 .05
45 Darrien Gordon .01 .05
46 Bryan Cox .01 .05
47 Junior Seau .08 .25
48 Al Smith .01 .05
49 Chris Slade .01 .05
50 Hardy Nickerson .01 .05
51 Brad Baxter .01 .05
52 Darryll Lewis .01 .05
53 Bryant Young .02 .10
54 Chris Warren .02 .10
55 Darion Conner .01 .05
56 Thomas Everett .01 .05
57 Charles Haley .02 .10
58 Chris Mims .01 .05
59 Sean Jones .01 .05
60 Tamarick Vanover RC .08 .25
61 Daryl Johnston .02 .10
62 Rashaan Salaam RC .02 .10
63 James Hasty .01 .05
64 Dante Jones .01 .05
65 Darren Perry UER .01 .05
Card is numbered as 367
66 Troy Drayton .01 .05
67 Mark Fields RC .08 .25
68 Brian Williams LB RC .01 .05
69 Steve Bono UER .02 .10
Name spelled Bond on card
70 Eric Allen .01 .05
71 Chris Zorich .01 .05
72 Dave Brown .02 .10
73 Ken Norton Jr. .02 .10
74 Wayne Martin .01 .05
75 Mo Lewis .01 .05
76 Johnny Mitchell .01 .05
77 Todd Lyght .01 .05
78 Erric Pegram .02 .10
79 Kevin Greene .02 .10
80 Randal Hill .01 .05
81 Brett Perriman .02 .10
82 Mike Sherrard .01 .05
83 Curtis Conway .08 .25
84 Mark Tuinei .01 .05
85 Mark Seay .02 .10
86 Randy Baldwin .01 .05
87 Ricky Ervins .01 .05
88 Chester McGlockton .02 .10
89 Tyrone Wheatley RC .40 1.00
90 Micheal Barrow UER .01 .05
91 Kenneth Davis .01 .05
92 Napoleon Kaufman RC .40 1.00
93 Webster Slaughter .01 .05
94 Darren Woodson .02 .10
95 Pete Stoyanovich .01 .05
96 Jimmie Jones .01 .05
97 Craig Erickson .01 .05
98 Michael Westbrook RC .08 .25
99 Steve McNair RC 1.00 2.50
100 Errict Rhett .02 .10
101 Devin Bush RC .01 .05
102 Dewayne Washington .02 .10
103 Bart Oates .01 .05
104 Aaron Pierce .01 .05
105 Warren Sapp RC .50 1.25
106 Eric Green .01 .05
107 Glyn Milburn .01 .05
108 Johnny Johnson .01 .05
109 Marshall Faulk .40 1.00
110 William Thomas .01 .05
111 George Koonce .01 .05
112 Dana Stubblefield .02 .10
113 Steve Tovar .01 .05
114 Steve Israel .01 .05
115 Brent Williams .01 .05
116 Shane Conlan .01 .05
117 Winston Moss .01 .05
118 Nate Newton .02 .10
119 Michael Irvin .08 .25
120 Jeff Lageman .01 .05
121 Ki-Jana Carter RC .08 .25
122 Dan Marino .60 1.50
123 Tony Casillas .01 .05
124 Kevin Carter RC .08 .25
125 Warren Moon .02 .10
126 Byron Bam Morris .01 .05
127 Ben Coates .02 .10
128 Michael Bankston .01 .05
129 Anthony Parker .01 .05
130 LeRoy Butler .01 .05
131 Tony Bennett .01 .05
132 Alvin Harper .01 .05
133 Tim Brown .08 .25
134 Tom Carter .01 .05
135 Lorenzo White .01 .05
136 Shane Dronett .01 .05
137 John Elliott UER .01 .05
138 Korey Stringer RC .07 .20
139 Jerry Rice .30 .75
140 Sherman Williams RC .01 .05
141 Kevin Turner .01 .05
142 Randall Cunningham .08 .25
143 Vinny Testaverde .02 .10
144 Tim Bowens .01 .05
145 Russell Maryland .01 .05
146 Chris Miller .01 .05
147 Vince Buck .01 .05
148 Willie Clay .01 .05
149 Jeff Graham .01 .05
150 Shannon Sharpe .02 .10
151 Carnell Lake .01 .05
152 Mark Bruener RC .02 .10
153 James Washington .01 .05
154 Pepper Johnson .01 .05
155 Bert Emanuel .08 .25
156 Mark Stepnoski .01 .05
157 Robert Jones .01 .05
158 Cris Dishman .01 .05
159 Henry Jones .01 .05
160 Henry Thomas .01 .05
161 John L. Williams .01 .05
162 Joe Cain .01 .05
163 Mike Johnson .01 .05
164 Merton Hanks .01 .05
165 Deion Sanders .15 .40
166 William Floyd .02 .10
167 Leroy Thompson .01 .05
168 Ray Childress .01 .05
169 Donnell Woolford .01 .05
170 Tony Siragusa .01 .05
171 Chad Brown .02 .10
172 Stanley Richard .01 .05
173 Rob Johnson RC .30 .75
174 Derrick Brooks RC .50 1.25
175 Drew Bledsoe .20 .50
176 Maurice Hurst .01 .05
177 Ricky Watters .02 .10
178 Myron Guyton .01 .05
179 Ricky Proehl .01 .05
180 Haywood Jeffires .01 .05
181 Michael Strahan .08 .25
182 Charles Wilson .01 .05
183 Mark Carrier DB .01 .05
184 James O. Stewart RC .40 1.00
185 Andy Harmon .01 .05
186 Ronnie Lott .02 .10
187 Clay Matthews .02 .10
188 John Carney .01 .05
189 Andre Rison .02 .10
190 Aeneas Williams .01 .05
191 Alexander Wright .01 .05
192 Desmond Howard .02 .10
193 Herman Moore .08 .25
194 Alfred Williams .01 .05
195 Tyrone Poole RC .08 .25
196 Darren Mickell RC .01 .05
197 Steve Young .25 .60
198 Roman Phifer .01 .05
199 Darrell Green .01 .05
200 Terry Wooden .01 .05
201 Chris Calloway .01 .05
202 Lewis Tillman .01 .05
203 Cris Carter .08 .25
204 Jim Everett .01 .05
205 Adrian Murrell .02 .10
206 Barry Sanders .50 1.25
207 Mario Bates .02 .10
208 Shawn Lee .01 .05
209 Charles Mincy .01 .05
210 Kerry Collins RC .75 2.00
211 Steve Walsh .01 .05
212 Chris Chandler .02 .10
213 Bennie Blades .01 .05
214 Kevin Williams WR .02 .10
215 Jim Kelly .08 .25
216 Marion Butts .01 .05
217 Jay Novacek .02 .10
218 Shawn Jefferson .01 .05
219 O.J. McDuffie .08 .25
220 Ray Seals .01 .05
221 Arthur Marshall .01 .05
222 Karl Mecklenburg .01 .05
223 Terance Mathis .02 .10
224 David Klingler .02 .10
225 Rod Woodson .02 .10
226 Quentin Coryatt .02 .10
227 Leroy Hoard .01 .05
228 Brian Blades .02 .10
229 Rob Moore .02 .10
230 Boomer Esiason .02 .10
231 Dave Krieg .01 .05
232 Sterling Sharpe .02 .10
233 Marcus Allen .08 .25
234 John Randle .02 .10
235 Craig Powell RC .01 .05
236 John Elway .60 1.50
237 Mark Ingram .01 .05
238 Cortez Kennedy .02 .10
239 Brent Jones .01 .05
240 Ken Harvey .01 .05
241 Keenan McCardell .08 .25
242 Dan Wilkinson .02 .10
243 Don Beebe .01 .05
244 Jack Del Rio .01 .05
245 Byron Evans .01 .05
246 Ronald Moore .01 .05
247 Edgar Bennett .02 .10
248 William Fuller .01 .05
249 James Williams .01 .05
250 Neil Smith .02 .10
251 Sam Mills .02 .10
252 Willie McGinest .02 .10
253 Howard Cross .01 .05
254 Troy Aikman .30 .75
255 Herschel Walker .02 .10
256 Dale Carter .02 .10
257 Sean Dawkins .02 .10
258 Greg Hill .02 .10
259 Stan Humphries .02 .10
260 Erik Kramer .01 .05
261 Leslie O'Neal .02 .10
262 Trezelle Jenkins RC .01 .05
263 Antonio Langham .01 .05
264 Bryce Paup .02 .10
265 Jake Reed .02 .10
266 Richmond Webb .01 .05
267 Eric Davis .01 .05
268 Mark McMillian .01 .05
269 John Walsh RC .01 .05
270 Irving Fryar .02 .10
271 Rocket Ismail .02 .10
272 Phil Hansen .01 .05
273 J.J. Stokes RC .08 .25
274 Craig Newsome RC .01 .05
275 Leonard Russell .01 .05
276 Derrick Deese .01 .05
277 Broderick Thomas .01 .05
278 Bobby Houston .01 .05
279 Lamar Lathon .01 .05
280 Eugene Robinson .01 .05
281 Dan Saleaumua .01 .05
282 Kyle Brady RC .08 .25
283 John Taylor UER .01 .05
Card lists him as a Tight End
284 Tony Boselli RC .08 .25
285 Seth Joyner .01 .05
286 Steve Beuerlein .02 .10
287 Sam Adams .01 .05
288 Frank Reich .01 .05
289 Patrick Hunter .01 .05
290 Sean Gilbert .02 .10
291 Dermontti Dawson UER .02 .10
292 Shaun Gayle .01 .05
293 Vincent Brown .01 .05
294 Terry Kirby .02 .10
295 Courtney Hawkins .01 .05
296 Carl Pickens .02 .10
297 Luther Elliss RC .01 .05
298 Steve Atwater .01 .05
299 James Francis .01 .05
300 Rob Burnett .01 .05
301 Keith Hamilton .01 .05
302 Rob Fredrickson .01 .05
303 Jerome Bettis .08 .25
304 Emmitt Smith .50 1.25
305 Clyde Simmons .01 .05
306 Reggie White .08 .25
307 Rodney Hampton .02 .10
308 Steve Emtman .01 .05
309 Hugh Douglas RC .08 .25
310 Bernie Parmalee .02 .10
311 Trent Dilfer .08 .25
312 Flipper Anderson .01 .05
313 Heath Shuler .02 .10
314 Rod Smith DB .02 .10
315 Ray Zellars RC .02 .10
316 Robert Brooks .08 .25
317 Lee Woodall .01 .05
318 Robert Porcher .01 .05
319 Todd Collins RC .30 .75
320 Willie Roaf .01 .05
321 Erik Williams .01 .05
322 Steve Wisniewski .01 .05
323 Derrick Alexander DE RC .01 .05
324 Frank Warren .01 .05
325 Kelvin Pritchett .01 .05
326 Dennis Gibson .01 .05
327 Jason Belser .01 .05
328 Vincent Brisby .01 .05
329 Calvin Williams .02 .10
330 Derek Brown RBK .01 .05
331 Blake Brockermeyer .01 .05
332 Jeff Herrod .01 .05
333 Darryl Williams .01 .05
334 Aaron Glenn .01 .05
335 Eric Metcalf .02 .10
336 Billy Milner .01 .05
337 Terry McDaniel .01 .05
338 Trace Armstrong .01 .05
339 Yancey Thigpen RC .02 .10
340 Jackie Harris .01 .05
341 Jeff George .02 .10
342 Darryl Talley .01 .05
343 Marcus Robertson .01 .05
344 Robert Massey .01 .05
345 Jessie Tuggle .01 .05
346 Scott Mitchell .02 .10
347 Harvey Williams .01 .05
348 Jack Jackson RC .01 .05
349 Brian Mitchell .01 .05
350 Lawrence Dawsey .01 .05
351 Erik Howard .01 .05
352 Quinn Early .02 .10
353 Terry Allen .02 .10
354 Simon Fletcher .01 .05
355 Eric Turner .01 .05
356 Natrone Means .02 .10
357 Frank Sanders RC .08 .25
358 Michael Timpson .01 .05
359 Michael Haynes .02 .10
360 Ruben Brown RC .08 .25
361 Troy Vincent UER .01 .05
Name spelled Vicent on back
362 Floyd Turner .01 .05
363 Larry Centers .02 .10
364 Eric Swann .02 .10
365 Albert Lewis .01 .05
366 Barry Foster .02 .10
367 Michael Dean Perry .01 .05
368 Jumpy Geathers UER .01 .05
Name spelled Jummpy on front
369 Kordell Stewart RC .50 1.25
370 Chuck Smith .01 .05
371 Lake Dawson .02 .10
372 Terry Hoage .01 .05
373 Jeff Cross .01 .05
374 Tony McGee .01 .05
375 Eric Curry .01 .05
376 Harold Green .01 .05
377 Eric Hill .01 .05
378 Ray Buchanan .01 .05
379 Willie Davis .02 .10
380 Chris T. Jones RC .01 .05
381 Martin Mayhew .01 .05
382 Anthony Pleasant .01 .05
383 Joey Galloway RC .50 1.25
384 Anthony Morgan .01 .05
385 Harlon Barnett .01 .05
386 Bruce Smith .08 .25
387 Jeff Hostetler .02 .10
388 Randall McDaniel .02 .10
389 Dave Meggett .01 .05
390 Bill Romanowski .01 .05
391 Gary Brown .01 .05
392 Charles Johnson .02 .10
393 Chris Doleman .01 .05
394 Tony Martin .02 .10
395 Raymont Harris .01 .05
396 John Copeland .01 .05
397 Emmitt Smith CL UER .08 .25
Several wrong names
398 Steve Young CL UER .02 .10
Many wrong names
399 Marshall Faulk CL UER .20 .50
Many wrong names
400 Ki-Jana Carter CL UER .02 .10
Many wrong names
HP1 Marshall Faulk Sample .60 1.50
GameBreakers card
P1 Marshall Faulk Promo .60 1.50
GameBreakers card/1995 National Convention back
P2 Jerome Bettis Promo .60 1.50
spin to win;
interactive game card;
from 1995 National Convention)

1995 Pro Line National Silver

COMPLETE SET (400) 100.00 200.00
*STARS: 4X TO 10X BASIC CARDS
*RCs: 2X TO 5X BASIC CARDS
ONE PER NATIONAL PACK

1995 Pro Line Printer's Proofs

COMPLETE SET (400) 100.00 200.00
*STARS: 4X TO 10X BASIC CARDS
*RCS: 2X to 5X BASIC CARDS
TWO PER HOBBY BOX

1995 Pro Line Printer's Proofs Silver

COMPLETE SET (400) 150.00 300.00
*PP SILVER STARS: 6X TO 15X BASIC CARDS
*PP SILVER RC's: 3X TO 8X BASIC CARDS
ONE PER HOBBY BOX
ANNOUNCE PRINT RUN 175 SETS

1995 Pro Line Silver

COMPLETE SET (400) 20.00 40.00
*STARS: .8X TO 2X BASIC CARDS
*RCs: .6X TO 1.5X BASIC CARDS
ONE PER PACK

1995 Pro Line Autographs

STATED ODDS 1:36H,1:24J,1:90R SER.1
1 Troy Aikman/500 25.00 60.00
2A Eric Allen/1225 5.00 12.00
2B Eric Allen/2398AP 5.00 12.00
2C Eric Allen/745AP 5.00 12.00
3 Flipper Anderson/1140 4.00 10.00
4A Randy Baldwin/1435 4.00 10.00
4B Randy Baldwin/2405AP 4.00 10.00
4C Randy Baldwin/760AP 4.00 10.00
5 Mario Bates/1480 4.00 10.00
6A Don Beebe/1200 5.00 12.00
6B Don Beebe/275AP 5.00 12.00
7A Cornelius Bennett/1200 6.00 15.00
7B Cornelius Bennett/255AP 6.00 15.00
8 Edgar Bennett/1475 6.00 15.00
9 Tony Bennett/1475 4.00 10.00
10 Steve Beuerlein/1465 5.00 12.00
11 J.J. Birden/775 4.00 10.00
12 Brian Blades/1465 5.00 12.00
13 Jeff Blake/1200 6.00 15.00
14 Drew Bledsoe/515 15.00 40.00
15A Blake Brockermeyer/1445 4.00 10.00
15B Blake Brockermeyer/2315AP 4.00 10.00
16 Derrick Brooks/1470 8.00 20.00
17 Tim Brown/2410 12.50 30.00
18 Dale Carter/1400 5.00 12.00
19A Ray Childress/1200 4.00 10.00
19B Ray Childress/235AP 4.00 10.00
20 Ben Coates/1175 6.00 15.00
21 Mark Collins/1430 4.00 10.00
22 Kerry Collins/3300 6.00 15.00
23 Curtis Conway/1200 5.00 12.00
24 Quentin Coryatt/1400 5.00 12.00
25 R. Cunningham/470 12.50 30.00
26A Jack Del Rio/1480 5.00 12.00
26B Jack Del Rio/930AP 5.00 12.00
27 Willie Davis/1500 5.00 12.00
28A Derrick Deese/1200 4.00 10.00
28B Derrick Deese/2375AP 4.00 10.00
28C Derrick Deese/735AP 4.00 10.00
29A Trent Dilfer/2010 6.00 15.00
29B Trent Dilfer/306AP 6.00 15.00
30 Troy Drayton/1375 4.00 10.00
31 Quinn Early/1200 5.00 12.00
32 Henry Ellard/1440 6.00 15.00
33 John Elliott/2380 4.00 10.00
34 Luther Elliss/1470 4.00 10.00
35 John Elway/50 125.00 250.00
36 Bert Emanuel/1445 5.00 12.00
37 Steve Emtman/2365 4.00 10.00
38A Craig Erickson/630 4.00 10.00
38B Craig Erickson/890AP 4.00 10.00
39 Boomer Esiason/1700 6.00 15.00
40 Marshall Faulk/1030 20.00 40.00
41 Barry Foster/1455 5.00 12.00
42 Mike Fox/1445 4.00 10.00
43 Irving Fryar/1500 6.00 15.00
44 Joey Galloway/1445 6.00 15.00
45A Shaun Gayle/1200 4.00 10.00
45B Shaun Gayle/265AP 4.00 10.00
46 Jeff George/1295 5.00 12.00
47 Darrien Gordon/2400 4.00 10.00
48 Jeff Graham/1465 4.00 10.00
49 Eric Green/1460 4.00 10.00
50 Charles Haley/1420 8.00 20.00
51 Rodney Hampton/1120 5.00 12.00
52 Andy Harmon/1200 4.00 10.00
53 Courtney Hawkins/1445 4.00 10.00
54 Michael Haynes/1180 4.00 10.00
55 Garrison Hearst/1460 6.00 15.00
56A Craig Heyward/1200 15.00 30.00
56B Craig Heyward/265AP 15.00 30.00
57 Greg Hill/1455 5.00 12.00
58 Pierce Holt/1440 4.00 10.00
59 Patrick Hunter/2375 4.00 10.00
60 Michael Irvin/1490 20.00 40.00
61 Sean Jones/2385 4.00 10.00
62 Qadry Ismail/1170 5.00 12.00
63A Steve Israel/1200 4.00 10.00
63B Steve Israel/2413AP 4.00 10.00
63C Steve Israel/750AP 4.00 10.00
64 Jack Jackson/1475 4.00 10.00
65 Michael Jackson/1200 5.00 12.00
66A Shawn Jefferson/1200 4.00 10.00
66B Shawn Jefferson/240AP 5.00 12.00
67 Haywood Jeffires/1470 5.00 12.00
68 Trezelle Jenkins/1470 4.00 10.00
69A Rob Johnson/2815 5.00 12.00
69B Rob Johnson/500 5.00 12.00
70 Seth Joyner/1480 6.00 15.00
71 Jim Kelly/470 15.00 40.00
72 Cortez Kennedy/1380 5.00 12.00
73 Terry Kirby/1450 4.00 10.00
74 Dave Krieg/1470 5.00 12.00
75A Antonio Langham/1200 4.00 10.00
75B Antonio Langham/260AP 4.00 10.00
76 Ty Law/1460 8.00 20.00
77 Leon Lett/1550 4.00 10.00
78 Ronnie Lott/1900 15.00 30.00
79A K.McCardell/1235 5.00 12.00
79B Keenan McCardell/2403AP 5.00 12.00
79C Keenan McCardell/754AP 5.00 12.00
80 Terry McDaniel/2340 4.00 10.00
81 Tony McGee/1385 5.00 12.00
82A Willie McGinest/1160 6.00 15.00
82B Willie McGinest/2407AP 6.00 15.00
82C Willie McGinest/754AP 6.00 15.00
83 Chester McGlockton/1280 4.00 10.00
84A Mark McMillian/1175 4.00 10.00
84B Mark McMillian/2400AP 4.00 10.00
84C Mark McMillian/825AP 4.00 10.00
85 Steve McNair/3490 12.50 30.00
86 Mike Mamula/1250 4.00 10.00
87A Arthur Marshall/1165 4.00 10.00
87B Arthur Marshall/2400AP 4.00 10.00
87C Arthur Marshall/870AP 4.00 10.00
88 Russell Maryland/1250 5.00 12.00
89 Clay Matthews/2385 10.00 25.00
90A Chad May/1180 4.00 10.00
90B Chad May/2410AP 4.00 10.00
91 Natrone Means/1058 5.00 12.00
92 Anthony Miller/2385 5.00 12.00
93 Sam Mills/1470 25.00 60.00
94 Herman Moore/2070 5.00 12.00
95 Byron Bam Morris/1430 4.00 10.00
96 Jay Novacek/1195 15.00 30.00
97A Brett Perriman/1380 4.00 10.00
97B Brett Perriman/935 4.00 10.00
98A Michael D. Perry/1200 6.00 15.00
98B Michael D.Perry/295AP 6.00 15.00
99 Roman Phifer/2395 4.00 10.00
100 Ricky Proehl/1475 5.00 12.00
101A John Randle/1170 6.00 15.00
101B John Randle/2400AP 6.00 15.00
101C John Randle/757AP 6.00 15.00
102 Andre Reed/1440 8.00 20.00
103 Jake Reed/1470 5.00 12.00
104 Errict Rhett/1400 5.00 12.00
105A Willie Roaf/1200 5.00 12.00
105B Willie Roaf/245AP 5.00 12.00
106 Bill Romanowski/1450 6.00 15.00
107 Rashaan Salaam/1320 5.00 12.00
108 Mike Sherrard/1450 4.00 10.00
109A Heath Shuler/2000 6.00 15.00
109B Heath Shuler/366AP 6.00 15.00
110 Clyde Simmons/735 6.00 15.00
111A Chris Slade/1100 4.00 10.00
111B Chris Slade/2417AP 4.00 10.00
111C Chris Slade/750AP 4.00 10.00
112 Al Smith/1360 4.00 10.00
113 Emmitt Smith/500 75.00 135.00
114 Neil Smith/1465 6.00 15.00
115 Mark Stepnoski/1500 4.00 10.00
116 J.J. Stokes/1435 5.00 12.00
117 Vinny Testaverde/1020 6.00 15.00
118 Henry Thomas/1420 4.00 10.00
119 Lewis Tillman/1170 4.00 10.00
120A Jessie Tuggle/1200 5.00 12.00
120B Jessie Tuggle/195AP 5.00 12.00
121 Tamarick Vanover/1155 5.00 12.00
122 Troy Vincent/1490 4.00 10.00
123 John Walsh/3340 4.00 10.00
124A Steve Walsh/1185 4.00 10.00
124B Steve Walsh/1015AP 4.00 10.00
125A Brian Williams 4.00 10.00
LB/1175
125B Brian Williams 4.00 10.00
LB/2670AP
125C Brian Williams 4.00 10.00
LB/865AP
126 Calvin Williams/1200 5.00 12.00
127 Sherman Williams/1460 4.00 10.00
128 Steve Young/500 20.00 40.00
129 Eric Zeier/500 5.00 12.00

1995 Pro Line Autograph Printer's Proofs

STATED PRINT RUN 50 NUMBERED SETS
99 Steve McNair 30.00 80.00
175 Drew Bledsoe 40.00 100.00
197 Steve Young 50.00 120.00
210 Kerry Collins 25.00 60.00
230 Boomer Esiason 15.00 40.00
254 Troy Aikman 75.00 150.00
304 Emmitt Smith 125.00 250.00
311 Trent Dilfer 15.00 40.00

1995 Pro Line Bonus Card Jumbos

COMPLETE SET (14) 20.00 50.00
1-3: INSERTED IN CLASSIC NFL ROOKIES
4-8: INSERTED IN PROLINE SERIES 1
9-11: INSERTED IN PROLINE SERIES 2
13-15: INSERTED IN 96 NFL EXPERIENCE
1 Ki-Jana Carter .30 .75
2 Steve McNair 3.00 8.00
3 Kerry Collins 1.50 4.00
4 Deion Sanders 1.25 3.00
5 Steve Young 2.00 5.00
6 Emmitt Smith 4.00 10.00
7 Natrone Means .30 .75

8 Drew Bledsoe 1.50 4.00
9 Troy Aikman 2.50 6.00
10 Marshall Faulk 3.00 8.00
11 J.J.Stokes .30 .75
13 Emmitt Smith 4.00 10.00
14 Rashaan Salaam .10 .30
15 Reggie White .75 2.00

1995 Pro Line Field Generals

COMPLETE SET (10) 30.00 80.00
STATED ODDS 1:60 SER.2
G1 Marshall Faulk 6.00 15.00
G2 Emmitt Smith 8.00 20.00
G3 Steve Young 4.00 10.00
G4 Ki-Jana Carter .75 2.00
G5 Rashaan Salaam .30 .75
G6 Dan Marino 10.00 25.00
G7 J.J. Stokes .75 2.00
G8 Drew Bledsoe 3.00 8.00
G9 Brett Favre 10.00 25.00
G10 Barry Sanders 8.00 20.00

1995 Pro Line Game of the Week Home

COMPLETE SET (60) 8.00 20.00
*VISITOR: .4X TO 1X HOME
ONE PER SPECIAL RETAIL PACK
*PRIZES: .6X TO 1.5X HOME
*PRIZES FOIL: 1X TO 2.5X HOME
H1 Barry Sanders .60 1.50
Reggie White
H2 Jeff Hostetler .75 2.00
John Elway
H3 Michael Westbrook .10 .30
Ricky Watters
H4 Jim Kelly .30 .75
Mo Lewis
H5 Marshall Faulk .50 1.25
Jerome Bettis
H6 Natrone Means .10 .30
Byron Bam Morris
H7 Seth Joyner .60 1.50
Emmitt Smith
H8 Errict Rhett .20 .50
Heath Shuler
H9 Junior Seau .20 .50
Randall Cunningham
H10 Drew Bledsoe .30 .75
Steve Young
H11 Dave Krieg .40 1.00
Kerry Collins
H12 Steve Beuerlein .20 .50
Alvin Harper
H13 Ben Coates .10 .30
Troy Vincent
H14 Jerry Rice .50 1.25
Michael Irvin
H15 Rodney Hampton .10 .30
Cortez Kennedy
H16 Steve McNair .60 1.50
Leroy Hoard
H17 Thurman Thomas .20 .50
Irving Fryar
H18 Andre Rison .10 .30
Ki-Jana Carter
H19 Dan Marino .75 2.00
Boomer Esiason
H20 Brett Favre 1.00 2.50
Warren Moon
H21 Anthony Miller .20 .50
Tim Brown
H22 Chris Warren .10 .30
Steve Bono
H23 Shannon Sharpe .20 .50
Neil Smith
H24 John Randle .10 .30
Dana Stubblefield
H25 Jim Everett .10 .30
Terance Mathis
H26 Troy Aikman .40 1.00
Mike Mamula
H27 Trent Dilfer .20 .50
Cris Carter
H28 Steve Walsh .08 .25
Scott Mitchell
H29 Greg Lloyd .10 .30
Vinny Testaverde
H30 Jeff George .10 .30
Garrison Hearst

1995 Pro Line GameBreakers

COMPLETE SET (30) 25.00 60.00
STATED ODDS 1:36HOB,1:30JUM SER.1
*GB PRINT.PROOF: 1.5X TO 3X BASIC INSERTS
STATED ODDS 1:432 SER.1 HOBBY
GB1 Troy Aikman 2.00 5.00
GB2 Drew Bledsoe 1.25 3.00
GB3 Tim Brown .60 1.50
GB4 Cris Carter .60 1.50
GB5 Ki-Jana Carter .30 .75
GB6 Kerry Collins 1.50 4.00
GB7 John Elway 4.00 10.00
GB8 Marshall Faulk 2.50 6.00
GB9 Brett Favre 4.00 10.00
GB10 Garrison Hearst .60 1.50
GB11 Michael Irvin .60 1.50
GB12 Jim Kelly .60 1.50
GB13 Dan Marino 4.00 10.00
GB14 Natrone Means .25 .60
GB15 Eric Metcalf .25 .60
GB16 J.J. Stokes .30 .75
GB17 Carl Pickens .25 .60
GB18 Jerry Rice 2.00 5.00
GB19 Andre Rison .25 .60
GB20 Barry Sanders 3.00 8.00
GB21 Deion Sanders 1.00 2.50
GB22 Junior Seau .60 1.50
GB23 Emmitt Smith 3.00 8.00
GB24 Thurman Thomas .60 1.50
GB25 Ricky Watters .25 .60
GB26 Reggie White .60 1.50
GB27 Rod Woodson .25 .60
GB28 Steve Young 1.50 4.00
GB29 Rashaan Salaam .10 .30
GB30 Michael Westbrook .30 .75

1995 Pro Line Grand Gainers

COMPLETE SET (30) 7.50 20.00
ONE PER SPECIAL RETAIL PACK
G1 Barry Sanders 1.00 2.50
G2 Emmitt Smith 1.00 2.50
G3 Natrone Means .07 .20
G4 Marshall Faulk .75 2.00
G5 Errict Rhett .07 .20
G6 Jerry Rice .60 1.50
G7 Tim Brown .20 .50
G8 Cris Carter .20 .50
G9 Irving Fryar .07 .20
G10 Ben Coates .07 .20
G11 Fred Barnett .07 .20
G12 Andre Rison .07 .20
G13 Drew Bledsoe .40 1.00
G14 Dan Marino 1.25 3.00
G15 Warren Moon .07 .20
G16 Steve Young .50 1.25
G17 Brett Favre 1.25 3.00
G18 John Elway 1.25 3.00
G19 Randall Cunningham .20 .50
G20 Stan Humphries .07 .20
G21 Jim Kelly .20 .50
G22 Ki-Jana Carter .08 .25
G23 Rodney Hampton .07 .20
G24 Tyrone Wheatley .40 1.00
G25 J.J. Stokes .08 .25
G26 Michael Irvin .20 .50
G27 Herman Moore .20 .50
G28 Kerry Collins .60 1.50
G29 Steve McNair 1.00 2.50
G30 Rob Johnson .30 .75

1995 Pro Line Images Previews

COMPLETE SET (5) 6.00 15.00
STATED ODDS 1:18 SERIES 2
1 Emmitt Smith 2.50 6.00
2 Steve Young 1.25 3.00
3 Drew Bledsoe 1.00 2.50
4 Kerry Collins 1.25 3.00
5 Marshall Faulk 2.00 5.00

1995 Pro Line Impact

COMPLETE SET (30) 15.00 40.00
SILVER/4500 ODDS 1:1 SER.1 RETAIL BOX
*GOLD/1750: .8X TO 2X SILVER/4500
GOLD/1750 ODDS 1:90 SER.1 RETAIL
1 Jim Kelly .40 1.00
2 Thurman Thomas .40 1.00
3 Troy Aikman 1.25 3.00
4 Michael Irvin .40 1.00
5 Emmitt Smith 2.00 5.00
6 John Elway 2.50 6.00
7 Barry Sanders 2.00 5.00
8 Brett Favre 2.50 6.00
9 Reggie White .40 1.00
10 Marshall Faulk 1.50 4.00
11 Ki-Jana Carter .20 .50
12 Tim Brown .40 1.00
13 Jeff Hostetler .15 .40
14 Dan Marino 2.50 6.00
15 Drew Bledsoe .75 2.00
16 Ben Coates .15 .40
17 Rodney Hampton .15 .40
18 Randall Cunningham .40 1.00
19 Ricky Watters .15 .40
20 Byron Bam Morris .07 .20
21 Natrone Means .15 .40
22 Junior Seau .40 1.00
23 Jerry Rice 1.25 3.00
24 Steve Young 1.00 2.50
25 William Floyd .15 .40
26 Rick Mirer .15 .40
27 Chris Warren .15 .40
28 Jerome Bettis .40 1.00
29 Alvin Harper .07 .20
30 Heath Shuler .15 .40

1995 Pro Line MVP Redemption

COMPLETE SET (35) 50.00 120.00
STATED ODDS 1:72H,1:60J,1:48SR SER.1
*NUMB.OF 200: 1.2X to 3X BASIC INSERTS
1 Garrison Hearst 1.00 2.50
2 Terance Mathis .40 1.00
3 Jim Kelly 1.00 2.50
4 Thurman Thomas 1.00 2.50
5 Kerry Collins 2.00 5.00
6 Rashaan Salaam .15 .40
7 Ki-Jana Carter .40 1.00
8 Andre Rison .40 1.00
9 Troy Aikman 3.00 8.00
10 Michael Irvin 1.00 2.50
11 Emmitt Smith 5.00 12.00
12 John Elway 6.00 15.00
13 Barry Sanders 5.00 12.00
14 Brett Favre WIN 6.00 15.00
15 Marshall Faulk 4.00 10.00
16 Marcus Allen 1.00 2.50
17 Jeff Hostetler .40 1.00
18 Dan Marino 6.00 15.00
19 Cris Carter 1.00 2.50
20 Warren Moon .40 1.00
21 Drew Bledsoe 2.00 5.00
22 Ben Coates .40 1.00
23 Rodney Hampton .40 1.00
24 Boomer Esiason .40 1.00
25 Ricky Watters .40 1.00
26 Barry Foster .40 1.00
27 Natrone Means .40 1.00
28 Rick Mirer .40 1.00
29 Chris Warren .40 1.00
30 Jerry Rice 3.00 8.00
31 Steve Young 2.50 6.00
32 Jerome Bettis 1.00 2.50
33 Errict Rhett .40 1.00
34 Heath Shuler .40 1.00
35 Field Card .20 .50
MVP Brett Favre MVP/2500 3.00 8.00

1995 Pro Line National Attention

COMPLETE SET (10) 10.00 25.00
STATED ODDS 1:18 NATIONAL
NA1 Jerome Bettis .75 2.00
NA2 Sean Gilbert .30 .75
NA3 Chris Miller .15 .40
NA4 Troy Aikman 2.50 6.00
NA5 Kevin Carter .75 2.00
NA6 Marshall Faulk 3.00 8.00
NA7 Drew Bledsoe 1.50 4.00
NA8 Shane Conlan .15 .40
NA9 Emmitt Smith 4.00 10.00
NA10 Steve Young 2.00 5.00

1995 Pro Line Phone Cards $1

COMPLETE SET (30) 4.00 10.00
ONE PER SERIES 2 PACK
*PRINT.PROOFS: 1.5X TO 4X BASIC INSERTS
PRINT.PROOF ODDS 1:44 SERIES 2
1 Kerry Collins .40 1.00
2 Barry Foster .05 .15
3 Jeff Blake .20 .50
4 Troy Aikman .50 1.25
5 Reggie White .15 .40
6 Marshall Faulk .60 1.50
7 Steve Bono .05 .15
8 Drew Bledsoe .30 .75
9 Byron Bam Morris .02 .10
10 Rodney Hampton .05 .15
11 Trent Dilfer .15 .40
12 Errict Rhett .05 .15
13 Heath Shuler .05 .15
14 Mike Mamula .02 .10
15 Ricky Watters .05 .15
16 Stan Humphries .05 .15
17 Natrone Means .05 .15
18 William Floyd .05 .15
19 Joey Galloway .40 1.00
20 Ki-Jana Carter .07 .20
21 Andre Rison .05 .15
22 Steve McNair .75 2.00
23 Napoleon Kaufman .30 .75
24 Kyle Brady .15 .40
25 Steve Beuerlein .05 .15
26 Ben Coates .05 .15
27 Eric Metcalf .05 .15
28 Desmond Howard .05 .15
29 Deion Sanders .25 .60
30 J.J. Stokes .07 .20
1P Kerry Collins Promo .60 1.50

1995 Pro Line Phone Cards $2

COMPLETE SET (25) 6.00 15.00
STATED ODDS 1:6 SER.2
*PRINT.PROOFS: 1.5X TO 4X BASIC INSERTS
PRINT.PROOF ODDS 1:75 SERIES 2
1 Kerry Collins .50 1.25
2 Barry Foster .10 .30
3 Andre Rison .10 .30
4 Troy Aikman 1.00 2.50
5 Steve McNair 1.00 2.50
6 Marshall Faulk 1.25 3.00
7 J.J. Stokes .08 .25
8 Drew Bledsoe .60 1.50
9 Byron Bam Morris .05 .15
10 Rodney Hampton .10 .30
11 Deion Sanders .50 1.25
12 Errict Rhett .10 .30
13 Heath Shuler .10 .30
14 Mike Mamula .05 .15
15 Ricky Watters .10 .30
16 Stan Humphries .10 .30
17 Natrone Means .10 .30
18 William Floyd .10 .30
19 Kyle Brady .30 .75
20 Ki-Jana Carter .08 .25
21 Jeff Blake .75 2.00
22 Eric Metcalf .10 .30
23 Steve Bono .10 .30
24 Steve Beuerlein .10 .30
25 Eric Green .05 .15

1995 Pro Line Phone Cards $5

COMPLETE SET (15) 25.00 50.00
STATED ODDS 1:18 SER.2
*PRINT.PROOFS: 1.5X TO 4X BASIC INSERTS
PRINT.PROOF ODDS 1:210 SERIES 2
1 Marshall Faulk 2.50 6.00
2 Troy Aikman 2.00 5.00
3 J.J. Stokes .20 .50
4 Kyle Brady .60 1.50
5 Steve McNair 2.00 5.00
6 Deion Sanders 1.00 2.50
7 Ki-Jana Carter .20 .50
8 Kerry Collins 1.00 2.50
9 Drew Bledsoe 1.25 3.00
10 Emmitt Smith 3.00 8.00
11 William Floyd .25 .60
12 Ricky Watters .25 .60
13 Reggie White .60 1.50
14 Steve Young 1.50 4.00
15 Warren Sapp 1.00 2.50

1995 Pro Line Phone Cards $20

COMPLETE SET (5) 25.00 60.00
STATED ODDS 1:144 SER.2
1 Steve Young 6.00 15.00
2 Drew Bledsoe 5.00 12.00
3 Marshall Faulk 10.00 25.00
4 Ki-Jana Carter 2.50 6.00
5 Kerry Collins 5.00 12.00

1995 Pro Line Phone Cards $100

COMPLETE SET (5) 50.00 120.00
STATED ODDS 1:266 SER.2
1 Emmitt Smith 20.00 50.00
2 Steve Young 10.00 25.00
3 Drew Bledsoe 8.00 20.00
4 Ki-Jana Carter 4.00 10.00
5 Troy Aikman 12.50 30.00

1995 Pro Line Phone Cards $1000/$1500

$1000 STATE ODDS 1:2995 SER.2 PACKS
$1500 STATE ODDS 1:11980 SER.2 PACKS
1 Steve Young 60.00 150.00
1B Emmitt Smith/$1500 125.00 300.00
2 Drew Bledsoe 60.00 150.00
3 Ki-Jana Carter 40.00 80.00
4 Troy Aikman 75.00 200.00

1995 Pro Line Pogs

COMPLETE SET (30) 2.50 6.00
RANDOM INS.IN SPECIAL RETAIL PACKS
C1 Garrison Hearst .05 .15
Seth Joyner
C2 Terance Mathis .01 .05
Jeff George
C3 Jim Kelly .05 .15
Thurman Thomas
C4 Kerry Collins .30 .75
Barry Foster
C5 Steve Walsh .01 .05
Rashaan .Salaam
C6 Barry Sanders .30 .75
Herman Moore
C7 John Elway .40 1.00
Shannon Sharpe
C8 Troy Aikman .30 .75
Emmitt Smith
C9 Leroy Hoard .01 .05
Andre Rison
C10 Jeff Blake .15 .40
Ki-Jana Carter
C11 Brett Favre .40 1.00
Reggie White
C12 Steve McNair .40 1.00
Gary Brown
C13 Marshall Faulk .25 .60
Quentin Coryatt
C14 Tony Boselli .01 .05
Steve Beuerlein
C15 Marcus Allen .05 .15
Steve Bono
C16 Jim Everett .01 .05
Mario Bates
C17 Drew Bledsoe .10 .30
Ben Coates
C18 Warren Moon .05 .15
Chris Carter
C19 Dan Marino .40 1.00
Irving Fryar
C20 Jeff Hostetler .05 .15
Tim Brown
C21 Kevin Greene .01 .05
Byron Bam Morris
C22 Dave Brown .01 .05
Rodney Hampton
C23 Boomer Esiason .01 .05
Mo Lewis
C24 Randall Cunningham .05 .15
Ricky Watters
C25 Natrone Means .05 .15
Junior Seau
C26 Heath Shuler .02 .10
Michael Westbrook
C27 Trent Dilfer .05 .15
Errict Rhett
C28 Jerome Bettis .05 .15
Kevin Carter
C29 Steve Young .20 .50
Jerry Rice
C30 Rick Mirer .01 .05
Chris Warren

1995 Pro Line Precision Cuts

COMPLETE SET (20) 50.00 120.00
STATED ODDS 1:45 SER.2
*SAMPLES: .2X TO .5X BASIC INSERTS
P1 Jim Kelly 2.50 6.00
P2 John Elway 8.00 20.00
P3 Kerry Collins 3.00 8.00
P4 Ki-Jana Carter .75 2.00
P5 Andre Rison 1.25 3.00
P6 Troy Aikman 5.00 12.00
P7 Emmitt Smith 8.00 20.00
P8 Barry Sanders 6.00 15.00
P9 Warren Moon 1.50 4.00
P10 Jeff Hostetler .75 2.00
P11 Dan Marino 8.00 20.00
P12 Drew Bledsoe 2.00 5.00
P13 Rodney Hampton 1.25 3.00
P14 Ricky Watters 1.25 3.00
P15 Byron Bam Morris .75 2.00
P16 Natrone Means 1.25 3.00
P17 Steve Young 4.00 10.00
P18 Jerry Rice 5.00 12.00
P19 J.J. Stokes .75 2.00
P20 Errict Rhett 1.25 3.00

1995 Pro Line Pro Bowl

COMPLETE SET (30) 7.50 20.00
ONE PER SPECIAL RETAIL PACK
PB1 Seth Joyner .02 .10
PB2 Andre Reed .07 .20
PB3 Bruce Smith .20 .50
PB4 Michael Irvin .20 .50
PB5 Troy Aikman .60 1.50
PB6 Emmitt Smith 1.00 2.50
PB7 Charles Haley .07 .20
PB8 Shannon Sharpe .07 .20
PB9 John Elway 1.25 3.00
PB10 Barry Sanders 1.00 2.50
PB11 Reggie White .20 .50
PB12 Marshall Faulk .75 2.00
PB13 Tim Brown .20 .50
PB14 Chester McGlockton .07 .20
PB15 Dan Marino 1.25 3.00
PB16 Cris Carter .20 .50
PB17 Warren Moon .07 .20
PB18 Ben Coates .07 .20
PB19 Drew Bledsoe .40 1.00
PB20 Rod Woodson .07 .20
PB21 Natrone Means .07 .20
PB22 Leslie O'Neal .07 .20
PB23 Junior Seau .20 .50
PB24 Jerry Rice .60 1.50
PB25 Chris Warren .07 .20
PB26 Brent Jones .02 .10
PB27 Steve Young .50 1.25
PB28 Dana Stubblefield .07 .20
PB29 Deion Sanders .30 .75
PB30 Jerome Bettis .20 .50

1995 Pro Line Record Breakers

COMPLETE SET (10) 50.00 120.00
HB1-HB5 INS.IN SER.1 HOBBY HOT BOXES
HB1-HB5 PRINT RUN 425 SERIAL #'d SETS
RB1-RB5 INS.IN SER.1 RETAIL HOT BOXES
RB1-RB5 PRINT RUN 350 SERIAL #'d SETS
HB1 Drew Bledsoe 5.00 12.00
HB2 Cris Carter 2.50 6.00
HB3 Jerry Rice 8.00 20.00
HB4 Steve Young 6.00 15.00
HB5 Marshall Faulk 10.00 25.00
RB1 Emmitt Smith 12.50 30.00
RB2 Barry Sanders 12.50 30.00
RB3 Natrone Means 1.00 2.50
RB4 Ben Coates 1.00 2.50
RB5 Bruce Smith 2.50 6.00

1995 Pro Line Series 2

Issued by Classic, this 75 card set came in 6 card packs and included one prepaid phone card per pack. Card fronts are similar to series one, but the player's name and team are against a blue holographic background at the bottom of the card. The "ProLine" emblem at the top left also shows the card as being a series 2 card. Terrell Fletcher is the only Rookie Card of note in this set. Card backs are numbered with a "II" prefix.

COMPLETE SET (75) 6.00 15.00
1 Jim Kelly .08 .25
2 Steve Walsh .01 .05
3 Jeff Blake .08 .25
4 Vinny Testaverde .02 .10
5 Jeff Hostetler .02 .10
6 Dan Marino .60 1.50
7 Cris Carter .08 .25
8 Drew Bledsoe .20 .50
9 Jim Everett .01 .05
10 Neil O'Donnell .02 .10
11 Rodney Hampton .02 .10
12 Troy Aikman .30 .75
13 John Elway .60 1.50
14 Barry Sanders .50 1.25
15 Reggie White .08 .25
16 Marshall Faulk .40 1.00
17 Marcus Allen .08 .25
18 James O. Stewart .08 .25
19 Randall Cunningham .08 .25
20 Natrone Means .02 .10
21 Rick Mirer .02 .10
22 Jerry Rice .30 .75
23 Errict Rhett .02 .10
24 Heath Shuler .02 .10
25 Jerome Bettis .08 .25
26 Garrison Hearst .08 .25
27 Jeff George .02 .10
28 Andre Reed .02 .10
29 Warren Moon .02 .10
30 Ben Coates .02 .10
31 Mario Bates .02 .10
32 Byron Bam Morris .01 .05
33 Dave Brown .02 .10
34 Emmitt Smith .50 1.25
35 Anthony Miller .02 .10
36 Herman Moore .08 .25
37 Brett Favre .60 1.50
38 Steve Bono .02 .10
39 Stan Humphries .02 .10
40 Steve Young .25 .60
41 Trent Dilfer .08 .25
42 Chris Miller .01 .05
43 Herschel Walker .02 .10
44 Michael Irvin .08 .25
45 Junior Seau .08 .25
46 Deion Sanders .15 .40
47 William Floyd .02 .10
48 Ki-Jana Carter .02 .10
49 Kerry Collins .30 .75
50 Steve McNair .30 .75
51 Tony Boselli .02 .10
52 Kyle Brady .08 .25
53 Mike Mamula .01 .05
54 Warren Sapp .08 .25
55 J.J. Stokes .02 .10
56 Joey Galloway .15 .40
57 Hugh Douglas .02 .10
58 Michael Westbrook .08 .25
59 Napoleon Kaufman .08 .25
60 Rashaan Salaam .02 .10
61 Tyrone Wheatley .08 .25
62 Terrell Fletcher RC .01 .05
63 Eric Metcalf .02 .10
64 Kevin Carter .08 .25
65 Andre Rison .02 .10
66 Eric Green .01 .05
67 Dave Meggett .01 .05
68 Ricky Watters .02 .10
69 Steve Beuerlein .02 .10
70 Craig Erickson .01 .05
71 Michael Dean Perry .01 .05
72 Alvin Harper .01 .05
73 Rob Moore .02 .10
74 Frank Reich .01 .05
75 Checklist .01 .05

1995 Pro Line Series 2 Printer's Proofs

COMPLETE SET (75) 100.00 200.00
*PRINTER'S PROOFS: 5X TO 12X BASIC CARDS
STATED ODDS 1:18

1995 Pro Line 5000

COMPLETE SET (5) 6.00 15.00
1 Emmitt Smith 2.50 6.00
2 Drew Bledsoe 1.25 3.00
3 Marshall Faulk 1.25 3.00
4 Kerry Collins 1.00 2.50
5 Steve Young 1.50 4.00

1996 Pro Line

The 1996 Pro Line set was issued in one series totalling 350 standard-size cards. The set was issued in 10 card packs (suggested retail price of $1.79) with 28 packs in a box and 12 boxes in a case. There is a Rookies subset as well as checklists that feature players on the front. An unnumbered Emmitt Smith Promo card was produced and priced below.

COMPLETE SET (350) 10.00 25.00
1 Troy Aikman .40 1.00
2 Steve Young .30 .75
3 John Elway .75 2.00
4 Jim Kelly .15 .40
5 Dan Marino .75 2.00
6 Brett Favre .75 2.00
7 Kerry Collins .15 .40
8 Jeff Blake .15 .40
9 Stan Humphries .07 .20
10 Steve Bono .02 .10
11 Jeff George .07 .20
12 Mark Brunell .25 .60
13 Scott Mitchell .07 .20
14 Steve McNair .30 .75
15 Jeff Hostetler .02 .10
16 Jim Everett .02 .10
17 Rick Mirer .07 .20
18 Boomer Esiason .07 .20
19 Neil O'Donnell .07 .20
20 Dave Brown .02 .10
21 Erik Kramer .02 .10
22 Trent Dilfer .15 .40
23 Jim Harbaugh .07 .20
24 Vinny Testaverde .07 .20
25 Thurman Thomas .15 .40
26 Rodney Peete .02 .10
27 Gus Frerotte .07 .20
28 Warren Moon .07 .20
29 Eric Zeier .02 .10
30 Randall Cunningham .15 .40
31 Heath Shuler .07 .20
32 John Friesz .02 .10
33 Tommy Maddox .15 .40
34 Glenn Foley .07 .20
35 Drew Bledsoe .25 .60
36 Kordell Stewart .15 .40
37 Natrone Means .07 .20
38 Errict Rhett .07 .20
39 Rashaan Salaam .07 .20
40 Emmitt Smith .60 1.50
41 Larry Centers .07 .20
42 Terrell Davis .30 .75
43 Marshall Faulk .20 .50
44 Rodney Hampton .07 .20
45 Byron Bam Morris .02 .10
46 Chris Warren .07 .20
47 Curtis Martin .30 .75
48 Ricky Watters .07 .20
49 Marcus Allen .15 .40
50 Barry Sanders .60 1.50
51 Edgar Bennett .07 .20
52 Adrian Murrell .07 .20
53 James O. Stewart .07 .20
54 Leroy Hoard .02 .10
55 Jerome Bettis .15 .40
56 Craig Heyward .02 .10
57 Harvey Williams .02 .10
58 Bernie Parmalee .02 .10
59 Garrison Hearst .07 .20
60 Terry Allen .07 .20
61 Charlie Garner .07 .20
62 Dorsey Levens .15 .40
63 Derek Loville .02 .10
64 Greg Hill .07 .20
65 Derrick Moore .02 .10
66 Rodney Thomas .02 .10
67 Daryl Johnston .07 .20
68 Mario Bates .07 .20
69 Aaron Hayden RC .02 .10
70 Napoleon Kaufman .15 .40
71 Terry Kirby .07 .20
72 Glyn Milburn .02 .10
73 Robert Smith .07 .20
74 Ki-Jana Carter .07 .20
75 Tyrone Wheatley .07 .20
76 Erric Pegram .02 .10
77 Brian Mitchell .02 .10
78 Vaughn Dunbar .02 .10
79 Dave Meggett .02 .10
80 Scottie Graham .02 .10
81 Darick Holmes .02 .10
82 Marion Butts .02 .10
83 Harold Green .02 .10
84 Zack Crockett .02 .10
85 Amp Lee .02 .10
86 Lamont Warren .02 .10
87 Mark Chmura .07 .20
88 Irving Fryar .07 .20
89 Tim Brown .15 .40
90 Michael Irvin .15 .40
91 Tony Martin .07 .20
92 Alvin Harper .02 .10
93 Darnay Scott .07 .20
94 Eric Metcalf .02 .10
95 Michael Timpson .02 .10
96 Sean Dawkins .02 .10
97 Qadry Ismail .07 .20
98 Yancey Thigpen .07 .20
99 Joey Galloway .15 .40
100 Herman Moore .07 .20
101 J.J. Stokes .15 .40
102 Wayne Chrebet .25 .60
103 Ernest Givins .02 .10
104 Michael Jackson .07 .20
105 Henry Ellard .02 .10
106 Thomas Lewis .02 .10
107 Anthony Miller .07 .20
108 Terance Mathis .02 .10
109 Horace Copeland .02 .10
110 Rocket Ismail .02 .10
111 Quinn Early .02 .10
112 Haywood Jeffires .02 .10
113 Mark Carrier WR .02 .10
114 Brent Jones .02 .10
115 Ben Coates .07 .20
116 Ken Dilger .07 .20
117 Irv Smith .02 .10
118 Jay Novacek .02 .10
119 Tony McGee .02 .10
120 Troy Drayton .02 .10
121 Johnny Mitchell .02 .10
122 Rob Moore .07 .20
123 Kevin Williams WR .02 .10
124 O.J. McDuffie .07 .20
125 Carl Pickens .07 .20
126 Curtis Conway .15 .40
127 Ed McCaffrey .07 .20
128 Arthur Marshall .02 .10
129 Ernie Mills .02 .10
130 Cris Carter .15 .40
131 Isaac Bruce .15 .40
132 Brian Blades .02 .10
133 Michael Westbrook .15 .40
134 Andre Reed .07 .20
135 Andre Rison .07 .20
136 Brett Perriman .02 .10
137 Willie Jackson .07 .20
138 Ryan Yarborough .02 .10
139 Chris T. Jones .07 .20
140 Jerry Rice .40 1.00
141 Lake Dawson .02 .10
142 Robert Brooks .15 .40
143 Vincent Brisby .02 .10
144 Desmond Howard .07 .20
145 Johnnie Morton .07 .20
146 Steve Tasker .02 .10
147 Ty Detmer .07 .20
148 Todd Kinchen .02 .10
149 Mike Sherrard .02 .10
150 Eric Green .02 .10
151 Mark Bruener .02 .10
152 Kyle Brady .02 .10
153 Frank Sanders .07 .20
154 Willie Green .02 .10
155 Jeff Graham .02 .10
156 Bert Emanuel .07 .20
157 Courtney Hawkins .02 .10
158 Mark Seay .02 .10
159 Chris Calloway .02 .10
160 John Taylor .02 .10
161 Fred Barnett .02 .10
162 Tamarick Vanover .07 .20
163 Keenan McCardell .15 .40
164 Bill Brooks .02 .10
165 Alexander Wright .02 .10
166 Jake Reed .07 .20
167 Floyd Turner .02 .10
168 Mike Pritchard .02 .10
169 Lawrence Dawsey .02 .10
170 Shawn Jefferson .02 .10
171 Michael Haynes .02 .10
172 Shannon Sharpe .07 .20
173 Jackie Harris .02 .10
174 Daryl Hobbs RC .02 .10
175 Chris Sanders .07 .20
176 Willie Davis .02 .10
177 Marco Coleman .02 .10
178 Pat Swilling .02 .10
179 Alonzo Spellman .02 .10
180 Simon Fletcher .02 .10
181 Sean Gilbert .02 .10
182 Tracy Scroggins .02 .10
183 Hugh Douglas .07 .20
184 Eric Swann .02 .10
185 Russell Maryland .02 .10
186 Warren Sapp .02 .10
187 Jim Flanigan .02 .10
188 Cortez Kennedy .02 .10
189 Andy Harmon .02 .10
190 Dan Saleaumua .02 .10
191 Kelvin Pritchett .02 .10
192 John Randle .07 .20
193 Dan Wilkinson .02 .10
194 Chester McGlockton .02 .10
195 Leon Lett .02 .10
196 Neil Smith .07 .20
197 Mike Mamula .02 .10
198 Mike Jones .02 .10
199 Reggie White .15 .40
200 Anthony Pleasant .02 .10
201 Phil Hansen .02 .10
202 Ray Seals .02 .10
203 Tony Bennett .02 .10
204 Leslie O'Neal .02 .10
205 Jeff Cross .02 .10
206 Anthony Cook .02 .10
207 Clyde Simmons .02 .10
208 Renaldo Turnbull .02 .10
209 Charles Haley .07 .20
210 John Copeland .02 .10
211 John Thierry .02 .10
212 Michael Strahan .07 .20
213 Jeff Lageman .02 .10
214 William Fuller .02 .10
215 Rickey Jackson .02 .10
216 Wayne Martin .02 .10
217 Steve Emtman .02 .10
218 Shawn Lee .02 .10
219 Chris Zorich .02 .10
220 Henry Thomas .02 .10
221 Dana Stubblefield .07 .20
222 D'Marco Farr .02 .10
223 Pierce Holt .02 .10
224 Sean Jones .02 .10
225 Robert Porcher .02 .10
226 Kevin Carter .02 .10
227 Chris Doleman .02 .10
228 Tony Tolbert .02 .10
229 Bruce Smith .07 .20
230 Marvin Washington .02 .10
231 Blaine Bishop .02 .10
232 Bryant Young .07 .20
233 Rob Burnett .02 .10
234 Lawrence Phillips RC .15 .40
235 Trev Alberts .02 .10
236 Eric Curry .02 .10
237 Anthony Smith .02 .10
238 Sam Mills .02 .10
239 Seth Joyner .02 .10
240 Quentin Coryatt .02 .10
241 Levon Kirkland .02 .10
242 Cornelius Bennett .02 .10
243 Chris Spielman .02 .10
244 Mo Lewis .02 .10
245 Lee Woodall .02 .10
246 Derrick Thomas .15 .40
247 Willie McGinest .02 .10
248 Terry Wooden .02 .10
249 Greg Lloyd .07 .20
250 Jack Del Rio .02 .10
251 Hardy Nickerson .02 .10
252 Micheal Barrow .02 .10
253 Lamar Lathon .02 .10
254 Bryan Cox .02 .10
255 Randy Kirk .02 .10
256 Jessie Tuggle .02 .10
257 Roman Phifer .02 .10
258 Ken Harvey .02 .10
259 Junior Seau .15 .40
260 Pepper Johnson .02 .10
261 Chris Slade .02 .10
262 Gary Plummer .02 .10
263 Wayne Simmons .02 .10
264 Bryce Paup .02 .10
265 William Thomas .02 .10
266 Kevin Greene .07 .20
267 Bobby Engram RC .15 .40
268 Ken Norton .02 .10
269 Eric Hill .02 .10
270 Darion Conner .02 .10
271 Tyrone Poole .02 .10
272 Cris Dishman .02 .10
273 Marcus Jones RC .02 .10
274 Rod Woodson .07 .20
275 Mark McMillian .02 .10
276 Dale Carter .02 .10
277 Darrell Green .02 .10
278 Donnell Woolford .02 .10
279 Troy Vincent .02 .10
280 Larry Brown .02 .10
281 Aeneas Williams .02 .10
282 Eric Allen .02 .10
283 Ray Buchanan .02 .10
284 Ty Law .15 .40
285 Eric Davis .02 .10
286 Todd Lyght .02 .10
287 Terry McDaniel .02 .10
288 Darryll Lewis .02 .10
289 Deion Sanders .25 .60
290 Phillippi Sparks .02 .10
291 Bobby Taylor .02 .10
292 Mark Collins .02 .10
293 Steve Atwater .02 .10
294 Stanley Richard .07 .20
295 Stevon Moore .02 .10
296 Bennie Blades .02 .10
297 Tim McDonald .02 .10
298 Shaun Gayle .02 .10
299 Darren Woodson .07 .20
300 Mark Carrier DB .02 .10
301 Carnell Lake .02 .10
302 James Washington .02 .10
303 LeRoy Butler .02 .10
304 Henry Jones .02 .10
305 Darryl Williams .02 .10
306 Darren Perry .02 .10
307 Merton Hanks .02 .10
308 Orlando Thomas .02 .10
309 Eric Turner .02 .10
310 Nate Newton .02 .10
311 Steve Wisniewski .02 .10
312 Derrick Deese .02 .10
313 Larry Allen .02 .10
314 Aaron Taylor .02 .10
315 Blake Brockermeyer .02 .10
316 William Roaf .02 .10
317 Jumbo Elliott .02 .10
318 Keyshawn Johnson RC .40 1.00
319 Karim Abdul-Jabbar RC .15 .40
320 Kevin Hardy RC .15 .40
321 Duane Clemons RC .02 .10
322 Jevon Langford RC .02 .10
323 Mike Alstott RC .40 1.00
324 Scott Greene RC .02 .10
325 Derrick Mayes RC .15 .40
326 Chris Doering RC .02 .10
327 Amani Toomer RC .40 1.00
328 Eric Moulds RC .50 1.25
329 Alex Molden RC .02 .10
330 Lawyer Milloy RC .20 .50
331 Daryl Gardener RC .02 .10
332 Randall Godfrey RC .02 .10
333 Willie Anderson RC .02 .10
334 Tony Banks RC .15 .40
335 Jeff Lewis RC .07 .20
336 Roman Oben RC .02 .10
337 Andre Johnson RC .02 .10
338 Brian Roche RC .02 .10
339 Johnny McWilliams RC .07 .20
340 Alex Van Dyke RC .07 .20
341 Ray Mickens RC .02 .10
342 Marvin Harrison RC 1.00 2.50
343 Terry Glenn RC .40 1.00
344 Tim Biakabutuka RC .15 .40
345 Simeon Rice RC .40 1.00
346 Cedric Jones RC .02 .10
347 Eddie George RC .50 1.25
348 Drew Bledsoe .15 .40
Checklist
349 Emmitt Smith .20 .50
Checklist
350 Keyshawn Johnson .15 .40
Checklist

1996 Pro Line Headliners

COMPLETE SET (350) 150.00 300.00
*STARS: 3X TO 8X BASIC CARDS
*RCs: 1.5X TO 4X BASIC CARDS
ONE PER JUMBO PACK

1996 Pro Line National

COMPLETE SET (350)	150.00	300.00
*NATIONAL STARS: 3X TO 8X BASIC CARDS		
*NATIONAL RCs: 1.5X TO 4X BASIC CARDS		
ONE PER NATIONAL PACK		

1996 Pro Line Printer's Proofs

COMPLETE SET (350)	250.00	500.00
*PP STARS: 5X TO 12X BASIC CARDS		
*PP RCs: 2.5X TO 6X BASIC CARDS		
STATED ODDS 1:10 SPECIAL RETAIL		

1996 Pro Line Autographs Gold

GOLD STAT.ODDS 1:170 HOB/RET, 1:200 JUM		
1 Troy Aikman	150.00	300.00
Emmitt Smith		
Gold Only		
2 Eric Allen	5.00	12.00
3 Mike Alstott	12.50	30.00
4 Tony Banks	8.00	20.00
5 Blaine Bishop	5.00	12.00
6 Drew Bledsoe	30.00	80.00
7 Tim Brown	15.00	40.00
8 Marion Butts	5.00	12.00
10 Sedric Clark	5.00	12.00
11 Duane Clemons	5.00	12.00
12 Marcus Coleman	5.00	12.00
13 Kerry Collins	12.50	30.00
14 Eric Davis	5.00	12.00
15 Derrick Deese	5.00	12.00
16 Jack Del Rio	5.00	12.00
17 Ty Detmer	8.00	20.00
18 Chris Doering	5.00	12.00
19 Jumbo Elliott	5.00	12.00
20 Marshall Faulk	25.00	50.00
21 Glenn Foley	5.00	12.00
22 John Friesz	5.00	12.00
23 Daryl Gardener	5.00	12.00
24 Randall Godfrey	5.00	12.00
25 Scott Greene	5.00	12.00
26 Rhett Hall	5.00	12.00
27 Merton Hanks	5.00	12.00
28 Kevin Hardy	5.00	12.00
29 Richard Huntley	5.00	12.00
30 Michael Jackson	5.00	12.00
31 Ron Jaworski	12.50	30.00
32 Andre Johnson	5.00	12.00
33 Keyshawn Johnson	12.50	30.00
34 Keyshawn Johnson	25.00	50.00
Neil O'Donnell		
Gold Only		
35 Mike Jones	5.00	12.00
36 Jim Kiick	12.50	30.00
37 Carnell Lake	5.00	12.00
38 Jeff Lewis	5.00	12.00
39 Tommy Maddox	12.50	30.00
40 Arthur Marshall	5.00	12.00
41 Russell Maryland	5.00	12.00
42 Derrick Mayes	5.00	12.00
43 Ed McCaffrey	8.00	20.00
44 Keenan McCardell	8.00	20.00
45 Terry McDaniel	5.00	12.00
46 Tim McDonald	5.00	12.00
47 Willie McGinest	12.50	30.00
48 Mark McMillian	5.00	12.00
49 Johnny McWilliams	5.00	12.00
50 Ray Mickens	5.00	12.00
51 Anthony Miller	5.00	12.00
52 Rick Mirer	8.00	20.00
53 Alex Molden	5.00	12.00
54 Johnnie Morton	8.00	20.00
55 Eric Moulds	8.00	20.00
56 Roman Oben	5.00	12.00
57 Neil O'Donnell	12.50	30.00
58 Leslie O'Neal	5.00	12.00
59 Roman Phifer	5.00	12.00
60 Gary Plummer	5.00	12.00
61 Jim Plunkett	12.50	30.00
62 Stanley Pritchett	5.00	12.00
63 John Randle	10.00	25.00
64 Brian Roche	5.00	12.00
65 Orpheus Roye	5.00	12.00
66 Mark Seay	5.00	12.00
67 Mike Sherrard	5.00	12.00
68 Chris Slade	5.00	12.00
69 Scott Slutzker	5.00	12.00
70 Emmitt Smith	100.00	250.00
Gold Only		
71 Steve Taneyhill	5.00	12.00
72 Robb Thomas	5.00	12.00
73 William Thomas	5.00	12.00
75 Alex Van Dyke	5.00	12.00
76 Randy White	12.50	30.00
77 Steve Young	40.00	100.00
Gold Only		

1996 Pro Line Autographs Blue

*BLUE CARDS: .25X TO .6X GOLDS		
74 Amani Toomer	15.00	30.00

1996 Pro Line Cels

COMPLETE SET (20)	60.00	150.00
STATED ODDS 1:75 HOBBY		
PC1 Bryce Paup	.60	1.50
PC2 Kerry Collins	2.50	6.00
PC3 Troy Aikman	6.00	15.00
PC4 Deion Sanders	4.00	10.00
PC5 Emmitt Smith	10.00	25.00
PC6 Steve McNair	3.00	8.00
PC7 Drew Bledsoe	4.00	10.00
PC8 Kordell Stewart	2.50	6.00
PC9 Ricky Watters	1.25	3.00
PC10 Jerry Rice	6.00	15.00
PC11 Steve Young	5.00	12.00
PC12 Errict Rhett	1.25	3.00
PC13 Brett Favre	12.50	30.00
PC14 Jeff Blake	2.50	6.00
PC15 Joey Galloway	2.50	6.00
PC16 Herman Moore	1.25	3.00
PC17 Curtis Martin	5.00	12.00
PC18 Keyshawn Johnson	2.50	6.00
PC19 Eddie George	3.00	8.00
PC20 Simeon Rice	1.25	3.00

1996 Pro Line Cover Story

COMPLETE SET (20)	20.00	50.00
STATED ODDS 1:30 JUMBO		
CS1 Bryce Paup	.30	.75
CS2 Kerry Collins	1.25	3.00
CS3 Rashaan Salaam	.60	1.50
CS4 Troy Aikman	3.00	8.00
CS5 Emmitt Smith	5.00	12.00
CS6 Herman Moore	.60	1.50
CS7 Curtis Martin	2.50	6.00
CS8 Kordell Stewart	1.25	3.00
CS9 Ricky Watters	.60	1.50
CS10 Carl Pickens	.60	1.50
CS11 Joey Galloway	1.25	3.00
CS12 Errict Rhett	.60	1.50
CS13 Deion Sanders	2.00	5.00
CS14 Reggie White	1.25	3.00
CS15 Hugh Douglas	.60	1.50
CS16 Tamarick Vanover	.60	1.50
CS17 Derrick Mayes	.60	1.50
CS18 Marvin Harrison	4.00	10.00
CS19 Tim Biakabutuka	.60	1.50
CS20 Terry Glenn	1.50	4.00

1996 Pro Line Rivalries

COMPLETE SET (20)	25.00	60.00
STATED ODDS 1:15		
R1 Drew Bledsoe	1.25	3.00
Jim Kelly		
R2 Dan Marino	4.00	10.00
Greg Lloyd		
R3 Kordell Stewart	1.00	2.50
Mark Brunell		
R4 Tamarick Vanover	.75	2.00
Napoleon Kaufman		
R5 John Elway	4.00	10.00
Jeff Blake		
R6 Emmitt Smith	3.00	8.00
Ricky Watters		
R7 Troy Aikman	2.00	5.00
Steve Young		
R8 Deion Sanders	1.25	3.00
Gus Frerotte		
R9 Brett Favre	4.00	10.00
Errict Rhett		
R10 Rashaan Salaam	.40	1.00
Warren Moon		
R11 Kerry Collins	.75	2.00
Ken Norton Jr.		
R12 Jeff George	.75	2.00
Isaac Bruce		
R13 Rod Woodson	.40	1.00
Rodney Thomas		
R14 Herman Moore	.40	1.00
Reggie White		
R15 Marshall Faulk	1.00	2.50
Curtis Martin		
R16 Keyshawn Johnson	2.50	6.00
Marvin Harrison		
R17 Kevin Hardy	.40	1.00
Alex Molden		
R18 Terry Glenn	1.00	2.50
Simeon Rice		
R19 Eddie George	1.00	2.50
Tim Biakabutuka		
R20 Karim Abdul-Jabbar	.40	1.00
Cedric Jones		

1996 Pro Line Touchdown Performers

COMPLETE SET (20)	25.00	60.00
STATED ODDS 1:75 RETAIL		
TD1 Kerry Collins	1.50	4.00
TD2 Troy Aikman	4.00	10.00
TD3 Deion Sanders	2.50	6.00
TD4 Emmitt Smith	6.00	15.00
TD5 Mark Brunell	1.50	4.00
TD6 Steve McNair	3.00	8.00
TD7 Marshall Faulk	2.00	5.00
TD8 Dan Marino	8.00	20.00
TD9 Cris Carter	1.50	4.00
TD10 Drew Bledsoe	2.50	6.00
TD11 Yancey Thigpen	.75	2.00
TD12 Jerry Rice	4.00	10.00
TD13 J.J. Stokes	1.50	4.00
TD14 Terrell Davis	3.00	8.00
TD15 Carl Pickens	.75	2.00
TD16 Joey Galloway	1.50	4.00
TD17 Kordell Stewart	1.50	4.00
TD18 Isaac Bruce	1.50	4.00
TD19 Keyshawn Johnson	1.50	4.00
TD20 Amani Toomer	1.50	4.00

1996 Pro Line National Laser Promos

These five promo cards were distributed at the 1996 National Card Collector's Convention in Anaheim. Each card was distributed during the show at the Classic booth. Complete sets framed in a lucite holder were also produced and individually numbered of 300.

COMPLETE SET (5)	8.00	20.00
COMP.FRAMED SET (5)	10.00	25.00
1 Kordell Stewart	1.60	4.00
2 Troy Aikman	2.00	5.00
3 Emmitt Smith	3.20	8.00
4 Lawrence Phillips	1.20	3.00
5 Keyshawn Johnson	1.60	4.00

1997 Pro Line

The 1997 Pro Line set was issued in one series totaling 300 cards and was distributed in eight-card packs with a suggested retail price of $2.79. The set features color player photos of the top NFL veterans, traded players, free agents, and rookies for 1997. Each box of 28 packs also contained at least one autographed card and a chance to win autographed memorabilia from two-time MVP Brett Favre.

COMPLETE SET (300)	10.00	25.00
1 Larry Centers	.10	.30
2 Kent Graham	.07	.20
3 LeShon Johnson	.07	.20
4 Leeland McElroy	.07	.20
5 Rob Moore	.10	.30
6 Simeon Rice	.10	.30
7 Frank Sanders	.10	.30
8 Eric Swann	.07	.20
9 Aeneas Williams	.07	.20
10 Jamal Anderson	.20	.50
11 Cornelius Bennett	.07	.20
12 Ray Buchanan	.07	.20
13 Bert Emanuel	.10	.30
14 Terance Mathis	.10	.30
15 Eric Metcalf	.10	.30
16 Jessie Tuggle	.07	.20
17 Derrick Alexander WR	.10	.30
18 Earnest Byner	.07	.20
19 Michael Jackson	.10	.30
20 Antonio Langham	.07	.20
21 Ray Lewis	.30	.75
22 Byron Bam Morris	.07	.20
23 Jonathan Ogden	.07	.20
24 Vinny Testaverde	.10	.30
25 Eric Moulds	.20	.50
26 Todd Collins	.07	.20
27 Quinn Early	.07	.20
28 Phil Hansen	.07	.20
29 Darick Holmes	.07	.20
30 Bryce Paup	.07	.20
31 Andre Reed	.10	.30
32 Bruce Smith	.10	.30
33 Chris Spielman	.07	.20
34 Matt Stevens	.07	.20
35 Steve Tasker	.07	.20
36 Thurman Thomas	.20	.50
37 Mark Carrier WR	.07	.20
38 Kerry Collins	.20	.50
39 Tim Biakabutuka	.10	.30
40 Eric Davis	.07	.20
41 Kevin Greene	.10	.30
42 Anthony Johnson	.07	.20
43 Lamar Lathon	.07	.20
44 Sam Mills	.07	.20
45 Wesley Walls	.10	.30
46 Muhsin Muhammad	.10	.30
47 Mark Carrier DB	.07	.20
48 Curtis Conway	.10	.30
49 Bryan Cox	.07	.20
50 Bobby Engram	.10	.30
51 Raymont Harris	.07	.20
52 Walt Harris	.07	.20
53 Rick Mirer	.07	.20
54 Rashaan Salaam	.10	.30
55 Alonzo Spellman	.07	.20
56 Ashley Ambrose	.07	.20
57 Jeff Blake	.10	.30
58 Ki-Jana Carter	.07	.20
59 John Copeland	.07	.20
60 James Francis	.07	.20
61 Tony McGee	.07	.20
62 Carl Pickens	.10	.30
63 Darnay Scott	.10	.30
64 Steve Tovar	.07	.20
65 Dan Wilkinson	.07	.20
66 Troy Aikman	.40	1.00
67 Eric Bjornson	.07	.20
68 Michael Irvin	.20	.50
69 Daryl Johnston	.10	.30
70 Nate Newton	.07	.20
71 Deion Sanders	.20	.50
72 Emmitt Smith	.60	1.50
73 Kevin Smith	.07	.20
74 Kevin Williams	.07	.20
75 Darren Woodson	.07	.20
76 Mark Tuinei	.07	.20
77 Steve Atwater	.07	.20
78 Terrell Davis	.25	.60
79 John Elway	.75	2.00
80 Ed McCaffrey	.10	.30
81 Anthony Miller	.07	.20
82 John Mobley	.07	.20
83 Michael Dean Perry	.07	.20
84 Shannon Sharpe	.10	.30
85 Alfred Williams	.07	.20
86 Reggie Brown LB	.10	.30
87 Luther Elliss	.07	.20
88 Scott Mitchell	.10	.30
89 Herman Moore	.10	.30
90 Johnnie Morton	.10	.30
91 Brett Perriman	.07	.20
92 Robert Porcher	.07	.20
93 Barry Sanders	.60	1.50
94 Henry Thomas	.07	.20
95 Edgar Bennett	.10	.30
96 Robert Brooks	.10	.30
97 Gilbert Brown	.10	.30
98 LeRoy Butler	.07	.20
99 Mark Chmura	.10	.30
100 Brett Favre	.75	2.00
101 Santana Dotson	.07	.20
102 Antonio Freeman	.20	.50
103 Dorsey Levens	.20	.50
104 Wayne Simmons	.07	.20
105 Reggie White	.20	.50
106 Willie Davis	.07	.20
107 Eddie George	.20	.50
108 Darryll Lewis	.07	.20
109 Steve McNair	.25	.60
110 Marcus Robertson	.07	.20
111 Chris Sanders	.07	.20
112 Al Smith	.07	.20
113 Tony Bennett	.07	.20
114 Quentin Coryatt	.07	.20
115 Ken Dilger	.07	.20
116 Sean Dawkins	.07	.20
117 Marshall Faulk	.25	.60
118 Jim Harbaugh	.10	.30
119 Marvin Harrison	.20	.50
120 Jeff Herrod	.07	.20
121 Tony Boselli	.07	.20
122 Tony Brackens	.07	.20
123 Mark Brunell	.25	.60
124 Kevin Hardy	.07	.20
125 Jeff Lageman	.07	.20
126 Keenan McCardell	.10	.30
127 Natrone Means	.10	.30
128 Eddie Robinson	.07	.20
129 Jimmy Smith	.10	.30
130 James O.Stewart	.10	.30
131 Marcus Allen	.20	.50
132 Dale Carter	.07	.20
133 Mark Collins	.07	.20
134 Lake Dawson	.07	.20
135 Greg Hill	.07	.20
136 Sean LaChapelle	.07	.20
137 Chris Penn	.07	.20
138 Derrick Thomas	.20	.50
139 Tamarick Vanover	.10	.30
140 Elvis Grbac	.10	.30
141 Karim Abdul-Jabbar	.20	.50
142 Fred Barnett	.07	.20
143 Terrell Buckley	.07	.20
144 Daryl Gardener	.07	.20
145 Randal Hill	.07	.20
146 Dan Marino	.75	2.00
147 O.J. McDuffie	.10	.30
148 Jerris McPhail	.07	.20
149 Zach Thomas	.20	.50
150 Cris Carter	.20	.50
151 Dixon Edwards	.07	.20
152 Leroy Hoard	.07	.20
153 Qadry Ismail	.10	.30
154 Brad Johnson	.20	.50
155 John Randle	.10	.30
156 Jake Reed	.10	.30
157 Robert Smith	.10	.30
158 Orlando Thomas	.07	.20
159 Dewayne Washington	.07	.20
160 Drew Bledsoe	.25	.60
161 Tedy Bruschi	.40	1.00
162 Willie Clay	.07	.20
163 Ben Coates	.10	.30
164 Terry Glenn	.20	.50
165 Shawn Jefferson	.07	.20
166 Ty Law	.10	.30
167 Curtis Martin	.25	.60
168 Willie McGinest	.07	.20
169 Chris Slade	.07	.20
170 Eric Allen	.07	.20
171 Mario Bates	.07	.20
172 Heath Shuler	.07	.20
173 Michael Haynes	.07	.20
174 Wayne Martin	.07	.20
175 Torrance Small	.07	.20
176 Dave Brown	.07	.20
177 Chris Calloway	.07	.20
178 Rodney Hampton	.10	.30
179 Danny Kanell	.10	.30
180 Thomas Lewis	.07	.20
181 Jason Sehorn	.10	.30
182 Amani Toomer	.10	.30
183 Charles Way	.10	.30
184 Tyrone Wheatley	.10	.30
185 Wayne Chrebet	.20	.50
186 Hugh Douglas	.07	.20
187 Aaron Glenn	.07	.20
188 Jeff Graham	.07	.20
189 Keyshawn Johnson	.20	.50
190 Mo Lewis	.07	.20
191 Adrian Murrell	.10	.30
192 Neil O'Donnell	.10	.30
193 Tim Brown	.20	.50
194 Rickey Dudley	.10	.30
195 Jeff George	.10	.30
196 Napoleon Kaufman	.20	.50
197 Russell Maryland	.07	.20
198 Terry McDaniel	.07	.20
199 Chester McGlockton	.07	.20
200 Desmond Howard	.10	.30
201 Pat Swilling	.07	.20
202 Ty Detmer	.10	.30
203 Jason Dunn	.07	.20
204 Ray Farmer	.07	.20
205 Irving Fryar	.10	.30
206 Chris T. Jones	.07	.20
207 Bobby Taylor	.07	.20
208 William Thomas	.07	.20
209 Hollis Thomas RC	.07	.20
210 Kevin Turner	.07	.20
211 Ricky Watters	.10	.30
212 Jerome Bettis	.20	.50
213 Andre Hastings	.07	.20
214 Charles Johnson	.10	.30
215 Levon Kirkland	.07	.20
216 Carnell Lake	.07	.20
217 Greg Lloyd	.07	.20
218 Darren Perry	.07	.20
219 Kordell Stewart	.20	.50
220 Rod Woodson	.10	.30
221 Andre Coleman	.07	.20
222 Marco Coleman	.07	.20
223 Leonard Russell	.07	.20
224 Stan Humphries	.10	.30
225 Shawn Lee	.07	.20
226 Tony Martin	.10	.30
227 Chris Mims	.07	.20
228 Junior Seau	.20	.50
229 Chris Doleman	.07	.20
230 William Floyd	.10	.30
231 Merton Hanks	.07	.20
232 Brent Jones	.10	.30
233 Terry Kirby	.10	.30
234 Ken Norton	.07	.20
235 Terrell Owens	.25	.60
236 Jerry Rice	.40	1.00
237 Bryant Young	.07	.20
238 Steve Young	.25	.60
239 Garrison Hearst	.10	.30
240 Brian Blades	.07	.20
241 Chad Brown	.07	.20
242 John Friesz	.07	.20
243 Joey Galloway	.10	.30
244 Cortez Kennedy	.07	.20
245 Chris Warren	.10	.30
246 Darryl Williams	.07	.20
247 Tony Banks	.10	.30
248 Isaac Bruce	.20	.50
249 Kevin Carter	.07	.20
250 Eddie Kennison	.10	.30
251 Todd Lyght	.07	.20
252 Leslie O'Neal	.07	.20
253 Anthony Parker	.07	.20
254 Roman Phifer	.07	.20
255 Lawrence Phillips	.07	.20
256 Mike Alstott	.20	.50
257 Derrick Brooks	.20	.50
258 Trent Dilfer	.20	.50
259 Jackie Harris	.07	.20
260 Hardy Nickerson	.07	.20
261 Errict Rhett	.07	.20
262 Warren Sapp	.10	.30
263 Terry Allen	.20	.50
264 Jamie Asher	.07	.20
265 Henry Ellard	.07	.20
266 Gus Frerotte	.07	.20
267 Sean Gilbert	.07	.20
268 Darrell Green	.10	.30
269 Ken Harvey	.07	.20
270 Brian Mitchell	.07	.20
271 Michael Westbrook	.10	.30
272 Koy Detmer RC	.40	1.00
273 Yatil Green RC	.10	.30
274 Troy Davis RC	.10	.30
275 Darrell Russell RC	.07	.20
276 Warrick Dunn RC	.60	1.50
277 David LaFleur RC	.07	.20
278 Tony Gonzalez RC	.75	2.00
279 Jake Plummer RC	.75	2.00
280 Antowain Smith RC	.50	1.25
281 Peter Boulware RC	.20	.50
282 Shawn Springs RC	.10	.30
283 Bryant Westbrook RC	.07	.20
284 Rae Carruth RC	.07	.20
285 Corey Dillon RC	.75	2.00
286 Byron Hanspard RC	.10	.30
287 Greg Jones RC	.07	.20
288 Trevor Pryce RC	.20	.50
289 Michael Booker RC	.07	.20
290 Orlando Pace RC	.20	.50
291 James Farrior RC	.20	.50
292 Walter Jones RC	.20	.50
293 Reinard Wilson RC	.10	.30
294 Ike Hilliard RC	.30	.75
295 Kenard Lang RC	.10	.30
296 Reidel Anthony RC	.20	.50
297 Brett Favre CL	.20	.50
298 Kerry Collins	.10	.30
Checklist back		
299 Drew Bledsoe	.10	.30
Checklist back		
300 Terrell Davis	.20	.50
Checklist back		

1997 Pro Line Autographs

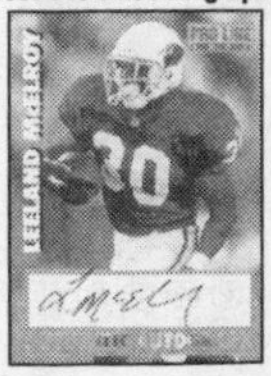

STATED ODDS 1:28		
1 Karim Abdul-Jabbar	8.00	20.00
2 Troy Aikman	60.00	120.00
3 Eric Allen	6.00	15.00
4 Mike Alstott	12.50	25.00
5 Marco Battaglia	4.00	10.00
6 Eric Bjornson	4.00	10.00
7 Peter Boulware	6.00	15.00
8 Ray Buchanon	8.00	20.00
9 Rae Carruth	4.00	10.00
10 Kerry Collins	8.00	20.00
11 Stephen Davis	12.00	30.00
12 Terrell Davis	15.00	40.00
13 Troy Davis/5000	4.00	10.00
14 Derrick Deese	4.00	10.00
15 Koy Detmer	6.00	15.00
16 Ken Dilger	6.00	15.00
17 Corey Dillon	12.00	30.00
18 Hugh Douglas	6.00	15.00
19 Jason Dunn	4.00	10.00
20 Warrick Dunn	10.00	25.00
21 Ray Farmer	4.00	10.00
22 Brett Favre	75.00	125.00
23 Joey Galloway	6.00	15.00
24 Norberto Garrido	4.00	10.00
25 Terry Glenn	10.00	25.00
26 Tony Gonzalez	20.00	40.00
27 Byron Hanspard	4.00	10.00
28 Kevin Hardy	6.00	15.00
29 Steve Israel	4.00	10.00
30 Brad Johnson	8.00	20.00
31 Keyshawn Johnson	8.00	20.00
32 Lance Johnstone	4.00	10.00
33 Greg Jones	4.00	10.00
34 Mike Jones	6.00	15.00
35 Danny Kanell	6.00	15.00
36 David LaFleur	4.00	10.00
37 Keenan McCardell	6.00	15.00
38 Leeland McElroy	4.00	10.00
39 Willie McGinest	8.00	20.00
40 Mark McMillian	4.00	10.00
41 Nate Newton	8.00	20.00
42 Jake Plummer	10.00	25.00
43 Trevor Pryce	8.00	20.00
44 John Randle	15.00	30.00
45 Simeon Rice	6.00	15.00
46 Jon Runyan	6.00	15.00
47 Chris Slade	4.00	10.00
48 Antowain Smith	8.00	20.00
49 Emmitt Smith	60.00	120.00
50 Jimmy Smith	8.00	20.00
51 Matt Stevens	4.00	10.00
52 Kordell Stewart	8.00	20.00
53 Mark Tuinei	15.00	30.00
54 Bryant Westbrook	4.00	10.00
55 Brian Williams LB	4.00	10.00
56 Dusty Zeigler	4.00	10.00

1997 Pro Line Autographs Emerald

STATED PRINT RUN 40-530		
1 Karim Abdul-Jabbar/190	12.00	30.00
2 Troy Aikman/40	125.00	250.00
3 Eric Allen/250	10.00	25.00
5 Marco Battaglia/500	7.50	20.00
6 Eric Bjornson/390	7.50	20.00
7A Peter Boulware/430	10.00	25.00
7B Peter Boulware/400	10.00	25.00
8 Ray Buchanon/390	12.00	30.00
9 Rae Carruth/525	7.50	20.00
10 Kerry Collins/170	20.00	40.00
11 Stephen Davis/530	12.00	30.00
12 Terrell Davis/100	30.00	60.00
13 Troy Davis/525	7.50	20.00
16 Ken Dilger/525	7.50	20.00
17 Corey Dillon/470	12.00	30.00
18 Hugh Douglas/400	7.50	20.00
19 Jason Dunn/525	7.50	20.00
20 Warrick Dunn/430	12.00	30.00
21 Ray Farmer/340	7.50	20.00
22 Brett Favre/100	125.00	250.00
23 Joey Galloway/300	10.00	25.00
25 Terry Glenn/380	12.00	30.00
27 Byron Hanspard/500	7.50	20.00
28 Kevin Hardy/500	7.50	20.00
30 Brad Johnson/410	12.00	30.00
31 Keyshawn Johnson/100	25.00	50.00
33 Greg Jones/470	7.50	20.00
35 Danny Kanell/450	10.00	25.00
36 David LaFleur/500	7.50	20.00
37 Keenan McCardell/220	10.00	25.00
38 Leeland McElroy/440	7.50	20.00
39 Willie McGinest/210	12.00	30.00
41 Nate Newton/340	10.00	25.00
42 Jake Plummer/440	12.00	30.00
44 John Randle/400	20.00	50.00
45 Simeon Rice/375	10.00	25.00
46 Jon Runyan/500	7.50	20.00
47 Chris Slade/260	7.50	20.00
49 Emmitt Smith/200	75.00	150.00
50 Jimmy Smith/280	10.00	25.00
51 Matt Stevens/450	7.50	20.00
52 Kordell Stewart/130	20.00	50.00
53 Mark Tuinei/400	12.00	30.00
54 Bryant Westbrook/525	10.00	25.00
56 Dusty Zeigler/480	7.50	20.00

1997 Pro Line Board Members

COMPLETE SET (15)	40.00	100.00
STATED ODDS 1:112		
BM1 Troy Aikman	6.00	15.00
BM2 Kerry Collins	3.00	8.00
BM3 Terrell Davis	4.00	10.00
BM4 Brett Favre	12.50	30.00
BM5 Gus Frerotte	1.25	3.00
BM6 Emmitt Smith	10.00	25.00
BM7 Kordell Stewart	3.00	8.00
BM8 Steve Young	4.00	10.00
BM9 Eddie George	3.00	8.00
BM10 Terry Glenn	3.00	8.00
BM11 Troy Davis	1.00	2.50
BM12 Darrell Russell	.60	1.50
BM13 Peter Boulware	1.50	4.00
BM14 Warrick Dunn	5.00	12.00
BM15 Rae Carruth	.60	1.50

1997 Pro Line Brett Favre

COMPLETE SET (9)	15.00	40.00
COMMON CARD (BF1-BF9)	2.00	5.00
1-9: STATED ODDS 1:28		
10: STATED ODDS 1:3024		
BF10 Brett Favre	50.00	120.00

1997 Pro Line Rivalries

COMPLETE SET (20)	25.00	60.00
STATED ODDS 1:35		
RV1 John Elway	6.00	15.00
Derrick Thomas		
RV2 Jeff Blake	.75	2.00
Vinny Testaverde		
RV3 Emmitt Smith	5.00	12.00
Ricky Watters		
RV4 Jim Harbaugh	.75	2.00
Thurman Thomas		
RV5 Barry Sanders	5.00	12.00
Reggie White		
RV6 Desmond Howard	1.25	3.00
Junior Seau		
RV7 Dan Marino	6.00	15.00
Hugh Douglas		
RV8 Jerome Bettis	1.25	3.00
Carl Pickens		
RV9 Mark Brunell	1.25	3.00
Kordell Stewart		
RV10 Karim Abdul-Jabbar	.75	2.00
Bruce Smith		
RV11 Rashaan Salaam	1.25	3.00
Brad Johnson		
RV12 Steve Young	3.00	8.00
Kerry Collins		
RV13 Brett Favre	6.00	15.00
Troy Aikman		
RV14 Drew Bledsoe	1.25	3.00
Marshall Faulk		
RV15 Steve McNair	1.25	3.00
Kevin Carter		
RV16 Jerry Rice	4.00	10.00
Terrell Davis		
RV17 Deion Sanders	1.25	3.00
Dave Brown		
RV18 Darrell Russell	.75	2.00
Orlando Pace		
RV19 Reidel Anthony	.60	1.50
Bryant Westbrook		
RV20 Yatil Green	3.00	8.00
Warrick Dunn		

1996 Pro Line DC3

The 1996 ProLine DC3 set was issued in one series totalling 100 cards. The first all-die cut series from Classic features the top 1995 NFL veterans and rookies. There are no Rookie Cards in this set. The set was issued in five-card packs. An Emmitt Smith Sample card was produced and priced below.

COMPLETE SET (100)	7.50	20.00
1 Emmitt Smith	.60	1.50
2 Larry Centers	.07	.20
3 Jeff George	.07	.20
4 Jim Kelly	.15	.40
5 Kerry Collins	.15	.40
6 Erik Kramer	.02	.10
7 Jeff Blake	.15	.40
8 Andre Rison	.07	.20
9 John Elway	.75	2.00
10 Herman Moore	.07	.20
11 Robert Brooks	.15	.40
12 Steve McNair	.30	.75
13 Jim Harbaugh	.07	.20
14 Mark Brunell	.25	.60
15 Steve Bono	.02	.10
16 Dan Marino	.75	2.00
17 Warren Moon	.07	.20
18 Drew Bledsoe	.25	.60
19 Jim Everett	.02	.10
20 Rodney Hampton	.07	.20
21 Kyle Brady	.02	.10
22 Jeff Hostetler	.02	.10
23 Neil O'Donnell	.07	.20
24 Ricky Watters	.07	.20
25 Isaac Bruce	.15	.40
26 Steve Young	.30	.75
27 Stan Humphries	.07	.20
28 Joey Galloway	.15	.40
29 Errict Rhett	.07	.20
30 Terry Allen	.07	.20
31 Eric Swann	.02	.10
32 Craig Heyward	.02	.10
33 Bryce Paup	.02	.10
34 Sam Mills	.02	.10
35 Jim Flanigan	.02	.10
36 Carl Pickens	.07	.20
37 Pepper Johnson	.02	.10
38 Troy Aikman	.40	1.00
39 Terrell Davis	.30	.75
40 Scott Mitchell	.07	.20
41 Brett Favre	.75	2.00
42 Chris Sanders	.07	.20
43 Marshall Faulk	.20	.50
44 James O. Stewart	.07	.20
45 Marcus Allen	.15	.40
46 Bernie Parmalee	.02	.10
47 Cris Carter	.15	.40
48 Ben Coates	.07	.20
49 Quinn Early	.02	.10
50 Tyrone Wheatley	.07	.20
51 Adrian Murrell	.07	.20
52 Tim Brown	.15	.40
53 Yancey Thigpen	.07	.20
54 Andy Harmon	.02	.10
55 Jerome Bettis	.15	.40
56 Jerry Rice	.40	1.00
57 Natrone Means	.07	.20
58 Chris Warren	.07	.20
59 Warren Sapp	.02	.10
60 Michael Westbrook	.15	.40
61 Aeneas Williams	.02	.10
62 Eric Metcalf	.02	.10
63 Bruce Smith	.07	.20
64 Rashaan Salaam	.07	.20
65 Michael Irvin	.15	.40
66 Anthony Miller	.07	.20
67 Barry Sanders	.60	1.50
68 Reggie White	.15	.40
69 Rodney Thomas	.02	.10
70 Zack Crockett	.02	.10
71 Neil Smith	.07	.20
72 Bryan Cox	.02	.10
73 Curtis Martin	.30	.75
74 Eric Allen	.02	.10
75 Hugh Douglas	.07	.20
76 Napoleon Kaufman	.15	.40
77 Greg Lloyd	.07	.20
78 Charlie Garner	.07	.20
79 Lee Woodall	.02	.10
80 Tony Martin	.07	.20
81 Cortez Kennedy	.02	.10
82 Gus Frerotte	.07	.20
83 Darick Holmes	.02	.10
84 Jay Novacek	.02	.10
85 Brett Perriman	.02	.10
86 Mark Chmura	.07	.20
87 Chester McGlockton	.02	.10
88 Dave Brown	.02	.10
89 William Thomas	.02	.10
90 Ken Norton	.02	.10
91 Junior Seau	.15	.40
92 Deion Sanders	.25	.60
93 J.J. Stokes	.15	.40
94 Kordell Stewart	.15	.40
95 Tamarick Vanover	.07	.20
96 Ken Harvey	.02	.10
97 John Randle	.07	.20
98 Lamont Warren	.02	.10
99 Dorsey Levens	.15	.40
100 Frank Sanders	.07	.20
S1 Emmitt Smith Sample	.80	2.00

1996 Pro Line DC3 All-Pros

COMPLETE SET (20)	30.00	80.00
STATED ODDS 1:100		
AP1 Bryce Paup	.60	1.50
AP2 Kerry Collins	1.25	3.00
AP3 Rashaan Salaam	.75	2.00
AP4 Emmitt Smith	5.00	12.00
AP5 Terrell Davis	2.00	5.00
AP6 Herman Moore	.75	2.00
AP7 Barry Sanders	4.00	10.00
AP8 Brett Favre	6.00	15.00
AP9 Marshall Faulk	1.50	4.00
AP10 Dan Marino	6.00	15.00
AP11 Cris Carter	1.25	3.00
AP12 Curtis Martin	2.50	6.00
AP13 Hugh Douglas	.75	2.00
AP14 Kordell Stewart	1.25	3.00
AP15 Jerry Rice	3.00	8.00
AP16 J.J. Stokes	1.25	3.00
AP17 Joey Galloway	1.25	3.00
AP18 Isaac Bruce	1.25	3.00
AP19 Steve McNair	2.00	5.00
AP20 Tim Brown	1.25	3.00

1996 Pro Line DC3 Road to the Super Bowl

COMPLETE SET (30)	30.00	80.00
STATED ODDS 1:15		
1 Larry Centers	.50	1.25
2 Eric Metcalf	.25	.60
3 Jim Kelly	1.00	2.50
4 Bryce Paup	.25	.60
5 Kerry Collins	1.00	2.50
6 Carl Pickens	.50	1.25
7 Emmitt Smith	4.00	10.00
8 Michael Irvin	1.00	2.50
9 Troy Aikman	2.50	6.00
10 Terrell Davis	2.00	5.00
11 Barry Sanders	4.00	10.00
12 Herman Moore	.50	1.25
13 Brett Favre	5.00	12.00
14 Robert Brooks	1.00	2.50
15 Jim Harbaugh	.50	1.25
16 Tony Bennett	.25	.60
17 Steve Bono	.25	.60
18 Dan Marino	5.00	12.00
19 Cris Carter	1.00	2.50
20 Curtis Martin	2.00	5.00
21 Tim Brown	1.00	2.50
22 Ricky Watters	.50	1.25
23 Yancey Thigpen	.50	1.25
24 Neil O'Donnell	.50	1.25
25 Kordell Stewart	1.00	2.50
26 Isaac Bruce	1.00	2.50
27 Tony Martin	.50	1.25
28 Steve Young	2.00	5.00
29 Jerry Rice	2.50	6.00
30 Chris Warren	.50	1.25

1997 Pro Line DC3

The 1997 Pro Line DC3 set was issued in one series totaling 100 cards and was distributed in four card packs with a suggested retail price of $3.99. The set features top NFL stars from the previous season on a unique die-cut design with detailed copy and statistical information that recaps the 1996 NFL season and allows the collector to accurately judge and compare the performances of offensive and defensive players. The set contains the topical subsets: DC Rewind (68-89) and DC Top Ten (90-100).

COMPLETE SET (100)	6.00	15.00
1 Emmitt Smith	.60	1.50
2 Rod Woodson	.10	.30
3 Eddie George	.20	.50
4 Ty Detmer	.10	.30
5 Zach Thomas	.20	.50
6 Kevin Greene	.10	.30
7 Michael Jackson	.10	.30
8 Isaac Bruce	.20	.50
9 Joey Galloway	.10	.30
10 Bryant Young	.07	.20
11 Terrell Davis	.25	.60
12 Mark Brunell	.25	.60
13 Marvin Harrison	.20	.50
14 Jake Reed	.10	.30
15 Terry Allen	.20	.50
16 Kordell Stewart	.20	.50
17 Reggie White	.20	.50
18 Michael Irvin	.20	.50
19 Tony Martin	.10	.30
20 Barry Sanders	.60	1.50
21 Tony Boselli	.07	.20
22 Carl Pickens	.10	.30
23 Simeon Rice	.10	.30
24 Adrian Murrell	.10	.30
25 Lamar Lathon	.07	.20
26 Thurman Thomas	.20	.50
27 Tim Brown	.20	.50
28 Karim Abdul-Jabbar	.20	.50
29 Brad Johnson	.20	.50
30 Keenan McCardell	.10	.30
31 Keyshawn Johnson	.20	.50
32 Ricky Watters	.10	.30
33 Michael McCrary	.07	.20
34 Brett Favre	.75	2.00
35 Steve McNair	.25	.60
36 Herman Moore	.10	.30
37 Tony Banks	.10	.30
38 Deion Sanders	.20	.50
39 Kerry Collins	.20	.50
40 Shannon Sharpe	.10	.30
41 Drew Bledsoe	.25	.60
42 Jim Everett	.07	.20
43 Jamal Anderson	.20	.50
44 Irving Fryar	.10	.30
45 Terry Glenn	.20	.50
46 Jerry Rice	.40	1.00
47 Curtis Martin	.25	.60
48 Curtis Conway	.10	.30
49 Jerome Bettis	.20	.50
50 Vinny Testaverde	.10	.30
51 Mike Alstott	.20	.50
52 Anthony Johnson	.07	.20
53 Dan Marino	.75	2.00
54 Junior Seau	.20	.50
55 Steve Young	.25	.60

56 Troy Aikman .40 1.00
57 Jimmy Smith .10 .30
58 Cris Carter .20 .50
59 Gus Frerotte .07 .20
60 Marcus Allen .20 .50
61 Rodney Hampton .10 .30
62 Bruce Smith .10 .30
63 LeRoy Butler .07 .20
64 Jeff Blake .10 .30
65 Antonio Freeman .20 .50
66 John Elway .75 2.00
67 B.Favre .20 .50
Rison CL
68 Barry Sanders REW .30 .75
69 Troy Aikman REW .20 .50
70 Jerome Bettis REW .10 .30
71 Mark Brunell REW .20 .50
72 Junior Seau REW .10 .30
73 John Elway REW .40 1.00
74 Chad Brown REW .07 .20
75 Irving Fryar REW .07 .20
76 Drew Bledsoe REW .20 .50
77 Jerry Rice REW .20 .50
78 Larry Centers REW .07 .20
79 Terrell Davis REW .20 .50
80 Carl Pickens REW .07 .20
81 Emmitt Smith REW .30 .75
82 Kerry Collins REW .10 .30
83 Eddie Kennison REW .10 .30
84 Kordell Stewart REW .10 .30
85 Natrone Means REW .10 .30
86 Curtis Martin REW UER .20 .50
back reads Curtin...
87 Dorsey Levens REW .20 .50
88 Desmond Howard REW .10 .30
89 Brett Favre REW CL .20 .50
90 Brett Favre T10 .40 1.00
91 Terrell Davis T10 .20 .50
92 Kevin Greene T10 .07 .20
93 Terry Allen T10 .07 .20
94 Barry Sanders T10 .30 .75
95 John Elway T10 .40 1.00
96 Ricky Watters T10 .07 .20
97 Reggie White T10 .10 .30
98 Jerome Bettis T10 .10 .30
99 Jerry Rice T10 .20 .50
100 Brett Favre T10 CL .20 .50

1997 Pro Line DC3 Autographs

STATED ODDS 1:240
STATED PRINT RUN 300 SER.#'d SETS
1 Kordell Stewart 15.00 40.00
2 Kerry Collins 7.50 20.00
3 Terrell Davis 25.00 60.00
4 Eddie George 12.50 30.00
5 Karim Abdul-Jabbar 6.00 15.00
6 Keyshawn Johnson 12.50 30.00

1997 Pro Line DC3 All-Pros

COMPLETE SET (20) 40.00 100.00
STATED ODDS 1:24
1 Emmitt Smith 5.00 12.00
2 Brett Favre 6.00 15.00
3 Jerry Rice 3.00 8.00
4 Steve Young 2.00 5.00
5 Barry Sanders 5.00 12.00
6 Reggie White 1.50 4.00
7 Ricky Watters 1.00 2.50
8 Lawrence Phillips 1.00 2.50
9 Kerry Collins 1.50 4.00
10 Mark Brunell 2.00 5.00
11 John Elway 6.00 15.00
12 Dan Marino 6.00 15.00
13 Drew Bledsoe 2.00 5.00
14 Curtis Martin 2.00 5.00
15 Terrell Davis 2.00 5.00
16 Karim Abdul-Jabbar 1.50 4.00
17 Marvin Harrison 1.50 4.00
18 Keyshawn Johnson 1.50 4.00
19 Terry Glenn 1.50 4.00
20 Eddie George 1.50 4.00

1997 Pro Line DC3 Draftnix Redemption

COMPLETE SET (3) 6.00 15.00
SILVER BASE STATED ODDS 1:24
1 Darrell Russell .75 2.00
2 Warrick Dunn 4.00 10.00
3 Tony Gonzalez 5.00 12.00

1997 Pro Line DC3 Road to the Super Bowl

COMPLETE SET (30) 40.00 100.00
STATED ODDS 1:12
SB1 Ricky Watters .75 2.00
SB2 Ty Detmer .75 2.00
SB3 Emmitt Smith 4.00 10.00
SB4 Troy Aikman 2.50 6.00
SB5 Kerry Collins 1.25 3.00
SB6 Kevin Greene .75 2.00
SB7 Steve Young 1.50 4.00
SB8 Jerry Rice 2.50 6.00
SB9 Brett Favre 5.00 12.00
SB10 Reggie White 1.25 3.00
SB11 Cris Carter 1.25 3.00
SB12 Brad Johnson 1.25 3.00
SB13 Drew Bledsoe 1.50 4.00
SB14 Curtis Martin 1.50 4.00
SB15 Bruce Smith .75 2.00
SB16 Thurman Thomas 1.25 3.00
SB17 Jim Harbaugh .75 2.00
SB18 Marshall Faulk 1.25 3.00
SB19 Mark Brunell 1.50 4.00
SB20 Natrone Means .75 2.00
SB21 John Elway 5.00 12.00
SB22 Terrell Davis 1.50 4.00
SB23 Kordell Stewart 1.25 3.00
SB24 Jerome Bettis 1.25 3.00
SB25 Eddie George 1.25 3.00
SB26 Dan Marino 5.00 12.00
SB27 Terry Glenn 1.25 3.00
SB28 Antonio Freeman 1.25 3.00
SB29 Anthony Johnson .50 1.25
SB30 Kevin Hardy .50 1.25

1998 Pro Line DC3

The 1998 Pro Line DC3 set was issued in one series totalling 100-cards and distributed in four-card hobby packs with a suggested retail price of $3.99. Retail blister 3-card packs were offered at $2.99 suggested retail. The fronts features color player photos on die-cut cards. The backs carry player information. Hobby packs contained cards printed with Gold foil fronts, while retail packs featured cardfronts with no foil layering. The set contains the topical subsets: DC Rewind (69-89), and Rookie Uprising (90-100).

COMPLETE SET (100) 10.00 25.00
1 Drew Bledsoe .50 1.25
2 Emmitt Smith 1.00 2.50
3 Dana Stubblefield .10 .30
4 Brett Favre 1.25 3.00
5 Derrick Alexander WR .20 .50
6 Bert Emanuel .20 .50
7 Joey Galloway .20 .50
8 Terrell Davis .30 .75
9 Mark Brunell .30 .75
10 Marshall Faulk .40 1.00
11 Jake Reed .20 .50
12 Terry Allen .30 .75
13 Kordell Stewart .30 .75
14 Reggie White .30 .75
15 Michael Irvin .30 .75
16 Tony Martin .20 .50
17 Barry Sanders 1.00 2.50
18 Carl Pickens .20 .50
19 Bobby Hoying .20 .50
20 Adrian Murrell .20 .50
21 Jeff George .20 .50
22 Tim Brown .30 .75
23 Karim Abdul-Jabbar .30 .75
24 Robert Smith .30 .75
25 Eddie George .30 .75
26 Corey Dillon .30 .75
27 Keyshawn Johnson .30 .75
28 Ricky Watters .20 .50
29 Robert Brooks .20 .50
30 Antonio Freeman .30 .75
31 Danny Kanell .20 .50
32 Steve McNair .30 .75
33 Antowain Smith .30 .75
34 Warrick Dunn .30 .75
35 Napoleon Kaufman .30 .75
36 Trent Dilfer .30 .75
37 Herman Moore .20 .50
38 Brad Johnson .30 .75
39 Deion Sanders .30 .75
40 Kerry Collins .20 .50
41 Shannon Sharpe .20 .50
42 Irving Fryar .20 .50
43 Dorsey Levens .30 .75
44 Jerry Rice .60 1.50
45 Curtis Martin .30 .75
46 Jerome Bettis .30 .75
47 Raymont Harris .10 .30
48 Vinny Testaverde .20 .50
49 Dan Marino 1.25 3.00
50 Junior Seau .30 .75
51 Steve Young .30 .75
52 Troy Aikman .60 1.50
53 Jimmy Smith .20 .50
54 Ben Coates .20 .50
55 Gus Frerotte .10 .30
56 Marcus Allen .30 .75
57 Bruce Smith .20 .50
58 Jeff Blake .20 .50
59 John Elway 1.25 3.00
60 Rod Smith WR .20 .50
61 Andre Rison .20 .50
62 Isaac Bruce .30 .75
63 Cris Carter .30 .75
64 Danny Wuerffel .20 .50
65 Rob Moore .20 .50
66 Garrison Hearst .30 .75
67 Warren Moon .30 .75
68 Jerome Bettis .10 .30
(checklist back)
69A Marcus Allen DCR .20 .50
69B Darrien Gordon DCR .10 .30
70 James O.Stewart DCR .20 .50
71 Karim Abdul-Jabbar DCR .20 .50
72 Joey Galloway DCR .20 .50
73 Corey Dillon DCR .20 .50
74 Andre Rison DCR .10 .30
75 Napoleon Kaufman DCR .20 .50
76 Dorsey Levens DCR .20 .50
77 Irving Fryar DCR .10 .30
78 Eric Metcalf DCR .10 .30
80 Neil O'Donnell DCR .20 .50
81 Rod Woodson DCR .20 .50
82 Rob Johnson DCR .20 .50
83 Michael Westbrook DCR .20 .50
84 Jake Plummer DCR .20 .50
85 Bobby Hoying DCR .10 .30
86 Adrian Murrell DCR .10 .30
87 Jim Druckenmiller DCR .10 .30
88 Warren Moon DCR .20 .50
89 Dorsey Levens .10 .30
(checklist back)
90 Tony Gonzalez RU .30 .75
91 Jim Druckenmiller RU .10 .30
92 Corey Dillon RU .20 .50
93 Darrell Russell RU .10 .30
94 Byron Hanspard RU .10 .30
95 Rae Carruth RU .10 .30
96 Peter Boulware RU .10 .30
97 Troy Davis RU .10 .30
98 Reidel Anthony RU .20 .50
99 Tiki Barber RU .30 .75
100 Jake Plummer .20 .50
(checklist back)

1998 Pro Line DC3 Gold

COMPLETE SET (100) 10.00 25.00
*GOLD FOIL HOBBY CARDS: SAME PRICE

1998 Pro Line DC3 Perfect Cut

STATED ODDS 1:2033

1998 Pro Line DC3 Choice Cuts

COMPLETE SET (10) 15.00 40.00
STATED ODDS 1:24 RETAIL
CHC1 Deion Sanders 1.50 4.00
CHC2 Jerome Bettis 1.50 4.00
CHC3 Troy Aikman 3.00 8.00
CHC4 Jerry Rice 3.00 8.00
CHC5 Mark Brunell 1.50 4.00
CHC6 Curtis Martin 1.50 4.00
CHC7 Cris Carter 1.50 4.00
CHC8 Steve Young 1.50 4.00
CHC9 Reggie White 1.50 4.00
CHC10 Dan Marino 6.00 15.00

1998 Pro Line DC3 Clear Cuts

COMPLETE SET (10) 60.00 150.00
STATED ODDS 1:95 HOBBY
STATED PRINT RUN 500 SERIAL #'d SETS
CLC1 John Elway 12.50 30.00
CLC2 Drew Bledsoe 5.00 12.00
CLC3 Terrell Davis 3.00 8.00
CLC4 Brett Favre 12.50 30.00
CLC5 Cris Carter 3.00 8.00
CLC6 Eddie George 3.00 8.00
CLC7 Kordell Stewart 3.00 8.00
CLC8 Warrick Dunn 3.00 8.00
CLC9 Tim Brown 3.00 8.00
CLC10 Barry Sanders 10.00 25.00

1998 Pro Line DC3 Decade Draft

COMPLETE SET (10) 25.00 60.00
STATED ODDS 1:24
DD1 Troy Aikman 5.00 12.00
Barry Sanders
DD2 Jeff George 5.00 12.00
Emmitt Smith
DD3 Russell Maryland 6.00 15.00
Brett Favre
DD4 Steve Emtman 1.00 2.50
Carl Pickens
DD5 Drew Bledsoe 2.50 6.00
Drew Bledsoe
DD6 Dan Wilkinson 2.00 5.00
Marshall Faulk
DD7 Ki-Jana Carter 1.50 4.00
Terrell Davis
DD8 Keyshawn Johnson 1.50 4.00
Eddie George
DD9 Orlando Pace 1.50 4.00
Warrick Dunn
DD10 Top Pick Redemption .20 .50

1998 Pro Line DC3 Team Totals

COMPLETE SET (30) 20.00 50.00
STATED ODDS 1:8
TT1 Ben Coates 1.00 2.50
Willie McGinest
TT2 Michael Irvin 1.50 4.00
Deion Sanders
TT3 Carl Pickens 1.00 2.50
Dan Wilkinson
TT4 Leroy Butler 1.50 4.00
Antonio Freeman
TT5 Adrian Murrell 1.00 2.50
Hugh Douglas
TT6 Raymont Harris .60 1.50
Bryan Cox
TT7 Ricky Watters 1.00 2.50
William Thomas
TT8 Neil Smith 1.00 2.50
Shannon Sharpe
TT9 Dana Stubblefield 1.50 4.00
Garrison Hearst
TT10 Keenan McCardell 1.00 2.50
Jeff Lageman
TT11 Rae Carruth .60 1.50
Lamar Lathon
TT12 Yancey Thigpen .60 1.50
Greg Lloyd
TT13 Chris Calloway 1.00 2.50
Michael Strahan
TT14 Troy Davis .60 1.50
Wayne Martin
TT15 Warren Moon 1.50 4.00
Cortez Kennedy
TT16 Rob Moore 1.00 2.50
Simeon Rice
TT17 O.J.McDuffie 1.50 4.00
Zach Thomas
TT18 John Randle 1.50 4.00
Robert Smith
TT19 Derrick Thomas 1.50 4.00
Elvis Grbac
TT20 Antowain Smith 1.50 4.00
Bruce Smith
TT21 Jeff George 1.00 2.50
Darrell Russell
TT22 Steve McNair 1.50 4.00
Darryll Lewis
TT23 Isaac Bruce 1.50 4.00
Leslie O'Neal
TT24 Junior Seau 1.50 4.00
Tony Martin
TT25 Warren Sapp 1.50 4.00
Mike Alstott
TT26 Jessie Tuggle 1.50 4.00
Jamal Anderson
TT27 Michael Jackson .60 1.50
Peter Boulware
TT28 Quentin Coryatt 1.50 4.00
Marvin Harrison
TT29 Bryant Westbrook 1.00 2.50
Scott Mitchell
TT30 Michael Westbrook 1.00 2.50
Darrell Green

1998 Pro Line DC3 X-Tra Effort

COMPLETE SET (20) 60.00 150.00
STATED ODDS 1:24 HOBBY
STATED PRINT RUN 1000 SER.#'d SETS
XE1 Reggie White 2.50 6.00
XE2 Emmitt Smith 8.00 20.00
XE3 Junior Seau 2.50 6.00
XE4 Brett Favre 10.00 25.00
XE5 Warrick Dunn 2.50 6.00
XE6 Keyshawn Johnson 2.50 6.00
XE7 Dan Marino 10.00 25.00
XE8 Thurman Thomas 2.50 6.00
XE9 Steve Young 2.50 6.00
XE10 Curtis Martin 2.50 6.00
XE11 Karim Abdul-Jabbar 2.50 6.00
XE12 John Elway 10.00 25.00
XE13 Marcus Allen 2.50 6.00
XE14 Napoleon Kaufman 2.50 6.00
XE15 Irving Fryar 1.50 4.00
XE16 Mark Brunell 2.50 6.00
XE17 Andre Rison 1.50 4.00
XE18 Herman Moore 1.50 4.00
XE19 Jerry Rice 5.00 12.00
XE20 Kordell Stewart 2.50 6.00

1997 Pro Line Gems

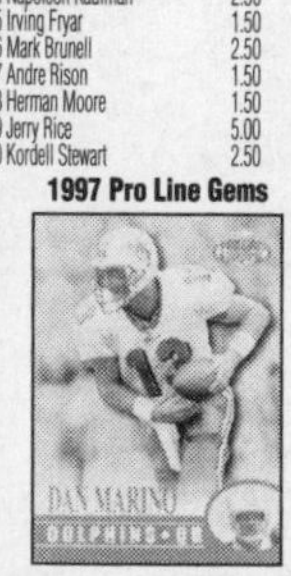

The 1997 ProLine Gems set was issued in one series totalling 100 cards and distributed in four-card packs. This limited edition three tiered set features color action photos printed on 18 pt. card stock of 60 of the top rated veteran players, 30 of the league's highest profile rookies, and 10 potential leaders. Each card in the three subsets carry an exclusive foil stamp design and color. A Brett Favre championship ring card was randomly inserted in packs at the rate of one in 240. It features a color photo of Brett Favre wearing his championship ring with an actual diamond embedded in the card. Only 1997 of these cards were produced.

COMPLETE SET (100) 10.00 20.00
1 Brett Favre .75 2.00
2 Robert Brooks .10 .30
3 Reggie White .20 .50
4 Drew Bledsoe .25 .60
5 Curtis Martin .25 .60
6 Terry Glenn .20 .50
7 Kerry Collins .20 .50
8 Kevin Greene .10 .30
9 Troy Aikman .40 1.00
10 Emmitt Smith .60 1.50
11 Deion Sanders .20 .50
12 John Elway .75 2.00
13 Terrell Davis .25 .60
14 Kordell Stewart .20 .50
15 Jerome Bettis .20 .50
16 Steve Young .25 .60
17 Jerry Rice .40 1.00
18 Bruce Smith .10 .30
19 Thurman Thomas .20 .50
20 Jim Harbaugh .10 .30
21 Marshall Faulk .25 .60
22 Marvin Harrison .20 .50
23 Ricky Watters .10 .30
24 Seth Joyner .07 .20
25 Mark Brunell .25 .60
26 Natrone Means .10 .30
27 Dan Marino .75 2.00
28 Zach Thomas .20 .50
29 Karim Abdul-Jabbar .20 .50
30 Isaac Bruce .20 .50
31 Eddie Kennison .10 .30
32 Tony Banks .10 .30
33 Tony Martin .10 .30
34 Junior Seau .20 .50
35 Barry Sanders .60 1.50
36 Herman Moore .10 .30
37 Leeland McElroy .07 .20
38 Jamal Anderson .20 .50
39 Rick Mirer .07 .20
40 Rashaan Salaam .07 .20
41 Vinny Testaverde .10 .30
42 Elvis Grbac .10 .30
43 Cris Carter .20 .50
44 Brad Johnson .20 .50
45 Keyshawn Johnson .20 .50
46 Adrian Murrell .10 .30
47 Joey Galloway .10 .30
48 Trent Dilfer .20 .50
49 Gus Frerotte .07 .20
50 Terry Allen .20 .50
51 Tim Brown .20 .50
52 Desmond Howard .10 .30
53 Jeff George .10 .30
54 Heath Shuler .07 .20
55 Steve McNair .25 .60
56 Eddie George .20 .50
57 Jeff Blake .10 .30
58 Carl Pickens .10 .30
59 Dave Brown .07 .20
60 Brett Favre CL .20 .50
61 Antowain Smith .20 .50
62 Emmitt Smith PL .30 .75
63 Terry Glenn PL .10 .30
64 Herman Moore PL .10 .30
65 Barry Sanders PL .30 .75
66 Derrick Thomas PL .20 .50
67 Brett Favre PL .40 1.00
68 Warrick Dunn .25 .60
69 Emmitt Smith PL .30 .75
70 Brett Favre CL .20 .50
71 Orlando Pace RC .20 .50
72 Darrell Russell RC .07 .20
73 Shawn Springs RC .10 .30
74 Warrick Dunn RC .60 1.50
75 Tiki Barber RC 1.25 3.00
76 Tom Knight RC .07 .20
77 Peter Boulware RC .20 .50
78 David LaFleur RC .07 .20
79 Tony Gonzalez RC .75 2.00
80 Yatil Green RC .10 .30
81 Ike Hilliard RC .30 .75
82 James Farrior RC .20 .50
83 Jim Druckenmiller RC .10 .30
84 Jon Harris RC .07 .20
85 Walter Jones RC .20 .50
86 Reidel Anthony RC .20 .50
87 Jake Plummer RC .75 2.00
88 Reinard Wilson RC .10 .30
89 Kevin Lockett RC .10 .30
90 Rae Carruth RC .07 .20
91 Byron Hanspard RC .10 .30
92 Renaldo Wynn RC .07 .20
93 Troy Davis RC .10 .30
94 Duce Staley RC 1.50 4.00
95 Kenard Lang RC .10 .30
96 Freddie Jones RC .10 .30
97 Corey Dillon RC .75 2.00
98 Antowain Smith RC .50 1.25
99 Dwayne Rudd RC .20 .50
100 Warrick Dunn CL .25 .60
CR1 Brett Favre Ring/1997 15.00 40.00

1997 Pro Line Gems Gems of the NFL 23K Gold

COMPLETE SET (15) 80.00 200.00
STATED ODDS 1:24
G1 Kerry Collins 3.00 8.00
G2 Troy Aikman 6.00 15.00
G3 Emmitt Smith 10.00 25.00
G4 Terrell Davis 4.00 10.00
G5 Barry Sanders 10.00 25.00
G6 Brett Favre 12.50 30.00
G7 Eddie George 3.00 8.00
G8 Mark Brunell 4.00 10.00
G9 Dan Marino 12.50 30.00
G10 Curtis Martin 4.00 10.00
G11 Terry Glenn 3.00 8.00
G12 Jerome Bettis 3.00 8.00
G13 Steve Young 4.00 10.00
G14 Jerry Rice 6.00 15.00
G15 Warrick Dunn 5.00 12.00
G16 John Elway 1999 Retirement 8.00 20.00
(released in 1999)

1997 Pro Line Gems Through the Years

COMPLETE SET (20) 20.00 50.00
STATED ODDS 1:12
TY1 Emmitt Smith 3.00 8.00
TY2 Brett Favre 4.00 10.00
TY3 Deion Sanders 1.00 2.50
TY4 Dan Marino 4.00 10.00
TY5 Barry Sanders 3.00 8.00
TY6 Herman Moore .60 1.50
TY7 Curtis Martin 1.25 3.00
TY8 Jerome Bettis 1.00 2.50
TY9 Mark Brunell 1.00 2.50
TY10 Jerry Rice 2.00 5.00
TY11 Warrick Dunn 1.50 4.00
TY12 Jim Druckenmiller .30 .75
TY13 Shawn Springs .30 .75
TY14 Tony Banks .60 1.50
TY15 Byron Hanspard .30 .75
TY16 Ike Hilliard .60 1.50
TY17 Antowain Smith 1.00 2.50
TY18 Eddie George 1.00 2.50
TY19 Jake Plummer 2.00 5.00
TY20 Terry Glenn 1.00 2.50

1996 Pro Line Intense

The 1996 Pro Line Intense set was issued in one series totalling 100-cards and was distributed in five-card packs. The fronts feature borderless color action player photos with the player's name and team helmet at the bottom. The backs carry player information and career statistics.

COMPLETE SET (100) 6.00 15.00
1 Kerry Collins .08 .25
2 Jeff George .02 .10
3 Mark Brunell .20 .50
4 Steve McNair .25 .60
5 Rick Mirer .02 .10
6 Dave Brown .01 .05
7 Rashaan Salaam .01 .05
8 Marshall Faulk .10 .30
9 Erric Pegram .01 .05
10 Cris Carter .08 .25
11 Eric Allen .01 .05
12 Jim Kelly .08 .25
13 Jeff Blake .08 .25
14 Stan Humphries .02 .10
15 Scott Mitchell .02 .10
16 Jeff Hostetler .01 .05
17 Rodney Peete .01 .05
18 Warren Moon .02 .10
19 Errict Rhett .02 .10
20 Terrell Davis .25 .60
21 J.J. Stokes .08 .25
22 Marco Coleman .01 .05
23 Heath Shuler .02 .10
24 Duane Clemons RC .01 .05
25 Amani Toomer RC .30 .75
26 Leslie O'Neal .01 .05
27 Tamarick Vanover .02 .10
28 Steve Bono .01 .05
29 Jim Everett .01 .05
30 Erik Kramer .01 .05
31 Trent Dilfer .08 .25
32 Jim Harbaugh .02 .10
33 Vinny Testaverde .02 .10
34 Rodney Hampton .02 .10
35 Chris Warren .02 .10
36 Curtis Martin .25 .60
37 Eddie Kennison RC .08 .25
38 Herman Moore .02 .10
39 Terance Mathis .01 .05
40 Carl Pickens .02 .10
41 Isaac Bruce .08 .25
42 Reggie White .08 .25
43 Junior Seau .08 .25
44 Bryce Paup .01 .05
45 Deion Sanders .10 .30
46 Thurman Thomas .08 .25
47 Gus Frerotte .02 .10
48 Tony Mandarich .01 .05
49 Michael Irvin .08 .25
50 Wayne Chrebet .10 .30
51 Bobby Engram RC .08 .25
52 Marcus Jones RC .01 .05
53 Daryl Gardener RC .01 .05
54 Alex Van Dyke RC .02 .10
55 Andre Rison .02 .10
56 Regan Upshaw RC .01 .05
57 Jason Dunn RC .02 .10
58 Mark Chmura .02 .10
59 Ray Lewis RC .75 2.00
60 Rickey Dudley RC .08 .25
61 Leeland McElroy RC .02 .10
62 Derrick Thomas .08 .25
63 Bobby Hoying RC .08 .25
64 Robert Brooks .02 .10
65 Tim Brown .08 .25
66 Michael Westbrook .08 .25
67 Jim Miller .08 .25
68 Aaron Hayden .01 .05
69 Marcus Allen .08 .25
70 Troy Aikman .30 .75
71 Steve Young .20 .50
72 Neil O'Donnell .02 .10
73 Drew Bledsoe .20 .50
74 Emmitt Smith .50 1.25
75 Ki-Jana Carter .02 .10
76 Irving Fryar .02 .10
77 Joey Galloway .08 .25
78 Russell Maryland .01 .05
79 Kordell Stewart .08 .25
80 Barry Sanders .50 1.25
81 Bryan Cox .01 .05
82 Keyshawn Johnson RC .30 .75
83 Karim Abdul-Jabbar RC .08 .25
84 Kevin Hardy RC .08 .25
85 Rodney Thomas .01 .05
86 John Elway .40 1.50
87 Dan Marino .60 1.50
88 Brett Favre .60 1.50
89 Eric Metcalf .01 .05
90 Jonathan Ogden RC .08 .25
91 Eddie George RC .40 1.00
92 Simeon Rice RC .25 .60
93 Tim Biakabutuka RC .08 .25
94 Terry Glenn RC .30 .75
95 Marvin Harrison RC .75 2.00
96 Lawrence Phillips RC .08 .25
97 Natrone Means .02 .10
98 Jerry Rice .30 .75
99 Ricky Watters .02 .10
100 Emmitt Smith .08 .25
Checklist card

1996 Pro Line Intense Double Intensity

COMPLETE SET (100) 40.00 100.00
*STARS: 2X TO 5X BASIC CARDS
*RCs: .8X TO 2X BASIC CARDS
STATED ODDS 1:5

1996 Pro Line Intense Determined

COMPLETE SET (20) 15.00 40.00
STATED ODDS 1:50
1 Kerry Collins .60 1.50
2 Troy Aikman 2.00 5.00
3 Herman Moore .25 .60
4 Mark Brunell 1.25 3.00
5 Dan Marino 4.00 10.00
6 Kordell Stewart .60 1.50
7 Junior Seau .60 1.50
8 Steve Young 1.25 3.00
9 John Elway 4.00 10.00
10 Emmitt Smith 3.00 8.00
11 Steve McNair 1.50 4.00
12 Drew Bledsoe 1.25 3.00
13 Joey Galloway .60 1.50
14 Deion Sanders .75 2.00
15 Kevin Hardy .30 .75
16 Keyshawn Johnson 1.00 2.50
17 Marvin Harrison 2.50 6.00
18 Tim Biakabutuka .30 .75
19 Eddie George 1.25 3.00
20 Terry Glenn 1.00 2.50

1996 Pro Line Intense Phone Cards $3

COMPLETE SET (50) 30.00 50.00
*PROOF CARDS: .6X TO 1.5X BASIC INSERTS
*TEST CARDS: 1.2X TO 3X BASIC INSERTS
1 Jim Kelly .40 1.00
2 Kerry Collins .40 1.00
3 Jeff George .20 .50
4 Troy Aikman .60 1.50
5 John Elway 1.25 3.00
6 Herman Moore .40 1.00
7 Barry Sanders 1.25 3.00
8 Brett Favre 1.25 3.00
9 Jim Harbaugh .20 .50
10 Steve Bono .20 .50
11 Dan Marino 1.25 3.00
12 Drew Bledsoe .60 1.50
13 Jim Everett .20 .50
14 Neil O'Donnell .20 .50
15 Ricky Watters .40 1.00
16 Junior Seau .40 1.00
17 Jerry Rice .60 1.50
18 Errict Rhett .20 .50
19 Joey Galloway .60 1.50
20 Steve Young .50 1.25
21 Kordell Stewart .60 1.50
22 Rodney Hampton .20 .50
23 Curtis Martin .60 1.50
24 Mark Brunell .60 1.50
25 Steve McNair .60 1.50
26 Deion Sanders .40 1.00
27 Carl Pickens .20 .50
28 Michael Irvin .40 1.00
29 Tamarick Vanover .20 .50
30 Trent Dilfer .40 1.00
31 Chris Warren .20 .50
32 Stan Humphries .20 .50
33 J.J. Stokes .40 1.00
34 Tim Biakabutuka .20 .50
35 Keyshawn Johnson .60 1.50
36 Simeon Rice .20 .50
37 Jonathan Ogden .20 .50
38 Rashaan Salaam .40 1.00
39 Bobby Engram .20 .50
40 Reggie White .40 1.00
41 Isaac Bruce .40 1.00
42 Eddie George 1.25 3.00
43 Marvin Harrison .50 1.25
44 Kevin Hardy .20 .50
45 Karim Abdul-Jabbar .40 1.00
46 Duane Clemons .20 .50
47 Terry Glenn .50 1.25
48 Marcus Allen .40 1.00
49 Rickey Dudley .20 .50
50 Lawrence Phillips .20 .50

1996 Pro Line Intense Phone Cards $5

COMPLETE SET (20) 30.00 60.00
*PROOFS: .6X TO 1.5X BASIC INSERTS
*TEST CARDS: 1.2X TO 3X BASIC INSERTS
1 Kerry Collins .30 .75
2 Troy Aikman 1.00 2.50
3 Reggie White .40 1.00
4 Mark Brunell 1.00 2.50
5 Dan Marino 2.00 5.00
6 Kordell Stewart .75 2.00
7 Junior Seau .30 .75
8 Steve Young .75 2.00
9 John Elway 2.00 5.00
10 Emmitt Smith 2.00 5.00
11 Steve McNair .75 2.00
12 Drew Bledsoe 1.00 2.50
13 Joey Galloway .50 1.25
14 Deion Sanders .40 1.00
15 Kevin Hardy .30 .75
16 Keyshawn Johnson .75 2.00
17 Marvin Harrison .75 2.00
18 Tim Biakabutuka .40 1.00
19 Eddie George 1.50 4.00
20 Terry Glenn .75 2.00

1996 Pro Line Intense Phone Cards $10

COMPLETE SET (10) 30.00 50.00
*PROOF CARDS: .6X TO 1.5X BASIC INSERTS
*TEST CARDS: 1.2X TO 3X BASIC INSERTS
1 Dan Marino 4.00 10.00
2 Jim Harbaugh 1.00 2.50
3 Troy Aikman 2.00 5.00
4 Curtis Martin 2.00 5.00
5 Kordell Stewart 2.00 5.00
6 Steve Young 1.50 4.00
7 Barry Sanders 4.00 10.00
8 Keyshawn Johnson 2.00 5.00
9 Lawrence Phillips .60 1.50
10 Eddie George 3.00 8.00

1996 Pro Line Intense Phone Cards $25 Die Cuts

COMPLETE SET (10) 60.00 100.00
*PROOF CARDS: .75X TO 1.5X BASIC CARDS
*TEST CARDS: 1X TO 2.5X BASIC INSERTS
1 Jim Kelly 1.50 4.00
2 Troy Aikman 4.00 10.00
3 John Elway 8.00 20.00
4 Kerry Collins 1.50 4.00
5 Barry Sanders 8.00 20.00
6 Drew Bledsoe 4.00 10.00
7 Keyshawn Johnson 4.00 10.00
8 Deion Sanders .30 8.00
9 Dan Marino 8.00 20.00
10 Brett Favre 8.00 20.00

1996 Pro Line Intense Phone Cards $1000

NOT PRICED DUE TO SCARCITY
1 John Elway
2 Keyshawn Johnson
3 Troy Aikman
4 Dan Marino
5 Brett Favre

1996 Pro Line Memorabilia

COMPLETE SET (100) 10.00 25.00
*MEMOR.CARDS: .6X to 1.5X INTENSE

1996 Pro Line Memorabilia Producers

COMPLETE SET (10) 12.50 30.00
STATED ODDS 1:6
*SILVER SIGS: 1.5X TO 4X BASIC INSERTS
SILVER STATED ODDS 1:100
P1 Keyshawn Johnson .75 2.00
P2 Barry Sanders 2.50 6.00
P3 Eddie George 1.00 2.50
P4 Emmitt Smith 2.50 6.00
P5 Jerry Rice 1.50 4.00
P6 Brett Favre 3.00 8.00
P7 Ricky Watters .20 .50
P8 Dan Marino 3.00 8.00
P9 Deion Sanders .60 1.50
P10 Marshall Faulk .60 1.50

1996 Pro Line Memorabilia Rookie Autographs

COMPLETE SET (16) 200.00 400.00
STATED ODDS 1:12
1 Tim Biakabutuka/210 12.50 30.00
2 Tim Biakabutuka/600 20.00 40.00
Eddie George
3 Duane Clemons/1255 6.00 15.00
4 Daryl Gardener/1390 6.00 15.00
5 Eddie George/395 20.00 40.00
6 Terry Glenn/600 15.00 40.00
Keyshawn Johnson
7 Kevin Hardy/940 7.50 20.00
8 Jeff Hartings/1370 10.00 25.00
9 Andre Johnson/1370 6.00 15.00
10 Keyshawn Johnson/195 25.00 50.00
11 Pete Kendall/1495 6.00 15.00
12 Alex Molden/1320 6.00 15.00
13 Eric Moulds/1010 12.50 30.00
14 Jamain Stephens/795 6.00 15.00
15 Regan Upshaw 6.00 15.00
(not serial numbered)
16 Jerome Woods/1375 6.00 15.00

1996 Pro Line Memorabilia Stretch Drive

COMPLETE SET (30) 15.00 40.00
STATED ODDS 1:3
*SILVER SIGS: .8X TO 2X BASIC INSERTS
SILVER STATED ODDS 1:25
DS1 Jim Kelly .30 .75
DS2 Kerry Collins .30 .75
DS3 Rashaan Salaam .10 .30
DS4 Jeff Blake .30 .75
DS5 Deion Sanders .40 1.00
DS6 Troy Aikman 1.00 2.50
DS7 Emmitt Smith 1.50 4.00
DS8 John Elway 2.00 5.00
DS9 Terrell Davis .75 2.00
DS10 Barry Sanders 1.50 4.00
DS11 Brett Favre 2.00 5.00
DS12 Steve McNair .75 2.00
DS13 Eddie George .60 1.50
DS14 Marshall Faulk .40 1.00
DS15 Marvin Harrison 1.25 3.00
DS16 Herman Moore .10 .30
DS17 Dan Marino 2.00 5.00
DS18 Curtis Martin .75 2.00
DS19 Drew Bledsoe .60 1.50
DS20 Terry Glenn .30 .75
DS21 Lawrence Phillips .10 .30
DS22 Neil O'Donnell .10 .30
DS23 Keyshawn Johnson .30 .75
DS24 Isaac Bruce .30 .75
DS25 Ricky Watters .10 .30
DS26 Kordell Stewart .30 .75
DS27 J.J. Stokes .30 .75
DS28 Steve Young .60 1.50
DS29 Joey Galloway .30 .75
DS30 Errict Rhett .10 .30

1997 Pro Line Memorabilia

Distributed in five-card packs, this 50-card set features color action photos of top players as selected by Score Board. The backs carry player information. A blue foil Signature Series parallel set was also produced and randomly inserted in 1:5 packs.

COMPLETE SET (50) 15.00 30.00
1 Jake Plummer RC .60 1.50
2 Byron Hanspard RC .10 .30
3 Vinny Testaverde .10 .30
4 Thurman Thomas .20 .50
5 Antowain Smith RC .50 1.25
6 Rae Carruth RC .07 .20
7 Kerry Collins .20 .50
8 Rashaan Salaam .10 .30
9 Rick Mirer .07 .20
10 Jeff Blake .10 .30
11 Troy Aikman .40 1.00
12 Emmitt Smith .60 1.50
13 John Elway .75 2.00
14 Terrell Davis .25 .60
15 Barry Sanders .60 1.50
16 Herman Moore .10 .30
17 Brett Favre .75 2.00
18 Reggie White .20 .50
19 Dorsey Levens .20 .50
20 Eddie George .20 .50
21 Jim Harbaugh .10 .30
22 Mark Brunell .25 .60
23 Tony Gonzalez RC .60 1.50
24 Elvis Grbac .10 .30
25 Dan Marino .75 2.00
26 Karim Abdul-Jabbar .20 .50
27 Brad Johnson .20 .50
28 Drew Bledsoe .25 .60
29 Curtis Martin .25 .60
30 Terry Glenn .20 .50
31 Heath Shuler .07 .20
32 Danny Wuerffel RC .20 .50
33 Ike Hilliard RC .30 .75
34 Keyshawn Johnson .20 .50
35 Darrell Russell RC .07 .20
36 Jeff George .10 .30
37 Ricky Watters .10 .30
38 Bobby Hoying .10 .30
39 Jerome Bettis .20 .50
40 Kordell Stewart .20 .50
41 Junior Seau .20 .50
42 Shawn Springs RC .10 .30
43 Jim Druckenmiller RC .10 .30
44 Steve Young .25 .60
45 Jerry Rice .40 1.00
46 Orlando Pace RC .20 .50
47 Isaac Bruce .20 .50

48 Warrick Dunn RC	.50	1.25
49 Gus Frerotte	.07	.20
50 Brett Favre CL	.20	.50

1997 Pro Line Memorabilia Signature Series

COMPLETE SET (50)	25.00	60.00
*SIG.SERIES STARS: 1.5X TO 4X BASIC CARDS		
*SIG.SERIES RCs: .8X TO 2X BASIC CARDS		
STATED ODDS 1:5		

1997 Pro Line Memorabilia Bustin' Out

COMPLETE SET (20)	40.00	100.00
STATED ODDS 1:20		
*GOLD CARDS: .8X TO 2X SILVERS		
GOLD STATED ODDS 1:65		
B1 Antowain Smith	2.00	5.00
B2 Kerry Collins	1.50	4.00
B3 Jeff Blake	1.00	2.50
B4 Emmitt Smith	5.00	12.00
B5 Troy Aikman	3.00	8.00
B6 Terrell Davis	2.00	5.00
B7 Barry Sanders	5.00	12.00
B8 Brett Favre	6.00	15.00
B9 Mark Brunell	2.00	5.00
B10 Dan Marino	6.00	15.00
B11 Brad Johnson	1.50	4.00
B12 Curtis Martin	2.00	5.00
B13 Keyshawn Johnson	1.50	4.00
B14 Darrell Russell	.60	1.50
B15 Reggie White	1.50	4.00
B16 Kordell Stewart	1.50	4.00
B17 Jerry Rice	3.00	8.00
B18 Isaac Bruce	1.50	4.00
B19 Warrick Dunn	2.50	6.00
B20 Eddie George	1.50	4.00

1997 Pro Line Memorabilia Rookie Autographs

COMPLETE SET (26)	125.00	250.00
STATED ODDS 1:10		
1 John Allred	2.50	6.00
2 Darnell Autry	2.50	6.00
3 Pat Barnes	2.50	6.00
4 Michael Booker	2.50	6.00
5 Peter Boulware	4.00	10.00
6 Rae Carruth	2.50	6.00
7 Troy Davis	4.00	10.00
8 Jim Druckenmiller	4.00	10.00
9 Warrick Dunn	10.00	25.00
10 James Farrior	6.00	15.00
11 Tony Gonzalez	10.00	25.00
12 Yatil Green	6.00	15.00
13 Byron Hanspard	4.00	10.00
14 Ike Hilliard	4.00	10.00
15 David LaFleur	2.50	6.00
16 Kevin Lockett	4.00	10.00
17 Jake Plummer	10.00	25.00
18 Trevor Pryce	6.00	15.00
19 Derrick Rodgers	2.50	6.00
20 Dwayne Rudd	2.50	6.00
21 Darrell Russell	2.50	6.00
22 Matt Russell	2.50	6.00
23 Sedrick Shaw	4.00	10.00
24 Antowain Smith	8.00	20.00
25 Reinard Wilson	2.50	6.00
26 Bryant Westbrook	4.00	10.00

1997 Pro Line Memorabilia Veteran Autographs

1 Eric Allen	6.00	15.00
2 Lamont Hollinquest SB (Score Board logo on front)	5.00	12.00
2 Randy Baldwin SB (Score Board logo on front)	5.00	12.00
3 Keenan McCardell	6.00	15.00
4 Willie McGinest	5.00	12.00
5 Chris Slade	5.00	12.00
6 Jimmy Smith	8.00	20.00

1994 Pro Mags

These magnets measure approximately 2 1/8" by 3 3/8" and have rounded corners. They were sold in five-magnet packs that included a free team magnet, measuring 2 1/8" by 3/4" and a checklist of all 140 players. Collectors could receive a special Warren Moon magnet by mailing in a redemption card that was included in every pack, three proofs of purchase, and 6.00. The fronts display borderless color action player photos. The player's last name in big letters appears along the right side. His first name in team color-coded letters is printed on the bottom, with the team logo next to it. There was a parallel set issued for Super Bowl XXIX, this set is valued at the same price as the regular set. The magnets are numbered on the front, grouped alphabetically within teams, and checklisted below according to teams. The team magnets are unnumbered and are checklisted below in alphabetical order with a "T" prefix. Troy Aikman and Chris Martin promo magnets were produced and are listed below. An oversized Warren Moon artist's rendering magnet was randomly inserted in boxes.

COMPLETE SET (168)	50.00	125.00
1 Rod Bernstine	.25	.60
2 John Elway	3.20	8.00
3 Glyn Milburn	.40	1.00
4 Shannon Sharpe	.40	1.00
5 Dennis Smith	.25	.60
6 Cody Carlson	.25	.60
7 Ernest Givins	.40	1.00
8 Haywood Jeffires	.40	1.00
9 Bruce Matthews	.25	.60
10 Webster Slaughter	.25	.60
11 O.J. McDuffie	.40	1.00
12 Keith Byars	.25	.60
13 Bryan Cox	.25	.60
14 Irving Fryar	.40	1.00
15 Dan Marino	3.20	8.00
16 Barry Foster	.25	.60
17 Kevin Greene	.14	.35
18 Greg Lloyd	.14	.35
19 Neil O'Donnell	.40	1.00
20 Rod Woodson	.14	.35
21 Steve Beuerlein	.14	.35
22 Chuck Cecil	.25	.60
23 Randal Hill	.25	.60
24 Ricky Proehl	.25	.60
25 Eric Swann	.40	1.00
26 Troy Aikman	1.60	4.00
27 Emmitt Smith	2.40	6.00
28 Michael Irvin	.60	1.50
29 Russell Maryland	.25	.60
30 Jay Novacek	.40	1.00
31 Jerome Bettis	.80	2.00
32 Sean Gilbert	.25	.60
33 Todd Lyght	.25	.60
34 Chris Martin	.25	.60
35 Roman Phifer	.25	.60
36 Neal Anderson	.25	.60
37 Quinn Early	.25	.60
38 Rickey Jackson	.25	.60
39 Sam Mills	.25	.60
40 Willie Roaf	.25	.60
41 Cornelius Bennett	.25	.60
42 Jim Kelly	.60	1.50
43 Kenneth Davis	.25	.60
44 Darryl Talley	.25	.60
45 Andre Reed	.40	1.00
46 Cris Carter	.60	1.50
47 Warren Moon	.60	1.50
48 Terry Allen	.40	1.00
49 Qadry Ismail	.40	1.00
50 Robert Smith	.60	1.50
51 Erric Pegram	.40	1.00
52 Andre Rison	.60	1.50
53 Deion Sanders	.80	2.00
54 Jessie Tuggle	.25	.60
55 Jeff George	.60	1.50
56 Brian Blades	.40	1.00
57 Rick Mirer	.40	1.00
58 Cortez Kennedy	.40	1.00
59 Chris Warren	.60	1.50
60 Eugene Robinson	.25	.60
61 Reggie Brooks	.25	.60
62 Ricky Ervins	.25	.60
63 Brian Mitchell	.25	.60
64 Ricky Sanders	.25	.60
65 Sterling Palmer	.25	.60
66 Tim Brown	.60	1.50
67 Jeff Hostetler	.40	1.00
68 Rocket Ismail	.40	1.00
69 Terry McDaniel	.25	.60
70 James Jett	.25	.60
71 Sterling Sharpe	.40	1.00
72 Brett Favre	3.20	8.00
73 Reggie White	.60	1.50
74 Terrell Buckley	.25	.60
75 Edgar Bennett	.40	1.00
76 Jerry Rice	1.60	4.00
77 Steve Young	1.20	3.00
78 Ricky Watters	.14	.35
79 Dana Stubblefield	.14	.35
80 John Taylor	.40	1.00
81 Ronnie Harmon	.25	.60
82 Stan Humphries	.14	.35
83 Natrone Means	.60	1.50
84 Junior Seau	.60	1.50
85 Eric Bieniemy	.25	.60
86 Dean Biasucci	.25	.60
87 Jim Harbaugh	.60	1.50
88 Roosevelt Potts	.25	.60
89 Scott Radecic	.25	.60
90 Rohn Stark	.25	.60
91 Eric Metcalf	.40	1.00
92 Michael Dean Perry	.25	.60
93 Vinny Testaverde	.40	1.00
94 Mark Carrier WR	.25	.60
95 Michael Jackson	.25	.60
96 Marcus Allen	.60	1.50
97 Dale Carter	.25	.60
98 Neil Smith	.25	.60
99 J.J. Birden	.25	.60
100 Willie Davis	.40	1.00
101 Rodney Hampton	.14	.35
102 Mark Jackson	.25	.60
103 Dave Meggett	.25	.60
104 Jumbo Elliott	.25	.60
105 Kenyon Rasheed	.25	.60
106 Boomer Esiason	.40	1.00
107 Johnny Johnson	.25	.60
108 Johnny Mitchell	.25	.60
109 Brad Baxter	.25	.60
110 Ronnie Lott	.40	1.00
111 Derrick Fenner	.25	.60
112 David Klingler	.25	.60
113 Bruce Pickens	.25	.60
114 Harold Green	.25	.60
115 Jeff Query	.25	.60
116 Leonard Russell	.25	.60
117 Drew Bledsoe	1.60	4.00
118 Marv Cook	.25	.60
119 Vincent Brisby	.14	.35
120 Vincent Brown	.25	.60
121 Trace Armstrong	.25	.60
122 Curtis Conway	.60	1.50
123 Dante Jones	.25	.60
124 Tim Worley	.25	.60
125 Chris Zorich	.25	.60
126 Ronald Moore	.25	.60
127 Barry Sanders	3.20	8.00
128 Pat Swilling	.25	.60
129 Brett Perriman	.25	.60
130 Chris Spielman	.25	.60
131 Mark Bavaro	.25	.60
132 Fred Barnett	.40	1.00
133 Randall Cunningham	.60	1.50
134 Herschel Walker	.40	1.00
135 Bubby Brister	.25	.60
136 Craig Erickson	.25	.60
137 Hardy Nickerson	.25	.60
138 Demetrius DuBose	.25	.60
139 Dan Stryzinski	.25	.60
140 Charles Wilson	.25	.60
T1 Arizona Cardinals	.14	.35
T2 Atlanta Falcons	.14	.35
T3 Buffalo Bills	.20	.50
T4 Chicago Bears	.20	.50
T5 Cincinnati Bengals	.14	.35
T6 Cleveland Browns	.20	.50
T7 Dallas Cowboys	.20	.50
T8 Denver Broncos	.20	.50
T9 Detroit Lions	.14	.35
T10 Green Bay Packers	.20	.50
T11 Houston Oilers	.14	.35
T12 Indianapolis Colts	.14	.35
T13 Kansas City Chiefs	.20	.50
T14 Los Angeles Raiders	.20	.50
T15 Los Angeles Rams	.14	.35
T16 Miami Dolphins	.20	.50
T17 Minnesota Vikings	.20	.50
T18 New England Patriots	.14	.35
T19 New Orleans Saints	.14	.35
T20 New York Giants	.20	.50
T21 New York Jets	.20	.50
T22 Philadelphia Eagles	.14	.35
T23 Pittsburgh Steelers	.20	.50
T24 San Diego Chargers	.14	.35
T25 San Francisco 49ers	.20	.50
T26 Seattle Seahawks	.14	.35
T27 Tampa Bay Buccaneers	.14	.35
T28 Washington Redskins	.20	.50
P3 Jim Kelly Promo	1.00	2.50
P1 Chris Martin Promo	.40	1.00
P2 Troy Aikman Promo	1.25	3.00
NNO Warren Moon/3 3/4-inch by 7-inch Bonus Magnet 3.20		8.00

1995 Pro Mags

Sold in packs of five and produced by Chris Martin Enterprises, this 150-magnet set features borderless color player photos with rounded corners. The magnets, measuring approximately 2 1/8" by 3 3/8," are grouped alphabetically within teams and checklisted below according to team. Some packs also contained a random assortment of insert magnets.

COMPLETE SET (150)	50.00	125.00
1 Larry Centers	.20	.50
2 Garrison Hearst	.40	1.00
3 Seth Joyner	.20	.50
4 Ronald Moore	.20	.50
5 Eric Swann	.20	.50
6 Chris Doleman	.20	.50
7 Jeff George	.40	1.00
8 Craig Heyward	.20	.50
9 Terance Mathis	.40	1.00
10 Jessie Tuggle	.20	.50
11 Cornelius Bennett	.40	1.00
12 Jim Kelly	.50	1.25
13 Andre Reed	.40	1.00
14 Bruce Smith	.50	1.25
15 Darryl Talley	.20	.50
16 Trace Armstrong	.20	.50
17 Dante Jones	.20	.50
18 Steve Walsh	.20	.50
19 Donnell Woolford	.20	.50
20 Tim Worley	.20	.50
21 Jeff Blake	.50	1.25
22 Harold Green	.20	.50
23 Carl Pickens	.40	1.00
24 Darnay Scott	.40	1.00
25 Dan Wilkinson	.20	.50
26 Derrick Alexander WR	.40	1.00
27 Leroy Hoard	.20	.50
28 Antonio Langham	.20	.50
29 Vinny Testaverde	.40	1.00
30 Eric Turner	.40	1.00
31 Troy Aikman	1.20	3.00
32 Michael Irvin	.50	1.25
33 Daryl Johnston	.40	1.00
34 Russell Maryland	.20	.50
35 Emmitt Smith	2.00	5.00
36 Rod Bernstine	.20	.50
37 John Elway	2.40	6.00
38 Glyn Milburn	.40	1.00
39 Anthony Miller	.40	1.00
40 Shannon Sharpe	.50	1.25
41 Scott Mitchell	.40	1.00
42 Herman Moore	.50	1.25
43 Brett Perriman	.40	1.00
44 Barry Sanders	2.40	6.00
45 Chris Spielman	.20	.50
46 Edgar Bennett	.40	1.00
47 Robert Brooks	.50	1.25
48 Brett Favre	2.40	6.00
49 Sean Jones	.40	1.00
50 Reggie White	.50	1.25
51 Gary Brown	.20	.50
52 Cody Carlson	.20	.50
53 Ernest Givins	.20	.50
54 Haywood Jeffires	.20	.50
55 Bruce Matthews	.20	.50
56 Quentin Coryatt	.20	.50
57 Steve Emtman	.20	.50
58 Marshall Faulk	1.00	2.50
59 Jim Harbaugh	.40	1.00
60 Roosevelt Potts	.20	.50
61 Marcus Allen	.50	1.25
62 Steve Bono	.40	1.00
63 Willie Davis	.40	1.00
64 Lake Dawson	.20	.50
65 Neil Smith	.40	1.00
66 Tim Brown	.50	1.25
67 Jeff Hostetler	.40	1.00
68 Rocket Ismail	.40	1.00
69 James Jett	.40	1.00
70 Harvey Williams	.40	1.00
71 Jerome Bettis	.50	1.25
72 Troy Drayton	.20	.50
73 Wayne Gandy	.20	.50
74 Sean Gilbert	.20	.50
75 Todd Lyght	.20	.50
76 Tim Bowens	.20	.50
77 Bryan Cox	.20	.50
78 Irving Fryar	.40	1.00
79 Dan Marino	2.40	6.00
80 Bernie Parmalee	.20	.50
81 Terry Allen	.50	1.25
82 Cris Carter	.50	1.25
83 Qadry Ismail	.40	1.00
84 Warren Moon	.50	1.25
85 John Randle	.40	1.00
86 Bruce Armstrong	.20	.50
87 Drew Bledsoe	1.20	3.00
88 Vincent Brisby	.20	.50
89 Marion Butts	.20	.50
90 Ben Coates	.40	1.00
91 Morten Andersen	.20	.50
92 Quinn Early	.20	.50
93 Jim Everett	.20	.50
94 Tyrone Hughes	.20	.50
95 Renaldo Turnbull	.20	.50
96 Michael Brooks	.20	.50
97 Dave Brown	.20	.50
98 Jumbo Elliott	.20	.50
99 Rodney Hampton	.40	1.00
100 Mike Sherrard	.20	.50
101 Boomer Esiason	.40	1.00
102 Johnny Johnson	.20	.50
103 Nick Lowery	.20	.50
104 Johnny Mitchell	.20	.50
105 Aaron Glenn	.20	.50
106 Fred Barnett	.40	1.00
107 Bubby Brister	.40	1.00
108 Randall Cunningham	.50	1.25
109 Charlie Garner	.50	1.25
110 Calvin Williams	.20	.50
111 Byron Bam Morris	.20	.50
112 Barry Foster	.20	.50
113 Kevin Greene	.40	1.00
114 Neil O'Donnell	.40	1.00
115 Rod Woodson	.40	1.00
116 Ronnie Harmon	.20	.50
117 Stan Humphries	.40	1.00
118 Tony Martin	.40	1.00
119 Natrone Means	.40	1.00
120 Junior Seau	.40	1.00
121 William Floyd	.40	1.00
122 Jerry Rice	1.20	3.00
123 Deion Sanders	.80	2.00
124 Dana Stubblefield	.40	1.00
125 Steve Young	1.00	2.50
126 Brian Blades	.20	.50
127 Cortez Kennedy	.40	1.00
128 Rick Mirer	.40	1.00
129 Eugene Robinson	.20	.50
130 Chris Warren	.40	1.00
131 Trent Dilfer	.50	1.25
132 Santana Dotson	.20	.50
133 Craig Erickson	.40	1.00
134 Thomas Everett	.20	.50
135 Errict Rhett	.40	1.00
136 Reggie Brooks	.20	.50
137 Ricky Ervins	.20	.50
138 Darrell Green	.20	.50
139 Brian Mitchell	.20	.50
140 Heath Shuler	.40	1.00
141 Randy Baldwin	.20	.50
142 Bob Christian	.20	.50
143 Kerry Collins	.50	1.25
144 Tyrone Poole	.50	1.25
145 Sam Mills	.20	.50
146 Steve Beuerlein	.40	1.00
147 Cedric Tillman	.20	.50
148 Reggie Cobb	.20	.50
149 Eugene Chung	.20	.50
150 Desmond Howard	.40	1.00
NNO Steve Young MVP Super Bowl XXIX MVP Promo	1.20	3.00
NNO Emmitt Smith Promo (no card number; slightly smaller than base card)	1.60	4.00

1995 Pro Mags Classics

This 12-card set was produced by Chris Martin Enterprises and features color action player photos over a background of columns with the team logo on a flexible magnet. The magnets were randomly inserted in packs of 1995 Pro Mags at the average rate of one per three packs.

COMPLETE SET (12)	10.00	25.00
CL1 Barry Sanders	2.00	5.00
CL2 Deion Sanders	.60	1.50
CL3 Dan Marino	2.00	5.00
CL4 Drew Bledsoe	1.00	2.50
CL5 Marcus Allen	.40	1.00
CL6 Jerome Bettis	.40	1.00
CL7 John Elway	2.00	5.00
CL8 Jerry Rice	1.00	2.50
CL9 Emmitt Smith	1.60	4.00
CL10 Steve Young	.80	2.00
CL11 Marshall Faulk	.40	1.00
CL12 Troy Aikman	1.00	2.50

1995 Pro Mags In The Zone

This 12-card In The Zone set features borderless color action player photos on a flexible magnet. The magnets were randomly inserted in packs of 1995 Pro Mags at the rate of 1:3 packs.

COMPLETE SET (12)	8.00	20.00
1 Troy Aikman	1.00	2.50
2 Drew Bledsoe	1.00	2.50
3 John Elway	2.00	5.00
4 Brett Favre	2.00	5.00
5 Jeff Hostetler	.30	.75
6 Stan Humphries	.30	.75
7 Dan Marino	2.00	5.00
8 Jim Kelly	.50	1.25
9 Warren Moon	.50	1.25
10 Neil O'Donnell	.30	.75
11 Rick Mirer	.40	1.00
12 Steve Young	.80	2.00

1995 Pro Mags Rookies

This 12-magnet set features top rookies from the 1994 NFL Draft. Each measures approximately 2-1/8" by 3-3/8" and includes a color player photo with the player's name printed in gold foil near the bottom of the card.

COMPLETE SET (12)	4.00	10.00
1 Trent Dilfer	.60	1.50
2 Heath Shuler	.40	1.00
3 John Thierry	.30	.75
4 Wayne Gandy	.30	.75
5 Errict Rhett	.50	1.25
6 David Palmer	.40	1.00
7 Andre Coleman	.30	.75
8 Lake Dawson	.40	1.00
9 Marshall Faulk	1.60	4.00
10 Dan Wilkinson	.30	.75
11 Greg Hill	.40	1.00
12 Willie McGinest	.40	1.00

1995 Pro Mags Superhero Jumbos

These three jumbo Pro Magnets were released one per box, as well as via mail order for $6 each directly from Chris Martin Enterprises, Inc. The offer could be found in packs of the 1995 Pro Magnets product. The jumbos feature an artist's rendering of the player, measure approximately 3-3/4" by 7" and have rounded corners.

COMPLETE SET (3)	8.00	20.00
1 Jerome Bettis	2.00	5.00
2 John Elway	4.80	12.00
3 Warren Moon	2.00	5.00

1995 Pro Mags Teams

This set of magnets was released as a 5-card promotional set. Each unnumbered magnet features color photos of three top players from one team along with an embossed team logo.

COMPLETE SET (5)	8.00	20.00
1 Junior Seau, Stan Humphries, Natrone Means	1.00	2.50
2 Michael Irvin, Troy Aikman, Emmitt Smith	2.40	6.00
3 Dan Marino, O.J. McDuffie, Bernie Parmalee	3.20	8.00
4 Ricky Watters, Steve Young, Jerry Rice	2.00	5.00
5 Barry Foster, Neil O'Donnell, Rod Woodson	1.00	2.50

1996 Pro Mags

Chris Martin Enterprises issued this set through five-magnet packs with 24-packs per box. Each magnet featured a borderless color player photo with rounded corners. The magnets, measuring approximately 2 1/8" by 3 3/8," are grouped alphabetically within teams below. Some hobby packs contained randomly inserted Draft Day Future Stars magnets, while retail packs had randomly inserted Destination All-Pro magnets.

COMPLETE SET (100)	40.00	100.00
1 Troy Aikman	1.00	2.50
2 Michael Irvin	.50	1.25
3 Emmitt Smith	1.60	4.00
4 Deion Sanders	.60	1.50
5 Jay Novacek	.40	1.00
6 Jerry Rice	1.00	2.50
7 Steve Young	.80	2.00
8 J.J. Stokes	.50	1.25
9 William Floyd	.40	1.00
10 Merton Hanks	.25	.60
11 Greg Lloyd	.40	1.00
12 Rod Woodson	.50	1.25
13 Kordell Stewart	.80	2.00
14 Yancey Thigpen	.50	1.25
15 Charles Johnson	.40	1.00
16 Richmond Webb	.25	.60
17 Eric Green	.25	.60
18 Bernie Parmalee	.25	.60
19 Dan Marino	2.00	5.00
20 O.J. McDuffie	.40	1.00
21 Brett Favre	2.00	5.00
22 Reggie White	.50	1.25
23 Robert Brooks	.50	1.25
24 Edgar Bennett	.40	1.00
25 Marcus Allen	.50	1.25
26 Tamarick Vanover	.40	1.00
27 Lake Dawson	.40	1.00
28 Neil Smith	.40	1.00
29 Steve Bono	.40	1.00
30 Harvey Williams	.40	1.00
31 Tim Brown	.50	1.25
32 Jeff Hostetler	.40	1.00
33 Drew Bledsoe	1.00	2.50
34 Vincent Brisby	.40	1.00
35 Curtis Martin	.80	2.00
36 Rashaan Salaam	.40	1.00
37 Erik Kramer	.40	1.00
38 Curtis Conway	.40	1.00
39 Kerry Collins	.50	1.25
40 Sam Mills	.25	.60
41 Mark Carrier	.25	.60
42 Dave Brown	.25	.60
43 Rodney Hampton	.40	1.00
44 Tyrone Wheatley	.50	1.25
45 Vinny Testaverde	.40	1.00
46 Andre Rison	.50	1.25
47 Eric Turner	.25	.60
48 Michael Jackson	.40	1.00
49 Mark Brunell	1.00	2.50
50 Jeff Lageman	.25	.60
51 Roman Phifer	.25	.60
52 Isaac Bruce	.50	1.25
53 Rodney Peete	.25	.60
54 Ricky Watters	.50	1.25
55 Calvin Williams	.25	.60
56 Warren Moon	.50	1.25
57 Cris Carter	.50	1.25
58 David Palmer	.25	.60
59 Scott Mitchell	.40	1.00
60 Barry Sanders	2.00	5.00
61 Herman Moore	.40	1.00
62 Brett Perriman	.40	1.00
63 Jim Kelly	.50	1.25
64 Bruce Smith	.40	1.00
65 Bryce Paup	.40	1.00
66 Junior Seau	.50	1.25
67 Stan Humphries	.40	1.00
68 Andre Coleman	.25	.60
69 Tony Martin	.50	1.25
70 Terry Allen	.50	1.25
71 Heath Shuler	.40	1.00
72 John Elway	2.00	5.00
73 Terrell Davis	2.00	5.00
74 Mike Pritchard	.25	.60
75 Neil O'Donnell	.40	1.00
76 Kyle Brady	.25	.60
77 Jim Harbaugh	.50	1.25
78 Marshall Faulk	.50	1.25
79 Zack Crockett	.25	.60
80 Quentin Coryatt	.25	.60
81 Jeff George	.50	1.25
82 Morten Andersen	.25	.60
83 Eric Metcalf	.40	1.00
84 Joey Galloway	.60	1.50
85 Rick Mirer	.40	1.00
86 Chris Warren	.40	1.00
87 Ray Zellars	.25	.60
88 Eric Allen	.25	.60
89 Jim Everett	.25	.60
90 Jeff Blake	.50	1.25
91 Carl Pickens	.40	1.00
92 Ki-Jana Carter	.40	1.00
93 Larry Centers	.40	1.00
94 Garrison Hearst	.50	1.25
95 Trent Dilfer	.50	1.25
96 Errict Rhett	.40	1.00
97 Hardy Nickerson	.25	.60
98 Alvin Harper	.25	.60
99 Steve McNair	.80	2.00
100 Haywood Jeffires	.25	.60

1996 Pro Mags Destination All-Pro

These magnets were randomly inserted in 1996 Chris Martin Enterprises Pro Mags retail packs. The odds of pulling one of the inserts was 1:4 packs.

COMPLETE SET (6)	10.00	25.00
PB1 Jim Harbaugh	1.20	3.00
PB2 Curtis Martin	1.60	4.00
PB3 Yancey Thigpen	.80	2.00
PB4 Brett Favre	3.20	8.00
PB5 Jerry Rice	2.00	5.00
PB6 Barry Sanders	3.20	8.00

1996 Pro Mags Die-Cut Magnets

Chris Martin Enterprises produced these fifteen Die-Cut Magnets packaged one per cello pack. Each measures roughly 3 1/2" by 3 1/2." The magnets are unnumbered and listed below alphabetically.

COMPLETE SET (15)	10.00	25.00
1 Troy Aikman	.75	2.00
2 Marcus Allen	.60	1.50
3 Drew Bledsoe	.60	1.50
4 John Elway	1.25	3.00
5 Marshall Faulk	.60	1.50
6 Brett Favre	1.50	4.00
7 Jeff Hostetler	.40	1.00
8 Keyshawn Johnson	.40	1.00
9 Dan Marino	1.50	4.00
10 Jerry Rice	.75	2.00
11 Rashaan Salaam	.40	1.00
12 Barry Sanders	1.00	2.50
13 Deion Sanders	.60	1.50
14 Emmitt Smith	1.25	3.00
15 Kordell Stewart	.50	1.25
16 Steve Young	.75	2.00

1996 Pro Mags Draft Day Future Stars

These magnets were randomly inserted in 1996 Chris Martin Enterprises Pro Mags hobby packs. The odds of pulling one of the inserts was 1:4 packs.

COMPLETE SET (6)	6.00	15.00
1 Kevin Hardy	.60	1.50
2 Eddie George	3.20	8.00
3 Keyshawn Johnson	2.00	5.00
4 Tim Biakabutuka	1.00	2.50
5 Lawrence Phillips	.60	1.50
6 Alex Molden	.60	1.50

1996 Pro Mags 12

Produced by Chris Martin Enterprises, these 12-magnets contain a player photo against a metallic foil background. They were issued one per cello pack and measure approximately 3 1/2" by 2 1/4."

COMPLETE SET (12)	4.00	10.00
1 Tim Brown	.20	.50
2 John Elway	.80	2.00
3 Marshall Faulk	.30	.75
4 Dan Marino	.80	2.00
5 Curtis Martin	.40	1.00
6 Rashaan Salaam	.10	.30
7 Barry Sanders	.80	2.00
8 Emmitt Smith	.80	2.00
9 Neil Smith	.10	.30
10 Reggie White	.20	.50
11 Rod Woodson	.10	.30
12 Steve Young	.30	.75

1997 Pro Magnets

This set of magnets was produced by Crown Pro and distributed through retail chains. Each magnet features a color player photo on the front printed on silver foil stock. The cards measure roughly 2 1/2" by 3 1/2" and feature rounded corners and blankbacks. The original retail price was $1.49 per magnet.

S1 Troy Aikman	1.50	4.00
S2 Emmitt Smith	2.50	6.00
S3 Brett Favre	2.50	6.00
S4 Barry Sanders	2.00	5.00
S6 Dan Marino	2.50	6.00

1997 Pro Magnets 4x5

This set of magnets was produced by Crown Pro and distributed through retail chains. Each magnet features a larger color player photo on the front along with a smaller photo and a team logo. The magnets measure roughly 3 1/2" by 4" and feature rounded corners and blankbacks. The original retail price was $1.99 per magnet.

PF1 Brett Favre	2.00	5.00
PF2 Barry Sanders	1.50	4.00
PF3 Emmitt Smith	2.00	5.00
PF4 Dan Marino	2.00	5.00
PF7 Mark Brunell	.75	2.00

1998 Pro Magnets

This set of magnets was produced by Crown Pro and distributed through retail chains. Each magnet features a color player photo on the front and a colorful team name and logo on the back. The cards measure roughly 2 1/2" by 3 1/2" and feature rounded corners.

COMPLETE SET (7)	10.00	25.00
1 Brett Favre	2.50	6.00
2 Dan Marino	2.50	6.00
3 Troy Aikman	1.25	3.00
4 Emmitt Smith	2.00	5.00
7 Barry Sanders	1.50	4.00
8 John Elway	2.00	5.00
9 Terrell Davis	1.00	2.50

1995 ProMint Marino Promo

ProMint released this Dan Marino Promo "gold" card. It was printed on front and back fully in gold foil with a 22 Karat Gold notation at the bottom of the cardfront. The back includes a write-up, the card number 1, and the Promo designation.

1 Dan Marino	6.00	15.00

1988 Pro Set Test

This eight-card standard-size set was reportedly produced as a give-away to show interested parties what the new "Pro Set" cards were going to be like. They were produced in limited quantities and merely given away primarily at the National Candy show in Phoenix. The only front photo that was the same in the actual set was Jerry Rice. This set is also distinguishable in that the backs are oriented vertically rather than horizontally as the regular set.

COMPLETE SET (8)	175.00	350.00
1 Dan Marino	60.00	150.00
2 Jerry Rice	30.00	80.00
3 Eric Dickerson	8.00	20.00
4 Reggie White	16.00	40.00
5 Mike Singletary	8.00	20.00
6 Frank Minnifield	6.00	15.00
7 Phil Simms	8.00	20.00
8 Jim Kelly	16.00	40.00

1989 Pro Set Promos

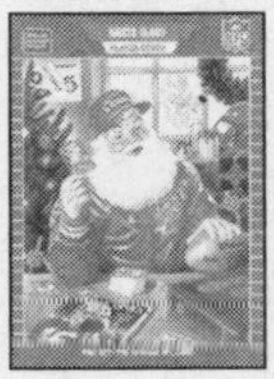

Cards 445, 455, and 463 were planned for inclusion in the Pro Set second series but were withdrawn before mass production began. Note, however, that Thomas Sanders was included in the set but as number 446. The Santa Claus card was mailed out to dealers and NFL dignitaries in December 1989. The Super Bowl Show card was given out to attendees at the show in New Orleans in late January 1990. All of these cards are standard size and utilize the 1989 Pro Set design.

COMPLETE SET (5)	40.00	100.00
445 Thomas Sanders	8.00	20.00
455 Blair Bush	8.00	20.00
463 James Lofton	10.00	25.00
1989 Santa Claus	16.00	40.00
NNO Super Bowl Card Show I New Orleans Super Bowl XXIV Logo/49ers vs. Broncos	.75	2.00

1989 Pro Set Test Designs

These five Randall Cunningham standard-size cards are the test designs for the 1990 Pro Set football cards. As tests, they were produced in very small quantities. It seems that all cards in this five-card set were printed at the same time and in the same (small) quantities. The five variations are basically experiments with and without borders and different color combinations. Horizontally oriented backs have a close-up photograph of player, statistical and biographical information, card number, and the Pro Set logo in a box enclosed in a white border. Player's name and personal statistics appear in reverse-out lettering in a colored band across the top of the card.

COMPLETE SET (5)	100.00	250.00
315A Randall Cunningham (No name or team designated on card front; borderless; vertical logo)	20.00	50.00
315B Randall Cunningham (No name or team designated on card front; silver border; vertical logo)	20.00	50.00
315C Randall Cunningham (Name and team designated on card front; borderless; horizontal logo)	20.00	50.00
315D Randall Cunningham (Name and team designated on card front; black border; horizontal logo)	20.00	50.00
315E Randall Cunningham (Name and team designated on card front; gray border; horizontal logo)	20.00	50.00

1989 Pro Set

Pro Set entered the football card market with a three series offering for 1989. A first series consisted of 440 cards followed by a 100-card second series offering. A Final Update set consisted of 21 cards for a total of 561 standard-size full-color cards. The backs are horizontal with a small photo, statistics and highlights. The first series is ordered numerically by teams and alphabetically within teams. The second series, issued five cards per Series II pack, includes first-round draft picks (485-515) from the previous spring's college draft and cards numbered 516-540 are "Pro Set Prospects". The second series cards differ in design by having a red border. The Final Update set includes Pro Set Prospects (542-549) and several cards (550-561) of players that were traded since the start of the season. These cards were also part of the second series offering. Complete Final Update sets were offered direct from Pro Set for $2.00 plus 50 Pro Set Play Book points. Rookie Cards include Troy Aikman, Flipper Anderson, Don Beebe, Brian Blades, Tim Brown, Cris Carter, Michael Irvin, Keith Jackson, Dave Meggett, Eric Metcalf, Anthony Miller, Jay Novacek, Rodney Peete, Andre Rison, Mark Rypien, Barry Sanders, Deion Sanders, Sterling Sharpe, Neil Smith, Chris Spielman, John Taylor, Derrick Thomas, Thurman Thomas and Rod Woodson. Card No. 47A William Perry, was pulled early in the initial production run creating a short print. He was replaced by Ron Morris (47B). A single print by design, the Pete Rozelle commemorative card was randomly inserted in one out of every 200 first series packs. The set is considered complete without either the Perry or the Rozelle cards.

COMPLETE SET (561) 10.00 25.00
COMP.SERIES 1 (440) 3.00 6.00
COMP.SERIES 2 (100) 10.00 20.00
COMP.FINAL FACT.SET (21) .75 2.00
1 Stacey Bailey .02 .10
2 Aundray Bruce RC .05 .15
3 Rick Bryan .02 .10
4 Bobby Butler .02 .10
5 Scott Case RC .02 .10
6 Tony Casillas .05 .15
7 Floyd Dixon .02 .10
8 Rick Donnelly .02 .10
9 Bill Fralic .05 .15
10 Mike Gann .02 .10
11 Mike Kenn .02 .10
12 Chris Miller RC .08 .25
13 John Rade .02 .10
14 Gerald Riggs UER .05 .15
(Uniform number is 42
but 43 on back)
15 John Settle RC .02 .10
16 Marion Campbell CO .02 .10
17 Cornelius Bennett .05 .15
18 Derrick Burroughs .02 .10
19 Shane Conlan .02 .10
20 Ronnie Harmon .05 .15
21 Kent Hull RC .05 .15
22 Jim Kelly .20 .50
23 Mark Kelso .05 .15
24 Pete Metzelaars .05 .15
25 Scott Norwood RC .05 .15
26 Andre Reed .08 .25
27 Fred Smerlas .02 .10
28 Bruce Smith .08 .25
29 Leonard Smith .02 .10
30 Art Still .02 .10
31 Darryl Talley .05 .15
32 Thurman Thomas RC .50 1.25
33 Will Wolford RC .05 .15
34 Marv Levy CO .05 .15
35 Neal Anderson .05 .15
36 Kevin Butler .02 .10
37 Jim Covert .05 .15
38 Richard Dent .05 .15
39 Dave Duerson .02 .10
40 Dennis Gentry .02 .10
41 Dan Hampton .05 .15
42 Jay Hilgenberg .02 .10
43 Dennis McKinnon UER .02 .10
(Caught 20 or 21
passes as a rookie)
44 Jim McMahon .05 .15
45 Steve McMichael .05 .15
46 Brad Muster RC .05 .15
47A William Perry SP 3.00 8.00
47B Ron Morris RC .02 .10
48 Ron Rivera .02 .10
49 Vestee Jackson RC .02 .10
50 Mike Singletary .05 .15
51 Mike Tomczak .05 .15
52 Keith Van Horne RC .02 .10
53A Mike Ditka CO .08 .25
(No HOF mention
on card front)
53B Mike Ditka CO .08 .25
(HOF banner on front)
54 Lewis Billups .02 .10
55 James Brooks .05 .15
56 Eddie Brown .02 .10
57 Jason Buck RC .02 .10
58 Boomer Esiason .05 .15
59 David Fulcher .05 .15
60A Rodney Holman RC .05 .15
(BENGALS on front)
60B Rodney Holman RC .08 .25
(Bengals on front)
61 Reggie Williams .05 .15
62 Joe Kelly RC .02 .10
63 Tim Krumrie .02 .10
64 Tim McGee .05 .15
65 Max Montoya .02 .10
66 Anthony Munoz .05 .15
67 Jim Skow .02 .10
68 Eric Thomas RC .02 .10
69 Leon White .02 .10
70 Ickey Woods RC .05 .15
71 Carl Zander .02 .10
72 Sam Wyche CO .02 .10
73 Brian Brennan .02 .10
74 Earnest Byner .05 .15
75 Hanford Dixon .02 .10
76 Mike Pagel .02 .10
77 Bernie Kosar .05 .15
78 Reggie Langhorne RC .05 .15
79 Kevin Mack .05 .15
80 Clay Matthews .05 .15
81 Gerald McNeil .02 .10
82 Frank Minnifield .02 .10
83 Cody Risien .02 .10
84 Webster Slaughter .05 .15
85 Felix Wright .02 .10
86 Bud Carson CO UER .02 .10
(NFLPA logo on back)
87 Bill Bates .05 .15
88 Kevin Brooks .02 .10
89 Michael Irvin RC .60 1.50
90 Jim Jeffcoat .02 .10
91 Ed Too Tall Jones .05 .15
92 Eugene Lockhart RC .02 .10
93 Nate Newton RC .05 .15
94 Danny Noonan .02 .10
95 Steve Pelluer .02 .10
96 Herschel Walker .05 .15
97 Everson Walls .02 .10
98 Jimmy Johnson CO RC .08 .25
99 Keith Bishop .02 .10
100A John Elway ERR 2.50 6.00
(Drafted 1st Round)
100B John Elway COR .75 2.00
(Acquired Trade)
101 Simon Fletcher RC .05 .15
102 Mike Harden .02 .10
103 Mike Horan .02 .10
104 Mark Jackson .05 .15
105 Vance Johnson .05 .15
106 Rulon Jones .02 .10
107 Clarence Kay .02 .10
108 Karl Mecklenburg .05 .15
109 Ricky Nattiel .02 .10
110 Steve Sewell RC .02 .10
111 Dennis Smith .05 .15
112 Gerald Willhite .02 .10
113 Sammy Winder .02 .10
114 Dan Reeves CO .05 .15
115 Jim Arnold .02 .10
116 Jerry Ball RC .05 .15
117 Bennie Blades RC .02 .10
118 Lomas Brown .05 .15
119 Mike Cofer .02 .10
120 Garry James .02 .10
121 James Jones .02 .10
122 Chuck Long .02 .10
123 Pete Mandley .02 .10
124 Eddie Murray .02 .10
125 Chris Spielman RC .08 .25
126 Dennis Gibson .02 .10
127 Wayne Fontes CO .02 .10
128 John Anderson .02 .10
129 Brent Fullwood RC .02 .10
130 Mark Cannon RC .02 .10
131 Tim Harris .02 .10
132 Mark Lee .02 .10
133 Don Majkowski RC .05 .15
134 Mark Murphy .02 .10
135 Brian Noble .02 .10
136 Ken Ruettgers RC .02 .10
137 Johnny Holland .02 .10
138 Randy Wright .02 .10
139 Lindy Infante CO .02 .10
140 Steve Brown .02 .10
141 Ray Childress .05 .15
(Sacking Joe Montana)
142 Jeff Donaldson .02 .10
143 Ernest Givins .05 .15
144 John Grimsley .02 .10
145 Alonzo Highsmith .05 .15
146 Drew Hill .05 .15
147 Robert Lyles .02 .10
148 Bruce Matthews RC .30 .75
149 Warren Moon .08 .25
150 Mike Munchak .05 .15
151 Allen Pinkett RC .05 .15
152 Mike Rozier .05 .15
153 Tony Zendejas .02 .10
154 Jerry Glanville CO .02 .10
155 Albert Bentley .02 .10
156 Dean Biasucci .02 .10
157 Duane Bickett .02 .10
158 Bill Brooks .05 .15
159 Chris Chandler RC .40 1.00
160 Pat Beach .02 .10
161 Ray Donaldson .02 .10
162 Jon Hand .02 .10
163 Chris Hinton .02 .10
164 Rohn Stark .02 .10
165 Fredd Young .02 .10
166 Ron Meyer CO .02 .10
167 Lloyd Burruss .02 .10
168 Carlos Carson .02 .10
169 Deron Cherry .05 .15
170 Irv Eatman .02 .10
171 Dino Hackett .02 .10
172 Steve DeBerg .05 .15
173 Albert Lewis .02 .10
174 Nick Lowery .02 .10
175 Bill Maas .02 .10
176 Christian Okoye .05 .15
177 Stephone Paige .05 .15
178 Mark Adickes RC .02 .10
(Out of alphabetical
sequence for his team)
179 Kevin Ross RC .05 .15
180 Neil Smith RC .20 .50
181 M. Schottenheimer CO .02 .10
182 Marcus Allen .08 .25
183 Tim Brown RC .60 1.50
184 Willie Gault .05 .15
185 Bo Jackson .10 .30
186 Howie Long .08 .25
187 Vann McElroy .02 .10
188 Matt Millen .05 .15
189 Don Mosebar RC .02 .10
190 Bill Pickel .02 .10
191 Jerry Robinson UER .02 .10
(Stats show 1 TD, but
text says 2 TD's)
192 Jay Schroeder .02 .10
193A Stacey Toran .02 .10
(No mention of death
on card front)
193B Stacey Toran .20 .50
(1961-1989 banner
on card front)
194 Mike Shanahan CO RC .05 .15
195 Greg Bell .02 .10
196 Ron Brown .02 .10
197 Aaron Cox RC .02 .10
198 Henry Ellard .08 .25
199 Jim Everett .05 .15
200 Jerry Gray .02 .10
201 Kevin Greene .08 .25
202 Pete Holohan .02 .10
203 LeRoy Irvin .05 .15
204 Mike Lansford .02 .10
205 Tom Newberry RC .02 .10
206 Mel Owens .02 .10
207 Jackie Slater .05 .15
208 Doug Smith .02 .10
209 Mike Wilcher .02 .10
210 John Robinson CO .02 .10
211 John Bosa .02 .10
212 Mark Brown .02 .10
213 Mark Clayton .05 .15
214A Ferrell Edmonds RC .20 .50
ERR, Misspelled Edmonds
on front and back)
214B Ferrell Edmonds RC .02 .10
COR, spelled correctly
215 Roy Foster .02 .10
216 Lorenzo Hampton .02 .10
217 Jim C. Jensen UER RC .02 .10
(Born Albington,
should be Abington)
218 William Judson .02 .10
219 Eric Kumerow RC .02 .10
220 Dan Marino .75 2.00
221 John Offerdahl .02 .10
222 Fuad Reveiz .02 .10
223 Reggie Roby .02 .10
224 Brian Sochia .02 .10
225 Don Shula CO RC .08 .25
226 Alfred Anderson .02 .10
227 Joey Browner .02 .10
228 Anthony Carter .05 .15
229 Chris Doleman .05 .15
230 Hassan Jones RC .02 .10
231 Steve Jordan .02 .10
232 Tommy Kramer .05 .15
233 Carl Lee RC .02 .10
234 Kirk Lowdermilk RC .02 .10
235 Randall McDaniel RC .50 1.25
236 Doug Martin .02 .10
237 Keith Millard .02 .10
238 Darrin Nelson .02 .10
239 Jesse Solomon .02 .10
240 Scott Studwell .02 .10
241 Wade Wilson .05 .15
242 Gary Zimmerman .08 .25
243 Jerry Burns CO .02 .10
244 Bruce Armstrong RC .05 .15
245 Raymond Clayborn .02 .10
246 Reggie Dupard .02 .10
247 Tony Eason .02 .10
248 Sean Farrell .02 .10
249 Doug Flutie .30 .75
250 Brent Williams RC .02 .10
251 Roland James .02 .10
252 Ronnie Lippett .02 .10
253 Fred Marion .02 .10
254 Larry McGrew .02 .10
255 Stanley Morgan .05 .15
256 Johnny Rembert RC .02 .10
257 John Stephens RC .02 .10
258 Andre Tippett .08 .25
259 Garin Veris .02 .10
260A Raymond Berry CO .05 .15
(No HOF mention
on card front)
260B Raymond Berry CO .05 .15
(HOF banner
on card front)
261 Morten Andersen .05 .15
262 Hoby Brenner .02 .10
263 Stan Brock .02 .10
264 Brad Edelman .02 .10
265 Jumpy Geathers .02 .10
266A Bobby Hebert ERR .20 .50
(passers in 42-0)
266B Bobby Hebert COR .05 .15
(passes in 42-0)
267 Craig Heyward RC .08 .25
268 Lonzell Hill .02 .10
269 Dalton Hilliard .02 .10
270 Rickey Jackson .05 .15
271 Steve Korte .02 .10
272 Eric Martin .02 .10
273 Rueben Mayes .02 .10
274 Sam Mills .05 .15
275 Brett Perriman RC .08 .25
276 Pat Swilling .05 .15
277 John Tice .02 .10
278 Jim Mora CO .02 .10
279 Eric Moore RC .02 .10
280 Carl Banks .05 .15
281 Mark Bavaro .05 .15
282 Maurice Carthon .02 .10
283 Mark Collins RC .05 .15
284 Erik Howard .02 .10
285 Terry Kinard .02 .10
286 Sean Landeta .02 .10
287 Lionel Manuel .05 .15
288 Leonard Marshall .05 .15
289 Joe Morris .05 .15
290 Bart Oates .02 .10
291 Phil Simms .05 .15
292 Lawrence Taylor .08 .25
293 Bill Parcells CO RC .05 .15
294 Dave Cadigan .02 .10
295 Kyle Clifton RC .02 .10
296 Alex Gordon .02 .10
297 James Hasty RC .02 .10
298 Johnny Hector .02 .10
299 Bobby Humphery .05 .15
300 Pat Leahy .02 .10
301 Marty Lyons .02 .10
302 Reggie McElroy RC .05 .15
303 Erik McMillan RC .02 .10
304 Freeman McNeil .05 .15
305 Ken O'Brien .05 .15
306 Pat Ryan .02 .10
307 Mickey Shuler .02 .10
308 Al Toon .05 .15
309 Jo Jo Townsell .02 .10
310 Roger Vick .02 .10
311 Joe Walton CO .02 .10
312 Jerome Brown .05 .15
313 Keith Byars .05 .15
314 Cris Carter RC .60 1.50
315 Randall Cunningham .15 .40
316 Terry Hoage .02 .10
317 Wes Hopkins .02 .10
318 Keith Jackson RC .08 .25
319 Mike Quick .05 .15
320 Mike Reichenbach .02 .10
321 Dave Rimington .02 .10
322 John Teltschik .02 .10
323 Anthony Toney .02 .10
324 Andre Waters .05 .15
325 Reggie White .08 .25
326 Luis Zendejas .02 .10
327 Buddy Ryan CO .05 .15
328 Robert Awalt .02 .10
329 Tim McDonald RC .05 .15
330 Roy Green .05 .15
331 Neil Lomax .05 .15
332 Cedric Mack .02 .10
333 Stump Mitchell .02 .10
334 Niko Noga RC .02 .10
335 Jay Novacek RC .08 .25
336 Freddie Joe Nunn .02 .10
337 Luis Sharpe .02 .10
338 Vai Sikahema .02 .10
339 J.T. Smith .02 .10
340 Ron Wolfley .02 .10
341 Gene Stallings CO RC .05 .15
342 Gary Anderson K .02 .10
343 Bubby Brister RC .08 .25
344 Dermontti Dawson RC .05 .15
345 Thomas Everett RC .02 .10
346 Delton Hall RC .02 .10
347 Bryan Hinkle RC .02 .10
348 Merril Hoge RC .05 .15
349 Tunch Ilkin RC .02 .10
350 Aaron Jones RC .02 .10
351 Louis Lipps .05 .15
352 David Little .02 .10
353 Hardy Nickerson RC .08 .25
354 Rod Woodson RC .40 1.00
355A Chuck Noll RC CO ERR .05 .15
(one of only three)
355B Chuck Noll RC CO COR .05 .15
(one of only two)
356 Gary Anderson RB .05 .15
357 Rod Bernstine RC .05 .15
358 Gill Byrd .02 .10
359 Vencie Glenn .02 .10
360 Dennis McKnight .02 .10
361 Lionel James .02 .10
362 Mark Malone .02 .10
363A Anthony Miller RC ERR .08 .25
(TD total 14.8)
363B Anthony Miller RC COR .08 .25
(TD total 3)
364 Ralf Mojsiejenko .02 .10
365 Leslie O'Neal .05 .15
366 Jamie Holland RC .02 .10
367 Lee Williams .02 .10
368 Dan Henning CO .02 .10
369 Harris Barton RC .02 .10
370 Michael Carter .02 .10
371 Mike Cofer RC .02 .10
(Joe Montana holding)
372 Roger Craig .08 .25
373 Riki Ellison RC .02 .10
374 Jim Fahnhorst .02 .10
375 John Frank .02 .10
376 Jeff Fuller .02 .10
377 Don Griffin .02 .10
378 Charles Haley .08 .25
379 Ronnie Lott .05 .15
380 Tim McKyer .02 .10
381 Joe Montana .75 2.00
382 Tom Rathman .05 .15
383 Jerry Rice .60 1.50
384 John Taylor RC .20 .50
385 Keena Turner .02 .10
386 Michael Walter .02 .10
387 Bubba Paris .02 .10
388 Steve Young .40 1.00
389 George Seifert .05 .15
CO RC UER
(NFLPA logo on back)
390 Brian Blades RC .08 .25
391A Brian Bosworth ERR .10 .30
(Seattle on front)
391B Brian Bosworth COR .05 .15
(Listed by team nick-
name on front)
392 Jeff Bryant .02 .10
393 Jacob Green .05 .15
394 Norm Johnson .02 .10
395 Dave Krieg .05 .15
396 Steve Largent .08 .25
397 Bryan Millard RC .02 .10
398 Paul Moyer .02 .10
399 Joe Nash .02 .10
400 Rufus Porter RC .02 .10
401 Eugene Robinson RC .08 .25
402 Bruce Scholtz .02 .10
403 Kelly Stouffer RC .02 .10
404A Curt Warner ERR .50 1.25
(yards 1455)
404B Curt Warner COR .05 .15
(yards 6074)
405 John L. Williams .02 .10
406 Tony Woods RC .05 .15
407 David Wyman .02 .10
408 Chuck Knox CO .05 .15
409 Mark Carrier RC .08 .25
410 Randy Grimes .02 .10
411 Paul Gruber RC .05 .15
412 Harry Hamilton .02 .10
413 Ron Holmes .02 .10
414 Donald Igwebuike .02 .10
415 Dan Turk .02 .10
416 Ricky Reynolds .02 .10
417 Bruce Hill RC .02 .10
418 Lars Tate .02 .10
419 Vinny Testaverde .10 .30
420 James Wilder .02 .10
421 Ray Perkins CO .02 .10
422 Jeff Bostic .02 .10
423 Kelvin Bryant .02 .10
424 Gary Clark .08 .25
425 Monte Coleman .02 .10
426 Darrell Green .05 .15
427 Joe Jacoby .05 .15
428 Jim Lachey .05 .15
429 Charles Mann .02 .10
430 Dexter Manley .05 .15
431 Darryl Grant .02 .10
432 Mark May RC .05 .15
433 Art Monk .05 .15
434 Mark Rypien RC .08 .25
435 Ricky Sanders .05 .15
436 Alvin Walton RC .02 .10
437 Don Warren .02 .10
438 Jamie Morris .02 .10
439 Doug Williams .05 .15
440 Joe Gibbs CO RC .08 .25
441 Marcus Cotton .02 .10
442 Joel Williams .02 .10
443 Joe Devlin .02 .10
444 Robb Riddick .02 .10
445 William Perry .05 .15
446 Thomas Sanders RC .02 .10
447 Brian Blados .02 .10
448 Cris Collinsworth .05 .15
449 Stanford Jennings .02 .10
450 Barry Krauss UER .02 .10
(Listed as playing for
Indianapolis 1979-88)
451 Ozzie Newsome .05 .15
452 Mike Oliphant RC .02 .10
453 Tony Dorsett .08 .25
454 Bruce McNorton .02 .10
455 Eric Dickerson .05 .15
456 Keith Bostic .02 .10
457 Sam Clancy RC .02 .10
458 Jack Del Rio RC .08 .25
459 Mike Webster .05 .15
460 Bob Golic .02 .10
461 Otis Wilson .02 .10
462 Mike Haynes .05 .15
463 Greg Townsend .05 .15
464 Mark Duper .05 .15
465 E.J. Junior .05 .15
466 Troy Stradford .02 .10
467 Mike Merriweather .05 .15
468 Irving Fryar .08 .25
469 Vaughan Johnson RC .05 .15
470 Pepper Johnson .05 .15
471 Gary Reasons RC .02 .10
472 Perry Williams RC .02 .10
473 Wesley Walker .05 .15
474 Anthony Bell RC .05 .15
475 Earl Ferrell .02 .10
476 Craig Wolfley .02 .10
477 Billy Ray Smith .02 .10
478A Jim McMahon .10 .30
(No mention of trade
on card front)
478B Jim McMahon .05 .15
(Traded banner
on card front)
478C Jim McMahon 15.00 40.00
(Traded banner
on card front but no
line on back saying
also see card 44)
479 Eric Wright .02 .10
480A Earnest Byner .05 .15
(No mention of trade
on card front but no
line on back saying
also see card 74)
480B Earnest Byner .10 .30
(Traded banner
on card front)
480C Earnest Byner 15.00 40.00
(Traded banner
on card front but no
line on back saying
also see card 74)
480D Earnest Byner 75.00 150.00
(No mention of trade
on card front with
line on back saying
to also see card 74)
481 Russ Grimm .05 .15
482 Wilber Marshall .05 .15
483A Gerald Riggs .05 .15
(No mention of trade
on card front but no
line on back saying
to also see card 14)
483B Gerald Riggs .10 .30
(Traded banner
on card front)
483C Gerald Riggs 15.00 40.00
(Traded banner
on card front but no
line on back saying
also see card 14)
483D Gerald Riggs 75.00 150.00
(No mention of trade
on card front with
line on back saying
to also see card 14)
484 Brian Davis RC .02 .10
485 Shawn Collins RC .02 .10
486 Deion Sanders RC .60 1.50
487 Trace Armstrong RC .05 .15
488 Donnell Woolford RC .05 .15
489 Eric Metcalf RC .08 .25
490 Troy Aikman RC 2.50 6.00
491 Steve Walsh RC .05 .15
492 Steve Atwater RC .08 .25
493 Bobby Humphrey RC .05 .15
494 Barry Sanders RC 2.50 6.00
495 Tony Mandarich RC .05 .15
496 David Williams RC .02 .10
497 Andre Rison UER RC .40 1.00
(Jersey number not
listed on back)
498 Derrick Thomas RC .60 1.50
499 Cleveland Gary RC .02 .10
500 Bill Hawkins RC .02 .10
501 Louis Oliver RC .05 .15
502 Sammie Smith RC .02 .10
503 Hart Lee Dykes RC .02 .10
504 Wayne Martin RC .02 .10
505 Brian Williams OL RC .02 .10
506 Jeff Lageman RC .05 .15
507 Eric Hill RC .05 .15
508 Joe Wolf RC .02 .10
509 Timm Rosenbach RC .05 .15
510 Tom Ricketts RC .02 .10
511 Tim Worley RC .02 .10
512 Burt Grossman RC .05 .15
513 Keith DeLong RC .02 .10
514 Andy Heck RC .02 .10
515 Broderick Thomas RC .08 .25
516 Don Beebe RC .08 .25
517 James Thornton RC .02 .10
518 Eric Kattus .02 .10
519 Bruce Kozerski RC .02 .10
520 Brian Washington RC .02 .10
521 Rodney Peete UER RC .20 .50
(Jersey 19 on back,
should be 9)
522 Erik Affholter RC .02 .10
523 Anthony Dilweg RC .02 .10
524 O'Brien Alston .02 .10
525 Mike Elkins RC .02 .10
526 Jonathan Hayes RC .02 .10
527 Terry McDaniel RC .02 .10
528 Frank Stams RC .02 .10
529 Darryl Ingram RC .02 .10
530 Henry Thomas .02 .10
531 Eric Coleman DB .02 .10
532 Sheldon White RC .02 .10
533 Eric Allen RC .08 .25
534 Robert Drummond .02 .10
535A Gizmo Williams RC 5.00 10.00
(Without Scouting Photo on front
and Footbal misspelled on back)
535B Gizmo Williams RC .08 .25
(Without Scouting Photo on front
but Canadian Football on back)
535C Gizmo Williams RC .05 .15
(With Scouting Photo on front)
536 Billy Joe Tolliver RC .05 .15
537 Daniel Stubbs RC .02 .10
538 Wesley Walls RC .15 .40
539A James Jefferson ERR RC .10 .30
539B James Jefferson RC COR .02 .10
Prospect banner
on card front
540 Tracy Rocker .02 .10
541 Art Shell CO .05 .15
542 Lemuel Stinson RC .02 .10
543 Tyrone Braxton UER RC .02 .10
(back photo actually
Ken Bell)
544 David Treadwell RC .02 .10
545 Flipper Anderson RC .08 .25
546 Dave Meggett RC .08 .25
547 Lewis Tillman RC .02 .10
548 Carnell Lake RC .08 .25
549 Marion Butts RC .05 .15
550 Sterling Sharpe RC .40 1.00
551 Ezra Johnson .02 .10
552 Clarence Verdin RC .02 .10
553 Mervyn Fernandez RC .02 .10
554 Ottis Anderson .05 .15
555 Gary Hogeboom .02 .10
556 Paul Palmer TR .02 .10
557 Jesse Solomon TR .02 .10
558 Chip Banks TR .05 .15
559 Steve Pelluer TR .02 .10
560 Darrin Nelson TR .02 .10
561 Herschel Walker TR .05 .15
CC1 Pete Rozelle COMM SP .20 .50

1989 Pro Set Announcers

COMPLETE SET (30) 1.25 3.00
1 Dan Dierdorf .07 .20
2 Frank Gifford .15 .40
3 Al Michaels .02 .10
4 Pete Axthelm .02 .10
5 Chris Berman .07 .20
6 Tom Jackson .07 .20
7 Mike Patrick .07 .20
8 John Saunders .02 .10
9 Joe Theismann .07 .20
10 Steve Sabol .02 .10
11 Jack Buck .02 .10
12 Terry Bradshaw .30 .75
13 James Brown .07 .20
14 Dan Fouts .07 .20
15 Dick Butkus .15 .40
16 Irv Cross .02 .10
17 Brent Musburger .02 .10
18 Ken Stabler .15 .40
19 Dick Stockton .02 .10
20 Hank Stram .07 .20
21 Verne Lundquist .02 .10
22 Will McDonough .02 .10
23 Bob Costas .02 .10
24 Dick Enberg .02 .10
25 Joe Namath .30 .75
26 Bob Trumpy .02 .10
27 Merlin Olsen .07 .20
28 Ahmad Rashad .07 .20
29 O.J. Simpson .07 .20
30 Bill Walsh .07 .20

1989 Pro Set Super Bowl Logos

This 23-card standard-size set contains a card for each Super Bowl played up through the production of the 1989 Pro Set regular set. These cards were inserted with the regular player cards in the wax packs of the 1989 Pro Set. The cards are unnumbered.

COMPLETE SET (23) 1.25 3.00
COMMON CARD (1-23) .07 .20

1989-90 Pro Set Super Bowl XXIV Binder

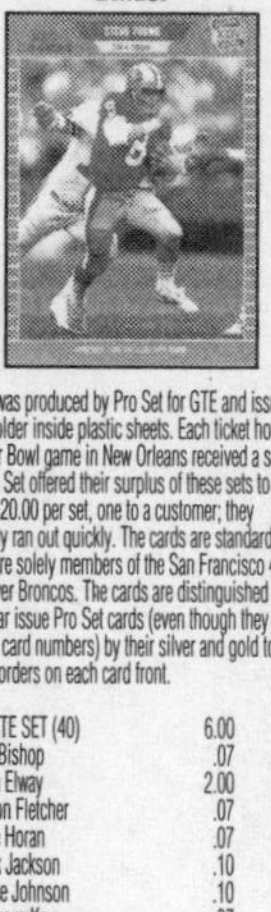

This set was produced by Pro Set for GTE and issued in a special folder inside plastic sheets. Each ticket holder at the Super Bowl game in New Orleans received a set. Later Pro Set offered their surplus of these sets to the public at 20.00 per set, one to a customer; they apparently ran out quickly. The cards are standard size and feature solely members of the San Francisco 49ers and Denver Broncos. The cards are distinguished from the regular issue Pro Set cards (even though they have the same card numbers) by their silver and gold top and bottom borders on each card front.

COMPLETE SET (40) 6.00 15.00
99 Keith Bishop .07 .20
100 John Elway 2.00 5.00
101 Simon Fletcher .07 .20
103 Mike Horan .07 .20
104 Mark Jackson .10 .30
105 Vance Johnson .10 .30
107 Clarence Kay .07 .20
108 Karl Mecklenburg .10 .30
109 Ricky Nattiel .07 .20
110 Steve Sewell .07 .20
111 Dennis Smith .07 .20
113 Sammy Winder .07 .20
114 Dan Reeves CO .10 .30
369 Harris Barton .07 .20
370 Michael Carter .07 .20
371 Mike Cofer .07 .20
372 Roger Craig .10 .30
374 Jim Fahnhorst .07 .20
377 Don Griffin .07 .20
378 Charles Haley .10 .30
379 Ronnie Lott .20 .50
380 Tim McKyer .07 .20
381 Joe Montana 2.50 6.00
382 Tom Rathman .10 .30
383 Jerry Rice 1.25 3.00
384 John Taylor .10 .30
385 Keena Turner .07 .20
386 Michael Walter .07 .20
387 Bubba Paris .07 .20
388 Steve Young .75 2.00
389 George Seifert CO .10 .30
479 Eric Wright .07 .20
492 Steve Atwater .07 .20
493 Bobby Humphrey .07 .20
537 Daniel Stubbs .07 .20
543 Tyrone Braxton .07 .20
544 David Treadwell .07 .20
NNO AFC Logo .07 .20
XXIV Collectible
NNO NFC Logo .07 .20
XXIV Collectible
NNO Superdome .07 .20
XXIV Collectible

1990 Pro Set Draft Day

This four-card standard-size set was issued by Pro Set on the date of the 1990 NFL draft. The cards feature action shots in the 1990 Pro Set design of potential number one draft picks with a yellow triangular shaped area in the lower right that reads "Number 1 Pick." The backs of the cards have a typical Pro Set format with one half of the card being a full-color portrait of the player and the other half consisting of biographical information. The fourth card in the set (Jeff George Colts) is not listed below but featured in the 1990 Pro Set regular issue checklist since it was also inserted into 1990 Pro Set first series packs. An additional blank backed version of each of the four cards surfaced much later that included a bronze colored top and bottom border and was printed without the yellow triangular area.

COMPLETE SET (3) 5.00 12.00
669A Jeff George Falcons 2.00 5.00
669B Jeff George Patriots 2.00 5.00
669C Keith McCants 1.25 3.00

1990 Pro Set

This set consists of 801 standard-size cards issued in three series. The first series contains 377 cards, the second series 392 and a 32-card Final Update. The set was issued in 14-card packs. The fronts have striking color action photos and team colored borders on the top and bottom edges. Cards 1-29 are special selections from Pro Set commemorating events or leaders from the previous year. Pro Set also produced and randomly inserted 10,000 Lombardi Trophy hologram cards, creating quite a hobby sensation. Speculation is that one special Lombardi card was inserted in every tenth case. These attractive cards were hand serial numbered out of 10,000 (printed as 10M) and feature the words "Collector Edition" on the back. An "Owner Edition" version (not serial numbered) exists but little is known about its origin. Due to a contractual dispute, the Pro Bowl card of Eric Dickerson (No. 338) was withdrawn early creating a short print, but quantities of this card were released after Pro Set closed and sold off old inventory. The set price below does not include any of the tougher variation cards: 1A Barry Sanders, 72A Dexter Manley and 75A Cody Risien. The 1990 Pro Set Final Update series was issued in a special mail-away offer. The series included a special Ronnie Lott Stay in School card and the 1990 Pro Set Rookie of the Year card which introduced the 1991 Pro Set design.

COMPLETE SET (801) 15.00 40.00
COMP.SERIES 1 (377) 8.00 20.00
COMP.SERIES 2 (392) 8.00 20.00
COMP.FINAL SERIES (32) 2.00 5.00
COMP.FINAL FACT. (32) 2.00 5.00
1A Barry Sanders ROY 100.00 200.00
(Issued at Hawaii Trade
Show in February 1990;
no ROY trophy on back:
gold border on front top and bottom)
1B Barry Sanders .25 .60
Rookie of the Year
2A Joe Montana ERR .20 .50
Player of the Year
(Jim Kelly's stats
in text)
2B Joe Montana COR .20 .50
Player of the Year
(Corrected from 3521
yards to 3130)
3 Lindy Infante UER .01 .05
Coach of the Year
(missing Coach next
to Packers)
4 Warren Moon UER .08 .25
Man of the Year
(missing R symbol)
5 Keith Millard .01 .05
Defensive Player
of the Year
6 Derrick Thomas UER .08 .25
Defensive Rookie
of the Year
(no 1989 on front
banner of card)
7 Ottis Anderson .02 .10
Comeback Player
of the Year
8 Joe Montana UER .20 .50
Passing Leader
9 Christian Okoye .01 .05
Rushing Leader
10 Thurman Thomas .08 .25
Total Yardage Leader
11 Mike Cofer .01 .05
Kick Scoring Leader
12 Dalton Hilliard UER .01 .05
TD Scoring Leader
(O.J. Simpson not
listed in stats, but
is mentioned in text)
13 Sterling Sharpe .08 .25
Receiving Leader
14 Rich Camarillo .01 .05
Punting Leader
15A Walter Stanley ERR .20 .50
Punt Return Leader
(jersey on front reads/87, back says 8 or 86)
15B Walter Stanley COR .01 .05
Punt Return Leader
16 Rod Woodson .08 .25
Kickoff Return Leader
17 Felix Wright .01 .05
Interception Leader
18A Chris Doleman ERR .20 .50
Sack Leader
(Townsent, Jeffcoact)
18B Chris Doleman COR .20 .50
Sack Leader
(Townsend, Jeffcoat)
19A Andre Ware RC .02 .10
Heisman Trophy
(No drafted stripe
on card front)
19B Andre Ware RC .02 .10
Heisman Trophy
(Drafted stripe
on card front)
20A Mo Elewonibi RC .01 .05
Outland Trophy
(No drafted stripe
on card front)

Card	Low	High
20B Mo Elewonibi RC	.01	.05
Outland Trophy		
(Drafted stripe		
on card front)		
21A Percy Snow	.20	.50
Lombardi Award		
(No drafted stripe		
on card front)		
21B Percy Snow	.01	.05
Lombardi Award		
(Drafted stripe		
on card front)		
22A Anthony Thompson RC	.01	.05
Maxwell Award		
(No drafted stripe		
on card front)		
22B Anthony Thompson RC	.01	.05
Maxwell Award		
(Drafted stripe		
on card front)		
23 Buck Buchanan	.01	.05
(Sacking Bart Starr)/1990 HOF Selection		
24 Bob Griese/1990 HOF Selection	.02	.10
25A Franco Harris ERR/1990 HOF Selection	.20	.50
(Born 2/7/50)		
25B Franco Harris COR	.02	.10
1990 HOF Selection		
(Born 3/7/50)		
26 Ted Hendricks/1990 HOF Selection	.01	.05
27A Jack Lambert ERR/1990 HOF Selection	.20	.50
(Born 7/2/52)		
27B Jack Lambert COR/1990 HOF Selection	.20	.50
(Born 7/8/52)		
28 Tom Landry/1990 HOF Selection	.02	.10
29 Bob St.Clair/1990 HOF Selection	.01	.05
30 Aundray Bruce UER	.01	.05
(Stats say Falcons)		
31 Tony Casillas UER	.01	.05
(Stats say Falcons)		
32 Shawn Collins	.01	.05
33 Marcus Cotton	.01	.05
34 Bill Fralic	.01	.05
35 Chris Miller	.02	.10
36 Deion Sanders UER	.20	.50
(Stats say Falcons)		
37 John Settle	.01	.05
38 Jerry Glanville CO	.01	.05
39 Cornelius Bennett	.02	.10
40 Jim Kelly	.08	.25
41 Mark Kelso UER	.01	.05
(No fumble rec. in 1988;		
mentioned in 1989)		
42 Scott Norwood	.01	.05
43 Nate Odomes RC	.02	.10
44 Scott Radecic	.01	.05
45 Jim Ritcher RC	.01	.05
46 Leonard Smith	.01	.05
47 Darryl Talley	.01	.05
48 Marv Levy CO	.01	.05
49 Neal Anderson	.02	.10
50 Kevin Butler	.01	.05
51 Jim Covert	.01	.05
52 Richard Dent	.02	.10
53 Jay Hilgenberg	.01	.05
54 Steve McMichael	.02	.10
55 Ron Morris	.01	.05
56 John Roper	.01	.05
57 Mike Singletary	.02	.10
58 Keith Van Horne	.01	.05
59A Mike Ditka CO	10.00	20.00
Hall of Fame printed in large letters		
59B Mike Ditka CO	.30	.75
Hall of Fame printed in small letters		
60 Lewis Billups	.01	.05
61 Eddie Brown	.01	.05
62 Jason Buck	.01	.05
63A Rickey Dixon RC ERR	.20	.50
(Info missing under bio notes)		
63B Rickey Dixon COR RC	.20	.50
64 Tim McGee	.01	.05
65 Eric Thomas	.01	.05
66 Ickey Woods	.01	.05
67 Carl Zander	.01	.05
68A Sam Wyche CO ERR	.20	.50
(Info missing under bio notes)		
68B Sam Wyche CO COR	.20	.50
69 Paul Farren	.01	.05
70 Thane Gash RC	.01	.05
71 David Grayson	.01	.05
72 Bernie Kosar	.02	.10
73 Reggie Langhorne	.01	.05
74 Eric Metcalf	.08	.25
75A Ozzie Newsome ERR	.20	.50
(Born Muscle Shoals)		
75B Ozzie Newsome COR	.20	.50
(Born Little Rock)		
75C Cody Risien SP	.20	.50
(initially withdrawn from pack;		
released in quantity years later)		
76 Felix Wright	.01	.05
77 Bud Carson CO	.01	.05
78 Troy Aikman	.30	.75
79 Michael Irvin	.08	.25
80 Jim Jeffcoat	.01	.05
81 Crawford Ker	.01	.05
82 Eugene Lockhart	.01	.05
83 Kelvin Martin RC	.01	.05
84 Ken Norton RC	.08	.25
85 Jimmy Johnson CO	.02	.10
86 Steve Atwater	.01	.05
87 Tyrone Braxton	.01	.05
88 John Elway	.50	1.25
89 Simon Fletcher	.01	.05
90 Ron Holmes	.01	.05
91 Bobby Humphrey	.01	.05
92 Vance Johnson	.01	.05
93 Ricky Nattiel	.01	.05
94 Dan Reeves CO	.01	.05
95 Jim Arnold	.01	.05
96 Jerry Ball	.01	.05
97 Bennie Blades	.01	.05
98 Lomas Brown	.01	.05
99 Michael Cofer	.01	.05
100 Richard Johnson	.01	.05
101 Eddie Murray	.01	.05
102 Barry Sanders	.50	1.25
103 Chris Spielman	.08	.25
104 William White RC	.01	.05
105 Eric Williams RC	.01	.05
106 Wayne Fontes CO UER	.01	.05
(Says born in MO,		
actually born in MA)		
107 Brent Fullwood	.01	.05
108 Ron Hallstrom RC	.01	.05
109 Tim Harris	.01	.05
110A Johnny Holland ERR	.20	.50
(No name or position		
at top of reverse)		
110B Johnny Holland COR	.20	.50
111A Perry Kemp ERR	.20	.50
(Photo on back is		
actually Ken Stiles,		
wearing gray shirt)		
111B Perry Kemp COR	.20	.50
(Wearing green shirt)		
112 Don Majkowski	.01	.05
113 Mark Murphy	.01	.05
114A Sterling Sharpe ERR	.08	.25
(Born Glenville, Ga.)		
114B Sterling Sharpe COR	.20	.50
(Born Chicago)		
115 Ed West RC	.01	.05
116 Lindy Infante CO	.01	.05
117 Steve Brown	.01	.05
118 Ray Childress	.01	.05
119 Ernest Givins	.02	.10
120 John Grimsley	.01	.05
121 Alonzo Highsmith	.01	.05
122 Drew Hill	.01	.05
123 Bubba McDowell	.01	.05
124 Dean Steinkuhler	.01	.05
125 Lorenzo White	.02	.10
126 Tony Zendejas	.01	.05
127 Jack Pardee CO	.01	.05
128 Albert Bentley	.01	.05
129 Dean Biasucci	.01	.05
130 Duane Bickett	.01	.05
131 Bill Brooks	.01	.05
132 Jon Hand	.01	.05
133 Mike Prior	.01	.05
134A Andre Rison	.08	.25
(No mention of trade		
on card front)		
134B Andre Rison	.08	.25
(Traded banner on card		
front; also reissued		
with Final Update)		
134C Andre Rison	.08	.25
(Traded banner on card		
front; message from		
Lud Denny on back)		
135 Rohn Stark	.01	.05
136 Donnell Thompson	.01	.05
137 Clarence Verdin	.01	.05
138 Fredd Young	.01	.05
139 Ron Meyer CO	.01	.05
140 John Alt RC	.01	.05
141 Steve DeBerg	.01	.05
142 Irv Eatman	.01	.05
143 Dino Hackett	.01	.05
144 Nick Lowery	.01	.05
145 Bill Maas	.01	.05
146 Stephone Paige	.01	.05
147 Neil Smith	.08	.25
148 Marty Schottenheimer CO	.01	.05
149 Steve Beuerlein	.02	.10
150 Tim Brown	.08	.25
151 Mike Dyal RC	.01	.05
152A Mervyn Fernandez ERR	.30	.75
(Acquired: Free		
Agent '87)		
152B Mervyn Fernandez COR	.30	.75
(Acquired: Drafted/10th Round, 1983)		
153 Willie Gault	.02	.10
154 Bob Golic	.01	.05
155 Bo Jackson	.10	.30
156 Don Mosebar	.01	.05
157 Steve Smith	.01	.05
158 Greg Townsend	.01	.05
159 Bruce Wilkerson RC	.01	.05
160 Steve Wisniewski	.02	.10
(Blocking for Bo Jackson)		
161A Art Shell CO ERR	.20	.50
(Born 11/25/46)		
161B Art Shell CO COR	3.00	8.00
(Born 11/26/46;		
large HOF print on front)		
161C Art Shell CO COR	4.00	10.00
(Born 11/26/46;		
small HOF print on front)		
162 Flipper Anderson	.01	.05
163 Greg Bell UER	.01	.05
(Stats have 5 catches,		
should be 9)		
164 Henry Ellard	.02	.10
165 Jim Everett	.02	.10
166 Jerry Gray	.01	.05
167 Kevin Greene	.02	.10
168 Pete Holohan	.01	.05
169 Larry Kelm RC	.01	.05
170 Tom Newberry	.01	.05
171 Vince Newsome RC	.01	.05
172 Irv Pankey	.01	.05
173 Jackie Slater	.01	.05
174 Fred Strickland RC	.01	.05
175 Mike Wilcher UER	.01	.05
(Fumble rec. number		
different from/1989 Pro Set card)		
176 John Robinson CO UER	.01	.05
(Stats say Rams,		
should say L.A. Rams)		
177 Mark Clayton	.02	.10
178 Roy Foster	.01	.05
179 Harry Galbreath RC	.01	.05
180 Jim C. Jensen	.01	.05
181 Dan Marino	.50	1.25
182 Louis Oliver	.01	.05
183 Sammie Smith	.01	.05
184 Brian Sochia	.01	.05
185 Don Shula CO	.02	.10
186 Joey Browner	.01	.05
187 Anthony Carter	.02	.10
188 Chris Doleman	.01	.05
189 Steve Jordan	.01	.05
190 Carl Lee	.01	.05
191 Randall McDaniel	.05	.15
192 Mike Merriweather	.01	.05
193 Keith Millard	.01	.05
194 Al Noga	.01	.05
195 Scott Studwell	.01	.05
196 Henry Thomas	.01	.05
197 Herschel Walker	.02	.10
198 Wade Wilson	.02	.10
199 Gary Zimmerman	.02	.10
200 Jerry Burns CO	.01	.05
201 Vincent Brown RC	.01	.05
202 Hart Lee Dykes	.01	.05
203 Sean Farrell	.01	.05
204A Fred Marion	40.00	100.00
(Belt visible on		
John Taylor in background)		
204B Fred Marion	.01	.05
(Belt not visible on		
John Taylor in background)		
205 Stanley Morgan UER	.01	.05
(Text says he reached/10,000 yards fastest;/		
3 players did it in 10 seasons)		
206 Eric Sievers RC	.01	.05
207 John Stephens	.01	.05
208 Andre Tippett	.01	.05
209 Rod Rust CO	.01	.05
210A Morten Andersen	.20	.50
(Card number and name		
on back in white)		
210B Morten Andersen	.20	.50
(Card number and name		
on back in black)		
211 Brad Edelman	.01	.05
212 John Fourcade	.01	.05
213 Dalton Hilliard	.01	.05
214 Rickey Jackson	.02	.10
(Forcing Jim Kelly fumble)		
215 Vaughan Johnson	.01	.05
216A Eric Martin	.20	.50
(Card number and name		
on back in white)		
216B Eric Martin	.20	.50
(Card number and name		
on back in black)		
217 Sam Mills	.02	.10
218 Pat Swilling UER	.02	.10
(Total fumble		
recoveries listed		
as 4, should be 5)		
219 Frank Warren RC	.01	.05
220 Jim Wilks	.01	.05
221A Jim Mora CO	.20	.50
(Card number and name		
on back in white)		
221B Jim Mora CO	.20	.50
(Card number and name		
on back in black)		
222 Raul Allegre	.01	.05
223 Carl Banks	.01	.05
224 John Elliott	.01	.05
225 Erik Howard	.01	.05
226 Pepper Johnson	.01	.05
227 Leonard Marshall UER	.01	.05
(In Super Bowl XXI		
George Martin had safety)		
228 Dave Meggett	.02	.10
229 Bart Oates	.01	.05
230 Phil Simms	.02	.10
231 Lawrence Taylor	.08	.25
232 Bill Parcells CO	.02	.10
233 Troy Benson	.01	.05
234 Kyle Clifton UER	.01	.05
(Born: Onley,		
should be Olney)		
235 Johnny Hector	.01	.05
236 Jeff Lageman	.01	.05
237 Pat Leahy	.01	.05
238 Freeman McNeil	.01	.05
239 Ken O'Brien	.01	.05
240 Al Toon	.02	.10
241 Jo Jo Townsell	.01	.05
242 Bruce Coslet CO	.01	.05
243 Eric Allen	.01	.05
244 Jerome Brown	.01	.05
245 Keith Byars	.01	.05
246 Cris Carter	.20	.50
247 Randall Cunningham	.08	.25
248 Keith Jackson	.02	.10
249 Mike Quick	.01	.05
(Darrell Green also in photo)		
250 Clyde Simmons	.01	.05
251 Andre Waters	.01	.05
252 Reggie White	.08	.25
253 Buddy Ryan CO	.01	.05
254 Rich Camarillo	.01	.05
255 Earl Ferrell	.01	.05
256 Roy Green	.02	.10
257 Ken Harvey RC	.08	.25
258 Ernie Jones RC	.01	.05
259 Tim McDonald	.01	.05
260 Timm Rosenbach UER	.01	.05
(Born 1967; should be 1966)		
261 Luis Sharpe	.01	.05
262 Vai Sikahema	.01	.05
263 J.T. Smith	.01	.05
264 Ron Wolfley UER	.01	.05
(Born Blaisdel,		
should be Blasdel)		
265 Joe Bugel CO	.01	.05
266 Gary Anderson K	.01	.05
267 Bubby Brister	.01	.05
268 Merril Hoge	.01	.05
269 Carnell Lake	.01	.05
270 Louis Lipps	.02	.10
271 David Little	.01	.05
272 Greg Lloyd	.08	.25
273 Keith Willis	.01	.05
274 Tim Worley	.01	.05
275 Chuck Noll CO	.02	.10
276 Marion Butts	.02	.10
277 Gill Byrd	.01	.05
278 Vencie Glenn UER	.01	.05
(Sack total should		
be 2, not 2.5)		
279 Burt Grossman	.01	.05
280 Gary Plummer	.01	.05
281 Billy Ray Smith	.01	.05
282 Billy Joe Tolliver	.01	.05
283 Dan Henning CO	.01	.05
284 Harris Barton	.01	.05
285 Michael Carter	.01	.05
286 Mike Cofer	.01	.05
287 Roger Craig	.02	.10
288 Don Griffin	.01	.05
289A Charles Haley ERR	4.00	10.00
(Fumble recoveries 1		
in '86 and 4 total)		
289B Charles Haley COR	.30	.75
(Fumble recoveries 2		
in '86 and 5 total)		
290 Pierce Holt RC	.01	.05
291 Ronnie Lott	.02	.10
292 Guy McIntyre	.01	.05
293 Joe Montana	.50	1.25
294 Tom Rathman	.01	.05
295 Jerry Rice	.30	.75
296 Jesse Sapolu RC	.01	.05
297 John Taylor	.02	.10
298 Michael Walter	.01	.05
299 George Seifert CO	.02	.10
300 Jeff Bryant	.01	.05
301 Jacob Green	.01	.05
302 Norm Johnson UER	.01	.05
(Card shop not in		
Garden Grove, should		
say Fullerton)		
303 Bryan Millard	.01	.05
304 Joe Nash	.01	.05
305 Eugene Robinson	.01	.05
306 John L. Williams	.01	.05
307 David Wyman	.01	.05
(NFL EXP is in caps,		
inconsistent with rest		
of the set)		
308 Chuck Knox CO	.01	.05
309 Mark Carrier WR	.08	.25
310 Paul Gruber	.01	.05
311 Harry Hamilton	.01	.05
312 Bruce Hill	.01	.05
313 Donald Igwebuike	.01	.05
314 Kevin Murphy	.01	.05
315 Ervin Randle	.01	.05
316 Mark Robinson	.01	.05
317 Lars Tate	.01	.05
318 Vinny Testaverde	.02	.10
319A Ray Perkins CO ERR	.30	.75
(No name or title		
at top of reverse)		
319B Ray Perkins CO COR	.01	.05
320 Earnest Byner	.01	.05
321 Gary Clark	.08	.25
322 Darryl Grant	.01	.05
323 Darrell Green	.02	.10
324 Jim Lachey	.01	.05
325 Charles Mann	.01	.05
326 Wilber Marshall	.01	.05
327 Ralf Mojsiejenko	.01	.05
328 Art Monk	.02	.10
329 Gerald Riggs	.02	.10
330 Mark Rypien	.02	.10
331 Ricky Sanders	.01	.05
332 Alvin Walton	.01	.05
333 Joe Gibbs CO	.02	.10
334 Aloha Stadium	.01	.05
335 Brian Blades PB	.01	.05
336 James Brooks PB	.01	.05
337 Shane Conlan PB	.01	.05
338A Eric Dickerson PB SP	1.25	3.00
(card withdrawn from packs;		
large quantities released years later)		
338B Lud Denny Promo	200.00	350.00
339 Ray Donaldson PB	.01	.05
340 Ferrell Edmunds PB	.01	.05
341 Boomer Esiason PB	.01	.05
342 David Fulcher PB	.01	.05
343A Chris Hinton PB	3.00	8.00
(No mention of trade		
on card front)		
343B Chris Hinton PB	.01	.05
(Traded banner		
on card front)		
344 Rodney Holman PB	.01	.05
345 Kent Hull PB	.01	.05
346 Tunch Ilkin PB	.01	.05
347 Mike Johnson PB	.01	.05
348 Greg Kragen PB	.01	.05
349 Dave Krieg PB	.02	.10
350 Albert Lewis PB	.01	.05
351 Howie Long PB	.02	.10
352 Bruce Matthews PB	.01	.05
353 Clay Matthews PB	.01	.05
354 Erik McMillan PB	.01	.05
355 Karl Mecklenburg PB	.01	.05
356 Anthony Miller PB	.01	.05
357 Frank Minnifield PB	.01	.05
358 Max Montoya PB	.01	.05
359 Warren Moon PB	.08	.25
360 Mike Munchak PB	.01	.05
361 Anthony Munoz PB	.01	.05
362 John Offerdahl PB	.01	.05
363 Christian Okoye PB	.01	.05
364 Leslie O'Neal PB	.01	.05
365 Rufus Porter PB UER	.01	.05
(TM logo missing)		
366 Andre Reed PB	.02	.10
367 Johnny Rembert PB	.01	.05
368 Reggie Roby PB	.01	.05
369 Kevin Ross PB	.01	.05
370 Webster Slaughter PB	.01	.05
371 Bruce Smith PB	.02	.10
372 Dennis Smith PB	.01	.05
373 Derrick Thomas PB	.02	.10
374 Thurman Thomas PB	.08	.25
375 David Treadwell PB	.01	.05
376 Lee Williams PB	.01	.05
377 Rod Woodson PB	.02	.10
378 Bud Carson CO PB	.01	.05
379 Eric Allen PB	.01	.05
380 Neal Anderson PB	.02	.10
381 Jerry Ball PB	.01	.05
382 Joey Browner PB	.01	.05
383 Rich Camarillo PB	.01	.05
384 Mark Carrier WR PB	.01	.05
385 Roger Craig PB	.02	.10
386A Randall Cunningham PB	.20	.50
Small print on front		
386B Randall Cunningham PB	.20	.50
Large print on front		
387 Chris Doleman PB	.01	.05
388 Henry Ellard PB	.01	.05
389 Bill Fralic PB	.01	.05
390 Brent Fullwood PB	.01	.05
391 Jerry Gray PB	.01	.05
392 Kevin Greene PB	.02	.10
393 Tim Harris PB	.01	.05
394 Jay Hilgenberg PB	.01	.05
395 Dalton Hilliard PB	.01	.05
396 Keith Jackson PB	.02	.10
397 Vaughan Johnson PB	.01	.05
398 Steve Jordan PB	.01	.05
399 Carl Lee PB	.01	.05
400 Ronnie Lott PB	.02	.10
401 Don Majkowski PB	.01	.05
402 Charles Mann PB	.01	.05
403 Randall McDaniel PB	.02	.10
404 Tim McDonald PB	.01	.05
405 Guy McIntyre PB	.01	.05
406 Dave Meggett PB	.01	.05
407 Keith Millard PB	.01	.05
408 Joe Montana PB UER	.20	.50
(incorrect uniform)		
409 Eddie Murray PB	.01	.05
410 Tom Newberry PB	.01	.05
411 Jerry Rice PB	.20	.50
412 Mark Rypien PB	.01	.05
413 Barry Sanders PB	.25	.60
414 Luis Sharpe PB	.01	.05
415 Sterling Sharpe PB	.01	.05
416 Mike Singletary PB	.02	.10
417 Jackie Slater PB	.01	.05
418 Doug Smith PB	.01	.05
419 Chris Spielman PB	.01	.05
420 Pat Swilling PB	.01	.05
421 John Taylor PB	.01	.05
422 Lawrence Taylor PB	.02	.10
423 Reggie White PB	.02	.10
424 Ron Wolfley PB	.01	.05
425 Gary Zimmerman PB	.02	.10
426 John Robinson CO PB	.01	.05
427 Scott Case UER	.01	.05
(front CB, back S)		
428 Mike Kenn	.01	.05
429 Mike Gann	.01	.05
430 Tim Green RC	.01	.05
431 Michael Haynes RC	.08	.25
432 Jessie Tuggle RC UER	.01	.05
(Front Jesse, back Jessie)		
433 John Rade	.01	.05
434 Andre Rison	.08	.25
435 Don Beebe	.02	.10
436 Ray Bentley	.01	.05
437 Shane Conlan	.01	.05
438 Kent Hull	.01	.05
439 Pete Metzelaars	.01	.05
440 Andre Reed UER	.08	.25
(Vance Johnson also had		
more catches in '85)		
441 Frank Reich	.08	.25
442 Leon Seals RC	.01	.05
443 Bruce Smith	.08	.25
444 Thurman Thomas	.08	.25
445 Will Wolford	.01	.05
446 Trace Armstrong	.01	.05
447 Mark Bortz RC	.01	.05
448 Tom Thayer RC	.01	.05
449A Dan Hampton	.20	.50
(Card back says DE)		
449B Dan Hampton	4.00	10.00
(Card back says DT)		
450 Shaun Gayle RC	.01	.05
451 Dennis Gentry	.01	.05
452 Jim Harbaugh	.08	.25
453 Vestee Jackson	.01	.05
454 Brad Muster	.01	.05
455 William Perry	.02	.10
456 Ron Rivera	.01	.05
457 James Thornton	.01	.05
458 Mike Tomczak	.02	.10
459 Donnell Woolford	.01	.05
460 Eric Ball	.01	.05
461 James Brooks	.02	.10
462 David Fulcher	.01	.05
463 Boomer Esiason	.02	.10
464 Rodney Holman	.01	.05
465 Bruce Kozerski	.01	.05
466 Tim Krumrie	.01	.05
467 Anthony Munoz	.02	.10
(Type on front smaller		
compared to other cards)		
468 Brian Blados	.01	.05
469 Mike Baab	.01	.05
470 Brian Brennan	.01	.05
471 Raymond Clayborn	.01	.05
472 Mike Johnson	.01	.05
473 Kevin Mack	.01	.05
474 Clay Matthews	.02	.10
475 Frank Minnifield	.01	.05
476 Gregg Rakoczy RC	.01	.05
477 Webster Slaughter	.02	.10
478 James Dixon	.01	.05
479 Robert Awalt	.01	.05
480 Dennis McKinnon UER	.01	.05
(front 81, back 85)		
481 Danny Noonan	.01	.05
482 Jesse Solomon	.01	.05
483 Daniel Stubbs UER	.01	.05
(front 66, back 96)		
484 Steve Walsh	.02	.10
485 Michael Brooks RC	.01	.05
486 Mark Jackson	.01	.05
487 Greg Kragen	.01	.05
488 Ken Lanier RC	.01	.05
489 Karl Mecklenburg	.01	.05
490 Steve Sewell	.01	.05
491 Dennis Smith	.01	.05
492 David Treadwell	.01	.05
493 Michael Young RC	.01	.05
494 Robert Clark RC	.01	.05
495 Dennis Gibson	.01	.05
496A Kevin Glover RC	.20	.50
(Card back says C		
G)		
496B Kevin Glover RC	.01	.05
(Card back says C)		
497 Mel Gray	.02	.10
498 Rodney Peete	.02	.10
499 Dave Brown DB	.01	.05
500 Jerry Holmes	.01	.05
501 Chris Jacke	.01	.05
502 Alan Veingrad	.01	.05
503 Mark Lee	.01	.05
504 Tony Mandarich	.01	.05
505 Brian Noble	.01	.05
506 Jeff Query	.01	.05
507 Ken Ruettgers	.01	.05
508 Patrick Allen	.01	.05
509 Curtis Duncan	.01	.05
510 William Fuller	.02	.10
511 Haywood Jeffires RC	.08	.25
512 Sean Jones	.02	.10
513 Terry Kinard	.01	.05
514 Bruce Matthews	.02	.10
515 Gerald McNeil	.01	.05
516 Greg Montgomery RC	.01	.05
517 Warren Moon	.08	.25
518 Mike Munchak	.02	.10
519 Allen Pinkett	.01	.05
520 Pat Beach	.01	.05
521 Eugene Daniel	.01	.05
522 Kevin Call	.01	.05
523 Ray Donaldson	.01	.05
524 Jeff Herrod RC	.01	.05
525 Keith Taylor	.01	.05
526 Jack Trudeau	.01	.05
527 Deron Cherry	.01	.05
528 Jeff Donaldson	.01	.05
529 Albert Lewis	.01	.05
530 Pete Mandley	.01	.05
531 Chris Martin RC	.01	.05
532 Christian Okoye	.01	.05
533 Steve Pelluer	.01	.05
534 Kevin Ross	.01	.05
535 Dan Saleaumua	.01	.05
536 Derrick Thomas	.08	.25
537 Mike Webster	.02	.10
538 Marcus Allen	.08	.25
539 Greg Bell	.01	.05
540 Thomas Benson RC	.01	.05
541 Ron Brown	.01	.05
542 Scott Davis	.01	.05
543 Riki Ellison	.01	.05
544 Jamie Holland	.01	.05
545 Howie Long	.08	.25
546 Terry McDaniel	.01	.05
547 Max Montoya	.01	.05
548 Jay Schroeder	.01	.05
549 Lionel Washington	.01	.05
550 Robert Delpino	.01	.05
551 Bobby Humphery	.01	.05
552 Mike Lansford	.01	.05
553 Michael Stewart RC	.01	.05
554 Doug Smith	.01	.05
555 Curt Warner	.01	.05
556 Alvin Wright RC	.01	.05
557 Jeff Cross	.01	.05
558 Jeff Dellenbach RC	.01	.05
559 Mark Duper	.02	.10
560 Ferrell Edmunds	.01	.05
561 Tim McKyer	.01	.05
562 John Offerdahl	.01	.05
563 Reggie Roby	.01	.05
564 Pete Stoyanovich	.01	.05
565 Alfred Anderson	.01	.05
566 Ray Berry	.01	.05
567 Rick Fenney	.01	.05
568 Rich Gannon RC	.60	1.50
569 Tim Irwin	.01	.05
570 Hassan Jones	.01	.05
571 Cris Carter	.20	.50
572 Kirk Lowdermilk	.01	.05
573 Reggie Rutland RC	.01	.05
574 Ken Stills	.01	.05
575 Bruce Armstrong	.01	.05
576 Irving Fryar	.02	.10
577 Roland James	.01	.05
578 Robert Perryman	.01	.05
579 Cedric Jones	.01	.05
580 Steve Grogan	.02	.10
581 Johnny Rembert	.01	.05
582 Ed Reynolds	.01	.05
583 Brent Williams	.01	.05
584 Marc Wilson	.01	.05
585 Hoby Brenner	.01	.05
586 Stan Brock	.01	.05
587 Jim Dombrowski RC	.01	.05
588 Joel Hilgenberg RC	.01	.05
589 Robert Massey	.01	.05
590 Floyd Turner	.01	.05
591 Ottis Anderson	.02	.10
592 Mark Bavaro	.01	.05
593 Maurice Carthon	.01	.05
594 Eric Dorsey RC	.01	.05
595 Myron Guyton	.01	.05
596 Jeff Hostetler RC	.08	.25
597 Sean Landeta	.01	.05
598 Lionel Manuel	.01	.05
599 Odessa Turner RC	.01	.05
600 Perry Williams	.01	.05
601 James Hasty	.01	.05
602 Erik McMillan	.01	.05
603 Alex Gordon UER	.01	.05
(reversed photo on back)		
604 Ron Stallworth	.01	.05
605 Byron Evans RC	.01	.05
606 Ron Heller RC	.01	.05
607 Wes Hopkins	.01	.05
(Hitting Ottis Anderson)		
608 Mickey Shuler UER	.01	.05
(Reversed photo on back)		
609 Seth Joyner	.02	.10
610 Jim McMahon	.02	.10
611 Mike Pitts	.01	.05
612 Izel Jenkins RC	.01	.05
613 Anthony Bell	.01	.05
614 David Galloway	.01	.05
615 Eric Hill	.01	.05
616 Cedric Mack	.01	.05
617 Freddie Joe Nunn	.01	.05
618 Tootie Robbins	.01	.05
619 Tom Tupa RC	.01	.05
620 Joe Wolf	.01	.05
621 Dermontti Dawson	.02	.10
622 Thomas Everett	.01	.05
623 Tunch Ilkin	.01	.05
624 Hardy Nickerson	.02	.10
625 Gerald Williams RC	.01	.05
626 Rod Woodson	.08	.25
627A Rod Bernstine TE	.20	.50
627B Rod Bernstine RB	.01	.05
628 Courtney Hall	.01	.05
629 Ronnie Harmon	.02	.10
630A Anthony Miller ERR	.08	.25
(Back says WR)		
630B Anthony Miller COR	.02	.10
(Back says WR-KR)		
631 Joe Phillips RC	.01	.05
632A Leslie O'Neal ERR	.05	.15
(LB-DE on front)		
632B Leslie O'Neal ERR	.02	.10
(LB on front)		
633A David Richards RC ERR	.05	.15
(Back says G-T)		
633B D.Richards RC COR	.05	.15
Back says G		
634 Mark Vlasic	.01	.05
635 Lee Williams	.01	.05
636 Chet Brooks	.01	.05
637 Keena Turner	.01	.05
638 Kevin Fagan RC	.01	.05
639 Brent Jones RC	.08	.25
640 Matt Millen	.02	.10
641 Bubba Paris	.01	.05
642 Bill Romanowski RC	.40	1.00
643 Fred Smerlas UER	.01	.05
(Front 67, back 76)		
644 Dave Waymer	.01	.05
645 Steve Young	.20	.50
646 Brian Blades	.02	.10
647 Andy Heck	.01	.05
648 Dave Krieg	.02	.10
649 Rufus Porter	.01	.05
650 Kelly Stouffer	.01	.05
651 Tony Woods	.01	.05
652 Gary Anderson RB	.01	.05
653 Reuben Davis	.01	.05
654 Randy Grimes	.01	.05
655 Ron Hall	.01	.05
656 Eugene Marve	.01	.05
657A Curt Jarvis ERR	.20	.50
(No 'Official NFL		
Card' on front)		
657B Curt Jarvis COR	4.00	10.00
(Includes 'Official NFL Card')		
658 Ricky Reynolds	.01	.05
659 Broderick Thomas	.01	.05
660 Jeff Bostic	.01	.05
661 Todd Bowles RC	.01	.05
662 Ravin Caldwell	.01	.05
663 Russ Grimm UER	.02	.10
(Back photo is Jeff Bostic)		
664 Joe Jacoby	.01	.05
665 Mark May	.01	.05
(Front G, back G		
T)		
666A Walter Stanley	.01	.05
666B Steven Young VP Promo	2.00	5.00
(Pro Set Vice President)		
667 Don Warren	.01	.05
668 Stan Humphries RC	.08	.25
669A Jeff George SP	.40	1.00
(Number 1 Pick; Illinois		
issued in first series)		
669B Jeff George RC	.20	.50
(First Pick; Colts		
issued in second series)		
670 Blair Thomas RC	.02	.10
(No color stripe along		
line with AFC symbol		
and Jets logo)		
671 Cortez Kennedy RC UER	.08	.25
(No scouting photo		
line on back)		
672 Keith McCants RC	.01	.05
673 Junior Seau RC	.50	1.25
674 Mark Carrier DB RC	.08	.25
675 Andre Ware	.02	.10
676 Chris Singleton RC UER	.01	.05
(Parsippany High,		
should be Parsippany		
Hills High)		
677 Richmond Webb RC	.01	.05
678 Ray Agnew RC	.01	.05
679 Anthony Smith RC	.01	.05
680 James Francis RC	.01	.05
681 Percy Snow RC	.01	.05
682 Renaldo Turnbull RC	.01	.05
683 Lamar Lathon RC	.02	.10
684 James Williams DB RC	.01	.05
685 Emmitt Smith RC	2.00	5.00
686 Tony Bennett RC	.08	.25
687 Darrell Thompson RC	.01	.05
688 Steve Broussard RC	.01	.05
689 Eric Green RC	.02	.10
690 Ben Smith RC	.01	.05
691 Bern Brostek RC UER	.01	.05
(Listed as Center but		
is playing Guard)		
692 Rodney Hampton RC	.08	.25
693 Dexter Carter RC	.01	.05
694 Rob Moore RC	.20	.50
695 Alexander Wright RC	.01	.05
696 Darion Conner RC	.02	.10
697 Reggie Rembert RC UER	.01	.05
(Missing Scouting Line		
credit on the front)		
698A Terry Wooden RC ERR	.20	.50
(Number on back is 51)		
698B Terry Wooden RC COR	.01	.05
(Number on back is 90)		
699 Reggie Cobb RC	.01	.05
700 Anthony Thompson	.01	.05
701 Fred Washington RC	.01	.05
(Final Update version		
mentions his death;		
this card does not)		
702 Ron Cox RC	.01	.05
703 Robert Blackmon RC	.01	.05
704 Dan Owens RC	.01	.05
705 Anthony Johnson RC	.08	.25
706 Aaron Wallace RC	.01	.05
707 Harold Green RC	.08	.25
708 Keith Sims RC	.01	.05
709 Tim Grunhard RC	.01	.05
710 Jeff Alm RC	.01	.05
711 Carwell Gardner RC	.01	.05
712 Kenny Davidson RC	.01	.05
713 Vince Buck RC	.01	.05
714 Leroy Hoard RC	.08	.25
715 Andre Collins RC	.01	.05
716 Dennis Brown RC	.01	.05
717 LeRoy Butler RC	.08	.25
718A Pat Terrell 41 ERR RC	.20	.50
718B Pat Terrell 37 COR RC	.01	.05
719 Mike Bellamy RC	.01	.05
720 Mike Fox RC	.01	.05
721 Alton Montgomery RC	.01	.05
722 Eric Davis RC	.02	.10
723A Oliver Barnett RC ERR	.20	.50
(Front says DT)		
723B Oliver Barnett RC COR	.01	.05
(Front says NT)		
724 Houston Hoover RC	.01	.05
725 Howard Ballard RC	.01	.05
726 Keith McKeller RC	.01	.05
727 Wendell Davis RC	.01	.05
(Pro Set Prospect in		
white, not black)		
728 Peter Tom Willis RC	.01	.05
729 Bernard Clark	.01	.05
730 Doug Widell RC	.01	.05
731 Eric Andolsek	.01	.05
732 Jeff Campbell RC	.01	.05
733 Marc Spindler RC	.01	.05
734 Keith Woodside	.01	.05
735 Willis Peguese RC	.01	.05
736 Frank Stams	.01	.05
737 Jeff Uhlenhake	.01	.05
738 Todd Kalis	.01	.05
739 Tommy Hodson RC UER	.01	.05
(Born Matthews,		
should be Mathews)		
740 Greg McMurtry RC	.01	.05
741 Mike Buck RC	.01	.05
742 Kevin Haverdink UER	.01	.05
(Jersey says 70,		
back says 74)		
743A Johnny Bailey RC	.02	.10
(Back says 46)		
743B Johnny Bailey RC	.02	.10
(Back says 22)		
744A Eric Moore	.05	.15
(No Pro Set Prospect		
on front of card)		
744B Eric Moore	4.00	10.00
(Pro Set Prospect		
on front of card)		
745 Tony Stargell RC	.01	.05
746 Fred Barnett RC	.08	.25
747 Walter Reeves	.01	.05
748 Derek Hill	.01	.05
749 Quinn Early	.08	.25
750 Ronald Lewis	.01	.05
751 Ken Clark RC	.01	.05
752 Garry Lewis RC	.01	.05
753 James Lofton	.02	.10
754 Steve Tasker UER	.08	.25
(Back says photo is		
against Raiders, but		
front shows a Steeler)		
755 Jim Shofner CO	.01	.05
756 Jimmie Jones RC	.01	.05
757 Jay Novacek	.08	.25
758 Jessie Hester RC	.01	.05
759 Barry Word RC	.01	.05
760 Eddie Anderson RC	.01	.05
761 Cleveland Gary	.01	.05
762 Marcus Dupree RC	.30	.75
763 David Griggs RC	.01	.05
764 Rueben Mayes	.01	.05
765 Stephen Baker	.01	.05
766 Reyna Thompson RC UER	.01	.05
(Front CB, back ST-CB)		
767 Everson Walls	.01	.05
768 Brad Baxter RC	.01	.05
769 Steve Walsh	.02	.10
770 Heath Sherman RC	.01	.05
771 Johnny Johnson RC	.02	.10
772A Dexter Manley	200.00	400.00
(Back mentions substance		
abuse violation)		
772B Dexter Manley	.01	.05
(Bio on back changed		
doesn't mention substance		
abuse violation)		
773 Ricky Proehl RC	.08	.25
774 Frank Cornish	.01	.05
775 Tommy Kane RC	.01	.05
776 Derrick Fenner RC	.01	.05
777 Steve Christie RC	.01	.05
778 Wayne Haddix RC	.01	.05
779 Richard Williamson UER	.01	.05
(Experience misspelled)		
780 Brian Mitchell RC	.08	.25
781 American Bowl	.01	.05
London		
Raiders vs. Saints		
782 American Bowl	.01	.04
Berlin		
Rams vs. Chiefs		

783 American Bowl Tokyo Broncos vs. Seahawks	.01	.04
784 American Bowl Montreal Steelers vs. Patriots	.01	.04
785A Berlin Wall Paul Tagliabue ('Peered through the Berlin Wall')	.30	.75
785B Berlin Wall Paul Tagliabue (...poses at historic Berlin Wall...)	.30	.75
786 Al Davis NEWS Raiders Stay in LA	.01	.04
787 Jerry Glanville Falcons Back in Black	.01	.04
788 NFL Goes International World League Spring Debut	.01	.04
789 Overseas Appeal (Cheerleaders)	.01	.04
790 Photo Contest (Mike Mularkey awash)	.01	.04
791 Photo Contest (Gary Reasons hitting Bobby Humphrey)	.01	.04
792 Photo Contest (Maurice Hurst covering Drew Hill)	.01	.04
793 Photo Contest (Ronnie Lott celebrating)	.01	.04
794 Photo Contest (Barry Sanders)	.20	.50
795 Photo Contest (George Seifert in Gatorade Shower)	.01	.04
796 Photo Contest (Doug Smith praying)	.01	.04
797 Photo Contest (Doug Widell keeping cool)	.01	.04
798 Photo Contest (Todd Bowles covering Cris Carter)	.01	.04
799 Ronnie Lott (Stay in School)	.02	.10
800D Mark Carrier DB D-ROY	.02	.10
800O Emmitt Smith (Offensive ROY)	.60	1.50
1990 Santa Claus SP (Second series only; No quote mark after Andre Ware)	.20	.50
CC2 Paul Tagliabue SP NFL Commissioner (First series only)	.15	.40
CC3 Joe Robbie Mem SP (Second series only)	.20	.50
SC Super Pro SP (Second series only)	.20	.50
SC4 Fred Washington UER (Memorial to his death; word patches repeated in fourth line of text)	.01	.04
SP1 Payne Stewart SP (First series only)	.40	1.00
NNO Lombardi Trophy Hologram (Collector Edition; hand serial numbered of 10,000)	50.00	100.00
NNO Super Bowl XXIV Logo	.01	.05

1990 Pro Set Super Bowl MVP's

COMPLETE SET (24)	1.50	4.00
1 Bart Starr	.15	.40
2 Bart Starr	.15	.40
3 Joe Namath	.15	.40
4 Len Dawson	.08	.25
5 Chuck Howley	.05	.15
6 Roger Staubach	.15	.40
7 Jake Scott	.05	.15
8 Larry Csonka	.08	.25
9 Franco Harris	.08	.25
10 Lynn Swann	.08	.25
11 Fred Biletnikoff	.08	.25
12 Harvey Martin	.05	.15
13 Terry Bradshaw	.15	.40
14 Terry Bradshaw	.15	.40
15 Jim Plunkett	.05	.15
16 Joe Montana	.30	.75
17 John Riggins	.08	.25
18 Marcus Allen	.08	.25
19 Joe Montana	.30	.75
20 Richard Dent	.05	.15
21 Phil Simms	.08	.25
22 Doug Williams	.05	.15
23 Jerry Rice	.30	.75
24 Joe Montana	.30	.75

1990 Pro Set Theme Art

The 1990 Pro Set Super Bowl Theme Art set contains 25 standard-size cards. The fronts have full color theme art from the Super Bowls; both sides have attractive silver borders. The horizontally-oriented backs have photos of the winning teams' rings and miscellaneous info about the games. These cards were distributed one per 1990 Pro Set Series I pack.

COMPLETE SET (24)	1.20	3.00
COMMON CARD (1-24)	.06	.15

1990 Pro Set Collect-A-Books

This 36-card (booklet) set, which measures the standard size, features some of the leading stars of the National Football League. The set features action photos of the players on the front of the card along with their name on the top of the front and the NFL Pro Set logo on the lower left hand corner. The cards have six pages including the outer cover photos and is interesting in that both Michael Dean Perry and Eric Dickerson have cards in this set but do not have cards in the regular Pro Set series. The set was released in three series of 12 cards each, with there being one rookie in each of the subsets. Not included in the complete set price below is a 1990-91 Pro Set Collect-A-Book Super Bowl XXV, numbered "SB" in the checklist below which presents color pictures with captions summarizing Super Bowls I-XXIV. The front and back cover form one painting of a wall and table covered with football memorabilia. This single item was apparently only available as part of the Super Bowl XXV Commemorative Tin.

COMPLETE SET (36)	3.20	8.00
1 Jim Kelly	.15	.40
2 Andre Ware	.05	.15
3 Phil Simms	.08	.25
4 Bubby Brister	.05	.15
5 Bernie Kosar	.08	.25
6 Eric Dickerson	.08	.25
7 Barry Sanders	1.00	2.50
8 Jerry Rice	.40	1.00
9 Keith Millard	.05	.15
10 Erik McMillan	.05	.15
11 Ickey Woods	.05	.15
12 Mike Singletary	.15	.40
13 Randall Cunningham	.15	.40
14 Boomer Esiason	.08	.25
15 John Elway	.80	2.00
16 Wade Wilson	.05	.15
17 Troy Aikman	.40	1.00
18 Dan Marino	.80	2.00
19 Lawrence Taylor	.08	.25
20 Roger Craig	.08	.25
21 Merril Hoge	.05	.15
22 Christian Okoye	.05	.15
23 Blair Thomas	.05	.15
24 William Perry	.05	.15
25 Bill Fralic	.05	.15
26 Warren Moon	.15	.40
27 Jim Everett	.08	.25
28 Jeff George	.08	.25
29 Shane Conlan	.05	.15
30 Carl Banks	.05	.15
31 Charles Mann	.05	.15
32 Anthony Munoz	.08	.25
33 Dan Hampton	.05	.15
34 Michael Dean Perry	.05	.15
35 Joey Browner	.05	.15
36 Ken O'Brien	.05	.15
SB Super Bowl Story/24 Years of Champions	.08	.25

1990-91 Pro Set Pro Bowl 106

This 106 standard-size set honored the Pro Bowl squad members. The set features regular cards already issued by Pro Set with no indication that these cards were specially issued for the Pro Bowl. There are no differences on most of these cards. The cards in the set are 39, 40, 49, 52, 53, 57, 86, 91, 96, 98, 102, 114, 118, 119, 122, 135, 137, 144, 155, 156, 158, 160, 173, 186, 188, 189, 190, 191, 210, 215, 218, 226, 229, 231, 244, 247, 248, 252, 271, 276, 289, 291, 292, 293, 295, 320, 321, 323, 324, 334, 434, 438, 440, 443, 444, 447, 462, 464, 467, 491, 497, 514, 517, 529, 534, 536, 557, 560, 562, 575, 597, 626, 630, 632, 677, 800D. The only exception are the four players who were in Pro Set's Final Update. These Pro Bowl cards show "1990 Final Update" on the front; this notation was not used on the regular issue Final Update cards. These are obviously the key cards in the set as they are distinguishable from regular Pro Set's issue whereas the other Pro Bowl cards are not. Therefore, we are only explicitly listing these four cards. In addition to the player cards, the 1990 Super Bowl Theme Art insert set was also issued. This set is housed in an attractive white binder with the identification of the Pro Bowl game on the front of the binder.

COMPLETE SET (106)	30.00	60.00
754 Steve Tasker (1990 Final Update on card front)	8.00	20.00
766 Reyna Thompson (1990 Final Update on card front)	6.00	15.00
771 Johnny Johnson (1990 Final Update on card front)	6.00	15.00
778 Wayne Haddix (1990 Final Update on card front)	6.00	15.00

1990-91 Pro Set Super Bowl 160

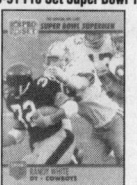

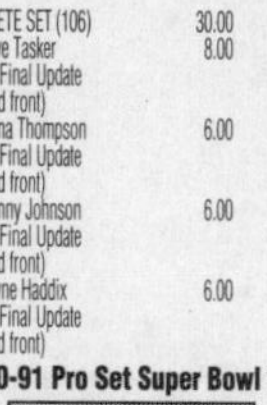

This 160-card standard-size set was issued by Pro Set as a complete set in a special commemorative box. Cards were also issued in eight-card wax packs along with six pieces of gum. The cards were introduced at the first Dallas Cowboys Pro Set Sports Collectors Show at Texas Stadium. The set features the highlights of the first 24 Super Bowls with the set being divided into the following sub-sets: Super Bowl Tickets (1-24), Super Bowl Supermen (25-135), Super Bowl Super Moments (136-151), and nine puzzle cards depicting the twenty-fifth Super Bowl Art (152-160).

COMP.FACT SET (160)	1.50	4.00
1 SB I Ticket	.01	.03
2 SB II Ticket	.01	.03
3 SB III Ticket	.01	.03
4 SB IV Ticket	.01	.03
5 SB V Ticket	.01	.03
6 SB VI Ticket	.01	.03
7 SB VII Ticket	.01	.03
8 SB VIII Ticket	.01	.03
9 SB IX Ticket	.01	.03
10 SB X Ticket	.01	.03
11 SB XI Ticket	.01	.03
12 SB XII Ticket	.01	.03
13 SB XIII Ticket	.01	.03
14 SB XIV Ticket	.01	.03
15 SB XV Ticket	.01	.03
16 SB XVI Ticket	.01	.03
17 SB XVII Ticket	.01	.03
18 SB XVIII Ticket	.01	.03
19 SB XIX Ticket	.01	.03
20 SB XX Ticket	.01	.03
21 SB XXI Ticket	.01	.03
22 SB XXII Ticket	.01	.03
23 SB XXIII Ticket	.01	.03
24 SB XXIV Ticket	.01	.03
25 Tom Flores CO	.01	.05
26 Joe Gibbs CO	.02	.10
27 Tom Landry CO	.08	.25
28 Vince Lombardi CO	.10	.30
29 Chuck Noll CO	.05	.15
30 Don Shula CO	.05	.15
31 Bill Walsh CO	.05	.15
32 Terry Bradshaw	.08	.25
33 Joe Montana	.40	1.00
34 Joe Namath	.20	.50
35 Jim Plunkett	.02	.10
36 Bart Starr	.10	.30
37 Roger Staubach	.10	.30
38 Marcus Allen	.07	.20
39 Roger Craig	.02	.10
40 Larry Csonka	.05	.15
41 Franco Harris	.02	.10
42 John Riggins	.02	.10
43 Timmy Smith	.01	.05
44 Matt Snell	.01	.05
45 Fred Biletnikoff	.05	.15
46 Cliff Branch	.02	.10
47 Max McGee	.01	.05
48 Jerry Rice	.20	.50
49 Ricky Sanders	.01	.05
50 George Sauer Jr.	.01	.05
51 John Stallworth	.02	.10
52 Lynn Swann	.05	.15
53 Dave Casper	.01	.05
54 Marv Fleming	.01	.05
55 Dan Ross	.01	.05
56 Forrest Gregg	.02	.10
57 Winston Hill	.01	.05
58 Joe Jacoby	.01	.05
59 Anthony Munoz	.02	.10
60 Art Shell	.02	.10
61 Rayfield Wright	.01	.05
62 Ron Yary	.02	.10
63 Randy Cross	.01	.05
64 Jerry Kramer	.02	.10
65 Bob Kuechenberg	.01	.05
66 Larry Little	.02	.10
67 Gerry Mullins	.01	.05
68 John Niland	.01	.05
69 Gene Upshaw	.02	.10
70 Dave Dalby	.01	.05
71 Jim Langer	.01	.05
72 Dwight Stephenson	.02	.10
73 Mike Webster	.02	.10
74 Ross Browner	.01	.05
75 Willie Davis	.02	.10
76 Richard Dent	.02	.10
77 L.C. Greenwood	.02	.10
78 Ed Too Tall Jones	.02	.10
79 Harvey Martin	.02	.10
80 Dwight White	.02	.10
81 Buck Buchanan	.02	.10
82 Curley Culp	.01	.05
83 Manny Fernandez	.01	.05
84 Joe Greene	.05	.15
85 Bob Lilly	.05	.15
86 Alan Page	.02	.10
87 Randy White	.05	.15
88 Nick Buoniconti	.02	.10
89 Lee Roy Jordan	.02	.10
90 Jack Lambert	.05	.15
91 Willie Lanier	.02	.10
92 Ray Nitschke	.02	.10
93 Mike Singletary	.02	.10
94 Carl Banks	.02	.10
95 Charles Haley	.02	.10
96 Jack Ham	.02	.10
97 Ted Hendricks	.02	.10
98 Chuck Howley	.01	.05
99 Rod Martin	.01	.05
100 Herb Adderley	.02	.10
101 Mel Blount	.02	.10
102 Willie Brown	.02	.10
103 Lester Hayes	.01	.05
104 Mike Haynes	.01	.05
105 Ronnie Lott	.02	.10
106 Mel Renfro	.02	.10
107 Eric Wright	.01	.05
108 Dick Anderson	.01	.05
109 David Fulcher	.01	.05
110 Cliff Harris	.02	.10
111 Johnny Robinson	.01	.05
112 Jake Scott	.01	.05
113 Donnie Shell	.02	.10
114 Mike Wagner	.01	.05
115 Willie Wood	.02	.10
116 Ray Guy	.02	.10
117 Lee Johnson	.01	.05
118 Larry Seiple	.01	.05
119 Jerrel Wilson	.01	.05
120 Kevin Butler	.01	.05
121 Don Chandler	.01	.05
122 Jan Stenerud	.02	.10
123 Jim Turner	.01	.05
124 Ray Wersching	.01	.05
125 Larry Anderson	.01	.05
126 Stanford Jennings	.01	.05
127 Mike Nelms	.01	.05
128 John Taylor	.02	.10
129 Fulton Walker	.01	.05
130 E.J. Holub	.01	.05
131 George Seifert CO	.02	.10
132 Jim Taylor	.05	.15
133 Joe Theismann	.05	.15
134 Johnny Unitas	.10	.30
135 Reggie Williams	.01	.05
136 Two Networks (Paul Christman and Frank Gifford)	.02	.10
137 First Fly-Over (Military jets)	.01	.05
138 Weeb Ewbank (Super Bowl Super Moment)	.01	.05
139 Otis Taylor (Super Bowl Super Moment)	.02	.10
140 Jim O'Brien (Super Bowl Super Moment)	.01	.05
141 Garo Yepremian (Super Bowl Super Moment)	.01	.05
142 Pete Rozelle and Art Rooney	.01	.05
143 Percy Howard (Super Bowl Super Moment)	.01	.05
144 Jackie Smith (Super Bowl Super Moment)	.02	.10
145 Record Crowd (Super Bowl Super Moment)	.01	.05
146 Yellow Ribbon UER (Fourth line says more than year, should say more than a year)	.01	.05
147 Dan Bunz and Charles Alexander (Super Bowl Super Moment)	.01	.05
148 Smurfs (Redskins) (Super Bowl Super Moment)	.01	.05
149 The Fridge	.02	.10
150 Phil McConkey (Super Bowl Super Moment)	.01	.05
151 Doug Williams (Super Bowl Super Moment)	.02	.10
152 Top row left XXV Theme Art Puzzle	.01	.03
153 Top row middle XXV Theme Art Puzzle	.01	.03
154 Top row right XXV Theme Art Puzzle	.01	.03
155 Center row left XXV Theme Art Puzzle	.01	.03
156 Center row middle XXV Theme Art Puzzle	.01	.03
157 Center row right XXV Theme Art Puzzle	.01	.03
158 Bottom row left XXV Theme Art Puzzle	.01	.03
159 Bottom row middle XXV Theme Art Puzzle	.01	.03
160 Bottom row right XXV Theme Art Puzzle	.01	.05
NNO Special Offer Card (SB Game Program direct from Pro Set)	.01	.05

1990-91 Pro Set Super Bowl XXV Binder

This set of 56 standard-size cards features members of the all-time Super Bowl team and members of the teams which competed in the 25th Super Bowl: the New York Giants and Buffalo Bills. This set also included card number 799 from the 1990 Pro Set Football set: the Ronnie Lott Stay in School Card. Published reports indicated that Pro Set made 125,000 of these sets, 90,000 for distribution at the Super Bowl and 35,000 for a special mail-away offer at $30.00 per set. The set is housed in an attractive binder with special plastic pages holding four cards per. The cards of the players playing in the Super Bowl have the same number on the back as their regular issue set but the fronts acknowledge their teams as champions of their conferences. Cards for players from the two losing teams in the Conference Championship games (49ers and Raiders) were also printed, but apparently where not destroyed as commonly thought since many of them surfaced some twenty years later.

COMPLETE SET (56)	8.00	20.00
1 Vince Lombardi CO	.20	.50
2 Joe Montana	3.20	8.00
3 Larry Csonka	.20	.50
4 Franco Harris	.20	.50
5 Jerry Rice	1.60	4.00
6 Lynn Swann	.20	.50
7 Forrest Gregg	.10	.30
8 Art Shell	.10	.30
9 Jerry Kramer	.07	.20
10 Gene Upshaw	.07	.20
11 Mike Webster	.07	.20
12 Dave Casper	.07	.20
13 Jan Stenerud	.07	.20
14 John Taylor	.07	.20
15 L.C. Greenwood	.07	.20
16 Ed Too Tall Jones	.10	.30
17 Joe Greene	.20	.50
18 Randy White	.20	.50
19 Jack Lambert	.20	.50
20 Mike Singletary	.10	.30
21 Jack Ham	.10	.30
22 Ted Hendricks	.10	.30
23 Mel Blount	.10	.30
24 Ronnie Lott	.10	.30
25 Donnie Shell	.07	.20
26 Willie Wood	.10	.30
27 Ray Guy	.07	.20
39 Cornelius Bennett	.10	.30
40 Jim Kelly	.40	1.00
47 Darryl Talley	.07	.20
48 Marv Levy CO	.07	.20
223 Carl Banks	.07	.20
226 Pepper Johnson	.07	.20
228 Dave Meggett	.10	.30
230 Phil Simms	.10	.30
231 Lawrence Taylor	.15	.40
232 Bill Parcells CO	.07	.20
437 Shane Conlan	.07	.20
438 Kent Hull	.07	.20
440 Andre Reed	.10	.30
443 Bruce Smith	.10	.30
444 Thurman Thomas	.40	1.00
591 Ottis Anderson	.07	.20
592 Mark Bavaro	.07	.20
596 Jeff Hostetler	.10	.30
692 Rodney Hampton	.20	.50
725 Howard Ballard	.07	.20
753 James Lofton	.10	.30
754 Steve Tasker	.07	.20
765 Stephen Baker	.07	.20
766 Reyna Thompson	.07	.20
799 Ronnie Lott Education	.10	.30
SC1 2,000,000th Fan	.07	.20
SC2 Buick Checklist Card	.07	.20
SC3 Lamar Hunt Trophy	.07	.20
SC4 George Halas Trophy	.07	.20

1990-91 Pro Set Super Bowl XXV 49ers

Pro Set created these cards in anticipation of the 49ers winning the NFC Championship game and making their way to Super Bowl XXV. If they had won the game, instead of the Giants, the cards would have been part of the Super Bowl XXV Binder set issued at the game. This set was thought to have been completely destroyed at the time, but a number of cards and sets surfaced some twenty years later. Just like the Giants and Bills Binder cards, these feature the Super Bowl XXV logo on the front but otherwise follow the basic style and card numbering of the 1990 Pro Set cards. New player photos, however, are also featured in this version.

COMPLETE SET (12)	100.00	200.00
287 Roger Craig	6.00	15.00
289 Charles Haley	8.00	20.00
290 Pierce Holt	4.00	10.00
291 Ronnie Lott	10.00	25.00
292 Guy McIntyre	4.00	10.00
293 Joe Montana	40.00	80.00
295 Jerry Rice	30.00	60.00
297 John Taylor	6.00	15.00
299 George Seifert CO	5.00	12.00
639 Brent Jones	5.00	12.00
640 Matt Millen	5.00	12.00
644 Dave Waymer	4.00	10.00

1990-91 Pro Set Super Bowl XXV Raiders

Pro Set created these cards in anticipation of the Raiders winning the AFC Championship game and making their way to Super Bowl XXV. If they had won the game, instead of the Bills, the cards would have been part of the Super Bowl XXV Binder set issued at the game. This set was thought to have been completely destroyed at the time, but a number of cards and sets surfaced some twenty years later. Just like the Giants and Bills Binder cards, these feature the Super Bowl XXV logo on the front but otherwise follow the basic style and card numbering of the 1990 Pro Set cards. New player photos, however, are also featured in this version.

COMPLETE SET (12)	60.00	120.00
152 Mervyn Fernandez	4.00	10.00
153 Willie Gault	5.00	12.00
155 Bo Jackson	*8.00	20.00
156 Don Mosebar	4.00	10.00
158 Greg Townsend	4.00	10.00
160 Steve Wisniewski	5.00	12.00
161 Art Shell	5.00	12.00
538 Marcus Allen	6.00	15.00
545 Howie Long	6.00	15.00
546 Terry McDaniel	4.00	10.00
547 Max Montoya	4.00	10.00
548 Jay Schroeder	4.00	10.00

1991 Pro Set Draft Day

This eight-card standard-size set was issued by Pro Set on April 21, 1991 the date of the NFL draft. The cards, which are all numbered 694, feature action shots in the 1991 Pro Set design of all the potential number one draft picks. The backs of the cards have a horizontal format, with one half of the card being a full-color portrait of the player and the other half consisting of biographical information. The set is checklisted below in alphabetical order. The Russell Maryland card was eventually released (on a somewhat limited basis) with the first series of 1991 Pro Set cards and is listed there rather than here.

COMPLETE SET (7)	125.00	250.00
694A Nick Bell	15.00	30.00
694B Mike Croel	20.00	40.00
694C Rocket Ismail	15.00	30.00
694D Rocket Ismail	50.00	100.00
694E Rocket Ismail	15.00	40.00
694F Todd Lyght	15.00	30.00
694G Dan McGwire	15.00	30.00

1991 Pro Set Promos

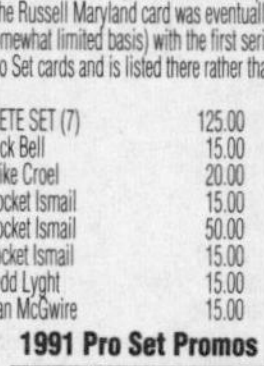

The Tele-Clinic card was given away as a promotion at Super Bowl XXV and was co-sponsored by NFL Pro Set, The Learning Channel, and Sports Illustrated for Kids. The card features a color photo on the front of an NFL player giving some football tips to a young kid. This card promotes the annual Super Bowl football clinic, in which current and former NFL stars talk to kids about football and life. The Super Bowl Card Show II card was issued in conjunction with the second annual Super Bowl show which was held in Tampa, Florida across the street from Tampa Stadium. The card is in the design on the Pro Set Super Bowl insert set from 1989 with a little inset on the bottom right hand corner of the card which states "Super Bowl Card Show II, January 24-27, 1991". The back of the card has information about the show and the other promotional activities which accompanied Super Bowl week. The Perry and Roberts cards were apparently planned but pulled from the Pro Bowl albums just prior to distribution. All of the above cards measure the standard size.

COMPLETE SET (6)	28.00	70.00
PSG1 Emmitt Smith Gazette	1.00	2.50
NNO NFL Kids on the Block (Tele-Clinic)	.20	.50
NNO Super Bowl XXV Card Show II	.20	.50
NNO Michael Dean Perry Pro Bowl Special (unnumbered; without Pro Set logo)	8.00	20.00
NNO Michael Dean Perry Pro Bowl Special (unnumbered; with Pro Set logo)	8.00	20.00
NNO William Roberts Pro Bowl Special (unnumbered)	12.00	30.00

1991 Pro Set

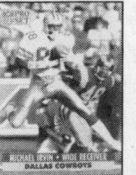

This set contains 850 standard-size cards issued in three series of 405, 407 and a 38-card Final Update set. The front design features full-bleed glossy color action photos with player, position and team name at the bottom in two stripes reflecting the team's colors. The horizontally oriented backs have a color head shot on the right side, with player profile highlights and statistics on the left. The set starts with NFL leaders (3-19), 1990 milestones (20-26), 1991 Hall of Fame inductees (27-31), college award winners (32-36), past Heisman trophy winners (37-45) and Super Bowl XXV highlights (46-54). Cards 55-324 and 433-684 are in team order. Further subsets include special games of the 1990 season (325-342), NFL officals (352-369), Stay in School (370-378) and 54 All-NFC (379-405) and All-AFC (406-432) drawings by artist Merv Corning, NFL Newsreel (685-693/813-815), Legends (694-702), World League Leaders (703-711), Hall of Fame Photo Contest (712-720), Think About It (721-729), first through third round Draft Choices (730-772) and a Super Bowl XXV Theme Art card. Since two #1 cards were issued, no #2 card exists.

COMPLETE SET (850)	15.00	35.00
COMP.SERIES 1 (405)	6.00	15.00
COMP.SERIES 2 (407)	6.00	15.00
COMP.FINAL FACT. (38)	2.00	5.00
1D Mark Carrier DB Defensive ROY	.02	.10
1O Emmitt Smith O-ROY	.50	1.25
3 Joe Montana NFL Player of the Year	.20	.50
4 Art Shell NFL Coach of the Year	.02	.10
5 Mike Singletary	.02	.10
6 Bruce Smith NFL Defensive Player of the Year	.02	.10
7 Barry Word NFL Comeback Player of the Year	.01	.05
8A Jim Kelly NFL Passing Leader (NFLPA logo on back)	.08	.25
8B Jim Kelly NFL Passing Leader (No NFLPA logo on back)	.08	.25
8C Jim Kelly NFL Passing Leader (No NFLPA logo on back but the registered symbol remains)	3.00	6.00
9 Warren Moon NFL Passing Yardage and TD Leader	.02	.10
10 Barry Sanders LL	.20	.50
11 Jerry Rice NFL Receiving and Receiving Yardage Leader	.15	.40
12 Jay Novacek Tight End Leader	.02	.10
13 Thurman Thomas NFL Total Yardage Leader	.02	.10
14 Nick Lowery NFL Scoring Leader, Kickers	.01	.05
15 Mike Horan NFL Punting Leader	.01	.05
16 Clarence Verdin NFL Punt Return Leader	.01	.05
17 Kevin Clark RC NFL Kickoff Return Leader	.01	.05
18 Mark Carrier DB NFL Interception Leader	.02	.10
19A Derrick Thomas ERR NFL Sack Leader (Bills helmet on front)	7.50	20.00
19B Derrick Thomas COR NFL Sack Leader (Chiefs helmet on front)	.02	.10
20 Ottis Anderson ML/10000 Career Rushing Yards	.02	.10
21 Roger Craig ML Most Career Receptions by RB	.02	.10
22 Art Monk ML 700 Career Receptions	.02	.10
23 Chuck Noll ML 200 Victories	.02	.10
24 Randall Cunningham ML Leads team in rushing, fourth straight year UER (586 rushes, should be 486 average 5.9, should be 7.1)	.02	.10
25 Dan Marino ML 7th 3000 yard season	.20	.50
26 49ers Road Record ML 18 victories in row still alive	.01	.05
27 Earl Campbell HOF	.01	.05
28 John Hannah HOF	.01	.05
29 Stan Jones HOF	.01	.05
30 Tex Schramm HOF	.01	.05
31 Jan Stenerud HOF	.01	.05
32 Russell Maryland RC	.02	.10
33 Chris Zorich RC	.02	.10
34 Darryll Lewis RC UER Thorpe Winner (Name misspelled Darryl on card)	.02	.10
35 Alfred Williams RC	.01	.05
36 Rocket Ismail RC Walter Camp POY	.40	1.00
37 Ty Detmer HH RC	.15	.40
38 Andre Ware HH	.02	.10
39 Barry Sanders HH	.20	.50
40 Tim Brown HH UER (No Official Photo and Stat Card of the NFL on card back)	.02	.10
41 Vinny Testaverde HH	.02	.10
42 Bo Jackson HH	.10	.30
43 Mike Rozier HH	.01	.05
44 Herschel Walker HH	.02	.10
45 Marcus Allen HH	.02	.10
46A James Lofton SB (NFLPA logo on back)	.02	.10
46B James Lofton SB (No NFLPA logo on back)	.02	.10
47A Bruce Smith SB (Official NFL Card in black letters)	.02	.10
47B Bruce Smith SB (Official NFL Card in white letters)	.02	.10
48 Myron Guyton SB	.01	.05
49 Stephen Baker SB	.01	.05
50 Mark Ingram SB UER (First repeated twice on back title)	.01	.05
51 Ottis Anderson SB	.02	.10
52 Thurman Thomas SB	.08	.25
53 Matt Bahr SB	.01	.05
54 Scott Norwood SB	.01	.05
55 Stephen Baker	.01	.05
56 Carl Banks	.01	.05
57 Mark Collins	.01	.05
58 Steve DeOssie	.01	.05
59 Eric Dorsey	.01	.05
60 John Elliott	.01	.05
61 Myron Guyton	.01	.05
62 Rodney Hampton	.08	.25
63 Jeff Hostetler	.02	.10
64 Erik Howard	.01	.05
65 Mark Ingram	.02	.10
66 Greg Jackson RC	.01	.05
67 Leonard Marshall	.01	.05
68 Dave Meggett	.02	.10
69 Eric Moore	.01	.05
70 Bart Oates	.01	.05
71 Gary Reasons	.01	.05
72 Bill Parcells CO	.02	.10
73 Howard Ballard	.01	.05
74A Cornelius Bennett (NFLPA logo on back)	.08	.25
74B Cornelius Bennett (No NFLPA logo on back)	.01	.05
75 Shane Conlan	.01	.05
76 Kent Hull	.01	.05
77 Kirby Jackson RC	.01	.05
78A Jim Kelly (NFLPA logo on back)	.25	.60
78B Jim Kelly (No NFLPA logo on back)	.08	.25
79 Mark Kelso	.01	.05
80 Nate Odomes	.01	.05
81 Andre Reed	.02	.10
82 Jim Ritcher	.01	.05
83 Bruce Smith	.08	.25
84 Darryl Talley	.01	.05
85 Steve Tasker	.02	.10
86 Thurman Thomas	.08	.25
87 James Williams	.01	.05
88 Will Wolford	.01	.05
89 Jeff Wright RC UER (Went to Central Missouri State, not Central Missouri)	.01	.05
90 Marv Levy CO	.01	.05
91 Steve Broussard	.01	.05
92A Darion Conner ERR (Drafted 1st round, 19'99)	4.00	10.00
92B Darion Conner COR (Drafted 2nd round, 1990)	.08	.25
93 Bill Fralic	.01	.05
94 Tim Green	.01	.05
95 Michael Haynes	.08	.25
96 Chris Hinton	.01	.05
97 Chris Miller UER (Two commas after city in his birth info)	.02	.10
98 Deion Sanders UER (Career TD's 3, but only 2 in yearly stats)	.15	.40
99 Jerry Glanville CO	.01	.05
100 Kevin Butler	.01	.05
101 Mark Carrier DB	.02	.10
102 Jim Covert	.01	.05
103 Richard Dent	.02	.10
104 Jim Harbaugh	.08	.25
105 Brad Muster	.01	.05
106 Lemuel Stinson	.01	.05
107 Keith Van Horne	.01	.05
108 Mike Ditka CO UER (Winning percent in '87 was .733, not .753)	.08	.25
109 Lewis Billups	.01	.05
110 James Brooks	.02	.10
111 Boomer Esiason	.02	.10
112 James Francis	.01	.05
113 David Fulcher	.01	.05
114 Rodney Holman	.01	.05
115 Tim McGee	.01	.05
116 Anthony Munoz	.02	.10
117 Sam Wyche CO	.01	.05
118 Paul Farren	.01	.05
119 Thane Gash	.01	.05
120 Mike Johnson	.01	.05
121A Bernie Kosar (NFLPA logo on back)	.02	.10
121B Bernie Kosar (No NFLPA logo on back)	.02	.10
122 Clay Matthews	.02	.10
123 Eric Metcalf	.02	.10
124 Frank Minnifield	.01	.05
125A Webster Slaughter (NFLPA logo on back)	.02	.10
125B Webster Slaughter (No NFLPA logo on back)	.02	.10
126 Bill Belichick CO RC	.60	1.50
127 Tommie Agee	.01	.05
128 Troy Aikman	.30	.75
129 Jack Del Rio	.02	.10
130 John Gesek RC	.01	.05
131 Issiac Holt	.01	.05
132 Michael Irvin	.08	.25
133 Ken Norton	.02	.10
134 Daniel Stubbs	.01	.05
135 Jimmy Johnson CO	.02	.10
136 Steve Atwater	.01	.05
137 Michael Brooks	.01	.05
138 John Elway	.50	1.25
139 Wymon Henderson	.01	.05
140 Bobby Humphrey	.01	.05
141 Mark Jackson	.01	.05
142 Karl Mecklenburg	.01	.05
143 Doug Widell	.01	.05
144 Dan Reeves CO	.01	.05
145 Eric Andolsek	.01	.05
146 Jerry Ball	.01	.05
147 Bennie Blades	.01	.05
148 Lomas Brown	.01	.05
149 Robert Clark	.01	.05
150 Michael Cofer	.01	.05
151 Dan Owens	.01	.05
152 Rodney Peete	.02	.10
153 Wayne Fontes CO	.01	.05
154 Tim Harris	.01	.05
155 Johnny Holland	.01	.05
156 Don Majkowski	.01	.05
157 Tony Mandarich	.01	.05
158 Mark Murphy	.01	.05
159 Brian Noble	.01	.05
160 Jeff Query	.01	.05
161 Sterling Sharpe	.08	.25
162 Lindy Infante CO	.01	.05
163 Ray Childress	.01	.05
164 Ernest Givins	.02	.10
165 Richard Johnson CB	.01	.05
166 Bruce Matthews	.02	.10
167 Warren Moon	.08	.25
168 Mike Munchak	.02	.10
169 Al Smith	.01	.05
170 Lorenzo White	.01	.05
171 Jack Pardee CO	.01	.05
172 Albert Bentley	.01	.05
173 Duane Bickett	.01	.05
174 Bill Brooks	.01	.05
175A Eric Dickerson (NFLPA logo on back)	.15	.40
175B Eric Dickerson (No NFLPA logo on back and 667 yards rushing for 1990 in text)	.50	1.25
175C Eric Dickerson (No NFLPA logo on back and 677 yards rushing for 1990 in text)	.08	.25

Card	Low	High
176 Ray Donaldson	.01	.05
177 Jeff George	.08	.25
178 Jeff Herrod	.01	.05
179 Clarence Verdin	.01	.05
180 Ron Meyer CO	.01	.05
181 John Alt	.01	.05
182 Steve DeBerg	.01	.05
183 Albert Lewis	.01	.05
184 Nick Lowery UER	.01	.05
(In his 13th year, not 12th)		
185 Christian Okoye	.01	.05
186 Stephone Paige	.01	.05
187 Kevin Porter	.01	.05
188 Derrick Thomas	.08	.25
189 Marty Schottenheimer CO	.01	.05
190 Willie Gault	.02	.10
191 Howie Long	.08	.25
192 Terry McDaniel	.01	.05
193 Jay Schroeder UER	.01	.05
(Passing total yards 13,863 should be 13,683)		
194 Steve Smith	.01	.05
195 Greg Townsend	.01	.05
196 Lionel Washington	.01	.05
197 Steve Wisniewski UER	.01	.05
(Back says drafted, should say traded to)		
198 Art Shell CO	.02	.10
199 Henry Ellard	.02	.10
200 Jim Everett	.02	.10
201 Jerry Gray	.01	.05
202 Kevin Greene	.02	.10
203 Buford McGee	.01	.05
204 Tom Newberry	.01	.05
205 Frank Stams	.01	.05
206 Alvin Wright	.01	.05
207 John Robinson CO	.01	.05
208 Jeff Cross	.01	.05
209 Mark Duper	.02	.10
210 Dan Marino	.50	1.25
211A Tim McKyer	.02	.10
(No Traded box on front)		
211B Tim McKyer	.08	.25
(Traded box on front)		
212 John Offerdahl	.01	.05
213 Sammie Smith	.01	.05
214 Richmond Webb	.01	.05
215 Jarvis Williams	.01	.05
216 Don Shula CO	.02	.10
217A Darrell Fullington ERR	.02	.10
(No registered symbol on back)		
217B Darrell Fullington COR	.02	.10
(Registered symbol on back)		
218 Tim Irwin	.01	.05
219 Mike Merriweather	.01	.05
220 Keith Millard	.01	.05
221 Al Noga	.01	.05
222 Henry Thomas	.01	.05
223 Wade Wilson	.02	.10
224 Gary Zimmerman	.02	.10
225 Jerry Burns CO	.01	.05
226 Bruce Armstrong	.01	.05
227 Marv Cook	.01	.05
228 Hart Lee Dykes	.01	.05
229 Tommy Hodson	.01	.05
230 Ronnie Lippett	.01	.05
231 Ed Reynolds	.01	.05
232 Chris Singleton	.01	.05
233 John Stephens	.01	.05
234 Dick MacPherson CO	.01	.05
235 Stan Brock	.01	.05
236 Craig Heyward	.02	.10
237 Vaughan Johnson	.01	.05
238 Robert Massey	.01	.05
239 Brett Maxie	.01	.05
240 Rueben Mayes	.01	.05
241 Pat Swilling	.02	.10
242 Ronaldo Turnbull	.01	.05
243 Jim Mora CO	.01	.05
244 Kyle Clifton	.01	.05
245 Jeff Criswell	.01	.05
246 James Hasty	.01	.05
247 Erik McMillan	.01	.05
248 Scott Mersereau RC	.01	.05
249 Ken O'Brien	.01	.05
250A Blair Thomas	.08	.25
(NFLPA logo on back)		
250B Blair Thomas	.02	.10
(No NFLPA logo on back)		
251 Al Toon	.02	.10
252 Bruce Coslet CO	.01	.05
253 Eric Allen	.01	.05
254 Fred Barnett	.08	.25
255 Keith Byars	.01	.05
256 Randall Cunningham	.08	.25
257 Seth Joyner	.02	.10
258 Clyde Simmons	.01	.05
259 Jessie Small	.01	.05
260 Andre Waters	.01	.05
261 Rich Kotite CO	.01	.05
262 Roy Green	.01	.05
263 Ernie Jones	.01	.05
264 Tim McDonald	.01	.05
265 Timm Rosenbach	.01	.05
266 Rod Saddler	.01	.05
267 Luis Sharpe	.01	.05
268 Anthony Thompson UER	.01	.05
(Terra Haute should be Terre...)		
269 Marcus Turner RC	.01	.05
270 Joe Bugel CO	.01	.05
271 Gary Anderson K	.01	.05
272 Dermontti Dawson	.01	.05
273 Eric Green	.01	.05
274 Merril Hoge	.01	.05
275 Tunch Ilkin	.01	.05
276 D.J. Johnson	.01	.05
277 Louis Lipps	.01	.05
278 Rod Woodson	.08	.25
279 Chuck Noll CO	.02	.10
280 Martin Bayless	.01	.05
281 Marion Butts UER	.02	.10
(2 years exp. should be 3)		
282 Gill Byrd	.01	.05
283 Burt Grossman	.01	.05
284 Courtney Hall	.01	.05
285 Anthony Miller	.02	.10
286 Leslie O'Neal	.02	.10
287 Billy Joe Tolliver	.01	.05
288 Dan Henning CO	.01	.05
289 Dexter Carter	.01	.05
290 Michael Carter	.01	.05
291 Kevin Fagan	.01	.05
292 Pierce Holt	.01	.05
293 Guy McIntyre	.01	.05
(Joe Montana also in photo)		
294 Tom Rathman	.01	.05
295 John Taylor	.02	.10
296 Steve Young	.30	.75
297 George Seifert CO	.02	.10
298 Brian Blades	.02	.10
299 Jeff Bryant	.01	.05
300 Norm Johnson	.01	.05
301 Tommy Kane	.01	.05
302 Cortez Kennedy UER	.08	.25
(Played for Seattle, not Miami)		
303 Bryan Millard	.01	.05
304 John L. Williams	.01	.05
305 David Wyman	.01	.05
306A Chuck Knox CO ERR	.01	.05
(Has NFLPA logo, but should not)		
306B Chuck Knox CO COR	.20	.50
(No NFLPA logo on back)		
307 Gary Anderson RB	.01	.05
308 Reggie Cobb	.01	.05
309 Randy Grimes	.01	.05
310 Harry Hamilton	.01	.05
311 Bruce Hill	.01	.05
312 Eugene Marve	.01	.05
313 Ervin Randle	.01	.05
314 Vinny Testaverde	.02	.10
315 Richard Williamson CO	.01	.05
UER (Coach: 1st year, should be 2nd year)		
316 Earnest Byner	.01	.05
317 Gary Clark	.08	.25
318A Andre Collins	.02	.10
(NFLPA logo on back)		
318B Andre Collins	.02	.10
(No NFLPA logo on back)		
319 Darryl Grant	.01	.05
320 Chip Lohmiller	.01	.05
321 Martin Mayhew	.01	.05
322 Mark Rypien	.02	.10
323 Alvin Walton	.01	.05
324 Joe Gibbs CO UER	.02	.10
(Has registered symbol but should not)		
325 Jerry Glanville REP	.01	.05
326A John Elway REP	2.00	4.00
(NFLPA logo on back)		
326B John Elway REP	.75	2.00
(No NFLPA logo on back)		
327 Boomer Esiason REP	.01	.05
328A Steve Tasker REP	2.00	4.00
(NFLPA logo on back)		
328B Steve Tasker REP	.75	2.00
(No NFLPA logo on back)		
329 Jerry Rice REP	.15	.40
330 Jeff Rutledge REP	.01	.05
331 K.C. Defense REP	.01	.05
332 49ers Streak REP	.01	.05
(Cleveland Gary)		
333 Monday Meeting REP	.01	.05
(John Taylor)		
334A Randall Cunningham REP	.01	.05
(NFLPA logo on back)		
334B Randall Cunningham REP	.01	.05
(No NFLPA logo on back)		
335A Bo Barry REP w LOGO	.20	.50
335B Bo Barry REP NO LOGO	.20	.50
336 Lawrence Taylor REP	.08	.25
337 Warren Moon REP	.08	.25
338 Alan Grant REP	.01	.05
339 Todd McNair REP	.01	.05
340A Miami Dolphins REP	.01	.05
(Mark Clayton; TM symbol on Chiefs player's shoulder)		
340B Miami Dolphins REP	.01	.05
(Mark Clayton; TM symbol off Chiefs player's shoulder)		
341A Highest Scoring REP	2.00	4.00
Jim Kelly Passing		
(NFLPA logo on back)		
341B Highest Scoring REP	.75	2.00
Jim Kelly Passing		
(No NFLPA logo on back)		
342 Matt Bahr REP	.01	.05
343 Robert Tisch NEW	.01	.05
(With Wellington Mara)		
344 Sam Jankovich NEW	.01	.05
345 In-the-Grasp NEW	.01	.05
(John Elway)		
346 Bo Jackson NEW	.02	.10
(Career in Jeopardy)		
347 NFL Teacher of the Year Jack Williams with Paul Tagliabue	.01	.05
348 Ronnie Lott NEW	.02	.10
(Plan B Free Agent)		
349 Super Bowl XXV	.02	.10
Teleclinic NEW Greg Gumbel with Warren Moon, Derrick Thomas, and Wade Wilson)		
350 Whitney Houston	.30	.75
351 U.S. Troops in Saudia Arabia NEW (Troops watching TV with gas masks)	.01	.05
352 Art McNally OFF	.01	.05
353 Dick Jorgensen OFF	.01	.05
354 Jerry Seeman OFF	.01	.05
355 Jim Tunney OFF	.01	.05
356 Gerry Austin OFF	.01	.05
357 Gene Barth OFF	.01	.05
358 Red Cashion OFF	.01	.05
359 Tom Dooley OFF	.01	.05
360 Johnny Grier OFF	.01	.05
361 Pat Haggerty OFF	.01	.05
362 Dale Hamer OFF	.01	.05
363 Dick Hantak OFF	.01	.05
364 Jerry Markbreit OFF	.01	.05
365 Gordon McCarter OFF	.01	.05
366 Bob McElwee OFF	.01	.05
367 Howard Roe OFF	.01	.05
(Illustrations on back smaller than other officials' cards)		
368 Tom White OFF	.01	.05
369 Norm Schachter OFF	.01	.05
370A Warren Moon	.08	.25
Crack Kills		
(Small type on back)		
370B Warren Moon	.08	.25
Crack Kills		
(Large type on back)		
371A Boomer Esiason	.20	.50
Don't Drink		
(Player and team name in upper and lower case type on back)		
371B Boomer Esiason	.02	.10
Don't Drink		
(Player and team name in all upper case type on back)		
372A Troy Aikman	.15	.40
Play It Straight		
(Small type on back)		
372B Troy Aikman	.15	.40
Play It Straight		
(Large type on back)		
373A Carl Banks	.20	.50
Read (Small type on back)		
373B Carl Banks	.01	.05
Read (Large type on back)		
374A Jim Everett	.20	.50
Study (Small type on back)		
374B Jim Everett	.02	.10
Study (Large type on back)		
375A Anthony Munoz	.02	.10
Quadante en la Escuela		
(Dificul; small type)		
375B Anthony Munoz	.02	.10
Quadante en la Escuela		
(Dificil; small type)		
375C Anthony Munoz	.02	.10
Quadante en la Escuela		
(Dificil; large type)		
375D Anthony Munoz	.02	.10
Quedate en la Escuela		
(Large type)		
376A Ray Childress	.50	1.25
Don't Pollute (Small type on back)		
376B Ray Childress	.01	.05
Don't Pollute (Large type on back)		
377A Charles Mann	.50	1.25
Steroids Destroy		
(Small type on back)		
377B Charles Mann	.01	.05
Steroids Destroy		
(Large type on back)		
378A Jackie Slater	.50	1.25
Keep the Peace		
(Small type on back)		
378B Jackie Slater	.01	.05
Keep the Peace		
(Large type on back)		
379 Jerry Rice NFC	.15	.40
380 Andre Rison NFC	.02	.10
381 Jim Lachey NFC	.01	.05
382 Jackie Slater NFC	.01	.05
383 Randall McDaniel NFC	.02	.10
384 Mark Bortz NFC	.01	.05
385 Jay Hilgenberg NFC	.01	.05
386 Keith Jackson NFC	.01	.05
387 Joe Montana NFC	.20	.50
388 Barry Sanders NFC	.20	.50
389 Neal Anderson NFC	.01	.05
390 Reggie White NFC	.08	.25
391 Chris Doleman NFC	.01	.05
392 Jerome Brown NFC	.01	.05
393 Charles Haley NFC	.01	.05
394 Lawrence Taylor NFC	.08	.25
395 Pepper Johnson NFC	.01	.05
396 Mike Singletary NFC	.02	.10
397 Darrell Green NFC	.01	.05
398 Carl Lee NFC	.01	.05
399 Joey Browner NFC	.01	.05
400 Ronnie Lott NFC	.02	.10
401 Sean Landeta NFC	.01	.05
402 Morten Andersen NFC	.01	.05
403 Mel Gray NFC	.01	.05
404 Reyna Thompson NFC	.01	.05
405 Jimmy Johnson CO NFC	.02	.10
406 Andre Reed AFC	.02	.10
407 Anthony Miller AFC	.02	.10
408 Anthony Munoz AFC	.02	.10
409 Bruce Armstrong AFC	.01	.05
410 Bruce Matthews AFC	.01	.05
411 Mike Munchak AFC	.01	.05
412 Kent Hull AFC	.01	.05
413 Rodney Holman AFC	.01	.05
414 Warren Moon AFC	.08	.25
415 Thurman Thomas AFC	.08	.25
416 Marion Butts AFC	.02	.10
417 Bruce Smith AFC	.02	.10
418 Greg Townsend AFC	.01	.05
419 Ray Childress AFC	.01	.05
420 Derrick Thomas AFC	.08	.25
421 Leslie O'Neal AFC	.02	.10
422 John Offerdahl AFC	.01	.05
423 Shane Conlan AFC	.01	.05
424 Rod Woodson AFC	.08	.25
425 Albert Lewis AFC	.01	.05
426 Steve Atwater AFC	.01	.05
427 David Fulcher AFC	.01	.05
428 Rohn Stark AFC	.01	.05
429 Nick Lowery AFC	.01	.05
430 Clarence Verdin AFC	.01	.05
431 Steve Tasker AFC	.01	.05
432 Art Shell CO AFC	.02	.10
433 Scott Case	.01	.05
434 Tory Epps UER	.01	.05
(No TM next to Pro Set on back)		
435 Mike Gann UER	.01	.05
(Text has 2 fumble recoveries, stats say 3)		
436 Brian Jordan UER	.02	.10
(No TM next to Pro Set on back)		
437 Mike Kenn	.01	.05
438 John Rade	.01	.05
439 Andre Rison	.02	.10
440 Mike Rozier	.01	.05
441 Jessie Tuggle	.01	.05
442 Don Beebe	.01	.05
443 John Davis RC	.01	.05
444 James Lofton	.02	.10
445 Keith McKeller	.01	.05
446 Jamie Mueller	.01	.05
447 Scott Norwood	.01	.05
448 Frank Reich	.02	.10
449 Leon Seals	.01	.05
450 Leonard Smith	.01	.05
451 Neal Anderson	.02	.10
452 Trace Armstrong	.01	.05
453 Mark Bortz	.01	.05
454 Wendell Davis	.01	.05
455 Shaun Gayle	.01	.05
456 Jay Hilgenberg	.01	.05
457 Steve McMichael	.02	.10
458 Mike Singletary	.02	.10
459 Donnell Woolford	.01	.05
460 Jim Breech	.01	.05
461 Eddie Brown	.01	.05
462 Barney Bussey RC	.01	.05
463 Bruce Kozerski	.01	.05
464 Tim Krumrie	.01	.05
465 Bruce Reimers	.01	.05
466 Kevin Walker RC	.01	.05
467 Ickey Woods	.01	.05
468 Carl Zander UER	.01	.05
(DOB: 4/12/63, should be 3/23/63)		
469 Mike Baab	.01	.05
470 Brian Brennan	.01	.05
471 Rob Burnett RC	.02	.10
472 Raymond Clayborn	.01	.05
473 Reggie Langhorne	.01	.05
474 Kevin Mack	.01	.05
475 Anthony Pleasant	.01	.05
476 Joe Morris	.01	.05
477 Dan Fike	.01	.05
478 Ray Horton	.01	.05
479 Jim Jeffcoat	.01	.05
480 Jimmie Jones	.01	.05
481 Kelvin Martin	.01	.05
482 Nate Newton	.02	.10
483 Danny Noonan	.01	.05
484 Jay Novacek	.08	.25
485 Emmitt Smith	1.00	2.50
486 James Washington RC	.01	.05
487 Simon Fletcher	.01	.05
488 Ron Holmes	.01	.05
489 Mike Horan	.01	.05
490 Vance Johnson	.01	.05
491 Keith Kartz	.01	.05
492 Greg Kragen	.01	.05
493 Ken Lanier	.01	.05
494 Warren Powers	.01	.05
495 Dennis Smith	.01	.05
496 Jeff Campbell	.01	.05
497 Ken Dallafior	.01	.05
498 Dennis Gibson	.01	.05
499 Kevin Glover	.01	.05
500 Mel Gray	.02	.10
501 Eddie Murray	.01	.05
502 Barry Sanders	.50	1.25
503 Chris Spielman	.02	.10
504 William White	.01	.05
505 Matt Brock RC	.01	.05
506 Robert Brown	.01	.05
507 LeRoy Butler	.02	.10
508 James Campen RC	.01	.05
509 Jerry Holmes	.01	.05
510 Perry Kemp	.01	.05
511 Ken Ruettgers	.01	.05
512 Scott Stephen RC	.01	.05
513 Ed West	.01	.05
514 Cris Dishman RC	.01	.05
515 Curtis Duncan	.01	.05
516 Drew Hill UER	.01	.05
(Text says 390 catches and 6368 yards, stats say 450 and 7715)		
517 Haywood Jeffires	.02	.10
518 Sean Jones	.02	.10
519 Lamar Lathon	.01	.05
520 Don Maggs	.01	.05
521 Bubba McDowell	.01	.05
522 Johnny Meads	.01	.05
523A Chip Banks ERR	1.25	3.00
(No textual information)		
523B Chip Banks ERR	.01	.05
(with textual information)		
524 Pat Beach	.01	.05
525 Sam Clancy	.01	.05
526 Eugene Daniel	.01	.05
527 Jon Hand	.01	.05
528 Jessie Hester	.01	.05
529A Mike Prior ERR	1.25	3.00
(No textual information)		
529B Mike Prior COR	.01	.05
(with textual information)		
530 Keith Taylor	.01	.05
531 Donnell Thompson	.01	.05
532 Dino Hackett	.01	.05
533 David Lutz RC	.01	.05
534 Chris Martin	.01	.05
535 Kevin Ross	.01	.05
536 Dan Saleaumua	.01	.05
537 Neil Smith	.08	.25
538 Percy Snow	.01	.05
539 Robb Thomas	.01	.05
540 Barry Word	.01	.05
541 Marcus Allen	.08	.25
542 Eddie Anderson	.01	.05
543 Scott Davis	.01	.05
544 Mervyn Fernandez	.01	.05
545 Ethan Horton	.01	.05
546 Ronnie Lott	.02	.10
547 Don Mosebar	.01	.05
548 Jerry Robinson	.01	.05
549 Aaron Wallace	.01	.05
550 Flipper Anderson	.01	.05
551 Cleveland Gary	.01	.05
552 Damone Johnson RC	.01	.05
553 Duval Love RC	.01	.05
554 Irv Pankey	.01	.05
555 Mike Piel	.01	.05
556 Jackie Slater	.01	.05
557 Michael Stewart	.01	.05
558 Pat Terrell	.01	.05
559 J.B. Brown	.01	.05
560 Mark Clayton	.02	.10
561 Ferrell Edmunds	.01	.05
562 Harry Galbreath	.01	.05
563 David Griggs	.01	.05
564 Jim C. Jensen	.01	.05
565 Louis Oliver	.01	.05
566 Tony Paige	.01	.05
567 Keith Sims	.01	.05
568 Joey Browner	.01	.05
569 Anthony Carter	.02	.10
570 Chris Doleman	.01	.05
571 Rich Gannon UER	.08	.25
(Acquired in '87, not '88 as in text)		
572 Hassan Jones	.01	.05
573 Steve Jordan	.01	.05
574 Carl Lee	.01	.05
575 Randall McDaniel	.02	.10
576 Herschel Walker	.02	.10
577 Ray Agnew	.01	.05
578 Vincent Brown	.01	.05
579 Irving Fryar	.02	.10
580 Tim Goad	.01	.05
581 Maurice Hurst	.01	.05
582 Fred Marion	.01	.05
583 Johnny Rembert	.01	.05
584 Andre Tippett	.01	.05
585 Brent Williams	.01	.05
586 Morten Andersen	.01	.05
587 Toi Cook RC	.01	.05
588 Jim Dombrowski	.01	.05
589 Dalton Hilliard	.01	.05
590 Rickey Jackson	.01	.05
591 Eric Martin	.01	.05
592 Sam Mills	.01	.05
593 Bobby Hebert	.01	.05
594 Steve Walsh	.01	.05
595 Ottis Anderson	.02	.10
596 Pepper Johnson	.01	.05
597 Bob Kratch RC	.01	.05
598 Sean Landeta	.01	.05
599 Doug Riesenberg	.01	.05
600 William Roberts	.01	.05
601 Phil Simms	.02	.10
602 Lawrence Taylor	.08	.25
603 Everson Walls	.01	.05
604 Brad Baxter	.01	.05
605 Dennis Byrd	.01	.05
606 Jeff Lageman	.01	.05
607 Pat Leahy	.01	.05
608 Rob Moore	.08	.25
609 Joe Mott	.01	.05
610 Tony Stargell	.01	.05
611 Brian Washington	.01	.05
612 Marvin Washington RC	.01	.05
613 David Alexander	.01	.05
614 Jerome Brown	.01	.05
615 Byron Evans	.01	.05
616 Ron Heller	.01	.05
617 Wes Hopkins	.01	.05
618 Keith Jackson	.02	.10
619 Heath Sherman	.01	.05
620 Reggie White	.08	.25
621 Calvin Williams	.02	.10
622 Ken Harvey	.02	.10
623 Eric Hill	.01	.05
624 Johnny Johnson	.01	.05
625 Freddie Joe Nunn	.01	.05
626 Ricky Proehl	.01	.05
627 Tootie Robbins	.01	.05
628 Jay Taylor RC	.01	.05
629 Tom Tupa	.01	.05
630 Jim Wahler RC	.01	.05
631 Bubby Brister	.01	.05
632 Thomas Everett	.01	.05
633 Bryan Hinkle	.01	.05
634 Carnell Lake	.01	.05
635 David Little	.01	.05
636 Hardy Nickerson	.02	.10
637 Gerald Williams	.01	.05
638 Keith Willis	.01	.05
639 Tim Worley	.01	.05
640 Rod Bernstine	.01	.05
641 Frank Cornish	.01	.05
642 Gary Plummer	.01	.05
643 Henry Rolling RC	.01	.05
644 Sam Seale	.01	.05
645 Junior Seau	.08	.25
646 Billy Ray Smith	.01	.05
647 Broderick Thompson	.01	.05
648 Derrick Walker RC	.01	.05
649 Todd Bowles	.01	.05
650 Don Griffin	.01	.05
651 Charles Haley	.02	.10
652 Brent Jones UER	.02	.10
(Born in Santa Clara, not San Jose)		
653 Joe Montana	.50	1.25
654 Jerry Rice	.30	.75
655 Bill Romanowski	.01	.05
656 Michael Walter	.01	.05
657 Dave Waymer	.01	.05
658 Jeff Chadwick	.01	.05
659 Derrick Fenner	.01	.05
660 Nesby Glasgow	.01	.05
661 Jacob Green	.01	.05
662 Dwayne Harper RC	.01	.05
663 Andy Heck	.01	.05
664 Dave Krieg	.02	.10
665 Rufus Porter	.01	.05
666 Eugene Robinson	.01	.05
667 Mark Carrier WR	.08	.25
668 Steve Christie	.01	.05
669 Reuben Davis	.01	.05
670 Paul Gruber	.01	.05
671 Wayne Haddix	.01	.05
672 Ron Hall	.01	.05
673 Keith McCants UER	.01	.05
(Senior All-American, sic, left school after junior year)		
674 Ricky Reynolds	.01	.05
675 Mark Robinson	.01	.05
676 Jeff Bostic	.01	.05
677 Darrell Green	.01	.05
678 Markus Koch	.01	.05
679 Jim Lachey	.01	.05
680 Charles Mann	.01	.05
681 Wilber Marshall	.01	.05
682 Art Monk	.02	.10
683 Gerald Riggs	.01	.05
684 Ricky Sanders	.01	.05
685 Ray Handley NEW	.01	.05
(Replaces Bill Parcells as Giants head coach)		
686 NFL expansion NEW	.01	.05
687 Super Bowl XXIX NEW	.01	.05
688 George Young GM NEW is named NFL Executive of the Year by Sporting News	.01	.05
689 HOF Five-millionth fan NEW	.01	.05
690 Sports Illustrated NEW	.01	.05
691 American Bowl NEW	.01	.05
London Theme Art		
692 American Bowl NEW	.01	.05
Berlin Theme Art		
693 American Bowl NEW	.01	.05
Tokyo Theme Art		
694A Russell Maryland	.08	.25
(Says he runs a 4.91/40, card 32 has 4.8)		
694B Joe Ferguson LEG	.01	.05
695 Carl Hairston LEG	.02	.10
696 Dan Hampton LEG	.02	.10
697 Mike Haynes LEG	.01	.05
698 Marty Lyons LEG	.01	.05
699 Ozzie Newsome LEG	.02	.10
700 Scott Studwell LEG	.01	.05
701 Mike Webster LEG	.01	.05
702 Dwayne Woodruff LEG	.01	.05
703 Larry Kennan CO	.01	.05
London Monarchs		
704 Stan Gelbaugh RC LL	.02	.10
London Monarchs		
705 John Brantley LL	.01	.05
Birmingham Fire		
706 Danny Lockett LL	.01	.05
London Monarchs		
707 Anthony Parker RC LL	.02	.10
NY/NJ Knights		
708 Dan Crossman LL	.01	.05
London Monarchs		
709 Eric Wilkerson LL	.01	.05
NY/NJ Knights		
710 Judd Garrett LL RC	.01	.05
711 Tony Baker LL	.01	.05
Frankfurt Galaxy		
712 1st Place BW PHOTO	.01	.05
Randall Cunningham		
713 2nd Place BW PHOTO	.01	.05
Mark Ingram		
714 3rd Place BW PHOTO	.01	.05
Pete Holohan		
Barney Bussey		
Carl Carter		
715 1st Place Color PHOTO	.01	.05
Action		
Sterling Sharpe		
716 2nd Place Color PHOTO	.01	.05
Action		
Jim Harbaugh		
717 3rd Place Color PHOTO	.01	.05
Action		
Anthony Miller		
David Fulcher		
718 1st Place Color PHOTO	.01	.05
Feature		
Bill Parcells CO		
Lawrence Taylor		
719 2nd Place Color PHOTO	.01	.05
Feature		
Patriotic Crowd		
720 3rd Place Color PHOTO	.01	.05
Feature		
Alfredo Roberts		
721 Ray Bentley	.01	.05
Read And Study		
722 Earnest Byner	.01	.05
Never Give Up		
723 Bill Fralic	.01	.05
Steroids Destroy		
724 Joe Jacoby	.01	.05
Don't Pollute		
725 Howie Long	.08	.25
Aids Kills		
726 Dan Marino	.20	.50
School's The Ticket		
727 Ron Rivera	.01	.05
Leer Y Estudiar		
728 Mike Singletary	.02	.10
729 Cornelius Bennett	.02	.10
Chill		
730 Russell Maryland	.08	.25
731 Eric Turner RC	.02	.10
732 Bruce Pickens RC UER	.01	.05
(Wearing 38, but card back lists 39)		
733 Mike Croel RC	.01	.05
734 Todd Lyght RC	.01	.05
735 Eric Swann RC	.08	.25
736 Charles McRae RC	.01	.05
737 Antone Davis RC	.01	.05
738 Stanley Richard RC	.01	.05
739 Herman Moore RC	.08	.25
740 Pat Harlow RC	.01	.05
741 Alvin Harper RC	.08	.25
742 Mike Pritchard RC	.08	.25
743 Leonard Russell RC	.08	.25
744 Huey Richardson RC	.01	.05
745 Dan McGwire RC	.01	.05
746 Bobby Wilson RC	.01	.05
747 Alfred Williams	.01	.05
748 Vinnie Clark RC	.01	.05
749 Kelvin Pritchett RC	.02	.10
750 Harvey Williams RC	.08	.25
751 Stan Thomas	.01	.05
752 Randal Hill RC	.02	.10
753 Todd Marinovich RC	.01	.05
754 Ted Washington RC	.01	.05
755 Henry Jones RC	.02	.10
756 Jarrod Bunch RC	.01	.05
757 Mike Dumas RC	.01	.05
758 Ed King RC	.01	.05
759 Reggie Johnson RC	.01	.05
760 Roman Phifer RC	.01	.05
761 Mike Jones DE RC	.01	.05
762 Brett Favre RC	3.00	8.00
763 Browning Nagle RC	.01	.05
764 Esera Tuaolo RC	.01	.05
765 George Thornton RC	.01	.05
766 Dixon Edwards RC	.01	.05
767 Darryll Lewis	.02	.10
768 Eric Bieniemy RC	.01	.05
769 Shane Curry	.01	.05
770 Jerome Henderson RC	.01	.05
771 Wesley Carroll RC	.01	.05
772 Nick Bell RC	.01	.05
773 John Flannery RC	.01	.05
774 Ricky Watters RC	.60	1.50
775 Jeff Graham RC	.08	.25
776 Eric Moten RC	.01	.05
777 Jesse Campbell RC	.01	.05
778 Chris Zorich	.02	.10
779 Joe Valerio RC	.01	.05
780 Doug Thomas RC	.01	.05
781 Lamar Rogers RC UER	.01	.05
(No 'Official Card of NFL' and TM on card front)		
782 John Johnson RC	.01	.05
783 Phil Hansen RC	.01	.05
784 Kanavis McGhee RC	.01	.05
785 Calvin Stephens RC UER	.01	.05
(Card says New England, others say New England Patriots)		
786 James Jones RC	.01	.05
787 Reggie Barrett	.01	.05
788 Aeneas Williams RC	.08	.25
789 Aaron Craver RC	.01	.05
790 Keith Traylor RC	.01	.05
791 Godfrey Myles RC	.01	.05
792 Mo Lewis RC	.02	.10
793 James Richard RC	.01	.05
794 Carlos Jenkins RC	.01	.05
795 Lawrence Dawsey RC	.02	.10
796 Don Davey	.01	.05
797 Jake Reed RC	.20	.50
798 Dave McCloughan	.01	.05
799 Erik Williams RC	.02	.10
800 Steve Jackson RC	.01	.05
801 Bob Dahl	.01	.05
802 Ernie Mills RC	.02	.10
803 David Daniels RC	.01	.05
804 Rob Selby RC	.01	.05
805 Ricky Ervins RC	.02	.10
806 Tim Barnett RC	.01	.05
807 Chris Gardocki RC	.08	.25
808 Kevin Donnalley RC	.01	.05
809 Robert Wilson RC	.01	.05
810 Chuck Webb RC	.01	.05
811 Darryl Wren RC	.01	.05
812 Ed McCaffrey RC	.75	2.00
813 Shula's 300th NEW	.01	.05
814 Raiders-49ers sell out NEW	.01	.05
815 NFL International NEW	.01	.05
816 Moe Gardner RC	.01	.05
817 Tim McKyer	.01	.05
818 Tom Waddle RC	.01	.05
819 Michael Jackson WR RC	.08	.25
820 Tony Casillas	.01	.05
821 Gaston Green	.01	.05
822 Kenny Walker RC	.01	.05
823 Willie Green RC	.01	.05
824 Erik Kramer RC	.08	.25
825 William Fuller	.02	.10
826 Allen Pinkett	.01	.05
827 Rick Venturi CO	.01	.05
828 Bill Maas	.01	.05
829 Jeff Jaeger	.01	.05
830 Robert Delpino	.01	.05
831 Mark Higgs RC	.01	.05
832 Reggie Roby	.01	.05
833 Terry Allen RC	.60	1.50
834 Cris Carter	.20	.50
(No indication when acquired on waivers)		
835 John Randle RC	.30	.75
836 Hugh Millen RC	.01	.05
837 Jon Vaughn RC	.01	.05
838 Gill Fenerty	.01	.05
839 Floyd Turner	.01	.05
840 Irv Eatman	.01	.05
841 Lonnie Young	.01	.05
842 Jim McMahon	.02	.10
843 Randal Hill UER	.01	.05
(Traded to Phoenix, not drafted)		
844 Barry Foster	.02	.10
845 Neil O'Donnell RC	.08	.25
846 John Friesz UER	.08	.25
(Wears 17, not 7)		
847 Broderick Thomas	.01	.05
848 Brian Mitchell	.02	.10
849 Mike Utley RC	.02	.10
850 Mike Croel ROY	.01	.05
SC1 Super Bowl XXVI	.08	.25
Theme Art UER		
(Says SB 26, should be 25)		
SC3 Jim Thorpe	.30	.75
Pioneers of the Game		
SC4 Otto Graham	.30	.75
Pioneers of the Game		
SC5 Paul Brown	.30	.75
Pioneers of the Game		
PSS1 Walter Payton Team 34	.20	.50
PSS2 Red Grange	.20	.50
MVPC25 Ottis Anderson	.08	.25
MVP Super Bowl XXV		
AU336 Lawrence Taylor	100.00	175.00
REP (autographed/500)		
AU394 Lawrence Taylor	100.00	175.00
PB (autographed/500)		
AU699 Ozzie Newsome	25.00	50.00
(Certified autograph)		
AU824 Erik Kramer	25.00	50.00
(Certified autograph)		
NNO Mini Pro Set Gazette	.08	.25
NNO Pro Set Gazette	.08	.25
NNO Santa Claus	.20	.50
NNO Super Bowl XXV Art	.08	.25
NNO Super Bowl XXV Logo	.08	.25

1991 Pro Set WLAF Helmets

This set of ten standard size cards features (on the front of each card) a helmet of the teams of the WLAF's first season. These cards were included in the 1991 Pro Set first series wax packs. The back has information about the teams.

Card	Low	High
COMPLETE SET (10)	.80	2.00
1 Barcelona Dragons Helmet	.08	.25
2 Birmingham Fire Helmet	.08	.25
3 Frankfurt Galaxy Helmet	.08	.25
4 London Monarchs Helmet	.08	.25
5 Montreal Machine Helmet	.08	.25
6 NY-NJ Knights Helmet	.08	.25
7 Orlando Thunder Helmet	.08	.25
8 Ral.-Durham Skyhawks Helmet	.08	.25
9 Sacramento Surge Helmet	.08	.25
10 San Antonio Riders Helmet	.08	.25

1991 Pro Set WLAF Inserts

This 32-card standard size set was issued by Pro Set as an insert to the 1991 Pro Set Football first series. This set features the leading players from the WLAF. All ten WLAF teams are represented, and each team's head coach and quarterback are depicted on a card.

Card	Low	High
COMPLETE SET (32)	1.60	4.00
1 Mike Lynn (President CEO)	.02	.10
2 London 24, Frankfurt/11 World League Opener Larry Kennan CO	.02	.10
3 Jack Bicknell CO	.02	.10
4 Scott Erney	.02	.10
5 A.J. Green (Anthony on card front)	.02	.10
6 Chan Gailey CO	.10	.30
7 Paul McGowan	.02	.10
8 Brent Pease	.02	.10
9 Jack Elway CO	.10	.30
10 Mike Perez	.02	.10
11 Mike Teeter	.02	.10
12 Larry Kennan CO UER (Coaching experience should say first year)	.02	.10
13 Corris Ervin	.02	.10
14 John Witkowski	.02	.10
15 Jacques Dussault CO	.02	.10
16 Ray Savage UER (Back should say DE, not Defensive End)	.02	.10
17 Kevin Sweeney	.02	.10
18 Mouse Davis CO	.10	.30
19 Todd Hammel UER (Missing TM on card front)	.02	.10
20 Anthony Parker	.10	.30
21 Don Matthews CO	.02	.10
22 Kerwin Bell	.10	.30
23 Wayne Davis	.02	.10
24 Roman Gabriel CO	.15	.40
25 Jon Carter	.02	.10
26 Mark Maye	.02	.10
27 Kay Stephenson CO	.02	.10
28 Ben Bennett	.02	.10
29 Shawn Knight UER (Back has NFL Exp. WLAF cards have Pro Exp.)	.02	.10
30 Mike Riley CO	.02	.10
31 Jason Garrett	1.25	3.00
32 Greg Gilbert UER (6th round choice, should say 5th)	.02	.10

1991 Pro Set Cinderella Story

This nine-card set was issued as a perforated insert sheet in The Official NFL Pro Set Card Book, which chronicles the history of NFL Pro Set cards. The unifying theme of this set is summed up by the words "Cinderella Story" on the card fronts. The set highlights players or teams who overcame formidable obstacles to become winners. After perforation, the cards measure the standard size. The front design is similar to the 1991 regular issue, with full-bleed player photos and player (or team) identification in colored stripes traversing the bottom of the card. All the cards feature color photos, with the exception of card numbers 4-6. The back has an extended caption for the card on the left portion, and a different photo on the right portion.

COMPLETE SET (9)	25.00	50.00
1 Rocky Bleier	3.00	6.00
2 Tom Dempsey	1.50	3.00
3 Dan Hampton	2.00	4.00
4 Charlie Hennigan	1.50	3.00
5 Dante Lavelli	2.00	4.00
6 Jim Plunkett	2.00	4.00
7 1968 New York Jets (Joe Namath handing off)	4.00	10.00
8 1981 San Francisco/49ers (Joe Montana passing)	10.00	20.00
9 1979 Tampa Bay Bucs (Ricky Bell running)	1.50	3.00

1991 Pro Set National Banquet

This five-card standard-size set was given away by Pro Set, one of the sponsors of the 1991 12th National Sports Collectors Convention in Anaheim, California. The cards have full-bleed color photos on the fronts. The horizontally oriented backs have other color photos and career summaries. The back of the ProFiles card has a picture of TV announcers Tim Brant and Craig James.

COMPLETE SET (5)	2.00	5.00
1 Ronnie Lott	.50	1.25
2 Roy Firestone	.40	1.00
3 Roger Craig	.50	1.25
4 ProFiles	.40	1.00
Television show (Craig James and Tim Brant)		
5 Title card	.40	1.00

1991 Pro Set Pro Files

These cards measure the standard size. The fronts have full-bleed color photos, with facsimile autographs inscribed across the bottom of the pictures. Reportedly only 150 of each were produced and approximately 100 of each were handed out as part of a contest on the Pro Files TV show. Each week viewers were invited to send in their names and addresses to a Pro Set post office box. All subjects in the set made appearances on the TV show. The show was hosted by Craig James and Tim Brant and was aired on Saturday nights in Dallas and sponsored by Pro Set. The cards were subtitled "Signature Series". The cards are unnumbered and are listed in alphabetical order by subject in the checklist below. All of the cards were facsimile autographed except for Anne Smith who signed all of her cards personally.

COMPLETE SET (13)	120.00	300.00
1 Troy Aikman FB	75.00	150.00

1991 Pro Set Super Bowl Tickets

This set was produced by Pro Set and distributed by Commemorative Sports Fragrances in factory set form. Each card features a replica Super Bowl ticket on the front and game stats on the back.

COMP.FACT SET (25)	20.00	50.00
COMMON CARD (1-25)	1.00	2.50

1991 Pro Set Spanish

The 1991 Pro Set Spanish football card set contains 300 standard-size cards selected from 1991 Pro Set Series I and II along with five special collectibles cards. Though the cards display the same player photos, the terminology has been translated into Spanish. The cards are numbered on the back and checklisted alphabetically according to teams.

COMPLETE SET (305)	25.00	50.00
1 Steve Broussard	.05	.15
2 Darion Conner	.05	.15
3 Tory Epps	.05	.15
4 Bill Fralic	.05	.15
5 Mike Gann	.05	.15
6 Chris Miller	.08	.25
7 Andre Rison	.20	.50
8 Deion Sanders	.50	1.25
9 Jessie Tuggle	.05	.15
10 Cornelius Bennett	.08	.25
11 Shane Conlan	.05	.15
12 Kent Hull	.05	.15
13 Kirby Jackson	.05	.15
14 James Lofton	.08	.25
15 Andre Reed	.08	.25
16 Bruce Smith	.20	.50
17 Darryl Talley	.05	.15
18 Thurman Thomas	.20	.50
19 Neal Anderson	.08	.25
20 Trace Armstrong	.05	.15
21 Mark Carrier DB	.08	.25
22 Wendell Davis	.05	.15
23 Richard Dent	.05	.15
24 Jim Harbaugh	.20	.50
25 Ron Rivera	.05	.15
26 Mike Singletary	.08	.25
27 Lemuel Stinson	.05	.15
28 James Brooks	.05	.15
29 Eddie Brown	.05	.15
30 Boomer Esiason	.08	.25
31 James Francis	.05	.15
32 David Fulcher	.05	.15
33 Rodney Holman	.05	.15
34 Anthony Munoz	.08	.25
35 Bruce Reimers	.05	.15
36 Ickey Woods	.05	.15
37 Mike Baab	.05	.15
38 Brian Brennan	.05	.15
39 Raymond Clayborn	.05	.15
40 Mike Johnson	.05	.15
41 Clay Matthews	.08	.25
42 Eric Metcalf	.20	.50
43 Frank Minnifield	.05	.15
44 Joe Morris	.05	.15
45 Anthony Pleasant	.05	.15
46 Troy Aikman	1.00	2.50
47 Jack Del Rio	.08	.25
48 Issiac Holt	.05	.15
49 Michael Irvin	.20	.50
50 Jimmie Jones	.05	.15
51 Nate Newton	.08	.25
52 Danny Noonan	.05	.15
53 Jay Novacek	.20	.50
54 Emmitt Smith	2.50	6.00
55 Steve Atwater	.05	.15
56 Michael Brooks	.05	.15
57 John Elway	3.00	6.00
58 Mike Horan	.05	.15
59 Mark Jackson	.05	.15
60 Karl Mecklenburg	.05	.15
61 Warren Powers	.05	.15
62 Dennis Smith	.05	.15
63 Doug Widell	.05	.15
64 Jerry Ball	.05	.15
65 Bennie Blades	.05	.15
66 Robert Clark	.05	.15
67 Ken Dallafior	.05	.15
68 Mel Gray	.08	.25
69 Eddie Murray	.05	.15
70 Rodney Peete	.08	.25
71 Barry Sanders	2.00	5.00
72 Chris Spielman	.08	.25
73 Robert Brown	.05	.15
74 LeRoy Butler	.08	.25
75 Perry Kemp	.05	.15
76 Don Majkowski	.05	.15
77 Tony Mandarich	.05	.15
78 Mark Murphy	.05	.15
79 Brian Noble	.05	.15
80 Sterling Sharpe	.20	.50
81 Ed West	.05	.15
82 Ray Childress	.08	.25
83 Cris Dishman	.05	.15
84 Ernest Givins	.08	.25
85 Drew Hill	.08	.25
86 Haywood Jeffires	.08	.25
87 Lamar Lathon	.05	.15
88 Bruce Matthews	.08	.25
89 Bubba McDowell	.05	.15
90 Warren Moon	.08	.25
91 Chip Banks	.05	.15
92 Albert Bentley	.05	.15
93 Duane Bickett	.05	.15
94 Bill Brooks	.05	.15
95 Sam Clancy	.05	.15
96 Ray Donaldson	.05	.15
97 Jeff George	.20	.50
98 Mike Prior	.05	.15
99 Clarence Verdin	.05	.15
100 Steve DeBerg	.08	.25
101 Albert Lewis	.05	.15
102 Christian Okoye	.05	.15
103 Kevin Ross	.05	.15
104 Stephone Paige	.05	.15
105 Kevin Porter	.05	.15
106 Percy Snow	.05	.15
107 Derrick Thomas	.20	.50
108 Barry Word	.05	.15
109 Marcus Allen	.20	.50
110 Mervyn Fernandez	.05	.15
111 Howie Long	.20	.50
112 Ronnie Lott	.08	.25
113 Terry McDaniel	.08	.25
114 Max Montoya	.05	.15
115 Don Mosebar	.05	.15
116 Jay Schroeder	.05	.15
117 Greg Townsend	.05	.15
118 Flipper Anderson	.05	.15
119 Henry Ellard	.08	.25
120 Jim Everett	.08	.25
121 Kevin Greene	.08	.25
122 Damone Johnson	.05	.15
123 Buford McGee	.05	.15
124 Tom Newberry	.05	.15
125 Michael Stewart	.05	.15
126 Alvin Wright	.05	.15
127 Mark Clayton	.08	.25
128 Jeff Cross	.05	.15
129 Mark Duper	.08	.25
130 Ferrell Edmunds	.05	.15
131 Dan Marino	3.00	6.00
132 Tim McKyer	.05	.15
133 John Offerdahl	.05	.15
134 Louis Oliver	.05	.15
135 Sammie Smith	.05	.15
136 Joey Browner	.05	.15
137 Anthony Carter	.08	.25
138 Chris Doleman	.08	.25
139 Hassan Jones	.05	.15
140 Steve Jordan	.05	.15
141 Carl Lee	.05	.15
142 Al Noga	.05	.15
143 Henry Thomas	.08	.25
144 Herschel Walker	.08	.25
145 Ray Agnew	.05	.15
146 Bruce Armstrong	.05	.15
147 Marv Cook	.05	.15
148 Irving Fryar	.08	.25
149 Tommy Hodson	.05	.15
150 Fred Marion	.05	.15
151 Johnny Rembert	.05	.15
152 Chris Singleton	.05	.15
153 Andre Tippett	.05	.15
154 Morten Andersen	.05	.15
155 Toi Cook	.05	.15
156 Craig Heyward	.08	.25
157 Dalton Hilliard	.05	.15
158 Rickey Jackson	.08	.25
159 Vaughan Johnson	.05	.15
160 Rueben Mayes	.05	.15
161 Pat Swilling	.08	.25
162 Bobby Hebert	.08	.25
163 Ottis Anderson	.08	.25
164 Carl Banks	.05	.15
165 Rodney Hampton	.20	.50
166 Jeff Hostetler	.08	.25
167 Mark Ingram	.05	.15
168 Leonard Marshall	.05	.15
169 Dave Meggett	.08	.25
170 Lawrence Taylor	.20	.50
171 Everson Walls	.05	.15
172 Brad Baxter	.05	.15
173 Jeff Lageman	.05	.15
174 Pat Leahy	.05	.15
175 Erik McMillan	.05	.15
176 Scott Mersereau	.05	.15
177 Rob Moore	.08	.25
178 Ken O'Brien	.05	.15
179 Blair Thomas	.05	.15
180 Al Toon	.05	.15
181 Eric Allen	.05	.15
182 Jerome Brown	.08	.25
183 Keith Byars	.08	.25
184 Randall Cunningham	.20	.50
185 Byron Evans	.05	.15
186 Keith Jackson	.08	.25
187 Heath Sherman	.05	.15
188 Clyde Simmons	.08	.25
189 Reggie White	.20	.50
190 Rich Camarillo	.05	.15
191 Johnny Johnson	.05	.15
192 Ernie Jones	.05	.15
193 Tim McDonald	.05	.15
194 Freddie Joe Nunn	.05	.15
195 Luis Sharpe	.05	.15
196 Jay Taylor	.05	.15
197 Anthony Thompson	.05	.15
198 Tom Tupa	.05	.15
199 Gary Anderson K	.05	.15
200 Bubby Brister	.08	.25
201 Eric Green	.08	.25
202 Bryan Hinkle	.05	.15
203 Merril Hoge	.05	.15
204 Carnell Lake	.08	.25
205 Louis Lipps	.05	.15
206 Keith Willis	.05	.15
207 Rod Woodson	.20	.50
208 Rod Bernstine	.05	.15
209 Marion Butts	.05	.15
210 Anthony Miller	.08	.25
211 Leslie O'Neal	.08	.25
212 Henry Rolling	.05	.15
213 Junior Seau	.20	.50
214 Billy Ray Smith	.05	.15
215 Broderick Thompson	.05	.15
216 Derrick Walker	.05	.15
217 Dexter Carter	.05	.15
218 Don Griffin	.05	.15
219 Charles Haley	.08	.25
220 Pierce Holt	.05	.15
221 Joe Montana	4.00	8.00
222 Jerry Rice	1.00	2.50
223 John Taylor	.08	.25
224 Michael Walter	.05	.15
225 Steve Young	.80	2.00
226 Brian Blades	.08	.25
227 Jeff Bryant	.05	.15
228 Jacob Green	.05	.15
229 Tommy Kane	.05	.15
230 Dave Krieg	.08	.25
231 Bryan Millard	.05	.15
232 Rufus Porter	.05	.15
233 Eugene Robinson	.05	.15
234 John L. Williams	.05	.15
235 Gary Anderson RB	.05	.15
236 Mark Carrier WR	.08	.25
237 Reggie Cobb	.05	.15
238 Reuben Davis	.05	.15
239 Paul Gruber	.05	.15
240 Harry Hamilton	.05	.15
241 Keith McCants	.05	.15
242 Ricky Reynolds	.05	.15
243 Vinny Testaverde	.08	.25
244 Earnest Byner	.06	.15
245 Gary Clark	.08	.25
246 Andre Collins	.06	.15
247 Darrell Green	.08	.25
248 Jim Lachey	.05	.15
249 Charles Mann	.05	.15
250 Wilber Marshall	.05	.15
251 Art Monk	.08	.25
252 Mark Rypien	.08	.25
253 Russell Maryland	.05	.15
254 Mike Croel	.05	.15
255 Stanley Richard	.08	.25
256 Leonard Russell	.20	.50
257 Dan McGwire	.05	.15
258 Todd Marinovich	.05	.15
259 Eric Swann	.20	.50
260 Mike Pritchard	.20	.50
261 Alfred Williams	.05	.15
262 Brett Favre	6.00	15.00
263 Browning Nagle	.05	.15
264 Darryll Lewis	.08	.25
265 Nick Bell	.05	.15
266 Jeff Graham	.20	.50
267 Eric Moten	.05	.15
268 Roman Phifer	.05	.15
269 Eric Bieniemy	.08	.25
270 Phil Hansen	.05	.15
271 Reggie Barrett	.05	.15
272 Aeneas Williams	.08	.25
273 Aaron Craver	.05	.15
274 Lawrence Dawsey	.08	.25
275 Ricky Ervins	.05	.15
276 Jake Reed	.20	.50
277 Erik Williams	.08	.25
278 Tim Barnett	.05	.15
279 Keith Traylor	.05	.15
280 Jerry Rice PB UER (Back color is AFC red, instead of NFC blue)	.50	1.25
281 Jim Lachey	.05	.15
282 Barry Sanders PB	1.00	2.50
283 Neal Anderson	.08	.25
284 Reggie White	.20	.50
285 Lawrence Taylor	.20	.50
286 Mike Singletary	.08	.25
287 Joey Browner	.05	.15
288 Morten Andersen SS	.05	.15
289 Andre Reed SS	.08	.25
290 Anthony Munoz SS	.08	.25
291 Warren Moon SS	.20	.50
292 Thurman Thomas SS	.20	.50
293 Ray Childress SS	.05	.15
294 Derrick Thomas SS	.20	.50
295 Rod Woodson SS	.20	.50
296 Steve Atwater SS	.05	.15
297 David Fulcher SS	.05	.15
298 Anthony Munoz Think	.08	.25
299 Ron Rivera Think	.05	.15
300 Cornelius Bennett Think	.08	.25
E1 Tom Flores	.40	1.00
E2 Anthony Munoz	.40	1.00
E3 Tony Casillas	.40	1.00
E4 Super Bowl XXVI Logo Minneapolis	.40	1.00
E5 Felicidades	.40	1.00

1991 Pro Set UK Sheets

This set of five (approximately) 5 1/8" by 11 3/4" six-card strips was issued by Pro Set in England as an advertisement in Today, a newspaper in Middlesex, England. The unperforated strips are numbered 1-5, and each presents a "collection" of six player cards that measure the standard size. The sheets were issued one per week in consecutive Sunday editions of the paper during the Fall of 1991. The cards and their numbering are identical to the 1991 regular issues. They are checklisted below by strips, and within strips listed beginning from the top left card and moving to the bottom right card.

COMPLETE SET (5)	25.00	60.00
1 200 Jim Everett/167 Warren Moon	8.00	20.00
111 Boomer Esiason/128 Troy Aikman		
726 Dan Marino/138 John Elway		
2 Running Backs/576 Herschel Walker	6.00	15.00
86 Thurman Thomas/213 Sammie Smith		
722 Earnest Byner/123 Eric Metcalf/485 Emmitt Smith		
3 209 Mark Duper/654 Jerry Rice	4.00	10.00
251 Al Toon/161 Sterling Sharpe		
618 Keith Jackson/115 Tim McGee		
4 460 Jim Breech/447 Scott Norwood	2.00	5.00
489 Mike Horan/300 Norm Johnson/		
184 Nick Lowery/401 Sean Landeta		
5 728 Mike Singletary/56 Carl Banks	4.00	10.00
98 Deion Sanders/191 Howie Long		
131 Issiac Holt/241 Pat Swilling		

1991 Pro Set WLAF 150

The premier edition of the 1991 Pro Set World League of American Football set contains 150 standard-size cards. The first 29 cards of the set are subdivided as follows: League Overview (1-3), World Bowl (4-9), Helmet Collectibles (10-19), and 1991 Statistical Leaders (20-29). The player cards are numbered 30-150, and they are checklisted below alphabetically within and according to teams.

COMPLETE SET (150)	1.60	4.00
1 World League Logo	.01	.05
2 Mike Lynn PRES	.01	.05
3 First Weekend	.01	.05
4 World Bowl Trophy	.01	.05
5 Jon Horton	.01	.05
6 Stan Gelbaugh	.07	.20
7 Dan Crossman	.01	.05
8 Marlon Brown	.01	.05
9 Judd Garrett	.02	.10
10 Barcelona Dragons Helmet	.02	.10
11 Birmingham Fire Helmet	.02	.10
12 Frankfurt Galaxy Helmet	.02	.10
13 London Monarchs Helmet	.02	.10
14 Montreal Machine Helmet	.02	.10
15 NY-NJ Knights Helmet	.02	.10
16 Orlando Thunder Helmet	.02	.10
17 Raleigh-Durham Skyhawks Helmet	.02	.10
18 Sacramento Surge Helmet	.02	.10
19 San Antonio Riders Helmet	.02	.10
20 Eric Wilkerson SL	.01	.05
21 Stan Gelbaugh SL	.07	.20
22 Judd Garrett SL	.01	.05
23 Tony Baker SL	.07	.20
24 Byron Williams SL	.01	.05
25 Chris Mohr SL	.01	.05
26 Errol Tucker SL	.01	.05
27 Carl Painter SL	.01	.05
28 Anthony Parker SL	.02	.10
29 Danny Lockett SL	.01	.05
30 Scott Adams	.01	.05
31 Jim Bell	.01	.05
32 Lydell Carr	.02	.10
33 Bruce Clark	.01	.05
34 Demetrius Davis	.02	.10
35 Scott Erney	.01	.05
36 Ron Goetz	.01	.05
37 Xisco Marcos	.01	.05
38 Paul Palmer	.01	.05
39 Tony Rice	.07	.20
40 Bobby Sign	.01	.05
41 Gene Taylor	.01	.05
42 Barry Voorhees	.01	.05
43 Jack Bicknell CO	.01	.05
44 Ken Bell	.01	.05
45 Willie Bouyer	.01	.05
46 John Brantley	.01	.05
47 Elroy Harris	.01	.05
48 James Henry	.01	.05
49 John Holland	.01	.05
50 Arthur Hunter	.01	.05
51 Eric Jones	.01	.05
52 Kirk Maggio	.01	.05
53 Paul McGowan	.01	.05
54 John Miller	.01	.05
55 Maurice Oliver	.01	.05
56 Darrell Phillips	.01	.05
57 Chan Gailey CO	.20	.50
58 Tony Baker	.07	.20
59 Tim Broady	.01	.05
60 Garry Frank	.01	.05
61 Jason Johnson	.01	.05
62 Stefan Maslo	.01	.05
63 Mark Mraz	.01	.05
64 Yepi Pau'u	.01	.05
65 Mike Perez	.01	.05
66 Mike Teeter	.01	.05
67 Chris Williams	.01	.05
68 Jack Elway CO	.02	.10
69 Theo Adams	.01	.05
70 Jeff Alexander	.01	.05
71 Phil Alexander	.01	.05
72 Paul Berardelli	.01	.05
73 Dana Brinson	.01	.05
74 Marlon Brown	.01	.05
75 Dedrick Dodge	.01	.05
76 Victor Ebubedike	.01	.05
77 Corris Ervin	.01	.05
78 Steve Gabbard	.01	.05
79 Judd Garrett	.02	.10
80 Stan Gelbaugh	.07	.20
81 Roy Hart	.01	.05
82 Jon Horton	.01	.05
83 Danny Lockett	.01	.05
84 Doug Marrone	.40	1.00
85 Ken Sale	.01	.05
86 Larry Kennan CO	.01	.05
87 Mike Cadore	.01	.05
88 K.D. Dunn	.02	.05
89 Ricky Johnson	.01	.05
90 Chris Mohr	.02	.10
91 Bjorn Nittmo	.01	.05
92 Michael Proctor	.01	.05
93 Richard Shelton	.01	.05
94 Tracy Simien	.07	.20
95 Jacques Dussault CO	.01	.05
96 Cornell Burbage	.01	.05
97 Joe Campbell	.01	.05
98 Monty Gilbreath	.01	.05
99 Jeff Graham	.20	.50
100 Kip Lewis	.01	.05
101 Bobby Lilljedahl	.01	.05
102 Falanda Newton	.01	.05
103 Anthony Parker	.07	.20
104 Caesar Rentie	.01	.05
105 Ron Sancho	.01	.05
106 Craig Schlicting	.01	.05
107 Lonnie Turner	.01	.05
108 Eric Wilkerson	.01	.05
109 Tony Woods	.02	.10
110 Darrell(Mouse) Davis CO	.02	.10
111 Kerwin Bell	.07	.20
112 Wayne Davis	.01	.05
113 John Guerrero	.01	.05
114 Myron Jones	.01	.05
115 Eric Mitchel	.01	.05
116 Billy Owens	.01	.05
117 Carl Painter	.01	.05
118 Rob Sterling	.01	.05
119 Errol Tucker	.01	.05
120 Byron Williams	.01	.05
121 Mike Withycombe	.01	.05
122 Don Matthews CO	.01	.05
123 Jon Carter	.01	.05
124 Marvin Hargrove	.01	.05
125 Clarkston Hines	.01	.05
126 Ray Jackson	.01	.05
127 Bobby McAllister	.01	.05
128 Darryl McGill	.01	.05
129 Pat McGuirk	.01	.05
130 Shawn Woodson	.01	.05
131 Roman Gabriel CO	.07	.20
132 Greg Coauette	.01	.05
133 Mike Elkins	.01	.05
134 Victor Floyd	.01	.05
135 Shawn Knight	.01	.05
136 Pete Najarian	.01	.05
137 Carl Parker	.01	.05
138 Richard Stephens	.01	.05
139 Curtis Wilson	.01	.05
140 Kay Stephenson CO	.01	.05
141 Ricky Blake	.02	.10
142 Donnie Gardner	.01	.05
143 Jason Garrett	1.25	3.00
144 Mike Johnson	.01	.05
145 Undra Johnson	.01	.05
146 John Layfield	.60	1.50
147 Mark Ledbetter	.01	.05
148 Gary Richard	.01	.05
149 Tim Walton	.01	.05
150 Mike Riley CO	.01	.05

1991 Pro Set WLAF World Bowl Combo

With a few subtle changes, this 43-card standard-size set is a reissue of the 1991 Pro Set WLAF Helmet and 1991 Pro Set WLAF sets. The first 32-cards are identical to the 1991 Pro Set WLAF Inserts set, except for card #28, so those have not been listed below. However, the helmet cards have been re-numbered and can also be distinguished on the back by the presence of a team narrative instead of a team schedule so those are priced below. Finally a newly created World Bowl Trophy card was added to round out the 43-card set. The set was passed out to attendees of the World Bowl Game in Wembley Stadium, London, England.

COMPLETE SET (43)	6.00	12.00
33 World Bowl Trophy	.40	1.00
34 Barcelona Dragons Helmet	.40	1.00
35 Birmingham Fire Helmet	.40	1.00
36 Frankfurt Galaxy Helmet	.40	1.00
37 London Monarchs Helmet	.40	1.00
38 Montreal Machine Helmet	.40	1.00
39 NY-NJ Knights Helmet	.40	1.00
40 Orlando Thunder Helmet	.40	1.00
41 Ral.-Durham Skyhawks Helmet	.40	1.00
42 Sacramento Surge Helmet	.40	1.00
43 San Antonio Riders Helmet	.40	1.00

1991-92 Pro Set Super Bowl XXVI Binder

This 49-card standard-size set was sponsored by American Express and produced by Pro Set to commemorate Super Bowl XXVI. The set was sold in a white binder that housed four cards per page. It includes five new cards (1-5), four Think About It cards (300, 370, 725-726), as well as player cards for the Buffalo Bills (73-77, 79-84, 86, 88-90, 444-445, 449-450) and Washington Redskins (316-318, 320-324, 676-684, 746, 805, 848). The player cards are the same as the regular issue (including numbering), except that the Bills' cards have a "1991 AFC Champs" logo on the front, while the Redskins' cards carry a "1991 NFC Champs" logo on their fronts. A Jim Kelly card was apparently produced separately (individually cellophane wrapped and unnumbered) and was only available at the Super Bowl with the seat-cushion sets. Kelly was not included in sets sent out as as part of the mail-away offer advertised after the Super Bowl. The Kelly card does not include the Pro Set logo on the back.

COMPLETE SET (49)	8.00	20.00
1 The NFL Experience	.20	.50
2 Super Bowl XXVI	.07	.20
3 AFC Standings	.07	.20
4 NFC Standings	.07	.20
5 The Metrodome	.07	.20
73 Howard Ballard	.07	.20
74 Cornelius Bennett	.20	.50
75 Shane Conlan	.07	.20
76 Kent Hull	.07	.20
77 Kirby Jackson	.07	.20
79 Mark Kelso	.07	.20
80 Nate Odomes	.10	.30
81 Andre Reed	.20	.50
82 Jim Ritcher	.07	.20
83 Bruce Smith	.20	.50
84 Darryl Talley	.07	.20
86 Thurman Thomas	.30	.75
88 Will Wolford	.07	.20
89 Jeff Wright	.07	.20
90 Marv Levy CO	.07	.20
300 Cornelius Bennett Piensalo	.10	.30
316 Earnest Byner	.10	.30
317 Gary Clark	.20	.50
318 Andre Collins	.10	.30
320 Chip Lohmiller	.07	.20
321 Martin Mayhew	.07	.20
322 Mark Rypien	.10	.30
323 Alvin Walton	.07	.20
324 Joe Gibbs CO	.20	.50
370 Warren Moon Think About It	.15	.40
444 James Lofton	.20	.50
445 Keith McKeller	.07	.20
449 Leon Seals	.07	.20
450 Leonard Smith	.07	.20
676 Jeff Bostic	.07	.20
677 Darrell Green	.10	.30
678 Markus Koch	.07	.20
679 Jim Lachey	.10	.30
680 Charles Mann	.10	.30
681 Wilber Marshall	.10	.30
682 Art Monk	.15	.40
683 Gerald Riggs	.07	.20
684 Ricky Sanders	.10	.30
725 Howie Long Think About It	.20	.50
726 Dan Marino Think About It	.80	2.00
746 Bobby Wilson	.07	.20
805 Ricky Ervins	.10	.30
848 Brian Mitchell	.20	.50
NNO Jim Kelly SP	6.00	15.00

1992 Pro Set

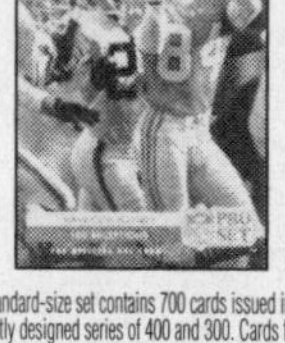

This standard-size set contains 700 cards issued in two differently designed series of 400 and 300. Cards for either series were issued in 15-card packs. First series fronts feature full-bleed color player photos with the player's name in a stripe at the bottom. The NFL Pro Set logo in the lower right corner. In a horizontal format, the backs have a close-up color player photo, biography, career highlights and complete statistical information. Second series cards are full-bleed on the right side with the players name running up the left border. A team logo is at the bottom left. Vertical backs have stats from the last three years, highlights and a small photo. Gray backgrounds contain all NFL team logos in white. The set opens with the following subsets: League Leaders (1-18), Milestones (19-27), Draft Day (28-33), Innovators (34-36), 1991 Replays (37-63), and Super Bowl XXVI Replays (64-72). Other than Washington and Buffalo leading off the first series, player cards are in team order by series. A number of subsets include Pro Set Newsreel (343-346), Magic Numbers (347-351), Play Smart (352-360), NFC Spirit of the Game (361-374), AFC Pro Bowl Stars (375-400), NFC Pro Bowl (401-427), Spirit of the Game (680-693) cards and some miscellaneous special cards (694-700). The key Rookie Cards in the set are Edgar Bennett, Steve Bono, Quentin Coryatt, Amp Lee and Carl Pickens. Randomly inserted in packs and listed at the end of the checklist below were Emmitt Smith and Erik Kramer autograph cards. Each player signed 1,000 cards that are individually numbered. Also inserted were a Smith Power Preview card, a Santa Claus card and Super Bowl XXVI logo card.

COMPLETE SET (700)	8.00	20.00
COMP.SERIES 1 (400)	4.00	10.00
COMP.SERIES 2 (300)	4.00	10.00
1 Mike Croel LL	.01	.05
2 Thurman Thomas LL Player of the Year	.08	.25
3 Wayne Fontes CO LL	.01	.05
4 Anthony Munoz LL Man of the Year	.02	.10
5 Steve Young LL Passing Leader	.10	.30
6 Warren Moon LL Passing Yardage Leader	.02	.10
7 Emmitt Smith LL Rushing Leader	.25	.60
8 Haywood Jeffires LL	.01	.05
9 Marv Cook LL	.01	.05
10 Michael Irvin LL Receiving Yardage Leader	.08	.25
11 Thurman Thomas LL UER Total Yardage Leader (Total combined yards should be 2,038)	.08	.25
12 Chip Lohmiller LL UER	.01	.05
13 Barry Sanders LL	.20	.50
14 Reggie Roby LL	.01	.05
15 Mel Gray LL	.01	.05
16 Ronnie Lott LL Interception Leader	.02	.10
17 Pat Swilling LL	.01	.05
18 Reggie White LL Defensive MVP	.02	.10
19 Haywood Jeffires ML	.01	.05
20 Pat Leahy MILE	.01	.05
21 James Lofton MILE/13,000 Yards	.02	.10
22 Art Monk MILE/800 Receptions	.02	.10
23 Don Shula MILE/300 Wins	.02	.10
24A Nick Lowery MILE ERR	.01	.05
24B Nick Lowery MILE COR	.01	.05
25 John Elway MILE 2,000 Completed Passes	.20	.50
26 Chicago Bears MILE	.01	.05
27 Marcus Allen MILE/ 2,000 Rushing Attempts	.02	.10
28 Terrell Buckley RC	.01	.05
29 Amp Lee RC	.01	.05
30 Chris Mims RC	.01	.05
31 Leon Searcy RC	.01	.05
32 Jimmy Smith RC	1.25	3.00
33 Siran Stacy RC	.01	.05
34 Pete Gogolak INN	.01	.05
35 Cheerleaders INN	.01	.05
36 Houston Astrodome INN	.01	.05
37 Week 1 REPLAY	.01	.05
38 Week 2 REPLAY	.01	.05
39 Week 3 REPLAY	.01	.05
40 Week 4 REPLAY	.01	.05
41 Week 5 REPLAY	.01	.05
42 Week 6 REPLAY	.01	.05
43 Week 7 REPLAY Bills 42, Colts 6 (Thurman Thomas)	.02	.10
44 Week 8 REPLAY	.01	.05
45 Week 9 REPLAY UER	.01	.05
46 Week 10 REPLAY	.01	.05
47 Week 11 REPLAY	.01	.05
48 Week 12 REPLAY	.01	.05
49 Week 13 REPLAY Cowboys 24 Redskins 21 (Steve Beuerlein and Michael Irvin)	.02	.10
50 Week 14 REPLAY	.01	.05
51 Week 15 REPLAY	.01	.05
52 Week 16 REPLAY	.01	.05
53 Week 17 REPLAY	.01	.05
54 AFC Wild Card REPLAY	.01	.05
55 AFC Wild Card REPLAY	.01	.05
56 NFC Wild Card REPLAY	.01	.05
57 NFC Wild Card REPLAY	.01	.05
58 AFC Divis. Playoff REPLAY	.01	.05
59 AFC Playoff REPLAY Bills 37 Chiefs 14 (Thurman Thomas)	.02	.10
60 Erik Kramer REP	.01	.05
61 NFC Divis. Playoff REPLAY	.01	.05
62 AFC Championship REPLAY	.01	.05
63 NFC Championship REPLAY	.01	.05
64 Super Bowl XXVI REPLAY	.01	.05
65 Super Bowl XXVI REPLAY	.01	.05
66 Super Bowl XXVI REPLAY	.01	.05
67 Super Bowl XXVI REPLAY	.01	.05
68 Super Bowl XXVI REPLAY	.01	.05
69 Super Bowl XXVI REPLAY Thomas Scores Bills' First TD	.02	.10
70 Super Bowl XXVI REPLAY	.01	.05
71 Super Bowl XXVI REPLAY	.01	.05
72 Super Bowl XXVI REPLAY	.01	.05
73 Jeff Bostic	.01	.05
74 Earnest Byner	.01	.05
75 Gary Clark	.08	.25
76 Andre Collins	.01	.05
77 Darrell Green	.01	.05
78 Joe Jacoby	.01	.05
79 Jim Lachey	.01	.05
80 Chip Lohmiller	.01	.05
81 Charles Mann	.01	.05
82 Martin Mayhew	.01	.05
83 Matt Millen	.02	.10
84 Brian Mitchell	.02	.10
85 Art Monk	.02	.10
86 Gerald Riggs	.01	.05
87 Mark Rypien	.01	.05
88 Fred Stokes	.01	.05
89 Bobby Wilson	.01	.05
90 Joe Gibbs CO	.02	.10
91 Howard Ballard	.01	.05
92 Cornelius Bennett UER (Interception total reads 0; he had 4)	.02	.10
93 Kenneth Davis	.01	.05
94 Al Edwards	.01	.05
95 Kent Hull	.01	.05
96 Kirby Jackson	.01	.05
97 Mark Kelso	.01	.05
98 James Lofton UER (Says he played in '75 Pro Bowl, but he wasn't in NFL until 1978)	.02	.10
99 Keith McKeller	.01	.05
100 Nate Odomes	.01	.05
101 Jim Ritcher	.01	.05
102 Leon Seals	.01	.05
103 Steve Tasker	.02	.10
104 Darryl Talley	.01	.05
105 Thurman Thomas	.08	.25
106 Will Wolford	.01	.05
107 Jeff Wright	.01	.05
108 Marv Levy CO	.01	.05
109 Darion Conner	.01	.05
110 Bill Fralic	.01	.05
111 Moe Gardner	.01	.05
112 Michael Haynes	.02	.10
113 Chris Miller	.02	.10
114 Erric Pegram	.02	.10
115 Bruce Pickens	.01	.05
116 Andre Rison	.02	.10
117 Jerry Glanville CO	.01	.05
118 Neal Anderson	.01	.05
119 Trace Armstrong	.01	.05
120 Wendell Davis	.01	.05
121 Richard Dent	.02	.10
122 Jay Hilgenberg	.01	.05
123 Lemuel Stinson	.01	.05
124 Stan Thomas	.01	.05
125 Tom Waddle	.01	.05
126 Mike Ditka CO	.08	.25
127 James Brooks	.02	.10
128 Eddie Brown	.01	.05
129 David Fulcher	.01	.05
130 Harold Green	.01	.05
131 Tim Krumrie UER	.01	.05
132 Anthony Munoz	.02	.10
133 Craig Taylor	.01	.05
134 Eric Thomas	.01	.05
135 David Shula CO RC	.01	.05
136 Mike Baab	.01	.05
137 Brian Brennan	.01	.05
138 Michael Jackson	.02	.10
139 James Jones DT UER (DL on front; DT on back)	.01	.05
140 Ed King	.01	.05
141 Clay Matthews	.02	.10
142 Eric Metcalf	.02	.10
143 Joe Morris	.01	.05
144A Bill Belichick CO ERR (No HC next to name on back)	.08	.25

144B Bill Belichick CO COR	.08	.25
(HC next to name on back)		
145 Steve Beuerlein	.02	.10
146 Larry Brown DB	.01	.05
147 Ray Horton	.01	.05
148 Ken Norton	.02	.10
149 Mike Saxon	.01	.05
150 Emmitt Smith	.60	1.50
151 Mark Stepnoski	.02	.10
152 Alexander Wright	.01	.05
153 Jimmy Johnson CO	.02	.10
154 Mike Croel	.01	.05
155 John Elway	.50	1.25
156 Gaston Green	.01	.05
157 Wymon Henderson	.01	.05
158 Karl Mecklenburg UER	.01	.05
159 Warren Powers	.01	.05
160 Steve Sewell UER	.01	.05
161 Doug Widell	.01	.05
162 Dan Reeves CO	.01	.05
163 Eric Andolsek	.01	.05
164 Jerry Ball	.01	.05
165 Bennie Blades	.01	.05
166 Ray Crockett	.01	.05
167 Willie Green	.01	.05
168 Erik Kramer	.02	.10
169 Barry Sanders	.50	1.25
170 Chris Spielman UER	.01	.05
171 Wayne Fontes CO	.01	.05
172 Vinnie Clark	.01	.05
173 Tony Mandarich	.01	.05
174 Brian Noble	.01	.05
175 Bryce Paup	.08	.25
176 Sterling Sharpe	.08	.25
177 Darrell Thompson	.01	.05
178 Esera Tuaolo UER	.01	.05
179 Ed West	.01	.05
180 Mike Holmgren CO RC	.08	.25
181 Ray Childress	.01	.05
182 Cris Dishman	.01	.05
183 Curtis Duncan	.01	.05
184 William Fuller	.01	.05
185 Lamar Lathon	.01	.05
186 Warren Moon	.08	.25
187 Bo Orlando RC	.01	.05
188 Lorenzo White	.01	.05
189 Jack Pardee CO	.01	.05
190 Chip Banks	.01	.05
191 Dean Biasucci UER	.01	.05
192 Bill Brooks	.01	.05
193 Ray Donaldson	.01	.05
194 Jeff Herrod	.01	.05
195 Mike Prior	.01	.05
196 Mark Vander Poel	.01	.05
197 Clarence Verdin	.01	.05
198 Ted Marchibroda CO	.01	.05
199 John Alt	.01	.05
200 Deron Cherry	.01	.05
201 Steve DeBerg	.01	.05
202 Nick Lowery	.01	.05
203 Neil Smith	.08	.25
204 Derrick Thomas	.08	.25
205 Joe Valerio	.01	.05
206 Barry Word	.01	.05
207 M. Schottenheimer CO	.01	.05
208 Marcus Allen	.08	.25
209 Nick Bell	.01	.05
210 Tim Brown	.08	.25
211 Howie Long	.08	.25
212 Ronnie Lott	.02	.10
213 Todd Marinovich	.01	.05
214 Greg Townsend	.01	.05
215 Steve Wright	.01	.05
216 Art Shell CO	.02	.10
217 Flipper Anderson	.01	.05
218 Robert Delpino	.01	.05
219 Henry Ellard	.02	.10
220 Kevin Greene	.02	.10
221 Todd Lyght	.01	.05
222 Tom Newberry	.01	.05
223 Roman Phifer	.01	.05
224 Michael Stewart	.01	.05
225 Chuck Knox CO	.01	.05
226 Aaron Craver	.01	.05
227 Jeff Cross	.01	.05
228 Mark Duper	.01	.05
229 Ferrell Edmunds	.01	.05
230 Jim C. Jensen	.01	.05
231 Louis Oliver UER	.01	.05
232 Reggie Roby	.01	.05
233 Sammie Smith	.01	.05
234 Don Shula CO	.02	.10
235 Joey Browner	.01	.05
236 Anthony Carter	.02	.10
237 Chris Doleman	.01	.05
238 Steve Jordan	.01	.05
239 Kirk Lowdermilk	.01	.05
240 Henry Thomas	.01	.05
241 Herschel Walker	.02	.10
242 Felix Wright	.01	.05
243 Dennis Green CO RC	.02	.10
244 Ray Agnew	.01	.05
245 Marv Cook	.01	.05
246 Irving Fryar UER	.02	.10
(WR KR on front, WR on back)		
247 Pat Harlow	.01	.05
248 Hugh Millen	.01	.05
249 Leonard Russell	.02	.10
250 Andre Tippett	.01	.05
251 Jon Vaughn	.01	.05
252 Dick MacPherson CO	.01	.05
253 Morten Andersen	.01	.05
254 Bobby Hebert	.01	.05
255 Joel Hilgenberg	.01	.05
256 Vaughan Johnson	.01	.05
257 Sam Mills	.01	.05
258 Pat Swilling	.01	.05
259 Floyd Turner	.01	.05
260 Steve Walsh	.01	.05
261 Jim Mora CO UER	.01	.05
262 Stephen Baker	.01	.05
263 Mark Collins	.01	.05
264 Rodney Hampton	.02	.10
265 Jeff Hostetler	.02	.10
266 Erik Howard	.01	.05
267 Sean Landeta	.01	.05
268 Gary Reasons UER	.01	.05
269 Everson Walls	.01	.05
270 Ray Handley CO	.01	.05
271 Louie Aguiar RC	.01	.05
272 Brad Baxter	.01	.05
273 Chris Burkett	.01	.05
274 Irv Eatman	.01	.05
275 Jeff Lageman	.01	.05
276 Freeman McNeil	.01	.05
277 Rob Moore	.02	.10
278 Lonnie Young	.01	.05
279 Bruce Coslet CO	.01	.05
280 Jerome Brown	.01	.05
281 Keith Byars	.01	.05
282 Bruce Collie UER	.01	.05
283 Keith Jackson	.02	.10
284 James Joseph	.01	.05
285 Seth Joyner	.01	.05
286 Andre Waters	.01	.05
287 Reggie White	.08	.25
288 Rich Kotite CO	.01	.05
289 Rich Camarillo	.01	.05
290 Garth Jax	.01	.05
291 Ernie Jones	.01	.05
292 Tim McDonald	.01	.05
293 Rod Saddler	.01	.05
294 Anthony Thompson UER	.01	.05
295 Tom Tupa UER	.01	.05
296 Ron Wolfley	.01	.05
297 Joe Bugel CO	.01	.05
298 Gary Anderson K	.01	.05
299 Jeff Graham	.08	.25
300 Eric Green	.01	.05
301 Bryan Hinkle	.01	.05
302 Tunch Ilkin	.01	.05
303 Louis Lipps	.01	.05
304 Neil O'Donnell	.02	.10
305 Rod Woodson	.08	.25
306 Bill Cowher CO RC	.30	.75
307 Eric Bieniemy	.01	.05
308 Marion Butts	.01	.05
309 John Friesz	.02	.10
310 Courtney Hall	.01	.05
311 Ronnie Harmon	.01	.05
312 Henry Rolling	.01	.05
313 Billy Ray Smith	.01	.05
314 George Thornton	.01	.05
315 Bobby Ross CO RC	.01	.05
316 Todd Bowles	.01	.05
317 Michael Carter	.01	.05
318 Don Griffin	.01	.05
319 Charles Haley	.02	.10
320 Brent Jones	.02	.10
321 John Taylor	.02	.10
322 Ted Washington	.01	.05
323 Steve Young	.25	.60
324 George Seifert CO	.02	.10
325 Brian Blades	.02	.10
326 Jacob Green	.01	.05
327 Patrick Hunter	.01	.05
328 Tommy Kane	.01	.05
329 Cortez Kennedy	.02	.10
330 Dave Krieg	.02	.10
331 Rufus Porter	.01	.05
332 John L. Williams	.01	.05
333 Tom Flores CO	.01	.05
334 Gary Anderson RB	.01	.05
335 Mark Carrier WR	.02	.10
336 Reuben Davis	.01	.05
337 Lawrence Dawsey	.02	.10
338 Keith McCants UER	.01	.05
(LB on front; DT on back)		
339 Vinny Testaverde	.02	.10
340 Broderick Thomas	.01	.05
341 Robert Wilson	.01	.05
342 Sam Wyche CO	.01	.05
343 1991 Teacher of	.01	.05
344 Owners Reject Instant	.01	.05
345 NFL Experience	.01	.05
346 Chuck Noll Retires	.02	.10
Tosses Coin NEWS		
347 Isaac Curtis	.01	.05
348 Drew Pearson	.02	.10
Michael Irvin MN		
349 Barry Sanders	.20	.50
B.Sims		
350 Todd Marinovich	.01	.05
K.Stable		
351 Craig James	.02	.10
Leonard Russell MN		
352 Bob Golic	.01	.05
353 Pat Harlow	.01	.05
354 Esera Tuaolo	.01	.05
355 Mark Schlereth RC	.01	.05
356 Trace Armstrong	.01	.05
357 Eric Bieniemy	.01	.05
358 Bill Romanowski	.01	.05
359 Irv Eatman	.01	.05
360 Jonathan Hayes	.01	.05
361 Atlanta Falcons	.01	.05
362 Chicago Bears	.01	.05
363 Dallas Cowboys	.01	.05
364 Detroit Lions	.01	.05
365 Green Bay Packers	.01	.05
366 Los Angeles Rams	.01	.05
367 Minnesota Vikings	.01	.05
368 New Orleans Saints UER	.01	.05
369 New York Giants	.01	.05
370 Philadelphia Eagles	.01	.05
371 Phoenix Cardinals	.01	.05
372 San Francisco 49ers	.01	.05
373 Tampa Bay Buccaneers	.01	.05
374 Washington Redskins	.01	.05
375 Steve Atwater PB UER	.01	.05
376 Cornelius Bennett PB	.02	.10
377 Tim Brown PB	.02	.10
378 Marion Butts PB	.01	.05
379 Ray Childress PB	.01	.05
380 Mark Clayton PB	.01	.05
381 Marv Cook PB	.01	.05
382 Cris Dishman PB	.01	.05
383 William Fuller PB	.01	.05
384 Gaston Green PB	.01	.05
385 Jeff Jaeger PB	.01	.05
386 Haywood Jeffires PB	.02	.10
387 James Lofton PB	.02	.10
388 Ronnie Lott PB	.02	.10
389 Karl Mecklenburg PB UER	.01	.05
(misspelled Meckleнberg on front)		
390 Warren Moon PB	.02	.10
391 Anthony Munoz PB	.01	.05
392 Dennis Smith PB	.01	.05
393 Neil Smith PB	.02	.10
394 Darryl Talley PB	.01	.05
395 Derrick Thomas PB	.02	.10
396 Thurman Thomas PB	.02	.10
397 Greg Townsend PB	.01	.05
398 Richmond Webb PB	.01	.05
399 Rod Woodson PB	.02	.10
400 Dan Reeves CO PB	.01	.05
401 Troy Aikman PB	.15	.40
402 Eric Allen PB	.01	.05
403 Bennie Blades PB	.01	.05
404 Lomas Brown PB	.01	.05
405 Mark Carrier DB PB	.01	.05
406 Gary Clark PB	.02	.10
407 Mel Gray PB	.01	.05
408 Darrell Green PB	.01	.05
409 Michael Irvin PB	.08	.25
410 Vaughan Johnson PB	.01	.05
411 Seth Joyner PB	.01	.05
412 Jim Lachey PB	.01	.05
413 Chip Lohmiller PB	.01	.05
414 Charles Mann PB	.01	.05
415 Chris Miller PB	.02	.10
416 Sam Mills PB	.01	.05
417 Bart Oates PB	.01	.05
418 Jerry Rice PB	.15	.40
419 Andre Rison PB	.02	.10
420 Mark Rypien PB	.01	.05
421 Barry Sanders PB	.20	.50
422 Deion Sanders PB	.08	.25
423 Mark Schlereth PB	.01	.05
424 Mike Singletary PB	.01	.05
425 Emmitt Smith PB	.25	.60
426 Pat Swilling PB	.01	.05
427 Reggie White PB	.02	.10
428 Rick Bryan	.01	.05
429 Tim Green	.01	.05
430 Drew Hill	.01	.05
431 Norm Johnson	.01	.05
432 Keith Jones	.01	.05
433 Mike Pritchard	.02	.10
434 Deion Sanders	.20	.50
435 Tony Smith RC	.01	.05
436 Jessie Tuggle	.01	.05
437 Steve Christie	.01	.05
438 Shane Conlan	.01	.05
439 Matt Darby RC	.01	.05
440 John Fina RC	.01	.05
441 Henry Jones	.01	.05
442 Jim Kelly	.08	.25
443 Pete Metzelaars	.01	.05
444 Andre Reed	.02	.10
445 Bruce Smith	.08	.25
446 Troy Auzenne RC	.01	.05
447 Mark Carrier DB	.01	.05
448 Will Furrer RC	.01	.05
449 Jim Harbaugh	.08	.25
450 Brad Muster	.01	.05
451 Darren Lewis	.01	.05
452 Mike Singletary	.02	.10
453 Alonzo Spellman RC	.02	.10
454 Chris Zorich	.02	.10
455 Jim Breech	.01	.05
456 Boomer Esiason	.02	.10
457 Derrick Fenner	.01	.05
458 James Francis	.01	.05
459 David Klingler RC	.01	.05
460 Tim McGee	.01	.05
461 Carl Pickens RC	.08	.25
462 Alfred Williams	.01	.05
463 Darryl Williams RC	.01	.05
464 Mark Bavaro	.01	.05
465 Jay Hilgenberg	.01	.05
466 Leroy Hoard	.02	.10
467 Bernie Kosar	.02	.10
468 Michael Dean Perry	.02	.10
469 Todd Philcox RC	.01	.05
470 Patrick Rowe RC	.01	.05
471 Tommy Vardell RC	.01	.05
472 Everson Walls	.01	.05
473 Troy Aikman	.30	.75
474 Kenneth Gant RC	.01	.05
475 Charles Haley	.02	.10
476 Michael Irvin	.08	.25
477 Robert Jones RC	.01	.05
478 Russell Maryland	.01	.05
479 Jay Novacek	.02	.10
480 Kevin Smith RC	.01	.05
481 Tony Tolbert	.01	.05
482 Steve Atwater	.01	.05
483 Shane Dronett RC	.01	.05
484 Simon Fletcher	.01	.05
485 Greg Lewis	.01	.05
486 Tommy Maddox RC	.75	2.00
487 Shannon Sharpe	.08	.25
488 Dennis Smith	.01	.05
489 Sammie Smith	.01	.05
490 Kenny Walker	.01	.05
491 Lomas Brown	.01	.05
492 Mike Farr	.01	.05
493 Mel Gray	.02	.10
494 Jason Hanson RC	.02	.10
495 Herman Moore	.08	.25
496 Rodney Peete	.02	.10
497 Robert Porcher RC	.08	.25
498 Kelvin Pritchett	.01	.05
499 Andre Ware	.01	.05
500 Sanjay Beach RC	.01	.05
501 Edgar Bennett RC	.08	.25
502 Lewis Billups	.01	.05
503 Torrell Buckley	.01	.05
504 Ty Detmer	.08	.25
505 Brett Favre	1.25	2.50
506 Johnny Holland	.01	.05
507 Dexter McNabb RC	.01	.05
508 Vince Workman	.01	.05
509 Cody Carlson	.01	.05
510 Ernest Givins	.02	.10
511 Jerry Gray	.01	.05
512 Haywood Jeffires	.02	.10
513 Bruce Matthews	.01	.05
514 Bubba McDowell	.01	.05
515 Bucky Richardson RC	.01	.05
516 Webster Slaughter	.01	.05
517 Al Smith	.01	.05
518 Mel Agee	.01	.05
519 Ashley Ambrose RC	.08	.25
520 Kevin Call	.01	.05
521 Ken Clark	.01	.05
522 Quentin Coryatt RC	.01	.05
523 Steve Emtman RC	.01	.05
524 Jeff George	.08	.25
525 Jessie Hester	.01	.05
526 Anthony Johnson	.02	.10
527 Tim Barnett	.01	.05
528 Martin Bayless	.01	.05
529 J.J. Birden	.01	.05
530 Dale Carter RC	.02	.10
531 Dave Krieg	.02	.10
532 Albert Lewis	.01	.05
533 Nick Lowery	.01	.05
534 Christian Okoye	.01	.05
535 Harvey Williams	.08	.25
536 Aundray Bruce	.01	.05
537 Eric Dickerson	.02	.10
538 Willie Gault	.02	.10
539 Ethan Horton	.01	.05
540 Jeff Jaeger	.01	.05
541 Napoleon McCallum	.01	.05
542 Chester McGlockton RC	.02	.10
543 Steve Smith	.01	.05
544 Steve Wisniewski	.01	.05
545 Marc Boutte RC	.01	.05
546 Pat Carter	.01	.05
547 Jim Everett	.02	.10
548 Cleveland Gary	.01	.05
549 Sean Gilbert RC	.02	.10
550 Steve Israel RC	.01	.05
551 Todd Kinchen RC	.01	.05
552 Jackie Slater	.01	.05
553 Tony Zendejas	.01	.05
554 Robert Clark	.01	.05
555 Mark Clayton	.02	.10
556 Marco Coleman RC	.01	.05
557 Bryan Cox	.02	.10
558 Keith Jackson UER	.02	.10
(Card says drafted in/'88, but acquired as free agent in '92)		
559 Dan Marino	.50	1.25
560 John Offerdahl	.01	.05
561 Troy Vincent RC	.01	.05
562 Richmond Webb	.01	.05
563 Terry Allen	.08	.25
564 Cris Carter	.20	.50
565 Roger Craig	.02	.10
566 Rich Gannon	.08	.25
567 Hassan Jones	.01	.05
568 Randall McDaniel	.02	.10
569 Al Noga	.01	.05
570 Todd Scott	.01	.05
571 Van Waiters RC	.01	.05
572 Bruce Armstrong	.01	.05
573 Gene Chilton RC	.01	.05
574 Eugene Chung RC	.01	.05
575 Todd Collins RC	.01	.05
576 Hart Lee Dykes	.01	.05
577 David Howard RC	.01	.05
578 Eugene Lockhart	.01	.05
579 Greg McMurtry	.01	.05
580 Rod Smith DB RC	.01	.05
581 Gene Atkins	.01	.05
582 Vince Buck	.01	.05
583 Wesley Carroll	.01	.05
584 Jim Dombrowski	.01	.05
585 Vaughn Dunbar RC	.01	.05
586 Craig Heyward	.02	.10
587 Dalton Hilliard	.01	.05
588 Wayne Martin	.01	.05
589 Renaldo Turnbull	.01	.05
590 Carl Banks	.01	.05
591 Derek Brown TE RC	.01	.05
592 Jarrod Bunch	.01	.05
593 Mark Ingram	.01	.05
594 Ed McCaffrey	.10	.30
595 Phil Simms	.02	.10
596 Phillippi Sparks RC	.01	.05
597 Lawrence Taylor	.08	.25
598 Lewis Tillman	.01	.05
599 Kyle Clifton	.01	.05
600 Mo Lewis	.01	.05
601 Terance Mathis	.02	.10
602 Scott Mersereau	.01	.05
603 Johnny Mitchell RC	.01	.05
604 Browning Nagle	.01	.05
605 Ken O'Brien	.01	.05
606 Al Toon	.02	.10
607 Marvin Washington	.01	.05
608 Eric Allen	.01	.05
609 Fred Barnett	.08	.25
610 John Booty	.01	.05
611 Randall Cunningham	.08	.25
612 Rich Miano	.01	.05
613 Clyde Simmons	.01	.05
614 Siran Stacy	.01	.05
615 Herschel Walker	.02	.10
616 Calvin Williams	.02	.10
617 Chris Chandler	.08	.25
618 Randal Hill	.01	.05
619 Johnny Johnson	.01	.05
620 Lorenzo Lynch	.01	.05
621 Robert Massey	.01	.05
622 Ricky Proehl	.01	.05
623 Timm Rosenbach	.01	.05
624 Tony Sacca RC	.01	.05
625 Aeneas Williams UER	.02	.10
(Name misspelled Aaneas)		
626 Bubby Brister	.01	.05
627 Barry Foster	.02	.10
628 Merril Hoge	.01	.05
629 D.J. Johnson	.01	.05
630 David Little	.01	.05
631 Greg Lloyd	.02	.10
632 Ernie Mills	.01	.05
633 Leon Searcy RC	.01	.05
634 Dwight Stone	.01	.05
635 Sam Anno RC	.01	.05
636 Burt Grossman	.01	.05
637 Stan Humphries	.08	.25
638 Nate Lewis	.01	.05
639 Anthony Miller	.02	.10
640 Chris Mims	.08	.25
641 Marquez Pope RC	.01	.05
642 Stanley Richard	.01	.05
643 Junior Seau	.08	.25
644 Brian Bollinger RC	.01	.05
645 Steve Bono RC	.08	.25
646 Dexter Carter	.01	.05
647 Dana Hall RC	.01	.05
648 Amp Lee	.01	.05
649 Joe Montana	.50	1.25
650 Tom Rathman	.01	.05
651 Jerry Rice	.30	.75
652 Ricky Watters	.08	.25
653 Robert Blackmon	.01	.05
654 John Kasay	.01	.05
655 Ronnie Lee RC	.01	.05
656 Dan McGwire	.01	.05
657 Ray Roberts RC	.01	.05
658 Kelly Stouffer	.01	.05
659 Chris Warren	.08	.25
660 Tony Woods	.01	.05
661 David Wyman	.01	.05
662 Reggie Cobb	.01	.05
663A Steve DeBerg ERR	.02	.10
(Career yardage 1455; found in foil packs)		
663B Steve DeBerg COR	.02	.10
(Career yardage 31,455; found in jumbo packs)		
664 Santana Dotson RC	.02	.10
665 Willie Drewery	.01	.05
666 Paul Gruber	.01	.05
667 Ron Hall	.01	.05
668 Courtney Hawkins RC	.02	.10
669 Charles McRae	.01	.05
670 Ricky Reynolds	.01	.05
671 Monte Coleman	.01	.05
672 Brad Edwards	.01	.05
673 Jumpy Geathers UER	.01	.05
674 Kelly Goodburn	.01	.05
675 Kurt Gouveia	.01	.05
676 Chris Hakel RC	.01	.05
677 Wilber Marshall	.01	.05
678 Ricky Sanders	.01	.05
679 Mark Schlereth	.01	.05
680 Buffalo Bills	.01	.05
681 Cincinnati Bengals	.01	.05
682 Cleveland Browns	.01	.05
683 Denver Broncos	.01	.05
684 Houston Oilers	.01	.05
685 Indianapolis Colts	.01	.05
686 Tracy Simien SG	.01	.05
687 Los Angeles Raiders	.01	.05
688 Miami Dolphins	.01	.05
689 New England Patriots	.01	.05
690 New York Jets	.01	.05
691 Pittsburgh Steelers	.01	.05
692 San Diego Chargers	.01	.05
693 Seattle Seahawks	.01	.05
694 Play Smart	.01	.05
695 Hank Williams Jr. NEW	.01	.05
696 3 Brothers in NFL NEWS	.01	.05
697 Japan Bowl NEWS	.01	.05
698 Georgia Dome NEWS	.01	.05
699 Theme Art NEWS	.01	.05
700 Mark Rypien SB MVP NEW	.01	.05
AU150 Emmitt Smith AU/1000	60.00	120.00
AU168 Erik Kramer AU/1000	12.50	30.00
NNO Emmitt Smith	.30	.75
Power Preview Card		
NNO Santa Claus	.20	.50
Spirit of the Season		
SC5 Super Bowl XXVI	.10	.30
Logo card		
P1 Cover Card Promo	.40	1.00
Hologram, numbered of 2000		

1992 Pro Set Emmitt Smith Holograms

COMPLETE SET (4)	20.00	50.00
RANDOM INSERTS IN SER.1 PACKS		
ES1 Statistics 1990-1999	2.50	6.00
ES2 Drafted by Cowboys	4.00	10.00
ES3 Rookie of the Year	7.50	20.00
ES4 NFL Rushing Leader	10.00	25.00

1992 Pro Set Gold MVPs

COMPLETE SET (30)	6.00	15.00
ONE PER JUMBO PACK		
MVP1 Thurman Thomas	.20	.50
MVP2 Anthony Munoz	.07	.20
MVP3 Clay Matthews	.07	.20
MVP4 John Elway	1.25	2.50
MVP5 Warren Moon	.20	.50
MVP6 Bill Brooks	.02	.10
MVP7 Derrick Thomas	.20	.50
MVP8 Todd Marinovich	.02	.10
MVP9 Mark Higgs	.02	.10
MVP10 Leonard Russell	.07	.20
MVP11 Rob Moore	.07	.20
MVP12 Rod Woodson	.20	.50
MVP13 Marion Butts	.02	.10
MVP14 Brian Blades	.07	.20
MVP15 Don Shula CO	.07	.20
MVP16 Deion Sanders	.40	1.00
MVP17 Neal Anderson	.02	.10
MVP18 Emmitt Smith	1.50	3.00
MVP19 Barry Sanders	1.25	2.50
MVP20 Brett Favre	2.50	5.00
MVP21 Kevin Greene	.07	.20
MVP22 Terry Allen	.20	.50
MVP23 Pat Swilling	.02	.10
MVP24 Rodney Hampton	.07	.20
MVP25 Randall Cunningham	.20	.50
MVP26 Randal Hill	.02	.10
MVP27 Jerry Rice	.75	1.50
MVP28 Vinny Testaverde	.10	.20
MVP29 Mark Rypien	.02	.10
MVP30 Jimmy Johnson CO	.07	.20

1992 Pro Set Ground Force

COMPLETE SET (6)	10.00	25.00
RANDOM INSERTS IN SER.1 PACKS		
86 Gerald Riggs	.15	.40
105 Thurman Thomas	1.00	2.50
118 Neal Anderson	.15	.40
150 Emmitt Smith	6.00	15.00
206 Barry Word	.15	.40
249 Leonard Russell	.40	1.00

1992 Pro Set HOF Inductees

COMPLETE SET (4)	.40	1.00
RANDOM INSERTS IN SERIES 1 PAC		
SC1 Lem Barney	.10	.30
SC2 Al Davis	.10	.30
SC3 John Mackey	.10	.30
SC4 John Riggins	.20	.50

1992 Pro Set HOF 2000

COMPLETE SET (10)	10.00	20.00
RANDOM INSERTS IN SER.2 FOIL P		
1 Marcus Allen	1.00	2.00
2 Richard Dent	.30	.75
3 Eric Dickerson	.30	.75
4 Ronnie Lott	.30	.75
5 Art Monk	.30	.75
6 Joe Montana	5.00	10.00
7 Warren Moon	1.00	2.00
8 Anthony Munoz	.30	.75
9 Mike Singletary	.30	.75
10 Lawrence Taylor	1.00	2.00

1992 Pro Set Club

The theme of the 1992 Pro Set Club set is "Football Practice." Each of the nine cards measures the standard-size. The full-bleed color photos on the fronts illustrate various aspects of the game. The card subtitle appears in a pastel purple bar superimposed over the picture toward the bottom. At the left end of the bar is the Pro Set Club logo. On a yellow panel inside a turquoise bordered speckled with green, the backs discuss how to play football and challenge the reader to "do it yourself," "think about it," "check it out," or "take a look."

COMPLETE SET (9)	2.00	5.00
1 Quarterback Throwing Pass	.40	1.00
2 Coach Reviewing Play Strategy	.30	.75
3 Team Stretching	.30	.75
4 Offensive Play	.30	.75
5 Kickoff	.30	.75
6 Player's Stance	.30	.75
7 Football Is a Spectator Sport	.30	.75
8 Defensive Practice	.30	.75
9 Play in Motion	.30	.75

1992 Pro Set Emmitt Smith Promo Sheet

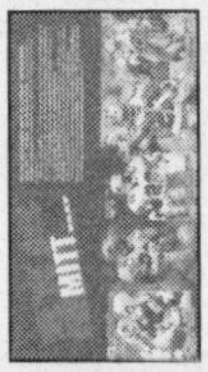

Pro Set produced this five-card sheet to announce Emmitt Smith as the company spokesman for Pro Set. The sheet features reprints of Smith's past Pro Set cards up to that time: 1990, 1991, 1991 Platinum, 1991 Platinum Game Breaker, and 1992 with a checklist back. Each sheet is numbered of 2000 produced and measures approximately 7" by 13."

NNO Emmitt Smith Sheet	4.00	10.00

1992-93 Pro Set Super Bowl XXVII

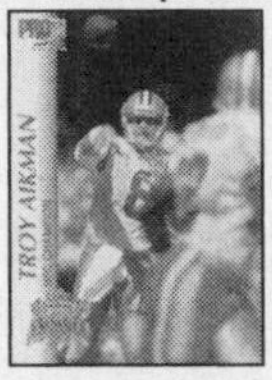

Produced by Pro Set to commemorate Super Bowl XXVII, this 38-card standard-size set was packaged in two cello packs. For those who paid admission to Super Bowl XXVII, January 31, 1993, in Pasadena, a set was inserted into the GTE seat cushion. The set was also available through mail-order for 22.00 plus either a Dallas Cowboys or Buffalo Bills mini-binder. Just 7,000 sets were produced for the mail-away offer. The cards have the same design as the regular issue except for the following differences: 1) all cards have a Super Bowl XXVII emblem on their fronts; 2) the Bills' and the Cowboys' cards have AFC Champion and NFC Champion respectively printed beneath the player's name; and 3) all the backs have a screened background of Super Bowl XXVII emblems. The set includes an AFL Conference logo card (1), Buffalo Bills (2-18), an NFL Conference logo card (19), Dallas Cowboys (20-36), a Newsreel card (37), and a card of Marco Coleman (701), the 1992 Pro Set Rookie of the Year. With the exception of the Coleman, all the cards are numbered on the back "XXVII" and checklisted below in alphabetical order within teams.

COMPLETE SET (38)	4.80	12.00
1 AFC Logo	.07	.20
2 Cornelius Bennett	.10	.30
3 Steve Christie	.07	.20
4 Shane Conlan	.07	.20
5 Matt Darby	.07	.20
6 Kenneth Davis	.07	.20
7 John Fina	.07	.20
8 Henry Jones	.07	.20
9 Jim Kelly	.30	.75
10 Marv Levy CO	.07	.20
11 James Lofton	.10	.30
12 Pete Metzelaars	.07	.20
13 Nate Odomes	.07	.20
14 Andre Reed	.20	.50
15 Bruce Smith	.20	.50
16 Darryl Talley	.07	.20
17 Steve Tasker	.07	.20
18 Thurman Thomas	.30	.75
19 NFC Logo	.07	.20
20 Troy Aikman	1.00	2.50
21 Steve Beuerlein	.10	.30
22 Tony Casillas	.07	.20
23 Kenneth Gant	.07	.20
24 Charles Haley	.10	.30
25 Alvin Harper	.07	.20
26 Michael Irvin	.30	.75
27 Jimmy Johnson CO	.10	.30
28 Robert Jones	.07	.20
29 Russell Maryland	.07	.20
30 Nate Newton	.07	.20
31 Ken Norton Jr.	.10	.30
32 Jay Novacek	.10	.30
33 Emmitt Smith	2.00	5.00
34 Kevin Smith	.07	.20
35 Mark Stepnoski	.07	.20
36 Tony Tolbert	.07	.20
37 Newsreel Art	.07	.20
Super Bowl XXVII		
701 Marco Coleman PS-ROY	.07	.20

1993 Pro Set Promos

These six standard-size cards were distributed to dealers, promoters, and card show attendees to promote the release of the 1993 Pro Set issue. The six cards were also issued in an uncut ten-card 8" by 13 1/2" sheet, the bottom row of which consisted of five copies of the Emmitt Smith card. The fronts feature color player action shots that are borderless, except at the bottom, where the photo appears to be torn away, revealing an irregular gray stripe that carries the player's name in team color-coded lettering. On the regular series cards, the color of this stripe varies, reflecting the team's primary color. The back appears to be torn away on the left edge, revealing a gray stripe that carries the player's name in vertical team color-coded lettering, and his position and team in black lettering. A color player action photo is displayed at the top, which blends into a grayish background that carries the player's biography, career highlights, and stats. On the regular cards, the stat box has a white background rather than a grayish one. The cards are unnumbered and checklisted below in alphabetical order.

COMPLETE SET (6)	2.40	6.00
1 Jerome Bettis	.60	1.50
2 Reggie Brooks	.40	1.00
3 Cortez Kennedy	.30	.75
4 Junior Seau	.40	1.00
5 Emmitt Smith	1.20	3.00
6 Wade Wilson	.30	.75

1993 Pro Set

The 1993 Pro Set football set was issued in one series of 449 standard-size cards. Including foil and jumbo cases, a total of 15,000 cases were reportedly produced. Cards were issued in 15-card foil packs and 32-card jumbo packs. After an 18-card Stat Leader subset (1-18) and an 11-card Replay 1992 subset (19-29), the cards are checklisted below according to teams. Rookie Cards include Jerome Bettis, Drew Bledsoe, Vincent Brisby, Reggie Brooks, Derek Brown, Mark Brunell, Curtis Conway, Garrison Hearst, Billy Joe Hobert, Qadry Ismail, Terry Kirby, O.J. McDuffie, Rick Mirer, Natrone Means, Glyn Milburn, Ronald Moore, Robert Smith, Dana Stubblefield and Kevin Williams.

COMPLETE SET (449)	8.00	20.00
1 Marco Coleman	.01	.05
Rookie of the Year		
2 Steve Young	.10	.30
Player of the Year		
3 Mike Holmgren	.02	.10
Coach of the Year		
4 John Elway	.30	.75
Man of the Year		
5 Steve Young	.10	.30
Passing Leader		
6 Dan Marino	.30	.75
Passing Yardage		
7 Emmitt Smith	.30	.75
Rushing Leader		
8 Sterling Sharpe	.02	.10
Receiving Leader		
9 Jay Novacek	.02	.10
Receiving TE		
10 Sterling Sharpe	.02	.10
Receiving Yardage		
11 Thurman Thomas	.02	.10
Total Yardage		
12 Pete Stoyanovich	.01	.05
Scoring Leader		
13 Greg Montgomery	.01	.05
Punting Leader		
14 Johnny Bailey	.01	.05
Punt Return		
15 Jon Vaughn	.01	.05
Kickoff Return		
16 Audrey McMillian	.01	.05
Henry Jones UER		
Interception		
(Name spelled McMillan on back)		
17 Clyde Simmons	.01	.05
Sack Leader		
18 Cortez Kennedy	.01	.05
Defensive MVP		
19 AFC Wildcard	.01	.05
(Stan Humphries)		
20 AFC Wildcard	.01	.05
(Don Beebe)		
21 NFC Wildcard	.01	.05
(Eric Allen)		
22 NFC Wildcard	.01	.05
(Brian Mitchell)		
23 AFC Divisional	.01	.05
(Frank Reich)		
24 AFC Divisional	.30	.75
(Dan Marino)		
25 NFC Divisional	.20	.50
(Troy Aikman)		
26 NFC Divisional	.02	.10
(Ricky Watters)		
27 AFC Championship	.01	.05
(Bruce Smith sacking/(Dan Marino)		
28 NFC Championship	.01	.05
(Tony Casillas sacking/(Steve Young)		
29 Super Bowl XXVIII Logo	.01	.05
30 Troy Aikman	.30	.75
31 Thomas Everett	.01	.05
32 Charles Haley	.02	.10
33 Alvin Harper	.02	.10
34 Michael Irvin	.08	.25
35 Robert Jones	.01	.05
36 Russell Maryland	.01	.05
37 Ken Norton	.02	.10
38 Jay Novacek	.02	.10
39 Emmitt Smith	.50	1.50
40 Darrin Smith RC	.02	.10
41 Mark Stepnoski	.01	.05
42 Kevin Williams RC	.08	.25
43 Daryl Johnston	.08	.25
44 Derrick Lassic RC	.01	.05
45 Don Beebe	.01	.05
46 Cornelius Bennett	.02	.10
47 Bill Brooks	.01	.05
48 Kenneth Davis	.01	.05
49 Jim Kelly	.08	.25
50 Andre Reed	.02	.10
51 Bruce Smith	.08	.25
52 Thomas Smith RC	.02	.10
53 Darryl Talley	.01	.05
54 Thurman Thomas	.08	.25
55 Russell Copeland RC	.02	.10
56 Steve Christie	.01	.05
57 Pete Metzelaars	.01	.05
58 Frank Reich	.02	.10
59 Henry Jones	.01	.05
60 Vinnie Clark	.01	.05
61 Eric Dickerson	.02	.10
62 Jumpy Geathers	.01	.05
63 Roger Harper RC	.01	.05
64 Michael Haynes	.02	.10
65 Bobby Hebert	.01	.05
66 Lincoln Kennedy RC	.01	.05
67 Chris Miller	.02	.10
68 Andre Rison	.02	.10
69 Deion Sanders	.20	.50
70 Jessie Tuggle	.01	.05
71 Ron George	.01	.05
72 Eric Pegram	.02	.10
73 Melvin Jenkins	.01	.05
74 Pierce Holt	.01	.05
75 Neal Anderson	.01	.05
76 Mark Carrier DB	.01	.05
77 Curtis Conway RC	.15	.40
78 Richard Dent	.02	.10
79 Jim Harbaugh	.08	.25
80 Craig Heyward	.02	.10
81 Darren Lewis	.01	.05
82 Alonzo Spellman	.01	.05
83 Tom Waddle	.01	.05

84 Wendell Davis .01 .05
85 Chris Zorich .01 .05
86 Carl Simpson RC .01 .05
87 Chris Gedney RC .01 .05
88 Trace Armstrong .01 .05
89 Peter Tom Willis .01 .05
90 John Copeland RC .02 .10
91 Derrick Fenner .01 .05
92 James Francis .01 .05
93 Harold Green .01 .05
94 David Klingler .01 .05
95 Tim Krumrie .01 .05
96 Tony McGee RC .02 .10
97 Carl Pickens .02 .10
98 Alfred Williams .01 .05
99 Doug Pelfrey RC .01 .05
100 Lance Gunn RC .01 .05
101 Jay Schroeder .01 .05
102 Steve Tovar RC .01 .05
103 Jeff Query .01 .05
104 Ty Parten RC .01 .05
105 Jerry Ball .01 .05
106 Mark Carrier WR .02 .10
107 Rob Burnett .01 .05
108 Michael Jackson .02 .10
109 Mike Johnson .01 .05
110 Bernie Kosar .02 .10
111 Clay Matthews .02 .10
112 Eric Metcalf .02 .10
113 Michael Dean Perry .02 .10
114 Vinny Testaverde .02 .10
115 Eric Turner .01 .05
116 Tommy Vardell .01 .05
117 Leroy Hoard .02 .10
118 Steve Everitt RC .01 .05
119 Everson Walls .01 .05
120 Steve Atwater .01 .05
121 Rod Bernstine .01 .05
122 Mike Croel .01 .05
123 John Elway .60 1.50
124 Simon Fletcher .01 .05
125 Glyn Milburn RC .08 .25
126 Reggie Rivers RC .01 .05
127 Shannon Sharpe .08 .25
128 Dennis Smith .01 .05
129 Dan Williams RC .01 .05
130 Rondell Jones RC .01 .05
131 Jason Elam RC .08 .25
132 Arthur Marshall RC .01 .05
133 Gary Zimmerman .01 .05
134 Karl Mecklenburg .01 .05
135 Bennie Blades .01 .05
136 Lomas Brown .01 .05
137 Bill Fralic .01 .05
138 Mel Gray .02 .10
139 Willie Green .01 .05
140 Ryan McNeil RC .08 .25
141 Rodney Peete .01 .05
142 Barry Sanders .50 1.25
143 Chris Spielman .02 .10
144 Pat Swilling .01 .05
145 Andre Ware .01 .05
146 Herman Moore .08 .25
147 Tim McKyer .01 .05
148 Brett Perriman .08 .25
149 Antonio London RC .01 .05
150 Edgar Bennett .08 .25
151 Terrell Buckley .01 .05
152 Brett Favre .75 2.00
153 Jackie Harris .01 .05
154 Johnny Holland .01 .05
155 Sterling Sharpe .08 .25
156 Tim Hauck .01 .05
157 George Teague RC .02 .10
158 Reggie White .08 .25
159 Mark Clayton .01 .05
160 Ty Detmer .08 .25
161 Wayne Simmons RC .01 .05
162 Mark Brunell RC .60 1.50
163 Tony Bennett .01 .05
164 Brian Noble .01 .05
165 Cody Carlson .01 .05
166 Ray Childress .01 .05
167 Cris Dishman .01 .05
168 Curtis Duncan .01 .05
169 Brad Hopkins RC .01 .05
170 Haywood Jeffires .02 .10
171 Wilber Marshall .01 .05
172 Micheal Barrow RC UER .08 .25
(Name spelled Michael on both sided)
173 Bubba McDowell .01 .05
174 Warren Moon .08 .25
175 Webster Slaughter .01 .05
176 Travis Hannah RC .01 .05
177 Lorenzo White .01 .05
178 Ernest Givins UER .02 .10
(Name spelled Givens on front)
179 Keith McCants .01 .05
180 Kerry Cash .01 .05
181 Quentin Coryatt .02 .10
182 Kirk Lowdermilk .01 .05
183 Rodney Culver .01 .05
184 Rohn Stark .01 .05
185 Steve Emtman .01 .05
186 Jeff George .08 .25
187 Jeff Herrod .01 .05
188 Reggie Langhorne .01 .05
189 Roosevelt Potts RC .01 .05
190 Jack Trudeau .01 .05
191 Will Wolford .01 .05
192 Jessie Hester .01 .05
193 Anthony Johnson .02 .10
194 Ray Buchanan RC .08 .25
195 Dale Carter .01 .05
196 Willie Davis .08 .25
197 John Alt .01 .05
198 Joe Montana .60 1.50
199 Will Shields RC .08 .25
200 Neil Smith .08 .25
201 Derrick Thomas .08 .25
202 Harvey Williams .02 .10
203 Marcus Allen .08 .25
204 J.J. Birden .01 .05
205 Tim Barnett .01 .05
206 Albert Lewis .01 .05
207 Nick Lowery .01 .05
208 Dave Krieg .02 .10
209 Keith Cash .01 .05
210 Patrick Bates RC .01 .05
211 Nick Bell .01 .05
212 Tim Brown .08 .25
213 Willie Gault .01 .05
214 Ethan Horton .01 .05
215 Jeff Hostetler .02 .10
216 Howie Long .08 .25
217 Greg Townsend .01 .05
218 Rocket Ismail .02 .10
219 Alexander Wright .01 .05
220 Greg Robinson RC .01 .05
221 Billy Joe Hobert RC .08 .25
222 Steve Wisniewski .01 .05
223 Steve Smith .01 .05
224 Vince Evans .01 .05
225 Flipper Anderson .01 .05
226 Jerome Bettis RC 1.50 4.00
227 Troy Drayton RC .02 .10
228 Henry Ellard .02 .10
229 Jim Everett .02 .10
230 Tony Zendejas .01 .05
231 Todd Lyght .01 .05
232 Todd Kinchen .01 .05
233 Jackie Slater .01 .05
234 Fred Stokes .01 .05
235 Russell White RC .02 .10
236 Cleveland Gary .01 .05
237 Sean LaChapelle RC .01 .05
238 Steve Israel .01 .05
239 Shane Conlan .01 .05
240 Keith Byars .01 .05
241 Marco Coleman .01 .05
242 Bryan Cox .01 .05
243 Irving Fryar .02 .10
244 Richmond Webb .01 .05
245 Mark Higgs .01 .05
246 Terry Kirby RC .08 .25
247 Mark Ingram .01 .05
248 John Offerdahl .01 .05
249 Keith Jackson .02 .10
250 Dan Marino .60 1.50
251 O.J. McDuffie RC .08 .25
252 Louis Oliver .01 .05
253 Pete Stoyanovich .01 .05
254 Troy Vincent .01 .05
255 Anthony Carter .02 .10
256 Cris Carter .08 .25
257 Roger Craig .02 .10
258 Jack Del Rio .01 .05
259 Chris Doleman .01 .05
260 Barry Word .01 .05
261 Qadry Ismail RC .08 .25
262 Jim McMahon .02 .10
263 Robert Smith RC .50 1.25
264 Fred Strickland .01 .05
265 Randall McDaniel .02 .10
266 Carl Lee .01 .05
267 Olanda Truitt RC UER .01 .05
(Name spelled Olanda on front)
268 Terry Allen .08 .25
269 Audray McMillian .01 .05
270 Drew Bledsoe RC 1.00 2.50
271 Eugene Chung .01 .05
272 Marv Cook .01 .05
273 Pat Harlow .01 .05
274 Greg McMurtry .01 .05
275 Leonard Russell .02 .10
276 Chris Slade RC .02 .10
277 Andre Tippett .01 .05
278 Vincent Brisby RC .08 .25
279 Ben Coates .20 .50
280 Sam Gash RC .08 .25
281 Bruce Armstrong .01 .05
282 Rod Smith DB .01 .05
283 Michael Timpson .01 .05
284 Scott Sisson RC .01 .05
285 Morten Andersen .01 .05
286 Reggie Freeman RC .01 .05
287 Dalton Hilliard .01 .05
288 Rickey Jackson .01 .05
289 Vaughan Johnson .01 .05
290 Eric Martin .01 .05
291 Sam Mills .01 .05
292 Brad Muster .01 .05
293 Willie Roaf RC .02 .10
294 Irv Smith RC .01 .05
295 Wade Wilson .01 .05
296 Derek Brown RBK RC .02 .10
297 Quinn Early .02 .10
298 Steve Walsh .01 .05
299 Renaldo Turnbull .01 .05
300 Jessie Armstead RC .02 .10
301 Carlton Bailey .01 .05
302 Michael Brooks .01 .05
303 Rodney Hampton .02 .10
304 Ed McCaffrey .08 .25
305 Dave Meggett .01 .05
306 Bart Oates .01 .05
307 Mike Sherrard .01 .05
308 Phil Simms .02 .10
309 Lawrence Taylor .08 .25
310 Mark Jackson .01 .05
311 Jarrod Bunch .01 .05
312 Howard Cross .01 .05
313 Michael Strahan RC .60 1.50
314 Marcus Buckley RC .01 .05
315 Brad Baxter .01 .05
316 Adrian Murrell RC .08 .25
317 Boomer Esiason .02 .10
318 Johnny Johnson .01 .05
319 Marvin Jones RC .01 .05
320 Jeff Lageman .01 .05
321 Ronnie Lott .02 .10
322 Leonard Marshall .01 .05
323 Johnny Mitchell .01 .05
324 Rob Moore .02 .10
325 Browning Nagle .01 .05
326 Blair Thomas .01 .05
327 Brian Washington .01 .05
328 Terance Mathis .02 .10
329 Kyle Clifton .01 .05
330 Eric Allen .01 .05
331 Victor Bailey RC .01 .05
332 Fred Barnett .02 .10
333 Mark Bavaro .01 .05
334 Randall Cunningham .08 .25
335 Ken O'Brien .01 .05
336 Seth Joyner .01 .05
337 Leonard Renfro RC .01 .05
338 Heath Sherman .01 .05
339 Clyde Simmons .01 .05
340 Herschel Walker .02 .10
341 Calvin Williams .02 .10
342 Bubby Brister .01 .05
343 Vaughn Hebron RC .01 .05
344 Keith Millard .01 .05
345 Johnny Bailey .01 .05
346 Steve Beuerlein .02 .10
347 Chuck Cecil .01 .05
348 Larry Centers RC .08 .25
349 Chris Chandler .02 .10
350 Ernest Dye RC .01 .05
351 Garrison Hearst RC .30 .75
352 Randal Hill .01 .05
353 John Booty .01 .05
354 Gary Clark .02 .10
355 Ronald Moore RC .02 .10
356 Ricky Proehl .01 .05
357 Eric Swann .02 .10
358 Ken Harvey .01 .05
359 Ben Coleman RC .01 .05
360 Deon Figures RC .01 .05
361 Barry Foster .02 .10
362 Jeff Graham .02 .10
363 Eric Green .01 .05
364 Kevin Greene .02 .10
365 Andre Hastings RC .02 .10
366 Greg Lloyd .02 .10
367 Neil O'Donnell .08 .25
368 Dwight Stone .01 .05
369 Mike Tomczak .01 .05
370 Rod Woodson .08 .25
371 Chad Brown RC .02 .10
372 Ernie Mills .01 .05
373 Darren Perry .01 .05
374 Leon Searcy .01 .05
375 Marion Butts .01 .05
376 John Carney .01 .05
377 Ronnie Harmon .01 .05
378 Stan Humphries .02 .10
379 Nate Lewis .01 .05
380 Natrone Means RC .08 .25
381 Anthony Miller .02 .10
382 Chris Mims .01 .05
383 Leslie O'Neal .02 .10
384 Joe Cocozzo RC .01 .05
385 Junior Seau .08 .25
386 Jerrol Williams .01 .05
387 John Friesz .02 .10
388 Darrien Gordon RC .01 .05
389 Derrick Walker .01 .05
390 Dana Hall .01 .05
391 Brent Jones .02 .10
392 Todd Kelly RC .01 .05
393 Amp Lee .01 .05
394 Tim McDonald .01 .05
395 Jerry Rice .40 1.00
396 Dana Stubblefield RC .08 .25
397 John Taylor .02 .10
398 Ricky Watters .08 .25
399 Steve Young .30 .75
400 Steve Bono .02 .10
401 Adrian Hardy .01 .05
402 Tom Rathman .01 .05
403 Elvis Grbac RC UER .60 1.50
(Name spelled Grabac on front)
404 Bill Romanowski .01 .05
405 Brian Blades .02 .10
406 Ferrell Edmunds .01 .05
407 Carlton Gray RC .01 .05
408 Cortez Kennedy .02 .10
409 Kelvin Martin .01 .05
410 Dan McGwire .01 .05
411 Rick Mirer RC .08 .25
412 Rufus Porter .01 .05
413 Chris Warren .02 .10
414 Jon Vaughn .01 .05
415 John L. Williams .01 .05
416 Eugene Robinson .01 .05
417 Michael McCrary RC .02 .10
418 Michael Bates RC .01 .05
419 Stan Gelbaugh .01 .05
420 Reggie Cobb .01 .05
421 Eric Curry RC .01 .05
422 Lawrence Dawsey .01 .05
423 Santana Dotson .02 .10
424 Craig Erickson .02 .10
425 Ron Hall .01 .05
426 Courtney Hawkins .01 .05
427 Broderick Thomas .01 .05
428 Vince Workman .01 .05
429 Demetrius DuBose RC .01 .05
430 Lamar Thomas RC .01 .05
431 John Lynch RC .25 .60
432 Hardy Nickerson .02 .10
433 Horace Copeland RC .02 .10
434 Steve DeBerg .01 .05
435 Joe Jacoby .01 .05
436 Tom Carter RC .02 .10
437 Andre Collins .01 .05
438 Darrell Green .01 .05
439 Desmond Howard .02 .10
440 Chip Lohmiller .01 .05
441 Charles Mann .01 .05
442 Tim McGee .01 .05
443 Art Monk .02 .10
444 Mark Rypien .01 .05
445 Ricky Sanders .01 .05
446 Brian Mitchell .02 .10
447 Reggie Brooks RC .02 .10
448 Carl Banks .01 .05
449 Cary Conklin .01 .05
NNO Santa Card .60 1.50

1993 Pro Set All-Rookies

COMPLETE SET (27) 3.00 8.00
RANDOM INSERTS IN FOIL PACKS
1 Rick Mirer .15 .40
2 Garrison Hearst .60 1.25
3 Jerome Bettis 2.00 5.00
4 Vincent Brisby .15 .40
5 O.J. McDuffie .15 .40
6 Curtis Conway .25 .60
7 Rocket Ismail .10 .15
8 Steve Everitt .02 .10
9 Ernest Dye .02 .10
10 Todd Rucci .02 .10
11 Willie Roaf .05 .15
12 Lincoln Kennedy .02 .10
13 Irv Smith .02 .10
14 Jason Elam .15 .40
15 Harold Alexander .02 .10
16 John Copeland .05 .15
17 Eric Curry .02 .10
18 Dana Stubblefield .15 .40
19 Leonard Renfro .02 .10
20 Marvin Jones .02 .10
21 Demetrius DuBose .02 .10
22 Chris Slade .05 .15
23 Darrin Smith .05 .15
24 Deon Figures .02 .10
25 Darrien Gordon .02 .10
26 Patrick Bates .02 .10
27 George Teague .05 .15

1993 Pro Set College Connections

COMPLETE SET (10) 8.00 20.00
RANDOM INSERTS IN JUMBO PACKS
CC1 Barry Sanders 3.00 6.00
Thurman Thomas
CC2 Jerome Bettis 1.00 2.50
Reggie Brooks
CC3 Emmitt Smith 3.00 6.00
Neal Anderson
CC4 Rocket Ismail .60 1.50
Tim Brown
CC5 Rodney Hampton .40 1.00
Garrison Hearst UER
(Hearst listed with Lions instead of Cardinals)
CC6 Derrick Thomas .50 1.25
Cornelius Bennett
CC7 Jim McMahon 1.50 3.00
Steve Young
CC8 Rick Mirer 2.50 5.00
Joe Montana
CC9 Terrell Buckley 1.50 3.00
Deion Sanders
CC10 Mark Rypien 2.00 5.00
Drew Bledsoe

1993 Pro Set Rookie Quarterbacks

COMPLETE SET (6) 4.00 10.00
RANDOM INSERTS IN JUMBO PACKS
RQ1 Drew Bledsoe 1.25 3.00
RQ2 Rick Mirer .20 .50
RQ3 Mark Brunell 1.00 2.50
RQ4 Billy Joe Hobert .08 .25
RQ5 Trent Green 2.50 6.00
RQ6 Elvis Grbac .75 2.00

1993 Pro Set Rookie Running Backs

COMPLETE SET (14) 3.00 8.00
RANDOM INSERTS IN FOIL PACKS
1 Derrick Lassic .02 .10
2 Reggie Brooks .05 .15
3 Garrison Hearst .60 1.25
4 Ronald Moore .05 .15
5 Robert Smith 1.00 2.00
6 Jerome Bettis 2.00 5.00
7 Russell White .05 .15
8 Derek Brown RBK .05 .15
9 Roosevelt Potts .02 .10
10 Terry Kirby .15 .40
11 Glyn Milburn .15 .40
12 Greg Robinson .02 .10
13 Natrone Means .15 .40
14 Vaughn Hebron .02 .10

1994 Pro Set National Promos

Distributed during the 1994 National Sports Collectors Convention, cards 1-5 and the letter-numbered cards feature prototype cards from Pro Set football, Power football, and Power racing. Cards 6 and 7 were inserted in Tuff Stuff and bear a gold foil "Tuff Stuff" emblem; they are part of a 5-card set made for that magazine and inserted one per month. The cards of Darrien Gordon and Joe Montana/Marcus Allen were released after Pro Set closed operations. The cardbacks feature a black diagonal "proto" stripe cutting across the lower right corner. The front of the title card has the convention logo on a blue screened background with the words Pro Set faintly detectible. The title card also carries the serial number "X" out of 10,000. The football cards are unnumbered and checklisted below in alphabetical order.

COMPLETE SET (10) 10.00 25.00
1 Jerome Bettis .80 2.00
Fire Power
2 Drew Bledsoe 1.60 4.00
3 Brett Favre 3.20 8.00
Sterling Sharpe
Air Power
4 Ronald Moore .30 .75
5 Willie Roaf .30 .75
Power Line
6 Garrison Hearst .60 1.50
7 Richmond Webb .30 .75
8 Darrien Gordon .30 .75
9 Joe Montana 5.00 10.00
Marcus Allen
Power Combos
NNO Title Card .30 .75
(1994 National)

1991 Pro Set Platinum

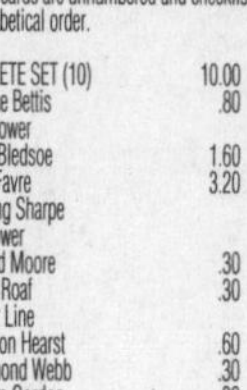

This set contains 315 standard-size cards. The cards were issued in series of 150 and 165. Cards were issued in 12-card packs for both series. The cards are checklisted below alphabetically according to teams. Special Collectibles (PC1-PC10) cards were randomly distributed in 12-card second series foil packs. Also randomly inserted in the packs were 2,150 bonus card certificates. One thousand five hundred could be redeemed for limited edition platinum cards of Paul Brown (first series) and 650 for Emmitt Smith (second series). Rookie Cards include Ricky Ervins, Brett Favre, Mike Pritchard, Leonard Russell and Harvey Williams.

COMPLETE SET (315) 5.00 10.00
COMP.SERIES 1 (150) 2.00 4.00
COMP.SERIES 2 (165) 3.00 6.00
1 Chris Miller .02 .10
2 Andre Rison .08 .25
3 Tim Green .01 .05
4 Jessie Tuggle .01 .05
5 Thurman Thomas .08 .25
6 Darryl Talley .01 .05
7 Kent Hull .01 .05
8 Bruce Smith .08 .25
9 Shane Conlan .01 .05
10 Jim Harbaugh .08 .25
11 Neal Anderson .02 .10
12 Mark Bortz .01 .05
13 Richard Dent .02 .10
14 Steve McMichael .01 .05
15 James Brooks .01 .05
16 Boomer Esiason .02 .10
17 Tim Krumrie .01 .05
18 James Francis .01 .05
19 Lewis Billups .01 .05
20 Eric Metcalf .08 .25
21 Kevin Mack .01 .05
22 Clay Matthews .02 .10
23 Mike Johnson .01 .05
24 Troy Aikman .30 .75
25 Emmitt Smith 1.00 2.50
26 Daniel Stubbs .01 .05
27 Ken Norton .02 .10
28 John Elway .50 1.25
29 Bobby Humphrey .01 .05
30 Simon Fletcher .01 .05
31 Karl Mecklenburg .01 .05
32 Rodney Peete .02 .10
33 Barry Sanders .50 1.25
34 Michael Cofer .01 .05
35 Jerry Ball .01 .05
36 Sterling Sharpe .08 .25
37 Tony Mandarich .01 .05
38 Brian Noble .01 .05
39 Tim Harris .01 .05
40 Warren Moon .02 .10
41 Ernest Givins UER .02 .10
(Misspelled Givens on card back)
42 Mike Munchak .02 .10
43 Sean Jones .02 .10
44 Ray Childress .02 .10
45 Jeff George .08 .25
46 Albert Bentley .01 .05
47 Duane Bickett .01 .05
48 Steve DeBerg .02 .10
49 Christian Okoye .02 .10
50 Neil Smith .08 .25
51 Derrick Thomas .08 .25
52 Willie Gault .02 .10
53 Don Mosebar .01 .05
54 Howie Long .08 .25
55 Greg Townsend .01 .05
56 Terry McDaniel .02 .10
57 Jackie Slater .01 .05
58 Jim Everett .02 .10
59 Cleveland Gary .01 .05
60 Mike Piel .01 .05
61 Jerry Gray .01 .05
62 Dan Marino .50 1.25
63 Sammie Smith .01 .05
64 Richmond Webb .01 .05
65 Louis Oliver .01 .05
66 Ferrell Edmunds .01 .05
67 Jeff Cross .01 .05
68 Wade Wilson .01 .05
69 Chris Doleman .02 .10
70 Joey Browner .01 .05
71 Keith Millard .01 .05
72 John Stephens .01 .05
73 Andre Tippett .01 .05
74 Brent Williams .01 .05
75 Craig Heyward .02 .10
76 Eric Martin .01 .05
77 Pat Swilling .02 .10
78 Sam Mills .02 .10
79 Jeff Hostetler .02 .10
80 Ottis Anderson .02 .10
81 Lawrence Taylor .08 .25
82 Pepper Johnson .01 .05
83 Blair Thomas .01 .05
84 Al Toon .02 .10
85 Ken O'Brien .01 .05
86 Erik McMillan .01 .05
87 Dennis Byrd .02 .10
88 Randall Cunningham .08 .25
89 Fred Barnett .08 .25
90 Seth Joyner .02 .10
91 Reggie White .08 .25
92 Timm Rosenbach .01 .05
93 Johnny Johnson .01 .05
94 Tim McDonald .01 .05
95 Freddie Joe Nunn .01 .05
96 Bubby Brister .02 .10
97 Gary Anderson K UER .01 .05
(Listed as RB)
98 Merril Hoge .01 .05
99 Keith Willis .01 .05
100 Rod Woodson .08 .25
101 Billy Joe Tolliver .01 .05
102 Marion Butts .02 .10
103 Rod Bernstine .01 .05
104 Lee Williams .01 .05
105 Burt Grossman UER .01 .05
(Photo on back is reversed)
106 Tom Rathman .01 .05
107 John Taylor .02 .10
108 Michael Carter .01 .05
109 Guy McIntyre .01 .05
110 Pierce Holt .01 .05
111 John L. Williams .01 .05
112 Dave Krieg .02 .10
113 Bryan Millard .01 .05
114 Cortez Kennedy .08 .25
115 Derrick Fenner .01 .05
116 Vinny Testaverde .02 .10
117 Reggie Cobb .01 .05
118 Gary Anderson RB .01 .05
119 Bruce Hill .01 .05
120 Wayne Haddix .01 .05
121 Broderick Thomas .01 .05
122 Keith McCants .01 .05
123 Andre Collins .02 .10
124 Earnest Byner .01 .05
125 Jim Lachey .01 .05
126 Mark Rypien .02 .10
127 Charles Mann .01 .05
128 Nick Lowery .01 .05
129 Chip Lohmiller .01 .05
130 Mike Horan .01 .05
131 Rohn Stark .01 .05
132 Sean Landeta .01 .05
133 Clarence Verdin .01 .05
134 Johnny Bailey .01 .05
135 Herschel Walker .02 .10
136 Bo Jackson PP .10 .30
137 Dexter Carter PP .01 .05
138 Warren Moon PP .02 .10
139 Joe Montana PP .50 1.25
140 Jerry Rice PP .30 .75
141 Deion Sanders PP .15 .40
142 Ronnie Lippett PP .01 .05
143 Terance Mathis PP .08 .25
144 Gaston Green PP .01 .05
145 Dean Biasucci PP .01 .05
146 Charles Haley PP .02 .10
147 Derrick Thomas PP .08 .25
148 Lawrence Taylor PP .02 .10
149 Art Shell CO PP .02 .10
150 Bill Parcells CO PP .02 .10
151 Steve Broussard .01 .05
152 Darion Conner .01 .05
153 Bill Fralic .01 .05
154 Mike Gann .01 .05
155 Tim McKyer .01 .05
156 Don Beebe UER .01 .05
(4 TD's against Dolphins, should be against Steelers)
157 Cornelius Bennett .02 .10
158 Andre Reed .08 .25
159 Leonard Smith .01 .05
160 Will Wolford .01 .05
161 Mark Carrier DB .02 .10
162 Wendell Davis .01 .05
163 Jay Hilgenberg .01 .05
164 Brad Muster .01 .05
165 Mike Singletary .02 .10
166 Eddie Brown .01 .05
167 David Fulcher .01 .05
168 Rodney Holman .01 .05
169 Anthony Munoz .02 .10
170 Craig Taylor RC .01 .05
171 Mike Baab .01 .05
172 David Grayson .01 .05
173 Reggie Langhorne .01 .05
174 Joe Morris .01 .05
175 Kevin Gogan RC .01 .05
176 Jack Del Rio .02 .10
177 Issiac Holt .01 .05
178 Michael Irvin .08 .25
179 Jay Novacek .08 .25
180 Steve Atwater .01 .05
181 Mark Jackson .01 .05
182 Ricky Nattiel .01 .05
183 Warren Powers .01 .05
184 Dennis Smith .01 .05
185 Bennie Blades .01 .05
186 Lomas Brown UER .01 .05
(Spent 6 seasons with Detroit, not 7)
187 Robert Clark UER .01 .05
(Plan B acquisition in 1989, not 1990)
188 Mel Gray .02 .10
189 Chris Spielman .02 .10
190 Johnny Holland .01 .05
191 Don Majkowski .01 .05
192 Bryce Paup RC .08 .25
193 Darrell Thompson .01 .05
194 Ed West UER .01 .05
(Photo on back is reversed)
195 Cris Dishman RC .02 .10
196 Drew Hill .02 .10
197 Bruce Matthews .02 .10
198 Bubba McDowell .01 .05
199 Allen Pinkett .01 .05
200 Bill Brooks .02 .10
201 Jeff Herrod .01 .05
202 Anthony Johnson .02 .10
203 Mike Prior .01 .05
204 John Alt .01 .05
205 Stephone Paige .01 .05
206 Kevin Ross .01 .05
207 Dan Saleaumua .01 .05
208 Barry Word .01 .05
209 Marcus Allen .08 .25
210 Roger Craig .02 .10
211 Ronnie Lott .02 .10
212 Winston Moss .01 .05
213 Jay Schroeder .01 .05
214 Robert Delpino .01 .05
215 Henry Ellard .02 .10
216 Kevin Greene .02 .10
217 Tom Newberry .01 .05
218 Michael Stewart .01 .05
219 Mark Duper .02 .10
220 Mark Higgs RC .01 .05
221 John Offerdahl UER .01 .05
(2nd round pick in/1986, not 6th)
222 Keith Sims .01 .05
223 Anthony Carter .02 .10
224 Cris Carter .20 .50
225 Steve Jordan .01 .05
226 Randall McDaniel .02 .10
227 Al Noga .01 .05
228 Ray Agnew .01 .05
229 Bruce Armstrong .01 .05
230 Irving Fryar .02 .10
231 Greg McMurtry .01 .05
232 Chris Singleton .01 .05
233 Morten Andersen .01 .05
234 Vince Buck .01 .05
235 Gill Fenerty .01 .05
236 Rickey Jackson .02 .10
237 Vaughan Johnson .01 .05
238 Carl Banks .01 .05
239 Mark Collins .01 .05
240 Rodney Hampton .08 .25
241 David Meggett .02 .10
242 Bart Oates .01 .05
243 Kyle Clifton .01 .05
244 Jeff Lageman .02 .10
245 Freeman McNeil UER .02 .10
(Drafted in 1981, not '80)
246 Rob Moore .08 .25
247 Eric Allen .01 .05
248 Keith Byars .02 .10
249 Keith Jackson .02 .10
250 Jim McMahon .02 .10
251 Andre Waters .01 .05
252 Ken Harvey .02 .10
253 Ernie Jones .01 .05
254 Luis Sharpe .01 .05
255 Anthony Thompson .01 .05
256 Tom Tupa .01 .05
257 Eric Green .02 .10
258 Barry Foster .02 .10
259 Bryan Hinkle .01 .05
260 Tunch Ilkin .01 .05
261 Louis Lipps .01 .05
262 Gill Byrd .01 .05
263 John Friesz .02 .10
264 Anthony Miller .02 .10
265 Junior Seau .08 .25
266 Ronnie Harmon .02 .10
267 Harris Barton .01 .05
268 Todd Bowles .01 .05
269 Don Griffin .01 .05
270 Bill Romanowski .01 .05
271 Steve Young .30 .75
272 Brian Blades .02 .10
273 Jacob Green .01 .05
274 Rufus Porter .01 .05
275 Eugene Robinson .01 .05
276 Mark Carrier WR .02 .10
277 Reuben Davis .01 .05
278 Paul Gruber .01 .05
279 Gary Clark .08 .25
280 Darrell Green .02 .10
281 Wilber Marshall .01 .05
282 Matt Millen .02 .10
283 Alvin Walton .01 .05
284 Joe Gibbs CO UER .02 .10
(NFLPA logo on back)
285 Don Shula CO UER .02 .10
(NFLPA logo on back)
286 Larry Brown DB RC .02 .10
287 Mike Croel RC .01 .05
288 Antone Davis RC .01 .05
289 Ricky Ervins RC UER .02 .10
(2nd round choice, should say 3rd)
290 Brett Favre RC 3.00 8.00
291 Pat Harlow RC .01 .05
292 Michael Jackson WR RC .08 .25
293 Henry Jones RC .02 .10
294 Aaron Craver RC .01 .05
295 Nick Bell RC .01 .05
296 Todd Lyght RC .02 .10
297 Todd Marinovich RC .01 .05
298 Russell Maryland RC .02 .10
299 Kanavis McGhee RC .01 .05
300 Dan McGwire RC .02 .10
301 Charles McRae RC .01 .05
302 Eric Moten RC .01 .05
303 Jerome Henderson RC .01 .05
304 Browning Nagle RC .01 .05
305 Mike Pritchard RC .08 .25
306 Stanley Richard RC .02 .10
307 Randal Hill RC .02 .10
308 Leonard Russell RC .02 .10
309 Eric Swann RC .02 .10
310 Phil Hansen RC .01 .05
311 Moe Gardner RC .01 .05
312 Jon Vaughn RC .01 .05
313 Aeneas Williams RC UER .08 .25
(Misspelled Aaneas on card back)
314 Alfred Williams RC .01 .05
315 Harvey Williams RC .08 .25
PM1 Emmitt Smith/650* 125.00 250.00
(1.28 grams actual platinum)
PM2 Paul Brown/1500* 25.00 60.00
(1.28 grams actual platinum)

1991 Pro Set Platinum PC

COMPLETE SET (10) 4.00 10.00
RANDOM INSERTS IN SER.2 PACKS
PC1 Bobby Hebert .05 .15
PC2 Art Monk .08 .25
PC3 Kenny Walker .05 .15
PC4 Low Fives .05 .15
PC5 Touchdown .05 .15
Kevin Mack
PC6 Neal Anderson .08 .25
PC7 Gaston Green .05 .15
PC8 Barry Sanders 1.25 3.00
PC9 Emmitt Smith 2.00 5.00
PC10 Thurman Thomas .25 .60

1991-92 Pro Set Platinum

The 1991-92 Pro Set Platinum hockey set was released in two series of 150 standard-size cards. The front design features full-bleed glossy color action player photos, with the Pro Set Platinum icon superimposed at the lower right corner. Player names do not appear on the front.

COMPLETE SET (300) 3.00 8.00
COMP.SERIES 1 (150) 1.50 4.00
COMP.SERIES 2 (150) 1.50 4.00
293 Jim Kelly CAP .07 .20

1995 Pro Stamps

Chris Martin Enterprises produced this stamp set with distribution in sheets of 12 stamps. Each stamp measures approximately 1 1/2" by 2." The first 140-stamps were included as part of the 12-stamp sheets with four stamps being double-printed.

COMPLETE SET (140) 16.00 40.00
1 Steve Young DP .30 .75
2 Jerry Rice .60 1.50
3 Deion Sanders .30 .75
4 Dana Stubblefield .05 .15
5 William Floyd .08 .25
6 Troy Aikman DP .50 1.25
7 Michael Irvin .20 .50
8 Emmitt Smith DP .80 2.00
9 Russell Maryland .05 .15
10 Daryl Johnston .08 .25
11 Dan Marino DP .80 2.00
12 Bernie Parmalee .05 .15
13 Tim Bowens .05 .15
14 Irving Fryar .08 .25
15 Bryan Cox .05 .15
16 Drew Bledsoe .60 1.50
17 Bruce Armstrong .05 .15
18 Vincent Brisby .05 .15
19 Marion Butts .05 .15
20 Ben Coates .08 .25
21 Dave Brown .05 .15
22 Michael Brooks .05 .15
23 Jumbo Elliott .05 .15
24 Rodney Hampton .08 .25
25 Mike Sherrard .05 .15
26 Jeff Hostetler .05 .15
27 Tim Brown .20 .50
28 Rocket Ismail .08 .25
29 James Jett .08 .25
30 Harvey Williams .05 .15
31 Heath Shuler .08 .25
32 Reggie Brooks .05 .15
33 Ricky Ervins .05 .15
34 Darrell Green UER .05 .15
Darryl on front
35 Brian Mitchell .05 .15
36 Trace Armstrong .05 .15
37 Dante Jones .05 .15
38 Steve Walsh .05 .15
39 Donnell Woolford .05 .15
40 Tim Worley .05 .15
41 Boomer Esiason .08 .25
42 Aaron Glenn .05 .15
43 Johnny Johnson .05 .15
44 Nick Lowery .05 .15
45 Johnny Mitchell .05 .15
46 Neil O'Donnell .08 .25
47 Barry Foster .05 .15
48 Byron Bam Morris .05 .15
49 Rod Woodson .08 .25
50 Kevin Greene .08 .25
51 Randall Cunningham .20 .50
52 Bubby Brister .05 .15
53 Fred Barnett .05 .15
54 Charlie Garner .05 .15
55 Calvin Williams .05 .15
56 Brett Favre 1.20 3.00
57 Reggie White .20 .50
58 Edgar Bennett .05 .15
59 Robert Brooks .08 .25
60 Sean Jones .05 .15
61 Ronnie Harmon .05 .15
62 Stan Humphries .08 .25
63 Natrone Means .08 .25
64 Tony Martin .20 .50
65 Junior Seau .20 .50
66 John Elway 1.20 3.00
67 Glyn Milburn .05 .15
68 Rod Bernstine .05 .15
69 Anthony Miller .08 .25
70 Shannon Sharpe .20 .50
71 Barry Sanders 1.20 3.00

72 Scott Mitchell	.08	.25
73 Herman Moore	.20	.50
74 Brett Perriman	.08	.25
75 Chris Spielman	.08	.25
76 Marcus Allen	.20	.50
77 Steve Bono	.08	.25
78 Willie Davis	.08	.25
79 Lake Dawson	.08	.25
80 Neil Smith	.08	.25
81 Vinny Testaverde	.08	.25
82 Eric Turner	.05	.15
83 Antonio Langham	.05	.15
84 Leroy Hoard	.05	.15
85 Derrick Alexander WR	.08	.25
86 Jim Kelly	.20	.50
87 Cornelius Bennett	.08	.25
88 Andre Reed	.08	.25
89 Bruce Smith	.20	.50
90 Darryl Talley	.05	.15
91 Warren Moon	.20	.50
92 Qadry Ismail	.05	.15
93 Terry Allen	.20	.50
94 Cris Carter	.20	.50
95 John Randle	.08	.25
96 Jeff George	.20	.50
97 Chris Doleman	.05	.15
98 Craig Heyward	.08	.25
99 Terance Mathis	.08	.25
100 Jessie Tuggle	.05	.15
101 Jerome Bettis	.20	.50
102 Sean Gilbert	.05	.15
103 Troy Drayton	.05	.15
104 Wayne Gandy	.05	.15
105 Todd Lyght	.05	.15
106 Jeff Blake	.20	.50
107 Harold Green	.05	.15
108 Carl Pickens	.08	.25
109 Dan Wilkinson	.05	.15
110 Darnay Scott	.08	.25
111 Cody Carlson	.05	.15
112 Gary Brown	.05	.15
113 Ernest Givins	.05	.15
114 Haywood Jeffires	.05	.15
115 Bruce Matthews	.05	.15
116 Jim Everett	.05	.15
117 Morten Andersen	.05	.15
118 Quinn Early	.05	.15
119 Tyrone Hughes	.05	.15
120 Renaldo Turnbull	.05	.15
121 Larry Centers	.08	.25
122 Garrison Hearst	.20	.50
123 Seth Joyner	.05	.15
124 Ronald Moore	.05	.15
125 Eric Swann	.05	.15
126 Rick Mirer	.08	.25
127 Chris Warren	.08	.25
128 Brian Blades	.05	.15
129 Cortez Kennedy	.05	.15
130 Eugene Robinson	.05	.15
131 Marshall Faulk	.20	.50
132 Quentin Coryatt	.05	.15
133 Jim Harbaugh	.20	.50
134 Roosevelt Potts	.05	.15
135 Steve Emtman	.05	.15
136 Trent Dilfer	.08	.25
137 Santana Dotson	.05	.15
138 Errict Rhett	.08	.25
139 Thomas Everett	.05	.15
140 Craig Erickson	.05	.15

1996 Pro Stamps

Chris Martin Enterprises released two different Pro Stamps sets in 1996. This set was sold in 12-stamp packages. They were essentially a re-make of the 1995 issue with the same stamp design and many of the same player photos. Some new players, however, were added for 1996 as were stamps for the two expansion teams. Each stamp measures approximately 1 1/2" by 2." Unlike the team set stamps, these are numbered in gold foil above the player's name.

COMPLETE SET (144)	14.00	35.00
1 Steve Young	.30	.75
2 Jerry Rice	.40	1.00
3 Merton Hanks	.05	.15
4 J.J.Stokes	.15	.40
5 William Floyd	.08	.25
6 Troy Aikman	.40	1.00
7 Michael Irvin	.15	.40
8 Emmitt Smith	.80	2.00
9 Deion Sanders	.25	.60
10 Daryl Johnston	.08	.25
11 Dan Marino	1.00	2.50
12 Bernie Parmalee	.05	.15
13 O.J. McDuffie	.08	.25
14 Richmond Webb	.05	.15
15 Eric Green	.05	.15
16 Drew Bledsoe	.30	.75
17 Bruce Armstrong	.05	.15
18 Dave Meggett	.05	.15
19 Curtis Martin	.30	.75
20 Ben Coates	.08	.25
21 Dave Brown	.05	.15
22 Michael Brooks	.05	.15
23 Tyrone Wheatley	.08	.25
24 Rodney Hampton	.08	.25
25 Jeff Hostetler	.05	.15
26 Tim Brown	.15	.40
27 Rocket Ismail	.08	.25
28 James Jett	.08	.25
29 Harvey Williams	.08	.25
30 Heath Shuler	.08	.25
31 Michael Westbrook	.15	.40
32 Terry Allen	.15	.40
33 Darrell Green	.08	.25
34 Brian Mitchell	.05	.15
35 Rashaan Salaam	.08	.25
36 Erik Kramer UER 37	.05	.15
37 Donnell Woolford	.05	.15
38 Alonzo Spellman	.05	.15
39 Kyle Brady	.08	.25
40 Aaron Glenn	.05	.15
41 Adrian Murrell	.08	.25
42 Nick Lowery	.05	.15
43 Charles Johnson	.08	.25
44 Kordell Stewart	.30	.75
45 Yancey Thigpen	.08	.25
46 Rod Woodson	.08	.25
47 Greg Lloyd	.15	.40
48 Randall Cunningham	.15	.40
49 Rodney Peete	.05	.15
50 Ricky Watters	.15	.40
51 Charlie Garner	.08	.25
52 Calvin Williams	.05	.15
53 Brett Favre	1.00	2.50
54 Reggie White	.15	.40
55 Edgar Bennett	.08	.25
56 Robert Brooks	.15	.40
57 Sean Jones	.05	.15
58 Ronnie Harmon	.05	.15
59 Stan Humphries	.08	.25
60 Andre Coleman	.05	.15
61 Tony Martin	.08	.25
62 Junior Seau	.15	.40
63 John Elway	1.00	2.50
64 Mike Pritchard	.05	.15
65 Terrell Davis	1.00	2.50
66 Anthony Miller	.08	.25
67 Shannon Sharpe	.15	.40
68 Barry Sanders	1.00	2.50
69 Scott Mitchell	.08	.25
70 Herman Moore	.08	.25
71 Brett Perriman	.08	.25
72 Johnnie Morton	.08	.25
73 Marcus Allen	.15	.40
74 Steve Bono	.08	.25
75 Tamarick Vanover	.08	.25
76 Lake Dawson	.08	.25
77 Neil Smith	.08	.25
78 Vinny Testaverde	.08	.25
79 Eric Turner	.05	.15
80 Michael Jackson	.08	.25
81 Leroy Hoard	.05	.15
82 Andre Rison	.15	.40
83 Jim Kelly	.15	.40
84 Carwell Gardner	.05	.15
85 Andre Reed	.08	.25
86 Bruce Smith	.15	.40
87 Bryce Paup	.08	.25
88 Warren Moon	.15	.40
89 Qadry Ismail	.08	.25
90 Robert Smith	.08	.25
91 Cris Carter	.15	.40
92 David Palmer	.05	.15
93 Jeff George	.15	.40
94 Morten Andersen	.05	.15
95 Craig Heyward	.05	.15
96 Eric Metcalf	.08	.25
97 Jessie Tuggle	.05	.15
98 Roman Phifer	.05	.15
99 Todd Lyght	.05	.15
100 Troy Drayton	.05	.15
101 Isaac Bruce	.15	.40
102 Sean Gilbert	.05	.15
103 Jeff Blake	.15	.40
104 Harold Green	.05	.15
105 Carl Pickens	.08	.25
106 Dan Wilkinson	.05	.15
107 Ki-Jana Carter	.08	.25
108 Steve McNair	.40	1.00
109 Gary Brown	.05	.15
110 Haywood Jeffires	.05	.15
111 Bruce Matthews	.05	.15
112 Jim Everett	.05	.15
113 Mario Bates	.08	.25
114 Ray Zellars	.05	.15
115 Tyrone Hughes	.05	.15
116 Eric Allen	.05	.15
117 Larry Centers	.08	.25
118 Garrison Hearst	.15	.40
119 Aeneas Williams	.05	.15
120 Rob Moore	.08	.25
121 Neil O'Donnell	.08	.25
122 Rick Mirer	.08	.25
123 Chris Warren	.08	.25
124 Eric Swann	.05	.15
125 Cortez Kennedy	.08	.25
126 Joey Galloway	.25	.60
127 Marshall Faulk	.15	.40
128 Quentin Coryatt	.05	.15
129 Jim Harbaugh	.15	.40
130 Trev Alberts	.05	.15
131 Zack Crockett	.05	.15
132 Trent Dilfer	.15	.40
133 Hardy Nickerson	.05	.15
134 Errict Rhett	.15	.40
135 Alvin Harper	.05	.15
136 Sam Mills	.05	.15
137 Tyrone Poole	.08	.25
138 Kerry Collins	.15	.40
139 Bob Christian	.05	.15
140 Randy Baldwin	.05	.15
141 Steve Beuerlein	.08	.25
142 Mark Brunell	.40	1.00
143 Tony Boselli	.08	.25
144 Jeff Lageman	.05	.15

1996 Pro Stamps Team Sets

Chris Martin Enterprises released a second version of some of its Pro Stamps from 1996. This set was sold as four different 6-stamp team sets. Five player stamps and one team logo stamp was included in each pack. They were essentially a re-make of the 1995 issue with the same stamp design and many of the same player photos. Some new players, however, were added for 1996 as were stamps for the two expansion teams. Each stamp measures approximately 1 1/2" by 2." These team set stamps are unnumbered, but have been assigned numbers below according to the alphabetical player list by team. The team logos were added to the end of the player listings.

COMPLETE SET (24)	6.00	15.00
CP1 Randy Baldwin	.14	.35
CP2 Bob Christian	.14	.35
CP3 Kerry Collins	.20	.50
CP4 Sam Mills	.14	.35
CP5 Tyrone Poole	.14	.35
CP6 Panthers Logo	.20	.50
DC1 Troy Aikman	.50	1.25
DC2 Michael Irvin	.20	.50
DC3 Daryl Johnston	.20	.50
DC4 Deion Sanders	.30	.75
DC5 Emmitt Smith	.80	2.00
DC6 Cowboys Logo	.20	.50
JJ1 Steve Beuerlein	.20	.50
JJ2 Tony Boselli	.20	.50
JJ3 Mark Brunell	.50	1.25
JJ4 Desmond Howard	.14	.35
JJ5 Jeff Lageman	.14	.35
JJ6 Jaguars Logo	.14	.35
SF1 William Floyd	.20	.50
SF2 Merton Hanks	.14	.35
SF3 Jerry Rice	.50	1.25
SF4 Dana Stubblefield	.20	.50
SF5 Steve Young	.40	1.00
SF6 49ers Logo	.20	.50

1998 Pro Stamps

These stamps were issued by Crown Pro in sheets of six with each sheet representing a category, such as NFC Quarterbacks. We've listed and priced them below in panels as this is the form in which they are most commonly traded. Each stamp measures roughly 1 13/16" by 1 3/8" while the entire panel along with the backer board measures 4 1/2" by 7 1/2."

COMPLETE SET (7)	5.60	14.00
1 Jake Plummer	1.20	3.00
Troy Aikman		
Brett Favre		
Danny Kanell		
Bobby Hoying		
Steve Young		
2 John Elway	1.20	3.00
Dan Marino		
Kordell Stewart		
Mark Brunell		
Jeff George		
Drew Bledsoe		
3 Emmitt Smith	1.20	3.00
Barry Sanders		
Warrick Dunn		
Terry Allen		
Jamaal Anderson		
Mike Alstott		
4 Jerome Bettis	.80	2.00
Terrell Davis		
Marcus Allen		
Antowain Smith		
Eddie George		
Corey Dillon		
5 Jerry Rice	.80	2.00
Robert Brooks		
Cris Carter		
Curtis Conway		
Isaac Bruce		
Herman Moore		
6 Andre Rison	1.20	3.00
Tim Brown		
Joey Galloway		
Terry Glenn		
Marvin Harrison		
Keyshawn Johnson		
7 John Randle	.80	2.00
Wayne Martin		
Lamar Lathon		
Junior Seau		
Derrick Thomas		
Peter Boulware		

1994 Pro Tags

This set of 168 Pro Tags marks the third consecutive year that Chris Martin Enterprises, Inc. has issued this line of sports collectibles. This first two sets were called Dog Tags. Measuring approximately 2 1/8" by 3 3/8", the plastic tags were sold six to a blister pack. A checklist card (printed on glossy paper) and a free team tag were included in each blister pack. Pro tags autographed by Jerome Bettis, J.J. Birden, Dale Carter, Keith Cash, Willie Davis, Sean Gilbert, Todd Lyght, Chris Martin, Roman Phifer, and Neil Smith were randomly seeded in packs. The set included an offer to receive 6 AFC or 6 NFC Super Rookie Pro Tags for $10.99 and 3 Proofs-of-Purchase for each set, or all 12 Super Rookies for $15.99 and 5 Proofs-of-Purchase. A parallel set was issued for Super Bowl XXIX in factory set form with an announced print run of just 750. The factory set included three autographed cards, all 168 base cards, 12 Super Rookies, and a Super Bowl XXIX logo card.

COMPLETE SET (168)	35.00	80.00
*SUPER BOWL XXIX: .4X TO 1X BASIC CARDS		
1 Steve Beuerlein	.40	1.00
2 Chuck Cecil	.20	.50
3 Randal Hill	.20	.50
4 Garrison Hearst	.20	.50
5 Ricky Proehl	.20	.50
6 Eric Swann	.40	1.00
7 Jeff George	.50	1.25
8 Drew Hill	.20	.50
9 Erric Pegram	.40	1.00
10 Andre Rison	.50	1.25
11 Deion Sanders	.80	2.00
12 Jessie Tuggle	.20	.50
13 Cornelius Bennett	.40	1.00
14 Kenneth Davis	.20	.50
15 Jim Kelly	.50	1.25
16 Andre Reed	.40	1.00
17 Darryl Talley	.20	.50
18 Steve Tasker	.40	1.00
19 Trace Armstrong	.20	.50
20 Curtis Conway UER (misnumbered 22)	.50	1.25
21 Dante Jones	.20	.50
22 Donnell Woolford	.20	.50
23 Tim Worley	.20	.50
24 Chris Zorich	.40	1.00
25 Derrick Fenner	.20	.50
26 Harold Green	.20	.50
27 David Klingler	.20	.50
28 Tony McGee	.20	.50
29 Carl Pickens	.40	1.00
30 Jeff Query	.20	.50
31 Mark Carrier WR	.40	1.00
32 Michael Jackson	.40	1.00
33 Eric Metcalf	.40	1.00
34 Michael Dean Perry	.40	1.00
35 Vinny Testaverde	.40	1.00
36 Tommy Vardell	.20	.50
37 Troy Aikman	1.20	3.00
38 Alvin Harper	.20	.50
39 Michael Irvin	.50	1.25
40 Russell Maryland	.40	1.00
41 Jay Novacek	.40	1.00
42 Emmitt Smith	2.00	5.00
43 Rod Bernstine	.20	.50
44 Mike Croel	.20	.50
45 John Elway	2.40	6.00
46 Glyn Milburn	.40	1.00
47 Shannon Sharpe	.50	1.25
48 Dennis Smith	.20	.50
49 Jason Hanson	.20	.50
50 Herman Moore	.50	1.25
51 Brett Perriman	.40	1.00
52 Barry Sanders	2.40	6.00
53 Chris Spielman	.40	1.00
54 Pat Swilling	.40	1.00
55 Edgar Bennett	.40	1.00
56 Terrell Buckley	.20	.50
57 Brett Favre	2.40	6.00
58 Chris Jacke	.20	.50
59 Sterling Sharpe	.40	1.00
60 Reggie White	.50	1.25
61 Gary Brown	.20	.50
62 Cody Carlson	.20	.50
63 Ernest Givins	.20	.50
64 Haywood Jeffires	.40	1.00
65 Bruce Matthews	.20	.50
66 Webster Slaughter	.20	.50
67 Jason Belser	.20	.50
68 Kerry Cash	.20	.50
69 Rodney Culver	.20	.50
70 Jim Harbaugh	.50	1.25
71 Scott Radecic	.20	.50
72 Roosevelt Potts	.20	.50
73 Marcus Allen	.50	1.25
74 J.J. Birden	.20	.50
75 Dale Carter	.20	.50
76 Keith Cash	.20	.50
77 Willie Davis	.40	1.00
78 Neil Smith	.40	1.00
79 Eddie Anderson	.20	.50
80 Tim Brown	.50	1.25
81 Jeff Hostetler	.40	1.00
82 Rocket Ismail	.50	1.25
83 James Jett	.20	.50
84 Terry McDaniel	.20	.50
85 Flipper Anderson	.20	.50
86 Jerome Bettis	.80	2.00
87 Troy Drayton	.40	1.00
88 Sean Gilbert UER (misnumbered 87)	.20	.50
89 Todd Lyght	.20	.50
90 Chris Martin	.20	.50
91 Keith Byars	.20	.50
92 Bryan Cox	.20	.50
93 Irving Fryar	.40	1.00
94 Terry Kirby	.40	1.00
95 Dan Marino	2.40	6.00
96 O.J. McDuffie	.50	1.25
97 Terry Allen	.50	1.25
98 Cris Carter	.50	1.25
99 Qadry Ismail	.40	1.00
100 Randall McDaniel	.20	.50
101 Warren Moon	.50	1.25
102 Robert Smith	.50	1.25
103 Drew Bledsoe	1.20	3.00
104 Vincent Brisby	.40	1.00
105 Vincent Brown	.20	.50
106 Marv Cook	.20	.50
107 Leonard Russell	.20	.50
108 Reyna Thompson	.20	.50
109 Morten Andersen	.20	.50
110 Quinn Early	.20	.50
111 Tyrone Hughes	.20	.50
112 Sam Mills	.20	.50
113 Willie Roaf	.20	.50
114 Renaldo Turnbull	.20	.50
115 Phil Simms	.40	1.00
116 John Elliott	.20	.50
117 Rodney Hampton	.40	1.00
118 Mark Jackson	.20	.50
119 Dave Meggett	.20	.50
120 Kenyon Rasheed	.20	.50
121 Brad Baxter	.20	.50
122 Boomer Esiason	.40	1.00
123 Johnny Johnson	.20	.50
124 Ronnie Lott	.40	1.00
125 Johnny Mitchell	.20	.50
126 Rob Moore	.40	1.00
127 Fred Barnett	.40	1.00
128 Mark Bavaro	.20	.50
129 Bubby Brister	.40	1.00
130 Randall Cunningham	.50	1.25
131 Tim Harris	.20	.50
132 Herschel Walker	.40	1.00
133 Gary Anderson K	.20	.50
134 Barry Foster	.20	.50
135 Kevin Greene	.40	1.00
136 Greg Lloyd	.40	1.00
137 Neil O'Donnell	.40	1.00
138 Rod Woodson	.40	1.00
139 Eric Bieniemy UER (misnumbered 189)	.20	.50
140 Ronnie Harmon UER (misnumbered 190)	.40	1.00
141 Stan Humphries UER (misnumbered 191)	.40	1.00
142 Natrone Means UER misnumbered 192)	.50	1.25
143 Leslie O'Neal UER misnumbered 193)	.40	1.00
144 Junior Seau UER misnumbered 194)	.50	1.25
145 Tim McDonald	.20	.50
146 Jerry Rice	1.20	3.00
147 Dana Stubblefield	.40	1.00
148 John Taylor	.40	1.00
149 Ricky Watters UER (misnumbered 147)	.40	1.00
150 Steve Young	1.00	2.50
151 Brian Blades	.40	1.00
152 Cortez Kennedy	.40	1.00
153 Rick Mirer	.40	1.00
154 Rufus Porter	.20	.50
155 Eugene Robinson	.20	.50
156 Chris Warren	.40	1.00
157 Santana Dotson	.40	1.00
158 Craig Erickson	.20	.50
159 Hardy Nickerson	.40	1.00
160 Dan Stryzinski	.20	.50
161 Charles Wilson	.20	.50
162 Thomas Everett UER (misnumbered 147)	.20	.50
163 Reggie Brooks	.20	.50
164 Darrell Green	.20	.50
165 Ricky Ervins	.20	.50
166 John Friesz	.40	1.00
167 Brian Mitchell	.40	1.00
168 Sterling Palmer	.20	.50
CL Chris Martin CL	.08	.25

1994 Pro Tags Super Rookies

COMPLETE SET (12)	4.00	10.00
*SUPER BOWL XXIX: .4X TO 1X		
1 Dan Wilkinson	.30	.75
2 Marshall Faulk	2.00	5.00
3 Johnnie Morton	.40	1.00
4 Trent Dilfer	.75	2.00
5A Greg Hill	.40	1.00
5B Errict Rhett	.40	1.00
6 Lake Dawson	.30	.75
7 Willie McGinest	.40	1.00
8 Andre Coleman	.20	.60
9 Heath Shuler	.50	1.25
10 Wayne Gandy	.20	.50
11 John Thierry	.20	.50

2000 Quad City Steamwheelers AF2

COMPLETE SET (35)	10.00	20.00
1 Corey Brown	.30	.75
2 Chad Buntin	.30	.75
3 Frank Carter	.30	.75
4 Cornelius Coe	.30	.75
5 Billy Dicken	.30	.75
6 Jesse Eaton	.30	.75
7 Jay Ellers	.30	.75
8 Josh Fourdyce	.30	.75
9 Eddie Gibson	.30	.75
10 Mike Gluski	.30	.75
11 Frank Haege CO	.30	.75
12 Brion Hurley	.30	.75
13 Scott Hvistendahl	.30	.75
14 Shon King	.30	.75
15 Sean McNamara	.30	.75
16 Xavier Patterson	.30	.75
17 Hiawatha Phifer	.30	.75
18 Spencer Stevens	.30	.75
19 Clarence Thompson	.30	.75
20 Russ Van Wetzinga	.30	.75
21 Jamarr Ward	.30	.75
22 Jeremy Wilkinson	.30	.75
23 Damon Williams	.30	.75
24 Jim Foster OWN	.30	.75
25 Asst Coaches	.30	.75
26 Steamwheeler (Mascot)	.30	.75
27 Broadcasters	.30	.75
28 Office Staff	.30	.75
29 Deckmates	.30	.75
Joanne Landis		
Kristina Lindquist		
30 Deckmates	.30	.75
Carolina Espinoza		
Deanna Ludin		
31 Deckmates	.30	.75
Jae Lynne McClellan		
Wendy Taets		
32 Deckmates	.30	.75
Shelly Engler		
Nicky Hyneck		
33 Deckmates	.30	.75
Jennifer Hopkins		
Julie Adams		
34 Deckmates	.30	.75
Sarah Widick		
Megan Linke		
35 Deckmates	.30	.75
Tennesha McCannon		
Allison Samson		

2002 Quad City Steamwheelers AF2

This set was sponsored by Sprint PCS and features members of the Quad City Steamrollers of the Arena Football League 2. Each card includes the team name and year running vertically on the left hand side of the front along with a color player photo. The cardbacks are also printed in color and feature another player photo and a player bio.

COMPLETE SET (40)	6.00	15.00
1 Chris Anthony	.30	.75
2 LaVance Banks	.20	.50
3 Cory Bern	.20	.50
4 Corey Brown	.20	.50
5 Brent Browner	.20	.50
6 Lamon Caldwell	.20	.50
7 Mike Cawley	.30	.75
8 Trent Clemen	.20	.50
9 Derrick Davison	.20	.50
10 Jay Eilers	.20	.50
11 Jim Foster OWN	.20	.50
12 Josh Fourdyce	.20	.50
13 Ira Gooch	.20	.50
14 Phil Hayek MGR	.20	.50
Phil Roehlk ASST CO		
15 Brian Hegnauer	.20	.50
16 Jeff Hewitt	.30	.75
17 Rich Ingold CO	.20	.50
18 Reggie Mathis ASST CO	.20	.50
19 Tim McGill	.20	.50
20 Dan McMullen	.20	.50
21 Shawn Orr	.20	.50
22 Hiawatha Phifer	.20	.50
23 Jon Roehlk ASST CO	.20	.50
24 Mike Schaefer	.20	.50
25 T.J. Schneckloth	.20	.50
26 Justin Thies	.20	.50
27 Eric Thigpen	.20	.50
28 Brett Thompson	.20	.50
29 Frank Trentadue	.30	.75
30 Damon Williams	.20	.50
31 Pee-Wee Woods	.20	.50
32 Tony Zimmerman	.40	1.00
33 Jim Albracht	.20	.50
John Furlong		
(Broadcast Team)		
34 DeckMates - First Year	.20	.50
35 DeckMates - Veterans	.20	.50
36 Front Office Staff	.20	.50
37 Physical Therapy	.20	.50
Training Staff		
38 Steamwheeler Willie/ MASCOT	.20	.50
39 Team Physicians	.20	.50
40 Cover Card	.20	.50

2003 Quad City Steamwheelers AF2

This set was sponsored by US Celular and features members of the Quad City Steamwheelers of the Arena Football League 2. Each card includes the team name below the player photo and the player's name above. The cardbacks are also feature a player photo as well as a player bio.

COMPLETE SET (39)	6.00	15.00
1 Brian Berg	.20	.50
2 Cory Bern	.20	.50
3 Corey Brown	.20	.50
4 Tony Burrier	.20	.50
5 Jamaal Cherry	.20	.50
6 LaRico Cole	.20	.50
7 Tim Dodge	.30	.75
8 Leo FenceRoy	.20	.50
9 Jim Foster AFL Founder	.20	.50
10 Matt Forbes	.20	.50
11 Josh Fourdyce	.20	.50
12 Asa Francis	.20	.50
13 Ira Gooch	.20	.50
14 Ronnie Gordon	.20	.50
15 Jeff Hewitt	.30	.75
16 James Houston	.20	.50
17 Rich Ingold CO	.20	.50
18 Randall Lane	.20	.50
19 Ed Lanford	.20	.50
Jon Roehlk Asst.CO		
20 Shawn Orr	.20	.50
21 O.J. Payne	.20	.50
22 Paul Savich	.20	.50
23 Michael Schaefer	.20	.50
24 T.J. Schneckloth	.20	.50
25 Justin Thies	.20	.50
26 Danny Thomas	.20	.50
27 Pete Traynor	.20	.50
28 Lee Wiggins	.20	.50
29 Damon Williams	.20	.50
30 Tony Zimmerman	.40	1.00
31 DeckMates	.20	.50
Janette Duhm		
Allie Toolate		
Ashley Wadsworth		
32 DeckMates	.20	.50
Steph Hillyer		
Kim Pierce		
Jen Hopkins-Tarchinski		
33 DeckMates	.20	.50
Julie Ziegenhorn		
Ashley Rubino		
AnMarie McCrery		
Brittany Corbett		
34 Quad Cities Arena	.20	.50
Cover Card		
35 Radio Broadcast Team	.20	.50
Jim Albracht		
John Furlong		
36 Senior Management	.20	.50
37 Steamwheelers Mascot	.20	.50
Jill Bartlett-Hill		
Cheerleading Coach		
38 Steamwheelers Staff	.20	.50
39 Craig Wainwright	.20	.50
Trainer		
Phil Hayek		
Equipment Manager		

2005 Quad City Steamwheelers AF2

COMPLETE SET (40)	7.50	15.00
1 Fred Barr	.20	.50
2 Nate Bell	.20	.50
3 Corey Brown	.20	.50
4 Travis Burns	.20	.50
5 Larry Bush Asst.CO	.20	.50
6 Jason Cedeno	.20	.50
7 Sam Clemons	.20	.50
8 John Culp	.20	.50
9 Giovanni Deloatch	.20	.50
10 Tim Dodge	.20	.50
11 Steve Fickert Ast.CO	.20	.50
12 Matt Forbes	.20	.50
13 Jim Foster OWN	.20	.50
14 Mike Fox Asst.CO	.20	.50
15 Rick Frazier CO	.20	.50
16 Nick Gatto	.20	.50
17 Jeff Hewitt	.30	.75
18 Pat Hughes	.20	.50
19 Johnathan Katona Asst.CO	.20	.50
20 Ed Langford Asst.CO	.20	.50
21 Torey Morris	.20	.50
22 A.J. Novak	.20	.50
23 Matt Pike	.20	.50
24 Scott Power	.20	.50
25 Jon Roehlk Asst.CO	.20	.50
26 Kofi Smith	.20	.50
27 DeOnte' Taylor	.20	.50
28 Mark Taylor Asst.CO	.20	.50
29 Pete Traynor	.30	.75
30 Jack Walker Jr.	.20	.50
31 Broadcasters	.20	.50
32 DeckMates	.20	.50
33 DeckMates	.20	.50
34 Steamwheeler (Mascot)	.20	.50
35 Trainers	.20	.50
36 Veteran Staff	.20	.50
37 First Year Staff	.20	.50
38 Intern Staff	.20	.50
39 Valley Bank Sponsor Coupon	.20	.50
40 Valley Bank Sponsor Locations	.20	.50

2006 Quad City Steamwheelers AF2

COMPLETE SET (29)	4.00	8.00
1 Shonn Bell	.20	.50
2 Larry Bush OWN	.20	.50
3 Chris Chandler	.20	.50
4 Mike Custer CO	.20	.50
5 Tim Dodge	.30	.75
6 Rick Frazier CO	.20	.50
7 Troy Graham	.20	.50
8 Tim Hicks	.30	.75
9 Patrick Horne	.20	.50
10 David Hurst	.20	.50
11 Chris Jahnke	.20	.50
12 Kika Kaululaau	.20	.50
13 Sidney Lewis	.20	.50
14 William Lobendahn	.20	.50
15 Jeff Macrea	.20	.50
16 Matt Manuma	.20	.50
17 Kimo Naehu	.20	.50
18 A.J. Novak	.20	.50
19 James Parham	.20	.50
20 Kris Peters	.20	.50
21 Matt Pike	.30	.75
22 Sean Ponder CO	.20	.50
23 Alfonso Pugh	.20	.50
24 Jon Roehlk CO	.20	.50
25 Mataese Togafau	.20	.50
26 Jack Walker	.20	.50
27 Adrian Wilson	.20	.50
28 Steamwheeler Willie (Mascot)	.20	.50
29 Deck Mates	.40	1.00
Cheerleaders; measures 3 1/2 x 5)		

1954 Quaker Sports Oddities

This 27-card set features strange moments in sports and was issued as an insert inside Quaker Puffed Rice cereal boxes. Fronts of the cards are drawings depicting the person or the event. In a stripe at the top of the card face appear the words "Sports Oddities." Two colorful drawings fill the remaining space: the left half is a portrait, while the right half is action-oriented. A variety of sports are included. The cards measure approximately 2 1/4" by 3 1/2" and have rounded corners. The last line on the back of each card declares, "It's Odd but True." A person could also buy the complete set for fifteen cents and two box tops from Quaker Puffed Wheat or Quaker Rice. If a collector did send in their material to Quaker Oats the set came back in a specially marked box with the cards in cellophane wrapping. Sets in original wrapping are valued at 1.25x to 1.5X the high column listings in our checklist.

COMPLETE SET (27)	125.00	250.00
1 Johnny Miller	3.00	6.00
(Incredible Punt)		
6 Wake Forest College	3.00	6.00
(Six Forward Passes)		
7 Amos Alonzo Stagg	12.50	25.00
(Three TD's No Score)		
19 George Halas	15.00	30.00
25 Texas University	3.00	6.00
Northwestern University		
26 Bronko Nagurski	30.00	60.00
(All-American Team)		

2000 Quantum Leaf Promos

QLP2 Ricky Williams	.50	1.25
QLP3 Terrell Davis	.50	1.25
QLP6 Tim Couch	.40	1.00
QLP9 Randy Moss	.50	1.25
QLP10 Dan Marino	1.50	4.00
QLP13 Marvin Harrison	.50	1.25
QLP14 Jerry Rice	1.00	2.50
QLP18 Marshall Faulk	.50	1.25

2000 Quantum Leaf

2000 Quantum Leaf was released as a 350-card base set containing 300 regular-issue veteran cards and 50 rookie subset cards seeded at one in two packs. Base cards feature full color player photos set a against a silver holographic fractal background, and rookie subset cards with the same format but enhanced with a gold stamp of the draft team and round drafted. Later in the season, card numbers 351-381 were issued as part of a wrapper redemption (24-wrappers plus $5.99) upon the initial release. Quantum Leaf was packaged in boxes containing 24-packs of four cards per pack which carried a suggested retail price of $2.99.

COMPLETE SET (350)	60.00	150.00
COMP.SET w/o SP's (300)	10.00	25.00
COMP.ROOKIE UPDATE (31)	10.00	20.00
ROOKIE SUBSET ODDS 1:2		
1 Frank Sanders	.25	.60
2 Adrian Murrell	.25	.60
3 Rob Moore	.25	.60
4 Simeon Rice	.30	.75
5 Michael Pittman	.25	.60
6 Jake Plummer	.30	.75
7 David Boston	.25	.60
8 Mario Bates	.25	.60
9 Chris Chandler	.30	.75
10 Tim Dwight	.30	.75
11 Chris Calloway	.25	.60
12 Terance Mathis	.25	.60

13 Jamal Anderson .30 .75
14 Byron Hanspard .25 .60
15 Ken Oxendine .25 .60
16 Tony Graziani .30 .75
17 Bob Christian .25 .60
18 Priest Holmes .40 1.00
19 Tony Banks .25 .60
20 Patrick Johnson .25 .60
21 Rod Woodson .40 1.00
22 Jermaine Lewis .25 .60
23 Errict Rhett .30 .75
24 Stoney Case .25 .60
25 Peter Boulware .25 .60
26 Qadry Ismail .30 .75
27 Brandon Stokley .30 .75
28 Andre Reed .40 1.00
29 Eric Moulds .30 .75
30 Doug Flutie .40 1.00
31 Bruce Smith .40 1.00
32 Jay Riemersma .25 .60
33 Antowain Smith .30 .75
34 Thurman Thomas .40 1.00
35 Jonathan Linton .25 .60
36 Peerless Price .30 .75
37 Rob Johnson .30 .75
38 Sam Gash .25 .60
39 Muhsin Muhammad .30 .75
40 Wesley Walls .25 .60
41 Fred Lane .25 .60
42 Kevin Greene .25 .60
43 Tim Biakabutuka .30 .75
44 Steve Beuerlein .30 .75
45 Donald Hayes .25 .60
46 Patrick Jeffers .30 .75
47 Curtis Enis .25 .60
48 Bobby Engram .30 .75
49 Curtis Conway .30 .75
50 Marcus Robinson .30 .75
51 Marty Booker .30 .75
52 Cade McNown .25 .60
53 Shane Matthews .25 .60
54 Jim Miller .25 .60
55 Darnay Scott .30 .75
56 Carl Pickens .30 .75
57 Corey Dillon .30 .75
58 Jeff Blake .30 .75
59 Akili Smith .25 .60
60 Michael Basnight .25 .60
61 Karim Abdul-Jabbar .25 .60
62 Tim Couch .30 .75
63 Kevin Johnson .25 .60
64 Terry Kirby .25 .60
65 Ty Detmer .30 .75
66 Leslie Shepherd .25 .60
67 Darrin Chiaverini .25 .60
68 Emmitt Smith 1.00 2.50
69 Deion Sanders .40 1.00
70 Michael Irvin .40 1.00
71 Rocket Ismail .30 .75
72 Troy Aikman .60 1.50
73 Daryl Johnston .40 1.00
74 Chris Warren .25 .60
75 Jason Garrett .40 1.00
76 Jason Tucker .25 .60
77 Lawyer Milloy .25 .60
78 Dexter Coakley .25 .60
79 Greg Ellis .25 .60
80 David LaFleur .25 .60
81 Todd Lyght .25 .60
82 Ernie Mills .25 .60
83 Wane McGarity .25 .60
84 Chris Brazzell RC .25 .60
85 Ed McCaffrey .30 .75
86 Rod Smith .30 .75
87 Shannon Sharpe .40 1.00
88 Brian Griese .30 .75
89 John Elway 1.00 2.50
90 Neil Smith .25 .60
91 Terrell Davis .40 1.00
92 Olandis Gary .30 .75
93 Derek Loville .25 .60
94 John Avery .25 .60
95 Bubby Brister .30 .75
96 Byron Chamberlain .25 .60
97 Dale Carter .25 .60
98 Johnnie Morton .30 .75
99 Charlie Batch .30 .75
100 Barry Sanders .75 2.00
101 Germane Crowell .25 .60
102 Gus Frerotte .30 .75
103 Desmond Howard .30 .75
104 Terry Fair .25 .60
105 Ron Rivers .25 .60
106 Greg Hill .25 .60
107 Sedrick Irvin .25 .60
108 David Sloan .25 .60
109 Herman Moore .30 .75
110 Robert Porcher .25 .60
111 Corey Bradford .25 .60
112 Dorsey Levens .30 .75
113 Antonio Freeman .30 .75
114 Brett Favre 1.25 3.00
115 De'Mond Parker .25 .60
116 Bill Schroeder .30 .75
117 Matt Hasselbeck .40 1.00
118 Donald Driver .60 1.50
119 Basil Mitchell .25 .60
120 E.G. Green .25 .60
121 Ken Dilger .25 .60
122 Marvin Harrison .40 1.00
123 Peyton Manning 1.00 2.50
124 Terrence Wilkins .25 .60
125 Edgerrin James .40 1.00
126 Jerome Pathon .25 .60
127 Marcus Pollard .25 .60
128 Keenan McCardell .30 .75
129 Mark Brunell .30 .75
130 Fred Taylor .40 1.00
131 Jimmy Smith .30 .75
132 James Stewart .25 .60
133 Kyle Brady .25 .60
134 Tony Brackens .25 .60
135 Derrick Thomas .40 1.00
136 Rashaan Shehee .25 .60
137 Derrick Alexander .25 .60
138 Bam Morris .25 .60
139 Andre Rison .30 .75
140 Elvis Grbac .25 .60
141 Tony Gonzalez .40 1.00
142 Donnell Bennett .25 .60
143 Warren Moon .40 1.00
144 Tamarick Vanover .25 .60
145 Kimble Anders .25 .60
146 Tony Richardson RC .30 .75
147 Zach Thomas .40 1.00
148 Oronde Gadsden .30 .75
149 Dan Marino 1.25 3.00
150 O.J. McDuffie .30 .75
151 Tony Martin .30 .75
152 Cecil Collins .25 .60
153 James Johnson .25 .60
154 Rob Konrad .25 .60
155 Yatil Green .25 .60
156 Damon Huard .30 .75
157 Nate Jacquet .25 .60
158 Stanley Pritchett .25 .60
159 Sam Madison .25 .60
160 Randy Moss .40 1.00
161 Cris Carter .40 1.00
162 Robert Smith .30 .75
163 Randall Cunningham .40 1.00
164 Jake Reed .30 .75
165 John Randle .30 .75
166 Leroy Hoard .25 .60
167 Jeff George .30 .75
168 Daunte Culpepper .30 .75
169 Matthew Hatchette .25 .60
170 Robert Tate .25 .60
171 Ty Law .30 .75
172 Troy Brown .30 .75
173 Tony Simmons .25 .60
174 Terry Glenn .30 .75
175 Ben Coates .25 .60
176 Drew Bledsoe .40 1.00
177 Terry Allen .30 .75
178 Kevin Faulk .30 .75
179 Shawn Jefferson .25 .60
180 Andy Katzenmoyer .25 .60
181 Willie McGinest .30 .75
182 Cameron Cleeland .25 .60
183 Eddie Kennison .25 .60
184 Ricky Williams .40 1.00
185 Danny Wuerffel .40 1.00
186 Brett Bech .25 .60
187 Billy Joe Hobert .25 .60
188 Jake Delhomme RC 1.00 2.50
189 Wilmont Perry .25 .60
190 Keith Poole .25 .60
191 Ashley Ambrose .25 .60
192 Amani Toomer .30 .75
193 Kerry Collins .30 .75
194 Tiki Barber .40 1.00
195 Ike Hilliard .30 .75
196 Jason Sehorn .25 .60
197 Joe Montgomery .25 .60
198 Joe Jurevicius .25 .60
199 Michael Strahan .30 .75
200 Sean Bennett .25 .60
201 Jessie Armstead .25 .60
202 Pete Mitchell .25 .60
203 Curtis Martin .40 1.00
204 Vinny Testaverde .30 .75
205 Keyshawn Johnson .30 .75
206 Wayne Chrebet .30 .75
207 Ray Lucas .25 .60
208 Tyrone Wheatley .25 .60
209 Napoleon Kaufman .30 .75
210 Tim Brown .40 1.00
211 Rickey Dudley .25 .60
212 James Jett .30 .75
213 Rich Gannon .30 .75
214 Charles Woodson .40 1.00
215 Zack Crockett .25 .60
216 Darrell Russell .25 .60
217 Duce Staley .30 .75
218 Donovan McNabb .40 1.00
219 Charles Johnson .25 .60
220 Dameane Douglas .25 .60
221 Doug Pederson .25 .60
222 Torrance Small .25 .60
223 Troy Vincent .25 .60
224 Na Brown .25 .60
225 Kordell Stewart .30 .75
226 Jerome Bettis .40 1.00
227 Hines Ward .40 1.00
228 Troy Edwards .25 .60
229 Richard Huntley .25 .60
230 Mark Bruener .30 .75
231 Pete Gonzalez .25 .60
232 Levon Kirkland .25 .60
233 Bobby Shaw RC .30 .75
234 Amos Zereoue .25 .60
235 Natrone Means .30 .75
236 Junior Seau .40 1.00
237 Jim Harbaugh .30 .75
238 Ryan Leaf .30 .75
239 Mikhael Ricks .25 .60
240 Jermaine Fazande .25 .60
241 Jeff Graham .25 .60
242 Tremayne Stephens .25 .60
243 Terrell Owens .40 1.00
244 J.J. Stokes .30 .75
245 Charlie Garner .30 .75
246 Jerry Rice .75 2.00
247 Garrison Hearst .25 .60
248 Steve Young .50 1.25
249 Jeff Garcia .30 .75
250 Fred Beasley .25 .60
251 Bryant Young .25 .60
252 Derrick Mayes .25 .60
253 Ahman Green .30 .75
254 Joey Galloway .30 .75
255 Ricky Watters .30 .75
256 Jon Kitna .30 .75
257 Sean Dawkins .25 .60
258 Sam Adams .25 .60
259 Christian Fauria .25 .60
260 Shawn Springs .25 .60
261 Az-Zahir Hakim .25 .60
262 Isaac Bruce .40 1.00
263 Marshall Faulk .40 1.00
264 Trent Green .30 .75
265 Kurt Warner .60 1.50
266 Torry Holt .40 1.00
267 Robert Holcombe .25 .60
268 Kevin Carter .25 .60
269 Amp Lee .25 .60
270 Roland Williams .25 .60
271 Jacquez Green .25 .60
272 Reidel Anthony .25 .60
273 Warren Sapp .30 .75
274 Mike Alstott .40 1.00
275 Warrick Dunn .30 .75
276 Trent Dilfer .30 .75
277 Shaun King .25 .60
278 Bert Emanuel .25 .60
279 Eric Zeier .25 .60
280 Neil O'Donnell .25 .60
281 Eddie George .30 .75
282 Yancey Thigpen .25 .60
283 Steve McNair .40 1.00
284 Kevin Dyson .30 .75
285 Frank Wycheck .30 .75
286 Jevon Kearse .30 .75
287 Bruce Matthews .30 .75
288 Lorenzo Neal .30 .75
289 Stephen Davis .30 .75
290 Stephen Alexander .25 .60
291 Darrell Green .30 .75
292 Skip Hicks .25 .60
293 Brad Johnson .30 .75
294 Michael Westbrook .25 .60
295 Albert Connell .25 .60
296 Irving Fryar .30 .75
297 Champ Bailey .30 .75
298 Larry Centers .25 .60
299 Brian Mitchell .25 .60
300 James Thrash .30 .75
301 LaVar Arrington RC 1.50 4.00
302 Peter Warrick RC 1.00 2.50
303 Courtney Brown RC .75 2.00
304 Plaxico Burress RC 1.00 2.50
305 Corey Simon RC .75 2.00
306 Thomas Jones RC 1.25 3.00
307 Travis Taylor RC .75 2.00
308 Shaun Alexander RC 1.25 3.00
309 Chris Redman RC .75 2.00
310 Chad Pennington RC 1.50 4.00
311 Jamal Lewis RC 1.00 2.50
312 Brian Urlacher RC 4.00 10.00
313 Keith Bulluck RC .75 2.00
314 Bubba Franks RC 1.00 2.50
315 Dez White RC .75 2.00
316 Ahmed Plummer RC .60 1.50
317 Ron Dayne RC 1.00 2.50
318 Shaun Ellis RC 1.00 2.50
319 Sylvester Morris RC .60 1.50
320 Deltha O'Neal RC .75 2.00
321 R.Jay Soward RC .60 1.50
322 Sherrod Gideon RC .60 1.50
323 John Abraham RC 1.00 2.50
324 Travis Prentice RC .75 2.00
325 Darrell Jackson RC .75 2.00
326 Giovanni Carmazzi RC .60 1.50
327 Anthony Lucas RC .60 1.50
328 Danny Farmer RC .60 1.50
329 Dennis Northcutt RC .75 2.00
330 Troy Walters RC .60 1.50
331 Laveranues Coles RC 1.00 2.50
332 Tee Martin RC 1.00 2.50
333 J.R. Redmond RC .60 1.50
334 Jerry Porter RC 1.00 2.50
335 Sebastian Janikowski RC 1.00 2.50
336 Michael Wiley RC .60 1.50
337 Reuben Droughns RC 1.00 2.50
338 Trung Canidate RC .75 2.00
339 Shyrone Stith RC .60 1.50
340 Trevor Gaylor RC .60 1.50
341 Rob Morris RC .75 2.00
342 Marc Bulger RC 1.00 2.50
343 Tom Brady RC 20.00 40.00
344 Todd Husak RC .60 1.50
345 Gari Scott RC .60 1.50
346 Erron Kinney RC .60 1.50
347 Julian Peterson RC 1.00 2.50
348 Doug Chapman RC .60 1.50
349 Ron Dugans RC .60 1.50
350 Todd Pinkston RC .60 1.50
351 Deon Grant RC .40 1.00
352 Na'il Diggs RC .40 1.00
353 Raynoch Thompson RC .40 1.00
354 Mario Edwards RC .40 1.00
355 John Engelberger RC .40 1.00
356 Dwayne Goodrich RC .40 1.00
357 Ben Kelly RC .40 1.00
358 Sekou Sanyika RC .40 1.00
359 Brandon Short RC .40 1.00
360 Jabari Issa RC .40 1.00
361 Darwin Walker RC .40 1.00
362 Jerry Johnson RC .40 1.00
363 Robaire Smith RC .40 1.00
364 Mark Roman RC .40 1.00
365 Leonardo Carson RC .40 1.00
366 Mark Simoneau RC .40 1.00
367 Hank Poteat RC .40 1.00
368 Darren Howard RC .40 1.00
369 David Macklin RC .40 1.00
370 Adalius Thomas RC 1.25 3.00
371 Ralph Brown RC .40 1.00
372 Mondriel Fulcher RC .40 1.00
373 Sammy Morris RC .50 1.25
374 Rondell Mealey RC .40 1.00
375 Deon Dyer RC .40 1.00
376 Mareno Philyaw RC .40 1.00
377 Thomas Hamner RC .40 1.00
378 Jarious Jackson RC .50 1.25
379 Joe Hamilton RC .40 1.00
380 Tim Rattay RC .50 1.25
381 Chris Hovan RC .50 1.25
SB1 Kurt Warner MVP/1000 3.00 8.00
SB1A Kurt Warner 40.00 80.00
MVP AUTO/100
NFL1 Kurt Warner MVP/1000 3.00 8.00
NFL1A Kurt Warner 40.00 80.00
MVP AUTO/100

2000 Quantum Leaf All-Millennium Team

COMPLETE SET (28) 60.00 120.00
STATED PRINT RUN 1000 SER.#'d SETS
FIRST 100 SER.#'d CARDS SIGNED
BS Barry Sanders 3.00 8.00
CC Cris Carter 1.50 4.00
DM Dan Marino 5.00 12.00
EC Earl Campbell 1.50 4.00
ED Eric Dickerson 1.25 3.00
ES Emmitt Smith 4.00 10.00
FB Fred Biletnikoff 1.50 4.00
GS Gale Sayers 2.50 6.00
JB Jim Brown 2.50 6.00
JE John Elway 4.00 10.00
JL James Lofton 1.00 2.50
JM Joe Montana 5.00 12.00
JR Jerry Rice 3.00 8.00
JU Johnny Unitas 4.00 10.00
KW Kellen Winslow 1.25 3.00
LA Lance Alworth 1.50 4.00
MA Marcus Allen 1.50 4.00
PH Paul Hornung 1.50 4.00
PW Paul Warfield 1.50 4.00
RB Raymond Berry 1.25 3.00
RM Randy Moss 1.50 4.00
RS Roger Staubach 3.00 8.00
SB Sammy Baugh 1.50 4.00
SL Steve Largent 1.50 4.00
TB Terry Bradshaw 4.00 10.00
TD Terrell Davis 1.50 4.00
BST Bart Starr 4.00 10.00
TDO Tony Dorsett 1.50 4.00

2000 Quantum Leaf All-Millennium Team Autographs

FIRST 100 SER.#'d CARDS SIGNED
BS Barry Sanders 75.00 150.00
CC Cris Carter 25.00 60.00
DM Dan Marino 125.00 200.00
EC Earl Campbell 25.00 60.00
ED Eric Dickerson 25.00 60.00
ES Emmitt Smith 125.00 200.00
FB Fred Biletnikoff 25.00 60.00
GS Gale Sayers 40.00 100.00
JB Jim Brown 40.00 100.00
JE John Elway 100.00 200.00
JL James Lofton 15.00 40.00
JM Joe Montana 100.00 200.00
JR Jerry Rice 75.00 150.00
JU Johnny Unitas 200.00 350.00
KW Kellen Winslow 20.00 50.00
LA Lance Alworth 25.00 60.00
MA Marcus Allen 40.00 80.00
PH Paul Hornung 40.00 80.00
PW Paul Warfield 25.00 60.00
RB Raymond Berry 20.00 50.00
RM Randy Moss 50.00 100.00
RS Roger Staubach 75.00 150.00
SB Sammy Baugh 100.00 175.00
SL Steve Largent 25.00 60.00
TB Terry Bradshaw 100.00 200.00
TD Terrell Davis 40.00 80.00
BST Bart Starr 125.00 200.00
TDO Tony Dorsett 40.00 80.00

2000 Quantum Leaf Banner Season

COMPLETE SET (40) 50.00 100.00
STATED PRINT RUN 1-4857
CARDS SER.#'d TO 1999 SEASON STAT
*CENT/99: 1.5X TO 4X BAN SEAS/2111-4857
*CENT/99: 1.2X TO 3X BAN SEAS/732-1663
*CENT/99: 1X TO 2.5X BAN SEASON/334
CENTURY PRINT RUN 99 SER.#'d SETS
BS1 Brett Favre/4091 3.00 8.00
BS2 Marvin Harrison/1663 1.25 3.00
BS3 Tim Brown/1344 1.25 3.00
BS4 Randy Moss/1413 1.25 3.00
BS5 Edgerrin James/2139 1.00 2.50
BS6 Kurt Warner/4353 1.50 4.00
BS7 Marshall Faulk/2429 1.00 2.50
BS8 Dan Marino/2448 3.00 8.00
BS9 Tim Couch/2447 .75 2.00
BS10 Ricky Williams/884 1.25 3.00
BS11 Eddie George/1304 1.00 2.50
BS12 Jerry Rice/830 2.50 6.00
BS13 Troy Aikman/2964 1.50 4.00
BS14 Emmitt Smith/1397 3.00 8.00
BS15 Antonio Freeman/1074 1.00 2.50
BS16 Jimmy Smith/1636 1.00 2.50
BS17 Charlie Batch/4857 .75 2.00
BS18 Jake Plummer/2111 .75 2.00
BS19 Drew Bledsoe/3985 1.00 2.50
BS20 Germane Crowell/1338 .75 2.00
BS21 Cris Carter/1241 1.25 3.00
BS22 Deion Sanders/334 1.50 4.00
BS23 Donovan McNabb/948 1.25 3.00
BS24 Mark Brunell/3060 .75 2.00
BS25 Fred Taylor/732 1.25 3.00
BS26 Stephen Davis/1405 1.00 2.50
BS27 Brad Johnson/4005 .75 2.00
BS28 Jon Kitna/3346 .75 2.00
BS29 Curtis Martin/1464 1.25 3.00
BS30 Key. Johnson/1170 1.00 2.50
BS31 Shaun King/875 .75 2.00
BS32 Isaac Bruce/1165 1.25 3.00
BS33 Kevin Johnson/986 .75 2.00
BS34 Steve McNair/2179 1.00 2.50
BS35 Eric Moulds/994 1.00 2.50
BS36 Peyton Manning/4136 2.50 6.00
BS37 Dorsey Levens/1607 1.00 2.50
BS38 Olandis Gary/1159 1.00 2.50
BS39 James Stewart/931 .75 2.00
BS40 Terry Glenn/1147 1.00 2.50

2000 Quantum Leaf Double Team

COMPLETE SET (30) 30.00 60.00
STATED PRINT RUN 1500 SER.#'d SETS
DT1 James Johnson 4.00 10.00
Dan Marino
DT2 Edgerrin James 3.00 8.00
Peyton Manning
DT3 Kevin Faulk 1.25 3.00
Drew Bledsoe
DT4 Antowain Smith 1.25 3.00
Doug Flutie
DT5 Curtis Martin 1.25 3.00
Vinny Testaverde
DT6 Jerome Bettis 1.25 3.00
Kordell Stewart
DT7 Eddie George 1.25 3.00
Steve McNair
DT8 Fred Taylor 1.25 3.00
Mark Brunell
DT9 Errict Rhett 1.00 2.50
Tony Banks
DT10 Karim Abdul-Jabbar 1.00 2.50
Tim Couch
DT11 Corey Dillon 1.00 2.50
Akili Smith
DT12 Terrell Davis 1.25 3.00
Brian Griese
DT13 Donnell Bennett .75 2.00
Elvis Grbac
DT14 Ricky Watters 1.00 2.50
Jon Kitna
DT15 Tyrone Wheatley 1.00 2.50
Rich Gannon
DT16 Natrone Means 1.00 2.50
Jim Harbaugh
DT17 Emmitt Smith 3.00 8.00
Troy Aikman
DT18 Stephen Davis 1.00 2.50
Brad Johnson
DT19 Duce Staley 1.25 3.00
Donovan McNabb
DT20 Michael Pittman 1.00 2.50
Jake Plummer
DT21 Dorsey Levens 4.00 10.00
Brett Favre
DT22 Robert Smith 1.00 2.50
Jeff George
DT23 Mike Alstott 1.25 3.00
Shaun King
DT24 Curtis Enis .75 2.00
Cade McNown
DT25 Barry Sanders 2.50 6.00
Charlie Batch
DT26 Marshall Faulk 2.00 5.00
Kurt Warner
DT27 Ricky Williams 1.25 3.00
Jeff Blake
DT28 Charlie Garner 1.50 4.00
Steve Young
DT29 Tim Biakabutuka 1.00 2.50
Steve Beuerlein
DT30 Jamal Anderson 1.00 2.50
Chris Chandler

2000 Quantum Leaf Gamers

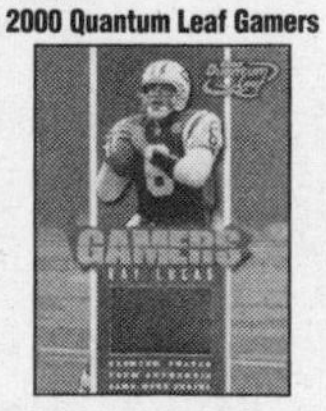

STATED PRINT RUN 25 SER.#'d SETS
G1 Brett Favre 60.00 150.00
G2 Dan Marino 60.00 150.00
G3 Barry Sanders 40.00 100.00
G4 John Elway 50.00 120.00
G5 Peyton Manning 50.00 120.00
G6 Terrell Davis 20.00 50.00
G7 Fred Taylor 20.00 50.00
G8 Drew Bledsoe 20.00 50.00
G9 Mark Brunell 15.00 40.00
G10 Eddie George 15.00 40.00
G11 Isaac Bruce 20.00 50.00
G12 Jerry Rice 40.00 100.00
G13 Ray Lucas 12.00 30.00
G14 Olandis Gary 15.00 40.00
G15 Emmitt Smith 50.00 120.00
G16 Shaun King 12.00 30.00
G17 Edgerrin James 20.00 50.00
G18 Cris Carter 20.00 50.00
G19 Jimmy Smith 15.00 40.00
G20 Brian Griese 15.00 40.00

2000 Quantum Leaf Hardwear

STATED PRINT RUN 125 SER.#'d SETS
HW1 Brett Favre 40.00 100.00
HW2 Dan Marino 40.00 100.00
HW3 Barry Sanders 25.00 60.00
HW4 John Elway 30.00 80.00
HW5 Terrell Davis 12.00 30.00
HW6 Troy Aikman 20.00 50.00
HW7 Steve Young 15.00 40.00
HW8 Eddie George 10.00 25.00
HW9 Brad Johnson 10.00 25.00
HW10 Herman Moore 10.00 25.00
HW11 Antowain Smith 10.00 25.00
HW12 Kordell Stewart 10.00 25.00
HW13 Dorsey Levens 10.00 25.00
HW14 Peyton Manning 30.00 80.00
HW15 Jerry Rice 25.00 60.00

2000 Quantum Leaf Infinity Green

*VETS 1-100: 6X TO 15X BASIC CARDS
1-100 VETERAN PRINT RUN 100
*VETS 101-200: 12X TO 30X BASIC CARDS
101-200 VETERAN PRINT RUN 25
*VETS 201-300: 8X TO 20X BASIC CARDS
201-300 VETERAN PRINT RUN 50
*ROOKIES 301-350: 2X TO 5X
*ROOKIES 351-381: 3X TO 8X
301-381 ROOKIE PRINT RUN 75
343 Tom Brady 300.00 500.00

2000 Quantum Leaf Infinity Purple

*VETS 1-100: 12X TO 30X BASIC CARDS
1-100 VETERAN PRINT RUN 25
*VETS 101-200: 8X TO 20X BASIC CARDS
101-200 VETERAN PRINT RUN 50
*VETS 201-300: 6X TO 15X BASIC CARDS
201-300 VETERAN PRINT RUN 100
*ROOKIES 301-350: 5X TO 12X
*ROOKIES 351-381: 8X TO 20X
301-381 ROOKIE PRINT RUN 15
343 Tom Brady 600.00 1,000.00

2000 Quantum Leaf Infinity Red

*VETS 1-100: 8X TO 20X BASIC CARDS
1-100 VETERAN PRINT RUN 50
*VETS 101-200: 6X TO 15X BASIC CARDS
101-200 VETERAN PRINT RUN 100
*VETS 201-300: 12X TO 30X BASIC CARDS
201-300 VETERAN PRINT RUN 25
*ROOKIES 301-350: 3X TO 8X
*ROOKIES 351-381: 5X TO 12X
301-381 ROOKIE PRINT RUN 35
343 Tom Brady 500.00 800.00

2000 Quantum Leaf Millennium Moments

COMPLETE SET (20) 40.00 80.00
STATED PRINT RUN 1000 SER.#'d SETS
MM1 Drew Bledsoe 1.25 3.00
MM2 Emmitt Smith 3.00 8.00
MM3 Mark Brunell 1.00 2.50
MM4 Brett Favre 4.00 10.00
MM5 Randy Moss 1.25 3.00
MM6 Kurt Warner 2.00 5.00
MM7 John Elway 3.00 8.00
MM8 Steve Young 1.50 4.00
MM9 Eddie George 1.00 2.50
MM10 Marshall Faulk 1.25 3.00
MM11 Edgerrin James 1.25 3.00
MM12 Antonio Freeman 1.00 2.50
MM13 Dan Marino 4.00 10.00
MM14 Terrell Davis 1.25 3.00
MM15 Doug Flutie 1.25 3.00
MM16 Jerry Rice 2.50 6.00
MM17 Fred Taylor 1.25 3.00
MM18 Peyton Manning 3.00 8.00
MM19 Troy Aikman 2.00 5.00
MM20 Barry Sanders 2.50 6.00

2000 Quantum Leaf Rookie Revolution

COMPLETE SET (20) 25.00 50.00
STATED PRINT RUN 5000 SER.#'d SETS
*FIRST STRIKE: 3X TO 8X BASIC INSERTS
FIRST STRIKE RANDOM INSERTS IN RETAIL
FIRST STRIKE PRINT RUN 50 SER.#'d SETS
RR1 Peter Warrick .75 2.00
RR2 J.R. Redmond .50 1.25
RR3 Chris Redman .60 1.50
RR4 R.Jay Soward .50 1.25
RR5 Ron Dayne .75 2.00
RR6 Chad Pennington 1.25 3.00
RR7 Anthony Lucas .50 1.25
RR8 Tim Rattay .60 1.50
RR9 Shaun Alexander 1.00 2.50
RR10 Dez White .60 1.50
RR11 Tee Martin .75 2.00
RR12 Travis Taylor .60 1.50
RR13 Travis Prentice .60 1.50
RR14 Sylvester Morris .50 1.25
RR15 Jamal Lewis .75 2.00
RR16 Plaxico Burress .75 2.00
RR17 Sherrod Gideon .50 1.25
RR18 Shyrone Stith .50 1.25
RR19 Thomas Jones 1.00 2.50
RR20 Kwame Cavil .50 1.25

2000 Quantum Leaf Shirt Off My Back

STATED PRINT RUN 100 SER.#'d SETS
SB1 Brett Favre 30.00 80.00
SB2 Dan Marino 30.00 80.00
SB3 Barry Sanders 20.00 50.00
SB4 John Elway 25.00 60.00
SB5 Peyton Manning 25.00 60.00
SB6 Terrell Davis 10.00 25.00
SB7 Fred Taylor 10.00 25.00
SB8 Drew Bledsoe 10.00 25.00
SB9 Mark Brunell 8.00 20.00
SB10 Eddie George 8.00 20.00
SB11 Isaac Bruce 10.00 25.00
SB12 Jerry Rice 20.00 50.00
SB13 Ray Lucas 6.00 15.00
SB14 Olandis Gary 8.00 20.00
SB15 Emmitt Smith 25.00 60.00
SB16 Shaun King 6.00 15.00
SB17 Edgerrin James 10.00 25.00
SB18 Cris Carter 10.00 25.00
SB19 Jimmy Smith 8.00 20.00
SB20 Brian Griese 8.00 20.00

2000 Quantum Leaf Star Factor

COMPLETE SET (40) 40.00 80.00
STATED PRINT RUN 2500 SER.#'d SETS
*QUASAR/50: 3X TO 8X BASIC INSERTS
QUASAR PRINT RUN 50 SER.#'d SETS
SF1 Edgerrin James .75 2.00
SF2 Cris Carter .75 2.00
SF3 Terrell Owens .75 2.00
SF4 Brett Favre 2.50 6.00
SF5 Tim Couch .60 1.50
SF6 Terry Glenn .60 1.50
SF7 John Elway 2.00 5.00
SF8 Troy Aikman 1.25 3.00
SF9 Charlie Batch .60 1.50
SF10 Steve McNair .75 2.00
SF11 Drew Bledsoe .75 2.00
SF12 Joey Galloway .60 1.50
SF13 Dan Marino 2.50 6.00
SF14 Marshall Faulk .75 2.00
SF15 Jamal Anderson .60 1.50
SF16 Jake Plummer .60 1.50
SF17 Curtis Martin .75 2.00
SF18 Peyton Manning 2.00 5.00
SF19 Keyshawn Johnson .60 1.50
SF20 Barry Sanders 1.50 4.00
SF21 Jerry Rice 1.50 4.00
SF22 Emmitt Smith 2.00 5.00
SF23 Daunte Culpepper .60 1.50
SF24 Brad Johnson .60 1.50
SF25 Kurt Warner 1.25 3.00
SF26 Steve Young 1.00 2.50
SF27 Eddie George .60 1.50
SF28 Fred Taylor .75 2.00
SF29 Randy Moss .75 2.00
SF30 Terrell Davis .75 2.00
SF31 Eric Moulds .60 1.50
SF32 Antonio Freeman .60 1.50
SF33 Isaac Bruce .75 2.00
SF34 Ricky Williams .75 2.00
SF35 Donovan McNabb .75 2.00
SF36 Stephen Davis .60 1.50
SF37 Jon Kitna .60 1.50
SF38 Marvin Harrison .75 2.00
SF39 Doug Flutie .75 2.00
SF40 Mark Brunell .60 1.50

2001 Quantum Leaf

2001 Quantum Leaf was initially released as a 260-card base set containing 200 veteran cards and 60 rookie subset cards seeded at one in two packs with an assortment of short-printed rookies seeded at 1:720 packs. The base veteran cards feature full color player photos set a against a blue background with silver glitter highlights. Some collectors have reported that the veterans can sometimes be found missing this silver glitter. The rookie subset cards follow the same basic format but are enhanced with gold foil of the draft team and round drafted, and a silver holographic fractal background. Later in the season, card numbers 261-290 were issued as part of a wrapper redemption (24-wrappers plus $6.99). Quantum Leaf was packaged in boxes containing 24-packs of five cards per pack which carried a suggested retail price of $2.99.

COMP.SET w/o SP's (200) 10.00 25.00
COMP.ROOKIE UPDATE (36) 6.00 15.00
201-260 ROOKIE ODDS 1:2
201-260 ROOKIE SP ODDS 1:720
1 David Boston .20 .50
2 Frank Sanders .20 .50
3 Jake Plummer .25 .60
4 Michael Pittman .25 .60
5 Rob Moore .20 .50
6 Thomas Jones .25 .60
7 Chris Chandler .25 .60
8 Doug Johnson .20 .50
9 Jamal Anderson .25 .60
10 Tim Dwight .25 .60
11 Chris Redman .30 .75
12 Jamal Lewis .30 .75
13 Qadry Ismail .25 .60
14 Ray Lewis .30 .75
15 Rod Woodson .30 .75
16 Shannon Sharpe .30 .75
17 Travis Taylor .20 .50
18 Trent Dilfer .25 .60
19 Doug Flutie .30 .75
20 Eric Moulds .25 .60
21 Jay Riemersma .20 .50
22 Peerless Price .20 .50
23 Rob Johnson .25 .60
24 Sammy Morris .25 .60
25 Shawn Bryson .20 .50
26 Donald Hayes .20 .50
27 Muhsin Muhammad .25 .60
28 Patrick Jeffers .20 .50
29 Reggie White DE .30 .75
30 Steve Beuerlein .25 .60
31 Tim Biakabutuka .20 .50
32 Wesley Walls .20 .50
33 Brian Urlacher .40 1.00
34 Cade McNown .25 .60
35 Dez White .25 .60
36 James Allen .20 .50
37 Marcus Robinson .25 .60
38 Marty Booker .25 .60
39 Akili Smith .20 .50
40 Corey Dillon .25 .60
41 Danny Farmer .20 .50
42 Peter Warrick .25 .60
43 Ron Dugans .20 .50
44 Courtney Brown .20 .50
45 Dennis Northcutt .20 .50
46 JaJuan Dawson .20 .50
47 Kevin Johnson .20 .50
48 Tim Couch .20 .50
49 Travis Prentice .20 .50
50 Anthony Wright .20 .50
51 Emmitt Smith .75 2.00
52 James McKnight .20 .50
53 Joey Galloway .25 .60
54 Rocket Ismail .25 .60
55 Randall Cunningham .30 .75
56 Troy Aikman .50 1.25
57 Brian Griese .25 .60
58 Ed McCaffrey .25 .60
59 Gus Frerotte .25 .60
60 John Elway .75 2.00
61 Mike Anderson .25 .60
62 Olandis Gary .20 .50
63 Rod Smith .25 .60
64 Terrell Davis .30 .75
65 Barry Sanders .75 2.00
66 Charlie Batch .25 .60
67 Germane Crowell .20 .50
68 Herman Moore .25 .60
69 James Stewart .20 .50
70 Johnnie Morton .25 .60
71 Ahman Green .30 .75
72 Antonio Freeman .30 .75
73 Bill Schroeder .25 .60
74 Brett Favre 1.00 2.50
75 Dorsey Levens .25 .60
76 Matt Hasselbeck .30 .75
77 Edgerrin James .30 .75
78 Jerome Pathon .20 .50
79 Ken Dilger .20 .50
80 Marvin Harrison .30 .75
81 Peyton Manning .75 2.00
82 Fred Taylor .30 .75
83 Hardy Nickerson .20 .50
84 Jimmy Smith .25 .60
85 Keenan McCardell .25 .60
86 Mark Brunell .25 .60
87 Tony Brackens .20 .50
88 Derrick Alexander .20 .50
89 Elvis Grbac .25 .60
90 Sylvester Morris .20 .50
91 Tony Gonzalez .30 .75
92 Tony Richardson .20 .50
93 Warren Moon .30 .75
94 Dan Marino .75 2.00
95 Jay Fiedler .25 .60
96 Lamar Smith .25 .60
97 Oronde Gadsden .20 .50
98 Sam Madison .20 .50
99 Thurman Thomas .30 .75
100 Tony Martin .25 .60
101 Zach Thomas .30 .75
102 Cris Carter .30 .75
103 Daunte Culpepper .25 .60
104 John Randle .25 .60
105 Randy Moss .30 .75
106 Robert Smith .25 .60
107 Drew Bledsoe .30 .75
108 J.R. Redmond .20 .50
109 Kevin Faulk .25 .60
110 Michael Bishop .25 .60
111 Terry Glenn .25 .60
112 Troy Brown .25 .60
113 Aaron Brooks .25 .60
114 Jake Reed .25 .60
115 Jeff Blake .25 .60
116 Joe Horn .25 .60
117 La'Roi Glover .20 .50
118 Ricky Williams .30 .75
119 Willie Jackson .20 .50
120 Amani Toomer .25 .60
121 Ike Hilliard .25 .60
122 Jason Sehorn .25 .60
123 Kerry Collins .25 .60
124 Michael Strahan .30 .75
125 Ron Dayne .25 .60
126 Ron Dixon .20 .50
127 Tiki Barber .30 .75
128 Chad Pennington .30 .75
129 Curtis Martin .30 .75
130 Dedric Ward .20 .50
131 Laveranues Coles .25 .60
132 Vinny Testaverde .25 .60
133 Wayne Chrebet .25 .60
134 Charles Woodson .30 .75
135 Napoleon Kaufman .20 .50
136 Rich Gannon .25 .60
137 Tim Brown .30 .75
138 Tyrone Wheatley .25 .60
139 Charles Johnson .20 .50
140 Donovan McNabb .30 .75
141 Duce Staley .25 .60
142 Hugh Douglas .20 .50
143 Na Brown .20 .50
144 Todd Pinkston .20 .50
145 Bobby Shaw .20 .50
146 Hines Ward .30 .75
147 Jerome Bettis .30 .75
148 Kordell Stewart .25 .60
149 Levon Kirkland .20 .50
150 Plaxico Burress .25 .60
151 Richard Huntley .20 .50
152 Troy Edwards .20 .50
153 Jim Harbaugh .25 .60
154 Junior Seau .30 .75
155 Ryan Leaf .20 .50
156 Charlie Garner .25 .60
157 Jeff Garcia .25 .60
158 Jerry Rice .60 1.50
159 Steve Young .40 1.00
160 Terrell Owens .30 .75
161 Brock Huard .20 .50
162 Darrell Jackson .25 .60
163 Derrick Mayes .20 .50
164 Ricky Watters .25 .60
165 Shaun Alexander .30 .75
166 Az-Zahir Hakim .20 .50
167 Isaac Bruce .30 .75
168 Kurt Warner .50 1.25
169 Marshall Faulk .30 .75
170 Torry Holt .25 .60
171 Trent Green .30 .75
172 Derrick Brooks .30 .75
173 Jacquez Green .20 .50
174 John Lynch .25 .60
175 Keyshawn Johnson .25 .60
176 Mike Alstott .25 .60
177 Reidel Anthony .20 .50
178 Shaun King .20 .50
179 Warren Sapp .25 .60
180 Warrick Dunn .30 .75
181 Carl Pickens .25 .60
182 Derrick Mason .25 .60
183 Eddie George .30 .75
184 Frank Wycheck .20 .50
185 Jevon Kearse .25 .60
186 Neil O'Donnell .25 .60
187 Steve McNair .30 .75
188 Yancey Thigpen .20 .50
189 Albert Connell .20 .50
190 Andre Reed .30 .75
191 Brad Johnson .25 .60
192 Bruce Smith .30 .75
193 Champ Bailey .30 .75
194 Darrell Green .30 .75
195 Deion Sanders .30 .75
196 Irving Fryar .25 .60
197 James Thrash .25 .60
198 Jeff George .25 .60
199 Michael Westbrook .20 .50
200 Stephen Davis .25 .60
201 Michael Vick RC 3.00 8.00
202 Drew Brees RC 5.00 12.00
203 Chris Weinke RC .60 1.50

204 Sage Rosenfels RC	.75	2.00
205 Josh Heupel RC	.75	2.00
206 Marques Tuiasosopo RC	.60	1.50
207 Mike McMahon SP RC	12.00	30.00
208 Deuce McAllister SP RC	15.00	40.00
209 LaMont Jordan RC	.75	2.00
210 LaDainian Tomlinson RC	2.50	6.00
211 James Jackson RC	.50	1.25
212 Anthony Thomas RC	.75	2.00
213 Travis Henry RC	.60	1.50
214 Travis Minor RC	.60	1.50
215 Rudi Johnson RC	.75	2.00
216 Michael Bennett RC	.60	1.50
217 Kevan Barlow RC	.60	1.50
218 Dan Alexander RC	.60	1.50
219 Correll Buckhalter SP RC	15.00	40.00
220 Moran Norris RC	.50	1.25
221 Jesse Palmer RC	.60	1.50
222 Heath Evans RC	.60	1.50
223 David Terrell SP RC	12.00	30.00
224 Santana Moss RC	1.00	2.50
225 Rod Gardner RC	.60	1.50
226 Quincy Morgan SP RC	12.00	30.00
227 Freddie Mitchell RC	.50	1.25
228 Reggie Wayne RC	1.50	4.00
229 Bobby Newcombe RC	.60	1.50
230 Casey Hampton RC	.75	2.00
231 Robert Ferguson RC	.75	2.00
232 Ken-Yon Rambo RC	.50	1.25
233 Alex Bannister RC	.50	1.25
234 Koren Robinson RC	.60	1.50
235 Chad Johnson RC	1.25	3.00
236 Chris Chambers RC	.75	2.00
237 Snoop Minnis RC	.50	1.25
238 Vinny Sutherland RC	.50	1.25
239 Cedrick Wilson RC	.60	1.50
240 T.J. Houshmandzadeh RC	1.00	2.50
241 Todd Heap RC	.75	2.00
242 Alge Crumpler RC	.75	2.00
243 Jabari Holloway RC	.50	1.25
244 Tony Stewart RC	.60	1.50
245 Jamal Reynolds RC	.50	1.25
246 Andre Carter SP RC	12.00	30.00
247 Justin Smith SP RC	15.00	40.00
248 Richard Seymour RC	.75	2.00
249 Marcus Stroud RC	.60	1.50
250 Damione Lewis RC	.60	1.50
251 Gerard Warren SP RC	12.00	30.00
252 Tommy Polley SP RC	10.00	25.00
253 Dan Morgan RC	.60	1.50
254 Jamar Fletcher RC	.50	1.25
255 Ken Lucas RC	.60	1.50
256 Fred Smoot SP RC	15.00	40.00
257 Nate Clements RC	.60	1.50
258 Will Allen RC	.75	2.00
259 Derrick Gibson RC	.50	1.25
260 Adam Archuleta RC	.60	1.50
261 Karon Riley RC	.25	.60
262 Cedric Scott RC	.25	.60
263 Kenny Smith RC	.25	.60
264 Willie Howard RC	.25	.60
265 Shaun Rogers RC	.40	1.00
266 Ennis Davis RC	.25	.60
267 Morlon Greenwood RC	.25	.60
268 Gary Baxter RC	.25	.60
269 Keith Adams RC	.25	.60
270 Brian Allen RC	.25	.60
271 Carlos Polk RC	.25	.60
272 Torrance Marshall RC	.25	.60
273 Jamie Winborn RC	.30	.75
274 Hakim Akbar RC	.25	.60
275 David Rivers RC	.25	.60
276 Ben Leard RC	.25	.60
277 Tim Hasselbeck RC	.30	.75
278 DeAngelo Evans RC	.30	.75
279 David Allen RC	.25	.60
280 Reggie White RC	.25	.60
281 Ja'Mar Toombs RC	.25	.60
282 Dustin McClintock RC	.30	.75
283 Boo Williams RC	.25	.60
284 Ronney Daniels RC	.25	.60
285 Daniel Guy RC	.25	.60
286 Javon Green RC	.25	.60
287 Marcellus Rivers RC	.25	.60
288 Rashon Burns RC	.25	.60
289 Jevaris Johnson RC	.25	.60
290 David Warren RC	.25	.60
291 John Capel RC	.25	.60
292 Kendrell Bell RC	.40	1.00
294 Willie Middlebrooks RC	.30	.75
295 Reggie Germany RC	.25	.60
296 Quincy Carter RC	.30	.75

2001 Quantum Leaf Autographs

202 Drew Brees/20	125.00	200.00

2001 Quantum Leaf Infinity Green

*VETS 1-100: 5X TO 12X BASIC CARDS
1-100 VETERAN PRINT RUN 100
*VETS 101-200: 12X TO 30X BASIC CARDS
101-200 VETERAN PRINT RUN 25
*ROOKIES 201-260: 3X TO 8X BASIC RC
*ROOKIES 201-260: .2X TO .5X RC SP
*ROOKIES 261-296: 6X TO 15X
201-296 ROOKIE PRINT RUN 75

2001 Quantum Leaf Infinity Purple

*VETS 1-100: 12X TO 30X BASIC CARDS
1-100 VETERAN PRINT RUN 25
*VETS 101-200: 8X TO 20X BASIC CARDS
101-200 VETERAN PRINT RUN 50
*ROOKIES 201-260: 8X TO 20X BASE RC
*ROOKIES 201-260: .4X TO 1X RC SP
*ROOKIES 261-296: 15X TO 40X
201-296 ROOKIE PRINT RUN 15

2001 Quantum Leaf Infinity Red

*VETS 1-100: 8X TO 20X BASIC CARDS
1-100 VETERAN PRINT RUN 50
*VETS 101-200: 5X TO 12X BASIC CARDS
101-200 VETERAN PRINT RUN 100
*ROOKIE 201-260: 5X TO 12X BASE RC
*ROOKIE 201-260: .25X TO .6X RC SP
*ROOKIES 261-296: 10X TO 25X
201-296 ROOKIE PRINT RUN 35

2001 Quantum Leaf All-Millennium Marks

COMPLETE SET (29)	50.00	100.00
STATED PRINT RUN 1000 SER.#'d SETS		
AMAR1 Walter Payton	6.00	15.00
AMAR2 Barry Sanders	4.00	10.00
AMAR3 Emmitt Smith	4.00	10.00
AMAR4 Eric Dickerson	1.50	4.00
AMAR5 Ricky Watters	1.25	3.00
AMAR6 Jim Brown	3.00	8.00
AMAR7 Marcus Allen	2.00	5.00
AMAR8 Jerome Bettis	1.50	4.00
AMAR9 Thurman Thomas	1.50	4.00
AMAR11 Jerry Rice	3.00	8.00
AMAR12 Ozzie Newsome	1.25	3.00
AMAR13 Henry Ellard	1.25	3.00
AMAR14 Charley Taylor	1.50	4.00
AMAR15 Steve Largent	2.00	5.00
AMAR16 Cris Carter	1.50	4.00
AMAR17 Art Monk	1.50	4.00
AMAR18 Irving Fryar	1.50	4.00
AMAR19 Michael Irvin	1.50	4.00
AMAR20 Tim Brown	1.50	4.00
AMAR21 Dan Marino	4.00	10.00
AMAR22 John Elway	4.00	10.00
AMAR23 Warren Moon	2.00	5.00
AMAR24 Fran Tarkenton	2.50	6.00
AMAR25 Dan Fouts	2.00	5.00
AMAR26 Joe Montana	4.00	10.00
AMAR27 Johnny Unitas	4.00	10.00
AMAR28 Boomer Esiason	1.25	3.00
AMAR29 Jim Kelly	2.00	5.00
AMAR30 Vinny Testaverde	1.25	3.00

2001 Quantum Leaf All-Millennium Marks Autographs

STATED PRINT RUN 100 SER.#'d SETS		
AMAR1 Walter Payton No AU	15.00	30.00
AMAR2 Barry Sanders	75.00	150.00
AMAR3 Emmitt Smith	125.00	200.00
AMAR4 Eric Dickerson	35.00	65.00
AMAR5 Ricky Watters	12.00	30.00
AMAR6 Jim Brown	50.00	100.00
AMAR7 Marcus Allen	30.00	80.00
AMAR8 Jerome Bettis	60.00	120.00
AMAR9 Thurman Thomas	15.00	40.00
AMAR11 Jerry Rice	75.00	150.00
AMAR12 Ozzie Newsome	15.00	40.00
AMAR13 Henry Ellard	10.00	25.00
AMAR14 Charley Taylor	12.00	30.00
AMAR15 Steve Largent	15.00	40.00
AMAR16 Cris Carter	15.00	40.00
AMAR17 Art Monk	15.00	40.00
AMAR18 Irving Fryar	12.00	30.00
AMAR19 Michael Irvin	20.00	50.00
AMAR20 Tim Brown	15.00	40.00
AMAR21 Dan Marino	100.00	200.00
AMAR22 John Elway	75.00	150.00
AMAR23 Warren Moon	15.00	40.00
AMAR24 Fran Tarkenton	20.00	50.00
AMAR25 Dan Fouts	30.00	60.00
AMAR26 Joe Montana	75.00	150.00
AMAR27 Johnny Unitas	175.00	300.00
AMAR28 Boomer Esiason	12.00	30.00
AMAR29 Jim Kelly	30.00	80.00
AMAR30 Vinny Testaverde	12.00	30.00

2001 Quantum Leaf All-Millennium Materials

STATED PRINT RUN 100 SERIAL #'d SETS		
AMAT1 Walter Payton	50.00	120.00
AMAT2 Barry Sanders	30.00	60.00
AMAT3 Emmitt Smith	25.00	60.00
AMAT4 Eric Dickerson	10.00	25.00
AMAT5 Ricky Watters	10.00	25.00
AMAT6 Jim Brown	25.00	60.00
AMAT7 Marcus Allen	12.00	30.00
AMAT8 Jerome Bettis	12.00	30.00
AMAT9 Thurman Thomas	12.00	30.00
AMAT11 Jerry Rice	25.00	60.00
AMAT12 Ozzie Newsome	8.00	20.00
AMAT13 Henry Ellard	8.00	20.00
AMAT14 Charley Taylor	10.00	25.00
AMAT15 Steve Largent	15.00	40.00
AMAT16 Cris Carter	12.00	30.00
AMAT17 Art Monk	10.00	25.00
AMAT18 Irving Fryar	10.00	25.00
AMAT19 Michael Irvin	12.00	30.00
AMAT20 Tim Brown	12.00	30.00
AMAT21 Dan Marino	40.00	100.00
AMAT22 John Elway	30.00	80.00
AMAT23 Warren Moon	12.00	30.00
AMAT24 Fran Tarkenton	15.00	40.00
AMAT25 Dan Fouts	12.00	30.00
AMAT26 Joe Montana	40.00	100.00
AMAT27 Johnny Unitas	30.00	80.00
AMAT28 Boomer Esiason	10.00	25.00
AMAT29 Jim Kelly	15.00	40.00
AMAT30 Vinny Testaverde	10.00	25.00

2001 Quantum Leaf All-Millennium Materials Autographs

FIRST 25 CARDS WERE SIGNED		
AMAT2 Barry Sanders	200.00	350.00
AMAT3 Emmitt Smith	250.00	400.00
AMAT4 Eric Dickerson	75.00	150.00
AMAT5 Ricky Watters	40.00	80.00
AMAT6 Jim Brown	175.00	300.00
AMAT7 Marcus Allen	75.00	150.00
AMAT8 Jerome Bettis	150.00	300.00
AMAT9 Thurman Thomas	50.00	100.00
AMAT11 Jerry Rice	200.00	350.00
AMAT12 Ozzie Newsome	50.00	100.00
AMAT14 Charley Taylor	40.00	80.00
AMAT15 Steve Largent	125.00	200.00
AMAT17 Art Monk	100.00	200.00
AMAT18 Irving Fryar	40.00	80.00
AMAT19 Michael Irvin	100.00	175.00
AMAT20 Tim Brown	125.00	200.00
AMAT21 Dan Marino	250.00	400.00
AMAT22 John Elway	200.00	350.00
AMAT23 Warren Moon	75.00	150.00
AMAT24 Fran Tarkenton	75.00	150.00
AMAT25 Dan Fouts	75.00	150.00
AMAT26 Joe Montana	250.00	400.00
AMAT27 Johnny Unitas	250.00	400.00
AMAT28 Boomer Esiason	40.00	80.00
AMAT29 Jim Kelly	125.00	200.00
AMAT30 Vinny Testaverde	40.00	80.00
AMAT16 Cris Carter	125.00	200.00

2001 Quantum Leaf All-Millennium Milestones

STATED PRINT RUN 1000 SERIAL #'d SETS		
AMILE1 John Elway	7.50	20.00
Dan Marino		
AMILE2 Cris Carter	5.00	12.00
Jerry Rice		
AMILE3 Emmitt Smith	7.50	20.00
Barry Sanders		
Walter Payton		
AMILE5 Dan Marino	7.50	20.00
Jerry Rice		
Emmitt Smith		

2001 Quantum Leaf All-Millennium Milestones Autographs

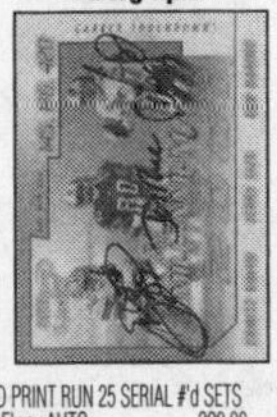

STATED PRINT RUN 25 SERIAL #'d SETS		
1 John Elway AUTO	200.00	350.00
Dan Marino AUTO		
2 Cris Carter	200.00	350.00
Jerry Rice AUTO		
3 Emmitt Smith AUTO	300.00	450.00
Barry Sanders AUTO		
Walter Payton No Auto		
5 Dan Marino AUTO	500.00	750.00
Jerry Rice AUTO		
Emmitt Smith AUTO		

2001 Quantum Leaf Century Season

COMPLETE SET (61)	100.00	200.00
STATED PRINT RUN 1000 SER.#'d SETS		
UNPRICED AUTO PRINT RUN 21		
CS1 Eric Dickerson	1.50	4.00
CS2 Barry Sanders	4.00	10.00
CS3 John Elway	4.00	10.00
CS4 Jim Brown	3.00	8.00
CS5 Sammy Baugh	2.00	5.00
CS6 Marcus Allen	2.00	5.00
CS7 Tony Gonzalez	1.50	4.00
CS8 Franco Harris	2.00	5.00
CS9 Dan Marino	4.00	10.00
CS10 Mike Singletary	2.00	5.00
CS11 Fred Biletnikoff	2.00	5.00
CS12 Warren Moon	2.00	5.00
CS13 Steve Largent	2.00	5.00
CS14 Fran Tarkenton	2.50	6.00
CS15 Lawrence Taylor	2.00	5.00
CS16 Roger Staubach	3.00	8.00
CS17 Roger Craig	1.50	4.00
CS18 Bart Starr	4.00	10.00
CS20 Steve Young	2.00	5.00
CS21 Don Maynard	1.50	4.00
CS22 Joe Montana	5.00	12.00
CS23 Tony Dorsett	2.00	5.00
CS24 Joe Namath	3.00	8.00
CS25 Johnny Unitas	4.00	10.00
CS26 Paul Hornung	2.00	5.00
CS27 Bob Griese	2.00	5.00
CS28 Isaac Bruce	1.50	4.00
CS29 Dan Fouts	2.00	5.00
CS31 Terry Bradshaw	3.00	8.00
CS32 Larry Csonka	2.00	5.00
CS33 Jim Kelly	2.00	5.00
CS34 Lance Alworth	1.50	4.00
CS36 Sonny Jurgensen	2.00	5.00
CS37 Ozzie Newsome	1.25	3.00
CS38 Kellen Winslow	1.50	4.00
CS39 Stephen Davis	1.25	3.00
CS40 Frank Gifford	2.00	5.00
CS41 Terrell Davis	1.50	4.00
CS43 Edgerrin James	1.50	4.00
CS44 Jerry Rice	3.00	8.00
CS45 Marshall Faulk	1.50	4.00
CS46 Kurt Warner	2.50	6.00
CS47 Cris Carter	1.50	4.00
CS48 Bruce Smith	1.50	4.00
CS49 Emmitt Smith	4.00	10.00
CS50 Ray Lewis	1.50	4.00
CS51 Jamal Lewis	1.50	4.00
CS52 Marvin Harrison	1.50	4.00
CS53 Eric Moulds	1.25	3.00
CS54 Eddie George	1.50	4.00
CS55 Ricky Williams	1.50	4.00
CS56 Mark Brunell	1.25	3.00
CS57 Brian Griese	1.25	3.00
CS58 Brett Favre	5.00	12.00
CS59 Daunte Culpepper	1.25	3.00
CS60 Mike Anderson	1.25	3.00
CS61 Donovan McNabb	1.50	4.00
CS62 Randall Cunningham	1.50	4.00
CS63 Drew Bledsoe	1.50	4.00
CS64 Troy Aikman	2.50	6.00
CS65 Randy Moss	1.50	4.00

2001 Quantum Leaf Gamers

STATED PRINT RUN 25 SER.#'d SETS		
G1 Akili Smith	15.00	40.00
G2 Corey Dillon	20.00	50.00
G3 Donovan McNabb	25.00	60.00
G4 Edgerrin James	25.00	60.00
G5 Fred Taylor	25.00	60.00
G6 Isaac Bruce	25.00	60.00
G7 Shaun King	15.00	40.00
G8 Tim Couch	15.00	40.00
G9 Jim Kelly	250.00	450.00
John Elway		
Dan Marino		
G10 Donovan McNabb	100.00	250.00
Dante Culpepper		
Tim Couch		
Cade McNown		
Akili Smith		
Shaun King		

2001 Quantum Leaf Hardwear

STATED PRINT RUN 100 SER.#'d SETS		
HW1 Akili Smith	10.00	25.00
HW2 Charlie Garner	12.00	30.00
HW3 Corey Dillon	12.00	30.00
HW4 Dan Marino	40.00	100.00
HW5 Donovan McNabb	15.00	40.00
HW6 Duce Staley		
HW7 Edgerrin James	15.00	40.00
HW8 Fred Taylor	15.00	40.00
HW9 Isaac Bruce	15.00	40.00
HW10 Jamal Anderson	12.00	30.00
HW11 Jason Sehorn	12.00	30.00
HW12 Jay Fiedler	12.00	30.00
HW13 Jerome Bettis	15.00	40.00
HW14 Jerry Rice	30.00	80.00
HW15 John Elway	40.00	100.00
HW16 Junior Seau	15.00	40.00
HW17 Ray Lewis	15.00	40.00
HW18 Reggie White DE	15.00	40.00
HW19 Ricky Watters	12.00	30.00
HW20 Ryan Leaf	10.00	25.00
HW21 Shaun King	10.00	25.00
HW22 Steve Young	20.00	50.00
HW23 Terrell Davis	15.00	40.00
HW24 Terry Glenn	12.00	30.00
HW25 Tim Couch	10.00	25.00
HW26 Torry Holt	12.00	30.00
HW27 Vinny Testaverde	12.00	30.00
HW28 Warren Sapp	12.00	30.00
HW29 Wayne Chrebet	12.00	30.00
HW30 Zach Thomas	15.00	40.00

2001 Quantum Leaf Hardwear Autographs

FIRST 25 CARDS WERE SIGNED		
HW4 Dan Marino	150.00	300.00
HW5 Donovan McNabb	60.00	120.00
HW7 Edgerrin James	40.00	80.00
HW9 Isaac Bruce	40.00	80.00
HW13 Jerome Bettis	75.00	150.00
HW14 Jerry Rice	125.00	250.00
HW15 John Elway	125.00	250.00
HW17 Ray Lewis	60.00	120.00
HW22 Steve Young	75.00	150.00

2001 Quantum Leaf Rookie Revolution

COMPLETE SET (20)	15.00	40.00
STATED PRINT RUN 4000 SER.#'d SETS		
RR1 Michael Vick	2.50	6.00
RR2 David Terrell	.50	1.25
RR3 Deuce McAllister	.60	1.50
RR4 Drew Brees	4.00	10.00
RR5 Santana Moss	.75	2.00
RR6 Anthony Thomas	.60	1.50
RR7 Chris Weinke	.50	1.25
RR8 Rod Gardner	.50	1.25
RR9 LaDainian Tomlinson	2.00	5.00
RR10 Quincy Carter	.50	1.25
RR11 Koren Robinson	.50	1.25
RR12 Travis Henry	.50	1.25
RR13 Quincy Morgan	.50	1.25
RR14 LaMont Jordan	.60	1.50
RR15 Rudi Johnson	.60	1.50
RR16 Reggie Wayne	1.25	3.00
RR17 Michael Bennett	.50	1.25
RR18 Freddie Mitchell	.40	1.00
RR19 Chris Chambers	.60	1.50
RR20 Chad Johnson	1.00	2.50

2001 Quantum Leaf Rookie Revolution Autographs

STATED PRINT RUN 50 SER.#'d SETS		
RR1 Michael Vick	80.00	200.00
RR2 David Terrell	15.00	40.00
RR3 Deuce McAllister	20.00	50.00
RR4 Drew Brees	100.00	175.00
RR5 Santana Moss	25.00	60.00
RR6 Anthony Thomas	20.00	50.00
RR7 Chris Weinke	15.00	40.00
RR8 Rod Gardner	15.00	40.00
RR9 LaDainian Tomlinson	100.00	200.00
RR11 Koren Robinson	15.00	40.00
RR12 Travis Henry	15.00	40.00
RR13 Quincy Morgan	15.00	40.00
RR14 LaMont Jordan	20.00	50.00
RR15 Rudi Johnson	20.00	50.00
RR16 Reggie Wayne	50.00	80.00
RR17 Michael Bennett	15.00	40.00
RR18 Freddie Mitchell	12.00	30.00
RR19 Chris Chambers	20.00	50.00
RR20 Chad Johnson	50.00	100.00

2001 Quantum Leaf Shirt Off My Back

STATED PRINT RUN 100 SER.#'d SETS		
SB1 Jamal Lewis	10.00	25.00
SB2 Mike Anderson	8.00	20.00
SB3 Ron Dayne	8.00	20.00
SB4 Peter Warrick	8.00	20.00
SB5 Shaun Alexander	10.00	25.00
SB6 Warrick Dunn	10.00	25.00
SB7 Shaun King	6.00	15.00
SB8 Tim Couch	6.00	15.00
SB9 Cade McNown	8.00	20.00
SB10 Akili Smith	6.00	15.00
SB11 Rich Gannon	8.00	20.00
SB12 Daunte Culpepper	8.00	20.00
SB13 Randy Moss	10.00	25.00
SB14 Cris Carter	10.00	25.00
SB15 Robert Smith	8.00	20.00
SB16 Kurt Warner	15.00	40.00
SB17 Marshall Faulk	10.00	25.00
SB18 Ricky Williams	10.00	25.00
SB19 Terrell Owens	10.00	25.00
SB20 Corey Dillon	8.00	20.00
SB21 Fred Taylor	10.00	25.00
SB22 Edgerrin James	10.00	25.00
SB23 Curtis Martin	10.00	25.00
SB24 Donovan McNabb	10.00	25.00
SB25 Steve McNair	10.00	25.00
SB26 Peyton Manning	25.00	60.00
SB27 Eric Moulds	8.00	20.00
SB28 Stephen Davis	8.00	20.00
SB29 Brian Griese	8.00	20.00
SB30 Isaac Bruce	10.00	25.00

2001 Quantum Leaf Shirt Off My Back Autographs

STATED PRINT RUN 25 SER.#'d SETS		
SB1 Jamal Lewis	30.00	80.00
SB2 Mike Anderson EXCH		
SB11 Rich Gannon	25.00	60.00
SB12 Daunte Culpepper	30.00	80.00
SB16 Kurt Warner	40.00	100.00
SB18 Ricky Williams	30.00	80.00
SB22 Edgerrin James	30.00	80.00
SB24 Donovan McNabb	75.00	150.00
SB28 Stephen Davis	25.00	60.00
SB30 Isaac Bruce	40.00	100.00

2001 Quantum Leaf Star Factor

COMPLETE SET (40)	25.00	60.00
STATED PRINT RUN 2000 SER.#'d SETS		
*X-FACTOR/25: 5X TO 12X BASIC INSERTS		
X-FACTOR PRINT RUN 25 SER.#'d SETS		
SF1 Peyton Manning	2.00	5.00
SF2 Edgerrin James	.75	2.00
SF3 Marvin Harrison	.75	2.00
SF4 Curtis Martin	.75	2.00
SF5 Eric Moulds	.60	1.50
SF6 Dan Marino	2.00	5.00
SF7 Jake Plummer	.60	1.50
SF8 Troy Aikman	1.25	3.00
SF9 Jamal Lewis	.75	2.00
SF10 Eddie George	.75	2.00
SF11 Steve McNair	.75	2.00
SF12 Steve Young	1.00	2.50
SF13 Jerome Bettis	.75	2.00
SF14 Tim Couch	.50	1.25
SF15 Mark Brunell	.60	1.50
SF16 Fred Taylor	.75	2.00
SF17 Corey Dillon	.60	1.50
SF18 Chad Pennington	.75	2.00
SF19 Brian Griese	.60	1.50
SF20 Mike Anderson	.60	1.50
SF21 John Elway	2.00	5.00
SF22 Terrell Owens	.75	2.00
SF23 Rich Gannon	.60	1.50
SF24 Jerry Rice	1.50	4.00
SF25 Ricky Williams	.75	2.00
SF26 Aaron Brooks	.60	1.50
SF27 Kurt Warner	1.25	3.00
SF28 Marshall Faulk	.75	2.00
SF29 Isaac Bruce	.75	2.00
SF30 Brett Favre	2.50	6.00
SF31 Antonio Freeman	.75	2.00
SF32 Daunte Culpepper	.60	1.50
SF33 Randy Moss	.75	2.00
SF34 Cris Carter	.75	2.00
SF35 Barry Sanders	2.00	5.00
SF36 Emmitt Smith	2.00	5.00
SF37 Stephen Davis	.60	1.50
SF38 Ron Dayne	.60	1.50
SF39 Donovan McNabb	.75	2.00
SF40 Peter Warrick	.60	1.50

2001 Quantum Leaf Touchdown Club

COMPLETE SET (40)	25.00	60.00
ODD #'s FOUND IN HOBBY PACKS		
EVEN #'s FOUND IN RETAIL PACKS		
STATED PRINT RUN 2000 SER.#'d SETS		
*TOTAL/266-429: 1X TO 2.5X BASIC INSERTS		
*TOTAL/109-187: 1.2X TO 3X BASIC INSERTS		
*TOTAL/62-90: 1.5X TO 4X BASIC INSERTS		
*TOTAL/40-50: 2X TO 5X BASIC INSERTS		
*TOTAL/35-38: 2.5X TO 6X BASIC INSERTS		
*TOTAL/24: 3X TO 8X BASIC INSERTS		
*TOTAL/11-15: 4X TO 10X BASIC INSERTS		
TOTALS PRINT RUN 5-429		
TC1 Marshall Faulk	.75	2.00
TC2 Edgerrin James	.75	2.00
TC3 Randy Moss	.75	2.00
TC4 Eddie George	.75	2.00
TC5 Terrell Owens	.75	2.00
TC6 Mike Anderson	.60	1.50
TC7 Stephen Davis	.60	1.50
TC8 Marvin Harrison	.75	2.00
TC9 Robert Smith	.60	1.50
TC10 Fred Taylor	.75	2.00
TC11 Daunte Culpepper	.60	1.50
TC12 Curtis Martin	.75	2.00
TC13 Emmitt Smith	2.00	5.00
TC14 Jamal Lewis	.75	2.00
TC15 Ricky Williams	.75	2.00
TC16 John Elway	2.00	5.00
TC17 Jerry Rice	1.50	4.00
TC18 Peyton Manning	2.00	5.00
TC19 Kurt Warner	1.25	3.00
TC20 Tim Brown	.75	2.00
TC21 Brett Favre	2.50	6.00
TC22 Jimmy Smith	.60	1.50
TC23 Cris Carter	.75	2.00
TC24 Terrell Davis	.75	2.00
TC25 Jeff Garcia	.60	1.50
TC26 Peter Warrick	.60	1.50
TC27 Ron Dayne	.60	1.50
TC28 Tony Gonzalez	.75	2.00
TC29 Isaac Bruce	.75	2.00
TC30 Drew Bledsoe	.75	2.00
TC31 Marcus Robinson	.60	1.50
TC32 Ricky Watters	.60	1.50
TC33 Ahman Green	.75	2.00
TC34 Dan Marino	2.00	5.00
TC35 Donovan McNabb	.75	2.00
TC36 Eric Moulds	.60	1.50
TC37 Aaron Brooks	.60	1.50
TC38 Steve McNair	.75	2.00
TC39 Barry Sanders	2.00	5.00
TC40 Brian Griese	.60	1.50

2001 Quantum Leaf X-ponential Power

COMPLETE SET (10)	20.00	40.00
EVEN #'d CARD HOBBY ONLY		
ODD #'d CARDS RETAIL ONLY		
STATED PRINT RUN 1000 SER.#'d SETS		
*X-FTR GREEN/75: 1.2X TO 3X BASIC INSERTS		
X-FACTOR GREEN PRINT RUN 75		
*X-FTR PRPL/15: 5X TO 12X BASIC INSERTS		
X-FACTOR PURPLE PRINT RUN 15		
*X-FCTR RED/35: 2.5X TO 6X BASIC INSERTS		
X-FACTOR RED PRINT RUN 35		
XP1 Kurt Warner	2.00	5.00
XP2 Peyton Manning	3.00	8.00
XP3 Steve Young	1.50	4.00
XP4 Dan Marino	3.00	8.00
XP5 Jerry Rice	2.50	6.00
XP6 John Elway	3.00	8.00
XP7 Barry Sanders	3.00	8.00
XP8 Steve McNair	1.25	3.00
XP9 Brett Favre	4.00	10.00
XP10 Terrell Davis	1.25	3.00

1991 Quarterback Legends

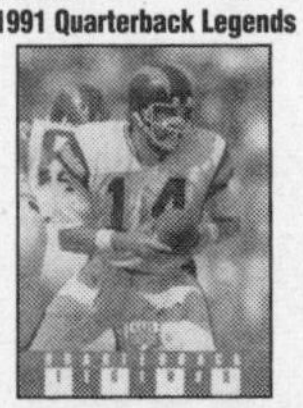

This 50-card set, measuring the standard size was produced by NFL Quarterback Legends and issued on high-quality card stock. The set is packaged in a red, white, and blue box. Card fronts feature a color action shot of the player. At the bottom of the card appears a red stripe and a blue and white checker board stripe, with the words "Quarterback Legends" reversed out in white and blue lettering. Card backs, printed horizontally, feature a full-bleed red stripe at the top with player's name in blue, another action photo, and statistical and biographical information. Sponsors' (QB Legends and Team NFL) logos and card number appear to the bottom right of card. The cards are numbered on the back. The first 46 cards in the set are ordered alphabetically by name. The last four cards depict legendary feats. The team name listed in the checklist below corresponds to uniform on front of cards; the photo on back of cards sometimes has player in a different team uniform. This set was introduced and distributed at the Quarterback Legends Show in Nashville, Tennessee in January, 1992.

COMPLETE SET (50)	12.50	25.00
1 Ken Anderson	.30	.75
2 Steve Bartkowski	.20	.50
3 George Blanda	.30	.75
4 Terry Bradshaw	.75	2.00
5 Zeke Bratkowski	.15	.40
6 John Brodie	.30	.75
7 Charley Conerly	.20	.50
8 Len Dawson	.30	.75
9 Lynn Dickey	.15	.40
10 Joe Ferguson	.15	.40
11 Vince Ferragamo	.15	.40
12 Tom Flores	.20	.50
13 Dan Fouts	.30	.75
14 Roman Gabriel	.20	.50
15 Otto Graham	.30	.75
16 Bob Griese	.40	1.00
17 Steve Grogan	.20	.50
18 John Hadl	.20	.50
19 James Harris	.15	.40
20 Jim Hart	.15	.40
21 Ron Jaworski	.15	.40
22 Charley Johnson	.15	.40
23 Bert Jones	.20	.50
24 Sonny Jurgensen	.30	.75
25 Joe Kapp	.15	.40
26 Billy Kilmer	.20	.50
27 Daryle Lamonica	.20	.50
28 Greg Landry	.15	.40
29 Neil Lomax	.15	.40
30 Archie Manning	.20	.50
31 Earl Morrall	.15	.40
32 Craig Morton	.20	.50
33 Gifford Nielsen	.15	.40
34 Dan Pastorini	.15	.40
35 Jim Plunkett	.20	.50
36 Norm Snead	.15	.40
37 Ken Stabler	.40	1.00
38 Bart Starr	.75	2.00
39 Roger Staubach	.75	2.00
40 Joe Theismann	.30	.75
41 Y.A. Tittle	.30	.75
42 Johnny Unitas	.75	2.00
43 Bill Wade	.15	.40
44 Danny White	.20	.50
45 Doug Williams	.20	.50
46 Jim Zorn	.20	.50
47 Otto Graham	.30	.75
Legendary Feats		
48 Johnny Unitas	.75	2.00
Legendary Feats		
49 Bart Starr	.75	2.00
Legendary Feats		
50 Terry Bradshaw	.75	2.00
Legendary Feats		

1992 Quarterback Greats GE

Produced by NFL Properties, this 12-card standard-size set was prepared for General Electric Silicones and features members of the Quarterback Club. The cards could be obtained by sending in proofs of purchase. The fronts carry action color player photos on a red face. The player's name is printed in white lettering above the picture. A blue and red bar icon containing the words "Quarterback Greats" runs horizontally from the top right and overlaps the picture. The backs carry statistics and career highlights. The GE logo and NFL Team Players logo appear at the bottom. The Quarterback Club icon (a black box with a brightly colored football player outline) is in the upper left corner.

COMPLETE SET (12)	12.00	30.00
1 Troy Aikman	1.60	4.00
2 Bubby Brister	.30	.75
3 Randall Cunningham	.40	1.00
4 John Elway	3.20	8.00
5 Boomer Esiason	.40	1.00
6 Jim Everett	.30	.75
7 Jim Kelly	.60	1.50
8 Bernie Kosar	.30	.75
9 Dan Marino	3.20	8.00
10 Warren Moon	.40	1.00
11 Phil Simms	.40	1.00
NNO Title Card	.30	.75
(Checklist)		

1993 Quarterback Legends

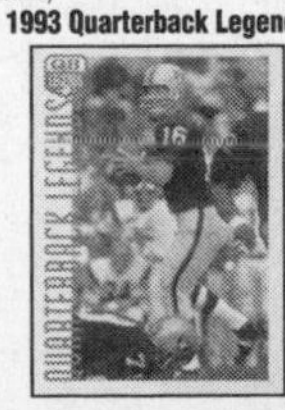

This 50-card standard-size set showcases outstanding quarterbacks throughout NFL history. The fronts feature action player photos in which the player appears in color against a sepia-toned background. The borders shade from white to pastel yellow as one moves from left to right, and the set title "Quarterback Legends" is printed vertically on the left edge in bronze lettering. The horizontal backs carry a close-up color player photo and career summary. The set closes with a Legendary Feats (48-50) subset.

COMPLETE SET (50)	6.00	15.00
1 Checklist Card	.14	.35
2 Ken Anderson	.25	.60
3 Steve Bartkowski	.14	.35
4 George Blanda	.25	.60
5 Terry Bradshaw	1.00	2.50
6 Zeke Bratkowski	.08	.25
7 John Brodie	.20	.50
8 Charley Conerly	.14	.35
9 Len Dawson	.20	.50
10 Lynn Dickey	.08	.25
11 Joe Ferguson	.08	.25
12 Vince Ferragamo	.08	.25
13 Tom Flores	.14	.35
14 Dan Fouts	.30	.75
15 Roman Gabriel	.14	.35
16 Otto Graham	.40	1.00
17 Bob Griese	.40	1.00
18 Steve Grogan	.14	.35
19 John Hadl	.14	.35
20 James Harris	.08	.25
21 Jim Hart	.08	.25
22 Ron Jaworski	.08	.25
23 Charley Johnson	.08	.25
24 Bert Jones	.14	.35
25 Sonny Jurgensen	.20	.50
26 Joe Kapp	.08	.25
27 Billy Kilmer	.14	.35
28 Daryle Lamonica	.14	.35
29 Greg Landry	.08	.25
30 Neil Lomax	.08	.25
31 Archie Manning	.20	.50
32 Earl Morrall	.08	.25
33 Craig Morton	.14	.35
34 Gifford Nielsen	.08	.25
35 Dan Pastorini	.08	.25
36 Jim Plunkett	.14	.35
37 Norm Snead	.08	.25
38 Ken Stabler	.40	1.00
39 Bart Starr	.60	1.50
40 Roger Staubach	1.00	2.50
41 Joe Theismann	.25	.60
42 Y.A. Tittle	.30	.75
43 Johnny Unitas	.60	1.50
44 Bill Wade	.08	.25
45 Danny White	.14	.35
46 Doug Williams	.08	.25
47 Jim Zorn	.08	.25
48 George Blanda	.25	.60
Miracle Streak		
49 Bob Griese	.20	.50
Earl Morrall		
Perfect Season		
50 Doug Williams	.08	.25
Record-setting Super		
Bowl XXII		

1935 R311-2 National Chicle Premiums

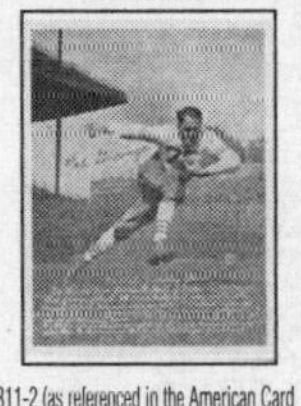

The R311-2 (as referenced in the American Card Catalog) Football Stars and Scenes set consists of 17 glossy, unnumbered, 6" by 8" photos. Both professional and collegiate players are pictured on these photos. These blank-back photos have been numbered in the checklist below alphabetically by the player's name or title. These premium photos were available from National Chicle with one premium given for every 20 wrappers turned in to the retailer.

COMPLETE SET (17)	3,000.00	4,500.00
1 Joe Bach	150.00	250.00
2 Eddie Casey	150.00	250.00
3 George Christensen	150.00	250.00
4 Red Grange	400.00	750.00
5 Stan Kostka	125.00	200.00
TD Next Stop		
6 Joe Maniaci	125.00	200.00
Fordham Back		
(26 with ball,		
shown trying to gain		
around left end)		
7 Harry Newman	125.00	200.00
8 Walter Switzer	125.00	200.00
Cornell QB vs. Columbia		
9 Chicago Bears/1934 Western Champs team photo		
250.00	400.00	
10 New York Giants/1934 World's Champs team photo		
200.00	350.00	
11 Bill Shakespeare punting	175.00	300.00
Notre Dame's Quick		
Kick Against		
Army, Nov. 24, 1934		
12 Pittsburgh U. in Rough	125.00	200.00
going Against the		
Navy 1934		
13 Pittsburgh Pirates/1935 team photo	175.00	300.00
14 S.L. Morton	125.00	200.00
Touchdown: Morton of Yale		
15 Dixie Howell	150.00	250.00
A Tight Spot		
16 Cotton Warburton	150.00	250.00
Cotton Goes Places/1935 East-West Shrine game		
(with Gerald Ford in photo)		
17 Ace Gutowsky	150.00	250.00
Steve Hokuf		
The Greatest Tackle		
Picture Ever Photographed		

1962 Raiders Team Issue

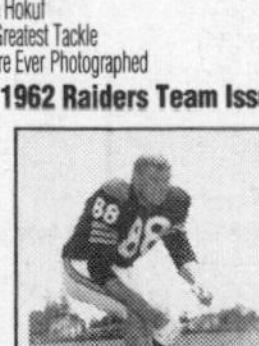

The Raiders likely released these photos over a number of seasons. Each measures approximately 8" by 10" and includes a black and white photo on the cardfront with a blank cardback. The team name, player's name, and position (abbreviated) appear below the photo from left to right. The checklist is thought to be incomplete. Any additions to this list are appreciated.

COMPLETE SET (4)	35.00	60.00
1 Wayne Hawkins	10.00	20.00
2 Jon Jelacic	7.50	15.00
3 Chuck McMurtry	7.50	15.00
4 Pete Nicklas	7.50	15.00

1964 Raiders Team Issue

The Raiders likely released these photos over a number of seasons. Each measures approximately 8" by 10" and includes a black and white photo on the front with a blank back. The player's name, position (spelled out in full) and team name appear below the photo. The text style and size varies slightly from photo to photo and the checklist is thought to be incomplete. Any additions to this list are appreciated.

COMPLETE SET (19)	150.00	250.00
1 Bill Budness	7.50	15.00
2 Billy Cannon	12.50	25.00
3 Clem Daniels	10.00	20.00
4 Ben Davidson	12.50	25.00
5 Cotton Davidson	10.00	20.00
6 Claude Gibson	7.50	15.00
7 Wayne Hawkins	10.00	20.00
8 Ken Herock	7.50	15.00
9 Jon Jelacic	7.50	15.00
10 Dick Klein	7.50	15.00
11 Joe Krakoski	7.50	15.00
12 Mike Mercer	7.50	15.00
13 Tommy Morrow	7.50	15.00
14 Clancy Osborne	7.50	15.00
15 Jim Otto (horizontal photo)	20.00	35.00
16 Art Powell (horizontal photo)	10.00	20.00
17 Ken Rice	7.50	15.00
18 Bo Roberson	7.50	15.00
19 Howie Williams	7.50	15.00

1968 Raiders Team Issue

The Raiders likely released these photos over a number of seasons. Each measures approximately 8" by 10 1/4" to 8 1/2" by 10 1/2" in size and includes a black and white photo on the cardfront with a blank cardback. All of the photos were taken outdoors with a rolling hillside in the far background. The player's name, position initials and team name appear below the photo. The text style and size varies slightly from photo to photo. The 1969 issue looks very similar to this set, but it was printed on slightly thicker, larger, and slightly less glossy paper stock than this 1968 release. Any additions to this list are appreciated.

COMPLETE SET (32)	200.00	400.00
1 Fred Biletnikoff	12.50	25.00
2 Dan Birdwell	6.00	12.00
3 Bill Budness	6.00	12.00
4 Billy Cannon	7.50	15.00
5 Dan Conners	6.00	12.00
6 Cotton Davidson	6.00	12.00
7 Eldridge Dickey	6.00	12.00
8A Hewritt Dixon (position is OT)	6.00	12.00
8B Hewritt Dixon (position omitted)	6.00	12.00
9 John Eason	6.00	12.00
10 Mike Eischeid	6.00	12.00
11 Dave Grayson (position listed is DB, charging to his left)	6.00	12.00
12 Roger Hagberg	6.00	12.00
13 James Harvey	6.00	12.00
14 Wayne Hawkins	6.00	12.00
15 Tom Keating	6.00	12.00
16 Bob Kruse	6.00	12.00
17A Daryle Lamonica (lateralling the ball)	10.00	20.00
17B Daryle Lamonica (passing pose)	10.00	20.00
18 Ike Lassiter	6.00	12.00
19 Kent McCloughan	6.00	12.00
20 Bill Miller	6.00	12.00
21 Carleton Oats (charging to his left)	6.00	12.00
22 Jim Otto	10.00	20.00
23 Gus Otto (charging to his right)	6.00	12.00
24 Warren Powers	6.00	12.00
25 John Rauch CO	6.00	12.00
26A Harry Schuh (position is OT)	6.00	12.00
26B Harry Schuh (position omitted)	6.00	12.00
27 Art Shell	15.00	30.00
28 Charlie Smith	6.00	12.00
29 Bob Svihus	6.00	12.00
30 Larry Todd	6.00	12.00
31 Warren Wells	6.00	12.00
32 Howie Williams	6.00	12.00

1969 Raiders Team Issue

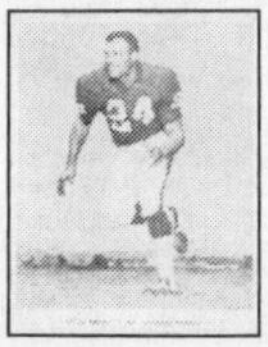

The Raiders issued these photos shrink wrapped in a package of 8 defensive or offensive players along with a small paper checklist. Each measures approximately 8 1/2" by 10 3/8" and includes a black and white photo on the cardfront with a blank cardback. The player's name, position initials (except Dave Grayson) and team name appear below the photo. The text style and size and some of the photos are nearly identical to the 1968 listing. This issue was printed on thicker, slightly less glossy, paper stock than the 1968 photos along with difference in size.

COMPLETE SET (8)	100.00	200.00
1 George Atkinson	6.00	12.00
2 Fred Biletnikoff	12.50	25.00
3 Willie Brown	10.00	20.00
4 Dan Conners (same photo as 1968, cropped slightly lower)	6.00	12.00
5 Ben Davidson	7.50	15.00
6 Hewritt Dixon	7.50	15.00
7 Dave Grayson (no position listed, charging to his right)	6.00	12.00
8 Tom Keating (same photo as 1968, cropped slightly more to the right)	6.00	12.00
9 Daryle Lamonica	10.00	20.00
10 Carleton Oats (hands in the air to block)	6.00	12.00
11 Gus Otto (running to his right, but looking back)	6.00	12.00
12 Jim Otto	10.00	20.00
13 Harry Schuh	6.00	12.00
14 Charlie Smith	6.00	12.00
15 Gene Upshaw	10.00	20.00
16 Warren Wells	6.00	12.00

1985 Raiders Shell Oil Posters

Available only at participating Southern California Shell stations during the 1985 season, these five posters measure approximately 11 5/8" by 18" and feature an artist's color renderings of the Raiders in action. The unnumbered posters are blank-backed, except for number 1 below, the back of which carries the Raiders and Shell logos along with the month in which each subsequent poster was released. The posters are listed below accordingly.

COMPLETE SET (5)	10.00	25.00
1 Pro Bowl (No release date)	3.00	8.00
2 Defensive Front (September)	2.00	5.00
3 Deep Secondary (October)	2.00	5.00
4 Big Offensive Line (November)	2.00	5.00
5 Scores (December)	2.00	5.00

1985 Raiders Fire Safety

This four-card set of Los Angeles Raiders was also sponsored by Kodak. The cards measure approximately 2 5/8" by 4 1/8". The cards are numbered (and dated) on the back. The fire safety tip on the back is in the form of a cartoon. There are also two or three paragraphs of biographical information about the player on the card backs. The card fronts show a full-color photo inside a white border. The player's name, team, position, height, and weight are given at the bottom of the card front.

COMPLETE SET (4)	1.50	4.00
1 Marcus Allen	.75	2.00
2 Tom Flores CO	.15	.40
3 Howie Long	.60	1.50
4 Rod Martin	.15	.40

1985 Raiders Police

This set of cards was distributed by Police Officers in the Los Angeles area and sponsored by KIIIS Radio. The unnumbered cards are listed alphabetically below. Uncut sheets of both the 1985 Rams and Raiders Police sets together are also on the market.

COMPLETE SET (15)	7.50	20.00
1 Marcus Allen	3.00	6.00
2 Lyle Alzado	1.25	3.00
3 Todd Christensen	.60	1.50
4 Dave Dalby	.40	1.00
5 Mike Davis	.40	1.00
6 Ray Guy	.60	1.50
7 Frank Hawkins	.40	1.00
8 Lester Hayes	.60	1.50
9 Mike Haynes	.60	1.50
10 Howie Long	3.00	6.00
11 Rod Martin	.40	1.00
12 Mickey Marvin	.40	1.00
13 Jim Plunkett	1.25	3.00
14 Brad Van Pelt	.40	1.00
15 Dokie Williams	.40	1.00

1987 Raiders Smokey Color-Grams

This set is actually a 14-page booklet featuring 13 player caricatures (all from the Los Angeles Raiders) and one of Smokey and Huddles. Each page includes a 5 5/8" by 3 11/16" postcard perforated with a card measuring 2 1/2" by 3 11/16". The booklet itself is approximately 8 1/8" by 3 11/16". The set is headlined as "Arsonbusters" in white over a black frame. The backs offer a fire prevention tip from Smokey. The cards are unnumbered, but are listed below according to booklet page number.

COMPLETE SET (14)	20.00	40.00
1 Smokey and Huddles	.60	1.50
2 Matt Millen	.75	2.00
3 Rod Martin	.75	2.00
4 Sean Jones	1.00	2.50
5 Dokie Williams	.60	1.50
6 Don Mosebar	.75	2.00
7 Todd Christensen	.75	2.00
8 Bill Pickel	.60	1.50
9 Marcus Allen	6.00	12.00
10 Charley Hannah	.60	1.50
11 Howie Long	4.00	8.00
12 Vann McElroy	.60	1.50
13 Reggie McKenzie	.60	1.50
14 Mike Haynes	1.25	3.00

1988 Raiders Ace Fact Pack

Cards from this 33-card set measure approximately 2 1/4" by 3 5/8". This set consists of 22-player cards and 11-additional informational cards about the Raiders team. We've checklisted the cards alphabetically beginning with the 22-players. The cards have square corners (as opposed to rounded like the 1987 sets) and a playing card design on the back printed in blue. These cards were manufactured in West Germany (by Ace Fact Pack) and released primarily in Great Britain.

COMPLETE SET (33)	200.00	350.00
1 Marcus Allen	40.00	80.00
2 Chris Bahr	2.00	5.00
3 Bob Buczkowski	2.00	5.00
4 Todd Christensen	4.00	10.00
5 John Clay	2.00	5.00
6 Vince Evans	2.50	6.00
7 Mervyn Fernandez	2.00	5.00
8 Mike Haynes	12.50	25.00
9 Jessie Hester	2.00	5.00
10 Brian Holloway	2.00	5.00
11 Bo Jackson	40.00	80.00
12 James Lofton	12.50	25.00
13 Howie Long	20.00	40.00
14 Rod Martin	2.50	6.00
15 Vann McElroy	2.00	5.00
16 Reggie McKenzie	2.00	5.00
17 Matt Millen	4.00	10.00
18 Don Mosebar	2.00	5.00
19 Bill Pickel	2.00	5.00
20 Jerry Robinson	2.50	6.00
21 Stacey Toran UER (first name spelled Tracey)	2.00	5.00
22 Greg Townsend	2.00	5.00
23 1987 Team Statistics	2.00	5.00
24 All-Time Greats	2.00	5.00
25 Career Record Holders	2.00	5.00
26 Coaching History	2.00	5.00
27 Game Record Holders	2.00	5.00
28 Memorial Coliseum	2.00	5.00
29 Record 1968-87	2.00	5.00
30 Raiders Helmet Cover card	2.00	5.00
31 Raiders Helmet Informational card	2.00	5.00
32 Raiders Uniform	2.00	5.00
33 Season Record Holders	2.00	5.00

1988 Raiders Police

The 1988 Police Los Angeles Raiders set contains 12 numbered cards measuring approximately 2 3/4" by 4 1/8". There are 11 player cards and one coach card. The backs have biographical information and safety tips. The set was sponsored by Texaco and the Los Angeles Raiders.

COMPLETE SET (12)	5.00	10.00
1 Vann McElroy	.25	.60
2 Bill Pickel	.25	.60
3 Marcus Allen	1.25	3.00
4 Rod Martin	.30	.75
5 Lionel Washington	.25	.60
6 Don Mosebar	.25	.60
7 Reggie McKenzie	.25	.60
8 Todd Christensen	.30	.75
9 Bo Jackson	.75	2.00
10 James Lofton	.40	1.00
11 Howie Long	.60	1.50
12 Mike Shanahan CO	.40	1.00

1988 Raiders Smokey

This 14-card set is distinguished by its thick black border on the front of every card as well as the presence of "Arsonbusters" in orange as a subtitle. The cards measure approximately 3" by 5". The set is not numbered although the players' uniform numbers are in small print on the back; the list below has been ordered alphabetically. Each card back features a different fire safety cartoon starring Smokey.

COMPLETE SET (14)	10.00	20.00
1 Marcus Allen	2.00	5.00
2 Todd Christensen	.60	1.50
3 Bo Jackson	1.25	3.00
4 James Lofton	.75	2.00
5 Howie Long	1.25	3.00
6 Rod Martin	.60	1.50
7 Vann McElroy	.50	1.25
8 Don Mosebar	.50	1.25
9 Bill Pickel	.50	1.25
10 Jerry Robinson	.50	1.25
11 Mike Shanahan CO	.60	1.50
12 Smokey Bear	.50	1.25
13 Stacey Toran	.50	1.25
14 Greg Townsend	.50	1.25

1989 Raiders Knudsen Bookmarks

This unnumbered 12-card set (of bookmarks) issued by Knudsen's Dairy in California measures approximately 2" by 8" and features members of the 1989 Los Angeles Raiders. These sets were distributed during the football season to those youngsters who checked out a book a week during the 1989 season from the Los Angeles Public Library. The backs of these bookmarks feature various reading tips for the youth to follow. The set is checklisted below by player's uniform number. The Shanahan card was apparently undistributed or withdrawn after he left the team.

COMPLETE SET (14)	20.00	50.00
6 Jeff Gossett	1.25	3.00
13 Jay Schroeder	1.50	4.00
26 Vann McElroy	1.25	3.00
35 Steve Smith	1.50	4.00
36 Terry McDaniel	1.50	4.00
70 Scott Davis	1.25	3.00
72 Don Mosebar	1.25	3.00
75 Howie Long	2.00	5.00
76 Steve Wisniewski	1.50	4.00
81 Tim Brown	5.00	12.00
83 Willie Gault	1.50	4.00
NNO Mike Shanahan SP CO	6.00	15.00
NNO Raiders Super Bowl	1.25	3.00
NNO Raiderettes SP	1.50	4.00

1989 Raiders Swanson

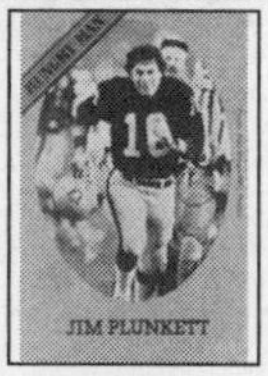

This three-card set was issued in a perforated strip containing five card slots; after perforation, the cards measure approximately 2 1/2" by 3 3/4". The first two slots consist of manufacturer's coupons to save 25 cents on the purchase of any variety of Swanson Hungry-Man dinners. The player cards feature an oval-shamped black and white player photo on a silver card face. A red diagonal with the words "Hungry-Man" cuts across the upper left corner, and the player's name appears in black lettering below the picture. The horizontal backs present biographical information and player profile. The cards are unnumbered and checklisted below in alphabetical order.

COMPLETE SET (3)	5.00	12.00
1 Marcus Allen	3.00	8.00
2 Howie Long	1.25	3.00
3 Jim Plunkett	1.00	2.50

1990 Raiders Smokey

This 16-card standard size set was issued by the USDA Forest Service in conjuction with the USDI Bureau of Land Management, USDI National Park Service, California Department of Forestry and Fire Prevention, and BDA. The set features solid black borders framing a full-color action shot with the Los Angeles Raiders team name in white. The player's name and uniform number is directly underneath the photo and there is a photo of the Smokey the Bear mascot in the lower left hand corner of the card. The back of the card has only the basic biographical information, as well as a fire safety tip. Surprisingly, there is no card of either Bo Jackson or Marcus Allen in this set. The set has been checklisted below in alphabetical order.

COMPLETE SET (16)	12.50	25.00
1 Eddie Anderson	.60	1.50
2 Thomas Benson	.60	1.50
3 Mervyn Fernandez	.75	2.00
4 Bob Golic	.60	1.50
5 Jeff Gossett	.60	1.50
6 Rory Graves	.60	1.50
7 Jeff Jaeger	.60	1.50
8 Howie Long	1.50	4.00
9 Don Mosebar	.60	1.50
10 Jay Schroeder	.75	2.00
11 Art Shell CO	1.00	2.50
12 Greg Townsend	.75	2.00
13 Lionel Washington	.60	1.50
14 Steve Wisniewski	.75	2.00
15 Commitment to Excellence (Helmet and Super Bowl trophies)	.60	1.50
16 Denise Franzen Cheerleader	.60	1.50

1990-91 Raiders Main Street Dairy Mile Cartons

This set of six half-pint milk cartons features the Raiders' team patch, a head shot of a player, and a safety tip to youngsters on one of its panels. When collapsed, the cartons measure approximately 4 1/2" by 6". The cartons were issued in the Los Angeles area and were printed in three colors, brown (chocolate lowfat), red (vitamin D), and blue (2 percent low fat). The primary color of the carton is given on the continuation line below.

COMPLETE SET (6)	12.00	30.00
1 Bob Golic (Blue)	2.40	6.00
2 Terry McDaniel (Brown)	2.00	5.00
3 Don Mosebar (Red)	2.00	5.00
4 Jay Schroeder (Blue)	2.40	6.00
5 Art Shell CO (Red)	3.20	8.00
6 Steve Wisniewski (Brown)	2.00	5.00

1991 Raiders Police

This 12-card standard-size set was sponsored by Clovis Police Department, REHCO Heating and Air Conditioning, and the Los Angeles Raiders. Five thousand sets were distributed throughout the Fresno/Clovis area as part of a sixth grade DARE (Drug Awareness Resistance Education) program. Card fronts feature color action player photos with white borders. The player's name appears in a gray stripe above the picture, while sponsor logos overlay another gray stripe at the bottom of the card face. The backs have biographical information and a safety tip printed in black lettering on a white background.

COMPLETE SET (12)	10.00	20.00
1 Art Shell CO	1.00	2.50
2 Marcus Allen	2.00	5.00
3 Mervyn Fernandez	.50	1.25
4 Willie Gault	.60	1.50
5 Howie Long	1.50	3.00
6 Don Mosebar	.50	1.25
7 Winston Moss	.50	1.25
8 Jay Schroeder	.60	1.50
9 Steve Wisniewski	.50	1.25
10 Ethan Horton	.50	1.25
11 Lionel Washington	.50	1.25
12 Greg Townsend	.50	1.25

1991-92 Raiders Adohr Farms Dairy

This set of ten half-pint milk cartons features the Raiders' team patch, a head shot of a player, and a safety message on one of its panels. When collapsed, the cartons measure approximately 4 1/2" by 6". The cartons were issued in the Los Angeles area and were printed in red (vitamin D) and blue (2 percent lowfat). Apparently only the Greg Townsend carton was issued in two varieties. The primary color of the carton is given on the continuation line. The cartons are unnumbered and checklisted below in alphabetical order. Apparently Adohr Farms Dairy bought out Main Street Dairy and with the buyout, obtained the rights to produce the selected Raiders.

COMPLETE SET (10)	20.00	40.00
1 Jeff Gossett (Red)	2.00	5.00
2 Ethan Horton (Blue)	2.00	5.00
3 Jeff Jaeger (Red)	2.00	5.00
4 Ronnie Lott (Blue)	3.00	8.00
5 Terry McDaniel (Red)	2.00	5.00
6 Don Mosebar (Red)	2.00	5.00
7 Jay Schroeder (Red)	2.00	5.00
8 Art Shell CO (Red)	2.50	6.00
9 Greg Townsend (Red or blue)	2.00	5.00
10 Steve Wisniewski (Red)	2.00	5.00

1993-94 Raiders Adohr Farms Dairy

This set of six half-pint vitamin D milk cartons features the Raiders team patch, a head shot of a player, and a message about education or crime prevention, all printed in red. When collapsed, the cartons measure approximately 4 1/2" by 6". Two million milk cartons were distributed only to Los Angeles area schools and hospitals in a two-week period during the season. Reportedly only 1,400 were produced flat and undistributed. The cartons are unnumbered and checklisted below in alphabetical order.

COMPLETE SET (6)	15.00	30.00
1 Jeff Gossett	2.00	5.00
2 Ethan Horton	2.00	5.00
3 Terry McDaniel	2.00	5.00
4 Don Mosebar	2.00	5.00
5 Art Shell CO	2.50	6.00
6 Steve Wisniewski	2.00	5.00

1994-95 Raiders Adohr Farms Dairy

This set of four half-pint Vitamin D milk cartons features the Raiders' team patch, a head shot of the player, and a safety tip on one of its panels. When collapsed, the cartons measure approximately 4 1/2" by 6". All cartons are printed in red with some black lettering. It was reported that 20,000,000 cartons (or five million sets) were issued in a three-week period. Ninety percent were distributed to hospitals, schools, and airlines, while ten percent were sold to the general public. Reportedly, 800 cartons (or 200 sets) were left flat and undistributed. The cartons are unnumbered and checklisted below in alphabetical order.

COMPLETE SET (4)	10.00	20.00
1 Jeff Jaeger	2.00	5.00
2 Terry McDaniel	2.00	5.00
3 Art Shell CO	2.50	6.00
4 Steve Wisniewski	2.00	5.00

2006 Raiders Topps

COMPLETE SET (12)	3.00	6.00
OAK1 LaMont Jordan	.25	.60
OAK2 Warren Sapp	.25	.60
OAK3 Kirk Morrison	.20	.50
OAK4 Jerry Porter	.20	.50
OAK5 Robert Gallery	.20	.50
OAK6 Ronald Curry	.25	.60
OAK7 Doug Gabriel	.20	.50
OAK8 Randy Moss	.30	.75
OAK9 Fabian Washington	.20	.50
OAK10 Derrick Burgess	.20	.50
OAK11 Aaron Brooks	.25	.60
OAK12 Michael Huff	.25	.60

2006 Raiders Topps Pepsi

These 6-cards were produced by Topps and inserted one card per 24-pack of Pepsi Cola product in the Oakland area. Each unnumbered card is completely redesigned compared to basic issue 2006 Topps football.

COMPLETE SET (6)	5.00	10.00
1 Aaron Brooks	.75	2.00
2 Derrick Gibson	.60	1.50
3 Michael Huff	.75	2.00
4 Randy Moss	1.00	2.50
5 Jerry Porter	.60	1.50
6 Warren Sapp	.75	2.00

2007 Raiders Topps

COMPLETE SET (12)	3.00	6.00
1 Andrew Walter	.20	.50
2 Nnamdi Asomugha	.30	.75
3 Kirk Morrison	.20	.50
4 Michael Huff	.25	.60
5 Ronald Curry	.25	.60
6 Derrick Burgess	.20	.50
7 Dominic Rhodes	.25	.60
8 LaMont Jordan	.25	.60
9 Warren Sapp	.25	.60
10 JaMarcus Russell	.20	.50
11 Zach Miller	.30	.75
12 Michael Bush	.30	.75

2008 Raiders Topps

COMPLETE SET (12)	2.50	5.00
1 DeAngelo Hall	.20	.50
2 Justin Fargas	.20	.50
3 Zach Miller	.25	.60
4 JaMarcus Russell	.25	.60
5 Ronald Curry	.25	.60
6 Daunte Culpepper	.25	.60
7 LaMont Jordan	.25	.60
8 Thomas Howard	.20	.50
9 Kirk Morrison	.20	.50
10 Derrick Burgess	.20	.50
11 Darren McFadden	1.00	2.50
12 Nnamdi Asomugha	.25	.60

1950 Rams Admiral

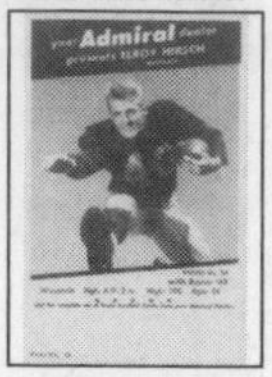

This 35-card set was sponsored by Admiral Televisions and features cards measuring approximately 3 1/2" by 5 1/2" (#1-25) and 3 1/8" by 5 3/8" (#26-35). The front design has a black and white action pose of the player, without borders on the sides of the picture. The words "Your Admiral dealer presents" followed by the player's name and position appear in the black stripe at the top of each card. A black border separates the bottom of the picture from the biographical information below. In a horizontal format, the backs are blank on the right half, and have a season schedule as well as Admiral advertisements on the left half (#1-25) or are blankbacked (#26-35). The cards are numbered on the front underneath the photos. Norm Van Brocklin appears in his Rookie Card year.

COMPLETE SET (35)	4,000.00	7,000.00
1 Joe Stydahar CO	125.00	200.00
2 Hampton Pool CO	100.00	175.00
3 Fred Naumetz	100.00	175.00
4 Jack Finlay	100.00	175.00
5 Gil Bouley	100.00	175.00
6 Bob Reinhard	100.00	175.00
7 Bob Boyd	100.00	175.00
8 Bob Waterfield	300.00	500.00
9 Mel Hein CO	125.00	200.00
10 Howard(Red) Hickey CO	100.00	175.00
11 Ralph Pasquariello	100.00	175.00
12 Jack Zilly	100.00	175.00
13 Tom Kalmanir	100.00	175.00
14 Norm Van Brocklin	400.00	750.00
15 Woodley Lewis	100.00	175.00
16 Glenn Davis	150.00	250.00
17 Dick Hoerner	100.00	175.00
18 Bob Kelley ANN	100.00	175.00
19 Paul(Tank) Younger	125.00	200.00
20 George Sims	100.00	175.00
21 Dick Huffman	100.00	175.00
22 Tom Fears	175.00	300.00
23 Vitamin T. Smith	100.00	175.00
24 Elroy Hirsch	350.00	600.00
25 Don Paul	100.00	175.00
26 Bill Lange	100.00	175.00
27 Paul Barry	100.00	175.00
28 Deacon Dan Towler	125.00	200.00
29 Vic Vasicek	100.00	175.00
30 Bill Smyth	100.00	175.00
31 Larry Brink	100.00	175.00
32 Jerry Williams	100.00	175.00
33 Stan West	100.00	175.00
34 Art Statuto	100.00	175.00
35 Ed Champagne	100.00	175.00

1950 Rams Matchbooks

These matchbook covers were produced by Universal Match Corporation around 1950 and feature members of the Los Angeles Rams. Each cover features a blue border and yellow-tinted player photo along with the Rams team logo. The inside or "back" of the covers is blank. Any additions to the list below are appreciated.

1 Bob Waterfield (punting pose)	20.00	40.00

1953 Rams Team Issue

This 36-card unnumbered set measures approximately 4 1/4" by 6 3/8" and was issued by the Los Angeles Rams for their fans. This set has black borders on the front framing posed action shots with the player's signature across the bottom portion of the picture. Biographical information on the back relating to the player pictured listing the player's name, height, weight, age, and college is also included. Among the interesting cards in this set are early cards of Dick "Night-Train" Lane and Andy Robustelli. The cards were available directly from the team as a complete set. We have checklisted this set in alphabetical order. Many cards from the 1953-1955 and 1957 Rams Team Issue Black Border sets are identical except for text differences on the card backs. Player stat lines are also helpful in identifying year of issue; the year of issue is typically the next year after the last year on the stats. The first few words of the first line of text is listed for players without stat lines.

COMPLETE SET (36)	250.00	400.00
1 Ben Agajanian	5.00	8.00
2 Bob Boyd	5.00	8.00
(Born in Riverside ...)		
3 Larry Brink	5.00	8.00
4 Rudy Bukich	5.00	8.00
5 Tom Dahms	5.00	8.00
(4 text lines)		
6 Dick Daugherty	5.00	8.00
(Regular Ram ...)		
7 Jack Dwyer	5.00	8.00
(Played 1951 ...)		
8 Tom Fears	15.00	30.00
(1952 stats)		
9 Bob Fry	5.00	8.00
(Was sprinter ...)		
10 Frank Fuller	5.00	8.00
(Attended ...)		
11 Norbert Hecker	5.00	8.00
12 Elroy Hirsch	25.00	40.00
(1952 stats)		
13 John Hock	5.00	8.00
(Just completed ...)		
14 Bob Kelley ANN	5.00	8.00
(Signature in dpper left of photo)		
15 Dick Lane	15.00	30.00
16 Woodley Lewis	5.00	8.00
(Ram utility ...)		
17 Tom McCormick	5.00	8.00
(Set three ...)		
18 Lewis(Bud) McFadin	5.00	8.00
(Came to Rams ...)		
19 Leon McLaughlin	5.00	8.00
(Played every ...)		
20 Brad Myers	5.00	8.00
21 Don Paul	5.00	8.00
(A five year ...)		
22 Hampton Pool CO	5.00	8.00
(Hampton Pool ...)		
23 Duane Putnam	5.00	8.00
(As rookie ...)		
24 Volney Quinlan	5.00	8.00
(Nickname ...)		
25 Herb Rich	5.00	8.00
26 Andy Robustelli	20.00	35.00
(Rams' regular ...)		
27 Vitamin T. Smith	5.00	8.00
28 Harland Svare	5.00	8.00
(Attended ...)		
29 Len Teeuws	5.00	8.00
30 Harry Thompson	5.00	8.00
(Used at ...)		
31 Charley Toogood	5.00	8.00
(Been defensive ...)		
32 Deacon Dan Towler	6.00	10.00
(National football ...)		
33 Norm Van Brocklin	35.00	60.00
(1952 stats)		
34 Stan West	5.00	8.00
(Rams' regular ...)		
35 Paul(Tank) Younger	6.00	10.00
(1952 stats)		
36 Coaches: John Sauer& William Battles& and Howard(Red) Hickey	5.00	8.00

1953-54 Rams Burgermeister Beer Team Photos

These oversized (roughly 6 1/4" by 9") color team photos were sponsored by Burgermeister Beer and distributed in the Los Angeles area. Each were printed on card stock and included advertising messages on the back.

1953 Los Angeles Rams	35.00	60.00
1954 Los Angeles Rams	35.00	60.00

1954 Rams Team Issue

This 36-card set measures approximately 4 1/4" by 6 3/8". The front features a black and white posed action photo enclosed by a black border, with the player's signature across the bottom portion of the picture. The back lists the player's name, height, weight, age, and college, along with basic biographical information. The set was available direct from the team as part of a package for their fans. The cards are listed alphabetically below since they are unnumbered. Many cards from the 1953-1955 and 1957 Rams Team Issue Black Border sets are identical except for text differences on the card backs. Player stat lines are also helpful in identifying year of issue; the year of issue is typically the next year after the last year on the stats. The first few words of the first line of text is listed for players without stat lines. The set features the first card appearance of Gene "Big Daddy" Lipscomb.

COMPLETE SET (36)	200.00	400.00
1 Bob Boyd	4.00	8.00
(One of fastest ...)		
2 Bob Carey	4.00	8.00
3 Bobby Cross	4.00	8.00
4 Tom Dahms	4.00	8.00
(5 text lines)		
5 Don Doll	4.00	8.00
6 Jack Dwyer	4.00	8.00
(Regular defensive ...)		
7 Tom Fears	12.50	25.00
(1953 stats)		
8 Bob Griffin	4.00	8.00
(All American ...)		
9 Art Hauser	4.00	8.00
(Was fastest ...)		
10 Hall Haynes	4.00	8.00
11 Elroy Hirsch	20.00	35.00
(1953 stats)		
12 Ed Hughes	4.00	8.00
13 Bob Kelley ANN	4.00	8.00
(Signature across photo)		
14 Woodley Lewis	4.00	8.00
(Established ...)		
15 Gene Lipscomb	10.00	20.00
16 Tom McCormick	4.00	8.00
(Rams' regular ...)		
17 Bud McFadin	4.00	8.00
(Although ...)		
18 Leon McLaughlin	4.00	8.00
(Started every ...)		
19 Paul Miller	4.00	8.00
(Lettered at ...)		
20 Don Paul	4.00	8.00
(One of two ...)		
21 Hampton Pool CO	4.00	8.00
(Since taking ...)		
22 Duane Putnam	4.00	8.00
(Offensive guard ...)		
23 Volney Quinlan	4.00	8.00
(Had best ...)		
24 Les Richter	4.00	8.00
(Rated one ...)		
25 Andy Robustelli	12.50	25.00
(L.A.'s regular ...)		
26 Willard Sherman	4.00	8.00
(Played at ...)		
27 Harland Svare	4.00	8.00
(An outside ...)		
28 Harry Thompson	4.00	8.00
(Played offensive ...)		
29 Charley Toogood	4.00	8.00
30 Deacon Dan Towler	5.00	10.00
(Since becoming ...)		
31 Norm Van Brocklin	25.00	50.00
(1953 stats)		
32 Bill Wade	7.50	15.00
(Selected as ...)		
33 Duane Wardlow	4.00	8.00
34 Stan West	4.00	8.00
(Virtually ...)		
35 Paul(Tank) Younger	5.00	10.00
(1953 stats)		
36 Coaches Card	4.00	8.00
Bill Battles		
Howard(Red) Hickey		
John Sauer		
Dick Voris		
Buck Weaver		
Hampton Pool		

1955 Rams Team Issue

This 37-card set measures approximately 4 1/4" by 6 3/8". The front features a black and white posed action photo enclosed by a black border, with the player's signature across the bottom portion of the picture. The back lists the player's name, height, weight, age, and college, along with basic biographical information. The set was available direct from the team as part of a package for their fans. The cards are listed alphabetically below since they are unnumbered. Many cards from the 1953-1955 and 1957 Rams Team Issue Black Border sets are identical except for text differences on the card backs. Player stat lines are also helpful in identifying year of issue; the year of issue is typically the next year after the last year on the stats. The first few words of the first line of text is listed for players without stat lines.

COMPLETE SET (37)	200.00	325.00
1 Jack Bighead	4.00	8.00
2 Bob Boyd	4.00	8.00
3 Don Burroughs	4.00	8.00
4 Jim Cason	4.00	8.00
5 Bobby Cross	4.00	8.00
6 Jack Ellena	4.00	8.00
7 Tom Fears	7.50	15.00
8 Sid Fournet	4.00	8.00
9 Frank Fuller	4.00	8.00
10 Sid Gillman and coaching staff	6.00	12.00
11 Bob Griffin	4.00	8.00
12 Art Hauser	4.00	8.00
13 Hall Haynes	4.00	8.00
14 Elroy Hirsch	15.00	30.00
15 John Hock	4.00	8.00
16 Glenn Holtzman	4.00	8.00
17 Ed Hughes	4.00	8.00
18 Woodley Lewis	4.00	8.00
19 Gene Lipscomb	7.50	15.00
20 Tom McCormick	4.00	8.00
21 Bud McFadin	4.00	8.00
22 Leon McLaughlin	4.00	8.00
23 Paul Miller	4.00	8.00
24 Larry Morris	4.00	8.00
25 Don Paul	4.00	8.00
26 Duane Putnam	4.00	8.00
27 Volney Quinlan	4.00	8.00
28 Les Richter	4.00	8.00
29 Andy Robustelli	7.50	15.00
30 Willard Sherman	4.00	8.00
31 Corky Taylor	4.00	8.00
32 Charley Toogood	4.00	8.00
33 Deacon Dan Towler	5.00	10.00
34 Norm Van Brocklin	20.00	40.00
35 Bill Wade	6.00	12.00
36 Ron Waller	4.00	8.00
37 Paul(Tank) Younger	5.00	10.00

1956 Rams Team Issue

This 37-card team-issued set measures approximately 4 1/4" by 6 3/8" and features members of the Los Angeles Rams. The set has posed action shots on the front framed by a white border with the player's signature across the picture, while the back has biographical information about the player listing the player's name, height, weight, age, number of years in NFL, and college. We have checklisted this (unnumbered) set in alphabetical order. The set was initially available for fans direct from the team for $1.

COMPLETE SET (37)	150.00	300.00
1 Bob Boyd	4.00	8.00
2 Rudy Bukich	4.00	8.00
3 Don Burroughs	4.00	8.00
4 Jim Cason	4.00	8.00
5 Leon Clarke	4.00	8.00
6 Dick Daugherty	4.00	8.00
7 Jack Ellena	4.00	8.00
8 Tom Fears	7.50	15.00
9 Sid Fournet	4.00	8.00
10 Bob Fry	4.00	8.00
11 Coaches:	6.00	12.00
Sid Gillman		
Joe Madro		
Jack Faulkner		
Joe Thomas		
Lowell Storm		
12 Bob Griffin	4.00	8.00
13 Art Hauser	4.00	8.00
14 Elroy Hirsch	12.50	25.00
15 John Hock	4.00	8.00
16 Bob Holladay	4.00	8.00
17 Glenn Holtzman	4.00	8.00
18 Bob Kelley ANN	4.00	8.00
19 Joe Marconi	4.00	8.00
20 Bud McFadin	4.00	8.00
21 Paul Miller	4.00	8.00
22 Ron Miller	4.00	8.00
23 Larry Morris	4.00	8.00
24 John Morrow	4.00	8.00
25 Brad Myers	4.00	8.00
26 Hugh Pitts	4.00	8.00
27 Duane Putnam	4.00	8.00
28 Les Richter	4.00	8.00
29 Willard Sherman	4.00	8.00
30 Charley Toogood	4.00	8.00
31 Norm Van Brocklin	17.50	05.00
32 Bill Wade	6.00	12.00
33 Ron Waller	4.00	8.00
34 Duane Wardlow	4.00	8.00
35 Jesse Whittenton	4.00	8.00
36 Tom Wilson	4.00	8.00
37 Paul(Tank) Younger	5.00	10.00

1957-61 Rams Falstaff Beer Team Photos

These oversized (roughly 6 1/4" by 9") color team photos were sponsored by Falstaff Beer and distributed in the Los Angeles area. Each was printed on card stock and included advertising and/or photos of the team's coaching staff on the back.

1957 Rams Team	30.00	50.00
1958 Rams Team	30.00	50.00
1959 Rams Team	30.00	50.00
1960 Rams Team	25.00	40.00
1961 Rams Team	25.00	40.00

1957 Rams Team Issue

This 38-card team-issued set measures approximately 4 1/4" by 6 3/8" and features posed action shots on the front surrounded by black borders with the player's signature across the picture. The card backs contain biographical information about the player listing the player's name, height, weight, age, number of years in NFL, and college. We have checklisted this (unnumbered) set in alphabetical order. The set was available direct from the team as part of a package for their fans. Many cards from the 1953-1955 and 1957 Rams Team Issue Black Border sets are identical except for text differences on the card backs. Player stat lines are also helpful in identifying year of issue; the year of issue is typically the next year after the last year on the stats. The first few words of the first line of text is listed for players without stat lines. The set features the first card appearance of Jack Pardee.

COMPLETE SET (38)	150.00	300.00
1 Jon Arnett	5.00	10.00
2 Bob Boyd	4.00	8.00
(Frequently called ...)		
3 Alex Bravo	4.00	8.00
4 Bill Brundige ANN	4.00	8.00
5 Don Burroughs	4.00	8.00
6 Jerry Castete	4.00	8.00
7 Leon Clarke	4.00	8.00
8 Paige Cothren	4.00	8.00
9 Dick Daugherty	4.00	8.00
(Has the ...)		
10 Bob Dougherty	4.00	8.00
11 Bob Fry	4.00	8.00
(One of the ...)		
12 Frank Fuller	4.00	8.00
(One of the ...)		
13 Coaches: Sid Gillman	12.50	25.00
Joe Madro		
George Allen		
Jack Faulkner		
Lowell Storm		
14 Bob Griffin	4.00	8.00
(After four ...)		
15 Art Hauser	4.00	8.00
(One of the ...)		
16 Elroy Hirsch	12.50	25.00
(A legendary ...)		
17 John Hock	4.00	8.00
(Teamed with ...)		
18 Glenn Holtzman	4.00	8.00
19 John Houser	4.00	8.00
20 Bob Kelley ANN	4.00	8.00
(Signature near right border of photo)		
21 Lamar Lundy	5.00	10.00
22 Joe Marconi	4.00	8.00
23 Paul Miller	4.00	8.00
(From a ...)		
24 Larry Morris	4.00	8.00
25 Ken Panfil	4.00	8.00
26 Jack Pardee	6.00	12.00
27 Duane Putnam	4.00	8.00
(Named to a ...)		
28 Les Richter	4.00	8.00
(One of the ...)		
29 Willard Sherman	4.00	8.00
(One of the ...)		
30 Del Shofner	5.00	10.00
31 Billy Ray Smith	4.00	8.00
32 George Strugar	4.00	8.00
33 Norm Van Brocklin	15.00	30.00
(When Van Brocklin ...)		
34 Bill Wade	6.00	12.00
(In the first ...)		
35 Ron Waller	4.00	8.00
36 Jesse Whittenton	4.00	8.00
37 Tom Wilson	4.00	8.00
38 Paul(Tank) Younger	5.00	10.00
(One of a ...)		

1959 Rams Bell Brand

The 1959 Bell Brand Los Angeles Rams set contains 40-regular issue standard-size cards. The catalog designation for this set is F387-1. The obverses contain white-bordered color photos of the player with a facsimile autograph. The backs contain the card number, a short biography and vital statistics of the player, a Bell Brand ad, and advertisements for Los Angeles Rams' merchandise. These cards were issued as inserts in potato chip and corn chip bags in the Los Angeles area and are frequently found with oil stains from the chips. Cards #41 Bill Jobko and #43 Tom Franckhauer were recently discovered. Much like the 1960 Gene Selawski card #2, it is thought that the Jobko and Franckhauser cards were withdrawn early in production and available only upon request from the company. It is not considered part of the complete set price below.

COMPLETE SET (40)	1,200.00	2,000.00
1 Bill Wade	40.00	75.00
2 Buddy Humphrey	30.00	50.00
3 Frank Ryan	35.00	60.00
4 Ed Meador	30.00	50.00
5 Tom Wilson	30.00	50.00
6 Don Burroughs	30.00	50.00
7 Jon Arnett	35.00	60.00
8 Del Shofner	35.00	60.00
9 Jack Pardee	35.00	60.00
10 Ollie Matson	60.00	100.00
11 Joe Marconi	30.00	50.00
12 Jim Jones	30.00	50.00
13 Jack Morris	30.00	50.00
14 Willard Sherman	30.00	50.00
15 Clendon Thomas	30.00	50.00
16 Les Richter	35.00	60.00
17 John Morrow	30.00	50.00
18 Lou Michaels	35.00	60.00
19 Bob Reifsnyder	30.00	50.00
20 John Guzik	30.00	50.00
21 Duane Putnam	30.00	50.00
22 John Houser	30.00	50.00
23 Buck Lansford	30.00	50.00
24 Gene Selawski	30.00	50.00
25 John Baker	30.00	50.00
26 Bob Fry	30.00	50.00
27 John Lovetere	30.00	50.00
28 George Strugar	30.00	50.00
29 Roy Wilkins	30.00	50.00
30 Charley Bradshaw	30.00	50.00
31 Gene Brito	30.00	50.00
32 Jim Phillips	35.00	60.00
33 Leon Clarke	30.00	50.00
34 Lamar Lundy	40.00	75.00
35 Sam Williams	30.00	50.00
36 Sid Gillman CO	50.00	00.00
37 Jack Faulkner CO	30.00	50.00
38 Joe Madro CO	30.00	50.00
39 Don Paul CO	30.00	50.00
40 Lou Rymkus CO	35.00	60.00
41 Bill Jobko SP	1,200.00	2,000.00
43 Tom Franckhauser SP	1,200.00	2,000.00

1960 Rams Bell Brand

The 1960 Bell Brand Los Angeles Rams Football set contains 39 standard-size cards in a format similar to the 1959 Bell Brand set. The fronts of the cards have distinctive yellow borders. The catalog designation for this set is F387-2. Card numbers 1-18, except number 2, are repeated photos from the 1959 set and were available throughout the season. Numbers 19-39 were available later in the 1960 season. These cards were issued as inserts in potato chip and corn chip bags in the Los Angeles area and are frequently found with oil stains from the chips. Card number 2 Selawski was withdrawn early in the year (after he was cut from the team) and was reportedly available only upon request from the company. It is not considered part of the complete set price below.

COMPLETE SET (38)	1,500.00	2,500.00
COMMON CARD (1-18)	30.00	50.00
COMMON CARD (19-39)	50.00	80.00
1 Joe Marconi	30.00	50.00
2 Gene Selawski SP	1,200.00	2,000.00
3 Frank Ryan	30.00	50.00
4 Ed Meador	35.00	60.00
5 Tom Wilson	30.00	50.00
6 Gene Brito	35.00	60.00
7 Jon Arnett	30.00	50.00
8 Buck Lansford	30.00	50.00
9 Jack Pardee	30.00	50.00
10 Ollie Matson	50.00	80.00
11 John Lovetere	30.00	50.00
12 Bill Jolko	30.00	50.00
13 Jim Phillips	35.00	60.00
14 Lamar Lundy	30.00	50.00
15 Del Shofner	30.00	50.00
16 Les Richter	35.00	60.00
17 Bill Wade	30.00	50.00
18 Lou Michaels	35.00	60.00
19 Dick Bass	60.00	100.00
20 Charley Britt	50.00	80.00
21 Willard Sherman	50.00	80.00
22 George Strugar	50.00	80.00
23 Bob Long	50.00	80.00
24 Danny Villanueva	50.00	80.00
25 Jim Boeke	50.00	80.00
26 Clendon Thomas	50.00	80.00
27 Art Hunter	50.00	80.00
28 Carl Karilivacz	50.00	80.00
29 John Baker	50.00	80.00
30 Charley Bradshaw	50.00	80.00
31 John Guzik	50.00	80.00
32 Buddy Humphrey	50.00	80.00
33 Carroll Dale	50.00	80.00
34 Don Ellersick	50.00	80.00
35 Roy Hord	50.00	80.00
36 Charlie Janerette	50.00	80.00
37 John Kennerson	50.00	80.00
38 Jerry Stalcup	50.00	80.00
39 Bob Waterfield CO	125.00	200.00

1967 Rams Team Issue

The Los Angeles Rams issued these black and white player photos around 1967. Each includes the player's name and team name below the photo, measures roughly 5 1/4" by 7" and is blankbacked.

COMPLETE SET (27)	125.00	250.00
1 Maxie Baughan	6.00	12.00
2 Joe Carollo	6.00	12.00
3 Bernie Casey	6.00	12.00
4 Don Chuy	6.00	12.00
5 Charlie Cowan	6.00	12.00
6 Irv Cross	6.00	12.00
7 Dan Currie	6.00	12.00
8 Willie Daniel	6.00	12.00
9 Willie Ellison	6.00	12.00
10 Roman Gabriel	7.50	15.00
11 Bruce Gossett	6.00	12.00
12 Roosevelt Grier	7.50	15.00
13 Anthony Guillory	6.00	12.00
14 Ken Iman	6.00	12.00
15 Deacon Jones	7.50	15.00
16 Les Josephson	6.00	12.00
17 Chuck Lamson	6.00	12.00
18 Tom Mack	7.50	15.00
19 Tommy Mason	6.00	12.00
20 Marlin McKeever	6.00	12.00
21 Bill Munson	6.00	12.00
22 Jack Pardee	6.00	12.00
23 Myron Pottios	6.00	12.00
24 Joe Scibelli	6.00	12.00
25 Jack Snow	6.00	12.00
26 Clancy Williams	6.00	12.00
27 Doug Woodlief	6.00	12.00

1968 Rams Team Issue

The Los Angeles Rams issued these black and white player photos. Each measures roughly 8" by 10" and is blank backed. The checklist below is thought to be incomplete.

COMPLETE SET (9)	50.00	100.00
1 George Allen CO	10.00	20.00
2 Dick Bass	5.00	10.00
3 Bernie Casey	5.00	10.00
4 Lamar Lundy	6.00	12.00
5 Deacon Jones	7.50	15.00
6 Les Josephson	5.00	10.00
7 Merlin Olsen	7.50	15.00
8 Jack Snow	5.00	10.00
9 Team Photo	5.00	10.00

1968 Rams Volpe Tumblers

These Rams artist's renderings were part of a plastic cup tumbler product produced in 1968 and distributed by White Front Stroes. The noted sports artist Volpe created the artwork which includes an action scene and a player portrait. The "cards" are unnumbered, each measures approximately 5" by 8 1/2" and is curved in the shape required to fit inside a plastic cup. The manufacturer notation PGC (programs General Corp) is printed on each piece as well. There are thought to be 6 cups included in this set. Any additions to this list are appreciated.

COMPLETE SET (6)	100.00	200.00
1 Dick Bass	15.00	30.00
2 Roger Brown	15.00	30.00
3 Roman Gabriel	25.00	50.00
4 Deacon Jones	25.00	50.00
5 Lamar Lundy	15.00	30.00
6 Merlin Olsen	30.00	60.00

1973 Rams Team Issue Color

The NFLPA worked with many teams in 1973 to issued photo packs to be sold at stadium concession stands. Each measures approximately 7" by 8-5/8" and features a color player photo with a blank back. A small sheet with a player checklist was included in each 6-photo pack.

COMPLETE SET (6)	25.00	50.00
1 Jim Bertelsen	4.00	8.00
2 John Hadl	6.00	12.00
3 Harold Jackson	5.00	10.00
4 Merlin Olsen	6.00	12.00
5 Isiah Robertson	4.00	8.00
6 Jack Snow	4.00	8.00

1974 Rams Team Issue

The Rams issued this group of photos around 1974. Each measures roughly 5" by 7 1/4" and features a black and white player photo on blankbacked paper stock. There is a thin white border on three sides with roughly a 1" border below the photo. The team's helmet logo, player's name and position (initials) are included in the border below the photo. The Rams' helmet logo has a single bar facemask, is oriented to the left on all the photos unless noted below, and measures roughly 5/8" high. The photos are identical in format to the 1978 team issue. Any additions to the list below are appreciated.

COMPLETE SET (30)	100.00	200.00
1 Larry Brooks	4.00	8.00
2 Mike Burke	4.00	8.00
3 Bud Carson CO	5.00	10.00
4 Al Clark	4.00	8.00
(helmet logo on the right)		
5 Bill Curry	4.00	8.00
6 Dave Elmendorf	4.00	8.00
7 Clyde Evans ASST	4.00	8.00
8 Jack Faulkner ASST	4.00	8.00
9 Chuck Knox CO	5.00	10.00
10 Paul Lanham CO	4.00	8.00
11 Frank Lauterbur CO	4.00	8.00
12 Tom Mack	6.00	12.00
13 Lawrence McCutcheon	5.00	10.00
14 Willie McGee	4.00	8.00
15 Eddie McMillan	4.00	8.00
16 Phil Olsen	4.00	8.00
(helmet logo on the right)		
17 Jim Peterson	4.00	8.00
18 Tony Plummer	4.00	8.00
19 Steve Preece	4.00	8.00
20 David Ray	4.00	8.00
(helmet logo on the right)		
21 Jack Reynolds	5.00	10.00
22 Isiah Robertson	5.00	10.00
23 Rich Saul	4.00	8.00
24 Rob Scribner	4.00	8.00
25 Bob Stein	4.00	8.00
26 Tim Stokes	4.00	8.00
27 Charlie Stukes	4.00	8.00
28 Lionel Taylor CO	5.00	10.00
29 LaVern Torgeson CO	4.00	8.00
30 John Williams G	4.00	8.00

1978 Rams Team Issue

The Rams issued this group of photos around 1978. Each measures roughly 5" by 7 1/4" and features a black and white player photo on blankbacked paper stock. There is a thin white border on three sides with roughly a 1" border below the photo. The team's helmet logo, player's name and position (initials) are included in the border below the photo. The Rams' helmet logo has a single bar facemask, is oriented to the left on all the photos unless noted below, and measures roughly 5/8" high. The photos are identical in format to the 1974 team issue. Any additions to the list below are appreciated.

COMPLETE SET (37)	100.00	200.00
1 Bob Brudzinski	3.00	6.00
2 Frank Corral	3.00	6.00
3 Nolan Cromwell	3.00	6.00
4 Reggie Doss	3.00	6.00
5 Fred Dryer	4.00	8.00
6 Carl Ekern	3.00	6.00
7 Mike Fanning	3.00	6.00
8 Vince Ferragamo	4.00	8.00
9 Doug France	3.00	6.00
10 Ed Fulton	3.00	6.00
11 Pat Haden	4.00	8.00
12 Dennis Harrah	3.00	6.00
13 Greg Horton	3.00	6.00
14 Ron Jaworski	5.00	10.00
15 Ron Jessie	3.00	6.00
16 Jim Jodat	3.00	6.00
17 Cody Jones	3.00	6.00
18 Lawrence McCutcheon	3.00	6.00
19 Kevin McLain	3.00	6.00
20 Willie Miller	3.00	6.00
21 Joe Namath	12.50	25.00
22 Terry Nelson	3.00	6.00
23 Rod Perry	3.00	6.00
24 Rod Phillips	3.00	6.00
25 Jack Reynolds	4.00	8.00
26 Dan Ryczek	3.00	6.00
27 Bill Simpson	3.00	6.00
28 Jackie Slater	6.00	12.00
29 Doug Smith C	3.00	6.00
30 Ron Smith WR	3.00	6.00
31 Pat Thomas	3.00	6.00
32 Wendell Tyler	3.00	6.00
33 Billy Waddy	3.00	6.00
34 Glen Walker	3.00	6.00
35 Charle Young	3.00	6.00
36 Jack Youngblood	5.00	10.00
37 Jim Youngblood	3.00	6.00

1979 Rams Team Issue

The Rams issued this group of photos around 1979. Each measures roughly 5" by 7 1/4" and features a black and white player photo on blankbacked paper stock. There is a thin white border on three sides with roughly a 1" border below the photo. The team's helmet logo, player's name and position (initials) are included in the border below the photo. The Rams' helmet logo has a double bar facemask that is oriented to the left on all of the photos and measures roughly 5/8" high. The photos are identical in format to the 1978 team issue except for the double bar facemask instead of single. Any additions to the list below are appreciated.

COMPLETE SET (34)	75.00	150.00
1 George Andrews	3.00	6.00
2 Larry Brooks	3.00	6.00
3 Dave Elmendorf	3.00	6.00
4 Doug France	3.00	6.00
5 Dennis Harrah	3.00	6.00
6 Drew Hill	5.00	10.00
7 Eddie Hill	3.00	6.00
8 Bill Hickman ASST	3.00	6.00
9 Kent Hill	3.00	6.00
10 Ron Jessie	4.00	8.00
11 Jim Jodat	3.00	6.00
12 Cody Jones	3.00	6.00
13 Sid Justin	3.00	6.00
14 Lawrence McCutcheon	4.00	8.00
15 Kevin McLain	3.00	6.00
16 Terry Nelson	3.00	6.00
17 Dwayne O'Steen	3.00	6.00
18 Elvis Peacock	3.00	6.00
19 Rod Perry	3.00	6.00
20 Dan Radakovich CO	3.00	6.00
21 Jack Reynolds	4.00	8.00
22 Jeff Rutledge	3.00	6.00
23 Dan Ryczek	3.00	6.00
24 Rich Saul	3.00	6.00
25 Jackie Slater	6.00	12.00
26 Doug Smith	3.00	6.00
27 Ron Smith WR	3.00	6.00
28 Pat Thomas	3.00	6.00
29 Wendell Tyler	4.00	8.00
30 Billy Waddy	4.00	8.00
31 Jerry Wilkinson	3.00	6.00
32 Charle Young	4.00	8.00
33 Jack Youngblood	6.00	12.00
34 Jim Youngblood	3.00	6.00

1980 Rams Police

This unnumbered, 14-card set has been listed in the checklist below by uniform number, which appears on the fronts of the cards. The cards measure approximately 2 5/8" by 4 1/8". The Kiwanis Club, who sponsored this set along with the local law enforcement agency and the Rams, has their logo on the fronts of the cards. These cards, which contain "Rams Tips" on the backs, were distributed by police officers, one per week over a 14-week period.

COMPLETE SET (14)	10.00	20.00
11 Pat Haden	2.00	4.00
15 Vince Ferragamo	1.25	2.50
21 Nolan Cromwell	1.25	2.50
26 Wendell Tyler	.75	2.00
32 Cullen Bryant	.50	1.25
53 Jim Youngblood	.50	1.25
59 Bob Brudzinski	.40	1.00
61 Rich Saul	.40	1.00
77 Doug France	.40	1.00
82 Willie Miller	.40	1.00
85 Jack Youngblood	2.50	5.00
88 Preston Dennard	.40	1.00
90 Larry Brooks	.40	1.00
NNO Ray Malavasi CO	.40	1.00

1980 Rams Team Issue

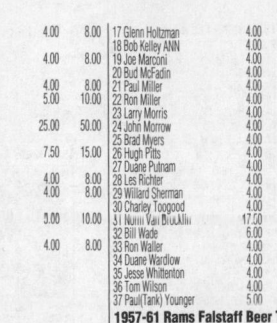

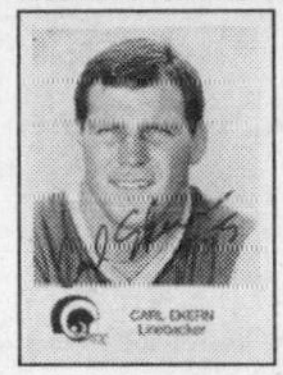

The Rams issued this group of photos around 1980. Each measures roughly 5" by 7" or 5" by 7 1/4" and features a black and white player photo on blankbacked paper stock. There is a thin white border on three sides with roughly a 1" border below the photo. The team's helmet logo, player's name and position (spelled out) are included in the border below the photo. The Rams' helmet logo has a double bar facemask that is oriented to the left on all of the photos and measures roughly 1" high. The photos are identical in format to the 1979 team issue except for the larger (1") helmet logo. Any additions to the list below are appreciated.

COMPLETE SET (52)	100.00	200.00
1 George Andrews	2.50	5.00
2 Walt Arnold	2.50	5.00
3 Bill Bain	2.50	5.00
4 Larry Brooks	2.50	5.00
5 Bob Brudzinski	2.50	5.00
6 Cullen Bryant	2.50	5.00
7 Howard Carson	2.50	5.00
8 Frank Corral	2.50	5.00
9 Nolan Cromwell	2.50	5.00
position safety spelled out)		
10 Nolan Cromwell	2.50	5.00
(position initial S)		
11 Jeff Delaney	2.50	5.00
12 Preston Dennard	2.50	5.00
13 Reggie Doss	2.50	5.00
14 Fred Dryer	3.00	6.00
15 Carl Ekern	2.50	5.00
16 Mike Fanning	2.50	5.00
17 Doug France	2.50	5.00
18 Mike Guman	2.50	5.00
19 Pat Haden	3.00	6.00
20 Dennis Harrah	2.50	5.00
21 Joe Harris	2.50	5.00
22 Victor Hicks	2.50	5.00
23 Drew Hill	4.00	8.00
24 Eddie Hill	2.50	5.00
25 Kent Hill	2.50	5.00
26 LeRoy Irvin	2.50	5.00
27 Johnnie Johnson	2.50	5.00
28 Cody Jones	2.50	5.00
29 Jeff Kemp	2.50	5.00
30 Bob Lee	2.50	5.00
31 Ray Malavasi CO	2.50	5.00
32 Willie Miller	2.50	5.00
33 Jeff Moore	2.50	5.00
34 Phil Murphy	2.50	5.00
35 Terry Nelson	2.50	5.00
36 Irv Pankey	2.50	5.00
37 Herb Paterra CO	2.50	5.00
38 Elvis Peacock	2.50	5.00
39 Rod Perry	2.50	5.00
40 Jack Reynolds	3.00	0.00
41 Jeff Rutledge	2.50	5.00
42 Rich Saul	2.50	5.00
43 Jackie Slater	4.00	8.00
44 Doug Smith C	2.50	5.00
45 Lucious Smith	2.50	5.00
46 Ivory Sully	2.50	5.00
47 Jewerl Thomas	2.50	5.00
48 Pat Thomas	2.50	5.00
49 Wendell Tyler	3.00	6.00
50 Billy Waddy	3.00	6.00
51 Jack Youngblood	4.00	8.00
52 Jim Youngblood	2.50	5.00

1981 Rams Team Issue

The Rams issued this group of photos around 1980. Each measures roughly 5" by 7" or 5" by 7 1/4" and features a black and white player photo on blankbacked paper stock. There is a thin white border on three sides with roughly a 1" border below the photo. The team's helmet logo, player's name and position (spelled out) are included in the border below the photo. The Rams' helmet logo has a double bar facemask that is oriented to the left on all of the photos and measures roughly 1 1/8" high. The photos are nearly identical in format to the 1980 team issue except for the larger (1 1/8") helmet logo and the much thinner white border that surrounds three sides of the photo. Any additions to the list below are appreciated.

COMPLETE SET (10)	20.00	40.00
1 Henry Childs	2.00	5.00
2 Kirk Collins	2.00	5.00
3 Nolan Cromwell	2.00	5.00
4 Johnnie Johnson	2.00	5.00
5 Jeff Kemp	2.00	5.00
6 Willie Miller	2.00	5.00
7 Mel Owens	2.00	5.00
8 Jairo Penaranda	2.00	5.00
9 Rod Perry	2.00	5.00
10 Lucious Smith	2.00	5.00

1984 Rams Team Issue

The Rams issued this group of photos around 1984. Each measures roughly 5" by 7" and features a black and white player photo on blankbacked paper stock. There is a thin white border on three sides with roughly a 1" border below the photo. The team's helmet logo, player's name and position (spelled out) are included in the border below the photo. The Rams' helmet logo has a double bar facemask that is oriented to the left on all of the photos and measures roughly 1" high. The photos are identical in format to the 1980 team issue except that each player was photographed in their training camp mesh jerseys. Any additions to the list below are appreciated.

COMPLETE SET (16)	30.00	50.00
1 Dieter Brock	3.00	5.00
2 Jim Collins	1.50	3.00
3 Nolan Cromwell	1.50	3.00
4 Steve Dils	1.50	3.00
5 Reggie Doss	1.50	3.00
6 Carl Ekern	1.50	3.00
7 Henry Ellard (name misspelled Ellerd)	3.00	5.00
8 Dennis Harrah	1.50	3.00
9 Drew Hill	2.50	4.00
10 Kent Hill	1.50	3.00
11 Johnnie Johnson	1.50	3.00
12A Mike Lansford (with copyright designation)	1.50	3.00
12B Mike Lansford (no copyright notation)	1.50	3.00
13 Vince Newsome	1.50	3.00
14 Joe Shearin	1.50	3.00
15 Doug Smith C	1.50	3.00

1985 Rams Police

This set of cards was distributed by Police Officers in the Los Angeles area and sponsored by KIIS Radio. The unnumbered cards are listed alphabetically below. Uncut sheets of both the 1985 Rams and Raiders Police sets together are also on the market.

COMPLETE SET (15)	3.00	8.00
1 Bill Bain	.20	.50
2 Mike Barber	.30	.75
3 Dieter Brock	.50	1.25
4 Nolan Cromwell	.30	.75
5 Eric Dickerson	1.00	2.50
6 Reggie Doss	.20	.50
7 Carl Ekern	.20	.50
8 Kent Hill	.20	.50
9 LeRoy Irvin	.30	.75
10 Johnnie Johnson	.20	.50
11 Jeff Kemp	.50	1.25
12 Mike Lansford	.20	.50
13 Mel Owens	.20	.50
14 Barry Redden	.20	.50
15 Mike Wilcher	.20	.50

1985 Rams Smokey

This set of 24 cards was issued in the Summer of 1985 and features players of the Los Angeles Rams. The cards measure approximately 4" by 6". Each card photo also features Smokey Bear. The cards are numbered on the back essentially in alphabetical order; there are a few exceptions and two Smokey cards are unnumbered (listed at the end of the checklist below). Supposedly, LeRoy Irvin is more difficult to find than the other cards in the set.

COMPLETE SET (24)	15.00	30.00
1 George Andrews	.40	1.00
2 Bill Bain	.40	1.00
3 Russ Bolinger	.40	1.00
4 Jim Collins	.40	1.00
5 Nolan Cromwell	.50	1.25
6 Reggie Doss	.40	1.00
7 Carl Ekern	.40	1.00
8 Vince Ferragamo	.60	1.50
9 Gary Green	.40	1.00
10 Mike Guman	.40	1.00
11 David Hill	.40	1.00
12 LeRoy Irvin SP	2.50	6.00
13 Mark Jerue	.40	1.00
14 Johnnie Johnson	.40	1.00
15 Jeff Kemp	.50	1.25
16 Mel Owens	.40	1.00
17 Irv Pankey	.40	1.00
18 Doug Smith	.40	1.00
19 Ivory Sully	.40	1.00
20 Jack Youngblood	.75	2.00
21 Mike McDonald	.40	1.00
22 Norwood Vann	.40	1.00
23 Smokey Bear (Unnumbered)	.40	1.00
24 Smokey Bear with Reggie Doss, Gary Green, Johnnie Johnson, and Carl Ekern (Unnumbered)	.40	1.00

1986 Rams Smokey Flipbooks

In conjunction with California Fire Prevention, the Rams issued these flipbooks in 1986. The books contain a black and white flip movie of the player on one side and a movie of Smokey on the other side, along with fire prevention tips. The books measure approximately 2 3/4" by 4 1/2" and are unnumbered. We have assigned card numbers to them alphabetically.

COMPLETE SET (2)	3.00	8.00
1 Steve Dils	1.50	4.00
2 Mike Lansford	1.50	4.00

1987 Rams Ace Fact Pack

This 33-card set measures approximately 2 1/4" by 3 5/8" and has rounded corners. This set was manufactured in West Germany (by Ace Fact Pack) for release in Great Britain. There are 22 player cards in the set, checklisted below in alphabetical order. The backs of the cards feature a playing card design. The set contains members of the Los Angeles Rams.

COMPLETE SET (33)	40.00	100.00
1 Nolan Cromwell	2.00	5.00
2 Eric Dickerson	7.50	20.00
3 Reggie Doss	1.25	3.00
4 Carl Ekern	1.25	3.00
5 Henry Ellard	4.00	10.00
6 Jim Everett	2.50	6.00
7 Jerry Gray	2.00	5.00
8 Dennis Harrah	1.25	3.00
9 David Hill	1.25	3.00
10 Kevin House	2.00	5.00
11 LeRoy Irvin	2.00	5.00
12 Mark Jerue	1.25	3.00
13 Shawn Miller	1.25	3.00
14 Tom Newberry	2.00	5.00
15 Vince Newsome	1.25	3.00
16 Mel Owens	1.25	3.00
17 Irv Pankey	1.25	3.00
18 Doug Reed	1.25	3.00
19 Doug Smith	2.00	5.00
20 Jackie Slater	3.00	8.00
21 Charles White	2.00	5.00
22 Mike Wilcher	1.25	3.00
23 Rams Helmet	1.25	3.00
24 Rams Information	1.25	3.00
25 Rams Uniform	1.25	3.00
26 Game Record Holders	1.25	3.00
27 Season Record Holders	1.25	3.00
28 Career Record Holders	1.25	3.00
29 Record 1967-86	1.25	3.00
30 1986 Team Statistics	1.25	3.00
31 All-Time Greats	1.25	3.00
32 Roll of Honour	1.25	3.00
33 Anaheim Stadium	1.25	3.00

1987 Rams Jello/General Foods

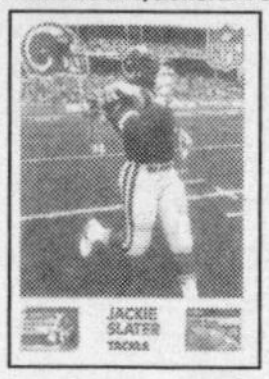

This ten-card standard-size set was sponsored by Jello and Birds Eye and features players of the Los Angeles Rams. The cards are numbered on the back; card backs are printed in black ink on heavy white card stock. The set comes as a perforated sheet including a coupon each for Birds Eye Cob Corn and any Jello product. This unnumbered set is listed below alphabetically.

COMPLETE SET (10)	6.00	12.00
1 Ron Brown	.40	1.00
2 Nolan Cromwell	.40	1.00
3 Eric Dickerson	1.25	3.00
4 Carl Ekern	.40	1.00
5 Jim Everett	.75	2.00
6 Dennis Harrah	.40	1.00
7 LeRoy Irvin	.40	1.00
8 Mike Lansford	.40	1.00
9 Jackie Slater	.50	1.25
10 Doug Smith	.40	1.00

1987 Rams Oscar Mayer

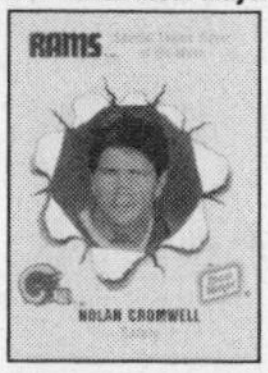

This 19-card standard-size set was sponsored by Oscar Mayer to honor the Special Teams Player of the Week. On a light blue background, the front features a color head shot inside a bullet hole design, with the jagged edges of the paper turned out. The team helmet and sponsor logo appear below the head shot. In dark blue print on white, the backs have biographical information as well as the Rams' helmet and the sponsor logo. The cards are unnumbered and checklisted below in alphabetical order.

COMPLETE SET (19)	25.00	50.00
1 Sam Anno	1.25	3.00
2 Ron Brown	1.50	4.00
3 Nolan Cromwell	1.50	4.00
4 Henry Ellard	2.00	5.00
5 Jerry Gray	1.50	4.00
6 Kevin Greene	2.50	6.00
7 Mike Guman	1.25	3.00
8 Dale Hatcher	1.25	3.00
9 Clifford Hicks	1.25	3.00
10 Mark Jerue	1.25	3.00
11 Johnnie Johnson	1.25	3.00
12 Larry Kelm	1.25	3.00
13 Mike Lansford	1.25	3.00
14 Vince Newsome	1.25	3.00
15 Michael Stewart	1.25	3.00
16 Mickey Sutton	1.25	3.00
17 Tim Tyrrell	1.25	3.00
18 Norwood Vann	1.25	3.00
19 Charles White	1.50	4.00

1989 Rams Police

This 16-card standard size set was issued in an uncut (perforated) sheet of 16 numbered cards which feature an action photo of various members of the 1989 Rams on the front and a football tip along with a safety tip on the back of the card. The safety tip features the popular anti-crime mascot McGruff. There was also a coupon for Frito-Lay products on the bottom of the sheet. The set was also sponsored by 7-Eleven stores.

COMPLETE SET (16)	5.00	12.00
1 John Robinson CO	.60	1.50
2 Jim Everett	.75	2.00
3 Doug Smith	.50	1.25
4 Duval Love	.40	1.00
5 Henry Ellard	1.00	2.50
6 Mel Owens	.40	1.00
7 Jerry Gray	.50	1.25
8 Kevin Greene	1.25	3.00
9 Vince Newsome	.40	1.00
10 Irv Pankey	.40	1.00
11 Tom Newberry	.50	1.25
12 Pete Holohan	.40	1.00
13 Mike Lansford	.40	1.00
14 Greg Bell	.50	1.25
15 Jackie Slater	.50	1.25
16 Dale Hatcher	.40	1.00

1990 Rams Knudsen

This six-card set (of bookmarks) which measures approximately 2" by 8" was produced by Knudsen's to help promote readership by people under 15 years old in the Los Angeles area. Between the Knudsen company name, the front features a color action photo of the player superimposed on a football stadium. The field is green, the bleachers are yellow with gray print, and the scoreboard above the player reads "The Reading Team". The box below the player gives brief biographical information and player highlights. The back has logos of the sponsors and describes two books that are available at the public library. We have checklisted this set in alphabetical order because they are otherwise unnumbered except for the player's uniform number displayed on the card front.

COMPLETE SET (6)	10.00	25.00
1 Henry Ellard	2.40	6.00
2 Jim Everett	2.40	6.00
3 Jerry Gray	2.00	5.00
4 Pete Holohan	2.00	5.00
5 Mike Lansford	2.00	5.00
6 Irv Pankey	2.00	5.00

1990 Rams Smokey

This 12-card set features members of the 1990 Rams and was sponsored by local Fire Departments. Borderless cardfronts feature a color player photo with backs including a small black and white photo and player bio. The cards measure approximately 3 3/4" by 5 3/4" and are unnumbered.

COMPLETE SET (12)	8.00	20.00
1 Aaron Cox	.60	1.50
2 Henry Ellard	1.20	3.00
3 Jim Everett	.80	2.00
4 Jerry Gray	.60	1.50
5 Kevin Greene	1.20	3.00
6 Pete Holohan	.60	1.50
7 Mike Lansford	.60	1.50
8 Vince Newsome	.60	1.50
9 Doug Reed	.60	1.50
10 Jackie Slater	.80	2.00
11 Fred Strickland	.60	1.50
12 Mike Wilcher	.60	1.50

1992 Rams Carl's Jr.

This 21-card safety standard-size set was sponsored by Carl's Jr. restaurants and distributed by the Orange County Sheriff's Department. It was reported that 80,000 sets were produced. Eleven Rams players participated in the program with autograph sessions at six Carl's Junior restaurants in Southern California. The fronts feature color action player photos inside a blue picture frame on a white card face. Player information appears below the photo between a Rams' helmet and a "Drug Use is Life Abuse" warning. Printed in black on white, the horizontal backs have a black-and-white headshot, biography, player profile, and an anti-drug or alcohol slogan.

COMPLETE SET (21)	10.00	20.00
1 Carl Karcher (Founder)	.40	1.00
2 Happy Star (Carl's Jr. symbol)	.40	1.00
3 Tony Zendejas	.40	1.00
4 Henry Ellard	.60	1.50
5 Jackie Slater	.50	1.25
6 Bern Brostek	.40	1.00
7 Cleveland Gary	.40	1.00
8 Larry Kelm	.40	1.00
9 Roman Phifer	.40	1.00
10 Jim Everett	.50	1.25
11 Anthony Newman	.40	1.00
12 Steve Israel	.40	1.00
13 Marc Boutte	.40	1.00
14 Darryl Henley	.40	1.00
15 Michael Stewart	.40	1.00
16 Flipper Anderson	.50	1.25
17 Kevin Greene	.75	2.00
18 Sean Gilbert	.50	1.25
NNO Skippy Be Drug Free	.40	1.00
NNO Spike Be Drug Free	.40	1.00
NNO Wise Owl Mike Be Drug Free	.40	1.00

1994 Rams L.A. Times

These 32 collector sheets were issued by the Los Angeles Times, were printed on semi-gloss paper, and measure approximately 5 1/2" by 8 1/2". The fronts feature color player action shots that are borderless, except at the bottom, where a yellow border carries the team name and helmet logo. The player's last name appears in large white vertical lettering near the right edge. The white back carries the player's name at the top, followed below by his uniform number, position, biography, head shot, career highlights and Rams 1994 game schedule. The sheets are numbered on the front as "X of 32." These sheets were distributed as inserts in weekend issues of the paper. Cleveland Gary and Marc Boutte were pulled from the set and not distributed since they were no longer with the Rams at the inception of the promotion.

COMPLETE SET (32)	4.80	12.00
1 Toby Wright	.15	.40
2 Tim Lester	.15	.40
3 Shane Conlan	.20	.50
4 Troy Drayton	.20	.50
5 Fred Stokes	.15	.40
6 Jerome Bettis	1.00	2.50
7 Jimmie Jones	.15	.40
8 Henry Rolling	.15	.40
9 Anthony Newman	.15	.40
10 Flipper Anderson	.30	.75
11 Steve Israel	.15	.40
12 Johnny Bailey	.15	.40
13 Jackie Slater	.20	.50
14 Chris Chandler	.20	.50
15 Sean Landeta	.15	.40
16 Bern Brostek	.15	.40
17 Roman Phifer	.15	.40
18 Robert Young	.20	.50
19 Leo Goeas	.15	.40
20 Chris Miller	.30	.75
21 Darryl Ashmore	.15	.40
22 Joe Kelly	.15	.40
23 Wayne Gandy	.20	.50
24 Tony Zendejas	.15	.40
25 Tom Newberry	.15	.40
26 David Lang	.15	.40
27 Sean Gilbert	.20	.50
28 Chris Martin	.15	.40
29 Thomas Homco	.15	.40
30 Chuck Knox CO	.20	.50
31 Todd Lyght	.20	.50
32 Jerome Bettis Sean Gilbert	.50	1.25

1995 Rams Upper Deck McDonald's

Upper Deck produced this set for distribution through McDonald's restaurants in the St.Louis area. The cards were sold in five-card packs for 79 cents per pack with the purchase of any McDonald's Value Meal. The cards were primarily available in the month of October and all royalties for the promotion were donated to Ronald McDonald Children's Charities. The phrases "Special Edition" and "Premiere Season" are printed in gold lettering running up the edge of the front, and the McDonald's logo appears in the upper right corner. The backs present biography, a second color photo, and a table displaying season-by-season statistics.

COMPLETE SET (26)	3.20	8.00
MCD1 Johnny Bailey	.08	.25
MCD2 Jerome Bettis	.50	1.25
MCD3 Isaac Bruce	1.20	3.00
MCD4 Kevin Carter	.50	1.25
MCD5 Shane Conlan	.08	.25
MCD6 Troy Drayton	.15	.40
MCD7 Wayne Gandy	.15	.40
MCD8 Sean Gilbert	.15	.40
MCD9 Jessie Hester	.08	.25
MCD10 Bern Brostek	.08	.25
MCD11 Jimmie Jones	.08	.25
MCD12 Todd Kinchen	.15	.40
MCD13 Sean Landeta	.08	.25
MCD14 Thomas Homco	.08	.25
MCD15 Todd Lyght	.08	.25
MCD16 Keith Lyle	.08	.25
MCD17 Chris Miller	.15	.40
MCD18 Toby Wright	.08	.25
MCD19 Anthony Parker	.08	.25
MCD20 Roman Phifer	.08	.25
MCD21 Leonard Russell	.08	.25
MCD22 Jackie Slater	.15	.40
MCD23 Fred Stokes	.08	.25
MCD24 Alexander Wright	.08	.25
MCD25 Robert Young	.15	.40
NNO Checklist Card	.15	.40

1996 Rams Team Issue

This 50-card set of the Los Angeles Rams features black-and-white player portaits in white borders measuring approximately 5" by 7" and sponsored by Northwest Plaza Mall. The team and sponsor logo is printed in the wide bottom margin. The backs carry player information and a large sponsor logo. The cards are unnumbered and checklisted below in alphabetical order.

COMPLETE SET (50)	20.00	50.00
1 Tony Banks	2.40	6.00
2 Chuck Belin	.40	1.00
3 Bern Brostek	.40	1.00
4 Isaac Bruce	2.40	6.00
5 Kevin Carter	.60	1.50
6 Hayward Clay	.40	1.00
7 Ernie Conwell	.40	1.00
8 Keith Crawford	.40	1.00
9 Torin Dorn	.40	1.00
10 D'Marco Farr	.40	1.00
11 Cedric Figaro	.40	1.00
12 Wayne Gandy	.40	1.00
13 Percell Gaskins	.40	1.00
14 Leo Goeas	.40	1.00
15 Harold Green	.40	1.00
16 Mike Gruttadauria	.40	1.00
17 Derrick Harris	.40	1.00
18 James Harris	.40	1.00
19 Tom Homco	.40	1.00
20 Carlos Jenkins	.40	1.00
21 Jimmie Jones	.40	1.00
22 Robert Jones	.40	1.00
23 Eddie Kennison	1.60	4.00
24 Jon Kirksey	.40	1.00
25 Aaron Laing	.40	1.00
26 Sean Landeta	.40	1.00
27 Jeremy Lincoln	.40	1.00
28 Chip Lohmiller	.40	1.00
29 Todd Lyght	.40	1.00
30 Keith Lyle	.40	1.00
31 Jamie Martin	1.25	3.00
32 Gerald McBurrows	.40	1.00
33 Fred Miller	.40	1.00
34 Jerald Moore	.60	1.50
35 Leslie O'Neal	.60	1.50
36 Chuck Osborne	.40	1.00
37 Anthony Parker	.40	1.00
38 Roman Phifer	.40	1.00
39 Lawrence Phillips	1.00	2.50
40 Greg Robinson	.40	1.00
41 Jermaine Ross	.40	1.00
42 Mike Scurlock	.40	1.00
43 J.T. Thomas	.40	1.00
44 Steve Walsh	.60	1.50
45 Alberto White	.40	1.00
46 Dwayne White	.40	1.00
47 Zach Wiegert	.40	1.00
48 Billy Williams	.40	1.00
49 Alexander Wright	.40	1.00
50 Toby Wright	.40	1.00

1997 Rams Team Issue

This 53-card set was released by the team for fans and player appearances. Each measures roughly 5" by 7" and features a black and white player photo on the front. The cardbacks include player information and the Northwest Plaza Mall sponsor logo. The unnumbered cards are listed below alphabetically.

COMPLETE SET (53)	20.00	50.00
1 Taje Allen	.40	1.00
2 Tony Banks	1.60	4.00
3 Will Brice	.40	1.00
4 Bern Brostek	.40	1.00
5 Isaac Bruce	2.40	6.00
6 Kevin Carter	.60	1.50
7 Charlie Clemons	.60	1.50
8 Ernie Conwell	.40	1.00
9 Keith Crawford	.40	1.00
10 Nate Dingle	.40	1.00
11 Ernest Dye	.40	1.00
12 D'Marco Farr	.40	1.00
13 Will Furrer	.40	1.00
14 Wayne Gandy	.40	1.00
15 John Gerak	.40	1.00
16 Mike Gruttadauria	.40	1.00
17 Britt Hager	.40	1.00
18 Derrick Harris	.40	1.00
19 Craig Heyward	.60	1.50
20 Mitch Jacoby	.40	1.00
21 Billy Jenkins Jr.	.40	1.00
22 Bill Johnson	.40	1.00
23 Mike Jones	.40	1.00
24 Robert Jones	.40	1.00
25 Muadianvita Kazadi	.40	1.00
26 Eddie Kennison	1.00	2.50
27 Aaron Laing	.40	1.00
28 Amp Lee	.40	1.00
29 Todd Lyght	.40	1.00
30 Keith Lyle	.40	1.00
31 Gerald McBurrows	.40	1.00
32 Dexter McCleon	1.00	2.50
33 Ryan McNeil	.40	1.00
34 Fred Miller	.40	1.00
35 Jerald Moore	.60	1.50
36 Ron Moore	.60	1.50
37 Leslie O'Neal	.40	1.00
38 Orlando Pace	1.00	2.50
39 Roman Phifer	.40	1.00
40 Lawrence Phillips	.60	1.50
41 Bryan Robinson	.40	1.00
42 Jeff Robinson	.40	1.00
43 Jermaine Ross	.40	1.00
44 Mark Rypien	.60	1.50
45 Torrance Small	.40	1.00
46 Vernice Smith	.40	1.00
47 J.T. Thomas	.40	1.00
48 Marquis Walker	.40	1.00
49 Zach Wiegert	.40	1.00
50 Jay Williams	.40	1.00
51 Jeff Wilkins	.40	1.00
52 Toby Wright	.40	1.00
53 Jeff Zgonina	.40	1.00

1998 Rams Team Issue

This set was released by the team for fans and player appearances. Each measures roughly 5" by 7" and features a black and white player photo on the front along with the title sponsor's logo - Sprint. The cardbacks include player information and additional sponsor logos. The unnumbered cards are listed below alphabetically.

COMPLETE SET (52)	60.00	100.00
1 Ray Agnew	.40	1.00
2 Taje Allen	.40	1.00
3 Tyji Armstrong	.40	1.00
4 Tony Banks	1.00	2.50
5 Steve Bono	.60	1.50
6 Ethan Brooks	.40	1.00
7 Issac Bruce	1.00	2.50
8 Kevin Carter	.60	1.50
9 Charlie Clemons	.60	1.50
10 Ernie Conwell	.40	1.00
11 D'Marco Farr	.40	1.00
12 John Flannery	.40	1.00
13 London Fletcher	1.00	2.50
14 Wayne Gandy	.40	1.00
15 Mike Gruttadauria	.40	1.00
16 Derrick Harris	.40	1.00
17 Az-Zahir Hakim	2.50	5.00
18 June Henley	.40	1.00
19 Eric Hill	.40	1.00
20 Greg Hill	.60	1.50
21 Robert Holcombe	1.25	3.00
22 Tony Horne	1.00	2.50
23 Billy Jenkins	.40	1.00
24 Mike Jones LB	.40	1.00
25 Mike Jones DE	.40	1.00
26 Eddie Kennison	1.00	2.50
27 Leonard Little	1.00	2.50
28 Todd Lyght	.40	1.00
29 Keith Lyle	.40	1.00
30 Gerald McBurrows	.40	1.00
31 Dexter McCleon	.60	1.50
32 Ryan McNeil	.40	1.00
33 Fred Miller	.40	1.00
34 Jerald Moore	.60	1.50
35 Tom Nutten	.40	1.00
36 Orlando Pace	.60	1.50
37 Roman Phifer	.40	1.00
38 Joe Phillips	.40	1.00
39 Ricky Proehl	.60	1.50
40 Jeff Robinson	.40	1.00
41 Mike Scurlock	.40	1.00
42 Lorenzo Styles	.40	1.00
43 J.T. Thomas	.40	1.00
44 Ryan Tucker	.40	1.00
45 Rick Tuten	.40	1.00
46 Kurt Warner	30.00	60.00
47 Zach Wiegert	.40	1.00
48 Jeff Wilkins	.40	1.00
49 Jay Williams	.40	1.00
50 Roland Williams	.40	1.00
51 Grant Wistrom	.60	1.50
52 Toby Wright	.40	1.00

1999 Rams Reader Team

These cards were produced by the Rams and distributed to school students as part of the Rams Reader Team program. Each unnumbered card features a color photo of the player on the cardfront with a brief bio on the back.

COMPLETE SET (5)	4.00	10.00
1 Tony Banks	1.20	3.00
2 Isaac Bruce	1.60	4.00
3 Kevin Carter	.60	1.50
4 Keith Lyle	.40	1.00
5 Jeff Wilkins	.40	1.00

1999 Rams Team Issue

These cards were released by the team for fans and player autograph appearances. Each measures roughly 5" by 7" and features a black and white player photo on the front. The cardbacks include player information and sponsor logos. The unnumbered cards are listed below alphabetically.

COMPLETE SET (53)	50.00	80.00
1 Ray Agnew	.40	1.00
2 Taje Allen	.40	1.00
3 Lionel Barnes	.40	1.00
4 Dre Bly	1.00	2.50
5 Isaac Bruce	2.00	4.00
6 Devin Bush	.40	1.00
7 Ron Carpenter DB	.40	1.00
8 Kevin Carter	.60	1.50
9 Charlie Clemons	.60	1.50
10 Rich Coady	.40	1.00
11 Todd Collins	.40	1.00
12 Ernie Conwell	.40	1.00
13 D'Marco Farr	.40	1.00
14 Marshall Faulk	4.00	8.00
15 London Fletcher	.40	1.00
16 Joe Germaine	1.50	4.00
17 Trent Green	1.00	2.50
18 Mike Gruttadauria	.40	1.00
19 Az-Zahir Hakim	1.00	2.50
20 James Hodgins	.40	1.00
21 Robert Holcombe	.60	1.50
22 Torry Holt	5.00	10.00
23 Tony Horne	1.00	2.50
24 Gaylon Hyder	.40	1.00
25 Billy Jenkins	.40	1.00
26 Willie Jones	.40	1.00
27 Paul Justin	.40	1.00
28 Amp Lee	.40	1.00
29 Chad Lewis	.40	1.00
30 Chad Levitt	.40	1.00
31 Todd Lyght	.40	1.00
32 Keith Lyle	.40	1.00
33 Dexter McCleon	.60	1.50
34 Andy McCollum	.40	1.00
35 Fred Miller	.40	1.00
36 Mike Morton	.40	1.00
37 Tom Nutten	.40	1.00
38 Orlando Pace	.60	1.50
39 Troy Pelshak	.40	1.00
40 Ricky Proehl	.60	1.50
41 Jeff Robinson	.40	1.00
42 Cameron Spikes	.40	1.00
43 Lorenzo Styles	.40	1.00
44 Adam Timmerman	.40	1.00
45 Ryan Tucker	.40	1.00
46 Rick Tuten	.40	1.00
47 Kurt Warner	12.50	25.00
48 Justin Watson	.40	1.00
49 Jeff Wilkins	.40	1.00
50 Jay Williams	.40	1.00
51 Roland Williams	.40	1.00
52 Grant Wistrom	.60	1.50
53 Jeff Zgonina	.40	1.00

2000 Rams Bank of America

This card was released in the seat cushions at Super Bowl XXXIV. It features 3-Rams players and was produced on a thick plastic stock with the "magic motion" style printing process.

1 Kurt Warner Isaac Bruce Marshall Faulk	24.00	60.00

2000 Rams Future and Hope

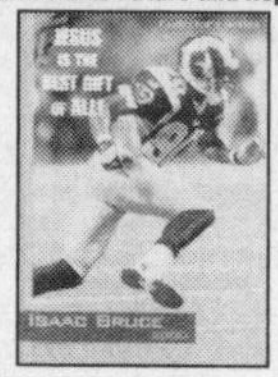

These three cards were produced and distributed by the religious organization www.futureandhope.org. Each card features a Rams player on the front along with the team name, year, and a short religious message. The unnumbered cardbacks include some brief player biographical information as well as a number of additional religious messages.

COMPLETE SET (3)	2.50	5.00
1 Isaac Bruce	.75	2.00
2 Ernie Conwell	.60	1.50
3 Kurt Warner	1.25	3.00

2000 Rams Team Issue

The Rams continued their oversized card program in 2000. These cards were released by the team to fulfill fan requests and for player appearances. Each measures roughly 5" by 7" and features a black and white player photo on the front along with the title sponsor's logo - Sega Sports. The cardbacks include player information and additional sponsor logos. The unnumbered cards are listed below alphabetically.

COMPLETE SET (54)	50.00	80.00
1 Ray Agnew	.40	1.00
2 Taje Allen	.40	1.00
3 John Baker	.40	1.00
4 Lionel Barnes	.40	1.00
5 Dre Bly	.40	1.00
6 Matt Bowen	.40	1.00
7 Isaac Bruce	2.00	4.00
8 Devin Bush	.40	1.00
9 Trung Canidate	2.00	5.00
10 Kevin Carter	.60	1.50
11 Rich Coady	.40	1.00
12 Todd Collins	.40	1.00
13 Ernie Conwell	.40	1.00
14 Steve Everitt	.40	1.00
15 D'Marco Farr	.40	1.00
16 Marshall Faulk	4.00	8.00
17 London Fletcher	.40	1.00
18 Joe Germaine	.60	1.50
19 Trent Green	1.00	2.50
20 Az-Zahir Hakim	.60	1.50
21 Nate Hobgood-Chittick	.40	1.00
22 James Hodgins	.40	1.00
23 Robert Holcombe	.60	1.50
24 Torry Holt	2.00	5.00
25 Tony Horne	.60	1.50
26 Mike Jones LB	.40	1.00
27 Leonard Little	1.00	2.50
28 Todd Lyght	.40	1.00
29 Keith Lyle	.40	1.00
30 Dexter McCleon	.40	1.00
31 Andy McCollum	.40	1.00
32 Keith Miller	.40	1.00
33 Sean Moran	.40	1.00
34 Kaulana Noa	.40	1.00

35 Tom Nutten	.40	1.00
36 Orlando Pace	.60	1.50
37 Ricky Proehl	.60	1.50
38 Jeff Robinson	.40	1.00
39 Jacoby Shepherd	.40	1.00
40 Jamel Smith	.40	1.00
41 Cameron Spikes	.40	1.00
42 John St.Clair	.40	1.00
43 Lorenzo Styles	.40	1.00
44 Pete Swanson	.40	1.00
45 Chris Thomas	.40	1.00
46 Adam Timmerman	.40	1.00
47 Ryan Tucker	.40	1.00
48 Kurt Warner	10.00	20.00
49 Justin Watson	.40	1.00
50 Jeff Wilkins	.40	1.00
51 Roland Williams	.40	1.00
52 Grant Wistrom	.60	1.50
53 Brian Young	.40	1.00
54 Jeff Zgonina	.40	1.00

2001 Rams Future and Hope

These three cards were produced and distributed by the religious organization www.futureandhope.org. Each card features a Rams player on the front along with the year printed in a small red box. The unnumbered cardbacks include some brief player biographical information as well as a number of religious messages.

COMPLETE SET (3)	2.50	5.00
1 Ray Agnew	.60	1.50
2 Trung Canidate	.75	2.00
3 Kurt Warner	1.25	3.00

2001 Rams Team Issue

Cards from this set were issued by the team for fan mail requests and player autograph appearances. Each measures roughly 5" by 7" and features a black and white player photo on the front along with the Rams helmet and Reebok logo. The cardbacks include player information and sponsor logos with Reebok being the main sponsor. The unnumbered cards are listed below alphabetically.

COMPLETE SET (54)	50.00	80.00
1 Chidi Ahanotu	.40	1.00
2 Brian Allen	.60	1.50
3 Adam Archuleta	1.00	2.50
4 Kole Ayi	.40	1.00
5 John Baker	.40	1.00
6 Dre Bly	.40	1.00
7 Matt Bowen	.40	1.00
8 Isaac Bruce	2.00	4.00
9 Marc Bulger	6.00	12.00
10 Jerametrius Butler	.40	1.00
11 Trung Canidate	.60	1.50
12 Rich Coady	.40	1.00
13 Dustin Cohen	.40	1.00
14 Ernie Conwell	.40	1.00
15 Don Davis	.40	1.00
16 Marshall Faulk	4.00	8.00
17 Mark Fields	.40	1.00
18 London Fletcher	.40	1.00
19 Frank Garcia	.40	1.00
20 Az-Zahir Hakim	.60	1.50
21 Kim Herring	.40	1.00
22 James Hodgins	.40	1.00
23 Robert Holcombe	.60	1.50
24 Torry Holt	1.50	4.00
25 Tyoka Jackson	.40	1.00
26 Rod Jones	.40	1.00
27 Paul Justin	.40	1.00
28 Damione Lewis	.40	1.00
29 Leonard Little	.60	1.50
30 Brandon Manumaleuna	.40	1.00
31 Jamie Martin	1.00	2.50
32 Dexter McCleon	.40	1.00
33 Andy McCollum	.40	1.00
34 Sean Moran	.40	1.00
35 Yo Murphy	.60	1.50
36 Kaulana Noa	.40	1.00
37 Tom Nutten	.40	1.00
38 Orlando Pace	.60	1.50
39 Ryan Pickett	.40	1.00
40 Tommy Polley	.60	1.50
41 Ricky Proehl	.60	1.50
42 Jeff Robinson	.40	1.00
43 Jacoby Shepherd	.40	1.00
44 John St.Clair	.40	1.00
45 Cameron Spikes	.40	1.00
46 Adam Timmerman	.40	1.00
47 Ryan Tucker	.40	1.00
48 Kurt Warner	6.00	15.00
49 Justin Watson	.40	1.00
50 Jeff Wilkins	.40	1.00
51 Aeneas Williams	.60	1.50
52 Grant Wistrom	.60	1.50
53 Brian Young	.40	1.00
54 Jeff Zgonina	.40	1.00

2002 Rams Team Issue

Cards from this set were issued by the team for fan mail requests and player autograph appearances. Each measures roughly 5" by 7" and features a color player photo on the front along with the Rams helmet and a Gatorade sponsorship logo. The cardbacks include a player bio and small black and white photo. The unnumbered cards are listed below alphabetically.

COMPLETE SET (53)	50.00	80.00
1 Adam Archuleta	.60	1.50
2 Kole Ayi	.40	1.00
3 Steve Bellisari	1.00	2.50
4 Mitch Berger	.40	1.00
5 Dre Bly	.40	1.00
6 Isaac Bruce	2.00	4.00
7 Marc Bulger	2.50	6.00
8 Courtland Bullard	.40	1.00
9 Jerametrius Butler	.40	1.00
10 Trung Canidate	1.00	2.50
11 Ernie Conwell	.40	1.00
12 Chad Cota	.40	1.00
13 Don Davis	.40	1.00
14 Jamie Duncan	.40	1.00
15 Troy Edwards	.40	1.00
16 Marshall Faulk	2.50	6.00
17 Bryce Fisher	1.00	2.50
18 Travis Fisher	.40	1.00
19 Frank Garcia	.40	1.00
20 Lamar Gordon	.50	1.25
21 Chris Hetherington	.40	1.00
22 Kim Herring	.40	1.00
23 James Hodgins	.40	1.00
24 Torry Holt	1.50	4.00
25 Heath Irwin	.40	1.00
26 Tyoka Jackson	.40	1.00
27 Damione Lewis	.40	1.00
28 Leonard Little	.40	1.00
29 Brandon Manumaleuna	.40	1.00
30 Chris Massey	.40	1.00
31 Jamie Martin	.60	1.50
32 Dexter McCleon	.40	1.00
33 Andy McCollum	.40	1.00
34 Yo Murphy	.40	1.00
35 Tom Nutten	.40	1.00
36 Orlando Pace	.60	1.50
37 Ryan Pickett	.40	1.00
38 Tommy Polley	.40	1.00
39 Ricky Proehl	.60	1.50
40 Travis Scott	.40	1.00
41 Nick Sorensen	.40	1.00
42 John St. Clair	.40	1.00
43 Robert Thomas	.60	1.50
44 Adam Timmerman	.40	1.00
45 Kurt Warner	6.00	12.00
46 James Whitley	.40	1.00
47 Jeff Wilkins	.40	1.00
48 Terrence Wilkins	.40	1.00
49 Aeneas Williams	.60	1.50
50 Grant Williams	.40	1.00
51 Grant Wistrom	.60	1.50
52 Brian Young	.40	1.00
53 Jeff Zgonina	.40	1.00

2006 Rams Topps

COMPLETE SET (12)	3.00	5.00
STL1 Marc Bulger	.25	.60
STL2 Isaac Bruce	.25	.60
STL3 Shaun McDonald	.20	.50
STL4 Kevin Curtis	.25	.60
STL5 Steven Jackson	.30	.75
STL6 Torry Holt	.25	.60
STL7 Marshall Faulk	.25	.60
STL8 Ryan Fitzpatrick	.30	.75
STL9 Jeff Wilkins	.20	.50
STL10 Orlando Pace	.20	.50
STL11 Tye Hill	.20	.50
STL12 Joe Klopfenstein	.20	.50

2007 Rams Topps

COMPLETE SET (12)	2.50	5.00
1 Marc Bulger	.25	.60
2 Torry Holt	.25	.60
3 Steven Jackson	.30	.75
4 Isaac Bruce	.25	.60
5 Leonard Little	.20	.50
6 Randy McMichael	.20	.50
7 Jeff Wilkins	.20	.50
8 Will Witherspoon	.20	.50
9 Joe Klopfenstein	.20	.50
10 Drew Bennett	.20	.50
11 Brian Leonard	.25	.60
12 Adam Carriker	.25	.60

2008 Rams Topps

COMPLETE SET (12)	2.50	5.00
1 Steven Jackson	.30	.75
2 Torry Holt	.25	.60
3 Marc Bulger	.25	.60
4 Trent Green	.25	.60
5 Randy McMichael	.20	.50
6 Corey Chavous	.20	.50
7 Brian Leonard	.20	.50
8 O.J. Atogwe	.20	.50
9 Drew Bennett	.20	.50
10 Will Witherspoon	.20	.50
11 Chris Long	.40	1.00
12 Donnie Avery	.30	.75

1961 Random House Football Portfolio

These color photos were issued as a set in the early 1960s by Random House. They were distributed in a colorful folder that featured the title "Football Portfolio" at the top and the Random House identification at the bottom. The body of the folder included the image of the Giants and Packers with Y.A. Tittle in the foreground. Each photo features a color image of a player or game action with only the photographer's notation on the front to use as identification. The backs are blank and the photos are borderless and measure roughly 7 7/8" by 11".

COMPLETE SET (6)	75.00	150.00
1 Bart Starr (photo by James Drake)	15.00	40.00
2 Jim Taylor running the ball (photo by Neil Leifer)	12.50	30.00
3 Jerry Kramer (kicking) Bart Starr (holding) (photo by James Drake)	12.50	30.00
4 Jim Taylor being tackled (photo by Neil Leifer)	10.00	25.00
5 Giants vs. Packers game action Y.A. Tittle in foreground with Hank Jordan and Willie Davis (photo by James Drake)	12.50	30.00
6 Don Chandler Phil King (photo by Walter Iooss Jr.)	7.50	20.00

1996 Ravens Score Board/Exxon

Score Board produced this team set for distribution by the Baltimore area Exxon stations. Each card appears similar to a 1996 Pro Line card, but contains the Score Board logo at the top. The Exxon sponsor logo appears only on the checklist card. Packs could be obtained, with the appropriate gasoline purchase, for 49-cents each and contained three-player cards and a checklist card.

COMPLETE SET (9)	1.50	4.00
BR1 Vinny Testaverde	.15	.40
BR2 Eric Zeier	.15	.40
BR3 Earnest Byner	.08	.25
BR4 Derrick Alexander WR	.30	.75
BR5 Michael Jackson	.15	.40
BR6 Jonathan Ogden	.15	.40
BR7 Ray Lewis	.50	1.25
BR8 Eric Turner	.08	.25
BR9 Ravens Checklist	.08	.25

2005 Ravens Activa Medallions

COMPLETE SET (22)	30.00	60.00
1 Kyle Boller	1.25	3.00
2 Orlando Brown	1.25	3.00
3 Mark Clayton	1.00	2.50
4 Will Demps	1.25	3.00
5 Mike Flynn	1.25	3.00
6 Kelly Gregg	1.25	3.00
7 Todd Heap	1.25	3.00
8 Jamal Lewis	1.50	4.00
9 Ray Lewis	1.50	4.00
10 Derrick Mason	1.25	3.00
11 Chris McCallister	1.25	3.00
12 Edwin Mulatalo	1.25	3.00
13 Jonathan Ogden	1.25	3.00
14 Ed Reed	1.25	3.00
15 Samari Rolle	1.25	3.00
16 Deion Sanders	1.50	4.00
17 Matt Stover	1.25	3.00
18 Terrell Suggs	1.25	3.00
19 Chester Taylor	1.25	3.00
20 Adalius Thomas	1.25	3.00
21 Anthony Weaver	1.25	3.00
22 Ravens Logo	1.00	2.50

2006 Ravens Topps

COMPLETE SET (12)	3.00	6.00
BAL1 Mike Anderson	.25	.60
BAL2 Ray Lewis	.30	.75
BAL3 Jonathan Ogden	.20	.50
BAL4 Kyle Boller	.25	.60
BAL5 Derrick Mason	.25	.60
BAL6 Mark Clayton	.25	.60
BAL7 Ed Reed	.25	.60
BAL8 Chris McAlister	.20	.50
BAL9 Jamal Lewis	.25	.60
BAL10 Todd Heap	.25	.60
BAL11 Haloti Ngata	.30	.75
BAL12 Demetrius Williams	.25	.60

2007 Ravens Topps

COMPLETE SET (12)	2.50	5.00
1 Willis McGahee	.25	.60
2 Todd Heap	.20	.50
3 Steve McNair	.25	.60
4 Mark Clayton	.25	.60
5 Ray Lewis	.30	.75
6 Ed Reed	.25	.60
7 Trevor Pryce	.20	.50
8 Terrell Suggs	.25	.60
9 Derrick Mason	.25	.60
10 Jonathan Ogden	.20	.50
11 Chris McAlister	.20	.50
12 Troy Smith	.30	.75

2008 Ravens Topps

COMPLETE SET (12)	3.00	6.00
1 Kyle Boller	.20	.50
2 Willis McGahee	.25	.60
3 Derrick Mason	.25	.60
4 Ray Lewis	.30	.75
5 Ed Reed	.25	.60
6 Todd Heap	.20	.50
7 Jonathan Ogden	.20	.50
8 Troy Smith	.25	.60
9 Mark Clayton	.25	.60
10 Terrell Suggs	.20	.50
11 Joe Flacco	1.25	3.00
12 Ray Rice	.75	2.00

2009 Ravens Breast Cancer Awareness

This three card set was issued at a home game in 2009. Each unnumbered card was created by one of the three NFL licensed manufacturers and features the pink ribbon breast cancer awareness logo on the fronts.

COMPLETE SET (3)	2.50	5.00
1 Joe Flacco Upper Deck	1.00	2.50
2 Ray Lewis Topps	1.00	2.50
3 Derrick Mason Panini	.75	2.00

1962-66 Rawlings Advisory Staff Photos

These photos were likely issued over a period of years in the early to mid-1960s. Each is unnumbered and checklisted below in alphabetical order. The cards measure roughly 8 1/8" by 10 1/8" and include a white box containing the player's facsimile autograph and Rawlings Advisory Staff identification lines. Any additions to the list below are appreciated.

COMMON CARD (1-13)	7.50	15.00
1 Jim Bakken	7.50	15.00
2 Billy Cannon (LSU Photo)	10.00	20.00
3 Roman Gabriel	15.00	25.00
4 John Hadl	15.00	25.00
5 Jim Hart	15.00	25.00
6 Harlon Hill	7.50	15.00
7 Bobby Layne	20.00	40.00
8 Don Meredith (SMU Photo)	20.00	40.00
9 Sonny Randle	7.50	15.00
10 Kyle Rote	10.00	20.00
11 Tobin Rote	7.50	15.00
12 John Stofa	7.50	15.00
13 Alex Webster	7.50	15.00

1976 RC Cola Colts Cans

This set of RC Cola cans was release in the Baltimore area and featured members of the Colts. The cans are blue and feature a black and white player photo. They are similar in design to the nationally issued 1977 set but include a red banner below the player's photo as well as different statistics for each player versus the 1977 release. Prices below reflect that of opened empty cans.

COMPLETE SET (43)	50.00	100.00
1 Mike Barnes	1.50	3.00
2 Tim Baylor	1.50	3.00
3 Forrest Blue	2.00	4.00
4 Roger Carr	1.50	3.00
5 Raymond Chester	2.00	4.00
6 Jim Cheyunski	1.50	3.00
7 Elmer Collett	1.50	3.00
8 Fred Cook	1.50	3.00
9 Dan Dickel	1.50	3.00
10 John Dutton	1.50	3.00
11 Joe Ehrmann	2.00	4.00
12 Ron Fernandes	1.50	3.00
13 Glenn Doughty	1.50	3.00
14 Randy Hall	1.50	3.00
15 Ken Huff	1.50	3.00
16 Bert Jones	3.00	6.00
17 Jimmie Kennedy	1.50	3.00
18 Mike Kirkland	1.50	3.00
19 George Kunz	1.50	3.00
20 Bruce Laird	1.50	3.00
21 Roosevelt Leaks	2.00	4.00
22 David Lee	2.00	4.00
23 Ron Lee	1.50	3.00
24 Toni Linhart	1.50	3.00
25 Derrel Luce	1.50	3.00
26 Don McCauley	2.00	4.00
27 Ken Mendenhall	1.50	3.00
28 Lydell Mitchell	3.00	6.00
29 Lloyd Mumphord	2.00	4.00
30 Nelson Munsey	1.50	3.00
31 Ken Novak	1.50	3.00
32 Ray Oldham	1.50	3.00
33 Robert Pratt	1.50	3.00
34 Sanders Shiver	1.50	3.00
35 Freddie Scott	1.50	3.00
36 Ed Simonini	1.50	3.00
37 Howard Stevens	1.50	3.00
38 David Taylor	1.50	3.00
39 Ricky Thompson	1.50	3.00
40 Bill Troup	1.50	3.00
41 Jackie Wallace	1.50	3.00
42 Bob Van Duyne	1.50	3.00
43 Stan White	2.00	4.00

1977 RC Cola Cans

RC Cola distributed this set of cans regionally in NFL team areas. Each can features a black and white NFL player photo along with a brief player summary. Ten players were issued for each NFL team, except for the Washington Redskins which featured over 40. We've catalogued the set below according to team (alphabetized). Prices below reflect opened empty cans.

COMPLETE SET (299)	500.00	1,000.00
1 Steve Bartkowski	3.00	6.00
2 Bubba Bean	2.00	4.00
3 Ray Brown	2.00	4.00
4 John Gilliam	2.00	4.00
5 Claude Humphrey	3.00	6.00
6 Alfred Jenkins	2.00	4.00
7 Nick Mike-Mayer	2.00	4.00
8 Jim Mitchell	2.00	4.00
9 Ralph Ortega	2.00	4.00
10 Jeff Van Note	2.00	4.00
11 Forrest Blue	1.50	3.00
12 Raymond Chester	2.00	4.00
13 Joe Ehrmann	1.50	3.00
14 Bert Jones	3.00	6.00
15 Roosevelt Leaks	2.00	4.00
16 David Lee	1.50	3.00
17 Don McCauley	1.50	3.00
18 Lydell Mitchell	2.00	4.00
19 Lloyd Mumphord	1.50	3.00
20 Stan White	1.50	3.00
21 Marv Bateman	2.00	4.00
22 Bob Chandler	3.00	6.00
23 Joe DeLamielleure	3.00	6.00
24 Joe Ferguson	3.00	6.00
25 Dave Foley	2.00	4.00
26 Steve Freeman	2.00	4.00
27 Mike Kadish	2.00	4.00
28 Jeff Lloyd	2.00	4.00
29 Reggie McKenzie	3.00	6.00
30 Bob Nelson	2.00	4.00
31 Lionel Antoine	1.50	3.00
32 Bob Avellini	1.50	3.00
33 Brian Baschnagel	1.50	3.00
34 Waymond Bryant	1.50	3.00
35 Doug Buffone	1.50	3.00
36 Wally Chambers	1.50	3.00
37 Virgil Livers	1.50	3.00
38 Johnny Musso	2.00	4.00
39 Walter Payton	20.00	40.00
40 Bo Rather	1.50	3.00
41 Ken Anderson	3.00	6.00
42 Coy Bacon	1.50	3.00
43 Tommy Casanova	1.50	3.00
44 Boobie Clark	1.50	3.00
45 Archie Griffin	3.00	6.00
46 Jim LeClair	1.50	3.00
47 Rufus Mayes	1.50	3.00
48 Chip Myers	1.50	3.00
49 Ken Riley	2.00	4.00
50 Bob Trumpy	2.00	4.00
51 Don Cockroft	1.50	3.00
52 Thom Darden	1.50	3.00
53 Tom DeLeone	1.50	3.00
54 John Garlington	1.50	3.00
55 Walter Johnson	1.50	3.00
56 Joe Jones	1.50	3.00
57 Cleo Miller	1.50	3.00
58 Greg Pruitt	3.00	6.00
59 Reggie Rucker	2.00	4.00
60 Paul Warfield	5.00	10.00
61 Cliff Harris	3.00	6.00
62 Ed Too Tall Jones	5.00	10.00
63 Ralph Neely	2.00	4.00
64 Robert Newhouse	2.00	4.00
65 Drew Pearson	4.00	8.00
66 Jethro Pugh	3.00	6.00
67 Mel Renfro	4.00	8.00
68 Golden Richards	2.00	4.00
69 Charlie Waters	3.00	6.00
70 Randy White	6.00	12.00
71 Otis Armstrong	2.00	4.00
72 Jon Keyworth	2.00	4.00
73 Jim Kiick	3.00	6.00
74 Craig Morton	3.00	6.00
75 Haven Moses	2.00	4.00
76 Riley Odoms	2.00	4.00
77 Bill Thompson	2.00	4.00
78 Jim Turner	2.00	4.00
79 Rick Upchurch	3.00	6.00
80 Louis Wright	3.00	6.00
81 Lem Barney	2.00	4.00
82 Larry Hand	1.50	3.00
83 J.D. Hill	1.50	3.00
84 Levi Johnson	1.50	3.00
85 Greg Landry	2.00	4.00
86 Jon Morris	1.50	3.00
87 Paul Naumoff	1.50	3.00
88 Charlie Sanders	2.00	4.00
89 Charlie West	1.50	3.00
90 Jim Yarbrough	1.50	3.00
91 John Brockington	2.00	4.00
92 Willie Buchanon	1.50	3.00
93 Fred Carr	1.50	3.00
94 Lynn Dickey	2.00	4.00
95 Bob Hyland	1.50	3.00
96 Chester Marcol	1.50	3.00
97 Mike McCoy	1.50	3.00
98 Rich McGeorge	1.50	3.00
99 Steve Odom	1.50	3.00
100 Clarence Williams	1.50	3.00
101 Willie Alexander	2.00	4.00
102 Duane Benson	2.00	4.00
103 Elvin Bethea	3.00	6.00
104 Ken Burrough	3.00	6.00
105 Skip Butler	2.00	4.00
106 Curley Culp	3.00	6.00
107 Elbert Drungo	2.00	4.00
108 Billy Johnson	3.00	6.00
109 Carl Mauck	2.00	4.00
110 Dan Pastorini	3.00	6.00
111 Tom Condon	2.00	4.00
112 MacArthur Lane	2.00	4.00
113 Willie Lee	2.00	4.00
114 Mike Livingston	2.00	4.00
115 Jim Nicholson	2.00	4.00
116 Jim Lynch	2.00	4.00
117 Barry Pearson	2.00	4.00
118 Ed Podolak	2.00	4.00
119 Jan Stenerud	4.00	8.00
120 Walter White	2.00	4.00
121 Jim Bertelsen	2.00	4.00
122 John Cappelletti	3.00	6.00
123 Fred Dryer	3.00	6.00
124 Pat Haden	3.00	6.00
125 Harold Jackson	3.00	6.00
126 Ron Jessie	2.00	4.00
127 Lawrence McCutcheon	2.00	4.00
128 Isiah Robertson	2.00	4.00
129 Bucky Scribner	2.00	4.00
130 Jack Youngblood	3.00	6.00
131 Dick Anderson	6.00	12.00
132 Norm Bulaich	5.00	10.00
133 Dave Foley	5.00	10.00
134 Vern Den Herder	5.00	10.00
135 Bob Kuechenberg	5.00	10.00
136 Larry Little	6.00	12.00
137 Jim Mandich	5.00	10.00
138 Don Nottingham	5.00	10.00
139 Larry Seiple	5.00	10.00
140 Howard Twilley	5.00	10.00
141 Bobby Bryant	1.50	3.00
142 Fred Cox	1.50	3.00
143 Carl Eller	3.00	6.00
144 Chuck Foreman	2.00	4.00
145 Paul Krause	3.00	6.00
146 Jeff Siemon	1.50	3.00
147 Mick Tingelhoff	2.00	4.00
148 Ed White	2.00	4.00
149 Nate Wright	1.50	3.00
150 Ron Yary	3.00	6.00
151 Marlin Briscoe	2.00	4.00
152 Sam Cunningham	2.00	4.00
153 Steve Grogan	3.00	6.00
154 John Hannah	4.00	8.00
155 Andy Johnson	2.00	4.00
156 Tony McGee DE	2.00	4.00
157 John Sanders	2.00	4.00
158 Randy Vataha	2.00	4.00
159 George Webster	2.00	4.00
160 Steve Zabel	2.00	4.00
161 Larry Burton	2.00	4.00
162 Tony Galbreath	2.00	4.00
163 Don Herrmann	2.00	4.00
164 Archie Manning	5.00	10.00
165 Alvin Maxson	2.00	4.00
166 Jim Merlo	2.00	4.00
167 Derland Moore	2.00	4.00
168 Chuck Muncie	3.00	6.00
169 Tom Myers	2.00	4.00
170 Bob Pollard	2.00	4.00
171 Rich Dvorak	2.00	4.00
172 Walker Gillette	2.00	4.00
173 Jack Gregory	2.00	4.00
174 John Hicks	2.00	4.00
175 Brian Kelley	2.00	4.00
176 John Mendenhall	2.00	4.00
177 Clyde Powers	2.00	4.00
178 Bob Tucker	3.00	6.00
179 Doug Van Horn	2.00	4.00
180 Brad Van Pelt	3.00	6.00
181 Jerome Barkum	2.00	4.00
182 Richard Caster	2.00	4.00
183 Clark Gaines	2.00	4.00
184 Pat Leahy	2.00	4.00
185 Ed Marinaro	3.00	6.00
186 Richard Neal	2.00	4.00
187 Lou Piccone	2.00	4.00
188 Walt Suggs	2.00	4.00
189 Richard Todd	3.00	6.00
190 Phil Wise	2.00	4.00
191 Fred Biletnikoff	6.00	12.00
192 Dave Casper	3.00	6.00
193 Ted Hendricks	4.00	8.00
194 Marv Hubbard	2.00	4.00
195 Ted Kwalick	2.00	4.00
196 Otis Sistrunk	3.00	6.00
197 Ken Stabler	10.00	20.00
198 Gene Upshaw	4.00	8.00
199 Mark Van Eeghen	3.00	6.00
200 Phil Villapiano	3.00	6.00
234 Bill Bergey	3.00	6.00
235 Harold Carmichael	3.00	6.00
236 Roman Gabriel	3.00	6.00
237 Art Malone	2.00	4.00
238 James McAlister	2.00	4.00
239 John Outlaw	2.00	4.00
240 Jerry Sisemore	2.00	4.00
241 Manny Sistrunk	2.00	4.00
242 Tom Sullivan	2.00	4.00
243 Will Wynn	2.00	4.00
244 Rocky Bleier	3.00	6.00
245 Mel Blount	4.00	8.00
246 Terry Bradshaw	12.50	25.00
247 Roy Gerela	1.50	3.00
248 Joe Greene	5.00	10.00
249 Jack Ham	4.00	8.00
250 Ernie Holmes	1.50	3.00
251 Jack Lambert	6.00	12.00
252 Ray Mansfield	1.50	3.00
253 Dwight White	2.00	4.00
254 Tom Banks	2.00	4.00
255 Dan Dierdorf	4.00	8.00
256 Conrad Dobler	2.00	4.00
257 Mel Gray	3.00	6.00
258 Terry Metcalf	3.00	6.00
259 Jackie Smith	4.00	8.00
260 Roger Wehrli	3.00	6.00
261 Ron Yankowski	2.00	4.00
262 Bob Young	2.00	4.00
263 John Zook	2.00	4.00
264 Pat Curran	2.00	4.00
265 Fred Dean	2.00	4.00
266 Ed Flanagan	2.00	4.00
267 Mike Fuller	2.00	4.00
268 Don Goode	2.00	4.00
269 Charlie Joiner	5.00	10.00
270 Louie Kelcher	3.00	6.00
271 Bo Matthews	2.00	4.00
272 Hal Stringert	2.00	4.00
273 Don Woods	2.00	4.00
274 Cas Banaszek	2.00	4.00
275 Cedrick Hardman	2.00	4.00
276 Tommy Hart	2.00	4.00
277 Wilbur Jackson	2.00	4.00
278 Mel Phillips	2.00	4.00
279 Jim Plunkett	4.00	8.00
280 Bruce Taylor	2.00	4.00
281 Gene Washington 49er	3.00	6.00
282 Delvin Williams	2.00	4.00
283 Skip Vanderbundt	2.00	4.00
284 Mike Curtis	3.00	6.00
285 Norm Evans	2.00	4.00
286 Don Hansen	2.00	4.00
287 Fred Hoaglin	2.00	4.00
288 Ron Howard	2.00	4.00
289 Al Matthews	2.00	4.00
290 Sam McCullum	2.00	4.00
291 Eddie McMillan	2.00	4.00
292 Steve Niehaus	2.00	4.00
293 Jim Zorn	3.00	6.00
294 Mike Boryla	2.00	4.00
295 Anthony Davis	3.00	6.00
296 Jimmy DuBose	2.00	4.00
297 Jimmy Gunn	2.00	4.00
298 Essex Johnson	2.00	4.00
299 Bob Moore TE	2.00	4.00
300 Jim Peterson	2.00	4.00
301 Dan Ryczek	2.00	4.00
302 Barry Smith	2.00	4.00
303 Ken Stone	2.00	4.00
304 Mike Bragg	1.50	3.00
305 Eddie Brown	1.50	3.00
306 Marlin Briscoe	1.50	3.00
307 Bill Brundige	1.50	3.00
308 Dave Butz	2.00	4.00
309 Brad Dusek	1.50	3.00
310 Pat Fischer	3.00	6.00
311 Jean Fugett	2.00	4.00
312 Frank Grant	1.50	3.00
313 Chris Hanburger	3.00	6.00
314 Len Hauss	2.00	4.00
315 Terry Hermeling	1.50	3.00
316 Calvin Hill	2.00	4.00
317 Ken Houston	3.00	6.00
318 Bob Kuziel	1.50	3.00
319 Joe Lavender	1.50	3.00
320 Mark Moseley	1.50	3.00
321 Dan Nugent	1.50	3.00
322 Brig Owens	2.00	4.00
323 John Riggins	6.00	12.00
324 Ron Saul	1.50	3.00
325 Jake Scott	3.00	6.00
326 George Starke	1.50	3.00
327 Tim Stokes	1.50	3.00
328 Diron Talbert	2.00	4.00
329 Charley Taylor	3.00	6.00
330 Joe Theismann	6.00	12.00
331 Mike Thomas	2.00	4.00
332 Pete Wysocki	1.50	3.00

2006 Reading Express AIFL

COMPLETE SET (2)	2.50	6.00
1 Sheet 1 Jon Broussard Dante Carter Ian Cooper Ollie Guidry CO Luis Figueroa, etc.	1.25	3.00
2 Sheet 2 Kenny Miller Asst.CO Tom Stetzer Mark Stout Steve Gaunt Asst.CO, etc.	1.25	3.00

2008 Reading Express AIFL

COMPLETE SET (30)	6.00	12.00
1 Michael Baldwin	.20	.50
2 Scott Blum	.20	.50
3 Tardon Brantley	.20	.50
4 Chad Clark	.20	.50
5 Ian Cooper	.20	.50
6 Robert Flowers	.20	.50
7 Shawn Foxworth	.20	.50
8 Corey Gipe	.20	.50
9 Jason Henley	.20	.50
10 Adam Hoffman	.20	.50
11 Trent Jones	.20	.50
12 Dan Kelly	.20	.50
13 Brett Kolk	.20	.50
14 Sean McKnight CO	.20	.50
15 Preston McKnight CO	.20	.50
16 Kenny Miller CO	.20	.50
17 Ronnie Montgomery	.20	.50
18 Bernie Nowotarski CO	.20	.50
19 Chris Nunn	.20	.50
20 Carmelo Ocasio	.20	.50
21 Mike Robinson CO	.20	.50
22 Erik Rockhold	.20	.50
23 Marcus Sargeant	.20	.50
24 Mike Schwebel	.20	.50
25 David Smith	.20	.50
26 Matt Sola	.20	.50
27 Mark Steinmeyer	.20	.50
28 Mark Stout	.20	.50
29 Chris Thompson GM	.20	.50
30 Jeff Willis	.20	.50

1995 Real Action Pop-Ups

COMPLETE SET (7)	2.50	6.00
2 John Elway	.60	1.50

1939 Redskins Matchbooks

Sponsored by Ross Jewelers, these 20 matchbooks measure approximately 1 1/2" by 4 1/2" (when completely folded out) and feature black-and-white photos of the 1939 Washington Redskins, with simulated autographs on the inside panel. The player's position and college, along with his height and weight, appear below the photo. The bottom half of the inside panel reads "This is one of 20 autographed pictures of the Washington Redskins compliments of the Ross Jewelry Co." In maroon lettering upon a gold background, the top half of the outside of the matchbook carries on its front the Ross Company name and address within a drawing of a football. the Redskins 1939 home game schedule is shown on the bottom half. This is the only distinguishing characteristic between the 1939 and 1940 issues. The covers of Jim Barber and Steve Slivinski are considered scarce. The matchbooks are unnumbered and checklisted below in alphabetical order. The prices given are for full covers (with strikers) missing the actual matches. This is the form in which the matchbooks are most commonly found. Complete books with matches typically carry a 50% premium. Books missing the striker are considered VG at best.

COMPLETE SET (20)	1,000.00	1,500.00
1 Jim Barber SP	250.00	400.00
2 Sammy Baugh	90.00	150.00
3 Hal Bradley	20.00	35.00
4 Vic Carroll	20.00	35.00
5 Bud Erickson	20.00	35.00
6 Andy Farkas	20.00	35.00
7 Frank Filchock	20.00	35.00
8 Ray Flaherty CO	25.00	40.00
9 Don Irwin	20.00	35.00
10 Ed Justice	20.00	35.00
11 Jim Karcher	20.00	35.00
12 Max Krause	20.00	35.00
13 Charley Malone	20.00	35.00
14 Bob Masterson	20.00	35.00
15 Wayne Millner	25.00	40.00
16 Mickey Parks	20.00	35.00
17 Erny Pinckert	20.00	35.00
18 Steve Slivinski SP	250.00	400.00
19 Clem Stralka	20.00	35.00
20 Jay Turner	20.00	35.00

1939 Redskins Postcards

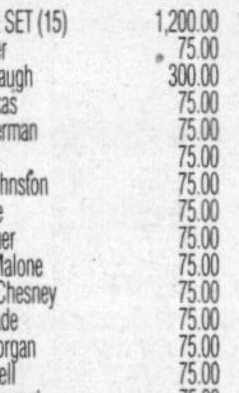

This series of postcards was produced for and issued by the team in 1939. Each card measures roughly 3 1/2" by 5 1/2" and features a typically postcard style back with a black and white player photo on the front. The player's name, position, and team name is included within the player photo.

COMPLETE SET (15)	1,200.00	1,800.00
1 Jim Barber	75.00	125.00
2 Sammy Baugh	300.00	500.00
3 Andy Farkas	75.00	125.00
4 Jimmy German	75.00	125.00
5 Don Irwin	75.00	125.00
6 Jimmy Johnston	75.00	125.00
7 Ed Justice	75.00	125.00
8 Jim Karcher	75.00	125.00
9 Charley Malone	75.00	125.00
10 Bob McChesney	75.00	125.00
11 Jim Meade	75.00	125.00
12 Boyd Morgan	75.00	125.00
13 Bo Russell	75.00	125.00
14 Clyde Shugart	75.00	125.00
15 Bill Young	75.00	125.00

1940 Redskins Matchbooks

Made for Ross Jewelers by the Universal Match Corp. of Philadelphia, these 20 matchbooks measure approximately 1 1/2" by 4 1/2" (when completely folded out) and feature black-and-white photos of the 1940 Washington Redskins, with simulated autographs, on the inside panel. The player's position and college, along with his height and weight, appear below the photo. The bottom half of the inside panel reads "This is one of 20 autographed pictures of the Washington Redskins compliments of Ross Jewelry Co." In maroon lettering upon a gold background, the top half of the outside of the matchbook carries on its front the Ross Company name and address within a drawing of a football. On the bottom half is shown the Redskins 1940 home game schedule. This is the only distinguishing characteristic between the 1939 and 1940 issues. The matchbooks are unnumbered and checklisted below in alphabetical order. The prices given are for full covers (with strikers) missing the actual matches. This is the form in which the matchbooks are most commonly found. Complete books with matches typically carry a 50% premium. Books missing the striker are considered VG at best.

COMPLETE SET (20)	200.00	350.00
1 Jim Barber	10.00	18.00
2 Sammy Baugh	50.00	80.00
3 Vic Carroll	10.00	18.00
4 Turk Edwards	18.00	30.00
5 Andy Farkas	10.00	18.00
6 Dick Farman	10.00	18.00
7 Bob Hoffman	10.00	18.00
8 Don Irwin	10.00	18.00
9 Charley Malone	10.00	18.00
10 Bob Masterson	10.00	18.00
11 Wayne Millner	12.00	20.00
12 Mickey Parks	10.00	18.00
13 Erny Pinckert	10.00	18.00
14 Bo Russell	10.00	18.00
15 Clyde Shugart	10.00	18.00
16 Steve Slivinski	10.00	18.00
17 Clem Stralka	10.00	18.00
18 Dick Todd	10.00	18.00
19 Bill Young	10.00	18.00
20 Roy Zimmerman	10.00	18.00

1941 Redskins Matchbooks

Made for Home Laundry by the Maryland Match Co. of Baltimore, these 20 matchbooks measure approximately 1 1/2" by 4 1/2" (when completely folded out) and feature black-and-white photos of the 1941 Washington Redskins, with simulated autographs on the inside panel. The player's position and college, along with his height and weight, appear below the photo. The bottom half of the inside panel reads "This is one of 20 autographed pictures of the Washington Redskins compliments of Home Laundry," followed by the business's 1941 six-digit phone number, ATlantic 2400. In gold lettering upon a maroon background, the outside of the matchbook carries on its front the Home Laundry name and telephone number within a drawing of a football. On the back is shown the Redskins 1941 home game schedule, which ended with a game against Philadelphia, on Sunday, Dec. 7, 1941. The matchbooks are unnumbered and checklisted below in alphabetical order. The prices given are for full covers (with strikers) missing the actual matches. This is the form in which the matchbooks are most commonly found. Complete books with matches typically carry a 50% premium. Books missing the striker are considered VG at best.

COMPLETE SET (20)	150.00	250.00
1 Ki Aldrich	7.00	12.00
2 Jim Barber	7.00	12.00
3 Sammy Baugh	35.00	60.00
4 Vic Carroll	7.00	12.00
5 Fred Davis	7.00	12.00
6 Andy Farkas	7.00	12.00
7 Dick Farman	7.00	12.00
8 Frank Filchock	7.00	12.00
9 Ray Flaherty CO	9.00	15.00
10 Bob Masterson	7.00	12.00
11 Bob McChesney	7.00	12.00
12 Wayne Millner	9.00	15.00
13 Wilbur Moore	7.00	12.00
14 Bob Seymour	7.00	12.00
15 Clyde Shugart	7.00	12.00
16 Clem Stralka	7.00	12.00
17 Robert Titchenal	7.00	12.00
18 Dick Todd	7.00	12.00
19 Bill Young	7.00	12.00
20 Roy Zimmerman	7.00	12.00

1942 Redskins Matchbooks

Made for Home Laundry by the Maryland Match Co. of Baltimore, these 20 matchbooks measure approximately 1 1/2" by 4 1/2" (when completely folded out) and feature black-and-white photos of the 1942 Washington Redskins, with simulated autographs, on the inside panel. The player's position and college, along with his height and weight, appear below the photo. The bottom half of the inside panel reads "This is one of 20 autographed pictures of the Washington Redskins compliments of Home Laundry," followed by the business's 1942 six-digit phone number, ATlantic 2400. In maroon lettering upon a yellow-orange background, the outside of the matchbook carries on its front the Home Laundry name and telephone number within a drawing of a football. On the back is shown the Redskins 1942 home game schedule. The matchbooks are unnumbered and checklisted below in alphabetical order. The prices given are for full covers (with strikers) missing the actual matches. This is the form in which the matchbooks are most commonly found. Complete books with matches typically carry a 50% premium. Books missing the striker are considered VG at best.

COMPLETE SET (20)	150.00	250.00
1 Ki Aldrich	7.00	12.00
2 Sammy Baugh	35.00	60.00
3 Joe Beinor	7.00	12.00
4 Vic Carroll	7.00	12.00
5 Ed Cifers	7.00	12.00
6 Fred Davis	7.00	12.00
7 Turk Edwards	12.00	20.00
8 Andy Farkas	7.00	12.00
9 Dick Farman	7.00	12.00
10 Ray Flaherty CO	9.00	15.00
11 Al Krueger	7.00	12.00
12 Bob Masterson	7.00	12.00
13 Bob McChesney	7.00	12.00
14 Wilbur Moore	7.00	12.00
15 Bob Seymour	7.00	12.00
16 Clyde Shugart	7.00	12.00
17 Clem Stralka	7.00	12.00
18 Dick Todd	7.00	12.00
19 Willie Wilkin	7.00	12.00
20 Bill Young	7.00	12.00

1951-52 Redskins Matchbooks

Sponsored by Arcade Pontiac and produced by the Universal Match Corp.,Washington D.C., these matchbooks measure approximately 1 1/2" by 4 1/2" (when completely folded out) and feature small black-and-white photos of Washington Redskins with simulated autographs on the inside panel. The player's position and college, along with his height and weight, appear below the photo. The bottom half of the inside panel reads "This is one of 20 autographed pictures of the Washington Redskins compliments of Jack Blank, President Arcade Pontiac Co.," followed by the business' 1950s six-digit phone number, ADams 8500. The outside of the matchbook carries on its top half the Arcade Pontiac name along with a logo on a black and gold background. On the bottom half is shown the Redskins logo on a gold background. The matchbooks are unnumbered and checklisted below in alphabetical order. Although the covers read "20" to the set, it is thought that only 17-matchbooks were released in 1951 and 19 in 1952. Many of the matchbooks were released in both 1951 and 1952 with a few containing only very minor differences in the photo cropping. Otherwise, the two sets are indistinguishable. Thus, we've listed the two sets together for ease in cataloging. Major variations between the two years (only the Herman Ball cover) and covers reportedly issued only one year are listed below as such. The prices given are for full covers (with strikers) missing the actual matches. This is the form in which the matchbooks are most commonly found. Complete books with matches typically carry a 50% premium. Books missing the striker are considered VG at best.

COMPLETE SET (25)	250.00	400.00
1 John Badaczewski	5.00	10.00
2A Herman Ball CO Head Coach	6.00	12.00
2B Herman Ball CO Assistant Coach	6.00	12.00
3 Sammy Baugh	25.00	50.00
4 Ed Berrang 1951	6.00	12.00
5 Dan Brown 1951	6.00	12.00
6 Al DeMao	5.00	10.00
7 Harry Dowda 1952	10.00	20.00
8 Chuck Drazenovich	5.00	10.00
9 Bill Dudley 1951	10.00	20.00
10 Harry Gilmer	7.50	15.00
11 Bob Goode 1951	6.00	12.00
12 Leon Heath 1952	10.00	20.00
13 Charlie Justice 1952	12.50	25.00
14 Lou Karras	5.00	10.00
15 Eddie LeBaron 1952	15.00	30.00
16 Paul Lipscomb	5.00	10.00
17 Laurie Niemi	5.00	10.00
18 Johnny Papit 1952	10.00	20.00
19 James Peebles 1951	6.00	12.00
20 Ed Quirk	5.00	10.00
21 Jim Ricca 1952	10.00	20.00
22 James Staton 1951	6.00	12.00
23 Hugh Taylor	6.00	12.00
24 Joe Tereshinski	5.00	10.00
25 Dick Todd CO 1952	10.00	20.00

1957 Redskins Team Issue 5x7

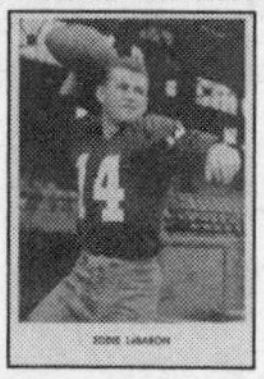

This set of 5x7 photos was issued by the team to fulfill fan requests and for player appearances. Each includes a black and white photo of a Redskins player with just his name below the image. The backs are blank and unnumbered.

COMPLETE SET (12)	75.00	150.00
1 Sam Baker	7.50	15.00
2 Don Bosseler	7.50	15.00
3 Gene Brito	7.50	15.00
4 John Carson	7.50	15.00
5 Chuck Drazenovich	7.50	15.00
6 Ralph Guglielmi	7.50	15.00
7 Dick James	7.50	15.00
8 Eddie LeBaron	12.50	25.00
9 Jim Podoley	7.50	15.00
10 Jim Schrader	7.50	15.00
11 Ed Sutton	7.50	15.00
12 Albert Zagers	7.50	15.00

1957 Redskins Team Issue 8x10

This set of black and white photos was issued by the team for fan requests and public appearances. Each measures roughly 8" by 10 1/4" with a 1/4" white border around all four sides. The team name and player name appear below the photo and the backs are blank and unnumbered.

COMPLETE SET (14)	125.00	250.00
1 Sam Baker	10.00	20.00
2 Gene Brito	10.00	20.00
3 John Carson	10.00	20.00
4 Bob Dee	10.00	20.00
5 Chuck Drazenovich	10.00	20.00
6 Ralph Felton	10.00	20.00
7 Norb Hecker	10.00	20.00
8 Dick James	10.00	20.00
9 Eddie LeBaron	15.00	30.00
10 Ray Lemek	10.00	20.00
11 Volney Peters	10.00	20.00
12 Joe Scudero	10.00	20.00
13 Dick Stanfel	12.50	25.00
14 Lavern Torgeson	10.00	20.00

1958-59 Redskins Matchbooks

Sponsored by First Federal Savings and produced by Universal Match Corp., Washington D.C., these 20 matchcovers measure approximately 1 1/2" by 4 1/2" (when completely folded out). Each front cover features a small black-and-white photo of a popular Washington Redskins player with the Redskins logo and the title "Famous Redskins" on the bottom half and a First Federal Savings advertisement on the top half. A player profile is given at the top of the matchcover back along with the words "This is one of twenty famous Redskins presented for you by your 1st Federal Savings and Loan Association of Washington& Bethesda Branch," followed by the address. The matchbooks are unnumbered and checklisted below in alphabetical order. It is most commonly thought that the set was issued in two ten-cover series over a two-year period. We've included the presumed year of issue after each cover. The matchbooks are very similar to the 1960-61 issue, but can be distinguished by their light gray colored paper stock instead of off-white. The prices given are for full covers (with strikers) missing the actual matches. This is the form in which the matchbooks are most commonly found. Complete books with matches typically carry a 50% premium. Books missing the striker are considered VG at best.

COMPLETE SET (20)	125.00	250.00
1 Steve Bagarus 58	5.00	10.00
2 Cliff Battles 58	10.00	20.00
3 Sammy Baugh 58	20.00	40.00
4 Gene Brito 58	5.00	10.00
5 Jim Castiglia 58	5.00	10.00
6 Al DeMao 58	5.00	10.00
7 Chuck Drazenovich 59	5.00	10.00
8 Bill Dudley 59	10.00	20.00
9 Al Fiorentino 59	5.00	10.00
10 Don Irwin 59	5.00	10.00
11 Eddie LeBaron 58	7.50	15.00
12 Wayne Millner 58	7.50	15.00
13 Wilbur Moore 58	5.00	10.00
14 Jim Schrader 59	5.00	10.00
15 Riley Smith 59	5.00	10.00
16 Mike Sommer 59	5.00	10.00
17 Joe Tereshinski 58	5.00	10.00
18 Dick Todd 59	6.00	12.00
19 Willie Wilkin 59	5.00	10.00
20 Casimir Witucki 59	5.00	10.00

1959 Redskins San Giorgio Flipbooks

This set features members of the Washington Redskins printed on velum type paper stock created in a multi-image action sequence. The set is commonly referenced as the San Giorgio Macaroni Football Flipbooks. Members of the Philadelphia Eagles, Pittsburgh Steelers, and Washington Redskins were produced regionally with 15-players, reportedly, issued per team. Some players were produced in more than one sequence of poses with different captions and/or slightly different photos used. When the flipbooks are still in uncut form (which is most desirable), they measure approximately 5 3/4" by 3 9/16". The sheets are blank backed, in black and white, and provide 14-small numbered pages when cut apart. Collectors were encouraged to cut out each photo and stack them in such a way as to create a moving image of the player when flipped with the fingers. Any additions to this list are appreciated.

1 Sam Baker	100.00	175.00
2 Don Bosseler	90.00	150.00
3 Eddei LeBaron	150.00	250.00
4 Mike Sommer	90.00	150.00

1960-61 Redskins Matchbooks

Sponsored by First Federal Savings and produced by Universal Match Corp., Washington D.C., these 20 matchcovers measure approximately 1 1/2" by 4 1/2" (when completely folded out). Each front cover features a small black-and-white photo of a popular Washington Redskins player with the Redskins logo and the title "Famous Redskins" on the bottom half and a First Federal Savings advertisement on the top half. A player profile is given at the top of the matchcover back along with the words "This is one of twenty famous Redskins presented for you by your 1st Federal Savings and Loan Association of Washington, Bethesda Branch," followed by the address and a Universal Match Corporation company logo. The matchbooks are unnumbered and checklisted below in alphabetical order. It is most commonly thought that the set was issued in two ten-cover series over a two-year period. We've included the presumed year of issue after each cover. The matchbooks are very similar to the 1958-59 issue& but can be distinguished by their off-white colored paper stock instead of light gray. The prices given are for full covers (with strikers) missing the actual matches. This is the form in which the matchbooks are most commonly found. Complete books with matches typically carry a 50% premium. Books missing the striker are considered VG at best.

COMPLETE SET (20)	100.00	200.00
1 Bill Anderson 61	6.00	12.00
2 Don Bosseler 60	6.00	12.00
3 Turk Edwards 60	12.50	25.00
4 Ralph Guglielmi 61	6.00	12.00
5 Bill Hartman 60	5.00	10.00
6 Norb Hecker 61	5.00	10.00
7 Dick James 61	6.00	12.00
8 Charlie Justice 60	10.00	20.00
9 Ray Krouse 61	5.00	10.00
10 Ray Lemek 61	5.00	10.00
11 Tommy Mont 60	5.00	10.00
12 John Olszewski 61	6.00	12.00
13 John Paluck 61	5.00	10.00
14 Jim Peebles 60	5.00	10.00
15 Bo Russell 60	5.00	10.00
16 Jim Schrader 61	5.00	10.00
17 Louis Stephens 61	5.00	10.00
18 Ed Sutton 60	5.00	10.00
19 Bob Toneff 60	6.00	12.00
20 Lavern Torgeson 60	6.00	12.00

1960 Redskins Jay Publishing

This 12-card set features (approximately) 5" by 7" black-and-white player photos. The photos show players in traditional poses with the quarterback preparing to throw, the runner heading downfield, and the defenseman ready for the tackle. These cards were packaged 12 to a packet and originally sold for 25 cents. The backs are blank. The cards are unnumbered and checklisted below in alphabetical order.

COMPLETE SET (12)	40.00	80.00
1 Sam Baker	4.00	8.00
2 Don Bosseler	4.00	8.00
3 Gene Brito	4.00	8.00
4 Johnny Carson	4.00	8.00
5 Chuck Drazenovich	4.00	8.00
6 Ralph Guglielmi	4.00	8.00
7 Dick James	4.00	8.00
8 Eddie LeBaron	6.00	12.00
9 Jim Podoley	4.00	8.00
10 Jim Schrader	4.00	8.00
11 Ed Sutton	4.00	8.00
12 Albert Zagers	4.00	8.00

1961 Redskins Jay Publishing

This 12-card set features 5" by 7" black-and-white player photos. The photos show players in traditional poses with the quarterback preparing to throw, the runner heading downfield, and the defenseman ready for the tackle. These cards were packaged 12 to a packet and originally sold for 25 cents through Jay Publishing's annual football magazine. The backs are blank. The cards are unnumbered and checklisted below in alphabetical order.

COMPLETE SET (12)	50.00	100.00
1 Don Bosseler	5.00	10.00
2 Eagle Day	4.00	8.00
3 Fred Dugan	4.00	8.00
4 Gary Glick	4.00	8.00
5 Sam Horner	4.00	8.00
6 Dick James	5.00	10.00
7 Bob Khayat	4.00	8.00
8 Bill McPeak CO	4.00	8.00
9 Jim Schrader	4.00	8.00
10 Norm Snead	7.50	15.00
11 Bob Toneff	4.00	8.00
12 Ed Vereb	4.00	8.00

1965 Redskins Team Issue

These black and white photos were issued by the Redskins in the mid-1960s. Each was printed on high gloss stock with a blankback and no identifying marks on the fronts. The Redskins often stamped the name of the player on the photo backs.

COMPLETE SET (10)	50.00	100.00
1 Willie Adams (jersey #50)	6.00	12.00
2 Len Hauss (jersey #56)	6.00	12.00
3 Bob Jencks (jersey #81)	6.00	12.00
4 Bob Pellegrini (jersey #53)	6.00	12.00
5 Jim Sleffen (jersey #41)	6.00	12.00
6 Pat Richter (jersey #88)	6.00	12.00
7 Fred Williams (jersey #75)	6.00	12.00
8 Unidentified Player #24	6.00	12.00
9 Unidentified Player #27	6.00	12.00
10 Unidentified Player #71	6.00	12.00

1965 Redskins Volpe Tumblers

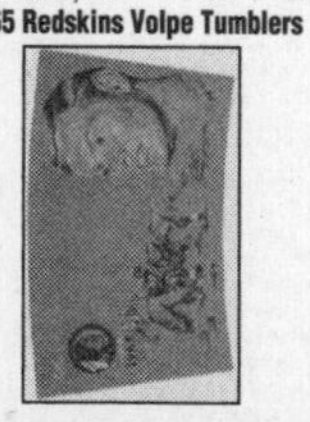

These Redskins artist's renderings were inserted into a plastic cup tumbler produced in 1965. The noted sports artist Volpe created the artwork which includes an action scene and a player portrait. The paper inserts are unnumbered, each measures approximately 5" by 8 1/2" and are curved in the shape required to fit inside the plastic cup. This set is believed to contain up to 12-cups. Any additions to this list are welcomed.

1 Sam Huff	50.00	80.00
2 Sonny Jurgensen	60.00	100.00
3 Paul Krause	30.00	50.00
4 Bobby Mitchell	35.00	60.00
5 John Paluck	25.00	40.00
6 Joe Rutgens	25.00	40.00
7 Charley Taylor	35.00	60.00

1966 Redskins Team Issue

This set of photos was issued in the mid-1960s and features a black and white photo of a Redskins player on each. The photos measure roughly 5" by 7" and include the player's name, his position (spelled out), and the team name below the each player image. The backs are blank. A complete set is thought to include 12-photos, therefore any additions to this list are appreciated.

COMPLETE SET (6)	40.00	80.00
1 Chris Hanburger	7.50	15.00
2 Sonny Jurgensen	12.50	25.00
3 Bobby Mitchell	10.00	20.00
4 Brig Owens	6.00	12.00
5 Joe Rutgens	6.00	12.00
6 Ron Snidow	6.00	12.00

1969 Redskins High's Dairy

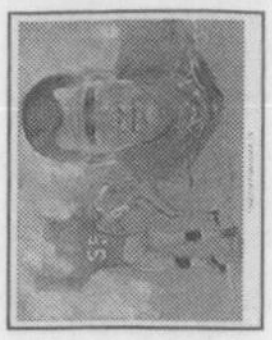

This eight-card set was sponsored by High's Dairy Stores and measures approximately 8" by 10". The front has white borders and a full color painting of the player by Alex Fournier, with the player's signature near the bottom of the portrait. The plain white back gives biographical and statistical information on the player on its left side, and information about Fournier on the right. Reportedly 70,000 of each photo was produced. Collectors could receive a free card for each two half gallons of milk they purchased or could buy them from High's Dairy Stores for ten cents each. The cards are unnumbered and checklisted below in alphabetical order. Reportedly, Bobby Mitchell was drawn for this set but never printed as he retired before the 1969 season began.

COMPLETE SET (8)	75.00	125.00
1 Chris Hanburger	7.50	15.00
2 Len Hauss	6.00	12.00
3 Sam Huff	10.00	20.00
4 Sonny Jurgensen	20.00	35.00
5 Carl Kammerer	6.00	12.00
6 Brig Owens	6.00	12.00
7 Pat Richter	6.00	12.00
8 Charley Taylor	10.00	20.00

1971 Redskins Team Issue

This set of black and white player photos was released around 1971. Each measures roughly 8" by 10 1/8" and features the player in the yellow Redskins helmet. No player names are identified on the fronts but either a stamped or written name was often included on the, otherwise blank, cardbacks. They look very similar to the 1973 set but can be identified by the yellow player helmets.

COMPLETE SET (20)	100.00	200.00
1 Verlon Biggs (jersey #89)	5.00	10.00
2 Larry Brown (jersey #43)	6.00	12.00
3 George Burman (jersey #58)	5.00	10.00
4 Boyd Dowler (jersey #86)	6.00	12.00
5 Pat Fischer (jersey #37)	5.00	10.00
6 Chris Hanburger (jersey #55)	6.00	12.00
7 Charlie Harraway (jersey #31)	5.00	10.00
8 Jon Jaqua (jersey #48)	5.00	10.00
9 Sonny Jurgensen (jersey #9)	10.00	20.00
10 Billy Kilmer (jersey #17)	7.50	15.00
11 Curt Knight (jersey #5)	5.00	10.00
12 Tommy Mason (jersey #20)	5.00	10.00
13 Clifton McNeil (jersey #85)	5.00	10.00
14 Brig Owens (jersey #23)	5.00	10.00
15 Jack Pardee (jersey #32)	6.00	12.00
16 Jerry Smith (jersey #87)	5.00	10.00
17 Diron Talbert (jersey #72)	5.00	10.00
18 Charley Taylor (jersey #42)	7.50	15.00
19 Ted Vactor (jersey #22)	5.00	10.00
20 John Wilbur (jersey #60)	5.00	10.00

1972 Redskins Characatures

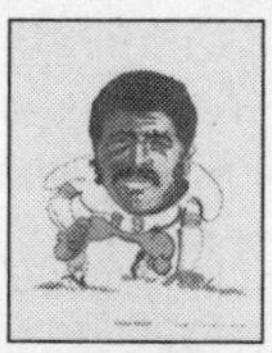

This set was produced by Dick Shuman and Compu-Set, Inc. in 1972 and features players of the Washington Redskins. Each card measures approxiamtely 8" by 10" and features a characature drawing of the player with his name printed below. The cards are unnumbered and blankbacked.

COMPLETE SET (31)	200.00	350.00
1 Mack Alston	6.00	12.00
2 Mike Bass	7.50	15.00
3 Verlon Biggs	6.00	12.00
4 Mike Bragg	6.00	12.00
5 Larry Brown	10.00	20.00
6 Speedy Duncan	7.50	15.00
7 Pat Fischer	7.50	15.00
8 Chris Hanburger	7.50	15.00
9 Charlie Harraway	6.00	12.00
10 Len Hauss	6.00	12.00
11 Roy Jefferson	7.50	15.00
12 Sonny Jurgensen	12.50	25.00
13 Billy Kilmer	10.00	20.00
14 Curt Knight	6.00	12.00
15 Ron McDole	6.00	12.00
16 Clifton McNeil	6.00	12.00
17 George Nock	6.00	12.00
18 Brig Owens	6.00	12.00
19 Jack Pardee	7.50	15.00
20 Richie Petitbon	7.50	15.00
21 Myron Pottios	6.00	12.00
22 Walter Rock	6.00	12.00
23 Ray Schoenke	6.00	12.00
24 Manny Sistrunk	6.00	12.00
25 Jerry Smith	6.00	12.00
26 Jim Snowden	6.00	12.00
27 Diron Talbert	6.00	12.00
28 Charley Taylor	10.00	20.00
29 Ted Vactor	6.00	12.00
30 John Wilbur	6.00	12.00
31 Cover Card Jack Pardee Mike Bass Manny Sistrunk Chris Hanburger	7.50	15.00

1972 Redskins Picture Pack

This set of 8 1/2" by 11" photos was distributed in two separate "picture packs" with 14-defensive players in one and 16-offensive players in the other envelope. The fronts feature a player photo with his jersey number and name below the photo and the team name below that. The backs are blank and unnumbered.

COMPLETE SET (30)	75.00	150.00
1 Mack Alston	2.50	5.00
2 Mike Bass	2.50	5.00
3 Verlon Biggs	2.50	5.00
4 Larry Brown	4.00	8.00
5 Bill Brundige	2.50	5.00
6 Bob Brunet	2.50	5.00
7 Pat Fischer	2.50	5.00
8 Chris Hanburger	3.00	6.00
9 Charlie Harraway	2.50	5.00
10 Len Hauss	2.50	5.00
11 Terry Hermeling	2.50	5.00
12 Jon Jaqua	2.50	5.00
13 Roy Jefferson	3.00	6.00
14 Sonny Jurgensen	6.00	12.00
15 Billy Kilmer	5.00	10.00
16 Paul Laaveg	2.50	5.00
17 Harold McLinton	2.50	5.00
18 Ron McDole	2.50	5.00
19 Clifton McNeil	2.50	5.00
20 Brig Owens	2.50	5.00
21 Jack Pardee	3.00	6.00
22 Myron Pottios	2.50	5.00
23 Walter Rock	2.50	5.00
24 Manny Sistrunk	2.50	5.00
25 Jerry Smith	2.50	5.00
26 Diron Talbert	2.50	5.00
27 Charley Taylor	5.00	10.00
28 Roosevelt Taylor	3.00	6.00
29 Ted Vactor	2.50	5.00
30 John Wilbur	2.50	5.00

1973 Redskins McDonald's

These 11" by 14" color posters were sponsored by and distributed through McDonald's stores. Each includes an artist's rendering of one Redskins player along with the year and the "McDonald's Superstars Collector's Series" notation below the picture. Reprints can often be found of these prints but can be identified by the new white flat finish paper stock. The originals were printed on glossy cream colored stock.

COMPLETE SET (4)	60.00	100.00
1 Chris Hanburger	12.00	20.00
2 Sonny Jurgensen	25.00	40.00
3 Billy Kilmer	15.00	25.00
4 Charley Taylor	15.00	25.00

1973 Redskins Newspaper Posters

These oversized (roughly 14 1/4" by 21 1/2") posters were inserted into issues of The Sunday Star and The Washington Daily News throughout the 1973 season. Each poster features an artist's rendering of a player with just his name printed inside the image. Within the border below the image are the names of the two newspapers. The backs feature newsprint from another page of the paper. There were thought to have been 26-different posters produced. Any additions to this list are appreciated.

COMPLETE SET (24)	175.00	300.00
1 George Allen CO	12.50	25.00
2 Mike Bass	6.00	12.00
3 Verlon Biggs	6.00	12.00
4 Mike Bragg	6.00	12.00
5 Larry Brown	10.00	20.00
6 Speedy Duncan	7.50	15.00
7 Pat Fischer	7.50	15.00
8 Chris Hanburger	7.50	15.00
9 Charlie Harraway	6.00	12.00
10 Len Hauss	6.00	12.00
11 Roy Jefferson	6.00	12.00
12 Sonny Jurgensen	12.50	25.00
13 Billy Kilmer	10.00	20.00
14 Curt Knight	6.00	12.00
15 Paul Laaveg	6.00	12.00
16 Ron McDole	6.00	12.00
17 Brig Owens	6.00	12.00
18 Walter Rock	6.00	12.00
19 Ray Schoenke	6.00	12.00
20 Manny Sistrunk	6.00	12.00
21 Jerry Smith	6.00	12.00
22 Diron Talbert	6.00	12.00
23 Charley Taylor	10.00	20.00
24 Roosevelt Taylor	7.50	15.00

1973 Redskins Team Issue

This set of black and white player photos was released around 1973. Each measures roughly 8" by 10 1/8" and features the player in the red Redskins helmet in a kneeling pose. No player names are identified on the fronts but either a stamped or written name was often included on the, otherwise blank, cardbacks. They look very similar to the 1971 set but can be identified by the red player helmets.

COMPLETE SET (43)	175.00	300.00
1 George Allen CO	10.00	20.00
2 Mike Bass (jersey #41)	5.00	10.00
3 Verlon Biggs (jersey #86)	5.00	10.00
4 Mike Bragg (jersey #4)	5.00	10.00
5 Larry Brown (jersey #43)	6.00	12.00
6 Bill Brundige (jersey #77)	5.00	10.00
7 Bob Brunet (jersey #26)	5.00	10.00
8 Speedy Duncan (jersey #45)	5.00	10.00
9 Brad Dusek (jersey #59)	5.00	10.00
10 Pat Fischer (jersey #37)	5.00	10.00
11 Frank Grant (jersey #46)	5.00	10.00
12 Charlie Harraway (jersey #31)	5.00	10.00
13 Chris Hanburger (jersey #55)	6.00	12.00
14 Mike Hancock (jersey #84)	5.00	10.00
15 Len Hauss (jersey #56)	5.00	10.00
16 Terry Hermeling (jersey #75)	5.00	10.00
17 Mike Hull (jersey #25)	5.00	10.00
18 Dennis Johnson (jersey #61)	5.00	10.00
19 Jimmie Jones (jersey #82)	5.00	10.00
20 Sonny Jurgensen (jersey #9)	10.00	20.00
21 Billy Kilmer (jersey #17)	7.50	15.00
22 Curt Knight (jersey #5)	5.00	10.00
23 Paul Laaveg (jersey #73)	5.00	10.00
24 Bill Malinchak (jersey #24)	5.00	10.00
25 Ron McDole (jersey #79)	5.00	10.00
26 Harold McLinton (jersey #53)	5.00	10.00
27 Herb Mul-Key (jersey #28)	5.00	10.00
28 Brig Owens (jersey #23)	5.00	10.00
29 Richie Petitbon (jersey #16)	5.00	10.00
30 Myron Pottios (jersey #66)	5.00	10.00
31 Walter Rock (jersey #76)	5.00	10.00
32 Dan Ryczek (jersey #51)	5.00	10.00
33 Ray Schoenke (jersey #62)	5.00	10.00
34 Manny Sistrunk (jersey #64)	5.00	10.00
35 Jerry Smith (jersey #87)	5.00	10.00
36 Diron Talbert (jersey #72)	5.00	10.00
37 Charley Taylor (jersey #42)	7.50	15.00
38 Roosevelt Taylor (jersey #22)	6.00	12.00
39 Duane Thomas (jersey #47)	5.00	10.00
40 Russell Tillman (jersey #67)	5.00	10.00
41 Ted Vactor (jersey #29)	5.00	10.00
42 John Wilbur (jersey #60)	5.00	10.00
43 Sam Wyche (jersey #18)	6.00	12.00

1973 Redskins Team Issue Color

The NFLPA worked with many teams in 1973 to issued photo packs to be sold at stadium concession stands. Each measures approximately 7" by 8-5/8" and features a color player photo with a blank back. A small sheet with a player checklist was included in each 6-photo pack.

COMPLETE SET (6)	25.00	40.00
1 Larry Brown	4.00	8.00
2 Chris Hanburger	4.00	8.00
3 Sonny Jurgensen	6.00	12.00
4 Billy Kilmer	5.00	10.00
5 Charley Taylor	5.00	10.00
6 Duane Thomas	4.00	8.00

1974 Redskins McDonald's

For the second year, these 11" by 14" color posters were sponsored by and distributed through McDonald's stores. Each includes an artist's rendering of a Redskins player along with the year and the "McDonald's Superstars Collector's Series" notation below the picture. Reprints can often be found of these prints but can be identified by the new white flat finish paper stock. The originals were printed on glossy cream colored stock.

COMPLETE SET (4)	35.00	60.00
1 Larry Brown	12.00	20.00
2 Roy Jefferson	12.00	20.00
3 Herb Mul-Key	10.00	15.00
4 Diron Talbert	10.00	15.00

1977 Redskins Team Issue

This set of photos was released by the Washington Redskins. Each measures roughly 5" by 7" and includes a player photo on the front with a 1/2" white border on the top and bottom and a 3/8" border on the left and right. There is no player identification except for the facsimile autograph that appears on some of the photos. The backs are blank and unnumbered. The photos are similar in appearance to the 1979 issue. Any additions to this list are appreciated.

COMPLETE SET (7)	30.00	60.00
1 Eddie Brown (Jersey #25, with facsimile auto)	4.00	8.00
2 Chris Hanburger (Jersey #55, no facsimile auto)	5.00	10.00
3 Terry Hermeling (Jersey #75, with facsimile auto)	4.00	8.00
4 Billy Kilmer (Jersey #17, with facsimile auto)	6.00	12.00
5 Joe Theismann (Jersey #7, no facsimile auto)	10.00	20.00
6 Pete Wysocki (Jersey #50, with facsimile auto)	4.00	8.00
7 Jersey #57 (with facsimile auto)	4.00	8.00

1979 Redskins Team Issue

This set of photos was released by the Washington Redskins. Each measures roughly 5" by 7" and includes a player photo on the front with a 1/4" white border on all four sides. There is no player identification except for the facsimile autograph that appears on the photo. The backs are blank and unnumbered. The photos are similar in appearance to the 1977 issue.

COMPLETE SET (14)	50.00	100.00
1 Coy Bacon	4.00	8.00
2 Mike Curtis	5.00	10.00
3 Fred Dean	5.00	10.00
4 Greg Dubinetz	4.00	8.00
5 Phil DuBois	4.00	8.00
6 Ted Fritsch	4.00	8.00
7 Don Harris	4.00	8.00
8 Don Hover	4.00	8.00
9 Benny Malone	4.00	8.00
10 Kim McQuilken	4.00	8.00
11 Jack Pardee CO	5.00	10.00
12 Paul Smith	4.00	8.00
13 Diron Talbert	4.00	8.00
14 Joe Theismann	10.00	20.00

1981 Redskins Frito Lay Schedules

This 30-card bi-fold schedule set sponsored by Frito Lay measures approximately standard card size when folded and opens to measure 3-1/2" by 7-1/2." Each schedule features a color action shot of a Washington Redskins player inside with sponsor logos on the back. When completely opened, the left panel contains the 1981 schedule. The center panel features a color action player shot with the player's name, biography, and profile appearing on another fold. The regular season schedule is printed on the right inside panel. The schedules are unnumbered and checklisted below in alphabetical order.

COMPLETE SET (30)	50.00	100.00
1 Coy Bacon	2.00	5.00
2 Perry Brooks	1.50	4.00
3 Dave Butz	2.00	5.00
4 Rickey Claitt	1.50	4.00
5 Monte Coleman	2.00	5.00
6 Mike Connell	1.50	4.00
7 Brad Dusek	2.00	5.00
8 Ike Forte	1.50	4.00
9 Clarence Harmon	1.50	4.00
10 Terry Hermeling	1.50	4.00
11 Wilbur Jackson	1.50	4.00
12 Mike Kruczek	1.50	4.00
13 Bob Kuziel	1.50	4.00
14 Joe Lavender	2.00	5.00
15 Karl Lorch	1.50	4.00
16 John McDaniel	1.50	4.00
17 Rich Milot	1.50	4.00
18 Art Monk	2.50	6.00
19 Mark Moseley	2.00	5.00
20 Mark Murphy	2.00	5.00
21 Mike Nelms	1.50	4.00
22 Neal Olkewicz	1.50	4.00
23 Lemar Parrish	2.00	5.00
24 Tony Peters	1.50	4.00
25 Ron Saul	1.50	4.00
26 George Starke	1.50	4.00
27 Joe Theismann	2.50	6.00
28 Ricky Thompson	1.50	4.00
29 Don Warren	2.00	5.00
30 Jeris White	1.50	4.00

1982 Redskins Frito Lay Schedules

This 15-card bi-fold schedule set measures the standard card size when folded and opens to measure 3-1/2" by 7-1/2." Each schedule features a color action shot of a Washington Redskins player inside with sponsor logos on the back. When completely opened, the left panel contains the preseason and postseason schedules. The center panel features a color action player shot with the player's name, biography, and profile appearing on another fold. The regular season schedule is printed on the right inside panel. The schedules are unnumbered and checklisted below in alphabetical order.

COMPLETE SET (15)	20.00	40.00
1 Dave Butz	1.50	4.00
2 Monte Coleman	1.50	4.00
3 Brad Dusek	1.25	3.00
4 Joe Lavender	1.50	4.00
5 Art Monk	2.00	5.00
6 Mark Moseley	1.50	4.00
7 Mark Murphy	1.50	4.00
8 Mike Nelms	1.25	3.00
9 Neal Olkewicz	1.25	3.00
10 Tony Peters	1.25	3.00
11 John Riggins	2.50	6.00
12 George Starke	1.25	3.00
13 Joe Theismann	2.00	5.00
14 Don Warren	1.25	3.00
15 Joe Washington	1.50	4.00

1982 Redskins Police

The 1982 Washington Redskins set contains 15 numbered (in very small print on the card backs) full-color cards. The cards measure approximately 2 5/8" by 4 1/8". The set was sponsored by Frito-Lay, the local law enforcement agency, the Washington Redskins, and an organization known as PACT (Police and Citizens Together). Logos of Frito-Lay and PACT appear on the backs of the cards as do "Redskins PACT Tips". A Redskins helmet appears on the fronts of the cards.

COMPLETE SET (15)	4.00	10.00
1 Dave Butz	.30	.75
2 Art Monk	.75	2.00
3 Mark Murphy	.20	.50
4 Monte Coleman	.30	.75
5 Mark Moseley	.30	.75
6 George Starke	.20	.50
7 Perry Brooks	.20	.50
8 Joe Washington	.30	.75
9 Don Warren	.30	.75
10 Joe Lavender	.20	.50
11 Joe Theismann	.75	2.00
12 Tony Peters	.20	.50
13 Neal Olkewicz	.20	.50
14 Mike Nelms	.20	.50
15 John Riggins	.75	2.00

1983 Redskins Frito Lay Schedules

This 15-card bi-fold schedule set measures 2 1/2" by 3 1/2" when folded and features the Super Bowl trophy and a Redskins helmet on front with sponsor logos on the back. When completely opened, the left panel contains the preseason and post season schedules. The center panel features a color action player shot with the player's name, biography, and profile appearing on another fold. The regular season schedule is printed on the right inside panel. The schedules are unnumbered and checklisted below in alphabetical order.

COMPLETE SET (15)	20.00	40.00
1 Charlie Brown	1.50	4.00
2 Dave Butz	1.50	4.00
3 The Hogs	1.50	4.00
4 Dexter Manley	1.50	4.00
5 Rich Milot	1.25	3.00
6 Art Monk	2.00	5.00
7 Mark Moseley	1.50	4.00
8 Mark Murphy	1.25	3.00
9 Mike Nelms	1.25	3.00
10 Neal Olkewicz	1.25	3.00
11 Tony Peters	1.25	3.00
12 John Riggins	2.50	6.00
13 Joe Theismann	2.00	5.00
14 Joe Washington	1.50	4.00
15 Jeris White	1.25	3.00

1983 Redskins Police

The 1983 Washington Redskins Police set consists of 16 numbered cards sponsored by Frito-Lay, the local law enforcement agency, PACT, and the Redskins. The cards measure 2 5/8" by 4 1/8" and were given out one per week (and are numbered according to that order) by the police department, except for week number 10, whose card featured Jeris White. White sat out the season and his card was not distributed; hence, it is available in lesser quantity than other cards in the set. Interestingly enough, the seventh week featured the issuance of Joe Theisman's card, who coincidentally, wears uniform number 7. The final card in this set, issued the 16th week, featured John Riggins. Logos of Frito-Lay and PACT appear on the back along with "Redskins/PACT Tips." The backs are printed in black with red accent on white card stock. There were some cards produced with a maroon color back. Although these maroon backs are more difficult to find, they are valued essentially the same.

COMPLETE SET (16)	4.00	10.00
1 Joe Washington	.40	1.00
2 The Hogs (Offensive Line)	.30	.75
3 Mark Moseley	.40	1.00
4 Monte Coleman	.20	.50
5 Mike Nelms	.20	.50
6 Neal Olkewicz	.20	.50
7 Joe Theismann	1.00	2.50
8 Charlie Brown	.30	.75
9 Dave Butz	.30	.75
10 Jeris White SP	.60	1.50
11 Mark Murphy	.20	.50
12 Dexter Manley	.30	.75
13 Art Monk	1.00	2.50
14 Rich Milot	.20	.50
15 Vernon Dean	.20	.50
16 John Riggins	1.00	2.50

1984 Redskins Frito Lay Schedules

This 15-card bi-fold schedule set measures the standard card size when folded and opens to measure 3-1/2" by 7-1/2." Each schedule features a color action shot of a Washington Redskins player inside with sponsor logos on the back. When completely opened, the left panel contains the preseason and postseason schedules. The center panel features a color action player shot with the player's name, biography, and profile appearing on another fold. The regular season schedule is printed on the right inside panel. The schedules are unnumbered and checklisted below in alphabetical order.

COMPLETE SET (15)	20.00	40.00
1 Charlie Brown	1.50	4.00
2 Dave Butz	1.50	4.00
3 Ken Coffey	1.25	3.00
4 Clint Didier	1.25	3.00
5 Darryl Grant	1.25	3.00
6 Darrell Green	2.00	5.00
7 Jeff Hayes	1.25	3.00
8 The Hogs	1.50	4.00
9 Rich Milot	1.25	3.00
10 Art Monk	2.00	5.00
11 Mark Murphy	1.25	3.00
12 John Riggins	2.50	6.00
13 Joe Theismann	2.00	5.00
14 Don Warren	1.50	4.00
15 Joe Washington	1.50	4.00

1984 Redskins Police

This numbered (on back) set of 16 cards features the Washington Redskins. Cards measure approximately 2 5/8" by 4 1/8". Backs are printed in black ink with a maroon accent. The set was sponsored by Frito-Lay, the local law enforcement agency, and the Washington Redskins.

COMPLETE SET (16)	3.00	8.00
1 John Riggins	.60	1.50
2 Darryl Grant	.15	.40
3 Art Monk	.60	1.50
4 Neal Olkewicz	.15	.40
5 The Hogs	.20	.50
6 Jeff Hayes	.15	.40
7 Joe Theismann	.50	1.25
8 Clint Didier	.15	.40
9 Mark Murphy	.15	.40
10 Don Warren	.20	.50
11 Darrell Green	.40	1.00
12 Dave Butz	.20	.50
13 Ken Coffey	.15	.40
14 Rich Milot	.15	.40
15 Charlie Brown	.20	.50
16 Joe Washington	.20	.50

1985 Redskins Police

This 16-card set of Washington Redskins is numbered on the back. Cards measure approximately 2 5/8" by 4 1/8" and the backs contain a "McGruff Says". Each player's uniform number is given on the card front. The set was sponsored by Frito-Lay, the Redskins, and local law enforcement agencies. Card backs are written in maroon and black on white card stock.

COMPLETE SET (16)	2.50	6.00
1 Darrell Green	.30	.75
2 Clint Didier	.15	.40
3 Neal Olkewicz	.15	.40
4 Darryl Grant	.15	.40
5 Joe Jacoby	.20	.50
6 Vernon Dean	.15	.40
7 Joe Theismann	.40	1.00
8 Mel Kaufman	.15	.40
9 Calvin Muhammad	.15	.40
10 Dexter Manley	.20	.50
11 John Riggins	.40	1.00
12 Mark May	.20	.50
13 Dave Butz	.20	.50
14 Art Monk	.50	1.25
15 Russ Grimm	.20	.50
16 Charles Mann	.20	.50

1986 Redskins Frito Lay Schedules

These schedules feature all-time great members of the Redskins in celebration of the team's 50th anniversary in Washington. They are standard schedule size and were sponsored by Frito Lay. The schedules measure 2 1/2" by 3 1/2" when folded and opens to approximately 3 1/2" by 7 1/2." The schedules feature the Redskins' 50th Anniversary logo against a yellow background on the front with Frito-Lay's sponsor logos on the back. When completely opened the left panel contains the preseason and post season schedules with the center panel featuring the player's photo. The regular season schedule is printed on the right inside panel with the player's profile featured on the other side. Each schedule is unnumbered and checklisted below in alphabetical order.

COMPLETE SET (16)	15.00	30.00
1 Cliff Battles	1.25	3.00
2 Sammy Baugh	1.50	4.00
3 Larry Brown	1.00	2.50
4 Bill Dudley	1.25	3.00
5 Turk Edwards	1.00	2.50
6 Pat Fischer	1.00	2.50
7 Chris Hanburger	1.00	2.50
8 Len Hauss	1.00	2.50
9 Sam Huff	1.50	4.00
10 Ken Houston	1.25	3.00
11 Sonny Jurgensen	1.50	4.00
12 Billy Kilmer	1.25	3.00
13 Wayne Millner	1.25	3.00
14 Bobby Mitchell	1.50	4.00
15 Brig Owens	1.00	2.50
16 Charley Taylor	.75	2.00

1986 Redskins Police

This 16-card set of Washington Redskins is numbered on the back. Cards measure approximately 2 5/8" by 4 1/8" and the backs contain a "Crime Prevention Tip". Each player's uniform number is given on the card front. The set was sponsored by Frito Lay, the Redskins, WMAL-AM63, and local law enforcement agencies. Card backs are printed in maroon and black on white card stock. The set commemorates the Redskins 50th Anniversary as a team.

COMPLETE SET (16)	2.50	6.00
1 Darrell Green	.30	.75
2 Joe Jacoby	.20	.50
3 Charles Mann	.20	.50
4 Jay Schroeder	.20	.50
5 Raphel Cherry	.15	.40
6 Russ Grimm	.20	.50
7 Mel Kaufman	.15	.40
8 Gary Clark	.50	1.25
9 Vernon Dean	.15	.40
10 Mark May	.20	.50
11 Dave Butz	.20	.50
12 Jeff Bostic	.20	.50
13 Dean Hamel	.15	.40
14 Dexter Manley	.20	.50
15 George Rogers	.20	.50
16 Art Monk	.40	1.00

1987 Redskins Ace Fact Pack

This 33-card set measures approximately 2 1/4" by 3 5/8" and features members of the Washington Redskins. This set was made in West Germany (by Ace Fact Pack) and the card design features rounded corners. We have checklisted the players portrayed in the set in alphabetical order.

COMPLETE SET (33)	100.00	200.00
1 Jeff Bostic	2.50	6.00
2 Dave Butz	2.50	6.00
3 Gary Clark	7.50	20.00
4 Monte Coleman	2.50	6.00
5 Vernon Dean	1.25	3.00
6 Clint Didier	1.25	3.00
7 Darryl Grant	2.50	6.00
8 Darrell Green	12.50	25.00
9 Russ Grimm	2.50	6.00
10 Joe Jacoby	2.50	6.00
11 Curtis Jordan	1.25	3.00
12 Dexter Manley	2.50	6.00
13 Charles Mann	2.50	6.00
14 Mark May	2.50	6.00
15 Rich Milot	1.25	3.00
16 Art Monk	20.00	50.00
17 Neal Olkewicz	1.25	3.00
18 George Rogers	2.50	6.00
19 Jay Schroeder	2.50	6.00
20 R.C. Thielemann	1.25	3.00
21 Alvin Walton	1.25	3.00
22 Don Warren	2.50	6.00
23 Redskins Helmet	1.25	3.00
24 Redskins Information	1.25	3.00
25 Redskins Uniform	1.25	3.00
26 Game Record Holders	1.25	3.00
27 Season Record Holders	1.25	3.00
28 Career Record Holders	1.25	3.00
29 Record 1967-86	1.25	3.00
30 1986 Team Statistics	1.25	3.00
31 All-Time Greats	1.25	3.00
32 Roll of Honour	1.25	3.00
33 Robert F. Kennedy Stadium	1.25	3.00

1987 Redskins Frito Lay Schedules

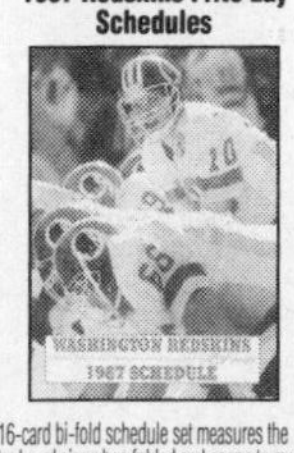

This 16-card bi-fold schedule set measures the standard card size when folded and opens to measure 3-1/2" by 7-1/2." Each schedule features a color action shot of a Washington Redskins player on the inside with sponsor logos on the back and Jay Schroeder on the front. When completely opened, the inside contains the season schedule. The schedules are unnumbered and checklisted below in alphabetical order.

COMPLETE SET (16)	15.00	30.00
1 Jeff Bostic	1.25	3.00
2 Kelvin Bryant	1.25	3.00
3 Dave Butz	1.25	3.00
4 Gary Clark	1.25	3.00
5 Steve Cox	1.00	2.50
6 Clint Didier	1.00	2.50
7 Darryl Grant	1.00	2.50
8 Darrell Green	1.25	3.00
9 Joe Jacoby	1.25	3.00
10 Dexter Manley	1.25	3.00
11 Charles Mann	1.25	3.00
12 Mark May	1.00	2.50
13 Art Monk	1.50	4.00
14 Jay Schroeder	1.00	2.50
15 Alvin Walton	1.00	2.50
16 Don Warren	1.00	2.50

1987 Redskins Police

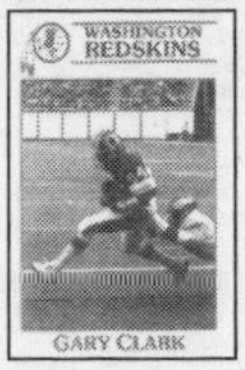

This 16-card set of Washington Redskins is numbered on the back. The cards measure approximately 2 5/8" by 4 1/8" and the backs contain a "McGruff Says" crime prevention tip. The set was sponsored by Frito Lay and PACT (Police and Citizens Together). Card backs are written in red and black on white card stock. The cards were given out one per week in the greater Washington metropolitan area.

COMPLETE SET (16)	2.00	5.00
1 Joe Jacoby	.15	.40
2 Gary Clark	.30	.75
3 Dexter Manley	.15	.40
4 Darrell Green	.15	.40
5 Alvin Walton	.10	.30
6 Clint Didier	.10	.30
7 Art Monk	.40	1.00
8 Darryl Grant	.10	.30
9 Kelvin Bryant	.15	.40
10 Jay Schroeder	.15	.40
11 Don Warren	.15	.40
12 Steve Cox	.10	.30
13 Mark May	.15	.40
14 Jeff Bostic	.15	.40
15 Charles Mann	.15	.40
16 Dave Butz	.15	.40

1988 Redskins Frito Lay Schedules

This 16-card bi-fold schedule set measures 2 1/2" by 3 1/2" when folded and opens to approximately 3 1/2" by 7 1/2." The schedules feature the Super Bowl trophy on front against a maroon background with Frito-Lay sponsor logos on the back. When completely opened the left panel contains the preseason schedule and the center panel features a color action player shot with the player's name, biography, and profile appearing on another fold. The regular season schedule is printed on the right inside panel. Each schedule is unnumbered and checklisted below in alphabetical order.

COMPLETE SET (16)	15.00	30.00
1 Jeff Bostic	1.00	2.50
2 Dave Butz	1.00	2.50
3 Gary Clark	1.25	3.00
4 Brian Davis	1.00	2.50
5 Joe Jacoby	1.00	2.50
6 Markus Koch	1.00	2.50
7 Charles Mann	1.25	3.00
8 Wilber Marshall	1.25	3.00
9 Mark May	1.00	2.50
10 Raleigh McKenzie	1.00	2.50
11 Art Monk	1.50	4.00
12 Ricky Sanders	1.25	3.00
13 Alvin Walton	1.00	2.50
14 Don Warren	1.00	2.50
15 Barry Wilburn	1.00	2.50
16 Doug Williams	.60	1.50

1988 Redskins Police

The 1988 Police Washington Redskins set contains 16 player cards measuring approximately 2 5/8" by 4 1/8". The fronts feature color action photos. The backs feature career highlights and safety tips. The Redskins team name appearing above the photo on the card front differentiates this set from other similar-looking Police Redskins sets.

COMPLETE SET (16)	2.00	5.00
1 Jeff Bostic	.15	.40
2 Dave Butz	.15	.40
3 Gary Clark	.30	.75
4 Brian Davis	.10	.30
5 Joe Jacoby	.15	.40
6 Markus Koch	.10	.30
7 Charles Mann	.15	.40
8 Wilber Marshall	.15	.40
9 Mark May	.15	.40
10 Raleigh McKenzie	.10	.30
11 Art Monk	.40	1.00
12 Ricky Sanders	.30	.75
13 Alvin Walton	.10	.30
14 Don Warren	.15	.40
15 Barry Wilburn	.10	.30
16 Doug Williams	.30	.75

1989 Redskins Mobil Schedules

This 16-card bi-fold schedule set sponsored by Mobil Oil measures the standard card size when folded and opens to measure 3-1/2" by 7-1/2." Each schedule features a color action shot of a Washington Redskins player with sponsor logos on the back. When completely opened, the inside contains the season schedule. The schedules are unnumbered and checklisted below in alphabetical order.

COMPLETE SET (16)	5.00	12.00
1 Ravin Caldwell	.30	.75
2 Gary Clark	.40	1.00
3 Monte Coleman	.30	.75
4 Brian Davis	.30	.75
5 Joe Jacoby	.40	1.00
6 Jim Lachey	.40	1.00
7 Chip Lohmiller	.30	.75
8 Charles Mann	.40	1.00
9 Wilber Marshall	.40	1.00
10 Mark May	.40	1.00
11 Raleigh McKenzie	.30	.75
12 Art Monk	.60	1.50
13 Mark Rypien	.40	1.00
14 Ricky Sanders	.30	.75
15 Don Warren	.30	.75
16 Doug Williams	.40	1.00

1989 Redskins Police

The 1989 Police Washington Redskins set contains 16 cards measuring approximately 2 5/8" by 4 1/8". The fronts have maroon borders and color action photos; the vertically oriented backs have safety tips, bios, and career highlights. These cards were printed on very thin stock. The cards are unnumbered, so therefore are listed below according to uniform number.

COMPLETE SET (16)	2.00	5.00
11 Mark Rypien	.25	.60
17 Doug Williams	.25	.60
21 Earnest Byner	.15	.40
22 Jamie Morris	.10	.30
28 Darrell Green	.15	.40
34 Brian Davis	.10	.30
37 Gerald Riggs	.15	.40
50 Ravin Caldwell	.10	.30
52 Neal Olkewicz	.10	.30
58 Wilber Marshall	.15	.40
73 Mark May	.15	.40
74 Markus Koch	.10	.30
81 Art Monk	.40	1.00
83 Ricky Sanders	.25	.60
84 Gary Clark	.30	.75
85 Don Warren	.15	.40

1990 Redskins Mobil Schedules

This 16-card bi-fold schedule set sponsored by Mobil Oil measures the standard card size when folded and opens to measure 3-1/2" by 7-1/2." Each schedule features a color action shot of a Washington Redskins player with sponsor logos on the back. When completely opened, the inside contains the season schedule. The schedules are unnumbered and checklisted below in alphabetical order.

COMPLETE SET (16)	4.80	12.00
1 Jeff Bostic	.30	.75
2 Earnest Byner	.40	1.00
3 Gary Clark	.40	1.00
4 Darryl Grant	.30	.75
5 Darrell Green	.40	1.00
6 Jim Lachey	.30	.75
7 Chip Lohmiller	.40	1.00
8 Charles Mann	.40	1.00
9 Wilber Marshall	.40	1.00
10 Ralf Mojsiejenko	.30	.75
11 Art Monk	.60	1.50
12 Gerald Riggs	.40	1.00
13 Mark Rypien	.40	1.00
14 Ricky Sanders	.40	1.00
15 Alvin Walton	.30	.75
16 Don Warren	.30	.75

1990 Redskins Police

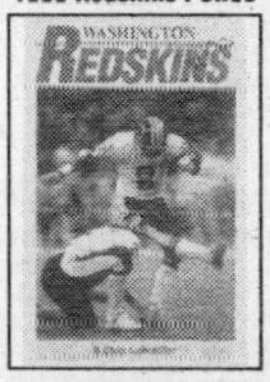

This 16-card set, which measures approximately 2 5/8" by 4 1/8", features members of the 1990 Washington Redskins. This set features white borders surrounding full-color photos on the front and biographical information on the back along with a safety tip. The set was sponsored by Mobil Oil, PACT (Police and Citizens Together), and Fox-5 of Washington WTIC. We have checklisted this set alphabetically.

COMPLETE SET (16)	2.00	5.00
1 Todd Bowles	.08	.25
2 Earnest Byner	.14	.35
3 Ravin Caldwell	.08	.25
4 Gary Clark	.25	.60
5 Darrell Green	.14	.35
6 Jimmie Johnson	.08	.25
7 Jim Lachey	.14	.35
8 Chip Lohmiller	.14	.35
9 Charles Mann	.14	.35
10 Greg Manusky	.08	.25
11 Wilber Marshall	.14	.35
12 Art Monk	.30	.75
13 Gerald Riggs	.14	.35
14 Mark Rypien	.14	.35
15 Alvin Walton	.08	.25
16 Don Warren	.14	.35

1991 Redskins Mobil Schedules

Distributed at area Mobil stations, this 16-piece tri-fold paper schedule set measures 2 1/2" by 3 1/2" when folded and features a color action shot of Art Monk on the front with the Mobil logo on the back. When completely opened, the left panel contains the preseason and postseason schedule while the right panel presents the regular season schedule. The center panel features a full color action player shot. The player's name, biography, and profile appear on the following fold. The schedules are unnumbered and checklisted below in alphabetical order.

COMPLETE SET (16)	4.80	12.00
1 Earnest Byner	.40	1.00
2 Gary Clark	.30	.75
3 Andre Collins	.30	.75
4 Kurt Gouveia	.30	.75
5 Darrell Green	.40	1.00
6 Jimmie Johnson	.30	.75
7 Markus Koch	.30	.75
8 Jim Lachey	.40	1.00
9 Chip Lohmiller	.30	.75
10 Charles Mann	.40	1.00
11 Martin Mayhew	.30	.75
12 Art Monk	.60	1.50
13 Mark Rypien	.40	1.00
14 Mark Schlereth	.30	.75
15 Ed Simmons	.30	.75
16 Eric Williams	.30	.75

1991 Redskins Police

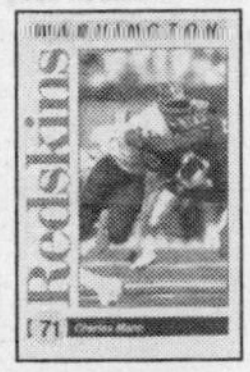

This 16-card set was jointly sponsored by Mobil, PACT (Police and Citizens Together), and WTTG Channel 5 TV. The set was released in the Washington area during the 1991 season. The cards measure approximately 2 5/8" by 4 1/8" and are printed on thin card stock. Card fronts carry a full-color player action shot on a white background. The word "Washington" is printed in black in a gold bar at top of card while the team name appears in large red print up the left side. Player's name is reversed out in a black stripe at bottom, while player's number appears in a gold circle to the left. Vertically printed backs present biographical information, player profile, an anti-drug message, and trivia question. Sponsors' logos appear at bottom. The cards are unnumbered and checklisted below in alphabetical order.

COMPLETE SET (16)	2.00	5.00
1 John Brandes	.08	.25
2 Earnest Byner	.14	.35
3 Gary Clark	.25	.60
4 Andre Collins	.14	.35
5 Darrell Green	.14	.35
6 Joe Howard	.08	.25
7 Tim Johnson	.08	.25
8 Jim Lachey	.14	.35
9 Chip Lohmiller	.08	.25
10 Charles Mann	.14	.35
11 Art Monk	.30	.75
12 Mark Rypien	.14	.35
13 Mark Schlereth	.08	.25
14 Fred Stokes	.08	.25
15 Don Warren	.14	.35
16 Eric Williams	.08	.25

1992 Redskins Mobil Schedules

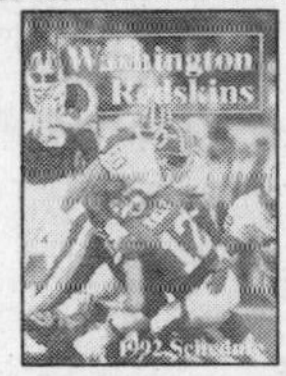

Distributed at area Mobil stations, this 16-piece bi-fold paper schedule set measures 2 1/2" by 3 1/2" when folded and features a color action shot of Fred Stokes sacking Jim Kelly on the front with the Mobil logo on the back. When completely opened, the left panel contains the preseason and postseason schedule while the right panel contains the regular season schedule. The center panel features a full color action player shot. The player's name, biography, and profile appear on the following fold. The schedules are unnumbered and checklisted below in alphabetical order.

COMPLETE SET (16)	4.00	10.00
1 Gary Clark	.30	.75
2 Brad Edwards	.25	.60
3 Ricky Ervins	.30	.75
4 Jumpy Geathers	.25	.60
5 Darrell Green	.30	.75
6 Joe Jacoby	.25	.60
7 Tim Johnson	.25	.60
8 Charles Mann	.30	.75
9 Wilber Marshall	.30	.75
10 Ron Middleton	.25	.60
11 Brian Mitchell	.30	.75
12 Art Monk	.40	1.00
13 Jim Lachey	.25	.60
14 Chip Lohmiller	.25	.60
15 Mark Rypien	.30	.75
16 Fred Stokes	.25	.60

1992 Redskins Police

This 16-card set was jointly sponsored by Mobil, PACT (Police and Citizens Together), and Fox WTTG Channel 5. The cards measure approximately 2 1/2" by 4 1/8" and feature action color player photos on a brick-red background. The pictures are offset, bleeding off the right edge of the card, and are framed on the other three sides in white. At the upper left corner of the picture is the Vince Lombardi trophy, and at the lower left corner is the uniform number in a circle. The team name appears at the top in mustard. The white backs feature biographical information, career highlights, and anti-drug and crime prevention tips in the form of player quotes. The cards are unnumbered and checklisted below in alphabetical order.

COMPLETE SET (16)	2.00	5.00
1 Jeff Bostic	.15	.40
2 Earnest Byner	.15	.40
3 Gary Clark	.25	.60
4 Monte Coleman	.15	.40

5 Andre Collins	.15	.40
6 Danny Copeland	.10	.30
7 Kurt Gouveia	.10	.30
8 Darrell Green	.15	.40
9 Jim Lachey	.15	.40
10 Charles Mann	.15	.40
11 Wilber Marshall	.15	.40
12 Raleigh McKenzie	.10	.30
13 Art Monk	.40	1.00
14 Mark Rypien	.15	.40
15 Mark Schlereth	.10	.30
16 Eric Williams	.10	.30

1993 Redskins Mobil Schedules

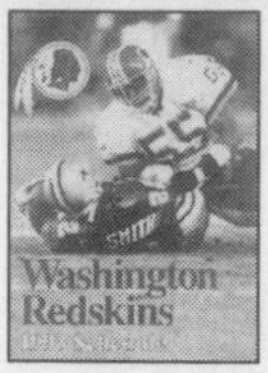

Distributed at area Mobil stations, this 16-piece tri-fold paper schedule set measures 2 1/2" by 3 1/2" when folded and features a color action shot of Andre Collins tackling Emmitt Smith on the front with the Mobil logo on the back. When completely opened, the left panel contains the preseason and postseason schedule while the right panel contains the regular season schedule. The center panel features a full color action player shot. The player's name, biography, and profile appear on the following fold. The schedules are unnumbered and checklisted below in alphabetical order.

COMPLETE SET (16)	4.00	10.00
1 Todd Bowles	.25	.60
2 Earnest Byner	.30	.75
3 Monte Coleman	.30	.75
4 Andre Collins	.30	.75
5 Shane Collins	.25	.60
6 Danny Copeland	.25	.60
7 Kurt Gouveia	.25	.60
8 Darrell Green	.30	.75
9 A.J. Johnson	.25	.60
10 Jim Lachey	.25	.60
11 Ron Middleton	.25	.60
12 Brian Mitchell	.40	1.00
13 Mark Rypien	.30	.75
14 Ricky Sanders	.30	.75
15 Mark Schlereth	.25	.60
16 Ed Simmons	.25	.60

1993 Redskins Police

These 16 cards measure approximately 2 3/4" by 4 1/8" and feature on their fronts yellow-bordered color player action shots. The player's name, team helmet, and uniform number rest within the bottom yellow margin. The white back carries the player's name and uniform number at the top, followed below by biography, career highlights, and safety message. The logos for Mobil, Cellular One, and Police and Citizens Together (PACT) at the bottom round out the card. The cards are unnumbered and checklisted below in alphabetical order.

COMPLETE SET (16)	2.00	5.00
1 Ray Brown	.10	.30
2 Andre Collins	.15	.40
3 Brad Edwards	.10	.30
4 Matt Elliott	.10	.30
5 Ricky Ervins	.15	.40
6 Darrell Green	.15	.40
7 Desmond Howard	.30	.75
8 Joe Jacoby	.15	.40
9 Tim Johnson	.10	.30
10 Jim Lachey	.15	.40
11 Chip Lohmiller	.10	.30
12 Charles Mann	.15	.40
13 Raleigh McKenzie	.10	.30
14 Brian Mitchell	.20	.50
15 Terry Orr	.10	.30
16 Mark Rypien	.15	.40

1994 Redskins Mobil Schedules

Distributed at area Mobil stations, this 16-piece bi-fold paper schedule set measures 2 1/2" by 3 1/2" when folded and features a color action shot on the front with the Mobil logo on the back. When completely opened, the left panel contains the preseason and postseason schedule while the right panel contains the regular season schedule. The center panel features a full color action player shot. The player's name, biography, and profile appear on the following fold. The schedules are unnumbered and checklisted below in alphabetical order.

COMPLETE SET (16)	3.20	8.00
1 Reggie Brooks	.30	.75
2 Ray Brown	.25	.60
3 Tom Carter	.30	.75
4 Shane Collins	.25	.60
5 Darrell Green	.30	.75
6 Ken Harvey	.30	.75
7 Lamont Hollinquest	.25	.60
8 Desmond Howard	.40	1.00
9 Tim Johnson	.25	.60
10 Jim Lachey	.25	.60
11 Chip Lohmiller	.25	.60
12 Brian Mitchell	.30	.75
13 Sterling Palmer	.25	.60
14 Heath Shuler	.50	1.25
15 Bobby Wilson	.25	.60
16 Frank Wycheck	.25	.60

1994 Redskins Police

These 16 cards measure approximately 2 3/4" by 4 1/8" and feature on their fronts maroon-bordered color player action shots. The player's name, team helmet, and uniform number rest within the bottom margin. The white back carries the player's name and uniform number at the top, followed below by biography, career highlights, and safety message. The cards are unnumbered and checklisted below in alphabetical order.

COMPLETE SET (16)	2.40	6.00
1 Tom Carter	.15	.40
2 Monte Coleman	.15	.40
3 Andre Collins	.10	.30
4 Pat Eilers	.10	.30
5 Henry Ellard	.30	.75
6 Ricky Ervins	.15	.40
7 Darrell Green	.30	.75
8 Ethan Horton	.10	.30
9 Desmond Howard	.30	.75
10 Jim Lachey	.15	.40
11 Alvoid Mays	.10	.30
12 Ron Middleton	.10	.30
13 Brian Mitchell	.15	.40
14 Raleigh McKenzie	.10	.30
15 Reggie Roby	.10	.30
16 Ed Simmons	.10	.30

1995 Redskins Program Sheets

These eight sheets measure approximately 8" by 10" and appeared in regular-season issues of the Redskins' GameDay program. The set features panoramic stadium photographs at which championship games involving the Washington Redskins were played. The sheets are listed below in chronological order.

COMPLETE SET (8)	10.00	25.00
1 9/3/95 vs. Cardinals Wrigley Field Redskins vs Bears 1937, 1943	1.40	3.50
2 9/10/95 vs. Raiders Griffith Stadium Redskins vs Bears, 1940, 1942	1.40	3.50
3 10/1/95 vs. Cowboys* Cleveland Stadium Redskins vs Rams, 1945	1.40	3.50
4 10/22/95 vs. Lions L.A. Coliseum Redskins vs Dolphins, S.B. VII	1.40	3.50
5 10/29/95 vs. Giants Rose Bowl Redskins vs Dolphins, S.B. XVII	1.40	3.50
6 11/19/95 vs. Seahawks Tampa Stadium Redskins vs Raiders, S.B. XVIII	1.40	3.50
7 11/26/95 vs. Eagles Jack Murphy Stadium Skins vs Broncos, S.B. XXII	1.40	3.50
8 12/24/95 vs. Panthers H.H.H. Metrodome Redskins vs Bills, S.B. XXVI	1.40	3.50

1996 Redskins Score Board/Exxon

Score Board produced this team set for distribution by the Washington D.C. area Exxon stations. Each card appears similar to a 1996 Pro Line card, but contains the Score Board logo at the top. The Exxon sponsor logo appears only on the checklist card. Packs could be obtained, with the appropriate gasoline purchase, for 49-cents each and contained three-player cards and a checklist card.

COMPLETE SET (9)	1.40	3.50
WR1 Gus Frerotte	.30	.75
WR2 Terry Allen	.30	.75
WR3 Henry Ellard	.15	.40
WR4 Michael Westbrook	.60	1.50
WR5 Brian Mitchell	.08	.25
WR6 Sean Gilbert	.08	.25
WR7 Ken Harvey	.08	.25
WR8 Darrell Green	.15	.40
WR9 Redskins Checklist	.08	.25

2001 Redskins Read Bookmarks

1 Jeff George	.75	2.00
2 Chris Samuels	.75	2.00

2006 Redskins Topps

COMPLETE SET (12)	3.00	6.00
WAS1 Clinton Portis	.30	.75
WAS2 Jason Campbell	.25	.60
WAS3 Carlos Rogers	.20	.50
WAS4 Shawn Springs	.20	.50
WAS5 Santana Moss	.25	.60
WAS6 Chris Cooley	.25	.60
WAS7 Antwaan Randle El	.25	.60
WAS8 Mark Brunell	.25	.60
WAS9 Brandon Lloyd	.20	.50
WAS10 Adam Archuleta	.20	.50
WAS11 Rocky McIntosh	.25	.60
WAS12 Sean Taylor	.30	.75

2007 Redskins Activa Medallions

COMPLETE SET (22)	30.00	60.00
1 George Allen	1.50	4.00
2 Sammy Baugh	1.50	4.00
3 Dave Butz	1.50	3.50
4 Gary Clark	1.50	3.50
5 Monte Coleman	1.50	3.50
6 Joe Gibbs	1.50	4.00
7 Russ Grimm	1.50	3.50
8 Joe Jacoby	1.50	3.50
9 Ken Houston	1.50	3.50
10 Sam Huff	1.50	4.00
11 Sonny Jurgensen	1.50	4.00
12 Billy Kilmer	1.50	3.50
13 Dexter Manley	1.50	3.50
14 Bobby Mitchell	1.50	4.00
15 Mark Moseley	1.50	3.50
16 John Riggins	1.50	4.00
17 Mark Rypien	1.50	3.50
18 Charley Taylor	1.50	3.50
19 Joe Theismann	1.50	4.00
20 Don Warren	1.50	3.50
21 Doug Williams	1.50	3.50
22 Super Bowl Wins	1.50	3.50

2007 Redskins Topps

COMPLETE SET (12)	2.50	5.00
1 London Fletcher	.20	.50
2 Antwaan Randle El	.20	.50
3 Jason Campbell	.25	.60
4 Sean Taylor	.30	.75
5 Clinton Portis	.25	.60
6 Santana Moss	.25	.60
7 Chris Cooley	.25	.60
8 Ladell Betts	.20	.50
9 Mark Brunell	.25	.60
10 Lemar Marshall	.20	.50
11 Carlos Rogers	.20	.50
12 LaRon Landry	.30	.75

2008 Redskins Topps

COMPLETE SET (12)	2.50	5.00
1 Jason Campbell	.25	.60
2 Clinton Portis	.25	.60
3 Chris Cooley	.25	.60
4 Santana Moss	.20	.50
5 Todd Collins	.20	.50
6 Ladell Betts	.20	.50
7 Antwaan Randle El	.20	.50
8 Andre Carter	.20	.50
9 London Fletcher	.20	.50
10 LaRon Landry	.25	.60
11 Devin Thomas	.30	.75
12 Malcolm Kelly	.30	.75

2004 Reflections

Reflections initially released in mid-August 2004. The base set consists of -294cards including 194-rookies numbered between 450 and 1150. Hobby boxes contained 8-packs of 4-cards and carried an S.R.P. of $14.99 per pack. Four parallel sets and a variety of inserts can be found seeded in hobby packs highlighted by the Signature Reflections and Signature Threads autograph inserts.

COMP.SET w/o SP's (100)	15.00	40.00
201-294 RC PRINT RUN 1150 SER.#'d SETS		
OVERALL RC STATED ODDS 1:1		
1 Emmitt Smith	1.50	4.00
2 Anquan Boldin	.60	1.50
3 Josh McCown	.50	1.25
4 Michael Vick	.75	2.00
5 Peerless Price	.40	1.00
6 T.J. Duckett	.50	1.25
7 Todd Heap	.50	1.25
8 Jamal Lewis	.50	1.25
9 Kyle Boller	.50	1.25
10 Drew Bledsoe	.60	1.50
11 Travis Henry	.40	1.00
12 Eric Moulds	.50	1.25
13 Jake Delhomme	.50	1.25
14 Steve Smith	.60	1.50
15 Stephen Davis	.50	1.25
16 Rex Grossman	.50	1.25
17 Brian Urlacher	.60	1.50
18 Anthony Thomas	.50	1.25
19 Rudi Johnson	.50	1.25
20 Carson Palmer	.60	1.50
21 Chad Johnson	.60	1.50
22 Jeff Garcia	.50	1.25
23 Andre Davis	.40	1.00
24 Quincy Morgan	.40	1.00
25 Keyshawn Johnson	.50	1.25
26 Roy Williams S	.50	1.25
27 Quincy Carter	.40	1.00
28 Ashley Lelie	.40	1.00
29 Champ Bailey	.50	1.25
30 Jake Plummer	.50	1.25
31 Az-Zahir Hakim	.40	1.00
32 Joey Harrington	.50	1.25
33 Charles Rogers	.40	1.00
34 Javon Walker	.40	1.00
35 Ahman Green	.50	1.25
36 Brett Favre	1.50	4.00
37 Domanick Davis	.40	1.00
38 David Carr	.40	1.00
39 Andre Johnson	.60	1.50
40 Edgerrin James	.50	1.25
41 Marvin Harrison	.60	1.50
42 Dwight Freeney	.50	1.25
43 Peyton Manning	1.25	3.00
44 Fred Taylor	.50	1.25
45 Jimmy Smith	.50	1.25
46 Byron Leftwich	.50	1.25
47 Dante Hall	.50	1.25
48 Tony Gonzalez	.60	1.50
49 Trent Green	.50	1.25
50 Priest Holmes	.60	1.50
51 Zach Thomas	.60	1.50
52 A.J. Feeley	.40	1.00
53 Chris Chambers	.50	1.25
54 Ricky Williams	.50	1.25
55 Randy Moss	.60	1.50
56 Onterrio Smith	.40	1.00
57 Daunte Culpepper	.50	1.25
58 Tom Brady	1.25	3.00
59 Troy Brown	.50	1.25
60 Corey Dillon	.50	1.25
61 Donte Stallworth	.40	1.00
62 Deuce McAllister	.50	1.25
63 Aaron Brooks	.50	1.25
64 Amani Toomer	.50	1.25
65 Jeremy Shockey	.50	1.25
66 Michael Strahan	.60	1.50
67 Curtis Martin	.60	1.50
68 Chad Pennington	.60	1.50
69 Santana Moss	.50	1.25
70 Jerry Porter	.40	1.00
71 Jerry Rice	1.25	3.00
72 Rich Gannon	.50	1.25
73 Tim Brown	.60	1.50
74 Terrell Owens	.60	1.50
75 Brian Westbrook	.60	1.50
76 Donovan McNabb	.60	1.50
77 Tommy Maddox	.50	1.25
78 Hines Ward	.60	1.50
79 Duce Staley	.50	1.25
80 Donnie Edwards	.50	1.25
81 LaDainian Tomlinson	.60	1.50
82 Drew Brees	.60	1.50
83 Brandon Lloyd	.50	1.25
84 Tim Rattay	.40	1.00
85 Kevan Barlow	.40	1.00
86 Koren Robinson	.40	1.00
87 Shaun Alexander	.50	1.25
88 Matt Hasselbeck	.50	1.25
89 Torry Holt	.50	1.25
90 Marc Bulger	.50	1.25
91 Marshall Faulk	.60	1.50
92 Brad Johnson	.50	1.25
93 Keenan McCardell	.40	1.00
94 Charlie Garner	.50	1.25
95 Steve McNair	.60	1.50
96 Chris Brown	.40	1.00
97 Eddie George	.50	1.25
98 Mark Brunell	.50	1.25
99 Laveranues Coles	.40	1.00
100 Clinton Portis	.60	1.50
101 Kris Wilson/750 RC	1.50	4.00
102 Carlos Francis/750 RC	1.25	3.00
103 D.J. Williams/750 RC	2.00	5.00
104 Devery Henderson/450 RC	2.50	6.00
105 Craig Krenzel/750 RC	1.50	4.00
106 Jonathan Vilma/750 RC	2.00	5.00
107 Luke McCown/750 RC	1.50	4.00
108 Michael Turner/750 RC	2.50	6.00
109 Richard Seigler/750 RC	1.25	3.00
110 Stuart Schweigert/750 RC	1.50	4.00
111 Ben Watson/750 RC	2.00	5.00
112 Chris Perry/450 RC	2.00	5.00
113 Jason Fife/750 RC	1.25	3.00
114 Eli Manning/450 RC	15.00	40.00
115 Matt Kegel/750 RC	2.00	5.00
116 Kellen Winslow/450 RC	2.50	6.00
117 Chris Cooley/750 RC	2.00	5.00
118 Quincy Wilson/750 RC	1.50	4.00
119 Samie Parker/750 RC	1.25	3.00
120 Vince Wilfork/750 RC	2.00	5.00
121 Bernard Berrian/750 RC	2.00	5.00
122 Ahmad Carroll/750 RC	1.25	3.00
123 Derrick Hamilton/750 RC	1.25	3.00
124 Rich Gardner/750 RC	1.50	4.00
125 Jeff Smoker/750 RC	1.50	4.00
126 Kenechi Udeze/750 RC	1.50	4.00
127 Mewelde Moore/750 RC	1.50	4.00
128 Keyaron Fox/750 RC	1.50	4.00
129 Sean Jones/750 RC	1.50	4.00
130 Will Poole/750 RC	2.00	5.00
131 Travelle Wharton/750 RC	1.25	3.00
132 Demorrio Williams/750 RC	2.00	5.00
133 Jason Babin/750 RC	2.00	5.00
134 Ernest Wilford/750 RC	1.50	4.00
135 Jerricho Cotchery/750 RC	1.50	4.00
136 Kevin Jones/450 RC	2.00	5.00
137 Michael Boulware/750 RC	2.00	5.00
138 D.J. Hackett/750 RC	1.50	4.00
139 Sean Taylor/450 RC	5.00	12.00
140 Will Smith/750 RC	1.50	4.00
141 John Standeford/750 RC	1.25	3.00
142 Max Starks/750 RC	1.50	4.00
143 Cody Pickett/750 RC	1.50	4.00
144 Derrick Strait/750 RC	1.25	3.00
145 Greg Jones/450 RC	1.50	4.00
146 John Navarre/750 RC	1.25	3.00
147 Larry Fitzgerald/450 RC	6.00	15.00
148 Michael Clayton/450 RC	2.00	5.00
149 Rashaun Woods/450 RC	1.50	4.00
150 Shawn Andrews/750 RC	1.50	4.00
151 B.J. Symons/750 RC	1.25	3.00
152 Cedric Cobbs/450 RC	1.50	4.00
153 Darius Watts/750 RC	1.25	3.00
154 B.J. Johnson/750 RC	1.25	3.00
155 Ricardo Colclough/750 RC	1.50	4.00
156 Josh Harris/750 RC	1.25	3.00
157 Derek Abney/750 RC	1.25	3.00
158 Kendrick Starling/750 RC	1.25	3.00
159 Robert Gallery/450 RC	2.50	6.00
160 Tatum Bell/450 RC	2.00	5.00
161 Ben Hartsock/750 RC	1.25	3.00
162 Dwan Edwards/750 RC	1.25	3.00
163 Darnell Dockett/750 RC	1.25	3.00
164 Igor Olshansky/750 RC	1.50	4.00
165 Justin Smiley/750 RC	1.50	4.00
166 Julius Jones/450 RC	2.00	5.00
167 Matt Mauck/750 RC	1.25	3.00
168 Derek McCoy/750 RC	1.25	3.00
169 Chris Pittman/750 RC	1.25	3.00
170 Teddy Lehman/750 RC	1.25	3.00
171 Ben Troupe/450 RC	2.00	5.00
172 Chris Gamble/750 RC	1.50	4.00
173 DeAngelo Hall/750 RC	2.00	5.00
174 Dunta Robinson/750 RC	1.25	3.00
175 Jason Shivers/750 RC	1.25	3.00
176 Keary Colbert/450 RC	1.50	4.00
177 Jared Lorenzen/750 RC	1.50	4.00
178 Philip Rivers/450 RC	10.00	25.00
179 Roy Williams/450 RC	2.50	6.00
180 Bob Sanders/750 RC	5.00	12.00
181 Antwan Odom/750 RC	1.50	4.00
182 Josh Davis/750 RC	1.50	4.00
183 Courtney Watson/750 RC	1.25	3.00
184 Devard Darling/750 RC	1.25	3.00
185 J.P. Losman/450 RC	2.00	5.00
186 Johnnie Morant/750 RC	1.25	3.00
187 Lee Evans/450 RC	2.50	6.00
188 Michael Jenkins/450 RC	2.50	6.00
189 Reggie Williams/450 RC	2.00	5.00
190 Steven Jackson/450 RC	4.00	10.00
191 Ben Roethlisberger/450 RC	15.00	40.00
192 P.K. Sam/750 RC	1.25	3.00
193 Derrick Knight/750 RC	1.25	3.00
194 Drew Henson/450 RC	1.50	4.00
195 Marquise Hill/750 RC	1.25	3.00
196 Karlos Dansby/750 RC	2.00	5.00
197 Matt Schaub/750 RC	4.00	10.00
198 Ben Utecht/750 RC	1.50	4.00
199 Darrion Scott/750 RC	1.50	4.00
200 Tommie Harris/750 RC	2.00	5.00
201 Andrae Thurman RC	1.00	2.50
202 Matt Kranchick RC	1.25	3.00
203 Shaun Phillips RC	1.50	4.00
204 Landon Johnson RC	1.00	2.50
205 Jeff Dugan RC	1.00	2.50
206 Wes Welker RC	6.00	15.00
207 Michael Gaines RC	1.00	2.50
208 Jamaar Taylor RC	1.00	2.50
209 Brandon Chillar RC	1.25	3.00
210 Jermaine Green RC	1.00	2.50
211 Triandos Luke RC	1.00	2.50
212 Brandon Miree RC	1.00	2.50
213 Dexter Reid RC	1.00	2.50
214 Isaac Hilton RC	1.25	3.00
215 Adrian Jones RC	1.00	2.50
216 Grant Wiley RC	1.00	2.50
217 Matt Cherry RC	1.00	2.50
218 Courtney Anderson RC	1.00	2.50
219 Antonio Smith RC	1.25	3.00
220 Sean Tufts RC	1.00	2.50
221 Johnny Lamar RC	1.00	2.50
222 Shawn Johnson RC	1.00	2.50
223 Jason Peters RC	1.25	3.00
224 Rodney Leisle RC	1.00	2.50
225 Lane Danielsen RC	1.00	2.50
226 Zack Abron RC	1.00	2.50
227 Romar Crenshaw RC	1.00	2.50
228 Keiwan Ratliff RC	1.00	2.50
229 Chad Lavalais RC	1.00	2.50
230 Jason Wright RC	1.00	2.50
231 Rayshun Reed RC	1.00	2.50
232 Patrick Crayton RC	1.50	4.00
233 Casey Bramlet RC	1.00	2.50
234 Nathaniel Adibi RC	1.00	2.50
235 Dontarrious Thomas RC	1.25	3.00
236 B.J. Sander RC	1.25	3.00
237 Ryan McGuffey RC	1.00	2.50
238 Shawntae Spencer RC	1.00	2.50
239 Amon Gordon RC	1.00	2.50
240 Vernon Carey RC	1.00	2.50
241 Stanford Samuels RC	1.00	2.50
242 Thomas Tapeh RC	1.25	3.00
243 Keith Smith RC	1.00	2.50
244 Casey Clausen RC	1.25	3.00
245 Jake Grove RC	1.00	2.50
246 Omar Nazel RC	1.00	2.50
247 Jammal Lord RC	1.00	2.50
248 Jeremy LeSueur RC	1.00	2.50
249 Daryl Smith RC	1.00	2.50
250 Nat Dorsey RC	1.00	2.50
251 Tim Anderson RC	1.25	3.00
252 Chris Snee RC	1.25	3.00
253 Sean Ryan RC	1.00	2.50
254 Tank Johnson RC	1.00	2.50
255 Marquis Cooper RC	1.00	2.50
256 Josh Scobee RC	1.25	3.00
257 Justin Jenkins RC	1.00	2.50
258 Nate Lawrie RC	1.00	2.50
259 Randy Starks RC	1.00	2.50
260 Caleb Miller RC	1.00	2.50
261 A.J. Ricker RC	1.00	2.50
262 Andy Hall RC	1.00	2.50
263 Troy Fleming RC	1.00	2.50
264 Matt Ware RC	1.50	4.00
265 Christian Ferrara RC	1.00	2.50
266 Stacy Andrews RC	1.00	2.50
267 Reggie Torbor RC	1.00	2.50
268 Jeris McIntyre RC	1.00	2.50
269 Jarrett Payton RC	1.25	3.00
270 Ronald Jones RC	1.00	2.50
271 Kelly Butler RC	1.00	2.50
272 Bryan Hickman RC	1.00	2.50
273 Chris Collins RC	1.00	2.50
274 Ryan Dinwiddie RC	1.00	2.50
275 Robert Geathers RC	1.00	2.50
276 Niko Koutouvides RC	1.00	2.50
277 Clarence Farmer RC	1.00	2.50
278 Jim Sorgi RC	1.25	3.00
279 Ran Carthon RC	1.00	2.50
280 Michael Waddell RC	1.00	2.50
281 Andrew Strojny RC	1.00	2.50
282 Sloan Thomas RC	1.25	3.00
283 Tim Euhus RC	1.00	2.50
284 Lawrence Richardson RC	1.00	2.50
285 Nate Kaeding RC	1.50	4.00
286 Ryan Krause RC	1.00	2.50
287 Derrick Ward RC	1.50	4.00
288 Nathan Vasher RC	1.50	4.00
289 Bobby McCray RC	1.00	2.50
290 Scott Rislov RC	1.00	2.50
291 Ryan Boschetti RC	1.00	2.50
292 Fred Russell RC	1.25	3.00
293 Von Hutchins RC	1.00	2.50
294 Derrick Crawford RC	1.00	2.50

2004 Reflections Black

UNPRICED BLACK PRINT RUN 1
NOT PRICED DUE TO SCARCITY

2004 Reflections Blue

*VETS: 6X TO 15X BASIC CARDS
*ROOKIES: 2X TO 5X ROOKIE/450
*ROOKIES: 2.5X TO 6X ROOKIE/750
*ROOKIES: 3X TO 8X ROOKIE/1150
BLUE STATED PRINT RUN 10

2004 Reflections Green

*VETS: 3X TO 8X BASIC CARDS
*ROOKIES: 1X TO 2.5X ROOKIE/450
*ROOKIES: 1.2X TO 3X ROOKIE/750
*ROOKIES: 1.5X TO 4X ROOKIE/1150
STATED PRINT RUN 50 SER.#'d SETS

2004 Reflections Red

*VETS: 2X TO 5X BASIC CARDS
*ROOKIES: .6X TO 1.5X ROOKIE/450
*ROOKIES: .8X TO 2X ROOKIE/750
*ROOKIES: 1X TO 2.5X ROOKIE/1150
STATED PRINT RUN 100 SER.#'d SETS

2004 Reflections Fantasy Fabrics

STATED PRINT RUN 99 SER.#'d SETS		
*LTD PATCH/21: 1X TO 2.5X BASIC JSY		
LTD PATCH PRINT RUN 21 SETS		
*RAINBOW/15: 1.2X TO 3X BASIC JSY		
RAINBOW PRINT RUN 15 SETS		
FFAB Anquan Boldin	5.00	12.00
FFAG Ahman Green	4.00	10.00
FFAR Antwaan Randle El	4.00	10.00
FFBF Brett Favre	12.00	30.00
FFCC Chris Chambers	4.00	10.00
FFCH Chad Pennington	5.00	12.00
FFCJ Chad Johnson	5.00	12.00
FFCM Curtis Martin	5.00	12.00
FFCP Clinton Portis	5.00	12.00
FFDA David Carr	3.00	8.00
FFDC Daunte Culpepper	4.00	10.00
FFDD Domanick Davis	3.00	8.00
FFDE Deuce McAllister	4.00	10.00
FFDM Donovan McNabb	5.00	12.00
FFEJ Edgerrin James	4.00	10.00
FFGR Trent Green	4.00	10.00
FFHW Hines Ward	5.00	12.00
FFJB Jerome Bettis	5.00	12.00
FFJL Jamal Lewis	4.00	10.00
FFJW Javon Walker	3.00	8.00
FFKR Koren Robinson	3.00	8.00
FFLC Laveranues Coles	3.00	8.00
FFLT LaDainian Tomlinson	5.00	12.00
FFMA Derrick Mason	4.00	10.00
FFMF Marshall Faulk	5.00	12.00
FFMH Marvin Harrison	5.00	12.00
FFMO Santana Moss	4.00	10.00
FFMV Michael Vick	6.00	15.00
FFPH Priest Holmes	5.00	12.00
FFPM Peyton Manning	10.00	25.00
FFPP Peerless Price	3.00	8.00
FFPR Patrick Ramsey	4.00	10.00
FFRJ Rudi Johnson	4.00	10.00
FFRM Randy Moss	5.00	12.00
FFRW Ricky Williams	4.00	10.00
FFSA Shaun Alexander	4.00	10.00
FFSD Stephen Davis	4.00	10.00
FFSM Steve McNair	5.00	12.00
FFTB Tom Brady	10.00	25.00
FFTG Tony Gonzalez	5.00	12.00
FFTH Torry Holt	4.00	10.00
FFTR Travis Henry	3.00	8.00

2004 Reflections Focus on the Future Jerseys Gold

GOLD STATED ODDS 1:3		
*RAINBOW/85: .6X TO 1.5X GOLD		
RAINBOW PRINT RUN 85		
FOAB Anquan Boldin	3.00	8.00
FOAJ Andre Johnson	3.00	8.00
FOAL Ashley Lelie	2.00	5.00
FOBJ Bethel Johnson	2.00	5.00
FOBL Byron Leftwich	2.50	6.00
FOBR Ben Roethlisberger	12.00	30.00
FOCB Chris Brown	2.00	5.00
FOCC Chris Chambers	2.50	6.00
FOCH Chris Perry	2.50	6.00
FOCP Carson Palmer	3.00	8.00
FOCR Charles Rogers	2.00	5.00
FODC David Carr	2.00	5.00
FODD Domanick Davis	2.00	5.00
FODH Dante Hall	2.50	6.00
FODS Donte Stallworth	2.00	5.00
FOEM Eli Manning	12.00	30.00
FOJH Joey Harrington	2.50	6.00
FOJJ Julius Jones	1.50	4.00
FOJP J.P. Losman	1.50	4.00
FOJS Jeremy Shockey	2.50	6.00
FOKB Kyle Boller	2.50	6.00
FOKJ Kevin Jones	2.50	6.00
FOKR Koren Robinson	2.00	5.00
FOKW Kellen Winslow Jr.	2.00	5.00
FOLC Laveranues Coles SP	2.00	5.00
FOLF Larry Fitzgerald	5.00	12.00
FOLS Lee Suggs SP	2.50	6.00
FOMB Marc Bulger	2.50	6.00
FOOS Onterrio Smith	2.00	5.00
FOPA Patrick Ramsey SP	2.50	6.00
FOPB Plaxico Burress	2.50	6.00
FOPR Philip Rivers	8.00	20.00
FORE Reggie Williams	2.50	6.00
FORG Rex Grossman	2.50	6.00
FORJ Rudi Johnson	2.50	6.00
FORO Roy Williams WR	2.00	5.00
FORW Roy Williams S	2.50	6.00
FOSJ Steven Jackson	3.00	8.00
FOTB Tatum Bell	2.50	6.00
FOTC Tyrone Calico	2.50	6.00
FOTH Todd Heap	2.50	6.00
FOTS Terrell Suggs	2.50	6.00

2004 Reflections Offensive Threads

STATED PRINT RUN 99 SER.#'d SETS		
*LTD PATCH/21: 1X TO 2.5X BASIC JSY		
LTD PATCH PRINT RUN 21 SETS		
*RAINBOW/15: 1.2X TO 3X BASIC JSY		
RAINBOW PRINT RUN 15 SETS		
OTAB Aaron Brooks	4.00	10.00
OTAG Ahman Green	4.00	10.00
OTAJ Andre Johnson	5.00	12.00
OTBF Brett Favre	12.00	30.00
OTBJ Brad Johnson	4.00	10.00
OTBL Byron Leftwich	4.00	10.00
OTCD Corey Dillon	4.00	10.00
OTCL Clinton Portis	5.00	12.00
OTCP Chad Pennington	5.00	12.00
OTCR Charles Rogers	3.00	8.00
OTDB David Boston	3.00	8.00
OTDC Daunte Culpepper	4.00	10.00
OTDE Deuce McAllister	4.00	10.00
OTDH Dante Hall	4.00	10.00
OTDM Donovan McNabb	5.00	12.00
OTDR Drew Bledsoe	5.00	12.00
OTEJ Edgerrin James	4.00	10.00
OTHA Matt Hasselbeck	4.00	10.00
OTJH Joey Harrington	4.00	10.00
OTJL Jamal Lewis	4.00	10.00
OTJP Jake Plummer	4.00	10.00
OTJR Jerry Rice	10.00	25.00
OTJS Jeremy Shockey	4.00	10.00
OTLT LaDainian Tomlinson	5.00	12.00
OTMA Derrick Mason	4.00	10.00
OTMB Marc Bulger	4.00	10.00
OTMF Marshall Faulk	5.00	12.00
OTMH Marvin Harrison	5.00	12.00
OTMV Michael Vick	6.00	15.00
OTPB Plaxico Burress	4.00	10.00
OTPH Priest Holmes	5.00	12.00
OTPM Peyton Manning	10.00	25.00
OTQC Quincy Carter	3.00	8.00
OTRM Randy Moss	5.00	12.00
OTRW Ricky Williams	4.00	10.00
OTSA Shaun Alexander	4.00	10.00
OTSD Stephen Davis	4.00	10.00
OTSM Steve McNair	5.00	12.00
OTTB Tom Brady	10.00	25.00
OTTH Torry Holt	4.00	10.00
OTTO Terrell Owens	5.00	12.00
OTTR Troy Brown	4.00	10.00

2004 Reflections Pro Cuts Jerseys Gold

OVERALL PRO CUTS ODDS 1:6		
*SILVER/85: .6X TO 1.5X GOLD		
SILVER PRINT RUN 85 SER.#'d SETS		
PCAB Aaron Brooks	3.00	8.00
PCAG Ahman Green	3.00	8.00
PCBF Brett Favre	10.00	25.00
PCBR Tim Brown	4.00	10.00
PCBU Brian Urlacher	4.00	10.00
PCCH Chad Pennington	4.00	10.00
PCCJ Chad Johnson	4.00	10.00
PCCM Curtis Martin	4.00	10.00
PCCP Clinton Portis	4.00	10.00
PCDC Daunte Culpepper	3.00	8.00
PCDM Deuce McAllister	3.00	8.00
PCDO Donovan McNabb	4.00	10.00
PCEG Eddie George	3.00	8.00
PCEJ Edgerrin James	3.00	8.00
PCES Emmitt Smith	10.00	25.00
PCJD Jake Delhomme SP	3.00	8.00
PCJH Joe Horn	3.00	8.00
PCJL Jamal Lewis	3.00	8.00
PCJR Jerry Rice	8.00	20.00
PCJS Junior Seau	4.00	10.00
PCKJ Keyshawn Johnson	3.00	8.00
PCLA LaVar Arrington SP	6.00	15.00
PCLT LaDainian Tomlinson	4.00	10.00
PCMF Marshall Faulk SP	4.00	10.00
PCMH Marvin Harrison	4.00	10.00
PCMS Michael Strahan	4.00	10.00
PCMV Michael Vick	5.00	12.00
PCPH Priest Holmes	4.00	10.00
PCPM Peyton Manning	8.00	20.00
PCRI Ricky Williams	3.00	8.00
PCRL Ray Lewis	4.00	10.00
PCRM Randy Moss	4.00	10.00
PCRW Roy Williams S	3.00	8.00
PCSM Santana Moss	3.00	8.00
PCST Steve McNair	4.00	10.00
PCTB Tom Brady	8.00	20.00
PCTG Tony Gonzalez	4.00	10.00
PCTH Torry Holt	3.00	8.00
PCTI Tiki Barber	4.00	10.00
PCTO Terrell Owens	4.00	10.00
PCWS Warren Sapp	3.00	8.00

2004 Reflections Select Swatch

STATED PRINT RUN 99 SER.#'d SETS		
*LTD PATCH/21: 1X TO 2.5X BASIC JSY		
LTD PATCH PRINT RUN 21 SETS		
*RAINBOW/15: 1.2X TO 3X BASIC JSY		
RAINBOW PRINT RUN 15 SETS		
SSAB Aaron Brooks	4.00	10.00
SSAG Ahman Green	4.00	10.00
SSAN Anquan Boldin	5.00	12.00
SSBF Brett Favre	12.00	30.00
SSBU Brian Urlacher	5.00	12.00
SSCJ Chad Johnson	5.00	12.00
SSCL Clinton Portis	5.00	12.00
SSCP Chad Pennington	5.00	12.00
SSDA David Carr	3.00	8.00
SSDC Daunte Culpepper	4.00	10.00
SSDD Domanick Davis	3.00	8.00
SSDE Deuce McAllister	4.00	10.00
SSDH Dante Hall	4.00	10.00
SSDM Donovan McNabb	5.00	12.00
SSEJ Edgerrin James	4.00	10.00
SSHW Hines Ward	5.00	12.00
SSJL Jamal Lewis	4.00	10.00
SSJR Jerry Rice	10.00	25.00
SSJS Jeremy Shockey	4.00	10.00
SSKR Koren Robinson	3.00	8.00
SSLA LaVar Arrington	4.00	10.00
SSLC Laveranues Coles	3.00	8.00
SSLT LaDainian Tomlinson	5.00	12.00
SSMA Matt Hasselbeck	4.00	10.00
SSMB Marc Bulger	4.00	10.00
SSMF Marshall Faulk	5.00	12.00
SSMH Marvin Harrison	5.00	12.00
SSMS Michael Strahan	5.00	12.00
SSMV Michael Vick	6.00	15.00
SSPH Priest Holmes	5.00	12.00
SSPM Peyton Manning	10.00	25.00
SSRL Ray Lewis	5.00	12.00
SSRM Randy Moss	5.00	12.00
SSRW Ricky Williams	4.00	10.00
SSSA Shaun Alexander	4.00	10.00
SSSM Steve McNair	5.00	12.00
SSTB Tom Brady	10.00	25.00
SSTG Tony Gonzalez	5.00	12.00
SSTH Torry Holt	4.00	10.00
SSTO Terrell Owens	5.00	12.00
SSWI Roy Williams S	4.00	10.00
SSZT Zach Thomas	5.00	12.00

2004 Reflections Signature Reflections

STATED ODDS 1:28		
SRAR Andy Reid	10.00	25.00
SRBB Bernard Berrian	10.00	25.00
SRBF Brett Favre	125.00	200.00
SRBP Bill Parcells	20.00	40.00
SRBR Ben Roethlisberger SP	100.00	200.00
SRBT Ben Troupe	8.00	20.00
SRCP Chris Perry	8.00	20.00
SRDC Daunte Culpepper	10.00	25.00
SRDE DeAngelo Hall	10.00	25.00
SRDH Drew Henson	6.00	15.00
SRDM Donovan McNabb SP	30.00	60.00
SRDV Devery Henderson	10.00	25.00
SRDW Darius Watts	6.00	15.00
SREM Eli Manning	90.00	150.00
SRGJ Greg Jones	6.00	15.00
SRGR Jon Gruden SP	20.00	35.00
SRJF John Fox	8.00	20.00
SRJO Joe Montana SP	150.00	250.00
SRJP J.P. Losman	8.00	20.00
SRKC Keary Colbert	6.00	15.00
SRKJ Kevin Jones	8.00	20.00
SRKW Kellen Winslow Jr.	10.00	25.00
SRLE Lee Evans	10.00	25.00
SRLF Larry Fitzgerald SP	75.00	150.00
SRLM Luke McCown	8.00	20.00
SRMC Michael Clayton	8.00	20.00
SRMJ Michael Jenkins	10.00	25.00
SRMS Matt Schaub	20.00	50.00
SRMV Michael Vick	25.00	50.00
SRPM Peyton Manning	50.00	100.00
SRPR Philip Rivers	35.00	60.00
SRRE Reggie Williams	8.00	20.00
SRRG Rex Grossman	10.00	25.00
SRRO Robert Gallery	10.00	25.00
SRRW Ricky Williams	10.00	25.00
SRSJ Steven Jackson	15.00	40.00
SRTB Tom Brady SP	150.00	250.00
SRTH Travis Henry SP	8.00	20.00
SRTR Troy Aikman SP	40.00	80.00
SRWI Roy Williams WR	10.00	25.00
SRWO Rashaun Woods	6.00	15.00

2004 Reflections Signature Threads

STATED PRINT RUN 99 SER.#'d SETS

STBF Brett Favre	125.00	250.00
STBL Byron Leftwich	12.00	30.00
STBR Ben Roethlisberger	100.00	200.00
STCB Chris Brown	8.00	20.00
STCH Chris Perry	10.00	25.00
STCJ Chad Johnson	15.00	40.00
STCPO Chad Pennington	15.00	40.00
STDB Drew Bledsoe	15.00	40.00
STDC David Carr	10.00	25.00
STDD Domanick Davis	10.00	25.00
STDH Dante Hall	12.00	30.00
STDM Donovan McNabb	35.00	60.00
STEM Eli Manning	125.00	200.00
STGA Robert Gallery	12.00	30.00
STJG Joey Galloway	12.00	30.00
STJM Josh McCown	10.00	25.00
STJP Jesse Palmer	10.00	25.00
STJT Joe Theismann	15.00	40.00
STKB Kyle Boller	12.00	30.00
STKE Kellen Winslow	12.00	30.00
STKJ Kevin Jones	10.00	25.00
STKW Kelley Washington	10.00	25.00
STLE Lee Evans	12.00	30.00
STLO J.P. Losman	10.00	25.00
STLT LaDainian Tomlinson	30.00	60.00
STMA Mark Brunell	12.00	30.00
STMC Deuce McAllister	12.00	30.00
STMV Michael Vick	30.00	60.00
STPM Peyton Manning	75.00	135.00
STPR Philip Rivers	50.00	120.00
STRG Rex Grossman	12.00	30.00
STRJ Rudi Johnson	12.00	30.00
STRO Roy Williams S	12.00	30.00
STRW Ricky Williams	12.00	30.00
STSM Steve McNair	25.00	50.00
STTB Tom Brady	125.00	250.00
STTG Tony Gonzalez	15.00	40.00
STTH Todd Heap	12.00	30.00
STTR Travis Henry	10.00	25.00
STWI Roy Williams WR	12.00	30.00
STWM Willis McGahee	15.00	40.00
STZT Zach Thomas	15.00	40.00

2004 Reflections Signature Threads LTD Patch

*LTD PATCH: .8X TO 2X BASIC INSERTS
STATED PRINT RUN 21 SER.#'d SETS

STPBF Brett Favre	150.00	300.00
STPBR Ben Roethlisberger	150.00	300.00
STPEM Eli Manning	175.00	300.00
STPPM Peyton Manning	125.00	250.00
STPPR Philip Rivers	75.00	200.00
STPTB Tom Brady	150.00	300.00

2004 Reflections Signature Threads Rainbow

*RAINBOW: 1.2X TO 3X BASIC INSERTS
RAINBOW STATED PRINT RUN 15

STBF Brett Favre	200.00	350.00
STBR Ben Roethlisberger	200.00	350.00
STEM Eli Manning	200.00	350.00
STPM Peyton Manning	150.00	300.00
STTB Tom Brady	200.00	350.00

2005 Reflections

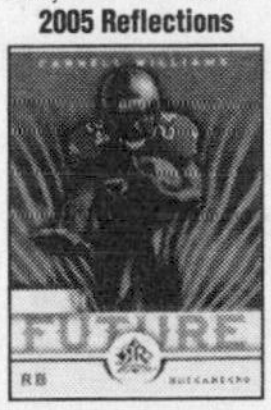

This 300-card set was released in October, 2005. The set was issued in the hobby through four-card packs with a $9.99 SRP which came 12 packs to a box. Cards numbered 1-100 were veterans in team alphabetical order while cards numbered 101-300 featured 2005 NFL rookies. Cards numbered 101-175 were printed to a stated print run of 899 serial numbered sets, cards numbered 176-225 were printed to a stated print run of 699 serial numbered sets, cards numbered 226-275 wewre printed to a stated print run of 499 and the final cards in the set (276-300) were printed to a stated print run of 299 serial numbered sets. The rookie cardxs were inserted into packs at an overall stated rate of one in three.

COMP.SET w/o SP's (100) 12.50 30.00
101-175 PRINT RUN 899 SER.#'d SETS
176-225 PRINT RUN 699 SER.#'d SETS
226-275 PRINT RUN 499 SER.#'d SETS
276-300 PRINT RUN 299 SER.#'d SETS
OVERALL DRAFT PICK ODDS 1:3
UNPRICED RAINBOW PRINT RUN 1 SET

1 Larry Fitzgerald	.50	1.25
2 Anquan Boldin	.40	1.00
3 Josh McCown	.40	1.00
4 Michael Vick	.50	1.25
5 Warrick Dunn	.40	1.00
6 Peerless Price	.30	.75
7 Ray Lewis	.50	1.25
8 Jamal Lewis	.40	1.00
9 Kyle Boller	.40	1.00
10 Derrick Mason	.40	1.00
11 J.P. Losman	.30	.75
12 Willis McGahee	.50	1.25
13 Lee Evans	.40	1.00
14 Eric Moulds	.30	.75
15 Jake Delhomme	.40	1.00
16 Keary Colbert	.30	.75
17 DeShaun Foster	.40	1.00
18 Brian Urlacher	.50	1.25
19 Rex Grossman	.40	1.00
20 Muhsin Muhammad	.40	1.00
21 Carson Palmer	.50	1.25
22 Rudi Johnson	.40	1.00
23 Chad Johnson	.40	1.00
24 Julius Jones	.30	.75
25 Keyshawn Johnson	.40	1.00
26 Drew Bledsoe	.50	1.25
27 Tatum Bell	.30	.75
28 Jake Plummer	.40	1.00
29 Ashley Lelie	.30	.75
30 Roy Williams WR	.40	1.00
31 Kevin Jones	.30	.75
32 Jeff Garcia	.40	1.00
33 Brett Favre	1.25	3.00
34 Ahman Green	.40	1.00
35 Javon Walker	.30	.75
36 David Carr	.30	.75
37 Andre Johnson	.50	1.25
38 Domanick Davis	.30	.75
39 Peyton Manning	1.00	2.50
40 Reggie Wayne	.50	1.25
41 Edgerrin James	.40	1.00
42 Marvin Harrison	.50	1.25
43 Byron Leftwich	.40	1.00
44 Fred Taylor	.40	1.00
45 Jimmy Smith	.40	1.00
46 Priest Holmes	.40	1.00
47 Larry Johnson	.40	1.00
48 Trent Green	.40	1.00
49 A.J. Feeley	.30	.75
50 Chris Chambers	.40	1.00
51 Randy McMichael	.30	.75
52 Daunte Culpepper	.40	1.00
53 Onterrio Smith	.30	.75
54 Nate Burleson	.30	.75
55 Tom Brady	1.00	2.50
56 Corey Dillon	.40	1.00
57 Deion Branch	.30	.75
58 David Givens	.30	.75
59 Aaron Brooks	.30	.75
60 Deuce McAllister	.40	1.00
61 Joe Horn	.40	1.00
62 Eli Manning	.75	2.00
63 Jeremy Shockey	.50	1.25
64 Tiki Barber	.50	1.25
65 Chad Pennington	.50	1.25
66 Curtis Martin	.50	1.25
67 Laveranues Coles	.30	.75
68 Kerry Collins	.40	1.00
69 Jerry Porter	.30	.75
70 Randy Moss	.50	1.25
71 Donovan McNabb	.50	1.25
72 Terrell Owens	.50	1.25
73 Brian Dawkins	.40	1.00
74 Brian Westbrook	.40	1.00
75 Ben Roethlisberger	.75	2.00
76 Jerome Bettis	.50	1.25
77 Hines Ward	.50	1.25
78 Duce Staley	.40	1.00
79 Drew Brees	.50	1.25
80 LaDainian Tomlinson	.50	1.25
81 Antonio Gates	.50	1.25
82 Tim Rattay	.30	.75
83 Kevan Barlow	.30	.75
84 Eric Johnson	.30	.75
85 Shaun Alexander	.40	1.00
86 Darrell Jackson	.30	.75
87 Matt Hasselbeck	.40	1.00
88 Marc Bulger	.40	1.00
89 Steven Jackson	.50	1.25
90 Marshall Faulk	.50	1.25
91 Torry Holt	.40	1.00
92 Michael Pittman	.30	.75
93 Brian Griese	.40	1.00
94 Michael Clayton	.30	.75
95 Steve McNair	.50	1.25
96 Billy Volek	.30	.75
97 Chris Brown	.30	.75
98 Clinton Portis	.40	1.00
99 Patrick Ramsey	.40	1.00
100 Santana Moss	.40	1.00
101 James Kilian RC	1.25	3.00
102 Matt Cassel RC	4.00	10.00
103 Keron Henry RC	1.25	3.00
104 Adrian McPherson RC	1.25	3.00
105 Marcus Randall RC	1.50	4.00
106 Roydel Williams RC	1.50	4.00
107 Dante Ridgeway RC	1.25	3.00
108 Marcus Maxwell RC	1.25	3.00
109 Paris Warren RC	1.50	4.00
110 Courtney Roby RC	1.50	4.00
111 Mark Bradley RC	1.25	3.00
112 Brandon Jones RC	1.50	4.00
113 Chase Lyman RC	1.25	3.00
114 LeRon McCoy RC	1.25	3.00
115 Adam Bergen RC	1.25	3.00
116 Harry Williams RC	1.50	4.00
117 Lance Moore RC	15.00	30.00
118 Jason Anderson RC	1.25	3.00
119 Lionel Gates RC	1.25	3.00
120 Darrell Shropshire RC	1.25	3.00
121 Will Matthews RC	1.25	3.00
122 Noah Herron RC	1.25	3.00
123 Jerome Collins RC	1.50	4.00
124 Stanford Routt RC	1.50	4.00
125 Nick Collins RC	2.00	5.00
126 Maurice Clarett	1.25	3.00
127 Kelvin Hayden RC	1.50	4.00
128 Bo Scaife RC	1.50	4.00
129 Eric King RC	1.25	3.00
130 Kerry Rhodes RC	1.50	4.00
131 Darrent Williams RC	2.00	5.00
132 Stanley Wilson RC	1.50	4.00
133 Nick Speegle RC	1.25	3.00
134 Brodney Pool RC	1.50	4.00
135 Ellis Hobbs RC	2.00	5.00
136 Sean Considine RC	1.25	3.00
137 Josh Bullocks RC	1.50	4.00
138 Jovan Haye RC	1.25	3.00
139 Jimmy Verdon RC	1.25	3.00
140 Ryan Riddle RC	1.25	3.00
141 Luis Castillo RC	1.50	4.00
142 Jesse Lumsden RC	1.25	3.00
143 David Baas RC	1.25	3.00
144 Chris Spencer RC	2.00	5.00
145 Jamaal Brown RC	2.00	5.00
146 Marcus Lawrence RC	1.25	3.00
147 Todd Mortensen RC	1.25	3.00
148 Shane Boyd RC	1.25	3.00
149 Darian Durant RC	1.25	3.00
150 Chance Mock RC	1.50	4.00
151 Damien Nash RC	1.50	4.00
152 Deandra Cobb RC	1.25	3.00
153 Jamaica Rector RC	1.25	3.00
154 Carlyle Holiday RC	1.50	4.00
155 Nehemiah Broughton RC	1.50	4.00
156 Efrem Hill RC	1.25	3.00
157 Dominic Robinson RC	1.25	3.00
158 Rick Razzano RC	1.25	3.00
159 Rasheed Marshall RC	1.50	4.00
160 Lofa Tatupu RC	2.00	5.00
161 Robert McCune RC	1.50	4.00
162 Channing Crowder RC	1.50	4.00
163 Ryan Claridge RC	1.25	3.00
164 Fred Amey RC	1.25	3.00
165 Jordan Beck RC	1.50	4.00
166 Leroy Hill RC	2.00	5.00
167 Travis Daniels RC	1.50	4.00
168 Jerome Carter RC	1.25	3.00
169 Chad Friehauf RC	1.50	4.00
170 Scott Starks RC	1.50	4.00
171 Marviel Underwood RC	1.50	4.00
172 Domonique Foxworth RC	1.50	4.00
173 Jon Goldsberry RC	2.00	5.00
174 Jonathan Babineaux RC	1.50	4.00
175 Sione Pouha RC	1.25	3.00
176 Kerry Wright RC	1.50	4.00
177 Jason White RC	2.00	5.00
178 Matt Jones RC	1.50	4.00
179 Gino Guidugli RC	1.25	3.00
180 Timmy Chang RC	1.50	4.00
181 Chris Rix RC	1.50	4.00
182 Ryan Fitzpatrick RC	3.00	8.00
183 Brock Berlin RC	1.50	4.00
184 Bryan Randall RC	1.50	4.00
185 Stefan LeFors RC	1.25	3.00
186 Larry Brackins RC	1.25	3.00
187 Charles Frederick RC	1.25	3.00
188 J.R. Russell RC	1.25	3.00
189 Vincent Jackson RC	2.50	6.00
190 Josh Davis RC	1.25	3.00
191 Chad Owens RC	1.50	4.00
192 Airese Currie RC	1.25	3.00
193 Chauncey Stovall RC	1.25	3.00
194 Jovan Witherspoon RC	1.25	3.00
195 Trent Cole RC	2.00	5.00
196 Tab Perry RC	1.25	3.00
197 Cedric Houston RC	2.00	5.00
198 Brandon Jacobs RC	2.50	6.00
199 Bobby Purify RC	1.50	4.00
200 Marion Barber RC	2.00	5.00
201 Alvin Pearman RC	1.25	3.00
202 Madison Hedgecock RC	2.00	5.00
203 Justin Green RC	2.00	5.00
204 Manuel White RC	1.50	4.00
205 Kevin Everett RC	2.00	5.00
206 Matthew Tant RC	1.25	3.00
207 Bryant McFadden RC	1.50	4.00
208 Ryan Moats RC	1.25	3.00
209 Fabian Washington RC	1.50	4.00
210 Oshiomogho Atogwe RC	2.00	5.00
211 Dustin Fox RC	1.50	4.00
212 Shaun Cody RC	1.50	4.00
213 Matt Roth RC	1.50	4.00
214 Vincent Burns RC	1.25	3.00
215 Bill Swancutt RC	1.25	3.00
216 Brady Poppinga RC	2.00	5.00
217 Logan Mankins RC	2.00	5.00
218 Michael Roos RC	1.25	3.00
219 Alfred Fincher RC	1.50	4.00
220 Darryl Blackstock RC	1.25	3.00
221 Jared Newberry RC	1.50	4.00
222 Khalif Barnes RC	1.25	3.00
223 Alex Barron RC	1.25	3.00
224 Patrick Estes RC	1.25	3.00
225 Elton Brown RC	1.25	3.00
226 David Greene RC	1.50	4.00
227 Dan Orlovsky RC	2.50	6.00
228 Derek Anderson RC	2.00	5.00
229 Kyle Orton RC	2.50	6.00
230 Chris Henry RC	2.50	6.00
231 Fred Gibson RC	2.00	5.00
232 Craphonso Thorpe RC	1.50	4.00
233 Terrence Murphy RC	1.50	4.00
234 Steve Savoy RC	1.50	4.00
235 Roscoe Parrish RC	1.50	4.00
236 Reggie Brown RC	1.50	4.00
237 Craig Bragg RC	1.50	4.00
238 Eric Shelton RC	1.50	4.00
239 T.A. McLendon RC	1.50	4.00
240 Walter Reyes RC	1.50	4.00
241 Anthony Davis RC	1.50	4.00
242 J.J. Arrington RC	2.00	5.00
243 Frank Gore RC	4.00	10.00
244 Alex Smith TE RC	1.50	4.00
245 Jeb Huckeba RC	2.00	5.00
246 Adam Jones RC	1.50	4.00
247 Brandon Browner RC	2.50	6.00
248 Carlos Rogers RC	2.50	6.00
249 Corey Webster RC	2.00	5.00
250 Justin Miller RC	2.00	5.00
251 Eric Green RC	1.50	4.00
252 Kurt Campbell RC	1.50	4.00
253 Ronald Bartell RC	2.00	5.00
254 Dilly Dajema RC	1.50	4.00
255 Vincent Fuller RC	2.00	5.00
256 Donte Nicholson RC	1.50	4.00
257 Derrick Johnson RC	2.00	5.00
258 Mike Patterson RC	1.50	4.00
259 Anttaj Hawthorne RC	1.50	4.00
260 Erasmus James RC	2.00	5.00
261 David Pollack RC	2.00	5.00
262 Garrett Cross RC	1.50	4.00
263 Justin Tuck RC	3.00	8.00
264 DeMarcus Ware RC	5.00	12.00
265 Odell Thurman RC	2.50	6.00
266 Barrett Ruud RC	2.50	6.00
267 Lance Mitchell RC	2.00	5.00
268 Kevin Burnett RC	2.00	5.00
269 Daven Holly RC	1.50	4.00
270 James Butler RC	2.00	5.00
271 Kirk Morrison RC	2.50	6.00
272 Mike Nugent RC	2.00	5.00
273 Zach Tuiasosopo RC	1.50	4.00
274 Kay-Jay Harris RC	1.50	4.00
275 Darren Sproles RC	2.50	6.00
276 Ciatrick Fason RC	2.00	5.00
277 Charlie Frye RC	3.00	8.00
278 Vernand Morency RC	2.00	5.00
279 Jason Campbell RC	4.00	10.00
280 Antrel Rolle RC	3.00	8.00
281 Derrick Johnson RC	2.50	6.00
282 Shawne Merriman RC	3.00	8.00
283 Marlin Jackson RC	2.00	5.00
284 Jerome Mathis RC	3.00	8.00
285 Mike Williams	3.00	8.00
286 Dan Cody RC	2.50	6.00
287 Travis Johnson RC	2.00	5.00
288 Thomas Davis RC	2.00	5.00
289 Marcus Spears RC	2.50	6.00
290 Andrew Walter RC	2.50	6.00
291 Heath Miller RC	4.00	10.00
292 Mark Clayton RC	2.50	6.00
293 Troy Williamson RC	2.50	6.00
294 Roddy White RC	4.00	10.00
295 Braylon Edwards RC	4.00	10.00
296 Cedric Benson RC	3.00	8.00
297 Cadillac Williams RC	3.00	8.00
298 Ronnie Brown RC	4.00	10.00
299 Alex Smith QB RC	5.00	12.00
300 Aaron Rodgers RC	40.00	80.00

2005 Reflections Black

*VETERANS 1-100: 6X TO 15X BASIC CARDS
*ROOKIES 101-175: 1.5X TO 4X BASIC CARDS
*ROOKIES 176-225: 1.5X TO 4X BASIC CARDS
*ROOKIES 226-275: 1.2X TO 3X BASIC CARDS
*ROOKIES 276-300: 1X TO 2.5X BASIC CARDS
STATED PRINT RUN 25 SER.#'d SETS
OVERALL PARALLEL ODDS 1:6

300 Aaron Rodgers	175.00	300.00

2005 Reflections Blue

*VETERANS 1-100: 2.5X TO 6X BASIC CARDS
*ROOKIES 101-175: .6X TO 1.5X
*ROOKIES 176-225: .6X TO 1.5X
*ROOKIES 226-275: .5X TO 1.2X
*ROOKIES 276-300: .4X TO 1X
STATED PRINT RUN 99 SER.#'d SETS

300 Aaron Rodgers	60.00	120.00

2005 Reflections Gold

*VETERANS 1-100: 4X TO 10X BASIC CARDS
*ROOKIES 101-175: 1X TO 2.5X BASIC CARDS
*ROOKIES 176-225: 1X TO 2.5X BASIC CARDS
*ROOKIES 226-275: .8X TO 2X BASIC CARDS
*ROOKIES 276-300: .6X TO 1.5X
STATED PRINT RUN 50 SER.#'d SETS

300 Aaron Rodgers	100.00	200.00

2005 Reflections Green

*VETERANS: 3X TO 8 BASIC CARDS
*ROOKIES 101-175: .8X TO 2X BASIC CARDS
*ROOKIES 176-225: .8X TO 2X BASIC CARDS
*ROOKIES 226-275: .6X TO 1.5X
*ROOKIES 276-300: .5X TO 1.2X
STATED PRINT RUN 75 SER.#'d SETS

300 Aaron Rodgers	125.00	200.00

2005 Reflections Cut From the Same Cloth Red

RED STATED ODDS 1:12
*BLUE: .6X TO 1.5X RED
BLUE PRINT RUN 50 SER.#'d SETS
UNPRICED AUTO PRINT RUN 10 SETS

CCBJ Marc Bulger	4.00	10.00
Steven Jackson		
CCBR Mark Bradley	2.50	6.00
Reggie Brown		
CCBT Tiki Barber SP	4.00	10.00
Fred Taylor		
CCBW Ronnie Brown	10.00	25.00
Cadillac Williams		
CCCJ Mark Clayton	3.00	8.00
Jamal Lewis		
CCCP Keary Colbert	4.00	10.00
Carson Palmer		
CCDM Domanick Davis	2.50	6.00
Vernand Morency		
CCEP Lee Evans	3.00	8.00
Roscoe Parrish		
CCET Braylon Edwards	6.00	15.00
Troy Williamson		
CCEW Braylon Edwards	6.00	15.00
Roy Williams WR		
CCFC Charlie Frye	6.00	15.00
Jason Campbell		
CCFL Charlie Frye	4.00	10.00
Byron Leftwich		
CCGB Antonio Gates	4.00	10.00
Drew Brees		
CCGF Ahman Green SP	12.50	30.00
Brett Favre		
CCGJ Antonio Gates	5.00	12.00
Vincent Jackson		
CCGS Frank Gore	10.00	25.00
Alex Smith QB		
CCJB Rudi Johnson	6.00	15.00
Ronnie Brown		
CCJD Julius Jones	10.00	25.00
Tony Dorsett		
CCJG Steven Jackson	4.00	10.00
Ahman Green		
CCJH Chad Johnson	3.00	8.00
Joe Horn		
CCJM Julius Jones	3.00	8.00
Deuce McAllister		
CCJR Adam Jones	4.00	10.00
Antrel Rolle		
CCJW Rudi Johnson	8.00	20.00
Cadillac Williams		
CCMB Donovan McNabb	4.00	10.00
Reggie Brown		
CCME Dan Marino	15.00	40.00
John Elway		
CCMF Peyton Manning	12.50	30.00
Brett Favre		
CCMG Terrence Murphy	3.00	8.00
Ahman Green		
CCML Joe Montana	15.00	40.00
Eli Manning		
CCMM Peyton Manning	15.00	40.00
Eli Manning		
CCMP Eli Manning	7.50	20.00
Carson Palmer		
CCMR Dan Marino	15.00	40.00
Ben Roethlisberger		
CCMS Peyton Manning	10.00	25.00
Alex Smith QB		
CCPW Andrew Walter	4.00	10.00
Carson Palmer		
CCRF Ben Roethlisbeger	10.00	25.00
Charlie Frye		
CCSA Barry Sanders	12.50	30.00
Troy Aikman		
CCSC Alex Smith QB	7.50	20.00
David Carr		
CCSM Barry Sanders	7.50	20.00
Vernand Morency		
CCSR Deion Sanders	5.00	12.00
Antrel Rolle		
CCTF Fred Taylor	3.00	8.00
Ciatrick Fason		
CCVM Michael Vick SP	5.00	12.00
Donovan McNabb		
CCWJ Troy Williamson	3.00	8.00
Chad Johnson		
CCWP Reggie Wayne	4.00	10.00
Roscoe Parrish		

2005 Reflections Dual Signature Reflections Red

STATED PRINT RUN 70 SER.#'d SETS
UNPRICED GOLD PRINT RUN 1 SET

DSAC Derek Anderson	15.00	40.00
Mark Clayton		
DSAR J.J. Arrington	125.00	200.00
Aaron Rodgers		
DSBB Nate Burleson	10.00	25.00
Drew Bennett		
DSBC Braylon Edwards	30.00	80.00
Mark Clayton		
DSBG Mark Bradley	10.00	25.00
Fred Gibson		
DSBJ Drew Bledsoe	25.00	60.00
Julius Jones		
DSBK Marion Barber	15.00	40.00
Kevin Burnett		
DSBM Reggie Brown	12.00	30.00
Ryan Moats		
DSBS Marion Barber	15.00	40.00
Eric Shelton		
DSBT Anquan Boldin	15.00	40.00
Craphonso Thorpe		
DSBW Nate Burleson	15.00	40.00
Reggie Wayne		
DSCB Mark Clayton	10.00	25.00
Mark Bradley		
DSCM Maurice Clarett	10.00	25.00
Ryan Moats		
DSDC Domanick Davis	10.00	25.00
Michael Clayton		
DSDP Thomas Davis	10.00	25.00
David Pollack		
DSEA Eli Manning	75.00	135.00
Alex Smith QB		
DSEC Lee Evans	10.00	25.00
Keary Colbert		
DSEF Braylon Edwards	30.00	80.00
Charlie Frye		
DSET Braylon Edwards	30.00	80.00
Troy Williamson		
DSFG Charlie Frye	10.00	25.00
David Greene		
DSFM Brett Favre	100.00	200.00
Terrence Murphy		
DSGG David Greene	10.00	25.00
Fred Gibson		
DSGS Antonio Gates	25.00	50.00
Darren Sproles		
DSGT Trent Green	10.00	25.00
Craphonso Thorpe		
DSHG Chris Henry	10.00	25.00
Fred Gibson		
DSJB Brandon Jacobs	30.00	60.00
Tiki Barber		
DSJC Rudi Johnson	15.00	40.00
Chris Henry		
DSJE Marlin Jackson	25.00	60.00
Braylon Edwards		
DSJH Adam Jones	15.00	40.00
Chris Henry		
DSKJ Kevin Burnett	15.00	40.00
Julius Jones		
DSMA Heath Miller	15.00	40.00
Alge Crumpler		
DSMD Deuce McAllister	15.00	40.00
Domanick Davis		
DSMM Mark Bradley	12.00	30.00
Muhsin Muhammad		
DSMP Marc Bulger	60.00	120.00
Peyton Manning		
DSOF Dan Orlovsky	10.00	25.00
Charlie Fyre		
DSOW Dan Orlovsky	15.00	40.00
Roy Williams WR		
DSPG David Pollack	12.00	30.00
David Greene		
DSRA Antrel Rolle	10.00	25.00
J.J. Arrington		
DSRC Charles Rogers	25.00	50.00
Jason Campbell		
DSRG Antrel Rolle	25.00	60.00
Frank Gore		
DSRJ Antrel Rolle	12.00	30.00
Adam Pacman Jones		
DSRS J.R. Russell	10.00	25.00
Eric Shelton		
DSRW Barrett Ruud	15.00	40.00
Jason White		
DSSD Darren Sproles	15.00	40.00
Anthony Davis		
DSTR Craphonso Thorpe	10.00	25.00
J.R. Russell		
DSVB Michael Vick	40.00	80.00
George Blanda		
DSWC Jason White	10.00	25.00
Mark Clayton		
DSWF Troy Williamson	10.00	25.00
Ciatrick Fason		
DSWH Jason White	20.00	50.00
Paul Hornung		
DSWO Andrew Walter	10.00	25.00
Dan Orlovsky		

2005 Reflections Fabrics

STATED ODDS 1:12

FRBF Brett Favre SP	10.00	25.00
FRBL Byron Leftwich	2.50	6.00
FRBR Ben Roethlisberger	5.00	12.00
FRBU Brian Urlacher	3.00	8.00
FRCH Chad Pennington	3.00	8.00
FRCL Clinton Portis	2.50	6.00
FRCM Curtis Martin	3.00	8.00
FRCP Carson Palmer	3.00	8.00
FRDA Daunte Culpepper	2.50	6.00
FRDB Drew Bledsoe	3.00	8.00
FRDC David Carr	2.00	5.00
FRDM Donovan McNabb	3.00	8.00
FRDR Drew Brees	3.00	8.00
FREJ Edgerrin James	2.50	6.00
FREM Eli Manning	5.00	12.00
FRJH Joey Harrington	2.50	6.00
FRJJ Julius Jones	2.00	5.00
FRJR Jerry Rice	6.00	15.00
FRLS Lee Suggs	2.00	5.00
FRLT LaDainian Tomlinson	3.00	8.00
FRMH Marvin Harrison	3.00	8.00
FRPH Priest Holmes	2.50	6.00
FRPM Peyton Manning	6.00	15.00
FRRM Randy Moss	3.00	8.00
FRSA Shaun Alexander	2.50	6.00
FRSM Steve McNair	3.00	8.00
FRTB Tom Brady	6.00	15.00
FRTO Terrell Owens	3.00	8.00

2005 Reflections Fabrics Gold

*GOLD: 1X TO 2.5X BASIC INSERTS
GOLD PRINT RUN 25 SER.#'d SETS

FRMV Michael Vick	8.00	20.00

2005 Reflections Fabrics Patches

*PATCH: 1.2X TO 3X BASIC JSYs
PATCH PRINT RUN 30 SER.#'d SETS

FRPAJ Andre Johnson	10.00	25.00
FRPMV Michael Vick	10.00	25.00

2005 Reflections Future Fabrics

STATED ODDS 1:12
*GOLD: 1.2X TO 3X BASIC JSYs
GOLD PRINT RUN 25 SER.#'d SETS
*PATCH: 1.2X TO 3X BASIC JSYs
PATCH PRINT RUN 30 SER.#'d SETS

FFRAN Antrel Rolle	3.00	8.00
FFRAS Alex Smith QB	8.00	20.00
FFRAW Andrew Walter	2.50	6.00
FFRBE Braylon Edwards	5.00	12.00
FFRCA Carlos Rogers	3.00	8.00
FFRCF Charlie Frye	3.00	8.00
FFRCI Ciatrick Fason	2.00	5.00
FFRCR Courtney Roby	2.50	6.00
FFRCW Cadillac Williams	8.00	20.00
FFRES Eric Shelton	2.00	5.00
FFRFG Frank Gore	5.00	12.00
FFRJC Jason Campbell	4.00	10.00
FFRJJ J.J. Arrington	2.50	6.00
FFRKO Kyle Orton	3.00	8.00
FFRMB Mark Bradley	2.00	5.00
FFRMC Mark Clayton	2.50	6.00
FFRMO Maurice Clarett	2.00	5.00
FFRRB Ronnie Brown	5.00	12.00
FFRRE Reggie Brown	2.00	5.00
FFRRM Ryan Moats	2.00	5.00
FFRRP Roscoe Parrish	2.00	5.00
FFRRW Roddy White	4.00	10.00
FFRSL Stefan LeFors	2.00	5.00
FFRTM Terrence Murphy	2.00	5.00
FFRTW Troy Williamson SP	2.50	6.00
FFRVJ Vincent Jackson	4.00	10.00
FFRVM Vernand Morency	2.00	5.00

2005 Reflections Rookie Exclusives Autographs Red

STATED PRINT RUN 100 SER.#'d SETS
UNPRICED GOLD PRINT RUN 1 SET

READ Anthony Davis	8.00	20.00
REAH Anttaj Hawthorne	8.00	20.00
REAJ Adam Jones	8.00	20.00
REAN Antrel Rolle	12.00	30.00
REAR Aaron Rodgers	175.00	300.00
REAS Alex Smith QB	30.00	60.00
REAW Andrew Walter	10.00	25.00
REBE Braylon Edwards	20.00	50.00
REBR Barrett Ruud	12.00	30.00
RECB Cedric Benson	12.00	30.00
RECF Charlie Frye	12.00	30.00
RECH Chris Henry	12.00	30.00
RECI Ciatrick Fason	8.00	20.00
RECR Carlos Rogers	12.00	30.00
RECT Craphonso Thorpe	8.00	20.00
RECW Cadillac Williams	25.00	60.00
REDA Derek Anderson	10.00	25.00
REDG David Greene	8.00	20.00
REDO Dan Orlovsky	12.00	30.00
REDP David Pollack	10.00	25.00
REDS Darren Sproles	15.00	40.00
REEJ Erasmus James	10.00	25.00
REES Eric Shelton	8.00	20.00
REFG Fred Gibson	10.00	25.00
REFR Frank Gore	20.00	50.00
REHM Heath Miller	25.00	50.00
REJC Jason Campbell	15.00	40.00
REJJ J.J. Arrington	10.00	25.00
REKH Kay-Jay Harris	8.00	20.00
REKO Kyle Orton	12.00	30.00
REMA Marion Barber	12.00	30.00
REMB Mark Bradley	8.00	20.00
REMC Mark Clayton	12.00	30.00
REMJ Marlin Jackson	8.00	20.00
REMO Maurice Clarett	10.00	25.00
RERB Ronnie Brown	30.00	80.00
RERE Reggie Brown	8.00	20.00
RERM Ryan Moats	10.00	25.00
RERP Roscoe Parrish	8.00	20.00
RERW Roddy White	15.00	40.00
RESL Stefan LeFors	8.00	20.00
RESM Shawne Merriman	15.00	40.00
RETD Thomas Davis	8.00	20.00
RETJ Travis Johnson	8.00	20.00
RETM Terrence Murphy	8.00	20.00
RETW Troy Williamson	10.00	25.00
REVJ Vincent Jackson	20.00	40.00
REVM Vernand Morency	10.00	25.00
REWE Corey Webster	10.00	25.00

2005 Reflections Signature Reflections Red

RED STATED ODDS 1:12
UNPRICED BLUE PRINT RUN 15 SETS
*GOLD: .5X TO 1.2X BASIC REDS
*GOLD: .4X TO 1X RED SP's
GOLD PRINT RUN 89 SER.#'d SETS

SRAB Aaron Brooks	5.00	12.00
SRAC Alge Crumpler	6.00	15.00
SRAD Anthony Davis	5.00	12.00
SRAF A.J. Feeley	5.00	12.00
SRAG Ahman Green	6.00	15.00
SRAH Anttaj Hawthorne	5.00	12.00
SRAJ Adam Jones	5.00	12.00
SRAN Antrel Rolle	8.00	20.00
SRAQ Anquan Boldin SP	8.00	20.00
SRAR Aaron Rodgers	175.00	300.00
SRAS Alex Smith QB SP	30.00	60.00
SRAT Antonio Gates SP	10.00	25.00
SRAW Andrew Walter	6.00	15.00
SRBD Brian Dawkins	6.00	15.00
SRBE Braylon Edwards	20.00	50.00
SRBF Brett Favre SP	100.00	175.00
SRBJ Brandon Jacobs	10.00	25.00
SRBL Byron Leftwich SP	8.00	20.00
SRBR Barrett Ruud	8.00	20.00
SRCB Chris Brown	5.00	12.00
SRCC Cris Collinsworth	8.00	20.00
SRCF Charlie Frye	8.00	20.00
SRCH Chris Henry	8.00	20.00
SRCI Ciatrick Fason SP	6.00	15.00
SRCJ Chad Johnson	6.00	15.00
SRCN Chuck Noll	15.00	40.00
SRCO Corey Webster	6.00	15.00
SRCT Craphonso Thorpe	5.00	12.00
SRCW Cadillac Williams SP	20.00	50.00
SRDA Derek Anderson	6.00	15.00
SRDB Drew Bennett	6.00	15.00
SRDC Dan Cody	6.00	15.00
SRDD Domanick Davis	5.00	12.00
SRDE Deuce McAllister SP	8.00	20.00
SRDG David Greene	5.00	12.00
SRDJ Deacon Jones	8.00	20.00
SRDO Dan Orlovsky	8.00	20.00
SRDP David Pollack	6.00	15.00
SRDR Drew Bledsoe SP	12.00	30.00
SRDS Darren Sproles	10.00	25.00
SREJ Edgerrin James SP	15.00	40.00
SREM Eli Manning SP	60.00	100.00
SRER Erasmus James	6.00	15.00
SRES Eric Shelton	5.00	12.00
SRFG Frank Gore	12.00	30.00
SRFR Fred Gibson	6.00	15.00
SRFR Charles Frederick	5.00	12.00
SRFT Fred Taylor	6.00	15.00
SRHM Heath Miller	10.00	25.00
SRJA James Butler	6.00	15.00
SRJB Jim Brown SP	50.00	120.00
SRJC Jason Campbell	10.00	25.00
SRJE John Elway SP	100.00	175.00
SRJH Joe Horn SP	8.00	20.00
SRJJ Julius Jones SP	6.00	15.00
SRJM Joe Montana SP	125.00	200.00
SRJP J.P. Losman SP	6.00	15.00
SRJR J.R. Russell	5.00	12.00
SRJW Jason White	8.00	20.00
SRKB Kevin Burnett	6.00	15.00
SRKC Keary Colbert	5.00	12.00
SRKH Kay-Jay Harris	5.00	12.00
SRKO Kyle Orton	8.00	20.00
SRLE Lee Evans SP	8.00	20.00
SRLJ LaMont Jordan	6.00	15.00
SRLY Larry Johnson	6.00	15.00
SRMB Marion Barber	10.00	25.00
SRMC Michael Clayton SP	6.00	15.00
SRMJ Marlin Jackson	5.00	12.00
SRMM Muhsin Muhhamad	6.00	15.00
SRMO Maurice Clarett	5.00	12.00
SRMU Marc Bulger SP	8.00	20.00
SRMW Mike Williams SP	10.00	25.00
SRNB Nate Burleson SP	6.00	15.00
SRPM Peyton Manning SP	60.00	100.00
SRRA Reggie Wayne SP	12.00	30.00
SRRB Ronnie Brown SP	20.00	50.00
SRRJ Rudi Johnson SP	8.00	20.00
SRRO Roy Williams WR	6.00	15.00
SRSM Shawne Merriman	8.00	20.00
SRTD Thomas Davis	5.00	12.00
SRTE Terrence Murphy	5.00	12.00
SRTG Trent Green SP	8.00	20.00
SRTJ Travis Johnson	5.00	12.00
SRTM T.A. McLendon	5.00	12.00
SRTS Taylor Stubblefield	5.00	12.00
SRTW Troy Williamson	6.00	15.00
SRVM Vernand Morency	6.00	15.00
SRWR Walter Reyes	5.00	12.00

2005 Reflections Super Swatch

STATED PRINT RUN 40 SER.#'d SETS
UNPRICED AUTOS PRINT RUN 10 SETS

SSAG Ahman Green	10.00	25.00
SSAN Antrel Rolle	8.00	20.00
SSAO Antonio Gates	12.00	30.00
SSAS Alex Smith QB	20.00	50.00
SSBE Braylon Edwards	15.00	40.00
SSBF Brett Favre	25.00	60.00
SSBL Byron Leftwich	10.00	25.00
SSBR Ben Roethlisberger	25.00	60.00
SSBS Barry Sanders	30.00	60.00
SSCA Carlos Rogers	8.00	20.00
SSCF Charlie Frye	8.00	20.00
SSCI Ciatrick Fason	5.00	12.00
SSCJ Chad Johnson	10.00	25.00
SSCP Carson Palmer	12.00	30.00
SSCW Cadillac Williams	15.00	40.00
SSDD Domanick Davis	8.00	20.00
SSDM Deuce McAllister	10.00	25.00
SSEM Eli Manning	20.00	50.00
SSES Eric Shelton	8.00	20.00
SSFT Fran Tarkenton	15.00	40.00
SSJC Jason Campbell	10.00	25.00
SSJH Joe Horn	10.00	25.00
SSJJ Julius Jones	15.00	40.00
SSJM Joe Montana	30.00	60.00
SSLE Lee Evans	10.00	25.00
SSLJ Larry Johnson	10.00	25.00
SSMA Mark Clayton	8.00	20.00
SSMB Marc Bulger	10.00	25.00
SSMC Michael Clayton	5.00	12.00
SSMO Maurice Clarett	8.00	20.00
SSNB Nate Burleson	8.00	20.00
SSPM Peyton Manning	20.00	50.00
SSRB Ronnie Brown	20.00	50.00
SSRJ Rudi Johnson	10.00	25.00
SSRP Roscoe Parrish	8.00	20.00
SSSJ Steven Jackson	12.00	30.00
SSSL Stefan LeFors	5.00	12.00
SSTW Troy Williamson	6.00	15.00

1997 Revolution

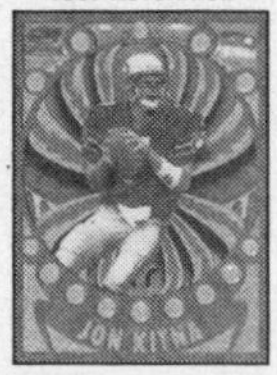

The 1997 Pacific Revolution set was issued in one series totalling 150 cards and distributed in three-card packs. The fronts feature color photos of prominent players with holographic foil, etching and embossing. The backs carry a small player head photo and career highlights.

COMPLETE SET (150)	40.00	80.00
1 Larry Centers	.30	.75
2 Kent Graham	.20	.50
3 Leeland McElroy	.20	.50
4 Rob Moore	.30	.75
5 Jake Plummer RC	2.50	6.00
6 Jamal Anderson	.50	1.25
7 Bert Emanuel	.30	.75
8 Byron Hanspard RC	.30	.75
9 Terance Mathis	.30	.75
10 O.J. Santiago RC	.30	.75
11 Derrick Alexander WR	.30	.75

12 Peter Boulware RC .50 1.25
13 Jay Graham RC .30 .75
14 Michael Jackson .30 .75
15 Vinny Testaverde .30 .75
16 Todd Collins .20 .50
17 Andre Reed .30 .75
18 Jay Riemersma .20 .50
19 Antowain Smith RC 1.50 4.00
20 Bruce Smith .30 .75
21 Thurman Thomas .50 1.25
22 Rae Carruth RC .20 .50
23 Kerry Collins .50 1.25
24 Anthony Johnson .20 .50
25 Muhsin Muhammad .30 .75
26 Wesley Walls .30 .75
27 Curtis Conway .30 .75
28 Bobby Engram .30 .75
29 Raymont Harris .20 .50
30 Rick Mirer .20 .50
31 Rashaan Salaam .20 .50
32 Jeff Blake .30 .75
33 Corey Dillon RC 2.50 6.00
34 Carl Pickens .30 .75
35 Darnay Scott .30 .75
36 Troy Aikman 1.00 2.50
37 Michael Irvin .50 1.25
38 Daryl Johnston .30 .75
39 Deion Sanders .50 1.25
40 Emmitt Smith 1.50 4.00
41 Terrell Davis .60 1.50
42 John Elway 2.00 5.00
43 Ed McCaffrey .30 .75
44 Shannon Sharpe .30 .75
45 Neil Smith .30 .75
46 Scott Mitchell .30 .75
47 Herman Moore .30 .75
48 Johnnie Morton .30 .75
49 Barry Sanders 1.50 4.00
50 Robert Brooks .30 .75
51 LeRoy Butler .20 .50
52 Brett Favre 2.00 5.00
53 Antonio Freeman .50 1.25
54 Dorsey Levens .50 1.25
55 Reggie White .50 1.25
56 Sean Dawkins .20 .50
57 Ken Dilger .20 .50
58 Marshall Faulk .60 1.50
59 Jim Harbaugh .30 .75
60 Marvin Harrison .50 1.25
61 Mark Brunell .60 1.50
62 Keenan McCardell .30 .75
63 Natrone Means .30 .75
64 Jimmy Smith .30 .75
65 James O.Stewart .30 .75
66 Marcus Allen .50 1.25
67 Tony Gonzalez RC 2.50 6.00
68 Elvis Grbac .30 .75
69 Greg Hill .20 .50
70 Andre Rison .30 .75
71 Karim Abdul-Jabbar .50 1.25
72 Fred Barnett .20 .50
73 Dan Marino 2.00 5.00
74 O.J. McDuffie .30 .75
75 Irving Spikes .20 .50
76 Cris Carter .50 1.25
77 Matthew Hatchette RC .30 .75
78 Brad Johnson .50 1.25
79 Jake Reed .30 .75
80 Robert Smith .30 .75
81 Drew Bledsoe .60 1.50
82 Ben Coates .30 .75
83 Terry Glenn .50 1.25
84 Curtis Martin .60 1.50
85 Dave Meggett .20 .50
86 Troy Davis RC .30 .75
87 Andre Hastings .20 .50
88 Heath Shuler .20 .50
89 Irv Smith .20 .50
90 Danny Wuerffel RC .50 1.25
91 Ray Zellars .20 .50
92 Tiki Barber RC 4.00 10.00
93 Dave Brown .20 .50
94 Chris Calloway .20 .50
95 Rodney Hampton .30 .75
96 Amani Toomer .30 .75
97 Wayne Chrebet .50 1.25
98 Keyshawn Johnson .50 1.25
99 Adrian Murrell .30 .75
100 Neil O'Donnell .30 .75
101 Dedric Ward RC .30 .75
102 Tim Brown .50 1.25
103 Rickey Dudley .30 .75
104 Jeff George .30 .75
105 Desmond Howard .30 .75
106 Napoleon Kaufman .50 1.25
107 Ty Detmer .30 .75
108 Jason Dunn .20 .50
109 Irving Fryar .30 .75
110 Rodney Peete .20 .50
111 Ricky Watters .30 .75
112 Jerome Bettis .50 1.25
113 Will Blackwell RC .30 .75
114 Charles Johnson .30 .75
115 Kordell Stewart .50 1.25
116 Tony Banks .30 .75
117 Isaac Bruce .50 1.25
118 Ernie Conwell .20 .50
119 Eddie Kennison .30 .75
120 Lawrence Phillips .20 .50
121 Stan Humphries .30 .75
122 Tony Martin .30 .75
123 Eric Metcalf .30 .75
124 Junior Seau .50 1.25
125 Jim Druckenmiller RC .30 .75
126 Kevin Greene .30 .75
127 Garrison Hearst .30 .75
128 Terrell Owens .60 1.50
129 Jerry Rice 1.00 2.50
130 J.J. Stokes .30 .75
131 Rod Woodson .30 .75
132 Steve Young .60 1.50
133 Joey Galloway .30 .75
134 Cortez Kennedy .20 .50
135 Jon Kitna RC 5.00 10.00
136 Warren Moon .50 1.25
137 Chris Warren .30 .75
138 Mike Alstott .50 1.25
139 Reidel Anthony RC .50 1.25
140 Trent Dilfer .50 1.25
141 Warrick Dunn RC 2.00 5.00
142 Willie Davis .20 .50
143 Eddie George .50 1.25
144 Steve McNair .60 1.50
145 Chris Sanders .20 .50
146 Terry Allen .50 1.25
147 Jamie Asher .20 .50
148 Henry Ellard .20 .50
149 Gus Frerotte .20 .50
150 Leslie Shepherd .20 .50
S1 Mark Brunell Sample .40 1.00

1997 Revolution Copper

COMPLETE SET (150) 150.00 300.00
*COPPER STARS: 1.5X TO 4X BASIC CARDS
*COPPER RCs: .6X TO 1.5X BASIC CARDS
STATED ODDS 2:25 HOBBY

1997 Revolution Platinum Blue

*PLAT.BLUE VETS: 2X TO 5X BASIC CARDS
*PLAT.BLUE RCs: 1X TO 2.5X
PLAT.BLUE STATED ODDS 1:49

1997 Revolution Red

COMPLETE SET (150) 125.00 250.00
*RED STARS: 1.2X TO 3X BASIC CARDS
*RED RCs: .6X TO 1.5X BASIC CARDS
STATED ODDS 2:25 SPECIAL RETAIL

1997 Revolution Silver

COMPLETE SET (150) 150.00 300.00
*SILVER STARS: 1.5X TO 4X BASIC CARDS
*SILVER RCs: .6X TO 1.5X BASIC CARDS
STATED ODDS 2:25 RETAIL

1997 Revolution Air Mail Die Cuts

COMPLETE SET (36) 50.00 120.00
STATED ODDS 1:25
1 Vinny Testaverde .75 2.00
2 Andre Reed .75 2.00
3 Kerry Collins 1.25 3.00
4 Jeff Blake .75 2.00
5 Troy Aikman 2.50 6.00
6 Deion Sanders 1.25 3.00
7 Emmitt Smith 4.00 10.00
8 Michael Irvin 1.25 3.00
9 Terrell Davis 1.50 4.00
10 John Elway 5.00 12.00
11 Barry Sanders 4.00 10.00
12 Brett Favre 5.00 12.00
13 Antonio Freeman 1.25 3.00
14 Mark Brunell 1.25 3.00
15 Marcus Allen 1.25 3.00
16 Elvis Grbac .75 2.00
17 Dan Marino 5.00 12.00
18 Brad Johnson 1.25 3.00
19 Drew Bledsoe 1.50 4.00
20 Terry Glenn 1.25 3.00
21 Curtis Martin 1.50 4.00
22 Danny Wuerffel .40 1.00
23 Jeff George .75 2.00
24 Napoleon Kaufman 1.25 3.00
25 Kordell Stewart 1.25 3.00
26 Tony Banks .75 2.00
27 Isaac Bruce 1.25 3.00
28 Jim Druckenmiller .40 1.00
29 Jerry Rice 2.50 6.00
30 Steve Young 1.50 4.00
31 Warren Moon 1.25 3.00
32 Trent Dilfer 1.25 3.00
33 Warrick Dunn 2.50 6.00
34 Eddie George 1.25 3.00
35 Steve McNair 1.50 4.00
36 Gus Frerotte .40 1.00

1997 Revolution Proteges

COMPLETE SET (20) 20.00 50.00
GOLD STATED ODDS 2:25
*SILVER CARDS: .25X TO .5X GOLDS
SILVERS ONE PER SPECIAL RETAIL BOX
1 Kent Graham 1.50 4.00
Jake Plummer
2 Jamal Anderson .60 1.50
Byron Hanspard
3 Thurman Thomas 1.25 3.00
Antowain Smith
4 Troy Aikman 2.50 6.00
Jason Garrett
5 Emmitt Smith 4.00 10.00
Sherman Williams
6 John Elway 5.00 12.00
Jeff Lewis
7 Barry Sanders 4.00 10.00
Ron Rivers
8 Brett Favre 5.00 12.00
Doug Pederson
9 Mark Brunell 2.00 5.00
Rob Johnson
10 Marcus Allen 1.00 2.50
Greg Hill
11 Dan Marino 5.00 12.00
Damon Huard
12 Curtis Martin 1.50 4.00
Mario Grier
13 Heath Shuler 1.00 2.50
Danny Wuerffel
14 Rodney Hampton 2.00 5.00
Tiki Barber
15 Jerome Bettis 1.00 2.50
George Jones
16 Jerry Rice 4.00 10.00
Terrell Owens
17 Steve Young 2.00 5.00
Jim Druckenmiller
18 Warren Moon 2.00 5.00
Jon Kitna
19 Errict Rhett 1.50 4.00
Warrick Dunn
20 Terry Allen 1.00 2.50
Stephen Davis

1997 Revolution Ring Bearers

COMPLETE SET (12) 50.00 120.00
STATED ODDS 1:121
1 Emmitt Smith 8.00 20.00
2 John Elway 6.00 15.00
3 Barry Sanders 6.00 15.00
4 Brett Favre 8.00 20.00
5 Mark Brunell 2.50 6.00
6 Dan Marino 8.00 20.00
7 Drew Bledsoe 3.00 8.00
8 Steve Young 4.00 10.00
9 Warrick Dunn 4.00 10.00
10 Eddie George 2.50 6.00
11 Troy Aikman 5.00 12.00
12 Jerry Rice 5.00 12.00

1997 Revolution Silks

COMPLETE SET (18) 20.00 50.00
STATED ODDS 1:49
1 Kerry Collins 1.00 2.50
2 Troy Aikman 2.00 5.00
3 Deion Sanders 1.50 4.00
4 Emmitt Smith 3.00 8.00
5 Terrell Davis 1.25 3.00
6 John Elway 2.50 6.00
7 Barry Sanders 2.50 6.00
8 Brett Favre 3.00 8.00
9 Mark Brunell 1.00 2.50
10 Marcus Allen 1.25 3.00
11 Dan Marino 3.00 8.00
12 Drew Bledsoe 1.25 3.00
13 Curtis Martin 1.25 3.00
14 Jerome Bettis 1.25 3.00
15 Jim Druckenmiller .75 2.00
16 Jerry Rice 2.00 5.00
17 Warrick Dunn 1.25 3.00
18 Eddie George 1.00 2.50
P1 Mark Brunell Promo 2.00 5.00

1998 Revolution

The 1998 Pacific Revolution set was issued in one series with a total of 150 cards. The fronts feature action player images printed using dual foiling, etching and embossing. The backs display full year-by-year career statistics for the pictured player.

COMPLETE SET (150) 40.00 100.00
1 Larry Centers .30 .75
2 Leeland McElroy .30 .75
3 Rob Moore .50 1.25
4 Jake Plummer .75 2.00
5 Frank Sanders .50 1.25
6 Jamal Anderson .75 2.00
7 Chris Chandler .50 1.25
8 Byron Hanspard .30 .75
9 Jay Graham .30 .75
10 Michael Jackson .30 .75
11 Vinny Testaverde .50 1.25
12 Eric Zeier .50 1.25
13 Todd Collins .30 .75
14 Quinn Early .30 .75
15 Andre Reed .50 1.25
16 Antowain Smith .75 2.00
17 Bruce Smith .50 1.25
18 Thurman Thomas .75 2.00
19 Rae Carruth .30 .75
20 Kerry Collins .50 1.25
21 Wesley Walls .50 1.25
22 Darnell Autry .30 .75
23 Curtis Conway .50 1.25
24 Bobby Engram .50 1.25
25 Curtis Enis RC .50 1.25
26 Raymont Harris .30 .75
27 Jeff Blake .50 1.25
28 Corey Dillon .75 2.00
29 Carl Pickens .50 1.25
30 Darnay Scott .50 1.25
31 Troy Aikman 1.50 4.00
32 Michael Irvin .75 2.00
33 Deion Sanders .75 2.00
34 Emmitt Smith 2.50 6.00
35 Steve Atwater .30 .75
36 Terrell Davis .75 2.00
37 John Elway 3.00 8.00
38 Brian Griese RC 2.00 5.00
39 Ed McCaffrey .50 1.25
40 Marcus Nash RC .50 1.25
41 Shannon Sharpe .50 1.25
42 Neil Smith .50 1.25
43 Rod Smith .50 1.25
44 Charlie Batch RC 1.00 2.50
45 Germane Crowell RC .75 2.00
46 Scott Mitchell .50 1.25
47 Herman Moore .50 1.25
48 Barry Sanders 2.50 6.00
49 Robert Brooks .50 1.25
50 Mark Chmura .50 1.25
51 Brett Favre 3.00 8.00
52 Antonio Freeman .75 2.00
53 Dorsey Levens .75 2.00
54 Aaron Bailey .30 .75
55 Ken Dilger .30 .75
56 Marshall Faulk 1.00 2.50
57 Marvin Harrison .75 2.00
58 Peyton Manning RC 12.50 25.00
59 Tavian Banks RC .75 2.00
60 Tony Brackens .30 .75
61 Mark Brunell .75 2.00
62 Keenan McCardell .50 1.25
63 Natrone Means .50 1.25
64 Jimmy Smith .50 1.25
65 James Stewart .50 1.25
66 Fred Taylor RC 1.50 4.00
67 Tony Gonzalez .75 2.00
68 Elvis Grbac .50 1.25
69 Greg Hill .30 .75
70 Andre Rison .50 1.25
71 Derrick Thomas .75 2.00
72 Karim Abdul-Jabbar .75 2.00
73 John Avery RC .75 2.00
74 Troy Drayton .30 .75
75 Dan Marino 3.00 8.00
76 O.J. McDuffie .50 1.25
77 Cris Carter .75 2.00
78 Brad Johnson .75 2.00
79 John Randle .50 1.25
80 Jake Reed .50 1.25
81 Robert Smith .75 2.00
82 Drew Bledsoe 1.25 3.00
83 Ben Coates .50 1.25
84 Robert Edwards RC .75 2.00
85 Terry Glenn .75 2.00
86 Tony Simmons RC .75 2.00
87 Troy Davis .30 .75
88 Heath Shuler .30 .75
89 Danny Wuerffel .50 1.25
90 Ray Zellars .30 .75
91 Tiki Barber .75 2.00
92 Joe Jurevicius RC 1.00 2.50
93 Danny Kanell .50 1.25
94 Charles Way .30 .75
95 Tyrone Wheatley .50 1.25
96 Wayne Chrebet .75 2.00
97 Glenn Foley .50 1.25
98 Keyshawn Johnson .75 2.00
99 Curtis Martin .75 2.00
100 Tim Brown .75 2.00
101 Rickey Dudley .30 .75
102 Jeff George .50 1.25
103 Desmond Howard .50 1.25
104 Napoleon Kaufman .75 2.00
105 Charles Woodson RC 1.25 3.00
106 Jason Dunn .30 .75
107 Irving Fryar .50 1.25
108 Charlie Garner .50 1.25
109 Bobby Hoying .50 1.25
110 Jerome Bettis .75 2.00
111 Mark Bruener .30 .75
112 Charles Johnson .30 .75
113 Levon Kirkland .30 .75
114 Kordell Stewart .75 2.00
115 Hines Ward RC 5.00 10.00
116 Tony Banks .50 1.25
117 Isaac Bruce .75 2.00
118 Robert Holcombe RC .75 2.00
119 Eddie Kennison .50 1.25
120 Freddie Jones .30 .75
121 Ryan Leaf RC 1.00 2.50
122 Tony Martin .50 1.25
123 Junior Seau .75 2.00
124 Jim Druckenmiller .30 .75
125 Garrison Hearst .75 2.00
126 Terrell Owens .75 2.00
127 Jerry Rice 1.50 4.00
128 J.J. Stokes .50 1.25
129 Steve Young 1.00 2.50
130 Joey Galloway .50 1.25
131 Ahman Green RC 2.50 6.00
132 Cortez Kennedy .30 .75
133 Jon Kitna .75 2.00
134 James McKnight .75 2.00
135 Warren Moon .75 2.00
136 Mike Alstott .75 2.00
137 Reidel Anthony .50 1.25
138 Trent Dilfer .75 2.00
139 Warrick Dunn .75 2.00
140 Warren Sapp .50 1.25
141 Kevin Dyson RC 1.00 2.50
142 Eddie George .75 2.00
143 Steve McNair .75 2.00
144 Chris Sanders .30 .75
145 Frank Wycheck .30 .75
146 Stephen Alexander RC .75 2.00
147 Terry Allen .75 2.00
148 Gus Frerotte .30 .75
149 Skip Hicks RC .75 2.00
150 Michael Westbrook .50 1.25
S1 Warrick Dunn Sample .40 1.00

1998 Revolution Shadows

*SHADOW STARS: 4X TO 10X BASIC CARDS
*SHADOW RCs: 1.5X TO 4X BASIC CARDS
SHADOW PRINT RUN 99 SERIAL #'d SETS

1998 Revolution Icons

COMPLETE SET (10) 125.00 250.00
STATED ODDS 1:121
1 Emmitt Smith 10.00 25.00
2 Terrell Davis 3.00 8.00
3 John Elway 12.50 30.00
4 Barry Sanders 10.00 25.00
5 Brett Favre 12.50 30.00
6 Mark Brunell 3.00 8.00
7 Dan Marino 12.50 30.00
8 Jerry Rice 6.00 15.00
9 Warrick Dunn 3.00 8.00
10 Eddie George 3.00 8.00

1998 Revolution Prime Time Performers

COMPLETE SET (20) 60.00 150.00
STATED ODDS 1:25
1 Jake Plummer 2.00 5.00
2 Corey Dillon 2.00 5.00
3 Troy Aikman 4.00 10.00
4 Deion Sanders 2.00 5.00
5 Emmitt Smith 6.00 15.00
6 Terrell Davis 2.00 5.00
7 John Elway 8.00 20.00
8 Barry Sanders 6.00 15.00
9 Brett Favre 8.00 20.00
10 Peyton Manning 15.00 40.00
11 Mark Brunell 2.00 5.00
12 Dan Marino 8.00 20.00
13 Drew Bledsoe 3.00 8.00
14 Jerome Bettis 2.00 5.00
15 Kordell Stewart 2.00 5.00
16 Jerry Rice 4.00 10.00
17 Steve Young 2.50 6.00
18 Warrick Dunn 2.00 5.00
19 Eddie George 2.00 5.00
20 Steve McNair 2.00 5.00

1998 Revolution Rookies and Stars

COMPLETE SET (30) 75.00 150.00
STATED ODDS 4:25
*GOLD/50: 6X TO 15X BASIC INSERTS
1 Michael Pittman .50 1.25
2 Curtis Enis .50 1.25
3 Takeo Spikes .50 1.25
4 Greg Ellis .50 1.25
5 Emmitt Smith 5.00 12.00
6 Terrell Davis 1.50 4.00
7 John Elway 6.00 15.00
8 Brian Griese 1.50 4.00
9 Marcus Nash .50 1.25
10 Charlie Batch 1.00 2.50
11 Barry Sanders 5.00 12.00
12 Brett Favre 6.00 15.00
13 Vonnie Holliday .50 1.25
14 E.G. Green .50 1.25
15 Peyton Manning 12.50 30.00
16 Fred Taylor 1.50 4.00
17 John Avery .50 1.25
18 Dan Marino 6.00 15.00
19 Drew Bledsoe 2.50 6.00
20 Robert Edwards .50 1.25
21 Joe Jurevicius 1.00 2.50
22 Charles Woodson 1.50 4.00
23 Kordell Stewart 1.50 4.00
24 Robert Holcombe .50 1.25
25 Ryan Leaf 1.00 2.50
26 Warrick Dunn 1.50 4.00
27 Jacquez Green 1.00 2.50
28 Kevin Dyson 1.00 2.50
29 Eddie George 1.50 4.00
30 Stephen Alexander .50 1.25

1998 Revolution Showstoppers

COMPLETE SET (36) 50.00 120.00
STATED ODDS 2:25
*RED: .4X TO 1X SILVER
1 Jake Plummer 1.50 4.00
2 Antowain Smith 1.50 4.00
3 Kerry Collins 1.00 2.50
4 Corey Dillon 1.50 4.00
5 Troy Aikman 3.00 8.00
6 Deion Sanders 1.50 4.00
7 Emmitt Smith 5.00 12.00
8 Terrell Davis 1.50 4.00
9 John Elway 6.00 15.00
10 Shannon Sharpe 1.00 2.50
11 Herman Moore 1.00 2.50
12 Barry Sanders 5.00 12.00
13 Brett Favre 6.00 15.00
14 Antonio Freeman 1.50 4.00
15 Dorsey Levens 1.50 4.00
16 Peyton Manning 12.50 25.00
17 Mark Brunell 1.50 4.00
18 Dan Marino 6.00 15.00
19 Robert Smith 1.50 4.00
20 Drew Bledsoe 2.50 6.00
21 Danny Kanell 1.00 2.50
22 Curtis Martin 1.50 4.00
23 Tim Brown 1.50 4.00
24 Napoleon Kaufman 1.50 4.00
25 Jerome Bettis 1.50 4.00
26 Kordell Stewart 1.50 4.00
27 Ryan Leaf 1.00 2.50
28 Terrell Owens 1.50 4.00
29 Jerry Rice 3.00 8.00
30 Steve Young 2.00 5.00
31 Ricky Watters 1.00 2.50
32 Mike Alstott 1.50 4.00
33 Trent Dilfer 1.50 4.00
34 Warrick Dunn 1.50 4.00
35 Eddie George 1.50 4.00
36 Steve McNair 1.50 4.00

1998 Revolution Touchdown

COMPLETE SET (20) 100.00 200.00
STATED ODDS 1:49
1 Jake Plummer 2.50 6.00
2 Corey Dillon 2.50 6.00
3 Troy Aikman 5.00 12.00
4 Emmitt Smith 8.00 20.00
5 Terrell Davis 2.50 6.00
6 John Elway 10.00 25.00
7 Barry Sanders 8.00 20.00
8 Brett Favre 10.00 25.00
9 Dorsey Levens 2.50 6.00
10 Peyton Manning 20.00 50.00
11 Mark Brunell 2.50 6.00
12 Marcus Allen 2.50 6.00
13 Dan Marino 10.00 25.00
14 Drew Bledsoe 4.00 10.00
15 Jerome Bettis 2.50 6.00
16 Kordell Stewart 2.50 6.00
17 Jerry Rice 5.00 12.00
18 Steve Young 3.00 8.00
19 Warrick Dunn 2.50 6.00
20 Eddie George 2.50 6.00

1999 Revolution

This 175 card set was issued by Pacific in three card packs and was released in July, 1999. Many of the Rookie Cards (45) in this set were shortprinted and released at a rate of one in four packs. Since the Rookie Cards were scattered throughout the set, we have identfied them with a SP next to their name.

COMPLETE SET (175) 50.00 100.00
1 David Boston RC .60 1.50
2 Joel Makovicka SP RC .75 2.00
3 Rob Moore .25 .60
4 Adrian Murrell .30 .75
5 Jake Plummer .30 .75
6 Frank Sanders .25 .60
7 Jamal Anderson .30 .75
8 Chris Chandler .30 .75
9 Tim Dwight .30 .75
10 Terance Mathis .25 .60
11 Jeff Paulk SP RC .75 2.00
12 O.J. Santiago .25 .60
13 Peter Boulware .25 .60
14 Priest Holmes .40 1.00
15 Michael Jackson .25 .60
16 Jermaine Lewis .25 .60
17 Doug Flutie .40 1.00
18 Eric Moulds .30 .75
19 Peerless Price SP RC 1.00 2.50
20 Andre Reed .40 1.00
21 Antowain Smith .25 .60
22 Bruce Smith .40 1.00
23 Steve Beuerlein .30 .75
24 Kevin Greene .30 .75
25 Fred Lane .25 .60
26 Muhsin Muhammad .30 .75
27 Wesley Walls .30 .75
28 Marty Booker SP RC 1.00 2.50
29 Curtis Conway .30 .75
30 Bobby Engram .30 .75
31 Curtis Enis .25 .60
32 Erik Kramer .30 .75
33 Cade McNown RC .60 1.50
34 Scott Covington RC .50 1.25
35 Corey Dillon .30 .75
36 Carl Pickens .30 .75
37 Darnay Scott .25 .60
38 Akili Smith RC .60 1.50
39 Craig Yeast SP RC .75 2.00
40 Darrin Chiaverini SP RC .75 2.00
41 Tim Couch RC .75 2.00
42 Ty Detmer .30 .75
43 Kevin Johnson RC .60 1.50
44 Terry Kirby .25 .60
45 Daylon McCutcheon SP RC .75 2.00
46 Irv Smith .25 .60
47 Troy Aikman .60 1.50
48 Michael Irvin .40 1.00
49 Wane McGarity SP RC .75 2.00
50 Dat Nguyen SP RC 1.25 3.00
51 Deion Sanders .40 1.00
52 Emmitt Smith 1.00 2.50
53 Terrell Davis .40 1.00
54 John Elway 1.25 3.00
55 Brian Griese .30 .75
56 Ed McCaffrey .30 .75
57 Travis McGriff SP RC .75 2.00
58 Shannon Sharpe .40 1.00
59 Rod Smith WR .30 .75
60 Charlie Batch .30 .75
61 Chris Claiborne RC .50 1.25
62 Sedrick Irvin RC .50 1.25
63 Herman Moore .30 .75
64 Johnnie Morton .30 .75
65 Barry Sanders 1.00 2.50
66 Aaron Brooks SP RC 1.25 3.00
67 Mark Chmura .25 .60
68 Brett Favre 1.25 3.00
69 Antonio Freeman .30 .75
70 Dorsey Levens .30 .75
71 De'Mond Parker SP RC .75 2.00
72 Marvin Harrison .40 1.00
73 Edgerrin James RC 1.00 2.50
74 Peyton Manning 1.25 3.00
75 Jerome Pathon .25 .60
76 Mike Peterson SP RC 1.00 2.50
77 Reggie Barlow .25 .60
78 Mark Brunell .30 .75
79 Keenan McCardell .30 .75
80 Jimmy Smith .30 .75
81 Fred Taylor .30 .75
82 Mike Cloud RC .50 1.25
83 Tony Gonzalez .40 1.00
84 Elvis Grbac .25 .60
85 Larry Parker RC SP 1.00 2.50
86 Andre Rison .30 .75
87 Brian Shay SP RC .75 2.00
88 Karim Abdul-Jabbar .30 .75
89 Oronde Gadsden .25 .60
90 James Johnson RC .50 1.25
91 Rob Konrad RC .50 1.25
92 Dan Marino 1.25 3.00
93 O.J. McDuffie .30 .75
94 Cris Carter .40 1.00
95 Daunte Culpepper RC .75 2.00
96 Randall Cunningham .40 1.00
97 Jim Kleinsasser SP RC 1.25 3.00
98 Randy Moss .40 1.00
99 Jake Reed .30 .75
100 Robert Smith .30 .75
101 Drew Bledsoe .40 1.00
102 Ben Coates .30 .75
103 Kevin Faulk RC .75 2.00
104 Terry Glenn .30 .75
105 Shawn Jefferson .25 .60
106 Andy Katzenmoyer SP RC 1.00 2.50
107 Cameron Cleeland .25 .60
108 Andre Hastings .25 .60
109 Billy Joe Tolliver .25 .60
110 Ricky Williams RC 1.25 3.00
111 Gary Brown .25 .60
112 Kent Graham .25 .60
113 Ike Hilliard .30 .75
114 Joe Montgomery SP RC .75 2.00
115 Amani Toomer .30 .75
116 Wayne Chrebet .30 .75
117 Keyshawn Johnson .30 .75
118 Leon Johnson .25 .60
119 Curtis Martin .40 1.00
120 Vinny Testaverde .30 .75
121 Dedric Ward .25 .60
122 Tim Brown .40 1.00
123 Dameane Douglas SP RC .75 2.00
124 Rickey Dudley .25 .60
125 James Jett .25 .60
126 Napoleon Kaufman .25 .60
127 Charles Woodson .40 1.00
128 Na Brown SP RC .75 2.00
129 Cecil Martin SP RC .75 2.00
130 Donovan McNabb RC 3.00 8.00
131 Duce Staley .30 .75
132 Kevin Turner .25 .60
133 Jerome Bettis .40 1.00
134 Troy Edwards RC .60 1.50
135 Courtney Hawkins .25 .60
136 Malcolm Johnson SP RC .75 2.00
137 Kordell Stewart .30 .75
138 Jerame Tuman SP RC .75 2.00
139 Amos Zereoue RC .60 1.50
140 Isaac Bruce .40 1.00
141 Joe Germaine RC .60 1.50
142 Torry Holt SP RC 2.00 5.00
143 Amp Lee .25 .60
144 Ricky Proehl .25 .60
145 Freddie Jones .25 .60
146 Ryan Leaf .30 .75
147 Natrone Means .30 .75
148 Mikhael Ricks .25 .60
149 Garrison Hearst .30 .75
150 Terry Jackson SP RC .75 2.00
151 Terrell Owens .40 1.00
152 Jerry Rice .75 2.00
153 J.J. Stokes .25 .60
154 Steve Young .50 1.25
155 Karsten Bailey RC .50 1.25
156 Joey Galloway .30 .75
157 Ahman Green .30 .75
158 Brock Huard RC .60 1.50
159 Jon Kitna .30 .75
160 Ricky Watters .30 .75
161 Mike Alstott .40 1.00
162 Reidel Anthony .25 .60
163 Trent Dilfer .30 .75
164 Warrick Dunn .30 .75
165 Shaun King RC .60 1.50
166 Anthony McFarland RC .60 1.50
167 Kevin Dyson .25 .60
168 Eddie George .30 .75
169 Darran Hall RC .50 1.25
170 Steve McNair .40 1.00
171 Frank Wycheck .30 .75
172 Stephen Alexander .25 .60
173 Champ Bailey RC 1.50 4.00
174 Skip Hicks .25 .60
175 Michael Westbrook .25 .60

1999 Revolution Opening Day

*STARS: 8X TO 20X BASIC CARDS
*RCs: 1.5X TO 4X BASIC CARDS
*RC SPs: 1.2X TO 3X BASIC CARDS
OPEN.DAY PRINT RUN 68 SER.#'d SETS

1999 Revolution Red

COMPLETE SET (175) 125.00 250.00
*STARS: 1.5X TO 4X BASIC CARDS
*RCs: .6X TO 1.5X BASIC CARDS
*RC SPs: .5X TO 1.2X BASIC CARDS
RED STATED PRINT RUN 299 SER.#'d SETS

1999 Revolution Shadows

*STARS: 5X TO 12X BASIC CARDS
*RCs: 1X TO 2.5X BASIC CARDS
*RC SPs: .8X TO 2X BASIC CARDS
SHADOWS PRINT RUN 99 SER.#'d SETS

1999 Revolution Chalk Talk

COMPLETE SET (20) 40.00 100.00
STATED ODDS 1:49
1 Jake Plummer 1.25 3.00
2 Jamal Anderson 2.00 5.00
3 Doug Flutie 2.00 5.00
4 Tim Couch 1.25 3.00
5 Troy Aikman 4.00 10.00
6 Emmitt Smith 4.00 10.00
7 Terrell Davis 2.00 5.00
8 John Elway 6.00 15.00
9 Barry Sanders 6.00 15.00
10 Brett Favre 6.00 15.00
11 Peyton Manning 6.00 15.00
12 Mark Brunell 2.00 5.00
13 Fred Taylor 2.00 5.00
14 Dan Marino 6.00 15.00
15 Randy Moss 5.00 12.00
16 Drew Bledsoe 2.50 6.00
17 Ricky Williams 2.00 5.00
18 Jerry Rice 4.00 10.00
19 Jon Kitna 2.00 5.00
20 Eddie George 2.00 5.00

1999 Revolution Icons

COMPLETE SET (10) 75.00 150.00
STATED ODDS 1:121
1 Emmitt Smith 6.00 15.00
2 Terrell Davis 3.00 8.00
3 John Elway 10.00 25.00
4 Barry Sanders 10.00 25.00
5 Brett Favre 10.00 25.00
6 Peyton Manning 10.00 25.00
7 Dan Marino 10.00 25.00
8 Randy Moss 8.00 20.00
9 Jerry Rice 6.00 15.00
10 Jon Kitna 3.00 8.00

1999 Revolution Showstoppers

COMPLETE SET (36) 75.00 150.00
STATED ODDS 2:25
1 Jake Plummer 1.00 2.50
2 Jamal Anderson 1.50 4.00
3 Priest Holmes 2.50 6.00
4 Doug Flutie 1.50 4.00
5 Antowain Smith 1.50 4.00
6 Cade McNown 1.00 2.50
7 Tim Couch 1.25 3.00
8 Corey Dillon 1.50 4.00
9 Akili Smith 1.00 2.50
10 Troy Aikman 3.00 8.00
11 Emmitt Smith 3.00 8.00
12 Terrell Davis 1.50 4.00
13 John Elway 5.00 12.00
14 Charlie Batch 1.50 4.00
15 Barry Sanders 5.00 12.00
16 Brett Favre 5.00 12.00
17 Antonio Freeman 1.50 4.00
18 Edgerrin James 4.00 10.00
19 Peyton Manning 5.00 12.00
20 Mark Brunell 1.50 4.00
21 Fred Taylor 1.50 4.00
22 Dan Marino 5.00 12.00
23 Randall Cunningham 1.50 4.00
24 Randy Moss 4.00 10.00
25 Drew Bledsoe 2.00 5.00
26 Ricky Williams 2.00 5.00
27 Curtis Martin 1.50 4.00
28 Napoleon Kaufman 1.50 4.00
29 Donovan McNabb 5.00 12.00
30 Kordell Stewart 1.00 2.50
31 Terrell Owens 1.50 4.00
32 Jerry Rice 3.00 8.00
33 Steve Young 2.00 5.00
34 Jon Kitna 1.50 4.00
35 Warrick Dunn 1.50 4.00
36 Eddie George 1.50 4.00

1999 Revolution Thorn in the Side

COMPLETE SET (20) 30.00 80.00
STATED ODDS 1:25
1 Jake Plummer .75 2.00
2 Jamal Anderson 1.25 3.00
3 Doug Flutie 1.25 3.00
4 Tim Couch 1.00 2.50
5 Troy Aikman 2.50 6.00
6 Emmitt Smith 2.50 6.00
7 Terrell Davis 1.25 3.00
8 John Elway 4.00 10.00
9 Barry Sanders 4.00 10.00
10 Brett Favre 4.00 10.00
11 Peyton Manning 4.00 10.00
12 Fred Taylor 1.25 3.00
13 Dan Marino 4.00 10.00
14 Randy Moss 3.00 8.00
15 Drew Bledsoe 1.50 4.00
16 Ricky Williams 1.50 4.00
17 Curtis Martin 1.25 3.00
18 Jerome Bettis 1.25 3.00
19 Jerry Rice 2.50 6.00
20 Jon Kitna 1.25 3.00

1999 Revolution Three-Deep Zone

COMPLETE SET (30) 25.00 60.00
GOLD STATED ODDS 4:25
*SILVERS 1-10: 5X TO 12X GOLDS
SILVER 1-10 PRINT RUN 99 SER.#'d SETS
*SILVERS 11-20: 1.25X TO 3X GOLDS
SILVER 11-20 PRINT RUN 199 SER.#'d SETS
*SILVERS 21-30: .6X TO 1.5X GOLDS
SILVER 21-30 PRINT RUN 299 SER.#'d SETS
1 Troy Aikman 1.25 3.00
2 Emmitt Smith 1.25 3.00
3 Terrell Davis .60 1.50
4 John Elway 2.00 5.00
5 Barry Sanders 2.00 5.00
6 Brett Favre 2.00 5.00
7 Peyton Manning 2.00 5.00
8 Dan Marino 2.00 5.00
9 Randy Moss 1.50 4.00
10 Drew Bledsoe .75 2.00
11 Jake Plummer .40 1.00
12 Jamal Anderson .60 1.50
13 Doug Flutie .60 1.50
14 Mark Brunell .60 1.50
15 Fred Taylor .60 1.50
16 Randall Cunningham .60 1.50
17 Terrell Owens .60 1.50
18 Jerry Rice 1.25 3.00
19 Steve Young .75 2.00
20 Jon Kitna .60 1.50
21 Antowain Smith .60 1.50
22 Antonio Freeman .60 1.50
23 Curtis Martin .60 1.50
24 Eddie George .60 1.50
25 Cade McNown .50 1.25
26 Tim Couch .60 1.50
27 Akili Smith .50 1.25
28 Edgerrin James 2.00 5.00
29 Ricky Williams 1.00 2.50
30 Donovan McNabb 2.50 6.00

2000 Revolution

Released in late November 2000, Revolution features a 150-card base set divided up into 100 veteran cards and 50 rookie cards sequentially numbered to 300. Base cards have a stadium backdrop colored to match each specific player's team and a team gold foil overlay behind full color player action photography. Revolution was offered in both Hobby and Retial versions. Hobby was packaged in a two card pack with one Beckett Grading Services graded card and carried a suggested retail price of $34.99. Hobby boxes also contained one BGS graded rookie card. Retail packs were released as a two card pack and carried a suggested retail price of $2.99.

COMP.SET w/o RC's (100) 20.00 40.00
1 David Boston .30 .76
2 Jake Plummer .40 1.00
3 Frank Sanders .30 .75
4 Jamal Anderson .40 1.00
5 Chris Chandler .40 1.00
6 Tim Dwight .40 1.00
7 Terance Mathis .30 .75
8 Tony Banks .30 .75
9 Qadry Ismail .40 1.00
10 Shannon Sharpe .50 1.25
11 Rob Johnson .40 1.00
12 Eric Moulds .40 1.00
13 Peerless Price .40 1.00
14 Antowain Smith .40 1.00
15 Steve Beuerlein .40 1.00

16 Tim Biakabutuka	.40	1.00
17 Muhsin Muhammad	.40	1.00
18 Curtis Enis	.30	.75
19 Cade McNown	.30	.75
20 Marcus Robinson	.40	1.00
21 Corey Dillon	.40	1.00
22 Akili Smith	.30	.75
23 Tim Couch	.40	1.00
24 Kevin Johnson	.30	.75
25 Troy Aikman	.75	2.00
26 Rocket Ismail	.40	1.00
27 Emmitt Smith	1.25	3.00
28 Terrell Davis	.50	1.25
29 Brian Griese	.40	1.00
30 Ed McCaffrey	.40	1.00
31 Charlie Batch	.40	1.00
32 Herman Moore	.40	1.00
33 James Stewart	.30	.75
34 Brett Favre	1.50	4.00
35 Antonio Freeman	.40	1.00
36 Dorsey Levens	.40	1.00
37 Marvin Harrison	.50	1.25
38 Edgerrin James	.50	1.25
39 Peyton Manning	1.25	3.00
40 Terrence Wilkins	.30	.75
41 Mark Brunell	.40	1.00
42 Keenan McCardell	.40	1.00
43 Jimmy Smith	.40	1.00
44 Fred Taylor	.50	1.25
45 Derrick Alexander	.30	.75
46 Tony Gonzalez	.50	1.25
47 Elvis Grbac	.30	.75
48 Damon Huard	.40	1.00
49 James Johnson	.30	.75
50 O.J. McDuffie	.40	1.00
51 Cris Carter	.50	1.25
52 Daunte Culpepper	.40	1.00
53 Randy Moss	.50	1.25
54 Robert Smith	.40	1.00
55 Drew Bledsoe	.50	1.25
56 Terry Glenn	.40	1.00
57 Jeff Blake	.40	1.00
58 Ricky Williams	.50	1.25
59 Tiki Barber	.50	1.25
60 Kerry Collins	.40	1.00
61 Ike Hilliard	.40	1.00
62 Amani Toomer	.40	1.00
63 Wayne Chrebet	.40	1.00
64 Curtis Martin	.50	1.25
65 Vinny Testaverde	.40	1.00
66 Dedric Ward	.30	.75
67 Tim Brown	.50	1.25
68 Napoleon Kaufman	.40	1.00
69 Tyrone Wheatley	.30	.75
70 Charles Johnson	.30	.75
71 Donovan McNabb	.50	1.25
72 Duce Staley	.40	1.00
73 Jerome Bettis	.50	1.25
74 Troy Edwards	.30	.75
75 Kordell Stewart	.40	1.00
76 Isaac Bruce	.50	1.25
77 Marshall Faulk	.50	1.25
78 Az-Zahir Hakim	.30	.75
79 Torry Holt	.50	1.25
80 Kurt Warner	.75	2.00
81 Curtis Conway	.40	1.00
82 Jermaine Fazande	.30	.75
83 Ryan Leaf	.40	1.00
84 Junior Seau	.50	1.25
85 Jeff Garcia	.40	1.00
86 Charlie Garner	.40	1.00
87 Terrell Owens	.50	1.25
88 Jerry Rice	1.00	2.50
89 Jon Kitna	.40	1.00
90 Derrick Mayes	.30	.75
91 Ricky Watters	.40	1.00
92 Mike Alstott	.50	1.25
93 Warrick Dunn	.40	1.00
94 Keyshawn Johnson	.40	1.00
95 Shaun King	.30	.75
96 Eddie George	.40	1.00
97 Jevon Kearse	.40	1.00
98 Steve McNair	.50	1.25
99 Stephen Davis	.40	1.00
100 Brad Johnson	.40	1.00
101 Thomas Jones RC	5.00	12.00
102 Doug Johnson RC	3.00	8.00
103 Jamal Lewis RC	4.00	10.00
104 Chris Redman RC	3.00	8.00
105 Travis Taylor RC	3.00	8.00
106 Troy Walters RC	2.50	6.00
107 Kwame Cavil RC	2.50	6.00
108 Sammy Morris RC	3.00	8.00
109 Dez White RC	3.00	8.00
110 Ron Dugans RC	2.50	6.00
111 Danny Farmer RC	2.50	6.00
112 Curtis Keaton RC	2.50	6.00
113 Peter Warrick RC	4.00	10.00
114 Dennis Northcutt RC	3.00	8.00
115 Travis Prentice RC	3.00	8.00
116 Kevin Thompson RC	2.50	6.00
117 Spergon Wynn RC	3.00	8.00
118 Michael Wiley RC	2.50	6.00
119 Mike Anderson RC	4.00	10.00
120 Chris Cole RC	3.00	8.00
121 Jarious Jackson RC	3.00	8.00
122 Charles Lee RC	2.50	6.00
123 Anthony Lucas RC	2.50	6.00
124 R.Jay Soward RC	2.50	6.00
125 Shyrone Stith RC	2.50	6.00
126 Sylvester Morris RC	3.00	8.00
127 Doug Chapman RC	2.50	6.00
128 Tom Brady RC	200.00	350.00
129 Gari Scott RC	2.50	6.00
130 J.R. Redmond RC	2.50	6.00
131 Ron Dayne RC	4.00	10.00
132 Ron Dixon RC	2.50	6.00
133 Laveranues Coles RC	4.00	10.00
134 Ronney Jenkins RC	2.50	6.00
135 Chad Pennington RC	6.00	15.00
136 Jerry Porter RC	4.00	10.00
137 Todd Pinkston RC	2.50	6.00
138 Plaxico Burress RC	4.00	10.00
139 Trung Canidate RC	3.00	8.00
140 Troy Walters RC	2.50	6.00
141 Giovanni Carmazzi RC	2.50	6.00
142 Tim Rattay RC	3.00	8.00
143 Shaun Alexander RC	5.00	12.00
144 Darrell Jackson RC	3.00	8.00
145 James Williams RC	2.50	6.00
146 Joe Hamilton RC	2.50	6.00
147 Aaron Stecker RC	3.00	8.00
148 Erron Kinney RC	2.50	6.00
149 Billy Volek RC	4.00	10.00
150 Todd Husak RC	2.50	6.00

2000 Revolution Premiere Date

*VETS: 5X TO 12X BASIC CARDS
PREMIERE DATE/85 ODDS 1:7 HOB
STATED PRINT RUN 85 SER.#'d SETS

2000 Revolution Red

*VETS 1-100: 5X TO 12X BASIC CARDS
RED/99 INSERTS IN RETAIL PACKS

2000 Revolution Silver

*VETS 1-100: 5X TO 12X BASIC CARDS
SILVER/80 INSERTS IN HOBBY PACKS

2000 Revolution First Look

COMPLETE SET (36)	40.00	80.00
STATED ODDS 4:25		
1 Thomas Jones	.50	1.25
2 Doug Johnson	.30	.75
3 Jamal Lewis	.40	1.00
4 Chris Redman	.30	.75
5 Travis Taylor	.30	.75
6 Sammy Morris	.30	.75
7 Dez White	.30	.75
8 Ron Dugans	.25	.60
9 Curtis Keaton	.25	.60
10 Peter Warrick	.40	1.00
11 Courtney Brown	.30	.75
12 Dennis Northcutt	.30	.75
13 Travis Prentice	.30	.75
14 Mike Anderson	.40	1.00
15 Jarious Jackson	.30	.75
16 Bubba Franks	.40	1.00
17 R.Jay Soward	.25	.60
18 Frank Moreau	.25	.60
19 Sylvester Morris	.25	.60
20 Deon Dyer	.25	.60
21 Doug Chapman	.25	.60
22 Tom Brady	40.00	80.00
23 Ron Dayne	.40	1.00
24 Laveranues Coles	.40	1.00
25 Chad Pennington	.60	1.50
26 Jerry Porter	.40	1.00
27 Todd Pinkston	.25	.60
28 Plaxico Burress	.40	1.00
29 Tee Martin	.40	1.00
30 Trung Canidate	.30	.75
31 JaJuan Seider	.25	.60
32 Giovanni Carmazzi	.25	.60
33 Tim Rattay	.30	.75
34 Darrell Jackson	.30	.75
35 Shaun Alexander	.50	1.25
36 Joe Hamilton	.25	.60

2000 Revolution First Look Super Bowl XXXV

22 Tom Brady	125.00	250.00

2000 Revolution Game Worn Jerseys

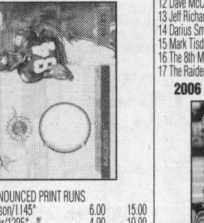

PACIFIC ANNOUNCED PRINT RUNS		
1 Rod Woodson/1145*	6.00	15.00
2 Jamir Miller/1295*	4.00	10.00
3 Olandis Gary/75*	8.00	20.00
4 Brett Favre/15*	100.00	200.00
5 Mark Brunell/735*	5.00	12.00
6 Keenan McCardell/679*	5.00	12.00
7 Fred Taylor/380*	6.00	15.00
8 Dan Marino/777*	20.00	50.00
9 Cris Carter/235*	15.00	40.00
10 Randy Moss/85*	15.00	40.00
11 Drew Bledsoe/645*	6.00	15.00
12 Ricky Williams/35*	10.00	25.00
13 Koy Detmer/726*	4.00	10.00
14 Torrance Small/481*	4.00	10.00
15 Duce Staley/35*	8.00	20.00
16 Jerome Bettis/65*	10.00	25.00
17 Junior Seau/60*	10.00	25.00
18 Jerry Rice/828*	12.00	30.00
19 Brock Huard/706*	4.00	10.00
20 Steve McNair/52*	10.00	25.00

2000 Revolution Making the Grade Black

COMPLETE SET (20)	15.00	40.00
BLACK 1-POINT ODDS 4:13 H, 2:25 R		
*RED: 1.2X TO 3X BLACK		
RED 5-POINT ODDS 1:49 H, 2:481 R		
*GOLD: 2X TO 5X BLACK		
GOLD 10-POINT ODDS 1:97 H, 1:481 R		
1 Peter Warrick	.60	1.50
2 Tim Couch	.50	1.25
3 Troy Aikman	1.00	2.50
4 Emmitt Smith	1.50	4.00
5 Terrell Davis	.60	1.50
6 Brian Griese	.50	1.25
7 Brett Favre	2.00	5.00
8 Peyton Manning	1.50	4.00
9 Edgerrin James	.60	1.50
10 Mark Brunell	.50	1.25
11 Fred Taylor	.60	1.50
12 Randy Moss	.60	1.50
13 Ricky Williams	.60	1.50
14 Ron Dayne	.60	1.50
15 Chad Pennington	1.00	2.50
16 Marshall Faulk	.60	1.50
17 Kurt Warner	1.00	2.50
18 Jerry Rice	1.25	3.00
19 Eddie George	.50	1.25
20 Steve McNair	.60	1.50

2000 Revolution Ornaments

COMPLETE SET (20)	25.00	60.00
STATED ODDS 1:25		
1 Thomas Jones	1.50	4.00
2 Jake Plummer	1.50	4.00
3 Jamal Anderson	1.50	4.00
4 Jamal Lewis	1.25	3.00
5 Cade McNown	1.25	3.00
6 Corey Dillon	1.50	4.00
7 Peter Warrick	1.25	3.00
8 Troy Aikman	3.00	8.00
9 Emmitt Smith	5.00	12.00
10 Mike Anderson	1.25	3.00
11 Marvin Harrison	2.00	5.00
12 Edgerrin James	2.00	5.00
13 Peyton Manning	5.00	12.00
14 Mark Brunell	1.50	4.00
15 Daunte Culpepper	1.50	4.00
16 Ron Dayne	2.00	5.00
17 Plaxico Burress	1.25	3.00
18 Marshall Faulk	2.00	5.00
19 Kurt Warner	3.00	8.00
20 Shaun King	1.25	3.00

2000 Revolution Shields

COMPLETE SET (20)	30.00	80.00
STATED ODDS 1:97		
1 Peter Warrick	1.50	4.00
2 Tim Couch	1.25	3.00
3 Troy Aikman	2.50	6.00
4 Emmitt Smith	4.00	10.00
5 Terrell Davis	1.50	4.00
6 Brett Favre	5.00	12.00
7 Edgerrin James	1.50	4.00
8 Peyton Manning	4.00	10.00
9 Mark Brunell	1.25	3.00
10 Daunte Culpepper	1.25	3.00
11 Randy Moss	1.50	4.00
12 Drew Bledsoe	1.50	4.00
13 Ricky Williams	1.50	4.00
14 Chad Pennington	2.00	5.00
15 Marshall Faulk	1.50	4.00
16 Kurt Warner	2.50	6.00
17 Eddie George	1.25	3.00
18 Steve McNair	1.50	4.00
19 Stephen Davis	1.25	3.00
20 Brad Johnson	1.25	3.00

1993 Rice Council

COMPLETE SET (10)	4.00	10.00
2 Troy Aikman FB	.75	2.00
5 Warren Moon FB	.40	1.00

2007 Rochester Raiders CIFL

COMPLETE SET (17)	7.50	15.00
1 Omar Baker	.40	1.00
2 Jeff Bruckman	.40	1.00
3 Jason Coley	.40	1.00
4 Mike Condello	.40	1.00
5 Matt Cottengim	.40	1.00
6 Reggie Cox	.40	1.00
7 Gerald Dias	.40	1.00
8 Noah Fehrenbach	.40	1.00
9 Dennis Greco CO	.40	1.00
10 Maurice Jackson	.40	1.00
11 Mike Kallfelz	.40	1.00
12 Dave McCarthy OWN	.40	1.00
13 Jeff Richardson	.40	1.00
14 Darius Smith	.40	1.00
15 Mark Tisdale	.40	1.00
16 The 8th Man	.40	1.00
17 The Raiderrettes	.40	1.00

2006 Rock River Raptors UIF

COMPLETE SET (31)	6.00	12.00
1 Ade Adeyemo	.20	.50
2 Brian Akins	.20	.50
3 Todd Allen Asst.CO	.20	.50
4 Ryan Aulenbacher	.20	.50
5 Randy Bell	.20	.50
6 Tyus Boyd	.20	.50
7 Tyrece Butler	.20	.50
8 Brian Ceaser	.20	.50
9 Billy Cook	.20	.50
10 Mike Davis	.20	.50
11 Roger Farrar Jr. Asst.CO	.20	.50
12 Keith Glover	.20	.50
13 Jermaine Hampton	.20	.50
14 Anthony Harris	.20	.50
15 Sean Hilliard	.20	.50
16 John Hollins	.20	.50
17 Craig Howard	.20	.50
18 Dave Jones Asst.CO	.20	.50
19 Markus Lewis	.20	.50
20 Luke McArdle	.20	.50
21 Ty Myers	.20	.50
22 Jack Phillips Jr. Asst.CO	.20	.50
23 Dillon Piefer	.20	.50
24 Rik Richards CO	.20	.50
25 Lance Samuseva	.20	.50
26 Billy Sanders Asst.CO	.20	.50
27 Ben Sankey	.20	.50
28 Fernandez Shaw	.20	.50
29 Anthony Stone	.20	.50
30 Jeremiah Thompson	.20	.50
31 Checklist Card	.20	.50

1930 Rogers Peet

The Rogers Peet Department Store in New York released this set in early 1930. The cards were given out four at time to employees at the store for enrolling boys in Ropeco (the store's magazine club). Employees who completed the set, and pasted them in the album designed to house the cards, were eligible to win prizes. The blankbacked cards measure roughly 1 3/4" by 2 1/2" and feature a black and white photo of the famous athlete with his name and card number below the picture. Additions to this list are appreciated.

31 Red Grange Football	800.00	1,200.00
33 Ken Strong Football	250.00	400.00
37 Ed Wittmer Football	100.00	175.00
41 Chris Cagle Football	125.00	200.00

2006 Rome Renegade AIFL

COMPLETE SET (34)	10.00	20.00
1 Danny Marshall	.30	.75
2 Courtney Stanley	.30	.75
3 Jason Colts	.30	.75
4 Lew Thomas	.30	.75
5 Gerald Gales	.30	.75
6 Gerald Gales	.30	.75
7 Bo Bartik	.30	.75
8 Reggie Jiles	.30	.75
9 T.J. Anderson	.30	.75
10 Bart Gloyd	.30	.75
11 Andrew Amerson	.30	.75
12 John Bowman	.30	.75
13 Marcus Brady	.30	.75
14 Marcus Brady	.30	.75
15 Joe Clark	.30	.75
16 Jermaine Collins	.30	.75
17 Jamaal Greer	.30	.75
18 Charles Jones	.30	.75
19 Lemar Parrish	.30	.75
20 Harold Lindsey	.30	.75
21 Leon Moore	.30	.75
22 Russell Green	.30	.75
23 Reggie Poole	.30	.75
24 Dwayne Morgan	.30	.75
25 Terel Toomer	.30	.75
26 Harry Pierce OWN	.30	.75
27 Renegade Race Car	.30	.75
28 Cheer Team	.30	.75
29 Richie The Renegade	.30	.75
30 David Humphrey CO	.30	.75
31 Scott Chandler CO	.30	.75
32 J.J. Owens CO	.30	.75
33 Greg Carter CO	.30	.75
34 Scott Hines CO	.30	.75

1998 Ron Mix HOF Platinum Autographs

NFL Hall of Famer Ron Mix produced this set in 1998 but released it in 1999. Each card features an artist's rendering of a Hall of Fame football player. These attractive, full color 4" by 6" cards were signed by the players and issued in factory set form only. Production was limited to 2500 sets with each card hand-numbered. Of the 116 cards, two players only signed their first name -- Sid Gillman and Doak Walker. The Doak Walker signature was apparantly done after his tragic skiing accident.

COMPLETE SET (116)	1,500.00	2,000.00
1 Herb Adderley	7.50	15.00
2 Lance Alworth	10.00	20.00
3 Doug Atkins	7.50	15.00
4 Lem Barney	8.00	20.00
5 Sammy Baugh	50.00	100.00
6 Chuck Bednarik	10.00	20.00
7 Bobby Bell	7.50	15.00
8 Raymond Berry	8.00	20.00
9 Fred Biletnikoff	12.50	25.00
10 George Blanda	25.00	50.00
11 Mel Blount	10.00	20.00
12 Roosevelt Brown	10.00	20.00
13 Willie Brown	7.50	15.00
14 Dick Butkus	20.00	40.00
15 Tony Canadeo	10.00	20.00
16 George Connor	12.50	25.00
17 Lou Creekmur	10.00	20.00
18 Larry Csonka	20.00	35.00
19 Willie Davis	7.50	15.00
20 Len Dawson	12.50	25.00
21 Dan Dierdorf	7.50	15.00
22 Mike Ditka	15.00	30.00
23 Art Donovan	7.50	15.00
24 Tony Dorsett	20.00	35.00
25 Bill Dudley	8.00	20.00
26 Weeb Ewbank	15.00	30.00
27 Tom Fears	20.00	35.00
28 Dan Fouts	12.50	30.00
29 Frank Gatski	10.00	20.00
30 Joe Gibbs	15.00	30.00
31 Sid Gillman (signed Sid)	12.50	25.00
32 Otto Graham	15.00	30.00
33 Bud Grant	20.00	40.00
34 Bob Griese	12.50	30.00
35 Lou Groza	15.00	30.00
36 Jack Ham	10.00	20.00
37 John Hannah	8.00	20.00
38 Franco Harris	20.00	40.00
39 Mike Haynes	8.00	20.00
40 Ted Hendricks	8.00	20.00
41 Crazylegs Hirsch	15.00	30.00
42 Paul Hornung	12.50	25.00
43 Ken Houston	7.50	15.00
44 Sam Huff	10.00	20.00
45 John Henry Johnson	12.50	25.00
46 Jimmy Johnson DB	7.50	15.00
47 Charlie Joiner	8.00	20.00
48 Deacon Jones	7.50	15.00
49 Stan Jones	10.00	20.00
50 Sonny Jurgensen	20.00	40.00
51 Leroy Kelly	8.00	20.00
52 Paul Krause	7.50	15.00
53 Tom Landry	50.00	80.00
54 Dick Lane	12.50	25.00
55 Jim Langer	7.50	15.00
56 Willie Lanier	7.50	15.00
57 Steve Largent	8.00	20.00
58 Yale Lary	7.50	15.00
59 Dante Lavelli	12.50	25.00
60 Bob Lilly	10.00	20.00
61 Larry Little	7.50	15.00
62 John Mackey	10.00	20.00
63 Gino Marchetti	10.00	20.00
64 Don Maynard	7.50	15.00
65 Mike McCormack	10.00	20.00
66 Tommy McDonald	7.50	15.00
67 Hugh McElhenny	10.00	20.00
68 Bobby Mitchell	12.50	25.00
69 Ron Mix	8.00	20.00
70 Lenny Moore	10.00	20.00
71 Marion Motley	25.00	50.00
72 Anthony Munoz	7.50	15.00
73 George Musso	12.50	25.00
74 Joe Namath	40.00	80.00
75 Chuck Noll CO	15.00	30.00
76 Leo Nomellini	12.50	25.00
77 Merlin Olsen	8.00	20.00
78 Jim Otto	7.50	15.00
79 Alan Page	8.00	20.00
80 Ace Parker	7.50	15.00
81 Jim Parker	12.50	25.00
82 Joe Perry	10.00	20.00
83 Pete Pihos	12.50	25.00
84 Mel Renfro	7.50	15.00
85 Jim Ringo	12.50	25.00
86 Andy Robustelli	7.50	15.00
87 Gale Sayers	20.00	40.00
88 Joe Schmidt	7.50	15.00
89 Tex Schramm	15.00	30.00
90 Lee Roy Selmon	7.50	15.00
91 Art Shell	8.00	20.00
92 Don Shula CO	25.00	50.00
93 Mike Singletary	10.00	20.00
94 O.J. Simpson	20.00	40.00
95 Jackie Smith	7.50	15.00
96 Bob St. Clair	7.50	15.00
97 Roger Staubach	30.00	60.00
98 Ernie Stautner	15.00	30.00
99 Jan Stenerud	7.50	15.00
100 Dwight Stephenson	7.50	15.00
101 Charley Taylor	7.50	15.00
102 Jim Taylor	10.00	20.00
103 Y.A. Tittle	10.00	25.00
104 Charley Trippi	7.50	15.00
105 Gene Upshaw	12.50	25.00
106 Steve Van Buren	10.00	20.00
107 Bill Walsh CO	30.00	50.00
108 Doak Walker	20.00	40.00
Post Accident-only signed Doak		
109 Paul Warfield	7.50	15.00
110 Mike Webster	25.00	50.00
111 Arnie Weinmeister	12.50	25.00
112 Randy White	12.50	25.00
113 Bill Willis	10.00	20.00
114 Larry Wilson	8.00	20.00
115 Kellen Winslow	8.00	20.00
116 Willie Wood	7.50	15.00

2003 Ron Mix HOF Gold

The Gold version of the Ron Mix art card set was issued in 2003 as a follow up to the 1998 Platinum release. Each card was printed with a gold colored stripe along the left edge instead of Platinum. Factory sets included all 115-cards with just one of those signed by a player. Two additional Platinum autographed cards were also included in each Gold factory set. Initial retail price for the factory set was $149.

COMPLETE SET (115)	75.00	150.00
1 Herb Adderley	.60	1.50
2 Lance Alworth	.75	2.00
3 Doug Atkins	.50	1.25
4 Red Badgro	.50	1.25
5 Lem Barney	.50	1.25
6 Sammy Baugh	1.50	4.00
7 Chuck Bednarik	.60	1.50
8 Bobby Bell	.60	1.50
9 Raymond Berry	.75	2.00
10 Fred Biletnikoff	.75	2.00
11 Mel Blount	.75	2.00
12 Roosevelt Brown	.50	1.25
13 Willie Brown	.60	1.50
14 Dick Butkus	1.50	4.00
15 Tony Canadeo	.60	1.50
16 George Connor	.60	1.50
17 Lou Creekmur	.50	1.25
18 Larry Csonka	.75	2.00
19 Willie Davis	.60	1.50
20 Len Dawson	1.00	2.50
21 Dan Dierdorf	.60	1.50
22 Mike Ditka	1.25	3.00
23 Art Donovan	.60	1.50
24 Tony Dorsett	1.25	3.00
25 Bill Dudley	.60	1.50
26 Weeb Ewbank	.50	1.25
27 Tom Fears	.60	1.50
28 Dan Fouts	.75	2.00
29 Frank Gatski	.50	1.25
30 Sid Gillman	.50	1.25
31 Otto Graham	1.00	2.50
32 Bud Grant	.50	1.25
33 Lou Groza	.75	2.00
34 Jack Ham	.75	2.00
35 John Hannah	.60	1.50
36 Franco Harris	1.25	3.00
37 Mike Haynes	.50	1.25
38 Ted Hendricks	.60	1.50
39 Elroy Hirsch	.75	2.00
40 Paul Hornung	1.00	2.50
41 Ken Houston	.50	1.25
42 Sam Huff	.75	2.00
43 John Henry Johnson	.75	2.00
44 Jimmy Johnson DB	.50	1.25
45 Charlie Joiner	.75	2.00
46 Stan Jones	.50	1.25
47 Sonny Jurgensen	.75	2.00
48 Leroy Kelly	.60	1.50
49 Paul Krause	.50	1.25
50 Tom Landry	1.00	2.50
51 Dick Lane	.60	1.50
52 Jim Langer	.50	1.25
53 Willie Lanier	.50	1.25
54 Steve Largent	.75	2.00
55 Yale Lary	.50	1.25
56 Dante Lavelli	.60	1.50
57 Bob Lilly	.75	2.00
58 Larry Little	.60	1.50
59 Sid Luckman	.75	2.00
60 John Mackey	.60	1.50
61 Gino Marchetti	.60	1.50
62 Ollie Matson	.75	2.00
63 Don Maynard	.75	2.00
64 George McAfee	.50	1.25
65 Mike McCormack	.50	1.25
66 Tommy McDonald	.50	1.25
67 Hugh McElhenny	.75	2.00
68 Bobby Mitchell	.75	2.00
69 Ron Mix	.60	1.50
70 Lenny Moore	.75	2.00
71 Marion Motley	.75	2.00
72 Anthony Munoz	.60	1.50
73 George Musso	.50	1.25
74 Chuck Noll CO	.75	2.00
75 Leo Nomellini	.60	1.50
76 Merlin Olsen	.75	2.00
77 Jim Otto	.75	2.00
78 Alan Page	.60	1.50
79 Ace Parker	.50	1.25
80 Jim Parker	.60	1.50
81 Joe Perry	.75	2.00
82 Pete Pihos	.60	1.50
83 Mel Renfro	.60	1.50
84 Jim Ringo	.60	1.50
85 Andy Robustelli	.60	1.50
86 Gale Sayers	1.50	4.00
87 Joe Schmidt	.60	1.50
88 Tex Schramm	.50	1.25
89 Lee Roy Selmon	.60	1.50
90 Art Shell	.75	2.00
91 Don Shula CO	.75	2.00
92 Mike Singletary	.75	2.00
93 O.J. Simpson	.75	2.00
94 Jackie Smith	.60	1.50
95 Bob St. Clair	.50	1.25
96 Roger Staubach	2.00	5.00
97 Ernie Stautner	.60	1.50
98 Jan Stenerud	.50	1.25
99 Dwight Stephenson	.50	1.25
100 Charley Taylor	.60	1.50
101 Jim Taylor	.75	2.00
102 Y.A. Tittle	.75	2.00
103 Charley Trippi	.60	1.50
104 Bulldog Turner	.60	1.50
105 Steve Van Buren	.75	2.00
106 Bill Walsh CO	.60	1.50
107 Doak Walker	.75	2.00
108 Paul Warfield	.75	2.00
109 Mike Webster	.60	1.50
110 Arnie Weinmeister	.60	1.50
111 Randy White	.75	2.00
112 Bill Willis	.50	1.25
113 Larry Wilson	.50	1.25
114 Kellen Winslow	.60	1.50
115 Willie Wood	.60	1.50

2010 Rookies and Stars

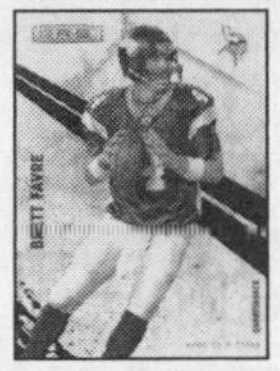

COMP.SET w/o RC's (150)	8.00	20.00
ROOKIE AUTO PRINT RUN 71-299		
EXCH EXPIRATION: 2/18/2012		
1 Chris Wells	.25	.60
2 Larry Fitzgerald	.30	.75
3 Matt Leinart	.25	.60
4 Steve Breaston	.20	.50
5 Matt Ryan	.30	.75
6 Michael Turner	.20	.50
7 Roddy White	.25	.60
8 Tony Gonzalez	.25	.60
9 Anquan Boldin	.25	.60
10 Derrick Mason	.25	.60
11 Joe Flacco	.30	.75
12 Ray Rice	.25	.60
13 Todd Heap	.20	.50
14 Fred Jackson	.30	.75
15 Lee Evans	.25	.60
16 Marshawn Lynch	.25	.60
17 Ryan Fitzpatrick	.30	.75
18 DeAngelo Williams	.25	.60
19 Jonathan Stewart	.25	.60
20 Matt Moore	.25	.60
21 Steve Smith	.25	.60
22 Brian Urlacher	.30	.75
23 Devin Hester	.30	.75
24 Greg Olsen	.20	.50
25 Jay Cutler	.30	.75
26 Matt Forte	.25	.60
27 Andre Caldwell	.20	.50
28 Antonio Bryant	.20	.50
29 Carson Palmer	.25	.60
30 Cedric Benson	.25	.60
31 Chad Ochocinco	.25	.60
32 Ben Watson	.20	.50
33 Jake Delhomme	.25	.60
34 Jerome Harrison	.20	.50
35 Josh Cribbs	.30	.75
36 Mohamed Massaquoi	.25	.60
37 Felix Jones	.25	.60
38 Jason Witten	.30	.75
39 Marion Barber	.25	.60
40 Miles Austin	.30	.75
41 Tony Romo	.40	1.00
42 Brandon Marshall	.25	.60
43 Eddie Royal	.20	.50
44 Jabar Gaffney	.20	.50
45 Knowshon Moreno	.25	.60
46 Kyle Orton	.25	.60
47 Brandon Pettigrew	.20	.50
48 Calvin Johnson	.30	.75
49 Matthew Stafford	.30	.75
50 Nate Burleson	.20	.50
51 Aaron Rodgers	.60	1.50
52 Donald Driver	.25	.60
53 Greg Jennings	.25	.60
54 Jermichael Finley	.25	.60
55 Ryan Grant	.25	.60
56 Andre Johnson	.25	.60
57 Kevin Walter	.25	.60
58 Matt Schaub	.25	.60
59 Owen Daniels	.20	.50
60 Steve Slaton	.20	.50
61 Pierre Garcon	.25	.60
62 Dallas Clark	.25	.60
63 Joseph Addai	.25	.60
64 Peyton Manning	.50	1.25
65 Reggie Wayne	.25	.60
66 David Garrard	.25	.60
67 Maurice Jones-Drew	.25	.60
68 Mike Sims-Walker	.25	.60
69 Mike Thomas	.25	.60
70 Torry Holt	.25	.60
71 Chris Chambers	.25	.60
72 Dwayne Bowe	.25	.60
73 Jamaal Charles	.25	.60
74 Matt Cassel	.25	.60
75 Thomas Jones	.25	.60
76 Brian Hartline	.25	.60
77 Chad Henne	.25	.60
78 Davone Bess	.20	.50
79 Greg Camarillo	.20	.50
80 Ronnie Brown	.25	.60
81 Adrian Peterson	.50	1.25
82 Brett Favre	.75	2.00
83 Percy Harvin	.30	.75
84 Sidney Rice	.25	.60
85 Visanthe Shiancoe	.25	.60
86 Laurence Maroney	.25	.60
87 Randy Moss	.30	.75
88 Tom Brady	.50	1.25
89 Wes Welker	.30	.75
90 Devery Henderson	.20	.50
91 Drew Brees	.30	.75
92 Jeremy Shockey	.25	.60
93 Marques Colston	.25	.60
94 Pierre Thomas	.25	.60
95 Brandon Jacobs	.25	.60
96 Eli Manning	.30	.75
97 Hakeem Nicks	.25	.60
98 Kevin Boss	.25	.60
99 Steve Smith USC	.25	.60
100 Braylon Edwards	.25	.60
101 Jerricho Cotchery	.25	.60
102 LaDainian Tomlinson	.30	.75
103 Mark Sanchez	.30	.75
104 Shonn Greene	.25	.60
105 Chaz Schilens	.20	.50
106 Darren McFadden	.25	.60
107 Jason Campbell	.25	.60
108 Louis Murphy	.25	.60
109 Zach Miller	.25	.60
110 Brent Celek	.25	.60
111 DeSean Jackson	.25	.60
112 Jeremy Maclin	.25	.60
113 Kevin Kolb	.25	.60
114 LeSean McCoy	.25	.60
115 Ben Roethlisberger	.30	.75
116 Heath Miller	.25	.60
117 Rashard Mendenhall	.25	.60
118 Santonio Holmes	.25	.60
119 Troy Polamalu	.30	.75
120 Antonio Gates	.25	.60
121 Darren Sproles	.25	.60
122 Philip Rivers	.30	.75
123 Vincent Jackson	.20	.50
124 Alex Smith QB	.25	.60
125 Frank Gore	.25	.60
126 Josh Morgan	.25	.60
127 Michael Crabtree	.30	.75
128 Vernon Davis	.25	.60
129 Deion Branch	.20	.50
130 John Carlson	.20	.50
131 Julius Jones	.20	.50
132 Matt Hasselbeck	.20	.50
133 T.J. Houshmandzadeh	.25	.60
134 Danny Amendola	.30	.75
135 Donnie Avery	.25	.60
136 James Laurinaitis	.25	.60
137 Steven Jackson	.25	.60
138 Cadillac Williams	.25	.60
139 Josh Freeman	.30	.75
140 Kellen Winslow Jr.	.25	.60
141 Sammie Stroughter	.20	.50
142 Bo Scaife	.20	.50
143 Chris Johnson	.30	.75
144 Kenny Britt	.25	.60
145 Vince Young	.20	.50
146 Chris Cooley	.25	.60
147 Clinton Portis	.25	.60
148 Donovan McNabb	.30	.75
149 Larry Johnson	.25	.60
150 Santana Moss	.25	.60
151 Dallas Clark ELE	1.00	2.50
152 Peyton Manning ELE	2.00	5.00
153 Lee Evans ELE	1.00	2.50
154 David Garrard ELE	1.00	2.50
155 Derrick Mason ELE	1.00	2.50
156 Calvin Johnson ELE	1.25	3.00
157 Joe Flacco ELE	1.25	3.00
158 Vince Young ELE	.75	2.00
159 Chris Johnson ELE	1.25	3.00
160 Tom Brady ELE	2.00	5.00
161 Wes Welker ELE	1.25	3.00
162 Ryan Fitzpatrick ELE	1.25	3.00
163 Fred Jackson ELE	1.25	3.00
164 Laurence Maroney ELE	1.00	2.50
165 Randy Moss ELE	1.25	3.00
166 A.J. Edds RC	1.50	4.00
167 Alterraun Verner RC	1.50	4.00
168 Amari Spievey RC	1.50	4.00
169 Andre Anderson RC	1.25	3.00
170 Andre Dixon RC	1.50	4.00
171 Anthony Davis RC	1.25	3.00
172 Anthony Dixon RC	1.50	4.00
173 Antonio Brown RC	2.50	6.00
174 Blair White RC	1.50	4.00
175 Brandon Ghee RC	1.25	3.00
176 Brandon Graham RC	1.25	3.00
177 Brian Price RC	1.50	4.00
178 Bryan Bulaga RC	1.50	4.00
179 Chad Jones RC	1.50	4.00
180 Charles Scott RC	1.25	3.00
181 Chris Cook RC	1.50	4.00
182 Chris McGaha RC	1.00	2.50
183 Corey Wootton RC	1.25	3.00
184 Dan Williams RC	1.25	3.00
185 Darrell Stuckey RC	1.00	2.50
186 Darryl Sharpton RC	1.00	2.50
187 Daryl Washington RC	1.25	3.00
188 David Gettis RC	1.50	4.00
189 Dennis Pitta RC	1.50	4.00
190 Devin McCourty RC	1.50	4.00
191 Dominique Franks RC	1.00	2.50
192 Donald Butler RC	1.00	2.50
193 Ed Dickson RC	1.50	4.00
194 Eric Norwood RC	1.25	3.00
195 Everson Griffen RC	1.50	4.00
196 Freddie Barnes RC	1.25	3.00
197 Garrett Graham RC	1.25	3.00
198 James Starks RC	2.50	6.00
199 Jared Odrick RC	1.50	4.00
200 Jarrett Brown RC	1.50	4.00
201 Jason Pierre-Paul RC	2.50	6.00
202 Jason Worilds RC	1.50	4.00
203 Javier Arenas RC	1.50	4.00
204 Jeremy Williams RC	1.00	2.50
205 Jermaine Cunningham RC	1.50	4.00
206 Jerome Murphy RC	1.25	3.00
207 Jerry Hughes RC	1.50	4.00
208 Jevan Snead RC	1.50	4.00
209 Jimmy Graham RC	3.00	8.00
210 Joique Bell RC	1.25	3.00
211 Kareem Jackson RC	1.50	4.00
212 Kevin Thomas RC	1.25	3.00
213 Koa Misi RC	1.50	4.00
214 Kyle Wilson RC	1.50	4.00
215 Lamarr Houston RC	1.50	4.00
216 LeGarrette Blount RC	2.50	6.00
217 Linval Joseph RC	1.25	3.00
218 Lonyae Miller RC	1.25	3.00
219 Major Wright RC	1.50	4.00
220 Maurkice Pouncey RC	1.50	4.00
221 Mike Hoomanawanui RC	1.50	4.00
222 Mike Iupati RC	1.50	4.00
223 Morgan Burnett RC	1.50	4.00
224 Myron Lewis RC	1.25	3.00
225 Nate Allen RC	1.50	4.00
226 NaVorro Bowman RC	1.50	4.00
227 Pat Angerer RC	1.50	4.00
228 Pat Paschall RC	1.25	3.00
229 Patrick Robinson RC	1.50	4.00
230 Perrish Cox RC	1.25	3.00
231 Perry Riley RC	1.50	4.00
232 Rennie Curran RC	1.25	3.00
233 Riley Cooper RC	1.50	4.00
234 Roddrick Muckelroy RC	1.25	3.00
235 Russell Okung RC	1.50	4.00
236 Sean Canfield RC	1.25	3.00
237 Sean Lee RC	1.50	4.00
238 Sean Weatherspoon RC	1.50	4.00
239 Sergio Kindle RC	1.50	4.00
240 Seyi Ajirotutu RC	1.50	4.00
241 T.J. Ward RC	1.50	4.00
242 Thaddeus Gibson RC	1.25	3.00
243 Tony Moeaki RC	1.50	4.00
244 Tony Pike RC	1.50	4.00
245 Torell Troup RC	1.25	3.00
246 Trent Williams RC	1.50	4.00
247 Trevard Lindley RC	1.00	2.50
248 Tyson Alualu RC	1.25	3.00
249 Walter Thurmond RC	1.00	2.50
250 Zac Robinson RC	1.25	3.00
251 Aaron Hernandez AU/299 RC	15.00	30.00
252 Andre Roberts AU/203 RC	8.00	20.00
253 Anthony McCoy AU/299 RC	6.00	15.00
254 Armanti Edwards AU/121 RC	8.00	20.00
255 Arrelious Benn AU/299 RC	8.00	20.00
256 Ben Tate AU/299 RC	10.00	25.00
257 Brandon LaFell AU/201 RC	8.00	20.00
258 Brandon Spikes AU/299 RC	8.00	20.00
259 C.J. Spiller AU/201 RC	20.00	50.00
260 Carlos Dunlap AU/299 RC	8.00	20.00
261 Carlton Mitchell AU/299 RC	6.00	15.00
262 Colt McCoy AU/201 RC	15.00	40.00
263 Damian Williams AU/121 RC	8.00	20.00
264 Dan LeFevour AU/299 RC	8.00	20.00

265 Demaryius Thomas AU/201 RC 10.00 25.00
266 Derrick Morgan AU/299 RC 6.00 15.00
267 Dexter McCluster AU/121 RC 10.00 25.00
268 Dez Bryant AU/200 RC 30.00 80.00
269 Dezmon Briscoe AU/299 RC 6.00 15.00
270 Earl Thomas AU/299 RC 8.00 20.00
271 Emmanuel Sanders AU/251 RC 8.00 20.00
272 Eric Berry AU/251 RC 15.00 40.00
273 Eric Decker AU/251 RC 10.00 25.00
274 Gerald McCoy AU/245 RC 8.00 20.00
275 Golden Tate AU/201 RC 8.00 20.00
276 Jacoby Ford AU/299 RC 8.00 20.00
277 Jahvid Best AU/299 RC 20.00 50.00
278 Jermaine Gresham AU/171 RC 10.00 25.00
279 Jimmy Clausen AU/199 RC 8.00 20.00
280 Joe Haden AU/299 RC 8.00 20.00
281 Joe McKnight AU/171 RC 8.00 20.00
282 John Skelton AU/299 RC 8.00 20.00
283 Jonathan Crompton AU/299 RC 6.00 15.00
284 Jonathan Dwyer AU/299 RC 8.00 20.00
285 Jordan Shipley AU/171 RC 8.00 20.00
286 Marcus Easley AU/251 RC 6.00 15.00
287 Mardy Gilyard AU/201 RC 8.00 20.00
288 Mike Kafka AU/251 RC 8.00 20.00
289 Mike Williams AU/170 RC 15.00 40.00
290 Montario Hardesty AU/121 RC 8.00 20.00
291 Ndamukong Suh AU/297 RC 15.00 40.00
292 Ricky Sapp AU/299 RC 6.00 15.00
293 Rob Gronkowski AU/71 RC 30.00 60.00
294 Rolando McClain AU/201 RC 8.00 20.00
295 Ryan Mathews AU/201 RC 25.00 60.00
296 Sam Bradford AU/202 RC 40.00 100.00
297 Taylor Mays AU/299 RC 8.00 20.00
298 Taylor Price AU/251 RC 8.00 20.00
299 Tim Tebow AU/201 RC 60.00 120.00
300 Toby Gerhart AU/200 RC 8.00 20.00

2010 Rookies and Stars Gold

*VETS 1-150: .8X TO 2X BASIC CARDS
*ELEMENT 151-165: .4X TO 1X BASIC CARDS
*ROOKIES 166-250: .4X TO 1X BASIC CARDS
RANDOM INSERTS IN RETAIL PACKS

2010 Rookies and Stars Longevity Parallel Gold

*VETS 1-150: 4X TO 10X BASIC CARDS
*ELEMENT 151-165: 1X TO 2.5X BASIC CARDS
*ROOKIES 166-250: 1.2X TO 3X BASIC CARDS
STATED PRINT RUN 49 SER.#'d SETS

2010 Rookies and Stars Longevity Parallel Platinum

*VETS 1-150: 5X TO 12X BASIC CARDS
*ELEMENT 151-165: 1.2X TO 3X BASIC CARDS
*ROOKIES 166-250: 1.5X TO 4X BASIC CARDS
STATED PRINT RUN 25 SER.#'d SETS

2010 Rookies and Stars Longevity Parallel Silver

*VETS 1-150: 2X TO 5X BASIC CARDS
*ELEMENT 151-165: .5X TO 1.2X BASIC CARDS
*ROOKIES 166-250: .8X TO 2X BASIC CARDS
STATED PRINT RUN 249 SER.#'d SETS

2010 Rookies and Stars Longevity Parallel Silver Holofoil

*VETS 1-150: 3X TO 8X BASIC CARDS
*ELEMENT 151-165: .8X TO 2X BASIC CARDS
*ROOKIES 166-250: 1X TO 2.5X BASIC CARDS
STATED PRINT RUN 99 SER.#'d SETS

2010 Rookies and Stars Autographs

STATED PRINT RUN 1-25
7 Roddy White/15 10.00 25.00
15 Lee Evans/15 10.00 25.00
37 Felix Jones/15 20.00 40.00
90 Devery Henderson/15 8.00 20.00
98 Kevin Boss/25 10.00 25.00
103 Mark Sanchez/20 30.00 60.00
108 Louis Murphy/20 10.00 25.00
112 Jeremy Maclin/15 12.00 30.00
116 Heath Miller/15 10.00 25.00
118 Santonio Holmes/25 10.00 25.00
127 Michael Crabtree/15 25.00 50.00

2010 Rookies and Stars Crosstraining

*BLACK/100: .6X TO 1.5X BASIC INSERTS
*GOLD/500: .5X TO 1.2X BASIC INSERTS
1 Jahvid Best 1.25 3.00
2 Jermaine Gresham 1.00 2.50
3 Jimmy Clausen .75 2.00
4 Joe McKnight .75 2.00
5 Jonathan Dwyer .75 2.00
6 Jordan Shipley .75 2.00
7 Mardy Gilyard .75 2.00
8 Mike Williams 1.25 3.00
9 Toby Gerhart .75 2.00
10 Tim Tebow 3.00 8.00
11 Sam Bradford 3.00 8.00
12 Ryan Mathews 1.50 4.00
13 Rolando McClain .75 2.00
14 Ndamukong Suh 1.50 4.00
15 Mike Kafka .75 2.00
16 Golden Tate .75 2.00
17 Eric Decker 1.00 2.50
18 Emmanuel Sanders .75 2.00
19 Eric Berry .75 2.00
20 Montario Hardesty .75 2.00
21 Taylor Price .75 2.00
22 Dez Bryant 2.50 6.00
23 Damian Williams .75 2.00
24 Colt McCoy 1.50 4.00
25 Dexter McCluster .75 2.00
26 Rob Gronkowski 2.00 5.00
27 Andre Roberts .75 2.00
28 Arrelious Benn .75 2.00
29 Armanti Edwards .75 2.00
30 Ben Tate 1.00 2.50
31 Brandon LaFell .75 2.00
32 C.J. Spiller 1.25 3.00
33 Demaryius Thomas 1.00 2.50
34 Gerald McCoy .75 2.00
35 Marcus Easley .60 1.50

2010 Rookies and Stars Crosstraining Materials

STATED PRINT RUN 299 SER.#'d SETS
*PRIME/50: .8X TO 2X BASIC JSY/299
*LONG/249: .4X TO 1X BASIC JSY/299
1 Jahvid Best 3.00 8.00
2 Jermaine Gresham 2.50 6.00
3 Jimmy Clausen 2.00 5.00
4 Joe McKnight 2.00 5.00
5 Jonathan Dwyer 2.00 5.00
6 Jordan Shipley 2.00 5.00
7 Mardy Gilyard 2.00 5.00
8 Mike Williams 3.00 8.00
9 Toby Gerhart 2.00 5.00
10 Tim Tebow 8.00 20.00
11 Sam Bradford 6.00 15.00
12 Ryan Mathews 4.00 10.00
13 Rolando McClain 2.00 5.00
14 Ndamukong Suh 4.00 10.00
15 Mike Kafka 2.00 5.00
16 Golden Tate 2.00 5.00
17 Eric Decker 2.50 6.00
18 Emmanuel Sanders 2.00 5.00
19 Eric Berry 2.00 5.00
20 Montario Hardesty 2.00 5.00
21 Taylor Price 2.00 5.00
22 Dez Bryant 6.00 15.00
23 Damian Williams 2.00 5.00
24 Colt McCoy 4.00 10.00
25 Dexter McCluster 2.00 5.00
26 Rob Gronkowski 5.00 12.00
27 Andre Roberts 2.00 5.00
28 Arrelious Benn 2.00 5.00
29 Armanti Edwards 2.00 5.00
30 Ben Tate 2.50 6.00
31 Brandon LaFell 2.00 5.00
32 C.J. Spiller 3.00 8.00
33 Demaryius Thomas 2.50 6.00
34 Gerald McCoy 2.00 5.00
35 Marcus Easley 1.50 4.00

2010 Rookies and Stars Crosstraining Materials Autographs

STATED PRINT RUN 25-100
1 Jahvid Best/25 25.00 60.00
2 Jermaine Gresham/100 8.00 20.00
3 Jimmy Clausen/25 12.00 30.00
4 Joe McKnight/100 6.00 15.00
5 Jonathan Dwyer/100 6.00 15.00
6 Jordan Shipley/50 8.00 20.00
7 Mardy Gilyard/100 6.00 15.00
8 Mike Williams/100 15.00 30.00
9 Toby Gerhart/50 8.00 20.00
10 Tim Tebow/25 75.00 150.00
11 Sam Bradford/25 60.00 120.00
12 Ryan Mathews/25 40.00 80.00
13 Rolando McClain/100 6.00 15.00
14 Ndamukong Suh/25 30.00 60.00
15 Mike Kafka/100 6.00 15.00
16 Golden Tate/25 12.00 30.00
17 Eric Decker/100 8.00 20.00
18 Emmanuel Sanders/100 6.00 15.00
19 Eric Berry/100 15.00 40.00
20 Montario Hardesty/100 6.00 15.00
21 Taylor Price/100 8.00 25.00
22 Dez Bryant/25 50.00 100.00
23 Damian Williams/50 8.00 20.00
24 Colt McCoy/25 40.00 80.00
25 Dexter McCluster/50 8.00 20.00
26 Rob Gronkowski/100 20.00 40.00
27 Andre Roberts/100 6.00 15.00
28 Arrelious Benn/25 12.00 30.00
29 Armanti Edwards/100 6.00 15.00
30 Ben Tate/100 8.00 20.00
31 Brandon LaFell/100 6.00 15.00
32 C.J. Spiller/25 30.00 80.00
33 Demaryius Thomas/25 15.00 40.00
34 Gerald McCoy/100 6.00 15.00
35 Marcus Easley/100 5.00 12.00

2010 Rookies and Stars Dress for Success Jerseys

STATED PRINT RUN 299 SER.#'d SETS
*PRIME/50: .8X TO 2X BASIC JSY/299
*LONG/249: .4X TO 1X BASIC JSY/299
1 Rob Gronkowski 5.00 12.00
2 Brandon LaFell 2.00 5.00
3 Toby Gerhart 2.00 5.00
4 Jermaine Gresham 2.50 6.00
5 Eric Berry 2.00 5.00
6 Ben Tate 2.50 6.00
7 Jimmy Clausen 2.00 5.00
8 Jordan Shipley 2.00 5.00
9 Emmanuel Sanders 2.00 5.00
10 Mike Williams 3.00 8.00
11 Mike Kafka 2.00 5.00
12 C.J. Spiller 3.00 8.00
13 Tim Tebow 8.00 20.00
14 Eric Decker 2.50 6.00
15 Rolando McClain 2.00 5.00
16 Gerald McCoy 2.00 5.00
17 Damian Williams 2.00 5.00
18 Ryan Mathews 4.00 10.00
19 Montario Hardesty 2.00 5.00
20 Taylor Price 2.00 5.00
21 Mardy Gilyard 2.00 5.00
22 Colt McCoy 4.00 10.00
23 Dez Bryant 6.00 15.00
24 Golden Tate 2.00 5.00
25 Jahvid Best 3.00 8.00
26 Armanti Edwards 2.00 5.00
27 Andre Roberts 2.00 5.00
28 Arrelious Benn 2.00 5.00
29 Dexter McCluster 2.00 5.00
30 Joe McKnight 2.00 5.00
31 Jonathan Dwyer 2.00 5.00
32 Demaryius Thomas 2.50 6.00
33 Ndamukong Suh 4.00 10.00
34 Sam Bradford 6.00 15.00
35 Marcus Easley 1.50 4.00

2010 Rookies and Stars Dress for Success Jerseys Autographs

STATED PRINT RUN 25-100
1 Rob Gronkowski/100 20.00 40.00
2 Brandon LaFell/100 6.00 15.00
3 Toby Gerhart/50 8.00 20.00
4 Jermaine Gresham/100 8.00 20.00
5 Eric Berry/100 15.00 40.00
6 Ben Tate/100 8.00 20.00
7 Jimmy Clausen/25 12.00 30.00
8 Jordan Shipley/50 8.00 20.00
9 Emmanuel Sanders/100 6.00 15.00
10 Mike Williams/100 15.00 30.00
11 Mike Kafka/100 6.00 15.00
12 C.J. Spiller/25 25.00 60.00
13 Tim Tebow/25 75.00 150.00
14 Eric Decker/100 8.00 20.00
15 Rolando McClain/100 6.00 15.00
16 Gerald McCoy/100 6.00 15.00
17 Damian Williams/50 8.00 20.00
18 Ryan Mathews/25 30.00 80.00
19 Montario Hardesty/100 6.00 15.00
20 Taylor Price/100 6.00 15.00
21 Mardy Gilyard/100 6.00 15.00
22 Colt McCoy/25 25.00 60.00
23 Dez Bryant/25 50.00 100.00
24 Golden Tate/25 12.00 30.00
25 Jahvid Best/25 25.00 60.00
26 Armanti Edwards/100 6.00 15.00
27 Andre Roberts/100 6.00 15.00
28 Arrelious Benn/25 12.00 30.00
29 Dexter McCluster/50 8.00 20.00
31 Jonathan Dwyer/100 6.00 15.00
32 Demaryius Thomas/25 15.00 40.00
33 Ndamukong Suh/25 30.00 60.00
34 Sam Bradford/25 60.00 120.00
35 Marcus Easley/100 5.00 12.00

2010 Rookies and Stars Elements Materials

STATED PRINT RUN 100-175
*FOIL: .5X TO 1.2X BASIC JSY
152 Peyton Manning/100 8.00 20.00
156 Calvin Johnson/175 4.00 10.00
157 Joe Flacco/100 5.00 12.00
158 Vince Young/175 2.50 6.00
159 Chris Johnson/100 5.00 12.00
160 Tom Brady/175 6.00 15.00
161 Wes Welker/100 5.00 12.00
165 Randy Moss/100 5.00 12.00

2010 Rookies and Stars Elements Materials Holofoil

STATED PRINT RUN 10-50
151 Dallas Clark/50 5.00 12.00
152 Peyton Manning/10
154 David Garrard/25 6.00 15.00
156 Calvin Johnson/50 6.00 15.00
157 Joe Flacco/15 8.00 20.00
158 Vince Young/50 4.00 10.00
159 Chris Johnson/50 6.00 15.00
160 Tom Brady/50 10.00 25.00
161 Wes Welker/50 6.00 15.00
164 Laurence Maroney/50 5.00 12.00
165 Randy Moss/50 6.00 15.00

2010 Rookies and Stars Freshman Orientation Materials Jerseys

STATED PRINT RUN 299 SER.#'d SETS
*PRIME/50: .8X TO 2X BASIC JSY/299
*LONG/249: .4X TO 1X BASIC JSY/299
1 Sam Bradford 6.00 15.00
2 Jonathan Dwyer 2.00 5.00
3 Dexter McCluster 2.00 5.00
4 Armanti Edwards 2.00 5.00
5 Dez Bryant 6.00 15.00
6 Montario Hardesty 2.00 5.00
7 Rolando McClain 2.00 5.00
8 C.J. Spiller 3.00 8.00
9 Jordan Shipley 2.00 5.00
10 Rob Gronkowski 5.00 12.00
11 Jermaine Gresham 2.50 6.00
12 Emmanuel Sanders 2.00 5.00
13 Gerald McCoy 2.00 5.00
14 Taylor Price 2.00 5.00
15 Tim Tebow 8.00 20.00
16 Colt McCoy 4.00 10.00
17 Arrelious Benn 2.00 5.00
18 Demaryius Thomas 2.50 6.00
19 Ndamukong Suh 4.00 10.00
20 Golden Tate 2.00 5.00
21 Jahvid Best 3.00 8.00
22 Toby Gerhart 2.00 5.00
23 Brandon LaFell 2.00 5.00
24 Mike Williams 3.00 8.00
25 Mike Kafka 2.00 5.00
26 Ryan Mathews 4.00 10.00
27 Mardy Gilyard 2.00 5.00
28 Damian Williams 2.00 5.00
29 Andre Roberts 2.00 5.00
30 Joe McKnight 2.00 5.00
31 Ben Tate 2.50 6.00
32 Marcus Easley 1.50 4.00
33 Eric Berry 2.00 5.00
34 Jimmy Clausen 2.00 5.00
35 Eric Decker 2.50 6.00

2010 Rookies and Stars Freshman Orientation Materials Jerseys Autographs

STATED PRINT RUN 25-100
1 Sam Bradford/25 60.00 120.00
2 Jonathan Dwyer/100 6.00 15.00
3 Dexter McCluster/50 8.00 20.00
4 Armanti Edwards/100 6.00 15.00
5 Dez Bryant/25 50.00 100.00
6 Montario Hardesty/100 6.00 15.00
7 Rolando McClain/100 6.00 15.00
8 C.J. Spiller/25 25.00 60.00
9 Jordan Shipley/50 8.00 20.00
10 Rob Gronkowski/100 20.00 40.00
11 Jermaine Gresham/100 8.00 20.00
12 Emmanuel Sanders/100 6.00 15.00
13 Gerald McCoy/100 6.00 15.00
14 Taylor Price/100 6.00 15.00
15 Tim Tebow/25 75.00 150.00
16 Colt McCoy/25 25.00 60.00
17 Arrelious Benn/25 12.00 30.00
18 Demaryius Thomas/25 15.00 40.00
19 Ndamukong Suh/25 30.00 60.00
20 Golden Tate/25 12.00 30.00
21 Jahvid Best/25 20.00 50.00
22 Toby Gerhart/50 8.00 20.00
23 Brandon LaFell/100 6.00 15.00
24 Mike Williams/100 15.00 30.00
25 Mike Kafka/100 6.00 15.00
26 Ryan Mathews/25 30.00 80.00
27 Mardy Gilyard/100 6.00 15.00
28 Damian Williams/50 8.00 20.00
29 Andre Roberts/100 6.00 15.00
30 Joe McKnight/100 6.00 15.00
31 Ben Tate/100 8.00 20.00
32 Marcus Easley/100 5.00 12.00
34 Jimmy Clausen/25 12.00 30.00
35 Eric Decker/100 8.00 20.00

2010 Rookies and Stars Gold Stars

*BLACK/100: .6X TO 1.5X BASIC INSERTS
*GOLD/500: .5X TO 1.2X BASIC INSERTS
1 Brent Celek .75 2.00
2 Carson Palmer .75 2.00
3 Philip Rivers 1.00 2.50
4 Larry Fitzgerald 1.00 2.50
5 Calvin Johnson 1.00 2.50
6 Drew Brees 1.00 2.50
7 Randy Moss 1.00 2.50
8 Chris Cooley .75 2.00
9 Troy Polamalu 1.00 2.50
10 Mark Sanchez 1.00 2.50
11 Jason Witten 1.00 2.50
12 Vince Young .60 1.50
13 LeSean McCoy .75 2.00
14 Ray Rice .75 2.00
15 Ben Roethlisberger 1.00 2.50

2010 Rookies and Stars Gold Stars Materials

STATED PRINT RUN 25-299
*PRIME/50: .8X TO 2X BASIC JSY/299
*PRIME/50: .6X TO 1.5X BASIC JSY/100-150
*PRIME/50: .4X TO 1X BASIC JSY/25
2 Carson Palmer/299 2.50 6.00
3 Philip Rivers/100 4.00 10.00
4 Larry Fitzgerald/100 4.00 10.00
5 Calvin Johnson/100 4.00 10.00
6 Drew Brees/299 3.00 8.00
7 Randy Moss/140 4.00 10.00
8 Chris Cooley/25 5.00 12.00
9 Troy Polamalu/150 5.00 12.00
10 Mark Sanchez/299 3.00 8.00
11 Jason Witten/125 4.00 10.00
12 Vince Young/299 2.00 5.00
13 LeSean McCoy/125 3.00 8.00
15 Ben Roethlisberger/125 4.00 10.00

2010 Rookies and Stars Materials Black Prime Longevity

COMMON CARD/15-25 5.00 12.00
SEMISTARS/15-25 6.00 15.00
UNL.STARS/15-25 8.00 20.00
STATED PRINT RUN 3-25
41 Tony Romo/25 10.00 25.00
81 Adrian Peterson/25 12.00 30.00
88 Tom Brady/25 12.00 30.00

2010 Rookies and Stars Materials Emerald Prime Longevity

COMMON CARD/35-50 4.00 10.00
SEMISTARS/35-50 5.00 12.00
UNL.STARS/35-50 6.00 15.00
COMMON CARD/12-25 8.00 20.00
STATED PRINT RUN 12-50
41 Tony Romo/50 8.00 20.00
64 Peyton Manning/25 12.00 30.00
81 Adrian Peterson/50 10.00 25.00
88 Tom Brady/50 10.00 25.00
103 Mark Sanchez/25 8.00 20.00

2010 Rookies and Stars Materials Gold

RANDOM INSERTS IN RETAIL PACKS
1 Chris Wells 2.50 6.00
2 Larry Fitzgerald 3.00 8.00
3 Matt Leinart 2.50 6.00
5 Matt Ryan 3.00 8.00
7 Roddy White 2.50 6.00
8 Tony Gonzalez 2.50 6.00
10 Derrick Mason 2.50 6.00
11 Joe Flacco 3.00 8.00
13 Todd Heap 2.00 5.00
16 Marshawn Lynch 2.50 6.00
18 DeAngelo Williams 2.50 6.00
23 Devin Hester 3.00 8.00
24 Greg Olsen 2.00 5.00
25 Jay Cutler 3.00 8.00
29 Carson Palmer 2.50 6.00
30 Cedric Benson 2.50 6.00
31 Chad Ochocinco 2.50 6.00
37 Felix Jones 2.50 6.00
38 Jason Witten 3.00 8.00
39 Marion Barber 2.50 6.00
41 Tony Romo 4.00 10.00
43 Eddie Royal 2.00 5.00
45 Knowshon Moreno 2.50 6.00
46 Kyle Orton 2.50 6.00
48 Calvin Johnson 3.00 8.00
49 Matthew Stafford 3.00 8.00
53 Greg Jennings 2.50 6.00
56 Andre Johnson 2.50 6.00
59 Owen Daniels 2.00 5.00
60 Steve Slaton 2.00 5.00
62 Dallas Clark 2.50 6.00
63 Joseph Addai 2.50 6.00
64 Peyton Manning 5.00 12.00
66 David Garrard 2.50 6.00
67 Maurice Jones-Drew 2.50 6.00
72 Dwayne Bowe 2.50 6.00
81 Adrian Peterson 5.00 12.00
82 Brett Favre 8.00 20.00
83 Percy Harvin 3.00 8.00
86 Laurence Maroney 2.50 6.00
87 Randy Moss 3.00 8.00
88 Tom Brady 5.00 12.00
90 Devery Henderson 2.00 5.00
91 Drew Brees 3.00 8.00
93 Marques Colston 2.50 6.00
96 Eli Manning 3.00 8.00
99 Steve Smith USC 2.50 6.00
101 Jerricho Cotchery 2.50 6.00
103 Mark Sanchez 3.00 8.00
104 Shonn Greene 2.50 6.00
106 Darren McFadden 2.50 6.00
108 Louis Murphy 2.50 6.00
109 Zach Miller 2.50 6.00
115 Ben Roethlisberger 3.00 8.00
117 Rashard Mendenhall 2.50 6.00
119 Troy Polamalu 3.00 8.00
120 Antonio Gates 2.50 6.00
121 Darren Sproles 2.50 6.00
122 Philip Rivers 3.00 8.00
123 Vincent Jackson 2.00 5.00
124 Alex Smith QB 2.50 6.00
125 Frank Gore 2.50 6.00
127 Michael Crabtree 3.00 8.00
128 Vernon Davis 2.50 6.00
132 Matt Hasselbeck 2.00 5.00
138 Cadillac Williams 2.50 6.00
139 Josh Freeman 3.00 8.00
144 Kenny Britt 2.50 6.00
145 Vince Young 2.00 5.00
146 Chris Cooley 2.50 6.00
147 Clinton Portis 2.50 6.00
150 Santana Moss 2.50 6.00

2010 Rookies and Stars Prime Cuts

STATED PRINT RUN 50 SER.#'d SETS
*COMBO/25: .5X TO 1.2X BASIC INSERTS
1 Chad Ochocinco 5.00 12.00
2 Dallas Clark 5.00 12.00
4 Michael Turner 4.00 10.00
5 DeAngelo Williams 5.00 12.00
6 Marques Colston 5.00 12.00
7 Eli Manning 6.00 15.00
8 Vernon Davis 5.00 12.00
9 Darren Sproles 5.00 12.00
10 Josh Cribbs 6.00 15.00

2010 Rookies and Stars Rookie Autographs Holofoil

STATED PRINT RUN 299 SER.#'d SETS
*LONGEVITY/249: .4X TO 1X R&S HOLO.AU/299
*LONGEVITY/49: .6X TO 1.5X R&S HOLO.AU/299
LONGEVITY ROOK.AU PRINT RUN 49-249
169 Andre Anderson 3.00 8.00
170 Andre Dixon 4.00 10.00
172 Anthony Dixon 4.00 10.00
173 Antonio Brown 8.00 20.00
174 Blair White 4.00 10.00
176 Brandon Graham 3.00 8.00
178 Bryan Bulaga 6.00 15.00
179 Chad Jones 4.00 10.00
180 Charles Scott 3.00 8.00
181 Chris Cook 4.00 10.00
182 Chris McGaha 2.50 6.00
183 Corey Wootton 3.00 8.00
187 Daryl Washington EXCH 3.00 8.00
188 David Gettis 4.00 10.00
190 Devin McCourty 4.00 10.00
191 Dominique Franks 2.50 6.00
193 Ed Dickson 4.00 10.00
195 Everson Griffen 4.00 10.00
196 Freddie Barnes 3.00 8.00
197 Garrett Graham 3.00 8.00
198 James Starks 12.00 30.00
200 Jarrett Brown 4.00 10.00
201 Jason Pierre-Paul 6.00 15.00
202 Jason Worilds 4.00 10.00
204 Jeremy Williams 2.50 6.00
207 Jerry Hughes 4.00 10.00
208 Jevan Snead 4.00 10.00
209 Jimmy Graham 15.00 30.00
210 Joique Bell 3.00 8.00
211 Kareem Jackson 4.00 10.00
216 LeGarrette Blount 12.00 30.00
218 Lonyae Miller 3.00 8.00
223 Morgan Burnett 4.00 10.00
225 Nate Allen 4.00 10.00
226 NaVorro Bowman 4.00 10.00
228 Pat Paschall 3.00 8.00
229 Patrick Robinson 4.00 10.00
230 Perrish Cox 3.00 8.00
233 Riley Cooper 4.00 10.00
235 Russell Okung 6.00 15.00
236 Sean Canfield 3.00 8.00
237 Sean Lee 5.00 12.00
238 Sean Weatherspoon 4.00 10.00
239 Sergio Kindle 4.00 10.00
240 Seyi Ajirotutu 4.00 10.00
244 Tony Pike 4.00 10.00
246 Trent Williams EXCH 6.00 15.00
250 Zac Robinson 3.00 8.00

2010 Rookies and Stars Rookie Jersey Jumbo Swatch

STATED PRINT RUN 50 SER.#'d SETS
*EMERALD/10: 1X TO 2.5X BASIC JSY/50
*GOLD/25: .5X TO 1.2X BASIC JSY/50
*LONGEVITY/50: .4X TO 1X BASIC JSY/50
252 Andre Roberts 5.00 12.00
254 Armanti Edwards 5.00 12.00
255 Arrelious Benn 5.00 12.00
256 Ben Tate 6.00 15.00
257 Brandon LaFell 5.00 12.00
259 C.J. Spiller 8.00 20.00
262 Colt McCoy 10.00 25.00
263 Damian Williams 5.00 12.00
265 Demaryius Thomas 6.00 15.00
267 Dexter McCluster 5.00 12.00
268 Dez Bryant 15.00 40.00
271 Emmanuel Sanders 5.00 12.00
272 Eric Berry 5.00 12.00
273 Eric Decker 6.00 15.00
274 Gerald McCoy 5.00 12.00
275 Golden Tate 5.00 12.00
277 Jahvid Best 8.00 20.00
278 Jermaine Gresham 6.00 15.00
279 Jimmy Clausen 5.00 12.00
281 Joe McKnight 5.00 12.00
284 Jonathan Dwyer 5.00 12.00
285 Jordan Shipley 5.00 12.00
286 Marcus Easley 4.00 10.00
287 Mardy Gilyard 5.00 12.00
288 Mike Kafka 5.00 12.00
289 Mike Williams 8.00 20.00
290 Montario Hardesty 5.00 12.00
291 Ndamukong Suh 10.00 25.00
293 Rob Gronkowski 12.00 30.00
294 Rolando McClain 5.00 12.00
295 Ryan Mathews 10.00 25.00
296 Sam Bradford 15.00 40.00
298 Taylor Price 5.00 12.00
299 Tim Tebow 20.00 50.00
300 Toby Gerhart 5.00 12.00

2010 Rookies and Stars Rookie Patch Autographs Blue NFL Logo

*ROOKIE AU: .6X TO 1.5X BASIC AU RC
STATED PRINT RUN 19-42
EXCH EXPIRATION: 2/18/2012
296 Sam Bradford/22 75.00 200.00
299 Tim Tebow/22 100.00 200.00

2010 Rookies and Stars Rookie Patch Autographs Blue Team Logo

*ROOKIE AU: .6X TO 1.5X BASIC AU RC
STATED PRINT RUN 25 SER.#'d SETS
EXCH EXPIRATION: 2/18/2012
296 Sam Bradford 75.00 200.00
299 Tim Tebow 100.00 200.00

2010 Rookies and Stars Statistical Standouts Materials Prime

STATED PRINT RUN 20-50
*BASE JSY/100-150: .25X TO .6X PRIME/50
*BASE JSY/100-150: .2X TO .5X PRIME/20-25
*BASE JSY/25: .4X TO 1X PRIME/50
1 Aaron Rodgers/50 12.00 30.00
2 Adrian Peterson/50 10.00 25.00
3 Andre Johnson/50 5.00 12.00
4 Chris Johnson/50 6.00 15.00
6 Maurice Jones-Drew/50 5.00 12.00
7 Miles Austin/20 8.00 20.00
8 Peyton Manning/15 12.00 30.00
9 Reggie Wayne/25 6.00 15.00
10 Ryan Grant/50 5.00 12.00
11 Sidney Rice/50 5.00 12.00
12 Steven Jackson/50 5.00 12.00
13 Tom Brady/50 10.00 25.00
14 Tony Romo/50 8.00 20.00
15 Wes Welker/50 6.00 15.00

2010 Rookies and Stars Studio Rookies

*BLACK/100: .6X TO 1.5X BASIC INSERTS
*GOLD/500: .5X TO 1.2X BASIC INSERTS
1 Tim Tebow 3.00 8.00
2 Sam Bradford 3.00 8.00
3 Rolando McClain .75 2.00
4 Ndamukong Suh 1.50 4.00
5 Golden Tate .75 2.00
6 Eric Decker 1.00 2.50
7 Eric Berry .75 2.00
8 Montario Hardesty .75 2.00
9 Gerald McCoy .75 2.00
10 Demaryius Thomas 1.00 2.50
11 Ben Tate 1.00 2.50
12 Arrelious Benn .75 2.00
13 Dexter McCluster .75 2.00
14 Damian Williams .75 2.00
15 Colt McCoy 1.50 4.00
16 Jermaine Gresham 1.00 2.50
17 Jimmy Clausen .75 2.00
18 Joe McKnight .75 2.00
19 Mike Williams 1.25 3.00
20 Toby Gerhart .75 2.00
21 Ryan Mathews 1.50 4.00
22 Armanti Edwards .75 2.00
23 C.J. Spiller 1.25 3.00
24 Brandon LaFell .75 2.00
25 Marcus Easley .60 1.50
26 Rob Gronkowski 2.00 5.00
27 Andre Roberts .75 2.00
28 Mike Kafka .75 2.00
29 Taylor Price .75 2.00
30 Mardy Gilyard .75 2.00
31 Jordan Shipley .75 2.00
32 Jonathan Dwyer .75 2.00
33 Jahvid Best 1.25 3.00
34 Emmanuel Sanders .75 2.00
35 Dez Bryant 2.50 6.00

2010 Rookies and Stars Studio Rookies Materials

STATED PRINT RUN 299 SER.#'d SETS
*PRIME/50: .8X TO 2X BASIC JSY/299
1 Tim Tebow 10.00 25.00
2 Sam Bradford 6.00 15.00
3 Rolando McClain 2.00 5.00
4 Ndamukong Suh 4.00 10.00
5 Golden Tate 2.00 5.00
6 Eric Decker 2.50 6.00
7 Eric Berry 2.00 5.00
8 Montario Hardesty 2.00 5.00
9 Gerald McCoy 2.00 5.00
10 Demaryius Thomas 2.50 6.00
11 Ben Tate 2.50 6.00
12 Arrelious Benn 2.00 5.00
13 Dexter McCluster 2.00 5.00
14 Damian Williams 2.00 5.00
15 Colt McCoy 5.00 12.00
16 Jermaine Gresham 2.50 6.00
17 Jimmy Clausen 2.00 5.00
18 Joe McKnight 2.00 5.00
19 Mike Williams 3.00 8.00
20 Toby Gerhart 2.00 5.00
21 Ryan Mathews 4.00 10.00
22 Armanti Edwards 2.00 5.00
23 C.J. Spiller 3.00 8.00
24 Brandon LaFell 2.00 5.00
25 Marcus Easley 1.50 4.00
26 Rob Gronkowski 5.00 12.00
27 Andre Roberts 2.00 5.00
28 Mike Kafka 2.00 5.00
29 Taylor Price 2.00 5.00
30 Mardy Gilyard 2.00 5.00
31 Jordan Shipley 2.00 5.00
32 Jonathan Dwyer 2.00 5.00
33 Jahvid Best 3.00 8.00
34 Emmanuel Sanders 2.00 5.00
35 Dez Bryant 6.00 15.00

2010 Rookies and Stars Studio Rookies Combos

*BLACK/100: .6X TO 1.5X BASIC INSERTS
*GOLD/500: .5X TO 1.2X BASIC INSERTS
1 Sam Bradford 3.00 8.00
Mardy Gilyard
2 Tim Tebow 3.00 8.00
Demaryius Thomas
3 Jimmy Clausen .75 2.00
Brandon LaFell
4 Colt McCoy 1.50 4.00
Montario Hardesty
5 Jermaine Gresham 1.00 2.50
Jordan Shipley
6 C.J. Spiller 1.25 3.00
Marcus Easley
7 Ndamukong Suh 1.50 4.00
Jahvid Best
8 Gerald McCoy 1.25 3.00
Mike Williams
9 Eric Berry .75 2.00
Dexter McCluster
10 Rob Gronkowski 2.00 5.00
Taylor Price

2010 Rookies and Stars Studio Rookies Combos Materials

STATED PRINT RUN 299 SER.#'d SETS
*PRIME/50: .6X TO 1.5X BASIC JSY/299
1 Sam Bradford 6.00 15.00
Mardy Gilyard
2 Tim Tebow 10.00 25.00
Demaryius Thomas
3 Jimmy Clausen 3.00 8.00
Brandon LaFell
4 Colt McCoy 5.00 12.00
Montario Hardesty
5 Jermaine Gresham 4.00 10.00
Jordan Shipley
6 C.J. Spiller 6.00 15.00
Marcus Easley
7 Ndamukong Suh 8.00 20.00
Jahvid Best
8 Gerald McCoy 4.00 10.00
Mike Williams
9 Eric Berry 3.00 8.00
Dexter McCluster
10 Rob Gronkowski 8.00 20.00
Taylor Price

2010 Rookies and Stars Team Chemistry Autographs

1 C.J. Spiller
Marcus Easley
2 Jimmy Clausen
Brandon LaFell
Armanti Edwards
3 Jermaine Gresham
Jordan Shipley
4 Colt McCoy
Montario Hardesty
6 Ndamukong Suh
Jahvid Best
7 Eric Berry
Dexter McCluster
8 Rob Gronkowski
Taylor Price
9 Sam Bradford
Mardy Gilyard
10 Arrelious Benn
Mike Williams

2011 Rookies and Stars

151-250 ROOKIES ONE PER PACK
251-300 ROOKIE AU PRINT RUN 299
1 Chris Wells .25 .60
2 Larry Fitzgerald .25 .60
3 Steve Breaston .20 .50
4 Tim Hightower .20 .50
5 Jason Snelling .25 .60
6 Matt Ryan .30 .75
7 Michael Turner .25 .60
8 Roddy White .25 .60
9 Tony Gonzalez .25 .60
10 Anquan Boldin .25 .60
11 Joe Flacco .30 .75
12 Ray Lewis .30 .75
13 Ray Rice .25 .60
14 Todd Heap .20 .50
15 C.J. Spiller .25 .60
16 Fred Jackson .30 .75
17 Lee Evans .25 .60
18 Ryan Fitzpatrick .25 .60
19 Steve Johnson .25 .60
20 DeAngelo Williams .25 .60
21 Jimmy Clausen .20 .50
22 Jonathan Stewart .25 .60
23 Steve Smith .25 .60
24 Brian Urlacher .30 .75
25 Devin Hester .30 .75
26 Jay Cutler .25 .60
27 Johnny Knox .25 .60
28 Matt Forte .25 .60
29 Carson Palmer .25 .60
30 Cedric Benson .25 .60
31 Chad Ochocinco .25 .60
32 Jordan Shipley .25 .60
33 Terrell Owens .30 .75
34 Ben Watson .20 .50
35 Colt McCoy .25 .60
36 Josh Cribbs .25 .60
37 Peyton Hillis .25 .60
38 Dez Bryant .30 .75
39 Felix Jones .25 .60
40 Jason Witten .30 .75
41 Miles Austin .25 .60
42 Tony Romo .30 .75
43 Brandon Lloyd .25 .60
44 Eddie Royal .20 .50
45 Jabar Gaffney .20 .50
46 Knowshon Moreno .25 .60
47 Tim Tebow .60 1.50
48 Brandon Pettigrew .20 .50
49 Calvin Johnson .30 .75
50 Jahvid Best .25 .60
51 Matthew Stafford .30 .75
52 Nate Burleson .20 .50
53 Aaron Rodgers .50 1.25
54 Clay Matthews .30 .75
55 Donald Driver .25 .60
56 Greg Jennings .25 .60
57 Jordy Nelson .25 .60
58 Andre Johnson .25 .60
59 Arian Foster .25 .60
60 Brian Cushing .20 .50
61 Kevin Walter .20 .50
62 Matt Schaub .25 .60
63 Austin Collie .25 .60
64 Dallas Clark .25 .60
65 Joseph Addai .25 .60
66 Peyton Manning .50 1.25
67 Reggie Wayne .25 .60
68 David Garrard .25 .60
69 Marcedes Lewis .20 .50
70 Maurice Jones-Drew .25 .60
71 Mike Sims-Walker .25 .60
72 Mike Thomas .25 .60
73 Dwayne Bowe .25 .60
74 Jamaal Charles .25 .60
75 Matt Cassel .25 .60
76 Tony Moeaki .20 .50
77 Brandon Marshall .25 .60
78 Brian Hartline .20 .50
79 Chad Henne .25 .60
80 Davone Bess .20 .50
81 Ronnie Brown .25 .60
82 Adrian Peterson .40 1.00
83 Percy Harvin .25 .60
84 Sidney Rice .25 .60
85 Joe Webb .20 .50
86 Visanthe Shiancoe .25 .60
87 BenJarvus Green-Ellis .25 .60
88 Danny Woodhead .30 .75
89 Deion Branch .20 .50
90 Tom Brady .50 1.25
91 Wes Welker .30 .75
92 Drew Brees .30 .75
93 Lance Moore .25 .60
94 Marques Colston .25 .60
95 Pierre Thomas .25 .60
96 Reggie Bush .25 .60
97 Ahmad Bradshaw .25 .60
98 Eli Manning .30 .75
99 Hakeem Nicks .25 .60
100 Mario Manningham .25 .60
101 Steve Smith USC .25 .60
102 Braylon Edwards .25 .60
103 LaDainian Tomlinson .30 .75
104 Mark Sanchez .30 .75
105 Santonio Holmes .25 .60
106 Shonn Greene .25 .60
107 Darren McFadden .25 .60
108 Darrius Heyward-Bey .20 .50
109 Louis Murphy .20 .50
110 Zach Miller .25 .60
111 DeSean Jackson .25 .60
112 Jeremy Maclin .25 .60
113 LeSean McCoy .25 .60
114 Michael Vick .30 .75
115 Ben Roethlisberger .30 .75
116 Hines Ward .25 .60
117 Mike Wallace .30 .75
118 Rashard Mendenhall .25 .60
119 Troy Polamalu .30 .75
120 Antonio Gates .25 .60
121 Malcom Floyd .25 .60
122 Mike Tolbert .25 .60
123 Philip Rivers .30 .75
124 Ryan Mathews .25 .60
125 Frank Gore .25 .60
126 Michael Crabtree .25 .60
127 Patrick Willis .25 .60
128 Vernon Davis .25 .60
129 John Carlson .20 .50
130 Marshawn Lynch .25 .60
131 Matt Hasselbeck .25 .60
132 Mike Williams USC .25 .60
133 Danny Amendola .25 .60
134 Donnie Avery .20 .50
135 Sam Bradford .30 .75
136 Steven Jackson .25 .60
137 Cadillac Williams .20 .50
138 Josh Freeman .30 .75
139 Kellen Winslow Jr. .25 .60
140 LeGarrette Blount .25 .60
141 Mike Williams .25 .60
142 Bo Scaife .20 .50
143 Chris Johnson .25 .60
144 Kenny Britt .25 .60
145 Nate Washington .20 .50
146 Randy Moss .25 .60
147 Chris Cooley .25 .60
148 Donovan McNabb .30 .75
149 Ryan Torain .20 .50
150 Santana Moss .25 .60
151 Aaron Williams RC .75 2.00
152 Adrian Clayborn RC 1.00 2.50
153 Ahmad Black RC .75 2.00
154 Akeem Ayers RC .75 2.00
155 Akeem Dent RC .75 2.00
156 Aldrick Robinson RC .60 1.50
157 Alex Henery RC .75 2.00
158 Allen Bailey RC .75 2.00
159 Allen Bradford RC .75 2.00

160 Anthony Allen RC .60 1.50
161 Anthony Castonzo RC .60 1.50
162 Anthony Sherman RC .75 2.00
163 Baron Batch RC 1.00 2.50
164 Brandon Harris RC .60 1.50
165 Brooks Reed RC 1.00 2.50
166 Bruce Carter RC 1.00 2.50
167 Cameron Heyward RC 1.00 2.50
168 Cameron Jordan RC .75 2.00
169 Casey Matthews RC 1.00 2.50
170 Chimdi Chekwa RC .75 2.00
171 Chris Conte RC .60 1.50
172 Chris Culliver RC .75 2.00
173 Christian Ballard RC .75 2.00
174 Colin McCarthy RC .75 2.00
175 Corey Liuget RC .60 1.50
176 Cortez Allen RC .60 1.50
177 Curtis Brown RC 1.00 2.50
178 Danny Watkins RC .75 2.00
179 Da'Norris Searcy RC .60 1.50
180 Da'Rel Scott RC .75 2.00
181 David Ausberry RC .75 2.00
182 DeMarco Sampson RC .60 1.50
183 Denarius Moore RC 1.25 3.00
184 Derek Sherrod RC 1.00 2.50
185 Dion Lewis RC 1.00 2.50
186 Dontay Moch RC .60 1.50
187 Drake Nevis RC 1.00 2.50
188 Dwayne Harris RC 1.00 2.50
189 Evan Royster RC 1.00 2.50
190 Gabe Carimi RC 1.00 2.50
191 Greg Jones RC .75 2.00
192 Greg McElroy RC 1.00 2.50
193 Jabaal Sheard RC 1.00 2.50
194 Jah Reid RC .60 1.50
195 Jaiquawn Jarrett RC .75 2.00
196 James Carpenter RC 1.00 2.50
197 Jarvis Jenkins RC .60 1.50
198 Jay Finley RC .75 2.00
199 Jimmy Smith RC 1.00 2.50
200 Johnny White RC .75 2.00
201 Jonas Mouton RC .75 2.00
202 Jordan Cameron RC .75 2.00
203 Julius Thomas RC .75 2.00
204 Justin Houston RC 1.00 2.50
205 Kealoha Pilares RC 1.00 2.50
206 Kelvin Sheppard RC 1.00 2.50
207 Kris Durham RC .75 2.00
208 Lee Smith RC .75 2.00
209 Luke Stocker RC .75 2.00
210 Marcus Cannon RC .60 1.50
211 Marcus Gilchrist RC .60 1.50
212 Martez Wilson RC 1.00 2.50
213 Marvin Austin RC .75 2.00
214 Mason Foster RC 1.00 2.50
215 Cheta Ozougwu RC .60 1.50
216 Mike Pouncey RC 1.00 2.50
217 Muhammad Wilkerson RC 1.00 2.50
218 Nate Irving RC .75 2.00
219 Nate Solder RC 1.00 2.50
220 Nathan Enderle RC 1.00 2.50
221 Nick Fairley RC 1.25 3.00
222 Owen Marecic RC 1.00 2.50
223 Patrick Peterson RC 1.50 4.00
224 Pernell McPhee RC 1.00 2.50
225 Phil Taylor RC .75 2.00
226 Prince Amukamara RC 1.00 2.50
227 Quan Sturdivant RC 1.00 2.50
228 Quinton Carter RC .60 1.50
229 Rahim Moore RC .75 2.00
230 Ras-I Dowling RC 1.00 2.50
231 Richard Gordon RC .75 2.00
232 Robert Housler RC .75 2.00
233 Robert Quinn RC 1.00 2.50
234 Robert Sands RC .75 2.00
235 Ronald Johnson RC .75 2.00
236 Ross Homan RC 1.00 2.50
237 Ryan Whalen RC .75 2.00
238 Sam Acho RC .75 2.00
239 Scotty McKnight RC .75 2.00
240 Terrelle Pryor RC 1.25 3.00
241 Sione Fua RC .75 2.00
242 Stanley Havili RC .60 1.50
243 Stefen Wisniewski RC 1.00 2.50
244 Stephen Burton RC .60 1.50
245 Stephen Paea RC 1.00 2.50
246 T.J. Yates RC 1.25 3.00
247 Tyler Sash RC 1.00 2.50
248 Tyrod Taylor RC 1.00 2.50
249 Tyron Smith RC 1.25 3.00
250 Virgil Green RC .75 2.00
251 Cam Newton AU RC 100.00 175.00
252 Blaine Gabbert AU RC 15.00 40.00
253 Jamie Harper AU RC 8.00 20.00
254 Leonard Hankerson AU RC 8.00 20.00
255 Mikel Leshoure AU RC 8.00 20.00
256 Ryan Mallett AU RC 20.00 40.00
257 Shane Vereen AU RC 8.00 20.00
258 Taiwan Jones AU RC 8.00 20.00
259 Mark Ingram AU RC 25.00 60.00
260 Colin Kaepernick AU RC 20.00 40.00
261 Jordan Todman AU RC 5.00 12.00
262 Titus Young AU RC 10.00 25.00
263 Clyde Gates AU RC 6.00 15.00
264 DeMarco Murray AU RC 25.00 60.00
265 Kyle Rudolph AU RC 8.00 20.00
266 Stevan Ridley AU RC 8.00 20.00
267 Von Miller AU RC 12.00 30.00
268 Andy Dalton AU RC 30.00 60.00
269 Jerrel Jernigan AU RC 6.00 15.00
270 Randall Cobb AU RC 10.00 25.00
271 A.J. Green AU RC 25.00 50.00
272 Marcell Dareus AU RC 8.00 20.00
273 Torrey Smith AU RC 10.00 25.00
274 Delone Carter AU RC 6.00 15.00
275 Bilal Powell AU RC 5.00 12.00
276 Jake Locker AU RC 40.00 80.00
277 Ryan Williams AU RC 10.00 25.00
278 Vincent Brown AU RC 8.00 20.00
279 Alex Green AU RC 8.00 20.00
280 Christian Ponder AU RC 25.00 60.00
281 Greg Little AU RC 8.00 20.00
282 Jonathan Baldwin AU RC 8.00 20.00
283 Daniel Thomas AU RC 12.00 30.00
284 Kendall Hunter AU RC 8.00 20.00
285 Austin Pettis AU RC 6.00 15.00
286 Julio Jones AU RC 20.00 50.00
287 Aldon Smith AU RC EXCH 12.00 30.00
288 Cecil Shorts AU RC EXCH 6.00 15.00
289 D.J. Williams AU RC EXCH 8.00 20.00
290 Da'Quan Bowers AU RC 8.00 20.00
291 Greg Salas AU RC 8.00 20.00
292 J.J. Watt AU RC 10.00 25.00
293 Jacquizz Rodgers AU RC 8.00 20.00
294 Jeremy Kerley AU RC 8.00 20.00
295 Lance Kendricks AU RC EXCH 6.00 15.00
296 Niles Paul AU RC 8.00 20.00
297 Ricky Stanzi AU RC 20.00 40.00
298 Roy Helu AU RC 15.00 40.00
299 Ryan Kerrigan AU RC 8.00 20.00
300 Tandon Doss AU RC 6.00 15.00

2011 Rookies and Stars Gold

*VETS 1-150: .8X TO 2X BASIC CARDS
*ROOKIES 151-250: .4X TO 1X BASIC CARDS
RANDOM INSERTS IN RETAIL PACKS

2011 Rookies and Stars Longevity Parallel Gold

*1-150 VETS/49: 4X TO 10X BASIC CARDS
*151-250 ROOKIES/49: 1.5X TO 4X BASIC CARDS
STATED PRINT RUN 49 SER.#'d SETS

2011 Rookies and Stars Longevity Parallel Silver Holofoil

*1-150 VETS/99: 3X TO 8X BASIC CARDS
*151-250 ROOKIES/99: 1.2X TO 3X BASIC CARDS
STATED PRINT RUN 99 SER.#'d SETS

2011 Rookies and Stars Longevity Parallel Platinum

*1-150 VETS/25: 5X TO 12X BASIC CARDS
*151-250 ROOKIES/25: 2X TO 5X BASIC R&S
STATED PRINT RUN 25 SER.#'d SETS

2011 Rookies and Stars Longevity Parallel Silver

*1-150 VETS/249: 2.5X TO 6X BASIC CARDS
*151-250 ROOKIES/249: 1X TO 2.5X BASIC CARDS
STATED PRINT RUN 249 SER.#'d SETS

2011 Rookies and Stars Rookie Patch Autographs Gold NFL Logo

*NFL LOGO/25: .8X TO 2X BASIC AU/299
STATED PRINT RUN 25 SER.#'d SETS
251 Cam Newton 175.00 300.00
276 Jake Locker 75.00 150.00

2011 Rookies and Stars All Americans

UNPRICED STATED PRINT RUN 10

2011 Rookies and Stars Dress for Success Jerseys

STATED PRINT RUN 299 SER.#'d SETS
*PRIME/50: .8X TO 2X BASIC JSY/299
*LONGEVITY/249: .4X TO 1X DRESS FOR SUCCESS
1 Jamie Harper 2.50 6.00
2 Stevan Ridley 2.50 6.00
3 Ryan Williams 3.00 8.00
4 Blaine Gabbert 4.00 10.00
5 Von Miller 4.00 10.00
6 Kyle Rudolph 2.50 6.00
7 Titus Young 3.00 8.00
8 Delone Carter 2.00 5.00
9 Randall Cobb 5.00 12.00
10 Bilal Powell 1.50 4.00
11 Alex Green 2.50 6.00
12 Mikel Leshoure 2.50 6.00
13 Colin Kaepernick 3.00 8.00
14 Cam Newton 12.00 30.00
15 Taiwan Jones 2.50 6.00
16 Andy Dalton 6.00 15.00
17 DeMarco Murray 5.00 12.00
18 Kendall Hunter 2.50 6.00
19 Torrey Smith 3.00 8.00
20 Julio Jones 6.00 15.00
21 Leonard Hankerson 2.50 6.00
22 Marcell Dareus 2.50 6.00
23 A.J. Green 5.00 12.00
24 Jake Locker 6.00 15.00
25 Greg Little 2.50 6.00
26 Austin Pettis 2.00 5.00
27 Christian Ponder 6.00 15.00
28 Ryan Mallett 5.00 12.00
29 Jonathan Baldwin 2.50 6.00
30 Jerrel Jernigan 2.00 5.00
31 Jordan Todman 1.50 4.00
32 Daniel Thomas 2.50 6.00
33 Mark Ingram 5.00 12.00
34 Shane Vereen 2.50 6.00
35 Vincent Brown 2.50 6.00
36 Clyde Gates 2.00 5.00

2011 Rookies and Stars Dress for Success Jerseys Autographs

STATED PRINT RUN 25-50
*PRIME/25: .6X TO 1.5X BASIC JSY AU/50
1 Jamie Harper/50 8.00 20.00
2 Stevan Ridley/50 8.00 20.00
3 Ryan Williams/25 15.00 40.00
4 Blaine Gabbert/25 40.00 80.00
5 Von Miller/25 15.00 40.00
6 Kyle Rudolph/50 8.00 20.00
7 Titus Young/25 15.00 40.00
8 Delone Carter/50 6.00 15.00
9 Randall Cobb/50 20.00 40.00
10 Bilal Powell/50 5.00 12.00
11 Alex Green/50 8.00 20.00
12 Mikel Leshoure/25 12.00 30.00
13 Colin Kaepernick/25 15.00 40.00
14 Cam Newton/25 125.00 250.00
15 Taiwan Jones/50 8.00 20.00
16 Andy Dalton/25 40.00 80.00
17 DeMarco Murray/25 40.00 80.00
18 Kendall Hunter/50 8.00 20.00
19 Torrey Smith/25 15.00 40.00
20 Julio Jones/25 40.00 80.00
21 Leonard Hankerson/50 8.00 20.00
22 Marcell Dareus/50 8.00 20.00
23 A.J. Green/25 30.00 80.00
24 Jake Locker/25 60.00 120.00
25 Greg Little/50 8.00 20.00
26 Austin Pettis/50 6.00 15.00
27 Christian Ponder/25 25.00 60.00
28 Ryan Mallett/25 25.00 60.00
29 Jonathan Baldwin/25 15.00 50.00
30 Jerrel Jernigan/50 6.00 15.00
31 Jordan Todman/25 8.00 20.00
32 Daniel Thomas/50 8.00 20.00
33 Mark Ingram/25 50.00 100.00
34 Shane Vereen/50 8.00 20.00
35 Vincent Brown/50 12.00 30.00
36 Clyde Gates/50 6.00 15.00

2011 Rookies and Stars Freshman Orientation Jerseys

*FRESH/299: .4X TO 1X DRESS FOR SUCCESS
STATED PRINT RUN 299 SER.#'d SETS
*PRIME/50: .8X TO 2X BASIC JSY/299
*LONGEVITY/249: .4X TO 1X DRESS FOR SUCCESS

2011 Rookies and Stars Freshman Orientation Jerseys Autographs

*FRESH: .4X TO 1X DRESS FOR SUCCESS
STATED PRINT RUN 25-50
*PRIME/25: .6X TO 1.5X BASIC JSY AU/50

2011 Rookies and Stars Materials Emerald Prime Longevity

STATED PRINT RUN 2-99
*BLACK/36-50: .5X TO 1.2X EMERALD/74-99
*BLACK/50: .4X TO 1X EMERALD/35
*BLACK/25: .6X TO 1.5X EMERALD/75-80
*BLACK/20: .4X TO 1X EMERALD/15
*BLACK/15-25: .5X TO 1.2X EMERALD/40-50
*BLACK/10-15: .4X TO 1X EMERALD/20-25
1 Chris Wells/99 4.00 10.00
2 Larry Fitzgerald/25 6.00 15.00
6 Matt Ryan/15 8.00 20.00
7 Michael Turner/99 4.00 10.00
8 Roddy White/99 4.00 10.00
9 Tony Gonzalez/99 4.00 10.00
10 Anquan Boldin/99 4.00 10.00
11 Joe Flacco/50 6.00 15.00
12 Ray Lewis/99 5.00 12.00
13 Ray Rice/99 4.00 10.00
14 Todd Heap/99 3.00 8.00
15 C.J. Spiller/99 4.00 10.00
16 Fred Jackson/99 6.00 15.00
17 Lee Evans/99 4.00 10.00
18 Ryan Fitzpatrick/99 6.00 15.00
20 DeAngelo Williams/99 4.00 10.00
21 Jimmy Clausen/99 3.00 8.00
22 Jonathan Stewart/99 4.00 10.00
23 Steve Smith/99 4.00 10.00
24 Brian Urlacher/99 5.00 12.00
25 Devin Hester/99 5.00 12.00
26 Jay Cutler/50 5.00 12.00
27 Johnny Knox/99 4.00 10.00
28 Matt Forte/99 4.00 10.00
29 Carson Palmer/50 5.00 12.00
30 Cedric Benson/99 4.00 10.00
31 Chad Ochocinco/99 4.00 10.00
32 Jordan Shipley/99 4.00 10.00
36 Josh Cribbs/99 4.00 10.00
39 Felix Jones/99 4.00 10.00
40 Jason Witten/99 5.00 12.00
41 Miles Austin/99 5.00 12.00
42 Tony Romo/99 5.00 12.00
43 Brandon Lloyd/99 4.00 10.00
44 Eddie Royal/99 3.00 8.00
45 Jabar Gaffney/99 3.00 8.00
46 Knowshon Moreno/99 4.00 10.00
47 Tim Tebow/50 12.00 30.00
49 Calvin Johnson/99 5.00 12.00
50 Jahvid Best/25 6.00 15.00
51 Matthew Stafford/99 5.00 12.00
53 Aaron Rodgers/50 12.00 30.00
54 Clay Matthews/99 6.00 15.00
55 Donald Driver/85 5.00 12.00
58 Andre Johnson/99 4.00 10.00
62 Matt Schaub/50 5.00 12.00
64 Dallas Clark/99 4.00 10.00
65 Joseph Addai/99 4.00 10.00
66 Peyton Manning/99 8.00 20.00
67 Reggie Wayne/25 6.00 15.00
68 David Garrard/75 4.00 10.00
70 Maurice Jones-Drew/99 4.00 10.00
71 Mike Sims-Walker/40 5.00 12.00
73 Dwayne Bowe/99 4.00 10.00
74 Jamaal Charles/99 4.00 10.00
75 Matt Cassel/2
77 Brandon Marshall/99 4.00 10.00
79 Chad Henne/99 4.00 10.00
81 Ronnie Brown/99 4.00 10.00
82 Adrian Peterson/99 6.00 15.00
83 Percy Harvin/99 4.00 10.00
84 Sidney Rice/99 4.00 10.00
86 Visanthe Shiancoe/99 4.00 10.00
90 Tom Brady/99 8.00 20.00
91 Wes Welker/99 5.00 12.00
92 Drew Brees/50 6.00 15.00
94 Marques Colston/99 4.00 10.00
95 Pierre Thomas/99 4.00 10.00
96 Reggie Bush/99 4.00 10.00
97 Ahmad Bradshaw/99 4.00 10.00
98 Eli Manning/95 5.00 12.00
99 Hakeem Nicks/99 4.00 10.00
101 Steve Smith USC/99 4.00 10.00
102 Braylon Edwards/50 5.00 12.00
103 LaDainian Tomlinson/99 5.00 12.00
104 Mark Sanchez/20 10.00 25.00
105 Santonio Holmes/99 4.00 10.00
106 Shonn Greene/99 4.00 10.00
107 Darren McFadden/75 4.00 10.00
111 DeSean Jackson/99 4.00 10.00
112 Jeremy Maclin/99 4.00 10.00
113 LeSean McCoy/99 4.00 10.00
114 Michael Vick/30 10.00 25.00
116 Hines Ward/80 4.00 10.00
117 Mike Wallace/99 5.00 12.00
118 Rashard Mendenhall/50 5.00 12.00
119 Troy Polamalu/99 6.00 15.00
120 Antonio Gates/99 4.00 10.00
121 Malcom Floyd/99 4.00 10.00
123 Philip Rivers/99 5.00 12.00
124 Ryan Mathews/90 4.00 10.00
125 Frank Gore/99 4.00 10.00
126 Michael Crabtree/99 4.00 10.00
127 Patrick Willis/99 4.00 10.00
128 Vernon Davis/74 4.00 10.00
131 Matt Hasselbeck/35 5.00 12.00
135 Sam Bradford/99 5.00 12.00
136 Steven Jackson/99 4.00 10.00
137 Cadillac Williams/99 3.00 8.00
139 Kellen Winslow Jr./99 4.00 10.00
143 Chris Johnson/99 4.00 10.00
145 Nate Washington/99 3.00 8.00
146 Randy Moss/99 4.00 10.00
147 Chris Cooley/99 4.00 10.00
148 Donovan McNabb/99 5.00 12.00
150 Santana Moss/99 4.00 10.00

2011 Rookies and Stars Prime Cuts

STATED PRINT RUN 20-50
*COMBOS/15-25: .5X TO 1.2X PRIME CUT/30-50
1 Aaron Rodgers/50 20.00 50.00
2 Joe Flacco/50 10.00 25.00
3 Rashard Mendenhall/50 8.00 20.00
4 Michael Vick/30 15.00 40.00
5 Mark Sanchez/20 15.00 40.00
6 Matt Ryan/30 10.00 25.00
7 Larry Fitzgerald/25 10.00 25.00
8 Steven Jackson/50 8.00 20.00

2011 Rookies and Stars Prime Cuts Autographs

STATED PRINT RUN 15-20
1 Aaron Rodgers/20 150.00 250.00
2 Joe Flacco/20
3 Rashard Mendenhall/20 EXCH
4 Michael Vick/20 30.00 60.00
5 Mark Sanchez/15
6 Matt Ryan/20 50.00 100.00
7 Larry Fitzgerald/15
8 Steven Jackson/20 25.00 50.00

2011 Rookies and Stars Rookie Autographs Holofoil

STATED PRINT RUN 300-350
151 Aaron Williams/300 5.00 12.00
152 Adrian Clayborn/300 8.00 20.00
153 Ahmad Black/350 5.00 12.00
154 Akeem Ayers/300 3.00 8.00
156 Aldrick Robinson/300 8.00 20.00
161 Anthony Castonzo/350 2.50 6.00
164 Brandon Harris/300 2.50 6.00
167 Cameron Heyward/300 8.00 20.00
168 Cameron Jordan/300 3.00 8.00
175 Corey Liuget/300 4.00 10.00
183 Denarius Moore/350 10.00 25.00
185 Dion Lewis/300 4.00 10.00
189 Evan Royster/350 4.00 10.00
191 Greg Jones/300 3.00 8.00
199 Jimmy Smith/300 4.00 10.00
200 Johnny White/350 3.00 8.00
202 Jordan Cameron/350 5.00 12.00
204 Justin Houston/350 4.00 10.00
207 Kris Durham/350 3.00 8.00
209 Luke Stocker/300 3.00 8.00
210 Marcus Cannon/350 4.00 10.00
212 Martez Wilson/300 5.00 12.00
225 Phil Taylor/300 5.00 12.00
226 Prince Amukamara/300 8.00 20.00
228 Quinton Carter/350 2.50 6.00
229 Rahim Moore/350 3.00 8.00
235 Ronald Johnson/300 3.00 8.00
237 Ryan Whalen/350 3.00 8.00
242 Stanley Havili/350 2.50 6.00
244 Stephen Burton/350 3.00 6.00
245 Stephen Paea/300 4.00 10.00
247 Tyler Sash/300 4.00 10.00
248 Tyrod Taylor/350 4.00 10.00

2011 Rookies and Stars Rookie Jersey Jumbo Swatch

*JUMBO/50: .6X TO 1.5X DRESS FOR SUCCESS
STATED PRINT RUN 50 SER.#'d SETS
*EMERALD/10: 1X TO 2.5X BASIC JUMBO/50
*GOLD/25: .5X TO 1.2X BASIC JUMBO/50
*LONGEVITY/50: .4X TO 1X JUMBO/50

2011 Rookies and Stars Rookie Revolution

RANDOM INSERTS IN PACKS
*BLACK/100: .6X TO 1.5X BASIC INSERTS
*GOLD/500: .5X TO 1.2X BASIC INSERTS
UNPRICED AUTO PRINT RUN 10
1 Blaine Gabbert 1.50 4.00
2 Daniel Thomas 1.00 2.50
3 Jamie Harper 1.00 2.50
4 Julio Jones 2.00 5.00
5 Mikel Leshoure 1.00 2.50
6 Taiwan Jones 1.00 2.50
7 Mark Ingram 2.00 5.00
8 DeMarco Murray 2.00 5.00
9 Shane Vereen 1.00 2.50
10 Stevan Ridley 1.00 2.50
11 Greg Little 1.00 2.50
12 Bilal Powell .60 1.50
13 A.J. Green 2.00 5.00
14 Jake Locker 2.50 6.00
15 Titus Young 1.25 3.00
16 Marcell Dareus 1.00 2.50
17 Kendall Hunter 1.00 2.50
18 Jonathan Baldwin 1.00 2.50
19 Von Miller 1.25 3.00
20 Alex Green 1.00 2.50
21 Christian Ponder 2.00 5.00
22 Jerrel Jernigan .75 2.00
23 Vincent Brown 1.00 2.50
24 Ryan Mallett 2.00 5.00
25 Austin Pettis .75 2.00
26 Delone Carter .75 2.00
27 Leonard Hankerson 1.00 2.50
28 Torrey Smith 1.25 3.00
29 Andy Dalton 2.50 6.00
30 Colin Kaepernick 1.25 3.00
31 Jordan Todman .60 1.50
32 Ryan Williams 1.25 3.00
33 Randall Cobb 1.25 3.00
34 Kyle Rudolph 1.00 2.50
35 Cam Newton 5.00 12.00
36 Clyde Gates .75 2.00

2011 Rookies and Stars Rookie Revolution Materials

*JSY/299: .4X TO 1X DRESS FOR SUCCESS
STATED PRINT RUN 299 SER.#'d SETS
*PRIME/50: .8X TO 2X BASIC JSY/299
*LONGEVITY/249: .4X TO 1X DRESS FOR SUCCESS

2011 Rookies and Stars Rookie Revolution Materials Autographs

*REVOLUTION: .4X TO 1X DRESS FOR SUCCESS
STATED PRINT RUN 25-50
*PRIME/25: .6X TO 1.5X BASIC JSY AU/50

2011 Rookies and Stars Statistical Standouts Materials

STATED PRINT RUN 95-299
*PRIME/30-50: .6X TO 1.5X BASIC JSY/200-299
*PRIME/25: .8X TO 2X BASIC JSY/299
1 Philip Rivers/299 4.00 10.00
2 Peyton Manning/299 6.00 15.00
3 Drew Brees/200 4.00 10.00
4 Matt Schaub/299 3.00 8.00
5 Eli Manning/299 4.00 10.00
6 Carson Palmer/299 3.00 8.00
7 Brandon Lloyd/299 3.00 8.00
8 Roddy White/299 3.00 8.00
9 Reggie Wayne/299 3.00 8.00
10 Ed Reed/200 3.00 8.00
11 Mike Wallace/299 4.00 10.00
12 Andre Johnson/299 3.00 8.00
14 Jamaal Charles/299 3.00 8.00
15 Michael Turner/299 3.00 8.00
16 Chris Johnson/299 3.00 8.00
17 Maurice Jones-Drew/299 3.00 8.00
18 Adrian Peterson/299 5.00 12.00
19 Tom Brady/299 6.00 15.00
20 Dwayne Bowe/200 3.00 8.00
21 Calvin Johnson/299 4.00 10.00
22 Arian Foster/95 5.00 12.00
23 DeMarcus Ware/299 3.00 8.00

2011 Rookies and Stars Statistical Standouts Materials Autographs

STATED PRINT RUN 10-20
EXCH EXPIRATION: 1/27/2013
1 Philip Rivers/20
2 Peyton Manning/15 75.00 150.00
3 Drew Brees/15 60.00 120.00
4 Matt Schaub/20
5 Eli Manning/20
6 Carson Palmer/20 EXCH
7 Brandon Lloyd/20 EXCH 15.00 40.00
8 Roddy White/15 25.00 50.00
9 Reggie Wayne/15 EXCH
11 Mike Wallace/25
12 Andre Johnson/20 EXCH 25.00 50.00
14 Jamaal Charles/20 EXCH 15.00 40.00
15 Michael Turner/20 15.00 40.00
17 Maurice Jones-Drew/20
18 Adrian Peterson/20 60.00 120.00
19 Tom Brady/20 EXCH 125.00 200.00
20 Dwayne Bowe/20 EXCH
21 Calvin Johnson/20 30.00 60.00

2011 Rookies and Stars Studio Rookies

*STUDIO: .4X TO 1X ROOKIE REVOLUTION
RANDOM INSERTS IN PACKS
*BLACK/100: .6X TO 1.5X BASIC INSERTS
*GOLD/500: .5X TO 1.2X BASIC INSERTS
UNPRICED AUTO PRINT RUN 10

2011 Rookies and Stars Studio Rookies Combos

RANDOM INSERTS IN PACKS
*BLACK/100: .6X TO 1.5X BASIC INSERTS
*GOLD/500: .5X TO 1.2X BASIC INSERTS
1 Cam Newton 4.00 10.00
Mark Ingram
2 Randall Cobb 1.00 2.50
Alex Green
3 Jordan Todman .75 2.00
Vincent Brown
4 Mikel Leshoure 1.00 2.50
Titus Young
5 Ryan Mallett 1.50 4.00
Shane Vereen
6 Christian Ponder 1.50 4.00
Kyle Rudolph
7 Jake Locker 2.00 5.00
Jamie Harper
8 A.J. Green 2.00 5.00
Andy Dalton
9 Colin Kaepernick 1.00 2.50
Kendall Hunter
10 Mark Ingram 1.50 4.00
Julio Jones

2011 Rookies and Stars Studio Rookies Combos Materials

STATED PRINT RUN 299 SER.#'d SETS
*PRIME/50 .8X TO 2X BASIC COMBO/299
1 Cam Newton 15.00 40.00
Mark Ingram
2 Randall Cobb 8.00 20.00
Alex Green
3 Jordan Todman 3.00 8.00
Vincent Brown
4 Mikel Leshoure 4.00 10.00
Titus Young
5 Ryan Mallett 6.00 15.00
Shane Vereen
6 Christian Ponder 6.00 15.00
Kyle Rudolph
7 Jake Locker 8.00 20.00
Jamie Harper
8 A.J. Green 8.00 20.00
Andy Dalton
9 Colin Kaepernick 4.00 10.00
Kendall Hunter
10 Mark Ingram 10.00 25.00
Julio Jones

2011 Rookies and Stars Studio Rookies Materials

*JSY/299: .4X TO 1X DRESS FOR SUCCESS
STATED PRINT RUN 299 SER.#'d SETS
*PRIME/50: .8X TO 2X BASIC JSY/299

2010 Rookies and Stars Longevity

COMP.SET w/o RC's (150) 8.00 20.00
*VETS 1-150: .4X TO 1X BASIC R&S
*ELE 151-165: .25X TO .6X BASIC R&S
*ROOKIES 166-250: .4X TO 1X BASIC R&S
251-300 UNPRICED ROOK.AU PRINT RUN 10
1 Chris Wells .25 .60
2 Larry Fitzgerald .30 .75
3 Matt Leinart .25 .60
4 Steve Breaston .20 .50
5 Matt Ryan .30 .75
6 Michael Turner .20 .50
7 Roddy White .25 .60
8 Tony Gonzalez .25 .60
9 Anquan Boldin .25 .60
10 Derrick Mason .25 .60
11 Joe Flacco .30 .75
12 Ray Rice .25 .60
13 Todd Heap .20 .50
14 Fred Jackson .30 .75
15 Lee Evans .25 .60
16 Marshawn Lynch .25 .60
17 Ryan Fitzpatrick .30 .75
18 DeAngelo Williams .25 .60
19 Jonathan Stewart .25 .60
20 Matt Moore .25 .60
21 Steve Smith .25 .60
22 Brian Urlacher .30 .75
23 Devin Hester .30 .75
24 Greg Olsen .20 .50
25 Jay Cutler .30 .75
26 Matt Forte .25 .60
27 Andre Caldwell .20 .50
28 Antonio Bryant .20 .50
29 Carson Palmer .25 .60
30 Cedric Benson .25 .60
31 Chad Ochocinco .25 .60
32 Ben Watson .20 .50
33 Jake Delhomme .25 .60
34 Jerome Harrison .20 .50
35 Josh Cribbs .30 .75
36 Mohamed Massaquoi .25 .60
37 Felix Jones .25 .60
38 Jason Witten .30 .75
39 Marion Barber .25 .60
40 Miles Austin .30 .75
41 Tony Romo .40 1.00
42 Brandon Marshall .25 .60
43 Eddie Royal .20 .50
44 Jabar Gaffney .20 .50
45 Knowshon Moreno .25 .60
46 Kyle Orton .25 .60
47 Brandon Pettigrew .20 .50
48 Calvin Johnson .30 .75
49 Matthew Stafford .30 .75
50 Nate Burleson .20 .50
51 Aaron Rodgers .60 1.50
52 Donald Driver .25 .60
53 Greg Jennings .25 .60
54 Jermichael Finley .25 .60
55 Ryan Grant .25 .60
56 Andre Johnson .25 .60
57 Kevin Walter .25 .60
58 Matt Schaub .25 .60
59 Owen Daniels .20 .50
60 Steve Slaton .20 .50
61 Pierre Garcon .25 .60
62 Dallas Clark .25 .60
63 Joseph Addai .25 .60
64 Peyton Manning .50 1.25
65 Reggie Wayne .25 .60
66 David Garrard .25 .60
67 Maurice Jones-Drew .25 .60
68 Mike Sims-Walker .25 .60
69 Mike Thomas .25 .60
70 Torry Holt .25 .60
71 Chris Chambers .25 .60
72 Dwayne Bowe .25 .60
73 Jamaal Charles .25 .60
74 Matt Cassel .25 .60
75 Thomas Jones .25 .60
76 Brian Hartline .25 .60
77 Chad Henne .25 .60
78 Davone Bess .20 .50
79 Greg Camarillo .20 .50
80 Ronnie Brown .25 .60
81 Adrian Peterson .50 1.25
82 Brett Favre .75 2.00
83 Percy Harvin .30 .75
84 Sidney Rice .25 .60
85 Visanthe Shiancoe .25 .60
86 Laurence Maroney .25 .60
87 Randy Moss .30 .75
88 Tom Brady .50 1.25
89 Wes Welker .30 .75
90 Devery Henderson .20 .50
91 Drew Brees .30 .75
92 Jeremy Shockey .25 .60
93 Marques Colston .25 .60
94 Pierre Thomas .25 .60
95 Brandon Jacobs .25 .60
96 Eli Manning .30 .75
97 Hakeem Nicks .25 .60
98 Kevin Boss .25 .60
99 Steve Smith USC .25 .60
100 Braylon Edwards .25 .60
101 Jerricho Cotchery .25 .60
102 LaDainian Tomlinson .30 .75
103 Mark Sanchez .30 .75
104 Shonn Greene .25 .60
105 Chaz Schilens .20 .50
106 Darren McFadden .25 .60
107 Jason Campbell .25 .60
108 Louis Murphy .25 .60
109 Zach Miller .25 .60
110 Brent Celek .25 .60
111 DeSean Jackson .25 .60
112 Jeremy Maclin .25 .60
113 Kevin Kolb .25 .60
114 LeSean McCoy .25 .60
115 Ben Roethlisberger .30 .75
116 Heath Miller .25 .60
117 Rashard Mendenhall .25 .60
118 Santonio Holmes .25 .60
119 Troy Polamalu .30 .75
120 Antonio Gates .25 .60
121 Darren Sproles .25 .60
122 Philip Rivers .30 .75
123 Vincent Jackson .20 .50
124 Alex Smith QB .25 .60
125 Frank Gore .25 .60
126 Josh Morgan .25 .60
127 Michael Crabtree .30 .75
128 Vernon Davis .25 .60
129 Deion Branch .20 .50
130 John Carlson .20 .50
131 Julius Jones .20 .50
132 Matt Hasselbeck .20 .50
133 T.J. Houshmandzadeh .25 .60
134 Danny Amendola .30 .75
135 Donnie Avery .25 .60
136 James Laurinaitis .25 .60
137 Steven Jackson .25 .60
138 Cadillac Williams .25 .60
139 Josh Freeman .30 .75
140 Kellen Winslow Jr. .25 .60
141 Sammie Stroughter .20 .50
142 Bo Scaife .20 .50
143 Chris Johnson .30 .75
144 Kenny Britt .25 .60
145 Vince Young .20 .50
146 Chris Cooley .25 .60
147 Clinton Portis .25 .60
148 Donovan McNabb .30 .75
149 Larry Johnson .25 .60
150 Santana Moss .25 .60
151 Dallas Clark ELE .60 1.50
152 Peyton Manning ELE 1.25 3.00
153 Lee Evans ELE .60 1.50
154 David Garrard ELE .60 1.50
155 Derrick Mason ELE .60 1.50
156 Calvin Johnson ELE .75 2.00
157 Joe Flacco ELE .75 2.00
158 Vince Young ELE .50 1.25
159 Chris Johnson ELE .75 2.00
160 Tom Brady ELE 1.25 3.00
161 Wes Welker ELE .75 2.00
162 Ryan Fitzpatrick ELE .75 2.00
163 Fred Jackson ELE .75 2.00
164 Laurence Maroney ELE .60 1.50
165 Randy Moss ELE .75 2.00
166 A.J. Edds RC 1.50 4.00
167 Alterraun Verner RC 1.50 4.00
168 Amari Spievey RC 1.50 4.00
169 Andre Anderson RC 1.25 3.00
170 Andre Dixon RC 1.50 4.00
171 Anthony Davis RC 1.25 3.00
172 Anthony Dixon RC 1.50 4.00
173 Antonio Brown RC 2.50 6.00
174 Blair White RC 1.50 4.00
175 Brandon Ghee RC 1.25 3.00
176 Brandon Graham RC 1.25 3.00
177 Brian Price RC 1.50 4.00
178 Bryan Bulaga RC 1.50 4.00
179 Chad Jones RC 1.50 4.00
180 Charles Scott RC 1.25 3.00
181 Chris Cook RC 1.50 4.00
182 Chris McGaha RC 1.00 2.50
183 Corey Wootton RC 1.25 3.00
184 Dan Williams RC 1.25 3.00
185 Darrell Stuckey RC 1.00 2.50
186 Darryl Sharpton RC 1.00 2.50
187 Daryl Washington RC 1.25 3.00
188 David Gettis RC 1.50 4.00
189 Dennis Pitta RC 1.50 4.00
190 Devin McCourty RC 1.50 4.00
191 Dominique Franks RC 1.00 2.50
192 Donald Butler RC 1.00 2.50
193 Ed Dickson RC 1.50 4.00
194 Eric Norwood RC 1.25 3.00
195 Everson Griffen RC 1.50 4.00
196 Freddie Barnes RC 1.25 3.00
197 Garrett Graham RC 1.25 3.00
198 James Starks RC 2.50 6.00
199 Jared Odrick RC 1.50 4.00
200 Jarrett Brown RC 1.50 4.00
201 Jason Pierre-Paul RC 2.50 6.00
202 Jason Worilds RC 1.50 4.00
203 Javier Arenas RC 1.50 4.00
204 Jeremy Williams RC 1.00 2.50
205 Jermaine Cunningham RC 1.50 4.00
206 Jerome Murphy RC 1.25 3.00
207 Jerry Hughes RC 1.50 4.00
208 Jevan Snead RC 1.50 4.00
209 Jimmy Graham RC 3.00 8.00
210 Joique Bell RC 1.25 3.00
211 Kareem Jackson RC 1.50 4.00
212 Kevin Thomas RC 1.25 3.00
213 Koa Misi RC 1.50 4.00
214 Kyle Wilson RC 1.50 4.00
215 Lamarr Houston RC 1.50 4.00
216 LeGarrette Blount RC 2.50 6.00
217 Linval Joseph RC 1.25 3.00
218 Lonyae Miller RC 1.25 3.00
219 Major Wright RC 1.50 4.00
220 Maurkice Pouncey RC 1.50 4.00
221 Mike Hoomanawanui RC 1.50 4.00
222 Mike Iupati RC 1.50 4.00
223 Morgan Burnett RC 1.50 4.00
224 Myron Lewis RC 1.25 3.00
225 Nate Allen RC 1.50 4.00
226 NaVorro Bowman RC 1.50 4.00
227 Pat Angerer RC 1.50 4.00
228 Pat Paschall RC 1.25 3.00
229 Patrick Robinson RC 1.50 4.00
230 Perrish Cox RC 1.25 3.00
231 Perry Riley RC 1.50 4.00
232 Rennie Curran RC 1.25 3.00
233 Riley Cooper RC 1.50 4.00
234 Roddrick Muckelroy RC 1.25 3.00
235 Russell Okung RC 1.50 4.00
236 Sean Canfield RC 1.25 3.00
237 Sean Lee RC 1.50 4.00
238 Sean Weatherspoon RC 1.50 4.00
239 Sergio Kindle RC 1.50 4.00
240 Seyi Ajirotutu RC 1.50 4.00
241 T.J. Ward RC 1.50 4.00
242 Thaddeus Gibson RC 1.25 3.00
243 Tony Moeaki RC 1.50 4.00
244 Tony Pike RC 1.50 4.00
245 Torell Troup RC 1.25 3.00
246 Trent Williams RC 1.50 4.00
247 Trevard Lindley RC 1.00 2.50
248 Tyson Alualu RC 1.25 3.00
249 Walter Thurmond RC 1.00 2.50
250 Zac Robinson RC 1.25 3.00

2010 Rookies and Stars Longevity Ruby

*VETS 1-150: 3X TO 8X BASIC R&S
*ELE 151-165: .8X TO 2X BASIC R&S
*ROOKIES 166-250: 1X TO 2.5X BASIC R&S
LONGEVITY RUBY PRINT RUN 100

2010 Rookies and Stars Longevity Sapphire

*VETS 1-150: 4X TO 10X BASIC R&S
*ELE 151-165: 1X TO 2.5X BASIC R&S
*ROOKIES 166-250: 1.2X TO 3X BASIC R&S
LONGEVITY SAPPHIRE PRINT RUN 50

2010 Rookies and Stars Longevity Materials Sapphire

LONG.MATER.SAPPHIRE PRINT RUN 5-75
*RUBY JSY/150-175: .3X TO .8X SAPP/75
*RUBY JSY/100-125: .4X TO 1X SAPP/75
*RUBY JSY/100: .3X TO .8X SAPP/50
*RUBY JSY/75: .25X TO .6X SAPP/25
*RUBY JSY/35: .6X TO 1.5X SAPP/75
LONG.MATER.RUBY PRINT RUN 12-175
1 Chris Wells/75 3.00 8.00
2 Larry Fitzgerald/75 4.00 10.00
3 Matt Leinart/75 3.00 8.00
5 Matt Ryan/75 4.00 10.00
7 Roddy White/50 4.00 10.00
8 Tony Gonzalez/75 3.00 8.00
10 Derrick Mason/75 3.00 8.00
11 Joe Flacco/75 4.00 10.00
13 Todd Heap/75 2.50 6.00
16 Marshawn Lynch/75 3.00 8.00
18 DeAngelo Williams/75 3.00 8.00
19 Jonathan Stewart/65 3.00 8.00
21 Steve Smith/75 3.00 8.00
22 Brian Urlacher/75 4.00 10.00
23 Devin Hester/75 4.00 10.00
24 Greg Olsen/75 2.50 6.00
25 Jay Cutler/75 4.00 10.00
29 Carson Palmer/75 3.00 8.00
30 Cedric Benson/75 3.00 8.00
31 Chad Ochocinco/75 3.00 8.00
35 Josh Cribbs/75 4.00 10.00
37 Felix Jones/75 3.00 8.00
38 Jason Witten/50 5.00 12.00
39 Marion Barber/75 3.00 8.00
41 Tony Romo/75 5.00 12.00
43 Eddie Royal/75 2.50 6.00
45 Knowshon Moreno/75 3.00 8.00
46 Kyle Orton/75 3.00 8.00
48 Calvin Johnson/75 4.00 10.00
49 Matthew Stafford/50 5.00 12.00
53 Greg Jennings/75 3.00 8.00
56 Andre Johnson/75 3.00 8.00
59 Owen Daniels/75 2.50 6.00
60 Steve Slaton/75 2.50 6.00
62 Dallas Clark/75 3.00 8.00
63 Joseph Addai/75 3.00 8.00
64 Peyton Manning/75 6.00 15.00
65 Reggie Wayne/75 3.00 8.00
66 David Garrard/75 3.00 8.00
67 Maurice Jones-Drew/75 3.00 8.00
72 Dwayne Bowe/75 3.00 8.00
80 Ronnie Brown/75 3.00 8.00
81 Adrian Peterson/75 6.00 15.00
82 Brett Favre/75 10.00 25.00
83 Percy Harvin/75 4.00 10.00
84 Sidney Rice/75 3.00 8.00
85 Visanthe Shiancoe/45 4.00 10.00
86 Laurence Maroney/75 3.00 8.00
87 Randy Moss/75 4.00 10.00
88 Tom Brady/75 6.00 15.00
90 Devery Henderson/75 2.50 6.00
91 Drew Brees/75 4.00 10.00
93 Marques Colston/75 3.00 8.00
96 Eli Manning/75 4.00 10.00
99 Steve Smith USC/75 3.00 8.00
101 Jerricho Cotchery/75 3.00 8.00
103 Mark Sanchez/75 4.00 10.00
104 Shonn Greene/75 3.00 8.00
106 Darren McFadden/75 3.00 8.00
108 Louis Murphy/75 3.00 8.00
109 Zach Miller/75 3.00 8.00
114 LeSean McCoy/75 3.00 8.00
115 Ben Roethlisberger/75 4.00 10.00
117 Rashard Mendenhall/50 4.00 10.00
119 Troy Polamalu/75 4.00 10.00
120 Antonio Gates/75 3.00 8.00
121 Darren Sproles/75 3.00 8.00
122 Philip Rivers/25 6.00 15.00
123 Vincent Jackson/75 2.50 6.00
124 Alex Smith QB/75 3.00 8.00
125 Frank Gore/75 3.00 8.00
127 Michael Crabtree/75 4.00 10.00
128 Vernon Davis/50 4.00 10.00
129 Deion Branch/75 2.50 6.00
132 Matt Hasselbeck/75 2.50 6.00
137 Steven Jackson/75 3.00 8.00
138 Cadillac Williams/75 3.00 8.00
139 Josh Freeman/75 4.00 10.00
143 Chris Johnson/50 5.00 12.00
144 Kenny Britt/75 3.00 8.00
145 Vince Young/75 2.50 6.00
146 Chris Cooley/75 3.00 8.00

147 Clinton Portis/75	3.00	8.00
148 Donovan McNabb/75	4.00	10.00
150 Santana Moss/75	3.00	8.00

2011 Rookies and Stars Longevity

*1-150 VETS: .4X TO 1X BASIC R&S
*151-250 ROOKIES: .4X TO 1X BASIC R&S
UNPRICED ROOKIE AU PRINT RUN 10
EXCH EXPIRATION: 1/27/2013

2011 Rookies and Stars Longevity Emerald

*1-150 VETS/25: 6X TO 15X BASIC R&S
*151-250 ROOKIES/25: 2X TO 5X BASIC R&S
STATED PRINT RUN 25 SER.#'d SETS

2011 Rookies and Stars Longevity Ruby

*1-150 VETS/150: 2.5X TO 6X BASIC R&S
*151-250 ROOKIES/150: .8X TO 2X BASIC R&S
STATED PRINT RUN 150 SER.#'d SETS

2011 Rookies and Stars Longevity Sapphire

*1-150 VETS/75: 4X TO 10X BASIC R&S
*151-250 ROOKIES/75: 1.2X TO 3X BASIC R&S
STATED PRINT RUN 75 SER.#'d SETS

2011 Rookies and Stars Longevity Rookie Autographs

STATED PRINT RUN 127-175

151 Aaron Williams/150	5.00	12.00
152 Adrian Clayborn/150	6.00	15.00
153 Ahmad Black/175	5.00	12.00
154 Akeem Ayers/150	3.00	8.00
156 Aldrick Robinson/150	6.00	15.00
159 Allen Bradford/150	3.00	8.00
160 Anthony Allen/150	3.00	8.00
161 Anthony Castonzo/175	2.50	6.00
164 Brandon Harris/150	2.50	6.00
167 Cameron Heyward/150	8.00	20.00
168 Cameron Jordan/150	3.00	8.00
175 Corey Liuget/150	4.00	10.00
180 Da'Rel Scott/175 EXCH	3.00	8.00
183 Denarius Moore/175	10.00	25.00
185 Dion Lewis/150	4.00	10.00
188 Dwayne Harris/150 EXCH	4.00	10.00
189 Evan Royster/175	4.00	10.00
191 Greg Jones/150	3.00	8.00
192 Greg McElroy/175	6.00	15.00
199 Jimmy Smith/150	4.00	10.00
200 Johnny White/175	3.00	8.00
202 Jordan Cameron/175	5.00	12.00
203 Julius Thomas/175 EXCH	3.00	8.00
204 Justin Houston/175	4.00	10.00
205 Kealoha Pilares/175 EXCH	4.00	10.00
207 Kris Durham/175	3.00	8.00
209 Luke Stocker/150	3.00	8.00
210 Marcus Cannon/175	4.00	10.00
212 Martez Wilson/150	5.00	12.00
220 Nathan Enderle/175 EXCH	4.00	10.00
222 Owen Marecic/175 EXCH	4.00	10.00
225 Phil Taylor/127	5.00	12.00
226 Prince Amukamara/150	8.00	20.00
228 Quinton Carter/175	2.50	6.00
229 Rahim Moore/175	3.00	8.00
232 Robert Housler/175	3.00	8.00
235 Ronald Johnson/150	3.00	8.00
237 Ryan Whalen/175 EXCH	3.00	8.00
239 Scotty McKnight/175 EXCH	3.00	8.00
242 Stanley Havili/175	2.50	6.00
244 Stephen Burton/175	3.00	8.00
245 Stephen Paea/150	4.00	10.00
246 T.J. Yates/175 EXCH	5.00	12.00
247 Tyler Sash/150	4.00	10.00
248 Tyrod Taylor/175	4.00	10.00
249 Tyron Smith/175 EXCH	5.00	12.00

2011 Rookies and Stars Longevity Materials Sapphire

STATED PRINT RUN 50-100
*RUBY/170-299: .3X TO .8X SAPP/75-100
*RUBY/130-145: .4X TO 1X SAPPHIRE/100
*RUBY/99-100: .4X TO 1X SAPP/50-100
*RUBY/49: .5X TO 1.2X SAPPHIRE/100

1 Beanie Wells/100	4.00	10.00
2 Larry Fitzgerald/100	4.00	10.00
6 Matt Ryan/100	5.00	12.00
7 Michael Turner/100	4.00	10.00
8 Roddy White/100	4.00	10.00
9 Tony Gonzalez/100	4.00	10.00
10 Anquan Boldin/100	4.00	10.00
11 Joe Flacco/100	5.00	12.00
12 Ray Lewis/100	5.00	12.00
13 Ray Rice/100	4.00	10.00
14 Todd Heap/100	3.00	8.00
15 C.J. Spiller/100	4.00	10.00
16 Fred Jackson/100	5.00	12.00
17 Lee Evans/100	4.00	10.00
18 Ryan Fitzpatrick/100	4.00	10.00
20 DeAngelo Williams/100	4.00	10.00
21 Jimmy Clausen/100	3.00	8.00
22 Jonathan Stewart/100	4.00	10.00
23 Steve Smith/100	4.00	10.00
24 Brian Urlacher/100	5.00	12.00
25 Devin Hester/100	5.00	12.00
26 Jay Cutler/100	4.00	10.00
27 Johnny Knox/100	4.00	10.00
28 Matt Forte/100	4.00	10.00
29 Carson Palmer/100	4.00	10.00
30 Cedric Benson/100	4.00	10.00
31 Chad Ochocinco/100	4.00	10.00
32 Jordan Shipley/100	4.00	10.00
33 Terrell Owens/80	5.00	12.00
36 Josh Cribbs/100	4.00	10.00
39 Felix Jones/100	4.00	10.00
41 Miles Austin/100	5.00	12.00
42 Tony Romo/100	5.00	12.00
43 Brandon Lloyd/100	4.00	10.00
44 Eddie Royal/100	3.00	8.00
45 Jabar Gaffney/100	3.00	8.00
46 Knowshon Moreno/100	4.00	10.00
47 Tim Tebow/100	10.00	25.00
49 Calvin Johnson/100	5.00	12.00
51 Matthew Stafford/100	5.00	12.00
53 Aaron Rodgers/100	12.00	30.00
54 Clay Matthews/100	5.00	12.00
55 Donald Driver/100	4.00	10.00
58 Andre Johnson/100	4.00	10.00
59 Arian Foster/100	4.00	10.00
62 Matt Schaub/100	4.00	10.00
64 Dallas Clark/100	4.00	10.00
65 Joseph Addai/100	4.00	10.00
66 Peyton Manning/100	8.00	20.00
67 Reggie Wayne/100	4.00	10.00
68 David Garrard/100	4.00	10.00
70 Maurice Jones-Drew/100	4.00	10.00
71 Mike Sims-Walker/75	4.00	10.00
73 Dwayne Bowe/100	4.00	10.00
74 Jamaal Charles/100	4.00	10.00
75 Matt Cassel/100	4.00	10.00
77 Brandon Marshall/100	4.00	10.00
79 Chad Henne/100	4.00	10.00
81 Ronnie Brown/100	4.00	10.00
82 Adrian Peterson/100	6.00	15.00
83 Percy Harvin/100	4.00	10.00
84 Sidney Rice/100	4.00	10.00
86 Visanthe Shiancoe/100	4.00	10.00
90 Tom Brady/100	8.00	20.00
91 Wes Welker/100	5.00	12.00
92 Drew Brees/100	5.00	12.00
94 Marques Colston/100	4.00	10.00
95 Pierre Thomas/100	4.00	10.00
96 Reggie Bush/100	4.00	10.00
97 Ahmad Bradshaw/100	4.00	10.00
98 Eli Manning/100	5.00	12.00
99 Hakeem Nicks/50	4.00	10.00
101 Steve Smith USC/100	4.00	10.00
102 Braylon Edwards/100	4.00	10.00
103 LaDainian Tomlinson/100	5.00	12.00
104 Mark Sanchez/100	5.00	12.00
105 Santonio Holmes/100	4.00	10.00
106 Shonn Greene/100	4.00	10.00
107 Darren McFadden/100	4.00	10.00
109 Louis Murphy/100	4.00	10.00
111 DeSean Jackson/100	4.00	10.00
112 Jeremy Maclin/100	4.00	10.00
113 LeSean McCoy/100	4.00	10.00
114 Michael Vick/100	5.00	12.00
116 Hines Ward/100	5.00	12.00
117 Mike Wallace/100	5.00	12.00
118 Rashard Mendenhall/100	4.00	10.00
119 Troy Polamalu/100	6.00	15.00
120 Antonio Gates/100	4.00	10.00
121 Malcom Floyd/100	4.00	10.00
123 Philip Rivers/100	5.00	12.00
124 Ryan Mathews/100	4.00	10.00
125 Frank Gore/100	4.00	10.00
126 Michael Crabtree/100	4.00	10.00
127 Patrick Willis/100	4.00	10.00
128 Vernon Davis/100	4.00	10.00
131 Matt Hasselbeck/100	4.00	10.00
135 Sam Bradford/100	5.00	12.00
136 Steven Jackson/100	4.00	10.00
137 Cadillac Williams/100	3.00	8.00
139 Kellen Winslow Jr./100	4.00	10.00
142 Bo Scaife/100	3.00	8.00
143 Chris Johnson/100	4.00	10.00
145 Nate Washington/100	3.00	8.00
146 Randy Moss/100	4.00	10.00
147 Chris Cooley/100	4.00	10.00
148 Donovan McNabb/100	5.00	12.00

1999 Ruffles QB Club Spanish

These unnumbered cards were sponsored by Ruffles Potato Chips and issued in potato chip bags in Mexico, The cards feature members of the Quarterback Club, both active and retired. Each card measures a small 1 5/16" by 1 15/16" and includes a color photo of the featured player (or team logo) on the front with a Ruffles logo, the QB Club logo, and the NFL logo on the cardfront. The cardbacks feature player stats and are written in Spanish.

COMPLETE SET (30)	25.00	50.00
1 Tony Banks	.75	2.00
2 Jeff Blake	.75	2.00
3 Drew Bledsoe	1.50	4.00
4 Chris Chandler	.75	2.00
5 Kerry Collins	1.00	2.50
6 Randall Cunningham	1.00	2.50
7 Jim Everett	.75	2.00
8 Brett Favre	5.00	10.00
9 Gus Frerotte	.75	2.00
10 Rich Gannon	1.00	2.50
11 Elvis Grbac	.75	2.00
12 Jim Harbaugh	.75	2.00
13 Brad Johnson	1.00	2.50
14 Rob Johnson	.75	2.00
15 Jim Kelly	2.00	5.00
16 Donovan McNabb	2.00	5.00
17 Steve McNair	1.25	3.00
18 Cade McNown	.75	2.00
19 Jake Plummer	1.00	2.50
20 Kordell Stewart	1.00	2.50
21 Vinny Testaverde	1.00	2.50
22 Ricky Williams	1.50	4.00
23 Broncos Logo	.75	2.00
24 Cowboys Logo	.75	2.00
25 Dolphins Logo	.75	2.00
26 49ers Logo	.75	2.00
27 Raiders Logo	.75	2.00
28 Rams Logo	.75	2.00
29 Redskins Logo	.75	2.00
30 Steelers Logo	.75	2.00

2002 Run With History Emmitt Smith

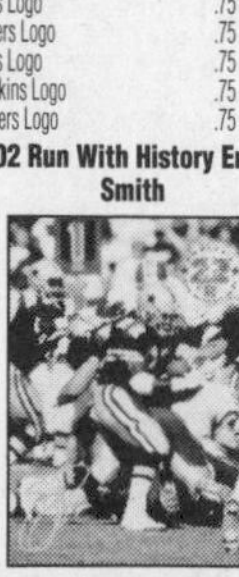

This set was licensed through Emmitt Smith and the Dallas Cowboys and was issued in box set form through traditional retail outlets. Each card takes an historical look at the career of Emmitt Smith. The stated print run was 16,727 sets.

COMPLETE SET (22)	8.00	12.00
COMMON CARD (1-22)	.30	.75

1979 Sacramento Buffaloes Schedules

This set of black and white cards features members of the California Football League Sacramento Buffaloes. Each features a game action photo on the front and the team's schedule on the back with the player identified at the bottom.

COMPLETE SET (6)	12.50	25.00
1 Wayne Dalkse	2.50	5.00
Bill Shiflett		
2 Jim Gabriel	2.50	5.00
Rod Lung		
3 Earl Green	2.50	5.00
4 Ron Killion	2.50	5.00
5 Rod Lung	2.50	5.00
6 Bob Morris	2.50	5.00

1991 Sacramento Surge Police

This 39-card set was sponsored by American Airlines and presents players of the WLAF Sacramento Surge. The cards measure approximately 2 3/8" by 3 1/2". The fronts feature a color posed photo of the player, with a drawing of the Sacramento helmet inside a triangle at the lower right hand corner. The backs have the Sacramento and WLAF logos at the top, biographical information, and a player quote consisting of an anti-drug message. The set was issued in the Summer of 1991. The cards are unnumbered and hence are listed alphabetically below for convenience.

COMPLETE SET (39)	20.00	40.00
1 Mike Adams	.60	1.50
2 Sam Archer	.60	1.50
3 John Buddenberg	.60	1.50
4 Jon Burman	.60	1.50
5 Tony Burse	.60	1.50
6 Ricardo Cartwright	.60	1.50
7 Greg Coauette	.60	1.50
8 Paco Craig	.60	1.50
9 John Dominic	.60	1.50
10 Mike Elkins	.60	1.50
11 Oliver Erhorn	.60	1.50
12 Mel Farr Jr.	.60	1.50
13 Victor Floyd	.60	1.50
14 Byron Forsythe	.60	1.50
15 Paul Frazier	.60	1.50
16 Tom Gerhart	.60	1.50
17 Mike Hall	.60	1.50
18 Anthony Henton	.60	1.50
19 Nate Hill	.60	1.50
20 Kubanai Kalombo	.60	1.50
21 Shawn Knight	.60	1.50
22 Sean Kugler	.60	1.50
23 Matti Lindholm	.60	1.50
24 Art Malone	.60	1.50
25 Robert McWright	.60	1.50
26 Tim Moore	.60	1.50
27 Pete Najarian	.60	1.50
28 Mark Nua	.60	1.50
29 Carl Parker	.60	1.50
30 Leon Perry	.60	1.50
31 Juha Salo	.60	1.50
32 Saute Sapolu	.60	1.50
33 Paul Soltis	.60	1.50
34 Richard Stephens	.60	1.50
35 Kay Stephenson CO	.60	1.50
36 Kendall Trainor	.60	1.50
37 Mike Wallace	.60	1.50
38 Curtis Wilson	.60	1.50
39 Rick Zumwalt	.60	1.50

1948-1950 Safe-T-Card

Cards from this set were issued in the Washington D.C. area in the late 1940s and early 1950s. Each card was printed in either black or red and features an artist's rendering of a famous area athlete or personality from a variety of sports. The card backs feature an ad for Jim Gibbons Cartoon-A-Quiz television show along with an ad from a local business. The player's facsimile autograph and team or sport affiliation is included on the fronts.

1 John Adams FB	15.00	30.00
5 Herman Ball FB	15.00	30.00
6 Sammy Baugh FB	50.00	100.00
7 Sammy Baugh QB FB	50.00	100.00
8 Bryan Bell FB	15.00	30.00
14 Billy Conn FB	15.00	30.00
16 Andy Davis FB	15.00	30.00
17 Doug DeGroot CO FB	15.00	30.00
18 Al Demao FB	15.00	30.00
20 Mush Dubofsky CO FB	15.00	30.00
22 Turk Edwards FB	30.00	60.00
24 Tom Farmer FB	15.00	30.00
26 Lou Gambino FB	15.00	30.00
27 Harry Gilmer Hel FB	20.00	40.00
28 Harry Gilmer No Hel FB	20.00	40.00
31 Art Guepe CO FB	15.00	30.00
39 Jan Jankowski CO FB	15.00	30.00
42 Bob Margarita CO FB	15.00	30.00
43 Corrine Griffith Marshall actress	15.00	30.00
44 Dick McCann GM FB	15.00	30.00
47 Wilbur Moore FB	20.00	40.00
51 Dick Poillon FB	15.00	30.00
53 Bo Rowland CO FB	15.00	30.00
54 Dan Sandifer FB	15.00	30.00
55 George Sauer CO FB	15.00	30.00
58 Jim Tatum CO FB	15.00	30.00
59 Joe Tereshinski FB	20.00	40.00
60 Dick Todd FB	15.00	30.00
61 Vic Turyn FB	15.00	30.00
63 Bob Waterfield FB	40.00	80.00
64 John Welchel CO FB	15.00	30.00

1976 Saga Discs

These cards parallel the 1976 Crane Discs set. Instead of the Crane sponsor logo on back, each features the "Saga" logo. The Saga versions are much more difficult to find than their Crane counterparts.

COMPLETE SET (30)	350.00	600.00
1 Ken Anderson	5.00	12.00
2 Otis Armstrong	3.00	8.00
3 Steve Bartkowski	4.00	10.00
4 Terry Bradshaw	25.00	60.00
5 John Brockington	2.50	6.00
6 Doug Buffone	2.50	6.00
7 Wally Chambers	2.50	6.00
8 Isaac Curtis	2.50	6.00
9 Chuck Foreman	3.00	8.00
10 Roman Gabriel	4.00	10.00
11 Mel Gray	3.00	8.00
12 Joe Greene	12.00	30.00
13 James Harris	2.50	6.00
14 Jim Hart	3.00	8.00
15 Billy Kilmer	4.00	10.00
16 Greg Landry	3.00	8.00
17 Ed Marinaro	2.50	6.00
18 Lawrence McCutcheon	3.00	8.00
19 Terry Metcalf	3.00	8.00
20 Lydell Mitchell	2.50	6.00
21 Jim Otis	2.50	6.00
22 Alan Page	4.00	10.00
23 Walter Payton	150.00	300.00
24 Greg Pruitt	3.00	8.00
25 Charlie Sanders	4.00	10.00
26 Ron Shanklin	2.50	6.00
27 Roger Staubach	25.00	60.00
28 Jan Stenerud	4.00	10.00
29 Charley Taylor	5.00	12.00
30 Roger Wehrli	3.00	8.00

2008 Saginaw Sting IFL

COMPLETE SET (9)	5.00	10.00
1 Damon Dowdell	.50	1.25
2 Ruben Gay	.50	1.25
3 Jeremiah McLaurin	.50	1.25
4 Jeff Dembowske	.50	1.25
5 Charles Barber	.50	1.25
6 Nicholas Body	.50	1.25
7 Nate Collins	.50	1.25
8 Brandon Genwright	.50	1.25
9 Corey Gonzales	.50	1.25

1967 Saints Team Doubloons

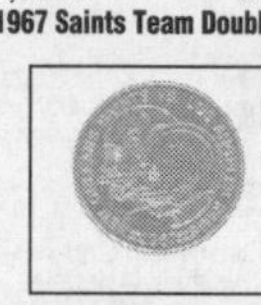

For a number of years, the New Orleans Saints included one Doubloon (coin) per game day program. The 1967 coins featured on the fronts a player wearing the team helmet for each home game match-up for the Saints season including one pre-season game. The coin backs included an advertisement for Jax Beer. The year of issue is also featured on the coin front and each was produced using a silver colored aluminum metal. We've numbered the set in the order of release.

COMPLETE SET (8)	15.00	30.00
1 Saints vs. Falcons	2.00	4.00
2 Saints vs. Rams	2.00	4.00
3 Saints vs. Redskins	2.50	5.00
4 Saints vs. Browns	2.50	5.00
5 Saints vs. Steelers	2.50	5.00
6 Saints vs. Eagles	2.00	4.00
7 Saints vs. Cowboys	2.50	5.00
8 Saints vs. Falcons	2.00	4.00

1967 Saints Team Issue 5X7 Bordered

The Saints issued several different sets of 5" by 7" photos, presumably over a period of years. Many of the photographs of the same players in either the bordered or borderless sets are identical. The text size and style of each photo in this release are exactly the same. The players full name is to the left, with his position initials in the center, and the full team name printed in all caps to the right. All are head and chest shots instead of action. Each is unnumbered and blankbacked.

COMPLETE SET (20)	75.00	150.00
1 Danny Abramowicz	5.00	10.00
2 Doug Atkins	6.00	12.00
3 Tom Barrington	4.00	8.00
4 Lou Cordileone	4.00	8.00
5 Bruce Cortez	4.00	8.00
6 Gary Cuozzo	5.00	10.00
7 Ted Davis	4.00	8.00
8 Jim Hester	4.00	8.00
9 Les Kelley	4.00	8.00
10 Kent Kramer	4.00	8.00
11 Jake Kupp	4.00	8.00
12 Obert Logan	4.00	8.00
13 Don McCall	4.00	8.00
14 Thomas McNeill	4.00	8.00
15 Ray Ogden	4.00	8.00
16 Ray Rissmiller	4.00	8.00
17 Walter Roberts	4.00	8.00
18 George Rose	4.00	8.00
19 Bill Sandeman	4.00	8.00
20 Phil Vandersea	4.00	8.00
21 Joe Wendryhoski	4.00	8.00
22 Dave Whitsell	4.00	8.00
23 Gary Wood	4.00	8.00

1967-68 Saints Team Issue 5X7 Borderless

The Saints issued two different sets of 5" by 7" photos, presumably over a period of years. The photographs of the same players in both sets are identical except for the white border or lack of a border. The text size and style varies from photo to photo as does the player information below the picture. All are head and chest shots instead of action. The two groups were likely issued together but have been separated for ease in cataloging. Each is unnumbered and blankbacked.

COMPLETE SET (28)	100.00	200.00
1 Charlie Brown RB	4.00	8.00
2 Vern Burke	4.00	8.00
3 Jackie Burkett	4.00	8.00
4 Bill Carr	4.00	8.00
5 Bill Cody	4.00	8.00
6 Ted Davis	4.00	8.00
7 Jim Garcia	4.00	8.00
8 Tom Hall	4.00	8.00
9 Jimmy Heidel	4.00	8.00
10 Les Kelley	4.00	8.00
11 Jake Kupp	4.00	8.00
12 Herman Lee	4.00	8.00
13 John Morrow	4.00	8.00
14 Ray Ogden	4.00	8.00
15 Ray Rissmiller	4.00	8.00
16 Bert Rose GM	4.00	8.00
17 Bill Sandeman	4.00	8.00
18 Roy Schmidt	4.00	8.00
19 Brian Schweda	4.00	8.00
20 Dave Simmons	4.00	8.00
21 Jerry Simmons	4.00	8.00
22 Mike Tilleman	4.00	8.00
23 Joe Wendryhoski	4.00	8.00
24 Ernie Wheelwright UER	4.00	8.00
misspelled Wheelright		
25 Fred Whittingham	4.00	8.00
26 Del Williams	4.00	8.00
27 Bo Wood	4.00	8.00
28 Gary Wood	4.00	8.00

1967-68 Saints Team Issue 8X10

The Saints released these posed action photos primarily for fans and to fulfill autograph requests. Each measures roughly 8" by 10" and features a black and white player photo with information in the border below the picture. They were likely released over a period of years as the type style and size used varies from photo to photo. There appear to be several distinct types issued with text as follows reading left to right: (1) player's name in all caps, position initials only, and team name in all caps, (2) player's name, position spelled out completely and team in all capital letters, (3) player's name in caps, position spelled out in upper and lower case letters, and team in upper and lower case letters, (4) player's name in all caps (no position) and team name in all caps, (5) player's name in all caps, position spelled out in caps, and team name in all caps, (6) player's name in all caps, no position, team name in upper and lower case letters. Some also appear to have been released through Maison Blanche department stores in New Orleans along with the store's logo stamped on front. These Maison Blanche variations typically sell for a premium as listed below. Any additions to this list and confirmation of Maison Blanche checklist is appreciated.

*MAISON BLANCHE: .75X TO 1.5X

1 Dan Abramowicz 1	6.00	12.00
2 Doug Atkins 1	7.50	15.00
3 Tony Baker 1	5.00	10.00
4B Tom Barrington 1	5.00	10.00
(running forward slightly to his right)		
4A Tom Barrington 1	5.00	10.00
(cutting with left leg off the ground)		
5 Jim Boeke 2	5.00	10.00
6 Johnny Brewer 2	5.00	10.00
7 Jackie Burkett 1	5.00	10.00
8 Bo Burris 4	5.00	10.00
9 Bill Cody 4	5.00	10.00
10 Gary Cuozzo 1	6.00	12.00
11 Ted Davis 1	5.00	10.00
12 Tom Dempsey 2	6.00	12.00
13 Al Dodd 1	5.00	10.00
14 John Douglas 1	5.00	10.00
15 Julian Fagan	5.00	10.00
16 Jim Garcia 1	5.00	10.00
17 John Gilliam 4	5.00	10.00
18A Tom Hall 1	5.00	10.00
18B Tom Hall 6	5.00	10.00
19 Kevin Hardy 2	5.00	10.00
20 Edd Hargett	5.00	10.00
21 George Harvey 1	5.00	10.00
22 Jimmy Heidel 1	5.00	10.00
23 Jim Hester 1	5.00	10.00
24 Paul Hornung 6	10.00	20.00
25 Gene Howard 3	5.00	10.00
26 Harry Jacobs	5.00	10.00
27A Les Kelley 1	5.00	10.00
(listed as RB)		
27B Les Kelley 3	5.00	10.00
(listed as Linebacker)		
28 Billy Kilmer	7.50	15.00
29 Elbert Kimbrough	5.00	10.00
30 Kent Kramer 1	5.00	10.00
31 Jake Kupp 1	5.00	10.00
32 Earl Leggett 1	5.00	10.00
33 Andy Livingston 1	5.00	10.00
34 Obert Logan 1	5.00	10.00
35 Tony Lorick 1	5.00	10.00
36 Ray Ogden 1	5.00	10.00
37 Don McCall 1	5.00	10.00
38A Tom McNeill 1	5.00	10.00
38B Tom McNeill 3	5.00	10.00
39 Mike Morgan	5.00	10.00
40 John Morrow 1	5.00	10.00
41 Elijah Nevett 5	5.00	10.00
42 Bob Newland	5.00	10.00
43 Ray Poage 4	5.00	10.00
44 Ray Rissmiller 1	5.00	10.00
45 Walter Roberts 1	5.00	10.00
46 George Rose 1	5.00	10.00
47 David Rowe 4	5.00	10.00
48 Roy Schmidt 4	5.00	10.00
49 Bob Scholtz 6	5.00	10.00
50 Randy Schultz 4	5.00	10.00
51 Brian Schweda 1	5.00	10.00
52 Dave Simmons 1	5.00	10.00
53 Larry Stephens 6	5.00	10.00
54 Monty Stickles 3	5.00	10.00
55 Steve Stonebreaker 1	5.00	10.00
56 Jim Taylor 1	7.50	15.00
57 Mike Tilleman 1	5.00	10.00
58 Willie Townes	5.00	10.00
59 Phil Vandersea 1	5.00	10.00
60 Joe Wendryhoski 1	5.00	10.00
61 Ernie Wheelwright	5.00	10.00
62 Dave Whitsell 1	5.00	10.00
63 Fred Whittingham 1	5.00	10.00
64 Del Williams 1	5.00	10.00
65 Gary Wood 1	5.00	10.00
66 Doug Wyatt	5.00	10.00
67 Team Photo	6.00	12.00

1968 Saints Team Doubloons

For a number of years, the New Orleans Saints included one Doubloon (coin) per game day program. The 1968 coins featured on the fronts the team helmets for each home game match-up for the Saints season including two pre-season games. The coin backs included an advertisement for Jax Beer. The year of issue is also featured on the coin front and each was produced using both a silver colored aluminum and a gold colored metal. We've numbered the set in the order of release.

COMPLETE SET (9)	20.00	40.00
*GOLD COINS: 1X TO 2X SILVERS		
1 Saints vs. Patriots	2.00	4.00
2 Saints vs. Browns	2.50	5.00
3 Saints vs. Browns	2.50	5.00
4 Saints vs. Redskins	2.50	5.00
5 Saints vs. Cardinals	2.00	4.00
6 Saints vs. Vikings	2.50	5.00
7 Saints vs. Cowboys	2.50	5.00
8 Saints vs. Bears	2.50	5.00
9 Saints vs. Steelers	2.50	5.00

1968 Saints Team Issue 5X7 Bordered

The Saints issued several different sets of 5" by 7" photos, presumably over a period of years. Many of the photographs of the same players in either the bordered or borderless sets are identical. The text size and style of each photo in this release are different than the 1967 set and differ from each other as noted below. Some photos in this group do not have the player identified at all, as noted below. These photos presumably were issued in haste by the team as several players didn't make the Saints rosters. All are head and chest shots instead of action. This group was not likely issued together but has been combined for ease in cataloging and identification. Each is unnumbered and blankbacked.

COMPLETE SET (17)	60.00	120.00
1 Tom Barrington	4.00	8.00
(no player ID, jersey #32)		
2 Charlie Brown RB	4.00	8.00
(no player ID, jersey #22)		
3 Bo Burris	4.00	8.00
4 Bill Cody	4.00	8.00
(no position identified)		
5 Willie Crittendon	4.00	8.00
(no player ID, jersey #71)		
6A Charles Durkee	4.00	8.00
(first and last name included)		
6B Charles Durkee	4.00	8.00
(last name only included)		
7 Jim Hester	4.00	8.00
(no player ID, jersey #84)		
8 Jerry Jones T	4.00	8.00
9 Elijah Nevett	4.00	8.00
(no player ID, jersey #24)		
10 Mike Rengel	4.00	8.00
(no player ID, jersey #79)		
11A Randy Schultz	4.00	8.00
(first and last name included)		
11B Randy Schultz	4.00	8.00
(last name only included)		
12 Brian Schweda	4.00	8.00
(no player ID, jersey #60)		
13 Jerry Sturm	4.00	8.00
(no player ID, jersey #73)		
14 Ernie Wheelwright	4.00	8.00
(last name only included)		
15 Del Williams G	4.00	8.00

1969 Saints Pro Players Doubloons

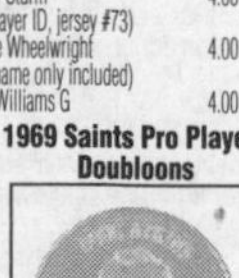

These coins were produced by Pro Players Doubloons, Inc. and distributed by the New Orleans Saints at games during the 1969 season. Each coin is unnumbered and measures approximately 1 1/2" in diameter. There were at least three different colored coins (silver, brass, and light gold) with each featuring a player bust on front with a short player bio and copyright information on back.

COMPLETE SET (24)	62.50	125.00
1 Dan Abramowicz	3.00	6.00
2 Doug Atkins	6.00	12.00
3 Tom Barrington	2.50	5.00
4 Johnny Brewer	2.50	5.00
5 Bo Burris	2.50	5.00
6 Ted Davis	2.50	5.00
7 John Douglas	2.50	5.00
8 Charlie Durkee	2.50	5.00
9 Gene Howard	2.50	5.00
10 Billy Kilmer	5.00	10.00
11 Jake Kupp	2.50	5.00
12 Errol Linden	2.50	5.00
13 Tony Lorick	2.50	5.00
14 Don McCall	2.50	5.00
15 Dave Parks	3.00	6.00
16 Dave Rowe	2.50	5.00
17 Brian Schweda	2.50	5.00
18 Monte Stickles	2.50	5.00
19 Jerry Sturm	2.50	5.00
20 Mike Tilleman	2.50	5.00
21 Joe Wendryhoski	2.50	5.00
22 Dave Whitsell	3.00	6.00
23 Fred Whittingham	2.50	5.00
24 Del Williams	2.50	5.00

1969 Saints Team Doubloons

For a number of years, the New Orleans Saints included one Doubloon (coin) per game day program. The 1969 coins featured on the fronts two footballs printed with the team names for each home game match-up for the Saints, as well as the team logos. Seven regular season games and two pre-season games were included. The coin backs included an advertisement for Volkswagon. The year of issue is also featured on the coin front and each was produced using both a silver colored aluminum and a gold colored metal. We've numbered the set in the order of release.

COMPLETE SET (9)	17.50	35.00
1 Saints vs. Falcons	2.00	4.00
2 Saints vs. Oilers	2.00	4.00
3 Saints vs. Redskins	2.50	5.00
4 Saints vs. Cowboys	2.50	5.00
5 Saints vs. Browns	2.50	5.00
6 Saints vs. Colts	2.00	4.00
7 Saints vs. 49ers	2.50	5.00
8 Saints vs. Eagles	2.00	4.00
9 Saints vs. Steelers	2.50	5.00

1970 Saints Team Doubloons

For a number of years, the New Orleans Saints included one Doubloon (coin) per game day program. The 1970 coins featured on the fronts a generic figure of a quarterback with the team names for each home game match-up for the Saints, as well as the team logos. Seven regular season games and two pre-season games were included. The coin backs included the crest of the NFL and the names of both conferences. The year of issue is also featured on the coin front and each was produced using both a silver colored aluminum and a gold colored metal. We've numbered the set in the order of release.

COMPLETE SET (9)	17.50	35.00
1 Saints vs. Lions	2.00	4.00
2 Saints vs. Chargers	2.00	4.00
3 Saints vs. Falcons	2.00	4.00
4 Saints vs. Giants	2.00	4.00
5 Saints vs. Rams	2.00	4.00
6 Saints vs. Lions	2.00	4.00
7 Saints vs. Broncos	2.00	4.00
8 Saints vs. 49ers	2.50	5.00
9 Saints vs. Bears	2.50	5.00

1971-76 Saints Circle Inset

Each of these photos measures approximately 8" by 10." The fronts feature black-and-white action player photos with white borders. Near one of the corners a black-and-white headshot photo appears within a circle. The player's name, position, and team name are typically printed in the lower border in a variety of different type sizes and styles. Some photos are horizontally oriented while others are vertical. The backs are blank. The photos are unnumbered and checklisted below in alphabetical order with some players having more than one type. The year of issue for this set is an estimate with the likelihood of the photos being released over a period of years.

1 Steve Baumgartner	4.00	8.00
2 John Beasley	4.00	8.00
3 Tom Blanchard	4.00	8.00
4 Larry Burton	4.00	8.00
5 Warren Capone	4.00	8.00
6 Rusty Chambers	4.00	8.00
7 Henry Childs	4.00	8.00
8 Larry Cipa	4.00	8.00
9 Don Coleman	4.00	8.00
10 Wayne Colman	4.00	8.00
11 Chuck Crist	4.00	8.00
12 Jack DeGrenier	4.00	8.00

13 Jim Deratt	4.00	8.00
14 John Didion	4.00	8.00
15 Andy Dorris	4.00	8.00
16 Bobby Douglass	5.00	10.00
17 Joe Federspiel	4.00	8.00
18 Jim Flanigan LB	4.00	8.00
19 Johnny Fuller	4.00	8.00
20 Elois Grooms	4.00	8.00
21 Andy Hamilton	4.00	8.00
22 Don Herrmann	4.00	8.00
23 Hugo Hollas	4.00	8.00
24 Ernie Jackson	4.00	8.00
26 Andrew Jones	4.00	8.00
26 Rick Kingrea	4.00	8.00
27 Jake Kupp	4.00	8.00
28 Phil LaPorta	4.00	8.00
29 Odell Lawson	4.00	8.00
30 Archie Manning	12.50	25.00
31 Andy Maurer	4.00	8.00
32 Alvin Maxson	4.00	8.00
33 Bill McClard	4.00	8.00
34 Rod McNeill	4.00	8.00
35 Leon McQuay	4.00	8.00
37 Rick Middleton	4.00	8.00
38 Mark Montgomery	4.00	8.00
39 Derland Moore	4.00	8.00
40 Jerry Moore	4.00	8.00
41 Chuck Muncie	6.00	12.00
43 Joe Owens	4.00	8.00
44 Tinker Owens	4.00	8.00
46 Jess Phillips	4.00	8.00
48 Elex Price	4.00	8.00
49 Ken Reaves	4.00	8.00
50 Steve Rogers	4.00	8.00
51 Terry Schmidt	4.00	8.00
52 Kurt Schumacher	4.00	8.00
53 Bobby Scott	4.00	8.00
54 Paul Seal	4.00	8.00
55 Royce Smith	4.00	8.00
56 Maurice Spencer	4.00	8.00
57 Mike Strachan	4.00	8.00
58 Hank Stram CO	6.00	12.00
59 Rich Szaro	4.00	8.00
60 Jim Thaxton	4.00	8.00
61 Dave Thompson	4.00	8.00
36A Jim Merlo	4.00	8.00
36B Jim Merlo	4.00	8.00
42A Tom Myers	4.00	8.00
42B Tom Myers	4.00	8.00
45A Joel Parker	4.00	8.00
45B Joel Parker	4.00	8.00
47A Bob Pollard	4.00	8.00
47B Bob Pollard	4.00	8.00
62A Greg Westbrooks	4.00	8.00
62B Greg Westbrooks	4.00	8.00
63A Emanuel Zanders	4.00	8.00
63B Emanuel Zanders	4.00	8.00

1971 Saints Team Doubloons

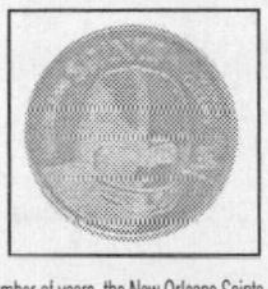

For a number of years, the New Orleans Saints included one Doubloon (coin) per game day program. The 1971 coins featured on the fronts a generic player profile with the team names for each home game match-up for the Saints. Seven regular season games and two pre-season games were included. The coin backs included an advertisement for New Orleans Magazine. The year of issue is also featured on the coin front and each was produced using a silver colored aluminum only. We've numbered the set in the order of release.

COMPLETE SET (9)	17.50	35.00
1 Saints vs. Eagles	2.00	4.00
2 Saints vs. Oilers	2.00	4.00
3 Saints vs. Rams	2.00	4.00
4 Saints vs. 49ers	2.50	5.00
5 Saints vs. Cowboys	2.50	5.00
6 Saints vs. Raiders	2.50	5.00
7 Saints vs. Vikings	2.50	5.00
8 Saints vs. Browns	2.50	5.00
9 Saints vs. Falcons	2.00	4.00

1971-72 Saints Team Issue 4X5

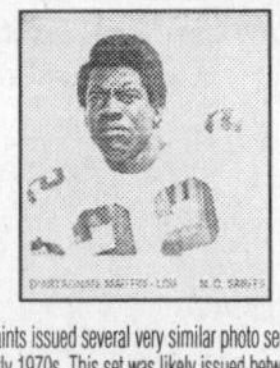

The Saints issued several very similar photo series in the early 1970s. This set was likely issued between 1971 and 1972. Each black and white portrait (no action) photo measures approximately 4" by 5" and carries the player's name and team in the border below the picture. Most include the player's name in large capital letters with the team name abbreviated "N.O. Saints." We've also included a few photos that feature the player's name and team in bold block letters. Any additions to this list are appreciated.

COMPLETE SET (14)	50.00	100.00
1 Carl Cunningham	4.00	8.00
2 Al Dodd	4.00	8.00
3 Julian Fagan	4.00	8.00
4 Edd Hargett	4.00	8.00
5 Glen Ray Hines	4.00	8.00
6 Jake Kupp	4.00	8.00
7 Bivian Lee	4.00	8.00
8 D'Artagnan Martin	4.00	8.00
9 Reynaud Moore	4.00	8.00
10 Don Morrison	4.00	8.00
11 Joe Owens	4.00	8.00
12 Dave Parks	4.00	8.00
13 John Shinners	4.00	8.00
14 Doug Wyatt UER	4.00	8.00

1972 Saints Square Inset

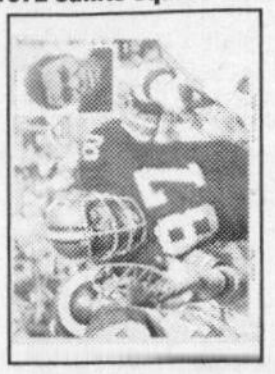

Each of these photos measures approximately 8" by 10." The fronts feature black-and-white action player photos with white borders. Near one of the corners, a black-and-white headshot appears within a square. The player's name, position initials, and team name are printed within one border. The backs are blank and the unnumbered photos are checklisted below in alphabetical order. The list below is thought to be incomplete. Any checklist additions would be appreciated.

COMPLETE SET (9)	30.00	60.00
1 Don Burchfield	4.00	8.00
2 John Didion	4.00	8.00
3 James Ford	4.00	8.00
4 Bob Gresham	4.00	8.00
5 Richard Neal	4.00	8.00
6 Bob Newland	4.00	8.00
7 Dave Parks	4.00	8.00
8 Virgil Robinson	4.00	8.00
9 Jim Strong	4.00	8.00

1972 Saints Team Doubloons

For a number of years, the New Orleans Saints included one Doubloon (coin) per game day program. The 1972 coins featured on the fronts a generic player profile with the team names for each home game match-up for the Saints. Seven regular season games and two pre-season games were included. The coin backs included an advertisement for Burger King. The year of issue is also featured on the coin front and each was produced using a silver colored aluminum only. We've numbered the set in the order of release.

COMPLETE SET (9)	17.50	35.00
1 Saints vs. Cowboys	2.50	5.00
2 Saints vs. Chargers	2.00	4.00
3 Saints vs. Chiefs	2.00	4.00
4 Saints vs. 49ers	2.50	5.00
5 Saints vs. Falcons	2.00	4.00
6 Saints vs. Eagles	2.00	4.00
7 Saints vs. Rams	2.00	4.00
8 Saints vs. Patriots	2.00	4.00
9 Saints vs. Packers	2.50	5.00

1972 Saints Team Issue

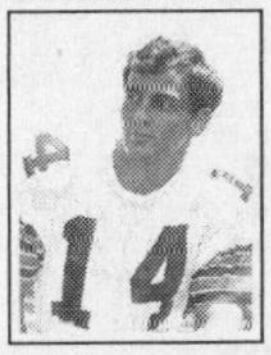

The Saints issued several very similar photo series in the early 1970s. This set was most likely released in 1972. Each black and white portrait (no action) photo measures approximately 4" by 5" and carries no pre-printed player identification nor team on the picture at all. Apparently, player names were sometimes written on the photo fronts by a New Orleans Saints employee prior to being shipped out to fans as many are found with this type of written ID.

COMPLETE SET (17)	60.00	120.00
1 Bill Butler	4.00	8.00
2 Al Dodd	4.00	8.00
3 Lawrence Estes	4.00	8.00
4 James Ford	4.00	8.00
5 Edd Hargett	4.00	8.00
6 Glen Ray Hines	4.00	8.00
7 Dave Kopay	4.00	8.00
8 Jake Kupp	4.00	8.00
9 Toni Linhart	4.00	8.00
10 Dave Long	4.00	8.00
11 Don Morrison	4.00	8.00
12 Richard Neal	4.00	8.00
13A Bob Newland (mouth opened)	4.00	8.00
13B Bob Newland (mouth closed)	4.00	8.00
14 Joe Owens	4.00	8.00
15 Virgil Robinson	4.00	8.00
16 Royce Smith	4.00	8.00

1973 Saints McDonald's

This set of four photos was sponsored by McDonald's. Each photo measures approximately 8" by 10" and features a posed color close-up photo bordered in white. The player's name and team name are printed in black in the bottom white border, and his facsimile autograph is inscribed across the photo. The top portion of the back has biographical information, career summary, and career statistics. The bottom portion includes a list of local McDonald's store addresses and presents the 1973 football schedule for the Saints, Tulane University and LSU. The photos are unnumbered and are checklisted below alphabetically.

COMPLETE SET (4)	17.50	35.00
1 Joe Federspiel	5.00	10.00
2 Jake Kupp	5.00	10.00
3 Joe Owens	5.00	10.00
4 Del Williams	5.00	10.00

1973 Saints Team Doubloons

For a number of years, the New Orleans Saints included one Doubloon (coin) per game day program. The 1973 coins featured on the fronts a generic player profile with the team names for each home game match-up for the Saints. Seven regular season games and two pre-season games were included. The coin backs included an advertisement for Burger King. The year of issue is also featured on the coin front and each was produced using a silver colored aluminum only. We've numbered the set in the order of release.

COMPLETE SET (9)	17.50	35.00
1 Saints vs. Patriots	2.00	4.00
2 Saints vs. Oilers	2.00	4.00
3 Saints vs. Falcons	2.00	4.00
4 Saints vs. Bears	2.50	5.00
5 Saints vs. Lions	2.00	4.00
6 Saints vs. Redskins	2.50	5.00
7 Saints vs. Bills	2.00	4.00
8 Saints vs. Rams	2.00	4.00
9 Saints vs. 49ers	2.50	5.00

1973 Saints Team Issue

The Saints issued several very similar photo series in the early 1970s. This set was most likely issued in 1973. Each black and white portrait (no action) photo measures approximately 4" by 5" and carries the player's name, position (initials) and team in the border below the picture. The type style used was small (all caps) block lettering with the team name spelled out completely.

COMPLETE SET (17)	60.00	120.00
1 Bill Butler	4.00	8.00
2 Drew Buie	4.00	8.00
3 Bob Davis	4.00	8.00
4 Ernie Jackson (facing right)	4.00	8.00
5 Ernie Jackson (facing left)	4.00	8.00
6 Mike Kelly	4.00	8.00
7 Jake Kupp	4.00	8.00
8 Jim Merlo	4.00	8.00
9 Don Morrison	4.00	8.00
10 Bob Newland	4.00	8.00
11 Joe Owens	4.00	8.00
12 Dick Palmer	4.00	8.00
13 Elex Price	4.00	8.00
14 Preston Riley	4.00	8.00
15 Bobby Scott	4.00	8.00
16 Royce Smith	4.00	8.00
17 Howard Stevens	4.00	8.00

1974 Saints Team Doubloons

For a number of years, the New Orleans Saints included one Doubloon (coin) per game day program. The 1974 coins featured on the fronts a generic player profile with the team names for each home game match-up for the Saints. Seven regular season games and two pre-season games were included. The coin backs included an advertisement for Burger King. The year of issue is also featured on the coin front and each was produced using a silver colored aluminum only. We've numbered the set in the order of release.

COMPLETE SET (9)	17.50	35.00
1 Saints vs. Cowboys	2.50	5.00
2 Saints vs. Steelers	2.50	5.00
3 Saints vs. 49ers	2.50	5.00
4 Saints vs. Falcons	2.00	4.00
5 Saints vs. Eagles	2.00	4.00
6 Saints vs. Dolphins	2.50	5.00
7 Saints vs. Rams	2.00	4.00
8 Saints vs. Steelers	2.50	5.00
9 Saints vs. Cardinals	2.00	4.00

1974 Saints Team Issue

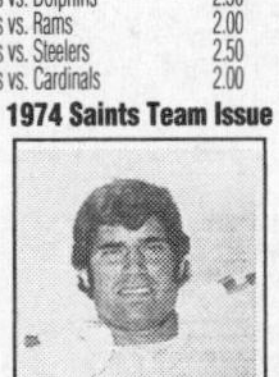

The Saints issued several very similar photo series in the early 1970s. This set was most likely issued in 1974. Each black and white portrait (no action) photo measures approximately 4" by 5" and carries the player's name, position (initials) and team in the border below the picture. The type style used was small italicized block lettering with the team name spelled out completely.

COMPLETE SET (13)	40.00	80.00
1 Andy Dorris	4.00	8.00
2 Paul Fersen	4.00	8.00
3 Len Garrett	4.00	8.00
4 Rick Kingrea	4.00	8.00
5 Odell Lawson	4.00	8.00
6 Jim Merlo	4.00	8.00
7 Jerry Moore	4.00	8.00
8 Don Morrison	4.00	8.00
9 Bob Newland	4.00	8.00
10 Joe Owens	4.00	8.00
11 Elex Price	4.00	8.00
12 Bobby Scott	4.00	8.00
13 Howard Stevens	4.00	8.00

1977 Saints Team Issue

This set of blankbacked photos issued by the Saints was most likely released in 1977. Each black and white action photo measures approximately 8" by 10" and includes the player's name, position (initials) and team name printed in all upper case letters. The player's facsimile autograph is also printed across the photo.

1 Tony Galbreath	4.00	8.00
2 Archie Manning	7.50	15.00
3 Bob Pollard / Mike Fultz	4.00	8.00
4 Bobby Scott	4.00	8.00
5 Kurt Schumacher / Chuck Muncie	5.00	10.00

1979 Saints Coke

The 1979 Coca-Cola New Orleans Saints set contains 45 black and white standard-size cards with red borders. The Coca-Cola logo appears in the upper right hand corner while a New Orleans Saints helmet appears in the lower left. The backs of this gray stock card contain minimal biographical data, the card number and the Coke logo. The cards were produced in conjunction with Topps. There were also unnumbered ad cards for Mr. Pibb and Sprite, one of which was included in each pack of cards.

COMPLETE SET (45)	40.00	80.00
1 Archie Manning	5.00	10.00
2 Ed Burns	1.00	2.00
3 Bobby Scott	1.00	2.00
4 Russell Erxleben	1.00	2.00
5 Eric Felton	1.00	2.00
6 David Gray	1.00	2.00
7 Ricky Ray	1.00	2.00
8 Clarence Chapman	1.00	2.00
9 Kim Jones	1.00	2.00
10 Mike Strachan	1.00	2.00
11 Tony Galbreath	1.25	2.50
12 Tom Myers	1.00	2.00
13 Chuck Muncie	2.50	5.00
14 Jack Holmes	1.00	2.00
15 Don Schwartz	1.00	2.00
16 Ralph McGill	1.00	2.00
17 Ken Bordelon	1.00	2.00
18 Jim Kovach	1.00	2.00
19 Pat Hughes	1.00	2.00
20 Reggie Mathis	1.00	2.00
21 Jim Merlo	1.00	2.00
22 Joe Federspiel	1.00	2.00
23 Don Reese	1.00	2.00
24 Roger Finnie	1.00	2.00
25 John Hill	1.00	2.00
26 Barry Bennett	1.00	2.00
27 Dave Lafary	1.00	2.00
28 Robert Woods	1.00	2.00
29 Conrad Dobler	1.50	3.00
30 John Watson	1.00	2.00
31 Fred Sturt	1.00	2.00
32 J.T. Taylor	1.00	2.00
33 Mike Fultz	1.00	2.00
34 Joe Campbell	1.00	2.00
35 Derland Moore	1.00	2.00
36 Elex Price	1.00	2.00
37 Elois Grooms	1.00	2.00
38 Emanuel Zanders	1.00	2.00
39 Ike Harris	1.00	2.00
40 Tinker Owens	1.00	2.00
41 Rich Mauti	1.00	2.00
42 Henry Childs	1.50	3.00
43 Larry Hardy	1.00	2.00
44 Brooks Williams	1.00	2.00
45 Wes Chandler	2.50	5.00
AD1 Mr.Pibb Ad Card	.20	.50
AD2 Sprite Ad Card	.20	.50

1980 Saints Team Issue

These photos were released by the Saints for fans and for player signing appearances. Each measures roughly 8" by 10" and includes a black and white photo of the player with the player's name (in all caps), his position (initials), and team name (New Orleans Saints stacked) below the picture. The backs are blank and unnumbered.

COMPLETE SET (7)	15.00	30.00
1 Russell Erxleben	2.50	5.00
2 Elois Grooms	2.50	5.00
3 Jack Holmes	2.50	5.00
4 Dave LaFary	2.50	5.00
5 Derland Moore	2.50	5.00
6 Benny Ricardo	2.50	5.00
7 Emanuel Zanders	2.50	5.00

1985 Saints Eckerd Posters

These large (18" by 25") color posters were sponsored by Eckerd Stores. Each was blankbacked and featured a strip of 11-coupons below the player image.

COMPLETE SET (8)	35.00	70.00
1 Hoby Brenner	4.00	8.00
2 Earl Campbell	10.00	20.00
3 Rickey Jackson	5.00	10.00
4 Dave Wilson	4.00	8.00
5 Dave Waymer	4.00	8.00
6 Russell Gary	4.00	8.00
7 Bruce Clark	4.00	8.00
8 Hokie Gajan	4.00	8.00

1992 Saints McDag

This 32-card safety standard-size set was produced by McDag Productions Inc. for the New Orleans Saints and Behavioral Health Inc. The cards feature posed color player photos with white borders. The pictures are studio shots with a blue background. Running horizontally down the left is a wide brown stripe with the team name and year in yellow outline lettering. A mustard stripe at the bottom of the photo intersects the brown stripe and contains the player's name. The backs are white with black print and carry biographical information, career highlights, and "Tips from the Team" in the form of public service messages. There is also an address and phone number for obtaining free cards. The cards are unnumbered and checklisted below in alphabetical order.

COMPLETE SET (32)	4.00	10.00
1 Morten Andersen	.20	.50
2 Gene Atkins	.15	.40
3 Toi Cook	.08	.25
4 Tommy Barnhardt	.08	.25
5 Hoby Brenner	.08	.25
6 Stan Brock	.08	.25
7 Vince Buck	.08	.25
8 Wesley Carroll	.15	.40
9 Jim Dombrowski	.08	.25
10 Vaughn Dunbar	.15	.40
11 Quinn Early	.30	.75
12 Bobby Hebert	.15	.40
13 Craig Heyward	.25	.60
14 Joel Hilgenberg	.08	.25
15 Dalton Hilliard	.08	.25
16 Rickey Jackson	.15	.40
17 Vaughan Johnson	.15	.40
18 Reginald Jones	.08	.25
19 Eric Martin	.15	.40
20 Wayne Martin	.15	.40
21 Brett Maxie	.08	.25
22 Fred McAfee	.08	.25
23 Sam Mills	.20	.50
24 Jim Mora CO	.15	.40
25 Pat Swilling	.15	.40
26 John Tice	.08	.25
27 Renaldo Turnbull	.15	.40
28 Floyd Turner	.15	.40
29 Steve Walsh	.15	.40
30 Frank Warren	.08	.25
31 Jim Wilks	.08	.25
32 Saints Cheerleaders	.08	.25

1993 Saints Team Issue

These photos were released by the Saints for fans and for player signing appearances. Each measures roughly 4" by 5" and includes a black and white photo of the player with the team helmet and player information below the picture. The backs are blank and unnumbered.

COMPLETE SET (6)	4.80	12.00
1 Derek Brown RBK	1.20	3.00
2 Tyrone Hughes	.80	2.00
3 Sean Lumpkin	.80	2.00
4 Jim Mora CO	.80	2.00
5 Willie Roaf	1.20	3.00
6 James Williams LB	.80	2.00

1994 Saints Team Issue

These photos were released by the Saints for fans and for player signing appearances. Each measures roughly 8" by 10" and includes a black and white photo of the player. The backs are blank and unnumbered and no player information is contained on the photos at all. These photos can be identified by the NFL 75th Anniversary patch on the player's sleeves.

COMPLETE SET (10)	8.00	20.00
1 Darion Conner	.80	2.00
2 Jim Everett	1.20	3.00
3 Joe Johnson	.80	2.00
4 J.J. McCleskey	.80	2.00
5 Derrick Ned	.80	2.00
6 Doug Nussmeier	.80	2.00
7 Chris Port	.80	2.00
8 Irv Smith	.80	2.00
9 Winfred Tubbs	.80	2.00
10 Wesley Walls	1.20	3.00

1996 Saints Team Issue

These photos were released by the Saints for fans and for player signing appearances. Each measures roughly 8" by 10" and includes a black and white photo of the player. The backs are blank and unnumbered and no player information is contained on the photos at all. They can be identified by the Saints 30th Anniversary patch on the player's jersey.

COMPLETE SET (10)	8.00	20.00
1 Mario Bates	1.20	3.00
2 Doug Brien	.80	2.00
3 Ernest Dixon	.80	2.00
4 Paul Green	.80	2.00
5 Richard Harvey	.80	2.00
6 Andy McCollum	.80	2.00
7 Darren Mickell	.80	2.00
8 Alex Molden	.80	2.00
9 Willie Roaf	1.20	3.00
10 Brady Smith	.80	2.00

2000 Saints Team Issue

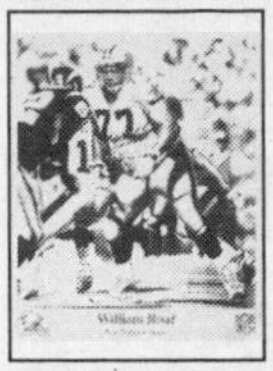

This large (roughly 8" by 10") black and white photos were issued by the Saints in 2000. Each includes a player photo with his name, team helmet, and NFL logo below the photo.

COMPLETE SET (11)	15.00	30.00
1 Jeff Blake	2.50	5.00
2 Jerry Fontenot	1.00	2.00
3 La'Roi Glover	1.00	2.00
4 Norman Hand	1.00	2.00
5 Sammy Knight	1.00	2.00
6 Keith Mitchell	1.00	2.00
7 Chad Morton	1.50	3.00
8 William Roaf	1.50	3.00
9 Ricky Williams	5.00	10.00
10 Wally Williams	1.00	2.00
11 Fred Weary	1.00	2.00

2001 Saints Team Issue

These blankbacked photos were issued in 2001 by the Saints for player appearances so they are often found signed. Each is black and white and measures roughly 3 1/2" by 5." Any additions to this list are appreciated.

COMPLETE SET (9)	12.50	25.00
1 Jake Delhomme	2.00	4.00
2 Norman Hand	1.00	2.50
3 Jim Haslett CO	1.50	3.00
4 Joe Horn	2.00	4.00
5 Fred McAfee	1.00	2.50
6 Deuce McAllister	5.00	12.00
7 Randy Mueller GM	1.00	2.50
8 Kenny Smith	1.50	3.00
9 Daryl Terrell	1.00	2.50

2002 Saints Team Issue

This set was issued by the Saints. Each card measures a large 3" by 4" and features a color image of a Saints player on the front with the team name above the photo and his name and position below. Each cardfront also includes a raised gold facsimile autograph. The cardbacks are black and white.

COMPLETE SET (8)	12.00	20.00
1 Aaron Brooks	1.50	4.00
2 Norman Hand	.75	2.00
3 Joe Horn	1.50	4.00
4 Darren Howard	.75	2.00
5 Sammy Knight	.75	2.00
6 Deuce McAllister	2.50	6.00
7 Terrelle Smith	.75	2.00
8 Kyle Turley	.75	2.00

2003 Saints Team Issue

This set was issued by the Saints. Each card measures a large 3" by 4" and features a color image of a Saints player on the front with the team name above the photo and his name and position below within a gold broder. Each cardfront also includes a raised gold facsimile autograph. The cardbacks are black and white.

COMPLETE SET (7)	7.50	15.00
1 Aaron Brooks	1.25	3.00
2 John Carney	.75	2.00
3 Charles Grant	.75	2.00
4 Joe Horn	1.25	3.00
5 Michael Lewis	1.25	3.00
6 Deuce McAllister	2.00	5.00
7 Donte Stallworth	1.25	3.00

2004 Saints Team Issue

This set was issued by the Saints with each card measuring standard size. The fronts feature a color image of a Saints player with the team name above the photo and his name and position below. Each cardfront also includes a raised gold facsimile autograph. The cardbacks are black and white and unnumbered.

COMPLETE SET (8)	3.00	6.00
1 Ashley Ambrose	.40	1.00
2 LeCharles Bentley	.40	1.00
3 Steve Gleason	.40	1.00
4 Joe Horn	.50	1.25
5 Darren Howard	.40	1.00
6 Michael Lewis	.50	1.25
7 Deuce McAllister	.50	1.25
8 Fred Thomas	.40	1.00

2006 Saints Team Issue

This set was issued by the Saints with each card measuring standard size. The fronts feature a color image of a Saints player with the team name above the photo and his name and position below. Each cardfront also includes a raised gold facsimile autograph. The cardbacks are black and white and unnumbered.

COMPLETE SET (9)	4.00	10.00
1 Drew Brees	.60	1.50
2 Reggie Bush	1.25	3.00
3 Charles Grant	.30	.75
4 Joe Horn	.50	1.25
5 Mike Karney	.40	1.00
6 Deuce McAllister	.50	1.25
7 Mike McKenzie	.40	1.00
8 Hollis Thomas	.40	1.00
9 Brian Young	.40	1.00

2006 Saints Topps

COMPLETE SET (12)	5.00	12.00
NO1 Joe Horn	.25	.60
NO2 Ernie Conwell	.20	.50
NO3 Donte Stallworth	.20	.50
NO4 Drew Brees	.30	.75
NO5 Deuce McAllister	.25	.60
NO6 Mike McKenzie	.20	.50
NO7 Aaron Stecker	.20	.50
NO8 Charles Grant	.15	.40
NO9 Will Smith	.20	.50
NO10 Devery Henderson	.20	.50
NO11A Reggie Bush 5 (wearing jersey #5)	4.00	10.00
NO11B Reggie Bush 25 (wearing jersey #25)	4.00	10.00
NO12 Mike Hass	.30	.75

2007 Saints Team Issue

This set was issued by the Saints with each card measuring standard size. The fronts feature a color image of a Saints player with the team name above the photo and his name and position below. Each cardfront also includes a raised gold facsimile autograph. The cardbacks are black and white and unnumbered.

COMPLETE SET (9)	4.00	10.00
1 Drew Brees	.60	1.50
2 Reggie Bush	.60	1.50
3 Marques Colston	.60	1.50
4 Scott Fujita	.40	1.00
5 Charles Grant	.40	1.00
6 Devery Henderson	.40	1.00
7 Deuce McAllister	.50	1.25
8 Mike McKenzie	.40	1.00
9 Will Smith	.40	1.00

2007 Saints Topps

COMPLETE SET (12)	2.50	5.00
1 Reggie Bush	.30	.75
2 Devery Henderson	.20	.50
3 Deuce McAllister	.25	.60
4 Marques Colston	.30	.75
5 Drew Brees	.30	.75
6 Eric Johnson	.20	.50
7 Will Smith	.20	.50
8 Mike McKenzie	.20	.50
9 Terrance Copper	.25	.60
10 Mike Karney	.20	.50
11 Charles Grant	.20	.50
12 Robert Meachem	.30	.75

2008 Saints Topps

COMPLETE SET (12)	2.50	5.00
1 Drew Brees	.30	.75
2 Marques Colston	.25	.60
3 Aaron Stecker	.20	.50
4 Reggie Bush	.30	.75
5 David Patten	.20	.50
6 Deuce McAllister	.25	.60
7 Devery Henderson	.20	.50
8 Will Smith	.20	.50
9 Mike McKenzie	.20	.50
10 Scott Fujita	.20	.50
11 Sedrick Ellis	.40	1.00
12 Tracy Porter	.40	1.00

2009 Saints Team Issue

This set was issued by the Saints with each card measuring standard size. The fronts feature a color image of a Saints player with the team name below the photo and his name and position above. Each cardfront also includes a raised gold facsimile autograph and a white border. The cardbacks are black and white and unnumbered.

COMPLETE SET (11)	5.00	12.00
1 Drew Brees	.60	1.50
2 Reggie Bush	.60	1.50
3 Marques Colston	.50	1.25
4 Sedrick Ellis	.40	1.00
5 Scott Fujita	.40	1.00
6 Roman Harper	.40	1.00
7 Lance Moore	.50	1.25
7 Will Smith	.40	1.00
8 Jon Stinchcomb	.40	1.00
9 Pierre Thomas	.50	1.25
10 Jonathan Vilma	.40	1.00

2010 Saints Upper Deck Super Bowl XLIV

COMP.FACT.SET (51)	10.00	20.00
1 Drew Brees	.40	1.00
2 Marques Colston	.30	.75
3 Reggie Bush	.40	1.00
4 Pierre Thomas	.30	.75
5 Mike Bell	.25	.60
6 Jeremy Shockey	.30	.75
7 Devery Henderson	.25	.60
8 Robert Meachem	.30	.75
9 David Thomas	.25	.60
10 Lance Moore	.30	.75
11 Heath Evans	.25	.60
12 Jonathan Vilma	.25	.60
13 Roman Harper	.25	.60
14 Darren Sharper	.30	.75
15 Scott Shanle	.25	.60
16 Will Smith	.25	.60
17 Malcolm Jenkins	.25	.60
18 Charles Grant	.25	.60
19 Tracy Porter	.25	.60
20 Jabari Greer	.25	.60
21 Jahri Evans	.25	.60
22 Jonathan Goodwin	.25	.60
23 Jon Stinchcomb	.25	.60
24 Lynell Hamilton	.25	.60
25 John Carney	.25	.60
26 Garrett Hartley	.25	.60
27 Thomas Morstead	.25	.60
28 Courtney Roby	.25	.60
29 Scott Fujita	.25	.60
30 Anthony Hargrove	.25	.60
31 Randall Gay	.25	.60
32 Sedrick Ellis	.25	.60
33 Remi Ayodele	.25	.60
34 Bobby McCray	.25	.60
35 Marvin Mitchell	.25	.60
36 Pierson Prioleau	.25	.60
37 Mark Brunell	.25	.60
38 Chase Daniel	.25	.60
39 Carl Nicks	.25	.60
40 Jermon Bushrod	.25	.60
41 Darren Sharper HL	.30	.75
42 Drew Brees HL	.40	1.00
43 Reggie Bush HL	.40	1.00
44 Robert Meachem HL	.30	.75
45 Jonathan Vilma HL	.25	.60
46 Chris Reis HL	.25	.60
47 Pierre Thomas HL	.30	.75
48 Jeremy Shockey HL	.30	.75
49 Tracy Porter HL	.25	.60
50 Drew Brees MVP	.40	1.00
SBXLIV Super Bowl Champs Jumbo	.60	1.50
Tracy Porter		
Jonathan Vilma		
Bobby McRay		
Scott Shanle		

1962-63 Salada Coins

This 154-coin set features popular NFL and AFL players from selected teams. Each team had a specific rim color. The numbering of the coins is essentially by teams, i.e., Colts (1-11 blue), Packers (12-22 green), 49ers (23-33 salmon), Bears (34-44 black), Rams (45-55 yellow), Browns (56-66 black), Steelers (67-77 yellow), Lions (78-88 blue), Redskins (89-99 yellow), Eagles (100-110 green), Giants (111-121 blue), Patriots (122-132 salmon), Titans (133-143 blue), and Bills (144-154 salmon). All players are pictured without their helmets. The coins measure approximately 1 1/2" in diameter. The coin backs give the player's name, position, pro team, college, height, and weight. The coins were originally produced on sheets measuring 31 1/2" by 25"; the 255 coins on the sheet included the complete set as well as duplicates and triplicates. Double prints (DP) and triple prints (TP) are listed below. The double-printed coins are generally from certain teams, i.e., Packers, Bears, Browns, Lions, Eagles, Giants, Patriots, Titans, and Bills. Those coins below not listed explicitly as to the frequency of printing are in fact single printed (SP) and hence more difficult to find. The set is sometimes found intact as a presentation set in its own custom box; such a set would be valued 25 percent higher than the complete set price below.

COMPLETE SET (154)	1,250.00	2,500.00
1 Johnny Unitas	75.00	150.00
2 Lenny Moore	40.00	80.00
3 Jim Parker	25.00	50.00
4 Gino Marchetti	25.00	50.00
5 Dick Szymanski	15.00	30.00
6 Alex Sandusky	15.00	30.00
7 Raymond Berry	40.00	80.00
8 Jimmy Orr	15.00	30.00
9 Ordell Braase	15.00	30.00
10 Bill Pellington	15.00	30.00
11 Bob Boyd	15.00	30.00
12 Paul Hornung DP	20.00	40.00
13 Jim Taylor DP	15.00	30.00
14 Hank Jordan DP	5.00	10.00
15 Dan Currie DP	4.00	8.00
16 Bill Forester DP	4.00	8.00
17 Dave Hanner DP	4.00	8.00
18 Bart Starr DP	25.00	50.00
19 Max McGee DP	5.00	10.00
20 Jerry Kramer DP	6.00	12.00
21 Forrest Gregg DP	6.00	12.00
22 Jim Ringo DP	6.00	12.00
23 Billy Kilmer	25.00	50.00
24 Charlie Krueger	15.00	30.00
25 Bob St. Clair	25.00	50.00
26 Abe Woodson	15.00	30.00
27 Jim Johnson	25.00	50.00
28 Matt Hazeltine	15.00	30.00
29 Bruce Bosley	15.00	30.00
30 Clyde Conner	15.00	30.00
31 John Brodie	30.00	60.00
32 J.D. Smith	15.00	30.00
33 Monty Stickles	15.00	30.00
34 Johnny Morris DP	3.00	6.00
35 Stan Jones DP	5.00	10.00
36 J.C. Caroline DP	2.50	5.00
37 Richie Petitbon DP	3.00	6.00
38 Joe Fortunato DP	3.00	6.00
39 Larry Morris DP	2.50	5.00
40 Doug Atkins DP	6.00	12.00
41 Bill Wade DP	3.00	6.00
42 Rick Casares DP	3.00	6.00
43 Willie Galimore DP	3.00	6.00
44 Angelo Coia DP	2.50	5.00
45 Ollie Matson	30.00	60.00
46 Carroll Dale	15.00	30.00
47 Ed Meador	15.00	30.00
48 Jon Arnett	15.00	30.00
49 Joe Marconi	15.00	30.00
50 John LoVetere	15.00	30.00
51 Red Phillips	15.00	30.00
52 Zeke Bratkowski	20.00	40.00
53 Dick Bass	15.00	30.00
54 Les Richter	15.00	30.00
55 Art Hunter	15.00	30.00
56 Jim Brown TP	25.00	50.00
57 Mike McCormack DP	5.00	10.00
58 Bob Gain DP	2.50	5.00
59 Paul Wiggin DP	2.50	5.00
60 Jim Houston DP	2.50	5.00
61 Ray Renfro DP	3.00	6.00
62 Galen Fiss DP	2.50	5.00
63 J.R. Smith DP	2.50	5.00
64 John Morrow DP	2.50	5.00
65 Gene Hickerson DP	3.00	6.00
66 Jim Ninowski DP	2.50	5.00
67 Tom Tracy	15.00	30.00
68 Buddy Dial	15.00	30.00
69 Mike Sandusky	15.00	30.00
70 Lou Michaels	15.00	30.00
71 Preston Carpenter	15.00	30.00
72 John Reger	15.00	30.00
73 John Henry Johnson	30.00	60.00
74 Gene Lipscomb	20.00	35.00
75 Mike Henry	15.00	30.00
76 George Tarasovic	15.00	30.00
77 Bobby Layne	50.00	100.00
78 Harley Sewell DP	2.50	5.00
79 Darris McCord DP	2.50	5.00
80 Yale Lary DP	5.00	10.00
81 Jim Gibbons DP	3.00	6.00
82 Gail Cogdill DP	2.50	5.00
83 Nick Pietrosante DP	2.50	5.00
84 Alex Karras DP	7.50	15.00
85 Dick Lane DP	5.00	10.00
86 Joe Schmidt DP	6.00	12.00
87 John Gordy DP	2.50	5.00
88 Milt Plum DP	3.00	6.00
89 Andy Stynchula	15.00	30.00
90 Bob Toneff	15.00	30.00
91 Bill Anderson	15.00	30.00
92 Sam Horner	15.00	30.00
93 Norm Snead	20.00	40.00
94 Bobby Mitchell	30.00	60.00
95 Bill Barnes	15.00	30.00
96 Rod Breedlove	15.00	30.00
97 Fred Hageman	15.00	30.00
98 Vince Promuto	15.00	30.00
99 Joe Rutgens	15.00	30.00
100 Maxie Baughan DP	2.50	5.00
101 Pete Retzlaff DP	3.00	6.00
102 Tom Brookshier DP	3.00	6.00
103 Sonny Jurgensen DP	9.00	18.00
104 Ed Khayat DP	2.50	5.00
105 Chuck Bednarik DP	7.50	15.00
106 Tommy McDonald DP	4.00	8.00
107 Bobby Walston DP	2.50	5.00
108 Ted Dean DP	2.50	5.00
109 Clarence Peaks DP	3.00	6.00
110 Jimmy Carr DP	2.50	5.00
111 Sam Huff DP	7.50	15.00
112 Erich Barnes DP	2.50	5.00
113 Del Shofner DP	3.00	6.00
114 Bob Gaiters DP	2.50	5.00
115 Alex Webster DP	3.00	6.00
116 Dick Modzelewski DP	2.50	5.00
117 Jim Katcavage DP	3.00	6.00
118 Roosevelt Brown DP	5.00	10.00
119 Y.A. Tittle DP	12.50	25.00
120 Andy Robustelli DP	6.00	12.00
121 Dick Lynch DP	2.50	5.00
122 Don Webb DP	2.50	5.00
123 Larry Eisenhauer DP	2.50	5.00
124 Babe Parilli DP	3.00	6.00
125 Charles Long DP	2.50	5.00
126 Billy Lott DP	2.50	5.00
127 Harry Jacobs DP	2.50	5.00
128 Bob Dee DP	2.50	5.00
129 Ron Burton DP	3.00	6.00
130 Jim Colclough TP	1.50	3.00
131 Gino Cappelletti DP	3.00	6.00
132 Tommy Addison DP	2.50	5.00
133 Larry Grantham DP	2.50	5.00
134 Dick Christy DP	2.50	5.00
135 Bill Mathis DP	3.00	6.00
136 Butch Songin DP	2.50	5.00
137 Dainard Paulson DP	2.50	5.00
138 Roger Ellis DP	2.50	5.00
139 Mike Hudock DP	2.50	5.00
140 Don Maynard DP	10.00	20.00
141 Al Dorow DP	2.50	5.00
142 Jack Klotz DP	2.50	5.00
143 Lee Riley DP	2.50	5.00
144 Bill Atkins DP	2.50	5.00
145 Art Baker DP	2.50	5.00
146 Stew Barber DP	2.50	5.00
147 Glenn Bass DP	2.50	5.00
148 Al Bemiller DP	2.50	5.00
149 Richie Lucas DP	2.50	5.00
150 Archie Matsos DP	2.50	5.00
151 Warren Rabb DP	2.50	5.00
152 Ken Rice DP	2.50	5.00
153 Billy Shaw DP	3.00	6.00
154 Laverne Torczon DP	2.50	5.00

2005 San Angelo Stampede Express NIFL

COMPLETE SET (34)	7.50	15.00
1 Jeff Anderson	.20	.50
2 Ray Brennan	.20	.50
3 Demont Burdine	.20	.50
4 Andre Cummings	.20	.50
5 Barrett Dallmeyer	.20	.50
6 Toby Davis	.20	.50
7 D'Ambrose Finch	.20	.50
8 David Guillen	.20	.50
9 Clay Hardt	.20	.50
10 Kito Hicks	.20	.50
11 Prescott Hill	.20	.50
12 Ryan Hunt	.20	.50
13 Tyrone Johnson	.20	.50
14 Terry Kilpatrick	.20	.50
15 Chuck Leonardis	.20	.50
16 Gary Love	.20	.50
17 Karson Lown	.20	.50
18 Marquez Reischl	.20	.50
19 Corey Roberson	.20	.50
20 Max Schug Asst.CO	.20	.50
21 Jessie Shields	.20	.50
22 Chris Simpson CO	.20	.50
23 Jeff Smith	.20	.50
24 Calvin Thomas	.20	.50
25 Brian Villanueva	.20	.50
26 Kailan Williams	.20	.50
27 Demont Burdine	.20	.50
Gary Love		
Prescott Hill		
28 Assistant Coaches	.20	.50
Jeff Mann		
Randy Matthews		
Joe Briley		
29 Jeff Smith	.20	.50
Clay Hardt		
30 Stomper (Mascot)	.20	.50
31 Team Card	.20	.50
32 Broadcast Team Ad Card	.20	.50
33 Gandy Ink Ad Card	.20	.50
34 Extreme Imaging Ad Card	.20	.50

2006 San Angelo Express IFL

COMPLETE SET (23)	6.00	12.00
1 Johnny Anderson	.20	.50
2 David Banks	.20	.50
3 Demont Burdine	.20	.50
4 James Cardenas	.20	.50
5 Barrett Dallmeyer	.20	.50
6 Michael Dansby	.20	.50
7 Toby Davis	.20	.50
8 Paul Francis	.20	.50
9 Bruce Hampton	.20	.50
10 Terrence Jefferson	.20	.50
11 Michael Johnson	.20	.50
12 Rashaad Lee	.20	.50
13 Quinton Morgan	.20	.50
14 Wali Mumin	.20	.50
15 Cody Munden (Trainer)	.20	.50
16 Sharif Najib	.20	.50
17 Jon Nielson	.20	.50
18 Larry Newton	.20	.50
19 Jaime Salazar	.20	.50
20 J.T. Smith CO	.20	.50
21 Derik Stotland	.20	.50
22 Jackie Warren	.20	.50
23 Cody Wilson	.20	.50

2007 San Antonio Steers NIFL

COMPLETE SET (4)	2.50	6.00
1 Bo Buescher	.60	1.50
2 Garyle Graham	.60	1.50
3 Mark Ricker CO	.60	1.50
4 Michael Ward	.60	1.50

1975 San Antonio Wings WFL Team Issue

This set of black and white photos was issued by the San Antonio Wings to fulfill fan requests and for player appearances. Each measures roughly 5" by 7" and includes the player's name, position, and team name below the photo in varying type styles and sizes. The photo backs are blank.

COMPLETE SET (5)	25.00	50.00
1 Rick Cash	5.00	10.00
2 Luther Palmer	5.00	10.00
3 Dick Pesonen CO	5.00	10.00
4 Lonnie Warwick	5.00	10.00
5 Craig Wiseman	5.00	10.00

2008 San Jose Sabercats AFL

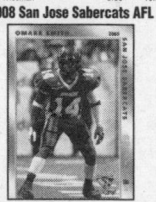

COMPLETE SET (38)	7.50	15.00
1 Darren Arbet CO	.20	.50
2 Frank Carter	.20	.50
3 Marquis Floyd	.20	.50
4 Gene Frederic	.20	.50
5 Jason Geathers	.20	.50
6 Trestin George	.20	.50
7 Mark Grieb	.20	.50
8 A.J. Haglund	.20	.50
9 Alan Harper	.20	.50
10 Brian Johnson	.20	.50
11 Ron Jones	.20	.50
12 Dan Loney	.20	.50
13 Garrett McIntyre	.20	.50
14 William Obeng	.20	.50
15 Scott Rislov	.20	.50
16 James Roe	.20	.50
17 Cleannord Saintil	.20	.50
18 Omarr Smith	.20	.50
19 Clevan Thomas	.30	.75
20 Jason Thomas	.20	.50
21 Steve Watson	.20	.50
22 George Williams	.20	.50
23 Rodney Wright	.20	.50
24 San Jose Saberkitten: Aimie	.20	.50
25 San Jose Saberkitten: Alexis	.20	.50
26 San Jose Saberkitten: Amber	.20	.50
27 San Jose Saberkitten: Andrea	.20	.50
28 San Jose Saberkitten: Charmaine	.20	.50
29 San Jose Saberkitten: Christi	.20	.50
30 San Jose Saberkitten: Desi	.20	.50
31 San Jose Saberkitten: Grecia	.20	.50
32 San Jose Saberkitten: Jenna	.20	.50
33 San Jose Saberkitten: Jennie	.20	.50
34 San Jose Saberkitten: Jennifer	.20	.50
35 San Jose Saberkitten: Krystle	.20	.50
36 San Jose Saberkitten: Leizl	.20	.50
37 San Jose Saberkitten: Meredith	.20	.50
38 Title Card	.20	.50

1954 Scoops

COMPLETE SET (156)	1,000.00	2,000.00
110 Notre Dame's Four Horsemen	40.00	80.00

1989 Score Promos

This set of six football standard-size full-color cards was intended as a preview of Score's first football set, after two years of baseball card issues. The cards were sent out to prospective dealers along with the ordering forms for Score's debut football set. The cards are distinguishable from the regular issue cards of the same numbers as indicated in the checklist below. One good way to recognize these promos is that the stats on the promo card backs are carried out to only one decimal place instead of two. In addition, the promo cards show a registered symbol (R with circle around it) rather than a trademark (TM) symbol.

COMPLETE SET (6)	80.00	200.00
1 Joe Montana	40.00	100.00
2 Bo Jackson	12.00	30.00
3 Boomer Esiason	8.00	20.00
4 Roger Craig	8.00	20.00
(Born: Preston, Mississippi, should be Davenport, Iowa)		
5 Ed Too Tall Jones	6.00	15.00
(Registered seven sacks, regular card issue has registered 7.0 sacks)		
6 Phil Simms	8.00	20.00
(Moorehead State, should read Morehead State; front photo cropped so that Score logo blocks part of the ball)		

1989 Score

This set of 330 standard-size full-color cards marks Score's entry into the football card market. The set was issued in 15-card packs along with a trivia card. The front has a player photo surrounded by a color border that differs according to team. The player's name and team helmet are at the bottom. The backs contain a photo, statistics and highlights. The first 244 cards in the set are regular player cards. Cards 245-272 are rookie cards of players selected in the '89 NFL draft. Other subsets are post-season action (273-275), combo cards (277-284), All-Pro selections (285-309), Speedburners (310-317), Predators (318-325) and Record Breakers (326-329). The last card in the set is a tribute to Tom Landry. Rookie Cards include Troy Aikman, Steve Atwater, Don Beebe, Steve Beuerlein, Brian Blades, Bubby Brister, Tim Brown, Mark (WR) Carrier, Cris Carter, Gaston Green, Michael Irvin, Keith Jackson, Eric Metcalf, Anthony Miller, Chris Miller, Andre Rison, Mark Rypien, Barry Sanders, Deion Sanders, Chris Spielman, John Taylor, Broderick Thomas, Derrick Thomas, Thurman Thomas, and Rod Woodson.

COMPLETE SET (330)	40.00	80.00
COMP.FACT.SET (330)	40.00	80.00
1 Joe Montana	1.50	4.00
2 Bo Jackson	.25	.60
3 Boomer Esiason	.07	.20
4 Roger Craig	.20	.50
5 Ed Too Tall Jones	.07	.20
6 Phil Simms	.07	.20
7 Dan Hampton	.07	.20
8 John Settle RC	.02	.10
9 Bernie Kosar	.07	.20
10 Al Toon	.07	.20
11 Bubby Brister RC	.40	1.00
12 Mark Clayton	.07	.20
13 Dan Marino	1.50	4.00
14 Joe Morris	.02	.10
15 Warren Moon	.20	.50
16 Chuck Long	.02	.10
17 Mark Jackson	.02	.10
18 Michael Irvin RC	4.00	10.00
19 Bruce Smith	.20	.50
20 Anthony Carter	.07	.20
21 Charles Haley	.20	.50
22 Dave Duerson	.02	.10
23 Troy Stradford	.02	.10
24 Freeman McNeil	.02	.10
25 Jerry Gray	.02	.10
26 Bill Maas	.02	.10
27 Chris Chandler RC	1.25	3.00
28 Tom Newberry RC	.02	.10
29 Albert Lewis	.02	.10
30 Jay Schroeder	.02	.10
31 Dalton Hilliard	.02	.10
32 Tony Eason	.02	.10
33 Rick Donnelly UER	.02	.10
(229.11 yards per punt)		
34 Herschel Walker	.07	.20
35 Wesley Walker	.02	.10
36 Chris Doleman	.07	.20
37 Pat Swilling	.07	.20
38 Joey Browner	.02	.10
39 Shane Conlan	.02	.10
40 Mike Tomczak	.07	.20
41 Webster Slaughter	.07	.20
42 Ray Donaldson	.02	.10
43 Christian Okoye	.02	.10
44 John Bosa	.02	.10
45 Aaron Cox RC	.02	.10
46 Bobby Hebert	.07	.20
47 Carl Banks	.02	.10
48 Jeff Fuller	.02	.10
49 Gerald Willhite	.02	.10
50 Mike Singletary	.07	.20
51 Stanley Morgan	.02	.10
52 Mark Bavaro	.07	.20
53 Mickey Shuler	.02	.10
54 Keith Millard	.02	.10
55 Andre Tippett	.02	.10
56 Vance Johnson	.07	.20
57 Bennie Blades RC	.07	.20
58 Tim Harris	.02	.10
59 Hanford Dixon	.02	.10
60 Chris Miller RC	.40	1.00
61 Cornelius Bennett	.20	.50
62 Neal Anderson	.07	.20
63 Ickey Woods UER RC	.20	.50
(Jersey is 31 but listed as 30 on card back)		
64 Gary Anderson RB	.02	.10
65 Vaughan Johnson RC	.02	.10
66 Ronnie Lippett	.02	.10
67 Mike Quick	.02	.10
68 Roy Green	.07	.20
69 Tim Krumrie	.02	.10
70 Mark Malone	.02	.10
71 James Jones	.02	.10
72 Cris Carter RC	4.00	10.00
73 Ricky Nattiel	.02	.10
74 Jim Arnold UER	.02	.10
(238.83 yards per punt)		
75 Randall Cunningham	.40	1.00
76 John L. Williams	.02	.10
77 Paul Gruber RC	.02	.10
78 Rod Woodson RC	2.00	5.00
79 Ray Childress	.02	.10
80 Doug Williams	.07	.20
81 Deron Cherry	.07	.20
82 John Offerdahl	.02	.10
83 Louis Lipps	.07	.20
84 Neil Lomax	.02	.10
85 Wade Wilson	.07	.20
86 Tim Brown RC	4.00	10.00
87 Chris Hinton	.02	.10
88 Stump Mitchell	.02	.10
89 Tunch Ilkin RC	.02	.10
90 Steve Pelluer	.02	.10
91 Brian Noble	.02	.10
92 Reggie White	.20	.50
93 Aundray Bruce RC	.02	.10
94 Garry James	.02	.10
95 Drew Hill	.02	.10
96 Anthony Munoz	.07	.20
97 James Wilder	.02	.10
98 Dexter Manley	.02	.10
99 Lee Williams	.02	.10
100 Dave Krieg	.07	.20
101A Keith Jackson RC ERR	.20	.50
(Listed as 84 on card back)		
101B Keith Jackson RC COR	.20	.50
(Listed as 88 on card back)		
102 Luis Sharpe	.02	.10
103 Kevin Greene	.20	.50
104 Duane Bickett	.02	.10
105 Mark Rypien RC	.20	.50
106 Curt Warner	.02	.10
107 Jacob Green	.02	.10
108 Gary Clark	.20	.50
109 Bruce Matthews RC	1.25	3.00
110 Bill Fralic	.02	.10
111 Bill Bates	.07	.20
112 Jeff Bryant	.02	.10
113 Charles Mann	.02	.10
114 Richard Dent	.07	.20
115 Bruce Hill RC	.02	.10
116 Mark May RC	.02	.10
117 Mark Collins RC	.02	.10
118 Ron Holmes	.02	.10
119 Scott Case RC	.02	.10
120 Tom Rathman	.02	.10
121 Dennis McKinnon	.02	.10
122A Ricky Sanders ERR	.08	.25
(Listed as 46 on card back)		
122B Ricky Sanders COR	.20	.50
(Listed as 83 on card back)		
123 Michael Carter	.02	.10
124 Ozzie Newsome	.07	.20
125 Irving Fryar UER	.07	.20
(wide reveiver)		
126A Ron Hall ERR RC	.08	.25
(wrong photos on card)		
126B Ron Hall COR RC	.20	.50
(correct photos used)		
127 Clay Matthews	.07	.20
128 Leonard Marshall	.02	.10
129 Kevin Mack	.02	.10
130 Art Monk	.07	.20
131 Garin Veris	.02	.10
132 Steve Jordan	.02	.10
133 Frank Minnifield	.02	.10
134 Eddie Brown	.02	.10
135 Stacey Bailey	.02	.10
136 Rickey Jackson	.07	.20
137 Henry Ellard	.07	.20
138 Jim Burt	.02	.10
139 Jerome Brown	.07	.20
140 Rodney Holman RC	.02	.10
141 Sammy Winder	.02	.10
142 Marcus Cotton	.02	.10
143 Jim Jeffcoat	.02	.10
144 Rueben Mayes	.02	.10
145 Jim McMahon	.07	.20
146 Reggie Williams	.02	.10
147 John Anderson	.02	.10
148 Harris Barton RC	.02	.10
149 Phillip Epps	.02	.10
150 Jay Hilgenberg	.02	.10
151 Earl Ferrell	.02	.10
152 Andre Reed	.20	.50
153 Dennis Gentry	.02	.10
154 Max Montoya	.02	.10
155 Darrin Nelson	.02	.10
156 Jeff Chadwick	.02	.10
157 James Brooks	.07	.20
158 Keith Bishop	.02	.10
159 Robert Awalt	.02	.10
160 Marty Lyons	.02	.10
161 Johnny Hector	.02	.10
162 Tony Casillas	.02	.10
163 Kyle Clifton RC	.02	.10
164 Cody Risien	.02	.10
165 Jamie Holland RC	.02	.10
166 Merril Hoge RC	.02	.10
167 Chris Spielman RC	.40	1.00
168 Carlos Carson	.02	.10
169 Jerry Ball RC	.02	.10
170 Don Majkowski RC	.20	.50
171 Everson Walls	.02	.10
172 Mike Rozier	.02	.10
173 Matt Millen	.07	.20
174 Karl Mecklenburg	.02	.10
175 Paul Palmer	.02	.10
176 Brian Blades RC UER	.20	.50
(Photo on back is reversed negative)		
177 Brent Fullwood RC	.02	.10
178 Anthony Miller RC	.20	.50
179 Brian Sochia	.02	.10
180 Stephen Baker RC	.02	.10
181 Jesse Solomon	.02	.10
182 John Grimsley	.02	.10
183 Timmy Newsome	.02	.10
184 Steve Sewell RC	.02	.10
185 Dean Biasucci	.02	.10
186 Alonzo Highsmith	.02	.10
187 Randy Grimes	.02	.10
188A Mark Carrier ERR RC	.40	1.00
Photo on back is actually Bruce Hill		
188B Mark Carrier COR RC	.40	1.00
(Wearing helmet in photo on back		
189 Vann McElroy	.02	.10
190 Greg Bell	.02	.10
191 Quinn Early RC	.40	1.00
192 Lawrence Taylor	.20	.50
193 Albert Bentley	.02	.10
194 Ernest Givins	.07	.20
195 Jackie Slater	.02	.10
196 Jim Sweeney	.02	.10
197 Freddie Joe Nunn	.02	.10
198 Keith Byars	.07	.20
199 Hardy Nickerson RC	.20	.50
200 Steve Beuerlein RC	1.25	3.00
201 Bruce Armstrong RC	.20	.50
202 Lionel Manuel	.02	.10
203 J.T. Smith	.02	.10
204 Mark Ingram RC	.20	.50
205 Fred Smerlas	.02	.10
206 Bryan Hinkle RC	.02	.10
207 Steve McMichael	.07	.20
208 Nick Lowery	.02	.10
209 Jack Trudeau	.02	.10
210 Lorenzo Hampton	.02	.10
211 Thurman Thomas RC	3.00	8.00
212 Steve Young	.60	1.50
213 James Lofton	.20	.50
214 Jim Covert	.02	.10
215 Ronnie Lott	.07	.20
216 Stephone Paige	.02	.10
217 Mark Duper	.07	.20
218A Willie Gault ERR	.08	.25
(Front photo actually/93 Greg Townsend)		
218B Willie Gault COR	.20	.50
(83 clearly visible)		
219 Ken Ruettgers RC	.02	.10
220 Kevin Ross RC	.02	.10
221 Jerry Rice	1.50	3.00
222 Billy Ray Smith	.02	.10
223 Jim Kelly	.40	1.00
224 Vinny Testaverde	.40	1.00
225 Steve Largent	.20	.50
226 Warren Williams RC	.02	.10
227 Morten Andersen	.02	.10
228 Bill Brooks	.07	.20
229 Reggie Langhorne RC	.02	.10
230 Pepper Johnson	.02	.10
231 Pat Leahy	.02	.10
232 Fred Marion	.02	.10
233 Gary Zimmerman	.07	.20
234 Marcus Allen	.20	.50
235 Gaston Green RC	.02	.10
236 John Stephens RC	.02	.10
237 Terry Kinard	.02	.10
238 John Taylor RC	.40	1.00
239 Brian Bosworth	.07	.20
240 Anthony Toney	.02	.10
241 Ken O'Brien	.02	.10
242 Howie Long	.20	.50
243 Doug Flutie	1.00	2.50
244 Jim Everett	.20	.50
245 Broderick Thomas RC	.02	.10
246 Deion Sanders RC	4.00	10.00
247 Donnell Woolford RC	.02	.10
248 Wayne Martin RC	.02	.10
249 David Williams RC	.02	.10
250 Bill Hawkins RC	.02	.10
251 Eric Hill RC	.02	.10
252 Burt Grossman RC	.02	.10
253 Tracy Rocker	.02	.10
254 Steve Wisniewski RC	.20	.50
255 Jessie Small RC	.02	.10
256 David Braxton	.02	.10
257 Barry Sanders RC	15.00	30.00
258 Derrick Thomas RC	3.00	8.00
259 Eric Metcalf RC	.40	1.00
260 Keith DeLong RC	.02	.10
261 Hart Lee Dykes RC	.02	.10
262 Sammie Smith RC	.02	.10
263 Steve Atwater RC	.20	.50
264 Eric Ball RC	.02	.10
265 Don Beebe RC	.20	.50
266 Brian Williams OL RC	.02	.10
267 Jeff Lageman RC	.02	.10
268 Tim Worley RC	.02	.10
269 Tony Mandarich RC	.02	.10
270 Troy Aikman RC	12.50	30.00
271 Andy Heck RC	.02	.10
272 Andre Rison RC	2.50	5.00
273 AFC Championship	.02	.10
Bengals over Bills (Ickey Woods and Boomer Esiason)		
274 NFC Championship/49ers over Bears	.40	1.00
(Joe Montana)		
275 Super Bowl XXIII/49ers over Bengals	.75	2.00
(Joe Montana and Jerry Rice)		
276 Rodney Carter	.02	.10
277 Mark Jackson	.02	.10
Vance Johnson		
Ricky Nattiel		
278 John L. Williams	.02	.10
and Curt Warner		
279 Joe Montana and	.75	2.00
Jerry Rice		
280 Roy Green	.02	.10
Neil Lomax		
281 Randall Cunningham	.02	.10
and Keith Jackson		
282 Chris Doleman and	.02	.10
Keith Millard		
283 Mark Duper and	.02	.10
Mark Clayton		
284 Marcus Allen and	.25	.60
Bo Jackson		
285 Frank Minnifield AP	.02	.10
286 Bruce Matthews AP	.15	.40
287 Joey Browner AP	.02	.10
288 Jay Hilgenberg AP	.02	.10
289 Carl Lee AP RC	.02	.10
290 Scott Norwood RC	.02	.10
291 John Taylor AP	.20	.50
292 Jerry Rice AP	.60	1.50
293A Keith Jackson AP ERR	.20	.50
(Listed as 84 on card back)		
293B Keith Jackson AP COR	.20	.50
(Listed as 88 on card back)		
294 Gary Zimmerman AP	.07	.20
295 Lawrence Taylor AP	.20	.50
296 Reggie White AP	.20	.50
297 Roger Craig AP	.07	.20
298 Boomer Esiason AP	.07	.20
299 Cornelius Bennett AP	.07	.20
300 Mike Horan AP	.02	.10
301 Deron Cherry AP	.02	.10
302 Tom Newberry AP	.02	.10
303 Mike Singletary AP	.07	.20
304 Shane Conlan AP	.02	.10
305A Tim Brown ERR AP	.75	2.00
Photo on front actually 80 James Lofton		
305B Tim Brown COR AP	.75	2.00
(Dark jersey 81)		
306 Henry Ellard AP	.07	.20
307 Bruce Smith AP	.07	.20
308 Tim Krumrie AP	.02	.10
309 Anthony Munoz AP	.07	.20
310 Darrell Green SPEED	.02	.10
311 Anthony Miller SPEED	.20	.50
312 Wesley Walker SPEED	.02	.10
313 Ron Brown SPEED	.02	.10
314 Bo Jackson SPEED	.25	.60
315 Phillip Epps SPEED	.02	.10
316A E.Thomas RC ERR SPEED	.08	.25
Listed as 31 on card back		
316B E.Thomas RC COR SPEED	.20	.50
Listed as 22 on card back		
317 Herschel Walker SPEED	.07	.20
318 Jacob Green PRED	.02	.10
319 Andre Tippett PRED	.02	.10
320 Freddie Joe Nunn PRED	.02	.10
321 Reggie White PRED	.20	.50
322 Lawrence Taylor PRED	.20	.50
323 Greg Townsend PRED	.02	.10
324 Tim Harris PRED	.02	.10
325 Bruce Smith PRED	.07	.20
326 Tony Dorsett RB	.20	.50
327 Steve Largent RB	.20	.50
328 Tim Brown RB	.75	2.00
329 Joe Montana RB	.60	1.50
330 Tom Landry Tribute	.40	1.00

1989 Score Trivia Quiz

COMPLETE SET (28)	1.50	4.00
1 Football Trivia Quiz	.08	.25
2 Football Trivia Quiz	.08	.25
3 Football Trivia Quiz	.08	.25
4 Football Trivia Quiz	.08	.25
5 Football Trivia Quiz	.08	.25
6 Football Trivia Quiz	.08	.25
7 Football Trivia Quiz	.08	.25
8 Football Trivia Quiz	.08	.25
9 Football Trivia Quiz	.08	.25
10 Football Trivia Quiz	.08	.25
11 Football Trivia Quiz	.08	.25
12 Football Trivia Quiz	.08	.25
13 Football Trivia Quiz	.08	.25
14 Football Trivia Quiz	.08	.25
15 Football Trivia Quiz	.08	.25
16 Football Trivia Quiz	.08	.25
17 Football Trivia Quiz	.08	.25
18 Football Trivia Quiz	.08	.25
19 Football Trivia Quiz	.08	.25
20 Football Trivia Quiz	.08	.25
21 Football Trivia Quiz	.08	.25
22 Football Trivia Quiz	.08	.25
23 Football Trivia Quiz	.08	.25
24 Football Trivia Quiz	.08	.25
25 Football Trivia Quiz	.08	.25
26 Football Trivia Quiz	.08	.25
27 Football Trivia Quiz	.08	.25
28 Football Trivia Quiz	.08	.25

1989 Score Supplemental

The 1989 Score Supplemental set contains 110 standard-size cards that were issued as a complete set through hobby dealers. The card numbering is a continuation of the basic set except for an "S" suffix. The fronts have purple borders, otherwise, the cards are identical to the regular issue 1989 Score football cards. There is a card of Bo Jackson in baseball regalia. Rookie Cards include Eric Allen, Jack Del Rio, Simon Fletcher, Dave Meggett, Rodney Peete, Frank Reich, Sterling Sharpe, Neil Smith, Steve Walsh and Lorenzo White.

COMP.FACT.SET (110)	5.00	12.00
331S Herschel Walker	.15	.40
332S Allen Pinkett RC	.02	.10
333S Sterling Sharpe RC	1.25	3.00
334S Alvin Walton RC	.02	.10
335S Frank Reich RC	.15	.40
336S Jim Thornton RC	.02	.10
337S David Fulcher	.07	.20
338S Raul Allegre	.02	.10
339S John Elway	2.00	4.00
340S Michael Cofer	.02	.10
341S Jim Skow	.02	.10
342S Steve DeBerg	.02	.10

343S Mervyn Fernandez RC .02 .10
344S Mike Lansford .02 .10
345S Reggie Roby .02 .10
346S Raymond Clayborn .02 .10
347S Lonzell Hill .02 .10
348S Ottis Anderson .07 .20
349S Erik McMillan RC .02 .10
350S Al Harris RC .02 .10
351S Jack Del Rio RC .15 .40
352S Gary Anderson K .02 .10
353S Jim McMahon .07 .20
354S Keena Turner .02 .10
355S Tony Woods RC .02 .10
356S Donald Igwebuike .02 .10
357S Gerald Riggs .07 .20
358S Eddie Murray .02 .10
359S Dino Hackett .02 .10
360S Brad Muster RC .02 .10
361S Paul Palmer .02 .10
362S Jerry Robinson .02 .10
363S Simon Fletcher RC .07 .20
364S Tommy Kramer .02 .10
365S Jim C. Jensen RC .02 .10
366S Lorenzo White RC .15 .40
367S Fredd Young .02 .10
368S Ron Jaworski .02 .10
369S Mel Owens .02 .10
370S Dave Waymer .02 .10
371S Sean Landeta .02 .10
372S Sam Mills .07 .20
373S Todd Blackledge .02 .10
374S Jo Jo Townsell .02 .10
375S Ron Wolfley .02 .10
376S Ralf Mojsiejenko .02 .10
377S Eric Wright .02 .10
378S Nesby Glasgow .02 .10
379S Darryl Talley .07 .20
380S Eric Allen RC .15 .40
381S Dennis Smith .07 .20
382S John Tice .02 .10
383S Jesse Solomon .02 .10
384S Bo Jackson .60 1.50
(FB
BB Pose)
385S Mike Merriweather .02 .10
386S Maurice Carthon .02 .10
387S David Grayson .02 .10
388S Wilber Marshall .02 .10
389S David Wyman .02 .10
390S Thomas Everett RC .02 .10
391S Alex Gordon .02 .10
392S D.J. Dozier .02 .10
393S Scott Radecic RC .02 .10
394S Eric Thomas .02 .10
395S Mike Gann .02 .10
396S William Perry .07 .20
397S Carl Hairston .02 .10
398S Billy Ard .02 .10
399S Donnell Thompson .02 .10
400S Mike Webster .07 .20
401S Scott Davis RC .02 .10
402S Sean Farrell .02 .10
403S Mike Golic RC .02 .10
404S Mike Kenn .02 .10
405S Keith Van Horne RC .02 .10
406S Bob Golic .02 .10
407S Neil Smith RC .75 2.00
408S Dermontti Dawson RC .07 .20
409S Leslie O'Neal .07 .20
410S Matt Bahr .02 .10
411S Guy McIntyre RC .02 .10
412S Bryan Millard .02 .10
413S Joe Jacoby .02 .10
414S Rob Taylor RC .02 .10
415S Tony Zendejas .02 .10
416S Vai Sikahema .02 .10
417S Gary Reasons RC .02 .10
418S Shawn Collins RC .02 .10
419S Mark Green RC .02 .10
420S Courtney Hall RC .02 .10
421S Bobby Humphrey RC .02 .10
422S Myron Guyton RC .02 .10
423S Darryl Ingram RC .02 .10
424S Chris Jacke RC .02 .10
425S Keith Jones RC .02 .10
426S Robert Massey RC .02 .10
427S Bubba McDowell RC .15 .40
428S Dave Meggett RC .15 .40
429S Louis Oliver RC .07 .20
430S Danny Peebles .02 .10
431S Rodney Peete RC .30 .75
432S Jeff Query RC .02 .10
433S Timm Rosenbach UER RC .02 .10
Photo actually
Gary Hogeboom
434S Frank Stams RC .02 .10
435S Lawyer Tillman RC .02 .10
436S Billy Joe Tolliver RC .02 .10
437S Floyd Turner RC .07 .20
438S Steve Walsh RC .07 .20
439S Joe Wolf RC .02 .10
440S Trace Armstrong RC .02 .10

1989-90 Score Franco Harris

These standard size cards were given away to all persons at the Super Bowl Show I in New Orleans who acquired Franco Harris' autograph while at the show. However, there were two different backs prepared and distributed since Franco's "Sure-shot" election was announced during the course of the show, after which time the "Hall of Famer" variety was passed out. The card fronts are exactly the same. The only difference in the two varieties on the back is essentially the presence of "Sure-shot" at the beginning of the narrative. The cards are unnumbered. The card fronts are in the style of the popular 1989 Score regular issue football cards. Although both varieties were produced on a limited basis, it is thought that the "Sure-shot" variety is the tougher of the two.

1A Franco Harris 40.00 80.00
(Sure-shot)
1B Franco Harris 30.00 75.00
(Hall of Famer)

1990 Score Promos

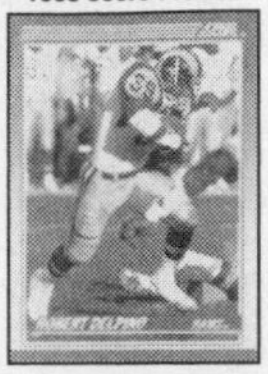

This set of standard-size full-color cards was intended as a preview of Score's football set. The cards were sent out to prospective dealers along with the ordering forms for Score's 1990 football set. The cards are distinguishable from the regular issue cards of the same numbers as indicated in the checklist below. The promo cards show a registered symbol (R with circle around it) rather than a trademark (TM) symbol as on the regular cards. In addition, these promos are cropped tighter than the regular issue cards.

COMPLETE SET (4) 4.80 12.00
20 Barry Sanders 4.00 10.00
24 Anthony Miller 2.00 5.00
184 Robert Delpino .80 2.00
256 Cornelius Bennett .80 2.00

1990 Score

The 1990 Score football set consists of 660 standard-size cards issued in two series of 330. The set was issued in 16-card packs along with a trivia card. The fronts have sharp color action photos and multicolored borders. The vertically oriented backs have color photos, stats and highlights. There are numerous subsets including Draft Picks (289-310/618-657), Hot Guns (311-320/563/564), Ground Force (321-330/561/562), Crunch Crew (551-555), Rocket Man (556-560), All-Pros (565-590), Record Breakers (591-594), Hall of Famers (595-601) and Class of '90 (606-617). Rookie Cards include Mark (DB) Carrier, Barry Foster, Barry Foster, Jeff George, Eric Green, Rodney Hampton, Haywood Jeffires, Cortez Kennedy, Scott Mitchell, Junior Seau and Andre Ware. The five-card "Final Five" set was a special insert in factory sets. These cards honor the final five picks of the 1990 National Football League Draft and are numbered with a "B" prefix. These cards have a "Final Five" logo on the front along with the photo of the player, while the back has a brief biographical description of the player.

COMPLETE SET (660) 6.00 15.00
COMP.FACT.SET (665) 7.50 20.00
1 Joe Montana .50 1.25
2 Christian Okoye .02 .10
3 Mike Singletary UER .02 .10
4 Jim Everett UER .02 .10
(Text says 415 yards
against Saints, should
be 454)
5 Phil Simms .02 .10
6 Brent Fullwood .01 .05
7 Bill Fralic .01 .05
8 Leslie O'Neal .02 .10
9 John Taylor .08 .25
10 Bo Jackson .10 .30
11 John Stephens .01 .05
12 Art Monk .02 .10
13 Dan Marino .50 1.25
14 John Settle .01 .05
15 Don Majkowski .01 .05
16 Bruce Smith .08 .25
17 Brad Muster .01 .05
18 Jason Buck .01 .05
19 James Brooks .02 .10
20 Barry Sanders .50 1.25
21 Troy Aikman .30 .75
22 Allen Pinkett .01 .05
23 Duane Bickett .01 .05
24 Kevin Ross .01 .05
25 John Elway .50 1.25
26 Jeff Query .01 .05
27 Eddie Murray .01 .05
28 Richard Dent .02 .10
29 Lorenzo White .01 .05
30 Eric Metcalf .08 .25
31 Jeff Dellenbach RC .01 .05
32 Leon White .01 .05
33 Jim Jeffcoat .01 .05
34 Herschel Walker .02 .10
35 Mike Johnson UER .01 .05
(Front photo actually/51 Eddie Johnson)
36 Joe Phillips RC .01 .05
37 Willie Gault .02 .10
38 Keith Millard .01 .05
39 Fred Marion .01 .05
40 Boomer Esiason .02 .10
41 Dermontti Dawson .02 .10
42 Dino Hackett .01 .05
43 Reggie Roby .01 .05
44 Roger Vick .01 .05
45 Bobby Hebert .01 .05
46 Don Beebe .02 .10
47 Neal Anderson .02 .10
48 Johnny Holland .01 .05
49 Bobby Humphery .01 .05
50 Lawrence Taylor .08 .25
51 Billy Ray Smith .01 .05
52 Robert Perryman .01 .05
53 Gary Anderson K .01 .05
54 Raul Allegre .01 .05
55 Pat Swilling .02 .10
56 Chris Doleman .01 .05
57 Andre Reed .08 .25
58 Seth Joyner .02 .10
59 Bart Oates .01 .05
60 Bernie Kosar .02 .10
61 Dave Krieg .02 .10
62 Lars Tate .01 .05
63 Scott Norwood .01 .05
64 Kyle Clifton .01 .05
65 Alan Veingrad .01 .05
66 Gerald Riggs UER .02 .10
(Text begins Depite,
should be Despite)
67 Tim Worley .01 .05
68 Rodney Holman .01 .05
69 Tony Zendejas .01 .05
70 Chris Miller .08 .25
71 Wilber Marshall .01 .05
72 Skip McClendon RC .01 .05
73 Jim Covert .01 .05
74 Sam Mills .02 .10
75 Chris Hinton .01 .05
76 Irv Eatman .01 .05
77 Bubba Paris UER .01 .05
(No draft team mentioned)
78 John Elliott UER .01 .05
(No draft team mentioned;
missing Team
FA status)
79 Thomas Everett .01 .05
80 Steve Smith .01 .05
81 Jackie Slater .01 .05
82 Kelvin Martin RC .01 .05
83 Jo Jo Townsell .01 .05
84 Jim C. Jensen .01 .05
85 Bobby Humphrey .01 .05
86 Mike Dyal RC .01 .05
87 Andre Rison UER .08 .25
(Front 87& back 85)
88 Brian Sochia .01 .05
89 Greg Bell .01 .05
90 Dalton Hilliard .01 .05
91 Carl Banks .01 .05
92 Dennis Smith .01 .05
93 Bruce Matthews .02 .10
94 Charles Haley .02 .10
95 Deion Sanders .20 .50
96 Stephone Paige .01 .05
97 Marion Butts .02 .10
98 Howie Long .08 .25
99 Donald Igwebuike .01 .05
100 Roger Craig UER .02 .10
(Text says 2 TD's in
SB XXIV, should be 1;
everything misspelled)
101 Charles Mann .01 .05
102 Fredd Young .01 .05
103 Chris Jacke .01 .05
104 Scott Case .01 .05
105 Warren Moon .08 .25
106 Clyde Simmons .01 .05
107 Steve Atwater .01 .05
108 Morten Andersen .01 .05
109 Eugene Marve .01 .05
110 Thurman Thomas .08 .25
111 Carnell Lake .01 .05
112 Jim Kelly .08 .25
113 Stanford Jennings .01 .05
114 Jacob Green .01 .05
115 Karl Mecklenburg .01 .05
116 Ray Childress .01 .05
117 Erik McMillan .01 .05
118 Harry Newsome .01 .05
119 James Dixon .01 .05
120 Hassan Jones .01 .05
121 Eric Allen .01 .05
122 Felix Wright .01 .05
123 Merril Hoge .01 .05
124 Eric Ball .01 .05
125 Flipper Anderson .01 .05
126 James Jefferson .01 .05
127 Tim McDonald .01 .05
128 Larry Kinnebrew .01 .05
129 Mark Collins .01 .05
130 Ickey Woods .01 .05
131 Jeff Donaldson UER .01 .05
(Stats say 0 int. and/0 fumble rec., text
says 4 and 1)
132 Rich Camarillo .01 .05
133 Melvin Bratton RC .01 .05
134A Kevin Butler .12 .35
(Photo on back
has helmet on)
134B Kevin Butler .20 .50
(Photo on back
has no helmet on)
135 Albert Bentley .01 .05
136A Vai Sikahema .12 .35
(Photo on back
has helmet on)
136B Vai Sikahema .20 .50
(Photo on back
has no helmet on)
137 Todd McNair RC .01 .05
138 Alonzo Highsmith .01 .05
139 Brian Blades .02 .10
140 Jeff Lageman .01 .05
141 Eric Thomas .01 .05
142 Derek Hill .01 .05
143 Rick Fenney .01 .05
144 Herman Heard .01 .05
145 Steve Young .20 .50
146 Kent Hull .01 .05
147A Joey Browner .12 .35
(Photo on back
looking to side)
147B Joey Browner .20 .50
(Photo on back
looking up)
148 Frank Minnifield .01 .05
149 Robert Massey .01 .05
150 Dave Meggett .02 .10
151 Bubba McDowell .01 .05
152 Rickey Dixon RC .01 .05
153 Ray Donaldson .01 .05
154 Alvin Walton .01 .05
155 Mike Cofer .01 .05
156 Darryl Talley .01 .05
157 A.J. Johnson .01 .05
158 Jerry Gray .01 .05
159 Keith Byars .01 .05
160 Andy Heck .01 .05
161 Mike Munchak .02 .10
162 Dennis Gentry .01 .05
163 Timm Rosenbach UER .01 .05
(Born 1967 in Everett,
Wa., should be 1966
in Missoula, Mont.)
164 Randall McDaniel .05 .15
165 Pat Leahy .01 .05
166 Bubby Brister .01 .05
167 Aundray Bruce .01 .05
168 Bill Brooks .01 .05
169 Eddie Anderson RC .01 .05
170 Ronnie Lott .02 .10
171 Jay Hilgenberg .01 .05
172 Joe Nash .01 .05
173 Simon Fletcher .01 .05
174 Shane Conlan .01 .05
175 Sean Landeta .01 .05
176 John Alt RC .01 .05
177 Clay Matthews .02 .10
178 Anthony Munoz .02 .10
179 Pete Holohan .01 .05
180 Robert Awalt .01 .05
181 Rohn Stark .01 .05
182 Vance Johnson .01 .05
183 David Fulcher .01 .05
184 Robert Delpino .01 .05
185 Drew Hill .01 .05
186 Reggie Langhorne UER .01 .05
(Stats read 1988,
not 1989)
187 Lonzell Hill .01 .05
188 Tom Rathman UER .01 .05
(On back, blocker
misspelled)
189 Greg Montgomery RC .01 .05
190 Leonard Smith .01 .05
191 Chris Spielman .08 .25
192 Tom Newberry .01 .05
193 Cris Carter .20 .50
194 Kevin Porter RC .01 .05
195 Donnell Thompson .01 .05
196 Vaughan Johnson .01 .05
197 Steve McMichael .02 .10
198 Jim Sweeney .01 .05
199 Rich Karlis UER .01 .05
(No comma between day
and year in birth data)
200 Jerry Rice .30 .75
201 Dan Hampton UER .02 .10
(Card says he's a DE,
should be DT)
202 Jim Lachey .01 .05
203 Reggie White .08 .25
204 Jerry Ball .01 .05
205 Russ Grimm .02 .10
206 Tim Green RC .01 .05
207 Shawn Collins .01 .05
208A Ralf Mojsiejenko ERR .05 .15
(Chargers stats)
208B Ralf Mojsiejenko COR .20 .50
(Redskins stats)
209 Trace Armstrong .01 .05
210 Keith Jackson .02 .10
211 Jamie Holland .01 .05
212 Mark Clayton .02 .10
213 Jeff Cross .01 .05
214 Bob Gagliano .01 .05
215 Louis Oliver UER .01 .05
(Text says played at
Miami, should be
Florida as in bio)
216 Jim Arnold .01 .05
217 Robert Clark RC .01 .05
218 Gill Byrd .01 .05
219 Rodney Peete .02 .10
220 Anthony Miller .08 .25
221 Steve Grogan .02 .10
222 Vince Newsome RC .01 .05
223 Thomas Benson RC .01 .05
224 Kevin Murphy .01 .05
225 Henry Ellard .02 .10
226 Richard Johnson .01 .05
227 Jim Skow .01 .05
228 Keith Jones .01 .05
229 Dave Brown DB .01 .05
230 Marcus Allen .08 .25
231 Steve Walsh .02 .10
232 Jim Harbaugh .08 .25
233 Mel Gray .02 .10
234 David Treadwell .01 .05
235 John Offerdahl .01 .05
236 Gary Reasons .01 .05
237 Tim Krumrie .01 .05
238 Dave Duerson .01 .05
239 Gary Clark UER .08 .25
(Stats read 1988,
not 1989)
240 Mark Jackson .01 .05
241 Mark Murphy .01 .05
242 Jerry Holmes .01 .05
243 Tim McGee .01 .05
244 Mike Tomczak .02 .10
245 Sterling Sharpe UER .08 .25
(Broke 47-yard-old
record, should be year)
246 Bennie Blades .01 .05
247 Ken Harvey RC UER .08 .25
(Sacks and fumble
recovery listings
are switched; dis-
appointing misspelled)
248 Ron Heller .01 .05
249 Louis Lipps .02 .10
250 Wade Wilson .02 .10
251 Freddie Joe Nunn .01 .05
252 Jerome Brown UER .01 .05
('89 stats show 2 fum-
ble rec., should be 1)
253 Myron Guyton .01 .05
254 Nate Odomes RC .02 .10
255 Rod Woodson .08 .25
256 Cornelius Bennett .02 .10
257 Keith Woodside .01 .05
258 Jeff Uhlenhake UER .01 .05
(Text calls him Ron)
259 Harry Hamilton .01 .05
260 Mark Bavaro .01 .05
261 Vinny Testaverde .02 .10
262 Steve DeBerg .01 .05
263 Steve Wisniewski UER .02 .10
(Drafted by Dallas,
not the Raiders)
264 Pete Mandley .01 .05
265 Tim Harris .01 .05
266 Jack Trudeau .01 .05
267 Mark Kelso .01 .05
268 Brian Noble .01 .05
269 Jessie Tuggle RC .01 .05
270 Ken O'Brien .01 .05
271 David Little .01 .05
272 Pete Stoyanovich .01 .05
273 Odessa Turner RC .01 .05
274 Anthony Toney .01 .05
275 Tunch Ilkin .01 .05
276 Carl Lee .01 .05
277 Hart Lee Dykes .01 .05
278 Al Noga .01 .05
279 Greg Lloyd .08 .25
280 Billy Joe Tolliver .01 .05
281 Kirk Lowdermilk .01 .05
282 Earl Ferrell .01 .05
283 Eric Sievers RC .01 .05
284 Steve Jordan .01 .05
285 Burt Grossman .01 .05
286 Johnny Rembert .01 .05
287 Jeff Jaeger RC .01 .05
288 James Hasty .01 .05
289 Tony Mandarich DP .01 .05
290 Chris Singleton RC .01 .05
291 Lynn James RC .01 .05
292 Andre Ware RC .08 .25
293 Ray Agnew RC .01 .05
294 Joel Smeenge RC .01 .05
295 Marc Spindler RC .01 .05
296 Renaldo Turnbull RC .01 .05
297 Reggie Rembert RC .01 .05
298 Jeff Alm RC .01 .05
299 Cortez Kennedy RC .08 .25
300 Blair Thomas RC .02 .10
301 Pat Terrell RC .01 .05
302 Junior Seau RC .50 1.25
303 Mo Elewonibi RC .01 .05
304 Tony Bennett RC .08 .25
305 Percy Snow RC .01 .05
306 Richmond Webb RC .01 .05
307 R.Hampton RC .08 .25
308 Barry Foster RC .08 .25
309 John Friesz RC .08 .25
310 Ben Smith RC .01 .05
311 Joe Montana HG .20 .50
312 Jim Everett HG .02 .10
313 Mark Rypien HG .02 .10
314 Phil Simms HG UER .02 .10
(Lists him as playing
in the AFC)
315 Don Majkowski HG .01 .05
316 Boomer Esiason HG .01 .05
317 Warren Moon HG .08 .25
(Moon on card)
318 Jim Kelly HG .08 .25
319 Bernie Kosar HG UER .02 .10
(Word just is mis-
spelled as justs)
320 Dan Marino HG UER .20 .50
(Text says 378 com-
pletions in 1984,
should be 1986)
321 Christian Okoye GF .01 .05
322 Thurman Thomas GF .08 .25
323 James Brooks GF .02 .10
324 Bobby Humphrey GF .01 .05
325 Barry Sanders GF .25 .60
326 Neal Anderson GF .01 .05
327 Dalton Hilliard GF .01 .05
328 Greg Bell GF .01 .05
329 Roger Craig GF UER .02 .10
(Text says 2 TD's in
SB XXIV, should be 1)
330 Bo Jackson GF .10 .30
331 Don Warren .01 .05
332 Rufus Porter .01 .05
333 Sammie Smith .01 .05
334 Lewis Tillman UER .01 .05
(Born 4/16/67, should
be 1966)
335 Michael Walter .01 .05
336 Marc Logan .01 .05
337 Ron Hallstrom RC .01 .05
338 Stanley Morgan .01 .05
339 Mark Robinson .01 .05
340 Frank Reich .08 .25
341 Chip Lohmiller .01 .05
342 Steve Beuerlein .02 .10
343 John L. Williams .01 .05
344 Irving Fryar .08 .25
345 Anthony Carter .02 .10
346 Al Toon .02 .10
347 J.T. Smith .01 .05
348 Pierce Holt RC .01 .05
349 Ferrell Edmunds .01 .05
350 Mark Rypien .02 .10
351 Paul Gruber .01 .05
352 Ernest Givins .02 .10
353 Ervin Randle .01 .05
354 Guy McIntyre .01 .05
355 Webster Slaughter .02 .10
356 Reuben Davis .01 .05
357 Rickey Jackson .02 .10
358 Earnest Byner .01 .05
359 Eddie Brown .01 .05
360 Troy Stradford .01 .05
361 Pepper Johnson .01 .05
362 Ravin Caldwell .01 .05
363 Chris Mohr RC .01 .05
364 Jeff Bryant .01 .05
365 Bruce Collie .01 .05
366 Courtney Hall .01 .05
367 Jerry Olsavsky .01 .05
368 David Galloway .01 .05
369 Wes Hopkins .01 .05
370 Johnny Hector .01 .05
371 Clarence Verdin .01 .05
372 Nick Lowery .01 .05
373 Tim Brown .08 .25
374 Kevin Greene .02 .10
375 Leonard Marshall .01 .05
376 Roland James .01 .05
377 Scott Studwell .01 .05
378 Jarvis Williams .01 .05
379 Mike Saxon .01 .05
380 Kevin Mack .01 .05
381 Joe Kelly .01 .05
382 Tom Thayer RC .01 .05
383 Roy Green .02 .10
384 Michael Brooks RC .01 .05
385 Michael Cofer .01 .05
386 Ken Ruettgers .01 .05
387 Dean Steinkuhler .01 .05
388 Maurice Carthon .01 .05
389 Ricky Sanders .01 .05
390 Winston Moss RC .01 .05
391 Tony Woods .01 .05
392 Keith DeLong .01 .05
393 David Wyman .01 .05
394 Vencie Glenn .01 .05
395 Harris Barton .01 .05
396 Bryan Hinkle .01 .05
397 Derek Kennard .01 .05
398 Heath Sherman RC .01 .05
399 Troy Benson .01 .05
400 Gary Zimmerman .02 .10
401 Mark Duper .02 .10
402 Eugene Lockhart .01 .05
403 Tim Manoa .01 .05
404 Reggie Williams .01 .05
405 Mark Bortz RC .01 .05
406 Mike Kenn .01 .05
407 John Grimsley .01 .05
408 Bill Romanowski RC .40 1.00
409 Perry Kemp .01 .05
410 Norm Johnson .01 .05
411 Broderick Thomas .01 .05
412 Joe Wolf .01 .05
413 Andre Waters .01 .05
414 Jason Staurovsky .01 .05
415 Eric Martin .01 .05
416 Joe Prokop .01 .05
417 Steve Sewell .01 .05
418 Cedric Jones .01 .05
419 Alphonso Carreker .01 .05
420 Keith Willis .01 .05
421 Bobby Butler .01 .05
422 John Roper .01 .05
423 Tim Spencer .01 .05
424 Jesse Sapolu RC .01 .05
425 Ron Wolfley .01 .05
426 Doug Smith .01 .05
427 William Howard .01 .05
428 Keith Van Horne .01 .05
429 Tony Jordan .01 .05
430 Mervyn Fernandez .01 .05
431 Shaun Gayle RC .01 .05
432 Ricky Nattiel .01 .05
433 Albert Lewis .01 .05
434 Fred Banks RC .01 .05
435 Henry Thomas .01 .05
436 Chet Brooks .01 .05
437 Mark Ingram .02 .10
438 Jeff Gossett .01 .05
439 Mike Wilcher .01 .05
440 Deron Cherry UER .01 .05
(Text says 7 cons. Pro
Bowls, but he didn't
play in 1989 Pro Bowl)
441 Mike Rozier .01 .05
442 Jon Hand .01 .05
443 Ozzie Newsome .02 .10
444 Danny Martin .01 .05
445 Luis Sharpe .01 .05
446 Lee Williams .01 .05
447 Chris Martin RC .01 .05
448 Kevin Fagan RC .01 .05
449 Gene Lang .01 .05
450 Greg Townsend .01 .05
451 Robert Lyles .01 .05
452 Eric Hill .01 .05
453 John Teltschik .01 .05
454 Vestee Jackson .01 .05
455 Bruce Reimers .01 .05
456 Butch Rolle RC .01 .05
457 Lawyer Tillman .01 .05
458 Andre Tippett .01 .05
459 James Thornton .01 .05
460 Randy Grimes .01 .05
461 Larry Roberts .01 .05
462 Ron Holmes .01 .05
463 Mike Wise .01 .05
464 Danny Copeland RC .01 .05
465 Bruce Wilkerson RC .01 .05
466 Mike Quick .01 .05
467 Mickey Shuler .01 .05
468 Mike Prior .01 .05
469 Ron Rivera .01 .05
470 Dean Biasucci .01 .05
471 Perry Williams .01 .05
472 Darren Comeaux UER .01 .05
(Front 53, back 52)
473 Freeman McNeil .01 .05
474 Tyrone Braxton .01 .05
475 Jay Schroeder .01 .05
476 Naz Worthen RC .01 .05
477 Lionel Washington .01 .05
478 Carl Zander .01 .05
479 Al(Bubba) Baker .02 .10
480 Mike Merriweather .01 .05
481 Mike Gann .01 .05
482 Brent Williams .01 .05
483 Eugene Robinson .01 .05
484 Ray Horton .01 .05
485 Bruce Armstrong .01 .05
486 John Fourcade .01 .05
487 Lewis Billups .01 .05
488 Scott Davis .01 .05
489 Kenneth Sims .01 .05
490 Chris Chandler .08 .25
491 Mark Lee .01 .05
492 Johnny Meads .01 .05
493 Tim Irwin .01 .05
494 E.J. Junior .01 .05
495 Hardy Nickerson .02 .10
496 Rob McGovern RC .01 .05
497 Fred Strickland RC .01 .05
498 Reggie Rutland RC .01 .05
499 Mel Owens .01 .05
500 Derrick Thomas .08 .25
501 Jerrol Williams .01 .05
502 Maurice Hurst RC .01 .05
503 Larry Kelm RC .01 .05
504 Herman Fontenot .01 .05
505 Pat Beach .01 .05
506 Haywood Jeffires RC .08 .25
507 Neil Smith .08 .25
508 Cleveland Gary .01 .05
509 William Perry .02 .10
510 Michael Carter .01 .05
511 Walker Lee Ashley RC .01 .05
512 Bob Golic .01 .05
513 Danny Villa RC .01 .05
514 Matt Millen .02 .10
515 Don Griffin .01 .05
516 Jonathan Hayes .01 .05
517 Gerald Williams RC .01 .05
518 Scott Fulhage .01 .05
519 Irv Pankey .01 .05
520 Randy Dixon RC .01 .05
521 Terry McDaniel .01 .05
522 Dan Saleaumua .01 .05
523 Darrin Nelson .01 .05
524 Leonard Griffin RC .01 .05
525 Michael Ball RC .01 .05
526 Ernie Jones RC .01 .05
527 Tony Eason UER .01 .05
(Drafted in 1963,
should be 1983)
528 Ed Reynolds .01 .05
529 Gary Hogeboom .01 .05
530 Don Mosebar .01 .05
531 Ottis Anderson .02 .10
532 Bucky Scribner .01 .05
533 Aaron Cox .01 .05
534 Sean Jones .02 .10
535 Doug Flutie .20 .50
536 Leo Lewis .01 .05
537 Art Still .01 .05
538 Matt Bahr .01 .05
539 Keena Turner .01 .05
540 Sammy Winder .01 .05
541 Mike Webster .02 .10
542 Doug Riesenberg RC .01 .05
543 Dan Fike .01 .05
544 Clarence Kay .01 .05
545 Jim Burt .01 .05
546 Mike Horan .01 .05
547 Al Harris .01 .05
548 Maury Buford .01 .05
549 Jerry Robinson .01 .05
550 Tracy Rocker .01 .05
551 Karl Mecklenburg CC .01 .05
552 Lawrence Taylor CC .08 .25
553 Derrick Thomas CC .08 .25
554 Mike Singletary CC .02 .10
555 Tim Harris CC .01 .05
556 Jerry Rice RM .20 .50
557 Art Monk RM .02 .10
558 Mark Carrier WR RM .02 .10
559 Andre Reed RM .02 .10
560 Sterling Sharpe RM .08 .25
561 Herschel Walker GF .02 .10
562 Ottis Anderson GF .02 .10
563 Randall Cunningham HG .02 .10
564 John Elway HG .20 .50
565 David Fulcher AP .01 .05
566 Ronnie Lott AP .02 .10
567 Jerry Gray AP .01 .05
568 Albert Lewis AP .01 .05
569 Karl Mecklenburg AP .01 .05
570 Mike Singletary AP .02 .10
571 Lawrence Taylor AP .08 .25
572 Tim Harris AP .01 .05
573 Keith Millard AP .01 .05
574 Reggie White AP .08 .25
575 Chris Doleman AP .01 .05
576 Dave Meggett AP .02 .10
577 Rod Woodson AP .08 .25
578 Sean Landeta AP .01 .05
579 Eddie Murray AP .01 .05
580 Barry Sanders AP .25 .60
581 Christian Okoye AP .01 .05
582 Joe Montana AP .20 .50
583 Jay Hilgenberg AP .01 .05
584 Bruce Matthews AP .02 .10
585 Tom Newberry AP .01 .05
586 Gary Zimmerman AP .02 .10
587 Anthony Munoz AP .02 .10
588 Keith Jackson AP .02 .10
589 Sterling Sharpe AP .08 .25
590 Jerry Rice AP .20 .50
591 Bo Jackson RB .10 .30
592 Steve Largent RB .08 .25
593 Flipper Anderson RB .01 .05
594 Joe Montana RB .20 .50
595 Franco Harris HOF .02 .10
596 Bob St. Clair HOF .01 .05
597 Tom Landry HOF .02 .10
598 Jack Lambert HOF .02 .10
599 Ted Hendricks HOF .01 .05
UER
(Int. avg. says 12.8,
should be 8.9)
600A Buck Buchanan HOF ERR .02 .10
(Drafted in 1983)
600B Buck Buchanan HOF COR .02 .10
(Drafted in 1963)
601 Bob Griese HOF .02 .10
602 Super Bowl Wrap .01 .05
603A Vince Lombardi UER .07 .20
Lombardi Legend
(Disciplinarian mis-
spelled; no logo for
Curtis Mgt. at bottom)
603B Vince Lombardi UER .07 .20
Lombardi Legend
(Disciplinarian mis-
spelled; logo for
Curtis Mgt. at bottom)
604 Mark Carrier UER .02 .10
(Front 88, back 89)
605 Randall Cunningham .08 .25
606 Percy Snow C90 .01 .05
607 Andre Ware C90 .08 .25
608 Blair Thomas C90 .02 .10
609 Eric Green C90 .01 .05
610 Reggie Rembert C90 .01 .05
611 Richmond Webb C90 .01 .05
612 Bern Brostek C90 .01 .05
613 James Williams C90 .01 .05
614 Mark Carrier DB C90 .02 .10
615 Renaldo Turnbull C90 .01 .05
616 Cortez Kennedy C90 .02 .10
617 Keith McCants C90 .01 .05
618 Anthony Thompson RC .01 .05
619 LeRoy Butler RC .08 .25
620 Aaron Wallace RC .01 .05
621 Alexander Wright RC .01 .05
622 Keith McCants RC .01 .05
623 Jimmie Jones RC UER .01 .05
January misspelled
624 Anthony Johnson RC .08 .25
625 Fred Washington RC .01 .05
626 Mike Bellamy RC .01 .05
627 Mark Carrier DB RC .08 .25
628 Harold Green RC .08 .25
629 Eric Green RC .02 .10
630 Andre Collins RC .01 .05
631 Lamar Lathon RC .02 .10
632 Terry Wooden RC .01 .05
633 Jesse Anderson RC .01 .05
634 Jeff George RC .20 .50
635 Carwell Gardner RC .01 .05
636 Darrell Thompson RC .01 .05
637 Vince Buck RC .01 .05
638 Mike Jones TE RC .01 .05
639 Charles Arbuckle RC .01 .05
640 Dennis Brown RC .01 .05
641 James Williams DB RC .01 .05
642 Bern Brostek RC .01 .05
643 Darion Conner RC .02 .10
644 Mike Fox RC .01 .05
645 Cary Conklin RC .01 .05
646 Tim Grunhard RC .01 .05
647 Ron Cox RC .01 .05
648 Keith Sims RC .01 .05
649 Alton Montgomery RC .01 .05
650 Greg McMurtry RC .01 .05
651 Scott Mitchell RC .08 .25
652 Tim Ryan DE RC .01 .05
653 Jeff Mills RC .01 .05
654 Ricky Proehl RC .08 .25
655 Steve Broussard RC .01 .05
656 Peter Tom Willis RC .01 .05
657 Dexter Carter RC .01 .05
658 Tony Casillas .01 .05
659 Joe Morris .01 .05
660 Greg Kragen .01 .05
B1 Matt Stover .08 .25
B2 Demetrius Davis .01 .05
B3 Ken McMichel .01 .05
B4 Judd Garrett .01 .05
B5 Elliott Searcy .01 .05

1990 Score Hot Cards

COMPLETE SET (10) 10.00 25.00
ONE PER BLISTER PACK
1 Joe Montana 3.00 6.00
2 Bo Jackson .75 1.50
3 Barry Sanders 3.00 6.00
4 Jerry Rice 2.00 4.00
5 Eric Metcalf .30 .75
6 Don Majkowski .20 .50
7 Christian Okoye .30 .75
8 Bobby Humphrey .20 .50
9 Dan Marino 3.00 6.00
10 Sterling Sharpe .60 1.25

1990 Score Supplemental

This 110-card standard size set was issued in the same design as the regular Score issue, but with blue and purple borders. The set included cards of rookies and cards of players who switched teams during the off-season. The set was released through Score's dealer outlets and was available only in complete set form. The key Rookie Card is Emmitt Smith. Other Rookie Cards include Reggie Cobb, Derrick Fenner, Stan Humphries, Johnny Johnson and Rob Moore. The cards are numbered on the back with a "T" suffix.

COMP.FACT.SET (110) 30.00 80.00
1T Marcus Dupree RC .30 .75
2T Jerry Kauric .05 .15
3T Everson Walls .05 .15

4T Elliott Smith	.05	.15
5T Donald Evans RC UER (Misspelled Pittsburg on card back)	.10	.30
6T Jerry Holmes	.05	.15
7T Dan Stryzinski RC	.05	.15
8T Gerald McNeil	.05	.15
9T Rick Tuten RC	.05	.15
10T Mickey Shuler	.05	.15
11T Jay Novacek	.25	.60
12T Eric Williams RC	.05	.15
13T Stanley Morgan	.05	.15
14T Wayne Haddix RC	.05	.15
15T Gary Anderson RB	.05	.15
16T Stan Humphries RC	.25	.60
17T Raymond Clayborn	.05	.15
18T Mark Boyer RC	.05	.15
19T Dave Waymer	.05	.15
20T Andre Rison	.25	.60
21T Daniel Stubbs	.05	.15
22T Mike Rozier	.05	.15
23T Damian Johnson	.05	.15
24T Don Smith RBK RC	.05	.15
25T Max Montoya	.05	.15
26T Terry Kinard	.05	.15
27T Herb Welch	.05	.15
28T Cliff Odom	.05	.15
29T John Kidd	.05	.15
30T Barry Word RC	.05	.15
31T Rich Karlis	.05	.15
32T Mike Baab	.05	.15
33T Ronnie Harmon	.10	.30
34T Jeff Donaldson	.05	.15
35T Riki Ellison	.05	.15
36T Steve Walsh	.10	.30
37T Bill Lewis RC	.05	.15
38T Tim McKyer	.05	.15
39T James Wilder	.05	.15
40T Tony Paige	.05	.15
41T Derrick Fenner RC	.05	.15
42T Thane Gash RC	.05	.15
43T Dave Duerson	.05	.15
44T Clarence Weathers	.05	.15
45T Matt Bahr	.05	.15
46T Alonzo Highsmith	.05	.15
47T Joe Kelly	.05	.15
48T Chris Hinton	.05	.15
49T Bobby Humphery	.05	.15
50T Greg Bell	.05	.15
51T Fred Smerlas	.05	.15
52T Walter Stanley	.05	.15
53T Jim Skow	.05	.15
54T Renaldo Turnbull	.05	.15
55T Bern Brostek	.05	.15
56T Charles Wilson RC	.05	.15
57T Keith McCants	.05	.15
58T Alexander Wright	.10	.30
59T Ian Beckles RC	.05	.15
60T Eric Davis RC	.10	.30
61T Chris Singleton	.05	.15
62T Rob Moore RC	1.00	2.50
63T Darion Conner	.10	.30
64T Tim Grunhard	.05	.15
65T Junior Seau	2.50	6.00
66T Tony Stargell RC	.05	.15
67T Anthony Thompson	.05	.15
68T Cortez Kennedy	.25	.60
69T Darrell Thompson	.05	.15
70T Calvin Williams RC	.25	.60
71T Rodney Hampton	.25	.60
72T Terry Wooden	.05	.15
73T Leo Goeas RC	.05	.15
74T Ken Willis	.05	.15
75T Ricky Proehl	.25	.60
76T Steve Christie RC	.05	.15
77T Andre Ware	.25	.60
78T Jeff George	1.00	2.50
79T Walter Wilson	.05	.15
80T Johnny Bailey RC	.05	.15
81T Harold Green	.10	.30
82T Mark Carrier	.25	.60
83T Frank Cornish	.05	.15
84T James Williams	.05	.15
85T James Francis RC	.05	.15
86T Percy Snow	.05	.15
87T Anthony Johnson	.25	.60
88T Tim Ryan	.05	.15
89T Dan Owens RC	.05	.15
90T Aaron Wallace RC	.05	.15
91T Steve Broussard	.05	.15
92T Eric Green	.05	.15
93T Blair Thomas	.10	.30
94T Robert Blackmon RC	.05	.15
95T Alan Grant RC	.05	.15
96T Andre Collins	.05	.15
97T Dexter Carter	.05	.15
98T Reggie Cobb RC	.05	.15
99T Dennis Brown	.05	.15
100T Kenny Davidson RC	.05	.15
101T Emmitt Smith RC	25.00	50.00
102T Jeff Alm	.05	.15
103T Alton Montgomery	.05	.15
104T Tony Bennett	.25	.60
105T Johnny Johnson RC	.10	.30
106T Leroy Hoard RC	.25	.60
107T Ray Agnew	.05	.15
108T Richmond Webb	.05	.15
109T Keith Sims	.05	.15
110T Barry Foster	.25	.60

1990 Score 100 Hottest

This 100-card standard size set, featuring some of the most popular football stars of 1990, was issued by Score in conjunction with Publications International, which issued an attractive magazine-style publication giving more biographical information about the players featured on the front. These cards have the same photos on the front as the regular issue Score Football cards with the only difference being the numbering on the back of the card.

COMPLETE SET (100)	6.00	15.00
1 Bo Jackson	.15	.40
2 Joe Montana	1.60	4.00
3 Deion Sanders	.40	1.00
4 Dan Marino	1.20	3.00
5 Barry Sanders	1.60	4.00
6 Neal Anderson	.07	.20
7 Phil Simms	.07	.20
8 Bobby Humphrey	.02	.10
9 Roger Craig	.07	.20
10 John Elway	1.20	3.00
11 James Brooks	.07	.20
12 Ken O'Brien	.02	.10
13 Thurman Thomas	.15	.40
14 Troy Aikman	.60	1.50
15 Karl Mecklenburg	.07	.20
16 Dave Krieg	.07	.20
17 Chris Spielman	.07	.20
18 Tim Harris	.02	.10
19 Tim Worley	.02	.10
20 Clay Matthews	.07	.20
21 Lars Tate	.02	.10
22 Hart Lee Dykes	.02	.10
23 Cornelius Bennett	.07	.20
24 Anthony Miller	.07	.20
25 Lawrence Taylor	.07	.20
26 Jay Hilgenberg	.02	.10
27 Tom Rathman	.07	.20
28 Brian Blades	.07	.20
29 David Fulcher	.02	.10
30 Cris Carter	.50	1.25
31 Marcus Allen	.15	.40
32 Eric Metcalf	.15	.40
33 Bruce Smith	.15	.40
34 Jim Kelly	.15	.40
35 Wade Wilson	.02	.10
36 Rich Camarillo	.02	.10
37 Boomer Esiason	.07	.20
38 John Offerdahl	.02	.10
39 Vance Johnson	.02	.10
40 Ronnie Lott	.07	.20
41 Kevin Ross	.02	.10
42 Greg Bell	.07	.20
43 Erik McMillan	.02	.10
44 Mike Singletary	.07	.20
45 Roger Vick	.02	.10
46 Keith Jackson	.15	.40
47 Henry Ellard	.07	.20
48 Gary Anderson RB	.07	.20
49 Art Monk	.07	.20
50 Jim Everett	.07	.20
51 Anthony Munoz	.07	.20
52 Ray Childress	.07	.20
53 Howie Long	.15	.40
54 Chris Hinton	.02	.10
55 John Stephens	.02	.10
56 Reggie White	.15	.40
57 Rodney Peete	.07	.20
58 Don Majkowski	.02	.10
59 Michael Cofer	.02	.10
60 Bubby Brister	.02	.10
61 Jerry Gray	.02	.10
62 Rodney Holman	.02	.10
63 Vinny Testaverde	.07	.20
64 Sterling Sharpe	.15	.40
65 Keith Millard	.02	.10
66 Jim Lachey	.02	.10
67 Dave Meggett	.07	.20
68 Brent Fullwood	.02	.10
69 Bobby Hebert	.07	.20
70 Joey Browner	.02	.10
71 Flipper Anderson	.07	.20
72 Tim McGee	.02	.10
73 Eric Allen	.07	.20
74 Charles Haley	.07	.20
75 Christian Okoye	.02	.10
76 Herschel Walker	.07	.20
77 Kelvin Martin	.02	.10
78 Bill Fralic	.02	.10
79 Leslie O'Neal	.07	.20
80 Bernie Kosar	.07	.20
81 Eric Sievers	.02	.10
82 Timm Rosenbach	.02	.10
83 Steve DeBerg	.07	.20
84 Duane Bickett	.02	.10
85 Chris Doleman	.07	.20
86 Carl Banks	.07	.20
87 Vaughan Johnson	.02	.10
88 Dennis Smith	.02	.10
89 Billy Joe Tolliver	.02	.10
90 Dalton Hilliard	.02	.10
91 John Taylor	.07	.20
92 Mark Rypien	.07	.20
93 Chris Miller	.07	.20
94 Mark Clayton	.07	.20
95 Andre Reed	.15	.40
96 Warren Moon	.15	.40
97 Bruce Matthews	.07	.20
98 Rod Woodson	.15	.40
99 Pat Swilling	.07	.20
100 Jerry Rice	.60	1.50

1990 Score Young Superstars

This 40-card standard size set was issued by Score in 1990 (via a mail-in offer), featuring forty of the leading young football players. This set features a glossy front with the player's photo being surrounded by black borders on the front of the card. The back, meanwhile, features a full color photo of the player along with seasonal and career statistics about the player.

COMPLETE SET (40)	4.00	10.00
1 Barry Sanders	2.40	6.00
2 Bobby Humphrey	.05	.15
3 Ickey Woods	.05	.15
4 Shawn Collins	.05	.15
5 Dave Meggett	.05	.15
6 Keith Jackson	.10	.30
7 Sterling Sharpe	.20	.50
8 Troy Aikman	1.20	3.00
9 Tim McDonald	.05	.15
10 Tim Brown	.40	1.00
11 Trace Armstrong	.05	.15
12 Eric Metcalf UER (Led Bears in rushing, should be Browns)	.10	.30
13 Derrick Thomas	.20	.50
14 Eric Hill	.05	.15
15 Deion Sanders	.60	1.50
16 Steve Atwater	.05	.15
17 Carnell Lake	.05	.15
18 Andre Reed	.10	.30
19 Chris Spielman	.10	.30
20 Eric Allen	.05	.15
21 Erik McMillan	.05	.15
22 Louis Oliver	.05	.15
23 Robert Massey	.05	.15
24 John Roper	.05	.15
25 Burt Grossman	.05	.15
26 Chris Jacke	.05	.15
27 Steve Wisniewski	.05	.15
28 Alonzo Highsmith	.05	.15
29 Mark Carrier WR	.10	.30
30 Bruce Armstrong	.05	.15
31 Jerome Brown	.10	.30
32 Cornelius Bennett	.10	.30
33 Flipper Anderson	.10	.30
34 Brian Blades	.10	.30
35 Anthony Miller	.10	.30
36 Thurman Thomas	.20	.50
37 Chris Miller	.10	.30
38 Aundray Bruce	.05	.15
39 Robert Clark	.05	.15
40 Robert Delpino	.05	.15

1990-91 Score Franco Harris

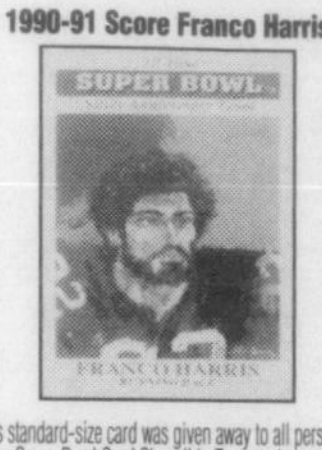

This standard-size card was given away to all persons at the Super Bowl Card Show II in Tampa who acquired Franco Harris' autograph while at the show. It was estimated that between 1500 and 5000 cards were printed. The card features a Leroy Nieman painting of Harris on the front which has the words "All-Time Super Bowl Silver Anniversary Team" on top of the portrait and Franco Harris' name and position underneath the drawing. The back of the card is split horizontally between a shot of Harris celebrating a Super Bowl victory and a brief Super Bowl history of Harris on the back. The card is unnumbered.

1 Franco Harris (Leroy Nieman's artistic rendition)	15.00	30.00

1991 Score Prototypes

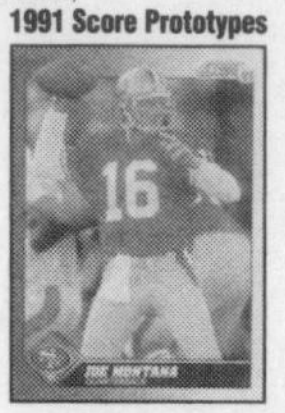

This six-card prototype standard-size set was issued to show the design of the 1991 Score regular series. As with the regular issue, the fronts display color action player photos with borders that shade from white to a solid color, while the horizontal backs carry biographical and statistical information on the left half and a color close-up photo on the right. The prototypes may be distinguished from the regular issues by noting the following minor differences: 1) the prototypes omit the tiny trademark symbol next to the Team NFL logo; 2) the shading of the borders on the front has been reversed on the Singletary and Cunningham cards; 3) statistics are printed in bluish-green on the prototypes rather than green as on the regular issues (except for Taylor, whose statistics are printed in red on his regular card); 4) on the Taylor prototype, his name appears in a blue (rather than a black) stripe on the back; and 5) the Montana, Esiason, and Thomas cards are cropped slightly differently. All cards are numbered on the back; the numbering of the prototype cards corresponds to their regular issue counterparts except for the Taylor card, who is card number 529 in the regular issue.

COMPLETE SET (6)	4.00	10.00
1 Joe Montana	3.20	8.00
4 Lawrence Taylor	.40	1.00
5 Derrick Thomas	.40	1.00
6 Mike Singletary	.40	1.00
7 Boomer Esiason	.40	1.00
12 Randall Cunningham	.60	1.50

1991 Score

The 1991 Score set consists of two series of 345 and 341 for a total of 686 standard size cards. Factory sets include four Super Bowl cards (B1-B4) for a total of 690. Cards were issued in 16-card packs. Subsets include 1991 Rookies (311-319/564-589/591-596/598-612/ 614-616), the players who had plays which resulted in 90 or more yards (320-328), Top Leaders (329-330/662-669), Dream Team (331-345/676-686), Team MVP's (620-647), Crunch Crew (648-654), Sack Attack (655-661), 1991 Hall of Fame (670-674). As part of a promotion, the 11 offensive Dream Team members each signed 500 of their cards. Of this total, 5,478 were randomly inserted in second series packs and 22 were given away in a mail-in sweepstakes. Rookie Cards include Mike Croel, Ricky Ervins, Brett Favre, Alvin Harper, Herman Moore, Mike Pritchard, Jake Reed, Ricky Watters and Harvey Williams.

COMPLETE SET (686)	7.50	20.00
COMP.FACT.SET (690)	12.50	25.00
1 Joe Montana	.50	1.25
2 Eric Allen	.01	.05
3 Rohn Stark	.01	.05
4 Frank Reich	.02	.10
5 Derrick Thomas	.08	.25
6 Mike Singletary	.02	.10
7 Boomer Esiason	.02	.10
8 Matt Millen	.02	.10
9 Chris Spielman	.02	.10
10 Gerald McNeil	.01	.05
11 Nick Lowery	.01	.05
12 Randall Cunningham	.08	.25
13 Marion Butts	.02	.10
14 Tim Brown	.08	.25
15 Emmitt Smith	1.00	2.50
16 Rich Camarillo	.01	.05
17 Mike Merriweather	.01	.05
18 Derrick Fenner	.01	.05
19 Clay Matthews	.02	.10
20 Barry Sanders	.50	1.25
21 James Brooks	.02	.10
22 Alton Montgomery	.01	.05
23 Steve Atwater	.01	.05
24 Ron Morris	.01	.05
25 Brad Muster	.01	.05
26 Andre Rison	.02	.10
27 Brian Brennan	.01	.05
28 Leonard Smith	.01	.05
29 Kevin Butler	.01	.05
30 Tim Harris	.01	.05
31 Jay Novacek	.08	.25
32 Eddie Murray	.01	.05
33 Keith Woodside	.01	.05
34 Ray Crockett RC	.01	.05
35 Eugene Lockhart	.01	.05
36 Bill Romanowski	.01	.05
37 Eddie Brown	.01	.05
38 Eugene Daniel	.01	.05
39 Scott Fulhage	.01	.05
40 Harold Green	.02	.10
41 Mark Jackson	.01	.05
42 Sterling Sharpe	.08	.25
43 Mel Gray	.02	.10
44 Jerry Holmes	.01	.05
45 Allen Pinkett	.01	.05
46 Warren Powers	.01	.05
47 Rodney Peete	.02	.10
48 Lorenzo White	.01	.05
49 Dan Owens	.01	.05
50 James Francis	.01	.05
51 Ken Norton	.02	.10
52 Ed West	.01	.05
53 Andre Reed	.02	.10
54 John Grimsley	.01	.05
55 Michael Cofer	.01	.05
56 Chris Doleman	.01	.05
57 Pat Swilling	.02	.10
58 Jessie Tuggle	.01	.05
59 Mike Johnson	.01	.05
60 Steve Walsh	.01	.05
61 Sam Mills	.01	.05
62 Don Mosebar	.01	.05
63 Jay Hilgenberg	.01	.05
64 Cleveland Gary	.01	.05
65 Andre Tippett	.01	.05
66 Tom Newberry	.01	.05
67 Maurice Hurst	.01	.05
68 Louis Oliver	.01	.05
69 Fred Marion	.01	.05
70 Christian Okoye	.01	.05
71 Marv Cook FSC	.01	.05
72 Darryl Talley	.01	.05
73 Rick Fenney	.01	.05
74 Kelvin Martin	.01	.05
75 Howie Long	.08	.25
76 Steve Wisniewski	.01	.05
77 Karl Mecklenburg	.01	.05
78 Dan Saleaumua	.01	.05
79 Ray Childress	.01	.05
80 Henry Ellard	.02	.10
81 Ernest Givins UER (3rd on Oilers in receiving, not 4th)	.02	.10
82 Ferrell Edmunds	.01	.05
83 Steve Jordan	.01	.05
84 Tony Mandarich	.01	.05
85 Eric Martin	.01	.05
86 Rich Gannon	.08	.25
87 Irving Fryar	.02	.10
88 Tom Rathman	.01	.05
89 Dan Hampton	.02	.10
90 Barry Word	.01	.05
91 Kevin Greene	.02	.10
92 Sean Landeta	.01	.05
93 Trace Armstrong	.01	.05
94 Dennis Byrd	.01	.05
95 Timm Rosenbach	.01	.05
96 Anthony Toney	.01	.05
97 Tim Krumrie	.01	.05
98 Jerry Ball	.01	.05
99 Tim Green	.01	.05
100 Bo Jackson	.10	.30
101 Myron Guyton	.01	.05
102 Mike Mularkey	.01	.05
103 Jerry Gray	.01	.05
104 Scott Stephen RC	.01	.05
105 Anthony Bell	.01	.05
106 Lomas Brown	.01	.05
107 David Little	.01	.05
108 Brad Baxter FSC	.01	.05
109 Freddie Joe Nunn	.01	.05
110 Dave Meggett	.02	.10
111 Mark Rypien	.02	.10
112 Warren Williams	.01	.05
113 Ron Rivera	.01	.05
114 Terance Mathis	.02	.10
115 Anthony Munoz	.02	.10
116 Jeff Bryant	.01	.05
117 Issiac Holt	.01	.05
118 Steve Sewell	.01	.05
119 Tim Newton RC	.01	.05
120 Emile Harry	.01	.05
121 Gary Anderson K	.01	.05
122 Mark Lee	.01	.05
123 Alfred Anderson	.01	.05
124 Anthony Blaylock	.01	.05
125 Earnest Byner	.01	.05
126 Bill Maas	.01	.05
127 Keith Taylor	.01	.05
128 Cliff Odom	.01	.05
129 Bob Golic	.01	.05
130 Bart Oates	.01	.05
131 Jim Arnold	.01	.05
132 Jeff Herrod	.01	.05
133 Bruce Armstrong	.01	.05
134 Craig Heyward	.02	.10
135 Joey Browner	.01	.05
136 Darren Comeaux	.01	.05
137 Pat Beach	.01	.05
138 Dalton Hilliard	.01	.05
139 David Treadwell	.01	.05
140 Gary Anderson RB	.01	.05
141 Eugene Robinson	.01	.05
142 Scott Case	.01	.05
143 Paul Farren	.01	.05
144 Gill Fenerty	.01	.05
145 Tim Irwin	.01	.05
146 Norm Johnson	.01	.05
147 Willie Gault	.02	.10
148 Clarence Verdin	.01	.05
149 Jeff Uhlenhake	.01	.05
150 Erik McMillan	.01	.05
151 Kevin Ross	.01	.05
152 Pepper Johnson	.01	.05
153 Bryan Hinkle	.01	.05
154 Gary Clark	.08	.25
155 Robert Delpino	.01	.05
156 Doug Smith	.01	.05
157 Chris Martin	.01	.05
158 Ray Berry	.01	.05
159 Steve Christie	.01	.05
160 Don Smith RB	.01	.05
161 Greg McMurtry	.01	.05
162 Jack Del Rio	.02	.10
163 Floyd Dixon	.01	.05
164 Buford McGee	.01	.05
165 Brett Maxie	.01	.05
166 Morten Andersen	.01	.05
167 Kent Hull	.01	.05
168 Skip McClendon	.01	.05
169 Keith Sims	.01	.05
170 Leonard Marshall	.01	.05
171 Tony Woods	.01	.05
172 Byron Evans	.01	.05
173 Rob Burnett RC	.02	.10
174 Tory Epps	.01	.05
175 Toi Cook RC	.01	.05
176 John Elliott	.01	.05
177 Tommie Agee	.01	.05
178 Keith Van Horne	.01	.05
179 Dennis Smith	.01	.05
180 James Lofton	.02	.10
181 Art Monk	.02	.10
182 Anthony Carter	.02	.10
183 Louis Lipps	.01	.05
184 Bruce Hill	.01	.05
185 Michael Young	.01	.05
186 Eric Green	.01	.05
187 Barney Bussey RC	.01	.05
188 Curtis Duncan	.01	.05
189 Robert Awalt	.01	.05
190 Johnny Johnson	.01	.05
191 Jeff Cross	.01	.05
192 Keith McKeller	.01	.05
193 Robert Brown	.01	.05
194 Vincent Brown	.01	.05
195 Calvin Williams	.02	.10
196 Sean Jones	.02	.10
197 Willie Drewrey	.01	.05
198 Bubba McDowell	.01	.05
199 Al Noga	.01	.05
200 Ronnie Lott	.02	.10
201 Warren Moon	.08	.25
202 Chris Hinton	.01	.05
203 Jim Sweeney	.01	.05
204 Wayne Haddix	.01	.05
205 Tim Jorden RC	.01	.05
206 Marvin Allen	.01	.05
207 Jim Morrissey RC	.01	.05
208 Ben Smith	.01	.05
209 William White	.01	.05
210 Jim C. Jensen	.01	.05
211 Doug Reed	.01	.05
212 Ethan Horton	.01	.05
213 Chris Jacke	.01	.05
214 Johnny Hector	.01	.05
215 Drew Hill UER	.01	.05
216 Roy Green	.01	.05
217 Dean Steinkuhler	.01	.05
218 Cedric Mack	.01	.05
219 Chris Miller	.02	.10
220 Keith Byars	.01	.05
221 Lewis Billups	.01	.05
222 Roger Craig	.02	.10
223 Shaun Gayle	.01	.05
224 Mike Rozier	.01	.05
225 Troy Aikman	.30	.75
226 Bobby Humphrey	.01	.05
227 Eugene Marve	.01	.05
228 Michael Carter	.01	.05
229 Richard Johnson CB RC	.01	.05
230 Billy Joe Tolliver	.01	.05
231 Mark Murphy	.01	.05
232 John L. Williams	.01	.05
233 Ronnie Harmon	.01	.05
234 Thurman Thomas	.08	.25
235 Martin Mayhew	.01	.05
236 Richmond Webb	.01	.05
237 Gerald Riggs UER (Earnest Byner misspelled as Ernest)	.02	.10
238 Mike Prior	.01	.05
239 Mike Gann	.01	.05
240 Alvin Walton	.01	.05
241 Tim McGee	.01	.05
242 Bruce Matthews	.02	.10
243 Johnny Holland	.01	.05
244 Martin Bayless	.01	.05
245 Eric Metcalf	.02	.10
246 John Alt	.01	.05
247 Max Montoya	.01	.05
248 Rod Bernstine	.01	.05
249 Paul Gruber	.01	.05
250 Charles Haley	.02	.10
251 Scott Norwood	.01	.05
252 Michael Haddix	.01	.05
253 Ricky Sanders	.01	.05
254 Ervin Randle	.01	.05
255 Duane Bickett	.01	.05
256 Mike Munchak	.02	.10
257 Keith Jones	.01	.05
258 Riki Ellison	.01	.05
259 Vince Newsome	.01	.05
260 Lee Williams	.01	.05
261 Steve Smith	.01	.05
262 Sam Clancy	.01	.05
263 Pierce Holt	.01	.05
264 Jim Harbaugh	.08	.25
265 Dino Hackett	.01	.05
266 Andy Heck	.01	.05
267 Leo Goeas	.01	.05
268 Russ Grimm	.02	.10
269 Gill Byrd	.01	.05
270 Neal Anderson	.02	.10
271 Jackie Slater	.01	.05
272 Joe Nash	.01	.05
273 Todd Bowles	.01	.05
274 D.J. Dozier	.01	.05
275 Kevin Fagan	.01	.05
276 Don Warren	.01	.05
277 Jim Jeffcoat	.01	.05
278 Bruce Smith	.08	.25
279 Cortez Kennedy	.08	.25
280 Thane Gash	.01	.05
281 Perry Kemp	.01	.05
282 John Taylor	.02	.10
283 Stephone Paige	.01	.05
284 Paul Skansi	.01	.05
285 Shawn Collins	.01	.05
286 Mervyn Fernandez	.01	.05
287 Daniel Stubbs	.01	.05
288 Chip Lohmiller	.01	.05
289 Brian Blades	.02	.10
290 Mark Carrier WR	.08	.25
291 Carl Zander	.01	.05
292 David Wyman	.01	.05
293 Jeff Bostic	.01	.05
294 Irv Pankey	.01	.05
295 Keith Millard	.01	.05
296 Jamie Mueller	.01	.05
297 Bill Fralic	.01	.05
298 Wendell Davis FSC	.01	.05
299 Ken Clarke	.01	.05
300 Wymon Henderson	.01	.05
301 Jeff Campbell	.01	.05
302 Cody Carlson RC	.01	.05
303 Matt Brock RC	.01	.05
304 Maurice Carthon	.01	.05
305 Scott Mersereau RC	.01	.05
306 Steve Wright RC	.01	.05
307 J.B. Brown	.01	.05
308 Ricky Reynolds	.01	.05
309 Darryl Pollard	.01	.05
310 Donald Evans	.01	.05
311 Nick Bell RC	.01	.05
312 Pat Harlow RC	.01	.05
313 Dan McGwire RC	.01	.05
314 Mike Dumas RC	.01	.05
315 Mike Croel RC	.01	.05
316 Chris Smith RC	.01	.05
317 Kenny Walker RC	.01	.05
318 Todd Lyght RC	.01	.05
319 Mike Stonebreaker	.01	.05
320 Randall Cunningham 90	.02	.10
321 Terance Mathis 90	.08	.25
322 Gaston Green 90	.01	.05
323 Johnny Bailey 90	.01	.05
324 Donnie Elder 90	.01	.05
325 Dwight Stone 90 UER	.01	.05
326 J.J.Birden RC	.02	.10
327 Alexander Wright 90	.01	.05
328 Eric Metcalf 90	.02	.10
329 Andre Rison TL	.02	.10
330 Warren Moon TL UER (Not Blanda's record, should be Van Brocklin)	.02	.10
331 Steve Tasker DT	.01	.05
332 Mel Gray DT	.02	.10
333 Nick Lowery DT	.01	.05
334 Sean Landeta DT	.01	.05
335 David Fulcher DT	.01	.05
336 Joey Browner DT	.01	.05
337 Albert Lewis DT	.01	.05
338 Rod Woodson DT	.02	.10
339 Shane Conlan DT	.01	.05
340 Pepper Johnson DT	.01	.05
341 Chris Spielman DT	.01	.05
342 Derrick Thomas DT	.02	.10
343 Ray Childress DT	.01	.05
344 Reggie White DT	.02	.10
345 Bruce Smith DT	.02	.10
346 Darrell Green	.01	.05
347 Ray Bentley	.01	.05
348 Herschel Walker	.02	.10
349 Rodney Holman	.01	.05
350 Al Toon	.02	.10
351 Harry Hamilton	.01	.05
352 Albert Lewis	.01	.05
353 Renaldo Turnbull	.01	.05
354 Junior Seau	.08	.25
355 Merril Hoge	.01	.05
356 Shane Conlan	.01	.05
357 Jay Schroeder	.01	.05
358 Steve Broussard	.01	.05
359 Mark Bavaro	.01	.05
360 Jim Lachey	.01	.05
361 Greg Townsend	.01	.05
362 Dave Krieg	.02	.10
363 Jessie Hester	.01	.05
364 Steve Tasker	.02	.10
365 Ron Hall	.01	.05
366 Pat Leahy	.01	.05
367 Jim Everett	.02	.10
368 Felix Wright	.01	.05
369 Ricky Proehl	.01	.05
370 Anthony Miller	.02	.10
371 Keith Jackson	.02	.10
372 Pete Stoyanovich	.01	.05
373 Tommy Kane	.01	.05
374 Richard Johnson	.01	.05
375 Randall McDaniel	.02	.10
376 John Stephens	.01	.05
377 Haywood Jeffires	.02	.10
378 Rodney Hampton	.08	.25
379 Tim Grunhard	.01	.05
380 Jerry Rice	.30	.75
381 Ken Harvey	.02	.10
382 Vaughan Johnson	.01	.05
383 J.T. Smith	.01	.05
384 Carnell Lake	.01	.05
385 Dan Marino	.50	1.25
386 Kyle Clifton	.01	.05
387 Wilber Marshall	.01	.05
388 Pete Holohan	.01	.05
389 Gary Plummer	.01	.05
390 William Perry	.02	.10
391 Mark Robinson	.01	.05
392 Nate Odomes	.01	.05
393 Ickey Woods	.01	.05
394 Reyna Thompson	.01	.05
395 Deion Sanders	.15	.40
396 Harris Barton	.01	.05
397 Sammie Smith	.01	.05
398 Vinny Testaverde	.02	.10
399 Ray Donaldson	.01	.05
400 Tim McKyer	.01	.05
401 Nesby Glasgow	.01	.05
402 Brent Williams	.01	.05
403 Rob Moore	.08	.25
404 Bubby Brister	.01	.05
405 David Fulcher	.01	.05
406 Reggie Cobb	.01	.05
407 Jerome Brown	.01	.05
408 Erik Howard	.01	.05
409 Tony Paige	.01	.05
410 John Elway	.50	1.25
411 Charles Mann	.01	.05
412 Luis Sharpe	.01	.05
413 Hassan Jones	.01	.05
414 Frank Minnifield	.01	.05
415 Steve DeBerg	.01	.05
416 Mark Carrier DB	.02	.10
417 Brian Jordan	.02	.10
418 Reggie Langhorne	.01	.05
419 Don Majkowski	.01	.05
420 Marcus Allen	.08	.25
421 Michael Brooks	.01	.05
422 Vai Sikahema	.01	.05
423 Dermontti Dawson	.01	.05
424 Jacob Green	.01	.05
425 Flipper Anderson	.01	.05
426 Bill Brooks	.01	.05
427 Keith McCants	.01	.05
428 Ken O'Brien	.01	.05
429 Fred Barnett	.08	.25
430 Mark Duper	.02	.10
431 Mark Kelso	.01	.05
432 Leslie O'Neal	.02	.10
433 Ottis Anderson	.02	.10
434 Jesse Sapolu	.01	.05
435 Gary Zimmerman	.02	.10
436 Kevin Porter	.01	.05
437 Anthony Thompson	.01	.05
438 Robert Clark	.01	.05
439 Chris Warren	.08	.25
440 Gerald Williams	.01	.05
441 Jim Skow	.01	.05
442 Rick Donnelly	.01	.05
443 Guy McIntyre	.01	.05
444 Jeff Lageman	.01	.05
445 John Offerdahl	.01	.05
446 Clyde Simmons	.01	.05
447 John Kidd	.01	.05
448 Chip Banks	.01	.05
449 Johnny Meads	.01	.05
450 Rickey Jackson	.01	.05
451 Lee Johnson	.01	.05
452 Michael Irvin	.08	.25
453 Leon Seals	.01	.05
454 Darrell Thompson	.01	.05
455 Everson Walls	.01	.05
456 LeRoy Butler	.02	.10
457 Marcus Dupree	.08	.25
458 Kirk Lowdermilk	.01	.05
459 Chris Singleton	.01	.05
460 Seth Joyner	.02	.10
461 Rueben Mayes UER	.01	.05
462 Ernie Jones	.01	.05
463 Greg Kragen	.01	.05
464 Bennie Blades	.01	.05
465 Mark Bortz	.01	.05
466 Tony Stargell	.01	.05
467 Mike Cofer	.01	.05
468 Randy Grimes	.01	.05
469 Tim Worley	.01	.05
470 Kevin Mack	.01	.05
471 Wes Hopkins	.01	.05
472 Will Wolford	.01	.05
473 Sam Seale	.01	.05
474 Jim Ritcher	.01	.05
475 Jeff Hostetler	.08	.25
476 Mitchell Price RC	.01	.05
477 Ken Lanier	.01	.05
478 Naz Worthen	.01	.05
479 Ed Reynolds	.01	.05
480 Mark Clayton	.02	.10
481 Matt Bahr	.01	.05
482 Gary Reasons	.01	.05
483 David Szott RC	.01	.05
484 Barry Foster	.02	.10
485 Bruce Reimers	.01	.05
486 Dean Biasucci	.01	.05
487 Cris Carter	.20	.50
488 Albert Bentley	.01	.05
489 Robert Massey	.01	.05
490 Al Smith	.01	.05
491 Greg Lloyd	.08	.25
492 Steve McMichael UER (Photo on back actually Dan Hampton)	.02	.10
493 Jeff Wright RC	.01	.05
494 Scott Davis	.01	.05
495 Freeman McNeil	.01	.05
496 Simon Fletcher	.01	.05
497 Terry McDaniel	.01	.05
498 Heath Sherman	.01	.05
499 Jeff Jaeger	.01	.05
500 Mark Collins	.01	.05
501 Tim Goad	.01	.05
502 Jeff George	.08	.25
503 Jimmie Jones	.01	.05
504 Henry Thomas	.01	.05
505 Steve Young	.30	.75
506 William Roberts	.01	.05
507 Neil Smith	.08	.25
508 Mike Saxon	.01	.05
509 Johnny Bailey	.01	.05
510 Broderick Thomas	.01	.05
511 Wade Wilson	.02	.10
512 Hart Lee Dykes	.01	.05
513 Hardy Nickerson	.02	.10
514 Tim McDonald	.01	.05
515 Frank Cornish	.01	.05
516 Jarvis Williams	.01	.05
517 Carl Lee	.01	.05
518 Carl Banks	.01	.05
519 Mike Golic	.01	.05
520 Brian Noble	.01	.05
521 James Hasty	.01	.05
522 Bubba Paris	.01	.05
523 Kevin Walker RC	.01	.05
524 William Fuller	.02	.10
525 Eddie Anderson	.01	.05
526 Roger Ruzek	.01	.05
527 Robert Blackmon	.01	.05
528 Vince Buck	.01	.05
529 Lawrence Taylor	.08	.25
530 Reggie Roby	.01	.05
531 Doug Riesenberg	.01	.05
532 Joe Jacoby	.01	.05
533 Kirby Jackson RC	.01	.05
534 Robb Thomas	.01	.05
535 Don Griffin	.01	.05
536 Andre Waters	.01	.05
537 Marc Logan	.01	.05
538 James Thornton	.01	.05
539 Ray Agnew	.01	.05
540 Frank Stams	.01	.05
541 Brett Perriman	.08	.25
542 Andre Ware	.02	.10
543 Kevin Haverdink	.01	.05
544 Greg Jackson RC	.01	.05
545 Tunch Ilkin	.01	.05
546 Dexter Carter	.01	.05
547 Rod Woodson	.08	.25
548 Donnell Woolford	.01	.05
549 Mark Boyer	.01	.05
550 Jeff Query	.01	.05
551 Burt Grossman	.01	.05
552 Mike Kenn	.01	.05
553 Richard Dent	.02	.10
554 Gaston Green	.01	.05
555 Phil Simms	.02	.10
556 Brent Jones	.08	.25
557 Ronnie Lippett	.01	.05
558 Mike Horan	.01	.05
559 Danny Noonan	.01	.05
560 Reggie White	.08	.25
561 Rufus Porter	.01	.05
562 Aaron Wallace	.01	.05
563 Vance Johnson	.01	.05
564A Aaron Craver ERR RC	.01	.05
564B Aaron Craver COR RC	.01	.05
565A Russell Maryland ERR RC No Highlight Line	.08	.25
565B Russell Maryland COR RC	.08	.25
566 Paul Justin RC	.01	.05
567 Walter Dean	.01	.05
568 Herman Moore RC	.08	.25
569 Bill Musgrave RC	.01	.05
570 Rob Carpenter RC	.01	.05
571 Greg Lewis RC	.01	.05
572 Ed King RC	.01	.05
573 Ernie Mills RC	.02	.10
574 Jake Reed RC	.20	.50
575 Ricky Watters RC	.60	1.50
576 Derek Russell RC	.01	.05
577 Shawn Moore RC	.01	.05
578 Eric Bieniemy RC	.01	.05
579 Chris Zorich RC	.08	.25
580 Scott Miller	.01	.05
581 Jarrod Bunch RC	.01	.05
582 Ricky Ervins RC	.02	.10
583 Browning Nagle RC	.01	.05
584 Eric Turner RC	.02	.10
585 William Thomas RC	.01	.05
586 Stanley Richard RC	.01	.05
587 Adrian Cooper RC	.01	.05
588 Harvey Williams RC	.08	.25
589 Alvin Harper RC	.08	.25
590 John Carney	.01	.05
591 Mark Vander Poel RC	.01	.05
592 Mike Pritchard RC	.08	.25
593 Eric Moten RC	.01	.05
594 Moe Gardner RC	.01	.05

595 Wesley Carroll RC	.01	.05
596 Eric Swann RC	.08	.25
597 Joe Kelly	.01	.05
598 Steve Jackson RC	.01	.05
599 Kelvin Pritchett RC	.02	.10
600 Jesse Campbell RC	.01	.05
601 Darryll Lewis RC UER (Name misspelled Darryl)	.02	.10
602 Howard Griffith	.01	.05
603 Blaise Bryant	.01	.05
604 Vinnie Clark RC	.01	.05
605 Mel Agee RC	.01	.05
606 Bobby Wilson RC	.01	.05
607 Kevin Donnalley RC	.01	.05
608 Randal Hill RC	.02	.10
609 Stan Thomas	.01	.05
610 Mike Heldt	.01	.05
611 Brett Favre RC	3.00	8.00
612 Lawrence Dawsey RC UER (Went to Florida State not Florida)	.02	.10
613 Dennis Gibson	.01	.05
614 Dean Dingman	.01	.05
615 Bruce Pickens RC	.01	.05
616 Todd Marinovich RC	.01	.05
617 Gene Atkins	.01	.05
618 Marcus Dupree	.08	.25
619 Warren Moon (Man of the Year)	.02	.10
620 Joe Montana MVP	.20	.50
621 Neal Anderson MVP	.01	.05
622 James Brooks MVP	.02	.10
623 Thurman Thomas MVP	.02	.10
624 Bobby Humphrey MVP	.01	.05
625 Kevin Mack MVP	.01	.05
626 Mark Carrier WR MVP	.01	.05
627 Johnny Johnson TM	.01	.05
628 Marion Butts MVP	.02	.10
629 Steve DeBerg MVP	.01	.05
630 Jeff George MVP	.02	.10
631 Troy Aikman MVP	.15	.40
632 Dan Marino MVP	.20	.50
633 R.Cunningham MVP	.02	.10
634 Andre Rison MVP	.02	.10
635 Pepper Johnson MVP	.01	.05
636 Pat Leahy MVP	.01	.05
637 Barry Sanders TM	.20	.50
638 Warren Moon MVP	.02	.10
639 Sterling Sharpe TM	.01	.05
640 Bruce Armstrong MVP	.01	.05
641 Bo Jackson MVP	.02	.10
642 Henry Ellard MVP	.02	.10
643 Earnest Byner MVP	.01	.05
644 Pat Swilling MVP	.01	.05
645 John L. Williams MVP	.01	.05
646 Rod Woodson MVP	.02	.10
647 Chris Doleman MVP	.01	.05
648 Joey Browner CC	.01	.05
649 Erik McMillan CC	.01	.05
650 David Fulcher CC	.01	.05
651A Ronnie Lott CC ERR (Front 47, back 42)	.02	.10
651B Ronnie Lott CC COR (Front 47, back 42 is now blacked out)	.02	.10
652 Louis Oliver CC	.01	.05
653 Mark Robinson CC	.01	.05
654 Dennis Smith CC	.01	.05
655 Reggie White SA ERR (listed as a QB)	.02	.10
656 Charles Haley SA	.01	.05
657 Leslie O'Neal SA	.02	.10
658 Kevin Greene SA	.02	.10
659 Dennis Byrd SA	.01	.05
660 Bruce Smith SA	.02	.10
661 Derrick Thomas SA	.02	.10
662 Steve DeBerg TL	.01	.05
663 Barry Sanders TL	.20	.50
664 Thurman Thomas TL	.02	.10
665 Jerry Rice TL	.15	.40
666 Derrick Thomas TL	.02	.10
667 Bruce Smith TL	.02	.10
668 Mark Carrier DB TL	.01	.05
669 Richard Johnson CB TL	.01	.05
670 Jan Stenerud HOF	.01	.05
671 Stan Jones HOF	.01	.05
672 John Hannah HOF	.01	.05
673 Tex Schramm HOF	.01	.05
674 Earl Campbell HOF	.08	.25
675 Emmitt Smith Carrier ROY	.30	.75
676 Warren Moon DT	.02	.10
677 Barry Sanders DT	.20	.50
678 Thurman Thomas DT	.08	.25
679 Andre Reed DT	.02	.10
680 Andre Rison DT	.02	.10
681 Keith Jackson DT	.01	.05
682 Bruce Armstrong DT	.01	.05
683 Jim Lachey DT	.01	.05
684 Bruce Matthews DT	.01	.05
685 Mike Munchak DT	.01	.05
686 Don Mosebar DT	.01	.05
B1 Jeff Hostetler SB	.08	.25
B2 Matt Bahr SB	.01	.05
B3 Ottis Anderson SB	.02	.10
B4 Ottis Anderson SB	.02	.10

1991 Score Dream Team Autographs

COMPLETE SET (11)	200.00	400.00
676 Warren Moon (signed on back)	20.00	50.00
677 Barry Sanders	50.00	120.00
678 Thurman Thomas (signed on front)	20.00	50.00
679 Andre Reed	20.00	50.00
680 Andre Rison	15.00	30.00
681 Keith Jackson (signed on back)	10.00	20.00
682 Bruce Armstrong	10.00	20.00
683 Jim Lachey	10.00	20.00
684 Bruce Matthews	25.00	50.00
685 Mike Munchak	15.00	30.00
686 Don Mosebar	10.00	20.00

1991 Score Hot Rookies

COMPLETE SET (10)	1.50	4.00
ONE PER BLISTER PACK		
1 Dan McGwire	.15	.40
2 Todd Lyght	.15	.40
3 Mike Dumas	.15	.40
4 Pat Harlow	.15	.40
5 Nick Bell	.15	.40
6 Chris Smith	.15	.40
7 Mike Stonebreaker	.15	.40
8 Mike Croel	.15	.40
9 Kenny Walker	.15	.40
10 Rob Carpenter	.15	.40

1991 Score Supplemental

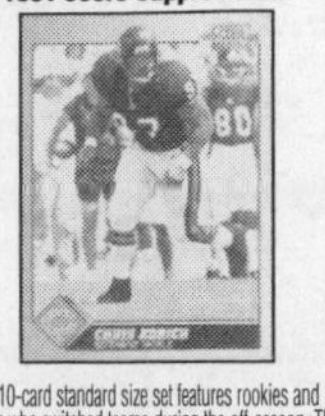

This 110-card standard size set features rookies and players who switched teams during the off-season. The set was issued only as a complete set. The cards are numbered on the back with a "T" suffix. Rookie Cards include Bryan Cox, Merton Hanks, Michael Jackson, Eric Pegram and Leonard Russell.

COMPLETE FACT.SET (110)	1.50	4.00
1T Ronnie Lott	.02	.10
2T Matt Millen	.02	.10
3T Tim McKyer	.01	.05
4T Vince Newsome	.01	.05
5T Gaston Green	.01	.05
6T Brett Perriman	.08	.25
7T Roger Craig	.02	.10
8T Pete Holohan	.01	.05
9T Tony Zendejas	.01	.05
10T Lee Williams	.01	.05
11T Mike Stonebreaker	.01	.05
12T Felix Wright	.01	.05
13T Lonnie Young	.01	.05
14T Hugh Millen RC	.01	.05
15T Roy Green	.01	.05
16T Greg Davis RC	.01	.05
17T Dexter Manley	.01	.05
18T Ted Washington RC	.01	.05
19T Norm Johnson	.01	.05
20T Joe Morris	.01	.05
21T Robert Perryman	.01	.05
22T Mike Iaquaniello RC UER (Free agent in '91, not '87)	.01	.05
23T Gerald Perry UER RC	.01	.05
24T Zeke Mowatt	.01	.05
25T Rich Miano RC	.01	.05
26T Nick Bell	.01	.05
27T Terry Orr RC	.01	.05
28T Matt Stover RC	.08	.25
29T Bubba Paris	.01	.05
30T Ron Brown	.01	.05
31T Don Davey	.01	.05
32T Lee Rouson	.01	.05
33T Terry Hoage UER	.01	.05
34T Tony Covington	.01	.05
35T John Rienstra	.01	.05
36T Charles Dimry RC	.01	.05
37T Todd Marinovich	.01	.05
38T Winston Moss	.01	.05
39T Vestee Jackson	.01	.05
40T Brian Hansen	.01	.05
41T Irv Eatman	.01	.05
42T Jarrod Bunch	.01	.05
43T Kanavis McGhee RC	.01	.05
44T Vai Sikahema	.01	.05
45T Charles McRae RC	.01	.05
46T Quinn Early	.02	.10
47T Jeff Faulkner RC	.01	.05
48T William Frizzell RC	.01	.05
49T John Booty	.01	.05
50T Tim Harris	.01	.05
51T Derek Russell	.01	.05
52T John Flannery RC	.01	.05
53T Tim Barnett RC	.01	.05
54T Alfred Williams RC	.01	.05
55T Dan McGwire	.01	.05
56T Ernie Mills	.01	.05
57T Stanley Richard	.01	.05
58T Huey Richardson RC	.01	.05
59T Jerome Henderson RC	.01	.05
60T Bryan Cox RC	.08	.25
61T Russell Maryland	.02	.10
62T Reginald Jones RC	.01	.05
63T Mo Lewis RC	.02	.10
64T Moe Gardner	.01	.05
65T Wesley Carroll	.01	.05
66T Michael Jackson WR RC	.08	.25
67T Shawn Jefferson RC	.02	.10
68T Chris Zorich	.02	.10
69T Kenny Walker	.01	.05
70T Erric Pegram RC	.08	.25
71T Alvin Harper	.08	.25
72T Harry Colon RC	.01	.05
73T Scott Miller	.01	.05
74T Lawrence Dawsey	.02	.10
75T Phil Hansen RC	.01	.05
76T Roman Phifer RC	.01	.05
77T Greg Lewis	.01	.05
78T Merton Hanks RC	.08	.25
79T James Jones RC	.01	.05
80T Vinnie Clark	.01	.05
81T R.J. Kors	.01	.05
82T Mike Pritchard	.08	.25
83T Stan Thomas	.01	.05
84T Lamar Rogers RC	.01	.05
85T Erik Williams RC	.02	.10
86T Keith Traylor RC	.01	.05
87T Mike Dumas	.01	.05
88T Mel Agee	.01	.05
89T Harvey Williams	.08	.25
90T Todd Lyght	.01	.05
91T Jake Reed	.15	.40
92T Pat Harlow	.01	.05
93T Antone Davis RC	.01	.05
94T Aeneas Williams RC	.08	.25
95T Eric Bieniemy	.01	.05
96T John Kasay RC	.02	.10
97T Robert Wilson RC	.01	.05
98T Ricky Ervins	.02	.10
99T Mike Croel	.01	.05
100T David Lang RC	.01	.05
101T Esera Tuaolo RC	.01	.05
102T Randal Hill	.02	.10
103T Jon Vaughn RC	.01	.05
104T Dave McCloughan	.01	.05
105T David Daniels RC	.01	.05
106T Eric Moten	.01	.05
107T Anthony Morgan RC	.01	.05
108T Ed King	.01	.05
109T Leonard Russell RC	.02	.10
110T Aaron Craver	.01	.05

1991 Score National 10

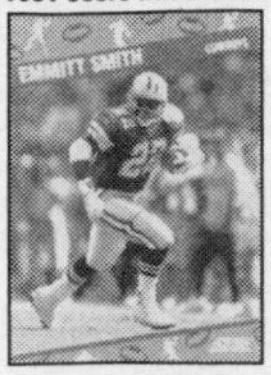

This set contains ten standard-size cards. The front design is distinctively colorful at the top and bottom of the obverse. In the middle of the back the cards are labeled as 12th National Sports Collectors Convention. The cards were given away as a complete set wrapped in its own cello wrapper.

COMPLETE SET (10)	4.00	10.00
1 Emmitt Smith	2.50	6.00
2 Mark Carrier DB	.30	.75
3 Steve Broussard	.20	.50
4 Johnny Johnson	.20	.50
5 Steve Christie	.20	.50
6 Richmond Webb	.20	.50
7 James Francis	.20	.50
8 Jeff George	.40	1.00
9 Rodney Hampton	.50	1.25
10 Calvin Williams	.30	.75

1991 Score Young Superstars

This 40-card standard-size set features some of the leading young players in football. The key player in the set is Emmitt Smith. This set was available from a mail-away offer on 1991 Score Football wax packs.

COMPLETE SET (40)	4.00	10.00
1 Johnny Bailey	.02	.10
2 Johnny Johnson	.02	.10
3 Fred Barnett	.15	.40
4 Keith McCants	.02	.10
5 Brad Baxter	.02	.10
6 Dan Owens	.02	.10
7 Steve Broussard	.02	.10
8 Ricky Proehl	.07	.20
9 Marion Butts	.07	.20
10 Reggie Cobb	.02	.10
11 Dennis Byrd	.07	.20
12 Emmitt Smith	2.50	6.00
13 Mark Carrier DB	.07	.20
14 Keith Sims	.02	.10
15 Dexter Carter	.02	.10
16 Chris Singleton	.02	.10
17 Steve Christie	.07	.20
18 Frank Cornish	.02	.10
19 Timm Rosenbach	.02	.10
20 Sammie Smith	.02	.10
21 Calvin Williams UER (Listed as WR on front, but back says FB)	.07	.20
22 Merril Hoge	.02	.10
23 Hart Lee Dykes	.02	.10
24 Darrell Thompson	.02	.10
25 James Francis	.07	.20
26 John Elliott	.02	.10
27 Jeff George	.40	1.00
28 Broderick Thomas	.02	.10
29 Eric Green	.07	.20
30 Steve Walsh	.07	.20
31 Harold Green	.07	.20
32 Andre Ware	.07	.20
33 Richmond Webb	.02	.10
34 Junior Seau	.30	.75
35 Tim Grunhard	.02	.10
36 Tim Worley	.02	.10
37 Haywood Jeffires	.07	.20
38 Rod Woodson	.15	.40
39 Rodney Hampton	.15	.40
40 David Szott	.02	.10

1992 Score

The 1992 Score football set contains 550 standard-size cards. Cards were issued in 16 and 35-card packs. Topical subsets featured include Draft Pick (476-514), Crunch Crew (515-519), Rookie of the Year (520-523), Little Big Men (524-528), Sack Attack (529-533), Hall of Fame (535-537), and 90 Plus Club (538-547). Rookie Cards include Edgar Bennett, Steve Bono, Terrell Buckley, Amp Lee, Derrick Moore, Michael Timpson and Tommy Vardell.

COMPLETE SET (550)	12.50	25.00
1 Barry Sanders	.75	2.00
2 Pat Swilling	.01	.05
3 Moe Gardner	.01	.05
4 Steve Young	.40	1.00
5 Chris Spielman	.02	.10
6 Richard Dent	.02	.10
7 Anthony Munoz	.02	.10
8 Martin Mayhew	.01	.05
9 Terry McDaniel	.01	.05
10 Thurman Thomas	.08	.25
11 Ricky Sanders	.01	.05
12 Steve Atwater	.01	.05
13 Tony Tolbert	.01	.05
14 Vince Workman	.01	.05
15 Haywood Jeffires	.02	.10
16 Duane Bickett	.01	.05
17 Jeff Uhlenhake	.01	.05
18 Tim McDonald	.01	.05
19 Cris Carter	.20	.50
20 Derrick Thomas	.08	.25
21 Hugh Millen	.01	.05
22 Bart Oates	.01	.05
23 Eugene Robinson	.01	.05
24 Jerrol Williams	.01	.05
25 Reggie White	.08	.25
26 Marion Butts	.01	.05
27 Jim Sweeney	.01	.05
28 Tom Newberry	.01	.05
29 Pete Stoyanovich	.01	.05
30 Ronnie Lott	.02	.10
31 Simon Fletcher	.01	.05
32 Dino Hackett	.01	.05
33 Morten Andersen	.01	.05
34 Clyde Simmons	.01	.05
35 Mark Rypien	.01	.05
36 Greg Montgomery	.01	.05
37 Nate Lewis	.01	.05
38 Henry Ellard	.02	.10
39 Luis Sharpe	.01	.05
40 Michael Irvin	.08	.25
41 Louis Lipps	.01	.05
42 John L. Williams	.01	.05
43 Broderick Thomas	.01	.05
44 Michael Haynes	.02	.10
45 Don Majkowski	.01	.05
46 William Perry	.02	.10
47 David Fulcher	.01	.05
48 Tony Bennett	.01	.05
49 Clay Matthews	.02	.10
50 Warren Moon	.08	.25
51 Bruce Armstrong	.01	.05
52 Harry Newsome	.01	.05
53 Bill Brooks	.01	.05
54 Greg Townsend	.01	.05
55 Tom Rathman	.01	.05
56 Sean Landeta	.01	.05
57 Kyle Clifton	.01	.05
58 Steve Broussard	.01	.05
59 Mark Carrier WR	.02	.10
60 Mel Gray	.02	.10
61 Tim Krumrie	.01	.05
62 Rufus Porter	.01	.05
63 Kevin Mack	.01	.05
64 Todd Bowles	.01	.05
65 Emmitt Smith	1.25	2.50
66 Mike Croel	.01	.05
67 Brian Mitchell	.02	.10
68 Bennie Blades	.01	.05
69 Carnell Lake	.01	.05
70 Cornelius Bennett	.02	.10
71 Darrell Thompson	.01	.05
72 Wes Hopkins	.01	.05
73 Jessie Hester	.01	.05
74 Irv Eatman	.01	.05
75 Marv Cook	.01	.05
76 Tim Brown	.08	.25
77 Pepper Johnson	.01	.05
78 Mark Duper	.01	.05
79 Robert Delpino	.01	.05
80 Charles Mann	.01	.05
81 Brian Jordan	.02	.10
82 Wendell Davis	.01	.05
83 Lee Johnson	.01	.05
84 Ricky Reynolds	.01	.05
85 Vaughan Johnson	.01	.05
86 Brian Blades	.02	.10
87 Sam Seale	.01	.05
88 Ed King	.01	.05
89 Gaston Green	.01	.05
90 Christian Okoye	.01	.05
91 Chris Jacke	.01	.05
92 Rohn Stark	.01	.05
93 Kevin Greene	.02	.10
94 Jay Novacek	.02	.10
95 Chip Lohmiller	.01	.05
96 Cris Dishman	.01	.05
97 Ethan Horton	.01	.05
98 Pat Harlow	.01	.05
99 Mark Ingram	.01	.05
100 Mark Carrier DB	.01	.05
101 Deron Cherry	.01	.05
102 Sam Mills	.01	.05
103 Mark Higgs	.01	.05
104 Keith Jackson	.02	.10
105 Steve Tasker	.02	.10
106 Ken Harvey	.01	.05
107 Bryan Hinkle	.01	.05
108 Anthony Carter	.02	.10
109 Johnny Hector	.01	.05
110 Randall McDaniel	.02	.10
111 Johnny Johnson	.01	.05
112 Shane Conlan	.01	.05
113 Ray Horton	.01	.05
114 Sterling Sharpe	.08	.25
115 Guy McIntyre	.01	.05
116 Tom Waddle	.01	.05
117 Albert Lewis	.01	.05
118 Riki Ellison	.01	.05
119 Chris Doleman	.01	.05
120 Andre Rison	.02	.10
121 Bobby Hebert	.01	.05
122 Dan Owens	.01	.05
123 Rodney Hampton	.02	.10
124 Ron Holmes	.01	.05
125 Ernie Jones	.01	.05
126 Michael Carter	.01	.05
127 Reggie Cobb	.01	.05
128 Esera Tuaolo	.01	.05
129 Wilber Marshall	.01	.05
130 Mike Munchak	.02	.10
131 Cortez Kennedy	.02	.10
132 Lamar Lathon	.01	.05
133 Todd Lyght	.01	.05
134 Jeff Feagles	.01	.05
135 Burt Grossman	.01	.05
136 Mike Cofer	.01	.05
137 Frank Warren	.01	.05
138 Jarvis Williams	.01	.05
139 Eddie Brown	.01	.05
140 John Elliott	.01	.05
141 Jim Everett	.02	.10
142 Hardy Nickerson	.02	.10
143 Eddie Murray	.01	.05
144 Andre Tippett	.01	.05
145 Heath Sherman	.01	.05
146 Ronnie Harmon	.01	.05
147 Eric Metcalf	.02	.10
148 Tony Martin	.02	.10
149 Chris Burkett	.01	.05
150 Andre Waters	.01	.05
151 Ray Donaldson	.01	.05
152 Paul Gruber	.01	.05
153 Chris Singleton	.01	.05
154 Clarence Kay	.01	.05
155 Ernest Givins	.02	.10
156 Eric Hill	.01	.05
157 Jesse Sapolu	.01	.05
158 Jack Del Rio	.01	.05
159 Erric Pegram	.02	.10
160 Joey Browner	.01	.05
161 Marcus Allen	.08	.25
162 Eric Moten	.01	.05
163 Donnell Thompson	.01	.05
164 Chuck Cecil	.01	.05
165 Matt Millen	.02	.10
166 Barry Foster	.02	.10
167 Kent Hull	.01	.05
168 Tony Jones	.01	.05
169 Mike Prior	.01	.05
170 Neal Anderson	.01	.05
171 Roger Craig	.02	.10
172 Felix Wright	.01	.05
173 James Francis	.01	.05
174 Eugene Lockhart	.01	.05
175 Dalton Hilliard	.01	.05
176 Nick Lowery	.01	.05
177 Tim McKyer	.01	.05
178 Lorenzo White	.01	.05
179 Jeff Hostetler	.02	.10
180 Jackie Harris RC	.08	.25
181 Ken Norton	.02	.10
182 Flipper Anderson	.01	.05
183 Don Warren	.01	.05
184 Brad Baxter	.01	.05
185 John Taylor	.02	.10
186 Harold Green	.01	.05
187 James Washington	.01	.05
188 Aaron Craver	.01	.05
189 Mike Merriweather	.01	.05
190 Gary Clark	.08	.25
191 Vince Buck	.01	.05
192 Cleveland Gary	.01	.05
193 Dan Saleaumua	.01	.05
194 Gary Zimmerman	.01	.05
195 Richmond Webb	.01	.05
196 Gary Plummer	.01	.05
197 Willie Green	.01	.05
198 Chris Warren	.08	.25
199 Mike Pritchard	.02	.10
200 Art Monk	.02	.10
201 Matt Stover	.01	.05
202 Tim Grunhard	.01	.05
203 Mervyn Fernandez	.01	.05
204 Mark Jackson	.01	.05
205 Freddie Joe Nunn	.01	.05
206 Stan Thomas	.01	.05
207 Keith McKeller	.01	.05
208 Jeff Lageman	.01	.05
209 Kenny Walker	.01	.05
210 Dave Krieg	.02	.10
211 Dean Biasucci	.01	.05
212 Herman Moore	.08	.25
213 Jon Vaughn	.01	.05
214 Howard Cross	.01	.05
215 Greg Davis	.01	.05
216 Bubby Brister	.01	.05
217 John Kasay	.01	.05
218 Ron Hall	.01	.05
219 Mo Lewis	.01	.05
220 Eric Green	.01	.05
221 Scott Case	.01	.05
222 Sean Jones	.01	.05
223 Winston Moss	.01	.05
224 Reggie Langhorne	.01	.05
225 Greg Lewis	.01	.05
226 Todd McNair	.01	.05
227 Rod Bernstine	.01	.05
228 Joe Jacoby	.01	.05
229 Brad Muster	.01	.05
230 Nick Bell	.01	.05
231 Terry Allen	.08	.25
232 Cliff Odom	.01	.05
233 Brian Hansen	.01	.05
234 William Fuller	.01	.05
235 Issiac Holt	.01	.05
236 Dexter Carter	.01	.05
237 Gene Atkins	.01	.05
238 Pat Beach	.01	.05
239 Tim McGee	.01	.05
240 Dermontti Dawson	.01	.05
241 Dan Fike	.01	.05
242 Don Beebe	.01	.05
243 Jeff Bostic	.01	.05
244 Mark Collins	.01	.05
245 Steve Sewell	.01	.05
246 Steve Walsh	.01	.05
247 Erik Kramer	.02	.10
248 Scott Norwood	.01	.05
249 Jesse Solomon	.01	.05
250 Jerry Ball	.01	.05
251 Eugene Daniel	.01	.05
252 Michael Stewart	.01	.05
253 Fred Barnett	.08	.25
254 Rodney Holman	.01	.05
255 Stephen Baker	.01	.05
256 Don Griffin	.01	.05
257 Will Wolford	.01	.05
258 Perry Kemp	.01	.05
259 Leonard Russell	.02	.10
260 Jeff Gossett	.01	.05
261 Dwayne Harper	.01	.05
262 Vinny Testaverde	.02	.10
263 Maurice Hurst	.01	.05
264 Tony Casillas	.01	.05
265 Louis Oliver	.01	.05
266 Jim Morrissey	.01	.05
267 Kenneth Davis	.01	.05
268 John Alt	.01	.05
269 Michael Zordich RC	.01	.05
270 Brian Brennan	.01	.05
271 Greg Kragen	.01	.05
272 Andre Collins	.01	.05
273 Dave Meggett	.02	.10
274 Scott Fulhage	.01	.05
275 Tony Zendejas	.01	.05
276 Herschel Walker	.02	.10
277 Keith Henderson	.01	.05
278 Johnny Bailey	.01	.05
279 Vince Newsome	.01	.05
280 Chris Hinton	.01	.05
281 Robert Blackmon	.01	.05
282 James Hasty	.01	.05
283 John Offerdahl	.01	.05
284 Wesley Carroll	.01	.05
285 Lomas Brown	.01	.05
286 Neil O'Donnell	.02	.10
287 Kevin Porter	.01	.05
288 Lionel Washington	.01	.05
289 Carlton Bailey RC	.01	.05
290 Leonard Marshall	.01	.05
291 John Carney	.01	.05
292 Bubba McDowell	.01	.05
293 Nate Newton	.01	.05
294 Dave Waymer	.01	.05
295 Rob Moore	.02	.10
296 Earnest Byner	.01	.05
297 Jason Staurovsky	.01	.05
298 Keith McCants	.01	.05
299 Floyd Turner	.01	.05
300 Steve Jordan	.01	.05
301 Nate Odomes	.01	.05
302 Gerald Riggs	.01	.05
303 Marvin Washington	.01	.05
304 Anthony Thompson	.01	.05
305 Steve DeBerg	.01	.05
306 Jim Harbaugh	.08	.25
307 Larry Brown DB	.01	.05
308 Roger Ruzek	.01	.05
309 Jessie Tuggle	.01	.05
310 Al Smith	.01	.05
311 Mark Kelso	.01	.05
312 Lawrence Dawsey	.02	.10
313 Steve Bono RC	.08	.25
314 Greg Lloyd	.02	.10
315 Steve Wisniewski	.01	.05
316 Gill Fenerty	.01	.05
317 Mark Stepnoski	.02	.10
318 Derek Russell	.01	.05
319 Chris Martin	.01	.05
320 Shaun Gayle	.01	.05
321 Bob Golic	.01	.05
322 Larry Kelm	.01	.05
323 Mike Brim RC	.01	.05
324 Tommy Kane	.01	.05
325 Mark Schlereth RC	.01	.05
326 Ray Childress	.01	.05
327 Richard Brown RC	.01	.05
328 Vincent Brown	.01	.05
329 Mike Farr UER (Back of card refers to him as Mel)	.01	.05
330 Eric Swann	.02	.10
331 Bill Fralic	.01	.05
332 Rodney Peete	.02	.10
333 Jerry Gray	.01	.05
334 Ray Berry	.01	.05
335 Dennis Smith	.01	.05
336 Jeff Herrod	.01	.05
337 Tony Mandarich	.01	.05
338 Matt Bahr	.01	.05
339 Mike Saxon	.01	.05
340 Bruce Matthews	.01	.05
341 Rickey Jackson	.01	.05
342 Eric Allen	.01	.05
343 Lonnie Young	.01	.05
344 Steve McMichael	.02	.10
345 Willie Gault	.02	.10
346 Barry Word	.01	.05
347 Rich Camarillo	.01	.05
348 Bill Romanowski	.01	.05
349 Jim Lachey	.01	.05
350 Jim Ritcher	.01	.05
351 Irving Fryar	.02	.10
352 Gary Anderson K	.01	.05
353 Henry Rolling	.01	.05
354 Mark Bortz	.01	.05
355 Mark Clayton	.02	.10
356 Keith Woodside	.01	.05
357 Jonathan Hayes	.01	.05
358 Derrick Fenner	.01	.05
359 Keith Byars	.01	.05
360 Drew Hill	.01	.05
361 Harris Barton	.01	.05
362 John Kidd	.01	.05
363 Aeneas Williams	.02	.10
364 Brian Washington	.01	.05
365 John Stephens	.01	.05
366 Norm Johnson	.01	.05
367 Darryl Henley	.01	.05
368 William White	.01	.05
369 Mark Murphy	.01	.05
370 Myron Guyton	.01	.05
371 Leon Seals	.01	.05
372 Rich Gannon	.08	.25
373 Toi Cook	.01	.05
374 Anthony Johnson	.02	.10
375 Rod Woodson	.08	.25
376 Alexander Wright	.01	.05
377 Kevin Butler	.01	.05
378 Neil Smith	.08	.25
379 Gary Anderson RB	.01	.05
380 Reggie Roby	.01	.05
381 Jeff Bryant	.01	.05
382 Ray Crockett	.01	.05
383 Richard Johnson	.01	.05
384 Hassan Jones	.01	.05
385 Karl Mecklenburg	.01	.05
386 Jeff Jaeger	.01	.05
387 Keith Willis	.01	.05
388 Phil Simms	.02	.10
389 Kevin Ross	.01	.05
390 Chris Miller	.02	.10
391 Brian Noble	.01	.05
392 Jamie Dukes RC	.01	.05
393 George Jamison	.01	.05
394 Rickey Dixon	.01	.05
395 Carl Lee	.01	.05
396 Jon Hand	.01	.05
397 Kirby Jackson	.01	.05
398 Pat Terrell	.01	.05
399 Howie Long	.08	.25
400 Michael Young	.01	.05
401 Keith Sims	.01	.05
402 Tommy Barnhardt	.01	.05
403 Greg McMurtry	.01	.05
404 Keith Van Horne	.01	.05
405 Seth Joyner	.01	.05
406 Jim Jeffcoat	.01	.05
407 Courtney Hall	.01	.05
408 Tony Covington	.01	.05
409 Jacob Green	.01	.05
410 Charles Haley	.02	.10
411 Darryl Talley	.01	.05
412 Jeff Cross	.01	.05
413 John Elway	.75	2.00
414 Donald Evans	.01	.05
415 Jackie Slater	.01	.05
416 John Friesz	.02	.10
417 Anthony Smith	.01	.05
418 Gill Byrd	.01	.05
419 Willie Drewrey	.01	.05
420 Jay Hilgenberg	.01	.05
421 David Treadwell	.01	.05
422 Curtis Duncan	.01	.05
423 Sammie Smith	.01	.05
424 Henry Thomas	.01	.05
425 James Lofton	.02	.10
426 Fred Marion	.01	.05
427 Bryce Paup	.08	.25
428 Michael Timpson RC	.01	.05
429 Reyna Thompson	.01	.05
430 Mike Kenn	.01	.05
431 Bill Maas	.01	.05
432 Quinn Early	.02	.10
433 Everson Walls	.01	.05
434 Jimmie Jones	.01	.05
435 Dwight Stone	.01	.05
436 Harry Colon	.01	.05
437 Don Mosebar	.01	.05
438 Calvin Williams	.02	.10
439 Tom Tupa	.01	.05
440 Darrell Green	.01	.05
441 Eric Thomas	.01	.05
442 Terry Wooden	.01	.05
443 Brett Perriman	.08	.25
444 Todd Marinovich	.01	.05
445 Jim Breech	.01	.05
446 Eddie Anderson	.01	.05
447 Jay Schroeder	.01	.05
448 William Roberts	.01	.05
449 Brad Edwards	.01	.05
450 Tunch Ilkin	.01	.05
451 Ivy Joe Hunter RC	.01	.05
452 Robert Clark	.01	.05
453 Tim Barnett	.01	.05
454 Jarrod Bunch	.01	.05
455 Tim Harris	.01	.05
456 James Brooks	.02	.10
457 Trace Armstrong	.01	.05
458 Michael Brooks	.01	.05
459 Andy Heck	.01	.05
460 Greg Jackson	.01	.05
461 Vance Johnson	.01	.05
462 Kirk Lowdermilk	.01	.05
463 Erik McMillan	.01	.05
464 Scott Mersereau	.01	.05
465 Jeff Wright	.01	.05
466 Mike Tomczak	.01	.05
467 David Alexander	.01	.05
468 Bryan Millard	.01	.05
469 John Randle	.02	.10
470 Joel Hilgenberg	.01	.05
471 Bennie Thompson RC	.01	.05
472 Freeman McNeil	.01	.05
473 Terry Orr RC	.01	.05
474 Mike Horan	.01	.05
475 Leroy Hoard	.02	.10
476 Patrick Rowe RC	.01	.05
477 Siran Stacy RC	.01	.05
478 Amp Lee RC	.01	.05
479 Eddie Blake RC	.01	.05
480 Joe Bowden RC	.01	.05
481 Rod Milstead RC	.01	.05
482 Keith Hamilton RC	.02	.10
483 Darryl Williams RC	.01	.05
484 Robert Porcher RC	.08	.25
485 Ed Cunningham RC	.01	.05
486 Chris Mims RC	.01	.05
487 Chris Hakel RC	.01	.05
488 Jimmy Smith RC	1.50	4.00
489 Todd Harrison RC	.01	.05
490 Edgar Bennett RC	.08	.25
491 Dexter McNabb RC	.01	.05
492 Leon Searcy RC	.01	.05
493 Tommy Vardell RC	.01	.05
494 Terrell Buckley RC	.01	.05
495 Kevin Turner RC	.01	.05
496 Russ Campbell RC	.01	.05
497 Torrance Small RC	.02	.10
498 Nate Turner RC	.01	.05
499 Cornelius Benton RC	.01	.05
500 Matt Elliott RC	.01	.05
501 Robert Stewart RC	.01	.05
502 Muhammad Shamsid-Deen RC	.01	.05
503 George Williams RC	.01	.05
504 Pumpy Tudors RC	.01	.05
505 Matt LaBounty RC	.01	.05
506 Darryl Hardy RC	.01	.05
507 Derrick Moore RC	.02	.10
508 Willie Clay RC	.01	.05
509 Bob Whitfield RC	.01	.05
510 Ricardo McDonald RC	.01	.05
511 Carlos Huerta RC	.01	.05
512 Selwyn Jones RC	.01	.05
513 Steve Gordon RC	.01	.05
514 Bob Meeks RC	.01	.05
515 Bennie Blades CC	.01	.05
516 Andre Waters CC	.01	.05
517 Bubba McDowell CC	.01	.05
518 Kevin Porter CC	.01	.05
519 Carnell Lake CC	.01	.05
520 Leonard Russell ROY	.02	.10
521 Mike Croel ROY	.01	.05
522 Lawrence Dawsey ROY	.01	.05
523 Moe Gardner ROY	.01	.05
524 Steve Broussard LBM	.01	.05
525 Dave Meggett LBM	.01	.05
526 Darrell Green LBM	.01	.05
527 Tony Jones LBM	.01	.05
528 Barry Sanders LBM	.40	1.00
529 Pat Swilling SA	.01	.05
530 Reggie White SA	.02	.10
531 William Fuller SA	.01	.05
532 Simon Fletcher SA	.01	.05
533 Derrick Thomas SA	.02	.10
534 Mark Rypien MOY	.01	.05
535 John Mackey HOF	.01	.05
536 John Riggins HOF	.02	.10
537 Lem Barney HOF	.01	.05
538 Shawn McCarthy 90 RC	.01	.05
539 Al Edwards 90	.01	.05
540 Alexander Wright 90	.01	.05
541 Ray Crockett 90	.01	.05
542 Steve Young 90 and John Taylor 90	.08	.25
543 Nate Lewis 90	.01	.05
544 Dexter Carter 90	.01	.05
545 Reggie Rutland 90	.01	.05
546 Jon Vaughn 90	.01	.05
547 Chris Martin 90	.01	.05
548 Warren Moon HL	.02	.10
549 Super Bowl Highlights	.01	.05
550 Robb Thomas	.01	.05
NNO Dick Butkus Promo	4.00	8.00

1992 Score Dream Team

COMPLETE SET (25)	30.00	60.00
RANDOM INSERTS IN FOIL PACKS		
1 Michael Irvin	.75	2.00
2 Haywood Jeffires	.30	.75
3 Emmitt Smith	8.00	20.00
4 Barry Sanders	6.00	15.00
5 Marv Cook	.15	.40
6 Bart Oates	.15	.40
7 Steve Wisniewski	.15	.40
8 Randall McDaniel	.15	.40
9 Jim Lachey	.15	.40
10 Lomas Brown	.15	.40
11 Reggie White	.75	2.00
12 Clyde Simmons	.15	.40
13 Jerome Brown	.75	2.00
14 Seth Joyner	.15	.40
15 Darryl Talley	.15	.40
16 Karl Mecklenburg	.15	.40
17 Sam Mills	.15	.40
18 Darrell Green	.15	.40
19 Steve Atwater	.15	.40
20 Mark Carrier DB	.15	.40
21 Jeff Gossett UER (Card says Rams, should say Raiders)	.15	.40
22 Chip Lohmiller	.15	.40
23 Mel Gray	.30	.75
24 Steve Tasker	.30	.75
25 Mark Rypien	.15	.40

1992 Score Gridiron Stars

COMPLETE SET (45)	3.00	8.00
1 Barry Sanders	.75	2.00
2 Mike Croel	.01	.05
3 Thurman Thomas	.08	.25
4 Lawrence Dawsey	.02	.10
5 Brad Baxter	.01	.05
6 Moe Gardner	.01	.05
7 Emmitt Smith	1.00	2.50

8 Sammie Smith	.01	.05
9 Rodney Hampton	.02	.10
10 Mark Carrier DB	.01	.05
11 Mo Lewis	.01	.05
12 Andre Rison	.02	.10
13 Eric Green	.01	.05
14 Richmond Webb	.01	.05
15 Johnny Bailey	.01	.05
16 Mike Pritchard	.02	.10
17 John Friesz	.02	.10
18 Leonard Russell	.02	.10
19 Derrick Thomas	.08	.25
20 Ken Harvey	.01	.05
21 Fred Barnett	.08	.25
22 Aeneas Williams	.02	.10
23 Marion Butts	.01	.05
24 Harold Green	.01	.05
25 Michael Irvin	.08	.25
26 Dan Owens	.01	.05
27 Curtis Duncan	.01	.05
28 Rodney Peete	.02	.10
29 Brian Blades	.02	.10
30 Marv Cook	.01	.05
31 Burt Grossman	.01	.05
32 Michael Haynes	.02	.10
33 Bennie Blades	.01	.05
34 Cornelius Bennett	.02	.10
35 Louis Oliver	.01	.05
36 Rod Woodson	.08	.25
37 Steve Wisniewski	.01	.05
38 Neil Smith	.08	.25
39 Gaston Green	.01	.05
40 Jeff Lageman	.01	.05
41 Chip Lohmiller	.01	.05
42 Tim McDonald	.01	.05
43 John Elliott	.01	.05
44 Steve Atwater	.01	.05
45 Flipper Anderson	.01	.05

1992 Score Young Superstars

This 40-card boxed standard-size set features some of the young stars in the NFL. The fronts feature glossy color action player photos inside a green inner border and a purple outer border speckled with black. The player's name appears in white lettering at the top, while the team name is printed at the lower left corner. On a gradated yellow background, the backs carry a color close-up photo, a scouting report feature, career highlights, biography, and statistics.

COMP. FACT SET (40)	2.40	6.00
1 Michael Irvin	.40	1.00
2 Cortez Kennedy	.07	.20
3 Ken Harvey	.02	.10
4 Bubba McDowell	.02	.10
5 Mark Higgs	.02	.10
6 Andre Rison	.15	.40
7 Lamar Lathon	.02	.10
8 Bennie Blades	.02	.10
9 Anthony Johnson	.02	.10
10 Vince Buck	.02	.10
11 Pat Harlow	.02	.10
12 Mike Croel	.02	.10
13 Myron Guyton	.02	.10
14 Curtis Duncan	.02	.10
15 Michael Haynes	.15	.40
16 Alexander Wright	.02	.10
17 Greg Lewis	.02	.10
18 Chip Lohmiller	.02	.10
19 Nate Lewis	.02	.10
20 Rodney Peete	.07	.20
21 Marv Cook	.02	.10
22 Lawrence Dawsey	.02	.10
23 Pat Terrell	.02	.10
24 John Friesz	.07	.20
25 Tony Bennett	.02	.10
26 Gaston Green	.02	.10
27 Kevin Porter	.02	.10
28 Mike Pritchard	.15	.40
29 Keith Henderson	.02	.10
30 Mo Lewis	.02	.10
31 John Randle	.07	.20
32 Aeneas Williams	.07	.20
33 Floyd Turner	.02	.10
34 Neil Smith	.07	.20
35 Tom Waddle	.02	.10
36 Jeff Lageman	.02	.10
37 Cris Carter	1.00	2.50
38 Leonard Russell	.02	.10
39 Terry McDaniel	.02	.10
40 Moe Gardner	.02	.10

1993 Score Samples

This six-card standard-size set was issued to preview the 1993 Score regular series. The fronts feature color action player photos bordered in white. The player's name appears in the bottom white border, while the team name is printed vertically in a team color-coded bar that edges the left side of the picture. On team color-coded and pastel panels, the backs present a color head shot, biography, statistics, and player profile. These cards are also issued as an uncut sheet. In a short yellow bar at the lower right corner, the cards are marked "sample card."

COMPLETE SET (6)	2.40	6.00
1 Barry Sanders	1.60	4.00
2 Moe Gardner	.20	.50
3 Ricky Watters	.40	1.00
4 Todd Lyght	.20	.50
5 Rodney Hampton	.30	.75
6 Curtis Duncan	.20	.50

1993 Score

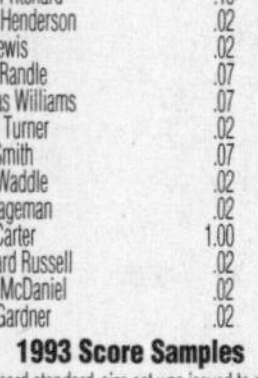

The 1993 Score football set consists of 440 standard-size cards. Cards were issued in 16 and 35-card packs. . Subsets featured are Rookies (306-315), Super Bowl Highlights (411-412), Double Trouble (413-416), Rookie of the Year (417-420), 90 Plus Club (421-430), Highlights (431-434), and Hall of Fame (436-439). The set concludes with a Man of the Year card (440), honoring Steve Young. Each 16-card pack included one Pinnacle card from a 55-card "Men of Autumn" set not found in regular Pinnacle packs. Dealers could receive one of 3,000 limited-edition autographed Dick Butkus cards for each order of 20 foil boxes. Rookie Cards include Jerome Bettis, Drew Bledsoe, Curtis Conway and Garrison Hearst.

COMPLETE SET (440)	6.00	15.00
1 Barry Sanders	.50	1.25
2 Moe Gardner	.01	.05
3 Ricky Watters	.08	.25
4 Todd Lyght	.01	.05
5 Rodney Hampton	.02	.10
6 Curtis Duncan	.01	.05
7 Barry Word	.01	.05
8 Reggie Cobb	.01	.05
9 Mike Kenn	.01	.05
10 Michael Irvin	.08	.25
11 Bryan Cox	.01	.05
12 Chris Doleman	.01	.05
13 Rod Woodson	.08	.25
14 Emmitt Smith	.60	1.50
15 Pete Stoyanovich	.01	.05
16 Steve Young	.30	.75
17 Randall McDaniel	.02	.10
18 Cortez Kennedy	.02	.10
19 Mel Gray	.02	.10
20 Barry Foster	.02	.10
21 Tim Brown	.08	.25
22 Todd McNair	.01	.05
23 Anthony Johnson	.02	.10
24 Nate Odomes	.01	.05
25 Brett Favre	.75	2.00
26 Jack Del Rio	.01	.05
27 Terry McDaniel	.01	.05
28 Haywood Jeffires	.02	.10
29 Jay Novacek	.02	.10
30 Wilber Marshall	.01	.05
31 Richmond Webb	.01	.05
32 Steve Atwater	.01	.05
33 James Lofton	.02	.10
34 Harold Green	.01	.05
35 Eric Metcalf	.02	.10
36 Bruce Matthews	.01	.05
37 Albert Lewis	.01	.05
38 Jeff Herrod	.01	.05
39 Vince Workman	.01	.05
40 John Elway	.60	1.50
41 Brett Perriman	.08	.25
42 Jon Vaughn	.01	.05
43 Terry Allen	.08	.25
44 Clyde Simmons	.01	.05
45 Bennie Thompson	.01	.05
46 Wendell Davis	.01	.05
47 Bobby Hebert	.01	.05
48 John Offerdahl	.01	.05
49 Jeff Graham	.02	.10
50 Steve Wisniewski	.01	.05
51 Louis Oliver	.01	.05
52 Rohn Stark	.01	.05
53 Cleveland Gary	.01	.05
54 John Randle	.02	.10
55 Jim Everett	.02	.10
56 Donnell Woolford	.01	.05
57 Pepper Johnson	.01	.05
58 Irving Fryar	.02	.10
59 Greg Townsend	.01	.05
60 Chris Burkett	.01	.05
61 Johnny Johnson	.01	.05
62 Ronnie Harmon	.01	.05
63 Don Griffin	.01	.05
64 Wayne Martin	.01	.05
65 John L. Williams	.01	.05
66 Brad Edwards	.01	.05
67 Toi Cook	.01	.05
68 Lawrence Dawsey	.01	.05
69 Johnny Bailey	.01	.05
70 Mike Brim	.01	.05
71 Andre Rison	.02	.10
72 Cornelius Bennett	.02	.10
73 Brad Muster	.01	.05
74 Broderick Thomas	.01	.05
75 Tom Waddle	.01	.05
76 Paul Gruber	.01	.05
77 Jackie Harris	.01	.05
78 Kenneth Davis	.01	.05
79 Norm Johnson	.01	.05
80 Jim Jeffcoat	.01	.05
81 Chris Warren	.02	.10
82 Greg Kragen	.01	.05
83 Ricky Reynolds	.01	.05
84 Hardy Nickerson	.02	.10
85 Brian Mitchell	.02	.10
86 Rufus Porter	.01	.05
87 Greg Jackson	.01	.05
88 Seth Joyner	.01	.05
89 Tim Grunhard	.01	.05
90 Tim Harris	.01	.05
91 Sterling Sharpe	.08	.25
92 Daniel Stubbs	.01	.05
93 Rob Burnett	.01	.05
94 Rich Camarillo	.01	.05
95 Al Smith	.01	.05
96 Thurman Thomas	.08	.25
97 Morten Andersen	.01	.05
98 Reggie White	.08	.25
99 Gill Byrd	.01	.05
100 Pierce Holt	.01	.05
101 Tim McGee	.01	.05
102 Rickey Jackson	.01	.05
103 Vince Newsome	.01	.05
104 Chris Spielman	.02	.10
105 Tim McDonald	.01	.05
106 James Francis	.01	.05
107 Andre Tippett	.01	.05
108 Sam Mills	.01	.05
109 Hugh Millen	.01	.05
110 Brad Baxter	.01	.05
111 Ricky Sanders	.01	.05
112 Marion Butts	.01	.05
113 Fred Barnett	.02	.10
114 Wade Wilson	.01	.05
115 Dave Meggett	.01	.05
116 Kevin Greene	.02	.10
117 Reggie Langhorne	.01	.05
118 Simon Fletcher	.01	.05
119 Tommy Vardell	.01	.05
120 Darion Conner	.01	.05
121 Darren Lewis	.01	.05
122 Charles Mann	.01	.05
123 David Fulcher	.01	.05
124 Tommy Kane	.01	.05
125 Richard Brown	.01	.05
126 Nate Lewis	.01	.05
127 Tony Tolbert	.01	.05
128 Greg Lloyd	.02	.10
129 Herman Moore	.08	.25
130 Robert Massey	.01	.05
131 Chris Jacke	.01	.05
132 Keith Byars	.01	.05
133 William Fuller	.01	.05
134 Rob Moore	.02	.10
135 Duane Bickett	.01	.05
136 Jarrod Bunch	.01	.05
137 Ethan Horton	.01	.05
138 Leonard Russell	.02	.10
139 Darryl Henley	.01	.05
140 Tony Bennett	.01	.05
141 Harry Newsome	.01	.05
142 Kelvin Martin	.01	.05
143 Audray McMillian	.01	.05
144 Chip Lohmiller	.01	.05
145 Henry Jones	.01	.05
146 Rod Bernstine	.01	.05
147 Darryl Talley	.01	.05
148 Clarence Verdin	.01	.05
149 Derrick Thomas	.08	.25
150 Raleigh McKenzie	.01	.05
151 Phil Hansen	.01	.05
152 Lin Elliott RC	.01	.05
153 Chip Banks	.01	.05
154 Shannon Sharpe	.08	.25
155 David Williams	.01	.05
156 Gaston Green	.01	.05
157 Trace Armstrong	.01	.05
158 Todd Scott	.01	.05
159 Stan Humphries	.02	.10
160 Christian Okoye	.01	.05
161 Dennis Smith	.01	.05
162 Derek Kennard	.01	.05
163 Melvin Jenkins	.01	.05
164 Tommy Barnhardt	.01	.05
165 Eugene Robinson	.01	.05
166 Tom Rathman	.01	.05
167 Chris Chandler	.02	.10
168 Steve Broussard	.01	.05
169 Wymon Henderson	.01	.05
170 Bryce Paup	.02	.10
171 Kent Hull	.01	.05
172 Willie Davis	.08	.25
173 Richard Dent	.02	.10
174 Rodney Peete	.01	.05
175 Clay Matthews	.02	.10
176 Erik Williams	.01	.05
177 Mike Cofer	.01	.05
178 Mark Kelso	.01	.05
179 Kurt Gouveia	.01	.05
180 Keith McCants	.01	.05
181 Jim Arnold	.01	.05
182 Sean Jones	.01	.05
183 Chuck Cecil	.01	.05
184 Mark Rypien	.01	.05
185 William Perry	.02	.10
186 Mark Jackson	.01	.05
187 Jim Dombrowski	.01	.05
188 Heath Sherman	.01	.05
189 Bubba McDowell	.01	.05
190 Fuad Reveiz	.01	.05
191 Darren Perry	.01	.05
192 Karl Mecklenburg	.01	.05
193 Frank Reich	.02	.10
194 Tony Casillas	.01	.05
195 Jerry Ball	.01	.05
196 Jessie Hester	.01	.05
197 David Lang	.01	.05
198 Sean Landeta	.01	.05
199 Jerry Gray	.01	.05
200 Mark Higgs	.01	.05
201 Bruce Armstrong	.01	.05
202 Vaughan Johnson	.01	.05
203 Calvin Williams	.02	.10
204 Leonard Marshall	.01	.05
205 Mike Munchak	.02	.10
206 Kevin Ross	.01	.05
207 Daryl Johnston	.08	.25
208 Jay Schroeder	.01	.05
209 Mo Lewis	.01	.05
210 Carlton Haselrig	.01	.05
211 Cris Carter	.08	.25
212 Marv Cook	.01	.05
213 Mark Duper	.01	.05
214 Jackie Slater	.01	.05
215 Mike Prior	.01	.05
216 Warren Moon	.08	.25
217 Mike Saxon	.01	.05
218 Derrick Fenner	.01	.05
219 Brian Washington	.01	.05
220 Jessie Tuggle	.01	.05
221 Jeff Hostetler	.02	.10
222 Deion Sanders	.20	.50
223 Neal Anderson	.01	.05
224 Kevin Mack	.01	.05
225 Tommy Maddox	.08	.25
226 Neil Smith	.08	.25
227 Ronnie Lott	.02	.10
228 Flipper Anderson	.01	.05
229 Keith Jackson	.02	.10
230 Pat Swilling	.01	.05
231 Carl Banks	.01	.05
232 Eric Allen	.01	.05
233 Randal Hill	.01	.05
234 Burt Grossman	.01	.05
235 Jerry Rice	.40	1.00
236 Santana Dotson	.02	.10
237 Andre Reed	.02	.10
238 Troy Aikman	.30	.75
239 Ray Childress	.01	.05
240 Phil Simms	.02	.10
241 Steve McMichael	.02	.10
242 Browning Nagle	.01	.05
243 Anthony Miller	.02	.10
244 Earnest Byner	.01	.05
245 Jay Hilgenberg	.01	.05
246 Jeff George	.08	.25
247 Marco Coleman	.01	.05
248 Mark Carrier DB	.01	.05
249 Howie Long	.08	.25
250 Ed McCaffrey	.08	.25
251 Jim Kelly	.08	.25
252 Henry Ellard	.02	.10
253 Joe Montana	.60	1.50
254 Dale Carter	.01	.05
255 Boomer Esiason	.02	.10
256 Gary Clark	.02	.10
257 Carl Pickens	.02	.10
258 Dave Krieg	.02	.10
259 Russell Maryland	.01	.05
260 Randall Cunningham	.08	.25
261 Leslie O'Neal	.02	.10
262 Vinny Testaverde	.02	.10
263 Ricky Ervins	.01	.05
264 Chris Mims	.01	.05
265 Dan Marino	.60	1.50
266 Eric Martin	.01	.05
267 Bruce Smith	.08	.25
268 Jim Harbaugh	.08	.25
269 Steve Emtman	.01	.05
270 Ricky Proehl	.01	.05
271 Vaughn Dunbar	.01	.05
272 Junior Seau	.08	.25
273 Sean Gilbert	.02	.10
274 Jim Lachey	.01	.05
275 Dalton Hilliard	.01	.05
276 David Klingler	.01	.05
277 Robert Jones	.01	.05
278 David Treadwell	.01	.05
279 Tracy Scroggins	.01	.05
280 Terrell Buckley	.01	.05
281 Quentin Coryatt	.02	.10
282 Jason Hanson	.01	.05
283 Shane Conlan	.01	.05
284 Guy McIntyre	.01	.05
285 Gary Zimmerman	.01	.05
286 Marty Carter	.01	.05
287 Jim Sweeney	.01	.05
288 Arthur Marshall RC	.01	.05
289 Eugene Chung	.01	.05
290 Mike Pritchard	.02	.10
291 Jim Ritcher	.01	.05
292 Todd Marinovich	.01	.05
293 Courtney Hall	.01	.05
294 Mark Collins	.01	.05
295 Troy Auzenne	.01	.05
296 Aeneas Williams	.01	.05
297 Andy Heck	.01	.05
298 Shaun Gayle	.01	.05
299 Kevin Fagan	.01	.05
300 Carnell Lake	.01	.05
301 Bernie Kosar	.02	.10
302 Maurice Hurst	.01	.05
303 Mike Merriweather	.01	.05
304 Reggie Roby	.01	.05
305 Darryl Williams	.01	.05
306 Jerome Bettis RC	2.50	5.00
307 Curtis Conway RC	.15	.40
308 Drew Bledsoe RC	1.00	2.50
309 John Copeland RC	.02	.10
310 Eric Curry RC	.01	.05
311 Lincoln Kennedy RC	.01	.05
312 Dan Williams RC	.01	.05
313 Patrick Bates RC	.01	.05
314 Tom Carter RC	.02	.10
315 Garrison Hearst RC	.30	.75
316 Joel Hilgenberg	.01	.05
317 Harris Barton	.01	.05
318 Jeff Lageman	.01	.05
319 Charles Mincy RC	.01	.05
320 Ricardo McDonald	.01	.05
321 Lorenzo White	.01	.05
322 Troy Vincent	.01	.05
323 Bennie Blades	.01	.05
324 Dana Hall	.01	.05
325 Ken Norton Jr.	.02	.10
326 Will Wolford	.01	.05
327 Neil O'Donnell	.08	.25
328 Tracy Simien	.01	.05
329 Darrell Green	.01	.05
330 Kyle Clifton	.01	.05
331 Elbert Shelley RC	.01	.05
332 Jeff Wright	.01	.05
333 Mike Johnson	.01	.05
334 John Gesek	.01	.05
335 Michael Brooks	.01	.05
336 George Jamison	.01	.05
337 Johnny Holland	.01	.05
338 Lamar Lathon	.01	.05
339 Bern Brostek	.01	.05
340 Steve Jordan	.01	.05
341 Gene Atkins	.01	.05
342 Aaron Wallace	.01	.05
343 Adrian Cooper	.01	.05
344 Amp Lee	.01	.05
345 Vincent Brown	.01	.05
346 James Hasty	.01	.05
347 Ron Hall	.01	.05
348 Matt Elliott	.01	.05
349 Tim Krumrie	.01	.05
350 Mark Stepnoski	.01	.05
351 Matt Stover	.01	.05
352 James Washington	.01	.05
353 Marc Spindler	.01	.05
354 Frank Warren	.01	.05
355 Vai Sikahema	.01	.05
356 Dan Saleaumua	.01	.05
357 Mark Clayton	.01	.05
358 Brent Jones	.02	.10
359 Andy Harmon RC	.02	.10
360 Anthony Parker	.01	.05
361 Chris Hinton	.01	.05
362 Greg Montgomery	.01	.05
363 Greg McMurtry	.01	.05
364 Craig Heyward	.02	.10
365 D.J. Johnson	.01	.05
366 Bill Romanowski	.01	.05
367 Steve Christie	.01	.05
368 Art Monk	.02	.10
369 Howard Ballard	.01	.05
370 Andre Collins	.01	.05
371 Alvin Harper	.02	.10
372 Blaise Winter RC	.01	.05
373 Al Del Greco	.01	.05
374 Eric Green	.01	.05
375 Chris Mohr	.01	.05
376 Tom Newberry	.01	.05
377 Cris Dishman	.01	.05
378 Jumpy Geathers	.01	.05
379 Don Mosebar	.01	.05
380 Andre Ware	.01	.05
381 Marvin Washington	.01	.05
382 Bobby Humphrey	.01	.05
383 Marc Logan	.01	.05
384 Lomas Brown	.01	.05
385 Steve Tasker	.02	.10
386 Chris Miller	.02	.10
387 Tony Paige	.01	.05
388 Charles Haley	.02	.10
389 Rich Moran	.01	.05
390 Mike Sherrard	.01	.05
391 Nick Lowery	.01	.05
392 Henry Thomas	.01	.05
393 Keith Sims	.01	.05
394 Thomas Everett	.01	.05
395 Steve Wallace	.01	.05
396 John Carney	.01	.05
397 Tim Johnson	.01	.05
398 Jeff Gossett	.01	.05
399 Anthony Smith	.01	.05
400 Kelvin Pritchett	.01	.05
401 Dermontti Dawson	.01	.05
402 Alfred Williams	.01	.05
403 Michael Haynes	.02	.10
404 Bart Oates	.01	.05
405 Ken Lanier	.01	.05
406 Vencie Glenn	.01	.05
407 John Taylor	.02	.10
408 Nate Newton	.02	.10
409 Mark Carrier WR	.02	.10
410 Ken Harvey	.01	.05
411 Troy Aikman SB	.15	.40
412 Charles Haley SB	.01	.05
413 Warren Moon DT Haywood Jeffires	.02	.10
414 Henry Jones DT Mark Kelso	.01	.05
415 Rickey Jackson DT Sam Mills	.01	.05
416 Clyde Simmons DT Reggie White	.01	.05
417 Dale Carter ROY	.01	.05
418 Carl Pickens ROY	.02	.10
419 Vaughn Dunbar ROY	.01	.05
420 Santana Dotson ROY	.01	.05
421 Steve Emtman 90	.01	.05
422 Louis Oliver 90	.01	.05
423 Carl Pickens 90	.02	.10
424 Eddie Anderson 90	.01	.05
425 Deion Sanders 90	.08	.25
426 Jon Vaughn 90	.01	.05
427 Darren Lewis 90	.01	.05
428 Kevin Ross 90	.01	.05
429 David Brandon 90	.01	.05
430 Dave Meggett 90	.01	.05
431 Jerry Rice HL	.20	.50
432 Sterling Sharpe HL	.02	.10
433 Art Monk HL	.01	.05
434 James Lofton HL	.01	.05
435 Lawrence Taylor	.02	.10
436 Bill Walsh HOF RC	.02	.10
437 Chuck Noll HOF	.02	.10
438 Dan Fouts HOF	.01	.05
439 Larry Little HOF	.01	.05
440 Steve Young MOY	.15	.40
NNO Dick Butkus AUTO/3000	25.00	40.00

1993 Score Dream Team

COMPLETE SET (26)	12.50	25.00
ONE PER SUPER PACK		
1 Steve Young	2.00	5.00
2 Emmitt Smith	4.00	10.00
3 Barry Foster	.25	.60
4 Sterling Sharpe	.60	1.50
5 Jerry Rice	2.50	6.00
6 Keith Jackson	.25	.60
7 Steve Wallace	.10	.30
8 Richmond Webb	.10	.30
9 Guy McIntyre	.10	.30
10 Carlton Haselrig	.10	.30
11 Bruce Matthews	.10	.30
12 Morten Andersen	.10	.30
13 Rich Camarillo	.10	.30
14 Deion Sanders	1.25	3.00
15 Steve Tasker	.25	.60
16 Clyde Simmons	.10	.30
17 Reggie White	.60	1.50
18 Cortez Kennedy	.25	.60
19 Rod Woodson	.60	1.50
20 Terry McDaniel	.10	.30
21 Chuck Cecil	.10	.30
22 Steve Atwater	.10	.30
23 Bryan Cox	.10	.30
24 Derrick Thomas	.60	1.50
25 Wilber Marshall	.10	.30
26 Sam Mills.	.10	.30

1993 Score Franchise

COMPLETE SET (28)	30.00	80.00
STATED ODDS 1:24		
1 Andre Rison	.50	1.25
2 Thurman Thomas	1.25	3.00
3 Richard Dent	.50	1.25
4 Harold Green	.25	.60
5 Eric Metcalf	.50	1.25
6 Emmitt Smith	8.00	20.00
7 John Elway	8.00	20.00
8 Barry Sanders	6.00	15.00
9 Sterling Sharpe	1.25	3.00
10 Warren Moon	1.25	3.00
11 Jeff Herrod	.25	.60
12 Derrick Thomas	1.25	3.00
13 Steve Wisniewski	.25	.60
14 Cleveland Gary	.25	.60
15 Dan Marino	8.00	20.00
16 Chris Doleman	.25	.60
17 Marv Cook	.25	.60
18 Rickey Jackson	.25	.60
19 Rodney Hampton	.50	1.25
20 Jeff Lageman	.25	.60
21 Clyde Simmons	.25	.60
22 Rich Camarillo	.25	.60
23 Rod Woodson	1.25	3.00
24 Ronnie Harmon	.25	.60
25 Steve Young	4.00	10.00
26 Cortez Kennedy	.50	1.25
27 Reggie Cobb	.25	.60
28 Mark Rypien	.25	.60

1993 Score Ore-Ida QB Club

This set of 18 standard-size cards could be obtained by the purchase of specially marked Ore-Ida products (Bagel Bites, Twice Baked, or Topped Baked Potatoes), filling out the order form on one of the packages, and mailing it plus six proofs-of-purchase and 1.50. Collectors would then receive two nine-card packs. For three proofs-of-purchase and 1.00, collectors could receive one nine-card set. The packs are sequentially numbered, with the first pack containing cards 1-9 and the second containing cards 10-18. Aside from sporting different color player action photos on their fronts (Hostetler and Esiason are pictured in their new Raiders and Jets uniforms, respectively), and the different numbering on the backs, the cards are identical in design to the regular 1993 Score issue.

COMPLETE SET (18)	16.00	40.00
1 John Elway	4.00	10.00
2 Steve Young	1.60	4.00
3 Warren Moon	.80	2.00
4 Randall Cunningham	.80	2.00
5 Jeff Hostetler	.30	.75
6 Phil Simms	.40	1.00
7 Jim Everett	.30	.75
8 David Klingler	.30	.75
9 Brett Favre	4.00	10.00
10 Troy Aikman	2.00	5.00
11 Dan Marino	4.00	10.00
12 Mark Rypien	.30	.75
13 Jim Kelly	.80	2.00
14 Jim Harbaugh	.40	1.00
15 Bernie Kosar	.30	.75
16 Boomer Esiason	.40	1.00
17 Chris Miller	.30	.75
18 Neil O'Donnell	.30	.75

1994 Score Samples

These ten sample standard-size cards were issued to herald the August release of the 1994 Score football set. The cards feature on their fronts color player action shots with irregular purple and teal borders, except for the Glyn Milburn card (112), which is a sample foil card from the parallel Gold Zone set. The player's name appears in white lettering below the photo; his position appears in white lettering within a black box at the upper left. The multicolored back carries the player's name and team logo at the top, followed below by his position, biography, profile, and statistics.

COMPLETE SET (10)	1.60	4.00
21 Jerome Bettis	.80	2.00
25 Steve Jordan	.15	.40
50 Shannon Sharpe	.15	.40
112 Glyn Milburn FOIL	.15	.40
161 Ronnie Lott	.15	.40
257 Derrick Thomas	.30	.75
0 Generic Rookie Card	.08	.25
NNO Sample Redemption Card	.08	.25
NNO Score Ad Card Retail	.08	.25
NNO Score Ad Card Hobby	.08	.25

1994 Score

The 1994 Score football set consists of 330 standard-size cards. Cards were issued in 14-card foil packs as well as in jumbo packs. Topical subsets featured are Rookies (276-305) and Team Checklists (306-319). Cards of players that were named All-Pro, have an All-Pro (AP) notation on front. Randomly inserted redemption cards gave collectors an opportunity to receive ten cards of top rookie players in their NFL uniforms. Rookie Cards include Derrick Alexander, Marshall Faulk, William Floyd, Greg Hill, Charles Johnson, Errict Rhett, Darnay Scott and Heath Shuler.

COMPLETE SET (330)	5.00	12.00
1 Barry Sanders	.50	1.25
2 Troy Aikman	.30	.75
3 Sterling Sharpe	.02	.10
4 Deion Sanders	.20	.50
5 Bruce Smith	.08	.25
6 Eric Metcalf	.02	.10
7 John Elway	.60	1.50
8 Bruce Matthews	.01	.05
9 Rickey Jackson	.01	.05
10 Cortez Kennedy	.02	.10
11 Jerry Rice	.30	.75
12 Stanley Richard	.01	.05
13 Rod Woodson	.02	.10
14 Eric Swann	.02	.10
15 Eric Allen	.01	.05
16 Richard Dent	.02	.10
17 Carl Pickens	.02	.10
18 Rohn Stark	.01	.05
19 Marcus Allen	.08	.25
20 Steve Wisniewski	.01	.05
21 Jerome Bettis	.20	.50
22 Darrell Green	.01	.05
23 Lawrence Dawsey	.01	.05
24 Larry Centers	.08	.25
25 Steve Jordan	.01	.05
26 Johnny Johnson	.01	.05
27 Phil Simms	.02	.10
28 Bruce Armstrong	.01	.05
29 Willie Roaf	.01	.05
30 Andre Rison	.02	.10
31 Henry Jones	.01	.05
32 Warren Moon	.08	.25
33 Sean Gilbert	.01	.05
34 Ben Coates	.02	.10
35 Seth Joyner	.01	.05
36 Ronnie Harmon	.01	.05
37 Quentin Coryatt	.01	.05
38 Ricky Sanders	.01	.05
39 Gerald Williams	.01	.05
40 Emmitt Smith	.40	1.00
41 Jason Hanson	.01	.05
42 Kevin Smith	.01	.05
43 Irving Fryar	.02	.10
44 Boomer Esiason	.02	.10
45 Darryl Talley	.01	.05
46 Paul Gruber	.01	.05
47 Anthony Smith	.01	.05
48 John Copeland	.01	.05
49 Michael Jackson	.02	.10
50 Shannon Sharpe	.02	.10
51 Reggie White	.08	.25
52 Andre Collins	.01	.05
53 Jack Del Rio	.01	.05
54 John Elliott	.01	.05
55 Kevin Greene	.02	.10
56 Steve Young	.25	.60
57 Erric Pegram	.01	.05
58 Donnell Woolford	.01	.05
59 Darryl Williams	.01	.05
60 Michael Irvin	.08	.25
61 Mel Gray	.01	.05
62 Greg Montgomery	.01	.05
63 Neil Smith	.02	.10
64 Andy Harmon	.01	.05
65 Dan Marino	.60	1.50
66 Leonard Russell	.01	.05
67 Joe Montana	.60	1.50
68 John Taylor	.02	.10
69 Cris Dishman	.01	.05
70 Cornelius Bennett	.02	.10
71 Harold Green	.01	.05
72 Anthony Pleasant	.01	.05
73 Dennis Smith	.01	.05
74 Bryce Paup	.02	.10
75 Jeff George	.08	.25
76 Henry Ellard	.02	.10
77 Randall McDaniel	.02	.10
78 Derek Brown RBK	.01	.05
79 Johnny Mitchell	.01	.05
80 Leroy Thompson	.01	.05
81 Junior Seau	.08	.25
82 Kelvin Martin	.01	.05
83 Guy McIntyre	.01	.05
84 Elbert Shelley	.01	.05
85 Louis Oliver	.01	.05
86 Tommy Vardell	.01	.05
87 Jeff Herrod	.01	.05
88 Edgar Bennett	.08	.25
89 Reggie Langhorne	.01	.05
90 Terry Kirby	.08	.25
91 Marcus Robertson	.01	.05
92 Mark Collins	.01	.05
93 Calvin Williams	.02	.10
94 Barry Foster	.01	.05
95 Brent Jones	.02	.10
96 Reggie Cobb	.01	.05
97 Ray Childress	.01	.05
98 Chris Miller	.01	.05
99 John Carney	.01	.05
100 Ricky Proehl	.01	.05
101 Renaldo Turnbull	.01	.05
102 John Randle	.02	.10
103 Flipper Anderson	.01	.05
104 Scottie Graham RC	.02	.10
105 Webster Slaughter	.01	.05
106 Tyrone Hughes	.02	.10
107 Ken Norton Jr.	.02	.10
108 Jim Kelly	.08	.25
109 Michael Haynes	.02	.10
110 Mark Carrier DB	.01	.05
111 Eddie Murray	.01	.05
112 Glyn Milburn	.02	.10
113 Jackie Harris	.01	.05
114 Dean Biasucci	.01	.05
115 Tim Brown	.08	.25
116 Mark Higgs	.01	.05
117 Steve Emtman	.01	.05
118 Clay Matthews	.01	.05
119 Clyde Simmons	.01	.05
120 Howard Ballard	.01	.05
121 Ricky Watters	.02	.10
122 William Fuller	.01	.05
123 Robert Brooks	.08	.25
124 Brian Blades	.02	.10
125 Leslie O'Neal	.01	.05
126 Gary Clark	.02	.10
127 Jim Sweeney	.01	.05
128 Vaughan Johnson	.01	.05
129 Gary Brown	.01	.05
130 Todd Lyght	.01	.05
131 Nick Lowery	.01	.05
132 Ernest Givins	.02	.10
133 Lomas Brown	.01	.05
134 Craig Erickson	.01	.05
135 James Francis	.01	.05
136 Andre Reed	.02	.10
137 Jim Everett	.02	.10
138 Nate Odomes	.01	.05
139 Tom Waddle	.01	.05
140 Stevon Moore	.01	.05
141 Rod Bernstine	.01	.05
142 Brett Favre	.60	1.50
143 Roosevelt Potts	.01	.05
144 Chester McGlockton	.01	.05
145 LeRoy Butler	.01	.05
146 Charles Haley	.02	.10
147 Rodney Hampton	.02	.10
148 George Teague	.01	.05
149 Gary Anderson K	.01	.05
150 Mark Stepnoski	.01	.05
151 Courtney Hawkins	.01	.05
152 Tim Grunhard	.01	.05
153 David Klingler	.01	.05
154 Erik Williams	.01	.05
155 Herman Moore	.08	.25
156 Daryl Johnston	.02	.10
157 Chris Zorich	.01	.05
158 Shane Conlan	.01	.05
159 Santana Dotson	.02	.10
160 Sam Mills	.01	.05
161 Ronnie Lott	.02	.10
162 Jesse Sapolu	.01	.05
163 Marion Butts	.01	.05
164 Eugene Robinson	.01	.05
165 Mark Schlereth	.01	.05
166 John L. Williams	.01	.05
167 Anthony Miller	.02	.10
168 Rich Camarillo	.01	.05
169 Jeff Lageman	.01	.05
170 Michael Brooks	.01	.05
171 Scott Mitchell	.02	.10
172 Duane Bickett	.01	.05
173 Willie Davis	.02	.10
174 Maurice Hurst	.01	.05
175 Brett Perriman	.02	.10
176 Jay Novacek	.02	.10
177 Terry Allen	.02	.10
178 Pete Metzelaars	.01	.05
179 Erik Kramer	.02	.10
180 Neal Anderson	.01	.05
181 Ethan Horton	.01	.05
182 Tony Bennett	.01	.05
183 Gary Zimmerman	.01	.05
184 Jeff Hostetler	.02	.10
185 Jeff Cross	.01	.05
186 Vincent Brown	.01	.05
187 Herschel Walker	.02	.10
188 Courtney Hall	.01	.05
189 Norm Johnson	.01	.05
190 Hardy Nickerson	.02	.10
191 Greg Townsend	.01	.05
192 Mike Munchak	.02	.10
193 Dante Jones	.01	.05
194 Vinny Testaverde	.02	.10
195 Vance Johnson	.01	.05
196 Chris Jacke	.01	.05
197 Will Wolford	.01	.05
198 Terry McDaniel	.01	.05
199 Bryan Cox	.01	.05
200 Nate Newton	.01	.05
201 Keith Byars	.01	.05
202 Neil O'Donnell	.08	.25
203 Harris Barton	.01	.05
204 Thurman Thomas	.08	.25
205 Jeff Query	.01	.05
206 Russell Maryland	.01	.05
207 Pat Swilling	.01	.05
208 Haywood Jeffires	.02	.10
209 John Alt	.01	.05
210 O.J. McDuffie	.08	.25
211 Keith Sims	.01	.05
212 Eric Martin	.01	.05
213 Kyle Clifton	.01	.05
214 Luis Sharpe	.01	.05
215 Thomas Everett	.01	.05
216 Chris Warren	.02	.10
217 Chris Doleman	.01	.05
218 Tony Jones	.01	.05
219 Karl Mecklenburg	.01	.05
220 Rob Moore	.02	.10
221 Jessie Hester	.01	.05
222 Jeff Jaeger	.01	.05
223 Keith Jackson	.01	.05
224 Mo Lewis	.01	.05
225 Mike Horan	.01	.05
226 Eric Green	.01	.05
227 Jim Ritcher	.01	.05
228 Eric Curry	.01	.05
229 Stan Humphries	.02	.10
230 Mike Johnson	.01	.05
231 Alvin Harper	.02	.10
232 Bennie Blades	.01	.05
233 Cris Carter	.20	.50
234 Morten Andersen	.01	.05
235 Brian Washington	.01	.05
236 Eric Hill	.01	.05
237 Natrone Means	.08	.25
238 Carlton Bailey	.01	.05
239 Anthony Carter	.02	.10
240 Jessie Tuggle	.01	.05
241 Tim Irwin	.01	.05
242 Mark Carrier WR	.02	.10
243 Steve Atwater	.01	.05
244 Sean Jones	.01	.05
245 Bernie Kosar	.02	.10
246 Richmond Webb	.01	.05
247 Dave Meggett	.01	.05
248 Vincent Brisby	.02	.10
249 Fred Barnett	.02	.10
250 Greg Lloyd	.02	.10
251 Tim McDonald	.01	.05
252 Mike Pritchard	.01	.05
253 Greg Robinson	.01	.05
254 Tony McGee	.01	.05

255 Chris Spielman .02 .10
256 Keith Loneker RC .01 .05
257 Derrick Thomas .08 .25
258 Wayne Martin .01 .05
259 Art Monk .02 .10
260 Andy Heck .01 .05
261 Chip Lohmiller .01 .05
262 Simon Fletcher .01 .05
263 Ricky Reynolds .01 .05
264 Chris Hinton .01 .05
265 Ronald Moore .01 .05
266 Rocket Ismail .02 .10
267 Pete Stoyanovich .01 .05
268 Mark Jackson .01 .05
269 Randall Cunningham .08 .25
270 Dermontti Dawson .01 .05
271 Bill Romanowski .01 .05
272 Tim Johnson .01 .05
273 Steve Tasker .02 .10
274 Keith Hamilton .01 .05
275 Pierce Holt .01 .05
276 Heath Shuler RC .08 .25
277 Marshall Faulk RC 2.00 5.00
278 Charles Johnson RC .08 .25
279 Sam Adams RC .02 .10
280 Trev Alberts RC .02 .10
281 Der. Alexander WR RC .08 .25
282 Bryant Young RC .15 .40
283 Greg Hill RC .08 .25
284 Darnay Scott RC .20 .50
285 Willie McGinest RC .08 .25
286 Thomas Randolph RC .01 .05
287 Errict Rhett RC .08 .25
288 Lamar Smith RC .50 1.25
289 William Floyd RC .08 .25
290 Johnnie Morton RC .20 .50
291 Jamir Miller RC .02 .10
292 David Palmer RC .08 .25
293 Dan Wilkinson RC .02 .10
294 Trent Dilfer RC .50 1.25
295 Antonio Langham RC .02 .10
296 Chuck Levy RC .01 .05
297 John Thierry RC .01 .05
298 Kevin Lee RC .01 .05
299 Aaron Glenn RC .08 .25
300 Charlie Garner RC .50 1.25
301 Lonnie Johnson RC .01 .05
302 LeShon Johnson RC .02 .10
303 Thomas Lewis RC .02 .10
304 Ryan Yarborough RC .01 .05
305 Mario Bates RC .08 .25
306 Buffalo Bills TC .01 .05
307 Cincinnati Bengals TC .01 .05
308 Cleveland Browns TC .01 .05
309 Denver Broncos TC .01 .05
310 Houston Oilers TC .01 .05
311 Indianapolis Colts TC .01 .05
312 Kansas City Chiefs TC .01 .05
313 Los Angeles Raiders TC .01 .05
314 Miami Dolphins TC .01 .05
315 New England Patriots TC .01 .05
316 New York Jets TC .01 .05
317 Pittsburgh Steelers TC .01 .05
318 San Diego Charges TC .01 .05
319 Seattle Seahawks TC .01 .05
320 Garrison Hearst FF .08 .25
321 Drew Bledsoe FF .30 .75
322 Tyrone Hughes FF .02 .10
323 James Jett FF .01 .05
324 Tom Carter FF .01 .05
325 Reggie Brooks FF .01 .05
326 Dana Stubblefield FF .02 .10
327 Jerome Bettis FF .08 .25
328 Chris Slade FF .01 .05
329 Rick Mirer FF .08 .25
330 Emmitt Smith NFL MVP .20 .50

1994 Score Gold Zone

COMPLETE SET (330) 50.00 100.00
*STARS: 3X TO 6X BASIC CARDS
*RCs: 1.5X TO 3X BASIC CARDS
ONE PER PACK

1994 Score Dream Team

COMPLETE SET (18) 30.00 80.00
STATED ODDS 1:72
DT1 Troy Aikman 6.00 15.00
DT2 Steve Atwater .40 1.00
DT3 Cornelius Bennett .75 2.00
DT4 Tim Brown 2.00 5.00
DT5 Michael Irvin 2.00 5.00
DT6 Bruce Matthews .40 1.00
DT7 Eric Metcalf .75 2.00
DT8 Anthony Miller .75 2.00
DT9 Jerry Rice 6.00 15.00
DT10 Andre Rison .75 2.00
DT11 Barry Sanders 10.00 25.00
DT12 Deion Sanders 4.00 10.00
DT13 Sterling Sharpe .75 2.00
DT14 Neil Smith .75 2.00
DT15 Derrick Thomas 2.00 5.00
DT16 Thurman Thomas 2.00 5.00
DT17 Rod Woodson .75 2.00
DT18 Steve Young 5.00 12.00

1994 Score Rookie Redemption

COMPLETE SET (10) 75.00 150.00
1 Heath Shuler 2.50 6.00
2 Trent Dilfer 12.00 30.00
3 Marshall Faulk 40.00 100.00
4 Charlie Garner 6.00 15.00
5 LeShon Johnson 1.25 3.00
6 Charles Johnson 2.50 6.00
7 Errict Rhett 2.50 6.00
8 Lake Dawson .60 1.50
9 Bert Emanuel 2.50 6.00
10 Greg Hill 2.50 6.00

1994 Score Sophomore Showcase

COMPLETE SET (18) 30.00 60.00
RANDOM INSERTS IN JUMBO PACKS
SS1 Jerome Bettis 4.00 10.00
SS2 Rick Mirer 2.00 5.00
SS3 Reggie Brooks .40 1.00
SS4 Drew Bledsoe 6.00 15.00
SS5 Ronald Moore .40 1.00
SS6 Derek Brown RBK .40 1.00
SS7 Roosevelt Potts .40 1.00
SS8 Terry Kirby 2.00 5.00
SS9 James Jett .40 1.00
SS10 Vincent Brisby .75 2.00
SS11 Tyrone Hughes .75 2.00
SS12 Rocket Ismail .75 2.00
SS13 Tony McGee .40 1.00
SS14 Garrison Hearst 2.00 5.00
SS15 Eric Curry .40 1.00
SS16 Dana Stubblefield .75 2.00
SS17 Tom Carter .40 1.00
SS18 Chris Slade .40 1.00

1995 Score Promos

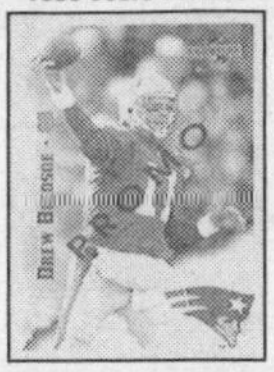

These cards were issued to preview the 1995 Score series. Four cards were packaged together in a cello wrapper. The Promos can easily be distinguished from their regular issue counterparts by the disclaimer "PROMO" stamped in black across their fronts or the word "Promotional" across the cardbacks.

10 Emmitt Smith 2.50 6.00
42 Drew Bledsoe 1.25 3.00
47 Barry Foster .20 .50
58 Steve Broussard .20 .50
167 Junior Seau .50 1.25
168 Ken Harvey .20 .50
178 Jessie Tuggle .20 .50
184 Willie Roaf .20 .50
187 Darren Woodson .40 1.00
191 Stan Humphies .20 .50
199 Kevin Turner .20 .50
204 Reggie Brooks .20 .50
206 Emmitt Smith SS 2.00 5.00
211 Jerry Rice SS 1.50 4.00
238 Emmitt Smith CL 2.00 5.00
246 Tony Boselli .40 1.00
256 Kerry Collins .40 1.00
260 Sherman Williams .20 .50
263 J.J. Stokes .40 1.00
265 Dave Barr .20 .50
266 Eddie Goines .20 .50
272 Mark Bruener .40 1.00
DT2 Troy Aikman Dream Team 1.25 3.00
NNO Title Card .20 .50

1995 Score

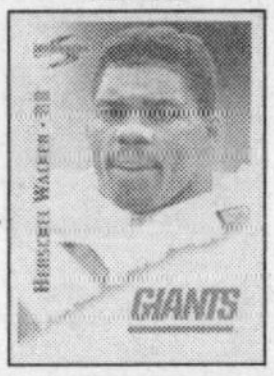

This 275-card standard-size set is issued in 12 card foil-packs (suggested retail price of 99 cents per pack) and 20-card jumbo packs. Rookie Cards in this set include Jeff Blake, Ki-Jana Carter, Kerry Collins, Joey Galloway, Steve McNair, Rashaan Salaam, Kordell Stewart, J.J Stokes and Michael Westbrook. A foil Steve Young card was distributed to collectors who correctly identified intentional errors from a Pinnacle print ad run throughout the season. The contest was the third part following two baseball ads, thus the AD3 card numbering.

COMPLETE SET (275) 6.00 15.00
1 Steve Young .25 .60
2 Barry Sanders .50 1.25
3 Jerry Rice .30 .75
4 Marshall Faulk .40 1.00
5 Terance Mathis .02 .10
6 Rod Woodson .02 .10
7 Seth Joyner .01 .05
8 Michael Timpson .01 .05
9 Deion Sanders .20 .50
10 Emmitt Smith .50 1.25
11 Cris Carter .08 .25
12 Jake Reed .02 .10
13 Reggie White .08 .25
14 Shannon Sharpe .02 .10
15 Troy Aikman .30 .75
16 Andre Reed .02 .10
17 Tyrone Hughes .02 .10
18 Sterling Sharpe .02 .10
19 Jerome Bettis .08 .25
20 Irving Fryar .02 .10
21 Warren Moon .02 .10
22 Ben Coates .02 .10
23 Frank Reich .01 .05
24 Henry Ellard .02 .10
25 Steve Atwater .01 .05
26 Willie Davis .02 .10
27 Michael Irvin .08 .25
28 Harvey Williams .01 .05
29 Aeneas Williams .01 .05
30 Errict Rhett .02 .10
31 Lorenzo White .01 .05
32 John Elway .60 1.50
33 Rodney Hampton .02 .10
34 Webster Slaughter .01 .05
35 Eric Turner .01 .05
36 Dan Marino .60 1.50
37 Daryl Johnston .02 .10
38 Bruce Smith .08 .25
39 Ronald Moore .01 .05
40 Larry Centers .02 .10
41 Curtis Conway .08 .25
42 Drew Bledsoe .20 .50
43 Quinn Early .02 .10
44 Marcus Allen .08 .25
45 Andre Rison .02 .10
46 Jeff Blake RC .20 .50
47 Barry Foster .02 .10
48 Antonio Langham .01 .05
49 Herman Moore .08 .25
50 Flipper Anderson .01 .05
51 Rick Mirer .02 .10
52 Jay Novacek .02 .10
53 Tim Bowens .01 .05
54 Carl Pickens .02 .10
55 Lewis Tillman .01 .05
56 Lawrence Dawsey .01 .05
57 Leroy Hoard .01 .05
58 Steve Broussard .01 .05
59 Dave Krieg .01 .05
60 John Taylor .01 .05
61 Johnny Mitchell .01 .05
62 Jessie Hester .01 .05
63 Johnny Bailey .01 .05
64 Brett Favre .60 1.50
65 Bryce Paup .02 .10
66 J.J. Birden .01 .05
67 Steve Tasker .02 .10
68 Edgar Bennett .02 .10
69 Ray Buchanan .01 .05
70 Brent Jones .01 .05
71 Dave Meggett .01 .05
72 Jeff Graham .01 .05
73 Michael Brooks .01 .05
74 Ricky Ervins .01 .05
75 Chris Warren .02 .10
76 Natrone Means .02 .10
77 Tim Brown .08 .26
78 Jim Everett .01 .05
79 Chris Calloway .01 .05
80 John L. Williams .01 .05
81 Chris Chandler .02 .10
82 Tim McDonald .01 .05
83 Calvin Williams .02 .10
84 Tony McGee .01 .05
85 Erik Kramer .01 .05
86 Eric Green .01 .05
87 Nate Newton .02 .10
88 Leonard Russell .01 .05
89 Jeff George .02 .10
90 Raymont Harris .01 .05
91 Darnay Scott .02 .10
92 Brian Mitchell .01 .05
93 Craig Erickson .01 .05
94 Cortez Kennedy .02 .10
95 Derrick Alexander WR .08 .25
96 Charles Haley .02 .10
97 Randall Cunningham .08 .25
98 Haywood Jeffires .01 .05
99 Ronnie Harmon .01 .05
100 Dale Carter .02 .10
101 Dave Brown .02 .10
102 Michael Haynes .02 .10
103 Johnny Johnson .01 .05
104 William Floyd .02 .10
105 Jeff Hostetler .02 .10
106 Bernie Parmalee .02 .10
107 Mo Lewis .01 .05
108 Byron Bam Morris .01 .05
109 Vincent Brisby .01 .05
110 John Randle .02 .10
111 Steve Walsh .01 .05
112 Terry Allen .02 .10
113 Greg Lloyd .02 .10
114 Merton Hanks .01 .05
115 Mel Gray .01 .05
116 Jim Kelly .08 .25
117 Don Beebe .01 .05
118 Floyd Turner .01 .05
119 Neil Smith .02 .10
120 Keith Byars .01 .05
121 Rocket Ismail .02 .10
122 Leslie O'Neal .02 .10
123 Mike Sherrard .01 .05
124 Marion Butts .01 .05
125 Andre Coleman .01 .05
126 Charles Johnson .02 .10
127 Derrick Fenner .01 .05
128 Vinny Testaverde .02 .10
129 Chris Spielman .02 .10
130 Bert Emanuel .08 .25
131 Craig Heyward .02 .10
132 Anthony Miller .02 .10
133 Rob Moore .02 .10
134 Gary Brown .01 .05
135 David Klingler UER .02 .10
Photo on back is Erik Wilhelm
136 Sean Dawkins .02 .10
137 Terry McDaniel .01 .05
138 Fred Barnett .02 .10
139 Bryan Cox .01 .05
140 Andrew Jordan .01 .05
141 Leroy Thompson .01 .05
142 Richmond Webb .01 .05
143 Kimble Anders .02 .10
144 Mario Bates .02 .10
145 Irv Smith .01 .05
146 Carnell Lake .01 .05
147 Mark Seay .02 .10
148 Dana Stubblefield .02 .10
149 Kelvin Martin .01 .05
150 Pete Metzelaars .01 .05
151 Roosevelt Potts .01 .05
152 Bubby Brister .01 .05
153 Trent Dilfer .08 .25
154 Ricky Proehl .01 .05
155 Aaron Glenn .01 .05
156 Eric Metcalf .02 .10
157 Kevin Williams WR .02 .10
158 Charlie Garner .08 .25
159 Glyn Milburn .01 .05
160 Fuad Reveiz .01 .05
161 Brett Perriman .02 .10
162 Neil O'Donnell .02 .10
163 Tony Martin .02 .10
164 Sam Adams .01 .05
165 John Friesz .02 .10
166 Bryant Young .02 .10
167 Junior Seau .08 .25
168 Ken Harvey .01 .05
169 Bill Brooks .01 .05
170 Eugene Robinson .01 .05
171 Ricky Sanders .02 .10
172 Rodney Peete .01 .05
173 Boomer Esiason .02 .10
174 Reggie Roby .01 .05
175 Michael Jackson .02 .10
176 Gus Frerotte .02 .10
177 Terry Kirby .02 .10
178 Jessie Tuggle .01 .05
179 Courtney Hawkins .01 .05
180 Heath Shuler .02 .10
181 Jack Del Rio .01 .05
182 O.J. McDuffie .08 .25
183 Ricky Watters .02 .10
184 Willie Roaf .01 .05
185 Glenn Foley .01 .05
186 Blair Thomas .01 .05
187 Darren Woodson .02 .10
188 Kevin Greene .02 .10
189 Jeff Burris .01 .05
190 Jay Schroeder .01 .05
191 Stan Humphries .02 .10
192 Irving Spikes .02 .10
193 Jim Harbaugh .02 .10
194 Robert Brooks .08 .25
195 Greg Hill .02 .10
196 Herschel Walker .02 .10
197 Brian Blades .02 .10
198 Mark Ingram .01 .05
199 Kevin Turner .01 .05
200 Lake Dawson .02 .10
201 Alvin Harper .01 .05
202 Derek Brown RBK .01 .05
203 Qadry Ismail .02 .10
204 Reggie Brooks .02 .10
205 Steve Young SS .10 .30
206 Emmitt Smith SS .25 .60
207 Stan Humphries SS .01 .05
208 Barry Sanders SS .25 .60
209 Marshall Faulk SS .15 .40
210 Drew Bledsoe SS .08 .25
211 Jerry Rice SS .15 .40
212 Tim Brown SS .02 .10
213 Cris Carter SS .08 .25
214 Dan Marino SS .30 .75
215 Troy Aikman SS .15 .40
216 Jerome Bettis SS .02 .10
217 Deion Sanders SS .08 .25
218 Junior Seau SS .02 .10
219 John Elway SS .30 .75
220 Warren Moon SS .01 .05
221 Sterling Sharpe SS .02 .10
222 Marcus Allen SS .08 .25
223 Michael Irvin SS .02 .10
224 Brett Favre SS .30 .75
225 Rodney Hampton SS .01 .05
226 Dave Brown SS .02 .10
227 Ben Coates SS .02 .10
228 Jim Kelly SS .08 .25
229 Heath Shuler SS .02 .10
230 Herman Moore SS .08 .25
231 Jeff Hostetler SS .02 .10
232 Rick Mirer SS .02 .10
233 Byron Bam Morris SS .01 .05
234 Terance Mathis SS .01 .05
235 John Elway CL .15 .40
Barry Sanders CL
236 Troy Aikman CL .08 .25
237 Jerry Rice CL .08 .25
238 Emmitt Smith CL .20 .50
239 Steve Young CL .08 .25
240 Drew Bledsoe CL .08 .25
241 Marshall Faulk CL .08 .25
242 Dan Marino CL .15 .40
243 Junior Seau CL .02 .10
244 Ray Zellars RC .02 .10
245 Rob Johnson RC .30 .75
246 Tony Boselli RC .08 .25
247 Kevin Carter RC .08 .25
248 Steve McNair RC 1.00 2.50
249 Tyrone Wheatley RC .30 .75
250 Steve Stenstrom RC .01 .05
251 Stoney Case RC .01 .05
252 Rodney Thomas RC .02 .10
253 Michael Westbrook RC .08 .25
254 Der.Alexander DE RC .01 .05
255 Kyle Brady RC .08 .25
256 Kerry Collins RC .75 2.00
257 Rashaan Salaam RC .02 .10
258 Frank Sanders RC .08 .25
259 John Walsh RC .01 .05
260 Sherman Williams RC .01 .05
261 Ki-Jana Carter RC .08 .25
262 Jack Jackson RC .01 .05
263 J.J. Stokes RC .08 .25
264 Kordell Stewart RC .50 1.25
265 Dave Barr RC .01 .05
266 Eddie Goines RC .01 .05
267 Warren Sapp RC .50 1.25
268 James O. Stewart RC .30 .75
269 Joey Galloway RC .50 1.25
270 Tyrone Davis RC .01 .05
271 Napoleon Kaufman RC .40 1.00
272 Mark Bruener RC .02 .10
273 Todd Collins RC .30 .75
274 Billy Williams RC .01 .05
275 James A.Stewart RC .01 .05
P264 Kordell Stewart PROMO 1.00 2.50
AD3 Steve Young 1.25 3.00
Ad Contest Redemption

1995 Score Red Siege

COMPLETE SET (275) 60.00 120.00
*STARS: 4X TO 8X BASIC CARDS
*RCs: 2X TO 4X BASIC CARDS
STATED ODDS 1:3

1995 Score Red Siege Artist's Proofs

*STARS: 12X TO 30X BASIC CARDS
*RCs: 0X TO 20X BASIC CARDS
STATED ODDS 1:36

1995 Score Dream Team

COMPLETE SET (10) 15.00 40.00
STATED ODDS 1:72 HOB/RET
DT1 Steve Young 1.50 4.00
DT2 Troy Aikman 2.00 5.00
DT3 Dan Marino 4.00 10.00
DT4 Drew Bledsoe 1.25 3.00
DT5 Emmitt Smith 3.00 8.00
DT6 Barry Sanders 3.00 8.00
DT7 Jerry Rice 2.00 5.00
DT8 Marshall Faulk 2.50 6.00
DT9 Deion Sanders 1.25 3.00
DT10 John Elway 4.00 10.00

1995 Score Offense Inc.

COMPLETE SET (30) 40.00 80.00
STATED ODDS 1:16 HOB, 1:8 JUM, 1:16 RET
1 Steve Young 1.50 4.00
2 Emmitt Smith 3.00 8.00
3 Dan Marino 4.00 10.00
4 Barry Sanders 3.00 8.00
5 Jeff Blake .50 1.25
6 Jerry Rice 2.00 5.00
7 Troy Aikman 2.00 5.00
8 Brett Favre 4.00 10.00
9 Marshall Faulk 2.50 6.00
10 Drew Bledsoe 1.25 3.00
11 Natrone Means .25 .60
12 John Elway 4.00 10.00
13 Chris Warren .25 .60
14 Michael Irvin .60 1.50
15 Mario Bates .25 .60
16 Warren Moon .25 .60
17 Jerome Bettis .60 1.50
18 Herman Moore .60 1.50
19 Barry Foster .25 .60
20 Jeff George .25 .60
21 Cris Carter .60 1.50
22 Sterling Sharpe .25 .60
23 Jim Kelly .60 1.50
24 Heath Shuler .25 .60
25 Marcus Allen .60 1.50
26 Dave Brown .25 .60
27 Rick Mirer .25 .60
28 Rodney Hampton .25 .60
29 Errict Rhett .25 .60
30 Ben Coates .25 .60

1995 Score Pass Time

COMPLETE SET (18) 75.00 150.00
STATED ODDS 1:18 JUMBO
PT1 Steve Young 5.00 12.00
PT2 Dan Marino 12.50 30.00
PT3 Drew Bledsoe 4.00 10.00
PT4 Troy Aikman 6.00 15.00
PT5 Glenn Foley .40 1.00
PT6 John Elway 12.50 30.00
PT7 Brett Favre 12.50 30.00
PT8 Heath Shuler .75 2.00
PT9 Warren Moon .75 2.00
PT10 Rick Mirer .75 2.00
PT11 Stan Humphries .75 2.00
PT12 Jeff Hostetler .75 2.00
PT13 Jim Kelly 2.00 5.00
PT14 Randall Cunningham 2.00 5.00
PT15 Jeff Blake 2.00 4.00
PT16 Trent Dilfer 2.00 5.00
PT17 Jeff George .75 2.00
PT18 Dave Brown .75 2.00

1995 Score Reflextions

COMPLETE SET (10) 30.00 60.00
STATED ODDS 1:36 HOBBY
RF1 Drew Bledsoe 6.00 15.00
Dan Marino
RF2 Charlie Garner 5.00 12.00
Barry Sanders
RF3 Rick Mirer 1.50 4.00
Warren Moon
RF4 Heath Shuler 2.50 6.00
Steve Young
RF5 Marshall Faulk 5.00 12.00
Emmitt Smith
RF6 Derrick Alexander WR 3.00 8.00
Jerry Rice
RF7 Barry Foster 1.00 2.50
Byron Bam Morris
RF8 Natrone Means 1.50 4.00
Chris Warren
RF9 Tim Brown 1.50 4.00
Lake Dawson
RF10 Mario Bates 1.00 2.50
Rodney Hampton

1995 Score Pin-Cards

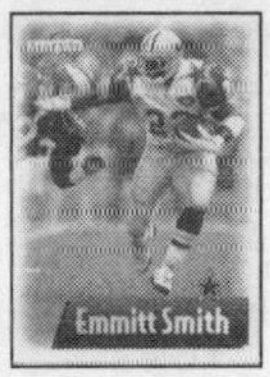

Sold in blister packs, each NFL team is represented by either one standard-size card depicting an NFL Quarterback Club member or a team helmet and a pin depicting the team logo. There are also 3 card sets in addition to regular cards for both expansion teams and the relocated St. Louis Rams, as well as a Super Bowl XXX card. The expansion and relocated team cards are black bordered with the team name repeated in the background on the front, and have copy relating to the teams' history, stadium, and logo lore on the back.These cards are also numbered 1 9. The other cards have fronts that feature color action photos of players or team helmets that fade to the surrounding white borders and are unnumbered. The player's or team's name appears on a rusty brown bar at the bottom. On a color panel, the backs present a color closeup photo and a brief player or team history. The cards are listed below by expansion and relocated teams, then alphabetically by player, and alphabetically by helmet. The prices below are for the trading cards only.

COMPLETE SET (40) 14.00 35.00
1 Jacksonville Jaguars-History .30 .75
2 Jacksonville Jaguars-Stadium .30 .75
3 Jacksonville Jaguars-Logo Lore .30 .75
4 Carolina Panthers-History .30 .75
5 Carolina Panthers-Stadium .30 .75
6 Carolina Panthers-Logo Lore .30 .75
7 St. Louis Rams-History .15 .40
8 St. Louis Rams-Stadium .15 .40
9 St. Louis Rams-Logo Lore .15 .40
10 Drew Bledsoe .80 2.00
11 Dave Brown .20 .50
12 Randall Cunningham .40 1.00
13 John Elway 1.60 4.00
14 Jim Everett .20 .50
15 Boomer Esiason .30 .75
16 Brett Favre 1.60 4.00
17 Jeff Hostetler .20 .50
18 Jim Kelly .40 1.00
19 David Klingler .20 .50
20 Dan Marino 1.60 4.00
21 Chris Miller .20 .50
22 Rick Mirer .30 .75
23 Warren Moon .40 1.00
24 Neil O'Donnell .30 .75
25 Jerry Rice .80 2.00
26 Barry Sanders 1.60 4.00
27 Junior Seau .30 .75
28 Heath Shuler .30 .75
29 Emmitt Smith 1.20 3.00
30 Arizona Cardinals .15 .40
31 Atlanta Falcons .15 .40
32 Carolina Panthers .30 .75
33 Chicago Bears .15 .40
34 Cleveland Browns .30 .75
35 Houston Oilers .15 .40
36 Indianapolis Colts .15 .40
37 Jacksonville Jaguars .30 .75
38 Kansas City Chiefs .15 .40
39 Tampa Bay Buccaneers .15 .40
40 Super Bowl XXX logo .15 .40

1995 Score Young Stars

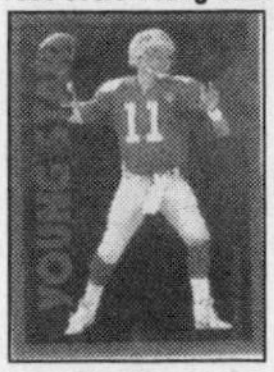

These standard size cards were available at the 1995 NFL Experience Super Bowl Card Show in exchange for three or five Pinnacle brand wrappers. Each day Pinnacle exchanged a Gold Zone or Platinum card of a different NFL star. Two thousand Gold Zone and one thousand Platinum cards were produced for each of the players listed below. We've included individual prices for the Gold Zone version. The Platinum version is valued using the multiplier line below.

COMPLETE SET (4) 10.00 25.00
*PLATINUM CARDS: 1X TO 2X GOLDS
YSG1 Marshall Faulk 3.20 8.00
YSG2 Jeff Blake 2.40 6.00
YSG3 Drew Bledsoe 4.80 12.00
YSG4 Natrone Means 2.00 5.00

1996 Score

The 1996 Score set was issued in one series totalling 275 standard-size cards. The set was issued in three different pack types: Hobby, Retail and Jumbo. The Hobby and Retail packs had a suggested retail price of .99 per pack and were packed with 10 cards in each pack, 36 packs in a box and 20 boxes in a case. Subsets include: Rookies 214-243, Second Effort 244-268, and Checklists 269-275. A Barry Sanders Dream Team Promo card was produced and priced below.

COMPLETE SET (275) 7.50 20.00
1 Emmitt Smith .50 1.25
2 Flipper Anderson .02 .10
3 Kordell Stewart .16 .40
4 Bruce Smith .07 .20
5 Marshall Faulk .20 .50
6 William Floyd .07 .20
7 Darren Woodson .07 .20
8 Lake Dawson .02 .10
9 Terry Allen .07 .20
10 Ki-Jana Carter .07 .20
11 Tony Boselli .02 .10
12 Christian Fauria .02 .10
13 Jeff George .07 .20
14 Dan Marino .60 1.50
15 Rodney Thomas .02 .10
16 Anthony Miller .07 .20
17 Chris Sanders .07 .20
18 Natrone Means .07 .20
19 Curtis Conway .15 .40
20 Ben Coates .07 .20
21 Alvin Harper .02 .10
22 Frank Sanders .07 .20
23 Boomer Esiason .07 .20
24 Lovell Pinkney .02 .10
25 Troy Aikman .30 .75
26 Quinn Early .02 .10
27 Adrian Murrell .07 .20
28 Chris Spielman .02 .10
29 Tyrone Wheatley .07 .20
30 Tim Brown .15 .40
31 Erik Kramer .02 .10
32 Warren Moon .07 .20
33 Jimmy Oliver .02 .10
34 Herman Moore .07 .20
35 Quentin Coryatt .02 .10
36 Heath Shuler .07 .20
37 Jim Kelly .15 .40
38 Mike Morris .02 .10
39 Harvey Williams .02 .10
40 Vinny Testaverde .07 .20
41 Steve McNair .25 .60
42 Jerry Rice .30 .75
43 Darick Holmes .02 .10
44 Kyle Brady .02 .10
45 Greg Lloyd .07 .20
46 Kerry Collins .15 .40
47 Willie McGinest .02 .10
48 Isaac Bruce .15 .40
49 Carnell Lake .02 .10
50 Charles Haley .07 .20
51 Troy Vincent .02 .10
52 Randall Cunningham .15 .40
53 Rashaan Salaam .07 .20
54 Willie Jackson .07 .20
55 Chris Warren .07 .20
56 Michael Irvin .15 .40
57 Mario Bates .07 .20
58 Warren Sapp .02 .10
59 John Elway .60 1.50
60 Shannon Sharpe .07 .20
61 Cornelius Bennett .02 .10
62 Robert Brooks .15 .40
63 Rodney Hampton .07 .20
64 Ken Norton Jr. .02 .10
65 Bryce Paup .02 .10
66 Eric Swann .02 .10
67 Rodney Peete .02 .10
68 Larry Centers .07 .20
69 Lamont Warren .02 .10
70 Jay Novacek .02 .10
71 Cris Carter .15 .40
72 Terrell Fletcher .02 .10
73 Andre Rison .07 .20
74 Ricky Watters .07 .20
75 Napoleon Kaufman .15 .40
76 Reggie White .15 .40
77 Yancey Thigpen .07 .20
78 Terry Kirby .07 .20
79 Deion Sanders .15 .40
80 Irving Fryar .07 .20
81 Marcus Allen .15 .40
82 Carl Pickens .07 .20
83 Drew Bledsoe .20 .50
84 Eric Metcalf .02 .10
85 Robert Smith .07 .20
86 Tamarick Vanover .07 .20
87 Henry Ellard .02 .10
88 Kevin Greene .07 .20
89 Mark Brunell .20 .50
90 Terrell Davis .25 .60
91 Brian Mitchell .02 .10
92 Aaron Bailey .02 .10
93 Rocket Ismail .02 .10
94 Dave Brown .02 .10
95 Rod Woodson .07 .20
96 Sean Gilbert .02 .10
97 Mark Seay .02 .10
98 Zack Crockett .02 .10
99 Scott Mitchell .07 .20
100 Eric Pegram .02 .10
101 David Palmer .02 .10
102 Vincent Brisby .02 .10
103 Brett Perriman .02 .10
104 Jim Everett .02 .10
105 Tony Martin .07 .20
106 Desmond Howard .07 .20
107 Stan Humphries .07 .20
108 Bill Brooks .02 .10
109 Neil Smith .07 .20
110 Michael Westbrook .15 .40
111 Herschel Walker .07 .20
112 Andre Coleman .02 .10
113 Derrick Alexander WR .07 .20
114 Jeff Blake .15 .40
115 Sherman Williams .02 .10
116 James O.Stewart .07 .20
117 Hardy Nickerson .02 .10
118 Elvis Grbac .07 .20
119 Brett Favre .60 1.50
120 Mike Sherrard .02 .10
121 Edgar Bennett .07 .20
122 Calvin Williams .02 .10
123 Brian Blades .02 .10
124 Jeff Graham .02 .10
125 Gary Brown .02 .10
126 Bernie Parmalee .02 .10
127 Kimble Anders .07 .20
128 Hugh Douglas .07 .20
129 James A.Stewart .02 .10
130 Eric Bjornson .02 .10
131 Ken Dilger .07 .20
132 Jerome Bettis .15 .40
133 Cortez Kennedy .02 .10
134 Bryan Cox .02 .10
135 Darnay Scott .07 .20
136 Bert Emanuel .07 .20
137 Steve Bono .02 .10
138 Charles Johnson .02 .10
139 Glyn Milburn .02 .10
140 Derrick Alexander DE .02 .10
141 Dave Meggett .02 .10
142 Trent Dilfer .15 .40
143 Eric Zeier .02 .10
144 Jim Harbaugh .07 .20
145 Antonio Freeman .15 .40
146 Orlando Thomas .02 .10
147 Russell Maryland .02 .10
148 Chad May .02 .10
149 Craig Heyward .02 .10
150 Aeneas Williams .02 .10
151 Kevin Williams WR .02 .10
152 Charlie Garner .07 .20
153 J.J. Stokes .15 .40
154 Stoney Case .02 .10
155 Mark Chmura .07 .20
156 Mark Bruener .02 .10
157 Derek Loville .02 .10
158 Justin Armour .02 .10
159 Brent Jones .02 .10
160 Aaron Craver .02 .10
161 Terance Mathis .02 .10
162 Chris Zorich .02 .10
163 Glenn Foley .07 .20
164 Johnny Mitchell .02 .10
165 Junior Seau .15 .40
166 Willie Davis .02 .10
167 Rick Mirer .07 .20
168 Mike Jones .02 .10
169 Greg Hill .07 .20
170 Steve Tasker .02 .10
171 Tony Bennett .02 .10
172 Jeff Hostetler .02 .10
173 Dave Krieg .02 .10
174 Mark Carrier WR .02 .10
175 Michael Haynes .02 .10
176 Chris Chandler .07 .20
177 Ernie Mills .02 .10
178 Jake Reed .07 .20
179 Errict Rhett .07 .20
180 Garrison Hearst .07 .20
181 Derrick Thomas .15 .40
182 Aaron Hayden RC .02 .10
183 Jackie Harris .02 .10
184 Curtis Martin .25 .60
185 Neil O'Donnell .07 .20
186 Derrick Moore .02 .10
187 Steve Young .25 .60
188 Pat Swilling .02 .10
189 Amp Lee .02 .10
190 Rob Johnson .15 .40
191 Todd Collins .07 .20
192 J.J. Birden .02 .10
193 O.J. McDuffie .07 .20
194 Shawn Jefferson .02 .10
195 Sean Dawkins .02 .10
196 Fred Barnett .02 .10
197 Roosevelt Potts .02 .10
198 Rob Moore .07 .20
199 Kevin Miniefield .02 .10
200 Barry Sanders .50 1.25
201 Floyd Turner .02 .10
202 Wayne Chrebet .25 .60
203 Andre Reed .07 .20
204 Tyrone Hughes .02 .10
205 Keenan McCardell .15 .40
206 Gus Frerotte .07 .20
207 Daryl Johnston .07 .20
208 Steve Broussard .02 .10
209 Steve Atwater .02 .10
210 Thurman Thomas .15 .40
211 Andre Hastings .02 .10
212 Joey Galloway .15 .40
213 Kevin Carter .02 .10
214 Keyshawn Johnson RC .40 1.00
215 Tony Brackens RC .15 .40
216 Stepfret Williams RC .07 .20
217 Mike Alstott RC .40 1.00
218 Terry Glenn RC .40 1.00
219 Tim Biakabutuka RC .15 .40
220 Eric Moulds RC .50 1.25
221 Jeff Lewis RC .07 .20
222 Bobby Engram RC .15 .40
223 Cedric Jones RC .02 .10
224 Stanley Pritchett RC .07 .20
225 Kevin Hardy RC .15 .40
226 Alex Van Dyke RC .07 .20
227 Willie Anderson RC .02 .10
228 Regan Upshaw RC .02 .10
229 Leeland McElroy RC .07 .20

230 Marvin Harrison RC 1.00 2.50
231 Eddie George RC .50 1.25
232 Lawrence Phillips RC .15 .40
233 Daryl Gardener RC .02 .10
234 Alex Molden RC .02 .10
235 Derrick Mayes RC .15 .40
236 John Mobley RC .02 .10
237 Israel Ifeanyi RC .02 .10
238 Pete Kendall RC .02 .10
239 Danny Kanell RC* .15 .40
240 Jonathan Ogden RC .15 .40
241 Reggie Brown LB RC .02 .10
242 Marcus Jones RC .02 .10
243 Jon Stark RC .02 .10
244 Barry Sanders SE .25 .60
245 Brett Favre SE .30 .75
246 John Elway SE .30 .75
247 Dan Marino SE .30 .75
248 Drew Bledsoe SE .15 .40
249 Michael Irvin SE .07 .20
250 Troy Aikman SE .15 .40
251 Emmitt Smith SE .20 .50
252 Steve Young SE .15 .40
253 Jerry Rice SE .15 .40
254 Jeff Blake SE .07 .20
255 Tim Brown SE .07 .20
256 Eric Metcalf SE .02 .10
257 Rodney Hampton SE .02 .10
258 Scott Mitchell SE .02 .10
259 Garrison Hearst SE .07 .20
260 Larry Centers SE .07 .20
261 Neil O'Donnell SE .07 .20
262 Orlando Thomas SE .02 .10
263 Hugh Douglas SE .02 .10
264 Bill Brooks SE .02 .10
265 Harvey Williams SE .02 .10
266 Charles Haley SE .07 .20
267 Greg Lloyd SE .07 .20
268 Daryl Johnston SE .07 .20
269 Dan Marino CL .15 .40
270 Jeff Blake CL .07 .20
271 John Elway CL .15 .40
272 Emmitt Smith CL .15 .40
273 Brett Favre CL .15 .40
274 Jerry Rice CL .15 .40
275 Dan Marino .15 .40
Jeff Blake
John Elway
Emmitt Smith
Brett Favre
Jerry Rice
Checklist Card
P1 Barry Sanders Promo .75 2.00
(Dream Team card)

1996 Score Artist's Proofs

COMPLETE SET (275) 250.00 500.00
*AP STARS: 5X TO 12X BASIC CARDS
*AP RCs: 2.5X TO 6X BASIC CARDS
STATED ODDS 1:36 H/R, 1:18 JUMBO

1996 Score Field Force

COMPLETE SET (275) 100.00 200.00
*STARS: 2X TO 5X BASIC CARDS
*RCs: 1X TO 2.5X BASIC CARDS
STATED ODDS 1:6 H/R, 1:3 JUMBO

1996 Score Dream Team

COMPLETE SET (10) 30.00 80.00
STATED ODDS 1:72
1 Troy Aikman 3.00 8.00
2 Michael Irvin 1.50 4.00
3 Emmitt Smith 5.00 12.00
4 John Elway 6.00 15.00
5 Barry Sanders 5.00 12.00
6 Brett Favre 6.00 15.00
7 Dan Marino 6.00 15.00
8 Drew Bledsoe 2.00 5.00
9 Jerry Rice 3.00 8.00
10 Steve Young 2.50 6.00

1996 Score Footsteps

COMPLETE SET (15) 60.00 120.00
STATED ODDS 1:35 HOBBY
1 Darick Holmes 1.25 2.50
Errict Rhett
2 Rashaan Salaam 2.00 4.00
Natrone Means
3 Ki-Jana Carter 7.50 20.00
Barry Sanders
4 Terrell Davis 7.50 20.00
Marshall Faulk
5 Rodney Thomas 1.25 2.50
Chris Warren
6 Curtis Martin 7.50 20.00
Emmitt Smith
7 Kerry Collins 6.00 15.00
Troy Aikman
8 Eric Zeier 3.00 8.00
Drew Bledsoe
9 Steve McNair 7.50 20.00
Brett Favre
10 Steve Young 5.00 12.00
Kordell Stewart
11 J.J.Stokes 6.00 12.00
Jerry Rice
12 Joey Galloway 2.00 4.00
Michael Irvin
13 Michael Westbrook 2.00 4.00
Cris Carter
14 Tamarick Vanover 2.00 4.00
Isaac Bruce
15 Orlando Thomas 3.00 6.00
Deion Sanders

1996 Score In The Zone

COMPLETE SET (20) 50.00 120.00
STATED ODDS 1:33 RETAIL
1 Brett Favre 10.00 25.00
2 Warren Moon 1.25 3.00
3 Erik Kramer .60 1.50
4 Scott Mitchell 1.25 3.00
5 Jeff Blake 2.50 6.00
6 Steve Bono .60 1.50
7 Dan Marino 10.00 25.00
8 Troy Aikman 5.00 12.00
9 Emmitt Smith 8.00 20.00
10 Curtis Martin 4.00 10.00
11 Errict Rhett 1.25 3.00
12 Terrell Davis 4.00 10.00
13 Derek Loville .60 1.50
14 Rodney Hampton 1.25 3.00
15 Cris Carter 2.50 6.00
16 Herman Moore 1.25 3.00
17 Jerry Rice 5.00 12.00
18 Ben Coates 1.25 3.00
19 Michael Irvin 2.50 6.00
20 Carl Pickens 1.25 3.00

1996 Score Numbers Game

COMPLETE SET (25) 40.00 80.00
STATED ODDS 1:17 HOB/RET, 1:9 JUM
1 Barry Sanders 4.00 8.00
2 Drew Bledsoe 2.00 4.00
3 Brett Favre 5.00 10.00
4 John Elway 5.00 10.00
5 Dan Marino 5.00 10.00
6 Michael Irvin 1.50 3.00
7 Troy Aikman 2.50 5.00
8 Emmitt Smith 4.00 8.00
9 Steve Young 2.00 4.00
10 Jerry Rice 2.50 5.00
11 Chris Sanders .75 1.50
12 Herman Moore .75 1.50
13 Frank Sanders .75 1.50
14 Kordell Stewart 1.50 3.00
15 Jeff Blake 1.50 3.00
16 Robert Brooks 1.50 3.00
17 Marshall Faulk 2.00 4.00
18 Carl Pickens .75 1.50
19 Greg Lloyd .75 1.50
20 Curtis Conway 1.50 3.00
21 Chris Warren .75 1.50
22 Natrone Means .75 1.50
23 Deion Sanders 1.50 3.00
24 Neil O'Donnell .75 1.50
25 Ricky Watters .75 1.50

1996 Score Settle the Score

COMPLETE SET (30) 150.00 400.00
STATED ODDS 1:36 JUM, 1:72 SPEC.RETAIL
1 Frank Sanders 2.50 6.00
Charlie Garner
2 Drew Bledsoe 5.00 12.00
Neil O'Donnell
3 Jerry Rice 6.00 15.00
Craig Heyward
4 Emmitt Smith 10.00 25.00
Rod Woodson
5 Derrick Holmes 12.50 30.00
Dan Marino
6 Kerry Collins 5.00 12.00
Steve Young
7 Rashaan Salaam 12.50 30.00
Brett Favre
8 Curtis Conway 12.50 30.00
Barry Sanders
9 Troy Aikman 15.00 30.00
Dan Marino
10 Dan Marino 12.50 30.00
Neil O'Donnell
11 Eric Zeier 4.00 10.00
Steve McNair
12 Jeff Blake 4.00 10.00
Kordell Stewart
13 Troy Aikman 6.00 15.00
Heath Shuler
14 Michael Irvin 6.00 15.00
Jerry Rice
15 Emmitt Smith 10.00 25.00
Ricky Watters
16 John Elway 12.50 30.00
Steve Bono
17 John Elway 12.50 30.00
Rick Mirer
18 John Elway 12.50 30.00
Tim Brown
19 Barry Sanders 20.00 40.00
Brett Favre
20 Barry Sanders 10.00 25.00
Warren Moon
21 Trent Dilfer 12.50 30.00
Brett Favre
22 Rodney Thomas 1.50 4.00
James O.Stewart
23 Jim Harbaugh 5.00 12.00
Drew Bledsoe
24 Marcus Allen 2.50 6.00
Harvey Williams
25 Tamarick Vanover 4.00 10.00
Joey Galloway
26 Dan Marino 12.50 30.00
Drew Bledsoe
27 Mario Bates 6.00 15.00
Jerry Rice
28 Tyrone Wheatley 2.50 6.00
Michael Westbrook
29 Napoleon Kaufman 4.00 10.00
Junior Seau
30 J.J.Stokes 2.50 6.00
Isaac Bruce

1996 Score WLAF

This 25-card set features players of the World League of American Football. The first six cards were printed using Pinnacle's lenticular technology and titled "Team Leaders." The fronts display color action player photos with the player's name below. The backs carry a head photo along with information about the player. The set was released in its own foil wrapper along with one of six Team Inserts.

COMPLETE SET (25) 15.00 30.00
1 Will Furrer TL .50 1.25
2 Kelly Holcomb TL 6.00 15.00
3 Steve Pelluer TL .40 1.00
4 William Perry TL .80 2.00
5 Manfred Burgsmuller TL .40 1.00
6 Siran Stacy TL .40 1.00
7 T.C. Wright .50 1.25
8 Malcolm Showell .40 1.00
9 Phillip Bobo .40 1.00
10 Marvin Marshall .40 1.00
11 Demetrius Davis .50 1.25
12 Mike Middleton .40 1.00
13 Nathaniel Bolton .40 1.00
14 Mario Bailey .40 1.00
15 George Hegamin .40 1.00
16 Preston Jones .40 1.00
17 Russell White .50 1.25
18 Victor X. Ebubedike .40 1.00
19 Andy Kelly .50 1.25
20 Tommie Boyd .40 1.00
21 Percy Snow .40 1.00
22 Gavin Hastings .40 1.00
23 Steve Matthews .40 1.00
24 George Coghill .40 1.00
NNO Cover Card .40 1.00

1996 Score WLAF Team Inserts

COMPLETE SET (6)
1 Mike Middleton 1.50 4.00
Kelly Holcomb
2 Steve Pelluer 2.00 5.00
Nathaniel Bolton
Mario Bailey
George Hegamin
5 Tommie Boyd 1.50 4.00
Manfred Burgsmuller
Andy Kelly
Percy Snow

1997 Score

The 1997 Score set was issued in one series totalling 330 cards. The fronts feature color action player photos in white borders. The backs carry player information and career statistics. The set contains the topical subsets: The Draft Class (273-307), and The Big Play (308-327). Cards were distributed in 20-card retail packs carrying a suggested price of $1.99, as well 27-card blister packs with a suggested retail of $2.99. Blister packs also contained one ad/cover promo card as listed below.

COMPLETE SET (330) 10.00 25.00
1 John Elway .75 2.00
2 Drew Bledsoe .25 .60
3 Brett Favre .75 2.00
4 Emmitt Smith .60 1.50
5 Kerry Collins .20 .50
6 Jerry Rice .40 1.00
7 Kordell Stewart .20 .50
8 Barry Sanders .60 1.50
9 Dan Marino .75 2.00
10 Steve Young .25 .60
11 Erik Kramer .07 .20
12 Warren Moon .20 .50
13 Chris Calloway .07 .20
14 Doug Evans .07 .20
15 Darren Woodson .07 .20
16 Alonzo Spellman .07 .20
17 Greg Hill .07 .20
18 Aaron Craver .07 .20
19 Jeff Hostetler .07 .20
20 William Thomas .07 .20
21 Marco Coleman .07 .20
22 Wayne Simmons .07 .20
23 Donnell Woolford .07 .20
24 Vinny Testaverde .10 .30
25 Ed McCaffrey .10 .30
26 Jim Everett .07 .20
27 Gilbert Brown .10 .30
28 Jason Dunn .07 .20
29 Stanley Pritchett .07 .20
30 Joey Galloway .10 .30
31 Amani Toomer .10 .30
32 Chris Penn .07 .20
33 Aeneas Williams .07 .20
34 Bobby Taylor .07 .20
35 Bryan Still .07 .20
36 Ty Law .10 .30
37 Shannon Sharpe .10 .30
38 Marty Carter .07 .20
39 Sam Mills .07 .20
40 William Floyd .10 .30
41 Brad Johnson .20 .50
42 Sean Dawkins .07 .20
43 Michael Irvin .20 .50
44 Jeff George .10 .30
45 Brent Jones .10 .30
46 Mark Brunell .25 .60
47 Rob Moore .10 .30
48 Hardy Nickerson .07 .20
49 Chris Chandler .10 .30
50 Willie Anderson .07 .20
51 Isaac Bruce .20 .50
52 Natrone Means .10 .30
53 Tony Banks .10 .30
54 Marshall Faulk .25 .60
55 Michael Westbrook .10 .30
56 Bruce Smith .10 .30
57 Jamal Anderson .20 .50
58 Jackie Harris .07 .20
59 Sean Gilbert .07 .20
60 Ki-Jana Carter .07 .20
61 Eric Moulds .20 .50
62 James O.Stewart .10 .30
63 Jeff Blake .10 .30
64 O.J. McDuffie .10 .30
65 Neil Smith .10 .30
66 Kevin Smith .07 .20
67 Terry Allen .20 .50
68 Sean LaChapelle .07 .20
69 Rashaan Salaam .07 .20
70 Jeff Graham .07 .20
71 Mark Carrier WR .07 .20
72 Allen Aldridge .07 .20
73 Keenan McCardell .10 .30
74 Willie McGinest .07 .20
75 Napoleon Kaufman .20 .50
76 Jerris McPhail .07 .20
77 Eric Swann .07 .20
78 Kimble Anders .10 .30
79 Charles Johnson .10 .30
80 Bryan Cox .07 .20
81 Johnnie Morton .10 .30
82 Andre Rison .10 .30
83 Corey Miller .07 .20
84 Troy Drayton .07 .20
85 Jim Harbaugh .10 .30
86 Wesley Walls .10 .30
87 Bryce Paup .07 .20
88 Curtis Martin .25 .60
89 Michael Sinclair .07 .20
90 Chris T. Jones .07 .20
91 Jake Reed .10 .30
92 LeRoy Butler .07 .20
93 Reggie Tongue .07 .20
94 Bert Emanuel .10 .30
95 Stan Humphries .10 .30
96 Neil O'Donnell .10 .30
97 Troy Vincent .07 .20
98 Mike Alstott .20 .50
99 Chad Cota .07 .20
100 Marvin Harrison .20 .50
101 Terrell Owens .25 .60
102 Dave Brown .07 .20
103 Harvey Williams .07 .20
104 Desmond Howard .10 .30
105 Carl Pickens .10 .30
106 Kent Graham .07 .20
107 Michael Bates .07 .20
108 Terrell Davis .25 .60
109 Marcus Allen .20 .50
110 Ray Zellars .07 .20
111 Chris Warren .10 .30
112 Phillippi Sparks .07 .20
113 Craig Erickson .07 .20
114 Eddie George .20 .50
115 Daryl Johnston .10 .30
116 Ricky Watters .10 .30
117 Tedy Bruschi .40 1.00
118 Mike Mamula .07 .20
119 Ken Harvey .07 .20
120 John Randle .10 .30
121 Mark Chmura .10 .30
122 Sam Gash .07 .20
123 John Kasay .07 .20
124 Barry Minter .07 .20
125 Raymont Harris .07 .20
126 Derrick Thomas .20 .50
127 Trent Dilfer .20 .50
128 Carnell Lake .07 .20
129 Brian Dawkins .20 .50
130 Tyronne Drakeford .07 .20
131 Daryl Gardener .07 .20
132 Fred Strickland .07 .20
133 Kevin Hardy .07 .20
134 Winslow Oliver .07 .20
135 Herman Moore .10 .30
136 Keith Byars .07 .20
137 Harold Green .07 .20
138 Ty Detmer .10 .30
139 Lamar Thomas .07 .20
140 Elvis Grbac .10 .30
141 Edgar Bennett .10 .30
142 Cornelius Bennett .07 .20
143 Tony Tolbert .07 .20
144 James Hasty .07 .20
145 Ben Coates .10 .30
146 Errict Rhett .07 .20
147 Jason Sehorn .10 .30
148 Michael Jackson .10 .30
149 John Mobley .07 .20
150 Walt Harris .07 .20
151 Terry Kirby .10 .30
152 Devin Wyman .07 .20
153 Ray Crockett .07 .20
154 Quinn Early .07 .20
155 Rodney Thomas .07 .20
156 Mark Seay .07 .20
157 Derrick Alexander WR .10 .30
158 Lamar Lathon .07 .20
159 Anthony Miller .07 .20
160 Shawn Wooden RC .07 .20
161 Antonio Freeman .20 .50
162 Cortez Kennedy .07 .20
163 Rickey Dudley .10 .30
164 Tony Carter .07 .20
165 Kevin Williams .07 .20
166 Reggie White .20 .50
167 Tim Bowens .07 .20
168 Roy Barker .07 .20
169 Adrian Murrell .10 .30
170 Anthony Johnson .07 .20
171 Terry Glenn .20 .50
172 Jeff Lewis .07 .20
173 Dorsey Levens .20 .50
174 Willie Jackson .07 .20
175 Willie Clay .07 .20
176 Richmond Webb .07 .20
177 Shawn Lee .07 .20
178 Joe Aska .07 .20
179 Rod Woodson .10 .30
180 Jim Schwantz RC .07 .20
181 Alfred Williams .07 .20
182 Ferric Collons .07 .20
183 Ken Norton Jr. .07 .20
184 Rick Mirer .07 .20
185 Leeland McElroy .07 .20
186 Rodney Hampton .10 .30
187 Ted Popson RC .07 .20
188 Fred Barnett .07 .20
189 Junior Seau .20 .50
190 Micheal Barrow .07 .20
191 Corey Widmer .07 .20
192 Rodney Peete .07 .20
193 Rod Smith WR .20 .50
194 Muhsin Muhammad .10 .30
195 Keith Jackson .07 .20
196 Jimmy Smith .10 .30
197 Dave Meggett .07 .20
198 Lawrence Phillips .07 .20
199 Chad Brown .07 .20
200 Darrin Smith .07 .20
201 Larry Centers .10 .30
202 Kevin Greene .10 .30
203 Sherman Williams .07 .20
204 Chris Sanders .07 .20
205 Shawn Jefferson .07 .20
206 Thurman Thomas .20 .50
207 Keyshawn Johnson .20 .50
208 Bryant Young .07 .20
209 Tim Biakabutuka .10 .30
210 Troy Aikman .40 1.00
211 Quentin Coryatt .07 .20
212 Karim Abdul-Jabbar .20 .50
213 Brian Blades .07 .20
214 Ray Farmer .07 .20
215 Simeon Rice .10 .30
216 Tyrone Braxton .07 .20
217 Jerome Woods .07 .20
218 Charles Way .10 .30
219 Garrison Hearst .10 .30
220 Bobby Engram .10 .30
221 Billy Davis RC .07 .20
222 Ken Dilger .07 .20
223 Robert Smith .10 .30
224 John Friesz .07 .20
225 Charlie Garner .10 .30
226 Jerome Bettis .20 .50
227 Darnay Scott .10 .30
228 Terance Mathis .10 .30
229 Brian Williams LB .07 .20
230 Cris Carter .20 .50
231 Michael Haynes .07 .20
232 Cedric Jones .07 .20
233 Danny Kanell .10 .30
234 Deion Sanders .20 .50
235 Steve Atwater .07 .20
236 Jonathan Ogden .07 .20
237 Lake Dawson .07 .20
238 Eric Allen .07 .20
239 Eddie Kennison .10 .30
240 Irving Fryar .10 .30
241 Michael Strahan .10 .30
242 Steve McNair .25 .60
243 Terrell Buckley .07 .20
244 Merton Hanks .07 .20
245 Jessie Armstead .07 .20
246 Dana Stubblefield .07 .20
247 Brett Perriman .07 .20
248 Mark Collins .07 .20
249 Willie Roaf .07 .20
250 Gus Frerotte .07 .20
251 William Fuller .07 .20
252 Tamarick Vanover .10 .30
253 Scott Mitchell .07 .20
254 Eric Metcalf .10 .30
255 Herschel Walker .10 .30
256 Robert Brooks .10 .30
257 Zach Thomas .20 .50
258 Alvin Harper .07 .20
259 Wayne Chrebet .20 .50
260 Bill Romanowski .07 .20
261 Willie Green .07 .20
262 Dale Carter .07 .20
263 Chris Slade .07 .20
264 J.J. Stokes .10 .30
265 Tim Brown .20 .50
266 Eric Davis .07 .20
267 Mark Carrier DB .07 .20
268 Tony Martin .10 .30
269 Tyrone Wheatley .10 .30
270 Eugene Robinson .07 .20
271 Curtis Conway .10 .30
272 Michael Timpson .07 .20
273 Orlando Pace RC .20 .50
274 Tiki Barber RC 1.25 3.00
275 Byron Hanspard RC .10 .30
276 Warrick Dunn RC .60 1.50
277 Rae Carruth RC .07 .20
278 Bryant Westbrook RC .07 .20
279 Antowain Smith RC .50 1.25
280 Peter Boulware RC .20 .50
281 Reidel Anthony RC .20 .50
282 Troy Davis RC .10 .30
283 Jake Plummer RC .75 2.00
284 Chris Canty RC .07 .20
285 Dwayne Rudd RC .20 .50
286 Ike Hilliard RC .30 .75
287 Reinard Wilson RC .10 .30
288 Corey Dillon RC .75 2.00
289 Tony Gonzalez RC .75 2.00
290 Darnell Autry RC .10 .30
291 Kevin Lockett RC .10 .30
292 Darrell Russell RC .07 .20
293 Jim Druckenmiller RC .10 .30
294 Simon Mitchell RC .07 .20
295 Joey Kent RC .20 .50
296 Shawn Springs RC .10 .30
297 James Farrior RC .20 .50
298 Sedrick Shaw RC .10 .30
299 Marcus Harris RC .07 .20
300 Danny Wuerffel RC .20 .50
301 Marc Edwards RC .07 .20
302 Michael Booker RC .07 .20
303 David LaFleur RC .07 .20
304 Mike Adams WR RC .07 .20
305 Pat Barnes RC .20 .50
306 George Jones RC .10 .30
307 Yatil Green RC .10 .30
308 Drew Bledsoe TBP .20 .50
309 Troy Aikman TBP .20 .50
310 Terrell Davis TBP .10 .30
311 Jim Everett TBP .07 .20
312 John Elway TBP .40 1.00
313 Barry Sanders TBP .30 .75
314 Jim Harbaugh TBP .10 .30
315 Steve Young TBP .20 .50
316 Dan Marino TBP .40 1.00
317 Michael Irvin TBP .20 .50
318 Emmitt Smith TBP .30 .75
319 Jeff Hostetler TBP .07 .20
320 Mark Brunell TBP .20 .50
321 Jeff Blake TBP .20 .50
322 Scott Mitchell TBP .07 .20
323 Boomer Esiason TBP .10 .30
324 Jerome Bettis TBP .20 .50
325 Warren Moon TBP .10 .30
326 Neil O'Donnell TBP .10 .30
327 Jim Kelly TBP .20 .50
328 Dan Marino CL .20 .50
329 John Elway CL .20 .50
330 Drew Bledsoe CL .10 .30
P1 Troy Aikman Promo .40 1.00
P2 Brett Favre Promo .75 2.00
P3 Dan Marino Promo .75 2.00
P4 Barry Sanders Promo .60 1.50

1997 Score Hobby Reserve

COMPLETE SET (330) 15.00 30.00
*HOBBY RESERVE: .6X TO 1.5X

1997 Score Reserve Collection

COMPLETE SET (330) 150.00 300.00
*RES.COLLECT.STARS: 6X TO 15X BASIC CARDS
*RES.COLLECT.RCs: 3X TO 8X BASIC CARDS
STATED ODDS 1:11 HOBBY RESERVE

1997 Score Showcase

COMPLETE SET (330) 60.00 120.00
*SHOWCASE STARS: 2.5X TO 6X BASIC CARDS
*SHOWCASE RCs: 1.2X TO 3X BASIC CARDS
STATED ODDS 1:4 HOB, 1:7 RET

1997 Score Showcase Artist's Proofs

COMPLETE SET (330) 200.00 400.00
*STARS: 8X TO 20X BASIC CARDS
*RCs: 4X TO 10X BASIC CARDS
STATED ODDS 1:17 H,1:35R, 1:23 HOB.RES.

1997 Score Franchise

COMPLETE SET (16) 75.00 150.00
STATED ODDS 1:47 HOBBY,1:30 RETAIL
*HOLO.ENHANCED: .6X TO 1.5X BASIC INS.
HOLO.ENHANCED STATED ODDS 1:125
1 Emmitt Smith 8.00 20.00
2 Barry Sanders 8.00 20.00
3 Brett Favre 10.00 25.00
4 Drew Bledsoe 3.00 8.00
5 Jerry Rice 5.00 12.00
6 Troy Aikman 5.00 12.00
7 Dan Marino 10.00 25.00
8 John Elway 10.00 25.00
9 Steve Young 3.00 8.00
10 Eddie George 2.50 6.00
11 Keyshawn Johnson 2.50 6.00
12 Terrell Davis 3.00 8.00
13 Marshall Faulk 3.00 8.00
14 Kerry Collins 2.50 6.00
15 Deion Sanders 2.50 6.00
16 Joey Galloway 1.50 4.00

1997 Score New Breed

COMPLETE SET (18) 35.00 70.00
COMP.SERIES 1 SET (9) 15.00 30.00
COMP.SERIES 2 SET (9) 20.00 40.00
1-9: STATED ODDS 1:12 RETAIL
10-18: STATED ODDS 1:15 HOBBY RESERVE
1 Eddie George 1.50 4.00
2 Terrell Davis 2.00 5.00
3 Curtis Martin 2.00 5.00
4 Tony Banks 1.00 2.50
5 Lawrence Phillips .60 1.50
6 Terry Glenn 1.50 4.00
7 Jerome Bettis 1.50 4.00
8 Karim Abdul-Jabbar 1.50 4.00
9 Napoleon Kaufman 1.50 4.00
10 Isaac Bruce 1.50 4.00
11 Keyshawn Johnson UER 1.50 4.00
(photo actually Bobby Hamilton)
12 Rickey Dudley 1.00 2.50
13 Eddie Kennison 1.00 2.50
14 Marvin Harrison 1.50 4.00
15 Emmitt Smith 5.00 12.00
16 Barry Sanders 5.00 12.00
17 Kerry Collins 1.50 4.00
18 Brett Favre 6.00 15.00

1997 Score Showdown in Titletown

COMPLETE SET (22) 10.00 25.00
1D Troy Aikman 1.25 3.00
1G Brett Favre 2.50 6.00
2D Emmitt Smith 2.00 5.00
2G Dorsey Levens .60 1.50
3D Daryl Johnston .60 1.50
3G Mark Chmura .50 1.25
4D Michael Irvin .75 2.00
4G Robert Brooks .60 1.50
5D Billy Davis .40 1.00
5G Antonio Freeman .60 1.50
6D Tony Tolbert .40 1.00
6G Reggie White .75 2.00
7D Fred Strickland .40 1.00
7G Brian Williams .40 1.00
8D Deion Sanders .75 2.00
8G LeRoy Butler .50 1.25
9D Kevin Smith .40 1.00
9G Doug Evans .40 1.00
10D Darren Woodson .60 1.50
10G Eugene Robinson .50 1.25
11D Troy Aikman CL .75 2.00
11G Brett Favre CL 1.25 3.00

1997 Score Specialists

COMPLETE SET (18) 50.00 100.00
STATED ODDS 1:15 HOBBY RESERVE
1 Brett Favre 6.00 15.00
2 Drew Bledsoe 2.00 5.00
3 Mark Brunell 2.00 5.00
4 Kerry Collins 1.50 4.00
5 John Elway 6.00 15.00
6 Barry Sanders 5.00 12.00
7 Troy Aikman 3.00 8.00
8 Jerry Rice 3.00 8.00
9 Dan Marino 6.00 15.00
10 Neil O'Donnell 1.00 2.50
11 Scott Mitchell 1.00 2.50
12 Jim Harbaugh 1.00 2.50
13 Emmitt Smith 5.00 12.00
14 Steve Young 2.00 5.00
15 Dave Brown .60 1.50
16 Jeff Blake 1.00 2.50
17 Jim Everett .60 1.50
18 Kordell Stewart 1.50 4.00

1998 Score

The 1998 Score set was issued in one series totalling 270 cards. The fronts feature action color player photos in black-and-white borders. The backs carry player information and career statistics. The set contains the topical subset, Off Season (253-267), and three checklist cards (268-270).

COMPLETE SET (270) 15.00 40.00
1 John Elway .75 2.00
2 Kordell Stewart .20 .50
3 Warrick Dunn .20 .50
4 Brad Johnson .20 .50
5 Kerry Collins .10 .30
6 Danny Kanell .10 .30
7 Emmitt Smith .60 1.50
8 Jamal Anderson .20 .50
9 Jim Harbaugh .10 .30
10 Tony Martin .10 .30
11 Rod Smith .10 .30
12 Dorsey Levens .20 .50
13 Steve McNair .20 .50
14 Derrick Thomas .20 .50
15 Rob Moore .10 .30
16 Peter Boulware .07 .20
17 Terry Allen .20 .50
18 Joey Galloway .10 .30
19 Jerome Bettis .20 .50
20 Carl Pickens .10 .30
21 Napoleon Kaufman .20 .50
22 Troy Aikman .40 1.00
23 Curtis Conway .10 .30
24 Adrian Murrell .10 .30
25 Elvis Grbac .10 .30
26 Garrison Hearst .20 .50
27 Chris Sanders .07 .20
28 Scott Mitchell .10 .30
29 Junior Seau .20 .50
30 Chris Chandler .10 .30
31 Kevin Hardy .07 .20
32 Terrell Davis .20 .50
33 Keyshawn Johnson .20 .50
34 Natrone Means .10 .30
35 Antowain Smith .20 .50
36 Jake Plummer .20 .50
37 Isaac Bruce .20 .50
38 Tony Banks .10 .30
39 Reidel Anthony .10 .30
40 Darren Woodson .07 .20
41 Corey Dillon .20 .50
42 Antonio Freeman .20 .50
43 Eddie George .20 .50
44 Yancey Thigpen .07 .20
45 Tim Brown .20 .50
46 Wayne Chrebet .20 .50
47 Andre Rison .10 .30
48 Michael Strahan .10 .30
49 Deion Sanders .20 .50
50 Eric Moulds .20 .50
51 Mark Brunell .20 .50
52 Rae Carruth .07 .20
53 Warren Sapp .10 .30
54 Mark Chmura .10 .30
55 Darrell Green .10 .30
56 Quinn Early .07 .20
57 Barry Sanders .60 1.50
58 Neil O'Donnell .10 .30
59 Tony Brackens .07 .20
60 Willie Davis .07 .20
61 Shannon Sharpe .10 .30
62 Shawn Springs .07 .20
63 Tony Gonzalez .20 .50
64 Rodney Harrison .07 .20
65 Terance Mathis .10 .30
66 Brett Favre .75 2.00
67 Eric Swann .07 .20
68 Kevin Turner .07 .20
69 Tyrone Wheatley .10 .30
70 Trent Dilfer .20 .50
71 Bryan Cox .07 .20
72 Lake Dawson .07 .20
73 Will Blackwell .07 .20
74 Fred Lane .07 .20
75 Ty Detmer .10 .30
76 Eddie Kennison .10 .30
77 Jimmy Smith .10 .30
78 Chris Calloway .07 .20
79 Shawn Jefferson .07 .20
80 Dan Marino .75 2.00
81 LeRoy Butler .07 .20
82 William Roaf .07 .20
83 Rick Mirer .07 .20
84 Dermontti Dawson .07 .20
85 Errict Rhett .10 .30
86 Lamar Thomas .07 .20
87 Lamar Lathon .07 .20
88 John Randle .10 .30
89 Darryl Williams .07 .20
90 Keenan McCardell .10 .30
91 Erik Kramer .07 .20
92 Ken Dilger .07 .20
93 Dave Meggett .07 .20
94 Jeff Blake .10 .30
95 Ed McCaffrey .10 .30
96 Charles Johnson .07 .20
97 Irving Spikes .07 .20
98 Mike Alstott .20 .50
99 Vincent Brisby .07 .20
100 Michael Westbrook .10 .30
101 Rickey Dudley .07 .20
102 Bert Emanuel .10 .30
103 Daryl Johnston .10 .30
104 Lawrence Phillips .07 .20
105 Eric Bieniemy .07 .20
106 Bryant Westbrook .07 .20
107 Rob Johnson .10 .30
108 Ray Zellars .07 .20
109 Anthony Johnson .07 .20
110 Reggie White .20 .50
111 Wesley Walls .10 .30
112 Amani Toomer .10 .30
113 Gary Brown .07 .20
114 Brian Blades .07 .20
115 Alex Van Dyke .07 .20
116 Michael Haynes .07 .20
117 Jessie Armstead .07 .20
118 James Jett .10 .30
119 Troy Drayton .07 .20
120 Craig Heyward .07 .20
121 Steve Atwater .07 .20
122 Tiki Barber .20 .50
123 Karim Abdul-Jabbar .20 .50
124 Kimble Anders .10 .30
125 Frank Sanders .10 .30
126 David Sloan .07 .20
127 Andre Hastings .07 .20
128 Vinny Testaverde .10 .30
129 Robert Smith .20 .50
130 Horace Copeland .07 .20
131 Larry Centers .07 .20
132 J.J. Stokes .10 .30
133 Ike Hilliard .10 .30
134 Muhsin Muhammad .10 .30
135 Sean Dawkins .07 .20
136 Raymont Harris .07 .20
137 Lamar Smith .10 .30
138 David Palmer .07 .20
139 Steve Young .25 .60
140 Bryan Still .07 .20
141 Keith Byars .07 .20
142 Cris Carter .20 .50
143 Charlie Garner .10 .30
144 Drew Bledsoe .30 .75
145 Simeon Rice .10 .30
146 Merton Hanks .07 .20
147 Aeneas Williams .07 .20
148 Rodney Hampton .10 .30
149 Zach Thomas .20 .50
150 Mark Bruener .07 .20
151 Jason Dunn .07 .20
152 Danny Wuerffel .10 .30
153 Jim Druckenmiller .07 .20
154 Greg Hill .07 .20
155 Earnest Byner .07 .20
156 Greg Lloyd .07 .20
157 John Mobley .07 .20
158 Tim Biakabutuka .10 .30
159 Terrell Owens .20 .50
160 O.J. McDuffie .10 .30
161 Glenn Foley .10 .30
162 Derrick Brooks .20 .50
163 Dave Brown .07 .20
164 Ki-Jana Carter .07 .20
165 Bobby Hoying .10 .30
166 Randal Hill .07 .20
167 Michael Irvin .20 .50
168 Bruce Smith .10 .30
169 Troy Davis .07 .20
170 Derrick Mayes .10 .30
171 Henry Ellard .10 .30
172 Dana Stubblefield .07 .20
173 Willie McGinest .07 .20
174 Leeland McElroy .07 .20
175 Edgar Bennett .07 .20
176 Robert Porcher .07 .20
177 Randall Cunningham .20 .50
178 Jim Everett .07 .20
179 Jake Reed .10 .30
180 Quentin Coryatt .07 .20
181 William Floyd .07 .20
182 Jason Sehorn .10 .30
183 Carnell Lake .07 .20
184 Dexter Coakley .07 .20
185 Derrick Alexander WR .10 .30
186 Johnnie Morton .10 .30
187 Irving Fryar .10 .30
188 Warren Moon .20 .50
189 Todd Collins .07 .20
190 Ken Norton .07 .20
191 Terry Glenn .20 .50
192 Rashaan Salaam .07 .20
193 Jerry Rice .40 1.00
194 James O.Stewart .10 .30
195 David LaFleur .07 .20
196 Eric Green .07 .20
197 Gus Frerotte .07 .20
198 Willie Green .07 .20
199 Marshall Faulk .25 .60
200 Brett Perriman .07 .20
201 Darnay Scott .10 .30
202 Marvin Harrison .20 .50
203 Joe Aska .07 .20
204 Darrien Gordon .07 .20
205 Herman Moore .10 .30
206 Curtis Martin .20 .50
207 Derek Loville .07 .20
208 Dale Carter .07 .20
209 Heath Shuler .07 .20
210 Jonathan Ogden .07 .20
211 Leslie Shepherd .07 .20
212 Tony Boselli .07 .20
213 Eric Metcalf .10 .30
214 Neil Smith .10 .30

215 Anthony Miller	.07	.20
216 Jeff George	.10	.30
217 Charles Way	.07	.20
218 Mario Bates	.10	.30
219 Ben Coates	.10	.30
220 Michael Jackson	.07	.20
221 Thurman Thomas	.20	.50
222 Kyle Brady	.07	.20
223 Marcus Allen	.20	.50
224 Robert Brooks	.10	.30
225 Yatil Green	.07	.20
226 Byron Hanspard	.07	.20
227 Andre Reed	.10	.30
228 Chris Warren	.10	.30
229 Jackie Harris	.07	.20
230 Ricky Watters	.10	.30
231 Bobby Engram	.10	.30
232 Tamarick Vanover	.07	.20
233 Peyton Manning RC	7.50	15.00
234 Curtis Enis RC	.30	.75
235 Randy Moss RC	4.00	10.00
236 Charles Woodson RC	.60	1.50
237 Robert Edwards RC	.40	1.00
238 Jacquez Green RC	.40	1.00
239 Keith Brooking RC	.60	1.50
240 Jerome Pathon RC	.60	1.50
241 Kevin Dyson RC	.60	1.50
242 Fred Taylor RC	.75	2.00
243 Tavian Banks RC	.40	1.00
244 Marcus Nash RC	.30	.75
245 Brian Griese RC	1.00	2.50
246 Andre Wadsworth RC	.40	1.00
247 Ahman Green RC	1.50	4.00
248 Joe Jurevicius RC	.60	1.50
249 Germane Crowell RC	.40	1.00
250 Skip Hicks RC	.40	1.00
251 Ryan Leaf RC	.60	1.50
252 Hines Ward RC	2.50	6.00
253 John Elway OS	.40	1.00
254 Mark Brunell OS	.20	.50
255 Brett Favre OS	.40	1.00
256 Troy Aikman OS	.20	.50
257 Warrick Dunn OS	.10	.30
258 Barry Sanders OS	.30	.75
259 Eddie George OS	.20	.50
260 Kordell Stewart OS	.20	.50
261 Emmitt Smith OS	.30	.75
262 Steve Young OS	.20	.50
263 Terrell Davis OS	.20	.50
264 Dorsey Levens OS	.10	.30
265 Dan Marino OS	.40	1.00
266 Jerry Rice OS	.20	.50
267 Drew Bledsoe OS	.20	.50
268 Brett Favre CL	.25	.60
269 Barry Sanders CL	.20	.50
270 Terrell Davis CL	.20	.50
251AU Ryan Leaf AUTO	15.00	40.00

1998 Score Showcase

COMPLETE SET (110) 75.00 150.00
*SHOWCASE STARS: 2.5X TO 6X BASIC CARDS
*SHOWCASE RCs: .6X TO 1.5X BASIC CARDS
SHOWCASE STATED ODDS 1:7

1998 Score Showcase One-of-One

STATED PRINT RUN 1 SET

1998 Score Showcase Artist's Proofs

*STARS: 4X TO 10X BASIC CARDS
*ROOKIES: 1.5X TO 4X BASIC CARDS
SHOWCASE STATED ODDS 1:35

1998 Score Complete Players

COMPLETE SET (30) 35.00 80.00
STATED ODDS 1:11

1A Brett Favre	2.00	5.00
1B Brett Favre	2.00	5.00
1C Brett Favre	2.00	5.00
2A John Elway	2.00	5.00
2B John Elway	2.00	5.00
2C John Elway	2.00	5.00
3A Emmitt Smith	1.50	4.00
3B Emmitt Smith	1.50	4.00
3C Emmitt Smith	1.50	4.00
4A Kordell Stewart	.50	1.25
4B Kordell Stewart	.50	1.25
4C Kordell Stewart	.50	1.25
5A Dan Marino	2.00	5.00
5B Dan Marino	2.00	5.00
5C Dan Marino	2.00	5.00
6A Mark Brunell	.50	1.25
6B Mark Brunell	.50	1.25
6C Mark Brunell	.50	1.25
7A Terrell Davis	.50	1.25
7B Terrell Davis	.50	1.25
7C Terrell Davis	.50	1.25
8A Barry Sanders	1.50	4.00
8B Barry Sanders	1.50	4.00
8C Barry Sanders	1.50	4.00
9A Warrick Dunn	.50	1.25
9B Warrick Dunn	.50	1.25
9C Warrick Dunn	.50	1.25
10A Jerry Rice	1.00	2.50
10B Jerry Rice	1.00	2.50
10C Jerry Rice	1.00	2.50

1998 Score Epix

COMP.ORANGE SET (24) 100.00 200.00
OVERALL STATED ODDS 1:61 HOBBY
*PURPLE CARDS: .75X TO 2X ORANGE
*EMERALD CARDS: 2X TO 4X ORANGE
ONLY ORANGE CARDS PRICED BELOW

E1 Emmitt Smith SEA	7.50	20.00
E2 Troy Aikman SEA	5.00	12.00
E3 Terrell Davis SEA	2.50	6.00
E4 Drew Bledsoe SEA	4.00	10.00
E5 Jeff George SEA	1.50	4.00
E6 Kerry Collins SEA	1.50	4.00
E7 Antonio Freeman SEA	2.00	5.00
E8 Herman Moore SEA	2.00	5.00
E9 Barry Sanders GAME	5.00	12.00
E10 Brett Favre GAME	6.00	15.00
E11 Michael Irvin GAME	1.25	3.00
E12 Steve Young GAME	2.00	5.00
E13 Mark Brunell GAME	2.50	6.00
E14 Jerome Bettis GAME	1.25	3.00
E15 Deion Sanders GAME	1.25	3.00
E16 Jeff Blake GAME	1.25	3.00
E17 Dan Marino MOM	10.00	25.00
E18 Eddie George MOM	2.00	5.00
E19 Jerry Rice MOM	5.00	12.00
E20 John Elway MOM	10.00	25.00
E21 Curtis Martin MOM	2.50	6.00
E22 Kordell Stewart MOM	2.00	5.00
E23 Junior Seau MOM	2.00	5.00
E24 Reggie White MOM	2.00	5.00

1998 Score Epix Hobby

COMPLETE SET (24) 60.00 120.00
RED IMAGE PRINT RUN 1500 SETS
RED MILESTONE PRINT RUN 500 SETS
RED JOURNEY PRINT RUN 3500 SETS
RED SHOWDOWN PRINT RUN 2500 SETS
*PURPLE CARDS: .6X TO 1.5X REDS
PURPLE IMAGE PRINT RUN 750 SETS
PURPLE MILESTONE PRINT RUN 200 SETS
PURPLE JOURNEY PRINT RUN 1750 SETS
PURPLE SHOWDOWN PRINT RUN 1250 SETS
*EMERALD 1-6/13-24: 1.5X TO 4X REDS
EMERALD IMAGE PRINT RUN 250 SETS
EMERALD JOURNEY PRINT RUN 500 SETS
EMERALD SHOWDOWN PRINT RUN 350 SETS
*EMERALD M7-M12: 4X TO 10X REDS
EMERALD MILESTONE PRINT RUN 30 SETS
OVERALL STATED ODDS 1:61

I1 Barry Sanders IMG	5.00	12.00
I2 Curtis Martin IMG	1.25	3.00
I3 John Elway IMG	6.00	15.00
I4 Jerome Bettis IMG	1.25	3.00
I5 Deion Sanders IMG	1.25	3.00
I6 Corey Dillon IMG	1.25	3.00
M7 Terrell Davis MILE	4.00	10.00
M8 Jerry Rice MILE	7.50	20.00
M9 Eddie George MILE	2.00	5.00
M10 Mark Brunell MILE	6.00	15.00
M11 Dorsey Levens MILE	3.00	8.00
M12 Kerry Collins MILE	1.25	3.00
J13 Brett Favre JRNY	3.00	8.00
J14 Kordell Stewart JRNY	1.25	3.00
J15 Steve Young JRNY	1.00	2.50
J16 Steve McNair JRNY	.60	1.50
J17 Emmitt Smith JRNY	2.50	6.00
J18 Terry Glenn JRNY	.60	1.50
S19 Warrick Dunn SHOW	1.25	3.00
S20 Dan Marino SHOW	4.00	10.00
S21 Drew Bledsoe SHOW	1.50	4.00
S22 Troy Aikman SHOW	2.00	5.00
S23 Antonio Freeman SHOW	.75	2.00
S24 Napoleon Kaufman SHOW	.75	2.00

1998 Score Rookie Autographs

STATED PRINT RUN 500 SETS

1 Stephen Alexander	10.00	25.00
2 Tavian Banks	10.00	25.00
3 Charlie Batch	12.50	30.00
4 Keith Brooking	12.50	30.00
5 Thad Busby	10.00	25.00
6 John Dutton	7.50	20.00
7 Tim Dwight	12.50	30.00
8 Kevin Dyson	10.00	25.00
9 Robert Edwards	10.00	25.00
10 Greg Ellis	7.50	20.00
12A Curtis Enis Black Ink	10.00	25.00
12B Curtis Enis Blue Ink	10.00	25.00
13 Chris Fuamatu-Ma'afala	10.00	25.00
14 Ahman Green	20.00	40.00
15 Jacquez Green	10.00	25.00
16 Brian Griese	15.00	40.00
17 Skip Hicks	10.00	25.00
18 Robert Holcombe	10.00	25.00
19 Tebucky Jones	10.00	25.00
20 Joe Jurevicius	12.50	30.00
21 Ryan Leaf	12.50	30.00
22 Leonard Little	12.50	30.00
23 Alonzo Mayes	7.50	20.00
24 Randy Moss	75.00	150.00
25 Michael Myers	7.50	20.00
26 Marcus Nash	7.50	20.00
27 Jerome Pathon	12.50	30.00
28 Jason Peter	7.50	20.00
29 Anthony Simmons	10.00	25.00
30 Tony Simmons	10.00	25.00
31 Takeo Spikes	12.50	30.00
32 Duane Starks	7.50	20.00
33 Fred Taylor	20.00	40.00
34 Hines Ward	50.00	80.00
35 Peyton Manning No Auto	4.00	10.00

1998 Score Star Salute

COMPLETE SET (20) 40.00 100.00
STATED ODDS 1:35
*PROMO: .3X TO .8X BASIC INSERTS

1 Terrell Davis	2.00	5.00
2 Barry Sanders	5.00	12.00
3 Steve Young	2.50	6.00
4 Drew Bledsoe	2.50	6.00
5 Kordell Stewart	1.25	3.00
6 Emmitt Smith	6.00	15.00
7 Dorsey Levens	1.25	3.00
8 Corey Dillon	2.00	5.00
9 Jerome Bettis	2.00	5.00
10 Herman Moore	1.00	2.50
11 Brett Favre	8.00	20.00
12 Antonio Freeman	1.25	3.00
13 Mark Brunell	2.00	5.00
14 John Elway	6.00	15.00
15 Terry Glenn	2.00	5.00
16 Warrick Dunn	2.00	5.00
17 Eddie George	2.00	5.00
18 Troy Aikman	3.00	8.00
19 Deion Sanders	2.00	5.00
20 Jerry Rice	4.00	10.00

1999 Score

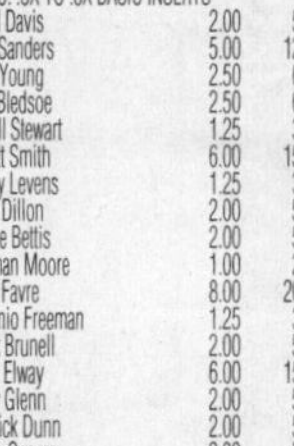

This 275 card set, released in June 1999, was issued in 10 card hobby and retail packs. The last 55 cards of the set feature either 1999 Rookies or subsets of popular players and were all short printed. These cards were released in a ratio of one every three hobby packs and one every nine retail packs. Notable Rookie Cards include Tim Couch, Edgerrin James and Ricky Williams.

COMPLETE SET (275) 25.00 60.00
COMP.SET w/o SP's (220) 6.00 15.00

1 Randy Moss	.25	.60
2 Randall Cunningham	.25	.60
3 Cris Carter	.25	.60
4 Robert Smith	.20	.50
5 Jake Reed	.20	.50
6 Leroy Hoard	.15	.40
7 John Randle	.20	.50
8 Brett Favre	.75	2.00
9 Antonio Freeman	.20	.50
10 Dorsey Levens	.20	.50
11 Robert Brooks	.20	.50
12 Derrick Mayes	.15	.40
13 Mark Chmura	.15	.40
14 Darick Holmes	.15	.40
15 Vonnie Holliday	.15	.40
16 Mike Alstott	.25	.60
17 Warrick Dunn	.20	.50
18 Trent Dilfer	.20	.50
19 Jacquez Green	.15	.40
20 Reidel Anthony	.15	.40
21 Warren Sapp	.20	.50
22 Bert Emanuel	.20	.50
23 Curtis Enis	.15	.40
24 Curtis Conway	.20	.50
25 Bobby Engram	.20	.50
26 Erik Kramer	.20	.50
27 Moses Moreno	.20	.50
28 Edgar Bennett	.20	.50
29 Barry Sanders	.60	1.50
30 Charlie Batch	.20	.50
31 Herman Moore	.20	.50
32 Johnnie Morton	.20	.50
33 Germane Crowell	.15	.40
34 Terry Fair	.15	.40
35 Gary Brown	.15	.40
36 Kent Graham	.15	.40
37 Kerry Collins	.20	.50
38 Charles Way	.15	.40
39 Tiki Barber	.25	.60
40 Ike Hilliard	.20	.50
41 Joe Jurevicius	.15	.40
42 Michael Strahan	.20	.50
43 Jason Sehorn	.20	.50
44 Brad Johnson	.20	.50
45 Terry Allen	.20	.50
46 Skip Hicks	.15	.40
47 Michael Westbrook	.15	.40
48 Leslie Shepherd	.15	.40
49 Stephen Alexander	.15	.40
50 Albert Connell	.15	.40
51 Darrell Green	.25	.60
52 Jake Plummer	.20	.50
53 Adrian Murrell	.20	.50
54 Frank Sanders	.15	.40
55 Rob Moore	.15	.40
56 Larry Centers	.20	.50
57 Simeon Rice	.15	.40
58 Andre Wadsworth	.15	.40
59 Duce Staley	.20	.50
60 Charles Johnson	.15	.40
61 Charlie Garner	.20	.50
62 Bobby Hoying	.15	.40
63 Daryl Johnston	.25	.60
64 Emmitt Smith	.60	1.50
65 Troy Aikman	.40	1.00
66 Michael Irvin	.25	.60
67 Deion Sanders	.25	.60
68 Chris Warren	.20	.50
69 Darren Woodson	.20	.50
70 Rod Woodson	.25	.60
71 Travis Jervey	.20	.50
72 Jerry Rice	.50	1.25
73 Terrell Owens	.25	.60
74 Steve Young	.30	.75
75 Garrison Hearst	.20	.50
76 J.J. Stokes	.15	.40
77 Ken Norton	.15	.40
78 R.W. McQuarters	.15	.40
79 Bryant Young	.20	.50
80 Jamal Anderson	.20	.50
81 Chris Chandler	.20	.50
82 Terance Mathis	.15	.40
83 Tim Dwight	.20	.50
84 O.J. Santiago	.15	.40
85 Chris Calloway	.15	.40
86 Keith Brooking	.20	.50
87 Eddie Kennison	.20	.50
88 Willie Roaf	.20	.50
89 Cam Cleeland	.15	.40
90 Lamar Smith	.15	.40
91 Sean Dawkins	.15	.40
92 Tim Biakabutuka	.20	.50
93 Muhsin Muhammad	.20	.50
94 Steve Beuerlein	.20	.50
95 Rae Carruth	.15	.40
96 Wesley Walls	.20	.50
97 Kevin Greene	.20	.50
98 Trent Green	.20	.50
99 Tony Banks	.20	.50
100 Greg Hill	.15	.40
101 Robert Holcombe	.15	.40
102 Isaac Bruce	.25	.60
103 Amp Lee	.15	.40
104 Az-Zahir Hakim	.15	.40
105 Warren Moon	.25	.60
106 Jeff George	.15	.40
107 Rocket Ismail	.20	.50
108 Kordell Stewart	.20	.50
109 Jerome Bettis	.25	.60
110 Courtney Hawkins	.15	.40
111 Chris Fuamatu-Ma'afala	.15	.40
112 Levon Kirkland	.15	.40
113 Hines Ward	.25	.60
114 Will Blackwell	.15	.40
115 Corey Dillon	.20	.50
116 Carl Pickens	.20	.50
117 Neil O'Donnell	.20	.50
118 Jeff Blake	.20	.50
119 Darnay Scott	.15	.40
120 Takeo Spikes	.15	.40
121 Steve McNair	.25	.60
122 Frank Wycheck	.20	.50
123 Eddie George	.20	.50
124 Chris Sanders	.15	.40
125 Yancey Thigpen	.15	.40
126 Kevin Dyson	.15	.40
127 Blaine Bishop	.15	.40
128 Fred Taylor	.20	.50
129 Mark Brunell	.20	.50
130 Jimmy Smith	.20	.50
131 Keenan McCardell	.20	.50
132 Kyle Brady	.15	.40
133 Tavian Banks	.15	.40
134 James Stewart	.15	.40
135 Kevin Hardy	.15	.40
136 Jonathan Quinn	.15	.40
137 Jermaine Lewis	.15	.40
138 Priest Holmes	.25	.60
139 Scott Mitchell	.15	.40
140 Eric Zeier	.15	.40
141 Patrick Johnson	.15	.40
142 Ray Lewis	.25	.60
143 Terry Kirby	.15	.40
144 Ty Detmer	.20	.50
145 Irv Smith	.15	.40
146 Chris Spielman	.20	.50
147 Antonio Langham	.15	.40
148 Dan Marino	.75	2.00
149 O.J. McDuffie	.20	.50
150 Oronde Gadsden	.15	.40
151 Karim Abdul-Jabbar	.20	.50
152 Yatil Green	.15	.40
153 Zach Thomas	.25	.60
154 John Avery	.15	.40
155 Lamar Thomas	.15	.40
156 Drew Bledsoe	.25	.60
157 Terry Glenn	.20	.50
158 Ben Coates	.20	.50
159 Shawn Jefferson	.15	.40
160 Sedrick Shaw	.15	.40
161 Tony Simmons	.15	.40
162 Ty Law	.20	.50
163 Robert Edwards	.15	.40
164 Curtis Martin	.25	.60
165 Keyshawn Johnson	.20	.50
166 Vinny Testaverde	.20	.50
167 Aaron Glenn	.15	.40
168 Wayne Chrebet	.20	.50
169 Dedric Ward	.15	.40
170 Peyton Manning	.75	2.00
171 Marshall Faulk	.25	.60
172 Marvin Harrison	.25	.60
173 Jerome Pathon	.15	.40
174 Ken Dilger	.15	.40
175 E.G. Green	.15	.40
176 Doug Flutie	.25	.60
177 Thurman Thomas	.25	.60
178 Andre Reed	.25	.60
179 Eric Moulds	.20	.50
180 Antowain Smith	.15	.40
181 Bruce Smith	.25	.60
182 Rob Johnson	.20	.50
183 Terrell Davis	.25	.60
184 John Elway	.75	2.00
185 Ed McCaffrey	.20	.50
186 Rod Smith	.20	.50
187 Shannon Sharpe	.25	.60
188 Marcus Nash	.15	.40
189 Brian Griese	.20	.50
190 Neil Smith	.15	.40
191 Bubby Brister	.15	.40
192 Ryan Leaf	.20	.50
193 Natrone Means	.20	.50
194 Mikhael Ricks	.15	.40
195 Junior Seau	.25	.60
196 Jim Harbaugh	.20	.50
197 Bryan Still	.15	.40
198 Freddie Jones	.15	.40
199 Andre Rison	.20	.50
200 Elvis Grbac	.15	.40
201 Byron Bam Morris	.15	.40
202 Rashaan Shehee	.15	.40
203 Kimble Anders	.15	.40
204 Donnell Bennett	.15	.40
205 Tony Gonzalez	.25	.60
206 Derrick Alexander WR	.15	.40
207 Jon Kitna	.20	.50
208 Ricky Watters	.20	.50
209 Joey Galloway	.20	.50
210 Ahman Green	.20	.50
211 Shawn Springs	.15	.40
212 Michael Sinclair	.15	.40
213 Napoleon Kaufman	.15	.40
214 Tim Brown	.25	.60
215 Charles Woodson	.25	.60
216 Harvey Williams	.15	.40
217 Jon Ritchie	.15	.40
218 Rich Gannon	.20	.50
219 Rickey Dudley	.15	.40
220 James Jett	.15	.40
221 Tim Couch RC	1.00	2.50
222 Ricky Williams RC	1.50	4.00
223 Donovan McNabb RC	2.50	6.00
224 Edgerrin James RC	1.25	3.00
225 Torry Holt RC	1.50	4.00
226 Daunte Culpepper RC	1.00	2.50
227 Akili Smith RC	.75	2.00
228 Champ Bailey RC	2.00	5.00
229 Chris Claiborne RC	.60	1.50
230 Chris McAlister RC	.75	2.00
231 Troy Edwards RC	.75	2.00
232 Jevon Kearse RC	1.00	2.50
233 Shaun King RC	.75	2.00
234 David Boston RC	.75	2.00
235 Peerless Price RC	.75	2.00
236 Cecil Collins RC	.60	1.50
237 Rob Konrad RC	.60	1.50
238 Cade McNown RC UER	.75	2.00
(college listed as UNLV)		
239 Shawn Bryson RC	.60	1.50
240 Kevin Faulk RC	1.00	2.50
241 Scott Covington RC	.60	1.50
242 James Johnson RC	.60	1.50
243 Mike Cloud RC	.60	1.50
244 Aaron Brooks RC	1.00	2.50
245 Sedrick Irvin RC	.60	1.50
246 Amos Zereoue RC	.75	2.00
247 Jermaine Fazande RC	.60	1.50
248 Joe Germaine RC	.75	2.00
249 Brock Huard RC	.75	2.00
250 Craig Yeast RC	.60	1.50
251 Travis McGriff RC	.60	1.50
252 D'Wayne Bates RC	.60	1.50
253 Na Brown RC	.60	1.50
254 Tai Streets RC	.75	2.00
255 Andy Katzenmoyer RC	.75	2.00
256 Kevin Johnson RC	.75	2.00
257 Joe Montgomery RC	.60	1.50
258 Karsten Bailey RC	.60	1.50
259 De'Mond Parker RC	.60	1.50
260 Reginald Kelly RC	.60	1.50
261 Eddie George AP	.50	1.25
262 Jamal Anderson AP	.50	1.25
263 Barry Sanders AP	1.50	4.00
264 Fred Taylor AP	.50	1.25
265 Keyshawn Johnson AP	.50	1.25
266 Jerry Rice AP	1.25	3.00
267 Doug Flutie AP	.60	1.50
268 Deion Sanders AP	.60	1.50
269 Randall Cunningham AP	.60	1.50
270 Steve Young AP	.75	2.00
271 John Elway GC	2.00	5.00
Terrell Davis GC		
272 Peyton Manning GC	2.00	5.00
Marshall Faulk GC		
273 Brett Favre GC	2.00	5.00
Antonio Freeman GC		
274 Troy Aikman GC	1.50	4.00
Emmitt Smith GC		
275 Cris Carter GC	.60	1.50
Randy Moss GC		

1999 Score Artist's Proofs

*STARS: 50X TO 120X BASIC CARDS
*RCs: 8X TO 20X BASIC CARDS
*APs/GCs: 15X TO 40X BASIC CARDS
STATED PRINT RUN 10 SERIAL #'d SETS

1999 Score Showcase

COMPLETE SET (275) 200.00 400.00
*STARS: 2.5X TO 6X BASIC CARDS
*RCs: .6X TO 1.5X BASIC CARDS
*APs/GCs: .8X TO 2X BASIC CARDS
STATED PRINT RUN 1989 SERIAL #'d SETS

1999 Score 10th Anniversary Reprints

COMPLETE SET (20) 30.00 60.00
STATED PRINT RUN 1989 SERIAL #'d SETS
FIRST 150-CARDS WERE SIGNED

1 Barry Sanders	5.00	12.00
2 Troy Aikman	3.00	8.00
3 John Elway	5.00	12.00
4 Cris Carter	1.50	4.00
5 Tim Brown	1.50	4.00
6 Doug Flutie	1.50	4.00
7 Chris Chandler	1.00	2.50
8 Thurman Thomas	1.00	2.50
9 Steve Young	2.00	5.00
10 Dan Marino	5.00	12.00
11 Derrick Thomas	1.00	2.50
12 Bubby Brister	.60	1.50
13 Jerry Rice	3.00	8.00
14 Andre Rison	1.00	2.50
15 Randall Cunningham	1.50	4.00
16 Vinny Testaverde	1.00	2.50
17 Michael Irvin	1.00	2.50
18 Rod Woodson	1.00	2.50
19 Neil Smith	1.00	2.50
20 Deion Sanders	1.50	4.00

1999 Score 10th Anniversary Reprints Autographs

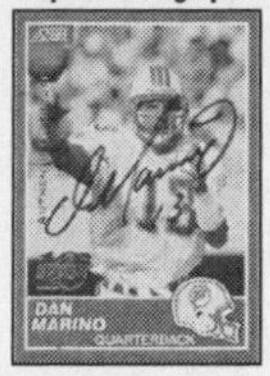

STATED PRINT RUN 150 SERIAL #'d SETS

1 Barry Sanders	200.00	350.00
2 Troy Aikman	125.00	250.00
3 John Elway	125.00	250.00
4 Cris Carter	60.00	120.00
5 Tim Brown	60.00	120.00
6 Doug Flutie	30.00	80.00
7 Chris Chandler	30.00	80.00
8 Thurman Thomas	60.00	120.00
9 Steve Young	100.00	200.00
10 Dan Marino	125.00	250.00
11 Derrick Thomas	200.00	350.00
12 Bubby Brister	25.00	60.00
13 Jerry Rice	125.00	250.00
14 Andre Rison	50.00	100.00
15 Randall Cunningham	50.00	100.00
16 Vinny Testaverde	30.00	80.00
17 Michael Irvin	60.00	120.00
18 Rod Woodson	90.00	150.00
19 Neil Smith	25.00	60.00
20 Deion Sanders	100.00	175.00

1999 Score Complete Players

COMPLETE SET (30) 25.00 60.00
STATED ODDS 1:17 HOB, 1:35 RET

1 Antonio Freeman	.75	2.00
2 Troy Aikman	1.50	4.00
3 Jerry Rice	1.50	4.00
4 Brett Favre	2.50	6.00
5 Cris Carter	.75	2.00
6 Jamal Anderson	.75	2.00
7 John Elway	2.50	6.00
8 Mark Brunell	.75	2.00
9 Steve McNair	.75	2.00
10 Kordell Stewart	.50	1.25
11 Drew Bledsoe	1.00	2.50
12 Tim Couch	.75	2.00
13 Dan Marino	2.50	6.00
14 Akili Smith	.50	1.25
15 Peyton Manning	2.50	6.00
16 Jake Plummer	.50	1.25
17 Jerome Bettis	.75	2.00
18 Randy Moss	2.00	5.00
19 Keyshawn Johnson	.75	2.00
20 Barry Sanders	2.50	6.00
21 Ricky Williams	1.00	2.50
22 Emmitt Smith	1.50	4.00
23 Corey Dillon	.75	2.00
24 Dorsey Levens	.75	2.00
25 Donovan McNabb	2.50	6.00
26 Curtis Martin	.75	2.00
27 Eddie George	.75	2.00
28 Fred Taylor	.75	2.00
29 Steve Young	1.00	2.50
30 Terrell Davis	.75	2.00

1999 Score Franchise

COMPLETE SET (31) 60.00 120.00
STATED ODDS 1:35

1 Brett Favre	6.00	15.00
2 Randy Moss	5.00	12.00
3 Mike Alstott	2.00	5.00
4 Barry Sanders	6.00	15.00
5 Curtis Enis	.75	2.00
6 Ike Hilliard	.75	2.00
7 Emmitt Smith	4.00	10.00
8 Jake Plummer	1.25	3.00
9 Brad Johnson	2.00	5.00
10 Duce Staley	2.00	5.00
11 Jamal Anderson	2.00	5.00
12 Steve Young	2.50	6.00
13 Eddie Kennison	1.25	3.00
14 Isaac Bruce	2.00	5.00
15 Muhsin Muhammad	1.25	3.00
16 Dan Marino	6.00	15.00
17 Drew Bledsoe	2.50	6.00
18 Curtis Martin	2.00	5.00
19 Doug Flutie	2.00	5.00
20 Peyton Manning	6.00	15.00
21 Kordell Stewart	1.25	3.00
22 Ty Detmer	.75	2.00
23 Corey Dillon	2.00	5.00
24 Mark Brunell	2.00	5.00
25 Priest Holmes	3.00	8.00
26 Eddie George	2.00	5.00
27 John Elway	6.00	15.00
28 Natrone Means	1.25	3.00
29 Tim Brown	2.00	5.00
30 Andre Rison	1.25	3.00
31 Joey Galloway	1.25	3.00

1999 Score Future Franchise

COMPLETE SET (31) 75.00 150.00
STATED ODDS 1:35 HOBBY

1 Aaron Brooks	5.00	12.00
Brett Favre		
2 Daunte Culpepper	4.00	10.00
Randy Moss		
3 Shaun King	1.50	4.00
Mike Alstott		
4 Sedrick Irvin	5.00	12.00
Barry Sanders		
5 Cade McNown	1.50	4.00
Curtis Enis		
6 Joe Montgomery	1.25	3.00
Ike Hilliard		
7 Wane McGarity	3.00	8.00
Emmitt Smith		
8 David Boston	1.50	4.00
Jake Plummer		
9 Champ Bailey	1.50	4.00
Brad Johnson		
10 Donovan McNabb	5.00	12.00
Duce Staley		
11 Reginald Kelly	1.50	4.00
Jamal Anderson		
12 Tai Streets	2.00	5.00
Steve Young		
13 Ricky Williams	2.50	6.00
Eddie Kennison		
14 Torry Holt	3.00	8.00
Isaac Bruce		
15 Mike Rucker	1.50	4.00
Mushin Muhammad		
16 James Johnson	5.00	12.00
Dan Marino		
17 Kevin Faulk	1.50	4.00
Drew Bledsoe		
18 Randy Thomas	1.25	3.00
Curtis Martin		
19 Peerless Price	2.50	6.00
Doug Flutie		
20 Edgerrin James	5.00	12.00
Peyton Manning		
21 Troy Edwards	1.50	4.00
Kordell Stewart		
22 Tim Couch	1.50	4.00
Ty Detmer		
23 Akili Smith	1.50	4.00
Corey Dillon		
24 Fernando Bryant	1.50	4.00
Mark Brunell		
25 Chris McAlister	2.50	6.00
Priest Holmes		
26 Jevon Kearse	1.50	4.00
Eddie George		
27 Travis McGriff	5.00	12.00
John Elway		
28 Jermaine Fazande	1.25	3.00
Natrone Means		
29 Dameane Douglas	1.50	4.00
Tim Brown		
30 Mike Cloud	1.25	3.00
Andre Rison		
31 Brock Huard	1.50	4.00
Joey Galloway		

1999 Score Millennium Men

COMPLETE SET (3) 30.00 60.00
STATED PRINT RUN 1000 SERIAL #'d SETS
FIRST 100-CARDS WERE SIGNED
INSERTED IN RETAIL PACKS ONLY

1 Barry Sanders	10.00	25.00
2 Ricky Williams	4.00	10.00
3 Barry Sanders	10.00	25.00
Ricky Williams		
1AU Barry Sanders AU	75.00	150.00
2AU Ricky Williams AU	30.00	80.00
3AU Barry Sanders AU	125.00	250.00
Ricky Williams AU		

1999 Score Numbers Game

COMPLETE SET (30) 25.00 60.00
RANDOM INSERTS IN HOBBY PACKS

1 Brett Favre/4212	2.50	6.00
2 Steve Young/4170	1.00	2.50
3 Jake Plummer/3737	1.00	2.50
4 Drew Bledsoe/3633	1.00	2.50
5 Dan Marino/3497	2.50	6.00
6 Peyton Manning/3739	2.00	5.00
7 Randall Cunningham/3704	.60	1.50
8 John Elway/2806	3.00	8.00
9 Doug Flutie/2711	1.00	2.50
10 Mark Brunell/2601	1.00	2.50
11 Troy Aikman/2330	2.00	5.00
12 Terrell Davis/2008	1.00	2.50
13 Jamal Anderson/1846	.75	2.00
14 Garrison Hearst/1570	.75	2.00
15 Barry Sanders/1491	4.00	10.00
16 Emmitt Smith/1332	2.50	6.00
17 Marshall Faulk/1319	1.50	4.00
18 Eddie George/1294	1.00	2.50
19 Curtis Martin/1287	.75	2.00
20 Fred Taylor/1223	.75	2.00
21 Corey Dillon/1130	.75	2.00
22 Antonio Freeman/1424	.75	2.00
23 Eric Moulds/1368	.75	2.00
24 Randy Moss/1313	2.50	6.00
25 Rod Smith/1222	.60	1.50
26 Jerry Rice/1157	2.50	6.00
27 Keyshawn Johnson/1131	.75	2.00
28 Terrell Owens/1097	1.00	2.50
29 Tim Brown/1012	1.00	2.50
30 Cris Carter/1011	1.00	2.50

1999 Score Rookie Preview Autographs

STATED PRINT RUN 600 SIGNED SETS
RANDOM INSERTS IN HOBBY PACKS

1 Champ Bailey	7.50	20.00
2 D'Wayne Bates	4.00	10.00
3 Michael Bishop	6.00	15.00
4 David Boston	6.00	15.00
5 Na Brown	4.00	10.00
6 Shawn Bryson	4.00	10.00
7 Chris Claiborne	4.00	10.00
8 Mike Cloud	4.00	10.00
9 Cecil Collins	3.00	8.00
10 Daunte Culpepper	20.00	40.00
11 Autry Denson	4.00	10.00
12 Troy Edwards	4.00	10.00
13 Kevin Faulk	6.00	15.00
14 Joe Germaine	4.00	10.00
15 Torry Holt	7.50	20.00
16 Sedrick Irvin	3.00	8.00
17 Edgerrin James	20.00	40.00
18 James Johnson	6.00	15.00
19 Kevin Johnson	4.00	10.00
20 Corby Jones	3.00	8.00
21 Jevon Kearse	10.00	25.00
22 Olandis Gary	6.00	15.00
23 Jim Kleinsasser	4.00	10.00
24 Rob Konrad	4.00	10.00
25 Chris McAlister	6.00	15.00
26 Darnell McDonald	4.00	10.00
27 Travis McGriff	3.00	8.00
28 Donovan McNabb	25.00	50.00
29 Cade McNown	4.00	10.00
30 De'Mond Parker	3.00	8.00
31 Peerless Price	6.00	15.00
32 Akili Smith	3.00	8.00
33 Tai Streets	6.00	15.00
34 Ricky Williams	10.00	25.00

1999 Score Scoring Core

COMPLETE SET (30) 25.00 60.00
STATED ODDS 1:17 HOB, 1:35 RET

1 Antonio Freeman	.75	2.00
2 Troy Aikman	1.50	4.00
3 Jerry Rice	1.50	4.00
4 Brett Favre	2.50	6.00
5 Cris Carter	.75	2.00
6 Jamal Anderson	.75	2.00
7 John Elway	2.50	6.00
8 Tim Brown	.75	2.00
9 Mark Brunell	.75	2.00
10 Terrell Owens	.75	2.00
11 Drew Bledsoe	1.00	2.50
12 Tim Couch	.60	1.50
13 Dan Marino	2.50	6.00
14 Marshall Faulk	1.00	2.50
15 Peyton Manning	2.50	6.00
16 Jake Plummer	.50	1.25
17 Jerome Bettis	.75	2.00
18 Randy Moss	2.00	5.00
19 Charlie Batch	.75	2.00
20 Barry Sanders	2.50	6.00
21 Ricky Williams	.75	2.00
22 Emmitt Smith	1.50	4.00
23 Joey Galloway	.50	1.25
24 Herman Moore	.50	1.25
25 Natrone Means	.50	1.25
26 Mike Alstott	.75	2.00
27 Eddie George	.75	2.00
28 Fred Taylor	.75	2.00
29 Steve Young	1.00	2.50
30 Terrell Davis	.75	2.00

1999 Score Settle the Score

COMPLETE SET (30) 30.00 60.00
STATED ODDS 1:17 RETAIL

1 Brett Favre	2.50	6.00
Randall Cunningham		
2 Dan Marino	2.50	6.00
Doug Flutie		
3 Emmitt Smith	1.50	4.00
Terry Allen		
4 Barry Sanders	2.50	6.00
Warrick Dunn		
5 Eddie George	.75	2.00
Corey Dillon		
6 Drew Bledsoe	1.00	2.50
Vinny Testaverde		
7 Troy Aikman	1.50	4.00
Jake Plummer		
8 Terrell Davis	.75	2.00
Jamal Anderson		
9 John Elway	2.50	6.00
Chris Chandler		
10 Mark Brunell	.75	2.00
Steve Young		
11 Cris Carter	.75	2.00
Herman Moore		
12 Kordell Stewart	.75	2.00
Steve McNair		
13 Natrone Means	.75	2.00
Napoleon Kaufman		
14 Curtis Martin	1.00	2.50
Marshall Faulk		
15 Antonio Freeman	.75	2.00
Terrell Owens		
16 Terry Glenn	.50	1.25
Wayne Chrebet		
17 Garrison Hearst	.50	1.25
Dorsey Levens		
18 Ryan Leaf	.75	2.00
Jon Kitna		
19 Robert Smith	.75	2.00
Mike Alstott		
20 Jerry Rice	2.00	5.00
Randy Moss		
21 Peyton Manning	2.50	6.00
Charlie Batch		
22 Fred Taylor	.75	2.00
Jerome Bettis		
23 Keyshawn Johnson	.75	2.00
Eric Moulds		
24 Tim Couch	1.50	4.00
Ricky Williams		
25 Carl Pickens	.75	2.00
Isaac Bruce		
26 Deion Sanders	.75	2.00
Charles Woodson		
27 Tim Brown	.75	2.00
Rod Smith		
28 Daunte Culpepper	3.00	8.00
Donovan McNabb		
29 Joey Galloway	.50	1.25
Ed McCaffrey		
30 Karim Abdul-Jabbar	.75	2.00
Antowain Smith		

1999 Score Supplemental

Released in complete set form only, the 1999 Score Supplemental set contains 110-cards intended to update the basic 1999 Score product. The set is broken down into 66 cards labeled 1999 Rookie, 24 Mid-Season update cards (which also included some 1999 rookies previously included in the base Score set), and 20 Star Salute veteran cards. Each sealed factory set also contained two packs of Score Supplemental Cards.

COMPLETE SET (110) 6.00 15.00
COMP.FACT.SET (110) 8.00 20.00

S1 Chris Greisen RC	.15	.40
S2 Sherdrick Bonner RC	.15	.40
S3 Joel Makovicka RC	.15	.40
S4 Andy McCullough RC	.15	.40
S5 Jeff Paulk RC	.15	.40
S6 Brandon Stokley RC	.25	.60
S7 Sheldon Jackson RC	.15	.40
S8 Bobby Collins RC	.15	.40
S9 Kamil Loud RC	.15	.40

S10 Antoine Winfield RC .15 .40
S11 Jerry Azumah RC .15 .40
S12 James Allen RC .15 .40
S13 Nick Williams RC .15 .40
S14 Michael Basnight RC .15 .40
S15 Damon Griffin RC .25 .60
S16 Ronnie Powell RC .15 .40
S17 Darrin Chiaverini RC .15 .40
S18 Mark Campbell RC .15 .40
S19 Mike Lucky RC .15 .40
S20 Wane McGarity RC .15 .40
S21 Jason Tucker RC .20 .50
S22 Ebenezer Ekuban RC .15 .40
S23 Robert Thomas RC .15 .40
S24 Dat Nguyen RC .25 .60
S25 Olandis Gary RC .25 .60
S26 Desmond Clark RC .20 .50
S27 Andre Cooper RC .15 .40
S28 Chris Watson RC .15 .40
S29 Al Wilson RC .25 .60
S30 Cory Sauter RC .15 .40
S31 Brock Olivo RC .15 .40
S32 Basil Mitchell RC .15 .40
S33 Matt Snider RC .15 .40
S34 Antuan Edwards RC .15 .40
S35 Mike McKenzie RC .25 .60
S36 Terrence Wilkins RC .20 .50
S37 Fernando Bryant RC .15 .40
S38 Larry Parker RC .20 .50
S39 Autry Denson RC .15 .40
S40 Jim Kleinsasser RC .25 .60
S41 Michael Bishop RC .20 .50
S42 Andy Katzenmoyer .20 .50
S43 Brett Bech RC .15 .40
S44 Sean Bennett RC .15 .40
S45 Dan Campbell RC .25 .60
S46 Ray Lucas RC .20 .50
S47 Scott Dreisbach RC .15 .40
S48 Cecil Martin RC .15 .40
S49 Dameane Douglas RC .15 .40
S50 Jed Weaver RC .15 .40
S51 Jerame Tuman RC .15 .40
S52 Steve Heiden RC .15 .40
S53 Jeff Garcia RC .75 2.00
S54 Terry Jackson RC .15 .40
S55 Charlie Rogers RC .15 .40
S56 Lamar King RC .15 .40
S57 Kurt Warner RC 2.00 5.00
S58 Dre Bly RC .25 .60
S59 Justin Watson RC .15 .40
S60 Rabih Abdullah RC .15 .40
S61 Martin Gramatica RC .15 .40
S62 Darnell McDonald RC .15 .40
S63 Anthony McFarland RC .20 .50
S64 Larry Brown TE RC .15 .40
S65 Kevin Daft RC .15 .40
S66 Mike Sellers .20 .50
S67 Ken Oxendine MS .15 .40
S68 Errict Rhett MS .15 .40
S69 Stoney Case MS .15 .40
S70 Jonathan Linton MS .15 .40
S71 Marcus Robinson MS .20 .50
S72 Shane Matthews MS .15 .40
S73 Cade McNown MS .20 .50
S74 Akili Smith MS .20 .50
S75 Karim Abdul-Jabbar MS .20 .50
S76 Tim Couch MS .25 .60
S77 Kevin Johnson MS .20 .50
S78 Ron Rivers MS .15 .40
S79 Bill Schroeder MS .20 .50
S80 Edgerrin James MS .30 .75
S81 Cecil Collins MS .15 .40
S82 Matthew Hatchette MS .20 .50
S83 Daunte Culpepper MS .25 .60
S84 Ricky Williams MS .40 1.00
S85 Tyrone Wheatley MS .20 .50
S86 Donovan McNabb MS 1.00 2.50
S87 Marshall Faulk MS .25 .60
S88 Torry Holt MS .40 1.00
S89 Stephen Davis MS .20 .50
S90 Brad Johnson MS .20 .50
S91 Jake Plummer SS .20 .50
S92 Emmitt Smith SS .60 1.50
S93 Troy Aikman SS .40 1.00
S94 John Elway SS .75 2.00
S95 Terrell Davis SS .25 .60
S96 Barry Sanders SS .60 1.50
S97 Brett Favre SS .75 2.00
S98 Antonio Freeman SS .20 .50
S99 Peyton Manning SS .75 2.00
S100 Fred Taylor SS .20 .50
S101 Mark Brunell SS .20 .50
S102 Dan Marino SS .75 2.00
S103 Randy Moss SS .25 .60
S104 Cris Carter SS .25 .60
S105 Drew Bledsoe SS .25 .60
S106 Terry Glenn SS .20 .50
S107 Keyshawn Johnson SS .20 .50
S108 Jerry Rice SS .50 1.25
S109 Steve Young SS .30 .75
S110 Eddie George SS .20 .50

1999 Score Supplemental Behind the Numbers

COMPLETE SET (30) 60.00 150.00
STATED PRINT RUN 1000 SER.#'d SETS
GOLDS RANDOM INSERTS IN PACKS
BN1 Kurt Warner 7.50 20.00
BN2 Tim Couch 2.50 6.00
BN3 Randy Moss 5.00 12.00
BN4 Brett Favre 6.00 15.00
BN5 Marvin Harrison 2.00 5.00
BN6 Terry Glenn 2.00 5.00
BN7 John Elway 6.00 15.00
BN8 Troy Aikman 4.00 10.00
BN9 Steve McNair 2.00 5.00
BN10 Kordell Stewart 2.00 5.00
BN11 Drew Bledsoe 2.50 6.00
BN12 Jon Kitna 2.00 5.00
BN13 Dan Marino 6.00 15.00
BN14 Jerry Rice 4.00 10.00
BN15 Edgerrin James 4.00 10.00
BN16 Jake Plummer 1.25 3.00
BN17 Antonio Freeman 2.00 5.00
BN18 Peyton Manning 6.00 15.00
BN19 Keyshawn Johnson 2.00 5.00
BN20 Barry Sanders 6.00 15.00
BN21 Cris Carter 2.00 5.00
BN22 Emmitt Smith 4.00 10.00
BN23 Steve Young 2.50 6.00
BN24 Ricky Williams 2.00 5.00
BN25 Doug Flutie 2.00 5.00
BN26 Mark Brunell 2.00 5.00
BN27 Eddie George 2.00 5.00
BN28 Fred Taylor 2.00 5.00
BN29 Donovan McNabb 5.00 12.00
BN30 Terrell Davis 2.00 5.00

1999 Score Supplemental Behind the Numbers Gold

GOLDS SERIAL #'d TO PLAYER'S JERSEY
CARDS SERIAL #'d UNDER 20 NOT PRICED
BN3 Randy Moss/84 20.00 50.00
BN5 Marvin Harrison/88 6.00 15.00
BN6 Terry Glenn/88 6.00 15.00
BN14 Jerry Rice/80 15.00 40.00
BN15 Edgerrin James/32 50.00 120.00
BN17 Antonio Freeman/86 6.00 15.00
BN20 Barry Sanders/20 60.00 150.00
BN21 Cris Carter/80 6.00 15.00
BN22 Emmitt Smith/22 75.00 150.00
BN24 Ricky Williams/34 30.00 60.00
BN27 Eddie George/27 20.00 50.00
BN28 Fred Taylor/28 20.00 50.00
BN30 Terrell Davis/30 30.00 80.00

1999 Score Supplemental Inscriptions

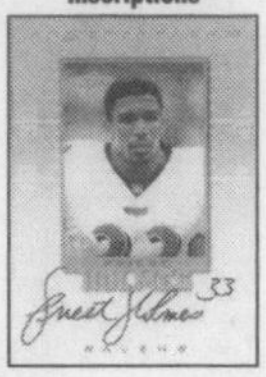

BG14 Brian Griese 7.50 20.00
BJ14 Brad Johnson 12.50 30.00
BS15 Bart Starr 60.00 100.00
CC12 Chris Chandler 6.00 15.00
CD28 Corey Dillon 12.50 30.00
DL25 Dorsey Levens 7.50 20.00
DS22 Duce Staley 12.50 30.00
EC34 Earl Campbell 20.00 40.00
EM79 Eric Moss 6.00 15.00
EM80 Eric Moulds 7.50 20.00
IB80 Isaac Bruce 12.50 30.00
JB32 Jim Brown 40.00 80.00
JG84 Joey Galloway 7.50 20.00
JK7 Jon Kitna 7.50 20.00
JU19 Johnny Unitas 175.00 300.00
KS10 Kordell Stewart 7.50 20.00
KW13 Kurt Warner 50.00 80.00
MH88 Marvin Harrison 12.50 30.00
NM20 Natrone Means 6.00 15.00
PH33 Priest Holmes 12.50 30.00
RW34 Ricky Williams 15.00 40.00
SD48 Stephen Davis 7.50 20.00
SH20 Skip Hicks 6.00 15.00
SM9 Steve McNair 12.50 30.00
TB21 Tim Biakabutuka 6.00 15.00
TB81 Tim Brown 20.00 40.00
TO81 Terrell Owens 20.00 40.00
TT34 Thurman Thomas 12.50 30.00
VT16 Vinny Testaverde 7.50 20.00
WW85 Wesley Walls 6.00 15.00

1999 Score Supplemental Quantum Leaf Previews

COMPLETE SET (18) 75.00 150.00
1 Barry Sanders 6.00 15.00
2 Ricky Williams 2.00 5.00
3 Terrell Davis 2.00 5.00
4 John Elway 6.00 15.00
5 Edgerrin James 4.00 10.00
6 Tim Couch 2.50 6.00
7 Peyton Manning 6.00 15.00
8 Kurt Warner 7.50 20.00
9 Randy Moss 5.00 12.00
10 Dan Marino 6.00 15.00
11 Brett Favre 6.00 15.00
12 Eddie George 2.00 5.00
13 Marvin Harrison 2.00 5.00
14 Jerry Rice 4.00 10.00
15 Emmitt Smith 4.00 10.00
16 Keyshawn Johnson 2.00 5.00
17 Drew Bledsoe 2.50 6.00
18 Marshall Faulk 2.50 6.00

1999 Score Supplemental Zenith Z-Team

COMPLETE SET (20) 250.00 500.00
STATED PRINT RUN 100 SER.#'d SETS
1 Steve Young 8.00 20.00
2 Barry Sanders 20.00 50.00
3 Fred Taylor 6.00 15.00
4 Marshall Faulk 8.00 20.00
5 Emmitt Smith 12.50 30.00
6 Brett Favre 20.00 50.00
7 Troy Aikman 12.50 30.00
8 Terrell Davis 6.00 15.00
9 Edgerrin James 40.00 100.00
10 Drew Bledsoe 8.00 20.00
11 Dan Marino 20.00 50.00
12 Randy Moss 15.00 40.00
13 Ricky Williams 20.00 50.00
14 Mark Brunell 6.00 15.00
15 Jake Plummer 4.00 10.00
16 Jerry Rice 12.50 30.00
17 Peyton Manning 20.00 50.00
18 Tim Couch 25.00 60.00
19 Eddie George 6.00 15.00
20 John Elway 20.00 50.00

2000 Score

Released as a 330-card set, 2000 Score contained 220 base issue cards and 110 short prints, 55 prospects, 25 All-Pros, 20 League Leaders, and 10 Sophomore Showcase cards. Due to a printing error, in packs, Drew Bledsoe was released both in the base set and parallel sets in twice the quantity of the other cards (no #118 was included in packs). The Playoff Corp. offered a redemption for those that pulled a Bledsoe card in exchange for number 118 Terry Allen which was not issued in packs. Several rookies were issued via redemption cards which carried an expiration date of 7/01/2001.

COMP.SET w/o SP's (220) 7.50 20.00
276-330 ROOKIE ODDS 1:2 HOB, 1:6 RET
ROOKIE SP PRINT RUN 500
1 Michael Pittman .15 .40
2 Jake Plummer .20 .50
3 Rob Moore .15 .40
4 David Boston .15 .40
5 Frank Sanders .15 .40
6 Jamal Anderson .20 .50
7 Chris Chandler .20 .50
8 Tim Dwight .20 .50
9 Terance Mathis .15 .40
10 Shawn Jefferson .15 .40
11 Ashley Ambrose .15 .40
12 Peter Boulware .15 .40
13 Priest Holmes .25 .60
14 Tony Banks .15 .40
15 Qadry Ismail .20 .50
16 Shannon Sharpe .25 .60
17 Rod Woodson .25 .60
18 Matt Stover .15 .40
19 Michael McCrary .15 .40
20 Doug Flutie .25 .60
21 Rob Johnson .20 .50
22 Eric Moulds .20 .50
23 Peerless Price .20 .50
24 Jonathan Linton .15 .40
25 Antowain Smith .20 .50
26 Jay Riemersma .15 .40
27 Muhsin Muhammad .20 .50
28 Tim Biakabutuka .20 .50
29 Patrick Jeffers .20 .50
30 Wesley Walls .15 .40
31 Steve Beuerlein .20 .50
32 John Kasay .15 .40
33 Curtis Enis .15 .40
34 Cade McNown .15 .40
35 Marcus Robinson .20 .50
36 Bobby Engram .20 .50
37 Eddie Kennison .15 .40
38 Akili Smith .15 .40
39 Carl Pickens .20 .50
40 Corey Dillon .20 .50
41 Darnay Scott .20 .50
42 Errict Rhett .20 .50
43 Karim Abdul-Jabbar .15 .40
44 Tim Couch .20 .50
45 Kevin Johnson .15 .40
46 Darrin Chiaverini .15 .40
47 Terry Kirby .15 .40
48 Jason Tucker .15 .40
49 Rocket Ismail .20 .50
50 Joey Galloway .20 .50
51 Michael Irvin .25 .60
52 Troy Aikman .40 1.00
53 Emmitt Smith .60 1.50
54 David LaFleur .15 .40
55 Trevor Pryce .15 .40
56 Brian Griese .20 .50
57 Olandis Gary .20 .50
58 Terrell Davis .25 .60
59 Rod Smith .20 .50
60 Ed McCaffrey .20 .50
61 Gus Frerotte .20 .50
62 Jason Elam .15 .40
63 Kavika Pittman .15 .40
64 James Stewart .15 .40
65 Charlie Batch .20 .50
66 Johnnie Morton .20 .50
67 Herman Moore .20 .50
68 Germane Crowell .15 .40
69 Barry Sanders .50 1.25
70 Chris Claiborne .15 .40
71 Brett Favre .75 2.00
72 Antonio Freeman .20 .50
73 Dorsey Levens .20 .50
74 De'Mond Parker .15 .40
75 Corey Bradford .15 .40
76 Basil Mitchell .15 .40
77 Bill Schroeder .20 .50
78 Peyton Manning .60 1.50
79 Marvin Harrison .25 .60
80 Terrence Wilkins .15 .40
81 Edgerrin James .25 .60
82 E.G. Green .15 .40
83 Chad Bratzke .15 .40
84 Mark Brunell .20 .50
85 Fred Taylor .25 .60
86 Jimmy Smith .20 .50
87 Keenan McCardell .20 .50
88 Kevin Hardy .15 .40
89 Aaron Beasley .15 .40
90 Elvis Grbac .15 .40
91 Derrick Alexander .15 .40
92 Tony Gonzalez .25 .60
93 Donnell Bennett .15 .40
94 Warren Moon .25 .60
95 Andre Rison .20 .50
96 James Hasty .15 .40
97 Dan Marino .75 2.00
98 Thurman Thomas .25 .60
99 James Johnson .15 .40
100 O.J. McDuffie .20 .50
101 Tony Martin .20 .50
102 Oronde Gadsden .20 .50
103 Zach Thomas .25 .60
104 Sam Madison .15 .40
105 Jay Fiedler .20 .50
106 Damon Huard .20 .50
107 Robert Smith .20 .50
108 Leroy Hoard .15 .40
109 Randy Moss .25 .60
110 Cris Carter .25 .60
111 Daunte Culpepper .20 .50
112 John Randle .20 .50
113 Randall Cunningham .25 .60
114 Gary Anderson .15 .40
115 Drew Bledsoe DP .25 .60
116 Terry Glenn .20 .50
117 Kevin Faulk .20 .50
118 Terry Allen SP 6.00 15.00
119 Adam Vinatieri .25 .60
120 Ty Law .20 .50
121 Lawyer Milloy .15 .40
122 Troy Brown .20 .50
123 Ben Coates .15 .40
124 Cam Cleeland .15 .40
125 Jeff Blake .20 .50
126 Ricky Williams .25 .60
127 Jake Reed .20 .50
128 Jake Delhomme RC .60 1.50
129 Andrew Glover .15 .40
130 Keith Poole .15 .40
131 Joe Horn .20 .50
132 Kerry Collins .20 .50
133 Joe Montgomery .15 .40
134 Sean Bennett .15 .40
135 Amani Toomer .20 .50
136 Ike Hilliard .20 .50
137 Joe Jurevicius .15 .40
138 Tiki Barber .25 .60
139 Victor Green .15 .40
140 Ray Lucas .15 .40
141 Vinny Testaverde .20 .50
142 Curtis Martin .25 .60
143 Wayne Chrebet .20 .50
144 Tyrone Wheatley .15 .40
145 Rich Gannon .20 .50
146 Napoleon Kaufman .20 .50
147 Tim Brown .25 .60
148 Rickey Dudley .15 .40
149 Charles Woodson .25 .60
150 James Jett .20 .50
151 Duce Staley .20 .50
152 Charles Johnson .15 .40
153 Donovan McNabb .25 .60
154 Troy Vincent .15 .40
155 Troy Edwards .15 .40
156 Jerome Bettis .25 .60
157 Kordell Stewart .20 .50
158 Richard Huntley .15 .40
159 Hines Ward .25 .60
160 Levon Kirkland .15 .40
161 Ryan Leaf .20 .50
162 Jim Harbaugh .20 .50
163 Jermaine Fazande .15 .40
164 Natrone Means .20 .50
165 Junior Seau .25 .60
166 Curtis Conway .20 .50
167 Freddie Jones .15 .40
168 Jeff Graham .15 .40
169 Terrell Owens .25 .60
170 Jeff Garcia .20 .50
171 Jerry Rice .50 1.25
172 Steve Young .30 .75
173 Garrison Hearst .15 .40
174 Charlie Garner .20 .50
175 Fred Beasley .15 .40
176 Bryant Young .15 .40
177 Derrick Mayes .15 .40
178 Sean Dawkins .15 .40
179 Jon Kitna .20 .50
180 Ricky Watters .20 .50
181 Charlie Rogers .15 .40
182 Kurt Warner .40 1.00
183 Marshall Faulk .25 .60
184 Isaac Bruce .25 .60
185 Az-Zahir Hakim .15 .40
186 Trent Green .20 .50
187 Jeff Wilkins .15 .40
188 Torry Holt .25 .60
189 London Fletcher RC .25 .60
190 Robert Holcombe .15 .40
191 Todd Lyght .15 .40
192 Keyshawn Johnson .20 .50
193 Derrick Brooks .25 .60
194 Warren Sapp .20 .50
195 Shaun King .15 .40
196 Warrick Dunn .20 .50
197 Mike Alstott .25 .60
198 Jacquez Green .15 .40
199 Reidel Anthony .15 .40
200 Martin Gramatica .15 .40
201 Donnie Abraham .15 .40
202 Steve McNair .25 .60
203 Eddie George .20 .50
204 Jevon Kearse .20 .50
205 Frank Wycheck .20 .50
206 Kevin Dyson .20 .50
207 Yancey Thigpen .15 .40
208 Al Del Greco .15 .40
209 Jeff George .20 .50
210 Adrian Murrell .15 .40
211 Brad Johnson .20 .50
212 Stephen Davis .20 .50
213 Stephen Alexander .15 .40
214 Michael Westbrook .15 .40
215 Darrell Green .20 .50
216 Champ Bailey .20 .50
217 Albert Connell .15 .40
218 Larry Centers .15 .40
219 Bruce Smith .25 .60
220 Deion Sanders .25 .60
221 Ricky Williams SS .30 .75
222 Edgerrin James SS .30 .75
223 Tim Couch SS .25 .60
224 Cade McNown SS .20 .50
225 Olandis Gary SS .25 .60
226 Torry Holt SS .30 .75
227 Donovan McNabb SS .30 .75
228 Shaun King SS .20 .50
229 Kevin Johnson SS .20 .50
230 Kurt Warner SS .50 1.25
231 Tony Gonzalez AP .30 .75
232 Frank Wycheck AP .25 .60
233 Eddie George AP .25 .60
234 Mark Brunell AP .25 .60
235 Corey Dillon AP .25 .60
236 Peyton Manning AP .75 2.00
237 Keyshawn Johnson AP .25 .60
238 Rich Gannon AP .25 .60
239 Terry Glenn AP .25 .60
240 Tony Brackens AP .20 .50
241 Edgerrin James AP .30 .75
242 Tim Brown AP .30 .75
243 Michael Strahan AP .25 .60
244 Kurt Warner AP .50 1.25
245 Brad Johnson AP .25 .60
246 Aeneas Williams AP .20 .50
247 Marshall Faulk AP .30 .75
248 Dexter Coakley AP .20 .50
249 Warren Sapp AP .25 .60
250 Mike Alstott AP .30 .75
251 David Sloan AP .20 .50
252 Cris Carter AP .30 .75
253 Muhsin Muhammad AP .25 .60
254 Isaac Bruce AP .30 .75
255 Wesley Walls AP .20 .50
256 Steve Beuerlein LL .25 .60
257 Kurt Warner LL .50 1.25
258 Peyton Manning LL .75 2.00
259 Brad Johnson LL .25 .60
260 Edgerrin James LL .30 .75
261 Curtis Martin LL .30 .75
262 Stephen Davis LL .25 .60
263 Emmitt Smith LL .75 2.00
264 Marvin Harrison LL .30 .75
265 Jimmy Smith LL .25 .60
266 Randy Moss LL .30 .75
267 Marcus Robinson LL .25 .60
268 Kevin Carter LL .20 .50
269 Simeon Rice LL .25 .60
270 Robert Porcher LL .20 .50
271 Jevon Kearse LL .25 .60
272 Mike Vanderjagt LL .20 .50
273 Olindo Mare LL .20 .50
274 Todd Peterson LL .20 .50
275 Mike Hollis LL .20 .50
276 Mike Anderson RC/500 8.00 20.00
277 Peter Warrick RC .75 2.00
278 Courtney Brown RC .60 1.50
279 Plaxico Burress RC .75 2.00
280 Corey Simon RC .60 1.50
281 Thomas Jones RC 1.00 2.50
282 Travis Taylor RC .60 1.50
283 Shaun Alexander RC 1.00 2.50
284 Patrick Pass RC/500 6.00 15.00
285 Chris Redman RC .60 1.50
286 Chad Pennington RC 1.25 3.00
287 Jamal Lewis RC .75 2.00
288 Brian Urlacher RC 3.00 8.00
289 Bubba Franks RC .75 2.00
290 Dez White RC .60 1.50
291 Frank Moreau RC/500 5.00 12.00
292 Ron Dayne RC .75 2.00
293 Sylvester Morris RC .50 1.25
294 R.Jay Soward RC .50 1.25
295 Curtis Keaton RC .50 1.25
296 Spergon Wynn RC/500 6.00 15.00
297 Rondell Mealey RC .50 1.25
298 Travis Prentice RC .60 1.50
299 Darrell Jackson RC .60 1.50
300 Giovanni Carmazzi RC .50 1.25
301 Anthony Lucas RC .50 1.25
302 Danny Farmer RC .50 1.25
303 Dennis Northcutt RC .60 1.50
304 Troy Walters RC .50 1.25
305 Laveranues Coles RC .75 2.00
306 Kwame Cavil RC .50 1.25
307 Tee Martin RC .75 2.00
308 J.R. Redmond RC .50 1.25
309 Tim Rattay RC .60 1.50
310 Jerry Porter RC .75 2.00
311 Michael Wiley RC .50 1.25
312 Reuben Droughns RC .75 2.00
313 Trung Canidate RC .60 1.50
314 Shyrone Stith RC .50 1.25
315 Marc Bulger RC .75 2.00
316 Tom Brady RC 15.00 30.00
317 Doug Johnson RC .60 1.50
318 Todd Husak RC .50 1.25
319 Gari Scott RC .50 1.25
320 Windrell Hayes RC/500 5.00 12.00
321 Chris Cole RC .60 1.50
322 Sammy Morris RC .60 1.50
323 Trevor Gaylor RC .50 1.25
324 Jarious Jackson RC .60 1.50
325 Doug Chapman RC/500 5.00 12.00
326 Ron Dugans RC .50 1.25
327 Ron Dixon RC/500 5.00 12.00
328 Joe Hamilton RC .50 1.25
329 Todd Pinkston RC .50 1.25
330 Chad Morton RC .75 2.00

2000 Score Final Score

*1-220 VET/54-66: 10X TO 25X BASIC CARDS
*1-220 VET/40-50: 12X TO 30X BASIC CARD
*1-220 VET/25-35: 15X TO 40X BASIC CARD
*221-275 SUBSET/54-66: 8X TO 20X
*221-275 SUBSET/40-50: 10X TO 25X
*221-275 SUBSET/25-35: 12X TO 30X
*277-330 ROOKIE/54-66: 3X TO 8X
*277-330 ROOKIE/40-50: 4X TO 10X
*277-330 ROOKIE/25-35: 5X TO 12X
*276/284/296/320/327 ROOKIE: .6X TO 1.2X
*291/325 ROOKIE/40-54: .5X TO 1X
CARDS SER.#'d TO A 1999 SEASON STAT
316 Tom Brady/32 400.00 700.00

2000 Score Scorecard

*VETS 1-220: 2X TO 5X BASIC CARDS
*SUBSET 221-275: .8X TO 2X
*ROOKIE 276-330: 1.2X TO 3X BASIC RC
*ROOKIE 276-330: .2X TO .5X BASE RC/500
STATED PRINT RUN 2000 SER.#'d SETS
316 Tom Brady 30.00 80.00

2000 Score Air Mail

COMPLETE SET (30) 60.00 120.00
STATED ODDS 1:70 HOB/RET
*FIRST CLASS/50: 1.5X TO 4X BASIC INSERTS
FIRST CLASS PRINT RUN 50
AM1 Isaac Bruce 1.50 4.00
AM2 Cris Carter 1.50 4.00
AM3 Tim Dwight 1.25 3.00
AM4 Joey Galloway 1.25 3.00
AM5 Marvin Harrison 1.50 4.00
AM6 Keyshawn Johnson 1.25 3.00
AM7 Jon Kitna 1.25 3.00
AM8 Steve McNair 1.50 4.00
AM9 Eric Moulds 1.25 3.00
AM10 Drew Bledsoe 1.50 4.00
AM11 John Elway 4.00 10.00
AM12 Brett Favre 5.00 12.00
AM13 Antonio Freeman 1.25 3.00
AM14 Peyton Manning 4.00 10.00
AM15 Randy Moss 1.50 4.00
AM16 Jake Plummer 1.25 3.00
AM17 Steve Young 2.00 5.00
AM18 Troy Aikman 2.50 6.00
AM19 Mark Brunell 1.25 3.00
AM20 Tim Couch 1.25 3.00
AM21 Dan Marino 5.00 12.00
AM22 Jerry Rice 3.00 8.00
AM23 Kevin Johnson 1.00 2.50
AM24 Michael Westbrook 1.00 2.50
AM25 Kurt Warner 2.50 6.00
AM26 Doug Flutie 1.50 4.00
AM27 Jimmy Smith 1.25 3.00
AM28 Germane Crowell 1.00 2.50
AM29 Cade McNown 1.00 2.50
AM30 Muhsin Muhammad 1.25 3.00

2000 Score Building Blocks

COMPLETE SET (30) 12.50 30.00
STATED ODDS 1:17 HOB, 1:35 RET
BB1 Cade McNown .40 1.00
BB2 Peerless Price .50 1.25
BB3 Akili Smith .40 1.00
BB4 Randy Moss .60 1.50
BB5 Edgerrin James .60 1.50
BB6 Kurt Warner 1.00 2.50
BB7 Ray Lucas .40 1.00
BB8 Jevon Kearse .50 1.25
BB9 Torry Holt .60 1.50
BB10 Ricky Williams .60 1.50
BB11 Daunte Culpepper .50 1.25
BB12 Fred Taylor .60 1.50
BB13 Brian Griese .50 1.25
BB14 Marcus Robinson .50 1.25
BB15 David Boston .40 1.00
BB16 James Johnson .40 1.00
BB17 Charlie Batch .50 1.25
BB18 Jake Plummer .50 1.25
BB19 Duce Staley .50 1.25
BB20 Germane Crowell .40 1.00
BB21 Curtis Enis .40 1.00
BB22 Donovan McNabb .60 1.50
BB23 Tim Couch .50 1.25
BB24 Stephen Davis .50 1.25
BB25 Jon Kitna .50 1.25
BB26 Shaun King .40 1.00
BB27 Kevin Johnson .40 1.00
BB28 Peyton Manning 1.50 4.00
BB29 Olandis Gary .50 1.25
BB30 Muhsin Muhammad .50 1.25

2000 Score Complete Players

COMPLETE SET (40) 25.00 60.00
STATED ODDS 1:17 HOB, 1:35 RET
*BLUE: 2.5X TO 6X BASIC INSERTS
BLUE ODDS 1:359 HOB, 1:718 RET
*GREEN: 4X TO 10X BASIC INSERTS
GREEN ODDS 1:718 HOB,1:1435 RET
CP1 Eric Moulds .50 1.25
CP2 Tim Couch .50 1.25
CP3 Marvin Harrison .60 1.50
CP4 Brett Favre 2.00 5.00
CP5 Steve Young .75 2.00
CP6 Brad Johnson .50 1.25
CP7 Randy Moss .60 1.50
CP8 Mark Brunell .50 1.25
CP9 Steve McNair .60 1.50
CP10 Donovan McNabb .60 1.50
CP11 Drew Bledsoe .60 1.50
CP12 Kurt Warner 1.00 2.50
CP13 Dan Marino 2.00 5.00
CP14 Muhsin Muhammad .50 1.25
CP15 Jimmy Smith .50 1.25
CP16 Fred Taylor .60 1.50
CP17 Corey Dillon .50 1.25
CP18 Peyton Manning 1.50 4.00
CP19 Keyshawn Johnson .50 1.25
CP20 Barry Sanders 1.25 3.00
CP21 Brian Griese .50 1.25
CP22 Emmitt Smith 1.50 4.00
CP23 Jerry Rice 1.25 3.00
CP24 Joey Galloway .50 1.25
CP25 Cris Carter .60 1.50
CP26 Robert Smith .50 1.25
CP27 Eddie George .50 1.25
CP28 Marshall Faulk .60 1.50
CP29 Tim Brown .60 1.50
CP30 Terrell Davis .60 1.50
CP31 Jamal Anderson .50 1.25
CP32 Edgerrin James .60 1.50
CP33 Antowain Smith .50 1.25
CP34 Antonio Freeman .50 1.25
CP35 Isaac Bruce .60 1.50
CP36 Stephen Davis .50 1.25
CP37 Troy Aikman 1.00 2.50
CP38 Kevin Johnson .40 1.00
CP39 Ricky Watters .50 1.25
CP40 Mike Alstott .60 1.50

2000 Score Franchise

COMPLETE SET (31) 30.00 60.00
STATED ODDS 1:35 RETAIL
F1 Emmitt Smith 2.50 6.00
F2 Amani Toomer .75 2.00
F3 Jake Plummer .75 2.00
F4 Brad Johnson .75 2.00
F5 Donovan McNabb 1.00 2.50
F6 Jerry Rice 2.00 5.00
F7 Jamal Anderson .75 2.00
F8 Marshall Faulk 1.00 2.50
F9 Steve Beuerlein .75 2.00
F10 Ricky Williams 1.00 2.50
F11 Brett Favre 3.00 8.00
F12 Barry Sanders 2.00 5.00
F13 Randy Moss 1.00 2.50
F14 Shaun King .60 1.50
F15 Cade McNown .60 1.50
F16 Dan Marino 3.00 8.00
F17 Drew Bledsoe 1.00 2.50
F18 Curtis Martin 1.00 2.50
F19 Peyton Manning 2.50 6.00
F20 Eric Moulds .75 2.00
F21 Mark Brunell .75 2.00
F22 Akili Smith .60 1.50
F23 Tim Couch .75 2.00
F24 Jerome Bettis 1.00 2.50
F25 Qadry Ismail .75 2.00
F26 Eddie George .75 2.00
F27 Jim Harbaugh .75 2.00
F28 Terrell Davis 1.00 2.50
F29 Elvis Grbac .60 1.50
F30 Tim Brown 1.00 2.50
F31 Jon Kitna .75 2.00

2000 Score Future Franchise

COMPLETE SET (30) 25.00 60.00
STATED ODDS 1:35 HOBBY
FF1 Michael Wiley .50 1.25
Emmitt Smith
FF2 Ron Dayne .75 2.00
Amani Toomer
FF3 Thomas Jones 1.00 2.50
Jake Plummer
FF4 Todd Husak .50 1.25
Brad Johnson
FF5 Todd Pinkston .50 1.25
Donovan McNabb
FF6 Giovanni Carmazzi 1.50 4.00
Jerry Rice
FF7 Mareno Philyaw .60 1.50
Jamal Anderson
FF8 Trung Canidate .75 2.00
Marshall Faulk
FF9 Deon Grant .50 1.25
Steve Beuerlein
FF10 Marc Bulger .75 2.00
Ricky Williams
FF11 Bubba Franks 2.50 6.00
Brett Favre
FF12 Reuben Droughns .75 2.00
Barry Sanders
FF13 Doug Chapman .75 2.00
Randy Moss
FF14 Joe Hamilton .50 1.25
Shaun King
FF15 Dez White .60 1.50
Cade McNown
FF16 Ben Kelly 2.50 6.00
Dan Marino
FF17 J.R. Redmond .50 1.25
Drew Bledsoe
FF18 Chad Pennington 1.25 3.00
Curtis Martin
FF19 Rob Morris .60 1.50
Peyton Manning
FF20 Sammy Morris .60 1.50
Eric Moulds
FF21 R.Jay Soward .50 1.25
Mark Brunell
FF22 Peter Warrick .75 2.00
Akili Smith
FF23 Courtney Brown .60 1.50
Tim Couch
FF24 Plaxico Burress .75 2.00
Jerome Bettis
FF25 Jamal Lewis .75 2.00
Qadry Ismail
FF26 Keith Bulluck .60 1.50
Eddie George
FF27 Trevor Gaylor .60 1.50
Jim Harbaugh
FF28 Chris Cole .75 2.00
Terrell Davis
FF29 Sylvester Morris .50 1.25
Elvis Grbac
FF30 Jerry Porter .75 2.00
Tim Brown
FF31 Shaun Alexander 1.00 2.50
Jon Kitna

2000 Score Millennium Men

COMPLETE SET (6) 40.00 80.00
STATED PRINT RUN 1000 SER.#'d SETS
FIRST 200-CARDS AUTOGRAPHED
MM4 Randy Moss 3.00 8.00
MM5 Chad Pennington 3.00 8.00
MM6 Randy Moss 3.00 8.00
Chad Pennington
MM7 Peyton Manning 8.00 20.00
MM8 Tee Martin 3.00 8.00
MM9 Tee Martin 3.00 8.00
Peyton Manning

2000 Score Millennium Men Autographs

FIRST 200-CARDS OF PRINT RUN
MM4 Randy Moss 25.00 50.00
MM5 Chad Pennington 20.00 50.00
MM6 Randy Moss 30.00 80.00
Chad Pennington
MM7 Peyton Manning 60.00 120.00
MM8 Tee Martin 15.00 30.00
MM9 Tee Martin 60.00 120.00
Peyton Manning

2000 Score Numbers Game Silver

CARDS SER.#'d TO A 1999 SEASON STAT
STATED PRINT RUN 732-4436
NG1 Kurt Warner/4353 1.00 2.50
NG2 Steve Beuerlein/4436 .50 1.25
NG3 Peyton Manning/4135 1.50 4.00
NG4 Brad Johnson/4005 .50 1.25
NG5 Steve McNair/2179 .75 2.00
NG6 Mark Brunell/3060 .50 1.25
NG7 Marvin Harrison/1663 .75 2.00
NG8 Isaac Bruce/1165 .75 2.00
NG9 Cris Carter/1241 .75 2.00
NG10 Randy Moss/1413 .75 2.00
NG11 Marcus Robinson/1444 .60 1.50
NG12 Terry Glenn/1147 .60 1.50
NG13 Edgerrin James/1553 .75 2.00
NG14 Curtis Martin/1464 .75 2.00
NG15 Stephen Davis/1405 .60 1.50
NG16 Emmitt Smith/1397 2.00 5.00
NG17 Marshall Faulk/1381 .75 2.00
NG18 Eddie George/1304 .60 1.50
NG19 Olandis Gary/1159 .60 1.50
NG20 Dorsey Levens/1034 .60 1.50
NG21 Robert Smith/1015 .60 1.50
NG22 Jerome Bettis/1091 .75 2.00
NG23 Corey Dillon/1200 .60 1.50
NG24 Drew Bledsoe/3985 .60 1.50
NG25 Fred Taylor/732 .75 2.00

2000 Score Numbers Game Gold

STATED PRINT RUN 69-369
CARDS SER.#'d TO A 1999 SEASON STAT
NG1 Kurt Warner/325 2.00 5.00
NG2 Steve Beuerlein/343 1.00 2.50
NG3 Peyton Manning/331 3.00 8.00
NG4 Brad Johnson/316 1.00 2.50
NG5 Steve McNair/187 1.25 3.00
NG6 Mark Brunell/259 1.00 2.50
NG7 Marvin Harrison/115 1.50 4.00
NG8 Isaac Bruce/77 1.50 4.00
NG9 Cris Carter/90 1.50 4.00
NG10 Randy Moss/80 1.50 4.00
NG11 Marcus Robinson/88 1.25 3.00
NG12 Terry Glenn/69 1.25 3.00
NG13 Edgerrin James/369 1.25 3.00
NG14 Curtis Martin/367 1.25 3.00
NG15 Stephen Davis/290 1.00 2.50
NG16 Emmitt Smith/329 3.00 8.00
NG17 Marshall Faulk/253 1.25 3.00
NG18 Eddie George/320 1.00 2.50
NG19 Olandis Gary/276 1.00 2.50
NG20 Dorsey Levens/279 1.00 2.50
NG21 Robert Smith/221 1.00 2.50
NG22 Jerome Bettis/299 1.25 3.00
NG23 Corey Dillon/263 1.00 2.50
NG24 Drew Bledsoe/305 1.25 3.00
NG25 Fred Taylor/159 1.25 3.00

2000 Score Rookie Preview Autographs

STATED ODDS 1:70 HOBBY
ANNOUNCED PRINT RUNS 300-700
SR2 Peter Warrick 10.00 25.00
SR3 Courtney Brown No AU 1.50 4.00
SR4 Plaxico Burress 10.00 25.00
SR5 Corey Simon 8.00 20.00
SR6 Thomas Jones 12.00 30.00
SR7 Travis Taylor 8.00 20.00
SR8 Shaun Alexander 12.00 30.00
SR9 Deon Grant 6.00 15.00
SR10 Chris Redman 8.00 20.00
SR11 Chad Pennington 15.00 40.00
SR12 Jamal Lewis 10.00 25.00
SR13 Brian Urlacher No AU 4.00 10.00
SR14 Bubba Franks No AU 2.00 5.00
SR15 Dez White 8.00 20.00
SR16 Ahmed Plummer 6.00 15.00
SR17 Ron Dayne 10.00 25.00
SR18 Sylvester Morris 6.00 15.00
SR19 R.Jay Soward 6.00 15.00
SR20 Sherrod Gideon 6.00 15.00
SR21 Ben Kelly No AU 1.25 3.00
SR22 Sekou Sanyika No AU 1.25 3.00
SR23 Travis Prentice 8.00 20.00
SR24 Darrell Jackson 8.00 20.00
SR25 Giovanni Carmazzi 6.00 15.00
SR26 Anthony Lucas 6.00 15.00
SR27 Danny Farmer 6.00 15.00
SR28 Dennis Northcutt 8.00 20.00
SR29 Troy Walters 6.00 15.00
SR30 Laveranues Coles 10.00 25.00
SR31 Kwame Cavil 6.00 15.00
SR32 Tee Martin 10.00 25.00
SR33 J.R. Redmond 6.00 15.00
SR34 Tim Rattay 8.00 20.00
SR35 Jerry Porter 10.00 25.00
SR36 Michael Wiley 6.00 15.00
SR37 Reuben Droughns 10.00 25.00
SR38 Trung Canidate 8.00 20.00
SR39 Shyrone Stith 6.00 15.00
SR40 Marc Bulger 10.00 25.00
SR41 Tom Brady 250.00 500.00
SR42 Doug Johnson 8.00 20.00
SR43 Todd Husak 6.00 15.00

SR44 Gari Scott 6.00 15.00
SR45 Chafie Fields 6.00 15.00
SR47 Sammy Morris 8.00 20.00
SR50 Trevor Gaylor 6.00 15.00
SR51 Ron Dugans 6.00 15.00
SR52 Chris Daniels 6.00 15.00
SR53 Joe Hamilton 6.00 15.00
SR54 Todd Pinkston 6.00 15.00

2000 Score Rookie Preview Autographs Roll Call

*AUTO/50: .8X TO 2X BASIC AU
ROLL CALL PRINT RUN 50 SER.#'d SETS
SR41 Tom Brady 800.00 1,200.00

2000 Score Team 2000

COMPLETE SET (20) 15.00 40.00
BLUE PRINT RUN 1500 SER.#'d SETS
BLUE/1500 HOBBY BOX TOPPER INSERT
*GOLD/1989-1999: .4X TO 1X BLUE/1500
GOLD STATED PRINT RUN 1989-1999
GOLDS RETAIL BOX TOPPER INSERT
*GREEN/200: 1X TO 2.5X BLUE/1500
GREEN PRINT RUN 200 SER.#'d SETS
*RED/500: .6X TO 1.5X BLUE/1500
RED PRINT RUN 500 SER.#'d SETS
TM1 Barry Sanders 1.50 4.00
TM2 Troy Aikman 1.25 3.00
TM3 Cris Carter .75 2.00
TM4 Emmitt Smith 2.00 5.00
TM5 Brett Favre 2.50 6.00
TM6 Jimmy Smith .60 1.50
TM7 Drew Bledsoe .75 2.00
TM8 Marshall Faulk .75 2.00
TM9 Steve McNair .75 2.00
TM10 Marvin Harrison .75 2.00
TM11 Eddie George .60 1.50
TM12 Eric Moulds .60 1.50
TM13 Jake Plummer .60 1.50
TM14 Antowain Smith .60 1.50
TM15 Fred Taylor .75 2.00
TM16 Randy Moss .75 2.00
TM17 Peyton Manning 2.00 5.00
TM18 Ricky Williams .75 2.00
TM19 Edgerrin James .75 2.00
TM20 Kurt Warner 1.25 3.00

2000 Score Team 2000 Autographs

AUTO PRINT RUN 50 SER.#'d SETS
TM1 Barry Sanders 150.00 300.00
TM2 Troy Aikman 125.00 200.00
TM3 Cris Carter 40.00 80.00
TM4 Emmitt Smith 200.00 350.00
TM5 Brett Favre 200.00 350.00
TM6 Jimmy Smith 15.00 40.00
TM7 Drew Bledsoe 20.00 50.00
TM8 Marshall Faulk 30.00 60.00
TM10 Marvin Harrison 40.00 80.00
TM11 Eddie George 40.00 80.00
TM12 Eric Moulds 15.00 40.00
TM13 Jake Plummer 15.00 40.00
TM14 Antowain Smith 15.00 40.00
TM15 Fred Taylor 20.00 50.00
TM16 Randy Moss 40.00 80.00
TM17 Peyton Manning 100.00 200.00
TM18 Ricky Williams 20.00 50.00
TM19 Edgerrin James 20.00 50.00
TM20 Kurt Warner 50.00 100.00

2001 Score

Playoff Inc. released Score as a retail only product on July 2, with a 99-cent per pack SRP. This 330-card set was highlighted by the short-printed rookies which were randomly inserted at a rate of 1:4. The base card design was a basic blue or green border for the standard cards and a red border for the short-printed base cards. The cardbacks featured a Pack Wars character that was assigned a value for playing the popular game. Many cards (possibly all of them) were issued with a tougher parallel variation on the Pack Wars character to include the word "Trump" as a wild card winner during the game. The packs were also distributed in two versions of retail boxes 15 packs for an SRP of $13.99 and 30 packs for $28.99. An exchange card was inserted in packs that was good for an option to purchase a 2001 Score Supplmental factory set. It carried an expiration date of 12/01/2001.

COMPLETE SET (330) 40.00 80.00
COMP.SET w/o SP's (220) 10.00 25.00
271-330 ROOKIE STATED ODDS 1:4
*TRUMP CARD BACKS: .6X TO 1.5X
1 David Boston .10 .25
2 Frank Sanders .10 .25
3 Jake Plummer .12 .30
4 Michael Pittman .12 .30
5 Rob Moore .10 .25
6 Thomas Jones .12 .30
7 Chris Chandler .12 .30
8 Doug Johnson .10 .25
9 Jamal Anderson .12 .30
10 Tim Dwight .12 .30
11 Brandon Stokley .12 .30
12 Chris Redman .15 .40
13 Jamal Lewis .15 .40
14 Qadry Ismail .12 .30
15 Ray Lewis .15 .40
16 Rod Woodson .15 .40
17 Shannon Sharpe .15 .40
18 Travis Taylor .10 .25
19 Trent Dilfer .12 .30
20 Elvis Grbac .12 .30
21 Eric Moulds .12 .30
22 Jay Riemersma .10 .25
23 Peerless Price .10 .25
24 Rob Johnson .12 .30
25 Sam Cowart .10 .25
26 Sammy Morris .12 .30
27 Shawn Bryson .10 .25
28 Donald Hayes .10 .25
29 Muhsin Muhammad .12 .30
30 Patrick Jeffers .10 .25
31 Reggie White DE .15 .40
32 Steve Beuerlein .12 .30
33 Tim Biakabutuka .10 .25
34 Wesley Walls .10 .25
35 Brian Urlacher .20 .50
36 Cade McNown .12 .30
37 Dez White .12 .30
38 James Allen .10 .25
39 Marcus Robinson .12 .30
40 Marty Booker .12 .30
41 Akili Smith .10 .25
42 Corey Dillon .12 .30
43 Danny Farmer .10 .25
44 Peter Warrick .12 .30
45 Ron Dugans .10 .25
46 Takeo Spikes .10 .25
47 Courtney Brown .10 .25
48 Dennis Northcutt .10 .25
49 JaJuan Dawson .10 .25
50 Kevin Johnson .10 .25
51 Tim Couch .10 .25
52 Travis Prentice .10 .25
53 Anthony Wright .10 .25
54 Emmitt Smith .40 1.00
55 James McKnight .10 .25
56 Joey Galloway .12 .30
57 Rocket Ismail .12 .30
58 Randall Cunningham .15 .40
59 Troy Aikman .25 .60
60 Brian Griese .12 .30
61 Ed McCaffrey .12 .30
62 Gus Frerotte .12 .30
63 John Elway .40 1.00
64 Mike Anderson .12 .30
65 Olandis Gary .10 .25
66 Rod Smith .12 .30
67 Terrell Davis .15 .40
68 Barry Sanders .40 1.00
69 Charlie Batch .12 .30
70 Germane Crowell .10 .25
71 Herman Moore .12 .30
72 James Stewart .10 .25
73 Johnnie Morton .12 .30
74 Robert Porcher .10 .25
75 Jim Harbaugh .12 .30
76 Ahman Green .15 .40
77 Antonio Freeman .15 .40
78 Bill Schroeder .12 .30
79 Brett Favre .50 1.25
80 Bubba Franks .12 .30
81 Dorsey Levens .12 .30
82 E.G. Green .10 .25
83 Edgerrin James .15 .40
84 Jerome Pathon .10 .25
85 Ken Dilger .10 .25
86 Marcus Pollard .10 .25
87 Marvin Harrison .15 .40
88 Peyton Manning .40 1.00
89 Terrence Wilkins .10 .25
90 Fred Taylor .15 .40
91 Hardy Nickerson .10 .25
92 Jimmy Smith .12 .30
93 Keenan McCardell .12 .30
94 Kyle Brady .10 .25
95 Mark Brunell .12 .30
96 Tony Brackens .10 .25
97 Derrick Alexander .10 .25
98 Sylvester Morris .10 .25
99 Tony Gonzalez .15 .40
100 Tony Richardson .10 .25
101 Kimble Anders .10 .25
102 Warren Moon .15 .40
103 Dan Marino .40 1.00
104 Jay Fiedler .12 .30
105 Lamar Smith .12 .30
106 O.J. McDuffie .10 .25
107 Oronde Gadsden .10 .25
108 Sam Madison .10 .25
109 Thurman Thomas .15 .40
110 Tony Martin .12 .30
111 Zach Thomas .15 .40
112 Cris Carter .15 .40
113 Daunte Culpepper .12 .30
114 Matthew Hatchette .10 .25
115 Randy Moss .15 .40
116 Robert Smith .12 .30
117 Drew Bledsoe .15 .40
118 J.R. Redmond .10 .25
119 Kevin Faulk .12 .30
120 Michael Bishop .12 .30
121 Terry Glenn .12 .30
122 Troy Brown .12 .30
123 Ty Law .12 .30
124 Aaron Brooks .12 .30
125 Darren Howard .10 .25
126 Jake Reed .12 .30
127 Jeff Blake .12 .30
128 Joe Horn .12 .30
129 La'Roi Glover .10 .25
130 Ricky Williams .15 .40
131 Willie Jackson .10 .25
132 Albert Connell .10 .25
133 Amani Toomer .12 .30
134 Ike Hilliard .12 .30
135 Jason Sehorn .12 .30
136 Jessie Armstead .10 .25
137 Kerry Collins .12 .30
138 Michael Strahan .15 .40
139 Ron Dayne .12 .30
140 Ron Dixon .10 .25
141 Tiki Barber .15 .40
142 Anthony Becht .10 .25
143 Chad Pennington .15 .40
144 Curtis Martin .15 .40
145 Dedric Ward .10 .25
146 Laveranues Coles .12 .30
147 Vinny Testaverde .12 .30
148 Wayne Chrebet .12 .30
149 Andre Rison .12 .30
150 Charles Woodson .15 .40
151 Darrell Russell .10 .25
152 Napoleon Kaufman .10 .25
153 Rich Gannon .12 .30
154 Tim Brown .15 .40
155 Tyrone Wheatley .12 .30
156 Chad Lewis .10 .25
157 Charles Johnson .10 .25
158 Donovan McNabb .15 .40
159 Duce Staley .12 .30
160 Hugh Douglas .10 .25
161 Na Brown .10 .25
162 Todd Pinkston .10 .25
163 James Thrash .12 .30
164 Bobby Shaw .10 .25
165 Hines Ward .15 .40
166 Jerome Bettis .15 .40
167 Kordell Stewart .12 .30
168 Levon Kirkland .10 .25
169 Plaxico Burress .12 .30
170 Richard Huntley .10 .25
171 Troy Edwards .10 .25
172 Jeff Graham .10 .25
173 Junior Seau .15 .40
174 Doug Flutie .15 .40
175 Charlie Garner .12 .30
176 Jeff Garcia .12 .30
177 Jerry Rice .30 .75
178 Steve Young .20 .50
179 Terrell Owens .15 .40
180 Brock Huard .10 .25
181 Darrell Jackson .12 .30
182 Derrick Mayes .10 .25
183 Ricky Watters .12 .30
184 Shaun Alexander .15 .40
185 Matt Hasselbeck .15 .40
186 John Randle .12 .30
187 Az-Zahir Hakim .10 .25
188 Isaac Bruce .15 .40
189 Kurt Warner .25 .60
190 Marshall Faulk .15 .40
191 Torry Holt .12 .30
192 Trent Green .15 .40
193 Derrick Brooks .15 .40
194 Jacquez Green .10 .25
195 John Lynch .12 .30
196 Keyshawn Johnson .12 .30
197 Mike Alstott .12 .30
198 Reidel Anthony .10 .25
199 Shaun King .10 .25
200 Warren Sapp .12 .30
201 Warrick Dunn .15 .40
202 Ryan Leaf .10 .25
203 Carl Pickens .12 .30
204 Derrick Mason .12 .30
205 Eddie George .15 .40
206 Frank Wycheck .10 .25
207 Jevon Kearse .12 .30
208 Neil O'Donnell .12 .30
209 Steve McNair .15 .40
210 Yancey Thigpen .10 .25
211 Andre Reed .15 .40
212 Brad Johnson .12 .30
213 Bruce Smith .15 .40
214 Champ Bailey .15 .40
215 Darrell Green .15 .40
216 Deion Sanders .15 .40
217 Irving Fryar .12 .30
218 Jeff George .12 .30
219 Michael Westbrook .10 .25
220 Stephen Davis .12 .30
221 Terrell Owens AP .25 .60
222 Peyton Manning AP .60 1.50
223 Stephen Davis AP .20 .50
224 Marvin Harrison AP .25 .60
225 Donovan McNabb AP .25 .60
226 Edgerrin James AP .25 .60
227 Eric Moulds AP .20 .50
228 Daunte Culpepper AP .20 .50
229 Eddie George AP .25 .60
230 Cris Carter AP .25 .60
231 Rich Gannon AP .20 .50
232 Jeff Garcia AP .20 .50
233 Jimmy Smith AP .20 .50
234 Tony Gonzalez AP .25 .60
235 Torry Holt AP .20 .50
236 Jevon Kearse AP .20 .50
237 Ray Lewis AP .25 .60
238 Warren Sapp AP .20 .50
239 Brian Urlacher AP .30 .75
240 Champ Bailey AP .25 .60
241 Peyton Manning LL .60 1.50
242 Jeff Garcia LL .20 .50
243 Elvis Grbac LL .20 .50
244 Daunte Culpepper LL .20 .50
245 Brett Favre LL .75 2.00
246 Edgerrin James LL .25 .60
247 Robert Smith LL .20 .50
248 Eddie George LL .25 .60
249 Mike Anderson LL .20 .50
250 Corey Dillon LL .20 .50
251 Torry Holt LL .20 .50
252 Rod Smith LL .20 .50
253 Isaac Bruce LL .25 .60
254 Terrell Owens LL .25 .60
255 Randy Moss LL .25 .60
256 La'Roi Glover LL .15 .40
257 Trace Armstrong LL .15 .40
258 Warren Sapp LL .20 .50
259 Hugh Douglas LL .15 .40
260 Jason Taylor LL .25 .60
261 Mike Anderson SS .20 .50
262 Jamal Lewis SS .25 .60
263 Sylvester Morris SS .15 .40
264 Darrell Jackson SS .20 .50
265 Peter Warrick SS .20 .50
266 Ron Dayne SS .20 .50
267 Shaun Alexander SS .25 .60
268 Plaxico Burress SS .20 .50
269 Brian Urlacher SS .30 .75
270 Courtney Brown SS .15 .40
271 Michael Vick RC 3.00 8.00
272 Drew Brees RC 5.00 12.00
273 Chris Weinke RC .60 1.50
274 Quincy Carter RC .60 1.50
275 Sage Rosenfels RC .75 2.00
276 Josh Heupel RC .75 2.00
277 David Rivers RC .50 1.25
278 Ben Leard RC .50 1.25
279 Marques Tuiasosopo RC .60 1.50
280 Mike McMahon RC .60 1.50
281 Deuce McAllister RC .75 2.00
282 LaMont Jordan RC .75 2.00
283 LaDainian Tomlinson RC 2.50 6.00
284 James Jackson RC .50 1.25
285 Anthony Thomas RC .75 2.00
286 Travis Henry RC .60 1.50
287 Travis Minor RC .60 1.50
288 Rudi Johnson RC .75 2.00
289 Michael Bennett RC .60 1.50
290 Kevan Barlow RC .60 1.50
291 Reggie White RC .50 1.25
292 Moran Norris RC .50 1.25
293 Ja'Mar Toombs RC .50 1.25
294 Heath Evans RC .60 1.50
295 David Terrell RC .60 1.50
296 Santana Moss RC 1.00 2.50
297 Rod Gardner RC .60 1.50
298 Quincy Morgan RC .60 1.50
299 Freddie Mitchell RC .50 1.25
300 Boo Williams RC .50 1.25
301 Reggie Wayne RC 1.50 4.00
302 Ronney Daniels RC .50 1.25
303 Bobby Newcombe RC .60 1.50
304 Vinny Sutherland RC .50 1.25
305 Cedrick Wilson RC .60 1.50
306 Robert Ferguson RC .75 2.00
307 Ken-Yon Rambo RC .50 1.25
308 Alex Bannister RC .50 1.25
309 Koren Robinson RC .60 1.50
310 Chad Johnson RC 1.25 3.00
311 Chris Chambers RC .75 2.00
312 Javon Green RC .50 1.25
313 Snoop Minnis RC .50 1.25
314 Scotty Anderson RC .50 1.25
315 Todd Heap RC .75 2.00
316 Alge Crumpler RC .75 2.00
317 Marcellus Rivers RC .50 1.25
318 Rashon Burns RC .50 1.25
319 Jamal Reynolds RC .50 1.25
320 Andre Carter RC .60 1.50
321 Justin Smith RC .75 2.00
322 Gerard Warren RC .60 1.50
323 Tommy Polley RC .50 1.25
324 Dan Morgan RC .60 1.50
325 Torrance Marshall RC .50 1.25
326 Correll Buckhalter RC .75 2.00
327 Derrick Gibson RC .50 1.25
328 Adam Archuleta RC .60 1.50
329 Jamar Fletcher RC .50 1.25
330 Nate Clements RC .60 1.50

2001 Score Scorecard

*VETS/307-540: 4X TO 10X BASIC CARD
*VETS/307-540: 2X TO 5X BASE SP
*ROOKIES/307-540: 1X TO 2.5X
*VETS/161-296: 5X TO 12X BASIC CARD
*VETS/161-296: 2.5X TO 6X BASE SP
*ROOKIES/161-296: 1.2X TO 3X
STATED PRINT RUN 161-540

2001 Score Complete Players

COMPLETE SET (30) 30.00 60.00
STATED ODDS 1:35
CP1 Edgerrin James 1.00 2.50
CP2 Marshall Faulk 1.00 2.50
CP3 Kurt Warner 1.50 4.00
CP4 Daunte Culpepper .75 2.00
CP5 Donovan McNabb 1.00 2.50
CP6 Koren Robinson .75 2.00
CP7 Peyton Manning 2.50 6.00
CP8 Eddie George 1.00 2.50
CP9 Fred Taylor 1.00 2.50
CP10 Drew Brees 3.00 8.00
CP11 Randy Moss 1.00 2.50
CP12 Cris Carter 1.00 2.50
CP13 Steve Young 1.25 3.00
CP14 Marvin Harrison 1.00 2.50
CP15 Isaac Bruce 1.00 2.50
CP16 Terrell Owens 1.00 2.50
CP17 Mike Anderson .75 2.00
CP18 Jamal Lewis 1.00 2.50
CP19 Curtis Martin 1.00 2.50
CP20 Ricky Williams 1.00 2.50
CP21 Jerry Rice 2.00 5.00
CP22 Steve McNair 1.00 2.50
CP23 Michael Vick 2.00 5.00
CP24 Brett Favre 3.00 8.00
CP25 John Elway 2.50 6.00
CP26 Dan Marino 2.50 6.00
CP27 Barry Sanders 2.50 6.00
CP28 Michael Bennett .75 2.00
CP29 David Terrell .75 2.00
CP30 Emmitt Smith 2.50 6.00

2001 Score Franchise

COMPLETE SET (31) 25.00 60.00
STATED ODDS 1:35 RETAIL
TF1 Tim Couch .60 1.50
TF2 Peter Warrick .75 2.00
TF3 Jerome Bettis 1.00 2.50
TF4 Fred Taylor 1.00 2.50
TF5 Eddie George 1.00 2.50
TF6 Jamal Lewis 1.00 2.50
TF7 Peyton Manning 2.50 6.00
TF8 Drew Bledsoe 1.00 2.50
TF9 Curtis Martin 1.00 2.50
TF10 Eric Moulds .75 2.00
TF11 Lamar Smith .75 2.00
TF12 Tony Gonzalez 1.00 2.50
TF13 Rich Gannon .75 2.00
TF14 Ricky Watters .75 2.00
TF15 Junior Seau 1.00 2.50
TF16 Brian Griese .75 2.00
TF17 Terrell Owens 1.00 2.50
TF18 Ricky Williams 1.00 2.50
TF19 Kurt Warner 1.50 4.00
TF20 Muhsin Muhammad .75 2.00
TF21 Jamal Anderson .75 2.00
TF22 Brett Favre 3.00 8.00
TF23 Randy Moss 1.00 2.50
TF24 Marcus Robinson .75 2.00
TF25 Warrick Dunn 1.00 2.50
TF26 James Stewart .60 1.50
TF27 Jake Plummer .75 2.00
TF28 Kerry Collins .75 2.00
TF29 Emmitt Smith 2.50 6.00
TF30 Stephen Davis .75 2.00
TF31 Donovan McNabb 1.00 2.50

2001 Score Franchise Fabrics

STATED ODDS 1:359
FF1 Daunte Culpepper 8.00 20.00
FF2 Stephen Davis 8.00 20.00
FF3 Kurt Warner 15.00 40.00
FF4 Ricky Williams 10.00 25.00
FF5 Terrell Owens 10.00 25.00
FF6 Ricky Watters 8.00 20.00
FF7 Rich Gannon 8.00 20.00
FF8 Mike Anderson 8.00 20.00
FF9 Tony Gonzalez 10.00 25.00
FF10 Jerome Bettis 10.00 25.00
FF11 Peter Warrick 8.00 20.00
FF12 Tim Couch 6.00 15.00
FF13 Mark Brunell 8.00 20.00
FF14 Edgerrin James 10.00 25.00
FF15 Curtis Martin 10.00 25.00
FF16 Brett Favre 30.00 80.00
FF17 Donovan McNabb 10.00 25.00
FF18 Drew Bledsoe 10.00 25.00
FF19 Jake Plummer 8.00 20.00
FF20 Eric Moulds 8.00 20.00
FF21 Lamar Smith 8.00 20.00
FF22 Junior Seau 10.00 25.00
FF23 Wesley Walls 6.00 15.00
FF24 Jamal Anderson 8.00 20.00
FF25 Warren Sapp 8.00 20.00
FF26 Ron Dayne 8.00 20.00
FF27 Jamal Lewis 10.00 25.00
FF28 Cade McNown 8.00 20.00
FF29 Charlie Batch 8.00 20.00
FF30 Eddie George 10.00 25.00
FF31 Troy Aikman 15.00 40.00

2001 Score Millennium Men

COMPLETE SET (40) 30.00 80.00
STATED PRINT RUN 1000 SER.#'d SETS
MM1 Michael Vick 3.00 8.00
MM2 Marvin Harrison 1.00 2.50
MM3 Curtis Martin 1.00 2.50
MM4 Eric Moulds .75 2.00
MM5 Dan Marino 2.50 6.00
MM6 Edgerrin James 1.00 2.50
MM7 Drew Bledsoe 1.00 2.50
MM8 Drew Brees 5.00 12.00
MM9 Jamal Lewis .75 2.00
MM10 Marshall Faulk 1.00 2.50
MM11 Eddie George 1.00 2.50
MM12 Koren Robinson .75 2.00
MM13 Peter Warrick .75 2.00
MM14 Jerome Bettis 1.00 2.50
MM15 Warren Sapp .75 2.00
MM16 Mark Brunell .75 2.00
MM17 David Terrell .75 2.00
MM18 Steve Young 1.25 3.00
MM19 Ron Dayne .75 2.00
MM20 Michael Bennett .60 1.50
MM21 Brian Griese .75 2.00
MM22 Deuce McAllister .75 2.00
MM23 Kurt Warner 1.50 4.00
MM24 Mike Anderson .75 2.00
MM25 Rudi Johnson .75 2.00
MM26 John Elway 2.50 6.00
MM27 Terrell Owens 1.00 2.50
MM28 Ricky Williams 1.00 2.50
MM29 Jerry Rice 2.00 5.00
MM30 Jeff Garcia .75 2.00
MM31 Isaac Bruce 1.00 2.50
MM32 Aaron Brooks .75 2.00
MM33 Brett Favre 3.00 8.00
MM34 Daunte Culpepper .75 2.00
MM35 Ricky Watters .75 2.00
MM36 Tony Gonzalez 1.00 2.50
MM37 Stephen Davis .75 2.00
MM38 Santana Moss 1.00 2.50
MM39 Cris Carter 1.00 2.50
MM40 Donovan McNabb 1.00 2.50

2001 Score Millennium Men Autographs

STATED PRINT RUN 25 SERIAL #'d SETS
1 Michael Vick 150.00 250.00
2 Marvin Harrison 25.00 60.00
3 Curtis Martin 30.00 80.00
5 Dan Marino 125.00 250.00
6 Edgerrin James 25.00 60.00
7 Drew Bledsoe 25.00 60.00
8 Drew Brees 175.00 300.00
9 Jamal Lewis 30.00 80.00
10 Marshall Faulk 25.00 60.00
11 Eddie George 20.00 50.00
14 Jerome Bettis 40.00 80.00
16 Mark Brunell 20.00 50.00
17 David Terrell 25.00 60.00
18 Steve Young 50.00 100.00
19 Ron Dayne 20.00 50.00
21 Brian Griese 20.00 50.00
23 Kurt Warner 25.00 60.00
24 Mike Anderson 25.00 60.00
25 Rudi Johnson 40.00 80.00
26 John Elway 125.00 250.00
27 Terrell Owens 30.00 80.00
28 Ricky Williams 25.00 60.00
29 Jerry Rice 125.00 250.00
30 Jeff Garcia 25.00 60.00
32 Aaron Brooks 25.00 60.00
33 Brett Favre 175.00 300.00
34 Daunte Culpepper 30.00 80.00
35 Ricky Watters 20.00 50.00
36 Tony Gonzalez 25.00 60.00
38 Santana Moss 25.00 60.00
39 Cris Carter 30.00 80.00
40 Donovan McNabb 60.00 120.00

2001 Score Numbers Game

COMPLETE SET (40) 30.00 80.00
CARDS SER.#'d TO 2000 SEASON STAT
STATED PRINT RUN 582-4413
NG1 Brett Favre/3812 2.00 5.00
NG2 Marshall Faulk/1359 .75 2.00
NG3 Michael Vick/1234 3.00 8.00
NG4 Peyton Manning/4413 1.50 4.00
NG5 David Terrell/994 .60 1.50
NG6 Randy Moss/1437 .75 2.00
NG7 Kurt Warner/3429 1.00 2.50
NG8 Edgerrin James/1709 .75 2.00
NG9 Drew Brees/3666 2.50 6.00
NG10 Daunte Culpepper/3937 .50 1.25
NG11 Jeff Garcia/4278 .50 1.25
NG12 Mike Anderson/1487 .60 1.50
NG13 Jamal Lewis/1364 .75 2.00
NG14 Eddie George/1509 .75 2.00
NG15 Michael Bennett/1681 .60 1.50
NG16 Emmitt Smith/1203 2.00 5.00
NG17 Chris Weinke/4167 .50 1.25
NG18 Tim Brown/1128 .75 2.00
NG19 Eric Moulds/1326 .60 1.50
NG20 Marvin Harrison/1413 .75 2.00
NG21 Deuce McAllister/582 .75 2.00
NG22 Donovan McNabb/3365 .60 1.50
NG23 Fred Taylor/1399 .75 2.00
NG24 Santana Moss/748 1.00 2.50
NG25 Cris Carter/1274 .75 2.00
NG26 Robert Smith/1521 .60 1.50
NG27 LaDainian Tomlinson/2158 1.25 3.00
NG28 Isaac Bruce/1471 .75 2.00
NG29 Terrell Owens/1451 .75 2.00
NG30 Torry Holt/1635 .60 1.50
NG31 Ricky Williams/1000 .75 2.00
NG32 Curtis Martin/1204 .75 2.00
NG33 Stephen Davis/1318 .60 1.50
NG34 Corey Dillon/1435 .60 1.50
NG35 Ed McCaffrey/1317 .60 1.50
NG36 Steve McNair/2847 .60 1.50
NG37 Rudi Johnson/1547 .75 2.00
NG38 Antonio Freeman/912 .75 2.00
NG39 Jerry Rice/805 1.50 4.00
NG40 Aaron Brooks/1514 .60 1.50

2001 Score Settle the Score

COMPLETE SET (30) 25.00 60.00
STATED ODDS 1:35 RETAIL
SS1 Kurt Warner .75 2.00
Steve McNair
SS2 Randy Moss 1.00 2.50
Isaac Bruce
SS3 Emmitt Smith 2.50 6.00
Stephen Davis
SS4 Marshall Faulk 1.00 2.50
Robert Smith
SS5 Eddie George 1.00 2.50
Ray Lewis
SS6 Fred Taylor 1.00 2.50
Jerome Bettis
SS7 Peyton Manning 2.50 6.00
Drew Bledsoe
SS8 Daunte Culpepper .75 2.00
Aaron Brooks
SS9 Marvin Harrison 1.00 2.50
Eric Moulds
SS10 Jerry Rice 2.00 5.00
Cris Carter
SS11 Curtis Martin 1.00 2.50
Edgerrin James
SS12 Donovan McNabb 1.00 2.50
Ron Dayne
SS13 Brett Favre 3.00 8.00
Warren Sapp
SS14 Tony Gonzalez 1.00 2.50
Shannon Sharpe
SS15 Wayne Chrebet .75 2.00
Kevin Johnson
SS16 Tim Couch .75 2.00
Cade McNown
SS17 Terell Davis 1.00 2.50
Jamal Anderson
SS18 Mike Anderson 1.00 2.50
Jamal Lewis
SS19 Terell Owens 1.00 2.50
Antonio Freeman
SS20 Brian Griese .75 2.00
Rich Gannon
SS21 Ricky Watters .75 2.00
Charlie Garner
SS22 Mushin Muhammad 1.00 2.50
Ricky Williams
SS23 Jeff Garcia .75 2.00
Elvis Grbac
SS24 Rod Smith .75 2.00
Jimmy Smith
SS25 Brian Urlacher 1.25 3.00
Ahman Green
SS26 Darrell Jackson .75 2.00
Sylvester Morris
SS27 Peter Warrick .75 2.00
Travis Taylor
SS28 Dan Marino 2.50 6.00
John Elway
SS29 Steve Young 1.25 3.00
Mark Brunell
SS30 Troy Aikman 1.50 4.00
Jake Plummer

2001 Score Chicago Collection

NOT PRICED DUE TO SCARCITY

2002 Score

This 330-card base set features 250 veterans and 80 rookies. Boxes contained 30 packs, each of which had an $1.99 SRP and contained seven cards.

COMPLETE SET (330) 20.00 50.00
1 David Boston .12 .30
2 Arnold Jackson .12 .30
3 MarTay Jenkins .12 .30
4 Thomas Jones .20 .50
5 Kwamie Lassiter .12 .30
6 Michael Pittman .15 .40
7 Jake Plummer .15 .40
8 Chris Chandler .15 .40
9 Alge Crumpler .15 .40
10 Terance Mathis .12 .30
11 Maurice Smith .12 .30
12 Ray Buchanan .12 .30
13 Jamal Anderson .15 .40
14 Keith Brooking .12 .30
15 Michael Vick .30 .75
16 Obafemi Ayanbadejo .12 .30
17 Jason Brookins .12 .30
18 Randall Cunningham .20 .50
19 Elvis Grbac .12 .30
20 Todd Heap .15 .40
21 Qadry Ismail .15 .40
22 Shannon Sharpe .20 .50
23 Travis Taylor .12 .30
24 Ray Lewis .20 .50
25 Jamal Lewis .15 .40
26 Larry Centers .15 .40
27 Rob Johnson .15 .40
28 Shawn Bryson .12 .30
29 Eric Moulds .15 .40
30 Peerless Price .12 .30
31 Nate Clements .12 .30
32 Travis Henry .12 .30
33 Isaac Byrd .12 .30
34 Nick Goings .12 .30
35 Donald Hayes .12 .30
36 Richard Huntley .12 .30
37 Muhsin Muhammad .15 .40
38 Steve Smith .20 .50
39 Wesley Walls .15 .40
40 Chris Weinke .12 .30
41 James Allen .12 .30
42 Marty Booker .15 .40
43 Jim Miller .12 .30
44 David Terrell .12 .30
45 Dez White .12 .30
46 Brian Urlacher .20 .50
47 Mike Brown .15 .40
48 Anthony Thomas .15 .40
49 T.J. Houshmandzadeh .20 .50
50 Chad Johnson .20 .50
51 Darnay Scott .15 .40
52 Peter Warrick .15 .40
53 Akili Smith .15 .40
54 Jon Kitna .15 .40
55 Justin Smith .12 .30
56 Corey Dillon .15 .40
57 Benjamin Gay .12 .30
58 Kevin Johnson .12 .30
59 Quincy Morgan .12 .30
60 James Jackson .12 .30
61 Anthony Henry .12 .30
62 Gerard Warren .12 .30
63 Jamir Miller .12 .30
64 Tim Couch .12 .30
65 Quincy Carter .12 .30
66 Joey Galloway .15 .40
67 Troy Hambrick .12 .30
68 Rocket Ismail .15 .40
69 Dexter Coakley .12 .30
70 Darren Woodson .15 .40
71 Emmitt Smith .50 1.25
72 Mike Anderson .15 .40
73 Terrell Davis .20 .50
74 Kevin Kasper .12 .30
75 Rod Smith .15 .40
76 Ed McCaffrey .15 .40
77 Olandis Gary .15 .40
78 Dwayne Carswell .12 .30
79 Deltha O'Neal .12 .30
80 Brian Griese .15 .40
81 Scotty Anderson .12 .30
82 Johnnie Morton .15 .40
83 Cory Schlesinger .12 .30
84 James Stewart .12 .30
85 Shaun Rogers .12 .30
86 Mike McMahon .12 .30
87 Charlie Batch .12 .30
88 Robert Porcher .12 .30
89 Bubba Franks .15 .40
90 Robert Ferguson .15 .40
91 Antonio Freeman .20 .50
92 Ahman Green .15 .40
93 Bill Schroeder .12 .30
94 Kabeer Gbaja-Biamila .15 .40
95 Jamal Reynolds .12 .30
96 Darren Sharper .15 .40
97 Brett Favre .50 1.25
98 Marvin Harrison .20 .50
99 Dominic Rhodes .15 .40
100 Edgerrin James .15 .40
101 Reggie Wayne .20 .50
102 Terrence Wilkins .12 .30
103 Ken Dilger .15 .40
104 Peyton Manning .40 1.00
105 Elvis Joseph .12 .30
106 Stacey Mack .12 .30
107 Fred Taylor .15 .40
108 Keenan McCardell .15 .40
109 Jimmy Smith .15 .40
110 Mark Brunell .15 .40
111 Derrick Alexander .12 .30
112 Tony Gonzalez .20 .50
113 Trent Green .15 .40
114 Snoop Minnis .12 .30
115 Priest Holmes .20 .50
116 Chris Chambers .15 .40
117 Jay Fiedler .15 .40
118 Oronde Gadsden .12 .30
119 Travis Minor .12 .30
120 Lamar Smith .15 .40
121 Zach Thomas .20 .50
122 Michael Bennett .15 .40
123 Todd Bouman .12 .30
124 Cris Carter .20 .50
125 Byron Chamberlain .12 .30
126 Randy Moss .20 .50
127 Jake Reed .15 .40
128 Daunte Culpepper .15 .40
129 Drew Bledsoe .20 .50
130 Troy Brown .15 .40
131 David Patten .12 .30
132 J.R. Redmond .12 .30
133 Antowain Smith .15 .40
134 Ty Law .15 .40
135 Richard Seymour .15 .40
136 Adam Vinatieri .20 .50
137 Tom Brady .50 1.25
138 Joe Horn .15 .40
139 Willie Jackson .12 .30
140 Deuce McAllister .15 .40
141 Boo Williams .12 .30
142 Ricky Williams .15 .40
143 La'Roi Glover .12 .30
144 Sammy Knight .12 .30
145 Aaron Brooks .15 .40
146 Tiki Barber .20 .50
147 Ron Dayne .15 .40
148 Ike Hilliard .15 .40
149 Amani Toomer .15 .40
150 Will Allen .12 .30
151 Michael Strahan .20 .50
152 Jason Sehorn .15 .40
153 Kerry Collins .15 .40
154 Anthony Becht .12 .30
155 Wayne Chrebet .15 .40
156 Laveranues Coles .15 .40
157 LaMont Jordan .15 .40
158 Santana Moss .15 .40
159 Chad Pennington .20 .50
160 John Abraham .15 .40
161 Vinny Testaverde .15 .40
162 Curtis Martin .20 .50
163 Tim Brown .20 .50
164 Rich Gannon .15 .40
165 Charlie Garner .15 .40
166 Jerry Porter .12 .30
167 Marques Tuiasosopo .12 .30
168 Tyrone Wheatley .15 .40
169 Charles Woodson .20 .50
170 Jerry Rice .40 1.00
171 Correll Buckhalter .15 .40
172 Chad Lewis .12 .30
173 Brian Mitchell .15 .40
174 Freddie Mitchell .12 .30
175 Todd Pinkston .12 .30
176 Duce Staley .15 .40
177 Tony Stewart .12 .30
178 James Thrash .15 .40
179 Hugh Douglas .12 .30
180 Donovan McNabb .20 .50
181 Plaxico Burress .15 .40
182 Chris Fuamatu-Ma'afala .12 .30
183 Kordell Stewart .15 .40
184 Hines Ward .20 .50
185 Amos Zereoue .12 .30
186 Kendrell Bell .12 .30
187 Casey Hampton .12 .30
188 Jerome Bettis .20 .50
189 Drew Brees .30 .75
190 Curtis Conway .15 .40
191 Tim Dwight .12 .30
192 Doug Flutie .20 .50
193 Junior Seau .20 .50
194 Marcellus Wiley .12 .30
195 Ryan McNeil .12 .30
196 Jeff Graham .12 .30
197 LaDainian Tomlinson .25 .60
198 Kevan Barlow .12 .30
199 Garrison Hearst .15 .40
200 Eric Johnson .12 .30
201 Terrell Owens .20 .50
202 J.J. Stokes .12 .30
203 Andre Carter .12 .30
204 Jeff Garcia .15 .40
205 Trent Dilfer .15 .40
206 Matt Hasselbeck .20 .50
207 Darrell Jackson .15 .40
208 Koren Robinson .12 .30
209 Ricky Watters .15 .40
210 John Randle .15 .40
211 Shaun Alexander .15 .40
212 Isaac Bruce .20 .50
213 Trung Canidate .12 .30
214 Marshall Faulk .20 .50
215 Az-Zahir Hakim .12 .30
216 Torry Holt .20 .50
217 Yo Murphy .12 .30
218 Ricky Proehl .15 .40
219 Adam Archuleta .12 .30
220 Dre Bly .12 .30
221 London Fletcher .12 .30
222 Tommy Polley .12 .30

223 Aeneas Williams	.15	.40
224 Kurt Warner	.20	.50
225 Mike Alstott	.15	.40
226 Warrick Dunn	.15	.40
227 Jacquez Green	.12	.30
228 Derrick Brooks	.20	.50
229 John Lynch	.15	.40
230 Warren Sapp	.15	.40
231 Ronde Barber	.15	.40
232 Brad Johnson	.15	.40
233 Keyshawn Johnson	.15	.40
234 Drew Bennett	.15	.40
235 Kevin Dyson	.15	.40
236 Eddie George	.15	.40
237 Derrick Mason	.15	.40
238 Justin McCareins	.15	.40
239 Frank Wycheck	.12	.30
240 Jevon Kearse	.15	.40
241 Samari Rolle	.12	.30
242 Steve McNair	.20	.50
243 Tony Banks	.12	.30
244 Stephen Davis	.15	.40
245 Michael Westbrook	.12	.30
246 Champ Bailey	.20	.50
247 Darrell Green	.20	.50
248 Bruce Smith	.20	.50
249 Fred Smoot	.15	.40
250 Rod Gardner	.12	.30
251 David Carr RC	.40	1.00
252 Joey Harrington RC	.40	1.00
253 Patrick Ramsey RC	.40	1.00
254 Kurt Kittner RC	.25	.60
255 Eric Crouch RC	.40	1.00
256 Josh McCown RC	.40	1.00
257 David Garrard RC	.50	1.25
258 Rohan Davey RC	.40	1.00
259 Ronald Curry RC	.30	.75
260 Chad Hutchinson RC	.25	.60
261 William Green RC	.30	.75
262 T.J. Duckett RC	.40	1.00
263 Clinton Portis RC	.50	1.25
264 DeShaun Foster RC	.40	1.00
265 Luke Staley RC	.25	.60
266 Wes Pate RC	.25	.60
267 Travis Stephens RC	.25	.60
268 Adrian Peterson RC	.40	1.00
269 Zak Kustok RC	.25	.60
270 Maurice Morris RC	.30	.75
271 Lamar Gordon RC	.30	.75
272 Chester Taylor RC	.40	1.00
273 Najeh Davenport RC	.40	1.00
274 Ladell Betts RC	.40	1.00
275 Ashley Lelie RC	.30	.75
276 Josh Reed RC	.30	.75
277 Cliff Russell RC	.25	.60
278 Javon Walker RC	.40	1.00
279 Ron Johnson RC	.30	.75
280 Antwaan Randle El RC	.40	1.00
281 Andre Davis RC	.30	.75
282 Marquise Walker RC	.25	.60
283 Kelly Campbell RC	.30	.75
284 Tavon Mason RC	.25	.60
285 Antonio Bryant RC	.40	1.00
286 Jabar Gaffney RC	.40	1.00
287 Donte Stallworth RC	.40	1.00
288 Tim Carter RC	.30	.75
289 Reche Caldwell RC	.40	1.00
290 Freddie Milons RC	.25	.60
291 Brian Poli-Dixon RC	.25	.60
292 Brian Westbrook RC	.60	1.50
293 Josh Scobey RC	.30	.75
294 Jeremy Shockey RC	.60	1.50
295 Daniel Graham RC	.30	.75
296 Deion Branch RC	.40	1.00
297 Julius Peppers RC	.75	2.00
298 Kalimba Edwards RC	.30	.75
299 Dwight Freeney RC	.50	1.25
300 Terry Charles RC	.25	.60
301 Alex Brown RC	.40	1.00
302 Jason McAddley RC	.30	.75
303 Michael Lewis RC	.40	1.00
304 Dennis Johnson RC	.25	.60
305 Albert Haynesworth RC	.40	1.00
306 Ryan Sims RC	.40	1.00
307 Larry Tripplett RC	.25	.60
308 Anthony Weaver RC	.25	.60
309 Wendell Bryant RC	.25	.60
310 John Henderson RC	.30	.75
311 Alan Harper RC	.25	.60
312 Napoleon Harris RC	.30	.75
313 Bryan Thomas RC	.25	.60
314 Andra Davis RC	.25	.60
315 Levar Fisher RC	.25	.60
316 Woody Dantzler RC	.30	.75
317 Robert Thomas RC	.25	.60
318 Quentin Jammer RC	.40	1.00
319 Lito Sheppard RC	.40	1.00
320 Travis Fisher RC	.30	.75
321 Roy Williams RC	.40	1.00
322 Phillip Buchanon RC	.40	1.00
323 Joseph Jefferson RC	.25	.60
324 Ed Reed RC	1.50	4.00
325 Lamont Thompson RC	.30	.75
326 Raonall Smith RC	.25	.60
327 Mike Rumph RC	.25	.60
328 Rocky Calmus RC	.30	.75
329 Bryant McKinnie RC	.25	.60
330 Mike Williams RC	.25	.60

2002 Score Final Score

*1-250 VETS: 6X TO 15X BASIC CARDS
*251-330 ROOKIES: 3X TO 8X
STATED PRINT RUN 100 SER.#'d SETS

2002 Score Scorecard

*1-250 VETS: 2.5X TO 6X BASIC CARDS
*251-330 ROOKIES: 1X TO 2.5X
STATED PRINT RUN 400 SER.#'d SETS

2002 Score Changing Stripes

STATED PRINT RUN 150 SER.#'d SETS

1 Curtis Martin	8.00	20.00
2 Doug Flutie	8.00	20.00
3 Eric Dickerson	6.00	15.00
4 Jerome Bettis	8.00	20.00
5 Jerry Rice	15.00	40.00
7 John Riggins	30.00	80.00
8 Kerry Collins	6.00	15.00
9 Keyshawn Johnson	6.00	15.00
10 Marcus Allen	12.00	30.00
11 Mark Brunell	6.00	15.00
12 Priest Holmes	8.00	20.00
13 Ricky Watters	6.00	15.00
14 Thurman Thomas	12.00	30.00
15 Warren Moon	12.00	30.00
P8 Kerry Collins Sample	6.00	15.00

2002 Score Franchise Fabrics

STATED ODDS 1:574 RETAIL

1 Ahman Green	5.00	12.00
2 Amani Toomer	5.00	12.00
3 Brad Johnson	5.00	12.00
4 Charles Woodson	6.00	15.00
5 Corey Dillon	5.00	12.00
6 Cris Carter	6.00	15.00
7 David Boston	4.00	10.00
8 Derrick Mason	5.00	12.00
9 Donovan McNabb	6.00	15.00
10 Emmitt Smith	20.00	50.00
11 Hines Ward	6.00	15.00
12 John Elway	15.00	40.00
13 Junior Seau	6.00	15.00
14 Kevin Johnson	4.00	10.00
16 LaDainian Tomlinson	8.00	20.00
17 Marvin Harrison	6.00	15.00
18 Michael Strahan	6.00	15.00
19 Mike Alstott	5.00	12.00
20 Ricky Williams	5.00	12.00
21 Rob Johnson	5.00	12.00
23 Stephen Davis	5.00	12.00
24 Troy Aikman	12.00	30.00
25 Zach Thomas	6.00	15.00

2002 Score In the Zone

COMPLETE SET (20)	15.00	40.00
STATED ODDS 1:35 HOB/RET		
1 Marshall Faulk	1.25	3.00
2 Terrell Owens	1.25	3.00
3 Shaun Alexander	1.00	2.50
4 Marvin Harrison	1.25	3.00
5 Antowain Smith	1.00	2.50
6 Corey Dillon	1.00	2.50
7 Mike Alstott	1.00	2.50
8 Rod Smith	1.00	2.50
9 Ahman Green	1.00	2.50
10 Derrick Mason	1.00	2.50
11 Tim Brown	1.25	3.00
12 Curtis Martin	1.25	3.00
13 Priest Holmes	1.25	3.00
14 Stacey Mack	.75	2.00
15 LaDainian Tomlinson	1.50	4.00
16 Dominic Rhodes	1.00	2.50
17 Randy Moss	1.25	3.00
18 Bill Schroeder	.75	2.00
19 Joe Horn	1.00	2.50
20 Jerry Rice	2.50	6.00

2002 Score Inscriptions

STATED ODDS 1:347
*PERSONAL/25: .8X TO 2X BASIC AU
PERSON/25: .6X TO 1.5X BASIC AU/75-125
PERSON/25: .4X TO 1X BASIC AU/25-50

1 Anthony Thomas	8.00	20.00
2 Brian Griese/50*	15.00	40.00
3 Brian Urlacher	15.00	40.00
4 Chad Johnson	10.00	25.00
5 Chad Pennington/100*	12.00	30.00
6 Chris Weinke	6.00	15.00
7 Corey Dillon/75*	10.00	25.00
8 Correll Buckhalter	8.00	20.00
9 Cris Carter/25*	30.00	60.00
10 Daunte Culpepper/75*	10.00	25.00
11 David Terrell/100*	8.00	20.00
12 Deuce McAllister/125*	10.00	25.00
13 Eric Moulds	8.00	20.00
14 Jamal Lewis/100*	10.00	25.00
15 James Jackson	6.00	15.00
16 Jimmy Smith	8.00	20.00
17 Kurt Warner/50*	20.00	50.00
18 Marshall Faulk/50*	20.00	50.00
19 Snoop Minnis/100* No Auto	8.00	20.00
20 Mike McMahon	6.00	15.00
21 Terrell Owens	15.00	40.00
22 Travis Henry/100* No Auto	8.00	20.00
23 Aaron Brooks/100*	10.00	25.00
24 Junior Seau	25.00	50.00
25 Troy Aikman/50*	40.00	80.00
26 Antwaan Randle El	10.00	25.00
27 Jeremy Shockey	15.00	40.00
28 Jabar Gaffney	10.00	25.00
29 Rocky Calmus	8.00	20.00
30 Donte Stallworth	10.00	25.00
31 Ashley Lelie	8.00	20.00
32 Marquise Walker	6.00	15.00
33 Javon Walker No Auto	10.00	25.00
34 Reche Caldwell	10.00	25.00
35 Daniel Graham	8.00	20.00
36 T.J. Duckett	10.00	25.00
37 Antonio Bryant	10.00	25.00
38 William Green	8.00	20.00
39 David Carr/150*	12.00	30.00
40 Ron Johnson	8.00	20.00

2002 Score Monday Matchups

COMPLETE SET (17)	15.00	40.00
ODDS 1:35 HOB/RET, 1:8 JUM		
1 Brian Griese	1.00	2.50
2 Ahman Green	1.00	2.50
3 Garrison Hearst	1.00	2.50
4 Kurt Warner	1.25	3.00
5 Emmitt Smith	3.00	8.00
6 James Thrash	1.00	2.50
7 Plaxico Burress	1.00	2.50
8 Tim Brown	1.25	3.00
9 Qadry Ismail	1.00	2.50
10 Randy Moss	1.25	3.00
11 Mike Alstott	1.00	2.50
12 Brett Favre	3.00	8.00
13 Jay Fiedler	1.00	2.50
14 Kurt Warner	1.25	3.00
15 Derrick Mason	1.00	2.50
16 Mike Alstott	1.00	2.50
17 Terry Allen	1.00	2.50

2002 Score Numbers Game

1-10 PRINT RUN 2843-4830
STATED ODDS 1:52 HOB, 1:13 JUM
11-30 PRINT RUN 729-1598

1 Kurt Warner/4830	1.50	4.00
2 Rich Gannon/3828	1.25	3.00
3 Trent Green/3783	1.25	3.00
4 Kerry Collins/3764	1.25	3.00
5 Jake Plummer/3653	1.25	3.00
6 Steve McNair/3350	1.50	4.00
7 Kordell Stewart/3109	1.25	3.00
8 Tim Couch/3040	1.00	2.50
9 Chris Weinke/2931	1.00	2.50
10 Tom Brady/2843	4.00	10.00
11 Priest Holmes/1555	2.00	5.00
12 Curtis Martin/1513	2.00	5.00
13 Ahman Green/1387	1.50	4.00
14 Marshall Faulk/1382	2.00	5.00
15 Shaun Alexander/1318	1.50	4.00
16 LaDainian Tomlinson/1236	2.50	6.00
17 Garrison Hearst/1206	1.50	4.00
18 Anthony Thomas/1183	1.50	4.00
19 Emmitt Smith/1021	5.00	12.00
20 Travis Henry/729	1.25	3.00
21 David Boston/1598	1.25	3.00
22 Marvin Harrison/1524	2.00	5.00
23 Terrell Owens/1412	2.00	5.00
24 Torry Holt/1363	2.00	5.00
25 Randy Moss/1224	2.00	5.00
26 Troy Brown/1199	1.50	4.00
27 Tim Brown/1165	2.00	5.00
28 Marty Booker/1071	1.50	4.00
29 Plaxico Burress/1008	1.50	4.00
30 Chris Chambers/883	1.50	4.00

2002 Score Originals Autographs

STATED PRINT RUN 1-100
SERIAL #'d UNDER 20 NOT PRICED

3 Kerry Collins 95Sco/100	15.00	40.00
5 Doug Flutie 89Sco/45	15.00	40.00
18 Ahman Green 98Sco/30	15.00	40.00
19 Bo Jackson 89ScoSup/22	40.00	80.00
25 Peyton Manning 98Sco/31	100.00	175.00
27 Warren Moon 89Sco/49	15.00	40.00
38 Jerry Rice 97Sco/69	50.00	100.00
42 Junior Seau 90Sco/30	30.00	60.00
49 Steve Young 89Sco/60	40.00	80.00

2002 Score The Franchise

STATED ODDS 1:35 HOB, 1:8 JUM

1 David Boston	.75	2.00
2 Michael Vick	2.00	5.00
3 Ray Lewis	1.25	3.00
4 Travis Henry	.75	2.00
5 Chris Weinke	.75	2.00
6 Anthony Thomas	1.00	2.50
7 Corey Dillon	1.00	2.50
8 Tim Couch	.75	2.00
9 Emmitt Smith	3.00	8.00
10 Rod Smith	1.00	2.50
11 Mike McMahon	.75	2.00
12 Ahman Green	1.00	2.50
13 Peyton Manning	2.50	6.00
14 Jimmy Smith	1.00	2.50
15 Priest Holmes	1.25	3.00
16 Chris Chambers	1.00	2.50
17 Randy Moss	1.25	3.00
18 Tom Brady	3.00	8.00
19 Aaron Brooks	1.00	2.50
20 Kerry Collins	1.00	2.50
21 Curtis Martin	1.25	3.00
22 Tim Brown	1.25	3.00
23 Donovan McNabb	1.25	3.00
24 Jerome Bettis	1.25	3.00
25 LaDainian Tomlinson	1.50	4.00
26 Jeff Garcia	1.00	2.50
27 Shaun Alexander	1.00	2.50
28 Marshall Faulk	1.25	3.00
29 Keyshawn Johnson	1.00	2.50
30 Steve McNair	1.25	3.00
31 Stephen Davis	1.00	2.50

2003 Score Atlantic City National Promos

STATED PRINT RUN 5 SER.#'d SETS
UNPRICED AC FINAL SCORE PRINT RUN 1

2003 Score

This set was issued in May, 2003. The cards were distributed in 18-card jumbo hobby packs which carried a $3 SRP and 7-card retail packs. Cards numbered 1-275 feature veterans while cards numbered 276-330 featured rookies. Please note that cards numbers 292, 323 and 328 were intended to have been pulled from packs but a very small number of the cards slipped through and made it onto the secondary market.

COMPLETE SET (327)	20.00	50.00
1 Jeff Blake	.15	.40
2 Todd Heap	.15	.40
3 Ron Johnson	.12	.30
4 Jamal Lewis	.15	.40
5 Ray Lewis	.20	.50
6 Chris Redman	.12	.30
7 Ed Reed	.20	.50
8 Travis Taylor	.12	.30
9 Anthony Weaver	.12	.30
10 Drew Bledsoe	.20	.50
11 Larry Centers	.15	.40
12 Nate Clements	.15	.40
13 Travis Henry	.12	.30
14 Eric Moulds	.15	.40
15 Peerless Price	.12	.30
16 Josh Reed	.12	.30
17 Coy Wire	.12	.30
18 Corey Dillon	.15	.40
19 T.J. Houshmandzadeh	.20	.50
20 Chad Johnson	.20	.50
21 Jon Kitna	.15	.40
22 Lorenzo Neal	.15	.40
23 Peter Warrick	.15	.40
24 Nicolas Luchey RC	.12	.30
25 Tim Couch	.12	.30
26 Andre Davis	.12	.30
27 William Green	.12	.30
28 Kevin Johnson	.12	.30
29 Quincy Morgan	.12	.30
30 Dennis Northcutt	.12	.30
31 Jamel White	.12	.30
32 Mike Anderson	.15	.40
33 Steve Beuerlein	.15	.40
34 Jason Elam	.15	.40
35 Olandis Gary	.12	.30
36 Brian Griese	.15	.40
37 Ashley Lelie	.12	.30
38 Ed McCaffrey	.15	.40
39 Clinton Portis	.15	.40
40 Shannon Sharpe	.20	.50
41 Rod Smith	.15	.40
42 James Allen	.12	.30
43 Corey Bradford	.12	.30
44 David Carr	.15	.40
45 JaJuan Dawson	.12	.30
46 Jabar Gaffney	.12	.30
47 Aaron Glenn	.12	.30
48 Billy Miller	.12	.30
49 Jonathan Wells	.12	.30
50 Dwight Freeney	.15	.40
51 Marvin Harrison	.20	.50
52 Qadry Ismail	.15	.40
53 Edgerrin James	.20	.50
54 Peyton Manning	.40	1.00
55 James Mungro	.12	.30
56 Marcus Pollard	.12	.30
57 Reggie Wayne	.20	.50
58 Kyle Brady	.12	.30
59 Mark Brunell	.15	.40
60 David Garrard	.20	.50
61 John Henderson	.15	.40
62 Stacey Mack	.12	.30
63 Jimmy Smith	.15	.40
64 Fred Taylor	.15	.40
65 Marc Boerigter	.12	.30
66 Tony Gonzalez	.20	.50
67 Trent Green	.15	.40
68 Priest Holmes	.20	.50
69 Eddie Kennison	.12	.30
70 Snoop Minnis	.12	.30
71 Johnnie Morton	.15	.40
72 Cris Carter	.20	.50
73 Chris Chambers	.15	.40
74 Robert Edwards	.15	.40
75 Jay Fiedler	.12	.30
76 Ray Lucas	.12	.30
77 Randy McMichael	.12	.30
78 Travis Minor	.12	.30
79 Zach Thomas	.20	.50
80 Ricky Williams	.15	.40
81 Tom Brady	.50	1.25
82 Deion Branch	.15	.40
83 Troy Brown	.15	.40
84 Tedy Bruschi	.20	.50
85 Kevin Faulk	.15	.40
86 Daniel Graham	.12	.30
87 David Patten	.12	.30
88 Antowain Smith	.15	.40
89 Adam Vinatieri	.20	.50
90 Donnie Abraham	.15	.40
91 Anthony Becht	.12	.30
92 Wayne Chrebet	.15	.40
93 Laveranues Coles	.12	.30
94 LaMont Jordan	.15	.40
95 Curtis Martin	.20	.50
96 Chad Morton	.12	.30
97 Santana Moss	.15	.40
98 Chad Pennington	.20	.50
99 Vinny Testaverde	.15	.40
100 Tim Brown	.20	.50
101 Phillip Buchanon	.12	.30
102 Rich Gannon	.15	.40
103 Charlie Garner	.15	.40
104 Doug Jolley	.12	.30
105 Jerry Porter	.12	.30
106 Jerry Rice	.40	1.00
107 Marques Tuiasosopo	.12	.30
108 Charles Woodson	.20	.50
109 Rod Woodson	.20	.50
110 Kendrell Bell	.12	.30
111 Jerome Bettis	.20	.50
112 Plaxico Burress	.15	.40
113 Tommy Maddox	.15	.40
114 Joey Porter	.20	.50
115 Antwaan Randle El	.15	.40
116 Kordell Stewart	.15	.40
117 Hines Ward	.20	.50
118 Amos Zereoue	.12	.30
119 Drew Brees	.20	.50
120 Reche Caldwell	.12	.30
121 Curtis Conway	.12	.30
122 Tim Dwight	.12	.30
123 Doug Flutie	.20	.50
124 Quentin Jammer	.12	.30
125 Ben Leber	.12	.30
126 Josh Norman	.12	.30
127 Junior Seau	.20	.50
128 LaDainian Tomlinson	.20	.50
129 Keith Bulluck	.12	.30
130 Rocky Calmus	.12	.30
131 Kevin Carter	.15	.40
132 Kevin Dyson	.12	.30
133 Eddie George	.15	.40
134 Albert Haynesworth	.20	.50
135 Jevon Kearse	.15	.40
136 Derrick Mason	.15	.40
137 Justin McCareins	.12	.30
138 Steve McNair	.20	.50
139 Frank Wycheck	.12	.30
140 David Boston	.12	.30
141 MarTay Jenkins	.12	.30
142 Freddie Jones	.12	.30
143 Thomas Jones	.20	.50
144 Jason McAddley	.12	.30
145 Josh McCown	.15	.40
146 Jake Plummer	.15	.40
147 Marcel Shipp	.12	.30
148 Alge Crumpler	.15	.40
149 T.J. Duckett	.15	.40
150 Warrick Dunn	.15	.40
151 Brian Finneran	.12	.30
152 Trevor Gaylor	.12	.30
153 Shawn Jefferson	.12	.30
154 Michael Vick	.25	.60
155 Randy Fasani	.12	.30
156 DeShaun Foster	.15	.40
157 Muhsin Muhammad	.15	.40
158 Rodney Peete	.12	.30
159 Julius Peppers	.20	.50
160 Lamar Smith	.15	.40
161 Steve Smith	.20	.50
162 Chris Weinke	.15	.40
163 Wesley Walls	.15	.40
164 Marty Booker	.15	.40
165 Mike Brown	.15	.40
166 Chris Chandler	.15	.40
167 Jim Miller	.12	.30
168 Marcus Robinson	.15	.40
169 David Terrell	.12	.30
170 Anthony Thomas	.15	.40
171 Brian Urlacher	.20	.50
172 Dez White	.12	.30
173 Antonio Bryant	.12	.30
174 Quincy Carter	.12	.30
175 Dexter Coakley	.15	.40
176 Joey Galloway	.15	.40
177 La'Roi Glover	.12	.30
178 Troy Hambrick	.12	.30
179 Chad Hutchinson	.12	.30
180 Rocket Ismail	.15	.40
181 Emmitt Smith	.50	1.25
182 Roy Williams	.15	.40
183 Scotty Anderson	.12	.30
184 Germane Crowell	.12	.30
185 Az-Zahir Hakim	.12	.30
186 Joey Harrington	.12	.30
187 Cory Schlesinger	.12	.30
188 Bill Schroeder	.12	.30
189 James Stewart	.12	.30
190 Marques Anderson	.12	.30
191 Najeh Davenport	.15	.40
192 Donald Driver	.20	.50
193 Brett Favre	.50	1.25
194 Bubba Franks	.15	.40
195 Terry Glenn	.15	.40
196 Ahman Green	.15	.40
197 Darren Sharper	.15	.40
198 Javon Walker	.15	.40
199 D'Wayne Bates	.12	.30
200 Michael Bennett	.15	.40
201 Todd Bouman	.12	.30
202 Byron Chamberlain	.12	.30
203 Daunte Culpepper	.15	.40
204 Randy Moss	.20	.50
205 Kelly Campbell	.12	.30
206 Aaron Brooks	.15	.40
207 Charles Grant	.15	.40
208 Joe Horn	.15	.40
209 Michael Lewis	.12	.30
210 Deuce McAllister	.15	.40
211 Jerome Pathon	.12	.30
212 Donte Stallworth	.12	.30
213 Boo Williams	.12	.30
214 Tiki Barber	.20	.50
215 Tim Carter	.12	.30
216 Kerry Collins	.15	.40
217 Ron Dayne	.15	.40
218 Jesse Palmer	.12	.30
219 Will Peterson	.15	.40
220 Jason Sehorn	.15	.40
221 Jeremy Shockey	.20	.50
222 Michael Strahan	.20	.50
223 Amani Toomer	.15	.40
224 Koy Detmer	.12	.30
225 Antonio Freeman	.15	.40
226 Dorsey Levens	.15	.40
227 Chad Lewis	.15	.40
228 Donovan McNabb	.20	.50
229 Freddie Mitchell	.15	.40
230 Duce Staley	.15	.40
231 James Thrash	.12	.30
232 Brian Westbrook	.20	.50
233 Kevan Barlow	.12	.30
234 Andre Carter	.12	.30
235 Jeff Garcia	.15	.40
236 Garrison Hearst	.15	.40
237 Eric Johnson	.15	.40
238 Terrell Owens	.20	.50
239 Jamal Robertson	.12	.30
240 Tai Streets	.12	.30
241 Shaun Alexander	.15	.40
242 Trent Dilfer	.15	.40
243 Bobby Engram	.12	.30
244 Matt Hasselbeck	.15	.40
245 Darrell Jackson	.15	.40
246 Maurice Morris	.12	.30
247 Koren Robinson	.15	.40
248 Jerramy Stevens	.15	.40
249 Isaac Bruce	.20	.50
250 Marc Bulger	.20	.50
251 Marshall Faulk	.20	.50
252 Lamar Gordon	.12	.30
253 Torry Holt	.20	.50
254 Ricky Proehl	.15	.40
255 Kurt Warner	.20	.50
256 Aeneas Williams	.15	.40
257 Mike Alstott	.20	.50
258 Ken Dilger	.15	.40
259 Brad Johnson	.15	.40
260 Keyshawn Johnson	.20	.50
261 Rob Johnson	.15	.40
262 John Lynch	.15	.40
263 Keenan McCardell	.15	.40
264 Michael Pittman	.12	.30
265 Warren Sapp	.15	.40
266 Marquise Walker	.12	.30
267 Champ Bailey	.20	.50
268 Stephen Davis	.15	.40
269 Rod Gardner	.12	.30
270 Darrell Green	.20	.50
271 Shane Matthews	.12	.30
272 Darnerien McCants	.12	.30
273 Patrick Ramsey	.15	.40
274 Bruce Smith	.15	.40
275 Kenny Watson	.12	.30
276 Carson Palmer RC	1.00	2.50
277 Byron Leftwich RC	.50	1.25
278 Kyle Boller RC	.50	1.25
279 Chris Simms RC	.50	1.25
280 Dave Ragone RC	.30	.75
281 Rex Grossman RC	.50	1.25
282 Brian St.Pierre RC	.40	1.00
283 Larry Johnson RC	.50	1.25
284 Lee Suggs RC	.40	1.00
285 Justin Fargas RC	.50	1.25
286 Onterrio Smith RC	.30	.75
287 Willis McGahee RC	.60	1.50
288 Chris Brown RC	.30	.75
289 Musa Smith RC	.30	.75
290 Artose Pinner RC	.30	.75
291 Cecil Sapp RC	.30	.75
292 Derek Watson SP RC	15.00	40.00
293 LaBrandon Toefield RC	.40	1.00
294 Charles Rogers RC	.40	1.00
295 Andre Johnson RC	1.25	3.00
296 Taylor Jacobs RC	.30	.75
297 Bryant Johnson RC	.50	1.25
298 Kelley Washington RC	.30	.75
299 Brandon Lloyd RC	.75	2.00
300 Justin Gage RC	.40	1.00
301 Tyrone Calico RC	.40	1.00
302 Kevin Curtis RC	.50	1.25
303 Sam Aiken RC	.40	1.00
304 Doug Gabriel RC	.40	1.00
305 Talman Gardner RC	.30	.75
306 Jason Witten RC	1.25	3.00
307 Mike Pinkard RC	.30	.75
308 Teyo Johnson RC	.40	1.00
309 Bennie Joppru RC	.30	.75
310 Dallas Clark RC	.75	2.00
311 Terrell Suggs RC	.50	1.25
312 Chris Kelsay RC	.40	1.00
313 Jerome McDougle RC	.30	.75
314 Andrew Williams RC	.30	.75
315 Michael Haynes RC	.30	.75
316 Jimmy Kennedy RC	.40	1.00
317 Kevin Williams RC	.50	1.25
318 Ken Dorsey RC	.40	1.00
319 William Joseph RC	.30	.75
320 Kenny Peterson RC	.40	1.00
321 Rien Long RC	.30	.75
322 Boss Bailey RC	.40	1.00
323 E.J. Henderson SP RC	15.00	40.00
324 Terence Newman RC	.40	1.00
325 Marcus Trufant RC	.40	1.00
326 Andre Woolfolk RC	.40	1.00
327 Dennis Weathersby RC	.30	.75
328 Eugene Wilson SP RC	15.00	40.00
329 Mike Doss RC	.50	1.25
330 Rashean Mathis RC	.40	1.00

2003 Score Final Score

UNPRICED FINAL SCORE PRINT RUN 2-12

2003 Score Scorecard

*VETS 1-275: 2.5X TO 6X BASIC CARDS
*ROOKIES 276-330: 1X TO 2.5X
STATED PRINT RUN 500 SER.#'d SETS

2003 Score Changing Stripes

STATED PRINT RUN 250 SER.#'d SETS

CS1 Drew Bledsoe		
CS2 Ricky Williams	6.00	15.00
CS3 Terry Glenn	6.00	15.00
CS4 Rich Gannon	6.00	15.00
CS5 Brad Johnson	6.00	15.00
CS6 James Stewart	5.00	12.00
CS7 Trent Green	6.00	15.00
CS8 Art Monk	10.00	25.00
CS9 Joe Montana	30.00	80.00
CS10 Warrick Dunn	6.00	15.00

2003 Score Franchise Fabrics

STATED PRINT RUN 250 SER.#'d SETS

FF1 Ahman Green		
FF2 Corey Dillon	4.00	10.00
FF3 Curtis Martin	5.00	12.00
FF4 Darrell Green	5.00	12.00
FF5 Emmitt Smith	12.00	30.00
FF6 Garrison Hearst	4.00	10.00
FF7 Jake Plummer	4.00	10.00
FF8 Jimmy Smith	4.00	10.00
FF9 Junior Seau	5.00	12.00
FF10 Kevin Johnson	3.00	8.00
FF11 Michael Strahan	5.00	12.00
FF12 Mike Alstott	5.00	12.00
FF13 Plaxico Burress	4.00	10.00
FF14 Ray Lewis	5.00	12.00
FF15 Rod Smith	4.00	10.00
FF16 Stephen Davis	4.00	10.00
FF17 Steve McNair	5.00	12.00
FF18 Tim Brown	5.00	12.00
FF19 Tony Gonzalez	5.00	12.00
FF20 Warren Sapp	4.00	10.00

2003 Score Inscriptions

STATED ODDS 1:65
*PERSONALIZED/25: .8X TO 2X BASIC AU
PERSONALIZED SER. #'d TO 25

1 Joe Montana	90.00	150.00
2 Kurt Warner	40.00	80.00
3 Jeff Garcia	10.00	25.00
4 Donald Driver	15.00	40.00
5 Shaun Alexander	10.00	25.00
6 Peerless Price	8.00	20.00
7 Derrick Mason	10.00	25.00
9 Boss Bailey	10.00	25.00
10 Chris Simms	10.00	25.00
11 Jason Witten	25.00	60.00
12 Jimmy Kennedy	10.00	25.00
13 Justin Fargas	10.00	25.00
14 Justin Gage	10.00	25.00
15 Kevin Curtis	12.00	30.00
16 Marcus Trufant	10.00	25.00
17 Mike Pinkard	8.00	20.00
18 Rex Grossman	10.00	25.00
19 Rien Long	8.00	20.00
20 Sam Aiken	10.00	25.00
21 Tyrone Calico	10.00	25.00
22 Willis McGahee	12.00	30.00

2003 Score Monday Night Heroes

COMPLETE SET (17)	10.00	25.00
STATED ODDS 1:9		
MN1 Tom Brady	2.00	5.00
MN2 Donovan McNabb	.75	2.00
MN3 Derrick Brooks	.60	1.50
MN4 Todd Heap	.60	1.50
MN5 Brett Favre	2.00	5.00
MN6 Terrell Owens	.75	2.00
MN7 Hines Ward	.75	2.00
MN8 Donovan McNabb	.75	2.00
MN9 Ahman Green	.60	1.50
MN10 Rich Gannon	.60	1.50
MN11 Marc Bulger	.75	2.00
MN12 Koy Detmer	.50	1.25
MN13 Tim Brown	.75	2.00
MN14 Ricky Williams	.60	1.50
MN15 Steve McNair	.75	2.00
MN16 Plaxico Burress	.60	1.50
MN17 Dre Bly	.50	1.25

2003 Score Numbers Game

COMPLETE SET (31)	30.00	80.00
STATED PRINT RUN 887-4689		
NG1 Rich Gannon/4689	.75	2.00
NG2 Drew Bledsoe/4359	1.00	2.50
NG3 Peyton Manning/4200	2.00	5.00
NG4 Tom Brady/3764	2.50	6.00
NG5 Joey Harrington/2294	.60	1.50
NG6 Brett Favre/3658	2.50	6.00
NG7 Aaron Brooks/3572	.75	2.00
NG8 Michael Vick/2936	1.25	3.00
NG9 Steve McNair/3387	1.00	2.50
NG10 David Carr/2592	.75	2.00
NG11 Priest Holmes/1615	1.25	3.00
NG12 LaDainian Tomlinson/1683	1.25	3.00
NG13 Ricky Williams/1853	1.00	2.50
NG14 Travis Henry/1438	.75	2.00
NG15 Deuce McAllister/1388	1.00	2.50
NG16 Clinton Portis/1508	1.00	2.50
NG17 William Green/887	.75	2.00
NG18 Jamal Lewis/1327	1.00	2.50
NG19 Michael Bennett/1296	1.00	2.50
NG20 Ahman Green/1240	1.00	2.50
NG21 Eddie George/1165	1.00	2.50
NG22 Marvin Harrison/1722	1.25	3.00
NG23 Hines Ward/1329	1.25	3.00
NG24 Rod Gardner/1006	.75	2.00
NG25 Jerry Rice/1211	2.50	6.00
NG26 Jeremy Shockey/894	1.25	3.00
NG27 Peerless Price/1252	.75	2.00
NG28 Eric Moulds/1287	1.00	2.50
NG29 Chad Johnson/1166	1.25	3.00
NG30 Donald Driver/1064	1.25	3.00
NG31 Koren Robinson/1240	1.00	2.50

2003 Score Reflextions

COMPLETE SET (20)	15.00	40.00
STATED ODDS 1:9		
R1 Terrell Owens David Boston	1.00	2.50
R2 Eddie George Anthony Thomas	.75	2.00
R3 Emmitt Smith LaDainian Tomlinson	2.50	6.00
R4 Marshall Faulk Priest Holmes	1.00	2.50
R5 Randy Moss Plaxico Burress	1.00	2.50
R6 Brett Favre Kurt Warner	2.50	6.00
R7 Zach Thomas Brian Urlacher	1.00	2.50
R8 Fred Taylor Micahel Bennett	.75	2.00
R9 Jerome Bettis T.J. Duckett	1.00	2.50
R10 Peyton Manning Joey Harrington	2.00	5.00
R11 Torry Holt Donte Stallworth	1.00	2.50
R12 Jerry Rice Marvin Harrison	2.00	5.00
R13 Keyshawn Johnson Rod Gardner	1.00	2.50
R14 Daunte Culpepper Aaron Brooks	.75	2.00
R15 Rich Gannon Jeff Garcia	.75	2.00
R16 Steve McNair Donovan McNabb	1.00	2.50
R17 Edgerrin James Deuce McAllister	1.00	2.50
R18 Eric Moulds Chris Chambers	.75	2.00
R19 Isaac Bruce Joe Horn	1.00	2.50
R20 Jevon Kearse Julius Peppers	1.00	2.50

2003 Score Reflextions Materials

STATED PRINT RUN 250 SER.#'d SETS

R1 Terrell Owens David Boston	6.00	15.00
R2 Eddie George Anthony Thomas	5.00	12.00
R3 Emmitt Smith LaDainian Tomlinson	15.00	40.00
R4 Marshall Faulk Priest Holmes	6.00	15.00
R5 Randy Moss Plaxico Burress	6.00	15.00
R6 Brett Favre Kurt Warner	15.00	40.00
R7 Zach Thomas Brian Urlacher	6.00	15.00
R8 Fred Taylor Micahel Bennett	5.00	12.00
R9 Jerome Bettis T.J. Duckett	6.00	15.00
R10 Peyton Manning Joey Harrington	12.00	30.00
R11 Torry Holt Donte Stallworth	6.00	15.00
R12 Jerry Rice Marvin Harrison	12.00	30.00
R13 Keyshawn Johnson Rod Gardner	6.00	15.00
R14 Daunte Culpepper Aaron Brooks	5.00	12.00
R15 Rich Gannon Jeff Garcia	5.00	12.00
R16 Steve McNair Donovan McNabb	6.00	15.00
R17 Edgerrin James Deuce McAllister	6.00	15.00
R18 Eric Moulds Chris Chambers	5.00	12.00
R19 Isaac Bruce Joe Horn	6.00	15.00
R20 Jevon Kearse Julius Peppers	6.00	15.00

2003 Score The Franchise

COMPLETE SET (32)	30.00	80.00
STATED ODDS 1:9		
TF1 David Boston	.75	2.00
TF2 Michael Vick	1.50	4.00
TF3 Jamal Lewis	1.00	2.50
TF4 Drew Bledsoe	1.25	3.00
TF5 Julius Peppers	1.25	3.00
TF6 Anthony Thomas	1.00	2.50
TF7 Chad Johnson	1.25	3.00
TF8 William Green	.75	2.00
TF9 Emmitt Smith	3.00	8.00
TF10 Clinton Portis	1.00	2.50
TF11 Joey Harrington	.75	2.00
TF12 Brett Favre	3.00	8.00
TF13 David Carr	1.00	2.50
TF14 Edgerrin James	1.25	3.00
TF15 Fred Taylor	1.00	2.50
TF16 Priest Holmes	1.25	3.00
TF17 Ricky Williams	1.00	2.50
TF18 Michael Bennett	1.00	2.50
TF19 Tom Brady	3.00	8.00
TF20 Deuce McAllister	1.00	2.50
TF21 Tiki Barber	1.25	3.00
TF22 Chad Pennington	1.25	3.00
TF23 Jerry Rice	2.50	6.00
TF24 Donovan McNabb	1.25	3.00
TF25 Tommy Maddox	1.00	2.50
TF26 Drew Brees	1.25	3.00
TF27 Terrell Owens	1.25	3.00
TF28 Shaun Alexander	1.00	2.50
TF29 Marshall Faulk	1.25	3.00
TF30 Warren Sapp	1.00	2.50
TF31 Eddie George	1.00	2.50
TF32 Patrick Ramsey	1.00	2.50

2004 Score

Score initially released in early September 2004. The base set consists of 440-cards including 70-rookies issued one per pack. The retail-only boxes contained 36-packs of 7-cards and carried an S.R.P. of $1 per pack. Three parallel sets and the Inscriptions autographs highlight the inserts.

COMPLETE SET (440)	40.00	80.00
UNPRICED FINAL SCORE #'d TO TEAM WINS		
1 Emmitt Smith	.50	1.25
2 Anquan Boldin	.20	.50
3 Bryant Johnson	.12	.30
4 Marcel Shipp	.12	.30
5 Josh McCown	.15	.40
6 Dexter Jackson	.12	.30
7 Bertrand Berry	.15	.40
8 Freddie Jones	.12	.30
9 Duane Starks	.12	.30
10 Michael Vick	.25	.60
11 T.J. Duckett	.15	.40
12 Warrick Dunn	.15	.40
13 Peerless Price	.12	.30
14 Alge Crumpler	.15	.40
15 Brian Finneran	.12	.30
16 Jason Webster	.12	.30
17 Dez White	.15	.40
18 Keith Brooking	.12	.30
19 Rod Coleman	.12	.30
20 Jamal Lewis	.15	.40
21 Kyle Boller	.15	.40
22 Todd Heap	.15	.40
23 Jonathan Ogden	.15	.40
24 Travis Taylor	.12	.30
25 Ray Lewis	.20	.50
26 Peter Boulware	.15	.40
27 Terrell Suggs	.15	.40
28 Chris McAlister	.12	.30
29 Ed Reed	.15	.40
30 Drew Bledsoe	.20	.50
31 Travis Henry	.12	.30
32 Eric Moulds	.15	.40
33 Josh Reed	.12	.30
34 Willis McGahee	.20	.50
35 Takeo Spikes	.12	.30
36 Lawyer Milloy	.12	.30
37 Troy Vincent	.15	.40
38 Sam Adams	.12	.30
39 Nate Clements	.15	.40
40 Jake Delhomme	.15	.40
41 Stephen Davis	.15	.40
42 DeShaun Foster	.15	.40
43 Muhsin Muhammad	.15	.40
44 Steve Smith	.20	.50
45 Ricky Proehl	.15	.40
46 Julius Peppers	.15	.40
47 Kris Jenkins	.15	.40
48 Dan Morgan	.15	.40
49 Ricky Manning	.12	.30
50 Brad Hoover	.15	.40
51 Carson Palmer	.20	.50
52 Rudi Johnson	.15	.40
53 Corey Dillon	.15	.40
54 Chad Johnson	.20	.50
55 Peter Warrick	.15	.40
56 Kelley Washington	.12	.30
57 Kevin Hardy	.15	.40
58 Tory James	.12	.30
59 Ickey Woods	.15	.40
60 Anthony Thomas	.15	.40
61 Thomas Jones	.20	.50
62 Rex Grossman	.15	.40
63 Marty Booker	.15	.40
64 Justin Gage	.15	.40
65 David Terrell	.12	.30
66 Brian Urlacher	.20	.50
67 Mike Brown	.15	.40
68 Charles Tillman	.15	.40
69 Jeff Garcia	.15	.40
70 Lee Suggs	.15	.40
71 William Green	.12	.30
72 Kelly Holcomb	.12	.30
73 Quincy Morgan	.12	.30
74 Andre Davis	.12	.30
75 Dennis Northcutt	.12	.30
76 Gerard Warren	.12	.30
77 Courtney Brown	.15	.40
78 Joey Harrington	.15	.40
79 Shawn Bryson	.12	.30
80 Charles Rogers	.12	.30
81 Mikhael Ricks	.12	.30
82 Artose Pinner	.12	.30
83 Az-Zahir Hakim	.12	.30
84 Dre Bly	.12	.30
85 Fernando Bryant	.12	.30
86 Boss Bailey	.12	.30
87 Tai Streets	.12	.30
88 Jake Plummer	.15	.40
89 Quentin Griffin	.12	.30
90 Mike Anderson	.15	.40
91 Garrison Hearst	.15	.40
92 Rod Smith	.15	.40
93 Ashley Lelie	.12	.30
94 Shannon Sharpe	.20	.50
95 Al Wilson	.12	.30
96 Champ Bailey	.15	.40
97 Jason Elam	.15	.40
98 John Lynch	.15	.40
99 Quincy Carter	.12	.30
100 Antonio Bryant	.15	.40
101 Terry Glenn	.15	.40
102 Keyshawn Johnson	.15	.40
103 Jason Witten	.20	.50
104 La'Roi Glover	.15	.40
105 Dat Nguyen	.12	.30
106 Dexter Coakley	.12	.30
107 Terence Newman	.15	.40
108 Darren Woodson	.15	.40
109 Roy Williams S	.15	.40
110 Brett Favre	.50	1.25
111 Ahman Green	.15	.40
112 Najeh Davenport	.15	.40
113 Donald Driver	.20	.50
114 Robert Ferguson	.12	.30
115 Javon Walker	.12	.30
116 Bubba Franks	.12	.30
117 Kabeer Gbaja-Biamila	.15	.40
118 Darren Sharper	.15	.40
119 Mike McKenzie	.15	.40
120 Nick Barnett	.15	.40
121 David Carr	.12	.30
122 Domanick Davis	.12	.30
123 Andre Johnson	.20	.50
124 Corey Bradford	.12	.30
125 Jabar Gaffney	.12	.30
126 Billy Miller	.12	.30
127 Gary Walker	.12	.30
128 Jamie Sharper	.12	.30
129 Aaron Glenn	.15	.40
130 Robaire Smith	.12	.30
131 Peyton Manning	.40	1.00
132 Edgerrin James	.15	.40
133 Dominic Rhodes	.15	.40
134 Marvin Harrison	.20	.50
135 Reggie Wayne	.20	.50
136 Brandon Stokley	.15	.40
137 Marcus Pollard	.12	.30
138 Dallas Clark	.20	.50
139 Mike Vanderjagt	.12	.30
140 Dwight Freeney	.15	.40
141 Mike Doss	.15	.40
142 Byron Leftwich	.15	.40
143 Fred Taylor	.15	.40
144 LaBrandon Toefield	.12	.30
145 Jimmy Smith	.15	.40
146 Kevin Johnson	.12	.30
147 Marcus Stroud	.12	.30
148 John Henderson	.12	.30
149 Donovin Darius	.12	.30
150 Deon Grant	.12	.30
151 Rashean Mathis	.12	.30
152 Trent Green	.15	.40
153 Priest Holmes	.20	.50
154 Johnnie Morton	.15	.40
155 Eddie Kennison	.15	.40
156 Marc Boerigter	.15	.40
157 Tony Gonzalez	.20	.50
158 Dante Hall	.15	.40
159 Tony Richardson	.12	.30
160 Gary Stills	.12	.30
161 Daunte Culpepper	.15	.40
162 Michael Bennett	.15	.40
163 Moe Williams	.12	.30
164 Onterrio Smith	.12	.30
165 Jim Kleinsasser	.12	.30
166 Antoine Winfield	.15	.40
167 Nate Burleson	.15	.40
168 Randy Moss	.20	.50
169 Marcus Robinson	.12	.30
170 Chris Hovan	.12	.30
171 Brian Russell RC	.12	.30
172 A.J. Feeley	.12	.30
173 Jay Fiedler	.12	.30
174 Ricky Williams	.15	.40
175 Chris Chambers	.15	.40
176 David Boston	.12	.30
177 Randy McMichael	.12	.30
178 Jason Taylor	.15	.40
179 Adewale Ogunleye	.15	.40
180 Zach Thomas	.20	.50
181 Junior Seau	.20	.50
182 Patrick Surtain	.12	.30
183 Tom Brady	.40	1.00
184 Kevin Faulk	.15	.40
185 Troy Brown	.15	.40
186 Deion Branch	.15	.40
187 David Givens	.12	.30
188 Bethel Johnson	.12	.30
189 Richard Seymour	.12	.30
190 Tedy Bruschi	.20	.50
191 Ty Law	.15	.40
192 Rodney Harrison	.15	.40
193 Willie McGinest	.15	.40
194 Adam Vinatieri	.20	.50
195 Aaron Brooks	.15	.40
196 Deuce McAllister	.15	.40
197 Joe Horn	.15	.40
198 Donte Stallworth	.12	.30
199 Jerome Pathon	.12	.30
200 Boo Williams	.12	.30
201 Charles Grant	.12	.30
202 Darren Howard	.12	.30
203 Michael Lewis	.15	.40
204 Johnathan Sullivan	.12	.30
205 LeCharles Bentley RC	.12	.30
206 Kerry Collins	.15	.40
207 Tiki Barber	.20	.50
208 Amani Toomer	.15	.40
209 Ike Hilliard	.15	.40
210 Tim Carter	.12	.30
211 Jeremy Shockey	.15	.40
212 Michael Strahan	.20	.50
213 Will Allen	.12	.30
214 Will Peterson	.12	.30
215 William Joseph	.12	.30
216 Chad Pennington	.20	.50
217 Curtis Martin	.20	.50
218 LaMont Jordan	.15	.40
219 Santana Moss	.15	.40
220 Justin McCareins	.12	.30
221 Wayne Chrebet	.15	.40
222 Anthony Becht	.12	.30
223 Shaun Ellis	.12	.30
224 John Abraham	.12	.30
225 DeWayne Robertson	.12	.30
226 Rich Gannon	.15	.40
227 Justin Fargas	.15	.40
228 Tyrone Wheatley	.15	.40
229 Jerry Rice	.40	1.00
230 Tim Brown	.20	.50
231 Jerry Porter	.12	.30
232 Teyo Johnson	.12	.30
233 Charles Woodson	.20	.50
234 Phillip Buchanon	.15	.40
235 Rod Woodson	.15	.40
236 Warren Sapp	.15	.40
237 Donovan McNabb	.20	.50
238 Brian Westbrook	.20	.50
239 Correll Buckhalter	.15	.40
240 Chad Lewis	.15	.40
241 L.J. Smith	.15	.40
242 Terrell Owens	.20	.50
243 Todd Pinkston	.12	.30
244 Freddie Mitchell	.12	.30
245 Jevon Kearse	.15	.40
246 Brian Dawkins	.15	.40
247 Corey Simon	.15	.40
248 Tommy Maddox	.15	.40
249 Duce Staley	.15	.40
250 Jerome Bettis	.20	.50
251 Hines Ward	.20	.50
252 Plaxico Burress	.15	.40
253 Antwaan Randle El	.15	.40
254 Kendrell Bell	.12	.30
255 Joey Porter	.15	.40
256 Alan Faneca	.20	.50
257 Casey Hampton	.12	.30
258 Drew Brees	.20	.50
259 Doug Flutie	.20	.50
260 LaDainian Tomlinson	.20	.50
261 Reche Caldwell	.15	.40
262 Tim Dwight	.12	.30
263 Eric Parker	.15	.40
264 Kevin Dyson	.12	.30
265 Antonio Gates	.20	.50
266 Quentin Jammer	.12	.30
267 Zeke Moreno	.12	.30
268 Tim Rattay	.12	.30
269 Kevan Barlow	.12	.30
270 Cedrick Wilson	.12	.30
271 Brandon Lloyd	.15	.40
272 Fred Beasley	.12	.30
273 Andre Carter	.12	.30
274 Julian Peterson	.15	.40
275 Ahmed Plummer	.12	.30
276 Tony Parrish	.12	.30
277 Bryant Young	.15	.40
278 Matt Hasselbeck	.15	.40
279 Shaun Alexander	.15	.40
280 Maurice Morris	.15	.40
281 Koren Robinson	.12	.30
282 Darrell Jackson	.15	.40
283 Bobby Engram	.15	.40
284 Grant Wistrom	.15	.40
285 Chad Brown	.12	.30
286 Marcus Trufant	.12	.30
287 Bobby Taylor	.15	.40
288 Marc Bulger	.15	.40
289 Kurt Warner	.20	.50
290 Marshall Faulk	.20	.50
291 Lamar Gordon	.12	.30
292 Torry Holt	.15	.40
293 Isaac Bruce	.15	.40
294 Leonard Little	.12	.30
295 Aeneas Williams	.12	.30
296 Orlando Pace	.15	.40
297 Tommy Polley	.12	.30
298 Pisa Tinoisamoa	.12	.30
299 Brad Johnson	.15	.40
300 Michael Pittman	.15	.40
301 Charlie Garner	.15	.40
302 Mike Alstott	.15	.40
303 Keenan McCardell	.12	.30
304 Joey Galloway	.15	.40
305 Joe Jurevicius	.12	.30
306 Anthony McFarland	.12	.30
307 Derrick Brooks	.15	.40
308 Ronde Barber	.15	.40
309 Shelton Quarles	.12	.30
310 Steve McNair	.20	.50
311 Eddie George	.15	.40
312 Chris Brown	.12	.30
313 Derrick Mason	.15	.40
314 Tyrone Calico	.15	.40
315 Drew Bennett	.15	.40
316 Kevin Carter	.15	.40
317 Keith Bulluck	.12	.30
318 Samari Rolle	.12	.30
319 Albert Haynesworth	.12	.30
320 Erron Kinney	.12	.30
321 Mark Brunell	.15	.40
322 Patrick Ramsey	.15	.40
323 Laveranues Coles	.12	.30
324 Rod Gardner	.12	.30
325 Darnerien McCants	.12	.30
326 Clinton Portis	.20	.50
327 LaVar Arrington	.15	.40
328 Shawn Springs	.12	.30
329 Fred Smoot	.12	.30
330 James Thrash	.12	.30
331 Marvin Harrison PB	.12	.30
332 Steve McNair PB	.12	.30
333 Ray Lewis PB	.12	.30
334 Trent Green PB	.10	.25
335 Peyton Manning PB	.25	.60
336 Priest Holmes PB	.12	.30
337 Clinton Portis PB	.12	.30
338 Torry Holt PB	.10	.25
339 Anquan Boldin PB	.12	.30
340 Daunte Culpepper PB	.10	.25
341 Ahman Green PB	.10	.25
342 Brian Urlacher PB	.12	.30
343 Donovan McNabb PB	.12	.30
344 Marc Bulger PB	.10	.25
345 Shaun Alexander PB	.10	.25
346 Peyton Manning LL	.25	.60
347 Daunte Culpepper LL	.10	.25
348 Brett Favre LL	.30	.75
349 Steve McNair LL	.12	.30
350 Tom Brady LL	.25	.60
351 Jamal Lewis LL	.10	.25
352 Deuce McAllister LL	.10	.25
353 Clinton Portis LL	.12	.30
354 Ahman Green LL	.10	.25
355 LaDainian Tomlinson LL	.12	.30
356 Torry Holt LL	.10	.25
357 Anquan Boldin LL	.12	.30
358 Randy Moss LL	.12	.30
359 Chad Johnson LL	.12	.30
360 Marvin Harrison LL	.12	.30
361 Peyton Manning HL	.25	.60
362 Jamal Lewis HL	.10	.25
363 Ray Lewis HL	.12	.30
364 Anquan Boldin HL	.12	.30
365 Terrell Suggs HL	.10	.25
366 Jamal Lewis HL	.10	.25
367 Priest Holmes HL	.12	.30
368 Tom Brady HL	.25	.60
369 Marc Bulger HL	.10	.25
370 Steve McNair HL	.12	.30
371 Eli Manning RC	3.00	8.00
372 Robert Gallery RC	.50	1.25
373 Larry Fitzgerald RC	1.25	3.00
374 Philip Rivers RC	2.00	5.00
375 Sean Taylor RC	1.00	2.50
376 Kellen Winslow RC	.50	1.25
377 Roy Williams RC	.50	1.25
378 DeAngelo Hall RC	.50	1.25
379 Reggie Williams RC	.40	1.00
380 Dunta Robinson RC	.30	.75
381 Ben Roethlisberger RC	3.00	8.00
382 Jonathan Vilma RC	.50	1.25
383 Lee Evans RC	.50	1.25
384 Tommie Harris RC	.50	1.25
385 Michael Clayton RC	.40	1.00
386 D.J. Williams RC	.50	1.25
387 Will Smith RC	.40	1.00
388 Kenechi Udeze RC	.40	1.00
389 Vince Wilfork RC	.50	1.25
390 J.P. Losman RC	.40	1.00
391 Marcus Tubbs RC	.30	.75
392 Steven Jackson RC	.75	2.00
393 Ahmad Carroll RC	.30	.75
394 Chris Perry RC	.40	1.00
395 Jason Babin RC	.50	1.25
396 Chris Gamble RC	.40	1.00
397 Michael Jenkins RC	.50	1.25
398 Kevin Jones RC	.40	1.00
399 Rashaun Woods RC	.30	.75
400 Ben Watson RC	.50	1.25
401 Karlos Dansby RC	.50	1.25
402 Igor Olshansky RC	.40	1.00
403 Junior Siavii RC	.30	.75
404 Teddy Lehman RC	.30	.75
405 Ricardo Colclough RC	.40	1.00
406 Daryl Smith RC	.30	.75
407 Ben Troupe RC	.40	1.00
408 Tatum Bell RC	.40	1.00
409 Travis LaBoy RC	.40	1.00
410 Julius Jones RC	.40	1.00
411 Mewelde Moore RC	.40	1.00
412 Drew Henson RC	.30	.75
413 Dontarrious Thomas RC	.40	1.00
414 Keiwan Ratliff RC	.30	.75
415 Devery Henderson RC	.50	1.25
416 Dwan Edwards RC	.30	.75
417 Michael Boulware RC	.50	1.25
418 Darius Watts RC	.30	.75
419 Greg Jones RC	.30	.75
420 Madieu Williams RC	.30	.75
421 Antwan Odom RC	.40	1.00
422 Shawntae Spencer RC	.30	.75
423 Sean Jones RC	.40	1.00
424 Courtney Watson RC	.30	.75
425 Kris Wilson RC	.40	1.00
426 Keary Colbert RC	.30	.75
427 Marquise Hill RC	.30	.75
428 Darnell Dockett RC	.30	.75
429 Stuart Schweigert RC	.40	1.00
430 Ben Hartsock RC	.30	.75
431 Joey Thomas RC	.30	.75
432 Randy Starks RC	.30	.75
433 Keith Smith RC	.30	.75
434 Derrick Hamilton RC	.30	.75
435 Bernard Berrian RC	.50	1.25
436 Chris Cooley RC	.50	1.25
437 Devard Darling RC	.30	.75
438 Matt Schaub RC	1.00	2.50
439 Luke McCown RC	.40	1.00
440 Cedric Cobbs RC	.30	.75

2004 Score Glossy

*VETS: 1.5X TO 4X BASIC CARDS
*ROOKIES: .6X TO 1.5X BASIC CARDS
ONE GLOSSY PER PACK

2004 Score Inscriptions

6 Dexter Jackson	8.00	20.00
7 Bertrand Berry	6.00	15.00
38 Sam Adams	6.00	15.00
59 Ickey Woods SP	10.00	25.00
147 Marcus Stroud No AU	3.00	8.00
170 Chris Hovan	6.00	15.00
265 Antonio Gates	30.00	60.00
267 Zeke Moreno	6.00	15.00
320 Erron Kinney	6.00	15.00

2004 Score Scorecard

*VETS: 2.5X TO 6X BASIC CARDS
*ROOKIES: 1.2X TO 3X BASIC CARDS
STATED PRINT RUN 625 SER.#'d SETS

2005 Score

This 385-card set was released in August, 2005. The set was issued into the hobby in seven-card packs which came 36 packs to a box. Cards numbered 1-300 feature veteran players sequenced in alphabetical order based on where they played in 2004; cards numbered 301-330 feature players who participated in the 2005 Pro Bowl and the set concludes with 2005 rookies. (Cards #331-385). The rookies were inserted at a stated rate of one per pack.

COMPLETE SET (385)	40.00	80.00
ONE ROOKIE PER PACK		
FINAL SCORE/2-17 TOO SCARCE TO PRICE		
1 Anquan Boldin	.15	.40
2 Bertrand Berry	.12	.30
3 Bryant Johnson	.12	.30
4 Darnell Dockett	.12	.30
5 Freddie Jones	.12	.30
6 Josh McCown	.15	.40
7 Karlos Dansby	.12	.30
8 Larry Fitzgerald	.20	.50
9 Alge Crumpler	.15	.40
10 DeAngelo Hall	.15	.40
11 Keith Brooking	.12	.30
12 Michael Jenkins	.15	.40
13 Michael Vick	.20	.50
14 Peerless Price	.12	.30
15 Rod Coleman	.12	.30
16 T.J. Duckett	.12	.30
17 Warrick Dunn	.15	.40
18 Chris McAlister	.12	.30
19 Clarence Moore	.12	.30
20 Ed Reed	.15	.40
21 Jamal Lewis	.15	.40
22 Jonathan Ogden	.12	.30
23 Kyle Boller	.15	.40
24 Peter Boulware	.12	.30
25 Ray Lewis	.20	.50
26 Terrell Suggs	.15	.40
27 Todd Heap	.15	.40
28 Drew Bledsoe	.20	.50
29 Eric Moulds	.12	.30
30 Josh Reed	.12	.30
31 Lee Evans	.15	.40
32 Nate Clements	.15	.40
33 Takeo Spikes	.12	.30
34 Travis Henry	.12	.30
35 Willis McGahee	.20	.50
36 Dan Morgan	.12	.30
37 DeShaun Foster	.15	.40
38 Jake Delhomme	.15	.40
39 Julius Peppers	.15	.40
40 Keary Colbert	.12	.30
41 Kris Jenkins	.12	.30
42 Muhsin Muhammad	.15	.40
43 Nick Goings	.12	.30
44 Stephen Davis	.15	.40
45 Steve Smith	.20	.50
46 Anthony Thomas	.12	.30
47 Adewale Ogunleye	.12	.30
48 Bernard Berrian	.15	.40
49 Brian Urlacher	.20	.50
50 David Terrell	.12	.30
51 Mike Brown	.12	.30
52 Rex Grossman	.15	.40
53 Thomas Jones	.20	.50
54 Tommie Harris	.12	.30
55 Carson Palmer	.20	.50
56 Chad Johnson	.15	.40
57 Chris Perry	.12	.30
58 Kelley Washington	.12	.30
59 Madieu Williams	.12	.30
60 Peter Warrick	.12	.30
61 Rudi Johnson	.15	.40
62 T.J. Houshmandzadeh	.15	.40
63 Tory James	.12	.30
64 Andre Davis	.12	.30
65 Antonio Bryant	.12	.30
66 Dennis Northcutt	.12	.30
67 Gerard Warren	.12	.30
68 Jeff Garcia	.15	.40
69 Kellen Winslow Jr.	.15	.40
70 Lee Suggs	.12	.30
71 William Green	.12	.30
72 Drew Henson	.12	.30
73 Jason Witten	.20	.50
74 Julius Jones	.12	.30
75 Keyshawn Johnson	.15	.40
76 La'Roi Glover	.12	.30
77 J.P. Losman	.12	.30
78 Roy Williams S	.12	.30
79 Terence Newman	.12	.30
80 Terry Glenn	.12	.30
81 Al Wilson	.12	.30
82 Ashley Lelie	.12	.30
83 Champ Bailey	.15	.40
84 D.J. Williams	.12	.30
85 Jake Plummer	.15	.40
86 Jason Elam	.12	.30
87 John Lynch	.15	.40
88 Reuben Droughns	.12	.30
89 Rod Smith	.15	.40
90 Tatum Bell	.12	.30
91 Trent Dilfer	.15	.40
92 Charles Rogers	.12	.30
93 Dre Bly	.12	.30
94 Joey Harrington	.15	.40
95 Kevin Jones	.12	.30
96 Roy Williams WR	.15	.40
97 Shawn Bryson	.12	.30
98 Tai Streets	.12	.30
99 Teddy Lehman	.12	.30
100 Ahman Green	.15	.40
101 Brett Favre	.50	1.25
102 Bubba Franks	.12	.30
103 Darren Sharper	.15	.40
104 Donald Driver	.20	.50
105 Javon Walker	.12	.30
106 Najeh Davenport	.15	.40
107 Nick Barnett	.15	.40
108 Robert Ferguson	.12	.30
109 Aaron Glenn	.12	.30
110 Andre Johnson	.20	.50
111 Corey Bradford	.12	.30
112 David Carr	.12	.30
113 Domanick Davis	.12	.30
114 Dunta Robinson	.12	.30
115 Jabar Gaffney	.12	.30
116 Jamie Sharper	.12	.30
117 Jason Babin	.12	.30
118 Brandon Stokley	.12	.30
119 Dallas Clark	.15	.40
120 Dwight Freeney	.15	.40
121 Edgerrin James	.15	.40
122 Marcus Pollard	.12	.30
123 Marvin Harrison	.20	.50
124 Peyton Manning	.40	1.00
125 Reggie Wayne	.20	.50
126 Robert Mathis RC	.60	1.50
127 Byron Leftwich	.15	.40
128 Daryl Smith	.12	.30
129 Donovan Darius	.12	.30
130 Ernest Wilford	.12	.30
131 Fred Taylor	.15	.40
132 Jimmy Smith	.15	.40
133 John Henderson	.12	.30
134 Marcus Stroud	.12	.30
135 Reggie Williams	.12	.30
136 Dante Hall	.12	.30
137 Eddie Kennison	.12	.30
138 Jared Allen	.20	.50
139 Johnnie Morton	.15	.40
140 Larry Johnson	.15	.40
141 Priest Holmes	.15	.40
142 Samie Parker	.12	.30
143 Tony Gonzalez	.15	.40
144 Trent Green	.15	.40
145 A.J. Feeley	.12	.30
146 Chris Chambers	.15	.40
147 Jason Taylor	.15	.40
148 Junior Seau	.20	.50
149 Marty Booker	.12	.30
150 Patrick Surtain	.12	.30
151 Randy McMichael	.12	.30
152 Sammy Morris	.12	.30
153 Zach Thomas	.20	.50
154 Daunte Culpepper	.15	.40
155 Jim Kleinsasser	.12	.30
156 Kelly Campbell	.12	.30
157 Kevin Williams	.12	.30
158 Marcus Robinson	.12	.30
159 Mewelde Moore	.12	.30
160 Michael Bennett	.15	.40
161 Nate Burleson	.12	.30
162 Onterrio Smith	.12	.30
163 Randy Moss	.20	.50
164 Adam Vinatieri	.20	.50
165 Corey Dillon	.15	.40
166 David Givens	.12	.30
167 David Patten	.12	.30
168 Deion Branch	.12	.30
169 Mike Vrabel	.20	.50
170 Richard Seymour	.12	.30
171 Tedy Bruschi	.20	.50
172 Tom Brady	.40	1.00
173 Troy Brown	.12	.30
174 Ty Law	.15	.40
175 Aaron Brooks	.12	.30
176 Charles Grant	.12	.30
177 Deuce McAllister	.15	.40
178 Devery Henderson	.12	.30
179 Donte Stallworth	.12	.30
180 Jerome Pathon	.12	.30
181 Joe Horn	.15	.40
182 Will Smith	.12	.30
183 Amani Toomer	.15	.40
184 Eli Manning	.30	.75
185 Gibril Wilson	.12	.30
186 Ike Hilliard	.12	.30
187 Jeremy Shockey	.20	.50
188 Michael Strahan	.20	.50
189 Tiki Barber	.20	.50
190 Jamaar Taylor	.12	.30
191 Tim Carter	.12	.30
192 Chad Pennington	.20	.50
193 DeWayne Robertson	.12	.30
194 Curtis Martin	.20	.50
195 John Abraham	.12	.30
196 Jonathan Vilma	.15	.40
197 Justin McCareins	.12	.30
198 LaMont Jordan	.15	.40
199 Santana Moss	.15	.40
200 Shaun Ellis	.12	.30
201 Wayne Chrebet	.15	.40
202 Charles Woodson	.20	.50
203 Doug Jolley	.12	.30
204 Jerry Porter	.12	.30
205 Justin Fargas	.15	.40
206 Kerry Collins	.15	.40
207 Robert Gallery	.12	.30
208 Ronald Curry	.12	.30
209 Sebastian Janikowski	.12	.30
210 Tyrone Wheatley	.12	.30
211 Warren Sapp	.15	.40
212 Brian Dawkins	.15	.40
213 Brian Westbrook	.15	.40
214 Chad Lewis	.12	.30
215 Corey Simon	.12	.30
216 Donovan McNabb	.20	.50
217 Freddie Mitchell	.12	.30
218 Jevon Kearse	.15	.40
219 L.J. Smith	.15	.40
220 Lito Sheppard	.15	.40
221 Terrell Owens	.20	.50
222 Todd Pinkston	.12	.30
223 Alan Faneca	.30	.75
224 Antwaan Randle El	.15	.40
225 Ben Roethlisberger	.30	.75
226 Duce Staley	.15	.40
227 Hines Ward	.20	.50
228 James Farrior	.12	.30
229 Jerome Bettis	.20	.50
230 Joey Porter	.12	.30
231 Kendrell Bell	.12	.30
232 Plaxico Burress	.15	.40
233 Troy Polamalu	.25	.60
234 Antonio Gates	.20	.50
235 Reche Caldwell	.12	.30
236 Doug Flutie	.20	.50
237 Drew Brees	.20	.50
238 Eric Parker	.12	.30
239 Keenan McCardell	.15	.40
240 LaDainian Tomlinson	.20	.50
241 Philip Rivers	.20	.50
242 Quentin Jammer	.12	.30
243 Tim Dwight	.12	.30
244 Brandon Lloyd	.12	.30
245 Bryant Young	.12	.30
246 Cedrick Wilson	.12	.30
247 Eric Johnson	.12	.30
248 Julian Peterson	.12	.30
249 Kevan Barlow	.12	.30
250 Rashaun Woods	.12	.30
251 Maurice Hicks RC	.12	.30
252 Tim Rattay	.12	.30
253 Bobby Engram	.15	.40
254 Chad Brown	.12	.30
255 Darrell Jackson	.12	.30
256 Grant Wistrom	.12	.30
257 Jerramy Stevens	.15	.40
258 Koren Robinson	.12	.30
259 Marcus Trufant	.12	.30
260 Matt Hasselbeck	.15	.40
261 Michael Boulware	.12	.30
262 Shaun Alexander	.15	.40
263 Isaac Bruce	.15	.40
264 Leonard Little	.12	.30
265 Marc Bulger	.15	.40
266 Marshall Faulk	.20	.50
267 Orlando Pace	.12	.30
268 Pisa Tinoisamoa	.12	.30
269 Shaun McDonald	.12	.30
270 Steven Jackson	.20	.50
271 Torry Holt	.15	.40
272 Anthony McFarland	.12	.30
273 Brian Griese	.15	.40
274 Charlie Garner	.15	.40
275 Derrick Brooks	.15	.40
276 Joe Jurevicius	.15	.40
277 Joey Galloway	.15	.40
278 Michael Clayton	.12	.30
279 Michael Pittman	.12	.30
280 Mike Alstott	.15	.40
281 Ronde Barber	.15	.40
282 Albert Haynesworth	.12	.30
283 Ben Troupe	.12	.30
284 Billy Volek	.12	.30
285 Chris Brown	.12	.30
286 Derrick Mason	.15	.40
287 Drew Bennett	.15	.40
288 Keith Bulluck	.12	.30
289 Kevin Carter	.12	.30
290 Samari Rolle	.12	.30
291 Steve McNair	.20	.50
292 Tyrone Calico	.12	.30
293 Chris Cooley	.15	.40
294 Clinton Portis	.15	.40
295 Fred Smoot	.12	.30
296 LaVar Arrington	.15	.40
297 Laveranues Coles	.12	.30
298 Patrick Ramsey	.15	.40
299 Rod Gardner	.12	.30
300 Sean Taylor	.20	.50
301 Michael Vick PB	.15	.40
302 Daunte Culpepper PB	.12	.30
303 Donovan McNabb PB	.15	.40
304 Brian Westbrook PB	.12	.30
305 Tiki Barber PB	.15	.40
306 Ahman Green PB	.12	.30
307 Joe Horn PB	.12	.30
308 Javon Walker PB	.10	.25
309 Torry Holt PB	.12	.30
310 Muhsin Muhammad PB	.12	.30
311 Jason Witten PB	.15	.40
312 Alge Crumpler PB	.12	.30
313 Peyton Manning PB	.30	.75
314 Tom Brady PB	.30	.75
315 Drew Brees PB	.15	.40
316 LaDainian Tomlinson PB	.15	.40
317 Rudi Johnson PB	.12	.30
318 Jerome Bettis PB	.15	.40
319 Marvin Harrison PB	.15	.40
320 Hines Ward PB	.15	.40
321 Andre Johnson PB	.15	.40
322 Chad Johnson PB	.12	.30
323 Tony Gonzalez PB	.12	.30
324 Adam Vinatieri PB	.15	.40
325 David Akers PB	.10	.25
326 Takeo Spikes PB	.10	.25
327 Joey Porter PB	.10	.25
328 Tedy Bruschi PB	.15	.40
329 Ed Reed PB	.12	.30
330 Terrell Owens PB	.15	.40
331 Alex Smith QB RC	.60	1.50
332 Ronnie Brown RC	.50	1.25
333 Braylon Edwards RC	.50	1.25
334 Cedric Benson RC	.40	1.00
335 Cadillac Williams RC	.40	1.00
336 Adam Jones RC	.30	.75
337 Troy Williamson RC	.30	.75
338 Antrel Rolle RC	.40	1.00
339 Carlos Rogers RC	.40	1.00
340 Mike Williams	.40	1.00
341 DeMarcus Ware RC	.75	2.00
342 Shawne Merriman RC	.40	1.00
343 Thomas Davis RC	.25	.60
344 Derrick Johnson RC	.30	.75
345 Travis Johnson RC	.25	.60
346 David Pollack RC	.30	.75
347 Erasmus James RC	.30	.75
348 Marcus Spears RC	.30	.75
349 Matt Jones RC	.40	1.00
350 Mark Clayton RC	.40	1.00
351 Fabian Washington RC	.30	.75
352 Aaron Rodgers RC	5.00	10.00
353 Jason Campbell RC	.50	1.25
354 Roddy White RC	.50	1.25
355 Marlin Jackson RC	.25	.60
356 Heath Miller RC	.50	1.25
357 Mike Patterson RC	.25	.60
358 Reggie Brown RC	.25	.60
359 Shaun Cody RC	.30	.75
360 Mark Bradley RC	.25	.60
361 J.J. Arrington RC	.30	.75
362 Dan Cody RC	.30	.75
363 Eric Shelton RC	.25	.60
364 Roscoe Parrish RC	.25	.60
365 Terrence Murphy RC	.25	.60
366 Vincent Jackson RC	.50	1.25
367 Frank Gore RC	.60	1.50
368 Charlie Frye RC	.40	1.00
369 Courtney Roby RC	.30	.75
370 Andrew Walter RC	.30	.75
371 Vernand Morency RC	.30	.75
372 Ryan Moats RC	.30	.75
373 Chris Henry RC	.40	1.00
374 David Greene RC	.25	.60
375 Brandon Jones RC	.30	.75
376 Maurice Clarett	.30	.75
377 Kyle Orton RC	.40	1.00
378 Marion Barber RC	.40	1.00
379 Brandon Jacobs RC	.50	1.25
380 Ciatrick Fason RC	.25	.60
381 Jerome Mathis RC	.40	1.00
382 Craphonso Thorpe RC	.25	.60
383 Stefan LeFors RC	.25	.60
384 Darren Sproles RC	.40	1.00
385 Fred Gibson RC	.30	.75

2005 Score Adrenaline

*VETERANS: 3X TO 8X BASIC CARDS
*ROOKIES: 1.2X TO 3X BASIC CARDS
STATED PRINT RUN 399 SER.#'d SETS

2005 Score Final Score

SERIAL #'d TO TEAM'S 2004 WIN TOTAL
NOT PRICED DUE TO SCARCITY

2005 Score Glossy

*VETERANS: 1.5X TO 4X BASIC CARDS
*ROOKIES: .8X TO 2X BASIC CARDS
ONE GLOSSY PER PACK

2005 Score Revolution

*VETERANS: 5X TO 12X BASIC CARDS
*ROOKIES: 2X TO 5X BASIC CARDS
STATED PRINT RUN 199 SER.#'d SETS

2005 Score Scorecard

*VETS: 5X TO 5X BASIC CARDS
*ROOKIES: 1X TO 2.5X BASIC CARDS
STATED PRINT RUN 599 SER.#'d SETS

2005 Score Inscriptions

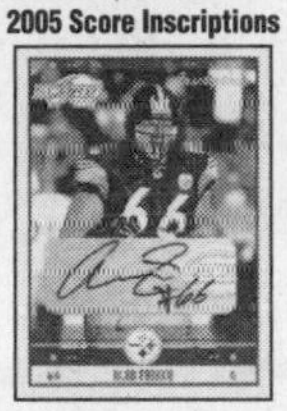

ANNOUNCED PRINT RUNS BELOW		
13 Michael Vick/25*	40.00	80.00
15 Rod Coleman/1000*	7.50	20.00
43 Nick Goings/1000*	7.50	20.00
138 Jared Allen/1000*	25.00	50.00
203 Doug Jolley/1000*	6.00	15.00
214 Chad Lewis/1000*	6.00	15.00
223 Alan Faneca/1000*	15.00	40.00

2006 Score

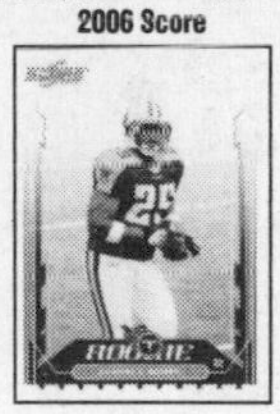

This 385-card set was released in July, 2006. This set was issued through retail outlets and those packs contained five packs, with an 99 cent SRP, and those packs came 20 to a box. Cards numbered 331-385 were inserted into packs at a stated rate of one per. Cards numbered 386-440 as well as some variations to cover issues such as switching teams were later issued in the factory set. The variations are priced at the same value as the cards found in packs. Please see our checklist for detailed information about the variations.

COMP.FACT.SET (440)	25.00	50.00
COMPLETE SET (385)	25.00	50.00
331-385 ROOKIE ODDS 1:1		
386-440 ROOKIES ISSUED IN FACT.SET		
FACTORY SET B VARIATIONS SAME PRICE		
1 Kurt Warner	.20	.50
2 J.J. Arrington	.12	.30
3 Anquan Boldin	.15	.40
4 Larry Fitzgerald	.20	.50
5 Marcel Shipp	.12	.30
6 Bryant Johnson	.12	.30
7 Bertrand Berry	.12	.30
8 John Navarre	.12	.30
9A Michael Vick Pro Bowl photo pack only	.20	.50
9B Michael Vick Falcons photo Factory Set only	.20	.50
10 Warrick Dunn	.15	.40
11 Roddy White	.15	.40
12 Alge Crumpler	.15	.40
13A T.J. Duckett Falcons photo pack only	.12	.30
13B T.J. Duckett Redskins photo Factory Set only	.12	.30
14 Michael Jenkins	.15	.40
15 DeAngelo Hall	.15	.40
16 Brian Finneran	.12	.30
17 Kyle Boller	.15	.40
18 Jamal Lewis	.15	.40
19A Chester Taylor Ravens photo pack only	.15	.40

19B Chester Taylor .15 .40
Vikings photo
Factory Set only
20 Derrick Mason .15 .40
21 Mark Clayton .15 .40
22 Todd Heap .15 .40
23 Ray Lewis .20 .50
24 Devard Darling .12 .30
25 J.P. Losman .15 .40
26 Willis McGahee .15 .40
27 Lee Evans .15 .40
28A Eric Moulds .12 .30
Bills photo
pack only
28B Eric Moulds .12 .30
Texans photo
Factory Set only
29A Lawyer Milloy .12 .30
Bills photo
pack only
29B Lawyer Milloy .12 .30
Falcons photo
Factory Set only
30 Josh Reed .12 .30
31 Kelly Holcomb .12 .30
32 Jake Delhomme .15 .40
33 DeShaun Foster .15 .40
34 Steve Smith .20 .50
35 Julius Peppers .15 .40
36 Drew Carter .12 .30
37 Chris Gamble .12 .30
38 Stephen Davis .15 .40
39 Keary Colbert .12 .30
40 Nick Goings .12 .30
41 Eric Shelton .12 .30
42 Rex Grossman .15 .40
43 Thomas Jones .15 .40
44 Cedric Benson .15 .40
45 Muhsin Muhammad .15 .40
46 Brian Urlacher .20 .50
47 Mark Bradley .12 .30
48 Kyle Orton .20 .50
49 Tommie Harris .12 .30
50 Adrian Peterson .15 .40
51 Bernard Berrian .15 .40
52 Justin Gage .12 .30
53 Carson Palmer .20 .50
54 Rudi Johnson .15 .40
55 Chad Johnson .15 .40
56 T.J. Houshmandzadeh .15 .40
57 Chris Henry .12 .30
58 Chris Perry .15 .40
59A Jon Kitna .15 .40
Bengals photo
pack only
59B Jon Kitna .15 .40
Lions photo
Factory Set only
60 Deltha O'Neal .12 .30
61 Charlie Frye .15 .40
62 Reuben Droughns .15 .40
63 Braylon Edwards .15 .40
64 Kellen Winslow .15 .40
65A Antonio Bryant .12 .30
Browns photo
pack only
65B Antonio Bryant/49ers photo .12 .30
Factory Set only
66A Trent Dilfer .15 .40
Browns photo
pack only
66B Trent Dilfer/49ers photo .15 .40
Factory Set only
67 Dennis Northcutt .12 .30
68 Drew Bledsoe .20 .50
69 Julius Jones .12 .30
70 Marion Barber .15 .40
71 Terry Glenn .15 .40
72A Keyshawn Johnson .15 .40
Cowboys photo
pack only
72B Keyshawn Johnson .15 .40
Panthers photo
Factory Set only
73 Roy Williams S .15 .40
74 Jason Witten .20 .50
75 Terence Newman .12 .30
76 Drew Henson .12 .30
77 Patrick Crayton .12 .30
78 Jake Plummer .15 .40
79A Mike Anderson .15 .40
Broncos photo
pack only
79B Mike Anderson .15 .40
Ravens photo
Factory Set only
80 Tatum Bell .12 .30
81A Ashley Lelie .12 .30
Broncos photo
pack only
81B Ashley Lelie .12 .30
Falcons photo
Factory Set only
82 Rod Smith .15 .40
83 D.J. Williams .12 .30
84 Darius Watts .12 .30
85 Ron Dayne .15 .40
86A Jeb Putzier .12 .30
Broncos photo
pack only
86B Jeb Putzier .12 .30
Texans photo
Factory Set only
87A Joey Harrington .12 .30
Lions photo
pack only
87B Joey Harrington .12 .30
Dolphins photo
Factory Set only
88 Kevin Jones .12 .30
89 Roy Williams WR .15 .40
90 Mike Williams .12 .30
91 Charles Rogers .15 .40
92 Teddy Lehman .12 .30
93 Marcus Pollard .12 .30
94 Artose Pinner .12 .30
95 Brett Favre .40 1.00
96 Ahman Green .15 .40
97 Najeh Davenport .15 .40
98 Samkon Gado .15 .40
99A Javon Walker .15 .40
Packers photo
pack only
99B Javon Walker .15 .40
Broncos photo
Factory Set only
100 Donald Driver .20 .50
101 Aaron Rodgers .40 1.00
102 Robert Ferguson .12 .30
103 David Carr .12 .30
104 Domanick Davis .12 .30
105 Andre Johnson .20 .50
106A Jabar Gaffney .12 .30
Texans photo
pack only
106B Jabar Gaffney .12 .30
Eagles photo
Factory Set only
107 Jonathan Wells .12 .30
108 Vernand Morency .12 .30
109A Corey Bradford .12 .30
Texans photo
pack only
109B Corey Bradford .12 .30
Lions photo
Factory Set only
110 Jerome Mathis .12 .30
111A Peyton Manning .30 .75
Pro Bowl photo
pack only
111B Peyton Manning .30 .75
Colts photo
Factory Set only
112A Edgerrin James .15 .40
Colts photo
pack only
112B Edgerrin James .15 .40
Cardinals photo
Factory Set only
113 Marvin Harrison .20 .50
114 Reggie Wayne .15 .40
115 Dwight Freeney .15 .40
116 Dallas Clark .15 .40
117 Dominic Rhodes .15 .40
118 Jim Sorgi .12 .30
119 Brandon Stokley .15 .40
120 Bob Sanders .15 .40
121 Mike Doss .12 .30
122 Marlin Jackson .12 .30
123 Byron Leftwich .15 .40
124 Fred Taylor .15 .40
125 Jimmy Smith .15 .40
126 Matt Jones .12 .30
127 Ernest Wilford .12 .30
128 Greg Jones .12 .30
129 Mike Peterson .12 .30
130 Reggie Williams .15 .40
131 Rashean Mathis .12 .30
132 Trent Green .15 .40
133 Larry Johnson .15 .40
134 Priest Holmes .15 .40
135 Eddie Kennison .12 .30
136 Tony Gonzalez .15 .40
137 Kendrell Bell .12 .30
138 Samie Parker .12 .30
139 Dante Hall .15 .40
140A Tony Richardson .12 .30
Chiefs photo
pack only
140B Tony Richardson .12 .30
Vikings photo
Factory Set only
141A Gus Frerotte .12 .30
Dolphins photo
pack only
141B Gus Frerotte .12 .30
Rams photo
Factory Set only
142 Ronnie Brown .20 .50
143A Neil Rackers .12 .30
Pro Bowl photo
pack only
143B Neil Rackers .12 .30
Cardinals photo
Factory Set only
144 Chris Chambers .15 .40
145 Zach Thomas .20 .50
146 Cliff Russell .12 .30
147A David Boston .12 .30
Dolphins photo
pack only
147B David Boston .12 .30
Buccaneers photo
Factory Set only
148 Wes Welker .20 .50
149 Marty Booker .12 .30
150 Randy McMichael .12 .30
151A Daunte Culpepper .15 .40
Vikings photo
pack only
151B Daunte Culpepper .15 .40
Dolphins photo
Factory Set only
152 Mewelde Moore .12 .30
153A Nate Burleson .12 .30
Vikings photo
pack only
153B Nate Burleson .12 .30
Seahawks photo
Factory Set only
154 Troy Williamson .12 .30
155 Koren Robinson .12 .30
156 Erasmus James .12 .30
157 Marcus Robinson .12 .30
158 E.J. Henderson .12 .30
159 Brad Johnson .15 .40
160A Michael Bennett .12 .30
Vikings photo
pack only
160B Michael Bennett .12 .30
Chiefs photo
Factory Set only
161 Travis Taylor .12 .30
162 Tom Brady .30 .75
163 Corey Dillon .15 .40
164 Deion Branch .15 .40
165 Tedy Bruschi .20 .50
166 Ben Watson .12 .30
167 Daniel Graham .12 .30
168A Bethel Johnson .12 .30
Patriots photo
pack only
168B Bethel Johnson .12 .30
Saints photo
Factory Set only
169 Kevin Faulk .15 .40
170A David Givens .15 .40
Patriots photo
pack only
170B David Givens .15 .40
Titans photo
Factory Set only
171 Troy Brown .12 .30
172A Aaron Brooks .15 .40
Saints photo
pack only
172B Aaron Brooks .15 .40
Raiders photo
Factory Set only
173 Deuce McAllister .15 .40
174 Joe Horn .15 .40
175A Donte Stallworth .12 .30
Saints photo
pack only
175B Donte Stallworth .12 .30
Eagles photo
Factory Set only
176A Antowain Smith .12 .30
Saints photo
pack only
176B Antowain Smith .12 .30
Texans photo
Factory Set only
177 Devery Henderson .12 .30
178 Eli Manning .25 .60
179 Tiki Barber .20 .50
180 Plaxico Burress .15 .40
181 Jeremy Shockey .20 .50
182A Osi Umenyiora .15 .40
Pro Bowl photo
pack only
182B Osi Umenyiora .15 .40
Giants photo
Factory Set only
183 Gibril Wilson .12 .30
184 Brandon Jacobs .20 .50
185 Michael Strahan .15 .40
186A Will Allen .12 .30
Giants photo
pack only
186B Will Allen .12 .30
Dolphins photo
Factory Set only
187 Amani Toomer .15 .40
188 Chad Pennington .15 .40
189 Curtis Martin .20 .50
190 Laveranues Coles .12 .30
191 Jonathan Vilma .15 .40
192A Ty Law .12 .30
Jets photo
pack only
192B Ty Law .12 .30
Chiefs photo
Factory Set only
193 Cedric Houston .12 .30
194 Justin McCareins .12 .30
195 Jerald Sowell .12 .30
196 Josh Brown .12 .30
197 LaMont Jordan .15 .40
198 Randy Moss .20 .50
199 Jerry Porter .12 .30
200 Doug Gabriel .12 .30
201 Johnnie Morant .12 .30
202 Zack Crockett .12 .30
203A Derrick Burgess .12 .30
Pro Bowl photo
pack only
203B Derrick Burgess .12 .30
Raiders photo
Factory Set only
204 Donovan McNabb .20 .50
205 Brian Westbrook .15 .40
206 Reggie Brown .12 .30
207A Terrell Owens .20 .50
Eagles photo
pack only
207B Terrell Owens .20 .50
Cowboys photo
Factory Set only
208 Ryan Moats .12 .30
209 Correll Buckhalter .12 .30
210 Jevon Kearse .15 .40
211 L.J. Smith .12 .30
212 Lamar Gordon .12 .30
213 Greg Lewis .12 .30
214 Ben Roethlisberger .25 .60
215 Willie Parker .15 .40
216 Jerome Bettis .20 .50
217 Hines Ward .20 .50
218 Troy Polamalu .25 .60
219 Heath Miller .15 .40
220A Antwaan Randle El .15 .40
Steelers photo
pack only
220B Antwaan Randle El .15 .40
Redskins photo
Factory Set only
221 Duce Staley .12 .30
222 Cedrick Wilson .12 .30
223 James Farrior .12 .30
224A Drew Brees .20 .50
Chargers
pack only
224B Drew Brees .20 .50
Saints photo
Factory Set only
225 LaDainian Tomlinson .20 .50
226 Keenan McCardell .15 .40
227 Antonio Gates .20 .50
228 Shawne Merriman .15 .40
229 Philip Rivers .20 .50
230 Vincent Jackson .15 .40
231 Donnie Edwards .12 .30
232 Eric Parker .12 .30
233A Reche Caldwell .12 .30
Chargers photo
pack only
233B Reche Caldwell .12 .30
Patriots photo
Factory Set only
234 Alex Smith QB .20 .50
235 Frank Gore .20 .50
236A Brandon Lloyd .12 .30
49ers photo
pack only
236B Brandon Lloyd .12 .30
Redskins photo
Factory Set only
237A Kevan Barlow .12 .30
49ers photo
pack only
237B Kevan Barlow .12 .30
Jets photo
Factory Set only
238A Rashaun Woods .12 .30
49ers pack only
238B Lorenzo Neal .12 .30
Factory Set only
239 Arnaz Battle .12 .30
240 Matt Hasselbeck .15 .40
241 Shaun Alexander .15 .40
242 Darrell Jackson .15 .40
243 Jerramy Stevens .15 .40
244 Lofa Tatupu .15 .40
245 D.J. Hackett .12 .30
246 Bobby Engram .12 .30
247A Joe Jurevicius .12 .30
Seahawks photo
pack only
247B Joe Jurevicius .12 .30
Browns photo
Factory Set only
248 Maurice Morris .12 .30
249 Marc Bulger .15 .40
250 Steven Jackson .20 .50
251 Torry Holt .15 .40
252 Isaac Bruce .15 .40
253 Kevin Curtis .15 .40
254 Marshall Faulk .15 .40
255 Shaun McDonald .12 .30
256 Chris Simms .15 .40
257 Cadillac Williams .15 .40
258 Joey Galloway .15 .40
259 Michael Clayton .12 .30
260 Derrick Brooks .15 .40
261 Ronde Barber .15 .40
262 Michael Pittman .12 .30
263 Alex Smith TE .12 .30
264 Simeon Rice .12 .30
265A Steve McNair .15 .40
Titans photo
pack only
265B Steve McNair .15 .40
Ravens photo
Factory Set only
266 Chris Brown .12 .30
267 Drew Bennett .15 .40
268 Brandon Jones .12 .30
269 Adam Jones .12 .30
270 Keith Bulluck .12 .30
271 Ben Troupe .12 .30
272 Jarrett Payton .12 .30
273 Tyrone Calico .12 .30
274 Bobby Wade .12 .30
275 Troy Fleming .12 .30
276 Mark Brunell .15 .40
277 Clinton Portis .20 .50
278 Santana Moss .15 .40
279 Jason Campbell .15 .40
280 Chris Cooley .15 .40
281 Carlos Rogers .12 .30
282 Ladell Betts .12 .30
283A Patrick Ramsey .15 .40
Redskins photo
pack only
283B Patrick Ramsey .15 .40
Jets photo
Factory Set only
284 Taylor Jacobs .12 .30
285 James Thrash .12 .30
286 Adrian Wilson .12 .30
287 London Fletcher .12 .30
288 Lance Briggs .15 .40
289 Robert Mathis .12 .30
290 Rod Coleman .12 .30
291 Bart Scott RC .60 1.50
292 Brian Moorman RC .20 .50
293 Shayne Graham RC .20 .50
294 Kevin Kaesviharn RC .20 .50
295 Leigh Bodden RC .25 .60
296 Lousaka Polite RC .20 .50
297 Todd Devoe RC .20 .50
298 Scottie Vines .20 .50
299 Cullen Jenkins RC .25 .60
300 Donovan Morgan RC .20 .50
301 C.C. Brown .20 .50
302 Demarcus Faggins RC .20 .50
303 Shantee Orr RC .20 .50
304 Vashon Pearson RC .20 .50
305 Reggie Hayward RC .20 .50
306 Paul Spicer RC .20 .50
307A Kenny Wright RC .20 .50
Jaguars photo
pack only
307B Kenny Wright .20 .50
Redskins photo
Factory Set only
308 Rich Alexis RC .20 .50
309 Terrence Melton RC .20 .50
310 Willie Whitehead RC .20 .50
311A Kendrick Clancy RC .20 .50
Giants photo
pack only
311B Kendrick Clancy .20 .50
Cardinals photo
Factory Set only
312 Mark Brown RC .20 .50
313 Tommy Kelly RC .20 .50
314 Josh Parry RC .20 .50
315 Malcom Floyd RC .40 1.00
316 Mike Adams RC .20 .50
317 Ben Emanuel RC .20 .50
318 Brandon Moore RC .20 .50
319 Chartric Darby RC .20 .50
320 Bryce Fisher RC .20 .50
321 D.D. Lewis RC .20 .50
322 Jimmy Williams DB RC .30 .75
323A Robert Pollard RC .20 .50
head and shoulders photo
pack only
323B Robert Pollard .20 .50
action photo
Factory Set only
324A Chris Johnson RC .30 .75
Rams photo
pack only
324B Chris Johnson .30 .75
Chiefs photo
Factory Set only
325 Edell Shepherd RC .20 .50
326 O.J. Small RC .20 .50
327A Brad Kassell RC .20 .50
Titans photo
pack only
327B Brad Kassell .20 .50
Jets photo
Factory Set only
328 Matt Leinart .60 1.50
Reggie Bush
329 Matt Leinart .40 1.00
Vince Young
330 LenDale White .60 1.50
Matt Leinart
Reggie Bush
331 Matt Leinart RC .50 1.25
332A Chad Greenway RC .50 1.25
training camp photo
pack only
332B Chad Greenway .50 1.25
updated game action photo
Factory Set only
333A Devin Aromashodu RC .50 1.25
training camp photo
pack only
333B Devin Aromashodu .50 1.25
updated game action photo
Factory Set only
334 DeAngelo Williams RC .60 1.50
335 Travis Wilson RC .30 .75
336 Leon Washington RC .40 1.00
337 Maurice Stovall RC .30 .75
338 Michael Huff SP RC .40 1.00
339 Charlie Whitehurst RC .50 1.25
340 Vince Young RC .60 1.50
341 Jerious Norwood RC .40 1.00
342A D'Brickashaw Ferguson RC .50 1.25
training camp photo
pack only
342B D'Brickashaw Ferguson .50 1.25
updated game action photo
Factory Set only
343A Taurean Henderson RC .50 1.25
pack only
343B Sam Hurd RC .30 .75
Factory Set only
344A Dominique Byrd RC .40 1.00
training camp photo
pack only
344B Dominique Byrd .40 1.00
updated game action photo
Factory Set only
345 Sinorice Moss SP RC .50 1.25
346A Martin Nance RC .40 1.00
training camp photo
pack only
346B Martin Nance .40 1.00
updated game action photo
Factory Set only
347 Vernon Davis RC .60 1.50
348 Ko Simpson RC .40 1.00
349A Jerome Harrison RC .50 1.25
training camp photo
pack only
349B Jerome Harrison .50 1.25
updated game action photo
Factory Set only
350A Jay Cutler RC 1.00 2.50
training camp photo
pack only
350B Jay Cutler 1.00 2.50
updated game action photo
Factory Set only
351A Alan Zemaitis RC .50 1.25
Penn State photo
pack only
351B Alan Zemaitis .50 1.25
updated Buccaneers photo
Factory Set only
352A Haloti Ngata SP RC .50 1.25
training camp photo
pack only
352B Haloti Ngata .50 1.25
updated game action photo
Factory Set only
353A Greg Lee RC .30 .75
training camp photo
pack only
353B Greg Lee .30 .75
updated game action photo
Factory Set only
354 Laurence Maroney RC .40 1.00
355A Bobby Carpenter SP RC .30 .75
training camp photo
pack only
355B Bobby Carpenter .30 .75
updated game action photo
Factory Set only
356A Jonathan Orr RC .40 1.00
training camp photo
pack only
356B Jonathan Orr .40 1.00
updated game action photo
Factory Set only
357 Marcedes Lewis RC .50 1.25
358A Brodrick Bunkley SP RC .40 1.00
training camp photo
pack only
358B Brodrick Bunkley .40 1.00
updated game action photo
Factory Set only
359A Todd Watkins RC .30 .75
training camp photo
pack only
359B Todd Watkins .30 .75
updated game action photo
Factory Set only
360 Reggie Bush RC 1.00 2.50
361A Jimmy Williams RC .50 1.25
training camp photo
pack only
361B Jimmy Williams .50 1.25
updated game action photo
Factory Set only
362 Maurice Drew RC .75 2.00
363 Mario Williams RC .50 1.25
364 Derek Hagan RC .40 1.00
365 Santonio Holmes RC .60 1.50
366A Tye Hill RC .30 .75
training camp photo
pack only
366B Tye Hill .30 .75
updated game action photo
Factory Set only
367 Jason Avant RC .30 .75
368A Tamba Hali SP RC .50 1.25
training camp photo
pack only
368B Tamba Hali .50 1.25
updated game action photo
Factory Set only
369 Joe Klopfenstein RC .30 .75
370 LenDale White RC .40 1.00
371A DeMeco Ryans RC .50 1.25
Alabama photo
pack only
371B DeMeco Ryans .50 1.25
updated Texans photo
Factory Set only
372A Bruce Gradkowski SP RC .50 1.25
training camp photo
pack only
372B Bruce Gradkowski .50 1.25
updated game action photo
Factory Set only
373 A.J. Hawk RC .50 1.25
374A Gabe Watson RC .30 .75
training camp photo
pack only
374B Gabe Watson 1.00 2.50
updated game action photo
Factory Set only
375A Devin Hester SP RC .75 2.00
training camp photo
pack only
375B Devin Hester .75 2.00
updated game action photo
Factory Set only
376 Demetrius Williams SP RC .40 1.00
377A Joseph Addai RC .50 1.25
training camp photo
pack only
377B Joseph Addai .50 1.25
updated game action photo
Factory Set only
378A Leonard Pope RC .50 1.25
training camp action photo
pack only
378B Leonard Pope .50 1.25
updated game action photo
Factory Set only
379 Omar Jacobs RC .30 .75
380A Brad Smith SP RC .50 1.25
training camp photo
pack only
380B Brad Smith .50 1.25
updated game action photo
Factory Set only
381 Michael Robinson RC .40 1.00
382A Brodie Croyle RC .50 1.25
training camp action photo
pack only
382B Brodie Croyle .50 1.25
updated game action photo
Factory Set only
383A Anthony Fasano RC .50 1.25
training camp action photo
pack only
383B Anthony Fasano .50 1.25
updated game action photo
Factory Set only
384 Brian Calhoun RC .30 .75
385 Chad Jackson RC .30 .75
386 Drew Olson RC .30 .75
387 Greg Jennings RC .75 2.00
388 Andre Hall RC .40 1.00
389 Mike Espy RC .50 1.25
390 Tim Day RC .40 1.00
391 Brandon Williams RC .30 .75
392 Mark Anderson RC 1.25 3.00
393 DonTrell Moore RC .50 1.25
394 Kellen Clemens RC .40 1.00
395 Ernie Sims RC .40 1.00
396 Cedric Humes RC .30 .75
397 Brandon Kirsch RC .40 1.00
398 Tony Scheffler RC .50 1.25
399 Kelly Jennings RC .40 1.00
400 Manny Lawson RC .40 1.00
401 Terrence Whitehead RC .40 1.00
402 Marcus Vick RC .30 .75
403 De'Arrius Howard RC .50 1.25
404 Wendell Mathis RC .40 1.00
405 Abdul Hodge RC .30 .75
406 Owen Daniels RC .50 1.25
407 Mike Hass RC .40 1.00
408 Brett Elliott RC .50 1.25
409 Kamerion Wimbley RC .50 1.25
410 Jeremy Bloom RC .40 1.00
411 D.J. Shockley RC .40 1.00
412 Darnell Bing RC .40 1.00
413 Miles Austin RC 1.25 3.00
414 D'Qwell Jackson RC .40 1.00
415 Tarvaris Jackson RC .50 1.25
416 Mathias Kiwanuka RC .50 1.25
417 Mike Bell RC .50 1.25
418 Paul Pinegar RC .30 .75
419 David Thomas RC .40 1.00
420 Hank Baskett RC .50 1.25
421 P.J. Daniels RC .30 .75
422 Jon Alston RC .30 .75
423 Reggie McNeal RC .40 1.00
424 Brandon Marshall RC .50 1.25
425 Gerald Riggs RC .40 1.00
426 Delanie Walker RC .50 1.25
427 Erik Meyer RC .40 1.00
428 Jeff Webb RC .40 1.00
429 Skyler Green RC .30 .75
430 Thomas Howard RC .40 1.00
431 Ashton Youboty RC .30 .75
432 Cedric Griffin RC .40 1.00
433 Donte Whitner RC .50 1.25
434 Jason Allen RC .40 1.00
435 Pat Watkins RC .40 1.00
436 Rocky McIntosh RC .40 1.00
437 Ingle Martin RC .40 1.00
438 John David Washington RC .40 1.00
439 Cory Rodgers RC .40 1.00
440 Willie Reid RC .40 1.00

2006 Score Artist's Proof

*VETS 1-290: 12X TO 30X BASIC CARDS
*VETS 291-327: 6X TO 15X BASIC CARDS
*ROOKIES 328-330: 2X TO 5X BASIC CARDS
*ROOKIES 331-385: 6X TO 15X BASIC CARDS
STATED PRINT RUN 32 SER.#'d SETS

2006 Score Black

UNPRICED BLACK PRINT RUN 6

2006 Score Glossy

*VETS 1-290: 1.5X TO 4X BASIC CARDS
*VETS 291-327: .8X TO 2X BASIC CARDS
*ROOKIES 328-330: .5X TO 1.2X
*ROOKIES 331-385: .5X TO 1.2X
ONE PER PACK

2006 Score Gold

*VETS 1-290: 3X TO 8X BASIC CARDS
*VETS 291-327: 1.5X TO 4X BASIC CARDS
*ROOKIES 328-330: .8X TO 2X BASIC CARDS
*ROOKIES 331-385: 1X TO 2.5X BASIC CARDS
STATED PRINT RUN 600 SER.#'d SETS

2006 Score Green

*ROOKIES 331-385: 1.5X TO 4X BASIC CARDS
INSERTS IN WAL-MART PACKS

2006 Score Red

*VETS 1-290: 5X TO 12X BASIC CARDS
*VETS 291-327: 2.5X TO 6X BASIC CARDS
*ROOKIES 328-330: 1.2X TO 3X BASIC CARDS
*ROOKIES 331-385: 1.5X TO 4X BASIC CARDS
STATED PRINT RUN 120 SER.#'d SETS

2006 Score Scorecard

*VETS 1-290: 2.5X TO 6X BASIC CARDS
*VETS 291-327: 1.2X TO 3X BASIC CARDS
*ROOKIES 328-330: .6X TO 1.5X
*ROOKIES 331-385: .8X TO 2X BASIC CARDS
STATED PRINT RUN 750 SER.#'d SETS

2006 Score Super Bowl XLI Embossed

*VETS/1-290: 4X TO 10X BASIC CARDS
*ROOKIES/328-330: 1X TO 2.5X
*ROOKIES/291-327/331-385: 2X TO 5X
ISSUED AT 2007 SUPER BOWL CARD SHOW

2006 Score Hot Rookies

COMPLETE SET (10) 8.00 20.00
*ART.PROOF/32: 4X TO 10X BASIC INSERTS
ARTIST PROOF PRINT RUN 32 SETS
UNPRICED BLACK PRINT RUN 6 SETS
*GLOSSY: .5X TO 1.2X BASIC INSERTS
*GOLD/600: .6X TO 1.5X BASIC INSERTS
*RED/120: 1.2X TO 3X BASIC INSERTS
*SCORECARD/750: .5X TO 1.2X
1 Matt Leinart .60 1.50
2 Vince Young .75 2.00
3 Jay Cutler 1.25 3.00
4 Reggie Bush 1.25 3.00
5 LenDale White .50 1.25
6 DeAngelo Williams .75 2.00
7 Laurence Maroney .50 1.25
8 Santonio Holmes .75 2.00
9 Sinorice Moss .60 1.50
10 Maurice Stovall .40 1.00

2006 Score Hot Rookies National Anaheim Embossed Promos

COMPLETE SET (10) 30.00 60.00
1 Matt Leinart 1.00 2.50
2 Vince Young 1.25 3.00
3 Jay Cutler 2.00 5.00
4 Reggie Bush 2.00 5.00
5 LenDale White .75 2.00
6 DeAngelo Williams 1.25 3.00
7 Laurence Maroney .75 2.00
8 Santonio Holmes 1.25 3.00
9 Sinorice Moss 1.00 2.50
10 Maurice Stovall .60 1.50

2006 Score Hot Rookies Super Bowl XLI Embossed Promos

COMPLETE SET (10) 40.00 80.00
1 Matt Leinart 1.25 3.00
2 Vince Young 1.50 4.00
3 Jay Cutler 2.50 6.00
4 Reggie Bush 2.50 6.00
5 LenDale White 1.00 2.50
6 DeAngelo Williams 1.50 4.00
7 Laurence Maroney 1.00 2.50
8 Santonio Holmes 1.50 4.00
9 Sinorice Moss 1.25 3.00
10 Maurice Stovall .75 2.00

2006 Score Inscriptions

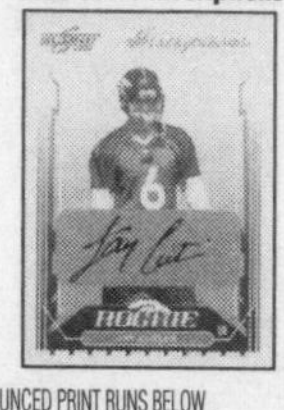

ANNOUNCED PRINT RUNS BELOW
PRINT RUNS UNDER 20 NOT PRICED
7 Bertrand Berry/50* 8.00 20.00
8 John Navarre/83*
15 DeAngelo Hall/44* 10.00 25.00
17 Kyle Boller/10*
19 Chester Taylor/20*
22 Todd Heap/100*
24 Devard Darling/47* 5.00 12.00
29 Lawyer Milloy/15*
37 Chris Gamble/30*
49 Tommie Harris/47* 6.00 15.00
50 Adrian Peterson/11*
51 Bernard Berrian/5*
57 Chris Henry/100* 6.00 15.00
58 Chris Perry/9*
62 Reuben Droughns/7*
75 Terence Newman/10*
76 Drew Henson/16*
77 Patrick Crayton/62*
78 Jake Plummer/5*
83 D.J. Williams/116* 6.00 15.00
84 Darius Watts/19*
85 Ron Dayne/2*
100 Donald Driver/2*
102 Robert Ferguson/15*
106 Jabar Gaffney/21*
107 Jonathan Wells/37* 5.00 12.00
116 Dallas Clark/20* 10.00 25.00
117 Dominic Rhodes/12*
118 Jim Sorgi/62* 5.00 12.00
130 Reggie Williams/9*
131 Rashean Mathis/30* 6.00 15.00
137 Kendrell Bell/39* 6.00 15.00
146 Cliff Russell/57* 6.00 15.00
147 David Boston/11*
148 Wes Welker/19* 35.00 60.00
156 Erasmus James/233* 6.00 15.00
157 Marcus Robinson/31*
158 E.J. Henderson/15*
166 Ben Watson/132* 6.00 15.00
167 Daniel Graham/90* 6.00 15.00
168 Bethel Johnson/11*
169 Kevin Faulk/15*
184 Brandon Jacobs/51* 8.00 20.00
186 Will Allen/69* 6.00 15.00
192 Ty Law/15*
200 Doug Gabriel/5*
201 Johnnie Morant/27*
209 Correll Buckhalter/14*
210 Jevon Kearse/25* 6.00 15.00
211 L.J. Smith/59* 10.00 25.00
212 Lamar Gordon/47*
230 Vincent Jackson/1*
231 Donnie Edwards/2*
232 Eric Parker/20*
233 Reche Caldwell/96*
235 Frank Gore/111* 10.00 25.00
238 Rashaun Woods/9*
245 D.J. Hackett/68*
255 Shaun McDonald/43*
256 Chris Simms/21* 20.00 40.00
259 Michael Clayton/64* 10.00 25.00
260 Derrick Brooks/100* 10.00 25.00
261 Ronde Barber/152* 20.00 40.00
271 Ben Troupe/186* 6.00 15.00
272 Jarrett Payton/21* 6.00 15.00
273 Tyrone Calico/57* 6.00 15.00
274 Bobby Wade/34*
275 Troy Fleming/35*
280 Chris Cooley/53* 10.00 25.00
282 Ladell Betts/40* 6.00 15.00
283 Patrick Ramsey/49* 6.00 15.00
325 Edell Shepherd/100*
331 Matt Leinart/5*
332 Chad Greenway/25* 12.50 30.00
333 Devin Aromashodu/50* 10.00 25.00
334 DeAngelo Williams/5*
335 Travis Wilson/10*
336 Leon Washington/10*
337 Maurice Stovall/5*
338 Michael Huff/10*
339 Charlie Whitehurst/10*
340 Vince Young/5*
341 Jerious Norwood/10*
342 D'Brickashaw Ferguson/50* 10.00 25.00
343 Taurean Henderson/50*
344 Dominique Byrd/10*
345 Sinorice Moss/5*
346 Martin Nance/50* 6.00 15.00
347 Vernon Davis/5*
348 Ko Simpson/50* 6.00 15.00

350 Jay Cutler/5*
351 Alan Zemaitis/10*
352 Haloti Ngata/50* 8.00 20.00
353 Greg Lee/50*
354 Laurence Maroney/10*
355 Bobby Carpenter/10*
356 Jonathan Orr/50* 10.00 25.00
357 Marcedes Lewis/25* 12.50 30.00
358 Brodrick Bunkley/10*
359 Todd Watkins/50*
360 Reggie Bush/5*
361 Jimmy Williams/50* 10.00 25.00
362 Maurice Drew/10*
363 Mario Williams/10*
364 Derek Hagan/10*
365 Santonio Holmes/5*
366 Tye Hill/25* 6.00 15.00
367 Jason Avant/10*
368 Tamba Hali/50* 8.00 20.00
369 Joe Klopfenstein/10*
370 LenDale White/5*
371 DeMeco Ryans/50* 12.50 30.00
372 Bruce Gradkowski/10*
373 A.J. Hawk/10*
374 Gabe Watson/10*
375 Devin Hester/10*
376 Demetrius Williams/10*
377 Joseph Addai/10*
378 Leonard Pope/10*
379 Omar Jacobs/10*
380 Brad Smith/50*
381 Michael Robinson/10*
382 Brodie Croyle/10*
383 Anthony Fasano/10*
384 Brian Calhoun/10*
385 Chad Jackson/10*

2006 Score 3-A-Day

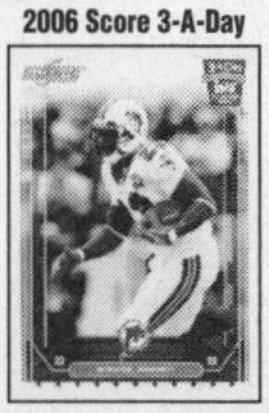

COMPLETE SET (5) 6.00 12.00
AR Allen Rossum 1.00 2.50
DF DeShaun Foster 1.00 2.50
EK Erron Kinney 1.00 2.50
RB Ronnie Brown 2.00 5.00
TS Takeo Spikes 1.00 2.50

2006 Score National Anaheim VIP Promos

COMPLETE SET (8) 20.00 40.00
1 Reggie Bush 2.00 5.00
2 Ben Roethlisberger 1.25 3.00
3 Peyton Manning 1.50 4.00
4 Carson Palmer 1.00 2.50
5 Michael Vick 1.00 2.50
6 Tom Brady 1.50 4.00
7 Eli Manning 1.25 3.00
8 Vince Young 1.25 3.00

2006 Score Pop Warner

COMPLETE SET (6) 6.00 12.00
1 Matt Leinart 1.25 3.00
Reggie Bush
2 Carson Palmer .60 1.50
3 Donovan McNabb .60 1.50
4 Tony Gonzalez .50 1.25
5 Matt Hasselbeck .50 1.25
6 Torry Holt .50 1.25

2007 Score

This 385-card set was released in July, 2007. The set was issued through retail channels in five-card packs, with a 99 cent SRP, which came 20 packs to a box. Cards numbered 1-288 feature veterans in team alphabetical order by division while cards numbered 289-385 feature 2007 NFL rookies. These Rookie Cards were inserted at a stated rate one per pack and three per jumbo pack. Cards numbered 386-440, which also feature 2007 NFL rookies, were all included in 2007 Score Factory sets.

COMPLETE SET (385) 25.00 50.00
COMP.FACT.SET (440) 30.00 50.00
ONE ROOKIE PER RETAIL PACK; THREE PER JUMBO
386-440 INSERTED IN FACTORY SETS
1 Tony Romo .25 .60
2 Julius Jones .12 .30
3 Terry Glenn .15 .40
4 Terrell Owens .20 .50
5 Jason Witten .20 .50
6 Marion Barber .20 .50
7 Patrick Crayton .12 .30
8 Bradie James .12 .30
9 DeMarcus Ware .15 .40
10 Roy Williams S .15 .40
11 Eli Manning .20 .50
12 Plaxico Burress .15 .40
13 Jeremy Shockey .15 .40
14 Brandon Jacobs .15 .40
15 Sinorice Moss .15 .40
16 Antonio Pierce .12 .30
17 David Tyree .12 .30
18 Donovan McNabb .20 .50
19 Brian Westbrook .15 .40
20 Reggie Brown .12 .30
21 L.J. Smith .12 .30
22 Hank Baskett .15 .40
23 Jeremiah Trotter .12 .30
24 Trent Cole .12 .30
25 Lito Sheppard .12 .30
26 Jason Campbell .15 .40
27 Clinton Portis .15 .40
28 Santana Moss .15 .40
29 Brandon Lloyd .15 .40
30 Chris Cooley .15 .40
31 Sean Taylor .20 .50
32 Lemar Marshall .12 .30
33 Ladell Betts .12 .30
34 London Fletcher .12 .30
35 Rex Grossman .15 .40
36 Cedric Benson .15 .40
37 Muhsin Muhammad .15 .40
38 Bernard Berrian .12 .30
39 Desmond Clark .12 .30
40 Lance Briggs .12 .30
41 Robbie Gould .12 .30
42 Devin Hester .20 .50
43 Mark Anderson .15 .40
44 Brian Urlacher .20 .50
45 Jon Kitna .12 .30
46 Kevin Jones .12 .30
47 Roy Williams WR .15 .40
48 Mike Furrey .15 .40
49 Cory Redding .12 .30
50 Ernie Sims .12 .30
51 Tatum Bell .12 .30
52 Brian Calhoun .12 .30
53 Brett Favre .40 1.00
54 Vernand Morency .15 .40
55 Donald Driver .20 .50
56 Greg Jennings .20 .50
57 Aaron Kampman .15 .40
58 Charles Woodson .20 .50
59 A.J. Hawk .15 .40
60 Nick Barnett .12 .30
61 Aaron Rodgers .50 1.25
62 Tarvaris Jackson .12 .30
63 Chester Taylor .12 .30
64 Troy Williamson .12 .30
65 Jim Kleinsasser .12 .30
66 Dwight Smith .12 .30
67 Antoine Winfield .12 .30
68 E.J. Henderson .12 .30
69 Mewelde Moore .12 .30
70 Michael Vick .20 .50
71 Warrick Dunn .15 .40
72 Joe Horn .15 .40
73 Michael Jenkins .15 .40
74 Alge Crumpler .15 .40
75 DeAngelo Hall .15 .40
76 Keith Brooking .12 .30
77 Lawyer Milloy .12 .30
78 Jerious Norwood .15 .40
79 Matt Schaub .15 .40
80 Jake Delhomme .15 .40
81 DeShaun Foster .15 .40
82 Steve Smith .15 .40
83 Keyshawn Johnson .15 .40
84 Julius Peppers .15 .40
85 DeAngelo Williams .20 .50
86 Chris Draft .12 .30
87 Drew Brees .20 .50
88 Deuce McAllister .15 .40
89 Scott Fujita .12 .30
90 Marques Colston .20 .50
91 Terrance Copper .15 .40
92 Will Smith .12 .30
93 Charles Grant .12 .30
94 Devery Henderson .12 .30
95 Reggie Bush .20 .50
96 Jeff Garcia .15 .40
97 Cadillac Williams .15 .40
98 Joey Galloway .15 .40
99 Michael Clayton .12 .30
100 Alex Smith TE .12 .30
101 Ronde Barber .15 .40
102 Jermaine Phillips .12 .30
103 Derrick Brooks .15 .40
104 Matt Leinart .15 .40
105 Edgerrin James .15 .40
106 Anquan Boldin .15 .40
107 Larry Fitzgerald .20 .50
108 Neil Rackers .12 .30
109 Adrian Wilson .12 .30
110 Karlos Dansby .12 .30
111 Chike Okeafor .12 .30
112 Marc Bulger .15 .40
113 Steven Jackson .20 .50
114 Torry Holt .15 .40
115 Isaac Bruce .15 .40
116 Joe Klopfenstein .12 .30
117 Randy McMichael .12 .30
118 Will Witherspoon .12 .30
119 Drew Bennett .12 .30
120 Alex Smith QB .20 .50
121 Frank Gore .20 .50
122 Arnaz Battle .12 .30
123 Ashley Lelie .15 .40
124 Vernon Davis .15 .40
125 Walt Harris .12 .30
126 Brandon Moore .12 .30
127 Nate Clements .12 .30
128 Matt Hasselbeck .15 .40
129 Shaun Alexander .15 .40
130 Deion Branch .15 .40
131 Darrell Jackson .12 .30
132 Nate Burleson .12 .30
133 Julian Peterson .12 .30
134 Lofa Tatupu .15 .40
135 Mack Strong .12 .30
136 Josh Brown .12 .30
137 J.P. Losman .12 .30
138 Anthony Thomas .12 .30
139 Lee Evans .15 .40
140 Josh Reed .12 .30
141 Roscoe Parrish .12 .30
142 Aaron Schobel .12 .30
143 Donte Whitner .12 .30
144 Shaud Williams .12 .30
145 Daunte Culpepper .15 .40
146 Ronnie Brown .15 .40
147 Chris Chambers .15 .40
148 Marty Booker .12 .30
149 Derek Hagan .12 .30
150 Jason Taylor .15 .40
151 Vonnie Holliday .12 .30
152 Zach Thomas .15 .40
153 Channing Crowder .12 .30
154 Joey Porter .12 .30
155 Tom Brady .30 .75
156 Laurence Maroney .15 .40
157 Chad Jackson .12 .30
158 Wes Welker .20 .50
159 Ben Watson .12 .30
160 Donte Stallworth .15 .40
161 Rosevelt Colvin .12 .30
162 Ty Warren .12 .30
163 Asante Samuel .12 .30
164 Adalius Thomas .12 .30
165 Tedy Bruschi .20 .50
166 Chad Pennington .15 .40
167 Thomas Jones .15 .40
168 Laveranues Coles .12 .30
169 Jerricho Cotchery .15 .40
170 Chris Baker .12 .30
171 Bryan Thomas .12 .30
172 Leon Washington .15 .40
173 Jonathan Vilma .15 .40
174 Eric Barton .12 .30
175 Erik Coleman .12 .30
176 Steve McNair .15 .40
177 Willis McGahee .15 .40
178 Derrick Mason .15 .40
179 Demetrius Williams .12 .30
180 Todd Heap .12 .30
181 Ray Lewis .20 .50
182 Trevor Pryce .12 .30
183 Bart Scott .15 .40
184 Terrell Suggs .15 .40
185 Mark Clayton .15 .40
186 Carson Palmer .15 .40
187 Rudi Johnson .15 .40
188 Chad Johnson .15 .40
189 T.J. Houshmandzadeh .15 .40
190 Robert Geathers .12 .30
191 Justin Smith .12 .30
192 Tory James .12 .30
193 Landon Johnson .12 .30
194 Shayne Graham .12 .30
195 Charlie Frye .15 .40
196 Reuben Droughns .15 .40
197 Braylon Edwards .15 .40
198 Travis Wilson .12 .30
199 Kellen Winslow .15 .40
200 Kamerion Wimbley .12 .30
201 Sean Jones .12 .30
202 Andra Davis .12 .30
203 Jamal Lewis .15 .40
204 Ben Roethlisberger .20 .50
205 Willie Parker .15 .40
206 Hines Ward .20 .50
207 Santonio Holmes .15 .40
208 Heath Miller .12 .30
209 Troy Polamalu .20 .50
210 James Farrior .12 .30
211 Cedrick Wilson .12 .30
212 Dunta Robinson .12 .30
213 Ahman Green .15 .40
214 Andre Johnson .15 .40
215 Jerome Mathis .12 .30
216 Owen Daniels .12 .30
217 DeMeco Ryans .15 .40
218 Wali Lundy .12 .30
219 Mario Williams .15 .40
220 Peyton Manning .30 .75
221 Joseph Addai .15 .40
222 Marvin Harrison .20 .50
223 Reggie Wayne .15 .40
224 Dallas Clark .12 .30
225 Robert Mathis .12 .30
226 Cato June .12 .30
227 Adam Vinatieri .15 .40
228 Bob Sanders .15 .40
229 Dwight Freeney .15 .40
230 Byron Leftwich .15 .40
231 Fred Taylor .15 .40
232 Matt Jones .15 .40
233 Reggie Williams .15 .40
234 Marcedes Lewis .12 .30
235 Bobby McCray .12 .30
236 Rashean Mathis .12 .30
237 Maurice Jones-Drew .20 .50
238 Ernest Wilford .12 .30
239 Daryl Smith .12 .30
240 Vince Young .15 .40
241 LenDale White .15 .40
242 Brandon Jones .12 .30
243 Bo Scaife .12 .30
244 Keith Bulluck .12 .30
245 Chris Hope .12 .30
246 Kyle Vanden Bosch .12 .30
247 Roydell Williams .12 .30
248 Jay Cutler .20 .50
249 Travis Henry .15 .40
250 Javon Walker .15 .40
251 Rod Smith .15 .40
252 Tony Scheffler .15 .40
253 Elvis Dumervil .12 .30
254 Champ Bailey .15 .40
255 Mike Bell .15 .40
256 Brandon Marshall .15 .40
257 Al Wilson .12 .30
258 Trent Green .15 .40
259 Larry Johnson .12 .30
260 Eddie Kennison .12 .30
261 Samie Parker .12 .30
262 Tony Gonzalez .15 .40
263 Jared Allen .20 .50
264 Kawika Mitchell .12 .30
265 Tamba Hali .12 .30
266 Dante Hall .15 .40
267 Brodie Croyle .15 .40
268 Andrew Walter .12 .30
269 LaMont Jordan .15 .40
270 Dominic Rhodes .15 .40
271 Randy Moss .20 .50
272 Ronald Curry .15 .40
273 Courtney Anderson .12 .30
274 Derrick Burgess .12 .30
275 Warren Sapp .15 .40
276 Michael Huff .15 .40
277 Thomas Howard .12 .30
278 Kirk Morrison .12 .30
279 Philip Rivers .20 .50
280 LaDainian Tomlinson .20 .50
281 Vincent Jackson .15 .40
282 Lorenzo Neal .12 .30
283 Antonio Gates .20 .50
284 Shawne Merriman .15 .40
285 Shaun Phillips .12 .30
286 Michael Turner .20 .50
287 Jamal Williams .12 .30
288 Nate Kaeding .12 .30
289 Michael Okwo RC .40 1.00
290 Gary Russell RC .40 1.00
291 Josh Wilson RC .40 1.00
292 Thomas Clayton RC .40 1.00
293 Jerard Rabb RC .40 1.00
294 Roy Hall RC .50 1.25
295 LaMarr Woodley RC .50 1.25
296 Eric Wright RC .50 1.25
297 Dan Bazuin RC .40 1.00
298 A.J. Davis RC .30 .75
299 Buster Davis RC .40 1.00
300 Stewart Bradley RC .40 1.00
301 Toby Korrodi RC .40 1.00
302 Marcus McCauley RC .40 1.00
303 Demarcus Tank Tyler RC .30 .75
304 Jon Abbate RC .30 .75
305 Ikaika Alama-Francis RC .50 1.25
306 Tim Crowder RC .50 1.25
307 D'Juan Woods RC .30 .75
308 Tim Shaw RC .40 1.00
309 Fred Bennett RC .30 .75
310 Victor Abiamiri RC .50 1.25
311 Eric Weddle RC .50 1.25
312 Danny Ware RC .50 1.25
313 Quentin Moses RC .40 1.00
314 Ryan McBean RC .50 1.25
315 David Harris RC .40 1.00
316 David Irons RC .30 .75
317 Syndric Steptoe RC .40 1.00
318 Eric Frampton RC .40 1.00
319 Jemalle Cornelius RC .40 1.00
320 Earl Everett RC .40 1.00
321 Alonzo Coleman RC .40 1.00
322 Josh Gattis RC .30 .75
323 Zak DeOssie RC .40 1.00
324 Jon Beason RC .40 1.00
325 Joe Staley RC .40 1.00
326 Aaron Rouse RC .40 1.00
327 Reggie Ball RC .40 1.00
328 Rufus Alexander RC .40 1.00
329 Daymeion Hughes RC .40 1.00
330 Justin Durant RC .40 1.00
331 JaMarcus Russell RC .30 .75
332 Paul Williams RC .30 .75
333 Kenny Irons RC .30 .75
334 Chris Davis RC .30 .75
335 Darius Walker RC .30 .75
336 Dwayne Bowe RC .60 1.50
337 Isaiah Stanback RC .30 .75
338 Leon Hall RC .40 1.00
339 Sidney Rice RC .60 1.50
340 Amobi Okoye RC .50 1.25
341 Adrian Peterson RC 2.00 5.00
342 LaRon Landry RC .50 1.25
343 Lorenzo Booker RC .40 1.00
344 Craig Buster Davis RC .40 1.00
345 Mike Walker RC .50 1.25
346 Zach Miller RC .50 1.25
347 Levi Brown RC .50 1.25
348 Brian Leonard RC .40 1.00
349 Aundrae Allison RC .30 .75
350 Brandon Siler RC .30 .75
351 Calvin Johnson RC 1.50 4.00
352 Gaines Adams RC .50 1.25
353 Anthony Gonzalez RC .50 1.25
354 John Beck RC .50 1.25
355 Joe Thomas RC .50 1.25
356 Michael Bush RC .50 1.25
357 Courtney Taylor RC .40 1.00
358 Lawrence Timmons RC .50 1.25
359 Drew Stanton RC .30 .75
360 Chansi Stuckey RC .50 1.25
361 Greg Olsen RC .40 1.00
362 Rhema McKnight RC .30 .75
363 Antonio Pittman RC .30 .75
364 Kevin Kolb RC .75 2.00
365 Alan Branch RC .40 1.00
366 Robert Meachem RC .50 1.25
367 Troy Smith RC .50 1.25
368 Jamaal Anderson RC .40 1.00
369 Tony Hunt RC .30 .75
370 David Clowney RC .40 1.00
371 Brady Quinn RC .50 1.25
372 Michael Griffin RC .50 1.25
373 Jared Zabransky RC .40 1.00
374 Jason Hill RC .50 1.25
375 Trent Edwards RC .50 1.25
376 Dwayne Jarrett RC .40 1.00
377 DeShawn Wynn RC .40 1.00
378 Patrick Willis RC 1.00 2.50
379 Steve Smith USC RC .50 1.25
380 David Ball RC .40 1.00
381 Marshawn Lynch RC .50 1.25
382 Paul Posluszny RC .50 1.25
383 Johnnie Lee Higgins RC .40 1.00
384 Kolby Smith RC .40 1.00
385 Ted Ginn Jr. RC .40 1.00
386 Adam Carriker RC .40 1.00
387 Tyler Palko RC .40 1.00
388 Joel Filani RC .40 1.00
389 Garrett Wolfe RC .30 .75
390 Ryne Robinson RC .40 1.00
391 Reggie Nelson RC .40 1.00
392 Dallas Baker RC .30 .75
393 Dwayne Wright RC .40 1.00
394 Scott Chandler RC .50 1.25
395 Jordan Kent RC .40 1.00
396 Jarvis Moss RC .40 1.00
397 Jonathan Wade RC .40 1.00
398 Ben Grubbs RC .40 1.00
399 Jason Snelling RC .50 1.25
400 Jeff Rowe RC .30 .75
401 Aaron Ross RC .50 1.25
402 Daniel Sepulveda RC .50 1.25
403 Chris Henry RC .30 .75
404 James Jones RC .50 1.25
405 Matt Spaeth RC .50 1.25
406 Brandon Meriweather RC .50 1.25
407 Nate Ilaoa RC .40 1.00
408 Mason Crosby RC .40 1.00
409 Ray McDonald RC .40 1.00
410 Chris Leak RC .40 1.00
411 Darrelle Revis RC .75 2.00
412 Ahmad Bradshaw RC .75 2.00
413 Tyler Thigpen RC .50 1.25
414 Justise Hairston RC .40 1.00
415 Charles Johnson RC .30 .75
416 Anthony Spencer RC .50 1.25
417 Legedu Naanee RC .50 1.25
418 Kenneth Darby RC .40 1.00
419 Steve Breaston RC .50 1.25
420 Ben Patrick RC .40 1.00
421 Chris Houston RC .40 1.00
422 Jordan Palmer RC .40 1.00
423 Laurent Robinson RC .50 1.25
424 Selvin Young RC .40 1.00
425 Justin Harrell RC .40 1.00
426 Sabby Piscitelli RC .50 1.25
427 Yamon Figurs RC .30 .75
428 Brandon Jackson RC .40 1.00
429 Jacoby Jones RC .50 1.25
430 H.B. Blades RC .30 .75
431 Tanard Jackson RC .30 .75
432 Matt Gutierrez RC .50 1.25
433 Matt Moore RC .50 1.25
434 Clifton Dawson RC .50 1.25
435 Marcus Mason RC .50 1.25
436 Pierre Thomas RC 2.00 5.00
437 Dante Rosario RC .50 1.25
438 Biren Ealy RC .40 1.00
439 John Broussard RC .40 1.00
440 Kenton Keith RC .50 1.25

2007 Score Artist's Proof

*VETS 1-288: 12X TO 30X BASIC CARDS
*ROOKIES 289-385: 5X TO 12X BASIC CARDS
STATED PRINT RUN 32 SER.#'d SETS

2007 Score Atomic

*VETS 1-288: 2.5X TO 6X BASIC CARDS
*ROOKIES 289-385: 1X TO 2.5X BASIC CARDS
TWO PER JUMBO PACK

2007 Score End Zone Black

UNPRICED BLACK SER.#'d TO 6

2007 Score Factory Set Updates

*VETS: .4X TO 1X BASIC CARDS
*ROOKIES: .4X TO 1X BASIC CARDS

2007 Score Glossy

*VETS 1-288: 1.5X TO 4X BASIC CARDS
*ROOKIES 289-385: .6X TO 1.5X BASIC CARDS
ONE PER RETAIL PACK; THREE PER JUMBO

2007 Score Gold Zone

*VETS 1-288: 3X TO 8X BASIC CARDS
*ROOKIES 289-385: 1.2X TO 3X BASIC CARDS
GOLD PRINT RUN 600 SER.#'d SETS

2007 Score Red Zone

*VETS 1-288: 6X TO 15X BASIC CARDS
*ROOKIES 289-385: 2.5X TO 6X BASIC CARDS
RED PRINT RUN 120 SER.#'d SETS

2007 Score Scorecard

*VETERANS 1-288: 2.5X TO 6X BASIC CARDS
*ROOKIES 289-385: 1X TO 2.5X BASIC CARDS
STATED PRINT RUN 750 SER.#'d SETS

2007 Score Franchise

COMPLETE SET (10) 6.00 15.00
*ATOMIC: .8X TO 2X BASIC INSERTS
*GLOSSY: .5X TO 1.2X BASIC INSERTS
*SCORECARD/750: .8X TO 2X BASIC INSERTS
SCORECARD PRINT RUN 750 SER.#'d SETS
*GOLD ZONE/600: 1X TO 2.5X BASIC INSERTS
GOLD ZONE PRINT RUN 600 SER.#'d SETS
*RED ZONE/120: 1.5 TO 4X BASIC INSERTS
RED ZONE PRINT RUN 120 SER.#'d SETS
*ARTIST PROOF/32: 3X TO 8X BASIC INSERTS
ARTIST'S PROOF PRINT RUN 32 SER.#'d SETS
UNPRICED BLACK PRINT RUN 6
1 LaDainian Tomlinson .60 1.50
2 Frank Gore .60 1.50
3 Shaun Alexander .50 1.25
4 Brett Favre 1.25 3.00
5 Reggie Bush .60 1.50
6 Jay Cutler .60 1.50
7 Larry Johnson .40 1.00
8 Maurice Jones-Drew .60 1.50
9 Carson Palmer .50 1.25
10 Vince Young .50 1.25

2007 Score Hot Rookies

*ATOMIC: .8X TO 2X BASIC INSERTS
*GLOSSY: .6X TO 1.5X BASIC INSERTS
*SCORECARD/750: .8X TO 2X BASIC INSERTS
SCORECARD PRINT RUN 750 SER.#'d SETS
*GOLD ZONE/600: 1X TO 2.5X BASIC INSERTS
GOLD ZONE PRINT RUN 600 SER.#'d SETS
*RED ZONE/120: 1.5X TO 4X BASIC INSERTS
RED ZONE PRINT RUN 120 SER.#'d SETS
*ARTIST PROOF/32: 3X TO 8X BASIC INSERTS
ARTIST'S PROOF PRINT RUN 32 SER.#'d SETS
UNPRICED BLACK PRINT RUN 6
INSCRIPTIONS TOO SCARCE TO PRICE
1 JaMarcus Russell .40 1.00
2 Brady Quinn .60 1.50
3 Adrian Peterson 2.50 6.00
4 Marshawn Lynch .60 1.50
5 Calvin Johnson 2.00 5.00
6 Ted Ginn Jr. .50 1.25
7 Dwayne Bowe .75 2.00
8 Robert Meachem .60 1.50
9 Dwayne Jarrett .50 1.25
10 Greg Olsen .50 1.25

2007 Score Inscriptions

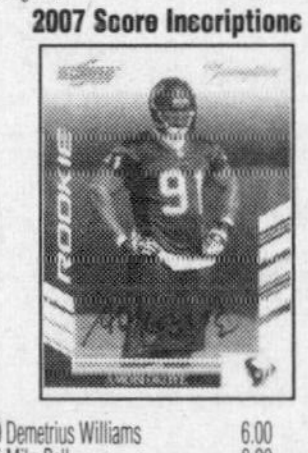

179 Demetrius Williams 6.00 15.00
255 Mike Bell 8.00 20.00
256 Brandon Marshall 8.00 20.00
289 Michael Okwo 8.00 20.00
290 Gary Russell 8.00 20.00
291 Josh Wilson 8.00 20.00
292 Thomas Clayton 8.00 20.00
293 Jerard Rabb 8.00 20.00
295 LaMarr Woodley 10.00 25.00
297 Dan Bazuin 8.00 20.00
298 A.J. Davis 6.00 15.00
299 Buster Davis 8.00 20.00
300 Stewart Bradley 8.00 20.00
301 Toby Korrodi 8.00 20.00
302 Marcus McCauley 8.00 20.00
306 Tim Crowder 10.00 25.00
307 D'Juan Woods 6.00 15.00
308 Tim Shaw 8.00 20.00
309 Fred Bennett 6.00 15.00
310 Victor Abiamiri 10.00 25.00
312 Danny Ware 10.00 25.00
313 Quentin Moses 8.00 20.00
314 Ryan McBean 10.00 25.00
315 David Harris 8.00 20.00
316 David Irons 6.00 15.00
317 Syndric Steptoe 8.00 20.00
318 Eric Frampton 8.00 20.00
319 Jemalle Cornelius 8.00 20.00
320 Earl Everett 8.00 20.00
321 Alonzo Coleman 8.00 20.00
322 Josh Gattis 6.00 15.00
323 Zak DeOssie 8.00 20.00
324 Jon Beason 8.00 20.00
326 Aaron Rouse 8.00 20.00
327 Reggie Ball 8.00 20.00
328 Rufus Alexander 8.00 20.00
329 Daymeion Hughes 8.00 20.00
331 JaMarcus Russell 6.00 15.00
332 Paul Williams 6.00 15.00
333 Kenny Irons 6.00 15.00
334 Chris Davis 6.00 15.00
335 Darius Walker 6.00 15.00
336 Dwayne Bowe 12.00 30.00
337 Isaiah Stanback 6.00 15.00
338 Leon Hall 8.00 20.00
340 Amobi Okoye 10.00 25.00
341 Adrian Peterson 150.00 250.00
342 LaRon Landry 10.00 25.00
343 Lorenzo Booker 8.00 20.00
345 Mike Walker 10.00 25.00
346 Zach Miller 10.00 25.00
347 Levi Brown 10.00 25.00
348 Brian Leonard 8.00 20.00
349 Aundrae Allison 6.00 15.00
350 Brandon Siler 6.00 15.00
351 Calvin Johnson 50.00 100.00
352 Gaines Adams 10.00 25.00
353 Anthony Gonzalez 10.00 25.00
354 John Beck 10.00 25.00
355 Joe Thomas 10.00 25.00
356 Michael Bush 10.00 25.00
357 Courtney Taylor 8.00 20.00
358 Lawrence Timmons 10.00 25.00
359 Drew Stanton 6.00 15.00
360 Chansi Stuckey 10.00 25.00
361 Greg Olsen 8.00 20.00
362 Rhema McKnight 6.00 15.00
363 Antonio Pittman 6.00 15.00
364 Kevin Kolb 15.00 40.00
366 Robert Meachem 10.00 25.00
367 Troy Smith 10.00 25.00
368 Jamaal Anderson 8.00 20.00
369 Tony Hunt 6.00 15.00
370 David Clowney 8.00 20.00
371 Brady Quinn 40.00 100.00
372 Michael Griffin 10.00 25.00
373 Jared Zabransky 8.00 20.00
374 Jason Hill 10.00 25.00
375 Trent Edwards 10.00 25.00
376 Dwayne Jarrett 8.00 20.00
377 DeShawn Wynn 8.00 20.00
378 Patrick Willis 20.00 50.00
379 Steve Smith USC 10.00 25.00
380 David Ball 8.00 20.00
381 Marshawn Lynch 10.00 25.00
382 Paul Posluszny 10.00 25.00
383 Johnnie Lee Higgins 8.00 20.00
384 Kolby Smith 8.00 20.00
385 Ted Ginn Jr. 8.00 20.00

2008 Score

COMPLETE SET (440) 30.00 60.00
COMP.FACT. SET (440) 30.00 50.00
COMP.SET w/o RC's (330) 15.00 30.00
1 Matt Leinart .20 .50
2 Kurt Warner .20 .50
3 Larry Fitzgerald .20 .50
4 Anquan Boldin .15 .40
5 Edgerrin James .15 .40
6 Neil Rackers .12 .30
7 Steve Breaston .12 .30
8 Antrel Rolle .12 .30
9 Karlos Dansby .12 .30
10 Joey Harrington .12 .30
11 Jerious Norwood .15 .40
12 Roddy White .15 .40
13 Michael Jenkins .12 .30
14 Joe Horn .15 .40
15 Keith Brooking .12 .30
16 Lawyer Milloy .12 .30
17 John Abraham .12 .30
18 Michael Turner .20 .50
19 Troy Smith .15 .40
20 Willis McGahee .15 .40
21 Musa Smith .12 .30
22 Derrick Mason .15 .40
23 Mark Clayton .15 .40
24 Bart Scott .12 .30
25 Demetrius Williams .12 .30
26 Yamon Figurs .12 .30
27 Ray Lewis .20 .50
28 Terrell Suggs .12 .30
29 Ed Reed .15 .40
30 Trent Edwards .12 .30
31 Marshawn Lynch .15 .40
32 Lee Evans .15 .40
33 Roscoe Parrish .12 .30
34 Paul Posluszny .15 .40
35 John DiGiorgio RC .15 .40
36 Angelo Crowell .12 .30
37 Jabari Greer RC .12 .30
38 Chris Kelsay .12 .30
39 Fred Jackson RC 1.25 3.00
40 Matt Moore .15 .40
41 Steve Smith .15 .40
42 DeAngelo Williams .15 .40
43 Brad Hoover .12 .30
44 Dante Rosario .12 .30
45 Julius Peppers .15 .40
46 Jon Beason .12 .30
47 Chris Harris .12 .30
48 D.J. Hackett .12 .30
49 Jake Delhomme .15 .40
50 Adrian Peterson .30 .75
51 Mark Anderson .12 .30
52 Desmond Clark .12 .30
53 Greg Olsen .15 .40
54 Devin Hester .20 .50
55 Brian Urlacher .20 .50
56 Jason McKie RC .15 .40
57 Lance Briggs .12 .30
58 Rex Grossman .15 .40
59 Carson Palmer .20 .50
60 Chad Johnson .15 .40
61 T.J. Houshmandzadeh .15 .40
62 Rudi Johnson .15 .40
63 Kenny Watson .12 .30
64 Dhani Jones .12 .30
65 Leon Hall .12 .30
66 Johnathan Joseph .12 .30
67 Derek Anderson .12 .30
68 Brady Quinn .15 .40
69 Jamal Lewis .15 .40
70 Josh Cribbs .20 .50
71 Kellen Winslow .15 .40
72 Braylon Edwards .15 .40
73 Joe Jurevicius .12 .30
74 D'Qwell Jackson .12 .30
75 Leigh Bodden .12 .30
76 Sean Jones .12 .30
77 Tony Romo .25 .60
78 Terrell Owens .20 .50
79 Marion Barber .15 .40
80 Jason Witten .20 .50
81 Patrick Crayton .15 .40
82 Anthony Henry .12 .30
83 DeMarcus Ware .15 .40
84 Terence Newman .12 .30
85 Greg Ellis .12 .30
86 Zach Thomas .15 .40
87 Keary Colbert .12 .30
88 Jay Cutler .20 .50
89 Tony Scheffler .12 .30
90 Selvin Young .12 .30
91 Brandon Marshall .15 .40
92 Brandon Stokley .15 .40
93 Champ Bailey .15 .40
94 John Lynch .15 .40
95 Dre Bly .12 .30
96 Elvis Dumervil .12 .30
97 Jon Kitna .15 .40
98 Tatum Bell .12 .30
99 Shaun McDonald .12 .30
100 Roy Williams WR .15 .40
101 Calvin Johnson .20 .50
102 Mike Furrey .15 .40
103 Ernie Sims .12 .30
104 Aveion Cason .12 .30
105 Aaron Rodgers .40 1.00
106 Brett Favre .50 1.25
107 Ryan Grant .20 .50
108 Greg Jennings .20 .50
109 Donald Driver .15 .40
110 Donald Lee .16 .40
111 James Jones .12 .30
112 Al Harris .12 .30
113 Nick Barnett .12 .30
114 Charles Woodson .20 .50
115 Aaron Kampman .15 .40
116 Mason Crosby .12 .30
117 Matt Schaub .15 .40
118 Ahman Green .15 .40
119 Andre Johnson .15 .40
120 Kevin Walter .15 .40
121 Owen Daniels .12 .30
122 Andre Davis .12 .30
123 DeMeco Ryans .15 .40
124 Mario Williams .15 .40
125 Dunta Robinson .12 .30
126 Chris Brown .12 .30
127 Peyton Manning .30 .75
128 Joseph Addai .15 .40
129 Marvin Harrison .20 .50
130 Reggie Wayne .15 .40
131 Dallas Clark .15 .40
132 Anthony Gonzalez .12 .30
133 Kenton Keith .12 .30
134 Adam Vinatieri .20 .50
135 Bob Sanders .15 .40
136 Kelvin Hayden .12 .30
137 Freddie Keiaho .12 .30
138 David Garrard .15 .40
139 Fred Taylor .15 .40
140 Maurice Jones-Drew .15 .40
141 Greg Jones .12 .30
142 Dennis Northcutt .12 .30
143 Reggie Williams .15 .40
144 Marcedes Lewis .12 .30
145 Matt Jones .15 .40
146 Reggie Nelson .12 .30
147 Cleo Lemon .12 .30
148 Jerry Porter .12 .30
149 Damon Huard .12 .30
150 Brodie Croyle .15 .40
151 Larry Johnson .15 .40
152 Kolby Smith .12 .30
153 Tony Gonzalez .15 .40
154 Dwayne Bowe .15 .40
155 Donnie Edwards .12 .30
156 Jared Allen .20 .50
157 Patrick Surtain .12 .30
158 Derrick Johnson .12 .30
159 Ernest Wilford .12 .30
160 John Beck .12 .30
161 Ronnie Brown .15 .40
162 Greg Camarillo RC .40 1.00
163 Ted Ginn Jr. .15 .40
164 Derek Hagan .12 .30
165 Channing Crowder .12 .30
166 Joey Porter .12 .30
167 Jason Taylor .15 .40
168 Josh McCown .12 .30
169 Bernard Berrian .15 .40
170 Maurice Hicks .12 .30
171 Tarvaris Jackson .15 .40
172 Adrian Peterson .30 .75
173 Chester Taylor .12 .30
174 Bobby Wade .12 .30
175 Sidney Rice .20 .50
176 Robert Ferguson .12 .30
177 Darren Sharper .15 .40
178 Visanthe Shiancoe .20 .50
179 E.J. Henderson .12 .30
180 Cedric Griffin .12 .30
181 Chad Greenway .12 .30
182 Tom Brady .30 .75
183 Randy Moss .20 .50
184 Laurence Maroney .15 .40
185 Wes Welker .20 .50
186 Sammy Morris .12 .30
187 Kevin Faulk .15 .40
188 Ben Watson .12 .30
189 Tedy Bruschi .20 .50
190 Rodney Harrison .12 .30
191 Mike Vrabel .12 .30
192 Drew Brees .20 .50
193 Reggie Bush .20 .50
194 Deuce McAllister .15 .40
195 Marques Colston .15 .40
196 David Patten .12 .30
197 Devery Henderson .12 .30
198 Scott Fujita .12 .30
199 Roman Harper .12 .30
200 Mike McKenzie .12 .30
201 Will Smith .12 .30
202 Billy Miller .12 .30
203 Sammy Knight .12 .30
204 Eli Manning .20 .50
205 Plaxico Burress .15 .40
206 Brandon Jacobs .15 .40
207 Ahmad Bradshaw .15 .40
208 David Tyree .15 .40
209 Amani Toomer .15 .40
210 Jeremy Shockey .15 .40
211 Steve Smith USC .15 .40
212 Aaron Ross .12 .30
213 Antonio Pierce .12 .30
214 Michael Strahan .15 .40
215 Jesse Chatman .12 .30
216 Calvin Pace .12 .30
217 Kellen Clemens .15 .40
218 Leon Washington .15 .40
219 Jerricho Cotchery .15 .40
220 Laveranues Coles .12 .30
221 Chris Baker .12 .30
222 Brad Smith .12 .30
223 Thomas Jones .15 .40
224 Darrelle Revis .15 .40
225 David Harris .12 .30
226 DeAngelo Hall .12 .30
227 Drew Carter .12 .30
228 Javon Walker .15 .40
229 JaMarcus Russell .15 .40
230 Justin Fargas .12 .30
231 Michael Bush .15 .40
232 Ronald Curry .15 .40
233 Zach Miller .15 .40
234 Thomas Howard .12 .30
235 Johnnie Lee Higgins .12 .30
236 Kirk Morrison .12 .30
237 Michael Huff .12 .30

238 Asante Samuel .12 .30
239 Donovan McNabb .20 .50
240 Brian Westbrook .15 .40
241 Correll Buckhalter .15 .40
242 Kevin Curtis .12 .30
243 Reggie Brown .12 .30
244 L.J. Smith .12 .30
245 Greg Lewis .12 .30
246 Lito Sheppard .12 .30
247 Omar Gaither .12 .30
248 Ben Roethlisberger .20 .50
249 Willie Parker .15 .40
250 Najeh Davenport .12 .30
251 Hines Ward .15 .40
252 Santonio Holmes .15 .40
253 Heath Miller .12 .30
254 Cedrick Wilson .12 .30
255 James Harrison RC 1.00 2.50
256 Ike Taylor .12 .30
257 James Farrior .12 .30
258 Troy Polamalu .20 .50
259 Philip Rivers .20 .50
260 LaDainian Tomlinson .20 .50
261 Darren Sproles .12 .30
262 Vincent Jackson .12 .30
263 Chris Chambers .15 .40
264 Antonio Gates .20 .50
265 Craig Buster Davis .12 .30
266 Malcom Floyd .15 .40
267 Antonio Cromartie .12 .30
268 Shawne Merriman .15 .40
269 DeShaun Foster .15 .40
270 Alex Smith QB .20 .50
271 Frank Gore .15 .40
272 Michael Robinson .12 .30
273 Vernon Davis .15 .40
274 Arnaz Battle .12 .30
275 Isaac Bruce .15 .40
276 Patrick Willis .15 .40
277 Nate Clements .12 .30
278 Jason Hill .12 .30
279 T.J. Duckett .12 .30
280 Matt Hasselbeck .15 .40
281 Julian Peterson .12 .30
282 Maurice Morris .12 .30
283 Bobby Engram .12 .30
284 Nate Burleson .12 .30
285 Deion Branch .15 .40
286 Lofa Tatupu .15 .40
287 Marcus Trufant .12 .30
288 Darryl Tapp .12 .30
289 Julius Jones .12 .30
290 Marc Bulger .15 .40
291 Steven Jackson .20 .50
292 Brian Leonard .12 .30
293 Torry Holt .15 .40
294 Dante Hall .12 .30
295 Randy McMichael .12 .30
296 Drew Bennett .12 .30
297 Will Witherspoon .12 .30
298 Tye Hill .12 .30
299 Corey Chavous .12 .30
300 Warrick Dunn .15 .40
301 Brian Griese .12 .30
302 Jeff Garcia .15 .40
303 Cadillac Williams .15 .40
304 Earnest Graham .12 .30
305 Joey Galloway .15 .40
306 Ike Hilliard .12 .30
307 Michael Clayton .12 .30
308 Derrick Brooks .15 .40
309 Phillip Buchanon .12 .30
310 Alex Smith TE .20 .50
311 Ronde Barber .12 .30
312 Justin McCareins .12 .30
313 Jevon Kearse .15 .40
314 Vince Young .15 .40
315 LenDale White .15 .40
316 Justin Gage .12 .30
317 Roydell Williams .12 .30
318 Alge Crumpler .15 .40
319 Brandon Jones .12 .30
320 Michael Griffin .12 .30
321 Keith Bulluck .12 .30
322 Jason Campbell .15 .40
323 Clinton Portis .15 .40
324 Ladell Betts .12 .30
325 Santana Moss .12 .30
326 Chris Cooley .15 .40
327 Antwaan Randle El .12 .30
328 London Fletcher .12 .30
329 Shawn Springs .12 .30
330 LaRon Landry .15 .40
331 Jake Long RC .50 1.25
332 Chris Long RC .50 1.25
333 Matt Ryan RC 2.00 5.00
334 Darren McFadden RC 1.25 3.00
335 Glenn Dorsey RC .50 1.25
336 Vernon Gholston RC .40 1.00
337 Sedrick Ellis RC .50 1.25
338 Derrick Harvey RC .30 .75
339 Keith Rivers RC .50 1.25
340 Jerod Mayo RC .50 1.25
341 Leodis McKelvin RC .40 1.00
342 Jonathan Stewart RC .75 2.00
343 Dominique Rodgers-Cromartie RC .50 1.25
344 Joe Flacco RC 1.50 4.00
345 Aqib Talib RC .50 1.25
346 Felix Jones RC .75 2.00
347 Rashard Mendenhall RC 1.00 2.50
348 Chris Johnson RC 1.25 3.00
349 Mike Jenkins RC .50 1.25
350 Antoine Cason RC .50 1.25
351 Lawrence Jackson RC .40 1.00
352 Kentwan Balmer RC .40 1.00
353 Dustin Keller RC .50 1.25
354 Kenny Phillips RC .50 1.25
355 Phillip Merling RC .40 1.00
356 Donnie Avery RC .40 1.00
357 Devin Thomas RC .40 1.00
358 Brandon Flowers RC .50 1.25
359 Jordy Nelson RC .60 1.50
360 Curtis Lofton RC .40 1.00
361 John Carlson RC .50 1.25
362 Tracy Porter RC .50 1.25
363 James Hardy RC .40 1.00
364 Eddie Royal RC .50 1.25
365 Matt Forte RC .75 2.00
366 Jordon Dizon RC .50 1.25
367 Jerome Simpson RC .50 1.25
368 Fred Davis RC .50 1.25
369 DeSean Jackson RC 1.00 2.50
370 Calais Campbell RC .40 1.00
371 Malcolm Kelly RC .40 1.00
372 Quentin Groves RC .40 1.00
373 Limas Sweed RC .50 1.25
374 Ray Rice RC 1.00 2.50
375 Brian Brohm RC .50 1.25
376 Chad Henne RC .50 1.25
377 Dexter Jackson RC .40 1.00
378 Martellus Bennett RC .40 1.00
379 Terrell Thomas RC .40 1.00
380 Kevin Smith RC .50 1.25
381 Anthony Alridge RC .40 1.00
382 Jacob Hester RC .50 1.25
383 Earl Bennett RC .50 1.25
384 Jamaal Charles RC .75 2.00
385 Dan Connor RC .50 1.25
386 Reggie Smith RC .40 1.00
387 Brad Cottam RC .40 1.00
388 Pat Sims RC .40 1.00
389 Dantrell Savage RC .40 1.00
390 Early Doucet RC .40 1.00
391 Harry Douglas RC .40 1.00
392 Steve Slaton RC .50 1.25
393 Jermichael Finley RC .50 1.25
394 Kevin O'Connell RC .40 1.00
395 Mario Manningham RC .50 1.25
396 Andre Caldwell RC .40 1.00
397 Will Franklin RC .40 1.00
398 Marcus Smith RC .40 1.00
399 Martin Rucker RC .40 1.00
400 Xavier Adibi RC .30 .75
401 Craig Steltz RC .40 1.00
402 Tashard Choice RC .40 1.00
403 Lavelle Hawkins RC .30 .75
404 Jacob Tamme RC .50 1.25
405 Keenan Burton RC .30 .75
406 John David Booty RC .40 1.00
407 Ryan Torain RC .50 1.25
408 Tim Hightower RC .50 1.25
409 Dennis Dixon RC .50 1.25
410 Kellen Davis RC .30 .75
411 Josh Johnson RC .50 1.25
412 Erik Ainge RC .50 1.25
413 Owen Schmitt RC .50 1.25
414 Marcus Thomas RC .40 1.00
415 Thomas Brown RC .40 1.00
416 Josh Morgan RC .50 1.25
417 Kevin Robinson RC .30 .75
418 Colt Brennan RC .50 1.25
419 Paul Hubbard RC .40 1.00
420 Andre Woodson RC .50 1.25
421 Mike Hart RC .50 1.25
422 Matt Flynn RC 1.00 2.50
423 Chauncey Washington RC .40 1.00
424 Caleb Campbell RC .50 1.25
425 Peyton Hillis RC 1.25 3.00
426 Justin Forsett RC .50 1.25
427 Adrian Arrington RC .40 1.00
428 Cory Boyd RC .30 .75
429 Allen Patrick RC .40 1.00
430 Marcus Monk RC .40 1.00
431 DJ Hall RC .40 1.00
432 Darrell Strong RC .40 1.00
433 Jason Rivers RC .40 1.00
434 Jed Collins RC .40 1.00
435 Paul Smith RC .50 1.25
436 Darius Reynaud RC .30 .75
437 Ali Highsmith RC .30 .75
438 Davone Bess RC .50 1.25
439 Erin Henderson RC .50 1.25
440 Kalvin McRae RC .30 .75

2008 Score Artist's Proof

*VETS 1-330: 12X TO 30X BASIC CARDS
*ROOKIES 331-440: 5X TO 12X
STATED PRINT RUN 32 SER.#'d SETS

2008 Score End Zone

UNPRICED END ZONE PRINT RUN 6

2008 Score Factory Set Updates

*VETS: .6X TO 1.5X BASIC CARDS
*ROOKIES: .4X TO 1X BASIC CARDS
INSERTED IN FACTORY SETS ONLY
18 Michael Turner .30 .75
21 Musa Smith .20 .50
48 D.J. Hackett .20 .50
75 Leigh Bodden .20 .50
86 Zach Thomas .25 .60
87 Keary Colbert .20 .50
94 John Lynch .25 .60
126 Chris Brown .20 .50
147 Cleo Lemon .20 .50
156 Jared Allen .30 .75
159 Ernest Wilford .20 .50
210 Jeremy Shockey .25 .60
215 Jesse Chatman .20 .50
216 Calvin Pace .20 .50
226 DeAngelo Hall .20 .50
227 Drew Carter .20 .50
228 Javon Walker .25 .60
238 Asante Samuel .20 .50
250 Byron Leftwich .25 .60
254 Ricky Williams .25 .60
269 Deshaun Foster .25 .60
275 Isaac Bruce .25 .60
279 T.J. Duckett .20 .50
289 Julius Jones .20 .50
300 Warrick Dunn .25 .60
301 Brian Griese .20 .50
312 Justin McCareins .20 .50
313 Jevon Kearse .25 .60
318 Alge Crumpler .25 .60
332 Chris Long .50 1.25
336 Vernon Gholston .40 1.00
337 Sedrick Ellis .50 1.25
338 Derrick Harvey .30 .75
339 Keith Rivers .50 1.25
340 Jerod Mayo .50 1.25
341 Leodis McKelvin .40 1.00
343 Dominique Rodgers-Cromartie .50 1.25
345 Aqib Talib .50 1.25
348 Chris Johnson 1.25 3.00
349 Mike Jenkins .50 1.25
350 Antoine Cason .50 1.25
351 Lawrence Jackson .40 1.00
354 Kenny Phillips .50 1.25
355 Phillip Merling .40 1.00
358 Brandon Flowers .50 1.25
360 Curtis Lofton .40 1.00
361 John Carlson .50 1.25
362 Tracy Porter .50 1.25
364 Eddie Royal .50 1.25
366 Jordon Dizon .50 1.25
368 Fred Davis .50 1.25
370 Calais Campbell .40 1.00
372 Quentin Groves .40 1.00
374 Ray Rice 1.00 2.50
377 Dexter Jackson .40 1.00
378 Martellus Bennett .40 1.00
379 Terrell Thomas .40 1.00
381 Anthony Alridge .40 1.00
382 Jacob Hester .50 1.25
384 Jamaal Charles .75 2.00
385 Dan Connor .50 1.25
386 Reggie Smith .40 1.00
387 Brad Cottam .40 1.00
388 Pat Sims .40 1.00
389 Dantrell Savage .40 1.00
393 Jermichael Finley .50 1.25
397 Will Franklin .40 1.00
398 Marcus Smith .40 1.00
399 Martin Rucker .40 1.00
400 Xavier Adibi .30 .75
401 Craig Steltz .40 1.00
402 Tashard Choice .40 1.00
403 Lavelle Hawkins .30 .75
404 Jacob Tamme .50 1.25
405 Keenan Burton .30 .75
408 Tim Hightower .50 1.25
409 Dennis Dixon .50 1.25
410 Kellen Davis .30 .75
411 Josh Johnson .50 1.25
412 Erik Ainge .50 1.25
413 Owen Schmitt .50 1.25
414 Marcus Thomas .40 1.00
415 Thomas Brown .40 1.00
416 Josh Morgan .50 1.25
418 Colt Brennan .50 1.25
419 Paul Hubbard .40 1.00
420 Andre Woodson .50 1.25
421 Mike Hart .50 1.25
422 Matt Flynn 1.00 2.50
423 Chauncey Washington .40 1.00
425 Peyton Hillis 1.25 3.00
426 Justin Forsett .50 1.25
427 Adrian Arrington .40 1.00
428 Jalen Parmele RC .40 1.00
429 Allen Patrick .40 1.00
430 Marcus Monk .40 1.00
431 DJ Hall .40 1.00
432 Darrell Strong .40 1.00
433 Xavier Omon RC .50 1.25
434 Jed Collins .40 1.00
435 Marcus Henry RC .40 1.00
436 Darius Reynaud .30 .75
437 Ali Highsmith .30 .75
438 Davone Bess .50 1.25
439 Erin Henderson .50 1.25
440 Kenneth Moore RC .40 1.00

2008 Score Glossy

*VETS 1-330: 1.2X TO 3X BASIC CARDS
*ROOKIES 331-440: .5X TO 1.2X
ONE PER RETAIL PACK; THREE PER HOBBY
106B Brett Favre Jets 2.50 6.00
(inserted in retail team set)

2008 Score Gold Zone

*VETS 1-330: 3X TO 8X BASIC CARDS
*ROOKIES 331-440: 1.2X TO 3X
STATED PRINT RUN 400 SER.#'d SETS

2008 Score Red Zone

*VETS 1-330: 5X TO 12X BASIC CARDS
*ROOKIES 331-440: 2X TO 5X
STATED PRINT RUN 100 SER.#'d SETS

2008 Score Scorecard

*VETS 1-330: 2.5X TO 6X BASIC CARDS
*ROOKIES 331-440: 1X TO 2.5X BASIC CARDS
STATED PRINT RUN 649 SER.#'d SETS

2008 Score Player Decals

COMPLETE SET (32) 10.00 25.00
1 Tom Brady 1.00 2.50
2 Reggie Bush .60 1.50
3 Kellen Clemens .50 1.25
4 Jay Cutler .60 1.50
5 Braylon Edwards .50 1.25
6 Joe Flacco 1.00 2.50
7 Jeff Garcia .50 1.25
8 Frank Gore .50 1.25
9 Matt Hasselbeck .50 1.25
10 Chad Henne .30 .75
11 Devin Hester .60 1.50
12 Torry Holt .50 1.25
13 Andre Johnson .50 1.25
14 Calvin Johnson .60 1.50
15 Larry Johnson .50 1.25
16 Matt Leinart .60 1.50
17 Marshawn Lynch .50 1.25
18 Eli Manning .60 1.50
19 Peyton Manning 1.00 2.50
20 Darren McFadden 2.00 5.00
21 Carson Palmer .60 1.50
22 Adrian Peterson 1.00 2.50
23 Aaron Rodgers 1.25 3.00
24 Ben Roethlisberger .60 1.50
25 Tony Romo .75 2.00
26 Matt Ryan 1.25 3.00
27 Jonathan Stewart .50 1.25
28 Fred Taylor .50 1.25
29 Devin Thomas .50 1.00
30 LaDainian Tomlinson .60 1.50
31 Brian Westbrook .50 1.25
32 Vince Young .50 1.25

2008 Score Team Logo Decals

COMPLETE SET (32) 5.00 12.00
1 Chicago Bears .40 1.00
2 Cincinnati Bengals .30 .75
3 Buffalo Bills .30 .75
4 Denver Broncos .40 1.00
5 Cleveland Browns .30 .75
6 Tampa Bay Buccaneers .30 .75
7 Arizona Cardinals .30 .75
8 San Diego Chargers .30 .75
9 Kansas City Chiefs .30 .75
10 Indianapolis Colts .40 1.00
11 Dallas Cowboys .50 1.25
12 Miami Dolphins .40 1.00
13 Philadelphia Eagles .30 .75
14 Atlanta Falcons .30 .75
15 San Francisco 49ers .40 1.00
16 New York Giants .40 1.00
17 Jacksonville Jaguars .30 .75
18 New York Jets .40 1.00
19 Detroit Lions .30 .75
20 Green Bay Packers .50 1.25
21 Carolina Panthers .30 .75
22 New England Patriots .40 1.00
23 Oakland Raiders .50 1.25
24 St. Louis Rams .30 .75
25 Baltimore Ravens .30 .75
26 Washington Redskins .40 1.00
27 New Orleans Saints .30 .75
28 Seattle Seahawks .30 .75
29 Pittsburgh Steelers .50 1.25
30 Houston Texans .30 .75
31 Tennessee Titans .30 .75
32 Minnesota Vikings .30 .75

2008 Score Franchise

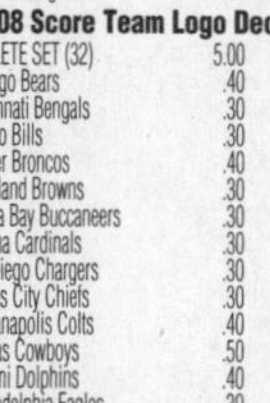

COMPLETE SET (25) 10.00 25.00
*GLOSSY: .5X TO 1.2X BASIC INSERTS
*SCORECARD/999: .6X TO 1.5X BASIC INSERTS
SCORECARD PRINT RUN 999 SER.#'d SETS
*GOLD ZONE/500: .8X TO 2X BASIC INSERTS
GOLD ZONE PRINT RUN 500 SER.#'d SETS
*RED ZONE/100: 1.5X TO 4X BASIC INSERTS
RED ZONE PRINT RUN 100 SER.#'d SETS
*ARTIST PROOF/32: 3X TO 8X BASIC INSERTS
ARTIST'S PROOF PRINT RUN 32 SER.#'d SETS
UNPRICED END ZONE PRINT RUN 6
1 Tony Romo .75 2.00
2 Tom Brady 1.00 2.50
3 Joseph Addai .50 1.25
4 Randy Moss .60 1.50
5 Terrell Owens .60 1.50
6 Aaron Rodgers 1.25 3.00
7 T.J. Houshmandzadeh .50 1.25
8 Ben Roethlisberger .60 1.50
9 Larry Johnson .50 1.25
10 Drew Brees .60 1.50
11 Jay Cutler .60 1.50
12 Eli Manning .60 1.50
13 Clinton Portis .50 1.25
14 Brian Westbrook .50 1.25
15 Torry Holt .50 1.25
16 Reggie Wayne .50 1.25
17 David Garrard .50 1.25
18 Steve Smith .50 1.25
19 Willie Parker .50 1.25
20 Edgerrin James .50 1.25
21 Andre Johnson .50 1.25
22 LaDainian Tomlinson .60 1.50
23 Donald Driver .50 1.25
24 Fred Taylor .50 1.25
25 Peyton Manning 1.00 2.50

2008 Score Future Franchise

*GLOSSY: .5X TO 1.2X BASIC INSERTS
*SCORECARD/999: .6X TO 1.5X BASIC INSERTS
SCORECARD PRINT RUN 999 SER.#'d SETS
*GOLD ZONE/500: .8X TO 2X BASIC INSERTS
GOLD ZONE PRINT RUN 500 SER.#'d SETS
*RED ZONE: 1.2X TO 3X BASIC INSERTS
RED ZONE PRINT RUN 100 SER.#'d SETS
*ARTIST'S PROOF: 2.5X TO 6X BASIC INSERTS
ARTIST'S PROOF PRINT RUN 32 SER.#'d SETS
UNPRICED END ZONE PRINT RUN 6
1 JaMarcus Russell .50 1.25
2 Brady Quinn .50 1.25
3 Brandon Jacobs .50 1.25
4 Adrian Peterson 1.00 2.50
5 Dallas Clark .50 1.25
6 Brandon Marshall .50 1.25
7 Santonio Holmes .50 1.25
8 Dwayne Bowe .50 1.25
9 Laurence Maroney .50 1.25
10 Marion Barber .50 1.25
11 Greg Jennings .60 1.50
12 Trent Edwards .40 1.00
13 Wes Welker .60 1.50
14 Michael Turner .60 1.50
15 Derek Anderson .40 1.00
16 Kevin Curtis .40 1.00
17 Reggie Bush .60 1.50
18 Chris Cooley .50 1.25
19 Maurice Jones-Drew .50 1.25
20 Braylon Edwards .50 1.25
21 Willis McGahee .50 1.25
22 Vince Young .50 1.25
23 Frank Gore .50 1.25
24 Roddy White .50 1.25
25 Marques Colston .50 1.25

2008 Score Hot Rookies

COMPLETE SET (25) 12.50 30.00
*GLOSSY: .5X TO 1.2X BASIC INSERTS
*SCORECARD/999: .6X TO 1.5X BASIC INSERTS
SCORECARD PRINT RUN 999 SER.#'d SETS
*GOLD ZONE/500: .8X TO 2X BASIC INSERTS
GOLD ZONE PRINT RUN 500 SER.#'d SETS
*RED ZONE/100: 1.2X TO 3X BASIC INSERTS
RED ZONE PRINT RUN 100 SER.#'d SETS
*ARTIST PROOF/32: 2.5X TO 6X BASIC INSERTS
ARTIST'S PROOF PRINT RUN 32 SER.#'d SETS
UNPRICED END ZONE PRINT RUN 6
1 Brian Brohm .60 1.50
2 Chad Henne .60 1.50
3 Chris Johnson 1.50 4.00
4 Darren McFadden 1.50 4.00
5 DeSean Jackson 1.25 3.00
6 Devin Thomas .50 1.25
7 Dexter Jackson .50 1.25
8 Donnie Avery .50 1.25
9 Eddie Royal .60 1.50
10 Felix Jones 1.00 2.50
11 Jamaal Charles 1.00 2.50
12 James Hardy .50 1.25
13 Jerome Simpson .60 1.50
14 Joe Flacco 2.00 5.00
15 Jonathan Stewart 1.00 2.50
16 Jordy Nelson .75 2.00
17 Kevin Smith .60 1.50
18 Limas Sweed .60 1.50
19 Malcolm Kelly .50 1.25
20 Mario Manningham .60 1.50
21 Matt Forte 1.00 2.50
22 Matt Ryan 2.50 6.00
23 Rashard Mendenhall 1.25 3.00
24 Ray Rice 1.25 3.00
25 Steve Slaton .60 1.50

2008 Score Inscriptions

STATED PRINT RUN 5-250
SERIAL #'d OF 5 NOT PRICED
362 Tracy Porter/100 8.00 20.00
366 Jordon Dizon/100 8.00 20.00
372 Quentin Groves/100 6.00 15.00
381 Anthony Alridge/250 6.00 15.00
387 Brad Cottam/100 6.00 15.00
389 Dantrell Savage/250 6.00 15.00
398 Marcus Smith/250 6.00 15.00
413 Owen Schmitt/242 8.00 20.00
416 Josh Morgan/250 8.00 20.00
419 Paul Hubbard/250 6.00 15.00
423 Chauncey Washington/100 6.00 15.00
424 Caleb Campbell/250 8.00 20.00
425 Peyton Hillis/125 15.00 40.00
426 Justin Forsett/100 8.00 20.00
427 Adrian Arrington/100 6.00 15.00
428 Cory Boyd/100 5.00 12.00
432 Darrell Strong/250 6.00 15.00
433 Jason Rivers/250 6.00 15.00
437 Ali Highsmith/250 5.00 12.00
439 Erin Henderson/250 8.00 20.00

2008 Score Young Stars

COMPLETE SET (25) 8.00 20.00
*GLOSSY: .5X TO 1.2X BASIC INSERTS
*SCORECARD/999: .6X TO 1.5X BASIC INSERTS
SCORECARD PRINT RUN 999 SER.#'d SETS
*GOLD ZONE/500: .8X TO 2X BASIC INSERTS
GOLD ZONE PRINT RUN 500 SER.#'d SETS
*RED ZONE/100: 1.2X TO 3X BASIC INSERTS
RED ZONE PRINT RUN 100 SER.#'d SETS
*ARTIST PROOF/32: 2.5X TO 6X BASIC INSERTS
ARTIST'S PROOF PRINT RUN 32 SER.#'d SETS
UNPRICED END ZONE PRINT RUN 6
1 Earnest Graham .50 1.25
2 Anthony Gonzalez .50 1.25
3 Ted Ginn Jr. .60 1.50
4 Marshawn Lynch .60 1.50
5 Calvin Johnson .75 2.00
6 Steve Smith USC .60 1.50
7 Kenny Watson .50 1.25
8 Vernon Davis .60 1.50
9 LenDale White .60 1.50
10 Vincent Jackson .40 1.00
11 Kolby Smith .50 1.25
12 Selvin Young .50 1.25
13 Patrick Willis .60 1.50
14 Lee Evans .60 1.50
15 Ahmad Bradshaw .60 1.50
16 Justin Fargas .50 1.25
17 Tarvaris Jackson .60 1.50
18 DeMeco Ryans .60 1.50
19 Fred Jackson 3.00 8.00
20 Patrick Crayton .60 1.50
21 James Jones .50 1.25
22 Michael Bush .60 1.50
23 Sidney Rice .75 2.00
24 LaRon Landry .60 1.50
25 Zach Miller .60 1.50

2008 Score Super Bowl XLIII

COMP.FACT.SET (440) 30.00 50.00
*RED: .4X TO 1X BASIC SCORE
BASE SET CARDS HAVE RED BORDER
*BLUE: .5X TO 1.2X RED BORDER
*GOLD: .6X TO 1.5X RED BORDER
*GREEN: .8X TO 2X RED BORDER
*BLACK: 1X TO 2.5X RED BORDER
*GLOSSY/250: 1.2X TO 3X RED

2009 Score

COMPLETE SET (400) 30.00 60.00
1 Adrian Wilson .12 .30
2 Anquan Boldin .15 .40
3 Dominique Rodgers-Cromartie .12 .30
4 Edgerrin James .15 .40
5 Kurt Warner .20 .50
6 Larry Fitzgerald .20 .50
7 Matt Leinart .15 .40
8 Steve Breaston .15 .40
9 Tim Hightower .12 .30
10 Chris Houston .12 .30
11 Curtis Lofton .12 .30
12 Harry Douglas .12 .30
13 Jerious Norwood .15 .40
14 John Abraham .12 .30
15 Matt Ryan .20 .50
16 Michael Jenkins .12 .30
17 Michael Turner .15 .40
18 Roddy White .15 .40
19 Demetrius Williams .12 .30
20 Derrick Mason .15 .40
21 Joe Flacco .20 .50
22 Le'Ron McClain .15 .40
23 Mark Clayton .12 .30
24 Ray Lewis .20 .50
25 Ray Rice .20 .50
26 Terrell Suggs .12 .30
27 Todd Heap .12 .30
28 Willis McGahee .15 .40
29 Derek Fine .12 .30
30 Fred Jackson .20 .50
31 James Hardy .15 .40
32 Lee Evans .15 .40
33 Leodis McKelvin .12 .30
34 Marshawn Lynch .15 .40
35 Paul Posluszny .15 .40
36 Steve Johnson .15 .40
37 Trent Edwards .12 .30
38 Charles Godfrey .12 .30
39 Chris Gamble .12 .30
40 Dante Rosario .12 .30
41 DeAngelo Williams .20 .50
42 Jake Delhomme .15 .40
43 Jon Beason .12 .30
44 Jonathan Stewart .15 .40
45 Muhsin Muhammad .15 .40
46 Steve Smith .15 .40
47 Alex Brown .12 .30
48 Brian Urlacher .20 .50
49 Desmond Clark .12 .30
50 Devin Hester .20 .50
51 Earl Bennett .15 .40
52 Greg Olsen .12 .30
53 Kyle Orton .15 .40
54 Lance Briggs .15 .40
55 Matt Forte .20 .50
56 Andre Caldwell .12 .30
57 Carson Palmer .20 .50
58 Cedric Benson .15 .40
59 Chad Ochocinco .15 .40
60 Dhani Jones .12 .30
61 Jerome Simpson .12 .30
62 Keith Rivers .12 .30
63 Reggie Kelly .12 .30
64 T.J. Houshmandzadeh .15 .40
65 Brady Quinn .15 .40
66 Braylon Edwards .15 .40
67 D'Qwell Jackson .12 .30
68 Jamal Lewis .15 .40
69 Jerome Harrison .12 .30
70 Josh Cribbs .20 .50
71 Kellen Winslow .15 .40
72 Shaun Rogers .12 .30
73 Steve Heiden .12 .30
74 DeMarcus Ware .15 .40
75 Felix Jones .20 .50
76 Jason Witten .20 .50
77 Marion Barber .15 .40
78 Patrick Crayton .12 .30
79 Roy Williams WR .15 .40
80 Tashard Choice .12 .30
81 Terrell Owens .20 .50
82 Terence Newman .12 .30
83 Tony Romo .30 .75
84 Brandon Marshall .15 .40
85 Brandon Stokley .15 .40
86 Champ Bailey .15 .40
87 Daniel Graham .12 .30
88 Eddie Royal .15 .40
89 Jay Cutler .20 .50
90 Peyton Hillis .20 .50
91 D.J. Williams .12 .30
92 Tony Scheffler .12 .30
93 Calvin Johnson .20 .50
94 Daunte Culpepper .15 .40
95 Ernie Sims .12 .30
96 Jerome Felton .12 .30
97 Jordon Dizon .12 .30
98 Kevin Smith .15 .40
99 Paris Lenon .12 .30
100 Rudi Johnson .12 .30
101 Shaun McDonald .12 .30
102 Aaron Rodgers .40 1.00
103 A.J. Hawk .15 .40
104 Brandon Jackson .15 .40
105 Donald Driver .15 .40
106 Donald Lee .12 .30
107 Greg Jennings .20 .50
108 James Jones .12 .30
109 Jermichael Finley .20 .50
110 Jordy Nelson .20 .50
111 Ryan Grant .15 .40
112 Amobi Okoye .12 .30
113 Andre Johnson .15 .40
114 Chester Pitts .12 .30
115 DeMeco Ryans .15 .40
116 Kevin Walter .15 .40
117 Kris Brown .12 .30
118 Mario Williams .15 .40
119 Matt Schaub .15 .40
120 Owen Daniels .12 .30
121 Steve Slaton .15 .40
122 Adam Vinatieri .15 .40
123 Anthony Gonzalez .12 .30
124 Dallas Clark .15 .40
125 Dominic Rhodes .12 .30
126 Dwight Freeney .15 .40
127 Joseph Addai .20 .50
128 Freddie Keiaho .12 .30
129 Mike Hart .15 .40
130 Peyton Manning .30 .75
131 Reggie Wayne .15 .40
132 David Garrard .15 .40
133 Dennis Northcutt .12 .30
134 Derrick Harvey .12 .30
135 Josh Scobee .12 .30
136 Marcedes Lewis .12 .30
137 Mike Peterson .12 .30
138 Maurice Jones-Drew .15 .40
139 Quentin Groves .12 .30
140 Reggie Nelson .12 .30
141 Brian Williams .12 .30
142 Derrick Johnson .12 .30
143 Matt Cassel .15 .40
144 Dwayne Bowe .15 .40
145 Jamaal Charles .20 .50
146 Kolby Smith .12 .30
147 Larry Johnson .15 .40
148 Mark Bradley .12 .30
149 Tony Gonzalez .15 .40
150 Tyler Thigpen .12 .30
151 Anthony Fasano .12 .30
152 Chad Henne .15 .40
153 Chad Pennington .15 .40
154 Davone Bess .12 .30
155 Joey Porter .15 .40
156 Greg Camarillo .15 .40
157 Jake Long .12 .30
158 Ricky Williams .15 .40
159 Ronnie Brown .15 .40
160 Ted Ginn .15 .40
161 Adrian Peterson .30 .75
162 Bernard Berrian .15 .40
163 Chad Greenway .12 .30
164 Chester Taylor .12 .30
165 Erin Henderson .12 .30
166 Jared Allen .20 .50
167 John David Booty .15 .40
168 Sidney Rice .15 .40
169 Tarvaris Jackson .15 .40
170 Visanthe Shiancoe .15 .40
171 Brandon Meriweather .12 .30
172 Jerod Mayo .15 .40
173 Kevin Faulk .12 .30
174 LaMont Jordan .12 .30
175 Laurence Maroney .15 .40
176 Randy Moss .20 .50
177 Tedy Bruschi .15 .40
178 Terrence Wheatley .12 .30
179 Tom Brady .30 .75
180 Wes Welker .20 .50
181 Adrian Arrington .12 .30
182 Devery Henderson .12 .30
183 Drew Brees .20 .50
184 Jeremy Shockey .12 .30
185 Jonathan Vilma .12 .30
186 Lance Moore .15 .40
187 Marques Colston .15 .40
188 Pierre Thomas .15 .40
189 Reggie Bush .20 .50
190 Scott Shanle .12 .30
191 Ahmad Bradshaw .15 .40
192 Antonio Pierce .12 .30
193 Brandon Jacobs .15 .40
194 Derrick Ward .12 .30
195 Domenik Hixon .12 .30
196 Eli Manning .20 .50
197 Justin Tuck .15 .40
198 Kenny Phillips .12 .30
199 Kevin Boss .15 .40
200 Steve Smith USC .15 .40
201 Calvin Pace .12 .30
202 Chansi Stuckey .12 .30
203 Dustin Keller .12 .30
204 Jerricho Cotchery .15 .40
205 Kellen Clemens .12 .30
206 Laveranues Coles .12 .30
207 Leon Washington .15 .40
208 Thomas Jones .15 .40
209 Vernon Gholston .12 .30
210 Chaz Schilens .12 .30
211 Darren McFadden .20 .50
212 JaMarcus Russell .12 .30
213 Johnnie Lee Higgins .12 .30
214 Justin Fargas .12 .30
215 Michael Bush .15 .40
216 Nnamdi Asomugha .15 .40
217 Sebastian Janikowski .12 .30
218 Zach Miller .12 .30
219 Brian Westbrook .15 .40
220 Correll Buckhalter .12 .30
221 DeSean Jackson .15 .40
222 Donovan McNabb .20 .50
223 Greg Lewis .12 .30
224 Hank Baskett .12 .30
225 Kevin Curtis .12 .30
226 Reggie Brown .12 .30
227 Stewart Bradley .12 .30
228 Ben Roethlisberger .20 .50
229 Heath Miller .15 .40
230 Hines Ward .15 .40
231 James Harrison .20 .50
232 Troy Polamalu .20 .50
233 Nate Washington .12 .30
234 Rashard Mendenhall .15 .40
235 Santonio Holmes .15 .40
236 Willie Parker .12 .30
237 Antonio Gates .15 .40
238 Chris Chambers .15 .40
239 Darren Sproles .15 .40
240 Eric Weddle .12 .30
241 Jacob Hester .12 .30
242 LaDainian Tomlinson .20 .50
243 Philip Rivers .20 .50
244 Shawne Merriman .15 .40
245 Vincent Jackson .15 .40
246 Brandon Jones .12 .30
247 Frank Gore .15 .40
248 Isaac Bruce .15 .40
249 Josh Morgan .12 .30
250 Michael Robinson .12 .30
251 Patrick Willis .15 .40
252 Reggie Smith .12 .30
253 Shaun Hill .12 .30
254 Vernon Davis .15 .40
255 Deion Branch .15 .40
256 John Carlson .15 .40
257 Julian Peterson .12 .30
258 Julius Jones .12 .30
259 Lofa Tatupu .15 .40
260 Matt Hasselbeck .15 .40
261 Nate Burleson .12 .30
262 Owen Schmitt .12 .30
263 T.J. Duckett .12 .30
264 Antonio Pittman .12 .30
265 Chris Long .15 .40
266 Donnie Avery .15 .40
267 Keenan Burton .12 .30
268 Marc Bulger .15 .40
269 Pisa Tinoisamoa .12 .30
270 Steven Jackson .15 .40
271 Torry Holt .15 .40
272 Antonio Bryant .12 .30
273 Aqib Talib .12 .30
274 Cadillac Williams .15 .40
275 Dexter Jackson .12 .30
276 Earnest Graham .12 .30
277 Gaines Adams .12 .30
278 Michael Clayton .12 .30
279 Ronde Barber .12 .30
280 Barrett Ruud .12 .30
281 Albert Haynesworth .12 .30
282 Bo Scaife .12 .30
283 Chris Johnson .20 .50
284 Justin Gage .12 .30
285 Keith Bulluck .12 .30
286 Kerry Collins .15 .40
287 LenDale White .15 .40
288 Rob Bironas .12 .30
289 Roydell Williams .12 .30
290 Vince Young .15 .40
291 Chris Cooley .15 .40
292 Chris Horton .15 .40
293 Clinton Portis .15 .40
294 Colt Brennan .15 .40
295 Devin Thomas .12 .30
296 Jason Campbell .12 .30
297 Kedric Golston RC .20 .50
298 Ladell Betts .12 .30
299 Malcolm Kelly .12 .30
300 Santana Moss .15 .40
301 Aaron Brown RC .50 1.25
302 Aaron Curry RC .50 1.25
303 Aaron Kelly RC .40 1.00
304 Aaron Maybin RC .40 1.00
305 Alphonso Smith RC .40 1.00
306 Andre Brown RC .30 .75
307 Andre Smith RC .40 1.00
308 Anthony Hill RC .30 .75
309 Arian Foster RC 1.00 2.50
310 Austin Collie RC .50 1.25
311 B.J. Raji RC .50 1.25
312 Brandon Gibson RC .50 1.25
313 Brandon Pettigrew RC .50 1.25
314 Brandon Tate RC .50 1.25
315 Brian Cushing RC .50 1.25
316 Brian Hartline RC .50 1.25
317 Brian Orakpo RC .50 1.25
318 Brian Robiskie RC .50 1.25
319 Brooks Foster RC .30 .75
320 Cameron Morrah RC .30 .75
321 Cedric Peerman RC .40 1.00
322 Chase Coffman RC .40 1.00
323 Chris Wells RC .75 2.00
324 Clay Matthews RC 1.25 3.00
325 Clint Sintim RC .50 1.25
326 Cornelius Ingram RC .30 .75
327 Curtis Painter RC .50 1.25
328 Darius Butler RC .50 1.25
329 Darius Passmore RC .40 1.00
330 Darrius Heyward-Bey RC .50 1.25
331 Davon Drew RC .40 1.00
332 Demetrius Byrd RC .40 1.00
333 Deon Butler RC .40 1.00
334 Derrick Williams RC .40 1.00
335 Devin Moore RC .40 1.00
336 Dominique Edison RC .30 .75
337 Donald Brown RC .50 1.25
338 Eugene Monroe RC .30 .75
339 Everette Brown RC .40 1.00
340 Gartrell Johnson RC .30 .75
341 Glen Coffee RC .40 1.00
342 Graham Harrell RC .50 1.25
343 Hakeem Nicks RC .75 2.00
344 Hunter Cantwell RC .50 1.25
345 Jairus Byrd RC .50 1.25
346 James Casey RC .40 1.00
347 James Davis RC .50 1.25
348 James Laurinaitis RC .50 1.25
349 Jared Cook RC .50 1.25
350 Jarett Dillard RC .50 1.25
351 Jason Smith RC .40 1.00
352 Javon Ringer RC .50 1.25
353 Jeremiah Johnson RC .50 1.25
354 Jeremy Childs RC .40 1.00
355 Jeremy Maclin RC .75 2.00
356 John Parker Wilson RC .50 1.25
357 Johnny Knox RC .75 2.00
358 Josh Freeman RC 1.00 2.50
359 Juaquin Iglesias RC .40 1.00
360 Keith Null RC .40 1.00
361 Kenny Britt RC .60 1.50
362 Kenny McKinley RC .50 1.25
363 Kevin Ogletree RC .50 1.25
364 Knowshon Moreno RC .50 1.25
365 Kory Sheets RC .40 1.00
366 Larry English RC .50 1.25
367 LeSean McCoy RC 1.00 2.50
368 Louis Murphy RC .50 1.25

369 Malcolm Jenkins RC .50 1.25
370 Mark Sanchez RC 1.50 4.00
371 Matthew Stafford RC 2.50 6.00
372 Michael Crabtree RC 1.00 2.50
373 Mike Goodson RC .50 1.25
374 Mike Thomas RC .50 1.25
375 Mike Wallace RC 1.00 2.50
376 Mohamed Massaquoi RC .40 1.00
377 Nate Davis RC .40 1.00
378 Nathan Brown RC .40 1.00
379 P.J. Hill RC .40 1.00
380 Pat White RC .50 1.25
381 Patrick Chung RC .50 1.25
382 Patrick Turner RC .40 1.00
383 Percy Harvin RC .75 2.00
384 Quan Cosby RC .40 1.00
385 Quinn Johnson RC .40 1.00
386 Quinten Lawrence RC .30 .75
387 Ramses Barden RC .30 .75
388 Rashad Jennings RC .50 1.25
389 Rey Maualuga RC .50 1.25
390 Rhett Bomar RC .40 1.00
391 Richard Quinn RC .40 1.00
392 Shawn Nelson RC .40 1.00
393 Shonn Greene RC .75 2.00
394 Stephen McGee RC .50 1.25
395 Tom Brandstater RC .50 1.25
396 Tony Fiammetta RC .40 1.00
397 Travis Beckum RC .40 1.00
398 Tyrell Sutton RC .40 1.00
399 Tyson Jackson RC .40 1.00
400 Vontae Davis RC .50 1.25

2009 Score Artist's Proof

*VETS 1-300: 12X TO 30X BASIC CARDS
*ROOKIES 301-400: 5X TO 12X BASIC CARDS
STATED PRINT RUN 32 SER.#'d SETS

2009 Score Glossy

*VETS 1-300: 1.2X TO 3X BASIC CARDS
*ROOKIES 301-400: .5X TO 1.2X BASIC CARDS
ONE GLOSSY PER SCORE PACK

2009 Score Gold Zone

*VETS 1-300: 4X TO 10X BASIC CARDS
*ROOKIES 301-400: 1.5X TO 4X BASIC CARDS
STATED PRINT RUN 249 SER.#'d SETS

2009 Score Red Zone

*VETS 1-300: 5X TO 12X BASIC CARDS
*ROOKIES 301-400: 2X TO 5X BASIC CARDS
STATED PRINT RUN 100 SER.#'d SETS

2009 Score Scorecard

*VETS 1-300: 3X TO 8X BASIC CARDS
*ROOKIES 301-400: 1.2X TO 3X BASIC CARDS
STATED PRINT RUN 299 SER.#'d SETS

2009 Score 1989 Score

*GLOSSY: .8X TO 2X BASIC INSERTS
1 Matthew Stafford 5.00 12.00
2 Mark Sanchez 3.00 8.00
3 Darrius Heyward-Bey 1.00 2.50
4 Michael Crabtree 2.00 5.00
5 Knowshon Moreno 1.00 2.50
6 Josh Freeman 2.00 5.00
7 Jeremy Maclin 1.50 4.00
8 Percy Harvin 1.50 4.00
9 Hakeem Nicks 1.50 4.00
10 Chris Wells 1.50 4.00

2009 Score 1989 Score Autographs

STATED PRINT RUN 20 SER.#'d SETS
1 Matthew Stafford 150.00 300.00
2 Mark Sanchez 150.00 300.00
3 Darrius Heyward-Bey 40.00 80.00
4 Michael Crabtree 100.00 200.00
5 Knowshon Moreno 100.00 200.00
6 Josh Freeman 75.00 150.00
7 Jeremy Maclin 60.00 120.00
8 Percy Harvin 150.00 250.00
9 Hakeem Nicks 40.00 80.00
10 Chris Wells 75.00 150.00

2009 Score Franchise

*ART.PROOF/32: 3X TO 8X BASIC INSERTS
*GLOSSY: .5X TO 1.2X BASIC INSERTS
*GOLD ZONE/299: 1.2X TO 3X BASIC INSERTS
*RED ZONE/100: 1.5X TO 4X BASIC INSERTS
*SCORECARD/499: .8X TO 2X BASIC INSERTS
1 Adrian Peterson 1.00 2.50
2 Andre Johnson .50 1.25
3 Brady Quinn .50 1.25
4 Brandon Jacobs .50 1.25
5 Brandon Marshall .50 1.25
6 Braylon Edwards .50 1.25
7 Brian Westbrook .50 1.25
8 Calvin Johnson .60 1.50
9 Clinton Portis .50 1.25
10 DeAngelo Williams .60 1.50
11 Frank Gore .50 1.25
12 Greg Jennings .60 1.50
13 Larry Fitzgerald .60 1.50
14 Lee Evans .50 1.25
15 Marion Barber .50 1.25
16 Maurice Jones-Drew .50 1.25
17 Philip Rivers .60 1.50
18 Roddy White .50 1.25
19 Santonio Holmes .50 1.25
20 Dwayne Bowe .50 1.25

2009 Score Future Franchise

*ART.PROOF/32: 2.5X TO 6X BASIC INSERTS
*GLOSSY: .5X TO 1.2X BASIC INSERTS
*GOLD ZONE/299: 1.2X TO 3X BASIC INSERTS
*RED ZONE/100: 1.5X TO 4X BASIC INSERTS
*SCORECARD/499: .8X TO 2X BASIC INSERTS
1 Brian Brohm .40 1.00
2 Chad Henne .50 1.25
3 Chris Johnson .60 1.50
4 Colt Brennan .50 1.25
5 Darren McFadden .60 1.50
6 Derrick Ward .40 1.00
7 DeSean Jackson .50 1.25
8 Eddie Royal .50 1.25
9 Erik Ainge .50 1.25
10 Joe Flacco .60 1.50
11 John David Booty .50 1.25
12 Jonathan Stewart .50 1.25
13 Kevin Smith .50 1.25
14 Matt Cassel .50 1.25
15 Matt Forte .60 1.50
16 Matt Ryan .60 1.50
17 Rashard Mendenhall .50 1.25
18 Ray Rice .60 1.50
19 Steve Slaton .50 1.25
20 Tashard Choice .40 1.00

2009 Score Hot Rookies

*ART.PROOF/32: 2.5X TO 6X BASIC INSERTS
*GLOSSY: .5X TO 1.2X BASIC INSERTS
*GOLD ZONE/299: 1X TO 2.5X BASIC INSERTS
*RED ZONE/100: 1.2X TO 3X BASIC INSERTS
*SCORECARD/499: .8X TO 2X BASIC INSERTS
1 Aaron Curry .60 1.50
2 Brandon Pettigrew .60 1.50
3 Brandon Tate .60 1.50
4 Brian Robiskie .60 1.50
5 Chris Wells 1.00 2.50
6 Darrius Heyward-Bey .60 1.50
7 Deon Butler .50 1.25
8 Derrick Williams .50 1.25
9 Donald Brown .60 1.50
10 Glen Coffee .50 1.25
11 Hakeem Nicks 1.00 2.50
12 Jeremy Maclin 1.00 2.50
13 Josh Freeman 1.25 3.00
14 Juaquin Iglesias .50 1.25
15 Kenny Britt .75 2.00
16 Knowshon Moreno .60 1.50
17 LeSean McCoy 1.25 3.00
18 Mark Sanchez 2.00 5.00
19 Matthew Stafford 3.00 8.00
20 Michael Crabtree 1.25 3.00
21 Mike Thomas .60 1.50
22 Mike Wallace 1.25 3.00
23 Mohamed Massaquoi .50 1.25
24 Pat White .60 1.50
25 Patrick Turner .50 1.25
26 Percy Harvin 1.00 2.50
27 Ramses Barden .40 1.00
28 Shonn Greene 1.00 2.50
29 Stephen McGee .60 1.50
30 Tyson Jackson .50 1.25

2009 Score Inscriptions Autographs Retail

RANDOM INSERTS IN SCORE PACKS
10 Chris Houston 4.00 10.00
11 Curtis Lofton 4.00 10.00
12 Harry Douglas 4.00 10.00
29 Derek Fine 4.00 10.00
30 Fred Jackson 12.00 30.00
36 Steve Johnson 8.00 20.00
38 Charles Godfrey 4.00 10.00
40 Dante Rosario 4.00 10.00
56 Andre Caldwell 4.00 10.00
58 Cedric Benson 5.00 12.00
96 Jerome Felton 4.00 10.00
103 A.J. Hawk 6.00 15.00
104 Brandon Jackson 5.00 12.00
112 Amobi Okoye 4.00 10.00
124 Dallas Clark 5.00 12.00
134 Derrick Harvey 4.00 10.00
139 Quentin Groves 4.00 10.00
165 Erin Henderson 4.00 10.00
171 Brandon Meriweather 4.00 10.00
178 Terrence Wheatley 4.00 10.00
181 Adrian Arrington 4.00 10.00
182 Devery Henderson 4.00 10.00
210 Chaz Schilens 4.00 10.00
223 Greg Lewis 4.00 10.00
262 Owen Schmitt 4.00 10.00
273 Aqib Talib 4.00 10.00
277 Gaines Adams 4.00 10.00
292 Chris Horton 5.00 12.00
303 Aaron Kelly 5.00 12.00
335 Devin Moore 5.00 12.00
363 Kevin Ogletree 6.00 15.00
365 Kory Sheets 5.00 12.00
379 P.J. Hill 5.00 12.00
384 Quan Cosby 5.00 12.00
398 Tyrell Sutton 5.00 12.00

2009 Score Young Stars

*ART.PRROF/32: 2.5X TO 6X BASIC INSERTS
*GLOSSY: .5X TO 1.2X BASIC INSERTS
*GOLD ZONE/299: 1X TO 2.5X BASIC INSERTS
*RED ZONE/100: 1.2X TO 3X BASIC INSERTS
*SCORECARD/499: .8X TO 2X BASIC INSERTS
1 Antoine Cason .50 1.25
2 Aqib Talib .50 1.25
3 Brandon Flowers .50 1.25
4 Chris Horton .60 1.50
5 Dan Connor .50 1.25
6 Davone Bess .50 1.25
7 Donnie Avery .60 1.50
8 Dustin Keller .50 1.25
9 Dwight Lowery .50 1.25
10 Felix Jones .75 2.00
11 Jerod Mayo .60 1.50
12 John Carlson .60 1.50
13 Josh Morgan .50 1.25
14 Leodis McKelvin .50 1.25
15 Le'Ron McClain .60 1.50
16 Malcolm Kelly .50 1.25
17 Martellus Bennett .50 1.25
18 Ryan Torain .50 1.25
19 Steve Johnson .60 1.50
20 Tim Hightower .50 1.25

2009 Score Atomic National Convention

COMPLETE SET (6) 8.00 20.00
*BLUE/50: .6X TO 1.5X
*GOLD/25: .8X TO 2X
*RED/50: .6X TO 1.5X
161 Adrian Peterson 1.50 4.00
323 Chris Wells 1.00 2.50
364 Knowshon Moreno .60 1.50
370 Mark Sanchez 2.00 5.00
371 Matthew Stafford 3.00 8.00
372 Michael Crabtree 1.25 3.00

2010 Score

COMPLETE SET (400) 25.00 50.00
COMP.FACT.HOBBY (400) 25.00 40.00
COMP.FACT.RETAIL (400) 25.00 40.00
COMP.FACT.w/JSYs (402) 35.00 50.00
1 Adrian Wilson .12 .30
2 Anquan Boldin .15 .40
3 Chris Wells .15 .40
4 Dominique Rodgers Cromartie .12 .30
5 Karlos Dansby .12 .30
6 Larry Fitzgerald .20 .50
7 Matt Leinart .15 .40
8 Steve Breaston .12 .30
9 Tim Hightower .12 .30
10 Curtis Lofton .12 .30
11 Jason Snelling .15 .40
12 Jerious Norwood .12 .30
13 Jonathan Babineaux .12 .30
14 Matt Ryan .20 .50
15 Michael Jenkins .12 .30
16 Michael Turner .12 .30
17 Roddy White .15 .40
18 Tony Gonzalez .15 .40
19 Derrick Mason .15 .40
20 Ed Reed .15 .40
21 Joe Flacco .20 .50
22 Mark Clayton .12 .30
23 Michael Oher .15 .40
24 Ray Lewis .20 .50
25 Ray Rice .15 .40
26 Terrell Suggs .12 .30
27 Todd Heap .12 .30
28 Willis McGahee .15 .40
29 Donte Whitner .12 .30
30 Fred Jackson .20 .50
31 Jairus Byrd .15 .40
32 Josh Reed .12 .30
33 Lee Evans .15 .40
34 Marshawn Lynch .15 .40
35 Paul Posluszny .15 .40
36 Ryan Fitzpatrick .20 .50
37 Aaron Schobel .12 .30
38 Chris Gamble .12 .30
39 DeAngelo Williams .15 .40
40 Matt Moore .15 .40
41 Jon Beason .12 .30
42 Jonathan Stewart .15 .40
43 Julius Peppers .15 .40
44 Richard Marshall .12 .30
45 Muhsin Muhammad .15 .40
46 Steve Smith .15 .40
47 Brian Urlacher .20 .50
48 Devin Hester .20 .50
49 Earl Bennett .15 .40
50 Garrett Wolfe .12 .30
51 Greg Olsen .12 .30
52 Jay Cutler .20 .50
53 Johnny Knox .15 .40
54 Lance Briggs .15 .40
55 Matt Forte .15 .40
56 Andre Caldwell .12 .30
57 Bernard Scott .12 .30
58 Carson Palmer .15 .40
59 Cedric Benson .15 .40
60 Chad Ochocinco .15 .40
61 Dhani Jones .12 .30
62 Johnathan Joseph .12 .30
63 Matt Jones .12 .30
64 Leon Hall .12 .30
65 Abram Elam RC .20 .50
66 Jake Delhomme .15 .40
67 James Davis .12 .30
68 Jerome Harrison .12 .30
69 Joe Thomas .12 .30
70 Josh Cribbs .20 .50
71 Kamerion Wimbley .12 .30
72 Mike Furrey .12 .30
73 Mohamed Massaquoi .15 .40
74 Bradie James .12 .30
75 DeMarcus Ware .15 .40
76 Felix Jones .15 .40
77 Jason Witten .20 .50
78 Jay Ratliff .15 .40
79 Marion Barber .15 .40
80 Mike Jenkins .12 .30
81 Miles Austin .20 .50
82 Roy Williams WR .15 .40
83 Tony Romo .25 .60
84 Brandon Marshall .15 .40
85 Champ Bailey .15 .40
86 Brian Dawkins .15 .40
87 Eddie Royal .12 .30
88 Elvis Dumervil .12 .30
89 Jabar Gaffney .12 .30
90 Knowshon Moreno .15 .40
91 Kyle Orton .15 .40
92 Tony Scheffler .12 .30
93 Brandon Pettigrew .12 .30
94 Bryant Johnson .12 .30
95 Calvin Johnson .20 .50
96 Dennis Northcutt .12 .30
97 Julian Peterson .12 .30
98 Kevin Smith .15 .40
99 Larry Foote .12 .30
100 Louis Delmas .12 .30
101 Matthew Stafford .20 .50
102 Aaron Rodgers .40 1.00
103 A.J. Hawk .15 .40
104 Charles Woodson .20 .50
105 Donald Driver .15 .40
106 Greg Jennings .15 .40
107 James Jones .12 .30
108 Jermichael Finley .15 .40
109 Jordy Nelson .20 .50
110 Ryan Grant .15 .40
111 Clay Matthews .20 .50
112 Andre Johnson .15 .40
113 Brian Cushing .12 .30
114 DeMeco Ryans .12 .30
115 Jacoby Jones .12 .30
116 Kevin Walter .15 .40
117 Mario Williams .15 .40
118 Matt Schaub .15 .40
119 Owen Daniels .12 .30
120 Steve Slaton .12 .30
121 Bob Sanders .15 .40
122 Austin Collie .15 .40
123 Clint Session .12 .30
124 Dallas Clark .15 .40
125 Donald Brown .15 .40
126 Dwight Freeney .15 .40
127 Joseph Addai .15 .40
128 Peyton Manning .30 .75
129 Pierre Garcon .15 .40
130 Reggie Wayne .15 .40
131 David Garrard .15 .40
132 Marcedes Lewis .12 .30
133 Maurice Jones-Drew .15 .40
134 Mike Sims-Walker .15 .40
135 Mike Thomas .15 .40
136 Rashean Mathis .12 .30
137 Aaron Kampman .15 .40
138 Torry Holt .15 .40
139 Zach Miller Jac .15 .40
140 Thomas Jones .15 .40
141 Brandon Flowers .12 .30
142 Chris Chambers .15 .40
143 Derrick Johnson .12 .30
144 Dwayne Bowe .15 .40
145 Jamaal Charles .15 .40
146 Matt Cassel .15 .40
147 Ryan Succop RC .12 .30
148 Tamba Hall .12 .30
149 Anthony Fasano .12 .30
150 Brian Hartline .15 .40
151 Chad Henne .15 .40
152 Davone Bess .12 .30
153 Greg Camarillo .12 .30
154 Chad Pennington .15 .40
155 Pat White .15 .40
156 Ricky Williams .15 .40
157 Ronnie Brown .15 .40
158 Ted Ginn .15 .40
159 Adrian Peterson .30 .75
160 Bernard Berrian .12 .30
161 Brett Favre .75 2.00
162 Cedric Griffin .12 .30
163 Chad Greenway .12 .30
164 Chester Taylor .12 .30
165 Jared Allen .20 .50
166 Percy Harvin .20 .50
167 Sidney Rice .15 .40
168 Visanthe Shiancoe .15 .40
169 Ben Watson .12 .30
170 Brandon Meriweather .12 .30
171 Vince Wilfork .12 .30
172 Julian Edelman .12 .30
173 Laurence Maroney .15 .40
174 Pierre Woods .12 .30
175 Randy Moss .20 .50
176 Tom Brady .30 .75
177 Wes Welker .20 .50
178 Darren Sharper .15 .40
179 Devery Henderson .12 .30
180 Drew Brees .20 .50
181 Garrett Hartley RC .12 .30
182 Jeremy Shockey .15 .40
183 Marques Colston .15 .40
184 Pierre Thomas .15 .40
185 Reggie Bush .20 .50
186 Robert Meachem .15 .40
187 Jonathan Vilma .12 .30
188 Ahmad Bradshaw .15 .40
189 Brandon Jacobs .15 .40
190 Eli Manning .20 .50
191 Hakeem Nicks .15 .40
192 Kenny Phillips .12 .30
193 Kevin Boss .15 .40
194 Justin Tuck .15 .40
195 Mario Manningham .15 .40
196 Steve Smith USC .15 .40
197 Terrell Thomas .12 .30
198 Brad Smith .12 .30
199 Braylon Edwards .15 .40
200 Darrelle Revis .15 .40
201 Dustin Keller .15 .40
202 Jerricho Cotchery .15 .40
203 Leon Washington .15 .40
204 Mark Sanchez .20 .50
205 Shonn Greene .15 .40
206 Antonio Cromartie .12 .30
207 Chaz Schilens .12 .30
208 Darren McFadden .15 .40
209 Jason Campbell .15 .40
210 Bruce Gradkowski .12 .30
211 Kirk Morrison .12 .30
212 Louis Murphy .15 .40
213 Michael Bush .12 .30
214 Nnamdi Asomugha .15 .40
215 Sebastian Janikowski .12 .30
216 Zach Miller .15 .40
217 Asante Samuel .12 .30
218 Brent Celek .15 .40
219 Kevin Kolb .15 .40
220 DeSean Jackson .15 .40
221 Donovan McNabb .20 .50
222 Jeremy Maclin .15 .40
223 Leonard Weaver .12 .30
224 LeSean McCoy .15 .40
225 Michael Vick .25 .60
226 Trent Cole .12 .30
227 Ben Roethlisberger .20 .50
228 Heath Miller .15 .40
229 Hines Ward .15 .40
230 James Harrison .20 .50
231 LaMarr Woodley .12 .30
232 Lawrence Timmons .12 .30
233 Mike Wallace .15 .40
234 Rashard Mendenhall .15 .40
235 Santonio Holmes .15 .40
236 Troy Polamalu .20 .50
237 Antonio Gates .15 .40
238 Darren Sproles .15 .40
239 Eric Weddle .12 .30
240 LaDainian Tomlinson .20 .50
241 Legedu Naanee .12 .30
242 Malcom Floyd .15 .40
243 Philip Rivers .20 .50
244 Shawne Merriman .15 .40
245 Vincent Jackson .12 .30
246 Alex Smith QB .15 .40
247 Dre Bly .12 .30
248 Frank Gore .15 .40
249 Glen Coffee .15 .40
250 Josh Morgan .15 .40
251 Manny Lawson .12 .30
252 Michael Crabtree .20 .50
253 Patrick Willis .15 .40
254 Vernon Davis .15 .40
255 Aaron Curry .15 .40
256 Deion Branch .12 .30
257 John Carlson .12 .30
258 Josh Wilson .12 .30
259 Julius Jones .12 .30
260 Justin Forsett .15 .40
261 Matt Hasselbeck .12 .30
262 Nate Burleson .12 .30
263 T.J. Houshmandzadeh .15 .40
264 Brandon Gibson .12 .30
265 Craig Dahl RC .15 .40
266 Danny Amendola .20 .50
267 Donnie Avery .15 .40
268 James Butler .12 .30
269 James Laurinaitis .15 .40
270 Chris Long .12 .30
271 Leonard Little .12 .30
272 Steven Jackson .15 .40
273 Antonio Bryant .12 .30
274 Aqib Talib .12 .30
275 Barrett Ruud .12 .30
276 Cadillac Williams .15 .40
277 Derrick Ward .12 .30
278 Josh Freeman .20 .50
279 Kellen Winslow Jr. .15 .40
280 Ronde Barber .12 .30
281 Sammie Stroughter .12 .30
282 Tanard Jackson .12 .30
283 Bo Scaife .12 .30
284 Chris Johnson .20 .50
285 Cortland Finnegan .12 .30
286 Justin Gage .12 .30
287 Kenny Britt .15 .40
288 LenDale White .12 .30
289 Nate Washington .12 .30
290 Rob Bironas .12 .30
291 Vince Young .12 .30
292 Antwaan Randle El .12 .30
293 Chris Cooley .15 .40
294 Chris Horton .12 .30
295 Clinton Portis .15 .40
296 Devin Thomas .12 .30
297 London Fletcher .12 .30
298 LaRon Landry .12 .30
299 Albert Haynesworth .12 .30
300 Santana Moss .15 .40
301 Aaron Hernandez RC .75 2.00
302 Andre Anderson RC .40 1.00
303 Andre Dixon RC .50 1.25
304 Andre Roberts RC .50 1.25
305 Anthony Dixon RC .50 1.25
306 Anthony McCoy RC .40 1.00
307 Antonio Brown RC .75 2.00
308 Arrelious Benn RC .50 1.25
309 Ben Tate RC .60 1.50
310 Blair White RC .50 1.25
311 Brandon Graham RC .40 1.00
312 Brandon LaFell RC .50 1.25
313 Brandon Spikes RC .50 1.25
314 Bryan Bulaga RC .50 1.25
315 C.J. Spiller RC .75 2.00
316 Carlos Dunlap RC .50 1.25
317 Carlton Mitchell RC .40 1.00
318 Chad Jones RC .50 1.25
319 Charles Scott RC .40 1.00
320 Armanti Edwards RC .50 1.25
321 Chris Cook RC .50 1.25
322 Chris McGaha RC .30 .75
323 Colt McCoy RC 1.00 2.50
324 Corey Wootton RC .40 1.00
325 Damian Williams RC .50 1.25
326 Dan LeFevour RC .50 1.25
327 Tyson Alualu RC .40 1.00
328 Daryl Washington RC .40 1.00
329 David Gettis RC .50 1.25
330 Demaryius Thomas RC .60 1.50
331 Derrick Morgan RC .40 1.00
332 Devin McCourty RC .50 1.25
333 Dexter McCluster RC .50 1.25
334 Dez Bryant RC 1.50 4.00
335 Dezmon Briscoe RC .40 1.00
336 Dominique Franks RC .30 .75
337 Earl Thomas RC .50 1.25
338 Ed Dickson RC .50 1.25
339 Eric Berry RC .50 1.25
340 Eric Decker RC .60 1.50
341 Everson Griffen RC .50 1.25
342 Freddie Barnes RC .40 1.00
343 Garrett Graham RC .40 1.00
344 Gerald McCoy RC .50 1.25
345 Golden Tate RC .50 1.25
346 Jacoby Ford RC .50 1.25
347 Jahvid Best RC .75 2.00
348 James Starks RC .75 2.00
349 Jarrett Brown RC .50 1.25
350 Jason Pierre-Paul RC .75 2.00
351 Jason Worilds RC .50 1.25
352 Jeremy Williams RC .30 .75
353 Jermaine Gresham RC .60 1.50
354 Jerry Hughes RC .50 1.25
355 Jevan Snead RC .50 1.25
356 Jimmy Clausen RC .50 1.25
357 Jimmy Graham RC 1.00 2.50
358 Joe Haden RC .50 1.25
359 Joe McKnight RC .50 1.25
360 John Skelton RC .50 1.25
361 Emmanuel Sanders RC .50 1.25
362 Jonathan Crompton RC .40 1.00
363 Jonathan Dwyer RC .50 1.25
364 Jordan Shipley RC .50 1.25
365 Kareem Jackson RC .50 1.25
366 Kyle Wilson RC .50 1.25
367 LeGarrette Blount RC .75 2.00
368 Lonyae Miller RC .40 1.00
369 Marcus Easley RC .40 1.00
370 Mardy Gilyard RC .50 1.25
371 Mike Kafka RC .50 1.25
372 Mike Williams RC .75 2.00
373 Montario Hardesty RC .50 1.25
374 Morgan Burnett RC .50 1.25
375 Nate Allen RC .50 1.25
376 NaVorro Bowman RC .50 1.25
377 Ndamukong Suh RC 1.00 2.50
378 Pat Paschall RC .40 1.00
379 Patrick Robinson RC .50 1.25
380 Perrish Cox RC .40 1.00
381 Ricky Sapp RC .40 1.00
382 Riley Cooper RC .50 1.25
383 Rob Gronkowski RC 1.25 3.00
384 Rolando McClain RC .50 1.25
385 Russell Okung RC .50 1.25
386 Ryan Mathews RC 1.00 2.50
387 Sam Bradford RC 2.00 5.00
388 Sean Canfield RC .40 1.00
389 Sean Lee RC .50 1.25
390 Sean Weatherspoon RC .50 1.25
391 Sergio Kindle RC .50 1.25
392 Seyi Ajirotutu RC .50 1.25
393 Shay Hodge RC .40 1.00
394 Taylor Mays RC .50 1.25
395 Taylor Price RC .50 1.25
396 Tim Tebow RC 3.00 6.00
397 Toby Gerhart RC .50 1.25
398 Tony Pike RC .50 1.25
399 Trent Williams RC .50 1.25
400 Zac Robinson RC .40 1.00

2010 Score Artist's Proof

*VETS 1-300: 12X TO 30X BASIC CARDS
*ROOKIES 301-400: 5X TO 12X BASIC CARDS
STATED PRINT RUN 32 SER.#'d SETS

2010 Score Glossy

*VETS 1-300: 1.2X TO 3X BASIC CARDS
*ROOKIES 301-400: .6X TO 1.5X BASIC CARDS
ONE PER PACK, SIX PER RACK PACK

2010 Score Gold Zone

*VETS 1-300: 3X TO 8X BASIC CARDS
*ROOKIES 301-400: 1.2X TO 3X BASIC CARDS
STATED PRINT RUN 299 SER.#'d SETS

2010 Score Red Zone

*VETS 1-300: 5X TO 12X BASIC CARDS
*ROOKIES 301-400: 1X TO 5X BASIC CARDS
STATED PRINT RUN 100 SER.#'d SETS

2010 Score Scorecard

*VETS 1-300: 2.5X TO 6X BASIC CARDS
*ROOKIES 301-400: 1X TO 2.5X BASIC CARDS
STATED PRINT RUN 499 SER.#'d SETS

2010 Score All Pro

COMPLETE SET (30) 8.00 20.00
*ARTIST PROOF/32: 3X TO 8X BASIC INSERT
*GLOSSY: .5X TO 1.2X BASIC INSERT
*GOLD ZONE/299: 1.2X TO 3X BASIC INSERT
*RED ZONE/100: 1.5X TO 4X BASIC INSERT
*SCORECARD/499: .8X TO 2X BASIC INSERT
1 Peyton Manning 1.00 2.50
2 Chris Johnson .60 1.50
3 Adrian Peterson 1.00 2.50
4 Leonard Weaver .40 1.00
5 Andre Johnson .50 1.25
6 Wes Welker .60 1.50
7 Dallas Clark .50 1.25
8 Jared Allen .60 1.50
9 Dwight Freeney .50 1.25
10 Jay Ratliff .50 1.25
11 Kevin Williams .40 1.00
12 Patrick Willis .50 1.25
13 Ray Lewis .60 1.50
14 Elvis Dumervil .40 1.00
15 DeMarcus Ware .50 1.25
16 Charles Woodson .60 1.50
17 Darrelle Revis .50 1.25
18 Darren Sharper .50 1.25
19 Adrian Wilson .40 1.00
20 Shane Lechler .40 1.00
21 Nate Kaeding .40 1.00
22 Josh Cribbs .60 1.50
23 Drew Brees .60 1.50
24 Ray Rice .50 1.25
25 Steven Jackson .50 1.25
26 Reggie Wayne .50 1.25
27 Larry Fitzgerald .60 1.50
28 Antonio Gates .50 1.25
29 DeSean Jackson .50 1.25
30 Brian Cushing .40 1.00

2010 Score All Pro Signatures

STATED PRINT RUN 10-25
EXCH EXPIRATION: 1/9/2012
1 Peyton Manning/10
2 Chris Johnson/10
3 Adrian Peterson/10
5 Andre Johnson/10 EXCH
7 Dallas Clark/10
15 DeMarcus Ware/25 15.00 40.00
17 Darrelle Revis/25 12.00 30.00
22 Josh Cribbs/10
23 Drew Brees/10
24 Ray Rice/10
26 Reggie Wayne/10
28 Antonio Gates/10
29 DeSean Jackson/15 12.00 30.00

2010 Score Franchise

COMPLETE SET (20) 8.00 20.00
*ARTIST PROOF/32: 3X TO 8X BASIC INSERT
*GLOSSY: .5X TO 1.2X BASIC INSERT
*GOLD ZONE/299: 1.2X TO 3X BASIC INSERT
*RED ZONE/100: 1.5X TO 4X BASIC INSERT
*SCORECARD/499: .8X TO 2X BASIC INSERT
1 Mark Sanchez .60 1.50
2 Matthew Stafford .60 1.50
3 Sidney Rice .50 1.25
4 Drew Brees .60 1.50
5 Michael Turner .40 1.00
6 DeAngelo Williams .50 1.25
7 LeSean McCoy .50 1.25
8 Steven Jackson .50 1.25
9 Peyton Manning 1.00 2.50
10 Jay Cutler .60 1.50
11 Chris Johnson .60 1.50
12 Miles Austin .60 1.50
13 Michael Crabtree .60 1.50
14 Aaron Rodgers 1.25 3.00
15 Josh Freeman .60 1.50
16 Knowshon Moreno .50 1.25
17 Tom Brady 1.00 2.50
18 Jamaal Charles .50 1.25
19 Chad Ochocinco .50 1.25
20 Eli Manning .60 1.50

2010 Score Franchise Signatures

STATED PRINT RUN 1-25
EXCH EXPIRATION: 1/9/2012
1 Mark Sanchez/25 30.00 60.00
2 Matthew Stafford/10
3 Sidney Rice/5
4 Drew Brees/5
5 Michael Turner/5 EXCH
6 DeAngelo Williams/10
9 Peyton Manning/5
10 Jay Cutler
11 Chris Johnson/5
13 Michael Crabtree/25 15.00 30.00
14 Aaron Rodgers/5
16 Knowshon Moreno/5 EXCH
17 Tom Brady/1
18 Jamaal Charles/5
19 Chad Ochocinco/5
20 Eli Manning/15 40.00 80.00

2010 Score Hot Rookies

COMPLETE SET (30) 25.00 50.00
*ARTIST PROOF/32: 2.5X TO 6X BASIC INSERT
*GLOSSY: .5X TO 1.2X BASIC INSERT
*GOLD ZONE/299: 1X TO 2.5X BASIC INSERT
*RED ZONE/100: 1.2X TO 3X BASIC INSERT
*SCORECARD/499: .8X TO 2X BASIC INSERT
1 Armanti Edwards .60 1.50
2 Tim Tebow 2.50 6.00
3 Sam Bradford 2.50 6.00
4 Rolando McClain .60 1.50
5 Ndamukong Suh 1.25 3.00
6 Mardy Gilyard .60 1.50
7 Jimmy Clausen .60 1.50
8 Jahvid Best 1.00 2.50
9 Gerald McCoy .60 1.50
10 Eric Berry .60 1.50
11 Dexter McCluster .60 1.50
12 Damian Williams .60 1.50
13 C.J. Spiller 1.00 2.50
14 Ben Tate .75 2.00
15 Andre Roberts .60 1.50
16 Arrelious Benn .60 1.50
17 Brandon LaFell .60 1.50
18 Colt McCoy 1.25 3.00
19 Demaryius Thomas .75 2.00
20 Dez Bryant 2.00 5.00
21 Eric Decker .75 2.00
22 Golden Tate .60 1.50
23 Jermaine Gresham .75 2.00
24 Jordan Shipley .60 1.50
25 Montario Hardesty .60 1.50
26 Rob Gronkowski 1.50 4.00
27 Ryan Mathews 1.25 3.00
28 Taylor Price .60 1.50
29 Toby Gerhart .60 1.50
30 Emmanuel Sanders .60 1.50

2010 Score Hot Rookies Signatures

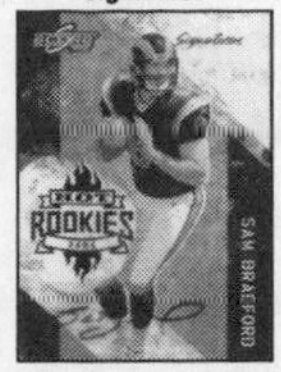

STATED PRINT RUN 25 SER.#'d SETS
EXCH EXPIRATION: 1/9/2012
1 Armanti Edwards 10.00 25.00
2 Tim Tebow 150.00 250.00
3 Sam Bradford 100.00 200.00
4 Rolando McClain 10.00 25.00
5 Ndamukong Suh 20.00 50.00
6 Mardy Gilyard 10.00 25.00
7 Jimmy Clausen 12.00 30.00
8 Jahvid Best 15.00 40.00
9 Gerald McCoy 10.00 25.00
10 Eric Berry 20.00 50.00
11 Dexter McCluster 10.00 25.00
12 Damian Williams 10.00 25.00
13 C.J. Spiller 20.00 50.00
14 Ben Tate 12.00 30.00
15 Andre Roberts 10.00 25.00
16 Arrelious Benn 10.00 25.00
17 Brandon LaFell 10.00 25.00
18 Colt McCoy 20.00 50.00
19 Demaryius Thomas 12.00 30.00
20 Dez Bryant 50.00 100.00
21 Eric Decker 12.00 30.00
22 Golden Tate 10.00 25.00
23 Jermaine Gresham 12.00 30.00
24 Jordan Shipley 10.00 25.00
25 Montario Hardesty 10.00 25.00
26 Rob Gronkowski 30.00 60.00
27 Ryan Mathews 40.00 100.00
28 Taylor Price 10.00 25.00
29 Toby Gerhart 10.00 25.00
30 Emmanuel Sanders 10.00 25.00

2010 Score NFL Players

COMPLETE SET (19) 8.00 20.00
*ARTIST PROOF/32: 3X TO 8X BASIC INSERT
*GLOSSY: .5X TO 1.2X BASIC INSERT
*GOLD ZONE/299: 1.2X TO 3X BASIC INSERT
*RED ZONE/100: 1.5X TO 4X BASIC INSERT
*SCORECARD/499: .8X TO 2X BASIC INSERT
1 Aaron Rodgers 1.25 3.00
2 Adrian Peterson 1.00 2.50
3 Andre Johnson .50 1.25
4 Ben Roethlisberger .60 1.50
5 Brandon Jacobs .50 1.25
6 Brett Favre 1.50 4.00
7 Brian Urlacher .60 1.50
8 Carson Palmer .50 1.25
9 Chad Ochocinco .50 1.25
10 Chad Pennington .50 1.25
11 Drew Brees .60 1.50
12 Jay Cutler .60 1.50
13 Larry Fitzgerald .60 1.50
14 Mark Sanchez .60 1.50
15 Matt Ryan .60 1.50
16 Peyton Manning 1.00 2.50
17 Ronde Barber .40 1.00
18 Tom Brady 1.00 2.50
19 Tony Romo .75 2.00

2010 Score NFL Players Signatures

STATED PRINT RUN 1-25
EXCH EXPIRATION: 1/9/2012
1 Aaron Rodgers/10
2 Adrian Peterson/10 EXCH
3 Andre Johnson/10 EXCH
4 Ben Roethlisberger/10
5 Brandon Jacobs/10 EXCH
6 Brett Favre/10
8 Carson Palmer/10
9 Chad Ochocinco/10
11 Drew Brees/10
12 Jay Cutler/10
14 Mark Sanchez/25 30.00 60.00
15 Matt Ryan/10
16 Peyton Manning/10
18 Tom Brady/1
19 Tony Romo/15 40.00 80.00

2010 Score Retail Factory Set Jerseys

ONE JSY PER RETAIL FACTORY SET
1 Michael Crabtree 3.00 8.00
2 LeSean McCoy 2.50 6.00
3 Percy Harvin 3.00 8.00
4 Chris Wells 2.50 6.00
5 Mark Sanchez 3.00 8.00
6 Shonn Greene 2.50 6.00
7 Knowshon Moreno 2.50 6.00
8 Matt Forte 2.50 6.00
9 Rashard Mendenhall 2.50 6.00
10 Chris Johnson 3.00 8.00
11 Felix Jones 2.50 6.00
12 Ray Rice 2.50 6.00
13 Sidney Rice 2.50 6.00
14 Adrian Peterson 5.00 12.00
15 Calvin Johnson 3.00 8.00
16 Maurice Jones-Drew 2.50 6.00
17 Kevin Kolb 2.50 6.00
18 Reggie Bush 3.00 8.00
19 Vernon Davis 2.50 6.00
20 DeAngelo Williams 2.50 6.00
21 Matt Ryan 3.00 8.00

2010 Score Retail Factory Set Rookie Jerseys

ONE JSY PER RETAIL FACTORY SET
1 Sam Bradford 6.00 15.00
2 Tim Tebow 8.00 20.00
3 Jimmy Clausen 1.50 4.00
4 Colt McCoy 3.00 8.00
5 Ndamukong Suh 3.00 8.00
6 Dez Bryant 5.00 12.00
7 Ryan Mathews 4.00 10.00
8 C.J. Spiller 2.50 6.00
9 Demaryius Thomas 2.00 5.00
10 Jahvid Best 2.50 6.00

2010 Score Select Factory Set Rookie Bonus

COMPLETE SET (10)	6.00	15.00
INSERTED IN SCORE FACTORY SET		
1 Sam Bradford	1.50	4.00
2 Jahvid Best	.60	1.50
3 Dez Bryant	1.25	3.00
4 Jimmy Clausen	.40	1.00
5 Ryan Mathews	.75	2.00
6 Colt McCoy	.75	2.00
7 C.J. Spiller	.60	1.50
8 Ndamukong Suh	.75	2.00
9 Tim Tebow	1.50	4.00
10 Demaryius Thomas	.50	1.25

2010 Score Signatures

EXCH EXPIRATION: 1/9/2012		
3 Chris Wells	6.00	15.00
10 Curtis Lofton	4.00	10.00
12 Jerious Norwood	4.00	10.00
17 Roddy White	5.00	12.00
21 Joe Flacco		
23 Michael Oher	15.00	30.00
39 DeAngelo Williams	6.00	15.00
46 Steve Smith	5.00	12.00
50 Garrett Wolfe	4.00	10.00
55 Matt Forte	6.00	15.00
57 Bernard Scott	4.00	10.00
58 Carson Palmer		
64 Leon Hall	4.00	10.00
67 James Davis	4.00	10.00
80 Mike Jenkins	4.00	10.00
83 Tony Romo		
87 Eddie Royal	4.00	10.00
91 Kyle Orton	5.00	12.00
93 Brandon Pettigrew	4.00	10.00
101 Matthew Stafford		
103 A.J. Hawk	6.00	15.00
107 James Jones	4.00	10.00
109 Jordy Nelson	6.00	15.00
114 DeMeco Ryans	4.00	10.00
118 Matt Schaub	6.00	15.00
122 Austin Collie	6.00	15.00
129 Pierre Garcon	6.00	15.00
144 Dwayne Bowe	5.00	12.00
155 Pat White	5.00	12.00
157 Ronnie Brown	6.00	15.00
161 Brett Favre		
164 Chester Taylor	4.00	10.00
176 Tom Brady		
179 Devery Henderson	4.00	10.00
190 Eli Manning	25.00	50.00
192 Kenny Phillips	4.00	10.00
193 Kevin Boss	5.00	12.00
197 Terrell Thomas	4.00	10.00
200 Darrelle Revis	5.00	12.00
201 Dustin Keller	5.00	12.00
204 Mark Sanchez	25.00	50.00
207 Chaz Schilens	4.00	10.00
212 Louis Murphy	5.00	12.00
220 DeSean Jackson	6.00	15.00
221 Donovan McNabb		
222 Jeremy Maclin	6.00	15.00
225 Michael Vick	25.00	50.00
227 Ben Roethlisberger		
232 Lawrence Timmons	4.00	10.00
233 Mike Wallace	6.00	15.00
237 Antonio Gates	5.00	12.00
239 Eric Weddle	4.00	10.00
241 Legedu Naanee	4.00	10.00
245 Vincent Jackson	4.00	10.00
249 Glen Coffee	6.00	15.00
252 Michael Crabtree	12.50	25.00
258 Josh Wilson	4.00	10.00
260 Justin Forsett	5.00	12.00
291 Vince Young		
294 Chris Horton	4.00	10.00
298 LaRon Landry	6.00	15.00
301 Aaron Hernandez	8.00	20.00
302 Andre Anderson	4.00	10.00
303 Andre Dixon	5.00	12.00
304 Andre Roberts	5.00	12.00
305 Anthony Dixon	5.00	12.00
306 Anthony McCoy	4.00	10.00
307 Antonio Brown	6.00	15.00
308 Arrelious Benn	5.00	12.00
309 Ben Tate	6.00	15.00
310 Blair White	5.00	12.00
311 Brandon Graham	4.00	10.00
312 Brandon LaFell	5.00	12.00
313 Brandon Spikes	5.00	12.00
314 Bryan Bulaga	5.00	12.00
315 C.J. Spiller	25.00	50.00
316 Carlos Dunlap	5.00	12.00
317 Carlton Mitchell	4.00	10.00
318 Chad Jones	5.00	12.00
319 Charles Scott	4.00	10.00
320 Armanti Edwards	5.00	12.00
321 Chris Cook	5.00	12.00
322 Chris McGaha	3.00	8.00
323 Colt McCoy	25.00	50.00
324 Corey Wootton	4.00	10.00
325 Damian Williams	5.00	12.00
326 Dan LeFevour	5.00	12.00
328 Daryl Washington No AU	1.25	3.00
329 David Gettis	5.00	12.00
330 Demaryius Thomas	6.00	15.00
331 Derrick Morgan	4.00	10.00
332 Devin McCourty	5.00	12.00
333 Dexter McCluster	5.00	12.00
334 Dez Bryant	30.00	60.00
335 Dezmon Briscoe	4.00	10.00
336 Dominique Franks	3.00	8.00
337 Earl Thomas	5.00	12.00
338 Ed Dickson	5.00	12.00
339 Eric Berry	12.00	30.00
340 Eric Decker	6.00	15.00
341 Everson Griffen	5.00	12.00
342 Freddie Barnes	4.00	10.00
343 Garrett Graham	4.00	10.00
344 Gerald McCoy	5.00	12.00
345 Golden Tate	5.00	12.00
346 Jacoby Ford	6.00	15.00
347 Jahvid Best	25.00	50.00
348 James Starks	10.00	25.00
349 Jarrett Brown	5.00	12.00
350 Jason Pierre-Paul	8.00	20.00
351 Jason Worilds	5.00	12.00
352 Jeremy Williams	3.00	8.00
353 Jermaine Gresham	6.00	15.00
354 Jerry Hughes	5.00	12.00
355 Jevan Snead	5.00	12.00
356 Jimmy Clausen	12.00	30.00
357 Jimmy Graham	15.00	30.00
358 Joe Haden	5.00	12.00
359 Joe McKnight	5.00	12.00
360 John Skelton	5.00	12.00
361 Emmanuel Sanders	5.00	12.00
362 Jonathan Crompton	4.00	10.00
363 Jonathan Dwyer	5.00	12.00
364 Jordan Shipley	5.00	12.00
365 Kareem Jackson	5.00	12.00
366 Kyle Wilson	5.00	12.00
367 LeGarrette Blount	12.00	30.00
368 Lonyae Miller	4.00	10.00
369 Marcus Easley	4.00	10.00
370 Mardy Gilyard	5.00	12.00
371 Mike Kafka	5.00	12.00
372 Mike Williams	8.00	20.00
373 Montario Hardesty	5.00	12.00
374 Morgan Burnett	5.00	12.00
375 Nate Allen	5.00	12.00
376 NaVorro Bowman	5.00	12.00
377 Ndamukong Suh	25.00	50.00
378 Pat Paschall	4.00	10.00
379 Patrick Robinson	5.00	12.00
380 Perrish Cox	4.00	10.00
381 Ricky Sapp	4.00	10.00
382 Riley Cooper	5.00	12.00
383 Rob Gronkowski	15.00	30.00
384 Rolando McClain	5.00	12.00
385 Russell Okung	5.00	12.00
386 Ryan Mathews	25.00	50.00
387 Sam Bradford	40.00	80.00
388 Sean Canfield	4.00	10.00
389 Sean Lee	5.00	12.00
390 Sean Weatherspoon	5.00	12.00
391 Sergio Kindle	5.00	12.00
392 Seyi Ajirotutu	5.00	12.00
393 Shay Hodge	4.00	10.00
394 Taylor Mays	5.00	12.00
395 Taylor Price	5.00	12.00
396 Tim Tebow	60.00	120.00
397 Toby Gerhart	5.00	12.00
398 Tony Pike	5.00	12.00
399 Trent Williams EXCH	5.00	12.00
400 Zac Robinson	4.00	10.00

2011 Score

COMP.SET w/o SP's (400)	25.00	50.00
COMP.RETAIL FACT.SET (402)	40.00	60.00
*ROOKIE VARIATION SP: 1.5X TO 4X		
ONE ROOKIE PER PACK		
1 Adrian Wilson	.12	.30
2 Chris Wells	.15	.40
3 Darnell Dockett	.12	.30
4 Dominique Rodgers-Cromartie	.12	.30
5 Jay Feely	.12	.30
6 LaRod Stephens-Howling	.12	.30
7 Larry Fitzgerald	.15	.40
8 Steve Breaston	.12	.30
9 Tim Hightower	.12	.30
10 Brent Grimes RC	.20	.50
11 Curtis Lofton	.12	.30
12 Eric Weems RC	.20	.50
13 Jason Snelling	.15	.40
14 John Abraham	.12	.30
15 Matt Ryan	.20	.50
16 Michael Jenkins	.12	.30
17 Michael Turner	.15	.40
18 Roddy White	.15	.40
19 Tony Gonzalez	.15	.40
20 Anquan Boldin	.15	.40
21 Derrick Mason	.12	.30
22 Ed Reed	.15	.40
23 Haloti Ngata	.12	.30
24 Joe Flacco	.20	.50
25 Michael Oher	.12	.30
26 Ray Lewis	.20	.50
27 Ray Rice	.15	.40
28 Terrell Suggs	.12	.30
29 Todd Heap	.12	.30
30 C.J. Spiller	.15	.40
31 Fred Jackson	.20	.50
32 Jairus Byrd	.12	.30
33 Kyle Williams	.12	.30
34 Lee Evans	.15	.40
35 Paul Posluszny	.12	.30
36 Roscoe Parrish	.12	.30
37 Ryan Fitzpatrick	.15	.40
38 Steve Johnson	.15	.40
39 Chris Gamble	.12	.30
40 David Gettis	.12	.30
41 DeAngelo Williams	.15	.40
42 Brandon LaFell	.12	.30
43 Jimmy Clausen	.12	.30
44 Jon Beason	.12	.30
45 Jonathan Stewart	.15	.40
46 Mike Goodson	.12	.30
47 Steve Smith	.15	.40
48 Brian Urlacher	.20	.50
49 Devin Hester	.20	.50
50 Earl Bennett	.12	.30
51 Greg Olsen	.12	.30
52 Jay Cutler	.15	.40
53 Johnny Knox	.15	.40
54 Julius Peppers	.15	.40
55 Lance Briggs	.15	.40
56 Matt Forte	.15	.40
57 Bernard Scott	.12	.30
58 Carson Palmer	.15	.40
59 Cedric Benson	.15	.40
60 Chad Johnson	.15	.40
61 Dhani Jones	.12	.30
62 Jermaine Gresham	.15	.40
63 Jordan Shipley	.15	.40
64 Leon Hall	.12	.30
65 Terrell Owens	.20	.50
66 Abram Elam	.12	.30
67 Ben Watson	.12	.30
68 Colt McCoy	.15	.40
69 Joe Haden	.12	.30
70 Joe Thomas	.12	.30
71 Josh Cribbs	.15	.40
72 Mohamed Massaquoi	.15	.40
73 Peyton Hillis	.15	.40
74 T.J. Ward	.12	.30
75 Bradie James	.12	.30
76 DeMarcus Ware	.15	.40
77 Dez Bryant	.20	.50
78 Felix Jones	.15	.40
79 Jason Witten	.20	.50
80 Jay Ratliff	.15	.40
81 Marion Barber	.15	.40
82 Miles Austin	.15	.40
83 Tony Romo	.20	.50
84 Brandon Lloyd	.15	.40
85 Champ Bailey	.15	.40
86 D.J. Williams	.12	.30
87 Eddie Royal	.12	.30
88 Elvis Dumervil	.12	.30
89 Jabar Gaffney	.12	.30
90 Knowshon Moreno	.15	.40
91 Kyle Orton	.15	.40
92 Tim Tebow	.40	1.00
93 Brandon Pettigrew	.12	.30
94 Calvin Johnson	.20	.50
95 Jahvid Best	.15	.40
96 Alphonso Smith	.12	.30
97 Louis Delmas	.12	.30
98 Matthew Stafford	.20	.50
99 Nate Burleson	.12	.30
100 Ndamukong Suh	.20	.50
101 Shaun Hill	.12	.30
102 A.J. Hawk	.15	.40
103 Aaron Rodgers	.30	.75
104 Charles Woodson	.20	.50
105 Clay Matthews	.20	.50
106 Donald Driver	.15	.40
107 Greg Jennings	.15	.40
108 James Starks	.15	.40
109 Jermichael Finley	.15	.40
110 Nick Collins	.12	.30
111 Ryan Grant	.15	.40
112 Tramon Williams	.20	.50
113 Andre Johnson	.15	.40
114 Arian Foster	.15	.40
115 Brian Cushing	.12	.30
116 DeMeco Ryans	.12	.30
117 Jacoby Jones	.12	.30
118 Kevin Walter	.15	.40
119 Mario Williams	.12	.30
120 Matt Schaub	.15	.40
121 Owen Daniels	.12	.30
122 Austin Collie	.15	.40
123 Dallas Clark	.15	.40
124 Donald Brown	.12	.30
125 Dwight Freeney	.15	.40
126 Jacob Tamme	.15	.40
127 Joseph Addai	.15	.40
128 Peyton Manning	.30	.75
129 Pierre Garcon	.15	.40
130 Reggie Wayne	.15	.40
131 Robert Mathis	.12	.30
132 Daryl Smith	.12	.30
133 David Garrard	.15	.40
134 Kirk Morrison	.12	.30
135 Marcedes Lewis	.12	.30
136 Maurice Jones-Drew	.15	.40
137 Mike Sims-Walker	.15	.40
138 Mike Thomas	.15	.40
139 Rashad Jennings	.12	.30
140 Rashean Mathis	.12	.30
141 Derrick Johnson	.12	.30
142 Dexter McCluster	.12	.30
143 Dwayne Bowe	.15	.40
144 Eric Berry	.15	.40
145 Jamaal Charles	.15	.40
146 Matt Cassel	.15	.40
147 Tamba Hali	.12	.30
148 Thomas Jones	.15	.40
149 Tony Moeaki	.12	.30
150 Anthony Fasano	.12	.30
151 Brandon Marshall	.15	.40
152 Cameron Wake	.12	.30
153 Chad Henne	.15	.40
154 Davone Bess	.12	.30
155 Jake Long	.12	.30
156 Karlos Dansby	.12	.30
157 Ricky Williams	.15	.40
158 Ronnie Brown	.15	.40
159 Adrian Peterson	.25	.60
160 Chad Greenway	.15	.40
161 E.J. Henderson	.12	.30
162 Jared Allen	.15	.40
163 Percy Harvin	.15	.40
164 Sidney Rice	.15	.40
165 Joe Webb	.12	.30
166 Toby Gerhart	.15	.40
167 Visanthe Shiancoe	.15	.40
168 Aaron Hernandez	.15	.40
169 Benjarvus Green-Ellis	.15	.40
170 Brandon Tate	.12	.30
171 Danny Woodhead	.20	.50
172 Deion Branch	.12	.30
173 Devin McCourty	.12	.30
174 Jerod Mayo	.12	.30
175 Rob Gronkowski	.20	.50
176 Tom Brady	.30	.75
177 Wes Welker	.20	.50
178 Chris Ivory	.15	.40
179 Drew Brees	.20	.50
180 Jimmy Graham	.20	.50
181 Jonathan Vilma	.12	.30
182 Lance Moore	.15	.40
183 Marques Colston	.15	.40
184 Reggie Bush	.15	.40
185 Robert Meachem	.15	.40
186 Roman Harper	.12	.30
187 Tracy Porter	.12	.30
188 Ahmad Bradshaw	.15	.40
189 Brandon Jacobs	.15	.40
190 Eli Manning	.20	.50
191 Hakeem Nicks	.15	.40
192 Justin Tuck	.15	.40
193 Kevin Boss	.15	.40
194 Mario Manningham	.15	.40
195 Osi Umenyiora	.12	.30
196 Steve Smith USC	.15	.40
197 Terrell Thomas	.12	.30
198 Brad Smith	.12	.30
199 Braylon Edwards	.15	.40
200 Darrelle Revis	.15	.40
201 David Harris	.12	.30
202 Dustin Keller	.15	.40
203 Jerricho Cotchery	.12	.30
204 LaDainian Tomlinson	.20	.50
205 Mark Sanchez	.20	.50
206 Santonio Holmes	.15	.40
207 Shonn Greene	.15	.40
208 Darren McFadden	.15	.40
209 Jacoby Ford	.15	.40
210 Jason Campbell	.15	.40
211 Louis Murphy	.15	.40
212 Michael Bush	.12	.30
213 Michael Huff	.12	.30
214 Nnamdi Asomugha	.15	.40
215 Rolando McClain	.12	.30
216 Tyvon Branch	.12	.30
217 Zach Miller	.15	.40
218 Asante Samuel	.12	.30
219 Brent Celek	.15	.40
220 DeSean Jackson	.15	.40
221 Jeremy Maclin	.15	.40
222 Kevin Kolb	.15	.40
223 LeSean McCoy	.15	.40
224 Michael Vick	.20	.50
225 Nate Allen	.12	.30
226 Trent Cole	.12	.30
227 Ben Roethlisberger	.20	.50
228 Brett Keisel	.15	.40
229 Heath Miller	.15	.40
230 Hines Ward	.15	.40
231 James Harrison	.20	.50
232 LaMarr Woodley	.12	.30
233 Lawrence Timmons	.12	.30
234 Mike Wallace	.20	.50
235 Rashard Mendenhall	.15	.40
236 Troy Polamalu	.20	.50
237 Antoine Cason	.12	.30
238 Antonio Gates	.15	.40
239 Darren Sproles	.15	.40
240 Malcom Floyd	.15	.40
241 Mike Tolbert	.15	.40
242 Philip Rivers	.20	.50
243 Ryan Mathews	.15	.40
244 Shaun Phillips	.12	.30
245 Vincent Jackson	.15	.40
246 Alex Smith QB	.15	.40
247 Frank Gore	.15	.40
248 Josh Morgan	.15	.40
249 Justin Smith	.12	.30
250 Michael Crabtree	.15	.40
251 Patrick Willis	.15	.40
252 Takeo Spikes	.12	.30
253 Troy Smith	.12	.30
254 Vernon Davis	.15	.40
255 Aaron Curry	.12	.30
256 Chris Clemons	.12	.30
257 Earl Thomas	.12	.30
258 John Carlson	.12	.30
259 Justin Forsett	.15	.40
260 Leon Washington	.12	.30
261 Marshawn Lynch	.15	.40
262 Matt Hasselbeck	.15	.40
263 Mike Williams USC	.15	.40
264 Brandon Gibson	.12	.30
265 Chris Long	.12	.30
266 Danny Amendola	.15	.40
267 Donnie Avery	.12	.30
268 James Hall	.12	.30
269 James Laurinaitis	.12	.30
270 Mark Clayton	.12	.30
271 Sam Bradford	.20	.50
272 Steven Jackson	.15	.40
273 Arrelious Benn	.15	.40
274 Barrett Ruud	.12	.30
275 Cadillac Williams	.12	.30
276 Gerald McCoy	.12	.30
277 Josh Freeman	.20	.50
278 Kellen Winslow	.15	.40
279 LeGarrette Blount	.15	.40
280 Mike Williams	.15	.40
281 Ronde Barber	.12	.30
282 Chris Johnson	.15	.40
283 Cortland Finnegan	.12	.30
284 Jason Babin	.12	.30
285 Kenny Britt	.15	.40
286 Marc Mariani	.15	.40
287 Michael Griffin	.12	.30
288 Nate Washington	.12	.30
289 Randy Moss	.15	.40
290 Stephen Tulloch	.12	.30
291 Rob Bironas	.12	.30
292 Anthony Armstrong	.15	.40
293 Brian Orakpo	.15	.40
294 Chris Cooley	.15	.40
295 DeAngelo Hall	.12	.30
296 Donovan McNabb	.20	.50
297 Keiland Williams	.12	.30
298 LaRon Landry	.12	.30
299 London Fletcher	.12	.30
300 Santana Moss	.15	.40
301A A.J. Green RC (field in background)	.75	2.00
301B A.J. Green SP (red stands in background)	3.00	8.00
301C A.J. Green SP (stairs in background)	3.00	8.00
302 Aaron Williams RC	.30	.75
303 Adrian Clayborn RC	.40	1.00
304 Ahmad Black RC	.30	.75
305 Akeem Ayers RC	.30	.75
306 Aldon Smith RC	.60	1.50
307A Alex Green RC (field in background)	.40	1.00
307B Alex Green SP (stands in background)	1.50	4.00
308A Andy Dalton RC (field in background)	1.00	2.50
308B Andy Dalton SP (stands in background, throwing right)	4.00	10.00
308C Andy Dalton SP (stands in background, throwing forward)	4.00	10.00
309A Austin Pettis RC (field in background)	.30	.75
309B Austin Pettis SP (stands in background)	1.25	3.00
310A Bilal Powell RC (left arm pointing up)	.25	.60
310B Bilal Powell SP (left arm pointing down)	1.00	2.50
311A Blaine Gabbert RC (field in background)	.60	1.50
311B Blaine Gabbert SP (stands and field, in background)	2.50	6.00
311C Blaine Gabbert SP (stands in background)	2.50	6.00
312 Brandon Harris RC	.25	.60
313 Brooks Reed RC	.40	1.00
314 Bruce Carter RC	.40	1.00
315A Cam Newton RC (field in background)	2.00	5.00
315B Cam Newton SP (red stands in background)	8.00	20.00
315C Cam Newton SP (steps in background)	8.00	20.00
316 Cameron Heyward RC	.40	1.00
317 Cameron Jordan RC	.30	.75
318 Cecil Shorts RC	.30	.75
319A Christian Ponder RC (field in background dropping back)	.75	2.00
319B Christian Ponder SP (stands in background)	3.00	8.00
319C Christian Ponder SP (field in background standing upright)	3.00	8.00
320A Colin Kaepernick RC (field in background, hashmarks)	.50	1.25
320B Colin Kaepernick SP (stands in background)	2.00	5.00
320C Colin Kaepernick SP (field in background, no hashmarks)	2.00	5.00
321 Colin McCarthy RC	.30	.75
322 Corey Liuget RC	.25	.60
323 Curtis Brown RC	.40	1.00
324 D.J. Williams RC	.40	1.00
325A Daniel Thomas RC (cutting pose)	.40	1.00
325B Daniel Thomas SP (running to his right)	1.50	4.00
326 Da'Quan Bowers RC	.40	1.00
327 Davon House RC	.30	.75
328A Delone Carter RC (field in background)	.30	.75
328B Delone Carter SP (stands in background)	1.25	3.00
329A DeMarco Murray RC (field in background)	.75	2.00
329B DeMarco Murray SP (stands in background)	3.00	8.00
330 Denarius Moore RC	.50	1.25
331 Dion Lewis RC	.40	1.00
332 Drake Nevis RC	.40	1.00
333 Dwayne Harris RC	.40	1.00
334A Clyde Gates RC (left knee raised)	.30	.75
334B Clyde Gates SP (left knee down)	1.25	3.00
335 Evan Royster RC	.40	1.00
336 Greg Jones RC	.30	.75
337A Greg Little RC (ball at stomach)	.40	1.00
337B Greg Little SP (ball away from body)	1.50	4.00
338 Greg McElroy RC	.40	1.00
339 Greg Salas RC	.40	1.00
340 J.J. Watt RC	.50	1.25
341 Jabaal Sheard RC	.40	1.00
342 Jacquizz Rodgers RC	.40	1.00
343A Jake Locker RC (ball in right hand only)	1.00	2.50
343B Jake Locker SP (ball in both hands)	4.00	10.00
343C Jake Locker SP (stands in background)	4.00	10.00
344A Jamie Harper RC (running forward)	.40	1.00
344B Jamie Harper SP (running to his right)	1.50	4.00
345 Jeremy Kerley RC	.40	1.00
346A Jerrel Jernigan RC (crouched pose)	.30	.75
346B Jerrel Jernigan SP (running upright)	1.25	3.00
347 Jimmy Smith RC	.40	1.00
348A Jonathan Baldwin RC (ball in both hands)	.40	1.00
348B Jonathan Baldwin SP (ball in right hand only)	1.50	4.00
349 Jordan Cameron RC	.30	.75
350A Jordan Todman RC (running forward)	.25	.60
350B Jordan Todman SP (cutting to his left)	1.00	2.50
351A Julio Jones RC (field in background)	.75	2.00
351B Julio Jones SP (stands in background ball in left hand)	3.00	8.00
351C Julio Jones SP (stands in background ball in right hand)	3.00	8.00
352 Justin Houston RC	.40	1.00
353 Kealoha Pilares RC	.40	1.00
354A Kendall Hunter RC (left arm at chest)	.40	1.00
354B Kendall Hunter SP (left arm down)	1.50	4.00
355 Kris Durham RC	.30	.75
356A Kyle Rudolph RC (field in background left arm at waist)	.40	1.00
356B Kyle Rudolph SP (field in background left arm at chest)	1.50	4.00
356C Kyle Rudolph SP (stands in background)	1.50	4.00
357 Lance Kendricks RC	.30	.75
358A Leonard Hankerson RC (left hand at thigh)	.40	1.00
358B Leonard Hankerson SP (left hand at waist)	1.50	4.00
359 Luke Stocker RC	.30	.75
360A Marcell Dareus RC (stands in background)	.40	1.00
360B Marcell Dareus SP (field in background)	1.50	4.00
361A Mark Ingram RC (field only in background)	.75	2.00
361B Mark Ingram SP (dark stands only in background)	3.00	8.00
361C Mark Ingram SP (red stands in background)	3.00	8.00
362 Martez Wilson RC	.40	1.00
363 Mike Pouncey RC	.40	1.00
364A Mikel Leshoure RC (field in background, left knee bent)	.40	1.00
364B Mikel Leshoure SP (field in background, left knee down)	1.50	4.00
364C Mikel Leshoure SP (stands in background)	1.50	4.00
365 Muhammad Wilkerson RC	.40	1.00
366 Nate Solder RC	.40	1.00
367 Nathan Enderle RC	.40	1.00
368 Nick Fairley RC	.50	1.25
369 Niles Paul RC	.40	1.00
370 Owen Marecic RC	.40	1.00
371 Patrick Peterson RC	.60	1.50
372 Phil Taylor RC	.30	.75
373 Prince Amukamara RC	.40	1.00
374 Quan Sturdivant RC	.40	1.00
375 Quinton Carter RC	.25	.60
376 Rahim Moore RC	.30	.75
377A Randall Cobb RC (football in right hand, facing forward)	.50	1.25
377B Randall Cobb SP (football in left hand)	2.00	5.00
377C Randall Cobb SP (football in right hand, facing sideways)	2.00	5.00
378 Ras-I Dowling RC	.40	1.00
379 Ricky Stanzi RC	.50	1.25
380 Robert Housler RC	.30	.75
381 Robert Quinn RC	.40	1.00
382 Ronald Johnson RC	.30	.75
383 Roy Helu RC	.75	2.00
384 Ryan Kerrigan RC	.40	1.00
385A Ryan Mallett RC (black stands in background)	.75	2.00
385B Ryan Mallett SP (red stands in background)	3.00	8.00
385C Ryan Mallett SP (field in background)	3.00	8.00
386 Ryan Whalen RC	.30	.75
387A Ryan Williams RC (football in left hand)	.50	1.25
387B Ryan Williams SP (football in right hand)	2.00	5.00
388A Shane Vereen RC (football in right hand)	.40	1.00
388B Shane Vereen SP (football in left hand)	1.50	4.00
389 Stanley Havili RC	.25	.60
390 Stephen Paea RC	.40	1.00
391A Stevan Ridley RC (football in left hand only)	.40	1.00
391B Stevan Ridley SP (football in both hands)	1.50	4.00
392 T.J. Yates RC	.50	1.25
393A Taiwan Jones RC (left hand pointing up)	.40	1.00
393B Taiwan Jones SP (left hand pointing down)	1.50	4.00
394 Tandon Doss RC	.30	.75
395A Titus Young RC (football in left hand)	.50	1.25
395B Titus Young SP (football in right hand)	2.00	5.00
396A Torrey Smith RC (football in both hands)	.50	1.25
396B Torrey Smith SP (football in right hand only)	2.00	5.00
397 Tyler Sash RC	.40	1.00
398 Tyron Smith RC	.50	1.25
399A Vincent Brown RC (ball in right hand; left hand at waist)	.40	1.00
399B Vincent Brown SP (football in both hands)	1.50	4.00
400A Von Miller RC (facing forward, field in background)	.50	1.25
400B Von Miller SP (red stands in background)	2.00	5.00
400C Von Miller SP (facing left, field in background)	2.00	5.00

2011 Score Artist's Proof

*VETS 1-300: 10X TO 25X BASIC CARDS
*ROOKIES 301-400: 5X TO 12X BASIC CARDS
RANDOM INSERTS IN PACKS

2011 Score End Zone

NOT PRICED DUE TO SCARCITY

2011 Score Factory Set Updates

*FACT.SET: .4X TO 1X BASIC CARDS

2011 Score Glossy

*VETS 1-300: 1X TO 2.5X BASIC CARDS
*ROOKIES 301-400: .6X TO 1.5X BASIC CARDS
ONE GLOSSY PER PACK

2011 Score Gold Zone

*VETS 1-300: 3X TO 8X BASIC CARDS
*ROOKIES 301-400: 1.5X TO 4X BASIC CARDS
RANDOM INSERTS IN PACKS

2011 Score Red Zone

*VETS 1-300: 4X TO 10X BASIC CARDS
*ROOKIES 301-400: 2X TO 5X BASIC CARDS
RANDOM INSERTS IN PACKS

2011 Score Scorecard

*VETS 1-300: 2.5X TO 6X BASIC CARDS
*ROOKIES 301-400: 1.2X TO 3X BASIC CARDS
RANDOM INSERTS IN PACKS

2011 Score Complete Players

COMPLETE SET (20)	5.00	12.00
*ARTIST PROOF: 4X TO 10X BASIC INSERT		
*GLOSSY: .6X TO 1.5X BASIC INSERT		
*GOLD ZONE: 1.5X TO 4X BASIC INSERT		
*RED ZONE: 2X TO 5X BASIC INSERT		
*SCORECARD: 1X TO 2.5X BASIC INSERT		
END ZONE TOO SCARCE TO PRICE		
SIGNATURES TOO SCARCE TO PRICE		
1 Carson Palmer	.40	1.00
2 Clay Matthews	.50	1.25
3 Dallas Clark	.40	1.00
4 Darrelle Revis	.40	1.00
5 David Harris	.30	.75
6 DeAngelo Williams	.40	1.00
7 DeSean Jackson	.40	1.00
8 Devin Hester	.50	1.25
9 Felix Jones	.40	1.00
10 Jason Witten	.50	1.25
11 Knowshon Moreno	.40	1.00
12 Michael Turner	.40	1.00
13 Michael Vick	.50	1.25
14 Patrick Willis	.40	1.00
15 Reggie Bush	.40	1.00
16 Reggie Wayne	.40	1.00
17 Tim Tebow	1.00	2.50
18 Vernon Davis	.40	1.00
19 Visanthe Shiancoe	.40	1.00
20 Wes Welker	.50	1.25

2011 Score Retail Factory Set Jerseys Prime

TWO PER RETAIL FACTORY SET		
CM Colt McCoy	2.50	6.00
CS C.J. Spiller	2.50	6.00
DJ DeSean Jackson	2.50	6.00
JF Josh Freeman	3.00	8.00
JF Joe Flacco	3.00	8.00
JM Jeremy Maclin	2.50	6.00
MS Mark Sanchez	3.00	8.00
NS Ndamukong Suh	3.00	8.00
RG Rob Gronkowski	3.00	8.00
RM Ryan Mathews	2.50	6.00
RM Rashard Mendenhall	2.50	6.00
RR Ray Rice	2.50	6.00
SB Sam Bradford	3.00	8.00
TT Tim Tebow	6.00	15.00

2011 Score Retail Factory Set Packers Super Bowl Bonus

ONE PER SPECIAL RETAIL FACT.SET		
SBCM Clay Matthews Prime	4.00	10.00
SBJN Jordy Nelson Prime	4.00	10.00
SBAR1 Aaron Rodgers SB patch	5.00	12.00
SBAR2 Aaron Rodgers MVP patch	5.00	12.00

2011 Score Retail Factory Set Rookie Jerseys

TWO PER RETAIL FACTORY SET		
AD Andy Dalton	3.00	8.00
AG A.J. Green	2.50	6.00
BG Blaine Gabbert	2.50	6.00
CN Cam Newton	6.00	15.00
CP Christian Ponder	2.50	6.00
DM DeMarco Murray	2.50	6.00
DT Daniel Thomas	2.00	5.00
JJ Julio Jones	2.50	6.00
JL Jake Locker	3.00	8.00
MI Mark Ingram	2.50	6.00
RM Ryan Mallett	2.50	6.00
VM Von Miller	2.00	5.00

2011 Score Hot Rookies

COMPLETE SET (30)	10.00	25.00
*ARTIST PROOF: 3X TO 8X BASIC INSERT		
*GLOSSY: .6X TO 1.5X BASIC INSERT		
*GOLD ZONE: 1.2X TO 3X BASIC INSERT		
*RED ZONE: 1.5X TO 4X BASIC INSERT		
*SCORECARD: 1X TO 2.5X BASIC INSERT		
END ZONE TOO SCARCE TO PRICE		
1 A.J. Green	.75	2.00
2 Alex Green	.40	1.00
3 Andy Dalton	1.00	2.50
4 Austin Pettis	.30	.75
5 Blaine Gabbert	.60	1.50
6 Cam Newton	2.00	5.00
7 Christian Ponder	.75	2.00
8 Colin Kaepernick	.50	1.25
9 Daniel Thomas	.40	1.00
10 Delone Carter	.30	.75
11 DeMarco Murray	.75	2.00
12 Greg Little	.40	1.00
13 Jake Locker	1.00	2.50
14 Jamie Harper	.40	1.00
15 Jerrel Jernigan	.30	.75
16 Jonathan Baldwin	.40	1.00
17 Julio Jones	.75	2.00
18 Kyle Rudolph	.40	1.00
19 Leonard Hankerson	.40	1.00
20 Mark Ingram	.75	2.00
21 Mikel LeShoure	.40	1.00
22 Randall Cobb	.50	1.25
23 Ryan Mallett	.75	2.00
24 Ryan Williams	.50	1.25
25 Shane Vereen	.40	1.00
26 Taiwan Jones	.40	1.00
27 Titus Young	.50	1.25
28 Torrey Smith	.50	1.25
29 Vincent Brown	.40	1.00
30 Von Miller	.50	1.25

2011 Score Hot Rookies Signatures

RANDOM INSERTS IN PACKS		
1 A.J. Green	25.00	60.00
2 Alex Green		
3 Andy Dalton		
4 Austin Pettis		
5 Blaine Gabbert		
6 Cam Newton	90.00	150.00
7 Christian Ponder		
8 Colin Kaepernick		
9 Daniel Thomas		
10 Delone Carter		
11 DeMarco Murray	40.00	80.00
12 Greg Little		
13 Jake Locker	40.00	100.00
14 Jamie Harper		
15 Jerrel Jernigan		
16 Jonathan Baldwin		
17 Julio Jones		
18 Kyle Rudolph		
19 Leonard Hankerson		
20 Mark Ingram		
21 Mikel Leshoure		
22 Randall Cobb	15.00	40.00
23 Ryan Mallett		
24 Ryan Williams		
25 Shane Vereen		
26 Taiwan Jones		
27 Titus Young		
28 Torrey Smith	15.00	40.00
30 Von Miller		

2011 Score In the Zone

COMPLETE SET (30)	6.00	15.00
*ARTIST PROOF: 4X TO 10X BASIC INSERT		
*GLOSSY: .6X TO 1.5X BASIC INSERT		
*GOLD ZONE: 1.5X TO 4X BASIC INSERT		
*RED ZONE: 2X TO 5X BASIC INSERT		
*SCORECARD: 1X TO 2.5X BASIC INSERT		
END ZONE TOO SCARCE TO PRICE		
SIGNATURES TOO SCARCE TO PRICE		
1 Andre Johnson	.40	1.00
2 Arian Foster	.40	1.00
3 Braylon Edwards	.40	1.00
4 Calvin Johnson	.50	1.25
5 Chad Johnson	.40	1.00
6 Darren McFadden	.40	1.00
7 DeMarcus Ware	.40	1.00
8 Dwayne Bowe	.40	1.00
9 Frank Gore	.40	1.00
10 Greg Jennings	.40	1.00
11 Jamaal Charles	.40	1.00
12 Jared Allen	.40	1.00
13 Jeremy Maclin	.40	1.00
14 Joe Flacco	.50	1.25
15 Josh Freeman	.50	1.25
16 Mark Sanchez	.50	1.25
17 Matt Cassel	.40	1.00
18 Matt Ryan	.50	1.25
19 Matt Schaub	.40	1.00
20 Mike Wallace	.50	1.25
21 Miles Austin	.40	1.00
22 Ndamukong Suh	.50	1.25
23 Percy Harvin	.40	1.00
24 Philip Rivers	.50	1.25
25 Rashard Mendenhall	.40	1.00
26 Roddy White	.40	1.00
27 Sam Bradford	.50	1.25
28 Shonn Greene	.40	1.00
29 Steve Smith	.40	1.00
30 Tony Romo	.50	1.25

2011 Score Millennium Men

COMPLETE SET (20)	6.00	15.00
*ARTIST PROOF: 4X TO 10X BASIC INSERT		
*GLOSSY: .6X TO 1.5X BASIC INSERT		
*GOLD ZONE: 1.5X TO 4X BASIC INSERT		
*RED ZONE: 2X TO 5X BASIC INSERT		
*SCORECARD: 1X TO 2.5X BASIC INSERT		
END ZONE TOO SCARCE TO PRICE		
SIGNATURES TOO SCARCE TO PRICE		
1 Aaron Rodgers	.75	2.00
2 Adrian Peterson	.60	1.50
3 Antonio Gates	.40	1.00
4 Ben Roethlisberger	.50	1.25
5 Brian Urlacher	.50	1.25
6 Chris Johnson	.40	1.00
7 Donovan McNabb	.50	1.25
8 Drew Brees	.50	1.25
9 Eli Manning	.50	1.25
10 Hines Ward	.40	1.00
11 LaDainian Tomlinson	.50	1.25
12 Larry Fitzgerald	.40	1.00
13 Maurice Jones-Drew	.40	1.00
14 Peyton Manning	.75	2.00
15 Randy Moss	.40	1.00
16 Ray Lewis	.50	1.25
17 Steven Jackson	.40	1.00
18 Tom Brady	.75	2.00
19 Tony Gonzalez	.40	1.00
20 Troy Polamalu	.50	1.25

2011 Score Millennium Men Signatures

RANDOM INSERTS IN PACKS		
10 Hines Ward	40.00	80.00
14 Peyton Manning	60.00	120.00
17 Steven Jackson		
19 Tony Gonzalez	20.00	40.00

2011 Score Signatures

RANDOM INSERTS IN PACKS		
20 Anquan Boldin	6.00	15.00
30 C.J. Spiller	8.00	20.00
42 Brandon LaFell	5.00	12.00
43 Jimmy Clausen	8.00	20.00
45 Jonathan Stewart	6.00	15.00
68 Colt McCoy	8.00	20.00
71 Josh Cribbs	6.00	15.00
77 Dez Bryant	12.00	30.00
91 Kyle Orton	6.00	15.00
93 Brandon Pettigrew	5.00	12.00

102 A.J. Hawk 6.00 15.00
111 Ryan Grant 8.00 20.00
116 DeMeco Ryans 5.00 12.00
124 Donald Brown 5.00 12.00
126 Jacob Tamme 6.00 15.00
128 Peyton Manning
142 Dexter McCluster 5.00 12.00
144 Eric Berry 8.00 20.00
149 Tony Moeaki 5.00 12.00
155 Jake Long 5.00 12.00
163 Percy Harvin 8.00 20.00
164 Sidney Rice 8.00 20.00
166 Toby Gerhart 6.00 15.00
193 Kevin Boss 6.00 15.00
200 Darrelle Revis 8.00 20.00
201 David Harris 5.00 12.00
205 Mark Sanchez
206 Santonio Holmes 8.00 20.00
207 Shonn Greene 8.00 20.00
215 Rolando McClain 5.00 12.00
216 Tyvon Branch 5.00 12.00
221 Jeremy Maclin 6.00 15.00
222 Kevin Kolb 6.00 15.00
229 Heath Miller 6.00 15.00
230 Hines Ward
237 Antoine Cason 5.00 12.00
241 Mike Tolbert 8.00 20.00
243 Ryan Mathews 8.00 20.00
245 Vincent Jackson 6.00 15.00
253 Troy Smith 5.00 12.00
260 Leon Washington 5.00 12.00
272 Steven Jackson 6.00 15.00
285 Kenny Britt 6.00 15.00
287 Michael Griffin 5.00 12.00
293 Brian Orakpo 6.00 15.00
301 A.J. Green 25.00 50.00
302 Aaron Williams 4.00 10.00
303 Adrian Clayborn 8.00 20.00
304 Ahmad Black 4.00 10.00
305 Akeem Ayers 4.00 10.00
306 Aldon Smith 10.00 25.00
307 Alex Green 8.00 20.00
308 Andy Dalton 40.00 80.00
309 Austin Pettis 4.00 10.00
310 Bilal Powell 5.00 12.00
311 Blaine Gabbert 20.00 50.00
312 Brandon Harris 3.00 8.00
315 Cam Newton 100.00 175.00
316 Cameron Heyward 5.00 12.00
317 Cameron Jordan 4.00 10.00
318 Cecil Shorts 4.00 10.00
319 Christian Ponder 25.00 60.00
320 Colin Kaepernick 25.00 60.00
322 Corey Liuget 3.00 8.00
324 D.J. Williams 5.00 12.00
325 Daniel Thomas 8.00 20.00
326 Da'Quan Bowers 8.00 20.00
328 Delone Carter 4.00 10.00
329 DeMarco Murray 30.00 60.00
331 Dion Lewis 5.00 12.00
333 Dwayne Harris 5.00 12.00
334 Clyde Gates 6.00 15.00
335 Evan Royster 5.00 12.00
336 Greg Jones 4.00 10.00
337 Greg Little 5.00 12.00
339 Greg Salas 8.00 20.00
340 J.J. Watt 6.00 15.00
342 Jacquizz Rodgers 5.00 12.00
343 Jake Locker 40.00 100.00
344 Jamie Harper 5.00 12.00
345 Jeremy Kerley 5.00 12.00
346 Jerrel Jernigan 4.00 10.00
347 Jimmy Smith 5.00 12.00
348 Jonathan Baldwin 8.00 20.00
350 Jordan Todman 3.00 8.00
351 Julio Jones 25.00 60.00
354 Kendall Hunter 6.00 15.00
356 Kyle Rudolph 5.00 12.00
357 Lance Kendricks 4.00 10.00
358 Leonard Hankerson 5.00 12.00
359 Luke Stocker 4.00 10.00
360 Marcell Dareus 6.00 15.00
361 Mark Ingram 40.00 80.00
362 Martez Wilson 5.00 12.00
364 Mikel Leshoure 8.00 20.00
369 Niles Paul 5.00 12.00
373 Prince Amukamara 8.00
375 Quinton Carter 5.00 12.00
377 Randall Cobb 20.00 50.00
379 Ricky Stanzi 15.00 30.00
382 Ronald Johnson 4.00 10.00
384 Ryan Korrigan 5.00 12.00
385 Ryan Mallett 20.00 50.00
387 Ryan Williams 20.00 50.00
388 Shane Vereen 8.00 20.00
389 Stanley Havili 3.00 8.00
390 Stephen Paea 5.00 12.00
391 Stevan Ridley 8.00 20.00
393 Taiwan Jones 6.00 15.00
394 Tandon Doss 6.00 15.00
395 Titus Young 8.00 20.00
396 Torrey Smith 8.00 20.00
397 Tyler Sash 5.00 12.00
400 Von Miller 12.00 30.00

2012 Score

COMP.SET w/o SPs (400) 40.00 80.00
*ROOKIE VARIATION SP: 1.5 TO 4X RC
1 Aaron Rodgers .30 .75
2 A.J. Hawk .15 .40
3 Charles Woodson .20 .50
4 Clay Matthews .20 .50
5 Desmond Bishop .12 .30
6 Greg Jennings .15 .40
7 James Starks .15 .40
8 Jermichael Finley .15 .40
9 Jordy Nelson .15 .40
10 Ryan Grant .15 .40
11 Aldon Smith .15 .40
12 Alex Smith QB .15 .40
13 Mario Williams .12 .30
14 Frank Gore .15 .40
15 Kendall Hunter .15 .40
16 Michael Crabtree .15 .40
17 NaVorro Bowman .12 .30
18 Patrick Willis .15 .40
19 Ted Ginn Jr. .12 .30
20 Vernon Davis .15 .40
21 Darren Sproles .15 .40
22 Drew Brees .20 .50
23 Jimmy Graham .15 .40
24 Jonathan Vilma .12 .30
25 Lance Moore .15 .40
26 Mark Ingram .15 .40
27 Marques Colston .15 .40
28 Pierre Thomas .15 .40
29 Robert Meachem .15 .40
30 Roman Harper .12 .30
31 Ahmad Bradshaw .15 .40
32 Antrel Rolle .12 .30
33 Brandon Jacobs .15 .40
34 Eli Manning .20 .50
35 Hakeem Nicks .15 .40
36 Jason Pierre-Paul .15 .40
37 Justin Tuck .12 .30
38 Mathias Kiwanuka .12 .30
39 Michael Boley .12 .30
40 Victor Cruz .20 .50
41 Curtis Lofton .12 .30
42 Harry Douglas .12 .30
43 Jacquizz Rodgers .12 .30
44 John Abraham .12 .30
45 Julio Jones .15 .40
46 Matt Ryan .15 .40
47 Michael Turner .15 .40
48 Roddy White .15 .40
49 Sean Weatherspoon .12 .30
50 Tony Gonzalez .15 .40
51 Brandon Pettigrew .12 .30
52 Calvin Johnson .20 .50
53 Sheldon Brown .12 .30
54 Jahvid Best .15 .40
55 Kevin Smith .12 .30
56 Matthew Stafford .20 .50
57 Nate Burleson .12 .30
58 Ndamukong Suh .20 .50
59 Stephen Tulloch .12 .30
60 Titus Young .12 .30
61 Brian Urlacher .20 .50
62 Devin Hester .20 .50
63 Jay Cutler .15 .40
64 Johnny Knox .15 .40
65 Julius Peppers .15 .40
66 Lance Briggs .12 .30
67 Kellen Davis .12 .30
68 Matt Forte .15 .40
69 Roy Williams .12 .30
70 Andre Roberts .12 .30
71 Beanie Wells .15 .40
72 Daryl Washington .12 .30
73 Early Doucet III .12 .30
74 Kevin Kolb .15 .40
75 LaRod Stephens-Howling .12 .30
76 Larry Fitzgerald .15 .40
77 Paris Lenon .12 .30
78 Patrick Peterson .15 .40
79 Asante Samuel .15 .40
80 Brent Celek .15 .40
81 DeSean Jackson .15 .40
82 Michael Huff .12 .30
83 Jason Babin .12 .30
84 Jeremy Maclin .15 .40
85 LeSean McCoy .15 .40
86 Michael Vick .20 .50
87 Nnamdi Asomugha .12 .30
88 DeMarco Murray .15 .40
89 DeMarcus Ware .15 .40
90 Dez Bryant .20 .50
91 Felix Jones .15 .40
92 Jason Witten .20 .50
93 Laurent Robinson .12 .30
94 Miles Austin .15 .40
95 Sean Lee .12 .30
96 Tony Romo .20 .50
97 Terrelle Pryor .15 .40
98 David Hawthorne .12 .30
99 Doug Baldwin .15 .40
100 Aaron Curry .12 .30
101 Golden Tate .15 .40
102 Leon Washington .15 .40
103 Marshawn Lynch .15 .40
104 Sidney Rice .15 .40
105 Tarvaris Jackson .12 .30
106 Brandon LaFell .12 .30
107 Cam Newton .30 .75
108 Charles Johnson .12 .30
109 DeAngelo Williams .15 .40
110 Greg Olsen .12 .30
111 James Anderson .12 .30
112 Jon Beason .12 .30
113 Jonathan Stewart .15 .40
114 Steve Smith WR .15 .40
115 DeAngelo Hall .12 .30
116 Fred Davis .12 .30
117 Jabar Gaffney .12 .30
118 London Fletcher .12 .30
119 Rex Grossman .15 .40
120 Roy Helu Jr. .15 .40
121 Ryan Kerrigan .12 .30
122 Santana Moss .15 .40
123 Tim Hightower .12 .30
124 Adrian Clayborn .12 .30
125 Dezmon Briscoe .12 .30
126 Josh Freeman .15 .40
127 Kellen Winslow Jr. .15 .40
128 LeGarrette Blount .12 .30
129 Mike Williams .15 .40
130 Preston Parker .12 .30
131 Ronde Barber .12 .30
132 Chris Canty .12 .30
133 Adrian Peterson .20 .50
134 Chad Greenway .15 .40
135 Christian Ponder .15 .40
136 E.J. Henderson .12 .30
137 Jared Allen .15 .40
138 Michael Jenkins .12 .30
139 Percy Harvin .15 .40
140 Toby Gerhart .12 .30
141 Visanthe Shiancoe .12 .30
142 Brandon Gibson .12 .30
143 Brandon Lloyd .15 .40
144 Chris Long .12 .30
145 Danario Alexander .12 .30
146 James Laurinaitis .12 .30
147 Lance Kendricks .12 .30
148 Eddie Royal .12 .30
149 Sam Bradford .20 .50
150 Steven Jackson .15 .40
151 Aaron Hernandez .15 .40
152 BenJarvus Green-Ellis .15 .40
153 Deion Branch .12 .30
154 Jerod Mayo .15 .40
155 Shaun Phillips .12 .30
156 Rob Gronkowski .15 .40
157 Stevan Ridley .12 .30
158 Tom Brady .30 .75
159 Wes Welker .20 .50
160 Anquan Boldin .15 .40
161 Ed Reed .15 .40
162 Haloti Ngata .12 .30
163 Joe Flacco .15 .40
164 Ray Lewis .20 .50
165 Ray Rice .15 .40
166 Ricky Williams .15 .40
167 Terrell Suggs .15 .40
168 Torrey Smith .12 .30
169 Andre Johnson .15 .40
170 Arian Foster .15 .40
171 Ben Tate .12 .30
172 Brian Cushing .12 .30
173 Brandon Carr .12 .30
174 DeMeco Ryans .12 .30
175 Kevin Walter .15 .40
176 Matt Schaub .15 .40
177 Owen Daniels .12 .30
178 Elvis Dumervil .12 .30
179 Champ Bailey .15 .40
180 Jay Ratliff .12 .30
181 Demaryius Thomas .15 .40
182 Eric Decker .15 .40
183 Knowshon Moreno .15 .40
184 Tim Tebow .30 .75
185 Von Miller .15 .40
186 Wesley Woodyard .12 .30
187 Willis McGahee .12 .30
188 Antonio Brown .15 .40
189 Ben Roethlisberger .20 .50
190 Heath Miller .15 .40
191 LaMarr Woodley .12 .30
192 James Harrison .20 .50
193 Lawrence Timmons .12 .30
194 Mike Wallace .15 .40
195 Rashard Mendenhall .15 .40
196 Ryan Clark .12 .30
197 Troy Polamalu .20 .50
198 A.J. Green .15 .40
199 Andre Caldwell .12 .30
200 Andy Dalton .20 .50
201 Brent Grimes .12 .30
202 Jermaine Gresham .15 .40
203 Jerome Simpson .12 .30
204 Lofa Tatupu .12 .30
205 Rey Maualuga .12 .30
206 Devery Henderson .12 .30
207 Chris Johnson .15 .40
208 Damian Williams .12 .30
209 Jake Locker .15 .40
210 Jared Cook .12 .30
211 Jason McCourty .20 .50
212 Jordan Babineaux .12 .30
213 Kenny Britt .15 .40
214 Matt Hasselbeck .15 .40
215 Nate Washington .12 .30
216 Darrelle Revis .15 .40
217 David Harris .12 .30
218 Dustin Keller .12 .30
219 Darnell Dockett .12 .30
220 LaDainian Tomlinson .20 .50
221 Mark Sanchez .15 .40
222 Plaxico Burress .15 .40
223 Santonio Holmes .15 .40
224 Shonn Greene .15 .40
225 Antonio Gates .15 .40
226 Antwan Barnes .12 .30
227 Eric Weddle .12 .30
228 Malcom Floyd .12 .30
229 Mike Tolbert .15 .40
230 Philip Rivers .15 .40
231 Ryan Mathews .15 .40
232 Takeo Spikes .12 .30
233 Vincent Jackson .15 .40
234 Carson Palmer .15 .40
235 Darren McFadden .15 .40
236 Darrius Heyward-Bey .12 .30
237 Denarius Moore .12 .30
238 Jacoby Ford .12 .30
239 Kamerion Wimbley .12 .30
240 Louis Murphy .12 .30
241 Michael Bush .12 .30
242 Rolando McClain .12 .30
243 Tyvon Branch .12 .30
244 Derrick Johnson .12 .30
245 Dexter McCluster .12 .30
246 Dwayne Bowe .15 .40
247 Jackie Battle .12 .30
248 Jamaal Charles .15 .40
249 Matt Cassel .15 .40
250 Steve Breaston .12 .30
251 Tamba Hali .12 .30
252 Thomas Jones .15 .40
253 Tony Moeaki .15 .40
254 Anthony Fasano .12 .30
255 Brandon Marshall .12 .30
256 Brian Hartline .12 .30
257 Cameron Wake .12 .30
258 Daniel Thomas .15 .40
259 Davone Bess .12 .30
260 Karlos Dansby .12 .30
261 Matt Moore .12 .30
262 Reggie Bush .15 .40
263 Yeremiah Bell .12 .30
264 C.J. Spiller .15 .40
265 David Nelson .12 .30
266 Fred Jackson .15 .40
267 George Wilson .12 .30
268 Marcell Dareus .12 .30
269 Nick Barnett .12 .30
270 Ryan Fitzpatrick .15 .40
271 Scott Chandler .12 .30
272 Steve Johnson .15 .40
273 Blaine Gabbert .15 .40
274 Daryl Smith .12 .30
275 Dawan Landry .12 .30
276 Jason Hill .12 .30
277 Jeremy Mincey .12 .30
278 Marcedes Lewis .12 .30
279 Maurice Jones-Drew .15 .40
280 Mike Thomas .15 .40
281 Paul Posluszny .15 .40
282 Ben Watson .12 .30
283 Colt McCoy .15 .40
284 D'Qwell Jackson .12 .30
285 Greg Little .12 .30
286 Jabaal Sheard .12 .30
287 Josh Cribbs .12 .30
288 Mohamed Massaquoi .12 .30
289 Montario Hardesty .12 .30
290 Peyton Hillis .12 .30
291 Antoine Bethea .12 .30
292 Austin Collie .15 .40
293 Dallas Clark .15 .40
294 Donald Brown .15 .40
295 Joseph Addai .12 .30
296 Pat Angerer .12 .30
297 Peyton Manning .50 1.25
298 Pierre Garcon .15 .40
299 Reggie Wayne .15 .40
300 Robert Mathis .12 .30
301A A.J. Jenkins RC .50 1.25
301B A.J. Jenkins SP 2.00 5.00
302A Alshon Jeffery RC .60 1.50
302B Alshon Jeffery SP 2.50 6.00
303 Andre Branch RC .30 .75
304A Andrew Luck RC 2.50 6.00
(scrambling pose)
304B Andrew Luck SP 12.00 30.00
(passing pose)
305 B.J. Coleman RC .50 1.25
306A Bernard Pierce RC .40 1.00
306B Bernard Pierce SP 1.50 4.00
307 Bobby Wagner RC .40 1.00
308A Brandon Weeden RC .75 2.00
(scrambling pose)
308B Brandon Weeden SP 3.00 8.00
(passing pose)
309A Brian Quick RC .50 1.25
309B Brian Quick SP 2.00 5.00
310A Brock Osweiler RC .50 1.25
310B Brock Osweiler SP 2.00 5.00
311 Case Keenum RC .50 1.25
312 Chandler Harnish RC .40 1.00
313A Chandler Jones RC .40 1.00
313B Chandler Jones SP 1.50 4.00
314A Chris Givens RC .30 .75
314B Chris Givens SP 1.25 3.00
315 Chris Rainey RC .40 1.00
316A Coby Fleener RC .50 1.25
316B Coby Fleener SP 2.00 5.00
317 Courtney Upshaw RC .50 1.25
318 Cyrus Gray RC .40 1.00
319 Dan Herron RC .40 1.00
320 Danny Coale RC .60 1.50
321 David DeCastro RC .50 1.25
322A David Wilson RC .75 2.00
(running pose)
322B David Wilson SP 3.00 8.00
(leaping pose)
323A DeVier Posey RC .40 1.00
323B DeVier Posey SP 1.50 4.00
324 Devon Still RC .40 1.00
325 Devon Wylie RC .40 1.00
326A Dont'a Hightower RC .60 1.50
326B Dont'a Hightower SP 2.50 6.00
327 Dontari Poe RC .40 1.00
328A Doug Martin RC .60 1.50
328B Doug Martin SP 2.50 6.00
329A Dre Kirkpatrick RC .60 1.50
329B Dre Kirkpatrick SP 2.50 6.00
330A Dwayne Allen RC .40 1.00
330B Dwayne Allen SP 1.50 4.00
331A Fletcher Cox RC .40 1.00
331B Fletcher Cox SP 1.50 4.00
332 George Iloka RC .30 .75
333A Isaiah Pead RC .40 1.00
333B Isaiah Pead SP 1.50 4.00
334 Janoris Jenkins RC .40 1.00
335 Jared Crick RC .40 1.00
336 Jarius Wright RC .40 1.00
337A Joe Adams RC .40 1.00
337B Joe Adams SP 1.50 4.00
338 Jonathan Martin RC .30 .75
339 Juron Criner RC .30 .75
340A Justin Blackmon RC .75 2.00
(running pose)
340B Justin Blackmon SP 3.00 8.00
(leaping pose)
341 Kellen Moore RC .60 1.50
342A Kendall Wright RC .50 1.25
342B Kendall Wright SP 2.00 5.00
343 Kirk Cousins RC .60* 1.50
344 Ladarius Green RC .40 1.00
345A Lamar Miller RC .50 1.25
345B Lamar Miller SP 2.00 5.00
346A LaMichael James RC .75 2.00
(running pose)
346B LaMichael James SP 3.00 8.00
(leaping pose)
347 Lavonte David RC .50 1.25
348A Luke Kuechly RC .50 1.25
348B Luke Kuechly SP 2.00 5.00
349A Mark Barron RC .60 1.50
349B Mark Barron SP 2.50 6.00
350 Marvin Jones RC .30 .75
351 Marvin McNutt RC .40 1.00
352A Matt Kalil RC .50 1.25
352B Matt Kalil SP 2.00 5.00
353A Melvin Ingram RC .50 1.25
353B Melvin Ingram SP 2.00 5.00
354A Michael Brockers RC .40 1.00
354B Michael Brockers SP 1.50 4.00
355A Michael Egnew RC .30 .75
355B Michael Egnew SP 1.25 3.00
356A Michael Floyd RC .75 2.00
(running pose)
356B Michael Floyd SP leap 3.00 8.00
(catching pose)
357A Mohamed Sanu RC .40 1.00
357B Mohamed Sanu SP 1.50 4.00
358A Morris Claiborne RC .75 2.00
358B Morris Claiborne SP 3.00 8.00
359 Mychal Kendricks RC .40 1.00
360A Nick Foles RC .60 1.50
360B Nick Foles SP 2.50 6.00
361 Nick Perry RC .40 1.00
362A Nick Toon RC .50 1.25
362B Nick Toon SP 2.00 5.00
363 Orson Charles RC .40 1.00
364A Quinton Coples RC .40 1.00
364B Quinton Coples SP 1.50 4.00
365A Rueben Randle RC .40 1.00
365B Rueben Randle SP 1.50 4.00
366 Riley Reiff RC .40 1.00
367 Rishard Matthews RC .40 1.00
368A Robert Griffin III RC 2.00 5.00
(scrambling pose)
368B Robert Griffin III SP 12.00 30.00
(passing pose)
369A Robert Turbin RC .40 1.00
369B Robert Turbin SP 1.50 4.00
370 Ronnell Lewis RC .40 1.00
371A Ronnie Hillman RC .50 1.25
371B Ronnie Hillman SP 2.00 5.00
372A Russell Wilson RC .60 1.50
372B Russell Wilson SP 2.50 6.00
373A Ryan Broyles RC .40 1.00
373B Ryan Broyles SP 1.50 4.00
374 Ryan Lindley RC .40 1.00
375A Ryan Tannehill RC 1.00 2.50
(scrambling pose)
375B Ryan Tannehill SP 4.00 10.00
(passing pose)
376A Shea McClellin RC .50 1.25
376B Shea McClellin SP 2.00 5.00
377A Stephen Hill RC .40 1.00
377B Stephen Hill SP 1.50 4.00
378A T.Y. Hilton RC .40 1.00
378B T.Y. Hilton SP 1.50 4.00
379 Terrance Ganaway RC .30 .75
380 Tommy Streeter RC .40 1.00
381A Trent Richardson RC 1.25 3.00
(running forward)
381B Trent Richardson SP 5.00 12.00
(running sideways)
382 Vick Ballard RC .30 .75
383 Vinny Curry RC .40 1.00
384A Whitney Mercilus RC .40 1.00
384B Whitney Mercilus SP 1.50 4.00
385 Zach Brown RC .30 .75
386 Alfred Morris RC .30 .75
387 B.J. Cunningham RC .30 .75
388 Bruce Irvin RC .50 1.25
389 Bryce Brown RC .40 1.00
390 Greg Childs RC .40 1.00
391A Harrison Smith RC .40 1.00
391B Harrison Smith SP 1.50 4.00
392 Jeff Fuller RC .50 1.25
393 Keshawn Martin RC .40 1.00
394 Kevin Zeitler RC .30 .75
395 LaVon Brazill RC .30 .75
396 Marc Tyler RC .40 1.00
397 Michael Smith RC .30 .75
398A Stephon Gilmore RC .40 1.00
398B Stephon Gilmore SP 1.50 4.00
399A T.J. Graham RC .40 1.00
399B T.J. Graham SP 1.50 4.00
400 Travis Benjamin RC .40 1.00

2012 Score Artist's Proof

*1-300 VETS/32: 10X TO 25X BASIC CARDS
*301-400 ROOKIES/32: 5X TO 12X BASIC RC
STATED PRINT RUN 32 SER.#'d SETS

2012 Score Glossy

*1-300 VETS: 1X TO 2.5X BASIC CARDS
*301-400 ROOKIES: .6X TO 1.5X BASIC CARDS
ONE GLOSSY PER PACK

2012 Score Gold Zone

*1-300 VETS: 3X TO 8X BASIC INSERTS
*301-400 ROOKIES: 1.5X TO 4X BASIC RC
RANDOM INSERTS IN PACKS

2012 Score Red Zone

*1-300 VETS/20: 12X TO 30X BASIC CARDS
*301-400 ROOKIES/20: 6X TO 15X BASIC RC
STATED PRINT RUN 20 SER.#'d SETS

2012 Score Scorecard

*1-300 VETS: 2.5X TO 6X BASIC CARDS
*301-400 ROOKIES: 1.2X TO 3X BASIC CARDS
RANDOM INSERTS IN PACKS

2012 Score Complete Players

COMPLETE SET (20) 4.00 10.00
*GLOSSY: .6X TO 1.5X BASIC INSERTS
1 Cam Newton .75 2.00
2 LeSean McCoy .40 1.00
3 Darren Sproles .40 1.00
4 Percy Harvin .40 1.00
5 Jason Pierre-Paul .40 1.00
6 Terrell Suggs .40 1.00
7 Ray Rice .40 1.00
8 Chris Johnson .40 1.00
9 Von Miller .40 1.00
10 Fred Jackson .40 1.00
11 Michael Vick .50 1.25
12 Maurice Jones-Drew .40 1.00
13 Matt Forte .40 1.00
14 Calvin Johnson .50 1.25
15 Jared Allen .40 1.00
16 Tamba Hali .30 .75
17 Darren McFadden .40 1.00
18 Jahvid Best .40 1.00
19 Wes Welker .50 1.25
20 Ryan Mathews .40 1.00

2012 Score Hot Rookies

COMPLETE SET (30) 10.00 25.00
*GLOSSY: .6X TO 1.5X BASIC INSERTS
1 Andrew Luck 3.00 8.00
2 Robert Griffin III 2.50 6.00
3 Trent Richardson 1.50 4.00
4 Justin Blackmon 1.00 2.50
5 Ryan Tannehill 1.25 3.00
6 Michael Floyd 1.00 2.50
7 Kendall Wright .60 1.50
8 Brandon Weeden 1.00 2.50
9 A.J. Jenkins .60 1.50
10 Doug Martin .75 2.00
11 David Wilson 1.00 2.50
12 Brian Quick .60 1.50
13 Coby Fleener .60 1.50
14 Stephen Hill .50 1.25
15 Bernard Pierce .50 1.25
16 Isaiah Pead .50 1.25
17 Ryan Broyles .50 1.25
18 Brock Osweiler .60 1.50
19 LaMichael James 1.00 2.50
20 Rueben Randle .50 1.25
21 Nick Toon .60 1.50
22 Russell Wilson .75 2.00
23 Mohamed Sanu .50 1.25
24 Lamar Miller .60 1.50
25 Chris Givens .40 1.00
26 Alshon Jeffery .75 2.00
27 DeVier Posey .50 1.25
28 T.J. Graham .50 1.25
29 Ronnie Hillman .60 1.50
30 Robert Turbin .50 1.25

2012 Score In the Zone

COMPLETE SET (30) 5.00 12.00
*GLOSSY: .6X TO 1.5X BASIC INSERTS
1 LeSean McCoy .40 1.00
2 Rob Gronkowski .40 1.00
3 Calvin Johnson .50 1.25
4 Jordy Nelson .40 1.00
5 Ray Rice .40 1.00
6 Cam Newton .75 2.00
7 Adrian Peterson .50 1.25
8 Marshawn Lynch .40 1.00
9 Arian Foster .40 1.00
10 Ahmad Bradshaw .40 1.00
11 BenJarvus Green-Ellis .40 1.00
12 Jimmy Graham .40 1.00
13 Laurent Robinson .30 .75
14 Maurice Jones-Drew .40 1.00
15 Michael Turner .40 1.00
16 Beanie Wells .40 1.00
17 Darren Sproles .40 1.00
18 Mike Tolbert .40 1.00
19 Dez Bryant .50 1.25
20 Eric Decker .40 1.00
21 Greg Jennings .40 1.00
22 Percy Harvin .40 1.00
23 Rashard Mendenhall .40 1.00
24 Victor Cruz .50 1.25
25 Vincent Jackson .40 1.00
26 Wes Welker .50 1.25
27 Frank Gore .40 1.00
28 Jermichael Finley .40 1.00
29 Larry Fitzgerald .40 1.00
30 Roddy White .40 1.00

2012 Score Numbers Game

COMPLETE SET (20) 4.00 10.00
*GLOSSY: .6X TO 1.5X BASIC INSERTS
1 Calvin Johnson .50 1.25
2 Wes Welker .50 1.25
3 Roddy White .40 1.00
4 Rob Gronkowski .40 1.00
5 Maurice Jones-Drew .40 1.00
6 Michael Turner .40 1.00
7 LeSean McCoy .40 1.00
8 Ray Rice .40 1.00
9 Drew Brees .50 1.25
10 Tom Brady .75 2.00
11 Aaron Rodgers .75 2.00
12 David Akers .30 .75
13 Brandon Banks .30 .75
14 Joe McKnight .30 .75
15 Patrick Peterson .40 1.00
16 Brandon Tate .30 .75
17 D'Qwell Jackson .30 .75
18 NaVorro Bowman .30 .75
19 Jared Allen .40 1.00
20 Terrell Suggs .40 1.00

2012 Score RC Flashbacks

18 Michael Irvin 1.25 3.00
57 Kurt Warner 1.25 3.00
72 Cris Carter 1.25 3.00
78 Rod Woodson 1.25 3.00
86 Tim Brown 1.25 3.00
101 Emmitt Smith 4.00 10.00
211 Thurman Thomas 1.25 3.00
214 Keyshawn Johnson 1.00 2.50
217 Mike Alstott .75 2.00
222 Ricky Williams 1.00 2.50
223 Donovan McNabb 1.00 2.50
228 Champ Bailey 1.00 2.50
230 Marvin Harrison 1.00 2.50
231 Eddie George 1.00 2.50
233 Peyton Manning 3.00 8.00
235 Randy Moss 1.00 2.50
236 Charles Woodson 1.50 4.00
246 Deion Sanders 1.50 4.00
252 Hines Ward 1.25 3.00
256 Kerry Collins 1.00 2.50
257 Barry Sanders 4.00 10.00
270 Troy Aikman 2.00 5.00
271 Michael Vick 1.25 3.00
272A Drew Brees 1.50 4.00
272B Andre Rison 1.00 2.50
274 Tiki Barber 1.00 2.50
276 Warrick Dunn .75 2.00
277 Marshall Faulk 1.25 3.00
283 LaDainian Tomlinson 1.25 3.00
288 Brian Urlacher 1.25 3.00
289 Tony Gonzalez 1.00 2.50
302 Junior Seau 1.00 2.50
306A Jason Witten 1.25 3.00
306B Jerome Bettis 1.25 3.00
310 Dallas Clark 1.00 2.50
316 Tom Brady 2.00 5.00
324 Ed Reed 1.00 2.50
331 Alex Smith QB 1.00 2.50
333 Sterling Sharpe 1.00 2.50
352 Aaron Rodgers 2.50 6.00
354 Roddy White 1.00 2.50
367 Frank Gore 1.00 2.50
371 Eli Manning 1.25 3.00
373 Larry Fitzgerald 1.00 2.50
374 Philip Rivers 1.00 2.50
381 Ben Roethlisberger 2.00 5.00
488 Jimmy Smith .75 2.00
506 Haywood Jeffires .75 2.00
611 Brett Favre 3.00 8.00
627 Mark Carrier .75 2.00

2012 Score Signatures

17 NaVorro Bowman 5.00 12.00
23 Jimmy Graham 6.00 15.00
26 Mark Ingram 8.00 20.00
43 Jacquizz Rodgers 5.00 12.00
79 Asante Samuel 8.00 20.00
107 Cam Newton 40.00 80.00
120 Roy Helu Jr. 6.00 15.00
145 Danario Alexander 5.00 12.00
147 Lance Kendricks 5.00 12.00
172 Brian Cushing 5.00 12.00
198 A.J. Green 6.00 15.00
208 Damian Williams 5.00 12.00
209 Jake Locker 15.00 30.00
256 Brian Hartline 5.00 12.00
301 A.J. Jenkins 6.00 15.00
304 Andrew Luck 125.00 200.00
307 Bobby Wagner 5.00 12.00
308 Brandon Weeden 20.00 40.00
310 Brock Osweiler 10.00 25.00
314 Chris Givens 4.00 10.00
316 Coby Fleener 6.00 15.00
318 Cyrus Gray 5.00 12.00
320 Danny Coale 8.00 20.00
321 David DeCastro 8.00 20.00
327 Dontari Poe 5.00 12.00
320 Doug Martin 8.00 20.00
330 Dwayne Allen 5.00 12.00
332 George Iloka 4.00 10.00
333 Isaiah Pead 6.00 15.00
335 Jared Crick 5.00 12.00
337 Joe Adams 5.00 12.00
338 Jonathan Martin 4.00 10.00
340 Justin Blackmon 15.00 40.00
341 Kellen Moore 8.00 20.00
342 Kendall Wright 6.00 15.00
343 Kirk Cousins 10.00 25.00
344 Ladarius Green 5.00 12.00
348 Luke Kuechly 6.00 15.00
350 Marvin Jones 4.00 10.00
351 Marvin McNutt 6.00 15.00
352 Matt Kalil 6.00 15.00
354 Michael Brockers 5.00 12.00
355 Michael Egnew 4.00 10.00
356 Michael Floyd 12.00 30.00
359 Mychal Kendricks 5.00 12.00
360 Nick Foles 8.00 20.00
362 Nick Toon 6.00 15.00
363 Orson Charles 5.00 12.00
366 Riley Reiff 6.00 15.00
368 Robert Griffin III 100.00 175.00
372 Russell Wilson 8.00 20.00
375 Ryan Tannehill 20.00 40.00
378 T.Y. Hilton 5.00 12.00
379 Terrance Ganaway 4.00 10.00
381 Trent Richardson 40.00 80.00
384 Whitney Mercilus 5.00 12.00
392 Jeff Fuller 6.00 15.00
396 Marc Tyler 5.00 12.00

2009 Score Inscriptions

COMP.SET w/o RC's (300) 20.00 40.00
ROOKIE PRINT RUN 999 SER.#'d SETS
1 Adrian Wilson .20 .50
2 Anquan Boldin .25 .60
3 Dominique Rodgers-Cromartie .20 .50
4 Edgerrin James .25 .60
5 Kurt Warner .30 .75
6 Larry Fitzgerald .30 .75
7 Matt Leinart .25 .60
8 Steve Breaston .25 .60
9 Tim Hightower .20 .50
10 Chris Houston .20 .50
11 Curtis Lofton .20 .50
12 Harry Douglas .20 .50
13 Jerious Norwood .25 .60
14 John Abraham .20 .50
15 Matt Ryan .30 .75
16 Michael Jenkins .20 .50
17 Michael Turner .25 .60
18 Roddy White .25 .60
19 Demetrius Williams .20 .50
20 Derrick Mason .25 .60
21 Joe Flacco .30 .75
22 Le'Ron McClain .25 .60
23 Mark Clayton .20 .50
24 Ray Lewis .30 .75
25 Ray Rice .30 .75
26 Terrell Suggs .20 .50
27 Todd Heap .20 .50
28 Willis McGahee .25 .60
29 Derek Fine .20 .50
30 Fred Jackson .30 .75
31 James Hardy .25 .60
32 Lee Evans .25 .60
33 Leodis McKelvin .20 .50
34 Marshawn Lynch .25 .60
35 Paul Posluszny .25 .60
36 Steve Johnson .25 .60
37 Trent Edwards .20 .50
38 Charles Godfrey .20 .50
39 Chris Gamble .20 .50
40 Dante Rosario .20 .50
41 DeAngelo Williams .30 .75
42 Jake Delhomme .25 .60
43 Jon Beason .20 .50
44 Jonathan Stewart .25 .60
45 Muhsin Muhammad .25 .60
46 Steve Smith .25 .60
47 Alex Brown .20 .50
48 Brian Urlacher .30 .75
49 Desmond Clark .20 .50
50 Devin Hester .30 .75
51 Earl Bennett .25 .60
52 Greg Olsen .20 .50
53 Kyle Orton .25 .60
54 Lance Briggs .25 .60
55 Matt Forte .30 .75
56 Andre Caldwell .20 .50
57 Carson Palmer .30 .75
58 Cedric Benson .25 .60
59 Chad Ochocinco .25 .60
60 Dhani Jones .20 .50
61 Jerome Simpson .20 .50
62 Keith Rivers .20 .50
63 Reggie Kelly .20 .50
64 T.J. Houshmandzadeh .25 .60
65 Brady Quinn .25 .60
66 Braylon Edwards .25 .60
67 D'Qwell Jackson .20 .50
68 Jamal Lewis .25 .60
69 Jerome Harrison .20 .50
70 Josh Cribbs .30 .75
71 Kellen Winslow .25 .60
72 Shaun Rogers .20 .50
73 Steve Heiden .20 .50
74 DeMarcus Ware .25 .60
75 Felix Jones .30 .75
76 Jason Witten .30 .75
77 Marion Barber .25 .60
78 Patrick Crayton .20 .50
79 Roy Williams WR .25 .60
80 Tashard Choice .20 .50
81 Terrell Owens .30 .75
82 Terence Newman .20 .50
83 Tony Romo .50 1.25
84 Brandon Marshall .25 .60
85 Brandon Stokley .25 .60
86 Champ Bailey .25 .60
87 Daniel Graham .20 .50
88 Eddie Royal .25 .60
89 Jay Cutler .30 .75
90 Peyton Hillis .30 .75
91 D.J. Williams .20 .50
92 Tony Scheffler .20 .50
93 Calvin Johnson .30 .75
94 Daunte Culpepper .25 .60
95 Ernie Sims .20 .50
96 Jerome Felton .20 .50
97 Jordon Dizon .20 .50
98 Kevin Smith .25 .60
99 Paris Lenon .20 .50
100 Rudi Johnson .20 .50
101 Shaun McDonald .20 .50
102 Aaron Rodgers .60 1.50
103 A.J. Hawk .25 .60
104 Brandon Jackson .25 .60
105 Donald Driver .25 .60
106 Donald Lee .20 .50
107 Greg Jennings .30 .75
108 James Jones .20 .50
109 Jermichael Finley .30 .75
110 Jordy Nelson .30 .75
111 Ryan Grant .25 .60
112 Amobi Okoye .20 .50
113 Andre Johnson .25 .60
114 Chester Pitts .20 .50
115 DeMeco Ryans .25 .60
116 Kevin Walter .25 .60
117 Kris Brown .20 .50
118 Mario Williams .25 .60
119 Matt Schaub .25 .60
120 Owen Daniels .20 .50
121 Steve Slaton .25 .60
122 Adam Vinatieri .25 .60
123 Anthony Gonzalez .20 .50
124 Dallas Clark .25 .60
125 Dominic Rhodes .20 .50
126 Dwight Freeney .25 .60
127 Joseph Addai .30 .75
128 Freddie Keiaho .20 .50
129 Mike Hart .25 .60
130 Peyton Manning .50 1.25
131 Reggie Wayne .25 .60
132 David Garrard .25 .60
133 Dennis Northcutt .20 .50
134 Derrick Harvey .20 .50
135 Josh Scobee .20 .50
136 Marcedes Lewis .20 .50
137 Mike Peterson .20 .50
138 Maurice Jones-Drew .25 .60
139 Quentin Groves .20 .50
140 Reggie Nelson .20 .50
141 Brian Williams .20 .50
142 Derrick Johnson .20 .50
143 Matt Cassel .25 .60
144 Dwayne Bowe .25 .60
145 Jamaal Charles .30 .75
146 Kolby Smith .20 .50
147 Larry Johnson .25 .60
148 Mark Bradley .20 .50
149 Tony Gonzalez .25 .60
150 Tyler Thigpen .20 .50
151 Anthony Fasano .20 .50
152 Chad Henne .25 .60
153 Chad Pennington .25 .60
154 Davone Bess .20 .50
155 Joey Porter .25 .60
156 Greg Camarillo .25 .60
157 Jake Long .20 .50
158 Ricky Williams .25 .60
159 Ronnie Brown .25 .60
160 Ted Ginn .25 .60
161 Adrian Peterson .50 1.25
162 Bernard Berrian .25 .60
163 Chad Greenway .20 .50
164 Chester Taylor .20 .50
165 Erin Henderson .20 .50
166 Jared Allen .30 .75

167 John David Booty .25 .60
168 Sidney Rice .25 .60
169 Tarvaris Jackson .25 .60
170 Visanthe Shiancoe .25 .60
171 Brandon Meriweather .20 .50
172 Jerod Mayo .25 .60
173 Kevin Faulk .20 .50
174 LaMont Jordan .20 .50
175 Laurence Maroney .25 .60
176 Randy Moss .30 .75
177 Tedy Bruschi .25 .60
178 Terrence Wheatley .20 .50
179 Tom Brady .50 1.25
180 Wes Welker .30 .75
181 Adrian Arrington .20 .50
182 Devery Henderson .20 .50
183 Drew Brees .30 .75
184 Jeremy Shockey .20 .50
185 Jonathan Vilma .20 .50
186 Lance Moore .25 .60
187 Marques Colston .25 .60
188 Pierre Thomas .25 .60
189 Reggie Bush .30 .75
190 Scott Shanle .20 .50
191 Ahmad Bradshaw .25 .60
192 Antonio Pierce .20 .50
193 Brandon Jacobs .25 .60
194 Derrick Ward .20 .50
195 Domenik Hixon .20 .50
196 Eli Manning .30 .75
197 Justin Tuck .25 .60
198 Kenny Phillips .20 .50
199 Kevin Boss .25 .60
200 Steve Smith USC .25 .60
201 Calvin Pace .20 .50
202 Chansi Stuckey .20 .50
203 Dustin Keller .20 .50
204 Jerricho Cotchery .25 .60
205 Kellen Clemens .20 .50
206 Laveranues Coles .20 .50
207 Leon Washington .25 .60
208 Thomas Jones .25 .60
209 Vernon Gholston .20 .50
210 Chaz Schilens .20 .50
211 Darren McFadden .30 .75
212 JaMarcus Russell .20 .50
213 Johnnie Lee Higgins .20 .50
214 Justin Fargas .20 .50
215 Michael Bush .25 .60
216 Nnamdi Asomugha .25 .60
217 Sebastian Janikowski .20 .50
218 Zach Miller .20 .50
219 Brian Westbrook .25 .60
220 Correll Buckhalter .20 .50
221 DeSean Jackson .25 .60
222 Donovan McNabb .30 .75
223 Greg Lewis .20 .50
224 Hank Baskett .20 .50
225 Kevin Curtis .20 .50
226 Reggie Brown .20 .50
227 Stewart Bradley .20 .50
228 Ben Roethlisberger .30 .75
229 Heath Miller .25 .60
230 Hines Ward .25 .60
231 James Harrison .30 .75
232 Troy Polamalu .30 .75
233 Nate Washington .20 .50
234 Rashard Mendenhall .25 .60
235 Santonio Holmes .25 .60
236 Willie Parker .20 .50
237 Antonio Gates .25 .60
238 Chris Chambers .25 .60
239 Darren Sproles .25 .60
240 Eric Weddle .20 .50
241 Jacob Hester .20 .50
242 LaDainian Tomlinson .30 .75
243 Philip Rivers .30 .75
244 Shawne Merriman .25 .60
245 Vincent Jackson .25 .60
246 Brandon Jones .20 .50
247 Frank Gore .25 .60
248 Isaac Bruce .25 .60
249 Josh Morgan .20 .50
250 Michael Robinson .20 .50
251 Patrick Willis .25 .60
252 Reggie Smith .20 .50
253 Shaun Hill .20 .50
254 Vernon Davis .25 .60
255 Deion Branch .25 .60
256 John Carlson .25 .60
257 Julian Peterson .20 .50
258 Julius Jones .20 .50
259 Lofa Tatupu .25 .60
260 Matt Hasselbeck .25 .60
261 Nate Burleson .20 .50
262 Owen Schmitt .20 .50
263 T.J. Duckett .20 .50
264 Antonio Pittman .20 .50
265 Chris Long .25 .60
266 Donnie Avery .25 .60
267 Keenan Burton .20 .50
268 Marc Bulger .25 .60
269 Pisa Tinoisamoa .20 .50
270 Steven Jackson .25 .60
271 Torry Holt .25 .60
272 Antonio Bryant .20 .50
273 Aqib Talib .20 .50
274 Cadillac Williams .25 .60
275 Dexter Jackson .20 .50
276 Earnest Graham .20 .50
277 Gaines Adams .20 .50
278 Michael Clayton .20 .50
279 Ronde Barber .20 .50
280 Barrett Ruud .20 .50
281 Albert Haynesworth .20 .50
282 Bo Scaife .20 .50
283 Chris Johnson .30 .75
284 Justin Gage .20 .50
285 Keith Bulluck .20 .50
286 Kerry Collins .25 .60
287 LenDale White .25 .60
288 Rob Bironas .20 .50
289 Roydell Williams .20 .50
290 Vince Young .25 .60
291 Chris Cooley .25 .60
292 Chris Horton .25 .60
293 Clinton Portis .25 .60
294 Colt Brennan .25 .60
295 Devin Thomas .20 .50
296 Jason Campbell .20 .50
297 Kedric Golston .30 .75
298 Ladell Betts .20 .50
299 Malcolm Kelly .20 .50
300 Santana Moss .25 .60
301 Aaron Brown RC 1.25 3.00
302 Aaron Curry RC 1.25 3.00
303 Aaron Kelly RC 1.00 2.50
304 Aaron Maybin RC 1.00 2.50
305 Alphonso Smith RC 1.00 2.50
306 Andre Brown RC .75 2.00
307 Andre Smith RC 1.00 2.50
308 Anthony Hill RC .75 2.00
309 Arian Foster RC 2.50 6.00
310 Austin Collie RC 1.25 3.00
311 B.J. Raji RC 1.25 3.00
312 Brandon Gibson RC 1.25 3.00
313 Brandon Pettigrew RC 1.25 3.00
314 Brandon Tate RC 1.25 3.00
315 Brian Cushing RC 1.25 3.00
316 Brian Hartline RC 1.25 3.00
317 Brian Orakpo RC 1.25 3.00
318 Brian Robiskie RC 1.25 3.00
319 Brooks Foster RC .75 2.00
320 Cameron Morrah RC .75 2.00
321 Cedric Peerman RC 1.00 2.50
322 Chase Coffman RC 1.00 2.50
323 Chris Wells RC 2.00 5.00
324 Clay Matthews RC 3.00 8.00
325 Clint Sintim RC 1.25 3.00
326 Cornelius Ingram RC .75 2.00
327 Curtis Painter RC 1.25 3.00
328 Darius Butler RC 1.25 3.00
329 Darius Passmore RC 1.00 2.50
330 Darrius Heyward-Bey RC 1.25 3.00
331 Davon Drew RC 1.00 2.50
332 Demetrius Byrd RC 1.00 2.50
333 Deon Butler RC 1.00 2.50
334 Derrick Williams RC 1.00 2.50
335 Devin Moore RC 1.00 2.50
336 Dominique Edison RC .75 2.00
338 Eugene Monroe RC .75 2.00
339 Everette Brown RC 1.00 2.50
340 Gartrell Johnson RC .75 2.00
341 Glen Coffee RC 1.00 2.50
342 Graham Harrell RC 1.25 3.00
343 Hakeem Nicks RC 2.00 5.00
344 Hunter Cantwell RC 1.25 3.00
345 Jairus Byrd RC 1.25 3.00
346 James Casey RC 1.00 2.50
347 James Davis RC 1.25 3.00
348 James Laurinaitis RC 1.25 3.00
349 Jared Cook RC 1.25 3.00
350 Jarett Dillard RC 1.25 3.00
351 Jason Smith RC 1.00 2.50
352 Javon Ringer RC 1.25 3.00
353 Jeremiah Johnson RC 1.25 3.00
354 Jeremy Childs RC 1.00 2.50
355 Jeremy Maclin RC 2.00 5.00
356 John Parker Wilson RC 1.25 3.00
357 Johnny Knox RC 2.00 5.00
358 Josh Freeman RC 2.50 6.00
359 Juaquin Iglesias RC 1.00 2.50
360 Keith Null RC 1.00 2.50
361 Kenny Britt RC 1.50 4.00
362 Kenny McKinley RC 1.25 3.00
363 Kevin Ogletree RC 1.25 3.00
364 Knowshon Moreno RC 1.25 3.00
365 Kory Sheets RC 1.00 2.50
366 Larry English RC* 1.25 3.00
367 LeSean McCoy RC 2.50 6.00
368 Louis Murphy RC 1.25 3.00
369 Malcolm Jenkins RC 1.25 3.00
370 Mark Sanchez RC 4.00 10.00
371 Matthew Stafford RC 6.00 15.00
372 Michael Crabtree RC 2.50 6.00
373 Mike Goodson RC 1.25 3.00
374 Mike Thomas RC 1.25 3.00
375 Mike Wallace RC 2.50 6.00
376 Mohamed Massaquoi RC 1.00 2.50
377 Nate Davis RC 1.00 2.50
378 Nathan Brown RC 1.00 2.50
379 P.J. Hill RC 1.00 2.50
380 Pat White RC 1.25 3.00
381 Patrick Chung RC 1.25 3.00
382 Patrick Turner RC 1.00 2.50
383 Percy Harvin RC 2.00 5.00
384 Quan Cosby RC 1.00 2.50
385 Quinn Johnson RC 1.00 2.50
386 Quinten Lawrence RC .75 2.00
387 Ramses Barden RC .75 2.00
388 Rashad Jennings RC 1.25 3.00
389 Rey Maualuga RC 1.25 3.00
390 Rhett Bomar RC 1.00 2.50
391 Richard Quinn RC 1.00 2.50
392 Shawn Nelson RC 1.00 2.50
393 Shonn Greene RC 2.00 5.00
394 Stephen McGee RC 1.25 3.00
395 Tom Brandstater RC 1.25 3.00
396 Tony Fiammetta RC 1.00 2.50
397 Travis Beckum RC 1.00 2.50
398 Tyrell Sutton RC 1.00 2.50
399 Tyson Jackson RC 1.00 2.50
400 Vontae Davis RC 1.25 3.00

2009 Score Inscriptions Artist's Proof

*VETS 1-300: 6X TO 15X BASIC CARDS
*ROOKIES 301-400: 1X TO 2.5X BASIC CARDS
ARTIST'S PROOF PRINT RUN 32

2009 Score Inscriptions Gold Zone

*VETS 1-300: 5X TO 12X BASIC CARDS
*ROOKIES 301-400: .8X TO 2X BASIC CARDS
GOLD ZONE PRINT RUN 50 SER.#'d SETS

2009 Score Inscriptions Red Zone

*VETS 1-300: 6X TO 15X BASIC CARDS
*ROOKIES 301-400: 1X TO 2.5X BASIC CARDS
RED ZONE PRINT RUN 30 SER.#'d SETS

2009 Score Inscriptions Scorecard

*VETS 1-300: 5X TO 12X BASIC CARDS
*ROOKIES 301-400: .8X TO 2X BASIC CARDS
STATED PRINT RUN 50 SER.#'d SETS

2009 Score Inscriptions 1989 Score

1 Matthew Stafford 6.00 15.00
2 Mark Sanchez 4.00 10.00
3 Darrius Heyward-Bey 1.25 3.00
4 Michael Crabtree 2.50 6.00
5 Knowshon Moreno 1.25 3.00
6 Josh Freeman 2.50 6.00
7 Jeremy Maclin 2.00 5.00
8 Percy Harvin 2.00 5.00
9 Hakeem Nicks 2.00 5.00
10 Chris Wells 2.00 5.00

2009 Score Inscriptions 1989 Score Autographs

STATED PRINT RUN 20 SER.#'d SETS
1 Matthew Stafford 150.00 300.00
2 Mark Sanchez 150.00 300.00
3 Darrius Heyward-Bey 40.00 80.00
4 Michael Crabtree 100.00 200.00
5 Knowshon Moreno 100.00 200.00
6 Josh Freeman 75.00 150.00
7 Jeremy Maclin 60.00 120.00
8 Percy Harvin 150.00 250.00
9 Hakeem Nicks 40.00 80.00
10 Chris Wells 75.00 150.00

2009 Score Inscriptions Autographs

VET PRINT RUN 10-499
*ROOK.AU/299-999: .25X TO .6X GOLD ZONE AU
*ROOK.AU/199: .3X TO .8X GOLD ZONE AU
*ROOK.AU/99: .4X TO 1X GOLD ZONE AU
ROOKIE PRINT RUN 45-999
SERIAL #'d UNDER 20 NOT PRICED
3 Dominique Rodgers-Cromartie/199 4.00 10.00
10 Chris Houston/182 4.00 10.00
12 Harry Douglas/50 5.00 12.00
19 Demetrius Williams/100 5.00 12.00
25 Ray Rice/299 5.00 12.00
29 Derek Fine/499 3.00 8.00
33 Leodis McKelvin/85 5.00 12.00
36 Steve Johnson/499 6.00 15.00
38 Charles Godfrey/399 3.00 8.00
40 Dante Rosario/499 3.00 8.00
51 Earl Bennett/399 4.00 10.00
56 Andre Caldwell/25 6.00 15.00
61 Jerome Simpson/299 3.00 8.00
70 Josh Cribbs/100 12.50 25.00
78 Patrick Crayton/100 5.00 12.00
90 Peyton Hillis/203 12.00 30.00
96 Jerome Felton/499 3.00 8.00
97 Jordon Dizon/22 6.00 15.00
100 Rudi Johnson/188 4.00 10.00
108 James Jones/100 5.00 12.00
109 Jermichael Finley/499 8.00 20.00
112 Amobi Okoye/499 3.00 8.00
115 DeMeco Ryans/249 5.00 12.00
129 Mike Hart/100 6.00 15.00
134 Derrick Harvey/499 3.00 8.00
139 Quentin Groves/449 3.00 8.00
140 Reggie Nelson/246 4.00 10.00
146 Kolby Smith/299 3.00 8.00
154 Davone Bess/100 5.00 12.00
157 Jake Long/499 3.00 8.00
167 John David Booty/199 5.00 12.00
168 Sidney Rice/75 6.00 15.00
171 Brandon Meriweather/499 3.00 8.00
174 LaMont Jordan/190 4.00 10.00
178 Terrence Wheatley/499 3.00 8.00
181 Adrian Arrington/214 4.00 10.00
182 Devery Henderson/499 3.00 8.00
187 Marques Colston/50 6.00 15.00
198 Kenny Phillips/499 3.00 8.00
209 Vernon Gholston/199 4.00 10.00
210 Chaz Schilens/499 3.00 8.00
215 Michael Bush/100 6.00 15.00
223 Greg Lewis/150 4.00 10.00
227 Stewart Bradley/126 4.00 10.00
241 Jacob Hester/499 3.00 8.00
249 Josh Morgan/263 3.00 8.00
264 Antonio Pittman/47 5.00 12.00
265 Chris Long/368 4.00 10.00
267 Keenan Burton/493 3.00 8.00
275 Dexter Jackson/499 3.00 8.00
277 Gaines Adams/499 3.00 8.00
292 Chris Horton/499 4.00 10.00
295 Devin Thomas/236 4.00 10.00
298 Ladell Betts/150 4.00 10.00
302 Aaron Curry/99 6.00 15.00
303 Aaron Kelly/799 3.00 8.00
306 Andre Brown/99 4.00 10.00
310 Austin Collie/599 5.00 12.00
311 B.J. Raji/299 6.00 15.00
312 Brandon Gibson/399 4.00 10.00
313 Brandon Pettigrew/99 6.00 15.00
314 Brandon Tate/99 6.00 15.00
315 Brian Cushing/99 6.00 15.00
317 Brian Orakpo/99 6.00 15.00
318 Brian Robiskie/99 6.00 15.00
319 Brooks Foster/499 2.50 6.00
320 Cameron Morrah/499 2.50 6.00
321 Cedric Peerman/99 5.00 12.00
322 Chase Coffman/99 5.00 12.00
324 Clay Matthews/99 20.00 50.00
325 Clint Sintim/99 6.00 15.00
326 Cornelius Ingram/499 2.50 6.00
329 Darius Passmore/999 3.00 8.00
332 Demetrius Byrd/499 3.00 8.00
333 Deon Butler/599 3.00 8.00
334 Derrick Williams/99 5.00 12.00
335 Devin Moore/799 3.00 8.00
336 Dominique Edison/599 2.50 6.00
339 Everette Brown/99 5.00 12.00
341 Glen Coffee/99 5.00 12.00
342 Graham Harrell/199 10.00 25.00
344 Hunter Cantwell/799 4.00 10.00
346 James Casey/399 3.00 8.00
348 James Laurinaitis/99 6.00 15.00
349 Jared Cook/299 4.00 10.00
350 Jarett Dillard/399 4.00 10.00
351 Jason Smith/99 5.00 12.00
352 Javon Ringer/99 6.00 15.00
353 Jeremiah Johnson/511 4.00 10.00
356 John Parker Wilson/99 6.00 15.00
357 Johnny Knox/299 6.00 15.00
358 Josh Freeman/99 20.00 50.00
362 Kenny McKinley/499 4.00 10.00
363 Kevin Ogletree/799 4.00 10.00
365 Kory Sheets/799 3.00 8.00
366 Larry English/99 6.00 15.00
367 LeSean McCoy/99 12.00 30.00
369 Malcolm Jenkins/99 6.00 15.00
370 Mark Sanchez/45 40.00 100.00
372 Michael Crabtree/199 15.00 40.00
373 Mike Goodson/599 4.00 10.00
374 Mike Thomas/99 6.00 15.00
375 Mike Wallace/599 10.00 25.00
376 Mohamed Massaquoi/99 5.00 12.00
377 Nate Davis/99 5.00 12.00
378 Nathan Brown/299 3.00 8.00
379 P.J. Hill/799 3.00 8.00
380 Pat White/99 6.00 15.00
382 Patrick Turner/599 3.00 8.00
383 Percy Harvin/99 25.00 60.00
384 Quan Cosby/799 3.00 8.00
385 Quinn Johnson/599 3.00 8.00
387 Ramses Barden/99 4.00 10.00
388 Rashad Jennings/99 6.00 15.00
389 Rey Maualuga/99 6.00 15.00
390 Rhett Bomar/99 5.00 12.00
392 Shawn Nelson/399 3.00 8.00
394 Stephen McGee/99 6.00 15.00
395 Tom Brandstater/99 6.00 15.00
396 Tony Fiammetta/599 3.00 8.00
397 Travis Beckum/499 3.00 8.00
398 Tyrell Sutton/590 3.00 8.00
399 Tyson Jackson/99 5.00 12.00
400 Vontae Davis/199 5.00 12.00

2009 Score Inscriptions Autographs Gold Zone

1-300 VET PRINT RUN 18-50
301-400 ROOKIE PRINT RUN 50
3 Dominique Rodgers-Cromartie/50 5.00 12.00
10 Chris Houston/50 5.00 12.00
12 Harry Douglas/50 5.00 12.00
19 Demetrius Williams/50 5.00 12.00
25 Ray Rice/50 8.00 20.00
29 Derek Fine/50 5.00 12.00
30 Fred Jackson/50 15.00 40.00
31 James Hardy/50 6.00 15.00
33 Leodis McKelvin/50 5.00 12.00
35 Paul Posluszny/50 6.00 15.00
36 Steve Johnson/50 10.00 25.00
38 Charles Godfrey/50 5.00 12.00
40 Dante Rosario/50 5.00 12.00
43 Jon Beason/44 5.00 12.00
51 Earl Bennett/50 6.00 15.00
56 Andre Caldwell/50 5.00 12.00
61 Jerome Simpson/50 5.00 12.00
70 Josh Cribbs/50 12.00 30.00
78 Patrick Crayton/50 5.00 12.00
90 Peyton Hillis/50 12.00 30.00
96 Jerome Felton/50 5.00 12.00
97 Jordon Dizon/50 5.00 12.00
100 Rudi Johnson/50 5.00 12.00
108 James Jones/50 5.00 12.00
109 Jermichael Finley/50 12.50 25.00
112 Amobi Okoye/50 5.00 12.00
115 DeMeco Ryans/50 6.00 15.00
121 Steve Slaton/50 6.00 15.00
129 Mike Hart/50 6.00 15.00
134 Derrick Harvey/50 5.00 12.00
139 Quentin Groves/50 5.00 12.00
140 Reggie Nelson/50 5.00 12.00
145 Jamaal Charles/50 8.00 20.00
146 Kolby Smith/50 5.00 12.00
150 Tyler Thigpen/50 5.00 12.00
152 Chad Henne/50 6.00 15.00
154 Davone Bess/50 5.00 12.00
157 Jake Long/50 5.00 12.00
165 Erin Henderson/50 5.00 12.00
167 John David Booty/50 6.00 15.00
168 Sidney Rice/50 6.00 15.00
169 Tarvaris Jackson/50 6.00 15.00
171 Brandon Meriweather/50 5.00 12.00
174 LaMont Jordan/50 5.00 12.00
178 Terrence Wheatley/50 5.00 12.00
181 Adrian Arrington/50 5.00 12.00
182 Devery Henderson/50 5.00 12.00
187 Marques Colston/50 6.00 15.00
188 Pierre Thomas/50 12.00 30.00
198 Kenny Phillips/50 5.00 12.00
203 Dustin Keller/50 5.00 12.00
209 Vernon Gholston/50 5.00 12.00
210 Chaz Schilens/50 5.00 12.00
215 Michael Bush/50 6.00 15.00
227 Stewart Bradley/50 5.00 12.00
234 Rashard Mendenhall/50 6.00 15.00
240 Eric Weddle/50 5.00 12.00
241 Jacob Hester/50 5.00 12.00
249 Josh Morgan/50 5.00 12.00
252 Reggie Smith/28 6.00 15.00
256 John Carlson/50 6.00 15.00
262 Owen Schmitt/50 5.00 12.00
264 Antonio Pittman/50 5.00 12.00
265 Chris Long/50 6.00 15.00
267 Keenan Burton/50 5.00 12.00
273 Aqib Talib/50 5.00 12.00
275 Dexter Jackson/50 5.00 12.00
277 Gaines Adams/50 5.00 12.00
292 Chris Horton/50 6.00 15.00
295 Devin Thomas/50 5.00 12.00
298 Ladell Betts/50 5.00 12.00
302 Aaron Curry/50 6.00 15.00
303 Aaron Kelly/50 5.00 12.00
306 Andre Brown/50 4.00 10.00
310 Austin Collie/50 8.00 20.00
311 B.J. Raji/50 8.00 20.00
312 Brandon Gibson/50 6.00 15.00
313 Brandon Pettigrew/50 6.00 15.00
314 Brandon Tate/50 6.00 15.00
315 Brian Cushing/50 6.00 15.00
317 Brian Orakpo/50 6.00 15.00
318 Brian Robiskie/50 6.00 15.00
319 Brooks Foster/50 4.00 10.00
320 Cameron Morrah/50 4.00 10.00
321 Cedric Peerman/50 5.00 12.00
322 Chase Coffman/50 5.00 12.00
323 Chris Wells/50 15.00 40.00
324 Clay Matthews/50 40.00 80.00
325 Clint Sintim/50 6.00 15.00
326 Cornelius Ingram/50 4.00 10.00
329 Darius Passmore/50 5.00 12.00
330 Darrius Heyward-Bey/50 6.00 15.00
332 Demetrius Byrd/50 5.00 12.00
333 Deon Butler/50 5.00 12.00
334 Derrick Williams/50 5.00 12.00
335 Devin Moore/50 5.00 12.00
336 Dominique Edison/50 4.00 10.00
337 Donald Brown/50 6.00 15.00
339 Everette Brown/50 5.00 12.00
341 Glen Coffee/50 5.00 12.00
342 Graham Harrell/50 12.50 25.00
343 Hakeem Nicks/50 10.00 25.00
344 Hunter Cantwell/50 6.00 15.00
346 James Casey/50 5.00 12.00
348 James Laurinaitis/50 6.00 15.00
349 Jared Cook/50 6.00 15.00
350 Jarett Dillard/50 6.00 15.00
351 Jason Smith/50 5.00 12.00
352 Javon Ringer/50 6.00 15.00
353 Jeremiah Johnson/50 6.00 15.00
355 Jeremy Maclin/50 10.00 25.00
356 John Parker Wilson/50 6.00 15.00
357 Johnny Knox/50 10.00 25.00
358 Josh Freeman/50 25.00 50.00
359 Juaquin Iglesias/50 5.00 12.00
361 Kenny Britt/50 8.00 20.00
362 Kenny McKinley/50 6.00 15.00
363 Kevin Ogletree/50 6.00 15.00
364 Knowshon Moreno/50 15.00 40.00
365 Kory Sheets/50 5.00 12.00
366 Larry English/50 6.00 15.00
367 LeSean McCoy/50 12.00 30.00
369 Malcolm Jenkins/50 6.00 15.00
370 Mark Sanchez/50 40.00 100.00
371 Matthew Stafford/50 60.00 120.00
372 Michael Crabtree/50 15.00 40.00
373 Mike Goodson/50 6.00 15.00
374 Mike Thomas/50 6.00 15.00
375 Mike Wallace/50 15.00 40.00
376 Mohamed Massaquoi/50 5.00 12.00
377 Nate Davis/50 5.00 12.00
378 Nathan Brown/50 5.00 12.00
379 P.J. Hill/50 5.00 12.00
380 Pat White/50 6.00 15.00
382 Patrick Turner/50 5.00 12.00
383 Percy Harvin/50 25.00 60.00
384 Quan Cosby/50 5.00 12.00
385 Quinn Johnson/50 5.00 12.00
387 Ramses Barden/50 4.00 10.00
388 Rashad Jennings/50 6.00 15.00
389 Rey Maualuga/50 6.00 15.00
390 Rhett Bomar/50 5.00 12.00
392 Shawn Nelson/50 5.00 12.00
393 Shonn Greene/50 10.00 25.00
394 Stephen McGee/50 6.00 15.00
395 Tom Brandstater/50 6.00 15.00
396 Tony Fiammetta/50 5.00 12.00
397 Travis Beckum/50 5.00 12.00
398 Tyrell Sutton/50 5.00 12.00
399 Tyson Jackson/50 5.00 12.00
400 Vontae Davis/50 6.00 15.00

2009 Score Inscriptions Autographs Red Zone

1-300 VET PRINT RUN 5-30
*ROOKIE/30: .5X TO 1.2X GOLD ZONE AU
301-400 ROOKIE PRINT RUN 30
SERIAL #'d UNDER 20 NOT PRICED
3 Dominique Rodgers-Cromartie/30 6.00 15.00
9 Tim Hightower/30 6.00 15.00
10 Chris Houston/30 6.00 15.00
11 Curtis Lofton/30 6.00 15.00
12 Harry Douglas/30 6.00 15.00
13 Jerious Norwood/30 8.00 20.00
19 Demetrius Williams/30 6.00 15.00
25 Ray Rice/30 10.00 25.00
29 Derek Fine/30 6.00 15.00
30 Fred Jackson/30 30.00 60.00
33 Leodis McKelvin/30 5.00 12.00
35 Paul Posluszny/30 8.00 20.00
36 Steve Johnson/30 12.00 30.00
37 Trent Edwards/30 6.00 15.00
38 Charles Godfrey/30 6.00 15.00
40 Dante Rosario/30 6.00 15.00
43 Jon Beason/30 6.00 15.00
51 Earl Bennett/30 8.00 20.00
56 Andre Caldwell/30 6.00 15.00
61 Jerome Simpson/30 6.00 15.00
62 Keith Rivers/30 6.00 15.00
64 T.J. Houshmandzadeh/30 8.00 20.00
70 Josh Cribbs/30 15.00 40.00
78 Patrick Crayton/30 6.00 15.00
88 Eddie Royal/30 8.00 20.00
90 Peyton Hillis/30 25.00 50.00
96 Jerome Felton/30 6.00 15.00
97 Jordon Dizon/30 6.00 15.00
98 Kevin Smith/30 8.00 20.00
100 Rudi Johnson/30 6.00 15.00
103 A.J. Hawk/30 8.00 20.00
107 Greg Jennings/30 10.00 25.00
109 Jermichael Finley/30 12.00 30.00
112 Amobi Okoye/30 6.00 15.00
115 DeMeco Ryans/30 8.00 20.00
121 Steve Slaton/20 8.00 20.00
129 Mike Hart/30 8.00 20.00
134 Derrick Harvey/30 6.00 15.00
139 Quentin Groves/30 6.00 15.00
140 Reggie Nelson/30 6.00 15.00
145 Jamaal Charles/30 10.00 25.00
146 Kolby Smith/30 6.00 15.00
147 Larry Johnson/30 8.00 20.00
150 Tyler Thigpen/30 6.00 15.00
154 Davone Bess/30 6.00 15.00
157 Jake Long/30 6.00 15.00
165 Erin Henderson/30 6.00 15.00
167 John David Booty/30 8.00 20.00
168 Sidney Rice/30 8.00 20.00
169 Tarvaris Jackson/30 8.00 20.00
171 Brandon Meriweather/30 6.00 15.00
172 Jerod Mayo/30 8.00 20.00
174 LaMont Jordan/20 6.00 15.00
178 Terrence Wheatley/30 6.00 15.00
181 Adrian Arrington/30 6.00 15.00
182 Devery Henderson/30 6.00 15.00
187 Marques Colston/30 8.00 20.00
188 Pierre Thomas/30 20.00 40.00
198 Kenny Phillips/30 6.00 15.00
203 Dustin Keller/30 6.00 15.00
209 Vernon Gholston /30 6.00 15.00
210 Chaz Schilens/30 6.00 15.00
214 Justin Fargas/30 6.00 15.00
215 Michael Bush/30 8.00 20.00
218 Zach Miller/30 6.00 15.00
224 Hank Baskett/30 6.00 15.00
227 Stewart Bradley/30 6.00 15.00
241 Jacob Hester/30 6.00 15.00
249 Josh Morgan/30 6.00 15.00
251 Patrick Willis/30 8.00 20.00
252 Reggie Smith/30 6.00 15.00
256 John Carlson/30 8.00 20.00
262 Owen Schmitt/30 6.00 15.00
264 Antonio Pittman/30 6.00 15.00
265 Chris Long/30 8.00 20.00
266 Donnie Avery/30 8.00 20.00
267 Keenan Burton/30 6.00 15.00
273 Aqib Talib/30 6.00 15.00
275 Dexter Jackson/30 6.00 15.00
277 Gaines Adams/30 6.00 15.00
292 Chris Horton/30 8.00 20.00
294 Colt Brennan/30 8.00 20.00
295 Devin Thomas/30 6.00 15.00
370 Mark Sanchez/30 60.00 120.00
371 Matthew Stafford/30 60.00 120.00
372 Michael Crabtree/30 30.00 80.00
383 Percy Harvin/30 40.00 80.00

2009 Score Inscriptions Franchise

STATED PRINT RUN 499 SER.#'d SETS
*ART.PROOF/32: 1.5X TO 4X BASIC INSERTS
*GOLD ZONE/50: 1.2X TO 3X BASIC INSERTS
*RED ZONE/30: 1.5X TO 4X BASIC INSERTS
*SCORECARD/100: .8X TO 2X BASIC INSERTS
1 Adrian Peterson 1.50 4.00
2 Andre Johnson .75 2.00
3 Brady Quinn .75 2.00
4 Brandon Jacobs .75 2.00
5 Brandon Marshall .75 2.00
6 Braylon Edwards .75 2.00
7 Brian Westbrook .75 2.00
8 Calvin Johnson 1.00 2.50
9 Clinton Portis .75 2.00
10 DeAngelo Williams 1.00 2.50
11 Frank Gore .75 2.00
12 Greg Jennings 1.00 2.50
13 Larry Fitzgerald 1.00 2.50
14 Lee Evans .75 2.00
15 Marion Barber .75 2.00
16 Maurice Jones-Drew .75 2.00
17 Philip Rivers 1.00 2.50
18 Roddy White .75 2.00
19 Santonio Holmes .75 2.00
20 Dwayne Bowe .75 2.00

2009 Score Inscriptions Future Franchise

STATED PRINT RUN 499 SER.#'d SETS
*ART.PROOF/32: 1.5X TO 4X BASIC INSERTS
*GOLD ZONE/50: 1.2X TO 3X BASIC INSERTS
*RED ZONE/30: 1.5X TO 4X BASIC INSERTS
*SCORECARD/100: .8X TO 2X BASIC INSERTS
1 Brian Brohm .60 1.50
2 Chad Henne .75 2.00
3 Chris Johnson 1.00 2.50
4 Colt Brennan .75 2.00
5 Darren McFadden 1.00 2.50
6 Derrick Ward .60 1.50
7 DeSean Jackson .75 2.00
8 Eddie Royal .75 2.00
9 Erik Ainge .75 2.00
10 Joe Flacco 1.00 2.50
11 John David Booty .75 2.00
12 Jonathan Stewart .75 2.00
13 Kevin Smith .75 2.00
14 Matt Cassel .75 2.00
15 Matt Forte 1.00 2.50
16 Matt Ryan 1.00 2.50
17 Rashard Mendenhall .75 2.00
18 Ray Rice 1.00 2.50
19 Steve Slaton .75 2.00
20 Tashard Choice .60 1.50

2009 Score Inscriptions Hot Rookies

STATED PRINT RUN 499 SER.#'d SETS
*ART.PROOF/32: 1X TO 2.5X BASIC INSERTS
*GOLD ZONE/50: .8X TO 2X BASIC INSERTS
*RED ZONE/30: 1X TO 2.5X BASIC INSERTS
*SCORECARD/100: .6X TO 1.5X BASIC INSERTS
1 Aaron Curry 1.00 2.50
2 Brandon Pettigrew 1.00 2.50
3 Brandon Tate 1.00 2.50
4 Brian Robiskie 1.00 2.50
5 Chris Wells 1.50 4.00
6 Darrius Heyward-Bey 1.00 2.50
7 Deon Butler .75 2.00
8 Derrick Williams .75 2.00
10 Glen Coffee .75 2.00
11 Hakeem Nicks 1.50 4.00
12 Jeremy Maclin 1.50 4.00
13 Josh Freeman 2.00 5.00
14 Juaquin Iglesias .75 2.00
15 Kenny Britt 1.25 3.00
16 Knowshon Moreno 1.00 2.50
17 LeSean McCoy 2.00 5.00
18 Mark Sanchez 3.00 8.00
19 Matthew Stafford 5.00 12.00
20 Michael Crabtree 2.00 5.00
21 Mike Thomas 1.00 2.50
22 Mike Wallace 2.00 5.00
23 Mohamed Massaquoi .75 2.00
24 Pat White 1.00 2.50
25 Patrick Turner .75 2.00
26 Percy Harvin 1.50 4.00
27 Ramses Barden .60 1.50
28 Shonn Greene 1.50 4.00
29 Stephen McGee 1.00 2.50
30 Tyson Jackson .75 2.00

2009 Score Inscriptions Hot Rookies Autographs Gold Zone

GOLD ZONE PRINT RUN 50
*RED ZONE/23-30: .5X TO 1.2X GOLD ZONE/50
1 Aaron Curry 6.00 15.00
2 Brandon Pettigrew 6.00 15.00
3 Brandon Tate 6.00 15.00
4 Brian Robiskie 6.00 15.00
5 Chris Wells 20.00 40.00
6 Darrius Heyward-Bey 6.00 15.00
7 Deon Butler 5.00 12.00
8 Derrick Williams 5.00 12.00
10 Glen Coffee 5.00 12.00
11 Hakeem Nicks 10.00 25.00
12 Jeremy Maclin 10.00 25.00
13 Josh Freeman 15.00 40.00
14 Juaquin Iglesias 5.00 12.00
15 Kenny Britt 8.00 20.00
16 Knowshon Moreno 20.00 50.00
17 LeSean McCoy 12.00 30.00
18 Mark Sanchez 50.00 100.00
19 Matthew Stafford 50.00 100.00
20 Michael Crabtree 25.00 60.00
21 Mike Thomas 6.00 15.00
22 Mike Wallace 12.00 30.00
23 Mohamed Massaquoi 5.00 12.00
24 Pat White 6.00 15.00
25 Patrick Turner 5.00 12.00
26 Percy Harvin 25.00 50.00
27 Ramses Barden 4.00 10.00
28 Shonn Greene 10.00 25.00
29 Stephen McGee 6.00 15.00
30 Tyson Jackson 5.00 12.00

2009 Score Inscriptions Young Stars

STATED PRINT RUN 499 SER.#'d SETS
*ART.PROOF/32: 1.5X TO 4X BASIC INSERTS
*GOLD ZONE/50: 1.2X TO 3X BASIC INSERTS
*RED ZONE/30: 1.5X TO 4X BASIC INSERTS
*SCORECARD/100: .8X TO 2X BASIC INSERTS
1 Antoine Cason .60 1.50
2 Aqib Talib .60 1.50
3 Brandon Flowers .60 1.50
4 Chris Horton .75 2.00
5 Dan Connor .60 1.50
6 Davone Bess .60 1.50
7 Donnie Avery .75 2.00
8 Dustin Keller .60 1.50
9 Dwight Lowery .60 1.50
10 Felix Jones 1.00 2.50
11 Jerod Mayo .75 2.00
12 John Carlson .75 2.00
13 Josh Morgan .60 1.50
14 Leodis McKelvin .60 1.50
15 Le'Ron McClain .75 2.00
16 Malcolm Kelly .60 1.50
17 Martellus Bennett .60 1.50
18 Ryan Torain .60 1.50
19 Steve Johnson .75 2.00
20 Tim Hightower .60 1.50

2009 Score National Convention VIP Promos

Cards from this set were available to VIP guests at the 2009 National Sports Collectors Convention in Cleveland, Ohio. Each card was produced in the style of the 1989 Score product.

COMPLETE SET (6) 10.00 20.00
1 Mark Sanchez 2.50 6.00
2 Matthew Stafford 4.00 10.00
3 Matt Ryan 1.25 3.00
4 Larry Fitzgerald 1.25 3.00
5 Ben Roethlisberger 1.25 3.00
6 Brady Quinn 1.00 2.50

2002 Score QBC Materials

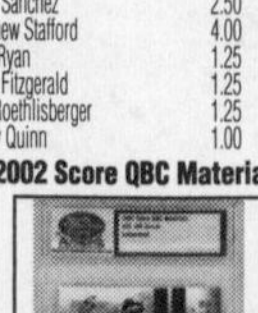

Issued in retail only blister packs, each card was slabbed by SCD Authentic and labeled as "Untouched." Packs contained one game-used jersey card or signed card and carried an initial SRP of $19.99. Signed cards were issued for the following players: Steve Young, Warren Moon, Jake Plummer, Aaron Brooks, and John Elway.

AUTOS TOO SCARCE TO PRICE
1 Donovan McNabb JSY 5.00 12.00
2 Jake Plummer JSY 4.00 10.00
3 Jeff Garcia JSY 4.00 10.00
4 Peyton Manning JSY 10.00 25.00
5 Rob Johnson JSY 4.00 10.00
6 Trent Dilfer JSY 4.00 10.00
7 Bernie Kosar JSY 5.00 12.00
8 Boomer Esiason JSY 5.00 12.00
9 Jim Everett JSY 5.00 12.00
10 Jim Kelly JSY 8.00 20.00
11 Steve Young JSY 8.00 20.00
12 Warren Moon JSY 6.00 15.00
13 Donovan McNabb FB 5.00 12.00
14 Jeff Garcia FB 4.00 10.00
15 Peyton Manning FB 10.00 25.00
16 Boomer Esiason FB 5.00 12.00
17 Jim Kelly FB 8.00 20.00
18 Steve Young FB 8.00 20.00
19 Warren Moon FB 6.00 15.00
20 Peyton Manning JSY 10.00 25.00
21 Doug Flutie JSY 6.00 15.00
22 Jeff Garcia JSY 4.00 10.00
23 Jake Plummer JSY 4.00 10.00
24 Aaron Brooks JSY 4.00 10.00
25 John Elway JSY 12.00 30.00
26 Boomer Esiason JSY 5.00 12.00
27 Warren Moon JSY 6.00 15.00
28 Jim Everett JSY 5.00 12.00
29 John Elway FB 12.00 30.00
30 Warren Moon FB 6.00 15.00
31 Jake Plummer FB 4.00 10.00
32 Peyton Manning FB 10.00 25.00
33 Jeff Garcia FB 4.00 10.00
34 Aaron Brooks FB 4.00 10.00
35 Doug Flutie FB 6.00 15.00
36 Boomer Esiason FB 5.00 12.00
37 Ken O'Brien JSY 4.00 10.00

1994 Score Board National Promos

COMPLETE SET (20) 20.00 40.00
10 Troy Aikman 1.00 2.50
12 Emmitt Smith 1.25 3.00
20A Troy Aikman CL 1.25 2.50
20E Emmitt Smith CL 1.25 3.00

1996-97 Score Board All Sport PPF

The 1996-97 All Sport Past Present and Future set was issued in two series in six-card packs. The product contains original vintage and rookie cards of the top athletes from baseball, basketball, football and hockey as well as new cards of tomorrow's stars from each sport. Release date for series one was October 1996; series two was February 1997. There was also a gold parallel produced for this set. Series one gold cards were inserted 1:10 packs while series two had gold cards inserted at a 1:5 ratio.

COMPLETE SET (200) 6.00 15.00
30 Troy Aikman .30 .75
31 Kerry Collins .15 .40
32 Steve Young .25 .60
33 Kordell Stewart .15 .40
34 Kevin Hardy .05 .15
35 Joey Galloway .15 .40
36 Simeon Rice .07 .20
37 Marcus Coleman .05 .15
38 Eric Moulds .20 .50
39 Ray Farmer .05 .15
40 Chris Darkins .05 .15
41 Amani Toomer .15 .40
42 Daryl Gardener .05 .15
43 Bobby Engram .08 .25
44 Stepfret Williams .07 .20
45 Eddie George .40 1.00
46 Tony Brackens .05 .15
47 Cedric Jones .05 .15
48 Jason Dunn .07 .20
49 Mike Alstott .20 .50
51 Danny Kanell .07 .20
52 Andre Johnson .07 .20
53 Rickey Dudley .07 .20
54 Jeff Hartings .07 .20
55 Regan Upshaw .05 .15
56 Alex Molden .07 .20
57 Terry Glenn .15 .40
58 Alex Van Dyke .07 .20
59 Karim Abdul-Jabbar .08 .25
87 Emmitt Smith .50 1.25
88 Drew Bledsoe .20 .50
89 Keyshawn Johnson .20 .50
90 Marshall Faulk .20 .50
91 Steve Young .25 .60
92 Lawrence Phillips .08 .25
93 Terry Glenn .15 .40
100 Troy Aikman CL (51-100) .15 .40
126 Emmitt Smith .50 1.25
127 Drew Bledsoe .20 .50
128 Steve McNair .15 .40
129 Marshall Faulk .20 .50
130 Keyshawn Johnson .20 .50
131 Lawrence Phillips .08 .25
132 Leeland McElroy .05 .15
133 Tony Banks .08 .25
134 Derrick Mayes .07 .20
135 Jonathan Ogden .15 .40
136 Zach Thomas .30 .75
137 Tim Biakabutuka .08 .25
138 Ray Mickens .05 .15
139 Ray Lewis .40 1.00
140 Marco Battaglia .05 .15
141 John Mobley .05 .15
142 Marvin Harrison .30 .75
143 Duane Clemons .07 .20
144 Lance Johnstone .07 .20
145 Eddie Kennison .10 .30
146 Bobby Hoying .10 .30
147 Brett Favre .40 1.00
148 Reggie Brown .05 .15
149 Walt Harris .05 .15
151 Marcus Jones .05 .15
152 Je'Rod Cherry .05 .15
153 Brian Dawkins .15 .40
154 Johnny McWilliams .07 .20
155 Brian Roche .05 .15
156 Muhsin Muhammad .15 .40
157 Lawyer Milloy .08 .25
158 Jermane Mayberry .05 .15
159 DeRon Jenkins .07 .20
187 Steve Young .25 .60
188 Kerry Collins .15 .40
189 Kevin Hardy .05 .15
190 Kordell Stewart .15 .40
191 Joey Galloway .15 .40

192 Simeon Rice	.08	.25
193 Eddie George	.40	1.00
194 Brett Favre	.40	1.00
195 Emmitt Smith	.50	1.25
200 Eddie George CL	.15	.40

1996-97 Score Board All Sport PPF Gold

*GOLDS: 1.2X TO 3X BASIC CARDS
GOLD STATED ODDS SER.1 1:10/SER.2 1:5

1996-97 Score Board All Sport PPF Retro

COMPLETE SET (10)	12.00	30.00
R2 Keyshawn Johnson	1.00	2.50
R4 Emmitt Smith	3.00	8.00
R7 Troy Aikman	2.00	5.00
R9 Lawrence Phillips	.40	2.00

1996-97 Score Board All Sport PPF Revivals

COMPLETE SET (10)	12.00	30.00
REV6 Emmitt Smith	2.50	6.00
REV7 Keyshawn Johnson	1.00	2.50
REV8 Eddie George	1.25	3.00
REV9 Brett Favre	3.00	8.00

1996-97 Score Board Autographed Collection

Each box of Score Board Autographed Collection contains 16 packs containing six cards. The 50-card regular set includes top athletes from all four major team sports. According to Score Board, a total of 1,500 sequentially numbered cases were produced.

COMPLETE SET (50)	5.00	12.00
18 Emmitt Smith	.50	1.25
19 Kordell Stewart	.15	.40
20 Lawrence Phillips	.07	.20
21 Kerry Collins	.15	.40
22 Drew Bledsoe	.20	.50
23 Marshall Faulk	.25	.60
24 Steve Young	.25	.60
25 Joey Galloway	.20	.50
26 Keyshawn Johnson	.20	.50
27 Eddie George	.75	2.00
28 Karim Abdul-Jabbar	.07	.20
29 Terry Glenn	.20	.50
30 Marvin Harrison	.30	.75
31 Tim Biakabutuka	.10	.30
32 Leeland McElroy	.07	.20
33 Simeon Rice	.07	.20
34 Kevin Hardy	.07	.20
35 Rickey Dudley	.07	.20
36 Zach Thomas	.30	.75
37 Bobby Engram	.07	.20

1996-97 Score Board Autographed Collection Autographs

1 Karim Abdul-Jabbar	2.00	5.00
5 Marco Battaglia	1.50	4.00
8 Michael Cheever	1.50	4.00
11 Chris Darkins	1.50	4.00
14 Donnie Edwards	1.50	4.00
15 Ray Farmer	1.50	4.00
17 Eddie George	15.00	40.00
19 Kevin Hardy	1.50	4.00
21 Jimmy Herndon	1.50	4.00
22 Bobby Hoying	2.00	5.00
24 Dietrich Jells	2.00	5.00
25 DeRon Jenkins	1.50	4.00
26 Andre Johnson	1.50	4.00
27 Danny Kanell	2.00	5.00
31 Derrick Mayes	2.00	5.00
33 Leeland McElroy	1.50	4.00
34 Ray Mickens	1.50	4.00
35 Roman Oben	1.50	4.00
36 Jason Odom	1.50	4.00
41 Jamain Stephens	1.50	4.00
42 Matt Stevens	1.50	4.00
43 Kordell Stewart	8.00	20.00
44 Zach Thomas	12.00	25.00

1996-97 Score Board Autographed Collection Autographs Gold

*UNLISTED GOLD: .6X TO 1.5X BASIC AU

1996-97 Score Board Autographed Collection Game Breakers

COMPLETE SET (30)	25.00	60.00
*GOLD: .8X TO 2X BASIC INSERTS		
GOLD STATED ODDS 1:50		
GB14 Emmitt Smith	3.00	8.00
GB15 Kordell Stewart	1.00	2.50
GB16 Kevin Hardy	.60	1.50
GB17 Kerry Collins	.75	2.00
GB18 Drew Bledsoe	1.25	3.00
GB19 Marshall Faulk	1.25	3.00
GB20 Steve Young	1.50	4.00
GB21 Lawrence Phillips	.60	1.50
GB22 Keyshawn Johnson	1.50	4.00
GB23 Eddie George	1.50	4.00
GB24 Karim Abdul-Jabbar	.60	1.50
GB25 Terry Glenn	1.00	2.50
GB26 Marvin Harrison	2.00	5.00
GB27 Tim Biakabutuka	.60	1.50

1997-98 Score Board Autographed Collection

The 1998 Autographed Collection set was issued in one series totaling 50 cards with players from baseball, basketball, football and hockey. The product's major draw was an average of five autographed cards and one memorabilia redemption card per 18-pack box. The regular autographs were inserted 1:4.5 packs, the Blue Ribbon autographs were inserted 1:18 packs. The one-per box memorabilia redemption cards were not all redeemed due to the fact that Score Board, Inc. filed for bankruptcy a few months after the product's release. Score Board also released a "Strongbox Collection" that original retailed for around $125. Each Strongbox included a parallel of this 50 card set, one star player autographed baseball with holder, one star player autographed 8" x 10", one Athletic Excellence card and One Sports City USA card.

COMPLETE SET (50)	5.00	12.00
2 Brett Favre	.60	1.50
6 Emmitt Smith	.50	1.25
8 Steve Young	.20	.50
10 Ike Hilliard	.15	.40
13 Darrell Russell	.07	.20
17 Jake Plummer	.20	.50
19 Danny Wuerffel	.10	.30
21 Kordell Stewart	.15	.40
26 Warrick Dunn	.30	.75
29 Rae Carruth	.07	.20
31 Troy Aikman	.25	.60
33 Peter Boulware	.08	.25
34 David LaFleur	.07	.20
35 Jim Druckenmiller	.07	.20
38 Yatil Green	.07	.20
40 Orlando Pace	.08	.25
42 Byron Hanspard	.08	.25
43 Troy Davis	.07	.20
44 Reidel Anthony	.07	.20
46 Tony Banks	.10	.30
48 Tony Gonzalez	.20	.50

1997-98 Score Board Autographed Collection Strongbox

*STRONGBOX: .8X TO 2X BASIC CARDS

1997-98 Score Board Autographed Collection Athletic Excellence

COMPLETE SET (12)	10.00	25.00
AE3 Warrick Dunn	1.50	4.00
AE7 Darrell Russell	.75	2.00

1997-98 Score Board Autographed Collection Autographs

1 John Allred	1.50	4.00
2 Darnell Autry	1.50	4.00
3 Pat Barnes	1.50	4.00
8 Jim Druckenmiller	1.50	4.00
13 Dexter McCleon	1.50	4.00
14 Brad Otton	1.50	4.00
17 Jake Plummer	8.00	20.00
18 Scot Pollard	2.50	6.00
19 Antowain Smith	4.00	10.00
22 Reinard Wilson	1.50	4.00

1997-98 Score Board Autographed Collection Blue Ribbon Autographs

8 Eddie George/240	30.00	60.00
13 Emmitt Smith/120	75.00	150.00
15 Steve Young/139	50.00	100.00
P1 Warrick Dunn/200	5.00	12.00

1997-98 Score Board Autographed Collection Sports City USA

COMPLETE SET (15)	10.00	25.00
*STRONGBOX/600: .8X to 2X BASIC INSERTS		
SC1 Adonal Foyle Joe Smith Steve Young	.75	2.00
SC2 Matt White Warrick Dunn Reidel Anthony	.75	2.00
SC4 Kerry Wood Scottie Pippen Darnell Autry	.60	1.50
SC5 Ray Allen Brett Favre	2.00	5.00
SC7 Tim Thomas Duce Staley J.D.Drew	1.00	2.50
SC8 Alonzo Mourning Yatil Green	.50	1.25
SC9 Joe Thornton Chauncey Billups	.40	1.00
SC10 Emmitt Smith Troy Aikman Richard Jackman	1.50	4.00
SC11 Kordell Stewart Robert Dome	.50	1.25
SC12 Wes Helms Bryan Hanspard Ed Gray	.40	1.00
SC13 Stephon Marbury Dwayne Rudd	.40	1.00
SC14 Jay Payton Tiki Barber Keith Van Horn	.75	2.00
SC15 Matt Drews Bryant Westbrook Scot Pollard	.75	2.00

1996 Score Board Lasers

The 1996 Score Board Lasers set consists of 100-cards distributed in six-card packs. Each card features a color action player photo of a top NFL player printed on 24-point foil board with special effects stamping.

COMPLETE SET (100)	8.00	20.00
1 Brett Favre	.75	2.00
2 Chris Warren	.07	.20
3 J.J. Stokes	.15	.40
4 Barry Sanders	.60	1.50
5 Ben Coates	.07	.20
6 Bryan Cox	.02	.10
7 Carl Pickens	.07	.20
8 Cris Carter	.15	.40
9 Curtis Martin	.30	.75
10 Dan Marino	.75	2.00
11 Dave Brown	.07	.20
12 Drew Bledsoe	.25	.60
13 Edgar Bennett	.07	.20
14 Herman Moore	.07	.20
15 Jeff Blake	.15	.40
16 Jerry Rice	.40	1.00
17 Jim Kelly	.15	.40
18 John Elway	.75	2.00
19 Junior Seau	.15	.40
20 Kerry Collins	.15	.40
21 Kordell Stewart	.15	.40
22 Leonard Russell	.02	.10
23 Mark Brunell	.25	.60
24 Marshall Faulk	.20	.50
25 Mike Tomczak	.02	.10
26 Reggie White	.15	.40
27 Ricky Watters	.07	.20
28 Rod Woodson	.07	.20
29 Rodney Peete	.02	.10
30 Stan Humphries	.07	.20
31 Steve McNair	.30	.75
32 Terry Allen	.07	.20
33 Thurman Thomas	.15	.40
34 Troy Aikman	.40	1.00
35 Vinny Testaverde	.07	.20
36 Chris T. Jones	.15	.40
37 Deion Sanders	.20	.50
38 Eric Metcalf	.07	.20
39 Erik Kramer	.02	.10
40 Emmitt Smith	.60	1.50
41 Gus Frerotte	.07	.20
42 Shannon Sharpe	.07	.20
43 Jerome Bettis	.15	.40
44 Jim Harbaugh	.07	.20
45 Isaac Bruce	.15	.40
46 Jeff Hostetler	.07	.20
47 Ki-Jana Carter	.07	.20
48 Marcus Allen	.15	.40
49 Neil O'Donnell	.07	.20
50 Rashaan Salaam	.07	.20
51 Robert Brooks	.15	.40
52 Steve Bono	.07	.20
53 Scott Mitchell	.07	.20
54 Terrell Davis	.30	.75
55 Tim Brown	.15	.40
56 Troy Vincent	.02	.10
57 Warren Moon	.07	.20
58 Tony Martin	.07	.20
59 Rodney Hampton	.07	.20
60 Steve Young	.30	.75
61 Rick Mirer	.07	.20
62 Mark Chmura	.07	.20
63 Larry Centers	.07	.20
64 Ken Dilger	.07	.20
65 Joey Galloway	.15	.40
66 Jim Everett	.02	.10
67 Chris Chandler	.07	.20
68 James O. Stewart	.07	.20
69 Robert Smith	.07	.20
70 Tamarick Vanover	.15	.40
71 Wayne Chrebet	.25	.60
72 Keyshawn Johnson RC	.40	1.00
73 Kevin Hardy RC	.15	.40
74 Lawrence Phillips RC	.15	.40
75 Jonathan Ogden RC	.15	.40
76 Terry Glenn RC	.40	1.00
77 Tim Biakabutuka RC	.15	.40
78 Eddie George RC	.50	1.25
79 Eric Moulds RC	.50	1.25
80 John Mobley RC	.02	.10
81 Amani Toomer RC	.40	1.00
82 Marvin Harrison RC	1.00	2.50
83 Leeland McElroy RC	.07	.20
84 Rickey Dudley RC	.15	.40
85 Tony Banks RC	.15	.40
86 Zach Thomas RC	.30	.75
87 Alex Molden RC	.02	.10
88 Daryl Gardener RC	.07	.20
89 Jamal Anderson RC	.20	.50
90 Karim Abdul-Jabbar RC	.15	.40
91 Simeon Rice RC	.40	1.00
92 Walt Harris RC	.02	.10
93 Bobby Engram RC	.15	.40
94 Kevin Williams	.02	.10
95 Sean Gilbert	.02	.10
96 Kevin Greene	.07	.20
97 Regan Upshaw RC	.02	.10
98 Marcus Jones RC	.02	.10
99 Ray Lewis RC	1.25	3.00
100 Keyshawn Johnson Checklist card	.07	.20
P1 Emmitt Smith Promo unnumbered Sample card	.30	.75
NNO Emmitt Smith JUMBO/10,000 Rushing Yards		

1996 Score Board Lasers Autographs

STATED ODDS 1:150
*DIE CUT/100: .6X TO 1.5X BASIC AU
DIE CUT/100 ODDS 1:930

1 Troy Aikman	30.00	80.00
2 Drew Bledsoe	12.00	30.00
3 Marshall Faulk	15.00	40.00
4 Keyshawn Johnson	10.00	25.00
5 Emmitt Smith	75.00	200.00
6 Kordell Stewart	10.00	25.00
7 Steve Young	20.00	50.00

1996 Score Board Lasers Images

COMPLETE SET (30)	20.00	50.00
STATED ODDS 1:7		
I1 Steve Bono	.30	.75
I2 Kerry Collins	.60	1.50
I3 Tim Biakabutuka	.30	.75
I4 Rashaan Salaam	.30	.75
I5 Jeff Blake	.40	1.00
I6 Emmitt Smith	2.50	6.00
I7 Troy Aikman	1.50	4.00
I8 Deion Sanders	.75	2.00
I9 John Elway	3.00	8.00
I10 Herman Moore	.30	.75
I11 Brett Favre	3.00	8.00
I12 Eddie George	.60	1.50
I13 Marvin Harrison	2.00	5.00
I14 Mark Brunell	.60	1.50
I15 Dan Marino	3.00	8.00
I16 Karim Abdul-Jabbar	.30	.75
I17 Cris Carter	.60	1.50
I18 Drew Bledsoe	1.00	2.50
I19 Curtis Martin	1.25	3.00
I20 Keyshawn Johnson	.60	1.50
I21 Chris T. Jones	.30	.75
I22 Kordell Stewart	.60	1.50
I23 Junior Seau	.60	1.50
I24 Steve Young	1.25	3.00
I25 Jerry Rice	1.50	4.00
I26 Joey Galloway	.40	1.00
I27 Lawrence Phillips	.40	1.00
I28 Jonathan Ogden	.40	1.00
I29 Jim Harbaugh	.30	.75
I30 Neil O'Donnell	.30	.75

1996 Score Board Lasers Sunday's Heroes

COMPLETE SET (25)	40.00	100.00
STATED ODDS 1:22		
SH1 Tim Brown	1.25	3.00
SH2 Kerry Collins	1.25	3.00
SH3 Tim Biakabutuka	.60	1.50
SH4 Rashaan Salaam	.60	1.50
SH5 Jeff Blake	1.25	3.00
SH6 Ki-Jana Carter	.60	1.50
SH7 Emmitt Smith	5.00	12.00
SH8 Troy Aikman	3.00	8.00
SH9 Deion Sanders	1.50	4.00
SH10 Terrell Davis	2.50	6.00
SH11 Barry Sanders	5.00	12.00
SH12 Brett Favre	6.00	15.00
SH13 Reggie White	1.25	3.00
SH14 Marshall Faulk	1.50	4.00
SH15 Mark Brunell	1.25	3.00
SH16 Kevin Hardy	1.25	3.00
SH17 Dan Marino	6.00	15.00
SH18 Drew Bledsoe	2.00	5.00
SH19 Curtis Martin	2.50	6.00
SH20 Keyshawn Johnson	1.25	3.00
SH21 Kordell Stewart	1.25	3.00
SH22 Steve Young	2.50	6.00
SH23 Jerry Rice	3.00	8.00
SH24 Chris Warren	.60	1.50
SH25 Karim Abdul-Jabbar	.60	1.50

1997 Score Board NFL Experience

The 1997 Score Board NFL Experience set was issued in 6-card packs with one series totaling 100-cards. A retail version and special Super Bowl Card Show version were produced with each box carrying a different assortment of insert cards. Score Board included a wide variety of "vintage" cards inserted in packs at the rate of 1:36. These included cards from the 1935 National Chicle set up to the near present. A blank-backed promo sheet was distributed at the 1997 NFL Experience Super Bowl Card Show in New Orleans. Each sheet features three members of the participating Super Bowl teams and is numbered of 5000 sheets produced.

COMPLETE SET (100)	5.00	12.00
1 Emmitt Smith	.50	1.25
2 Kordell Stewart	.15	.40
3 Antonio Freeman	.15	.40
4 William Thomas	.05	.15
5 Simeon Rice	.08	.25
6 Drew Bledsoe	.20	.50
7 Elvis Grbac	.08	.25
8 Ken Dilger	.05	.15
9 John Elway	.60	1.50
10 Curtis Conway	.08	.25
11 Adrian Murrell	.08	.25
12 Karim Abdul-Jabbar	.15	.40
13 Terry Allen	.15	.40
14 Lawrence Phillips	.05	.15
15 Barry Sanders	.50	1.25
16 Shannon Sharpe	.08	.25
17 Troy Aikman	.30	.75
18 Kevin Greene	.08	.25
19 Cris Carter	.15	.40
20 Jim Kelly	.15	.40
21 Eric Metcalf	.08	.25
22 Joey Galloway	.08	.25
23 Eddie George	.15	.40
24 Scott Mitchell	.08	.25
25 Neil O'Donnell	.08	.25
26 Ben Coates	.08	.25
27 Andre Reed	.08	.25
28 Michael Jackson	.08	.25
29 Keith Jackson	.05	.15
30 J.J. Stokes	.08	.25
31 Rickey Dudley	.08	.25
32 Ricky Watters	.08	.25
33 Marcus Allen	.15	.40
34 Brett Favre	.60	1.50
35 Kevin Hardy	.05	.15
36 Jim Everett	.05	.15
37 Zach Thomas	.15	.40
38 Lamar Lathon	.05	.15
39 LeShon Johnson	.05	.15
40 Bruce Smith	.08	.25
41 Junior Seau	.15	.40
42 Tony Banks	.08	.25
43 Brian Mitchell	.05	.15
44 Chris T. Jones	.05	.15
45 Ty Detmer	.08	.25
46 Robert Brooks	.08	.25
47 Derrick Thomas	.15	.40
48 Dan Wilkinson	.05	.15
49 Michael Sinclair	.05	.15
50 Dave Brown	.05	.15
51 Carl Pickens	.08	.25
52 Jim Harbaugh	.08	.25
53 Wayne Chrebet	.15	.40
54 Warren Moon	.15	.40
55 Steve Young	.20	.50
56 Sean Gilbert	.05	.15
57 Jerome Bettis	.15	.40
58 Dan Marino	.60	1.50
59 Terrell Davis	.25	.60
60 Mark Brunell	.20	.50
61 Kent Graham	.05	.15
62 Rashaan Salaam	.08	.25
63 Tony Martin	.08	.25
64 Robert Smith	.08	.25
65 Thurman Thomas	.15	.40
66 Marshall Faulk	.20	.50
67 Dale Carter	.05	.15
68 Stan Humphries	.08	.25
69 Isaac Bruce	.15	.40
70 Warren Sapp	.08	.25
71 Kerry Collins	.15	.40
72 Jamal Anderson	.15	.40
73 Chris Chandler	.08	.25
74 Herman Moore	.08	.25
75 Rodney Hampton	.08	.25
76 Tim Brown	.15	.40
77 Keenan McCardell	.08	.25
78 Anthony Miller	.05	.15
79 Jake Reed	.08	.25
80 Earnest Byner	.05	.15
81 Chris Warren	.08	.25
82 Deion Sanders	.15	.40
83 Mike Tomczak	.05	.15
84 Curtis Martin	.20	.50
85 John Friesz	.05	.15
86 Gus Frerotte	.05	.15
87 Vinny Testaverde	.08	.25
88 Jason Dunn	.05	.15
89 James O.Stewart	.08	.25
90 Steve Bono	.08	.25
91 Levon Kirkland	.05	.15
92 Merton Hanks	.05	.15
93 Marvin Harrison	.15	.40
94 Reggie Brooks	.05	.15
95 Reggie White	.15	.40
96 Jeff Blake	.08	.25
97 Terry Glenn	.15	.40
98 Jerry Rice	.30	.75
99 Keyshawn Johnson	.15	.40
100 Edgar Bennett Checklist back	.05	.15
P1 Promo Sheet	1.20	3.00
NNO Barry Sanders JUMBO/2053	7.50	15.00

1997 Score Board NFL Experience Bayou Country

COMPLETE SET (10)	25.00	60.00
STATED ODDS 1:35 SUPER BOWL PACKS		
BC1 Terry Allen	1.50	4.00
BC2 Emmitt Smith	5.00	12.00
BC3 Troy Aikman	3.00	8.00
BC4 Brett Favre	6.00	15.00
BC5 Jerry Rice	3.00	8.00
BC6 Curtis Martin	2.00	5.00
BC7 John Elway	6.00	15.00
BC8 Jerome Bettis	1.50	4.00
BC9 Kevin Greene	1.00	2.50
BC10 Karim Abdul-Jabbar	1.50	4.00

1997 Score Board NFL Experience Foundations

COMPLETE SET (30)	40.00	100.00
STATED ODDS 1:12		
F1 Ray Lewis	1.50	4.00
F2 Bruce Smith	.75	2.00
F3 Jeff Blake	.75	2.00
F4 Terrell Davis	2.00	5.00
F5 Steve McNair	1.50	4.00
F6 Marshall Faulk	1.50	4.00
F7 Mark Brunell	1.50	4.00
F8 Derrick Thomas	1.25	3.00
F9 Karim Abdul-Jabbar	1.25	3.00
F10 Curtis Martin	1.50	4.00
F11 Keyshawn Johnson	1.25	3.00
F12 Tim Brown	1.25	3.00
F13 Kordell Stewart	1.25	3.00
F14 Junior Seau	1.25	3.00
F15 Joey Galloway	.75	2.00
F16 Simeon Rice	.75	2.00
F17 Jessie Tuggle	.50	1.25
F18 Kerry Collins	1.25	3.00
F19 Rashaan Salaam	.75	2.00
F20 Emmitt Smith	4.00	10.00
F21 Barry Sanders	4.00	10.00
F22 Brett Favre	5.00	12.00
F23 Cris Carter	1.25	3.00
F24 Jim Everett	.50	1.25
F25 Amani Toomer	1.25	3.00
F26 Ricky Watters	.75	2.00
F27 Tony Banks	.75	2.00
F28 Jerry Rice	2.50	6.00
F29 Warren Sapp	.75	2.00
F30 Terry Allen	1.25	3.00

1997 Score Board NFL Experience Season's Heroes

COMPLETE SET (20)	30.00	80.00
STATED ODDS 1:18 SUPER BOWL PACKS		
SH1 Gus Frerotte	.60	1.50
SH2 Terry Allen	1.50	4.00
SH3 Troy Aikman	3.00	8.00
SH4 Emmitt Smith	5.00	12.00
SH5 Ricky Watters	1.00	2.50
SH6 Brett Favre	6.00	15.00
SH7 Reggie White	1.50	4.00
SH8 Steve Young	2.00	5.00
SH9 Jerry Rice	3.00	8.00
SH10 Kevin Greene	1.00	2.50
SH11 Anthony Johnson	.60	1.50
SH12 Thurman Thomas	1.50	4.00
SH13 Bruce Smith	1.00	2.50
SH14 Jerome Bettis	1.50	4.00
SH15 Rod Woodson	1.00	2.50
SH16 Eddie George	1.50	4.00
SH17 Terrell Davis	2.50	6.00
SH18 John Elway	6.00	15.00
SH19 Drew Bledsoe	2.00	5.00
SH20 Junior Seau	1.50	4.00

1997 Score Board NFL Experience Teams of the '90s

COMPLETE SET (15)	40.00	100.00
STATED ODDS 1:100		
WC1 Emmitt Smith	10.00	25.00
WC2 Bruce Smith	2.00	5.00
WC3 Steve Young	4.00	10.00
WC4 Thurman Thomas	3.00	8.00
WC5 Kordell Stewart	3.00	8.00
WC6 Ricky Watters	2.00	5.00
WC7 Ken Norton	1.25	3.00
WC8 Jeff Hostetler	2.00	5.00
WC9 Jim Kelly	3.00	8.00
WC10 Troy Aikman	6.00	15.00
WC11 Jerry Rice	6.00	15.00
WC12 Mark Rypien	2.00	5.00
WC13 Stan Humphries	2.00	5.00
WC14 Deion Sanders	3.00	8.00
WC15 Andre Reed	2.00	5.00

1997 Score Board NFL Experience Hard Target

These oversized (approximately 5" by 7") cards were distributed by Score Board at the 1997 NFL Experience Super Bowl Card Show in New Orleans. Each card is unnumbered and features a top NFL player on the cardfront with an explanation of Score Board's Wrapper Redemption program on the cardbacks. A different player was distributed each day of the card show.

COMPLETE SET (5)	6.00	15.00
1 Terrell Davis	2.00	5.00
2 Brett Favre	2.00	5.00
3 Eddie George	1.20	3.00
4 Keyshawn Johnson	1.00	2.50
5 Emmitt Smith	1.60	4.00

1997 Score Board Playbook

The 1997 Score Board Playbook set was issued in one series totaling 100-cards and was distributed in five-card packs with a suggested retail price of $3.99. The fronts feature color action player photos in four unique designs based on the player's playing position. The backs carry player information and statistical graphs and charts. Only 1,500 sequentially numbered cases were produced. A By the Numbers partial (50-cards) parallel set was later released in its own separate packaging.

COMPLETE SET (100)	6.00	15.00
1 Warren Moon	.15	.40
2 Troy Aikman	.30	.75
3 Jeff George	.08	.25
4 Brett Favre	.60	1.50
5 Jim Harbaugh	.08	.25
6 Jeff Blake	.08	.25
7 John Elway	.60	1.50
8 Mark Brunell	.20	.50
9 Steve McNair	.20	.50
10 Kordell Stewart	.15	.40
11 Drew Bledsoe	.20	.50
12 Kerry Collins	.15	.40
13 Dan Marino	.60	1.50
14 Jim Druckenmiller RC	.08	.25
15 Todd Collins QB	.05	.15
16 Jake Plummer RC	.60	1.50
17 Pat Barnes RC	.05	.15
18 Vinny Testaverde	.08	.25
19 Scott Mitchell	.08	.25
20 Rob Johnson	.15	.40
21 Elvis Grbac	.08	.25
22 Danny Wuerffel RC	.15	.40
23 Neil O'Donnell	.08	.25
24 Tony Banks	.08	.25
25 Stan Humphries	.08	.25
26 Brad Johnson	.15	.40
27 Trent Dilfer	.15	.40
28 Ty Detmer	.08	.25
29 Steve Young	.20	.50
30 Gus Frerotte	.05	.15
31 Leeland McElroy	.05	.15
32 Byron Hanspard RC	.08	.25
33 Jamal Anderson	.15	.40
34 Thurman Thomas	.15	.40
35 Antowain Smith RC	.40	1.00
36 Tim Biakabutuka	.08	.25
37 Raymont Harris	.05	.15
38 Corey Dillon RC	.60	1.50
39 Emmitt Smith	.50	1.25
40 Terrell Davis	.20	.50
41 Barry Sanders	.50	1.25
42 Dorsey Levens	.15	.40
43 Marshall Faulk	.20	.50
44 Natrone Means	.08	.25
45 Marcus Allen	.15	.40
46 Karim Abdul-Jabbar	.15	.40
47 Robert Smith	.08	.25
48 Curtis Martin	.20	.50
49 Troy Davis RC	.08	.25
50 Tiki Barber RC	1.00	2.50
51 Adrian Murrell	.08	.25
52 Napoleon Kaufman	.15	.40
53 Ricky Watters	.08	.25
54 Jerome Bettis	.15	.40
55 Lawrence Phillips	.05	.15
56 Garrison Hearst	.08	.25
57 Warrick Dunn RC	.50	1.25
58 Eddie George	.15	.40
59 Terry Allen	.15	.40
60 Michael Jackson	.08	.25
61 Rae Carruth RC	.05	.15
62 Carl Pickens	.08	.25
63 Michael Irvin	.15	.40
64 Shannon Sharpe	.08	.25
65 Herman Moore	.08	.25
66 Robert Brooks	.08	.25
67 Antonio Freeman	.15	.40
68 Marvin Harrison	.15	.40
69 Keenan McCardell	.08	.25
70 Jimmy Smith	.08	.25
71 Cris Carter	.15	.40
72 Ben Coates	.08	.25
73 Terry Glenn	.15	.40
74 Ike Hilliard RC	.25	.60
75 Keyshawn Johnson	.15	.40
76 Eddie Kennison	.08	.25
77 Tim Brown	.15	.40
78 Irving Fryar	.08	.25
79 Jake Reed	.08	.25
80 Isaac Bruce	.15	.40
81 Tony Martin	.08	.25
82 Jerry Rice	.30	.75
83 Joey Galloway	.08	.25
84 Reidel Anthony RC	.15	.40
85 Yatil Green RC	.08	.25
86 Tony Gonzalez RC	.60	1.50
87 Simeon Rice	.08	.25
88 Peter Boulware RC	.15	.40
89 Bruce Smith	.08	.25
90 Reinard Wilson RC	.08	.25
91 Deion Sanders	.15	.40
92 Dryant Westbrook RC	.05	.15
93 Reggie White	.15	.40
94 Dwayne Rudd RC	.05	.15
95 Darrell Russell RC	.05	.15
96 Greg Lloyd	.05	.15
97 Junior Seau	.15	.40
98 Shawn Springs RC	.08	.25
99 Cortez Kennedy	.05	.15
100 Kordell Stewart Checklist back	.08	.25

1997 Score Board Playbook Franchise Player

COMPLETE SET (30)	20.00	50.00
STATED ODDS 1:6 PLAYBOOK		
FP1 Simeon Rice	.50	1.25
FP2 Jamal Anderson	.75	2.00
FP3 Peter Boulware	.75	2.00
FP4 Bruce Smith	.50	1.25
FP5 Kerry Collins	.75	2.00
FP6 Rashaan Salaam	.50	1.25
FP7 Jeff Blake	.50	1.25
FP8 Emmitt Smith	2.50	6.00
FP9 Terrell Davis	1.00	2.50
FP10 Barry Sanders	2.50	6.00
FP11 Brett Favre	3.00	8.00
FP12 Marshall Faulk	1.00	2.50
FP13 Mark Brunell	1.00	2.50
FP14 Derrick Thomas	.75	2.00
FP15 Dan Marino	3.00	8.00
FP16 Brad Johnson	.75	2.00
FP17 Drew Bledsoe	1.00	2.50
FP18 Troy Davis	.50	1.25
FP19 Ike Hilliard	.60	1.50
FP20 Keyshawn Johnson	.75	2.00
FP21 Tim Brown	.75	2.00
FP22 Ricky Watters	.50	1.25
FP23 Jerome Bettis	.75	2.00
FP24 Isaac Bruce	.75	2.00
FP25 Junior Seau	.75	2.00
FP26 Jerry Rice	1.50	4.00
FP27 Joey Galloway	.50	1.25
FP28 Warrick Dunn	1.25	3.00
FP29 Eddie George	.75	2.00
FP30 Gus Frerotte	.30	.75

1997 Score Board Playbook Mirror Image

COMPLETE SET (20)	40.00	100.00
STATED ODDS 1:24 PLAYBOOK		
1 Brett Favre	6.00	15.00
2 Warrick Dunn	2.50	6.00
3 Emmitt Smith	5.00	12.00
4 Steve Young	2.00	5.00
5 Terrell Davis	2.00	5.00
6 Kordell Stewart	1.50	4.00
7 Kerry Collins	1.50	4.00
8 John Elway	6.00	15.00
9 Barry Sanders	5.00	12.00
10 Drew Bledsoe	2.00	5.00
11 Troy Aikman	3.00	8.00
12 Curtis Martin	2.00	5.00
13 Mark Brunell	2.00	5.00
14 Terry Glenn	1.50	4.00
15 Antowain Smith	2.00	5.00
16 Reggie White	1.50	4.00
17 Jeff Blake	1.00	2.50
18 Darrell Russell	.60	1.50
19 Terry Allen	1.50	4.00
20 Keyshawn Johnson	1.50	4.00

1997 Score Board Playbook Mirror Image Autographs

AUTO/110-915 ODDS 1:192 PLAYBOOK		
MI1 Brett Favre/110	75.00	150.00
MI2 Warrick Dunn/915	12.00	30.00
MI3 Emmitt Smith/410	50.00	120.00
MI4 Steve Young/360	20.00	50.00
MI5 Terrell Davis/590	12.00	30.00
MI6 Kordell Stewart/550	10.00	25.00
MI7 Kerry Collins/200	12.00	30.00

1997 Score Board Playbook Title Quest

COMPLETE SET (12)	20.00	50.00
TQ1-TQ2: ODDS 1:192 PLAYBOOK		
TQ3-TQ12: ODDS 1:32 PLAYBOOK		
TQ1 Brett Favre	5.00	12.00
TQ2 Terrell Davis	1.50	4.00
TQ3 Emmitt Smith	4.00	10.00
TQ4 Drew Bledsoe	1.50	4.00
TQ5 Mark Brunell	1.50	4.00
TQ6 Warrick Dunn	2.00	5.00
TQ7 Jim Druckenmiller	.75	2.00
TQ8 Derrick Thomas	1.25	3.00
TQ9 Rae Carruth	.50	1.25
TQ10 Jerome Bettis	1.25	3.00
TQ11 Dan Marino	5.00	12.00
TQ12 Barry Sanders	4.00	10.00

1997 Score Board Playbook By The Numbers

COMPLETE SET (50)	5.00	12.00
*BY THE NUMB: SAME PRICE AS PLAYBOOK		
GOLD MAG.ODDS 1:21 BY THE NUMBERS		
SILVER MAG.ODDS 1:2 BY THE NUMBERS		

1997 Score Board Playbook By The Numbers Magnified Gold

COMPLETE SET (50)	30.00	80.00
*MAG.GOLD STARS: 3X TO 8X BASIC CARDS		
*MAG.GOLD RCs: 1.5X TO 4X BASIC CARDS		
STATED PRINT RUN 200 SERIAL #'d SETS		
STATED ODDS 1:21 BY THE NUMBERS		

1997 Score Board Playbook By The Numbers Magnified Silver

COMPLETE SET (50)	10.00	25.00
*MAG SILV.STARS: .8X TO 2X BASIC CARDS		
*MAG SILV.RCs: .8X TO 2X BASIC CARDS		
STATED PRINT RUN 2000 SERIAL #'d SETS		
STATED ODDS 1:2 BY THE NUMBERS		

1997 Score Board Playbook By The Numbers Red Zone Stats

COMPLETE SET (10)	10.00	25.00
STATED ODDS 1:20 BY THE NUMBERS		
*MAGNIFIED GOLD/100: 2.5X TO 6X		
*MAGNIFIED SILVER/1000: .4X TO 1X		
RZ1 Emmitt Smith	2.50	6.00
RZ2 Terry Allen	.50	1.25
RZ3 Troy Aikman	1.50	4.00
RZ4 Brett Favre	3.00	8.00
RZ5 John Elway	3.00	8.00
RZ6 Drew Bledsoe	1.00	2.50
RZ7 Terrell Davis	1.00	2.50
RZ8 Karim Abdul-Jabbar	.50	1.25
RZ9 Curtis Martin	1.00	2.50
RZ10 Warrick Dunn	1.25	3.00

1997 Score Board Playbook By The Numbers Standout Numbers

COMPLETE SET (30)	15.00	40.00
STATED ODDS 1:4 BY THE NUMBERS		
*MAG.GOLDS: 1.2X TO 3X BASIC INSERTS		
MAG.GOLD ODDS 1:26 BY THE NUMBERS		
MAG.GOLD PRINT RUN 270 SER.#'d SETS		
*MAG.SILVERS: .4X TO 1X BASIC INSERTS		
MAG.SILVER ODDS 1:3 BY THE NUMBERS		
MAG.SILVER PRINT RUN 2700 SER.#'d SETS		
SN1 Drew Bledsoe	.75	2.00
SN2 Emmitt Smith	2.00	5.00
SN3 Cris Carter	.60	1.50
SN4 Brett Favre	2.50	6.00
SN5 Jerome Bettis	.60	1.50
SN6 Mark Brunell	.60	1.50
SN7 John Elway	2.50	6.00
SN8 Troy Aikman	1.25	3.00
SN9 Steve Young	.75	2.00
SN10 Kordell Stewart	.60	1.50
SN11 Reggie White	.60	1.50
SN12 Isaac Bruce	.60	1.50
SN13 Dan Marino	2.50	6.00
SN14 Kevin Greene	.60	1.50
SN15 Tim Brown	.60	1.50
SN16 Terry Glenn	.60	1.50
SN17 Ricky Watters	.40	1.00
SN18 Carl Pickens	.40	1.00
SN19 Keyshawn Johnson	.60	1.50
SN20 Barry Sanders	2.00	5.00
SN21 Marshall Faulk	.75	2.00
SN22 James O.Stewart	.60	1.50
SN23 Jerry Rice	1.25	3.00
SN24 Curtis Martin	.75	2.00
SN25 Herman Moore	.40	1.00
SN26 Terry Allen	.60	1.50
SN27 Eddie George	.60	1.50
SN28 Warrick Dunn	1.00	2.50
SN29 Marcus Allen	.60	1.50
SN30 Terrell Davis	.75	2.00

1997 Score Board Players Club

The 70 cards that make-up this set are a grouping from baseball, basketball, football and hockey players. Card fronts are full colored action shots, with professional team names air-brushed out. The card backs contain 1997 projected statistics and biographical information. Along with the number 1 Die-Cuts and Play Back inserts, vintage cards were the major draw to this product. One in 32 packs contained a vintage card from 1909-1979 from any of the four sports. An original Honus Wagner T206 card was offered as a redemption in 1:153,600 packs. Also, one vintage wax pack was available via redemption card in one in every 32 packs.

COMPLETE SET (70)	5.00	12.00
1 Brett Favre	.60	1.50
2 Duce Staley	.20	.50
5 Karim Abdul-Jabbar	.08	.25
10 Kordell Stewart	.08	.25
11 Mike Alstott	.08	.25
13 Peter Boulware	.08	.25
R.Wilson		
14 Troy Davis	.07	.20
20 Emmitt Smith	.50	1.25
21 Troy Aikman	.25	.60
25 Warrick Dunn	.30	.75
26 Eddie George	.20	.50
28 Joey Galloway	.08	.25
33 Darnell Autry	.07	.20
34 Steve Young	.20	.50
38 Tony Gonzalez	.30	.75
39 Jim Druckenmiller	.07	.20
44 Corey Dillon	.30	.75
46 Kerry Collins	.08	.25
47 Byron Hanspard	.08	.25
50 Rae Carruth	.07	.20
51 Jake Plummer	.20	.50
53 Darrell Russell	.07	.20
54 Shawn Springs	.07	.20
56 Bryant Westbrook	.07	.20
59 Orlando Pace	.08	.25
61 Ike Hilliard	.08	.25
63 Reidel Anthony	.07	.20
67 Zach Thomas	.20	.50
70 Brett Favre CL	.25	.60

1997 Score Board Players Club #1 Die-Cuts

COMPLETE SET (20)	25.00	60.00
D2 Troy Aikman	2.50	6.00
D3 Darrell Russell	1.25	3.00
D7 Orlando Pace	1.25	3.00
D15 Jim Druckenmiller	1.25	"3.00
D18 Warrick Dunn	1.50	4.00
D19 Emmitt Smith	4.00	10.00

1997 Score Board Players Club Play Backs

COMPLETE SET (15)	30.00	80.00
STATED ODDS 1:32		
PB1 Brett Favre	5.00	12.00
PB2 Kordell Stewart	1.25	3.00
PB3 Emmitt Smith	4.00	10.00
PB4 Troy Aikman	2.50	6.00
PB6 Steve Young	2.00	5.00
PB13 Kerry Collins	1.50	4.00

1997 Score Board Brett Favre Super Bowl XXXI

Special retail boxes of 1997 Pro Line contained one of these five Brett Favre Super Bowl XXXI cards. Each box included packs with 112-Pro Line cards along with one autographed card and one of these Favre cards. Each card features Favre along with "Super Bowl XXXI Champion" printed below the player image. Score Board logos are included on the cards instead of Pro Line.

COMPLETE SET (5)	3.00	8.00
COMMON CARD (BF1-BF5)	.75	2.00

1997 Score Board Talk N' Sports

This product features phone cards with a couple twists, including trivia contests to win memorabilia and to check current sports scores. The 50-card regular set includes stars and prospects from all four major team sports. According to Score Board, a total of 1,500 sequentially numbered cases were produced.

COMPLETE SET (50)	4.00	10.00
1 Brett Favre	.50	1.25
2 Marshall Faulk	.15	.40
3 Steve Young	.20	.50
4 Troy Aikman	.25	.60
5 Kordell Stewart	.08	.25
6 Kerry Collins	.10	.30
7 Keyshawn Johnson	.08	.25
8 Eddie George	.10	.30
9 Terry Glenn	.10	.30
10 Kevin Hardy	.07	.20
11 Emmitt Smith	.40	1.00
12 Karim Abdul-Jabbar	.08	.25
13 Tony Banks	.08	.25
14 Zach Thomas	.20	.50
15 Mike Alstott	.10	.30
16 Matt Stevens	.07	.20
17 Troy Davis	.07	.20
18 Warrick Dunn	.25	.60
19 Yatil Green	.07	.20
20 Rae Carruth	.07	.20
21 Darrell Russell	.07	.20
22 Peter Boulware	.07	.20
23 Shawn Springs	.07	.20

1997 Score Board Talk N' Sports Essentials

COMPLETE SET (10)	25.00	60.00
E1 Brett Favre	5.00	12.00
E4 Emmitt Smith	4.00	10.00
E7 Eddie George	3.00	8.00
E8 Troy Davis	1.50	4.00
E9 Darrell Russell	1.50	4.00

1997 Score Board Talk N' Sports Phone Cards $1

COMPLETE SET (50)	8.00	20.00
*PIN NUMBER REVEALED: HALF VALUE		

1997 Score Board Talk N' Sports Phone Cards $10

COMPLETE SET (10)	12.00	30.00
*PIN NUMBER REVEALED: HALF VALUE		
1 Brett Favre	3.00	8.00
3 Keyshawn Johnson	1.25	3.00
4 Steve Young	1.50	4.00
5 Kordell Stewart	1.00	2.50
7 Eddie George	1.25	3.00
8 Troy Aikman	2.00	5.00

1997 Score Board Talk N' Sports Phone Cards $20

COMPLETE SET (10)	25.00	60.00
*PIN NUMBER REVEALED: HALF VALUE		
1 Brett Favre	5.00	12.00
7 Eddie George	2.50	6.00
8 Troy Davis	2.00	5.00
9 Darrell Russell	2.00	5.00

1997 Score Board Talk N' Sports Phone Cards $1000

These rare cards are inserted at a rate of 1:11,000 packs. They are sequentially numbered out of 10. The phone time expired ON 7/31/1998.

PIN NUMBER REVEALED: HALF VALUE
3 Brett Favre
5 Eddie George

1998 Score Board Jumbos

Score Board released these cards as singles direct to the public for $19.75 each. Each measures roughly 3 1/2" by 5," is die cut, and carries and announced print run.

COMPLETE SET (2)	12.00	30.00
JE7 John Elway	6.00	15.00
Mile High Salute		
MVP3 Brett Favre/3-Time MVP	6.00	15.00
SB Super Bowl XXXII/5000	8.00	20.00
Terrell Davis		
John Elway		
Dorsey Levens		
Brett Favre		

1976 Seahawks Post-Intelligencer

This 57-card set was issued at the start of training camp for the Seattle Seahawks first season. The cards measure approximately 6 1/2" by 3" and were printed in the sports section of the local newspaper. The fronts feature headshot drawings of the player and his background and have a black dotted line to help cut them out of the newspaper.

COMPLETE SET (57)	125.00	250.00
1 Jack Patera	3.00	6.00
2 Dave Williams WR	3.00	6.00
3 Bill Olds	3.00	6.00
4 Mike Curtis	4.00	8.00
5 Norm Evans	3.00	6.00
6 Ron Howard	3.00	6.00
7 John Demarie	3.00	6.00
8 Ken Geddes	3.00	6.00
9 Don Hansen	3.00	6.00
10 Rollie Woolsey	3.00	6.00
11 Sam McCullum	3.00	6.00
12 Eddie McMillan	3.00	6.00
13 Gordon Jolley	3.00	6.00
14 John McMakin	3.00	6.00
15 Nick Bebout	3.00	6.00
16 Carl Barisich	3.00	6.00
17 Gary Hayman	3.00	6.00
18 Al Matthews	3.00	6.00
19 Fred Hoaglin	3.00	6.00
20 Ahmad Rashad	6.00	12.00
21 Wayne Baker	3.00	6.00
22 Dave Brown	3.00	6.00
23 Larry Woods	3.00	6.00
24 Dave Tipton	3.00	6.00
25 Ed Bradley	3.00	6.00
26 Bob Penchion	3.00	6.00
27 Steve Niehaus	3.00	6.00
28 Gary Keithley	3.00	6.00
29 Bob Picard	3.00	6.00
30 Joe Owens	3.00	6.00
31 Steve Myer	3.00	6.00
32 Lyle Blackwood	3.00	6.00
33 Sherman Smith	3.00	6.00
34 Don Bitterlich	3.00	6.00
35 Neil Graff	3.00	6.00
36 Steve Taylor	3.00	6.00
37 Kerry Marbury	3.00	6.00
38 Charles Waddell	3.00	6.00
39 Art Kuehn	3.00	6.00
40 Jerry Davis	3.00	6.00
41 Sammy Green	3.00	6.00
42 Rocky Rasley	3.00	6.00
43 Ken Hutcherson	3.00	6.00
44 Dwayne Crump	3.00	6.00
45 Steve Raible	3.00	6.00
45 Larry Bates	3.00	6.00
46 Rondy Colbert	3.00	6.00
47 Randy Johnson	3.00	6.00
48 Andy Bolton	3.00	6.00
49 Jeff Lloyd	3.00	6.00
50 Don Dufek Jr.	3.00	6.00
51 Rick Engles	3.00	6.00
52 Alvis Darby	3.00	6.00
53 Ernie Jones DB	3.00	6.00
55 Jim Zorn	5.00	10.00
56 Don Clune	3.00	6.00
57 Bill Munson	4.00	8.00

1976 Seahawks Team Issue 8.5x11

These blank-backed photos measure approximately 8 1/2" by 11" and feature black-and-white full-bleed head shots of Seattle Seahawks players. The player's name, team name, facsimile autograph, and Seahawks logo appear near the bottom. The photos are unnumbered and checklisted below in alphabetical order. We've included all known photos. Any addtions to this list are appreciated.

COMPLETE SET (12)	60.00	120.00
1 Ed Bradley	5.00	10.00
2 Mike Curtis	6.00	12.00
3 Norm Evans	5.00	10.00
4 Ken Geddes	5.00	10.00
5 Sammy Green	5.00	10.00
6 Fred Hoaglin	5.00	10.00
7 Ron Howard	5.00	10.00
8 Eddie McMillan	5.00	10.00
9 Steve Niehaus	5.00	10.00
10 Jack Patera	5.00	10.00
11 Bob Penchion	5.00	10.00
12 Jim Zorn	7.50	15.00

1976-77 Seahawks Team Issue 5x7

These blank-backed photos measure approximately 5" by 7" and feature black-and-white full-bleed head shots of Seattle Seahawks players. The player's name, team, facsimile autograph, and Seahawks logo appear near the bottom. Some of the photos have the text and helmet printed in black ink while others use white ink. The photos are unnumbered and checklisted below in alphabetical order. We've included all known photos. Any addtions to this list are appreciated.

COMPLETE SET (37)	150.00	300.00
1 Sam Adkins	4.00	8.00
2 Steve August	4.00	8.00
3 Carl Barisich	4.00	8.00
4 Nick Bebout	4.00	8.00
5 Dennis Boyd	4.00	8.00
6 Dave Brown	4.00	8.00
7 Ron Coder	4.00	8.00
8 Mike Curtis	5.00	10.00
9 John DeMarie	4.00	8.00
10 Dan Doornink	4.00	8.00
11 Norm Evans	4.00	8.00
12 Efren Herrera	4.00	8.00
13 Fred Hoaglin	4.00	8.00
14 Ron Howard	4.00	8.00
15 Steve Largent	15.00	25.00
(jersey no. partially in view)		
16 Steve Largent	15.00	25.00
(no jersey no. showing)		
17 John Leypoldt	4.00	8.00
18 Bob Lurtsema	4.00	8.00
19 Al Matthews	4.00	8.00
20 Sam McCullum	4.00	8.00
21 John McMakin	4.00	8.00
22 Bill Munson	5.00	10.00
23 Steve Myer	4.00	8.00
24 Steve Niehaus	4.00	8.00
25 Jack Patera CO	4.00	8.00
26 Steve Raible	4.00	8.00
27 John Sawyer	4.00	8.00
28 Sherman Smith	4.00	8.00
29 Don Testerman	4.00	8.00
30 Dave Tipton	4.00	8.00
31 Manu Tuiasosopo	4.00	8.00
32 Herman Weaver	4.00	8.00
33 Cornell Webster	4.00	8.00
34 Rollie Woolsey	4.00	8.00
35 Jim Zorn	7.50	15.00
(jersey no. partially in view)		
36 Jim Zorn	7.50	15.00
(no jersey # showing)		
37 Seahawk Mascot	4.00	8.00

1977 Seahawks Fred Meyer

Sponsored by Fred Meyer Department Stores and subtitled "Savings Selections Quality Service," this set consists of 14 photos (approximately 6" by 7 1/4") printed on thin glossy paper stock. The cards were reportedly given out one per week. The fronts feature either posed or action color player photos with black borders. The player's name, uniform number, and brief player information appear in one of the bottom corners. Most photos have a small color closeup in one of the lower corners; several others do not (photo numbers 3, 5, 12, 13A). Only Jim Zorn is represented twice in the set, by an action photo with a small color closeup and a portrait without an inset closeup. The backs are blank. The cards are unnumbered and checklisted below in alphabetical order. The set features a card of Steve Largent in his Rookie Card year.

COMPLETE SET (14)	75.00	150.00
1 Steve August	5.00	10.00
2 Autry Beamon	5.00	10.00
3 Terry Beeson	5.00	10.00
4 Dennis Boyd	5.00	10.00
5 Norm Evans	5.00	10.00
6 Sammy Green	5.00	10.00
7 Ron Howard	5.00	10.00
8 Steve Largent	20.00	40.00
9 Steve Myer	5.00	10.00
10 Steve Niehaus	5.00	10.00
11 Sherman Smith	5.00	10.00
12 Don Testerman	5.00	10.00
13A Jim Zorn	7.50	15.00
(No inset photo)		
13B Jim Zorn	7.50	15.00
(With inset photo)		

1978 Seahawks Nalley's

The 1978 Nalley's Chips Seattle Seahawks cards are actually the back panels of large (nine ounce) Nalley's boxes of Dippers, Barbecue Chips, and Potato Chips. The cards themselves measure approximately 9" by 10 3/4" and include a facsimile autograph. The back of the potato chip box features a color posed photo of the player with his facsimile autograph. One side of the box has the Seahawks game schedule, while the other side provides biographical and statistical information on the player. The front of the box includes the player's name and card number. The prices listed below refer to complete boxes.

COMPLETE SET (8)	350.00	500.00
1 Steve Largent	200.00	350.00
2 Autry Beamon	15.00	25.00
3 Jim Zorn	35.00	60.00
4 Sherman Smith	18.00	30.00
5 Ron Coder	15.00	25.00
6 Terry Beeson	15.00	25.00
7 Steve Niehaus	15.00	25.00
8 Ron Howard	15.00	25.00

1979 Seahawks Nalley's

The 1979 Nalley's Chips Seattle Seahawks cards are actually the back panels of large (nine ounce) Nalley's boxes of Dippers, Barbecue Chips, and Potato Chips. The cards themselves measure approximately 9" by 10 3/4" and include a facsimile autograph. The back of the potato chip box features a color photo of the player with his facsimile autograph. One side of the box has the Seahawks game schedule, while the other side provides biographical and statistical information on the player. The front of the box features the player's name and a card number that is a continuation of previous year's cards. The prices listed below refer to complete boxes.

COMPLETE SET (8)	75.00	135.00
9 Steve Myer	12.00	20.00
10 Tom Lynch	12.00	20.00
11 David Sims	12.00	20.00
12 John Yarno	12.00	20.00
13 Bill Gregory	12.00	20.00
14 Steve Raible	12.00	20.00
15 Dennis Boyd	12.00	20.00
16 Steve August	12.00	20.00

1979 Seahawks Police

The 1979 Seattle Seahawks Police set consists of 16 cards each measuring approximately 2 5/8" by 4 1/8". In addition to the local law enforcement agency, the set was sponsored by the Washington State Crime Prevention Association, the Kiwanis Club, and Coca-Cola, the logos of which all appear on the back of the cards. In addition to the 13 player cards, cards for the mascot, coach, and Sea Gal were issued. The set is unnumbered but has been listed below in alphabetical order by subject. The backs contain "Tips from the Seahawks". A 1979 copyright date can be found on the back of the cards.

COMPLETE SET (16)	12.50	25.00
1 Steve August	.50	1.00
2 Autry Beamon	.50	1.00
3 Terry Beeson	.50	1.00
4 Dennis Boyd	.50	1.00
5 Dave Brown	.63	1.25
6 Efren Herrera	.50	1.00
7 Steve Largent	6.00	12.00
8 Tom Lynch	.50	1.00
9 Bob Newton	.50	1.00
10 Jack Patera CO	.63	1.25
11 Sea Gal (Keri Truscan)	.50	1.00
12 Seahawk (Mascot)	.50	1.00
13 David Sims	.50	1.00
14 Sherman Smith	.63	1.25
15 John Yarno	.50	1.00
16 Jim Zorn	1.50	3.00

1980 Seahawks Nalley's

The 1980 Nalley's Chips Seattle Seahawks cards are actually the back panels of large (nine ounce) Nalley's boxes of Dippers, Barbecue Chips, and Potato Chips. The cards themselves measure approximately 9" by 10 3/4" and include a facsimile autograph. The back of the potato chip box features a color photo of the player with his facsimile autograph. One side of the box has the Seahawks game schedule, while the other side provides biographical and statistical information on the player. The front of the box features the player's name and a card number that is a continuation of previous year's cards. The prices listed below refer to complete boxes.

COMPLETE SET (8)	75.00	135.00
17 Keith Simpson	12.00	20.00
18 Michael Jackson	12.00	20.00
19 Manu Tuiasosopo	12.00	20.00
20 Sam McCullum	12.00	20.00
21 Keith Butler	12.00	20.00
22 Sam Adkins	12.00	20.00
23 Dan Doornink	12.00	20.00
24 Dave Brown	12.00	20.00

1980 Seahawks Police

The 1980 Seattle Seahawks set of 16 cards is numbered and contains the 1980 date on the back. The cards measure approximately 2 5/8" by 4 1/8". In addition to the local law enforcement agency, the set is sponsored by the Washington State Crime Prevention Association, the Kiwanis Club, Coca-Cola, and the Ernst Home Centers, each of which has their logo appearing on the back. Also appearing on the backs of the cards are "Tips from the Seahawks". The card backs have blue printing with red accent on white card stock. A stylized Seahawks helmet logo appears on the front.

COMPLETE SET (16)	7.50	15.00
1 Sam McCullum	.30	.75
2 Dan Doornink	.25	.60
3 Sherman Smith	.40	1.00
4 Efren Herrera	.25	.60
5 Bill Gregory	.25	.60
6 Keith Simpson	.25	.60
7 Manu Tuiasosopo	.30	.75
8 Michael Jackson	.25	.60
9 Steve Raible	.25	.60
10 Steve Largent	3.00	6.00
11 Jim Zorn	.75	2.00
12 Nick Bebout	.25	.60
13 The Seahawk (mascot)	.25	.60
14 Jack Patera CO	.30	.75
15 Robert Hardy	.25	.60
16 Keith Butler	.25	.60

1980 Seahawks 7-Up

This "7-Up/Seahawks Collectors Series" (as noted on the cardbacks) measures approximately 2 3/8" by 3 1/4" and is printed on thin card stock. Each card was issued on a slightly larger panel (roughly 3 7/8" by 3 1/4") with both the left and right side of the panel being intended to be removed leaving a perforation on both sides of the final separated card. The cardfronts carry a color player photo enclosed in a white border with the Seahawks' helmet, player's name, and 7-Up logo in the bottom border. The card backs feature brief player vital statistics and sponsor logos. The cards are unnumbered and checklisted below alphabetically. Steve Largent and Jim Zorn were not included in the set due to their sponsorship of Darigold Dairy Products.

COMPLETE SET (10)	75.00	150.00
1 Steve August	7.50	15.00
2 Terry Beeson	7.50	15.00
3 Dan Doornink	7.50	15.00
4 Michael Jackson	7.50	15.00
5 Tom Lynch	7.50	15.00
6 Steve Myer	7.50	15.00
7 Steve Raible	7.50	15.00
8 Sherman Smith	10.00	20.00
9 Manu Tuiasosopo	7.50	15.00
10 John Yarno	7.50	15.00

1981 Seahawks 7-Up

Sponsored by 7-Up and issued by the Seahawks, usually through mail requests, these cards measure approximately 3 1/2" by 5 1/2" and are made of thin stock. The borderless cardfronts feature color player photos with the words "Seahawks Fan Mail Courtesy..." and the 7-Up logo. A facsimile autograph can also be found on the photo. However, the Steve Largent and Jim Zorn photos do not have the 7-Up logo due to their association with Darigold Milk products at the time. The backs carry a brief player biography. The cards are unnumbered and checklisted below in alphabetical order.

COMPLETE SET (31)	48.00	120.00
1 Sam Adkins	1.50	4.00
2 Steve August	1.50	4.00
3 Terry Beeson	1.50	4.00
4 Dennis Boyd	1.50	4.00
5 Dave Brown	2.50	6.00
6 Louis Bullard	1.50	4.00
7 Keith Butler	1.50	4.00
8 Ron Coder		
9 Peter Cronan	1.50	4.00
10 Dan Doornink	1.50	4.00
11 Jacob Green	2.50	6.00
12 Bill Gregory	1.50	4.00
13 Robert Hardy	1.50	4.00
14 Efren Herrera	1.50	4.00
15 Michael Jackson	2.50	6.00
16 Art Kuehn	1.50	4.00
17 Steve Largent	10.00	25.00
18 Tom Lynch	1.50	4.00
19 Sam McCullum	2.50	6.00
20 Steve Myer	1.50	4.00
21 Jack Patera CO	1.50	4.00
22 Steve Raible	1.50	4.00
23 The Sea Gals	1.50	4.00
24 The Seahawk Mascot	1.50	4.00
25 Keith Simpson	1.50	4.00
26 Sherman Smith	2.50	6.00
27 Manu Tuiasosopo	2.50	6.00
28 Herman Weaver	1.50	4.00
29 Cornell Webster	1.50	4.00
30 John Yarno	1.50	4.00
31 Jim Zorn	4.00	10.00

1982 Seahawks Police

Similar to the 1980 set in design, this 16-card, numbered set is sponsored by the Washington State Crime Prevention Association, the Kiwanis Club, Coca-Cola, and Ernst Home Centers in addition to the local law enforcement agency. The cards measure approximately 2 5/8" by 4 1/8". A 1982 date and short "Tips from the Seahawks" appear on the backs. Card backs have blue print with red trim on white card stock. Cards of Jack Patera and Sam McCullum are reported to be more difficult to obtain than other cards in this set.

COMPLETE SET (16)	4.00	10.00
1 Sam McCullum SP	.60	1.50
2 Manu Tuiasosopo	.20	.50
3 Sherman Smith	.30	.75
4 Karen Godwin (Sea Gal)	.15	.40
5 Dave Brown	.30	.75
6 Keith Simpson	.15	.40
7 Steve Largent	1.50	4.00
8 Michael Jackson	.15	.40
9 Kenny Easley	.30	.75
10 Dan Doornink	.15	.40
11 Jim Zorn	.50	1.25
12 Jack Patera CO SP	.60	1.50
13 Jacob Green	.30	.75
14 Dave Krieg	.60	1.50
15 Steve August	.15	.40
16 Keith Butler	.15	.40

1982 Seahawks 7-Up

Sponsored by 7-Up and issued by the Seahawks, usually through mail requests, these 15 cards measure approximately 3 1/2" by 5 1/2" and are printed on thin stock. The fronts feature color player action shots with "Seahawks Fan Mail Courtesy," the 7-Up logo, and a facsimile autograph (which sometimes appears on the card back). The Steve Largent and Jim Zorn cards carry the Darigold logo, "Gold-n-Soft Margarine," due to their association with Darigold Milk products at the time. The back carries a brief player biography, career highlights, or personal message. Some of the cards are horizontally oriented and some are vertically oriented. The cards are unnumbered and checklisted below in alphabetical order.

COMPLETE SET (15)	50.00	100.00
1 Edwin Bailey	2.50	6.00
2 Dave Brown	2.50	6.00
3 Kenny Easley	3.00	8.00
4 Ron Essink	2.50	6.00
5 Jacob Green	3.00	8.00
(No facsimile autograph)		
6 Robert Hardy	2.50	6.00
7 John Harris	2.50	6.00
8 David Hughes	2.50	6.00
9 Paul Johns HOR	2.50	6.00
10 Kerry Justin	2.50	6.00
11 Dave Krieg	4.00	10.00
12 Steve Largent	8.00	20.00
(Darigold logo or		
Gold-n-Soft)		
13 Keith Simpson	2.50	6.00
14 Manu Tuiasosopo	2.50	6.00
15 Jim Zorn HOR	3.00	8.00
(Darigold logo or		
Gold-n-Soft)		

1984 Seahawks GTE

Sponsored by GTE Communications and issued by the Seahawks, usually through mail requests or player appearances, these cards measure approximately 3 1/2" by 5 1/2" and are printed on thin stock. The fronts feature color player action shots with the GTE logo and facsimile autograph. The back carries a brief player biography. They are very similar to the 1988 set and may have been released over a period of years. The card's year can be determined by the varying information in the player bios on the backs or in very slight differences in the cropping of the player photos. The cards are unnumbered and checklisted below in alphabetical order. Any additions to the list below are appreciated.

COMPLETE SET (13)	40.00	80.00
1 Dan Doornink	2.50	5.00
2 Kenny Easley	2.50	5.00
3 Jacob Green	3.00	6.00
4 John Harris	2.50	5.00
5 Norm Johnson	2.50	5.00
6 Chuck Knox CO	3.00	6.00
7 Dave Krieg	4.00	8.00
8 Steve Largent	10.00	20.00
(I in photo positioned		
at back edge of left leg)		
9 Joe Nash	2.50	5.00
10 Keith Simpson	2.50	5.00
11 Mike Tice	2.50	5.00
12 Curt Warner	4.00	8.00
13 Charle Young	2.50	5.00

1984 Seahawks Nalley's

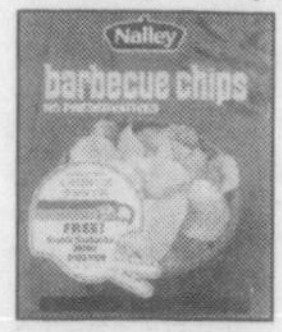

The 1984 Nalley's Seahawks set was issued on large Nalley's Potato Chip boxes. The back of the box features a color photo of the player, with his facsimile autograph. One side of the box has the Seahawks 1984 schedule, while the other side provides biographical and statistical information on the player. The prices listed below refer to complete boxes. These cards are unnumbered and are listed below alphabetically.

COMPLETE SET (4)	30.00	80.00
1 Kenny Easley	5.00	12.00
2 Dave Krieg	6.00	15.00
3 Steve Largent	20.00	40.00
4 Curt Warner	8.00	20.00

1984 Seahawks Team Issue

These photos were issued by the Seahawks around 1984. Each measures roughly 8" by 10" and includes a black and white player photo and a blank cardback. The player's name, position and Seahawks helmet logo appear below the photo.

COMPLETE SET (23)	35.00	60.00
1 Edwin Bailey	1.25	3.00
2 Cullen Bryant	1.25	3.00
3 Keith Butler	1.25	3.00
4 Chris Castor	1.25	3.00
5 Bob Cryder	1.25	3.00
6 Zachary Dixon	1.25	3.00
7 Randy Edwards	1.25	3.00
8 John Harris S	1.25	3.00
9 David Hughes	1.25	3.00
10 Terry Jackson CB	1.25	3.00
11 Paul Johns	1.25	3.00
12 John Kaiser	1.25	3.00
13 Reggie McKenzie	1.50	4.00
14 Sam Merriman	1.25	3.00
15 Bryan Millard	1.50	4.00
16 Joe Nash	1.25	3.00
17 Shelton Robinson	1.25	3.00
18 Bruce Scholtz	1.25	3.00
19 Keith Simpson	1.25	3.00
20 Terry Taylor	1.25	3.00
21 Mike Tice	1.25	3.00
22 Daryl Turner	1.25	3.00
23 Jeff West	1.25	3.00

1985 Seahawks Police

This 16-card set of Seattle Seahawks is unnumbered; not even the uniform number is given. Cards measure approximately 2 5/8" by 4 1/8" and the backs contain "Tips from the Seahawks". The set was sponsored by Coca-Cola, McDonald's, KOMO-TV4, Kiwanis, the Washington State Crime Prevention Association, and local law enforcement agencies. Card backs are written in red and blue on white card stock. The year of issue is printed in the bottom right corner of the reverse.

COMPLETE SET (16)	3.00	8.00
1 Dave Brown	.25	.60
2 Jeff Bryant	.20	.50
3 Blair Bush	.20	.50
4 Keith Butler	.15	.40
5 Dan Doornink	.15	.40
6 Kenny Easley	.25	.60
7 Jacob Green	.25	.60
8 John Harris	.15	.40
9 Norm Johnson	.25	.60
10 Chuck Knox CO	.25	.60
11 Dave Krieg	.60	1.50
12 Steve Largent	1.25	3.00
13 Joe Nash	.20	.50
14 Bruce Scholtz	.15	.40
15 Curt Warner	.40	1.00
16 Fredd Young	.25	.60

1986 Seahawks Police

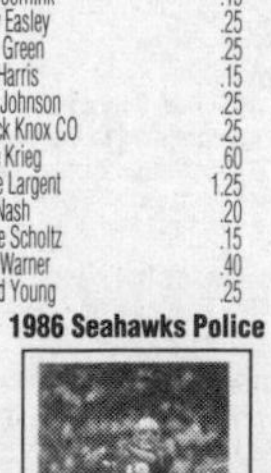

This 16-card set of Seattle Seahawks is unnumbered; not even the uniform number is given explicitly on the front of the card. Cards measure approximately 2 5/8" by 4 1/8" and the backs contain "Tips from the Seahawks". The year of issue is not printed anywhere on the cards. The cards are unnumbered so they are ordered below alphabetically.

COMPLETE SET (16)	3.00	8.00
1 Edwin Bailey	.15	.40
2 Dave Brown	.25	.60
3 Jeff Bryant	.20	.50
4 Blair Bush	.20	.50

5 Keith Butler	.15	.40
6 Kenny Easley	.25	.60
7 Jacob Green	.25	.60
8 Michael Jackson	.15	.40
9 Chuck Knox CO	.25	.60
10 Dave Krieg	.40	1.00
11 Steve Largent	1.40	3.50
12 Joe Nash	.20	.50
13 Bruce Scholtz	.15	.40
14 Terry Taylor	.15	.40
15 Curt Warner	.30	.75
16 Fredd Young	.25	.60

1987 Seahawks Ace Fact Pack

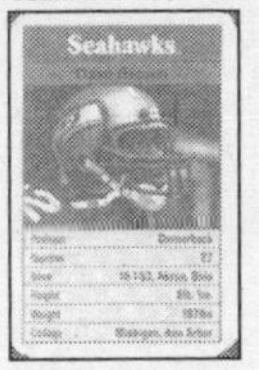

This 33-card set measures approximately 2 1/4" by 3 5/8". This set consists of 33 cards of which 22 are player cards and we have checklisted those cards alphabetically. The cards have rounded corners and a playing card type of design on the back. These cards were manufactured in West Germany (by Ace Fact Pack) and released in Great Britain. The set contains members of the Seattle Seahawks.

COMPLETE SET (33)	50.00	120.00
1 Edwin Bailey	1.25	3.00
2 Dave Brown	1.25	3.00
3 Jeff Bryant	1.25	3.00
4 Blair Bush	1.25	3.00
5 Keith Butler	1.25	3.00
6 Kenny Easley	2.00	5.00
7 Greg Gaines	1.25	3.00
8 Jacob Green	2.00	5.00
9 Norm Johnson	2.00	5.00
10 Dave Krieg	3.00	8.00
11 Steve Largent	12.50	30.00
12 Reggie Kinlaw	1.25	3.00
13 Ron Mattes	1.25	3.00
14 Bryan Millard	1.25	3.00
15 Eugene Robinson	2.00	5.00
16 Bruce Scholtz	1.25	3.00
17 Terry Taylor	1.25	3.00
18 Mike Tice	2.00	5.00
19 Daryl Turner	1.25	3.00
20 Curt Warner	2.50	6.00
21 John L. Williams	2.00	5.00
22 Fredd Young	2.00	5.00
23 Seahawks Helmet	1.25	3.00
24 Seahawks Information	1.25	3.00
25 Seahawks Uniform	1.25	3.00
26 Game Record Holders	1.25	3.00
27 Season Record Holders	1.25	3.00
28 Career Record Holders	1.25	3.00
29 Record 1977-86	1.25	3.00
30 1986 Team Statistics	1.25	3.00
31 All-Time Greats	1.25	3.00
32 Roll of Honour	1.25	3.00
33 Kingdome	1.25	3.00

1987 Seahawks Police

This 16-card set of Seattle Seahawks is unnumbered; not even the uniform number is given explicitly on the front of the card. Cards measure approximately 2 5/8" by 4 1/8". The backs contain a safety tip. The year of issue is not printed anywhere on the cards. The card fronts have a silver border and feature a blue and green Seahawks logo. The cards are listed below alphabetically for convenience.

COMPLETE SET (16)	3.00	8.00
1 Jeff Bryant	.20	.50
2 Kenny Easley	.25	.60
3 Bobby Joe Edmonds	.15	.40
4 Jacob Green	.25	.60
5 Chuck Knox CO	.25	.60
6 Dave Krieg	.50	1.25
7 Steve Largent	1.25	3.00
8 Ron Mattes	.15	.40
9 Bryan Millard	.15	.40
10 Eugene Robinson	.25	.60
11 Bruce Scholtz	.15	.40
12 Paul Skansi	.15	.40
13 Curt Warner	.25	.60
14 John L. Williams	.25	.60
15 Mike Wilson	.15	.40
16 Fredd Young	.20	.50

1987 Seahawks Snyder's/Franz

This 12-card set features players of the Seattle Seahawks. Cards were available only in Snyder's (distributed in the Spokane area) or Franz Bread (distributed in the Portland area) loaves. The set was co-produced by Mike Schechter Associates on behalf of the NFL Players Association. Cards are standard size, 2 1/2" by 3 1/2", in full color, and are numbered on the back. The card fronts have a color photo within a blue border and the backs are printed in black ink on white card stock.

COMPLETE SET (12)	30.00	75.00
1 Jeff Bryant	2.50	6.00
2 Keith Butler	2.50	6.00
3 Randy Edwards	2.50	6.00
4 Byron Franklin	2.50	6.00
5 Jacob Green	2.50	6.00
6 Dave Krieg	3.00	8.00
7 Bryan Millard	2.50	6.00
8 Paul Moyer	2.50	6.00
9 Eugene Robinson	3.00	8.00
10 Mike Tice	2.50	6.00
11 Daryl Turner	2.50	6.00
12 Curt Warner	3.00	8.00

1988 Seahawks Ace Fact Pack

Cards from this 33-card set measure approximately 2 1/4" by 3 5/8". This set consists of 22-player cards and 11-additional informational cards about the Seahawks team. We've checklisted the cards alphabetically beginning with the 22-players. The cards have square corners (as opposed to rounded like the 1987 sets) and a playing card design on the back printed in red. These cards were manufactured in West Germany (by Ace Fact Pack) and released primarily in Great Britain.

COMPLETE SET (33)	75.00	150.00
1 Edwin Bailey	1.50	4.00
2 Brian Bosworth	7.50	15.00
3 Jeff Bryant	1.50	4.00
4 Blair Bush	1.50	4.00
5 Raymond Butler	2.00	5.00
6 Bobby Joe Edmonds	1.50	4.00
7 Greg Gaines	1.50	4.00
8 Jacob Green	2.00	5.00
9 Norm Johnson	1.50	4.00
10 Dave Krieg	3.00	8.00
11 Steve Largent	25.00	50.00
12 Ron Mattes	1.50	4.00
13 Bryan Millard	1.50	4.00
14 Paul Moyer	1.50	4.00
15 Eugene Robinson	2.00	5.00
16 Bruce Scholtz	1.50	4.00
17 Terry Taylor	1.50	4.00
18 Mike Tice	1.50	4.00
19 Daryl Turner	1.50	4.00
20 Curt Warner	3.00	8.00
21 John L. Williams	2.00	5.00
22 Fredd Young	1.50	4.00
23 1987 Team Statistics	1.50	4.00
24 All-Time Greats	1.50	4.00
25 Career Record Holders	1.50	4.00
26 Game Record Holders	1.50	4.00
27 Kingdome	1.50	4.00
28 Record 1976-87	1.50	4.00
29 Roll Of Honour	1.50	4.00
30 Seahawks Helmet	1.50	4.00
(Cover Card)		
31 Seahawks Helmet	1.50	4.00
(Informational card)		
32 Seahawks Uniform	1.50	4.00
33 Season Record Holders	1.50	4.00

1988 Seahawks Domino's

This 50-card set was sponsored by Domino's Pizza and features Seattle Seahawks players and personnel. The cards were first distributed as a starter set of nine cards (1-9) perforated along with a team photo. Later cards were issued in strips of four or five players (10-13,*14-17, 18-21, 22-25, 26-29, 30-33, 34-38, 39-42, 43-46, and 47-50) along with a promotional coupon for a discount on pizza at Domino's. One strip was available each week with every Domino's pizza ordered. The discount coupons on strips 5, 6, and 8 were supposedly removed prior to distribution to the general public. The cards measure approximately 2 1/2" by 3" whereas the team photo is approximately 12 1/2" by 8 1/2". The set was also partially sponsored by Coca-Cola Classic and KING-5 TV.

COMPLETE SET (51)	16.00	40.00
1 Steve Largent	4.00	10.00
2 Kelly Stouffer	.30	.75
3 Bobby Joe Edmonds	.30	.75
4 Patrick Hunter	.20	.50
5 Ventrella	.20	.50
Valle		
Gellos		
6 Edwin Bailey	.20	.50
7 Alonzo Mitz	.20	.50
8 Tommy Kane	.30	.75
9 Chuck Knox CO	.30	.75
10 Curt Warner	.40	1.00
11 Alvin Powell	.20	.50
12 Joe Nash	.20	.50
13 Brian Blades	1.25	3.00
14 Blair Bush	.30	.75
15 Melvin Jenkins	.20	.50
16 Ruben Rodriguez	.20	.50
17 Tommie Agee	.20	.50
18 Eugene Robinson	.40	1.00
19 Dwayne Harper	.20	.50
20 Raymond Butler	.20	.50
21 Jeff Kemp	.40	1.00
22 Norm Johnson	.30	.75
23 Bryan Millard	.20	.50
24 Tony Woods	.20	.50
25 Paul Skansi	.20	.50
26 Jacob Green	.30	.75
27 Randall Morris	.20	.50
28 Mike Tice	.30	.75
29 Kevin Harmon	.20	.50
30 Dave Krieg	.75	2.00
31 Nesby Glasgow	.20	.50
32 Bruce Scholtz	.20	.50
33 John Spagnola	.20	.50
34 Jeff Bryant	.30	.75
35 Stan Eisenhooth	.20	.50
36 David Wyman	.20	.50
37 Greg Gaines	.20	.50
38 Charlie Jones NBC ANN	.20	.50
39 Terry Taylor	.20	.50
40 Vernon Dean	.20	.50
41 Mike Wilson	.20	.50
42 Darrin Miller	.20	.50
43 John L. Williams	.40	1.00
44 Grant Feasel	.20	.50
45 M.L. Johnson	.20	.50
46 Ken Clarke	.20	.50
47 Brian Bosworth	1.25	3.00
48 Ron Mattes	.20	.50
49 Paul Moyer	.20	.50
50 Rufus Porter	.30	.75
NNO Team Photo	2.50	6.00
(Large size)		

1988 Seahawks GTE

This 24-card set was sponsored by GTE and features members of the Seattle Seahawks. The cards measure approximately 3 5/8" by 5 1/2" and were used primarily for player appearances and for fan mailings. The fronts show full-bleed color player photos with the player's signature and uniform number inscribed across the picture. The horizontal backs have a brief career summary on the left portion; the right portion is blank but often has a greeting and/or the player's signature if the player or team signed and mailed out the card. They are very similar to the 1984 set and may have been released over a period of years. The card's year can be determined by the varying information in the player bios on the backs.

COMPLETE SET (24)	40.00	80.00
1 Edwin Bailey	1.25	3.00
2 Brian Bosworth	4.00	8.00
3 Dave Brown	1.25	3.00
4 Jeff Bryant	1.25	3.00
5 Bobby Joe Edmonds	1.25	3.00
(hands on hips)		
6 Jacob Green	1.50	4.00
7 Michael Jackson	1.50	4.00
8 Norm Johnson	1.25	3.00
9 Jeff Kemp	1.50	4.00
10 Chuck Knox CO	1.50	4.00
11 Dave Krieg	4.00	8.00
12 Steve Largent	10.00	20.00
(I in photo positioned		
at center knee of left leg)		
13 Ron Mattes	1.25	3.00
14 Bryan Millard	1.25	3.00
15 Paul Moyer	1.25	3.00
16 Eugene Robinson	1.50	4.00
17 Paul Skansi	1.25	3.00
18 Kelly Stouffer	1.25	3.00
19 Terry Taylor	1.25	3.00
20 Mike Tice	1.25	3.00
21 Daryl Turner	1.25	3.00
22 Curt Warner	2.00	5.00
23 John L. Williams	2.00	5.00
24 Fredd Young	1.25	3.00

1988 Seahawks Police

The 1988 Police Seattle Seahawks set contains 16 cards measuring approximately 2 5/8" by 4 1/8". There are 15 player cards and one coach card. The fronts have gray borders and color photos. The backs have safety tips. Terry Taylor's card was pulled from distribution after his suspension from the team. This unnumbered set is listed alphabetically below for convenience.

COMPLETE SET (15)	4.00	10.00
1 Brian Bosworth	.25	.60
2 Jeff Bryant	.15	.40
3 Raymond Butler	.10	.30
4 Jacob Green	.15	.40
5 Patrick Hunter	.10	.30
6 Norm Johnson	.15	.40
7 Chuck Knox CO	.15	.40
8 Dave Krieg	.25	.60
9 Steve Largent	.75	2.00
10 Ron Mattes	.10	.30
11 Bryan Millard	.10	.30
12 Paul Moyer	.10	.30
13 Terry Taylor SP	1.25	3.00
14 Curt Warner	.25	.60
15 John L. Williams	.25	.60
16 Fredd Young SP	1.25	3.00

1988 Seahawks Snyder's/Franz

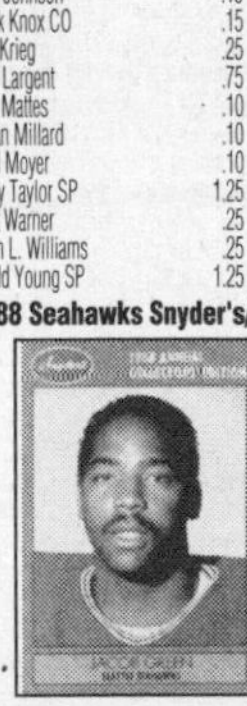

This 12-card standard-size full-color set features players of the Seattle Seahawks. Cards were available only in Snyder's (distributed in the Spokane area) or Franz Bread (distributed in the Portland area) loaves. The set was co-produced by Mike Schechter Associates on behalf of the NFL Players Association. The card fronts have a color photo within a blue border and the backs are printed in black ink on white card stock.

COMPLETE SET (12)	30.00	60.00
1 Dave Krieg	4.00	10.00
2 Curt Warner	3.00	8.00
3 Byron Franklin	2.00	5.00
4 Eugene Robinson	2.50	6.00
5 Mike Tice	2.50	6.00
6 Daryl Turner	2.00	5.00
7 Paul Moyer	2.00	5.00
8 Bryan Millard	2.00	5.00
9 Jeff Bryant	2.00	5.00
10 Keith Butler	2.00	5.00
11 Randy Edwards	2.00	5.00
12 Jacob Green	2.50	6.00

1988 Seahawks Team Issue

This set of photos was issued by the Seahawks. Each measures roughly 8" by 10" and includes a black and white player photo on the front with his name, position, and team name below the photo. These were likely released over a period of years since many vary slightly in regards to type style and size. The backs are blank and unnumbered.

COMPLETE SET (15)	20.00	50.00
1 Brian Bosworth	4.00	10.00
2 Jacob Green	1.50	4.00
3 David Hollis	1.25	3.00
4 Melvin Jenkins	1.25	3.00
5 Norm Johnson	1.25	3.00
6 Jeff Kemp	1.50	4.00
7 Chuck Knox CO	1.50	4.00
8 David Krieg	1.50	4.00
9 Ron Mattes	1.25	3.00
10 Paul Moyer	1.25	3.00
11 Eugene Robinson	2.50	6.00
12 Paul Skansi	1.25	3.00
13 John L. Williams	1.50	4.00
14 Curt Warner	2.50	6.00
15 Tony Woods LB	1.25	3.00

1989 Seahawks Oroweat

The 1989 Oroweat Seahawks set contains 20 standard-size cards. The cards have attractive silver borders and color action shots and were produced by Pacific Trading Cards for Oroweat. The horizontally-oriented backs have light blue borders with bios, stats, and career highlights. One card was distributed in each specially marked loaf of Oroweat's Oatnut Bread, sold only in the Pacific Northwest. It has been reported that 1.5 million cards were distributed.

COMPLETE SET (20)	25.00	60.00
1 Paul Moyer	.40	1.00
2 David Wyman	.40	1.00
3 Tony Woods	.60	1.50
4 Kelly Stouffer	.40	1.00
5 Brian Blades	4.00	10.00
6 Norm Johnson	.60	1.50
7 Curt Warner	1.00	2.50
8 John L. Williams	1.00	2.50
9 Edwin Bailey	.40	1.00
10 Jacob Green	.60	1.50
11 Paul Skansi	.40	1.00
12 Jeff Bryant	.40	1.00
13 Bruce Scholtz	.40	1.00
14 Dave Krieg	2.00	5.00
15 Steve Largent	6.00	15.00
16 Joe Nash	.40	1.00
17 Mike Wilson	.40	1.00
18 Ron Mattes	.40	1.00
19 Grant Feasel	.40	1.00
20 Bryan Millard	.40	1.00

1989 Seahawks Police

The 1989 Police Seattle Seahawks set contains 16 cards measuring approximately 2 5/8" by 4 1/8". The fronts have light blue borders and color action photos; the vertically-oriented backs have safety tips. These cards were printed on very thin stock. The cards are unnumbered, so therefore are listed alphabetically by subject's name. The Largent card contains a list of Steve's records on the back instead of the typical safety tip found on all the other cards in the set.

COMPLETE SET (16)	2.50	6.00
1 Brian Blades	.25	.60
2 Brian Bosworth	.40	1.00
3 Jeff Bryant	.10	.30
4 Jacob Green	.15	.40
5 Chuck Knox CO	.15	.40
6 Dave Krieg	.30	.75
7 Steve Largent	.75	2.00
8 Bryan Millard	.10	.30
9 Rufus Porter	.10	.30
10 Paul Moyer	.10	.30
11 Eugene Robinson	.25	.60
12 Ruben Rodriguez	.10	.30
13 Kelly Stouffer	.15	.40
14 Curt Warner	.25	.60
15 John L. Williams	.25	.60
16 Tony Woods	.15	.40

1990 Seahawks Oroweat

This 50-card set of Seattle Seahawks was released in the Seattle area in various loaves of Oroweat products, Oat Nut, Health Nut, and Twelve Grain bread. The set was released in two series, 20 cards issued before the 1990 NFL season began and 30 cards released during the season. The fronts of the set feature full-color action shots within a silver border while the back of the card features a mix of statistical and biographical information. The cards each measure approximately 2 1/2" by 3 1/2" and were produced by Pacific Trading Cards for Oroweat. There are two #24 cards and no card #25.

COMPLETE SET (50)	20.00	50.00
1 Dave Krieg	1.00	2.50
2 Rick Donnelly	.30	.75
3 Brian Blades	1.25	3.00
4 Cortez Kennedy	1.20	3.00
5 John L. Williams	.80	2.00
6 Jeff Chadwick	.00	1.50
7 Thom Kaumeyer	.30	.75
8 Bryan Millard	.30	.75
9 Eugene Robinson	.60	1.50
10 Jacob Green	.60	1.50
11 Willie Bouyer	.30	.75
12 Jeff Bryant	.30	.75
13 Chris Warren	3.20	8.00
14 Derrick Fenner	.60	1.50
15 Paul Skansi	.30	.75
16 Joe Cain	.30	.75
17 Tommy Kane	.30	.75
18 Tom Flores GM	.60	1.50
19 Terry Wooden	.30	.75
20 Tony Woods	.80	2.00
21 Ricky Andrews	.40	1.00
22 Joe Tofflemire	.40	1.00
23 Ned Bolcar	.40	1.00
24A Kelly Stouffer	.80	2.00
24B Melvin Jenkins	.40	1.00
26 Norm Johnson	.80	2.00
27 Eric Hayes	.40	1.00
28 Mike Morris	.40	1.00
29 Edwin Bailey	.40	1.00
30 Ron Heller	.40	1.00
31 Darren Comeaux	.40	1.00
32 Andy Heck	.40	1.00
33 Ronnie Lee	.40	1.00
34 Robert Blackmon	.40	1.00
35 Joe Nash	.40	1.00
36 Patrick Hunter	.40	1.00
37 Darrick Brilz	.40	1.00
38 Ron Mattes	.40	1.00
39 Nesby Glasgow	.40	1.00
40 Dwayne Harper	.40	1.00
41 Chuck Knox CO	.80	2.00
42 Travis McNeal	.80	2.00
43 Derek Loville	.80	2.00
44 David Wyman	.80	2.00
45 Louis Clark	.40	1.00
46 Grant Feasel	.40	1.00
47 James Jones	.40	1.00
48 Rufus Porter	.80	2.00
49 Jeff Kemp	.80	2.00
50 James Jefferson	.80	2.00
NNO Title Card	1.60	4.00

1990 Seahawks Police

This 16-card set was issued in the Seattle area to promote the various saftey tips using members of the 1990 Seattle Seahawks. The cards measure approximately 2 5/8" by 4 1/8" and have solid green borders which frame a full-color photo of the player pictured. On the back is a safety tip. Since the cards are unnumbered, we have checklisted this set in alphabetical order.

COMPLETE SET (16)	2.40	6.00
1 Brian Blades	.40	1.00
2 Grant Feasel	.10	.30
3 Jacob Green	.15	.40
4 Andy Heck	.10	.30
5 James Jefferson	.10	.30
6 Norm Johnson	.15	.40
7 Cortez Kennedy	.40	1.00
8 Chuck Knox CO	.15	.40
9 Dave Krieg	.25	.60
10 Travis McNeal	.10	.30
11 Bryan Millard	.10	.30
12 Rufus Porter	.10	.30
13 Paul Skansi	.10	.30
14 John L. Williams	.25	.60
15 Tony Woods	.15	.40
16 David Wyman	.10	.30

1991 Seahawks Oroweat

This 50-card standard-size set was sponsored by Oroweat and produced by Pacific. One card was included in every Oroweat loaf of bread throughout Washington, Oregon, and western portions of Idaho. Although cards were not sold in complete sets, five-card packs were given out at one of the Seahawks' games. The title cards were only available in the five-card packs. The fronts of these cards feature glossy color action player photos, with the player's name written vertically in a purple stripe at the left side of the picture. The team name and position appear in a silver stripe below the picture. In a diagonal design, the horizontally oriented backs have biography, a color headshot of the player, statistics, and career summary.

COMPLETE SET (51)	16.00	40.00
1 Tommy Kane	.40	1.00
2 Norm Johnson	.40	1.00
3 Robert Blackmon	.40	1.00
4 Mike Tice	.40	1.00
5 Cortez Kennedy	.80	2.00
6 Bryan Millard	.40	1.00
7 Tony Woods	.50	1.25
8 Paul Skansi	.40	1.00
9 John L. Williams	.80	2.00
10 Terry Wooden	.40	1.00
11 Brian Blades	.80	2.00
12 Jacob Green	.40	1.00
13 Joe Nash	.40	1.00
14 Eugene Robinson	.80	2.00
15 Rufus Porter	.40	1.00
16 Andy Heck	.40	1.00
17 Derrick Fenner	.80	2.00
18 Nesby Glasgow	.40	1.00
19 Chris Warren	3.20	8.00
20 Dave Krieg	1.00	2.50
21 Vann McElroy	.40	1.00
22 Jeff Bryant	.40	1.00
23 Warren Wheat	.40	1.00
24 Marcus Cotton	.40	1.00
25 David Wyman	.40	1.00
26 Joe Cain	.40	1.00
27 Darrick Brilz	.40	1.00
28 Eric Hayes	.40	1.00
29 Ronnie Lee	.40	1.00
30 Louis Clark	.40	1.00
31 James Jones	.40	1.00
32 Dwayne Harper	.40	1.00
33 Grant Feasel	.40	1.00
34 Trey Junkin	.40	1.00
35 James Jefferson	.40	1.00
36 Edwin Bailey	.40	1.00
37 Derek Loville	.80	2.00
38 Travis McNeal	.40	1.00
39 Rick Donnelly	.40	1.00
40 Rod Stephens	.40	1.00
41 Darren Comeaux	.40	1.00
42 Brian Davis	.40	1.00
43 Bill Hitchcock	.40	1.00
44 Jeff Chadwick	.50	1.25
45 Patrick Hunter	.50	1.25
46 David Daniels	.40	1.00
47 Doug Thomas	.40	1.00
48 Dan McGwire	.50	1.25
49 John Kasay	.80	2.00
50 Jeff Kemp	.50	1.25
NNO Title Card	1.60	4.00

1992 Seahawks Oroweat

Inserted one card per Oroweat bread loaf, these 50 standard-size cards feature on their fronts white-bordered color player action shots. The player's name and position appear vertically in green lettering within a gray stripe on the left. The white-bordered horizontal back carries a color player close-up on the left and, alongside on the right, the player's name and position within a white strip near the top, followed below by biography, statistics, and career highlights within a green panel. The Oroweat and KIRO Newsradio logos on the back round out the card.

COMPLETE SET (51)	60.00	100.00
1 Brian Blades	2.00	4.00
2 Patrick Hunter	.75	2.00
3 Jeff Bryant	.75	2.00
4 Robert Blackmon	.75	2.00
5 Joe Cain	.75	2.00
6 Grant Feasel	.75	2.00
7 Dan McGwire	1.25	2.50
8 David Wyman	.75	2.00
9 Jacob Green	1.25	2.50
10 Theo Adams	.75	2.00
11 Brian Davis	.75	2.00
12 Andy Heck	.75	2.00
13 Bill Hitchcock	.75	2.00
14 Joe Nash	.75	2.00
15 Rod Stephens	.75	2.00
16 John Hunter	.75	2.00
17 Paul Green	.75	2.00
18 James Jones	.75	2.00
19 Robb Thomas	.75	2.00
20 Tony Woods	.75	2.00
21 Dedrick Dodge	.75	2.00
22 Tracy Johnson	.75	2.00
23 Darrick Brilz	.75	2.00
24 Joe Tofflemire	.75	2.00
25 Louis Clark	.75	2.00
26 Rueben Mayes	1.25	2.50
27 Natu Tuatagaloa	.75	2.00
28 Terry Wooden	.75	2.00
29 Tommy Kane	.75	2.00
30 Stan Gelbaugh	.75	2.00
31 Nesby Glasgow	.75	2.00
32 Kelly Stouffer	.75	2.00
33 Ray Roberts	.75	2.00
34 Doug Thomas	.75	2.00
35 David Daniels	.75	2.00
36 John Kasay	2.00	4.00
37 Cortez Kennedy	1.25	2.50
38 Tyrone Rodgers	.75	2.00
39 Bryan Millard	.75	2.00
40 Eugene Robinson	2.00	4.00
41 Malcolm Frank	.75	2.00
42 Dwayne Harper	.75	2.00
43 Ron Heller	.75	2.00
44 Rick Tuten	.75	2.00
45 Trey Junkin	.75	2.00
46 Bob Spitulski	.75	2.00
47 Chris Warren	2.00	4.00
48 John L. Williams	1.25	2.50
49 Ronnie Lee	.75	2.00
50 Rufus Porter	.75	2.00
NNO Title	2.00	4.00
ad card		

1993 Seahawks Oroweat

Produced by Pacific, this 50-card standard-size set was co-sponsored by Oroweat and KIRO News 710 AM. One card was included in each Oroweat loaf of bread throughout Washington, Oregon, and western portions of Idaho. Moreover, cello packs containing three player cards and one ad card were given away at home games. The fronts feature color action player photos that are tilted slightly to the left and set on a team color-coded gray and blue marbleized card face. The team helmet appears at the lower left corner, and the player's name and position are printed across the bottom of the picture. On a marbleized gray and blue background, the backs carry a second color player photo, biography, statistics, and player profile.

COMPLETE SET (50)	50.00	100.00
1 Cortez Kennedy	1.25	2.50
2 Robb Thomas	1.00	2.00
3 Rueben Mayes	1.00	2.00
4 Rick Tuten	1.00	2.00
5 Tracy Johnson	1.00	2.00
6 Michael Bates	1.00	2.00
7 Andy Heck	1.00	2.00
8 Stan Gelbaugh	1.00	2.00
9 Dan McGwire	1.25	2.50
10 Mike Keim	1.00	2.00
11 Grant Feasel	1.00	2.00
12 Brian Blades	2.00	4.00
13 Tyrone Rodgers	1.00	2.00
14 Paul Green	1.00	2.00
15 Rafael Robinson	1.00	2.00
16 John Kasay	2.00	4.00
17 Chris Warren	2.00	4.00
18 Michael Sinclair	1.25	2.50
19 John L. Williams	1.25	2.50
20 Bob Spitulski	1.00	2.00
21 Eugene Robinson	2.00	4.00
22 Patrick Hunter	1.00	2.00
23 Kevin Murphy	1.00	2.00
24 Dave McCloughan	1.00	2.00
25 Rick Mirer	4.00	8.00
26 Ray Donaldson	1.00	2.00
27 E.J. Junior	1.00	2.00
28 Jeff Bryant	1.00	2.00
29 Ferrell Edmunds	1.00	2.00
30 Tommy Kane	1.00	2.00
31 Terry Wooden	1.00	2.00
32 Doug Thomas	1.00	2.00
33 Carlton Gray	1.00	2.00
34 Kelvin Martin	1.00	2.00
35 Rod Stephens	1.00	2.00
36 Darrick Brilz	1.00	2.00
37 Joe Tofflemire	1.00	2.00
38 James Jefferson	1.00	2.00
39 Rufus Porter	1.00	2.00
40 Jeff Blackshear	1.00	2.00
41 Dwayne Harper	1.00	2.00
42 Ray Roberts	1.00	2.00
43 Robert Blackmon	1.00	2.00
44 Joe Nash	1.00	2.00
45 Michael McCrary	2.00	4.00
46 Trey Junkin	1.00	2.00
47 Natu Tuatagaloa	1.00	2.00
48 Bill Hitchcock	1.00	2.00
49 Jon Vaughn	1.00	2.00
50 Dean Wells	1.00	2.00

1994 Seahawks Oroweat

These 50 standard-size cards were produced by Pacific Trading Cards, Inc. for Oroweat. This occasion marks the sixth straight year that these two companies have worked together in a promotion. Seven different players were issued every two weeks throughout the regular season. The cards were found in loaves of Oatnut, Health Nut, and other variety breads sold throughout Washington, Oregon, Idaho, and Alaska. The fronts feature color player action shots on their blue-bordered fronts. The player's name and position appear at the lower right. The horizontal white-bordered back carries a color player close-up on the left, with the player's name, position, biography, and career highlights displayed alongside on the right within a gray panel highlighted by a ghosted Seahawks helmet. The cards are numbered on the back as "X of 50."

COMPLETE SET (50)	50.00	100.00
1 Brian Blades	1.25	2.50
2 Terrence Warren	1.00	2.00
3 Carlton Gray	1.00	2.00
4 Bob Spitulski	1.00	2.00
5 Dean Wells	1.00	2.00
6 Lamar Smith	7.50	15.00
7 Michael Bates	1.00	2.00
8 Duane Bickett	1.00	2.00
9 Cortez Kennedy	1.25	2.50
10 Dave McCloughan	1.00	2.00
11 Tracy Johnson	1.00	2.00
12 Eugene Robinson	2.00	4.00
13 Jeff Blackshear	1.00	2.00
14 Tyrone Rodgers	1.00	2.00
15 Trey Junkin	1.00	2.00
16 Ferrell Edmunds	1.00	2.00
17 Tony Brown	1.00	2.00
18 Orlando Watters	1.00	2.00
19 John Kasay	2.00	4.00
20 Rafael Robinson	1.00	2.00
21 Kelvin Martin	1.00	2.00
22 Stan Gelbaugh	1.00	2.00
23 Steve Smith	1.00	2.00
24 Ray Donaldson	1.00	2.00
25 Rufus Porter	1.00	2.00
26 Patrick Hunter	1.00	2.00
27 Terry Wooden	1.00	2.00
28 Sam Adams	2.00	4.00
29 Mack Strong	2.50	6.00
30 Chris Warren	1.25	2.50
31 Bill Hitchcock	1.00	2.00
32 David Brandon	1.00	2.00
33 Michael McCrary	2.00	4.00
34 Jon Vaughn	1.00	2.00
35 Paul Green	1.00	2.00
36 Mike Keim	1.00	2.00
37 Joe Tofflemire	1.00	2.00
38 Rick Tuten	1.00	2.00
39 Rick Mirer	2.00	4.00
40 Rod Stephens	1.00	2.00
41 Robert Blackmon	1.00	2.00
42 Howard Ballard	1.00	2.00
43 Michael Sinclair	1.00	2.00
44 Kevin Mawae	2.00	4.00

45 Brent Williams	1.00	2.00
46 Ray Roberts	1.00	2.00
47 Robb Thomas	1.00	2.00
48 Antonio Edwards	1.00	2.00
49 Dan McGwire	1.00	2.00
50 Joe Nash	1.00	2.00

1994 Seahawks Pacific Prisms Promos

COMPLETE SET (5)	5.00	12.00
1 Sam Adams	.75	2.00
2 Dave Brown	.75	2.00
3 Cortez Kennedy	1.00	2.50
4 Steve Largent	2.00	5.00
5 Rick Mirer	1.25	3.00

1997 Seahawks Pacific Franz

This set was produced by Pacific Trading Cards and released in Franz Bread packages one card at a time. The card fronts feature both the Pacific Crown and Seattle Seahawks logos.

COMPLETE SET (16)	60.00	100.00
1 Howard Ballard	2.00	5.00
2 Bennie Blades	2.00	5.00
3 Brian Blades	2.50	6.00
4 Chad Brown	2.50	6.00
5 John Friesz	2.50	6.00
6 Joey Galloway	4.00	10.00
7 Walter Jones	2.00	5.00
8 Pete Kendall	2.00	5.00
9 Cortez Kennedy	2.50	6.00
10 Warren Moon	5.00	12.00
11 Winston Moss	2.00	5.00
12 Michael Sinclair	2.00	5.00
13 Shawn Springs	2.50	6.00
14 Chris Warren	3.00	8.00
15 Darryl Williams	2.00	5.00
16 Willie Williams	2.00	5.00

2006 Seahawks DAV

COMPLETE SET (10)	4.00	10.00
1 Shaun Alexander	.50	1.50
2 Michael Boulware	.40	1.00
3 Josh Brown	.40	1.00
4 Bobby Engram	.40	1.00
5 Bryce Fisher	.30	.75
6 Matt Hasselbeck	.60	1.50
7 Mack Strong	.40	1.00
8 Lofa Tatupu	.60	1.50
9 Marcus Trufant	.40	1.00
10 Grant Wistrom	.40	1.00

2006 Seahawks Topps

COMPLETE SET (12)	3.00	6.00
SEA1 Lofa Tatupu	.25	.60
SEA2 Bobby Engram	.20	.50
SEA3 Leroy Hill	.20	.50
SEA4 Jerramy Stevens	.25	.60
SEA5 Michael Boulware	.20	.50
SEA6 Matt Hasselbeck	.25	.60
SEA7 Shaun Alexander	.25	.60
SEA8 Darrell Jackson	.25	.60
SEA9 Marcus Trufant	.20	.50
SEA10 Walter Jones	.20	.50
SEA11 Nate Burleson	.20	.50
SEA12 Kelly Jennings	.25	.60

2007 Seahawks Topps

COMPLETE SET (12)	2.50	5.00
1 Shaun Alexander	.25	.60
2 Matt Hasselbeck	.25	.60
3 Deion Branch	.25	.60
4 Lofa Tatupu	.25	.60
5 Seneca Wallace	.20	.50
6 Maurice Morris	.20	.50
7 Marcus Pollard	.20	.50
8 D.J. Hackett	.20	.50
9 Walter Jones	.20	.50
10 Julian Peterson	.20	.50
11 Josh Brown	.20	.50
12 Patrick Kerney	.20	.50

2008 Seahawks Topps

COMPLETE SET (12)	2.00	4.00
1 Lawrence Jackson	.25	.60
2 Bobby Engram	.20	.50
3 Patrick Kerney	.20	.50
4 Lofa Tatupu	.25	.60
5 Matt Hasselbeck	.25	.60
6 Julius Jones	.20	.50
7 Maurice Morris	.20	.50
8 Deion Branch	.25	.60
9 Julian Peterson	.20	.50
10 Nate Burleson	.20	.50
11 Marcus Trufant	.20	.50
12 Walter Jones	.20	.50

1982 Sears-Roebuck

These oversized 5" by 7" cards feature player photos on fronts. Reportedly these cards were issued in Sears 37 District Stores from January to December 1982. Reportedly because of the football players' strike, the promotion flopped, and consequently many cards were destroyed or thrown out. These cards look almost exactly like the Marketcom cards but say Sears Roebuck at the bottom of the reverse. These unnumbered cards are checklisted below in alphabetical order.

COMPLETE SET (14)	150.00	300.00
1 Ken Anderson	5.00	12.00
2 Terry Bradshaw	12.00	30.00
3 Earl Campbell	8.00	20.00
4 Rob Carpenter	4.00	10.00
5 Dwight Clark	4.00	10.00
6 Cris Collinsworth	4.00	10.00
7 Tony Dorsett	8.00	20.00
8 Dan Fouts	6.00	15.00
9 Mark Gastineau	5.00	12.00
10 Franco Harris	8.00	20.00
11 Joe Montana	50.00	125.00
12 Walter Payton	20.00	50.00
13 Randy White	6.00	15.00
14 Kellen Winslow	5.00	12.00

1993 Select

The 1993 Select set consists of 200 standard-size cards. Production was reportedly limited to 2,950 cases and cards were issued in 12-card packs. Rookie Cards include Jerome Bettis, Drew Bledsoe, Curtis Conway, Garrison Hearst, O.J. McDuffie, Natrone Means, Glyn Milburn and Rick Mirer.

COMPLETE SET (200)	7.50	20.00
1 Steve Young	.75	2.00
2 Andre Reed	.15	.40
3 Deion Sanders	.50	1.25
4 Harold Green	.07	.20
5 Wendell Davis	.07	.20
6 Mike Johnson	.07	.20
7 Troy Aikman	.75	2.00
8 Johnny Mitchell	.07	.20
9 Dale Carter	.07	.20
10 Bruce Matthews	.07	.20
11 Terrell Buckley	.07	.20
12 Steve Emtman	.07	.20
13 Neil Smith	.30	.75
14 Tim Brown	.30	.75
15 Chris Doleman	.07	.20
16 Dan Marino	1.50	4.00
17 Terry McDaniel	.07	.20
18 Neal Anderson	.07	.20
19 Phil Simms	.15	.40
20 Jeff Lageman	.07	.20
21 Jerry Rice	1.00	2.50
22 Dermontti Dawson	.07	.20
23 Reggie Cobb	.07	.20
24 Junior Seau	.30	.75
25 Darrell Green	.07	.20
26 Chris Warren	.15	.40
27 Randall Cunningham	.30	.75
28 Bruce Smith	.30	.75
29 Bryan Cox	.07	.20
30 David Klingler	.07	.20
31 Chip Lohmiller	.07	.20
32 Eric Metcalf	.15	.40
33 Ken Norton Jr.	.15	.40
34 John Elway	1.50	4.00
35 Harris Barton	.07	.20
36 Tim Barnett	.07	.20
37 Rodney Hampton	.15	.40
38 Desmond Howard	.15	.40
39 Tom Rathman	.07	.20
40 Derrick Thomas	.30	.75
41 Randal Hill	.07	.20
42 Steve Wisniewski	.07	.20
43 Brett Favre	2.00*	5.00
44 Darryl Talley	.07	.20
45 Shane Conlan	.07	.20
46 Anthony Miller	.15	.40
47 Randall McDaniel	.07	.20
48 Rod Woodson	.30	.75
49 Eric Martin	.07	.20
50 Ronnie Lott	.15	.40
51 Chris Spielman	.15	.40
52 Vincent Brown	.07	.20
53 Donnell Woolford	.07	.20
54 Richmond Webb	.07	.20
55 Emmitt Smith	1.25	3.00
56 Haywood Jeffires	.15	.40
57 Jim Kelly	.30	.75
58 James Francis	.07	.20
59 Steve Wallace	.07	.20
60 Jarrod Bunch	.07	.20
61 Lawrence Dawsey	.07	.20
62 Steve Atwater	.07	.20
63 Art Monk	.15	.40
64 Eric Green	.07	.20
65 Lawrence Taylor	.30	.75
66 Ronnie Harmon	.07	.20
67 Fred Barnett	.15	.40
68 Cortez Kennedy	.15	.40
69 Mark Collins	.07	.20
70 Howie Long	.30	.75
71 Jackie Harris	.07	.20
72 Irving Fryar	.15	.40
73 Jim Everett	.15	.40
74 Troy Vincent	.07	.20
75 Cris Carter	.30	.75
76 Boomer Esiason	.15	.40
77 Sam Mills	.07	.20
78 Lorenzo White	.07	.20
79 Andre Rison	.15	.40
80 Quentin Coryatt	.15	.40
81 Steve McMichael	.15	.40
82 Nick Lowery	.07	.20
83 Michael Irvin	.30	.75
84 Thurman Thomas	.30	.75
85 Bill Romanowski	.07	.20
86 Carl Pickens	.15	.40
87 Tim McDonald	.07	.20
88 Bernie Kosar	.15	.40
89 Greg Lloyd	.15	.40
90 Barry Sanders	1.25	3.00
91 Shannon Sharpe	.30	.75
92 Henry Thomas	.07	.20
93 Barry Foster	.15	.40
94 Antone Davis	.07	.20
95 Stan Humphries	.15	.40
96 Eric Swann	.15	.40
97 Mike Pritchard	.15	.40
98 Reggie White	.30	.75
99 Jeff Hostetler	.15	.40
100 Flipper Anderson	.07	.20
101 Gary Clark	.15	.40
102 Morten Andersen	.07	.20
103 Leonard Russell	.15	.40
104 Chris Hinton	.07	.20
105 John Stephens	.07	.20
106 Byron Evans	.07	.20
107 Warren Moon	.30	.75
108 Marv Cook	.07	.20
109 Carlton Gray RC	.07	.20
110 Jay Novacek	.15	.40
111 Gary Anderson K	.07	.20
112 Andre Tippett	.07	.20
113 Cornelius Bennett	.15	.40
114 Clyde Simmons	.07	.20
115 Jeff George	.30	.75
116 Audray McMillian	.07	.20
117 Mark Carrier WR	.15	.40
118 Vaughan Johnson	.07	.20
119 Kevin Greene	.15	.40
120 John Taylor	.15	.40
121 Jerry Ball	.07	.20
122 Pat Swilling	.07	.20
123 George Teague RC	.15	.40
124 Ricky Reynolds	.07	.20
125 Marcus Allen	.30	.75
126 Henry Jones	.07	.20
127 Ricky Watters	.30	.75
128 Leon Searcy	.07	.20
129 Chris Miller	.15	.40
130 Jim Harbaugh	.30	.75
131 Luis Sharpe	.07	.20
132 Simon Fletcher	.07	.20
133 Eric Allen	.07	.20
134 Carlton Haselrig	.07	.20
135 Harvey Williams	.15	.40
136 Leslie O'Neal	.15	.40
137 Sterling Sharpe	.30	.75
138 Tim Harris	.07	.20
139 Mark Rypien	.07	.20
140 Harry Galbreath	.07	.20
141 Sean Gilbert	.15	.40
142 Keith Jackson	.15	.40
143 Mark Clayton	.07	.20
144 Guy McIntyre	.07	.20
145 Jessie Tuggle	.07	.20
146 Leonard Marshall	.07	.20
147 Willie Davis	.30	.75
148 Herman Moore	.30	.75
149 Charles Haley	.15	.40
150 Amp Lee	.07	.20
151 Gary Zimmerman	.07	.20
152 Bennie Blades	.07	.20
153 Pierce Holt	.07	.20
154 Edgar Bennett	.30	.75
155 Joe Montana	1.50	4.00
156 Ted Washington	.07	.20
157 Hardy Nickerson	.15	.40
158 Rohn Stark	.07	.20
159 Brent Jones	.15	.40
160 Eugene Robinson	.07	.20
161 Pepper Johnson	.07	.20
162 Dan Saleaumua	.07	.20
163 Seth Joyner	.07	.20
164 Bruce Armstrong	.07	.20
165 Mike Munchak	.15	.40
166 Drew Bledsoe RC	2.00	5.00
167 Curtis Conway RC	.50	1.25
168 Lincoln Kennedy RC	.07	.20
169 Dana Stubblefield RC	.30	.75
170 Wayne Simmons RC	.07	.20
171 Garrison Hearst RC	.75	2.00
172 Jerome Bettis RC	3.00	8.00
173 Eric Curry RC	.07	.20
174 Natrone Means RC	.30	.75
175 Glyn Milburn RC	.30	.75
176 Marvin Jones RC	.07	.20
177 O.J. McDuffie RC	.30	.75
178 Dan Williams RC	.07	.20
179 Rick Mirer RC	.30	.75
180 John Copeland RC	.15	.40
181 Willie Roaf RC	.15	.40
182 Patrick Bates RC	.07	.20
183 Troy Drayton RC	.15	.40
184 Vincent Brisby RC	.30	.75
185 Irv Smith RC	.07	.20
186 Marion Butts	.07	.20
187 Wayne Martin	.07	.20
188 Brian Blades	.15	.40
189 Mel Gray	.15	.40
190 Mark Stepnoski	.07	.20
191 Ernest Givins	.15	.40
192 Steve Tasker	.15	.40
193 Tim Grunhard	.07	.20
194 Stanley Richard	.07	.20
195 Jeff Wright	.07	.20
196 Rodney Peete	.07	.20
197 Tunch Ilkin	.07	.20
198 Rich Camarillo	.07	.20
199 Erik Williams	.07	.20
200 Pete Stoyanovich	.07	.20
S21 Jerry Rice SAMPLE	1.00	2.50

1993 Select Gridiron Skills

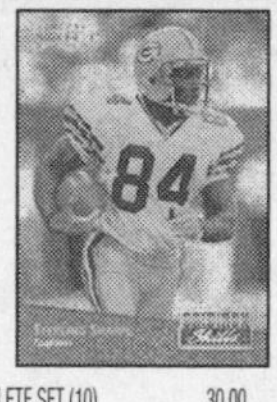

COMPLETE SET (10)	30.00	80.00
1 Warren Moon	2.00	5.00
2 Steve Young	5.00	12.00
3 Dan Marino	10.00	25.00
4 John Elway	10.00	25.00
5 Troy Aikman	5.00	12.00
6 Sterling Sharpe	2.00	5.00
7 Jerry Rice	6.00	15.00
8 Andre Rison	1.00	2.50
9 Haywood Jeffires	1.00	2.50
10 Michael Irvin	2.00	5.00

1993 Select Young Stars

This 38-card standard-size set was sold in a hinged black leatherette box. Each set included a certificate of authenticity, providing the set serial number out of a total of 5,900 sets produced. Using Score's FX printing technology, the fronts display color action cutouts that extend beyond the arched-shape background. The cards are numbered on the back "X of 38."

COMP.FACT SET (38)	15.00	40.00
1 Brett Favre	4.00	10.00
2 Anthony Miller	.30	.75
3 Rodney Hampton	.30	.75
4 Cortez Kennedy	.30	.75
5 Junior Seau	.40	1.00
6 Ricky Watters	.30	.75
7 Terry Allen	.30	.75
8 Drew Bledsoe	6.00	15.00
9 Rick Mirer	.40	1.00
10 Jeff Graham	.30	.75
11 Barry Foster	.30	.75
12 Eric Green	.20	.50
13 Troy Aikman	2.50	6.00
14 Michael Haynes	.30	.75
15 Johnny Mitchell	.20	.50
16 Lawrence Dawsey	.20	.50
17 Mo Lewis	.20	.50
18 Andre Ware	.30	.75
19 Neil O'Donnell	.30	.75
20 Broderick Thomas	.20	.50
21 Tim Barnett	.20	.50
22 Fred Barnett	.30	.75
23 Carl Pickens	.30	.75
24 Santana Dotson	.30	.75
25 Sean Gilbert	.20	.50
26 Quentin Coryatt	.20	.50
27 Arthur Marshall	.20	.50
28 Dale Carter	.20	.50
29 Henry Jones	.20	.50
30 Terrell Buckley	.20	.50
31 Tommy Vardell	.20	.50
32 Russell Maryland	.20	.50
33 Steve Emtman	.20	.50
34 Jarrod Bunch	.20	.50
35 Alfred Williams	.20	.50
36 Brian Mitchell	.20	.50
37 Chris Warren	.30	.75
38 Deion Sanders	1.25	3.00

1994 Select Samples

These sample cards measure the standard size and preview the style of the 1994 Select football set and include four regular issue cards, one "Canton Bound" and one "Future Force" card. The fronts feature full-bleed color action player photos. A small, oval-shaped black-and-white action player photo with a gold-foil border carrying the team name appears in the lower left corner. Select's logo is superimposed in the lower right corner, with the player's last name printed in gold-foil letters over it. The horizontal backs carry a second color action photo on the left, with 1993 highlights, statistics and career totals on the right. The upper right corner of each card is cut off.

COMPLETE SET (7)	4.80	12.00
5 Rod Woodson	.40	1.00
19 Junior Seau	.50	1.25
33 Mark Carrier DB	.40	1.00
218 Charlie Garner	.60	1.50
CB4 Barry Sanders	2.00	5.00
FF2 Drew Bledsoe	1.20	3.00
NNO Title Card	.40	1.00

1994 Select

The 1994 Select football set consists of 225 standard-size cards. Production was reportedly limited to 3,950 individually numbered boxes and cases. Top rookie prospects are showcased in a Rookie (199-223) subset. Rookie cards include Derrick Alexander, Mario Bates, Trent Dilfer, Marshall Faulk, William Floyd, Greg Hill, Charles Johnson, Errict Rhett, Darnay Scott and Heath Shuler.

COMPLETE SET (225)	6.00	15.00
1 Emmitt Smith	1.00	2.50
2 Bruce Smith	.15	.40
3 Randall McDaniel	.05	.15
4 Drew Bledsoe	.50	1.25
5 Rod Woodson	.07	.20
6 Richard Dent	.07	.20
7 Norm Johnson	.02	.10
8 Jim Everett	.07	.20
9 Harold Green	.02	.10
10 John Elway	1.25	3.00
11 Barry Sanders	1.00	2.50
12 Sterling Sharpe	.07	.20
13 Marcus Robertson	.02	.10
14 Steve Wisniewski	.02	.10
15 Irving Fryar	.07	.20
16 Tyrone Hughes	.07	.20
17 Garrison Hearst	.15	.40
18 Randall Cunningham	.15	.40
19 Junior Seau	.15	.40
20 Rick Mirer	.15	.40
21 Jerry Rice	.60	1.50
22 Eric Metcalf	.07	.20
23 Roosevelt Potts	.02	.10
24 Neil Smith	.07	.20
25 Jerome Bettis	.30	.75
26 Keith Hamilton	.02	.10
27 Hardy Nickerson	.07	.20
28 Steve Tasker	.07	.20
29 Johnny Johnson	.02	.10
30 Tom Carter	.02	.10
31 Andre Rison	.07	.20
32 Cortez Kennedy	.07	.20
33 Mark Carrier DB	.02	.10
34 Shannon Sharpe	.07	.20
35 Eric Swann	.07	.20
36 Steve Young	.50	1.25
37 Johnny Mitchell	.02	.10
38 Dermontti Dawson	.02	.10
39 Mike Johnson	.02	.10
40 Troy Aikman	.60	1.50
41 Pierce Holt	.02	.10
42 Derrick Thomas	.15	.40
43 Reggie Cobb	.02	.10
44 Michael Jackson	.07	.20
45 Lomas Brown	.02	.10
46 Jeff Hostetler	.07	.20
47 Pete Stoyanovich	.02	.10
48 Reggie White	.15	.40
49 Quentin Coryatt	.02	.10
50 Cris Carter	.30	.75
51 Sean Gilbert	.02	.10
52 Chris Slade	.02	.10
53 Ronnie Harmon	.02	.10
54 Renaldo Turnbull	.02	.10
55 Fred Barnett	.07	.20
56 John Elliott	.02	.10
57 Deion Sanders	.30	.75
58 John Carney	.02	.10
59 Louis Oliver	.02	.10
60 Greg Lloyd	.07	.20
61 Chris Hinton	.02	.10
62 Ronald Moore	.02	.10
63 Vincent Brown	.02	.10
64 Tony McGee	.02	.10
65 Erik Williams	.02	.10
66 Thurman Thomas	.15	.40
67 Neil O'Donnell	.15	.40
68 Scott Mitchell	.07	.20
69 Keith Byars	.02	.10
70 Henry Ellard	.07	.20
71 Chris Spielman	.07	.20
72 LeRoy Butler	.02	.10
73 Tim Brown	.15	.40
74 Darrell Green	.02	.10
75 Bruce Matthews	.02	.10
76 Stan Humphries	.07	.20
77 Will Wolford	.02	.10
78 John Taylor	.07	.20
79 Joe Montana	1.25	3.00
80 Chris Warren	.07	.20
81 Michael Brooks	.02	.10
82 Vance Johnson	.02	.10
83 Rob Moore	.07	.20
84 Herschel Walker	.07	.20
85 Alvin Harper	.07	.20
86 Wayne Martin	.02	.10
87 Leslie O'Neal	.02	.10
88 Flipper Anderson	.02	.10
89 Tommy Vardell	.02	.10
90 Mike Sherrard	.02	.10
91 Chris Jacke	.02	.10
92 Jim Kelly	.15	.40
93 Jeff Graham	.02	.10
94 Bryan Cox	.02	.10
95 Michael Irvin	.15	.40
96 Jeff Lageman	.02	.10
97 Webster Slaughter	.02	.10
98 Eugene Robinson	.02	.10
99 Vencie Glenn	.02	.10
100 Sean Jones	.02	.10
101 Calvin Williams	.07	.20
102 Jim Harbaugh	.15	.40
103 Eric Curry	.02	.10
104 Terry Allen	.07	.20
105 Darryl Williams	.02	.10
106 Gary Clark	.07	.20
107 Marcus Allen	.15	.40
108 Chip Lohmiller	.02	.10
109 Vaughan Johnson	.02	.10
110 Herman Moore	.15	.40
111 Barry Foster	.02	.10
112 Rocket Ismail	.07	.20
113 Erric Pegram	.02	.10
114 Anthony Miller	.07	.20
115 Shane Conlan	.02	.10
116 David Klingler	.02	.10
117 Mark Collins	.02	.10
118 Tony Bennett	.02	.10
119 Donnell Woolford	.02	.10
120 Reggie Brooks	.07	.20
121 Sam Mills	.02	.10
122 Greg Montgomery	.02	.10
123 Kevin Greene	.07	.20
124 Terry McDaniel	.02	.10
125 Henry Jones	.02	.10
126 Ricky Watters	.07	.20
127 Dan Marino	1.25	3.00
128 Steve Atwater	.02	.10
129 Ricky Proehl	.02	.10
130 Ernest Givins	.07	.20
131 John L. Williams	.02	.10
132 John Randle	.07	.20
133 Jay Novacek	.07	.20
134 Boomer Esiason	.07	.20
135 Jessie Hester	.02	.10
136 Courtney Hawkins	.02	.10
137 Ben Coates	.07	.20
138 Stevon Moore	.02	.10
139 Eric Allen	.02	.10
140 Jessie Tuggle	.02	.10
141 Marion Butts	.02	.10
142 Brett Favre	1.25	3.00
143 Andre Reed	.07	.20
144 Rodney Hampton	.07	.20
145 Keith Sims	.02	.10
146 Derek Brown RBK	.02	.10
147 Eric Green	.02	.10
148 Greg Robinson	.02	.10
149 Nate Newton	.02	.10
150 Mark Higgs	.02	.10
151 Nick Lowery	.02	.10
152 Craig Erickson	.02	.10
153 Anthony Carter	.07	.20
154 Simon Fletcher	.02	.10
155 Ronnie Lott	.07	.20
156 Gary Brown	.02	.10
157 Brent Jones	.07	.20
158 Jim Sweeney	.02	.10
159 Robert Brooks	.15	.40
160 Keith Jackson	.02	.10
161 Daryl Johnston	.07	.20
162 Tom Waddle	.02	.10
163 Eric Martin	.02	.10
164 Cornelius Bennett	.07	.20
165 Tim McDonald	.02	.10
166 Chris Doleman	.02	.10
167 Gary Zimmerman	.02	.10
168 Al Smith	.02	.10
169 Mark Carrier WR	.07	.20
170 Harris Barton	.02	.10
171 Ray Childress	.02	.10
172 Darryl Talley	.02	.10
173 James Jett	.02	.10
174 Mark Stepnoski	.02	.10
175 Jeff Query	.02	.10
176 Charles Haley	.07	.20
177 Rod Bernstine	.02	.10
178 Richmond Webb	.02	.10
179 Rich Camarillo	.02	.10
180 Pat Swilling	.02	.10
181 Chris Miller	.02	.10
182 Mike Pritchard	.02	.10
183 Checklist NFC	.02	.10
184 Natrone Means	.15	.40
185 Erik Kramer	.07	.20
186 Clyde Simmons	.02	.10
187 Checklist AFC NFC	.02	.10
188 Warren Moon	.15	.40
189 Michael Haynes	.07	.20
190 Terry Kirby	.15	.40
191 Brian Blades	.07	.20
192 Haywood Jeffires	.07	.20
193 Thomas Everett	.02	.10
194 Morten Andersen	.02	.10
195 Dana Stubblefield	.07	.20
196 Ken Norton	.07	.20
197 Art Monk	.07	.20
198 Seth Joyner	.02	.10
199 Heath Shuler RC	.15	.40
200 Marshall Faulk RC	2.50	6.00
201 Charles Johnson RC	.15	.40
202 Der.Alexander WR RC	.15	.40
203 Greg Hill RC	.15	.40
204 Darnay Scott RC	.40	1.00
205 Willie McGinest RC	.15	.40
206 Thomas Randolph RC	.02	.10
207 Errict Rhett RC	.15	.40
208 William Floyd RC	.15	.40
209 Johnnie Morton RC	.75	2.00
210 David Palmer RC	.15	.40
211 Dan Wilkinson RC	.07	.20
212 Trent Dilfer RC	.50	1.25
213 Antonio Langham RC	.07	.20
214 Chuck Levy RC	.02	.10
215 John Thierry RC	.02	.10
216 Kevin Lee RC	.02	.10
217 Aaron Glenn RC	.15	.40
218 Charlie Garner RC	.60	1.50
219 Jeff Burris RC	.07	.20
220 LeShon Johnson RC	.07	.20
221 Thomas Lewis RC	.07	.20
222 Ryan Yarborough RC	.02	.10
223 Mario Bates RC	.15	.40
224 Checklist NFC AFC	.02	.10
225 Checklist AFC	.02	.10
SR1 Marshall Faulk SR	15.00	40.00
SR2 Dan Wilkinson SR	3.00	8.00

1994 Select Canton Bound

COMPLETE SET (12)	40.00	100.00
STATED ODDS 1:48		
CB1 Emmitt Smith	8.00	20.00
CB2 Sterling Sharpe	.60	1.50
CB3 Joe Montana	10.00	25.00
CB4 Barry Sanders	8.00	20.00
CB5 Jerry Rice	5.00	12.00
CB6 Ronnie Lott	.60	1.50
CB7 Reggie White	1.25	3.00
CB8 Steve Young	4.00	10.00
CB9 Jerome Bettis	2.50	6.00
CB10 Bruce Smith	1.25	3.00
CB11 Troy Aikman	5.00	12.00
CB12 Thurman Thomas	1.25	3.00

1994 Select Future Force

COMPLETE SET (12)	7.50	20.00
STATED ODDS 1:48		
FF1 Rick Mirer	1.25	3.00
FF2 Drew Bledsoe	4.00	10.00
FF3 Jerome Bettis	2.50	6.00
FF4 Reggie Brooks	.60	1.50
FF5 Natrone Means	1.25	3.00
FF6 James Jett	.30	.75
FF7 Terry Kirby	1.25	3.00
FF8 Vincent Brisby	.30	.75
FF9 Gary Brown	.30	.75
FF10 Tyrone Hughes	.60	1.50
FF11 Dana Stubblefield	.60	1.50
FF12 Garrison Hearst	1.25	3.00

1994 Select Franco Harris Autograph

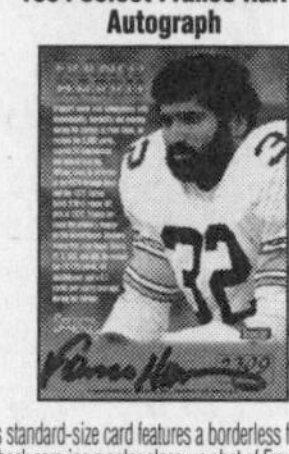

This standard-size card features a borderless front with the back carrying a color close-up shot of Franco on the right and bio information on the left. This card was given away at the Pinnacle Party at the 15th National Sports Card Convention. Harris' autograph appears in black felt-tip pen in the brown bottom margin, along with hand serial numbering of a total of 5,000 produced.

1 Franco Harris	10.00	25.00

1996 Select Promos

These three promos were sent out to promote the 1996 Select release. Two base brand promo cards were produced and one Prime Cut insert promo (Dan Marino).

COMPLETE SET (3)	4.00	10.00
1 Troy Aikman	.75	2.00
10 Dan Marino Prime Cut card	1.50	4.00
19 Brett Favre	1.50	4.00*

1996 Select

The 1996 Select set was issued in one hobby series totalling 200 standard-size cards. The set was issued in 10-card packs which had a suggested retail price of $1.99 each. Among the topical subsets are 1996 Rookies (151-180), Fluid and Fleet (181-195) and Checklists (196-200). Rookie Cards in this set include Tim Biakabutuka, Terry Glenn, Eddie George, Keyshawn Johnson, Leeland McElroy and Lawrence Phillips.

COMPLETE SET (200)	8.00	20.00
1 Troy Aikman	.40	1.00
2 Marshall Faulk	.20	.50
3 Kordell Stewart	.15	.40
4 Larry Centers	.07	.20
5 Tamarick Vanover	.07	.20
6 Ken Norton Jr.	.02	.10
7 Steve Tasker	.02	.10
8 Dan Marino	.75	2.00
9 Heath Shuler	.07	.20
10 Anthony Miller	.07	.20
11 Mario Bates	.07	.20
12 Natrone Means	.07	.20
13 Darren Woodson	.07	.20
14 Chris Sanders	.07	.20
15 Chris Warren	.07	.20
16 Eric Metcalf	.02	.10
17 Quentin Coryatt	.02	.10
18 Jeff Hostetler	.02	.10
19 Brett Favre	.75	2.00
20 Curtis Martin	.30	.75
21 Floyd Turner	.02	.10
22 Curtis Conway	.15	.40
23 Orlando Thomas	.02	.10
24 Lee Woodall	.02	.10
25 Darick Holmes	.02	.10
26 Marcus Allen	.15	.40
27 Ricky Watters	.07	.20
28 Herman Moore	.07	.20
29 Rodney Hampton	.07	.20
30 Alvin Harper	.02	.10
31 Jeff Blake	.15	.40
32 Wayne Chrebet	.25	.60
33 Jerry Rice	.40	1.00
34 Dave Krieg	.02	.10
35 Mark Brunell	.25	.60
36 Terry Allen	.07	.20
37 Emmitt Smith	.60	1.50
38 Bryan Cox	.02	.10
39 Tony Martin	.07	.20
40 John Elway	.75	2.00
41 Warren Moon	.07	.20
42 Yancey Thigpen	.07	.20
43 Jeff George	.07	.20
44 Rodney Thomas	.02	.10
45 Joey Galloway	.15	.40
46 Jim Kelly	.15	.40
47 Drew Bledsoe	.25	.60
48 Greg Lloyd	.07	.20
49 Michael Irvin	.15	.40
50 Quinn Early	.02	.10
51 Brent Jones	.02	.10
52 Rashaan Salaam	.07	.20
53 James O.Stewart	.07	.20
54 Gus Frerotte	.07	.20
55 Edgar Bennett	.07	.20
56 Lamont Warren	.02	.10
57 Napoleon Kaufman	.15	.40
58 Kevin Williams	.02	.10
59 Irving Fryar	.07	.20
60 Trent Dilfer	.15	.40
61 Eric Zeier	.02	.10
62 Tyrone Wheatley	.07	.20
63 Isaac Bruce	.15	.40
64 Terrell Davis	.30	.75
65 Lake Dawson	.02	.10
66 Carnell Lake	.02	.10
67 Kerry Collins	.15	.40
68 Kyle Brady	.02	.10
69 Rodney Peete	.02	.10
70 Carl Pickens	.07	.20
71 Robert Smith	.07	.20
72 Rod Woodson	.07	.20
73 Deion Sanders	.25	.60
74 Sean Dawkins	.02	.10
75 William Floyd	.07	.20
76 Barry Sanders	.60	1.50
77 Ben Coates	.07	.20
78 Neil O'Donnell	.07	.20
79 Bill Brooks	.02	.10
80 Steve Bono	.02	.10
81 Jay Novacek	.02	.10
82 Bernie Parmalee	.02	.10
83 Derek Loville	.02	.10
84 Frank Sanders	.07	.20
85 Robert Brooks	.15	.40
86 Jim Harbaugh	.07	.20
87 Rick Mirer	.07	.20
88 Craig Heyward	.02	.10
89 Greg Hill	.07	.20
90 Andre Coleman	.02	.10
91 Shannon Sharpe	.07	.20
92 Hugh Douglas	.07	.20
93 Andre Hastings	.02	.10
94 Bryce Paup	.02	.10
95 Jim Everett	.02	.10
96 Brian Mitchell	.02	.10
97 Jeff Graham	.02	.10
98 Steve McNair	.30	.75
99 Charlie Garner	.07	.20
100 Willie McGinest	.02	.10
101 Harvey Williams	.02	.10
102 Daryl Johnston	.07	.20
103 Cris Carter	.15	.40
104 J.J. Stokes	.15	.40
105 Garrison Hearst	.07	.20
106 Mark Chmura	.07	.20
107 Derrick Thomas	.15	.40
108 Errict Rhett	.07	.20
109 Terance Mathis	.02	.10
110 Dave Brown	.02	.10
111 Eric Pegram	.02	.10
112 Scott Mitchell	.07	.20
113 Aaron Bailey	.02	.10
114 Stan Humphries	.07	.20
115 Bruce Smith	.07	.20
116 Rob Johnson	.15	.40
117 O.J. McDuffie	.07	.20
118 Brian Blades	.02	.10
119 Steve Atwater	.02	.10
120 Tyrone Hughes	.02	.10
121 Michael Westbrook	.15	.40
122 Ki-Jana Carter	.07	.20
123 Adrian Murrell	.07	.20
124 Steve Young	.30	.75
125 Charles Haley	.07	.20
126 Vincent Brisby	.02	.10
127 Jerome Bettis	.15	.40
128 Erik Kramer	.02	.10
129 Roosevelt Potts	.02	.10
130 Tim Brown	.15	.40
131 Reggie White	.15	.40
132 Jake Reed	.07	.20
133 Junior Seau	.15	.40
134 Stoney Case	.02	.10
135 Kimble Anders	.07	.20
136 Brett Perriman	.02	.10
137 Todd Collins	.07	.20
138 Sherman Williams	.02	.10
139 Hardy Nickerson	.02	.10
140 Ernie Mills	.02	.10
141 Glyn Milburn	.02	.10
142 Terry Kirby	.07	.20
143 Bert Emanuel	.07	.20
144 Aeneas Williams	.02	.10
145 Aaron Craver	.02	.10

146 Jackie Harris	.02	.10
147 Thurman Thomas	.15	.40
148 Aaron Hayden RC	.02	.10
149 Antonio Freeman	.15	.40
150 Kevin Greene	.07	.20
151 Kevin Hardy RC	.15	.40
152 Eric Moulds RC	.60	1.50
153 Tim Biakabutuka RC	.15	.40
154 Keyshawn Johnson RC	.50	1.25
155 Jeff Lewis RC	.07	.20
156 Stepfret Williams RC	.07	.20
157 Tony Brackens RC	.15	.40
158 Mike Alstott RC	.50	1.25
159 Willie Anderson RC	.02	.10
160 Marvin Harrison RC	1.25	3.00
161 Regan Upshaw RC	.02	.10
162 Bobby Engram RC	.15	.40
163 Leeland McElroy RC	.07	.20
164 Alex Van Dyke RC	.07	.20
165 Stanley Pritchett RC	.07	.20
166 Cedric Jones RC	.02	.10
167 Terry Glenn RC	.50	1.25
168 Eddie George RC	.60	1.50
169 Lawrence Phillips RC	.15	.40
170 Jonathan Ogden RC	.15	.40
171 Danny Kanell RC	.15	.40
172 Alex Molden RC	.02	.10
173 Daryl Gardener RC	.02	.10
174 Derrick Mayes RC	.15	.40
175 Marco Battaglia RC	.02	.10
176 Jon Stark RC	.02	.10
177 Karim Abdul-Jabbar RC	.15	.40
178 Stephen Davis RC	.75	2.00
179 Rickey Dudley RC	.15	.40
180 Eddie Kennison RC	.15	.40
181 Barry Sanders FF	.30	.75
182 Brett Favre FF	.40	1.00
183 John Elway FF	.40	1.00
184 Steve Young FF	.15	.40
185 Michael Irvin FF	.07	.20
186 Jerry Rice FF	.20	.50
187 Emmitt Smith FF	.30	.75
188 Isaac Bruce FF	.15	.40
189 Chris Warren FF	.07	.20
190 Errict Rhett FF	.07	.20
191 Herman Moore FF	.07	.20
192 Carl Pickens FF	.07	.20
193 Cris Carter FF	.15	.40
194 Terrell Davis FF	.15	.40
195 Rodney Thomas FF	.02	.10
196 Dan Marino CL	.15	.40
197 Drew Bledsoe CL	.07	.20
198 Emmitt Smith CL	.15	.40
199 Jerry Rice CL	.15	.40
200 Barry Sanders CL John Elway	.15	.40

1996 Select Artist's Proofs

*AP STARS: 6X TO 15X BASIC CARDS
*AP RCs: 3X TO 8X BASIC CARDS
STATED ODDS 1:23

1996 Select Building Blocks

COMPLETE SET (20)	50.00	100.00
STATED ODDS 1:48		
1 Curtis Martin	5.00	12.00
2 Terrell Davis	5.00	12.00
3 Darick Holmes	.60	1.50
4 Rashaan Salaam	1.25	3.00
5 Ki-Jana Carter	1.25	3.00
6 Rodney Thomas	.60	1.50
7 Kerry Collins	2.50	6.00
8 Eric Zeier	.60	1.50
9 Steve McNair	5.00	12.00
10 Kordell Stewart	2.50	6.00
11 J.J. Stokes	2.50	6.00
12 Joey Galloway	2.50	6.00
13 Michael Westbrook	2.50	6.00
14 Mike Alstott	2.50	6.00
15 Tony Brackens	.75	2.00
16 Terry Glenn	2.50	6.00
17 Kevin Hardy	.75	2.00
18 Leeland McElroy	.40	1.00
19 Tim Biakabutuka	.75	2.00
20 Keyshawn Johnson	2.50	6.00

1996 Select Four-midable

COMPLETE SET (16)	20.00	40.00
STATED ODDS 1:18		
1 Troy Aikman	2.50	5.00
2 Michael Irvin	1.00	2.00
3 Emmitt Smith	4.00	8.00
4 Deion Sanders	1.50	3.00
5 Brett Favre	5.00	10.00
6 Robert Brooks	1.00	2.00
7 Edgar Bennett	.40	1.00
8 Reggie White	1.00	2.00
9 Kordell Stewart	1.00	2.00
10 Yancey Thigpen	.40	1.00
11 Neil O'Donnell	.40	1.00
12 Greg Lloyd	.40	1.00
13 Jim Harbaugh	.40	1.00
14 Sean Dawkins	.20	.50
15 Marshall Faulk	1.25	2.50
16 Quentin Coryatt	.20	.50

1996 Select Prime Cuts

COMPLETE SET (18)	100.00	200.00
STATED ODDS 1:80		
1 Emmitt Smith	8.00	20.00
2 Troy Aikman	5.00	12.00
3 Michael Irvin	2.00	5.00
4 Steve Young	4.00	10.00
5 Jerry Rice	5.00	12.00
6 Drew Bledsoe	3.00	8.00
7 Brett Favre	10.00	25.00
8 John Elway	10.00	25.00
9 Barry Sanders	8.00	20.00
10 Dan Marino	10.00	25.00
11 Isaac Bruce	2.00	5.00
12 Marshall Faulk	2.50	6.00
13 Errict Rhett	1.00	2.50
14 Chris Warren	1.00	2.50
15 Herman Moore	1.00	2.50
16 Deion Sanders	3.00	8.00
17 Joey Galloway	2.00	5.00
18 Curtis Martin	4.00	10.00

2001 Select

Playoff released Score Select as the hobby version of the basic Score product. This 330-card set was highlighted by the serial numbered rookies (numbered of 275-325) which were randomly inserted. The base card design follows that of the Score set along with a glossy coating on the cardfront. The cards were also printed on much thicker paper stock. An exchange card was inserted in packs that was good for an option to purchase a 2001 Score Supplemental factory set. It carried an expiration date of 12/01/2001.

COMP.SET w/o SPs (220)	12.50	30.00
271-330 ROOKIE PRINT RUN 275		
1 David Boston	.20	.50
2 Frank Sanders	.20	.50
3 Jake Plummer	.25	.60
4 Michael Pittman	.25	.60
5 Rob Moore	.20	.50
6 Thomas Jones	.25	.60
7 Chris Chandler	.25	.60
8 Doug Johnson	.20	.50
9 Jamal Anderson	.25	.60
10 Tim Dwight	.25	.60
11 Brandon Stokley	.25	.60
12 Chris Redman	.30	.75
13 Jamal Lewis	.30	.75
14 Qadry Ismail	.25	.60
15 Ray Lewis	.30	.75
16 Rod Woodson	.30	.75
17 Shannon Sharpe	.30	.75
18 Travis Taylor	.20	.50
19 Trent Dilfer	.25	.60
20 Elvis Grbac	.25	.60
21 Eric Moulds	.25	.60
22 Jay Riemersma	.20	.50
23 Peerless Price	.20	.50
24 Rob Johnson	.25	.60
25 Sam Cowart	.20	.50
26 Sammy Morris	.25	.60
27 Shawn Bryson	.20	.50
28 Donald Hayes	.20	.50
29 Muhsin Muhammad	.25	.60
30 Patrick Jeffers	.20	.50
31 Reggie White DE	.30	.75
32 Steve Beuerlein	.25	.60
33 Tim Biakabutuka	.20	.50
34 Wesley Walls	.20	.50
35 Brian Urlacher	.40	1.00
36 Cade McNown	.25	.60
37 Dez White	.25	.60
38 James Allen	.20	.50
39 Marcus Robinson	.25	.60
40 Marty Booker	.25	.60
41 Akili Smith	.20	.50
42 Corey Dillon	.25	.60
43 Danny Farmer	.20	.50
44 Peter Warrick	.25	.60
45 Ron Dugans	.20	.50
46 Takeo Spikes	.20	.50
47 Courtney Brown	.20	.50
48 Dennis Northcutt	.20	.50
49 JaJuan Dawson	.20	.50
50 Kevin Johnson	.20	.50
51 Tim Couch	.20	.50
52 Travis Prentice	.20	.50
53 Anthony Wright	.20	.50
54 Emmitt Smith	.75	2.00
55 James McKnight	.20	.50
56 Joey Galloway	.25	.60
57 Rocket Ismail	.25	.60
58 Randall Cunningham	.30	.75
59 Troy Aikman	.50	1.25
60 Brian Griese	.25	.60
61 Ed McCaffrey	.25	.60
62 Gus Frerotte	.25	.60
63 John Elway	.75	2.00
64 Mike Anderson	.25	.60
65 Olandis Gary	.20	.50
66 Rod Smith	.25	.60
67 Terrell Davis	.30	.75
68 Barry Sanders	.75	2.00
69 Charlie Batch	.25	.60
70 Germane Crowell	.20	.50
71 Herman Moore	.25	.60
72 James Stewart	.20	.50
73 Johnnie Morton	.25	.60
74 Robert Porcher	.20	.50
75 Jim Harbaugh	.25	.60
76 Ahman Green	.30	.75
77 Antonio Freeman	.30	.75
78 Bill Schroeder	.25	.60
79 Brett Favre	1.00	2.50
80 Bubba Franks	.25	.60
81 Dorsey Levens	.25	.60
82 E.G. Green	.20	.50
83 Edgerrin James	.30	.75
84 Jerome Pathon	.20	.50
85 Ken Dilger	.20	.50
86 Marcus Pollard	.20	.50
87 Marvin Harrison	.30	.75
88 Peyton Manning	.75	2.00
89 Terrence Wilkins	.20	.50
90 Fred Taylor	.30	.75
91 Hardy Nickerson	.20	.50
92 Jimmy Smith	.25	.60
93 Keenan McCardell	.25	.60
94 Kyle Brady	.20	.50
95 Mark Brunell	.25	.60
96 Tony Brackens	.20	.50
97 Derrick Alexander WR	.20	.50
98 Sylvester Morris	.20	.50
99 Tony Gonzalez	.30	.75
100 Tony Richardson	.20	.50
101 Kimble Anders	.20	.50
102 Warren Moon	.30	.75
103 Dan Marino	.75	2.00
104 Jay Fiedler	.25	.60
105 Lamar Smith	.25	.60
106 O.J. McDuffie	.20	.50
107 Oronde Gadsden	.20	.50
108 Sam Madison	.20	.50
109 Thurman Thomas	.30	.75
110 Tony Martin	.25	.60
111 Zach Thomas	.30	.75
112 Cris Carter	.30	.75
113 Daunte Culpepper	.25	.60
114 Matthew Hatchette	.20	.50
115 Randy Moss	.30	.75
116 Robert Smith	.25	.60
117 Drew Bledsoe	.30	.75
118 J.R. Redmond	.20	.50
119 Kevin Faulk	.25	.60
120 Michael Bishop	.25	.60
121 Terry Glenn	.25	.60
122 Troy Brown	.25	.60
123 Ty Law	.25	.60
124 Aaron Brooks	.25	.60
125 Darren Howard	.20	.50
126 Jake Reed	.25	.60
127 Jeff Blake	.25	.60
128 Joe Horn	.25	.60
129 La'Roi Glover	.20	.50
130 Ricky Williams	.30	.75
131 Willie Jackson	.20	.50
132 Albert Connell	.20	.50
133 Amani Toomer	.25	.60
134 Ike Hilliard	.25	.60
135 Jason Sehorn	.25	.60
136 Jessie Armstead	.20	.50
137 Kerry Collins	.25	.60
138 Michael Strahan	.30	.75
139 Ron Dayne	.25	.60
140 Ron Dixon	.20	.50
141 Tiki Barber	.30	.75
142 Anthony Becht	.20	.50
143 Chad Pennington	.30	.75
144 Curtis Martin	.30	.75
145 Dedric Ward	.20	.50
146 Laveranues Coles	.25	.60
147 Vinny Testaverde	.25	.60
148 Wayne Chrebet	.25	.60
149 Andre Rison	.25	.60
150 Charles Woodson	.30	.75
151 Darrell Russell	.20	.50
152 Napoleon Kaufman	.20	.50
153 Rich Gannon	.25	.60
154 Tim Brown	.30	.75
155 Tyrone Wheatley	.25	.60
156 Chad Lewis	.20	.50
157 Charles Johnson	.20	.50
158 Donovan McNabb	.30	.75
159 Duce Staley	.25	.60
160 Hugh Douglas	.20	.50
161 Na Brown	.20	.50
162 Todd Pinkston	.20	.50
163 James Thrash	.25	.60
164 Bobby Shaw	.20	.50
165 Hines Ward	.30	.75
166 Jerome Bettis	.30	.75
167 Kordell Stewart	.25	.60
168 Levon Kirkland	.20	.50
169 Plaxico Burress	.25	.60
170 Richard Huntley	.20	.50
171 Troy Edwards	.20	.50
172 Jeff Graham	.20	.50
173 Junior Seau	.30	.75
174 Doug Flutie	.30	.75
175 Charlie Garner	.25	.60
176 Jeff Garcia	.25	.60
177 Jerry Rice	.60	1.50
178 Steve Young	.40	1.00
179 Terrell Owens	.30	.75
180 Brock Huard	.20	.50
181 Darrell Jackson	.25	.60
182 Derrick Mayes	.20	.50
183 Ricky Watters	.25	.60
184 Shaun Alexander	.30	.75
185 Matt Hasselbeck	.30	.75
186 John Randle	.25	.60
187 Az-Zahir Hakim	.20	.50
188 Isaac Bruce	.30	.75
189 Kurt Warner	.50	1.25
190 Marshall Faulk	.30	.75
191 Torry Holt	.25	.60
192 Trent Green	.30	.75
193 Derrick Brooks	.30	.75
194 Jacquez Green	.20	.50
195 John Lynch	.25	.60
196 Keyshawn Johnson	.25	.60
197 Mike Alstott	.25	.60
198 Reidel Anthony	.20	.50
199 Shaun King	.20	.50
200 Warren Sapp	.25	.60
201 Warrick Dunn	.30	.75
202 Ryan Leaf	.20	.50
203 Carl Pickens	.25	.60
204 Derrick Mason	.25	.60
205 Eddie George	.30	.75
206 Frank Wycheck	.20	.50
207 Jevon Kearse	.25	.60
208 Neil O'Donnell	.25	.60
209 Steve McNair	.30	.75
210 Yancey Thigpen	.20	.50
211 Andre Reed	.30	.75
212 Brad Johnson	.25	.60
213 Bruce Smith	.30	.75
214 Champ Bailey	.30	.75
215 Darrell Green	.30	.75
216 Deion Sanders	.30	.75
217 Irving Fryar	.25	.60
218 Jeff George	.25	.60
219 Michael Westbrook	.20	.50
220 Stephen Davis	.25	.60
221 Terrell Owens AP	.75	2.00
222 Peyton Manning AP	2.00	5.00
223 Stephen Davis AP	.60	1.50
224 Marvin Harrison AP	.75	2.00
225 Donovan McNabb AP	.75	2.00
226 Edgerrin James AP	.75	2.00
227 Eric Moulds AP	.60	1.50
228 Daunte Culpepper AP	.60	1.50
229 Eddie George AP	.75	2.00
230 Cris Carter AP	.75	2.00
231 Rich Gannon AP	.60	1.50
232 Jeff Garcia AP	.60	1.50
233 Jimmy Smith AP	.60	1.50
234 Tony Gonzalez AP	.75	2.00
235 Torry Holt AP	.60	1.50
236 Jevon Kearse AP	.60	1.50
237 Ray Lewis AP	.75	2.00
238 Warren Sapp AP	.60	1.50
239 Brian Urlacher AP	1.00	2.50
240 Champ Bailey AP	.75	2.00
241 Peyton Manning LL	2.00	5.00
242 Jeff Garcia LL	.60	1.50
243 Elvis Grbac LL	.60	1.50
244 Daunte Culpepper LL	.60	1.50
245 Brett Favre LL	2.50	6.00
246 Edgerrin James LL	.75	2.00
247 Robert Smith LL	.60	1.50
248 Eddie George LL	.75	2.00
249 Mike Anderson LL	.60	1.50
250 Corey Dillon LL	.60	1.50
251 Torry Holt LL	.60	1.50
252 Rod Smith LL	.60	1.50
253 Isaac Bruce LL	.75	2.00
254 Terrell Owens LL	.75	2.00
255 Randy Moss LL	.75	2.00
256 La'Roi Glover LL	.50	1.25
257 Trace Armstrong LL	.50	1.25
258 Warren Sapp LL	.60	1.50
259 Hugh Douglas LL	.50	1.25
260 Jason Taylor LL	.75	2.00
261 Mike Anderson SS	.60	1.50
262 Jamal Lewis SS	.75	2.00
263 Sylvester Morris SS	.50	1.25
264 Darrell Jackson SS	.60	1.50
265 Peter Warrick SS	.60	1.50
266 Ron Dayne SS	.60	1.50
267 Shaun Alexander SS	.75	2.00
268 Plaxico Burress SS	.60	1.50
269 Brian Urlacher SS	1.00	2.50
270 Courtney Brown SS	.50	1.25
271 Michael Vick RC	12.00	30.00
272 Drew Brees RC	25.00	50.00
273 Chris Weinke RC	2.50	6.00
274 Quincy Carter RC	2.50	6.00
275 Sage Rosenfels RC	3.00	8.00
276 Josh Heupel RC	3.00	8.00
277 David Rivers RC	2.00	5.00
278 Ben Leard RC	2.00	5.00
279 Marques Tuiasosopo RC	2.50	6.00
280 Mike McMahon RC	2.50	6.00
281 Deuce McAllister RC	3.00	8.00
282 LaMont Jordan RC	3.00	8.00
283 LaDainian Tomlinson RC	10.00	25.00
284 James Jackson RC	2.00	5.00
285 Anthony Thomas RC	3.00	8.00
286 Travis Henry RC	2.50	6.00
287 Travis Minor RC	2.50	6.00
288 Rudi Johnson RC	3.00	8.00
289 Michael Bennett RC	2.50	6.00
290 Kevan Barlow RC	2.50	6.00
291 Reggie White RC	2.00	5.00
292 Moran Norris RC	2.00	5.00
293 Ja'Mar Toombs RC	2.00	5.00
294 Heath Evans RC	2.50	6.00
295 David Terrell RC	2.50	6.00
296 Santana Moss RC	4.00	10.00
297 Rod Gardner RC	2.50	6.00
298 Quincy Morgan RC	2.50	6.00
299 Freddie Mitchell RC	2.00	5.00
300 Boo Williams RC	2.00	5.00
301 Reggie Wayne RC	6.00	15.00
302 Ronney Daniels RC	2.00	5.00
303 Bobby Newcombe RC	2.50	6.00
304 Vinny Sutherland RC	2.00	5.00
305 Cedrick Wilson RC	2.50	6.00
306 Robert Ferguson RC	3.00	8.00
307 Ken-Yon Rambo RC	2.00	5.00
308 Alex Bannister RC	2.00	5.00
309 Koren Robinson RC	2.50	6.00
310 Chad Johnson RC	6.00	15.00
311 Chris Chambers RC	3.00	8.00
312 Javon Green RC	2.00	5.00
313 Snoop Minnis RC	2.00	5.00
314 Scotty Anderson RC	2.00	5.00
315 Todd Heap RC	3.00	8.00
316 Algé Crumpler RC	3.00	8.00
317 Marcellus Rivers RC	2.00	5.00
318 Rashon Burns RC	2.00	5.00
319 Jamal Reynolds RC	2.00	5.00
320 Andre Carter RC	2.50	6.00
321 Justin Smith RC	3.00	8.00
322 Gerard Warren RC	2.50	6.00
323 Tommy Polley RC	2.00	5.00
324 Dan Morgan RC	2.50	6.00
325 Torrance Marshall RC	2.00	5.00
326 Correll Buckhalter RC	3.00	8.00
327 Derrick Gibson RC	2.00	5.00
328 Adam Archuleta RC	2.50	6.00
329 Jamar Fletcher RC	2.00	5.00
330 Nate Clements RC	2.50	6.00

2001 Select Chicago Collection

NOT PRICED DUE TO SCARCITY

2001 Select Final Score

STATED PRINT RUNS VARY ACCORDING
UNPRICED FINAL SCORE PRINT RUN 1-13

2001 Select Behind the Numbers

STATED PRINT RUN 45-403		
BN1 Brett Favre/338	5.00	12.00
BN2 Marshall Faulk/253	1.50	4.00
BN3 Michael Vick/87	5.00	12.00
BN4 Peyton Manning/357	4.00	10.00
BN5 David Terrell/63	1.50	4.00
BN6 Randy Moss/77	2.00	5.00
BN7 Kurt Warner/235	2.50	6.00
BN8 Edgerrin James/387	1.50	4.00
BN9 Drew Brees/309	6.00	15.00
BN10 Daunte Culpepper/297	1.25	3.00
BN11 Jeff Garcia/355	1.25	3.00
BN12 Mike Anderson/297	1.25	3.00
BN13 Jamal Lewis/309	1.50	4.00
BN14 Eddie George/403	1.50	4.00
BN15 Michael Bennett/310	1.25	3.00
BN16 Emmitt Smith/294	4.00	10.00
BN17 Chris Weinke/266	1.25	3.00
BN18 Tim Brown/76	2.00	5.00
BN19 Eric Moulds/94	1.50	4.00
BN20 Marvin Harrison/102	2.00	5.00
BN21 Deuce McAllister/105	2.00	5.00
BN22 Donovan McNabb/330	1.50	4.00
BN23 Fred Taylor/282	1.50	4.00
BN24 Santana Moss/45	2.50	6.00
BN25 Cris Carter/96	2.00	5.00
BN26 Robert Smith/295	1.25	3.00
BN27 LaDainian Tomlinson/369	3.00	8.00
BN28 Isaac Bruce/87	2.00	5.00
BN29 Terrell Owens/97	2.00	5.00
BN30 Torry Holt/82	1.50	4.00
BN31 Ricky Williams/248	1.50	4.00
BN32 Curtis Martin/316	1.50	4.00
BN33 Stephen Davis/332	1.25	3.00
BN34 Corey Dillon/315	1.25	3.00
BN35 Ed McCaffrey/101	1.50	4.00
BN36 Steve McNair/248	1.50	4.00
BN37 Rudi Johnson/324	1.50	4.00
BN38 Antonio Freeman/62	2.00	5.00
BN39 Jerry Rice/75	4.00	10.00
BN40 Aaron Brooks/113	1.50	4.00

2001 Select Complete Players

COMPLETE SET (30)	40.00	100.00
STATED PRINT RUN 550 SER.#'d SETS		
CP1 Edgerrin James	1.25	3.00
CP2 Marshall Faulk	1.25	3.00
CP3 Kurt Warner	2.00	5.00
CP4 Daunte Culpepper	1.00	2.50
CP5 Donovan McNabb	1.25	3.00
CP6 Koren Robinson	1.00	2.50
CP7 Peyton Manning	3.00	8.00
CP8 Eddie George	1.25	3.00
CP9 Fred Taylor	1.25	3.00
CP10 Drew Brees	5.00	12.00
CP11 Randy Moss	1.25	3.00
CP12 Cris Carter	1.25	3.00
CP13 Steve Young	1.50	4.00
CP14 Marvin Harrison	1.25	3.00
CP15 Isaac Bruce	1.25	3.00
CP16 Terrell Owens	1.25	3.00
CP17 Mike Anderson	1.00	2.50
CP18 Jamal Lewis	1.25	3.00
CP19 Curtis Martin	1.25	3.00
CP20 Ricky Williams	1.25	3.00
CP21 Jerry Rice	2.50	6.00
CP22 Steve McNair	1.25	3.00
CP23 Michael Vick	3.00	8.00
CP24 Brett Favre	4.00	10.00
CP25 John Elway	3.00	8.00
CP26 Dan Marino	3.00	8.00
CP27 Barry Sanders	3.00	8.00
CP28 Michael Bennett	1.00	2.50
CP29 David Terrell	1.00	2.50
CP30 Emmitt Smith	3.00	8.00

2001 Select Franchise Tags Autographs

STATED PRINT RUN 50 SER.#'d SETS		
FT1 Daunte Culpepper	20.00	50.00
FT2 Stephen Davis	20.00	50.00
FT3 Kurt Warner	40.00	100.00
FT4 Ricky Williams	25.00	60.00
FT5 Terrell Owens	25.00	60.00
FT6 Ricky Watters	20.00	50.00
FT7 Rich Gannon	20.00	50.00
FT8 Mike Anderson	20.00	50.00
FT9 Tony Gonzalez	25.00	60.00
FT10 Jerome Bettis	100.00	175.00
FT11 Peter Warrick		
FT12 Tim Couch No Auto	10.00	25.00
FT13 Mark Brunell	20.00	50.00
FT14 Edgerrin James	25.00	60.00
FT15 Curtis Martin No Auto	15.00	40.00
FT16 Brett Favre	150.00	300.00
FT17 Donovan McNabb	25.00	60.00
FT18 Drew Bledsoe	25.00	60.00
FT19 Jake Plummer	20.00	50.00
FT20 Eric Moulds	20.00	50.00
FT21 Lamar Smith No Auto	12.00	30.00
FT22 Junior Seau	40.00	80.00
FT23 Wesley Walls	15.00	40.00
FT24 Jamal Anderson	20.00	50.00
FT25 Warren Sapp No Auto	12.00	30.00
FT26 Ron Dayne	20.00	50.00
FT27 Jamal Lewis	25.00	60.00
FT28 Cade McNown	20.00	50.00
FT29 Charlie Batch	15.00	40.00
FT30 Eddie George	25.00	60.00
FT31 Troy Aikman	90.00	150.00

2001 Select Future Franchise

COMPLETE SET (31)	50.00	120.00
STATED PRINT RUN 550 SER.#'d SETS		
FF1 Tim Couch Jarius Jackson	.75	2.00
FF2 Peter Warrick Justin Smith	1.25	3.00
FF3 Jerome Bettis Casey Hampton	1.25	3.00
FF4 Fred Taylor Marcus Stroud	1.25	3.00
FF5 Eddie George Dan Alexander	1.25	3.00
FF6 Jamal Lewis Todd Heap	1.25	3.00
FF7 Peyton Manning Reggie Wayne	3.00	8.00
FF8 Drew Bledsoe Jabari Holloway	1.25	3.00
FF9 Curtis Martin Santana Moss	1.00	2.50
FF10 Eric Moulds Travis Henry	1.00	2.50
FF11 Lamar Smith Chris Chambers	1.25	3.00
FF12 Tony Gonzalez Snoop Minnis	1.25	3.00
FF13 Rich Gannon Marques Tuiasosopo	1.00	2.50
FF14 Ricky Watters Koren Robinson	1.00	2.50
FF15 Junior Seau LaDainian Tomlinson	2.50	6.00
FF16 Brian Griese Kevin Kasper	1.00	2.50
FF17 Terell Owens Kevan Barlow	1.25	3.00
FF18 Ricky Williams Deuce McAllister	1.25	3.00
FF19 Kurt Warner Damoine Lewis	2.00	5.00
FF20 Mushin Muhammad Chris Weinke	1.00	2.50
FF21 Jamal Anderson Michael Vick	3.00	8.00
FF22 Brett Favre Robert Ferguson	4.00	10.00
FF23 Randy Moss Michael Bennett	1.25	3.00
FF24 Marcus Robinson David Terrell	1.00	2.50
FF25 Warrick Dunn Kenyatta Walker	1.25	3.00
FF26 James Stewart Mike McMahon	1.00	2.50
FF27 Jake Plummer Bobby Newcombe	1.00	2.50
FF28 Kerry Collins Jesse Palmer	1.00	2.50
FF29 Emmitt Smith Quincy Carter	3.00	8.00
FF30 Stephen Davis Rod Gardner	1.00	2.50
FF31 Donovan McNabb Freddie Mitchell	1.25	3.00

2001 Select Rookie Preview Autographs

RP1 Michael Vick/150	75.00	150.00
RP2 Drew Brees/150	90.00	150.00
RP3 Chris Weinke/250	5.00	12.00
RP5 Josh Heupel/450	5.00	12.00
RP6 David Terrell/150	5.00	12.00
RP7 Santana Moss/250	8.00	20.00
RP8 Freddie Mitchell/350	3.00	8.00
RP9 Reggie Wayne/250	25.00	50.00
RP10 Rod Gardner/50	6.00	15.00
RP11 Chris Chambers/450	5.00	12.00
RP12 Chad Johnson/450	8.00	20.00
RP13 Ken-Yon Rambo/550	3.00	8.00
RP14 Deuce McAllister/150	6.00	15.00
RP15 LaDainian Tomlinson/250	60.00	120.00
RP16 Travis Henry/450	4.00	10.00
RP17 Anthony Thomas/250	6.00	15.00
RP18 Michael Bennett/250	5.00	12.00
RP19 LaMont Jordan/350	5.00	12.00
RP20 Kevan Barlow/450	4.00	10.00
RP21 Reggie White/550	3.00	8.00
RP22 Sage Rosenfels/50	8.00	20.00
RP24 Mike McMahon/450	4.00	10.00
RP25 Quincy Morgan/450	4.00	10.00
RP28 Alex Bannister/450	3.00	8.00
RP29 Snoop Minnis/450	3.00	8.00
RP30 Cedrick Wilson/450	4.00	10.00
RP34 Correll Buckhalter/550	5.00	12.00
RP36 Jamal Reynolds/350	3.00	8.00
RP37 Richard Seymour/350 No Auto	2.50	6.00
RP42 James Jackson/350	3.00	8.00
RP43 Rudi Johnson/350	5.00	12.00
RP45 Travis Minor/750	4.00	10.00
RP46 Robert Ferguson/350	5.00	12.00
RP49 Justin Smith/350	5.00	12.00
RP50 Gerard Warren/350	4.00	10.00
RP51 Koren Robinson/50	6.00	15.00
RP52 T.J. Houshmandzadeh/450	6.00	15.00
RP53 Todd Heap/750	5.00	12.00
RP55 Alge Crumpler/750	5.00	12.00
RP60 Will Allen/750	5.00	12.00

2001 Select Rookie Roll Call Autographs

STATED PRINT RUN 50 SER.#'d SETS		
RP1 Michael Vick	125.00	200.00
RP2 Drew Brees	125.00	200.00
RP3 Chris Weinke	6.00	15.00
RP5 Josh Heupel	8.00	20.00
RP6 David Terrell	6.00	15.00
RP7 Santana Moss	10.00	25.00
RP8 Freddie Mitchell	5.00	12.00
RP9 Reggie Wayne	40.00	80.00
RP10 Rod Gardner	6.00	15.00
RP11 Chris Chambers	8.00	20.00
RP12 Chad Johnson	12.00	30.00
RP13 Ken-Yon Rambo	5.00	12.00
RP14 Deuce McAllister	8.00	20.00
RP15 LaDainian Tomlinson	100.00	200.00
RP16 Travis Henry	6.00	15.00
RP17 Anthony Thomas	8.00	20.00
RP18 Michael Bennett	6.00	15.00
RP19 LaMont Jordan	8.00	20.00
RP20 Kevan Barlow	6.00	15.00
RP21 Reggie White	5.00	12.00
RP22 Sage Rosenfels	8.00	20.00
RP24 Mike McMahon	6.00	15.00
RP25 Quincy Morgan	6.00	15.00
RP28 Alex Bannister	5.00	12.00
RP29 Snoop Minnis	5.00	12.00
RP30 Cedrick Wilson	6.00	15.00
RP34 Correll Buckhalter	8.00	20.00
RP36 Jamal Reynolds	5.00	12.00
RP37 Richard Seymour No Auto	4.00	10.00
RP42 James Jackson	5.00	12.00
RP43 Rudi Johnson	8.00	20.00
RP45 Travis Minor	6.00	15.00
RP46 Robert Ferguson	8.00	20.00
RP49 Justin Smith	8.00	20.00
RP50 Gerard Warren	6.00	15.00
RP51 Koren Robinson	6.00	15.00
RP52 T.J. Houshmandzadeh	10.00	25.00
RP53 Todd Heap	8.00	20.00
RP55 Alge Crumpler	8.00	20.00
RP60 Will Allen	8.00	20.00

2001 Select Settle the Score

COMPLETE SET (30)	40.00	100.00
STATED PRINT RUN 550 SER.#'d SETS		
SS1 Kurt Warner Steve McNair	2.00	5.00
SS2 Randy Moss Isaac Bruce	1.25	3.00
SS3 Emmitt Smith Stephen Davis	3.00	8.00
SS4 Marshall Faulk Robert Smith	1.25	3.00
SS5 Eddie George Ray Lewis	1.25	3.00
SS6 Fred Taylor Jerome Bettis	1.25	3.00
SS7 Peyton Manning Drew Bledsoe	3.00	8.00
SS8 Daunte Culpepper Aaron Brooks	1.00	2.50
SS9 Marvin Harrison Eric Moulds	1.25	3.00
SS10 Jerry Rice Cris Carter	2.50	6.00
SS11 Curtis Martin Edgerrin James	1.25	3.00
SS12 Donovan McNabb Ron Dayne	1.25	3.00
SS13 Brett Favre Warren Sapp	4.00	10.00
SS14 Tony Gonzalez Shannon Sharpe	1.25	3.00
SS15 Wayne Chrebet Kevin Johnson	1.00	2.50
SS16 Tim Couch Cade McNown	1.00	2.50
SS17 Terell Davis Jamal Anderson	1.25	3.00
SS18 Mike Anderson Jamal Lewis	1.25	3.00
SS19 Terell Owens Antonio Freeman	1.25	3.00
SS20 Brian Griese Rich Gannon	1.00	2.50
SS21 Ricky Watters Charlie Garner	1.00	2.50
SS22 Mushin Muhammad Ricky Williams	1.25	3.00
SS23 Jeff Garcia Elvis Grbac	1.00	2.50
SS24 Rod Smith Jimmy Smith	1.00	2.50
SS25 Brian Urlacher Ahman Green	1.50	4.00
SS26 Darrell Jackson Sylvester Morris	1.00	2.50
SS27 Peter Warrick Travis Taylor	1.00	2.50
SS28 Dan Marino John Elway	3.00	8.00
SS29 Steve Young Mark Brunell	1.50	4.00
SS30 Troy Aikman Jake Plummer	2.00	5.00

2001 Select Zenith Z-Team

STATED PRINT RUN 100 SER.#'d SETS		
ZT1 Michael Vick	8.00	20.00
ZT2 Donovan McNabb	4.00	10.00
ZT3 Daunte Culpepper	3.00	8.00
ZT4 Kurt Warner	6.00	15.00
ZT5 Peyton Manning	10.00	25.00
ZT6 Brett Favre	12.00	30.00
ZT7 Dan Marino	10.00	25.00
ZT8 John Elway	10.00	25.00
ZT9 Steve Young	5.00	12.00
ZT10 Troy Aikman	6.00	15.00
ZT11 Chad Pennington	4.00	10.00
ZT12 Brian Griese	3.00	8.00
ZT13 Drew Brees	12.00	30.00
ZT14 David Terrell	3.00	8.00
ZT15 Eric Moulds	3.00	8.00
ZT16 Marvin Harrison	4.00	10.00
ZT17 Randy Moss	4.00	10.00
ZT18 Reggie Wayne	4.00	10.00
ZT19 Terrell Owens	4.00	10.00
ZT20 Jerry Rice	8.00	20.00
ZT21 Cris Carter	4.00	10.00
ZT22 Isaac Bruce	4.00	10.00
ZT23 Peter Warrick	3.00	8.00
ZT24 Deuce McAllister	4.00	10.00
ZT25 Edgerrin James	4.00	10.00
ZT26 Robert Smith	3.00	8.00
ZT27 Marshall Faulk	4.00	10.00
ZT28 Ricky Williams	4.00	10.00
ZT29 Michael Bennett	3.00	8.00
ZT30 Emmitt Smith	10.00	25.00
ZT31 Eddie George	4.00	10.00
ZT32 Jamal Lewis	4.00	10.00
ZT33 Ron Dayne	3.00	8.00
ZT34 Mike Anderson	3.00	8.00
ZT35 Barry Sanders	10.00	25.00
ZT36 Stephen Davis	3.00	8.00
ZT37 Koren Robinson	3.00	8.00
ZT38 LaDainian Tomlinson	6.00	15.00

2006 Select

This 430-card set was released in July, 2006. The set was issued into hobby outlets in five-card packs which came 20 packs to a box. Cards numbered 1-290 feature players sequenced in team alphabetical order by where they played in 2005. Cards numbered 291-330 featured rookies also in team alphabetical order while cards numbered 331-430 also featured 2006 NFL rookies. Cards numbered 331-430 were issued to a stated print run of 599 serial numbered copies.

COMP.SET w/o RC's (330)	25.00	50.00
331-430 RC PRINT RUN 599 SETS		
UNPRICED BLACK PRINT RUN 6 SETS		
1 Kurt Warner	.30	.75
2 J.J. Arrington	.20	.50
3 Anquan Boldin	.25	.60
4 Larry Fitzgerald	.30	.75
5 Marcel Shipp	.20	.50
6 Bryant Johnson	.20	.50
7 Bertrand Berry	.20	.50
8 John Navarre	.20	.50
9 Michael Vick	.30	.75
10 Warrick Dunn	.25	.60
11 Roddy White	.25	.60
12 Alge Crumpler	.25	.60
13 T.J. Duckett	.20	.50
14 Michael Jenkins	.25	.60
15 DeAngelo Hall	.25	.60
16 Brian Finneran	.20	.50
17 Kyle Boller	.25	.60
18 Jamal Lewis	.25	.60
19 Chester Taylor	.25	.60
20 Derrick Mason	.25	.60
21 Mark Clayton	.25	.60
22 Todd Heap	.25	.60
23 Ray Lewis	.30	.75
24 Devard Darling	.20	.50
25 J.P. Losman	.25	.60
26 Willis McGahee	.25	.60
27 Lee Evans	.25	.60
28 Eric Moulds	.20	.50
29 Lawyer Milloy	.20	.50
30 Josh Reed	.20	.50
31 Kelly Holcomb	.20	.50
32 Jake Delhomme	.25	.60
33 DeShaun Foster	.25	.60
34 Steve Smith	.30	.75
35 Julius Peppers	.25	.60
36 Drew Carter	.20	.50
37 Chris Gamble	.20	.50
38 Stephen Davis	.25	.60
39 Keary Colbert	.20	.50
40 Nick Goings	.20	.50
41 Eric Shelton	.20	.50
42 Rex Grossman	.25	.60
43 Thomas Jones	.25	.60
44 Cedric Benson	.25	.60
45 Muhsin Muhammad	.25	.60
46 Brian Urlacher	.30	.75
47 Mark Bradley	.20	.50
48 Kyle Orton	.30	.75
49 Tommie Harris	.20	.50
50 Adrian Peterson	.25	.60
51 Bernard Berrian	.25	.60
52 Justin Gage	.20	.50
53 Carson Palmer	.30	.75
54 Rudi Johnson	.25	.60
55 Chad Johnson	.25	.60
56 T.J. Houshmandzadeh	.25	.60
57 Chris Henry	.20	.50
58 Chris Perry	.25	.60
59 Jon Kitna	.25	.60
60 Deltha O'Neal	.20	.50
61 Charlie Frye	.25	.60
62 Reuben Droughns	.25	.60
63 Braylon Edwards	.25	.60
64 Kellen Winslow	.25	.60
65 Antonio Bryant	.20	.50
66 Trent Dilfer	.25	.60
67 Dennis Northcutt	.20	.50
68 Drew Bledsoe	.30	.75
69 Julius Jones	.20	.50
70 Marion Barbor	.25	.60
71 Terry Glenn	.25	.60
72 Keyshawn Johnson	.25	.60
73 Roy Williams S	.25	.60
74 Jason Witten	.30	.75
75 Terence Newman	.20	.50
76 Drew Henson	.20	.50
77 Patrick Crayton	.20	.50
78 Jake Plummer	.25	.60
79 Mike Anderson	.25	.60
80 Tatum Bell	.20	.50
81 Ashley Lelie	.20	.50
82 Rod Smith	.25	.60
83 D.J. Williams	.20	.50
84 Darius Watts	.20	.50

85 Ron Dayne	.25	.60
86 Jeb Putzier	.20	.50
87 Joey Harrington	.20	.50
88 Kevin Jones	.20	.50
89 Roy Williams WR	.25	.60
90 Mike Williams	.20	.50
91 Charles Rogers	.25	.60
92 Teddy Lehman	.20	.50
93 Marcus Pollard	.20	.50
94 Artose Pinner	.20	.50
95 Brett Favre	.60	1.50
96 Ahman Green	.25	.60
97 Najeh Davenport	.25	.60
98 Samkon Gado	.25	.60
99 Javon Walker	.25	.60
100 Donald Driver	.30	.75
101 Aaron Rodgers	.60	1.50
102 Robert Ferguson	.20	.50
103 David Carr	.20	.50
104 Domanick Davis	.20	.50
105 Andre Johnson	.30	.75
106 Jabar Gaffney	.20	.50
107 Jonathan Wells	.20	.50
108 Vernand Morency	.20	.50
109 Corey Bradford	.20	.50
110 Jerome Mathis	.20	.50
111 Peyton Manning	.50	1.25
112 Edgerrin James	.25	.60
113 Marvin Harrison	.30	.75
114 Reggie Wayne	.25	.60
115 Dwight Freeney	.25	.60
116 Dallas Clark	.25	.60
117 Dominic Rhodes	.25	.60
118 Jim Sorgi	.20	.50
119 Brandon Stokley	.25	.60
120 Bob Sanders	.25	.60
121 Mike Doss	.20	.50
122 Marlin Jackson	.20	.50
123 Byron Leftwich	.25	.60
124 Fred Taylor	.25	.60
125 Jimmy Smith	.25	.60
126 Matt Jones	.20	.50
127 Ernest Wilford	.20	.50
128 Greg Jones	.20	.50
129 Mike Peterson	.20	.50
130 Reggie Williams	.25	.60
131 Rashean Mathis	.20	.50
132 Trent Green	.25	.60
133 Larry Johnson	.25	.60
134 Priest Holmes	.25	.60
135 Eddie Kennison	.20	.50
136 Tony Gonzalez	.25	.60
137 Kendrell Bell	.20	.50
138 Samie Parker	.20	.50
139 Dante Hall	.25	.60
140 Tony Richardson	.20	.50
141 Gus Frerotte	.20	.50
142 Ronnie Brown	.30	.75
143 Neil Rackers	.20	.50
144 Chris Chambers	.25	.60
145 Zach Thomas	.30	.75
146 Cliff Russell	.20	.50
147 David Boston	.20	.50
148 Wes Welker	.30	.75
149 Marty Booker	.20	.50
150 Randy McMichael	.20	.50
151 Daunte Culpepper	.25	.60
152 Mewelde Moore	.20	.50
153 Nate Burleson	.20	.50
154 Troy Williamson	.20	.50
155 Koren Robinson	.20	.50
156 Erasmus James	.20	.50
157 Marcus Robinson	.20	.50
158 E.J. Henderson	.20	.50
159 Brad Johnson	.25	.60
160 Michael Bennett	.20	.50
161 Travis Taylor	.20	.50
162 Tom Brady	.50	1.25
163 Corey Dillon	.25	.60
164 Deion Branch	.25	.60
165 Tedy Bruschi	.30	.75
166 Ben Watson	.20	.50
167 Daniel Graham	.20	.50
168 Bethel Johnson	.20	.50
169 Kevin Faulk	.25	.60
170 David Givens	.25	.60
171 Troy Brown	.20	.50
172 Aaron Brooks	.25	.60
173 Deuce McAllister	.25	.60
174 Joe Horn	.25	.60
175 Donte Stallworth	.20	.50
176 Antowain Smith	.20	.50
177 Devery Henderson	.20	.50
178 Eli Manning	.40	1.00
179 Tiki Barber	.30	.75
180 Plaxico Burress	.25	.60
181 Jeremy Shockey	.30	.75
182 Osi Umenyiora	.25	.60
183 Gibril Wilson	.20	.50
184 Brandon Jacobs	.30	.75
185 Michael Strahan	.25	.60
186 Will Allen	.20	.50
187 Amani Toomer	.25	.60
188 Chad Pennington	.25	.60
189 Curtis Martin	.30	.75
190 Laveranues Coles	.20	.50
191 Jonathan Vilma	.25	.60
192 Ty Law	.20	.50
193 Cedric Houston	.20	.50
194 Justin McCareins	.20	.50
195 Jerald Sowell	.20	.50
196 Josh Brown	.20	.50
197 LaMont Jordan	.25	.60
198 Randy Moss	.30	.75
199 Jerry Porter	.20	.50
200 Doug Gabriel	.20	.50
201 Johnnie Morant	.20	.50
202 Zack Crockett	.20	.50
203 Derrick Burgess	.20	.50
204 Donovan McNabb	.30	.75
205 Brian Westbrook	.25	.60
206 Reggie Brown	.20	.50
207 Terrell Owens	.30	.75
208 Ryan Moats	.20	.50
209 Correll Buckhalter	.20	.50
210 Jevon Kearse	.25	.60
211 L.J. Smith	.20	.50
212 Lamar Gordon	.20	.50
213 Greg Lewis	.20	.50
214 Ben Roethlisberger	.40	1.00
215 Willie Parker	.25	.60
216 Jerome Bettis	.30	.75
217 Hines Ward	.30	.75
218 Troy Polamalu	.40	1.00
219 Heath Miller	.25	.60
220 Antwaan Randle El	.25	.60
221 Duce Staley	.20	.50
222 Cedrick Wilson	.20	.50
223 James Farrior	.20	.50
224 Drew Brees	.30	.75
225 LaDainian Tomlinson	.30	.75
226 Keenan McCardell	.25	.60
227 Antonio Gates	.30	.75
228 Shawne Merriman	.25	.60
229 Philip Rivers	.30	.75
230 Vincent Jackson	.25	.60
231 Donnie Edwards	.20	.50
232 Eric Parker	.20	.50
233 Reche Caldwell	.20	.50
234 Alex Smith QB	.30	.75
235 Frank Gore	.30	.75
236 Brandon Lloyd	.20	.50
237 Kevan Barlow	.20	.50
238 Rashaun Woods	.20	.50
239 Arnaz Battle	.20	.50
240 Matt Hasselbeck	.25	.60
241 Shaun Alexander	.25	.60
242 Darrell Jackson	.25	.60
243 Jerramy Stevens	.25	.60
244 Lofa Tatupu	.25	.60
245 D.J. Hackett	.20	.50
246 Bobby Engram	.20	.50
247 Joe Jurevicius	.20	.50
248 Maurice Morris	.20	.50
249 Marc Bulger	.25	.60
250 Steven Jackson	.30	.75
251 Torry Holt	.25	.60
252 Isaac Bruce	.25	.60
253 Kevin Curtis	.25	.60
254 Marshall Faulk	.25	.60
255 Shaun McDonald	.20	.50
256 Chris Simms	.25	.60
257 Cadillac Williams	.25	.60
258 Joey Galloway	.25	.60
259 Michael Clayton	.20	.50
260 Derrick Brooks	.25	.60
261 Ronde Barber	.25	.60
262 Michael Pittman	.20	.50
263 Alex Smith TE	.20	.50
264 Simeon Rice	.20	.50
265 Steve McNair	.25	.60
266 Chris Brown	.20	.50
267 Drew Bennett	.25	.60
268 Brandon Jones	.20	.50
269 Adam Jones	.20	.50
270 Keith Bulluck	.20	.50
271 Ben Troupe	.20	.50
272 Jarrett Payton	.20	.50
273 Tyrone Calico	.20	.50
274 Bobby Wade	.20	.50
275 Troy Fleming	.20	.50
276 Mark Brunell	.25	.60
277 Clinton Portis	.30	.75
278 Santana Moss	.25	.60
279 Jason Campbell	.25	.60
280 Chris Cooley	.25	.60
281 Carlos Rogers	.20	.50
282 Ladell Betts	.20	.50
283 Patrick Ramsey	.25	.60
284 Taylor Jacobs	.20	.50
285 James Thrash	.20	.50
286 Adrian Wilson	.20	.50
287 London Fletcher	.20	.50
288 Lance Briggs	.25	.60
289 Robert Mathis	.20	.50
290 Rod Coleman	.20	.50
291 Bart Scott RC	1.00	2.50
292 Brian Moorman RC	.30	.75
293 Shayne Graham RC	.30	.75
294 Kevin Kaesviharn RC	.30	.75
295 Leigh Bodden RC	.40	1.00
296 Lousaka Polite RC	.30	.75
297 Todd Devoe RC	.30	.75
298 Scottie Vines	.30	.75
299 Cullen Jenkins RC	.40	1.00
300 Donovan Morgan RC	.30	.75
301 C.C. Brown	.30	.75
302 Demarcus Faggins RC	.30	.75
303 Shantee Orr RC	.30	.75
304 Vashon Pearson RC	.30	.75
305 Reggie Hayward RC	.30	.75
306 Paul Spicer RC	.30	.75
307 Kenny Wright RC	.30	.75
308 Rich Alexis RC	.30	.75
309 Terrence Melton RC	.30	.75
310 Willie Whitehead RC	.30	.75
311 Kendrick Clancy RC	.30	.75
312 Mark Brown RC	.30	.75
313 Tommy Kelly	.30	.75
314 Josh Parry RC	.30	.75
315 Malcom Floyd RC	.60	1.50
316 Mike Adams RC	.30	.75
317 Ben Emanuel RC	.30	.75
318 Brandon Moore RC	.30	.75
319 Chartric Darby RC	.30	.75
320 Bryce Fisher RC	.30	.75
321 D.D. Lewis RC	.30	.75
322 Jimmy Williams DB RC	.30	.75
323 Robert Pollard RC	.30	.75
324 Chris Johnson RC	.50	1.25
325 Edell Shepherd RC	.30	.75
326 O.J. Small RC	.30	.75
327 Brad Kassell RC	.30	.75
328 Matt Leinart Reggie Bush	1.00	2.50
329 Matt Leinart Vince Young	.60	1.50
330 LenDale White Matt Leinart Reggie Bush	1.00	2.50
331 Matt Leinart RC	2.50	6.00
332 Chad Greenway RC	2.50	6.00
333 Devin Aromashodu RC	2.50	6.00
334 DeAngelo Williams RC	3.00	8.00
335 Travis Wilson RC	1.50	4.00
336 Leon Washington RC	2.00	5.00
337 Maurice Stovall RC	1.50	4.00
338 Michael Huff RC	2.00	5.00
339 Charlie Whitehurst RC	2.50	6.00
340 Vince Young RC	3.00	8.00
341 Jerious Norwood RC	2.00	5.00
342 D'Brickashaw Ferguson RC	2.50	6.00
343 Taurean Henderson RC	2.50	6.00
344 Dominique Byrd RC	2.00	5.00
345 Sinorice Moss RC	2.50	6.00
346 Martin Nance RC	2.00	5.00
347 Vernon Davis RC	3.00	8.00
348 Ko Simpson RC	2.00	5.00
349 Jerome Harrison RC	2.50	6.00
350 Jay Cutler RC	5.00	12.00
351 Alan Zemaitis RC	2.50	6.00
352 Haloti Ngata RC	2.50	6.00
353 Greg Lee RC	1.50	4.00
354 Laurence Maroney RC	2.00	5.00
355 Bobby Carpenter RC	1.50	4.00
356 Jonathan Orr RC	2.00	5.00
357 Marcedes Lewis RC	2.50	6.00
358 Brodrick Bunkley RC	2.00	5.00
359 Todd Watkins RC	1.50	4.00
360 Reggie Bush RC	5.00	12.00
361 Jimmy Williams RC	2.50	6.00
362 Maurice Drew RC	4.00	10.00
363 Mario Williams RC	2.50	6.00
364 Derek Hagan RC	2.00	5.00
365 Santonio Holmes RC	3.00	8.00
366 Tye Hill RC	1.50	4.00
367 Jason Avant RC	1.50	4.00
368 Tamba Hali RC	2.50	6.00
369 Joe Klopfenstein RC	1.50	4.00
370 LenDale White RC	2.00	5.00
371 DeMeco Ryans RC	2.50	6.00
372 Bruce Gradkowski RC	2.50	6.00
373 A.J. Hawk RC	2.50	6.00
374 Gabe Watson RC	1.50	4.00
375 Devin Hester RC	4.00	10.00
376 Demetrius Williams RC	2.00	5.00
377 Joseph Addai RC	2.50	6.00
378 Leonard Pope RC	2.50	6.00
379 Omar Jacobs RC	1.50	4.00
380 Brad Smith RC	2.50	6.00
381 Michael Robinson RC	2.00	5.00
382 Brodie Croyle RC	2.50	6.00
383 Anthony Fasano RC	2.50	6.00
384 Brian Calhoun RC	1.50	4.00
385 Chad Jackson RC	1.50	4.00
386 Drew Olson RC	1.50	4.00
387 Greg Jennings RC	4.00	10.00
388 Andre Hall RC	2.00	5.00
389 Ryan Gilbert RC	2.00	5.00
390 Tim Day RC	2.00	5.00
391 Brandon Williams RC	1.50	4.00
392 Mark Anderson RC	6.00	15.00
393 DonTrell Moore RC	2.00	5.00
394 Kellen Clemens RC	2.00	5.00
395 Ernie Sims RC	2.00	5.00
396 Cedric Humes RC	1.50	4.00
397 Brandon Kirsch RC	2.00	5.00
398 Tony Scheffler RC	2.50	6.00
399 Kelly Jennings RC	2.00	5.00
400 Manny Lawson RC	2.00	5.00
401 Terrence Whitehead RC	2.00	5.00
402 Marcus Vick RC	1.50	4.00
403 De'Arrius Howard RC	2.50	6.00
404 Wendell Mathis RC	2.00	5.00
405 Abdul Hodge RC	1.50	4.00
406 Owen Daniels RC	2.50	6.00
407 Mike Hass RC	2.00	5.00
408 Brett Elliott RC	2.50	6.00
409 Kamerion Wimbley RC	2.50	6.00
410 Jeremy Bloom RC	2.00	5.00
411 D.J. Shockley RC	2.00	5.00
412 Darnell Bing RC	2.00	5.00
413 Miles Austin RC	6.00	15.00
414 D'Qwell Jackson RC	2.00	5.00
415 Tarvaris Jackson RC	2.50	6.00
416 Mathias Kiwanuka RC	2.50	6.00
417 Mike Bell RC	2.50	6.00
418 Paul Pinegar RC	1.50	4.00
419 David Thomas RC	2.00	5.00
420 Hank Baskett RC	2.50	6.00
421 P.J. Daniels RC	1.50	4.00
422 Jon Alston RC	1.50	4.00
423 Reggie McNeal RC	2.00	5.00
424 Brandon Marshall RC	2.50	6.00
425 Gerald Riggs RC	2.00	5.00
426 Delanie Walker RC	2.50	6.00
427 Erik Meyer RC	2.00	5.00
428 Jeff Webb RC	2.00	5.00
429 Skyler Green RC	1.50	4.00
430 Thomas Howard RC	2.00	5.00

2006 Select Artist's Proof

*VETS 1-290: 10X TO 25X BASIC CARDS
*VETS 291-327: 6X TO 15X BASIC CARDS
*ROOKIES 328-330: 2X TO 5X BASIC CARDS
*ROOKIES 331-385: .8X TO 2X BASIC CARDS
STATED PRINT RUN 32 SER.#'d SETS

2006 Select Gold

*VETS 1-290: 6X TO 15X BASIC CARDS
*VETS 291-327: 4X TO 10X BASIC CARDS
*ROOKIES 328-330: 1.2X TO 3X BASIC CARDS
*ROOKIES 331-385: .6X TO 1.5X
GOLD PRINT RUN 50 SER.#'d SETS

2006 Select Red

*VETS 1-290: 10X TO 25X BASIC CARDS
*VETS 291-327: 6X TO 15X BASIC CARDS
*ROOKIES 328-330: 2X TO 5X BASIC CARDS
*ROOKIES 331-385: 1X TO 2.5X BASIC CARDS
RED PRINT RUN 25 SER.#'d SETS

360 Reggie Bush	12.00	30.00

2006 Select Scorecard

*VETS 1-290: 4X TO 10X BASIC CARDS
*VETS 291-327: 2.5X TO 6X BASIC CARDS
*ROOKIES 328-330: 1X TO 2.5X BASIC CARDS
*ROOKIES 331-385: .5X TO 1.2X
SCORECARD PRINT RUN 100 SER.#'d SETS

2006 Select Autographs Red

SERIAL #'d UNDER 25 NOT PRICED
UNPRICED BLACK SER.#'d TO 6

332 Chad Greenway/25	12.00	30.00
335 Travis Wilson/25	12.00	30.00
336 Leon Washington/25	25.00	60.00
341 Jerious Norwood/25	25.00	60.00
352 Haloti Ngata/25	12.00	30.00
355 Bobby Carpenter/25	12.00	30.00
367 Jason Avant/25	12.00	30.00
368 Tamba Hali/25	15.00	40.00
381 Michael Robinson/25	12.00	30.00
387 Greg Jennings/25	35.00	60.00
394 Kellen Clemens/25	25.00	60.00
399 Kelly Jennings/25	12.00	30.00
400 Manny Lawson/25	12.00	30.00
415 Tarvaris Jackson/25	12.00	30.00
416 Mathias Kiwanuka/25	20.00	50.00
424 Brandon Marshall/25	20.00	40.00

2006 Select Hot Rookies

STATED PRINT RUN 749 SER.#'d SETS
*ART.PROOF: 1X TO 2.5X BASIC INSERTS
ART.PROOF PRINT RUN 32 SER.#'d SETS
UNPRICED BLACK PRINT RUN 6 SETS
*GOLD: .8X TO 2X BASIC INSERTS
GOLD PRINT RUN 75 SER.#'d SETS
*RED: 1.2X TO 3X BASIC INSERTS
RED PRINT RUN 25 SER.#'d SETS
*SCORECARD: .6X TO 1.5X BASIC INSERTS
SCORECARD PRINT RUN 125 SER.#'d SETS

1 Matt Leinart	1.25	3.00
2 Vince Young	1.50	4.00
3 Jay Cutler	2.50	6.00
4 Reggie Bush	2.50	6.00
5 LenDale White	1.00	2.50
6 DeAngelo Williams	1.50	4.00
7 Laurence Maroney	1.00	2.50
8 Santonio Holmes	1.50	4.00
9 Sinorice Moss	1.25	3.00
10 Maurice Stovall	.75	2.00
11 Brodie Croyle	1.25	3.00
12 Charlie Whitehurst	1.25	3.00
13 Reggie McNeal	1.00	2.50
14 Joseph Addai	1.25	3.00
15 Brian Calhoun	.75	2.00
16 Maurice Drew	2.00	5.00
17 Vernon Davis	1.50	4.00
18 Chad Jackson	.75	2.00
19 Demetrius Williams	1.00	2.50
20 Brandon Marshall	1.25	3.00

2006 Select Hot Rookies Inscriptions

STATED PRINT RUN 25 SER.#'d SETS

1 Matt Leinart	20.00	50.00
2 Vince Young	25.00	60.00
3 Jay Cutler	40.00	100.00
4 Reggie Bush	40.00	100.00
5 LenDale White	15.00	40.00
6 DeAngelo Williams	25.00	60.00
7 Laurence Maroney	15.00	40.00
8 Santonio Holmes	25.00	60.00
9 Sinorice Moss		
10 Maurice Stovall	12.00	30.00
11 Brodie Croyle	20.00	50.00
12 Charlie Whitehurst	20.00	50.00
13 Reggie McNeal	15.00	40.00
14 Joseph Addai	20.00	50.00
15 Brian Calhoun	12.00	30.00
16 Maurice Drew	30.00	80.00
17 Vernon Davis	40.00	80.00
18 Chad Jackson	12.00	30.00
19 Demetrius Williams	15.00	40.00
20 Brandon Marshall	20.00	50.00

2006 Select Inscriptions

VETERAN STATED PRINT RUN 5-50
SERIAL #'d UNDER 25 NOT PRICED

32 Jake Delhomme/50	8.00	20.00
56 T.J. Houshmandzadeh/25	8.00	20.00
80 Tatum Bell/25	10.00	25.00
88 Kevin Jones/25	15.00	40.00
98 Samkon Gado/100	10.00	25.00
104 Domanick Davis/50	8.00	20.00
114 Reggie Wayne/50	8.00	20.00
116 Dallas Clark/25	10.00	25.00
123 Byron Leftwich/50	8.00	20.00
125 Jimmy Smith/25	10.00	25.00
188 Chad Pennington/30	12.00	30.00
190 Laveranues Coles/35	8.00	20.00
218 Troy Polamalu/37	100.00	200.00
227 Antonio Gates/34	12.00	30.00
253 Kevin Curtis/59	8.00	20.00
266 Chris Brown/50	6.00	15.00
331 Matt Leinart/100	10.00	25.00
332 Chad Greenway/250	8.00	20.00
333 Devin Aromashodu/250	8.00	20.00
334 DeAngelo Williams/100	12.00	30.00
335 Travis Wilson/100	6.00	15.00
336 Leon Washington/50	8.00	20.00
337 Maurice Stovall/100	6.00	15.00
338 Michael Huff/50	8.00	20.00
339 Charlie Whitehurst/50	10.00	25.00
340 Vince Young/100	12.00	30.00
341 Jerious Norwood/100	8.00	20.00
342 D'Brickashaw Ferguson/250	8.00	20.00
343 Taurean Henderson/250	8.00	20.00
344 Dominique Byrd/100	8.00	20.00
345 Sinorice Moss/100	10.00	25.00
346 Martin Nance/250	6.00	15.00
347 Vernon Davis/100	12.00	30.00
348 Ko Simpson/250	6.00	15.00
349 Jerome Harrison/200	8.00	20.00
350 Jay Cutler/100	30.00	80.00
351 Alan Zemaitis/100	10.00	25.00
352 Haloti Ngata/150	8.00	20.00
353 Greg Lee/250	5.00	12.00
354 Laurence Maroney/100	8.00	20.00
355 Bobby Carpenter/100	6.00	15.00
356 Jonathan Orr/250	6.00	15.00
357 Marcedes Lewis/250	8.00	20.00
358 Brodrick Bunkley/50	8.00	20.00
359 Todd Watkins/250	5.00	12.00
360 Reggie Bush/100		80.00
361 Jimmy Williams/250	8.00	20.00
362 Maurice Drew/100	15.00	40.00
363 Mario Williams/50	10.00	25.00
364 Derek Hagan/100	8.00	20.00
365 Santonio Holmes/100	12.00	30.00
366 Tye Hill/50	6.00	15.00
367 Jason Avant/125	6.00	15.00
368 Tamba Hali/250	8.00	20.00
369 Joe Klopfenstein/50	6.00	15.00
370 LenDale White/100	8.00	20.00
371 DeMeco Ryans/250	8.00	20.00
372 Bruce Gradkowski/100	10.00	25.00
373 A.J. Hawk/50	15.00	40.00
374 Gabe Watson/200	5.00	12.00
375 Devin Hester/50	25.00	50.00
376 Demetrius Williams/50	8.00	20.00
377 Joseph Addai/100	10.00	25.00
378 Leonard Pope/100	10.00	25.00
379 Omar Jacobs/125	6.00	15.00
380 Brad Smith/250	8.00	20.00
381 Michael Robinson/50	8.00	20.00
382 Brodie Croyle/100	10.00	25.00
383 Anthony Fasano/50	10.00	25.00
384 Brian Calhoun/100	6.00	15.00
385 Chad Jackson/100	6.00	15.00
386 Drew Olson/250	5.00	12.00
387 Greg Jennings/100	20.00	50.00
388 Andre Hall/250	6.00	15.00
391 Brandon Williams/50	6.00	15.00
394 Kellen Clemens/50	8.00	20.00
396 Cedric Humes/250	5.00	12.00
397 Brandon Kirsch/250	6.00	15.00
398 Tony Scheffler/250	8.00	20.00
399 Kelly Jennings/100	8.00	20.00
400 Manny Lawson/50	8.00	20.00
403 De'Arrius Howard/250	8.00	20.00
404 Wendell Mathis/250	6.00	15.00
405 Abdul Hodge/250	5.00	12.00
407 Mike Hass/250	6.00	15.00
409 Kamerion Wimbley/100	10.00	25.00
410 Jeremy Bloom/25	10.00	25.00
411 D.J. Shockley/100	8.00	20.00
412 Darnell Bing/100	8.00	20.00
413 Miles Austin/250	30.00	80.00
414 D'Qwell Jackson/100	8.00	20.00
415 Tarvaris Jackson/100	10.00	25.00
416 Mathias Kiwanuka/100	10.00	25.00
417 Mike Bell/250	8.00	20.00
418 Paul Pinegar/250	5.00	12.00
419 David Thomas/100	8.00	20.00
420 Hank Baskett/250	8.00	20.00
421 P.J. Daniels/250	5.00	12.00
422 Jon Alston/250	5.00	12.00
423 Reggie McNeal/250	6.00	15.00
424 Brandon Marshall/100	10.00	25.00
425 Gerald Riggs/250	6.00	15.00
426 Delanie Walker/250	8.00	20.00
427 Erik Meyer/250	6.00	15.00
428 Jeff Webb/250	6.00	15.00
429 Skyler Green/250	5.00	12.00
430 Thomas Howard/25	12.00	30.00

2006 Select Hot Rookies National Anaheim Embossed Promos

COMPLETE SET (10)	30.00	60.00
11 Brodie Croyle	1.50	4.00
12 Charlie Whitehurst	1.50	4.00
13 Reggie McNeal	1.25	3.00
14 Joseph Addai	1.50	4.00
15 Brian Calhoun	1.00	2.50
16 Maurice Drew	2.50	6.00
17 Vernon Davis	2.00	5.00
18 Chad Jackson	1.00	2.50
19 DeMetrius Williams	1.25	3.00
20 Brandon Marshall	1.50	4.00

2006 Select National Anaheim Blue Promos

COMPLETE SET (12)	30.00	60.00
*GOLD/100: .8X TO 2X BLUE		
1 Mario Williams	1.00	2.50
2 Reggie Bush	2.00	5.00
3 Vince Young	1.25	3.00
4 A.J. Hawk	1.00	2.50
5 Vernon Davis	1.25	3.00
6 Matt Leinart	1.00	2.50
7 Jay Cutler	2.00	5.00
8 Laurence Maroney	.75	2.00
9 Santonio Holmes	1.25	3.00
10 Chad Jackson	.60	1.50
11 LenDale White	.75	2.00
12 DeAngelo Williams	1.25	3.00

2007 Select

This 430-card set was released in July, 2007. The set was issued into the hobby in five-card packs, with a $4 SRP, which came 20 packs to a box. Cards numbered 1-288 feature veterans in team alphabetical order by division while cards numbered 289-430 feature 2007 NFL rookies. The rookie cards are broken up into two groups: Cards numbered 289-330 and cards numbered 331-430 which were issued to a stated print run of 599 serial numbered sets.

COMP.SET w/o RC's (288)	25.00	50.00
331-430 RC PRINT RUN 599 SER.#'d SETS		
1 Tony Romo	.40	1.00
2 Julius Jones	.20	.50
3 Terry Glenn	.25	.60
4 Terrell Owens	.30	.75
5 Jason Witten	.30	.75
6 Marion Barber	.30	.75
7 Patrick Crayton	.20	.50
8 Bradie James	.20	.50
9 DeMarcus Ware	.25	.60
10 Roy Williams S	.25	.60
11 Eli Manning	.30	.75
12 Plaxico Burress	.25	.60
13 Jeremy Shockey	.25	.60
14 Brandon Jacobs	.25	.60
15 Sinorice Moss	.25	.60
16 Antonio Pierce	.20	.50
17 David Tyree	.20	.50
18 Donovan McNabb	.30	.75
19 Brian Westbrook	.25	.60
20 Reggie Brown	.20	.50
21 L.J. Smith	.20	.50
22 Hank Baskett	.25	.60
23 Jeremiah Trotter	.20	.50
24 Trent Cole	.20	.50
25 Lito Sheppard	.20	.50
26 Jason Campbell	.25	.60
27 Clinton Portis	.25	.60
28 Santana Moss	.25	.60
29 Brandon Lloyd	.25	.60
30 Chris Cooley	.25	.60
31 Sean Taylor	.30	.75
32 Lemar Marshall	.20	.50
33 Ladell Betts	.20	.50
34 London Fletcher	.20	.50
35 Rex Grossman	.25	.60
36 Cedric Benson	.25	.60
37 Muhsin Muhammad	.25	.60
38 Bernard Berrian	.20	.50
39 Desmond Clark	.20	.50
40 Lance Briggs	.20	.50
41 Robbie Gould	.20	.50
42 Devin Hester	.30	.75
43 Mark Anderson	.25	.60
44 Brian Urlacher	.30	.75
45 Jon Kitna	.20	.50
46 Kevin Jones	.20	.50
47 Roy Williams WR	.25	.60
48 Mike Furrey	.25	.60
49 Cory Redding	.20	.50
50 Ernie Sims	.20	.50
51 Tatum Bell	.20	.50
52 Brian Calhoun	.20	.50
53 Brett Favre	.60	1.50
54 Vernand Morency	.25	.60
55 Donald Driver	.30	.75
56 Greg Jennings	.30	.75
57 Aaron Kampman	.25	.60
58 Charles Woodson	.30	.75
59 A.J. Hawk	.25	.60
60 Nick Barnett	.20	.50
61 Aaron Rodgers	.75	2.00
62 Tarvaris Jackson	.20	.50
63 Chester Taylor	.20	.50
64 Troy Williamson	.20	.50
65 Jim Kleinsasser	.20	.50
66 Dwight Smith	.20	.50
67 Antoine Winfield	.20	.50
68 E.J. Henderson	.20	.50
69 Mewelde Moore	.20	.50
70 Michael Vick	.30	.75
71 Warrick Dunn	.25	.60
72 Joe Horn	.25	.60
73 Michael Jenkins	.25	.60
74 Alge Crumpler	.25	.60
75 DeAngelo Hall	.25	.60
76 Keith Brooking	.20	.50
77 Lawyer Milloy	.20	.50
78 Jerious Norwood	.25	.60
79 Matt Schaub	.25	.60
80 Jake Delhomme	.25	.60
81 DeShaun Foster	.25	.60
82 Steve Smith	.25	.60
83 Keyshawn Johnson	.25	.60
84 Julius Peppers	.25	.60
85 DeAngelo Williams	.30	.75
86 Chris Draft	.20	.50
87 Drew Brees	.30	.75
88 Deuce McAllister	.25	.60
89 Scott Fujita	.20	.50
90 Marques Colston	.30	.75
91 Terrance Copper	.25	.60
92 Will Smith	.20	.50
93 Charles Grant	.20	.50
94 Devery Henderson	.20	.50
95 Reggie Bush	.30	.75
96 Jeff Garcia	.25	.60
97 Cadillac Williams	.25	.60
98 Joey Galloway	.25	.60
99 Michael Clayton	.20	.50
100 Alex Smith TE	.20	.50
101 Ronde Barber	.25	.60
102 Jermaine Phillips	.20	.50
103 Derrick Brooks	.25	.60
104 Matt Leinart	.25	.60
105 Edgerrin James	.25	.60
106 Anquan Boldin	.25	.60
107 Larry Fitzgerald	.30	.75
108 Neil Rackers	.20	.50
109 Adrian Wilson	.20	.50
110 Karlos Dansby	.20	.50
111 Chike Okeafor	.20	.50
112 Marc Bulger	.25	.60
113 Steven Jackson	.30	.75
114 Torry Holt	.25	.60
115 Isaac Bruce	.25	.60
116 Joe Klopfenstein	.20	.50
117 Randy McMichael	.20	.50
118 Will Witherspoon	.20	.50
119 Drew Bennett	.20	.50
120 Alex Smith QB	.30	.75
121 Frank Gore	.30	.75
122 Arnaz Battle	.20	.50
123 Ashley Lelie	.25	.60
124 Vernon Davis	.25	.60
125 Walt Harris	.20	.50
126 Brandon Moore	.20	.50
127 Nate Clements	.20	.50
128 Matt Hasselbeck	.25	.60
129 Shaun Alexander	.25	.60
130 Deion Branch	.25	.60
131 Darrell Jackson	.20	.50
132 Nate Burleson	.20	.50
133 Julian Peterson	.20	.50
134 Lofa Tatupu	.25	.60
135 Mack Strong	.20	.50
136 Josh Brown	.20	.50
137 J.P. Losman	.20	.50
138 Anthony Thomas	.20	.50
139 Lee Evans	.25	.60
140 Josh Reed	.20	.50
141 Roscoe Parrish	.20	.50
142 Aaron Schobel	.20	.50
143 Donte Whitner	.20	.50
144 Shaud Williams	.20	.50
145 Daunte Culpepper	.25	.60
146 Ronnie Brown	.25	.60
147 Chris Chambers	.25	.60
148 Marty Booker	.20	.50
149 Derek Hagan	.20	.50
150 Jason Taylor	.25	.60
151 Vonnie Holliday	.20	.50
152 Zach Thomas	.25	.60
153 Channing Crowder	.20	.50
154 Joey Porter	.20	.50
155 Tom Brady	.50	1.25
156 Laurence Maroney	.25	.60
157 Chad Jackson	.20	.50
158 Wes Welker	.30	.75
159 Ben Watson	.20	.50
160 Donte Stallworth	.25	.60
161 Rosevelt Colvin	.20	.50
162 Ty Warren	.20	.50
163 Asante Samuel	.20	.50
164 Adalius Thomas	.20	.50
165 Tedy Bruschi	.30	.75
166 Chad Pennington	.25	.60
167 Thomas Jones	.25	.60
168 Laveranues Coles	.20	.50
169 Jerricho Cotchery	.25	.60
170 Chris Baker	.20	.50
171 Bryan Thomas	.20	.50
172 Leon Washington	.25	.60
173 Jonathan Vilma	.25	.60
174 Eric Barton	.20	.50
175 Erik Coleman	.20	.50
176 Steve McNair	.25	.60
177 Willis McGahee	.25	.60
178 Derrick Mason	.25	.60
179 Demetrius Williams	.20	.50
180 Todd Heap	.20	.50
181 Ray Lewis	.30	.75
182 Trevor Pryce	.20	.50
183 Bart Scott	.25	.60
184 Terrell Suggs	.25	.60
185 Mark Clayton	.25	.60
186 Carson Palmer	.25	.60
187 Rudi Johnson	.25	.60
188 Chad Johnson	.25	.60
189 T.J. Houshmandzadeh	.25	.60
190 Robert Geathers	.20	.50
191 Justin Smith	.20	.50
192 Tory James	.20	.50
193 Landon Johnson	.20	.50
194 Shayne Graham	.20	.50
195 Charlie Frye	.25	.60
196 Reuben Droughns	.25	.60
197 Braylon Edwards	.25	.60
198 Travis Wilson	.20	.50
199 Kellen Winslow	.25	.60
200 Kamerion Wimbley	.20	.50
201 Sean Jones	.20	.50
202 Andra Davis	.20	.50
203 Jamal Lewis	.25	.60
204 Ben Roethlisberger	.30	.75
205 Willie Parker	.25	.60
206 Hines Ward	.30	.75
207 Santonio Holmes	.25	.60
208 Heath Miller	.20	.50
209 Troy Polamalu	.30	.75
210 James Farrior	.20	.50
211 Cedrick Wilson	.20	.50
212 Dunta Robinson	.20	.50
213 Ahman Green	.25	.60
214 Andre Johnson	.25	.60
215 Jerome Mathis	.20	.50
216 Owen Daniels	.20	.50
217 DeMeco Ryans	.25	.60
218 Wali Lundy	.20	.50
219 Mario Williams	.25	.60
220 Peyton Manning	.50	1.25
221 Joseph Addai	.25	.60
222 Marvin Harrison	.30	.75
223 Reggie Wayne	.25	.60
224 Dallas Clark	.20	.50
225 Robert Mathis	.20	.50
226 Cato June	.20	.50
227 Adam Vinatieri	.25	.60
228 Bob Sanders	.25	.60
229 Dwight Freeney	.25	.60
230 Byron Leftwich	.25	.60
231 Fred Taylor	.25	.60
232 Matt Jones	.25	.60
233 Reggie Williams	.25	.60
234 Marcedes Lewis	.20	.50
235 Bobby McCray	.20	.50
236 Rashean Mathis	.20	.50
237 Maurice Jones-Drew	.30	.75
238 Ernest Wilford	.20	.50
239 Daryl Smith	.20	.50
240 Vince Young	.25	.60
241 LenDale White	.25	.60
242 Brandon Jones	.20	.50
243 Bo Scaife	.20	.50
244 Keith Bulluck	.20	.50
245 Chris Hope	.20	.50
246 Kyle Vanden Bosch	.20	.50
247 Roydell Williams	.20	.50
248 Jay Cutler	.30	.75
249 Travis Henry	.25	.60
250 Javon Walker	.25	.60
251 Rod Smith	.25	.60
252 Tony Scheffler	.25	.60
253 Elvis Dumervil	.20	.50
254 Champ Bailey	.25	.60
255 Mike Bell	.25	.60
256 Brandon Marshall	.25	.60
257 Al Wilson	.20	.50
258 Trent Green	.25	.60
259 Larry Johnson	.20	.50
260 Eddie Kennison	.20	.50
261 Samie Parker	.20	.50
262 Tony Gonzalez	.25	.60
263 Jared Allen	.30	.75
264 Kawika Mitchell	.20	.50
265 Tamba Hali	.20	.50
266 Dante Hall	.25	.60
267 Brodie Croyle	.25	.60
268 Andrew Walter	.20	.50
269 LaMont Jordan	.25	.60
270 Dominic Rhodes	.25	.60
271 Randy Moss	.30	.75
272 Ronald Curry	.25	.60
273 Courtney Anderson	.20	.50
274 Derrick Burgess	.20	.50
275 Warren Sapp	.25	.60
276 Michael Huff	.25	.60
277 Thomas Howard	.20	.50
278 Kirk Morrison	.20	.50
279 Philip Rivers	.30	.75
280 LaDainian Tomlinson	.30	.75
281 Vincent Jackson	.25	.60
282 Lorenzo Neal	.20	.50
283 Antonio Gates	.30	.75
284 Shawne Merriman	.25	.60
285 Shaun Phillips	.20	.50
286 Michael Turner	.30	.75
287 Jamal Williams	.20	.50
288 Nate Kaeding	.20	.50
289 Michael Okwo RC	.60	1.50
290 Gary Russell RC	.60	1.50
291 Josh Wilson RC	.60	1.50
292 Thomas Clayton RC	.60	1.50
293 Jerard Rabb RC	.60	1.50
294 Roy Hall RC	.75	2.00
295 LaMarr Woodley RC	.75	2.00
296 Eric Wright RC	.75	2.00
297 Dan Bazuin RC	.60	1.50
298 A.J. Davis RC	.50	1.25
299 Buster Davis RC	.60	1.50
300 Stewart Bradley RC	.60	1.50
301 Toby Korrodi RC	.60	1.50
302 Marcus McCauley RC	.60	1.50
303 DeMarcus Tank Tyler RC	.50	1.25
304 Jon Abbate RC	.50	1.25
305 Ikaika Alama-Francis RC	.75	2.00
306 Tim Crowder RC	.75	2.00
307 D'Juan Woods RC	.50	1.25
308 Tim Shaw RC	.60	1.50
309 Fred Bennett RC	.50	1.25
310 Victor Abiamiri RC	.75	2.00
311 Eric Weddle RC	.75	2.00
312 Danny Ware RC	.75	2.00
313 Quentin Moses RC	.60	1.50
314 Ryan McBean RC	.75	2.00
315 David Harris RC	.60	1.50
316 David Irons RC	.50	1.25
317 Syndric Steptoe RC	.60	1.50
318 Eric Frampton RC	.60	1.50
319 Jemalle Cornelius RC	.60	1.50
320 Earl Everett RC	.60	1.50
321 Alonzo Coleman RC	.60	1.50
322 Josh Gattis RC	.50	1.25
323 Zak DeOssie RC	.60	1.50
324 Jon Beason RC	.60	1.50
325 Joe Staley RC	.60	1.50
326 Aaron Rouse RC	.60	1.50
327 Reggie Ball RC	.60	1.50
328 Rufus Alexander RC	.60	1.50
329 Daymeion Hughes RC	.60	1.50
330 Justin Durant RC	.60	1.50
331 JaMarcus Russell RC	1.50	4.00
332 Paul Williams RC	1.50	4.00
333 Kenny Irons RC	1.50	4.00
334 Chris Davis RC	1.50	4.00
335 Darius Walker RC	1.50	4.00
336 Dwayne Bowe RC	3.00	8.00
337 Isaiah Stanback RC	1.50	4.00
338 Leon Hall RC	2.00	5.00
339 Sidney Rice RC	3.00	8.00
340 Amobi Okoye RC	2.50	6.00
341 Adrian Peterson RC	10.00	25.00
342 LaRon Landry RC	2.50	6.00
343 Lorenzo Booker RC	2.00	5.00
344 Craig Buster Davis RC	2.00	5.00
345 Mike Walker RC	2.50	6.00
346 Zach Miller RC	2.50	6.00
347 Levi Brown RC	2.50	6.00
348 Brian Leonard RC	2.00	5.00
349 Aundrae Allison RC	1.50	4.00
350 Brandon Siler RC	1.50	4.00
351 Calvin Johnson RC	8.00	20.00
352 Gaines Adams RC	2.50	6.00
353 Anthony Gonzalez RC	2.50	6.00
354 John Beck RC	2.50	6.00
355 Joe Thomas RC	2.50	6.00
356 Michael Bush RC	2.50	6.00
357 Courtney Taylor RC	2.00	5.00

358 Lawrence Timmons RC	2.50	6.00
359 Drew Stanton RC	1.50	4.00
360 Chansi Stuckey RC	2.50	6.00
361 Greg Olsen RC	2.00	5.00
362 Rhema McKnight RC	1.50	4.00
363 Antonio Pittman RC	1.50	4.00
364 Kevin Kolb RC	4.00	10.00
365 Alan Branch RC	2.00	5.00
366 Robert Meachem RC	2.50	6.00
367 Troy Smith RC	2.50	6.00
368 Jamaal Anderson RC	2.00	5.00
369 Tony Hunt RC	1.50	4.00
370 David Clowney RC	2.00	5.00
371 Brady Quinn RC	2.50	6.00
372 Michael Griffin RC	2.50	6.00
373 Jared Zabransky RC	2.00	5.00
374 Jason Hill RC	2.50	6.00
375 Trent Edwards RC	2.50	6.00
376 Dwayne Jarrett RC	2.00	5.00
377 DeShawn Wynn RC	2.00	5.00
378 Patrick Willis RC	5.00	12.00
379 Steve Smith USC RC	2.50	6.00
380 David Ball RC	2.00	5.00
381 Marshawn Lynch RC	2.50	6.00
382 Paul Posluszny RC	2.50	6.00
383 Johnnie Lee Higgins RC	2.00	5.00
384 Kolby Smith RC	2.00	5.00
385 Ted Ginn Jr. RC	2.00	5.00
386 Adam Carriker RC	2.00	5.00
387 Tyler Palko RC	2.00	5.00
388 Joel Filani RC	2.00	5.00
389 Garrett Wolfe RC	1.50	4.00
390 Ryne Robinson RC	2.00	5.00
391 Reggie Nelson RC	2.00	5.00
392 Dallas Baker RC	1.50	4.00
393 Dwayne Wright RC	2.00	5.00
394 Scott Chandler RC	2.50	6.00
395 Jordan Kent RC	2.00	5.00
396 Jarvis Moss RC	2.00	5.00
397 Jonathan Wade RC	2.00	5.00
398 Ben Grubbs RC	2.00	5.00
399 Jason Snelling RC	2.50	6.00
400 Jeff Rowe RC	1.50	4.00
401 Aaron Ross RC	2.50	6.00
402 Jarrett Hicks RC	2.00	5.00
403 Chris Henry RC	1.50	4.00
404 James Jones RC	2.50	6.00
405 Matt Spaeth RC	2.50	6.00
406 Brandon Meriweather RC	2.50	6.00
407 Nate Ilaoa RC	2.00	5.00
408 Brandon Myles RC	2.00	5.00
409 Ray McDonald RC	2.00	5.00
410 Chris Leak RC	2.00	5.00
411 Darrelle Revis RC	4.00	10.00
412 Ahmad Bradshaw RC	4.00	10.00
413 Tyler Thigpen RC	2.50	6.00
414 Justise Hairston RC	2.00	5.00
415 Charles Johnson RC	1.50	4.00
416 Anthony Spencer RC	2.50	6.00
417 Legedu Naanee RC	2.50	6.00
418 Kenneth Darby RC	2.00	5.00
419 Steve Breaston RC	2.50	6.00
420 Ben Patrick RC	2.00	5.00
421 Chris Houston RC	2.00	5.00
422 Jordan Palmer RC	2.00	5.00
423 Laurent Robinson RC	2.50	6.00
424 Selvin Young RC	2.00	5.00
425 Justin Harrell RC	2.00	5.00
426 Sabby Piscitelli RC	2.50	6.00
427 Yamon Figurs RC	1.50	4.00
428 Brandon Jackson RC	2.00	5.00
429 Jacoby Jones RC	2.50	6.00
430 H.B. Blades RC	1.50	4.00

2007 Select Artist's Proof

*VETS 1-288: 8X TO 20X BASIC CARDS
*ROOKIES 289-330: 2.5X TO 6X BASIC CARDS
*ROOKIES 331-430: .8X TO 2X BASIC CARDS
STATED PRINT RUN 32 SER.#'d SETS

2007 Select End Zone

UNPRICED END ZONE PRINT RUN 6

2007 Select Gold Zone

*VETS 1-288: 5X TO 12X BASIC CARDS
*ROOKIES 289-330: 2X TO 5X BASIC CARDS
*ROOKIES 331-430: .6X TO 1.5X BASIC CARDS
STATED PRINT RUN 50 SER.#'d SETS

2007 Select Red Zone

*VETS 1-288: 8X TO 20X BASIC CARDS
*ROOKIES 289-330: 2.5X TO 6X BASIC CARDS
*ROOKIES 331-430: .8X TO 2X BASIC CARDS
STATED PRINT RUN 30 SER.#'d SETS

2007 Select Scorecard

*VETS 1-288: 4X TO 10X BASIC CARDS
*ROOKIES 289-330: 1.5X TO 4X BASIC CARDS
*ROOKIES 331-430: .5X TO 1.2X BASIC CARDS
STATED PRINT RUN 100 SER.#'d SETS

2007 Select Autographs Gold Zone

GOLD ZONE PRINT RUN 10-40
*RED ZONE/25: .5X TO 1.2X GOLD AU/40
RED ZONE PRINT RUN 5-25
UNPRICED END ZONE PRINT RUN 1-5
SERIAL #'d UNDER 25 NOT PRICED

289 Michael Okwo/40	10.00	25.00
290 Gary Russell/40	10.00	25.00
291 Josh Wilson/40	10.00	25.00
292 Thomas Clayton/40	10.00	25.00
293 Jerard Rabb/40	10.00	25.00
295 LaMarr Woodley/40	12.00	30.00
297 Dan Bazuin/40	10.00	25.00
298 A.J. Davis/40	8.00	20.00
299 Buster Davis/40	10.00	25.00
300 Stewart Bradley/40	10.00	25.00
301 Toby Korrodi/40	10.00	25.00
302 Marcus McCauley/40	10.00	25.00
306 Tim Crowder/40	12.00	30.00
307 D'Juan Woods/40	8.00	20.00
308 Tim Shaw/40	10.00	25.00
309 Fred Bennett/40	8.00	20.00
310 Victor Abiamiri/40	12.00	30.00
312 Danny Ware/40	12.00	30.00
313 Quentin Moses/40	10.00	25.00
314 Ryan McBean/40	12.00	30.00
315 David Harris/40	10.00	25.00
316 David Irons/40	8.00	20.00
317 Syndric Steptoe/40	10.00	25.00
318 Eric Frampton/40	10.00	25.00
319 Jemalle Cornelius/40	10.00	25.00
320 Earl Everett/40	10.00	25.00
321 Alonzo Coleman/40	10.00	25.00
322 Josh Gattis/40	8.00	20.00
323 Zak DeOssie/40	10.00	25.00
324 Jon Beason/25	12.00	30.00
326 Aaron Rouse/40	10.00	25.00
327 Reggie Ball/40	10.00	25.00
328 Rufus Alexander/40	10.00	25.00
329 Daymeion Hughes/40	10.00	25.00
331 JaMarcus Russell/25	10.00	25.00
332 Paul Williams/25	10.00	25.00
333 Kenny Irons/25	10.00	25.00
334 Chris Davis/40	8.00	20.00
335 Darius Walker/40	8.00	20.00
336 Dwayne Bowe/25	20.00	50.00
337 Isaiah Stanback/40	8.00	20.00
338 Leon Hall/25	12.00	30.00
339 Sidney Rice/25	20.00	50.00
340 Amobi Okoye/25	15.00	40.00
341 Adrian Peterson/25	125.00	250.00
342 LaRon Landry/40	12.00	30.00
343 Lorenzo Booker/25	12.00	30.00
345 Mike Walker/40	12.00	30.00
346 Zach Miller/25	15.00	40.00
347 Levi Brown/40	12.00	30.00
348 Brian Leonard/25	12.00	30.00
349 Aundrae Allison/40	8.00	20.00
350 Brandon Siler/40	8.00	20.00
351 Calvin Johnson/25	50.00	125.00
352 Gaines Adams/25	15.00	40.00
353 Anthony Gonzalez/25	15.00	40.00
354 John Beck/25	15.00	40.00
355 Joe Thomas/40	12.00	30.00
356 Michael Bush/25	15.00	40.00
357 Courtney Taylor/40	10.00	25.00
358 Lawrence Timmons/25	15.00	40.00
359 Drew Stanton/25	10.00	25.00
360 Chansi Stuckey/40	12.00	30.00
361 Greg Olsen/25	12.00	30.00
362 Rhema McKnight/40	8.00	20.00
363 Antonio Pittman/25	10.00	25.00
364 Kevin Kolb/25	25.00	60.00
366 Robert Meachem/25	15.00	40.00
367 Troy Smith/25	15.00	40.00
368 Jamaal Anderson/40	10.00	25.00
369 Tony Hunt/25	10.00	25.00
370 David Clowney/40	10.00	25.00
371 Brady Quinn/25	15.00	40.00
372 Michael Griffin/40	12.00	30.00
373 Jared Zabransky/40	10.00	25.00
374 Jason Hill/25	15.00	40.00
375 Trent Edwards/25	15.00	40.00
376 Dwayne Jarrett/25	12.00	30.00
377 DeShawn Wynn/25	10.00	25.00
378 Patrick Willis/25	30.00	80.00
379 Steve Smith USC/25	15.00	40.00
380 David Ball/40	10.00	25.00
381 Marshawn Lynch/25	15.00	40.00
382 Paul Posluszny/25	15.00	40.00
383 Johnnie Lee Higgins/25	12.00	30.00
384 Kolby Smith/40	10.00	25.00
385 Ted Ginn Jr./25	12.00	30.00
386 Adam Carriker/40	10.00	25.00
387 Tyler Palko/40	10.00	25.00
388 Joel Filani/40	10.00	25.00
389 Garrett Wolfe/25	10.00	25.00
390 Ryne Robinson/40	10.00	25.00
391 Reggie Nelson/40	10.00	25.00
392 Dallas Baker/40	8.00	20.00
393 Dwayne Wright/40	10.00	25.00
394 Scott Chandler/40	12.00	30.00
395 Jordan Kent/40	10.00	25.00
397 Jonathan Wade/40	10.00	25.00
399 Jason Snelling/40	12.00	30.00
400 Jeff Rowe/40	8.00	20.00
401 Aaron Ross/40	12.00	30.00
402 Jarrett Hicks/40	10.00	25.00
403 Chris Henry/25	10.00	25.00
404 James Jones/40	12.00	30.00
405 Matt Spaeth/40	12.00	30.00
406 Brandon Meriweather/40	12.00	30.00
407 Nate Ilaoa/40	10.00	25.00
408 Brandon Myles/40	10.00	25.00
409 Ray McDonald/40	10.00	25.00
410 Chris Leak/25	12.00	30.00
411 Darrelle Revis/40	20.00	50.00
412 Ahmad Bradshaw/40	20.00	50.00
416 Anthony Spencer/40	12.00	30.00
418 Kenneth Darby/40	10.00	25.00
419 Steve Breaston/40	12.00	30.00
420 Ben Patrick/40	10.00	25.00
421 Chris Houston/40	10.00	25.00
422 Jordan Palmer/25	12.00	30.00
423 Laurent Robinson/40	12.00	30.00
424 Selvin Young/40	10.00	25.00
426 Sabby Piscitelli/40	12.00	30.00
427 Yamon Figurs/25	10.00	25.00
428 Brandon Jackson/25	12.00	30.00
429 Jacoby Jones/40	12.00	30.00
430 H.B. Blades/40	8.00	20.00

2007 Select Franchise

STATED PRINT RUN 749 SER.#'d SETS
*SCORECARD/100: .6X TO 1.5X BASIC INSERTS
SCORECARD PRINT RUN 100 SER.#'d SETS
*GOLD ZONE/50: 1X TO 2.5X BASIC INSERTS
GOLD ZONE PRINT RUN 50 SER.#'d SETS
*ART.PROOF/32: 1.5X TO 4X BASIC INSERTS
ARTIST'S PROOF PRINT RUN 32 SER.#'d SETS
*RED ZONE/30: 1.5X TO 4X BASIC INSERTS
RED ZONE PRINT RUN 30 SER.#'d SETS
UNPRICED END ZONE PRINT RUN 6
UNPRICED AUTO END ZONE PRINT RUN 1
UNPRICED AUTO RED ZONE PRINT RUN 5

1 LaDainian Tomlinson	1.00	2.50
2 Frank Gore	1.00	2.50
3 Shaun Alexander	.75	2.00
4 Brett Favre	2.00	5.00
5 Reggie Bush	1.00	2.50
6 Jay Cutler	1.00	2.50
7 Larry Johnson	.60	1.50
8 Maurice Jones-Drew	1.00	2.50
9 Carson Palmer	.75	2.00
10 Vince Young	.75	2.00
11 Matt Leinart	.75	2.00
12 Tom Brady	1.50	4.00
13 Tony Romo	1.25	3.00
14 Willie Parker	.75	2.00
15 Brian Urlacher	1.00	2.50
16 Roy Williams WR	.75	2.00
17 Steven Jackson	1.00	2.50
18 Peyton Manning	1.50	4.00
19 Brian Westbrook	.75	2.00
20 Steve Smith	.75	2.00

2007 Select Hot Rookies

STATED PRINT RUN 749 SER.#'d SETS
*SCORECARD/100: .6X TO 1.5X BASIC INSERTS
SCORECARD PRINT RUN 100 SER.#'d SETS
*GOLD ZONE/50: 1X TO 2.5X BASIC INSERTS
GOLD ZONE PRINT RUN 50 SER.#'d SETS
*ART.PROOF/32: 1.2X TO 3X BASIC INSERTS
ARTIST'S PROOF PRINT RUN 32 SER.#'d SETS
*RED ZONE/25: 1.2X TO 3X BASIC INSERTS
RED ZONE PRINT RUN 25 SER.#'d SETS
UNPRICED END ZONE PRINT RUN 6

1 JaMarcus Russell	.75	2.00
2 Brady Quinn	1.25	3.00
3 Adrian Peterson	5.00	12.00
4 Marshawn Lynch	1.25	3.00
5 Calvin Johnson	4.00	10.00
6 Ted Ginn Jr.	1.00	2.50
7 Dwayne Bowe	1.50	4.00
8 Robert Meachem	1.25	3.00
9 Dwayne Jarrett	1.00	2.50
10 Greg Olsen	1.00	2.50
11 Kevin Kolb	2.00	5.00
12 John Beck	1.25	3.00
13 Drew Stanton	.75	2.00
14 Kenny Irons	.75	2.00
15 Chris Henry	.75	2.00
16 Brandon Jackson	1.00	2.50
17 Craig Buster Davis	1.00	2.50
18 Anthony Gonzalez	1.25	3.00
19 Sidney Rice	1.50	4.00
20 Steve Smith USC	1.25	3.00

2007 Select Hot Rookies Autographs Gold Zone

GOLD ZONE PRINT RUN 20 SER.#'d SETS
UNPRICED RED ZONE PRINT RUN 10
UNPRICED END ZONE PRINT RUN 5

1 JaMarcus Russell	10.00	25.00
2 Brady Quinn	40.00	100.00
3 Adrian Peterson	150.00	300.00
4 Marshawn Lynch	15.00	40.00
5 Calvin Johnson	60.00	120.00
6 Ted Ginn Jr.	12.00	30.00
7 Dwayne Bowe	20.00	50.00
8 Robert Meachem	15.00	40.00
9 Dwayne Jarrett	12.00	30.00
10 Greg Olsen	12.00	30.00
11 Kevin Kolb	25.00	60.00
12 John Beck	15.00	40.00
13 Drew Stanton	10.00	25.00
14 Kenny Irons	10.00	25.00
15 Chris Henry	10.00	25.00
16 Brandon Jackson	12.00	30.00
18 Anthony Gonzalez	15.00	40.00
19 Sidney Rice	20.00	50.00
20 Steve Smith USC	15.00	40.00

2007 Select Hot Rookies Inscriptions

STATED PRINT RUN 40 SER.#'d SETS

1 JaMarcus Russell	8.00	20.00
2 Brady Quinn	12.00	30.00
3 Adrian Peterson	125.00	250.00
4 Marshawn Lynch	12.00	30.00
5 Calvin Johnson	40.00	100.00
6 Ted Ginn Jr.	10.00	25.00
7 Dwayne Bowe	15.00	40.00
8 Robert Meachem	12.00	30.00
9 Dwayne Jarrett	10.00	25.00
10 Greg Olsen	10.00	25.00
11 Kevin Kolb	20.00	50.00
12 John Beck	12.00	30.00
13 Drew Stanton	8.00	20.00
14 Kenny Irons	8.00	20.00
15 Chris Henry	8.00	20.00
16 Brandon Jackson	10.00	25.00
18 Anthony Gonzalez	12.00	30.00
19 Sidney Rice	15.00	40.00
20 Steve Smith USC	12.00	30.00

2007 Select Inscriptions

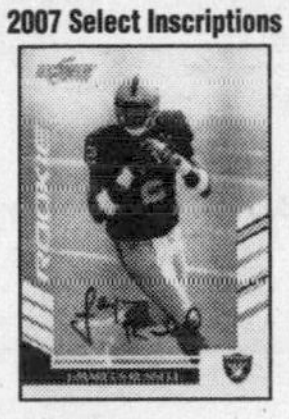

STATED PRINT RUN 20-100

7 Patrick Crayton/20	8.00	20.00
38 Bernard Berrian/20	8.00	20.00
48 Mike Furrey/20	10.00	25.00
78 Jerious Norwood/20	10.00	25.00
90 Marques Colston/20	12.00	30.00
94 Devery Henderson/20	8.00	20.00
179 Demetrius Williams/20	8.00	20.00
217 DeMeco Ryans/20	10.00	25.00
255 Mike Bell/20	10.00	25.00
256 Brandon Marshall/20	10.00	25.00
281 Vincent Jackson/20	10.00	25.00
286 Michael Turner/20	12.00	30.00
289 Michael Okwo/100	6.00	15.00
290 Gary Russell/100	6.00	15.00
291 Josh Wilson/50	10.00	25.00
292 Thomas Clayton/50	10.00	25.00
293 Jerard Rabb/100	6.00	15.00
295 LaMarr Woodley/50	12.00	30.00
297 Dan Bazuin/100	6.00	15.00
298 A.J. Davis/50	8.00	20.00
299 Buster Davis/100	6.00	15.00
300 Stewart Bradley/100	6.00	15.00
301 Toby Korrodi/50	10.00	25.00
302 Marcus McCauley/50	10.00	25.00
306 Tim Crowder/50	12.00	30.00
307 D'Juan Woods/100	5.00	12.00
308 Tim Shaw/50	10.00	25.00
309 Fred Bennett/100	5.00	12.00
310 Victor Abiamiri/50	12.00	30.00
312 Danny Ware/100	8.00	20.00
313 Quentin Moses/50	10.00	25.00
314 Ryan McBean/100	8.00	20.00
315 David Harris/50	10.00	25.00
316 David Irons/100	5.00	12.00
317 Syndric Steptoe/100	6.00	15.00
318 Eric Frampton/100	6.00	15.00
319 Jemalle Cornelius/100	6.00	15.00
320 Earl Everett/50	10.00	25.00
321 Alonzo Coleman/50	10.00	25.00
322 Josh Gattis/50	8.00	20.00
323 Zak DeOssie/100	6.00	15.00
324 Jon Beason/40	10.00	25.00
326 Aaron Rouse/50	10.00	25.00
327 Reggie Ball/100	6.00	15.00
328 Rufus Alexander/100	6.00	15.00
329 Daymeion Hughes/100	6.00	15.00
331 JaMarcus Russell/40	8.00	20.00
332 Paul Williams/40	8.00	20.00
333 Kenny Irons/40	8.00	20.00
334 Chris Davis/50	8.00	20.00
335 Darius Walker/50	8.00	20.00
336 Dwayne Bowe/40	15.00	40.00
337 Isaiah Stanback/50	8.00	20.00
338 Leon Hall/40	10.00	25.00
339 Sidney Rice/40	15.00	40.00
340 Amobi Okoye/40	12.00	30.00
341 Adrian Peterson/40	125.00	250.00
342 LaRon Landry/50	12.00	30.00
343 Lorenzo Booker/40	10.00	25.00
345 Mike Walker/50	12.00	30.00
346 Zach Miller/40	12.00	30.00
347 Levi Brown/100	8.00	20.00
348 Brian Leonard/40	10.00	25.00
349 Aundrae Allison/50	8.00	20.00
350 Brandon Siler/100	5.00	12.00
351 Calvin Johnson/40	40.00	100.00
352 Gaines Adams/40	12.00	30.00
353 Anthony Gonzalez/40	12.00	30.00
354 John Beck/40	12.00	30.00
355 Joe Thomas/50	12.00	30.00
356 Michael Bush/40	12.00	30.00
357 Courtney Taylor/50	10.00	25.00
358 Lawrence Timmons/40	12.00	30.00
359 Drew Stanton/40	8.00	20.00
360 Chansi Stuckey/50	12.00	30.00
361 Greg Olsen/40	10.00	25.00
362 Rhema McKnight/100	5.00	12.00
363 Antonio Pittman/40	8.00	20.00
364 Kevin Kolb/40	20.00	50.00
366 Robert Meachem/40	12.00	30.00
367 Troy Smith/40	12.00	30.00
368 Jamaal Anderson/50	10.00	25.00
369 Tony Hunt/40	8.00	20.00
370 David Clowney/50	10.00	25.00
371 Brady Quinn/40	40.00	100.00
372 Michael Griffin/50	12.00	30.00
373 Jared Zabransky/50	10.00	25.00
374 Jason Hill/40	12.00	30.00
375 Trent Edwards/40	12.00	30.00
376 Dwayne Jarrett/40	10.00	25.00
377 DeShawn Wynn/40	10.00	25.00
378 Patrick Willis/40	25.00	60.00
379 Steve Smith USC/40	12.00	30.00
380 David Ball/50	10.00	25.00
381 Marshawn Lynch/40	12.00	30.00
382 Paul Posluszny/40	12.00	30.00
383 Johnnie Lee Higgins/40	10.00	25.00
384 Kolby Smith/50	10.00	25.00
385 Ted Ginn Jr./40	10.00	25.00
386 Adam Carriker/50	10.00	25.00
387 Tyler Palko/50	10.00	25.00
388 Joel Filani/50	10.00	25.00
389 Garrett Wolfe/40	8.00	20.00
390 Ryne Robinson/50	10.00	25.00
391 Reggie Nelson/50	10.00	25.00
392 Dallas Baker/50	8.00	20.00
393 Dwayne Wright/100	6.00	15.00
394 Scott Chandler/50	12.00	30.00
395 Jordan Kent/50	10.00	25.00
397 Jonathan Wade/100	6.00	15.00
399 Jason Snelling/50	12.00	30.00
400 Jeff Rowe/50	8.00	20.00
401 Aaron Ross/50	12.00	30.00
402 Jarrett Hicks/100	6.00	15.00
403 Chris Henry/40	8.00	20.00
404 James Jones/50	12.00	30.00
405 Matt Spaeth/50	12.00	30.00
406 Brandon Meriweather/50	12.00	30.00
407 Nate Ilaoa/100	6.00	15.00
408 Brandon Myles/100	6.00	15.00
409 Ray McDonald/50	10.00	25.00
410 Chris Leak/40	10.00	25.00
411 Darrelle Revis/50	20.00	50.00
412 Ahmad Bradshaw/100	12.00	30.00
416 Anthony Spencer/50	12.00	30.00
418 Kenneth Darby/100	6.00	15.00
419 Steve Breaston/50	12.00	30.00
420 Ben Patrick/50	10.00	25.00
421 Chris Houston/50	10.00	25.00
422 Jordan Palmer/40	10.00	25.00
423 Laurent Robinson/50	12.00	30.00
424 Selvin Young/50	10.00	25.00
426 Sabby Piscitelli/100	8.00	20.00
427 Yamon Figurs/40	8.00	20.00
428 Brandon Jackson/40	10.00	25.00
429 Jacoby Jones/50	12.00	30.00
430 H.B. Blades/100	5.00	12.00

2007 Select National Convention

COMPLETE SET (12)	10.00	25.00
1 Brett Favre	1.25	3.00
2 Reggie Bush	.60	1.50
3 Peyton Manning	1.00	2.50
4 Vince Young	.50	1.25
5 LaDainian Tomlinson	.60	1.50
6 JaMarcus Russell	.50	1.25
7 Adrian Peterson	3.00	8.00
8 Calvin Johnson	2.50	6.00
9 Brady Quinn	.75	2.00
10 Ted Ginn Jr.	.60	1.50
11 Marshawn Lynch	.75	2.00
12 Troy Smith	.75	2.00

2008 Select

This set was released on August 27, 2008. The base set consists of 440 cards. Cards 1-330 feature veterans, and cards 331-440 are rookies serial numbered of 999.

COMP.SET w/o RC's (330)	25.00	50.00
ROOKIE PRINT RUN 999 SER.#'d SETS		
UNPRICED END ZONE PRINT RUN 6		
1 Matt Leinart	.30	.75
2 Kurt Warner	.30	.75
3 Larry Fitzgerald	.30	.75
4 Anquan Boldin	.25	.60
5 Edgerrin James	.25	.60
6 Neil Rackers	.20	.50
7 Steve Breaston	.20	.50
8 Antrel Rolle	.20	.50
9 Karlos Dansby	.20	.50
10 Joey Harrington	.20	.50
11 Jerious Norwood	.25	.60
12 Roddy White	.25	.60
13 Michael Jenkins	.20	.50
14 Joe Horn	.25	.60
15 Keith Brooking	.20	.50
16 Lawyer Milloy	.20	.50
17 John Abraham	.20	.50
18 Michael Turner	.30	.75
19 Troy Smith	.25	.60
20 Willis McGahee	.25	.60
21 Musa Smith	.20	.50
22 Derrick Mason	.25	.60
23 Mark Clayton	.25	.60
24 Bart Scott	.20	.50
25 Demetrius Williams	.20	.50
26 Yamon Figurs	.20	.50
27 Ray Lewis	.30	.75
28 Terrell Suggs	.20	.50
29 Ed Reed	.25	.60
30 Trent Edwards	.20	.50
31 Marshawn Lynch	.25	.60
32 Lee Evans	.25	.60
33 Roscoe Parrish	.20	.50
34 Paul Posluszny	.25	.60
35 John DiGiorgio RC	.25	.60
36 Angelo Crowell	.20	.50
37 Jabari Greer RC	.20	.50
38 Chris Kelsay	.20	.50
39 Fred Jackson RC	2.00	5.00
40 Matt Moore	.25	.60
41 Steve Smith	.25	.60
42 DeAngelo Williams	.25	.60
43 Brad Hoover	.20	.50
44 Dante Rosario	.20	.50
45 Julius Peppers	.25	.60
46 Jon Beason	.20	.50
47 Chris Harris	.20	.50
48 D.J. Hackett	.20	.50
49 Jake Delhomme	.25	.60
50 Adrian Peterson	.50	1.25
51 Mark Anderson	.20	.50
52 Desmond Clark	.20	.50
53 Greg Olsen	.25	.60
54 Devin Hester	.30	.75
55 Brian Urlacher	.30	.75
56 Jason McKie RC	.25	.60
57 Lance Briggs	.20	.50
58 Rex Grossman	.25	.60
59 Carson Palmer	.30	.75
60 Chad Johnson	.25	.60
61 T.J. Houshmandzadeh	.25	.60
62 Rudi Johnson	.25	.60
63 Kenny Watson	.20	.50
64 Dhani Jones	.20	.50
65 Leon Hall	.20	.50
66 Johnathan Joseph	.20	.50
67 Derek Anderson	.20	.50
68 Brady Quinn	.25	.60
69 Jamal Lewis	.25	.60
70 Josh Cribbs	.30	.75
71 Kellen Winslow	.25	.60
72 Braylon Edwards	.25	.60
73 Joe Jurevicius	.20	.50
74 D'Qwell Jackson	.20	.50
75 Leigh Bodden	.20	.50
76 Sean Jones	.20	.50
77 Tony Romo	.40	1.00
78 Terrell Owens	.30	.75
79 Marion Barber	.25	.60
80 Jason Witten	.30	.75
81 Patrick Crayton	.25	.60
82 Anthony Henry	.20	.50
83 DeMarcus Ware	.25	.60
84 Terence Newman	.20	.50
85 Greg Ellis	.20	.50
86 Zach Thomas	.25	.60
87 Keary Colbert	.20	.50
88 Jay Cutler	.30	.75
89 Tony Scheffler	.20	.50
90 Selvin Young	.20	.50
91 Brandon Marshall	.25	.60
92 Brandon Stokley	.25	.60
93 Champ Bailey	.25	.60
94 John Lynch	.25	.60
95 Dre Bly	.20	.50
96 Elvis Dumervil	.20	.50
97 Jon Kitna	.25	.60
98 Tatum Bell	.20	.50
99 Shaun McDonald	.20	.50
100 Roy Williams WR	.25	.60
101 Calvin Johnson	.30	.75
102 Mike Furrey	.25	.60
103 Ernie Sims	.20	.50
104 Aveion Cason	.20	.50
105 Aaron Rodgers	.60	1.50
106 Brett Favre	.75	2.00
107 Ryan Grant	.30	.75
108 Greg Jennings	.30	.75
109 Donald Driver	.25	.60
110 Donald Lee	.25	.60
111 James Jones	.20	.50
112 Al Harris	.20	.50
113 Nick Barnett	.20	.50
114 Charles Woodson	.30	.75
115 Aaron Kampman	.25	.60
116 Mason Crosby	.20	.50
117 Matt Schaub	.25	.60
118 Ahman Green	.25	.60
119 Andre Johnson	.25	.60
120 Kevin Walter	.25	.60
121 Owen Daniels	.20	.50
122 Andre Davis	.20	.50
123 DeMeco Ryans	.25	.60
124 Mario Williams	.25	.60
125 Dunta Robinson	.20	.50
126 Chris Brown	.20	.50
127 Peyton Manning	.50	1.25
128 Joseph Addai	.25	.60
129 Marvin Harrison	.30	.75
130 Reggie Wayne	.25	.60
131 Dallas Clark	.25	.60
132 Anthony Gonzalez	.20	.50
133 Kenton Keith	.20	.50
134 Adam Vinatieri	.30	.75
135 Bob Sanders	.25	.60
136 Kelvin Hayden	.20	.50
137 Freddie Keiaho	.20	.50
138 David Garrard	.25	.60
139 Fred Taylor	.25	.60
140 Maurice Jones-Drew	.25	.60
141 Greg Jones	.20	.50
142 Dennis Northcutt	.20	.50
143 Reggie Williams	.25	.60
144 Marcedes Lewis	.20	.50
145 Matt Jones	.25	.60
146 Reggie Nelson	.20	.50
147 Cleo Lemon	.20	.50
148 Jerry Porter	.20	.50
149 Damon Huard	.20	.50
150 Brodie Croyle	.25	.60
151 Larry Johnson	.25	.60
152 Kolby Smith	.20	.50
153 Tony Gonzalez	.25	.60
154 Dwayne Bowe	.25	.60
155 Donnie Edwards	.20	.50
156 Jared Allen	.30	.75
157 Patrick Surtain	.20	.50
158 Derrick Johnson	.20	.50
159 Ernest Wilford	.20	.50
160 John Beck	.20	.50
161 Ronnie Brown	.25	.60
162 Greg Camarillo RC	.60	1.50
163 Ted Ginn Jr.	.25	.60
164 Derek Hagan	.20	.50
165 Channing Crowder	.20	.50
166 Joey Porter	.20	.50
167 Jason Taylor	.25	.60
168 Josh McCown	.20	.50
169 Bernard Berrian	.25	.60
170 Maurice Hicks	.20	.50
171 Tarvaris Jackson	.25	.60
172 Adrian Peterson	.50	1.25
173 Chester Taylor	.20	.50
174 Bobby Wade	.20	.50
175 Sidney Rice	.30	.75
176 Robert Ferguson	.20	.50
177 Darren Sharper	.25	.60
178 Visanthe Shiancoe	.30	.75
179 E.J. Henderson	.20	.50
180 Cedric Griffin	.20	.50
181 Chad Greenway	.20	.50
182 Tom Brady	.50	1.25
183 Randy Moss	.30	.75
184 Laurence Maroney	.25	.60
185 Wes Welker	.30	.75
186 Sammy Morris	.20	.50
187 Kevin Faulk	.25	.60
188 Ben Watson	.20	.50
189 Tedy Bruschi	.30	.75
190 Rodney Harrison	.20	.50
191 Mike Vrabel	.20	.50
192 Drew Brees	.30	.75
193 Reggie Bush	.30	.75
194 Deuce McAllister	.25	.60
195 Marques Colston	.25	.60
196 David Patten	.20	.50
197 Devery Henderson	.20	.50
198 Scott Fujita	.20	.50
199 Roman Harper	.20	.50
200 Mike McKenzie	.20	.50
201 Will Smith	.20	.50
202 Billy Miller	.20	.50
203 Sammy Knight	.20	.50
204 Eli Manning	.30	.75
205 Plaxico Burress	.25	.60
206 Brandon Jacobs	.25	.60
207 Ahmad Bradshaw	.25	.60
208 David Tyree	.25	.60
209 Amani Toomer	.25	.60
210 Jeremy Shockey	.25	.60
211 Steve Smith USC	.25	.60
212 Aaron Ross	.20	.50
213 Antonio Pierce	.20	.50
214 Michael Strahan	.25	.60
215 Jesse Chatman	.20	.50
216 Calvin Pace	.20	.50
217 Kellen Clemens	.25	.60
218 Leon Washington	.25	.60
219 Jerricho Cotchery	.25	.60
220 Laveranues Coles	.20	.50
221 Chris Baker	.20	.50
222 Brad Smith	.20	.50
223 Thomas Jones	.25	.60
224 Darrelle Revis	.25	.60
225 David Harris	.20	.50
226 DeAngelo Hall	.20	.50
227 Drew Carter	.20	.50
228 Javon Walker	.25	.60
229 JaMarcus Russell	.25	.60
230 Justin Fargas	.20	.50
231 Michael Bush	.25	.60
232 Ronald Curry	.25	.60
233 Zach Miller	.25	.60
234 Thomas Howard	.20	.50
235 Johnnie Lee Higgins	.20	.50
236 Kirk Morrison	.20	.50
237 Michael Huff	.20	.50
238 Asante Samuel	.20	.50
239 Donovan McNabb	.30	.75
240 Brian Westbrook	.25	.60
241 Correll Buckhalter	.25	.60
242 Kevin Curtis	.20	.50
243 Reggie Brown	.20	.50
244 L.J. Smith	.20	.50
245 Greg Lewis	.20	.50
246 Lito Sheppard	.20	.50
247 Omar Gaither	.20	.50
248 Ben Roethlisberger	.30	.75
249 Willie Parker	.25	.60
250 Najeh Davenport	.20	.50
251 Hines Ward	.25	.60
252 Santonio Holmes	.25	.60
253 Heath Miller	.20	.50
254 Cedrick Wilson	.20	.50
255 James Harrison RC	1.25	3.00
256 Ike Taylor	.20	.50
257 James Farrior	.20	.50
258 Troy Polamalu	.30	.75
259 Philip Rivers	.30	.75
260 LaDainian Tomlinson	.30	.75
261 Darren Sproles	.20	.50
262 Vincent Jackson	.20	.50
263 Chris Chambers	.25	.60
264 Antonio Gates	.30	.75
265 Craig Buster Davis	.20	.50
266 Malcom Floyd	.25	.60
267 Antonio Cromartie	.20	.50
268 Shawne Merriman	.25	.60
269 DeShaun Foster	.25	.60
270 Alex Smith QB	.30	.75
271 Frank Gore	.25	.60
272 Michael Robinson	.20	.50
273 Vernon Davis	.25	.60
274 Arnaz Battle	.20	.50
275 Isaac Bruce	.25	.60
276 Patrick Willis	.25	.60
277 Nate Clements	.20	.50
278 Jason Hill	.20	.50
279 T.J. Duckett	.20	.50
280 Matt Hasselbeck	.25	.60
281 Julian Peterson	.20	.50
282 Maurice Morris	.20	.50
283 Bobby Engram	.20	.50
284 Nate Burleson	.20	.50
285 Deion Branch	.25	.60
286 Lofa Tatupu	.25	.60
287 Marcus Trufant	.20	.50
288 Darryl Tapp	.20	.50
289 Julius Jones	.20	.50
290 Marc Bulger	.25	.60
291 Steven Jackson	.30	.75
292 Brian Leonard	.20	.50
293 Torry Holt	.25	.60
294 Dante Hall	.20	.50
295 Randy McMichael	.20	.50
296 Drew Bennett	.20	.50
297 Will Witherspoon	.20	.50
298 Tye Hill	.20	.50
299 Corey Chavous	.20	.50
300 Warrick Dunn	.25	.60
301 Brian Griese	.20	.50
302 Jeff Garcia	.25	.60
303 Cadillac Williams	.25	.60
304 Earnest Graham	.20	.50
305 Joey Galloway	.25	.60
306 Ike Hilliard	.20	.50
307 Michael Clayton	.20	.50
308 Derrick Brooks	.25	.60
309 Phillip Buchanon	.20	.50
310 Alex Smith TE	.30	.75
311 Ronde Barber	.20	.50
312 Justin McCareins	.20	.50
313 Jevon Kearse	.25	.60
314 Vince Young	.25	.60
315 LenDale White	.25	.60
316 Justin Gage	.20	.50
317 Roydell Williams	.20	.50
318 Alge Crumpler	.25	.60
319 Brandon Jones	.20	.50
320 Michael Griffin	.20	.50
321 Keith Bulluck	.20	.50
322 Jason Campbell	.25	.60
323 Clinton Portis	.25	.60
324 Ladell Betts	.20	.50
325 Santana Moss	.20	.50
326 Chris Cooley	.25	.60
327 Antwaan Randle El	.20	.50
328 London Fletcher	.20	.50
329 Shawn Springs	.20	.50
330 LaRon Landry	.25	.60
331 Jake Long RC	1.50	4.00
332 Chris Long RC	1.50	4.00
333 Matt Ryan RC	6.00	15.00
334 Darren McFadden RC	4.00	10.00
335 Glenn Dorsey RC	1.50	4.00
336 Vernon Gholston RC	1.25	3.00
337 Sedrick Ellis RC	1.50	4.00
338 Derrick Harvey RC	1.00	2.50
339 Keith Rivers RC	1.50	4.00
340 Jerod Mayo RC	1.50	4.00
341 Leodis McKelvin RC	1.25	3.00
342 Jonathan Stewart RC	2.50	6.00
343 Dominique Rodgers-Cromartie RC	1.50	4.00
344 Joe Flacco RC	5.00	12.00
345 Aqib Talib RC	1.50	4.00
346 Felix Jones RC	2.50	6.00
347 Rashard Mendenhall RC	3.00	8.00
348 Chris Johnson RC	4.00	10.00
349 Mike Jenkins RC	1.50	4.00
350 Antoine Cason RC	1.50	4.00
351 Lawrence Jackson RC	1.25	3.00
352 Kentwan Balmer RC	1.25	3.00
353 Dustin Keller RC	1.50	4.00
354 Kenny Phillips RC	1.50	4.00
355 Phillip Merling RC	1.25	3.00
356 Donnie Avery RC	1.25	3.00
357 Devin Thomas RC	1.25	3.00
358 Brandon Flowers RC	1.50	4.00
359 Jordy Nelson RC	2.00	5.00
360 Curtis Lofton RC	1.25	3.00
361 John Carlson RC	1.50	4.00
362 Tracy Porter RC	1.50	4.00
363 James Hardy RC	1.25	3.00
364 Eddie Royal RC	1.50	4.00
365 Matt Forte RC	2.50	6.00
366 Jordon Dizon RC	1.50	4.00
367 Jerome Simpson RC	1.50	4.00
368 Fred Davis RC	1.50	4.00
369 DeSean Jackson RC	3.00	8.00
370 Calais Campbell RC	1.25	3.00
371 Malcolm Kelly RC	1.25	3.00
372 Quentin Groves RC	1.25	3.00
373 Limas Sweed RC	1.50	4.00
374 Ray Rice RC	3.00	8.00
375 Brian Brohm RC	1.50	4.00
376 Chad Henne RC	1.50	4.00
377 Dexter Jackson RC	1.25	3.00
378 Martellus Bennett RC	1.25	3.00
379 Terrell Thomas RC	1.25	3.00
380 Kevin Smith RC	1.50	4.00
381 Anthony Alridge RC	1.25	3.00
382 Jacob Hester RC	1.50	4.00
383 Earl Bennett RC	1.50	4.00
384 Jamaal Charles RC	2.50	6.00
385 Dan Connor RC	1.50	4.00
386 Reggie Smith RC	1.25	3.00
387 Brad Cottam RC	1.25	3.00
388 Pat Sims RC	1.25	3.00
389 Dantrell Savage RC	1.25	3.00
390 Early Doucet RC	1.25	3.00
391 Harry Douglas RC	1.25	3.00
392 Steve Slaton RC	1.50	4.00
393 Jermichael Finley RC	1.50	4.00
394 Kevin O'Connell RC	1.25	3.00
395 Mario Manningham RC	1.50	4.00
396 Andre Caldwell RC	1.25	3.00
397 Will Franklin RC	1.25	3.00
398 Marcus Smith RC	1.25	3.00
399 Martin Rucker RC	1.25	3.00
400 Xavier Adibi RC	1.00	2.50
401 Craig Steltz RC	1.25	3.00
402 Tashard Choice RC	1.25	3.00
403 Lavelle Hawkins RC	1.00	2.50
404 Jacob Tamme RC	1.50	4.00
405 Keenan Burton RC	1.00	2.50
406 John David Booty RC	1.25	3.00
407 Ryan Torain RC	1.50	4.00
408 Tim Hightower RC	1.50	4.00
409 Dennis Dixon RC	1.50	4.00
410 Kellen Davis RC	1.00	2.50
411 Josh Johnson RC	1.50	4.00
412 Erik Ainge RC	1.50	4.00
413 Owen Schmitt RC	1.50	4.00
414 Marcus Thomas RC	1.25	3.00
415 Thomas Brown RC	1.25	3.00
416 Josh Morgan RC	1.50	4.00
417 Kevin Robinson RC	1.00	2.50
418 Colt Brennan RC	1.50	4.00
419 Paul Hubbard RC	1.25	3.00
420 Andre Woodson RC	1.50	4.00
421 Mike Hart RC	1.50	4.00
422 Matt Flynn RC	3.00	8.00
423 Chauncey Washington RC	1.25	3.00
424 Caleb Campbell RC	1.50	4.00
425 Peyton Hillis RC	3.00	8.00
426 Justin Forsett RC	1.50	4.00
427 Adrian Arrington RC	1.25	3.00
428 Cory Boyd RC	1.00	2.50
429 Allen Patrick RC	1.25	3.00
430 Marcus Monk RC	1.25	3.00
431 DJ Hall RC	1.25	3.00
432 Darrell Strong RC	1.25	3.00
433 Jason Rivers RC	1.25	3.00
434 Jed Collins RC	1.25	3.00
435 Paul Smith RC	1.50	4.00
436 Darius Reynaud RC	1.00	2.50
437 Ali Highsmith RC	1.00	2.50
438 Davone Bess RC	1.50	4.00
439 Erin Henderson RC	1.50	4.00
440 Kalvin McRae RC	1.00	2.50

2008 Select Artist's Proof

*VETS 1-330: 6X TO 15X BASIC CARDS
*ROOKIES 331-440: .8X TO 2X BASIC CARDS
STATED PRINT RUN 32 SER.#'d SETS

2008 Select Gold Zone

*VETS 1-330: 5X TO 12X BASIC CARDS
*ROOKIES 331-440: .6X TO 1.5X BASIC CARDS
STATED PRINT RUN 50 SER.#'d SETS

2008 Select Red Zone

*VETS 1-330: 6X TO 15X BASIC CARDS
*ROOKIES 331-440: .8X TO 2X BASIC CARDS
STATED PRINT RUN 30 SER.#'d SETS

2008 Select Scorecard

*VETS 1-330: 4X TO 10X BASIC CARDS
*ROOKIES 331-440: .5X TO 1.2X BASIC CARDS
STATED PRINT RUN 100 SER.#'d SETS

2008 Select Autographs Gold Zone

GOLD ZONE PRINT RUN 40-50
*RED ZONE/25-30: .5X TO 1.2X GOLD/40-50
RED ZONE PRINT RUN 25-30
UNPRICED END ZONE PRINT RUN 6

331 Jake Long/40	8.00	20.00
332 Chris Long/40	8.00	20.00
333 Matt Ryan/50	60.00	120.00
334 Darren McFadden/50	20.00	50.00
335 Glenn Dorsey/50 EXCH	8.00	20.00

336 Vernon Gholston/40 6.00 15.00
337 Sedrick Ellis/40 8.00 20.00
338 Derrick Harvey/40 5.00 12.00
339 Keith Rivers/40 8.00 20.00
340 Jerod Mayo/40 8.00 20.00
341 Leodis McKelvin/50 6.00 15.00
342 Jonathan Stewart/50 12.00 30.00
343 Dominique Rodgers-Cromartie/40 8.00 20.00
344 Joe Flacco/50 40.00 80.00
345 Aqib Talib/50 8.00 20.00
346 Felix Jones/50 25.00 50.00
347 Rashard Mendenhall/50 15.00 40.00
348 Chris Johnson/40 40.00 80.00
349 Mike Jenkins/50 8.00 20.00
350 Antoine Cason/50 8.00 20.00
351 Lawrence Jackson/50 6.00 15.00
352 Kentwan Balmer/50 6.00 15.00
353 Dustin Keller/40 8.00 20.00
354 Kenny Phillips/40 8.00 20.00
355 Phillip Merling/50 6.00 15.00
356 Donnie Avery/40 6.00 15.00
357 Devin Thomas/40 6.00 15.00
358 Brandon Flowers/50 8.00 20.00
359 Jordy Nelson/40 20.00 40.00
360 Curtis Lofton/50 6.00 15.00
361 John Carlson/50 8.00 20.00
362 Tracy Porter/50 8.00 20.00
363 James Hardy/40 6.00 15.00
364 Eddie Royal/40 8.00 20.00
365 Matt Forte/50 20.00 50.00
366 Jordon Dizon/50 8.00 20.00
367 Jerome Simpson/40 8.00 20.00
368 Fred Davis/50 8.00 20.00
369 DeSean Jackson/40 20.00 50.00
370 Calais Campbell/50 6.00 15.00
371 Malcolm Kelly/40 6.00 15.00
372 Quentin Groves/50 6.00 15.00
373 Limas Sweed/40 8.00 20.00
374 Ray Rice/40 20.00 50.00
375 Brian Brohm/50 8.00 20.00
376 Chad Henne/50 8.00 20.00
377 Dexter Jackson/50 6.00 15.00
378 Martellus Bennett/50 6.00 15.00
379 Terrell Thomas/50 6.00 15.00
380 Kevin Smith/40 8.00 20.00
381 Anthony Alridge/50 6.00 15.00
382 Jacob Hester/50 8.00 20.00
383 Earl Bennett/40 8.00 20.00
384 Jamaal Charles/40 12.00 30.00
385 Dan Connor/50 8.00 20.00
386 Reggie Smith/50 6.00 15.00
387 Brad Cottam/50 6.00 15.00
388 Pat Sims/50 6.00 15.00
389 Dantrell Savage/50 6.00 15.00
390 Early Doucet/40 EXCH 6.00 15.00
391 Harry Douglas/40 EXCH 6.00 15.00
392 Steve Slaton/40 8.00 20.00
393 Jermichael Finley/50 15.00 40.00
394 Kevin O'Connell/40 6.00 15.00
395 Mario Manningham/40 12.50 25.00
396 Andre Caldwell/40 6.00 15.00
397 Will Franklin/50 6.00 15.00
398 Marcus Smith/50 6.00 15.00
399 Martin Rucker/50 6.00 15.00
400 Xavier Adibi/50 5.00 12.00
401 Craig Steltz/50 6.00 15.00
402 Tashard Choice/50 6.00 15.00
403 Lavelle Hawkins/50 5.00 12.00
404 Jacob Tamme/50 8.00 20.00
405 Keenan Burton/50 5.00 12.00
406 John David Booty/40 6.00 15.00
407 Ryan Torain/50 8.00 20.00
408 Tim Hightower/50 12.00 30.00
409 Dennis Dixon/40 12.00 30.00
410 Kellen Davis/50 5.00 12.00
411 Josh Johnson/40 8.00 20.00
412 Erik Ainge/40 8.00 20.00
413 Owen Schmitt/50 8.00 20.00
414 Marcus Thomas/50 6.00 15.00
415 Thomas Brown/50 6.00 15.00
416 Josh Morgan/50 8.00 20.00
417 Kevin Robinson/50 5.00 12.00
418 Colt Brennan/40 15.00 40.00
419 Paul Hubbard/50 6.00 15.00
420 Andre Woodson/40 8.00 20.00
421 Mike Hart/40 8.00 20.00
422 Matt Flynn/40 25.00 60.00
423 Chauncey Washington/50 6.00 15.00
424 Caleb Campbell/50 8.00 20.00
425 Peyton Hillis/50 20.00 50.00
426 Justin Forsett/50 8.00 20.00
427 Adrian Arrington/50 6.00 15.00
428 Cory Boyd/50 5.00 12.00
429 Allen Patrick/50 6.00 15.00
430 Marcus Monk/50 6.00 15.00
431 DJ Hall/50 6.00 15.00
432 Darrell Strong/50 6.00 15.00
433 Jason Rivers/50 6.00 15.00
434 Jed Collins/50 6.00 15.00
435 Paul Smith/50 8.00 20.00
436 Darius Reynaud/50 5.00 12.00
437 Ali Highsmith/50 5.00 12.00
438 Davone Bess/50 8.00 20.00
439 Erin Henderson/50 8.00 20.00
440 Kalvin McRae/50 5.00 12.00

2008 Select Franchise

STATED PRINT RUN 999 SER.#'d SETS
*SCORECARD/100: .8X TO 2X BASIC INSERTS
SCORECARD PRINT RUN 100 SER.#'d SETS
*GOLD ZONE/50: 1.2X TO 3X BASIC INSERTS
GOLD ZONE PRINT RUN 50 SER.#'d SETS
*ARTIST PROOF/32: 1.5X TO 4X BASIC INSERTS
ARTIST'S PROOF PRINT RUN 32 SER.#'d SETS
*RED ZONE/30: 1.5X TO 4X BASIC INSERTS
RED ZONE PRINT RUN 30 SER.#'d SETS
UNPRICED END ZONE PRINT RUN 6
1 Tony Romo 1.25 3.00
2 Tom Brady 1.50 4.00
3 Joseph Addai .75 2.00
4 Randy Moss 1.00 2.50
5 Terrell Owens 1.00 2.50
6 Aaron Rodgers 2.00 5.00
7 T.J. Houshmandzadeh .75 2.00
8 Ben Roethlisberger 1.00 2.50
9 Larry Johnson .75 2.00
10 Drew Brees 1.00 2.50
11 Jay Cutler 1.00 2.50
12 Eli Manning 1.00 2.50
13 Clinton Portis .75 2.00
14 Brian Westbrook .75 2.00
15 Torry Holt .75 2.00
16 Reggie Wayne .75 2.00
17 David Garrard .75 2.00
18 Steve Smith .75 2.00
19 Willie Parker .75 2.00
20 Edgerrin James .75 2.00
21 Andre Johnson .75 2.00
22 LaDainian Tomlinson 1.00 2.50
23 Donald Driver .75 2.00
24 Fred Taylor .75 2.00
25 Peyton Manning 1.50 4.00

2008 Select Future Franchise

STATED PRINT RUN 999 SER.#'d SETS
*SCORECARD/100: .8X TO 2X BASIC INSERTS
SCORECARD PRINT RUN 100 SER.#'d SETS
*GOLD ZONE/50: 1.2X TO 3X BASIC INSERTS
GOLD ZONE PRINT RUN 50 SER.#'d SETS
*ARTIST PROOF/32: 1.5X TO 4X BASIC INSERTS
ARTIST'S PROOF PRINT RUN 32 SER.#'d SETS
*RED ZONE/30: 1.5X TO 4X BASIC INSERTS
RED ZONE PRINT RUN 30 SER.#'d SETS
UNPRICED END ZONE PRINT RUN 6
1 JaMarcus Russell .75 2.00
2 Brady Quinn .75 2.00
3 Brandon Jacobs .75 2.00
4 Adrian Peterson 1.50 4.00
5 Dallas Clark .75 2.00
6 Brandon Marshall .75 2.00
7 Santonio Holmes .75 2.00
8 Dwayne Bowe .75 2.00
9 Laurence Maroney .75 2.00
10 Marion Barber .75 2.00
11 Greg Jennings 1.00 2.50
12 Trent Edwards .60 1.50
13 Wes Welker 1.00 2.50
14 Michael Turner 1.00 2.50
15 Derek Anderson .60 1.50
16 Kevin Curtis .60 1.50
17 Reggie Bush 1.00 2.50
18 Chris Cooley .75 2.00
19 Maurice Jones-Drew .75 2.00
20 Braylon Edwards .75 2.00
21 Willis McGahee .75 2.00
22 Vince Young .75 2.00
23 Frank Gore .75 2.00
24 Roddy White .75 2.00
25 Marques Colston .75 2.00

2008 Select Hot Rookies

STATED PRINT RUN 999 SER.#'d SETS
*SCORECARD/100: .6X TO 1.5X BASIC INSERTS
SCORECARD PRINT RUN 100 SER.#'d SETS
*GOLD ZONE/50: .8X TO 2X BASIC INSERTS
GOLD ZONE PRINT RUN 50 SER.#'d SETS
*ARTIST PROOF/32: 1X TO 2.5X BASIC INSERTS
ARTIST'S PROOF PRINT RUN 32 SER.#'d SETS
*RED ZONE/30: 1X TO 2.5X BASIC INSERTS
RED ZONE PRINT RUN 30 SER.#'d SETS
UNPRICED END ZONE PRINT RUN 6
1 Brian Brohm 1.00 2.50
2 Chad Henne 1.00 2.50
3 Chris Johnson 2.50 6.00
4 Darren McFadden 2.50 6.00
5 DeSean Jackson 2.00 5.00
6 Devin Thomas .75 2.00
7 Dexter Jackson .75 2.00
8 Donnie Avery .75 2.00
9 Eddie Royal 1.00 2.50
10 Felix Jones 1.50 4.00
11 Jamaal Charles 1.50 4.00
12 James Hardy .75 2.00
13 Jerome Simpson 1.00 2.50
14 Joe Flacco 3.00 8.00
15 Jonathan Stewart 1.50 4.00
16 Jordy Nelson 1.25 3.00
17 Kevin Smith 1.00 2.50
18 Limas Sweed 1.00 2.50
19 Malcolm Kelly .75 2.00
20 Mario Manningham 1.00 2.50
21 Matt Forte 1.50 4.00
22 Matt Ryan 4.00 10.00
23 Rashard Mendenhall 2.00 5.00
24 Ray Rice 2.00 5.00
25 Steve Slaton 1.00 2.50

2008 Select Hot Rookies Autographs Gold Zone

GOLD ZONE PRINT RUN 40 SER.#'d SETS
*RED ZONE/25: .5X TO 1.2X GOLD/40
RED ZONE PRINT RUN 25 SER.#'d SETS
UNPRICED END ZONE PRINT RUN 6
1 Brian Brohm 8.00 20.00
2 Chad Henne 8.00 20.00
3 Chris Johnson 40.00 80.00
4 Darren McFadden 20.00 50.00
5 DeSean Jackson 20.00 50.00
6 Devin Thomas 6.00 15.00
7 Dexter Jackson 6.00 15.00
8 Donnie Avery 6.00 15.00
9 Eddie Royal 8.00 20.00
10 Felix Jones 20.00 50.00
11 Jamaal Charles 12.00 30.00
12 James Hardy 6.00 15.00
13 Jerome Simpson 8.00 20.00
14 Joe Flacco 50.00 100.00
15 Jonathan Stewart 12.00 30.00
16 Jordy Nelson 20.00 40.00
17 Kevin Smith 8.00 20.00
18 Limas Sweed 8.00 20.00
19 Malcolm Kelly 6.00 15.00
20 Mario Manningham 12.50 25.00
21 Matt Forte 20.00 50.00
22 Matt Ryan 60.00 120.00
23 Rashard Mendenhall 15.00 40.00
24 Ray Rice 20.00 50.00
25 Steve Slaton 8.00 20.00

2008 Select Inscriptions

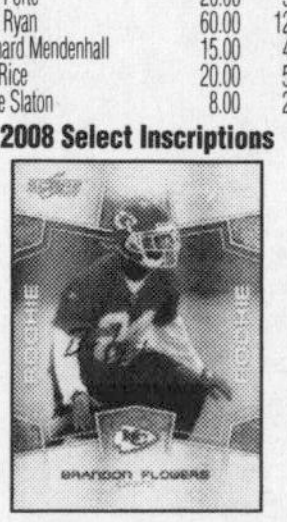

STATED PRINT RUN 25-750
331 Jake Long/375 4.00 10.00
332 Chris Long/50 6.00 15.00
333 Matt Ryan/25 75.00 150.00
334 Darren McFadden/25 30.00 80.00
335 Glenn Dorsey/500 No AU 2.00 5.00
336 Vernon Gholston/50 5.00 12.00
337 Sedrick Ellis/375 4.00 10.00
338 Derrick Harvey/450 2.50 6.00
339 Keith Rivers/50 6.00 15.00
340 Jerod Mayo/375 4.00 10.00
341 Leodis McKelvin/500 3.00 8.00
342 Jonathan Stewart/25 15.00 40.00
343 Dominique Rodgers-Cromartie/375 4.00 10.00
344 Joe Flacco/25 50.00 100.00
345 Aqib Talib/500 4.00 10.00
346 Felix Jones/25 30.00 80.00
347 Rashard Mendenhall/25 30.00 80.00
348 Chris Johnson/50 30.00 80.00
349 Mike Jenkins/375 4.00 10.00
350 Antoine Cason/500 4.00 10.00
351 Lawrence Jackson/500 3.00 8.00
352 Kentwan Balmer/500 3.00 8.00
353 Dustin Keller/50 6.00 15.00
354 Kenny Phillips/375 4.00 10.00
355 Phillip Merling/500 3.00 8.00
356 Donnie Avery/25 8.00 20.00
357 Devin Thomas/50 5.00 12.00
358 Brandon Flowers/500 4.00 10.00
359 Jordy Nelson/25 30.00 60.00
360 Curtis Lofton/750 3.00 8.00
361 John Carlson/375 4.00 10.00
362 Tracy Porter/750 5.00 12.00
363 James Hardy/25 8.00 20.00
364 Eddie Royal/25 12.00 30.00
365 Matt Forte/100 20.00 50.00
366 Jordon Dizon/750 4.00 10.00
367 Jerome Simpson/50 6.00 15.00
368 Fred Davis/375 4.00 10.00
369 DeSean Jackson/25 30.00 60.00
370 Calais Campbell/750 3.00 8.00
371 Malcolm Kelly/25 8.00 20.00
372 Quentin Groves/750 3.00 8.00
373 Limas Sweed/25 10.00 25.00
374 Ray Rice/50 20.00 50.00
375 Brian Brohm/25 10.00 25.00
376 Chad Henne/25 10.00 25.00
377 Dexter Jackson/50 5.00 12.00
378 Martellus Bennett/375 3.00 8.00
379 Terrell Thomas/500 3.00 8.00
380 Kevin Smith/50 6.00 15.00
381 Anthony Alridge/750 3.00 8.00
382 Jacob Hester/500 4.00 10.00
383 Earl Bennett/50 6.00 15.00
384 Jamaal Charles/50 15.00 30.00
385 Dan Connor/50 6.00 15.00
386 Reggie Smith/500 3.00 8.00
387 Brad Cottam/750 3.00 8.00
388 Pat Sims/500 3.00 8.00
389 Dantrell Savage/750 3.00 8.00
390 Early Doucet/50 EXCH 5.00 12.00
391 Harry Douglas/50 EXCH 5.00 12.00
392 Steve Slaton/50 6.00 15.00
393 Jermichael Finley/375 12.00 30.00
394 Kevin O'Connell/50 5.00 12.00
395 Mario Manningham/50 8.00 20.00
396 Andre Caldwell/50 5.00 12.00
397 Will Franklin/750 3.00 8.00
398 Marcus Smith/750 3.00 8.00
399 Martin Rucker/750 3.00 8.00
400 Xavier Adibi/375 2.50 6.00
401 Craig Steltz/76 5.00 12.00
402 Tashard Choice/100 5.00 12.00
403 Lavelle Hawkins/500 2.50 6.00
404 Jacob Tamme/500 4.00 10.00
405 Keenan Burton/500 2.50 6.00
406 John David Booty/50 5.00 12.00
407 Ryan Torain/500 4.00 10.00
408 Tim Hightower/750 6.00 15.00
409 Dennis Dixon/25 15.00 40.00
410 Kellen Davis/750 2.50 6.00
411 Josh Johnson/50 6.00 15.00
412 Erik Ainge/50 6.00 15.00
413 Owen Schmitt/750 4.00 10.00
414 Marcus Thomas/500 3.00 8.00
415 Thomas Brown/375 3.00 8.00
416 Josh Morgan/750 4.00 10.00
417 Kevin Robinson/750 2.50 6.00
418 Colt Brennan/25 15.00 40.00
419 Paul Hubbard/750 3.00 8.00
420 Andre Woodson/25 10.00 25.00
421 Mike Hart/50 6.00 15.00
422 Matt Flynn/50 25.00 60.00
423 Chauncey Washington/750 3.00 8.00
424 Caleb Campbell/750 4.00 10.00
425 Peyton Hillis/750 12.00 30.00
426 Justin Forsett/750 4.00 10.00
427 Adrian Arrington/750 3.00 8.00
428 Cory Boyd/750 2.50 6.00
429 Allen Patrick/500 3.00 8.00
430 Marcus Monk/656 3.00 8.00
431 DJ Hall/520 3.00 8.00
432 Darrell Strong/750 3.00 8.00
433 Jason Rivers/750 3.00 8.00
434 Jed Collins/604 3.00 8.00
435 Paul Smith/750 4.00 10.00
436 Darius Reynaud/375 2.50 6.00
437 Ali Highsmith/750 2.50 6.00
438 Davone Bess/750 4.00 10.00
439 Erin Henderson/750 4.00 10.00
440 Kalvin McRae/535 2.50 6.00

2008 Select Young Stars

STATED PRINT RUN 999 SER.#'d SETS
*SCORECARD/100: .8X TO 2X BASIC INSERTS
SCORECARD PRINT RUN 100 SER.#'d SETS
*GOLD ZONE/50: 1.2X TO 3X BASIC INSERTS
GOLD ZONE PRINT RUN 50 SER.#'d SETS
*ARTIST PROOF/32: 1.5X TO 4X BASIC INSERTS
ARTIST'S PROOF PRINT RUN 32 SER.#'d SETS
*RED ZONE/30: 1.5X TO 4X BASIC INSERTS
RED ZONE PRINT RUN 30 SER.#'d SETS
END ZONE PRINT RUN 6 SER.#'d SETS
1 Earnest Graham .60 1.50
2 Anthony Gonzalez .60 1.50
3 Ted Ginn Jr. .75 2.00
4 Marshawn Lynch .75 2.00
5 Calvin Johnson 1.00 2.50
6 Steve Smith USC .75 2.00
7 Kenny Watson .60 1.50
8 Vernon Davis .75 2.00
9 LenDale White .75 2.00
10 Vincent Jackson .60 1.50
11 Kolby Smith .60 1.50
12 Selvin Young .60 1.50
13 Patrick Willis .75 2.00
14 Lee Evans .75 2.00
15 Ahmad Bradshaw .75 2.00
16 Justin Fargas .60 1.50
17 Tarvaris Jackson .75 2.00
18 DeMeco Ryans .75 2.00
19 Fred Jackson 4.00 10.00
20 Patrick Crayton .75 2.00
21 James Jones .60 1.50
22 Michael Bush .75 2.00
23 Sidney Rice 1.00 2.50
24 LaRon Landry .75 2.00
25 Zach Miller .75 2.00

1995 Select Certified

The first year product from Pinnacle was offered in six card packs with a suggested retail price of $4.99/pack. The set contains 135 cards with seven checklist cards inserted at one per pack. Card fronts feature an all-foil silver black and white background with the player shot in color. The player's name is located at the bottom right. Card backs are horizontal with statistical and biographical information. Also, a NFL Super Bowl Instant Win Card was randomly inserted at a rate of one in 1,264,000 packs. Card #78 (Deion Sanders) was not issued in pack form, rather he was issued later in December '95 through a mail offering to Pinnacle direct dealers. Rookie cards include Jeff Blake, Ki-Jana Carter, Kerry Collins, Terrell Davis, Joey Galloway, Curtis Martin, Napoleon Kaufman, Rashaan Salaam, Kordell Stewart, J.J. Stokes, Rodney Thomas and Michael Westbrook. Three promo card were produced and priced below.

COMPLETE SET (135) 15.00 40.00
1 Marshall Faulk 1.50 4.00
2 Heath Shuler .20 .50
3 Garrison Hearst .40 1.00
4 Errict Rhett .20 .50
5 Jeff George .20 .50
6 Jerome Bettis .40 1.00
7 Jim Kelly .40 1.00
8 Rick Mirer .20 .50
9 Willie Davis .20 .50
10 Steve Young 1.00 2.50
11 Erik Kramer .08 .25
12 Natrone Means .20 .50
13 Jeff Blake RC 1.25 3.00
14 Neil O'Donnell .20 .50
15 Andre Rison .20 .50
16 Randall Cunningham .40 1.00
17 Emmitt Smith 2.00 5.00
18 Tim Brown .40 1.00
19 Shannon Sharpe .20 .50
20 Boomer Esiason .20 .50
21 Barry Sanders 2.00 5.00
22 Rodney Hampton .20 .50
23 Robert Brooks .40 1.00
24 Jim Everett .08 .25
25 Gary Brown .08 .25
26 Drew Bledsoe .50 1.25
27 Desmond Howard .20 .50
28 Cris Carter .40 1.00
29 Marcus Allen .40 1.00
30 Dan Marino 2.50 6.00
31 Warren Moon .20 .50
32 Dave Krieg .08 .25
33 Ben Coates .20 .50
34 Terance Mathis .20 .50
35 Mario Bates .20 .50
36 Andre Reed .20 .50
37 Dave Brown .20 .50
38 Jeff Graham .08 .25
39 Johnny Mitchell .08 .25
40 Carl Pickens .20 .50
41 Jeff Hostetler .20 .50
42 Vinny Testaverde .20 .50
43 Ricky Watters .20 .50
44 Troy Aikman 1.25 3.00
45 Byron Bam Morris .08 .25
46 John Elway 2.50 6.00
47 Junior Seau .40 1.00
48 Scott Mitchell .20 .50
49 Jerry Rice 1.25 3.00
50 Brett Favre 2.50 6.00
51 Chris Warren .20 .50
52 Chris Chandler .20 .50
53 Lorenzo White .08 .25
54 Craig Erickson .08 .25
55 Alvin Harper .08 .25
56 Steve Beuerlein .20 .50
57 Edgar Bennett .20 .50
58 Steve Bono .20 .50
59 Eric Green .08 .25
60 Jake Reed .20 .50
61 Terry Kirby .20 .50
62 Vincent Brisby .08 .25
63 Lake Dawson .20 .50
64 Torrance Small .08 .25
65 Mark Brunell .50 1.25
66 Haywood Jeffires .08 .25
67 Flipper Anderson .08 .25
68 Ronald Moore .08 .25
69 LeShon Johnson .20 .50
70 Rocket Ismail .20 .50
71 Herman Moore .40 1.00
72 Charlie Garner .40 1.00
73 Anthony Miller .20 .50
74 Greg Lloyd .20 .50
75 Michael Irvin .40 1.00
76 Stan Humphries .20 .50
77 Leroy Hoard .08 .25
78 Deion Sanders 1.25 3.00
Card mailed to dealers
79 Darnay Scott .20 .50
80 Chris Miller .08 .25
81 Curtis Conway .40 1.00
82 Trent Dilfer .40 1.00
83 Bruce Smith .40 1.00
84 Reggie Brooks .20 .50
85 Frank Reich .08 .25
86 Henry Ellard .20 .50
87 Eric Metcalf .20 .50
88 Sean Gilbert .20 .50
89 Larry Centers .20 .50
90 Ricky Ervins .08 .25
91 Craig Heyward .20 .50
92 Rod Woodson .20 .50
93 Steve Walsh .08 .25
94 Fred Barnett .20 .50
95 William Floyd .20 .50
96 Harvey Williams .08 .25
97 Greg Hill .20 .50
98 Irving Fryar .20 .50
99 Kevin Williams .20 .50
100 Herschel Walker .20 .50
101 Sean Dawkins .20 .50
102 Michael Haynes .20 .50
103 Reggie White .40 1.00
104 Robert Smith .40 1.00
105 Todd Collins RC 2.50 6.00
106 Michael Westbrook RC .75 2.00
107 Frank Sanders RC .75 2.00
108 Christian Fauria RC .40 1.00
109 Stoney Case RC .20 .50
110 Jimmy Oliver RC .20 .50
111 Mark Bruener RC .40 1.00
112 Rodney Thomas RC .40 1.00
113 Chris T.Jones RC .20 .50
114 James A.Stewart RC .20 .50
115 Kevin Carter RC .75 2.00
116 Eric Zeier RC .75 2.00
117 Curtis Martin RC 6.00 15.00
118 James O. Stewart RC 2.00 5.00
119 Joe Aska RC .20 .50
120 Ken Dilger RC .75 2.00
121 Tyrone Wheatley RC 2.00 5.00
122 Ray Zellars RC .40 1.00
123 Kyle Brady RC .75 2.00
124 Chad May RC .20 .50
125 Napoleon Kaufman RC 2.00 5.00
126 Terrell Davis RC 5.00 12.00
127 Warren Sapp RC 2.50 6.00
128 Sherman Williams RC .20 .50
129 Kordell Stewart RC 3.00 8.00
130 Ki-Jana Carter RC .75 2.00
131 Terrell Fletcher RC .20 .50
132 Rashaan Salaam RC .40 1.00
133 J.J. Stokes RC .75 2.00
134 Kerry Collins RC 4.00 8.00
135 Joey Galloway RC 3.00 8.00
P7 Dan Marino Promo 2.00 5.00
Gold Team Card
P10 Steve Young Promo .75 2.00
P44 Troy Aikman Promo 1.00 2.50

1995 Select Certified Mirror Gold

COMPLETE SET (135) 125.00 300.00
*MIRROR GOLD STARS: 2X TO 5X BASIC CARDS
*MIRROR GOLD RCs: 1X TO 2.5X BASIC CARDS
MIRROR GOLDS: STATED ODDS 1:5

1995 Select Certified Checklists

These cards were inserted one per pack in Select Certified and feature different members of the Quarterback Club on the card fronts with numerical checklists on the back.

COMPLETE SET (7) .60 1.50
1 Drew Bledsoe .15 .40
2 John Elway .25 .60
3 Dan Marino .25 .60
4 Brett Favre .25 .60
5 Troy Aikman .15 .40
6 Steve Young .10 .30
7 Rick Mirer UER .07 .20
Randall Cunningham
Gold Team list incorrect

1995 Select Certified Future

COMPLETE SET (10) 20.00 50.00
STATED ODDS 1:19
1 Ki-Jana Carter .75 2.00
2 Steve McNair 6.00 15.00
3 Kerry Collins 3.00 8.00
4 Michael Westbrook 1.25 3.00
5 Joey Galloway 3.00 8.00
6 J.J. Stokes 1.25 3.00
7 Rashaan Salaam .75 2.00
8 Tyrone Wheatley 2.00 5.00
9 Todd Collins 3.00 8.00
10 Curtis Martin 6.00 15.00

1995 Select Certified Gold Team

COMPLETE SET (10) 50.00 120.00
STATED ODDS 1:41
1 Jerry Rice 5.00 12.00
2 Emmitt Smith 8.00 20.00
3 Drew Bledsoe 2.00 5.00
4 Marshall Faulk 6.00 15.00
5 Troy Aikman 5.00 12.00
6 Barry Sanders 8.00 20.00
7 Dan Marino 10.00 25.00
8 Errict Rhett .75 2.00
9 Brett Favre 10.00 25.00
10 Steve McNair 7.50 20.00

1995 Select Certified Select Few

COMPLETE SET (20) 50.00 120.00
STATED ODDS 1:32
PRICED CARDS ARE NUMBERED OF 2250
*1028 CARDS: .8X TO 2X BASIC INSERTS
1 Dan Marino 10.00 25.00
2 Emmitt Smith 8.00 20.00
3 Marshall Faulk 6.00 15.00
4 Barry Sanders 8.00 20.00
5 Drew Bledsoe 2.00 5.00
6 Brett Favre 10.00 25.00
7 Troy Aikman 5.00 12.00
8 Jerry Rice 5.00 12.00
9 Steve Young 4.00 10.00
10 Natrone Means .75 2.00
11 Byron Bam Morris .40 1.00
12 Errict Rhett .75 2.00
13 John Elway 10.00 25.00
14 Heath Shuler .75 2.00
15 Ki-Jana Carter 1.25 3.00
16 Kerry Collins 5.00 12.00
17 Steve McNair 7.50 20.00
18 Rashaan Salaam .60 1.50
19 Tyrone Wheatley 3.00 8.00
20 J.J. Stokes 1.25 3.00

1996 Select Certified

The 1996 Select Certified set was issued in one series totalling 125 cards. The six-card packs retail for $4.99 each. The cards feature color player photos on 24-point silver mirror card stock. The set includes 30 rookie cards and a special Silver Spiral subset (116-125) which honors ten of the Quarterback Club's superstar elite. Too many promos were produced to properly catalog for this book. Many of the promos apparently were made for the various Mirror parallels and usually sell at a heavy discount over the base cards.

COMPLETE SET (125) 20.00 50.00
1 Isaac Bruce .30 .75
2 Rick Mirer .15 .40
3 Jake Reed .15 .40
4 Reggie White .30 .75
5 Harvey Williams .07 .20
6 Jim Everett .07 .20
7 Tony Martin .15 .40
8 Craig Heyward .07 .20
9 Tamarick Vanover .15 .40
10 Hugh Douglas .15 .40
11 Erik Kramer .07 .20
12 Charlie Garner .15 .40
13 Erric Pegram .07 .20
14 Scott Mitchell .15 .40
15 Michael Westbrook .30 .75
16 Robert Smith .15 .40
17 Kerry Collins .30 .75
18 Derek Loville .07 .20
19 Jeff Blake .30 .75
20 Terry Kirby .15 .40
21 Bruce Smith .15 .40
22 Stan Humphries .15 .40
23 Rodney Thomas .07 .20
24 Wayne Chrebet .30 .75
25 Napoleon Kaufman .30 .75
26 Marshall Faulk .40 1.00
27 Emmitt Smith 1.25 3.00
28 Natrone Means .15 .40
29 Neil O'Donnell .15 .40
30 Warren Moon .15 .40
31 Junior Seau .30 .75
32 Chris Sanders .15 .40
33 Barry Sanders 1.25 3.00
34 Jeff Graham .07 .20
35 Kordell Stewart .30 .75
36 Jim Harbaugh .15 .40
37 Chris Warren .15 .40
38 Cris Carter .30 .75
39 J.J. Stokes .30 .75
40 Tyrone Wheatley .15 .40
41 Terrell Davis .60 1.50
42 Mark Brunell .30 .75
43 Steve Young .60 1.50
44 Rodney Hampton .15 .40
45 Drew Bledsoe .50 1.25
46 Larry Centers .15 .40
47 Ken Norton Jr. .07 .20
48 Deion Sanders .50 1.25
49 Alvin Harper .07 .20
50 Trent Dilfer .30 .75
51 Steve McNair .60 1.50
52 Robert Brooks .30 .75
53 Edgar Bennett .15 .40
54 Troy Aikman .75 2.00
55 Dan Marino 1.50 4.00
56 Steve Bono .07 .20
57 Marcus Allen .30 .75
58 Rodney Peete .07 .20
59 Ben Coates .15 .40
60 Yancey Thigpen .15 .40
61 Tim Brown .30 .75
62 Jerry Rice .75 2.00
63 Quinn Early .07 .20
64 Ricky Watters .15 .40
65 Thurman Thomas .30 .75
66 Greg Lloyd .15 .40
67 Eric Metcalf .07 .20
68 Jeff George .15 .40
69 John Elway 1.50 4.00
70 Frank Sanders .15 .40
71 Curtis Conway .30 .75
72 Greg Hill .15 .40
73 Darick Holmes .07 .20
74 Herman Moore .15 .40
75 Carl Pickens .15 .40
76 Eric Zeier .07 .20
77 Curtis Martin .60 1.50
78 Rashaan Salaam .15 .40
79 Joey Galloway .30 .75
80 Jeff Hostetler .07 .20
81 Jim Kelly .30 .75
82 Dave Brown .07 .20
83 Sean Dawkins .07 .20
84 Michael Irvin .30 .75
85 Brett Favre 1.50 4.00
86 Cedric Jones RC .08 .25
87 Jeff Lewis RC .20 .50
88 Alex Van Dyke RC .20 .50
89 Regan Upshaw RC .08 .25
90 Karim Abdul-Jabbar RC .40 1.00
91 Marvin Harrison RC 3.00 8.00
92 Stephen Davis RC 1.50 4.00
93 Terry Glenn RC 1.00 2.50
94 Kevin Hardy RC .40 1.00
95 Stanley Pritchett RC .08 .25
96 Willie Anderson RC .08 .25
97 Lawrence Phillips RC .20 .50
98 Bobby Hoying RC .40 1.00
99 Amani Toomer RC 1.25 3.00
100 Eddie George RC 2.00 5.00
101 Stepfret Williams RC .08 .25
102 Eric Moulds RC .40 1.00
103 Simeon Rice RC .75 2.00
104 John Mobley RC .08 .25
105 Keyshawn Johnson RC 1.25 3.00
106 Daryl Gardener RC .08 .25
107 Tony Banks RC .40 1.00
108 Bobby Engram RC .40 1.00
109 Jonathan Ogden RC .40 1.00
110 Eddie Kennison RC .40 1.00
111 Danny Kanell RC .40 1.00
112 Tony Brackens RC .40 1.00
113 Tim Biakabutuka RC .40 1.00
114 Leeland McElroy RC .20 .50
115 Rickey Dudley RC .40 1.00
116 Troy Aikman SS .40 1.00
117 Brett Favre SS .75 2.00
118 Drew Bledsoe SS .30 .75
119 Steve Young SS .30 .75
120 Kerry Collins SS .30 .75
121 John Elway SS .75 2.00
122 Dan Marino SS .75 2.00
123 Kordell Stewart SS .30 .75
124 Jeff Blake SS .15 .40
125 Jim Harbaugh SS .15 .40

1996 Select Certified Artist's Proofs

COMPLETE SET (125) 200.00 400.00
*STARS: 2.5X TO 6X BASIC CARDS
*RCs: 1.2X TO 3X BASIC CARDS
STATED ODDS 1:18
STATED PRINT RUN 500 SETS

1996 Select Certified Blue

COMPLETE SET (125) 500.00 1,000.00
*STARS: 6X TO 15X BASIC CARDS
*RCs: 2.5X TO 6X
STATED ODDS 1:50
STATED PRINT RUN 200 SETS

1996 Select Certified Mirror Blue

*MIR.BLUE STARS: 15X TO 40X BASIC CARDS
*MIR.BLUE RC'S: 6X TO 15X
STATED ODDS 1:200
STATED PRINT RUN 50 SETS

1996 Select Certified Mirror Gold

*1-125 VETS: 20X TO 50X BASIC CARDS
*86-115 ROOKIE STARS: 6X TO 15X
STATED ODDS 1:300
STATED PRINT RUN 35 SETS

1996 Select Certified Mirror Red

COMPLETE SET (125)
*MIR.RED STARS: 8X TO 20X BASIC CARDS
*MIR.RED RCs: 3X TO 8X
MIRROR RED STATED ODDS 1:100
MIRROR RED STATED PRINT RUN 90 SETS

1996 Select Certified Mirror Red Premium Stock

*1-125 VETS: 40X TO 100X BASIC CARDS
*ROOKIE STARS: 12X TO 30X
RED PS ANNOUNCED PRINT RUN 20

1996 Select Certified Premium Stock

COMPLETE SET (125) 30.00 8.00
*PREM.STOCK: .8X TO 2X BASIC CARDS
STATED PRINT RUN LESS THAN 7000 SETS

1996 Select Certified Red

COMPLETE SET (125) 150.00 300.00
*STARS: 2X TO 5X BASIC CARDS
*RCs: 1X TO 2.5X BASIC CARDS
STATED ODDS 1:5
STATED PRINT RUN 2000 SETS

1996 Select Certified Gold Team

COMPLETE SET (18) 75.00 150.00
STATED ODDS 1:38
1 Emmitt Smith 6.00 15.00
2 Barry Sanders 6.00 15.00
3 Dan Marino 8.00 20.00
4 Steve Young 3.00 8.00
5 Troy Aikman 4.00 10.00
6 Jerry Rice 4.00 10.00
7 Rashaan Salaam .75 2.00
8 Marshall Faulk 2.00 5.00
9 Drew Bledsoe 2.50 6.00
10 Steve McNair 3.00 8.00
11 Brett Favre 8.00 20.00
12 Terrell Davis 3.00 8.00
13 Kordell Stewart 1.50 4.00
14 Keyshawn Johnson 3.00 8.00
15 Kerry Collins 1.50 4.00
16 Curtis Martin 3.00 8.00
17 Isaac Bruce 1.50 4.00
18 Terry Glenn 3.00 8.00

1996 Select Certified Thumbs Up

COMPLETE SET (24) 125.00 250.00
STATED ODDS 1:41
1 Steve Young 4.00 10.00
2 Jeff Blake 2.00 5.00
3 Dan Marino 10.00 25.00
4 Kerry Collins 2.00 5.00
5 John Elway 10.00 25.00
6 Neil O'Donnell 1.00 2.50
7 Brett Favre 10.00 25.00
8 Scott Mitchell 1.00 2.50
9 Troy Aikman 5.00 12.00
10 Jim Harbaugh 1.00 2.50
11 Drew Bledsoe 3.00 8.00
12 Jeff Hostetler .50 1.25
13 Marvin Harrison 10.00 25.00
14 Tim Biakabutuka .75 2.00
15 Eddie George 5.00 12.00
16 Tony Brackens .75 2.00
17 Karim Abdul-Jabbar .75 2.00
18 Daryl Gardener .20 .50
19 Alex Van Dyke .40 1.00
20 Terry Glenn 3.00 8.00
21 Eric Moulds 4.00 10.00
22 Eddie Kennison .75 2.00
23 Regan Upshaw .20 .50
24 Mike Alstott 3.00 8.00

1972 7-Eleven Slurpee Cups

Seven-Eleven stores released two series of football player cups in the early 1970s. Each white plastic cup measures roughly 5-1/4" tall, 3-1/4" in diameter at the mouth and 2" at the base. The fronts feature a color portrait of a player along with his name and team name. In many cases, a facsimile autograph appears between the bottom of the portrait and the player's name. All of the players pictured are helmetless. The backs include basic biographical information along with the 7-Eleven logo at the top and the player's team helmet at the bottom. The unnumbered cups are arranged below alphabetically. Both years are very similar in design. The 1972 release is distinguished by the smaller type face used on the player's name (1/16" tall) and the lack of the "Made in USA" tag that runs down the sides of the 1973 cups.

COMPLETE SET (60) 75.00 150.00
1 Donny Anderson 1.00 2.50
2 Elvin Bethea 1.00 2.50
3 Fred Biletnikoff 2.00 5.00
4 Bill Bradley .75 2.00
5 Terry Bradshaw 5.00 12.00
6 Larry Brown 1.00 2.50
7 Willie Brown 1.25 3.00
8 Norm Bulaich .75 2.00
9 Dick Butkus 3.00 8.00
10 Ray Chester .75 2.00
11 Bill Curry .75 2.00
12 Len Dawson 1.50 4.00
13 Willie Ellison .75 2.00
14 Ed Flanagan .75 2.00
15 Gary Garrison .75 2.00
16 Gale Gillingham .75 2.00
17 Joe Greene 1.50 4.00
18 Cedrick Hardman .75 2.00
19 Jim Hart 1.25 3.00
20 Ted Hendricks 1.25 3.00
21 Winston Hill .75 2.00
22 Ken Houston 1.25 3.00
23 Chuck Howley 1.00 2.50
24 Claude Humphrey .75 2.00
25 Roy Jefferson .75 2.00
26 Sonny Jurgensen 1.50 4.00
27 Leroy Kelly 1.25 3.00
28 Paul Krause 1.00 2.50
29 George Kunz .75 2.00
30 Jake Kupp .75 2.00
31 Ted Kwalick .75 2.00
32 Willie Lanier 1.25 3.00
33 Bob Lilly 1.50 4.00
34 Floyd Little 1.00 2.50
35 Larry Little 1.25 3.00
36 Tom Mack 1.00 2.50
37 Milt Morin .75 2.00
38 Mercury Morris 1.25 3.00
39 John Niland .75 2.00
40 Jim Otto 1.25 3.00

41 Steve Owens	1.00	2.50
42 Alan Page	1.25	3.00
43 Jim Plunkett	1.25	3.00
44 Mike Reid	1.25	3.00
45 Mel Renfro	1.25	3.00
46 Isiah Robertson	.75	2.00
47 Andy Russell	1.00	2.50
48 Charlie Sanders	1.00	2.50
49 O.J. Simpson	2.50	6.00
50 Bubba Smith	1.25	3.00
51 Bill Stanfill	1.00	2.50
52 Jan Stenerud	1.25	3.00
53 Walt Sweeney	.75	2.00
54 Bob Tucker	.75	2.00
55 Jim Tyrer	.75	2.00
56 Rick Volk	.75	2.00
57 Gene Washington 49er	1.00	2.50
58 Dave Wilcox	1.00	2.50
59 Del Williams	.75	2.00
60 Ron Yary	1.25	3.00
NNO Picture Checklist	6.00	15.00

1973 7-Eleven Slurpee Cups

Seven-Eleven stores released two series of football player cups in the early 1970s. Each white plastic cup measures roughly 5-1/4" tall, 3-1/4" in diameter at the mouth and 2" at the base. The fronts feature a color portrait of a player along with his name and team name. In many cases, a facsimile autograph appears between the bottom of the portrait and the player's name. All of the players pictured are helmetless. The backs include basic biographical information along with the 7-Eleven logo at the top and the player's team helmet at the bottom. The unnumbered cups are arranged below alphabetically. Both years are very similar in design. The 1973 issue is distinguished by the larger type face used on the player's name (1/8" tall) and the words "Made in USA" that run down the sides of the cups.

COMPLETE SET (1-80)	125.00	250.00
1 Dan Abramowicz	1.25	3.00
2 Ken Anderson	2.00	5.00
3 Jim Beirne	1.00	2.50
4 Ed Bell	1.00	2.50
5 Bob Berry	1.00	2.50
6 Jim Bertelsen	1.00	2.50
7 Marlin Briscoe	1.00	2.50
8 John Brockington	1.00	2.50
9 Larry Brown	1.25	3.00
10 Buck Buchanan	1.50	4.00
11 Dick Butkus	5.00	12.00
12 Larry Carwell	1.00	2.50
13 Rich Caster	1.00	2.50
14 Bobby Douglass	1.00	2.50
15 Pete Duranko	1.00	2.50
16 Cid Edwards	1.00	2.50
17 Mel Farr	1.00	2.50
18 Pat Fischer	1.00	2.50
19 Mike Garrett	1.25	3.00
20 Walt Garrison	1.25	3.00
21 George Goeddeke	1.00	2.50
22 Bob Gresham	1.00	2.50
23 Jack Ham	2.50	6.00
24 Chris Hanburger	1.25	3.00
25 Franco Harris	5.00	12.00
26 Calvin Hill	1.25	3.00
27 J.D. Hill	1.00	2.50
28 Marv Hubbard	1.00	2.50
29 Scott Hunter	1.00	2.50
30 Harold Jackson	1.25	3.00
31 Randy Jackson	1.00	2.50
32 Bob Johnson	1.00	2.50
33 Jim Johnson	1.50	4.00
34 Ron Johnson	1.00	2.50
35 Leroy Keyes	1.00	2.50
36 Greg Landry	1.25	3.00
37 Gary Larsen	1.00	2.50
38 Frank Lewis	1.00	2.50
39 Bob Lilly	2.00	5.00
40 Dale Lindsey	1.00	2.50
41 Larry Little	1.50	4.00
42 Spider Lockhart	1.00	2.50
43 Mike Lucci	1.00	2.50
44 Jim Lynch	1.00	2.50
45 Art Malone	1.00	2.50
46 Ed Marinaro	1.25	3.00
47 Jim Marshall	1.50	4.00
48 Ray May	1.00	2.50
49 Don Maynard	2.00	5.00
50 Don McCauley	1.00	2.50
51 Mike McCoy	1.00	2.50
52 Tom Mitchell	1.00	2.50
53 Tommy Nobis	1.25	3.00
54 Dan Pastorini	1.25	3.00
55 Mac Percival	1.00	2.50
56 Mike Phipps	1.25	3.00
57 Ed Podolak	1.00	2.50
58 John Reaves	1.00	2.50
59 Tim Rossovich	1.00	2.50
60 Bo Scott	1.00	2.50
61 Ron Sellers	1.00	2.50
62 Dennis Shaw	1.00	2.50
63 Mike Siani	1.00	2.50
64 O.J. Simpson	3.00	8.00
65 Bubba Smith	1.50	4.00
66 Larry Smith	1.00	2.50
67 Jackie Smith	1.50	4.00
68 Norm Snead	1.25	3.00
69 Jack Snow	1.25	3.00
70 Steve Spurrier	2.50	6.00
71 Doug Swift	1.00	2.50
72 Jack Tatum	1.50	4.00
73 Bruce Taylor	1.00	2.50
74 Otis Taylor	1.25	3.00
75 Bob Trumpy	1.25	3.00
76 Jim Turner	1.00	2.50
77 Phil Villapiano	1.25	3.00
78 Roger Wehrli	1.25	3.00
79 Ken Willard	1.00	2.50
80 Jack Youngblood	1.50	4.00
NNO Picture Checklist	10.00	25.00

1983 7-Eleven Discs

This set of 15 discs, each measuring approximately 1 3/4" in diameter, features an alternating portrait and action picture of each of the players listed below. The set was sponsored by 7-Eleven Stores (Southland Corporation) and distributed through an in-store promotion.

COMPLETE SET (15)	12.50	25.00
1 Franco Harris	.75	2.00
2 Dan Fouts	.75	2.00
3 Lee Roy Selmon	.50	1.25
4 Nolan Cromwell	.30	.75
5 Marcus Allen	2.50	6.00
6 Joe Montana	4.00	10.00
7 Kellen Winslow	.50	1.25
8 Hugh Green	.30	.75
9 Ted Hendricks	.50	1.25
10 Danny White	.50	1.25
11 Wes Chandler	.30	.75
12 Jimmie Giles	.30	.75
13 Jack Youngblood	.40	1.00
14 Lester Hayes	.40	1.00
15 Vince Ferragamo	.40	1.00

1984 7-Eleven Discs

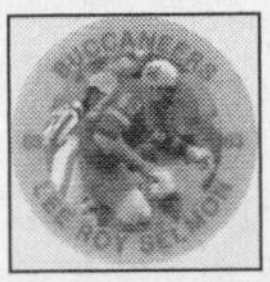

This set of 40 discs, each measuring approximately 1 3/4" in diameter, features an alternating portrait and action picture of each of the players listed below. The set was sponsored by 7-Eleven Stores (Southland Corporation) and distributed through an in-store promotion. The discs in the set are grouped into two subsets, East (E prefix) and West (W prefix). Some players were included in both subsets.

COMPLETE SET (40)	25.00	50.00
E1 Franco Harris	.50	1.25
E2 Lawrence Taylor	.50	1.25
E3 Mark Gastineau	.20	.50
E4 Lee Roy Selmon	.30	.75
E5 Ken Anderson	.30	.75
E6 Walter Payton	2.00	5.00
E7 Ken Stabler	.50	1.25
E8 Marcus Allen	.60	1.50
E9 Fred Smerlas	.20	.50
E10 Ozzie Newsome	.30	.75
E11 Steve Bartkowski	.30	.75
E12 Tony Dorsett	.50	1.25
E13 John Riggins	.40	1.00
E14 Billy Sims	.30	.75
E15 Dan Marino	5.00	12.00
E16 Tony Collins	.20	.50
E17 Curtis Dickey	.20	.50
E18 Ron Jaworski	.20	.50
E19 William Andrews	.20	.50
E20 Joe Theismann	.40	1.00
W1 Franco Harris	.50	1.25
W2 Joe Montana	4.00	10.00
W3 Matt Blair	.20	.50
W4 Warren Moon	.40	1.00
W5 Marcus Allen	.60	1.50
W6 John Riggins	.40	1.00
W7 Walter Payton	2.00	5.00
W8 Vince Ferragamo	.20	.50
W9 Billy Sims	.30	.75
W10 Ken Anderson	.30	.75
W11 Lynn Dickey	.20	.50
W12 Tony Dorsett	.50	1.25
W13 Bill Kenney	.20	.50
W14 Ottis Anderson	.30	.75
W15 Dan Fouts	.40	1.00
W16 Eric Dickerson	.40	1.00
W17 John Elway	5.00	12.00
W18 Ozzie Newsome	.30	.75
W19 Curt Warner	.20	.50
W20 Joe Theismann	.40	1.00
NNO West Display Board	6.00	15.00
NNO East Display Board	6.00	15.00

1996 7-Eleven Sprint Phone Cards

7-Eleven stores distributed these Sprint 15-minute phone cards. Each includes a photo of the player on front with the phone card use instructions on back. The cards are priced below in unused condition and originally carried an SRP of $5.99 each.

COMPLETE SET (12)	32.00	80.00
1 Troy Aikman	3.20	8.00
2 Drew Bledsoe	3.20	8.00
3 John Elway	4.80	12.00
4 Brett Favre	4.80	12.00
5 Jim Kelly	2.00	5.00
6 Erik Kramer	2.00	5.00
7 Dan Marino	4.80	12.00
8 Barry Sanders	4.80	12.00
9 Jerry Rice	3.20	8.00
10 Junior Seau	2.00	5.00
11 Emmitt Smith	4.80	12.00
12 Steve Young	2.40	6.00

1997 7-Eleven Promotion

This set was released 3-cards at a time via a 7-Eleven Stores wrapper redemption program from November 1997 to January 1998. For $1 and two wrappers from football card packs purchased at 7-Eleven stores, the collector would receive the 3-cards. Each was produced by a major card manufacturer and features a unique card design. Some include card numbers while others do not. We've cataloged the set below in the order of card release and/or card number.

COMPLETE SET (9)	4.80	12.00
1 John Elway (Checklist Card)	.50	1.25
2 Barry Sanders	1.20	3.00
3 Steve Young	.40	1.00
4 Troy Aikman	.60	1.50
5 Terrell Davis	.80	2.00
6 Junior Seau	.30	.75
7 Drew Bledsoe	.60	1.50
8 Rae Carruth	.30	.75
9 Dan Marino	1.20	3.00

1981 Shell Posters

This set of 96 posters was distributed by Shell Oil Co. across the country, with each major city distributing players from the local team. Those cities without a close NFL issuing team distributed the National set of six popular players (indicated as "National" in the checklist below: numbers 18, 21, 28, 35, 45, and 79). The pictures used are actually black and white drawings by artists, suitable for framing. These posters measure approximately 10 7/8" by 13 7/8"; most were (facsimile) signed by the artist. They are frequently available and offered by the team set of six. Several different artists are responsible for the artwork; they are K. Akins (KA), Nick Galloway (NG) and Tanenbawm (T). Those drawings which are not signed are asterisked in the checklist below. New Orleans and Houston are supposedly tougher to find than the other teams. The posters are numbered below alphabetically by team and then player.

COMPLETE SET (96)	100.00	200.00
1 William Andrews NG	1.25	3.00
2 Steve Bartkowski NG	1.25	3.00
3 Buddy Curry NG	1.00	2.50
4 Wallace Francis NG	1.25	3.00
5 Mike Kenn NG	1.00	2.50
6 Jeff Van Note NG	1.00	2.50
7 Mike Barnes *	1.00	2.50
8 Roger Carr KA	1.00	2.50
9 Curtis Dickey KA	1.25	3.00
10 Bert Jones KA	1.25	3.00
11 Bruce Laird *	1.00	2.50
12 Randy McMillan *	1.00	2.50
13 Brian Baschnagel T	1.00	2.50
14 Vince Evans T	1.00	2.50
15 Gary Fencik T	1.00	2.50
16 Roland Harper T	1.00	2.50
17 Alan Page T	1.25	3.00
18 Walter Payton T (National)	4.00	10.00
19 Ken Anderson T	1.50	4.00
20 Ross Browner T	1.00	2.50
21 Archie Griffin T (National)	1.00	2.50
22 Pat McInally T	1.00	2.50
23 Anthony Munoz T	1.50	4.00
24 Reggie Williams T	1.25	3.00
25 Lyle Alzado KA	1.25	3.00
26 Joe DeLamielleure KA	1.25	3.00
27 Doug Dieken KA	1.00	2.50
28 Dave Logan KA (National)	1.00	2.50
29 Reggie Rucker KA	1.25	3.00
30 Brian Sipe KA	1.25	3.00
31 Benny Barnes T	1.00	2.50
32 Bob Breunig T	1.00	2.50
33 D.D. Lewis T	1.00	2.50
34 Harvey Martin T	1.25	3.00
35 Drew Pearson T (National)	1.25	3.00
36 Rafael Septien T	1.00	2.50
37 Al(Bubba) Baker KA	1.25	3.00
38 Dexter Bussey KA	1.00	2.50
39 Gary Danielson KA	1.00	2.50
40 Freddie Scott KA	1.00	2.50
41 Billy Sims KA	1.50	4.00
42 Tom Skladany KA	1.00	2.50
43 Robert Brazile T	1.25	3.00
44 Ken Burrough T	1.25	3.00
45 Earl Campbell T (National)	2.50	6.00
46 Leon Gray T	1.00	2.50
47 Carl Mauck T	1.00	2.50
48 Ken Stabler T	4.00	4.00
49 Bob Baumhower NG	1.25	3.00
50 Jimmy Cefalo NG	1.25	3.00
51 A.J. Duhe NG	1.00	2.50
52 Nat Moore NG	1.25	3.00
53 Ed Newman NG	1.00	2.50
54 Uwe Von Schamann NG	1.00	2.50
55 Steve Grogan NG	1.25	3.00
56 John Hannah NG	1.25	3.00
57 Don Hasselbeck NG	1.00	2.50
58 Mike Haynes NG	1.25	3.00
59 Harold Jackson NG	1.25	3.00
60 Steve Nelson NG	1.00	2.50
61 Elois Grooms	1.25	3.00
62 Rickey Jackson NG	1.50	4.00
63 Archie Manning T	1.50	4.00
64 Tom Myers	1.25	3.00
65 Benny Ricardo T	1.25	3.00
66 George Rogers NG	1.25	3.00
67 Harry Carson NG	1.50	4.00
68 Dave Jennings NG	1.00	2.50
69 Gary Jeter NG	1.00	2.50
70 Phil Simms NG	1.50	4.00
71 Lawrence Taylor NG	2.00	5.00
72 Brad Van Pelt NG	1.25	3.00
73 Greg Buttle NG	1.00	2.50
74 Bruce Harper NG	1.00	2.50
75 Joe Klecko NG	1.25	3.00
76 Randy Rasmussen NG	1.00	2.50
77 Richard Todd NG	1.25	3.00
78 Wesley Walker NG	1.25	3.00
79 Ottis Anderson NG (National)	1.00	2.50
80 Dan Dierdorf NG	1.25	3.00
81 Mel Gray NG	1.25	3.00
82 Jim Hart NG	1.25	3.00
83 E.J. Junior NG	1.25	3.00
84 Pat Tilley NG	1.25	3.00
85 Jimmie Giles NG	1.25	3.00
86 Charley Hannah NG	1.00	2.50
87 Bill Kollar NG	1.00	2.50
88 David Lewis NG	1.00	2.50
89 Lee Roy Selmon NG	1.50	4.00
90 Doug Williams NG	1.25	3.00
91 Joe Lavender T	1.00	2.50
92 Mark Moseley T	1.00	2.50
93 Mark Murphy *	1.00	2.50
94 Lemar Parrish T	1.00	2.50
95 John Riggins T	2.00	5.00
96 Joe Washington T	1.25	3.00

1926 Shotwell Red Grange Ad Back

Shotwell Candy issued two different sets featuring Red Grange. Each card in the "ad back" version measures roughly 2" by 3 1/8" (slightly larger than the blankbacks) and was printed on very thin newspaper type paper stock. Each features Red Grange in a black and white photo from the motion picture "One Minute to Play." The cards were issued as inserts into Shotwell Candies so many are found with creases and other damage from the original packaging. Many of the same photos were used in this version as the first 12-cards of the blankbacked set. However, the captions are worded differently. Each also includes an advertisement on the cardback for Shotwell Candies, a Grange album, and Grange photos. A second, presumably much more scarce, version of card #9 was confirmed in 2011 featuring a photo of Grange wearing his famous jersey #77. It has been speculated that this card may have been pulled early in production or issued very late in the promotion or even issued as a seperate sample card.

COMPLETE SET (12)	2,500.00	4,000.00
1 Red Grange (Getting Under Way)	250.00	400.00
2 Red Grange (A Forward Pass)	200.00	350.00
3 Red Grange (The start of one of those famous 50-yard runs)	200.00	350.00
4 Red Grange (Passing it Along)	250.00	400.00
5 Red Grange (Picking a High One)	200.00	350.00
6 Red Grange (Raccoon coat photo)	250.00	400.00
7 Red Grange (America's Most Famous Ice Man)	200.00	350.00
8 Red Grange (The Famous Smile)	200.00	350.00
9A Red Grange (Illinois Famous Half Back)	250.00	400.00
9B Red Grange SP (Red calls this his lucky number)		
10 Red Grange (The Kick That Put it Over)	250.00	400.00
11 Red Grange (On the Run)	250.00	400.00
12 Red Grange (Himself)	250.00	400.00

1926 Shotwell Red Grange Blankbacked

Shotwell Candy issued two different sets featuring Red Grange. Each card in the blankbacked version measures roughly 1-15/16" by 3" and features a black and white photo from the motion picture "One Minute to Play." The cards were issued as inserts into Shotwell Candies. Photos that feature Grange in football attire generally fetch a slight premium over the movie photo cards.

COMPLETE SET (24)	5,000.00	8,000.00
WRAPPER	1,000.00	1,500.00
1 Red Grange (with actress)	250.00	400.00
2 Red Grange (with actress)	200.00	350.00
3 Red Grange (standing with actress)	200.00	350.00
4 Red Grange (standing with actress)	200.00	350.00
5 Red Grange (In white shirt and bow tie)	200.00	350.00
6 Red Grange (with another player in college sweaters)	200.00	350.00
7 Red Grange In uniform, ready to pass	250.00	400.00
8 Red Grange (with coach)	200.00	350.00
9 Red Grange (carrying books)	200.00	350.00
10 Red Grange (with two actors)	200.00	350.00
11 Red Grange (with actress)	200.00	350.00
12 Red Grange (with coach in uniform)	200.00	350.00
13 Red Grange (running the ball)	250.00	400.00
14 Red Grange (Punting the ball)	250.00	400.00
15 Red Grange (Reaching for ball)	250.00	400.00
16 Red Grange (with actress)	200.00	350.00
17 Red Grange (with coach and actress)	200.00	350.00
18 Red Grange (with actress)	200.00	350.00
19 Red Grange (with actors)	200.00	350.00
20 Red Grange (Running the ball)	250.00	400.00
21 Red Grange (with actress)	200.00	350.00
22 Red Grange (Portrait shot, facing left)	200.00	350.00
23 Red Grange (portrait shot)	200.00	350.00
24 Red Grange (Running to right in uniform)	250.00	400.00

2005 Sioux City Bandits UIF

COMPLETE SET (30)	7.50	15.00
1 Nick Allison	.30	.75
2 Jamal Argrow	.30	.75
3 John Bowman	.30	.75
4 Cody Butler	.30	.75
5 Keith Chapman	.30	.75
6 Jarrod DeGeorgia	.30	.75
7 Clint Harrison	.30	.75
8 Kenneth Horton	.30	.75
9 Fred Jackson	.30	.75
10 Patrick Jackson	.30	.75
11 Jose Jefferson CO	.30	.75
12 Jose Jefferson CO	.30	.75
13 Cori Johnson	.30	.75
14 Tristan Johnson	.30	.75
15 Donavan Laviness	.30	.75
16 Adam Lloyd	.30	.75
17 Art Maulupe	.30	.75
18 Corey Mayes	.30	.75
19 Johnnie Ostermeyer	.30	.75
20 Jon Paulsen	.30	.75
21 David Perrigo	.30	.75
22 Deron Rush	.30	.75
23 Steve Schmidt	.30	.75
24 Willie Simmons	.30	.75
25 Derrick Smith Jr.	.30	.75
26 Erv Strohbeen	.30	.75
27 Anthony Thomas	.30	.75
28 Spetlar Tonga	.30	.75
29 Ken Ware	.30	.75
30 Jesse Wavrunek	.30	.75

2005 Sioux Falls Storm UIF

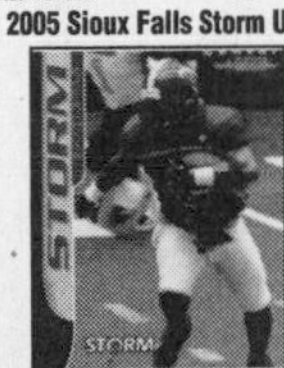

COMPLETE SET (6)	4.00	8.00
1 Shannon Poppinga	.60	1.50
2 Adam Hicks	.60	1.50
3 Mark Blackburn	.60	1.50
4 Nate Fluit	.60	1.50
5 James Jones	.60	1.50
6 John Semchenko	.60	1.50

2007 Sioux Falls Storm UIF

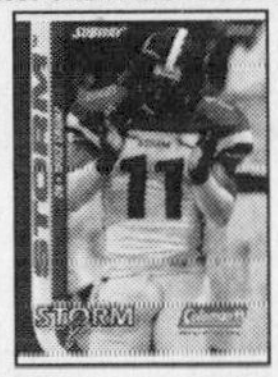

COMPLETE SET (6)	4.00	8.00
1 Trice Crump	.60	1.50
2 Leo Hall Jr.	.60	1.50
3 Paul Keizer	.60	1.50
4 Justin Landis	.60	1.50
5 Leif Murphy	.60	1.50
6 James Terry	.60	1.50

2008 Sioux Falls Storm UIF

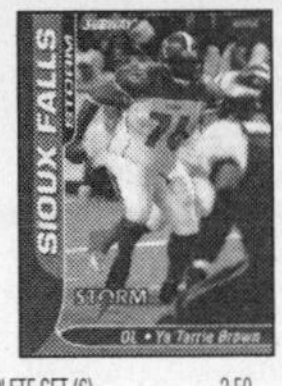

COMPLETE SET (6)	2.50	6.00
1 Bryan Alberty	.40	1.00
2 Mark Blackburn	.40	1.00
3 Ya'Tarrie Brown	.40	1.00
4 Cory Johnsen	.40	1.00
5 Anthony Thomas	.40	1.00
6 Sean Treasure	.40	1.00

1993 SkyBox Celebrity Cycle Prototypes

Measuring the standard size, these two prototype cards feature celebrities and their bikes. On the fronts, the featured celebrity is pictured on his bike, and the varying backgrounds have a metallic sheen to them. The celebrity is identified by his name, position, and his team. (The mystery card pictures a Harley Davidson motocycle against an American flag background.) The backs are blank except for a red-inked stamp that reads "Unfinished SkyBox Prototype." The cards are unnumbered and checklisted below in alphabetical order.

1 Mitch Frerotte	.80	2.00
2 Jerry Glanville CO	.75	2.00

2000 SkyBox

Released as a 300-card base set, Skybox features 200-veteran cards, 50-base rookie cards and the same 50-rookies again in a short printed version. The Short Printed rookies (noted below with an "H" suffix on the card number) feature a horizontal photo on the cardfront instead of vertical and are sequentially numbered to 2000. SkyBox was packaged in 24-pack boxes with packs containing 10 cards and carried a suggested retail price of $2.99.

COMPLETE SET (300)	250.00	400.00
COMP.SET w/o SPs (250)	12.50	30.00
201-250 ROOKIE SP PRINT RUN 2000		
1 Tim Couch	.20	.50
2 Edgerrin James	.25	.60
3 Wesley Walls	.15	.40
4 Brian Griese	.20	.50
5 Herman Moore	.20	.50
6 Mark Brunell	.20	.50
7 John Randle	.20	.50
8 Victor Green	.15	.40
9 Michael Sinclair	.15	.40
10 Jevon Kearse	.20	.50
11 Peter Boulware	.15	.40
12 Kevin Johnson	.15	.40
13 Vonnie Holliday	.15	.40
14 Jason Taylor	.20	.50
15 Cam Cleeland	.15	.40
16 Jeff Graham	.15	.40
17 Jacquez Green	.15	.40
18 Chris McAlister	.15	.40
19 Takeo Spikes	.15	.40
20 Marvin Harrison	.25	.60
21 Jay Fiedler	.20	.50
22 Jake Reed	.20	.50
23 Jerry Rice	.50	1.25
24 Shaun King	.15	.40
25 Donovan McNabb	.25	.60
26 David Boston	.15	.40
27 Curtis Enis	.15	.40
28 Olandis Gary	.20	.50
29 James Stewart	.15	.40
30 Jimmy Smith	.20	.50
31 Randy Moss	.25	.60
32 Keyshawn Johnson	.20	.50
33 Kevin Carter	.15	.40
34 Stephen Davis	.20	.50
35 Jay Riemersma	.15	.40
36 Emmitt Smith	.60	1.50
37 E.G. Green	.15	.40
38 Dwayne Rudd	.15	.40
39 Michael Strahan	.20	.50
40 Troy Edwards	.15	.40
41 Derrick Mayes	.15	.40
42 Eddie George	.20	.50
43 Bruce Smith	.25	.60
44 Andre Wadsworth	.15	.40
45 Bobby Engram	.20	.50
46 Byron Chamberlain	.15	.40
47 Antonio Freeman	.20	.50
48 Hardy Nickerson	.15	.40
49 Terry Glenn	.20	.50
50 Wayne Chrebet	.20	.50
51 London Fletcher RC	.25	.60
52 Michael Westbrook	.15	.40
53 Rob Moore	.15	.40
54 Eddie Kennison	.15	.40
55 Ed McCaffrey	.20	.50
56 Dorsey Levens	.20	.50
57 Andre Rison	.20	.50
58 Willie McGinest	.20	.50
59 Tyrone Wheatley	.15	.40
60 Kurt Warner	.40	1.00
61 Stephen Alexander	.15	.40
62 Jessie Tuggle	.15	.40
63 Jim Miller	.15	.40
64 Luther Elliss	.15	.40
65 Bill Schroeder	.20	.50
66 Elvis Grbac	.15	.40
67 Ty Law	.20	.50
68 Tim Brown	.25	.60
69 Marshall Faulk	.25	.60
70 Champ Bailey	.20	.50
71 Charlie Batch	.20	.50
72 Steve Beuerlein	.20	.50
73 Rocket Ismail	.20	.50
74 Kevin Hardy	.15	.40
75 Zach Thomas	.25	.60
76 Aaron Glenn	.15	.40
77 Jerome Bettis	.25	.60
78 Chris Chandler	.20	.50
79 Marcus Robinson	.20	.50
80 Derrick Alexander	.15	.40
81 Drew Bledsoe	.25	.60
82 Charles Woodson	.25	.60
83 Isaac Bruce	.25	.60
84 Darrell Green	.20	.50
85 Tim Dwight	.20	.50
86 Darnay Scott	.20	.50
87 Chris Claiborne	.15	.40
88 Tony Gonzalez	.25	.60
89 Tony Simmons	.15	.40
90 Rich Gannon	.20	.50
91 Torry Holt	.25	.60
92 Jamal Anderson	.20	.50
93 Akili Smith	.15	.40
94 Germane Crowell	.15	.40
95 Lawyer Milloy	.15	.40
96 Napoleon Kaufman	.20	.50
97 Grant Wistrom	.15	.40
98 Terance Mathis	.15	.40
99 Karim Abdul-Jabbar	.15	.40
100 Kerry Collins	.20	.50
101 Troy Vincent	.15	.40
102 Jermaine Fazande	.15	.40
103 Warren Sapp	.20	.50
104 Tony Banks	.15	.40
105 Darrin Chiaverini	.15	.40
106 Corey Bradford	.15	.40
107 Tony Martin	.20	.50
108 Jeff Blake	.20	.50
109 Torrance Small	.15	.40
110 Freddie Jones	.15	.40
111 Warrick Dunn	.20	.50
112 Tim Biakabutuka	.20	.50
113 Rod Smith	.20	.50
114 Kyle Brady	.15	.40
115 Oronde Gadsden	.20	.50
116 Dedric Ward	.15	.40
117 Mikhael Ricks	.15	.40
118 Bryant Young	.15	.40
119 Michael Bates	.15	.40
120 Junior Seau	.25	.60
121 Bill Romanowski	.15	.40
122 Reggie Barlow	.15	.40
123 Jeff Garcia	.20	.50
124 Peerless Price	.20	.50
125 Jeff George	.20	.50
126 Cornelius Bennett	.15	.40
127 Amani Toomer	.20	.50
128 Charles Johnson	.15	.40
129 Cortez Kennedy	.15	.40
130 Samari Rolle	.15	.40
131 Eric Moulds	.20	.50
132 Joey Galloway	.20	.50
133 Peyton Manning	.60	1.50
134 Robert Smith	.20	.50
135 Jessie Armstead	.15	.40
136 Will Blackwell	.15	.40
137 Jon Kitna	.20	.50
138 Kevin Dyson	.20	.50
139 Jake Plummer	.20	.50
140 Cade McNown	.15	.40
141 Terrell Davis	.25	.60
142 Johnnie Morton	.20	.50
143 Fred Taylor	.25	.60
144 Ed McDaniel	.15	.40
145 Vinny Testaverde	.20	.50
146 Az-Zahir Hakim	.15	.40
147 Brad Johnson	.20	.50
148 Antowain Smith	.20	.50
149 Rob Konrad	.15	.40
150 Sam Cowart	.15	.40
151 Cris Carter	.25	.60
152 Jason Sehorn	.15	.40
153 Levon Kirkland	.15	.40
154 Shawn Springs	.15	.40
155 Frank Wycheck	.20	.50
156 Troy Aikman	.40	1.00
157 Keenan McCardell	.20	.50
158 Sam Madison	.15	.40
159 Curtis Martin	.25	.60
160 Hines Ward	.25	.60
161 Steve Young	.30	.75
162 Blaine Bishop	.15	.40
163 Shannon Sharpe	.25	.60
164 Michael Pittman	.15	.40
165 Brett Favre	.75	2.00
166 Damon Huard	.20	.50
167 Keith Poole	.15	.40
168 Curtis Conway	.20	.50
169 Derrick Brooks	.25	.60
170 Duce Staley	.20	.50
171 Rob Johnson	.20	.50
172 Pete Gonzalez	.15	.40
173 Ken Dilger	.15	.40
174 Ike Hilliard	.20	.50
175 Bobby Taylor	.15	.40
176 Ricky Watters	.20	.50
177 Steve McNair	.25	.60
178 Pat Johnson	.15	.40
179 Carl Pickens	.20	.50
180 Terrence Wilkins	.15	.40
181 Rashaan Shehee	.15	.40
182 Ricky Williams	.25	.60
183 James Jett	.20	.50
184 Terrell Owens	.25	.60
185 John Lynch	.20	.50
186 Muhsin Muhammad	.20	.50
187 Ryan McNeil	.15	.40
188 Jerome Pathon	.15	.40
189 Daunte Culpepper	.20	.50
190 Joe Jurevicius	.15	.40
191 Kordell Stewart	.20	.50
192 Christian Fauria	.15	.40
193 Yancey Thigpen	.15	.40
194 Patrick Jeffers	.20	.50
195 Corey Dillon	.20	.50
196 Tamarick Vanover	.15	.40
197 Doug Flutie	.25	.60
198 Rickey Dudley	.15	.40
199 Charlie Garner	.20	.50
200 Mike Alstott	.25	.60
201 Courtney Brown RC	.25	.60
201H Courtney Brown SP	2.00	5.00
202 Peter Warrick RC	.30	.75
202H Peter Warrick SP	2.50	6.00
203 Thomas Jones RC	.40	1.00
203H Thomas Jones SP	3.00	8.00
204 Sylvester Morris RC	.20	.50
204H Sylvester Morris SP	1.50	4.00
205 Chad Pennington RC	.50	1.25
205H Chad Pennington SP	4.00	10.00
206 Ron Dayne RC	.30	.75
206H Ron Dayne SP	2.50	6.00
207 Todd Pinkston RC	.20	.50
207H Todd Pinkston SP	1.50	4.00
208 Todd Husak RC	.20	.50
208H Todd Husak SP	1.50	4.00
209 Chris Redman RC	.25	.60
209H Chris Redman SP	2.00	5.00
210 Jerry Porter RC	.30	.75
210H Jerry Porter SP	2.50	6.00
211 Michael Wiley RC	.20	.50
211H Michael Wiley SP	1.50	4.00
212 J.R. Redmond RC	.20	.50
212H J.R. Redmond SP	1.50	4.00
213 Dennis Northcutt RC	.25	.60
213H Dennis Northcutt SP	2.00	5.00
214 Gari Scott RC	.20	.50
214H Gari Scott SP	1.50	4.00
215 Bashir Yamini RC	.20	.50
215H Bashir Yamini SP	1.50	4.00
216 Danny Farmer RC	.20	.50
216H Danny Farmer SP	1.50	4.00
217 Corey Simon RC	.25	.60
217H Corey Simon SP	2.00	5.00
218 Plaxico Burress RC	.30	.75
218H Plaxico Burress SP	2.50	6.00
219 Chad Morton RC	.30	.75
219H Chad Morton SP	2.50	6.00
220 Bubba Franks RC	.30	.75
220H Bubba Franks SP	2.50	6.00
221 Shaun Alexander RC	.40	1.00
221H Shaun Alexander SP	3.00	8.00
222 Dez White RC	.25	.60
222H Dez White SP	2.00	5.00
223 Mareno Philyaw RC	.20	.50
223H Mareno Philyaw SP	1.50	4.00
224 Travis Taylor RC	.25	.60
224H Travis Taylor SP	2.00	5.00
225 Brian Urlacher RC	1.25	3.00
225H Brian Urlacher SP	10.00	25.00
226 Jamal Lewis RC	.30	.75
226H Jamal Lewis SP	2.50	6.00
227 Sherrod Gideon RC	.20	.50
227H Sherrod Gideon SP	1.50	4.00
228 Shyrone Stith RC	.20	.50
228H Shyrone Stith SP	1.50	4.00
229 Chris Cole RC	.25	.60
229H Chris Cole SP	2.00	5.00
230 Darrell Jackson RC	.25	.60
230H Darrell Jackson SP	2.00	5.00
231 Quinton Spotwood RC	.20	.50
231H Quinton Spotwood SP	1.50	4.00
232 Tee Martin RC	.30	.75
232H Tee Martin SP	2.50	6.00
233 Tim Rattay RC	.25	.60
233H Tim Rattay SP	2.00	5.00
234 Marc Bulger RC	.30	.75
234H Marc Bulger SP	2.50	6.00
235 Doug Johnson RC	.25	.60
235H Doug Johnson SP	2.00	5.00
236 Joe Hamilton RC	.20	.50
236H Joe Hamilton SP	1.50	4.00
237 Trevor Gaylor RC	.20	.50
237H Trevor Gaylor SP	1.50	4.00
238 Travis Prentice RC	.25	.60
238H Travis Prentice SP	2.00	5.00
239 R.Jay Soward RC	.20	.50
239H R.Jay Soward SP	1.50	4.00

240 Trung Canidate RC .25 .60
240H Trung Canidate SP 2.00 5.00
241 Giovanni Carmazzi RC .20 .50
241H Giovanni Carmazzi SP 1.50 4.00
242 Reuben Droughns RC .30 .75
242H Reuben Droughns SP 2.50 6.00
243 Curtis Keaton RC .20 .50
243H Curtis Keaton SP 1.50 4.00
244 Laveranues Coles RC .30 .75
244H Laveranues Coles SP 2.50 6.00
245 Ron Dugans RC .20 .50
245H Ron Dugans SP 1.50 4.00
246 Mike Anderson RC .30 .75
246H Mike Anderson SP 2.50 6.00
247 Anthony Becht RC .25 .60
247H Anthony Becht SP 2.00 5.00
248 Raynoch Thompson RC .20 .50
248H Raynoch Thompson SP 1.50 4.00
249 Rob Morris RC .25 .60
249H Rob Morris SP 2.00 5.00
250 Chafie Fields RC .20 .50
250H Chafie Fields SP 1.50 4.00
P1 Tim Couch Promo .40 1.00

2000 SkyBox Star Rubies

COMPLETE SET (250) 60.00 120.00
*VETS 1-200: 2.5X TO 6X BASIC CARDS
*ROOKIES 201-250: 2X TO 5X
STAR RUBY STATED ODDS 1:12

2000 SkyBox Star Rubies Extreme

*VETS 1-200: 12X TO 30X BASIC CARDS
*ROOKIES 201-250: 10X TO 25X
EXTREME PRINT RUN 50 SER.#'d SETS

2000 SkyBox Preemptive Strike

COMPLETE SET (15) 5.00 12.00
STATED ODDS 1:4
*STAR RUBIES/100: 5X TO 12X BASIC INSERTS
STAR RUBIES PRINT RUN 100 SER.#'d SETS
1 Tim Couch .30 .75
2 Edgerrin James .40 1.00
3 Jake Plummer .30 .75
4 Akili Smith .25 .60
5 Cade McNown .25 .60
6 Isaac Bruce .40 1.00
7 Marvin Harrison .40 1.00
8 Troy Aikman .60 1.50
9 Germane Crowell .25 .60
10 Cris Carter .40 1.00
11 Keyshawn Johnson .30 .75
12 Donovan McNabb .40 1.00
13 Charlie Batch .30 .75
14 Muhsin Muhammad .30 .75
15 Marcus Robinson .30 .75

2000 SkyBox Skylines

COMPLETE SET (10) 7.50 20.00
STATED ODDS 1:11
*STAR RUBIES/50: 5X TO 12X BASIC INSERTS
STAR RUBIES PRINT RUN 50 SER.#'d SETS
1 Tim Couch .50 1.25
2 Edgerrin James .60 1.50
3 Terrell Davis .60 1.50
4 Jamal Anderson .50 1.25
5 Kurt Warner 1.00 2.50
6 Charlie Batch .50 1.25
7 Emmitt Smith 1.50 4.00
8 Peyton Manning 1.50 4.00
9 Cade McNown .40 1.00
10 Mark Brunell .50 1.25

2000 SkyBox Sole Train

COMPLETE SET (10) 5.00 12.00
STATED ODDS 1:8
*STAR RUBIES/100: 4X TO 10X BASIC INSERTS
STAR RUBIES PRINT RUN 100 SER.#'d SETS
1 Edgerrin James .50 1.25
2 Eddie George .40 1.00
3 Marshall Faulk .50 1.25
4 Emmitt Smith 1.25 3.00
5 Fred Taylor .50 1.25
6 Stephen Davis .40 1.00
7 Ricky Williams .50 1.25
8 Jamal Anderson .40 1.00
9 Warrick Dunn .40 1.00
10 Jerome Bettis .50 1.25

2000 SkyBox Sunday's Best

COMPLETE SET (10) 12.50 30.00
STATED ODDS 1:24
*STAR RUBIES/50: 4X TO 10X BASIC INSERTS
STAR RUBIES PRINT RUN 50 SER.#'d SETS
1 Tim Couch .60 1.50
2 Edgerrin James .75 2.00
3 Terrell Davis .75 2.00
4 Peyton Manning 2.00 5.00
5 Marshall Faulk .75 2.00
6 Brett Favre 2.50 6.00
7 Emmitt Smith 2.00 5.00
8 Randy Moss .75 2.00
9 Fred Taylor .75 2.00
10 Ricky Williams .75 2.00

2000 SkyBox Superlatives

COMPLETE SET (15) 10.00 25.00
STATED ODDS 1:11
*STAR RUBIES/50: 5X TO 12X BASIC INSERTS
STAR RUBIES PRINT RUN 50 SER.#'d SETS
1 Tim Couch .50 1.25
2 Edgerrin James .60 1.50
3 Randy Moss .60 1.50
4 Marshall Faulk .60 1.50
5 Fred Taylor .60 1.50
6 Jake Plummer .50 1.25
7 Vinny Testaverde .50 1.25
8 Troy Aikman 1.00 2.50
9 Drew Bledsoe .60 1.50
10 Stephen Davis .50 1.25
11 Marvin Harrison .60 1.50
12 Steve Young .75 2.00
13 Jimmy Smith .50 1.25
14 Ricky Williams .60 1.50
15 Kurt Warner 1.00 2.50

2000 SkyBox The Bomb

COMPLETE SET (10) 12.00 30.00
STATED ODDS 1:24
*STAR RUBIES/50: 4X TO 10X BASIC INSERTS
STAR RUBIES PRINT RUN 50
1 Tim Couch .60 1.50
2 Kurt Warner 1.25 3.00
3 Edgerrin James .75 2.00
4 Randy Moss .75 2.00
5 Keyshawn Johnson .60 1.50
6 Brett Favre 2.50 6.00
7 Peyton Manning 2.00 5.00
8 Eddie George .60 1.50
9 Isaac Bruce .75 2.00
10 Marvin Harrison .75 2.00

1999 SkyBox Dominion

Released as a 250-card set, the 1999 Skybox Dominion is comprised of 200 veteran player cards an 50 rookie cards. Base cards are accented with gray tone backgrounds and silver foil highlights. Skybox Dominion was packaged in 36-pack boxes with 10 cards per pack. Also inserted were the cross brand autographics cards which features hand signed cards of various players.

COMPLETE SET (250) 15.00 40.00
1 Randy Moss .20 .50
2 James Jett .12 .30
3 Lawyer Milloy .15 .40
4 Mike Alstott .20 .50
5 Courtney Hawkins .12 .30
6 Carl Pickens .15 .40
7 Marvin Harrison .20 .50
8 Robert Smith .15 .40
9 Fred Taylor .15 .40
10 Barry Sanders .50 1.25
11 Tony Gonzalez .20 .50
12 Leroy Hoard .12 .30
13 Drew Bledsoe .20 .50
14 Cam Cleeland .12 .30
15 Steve Atwater .15 .40
16 Eric Moulds .15 .40
17 Herman Moore .15 .40
18 Rickey Dudley .12 .30
19 Jeff Blake .15 .40
20 Eddie George .15 .40
21 Antonio Freeman .15 .40
22 Stephen Alexander .12 .30
23 Larry Centers .15 .40
24 Chris Chandler .15 .40
25 James Stewart .12 .30
26 Randall Cunningham .20 .50
27 Mark Brunell .15 .40
28 David Palmer .12 .30
29 Eric Green .12 .30
30 Terry Glenn .15 .40
31 Jerry Rice .40 1.00
32 Ricky Proehl .12 .30
33 Tony Banks .15 .40
34 John Elway .60 1.50
35 Johnnie Morton .15 .40
36 Tony Simmons .12 .30
37 Jon Kitna .15 .40
38 Trent Green .15 .40
39 Peyton Manning .60 1.50
40 Emmitt Smith .50 1.25
41 Warrick Dunn .15 .40
42 Jerome Bettis .20 .50
43 Ricky Watters .15 .40
44 Rocket Ismail .15 .40
45 Ryan Leaf .15 .40
46 Jackie Harris .15 .40
47 Robert Holcombe .12 .30
48 Dorsey Levens .15 .40
49 Duce Staley .15 .40
50 Brett Favre .60 1.50
51 Andre Rison .15 .40
52 Curtis Conway .15 .40
53 Mark Chmura .12 .30
54 Doug Flutie .20 .50
55 Ernie Mills .12 .30
56 Jeff George .12 .30
57 Chris Warren .15 .40
58 Alonzo Mayes .12 .30
59 Freddie Jones .12 .30
60 Shannon Sharpe .20 .50
61 O.J. Santiago .12 .30
62 Shawn Springs .12 .30
63 Kent Graham .12 .30
64 Muhsin Muhammad .15 .40
65 Keith Poole .12 .30
66 Chris Spielman .15 .40
67 Curtis Enis .12 .30
68 Lamar Smith .12 .30
69 Charles Johnson .12 .30
70 Kerry Collins .15 .40
71 Charlie Batch .15 .40
72 Keenan McCardell .15 .40
73 Ty Detmer .15 .40
74 Mark Bruener .12 .30
75 Lamar Thomas .12 .30
76 Kwamie Lassiter RC .12 .30
77 Byron Bam Morris .12 .30
78 Michael Sinclair .12 .30
79 Darnay Scott .12 .30
80 Napoleon Kaufman .12 .30
81 Ed McCaffrey .15 .40
82 Reidel Anthony .12 .30
83 Kevin Greene .15 .40
84 Michael Irvin .20 .50
85 Charles Way .12 .30
86 Tim Brown .20 .50
87 Johnny McWilliams .12 .30
88 Brad Johnson .15 .40
89 Antonio Langham .12 .30
90 Bruce Smith .20 .50
91 Reggie Barlow .12 .30
92 Ty Law .15 .40
93 Bobby Engram .15 .40
94 Kimble Anders .12 .30
95 Dale Carter .12 .30
96 Jimmy Smith .15 .40
97 Marc Edwards .15 .40
98 Ken Dilger .12 .30
99 Adrian Murrell .15 .40
100 Terance Mathis .12 .30
101 Gary Anderson .12 .30
102 Garrison Hearst .15 .40
103 Ahman Green .15 .40
104 Daryl Johnston .20 .50
105 O.J. McDuffie .15 .40
106 Matthew Hatchette .15 .40
107 Chris Doleman .12 .30
108 Steve McNair .20 .50
109 Leon Johnson .12 .30
110 Terrell Davis .20 .50
111 Rob Moore .12 .30
112 Troy Aikman .30 .75
113 John Avery .12 .30
114 Frank Wycheck .15 .40
115 Curtis Martin .20 .50
116 Jim Harbaugh .15 .40
117 Sean Dawkins .12 .30
118 Glenn Foley .12 .30
119 Warren Sapp .15 .40
120 R.W. McQuarters .12 .30
121 Yancey Thigpen .12 .30
122 Frank Sanders .12 .30
123 Tim Dwight .15 .40
124 Pete Mitchell .12 .30
125 Steve Beuerlein .15 .40
126 Tyrone Davis .12 .30
127 Jamie Asher .12 .30
128 Corey Dillon .15 .40
129 Doug Pederson .12 .30
130 Deion Sanders .20 .50
131 J.J. Stokes .12 .30
132 Jermaine Lewis .12 .30
133 Gary Brown .12 .30
134 Derrick Alexander .12 .30
135 Tony McGee .12 .30
136 Kyle Brady .12 .30
137 Mikhael Ricks .12 .30
138 Germane Crowell .12 .30
139 Skip Hicks .12 .30
140 Ben Coates .15 .40
141 Will Blackwell .12 .30
142 Al Del Greco .12 .30
143 Jake Plummer .15 .40
144 Marshall Faulk .20 .50
145 Antowain Smith .12 .30
146 Corey Fuller .12 .30
147 Keyshawn Johnson .15 .40
148 John Randle .15 .40
149 Terrell Buckley .15 .40
150 Terry Kirby .12 .30
151 Robert Brooks .15 .40
152 Karim Abdul-Jabbar .15 .40
153 Jason Sehorn .15 .40
154 Elvis Grbac .12 .30
155 Andre Reed .20 .50
156 Ike Hilliard .15 .40
157 Jamal Anderson .15 .40
158 Jake Reed .15 .40
159 Rich Gannon .15 .40
160 Michael Jackson .12 .30
161 Bert Emanuel .15 .40
162 Charles Woodson .20 .50
163 Ray Lewis .20 .50
164 Trent Dilfer .15 .40
165 Oronde Gadsden .12 .30
166 Wesley Walls .15 .40
167 Joey Galloway .15 .40
168 Mo Lewis .12 .30
169 Darren Woodson .15 .40
170 Cris Carter .20 .50
171 Brian Mitchell .15 .40
172 Tim Biakabutuka .15 .40
173 Michael Westbrook .12 .30
174 Dan Marino .60 1.50
175 Greg Hill .12 .30
176 Priest Holmes .20 .50
177 Fred Lane .12 .30
178 Isaac Bruce .20 .50
179 Erik Kramer .15 .40
180 Steve Young .25 .60
181 Terry Fair .12 .30
182 Brian Griese .15 .40
183 Leslie Shepherd .12 .30
184 Kordell Stewart .15 .40
185 Charlie Jones .12 .30
186 Chris Calloway .12 .30
187 Wayne Chrebet .15 .40
188 Natrone Means .15 .40
189 David LaFleur .12 .30
190 Rod Smith WR .15 .40
191 Kevin Dyson .12 .30
192 Scott Mitchell .12 .30
193 Andre Wadsworth .12 .30
194 Vinny Testaverde .15 .40
195 Az-Zahir Hakim .12 .30
196 Joe Jurevicius .12 .30
197 Junior Seau .20 .50
198 Jason Elam .12 .30
199 Terrell Owens .20 .50
200 Jacquez Green .12 .30
201 Tim Couch RC .30 .75
202 Donovan McNabb RC 2.00 5.00
203 Cade McNown RC .25 .60
204 Akili Smith RC .25 .60
205 Kevin Faulk RC .30 .75
206 Sedrick Irvin RC .20 .50
207 Edgerrin James RC .40 1.00
208 Ricky Williams RC .50 1.25
209 D'Wayne Bates RC .20 .50
210 David Boston RC .25 .60
211 Torry Holt RC .50 1.25
212 Peerless Price RC .25 .60
213 Daunte Culpepper RC .30 .75
214 Troy Edwards RC .25 .60
215 Rob Konrad RC .20 .50
216 Joe Germaine RC .25 .60
217 James Johnson RC .20 .50
218 Brock Huard RC .25 .60
219 Cecil Collins RC .20 .50
220 Jeff Paulk RC .20 .50
Eugene Baker RC
221 Marty Booker RC .25 .60
Jim Finn RC
222 Scott Covington RC .20 .50
Nick Williams RC
223 Kevin Johnson RC .25 .60
Darrin Chiaverini RC
224 Ebenezer Ekuban RC .30 .75
Dat Nguyen RC
225 Al Wilson RC .30 .75
Chad Plummer RC
226 Chris Claiborn RC .20 .50
Aaron Gibson RC
227 Aaron Brooks RC .30 .75
De'Mond Parker RC
228 John Tait RC .20 .50
Mike Cloud RC
229 Andy Katzenmoyer RC .25 .60
Michael Bishop RC
230 Joe Montgomery RC .30 .75
Dan Campbell RC
231 Na Brown RC .20 .50
Cecil Martin RC
232 Amos Zereoue RC .25 .60
Jerame Tuman RC
233 Jermaine Fazande RC .20 .50
Steve Heiden RC
234 Karsten Bailey RC .20 .50
Charlie Rogers RC
235 Shaun King RC .25 .60
Martin Gramatica RC
236 Jevon Kearse RC .30 .75
Kevin Daft RC
237 Champ Bailey RC .60 1.50
Tim Alexander RC
238 Karsten Bailey RC .20 .50
Darnell McDonald RC
239 Lamarr Glenn RC .20 .50
Terry Jackson RC
240 Troy Smith RC .25 .60
Malcolm Johnson RC
241 Rondel Menendez RC .20 .50
Craig Yeast RC
242 Jed Weaver RC .20 .50
James Dearth RC
243 Joel Makovicka RC .20 .50
Shawn Bryson RC
244 Desmond Clark RC .30 .75
Jim Kleinsasser RC
245 Sean Bennett RC .20 .50
Autry Denson RC
246 Billy Miller RC .20 .50
Wane McGarity RC
247 Mike Lucky RC .20 .50
Justin Swift RC
248 Travis McGriff RC .25 .60
MarTay Jenkins RC
249 Donald Driver RC 4.00 10.00
Larry Parker RC
250 Antoine Winfield RC .30 .75
Dre Bly RC
P54 Doug Flutie Promo .40 1.00

1999 SkyBox Dominion Atlantattitude

COMPLETE SET (15) 40.00 80.00
STATED ODDS 1:24
*PLUS CARDS: 1.2X TO 3X BASIC INSERT
PLUS STATED ODDS 1:240
1 Charlie Batch 1.50 4.00
2 Mark Brunell 1.50 4.00
3 Tim Couch .75 2.00
4 Terrell Davis 1.50 4.00
5 Warrick Dunn 1.50 4.00
6 Brett Favre 5.00 12.00
7 Peyton Manning 5.00 12.00
8 Dan Marino 5.00 12.00
9 Randy Moss 4.00 10.00
10 Jake Plummer 1.00 2.50
11 Barry Sanders 5.00 12.00
12 Akili Smith .60 1.50
13 Emmitt Smith 3.00 8.00
14 Fred Taylor 1.50 4.00
15 Ricky Williams 2.00 5.00

1999 SkyBox Dominion Atlantattitude Warp Tek

CARDS SERIAL #'d UNDER 20 NOT PRICED
4 Terrell Davis/30 30.00 80.00
5 Warrick Dunn/28 30.00 60.00
9 Randy Moss/84 40.00 80.00
11 Barry Sanders/20 125.00 250.00
13 Emmitt Smith/22 75.00 150.00
14 Fred Taylor/28 40.00 100.00
15 Ricky Williams/34 30.00 80.00

1999 SkyBox Dominion Gen Next

COMPLETE SET (20) 10.00 25.00
STATED ODDS 1:3
*PLUS CARDS: 1X TO 2.5X BASIC INSERT
PLUS STATED ODDS 1:30
*WARP TEK CARDS: 3X TO 8X BASIC INSERT
WARP TEK STATED ODDS 1:300
1 D'Wayne Bates .20 .50
2 David Boston .25 .60
3 Cecil Collins .10 .30
4 Tim Couch .25 .60
5 Daunte Culpepper 1.25 3.00
6 Troy Edwards .20 .50
7 Kevin Faulk .25 .60
8 Joe Germaine .20 .50
9 Torry Holt .60 1.50
10 Brock Huard .25 .60
11 Sedrick Irvin .10 .30
12 Edgerrin James 1.25 3.00
13 James Johnson .20 .50
14 Kevin Johnson .25 .60
15 Shaun King .20 .50
16 Donovan McNabb 1.50 4.00
17 Cade McNown .20 .50
18 Akili Smith .20 .50
19 Ricky Williams .60 1.50
20 Amos Zereoue .25 .60

1999 SkyBox Dominion Goal 2 Go

COMPLETE SET (10) 10.00 25.00
STATED ODDS 1:9
*PLUS CARDS: 1.25X TO 3X BASIC INSERT
PLUS STATED ODDS 1:90
*WARP TEK CARDS: 3X TO 8X BASIC INSERT
WARP TEK STATED ODDS 1:900
1 Terrell Davis .60 1.50
Jamal Anderson
2 Brett Favre 2.00 5.00
Jake Plummer
3 Randy Moss 1.50 4.00
Jerry Rice
4 Warrick Dunn 2.00 5.00
Barry Sanders
5 Eddie George .60 1.50
Fred Taylor
6 Emmitt Smith 1.25 3.00
Marshall Faulk
7 Keyshawn Johnson .60 1.50
Terrell Owens
8 Peyton Manning 2.00 5.00
Ryan Leaf
9 Dan Marino 2.00 5.00
John Elway
10 Cade McNown .60 1.50
Charlie Batch

1999 SkyBox Dominion Hats Off

1 Tim Couch/135 15.00 40.00
2 Donovan McNabb/130 30.00 80.00
3 Akili Smith/85 15.00 40.00
4 Ricky Williams/130 25.00 60.00
5 Daunte Culpepper/100 20.00 50.00
6 Cade McNown/120 20.00 50.00

2000 SkyBox Dominion

Released as a 243-card set, 2000 Dominion is composed of 195 Veteran cards, 33 Rookies, and 15 Rookie Pairs cards. Base cards contain full color action photograpy that fades away into an all white border, and are accented with silver foil stamping. Dominion was packaged in 20-pack boxes with packs containing 10 cards and carried a suggested retail price of $1.49. Card numbers 214 and 226 were not released.

COMPLETE SET (243) 12.50 30.00
1 Tim Couch .15 .40
2 Byron Hanspard .12 .30
3 Jay Riemersma .12 .30
4 Cade McNown .12 .30
5 Darnay Scott .15 .40
6 Emmitt Smith .50 1.25
7 Rod Smith .15 .40
8 James Stewart .12 .30
9 Marvin Harrison .20 .50
10 Keenan McCardell .15 .40
11 Andre Rison .15 .40
12 Jeff George .15 .40
13 Terry Glenn .15 .40
14 Cam Cleeland .12 .30
15 Curtis Martin .20 .50
16 Troy Edwards .12 .30
17 Mikhael Ricks .12 .30
18 Joey Galloway .15 .40
19 Az-Zahir Hakim .12 .30
20 Mike Alstott .20 .50
21 Samari Rolle .12 .30
22 Michael Pittman .12 .30
23 Tony Banks .12 .30
24 Bruce Smith .20 .50
25 Curtis Enis .12 .30
26 Jake Plummer .15 .40
27 Darren Woodson .12 .30
28 Bill Romanowski .12 .30
29 Antonio Freeman .15 .40
30 Terrence Wilkins .12 .30
31 Kevin Hardy .12 .30
32 Peerless Price .15 .40
33 Cris Carter .20 .50
34 Willie McGinest .15 .40
35 Kerry Collins .15 .40
36 Bryan Cox .12 .30
37 Tyrone Wheatley .12 .30
38 Jason Sehorn .12 .30
39 Jerry Rice .40 1.00
40 Christian Fauria .12 .30
41 Kevin Carter .12 .30
42 John Lynch .15 .40
43 Brad Johnson .15 .40
44 David Boston .12 .30
45 Peter Boulware .12 .30
46 Muhsin Muhammad .15 .40
47 Bobby Engram .15 .40
48 Kevin Johnson .12 .30
49 Charlie Batch .15 .40
50 Dorsey Levens .15 .40
51 Cornelius Bennett .12 .30
52 Kyle Brady .12 .30
53 Damon Huard .15 .40
54 Robert Smith .15 .40
55 Ty Law .15 .40
56 Amani Toomer .15 .40
57 Aaron Glenn .12 .30
58 Donovan McNabb .20 .50
59 Levon Kirkland .12 .30
60 Terrell Owens .20 .50
61 Sam Adams .12 .30
62 London Fletcher RC .20 .50
63 Steve McNair .20 .50
64 Stephen Davis .15 .40
65 Daunte Culpepper .15 .40
66 Andre Wadsworth .12 .30
67 Priest Holmes .20 .50
68 Patrick Jeffers .15 .40
69 Walt Harris .12 .30
70 Darrin Chiaverini .12 .30
71 Dat Nguyen .12 .30
72 Robert Porcher .12 .30
73 Bill Schroeder .15 .40
74 Tyrone Poole .12 .30
75 Bryce Paup .12 .30
76 O.J. McDuffie .15 .40
77 Jake Reed .15 .40
78 Ike Hilliard .15 .40
79 Victor Green .12 .30
80 Duce Staley .15 .40
81 Amos Zereoue .12 .30
82 Charlie Garner .15 .40
83 Shawn Springs .12 .30
84 Shaun King .12 .30
85 Eddie George .15 .40
86 Michael Westbrook .12 .30
87 Ricky Williams .20 .50
88 Chris Chandler .15 .40
89 Chris McAlister .12 .30
90 Steve Beuerlein .15 .40
91 Marty Booker .15 .40
92 Karim Abdul-Jabbar .12 .30
93 Brian Griese .15 .40
94 Germane Crowell .12 .30
95 Mark Chmura .12 .30
96 E.G. Green .12 .30
97 Elvis Grbac .12 .30
98 Tony Martin .15 .40
99 John Randle .15 .40
100 Michael Strahan .15 .40
101 Tim Brown .20 .50
102 Torrance Small .12 .30
103 Junior Seau .20 .50
104 Bryant Young .12 .30
105 Kurt Warner .30 .75
106 Trent Dilfer .15 .40
107 Kevin Dyson .15 .40
108 Stephen Alexander .12 .30
109 Tim Dwight .15 .40
110 Rob Johnson .15 .40
111 Tim Biakabutuka .15 .40
112 Akili Smith .12 .30
113 Terry Kirby .12 .30
114 Terrell Davis .20 .50
115 Herman Moore .15 .40
116 Vonnie Holliday .12 .30
117 Mark Brunell .15 .40
118 Derrick Alexander .12 .30
119 Oronde Gadsden .15 .40
120 Ed McDaniel .12 .30
121 Eddie Kennison .12 .30
122 Jessie Armstead .12 .30
123 Charles Woodson .20 .50
124 Troy Vincent .12 .30
125 Jeff Garcia .15 .40
126 Marshall Faulk .20 .50
127 Jacquez Green .12 .30
128 Frank Wycheck .15 .40
129 Champ Bailey .15 .40
130 Natrone Means .15 .40
131 Jamal Anderson .15 .40
132 Doug Flutie .20 .50
133 Michael Bates .12 .30
134 Corey Dillon .15 .40
135 Corey Fuller .12 .30
136 Olandis Gary .15 .40
137 Johnnie Morton .15 .40
138 Peyton Manning .50 1.25
139 Fred Taylor .20 .50
140 Tony Gonzalez .20 .50
141 Zach Thomas .20 .50
142 Drew Bledsoe .20 .50
143 Keith Poole .12 .30
144 Vinny Testaverde .15 .40
145 Rich Gannon .15 .40
146 Jeremiah Trotter RC .40 1.00
147 Freddie Jones .12 .30
148 Jon Kitna .15 .40
149 Isaac Bruce .20 .50
150 Warrick Dunn .15 .40
151 Yancey Thigpen .12 .30
152 Darrell Green .15 .40
153 Terance Mathis .12 .30
154 Eric Moulds .15 .40
155 Wesley Walls .12 .30
156 Carl Pickens .15 .40
157 Troy Aikman .30 .75
158 Dwayne Carswell .12 .30
159 David Sloan .12 .30
160 Edgerrin James .20 .50
161 Jimmy Smith .15 .40
162 Tamarick Vanover .12 .30
163 Sam Madison .12 .30
164 Tony Simmons .12 .30
165 Andre Hastings .12 .30
166 Keyshawn Johnson .15 .40
167 Napoleon Kaufman .15 .40
168 Hines Ward .20 .50
169 Jeff Graham .12 .30
170 Derrick Mayes .12 .30
171 Torry Holt .20 .50
172 Blaine Bishop .12 .30
173 Rob Moore .12 .30
174 Pat Johnson .12 .30
175 Antowain Smith .15 .40
176 Marcus Robinson .15 .40
177 Takeo Spikes .12 .30
178 Rocket Ismail .15 .40
179 Ed McCaffrey .15 .40
180 Brett Favre .60 1.50
181 Ken Dilger .12 .30
182 Carnell Lake .12 .30
183 Cris Dishman .12 .30
184 Randy Moss .20 .50
185 Lawyer Milloy .12 .30
186 Jake Delhomme RC .50 1.25
187 Wayne Chrebet .15 .40
188 Darrell Russell .12 .30
189 Jerome Bettis .20 .50
190 Steve Young .25 .60
191 Ricky Watters .15 .40
192 Grant Wistrom .12 .30
193 Warren Sapp .15 .40
194 Jevon Kearse .15 .40
195 James Jett .15 .40
196 Courtney Brown RC .20 .50
197 Peter Warrick RC .25 .60
198 Thomas Jones RC .30 .75
199 Sylvester Morris RC .15 .40
200 Chad Pennington RC .40 1.00
201 Ron Dayne RC .25 .60
202 Todd Pinkston RC .15 .40
203 Deon Dyer RC .15 .40
204 Chris Redman RC .20 .50
205 Jerry Porter RC .25 .60
206 Michael Wiley RC .15 .40
207 J.R. Redmond RC .15 .40
208 Dennis Northcutt RC .20 .50
209 Gari Scott RC .15 .40
210 Anthony Lucas RC .15 .40
211 Danny Farmer RC .15 .40
212 Marcus Knight RC .15 .40
213 Plaxico Burress RC .25 .60
215 Bubba Franks RC .25 .60
216 Shaun Alexander RC .30 .75
217 Dez White RC .20 .50
218 Mareno Philyaw RC .15 .40
219 Travis Taylor RC .20 .50
220 Kwame Cavil RC .15 .40
221 Jamal Lewis RC .25 .60
222 Sebastian Janikowski RC .25 .60
223 Shyrone Stith RC .15 .40
224 Ron Dugans RC .15 .40
225 Darrell Jackson RC .20 .50
227 Tee Martin RC .25 .60
228 Tim Rattay RC .20 .50
229 Marc Bulger RC .25 .60
230 Doug Johnson RC .20 .50
231 Joe Hamilton RC .15 .40
Todd Husak RC
232 Travis Prentice RC .20 .50
R.Jay Soward RC
233 Trung Canidate RC .25 .60
Reuben Droughns RC
234 Tom Brady RC 7.50 15.00
Giovanni Carmazzi RC
235 Laveranues Coles RC .25 .60
Chafie Fields RC
236 Jarious Jackson RC .20 .50
Sherrod Gideon RC
237 Troy Walters RC .15 .40
Erron Kinney RC
238 Ronell Mealey RC .15 .40
Joey Goodspeed RC
239 Anthony Becht RC .20 .50
Quinton Spotwood RC
240 Deltha O'Neal RC .20 .50
Na'il Diggs RC
241 Corey Simon RC .20 .50
Chris Hovan RC
242 Brian Urlacher RC 1.00 2.50
Corey Moore RC
243 Keith Bulluck RC .20 .50
Rob Morris RC
244 Raynoch Thompson RC .15 .40
Deon Grant RC
245 John Abraham RC .25 .60
Shaun Ellis RC
P1 Tim Couch Promo .40 1.00

2000 SkyBox Dominion Extra

COMPLETE SET (243) 40.00 100.00
*VETS 1-195: 1X TO 2.5X BASIC CARDS
*ROOKIES 196-245: .8X TO 25X
STATED ODDS 1:2

2000 SkyBox Dominion Characteristics

COMPLETE SET (10) 10.00 25.00
STATED ODDS 1:35
1 Brett Favre 2.50 6.00
2 Troy Aikman 1.25 3.00
3 Terrell Davis .75 2.00
4 Emmitt Smith 2.00 5.00
5 Peyton Manning 2.00 5.00
6 Randy Moss .75 2.00
7 Tim Couch .60 1.50
8 Eddie George .60 1.50
9 Kurt Warner 1.25 3.00
10 Edgerrin James .75 2.00

2000 SkyBox Dominion Go-To Guys

COMPLETE SET (20) 7.50 20.00
STATED ODDS 1:12
1 Peyton Manning 1.50 4.00
2 Brett Favre 2.00 5.00
3 Troy Aikman 1.00 2.50
4 Kurt Warner 1.00 2.50
5 Randy Moss .60 1.50
6 Germane Crowell .40 1.00
7 Marvin Harrison .60 1.50
8 Jerry Rice 1.25 3.00
9 Muhsin Muhammad .50 1.25
10 Marcus Robinson .50 1.25
11 Isaac Bruce .60 1.50
12 Tim Brown .60 1.50
13 Stephen Davis .50 1.25
14 Cris Carter .60 1.50
15 Tim Couch .50 1.25
16 Ricky Williams .60 1.50
17 Dorsey Levens .50 1.25
18 Keyshawn Johnson .50 1.25
19 Mark Brunell .50 1.25
20 Jimmy Smith .50 1.25

2000 SkyBox Dominion Hard Corps

COMPLETE SET (10) 2.50 6.00
STATED ODDS 1:6
1 Brett Favre .75 2.00
2 Eddie George .20 .50
3 Terrell Davis .25 .60
4 Randy Moss .25 .60
5 Marshall Faulk .25 .60
6 Ricky Williams .25 .60
7 Keyshawn Johnson .20 .50
8 Fred Taylor .25 .60
9 Steve Young .30 .75
10 Edgerrin James .25 .60

2000 SkyBox Dominion Turfs Up

COMPLETE SET (10) 6.00 15.00
STATED ODDS 1:18
1 Terrell Davis .60 1.50
2 Ricky Williams .60 1.50
3 Jamal Anderson .50 1.25
4 Marshall Faulk .60 1.50
5 Emmitt Smith 1.50 4.00
6 Eddie George .50 1.25
7 Fred Taylor .60 1.50
8 Edgerrin James .60 1.50
9 Warrick Dunn .50 1.25
10 Stephen Davis .50 1.25

1998 SkyBox Double Vision

This 32-card set was distributed in one-card packs with a suggested retail price of $5.99. The cards feature player color action photos and portraits printed on a large interactive slide that makes images appear and disappear. The slide mechanism combined with an acetate window background magically disappears. The borders are illustrated with team logos and colors. Every slide is sequentially numbered to 5000. The set includes the subset, "Strange but True" (Cards #22-32).

COMPLETE SET (32) 40.00 80.00
1 Dan Marino 3.00 8.00
2 John Elway 3.00 8.00
3 Troy Aikman 2.00 5.00
4 Steve Young 1.25 3.00
5 Terrell Davis 2.00 5.00
6 Barry Sanders 3.00 8.00
7 Jerry Rice 2.00 5.00
8 Kordell Stewart .60 1.50
9 Jake Plummer .60 1.50
10 Brett Favre 3.00 8.00
11 Drew Bledsoe 1.25 3.00
12 Tony Banks .40 1.00
13 Kerry Collins .40 1.00
14 Steve McNair .60 1.50
15 Warren Moon .40 1.00
16 Ryan Leaf .60 1.50
17 Peyton Manning 4.00 10.00
18 Elvis Grbac .40 1.00
19 Jeff Blake .40 1.00
20 Brad Johnson .60 1.50
21 Trent Dilfer .40 1.00
22 Scott Mitchell .30 .75
23 Dan Marino 3.00 8.00
24 John Elway 3.00 8.00
25 Troy Aikman 2.00 5.00
26 Steve Young 1.25 3.00
27 Terrell Davis 2.00 5.00
28 Barry Sanders 3.00 8.00
29 Jerry Rice 2.00 5.00
30 Kordell Stewart .60 1.50
31 Jake Plummer .60 1.50
32 Brett Favre 3.00 8.00

1992 SkyBox/Impel Impact/Primetime Promos

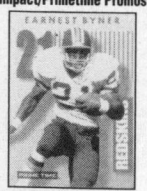

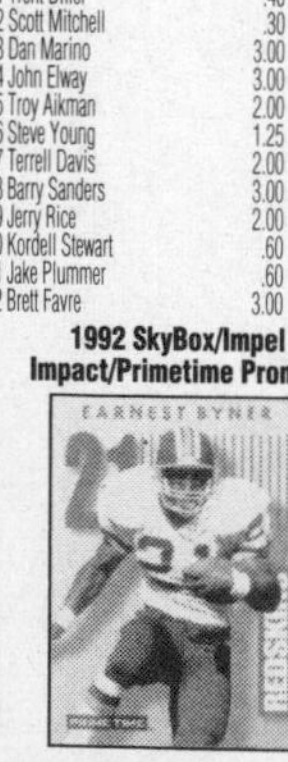

This two-card promotional standard-size set was distributed at the Super Bowl XXVI Show in Minneapolis in January, 1992. These cards were issued before Impel changed their corporate name to SkyBox and hence made some subtle changes in the promo cards to reflect their new identity. The Byner card displays a full-bleed photo of him running with the ball, superimposed on a gray background. His name and jersey number are printed in maroon, with the team name in white on a maroon bar. Against the background of a crowd, the Kelly card shows him with the ball cocked, ready to pass. The backs of both cards have an advertisement for Impel's new Impact and Primetime series. The Byner card is trimmed in red, while the Kelly card is trimmed in blue. The cards are unnumbered.

NNO Jim Kelly 1.20 3.00
Impact
NNO Earnest Byner .50 1.25
PrimeTime

1992 SkyBox Impact Promos

These three standard-size cards were issued as a promo pack to show what the then-upcoming SkyBox Impact cards would be like. The fronts feature full-bleed color action photos, with the player's name in block lettering across the top of the picture. The team logo is superimposed at the lower left corner, and the SkyBox logo appears in the lower right corner. The backs show another color photo, career highlights, statistics, and the player's position by a diagram of "X's" and "O's." The photo displayed on the front of the Kelly card is almost identical to that used on the Impel promo given away at the Super Bowl XXVI card show.

COMPLETE SET (3)	1.60	4.00
1 Jim Kelly	1.00	2.50
2 Michael Dean Perry	.40	1.00
3 Reggie Roby	.40	1.00

1992 SkyBox Impact

The 1992 SkyBox Impact set consists of 350 standard-size cards that were issued in 12 and 24-card packs. The set includes the following subsets: Team Checklists (277-304), High Impact League Leaders (305-314), Sudden Impact Hardest Hitters (315-320), and Instant Impact Rookies (321-350). The key Rookie Cards in this set are Edgar Bennett, Steve Bono, Robert Brooks, Terrell Buckley, Marco Coleman, Steve Emtman and Carl Pickens. Five hundred Impact Playmakers cards featuring Magic Johnson and Jim Kelly bear autographs by both stars. These cards were randomly inserted in foil packs. Also, 2,500 gold foil-stamped Total Impact cards were autographed by Jim Kelly and randomly inserted in the foil packs.

COMPLETE SET (350)	5.00	12.00
1 Jim Kelly	.08	.25
2 Andre Rison	.02	.10
3 Michael Dean Perry	.02	.10
4 Herman Moore	.08	.25
5 Fred McAfee RC	.01	.05
6 Ricky Proehl	.01	.05
7 Jim Everett	.02	.10
8 Mark Carrier DB	.01	.05
9 Eric Martin	.01	.05
10 John Elway	.50	1.25
11 Michael Irvin	.08	.25
12 Keith McCants	.01	.05
13 Greg Lloyd	.02	.10
14 Lawrence Taylor	.08	.25
15 Mike Tomczak	.01	.05
16 Cortez Kennedy	.02	.10
17 William Fuller	.01	.05
18 James Lofton	.02	.10
19 Kevin Fagan	.01	.05
20 Bill Brooks	.01	.05
21 Roger Craig UER (Text is about Vikings, but Raiders logo still on card)	.02	.10
22 Jay Novacek	.02	.10
23 Steve Sewell	.01	.05
24 William Perry UER (Card has him injured for 1988, but he did play)	.02	.10
25 Jerry Rice	.30	.75
26 James Joseph	.01	.05
27 Timm Rosenbach	.01	.05
28 Pat Terrell	.01	.05
29 Jon Vaughn	.01	.05
30 Steve Walsh	.01	.05
31 James Hasty	.01	.05
32 Dwight Stone	.01	.05
33 Derrick Fenner UER (Text mentions Bengals, but Seahawks logo still on front)	.01	.05
34 Mark Bortz	.01	.05
35 Dan Saleaumua	.01	.05
36 Sammie Smith UER (Text mentions Broncos, but Dolphins logo still on front)	.01	.05
37 Antone Davis	.01	.05
38 Steve Young	.25	.60
39 Mike Baab	.01	.05
40 Rick Fenney	.01	.05
41 Chris Hinton	.01	.05
42 Bart Oates	.01	.05
43 Bryan Hinkle	.01	.05
44 James Francis	.01	.05
45 Ray Crockett	.01	.05
46 Eric Dickerson UER (Text mentions Raiders, but Colts logo still on front)	.02	.10
47 Hart Lee Dykes	.01	.05
48 Percy Snow	.01	.05
49 Ron Hall	.01	.05
50 Warren Moon	.08	.25
51 Ed West	.01	.05
52 Clarence Verdin	.01	.05
53 Eugene Lockhart	.01	.05
54 Andre Reed	.02	.10
55 Kevin Ross	.01	.05
56 Al Noga	.01	.05
57 Wes Hopkins	.01	.05
58 Rufus Porter	.01	.05
59 Brian Mitchell	.02	.10
60 Reggie Roby	.01	.05
61 Rodney Peete	.02	.10
62 Jeff Herrod	.01	.05
63 Anthony Smith	.01	.05
64 Brad Muster	.01	.05
65 Jessie Tuggle	.01	.05
66 Al Smith	.01	.05
67 Jeff Hostetler	.02	.10
68 John L. Williams	.01	.05
69 Paul Gruber	.01	.05
70 Cornelius Bennett	.02	.10
71 William White	.01	.05
72 Tom Rathman	.01	.05
73 Boomer Esiason	.02	.10
74 Neil Smith	.08	.25
75 Sterling Sharpe	.08	.25
76 James Jones	.01	.05
77 David Treadwell	.01	.05
78 Flipper Anderson	.01	.05
79 Eric Allen	.01	.05
80 Joe Jacoby	.01	.05
81 Keith Sims	.01	.05
82 Bubba McDowell	.01	.05
83 Ronnie Lippett	.01	.05
84 Cris Carter	.20	.50
85 Chris Burkett	.01	.05
86 Issiac Holt.	.01	.05
87 Duane Bickett	.01	.05
88 Leslie O'Neal	.02	.10
89 Gill Fenerty	.01	.05
90 Pierce Holt	.01	.05
91 Willie Drewrey	.01	.05
92 Brian Blades	.02	.10
93 Tony Martin	.02	.10
94 Jessie Hester	.01	.05
95 John Stephens	.01	.05
96 Keith Willis UER (Text mentions Redskins, but Steelers logo still on front)	.01	.05
97 Vai Sikahema UER (Text mentions Eagles, but Cardinals logo still on front)	.01	.05
98 Mark Higgs	.01	.05
99 Steve McMichael	.02	.10
100 Deion Sanders	.20	.50
101 Marvin Washington	.01	.05
102 Ken Norton	.02	.10
103 Barry Word	.01	.05
104 Sean Jones	.01	.05
105 Ronnie Harmon	.01	.05
106 Donnell Woolford	.01	.05
107 Ray Agnew	.01	.05
108 Lemuel Stinson	.01	.05
109 Dennis Smith	.01	.05
110 Lorenzo White	.01	.05
111 Craig Heyward	.02	.10
112 Jeff Query UER (Text mentions Oilers, but Packers logo still on front)	.01	.05
113 Gary Plummer	.01	.05
114 John Taylor	.02	.10
115 Rohn Stark	.01	.05
116 Tom Waddle	.01	.05
117 Jeff Cross	.01	.05
118 Tim Green	.01	.05
119 Anthony Munoz	.02	.10
120 Mel Gray	.02	.10
121 Ray Donaldson	.01	.05
122 Dennis Byrd	.01	.05
123 Carnell Lake	.01	.05
124 Broderick Thomas	.01	.05
125 Charles Mann	.01	.05
126 Darion Conner	.01	.05
127 John Roper	.01	.05
128 Jack Del Rio UER (Text mentions Vikings, but Cowboys logo still on front)	.01	.05
129 Rickey Dixon	.01	.05
130 Eddie Anderson	.01	.05
131 Steve Broussard	.01	.05
132 Michael Young	.01	.05
133 Lamar Lathon	.01	.05
134 Rickey Jackson	.01	.05
135 Billy Ray Smith	.01	.05
136 Tony Casillas	.01	.05
137 Ickey Woods	.01	.05
138 Ray Childress	.01	.05
139 Vance Johnson	.01	.05
140 Brett Perriman	.08	.25
141 Calvin Williams	.02	.10
142 Dino Hackett	.01	.05
143 Jacob Green	.01	.05
144 Robert Delpino	.01	.05
145 Marv Cook	.01	.05
146 Dwayne Harper	.01	.05
147 Ricky Ervins	.01	.05
148 Kelvin Martin	.01	.05
149 Leroy Hoard	.02	.10
150 Dan Marino	.50	1.25
151 Richard Johnson UER (He and Carrier had 2 interceptions, only given credit for 1 on card)	.01	.05
152 Henry Ellard	.02	.10
153 Al Toon	.02	.10
154 Dermontti Dawson	.01	.05
155 Robert Blackmon	.01	.05
156 Howie Long	.08	.25
157 David Fulcher	.01	.05
158 Mike Merriweather	.01	.05
159 Gary Anderson K	.01	.05
160 John Friesz	.02	.10
161 Eugene Robinson	.01	.05
162 Brad Baxter	.01	.05
163 Bennie Blades	.01	.05
164 Harold Green	.01	.05
165 Ernest Givins	.02	.10
166 Deron Cherry	.01	.05
167 Carl Banks	.01	.05
168 Keith Jackson	.02	.10
169 Pat Leahy	.01	.05
170 Alvin Harper	.02	.10
171 David Little	.01.	.05
172 Anthony Carter	.02	.10
173 Willie Gault	.02	.10
174 Bruce Armstrong	.01	.05
175 Junior Seau	.08	.25
176 Eric Metcalf	.02	.10
177 Tony Mandarich	.01	.05
178 Ernie Jones	.01	.05
179 Albert Bentley	.01	.05
180 Mike Pritchard	.02	.10
181 Bubby Brister	.01	.05
182 Vaughan Johnson	.01	.05
183 Robert Clark UER (Text mentions Dolphins, but Seahawks logo on front)	.01	.05
184 Lawrence Dawsey	.02	.10
185 Eric Green	.01	.05
186 Jay Schroeder	.01	.05
187 Andre Tippett	.01	.05
188 Vinny Testaverde	.02	.10
189 Wendell Davis	.01	.05
190 Russell Maryland	.01	.05
191 Chris Singleton	.01	.05
192 Ken O'Brien	.01	.05
193 Merril Hoge	.01	.05
194 Steve Bono RC	.08	.25
195 Earnest Byner	.01	.05
196 Mike Singletary	.02	.10
197 Gaston Green	.01	.05
198 Mark Carrier WR	.02	.10
199 Harvey Williams	.08	.25
200 Randall Cunningham	.08	.25
201 Cris Dishman	.01	.05
202 Greg Townsend	.01	.05
203 Christian Okoye	.01	.05
204 Sam Mills	.01	.05
205 Kyle Clifton	.01	.05
206 Jim Harbaugh	.08	.25
207 Anthony Thompson	.01	.05
208 Rob Moore	.02	.10
209 Irving Fryar	.02	.10
210 Derrick Thomas	.08	.25
211 Chris Miller	.02	.10
212 Doug Smith	.01	.05
213 Michael Haynes	.02	.10
214 Phil Simms	.02	.10
215 Charles Haley	.02	.10
216 Burt Grossman	.01	.05
217 Rod Bernstine	.01	.05
218 Louis Lipps	.01	.05
219 Dan McGwire UER (Actually drafted in/1991, not 1990)	.01	.05
220 Ethan Horton	.01	.05
221 Michael Carter	.01	.05
222 Neil O'Donnell	.02	.10
223 Anthony Miller	.02	.10
224 Eric Swann	.02	.10
225 Thurman Thomas	.08	.25
226 Jeff George	.08	.25
227 Joe Montana	.50	1.25
228 Leonard Marshall	.01	.05
229 Haywood Jeffires	.02	.10
230 Mark Clayton	.02	.10
231 Chris Doleman	.01	.05
232 Troy Aikman	.30	.75
233 Gary Anderson RB	.01	.05
234 Pat Swilling	.01	.05
235 Ronnie Lott	.02	.10
236 Brian Jordan	.02	.10
237 Bruce Smith	.08	.25
238 Tony Jones UER (Text mentions Falcons, but Oilers logo still on front)	.01	.05
239 Tim McKyer	.01	.05
240 Gary Clark	.08	.25
241 Mitchell Price	.01	.05
242 John Kasay	.01	.05
243 Stephone Paige	.01	.05
244 Jeff Wright	.01	.05
245 Shannon Sharpe	.08	.25
246 Keith Byars	.01	.05
247 Charles Dimry	.01	.05
248 Steve Smith	.01	.05
249 Eric Pegram	.02	.10
250 Bernie Kosar	.02	.10
251 Peter Tom Willis	.01	.05
252 Mark Ingram	.01	.05
253 Keith McKeller	.01	.05
254 Lewis Billups UER (Text mentions Packers, but Bengals logo still on front)	.01	.05
255 Alton Montgomery	.01	.05
256 Jimmie Jones	.01	.05
257 Brent Williams	.01	.05
258 Gene Atkins	.01	.05
259 Reggie Rutland	.01	.05
260 Sam Seale UER (Text mentions Raiders, but Chargers logo still on back)	.01	.05
261 Andre Ware	.01	.05
262 Fred Barnett	.08	.25
263 Randal Hill	.01	.05
264 Patrick Hunter	.01	.05
265 Johnny Rembert UER (Card says DNP in 1991, but he played 12 games)	.01	.05
266 Monte Coleman	.01	.05
267 Aaron Wallace	.01	.05
268 Ferrell Edmunds	.01	.05
269 Stan Thomas	.01	.05
270 Robb Thomas	.01	.05
271 Martin Bayless UER (Text mentions Chiefs, but Chargers logo still on front)	.01	.05
272 Dean Biasucci	.01	.05
273 Keith Henderson	.01	.05
274 Vinnie Clark	.01	.05
275 Emmitt Smith	.60	1.50
276 Mark Rypien	.01	.05
277 Atlanta Falcons CL Wing and a Prayer (Michael Haynes)	.01	.05
278 Buffalo Bills CL Machine Gun (Jim Kelly)	.02	.10
279 Chicago Bears CL Grizzly (Tom Waddle)	.01	.05
280 Cincinnati Bengals CL Price is Right (Mitchell Price)	.01	.05
281 Cleveland Browns CL Coasting (Bernie Kosar)	.01	.05
282 Dallas Cowboys CL Gunned Down (Michael Irvin)	.02	.10
283 Denver Broncos CL The Drive II (John Elway)	.20	.50
284 Detroit Lions CL Lions Roar (Mel Gray)	.01	.05
285 Green Bay Packers CL Razor Sharpe (Sterling Sharpe)	.02	.10
286 Houston Oilers CL Oil's Well (Warren Moon)	.02	.10
287 Indianapolis Colts CL Whew (Jeff George)	.02	.10
288 Kansas City Chiefs CL Ambush (Derrick Thomas)	.02	.10
289 Los Angeles Raiders CL Lott of Defense (Ronnie Lott)	.01	.05
290 Los Angeles Rams CL Ram It (Robert Delpino)	.01	.05
291 Miami Dolphins CL Miami Ice (Dan Marino)	.20	.50
292 Minnesota Vikings CL Purple Blaze (Cris Carter)	.08	.25
293 New England Patriots CL Surprise Attack (Irving Fryar)	.01	.05
294 New Orleans Saints CL Marching In (Gene Atkins)	.01	.05
295 New York Giants CL Almost Perfect (Phil Simms)	.01	.05
296 New York Jets CL Playoff Bound (Ken O'Brien)	.01	.05
297 Philadelphia Eagles CL Flying High (Keith Jackson)	.01	.05
298 Phoenix Cardinals CL Airborne (Ricky Proehl)	.01	.05
299 Pittsburgh Steelers CL Steel Curtain (Bryan Hinkle)	.01	.05
300 San Diego Chargers CL Lightning (John Friesz)	.01	.05
301 San Francisco 49ers CL Instant Rice (Jerry Rice)	.20	.50
302 Seattle Seahawks CL Defense Never Rests (Eugene Robinson)	.01	.05
303 T.Bay Buccaneers CL Stunned Broderick Thomas	.01	.05
304 Washington Redskins CL Super (Mark Rypien)	.01	.05
305 Jim Kelly LL	.02	.10
306 Steve Young LL	.10	.30
307 Thurman Thomas LL	.02	.10
308 Emmitt Smith LL	.30	.75
309 Haywood Jeffires LL	.01	.05
310 Michael Irvin LL	.02	.10
311 William Fuller LL	.01	.05
312 Pat Swilling LL	.01	.05
313 Ronnie Lott LL	.01	.05
314 Deion Sanders LL	.08	.25
315 Cornelius Bennett HH	.01	.05
316 David Fulcher HH	.01	.05
317 Ronnie Lott HH	.01	.05
318 Pat Swilling HH	.01	.05
319 Lawrence Taylor HH	.02	.10
320 Derrick Thomas HH	.02	.10
321 Steve Emtman RC	.01	.05
322 Carl Pickens RC	.08	.25
323 David Klingler RC	.01	.05
324 Dale Carter RC	.02	.10
325 Mike Gaddis RC	.01	.05
326 Quentin Coryatt RC	.01	.05
327 Darryl Williams RC	.01	.05
328 Jeremy Lincoln RC	.01	.05
329 Robert Jones RC	.01	.05
330 Bucky Richardson RC	.01	.05
331 Tony Brooks RC	.01	.05
332 Alonzo Spellman RC	.02	.10
333 Robert Brooks RC	.25	.60
334 Marco Coleman RC	.01	.05
335 Siran Stacy RC UER (Misspelled Stacey)	.01	.05
336 Tommy Maddox RC	.60	1.50
337 Steve Israel RC	.01	.05
338 Vaughn Dunbar RC	.01	.05
339 Shane Collins RC	.01	.05
340 Kevin Smith RC	.01	.05
341 Chris Mims RC	.01	.05
342 C.McGlockton RC UER Misspelled McGlokton on both sides	.02	.10
343 Tracy Scroggins RC	.01	.05
344 Howard Dinkins RC	.01	.05
345 Levon Kirkland RC	.01	.05
346 Terrell Buckley RC	.01	.05
347 Marquez Pope RC	.01	.05
348 Phillippi Sparks RC	.01	.05
349 Joe Bowden RC	.01	.05
350 Edgar Bennett RC	.08	.25
SP1 Jim Kelly	3.00	8.00
SP1AU Jim Kelly AUTO	15.00	40.00
SP2AU Kelly Magic AUTO	100.00	250.00

1992 SkyBox Impact Holograms

COMPLETE SET (6)	8.00	20.00
H1-H2 RANDOM INSERTS IN PACKS		
H3-H6 AVAILABLE VIA MAIL REDEMPT.		
H1 Jim Kelly	1.00	2.50
H2 Lawrence Taylor	1.00	2.50
H3 Christian Okoye	2.00	4.00
H4 Mark Rypien	2.00	4.00
H5 Pat Swilling	2.00	4.00
H6 Ricky Ervins	2.00	4.00

1992 SkyBox Impact Major Impact

COMPLETE SET (20)	6.00	15.00
RANDOM INSERTS IN JUMBO PACKS		
M1 Cornelius Bennett	.08	.25
M2 David Fulcher	.05	.15
M3 Haywood Jeffires	.08	.25
M4 Ronnie Lott	.08	.25
M5 Dan Marino	1.25	3.00
M6 Warren Moon	.25	.60
M7 Christian Okoye	.05	.15
M8 Andre Reed	.08	.25
M9 Derrick Thomas	.25	.60
M10 Thurman Thomas	.25	.60
M11 Troy Aikman	.75	2.00
M12 Randall Cunningham	.25	.60
M13 Michael Irvin	.25	.60
M14 Jerry Rice	.75	2.00
M15 Joe Montana	1.25	3.00
M16 Mark Rypien	.05	.15
M17 Deion Sanders	.50	1.25
M18 Emmitt Smith	1.50	4.00
M19 Pat Swilling	.05	.15
M20 Lawrence Taylor	.25	.60

1993 SkyBox Impact Promos

These two standard-size cards were issued to preview the design of the 1993 SkyBox Impact football set. The fronts feature full-bleed color action player photos with an unfocused background to make the featured player stand out. The player's name is printed vertically with the team logo beneath it. The top of the back has a second color photo, with biography, expanded four-year statistics, and career totals filling out the rest of the back. The cards are numbered on the back. A version of Jim Kelly was also issued at the 1993 Chicago National with a stamp commemorating that event on the card front.

COMPLETE SET (2)	1.20	3.00
IP1 Jim Kelly	.80	2.00
IP2 Lawrence Taylor	.40	1.00

1993 SkyBox Impact

The 1993 SkyBox Impact football set consists of 400 standard-size cards. Cards were issued in 12-card packs that included one Impact Colors card. The cards are checklisted below alphabetically according to teams. Subsets include Class of '83 (341-352), and Impact Rookies (361-400) which represents first and second round draft picks. Rookie Cards include Jerome Bettis, Drew Bledsoe, Curtis Conway, Garrison Hearst, O.J. McDuffie, Natrone Means, Glyn Milburn, Rick Mirer and Robert Smith. Randomly inserted in foil packs were 500 individually numbered redemption certificates that entitled the collector to an Impact Jim Kelly/Magic Johnson Header card signed by Kelly. As a bonus, certificates number 12 and number 32, which correspond to Kelly and Johnson's uniform numbers, respectively, received the autographed cards personally presented by the superstar.

COMPLETE SET (400)	6.00	15.00
1 Steve Broussard	.01	.05
2 Michael Haynes	.02	.10
3 Tony Smith	.01	.05
4 Tory Epps	.01	.05
5 Chris Hinton	.01	.05
6 Bobby Hebert	.01	.05
7 Tim McKyer	.01	.05
8 Chris Miller	.02	.10
9 Bruce Pickens	.01	.05
10 Mike Pritchard	.02	.10
11 Andre Rison	.02	.10
12 Deion Sanders	.20	.50
13 Pierce Holt	.01	.05
14 Jessie Tuggle	.01	.05
15 Don Beebe	.01	.05
16 Cornelius Bennett	.02	.10
17 Kenneth Davis	.01	.05
18 Kent Hull	.01	.05
19 Jim Kelly	.08	.25
20 Mark Kelso	.01	.05
21 Keith McKeller UER (Name misspelled McKellar on front)	.01	.05
22 Andre Reed	.02	.10
23 Jim Ritcher	.01	.05
24 Bruce Smith	.08	.25
25 Thurman Thomas	.08	.25
26 Steve Christie	.01	.05
27 Darryl Talley UER (Name misspelled Darrell on front)	.01	.05
28 Pete Metzelaars	.01	.05
29 Steve Tasker	.02	.10
30 Henry Jones	.01	.05
31 Neal Anderson	.01	.05
32 Trace Armstrong	.01	.05
33 Mark Bortz	.01	.05
34 Mark Carrier DB	.01	.05
35 Wendell Davis	.01	.05
36 Richard Dent	.02	.10
37 Jim Harbaugh	.08	.25
38 Steve McMichael	.02	.10
39 Craig Heyward	.02	.10
40 William Perry	.02	.10
41 Donnell Woolford	.01	.05
42 Tom Waddle	.01	.05
43 Anthony Morgan	.01	.05
44 Jim Breech	.01	.05
45 David Klingler	.01	.05
46 Derrick Fenner	.01	.05
47 David Fulcher	.01	.05
48 James Francis	.01	.05
49 Harold Green	.01	.05
50 Carl Pickens	.02	.10
51 Jay Schroeder	.01	.05
52 Alex Gordon	.01	.05
53 Eric Ball	.01	.05
54 Eddie Brown	.01	.05
55 Jay Hilgenberg UER (Name misspelled Hilgenburg on front)	.01	.05
56 Michael Jackson	.02	.10
57 Bernie Kosar	.02	.10
58 Kevin Mack	.01	.05
59 Eric Metcalf	.02	.10
60 Michael Dean Perry	.02	.10
61 Tommy Vardell	.01	.05
62 Leroy Hoard	.02	.10
63 Clay Matthews	.02	.10
64 Vinny Testaverde	.02	.10
65 Mark Carrier WR	.02	.10
66 Troy Aikman	.30	.75
67 Lin Elliott RC UER (Name misspelled Elliot on front)	.01	.05
68 Thomas Everett	.01	.05
69 Alvin Harper	.02	.10
70 Ray Horton	.01	.05
71 Michael Irvin	.08	.25
72 Russell Maryland	.01	.05
73 Jay Novacek	.02	.10
74 Emmitt Smith	.60	1.50
75 Tony Casillas	.01	.05
76 Robert Jones	.01	.05
77 Ken Norton Jr.	.02	.10
78 Daryl Johnston	.08	.25
79 Charles Haley	.02	.10
80 Leon Lett RC	.02	.10
81 Steve Atwater	.01	.05
82 Mike Croel	.01	.05
83 John Elway	.60	1.50
84 Simon Fletcher	.01	.05
85 Vance Johnson	.01	.05
86 Shannon Sharpe	.08	.25
87 Rod Bernstine	.01	.05
88 Robert Delpino	.01	.05
89 Karl Mecklenburg	.01	.05
90 Steve Sewell	.01	.05
91 Tommy Maddox UER (Name misspelled Maddux on front and back)	.08	.25
92 Arthur Marshall RC	.01	.05
93 Dennis Smith	.01	.05
94 Derek Russell	.01	.05
95 Bennie Blades	.01	.05
96 Michael Cofer	.01	.05
97 Willie Green	.01	.05
98 Herman Moore	.08	.25
99 Rodney Peete	.01	.05
100 Andre Ware	.01	.05
101 Barry Sanders UER	.50	1.25
102 Chris Spielman	.02	.10
103 Jason Hanson	.01	.05
104 Mel Gray	.02	.10
105 Pat Swilling	.01	.05
106 Bill Fralic	.01	.05
107 Rodney Holman	.01	.05
108 Brett Favre	.75	2.00
109 Sterling Sharpe	.08	.25
110 Reggie White	.08	.25
111 Terrell Buckley	.01	.05
112 Sanjay Beach	.01	.05
113 Tony Bennett	.01	.05
114 Jackie Harris	.01	.05
115 Bryce Paup	.02	.10
116 Shawn Patterson	.01	.05
117 John Stephens	.01	.05
118 Cris Dishman	.01	.05
119 Ernest Givins	.02	.10
120 Haywood Jeffires	.02	.10
121 Lamar Lathon	.01	.05
122 Warren Moon	.08	.25
123 Lorenzo White	.01	.05
124 Curtis Duncan	.01	.05
125 Webster Slaughter	.01	.05
126 Cody Carlson	.01	.05
127 Leonard Harris	.01	.05
128 Bruce Matthews	.01	.05
129 Ray Childress	.01	.05
130 Al Smith	.01	.05
131 Jeff George	.08	.25
132 Anthony Johnson	.02	.10
133 Steve Emtman	.01	.05
134 Quentin Coryatt	.02	.10
135 Rodney Culver	.01	.05
136 Jessie Hester	.01	.05
137 Aaron Cox	.01	.05
138 Clarence Verdin	.01	.05
139 Joe Montana	.60	1.50
140 Dave Krieg	.02	.10
141 Harvey Williams	.02	.10
142 Derrick Thomas	.08	.25
143 Barry Word	.01	.05
144 Christian Okoye	.01	.05
145 Nick Lowery	.01	.05
146 Dale Carter	.01	.05
147 Willie Davis	.08	.25
148 Tim Barnett	.01	.05
149 Neil Smith UER (Name misspelled Neal on front)	.08	.25
150 Marcus Allen	.08	.25
151 Nick Bell	.01	.05
152 Tim Brown	.08	.25
153 Eric Dickerson	.02	.10
154 Willie Gault	.01	.05
155 Howie Long	.08	.25
156 Gaston Green	.01	.05
157 Chester McGlockton	.02	.10
158 Eddie Anderson	.01	.05
159 Ethan Horton	.01	.05
160 James Lofton	.02	.10
161 Jeff Hostetler	.02	.10
162 Terry McDaniel	.01	.05
163 Flipper Anderson	.01	.05
164 Shane Conlan	.01	.05
165 Jim Everett	.02	.10
166 Henry Ellard	.02	.10
167 Cleveland Gary	.01	.05
168 Todd Lyght	.01	.05
169 Sean Gilbert	.02	.10
170 Jim Price	.01	.05
171 Bill Hawkins	.01	.05
172 Mark Clayton	.01	.05
173 Mark Higgs	.01	.05
174 Dan Marino	.60	1.50
175 Louis Oliver	.01	.05
176 Reggie Roby	.01	.05
177 Bobby Humphrey	.01	.05
178 Troy Vincent	.01	.05
179 Marco Coleman	.01	.05
180 Aaron Craver	.01	.05
181 Keith Jackson	.02	.10
182 Mark Duper	.01	.05
183 Pete Stoyanovich	.01	.05
184 Irving Fryar	.02	.10
185 Bryan Cox UER (Name misspelled Brian on front and back)	.01	.05
186 Terry Allen	.08	.25
187 Anthony Carter	.02	.10
188 Cris Carter	.08	.25
189 Chris Doleman	.01	.05
190 Rich Gannon	.08	.25
191 Sean Salisbury	.01	.05
192 Hassan Jones	.01	.05
193 Steve Jordan	.01	.05
194 Roger Craig	.02	.10
195 Todd Scott	.01	.05
196 Esera Tuaolo	.01	.05
197 Ray Agnew	.01	.05
198 Marv Cook	.01	.05
199 Tommy Hodson	.01	.05
200 Chris Singleton	.01	.05
201 Michael Timpson	.01	.05
202 Jon Vaughn ERR (Photo on back is Keith Byars)	.01	.05
203 Leonard Russell	.02	.10
204 Scott Zolak	.01	.05
205 Reyna Thompson	.01	.05
206 Andre Tippett	.01	.05
207 Morten Andersen UER (Name misspelled Morton Anderson on front)	.01	.05
208 Wesley Carroll	.01	.05
209 Vince Buck	.01	.05
210 Rickey Jackson	.01	.05
211 Vaughan Johnson UER (Name misspelled Vaughn on front)	.01	.05
212 Eric Martin	.01	.05
213 Sam Mills	.01	.05
214 Steve Walsh	.01	.05
215 Wade Wilson	.01	.05
216 Vaughn Dunbar	.01	.05
217 Brad Muster	.01	.05
218 Dalton Hilliard	.01	.05
219 Floyd Turner	.01	.05
220 Stephen Baker	.01	.05
221 Mark Jackson	.01	.05
222 Jarrod Bunch	.01	.05
223 Mark Collins	.01	.05
224 Rodney Hampton	.02	.10
225 Phil Simms	.02	.10
226 Pepper Johnson	.01	.05
227 Dave Meggett	.01	.05
228 Derek Brown TE	.01	.05
229 Mike Sherrard	.01	.05
230 Lawrence Taylor	.08	.25
231 Leonard Marshall	.01	.05
232 Brad Baxter	.01	.05
233 Dennis Byrd	.01	.05
234 Ronnie Lott	.02	.10
235 Boomer Esiason	.02	.10
236 Browning Nagle	.01	.05
237 Rob Moore	.02	.10
238 Jeff Lageman	.01	.05
239 Johnny Mitchell	.01	.05
240 Chris Burkett	.01	.05
241 Eric Thomas	.01	.05
242 Johnny Johnson	.01	.05
243 Eric Allen	.01	.05
244 Fred Barnett	.02	.10
245 Keith Byars	.01	.05
246 Randall Cunningham	.08	.25
247 Heath Sherman	.01	.05
248 Calvin Williams	.02	.10
249 Erik McMillan	.01	.05
250 Byron Evans	.01	.05
251 Seth Joyner	.01	.05
252 Vai Sikahema	.01	.05
253 Andre Waters	.01	.05
254 Tim Harris	.01	.05
255 Mark Bavaro	.01	.05
256 Clyde Simmons	.01	.05
257 Steve Beuerlein	.02	.10
258 Randal Hill UER (Name misspelled Randall on front)	.01	.05
259 Ernie Jones	.01	.05
260 Robert Massey	.01	.05
261 Ricky Proehl UER (Name misspelled Rickey on front)	.01	.05
262 Aeneas Williams	.01	.05
263 Johnny Bailey	.01	.05
264 Chris Chandler UER (Name misspelled Cris on front)	.02	.10
265 Anthony Thompson	.01	.05
266 Gary Clark	.02	.10
267 Chuck Cecil	.01	.05
268 Rich Camarillo	.01	.05
269 Neil O'Donnell	.08	.25
270 Gerald Williams	.01	.05
271 Greg Lloyd	.02	.10
272 Eric Green	.01	.05
273 Merril Hoge	.01	.05
274 Ernie Mills	.01	.05
275 Rod Woodson	.08	.25
276 Gary Anderson K	.01	.05
277 Barry Foster	.02	.10
278 Jeff Graham	.02	.10
279 Dwight Stone	.01	.05
280 Kevin Greene	.02	.10
281 Eric Bieniemy	.01	.05
282 Marion Butts	.01	.05
283 Gill Byrd	.01	.05
284 Stan Humphries	.02	.10
285 Anthony Miller	.02	.10
286 Leslie O'Neal	.02	.10
287 Junior Seau	.08	.25
288 Ronnie Harmon	.01	.05
289 Nate Lewis	.01	.05
290 John Kidd	.01	.05
291 Steve Young	.30	.75
292 John Taylor	.02	.10
293 Jerry Rice	.40	1.00
294 Tim McDonald	.01	.05
295 Brent Jones	.02	.10
296 Tom Rathman	.01	.05
297 Dexter Carter	.01	.05
298 Mike Cofer	.01	.05
299 Ricky Watters	.08	.25
300 Mervyn Fernandez	.01	.05
301 Amp Lee	.01	.05
302 Kevin Fagan	.01	.05
303 Roy Foster	.01	.05
304 Bill Romanowski	.01	.05
305 Brian Blades	.02	.10
306 John L. Williams	.01	.05
307 Tommy Kane	.01	.05
308 John Kasay	.01	.05
309 Chris Warren	.02	.10
310 Rufus Porter	.01	.05
311 Cortez Kennedy	.02	.10
312 Dan McGwire UER (Name misspelled McGuire on front)	.01	.05
313 Stan Gelbaugh	.01	.05
314 Kelvin Martin	.01	.05
315 Ferrell Edmunds	.01	.05
316 Eugene Robinson	.01	.05
317 Gary Anderson RB	.01	.05
318 Reggie Cobb	.01	.05
319 Lawrence Dawsey	.01	.05
320 Courtney Hawkins	.01	.05
321 Santana Dotson	.02	.10
322 Ron Hall	.01	.05
323 Keith McCants	.01	.05
324 Martin Mayhew	.01	.05
325 Anthony Munoz	.02	.10
326 Steve DeBerg	.01	.05
327 Vince Workman	.01	.05
328 Earnest Byner	.01	.05
329 Ricky Ervins	.01	.05
330 Jim Lachey	.01	.05
331 Chip Lohmiller	.01	.05
332 Ricky Sanders UER (Name misspelled Rickey on front)	.01	.05
333 Brad Edwards	.01	.05
334 Tim McGee	.01	.05
335 Darrell Green	.01	.05
336 Charles Mann	.01	.05
337 Wilber Marshall	.01	.05
338 Brian Mitchell	.02	.10
339 Art Monk	.02	.10
340 Mark Rypien	.01	.05
341 John Elway C83	.30	.75
342 Jim Kelly C83	.02	.10
343 Dan Marino C83	.30	.75
344 Eric Dickerson C83	.02	.10
345 Willie Gault C83	.01	.05
346 Ken O'Brien C83	.01	.05
347 Darrell Green C83	.01	.05
348 Richard Dent C83	.01	.05
349 Karl Mecklenburg C83	.01	.05
350 Henry Ellard C83	.01	.05
351 Roger Craig C83	.01	.05
352 Charles Mann C83	.01	.05
353 Checklist A UER (Misspellings)	.01	.05
354 Checklist B UER (Misspellings)	.01	.05
355 Checklist C UER (Numbering out of order)	.01	.05
356 Checklist D UER (Misspellings and numbering out of order)	.01	.05

357 Checklist E UER .01 .05
(Misspelling and
numbering out of order)
358 Checklist F UER .01 .05
(Misspelling and
numbering out of order)
359 Checklist G UER .01 .05
(Misspellings and
numbering out of order)
360 Rookies Checklist UER .01 .05
(Misspelling on 391)
361 Drew Bledsoe RC 1.00 2.50
Text indicates drafted
in '92; should be '93
362 Rick Mirer RC .08 .25
363 Garrison Hearst RC .30 .75
364 Marvin Jones RC .01 .05
365 John Copeland RC .02 .10
366 Eric Curry RC .01 .05
367 Curtis Conway RC .15 .40
368 Willie Roaf RC .02 .10
369 Lincoln Kennedy RC .01 .05
370 Jerome Bettis RC 1.50 4.00
371 Dan Williams IR RC .01 .05
372 Patrick Bates RC .01 .05
373 Brad Hopkins RC .01 .05
374 Steve Everitt RC .01 .05
375 Wayne Simmons RC .01 .05
376 Tom Carter RC .02 .10
377 Ernest Dye IR RC .01 .05
378 Lester Holmes IR RC .01 .05
379 Irv Smith RC .01 .05
380 Robert Smith RC .50 1.25
381 Darrien Gordon IR RC .01 .05
382 Deon Figures RC .01 .05
383 O.J.McDuffie RC .08 .25
384 Dana Stubblefield RC .08 .25
385 Todd Kelly IR RC .01 .05
386 Thomas Smith RC .02 .10
387 George Teague RC .02 .10
388 Carlton Gray IR RC .01 .05
389 Chris Slade RC .02 .10
390 Ben Coleman IR RC .01 .05
391 Ryan McNeil IR RC UER .08 .25
(Name misspelled
McNeill on front)
392 Demetrius DuBose RC .01 .05
393 Carl Simpson RC .01 .05
394 Coleman Rudolph RC .01 .05
395 Tony McGee IR RC .02 .10
396 Roger Harper RC .01 .05
397 Troy Drayton RC .02 .10
398 Michael Strahan RC .60 1.50
399 Natrone Means RC .08 .25
400 Glyn Milburn IR RC .08 .25

1993 SkyBox Impact Colors

COMPLETE SET (392) 30.00 60.00
*COLOR STARS: 1.5X TO 4X BASIC CARDS
*COLOR RCs: 1X TO 2.5X BASIC CARDS
ONE PER PACK

1993 SkyBox Impact Kelly/Magic

COMPLETE SET (12) 8.00 20.00
STATED ODDS 1:12
AUTO.STATED ODDS 1:2071
1 Jim Kelly .75 2.00
Magic Johnson Header
2 Dan Marino 2.00 5.00
Jim Kelly
3 Jay Novacek .40 1.00
Keith Jackson
4 Barry Sanders 2.00 5.00
Thurman Thomas
5 Emmitt Smith 3.00 6.00
Barry Sanders
6 Jerry Rice 1.50 3.00
Sterling Sharpe
7 Andre Reed 1.50 3.00
Jerry Rice
8 Derrick Thomas .75 2.00
Pat Swilling
9 Darryl Talley .75 2.00
Lawrence Taylor
10 Rod Woodson .75 2.00
Darrell Green
11 Steve Tasker .40 1.00
Elvis Patterson
12 Chip Lohmiller .40 1.00
Morten Andersen
AU1 Jim Kelly 12.50 30.00
Magic Johnson Header AU/2500 signed by Jim Kelly

1993 SkyBox Impact Update

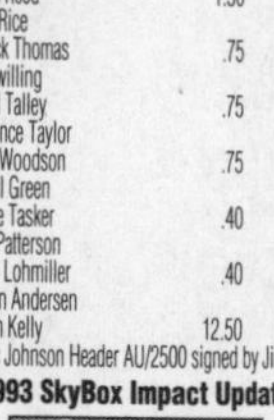

COMPLETE SET (20) 5.00 10.00
SET AVAILABLE VIA MAIL OFFER
U1 Pierce Holt .08 .25
U2 Vinny Testaverde .20 .50
U3 Rod Bernstine .08 .25
U4 Reggie White .60 1.25
U5 Mark Clayton .08 .25
U6 Joe Montana 4.00 8.00
U7 Marcus Allen .60 1.25
U8 Jeff Hostetler .20 .50
U9 Shane Conlan .08 .25
U10 Brad Muster .08 .25
U11 Mike Sherrard .08 .25
U12 Ronnie Lott .20 .50
U13 Steve Beuerlein .20 .50
U14 Gary Clark .20 .50
U15 Kevin Greene .20 .50
U16 Tim McDonald .08 .25
U17 Wilber Marshall .08 .25
U18 Keith Byars .08 .25
U19 Pat Swilling .08 .25
U20 Boomer Esiason .20 .50

1993 SkyBox Impact Rookie Redemption

COMPLETE SET (29) 5.00 12.00
ONE SET PER REDEMPTION CARD BY
R1 Drew Bledsoe CL 1.00 2.50
R2 Drew Bledsoe 1.50 4.00
R3 Rick Mirer .15 .40
R4 Garrison Hearst .50 1.25
R5 Marvin Jones .02 .10
R6 John Copeland .05 .15
R7 Eric Curry .02 .10
R8 Curtis Conway .25 .60
R9 Willie Roaf .05 .15
R10 Lincoln Kennedy .02 .10
R11 Jerome Bettis 2.50 6.00
R12 Dan Williams .02 .10
R13 Patrick Bates .02 .10
R14 Brad Hopkins .02 .10
R15 Steve Everitt .02 .10
R16 Wayne Simmons .02 .10
R17 Tom Carter .05 .15
R18 Ernest Dye .02 .10
R19 Lester Holmes .02 .10
R20 Irv Smith .02 .10
R21 Robert Smith .75 2.00
R22 Darrien Gordon .02 .10
R23 Deon Figures .02 .10
R24 Leonard Renfro .02 .10
R25 O.J.McDuffie .15 .40
R26 Dana Stubblefield .15 .40
R27 Todd Kelly .02 .10
R28 Thomas Smith .05 .15
R29 George Teague .05 .15
NNO Rookie Redempt.Expired .02 .10

1994 SkyBox Impact Promos

These six standard-size promo cards feature on their fronts borderless color player action shots. The featured players stand out against faded backgrounds. The player's name appears within team-colored boxes in an upper corner. The horizontal back carries a color player action shot on the right, and upon which the player's NFL stats appear. His biography and career highlights appear to the left of the photo. The cards are numbered on the back with an "S" prefix. These six promo cards were also issued as a 7 1/2" by 8 1/2" unperforated sheet. Reportedly 55,000 sheets were produced to be given away at the National Sports Collectors Convention (August 2, 4-7, 1994).

COMPLETE SET (6) 3.20 8.00
S1 Marcus Allen 1.20 3.00
S2 Chris Doleman .30 .75
S3 Craig Erickson .30 .75
S4 Jim Kelly 1.20 3.00
S5 Reggie Roby .30 .75
S6 Rod Woodson .50 1.25
NNO National Promo Sheet 2.00 5.00

1994 SkyBox Impact

These 300 standard-size cards were issued in 12-card foil and 20-card jumbo packs. The checklist is alphabetical by team. Randomly inserted in packs and listed at the end of the checklist below is a Carolina Panthers Hologram card. Rookie Cards include Derrick Alexander, Marshall Faulk, William Floyd, Greg Hill, Charles Johnson and Heath Shuler. A Jim Kelly promo card was produced and given away at the 1994 Super Bowl Card Show in Atlanta.

COMPLETE SET (300) 6.00 15.00
1 Johnny Bailey .01 .05
2 Steve Beuerlein .02 .10
3 Gary Clark .02 .10
4 Garrison Hearst .08 .25
5 Ronald Moore .01 .05
6 Ricky Proehl .01 .05
7 Eric Swann .02 .10
8 Aeneas Williams .01 .05
9 Robert Massey .01 .05
10 Chuck Cecil .01 .05
11 Ken Harvey .01 .05
12 Michael Haynes .02 .10
13 Tony Smith .01 .05
14 Bobby Hebert .01 .05
15 Mike Pritchard .01 .05
16 Andre Rison .02 .10
17 Deion Sanders .15 .40
18 Pierce Holt .01 .05
19 Erric Pegram .01 .05
20 Jessie Tuggle .01 .05
21 Steve Broussard .01 .05
22 Don Beebe .01 .05
23 Cornelius Bennett .02 .10
24 Kenneth Davis .01 .05
25 Bill Brooks .01 .05
26 Jim Kelly .08 .25
27 Andre Reed .02 .10
28 Bruce Smith .08 .25
29 Darryl Talley .01 .05
30 Thurman Thomas .08 .25
31 Steve Tasker .02 .10
32 Neal Anderson .01 .05
33 Mark Carrier DB .01 .05
34 Richard Dent .02 .10
35 Jim Harbaugh .08 .25
36 Chris Gedney .01 .05
37 Tom Waddle .01 .05
38 Curtis Conway .08 .25
39 Dante Jones .01 .05
40 Donnell Woolford .01 .05
41 Tim Worley .01 .05
42 John Copeland .01 .05
43 David Klingler .01 .05
44 Derrick Fenner .01 .05
45 Harold Green .01 .05
46 Carl Pickens .02 .10
47 Tony McGee .01 .05
48 Darryl Williams .01 .05
49 Steve Everitt .01 .05
50 Michael Jackson .02 .10
51 Eric Metcalf .02 .10
52 Tommy Vardell .01 .05
53 Vinny Testaverde .02 .10
54 Mark Carrier WR .02 .10
55 Michael Dean Perry .02 .10
56 Eric Turner .01 .05
57 Troy Aikman .30 .75
58 Alvin Harper .02 .10
59 Michael Irvin .08 .25
60 Leon Lett .01 .05
61 Russell Maryland .01 .05
62 Jay Novacek .02 .10
63 Emmitt Smith .50 1.25
64 Ken Norton .02 .10
65 Charles Haley .02 .10
66 Daryl Johnston .02 .10
67 Kevin Smith .01 .05
68 James Washington .01 .05
69 Kevin Williams .02 .10
70 Bernie Kosar .02 .10
71 Mike Croel .01 .05
72 John Elway .60 1.50
73 Shannon Sharpe .02 .10
74 Rod Bernstine .01 .05
75 Simon Fletcher .01 .05
76 Arthur Marshall .01 .05
77 Glyn Milburn .02 .10
78 Dennis Smith .01 .05
79 Herman Moore .08 .25
80 Rodney Peete .01 .05
81 Barry Sanders .50 1.25
82 Mel Gray .01 .05
83 Erik Kramer .02 .10
84 Pat Swilling .01 .05
85 Willie Green .01 .05
86 Chris Spielman .02 .10
87 Robert Porcher .01 .05
88 Derrick Moore .01 .05
89 Edgar Bennett .08 .25
90 Tony Bennett .01 .05
91 LeRoy Butler .01 .05
92 Brett Favre .60 1.50
93 Jackie Harris .01 .05
94 Sterling Sharpe .02 .10
95 Darrell Thompson .01 .05
96 Reggie White .08 .25
97 Terrell Buckley .01 .05
98 Cris Dishman .01 .05
99 Ernest Givins .02 .10
100 Haywood Jeffires .02 .10
101 Warren Moon .08 .25
102 Lorenzo White .01 .05
103 Webster Slaughter .01 .05
104 Ray Childress .01 .05
105 Wilber Marshall .01 .05
106 Gary Brown .01 .05
107 Marcus Robertson .01 .05
108 Sean Jones .01 .05
109 Jeff George .08 .25
110 Steve Emtman .01 .05
111 Quentin Coryatt .01 .05
112 Sean Dawkins RC .08 .25
113 Jeff Herrod .01 .05
114 Roosevelt Potts .01 .05
115 Marcus Allen .08 .25
116 Kimble Anders .02 .10
117 Tim Barnett .01 .05
118 J.J. Birden .01 .05
119 Dale Carter .01 .05
120 Willie Davis .02 .10
121 Nick Lowery .01 .05
122 Joe Montana .60 1.50
123 Kevin Ross .01 .05
124 Neil Smith .02 .10
125 Derrick Thomas .08 .25
126 Keith Cash .01 .05
127 Tim Brown .08 .25
128 Rocket Ismail .02 .10
129 Ethan Horton .01 .05
130 Jeff Hostetler .02 .10
131 Patrick Bates .01 .05
132 Terry McDaniel .01 .05
133 Anthony Smith .01 .05
134 Greg Robinson .01 .05
135 James Jett .01 .05
136 Alexander Wright .01 .05
137 Flipper Anderson .01 .05
138 Shane Conlan .01 .05
139 Jim Everett .02 .10
140 Henry Ellard .02 .10
141 Jerome Bettis .20 .50
142 Troy Drayton .01 .05
143 Sean Gilbert .01 .05
144 Chris Miller .01 .05
145 Keith Byars .01 .05
146 Marco Coleman .01 .05
147 Bryan Cox .01 .05
148 Irving Fryar .02 .10
149 Mark Ingram .01 .05
150 Keith Jackson .01 .05
151 Terry Kirby .08 .25
152 Dan Marino .60 1.50
153 O.J. McDuffie .08 .25
154 Scott Mitchell .02 .10
155 Anthony Carter .02 .10
156 Cris Carter .15 .40
157 Chris Doleman .01 .05
158 Steve Jordan .01 .05
159 Qadry Ismail .08 .25
160 Randall McDaniel .02 .10
161 John Randle .02 .10
162 Robert Smith .08 .25
163 Henry Thomas .01 .05
164 Terry Allen .02 .10
165 Scottie Graham RC .02 .10
166 Drew Bledsoe .30 .75
167 Vincent Brown .01 .05
168 Ben Coates .02 .10
169 Leonard Russell .01 .05
170 Andre Tippett .01 .05
171 Vincent Brisby .02 .10
172 Michael Timpson .01 .05
173 Bruce Armstrong .01 .05
174 Morten Andersen UER .01 .05
(Morton on front)
175 Derek Brown RBK .01 .05
176 Quinn Early .02 .10
177 Rickey Jackson .01 .05
178 Vaughan Johnson .01 .05
179 Lorenzo Neal .01 .05
180 Sam Mills .01 .05
181 Irv Smith .01 .05
182 Renaldo Turnbull .01 .05
183 Wade Wilson .01 .05
184 Willie Roaf .01 .05
185 Michael Brooks .01 .05
186 Mark Jackson .01 .05
187 Rodney Hampton .02 .10
188 Phil Simms .02 .10
189 Dave Meggett .01 .05
190 Mike Sherrard .01 .05
191 Chris Calloway .01 .05
192 Brad Baxter .01 .05
193 Ronnie Lott .02 .10
194 Boomer Esiason .02 .10
195 Rob Moore .02 .10
196 Johnny Johnson .01 .05
197 Marvin Jones .01 .05
198 Mo Lewis .01 .05
199 Johnny Mitchell .01 .05
200 Brian Washington .01 .05
201 Eric Allen .01 .05
202 Fred Barnett .02 .10
203 Mark Bavaro .01 .05
204 Randall Cunningham .08 .25
205 Vaughn Hebron .01 .05
206 Seth Joyner .01 .05
207 Clyde Simmons .01 .05
208 Herschel Walker .02 .10
209 Calvin Williams .02 .10
210 Neil O'Donnell .08 .25
211 Eric Green .01 .05
212 Leroy Thompson .01 .05
213 Rod Woodson .02 .10
214 Barry Foster .01 .05
215 Jeff Graham .01 .05
216 Kevin Greene .02 .10
217 Deon Figures .01 .05
218 Greg Lloyd .02 .10
219 Marion Butts .01 .05
220 Chris Mims .01 .05
221 Eric Curry .01 .05
222 Ronnie Harmon .01 .05
223 Stan Humphries .02 .10
224 Nate Lewis .01 .05
225 Natrone Means .08 .25
226 Anthony Miller .02 .10
227 Leslie O'Neal .01 .05
228 Junior Seau .08 .25
229 Brent Jones .02 .10
230 Tim McDonald .01 .05
231 Tom Rathman .01 .05
232 Jerry Rice .30 .75
233 Dana Stubblefield .02 .10
234 John Taylor .02 .10
235 Ricky Watters .02 .10
236 Steve Young .25 .60
237 Amp Lee .01 .05
238 Robert Blackmon .01 .05
239 Brian Blades .02 .10
240 Cortez Kennedy .02 .10
241 Kelvin Martin .01 .05
242 Rick Mirer .08 .25
243 Eugene Robinson .01 .05
244 Chris Warren .02 .10
245 John L. Williams .01 .05
246 Jon Vaughn .01 .05
247 Reggie Cobb .01 .05
248 Horace Copeland .01 .05
249 Der. Alexander WR RC .08 .25
250 Santana Dotson .02 .10
251 Craig Erickson .01 .05
252 Courtney Hawkins .01 .05
253 Hardy Nickerson .02 .10
254 Vince Workman .01 .05
255 Paul Gruber .01 .05
256 Reggie Brooks .02 .10
257 Tom Carter .01 .05
258 Andre Collins .01 .05
259 Darrell Green .01 .05
260 Desmond Howard .02 .10
261 Tim McGee .01 .05
262 Brian Mitchell .01 .05
263 Art Monk .02 .10
264 John Friesz .02 .10
265 Ricky Sanders .01 .05
266 Checklist .01 .05
267 Checklist .01 .05
268 Checklist .01 .05
269 Checklist .01 .05
270 Checklist .01 .05
271 Carolina Panthers .05 .15
Logo Card
272 Jacksonville Jaguars .05 .15
Logo Card
273 Dan Wilkinson RC .02 .10
274 Marshall Faulk RC 2.00 5.00
275 Heath Shuler RC .08 .25
276 Willie McGinest RC .08 .25
277 Trev Alberts RC .02 .10
278 Trent Dilfer RC .50 1.25
279 Bryant Young RC .15 .40
280 Sam Adams RC .02 .10
281 Antonio Langham RC .02 .10
282 Jamir Miller RC .02 .10
283 John Thierry RC .01 .05
284 Aaron Glenn RC .08 .25
285 Joe Johnson RC .01 .05
286 Bernard Williams RC .01 .05
287 Wayne Gandy RC .01 .05
288 Aaron Taylor RC .01 .05
289 Charles Johnson RC .08 .25
290 Dewayne Washington RC .02 .10
291 Todd Steussie RC .02 .10
292 Tim Bowens RC .02 .10
293 Johnnie Morton RC .20 .50
294 Rob Fredrickson RC .02 .10
295 Shante Carver RC .01 .05
296 Thomas Lewis RC .02 .10
297 Greg Hill RC .08 .25
298 Henry Ford RC .01 .05
299 Jeff Burris RC .02 .10
300 William Floyd RC .08 .25
NNO Carolina Panthers 7.50 20.00
Hologram Logo
P1 Jim Kelly Promo .30 .75

1994 SkyBox Impact Instant Impact

COMPLETE SET (12) 7.50 20.00
STATED ODDS 1:30
R1 Rick Mirer 1.25 2.50
R2 Jerome Bettis 2.50 5.00
R3 Reggie Brooks .40 1.00
R4 Terry Kirby 1.25 2.50
R5 Vincent Brisby .40 1.00
R6 James Jett .20 .50
R7 Drew Bledsoe 4.00 8.00
R8 Dana Stubblefield .40 1.00
R9 Natrone Means 1.25 2.50
R10 Curtis Conway 1.25 2.50
R11 O.J. McDuffie 1.25 2.50
R12 Garrison Hearst 1.25 2.50

1994 SkyBox Impact Quarterback Update

COMPLETE SET (11) 1.50 4.00
SET AVAILABLE VIA MAIL REDEMPT
ONE SET PER SPECIAL SKYBOX RET
1 Warren Moon .30 .75
2 Trent Dilfer .60 1.50
3 Jeff George .20 .50
4 Heath Shuler .30 .75
5 Jim Harbaugh .20 .50
6 Rodney Peete .08 .25
7 Chris Miller .08 .25
8 Jim Everett .08 .25
9 Scott Mitchell .20 .50
10 Erik Kramer .08 .25
NNO Checklist .08 .25

1994 SkyBox Impact Rookie Redemption

COMPLETE SET (30) 7.50 15.00
SET AVAILABLE VIA MAIL REDEMPT
1 Dan Wilkinson .07 .20
2 Marshall Faulk 5.00 10.00
3 Heath Shuler .20 .50
4 Willie McGinest .20 .50
5 Trev Alberts .07 .20
6 Trent Dilfer 1.25 2.50
7 Bryant Young .30 .75
8 Sam Adams .07 .20
9 Antonio Langham .07 .20
10 Jamir Miller .07 .20
11 John Thierry .02 .10
12 Aaron Glenn .20 .50
13 Joe Johnson .02 .10
14 Bernard Williams .02 .10
15 Wayne Gandy .02 .10
16 Aaron Taylor .02 .10
17 Charles Johnson .20 .50
18 Dewayne Washington .07 .20
19 Todd Steussie .07 .20
20 Tim Bowens .07 .20
21 Johnnie Morton .40 1.00
22 Rob Fredrickson .07 .20
23 Shante Carver .02 .10
24 Thomas Lewis .07 .20
25 Greg Hill .20 .50
26 Henry Ford .02 .10
27 Jeff Burris .07 .20
28 William Floyd .20 .50
29 Derrick Alexander WR .20 .50
30 Title .02 .10
Checklist Card
NNO Redemption Card .02 .10
Expired 1/31/1995

1994 SkyBox Impact Ultimate Impact

COMPLETE SET (15) 25.00 60.00
STATED ODDS 1:15
U1 Troy Aikman 2.50 6.00
U2 Emmitt Smith UER 4.00 10.00
U3 Michael Irvin .75 2.00
U4 Joe Montana 5.00 12.00
U5 Jerry Rice 2.50 6.00
U6 Sterling Sharpe .30 .75
U7 Steve Young 2.00 5.00
U8 Ricky Watters .30 .75
U9 Barry Sanders 4.00 10.00
U10 John Elway 5.00 12.00
U11 Reggie White .75 2.00
U12 Jim Kelly .75 2.00
U13 Thurman Thomas .75 2.00
U14 Dan Marino 5.00 12.00
U15 Brett Favre 5.00 12.00

1995 SkyBox Impact Samples

This 6-card promotion or sample panel was issued to promote the 1995 SkyBox Impact product. Each card includes a card number on the back and could be detached individually using the perforations applied in the printing process. A seventh card was issued separately to round out the set.

COMPLETE SET (7) 2.00 5.00
S1 Chris Spielman .30 .75
S2 Ronald Moore .20 .50
S3 Bernie Parmalee .20 .50
S4 Tyrone Hughes .20 .50
S5 Brett Favre Countdown 1.25 3.00
S6 Bryan Cox Impact Power .20 .50
S7 William Floyd More Attitude .40 1.00
NNO Uncut Panel S1-S6 1.50 4.00

1995 SkyBox Impact

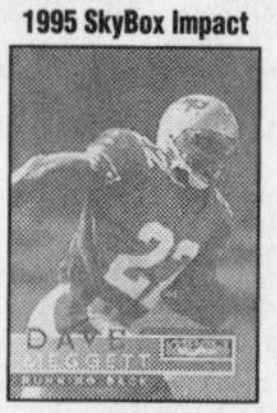

This 200-card standard-size set is considered the base issue released by SkyBox.. The cards were issued in 12-card foil packs with a suggested retail price of $1.29 or 20-card jumbo packs with a suggested retail price of $1.99. . Featured in the set are 148 player cards. The set is broken down by teams and includes these subsets: Something Special (149-158), Sophomores (159-168), Impact Rookies (169-198) and Checklists (199-200). Rookie Cards in this set include Jeff Blake, Ki-Jana Carter, Kerry Collins, Joey Galloway, Steve McNair, and Rashaan Salaam. There was also a rookie running back set randomly inserted at a rate of one set per special retail box. A promo sheet was produced and is priced below in complete sheet form.

COMPLETE SET (200) 6.00 15.00
1 Garrison Hearst .08 .25
2 Ronald Moore .01 .05
3 Eric Swann .02 .10
4 Aeneas Williams .01 .05
5 Jeff George .02 .10
6 Craig Heyward .02 .10
7 Terance Mathis .02 .10
8 Andre Rison .02 .10
9 Cornelius Bennett .02 .10
10 Jim Kelly .08 .25
11 Andre Reed .02 .10
12 Bruce Smith .08 .25
13 Thurman Thomas .08 .25
14 Frank Reich .01 .05
15 Lamar Lathon .01 .05
16 Darion Conner .01 .05
17 Randy Baldwin .01 .05
18 Don Beebe .01 .05
19 Mark Carrier DB .01 .05
20 Jeff Graham .01 .05
21 Raymont Harris .01 .05
22 Alonzo Spellman .01 .05
23 Lewis Tillman .01 .05
24 Steve Walsh .01 .05
25 Jeff Blake RC .25 .60
26 Carl Pickens .02 .10
27 Darnay Scott .02 .10
28 Dan Wilkinson .02 .10
29 Derrick Alexander WR .08 .25
30 Leroy Hoard .01 .05
31 Antonio Langham .01 .05
32 Vinny Testaverde .02 .10
33 Eric Turner .01 .05
34 Troy Aikman .30 .75
35 Charles Haley .02 .10
36 Alvin Harper .01 .05
37 Michael Irvin .08 .25
38 Daryl Johnston .02 .10
39 Jay Novacek .02 .10
40 Leon Lett .01 .05
41 Emmitt Smith .50 1.25
42 John Elway .60 1.50
43 Glyn Milburn .01 .05
44 Anthony Miller .02 .10
45 Leonard Russell .01 .05
46 Shannon Sharpe .02 .10
47 Scott Mitchell .02 .10
48 Herman Moore .08 .25
49 Barry Sanders .50 1.25
50 Chris Spielman .02 .10
51 Edgar Bennett .02 .10
52 Robert Brooks .08 .25
53 Brett Favre .60 1.50
54 Bryce Paup .02 .10
55 Sterling Sharpe .02 .10
56 Reggie White .08 .25
57 Ray Childress .01 .05
58 Haywood Jeffires .01 .05
59 Webster Slaughter .01 .05
60 Lorenzo White .01 .05
61 Trev Alberts .01 .05
62 Quentin Coryatt .02 .10
63 Sean Dawkins .02 .10
64 Marshall Faulk .40 1.00
65 Jeff Lageman .01 .05
66 Steve Beuerlein .02 .10
67 Desmond Howard .02 .10
68 Kelvin Martin .01 .05
69 Reggie Cobb .01 .05
70 Marcus Allen .08 .25
71 Greg Hill .02 .10
72 Joe Montana .60 1.50
73 Neil Smith .02 .10
74 Derrick Thomas .08 .25
75 Tim Brown .08 .25
76 Rocket Ismail .02 .10
77 Jeff Hostetler .02 .10
78 Chester McGlockton .02 .10
79 Harvey Williams .01 .05
80 Tim Bowens .01 .05
81 Irving Fryar .02 .10
82 Keith Jackson .01 .05
83 Terry Kirby .02 .10
84 Dan Marino .60 1.50
85 O.J. McDuffie .08 .25
86 Bernie Parmalee .02 .10
87 Terry Allen .02 .10
88 Cris Carter .08 .25
89 Qadry Ismail .02 .10
90 Warren Moon .02 .10
91 Jake Reed .02 .10
92 Drew Bledsoe .20 .50
93 Vincent Brisby .01 .05
94 Ben Coates .02 .10
95 Michael Timpson .01 .05
96 Jim Everett .01 .05
97 Michael Haynes .02 .10
98 Willie Roaf .01 .05
99 Michael Brooks .01 .05
100 Dave Brown .02 .10
101 Rodney Hampton .02 .10
102 Thomas Lewis .02 .10
103 Dave Meggett .01 .05
104 Boomer Esiason .02 .10
105 Johnny Johnson .01 .05
106 Johnny Mitchell .01 .05
107 Rob Moore .02 .10
108 Fred Barnett .02 .10
109 Randall Cunningham .08 .25
110 Charlie Garner .08 .25
111 Herschel Walker .02 .10
112 Barry Foster .02 .10
113 Eric Green .01 .05
114 Charles Johnson .02 .10
115 Greg Lloyd .02 .10
116 Byron Bam Morris .01 .05
117 Neil O'Donnell .02 .10
118 Rod Woodson .02 .10
119 Flipper Anderson .01 .05
120 Jerome Bettis .08 .25
121 Troy Drayton .01 .05
122 Sean Gilbert .02 .10
123 Ronnie Harmon .01 .05
124 Stan Humphries .02 .10
125 Shawn Jefferson .01 .05
126 Natrone Means .02 .10
127 Leslie O'Neal .02 .10
128 Junior Seau .08 .25
129 William Floyd .02 .10
130 Brent Jones .01 .05
131 Jerry Rice .30 .75
132 Deion Sanders .20 .50
133 Dana Stubblefield .02 .10
134 Ricky Watters .02 .10
135 Bryant Young .02 .10
136 Steve Young .25 .60
137 Brian Blades .02 .10
138 Cortez Kennedy .02 .10
139 Rick Mirer .02 .10
140 Chris Warren .02 .10
141 Horace Copeland .01 .05
142 Trent Dilfer .08 .25
143 Hardy Nickerson .01 .05
144 Errict Rhett .02 .10
145 Henry Ellard .02 .10
146 Brian Mitchell .01 .05
147 Heath Shuler .02 .10
148 Tydus Winans .01 .05
149 Steve Tasker .02 .10
150 Jeff Burris .01 .05
151 Tyrone Hughes .02 .10
152 Mel Gray .01 .05
153 Kevin Williams WR .02 .10
154 Andre Coleman .01 .05
155 Corey Sawyer .01 .05
156 Darrien Gordon .01 .05
157 Aaron Glenn .01 .05
158 Eric Metcalf .02 .10
159 Errict Rhett SS .02 .10
160 Marshall Faulk SS .15 .40
161 Darnay Scott SS .02 .10
162 William Floyd SS .01 .05
163 Charlie Garner SS .02 .10
164 Heath Shuler SS .02 .10
165 Trent Dilfer SS .08 .25
166 Willie McGinest SS .02 .10
167 Byron Bam Morris SS .01 .05
168 Mario Bates SS .02 .10
169 Ki-Jana Carter RC .08 .25
170 Tony Boselli RC .08 .25
171 Steve McNair RC 1.00 2.50
172 Michael Westbrook RC .08 .25
173 Kerry Collins RC .75 2.00
174 Kevin Carter RC .08 .25
175 Mike Mamula RC .01 .05
176 Joey Galloway RC .50 1.25
177 Kyle Brady RC .08 .25
178 J.J. Stokes RC .08 .25
179 Warren Sapp RC .50 1.25
180 Rob Johnson RC .30 .75
181 Tyrone Wheatley RC .40 1.00
182 Napoleon Kaufman RC .40 1.00
183 James O. Stewart RC .40 1.00
184 Dino Philyaw RC .01 .05
185 Rashaan Salaam RC .02 .10
186 Tyrone Poole RC .08 .25
187 Ty Law RC .50 1.25
188 Joe Aska RC .01 .05
189 Mark Bruener RC .02 .10
190 Derrick Brooks RC .50 1.25
191 Jack Jackson RC .01 .05
192 Ray Zellars RC .02 .10
193 Eddie Goines RC .01 .05
194 Chris Sanders RC .02 .10
195 Charlie Simmons RC .01 .05
196 Lee DeRamus RC .01 .05
197 Frank Sanders RC .08 .25
198 Rodney Thomas RC .02 .10
199 Checklist A 1-128 .01 .05
200 Checklist B 129-200 .01 .05
M1 Brett Favre SkyMotion 15.00 30.00
M2 Brett Favre SkyMotion 15.00 30.00

1995 SkyBox Impact Countdown

COMPLETE SET (10) 20.00 50.00
STATED ODDS 1:20 H/R, 1:60 SPEC.RET
C1 Barry Sanders 5.00 10.00
C2 Jerry Rice 3.00 6.00
C3 Steve Young 2.50 5.00
C4 Troy Aikman 3.00 6.00
C5 Dan Marino 6.00 12.00
C6 Emmitt Smith 5.00 10.00
C7 Junior Seau .75 2.00
C8 Drew Bledsoe 2.00 4.00
C9 Brett Favre 6.00 12.00
C10 Deion Sanders 2.00 4.00

1995 SkyBox Impact Future Hall of Famers

COMP.SHORT SET (7) 30.00 80.00
STATED ODDS 1:60 HOBBY
HF1 Jerry Rice 5.00 12.00
HF2 Joe Montana SP 600.00 1,000.00
HF3 Steve Young 4.00 10.00
HF4 John Elway 10.00 25.00
HF5 Dan Marino 10.00 25.00
HF6 Emmitt Smith 8.00 20.00
HF7 Barry Sanders 8.00 20.00
HF8 Troy Aikman 5.00 12.00

1995 SkyBox Impact More Attitude

COMPLETE SET (15) 10.00 25.00
STATED ODDS 1:9 H/R, 1:27 SPEC.RET
F1 Ki-Jana Carter .25 .60
F2 Steve McNair 3.00 6.00
F3 Michael Westbrook .25 .60
F4 Kerry Collins 1.50 4.00
F5 Joey Galloway 1.50 3.00
F6 J.J. Stokes .25 .60
F7 James O. Stewart 1.25 2.50
F8 Rashaan Salaam .08 .25
F9 Trent Dilfer 1.00 2.00
F10 William Floyd .30 .75
F11 Marshall Faulk 4.00 8.00
F12 Errict Rhett .30 .75
F13 Heath Shuler .30 .75
F14 Drew Bledsoe 2.00 4.00
F15 Ben Coates .30 .75

1995 SkyBox Impact Power

COMP.SHORT SET (29) 10.00 25.00
STATED ODDS 1:3 H/R, 1:9 SPEC.RET
IP1 Junior Seau .40 1.00
IP2 Reggie White .40 1.00
IP3 Eric Swann .15 .40
IP4 Bruce Smith .40 1.00
IP5 Rod Woodson .15 .40
IP6 Derrick Thomas .40 1.00
IP7 Chester McGlockton .15 .40
IP8 Cortez Kennedy .15 .40
IP9 Deion Sanders 1.00 2.00
IP10 Bryan Cox .07 .20
IP11 Jerry Rice 1.50 3.00
IP12 Sterling Sharpe .15 .40
IP13 Tim Brown .40 1.00
IP14 Marshall Faulk 2.00 4.00
IP15 Brett Favre 3.00 6.00
IP16 Chris Warren .15 .40
IP17 Herman Moore .40 1.00
IP18 Steve Young 1.25 2.50
IP19 Andre Rison .15 .40
IP20 Thurman Thomas .40 1.00
IP21 Marcus Allen .40 1.00
IP22 Michael Irvin .40 1.00
IP23 Emmitt Smith 2.50 5.00
IP24 John Elway 3.00 6.00
IP25 Joe Montana SP 300.00 600.00
IP26 Barry Sanders 2.50 5.00
IP27 Troy Aikman 1.50 3.00
IP28 Natrone Means .15 .40
IP29 Ben Coates .15 .40
IP30 Errict Rhett .15 .40

1995 SkyBox Impact Rookie Running Backs

COMPLETE SET (9) 4.00 8.00
ONE SET PER SPECIAL RETAIL BOX
1 Ki-Jana Carter .30 .75
2 Tyrone Wheatley .60 1.50
3 Napoleon Kaufman .60 1.50
4 James O. Stewart .60 1.50
5 Rashaan Salaam .30 .75
6 Ray Zellars .20 .50
7 Rodney Thomas .20 .50
8 Curtis Martin 1.50 4.00
NNO Cover .10 .30
Checklist Card

1995 SkyBox Impact Fox Announcers

SkyBox issued this promo set to announce its affiliation with Fox. The seven-card set features the Fox Network NFL Sunday announcers. The fronts display photos of the announcers while the backs carry information about them.

COMPLETE SET (8) 8.00 20.00
1 Pat Summerall 2.00 5.00
John Madden
2 James Brown 2.00 5.00
Jimmy Johnson
Terry Bradshaw
Howie Long
3 Dick Stockton .80 2.00
Matt Millen
4 Kevin Harlan .80 2.00
Jerry Glanville
5 Joe Buck .80 2.00
Tim Green
6 Kenny Albert 1.20 3.00
Anthony Munoz
7 Thom Brennaman .80 2.00
Ron Pitts
NNO Cover Card .40 1.00

1996 SkyBox Impact Samples

This 3-card promotion or sample panel was issued to promote the 1996 SkyBox Impact product. Each card includes a card number on the back and could be detached individually using the perforations applied in the printing process.

COMPLETE SET (3)	1.50	4.00
S1 Brett Favre	1.25	3.00
S2 William Floyd Excelerators	.20	.50
S3 Daryl Johnston Inspiration	.30	.75
NNO Uncut Panel	1.50	4.00

1996 SkyBox Impact

The 1996 Skybox Impact set was issued in one series totalling 200 cards. The 10-card packs retail for $1.49 each. Dealers had the option of ordering either a 30 box case or a 12 box case. Each box contains 24 packs. The set contains the topical subsets: Rookies (149-188), Inspirations (189-193) and Brett Favre Highlights (194-198). The regular cards are grouped alphabetically within teams and checklisted below alphabetically according to teams. A Brett Favre instant win card is included in every pack. Among the prizes available were 1,995 Favre SkyMotion cards, 1,995 Favre Lenticular Cards and 1995 Favre Season Highlight All-In-One Cards. These winning cards were exchanged one every 480 packs. Exchange cards for the SkyMotion card as well as a SkyMint Coin were inserted one every 360 packs. These two cards expired on 1/24/97. Rookie Cards in this set include Karim Abdul-Jabbar, Tim Biakabutuka, Tommie Frazier, Eddie George, Terry Glenn, Keyshawn Johnson, Danny Kanell, and Leeland McElroy. A 3-card (cards numbered S1-S3) promo sheet was produced as well and priced below in complete sheet form.

COMPLETE SET (200)	6.00	15.00
1 Garrison Hearst	.07	.20
2 Rob Moore	.07	.20
3 Frank Sanders	.07	.20
4 Eric Swann	.02	.10
5 Aeneas Williams	.02	.10
6 Bert Emanuel	.07	.20
7 Jeff George	.07	.20
8 Craig Heyward	.02	.10
9 Terance Mathis	.02	.10
10 Eric Metcalf	.02	.10
11 Leroy Hoard	.02	.10
12 Michael Jackson	.07	.20
13 Andre Rison	.07	.20
14 Vinny Testaverde	.07	.20
15 Eric Turner	.02	.10
16 Darick Holmes	.02	.10
17 Jim Kelly	.10	.30
18 Bryce Paup	.02	.10
19 Bruce Smith	.07	.20
20 Thurman Thomas	.10	.30
21 Mark Carrier WR	.02	.10
22 Kerry Collins	.10	.30
23 Derrick Moore	.02	.10
24 Tyrone Poole	.02	.10
25 Curtis Conway	.10	.30
26 Jeff Graham	.02	.10
27 Erik Kramer	.02	.10
28 Rashaan Salaam	.07	.20
29 Jeff Blake	.10	.30
30 Ki-Jana Carter	.07	.20
31 Carl Pickens	.07	.20
32 Darnay Scott	.07	.20
33 Troy Aikman	.30	.75
34 Charles Haley	.07	.20
35 Michael Irvin	.10	.30
36 Daryl Johnston	.07	.20
37 Jay Novacek	.02	.10
38 Deion Sanders	.15	.40
39 Emmitt Smith	.50	1.25
40 Steve Atwater	.02	.10
41 Terrell Davis	.25	.60
42 John Elway	.60	1.50
43 Anthony Miller	.07	.20
44 Shannon Sharpe	.07	.20
45 Scott Mitchell	.07	.20
46 Herman Moore	.07	.20
47 Brett Perriman	.02	.10
48 Barry Sanders	.50	1.25
49 Edgar Bennett	.07	.20
50 Robert Brooks	.10	.30
51 Mark Chmura	.07	.20
52 Brett Favre	.60	1.50
53 Reggie White	.10	.30
54 Mel Gray	.02	.10
55 Steve McNair	.25	.60
56 Chris Sanders	.07	.20
57 Rodney Thomas	.02	.10
58 Quentin Coryatt	.02	.10
59 Sean Dawkins	.02	.10
60 Ken Dilger	.07	.20
61 Marshall Faulk	.15	.40
62 Jim Harbaugh	.07	.20
63 Tony Boselli	.02	.10
64 Mark Brunell	.20	.50
65 Keenan McCardell	.10	.30
66 James O.Stewart	.07	.20
67 Marcus Allen	.10	.30
68 Steve Bono	.02	.10
69 Neil Smith	.07	.20
70 Derrick Thomas	.10	.30
71 Tamarick Vanover	.07	.20
72 Bryan Cox	.02	.10
73 Irving Fryar	.07	.20
74 Eric Green	.02	.10
75 Dan Marino	.60	1.50
76 O.J. McDuffie	.07	.20
77 Bernie Parmalee	.02	.10
78 Cris Carter	.10	.30
79 Qadry Ismail	.07	.20
80 Warren Moon	.07	.20
81 Jake Reed	.07	.20
82 Robert Smith	.07	.20
83 Drew Bledsoe	.20	.50
84 Ben Coates	.07	.20
85 Curtis Martin	.25	.60
86 Willie McGinest	.02	.10
87 Dave Meggett	.02	.10
88 Mario Bates	.07	.20
89 Quinn Early	.02	.10
90 Jim Everett	.02	.10
91 Michael Haynes	.02	.10
92 Renaldo Turnbull	.02	.10
93 Dave Brown	.02	.10
94 Rodney Hampton	.07	.20
95 Thomas Lewis	.02	.10
96 Phillippi Sparks	.02	.10
97 Tyrone Wheatley	.07	.20
98 Kyle Brady	.02	.10
99 Hugh Douglas	.07	.20
100 Mo Lewis	.02	.10
101 Adrian Murrell	.07	.20
102 Tim Brown	.10	.30
103 Jeff Hostetler	.02	.10
104 Rocket Ismail	.02	.10
105 Chester McGlockton	.02	.10
106 Harvey Williams	.02	.10
107 Fred Barnett	.02	.10
108 William Fuller	.02	.10
109 Charlie Garner	.07	.20
110 Rodney Peete	.02	.10
111 Ricky Watters	.07	.20
112 Calvin Williams	.02	.10
113 Byron Bam Morris	.02	.10
114 Neil O'Donnell	.07	.20
115 Erric Pegram	.02	.10
116 Kordell Stewart	.10	.30
117 Yancey Thigpen	.07	.20
118 Rod Woodson	.07	.20
119 Jerome Bettis	.10	.30
120 Isaac Bruce	.10	.30
121 Troy Drayton	.02	.10
122 Leslie O'Neal	.02	.10
123 Aaron Hayden RC	.02	.10
124 Stan Humphries	.07	.20
125 Natrone Means	.07	.20
126 Junior Seau	.10	.30
127 William Floyd	.07	.20
128 Brent Jones	.02	.10
129 Derek Loville	.02	.10
130 Ken Norton	.02	.10
131 Jerry Rice	.30	.75
132 J.J. Stokes	.10	.30
133 Steve Young	.25	.60
134 Brian Blades	.02	.10
135 Joey Galloway	.10	.30
136 Cortez Kennedy	.02	.10
137 Rick Mirer	.07	.20
138 Chris Warren	.07	.20
139 Trent Dilfer	.10	.30
140 Alvin Harper	.02	.10
141 Jackie Harris	.02	.10
142 Hardy Nickerson	.02	.10
143 Errict Rhett	.07	.20
144 Terry Allen	.07	.20
145 Henry Ellard	.02	.10
146 Brian Mitchell	.02	.10
147 Heath Shuler	.07	.20
148 Michael Westbrook	.10	.30
149 Karim Abdul-Jabbar RC	.10	.30
150 Mike Alstott RC	.40	1.00
151 Marco Battaglia RC	.02	.10
152 Tim Biakabutuka RC	.10	.30
153 Sean Boyd RC	.07	.20
154 Tony Brackens RC	.10	.30
155 Duane Clemons RC	.02	.10
156 Marcus Coleman RC	.02	.10
157 Chris Darkins RC	.02	.10
158 Rickey Dudley RC	.10	.30
159 Jason Dunn RC	.07	.20
160 Bobby Engram RC	.10	.30
161 Daryl Gardener RC	.02	.10
162 Eddie George RC	.50	1.25
163 Terry Glenn RC	.40	1.00
164 Kevin Hardy RC	.10	.30
165 Marvin Harrison RC	1.00	2.50
166 Dietrich Jells RC	.02	.10
167 DeRon Jenkins RC	.07	.20
168 Darrius Johnson RC	.02	.10
169 Keyshawn Johnson RC	.40	1.00
170 Lance Johnstone RC	.07	.20
171 Cedric Jones RC	.02	.10
172 Marcus Jones RC	.02	.10
173 Danny Kanell RC	.10	.30
174 Eddie Kennison RC	.10	.30
175 Jevon Langford RC	.02	.10
176 Markco Maddox RC	.07	.20
177 Derrick Mayes RC	.10	.30
178 Leeland McElroy RC	.07	.20
179 Dell McGee RC	.02	.10
180 Johnny McWilliams RC	.07	.20
181 Alex Molden RC	.02	.10
182 Eric Moulds RC	.50	1.25
183 Jonathan Ogden RC	.10	.30
184 Lawrence Phillips RC	.10	.30
185 Simeon Rice RC	.30	.75
186 Amani Toomer RC	.40	1.00
187 Regan Upshaw RC	.02	.10
188 Jerome Woods RC	.02	.10
189 Darrell Green I	.02	.10
190 Daryl Johnston I	.07	.20
191 Sam Mills I	.02	.10
192 Earnest Byner I	.02	.10
193 Herschel Walker I	.07	.20
194 Brett Favre Highlights	.20	.50
195 Brett Favre Highlights	.20	.50
196 Brett Favre Highlights	.20	.50
197 Brett Favre Highlights	.20	.50
198 Brett Favre Highlights	.20	.50
199 Checklist	.02	.10
200 Checklist	.02	.10
BF1 Brett Favre SkyMotion	5.00	12.00
BF1X Brett Favre Expired SkyMotion Exchange Card	.40	1.00
BF2 Brett Favre SkyMint	12.50	30.00
BF2X Favre SkyMint EXCH	.40	1.00

1996 SkyBox Impact Excelerators

COMPLETE SET (15)	12.50	30.00
STATED ODDS 1:12		
1 Robert Brooks	1.00	2.00
2 Isaac Bruce	1.00	2.00
3 William Floyd	.60	1.25
4 Joey Galloway	1.00	2.00
5 Michael Irvin	1.00	2.00
6 Napoleon Kaufman	1.00	2.00
7 Anthony Miller	.60	1.25
8 Herman Moore	.60	1.25
9 Barry Sanders	4.00	8.00
10 Chris Sanders	.60	1.25
11 Kordell Stewart	1.00	2.00
12 Rodney Thomas	.25	.60
13 Tamarick Vanover	.60	1.25
14 Ricky Watters	.60	1.25
15 Michael Westbrook	1.00	2.00

1996 SkyBox Impact Intimidators

COMPLETE SET (10)	20.00	50.00
STATED ODDS 1:20		
1 Terrell Davis	3.00	6.00
2 Hugh Douglas	1.00	2.00
3 Dan Marino	8.00	15.00
4 Curtis Martin	3.00	6.00
5 Carl Pickens	1.00	2.00
6 Errict Rhett	1.00	2.00
7 Jerry Rice	4.00	8.00
8 Emmitt Smith	6.00	12.00
9 Eric Swann	.40	1.00
10 Chris Warren	1.00	2.00

1996 SkyBox Impact More Attitude

COMPLETE SET (20)	12.50	25.00
STATED ODDS 1:3		
1 Karim Abdul-Jabbar	.25	.60
2 Tim Biakabutuka	.25	.60
3 Bobby Engram	.25	.60
4 Daryl Gardener	.07	.20
5 Eddie George	1.25	2.50
6 Terry Glenn	1.00	2.00
7 Kevin Hardy	.25	.60
8 Marvin Harrison	2.50	5.00
9 DeRon Jenkins	.15	.40
10 Keyshawn Johnson	1.00	2.00
11 Cedric Jones	.07	.20
12 Eddie Kennison	.25	.60
13 Jevon Langford	.07	.20
14 Leeland McElroy	.15	.40
15 Johnny McWilliams	.15	.40
16 Eric Moulds	1.25	2.50
17 Lawrence Phillips	.25	.60
18 Jonathan Ogden	.25	.60
19 Simeon Rice	.75	1.50
20 Amani Toomer	1.00	2.00

1996 SkyBox Impact No Surrender

COMPLETE SET (20)	30.00	80.00
STATED ODDS 1:40 HOBBY		
1 Marcus Allen	2.00	5.00
2 Jeff Blake	2.00	5.00
3 Drew Bledsoe	3.00	8.00
4 Ben Coates	1.25	3.00
5 Brett Favre	10.00	25.00
6 Terry Glenn	5.00	10.00
7 Jim Harbaugh	1.25	3.00
8 Kevin Hardy	1.50	3.00
9 Keyshawn Johnson	5.00	10.00
10 Dan Marino	10.00	25.00
11 Leeland McElroy	1.00	2.00
12 Steve McNair	4.00	10.00
13 Herman Moore	1.25	3.00
14 Lawrence Phillips	1.50	3.00
15 Errict Rhett	1.25	3.00
16 Jerry Rice	5.00	12.00
17 Simeon Rice	4.00	8.00
18 Barry Sanders	8.00	20.00
19 Rodney Thomas	.60	1.50
20 Tyrone Wheatley	1.25	3.00

1996 SkyBox Impact VersaTeam

COMPLETE SET (10)	30.00	80.00
STATED ODDS 1:120		
1 Tim Brown	2.50	6.00
2 Terrell Davis	5.00	12.00
3 John Elway	12.50	30.00
4 Marshall Faulk	3.00	8.00
5 Joey Galloway	2.50	6.00
6 Curtis Martin	5.00	12.00
7 Deion Sanders	3.00	8.00
8 Kordell Stewart	2.50	6.00
9 Chris Warren	1.50	4.00
10 Steve Young	5.00	12.00

1996 SkyBox Impact Rookies

The SkyBox Impact Rookies set was issued in one series totalling 150 cards. The set contains the topical subsets: All-Time Impact Rookies (71-120), Rookie Sleepers (121-140) and Rookie Record Holders (141-148). The cards were packaged 10-cards per pack with 36-packs per box and carried a suggested retail price of $1.49 per pack. The Draft Exchange card (expired 7/22/97) mentions several prize levels on the cardback instructions in error. In fact, there was only one Draft Exchange card which was good for all five prize cards.

COMPLETE SET (150)	5.00	12.00
1 Leeland McElroy RC	.02	.10
2 Johnny McWilliams	.01	.05
3 Simeon Rice RC	.20	.50
4 DeRon Jenkins	.01	.05
5 Jermaine Lewis RC	.07	.20
6 Ray Lewis RC	.75	2.00
7 Jonathan Ogden	.07	.20
8 Eric Moulds RC UER card misnumbered 123	.40	1.00
9 Tim Biakabutuka RC	.07	.20
10 Muhsin Muhammad RC	.40	1.00
11 Winslow Oliver	.01	.05
12 Bobby Engram RC	.07	.20
13 Walt Harris	.01	.05
14 Willie Anderson	.01	.05
15 Marco Battaglia	.01	.05
16 Jevon Langford	.01	.05
17 Kavika Pittman RC	.01	.05
18 Stephen Williams	.01	.05
19 Tory James RC	.02	.10
20 Jeff Lewis RC	.02	.10
21 John Mobley	.01	.05
22 Detron Smith	.01	.05
23 Derrick Mayes RC	.07	.20
24 Eddie George RC	.40	1.00
25 Marvin Harrison RC	.75	2.00
26 Dedric Mathis	.01	.05
27 Tony Brackens RC	.07	.20
28 Kevin Hardy RC	.07	.20
29 Jerome Woods	.01	.05
30 Karim Abdul-Jabbar RC	.07	.20
31 Daryl Gardener	.01	.05
32 Jerris McPhail	.01	.05
33 Stanley Pritchett	.01	.05
34 Zach Thomas RC	.20	.50
35 Duane Clemons	.01	.05
36 Moe Williams RC	.20	.50
37 Tedy Bruschi RC	1.50	4.00
38 Terry Glenn RC	.30	.75
39 Alex Molden	.01	.05
40 Ricky Whittle	.01	.05
41 Cedric Jones	.01	.05
42 Danny Kanell RC	.07	.20
43 Amani Toomer RC	.30	.75
44 Marcus Coleman	.01	.05
45 Keyshawn Johnson RC	.30	.75
46 Ray Mickens	.01	.05
47 Alex Van Dyke RC	.02	.10
48 Rickey Dudley RC	.07	.20
49 Lance Johnstone	.02	.10
50 Brian Dawkins RC	.40	1.00
51 Jason Dunn	.01	.05
52 Ray Farmer	.01	.05
53 Bobby Hoying RC	.07	.20
54 Jermane Mayberry	.01	.05
55 Bryan Still RC	.02	.10
56 Tony Banks RC	.07	.20
57 Ernie Conwell	.01	.05
58 Eddie Kennison RC	.07	.20
59 Jerald Moore RC	.02	.10
60 Lawrence Phillips RC	.07	.20
61 Israel Ifeanyi	.01	.05
62 Terrell Owens RC	.75	2.00
63 Iheanyi Uwaezuoke RC	.07	.20
64 Mike Alstott RC	.30	.75
65 Marcus Jones	.01	.05
66 Nilo Silvan	.01	.05
67 Regan Upshaw	.01	.05
68 Stephen Davis RC	.50	1.25
69 Troy Aikman AIR	.20	.50
70 Terry Allen AIR	.02	.10
71 Edgar Bennett AIR	.02	.10
72 Jerome Bettis AIR	.02	.10
73 Drew Bledsoe AIR	.15	.40
74 Tim Brown AIR	.07	.20
75 Mark Brunell AIR	.15	.40
76 Cris Carter AIR	.07	.20
77 Kerry Collins AIR	.07	.20
78 Terrell Davis AIR	.15	.40
79 John Elway AIR	.40	1.00
80 Marshall Faulk AIR	.07	.20
81 Brett Favre AIR	.40	1.00
82 Joey Galloway AIR	.07	.20
83 Rodney Hampton AIR	.01	.05
84 Jim Harbaugh AIR	.02	.10
85 Michael Irvin AIR	.02	.10
86 Chris T. Jones AIR	.07	.20
87 Napoleon Kaufman AIR	.07	.20
88 Jim Kelly AIR	.07	.20
89 Dan Marino AIR	.40	1.00
90 Curtis Martin AIR	.15	.40
91 Terance Mathis AIR	.01	.05
92 Steve McNair AIR	.20	.50
93 Anthony Miller AIR	.02	.10
94 Scott Mitchell AIR	.01	.05
95 Herman Moore AIR	.02	.10
96 Brett Perriman AIR	.01	.05
97 Carl Pickens AIR	.02	.10
98 Jerry Rice AIR	.20	.50
99 Andre Rison AIR	.02	.10
100 Rashaan Salaam AIR	.02	.10
101 Barry Sanders AIR	.30	.75
102 Chris Sanders AIR	.02	.10
103 Deion Sanders AIR	.07	.20
104 Frank Sanders AIR	.02	.10
105 Bruce Smith AIR	.02	.10
106 Emmitt Smith AIR	.30	.75
107 Robert Smith AIR	.02	.10
108 Kordell Stewart AIR	.07	.20
109 J.J. Stokes AIR	.07	.20
110 Yancey Thigpen AIR	.02	.10
111 Thurman Thomas AIR	.02	.10
112 Eric Turner AIR	.01	.05
113 Tamarick Vanover AIR	.02	.10
114 Chris Warren AIR	.02	.10
115 Ricky Watters AIR	.02	.10
116 Michael Westbrook AIR	.07	.20
117 Reggie White AIR	.07	.20
118 Steve Young AIR	.15	.40
119 Jeff Blake AIR	.02	.10
120 Robert Brooks AIR	.02	.10
121 Isaac Bruce RS	.07	.20
122 Mark Chmura RS	.02	.10
123 Wayne Chrebet RS see card #8	.10	.30
124 Ben Coates RS	.02	.10
125 Ken Dilger RS	.02	.10
126 Bert Emanuel RS	.02	.10
127 Gus Frerotte RS	.02	.10
128 Kevin Greene RS	.02	.10
129 Erik Kramer RS	.01	.05
130 Greg Lloyd RS	.02	.10
131 Tony Martin RS	.01	.05
132 Brian Mitchell RS	.01	.05
133 Bryce Paup RS	.01	.05
134 Jake Reed RS	.02	.10
135 Errict Rhett RS	.02	.10
136 Yancey Thigpen RS	.02	.10
137 Tamarick Vanover RS	.02	.10
138 Chris Warren RS	.02	.10
139 Marcus Allen RS	.07	.20
140 Jerome Bettis RS	.07	.20
141 Tim Brown RRH	.07	.20
142 Mark Carrier RRH	.01	.05
143 Marshall Faulk RRH	.07	.20
144 Tyrone Hughes RRH	.01	.05
145 Dan Marino RRH	.40	1.00
146 Curtis Martin RRH	.15	.40
147 Barry Sanders RRH	.30	.75
148 Orlando Thomas RRH	.01	.05
149 Checklist (1-107) UER card #24 missing from list	.01	.05
150 Checklist/108-150 inserts	.01	.05
NNO Draft Exchange Card Expired 7/22/97	.40	1.00

1996 SkyBox Impact Rookies All-Rookie Team

COMPLETE SET (10)	5.00	12.00
STATED ODDS 1:6		
1 Karim Abdul-Jabbar	.25	.60
2 Tim Biakabutuka	.25	.60
3 Eddie George	1.50	3.00
4 Marvin Harrison	3.00	6.00
5 Keyshawn Johnson	1.25	2.50
6 Eddie Kennison	.25	.60
7 Lawrence Phillips	.25	.60
8 Zach Thomas	.75	1.50
9 Amani Toomer	1.25	2.50
10 Simeon Rice	.75	1.50

1996 SkyBox Impact Rookies Draft Board

COMPLETE SET (20)	50.00	100.00
STATED ODDS 1:48		
1 Terry Glenn	2.50	6.00
Rickey Dudley		
Bobby Hoying		
2 Simeon Rice	4.00	10.00
Kevin Hardy		
3 Emmitt Smith	7.50	15.00
Errict Rhett		
4 Deion Sanders	3.00	6.00
Corey Sawyer		
Derrick Brooks		
5 Terry Allen	2.00	5.00
Marcus Allen		
6 John Mobley	1.25	3.00
Andre Reed		
7 Drew Bledsoe	3.00	8.00
Rick Mirer		
Mark Brunell		
8 John Elway	6.00	15.00
Jim Kelly		
Dan Marino		
9 Carl Pickens	1.25	3.00
Anthony Miller		
10 Antonio Freeman	2.00	5.00
Robert Brooks		
Cedric Jones		
11 Jerome Bettis	2.00	5.00
Ricky Watters		
Tim Brown		
12 Jerry Rice	5.00	10.00
Herman Moore		
Michael Irvin		
13 Terrell Davis	3.00	8.00
Rodney Hampton		
Garrison Hearst		
14 Kerry Collins	2.00	5.00
Ki-Jana Carter		
Kyle Brady		
15 Barry Sanders	6.00	15.00
Thurman Thomas		
16 Jermaine Lewis	3.00	8.00
Jeff Lewis		
Ray Lewis		
17 Steve Young	5.00	10.00
Troy Aikman		
18 Curtis Martin	3.00	8.00
Chris Warren		
Jamal Anderson		
19 Kordell Stewart	2.00	5.00
Rashaan Salaam		
Michael Westbrook		
20 Tony Banks	2.50	6.00
Muhsin Muhammad		

1996 SkyBox Impact Rookies 1996 Rookies

COMPLETE SET (10)	40.00	100.00
STATED ODDS 1:144		
STATED PRINT RUN 1996 SER.#'d SETS		
1 Karim Abdul-Jabbar	1.50	4.00
2 Tim Biakabutuka	1.50	4.00
3 Rickey Dudley	1.50	4.00
4 Eddie George	8.00	20.00
5 Terry Glenn	6.00	15.00
6 Marvin Harrison	15.00	40.00
7 Keyshawn Johnson	6.00	15.00
8 Eddie Kennison	1.50	4.00
9 Lawrence Phillips	1.50	4.00
10 Amani Toomer	6.00	15.00

1996 SkyBox Impact Rookies 1996 Rookies Autographs

A1 Karim Abdul-Jabbar	7.50	20.00
A2 Rickey Dudley	7.50	20.00
A3 Marvin Harrison	25.00	60.00
A4 Eddie Kennison	10.00	25.00
A5 Lawrence Phillips	7.50	20.00
A6 Amani Toomer	10.00	25.00

1996 SkyBox Impact Rookies Rookie Rewind

COMPLETE SET (10)	15.00	30.00
STATED ODDS 1:36 HOBBY		
1 Jamal Anderson	.60	1.50
2 Jeff Blake	1.00	2.50
3 Robert Brooks	1.00	2.50
4 Mark Brunell	1.50	4.00
5 Brett Favre	5.00	12.00
6 Aaron Hayden	.30	.75
7 Derek Loville	.30	.75
8 Emmitt Smith	4.00	10.00
9 Robert Smith	.60	1.50
10 Tamarick Vanover	.60	1.50

1997 SkyBox Impact

The 1997 SkyBox Impact set was issued in one series totalling 250 cards and was distributed in eight-card packs with a suggested retail of $1.59. The fronts features a color player image with 3-D illustrated graphics. The backs carry another player image, player information and key statistics. In addition to the popular Autographics inserts, a separate Karim Abdul-Jabbar Sample signed card was randomly insderted into packs. SkyBox Impact included 250 of the 500 signed cards, with the balance being distributed as a chiptopper through the Fleer/SkyBox Surprise insert program across various card brands..

COMPLETE SET (250)	6.00	15.00
1 Carl Pickens	.10	.30
2 Ray Lewis	.30	.75
3 Darrell Green	.10	.30
4 Brett Favre	.75	2.00
5 Todd Collins	.07	.20
6 Errict Rhett	.07	.20
7 John Elway	.75	2.00
8 Troy Aikman	.40	1.00
9 Steve McNair	.25	.60
10 Kordell Stewart	.20	.50
11 Drew Bledsoe	.25	.60
12 Kerry Collins	.20	.50
13 Dan Marino	.75	2.00
14 Ricky Watters	.10	.30
15 Marvin Harrison	.20	.50
16 Simeon Rice	.10	.30
17 Qadry Ismail	.10	.30
18 Andre Coleman	.07	.20
19 Keyshawn Johnson	.20	.50
20 Barry Sanders	.60	1.50
21 Rickey Dudley	.10	.30
22 Emmitt Smith	.60	1.50
23 Erik Kramer	.07	.20
24 Tony Boselli	.07	.20
25 Steve Young	.25	.60
26 Rod Woodson	.10	.30
27 Eddie George	.20	.50
28 Curtis Martin	.25	.60
29 Amani Toomer	.10	.30
30 Terrell Davis	.25	.60
31 Jim Everett	.07	.20
32 Marcus Allen	.20	.50
33 Karim Abdul-Jabbar	.20	.50
34 Thurman Thomas	.20	.50
35 Cortez Kennedy	.07	.20
36 Jerome Bettis	.20	.50
37 Kevin Carter	.07	.20
38 Gilbert Brown	.10	.30
39 Bert Emanuel	.10	.30
40 Kyle Brady	.07	.20
41 Trent Dilfer	.20	.50
42 Garrison Hearst	.10	.30
43 Kevin Greene	.10	.30
44 Bryan Cox	.07	.20
45 Desmond Howard	.10	.30
46 Larry Centers	.10	.30
47 Quentin Coryatt	.07	.20
48 Michael Jackson	.10	.30
49 John Randle	.10	.30
50 Mark Brunell	.25	.60
51 William Thomas	.07	.20
52 Glyn Milburn	.07	.20
53 Mike Alstott	.20	.50
54 Chris Spielman	.07	.20
55 Junior Seau	.20	.50
56 Brian Blades	.07	.20
57 Lamar Lathon	.07	.20
58 Derrick Thomas	.20	.50
59 Dave Brown	.07	.20
60 Frank Wycheck	.07	.20
61 Chris Slade	.07	.20
62 Neil Smith	.10	.30
63 Ashley Ambrose	.07	.20
64 Alex Molden	.07	.20
65 Edgar Bennett	.10	.30
66 Alvin Harper	.07	.20
67 Jamal Anderson	.20	.50
68 Eddie Kennison	.10	.30
69 Ken Norton	.07	.20
70 Zach Thomas	.20	.50
71 Leeland McElroy	.07	.20
72 Terry Allen	.20	.50
73 Raymont Harris	.07	.20
74 Ken Dilger	.07	.20
75 Jason Dunn	.07	.20
76 Robert Smith	.10	.30
77 William Roaf	.07	.20
78 Bruce Smith	.10	.30
79 Vinny Testaverde	.10	.30
80 Jerry Rice	.40	1.00
81 Tim Brown	.20	.50
82 James O.Stewart	.10	.30
83 Andre Reed	.10	.30
84 Herman Moore	.10	.30
85 Stan Humphries	.10	.30
86 Chris Warren	.10	.30
87 Tyrone Wheatley	.10	.30
88 Michael Irvin	.20	.50
89 Dan Wilkinson	.07	.20
90 Tony Banks	.10	.30
91 Chester McGlockton	.07	.20
92 Reggie White	.20	.50
93 Elvis Grbac	.10	.30
94 Willie Davis	.07	.20
95 Greg Lloyd	.07	.20
96 Ben Coates	.10	.30
97 Rashaan Salaam	.07	.20
98 Eric Swann	.07	.20
99 Hugh Douglas	.07	.20
100 Henry Ellard	.07	.20
101 Rod Smith WR	.20	.50
102 Tim Biakabutuka	.10	.30
103 Chad Brown	.07	.20
104 Kevin Hardy	.07	.20
105 Chris T. Jones	.07	.20
106 Antonio Freeman	.20	.50
107 Lamont Warren	.07	.20
108 Derrick Alexander DE	.07	.20
109 Brett Perriman	.07	.20
110 Antonio Langham	.07	.20
111 Eric Moulds	.20	.50
112 O.J. McDuffie	.10	.30
113 Eric Metcalf	.10	.30
114 Ray Zellars	.07	.20
115 Marco Coleman	.07	.20
116 Terry Kirby	.10	.30
117 Darren Woodson	.07	.20
118 Charles Johnson	.10	.30
119 Sam Mills	.07	.20
120 Rodney Hampton	.10	.30
121 Rick Mirer	.07	.20
122 Derrick Brooks	.20	.50
123 Greg Hill	.07	.20
124 John Mobley	.07	.20
125 Chris Sanders	.07	.20
126 Kent Graham	.07	.20
127 Michael Westbrook	.10	.30
128 Harvey Williams	.07	.20
129 Keenan McCardell	.10	.30
130 Neil O'Donnell	.10	.30
131 LeRoy Butler	.07	.20
132 Willie McGinest	.07	.20
133 Ki-Jana Carter	.07	.20
134 Robert Jones	.07	.20
135 Jim Harbaugh	.10	.30
136 Wesley Walls	.10	.30
137 Jackie Harris	.07	.20
138 Jermaine Lewis	.20	.50
139 Jake Reed	.10	.30
140 John Friesz	.07	.20
141 Jerris McPhail	.07	.20
142 Charlie Garner	.10	.30
143 Bryce Paup	.07	.20
144 Tony Martin	.10	.30
145 Shannon Sharpe	.10	.30
146 Terrell Owens	.25	.60
147 Curtis Conway	.10	.30
148 Jamie Asher	.07	.20
149 Lawrence Phillips	.07	.20
150 Deion Sanders	.20	.50
151 Frank Sanders	.10	.30
152 Joey Galloway	.10	.30
153 Mel Gray	.07	.20
154 Robert Brooks	.10	.30
155 Jeff George	.10	.30
156 Michael Haynes	.07	.20
157 Chris Chandler	.10	.30
158 Adrian Murrell	.10	.30
159 Tamarick Vanover	.10	.30
160 Marshall Faulk	.25	.60
161 Thomas Lewis	.07	.20
162 Ty Detmer	.10	.30
163 Darnay Scott	.10	.30
164 Byron Bam Morris	.07	.20
165 Scott Mitchell	.10	.30
166 Brad Johnson	.20	.50
167 Dave Meggett	.07	.20
168 Bobby Engram	.10	.30
169 Natrone Means	.10	.30
170 Erric Pegram	.07	.20
171 Leonard Russell	.07	.20
172 Muhsin Muhammad	.10	.30
173 Aeneas Williams	.07	.20
174 Fred Barnett	.07	.20
175 William Floyd	.10	.30
176 Kimble Anders	.10	.30
177 Darick Holmes	.07	.20
178 Willie Green	.07	.20
179 Rodney Thomas	.07	.20
180 Derrick Alexander WR	.10	.30
181 Sean Dawkins	.07	.20
182 Dorsey Levens	.20	.50
183 Napoleon Kaufman	.20	.50
184 Mario Bates	.07	.20
185 Yancey Thigpen	.10	.30
186 Johnnie Morton	.10	.30
187 Gus Frerotte	.07	.20
188 Terance Mathis	.10	.30
189 Tyrone Hughes	.07	.20
190 Wayne Chrebet	.20	.50
191 Tony Brackens	.07	.20
192 Hardy Nickerson	.07	.20
193 Daryl Johnston	.10	.30
194 Irving Fryar	.10	.30
195 Jeff Blake	.10	.30
196 Charles Way	.10	.30
197 Brian Mitchell	.07	.20
198 Brent Jones	.10	.30
199 Mark Chmura	.10	.30
200 Terry Glenn	.20	.50
201 Cris Carter	.20	.50
202 Steve Atwater	.07	.20
203 Rob Moore	.10	.30
204 Anthony Johnson	.07	.20
205 Warren Moon	.20	.50
206 Darrien Gordon	.07	.20
207 Isaac Bruce	.20	.50
208 Reidel Anthony RC	.20	.50
209 Darnell Autry RC	.10	.30
210 Tiki Barber RC	1.25	3.00
211 Pat Barnes RC	.20	.50
212 Terry Battle RC	.07	.20
213 Michael Booker RC	.07	.20
214 Peter Boulware RC	.20	.50
215 Chris Canty RC	.07	.20
216 Rae Carruth RC	.07	.20
217 Troy Davis RC	.10	.30
218 Corey Dillon RC	.75	2.00
219 Jim Druckenmiller RC	.10	.30
220 Warrick Dunn RC	.60	1.50
221 James Farrior RC	.20	.50
222 Tarik Glenn RC	.20	.50
223 Tony Gonzalez RC	.75	2.00
224 Yatil Green RC	.10	.30
225 Byron Hanspard RC	.10	.30
226 Ike Hilliard RC	.30	.75
227 Kenny Holmes RC	.20	.50
228 Walter Jones RC	.20	.50
229 Tom Knight RC	.07	.20
230 David LaFleur RC	.07	.20
231 Kenard Lang RC	.10	.30
232 Kevin Lockett RC	.10	.30
233 Tremain Mack RC	.07	.20
234 Sam Madison RC	.20	.50
235 Chris Naeole RC	.07	.20
236 Orlando Pace RC	.20	.50
237 Jake Plummer RC	.75	2.00
238 Dwayne Rudd RC	.20	.50
239 Darrell Russell RC	.07	.20
240 Jamie Sharper RC	.10	.30
241 Sedrick Shaw RC	.10	.30
242 Antowain Smith RC	.50	1.25
243 Shawn Springs RC	.10	.30
244 Bryant Westbrook RC	.07	.20
245 Reinard Wilson RC	.10	.30
246 Danny Wuerffel RC	.20	.50
247 Renaldo Wynn RC	.07	.20
248 Checklist	.07	.20
249 Checklist	.07	.20
250 Checklist	.07	.20
S1 Karim Abdul-Jabbar Sample Card	.10	.30
S1AU K.Abdul-Jabbar AUTO (Sample Card Signed; Numbered of 500)	25.00	50.00

1997 SkyBox Impact Rave

*STARS: 10X TO 25X BASIC CARDS
*RCs: 8X TO 20X BASIC CARDS
STATED ODDS 1:36 HOBBY
STATED PRINT RUN 150 SERIAL #'d SETS

1997 SkyBox Impact Boss

COMPLETE SET (20)	15.00	40.00
STATED ODDS 1:6		
*SUPER BOSS: 1.5X TO 3X BASIC INSERTS		
1 Karim Abdul-Jabbar	.60	1.50
2 Troy Aikman	1.25	3.00
3 Tim Biakabutuka	.40	1.00
4 Mark Brunell	.75	2.00
5 Rae Carruth	.15	.40
6 Kerry Collins	.60	1.50
7 Corey Dillon	2.50	6.00
8 Jim Druckenmiller	.25	.60
9 Warrick Dunn	1.25	3.00
10 Brett Favre	2.50	6.00
11 Eddie George	.60	1.50

12 Marvin Harrison .60 1.50
13 Keyshawn Johnson .60 1.50
14 Eddie Kennison .40 1.00
15 Dan Marino 2.50 6.00
16 Curtis Martin .75 2.00
17 Steve McNair .75 2.00
18 Orlando Pace .40 1.00
19 Barry Sanders 2.00 5.00
20 Steve Young .75 2.00

1997 SkyBox Impact Excelerators

COMPLETE SET (12) 30.00 60.00
STATED ODDS 1:48
1 Mark Brunell 3.00 8.00
2 Rae Carruth 1.00 2.50
3 Terrell Davis 3.00 8.00
4 Joey Galloway 1.50 4.00
5 Marvin Harrison 2.50 6.00
6 Keyshawn Johnson 2.50 6.00
7 Eddie Kennison 1.50 4.00
8 Steve McNair 3.00 8.00
9 Jerry Rice 5.00 12.00
10 Emmitt Smith 8.00 20.00
11 Shawn Springs 1.50 4.00
12 Kordell Stewart 2.50 6.00

1997 SkyBox Impact Instant Impact

COMPLETE SET (15) 15.00 40.00
STATED ODDS 1:24
1 Reidel Anthony 1.50 4.00
2 Darnell Autry 1.00 2.50
3 Tiki Barber 10.00 25.00
4 Peter Boulware 1.50 4.00
5 Troy Davis 1.00 2.50
6 Jim Druckenmiller 1.00 2.50
7 Warrick Dunn 5.00 12.00
8 Yatil Green 1.00 2.50
9 Ike Hilliard 2.50 6.00
10 Orlando Pace 1.50 4.00
11 Darrell Russell .60 1.50
12 Sedrick Shaw 1.00 2.50
13 Shawn Springs 1.00 2.50
14 Bryant Westbrook .60 1.50
15 Danny Wuerffel 1.50 4.00

1997 SkyBox Impact Rave Reviews

COMPLETE SET (12) 125.00 250.00
STATED ODDS 1:288
1 Terrell Davis 5.00 12.00
2 John Elway 15.00 40.00
3 Brett Favre 15.00 40.00
4 Joey Galloway 2.50 6.00
5 Eddie George 4.00 10.00
6 Terry Glenn 4.00 10.00
7 Dan Marino 15.00 40.00
8 Curtis Martin 5.00 12.00
9 Jerry Rice 8.00 20.00
10 Barry Sanders 12.50 30.00
11 Deion Sanders 4.00 10.00
12 Emmitt Smith 12.50 30.00

1997 SkyBox Impact Total Impact

COMPLETE SET (10) 25.00 60.00
STATED ODDS 1:36 RETAIL
1 Karim Abdul-Jabbar 2.50 6.00
2 Troy Aikman 5.00 12.00
3 Drew Bledsoe 3.00 8.00
4 Isaac Bruce 2.50 6.00
5 Kerry Collins 2.50 6.00
6 John Elway 10.00 25.00
7 Terry Glenn 2.50 6.00
8 Lawrence Phillips 1.00 2.50
9 Deion Sanders 2.50 6.00
10 Kordell Stewart 2.50 6.00

2003 SkyBox LE

Released in January of 2004, this set contains 160 cards including 60 veterans and 100 rookies. Rookies are serial numbered to 99. Boxes contained 18 packs of 3 cards. SRP was $3.99.

COMP.SET w/o RC's (60) 8.00 20.00
61-160 ROOKIE PRINT RUN 99
1 Emmitt Smith .75 2.00
2 Eric Moulds .25 .60
3 William Green .20 .50
4 Clinton Portis .25 .60
5 Tony Gonzalez .30 .75
6 Aaron Brooks .25 .60
7 Chad Pennington .30 .75
8 Jerry Rice .60 1.50
9 LaDainian Tomlinson .30 .75
10 Torry Holt .30 .75
11 Warren Sapp .25 .60
12 Steve McNair .30 .75
13 Marc Bulger .30 .75
14 Patrick Ramsey .25 .60
15 Peerless Price .20 .50
16 Jamal Lewis .25 .60
17 Rich Gannon .25 .60
18 Plaxico Burress .25 .60
19 Drew Brees .30 .75
20 Eddie George .25 .60
21 Ray Lewis .30 .75
22 Drew Bledsoe .30 .75
23 Antonio Bryant .20 .50
24 David Carr .25 .60
25 Priest Holmes .30 .75
26 Ricky Williams .25 .60
27 Peyton Manning .60 1.50
28 Daunte Culpepper .25 .60
29 Jeremy Shockey .30 .75
30 Tiki Barber .30 .75
31 Koren Robinson .25 .60
32 Keyshawn Johnson .30 .75
33 Laveranues Coles .20 .50
34 Brian Urlacher .30 .75
35 Jake Plummer .25 .60
36 Edgerrin James .30 .75
37 Marvin Harrison .30 .75
38 Tom Brady .75 2.00
39 Curtis Martin .30 .75
40 Donovan McNabb .30 .75
41 Hines Ward .30 .75
42 Charlie Garner .25 .60
43 Tommy Maddox .25 .60
44 Terrell Owens .30 .75
45 Shaun Alexander .25 .60
46 Ahman Green .25 .60
47 Fred Taylor .25 .60
48 Randy Moss .30 .75
49 Deuce McAllister .25 .60
50 Quincy Carter .20 .50
51 Jeff Garcia .25 .60
52 Marshall Faulk .30 .75
53 Dante Hall .25 .60
54 Michael Vick .40 1.00
55 Stephen Davis .25 .60
56 Corey Dillon .25 .60
57 Travis Henry .20 .50
58 Chad Johnson .30 .75
59 Joey Harrington .20 .50
60 Brett Favre .75 2.00
61 Bryant Johnson RC 10.00 25.00
62 Terence Newman RC 8.00 20.00
63 Labrandon Toefield RC 8.00 20.00
64 Visanthe Shiancoe RC 10.00 25.00
65 Josh Brown RC 12.00 30.00
66 Andre Woolfolk RC 8.00 20.00
67 Jeremi Johnson RC 6.00 15.00
68 Michael Doss RC 10.00 25.00
69 Talman Gardner RC 6.00 15.00
70 Arnaz Battle RC 10.00 25.00
71 Troy Polamalu RC 75.00 135.00
72 Brock Forsey RC 8.00 20.00
73 Domanick Davis RC 8.00 20.00
74 Onterrio Smith RC 6.00 15.00
75 Kassim Osgood RC 10.00 25.00
76 Asante Samuel RC 20.00 50.00
77 Terrell Suggs RC 10.00 25.00
78 Boss Bailey RC 8.00 20.00
79 Larry Johnson RC 10.00 25.00
80 Teyo Johnson RC 8.00 20.00
81 Chris Simms RC 10.00 25.00
82 Walter Young RC 6.00 15.00
83 Dave Ragone RC 6.00 15.00
84 E.J. Henderson RC 8.00 20.00
85 Billy McMullen RC 6.00 15.00
86 Taylor Jacobs RC 6.00 15.00
87 Sam Aiken RC 8.00 20.00
88 Avon Cobourne RC 6.00 15.00
89 J.R. Tolver RC 8.00 20.00
90 Doug Gabriel RC 8.00 20.00
91 Chris Brown RC 6.00 15.00
92 Musa Smith RC 6.00 15.00
93 Charles Rogers RC 8.00 20.00
94 Seth Marler RC 6.00 15.00
95 DeWayne Robertson RC 8.00 20.00
96 Shaun McDonald RC 8.00 20.00
97 Reno Mahe RC 8.00 20.00
98 Carson Palmer RC 40.00 80.00
99 Dallas Clark RC 15.00 40.00
100 Johnathan Sullivan RC 6.00 15.00
101 Brandon Lloyd RC 15.00 40.00
102 Ken Dorsey RC 8.00 20.00
103 Kelley Washington RC 6.00 15.00
104 Tony Hollings RC 8.00 20.00
105 Bethel Johnson RC 6.00 15.00
106 Antonio Gates RC 60.00 120.00
107 Tyler Brayton RC 8.00 20.00
108 Michael Haynes RC 6.00 15.00
109 Andre Johnson RC 25.00 60.00
110 Nate Burleson RC 8.00 20.00
111 Sammy Davis RC 8.00 20.00
112 Nick Barnett RC 10.00 25.00
113 Willis McGahee RC 12.00 30.00
114 Casey Fitzsimmons RC 8.00 20.00
115 Donald Lee RC 8.00 20.00
116 L.J. Smith RC 10.00 25.00
117 Tyrone Calico RC 8.00 20.00
118 Anquan Boldin RC 15.00 40.00
119 Jason Witten RC 25.00 60.00
120 George Wrighster RC 6.00 15.00
121 William Joseph RC 6.00 15.00
122 Kevin Curtis RC 10.00 25.00
123 Anthony Adams RC 8.00 20.00
124 Kyle Boller RC 10.00 25.00
125 Artose Pinner RC 6.00 15.00
126 Rashean Mathis RC 8.00 20.00
127 Justin Fargas RC 10.00 25.00
128 Pisa Tinoisamoa RC 10.00 25.00
129 Justin Griffith RC 8.00 20.00
130 Quentin Griffin RC 8.00 20.00
131 Cortez Hankton RC 8.00 20.00
132 B.J. Askew RC 8.00 20.00
133 Arlen Harris RC 6.00 15.00
134 Dan Klecko RC 8.00 20.00
135 Lee Suggs RC 8.00 20.00
136 Byron Leftwich RC 10.00 25.00
137 David Tyree RC 10.00 25.00
138 Aaron Walker RC 8.00 20.00
139 Marcus Trufant RC 8.00 20.00
140 Rex Grossman RC 10.00 25.00
141 Bennie Joppru RC 6.00 15.00
142 Kevin Williams RC 10.00 25.00
143 Jerome McDougle RC 6.00 15.00
144 Ken Hamlin RC 10.00 25.00
145 Zuriel Smith RC 6.00 15.00
146 Brooks Bollinger RC 8.00 20.00
147 Ike Taylor RC 20.00 50.00
148 Brad Pyatt RC 6.00 15.00
149 DeJuan Groce RC 10.00 25.00
150 Keenan Howry RC 6.00 15.00
151 Seneca Wallace RC 10.00 25.00
152 Richard Angulo RC 6.00 15.00
153 Jimmy Kennedy RC 8.00 20.00
154 Ty Warren RC 8.00 20.00
155 Nnamdi Asomugha RC 25.00 50.00
156 Chris Kelsay RC 8.00 20.00
157 Terry Pierce RC 6.00 15.00
158 Victor Hobson RC 6.00 15.00
159 Brian St.Pierre RC 8.00 20.00
160 Dewayne White RC 6.00 15.00

2003 SkyBox LE Artist Proofs

*VETS 1-60: 8X TO 20X BASIC CARDS
STATED PRINT RUN 50 SER.#'d SETS

2003 SkyBox LE Executive Proofs

PRINT RUN 1 SERIAL #'d SET

2003 SkyBox LE Gold Proofs

*VETS 1-60: 4X TO 10X BASIC CARDS
STATED PRINT RUN 150 SER.#'d SETS

2003 SkyBox LE Jersey Proofs

STATED PRINT RUN 175 SER.#'d SETS
UNPRICED GOLD PRINT RUN 10
1 Emmitt Smith 15.00 40.00
2 Eric Moulds 5.00 12.00
4 Clinton Portis 5.00 12.00
5 Tony Gonzalez 6.00 15.00
7 Chad Pennington 6.00 15.00
8 Jerry Rice 12.00 30.00
9 LaDainian Tomlinson 6.00 15.00
10 Torry Holt 6.00 15.00
11 Warren Sapp 5.00 12.00
12 Steve McNair 6.00 15.00
21 Ray Lewis 6.00 15.00
22 Drew Bledsoe 6.00 15.00
24 David Carr 5.00 12.00
25 Priest Holmes 6.00 15.00
26 Ricky Williams 5.00 12.00
27 Peyton Manning 12.00 30.00
28 Daunte Culpepper 5.00 12.00
29 Jeremy Shockey 6.00 15.00
30 Tiki Barber 6.00 15.00
32 Keyshawn Johnson 6.00 15.00
34 Brian Urlacher 6.00 15.00
35 Jake Plummer 5.00 12.00
36 Edgerrin James 6.00 15.00
37 Marvin Harrison 6.00 15.00
39 Curtis Martin 6.00 15.00
40 Donovan McNabb 6.00 15.00
41 Hines Ward 6.00 15.00
42 Charlie Garner 5.00 12.00
44 Terrell Owens 6.00 15.00
45 Shaun Alexander 5.00 12.00
46 Ahman Green 5.00 12.00
47 Fred Taylor 5.00 12.00
48 Randy Moss 6.00 15.00
49 Deuce McAllister 5.00 12.00
52 Marshall Faulk 6.00 15.00
54 Michael Vick 8.00 20.00
55 Stephen Davis 5.00 12.00
56 Corey Dillon 5.00 12.00
59 Joey Harrington 4.00 10.00
60 Brett Favre 15.00 40.00

2003 SkyBox LE Photographer's Proofs

*VETS 1-60: 15X TO 40X BASIC CARDS
STATED PRINT RUN 25 SER.#'d SETS

2003 SkyBox LE Retail

COMPLETE SET (60) 8.00 20.00
*VETS 1-60: .3X TO .8X BASIC CARDS

2003 SkyBox LE History of the Draft Jerseys

STATED PRINT RUN 90-99
*SILVER/50: .5X TO 1.2X JSY/90-99
SILVER PRINT RUN 50 SER.#'d SETS
UNPRICED GOLD PRINT RUN 10
HDAG Ahman Green/98 6.00 15.00
HDAT Amani Toomer/96 6.00 15.00
HDBF Brett Favre/91 20.00 50.00
HDCD Corey Dillon/97 6.00 15.00
HDCG Charlie Garner/94 6.00 15.00
HDCM Curtis Martin/95 8.00 20.00
HDCW Charles Woodson/98 8.00 20.00
HDDB Derrick Brooks/95 6.00 15.00
HDDB Drew Bledsoe/93 8.00 20.00
HDDC Daunte Culpepper/99 6.00 15.00
HDDM Donovan McNabb/99 8.00 20.00
HDEG Eddie George/96 6.00 15.00
HDEJ Edgerrin James/99 8.00 20.00
HDEM Eric Moulds/96 6.00 15.00
HDES Emmitt Smith/90 20.00 50.00
HDFT Fred Taylor/98 6.00 15.00
HDHW Hines Ward/98 8.00 20.00
HDIB Isaac Bruce/94 8.00 20.00
HDJG Joey Galloway/95 6.00 15.00
HDJK Jevon Kearse/99 6.00 15.00
HDJP Jake Plummer/97 6.00 15.00
HDKC Kerry Collins/95 6.00 15.00
HDKJ Keyshawn Johnson/96 8.00 20.00
HDMA Mike Alstott/96 8.00 20.00
HDMF Marshall Faulk/94 8.00 20.00
HDMH Marvin Harrison/96 8.00 20.00
HDPM Peyton Manning/98 15.00 40.00
HDRL Ray Lewis/96 8.00 20.00
HDRM Randy Moss/98 8.00 20.00
HDRW Ricky Williams/99 6.00 15.00
HDSD Stephen Davis/96 6.00 15.00
HDSM Steve McNair/95 8.00 20.00
HDSR Simeon Rice/96 5.00 12.00
HDTB Tiki Barber/97 8.00 20.00
HDTC Tim Couch/99 5.00 12.00
HDTG Tony Gonzalez/97 8.00 20.00
HDTH Torry Holt/99 8.00 20.00
HDTO Terrell Owens/96 8.00 20.00
HDWS Warren Sapp/95 6.00 15.00
HDZT Zach Thomas/96 8.00 20.00

2003 SkyBox LE League Leaders

COMPLETE SET (10) 12.00 30.00
STATED ODDS 1:18
UNPRICED EXEC.PROOF PRINT RUN 1
1 Ricky Williams 1.00 2.50
2 Marvin Harrison 1.25 3.00
3 Chad Pennington 1.25 3.00
4 Terrell Owens 1.25 3.00
5 Brian Urlacher 1.25 3.00
6 Shaun Alexander 1.00 2.50
7 Marshall Faulk 1.25 3.00
8 Ray Lewis 1.25 3.00
9 Randy Moss 1.25 3.00
10 Peyton Manning 2.50 6.00

2003 SkyBox LE League Leaders Jerseys

STATED PRINT RUN 75 SER.#'d SETS
*SILVER/50: .5X TO 1.2X BASE JSY/75
SILVER PRINT RUN 50 SER.#'d SETS
UNPRICED GOLD PRINT RUN 10
LLBU Brian Urlacher 8.00 20.00
LLCP Chad Pennington 8.00 20.00
LLMF Marshall Faulk 8.00 20.00
LLMH Marvin Harrison 8.00 20.00
LLPM Peyton Manning 15.00 40.00
LLRL Ray Lewis 8.00 20.00
LLRM Randy Moss 8.00 20.00
LLRW Ricky Williams 6.00 15.00
LLSA Shaun Alexander 6.00 15.00
LLTO Terrell Owens 8.00 20.00

2003 SkyBox LE Rare Form

STATED ODDS 1:288
UNPRICED EXEC.PROOF PRINT RUN 1
1 Brett Favre 10.00 25.00
2 Emmitt Smith 10.00 25.00
3 Michael Vick 5.00 12.00
4 Clinton Portis 3.00 8.00
5 Jeremy Shockey 4.00 10.00
6 Jerry Rice 8.00 20.00
7 David Carr 3.00 8.00
8 Peyton Manning 8.00 20.00
9 Randy Moss 4.00 10.00
10 Brian Urlacher 4.00 10.00

2003 SkyBox LE Rare Form Jerseys Silver Proofs

SILVER PRINT RUN 50 SER.#'d SETS
*BASE JSY/54-84: .4X TO 1X JSY/50
*BASE JSY/22-26: .6X TO 1.5X JSY/50
BASE JSY PRINT RUN 4-84
UNPRICED GOLD PRINT RUN 10
RFBF Brett Favre 25.00 60.00
RFBU Brian Urlacher 10.00 25.00
RFCP Clinton Portis 8.00 20.00
RFDC David Carr 8.00 20.00
RFES Emmitt Smith 25.00 60.00
RFJR Jerry Rice 20.00 50.00
RFJS Jeremy Shockey 10.00 25.00
RFMV Michael Vick 12.00 30.00
RFPM Peyton Manning 20.00 50.00
RFRM Randy Moss 10.00 25.00

2003 SkyBox LE Sky's the Limit

COMPLETE SET (20) 25.00 60.00
STATED ODDS 1:6
UNPRICED EXEC.PROOF PRINT RUN 1
1 Donovan McNabb 1.25 3.00
2 Jeremy Shockey 1.25 3.00
3 Michael Vick 1.50 4.00
4 Peyton Manning 2.50 6.00
5 Randy Moss 1.25 3.00
6 Clinton Portis 1.00 2.50
7 Joey Harrington .75 2.00
8 Ricky Williams 1.00 2.50
9 Deuce McAllister 1.00 2.50
10 LaDainian Tomlinson 1.25 3.00
11 Priest Holmes 1.25 3.00
12 Carson Palmer 1.50 4.00
13 Byron Leftwich .75 2.00
14 Andre Johnson 2.00 5.00
15 Larry Johnson .75 2.00
16 Rex Grossman .75 2.00
17 Terence Newman .60 1.50
18 David Carr 1.00 2.50
19 Daunte Culpepper 1.00 2.50
20 Brian Urlacher 1.25 3.00

2003 SkyBox LE Sky's the Limit Jerseys

PRINT RUN 99 SERIAL #'d SETS
*SILVER/50: .5X TO 1.2X JSY/99
SILVER PRINT RUN 50 SER.#'d SETS
UNPRICED GOLD PRINT RUN 10
SLAJ Andre Johnson 12.00 30.00
SLBL Byron Leftwich 5.00 12.00
SLBU Brian Urlacher 8.00 20.00
SLCP Carson Palmer 10.00 25.00
SLCP Clinton Portis 6.00 15.00
SLDC David Carr 6.00 15.00
SLDC Daunte Culpepper 6.00 15.00
SLDM Deuce McAllister 6.00 15.00
SLDM Donovan McNabb 8.00 20.00
SLJH Joey Harrington 5.00 12.00
SLJS Jeremy Shockey 8.00 20.00
SLLJ Larry Johnson 5.00 12.00
SLLT LaDainian Tomlinson 8.00 20.00
SLMV Michael Vick 10.00 25.00
SLPH Priest Holmes 8.00 20.00
SLPM Peyton Manning 15.00 40.00
SLRG Rex Grossman 5.00 12.00
SLRM Randy Moss 8.00 20.00
SLRW Ricky Williams 6.00 15.00
SLTN Terence Newman 4.00 10.00

2004 SkyBox LE

SkyBox LE was produced by Fleer and initially released in late September 2004. The base set consists of 160-cards including 100-rookies serial numbered of 99. Hobby boxes contained 16-packs of 3-cards and retail boxes contained 24-packs of 5-cards each. Four parallel sets and a variety of inserts can be found seeded in hobby and retail packs highlighted by the Future Legends Autographed Patches and a variety of other game used jersey inserts. Some signed cards were issued via mail-in exchange or redemption cards with a number of those EXCH cards not yet appearing live on the secondary market as of the printing of this book.

COMP.SET w/o SP's (60) 7.50 20.00
ROOKIE/99 ODDS 1:29 HOB
ROOKIE PRINT RUN 99 SER.#'d SETS
UNPRICED PURPLE PRINT RUN 1
1 Anquan Boldin .30 .75
2 Quincy Carter .20 .50
3 Chad Pennington .30 .75
4 Brett Favre .75 2.00
5 Marc Bulger .25 .60
6 David Carr .20 .50
7 Byron Leftwich .25 .60
8 Hines Ward .30 .75
9 Drew Bledsoe .30 .75
10 Domanick Davis .20 .50
11 Plaxico Burress .25 .60
12 Mark Brunell .25 .60
13 Terrell Owens .30 .75
14 Peyton Manning .60 1.50
15 Matt Hasselbeck .25 .60
16 Willis McGahee .30 .75
17 Fred Taylor .25 .60
18 Torry Holt .25 .60
19 Priest Holmes .30 .75
20 Charlie Garner .25 .60
21 Brian Urlacher .30 .75
22 Corey Dillon .25 .60
23 Daunte Culpepper .25 .60
24 Clinton Portis .30 .75
25 Chad Johnson .30 .75
26 Tom Brady .60 1.50
27 Deuce McAllister .25 .60
28 Randy Moss .30 .75
29 A.J. Feeley .20 .50
30 Steve McNair .30 .75
31 Aaron Brooks .25 .60
32 Carson Palmer .30 .75
33 Jeremy Shockey .25 .60
34 Emmitt Smith .75 2.00
35 Jeff Garcia .25 .60
36 Kurt Warner .30 .75
37 Andre Johnson .30 .75
38 LaDainian Tomlinson .30 .75
39 Ray Lewis .30 .75
40 Charles Rogers .20 .50
41 Rich Gannon .25 .60
42 Jake Delhomme .25 .60
43 Marvin Harrison .30 .75
44 Shaun Alexander .25 .60
45 Ricky Williams .25 .60
46 Eddie George .25 .60
47 Edgerrin James .25 .60
48 Chris Chambers .25 .60
49 Jamal Lewis .25 .60
50 Joey Harrington .25 .60
51 Jerry Rice .60 1.50
52 Kyle Boller .25 .60
53 Ahman Green .25 .60
54 Donovan McNabb .30 .75
55 Stephen Davis .25 .60
56 Tony Gonzalez .30 .75
57 Marshall Faulk .30 .75
58 Michael Vick .40 1.00
59 Jake Plummer .25 .60
60 Curtis Martin .30 .75
61 Eli Manning RC 25.00 60.00
62 Robert Gallery RC 4.00 10.00
63 Larry Fitzgerald RC 10.00 25.00
64 Philip Rivers RC 15.00 40.00
65 Sean Taylor RC 8.00 20.00
66 Kellen Winslow RC 4.00 10.00
67 Roy Williams RC 4.00 10.00
68 DeAngelo Hall RC 4.00 10.00
69 Reggie Williams RC 3.00 8.00
70 Dunta Robinson RC 2.50 6.00
71 Ben Roethlisberger RC 25.00 60.00
72 Jonathan Vilma RC 4.00 10.00
73 Lee Evans RC 4.00 10.00
74 Tommie Harris RC 4.00 10.00
75 Michael Clayton RC 3.00 8.00
76 D.J. Williams RC 4.00 10.00
77 Tim Euhus RC 2.50 6.00
78 Kenechi Udeze RC 3.00 8.00
79 Vince Wilfork RC 4.00 10.00
80 J.P. Losman RC 3.00 8.00
81 Jared Lorenzen RC 3.00 8.00
82 Steven Jackson RC 6.00 15.00
83 Ricky Ray RC 4.00 10.00
84 Chris Perry RC 3.00 8.00
85 Jason Babin RC 4.00 10.00
86 Chris Gamble RC 3.00 8.00
87 Michael Jenkins RC 4.00 10.00
88 Kevin Jones RC 3.00 8.00
89 Rashaun Woods RC 2.50 6.00
90 Ben Watson RC 4.00 10.00
91 Karlos Dansby RC 4.00 10.00
92 Teddy Lehman RC 2.50 6.00
93 Ben Troupe RC 3.00 8.00
94 Tatum Bell RC 3.00 8.00
95 Julius Jones RC 3.00 8.00
96 Devery Henderson RC 4.00 10.00
97 Drew Henson RC 2.50 6.00
98 Darius Watts RC 2.50 6.00
99 Greg Jones RC 2.50 6.00
100 Luke McCown RC 3.00 8.00
101 Keary Colbert RC 2.50 6.00
102 Mewelde Moore RC 3.00 8.00
103 Ben Hartsock RC 2.50 6.00
104 Derrick Hamilton RC 2.50 6.00
105 Bernard Berrian RC 4.00 10.00
106 Chris Cooley RC 4.00 10.00
107 Devard Darling RC 2.50 6.00
108 Matt Schaub RC 8.00 20.00
109 Carlos Francis RC 2.50 6.00
110 Will Poole RC 4.00 10.00
111 Samie Parker RC 2.50 6.00
112 Derrick Knight RC 2.50 6.00
113 Jerricho Cotchery RC 3.00 8.00
114 Rod Rutherford RC 2.50 6.00
115 Ernest Wilford RC 3.00 8.00
116 Cedric Cobbs RC 2.50 6.00
117 Johnnie Morant RC 2.50 6.00
118 Craig Krenzel RC 3.00 8.00
119 Maurice Mann RC 2.50 6.00
120 Michael Turner RC 5.00 12.00
121 Ryan Dinwiddie RC 2.50 6.00
122 Drew Carter RC 3.00 8.00
123 P.K. Sam RC 2.50 6.00
124 Jamaar Taylor RC 2.50 6.00
125 Ryan Krause RC 2.50 6.00
126 Triandos Luke RC 2.50 6.00
127 Andy Hall RC 2.50 6.00
128 Josh Harris RC 2.50 6.00
129 Jim Sorgi RC 3.00 8.00
130 Jason Fife RC 2.50 6.00
131 Clarence Moore RC 2.50 6.00
132 Jeff Smoker RC 3.00 8.00
133 John Navarre RC 2.50 6.00
134 Justin Jenkins RC 2.50 6.00
135 Adimchinobe Echemandu RC 3.00 8.00
136 Jammal Lord RC 2.50 6.00
137 Erik Jensen RC 2.50 6.00
138 Cody Pickett RC 3.00 8.00
139 Casey Bramlet RC 2.50 6.00
140 Quincy Wilson RC 3.00 8.00
141 Thomas Tapeh RC 3.00 8.00
142 Matt Brandt RC 2.50 6.00
143 Bruce Perry RC 2.50 6.00
144 Mark Jones RC 2.50 6.00
145 Keith Smith RC 2.50 6.00
146 B.J. Symons RC 2.50 6.00
147 Patrick Crayton RC 4.00 10.00
148 Daryl Smith RC 2.50 6.00
149 Demorrio Williams RC 4.00 10.00
150 Casey Clausen RC 3.00 8.00
151 Jarrett Payton RC 3.00 8.00
152 Kris Wilson RC 3.00 8.00
153 Renaldo Works RC 2.50 6.00
154 Shawn Andrews RC 3.00 8.00
155 Ricardo Colclough RC 3.00 8.00
156 Travis LaBoy RC 3.00 8.00
157 Bob Sanders RC 10.00 25.00
158 Chad Lavalais RC 2.50 6.00
159 Derrick Strait RC 2.50 6.00
160 Darnell Dockett RC 2.50 6.00

2004 SkyBox LE Black Border Red

*VETS: 6X TO 15X BASIC CARDS
*ROOKIES: .4X TO 1X BASIC CARDS
STATED PRINT RUN 50 SER.#'d SETS

2004 SkyBox LE Gold

*VETS: 3X TO 8X BASIC CARDS
*ROOKIES: .25X TO .6X BASIC CARDS
STATED PRINT RUN 150 SER.#'d SETS

2004 SkyBox LE Black Border Platinum

*VETS: 8X TO 20X BASIC CARDS
*ROOKIES: .5X TO 1.2X BASIC CARDS
STATED PRINT RUN 35 SER.#'d SETS

2004 SkyBox LE Future Legends

STATED ODDS 1:16
UNPRICED EXEC.PROOF #'d OF 1
1FL Tatum Bell .75 2.00
2FL Bernard Berrian 1.00 2.50
3FL Michael Clayton .75 2.00
4FL Lee Evans 1.00 2.50
5FL Devery Henderson 1.00 2.50
6FL Michael Jenkins 1.00 2.50
7FL Greg Jones .60 1.50
8FL Julius Jones .75 2.00
9FL Kevin Jones .75 2.00
10FL J.P. Losman .75 2.00
11FL Eli Manning 6.00 15.00
12FL Chris Perry .75 2.00
13FL Ben Troupe .75 2.00
14FL Philip Rivers 4.00 10.00
15FL Ben Roethlisberger 6.00 15.00
16FL Matt Schaub 2.00 5.00
17FL Sean Taylor 2.00 5.00
18FL Roy Williams WR 1.00 2.50
19FL Kellen Winslow Jr. 1.00 2.50
20FL Rashaun Woods .60 1.50
21FL Reggie Williams .75 2.00
22FL Steven Jackson 1.50 4.00
23FL Larry Fitzgerald 2.50 6.00
24FL Drew Henson .60 1.50
25FL Luke McCown .75 2.00

2004 SkyBox LE Future Legends Autographed Patches

STATED PRINT RUN 25 SER.#'d SETS
UNPRICED DUAL AU PRINT RUN 1
BR Ben Roethlisberger 150.00 300.00
CP Chris Perry 15.00 40.00
DH Devery Henderson 20.00 50.00
EM Eli Manning 175.00 300.00
JL J.P. Losman 15.00 40.00
KW Kellen Winslow Jr. 20.00 50.00
MC Michael Clayton 15.00 40.00
PR Philip Rivers 60.00 100.00
RW Roy Williams WR 20.00 50.00
RW2 Rashaun Woods 12.00 30.00
RW3 Reggie Williams 15.00 40.00
WP Will Poole 20.00 50.00

2004 SkyBox LE Future Legends Jerseys Silver

SILVER PRINT RUN 75
*COPPER/50: .5X TO 1.2X SLVR/75
COPPER PRINT RUN 50
*GOLD PATCH/25: .8X TO 2X SLVR/75
GOLD PROOF PATCH PRINT RUN 25
FLBB Bernard Berrian 4.00 10.00
FLBR Ben Roethlisberger 15.00 40.00
FLBT Ben Troupe 3.00 8.00
FLCP Chris Perry 3.00 8.00
FLDH Drew Henson 2.50 6.00
FLDH Devery Henderson 4.00 10.00
FLEM Eli Manning 15.00 40.00
FLGJ Greg Jones 2.50 6.00
FLJJ Julius Jones 3.00 8.00
FLJL J.P. Losman 3.00 8.00
FLKJ Kevin Jones 3.00 8.00
FLKW Kellen Winslow Jr. 4.00 10.00
FLLE Lee Evans 4.00 10.00
FLLF Larry Fitzgerald 10.00 25.00
FLLM Luke McCown 3.00 8.00
FLMC Michael Clayton 3.00 8.00
FLMJ Michael Jenkins 4.00 10.00
FLMS Matt Schaub 8.00 20.00
FLPR Philip Rivers 12.00 30.00
FLRW Rashaun Woods 2.50 6.00
FLRW2 Reggie Williams 3.00 8.00
FLRW3 Roy Williams WR 4.00 10.00
FLSJ Steven Jackson 6.00 15.00
FLST Sean Taylor 12.00 30.00
FLTB Tatum Bell 3.00 8.00

2004 SkyBox LE Jersey Silver

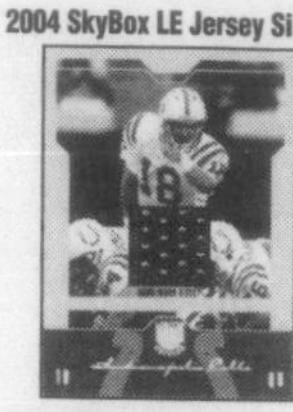

SILVER PRINT RUN 250 SER.#'d SETS
*COPPER/99: .6X TO 1.5X SILVER/250
COPPER PRINT RUN 99 SER.#'d SETS
UNPRICED EXEC.PRPL PRINT RUN 1
*GOLD PATCH/50: 1X TO 2.5X SILVER/250
GOLD PATCH SER.#'d OF 50 SETS
*PLATINUM/15: 1.5X TO 4X SLVR/250
PLATINUM PATCH PRINT RUN 15
1 Anquan Boldin 3.00 8.00
2 Quincy Carter 2.00 5.00
3 Chad Pennington 3.00 8.00
4 Brett Favre 8.00 20.00
5 Marc Bulger 2.50 6.00
6 David Carr 2.00 5.00
7 Byron Leftwich 2.50 6.00
8 Hines Ward 3.00 8.00
9 Drew Bledsoe 3.00 8.00
10 Domanick Davis 2.00 5.00
11 Plaxico Burress 2.50 6.00
12 Mark Brunell 2.50 6.00
13 Terrell Owens 3.00 8.00
14 Peyton Manning 6.00 15.00
15 Matt Hasselbeck 2.50 6.00
16 Willis McGahee 3.00 8.00
17 Fred Taylor 2.50 6.00
18 Torry Holt 2.50 6.00
19 Priest Holmes 3.00 8.00
20 Charlie Garner 2.50 6.00
21 Brian Urlacher 3.00 8.00
22 Corey Dillon 2.50 6.00
23 Daunte Culpepper 2.50 6.00
24 Clinton Portis 3.00 8.00
25 Chad Johnson 3.00 8.00
26 Tom Brady 6.00 15.00
27 Deuce McAllister 2.50 6.00
28 Randy Moss 3.00 8.00
29 A.J. Feeley 2.00 5.00
30 Steve McNair 3.00 8.00
31 Aaron Brooks 2.50 6.00
32 Carson Palmer 3.00 8.00
33 Jeremy Shockey 2.50 6.00
34 Emmitt Smith 8.00 20.00
35 Jeff Garcia 2.50 6.00
36 Kurt Warner 3.00 8.00
37 Andre Johnson 3.00 8.00
38 LaDainian Tomlinson 3.00 8.00
39 Ray Lewis 3.00 8.00
40 Charles Rogers 2.00 5.00
41 Rich Gannon 2.50 6.00
42 Jake Delhomme 2.50 6.00
43 Marvin Harrison 3.00 8.00
44 Shaun Alexander 2.50 6.00
45 Ricky Williams 2.50 6.00
46 Eddie George 2.50 6.00
47 Edgerrin James 2.50 6.00
48 Chris Chambers 2.50 6.00
49 Jamal Lewis 2.50 6.00
50 Joey Harrington 2.50 6.00
51 Jerry Rice 6.00 15.00
52 Kyle Boller 2.50 6.00
53 Ahman Green 2.50 6.00
54 Donovan McNabb 3.00 8.00
55 Stephen Davis 2.50 6.00
56 Tony Gonzalez 3.00 8.00
57 Marshall Faulk 3.00 8.00
58 Michael Vick 4.00 10.00
59 Jake Plummer 2.50 6.00
60 Curtis Martin 3.00 8.00

2004 SkyBox LE LEgends of the Draft Autographed Patches

STATED PRINT RUN 25 SER.#'d SETS
UNPRICED DUAL AU PRINT RUN 1
AJ Andre Johnson 20.00 50.00
BL Byron Leftwich 15.00 40.00
JL Jamal Lewis 15.00 40.00
KB Kyle Boller 15.00 40.00
PM Peyton Manning 75.00 150.00

2004 SkyBox LE LEgends of the Draft Jerseys Silver

SILVER PRINT RUN 81-103
*COPPER/50: .5X TO 1.2X SILVER
COPPER PRINT RUN 50
*GOLD PATCH/25: 1X TO 2.5X SILVER
GOLD PROOF PATCH PRINT RUN 25
LDAB Anquan Boldin/103 5.00 12.00
LDAF A.J. Feeley/101 3.00 8.00
LDAJ Andre Johnson/103 5.00 12.00
LDBF Brett Favre/91 12.00 30.00
LDBL Byron Leftwich/103 4.00 10.00
LDBS Barry Sanders/89 15.00 40.00
LDBU Brian Urlacher/100 5.00 12.00
LDBW Brian Westbrook/102 5.00 12.00
LDCC Chris Chambers/101 4.00 10.00
LDCJ Chad Johnson/101 5.00 12.00
LDCP Bo Jackson/87 12.00 30.00
LDCP Clinton Portis/102 5.00 12.00
LDDC David Carr/102 3.00 8.00
LDDD Domanick Davis/103 3.00 8.00
LDDF DeShaun Foster/102 4.00 10.00
LDDM Donovan McNabb/99 5.00 12.00
LDDM Dan Marino/83 20.00 50.00
LDDM2 Deuce McAllister/100 4.00 10.00
LDDS Deion Sanders/89 8.00 20.00
LDES Emmitt Smith/90 12.00 30.00
LDJE John Elway/83 20.00 50.00
LDJH Joey Harrington/100 4.00 10.00
LDJL Jamal Lewis/100 4.00 10.00
LDJM Joe Montana/86 20.00 50.00
LDJR Jerry Rice/85 10.00 25.00
LDJS Jeremy Shockey/102 4.00 10.00
LDKB Kyle Boller/103 4.00 10.00
LDLA LaVar Arrington/100 4.00 10.00
LDLT Lawrence Taylor/81 8.00 20.00

LDLT2 LaDainian Tomlinson/101 5.00 12.00
LDMV Michael Vick/101 6.00 15.00
LDPM Peyton Manning/98 10.00 25.00
LDRJ Rudi Johnson/101 4.00 10.00
LDRM Randy Moss/98 5.00 12.00
LDSM Santana Moss/101 4.00 10.00
LDSY Steve Young/84 10.00 25.00
LDTA Troy Aikman/89 12.00 30.00
LDTB Tom Brady/100 10.00 25.00
LDTC Tyrone Calico/103 4.00 10.00
LDWM Willis McGahee/100 5.00 12.00

2004 SkyBox LE Rare Form

STATED ODDS 1:256
UNPRICED EXECUTIVE PROOF #'d TO 1
1RF Randy Moss 2.50 6.00
2RF Donovan McNabb 2.50 6.00
3RF Chad Pennington 2.50 6.00
4RF Tom Brady 5.00 12.00
5RF Brett Favre 6.00 15.00
6RF Priest Holmes 2.50 6.00
7RF Ricky Williams 2.00 5.00
8RF Byron Leftwich 2.00 5.00
9RF Carson Palmer 2.50 6.00
10RF Michael Vick 3.00 8.00

2004 SkyBox LE Rare Form Jerseys Copper

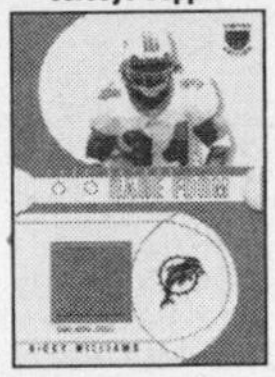

COPPER PRINT RUN 50 SER.#'d SETS
*GOLD PATCH/25: .8X TO 2X COP/50
GOLD PATCH PRINT RUN 25
*SILVER/84: .4X TO 1X COP/50
*SILVER/31-34: .5X TO 1.2X COP/50
SILVER STATED PRINT RUN 4-84
RFBF Brett Favre 15.00 40.00
RFBL Byron Leftwich 5.00 12.00
RFCP Chad Pennington 6.00 15.00
RFCP2 Carson Palmer 6.00 15.00
RFDM Donovan McNabb 6.00 15.00
RFMV Michael Vick 8.00 20.00
RFPH Priest Holmes 6.00 15.00
RFRM Randy Moss 6.00 15.00
RFRW Ricky Williams 5.00 12.00
RFTB Tom Brady 12.00 30.00

2004 SkyBox LE Sky's the Limit

COMPLETE SET (20) 15.00 40.00
STATED ODDS 1:4
UNPRICED EXEC.PROOF #'d TO 1
1SL Eli Manning 4.00 10.00
2SL Peyton Manning 1.50 4.00
3SL Philip Rivers 2.50 6.00
4SL LaDainian Tomlinson .75 2.00
5SL Steven Jackson 1.00 2.50
6SL Marshall Faulk .75 2.00
7SL Ben Roethlisberger 4.00 10.00
8SL Hines Ward .75 2.00
9SL Reggie Williams .50 1.25
10SL Byron Leftwich .60 1.50
11SL Kevin Jones .50 1.25
12SL Joey Harrington .60 1.50
13SL Larry Fitzgerald 1.50 4.00
14SL Anquan Boldin .75 2.00
15SL Roy Williams WR .60 1.50
16SL Charles Rogers .50 1.25
17SL Julius Jones .50 1.25
18SL Emmitt Smith 2.00 5.00
19SL Tatum Bell .50 1.25
20SL Clinton Portis .75 2.00

2004 SkyBox LE Sky's the Limit Jerseys Silver

STATED PRINT RUN 99 SER.#'d SETS
*COPPER/50: .5X TO 1.2X SLVR/99
COPPER PRINT RUN 50 SER.#'d SETS
*GOLD PATCH/25: .8X TO 2X SLVR/99
GOLD PATCH SER.#'d OF 25 SETS
UNPRICED DUAL PLATINUM #'d TO 10
UNPRICED DUAL PURPLE #'d TO 1
SLAB Anquan Boldin 5.00 12.00
SLBL Byron Leftwich 4.00 10.00
SLBR Ben Roethlisberger 15.00 40.00
SLCP Clinton Portis 5.00 12.00
SLCR Charles Rogers 3.00 8.00
SLEM Eli Manning 20.00 40.00
SLES Emmitt Smith 12.00 30.00
SLHW Hines Ward 5.00 12.00
SLJH Joey Harrington 4.00 10.00
SLJJ Julius Jones 2.50 6.00
SLKJ Kevin Jones 3.00 8.00
SLLF Larry Fitzgerald 8.00 20.00
SLLT LaDainian Tomlinson 5.00 12.00
SLMF Marshall Faulk 5.00 12.00
SLPM Peyton Manning 10.00 25.00
SLPR Philip Rivers 10.00 25.00
SLRW Reggie Williams 3.00 8.00
SLRW2 Roy Williams WR 3.00 8.00
SLSJ Steven Jackson 5.00 12.00
SLTB Tatum Bell 3.00 8.00

1999 SkyBox Molten Metal

Released as a 151-card set, 1999 Skybox Molten Metal is comprised of 125 veteran cards and 26 short-printed rookies found one in every five packs. Rookie cards are printed on actual metal cards. Packaged in five card packs, Molten Metal carried a suggested retail of $5.99.

COMPLETE SET (151) 40.00 100.00
COMP.SET w/o SP's (125) 12.50 30.00
1 Terrell Davis .40 1.00
2 Chris Chandler .30 .75
3 Terry Glenn .30 .75
4 Jon Kitna .30 .75
5 Bubby Brister .25 .60
6 Jermaine Lewis .25 .60
7 Doug Flutie .40 1.00
8 Napoleon Kaufman .25 .60
9 Yancey Thigpen .25 .60
10 Bobby Engram .30 .75
11 Barry Sanders 1.00 2.50
12 Ben Coates .30 .75
13 Joey Galloway .30 .75
14 Charlie Batch .30 .75
15 Jerome Bettis .40 1.00
16 Brad Johnson .30 .75
17 Brian Griese .30 .75
18 Jeff Lewis .25 .60
19 Jake Plummer .30 .75
20 Mark Brunell .30 .75
21 Robert Smith .30 .75
22 Steve Young .50 1.25
23 Derrick Mayes .25 .60
24 Wayne Chrebet .30 .75
25 Rich Gannon .30 .75
26 Steve McNair .40 1.00
27 Charles Johnson .25 .60
28 Stephen Alexander .25 .60
29 Jeff Blake .30 .75
30 Tony Gonzalez .40 1.00
31 Eddie Kennison .30 .75
32 Hines Ward .40 1.00
33 Isaac Bruce .40 1.00
34 Peyton Manning 1.25 3.00
35 Doug Pederson .25 .60
36 Stephen Davis .30 .75
37 Terance Mathis .25 .60
38 Herman Moore .30 .75
39 Fred Taylor .30 .75
40 Courtney Hawkins .25 .60
41 Michael Westbrook .25 .60
42 Vinny Testaverde .30 .75
43 Jacquez Green .25 .60
44 Rocket Ismail .30 .75
45 Curtis Martin .40 1.00
46 Tim Brown .40 1.00
47 Kevin Dyson .25 .60
48 Steve Beuerlein .30 .75
49 Adrian Murrell .30 .75
50 Randall Cunningham .40 1.00
51 Jerry Rice .75 2.00
52 Tim Biakabutuka .30 .75
53 Muhsin Muhammad .30 .75
54 Antonio Freeman .30 .75
55 Cris Carter .40 1.00
56 Lawrence Phillips .30 .75
57 Michael Irvin .40 1.00
58 Terrell Owens .40 1.00
59 Warrick Dunn .30 .75
60 Leslie Shepherd .25 .60
61 O.J. McDuffie .30 .75
62 Byron Hanspard .25 .60
63 Trent Dilfer .30 .75
64 Eric Moulds .30 .75
65 Scott Mitchell .25 .60
66 Marc Edwards .30 .75
67 Dorsey Levens .30 .75
68 Dan Marino 1.25 3.00
69 Jason Sehorn .30 .75
70 Junior Seau .40 1.00
71 Reidel Anthony .25 .60
72 Rob Moore .25 .60
73 Deion Sanders .40 1.00
74 Rickey Dudley .25 .60
75 Keyshawn Johnson .30 .75
76 Eddie George .30 .75
77 E.G. Green .25 .60
78 Terry Kirby .25 .60
79 John Avery .25 .60
80 Pete Mitchell .25 .60
81 Natrone Means .30 .75
82 Mike Alstott .40 1.00
83 Carl Pickens .30 .75
84 Karim Abdul-Jabbar .30 .75
85 Kerry Collins .30 .75
86 Erik Kramer .30 .75
87 Robert Holcombe .25 .60
88 Willie Jackson .25 .60
89 Marcus Pollard .25 .60
90 Dam Morris .25 .60
91 Gary Brown .25 .60
92 Freddie Jones .25 .60
93 Kurt Warner RC 4.00 10.00
94 Priest Holmes .40 1.00
95 Duce Staley .30 .75
96 Skip Hicks .25 .60
97 Frank Sanders .25 .60
98 Corey Dillon .30 .75
99 Shannon Sharpe .40 1.00
100 Randy Moss .40 1.00
101 Sean Dawkins .25 .60
102 Marshall Faulk .40 1.00
103 Mark Chmura .25 .60
104 Keenan McCardell .30 .75
105 Jimmy Smith .30 .75
106 Jim Harbaugh .30 .75
107 Jamal Anderson .30 .75
108 Elvis Grbac .25 .60
109 Ed McCaffrey .30 .75
110 Drew Bledsoe .40 1.00
111 Curtis Conway .30 .75
112 Billy Joe Tolliver .25 .60
113 J.J. Stokes .25 .60
114 Curtis Enis .25 .60
115 Antowain Smith .25 .60
116 Troy Aikman .60 1.50
117 Ricky Watters .30 .75
118 Kordell Stewart .30 .75
119 Derrick Alexander .25 .60
120 Emmitt Smith 1.00 2.50
121 Billy Joe Hobert .25 .60
122 Johnnie Morton .30 .75
123 Rod Smith .30 .75
124 Marvin Harrison .40 1.00
125 Brett Favre 1.25 3.00
126 Craig Yeast RC .60 1.50
127 Ricky Williams RC 1.50 4.00
128 Brandon Stokley RC 1.00 2.50
129 Akili Smith RC .75 2.00
130 Peerless Price RC .75 2.00
131 Joe Montgomery RC .60 1.50
132 Cade McNown RC .75 2.00
133 Donovan McNabb RC 2.50 6.00
134 Shaun King RC .75 2.00
135 James Johnson RC .60 1.50
136 Kevin Johnson RC .75 2.00
137 Edgerrin James RC 1.25 3.00
138 Terry Jackson RC .60 1.50
139 Sedrick Irvin RC .60 1.50
140 Brock Huard RC .75 2.00
141 Torry Holt RC 1.50 4.00
142 Amos Zereoue RC .75 2.00
143 Kevin Faulk RC 1.00 2.50
144 Troy Edwards RC .75 2.00
145 Donald Driver RC 8.00 20.00
146 Daunte Culpepper RC 1.00 2.50
147 Tim Couch RC 1.00 2.50
148 Cecil Collins RC .60 1.50
149 David Boston RC .75 2.00
150 Champ Bailey RC 2.00 5.00
151 Olandis Gary RC 1.00 2.50
P133 Donovan McNabb Promo 1.25 3.00

1999 SkyBox Molten Metal Gridiron Gods

COMPLETE SET (20) 25.00 50.00
STATED ODDS 1:6
*BLUE CARDS: 2.5X TO 6X BRONZE
BLUE STATED PRINT RUN 99 SER.#'d SETS
*GOLD CARDS: 1.5X TO 4X BRONZE
GOLD STATED ODDS 1:72
*SILVER CARDS: .6X TO 2X BRONZE
SILVER STATED ODDS 1:24
GG1 Randy Moss 2.50 6.00
GG2 Keyshawn Johnson 1.00 2.50
GG3 Mike Alstott 1.00 2.50
GG4 Brian Griese 1.00 2.50
GG5 Tim Couch .75 2.00
GG6 Troy Aikman 2.00 5.00
GG7 Warrick Dunn 1.00 2.50
GG8 Mark Brunell 1.00 2.50
GG9 Jerry Rice 2.00 5.00
GG10 Dorsey Levens 1.00 2.50
GG11 Fred Taylor 1.00 2.50
GG12 Emmitt Smith 2.00 5.00
GG13 Edgerrin James 2.50 6.00
GG14 Eddie George 1.00 2.50
GG15 Drew Bledsoe 1.25 3.00
GG16 Deion Sanders 1.00 2.50
GG17 Charlie Batch 1.00 2.50
GG18 Kordell Stewart .60 1.50
GG19 Brad Johnson 1.00 2.50
GG20 Akili Smith .60 1.50

1999 SkyBox Molten Metal Patchworks

STATED ODDS 1:360 HOBBY
1 Drew Bledsoe 12.00 30.00
2 Mark Brunell 12.00 30.00
3 Randall Cunningham FS 12.00 30.00
4 Terrell Davis 12.00 30.00
5 Marshall Faulk FS 12.00 30.00
6 Brett Favre 50.00 100.00
7 Antonio Freeman FS 12.00 30.00
8 Dorsey Levens FS 12.00 30.00
9 Peyton Manning 30.00 100.00
10 Dan Marino 40.00 100.00
11 Curtis Martin 15.00 40.00
12 Keenan McCardell FS 8.00 20.00
13 Herman Moore 8.00 20.00
14 Johnnie Morton 8.00 20.00
15 Randy Moss 15.00 40.00
16 Jake Plummer FS 10.00 25.00
17 Jerry Rice 30.00 80.00
18 Fred Taylor FS 10.00 25.00
19 Steve Young 20.00 50.00

1999 SkyBox Molten Metal Perfect Fit

COMPLETE SET (10) 30.00 60.00
STATED ODDS 1:24
*GOLD CARDS: 1.2X TO 3X BRONZE
GOLD STATED ODDS 1:216
*RED CARDS: 6X TO 12X BRONZE
RED STATED PRINT RUN 25 SER.#'d SETS
*SILVER CARDS: .6X TO 1.5X BRONZE
SILVER STATED ODDS 1:72
PF1 Barry Sanders 5.00 12.00
PF2 Brett Favre 5.00 12.00
PF3 Dan Marino 5.00 12.00
PF4 Edgerrin James 5.00 12.00
PF5 Emmitt Smith 3.00 8.00
PF6 Fred Taylor 1.50 4.00
PF7 Randy Moss 4.00 10.00
PF8 Torrell Davis 1.50 4.00
PF9 Tim Couch 1.50 4.00
PF10 Peyton Manning 5.00 12.00

1999 SkyBox Molten Metal Top Notch

COMPLETE SET (15) 25.00 50.00
STATED ODDS 1:12
*GOLD CARDS: 1.2X TO 3X BRONZE
GOLD STATED ODDS 1:108
*GREEN CARDS: 3X TO 8X BRONZE
GREEN STATED PRINT RUN 75 SER.#'d SETS
*SILVER CARDS: .6X TO 1.5X BRONZE
SILVER STATED ODDS 1:36
TN1 Jake Plummer .75 2.00
TN2 Cade McNown 1.00 2.50
TN3 Tim Couch 1.25 3.00
TN4 Emmitt Smith 2.50 6.00
TN5 Charlie Batch 1.25 3.00
TN6 Donovan McNabb 5.00 12.00
TN7 Steve Young 1.50 4.00
TN8 Brian Griese 1.25 3.00
TN9 Doug Flutie 1.25 3.00
TN10 Edgerrin James 4.00 10.00
TN11 Fred Taylor 1.25 3.00
TN12 Keyshawn Johnson 1.25 3.00
TN13 Mark Brunell 1.25 3.00
TN14 Randy Moss 3.00 8.00
TN15 Ricky Williams 2.00 5.00

1999 SkyBox Molten Metal Millennium Gold

COMP.FACT.SET (127) 25.00 60.00
*GOLD STARS: .6X TO 1.5X BASIC CARDS
STATED PRINT RUN 2000 SETS

1999 SkyBox Molten Metal Millennium Silver

COMPLETE SET (125) 12.50 30.00
*MILL.SILVERS: .4X TO 1X BASIC CARDS
STATED PRINT RUN 3400 SETS

1999 SkyBox Molten Metal Player's Party

COMPLETE SET (125) 30.00 50.00
*SINGLES: .5X TO 1.2X BASIC CARDS

1993 SkyBox Premium

Having dropped "Primetime" from the set name, the 1993 Skybox Premium set consists of 270 standard-size cards. Cards were issued in 10-card packs. The fronts display borderless color action player photos with backgrounds that are split horizontally or vertically into team colors. The player's name and team logo appear near the top. The backs carry a second color action photo, career synopsis, biography, four-year stats and career totals. Rookie Cards include Jerome Bettis, Drew Bledsoe, Curtis Conway, Garrison Hearst, O.J. McDuffie, Natrone Means, Rick Mirer and Robert Smith. Two 6-card promo panel sheets were produced and are listed below. The sheets were given away at the 1993 National Sports Collectors Convention in Chicago.

COMPLETE SET (270) 10.00 25.00
1 Eric Martin .02 .10
2 Earnest Byner .02 .10
3 Ricky Proehl .02 .10
4 Mark Carrier WR .07 .20
5 Shannon Sharpe .15 .40
6 Anthony Thompson .02 .10
7 Drew Bledsoe RC 2.00 5.00
8 Tom Carter RC .07 .20
9 Ryan McNeil RC .15 .40
10 Troy Aikman .60 1.50
11 Robert Jones .02 .10
12 Rodney Peete .02 .10
13 Wendell Davis .02 .10
14 Thurman Thomas .15 .40
15 John Stephens .02 .10
16 Rodney Hampton .07 .20
17 Eric Bieniemy .02 .10
18 Santana Dotson .07 .20
19 Jeff George .15 .40
20 John L. Williams .02 .10
21 Barry Word .02 .10
22 Chris Miller .07 .20
23 Jeff Hostetler .07 .20
24 Dwight Stone .02 .10
25 Brad Baxter .02 .10
26 Randall Cunningham .15 .40
27 Mark Higgs .02 .10
28 Vaughn Dunbar .02 .10
29 Ricky Ervins .02 .10
30 Johnny Bailey .02 .10
31 Michael Jackson .07 .20
32 Mike Croel .02 .10
33 Steve Young .60 1.50
34 Deon Figures RC .02 .10
35 Robert Smith RC 1.00 2.50
36 Irv Smith RC .02 .10
37 Charles Haley .07 .20
38 Cris Dishman .02 .10
39 Barry Sanders 1.00 2.50
40 Jim Harbaugh .15 .40
41 Darryl Talley .02 .10
42 Jackie Harris .02 .10
43 Phil Simms .07 .20
44 Marion Butts .02 .10
45 Anthony Munoz .07 .20
46 Steve Emtman .02 .10
47 Kelvin Martin .02 .10
48 Joe Montana 1.25 3.00
49 Andre Rison .07 .20
50 Ethan Horton .02 .10
51 Kevin Greene .07 .20
52 Browning Nagle .02 .10
53 Tim Harris .02 .10
54 Keith Byars .02 .10
55 Terry Allen .15 .40
56 Chip Lohmiller .02 .10
57 Robert Massey .02 .10
58 Michael Dean Perry .07 .20
59 Tommy Maddox .15 .40
60 Jerry Rice .75 2.00
61 Lincoln Kennedy RC .02 .10
62 Jerome Bettis RC 3.00 8.00
63 Coleman Rudolph RC .02 .10
64 Emmitt Smith 1.50 3.00
65 Curtis Duncan .02 .10
66 Andre Ware .02 .10
67 Neal Anderson .02 .10
68 Jim Kelly .15 .40
69 Reggie White .15 .40
70 Dave Meggett .02 .10
71 Junior Seau .15 .40
72 Courtney Hawkins .02 .10
73 Clarence Verdin .02 .10
74 Tommy Kane .02 .10
75 Dale Carter .02 .10
76 Michael Haynes .07 .20
77 Willie Gault .02 .10
78 Eric Green .02 .10
79 Ronnie Lott .07 .20
80 Vai Sikahema .02 .10
81 Mark Ingram .02 .10
82 Anthony Carter .07 .20
83 Mark Rypien .02 .10
84 Gary Clark .07 .20
85 Bernie Kosar .07 .20
86 Cleveland Gary .02 .10
87 Tom Rathman .02 .10
88 Tony McGee RC .07 .20
89 Rick Mirer RC .15 .40
90 John Copeland RC .07 .20
91 Michael Irvin .15 .40
92 Wilber Marshall .02 .10
93 Mel Gray .07 .20
94 Craig Heyward .07 .20
95 Don Beebe .02 .10
96 Andre Tippett .02 .10
97 Derek Brown TE .02 .10
98 Ronnie Harmon .02 .10
99 Derrick Fenner .02 .10
100 Rodney Culver .02 .10
101 Cortez Kennedy .07 .20
102 Marcus Allen .15 .40
103 Steve Broussard .02 .10
104 Tim Brown .15 .40
105 Merril Hoge .02 .10
106 Chris Burkett .02 .10
107 Fred Barnett .07 .20
108 Dan Marino 1.25 3.00
109 Chris Doleman .02 .10
110 Art Monk .07 .20
111 Ernie Jones .02 .10
112 Jay Hilgenberg .02 .10
113 Jim Everett .07 .20
114 John Taylor .07 .20
115 Steve Everitt RC .02 .10
116 Carlton Gray RC .02 .10
117 Eric Curry RC .02 .10
118 Ken Norton Jr. .07 .20
119 Lorenzo White .02 .10
120 Pat Swilling .02 .10
121 William Perry .07 .20
122 Brett Favre 2.00 4.00
123 Jon Vaughn .02 .10
124 Mark Jackson .02 .10
125 Stan Humphries .07 .20
126 Harold Green .02 .10
127 Anthony Johnson .07 .20
128 Brian Blades .07 .20
129 Willie Davis .15 .40
130 Bobby Hebert .02 .10
131 Terry McDaniel .02 .10
132 Jeff Graham .07 .20
133 Jeff Lageman .02 .10
134 Andre Waters .02 .10
135 Steve Walsh .02 .10
136 Cris Carter .15 .40
137 Tim McGee .02 .10
138 Chuck Cecil .02 .10
139 John Elway 1.25 3.00
140 Todd Lyght .02 .10
141 Brent Jones .07 .20
142 Patrick Bates RC .02 .10
143 Darrien Gordon RC .02 .10
144 Michael Strahan RC 1.25 3.00
145 Jay Novacek .07 .20
146 Warren Moon .15 .40
147 Rodney Holman .02 .10
148 Anthony Morgan .02 .10
149 Sterling Sharpe .15 .40
150 Leonard Russell .07 .20
151 Lawrence Taylor .15 .40
152 Leslie O'Neal .07 .20
153 Carl Pickens .07 .20
154 Aaron Cox .02 .10
155 Ferrell Edmunds .02 .10
156 Neil O'Donnell .15 .40
157 Tony Smith .02 .10
158 James Lofton .07 .20
159 George Teague RC .07 .20
160 Boomer Esiason .07 .20
161 Eric Allen .02 .10
162 Floyd Turner .02 .10
163 Esera Tuaolo .02 .10
164 Darrell Green .02 .10
165 Steve Beuerlein .07 .20
166 Vance Johnson .02 .10
167 Flipper Anderson .02 .10
168 Ricky Watters .15 .40
169 Marvin Jones RC .02 .10
170 Dana Stubblefield RC .15 .40
171 Willie Roaf RC .07 .20
172 Russell Maryland .02 .10
173 Ernest Givins .07 .20
174 Willie Green .02 .10
175 Bruce Smith .15 .40
176 Terrell Buckley .02 .10
177 Scott Zolak .02 .10
178 Mike Sherrard .02 .10
179 Lawrence Dawsey .02 .10
180 Jay Schroeder .02 .10
181 Quentin Coryatt .07 .20
182 Harvey Williams .07 .20
183 Natrone Means RC .15 .40
184 Eric Dickerson .07 .20
185 Gaston Green .02 .10
186 Thomas Smith RC .07 .20
187 Johnny Johnson .02 .10
188 Marco Coleman .02 .10
189 Wade Wilson .02 .10
190 Rich Gannon .15 .40
191 Brian Mitchell .07 .20
192 Eric Metcalf .07 .20
193 Robert Delpino .02 .10
194 Shane Conlan .02 .10
195 Dexter Carter .02 .10
196 Garrison Hearst RC .60 1.50
197 Chris Slade RC .07 .20
198 Troy Drayton RC .07 .20
199 Lin Elliott .02 .10
200 Haywood Jeffires .07 .20
201 Herman Moore .15 .40
202 Cornelius Bennett .07 .20
203 Mark Clayton .02 .10
204 Marv Cook .02 .10
205 Stephen Baker .02 .10
206 Gary Anderson RB .02 .10
207 Eddie Brown .02 .10
208 Will Wolford .02 .10
209 Derrick Thomas .15 .40
210 Seth Joyner .02 .10
211 Mike Pritchard .07 .20
212 Rod Woodson .15 .40
213 Todd Kelly RC .02 .10
214 Rob Moore .07 .20
215 Keith Jackson .07 .20
216 Wesley Carroll .02 .10
217 Steve Jordan .02 .10
218 Ricky Sanders .02 .10
219 Tommy Vardell .02 .10
220 Rod Bernstine .02 .10
221 Henry Ellard .07 .20
222 Amp Lee .02 .10
223 O.J. McDuffie RC .15 .40
224 Carl Simpson RC .02 .10
225 Dan Williams RC .02 .10
226 Thomas Everett .02 .10
227 Webster Slaughter .02 .10
228 Trace Armstrong .02 .10
229 Kenneth Davis .02 .10
230 Tony Bennett .02 .10
231 Reyna Thompson .02 .10
232 Anthony Miller .07 .20
233 Reggie Cobb .02 .10
234 Mark Duper .02 .10
235 Chris Warren .07 .20
236 Christian Okoye .02 .10
237 Irving Fryar .07 .20
238 Deion Sanders .30 .75
239 Barry Foster .07 .20
240 Ernest Dye RC .02 .10
241 Calvin Williams .07 .20
242 Louis Oliver .02 .10
243 Dalton Hilliard .02 .10
244 Roger Craig .07 .20
245 Randal Hill .02 .10
246 Vinny Testaverde .07 .20
247 Steve Atwater .02 .10
248 Jim Price .02 .10
249 Martin Harrison RC .02 .10
250 Curtis Conway RC .30 .75
251 Demetrius DuBose RC .02 .10
252 Leonard Renfro RC .02 .10
253 Alvin Harper .07 .20
254 Leonard Harris .02 .10
255 Tom Waddle .02 .10
256 Andre Reed .07 .20
257 Sanjay Beach .02 .10
258 Michael Timpson .02 .10
259 Nate Lewis .02 .10
260 Steve DeBerg .02 .10
261 David Klingler .02 .10
262 Dan McGwire .02 .10
263 Dave Krieg .07 .20
264 Brad Muster .02 .10
265 Nick Bell .02 .10
266 Checklist 1 .02 .10
267 Checklist 2 .02 .10
268 Checklist 3 .02 .10
269 Checklist 4 .02 .10
270 Checklist 5 .02 .10
P1 Promo Panel .75 2.00
Jim Kelly
Derrick Thomas
Lawrence Taylor
Neal Anderson
Marco Coleman
Chris Doleman
P2 Promo Panel .75 2.00
Lawrence Taylor
Chris Doleman
Jim Kelly
Michael Irvin
Neal Anderson
Derrick Thomas

1993 SkyBox Premium Poster Cards

COMPLETE SET (10) 2.00 5.00
CB1 Dallas Cowboys Defense .15 .40
Doomsday Afternoon
Leon Lett
Tony Casillas
Tony Tolbert
Russell Maryland
Jimmie Jones
Charles Haley
Jim Jeffcoat
CB2 Dallas Cowboys .50 1.25
1993 Word Champions
Troy Aikman
Michael Irvin
Emmitt Smith
Russell Maryland
CB3 Barry Foster .08 .25
Steel Wheels
CB4 Art Monk .08 .25
The Art of Receiving
CB5 Jerry Rice .40 1.00
Wide Receiver
CB6 Barry Sanders .75 2.00
CB7 Deion Sanders .20 .50
Big Time
CB8 Junior Seau .20 .50
Shock Treatment
CB9 Derrick Thomas .20 .50
Neil Smith
Rush Hour
CB10 Steve Young .25 .60
Run and Gun

1993 SkyBox Premium Prime Time Rookies

COMPLETE SET (10) 15.00 30.00
1 Patrick Bates .75 2.00
2 Drew Bledsoe 6.00 15.00
3 Darrien Gordon .75 2.00
4 Garrison Hearst 2.50 6.00
5 Marvin Jones .75 2.00
6 Terry Kirby .75 2.00
7 Natrone Means 1.50 4.00
8 Rick Mirer 1.25 3.00
9 Willie Roaf 1.25 3.00
10 Dan Williams .75 2.00

1993 SkyBox Premium Thunder and Lightning

COMPLETE SET (9) 7.50 20.00
1 Jim Kelly 1.50 4.00
Thurman Thomas
2 Randall Cunningham 1.50 4.00
Fred Barnett
3 Dan Marino 3.00 8.00
Keith Jackson
4 Sam Mills .60 1.50
Vaughan Johnson
5 Warren Moon 1.00 2.50
Haywood Jeffires
6 Troy Aikman 2.00 5.00
Michael Irvin
7 Brett Favre 3.00 8.00
Sterling Sharpe
8 Steve Young 2.50 6.00
Jerry Rice
9 Dennis Smith .60 1.50
Steve Atwater

1994 SkyBox Premium Promos

Issued to preview the design of SkyBox's '94 Premium set, these seven standard-size promo cards feature on their borderless fronts color player action shots set on ghosted and colorized backgrounds. The player's name, position, and ghosted team logo appear in a white rectangle in an upper corner. The back carries a color player close-up on the right, with the player's team logo, name, position, career highlights, and statistics displayed alongside on the left. The S4 Jim Kelly card was also given away in Tuff Stuff.

COMPLETE SET (7) 3.20 8.00
S1 Tom Carter .40 1.00
S2 Gary Clark .40 1.00
S3 James Jett .50 1.25
S4 Jim Kelly 1.00 2.50
S5 Ronnie Lott .50 1.25
S6 John Taylor .40 1.00
NNO Sample Commemorative Game Card .20 .50

1994 SkyBox Premium

These 200 standard-size cards feature borderless color player action photos. The featured players stand out against a faded background. The player's name appears in either upper corner with the SkyBox logo in either lower corner. The cards were issued in 10-card foil packs with a suggested retail price of $1.99. The cards are grouped alphabetically within teams, and checklisted below alphabetically according to teams. The set closes with Rookies (157-200). Rookie Cards include Mario Bates, Trent Dilfer, Marshall Faulk, William Floyd, Byron Bam Morris, Errict Rhett, Darnay Scott and Heath Shuler.

COMPLETE SET (200) 7.50 20.00
1 Steve Beuerlein .05 .15
2 Gary Clark .05 .15
3 Garrison Hearst .10 .30
4 Ronald Moore .01 .05
5 Eric Swann .05 .15
6 Chuck Cecil .01 .05
7 Seth Joyner .01 .05
8 Clyde Simmons .01 .05
9 Andre Rison .05 .15
10 Deion Sanders .15 .40
11 Erric Pegram .01 .05
12 Steve Broussard .01 .05
13 Chris Doleman .01 .05
14 Jeff George .10 .30
15 Cornelius Bennett .05 .15
16 Jim Kelly .10 .30
17 Andre Reed .05 .15
18 Bruce Smith .10 .30
19 Darryl Talley .01 .05
20 Thurman Thomas .10 .30
21 Mark Carrier DB .01 .05
22 Dante Jones .01 .05
23 Curtis Conway .10 .30
24 Tim Worley .01 .05
25 Erik Kramer .05 .15
26 John Copeland .01 .05
27 David Klingler .01 .05
28 Derrick Fenner .01 .05
29 Harold Green .01 .05
30 Carl Pickens .05 .15
31 Tony McGee .01 .05
32 Steve Everitt .01 .05
33 Michael Jackson .05 .15
34 Eric Metcalf .05 .15
35 Vinny Testaverde .05 .15
36 Michael Dean Perry .05 .15
37 Troy Aikman .50 1.25
38 Alvin Harper .05 .15
39 Michael Irvin .10 .30
40 Jay Novacek .05 .15
41 Emmitt Smith .75 2.00
42 Charles Haley .05 .15
43 Daryl Johnston .05 .15
44 Kevin Williams .05 .15
45 Rodney Peete .01 .05
46 John Elway 1.00 2.50
47 Shannon Sharpe .05 .15
48 Rod Bernstine .01 .05
49 Glyn Milburn .05 .15
50 Mike Pritchard .01 .05
51 Anthony Miller .05 .15
52 Herman Moore .10 .30
53 Barry Sanders .75 2.00
54 Scott Mitchell .05 .15
55 Pat Swilling .01 .05
56 Willie Green .01 .05
57 Edgar Bennett .10 .30
58 Brett Favre 1.00 2.50
59 Sterling Sharpe .05 .15
60 Reggie White .10 .30
61 Sean Jones .01 .05
62 Reggie Cobb .01 .05
63 Haywood Jeffires .05 .15
64 Lorenzo White .01 .05
65 Webster Slaughter .01 .05
66 Gary Brown .01 .05
67 Steve Emtman .01 .05
68 Quentin Coryatt .01 .05
69 Sean Dawkins RC .10 .30
70 Jim Harbaugh .10 .30
71 Tony Bennett .01 .05
72 Marcus Allen .10 .30
73 Steve Bono .05 .15
74 Dale Carter .01 .05
75 Joe Montana 1.00 2.50
76 Neil Smith .05 .15
77 Derrick Thomas .10 .30
78 Keith Cash .01 .05
79 Tim Brown .10 .30
80 Rocket Ismail .05 .15
81 Jeff Hostetler .05 .15
82 Patrick Bates .01 .05
83 James Jett .01 .05
84 Jerome Bettis .25 .60
85 Chris Miller .01 .05
86 Marc Boutte .01 .05
87 Sean Gilbert .01 .05
88 Keith Jackson .01 .05
89 Terry Kirby .10 .30
90 Dan Marino 1.00 2.50
91 Bryan Cox .01 .05
92 Bernie Kosar .05 .15
93 Qadry Ismail .10 .30
94 Robert Smith .10 .30
95 Terry Allen .05 .15
96 Scottie Graham RC .05 .15
97 Warren Moon .10 .30
98 Drew Bledsoe .40 1.00
99 Ben Coates .05 .15
100 Leonard Russell .01 .05
101 Vincent Brisby .05 .15
102 Marion Butts .01 .05
103 Morten Andersen .01 .05
104 Derek Brown RBK .01 .05
105 Michael Haynes .05 .15
106 Sam Mills .01 .05
107 Lorenzo Neal .01 .05
108 Willie Roaf .01 .05
109 Jim Everett .05 .15
110 Michael Brooks .01 .05
111 Rodney Hampton .05 .15
112 Dave Brown .05 .15
113 Dave Meggett .01 .05
114 Ronnie Lott .05 .15
115 Boomer Esiason .05 .15
116 Rob Moore .05 .15
117 Johnny Johnson .01 .05
118 Marvin Jones .01 .05
119 Johnny Mitchell .01 .05
120 Fred Barnett .05 .15
121 Randall Cunningham .10 .30
122 Herschel Walker .05 .15
123 Calvin Williams .05 .15
124 Neil O'Donnell .10 .30
125 Eric Green .01 .05
126 Leroy Thompson .01 .05
127 Rod Woodson .05 .15
128 Barry Foster .01 .05
129 Deon Figures .01 .05
130 John L. Williams .01 .05
131 Chris Mims .01 .05
132 Darrien Gordon .01 .05
133 Stan Humphries .05 .15
134 Natrone Means .10 .30
135 Junior Seau .10 .30
136 Brent Jones .05 .15
137 Jerry Rice .50 1.25
138 Dana Stubblefield .05 .15
139 John Taylor .05 .15
140 Ricky Watters .05 .15
141 Steve Young .40 1.00
142 Ken Norton Jr. .05 .15
143 Brian Blades .05 .15
144 Cortez Kennedy .05 .15
145 Kelvin Martin .01 .05
146 Rick Mirer .10 .30
147 Chris Warren .05 .15
148 Eric Curry .01 .05
149 Santana Dotson .05 .15
150 Craig Erickson .01 .05
151 Hardy Nickerson .05 .15
152 Paul Gruber .01 .05
153 Reggie Brooks .05 .15
154 Tom Carter .01 .05
155 Desmond Howard .05 .15
156 Ken Harvey .01 .05
157 Dan Wilkinson RC .05 .15
158 Marshall Faulk RC 2.00 5.00
159 Heath Shuler RC .10 .30
160 Willie McGinest RC .10 .30
161 Trev Alberts RC .10 .30
162 Trent Dilfer RC .50 1.25

163 Bryant Young RC	.20	.50
164 Sam Adams RC	.05	.15
165 Antonio Langham RC	.05	.15
166 Jamir Miller RC	.05	.15
167 John Thierry RC	.01	.05
168 Aaron Glenn RC	.10	.30
169 Joe Johnson RC	.01	.05
170 Bernard Williams RC	.01	.05
171 Wayne Gandy RC	.01	.05
172 Aaron Taylor RC	.01	.05
173 Charles Johnson RC	.10	.30
174 Dewayne Washington RC	.05	.15
175 Todd Steussie RC	.05	.15
176 Tim Bowens RC	.05	.15
177 Johnnie Morton RC	.50	1.25
178 Rob Fredrickson	.05	.15
179 Shante Carver RC	.01	.05
180 Thomas Lewis RC	.05	.15
181 Greg Hill RC	.10	.30
182 Henry Ford RC	.01	.05
183 Jeff Burris RC	.05	.15
184 William Floyd RC	.10	.30
185 Der. Alexander WR RC	.10	.30
186 Glenn Foley RC	.10	.30
187 Charlie Garner RC	.50	1.25
188 Errict Rhett RC	.10	.30
189 Chuck Levy RC	.01	.05
190 Byron Bam Morris RC	.05	.15
191 Donnell Bennett RC	.10	.30
192 LeShon Johnson RC	.05	.15
193 Mario Bates RC	.10	.30
194 David Palmer RC	.10	.30
195 Darnay Scott RC	.25	.60
196 Lake Dawson RC	.05	.15
197 Checklist	.01	.05
198 Checklist	.01	.05
199 Checklist	.01	.05
200 Checklist for Inserts	.01	.05
NNO NFL Anniversary Commemorative	.10	.30

1994 SkyBox Premium Inside the Numbers

COMPLETE SET (20)	4.00	10.00
ONE PER SPECIAL RETAIL PACK		
1 Jim Kelly	.25	.60
2 Ronnie Lott	.10	.30
3 Morten Andersen	.02	.10
4 Reggie White	.25	.60
5 Terry Kirby	.25	.60
6 Marcus Allen	.25	.60
7 Thurman Thomas	.25	.60
8 Joe Montana	2.00	5.00
9 Tom Carter	.02	.10
10 Jerome Bettis	.50	1.25
11 Sterling Sharpe	.10	.30
12 Andre Rison	.10	.30
13 Reggie Brooks	.10	.30
14 Hardy Nickerson	.10	.30
15 Ricky Watters	.10	.30
16 Gary Brown	.02	.10
17 Natrone Means	.25	.60
18 LeShon Johnson	.07	.20
19 Errict Rhett	.15	.40
20 Trent Dilfer	.60	1.50

1994 SkyBox Premium Quarterback Autographs

1 Trent Dilfer	25.00	50.00
2 Jim Kelly	40.00	80.00
3 Ken Stabler	20.00	50.00

1994 SkyBox Premium Revolution

COMPLETE SET (15)	12.50	30.00
STATED ODDS 1:20		
R1 Jim Kelly	.40	1.00
R2 Thurman Thomas	.40	1.00
R3 Troy Aikman	1.50	4.00
R4 Michael Irvin	.40	1.00
R5 Emmitt Smith	2.50	6.00
R6 John Elway	3.00	8.00
R7 Barry Sanders	2.50	6.00
R8 Sterling Sharpe	.30	.75
R9 Joe Montana	3.00	8.00
R10 Jerome Bettis	.75	2.00
R11 Dan Marino	3.00	8.00
R12 Drew Bledsoe	1.25	3.00
R13 Jerry Rice	1.50	4.00
R14 Steve Young	1.25	3.00
R15 Rick Mirer	.30	.75

1994 SkyBox Premium Prime Time Rookies

COMPLETE SET (10)	20.00	40.00
STATED ODDS 1:96		
PT1 Trent Dilfer	2.50	6.00
PT2 Heath Shuler	.60	1.50
PT3 Marshall Faulk	8.00	20.00
PT4 Charlie Garner	1.50	4.00
PT5 Errict Rhett	.60	1.50
PT6 Greg Hill	.60	1.50
PT7 William Floyd	.60	1.50
PT8 Charles Johnson	.60	1.50
PT9 Derrick Alexander WR	.60	1.50
PT10 David Palmer	.60	1.50

1994 SkyBox Premium SkyTech Stars

COMPLETE SET (30)	12.50	30.00
STATED ODDS 1:6		
ST1 Troy Aikman	1.25	3.00
ST2 Emmitt Smith	2.00	5.00
ST3 Michael Irvin	.30	.75
ST4 John Elway	2.50	6.00
ST5 Sterling Sharpe	.15	.40
ST6 Joe Montana	2.50	6.00
ST7 Drew Bledsoe	1.00	2.50
ST8 Rick Mirer	.30	.75
ST9 Junior Seau	.30	.75
ST10 Jerome Bettis	.60	1.50
ST11 Rod Woodson	.15	.40
ST12 Tim Brown	.30	.75
ST13 Jeff George	.30	.75
ST14 Brett Favre	2.50	6.00
ST15 Reggie White	.30	.75
ST16 Cortez Kennedy	.15	.40
ST17 Ricky Watters	.15	.40
ST18 Shannon Sharpe	.15	.40
ST19 Reggie Brooks	.15	.40
ST20 Heath Shuler	.15	.40
ST21 Marshall Faulk	2.50	6.00
ST22 Thurman Thomas	.30	.75
ST23 Barry Foster	.05	.15
ST24 Sean Gilbert	.05	.15
ST25 Jerry Rice	1.25	3.00
ST26 Andre Rison	.15	.40
ST27 Barry Sanders	2.00	5.00
ST28 Jim Kelly	.30	.75
ST29 Steve Young	1.00	2.50
ST30 Dan Marino	2.50	6.00

1995 SkyBox Premium Samples

This 6-card promotion or sample panel was issued to promote the 1995 SkyBox Premium product. Each card includes a card number on the back and could be detached individually using the perforations applied in the printing process.

COMPLETE SET (6)	2.00	5.00
S1 Trent Dilfer Promise	.40	1.00
S2 Eric Turner Quickstrike	.30	.75
S3 William Floyd	.30	.75
S4 Dave Meggett	.30	.75
S5 Daryl Johnston Mirror Image William Floyd	.30	.75
S6 Brett Favre Style Points Trent Dilfer	1.25	3.00
NNO Uncut Panel	2.00	5.00

1995 SkyBox Premium

Issued as a 200 card set in 10 card packs with a suggested retail price of $2.19/pack. Card fronts have a borderless design featuring the player on a half-action half metallic background with a "ripped" effect dividing the two sections, along with a gold foil logo and player name. Card backs show a headshot with biographical and career statistics. Subsets include: Stylepoints (139-148), Mirror Image (149-158) and Rookies (159-198). Rookie Cards include Jeff Blake, Ki-Jana Carter, Kerry Collins, Joey Galloway, Napoleon Kaufman, Steve McNair, Rashaan Salaam, Chris Sanders, Kordell Stewart, J.J Stokes, Rodney Thomas and Michael Westbrook. A complete rookie receiver set was also available at one set per special retail box. A 6-card SkyBox promo sheet was produced and priced below as an uncut sheet. A number of John Elway cards (#36) were signed and released through SkyBox's instant win contest. Each autographed card was embossed with a SkyBox stamp.

COMPLETE SET (200)	7.50	20.00
1 Garrison Hearst	.15	.40
2 Dave Krieg	.02	.10
3 Rob Moore	.07	.20
4 Eric Swann	.07	.20
5 Larry Centers	.07	.20
6 Jeff George	.07	.20
7 Craig Heyward	.07	.20
8 Terance Mathis	.07	.20
9 Eric Metcalf	.07	.20
10 Jim Kelly	.15	.40
11 Andre Reed	.07	.20
12 Bruce Smith	.15	.40
13 Cornelius Bennett	.07	.20
14 Randy Baldwin	.02	.10
15 Don Beebe	.02	.10
16 Barry Foster	.07	.20
17 Lamar Lathon	.02	.10
18 Frank Reich	.02	.10
19 Jeff Graham	.02	.10
20 Raymont Harris	.02	.10
21 Lewis Tillman	.02	.10
22 Michael Timpson	.02	.10
23 Jeff Blake RC	.40	1.00
24 Carl Pickens	.07	.20
25 Darnay Scott	.07	.20
26 Dan Wilkinson	.07	.20
27 Derrick Alexander WR	.15	.40
28 Leroy Hoard	.02	.10
29 Antonio Langham	.02	.10
30 Andre Rison	.07	.20
31 Eric Turner	.02	.10
32 Troy Aikman	.50	1.25
33 Michael Irvin	.15	.40
34 Daryl Johnston	.07	.20
35 Emmitt Smith	.75	2.00
36 John Elway	1.00	2.50
37 Glyn Milburn	.02	.10
38 Anthony Miller	.07	.20
39 Shannon Sharpe	.07	.20
40 Scott Mitchell	.07	.20
41 Herman Moore	.15	.40
42 Barry Sanders	.75	2.00
43 Chris Spielman	.07	.20
44 Edgar Bennett	.07	.20
45 Robert Brooks	.15	.40
46 Brett Favre	1.00	2.50
47 Reggie White	.15	.40
48 Mel Gray	.02	.10
49 Haywood Jeffires	.02	.10
50 Gary Brown	.02	.10
51 Craig Erickson	.02	.10
52 Quentin Coryatt	.07	.20
53 Sean Dawkins	.07	.20
54 Marshall Faulk	.60	1.50
55 Steve Beuerlein	.07	.20
56 Reggie Cobb	.02	.10
57 Desmond Howard	.07	.20
58 Ernest Givins	.02	.10
59 Jeff Lageman	.02	.10
60 Marcus Allen	.15	.40
61 Steve Bono	.07	.20
62 Greg Hill	.07	.20
63 Willie Davis	.07	.20
64 Tim Brown	.15	.40
65 Rocket Ismail	.07	.20
66 Jeff Hostetler	.07	.20
67 Chester McGlockton	.07	.20
68 Tim Bowens	.02	.10
69 Irving Fryar	.07	.20
70 Eric Green	.02	.10
71 Terry Kirby	.07	.20
72 Dan Marino	1.00	2.50
73 O.J. McDuffie	.15	.40
74 Bernie Parmalee	.07	.20
75 Dewayne Washington	.07	.20
76 Cris Carter	.15	.40
77 Qadry Ismail	.07	.20
78 Warren Moon	.07	.20
79 Jake Reed	.07	.20
80 Drew Bledsoe	.30	.75
81 Vincent Brisby	.02	.10
82 Ben Coates	.07	.20
83 Dave Meggett	.02	.10
84 Mario Bates	.07	.20
85 Jim Everett	.02	.10
86 Michael Haynes	.07	.20
87 Tyrone Hughes	.07	.20
88 Dave Brown	.07	.20
89 Rodney Hampton	.07	.20
90 Thomas Lewis	.07	.20
91 Herschel Walker	.07	.20
92 Mike Sherrard	.02	.10
93 Boomer Esiason	.07	.20
94 Aaron Glenn	.02	.10
95 Johnny Johnson	.02	.10
96 Johnny Mitchell	.02	.10
97 Ronald Moore	.02	.10
98 Fred Barnett	.07	.20
99 Randall Cunningham	.15	.40
100 Charlie Garner	.15	.40
101 Ricky Watters	.07	.20
102 Calvin Williams	.15	.40
103 Charles Johnson	.07	.20
104 Byron Bam Morris	.02	.10
105 Neil O'Donnell	.07	.20
106 Rod Woodson	.07	.20
107 Jerome Bettis	.15	.40
108 Troy Drayton	.02	.10
109 Sean Gilbert	.07	.20
110 Chris Miller	.02	.10
111 Leonard Russell	.02	.10
112 Ronnie Harmon	.02	.10
113 Stan Humphries	.07	.20
114 Shawn Jefferson	.02	.10
115 Natrone Means	.07	.20
116 Junior Seau	.15	.40
117 William Floyd	.07	.20
118 Brent Jones	.02	.10
119 Jerry Rice	.50	1.25
120 Deion Sanders	.30	.75
121 Dana Stubblefield	.07	.20
122 Bryant Young	.07	.20
123 Steve Young	.40	1.00
124 Brian Blades	.07	.20
125 Cortez Kennedy	.07	.20
126 Rick Mirer	.07	.20
127 Ricky Proehl	.02	.10
128 Chris Warren	.07	.20
129 Horace Copeland	.02	.10
130 Trent Dilfer	.15	.40
131 Alvin Harper	.02	.10
132 Jackie Harris	.02	.10
133 Hardy Nickerson	.02	.10
134 Errict Rhett	.07	.20
135 Henry Ellard	.07	.20
136 Brian Mitchell	.02	.10
137 Heath Shuler	.07	.20
138 Tydus Winans	.02	.10
139 Brett Favre Drew Bledsoe	.40	1.00
140 Marshall Faulk William Floyd	.25	.60
141 Brett Favre Trent Dilfer	.30	.75
142 Dan Marino Brett Favre	.40	1.00
143 Trent Dilfer Errict Rhett	.15	.40
144 Jerry Rice Eric Turner	.20	.50
145 Andre Rison Eric Turner	.07	.20
146 Barry Sanders Dave Meggett	.25	.60
147 Emmitt Smith Daryl Johnston	.25	.60
148 Steve Young Brett Favre	.40	1.00
149 Emmitt Smith Errict Rhett	.25	.60
150 Marshall Faulk Barry Sanders	.30	.75
151 Jerry Rice Darnay Scott	.20	.50
152 William Floyd Daryl Johnston	.07	.20
153 Dan Marino Trent Dilfer	.30	.75
154 John Elway Heath Shuler	.30	.75
155 Byron Bam Morris Natrone Means	.02	.10
156 Dan Wilkinson Reggie White	.07	.20
157 Mario Bates Rodney Hampton	.07	.20
158 Junior Seau Marvin Jones	.15	.40
159 Ki-Jana Carter RC	.15	.40
160 Tony Boselli RC	.15	.40
161 Steve McNair RC	1.50	4.00
162 Michael Westbrook RC	.15	.40
163 Kerry Collins RC	.75	2.00
164 Kevin Carter RC	.15	.40
165 Mike Mamula RC	.02	.10
166 Joey Galloway RC	.75	2.00
167 Kyle Brady RC	.15	.40
168 J.J. Stokes RC	.15	.40
169 Warren Sapp RC	.75	2.00
170 Rob Johnson RC	.50	1.25
171 Tyrone Wheatley RC	.60	1.50
172 Napoleon Kaufman RC	.60	1.50
173 James O. Stewart RC	.60	1.50
174 Joe Aska RC	.02	.10
175 Rashaan Salaam RC	.07	.20
176 Tyrone Poole RC	.15	.40
177 Ty Law RC	.75	2.00
178 Dino Philyaw RC	.02	.10
179 Mark Bruener RC	.07	.20
180 Derrick Brooks RC	.75	2.00
181 Jack Jackson RC	.02	.10
182 Ray Zellars RC	.07	.20
183 Eddie Goines RC	.02	.10
184 Chris Sanders RC	.07	.20
185 Charlie Simmons RC	.02	.10
186 Lee DeRamus RC	.02	.10
187 Frank Sanders RC	.15	.40
188 Rodney Thomas RC	.07	.20
189 Steve Stenstrom RC	.02	.10
190 Stoney Case RC	.02	.10
191 Tyrone Davis RC	.02	.10
192 Kordell Stewart RC	.75	2.00
193 Christian Fauria RC	.07	.20
194 Todd Collins RC	.50	1.25
195 Sherman Williams RC	.02	.10
196 Lovell Pinkney RC	.02	.10
197 Eric Zeier RC	.15	.40
198 Zack Crockett RC	.07	.20
199 Checklist A	.02	.10
200 Checklist B	.02	.10
AU36 John Elway AUTO	75.00	150.00
AU46 Brett Favre AUTO/250	125.00	250.00

1995 SkyBox Premium Inside the Numbers

COMPLETE SET (20)	10.00	20.00
ONE PER SPECIAL RETAIL PACK		
1 William Floyd	.10	.30
2 Marshall Faulk	1.00	2.50
3 Warren Moon	.10	.30
4 Cris Carter	.25	.60
5 Deion Sanders	.50	1.25
6 Drew Bledsoe	.50	1.25
7 Natrone Means	.10	.30
8 Herschel Walker	.10	.30
9 Ben Coates	.10	.30
10 Mel Gray	.05	.15
11 Barry Sanders	1.25	3.00
12 Steve Young	.60	1.50
13 Rashaan Salaam	.10	.30
14 Andre Reed	.10	.30
15 Tyrone Hughes	.10	.30
16 Eric Turner	.05	.15
17 Ki-Jana Carter	.25	.60
18 Dan Marino	1.50	4.00
19 Errict Rhett	.10	.30
20 Jerry Rice	.75	2.00

1995 SkyBox Premium Paydirt Gold

COMPLETE GOLD SET (30)	20.00	50.00
STATED ODDS 1:4		
*COLORS: 2.5X TO 6X BASIC INSERTS		
*COLOR ROOKIES: 2.5X TO 6X BASE CARD HI		
COLORS STATED PRINT RUN 5% OF TOTAL		
PD1 Troy Aikman	1.25	3.00
PD2 J.J. Stokes	.08	.25
PD3 Ki-Jana Carter	.08	.25
PD4 Steve McNair	2.00	4.00
PD5 Jerome Bettis	.40	1.00
PD6 Tim Brown	.40	1.00
PD7 Cris Carter	.40	1.00
PD8 John Elway	2.50	6.00
PD9 Marshall Faulk	1.50	4.00
PD10 Brett Favre	2.50	6.00
PD11 Michael Westbrook	.08	.25
PD12 Rodney Hampton	.20	.50
PD13 Michael Irvin	.40	1.00
PD14 Dan Marino	2.50	6.00
PD15 Natrone Means	.20	.50
PD16 Dave Meggett	.08	.25
PD17 Joey Galloway	1.00	2.00
PD18 Herman Moore	.40	1.00
PD19 Byron Bam Morris	.08	.25
PD20 Carl Pickens	.20	.50
PD21 Errict Rhett	.20	.50
PD22 Kerry Collins	1.00	2.00
PD23 Barry Sanders	2.00	5.00
PD24 Deion Sanders	.75	2.00
PD25 Emmitt Smith	2.00	5.00
PD26 Drew Bledsoe	.75	2.00
PD27 Ricky Watters	.20	.50
PD28 Rod Woodson	.20	.50
PD29 Chris Warren	.20	.50
PD30 Steve Young	1.00	2.50

1995 SkyBox Premium Promise

COMPLETE SET (14)	12.50	25.00
STATED ODDS 1:24		
P1 Derrick Alexander WR	1.25	3.00
P2 Mario Bates	.75	2.00
P3 Trent Dilfer	1.50	4.00
P4 Marshall Faulk	5.00	12.00
P5 William Floyd	.75	2.00
P6 Aaron Glenn	.75	2.00
P7 Raymont Harris	.75	2.00
P8 Greg Hill	.75	2.00
P9 Charles Johnson	1.25	3.00
P10 Byron Bam Morris	.75	2.00
P11 Errict Rhett	1.25	3.00
P12 Darnay Scott	1.25	3.00
P13 Heath Shuler	1.25	3.00
P14 Dan Wilkinson	.75	2.00

1995 SkyBox Premium Quickstrike

COMPLETE SET (10)	8.00	20.00
STATED ODDS 1:15		
Q1 Chris Warren	.25	.60
Q2 Marshall Faulk	2.00	5.00
Q3 William Floyd	.25	.60
Q4 Jerry Rice	1.50	4.00
Q5 Eric Turner	.10	.30
Q6 Tim Brown	.50	1.25
Q7 Deion Sanders	1.00	2.50
Q8 Emmitt Smith	2.50	6.00
Q9 Rod Woodson	.25	.60
Q10 Steve Young	1.25	3.00

1995 SkyBox Premium Rookie Receivers

COMPLETE SET (8)	2.50	6.00
ONE SET PER SPECIAL RETAIL BOX		
1 Michael Westbrook	.50	1.25
2 Joey Galloway	.75	2.00
3 J.J.Stokes	.30	.75
4 Frank Sanders	.30	.75
5 Chris Sanders	.20	.50
6 Tyrone Davis	.20	.50
7 Jimmy Oliver	.20	.50
NNO Cover Checklist Card	.10	.30

1995 SkyBox Premium Prime Time Rookies

COMPLETE SET (10)	25.00	60.00
STATED ODDS 1:96		
PT1 Ki-Jana Carter	1.00	2.50
PT2 Kerry Collins	5.00	12.00
PT3 Joey Galloway	5.00	12.00
PT4 Steve McNair	10.00	25.00
PT5 Rashaan Salaam	.50	1.25
PT6 James O. Stewart	4.00	10.00
PT7 J.J. Stokes	1.00	2.50
PT8 Rodney Thomas	.50	1.25
PT9 Michael Westbrook	1.00	2.50
PT10 Tyrone Wheatley	4.00	10.00

1996 SkyBox Premium Samples

This 3-card promotion or sample panel was issued to promote the 1996 SkyBox Premium product. Each card includes a card number on the back and could be detached individually using the perforations applied in the printing process.

COMPLETE SET (3)	1.50	4.00
S1 Brett Favre	1.25	3.00
S2 Leeland McElroy	.20	.50
S3 Kordell Stewart Panorama Quentin Coryatt	.30	.75
NNO Uncut Panel	1.50	4.00

1996 SkyBox Premium

The 1996 Skybox set was issued in one series totalling 250 cards. The fronts feature borderless color player photos with foil stamping and UV coating. The set contains the topical subsets: Rookies (179-228), PrimeTime Rookie Retrospective (229-238) and Panorama (239-248). A 3-card (cards numbered S1-S3) promo sheet was produced and is priced below in complete sheet form.

COMPLETE SET (250)	7.50	20.00
1 Larry Centers	.08	.25
2 Boomer Esiason	.08	.25
3 Garrison Hearst	.08	.25
4 Rob Moore	.08	.25
5 Frank Sanders	.08	.25
6 Eric Swann	.02	.10
7 Bert Emanuel	.08	.25
8 Jeff George	.08	.25
9 Craig Heyward	.02	.10
10 Terance Mathis	.02	.10
11 Eric Metcalf	.02	.10
12 Derrick Alexander WR	.08	.25
13 Leroy Hoard	.02	.10
14 Michael Jackson	.08	.25
15 Vinny Testaverde	.08	.25
16 Eric Turner	.02	.10
17 Darick Holmes	.02	.10
18 Jim Kelly	.20	.50
19 Bryce Paup	.02	.10
20 Andre Reed	.08	.25
21 Bruce Smith	.08	.25
22 Thurman Thomas	.20	.50
23 Tim Tindale RC	.02	.10
24 Mark Carrier WR	.02	.10
25 Kerry Collins	.20	.50
26 Willie Green	.02	.10
27 Kevin Greene	.08	.25
28 Tyrone Poole	.02	.10
29 Curtis Conway	.20	.50
30 Bryan Cox	.02	.10
31 Erik Kramer	.02	.10
32 Nate Lewis	.02	.10
33 Rashaan Salaam	.08	.25
34 Alonzo Spellman	.02	.10
35 Michael Timpson	.02	.10
36 Jeff Blake	.20	.50
37 Ki-Jana Carter	.08	.25
38 David Dunn	.02	.10
39 Carl Pickens	.08	.25
40 Darnay Scott	.08	.25
41 Troy Aikman	.50	1.25
42 Charles Haley	.08	.25
43 Michael Irvin	.20	.50
44 Daryl Johnston	.08	.25
45 Jay Novacek	.02	.10
46 Deion Sanders	.30	.75
47 Emmitt Smith	.75	2.00
48 Kevin Williams	.02	.10
49 Steve Atwater	.02	.10
50 Terrell Davis	.40	1.00
51 John Elway	1.00	2.50
52 Anthony Miller	.08	.25
53 Shannon Sharpe	.08	.25
54 Mike Sherrard	.02	.10
55 Scott Mitchell	.08	.25
56 Herman Moore	.08	.25
57 Johnnie Morton	.08	.25
58 Brett Perriman	.02	.10
59 Barry Sanders	.75	2.00
60 Edgar Bennett	.08	.25
61 Robert Brooks	.20	.50
62 Mark Chmura	.08	.25
63 Brett Favre	1.00	2.50
64 Antonio Freeman	.20	.50
65 Keith Jackson	.02	.10
66 Reggie White	.20	.50
67 Chris Chandler	.08	.25
68 Mel Gray	.02	.10
69 Steve McNair	.40	1.00
70 Chris Sanders	.08	.25
71 Rodney Thomas	.02	.10
72 Quentin Coryatt	.02	.10
73 Sean Dawkins	.02	.10
74 Ken Dilger	.08	.25
75 Marshall Faulk	.25	.60
76 Jim Harbaugh	.08	.25
77 Lamont Warren	.02	.10
78 Tony Boselli	.02	.10
79 Mark Brunell	.30	.75
80 Willie Jackson	.08	.25
81 Natrone Means	.08	.25
82 James O.Stewart	.08	.25
83 Marcus Allen	.20	.50
84 Kimble Anders	.08	.25
85 Steve Bono	.02	.10
86 Lake Dawson	.02	.10
87 Neil Smith	.08	.25
88 Derrick Thomas	.20	.50
89 Tamarick Vanover	.08	.25
90 Fred Barnett	.02	.10
91 Terry Kirby	.08	.25
92 Dan Marino	1.00	2.50
93 O.J. McDuffie	.08	.25
94 Bernie Parmalee	.02	.10
95 Richmond Webb	.02	.10
96 Cris Carter	.20	.50
97 Scottie Graham	.02	.10
98 Qadry Ismail	.08	.25
99 Warren Moon	.08	.25
100 Jake Reed	.08	.25
101 Robert Smith	.08	.25
102 Drew Bledsoe	.30	.75
103 Vincent Brisby	.02	.10
104 Ben Coates	.08	.25
105 Curtis Martin	.40	1.00
106 Dave Meggett	.02	.10
107 Chris Slade	.02	.10
108 Mario Bates	.08	.25
109 Jim Everett	.02	.10
110 Michael Haynes	.02	.10
111 Tyrone Hughes	.02	.10
112 Renaldo Turnbull	.02	.10
113 Dave Brown	.02	.10
114 Chris Calloway	.02	.10
115 Rodney Hampton	.08	.25
116 Thomas Lewis	.02	.10
117 Tyrone Wheatley	.08	.25
118 Kyle Brady	.02	.10
119 Hugh Douglas	.08	.25
120 Aaron Glenn	.02	.10
121 Jeff Graham	.02	.10
122 Adrian Murrell	.08	.25
123 Neil O'Donnell	.08	.25
124 Tim Brown	.20	.50
125 Nolan Harrison	.02	.10
126 Billy Joe Hobert	.08	.25
127 Jeff Hostetler	.02	.10
128 Napoleon Kaufman	.20	.50
129 Chester McGlockton	.02	.10
130 Harvey Williams	.02	.10
131 Charlie Garner	.08	.25
132 Andy Harmon	.02	.10
133 Chris T. Jones	.08	.25
134 Mike Mamula	.02	.10
135 Rodney Peete	.02	.10
136 Bobby Taylor	.02	.10
137 Ricky Watters	.08	.25
138 Jerome Bettis	.20	.50
139 Greg Lloyd	.08	.25
140 Jim Miller	.20	.50
141 Ernie Mills	.02	.10
142 Kordell Stewart	.20	.50
143 Yancey Thigpen	.08	.25
144 Rod Woodson	.08	.25
145 Andre Coleman	.02	.10
146 Terrell Fletcher	.02	.10
147 Aaron Hayden RC	.02	.10
148 Stan Humphries	.08	.25
149 Junior Seau	.20	.50
150 Isaac Bruce	.20	.50
151 Kevin Carter	.02	.10
152 Todd Kinchen	.02	.10
153 Leslie O'Neal	.02	.10
154 Steve Walsh	.02	.10
155 William Floyd	.08	.25
156 Merton Hanks	.02	.10
157 Brent Jones	.02	.10
158 Derek Loville	.02	.10
159 Ken Norton	.02	.10
160 Jerry Rice	.50	1.25
161 J.J. Stokes	.20	.50
162 Steve Young	.40	1.00
163 Brian Blades	.02	.10
164 Christian Fauria	.02	.10
165 Joey Galloway	.20	.50
166 Rick Mirer	.08	.25
167 Chris Warren	.08	.25
168 Trent Dilfer	.20	.50
169 Alvin Harper	.02	.10
170 Jackie Harris	.02	.10
171 Hardy Nickerson	.02	.10
172 Errict Rhett	.08	.25
173 Terry Allen	.08	.25
174 Henry Ellard	.02	.10
175 Gus Frerotte	.08	.25
176 Brian Mitchell	.02	.10
177 Heath Shuler	.08	.25
178 Michael Westbrook	.20	.50
179 Karim Abdul-Jabbar RC	.20	.50
180 Mike Alstott RC	.50	1.25
181 Willie Anderson RC	.02	.10
182 Marco Battaglia RC	.02	.10
183 Tim Biakabutuka RC	.20	.50
184 Tony Brackens RC	.20	.50
185 Duane Clemons RC	.02	.10
186 Marcus Coleman RC	.02	.10
187 Ernie Conwell RC	.02	.10
188 Chris Darkins RC	.02	.10
189 Stephen Davis RC	.75	2.00
190 Brian Dawkins RC	.60	1.50
191 Rickey Dudley RC	.20	.50
192 Jason Dunn RC	.08	.25
193 Bobby Engram RC	.20	.50
194 Daryl Gardener RC	.02	.10
195 Eddie George RC	.60	1.50
196 Terry Glenn RC	.50	1.25
197 Kevin Hardy RC	.20	.50
198 Walt Harris RC	.02	.10
199 Marvin Harrison RC	1.25	3.00
200 Bobby Hoying RC	.20	.50
201 Israel Ifeanyi RC	.02	.10
202 DeRon Jenkins RC	.02	.10
203 Keyshawn Johnson RC	.50	1.25
204 Lance Johnstone RC	.08	.25
205 Cedric Jones RC	.02	.10
206 Marcus Jones RC	.02	.10
207 Eddie Kennison RC	.20	.50
208 Jevon Langford RC	.02	.10
209 Dedric Mathis RC	.02	.10
210 Jermane Mayberry RC	.02	.10
211 Leeland McElroy RC	.08	.25
212 Johnny McWilliams RC	.08	.25
213 Ray Mickens RC	.02	.10
214 John Mobley RC	.02	.10
215 Jerald Moore RC	.08	.25
216 Eric Moulds RC	.60	1.50
217 Muhsin Muhammad RC (UER,photo is Tim Biakabutuka)	.50	1.25
218 Jonathan Ogden RC	.20	.50
219 Lawrence Phillips RC	.20	.50
220 Kavika Pittman RC	.02	.10
221 Stanley Pritchett RC	.08	.25
222 Simeon Rice RC	.50	1.25
223 Detron Smith RC	.02	.10
224 Bryan Still RC	.08	.25
225 Amani Toomer RC	.50	1.25
226 Regan Upshaw RC	.02	.10
227 Alex Van Dyke RC	.08	.25
228 Stepfret Williams RC	.08	.25
229 Retrospective Quentin Coryatt Chester McGlockton Carl Pickens Robert Brooks	.08	.25
230 Retrospective Dale Carter Edgar Bennett Drew Bledsoe Garrison Hearst	.20	.50
231 Retrospective Natrone Means Rick Mirer Jerome Bettis Robert Smith	.08	.25
232 Retrospective O.J.McDuffie Curtis Conway Marshall Faulk Greg Hill	.20	.50
233 Retrospective Heath Shuler Trent Dilfer William Floyd Charles Johnson	.08	.25
234 Retrospective Errict Rhett Sean Dawkins Mario Bates Ki-Jana Carter	.08	.25
235 Retrospective Kerry Collins Steve McNair Joey Galloway Rashaan Salaam	.20	.50
236 Retrospective J.J.Stokes Michael Westbrook Kyle Brady Kordell Stewart	.20	.50
237 Retrospective Keyshawn Johnson Eddie George Leeland McElroy Lawrence Phillips	.08	.25
238 Retrospective Bobby Engram Rickey Dudley Eric Moulds Tim Biakabutuka	.08	.25
239 Panorama Jan.14, 1996 Kordell Stewart Quentin Coryatt	.20	.50
240 Panorama Nov.26, 1995 Robert Brooks	.08	.25
241 Panorama Nov.12, 1995 Henry Jones Terance Mathis	.02	.10
242 Panorama Dec.9, 1995 Mark Seay Alfred Pupunu	.02	.10
243 Panorama Sept.17, 1995 Robert Brooks Willie Beamon	.08	.25
244 Panorama Oct.29, 1995/49ers Halloween	.02	.10
245 Panorama Oct.15, 1995	.02	.10
246 Panorama Dec.31, 1995 Zack Crockett Junior Seau	.20	.50
247 Panorama Jan.14, 1996 Kevin Williams Doug Evans	.02	.10
248 Panorama Nov.19, 1995 Tim Jacobs Antonio Freeman	.08	.25
249 Checklist Card 1	.02	.10
250 Checklist Card 2	.02	.10

1996 SkyBox Premium Rubies

COMP.RUBY SET (248)	250.00	500.00
*RUBY STARS: 10X TO 25X BASIC CARDS		
*RUBY RCs: 5X TO 12X BASIC CARDS		
ONE PER HOBBY BOX		

1996 SkyBox Premium Close-ups

COMPLETE SET (10)	20.00	50.00
RANDOM INS.IN RETAIL PACKS		
1 Troy Aikman	4.00	10.00
2 Drew Bledsoe	2.50	6.00
3 Isaac Bruce	1.50	4.00
4 Terrell Davis	3.00	8.00
5 John Elway	8.00	20.00
6 Barry Sanders	6.00	15.00
7 Emmitt Smith	6.00	15.00
8 Kordell Stewart	1.50	4.00
9 Tamarick Vanover	.75	2.00
10 Ricky Watters	.75	2.00

1996 SkyBox Premium Brett Favre MVP

COMPLETE SET (6)	30.00	80.00
1-3A: RANDOM INSERTS IN IMPACT PACKS		
3B-5: RANDOM INSERTS IN SKYBOX PACKS		
1 Brett Favre Foil	5.00	12.00
2 Brett Favre Acrylic	5.00	12.00
3A Brett Favre Lent.Exch.A	.10	.30
3B Brett Favre Lent.Exch.B	.10	.30
3C Brett Favre Lent.Prize	15.00	40.00
4 Brett Favre Die Cut	6.00	15.00
5 Brett Favre Leather	6.00	15.00

1996 SkyBox Premium Inside the Numbers

COMPLETE SET (20)	10.00	25.00
ONE PER SPECIAL RETAIL PACK		
1 Troy Aikman	1.25	3.00
2 Robert Brooks	.50	1.25
3 Mark Brunell	.50	1.25
4 Larry Centers	.25	.60
5 Andre Coleman	.08	.25
6 Brett Favre	2.50	6.00
7 Charlie Garner	.25	.60
8 Mel Gray	.08	.25
9 Greg Lloyd	.25	.60
10 Dan Marino	2.50	6.00
11 Warren Moon	.25	.60
12 Bryce Paup	.08	.25
13 Carl Pickens	.25	.60
14 Barry Sanders	2.00	5.00
15 Deion Sanders	.75	2.00
16 Eric Swann	.08	.25
17 Thurman Thomas	.50	1.25
18 Tamarick Vanover	.25	.60
19 Reggie White	.50	1.25
20 Steve Young	1.00	2.50

1996 SkyBox Premium Next Big Thing

COMPLETE SET (15)	25.00	60.00
STATED ODDS 1:40		
1 Mark Brunell	3.00	8.00
2 Rickey Dudley	1.25	3.00
3 Bobby Engram	1.25	3.00
4 Antonio Freeman	2.00	5.00
5 Eddie George	4.00	10.00
6 Terry Glenn	3.00	8.00
7 Marvin Harrison	8.00	20.00
8 Keyshawn Johnson	3.00	8.00
9 Napoleon Kaufman	2.00	5.00
10 Steve McNair	4.00	10.00
11 Alex Molden	.40	1.00
12 Frank Sanders	1.00	2.50
13 Kordell Stewart	2.00	5.00
14 Amani Toomer	3.00	8.00
15 Alex Van Dyke	.60	1.50

1996 SkyBox Premium Prime Time Rookies

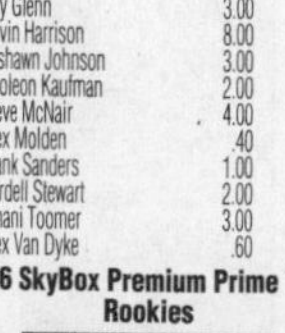

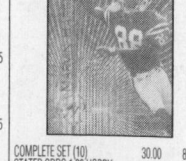

COMPLETE SET (10)	30.00	80.00
STATED ODDS 1:96 HOBBY		
1 Tim Biakabutuka	2.00	5.00

2 Rickey Dudley	2.00	5.00
3 Bobby Engram	2.00	5.00
4 Eddie George	6.00	15.00
5 Terry Glenn	5.00	12.00
6 Marvin Harrison	12.50	30.00
7 Keyshawn Johnson	5.00	12.00
8 Leeland McElroy	1.00	2.50
9 Eric Moulds	6.00	15.00
10 Lawrence Phillips	2.00	5.00

1996 SkyBox Premium Autographs

COMPLETE SET (6)	100.00	200.00
STATED ODDS 1:900		
A1 Trent Dilfer	20.00	40.00
A2 Brett Favre	75.00	150.00
A3 William Floyd	7.50	20.00
A4 Daryl Johnston	20.00	40.00
A5 Dave Meggett	7.50	20.00
A6 Eric Turner	20.00	40.00

1996 SkyBox Premium Thunder and Lightning

COMPLETE SET (10)	75.00	150.00
STATED ODDS 1:72		
1 Emmitt Smith Troy Aikman	7.50	20.00
2 Barry Sanders Scott Mitchell	7.50	20.00
3 Marshall Faulk Jim Harbaugh	7.50	20.00
4 Dan Marino O.J.McDuffie	10.00	25.00
5 Jerry Rice Steve Young	10.00	25.00
6 Jeff Blake Carl Pickens	5.00	12.00
7 Brett Favre Robert Brooks	10.00	25.00
8 Curtis Martin Drew Bledsoe	7.50	20.00
9 Errict Rhett Trent Dilfer	4.00	10.00
10 Rick Mirer Chris Warren	4.00	10.00

1996 SkyBox Premium V

COMPLETE SET (10)	15.00	30.00
STATED ODDS 1:18		
1 Ki-Jana Carter	1.00	2.50
2 Kerry Collins	2.00	5.00
3 Trent Dilfer	2.00	5.00
4 Joey Galloway	2.00	5.00
5 Herman Moore	1.00	2.50
6 Errict Rhett	1.00	2.50
7 Rashaan Salaam	1.00	2.50
8 Deion Sanders	3.00	8.00
9 Thurman Thomas	2.00	5.00
10 Reggie White	2.00	5.00

1997 SkyBox Premium

The 1997 SkyBox set was issued in one series totalling 250 cards. The set features color action player images printed on 20 pt. card stock with colorful holographic foil enhancements. The backs carry player information and career statistics with a faint player photo in the background. The set features 40-rookies (208-247) and 3-checklists (248-250)

COMPLETE SET (250)	12.50	30.00
1 Brett Favre	1.25	2.50
2 Michael Bates	.08	.25
3 Jeff Graham	.08	.25
4 Terry Glenn	.25	.60
5 Stephen Davis	.25	.60
6 Wesley Walls	.15	.40
7 Barry Sanders	.75	2.00
8 Chris Sanders	.08	.25
9 O.J. McDuffie	.15	.40
10 Ken Dilger	.08	.25
11 Kimble Anders	.15	.40
12 Keenan McCardell	.15	.40
13 Ki-Jana Carter	.08	.25
14 Gary Brown	.08	.25
15 Andre Rison	.15	.40
16 Edgar Bennett	.15	.40
17 Jerome Bettis	.25	.60
18 Ted Johnson	.08	.25
19 John Friesz	.08	.25
20 Tony Brackens	.08	.25
21 Bryan Cox	.08	.25
22 Eric Moulds	.25	.60
23 Johnnie Morton	.15	.40
24 Brad Johnson	.25	.60
25 Byron Bam Morris	.08	.25
26 Anthony Johnson	.08	.25
27 Jim Harbaugh	.15	.40
28 Keyshawn Johnson	.25	.60
29 Cary Blanchard	.08	.25
30 Curtis Conway	.15	.40
31 Herschel Walker	.15	.40
32 Thurman Thomas	.25	.60
33 Frank Sanders	.15	.40
34 Lawrence Phillips	.08	.25
35 Scottie Graham	.08	.25
36 Jim Everett	.08	.25
37 Dale Carter	.08	.25
38 Ashley Ambrose	.08	.25
39 Mark Chmura	.15	.40
40 James O.Stewart	.15	.40
41 John Mobley	.08	.25
42 Terrell Davis	.30	.75
43 Ben Coates	.15	.40
44 Jeff George	.15	.40
45 Ty Detmer	.15	.40
46 Isaac Bruce	.25	.60
47 Chris Warren	.15	.40
48 Steve Walsh	.08	.25
49 Bruce Smith	.15	.40
50 Cris Carter	.25	.60
51 Jamal Anderson	.25	.60
52 Tim Biakabutuka	.15	.40
53 Steve Young	.30	.75
54 Eric Turner	.08	.25
55 Jessie Tuggle	.08	.25
56 Chris T. Jones	.08	.25
57 Daryl Johnston	.15	.40
58 Randall Cunningham	.25	.60
59 Trent Dilfer	.25	.60
60 Mark Brunell	.30	.75
61 Warren Moon	.25	.60
62 Terry Kirby	.15	.40
63 Eddie George	.25	.60
64 Neil Smith	.15	.40
65 Gilbert Brown	.15	.40
66 Emmitt Smith	.75	2.00
67 Chad Brown	.08	.25
68 Jamie Asher	.08	.25
69 Willie McGinest	.08	.25
70 Tim Brown	.25	.60
71 Quentin Coryatt	.08	.25
72 Mario Bates	.08	.25
73 Fred Barnett	.08	.25
74 Hugh Douglas	.08	.25
75 Eric Swann	.08	.25
76 Chris Chandler	.15	.40
77 Larry Centers	.15	.40
78 Vinny Testaverde	.15	.40
79 Jermaine Lewis	.25	.60
80 Junior Seau	.25	.60
81 Kevin Greene	.15	.40
82 Ricky Watters	.15	.40
83 Billy Davis RC	.08	.25
84 Michael Westbrook	.15	.40
85 Charles Way	.15	.40
86 Andre Reed	.15	.40
87 Darrell Green	.15	.40
88 Troy Aikman	.50	1.25
89 Jim Pyne	.08	.25
90 Dan Marino	1.00	2.50
91 Elvis Grbac	.15	.40
92 Mel Gray	.08	.25
93 Marcus Allen	.25	.60
94 Terry Allen	.25	.60
95 Karim Abdul-Jabbar	.25	.60
96 Rick Mirer	.08	.25
97 Bert Emanuel	.15	.40
98 John Elway	1.00	2.50
99 Tony Martin	.15	.40
100 Zach Thomas	.25	.60
101 Harvey Williams	.08	.25
102 Jason Sehorn	.15	.40
103 Lawyer Milloy	.15	.40
104 Thomas Lewis	.08	.25
105 Michael Irvin	.25	.60
106 James Hundon RC	.25	.60
107 Willie Green	.08	.25
108 Bobby Engram	.15	.40
109 Mike Alstott	.25	.60
110 Greg Lloyd	.08	.25
111 Shannon Sharpe	.15	.40
112 Desmond Howard	.15	.40
113 Jason Elam	.15	.40
114 Qadry Ismail	.15	.40
115 William Thomas	.08	.25
116 Marshall Faulk	.30	.75
117 Tyrone Wheatley	.15	.40
118 Tommy Vardell	.08	.25
119 Rashaan Salaam	.08	.25
120 Brian Mitchell	.08	.25
121 Terance Mathis	.15	.40
122 Dorsey Levens	.25	.60
123 Todd Collins	.08	.25
124 Derrick Alexander WR	.15	.40
126 Stan Humphries	.15	.40
126 Kordell Stewart	.25	.60
127 Kent Graham	.08	.25
128 Yancey Thigpen	.15	.40
129 Bryan Still	.08	.25
130 Carl Pickens	.15	.40
131 Ray Lewis	.40	1.00
132 Curtis Martin	.30	.75
133 Kerry Collins	.25	.60
134 Ed McCaffrey	.15	.40
135 Darick Holmes	.08	.25
136 Glyn Milburn	.08	.25
137 Rickey Dudley	.15	.40
138 Terrell Owens	.30	.75
139 Kevin Williams	.08	.25
140 Reggie White	.25	.60
141 Darnay Scott	.15	.40
142 Brett Perriman	.08	.25
143 Neil O'Donnell	.15	.40
144 Natrone Means	.15	.40
145 Jerris McPhail	.08	.25
146 Lamar Lathon	.08	.25
147 Michael Jackson	.15	.40
148 Simeon Rice	.15	.40
149 Greg Hill	.08	.25
150 Erik Kramer	.08	.25
151 Quinn Early	.08	.25
152 Tamarick Vanover	.15	.40
153 Derrick Thomas	.25	.60
154 Nilo Silvan	.08	.25
155 Deion Sanders	.25	.60
156 Lorenzo Neal	.08	.25
157 Steve McNair	.30	.75
158 Levon Kirkland	.08	.25
159 Bobby Hebert	.08	.25
160 William Floyd	.15	.40
161 Leeland McElroy	.08	.25
162 Chester McGlockton	.08	.25
163 Michael Haynes	.08	.25
164 Aeneas Williams	.08	.25
165 Hardy Nickerson	.08	.25
166 Ray Zellars	.08	.25
167 Iheanyi Uwaezuoke	.15	.40
168 Chris Slade	.08	.25
169 Herman Moore	.15	.40
170 Rob Moore	.15	.40
171 Andre Hastings	.08	.25
172 Antonio Freeman	.25	.60
173 Tony Boselli	.08	.25
174 Drew Bledsoe	.30	.75
175 Sam Mills	.08	.25
176 Robert Smith	.15	.40
177 Jimmy Smith	.15	.40
178 Alex Molden	.08	.25
179 Joey Galloway	.15	.40
180 Irving Fryar	.15	.40
181 Wayne Chrebet	.25	.60
182 Dave Brown	.08	.25
183 Robert Brooks	.15	.40
184 Tony Banks	.15	.40
185 Eric Metcalf	.15	.40
186 Napoleon Kaufman	.25	.60
187 Frank Wycheck	.08	.25
188 Donnell Woolford	.08	.25
189 Kevin Turner	.08	.25
190 Eddie Kennison	.15	.40
191 Cortez Kennedy	.08	.25
192 Raymont Harris	.08	.25
193 Ronnie Harmon	.08	.25
194 Kevin Hardy	.08	.25
195 Gus Frerotte	.08	.25
196 Marvin Harrison	.25	.60
197 Jeff Blake	.15	.40
198 Mike Tomczak	.08	.25
199 William Roaf	.08	.25
200 Jerry Rice	.50	1.25
201 Jake Reed	.15	.40
202 Ken Norton	.08	.25
203 Errict Rhett	.08	.25
204 Adrian Murrell	.15	.40
205 Rodney Hampton	.15	.40
206 Scott Mitchell	.15	.40
207 Jason Dunn	.08	.25
208 Mike Adams RC	.08	.25
209 John Allred RC	.08	.25
210 Reidel Anthony RC	.25	.60
211 Darnell Autry RC	.15	.40
212 Tiki Barber RC	1.50	4.00
213 Will Blackwell RC	.15	.40
214 Peter Boulware RC	.25	.60
215 Macey Brooks RC	.25	.60
216 Rae Carruth RC	.08	.25
217 Troy Davis RC	.15	.40
218 Corey Dillon RC	1.00	2.50
219 Jim Druckenmiller RC	.15	.40
220 Warrick Dunn RC	.75	2.00
221 Marc Edwards RC	.08	.25
222 James Farrior RC	.25	.60
223 Tony Gonzalez RC	1.00	2.50
224 Jay Graham RC	.15	.40
225 Yatil Green RC	.15	.40
226 Byron Hanspard RC	.15	.40
227 Ike Hilliard RC	.30	.75
228 Leon Johnson RC	.15	.40
229 Damon Jones RC	.08	.25
230 Freddie Jones RC	.15	.40
231 Joey Kent RC	.25	.60
232 David LaFleur RC	.08	.25
233 Kevin Lockett RC	.15	.40
234 Sam Madison RC	.25	.60
235 Brian Manning RC	.08	.25
236 Ronnie McAda RC	.08	.25
237 Orlando Pace RC	.25	.60
238 Jake Plummer RC	1.00	2.50
239 Keith Poole RC	.25	.60
240 Darrell Russell RC	.08	.25
241 Sedrick Shaw RC	.15	.40
242 Antowain Smith RC	.60	1.50
243 Shawn Springs RC	.15	.40
244 Duce Staley RC	2.00	5.00
245 Dedric Ward RC	.15	.40
246 Bryant Westbrook RC	.08	.25
247 Danny Wuerffel RC	.25	.60
248 Checklist	.08	.25
249 Checklist	.08	.25
250 Checklist	.08	.25
S1 Terrell Davis Sample	.75	2.00

1997 SkyBox Premium Rubies

*RUBY STARS: 40X TO 100X BASIC CARDS
*RUBY RCs: 15X TO 40X BASIC CARDS
STATED PRINT RUN 50 SERIAL #'d SETS

1997 SkyBox Premium Autographics

ODDS: 1:120 IMPACT/1:500 METAL UNIV		
1:72 SKYBOX/1:60 E-X2000		
5-CARDS/SKYBOX HOT PACK 1:288 ODDS		
1 Karim Abdul-Jabbar (EX/IM/MU/S)	10.00	25.00
2 Larry Allen IM/S	12.00	30.00
3 Terry Allen IM/S	10.00	25.00
4 Mike Alstott IM/MU/S	10.00	25.00
5 Darnell Autry EX/IM/MU/S	4.00	10.00
6 Tony Banks IM	6.00	15.00
7 Pat Barnes EX/S	4.00	10.00
8 Jeff Blake S	10.00	25.00
9 Michael Booker IM/S	4.00	10.00
10 Rueben Brown EX/S	4.00	10.00
11 Rae Carruth EX/IM/MU/S	4.00	10.00
12 Cris Carter EX/IM/S	20.00	40.00
13 Ben Coates EX/IM/S	6.00	15.00
14 Ernie Conwell EX/IM/S	4.00	10.00
15 Terrell Davis EX/IM/S	12.50	30.00
16 Ty Detmer EX/IM/MU/S	6.00	15.00
17 Ken Dilger EX/IM/S	4.00	10.00
18 Corey Dillon IM/S	10.00	25.00
19 Jim Druckenmiller EX/S	6.00	15.00
20 Rickey Dudley EX/IM/S	6.00	15.00
22 Antonio Freeman EX/IM/S	10.00	25.00
23 Daryl Gardener EX/IM/S	4.00	10.00
24 Chris Gedney IM/S	4.00	10.00
25 Eddie George S	10.00	25.00
26 Hunter Goodwin EX/IM/S	4.00	10.00
27 Marvin Harrison EX/S	12.00	30.00
28 Garrison Hearst EX/S	6.00	15.00
29 William Henderson/EX/IM/S	10.00	25.00
30 Michael Jackson EX/IM/S	6.00	15.00
31 Tory James EX/IM/S	4.00	10.00
32 Rob Johnson EX/IM/S	10.00	25.00
33 Chris T. Jones IM/S	4.00	10.00
34 Pete Kendall EX/S	4.00	10.00
35 Eddie Kennison EX/MU/S	6.00	15.00
36 David LaFleur EX/IM/S	4.00	10.00
37 Jeff Lewis EX/IM/S	4.00	10.00
38 Thomas Lewis IM/S	4.00	10.00
39 Kevin Lockett EX/IM/S	4.00	10.00
40 Brian Manning IM/MU/S	4.00	10.00
41 Dan Marino S	200.00	400.00
42 Ed McCaffrey/EX/IM/MU/S	10.00	25.00
43 Keenan McCardell EX/S	10.00	25.00
44 Glyn Milburn EX/IM/S	4.00	10.00
45 Alex Molden EX/IM/S	4.00	10.00
46 Johnnie Morton IM/S	6.00	15.00
47 Winslow Oliver EX/S	4.00	10.00
48 Jerry Rice MU	125.00	200.00
49 Rashaan Salaam EX/S	4.00	10.00
50 Frank Sanders EX/IM/S	6.00	15.00
51 Shannon Sharpe/EX/IM/MU/S	15.00	40.00
52 Sedrick Shaw EX/IM/S	6.00	15.00
53 Alex Smith EX/IM/S	4.00	10.00
54 Antowain Smith EX/S	10.00	25.00
55 Emmitt Smith EX	100.00	200.00
56 Jimmy Smith IM/S	6.00	15.00
57 Shawn Springs S	6.00	15.00
58 James O.Stewart EX/IM/S	6.00	15.00
59 Kordell Stewart IM	10.00	25.00
60 Rodney Thomas EX/S	4.00	10.00
61 Amani Toomer EX/IM/S	10.00	25.00
62 Floyd Turner EX/IM/S	4.00	10.00
63 Alex Van Dyke EX/IM/S	4.00	10.00
64 Mike Vrabel IM/MU/S	25.00	50.00
65 Charles Way EX/S	4.00	10.00
66 Chris Warren EX/MU/S	4.00	10.00
68 Ricky Whittle EX/IM/S	4.00	10.00
69 Sherman Williams/EX/IM/S	4.00	10.00
70 Jon Witman EX/IM/S	6.00	15.00

1997 SkyBox Premium Autographics Century Mark

*CENT.MARKS: .5X TO 1.2X BASIC AUTOS		
21 Brett Favre EX	250.00	400.00
41 Dan Marino S	200.00	400.00
48 Jerry Rice MU	125.00	250.00
55 Emmitt Smith EX	150.00	250.00
67 Reggie White EX/S	75.00	135.00

1997 SkyBox Premium Close-ups

COMPLETE SET (10)	25.00	60.00
STATED ODDS 1:18		
1 Terrell Davis	3.00	8.00
2 Troy Aikman	5.00	12.00
3 Drew Bledsoe	3.00	8.00
4 Steve McNair	3.00	8.00
5 Jerry Rice	5.00	12.00
6 Kordell Stewart	2.50	6.00
7 Kerry Collins	2.50	6.00
8 John Elway	10.00	25.00
9 Deion Sanders	2.50	6.00
10 Joey Galloway	1.50	4.00

1997 SkyBox Premium Inside the Numbers

COMPLETE SET (8)	6.00	15.00
ONE PER SPECIAL RETAIL PACK		
1 Brett Favre	2.00	5.00
32 Thurman Thomas	.50	1.25
46 Isaac Bruce	.50	1.25
47 Chris Warren	.30	.75
49 Bruce Smith	.30	.75
66 Emmitt Smith	1.50	4.00
98 John Elway	2.00	5.00
140 Reggie White	.50	1.25

1997 SkyBox Premium Larger Than Life

COMPLETE SET (10)	125.00	250.00
STATED ODDS 1:360		
1 Emmitt Smith	15.00	40.00
2 Barry Sanders	15.00	40.00
3 Curtis Martin	6.00	15.00
4 Dan Marino	20.00	50.00
5 Keyshawn Johnson	5.00	12.00
6 Marvin Harrison	5.00	12.00
7 Terry Glenn	5.00	12.00
8 Eddie George	5.00	12.00
9 Brett Favre	20.00	50.00
10 Karim Abdul-Jabbar	5.00	12.00

1997 SkyBox Premium Players

COMPLETE SET (15)	100.00	250.00
STATED ODDS 1:192		
1 Eddie George	4.00	10.00
2 Terry Glenn	4.00	10.00
3 Karim Abdul-Jabbar	4.00	10.00
4 Emmitt Smith	12.50	30.00
5 Dan Marino	15.00	40.00
6 Brett Favre	15.00	40.00
7 Keyshawn Johnson	4.00	10.00
8 Curtis Martin	5.00	12.00
9 Marvin Harrison	4.00	10.00
10 Barry Sanders	12.50	30.00
11 Jerry Rice	8.00	20.00
12 Terrell Davis	5.00	12.00
13 Troy Aikman	8.00	20.00
14 Drew Bledsoe	5.00	12.00
15 John Elway	15.00	40.00

1997 SkyBox Premium Prime Time Rookies

COMPLETE SET (10)	30.00	80.00
STATED ODDS 1:96		
1 Jim Druckenmiller	2.50	6.00
2 Antowain Smith	10.00	25.00
3 Rae Carruth	1.50	4.00
4 Yatil Green	2.50	6.00
5 Ike Hilliard	5.00	12.00
6 Reidel Anthony	4.00	10.00
7 Orlando Pace	4.00	10.00
8 Peter Boulware	4.00	10.00
9 Warrick Dunn	12.50	30.00
10 Troy Davis	2.50	6.00

1997 SkyBox Premium Reebok

COMP.BRONZE SET (15)	1.25	3.00
*REEBOK GREENS: 25X TO 50X BRONZES		
*REEBOK GOLDS: 2X TO 5X BRONZES		
*REEBOK REDS: 12.5X TO 25X BRONZES		
*REEBOK SILVERS: .8X TO 2X BRONZES		
OVERALL REEBOK ODDS ONE PER PACK		
12 Keenan McCardell	.10	.30
37 Dale Carter	.07	.20
38 Ashley Ambrose	.07	.20
43 Ben Coates	.10	.30
66 Emmitt Smith	.40	1.00
95 Karim Abdul-Jabbar	.15	.40
98 John Elway	.50	1.25
110 Greg Lloyd	.07	.20
123 Todd Collins	.07	.20
161 Leeland McElroy	.07	.20
169 Herman Moore	.10	.30
175 Sam Mills	.07	.20
180 Irving Fryar	.10	.30
202 Ken Norton	.07	.20
205 Rodney Hampton	.10	.30

1997 SkyBox Premium Rookie Preview

COMPLETE SET (15)	6.00	15.00
STATED ODDS 1:6		
1 Reidel Anthony	.60	1.50
2 Tiki Barber	4.00	10.00
3 Peter Boulware	.60	1.50
4 Rae Carruth	.25	.60
5 Jim Druckenmiller	.40	1.00
6 Warrick Dunn	2.00	5.00
7 James Farrior	.60	1.50
8 Yatil Green	.40	1.00
9 Byron Hanspard	.40	1.00
10 Ike Hilliard	.75	2.00
11 Orlando Pace	.60	1.50
12 Darrell Russell	.25	.60
13 Antowain Smith	1.50	4.00
14 Shawn Springs	.40	1.00
15 Bryant Westbrook	.25	.60

1998 SkyBox Premium

The 1998 SkyBox set was issued in one series totalling 250 cards and was distributed in eight-card packs with a suggested retail price of $2.69. The set features color action player photos highlighted by gold holo-foil stamping on thick 20 pt. card stock. The set contains the topical subsets: One for the Ages (196-210), and Rookies (211-250) seeded 1:4 packs.

COMPLETE SET (250)	30.00	80.00
1 John Elway	1.00	2.50
2 Drew Bledsoe	.40	1.00
3 Antonio Freeman	.25	.60
4 Merton Hanks	.08	.25
5 James Jett	.15	.40
6 Ricky Proehl	.08	.25
7 Deion Sanders	.25	.60
8 Frank Sanders	.15	.40
9 Bruce Smith	.15	.40
10 Tiki Barber	.25	.60
11 Isaac Bruce	.25	.60
12 Mark Brunell	.25	.60
13 Quinn Early	.08	.25
14 Terry Glenn	.25	.60
15 Darrien Gordon	.08	.25
16 Keith Byars	.08	.25
17 Terrell Davis	.25	.60
18 Charlie Garner	.15	.40
19 Eddie Kennison	.15	.40
20 Keenan McCardell	.15	.40
21 Eric Moulds	.25	.60
22 Jimmy Smith	.15	.40
23 Reidel Anthony	.15	.40
24 Rae Carruth	.08	.25
25 Michael Irvin	.25	.60
26 Dorsey Levens	.25	.60
27 Derrick Mayes	.15	.40
28 Adrian Murrell	.15	.40
29 Dwayne Rudd	.08	.25
30 Leslie Shepherd	.08	.25
31 Jamal Anderson	.25	.60
32 Robert Brooks	.15	.40
33 Sean Dawkins	.08	.25
34 Cris Dishman	.08	.25
35 Rickey Dudley	.08	.25
36 Bobby Engram	.15	.40
37 Chester McGlockton	.08	.25
38 Terrell Owens	.25	.60
39 Wayne Chrebet	.25	.60
40 Dexter Coakley	.08	.25
41 Kerry Collins	.15	.40
42 Trent Dilfer	.25	.60
43 Bobby Hoying	.15	.40
44 Glyn Milburn	.08	.25
45 Rob Moore	.15	.40
46 Jake Reed	.15	.40
47 Dana Stubblefield	.08	.25
48 Reggie White	.25	.60
49 Natrone Means	.15	.40
50 Troy Aikman	.50	1.25
51 Aaron Bailey	.08	.25
52 William Floyd	.08	.25
53 Eric Metcalf	.08	.25
54 Warrick Dunn	.25	.60
55 Chad Lewis	.15	.40
56 Curtis Martin	.25	.60
57 Tony Martin	.15	.40
58 John Randle	.15	.40
59 Jeff Burris	.08	.25
60 Larry Centers	.08	.25
61 Bert Emanuel	.15	.40
62 Sean Gilbert	.08	.25
63 David Palmer	.08	.25
64 Eric Bieniemy	.08	.25
65 Peter Boulware	.08	.25
66 Charles Johnson	.08	.25
67 Jerris McPhail	.08	.25
68 Scott Mitchell	.15	.40
69 Chris Sanders	.08	.25
70 Ken Dilger	.08	.25
71 Brad Johnson	.25	.60
72 Danny Kanell	.15	.40
73 Fred Lane	.08	.25
74 Warren Sapp	.15	.40
75 Carl Pickens	.15	.40
76 Cris Carter	.25	.60
77 Marshall Faulk	.30	.75
78 Keyshawn Johnson	.25	.60
79 Tony McGee	.08	.25
80 Muhsin Muhammad	.15	.40
81 Kordell Stewart	.25	.60
82 Karl Williams	.08	.25
83 Willie Davis	.08	.25
84 David Dunn	.08	.25
85 Marvin Harrison	.25	.60
86 Michael Jackson	.08	.25
87 John Mobley	.08	.25
88 Shawn Springs	.08	.25
89 Wesley Walls	.15	.40
90 Jermaine Lewis	.15	.40
91 Ed McCaffrey	.15	.40
92 Chris Calloway	.08	.25
93 Lamont Warren	.08	.25
94 Ricky Watters	.15	.40
95 Tony Banks	.15	.40
96 Tony Brackens	.08	.25
97 Gary Brown	.08	.25
98 Howard Griffith	.08	.25
99 Ray Lewis	.25	.60
100 Jeff Blake	.15	.40
101 Charlie Jones	.08	.25
102 Glenn Foley	.15	.40
103 Jay Graham	.08	.25
104 James McKnight	.25	.60
105 Steve McNair	.25	.60
106 Chad Scott	.08	.25
107 Rod Smith WR	.15	.40
108 Jason Taylor	.15	.40
109 Corey Dillon	.25	.60
110 Eddie George	.25	.60
111 Jim Harbaugh	.15	.40
112 Warren Moon	.25	.60
113 Shannon Sharpe	.15	.40
114 Darnell Autry	.08	.25
115 Brett Favre	1.25	2.50
116 Jeff George	.15	.40
117 Tony Gonzalez	.25	.60
118 Garrison Hearst	.25	.60
119 Randal Hill	.08	.25
120 Eric Swann	.08	.25
121 Jamie Asher	.08	.25
122 Tim Brown	.25	.60
123 Stephen Davis	.08	.25
124 Chris Chandler	.15	.40
125 Jerry Rice	.50	1.25
126 Troy Davis	.08	.25
127 Ronnie Harmon	.08	.25
128 Andre Rison	.15	.40
129 Duce Staley	.30	.75
130 Charles Way	.08	.25
131 Bryant Westbrook	.08	.25
132 Mike Alstott	.25	.60
133 Gus Frerotte	.08	.25
134 Travis Jervey	.15	.40
135 Daryl Johnston	.15	.40
136 Jake Plummer	.25	.60
137 Junior Seau	.25	.60
138 Robert Smith	.25	.60
139 Thurman Thomas	.25	.60
140 Karim Abdul-Jabbar	.25	.60
141 Jerome Bettis	.25	.60
142 Byron Hanspard	.08	.25
143 Raymont Harris	.08	.25
144 Willie McGinest	.08	.25
145 Barry Sanders	.75	2.00
146 Irv Smith	.08	.25
147 Michael Strahan	.15	.40
148 Frank Wycheck	.08	.25
149 Steve Broussard	.08	.25
150 Joey Galloway	.15	.40
151 Courtney Hawkins	.08	.25
152 O.J. McDuffie	.15	.40
153 Herman Moore	.15	.40
154 Chris Penn	.08	.25
155 O.J. Santiago	.08	.25
156 Yancey Thigpen	.08	.25
157 Jason Sehorn	.15	.40
158 Ben Coates	.15	.40
159 Ernie Conwell	.08	.25
160 Dale Carter	.08	.25
161 Jeff Graham	.08	.25
162 Rob Johnson	.15	.40
163 Damon Jones	.08	.25
164 Mark Chmura	.15	.40
165 Curtis Conway	.15	.40
166 Elvis Grbac	.15	.40
167 Andre Hastings	.08	.25
168 Terry Kirby	.08	.25
169 Aeneas Williams	.08	.25
170 Derrick Alexander WR	.15	.40
171 Troy Brown	.15	.40
172 Irving Fryar	.15	.40
173 Jerald Moore	.08	.25
174 Andre Reed	.15	.40
175 James Stewart	.15	.40
176 Chris Warren	.15	.40
177 Will Blackwell	.08	.25
178 Erik Kramer	.08	.25
179 Dan Marino	1.00	2.50
180 Terance Mathis	.15	.40
181 Johnnie Morton	.15	.40
182 J.J. Stokes	.15	.40
183 Rodney Thomas	.08	.25
184 Steve Young	.30	.75
185 Kimble Anders	.15	.40
186 Napoleon Kaufman	.25	.60
187 Orlando Pace	.08	.25
188 Antowain Smith	.25	.60
189 Emmitt Smith	.75	2.00
190 Terry Allen	.25	.60
191 Mark Bruener	.08	.25
192 Rodney Harrison	.15	.40
193 Billy Joe Hobert	.08	.25
194 Leon Johnson	.08	.25
195 Freddie Jones	.08	.25
196 John Elway OFA	.40	1.00
197 Brett Favre OFA Steve Atwater OFA	.30	.75
198 Brett Favre OFA Steve Atwater OFA	.30	.75
199 Dorsey Levens OFA Keith Traylor OFA	.15	.40
200 Packers Offense OFA Broncos Defense OFA	.25	.60
201 Mark Chmura OFA Tyrone Braxton OFA	.08	.25
202 Dorsey Levens OFA Steve Atwater OFA Bill Romanowski OFA	.15	.40
203 Robert Brooks OFA Ray Crockett OFA	.15	.40
204 Tim McKyer OFA	.08	.25
205 Allen Aldridge OFA	.08	.25
206 Terrell Davis OFA Rod Smith WR OFA	.25	.60
207 Bill Romanowski OFA	.08	.25
208 John Elway OFA Rod Smith WR OFA Ed McCaffrey OFA	.40	1.00
209 Ray Crockett OFA	.08	.25
210 John Elway OFA	.40	1.00
211 Robert Edwards RC	1.00	2.50
212 Roland Williams RC	.75	2.00
213 Joe Jurevicius RC	1.50	4.00
214 Wilmont Perry RC	.75	2.00
215 Robert Holcombe RC	1.00	2.50
216 Larry Shannon RC	.75	2.00
217 Skip Hicks RC	1.00	2.50
218 Pat Johnson RC	1.00	2.50
219 Pat Palmer RC	.75	2.00
220 John Dutton RC	.75	2.00
221 Az-Zahir Hakim RC	1.50	4.00
222 Mikhael Ricks RC	1.00	2.50
223 Rashaan Shehee RC	1.00	2.50
224 Ryan Leaf RC	1.50	4.00
225 Alvis Whitted RC	1.00	2.50
226 Marcus Nash RC	.75	2.00
227 Fred Taylor RC	2.50	6.00
228 Hines Ward RC	7.50	15.00
229 C.Fuamatu-Ma'afala RC	1.00	2.50
230 Jerome Pathon RC	1.50	4.00
231 Peyton Manning RC	15.00	40.00
232 Charles Woodson RC	2.00	5.00
233 Jon Ritchie RC	1.00	2.50
234 Scott Frost R RC	.75	2.00
235 John Avery RC	1.00	2.50
236 Jonathan Linton RC	1.00	2.50
237 Jacquez Green RC	1.00	2.50
238 Andre Wadsworth RC	1.00	2.50
239 Cam Quayle RC	.75	2.00
240 Randy Moss RC	8.00	20.00
241 Raymond Priester RC	.75	2.00
242 Donald Hayes RC	1.00	2.50
243 Brian Griese RC	3.00	8.00
244 Brian Alford RC	.75	2.00
245 Kevin Dyson RC	1.50	4.00
246 Jammi German RC	.75	2.00
247 Cameron Cleeland RC	.75	2.00
248 Curtis Enis RC	.75	2.00
249 Terry Hardy RC	.75	2.00
250 Tony Simmons RC	1.00	2.50
NNO Checklist Card	.08	.25
P136 Jake Plummer Promo	.60	1.50

1998 SkyBox Premium Fleet Farms

COMPLETE SET (250)	90.00	150.00
*STARS: 1.5X TO 4X BASIC CARDS		
*ROOKIES: .15X TO .4X BASIC CARDS		
ONE PER FLEET FARMS PACK		

1998 SkyBox Premium Star Rubies

*RUBY STARS: 40X TO 100X		
1-210 PRINT RUN 50 SERIAL #'d SETS		
*RUBY RCs: 4X TO 10X		
211-250 PRINT RUN 35 SERIAL #'d SETS		
115 Brett Favre	100.00	200.00
231 Peyton Manning	250.00	400.00

1998 SkyBox Premium Autographics

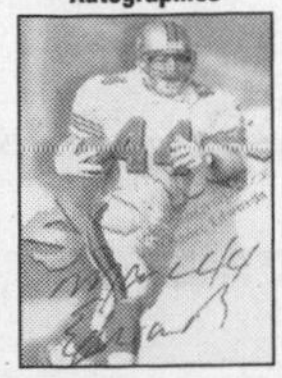

ODDS: 1:48 E-X2001/1:68 METAL UNIVERSE		
1:68 SKYBOX PREMIUM/1:112 SKY.THUNDER		
*BLUE SIGS/50: .8X TO 2X BASIC AU		
BLUE SIGNATURES PRINT RUN 50 SETS		
1 Kevin Abrams S/ST	4.00	10.00
2 Mike Alstott MU/S	10.00	25.00
3 Jamie Asher MU/S/ST*	4.00	10.00
4 John Avery S	6.00	15.00
5 Tavian Banks MU/S/ST*	6.00	15.00
6 Pat Barnes MU/ST	4.00	10.00
7 Jerome Bettis MU/S*	50.00	100.00
8 Eric Bjornson MU/S*	4.00	10.00
9 Peter Boulware MU/ST*	4.00	10.00
10 Troy Brown MU/S/ST	10.00	25.00
11 Mark Bruener MU/S*	4.00	10.00
12 Mark Brunell MU/ST*	12.50	30.00
13 Rae Carruth MU/S/ST	4.00	10.00
14 Ray Crockett S/ST*	4.00	10.00
15 Germane Crowell S/ST	6.00	15.00
16 Stephen Davis MU/S*	10.00	25.00
17 Troy Davis MU/ST	4.00	10.00
18 Sean Dawkins MU/ST	4.00	10.00
19 Trent Dilfer S/ST	10.00	25.00
20 Corey Dillon MU/S	10.00	25.00
21 Jim Druckenmiller S/ST	4.00	10.00
22 Kevin Dyson MU/S/ST	6.00	15.00
23 Marc Edwards S/ST	4.00	10.00
24 Robert Edwards S/ST	6.00	15.00
25 Bobby Engram MU/S/ST	6.00	15.00
26 Curtis Enis S/ST	4.00	10.00
27 William Floyd MU/ST	6.00	15.00
28 Glenn Foley MU/ST	6.00	15.00
29 Chris Fuamatu-Ma'afala MU/S/ST*	6.00	15.00
30 Joey Galloway MU/S/ST*	6.00	15.00
31 Jeff George MU/ST	10.00	25.00
32 Ahman Green S/ST	20.00	50.00
33 Jacquez Green S/ST	6.00	15.00
34 Yatil Green MU/S/ST	4.00	10.00
35 Byron Hanspard MU/S*	4.00	10.00
36 Marvin Harrison MU/S*	15.00	30.00
37 Skip Hicks S/ST	6.00	15.00
38 Robert Holcombe MU/S	6.00	15.00
39 Bobby Hoying MU/S	6.00	15.00
40 Travis Jervey MU/S/ST	4.00	10.00
41 Rob Johnson MU/S	6.00	15.00
42 Freddie Jones MU/S/ST	4.00	10.00
43 Eddie Kennison S/ST	6.00	15.00
44 Fred Lane MU/S	10.00	25.00
45 Ryan Leaf EX	6.00	15.00
46 Dorsey Levens MU/ST	6.00	15.00
47 Jeff Lewis S	4.00	10.00
48 Jermaine Lewis MU/ST	6.00	15.00
49 Dan Marino S	75.00	150.00
50 Curtis Martin MU/S/ST*	30.00	80.00
51 Steve Matthews MU/ST	4.00	10.00
52 Alonzo Mayes S/ST	4.00	10.00
53 Keenan McCardell MU/ST*	6.00	15.00
54 Willie McGinest S/ST*	10.00	25.00
55 James McKnight S	6.00	15.00
56 Glyn Milburn MU/ST*	4.00	10.00
57 Randy Moss MU/ST	125.00	200.00
58 Marcus Nash MU/S/ST	4.00	10.00
59 Terrell Owens S/ST*	20.00	40.00
60 Jason Peter S/ST	4.00	10.00
61 Jake Plummer MU	10.00	25.00
62 John Randle MU/ST	10.00	25.00
63 Shannon Sharpe MU/S*	15.00	40.00
64 Jimmy Smith MU/ST	6.00	15.00
65 Robert Smith MU/ST	6.00	15.00
66 Duce Staley MU/S	10.00	25.00
67 Kordell Stewart S*	10.00	25.00
68 Fred Taylor MU/S/ST	10.00	25.00
69 Rodney Thomas MU/S/ST*	4.00	10.00
70 Kevin Turner MU/S/ST	4.00	10.00
71 Hines Ward MU/S/ST*	35.00	60.00
72 Charles Way MU/S*	4.00	10.00
73 Frank Wycheck MU/ST	4.00	10.00
NNO E-X2001 Checklist Card	.02	.10
NNO Premium Checklist Card	.02	.10
NNO Premium Retail Checklist	.02	.10

1998 SkyBox Premium D'stroyers

COMPLETE SET (15)	12.50	30.00
STATED ODDS 1:6		
1D Antowain Smith	.60	1.50
2D Corey Dillon	1.00	2.50
3D Charles Woodson	.60	1.50
4D Randy Moss	3.00	8.00
5D Deion Sanders	1.00	2.50
6D Robert Edwards	.30	.75
7D Herman Moore	.30	.75
8D Mark Brunell	1.00	2.50
9D Dorsey Levens	.30	.75
10D Curtis Enis	.30	.75
11D Drew Bledsoe	1.50	4.00
12D Steve McNair	1.00	2.50
13D Keyshawn Johnson	.60	1.50
14D Bobby Hoying	.30	.75
15D Trent Dilfer	.60	1.50

1998 SkyBox Premium Intimidation Nation

COMPLETE SET (15)	125.00	250.00
STATED ODDS 1:360		
1IN Terrell Davis	4.00	10.00
2IN Emmitt Smith	12.50	30.00
3IN Barry Sanders	12.50	30.00
4IN Brett Favre	15.00	40.00
5IN Eddie George	4.00	10.00
6IN Jerry Rice	8.00	20.00
7IN John Elway	15.00	40.00
8IN Mark Brunell	4.00	10.00

9IN Troy Aikman 8.00 20.00
10IN Peyton Manning 50.00 100.00
11IN Ryan Leaf 4.00 10.00
12IN Curtis Martin 4.00 10.00
13IN Dan Marino 15.00 40.00
14IN Warrick Dunn 4.00 10.00
15IN Jake Plummer 4.00 10.00

1998 SkyBox Premium Prime Time Rookies

COMPLETE SET (10) 60.00 120.00
STATED ODDS 1:96
1PT Curtis Enis 2.00 5.00
2PT Robert Edwards 3.00 8.00
3PT Fred Taylor 4.00 10.00
4PT Robert Holcombe 3.00 8.00
5PT Ryan Leaf 4.00 10.00
6PT Peyton Manning 15.00 40.00
7PT Randy Moss 10.00 25.00
8PT Charles Woodson 5.00 12.00
9PT Andre Wadsworth 3.00 8.00
10PT Kevin Dyson 4.00 10.00

1998 SkyBox Premium Rap Show

COMPLETE SET (15) 30.00 60.00
STATED ODDS 1:36
1 John Elway 5.00 12.00
2 Drew Bledsoe 2.00 5.00
3 Corey Dillon 1.25 3.00
4 Brett Favre 5.00 12.00
5 Barry Sanders 4.00 10.00
6 Eddie George 1.25 3.00
7 Emmitt Smith 4.00 10.00
8 Jake Plummer 1.25 3.00
9 Joey Galloway .75 2.00
10 Ricky Watters .75 2.00
11 Mike Alstott 1.25 3.00
12 Kordell Stewart 1.25 3.00
13 Antonio Freeman 1.25 3.00
14 Terrell Davis 1.25 3.00
15 Warrick Dunn 1.25 3.00

1998 SkyBox Premium Soul of the Game

COMPLETE SET (15) 15.00 30.00
STATED ODDS 1:18
1 Troy Aikman 2.00 5.00
2 Dorsey Levens 1.00 2.50
3 Deion Sanders 1.00 2.50
4 Antonio Freeman 1.00 2.50
5 Dan Marino 4.00 10.00
6 Keyshawn Johnson 1.00 2.50
7 Terry Glenn 1.00 2.50
8 Tim Brown 1.00 2.50
9 Curtis Martin 1.00 2.50
10 Bobby Hoying .60 1.50
11 Kordell Stewart 1.00 2.50
12 Jerry Rice 2.00 5.00
13 Steve McNair 1.00 2.50
14 Joey Galloway .60 1.50
15 Steve Young 1.25 3.00

1999 SkyBox Premium

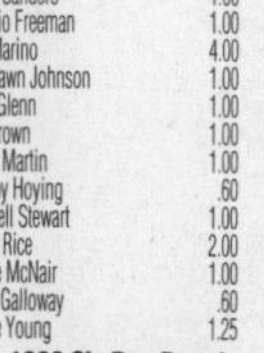

Issued in late October of 1999, This set contained 210 veteran player cards with 40 rookie cards also availble. The rookie cards were available in two forms a regular issue which featured a head shot non action photo and a short printed version with a full player action shot which was inserted 1 in 8 packs. Also randomly inserted were the Autographics cross brand insert of hand signed autographs at a rate of 1 in 68 packs. Boxes contained 24 packs with 8 cards per pack.

COMPLETE SET (290) 150.00 300.00
COMP.SET w/o SPs (250) 25.00 50.00
1 Randy Moss .25 .60
2 Jamie Asher .15 .40
3 Joey Galloway .20 .50
4 Kent Graham .15 .40
5 Leslie Shepherd .15 .40
6 Levon Kirkland .15 .40
7 Marcus Pollard .15 .40
8 O.J. McDuffie .20 .50
9 Bill Romanowski .20 .50
10 Priest Holmes .25 .60
11 Tim Biakabutuka .20 .50
12 Duce Staley .20 .50
13 Isaac Bruce .25 .60
14 Jay Riemersma .15 .40
15 Karim Abdul-Jabbar .20 .50
16 Kevin Dyson .15 .40
17 Rickey Dudley .15 .40
18 Rocket Ismail .20 .50
19 Billy Davis .15 .40
20 James Jett .15 .40
21 Jerome Bettis .25 .60
22 Michael McCrary .15 .40
23 Michael Westbrook .15 .40
24 Oronde Gadsden .15 .40
25 Brad Johnson .20 .50
26 Shawn Springs .15 .40
27 Cris Carter .25 .60
28 Ed McCaffrey .20 .50
29 Gary Brown .15 .40
30 Hines Ward .25 .60
31 Hugh Douglas .20 .50
32 Jamir Miller .15 .40
33 Michael Bates .15 .40
34 Peyton Manning .75 2.00
35 Tony Banks .20 .50
36 Charles Way .15 .40
37 Charlie Batch .20 .50
38 Jake Reed .20 .50
39 Mark Brunell .20 .50
40 Skip Hicks .15 .40
41 Steve Young .30 .75
42 Wesley Walls .20 .50
43 Antonio Langham .15 .40
44 Antowain Smith .15 .40
45 Brian Griese .20 .50
46 Jessie Armstead .20 .50
47 Thurman Thomas .25 .60
48 Jeff George .15 .40
49 Jessie Tuggle .15 .40
50 Jim Harbaugh .20 .50
51 Marvin Harrison .25 .60
52 Randall Cunningham .25 .60
53 Stephen Alexander .15 .40
54 Tiki Barber .25 .60
55 Billy Joe Tolliver .15 .40
56 Bruce Smith .25 .60
57 Eddie George .20 .50
58 Eugene Robinson .20 .50
59 John Elway .75 2.00
60 Kent Dilger .15 .40
61 Rodney Harrison .20 .50
62 Ty Detmer .20 .50
63 Andre Reed .25 .60
64 Dorsey Levens .20 .50
65 Eddie Kennison .20 .50
66 Freddie Jones .15 .40
67 Jacquez Green .15 .40
68 Jason Elam .15 .40
69 Marc Edwards .20 .50
70 Terance Mathis .15 .40
71 Alonzo Mayes .15 .40
72 Andre Wadsworth .15 .40
73 Barry Sanders .60 1.50
74 Derrick Alexander .15 .40
75 Garrison Hearst .20 .50
76 Leon Johnson .15 .40
77 Mike Alstott .25 .60
78 Shawn Jefferson .15 .40
79 Andre Hastings .15 .40
80 Eric Moulds .20 .50
81 Ryan Leaf .20 .50
82 Takeo Spikes .15 .40
83 Terrell Davis .25 .60
84 Tim Dwight .20 .50
85 Trent Dilfer .20 .50
86 Vonnie Holliday .15 .40
87 Antonio Freeman .20 .50
88 Carl Pickens .20 .50
89 Chris Chandler .20 .50
90 Dale Carter .15 .40
91 La'Roi Glover RC .40 1.00
92 Natrone Means .20 .50
93 Reidel Anthony .15 .40
94 Brett Favre .75 2.00
95 Bubby Brister .15 .40
96 Cameron Cleeland .15 .40
97 Chris Calloway .15 .40
98 Corey Dillon .20 .50
99 Greg Hill .15 .40
100 Vinny Testaverde .20 .50
101 Trent Green .20 .50
102 Sam Gash .15 .40
103 Mikhael Ricks .15 .40
104 Emmitt Smith .60 1.50
105 Doug Flutie .25 .60
106 Deion Sanders .25 .60
107 Charles Johnson .15 .40
108 Byron Bam Morris .15 .40
109 Andre Rison .20 .50
110 Doug Pederson .15 .40
111 Marshall Faulk .25 .60
112 Tim Brown .25 .60
113 Warren Sapp .20 .50
114 Bryan Still .15 .40
115 Chris Penn .15 .40
116 Jamal Anderson .20 .50
117 Keyshawn Johnson .20 .50
118 Ricky Proehl .15 .40
119 Robert Brooks .20 .50
120 Tony Gonzalez .25 .60
121 Ty Law .20 .50
122 Elvis Grbac .15 .40
123 Jeff Blake .20 .50
124 Mark Chmura .15 .40
125 Junior Seau .25 .60
126 Mo Lewis .15 .40
127 Ray Buchanan .15 .40
128 Robert Holcombe .15 .40
129 Tony Simmons .15 .40
130 David Palmer .15 .40
131 Ike Hilliard .20 .50
132 Mike Vanderjagt .15 .40
133 Rae Carruth .15 .40
134 Sean Dawkins .15 .40
135 Shannon Sharpe .25 .60
136 Curtis Conway .20 .50
137 Darrell Green .25 .60
138 Germane Crowell .15 .40
139 J.J. Stokes .15 .40
140 Kevin Hardy .15 .40
141 Rob Moore .15 .40
142 Robert Smith .20 .50
143 Wayne Chrebet .20 .50
144 Yancey Thigpen .15 .40
145 Jerome Pathon .15 .40
146 John Mobley .15 .40
147 Kerry Collins .20 .50
148 Peter Boulware .15 .40
149 Matthew Hatchette .20 .50
150 Kordell Stewart .20 .50
151 Koy Detmer .15 .40
152 Sedrick Shaw .15 .40
153 Steve Beuerlein .20 .50
154 Zach Thomas .25 .60
155 Adrian Murrell .20 .50
156 Bobby Engram .20 .50
157 Bryan Cox .20 .50
158 Drew Bledsoe .25 .60
159 Jerry Rice .50 1.25
160 Keenan McCardell .20 .50
161 Steve McNair .25 .60
162 Terry Fair .15 .40
163 Derrick Brooks .25 .60
164 Eric Green .15 .40
165 Erik Kramer .20 .50
166 Frank Sanders .15 .40
167 Fred Taylor .20 .50
168 Johnnie Morton .20 .50
169 R.W. McQuarters .15 .40
170 Terry Glenn .20 .50
171 Frank Wycheck .20 .50
172 John Avery .15 .40
173 Kevin Turner .15 .40
174 Larry Centers .20 .50
175 Michael Irvin .25 .60
176 Rich Gannon .20 .50
177 Ricky Watters .20 .50
178 Rodney Thomas .15 .40
179 Scott Mitchell .15 .40
180 Chad Brown .15 .40
181 John Randle .20 .50
182 Michael Strahan .20 .50
183 Muhsin Muhammad .20 .50
184 Reggie Barlow .15 .40
185 Rod Smith .20 .50
186 Dan Marino .75 2.00
187 Dexter Coakley .15 .40
188 Jermaine Lewis .15 .40
189 Jon Kitna .20 .50
190 Napoleon Kaufman .15 .40
191 Will Blackwell .15 .40
192 Aaron Glenn .15 .40
193 Ben Coates .20 .50
194 Curtis Enis .15 .40
195 Herman Moore .20 .50
196 Jake Plummer .20 .50
197 Jimmy Smith .20 .50
198 Terrell Owens .25 .60
199 Warrick Dunn .20 .50
200 Charles Woodson .25 .60
201 Ahman Green .20 .50
202 Mark Bruener .15 .40
203 Ray Lewis .25 .60
204 Tony Martin .20 .50
205 Troy Aikman .40 1.00
206 Curtis Martin .25 .60
207 Darnay Scott .15 .40
208 Derrick Mayes .15 .40
209 Keith Poole .15 .40
210 Warren Moon .25 .60
211 Chris Claiborne RC .25 .60
211S Chris Claiborne SP .60 1.50
212 Ricky Williams RC .60 1.50
212S Ricky Williams SP 1.50 4.00
213 Tim Couch RC .40 1.00
213S Tim Couch SP 1.00 2.50
214 Champ Bailey RC .75 2.00
214S Champ Bailey SP 2.00 5.00
215 Torry Holt RC .60 1.50
215S Torry Holt SP 1.50 4.00
216 Donovan McNabb RC 1.50 4.00
216S Donovan McNabb SP 4.00 10.00
217 David Boston RC .30 .75
217S David Boston SP .75 2.00
218 Chris McAlister RC .30 .75
218S Chris McAlister SP .75 2.00
219 Michael Bishop RC .30 .75
219S Michael Bishop SP .75 2.00
220 Daunte Culpepper RC .40 1.00
220S Daunte Culpepper SP 1.00 2.50
221 Joe Germaine RC .30 .75
221S Joe Germaine SP .75 2.00
222 Edgerrin James RC .50 1.25
222S Edgerrin James SP 1.25 3.00
223 Jevon Kearse RC .40 1.00
223S Jevon Kearse SP 1.00 2.50
224 Ebenezer Ekuban RC .25 .60
224S Ebenezer Ekuban SP .60 1.50
225 Scott Covington RC .25 .60
225S Scott Covington SP .60 1.50
226 Aaron Brooks RC .40 1.00
226S Aaron Brooks SP 1.00 2.50
227 Cecil Collins RC .25 .60
227S Cecil Collins SP .60 1.50
228 Akili Smith RC .30 .75
228S Akili Smith SP .75 2.00
229 Shaun King RC .30 .75
229S Shaun King SP .75 2.00
230 Chad Plummer RC .25 .60
230S Chad Plummer SP .60 1.50
231 Peerless Price RC .30 .75
231S Peerless Price SP .75 2.00
232 Antoine Winfield RC .25 .60
232S Antoine Winfield SP .60 1.50
233 Antuan Edwards RC .25 .60
233S Antuan Edwards SP .60 1.50
234 Rob Konrad RC .25 .60
234S Rob Konrad SP .60 1.50
235 Troy Edwards RC .30 .75
235S Troy Edwards SP .75 2.00
236 Terry Jackson RC .25 .60
236S Terry Jackson SP .60 1.50
237 Jim Kleinsasser RC .40 1.00
237S Jim Kleinsasser SP 1.00 2.50
238 Joe Montgomery RC .25 .60
238S Joe Montgomery SP .60 1.50
239 Desmond Clark RC .30 .75
239S Desmond Clark SP .75 2.00
240 Lamar King RC .25 .60
240S Lamar King SP .60 1.50
241 Dameane Douglas RC .25 .60
241S Dameane Douglas SP .60 1.50
242 Martin Gramatica RC .25 .60
242S Martin Gramatica SP .60 1.50
243 Jim Finn RC .25 .60
243S Jim Finn SP .60 1.50
244 Andy Katzenmoyer RC .30 .75
244S Andy Katzenmoyer SP .75 2.00
245 Dee Miller RC .25 .60
245S Dee Miller SP .60 1.50
246 D'Wayne Bates RC .25 .60
246S D'Wayne Bates SP .60 1.50
247 Amos Zereoue RC .30 .75
247S Amos Zereoue SP .75 2.00
248 Karsten Bailey RC .25 .60
248S Karsten Bailey SP .60 1.50
249 Kevin Johnson RC .30 .75
249S Kevin Johnson SP .75 2.00
250 Cade McNown RC .30 .75
250S Cade McNown SP .75 2.00

1999 SkyBox Premium Shining Star Rubies

*RUBY VETS/30: 30X TO 80X BASIC CARDS
*RUBY ROOKIES/30: 10X TO 25X
*RUBY SINGLES/15: 4X TO 10X BASE SPs

1999 SkyBox Premium 2000 Men

COMPLETE SET (15) 150.00 400.00
STATED PRINT RUN 100 SER.#'d SETS
1TM Warrick Dunn 8.00 20.00
2TM Tim Couch 3.00 8.00
3TM Fred Taylor 8.00 20.00
4TM Jake Plummer 5.00 12.00
5TM Jerry Rice 15.00 40.00
6TM Edgerrin James 12.50 30.00
7TM Mark Brunell * 8.00 20.00
8TM Peyton Manning 25.00 60.00
9TM Randy Moss 20.00 50.00
10TM Terrell Davis 8.00 20.00
11TM Charlie Batch 8.00 20.00
12TM Dan Marino 25.00 60.00
13TM Emmitt Smith 15.00 40.00
14TM Brett Favre 25.00 60.00
15TM Barry Sanders 25.00 60.00

1999 SkyBox Premium Autographics

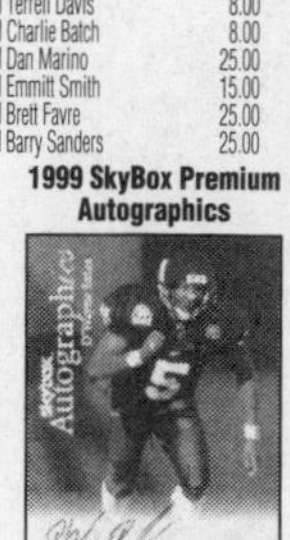

STATED ODDS 1:68H, 1:90R
*RED FOIL STARS: 1X TO 2.5X BASIC AUTOS
*RED FOIL ROOKIES: .8X TO 2X BASIC AUTOS
RED FOIL STATED PRINT RUN 50 SER.#'d SETS
1 Stephen Alexander EX/MM/MU/S 5.00 12.00
2 Mike Alstott D/EX/S 12.50 30.00
3 Champ Bailey/D/EX/MM/MU/S 20.00 40.00
4 Karsten Bailey/EX/MM/MU/S 5.00 12.00
5 Charlie Batch/EX/MM/MU/S 7.50 20.00
6 D'Wayne Bates D/EX/MM/MU/S 5.00 12.00
7 Michael Bishop/D/EX/MM/S 7.50 20.00
8 Dre Bly D/EX/MM/MU/S 7.50 20.00
9 David Boston/D/EX/MM/S 12.50 30.00
10 Gary Brown D/EX/MM/S 5.00 12.00
11 Na Brown D/EX/MM/S 5.00 12.00
12 Tim Brown D/EX/MM/S 12.50 30.00
13 Troy Brown/EX/MM/MU/S 12.50 30.00
14 Mark Bruener D/EX/MM/MU/S 5.00 12.00
15 Mark Brunell/D/EX/MM/S 7.50 20.00
16 Shawn Bryson EX 5.00 12.00
17 Wayne Chrebet EX/MM/MU/S 12.50 30.00
18 Chris Claiborne/D/EX/MM/S 5.00 12.00
19 Cam Cleeland D/EX/MM/MU/S 5.00 12.00
20 Cecil Collins/D/EX/MM/S 5.00 12.00
21 Daunte Culpepper/D/EX/MM 15.00 40.00
22 Randall Cunningham D/EX/MM 12.50 30.00
23 Terrell Davis EX/MU/S 15.00 40.00
24 Ty Detmer D/EX/MM/S 5.00 12.00
25 Jared DeVries D/EX/MM/MU/S 5.00 12.00
26 Troy Edwards/D/EX/MM/S 5.00 12.00
27 Kevin Faulk D/EX/MM/S 7.50 20.00
28 Marshall Faulk/D/EX/MM/S 15.00 40.00
29 Doug Flutie/EX/MM/MU/S 12.50 30.00
30 Oronde Gadsden MU/S 7.50 20.00
31 Joey Galloway/D/EX/MM/S 7.50 20.00
32 Eddie George D/MM/S 12.50 30.00
33 Martin Gramatica EX/MM/MU/S 5.00 12.00
34 Anthony Gray MM/MU/S 5.00 12.00
35 Ahman Green/D/EX/MM/S 12.50 30.00
36 Brian Griese D/EX/MM/S 12.50 30.00
37 Howard Griffith EX/MM/MU/S 5.00 12.00
38 Marvin Harrison/MM/MU/S 12.00 30.00
39 Courtney Hawkins D/MM/MU/S 5.00 12.00
40 Vonnie Holliday D/EX/MM/MU/S 5.00 12.00
41 Priest Holmes MM 12.50 30.00
42 Torry Holt D/EX/MM 12.50 30.00
43 Sedrick Irvin D/S 5.00 12.00
44 Edgerrin James D/EX/MM/MU 25.00 50.00
45 Patrick Jeffers D/MU/S 5.00 12.00
46 James Johnson D/MM/S 5.00 12.00
47 Kevin Johnson/D/EX/MM/S 7.50 20.00
48 Freddie Jones/D/EX/MM/S 5.00 12.00
49 Jevon Kearse/D/EX/MM/S 12.50 30.00
50 Shaun King D/EX/MM/S 5.00 12.00
51 Jon Kitna EX/MM/MU/S 7.50 20.00
52 Rob Konrad D/EX/MM/S 5.00 12.00
53 Dorsey Levens MU/S 7.50 20.00
54 Peyton Manning/D/EX/MM 75.00 150.00
55 Darnell McDonald D/EX/MM/MU/S 5.00 12.00
56 Donovan McNabb D/EX/MM/S 30.00 60.00
57 Cade McNown/D/EX/MM/S 5.00 12.00
58 Eric Moss D/MM/S 5.00 12.00
59 Randy Moss EX/MM/S 40.00 80.00
60 Eric Moulds EX/MM/S 7.50 20.00
61 Marcus Nash/EX/MM/MU/S 5.00 12.00
62 Terrell Owens D/EX/MM 15.00 40.00
63 Jerome Pathon EX/MM/MU/S 5.00 12.00
64 Jake Plummer D/EX/MM 12.50 30.00
65 Peerless Price EX/MM 12.50 30.00
66 Mikhael Ricks D/EX/MM/MU/S 5.00 12.00
67 Frank Sanders/EX/MM/MU/S 5.00 12.00
68 Tony Simmons D/EX/MM/MU/S 5.00 12.00
69 Akili Smith D/S 5.00 12.00
70 Antowain Smith EX/MM/MU/S 7.50 20.00
71 L.C. Stevens/D/EX/MM/S 5.00 12.00
72 Michael Strahan EX/MM/MU/S 25.00 50.00
73 Tai Streets/D/EX/MM/MU/S 7.50 20.00
74 Fred Taylor MM 12.50 30.00
75 Lamar Thomas EX/MM 5.00 12.00
76 Jerame Tuman/D/EX/MM/S 12.50 30.00
77 Kevin Turner D/EX/MM/MU/S 5.00 12.00
78 Kurt Warner MM 50.00 100.00
79 Tyrone Wheatley D/EX/MM/MU/S 7.50 20.00
80 Ricky Williams/D/EX/MM/S 12.50 30.00
81 Frank Wycheck D/EX/MM/MU/S 5.00 12.00
82 Amos Zereoue/EX/MM/MU/S 7.50 20.00
CL1 Dominion CL .02 .10
CL2 E-X Century CL .02 .10
CL3 Metal Universe CL .02 .10
CL4 Premium CL .02 .10

1999 SkyBox Premium Box Tops

COMPLETE SET (15) 20.00 40.00
STATED ODDS 1:12
1BT Terrell Davis .75 2.00
2BT Troy Aikman 1.50 4.00
3BT Peyton Manning 2.50 6.00
4BT Mark Brunell .75 2.00
5BT Eddie George .75 2.00
6BT Corey Dillon .75 2.00
7BT Dan Marino 2.50 6.00
8BT Brett Favre 2.50 6.00
9BT Barry Sanders 2.50 6.00
10BT Emmitt Smith 1.50 4.00
11BT Fred Taylor .75 2.00
12BT Jerry Rice 1.50 4.00
13BT Jamal Anderson .75 2.00
14BT Joey Galloway .50 1.25
15BT Randy Moss 2.00 5.00

1999 SkyBox Premium DejaVu

COMPLETE SET (15) 25.00 50.00
STATED ODDS 1:36
*DIE CUTS: 2X TO 5X BASIC INSERTS
DIE CUTS PRINT RUN 99 SER.#'d SETS
1DV Akili Smith / Barry Sanders 3.00 8.00
2DV Cade McNown / Warrick Dunn .75 2.00
3DV Cecil Collins / Jerris McPhail .60 1.50
4DV Champ Bailey / Curtis Conway .75 2.00
5DV Daunte Culpepper / Michael Irvin 2.00 5.00
6DV David Boston / Tim Biakabutuka .75 2.00
7DV Donovan McNabb / Marshall Faulk 2.50 6.00
8DV Edgerrin James / Michael Westbrook 2.00 5.00
9DV Kevin Faulk / Joey Kent .75 2.00
10DV Kevin Johnson / Jerome Pathon .75 2.00
11DV Ricky Williams / Deion Sanders 1.00 2.50
12DV Shaun King / Germane Crowell .60 1.50
13DV Tim Couch / Troy Aikman 3.00 8.00
14DV Torry Holt / Tim Brown 1.50 4.00
15DV Troy Edwards / Eric Metcalf .60 1.50

1999 SkyBox Premium Genuine Coverage

COMPLETE SET (6) 75.00 150.00
*MULTI-COLORED SWATCHES: .6X TO 1.5X
1GC Mark Brunell/420 10.00 25.00
2GC Randy Moss/265 15.00 40.00
3GC Herman Moore/400 7.50 20.00
4GC Brett Favre/410 20.00 50.00
5GC R.Cunningham/425 7.50 20.00
6GC Drew Bledsoe/440 12.50 30.00

1999 SkyBox Premium Prime Time Rookies

COMPLETE SET (15) 75.00 150.00
STATED ODDS 1:96
1PR Ricky Williams 4.00 10.00
2PR Tim Couch 2.00 5.00
3PR Edgerrin James 8.00 20.00
4PR Daunte Culpepper 8.00 20.00
5PR David Boston 2.00 5.00
6PR Akili Smith .75 2.00
7PR Cecil Collins .75 2.00
8PR Cade McNown 1.25 3.00
9PR Torry Holt 5.00 12.00
10PR Donovan McNabb 10.00 25.00
11PR Kevin Johnson .75 2.00
12PR Shaun King .75 2.00
13PR Champ Bailey 2.50 6.00
14PR Troy Edwards 1.25 3.00
15PR Kevin Faulk 1.25 3.00

1999 SkyBox Premium Prime Time Rookies Autographs

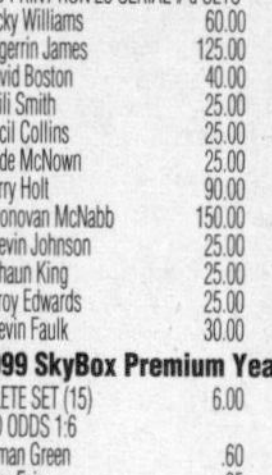

STATED PRINT RUN 25 SERIAL #'d SETS
1PR Ricky Williams 60.00 150.00
3PR Edgerrin James 125.00 250.00
5PR David Boston 40.00 100.00
6PR Akili Smith 25.00 60.00
7PR Cecil Collins 25.00 60.00
8PR Cade McNown 25.00 60.00
9PR Torry Holt 90.00 150.00
10PR Donovan McNabb 150.00 300.00
11PR Kevin Johnson 25.00 60.00
12PR Shaun King 25.00 60.00
14PR Troy Edwards 25.00 60.00
15PR Kevin Faulk 30.00 80.00

1999 SkyBox Premium Year 2

COMPLETE SET (15) 6.00 15.00
STATED ODDS 1:6
1Y2 Ahman Green .60 1.50
2Y2 Terry Fair .25 .60
3Y2 Charlie Batch .60 1.50
4Y2 Ryan Leaf .60 1.50
5Y2 Skip Hicks .25 .60
6Y2 John Avery .25 .60
7Y2 Charles Woodson .60 1.50
8Y2 Jacquez Green .25 .60
9Y2 Kevin Dyson .40 1.00
10Y2 Marcus Nash .40 1.00
11Y2 Robert Holcombe .25 .60
12Y2 Germane Crowell .25 .60
13Y2 Curtis Enis .25 .60
14Y2 Tim Dwight .60 1.50
15Y2 Brian Griese .60 1.50

1992 SkyBox Prime Time Previews

This five-card standard-size set was issued in cello packs to provide collectors with samples of SkyBox's Prime Time series. The fronts feature cut-out action color player photos superimposed on a computer generated gray background accented with a row of thin black lines. The player's name is printed across the top. The player's jersey number is team color-coded while his team name is printed vertically in a team color-coded bar along the edge of the card. For example, the Elway card has a Broncos "purple" background featuring the picture of a horse. The backs display action color player photos on the upper half of the card. Biographical information, statistics, and career highlights appear below a team color-coded stripe on a white background. Except for the title card, the cards are numbered on the back at the upper right corner.

COMPLETE SET (5) 4.00 10.00
A Jerry Rice 1.20 3.00
B Deion Sanders .60 1.50
C John Elway 2.40 6.00
D Vaughn Dunbar .20 .50
NNO Title Card (Advertisement) .20 .50

1992 SkyBox Prime Time

The 1992 SkyBox Prime Time football set consists of 360 standard-size cards. The cards were issued in 12-card packs. . The player's jersey number is team color-coded while his team name is printed vertically in a team color-coded bar along the edge of the card. The cards of rookies, including many in their NFL uniforms, have the round and the draft pick number on their fronts. The backs display action color player photos on the upper half of the card. Team MVP's (four of them without player photos) and Costacos Poster Art cards (PC) are scattered throughout the set. There are five uncorrected errors involving misnumbered cards: see card numbers 38, 61, 138, 216, and 267. Rookie Cards include Edgar Bennett, Robert Brooks, Terrell Buckley, Robert Brooks, Dale Carter, Marco Coleman, Quentin Coryatt, Steve Emtman and Carl Pickens. Randomly inserted in packs and listed at the end of the checklist below are a Jim Kelly hologram card (H1) and a Steve Emtman Horse-Power card (S1).

COMPLETE SET (360) 10.00 25.00
1 Deion Sanders .40 1.00
2 Shane Collins RC UER (Photo actually Terry Smith; see also number 216) .02 .10
3 James Patton RC .02 .10
4 Reggie Roby .02 .10
5 Merril Hoge .02 .10
6 Vinny Testaverde .07 .20
7 Boomer Esiason .07 .20
8 Troy Aikman .75 2.00
9 Tommy Jeter RC .02 .10
10 Brent Williams .02 .10
11 Mark Rypien .02 .10
12 Jim Kelly .15 .40
13 Dan Marino 1.25 3.00
14 Bill Cowher CO RC .30 .75
15 Leslie O'Neal .07 .20
16 Joe Montana 1.25 3.00
17 William Fuller .02 .10
18 Paul Gruber .02 .10
19 Bernie Kosar .07 .20
20 Rickey Jackson .02 .10
21 Earnest Byner .02 .10
22 Emmitt Smith 1.50 4.00
23 Neal Anderson PC .02 .10
24 Greg Lloyd .07 .20
25 Ronnie Harmon .02 .10
26 Ray Donaldson .02 .10
27 Kevin Ross .02 .10
28 Irving Fryar .07 .20
29 John L. Williams .02 .10
30 Chris Hinton .02 .10
31 Tracy Scroggins RC .02 .10
32 Rohn Stark .02 .10
33 David Fulcher .02 .10
34 Thurman Thomas .15 .40
35 Christian Okoye .02 .10
36 Vaughn Dunbar RC .02 .10
37 Joel Steed RC .02 .10
38 James Francis UER (card number on back is actually 354) .02 .10
39 Dermontti Dawson .02 .10
40 Mark Higgs .02 .10
41 Flipper Anderson UER/5,301 receiving yards in 1991 .02 .10
42 Ronnie Lott .07 .20
43 Jim Everett .07 .20
44 Burt Grossman .02 .10
45 Charles Haley .07 .20
46 Ricky Proehl .02 .10
47 Marquez Pope RC .02 .10
48 David Treadwell .02 .10
49 William White .02 .10
50 John Elway 1.25 3.00
51 Mark Carrier WR .07 .20
52 Brian Blades .07 .20
53 Keith McKeller .02 .10
54 Art Monk .07 .20
55 Lamar Lathon .02 .10
56 Pat Swilling .02 .10
57 Steve Broussard .02 .10
58 Derrick Thomas .15 .40
59 Keith Jackson .07 .20
60 Leonard Marshall .02 .10
61 Eric Metcalf UER (card number on back is actually 350) .15 .40
62 Andy Heck .02 .10
63 Mark Carrier DB .02 .10
64 Neil O'Donnell .07 .20
65 Broderick Thomas MVP .02 .10
66 Eric Kramer .07 .20
67 Joe Montana PC .60 1.50
68 Robert Delpino MVP .02 .10
69 Steve Israel RC .02 .10
70 Herman Moore .15 .40
71 Jacob Green .02 .10
72 Lorenzo White .02 .10
73 Nick Lowery .02 .10
74 Eugene Robinson .02 .10
75 Carl Banks .02 .10
76 Bruce Smith .15 .40
77 Mark Rypien MVP .02 .10
78 Anthony Munoz .07 .20
79 Clayton Holmes RC .02 .10
80 Jerry Rice .75 2.00
81 Henry Ellard .07 .20
82 Tim McGee .02 .10
83 Al Toon .07 .20
84 Haywood Jeffires .07 .20
85 Mike Singletary .07 .20
86 Thurman Thomas PC .07 .20
87 Jessie Hester .02 .10
88 Michael Irvin .15 .40
89 Jack Del Rio .02 .10
90 Eagles MVP Seth Joyner listed .02 .10
91 Jeff Herrod .02 .10
92 Michael Dean Perry .07 .20
93 Louis Oliver .02 .10
94 Dan McGwire .02 .10
95 Cris Carter MVP .07 .20
96 Dale Carter RC .07 .20
97 Cornelius Bennett .07 .20
98 Edgar Bennett RC .15 .40
99 Steve Young .60 1.50
100 Warren Moon .15 .40
101 Deion Sanders MVP .25 .60
102 Mel Gray .07 .20
103 Mark Murphy .02 .10
104 Jeff George .15 .40
105 Anthony Miller .07 .20
106 Tom Rathman .02 .10
107 Fred McAfee RC .02 .10
108 Paul Siever RC .02 .10
109 Lemuel Stinson .02 .10
110 Vance Johnson .02 .10
111 Jay Schroeder .02 .10
112 Calvin Williams .07 .20
113 Cortez Kennedy .07 .20
114 Quentin Coryatt RC .02 .10
115 Ronnie Lippett .02 .10
116 Brad Baxter .02 .10
117 Bubba McDowell .02 .10
118 Cris Carter .40 1.00
119 John Stephens .02 .10
120 James Hasty .02 .10
121 Bubby Brister .02 .10
122 Robert Jones RC .02 .10
123 Sterling Sharpe .15 .40
124 Jason Hanson RC .07 .20
125 Sam Mills .02 .10
126 Ernie Jones .02 .10
127 Chester McGlockton RC .07 .20
128 Troy Vincent RC .02 .10
129 Chuck Smith RC .02 .10
130 Tim McKyer .02 .10
131 Tom Newberry .02 .10
132 Leonard Wheeler RC .02 .10
133 Patrick Rowe RC .02 .10
134 Eric Swann .07 .20
135 Jeremy Lincoln RC .02 .10
136 Brian Noble .02 .10
137 Allen Pinkett .02 .10
138 Carl Pickens RC UER (card number on back is actually 358) .15 .40
139 Eric Green .02 .10
140 Louis Lipps .02 .10
141 Chris Singleton .02 .10
142 Gary Clark .15 .40
143 Tim Green .02 .10
144 Dennis Green CO RC .07 .20
145 Gary Anderson K .02 .10
146 Mark Clayton .07 .20
147 Kelvin Martin .02 .10
148 Mike Holmgren CO RC .15 .40
149 Gaston Green .02 .10
150 Terrell Buckley RC .02 .10
151 Robert Brooks RC .50 1.25
152 Anthony Smith .02 .10
153 Jay Novacek .07 .20
154 Webster Slaughter .02 .10
155 John Roper .02 .10
156 Steve Emtman RC .02 .10
157 Tony Sacca RC .02 .10
158 Ray Crockett .02 .10
159 Jerry Rice MVP .40 1.00
160 Alonzo Spellman RC .07 .20
161 Deion Sanders PC .25 .60
162 Robert Clark .02 .10
163 Mark Ingram .02 .10
164 Ricardo McDonald RC .02 .10
165 Emmitt Smith PC .75 2.00
166 Tommy Maddox RC 1.25 3.00
167 Tom Myslinski RC .02 .10
168 Packers MVP Tony Bennett listed .02 .10
169 Ernest Givins .07 .20
170 Eugene Robinson MVP .02 .10
171 Roger Craig .07 .20
172 Irving Fryar MVP .02 .10
173 Jeff Herrod MVP .02 .10
174 Chris Mims RC .02 .10
175 Bart Oates .02 .10
176 Michael Irvin MVP .15 .40
177 Lawrence Dawsey .07 .20
178 Warren Moon MVP .07 .20
179 Timm Rosenbach .02 .10
180 Bobby Ross CO RC .02 .10
181 Chris Burkett MVP .02 .10
182 Tony Brooks RC .02 .10
183 Clarence Verdin .02 .10
184 Bernie Kosar PC .02 .10
185 Eric Martin .02 .10
186 Jeff Bryant .02 .10
187 Carnell Lake .02 .10
188 Darren Woodson RC .15 .40
189 Dwayne Harper .02 .10
190 Bernie Kosar MVP .02 .10
191 Keith Sims .02 .10
192 Rich Gannon .15 .40
193 Broderick Thomas .02 .10
194 Michael Young .02 .10
195 Cris Dishman .02 .10
196 Wes Hopkins .02 .10
197 Christian Okoye PC .02 .10
198 David Little .02 .10
199 Chris Crooms RC .02 .10
200 Lawrence Taylor .15 .40
201 Marc Boutte RC .02 .10
202 Mark Carrier DB PC .02 .10
203 Keith McCants .02 .10
204 Dwayne Sabb RC .02 .10
205 Brian Mitchell .07 .20
206 Keith Byars .02 .10
207 Jeff Hostetler .07 .20
208 Percy Snow .02 .10
209 Lawrence Taylor MVP .07 .20
210 Troy Auzenne RC .02 .10
211 Warren Moon PC .07 .20
212 Mike Pritchard .07 .20
213 Eric Dickerson .07 .20
214 Harvey Williams .15 .40
215 Phil Simms UER (Misspelled Sims on card front) .07 .20
216 Sean Lumpkin RC UER (Card number on back is actually 002) .02 .10
217 Marco Coleman RC .02 .10
218 Phillippi Sparks RC .02 .10
219 Gerald Dixon RC .02 .10
220 Steve Walsh .02 .10
221 Russell Maryland .02 .10
222 Eddie Anderson .02 .10
223 Shane Dronett RC .02 .10
224 Todd Collins RC .02 .10
225 Leon Searcy RC .02 .10
226 Andre Rison .07 .20
227 James Lofton .07 .20
228 Ken O'Brien .02 .10
229 Mike Tomczak .02 .10
230 Nick Bell .02 .10
231 Ben Smith .02 .10
232 Wendell Davis MVP .02 .10
233 Craig Thompson RC .02 .10
234 Dana Hall RC .02 .10
235 Larry Webster RC .02 .10
236 Jerry Rice PC .40 1.00
237 Rod Bernstine .02 .10
238 David Klingler RC .02 .10
239 Greg Skrepenak RC .02 .10
240 Mark Wheeler RC .02 .10
241 Kevin Smith RC .02 .10
242 Charles Mann .02 .10
243 Lions MVP Barry Sanders listed .02 .10
244 Curtis Whitley RC .02 .10
245 Ronnie Harmon MVP .02 .10
246 Brent Jones .07 .20
247 Robert Harris RC .02 .10
248 Ted Marchibroda CO .02 .10
249 Willie Gault .07 .20
250 Siran Stacy RC .02 .10
251 Dennis Byrd .02 .10
252 Corey Harris RC .02 .10

253 Al Noga .02 .10
254 David Shula CO RC .02 .10
255 Rob Moore .07 .20
256 Marv Cook .02 .10
257 John Elway MVP .60 1.50
258 Harold Green .02 .10
259 Tom Flores CO .02 .10
260 Andre Reed .07 .20
261 Anthony Thompson .02 .10
262 Issiac Holt .02 .10
263 Mike Evans RC .02 .10
264 Jimmy Smith RC 2.00 5.00
265 Anthony Carter .07 .20
266 Ashley Ambrose RC .15 .40
267 John Fina RC .02 .10
(card number on back
is actually 357)
268 Sean Gilbert RC .07 .20
269 Ken Norton Jr. .07 .20
270 Barry Word .02 .10
271 Pat Swilling MVP .02 .10
272 Dan Marino PC .60 1.50
273 David Fulcher MVP .02 .10
274 William Perry .07 .20
275 Ed West .02 .10
276 Gene Atkins .02 .10
277 Neal Anderson .02 .10
278 Dino Hackett .02 .10
279 Greg Townsend .02 .10
280 Andre Tippett .02 .10
281 Darryl Williams RC .02 .10
282 Kurt Barber RC .02 .10
283 Pat Terrell .02 .10
284 Derrick Thomas PC .07 .20
285 Eddie Robinson RC .02 .10
286 Howie Long .15 .40
287 Cardinals MVP .02 .10
Tim McDonald listed
288 Thurman Thomas MVP .07 .20
289 Wendell Davis .02 .10
290 Jeff Cross .02 .10
291 Duane Bickett .02 .10
292 Tony Smith RC .02 .10
293 Jerry Ball .02 .10
294 Jessie Tuggle .02 .10
295 Chris Burkett .02 .10
296 Eugene Chung RC .02 .10
297 Chris Miller .07 .20
298 Albert Bentley .02 .10
299 Richard Johnson .02 .10
300 Randall Cunningham .15 .40
301 Courtney Hawkins RC .07 .20
302 Ray Childress .02 .10
303 Rodney Peete .07 .20
304 Kevin Fagan .02 .10
305 Ronnie Lott MVP .02 .10
306 Michael Carter .02 .10
307 Derrick Thomas MVP .07 .20
308 Jarvis Williams .02 .10
309 Greg Lloyd MVP .07 .20
310 Ethan Horton .02 .10
311 Ricky Ervins .02 .10
312 Bennie Blades .02 .10
313 Troy Aikman PC .40 1.00
314 Bruce Armstrong .02 .10
315 Leroy Hoard .07 .20
316 Gary Anderson RB .02 .10
317 Steve McMichael .07 .20
318 Junior Seau .15 .40
319 Mark Thomas RC .02 .10
320 Fred Barnett .15 .40
321 Mike Merriweather .02 .10
322 Keith Willis .02 .10
323 Brett Perriman .15 .40
324 Michael Haynes .07 .20
325 Jim Harbaugh .15 .40
326 Sammie Smith .02 .10
327 Robert Delpino .02 .10
328 Tony Mandarich .02 .10
329 Mark Bortz .02 .10
330 Ray Etheridge RC UER .02 .10
(Name misspelled Ethridge)
331 Jarvis Williams PC .02 .10
Louis Oliver
332 Dan Marino MVP .60 1.50
333 Dwight Stone .02 .10
334 Billy Ray Smith .02 .10
335 Darion Conner .02 .10
336 Howard Dinkins RC .02 .10
337 Robert Porcher RC .15 .40
338 Chris Doleman .02 .10
339 Alvin Harper .07 .20
340 John Taylor .07 .20
341 Ray Agnew .02 .10
342 Jon Vaughn .02 .10
343 James Brown RC .02 .10
344 Michael Irvin PC .15 .40
345 Neil Smith .15 .40
346 Vaughan Johnson .02 .10
347 Checklist .02 .10
348 Checklist .02 .10
349 Checklist .02 .10
350 Checklist .02 .10
(See also number 61)
351 Checklist .02 .10
352 Checklist .02 .10
353 Checklist .02 .10
354 Checklist .02 .10
(See also number 38)
355 Checklist .02 .10
356 Checklist .02 .10
357 Checklist .02 .10
(See also number 267)
358 Checklist .02 .10
(See also number 138)
359 Checklist .02 .10
360 Checklist .02 .10
H1 Jim Kelly 1.00 2.50
(Flip Hologram)
S1 Steve Emtman .30 .75
Poster Card
(Horse Power)

1992 SkyBox Prime Time Poster Cards

COMPLETE SET (16) 12.00 30.00
RANDOM INSERTS IN FOIL PACKS
M1 Bernie Kosar .15 .40
Air Raid 19
M2 Mark Carrier DB .07 .20
Monster of the Midway
M3 Neal Anderson .07 .20
The Bear Necessity
M4 Thurman Thomas .30 .75
Thurmanator
M5 Deion Sanders .75 2.00
PrimeTime
M6 Joe Montana 2.50 6.00
Sweet Sixteen
M7 Jerry Rice 1.50 4.00
Speed of Light
M8 Jarvis Williams .07 .20
Louis Oliver
B2 Bombers
M9 Dan Marino 2.50 6.00
Armed and Dangerous
M10 Derrick Thomas .30 .75
Sacred Ground
M11 Christian Okoye .07 .20
Nigerian Nightmare
M12 Warren Moon .30 .75
Moonlighting
M13 Michael Irvin .30 .75
Playmaker
M14 Troy Aikman 1.50 4.00
Strong Arm of the Law
M15 Emmitt Smith 3.00 8.00
Catch 22
M16 Checklist .07 .20

1996 SkyBox SkyMotion

The 1996 Skybox SkyMotion is a hobby only set issued in one series totalling 60 cards. The two-card packs retail for $4.99 each. The fronts feature color player motion-photos on paper stock with 3.5 seconds of game action. The four-color backs carry action photos plus career statistics and player biographical information.

COMPLETE SET (60) 15.00 40.00
1 Troy Aikman .75 2.00
2 Marcus Allen .30 .75
3 Jeff Blake .30 .75
4 Drew Bledsoe .50 1.25
5 Tim Brown .30 .75
6 Isaac Bruce .30 .75
7 Mark Brunell .50 1.25
8 Cris Carter .30 .75
9 Ben Coates .15 .40
10 Kerry Collins .30 .75
11 Curtis Conway .30 .75
12 Terrell Davis .60 1.50
13 Trent Dilfer .30 .75
14 Hugh Douglas .15 .40
15 John Elway 1.50 4.00
16 Marshall Faulk .40 1.00
17 Brett Favre 1.50 4.00
18 William Floyd .07 .20
19 Joey Galloway .30 .75
20 Jeff George .15 .40
21 Rodney Hampton .15 .40
22 Jim Harbaugh .15 .40
23 Aaron Hayden RC .07 .20
24 Jeff Hostetler .07 .20
25 Tyrone Hughes .07 .20
26 Michael Irvin .30 .75
27 Daryl Johnston .15 .40
28 Jim Kelly .30 .75
29 Greg Lloyd .15 .40
30 Dan Marino 1.50 4.00
31 Curtis Martin .60 1.50
32 Chester McGlockton .07 .20
33 Steve McNair .60 1.50
34 Eric Metcalf .07 .20
35 Scott Mitchell .15 .40
36 Herman Moore .15 .40
37 Bryce Paup .07 .20
38 Carl Pickens .15 .40
39 Errict Rhett .15 .40
40 Jerry Rice .75 2.00
41 Rashaan Salaam .15 .40
42 Barry Sanders 1.25 3.00
43 Chris Sanders .15 .40
44 Deion Sanders .50 1.25
45 Junior Seau .30 .75
46 Heath Shuler .15 .40
47 Bruce Smith .15 .40
48 Emmitt Smith 1.25 3.00
49 Kordell Stewart .30 .75
50 Eric Swann .07 .20
51 Derrick Thomas .30 .75
52 Thurman Thomas .30 .75
53 Eric Turner .07 .20
54 Tamarick Vanover .15 .40
55 Chris Warren .15 .40
56 Ricky Watters .15 .40
57 Michael Westbrook .30 .75
58 Reggie White .30 .75
59 Rod Woodson .15 .40
60 Steve Young .60 1.50
P1 Trent Dilfer Promo .40 1.00
Advertisement back
unnumbered
SM1 Trent Dilfer Promo .40 1.00
Standard card back

1996 SkyBox SkyMotion Gold

COMPLETE SET (60) 200.00 400.00
*GOLDS: 2.5X TO 6X BASIC CARDS
STATED ODDS 1:2 BOXES

1996 SkyBox SkyMotion Big Bang

COMPLETE SET (10) 12.50 30.00
STATED ODDS 1:9
1 Tim Biakabutuka 1.00 2.50
2 Rickey Dudley 1.00 2.50
3 Eddie George 4.00 10.00
4 Terry Glenn 2.50 6.00
5 Kevin Hardy .60 1.50
6 Marvin Harrison 6.00 15.00
7 Keyshawn Johnson 2.00 5.00
8 Leeland McElroy .60 1.50
9 Lawrence Phillips UER .60 1.50
name misspelled Philiips
10 Simeon Rice 1.25 3.00

1996 SkyBox SkyMotion Team Galaxy

COMPLETE SET (5) 12.50 30.00
STATED ODDS 1:35
1 Karim Abdul-Jabbar 1.50 4.00
2 Brett Favre 8.00 20.00
3 Curtis Martin 2.50 6.00
4 Jerry Rice 4.00 10.00
5 Emmitt Smith 5.00 12.00

1998 SkyBox Thunder

The 1998 SkyBox Thunder set was issued in one series totalling 250 cards. The fronts feature color player photos. The backs carry player information. The base set was broken down into three tiers: 1-100 (3-4 perpack), 101-200 (3 per pack), and 201-250 (1 per pack).

COMPLETE SET (250) 25.00 50.00
1 Reggie White .20 .50
2 Elvis Grbac .10 .30
3 Ed McCaffrey .10 .30
4 O.J. McDuffie .10 .30
5 Scott Mitchell .10 .30
6 Byron Hanspard .07 .20
7 John Randle .10 .30
8 Shawn Jefferson .07 .20
9 Peter Boulware .07 .20
10 Karl Williams .07 .20
11 Napoleon Kaufman .20 .50
UER front Napolean
12 Barry Minter .07 .20
13 Cris Dishman .07 .20
14 James Stewart .10 .30
15 Marcus Robertson .07 .20
16 Rodney Harrison .10 .30
17 Michael Barrow .07 .20
UER front Micheal
18 Michael Sinclair .07 .20
19 Dewayne Washington .07 .20
20 Phillippi Sparks .07 .20
21 Ernie Conwell .07 .20
22 Ken Dilger .07 .20
23 Johnnie Morton .10 .30
24 Eric Swann .07 .20
25 Curtis Conway .10 .30
26 Duce Staley .30 .75
27 Darrell Green .10 .30
28 Quinn Early .07 .20
29 LeRoy Butler .07 .20
30 Winfred Tubbs .07 .20
31 Darren Woodson .07 .20
32 Marcus Allen .20 .50
33 Glenn Foley .10 .30
34 Tom Knight .07 .20
35 Sam Shade .07 .20
36 James McKnight .20 .50
37 Leeland McElroy .07 .20
38 Earl Holmes RC .25 .60
39 Ryan McNeil .07 .20
40 Cris Carter .20 .50
41 Jessie Armstead .07 .20
42 Bryce Paup .07 .20
43 Chris Slade .07 .20
44 Eric Metcalf .07 .20
45 Jim Harbaugh .10 .30
46 Terry Kirby .07 .20
47 Donnie Edwards .07 .20
48 Darryl Williams .07 .20
49 Neil Smith .10 .30
50 Warren Sapp .10 .30
51 Jason Taylor .10 .30
52 Irving Fryar .10 .30
53 Jeff George .10 .30
54 Yancey Thigpen .07 .20
55 Ricky Proehl .07 .20
56 Kevin Greene .10 .30
57 Joel Steed .07 .20
58 Larry Allen .07 .20
59 Thurman Thomas .20 .50
60 Aaron Glenn .07 .20
61 Natrone Means .10 .30
62 Chris Calloway .07 .20
63 Chuck Smith .07 .20
64 Chidi Ahanotu .07 .20
65 Mario Bates .10 .30
66 Jonathan Ogden .07 .20
67 Drew Bledsoe CL .20 .50
68 John Mobley CL .07 .20
69 Antowain Smith CL .10 .30
70 Aeneas Williams .07 .20
71 Brian Williams .07 .20
72 Derrick Thomas .20 .50
73 Ted Johnson .07 .20
74 Troy Drayton .07 .20
75 Mike Pritchard .07 .20
76 Darnay Scott .10 .30
77 James Jett .10 .30
78 Dwayne Rudd .07 .20
79 Marvin Harrison .20 .50
80 Dermontti Dawson .07 .20
81 Keith Lyle .07 .20
82 Steve Atwater .07 .20
83 Tyrone Wheatley .10 .30
84 Tony Brackens .07 .20
85 Dale Carter .07 .20
86 Robert Porcher .07 .20
87 Merton Hanks .07 .20
88 Leon Johnson .07 .20
89 Simeon Rice .10 .30
90 Robert Brooks .10 .30
91 William Thomas .07 .20
92 Wesley Walls .10 .30
93 Chester McGlockton .07 .20
94 Chris Chandler .10 .30
95 Michael Strahan .10 .30
96 Ray Zellars .07 .20
97 Dexter Coakley .07 .20
98 Rob Johnson .10 .30
99 Eric Green .07 .20
100 Darrien Gordon .07 .20
101 Gary Brown .07 .20
102 Reidel Anthony .10 .30
103 Keenan McCardell .10 .30
104 Leslie O'Neal .07 .20
105 Bryant Westbrook .07 .20
106 Derrick Alexander .10 .30
107 Jeff Blake .10 .30
108 Ben Coates .10 .30
109 Shawn Springs .07 .20
110 Robert Smith .20 .50
111 Karim Abdul-Jabbar .20 .50
112 Willie Davis .07 .20
113 Mark Chmura .10 .30
114 Terry Allen .20 .50
115 Will Blackwell .07 .20
116 Jamal Anderson .20 .50
117 Dana Stubblefield .07 .20
118 Trent Dilfer .20 .50
119 Jermaine Lewis .10 .30
120 Chad Brown .07 .20
121 Tamarick Vanover .07 .20
122 Tony Martin .10 .30
123 Larry Centers .07 .20
124 J.J. Stokes .10 .30
125 Danny Kanell .10 .30
126 Wayne Chrebet .20 .50
127 Kerry Collins .10 .30
128 Tony Banks .10 .30
129 Randal Hill .07 .20
130 Jimmy Smith .10 .30
131 Tim Brown .20 .50
132 Zach Thomas .20 .50
133 Rod Smith .10 .30
134 Frank Wycheck .07 .20
135 Garrison Hearst .20 .50
136 Bruce Smith .10 .30
137 Hardy Nickerson .07 .20
138 Sean Dawkins .07 .20
139 Willie McGinest .07 .20
140 Kimble Anders .10 .30
141 Michael Westbrook .10 .30
142 Chris Doleman .07 .20
143 Ricky Watters .10 .30
144 Levon Kirkland .07 .20
145 Rob Moore .10 .30
146 Eddie Kennison .10 .30
147 Rickey Dudley .07 .20
148 Jay Graham .07 .20
149 Brad Johnson .20 .50
150 Bobby Hoying .10 .30
151 Sherman Williams .07 .20
152 Charles Way .07 .20
153 Adrian Murrell .10 .30
154 Chris Sanders .07 .20
155 Greg Hill .07 .20
156 Rae Carruth .07 .20
157 Mike Alstott .20 .50
158 Terance Mathis .10 .30
159 Antonio Freeman .20 .50
160 Junior Seau .20 .50
161 Chris Warren .10 .30
162 Shannon Sharpe .10 .30
163 Derrick Rodgers .07 .20
164 Charles Johnson .07 .20
165 Marshall Faulk .25 .60
166 Jamie Asher .07 .20
167 Michael Jackson .07 .20
168 Terrell Owens .20 .50
169 Jason Sehorn .10 .30
170 Raymont Harris .07 .20
171 Jake Reed .10 .30
172 Kevin Hardy .07 .20
173 Jerald Moore .07 .20
174 Michael Irvin .20 .50
175 Freddie Jones .07 .20
176 Steve McNair .20 .50
177 Carnell Lake .07 .20
178 Troy Brown .10 .30
179 Hugh Douglas .07 .20
180 Andre Rison .10 .30
181 Leslie Shepherd .07 .20
182 Andre Hastings .07 .20
183 Fred Lane .07 .20
184 Andre Reed .10 .30
185 Darrell Russell .07 .20
186 Frank Sanders .10 .30
187 Derrick Brooks .20 .50
188 Charlie Garner .10 .30
189 Bert Emanuel .10 .30
190 Terrell Buckley .07 .20
191 Carl Pickens .10 .30
192 Tiki Barber .20 .50
193 Pete Mitchell .07 .20
194 Gilbert Brown .07 .20
195 Isaac Bruce .20 .50
196 Ray Lewis .20 .50
197 Warren Moon .20 .50
198 Tony Gonzalez .20 .50
199 John Mobley .07 .20
200 Gus Frerotte .07 .20
201 Brett Favre 1.50 3.00
202 Terrell Davis .20 .50
203 Dan Marino 1.50 3.00
204 Barry Sanders 1.00 2.50
205 Steve Young .30 .75
206 Deion Sanders .25 .60
207 Kordell Stewart .25 .60
208 Eddie George .20 .50
209 Jake Plummer .20 .50
210 Warrick Dunn .25 .60
211 John Elway 1.50 3.00
212 Terry Glenn .25 .60
213 Mark Brunell .20 .50
214 Corey Dillon .20 .50
215 Joey Galloway .25 .60
216 Dorsey Levens .25 .60
217 Troy Aikman .60 1.50
218 Keyshawn Johnson .25 .60
219 Jerome Bettis .25 .60
220 Curtis Martin .25 .60
221 Herman Moore .25 .60
222 Emmitt Smith 1.00 2.50
223 Jerry Rice .60 1.50
224 Drew Bledsoe .50 1.25
225 Antowain Smith .25 .60
226 Stephen Alexander RC .50 1.25
227 John Avery RC .25 .60
228 Kevin Dyson RC .75 2.00
229 Robert Edwards RC .25 .60
230 Greg Ellis RC .40 1.00
231 Curtis Enis RC .25 .60
232 C.Fuamatu-Ma'afala RC .50 1.25
233 Ahman Green RC 2.00 5.00
234 Jacquez Green RC .50 1.25
235 Az-Zahir Hakim RC .75 2.00
236 Skip Hicks RC .50 1.25
237 Joe Jurevicius RC .25 .60
238 Ryan Leaf RC .75 2.00
239 Peyton Manning RC 10.00 20.00
240 Alonzo Mayes RC .40 1.00
241 R.W. McQuarters RC .50 1.25
242 Randy Moss RC 5.00 12.00
243 Marcus Nash RC .40 1.00
244 Jerome Pathon RC .75 2.00
245 Jason Peter RC .40 1.00
246 Brian Simmons RC .50 1.25
247 Takeo Spikes RC .75 2.00
248 Fred Taylor RC 1.25 3.00
249 Andre Wadsworth RC .50 1.25
250 Charles Woodson RC 1.00 2.50
P162 Shannon Sharpe Promo .30 .75

1998 SkyBox Thunder Rave

*1-200 VETS: 30X TO 60X BASE CARDS
*201-225 VETS: 20X TO 40X BASIC CARDS
*226-250 ROOKIES: 3X TO 8X
STATED PRINT RUN 150 SER.#'d SETS

1998 SkyBox Thunder Super Rave

*1-200 STARS: 40X TO 100X BASIC CARDS
*201-225 STARS: 30X TO 80X BASIC CARDS
STATED PRINT RUN 25 SER.#'d SETS
*226-250 ROOKIES: 10X TO 25X BASIC CARDS

1998 SkyBox Thunder Boss

COMPLETE SET (20) 15.00 30.00
STATED ODDS 1:8
1B Troy Aikman 2.50 6.00
2B Drew Bledsoe 2.00 5.00
3B Tim Brown .75 2.00
4B Antonio Freeman .75 2.00
5B Joey Galloway 1.00 2.50
6B Terry Glenn 1.00 2.50
7B Bobby Hoying .50 1.25
8B Michael Irvin .75 2.00
9B Keyshawn Johnson 1.00 2.50
10B Dorsey Levens 1.00 2.50
11B Curtis Martin 1.00 2.50
12B John Mobley .30 .75
13B Jake Plummer .75 2.00
14B John Randle .50 1.25
15B Deion Sanders 1.00 2.50
16B Junior Seau .75 2.00
17B Shannon Sharpe .50 1.25
18B Bruce Smith .50 1.25
19B Robert Smith .75 2.00
20B Dana Stubblefield .30 .75

1998 SkyBox Thunder Destination Endzone

COMPLETE SET (15) 125.00 250.00
STATED ODDS 1:96
1DE Jerome Bettis 3.00 8.00
2DE Mark Brunell 3.00 8.00
3DE Terrell Davis 3.00 8.00
4DE Corey Dillon 3.00 8.00
5DE Warrick Dunn 3.00 8.00
6DE John Elway 15.00 40.00
7DE Brett Favre 15.00 40.00
8DE Eddie George 2.00 5.00
9DE Dorsey Levens 1.25 3.00
10DE Curtis Martin 3.00 8.00
11DE Herman Moore 1.25 3.00
12DE Barry Sanders 12.50 30.00
13DE Emmitt Smith 12.50 30.00
14DE Kordell Stewart 2.00 5.00
15DE Steve Young 4.00 10.00

1998 SkyBox Thunder Number Crushers

COMPLETE SET (10) 15.00 35.00
STATED ODDS 1:16
1NC Troy Aikman 2.50 6.00
2NC Jerome Bettis 1.25 3.00
3NC Tim Brown 1.25 3.00
4NC Mark Brunell 1.25 3.00
5NC Dan Marino 5.00 12.00
6NC Herman Moore .50 1.25
7NC Rob Moore .50 1.25
8NC Jerry Rice 2.50 6.00
9NC Shannon Sharpe .75 2.00
10NC Emmitt Smith 4.00 10.00

1998 SkyBox Thunder Quick Strike

COMPLETE SET (12) 125.00 250.00
STATED ODDS 1:300
1QS Terrell Davis 5.00 12.00
2QS John Elway 20.00 60.00
3QS Brett Favre 20.00 50.00
4QS Joey Galloway 3.00 8.00
5QS Eddie George 3.00 8.00
6QS Keyshawn Johnson 3.00 8.00
7QS Dan Marino 20.00 50.00
8QS Jerry Rice 10.00 25.00
9QS Barry Sanders 15.00 40.00
10QS Deion Sanders 5.00 12.00
11QS Kordell Stewart 3.00 8.00
12QS Steve Young 6.00 15.00

1998 SkyBox Thunder StarBurst

COMPLETE SET (10) 30.00 60.00
STATED ODDS 1:32
1SB Tiki Barber 1.25 3.00
2SB Corey Dillon 1.25 3.00
3SB Warrick Dunn 1.25 3.00
4SB Curtis Enis .60 1.50
5SB Ryan Leaf .60 1.50
6SB Peyton Manning 10.00 20.00
7SB Randy Moss 5.00 12.00
8SB Jake Plummer 1.25 3.00
9SB Antowain Smith 1.25 3.00
10SB Charles Woodson 1.25 3.00

1992 Slam Thurman Thomas

This ten-card set showcases Thurman Thomas, the All-Pro Buffalo Bills' running back. The backs combine to present a biography of Thomas' life. The production run was reportedly 25,000 sets, and for every 25 sets ordered, the dealer received a limited edition (only 1,000 were reportedly produced) autograph card. Also a free promo card, numbered "Promo 1" in the upper right corner, was issued with every ten-card set. The fronts feature mostly color action or posed player photos inside a white frame. The card face shades from purple to white and back to purple. The player's name and the card subtitle are gold foil stamped in the bottom border. On a blue background inside a white frame, the backs carry career highlights, statistics, and a special "Slam-O-Meter" feature that summarizes his performance at that level.

COMPLETE SET (11) 4.00 10.00
COMMON THOMAS (1-10) .40 1.00
AU Thurman Thomas AUTO 20.00 50.00

1993 Slam Jerome Bettis

This six-card set is comprised of five numbered cards and one unnumbered promo, and spotlights Jerome Bettis. One card in each sealed factory set was hand autographed by Bettis. A promo card and the four other numbered cards were included with each factory set. Each factory set also came with a certificate of authenticity, which carried the production number out of 5,000 numbered sets produced. The cards measure 2 1/2" by 3 5/8" and feature on their fronts blue-bordered color action shots of Bettis in his Notre Dame uniform. His name and the card's title appear in gold foil within the bottom margin. The words "1st Round Pick" appear in gold foil within the top margin. The blue back is framed by a white line and carries a quote about Bettis from his coach at Notre Dame, Lou Holtz. Below this, each card carries stats and a graph representing Jerome's on-field yearly performance. Aside from the promo card, the cards are numbered on the back.

COMPLETE SET (6) 4.00 10.00
COMPLETE FACT.SET (6) 10.00 25.00
1AU Jerome Bettis AUTO 8.00 20.00
High School
All-American
2AU Jerome Bettis AUTO 8.00 20.00
Freshman Notre Dame
3AU Jerome Bettis AUTO 8.00 20.00
1991 Notre Dame Co-MVP
4AU Jerome Bettis AUTO 8.00 20.00
All-American
5AU Jerome Bettis AUTO 8.00 20.00
10th Pick Overall

1978 Slim Jim

The 1978 Slim Jim football discs were issued on the backs of Slim Jim packages with each package back containing two discs. There were six package colors (flavors): blue (mild), green (pizza), dark green (pepperoni), maroon (salami), orange (bacon), and red (spicy). The large display boxes originally contained 12 small packages and each large box featured one Slim Jim player disc. It is thought that all 70 discs appeared on at least one large box. The complete set consists of 35 connected pairs or 70 individual discs. The individual discs measure approximately 2 3/8" in diameter whereas the complete panel is 3" by 5 3/4". The discs themselves are either yellow, red or brown with black lettering. The same two players are always paired on a particular package. The discs are numbered for convenience in alphabetical order below and prices are for single punched or neatly cut out discs.

COMPLETE SET (70) 200.00 400.00
*UNCUT BOXES: .6X TO 1.5X PAIRS
*LARGE OUTER BOXES: 2X TO 4X
1 Lyle Alzado 3.00 8.00
2 Otis Armstrong 2.50 6.00
3 Jerome Barkum 1.50 4.00
4 Bill Bergey 2.00 5.00
5 Elvin Bethea 3.00 8.00
6 Fred Biletnikoff 6.00 15.00
7 Rocky Bleier 5.00 12.00
8 Willie Buchanon 1.50 4.00
9 Doug Buffone 1.50 4.00
10 Dexter Bussey 1.50 4.00
11 John Cappelletti 3.00 8.00
12 Fred Carr 1.50 4.00
13 Tommy Casanova 1.50 4.00
14 Richard Caster 1.50 4.00
15 Bob Chandler 1.50 4.00
16 Larry Csonka 10.00 20.00
17 Isaac Curtis 2.00 5.00
18 Joe DeLamielleure 3.00 8.00
19 Dan Dierdorf 3.00 8.00
20 Glenn Doughty 1.50 4.00
21 Billy Joe DuPree 2.00 5.00
22 John Dutton 1.50 4.00
23 Glen Edwards 1.50 4.00
24 Leon Gray 1.50 4.00
25 Mel Gray 2.00 5.00
26 Joe Greene 6.00 15.00
27 Jack Gregory 1.50 4.00
28 Steve Grogan 3.00 8.00
29 John Hannah 4.00 10.00
30 Jim Hart 2.50 6.00
31 Tommy Hart 1.50 4.00
32 Ron Howard 1.50 4.00
33 Claude Humphrey 2.00 5.00
34 Wilbur Jackson 1.50 4.00
35 Ron Jaworski 3.00 8.00
36 Ron Jessie 1.50 4.00
37 Billy Johnson 2.00 5.00
38 Charlie Joiner 3.00 8.00
39 Paul Krause 3.00 8.00
40 Larry Little 4.00 10.00
41 Archie Manning 5.00 12.00
42 Ron McDole 1.50 4.00
43 Lydell Mitchell 2.00 5.00
44 Nat Moore 2.00 5.00
45 Robert Newhouse 2.50 6.00
46 Riley Odoms 1.50 4.00
47 Alan Page 4.00 10.00
48 Lemar Parrish 2.00 5.00
49 Walter Payton 30.00 60.00
50 Greg Pruitt 2.00 5.00
51 Ahmad Rashad 4.00 10.00
52 Golden Richards 2.00 5.00
53 John Riggins 6.00 15.00
54 Isiah Robertson 1.50 4.00
55 Charlie Sanders 2.50 6.00
56 Clarence Scott 1.50 4.00
57 Lee Roy Selmon 6.00 15.00
58 Otis Sistrunk 2.50 6.00
59 Darryl Stingley 2.50 6.00
60 Bruce Taylor 1.50 4.00
61 Emmitt Thomas 2.00 5.00
62 Mike Thomas 1.50 4.00
63 Gene Upshaw 3.00 8.00
64 Jeff Van Note 1.50 4.00
65 Brad Van Pelt 1.50 4.00
66 Gene Washington 49ers 2.00 5.00
67 Ted Washington 1.50 4.00
68 Roger Wehrli 2.00 5.00
69 Clarence Williams 1.50 4.00
70 Don Woods 1.50 4.00

1974 Southern California Sun WFL Team Issue 8X10

These photos measure roughly 8" x 10" and include black and white images with the player's name in the lower right below the photo and the team name in the upper left corner above the photo. The backs are blank.

1 Anthony Davis 10.00 20.00
2 Dave Roller 7.50 15.00

1974 Southern California Sun WFL Team Sheets

These team issued sheets feature player photos, measuring roughly 8" x 10" overall, with black and white images of either three or four players. The format varies from eight small photos of four players to a sheet to three larger photos on one sheet. The team name and year are included near the bottom and each player's name is printed below his image.

COMPLETE SET (11) 75.00 125.00
1 Booker Brown 7.50 15.00
Joe Carollo
Jack Conners
Dennis Crane
2 Alonzo Emery 7.50 15.00
Wayne Estabrook
Kevin Fletcher
Kevin Grady
3 Steve Gunther 7.50 15.00
Tim Guy
Ike Harris
John Hoffman DE
4 Gene Howard 7.50 15.00
Clay Jefferies
Eric Johnson DB
Kermit Johnson
5 Jimmie Jones RB 7.50 15.00
Durwood Keeton
Younger Klippert
Ed Kezirian
6 Ken Lee 7.50 15.00
Terry Lindsey
Jacque MacKinnon
Greg Mason
7 Ralph Nelson 7.50 15.00
Jim Bowman
Charles DeJurnett
8 Eric Patton 7.50 15.00
Ed Philpott
Dan Pride
Bill Reid
9 Dave Roller 7.50 15.00
Mike Ryan
Steve Schroder
Ted Seifert
10 Neal Skarin 7.50 15.00
Dave Szymakowski
Ron Thomas WR
Gary Valbuena
11 Cleveland Vann 7.50 15.00
Jim Williams DB
Dave Williams WR

1975 Southern California Sun WFL Team Issue 5X7

These photos were released by the team to fulfill fan requests. Each measures roughly 5" x 7" and includes a black and white image with no player names or writing on the fronts. The backs are blank.

1 Kevin Fletcher 6.00 12.00
2 Jim Jones 6.00 12.00
3 Jim Norton 6.00 12.00
4 Scott Palmer 6.00 12.00
5 Don Parish 6.00 12.00
6 Ron Thomas 6.00 12.00

1975 Southern California Sun WFL Team Issue 8X10

These team issued photos measure roughly 8" x 10" and feature black and white player images with no names or identification on the fronts. The photo backs sometimes contain hand written player identification.

1 Kermit Johnson 7.50 15.00
2 Jimmie Lee Jones 7.50 15.00
3 Younger Klippert 7.50 15.00
4 Daryle Lamonica 10.00 20.00
5 James McAlister 7.50 15.00
6 Bill Reid 7.50 15.00
7 Paul Seiler 7.50 15.00
8 Dave Williams 7.50 15.00

1993 SP

The 270 standard-size cards comprising Upper Deck's SP set were issued in 12-card packs. After a Premier Prospects (1-18) subset, the cards are arranged alphabetically according to and within teams. Rookie Cards include Jerome Bettis, Drew Bledsoe, Reggie Brooks, Mark Brunell, Curtis Conway, Garrison Hearst, Qadry Ismail, O.J. McDuffie, Rick Mirer, Dana Stubblefield and Kevin Williams. A Joe Montana promo card was issued to promote the debut of the set and closely resembles his regular 1993 SP card. The promo card is not marked as such, but its card number

(19) contrasts with Montana's card number (122) in the regular series.

COMPLETE SET (270)	25.00	60.00
1 Curtis Conway RC	1.25	3.00
2 John Copeland RC	.30	.75
3 Kevin Williams RC	.60	1.50
4 Dan Williams RC	.30	.75
5 Patrick Bates RC	.30	.75
6 Jerome Bettis RC	8.00	20.00
7 O.J.McDuffie RC	1.25	3.00
8 Robert Smith RC	2.00	5.00
9 Drew Bledsoe RC	6.00	15.00
10 Irv Smith RC	.30	.75
11 Marvin Jones RC	.30	.75
12 Victor Bailey RC	.30	.75
13 Garrison Hearst RC	2.00	5.00
14 Natrone Means RC	1.25	3.00
15 Todd Kelly RC	.30	.75
16 Rick Mirer RC	1.25	3.00
17 Eric Curry RC	.30	.75
18 Reggie Brooks RC	.60	1.50
19 Eric Dickerson	.20	.50
20 Roger Harper RC	.10	.30
21 Michael Haynes	.20	.50
22 Bobby Hebert	.10	.30
23 Lincoln Kennedy RC	.10	.30
24 Chris Miller	.20	.50
25 Mike Pritchard	.20	.50
26 Andre Rison	.20	.50
27 Deion Sanders	.60	1.50
28 Cornelius Bennett	.20	.50
29 Kenneth Davis	.10	.30
30 Henry Jones	.10	.30
31 Jim Kelly	.40	1.00
32 John Parrella RC	.10	.30
33 Andre Reed	.20	.50
34 Bruce Smith	.40	1.00
35 Thomas Smith RC	.20	.50
36 Thurman Thomas	.40	1.00
37 Neal Anderson	.10	.30
38 Myron Baker RC	.10	.30
39 Mark Carrier DB	.10	.30
40 Richard Dent	.20	.50
41 Chris Gedney RC	.10	.30
42 Jim Harbaugh	.40	1.00
43 Craig Heyward	.20	.50
44 Carl Simpson RC	.10	.30
45 Alonzo Spellman	.10	.30
46 Derrick Fenner	.10	.30
47 Harold Green	.10	.30
48 David Klingler	.10	.30
49 Ricardo McDonald	.10	.30
50 Tony McGee RC	.20	.50
51 Carl Pickens	.20	.50
52 Steve Tovar RC	.10	.30
53 Alfred Williams	.10	.30
54 Darryl Williams	.10	.30
55 Jerry Ball	.10	.30
56 Mike Caldwell RC	.10	.30
57 Mark Carrier WR	.20	.50
58 Steve Everitt RC	.10	.30
59 Dan Footman RC	.10	.30
60 Pepper Johnson	.10	.30
61 Bernie Kosar	.20	.50
62 Eric Metcalf	.20	.50
63 Michael Dean Perry	.20	.50
64 Troy Aikman	1.25	2.50
65 Charles Haley	.20	.50
66 Michael Irvin	.40	1.00
67 Robert Jones	.10	.30
68 Derrick Lassic RC	.10	.30
69 Russell Maryland	.10	.30
70 Ken Norton Jr.	.20	.50
71 Darrin Smith RC	.20	.50
72 Emmitt Smith	2.50	5.00
73 Steve Atwater	.10	.30
74 Rod Bernstine	.10	.30
75 Jason Elam RC	.40	1.00
76 John Elway	2.00	5.00
77 Simon Fletcher	.10	.30
78 Tommy Maddox	.40	1.00
79 Glyn Milburn RC	.40	1.00
80 Derek Russell	.10	.30
81 Shannon Sharpe	.40	1.00
82 Bennie Blades	.10	.30
83 Willie Green	.10	.30
84 Antonio London RC	.10	.30
85 Ryan McNeil RC	.40	1.00
86 Herman Moore	.40	1.00
87 Rodney Peete	.10	.30
88 Barry Sanders	1.50	4.00
89 Chris Spielman	.20	.50
90 Pat Swilling	.10	.30
91 Mark Brunell RC	5.00	12.00
92 Terrell Buckley	.10	.30
93 Brett Favre	3.00	6.00
94 Jackie Harris	.10	.30
95 Sterling Sharpe	.40	1.00
96 John Stephens	.10	.30
97 Wayne Simmons RC	.10	.30
98 George Teague RC	.20	.50
99 Reggie White	.40	1.00
100 Micheal Barrow RC	.40	1.00
101 Cody Carlson	.10	.30
102 Ray Childress	.10	.30
103 Brad Hopkins RC	.10	.30
104 Haywood Jeffires	.20	.50
105 Wilber Marshall	.10	.30
106 Warren Moon	.40	1.00
107 Webster Slaughter	.10	.30
108 Lorenzo White	.10	.30
109 John Baylor	.10	.30
110 Duane Bickett	.10	.30
111 Quentin Coryatt	.20	.50
112 Steve Emtman	.10	.30
113 Jeff George	.40	1.00
114 Jessie Hester	.10	.30
115 Anthony Johnson	.20	.50
116 Reggie Langhorne	.10	.30
117 Roosevelt Potts RC	.10	.30
118 Marcus Allen	.40	1.00
119 J.J. Birden	.10	.30
120 Willie Davis	.40	1.00
121 Jaime Fields RC	.10	.30
122 Joe Montana	2.00	5.00
123 Will Shields RC	.40	1.00
124 Neil Smith	.40	1.00
125 Derrick Thomas	.40	1.00
126 Harvey Williams	.20	.50
127 Tim Brown	.40	1.00
128 Billy Joe Hobert RC	.40	1.00
129 Jeff Hostetler	.20	.50
130 Ethan Horton	.10	.30
131 Rocket Ismail	.20	.50
132 Howie Long	.40	1.00
133 Terry McDaniel	.10	.30
134 Greg Robinson RC	.10	.30
135 Anthony Smith	.10	.30
136 Flipper Anderson	.10	.30
137 Marc Boutte	.10	.30
138 Shane Conlan	.10	.30
139 Troy Drayton RC	.20	.50
140 Henry Ellard	.20	.50
141 Jim Everett	.20	.50
142 Cleveland Gary	.10	.30
143 Sean Gilbert	.20	.50
144 Robert Young	.10	.30
145 Marco Coleman	.10	.30
146 Bryan Cox	.10	.30
147 Irving Fryar	.20	.50
148 Keith Jackson	.20	.50
149 Terry Kirby RC	.40	1.00
150 Dan Marino	2.00	5.00
151 Scott Mitchell	.40	1.00
152 Louis Oliver	.10	.30
153 Troy Vincent	.10	.30
154 Anthony Carter	.20	.50
155 Cris Carter	.40	1.00
156 Roger Craig	.20	.50
157 Chris Doleman	.10	.30
158 Qadry Ismail RC	.75	2.00
159 Steve Jordan	.10	.30
160 Randall McDaniel	.10	.30
161 Audray McMillian	.10	.30
162 Barry Word	.10	.30
163 Vincent Brown	.10	.30
164 Marv Cook	.10	.30
165 Sam Gash RC	.40	1.00
166 Pat Harlow	.10	.30
167 Greg McMurtry	.10	.30
168 Todd Rucci RC	.10	.30
169 Leonard Russell	.20	.50
170 Scott Sisson RC	.10	.30
171 Chris Slade RC	.20	.50
172 Morten Andersen	.10	.30
173 Derek Brown RBK RC	.20	.50
174 Reggie Freeman RC	.10	.30
175 Rickey Jackson	.10	.30
176 Eric Martin	.10	.30
177 Wayne Martin	.10	.30
178 Brad Muster	.10	.30
179 Willie Roaf RC	.20	.50
180 Renaldo Turnbull	.10	.30
181 Derek Brown TE	.10	.30
182 Marcus Buckley RC	.10	.30
183 Jarrod Bunch	.10	.30
184 Rodney Hampton	.20	.50
185 Ed McCaffrey	.40	1.00
186 Kanavis McGhee	.10	.30
187 Mike Sherrard	.10	.30
188 Phil Simms	.20	.50
189 Lawrence Taylor	.40	1.00
190 Kurt Barber	.10	.30
191 Boomer Esiason	.20	.50
192 Johnny Johnson	.10	.30
193 Ronnie Lott	.20	.50
194 Johnny Mitchell	.10	.30
195 Rob Moore	.20	.50
196 Adrian Murrell RC	.40	1.00
197 Browning Nagle	.10	.30
198 Marvin Washington	.10	.30
199 Eric Allen	.10	.30
200 Fred Barnett	.20	.50
201 Randall Cunningham	.40	1.00
202 Byron Evans	.10	.30
203 Tim Harris	.10	.30
204 Seth Joyner	.10	.30
205 Leonard Renfro RC	.10	.30
206 Heath Sherman	.10	.30
207 Clyde Simmons	.10	.30
208 Johnny Bailey	.10	.30
209 Steve Beuerlein	.20	.50
210 Chuck Cecil	.10	.30
211 Larry Centers RC	.40	1.00
212 Gary Clark	.20	.50
213 Ernest Dye RC	.10	.30
214 Ken Harvey	.10	.30
215 Randal Hill	.10	.30
216 Ricky Proehl	.10	.30
217 Deon Figures RC	.10	.30
218 Barry Foster	.20	.50
219 Eric Green	.10	.30
220 Kevin Greene	.20	.50
221 Carlton Haselrig	.10	.30
222 Andre Hastings RC	.20	.50
223 Greg Lloyd	.20	.50
224 Neil O'Donnell	.40	1.00
225 Rod Woodson	.40	1.00
226 Marion Butts	.10	.30
227 Darren Carrington RC	.10	.30
228 Darrien Gordon RC	.10	.30
229 Ronnie Harmon	.10	.30
230 Stan Humphries	.20	.50
231 Anthony Miller	.20	.50
232 Chris Mims	.10	.30
233 Leslie O'Neal	.20	.50
234 Junior Seau	.40	1.00
235 Dana Hall	.10	.30
236 Adrian Hardy	.10	.30
237 Brent Jones	.20	.50
238 Tim McDonald	.10	.30
239 Tom Rathman	.10	.30
240 Jerry Rice	1.50	3.00
241 Dana Stubblefield RC	.40	1.00
242 Ricky Watters	.40	1.00
243 Steve Young	1.25	2.50
244 Brian Blades	.20	.50
245 Ferrell Edmunds	.10	.30
246 Carlton Gray RC	.10	.30
247 Cortez Kennedy	.20	.50
248 Kelvin Martin	.10	.30
249 Dan McGwire	.10	.30
250 Jon Vaughn	.10	.30
251 Chris Warren	.20	.50
252 John L. Williams	.10	.30
253 Reggie Cobb	.10	.30
254 Horace Copeland RC	.20	.50
255 Lawrence Dawsey	.10	.30
256 Demetrius DuBose RC	.10	.30
257 Craig Erickson	.20	.50
258 Courtney Hawkins	.10	.30
259 John Lynch RC	3.00	8.00
260 Hardy Nickerson	.20	.50
261 Lamar Thomas RC	.10	.30
262 Carl Banks	.10	.30
263 Tom Carter RC	.20	.50
264 Brad Edwards	.10	.30
265 Kurt Gouveia	.10	.30
266 Desmond Howard	.20	.50
267 Charles Mann	.10	.30
268 Art Monk	.20	.50
269 Mark Rypien	.10	.30
270 Ricky Sanders	.10	.30
P1 Joe Montana Promo	2.00	5.00
numbered 19		

1993 SP All-Pros

COMPLETE SET (15)	50.00	120.00
STATED ODDS 1:15		
AP1 Steve Young	5.00	12.00
AP2 Warren Moon	2.50	6.00
AP3 Troy Aikman	6.00	15.00
AP4 Dan Marino	10.00	25.00
AP5 Barry Sanders	8.00	20.00
AP6 Barry Foster	2.00	5.00
AP7 Emmitt Smith	10.00	25.00
AP8 Thurman Thomas	3.00	8.00
AP9 Jerry Rice	8.00	20.00
AP10 Sterling Sharpe	3.00	8.00
AP11 Anthony Miller	2.00	5.00
AP12 Haywood Jeffires	2.00	5.00
AP13 Junior Seau	3.00	8.00
AP14 Reggie White	3.00	8.00
AP15 Derrick Thomas	3.00	8.00

1994 SP

These 200 standard-size cards feature all-foil player photos that are full-bleed except on the right where a black-and-gold variegated strip carrying the "Upper Deck SP" logo edges the picture. The small hologram on the cardbacks were printed primarily in gold foil (with two variations on the gold Upper Deck name -- either horizontal or vertical) but silver foil holograms are known to exist. The silver hologram was used on the Die Cut parallels. After beginning with Premier Prospects (1-20), the cards are checklisted according to teams. Inserted approximately one in every other case, are special Dan Marino (300th touchdown pass) and Jerry Rice (127th touchdown) cards. Numbered RB1 and RB2, respectively, the cards are horizontal with a gold die cut design. A Joe Montana Promo card was produced and priced below.

COMPLETE SET (200)	25.00	50.00
1 Dan Wilkinson RC	.50	1.25
2 Heath Shuler RC	.30	.75
3 Marshall Faulk RC	6.00	15.00
4 Willie McGinest RC	.75	2.00
5 Trent Dilfer RC	2.00	5.00
6 Bryant Young RC	.75	2.00
7 Antonio Langham RC	.15	.40
8 John Thierry RC	.15	.40
9 Aaron Glenn RC	.50	1.25
10 Charles Johnson RC	.50	1.25
11 Dewayne Washington RC	.15	.40
12 Johnnie Morton RC	1.25	3.00
13 Greg Hill RC	.30	.75
14 William Floyd RC	.30	.75
15 Derrick Alexander WR RC	.50	1.25
16 Darnay Scott RC	.50	1.25
17 Errict Rhett RC	.50	1.25
18 Charlie Garner RC	1.25	3.00
19 Thomas Lewis RC	.15	.40
20 David Palmer RC	.50	1.25
21 Andre Reed	.10	.30
22 Thurman Thomas	.20	.50
23 Bruce Smith	.20	.50
24 Jim Kelly	.20	.50
25 Cornelius Bennett	.10	.30
26 Bucky Brooks RC	.05	.15
27 Jeff Burris RC	.10	.30
28 Jim Harbaugh	.20	.50
29 Tony Bennett	.05	.15
30 Quentin Coryatt	.05	.15
31 Floyd Turner	.05	.15
32 Roosevelt Potts	.05	.15
33 Jeff Herrod	.05	.15
34 Irving Fryar	.10	.30
35 Bryan Cox	.05	.15
36 Dan Marino	1.50	4.00
37 Terry Kirby	.20	.50
38 Michael Stewart	.05	.15
39 Bernie Kosar	.10	.30
40 Aubrey Beavers RC	.05	.15
41 Vincent Brisby	.10	.30
42 Ben Coates	.10	.30
43 Drew Bledsoe	.75	2.00
44 Marion Butts	.05	.15
45 Chris Slade	.05	.15
46 Michael Timpson	.05	.15
47 Ray Crittenden RC	.05	.15
48 Rob Moore	.10	.30
49 Johnny Mitchell	.05	.15
50 Art Monk	.10	.30
51 Boomer Esiason	.10	.30
52 Ronnie Lott	.10	.30
53 Ryan Yarborough RC	.05	.15
54 Carl Pickens	.10	.30
55 David Klingler	.05	.15
56 Harold Green	.05	.15
57 John Copeland	.05	.15
58 Louis Oliver	.05	.15
59 Corey Sawyer	.10	.30
60 Michael Jackson	.10	.30
61 Mark Rypien	.05	.15
62 Vinny Testaverde	.10	.30
63 Eric Metcalf	.10	.30
64 Eric Turner	.05	.15
65 Haywood Jeffires	.10	.30
66 Micheal Barrow	.05	.15
67 Cody Carlson	.05	.15
68 Gary Brown	.05	.15
69 Bucky Richardson	.05	.15
70 Al Smith	.05	.15
71 Eric Green	.05	.15
72 Neil O'Donnell	.20	.50
73 Barry Foster	.05	.15
74 Greg Lloyd	.10	.30
75 Rod Woodson	.10	.30
76 Byron Bam Morris RC	.10	.30
77 John L. Williams	.05	.15
78 Anthony Miller	.10	.30
79 Mike Pritchard	.05	.15
80 John Elway	1.50	4.00
81 Shannon Sharpe	.10	.30
82 Steve Atwater	.05	.15
83 Simon Fletcher	.05	.15
84 Glyn Milburn	.10	.30
85 Mark Collins	.05	.15
86 Keith Cash	.05	.15
87 Willie Davis	.10	.30
88 Joe Montana	1.50	4.00
89 Marcus Allen	.20	.50
90 Neil Smith	.10	.30
91 Derrick Thomas	.20	.50
92 Tim Brown	.20	.50
93 Jeff Hostetler	.10	.30
94 Terry McDaniel	.05	.15
95 Rocket Ismail	.10	.30
96 Rob Fredrickson RC	.10	.30
97 Harvey Williams	.10	.30
98 Steve Wisniewski	.05	.15
99 Stan Humphries	.10	.30
100 Natrone Means	.20	.50
101 Leslie O'Neal	.05	.15
102 Junior Seau	.20	.50
103 Ronnie Harmon	.05	.15
104 Shawn Jefferson	.05	.15
105 Howard Ballard	.05	.15
106 Rick Mirer	.20	.50
107 Cortez Kennedy	.10	.30
108 Chris Warren	.10	.30
109 Brian Blades	.10	.30
110 Sam Adams RC	.10	.30
111 Gary Clark	.10	.30
112 Steve Beuerlein	.10	.30
113 Ronald Moore	.05	.15
114 Eric Swann	.10	.30
115 Clyde Simmons	.05	.15
116 Seth Joyner	.05	.15
117 Troy Aikman	.75	2.00
118 Charles Haley	.10	.30
119 Alvin Harper	.10	.30
120 Michael Irvin	.20	.50
121 Daryl Johnston	.10	.30
122 Emmitt Smith	1.25	3.00
123 Shante Carver RC	.05	.15
124 Dave Brown	.10	.30
125 Rodney Hampton	.10	.30
126 Dave Meggett	.05	.15
127 Chris Calloway	.05	.15
128 Mike Sherrard	.05	.15
129 Carlton Bailey	.05	.15
130 Randall Cunningham	.20	.50
131 William Fuller	.05	.15
132 Eric Allen	.05	.15
133 Calvin Williams	.10	.30
134 Herschel Walker	.10	.30
135 Bernard Williams RC	.05	.15
136 Henry Ellard	.10	.30
137 Ethan Horton	.05	.15
138 Desmond Howard	.10	.30
139 Reggie Brooks	.10	.30
140 John Friesz	.10	.30
141 Tom Carter	.05	.15
142 Terry Allen	.10	.30
143 Adrian Cooper	.05	.15
144 Qadry Ismail	.20	.50
145 Warren Moon	.20	.50
146 Henry Thomas	.05	.15
147 Todd Steussie RC	.10	.30
148 Cris Carter	.30	.75
149 Andy Heck	.05	.15
150 Curtis Conway	.20	.50
151 Erik Kramer	.10	.30
152 Lewis Tillman	.05	.15
153 Dante Jones	.05	.15
154 Alonzo Spellman	.05	.15
155 Herman Moore	.20	.50
156 Broderick Thomas	.05	.15
157 Scott Mitchell	.10	.30
158 Barry Sanders	1.25	3.00
159 Chris Spielman	.10	.30
160 Pat Swilling	.05	.15
161 Bennie Blades	.05	.15
162 Sterling Sharpe	.10	.30
163 Brett Favre	1.50	4.00
164 Reggie Cobb	.05	.15
165 Reggie White	.20	.50
166 Sean Jones	.05	.15
167 George Teague	.05	.15
168 LeShon Johnson RC	.10	.30
169 Courtney Hawkins	.05	.15
170 Jackie Harris	.05	.15
171 Craig Erickson	.05	.15
172 Santana Dotson	.10	.30
173 Eric Curry	.05	.15
174 Hardy Nickerson	.10	.30
175 Derek Brown RBK	.05	.15
176 Jim Everett	.10	.30
177 Michael Haynes	.10	.30
178 Tyrone Hughes	.10	.30
179 Wayne Martin	.05	.15
180 Willie Roaf	.05	.15
181 Irv Smith	.05	.15
182 Jeff George	.20	.50
183 Andre Rison	.10	.30
184 Erric Pegram	.05	.15
185 Bret Emanuel RC	.40	1.00
186 Chris Doleman	.05	.15
187 Ron George	.05	.15
188 Chris Miller	.05	.15
189 Troy Drayton	.05	.15
190 Chris Chandler	.10	.30
191 Jerome Bettis	.40	1.00
192 Jimmie Jones	.05	.15
193 Sean Gilbert	.05	.15
194 Jerry Rice	.75	2.00
195 Brent Jones	.10	.30
196 Deion Sanders	.40	1.00
197 Steve Young	.60	1.50
198 Ricky Watters	.10	.30
199 Dana Stubblefield	.10	.30
200 Ken Norton Jr.	.10	.30
RB1 Dan Marino RB	10.00	25.00
RB2 Jerry Rice RB	12.50	25.00
P16 Joe Montana Promo	1.50	4.00

1994 SP Die Cuts

COMPLETE SET (200)	40.00	80.00
*STARS: .8X TO 2X BASIC CARDS		
*RCs: .5X TO 1.2X BASIC CARDS		
ONE PER PACK		

1994 SP Holoviews

COMPLETE SET (40)	20.00	40.00
STATED ODDS 1:5		
*DIE CUTS: 3X TO 8X BASIC INSERTS		
DIE CUT STATED ODDS 1:75		
PB1 Jamir Miller	.50	1.25
PB2 Andre Rison	.75	2.00
PB3 Bucky Brooks	.50	1.25
PB4 Thurman Thomas	.75	2.00
PB5 John Thierry	.50	1.25
PB6 Dan Wilkinson	.50	1.25
PB7 Darnay Scott	.60	1.50
PB8 Antonio Langham	.50	1.25
PB9 Troy Aikman	2.00	5.00
PB10 Emmitt Smith	3.00	8.00
PB11 John Elway	4.00	10.00
PB12 Barry Sanders	3.00	8.00
PB13 Johnnie Morton	.60	1.50
PB14 Reggie White	1.00	2.50
PB15 Brett Favre	4.00	10.00
PB16 LeShon Johnson	.50	1.25
PB17 Joe Montana	4.00	10.00
PB18 Greg Hill	.50	1.25
PB19 Calvin Jones	.50	1.25
PB20 Tim Brown	.75	2.00
PB21 Isaac Bruce	.75	2.00
PB22 Jerome Bettis	1.25	3.00
PB23 Dan Marino	4.00	10.00
PB24 O.J.McDuffie	.50	1.25
PB25 Willie McGinest	.50	1.25
PB26 Mario Bates	.50	1.25
PB27 Rodney Hampton	.50	1.25
PB28 Thomas Lewis	.50	1.25
PB29 Aaron Glenn	.50	1.25
PB30 Barry Foster	.50	1.25
PB31 Charles Johnson	.50	1.25
PB32 Steve Young	1.50	4.00
PB33 Jerry Rice	2.50	6.00
PB34 Bryant Young	.60	1.50
PB35 William Floyd	.60	1.50
PB36 Sam Adams	.50	1.25
PB37 Rick Mirer	.60	1.50
PB38 Errict Rhett	.60	1.50
PB39 Reggie Brooks	.50	1.25
PB40 Heath Shuler	.60	1.50

1995 SP

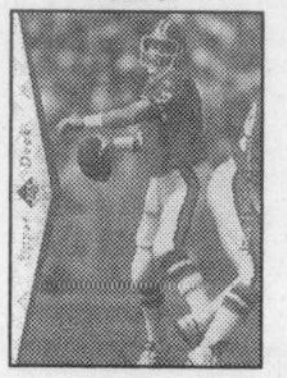

Issued as a 200 card set, these cards were available in eight card packs at a suggested retail price of $4.19/pack. The set is broken down into 180 player cards and 20 Premier Prospect cards, which features top rookies. Rookie Cards include Jeff Blake, Ki-Jana Carter, Kerry Collins, Terrell Davis, Joey Galloway, Curtis Martin, Steve McNair, Rashaan Salaam, J.J. Stokes, Tamarick Vanover and Michael Westbrook. A couple of "one-shot" inserts were also available: a Dan Marino Record Breaker and a Joe Montana Tribute. The Marino Record Breaker card is a horizontal etched-foil card saluting his record breaking 343 career touchdown passes. This card was randomly inserted at a rate of one in 383 packs. The Montana Tribute card is also a horizontal etched-foil card showcasing his extraordinary career. It was also randomly inserted at a rate of one in 383 packs. A Joe Montana All-Pro Promo card was produced and priced below.

COMPLETE SET (200)	20.00	50.00
1 Ki-Jana Carter RC	.75	2.00
2 Eric Zeier RC	.75	2.00
3 Steve McNair RC	4.00	10.00
4 Michael Westbrook RC	.75	2.00
5 Kerry Collins RC	2.50	6.00
6 Joey Galloway RC	2.00	5.00
7 Kevin Carter RC	.75	2.00
8 Mike Mamula RC	.20	.50
9 Kyle Brady RC	.75	2.00
10 J.J. Stokes RC	.75	2.00
11 Tyrone Poole RC	.75	2.00
12 Rashaan Salaam RC	.40	1.00
13 Sherman Williams RC	.20	.50
14 Luther Elliss RC	.20	.50
15 James O. Stewart RC	1.25	3.00
16 Tamarick Vanover RC	.75	2.00
17 Napoleon Kaufman RC	1.25	3.00
18 Curtis Martin RC	6.00	12.00
19 Tyrone Wheatley RC	1.25	3.00
20 Frank Sanders RC	.75	2.00
21 Devin Bush	.07	.20
22 Terance Mathis	.15	.40
23 Bert Emanuel	.30	.75
24 Eric Metcalf	.15	.40
25 Craig Heyward	.15	.40
26 Jeff George	.15	.40
27 Mark Carrier WR	.15	.40
28 Pete Metzelaars	.07	.20
29 Frank Reich	.07	.20
30 Sam Mills	.15	.40
31 John Kasay	.07	.20
32 Willie Green	.15	.40
33 Jeff Graham	.07	.20
34 Curtis Conway	.30	.75
35 Steve Walsh	.07	.20
36 Erik Kramer	.07	.20
37 Michael Timpson	.07	.20
38 Mark Carrier	.07	.20
39 Troy Aikman	.75	2.00
40 Michael Irvin	.30	.75
41 Charles Haley	.15	.40
42 Deion Sanders	.50	1.25
43 Jay Novacek	.15	.40
44 Emmitt Smith	1.25	3.00
45 Herman Moore	.30	.75
46 Scott Mitchell UER	.15	.40
front reads Mitcehill		
47 Bennie Blades	.07	.20
48 Johnnie Morton	.15	.40
49 Chris Spielman	.15	.40
50 Barry Sanders	1.25	3.00
51 Edgar Bennett	.15	.40
52 Reggie White	.30	.75
53 Sean Jones	.07	.20
54 Mark Ingram	.07	.20
55 Robert Brooks	.30	.75
56 Brett Favre	1.50	4.00
57 Lovell Pinkney RC	.20	.50
58 Chris Miller	.07	.20
59 Isaac Bruce	.50	1.25
60 Roman Phifer	.07	.20
61 Sean Gilbert	.15	.40
62 Jerome Bettis	.30	.75
63 Derrick Alexander DE RC	.20	.50
64 Cris Carter	.30	.75
65 Jake Reed	.15	.40
66 Robert Smith	.30	.75
67 David Palmer	.15	.40
68 Warren Moon	.15	.40
69 Ray Zellars RC	.40	1.00
70 Jim Everett	.07	.20
71 Michael Haynes	.15	.40
72 Quinn Early	.15	.40
73 Willie Roaf	.07	.20
74 Mario Bates	.15	.40
75 Mike Sherrard	.07	.20
76 Chris Calloway	.07	.20
77 Dave Brown	.15	.40
78 Thomas Lewis	.15	.40
79 Herschel Walker	.15	.40
80 Rodney Hampton	.15	.40
81 Fred Barnett	.15	.40
82 Calvin Williams	.15	.40
83 Randall Cunningham	.30	.75
84 Charlie Garner	.30	.75
85 Bobby Taylor RC	1.25	3.00
86 Ricky Watters	.15	.40
87 Dave Krieg	.07	.20
88 Rob Moore	.15	.40
89 Eric Swann	.15	.40
90 Clyde Simmons	.07	.20
91 Seth Joyner	.07	.20
92 Garrison Hearst	.30	.75
93 Jerry Rice	.75	2.00
94 Bryant Young	.15	.40
95 Brent Jones	.07	.20
96 Ken Norton	.15	.40
97 William Floyd	.15	.40
98 Steve Young	.60	1.50
99 Warren Sapp RC	2.00	5.00
100 Trent Dilfer	.30	.75
101 Alvin Harper	.07	.20
102 Hardy Nickerson	.07	.20
103 Derrick Brooks RC	2.00	5.00
104 Errict Rhett	.15	.40
105 Henry Ellard	.15	.40
106 Ken Harvey	.07	.20
107 Gus Frerotte	.15	.40
108 Brian Mitchell	.07	.20
109 Terry Allen	.15	.40
110 Heath Shuler	.15	.40
111 Jim Kelly	.30	.75
112 Andre Reed	.15	.40
113 Bruce Smith	.30	.75
114 Darick Holmes RC	.40	1.00
115 Bryce Paup	.15	.40
116 Cornelius Bennett	.15	.40
117 Carl Pickens	.15	.40
118 Darnay Scott	.15	.40
119 Jeff Blake RC	.75	2.00
120 Steve Tovar	.07	.20
121 Tony McGee	.07	.20
122 Dan Wilkinson	.15	.40
123 Craig Powell RC	.07	.20
124 Vinny Testaverde	.15	.40
125 Eric Turner	.07	.20
126 Leroy Hoard	.07	.20
127 Lorenzo White	.07	.20
128 Andre Rison	.15	.40
129 Shannon Sharpe	.15	.40
130 Terrell Davis RC	3.00	8.00
131 Anthony Miller	.15	.40
132 Mike Pritchard	.07	.20
133 Steve Atwater	.07	.20
134 John Elway	1.50	4.00
135 Haywood Jeffires	.07	.20
136 Gary Brown	.07	.20
137 Al Smith	.07	.20
138 Rodney Thomas RC	.40	1.00
139 Chris Chandler	.15	.40
140 Mel Gray	.07	.20
141 Craig Erickson	.07	.20
142 Sean Dawkins	.15	.40
143 Ken Dilger RC	.75	2.00
144 Ellis Johnson RC UER	.20	.50
front reads Elliss		
145 Quentin Coryatt	.15	.40
146 Marshall Faulk	1.00	2.50
147 Tony Boselli RC	.75	2.00
148 Rob Johnson RC	1.25	3.00
149 Desmond Howard	.15	.40
150 Steve Beuerlein	.15	.40
151 Reggie Cobb	.07	.20
152 Jeff Lageman	.07	.20
153 Willie Davis	.15	.40
154 Marcus Allen	.30	.75
155 Neil Smith	.15	.40
156 Greg Hill	.15	.40
157 Steve Bono	.15	.40
158 Derrick Thomas	.30	.75
159 Jeff Hostetler	.15	.40
160 Harvey Williams	.07	.20
161 Rocket Ismail	.15	.40
162 Chester McGlockton	.15	.40
163 Terry McDaniel	.07	.20
164 Tim Brown	.30	.75
165 Terry Kirby	.15	.40
166 Irving Fryar	.15	.40
167 O.J. McDuffie	.30	.75
168 Bryan Cox	.07	.20
169 Eric Green	.07	.20
170 Dan Marino	1.50	4.00
171 Ben Coates	.15	.40
172 Vincent Brisby	.07	.20
173 Chris Slade	.07	.20
174 Ty Law RC	1.50	4.00
175 Vincent Brown	.07	.20
176 Drew Bledsoe	.50	1.25
177 Johnny Mitchell	.07	.20
178 Boomer Esiason	.15	.40
179 Wayne Chrebet RC	2.00	5.00
180 Mo Lewis	.07	.20
181 Ronald Moore	.07	.20
182 Aaron Glenn	.07	.20
183 Mark Bruener RC	.40	1.00
184 Neil O'Donnell	.15	.40
185 Charles Johnson	.15	.40
186 Greg Lloyd	.15	.40
187 Rod Woodson	.15	.40
188 Byron Bam Morris	.07	.20
189 Terrell Fletcher RC	.20	.50
190 Terrance Shaw RC UER	.20	.50
front reads Terrence		
191 Stan Humphries	.15	.40
192 Junior Seau	.30	.75
193 Leslie O'Neal	.15	.40
194 Natrone Means	.15	.40
195 Christian Fauria RC	.40	1.00
196 Rick Mirer	.15	.40
197 Sam Adams	.07	.20
198 Cortez Kennedy	.15	.40
199 Eugene Robinson	.07	.20
200 Chris Warren	.15	.40
DM1 Dan Marino Tribute	7.50	20.00
JM1 Joe Montana Salute	7.50	20.00
JMAP Joe Montana Promo	1.50	4.00
All-Pro Silver card		
NNO Dan Marino TRI Jumbo	10.00	25.00
Card measures 3 1/2 x 5		
Issued by Upper Deck Authenticated		
Numbered of 10,000		
NNO J.Montana SAL Jumbo	10.00	25.00
Card meaures 3 1/2 x 5		
Issued by Upper Deck Authenticated		
Numbered of 10,000		
P113 Dan Marino Promo	1.25	3.00

1995 SP All-Pros

COMPLETE SET (20)	15.00	40.00
SILVER STATED ODDS 1:5		
*GOLD: 1.2X TO 3X SILVER		
GOLD STATED ODDS 1:62		
1 Marshall Faulk	1.50	4.00
2 Natrone Means	.75	2.00
3 Emmitt Smith	3.00	8.00
4 Brett Favre	4.00	10.00
5 Michael Westbrook	.75	2.00
6 Jerry Rice	2.50	6.00
7 John Elway	4.00	10.00
8 Troy Aikman	2.00	5.00
9 Rashaan Salaam	.60	1.50
10 Jerome Bettis	1.00	2.50
11 Drew Bledsoe	1.00	2.50
12 Kerry Collins	1.00	2.50
13 Dan Marino	4.00	10.00
14 Tyrone Wheatley	.75	2.00
15 Steve McNair	2.50	6.00
16 Steve Young	1.50	4.00
17 Eric Zeier	.60	1.50
18 Errict Rhett	.75	2.00
19 Michael Irvin	1.25	3.00
20 Barry Sanders	3.00	8.00

1995 SP Holoviews

COMPLETE SET (40)	25.00	60.00
STATED ODDS 1:5		
*DIE CUTS: .8X TO 2X BASIC INSERTS		
DIE CUT STATED ODDS 1:75		
1 Joe Montana	3.00	8.00
2 Dan Marino	4.00	10.00
3 Drew Bledsoe	1.25	3.00
4 Ben Coates	.40	1.00
5 Curtis Martin	4.00	10.00
6 Kyle Brady	.60	1.50
7 Marshall Faulk	2.50	6.00
8 Ki-Jana Carter	.60	1.50
9 Leroy Hoard	.20	.50
10 James O. Stewart	1.25	3.00
11 Mark Bruener	.30	.75
12 Charles Johnson	.40	1.00
13 Rod Woodson	.40	1.00
14 John Elway	4.00	10.00
15 Tim Brown	.75	2.00
16 Napoleon Kaufman	1.25	3.00
17 Natrone Means	.40	1.00
18 Jimmy Oliver	.05	.15
19 Christian Fauria	.30	.75
20 Joey Galloway	1.50	4.00
21 Chris Warren	.40	1.00
22 Kerry Collins	2.00	5.00
23 Mario Bates	.40	1.00
24 Jerome Bettis	.75	2.00
25 William Floyd	.40	1.00
26 Jerry Rice	2.00	5.00
27 J.J. Stokes	.60	1.50
28 Steve Young	1.50	4.00
29 Troy Aikman	2.00	5.00
30 Michael Irvin	.75	2.00
31 Emmitt Smith	3.00	8.00
32 Rodney Hampton	.40	1.00
33 Heath Shuler	.40	1.00
34 Michael Westbrook	.60	1.50
35 Barry Sanders	3.00	8.00
36 Brett Favre	4.00	10.00
37 Cris Carter	.75	2.00
38 Warren Moon	.40	1.00
39 James A.Stewart	.05	.15
40 Errict Rhett	.40	1.00

1995 SP Championship

This is the first effort for the retail version of SP and comes as a 225 card set in six card packs with a suggested retail price of $2.99. The set breaks down into 180 regular player cards and 45 Future Champions cards which highlight the top 1995 rookies in game-action photographs. Rookies include Jeff Blake, Ki-Jana Carter, Kerry Collins, Terrell Davis, Joey Galloway, Steve McNair, Kordell Stewert, J.J. Stokes, Tamarick Vanover and Michael Westbrook. A Joe Montana promo card (#116) was produced and priced below.

COMPLETE SET (225)	20.00	50.00
1 Frank Sanders RC	.30	.75
2 Stoney Case RC	.07	.20
3 Lorenzo Styles RC	.07	.20
4 Todd Collins RC	1.00	2.50
5 Darick Holmes RC	.15	.40
6 Brian DeMarco RC	.07	.20
7 Tyrone Poole RC	.30	.75
8 Kerry Collins RC	1.50	4.00
9 Rashaan Salaam RC	.15	.40
10 Steve Stenstrom RC	.07	.20
11 Ki-Jana Carter RC	.30	.75
12 Eric Zeier RC	.30	.75
13 Sherman Williams RC	.07	.20
14 Terrell Davis RC	2.00	5.00
15 David Dunn RC	.07	.20
16 Luther Elliss RC	.07	.20
17 Craig Newsome RC	.07	.20
18 Antonio Freeman RC	.75	2.00
19 Steve McNair RC	2.50	6.00
20 Anthony Cook RC	.07	.20
21 Rodney Thomas RC	.15	.40
22 Ellis Johnson RC	.07	.20
23 Ken Dilger RC	.30	.75
24 James O. Stewart RC	.75	2.00
25 Pete Mitchell RC	.15	.40
26 Tamarick Vanover RC	.30	.75
27 Orlando Thomas RC	.07	.20
28 Corey Fuller RC	.07	.20
29 Curtis Martin RC	2.50	6.00
30 Ty Law RC	1.00	2.50
31 Roell Preston RC	.10	.30
32 Mark Fields RC	.30	.75
33 Tyrone Wheatley RC	.75	2.00
34 Kyle Brady RC	.30	.75
35 Napoleon Kaufman RC	1.00	2.50
36 Kordell Stewart RC	1.25	3.00
37 Mark Bruener RC	.15	.40
38 Terrance Shaw RC	.07	.20
39 Terrell Fletcher RC	.07	.20
40 J.J. Stokes RC	.30	.75
41 Christian Fauria RC	.15	.40
42 Joey Galloway RC	1.25	3.00
43 Kevin Carter RC	.30	.75
44 Warren Sapp RC	1.25	3.00
45 Michael Westbrook RC	.30	.75
46 Clyde Simmons	.05	.15
47 Rob Moore	.10	.30
48 Seth Joyner	.05	.15

49 Dave Krieg	.05	.15
50 Garrison Hearst	.20	.50
51 Aeneas Williams	.05	.15
52 Terance Mathis	.10	.30
53 Bert Emanuel UER	.20	.50
Name spelled Emanual		
54 Chris Doleman	.05	.15
55 Craig Heyward	.10	.30
56 Jeff George	.10	.30
57 Eric Metcalf	.10	.30
58 Jim Kelly	.20	.50
59 Andre Reed	.10	.30
60 Russell Copeland	.05	.15
61 Bruce Smith	.20	.50
62 Cornelius Bennett	.10	.30
63 Jeff Burris	.05	.15
64 Mark Carrier WR	.10	.30
65 Pete Metzelaars	.05	.15
66 Frank Reich	.05	.15
67 Sam Mills	.10	.30
68 John Kasay	.05	.15
69 Willie Green	.10	.30
70 Curtis Conway	.20	.50
71 Erik Kramer	.05	.15
72 Donnell Woolford	.05	.15
73 Mark Carrier	.05	.15
74 Jeff Graham	.05	.15
75 Raymont Harris	.05	.15
76 Carl Pickens	.10	.30
77 Darnay Scott	.10	.30
78 Jeff Blake RC	.50	1.25
79 Dan Wilkinson	.10	.30
80 Tony McGee	.05	.15
81 Eric Bieniemy	.05	.15
82 Vinny Testaverde	.10	.30
83 Eric Turner	.05	.15
84 Leroy Hoard	.05	.15
85 Lorenzo White	.05	.15
86 Antonio Langham	.05	.15
87 Andre Rison	.10	.30
88 Troy Aikman	.60	1.50
89 Michael Irvin	.20	.50
90 Charles Haley	.10	.30
91 Daryl Johnston	.10	.30
92 Jay Novacek	.10	.30
93 Emmitt Smith	1.00	2.50
94 Shannon Sharpe	.10	.30
95 Anthony Miller	.10	.30
96 Mike Pritchard	.05	.15
97 Glyn Milburn	.05	.15
98 Simon Fletcher	.05	.15
99 John Elway	1.25	3.00
100 Henry Thomas	.05	.15
101 Herman Moore	.20	.50
102 Scott Mitchell	.10	.30
103 Bennie Blades	.05	.15
104 Chris Spielman	.10	.30
105 Barry Sanders	1.00	2.50
106 Mark Ingram	.05	.15
107 Edgar Bennett	.10	.30
108 Reggie White	.20	.50
109 Sean Jones	.05	.15
110 Robert Brooks	.20	.50
111 Brett Favre	1.25	3.00
112 Chris Chandler	.10	.30
113 Haywood Jeffires	.05	.15
114 Gary Brown	.05	.15
115 Al Smith	.05	.15
116 Ray Childress	.05	.15
117 Mel Gray	.05	.15
118 Jim Harbaugh	.10	.30
119 Sean Dawkins	.10	.30
120 Roosevelt Potts	.05	.15
121 Marshall Faulk	.75	2.00
122 Tony Bennett	.05	.15
123 Quentin Coryatt	.10	.30
124 Desmond Howard	.10	.30
125 Tony Boselli	.20	.50
126 Steve Beuerlein	.10	.30
127 Jeff Lageman	.05	.15
128 Rob Johnson RC	.75	2.00
129 Ernest Givins	.05	.15
130 Willie Davis	.10	.30
131 Marcus Allen	.20	.50
132 Neil Smith	.10	.30
133 Greg Hill	.10	.30
134 Steve Bono	.10	.30
135 Lake Dawson	.10	.30
136 Dan Marino	1.25	3.00
137 Terry Kirby	.10	.30
138 Irving Fryar	.10	.30
139 O.J. McDuffie	.20	.50
140 Bryan Cox	.05	.15
141 Eric Green	.05	.15
142 Cris Carter	.20	.50
143 Robert Smith	.20	.50
144 John Randle	.10	.30
145 Jake Reed	.10	.30
146 Dewayne Washington	.10	.30
147 Warren Moon	.10	.30
148 Dave Meggett	.05	.15
149 Ben Coates	.10	.30
150 Vincent Brisby	.05	.15
151 Willie McGinest	.10	.30
152 Chris Slade	.05	.15
153 Drew Bledsoe	.40	1.00
154 Eric Allen	.05	.15
155 Mario Bates	.10	.30
156 Jim Everett	.05	.15
157 Renaldo Turnbull	.05	.15
158 Tyrone Hughes	.10	.30
159 Michael Haynes	.10	.30
160 Mike Sherrard	.05	.15
161 Dave Brown	.10	.30
162 Chris Calloway	.05	.15
163 Keith Hamilton	.05	.15
164 Rodney Hampton	.10	.30
165 Herschel Walker	.10	.30
166 Adrian Murrell	.10	.30
167 Johnny Mitchell	.05	.15
168 Boomer Esiason	.10	.30
169 Mo Lewis	.05	.15
170 Brad Baxter	.05	.15
171 Aaron Glenn	.05	.15
172 Jeff Hostetler	.10	.30
173 Harvey Williams	.05	.15
174 Tim Brown	.20	.50
175 Terry McDaniel	.05	.15
176 Pat Swilling	.05	.15
177 Rocket Ismail	.10	.30
178 Randall Cunningham	.20	.50
179 Calvin Williams	.10	.30
180 Ricky Watters	.10	.30
181 Charlie Garner	.20	.50
182 Fred Barnett	.10	.30
183 Rodney Peete	.05	.15
184 Neil O'Donnell	.10	.30
185 Charles Johnson	.10	.30
186 Rod Woodson	.10	.30
187 Byron Bam Morris	.05	.15
188 Kevin Greene	.10	.30
189 Greg Lloyd	.10	.30
190 Chris Miller	.05	.15
191 Isaac Bruce	.30	.75
192 Roman Phifer	.05	.15
193 Jerome Bettis	.20	.50
194 Carlos Jenkins	.05	.15
195 Troy Drayton	.05	.15
196 Andre Coleman	.05	.15
197 Natrone Means	.10	.30
198 Leslie O'Neal	.10	.30
199 Junior Seau	.20	.50
200 Tony Martin	.10	.30
201 Stan Humphries	.10	.30
202 Steve Young	.50	1.25
203 Jerry Rice	.60	1.50
204 Brent Jones	.05	.15
205 Dana Stubblefield	.10	.30
206 Lee Woodall	.05	.15
207 Merton Hanks	.05	.15
208 Rick Mirer	.10	.30
209 Brian Blades	.10	.30
210 Chris Warren	.10	.30
211 Sam Adams	.05	.15
212 Cortez Kennedy	.10	.30
213 Eugene Robinson	.05	.15
214 Alvin Harper	.05	.15
215 Trent Dilfer	.20	.50
216 Hardy Nickerson	.05	.15
217 Errict Rhett	.10	.30
218 Eric Curry	.05	.15
219 Jackie Harris	.05	.15
220 Henry Ellard	.10	.30
221 Terry Allen	.10	.30
222 Brian Mitchell	.05	.15
223 Ken Harvey	.05	.15
224 Gus Frerotte	.10	.30
225 Heath Shuler	.10	.30
P116 Joe Montana Promo	1.25	3.00
Numbered 116		

1995 SP Championship Die Cuts

COMPLETE SET (225)	75.00	150.00
*STARS: 1.5X TO 3X BASIC CARDS		
*RCs: .6X TO 1.5X BASIC CARDS		
ONE PER PACK		

1995 SP Championship Playoff Showcase

COMPLETE SET (20)	50.00	100.00
STATED ODDS 1:15		
*DIE CUTS: .6X TO 1.5X BASIC INSERTS		
DIE CUTS: STATED ODDS 1:20		
PS1 Troy Aikman	5.00	10.00
PS2 Jerry Rice	5.00	10.00
PS3 Isaac Bruce	2.50	5.00
PS4 Rodney Peete	.40	1.00
PS5 Rashaan Salaam	.60	1.25
PS6 Brett Favre	10.00	20.00
PS7 Alvin Harper	.40	1.00
PS8 Cris Carter	1.50	3.00
PS9 Michael Westbrook	1.25	2.50
PS10 Jeff George	1.00	2.00
PS11 Natrone Means	1.00	2.00
PS12 Dan Marino	10.00	20.00
PS13 Steve Bono	1.00	2.00
PS14 Greg Lloyd	1.00	2.00
PS15 Jim Kelly	1.50	3.00
PS16 Jeff Hostetler	1.00	2.00
PS17 Marshall Faulk	6.00	12.00
PS18 John Elway	10.00	20.00
PS19 Jeff Blake	2.00	4.00
PS20 Andre Rison	1.00	2.00

1996 SP

The 1996 SP set was issued in one series totalling 188 cards. The 8-card packs retail for $4.39 each. The set contains the topical subset Premier Prospects (1-20). The fronts feature color action player photos with a small player head portrait insert and a silver foil border around two-thirds of the card. The backs display another player photo with biographical information and statistics.

COMPLETE SET (188)	40.00	100.00
1 Keyshawn Johnson RC	3.00	8.00
2 Kevin Hardy RC	.30	.75
3 Simeon Rice RC	1.25	3.00
4 Jonathan Ogden RC	.50	1.25
5 Eddie George RC	4.00	10.00
6 Terry Glenn RC	2.50	6.00
7 Terrell Owens RC	8.00	20.00
8 Tim Biakabutuka RC	.75	2.00
9 Lawrence Phillips RC	.30	.75
10 Alex Molden RC	.15	.40
11 Regan Upshaw RC	.15	.40
12 Rickey Dudley RC	.50	1.25
13 Duane Clemons RC	.15	.40
14 John Mobley RC	.30	.75
15 Eddie Kennison RC	.75	2.00
16 Karim Abdul-Jabbar RC	.50	1.25
17 Eric Moulds RC	1.50	4.00
18 Marvin Harrison RC	6.00	15.00
19 Stepfret Williams RC	.15	.40
20 Stephen Davis RC	3.00	8.00
21 Deion Sanders	.50	1.25
22 Emmitt Smith	1.25	3.00
23 Troy Aikman	.75	2.00
24 Michael Irvin	.30	.75
25 Herschel Walker	.15	.40
26 Kavika Pittman RC	.07	.20
27 Andre Hastings	.07	.20
28 Jerome Bettis	.30	.75
29 Mike Tomczak	.07	.20
30 Kordell Stewart	.30	.75
31 Charles Johnson	.07	.20
32 Greg Lloyd	.15	.40
33 Brett Favre	1.50	4.00
34 Mark Chmura	.15	.40
35 Edgar Bennett	.15	.40
36 Robert Brooks	.15	.40
37 Craig Newsome	.07	.20
38 Reggie White UER	.30	.75
(birth year incorrect on back as well as college)		
39 Jim Harbaugh	.15	.40
40 Marshall Faulk	.40	1.00
41 Sean Dawkins	.07	.20
42 Quentin Coryatt	.07	.20
43 Ray Buchanan	.07	.20
44 Ken Dilger	.15	.40
45 Jerry Rice	.75	2.00
46 J.J. Stokes	.30	.75
47 Steve Young	.60	1.50
48 Derek Loville	.07	.20
49 Terry Kirby	.15	.40
50 Ken Norton	.07	.20
51 Tamarick Vanover	.15	.40
52 Marcus Allen	.30	.75
53 Steve Bono	.07	.20
54 Neil Smith	.15	.40
55 Derrick Thomas	.30	.75
56 Dale Carter	.07	.20
57 Terance Mathis	.07	.20
58 Eric Metcalf	.07	.20
59 Jamal Anderson RC	.60	1.50
60 Bert Emanuel	.15	.40
61 Craig Heyward	.07	.20
62 Cornelius Bennett	.07	.20
63 Tony Martin	.15	.40
64 Stan Humphries	.15	.40
65 Andre Coleman	.07	.20
66 Junior Seau	.30	.75
67 Terrell Fletcher	.07	.20
68 John Carney	.07	.20
69 Charlie Jones RC	.15	.40
70 Ricky Watters	.15	.40
71 Charlie Garner	.15	.40
72 Bobby Hoying RC	.30	.75
73 Jason Dunn RC	.15	.40
74 Bobby Taylor	.07	.20
75 Irving Fryar	.15	.40
76 Jim Kelly	.30	.75
77 Thurman Thomas	.30	.75
78 Bruce Smith	.15	.40
79 Bryce Paup	.07	.20
80 Darick Holmes	.07	.20
81 Andre Reed	.15	.40
82 Glyn Milburn	.07	.20
83 Brett Perriman	.07	.20
84 Herman Moore	.15	.40
85 Scott Mitchell	.15	.40
86 Barry Sanders	1.25	3.00
87 Johnnie Morton	.15	.40
88 Dan Marino	1.50	4.00
89 O.J. McDuffie	.15	.40
90 Stanley Pritchett RC	.07	.20
91 Zach Thomas RC	2.00	5.00
92 Daryl Gardener RC	.07	.20
93 Rashaan Salaam	.15	.40
94 Erik Kramer	.07	.20
95 Curtis Conway	.30	.75
96 Bobby Engram RC	.30	.75
97 Walt Harris RC	.07	.20
98 Bryan Cox	.07	.20
99 John Elway	1.50	4.00
100 Terrell Davis	.60	1.50
101 Anthony Miller	.15	.40
102 Shannon Sharpe	.15	.40
103 Tory James RC	.30	.75
104 Jeff Lewis RC	.15	.40
105 Joey Galloway	.30	.75
106 Chris Warren	.15	.40
107 Rick Mirer	.15	.40
108 Cortez Kennedy	.07	.20
109 Michael Sinclair	.07	.20
110 John Friesz	.07	.20
111 Warren Moon	.15	.40
112 Cris Carter	.30	.75
113 Jake Reed	.15	.40
114 Robert Smith	.15	.40
115 John Randle	.15	.40
116 Orlando Thomas	.07	.20
117 Jeff Hostetler	.07	.20
118 Tim Brown	.30	.75
119 Joe Aska	.07	.20
120 Napoleon Kaufman	.30	.75
121 Terry McDaniel	.07	.20
122 Harvey Williams	.07	.20
123 Trent Dilfer	.30	.75
124 Reggie Brooks	.07	.20
125 Alvin Harper	.07	.20
126 Mike Alstott RC	2.00	5.00
127 Hardy Nickerson	.07	.20
128 Mario Bates	.15	.40
129 Jim Everett	.07	.20
130 Tyrone Hughes	.07	.20
131 Michael Haynes	.07	.20
132 Eric Allen	.07	.20
133 Isaac Bruce	.30	.75
134 Kevin Carter	.07	.20
135 Leslie O'Neal	.07	.20
136 Tony Banks RC	.30	.75
137 Chris Chandler	.15	.40
138 Steve McNair	.60	1.50
139 Chris Sanders	.15	.40
140 Ronnie Harmon	.07	.20
141 Willie Davis	.07	.20
142 Michael Westbrook	.30	.75
143 Terry Allen	.15	.40
144 Brian Mitchell	.07	.20
145 Henry Ellard	.07	.20
146 Gus Frerotte	.15	.40
147 Kerry Collins	.30	.75
148 Sam Mills	.07	.20
149 Wesley Walls	.15	.40
150 Kevin Greene	.15	.40
151 Muhsin Muhammad RC	1.50	4.00
152 Winslow Oliver	.07	.20
153 Jeff Blake	.30	.75
154 Carl Pickens	.15	.40
155 Darnay Scott	.15	.40
156 Garrison Hearst	.15	.40
157 Marco Battaglia RC	.07	.20
158 Drew Bledsoe	.50	1.25
159 Curtis Martin	.60	1.50
160 Shawn Jefferson	.07	.20
161 Ben Coates	.15	.40
162 Lawyer Milloy RC	.75	2.00
163 Tyrone Wheatley	.15	.40
164 Rodney Hampton	.15	.40
165 Chris Calloway	.07	.20
166 Dave Brown	.07	.20
167 Amani Toomer RC	1.50	4.00
168 Vinny Testaverde	.15	.40
169 Michael Jackson	.15	.40
170 Eric Turner	.07	.20
171 DeRon Jenkins	.07	.20
172 Jermaine Lewis RC	.30	.75
173 Frank Sanders	.15	.40
174 Rob Moore	.15	.40
175 Kent Graham	.07	.20
176 Leeland McElroy RC	.15	.40
177 Larry Centers	.15	.40
178 Eric Swann	.07	.20
179 Mark Brunell	.50	1.25
180 Willie Jackson	.15	.40
181 James O. Stewart	.15	.40
182 Natrone Means	.15	.40
183 Tony Brackens RC	.30	.75
184 Adrian Murrell	.15	.40
185 Neil O'Donnell	.15	.40
186 Hugh Douglas	.15	.40
187 Wayne Chrebet	.40	1.00
188 Alex Van Dyke RC	.15	.40
SP13 Dan Marino Promo	1.25	3.00

1996 SP Explosive

STATED ODDS 1:360		
X1 Emmitt Smith	50.00	120.00
X2 Jerry Rice	30.00	80.00
X3 Rashaan Salaam	10.00	25.00
X4 Brett Favre	50.00	120.00
X5 Napoleon Kaufman	10.00	25.00
X6 Tim Biakabutuka	10.00	25.00
X7 John Elway	40.00	100.00
X8 Steve Young	25.00	60.00
X9 Isaac Bruce	12.00	30.00
X10 Troy Aikman	30.00	80.00
X11 Drew Bledsoe	15.00	40.00
X12 Carl Pickens	10.00	25.00
X13 Dan Marino	50.00	120.00
X14 Eddie George	12.00	30.00
X15 Joey Galloway	12.00	30.00
X16 Deion Sanders	25.00	60.00
X17 Curtis Martin	25.00	60.00
X18 Marshall Faulk	12.00	30.00
X19 Keyshawn Johnson	15.00	40.00
X20 Barry Sanders	40.00	100.00

1996 SP Focus on the Future

COMPLETE SET (30)	75.00	200.00
STATED ODDS 1:30		
F1 Leeland McElroy	.60	1.50
F2 Frank Sanders	.60	1.50
F3 Darick Holmes	.60	1.50
F4 Eric Moulds	4.00	10.00
F5 Kerry Collins	4.00	10.00
F6 Tim Biakabutuka	.60	1.50
F7 Ki-Jana Carter	.60	1.50
F8 Jeff Blake	2.50	6.00
F9 John Mobley	.60	1.50
F10 Johnnie Morton	.60	1.50
F11 Eddie George	5.00	12.00
F12 Steve McNair	5.00	12.00
F13 Marshall Faulk	4.00	10.00
F14 Kevin Hardy	.60	1.50
F15 Greg Hill	.60	1.50
F16 Karim Abdul-Jabbar	1.25	3.00
F17 Drew Bledsoe	4.00	10.00
F18 Curtis Martin	5.00	12.00
F19 Mario Bates	.60	1.50
F20 Danny Kanell	.60	1.50
F21 Keyshawn Johnson	4.00	10.00
F22 Napoleon Kaufman	1.25	3.00
F23 Rickey Dudley	.60	1.50
F24 Kordell Stewart	2.50	6.00
F25 Lawrence Phillips	.60	1.50
F26 Isaac Bruce	2.50	6.00
F27 J.J. Stokes	1.25	3.00
F28 Joey Galloway	2.50	6.00
F29 Errict Rhett	.60	1.50
F30 Mike Alstott	2.50	6.00

1996 SP Holoviews

COMPLETE SET (48)	75.00	150.00
STATED ODDS 1:7		
*DIE CUTS: .8X TO 2X BASIC INSERTS		
DIE CUT STATED ODDS 1:74		
1 Jerry Rice	2.50	6.00
2 Herman Moore	.50	1.25
3 Kerry Collins	1.00	2.50
4 Brett Favre	5.00	12.00
5 Junior Seau	1.00	2.50
6 Troy Aikman	2.50	6.00
7 John Elway	5.00	12.00
8 Steve Young	2.00	5.00
9 Reggie White	1.00	2.50
10 Kordell Stewart	1.00	2.50
11 Drew Bledsoe	1.50	4.00
12 Jeff Blake	1.00	2.50
13 Dan Marino	5.00	12.00
14 Curtis Martin	2.00	5.00
15 Marshall Faulk	1.25	3.00
16 Greg Lloyd	.50	1.25
17 Cris Carter	1.00	2.50
18 Isaac Bruce	1.00	2.50
19 Joey Galloway	1.00	2.50
20 Barry Sanders	4.00	10.00
21 Emmitt Smith	4.00	10.00
22 Edgar Bennett	.50	1.25
23 Rashaan Salaam	.50	1.25
24 Steve McNair	2.00	5.00
25 Tamarick Vanover	.50	1.25
26 Deion Sanders	1.50	4.00
27 Keyshawn Johnson	2.50	6.00
28 Kevin Hardy	.25	.60
29 Simeon Rice	.50	1.25
30 Lawrence Phillips	.25	.60
31 Tim Biakabutuka	.50	1.25
32 Terry Glenn	2.00	5.00
33 Rickey Dudley	.25	.60
34 Regan Upshaw	.25	.60
35 Eddie George	3.00	8.00
36 John Mobley	.25	.60
37 Eddie Kennison	.50	1.25
38 Marvin Harrison	6.00	15.00
39 Leeland McElroy	.25	.60
40 Eric Moulds	2.50	6.00
41 Alex Van Dyke	.25	.60
42 Mike Alstott	1.50	4.00
43 Jeff Lewis	.25	.60
44 Bobby Engram	.25	.60
45 Derrick Mayes	.25	.60
46 Karim Abdul-Jabbar	.50	1.25
47 Stepfret Williams	.25	.60
48 Stephen Davis	4.00	10.00

1996 SP SPx Force

COMPLETE SET (4)	40.00	100.00
STATED ODDS 1:950		
AUTO STATED ODDS 1:8820		
FR1 Keyshawn Johnson	7.50	20.00
Lawrence Phillips		
Terry Glenn		
Tim Biakabutuka		
FR2 Barry Sanders	15.00	40.00
Emmitt Smith		
Marshall Faulk		
Curtis Martin		
FR3 Dan Marino	15.00	40.00
Brett Favre		
Drew Bledsoe		
Troy Aikman		
FR4 Jerry Rice	10.00	25.00
Herman Moore		
Carl Pickens		
Isaac Bruce		
SPX5A Keyshawn Johnson AUTO	50.00	120.00
(signed card number 5)		
SPX5B Dan Marino AUTO	100.00	250.00
(signed card number 5)		
SPX5C Jerry Rice AUTO	60.00	150.00
(signed card number 5)		
SPX5D Barry Sanders AUTO	125.00	250.00

1997 SP Authentic

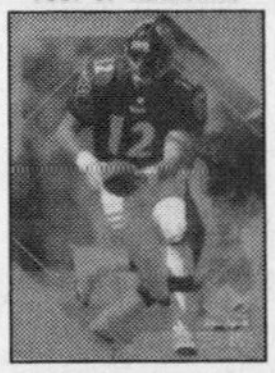

The 1997 SP Authentic set was issued in one series totalling 198 cards and distributed in five-card packs with a suggested retail price of $4.99. The fronts features color player photos, while the backs carry player information. The set contains the topical subset: Future Watch (1-30).

COMPLETE SET (198)	50.00	100.00
1 Orlando Pace RC	.75	2.00
2 Darrell Russell RC	.20	.50
3 Shawn Springs RC	.40	1.00
4 Peter Boulware RC	1.50	4.00
5 Bryant Westbrook RC	.40	1.00
6 Walter Jones RC	.75	2.00
7 Ike Hilliard RC	1.50	4.00
8 James Farrior RC	1.25	3.00
9 Tom Knight RC	.20	.50
10 Warrick Dunn RC	4.00	10.00
11 Tony Gonzalez RC	8.00	20.00
12 Reinard Wilson RC	.40	1.00
13 Yatil Green RC	.40	1.00
14 Reidel Anthony RC	.75	2.00
15 Kenny Holmes RC	.20	.50
16 Dwayne Rudd RC	.20	.50
17 Renaldo Wynn RC	.20	.50
18 David LaFleur RC	.20	.50
19 Antowain Smith RC	2.50	6.00
20 Jim Druckenmiller RC	.40	1.00
21 Rae Carruth RC	.20	.50
22 Byron Hanspard RC	.40	1.00
23 Jake Plummer RC	4.00	10.00
24 Joey Kent RC	.40	1.00
25 Corey Dillon RC	4.00	10.00
26 Danny Wuerffel RC	2.00	5.00
27 Will Blackwell RC	.20	.50
28 Troy Davis RC	.40	1.00
29 Darnell Autry RC	.40	1.00
30 Pat Barnes RC	.40	1.00
31 Kent Graham	.20	.50
32 Simeon Rice	.30	.75
33 Frank Sanders	.30	.75
34 Rob Moore	.30	.75
35 Eric Swann	.20	.50
36 Chris Chandler	.30	.75
37 Jamal Anderson	.50	1.25
38 Terance Mathis	.30	.75
39 Bert Emanuel	.30	.75
40 Michael Booker	.20	.50
41 Vinny Testaverde	.30	.75
42 Byron Bam Morris	.20	.50
43 Michael Jackson	.30	.75
44 Derrick Alexander WR	.30	.75
45 Jamie Sharper RC	.75	2.00
46 Kim Herring RC	.20	.50
47 Todd Collins	.20	.50
48 Thurman Thomas	.50	1.25
49 Andre Reed	.30	.75
50 Quinn Early	.20	.50
51 Bryce Paup	.20	.50
52 Lonnie Johnson	.20	.50
53 Kerry Collins	.50	1.25
54 Anthony Johnson	.20	.50
55 Tim Biakabutuka	.30	.75
56 Muhsin Muhammad	.30	.75
57 Sam Mills	.20	.50
58 Wesley Walls	.30	.75
59 Rick Mirer	.20	.50
60 Raymont Harris	.20	.50
61 Curtis Conway	.30	.75
62 Bobby Engram	.30	.75
63 Bryan Cox	.20	.50
64 John Allred RC	.20	.50
65 Jeff Blake	.30	.75
66 Ki-Jana Carter	.20	.50
67 Darnay Scott	.30	.75
68 Carl Pickens	.30	.75
69 Dan Wilkinson	.20	.50
70 Troy Aikman	1.25	2.50
71 Emmitt Smith	2.00	4.00
72 Michael Irvin	.50	1.25
73 Deion Sanders	.50	1.25
74 Anthony Miller	.20	.50
75 Antonio Anderson RC	.20	.50
76 John Elway	2.00	5.00
77 Terrell Davis	.60	1.50
78 Rod Smith WR	.50	1.25
79 Shannon Sharpe	.30	.75
80 Neil Smith	.30	.75
81 Trevor Pryce RC	.75	2.00
82 Scott Mitchell	.30	.75
83 Barry Sanders	1.50	4.00
84 Herman Moore	.30	.75
85 Johnnie Morton	.30	.75
86 Matt Russell RC	.20	.50
87 Brett Favre	2.50	5.00
88 Edgar Bennett	.30	.75
89 Robert Brooks	.30	.75
90 Antonio Freeman	.50	1.25
91 Reggie White	.50	1.25
92 Craig Newsome	.20	.50
93 Jim Harbaugh	.30	.75
94 Marshall Faulk	.60	1.50
95 Sean Dawkins	.20	.50
96 Marvin Harrison	.50	1.25
97 Quentin Coryatt	.20	.50
98 Tarik Glenn RC	.40	1.00
99 Mark Brunell	.60	1.50
100 Natrone Means	.30	.75
101 Keenan McCardell	.30	.75
102 Jimmy Smith	.30	.75
103 Tony Brackens	.20	.50
104 Kevin Hardy	.20	.50
105 Elvis Grbac	.30	.75
106 Marcus Allen	.50	1.25
107 Greg Hill	.20	.50
108 Derrick Thomas	.50	1.25
109 Dale Carter	.20	.50
110 Dan Marino	2.00	5.00
111 Karim Abdul-Jabbar	.30	.75
112 Brian Manning RC	.20	.50
113 Daryl Gardener	.20	.50
114 Troy Drayton	.20	.50
115 Zach Thomas	.50	1.25
116 Jason Taylor RC	6.00	15.00
117 Brad Johnson	.50	1.25
118 Robert Smith	.30	.75
119 John Randle	.30	.75
120 Cris Carter	.50	1.25
121 Jake Reed	.30	.75
122 Randall Cunningham	.50	1.25
123 Drew Bledsoe	.60	1.50
124 Curtis Martin	.60	1.50
125 Terry Glenn	.50	1.25
126 Willie McGinest	.20	.50
127 Chris Canty RC	.20	.50
128 Sedrick Shaw RC	.40	1.00
129 Heath Shuler	.20	.50
130 Mario Bates	.20	.50
131 Ray Zellars	.20	.50
132 Andre Hastings	.20	.50
133 Dave Brown	.20	.50
134 Tyrone Wheatley	.30	.75
135 Rodney Hampton	.30	.75
136 Chris Calloway	.20	.50
137 Tiki Barber RC	8.00	20.00
138 Neil O'Donnell	.30	.75
139 Adrian Murrell	.30	.75
140 Wayne Chrebet	.50	1.25
141 Keyshawn Johnson	.50	1.25
142 Hugh Douglas	.20	.50
143 Jeff George	.30	.75
144 Napoleon Kaufman	.50	1.25
145 Tim Brown	.50	1.25
146 Desmond Howard	.30	.75
147 Rickey Dudley	.30	.75
148 Terry McDaniel	.20	.50
149 Ty Detmer	.30	.75
150 Ricky Watters	.30	.75
151 Chris T. Jones	.20	.50
152 Irving Fryar	.30	.75
153 Mike Mamula	.20	.50
154 Jon Harris RC	.20	.50
155 Kordell Stewart	.50	1.25
156 Jerome Bettis	.50	1.25
157 Charles Johnson	.30	.75
158 Greg Lloyd	.20	.50
159 George Jones RC	.20	.50
160 Terrell Fletcher	.20	.50
161 Stan Humphries	.30	.75
162 Tony Martin	.30	.75
163 Eric Metcalf	.30	.75
164 Junior Seau	.50	1.25
165 Rod Woodson	.30	.75
166 Steve Young	.60	1.50
167 Terry Kirby	.30	.75
168 Garrison Hearst	.30	.75
169 Jerry Rice	1.25	2.50
170 Ken Norton	.20	.50
171 Kevin Greene	.30	.75
172 Lamar Smith	.50	1.25
173 Warren Moon	.50	1.25
174 Chris Warren	.30	.75
175 Cortez Kennedy	.20	.50
176 Joey Galloway	.30	.75
177 Tony Banks	.30	.75
178 Isaac Bruce	.50	1.25
179 Eddie Kennison	.30	.75
180 Kevin Carter	.20	.50
181 Craig Heyward	.20	.50
182 Trent Dilfer	.50	1.25
183 Errict Rhett	.20	.50
184 Mike Alstott	.50	1.25
185 Hardy Nickerson	.20	.50
186 Ronde Barber RC	4.00	10.00
187 Steve McNair	.60	1.50
188 Eddie George	.50	1.25
189 Chris Sanders	.20	.50
190 Blaine Bishop	.20	.50
191 Derrick Mason RC	5.00	12.00
192 Gus Frerotte	.20	.50
193 Terry Allen	.50	1.25
194 Brian Mitchell	.20	.50
195 Alvin Harper	.20	.50
196 Jeff Hostetler	.20	.50
197 Leslie Shepherd	.20	.50
198 Stephen Davis	.50	1.25
A1 Aikman Audio Blue	1.50	4.00
A2 Aikman Audio Pro Bowl	4.00	10.00
A3 Aikman Audio White	15.00	30.00
(500 cards made)		

1997 SP Authentic Mark of a Legend

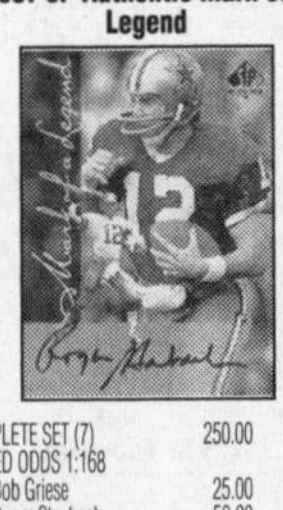

COMPLETE SET (7)	250.00	400.00
STATED ODDS 1:168		
ML1 Bob Griese	25.00	50.00
ML2 Roger Staubach	50.00	80.00
ML3 Joe Montana	60.00	120.00
ML4 Franco Harris	30.00	60.00
ML5A Gale Sayers Wht	30.00	60.00
ML5B Gale Sayers Silv	30.00	60.00
ML6 Steve Largent	25.00	50.00
ML7 Tony Dorsett	30.00	60.00

1997 SP Authentic ProFiles

COMPLETE SET (40)	30.00	80.00
STATED ODDS 1:5		
*DIE CUTS: .6X TO 1.5X BASIC INSERTS		
DIE CUT STATED ODDS 1:12		
*DIE CUT 100: 2.5X TO 6X BASIC INSERTS		
STATED PRINT RUN 100 SERIAL #'d SETS		
P1 Dan Marino	5.00	12.00
P2 Kordell Stewart	1.25	3.00
P3 Emmitt Smith	4.00	10.00
P4 Brett Favre	5.00	12.00
P5 Marcus Allen	1.25	3.00
P6 Jerry Rice	2.50	6.00
P7 Jeff George	.75	2.00
P8 Mark Brunell	1.50	4.00
P9 Eddie George	1.25	3.00
P10 Cris Carter	1.25	3.00
P11 Tim Biakabutuka	.75	2.00
P12 Ike Hilliard	.75	2.00
P13 Darrell Russell	.08	.25
P14 Jim Druckenmiller	.20	.50
P15 Rae Carruth	.08	.25
P16 Warrick Dunn	5.00	12.00
P17 Herman Moore	.75	2.00
P18 Deion Sanders	1.25	3.00
P19 Drew Bledsoe	1.50	4.00
P20 Jeff Blake	.75	2.00
P21 Keyshawn Johnson	1.25	3.00
P22 Curtis Martin	1.50	4.00
P23 Michael Irvin	1.25	3.00
P24 Barry Sanders	4.00	10.00
P25 Carl Pickens	.75	2.00
P26 Steve McNair	1.50	4.00
P27 Terry Allen	1.25	3.00
P28 Terrell Davis	1.50	4.00
P29 Lawrence Phillips	.50	1.25
P30 Marshall Faulk	1.50	4.00
P31 Karim Abdul-Jabbar	.75	2.00
P32 Steve Young	1.50	4.00
P33 Tim Brown	1.25	3.00
P34 Antowain Smith	2.50	6.00
P35 Kerry Collins	1.25	3.00
P36 Reggie White	1.25	3.00
P37 John Elway	5.00	12.00
P38 Jerome Bettis	1.25	3.00
P39 Troy Aikman	2.50	6.00
P40 Junior Seau	1.25	3.00

1997 SP Authentic Sign of the Times

STATED ODDS 1:24		
1 Karim Abdul-Jabbar	7.50	20.00
(white stock)		
2 Troy Aikman	40.00	80.00
3 Terry Allen	7.50	20.00
4 Reidel Anthony	6.00	15.00
5 Jerome Bettis	50.00	100.00
6 Will Blackwell	6.00	15.00
7 Jeff Blake	7.50	20.00
8 Robert Brooks	7.50	20.00
9 Tim Brown	12.00	30.00
10 Isaac Bruce	10.00	25.00
11 Rae Carruth	7.50	20.00
(white stock)		
12 Kerry Collins	10.00	25.00
13 Terrell Davis	12.00	30.00
14 Jim Druckenmiller	6.00	15.00
15 Warrick Dunn	12.00	30.00
16 Marshall Faulk	15.00	40.00
17 Joey Galloway	7.50	20.00
18 Eddie George	10.00	25.00
(silver foil stock)		
19 Tony Gonzalez	25.00	50.00
20 George Jones	6.00	15.00
21 Napoleon Kaufman	7.50	20.00
22A Dan Marino	75.00	125.00
(silver foil stock)		
22B Dan Marino	75.00	125.00
(white stock)		
23 Curtis Martin SP	25.00	50.00
24 Herman Moore	7.50	20.00
25A Jerry Rice	75.00	150.00
(silver foil stock)		
25B Jerry Rice	75.00	150.00
(white stock)		
26 Rashaan Salaam	6.00	15.00
27 Antowain Smith	10.00	25.00
28 Emmitt Smith	150.00	250.00
(silver foil stock)		

1997 SP Authentic Traditions

STATED ODDS 1:1440		
TD1 Dan Marino	250.00	400.00
Bob Griese		
TD2 Troy Aikman	125.00	250.00
Roger Staubach		
TD3 Jerry Rice	300.00	500.00
Joe Montana		
TD4 Jerome Bettis	125.00	250.00
Franco Harris		
TD5 Emmitt Smith	250.00	400.00
Tony Dorsett		
TD6 Joey Galloway	75.00	135.00
Steve Largent		

1998 SP Authentic

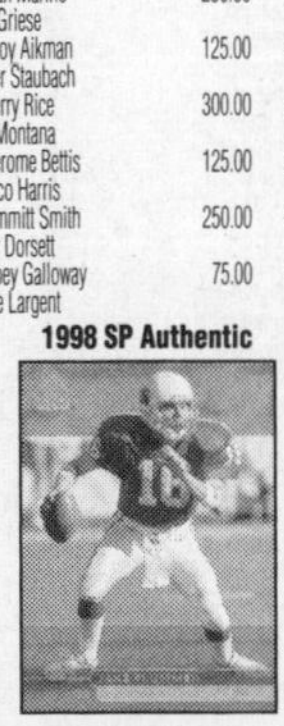

This set was released in one series with a total of 126-cards. The first 42-cards (1998 draft picks and Time Warp subsets) were short-printed and serial numbered to 2000-sets produced. A Die Cut parallel of all cards was produced and numbered of 500-sets.

COMP.SET w/o SP's (84)	20.00	40.00
*HAND NUMBERED RC: .3X TO .8X		
1 Andre Wadsworth RC	8.00	20.00
2 Corey Chavous RC	8.00	20.00
3 Keith Brooking RC	12.00	30.00
4 Duane Starks RC	5.00	12.00
5 Pat Johnson RC	5.00	12.00
6 Jason Peter RC	5.00	12.00
7 Curtis Enis RC	6.00	15.00
8 Takeo Spikes RC	8.00	20.00

9 Greg Ellis RC 6.00 15.00
10 Marcus Nash RC 5.00 12.00
11 Brian Griese RC 12.00 30.00
12 Germane Crowell RC 6.00 15.00
13 Vonnie Holliday RC 8.00 20.00
14 Peyton Manning RC 450.00 800.00
15 Jerome Pathon RC 5.00 12.00
16 Fred Taylor RC 20.00 40.00
17 John Avery RC 5.00 12.00
18 Randy Moss RC 50.00 120.00
19 Robert Edwards RC 5.00 12.00
20 Tony Simmons RC 5.00 12.00
21 Shaun Williams RC 5.00 12.00
22 Joe Jurevicius RC 8.00 20.00
23 Charles Woodson RC 30.00 60.00
24 Tra Thomas RC 5.00 12.00
25 Grant Wistrom RC 6.00 15.00
26 Ryan Leaf RC 8.00 20.00
27 Ahman Green RC 15.00 40.00
28 Jacquez Green RC 5.00 12.00
29 Kevin Dyson RC 8.00 20.00
30 Stephen Alexander RC 6.00 15.00
31 John Elway TW 6.00 15.00
32 Jerry Rice TW 5.00 12.00
33 Emmitt Smith TW 6.00 15.00
34 Steve Young TW 3.00 8.00
35 Jerome Bettis TW 2.50 6.00
36 Deion Sanders TW 2.50 6.00
37 Andre Rison TW 1.50 4.00
38 Warren Moon TW 2.50 6.00
39 Mark Brunell TW 2.00 5.00
40 Ricky Watters TW 1.50 4.00
41 Dan Marino TW 8.00 20.00
42 Brett Favre TW 10.00 25.00
43 Jake Plummer .40 1.00
44 Adrian Murrell .25 .60
45 Eric Swann .15 .40
46 Jamal Anderson .40 1.00
47 Chris Chandler .25 .60
48 Jim Harbaugh .25 .60
49 Michael Jackson .15 .40
50 Jermaine Lewis .25 .60
51 Rob Johnson .25 .60
52 Antowain Smith .40 1.00
53 Thurman Thomas .40 1.00
54 Kerry Collins .25 .60
55 Fred Lane .15 .40
56 Rae Carruth .15 .40
57 Erik Kramer .15 .40
58 Curtis Conway .25 .60
59 Corey Dillon .40 1.00
60 Neil O'Donnell .25 .60
61 Carl Pickens .25 .60
62 Troy Aikman .75 2.00
63 Emmitt Smith 1.25 3.00
64 Deion Sanders .40 1.00
65 Terrell Davis .40 1.00
66 John Elway 1.50 4.00
67 Rod Smith .25 .60
68 Scott Mitchell .25 .60
69 Barry Sanders 1.25 3.00
70 Herman Moore .25 .60
71 Brett Favre 1.50 4.00
72 Dorsey Levens .40 1.00
73 Antonio Freeman .40 1.00
74 Marshall Faulk .50 1.25
75 Marvin Harrison .40 1.00
76 Mark Brunell .40 1.00
77 Keenan McCardell .25 .60
78 Jimmy Smith .25 .60
79 Andre Rison .25 .60
80 Elvis Grbac .25 .60
81 Derrick Alexander .25 .60
82 Dan Marino 1.50 4.00
83 Karim Abdul-Jabbar .40 1.00
84 O.J. McDuffie .25 .60
85 Brad Johnson .40 1.00
86 Cris Carter .40 1.00
87 Robert Smith .40 1.00
88 Drew Bledsoe .60 1.50
89 Terry Glenn .40 1.00
90 Ben Coates .25 .60
91 Lamar Smith .25 .60
92 Danny Wuerffel .25 .60
93 Tiki Barber .40 1.00
94 Danny Kanell .25 .60
95 Ike Hilliard .25 .60
96 Curtis Martin .40 1.00
97 Keyshawn Johnson .40 1.00
98 Glenn Foley .25 .60
99 Jeff George .25 .60
100 Tim Brown .40 1.00
101 Napoleon Kaufman .40 1.00
102 Bobby Hoying .25 .60
103 Charlie Garner .25 .60
104 Irving Fryar .25 .60
105 Kordell Stewart .40 1.00
106 Jerome Bettis .40 1.00
107 Charles Johnson .15 .40
108 Tony Banks .25 .60
109 Isaac Bruce .40 1.00
110 Natrone Means .25 .60
111 Junior Seau .40 1.00
112 Steve Young .50 1.25
113 Jerry Rice .75 2.00
114 Garrison Hearst .40 1.00
115 Ricky Watters .25 .60
116 Warren Moon .40 1.00
117 Joey Galloway .25 .60
118 Trent Dilfer .40 1.00
119 Warrick Dunn .50 1.25
120 Mike Alstott .40 1.00
121 Steve McNair .40 1.00
122 Eddie George .40 1.00
123 Yancey Thigpen .15 .40
124 Gus Frerotte .15 .40
125 Terry Allen .40 1.00
126 Michael Westbrook .25 .60
AE13 Dan Marino SAMPLE 1.25 3.00

1998 SP Authentic Die Cuts

*DIE CUT VETS 43-126: 3X TO 8X
*DIE CUT TIME WARP 31-42: .6X TO 1.5X
*DIE CUT ROOKIE 1-30: .3X TO .8X
DIE CUT PRINT RUN 500 SER.#'d SETS
14 Peyton Manning 400.00 750.00
18 Randy Moss 50.00 120.00

1998 SP Authentic Maximum Impact

COMPLETE SET (30) 20.00 50.00
STATED ODDS 1:4
SE1 Brett Favre 2.00 5.00
SE2 Warrick Dunn .60 1.50
SE3 Junior Seau .50 1.25
SE4 Steve Young .60 1.50
SE5 Herman Moore .30 .75
SE6 Antowain Smith .50 1.25
SE7 John Elway 2.00 5.00
SE8 Troy Aikman 1.00 2.50
SE9 Dorsey Levens .50 1.25
SE10 Kordell Stewart .50 1.25
SE11 Peyton Manning 8.00 20.00
SE12 Eddie George .50 1.25
SE13 Dan Marino 2.00 5.00
SE14 Joey Galloway .30 .75
SE15 Mark Brunell .50 1.25
SE16 Jake Plummer .50 1.25
SE17 Curtis Enis .30 .75
SE18 Corey Dillon .50 1.25
SE19 Rob Johnson .30 .75
SE20 Barry Sanders 1.50 4.00
SE21 Deion Sanders .50 1.25
SE22 Napoleon Kaufman .50 1.25
SE23 Ryan Leaf .50 1.25
SE24 Jerry Rice 1.00 2.50
SE25 Drew Bledsoe .50 1.25
SE26 Jerome Bettis .50 1.25
SE27 Emmitt Smith 1.50 4.00
SE28 Tim Brown .50 1.25
SE29 Curtis Martin .50 1.25
SE30 Terrell Davis .50 1.25

1998 SP Authentic Player's Ink Green

STATED ODDS 1:23 OVERALL
AW Andre Wadsworth 7.50 20.00
BG Brian Griese 10.00 25.00
BH Bobby Hoying 7.50 20.00
CD Corey Dillon 10.00 25.00
CE Curtis Enis 7.50 20.00
DL Dorsey Levens 7.50 20.00
DM Dan Marino 75.00 150.00
EG Eddie George 10.00 25.00
FL Fred Lane 10.00 25.00
FT Fred Taylor 15.00 30.00
GC Germane Crowell 5.00 12.00
JA Jamal Anderson 7.50 20.00
JM Johnnie Morton 7.50 20.00
JP Jake Plummer 10.00 25.00
JR Jerry Rice 100.00 200.00
KJ Keyshawn Johnson 10.00 25.00
KM Keenan McCardell 7.50 20.00
KS Kordell Stewart 7.50 20.00
MA Mike Alstott 10.00 25.00
MJ Michael Jackson 5.00 12.00
MN Marcus Nash 5.00 12.00
PA Jerome Pathon 5.00 12.00
RE Robert Edwards 7.50 20.00
RL Ryan Leaf 7.50 20.00
RM Randy Moss 50.00 100.00
SH Skip Hicks 7.50 20.00
SS Shannon Sharpe 10.00 25.00
TA Troy Aikman 30.00 60.00
TS Takeo Spikes 7.50 20.00
TV Tamarick Vanover 5.00 12.00

1998 SP Authentic Player's Ink Gold

GOLDS SERIAL #'d TO PLAYER'S JERSEY NO.
CARDS SERIAL #'d UNDER 25 NOT PRICED
AW Andre Wadsworth/90 20.00 50.00
CD Corey Dillon/28 25.00 60.00
CE Curtis Enis/39 25.00 60.00
DL Dorsey Levens/25 25.00 60.00
EG Eddie George/27 50.00 100.00
FL Fred Lane/32 20.00 50.00
FT Fred Taylor/28 60.00 120.00
JA Jamal Anderson/32 25.00 60.00
JM Johnnie Morton/87 20.00 50.00
JR Jerry Rice/80 125.00 250.00
KM Keenan McCardell/87 20.00 50.00
MA Mike Alstott/40 30.00 80.00
MJ Michael Jackson/81 20.00 50.00
RE Robert Edwards/47 20.00 50.00
SS Shannon Sharpe/84 20.00 50.00
TS Takeo Spikes/51 20.00 50.00
TV Tamarick Vanover/87 20.00 50.00

1998 SP Authentic Player's Ink Silver

*SILVERS: .8X TO 2X GREENS
JR Jerry Rice 100.00 250.00
RM Randy Moss 50.00 120.00

1998 SP Authentic Special Forces

COMPLETE SET (30) 100.00 200.00
STATED PRINT RUN 1000 SERIAL #'d SETS
S1 Kordell Stewart 2.00 5.00
S2 Charles Woodson 3.00 8.00
S3 Terrell Davis 2.00 5.00
S4 Brett Favre 8.00 20.00
S5 Joey Galloway 1.25 3.00
S6 Warrick Dunn 2.50 6.00
S7 Ryan Leaf 2.00 5.00
S8 Drew Bledsoe 3.00 8.00
S9 Takeo Spikes 1.25 3.00
S10 Barry Sanders 6.00 15.00
S11 Troy Aikman 4.00 10.00
S12 John Elway 8.00 20.00
S13 Jerome Bettis 2.00 5.00
S14 Karim Abdul-Jabbar 2.00 5.00
S15 Tony Gonzalez 2.00 5.00
S16 Steve Young 2.50 6.00
S17 Napoleon Kaufman 2.00 5.00
S18 Andre Wadsworth 1.25 3.00
S19 Herman Moore 1.25 3.00
S20 Fred Taylor 4.00 10.00
S21 Deion Sanders 2.00 5.00
S22 Peyton Manning 20.00 40.00
S23 Jerry Rice 4.00 10.00
S24 Dan Marino 8.00 20.00
S25 Antonio Freeman 2.00 5.00
S26 Curtis Enis 1.25 3.00
S27 Jake Plummer 2.00 5.00
S28 Steve McNair 2.00 5.00
S29 Mark Brunell 2.00 5.00
S30 Robert Edwards 1.25 3.00

1999 SP Authentic

Released as a 145-card base set, the 1999 SP Authentic set features 90 veteran cards and 55 rookie cards. Base cards are printed on white card stock with gold foil highlights. Rookie cards are sequentially numbered out of 1999. The set was released in boxes containing 24 packs of 5 cards each, and carried a suggested retail price of $4.99.

COMP.SET w/o SPs (90) 12.00 30.00
*HAND NUMBERED RCs: .3X TO .8X
1 Jake Plummer .30 .75
2 Adrian Murrell .30 .75
3 Frank Sanders .25 .60
4 Jamal Anderson .30 .75
5 Chris Chandler .30 .75
6 Terance Mathis .25 .60
7 Priest Holmes .40 1.00
8 Jermaine Lewis .25 .60
9 Antowain Smith .25 .60
10 Doug Flutie .40 1.00
11 Eric Moulds .30 .75
12 Muhsin Muhammad .30 .75
13 Tim Biakabutuka .30 .75
14 Wesley Walls .30 .75
15 Curtis Enis .25 .60
16 Bobby Engram .30 .75
17 Corey Dillon .30 .75
18 Darnay Scott .25 .60
19 Terry Kirby .25 .60
20 Ty Detmer .30 .75
21 Troy Aikman .60 1.50
22 Michael Irvin .40 1.00
23 Emmitt Smith 1.00 2.50
24 Terrell Davis .40 1.00
25 Brian Griese .30 .75
26 Rod Smith .30 .75
27 Shannon Sharpe .40 1.00
28 Barry Sanders 1.00 2.50
29 Charlie Batch .30 .75
30 Herman Moore .30 .75
31 Johnnie Morton .30 .75
32 Brett Favre 1.25 3.00
33 Antonio Freeman .30 .75
34 Dorsey Levens .30 .75
35 Mark Chmura .25 .60
36 Peyton Manning 1.25 3.00
37 Marvin Harrison .40 1.00
38 Mark Brunell .30 .75
39 Fred Taylor .30 .75
40 Jimmy Smith .30 .75
41 Elvis Grbac .25 .60
42 Andre Rison .30 .75
43 Dan Marino 1.25 3.00
44 O.J. McDuffie .30 .75
45 Yatil Green .25 .60
46 Randall Cunningham .40 1.00
47 Randy Moss .40 1.00
48 Robert Smith .30 .75
49 Cris Carter .40 1.00
50 Drew Bledsoe .40 1.00
51 Ben Coates .30 .75
52 Terry Glenn .30 .75
53 Eddie Kennison .30 .75
54 Cam Cleeland .25 .60
55 Ike Hilliard .30 .75
56 Gary Brown .25 .60
57 Kerry Collins .30 .75
58 Vinny Testaverde .30 .75
59 Keyshawn Johnson .30 .75
60 Wayne Chrebet .30 .75
61 Curtis Martin .40 1.00
62 Tim Brown .40 1.00
63 Napoleon Kaufman .25 .60
64 Charles Woodson .40 1.00
65 Duce Staley .30 .75
66 Charles Johnson .25 .60
67 Kordell Stewart .30 .75
68 Jerome Bettis .40 1.00
69 Marshall Faulk .40 1.00
70 Isaac Bruce .40 1.00
71 Trent Green .30 .75
72 Jim Harbaugh .30 .75
73 Junior Seau .40 1.00
74 Natrone Means .30 .75
75 Steve Young .50 1.25
76 Jerry Rice .75 2.00
77 Terrell Owens .40 1.00
78 Lawrence Phillips .30 .75
79 Joey Galloway .30 .75
80 Ricky Watters .30 .75
81 Jon Kitna .30 .75
82 Warrick Dunn .30 .75
83 Trent Dilfer .30 .75
84 Mike Alstott .40 1.00
85 Eddie George .30 .75
86 Steve McNair .40 1.00
87 Yancey Thigpen .25 .60
88 Brad Johnson .30 .75
89 Skip Hicks .25 .60
90 Michael Westbrook .25 .60
91 Ricky Williams RC 8.00 20.00
92 Tim Couch RC 5.00 12.00
93 Akili Smith RC 4.00 10.00
94 Edgerrin James RC 6.00 15.00
95 Donovan McNabb RC 20.00 50.00
96 Torry Holt RC 10.00 25.00
97 Cade McNown RC 4.00 10.00
98 Shaun King RC 4.00 10.00
99 Daunte Culpepper RC 5.00 12.00
100 Brock Huard RC 4.00 10.00
101 Chris Claiborne RC 3.00 8.00
102 James Johnson RC 3.00 8.00
103 Rob Konrad RC 3.00 8.00
104 Peerless Price RC 4.00 10.00
105 Kevin Faulk RC 6.00 15.00
106 Andy Katzenmoyer RC 4.00 10.00
107 Troy Edwards RC 4.00 10.00
108 Kevin Johnson RC 4.00 10.00
109 Mike Cloud RC 3.00 8.00
110 David Boston RC 4.00 10.00
111 Champ Bailey RC 10.00 25.00
112 D'Wayne Bates RC 3.00 8.00
113 Joe Germaine RC 4.00 10.00
114 Antoine Winfield RC 3.00 8.00
115 Fernando Bryant RC 3.00 8.00
116 Jevon Kearse RC 5.00 12.00
117 Chris McAlister RC 4.00 10.00
118 Brandon Stokley RC 5.00 12.00
119 Karsten Bailey RC 3.00 8.00
120 Daylon McCutcheon RC 3.00 8.00
121 Jermaine Fazande RC 3.00 8.00
122 Joel Makovicka RC 3.00 8.00
123 Ebenezer Ekuban RC 3.00 8.00
124 Joe Montgomery RC 3.00 8.00
125 Sean Bennett RC 3.00 8.00
126 Na Brown RC 3.00 8.00
127 De'Mond Parker RC 3.00 8.00
128 Sedrick Irvin RC 3.00 8.00
129 Terry Jackson RC 3.00 8.00
130 Jeff Paulk RC 3.00 8.00
131 Cecil Collins RC 3.00 8.00
132 Bobby Collins RC 3.00 8.00
133 Amos Zereoue RC 4.00 10.00
134 Travis McGriff RC 3.00 8.00
135 Larry Parker RC 4.00 10.00
136 Wane McGarity RC 3.00 8.00
137 Cecil Martin RC 3.00 8.00
138 Al Wilson RC 5.00 12.00
139 Jim Kleinsasser RC 5.00 12.00
140 Dat Nguyen RC 5.00 12.00
141 Marty Booker RC 4.00 10.00
142 Reginald Kelly RC 3.00 8.00
143 Scott Covington RC 3.00 8.00
144 Antuan Edwards RC 3.00 8.00
145 Craig Yeast RC 3.00 8.00
WPA Walter Payton AU/100 400.00 600.00
WPSP Walter Payton Jsy AU/34 1,000.00 1,500.00

1999 SP Authentic Excitement

*VETS: 5X TO 12X BASIC CARDS
STATED PRINT RUN 250 SER.#'d SETS
91 Ricky Williams 30.00 80.00
92 Tim Couch 12.50 30.00
93 Akili Smith 10.00 25.00
94 Edgerrin James 30.00 80.00
95 Donovan McNabb 50.00 120.00
96 Torry Holt 15.00 40.00
97 Cade McNown 10.00 25.00
98 Shaun King 10.00 25.00
99 Daunte Culpepper 25.00 60.00
100 Brock Huard 12.50 30.00
101 Chris Claiborne 6.00 15.00
102 James Johnson 10.00 25.00
103 Rob Konrad 12.50 30.00
104 Peerless Price 12.50 30.00
105 Kevin Faulk 15.00 40.00
106 Andy Katzenmoyer 10.00 25.00
107 Troy Edwards 10.00 25.00
108 Kevin Johnson 12.50 30.00
109 Mike Cloud 10.00 25.00
110 David Boston 12.50 30.00
111 Champ Bailey 15.00 40.00
112 D'Wayne Bates 10.00 25.00
113 Joe Germaine 10.00 25.00
114 Antoine Winfield 10.00 25.00
115 Fernando Bryant 10.00 25.00
116 Jevon Kearse 20.00 50.00
117 Chris McAlister 10.00 25.00
118 Brandon Stokley 15.00 40.00
119 Karsten Bailey 10.00 25.00
120 Daylon McCutcheon 10.00 25.00
121 Jermaine Fazande 10.00 25.00
122 Joel Makovicka 12.50 30.00
123 Ebenezer Ekuban 10.00 25.00
124 Joe Montgomery 10.00 25.00
125 Sean Bennett 6.00 15.00
126 Na Brown 10.00 25.00
127 De'Mond Parker 6.00 15.00
128 Sedrick Irvin 6.00 15.00
129 Terry Jackson 10.00 25.00
130 Jeff Paulk 6.00 15.00
131 Cecil Collins 6.00 15.00
132 Bobby Collins 6.00 15.00
133 Amos Zereoue 12.50 30.00
134 Travis McGriff 6.00 15.00
135 Larry Parker 12.50 30.00
136 Wane McGarity 6.00 15.00
137 Cecil Martin 10.00 25.00
138 Al Wilson 10.00 25.00
139 Jim Kleinsasser 10.00 25.00
140 Dat Nguyen 10.00 25.00
141 Marty Booker 12.50 30.00
142 Reginald Kelly 6.00 15.00
143 Scott Covington 12.50 30.00
144 Antuan Edwards 10.00 25.00
145 Craig Yeast 10.00 25.00

1999 SP Authentic Excitement Gold

*VETS: 30X TO 80X BASIC CARDS
STATED PRINT RUN 25 SER.#'d SETS
91 Ricky Williams 125.00 250.00
92 Tim Couch 30.00 80.00
93 Akili Smith 25.00 50.00
94 Edgerrin James 100.00 250.00
95 Donovan McNabb 150.00 300.00
96 Torry Holt 100.00 200.00
97 Cade McNown 25.00 50.00
98 Shaun King 25.00 50.00
99 Daunte Culpepper 75.00 150.00
100 Brock Huard 30.00 60.00
101 Chris Claiborne 15.00 30.00
102 James Johnson 25.00 50.00
103 Rob Konrad 30.00 60.00
104 Peerless Price 30.00 60.00
105 Kevin Faulk 30.00 60.00
106 Andy Katzenmoyer 25.00 50.00
107 Troy Edwards 25.00 50.00
108 Kevin Johnson 30.00 60.00
109 Mike Cloud 25.00 50.00
110 David Boston 30.00 60.00
111 Champ Bailey 30.00 80.00
112 D'Wayne Bates 25.00 50.00
113 Joe Germaine 25.00 50.00
114 Antoine Winfield 25.00 50.00
115 Fernando Bryant 25.00 50.00
116 Jevon Kearse 40.00 100.00
117 Chris McAlister 25.00 50.00
118 Brandon Stokley 30.00 80.00
119 Karsten Bailey 25.00 50.00
120 Daylon McCutcheon 25.00 50.00
121 Jermaine Fazande 25.00 50.00
122 Joel Makovicka 30.00 60.00
123 Ebenezer Ekuban 25.00 50.00
124 Joe Montgomery 25.00 50.00
125 Sean Bennett 15.00 30.00
126 Na Brown 25.00 50.00
127 De'Mond Parker 15.00 30.00
128 Sedrick Irvin 15.00 30.00
129 Terry Jackson 25.00 50.00
130 Jeff Paulk 15.00 30.00
131 Cecil Collins 15.00 30.00
132 Bobby Collins 15.00 30.00
133 Amos Zereoue 30.00 60.00
134 Travis McGriff 15.00 30.00
135 Larry Parker 30.00 60.00
136 Wane McGarity 15.00 30.00
137 Cecil Martin 25.00 50.00
138 Al Wilson 25.00 50.00
139 Jim Kleinsasser 25.00 50.00
140 Dat Nguyen 25.00 50.00
141 Marty Booker 30.00 60.00
142 Reginald Kelly 15.00 30.00
143 Scott Covington 30.00 60.00
144 Antuan Edwards 25.00 50.00
145 Craig Yeast 25.00 50.00

1999 SP Authentic Athletic

COMPLETE SET (10) 15.00 30.00
STATED ODDS 1:10
A1 Randy Moss 4.00 10.00
A2 Steve McNair 1.25 3.00
A3 Jamal Anderson 1.25 3.00
A4 Curtis Martin 1.25 3.00
A5 Kordell Stewart .75 2.00
A6 Barry Sanders 4.00 10.00
A7 Fred Taylor 1.25 3.00
A8 Doug Flutie 1.25 3.00
A9 Emmitt Smith 2.50 6.00
A10 Steve Young 1.50 4.00

1999 SP Authentic Buy Back Autographs

BUY BACK AU/1-117 ODDS 1:576
SERIAL #'d UNDER 12 NOT PRICED
1 T.Aikman 93SP/12 60.00 150.00
2 T.Aikman 94SP/42 40.00 80.00
3 T.Aikman 95SP/94 25.00 60.00
4 T.Aikman 95SPC/24 50.00 100.00
6 T.Aikman 96SP/28 50.00 100.00
8 T.Aikman 98SPA/24 50.00 100.00
10 J.Anderson 96SP/15 30.00 60.00
12 J.Anderson 98SPA/20 25.00 60.00
13 J.Bettis 93SP/25 90.00 150.00
14 J.Bettis 94SP/42 50.00 80.00
15 J.Bettis 95SP/93 50.00 80.00
16 J.Bettis 95SPC/25 60.00 100.00
19 J.Bettis 98SPA/63 50.00 80.00
20 D.Bledsoe 93SP/14 60.00 120.00
21 D.Bledsoe 94SP/28 30.00 80.00
22 D.Bledsoe 95SP/98 20.00 50.00
23 D.Bledsoe 95SPC/25 40.00 100.00
28 D.Bledsoe 98SPA/117 20.00 50.00
30 T.Brown 93SP/19 30.00 80.00
31 T.Brown 94SP/36 25.00 60.00
32 T.Brown 95SPC/25 25.00 60.00
34 T.Brown 98SP/25 25.00 60.00
38 M.Brunell 98SPA/21 60.00 120.00
39 W.Chrebet 95SP/43 25.00 60.00
40 W.Chrebet 96SP/14 30.00 80.00
41 T.Davis 96SP/14 150.00 300.00
43 T.Davis 98SPA/62 25.00 60.00
45 W.Dunn 98SPAMI/50 20.00 50.00
46 M.Faulk 94SP/28 125.00 250.00
47 M.Faulk 95SP/17 60.00 120.00
48 M.Faulk 95SPC/23 30.00 80.00
50 M.Faulk 96SP/40 25.00 60.00
51 M.Faulk 98SPA/28 60.00 120.00
52 J.Galloway 95SP/30 20.00 50.00
53 J.Galloway 95SPC/48 20.00 50.00
55 J.Galloway 98SPA/68 20.00 50.00
56 E.George 96SP/17 175.00 300.00
58 E.George 98SPA/65 20.00 50.00
59 E.George 98SPAMI/48 20.00 50.00
60 B.Johnson 98SPA/70 20.00 50.00
61 P.Manning 98UDEnc/60 175.00 300.00
62 P.Manning 98UDECT/16 300.00 500.00
63 D.Marino 95SP/100 50.00 100.00
64 D.Marino 95SPC/25 75.00 150.00
65 D.Marino 96SP/37 60.00 120.00
67 D.Marino 98SPA/44 60.00 120.00
68 D.Marino 99SP/28 60.00 120.00
69 N.Means 95SP/64 15.00 40.00
70 H.Moore 93SP/18 20.00 50.00
71 H.Moore 94SP/45 15.00 40.00
72 H.Moore 95SP/84 15.00 40.00
73 H.Moore 95SPC/25 15.00 40.00
74 H.Moore 96SP/40 15.00 40.00
75 H.Moore 98SPA/30 15.00 40.00
76 J.Plummer 98SPA/112 20.00 50.00
78 J.Plummer 98SPAMI/98 20.00 50.00
80 J.Rice 95SP/80 60.00 120.00
81 J.Rice 95SPC/28 100.00 200.00
85 J.Rice 98SPA/61 75.00 150.00

1999 SP Authentic Maximum Impact

COMPLETE SET (10) 6.00 15.00
STATED ODDS 1:4
MI1 Jerry Rice 1.25 3.00
MI2 Eddie George .60 1.50
MI3 Marshall Faulk .75 2.00
MI4 Keyshawn Johnson .60 1.50
MI5 Terrell Davis .60 1.50
MI6 Warrick Dunn .60 1.50
MI7 Jerome Bettis .60 1.50
MI8 Drew Bledsoe .75 2.00
MI9 Curtis Martin .60 1.50
MI10 Brett Favre 2.00 5.00

1999 SP Authentic New Classics

COMPLETE SET (10) 15.00 40.00
STATED ODDS 1:23
NC1 Steve McNair 1.50 4.00
NC2 Jon Kitna 1.50 4.00
NC3 Curtis Enis .60 1.50
NC4 Peyton Manning 5.00 12.00
NC5 Fred Taylor 1.50 4.00
NC6 Randy Moss 5.00 12.00
NC7 Donovan McNabb 6.00 15.00
NC8 Terrell Owens 1.50 4.00
NC9 Keyshawn Johnson 1.50 4.00
NC10 Ricky Williams 2.50 6.00

1999 SP Authentic NFL Headquarters

COMPLETE SET (10) 15.00 40.00
STATED ODDS 1:10
HQ1 Brett Favre 4.00 10.00
HQ2 Jake Plummer .75 2.00
HQ3 Charlie Batch 1.25 3.00
HQ4 Akili Smith 1.00 2.50
HQ5 Troy Aikman 2.50 6.00
HQ6 Drew Bledsoe 1.50 4.00
HQ7 Dan Marino 4.00 10.00
HQ8 Jon Kitna 1.25 3.00
HQ9 Mark Brunell 1.25 3.00
HQ10 Tim Couch 1.25 3.00

1999 SP Authentic Player's Ink Green

STATED ODDS 1:23
AFA Antonio Freeman 10.00 25.00
ASA Akili Smith 6.00 15.00
BHA Brock Huard 6.00 15.00
BJA Brad Johnson 10.00 25.00
BRA Mark Brunell 10.00 25.00
CBA Champ Bailey 15.00 40.00
CDA Corey Dillon 10.00 25.00
CHA Charlie Batch 10.00 25.00
CLA Mike Cloud 6.00 15.00
CMA Cade McNown 6.00 15.00
DBA David Boston 10.00 25.00
DCA Daunte Culpepper 12.00 30.00
DFA Doug Flutie 12.00 30.00
DMA Dan Marino 75.00 150.00
DRA Drew Bledsoe 12.00 30.00
EDA Ed McCaffrey 10.00 25.00
EGA Eddie George 10.00 25.00
EJA Edgerrin James 12.00 30.00
EMA Eric Moulds 10.00 25.00
HMA Herman Moore 6.00 15.00
JAA Jamal Anderson 10.00 25.00
JBA Jerome Bettis 40.00 80.00
JGA Joey Galloway 10.00 25.00
JPA Jake Plummer 12.00 30.00
JRA Jerry Rice 90.00 150.00
KFA Kevin Faulk 10.00 25.00
MBA Michael Bishop 6.00 15.00
MFA Marshall Faulk 15.00 40.00
NMA Natrone Means 6.00 15.00
PMA Peyton Manning 60.00 120.00
RMA Randy Moss 25.00 60.00
SKA Shaun King 10.00 25.00
SSA Shannon Sharpe 15.00 40.00
TAA Troy Aikman 40.00 80.00
TCA Tim Couch 10.00 25.00
TDA Terrell Davis 15.00 40.00
TEA Troy Edwards 10.00 25.00
THA Torry Holt 12.00 30.00
TOA Terrell Owens 12.00 30.00
WCA Wayne Chrebet 10.00 25.00
DRAX Drew Bledsoe EXCH 2.00 5.00

1999 SP Authentic Player's Ink Purple

*LEVEL 2 PURPLE/100: .8X TO 2X GREEN AU
RWA Ricky Williams 40.00 100.00

1999 SP Authentic Rookie Blitz

COMPLETE SET (19) 20.00 50.00
STATED ODDS 1:11
RB1 Edgerrin James 4.00 10.00
RB2 Tim Couch 1.00 2.50
RB3 Daunte Culpepper 4.00 10.00
RB4 Champ Bailey 1.25 3.00
RB5 Donovan McNabb 5.00 12.00
RB6 Kevin Johnson 1.00 2.50
RB7 Shaun King 1.00 2.50
RB8 Peerless Price 1.00 2.50
RB9 David Boston 1.00 2.50
RB10 Ricky Williams 2.00 5.00
RB11 Akili Smith 1.00 2.50
RB12 Kevin Faulk 1.00 2.50
RB13 D'Wayne Bates .75 2.00
RB14 Brock Huard 1.00 2.50
RB15 Rob Konrad .75 2.00
RB16 Torry Holt 2.50 6.00
RB17 Troy Edwards 1.00 2.50
RB18 Cade McNown 1.00 2.50
RB19 Cecil Collins .75 2.00

1999 SP Authentic Supremacy

COMPLETE SET (12) 30.00 60.00
STATED ODDS 1:23
S1 Terrell Davis 1.50 4.00
S2 Joey Galloway 1.00 2.50
S3 Dan Marino 5.00 12.00
S4 Brett Favre 5.00 12.00
S5 Emmitt Smith 3.00 8.00
S6 Barry Sanders 5.00 12.00
S7 Curtis Martin 1.50 4.00
S8 Jamal Anderson 1.50 4.00
S9 Jake Plummer 1.00 2.50
S10 Randy Moss 5.00 12.00
S11 Tim Couch 1.50 4.00
S12 Peyton Manning 5.00 12.00

2000 SP Authentic

Released as a 150-card set, SP Authentic is comprised of 90 veteran base cards and 60 shortprinted rookie cards sequentially numbered to 1250. Card stock is white bordered and embossed along the edges of the cards with full color player action photography and silver foil highlights. SP Authentic was packaged in 24-pack boxes with packs containing five cards each and carried a suggested retail price of $4.99. An Update set of 21-cards was issued in April 2001 as part of 3-card packs distributed directly to Upper Deck hobby accounts.

COMP.SET w/o RC's (90) 6.00 15.00
91-171 ROOKIE PRINT RUN 1250
1 Jake Plummer .25 .60
2 David Boston .20 .50
3 Frank Sanders .20 .50
4 Chris Chandler .25 .60
5 Jamal Anderson .25 .60
6 Shawn Jefferson .20 .50
7 Tony Banks .20 .50
8 Shannon Sharpe .30 .75
9 Rob Johnson .25 .60
10 Antowain Smith .25 .60
11 Muhsin Muhammad .25 .60
12 Steve Beuerlein .25 .60
13 Cade McNown .20 .50
14 Curtis Enis .20 .50
15 Marcus Robinson .25 .60
16 Akili Smith .20 .50
17 Corey Dillon .25 .60
18 Tim Couch .25 .60
19 Kevin Johnson .20 .50
20 Errict Rhett .25 .60
21 Troy Aikman .50 1.25
22 Emmitt Smith .75 2.00
23 Rocket Ismail .25 .60
24 Joey Galloway .25 .60
25 Terrell Davis .30 .75
26 Olandis Gary .25 .60
27 Ed McCaffrey .25 .60
28 Brian Griese .25 .60
29 Charlie Batch .25 .60
30 Germane Crowell .20 .50
31 James O. Stewart .20 .50
32 Brett Favre 1.00 2.50
33 Antonio Freeman .25 .60
34 Dorsey Levens .25 .60
35 Peyton Manning .75 2.00
36 Edgerrin James .30 .75
37 Marvin Harrison .30 .75
38 Mark Brunell .25 .60
39 Fred Taylor .30 .75
40 Jimmy Smith .25 .60
41 Elvis Grbac .20 .50
42 Tony Gonzalez .30 .75
43 James Johnson .20 .50
44 Oronde Gadsden .25 .60
45 Damon Huard .25 .60
46 Randy Moss .30 .75
47 Cris Carter .30 .75
48 Daunte Culpepper .25 .60
49 Drew Bledsoe .30 .75
50 Terry Glenn .25 .60
51 Ricky Williams .30 .75
52 Jeff Blake .25 .60
53 Keith Poole .20 .50
54 Kerry Collins .25 .60
55 Amani Toomer .25 .60
56 Ike Hilliard .25 .60
57 Wayne Chrebet .25 .60
58 Curtis Martin .30 .75
59 Vinny Testaverde .25 .60
60 Tim Brown .30 .75
61 Rich Gannon .25 .60
62 Tyrone Wheatley .20 .50
63 Duce Staley .25 .60
64 Donovan McNabb .30 .75
65 Troy Edwards .20 .50
66 Jerome Bettis .30 .75
67 Kordell Stewart .25 .60
68 Marshall Faulk .30 .75
69 Kurt Warner .50 1.25
70 Isaac Bruce .30 .75
71 Torry Holt .30 .75
72 Ryan Leaf .25 .60
73 Jim Harbaugh .25 .60
74 Jermaine Fazande .20 .50
75 Jerry Rice .60 1.50
76 Terrell Owens .30 .75
77 Jeff Garcia .25 .60
78 Ricky Watters .25 .60
79 Jon Kitna .25 .60
80 Derrick Mayes .20 .50
81 Shaun King .20 .50
82 Mike Alstott .30 .75
83 Keyshawn Johnson .25 .60
84 Warrick Dunn .25 .60
85 Eddie George .25 .60
86 Steve McNair .30 .75
87 Jevon Kearse .25 .60
88 Brad Johnson .25 .60
89 Stephen Davis .25 .60
90 Michael Westbrook .20 .50
91 Anthony Lucas RC 2.50 6.00
92 Avion Black RC 2.50 6.00
93 Dante Hall RC 4.00 10.00
94 Darrell Jackson RC 3.00 8.00
95 Deltha O'Neal RC 3.00 8.00
96 Erron Kinney RC 2.50 6.00
97 Doug Chapman RC 2.50 6.00
98 Frank Murphy RC 2.50 6.00
99 Gari Scott RC 2.50 6.00
100 Giovanni Carmazzi RC 2.50 6.00
101 JaJuan Dawson RC 2.50 6.00
102 Jarious Jackson RC 3.00 8.00
103 Rashard Anderson RC 2.50 6.00
104 Michael Wiley RC 2.50 6.00
105 Spergon Wynn RC 3.00 8.00
106 Muneer Moore RC 2.50 6.00
107 Ahmed Plummer RC 2.50 6.00
108 Chad Morton RC 4.00 10.00
109 Rob Morris RC 3.00 8.00
110 Ron Dixon RC 2.50 6.00
111 Rondell Mealey RC 2.50 6.00
112 Sebastian Janikowski RC 4.00 10.00
113 Shaun Ellis RC 4.00 10.00
114 Rogers Beckett RC 2.50 6.00
115 Shyrone Stith RC 2.50 6.00
116 Tim Rattay RC 3.00 8.00
117 Todd Husak RC 2.50 6.00
118 Tom Brady RC 600.00 900.00
119 Trevor Gaylor RC 2.50 6.00
120 Windrell Hayes RC 2.50 6.00
121 Anthony Becht RC 3.00 8.00
122 Brian Urlacher RC 30.00 60.00
123 Bubba Franks RC 4.00 10.00
124 Chad Pennington RC 6.00 15.00
125 Chris Redman RC 3.00 8.00
126 Corey Simon RC 3.00 8.00
127 Curtis Keaton RC 2.50 6.00
128 Danny Farmer RC 2.50 6.00
129 Dennis Northcutt RC 3.00 8.00
130 Dez White RC 3.00 8.00
131 J.R. Redmond RC 2.50 6.00
132 Jamal Lewis RC 4.00 10.00
133 Jerry Porter RC 4.00 10.00
134 Joe Hamilton RC 2.50 6.00
135 Laveranues Coles RC 4.00 10.00
136 R.Jay Soward RC 2.50 6.00
137 Reuben Droughns RC 4.00 10.00
138 Ron Dayne RC 4.00 10.00
139 Ron Dugans RC 2.50 6.00
140 Shaun Alexander RC 5.00 12.00
141 Sylvester Morris RC 2.50 6.00
142 Tee Martin RC 4.00 10.00
143 Thomas Jones RC 5.00 12.00
144 Todd Pinkston RC 2.50 6.00
145 Travis Prentice RC 3.00 8.00
146 Travis Taylor RC 3.00 8.00
147 Trung Canidate RC 3.00 8.00
148 Courtney Brown RC 3.00 8.00
149 Plaxico Burress RC 6.00 12.00
150 Peter Warrick RC 4.00 10.00
151 Billy Volek RC 4.00 10.00
152 Bobby Shaw RC 3.00 8.00
153 Brad Hoover RC 3.00 8.00
154 Brian Finneran RC 4.00 10.00
155 Charles Lee RC 2.50 6.00
156 Chris Cole RC 3.00 8.00
157 Clint Stoerner RC 5.00 12.00
158 Doug Johnson RC 3.00 8.00
159 Frank Moreau RC 2.50 6.00
160 Jake Delhomme RC 12.00 30.00
161 KaRon Coleman RC 2.50 6.00
162 Kevin McDougal RC 2.50 6.00
163 Larry Foster RC 2.50 6.00
164 Mike Anderson RC 4.00 10.00
165 Patrick Pass RC 3.00 8.00
166 Reggie Jones RC 2.50 6.00
167 Sammy Morris RC 3.00 8.00
168 Shockmain Davis RC 2.50 6.00
169 Terrelle Smith RC 2.50 6.00
170 Ronney Jenkins RC 2.50 6.00

171 Troy Walters RC 2.50 6.00
PM Peyton Manning Sample 1.00 2.50

2000 SP Authentic Buy Back Autographs

STATED ODDS 1:71
1 T.Aikman 94SP/55 30.00 60.00
2 T.Aikman 96SP/27 30.00 80.00
3 T.Aikman 98SPA/65 30.00 60.00
4 T.Aikman 99SPA/385 25.00 50.00
5 M.Alstott 98SPA/204 15.00 40.00
6 M.Alstott 99SPA/400 15.00 40.00
7 J.Anderson 97SPA
8 J.Anderson 98SPA/133 10.00 25.00
9 J.Anderson 99SPA/584 6.00 15.00
10 C.Bailey 99SPARB/426 10.00 25.00
11 C.Batch 99SPA/285 7.50 20.00
12 C.Batch 99SPANFL/354 7.50 20.00
13 D.Bledsoe 94SP/50 40.00 80.00
14 D.Bledsoe 96SP/21 50.00 120.00
15 D.Bledsoe 95SP/74 25.00 50.00
16 D.Bledsoe 99SPA/156 20.00 50.00
17 T.Brown 93SP/26 30.00 60.00
18 T.Brown 94SP/302 7.50 20.00
19 T.Brown 95SP/123 10.00 25.00
20 T.Brown 96SP/24 30.00 60.00
22 T.Brown 98SPA/121 10.00 25.00
23 T.Brown 99SPA/464 7.50 20.00
24 I.Bruce 95SP/217 10.00 25.00
25 I.Bruce 96SP/33 30.00 60.00
26 I.Bruce 97SPA/16 40.00 80.00
27 I.Bruce 98SPA/147 10.00 25.00
28 I.Bruce 99SPA/555 7.50 20.00
29 M.Brunell 96SP/46 20.00 50.00
30 M.Brunell 97SPA/11 100.00 200.00
31 M.Brunell 99SPA/620 8.00 20.00
32 C.Carter 93SP/21 50.00 100.00
33 C.Carter 98SPA/68 15.00 30.00
34 C.Carter 99SPA/300 15.00 30.00
35 C.Carter 00SPA/180 15.00 30.00
36 C.Chandler 94SP/35 10.00 25.00
37 C.Chandler 95SP/361 6.00 15.00
38 C.Chandler 96SP/18 15.00 40.00
40 C.Chandler 98SPA/153 6.00 15.00
41 C.Chandler 99SPA/595 6.00 15.00
42 W.Chrebet 99SPA/267 7.50 20.00
43 K.Collins 95SP/114 30.00 80.00
44 K.Collins 96SP/32 15.00 40.00
45 K.Collins 98SPA/202 7.50 20.00
46 K.Collins 99SPA/605 7.50 20.00
47 T.Couch 99SPARB/400 7.50 20.00
48 T.Couch 99SPANFL/251 7.50 20.00
49 T.Davis 99SPA/237 20.00 40.00
51 T.Davis 98SPA/43 40.00 80.00
52 T.Dilfer 96SP/12 30.00 60.00
53 T.Dilfer 98SPA/65 10.00 25.00
54 T.Dilfer 99SPA/288 6.00 15.00
55 K.Faulk 99SPARB/394 7.50 20.00
56 M.Faulk 95SP/38 30.00 80.00
57 M.Faulk 96SP/25 50.00 100.00
58 M.Faulk 98SPA/65 25.00 50.00
59 M.Faulk 99SPA/74 25.00 50.00
60 D.Flutie 99SPA/293 10.00 25.00
61 D.Flutie 99SPAA/395 10.00 25.00
63 A.Freeman 98SPA/137 10.00 25.00
64 A.Freeman 99SPA/507 7.50 20.00
66 J.Galloway 96SP/123 10.00 25.00
67 J.Galloway 98SPA/200 10.00 25.00
68 J.Galloway 99SPA/273 10.00 25.00
69 J.Galloway 99SPAS/415 7.50 20.00
71 E.George 98SPA/121 10.00 25.00
72 E.George 99SPA/155 10.00 25.00
73 T.Holt 99SPARB/400 10.00 25.00
74 B.Johnson 99SPA/381 10.00 25.00
76 Ky.Johnson 98SPA/102 10.00 25.00
77 Ky.Johnson 99SPA/310 7.50 20.00
78 J.Kitna 99SPA/240 6.00 15.00
79 J.Kitna 99SPANC/396 6.00 15.00
80 D.Levens 98SPA/196 10.00 25.00
81 D.Levens 99SPA/620 6.00 15.00
82 P.Manning 99SPA/131 30.00 80.00
83 H.Moore 94SP/333 7.50 20.00
84 H.Moore 96SP/221 7.50 20.00
85 H.Moore 99SPA/270 7.50 20.00
86 E.Moulds 99SPA/291 7.50 20.00
87 R.Moss 99SPA/50 60.00 120.00
88 T.Owens 99SPA/450 15.00 40.00
89 T.Owens 99SPANC/282 15.00 40.00
90 J.Plummer 99SPA/280 10.00 25.00
91 J.Plummer 99SPASUP/165 10.00 25.00
92 S.Sharpe 94SP/77 12.00 30.00
93 S.Sharpe 95SP/281 10.00 25.00
94 S.Sharpe 96SP/62 12.00 30.00
96 S.Sharpe 99SPA/554 10.00 25.00
97 Ak.Smith 99SPARB/417 10.00 25.00
98 K.Stewart 96SP/67 30.00 60.00
99 K.Stewart 98SPA/169 10.00 25.00
100 K.Stewart 99SPA/600 10.00 25.00
101 V.Testeverde 99SPA/290 7.50 20.00
103 R.Watters 94SP/45 10.00 25.00
104 R.Watters 96SP/39 10.00 25.00
105 R.Watters 98SPA/148 7.50 20.00
106 R.Watters 99SPA/430 7.50 20.00

2000 SP Authentic New Classics

COMPLETE SET (10) 5.00 12.00
STATED ODDS 1:11
NC1 Peter Warrick .60 1.50
NC2 Courtney Brown .50 1.25
NC3 Trung Canidate .50 1.25
NC4 Dennis Northcutt .50 1.25
NC5 J.R. Redmond .40 1.00
NC6 Daunte Culpepper .50 1.25
NC7 Edgerrin James .60 1.50
NC8 Marcus Robinson .50 1.25
NC9 Shaun King .40 1.00
NC10 Ricky Williams .60 1.50

2000 SP Authentic Rookie Fusion

COMPLETE SET (7) 6.00 15.00
STATED ODDS 1:18
RF1 Plaxico Burress .75 2.00
RF2 Chad Pennington 1.25 3.00
RF3 Travis Taylor .60 1.50
RF4 Ron Dayne .75 2.00
RF5 Thomas Jones 1.00 2.50
RF6 Jamal Lewis .75 2.00
RF7 Sylvester Morris .50 1.25

2000 SP Authentic Sign of the Times

STATED ODDS 1:23
AF Antonio Freeman 6.00 15.00
AL Anthony Lucas 5.00 12.00
AS Akili Smith 5.00 12.00
BF Bubba Franks 8.00 20.00
BG Brian Griese 6.00 15.00
BJ Brad Johnson 6.00 15.00
BU Brian Urlacher 20.00 50.00
CA Trung Canidate 6.00 15.00
CB Charlie Batch 6.00 15.00
CH Champ Bailey 6.00 15.00
CK Curtis Keaton 5.00 12.00
CL Chris Coleman UER 5.00 12.00
(name misspelled on front Colleman)
CM Cade McNown 5.00 12.00
CO Courtney Brown 6.00 15.00
CP Chad Pennington 20.00 40.00
CR Chris Chandler/7*
CS Corey Simon 6.00 15.00
DB David Boston 5.00 12.00
DC Daunte Culpepper 6.00 15.00
DF Danny Farmer 5.00 12.00
DJ Darrell Jackson 6.00 15.00
DL Chris Claiborne 5.00 12.00
DM Dan Marino/23*
DN Dennis Northcutt 6.00 15.00
DR Reuben Droughns 8.00 20.00
DU Ron Dugans 5.00 12.00
DW Dez White 6.00 15.00
EG Eddie George 6.00 15.00
EJ Edgerrin James 8.00 20.00
EM Eric Moulds 6.00 15.00
FB Mike Alstott 8.00 20.00
FL Doug Flutie 8.00 20.00
GC Giovanni Carmazzi 5.00 12.00
GF Gus Frerotte 6.00 15.00
GO Tony Gonzalez 10.00 25.00
HM Herman Moore 6.00 15.00
JD JaJuan Dawson 5.00 12.00
JH Joe Hamilton 5.00 12.00
JJ J.J. Stokes 6.00 15.00
JK Jon Kitna 6.00 15.00
JL Jamal Lewis 8.00 20.00
JN Joe Namath 40.00 80.00
JO Kevin Johnson 5.00 12.00
JR J.R. Redmond 5.00 12.00
KC Kwame Cavil 5.00 12.00
KE Kerry Collins 6.00 15.00
KF Kevin Faulk 6.00 15.00
KJ Keyshawn Johnson 6.00 15.00
KS Kordell Stewart 6.00 15.00
KW Kurt Warner 12.00 30.00
LC Laveranues Coles 8.00 20.00
MB Mark Brunell 6.00 15.00
MH Marvin Harrison 8.00 20.00
MO Corey Moore 5.00 12.00
MW Michael Wiley 5.00 12.00
OG Olandis Gary 6.00 15.00
PB Plaxico Burress 12.50 25.00
PM Peyton Manning 50.00 100.00
QI Qadry Ismail 6.00 15.00
RB Rob Johnson 6.00 15.00
RD Ron Dayne 8.00 20.00
RE Chris Redman 6.00 15.00
RL Ray Lucas 5.00 12.00
RM Randy Moss 40.00 80.00
SA Shaun Alexander 25.00 50.00
SD Stephen Davis 6.00 15.00
SG Sherrod Gideon 5.00 12.00
SM Sylvester Morris 5.00 12.00
SY Steve Young 40.00 80.00
TC Tim Couch 6.00 15.00
TD Trent Dilfer 6.00 15.00
TE Troy Edwards 5.00 12.00
TG Trevor Gaylor 5.00 12.00
TH Torry Holt 8.00 20.00
TM1 Tee Martin 8.00 20.00
TP Travis Prentice 6.00 15.00
TR Tim Rattay 6.00 15.00
TT Travis Taylor 6.00 15.00
TW Troy Walters 5.00 12.00
WC Wayne Chrebet 6.00 15.00
WH Windrell Hayes 5.00 12.00
RJ R.Jay Soward EXCH
RW Ricky Williams EXCH
SJ Sebastian Janikowski EXCH 2.00 5.00
TJ Thomas Jones EXCH 2.50 6.00
TO Terrell Owens EXCH 4.00 10.00
(no auto; no sticker on front)

2000 SP Authentic Sign of the Times Gold

STATED PRINT RUN 5-92
SERIAL #'d UNDER 20 NOT PRICED
AF Antonio Freeman/86 10.00 25.00
AL Anthony Lucas/87 8.00 20.00
BF Bubba Franks/88 12.00 30.00
BU Brian Urlacher/54 50.00 100.00
CH Champ Bailey/24 25.00 60.00
CK Curtis Keaton/29 15.00 40.00
CO Courtney Brown/92 10.00 25.00
CS Corey Simon/90 10.00 25.00
DB David Boston/89 8.00 20.00
DJ Darrell Jackson/82 10.00 25.00
DL Chris Claiborne/50 10.00 25.00
DN Dennis Northcutt/86 10.00 25.00
DR Reuben Droughns/21 25.00 60.00
EG Eddie George/27 20.00 50.00
EJ Edgerrin James/32 20.00 50.00
EM Eric Moulds/80 10.00 25.00
FB Mike Alstott/40 15.00 40.00
GO Tony Gonzalez/88 15.00 40.00
JD JaJuan Dawson/88 8.00 20.00
JJ J.J. Stokes/83 10.00 25.00
JL Jamal Lewis/31 15.00 40.00
JO Kevin Johnson/85 8.00 20.00
JR J.R. Redmond/21 15.00 40.00
KC Kwame Cavil/82 8.00 20.00
LC Laveranues Coles/87 12.00 30.00
MH Marvin Harrison/88 15.00 40.00
MW Michael Wiley/33 12.00 30.00
OG Olandis Gary/22 20.00 50.00
PB Plaxico Burress/88 15.00 40.00
QI Qadry Ismail/87 10.00 25.00
RD Ron Dayne/27 25.00 60.00
SA Shaun Alexander/37 20.00 50.00
SD Stephen Davis/46 12.00 30.00
SM Sylvester Morris/82 8.00 20.00
TE Troy Edwards/81 8.00 20.00
TH Torry Holt/88 15.00 40.00
TW Troy Walters/82 8.00 20.00
WC Wayne Chrebet/80 10.00 25.00
WH Windrell Hayes/86 8.00 20.00

2000 SP Authentic SP Athletic

COMPLETE SET (10) 3.00 8.00
STATED ODDS 1:11
A1 Marshall Faulk .60 1.50
A2 Kevin Johnson .40 1.00
A3 Olandis Gary .50 1.25
A4 Jeff Garcia .50 1.25
A5 Akili Smith .40 1.00
A6 Donovan McNabb .60 1.50
A7 Rob Johnson .50 1.25
A8 Marcus Robinson .50 1.25
A9 Shaun King .40 1.00
A10 Troy Edwards .40 1.00

2000 SP Authentic Supremacy

COMPLETE SET (15) 10.00 25.00
STATED ODDS 1:8
S1 Mark Brunell .60 1.50
S2 Terrell Davis .75 2.00
S3 Jamal Anderson .60 1.50
S4 Jerry Rice 1.50 4.00
S5 Emmitt Smith 2.00 5.00
S6 Troy Aikman 1.25 3.00
S7 Randy Moss .75 2.00
S8 Brad Johnson .60 1.50
S9 Brett Favre 2.50 6.00
S10 Keyshawn Johnson .60 1.50
S11 Fred Taylor .75 2.00
S12 Kurt Warner 1.25 3.00
S13 Tim Couch .60 1.50
S14 Eddie George .60 1.50
S15 Drew Bledsoe .75 2.00

2001 SP Authentic

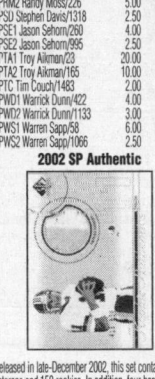

This set was issued in December, 2001. The set was issued in five card packs which were packed 24 to a box. Cards numbered 91-190 featured rookies and were printed to different amounts. Cards numbered 91-93, which had a jersey swatch and an autograph, had a print run of 250 sets. Cards numbered 94-120 had a jersey swatch and were printed to 800 (except for a few cards which we have notated specific print runs in our checklist). Cards number 121-150 had a stated print run of 550 sets and were autographed. Cards numbered 151-190 also had a print run of 800 sets. Some cards were issued in packs via mail redemptions. Of those, cards #121 Adam Archuleta and #122 Alex Bannister were never fulfilled.

COMP.SET w/o SP's (90) 7.50 20.00
91-93 JSY AU RC PRINT RUN 250
94-120 JSY RC PRINT RUN 106-800
151-190 ROOKIE PRINT RUN 800
1 Jake Plummer .25 .60
2 Thomas Jones .25 .60
3 Frank Sanders .20 .50
4 Jamal Anderson .25 .60
5 Chris Chandler .25 .60
6 Tony Martin .25 .60
7 Jamal Lewis .30 .75
8 Elvis Grbac .25 .60
9 Travis Taylor .20 .50
10 Peerless Price .20 .50
11 Rob Johnson .25 .60
12 Eric Moulds .25 .60
13 Muhsin Muhammad .25 .60
14 Isaac Byrd .20 .50
15 Wesley Walls .20 .50
16 James Allen .20 .50
17 Marcus Robinson .25 .60
18 Brian Urlacher .40 1.00
19 Jon Kitna .25 .60
20 Peter Warrick .25 .60
21 Corey Dillon .25 .60
22 Kevin Johnson .20 .50
23 JaJuan Dawson .20 .50
24 Tim Couch .20 .50
25 Rocket Ismail .25 .60
26 Emmitt Smith .75 2.00
27 Joey Galloway .25 .60
28 Terrell Davis .30 .75
29 Mike Anderson .25 .60
30 Brian Griese .25 .60
31 Ed McCaffrey .25 .60
32 Charlie Batch .25 .60
33 James O. Stewart .20 .50
34 Johnnie Morton .25 .60
35 Brett Favre 1.00 2.50
36 Antonio Freeman .30 .75
37 Bill Schroeder .25 .60
38 Ahman Green .30 .75
39 Peyton Manning .75 2.00
40 Edgerrin James .30 .75
41 Marvin Harrison .30 .75
42 Mark Brunell .25 .60
43 Fred Taylor .30 .75
44 Jimmy Smith .25 .60
45 Tony Gonzalez .30 .75
46 Trent Green .30 .75
47 Oronde Gadsden .20 .50
48 Jay Fiedler .25 .60
49 Lamar Smith .25 .60
50 Randy Moss .30 .75
51 Cris Carter .30 .75
52 Daunte Culpepper .25 .60
53 Drew Bledsoe .30 .75
54 Terry Glenn .25 .60
55 Antowain Smith .25 .60
56 Ricky Williams .30 .75
57 Joe Horn .25 .60
58 Aaron Brooks .25 .60
59 Kerry Collins .25 .60
60 Tiki Barber .30 .75
61 Ron Dayne .25 .60
62 Vinny Testaverde .25 .60
63 Wayne Chrebet .25 .60
64 Curtis Martin .30 .75
65 Tim Brown .30 .75
66 Rich Gannon .25 .60
67 Jerry Rice .60 1.50
68 Duce Staley .25 .60
69 Donovan McNabb .30 .75
70 Kordell Stewart .25 .60
71 Jerome Bettis .30 .75
72 Marshall Faulk .30 .75
73 Kurt Warner .50 1.25
74 Isaac Bruce .30 .75
75 Doug Flutie .30 .75
76 Junior Seau .30 .75
77 Jeff Garcia .25 .60
78 Garrison Hearst .25 .60
79 Terrell Owens .30 .75
80 Ricky Watters .25 .60
81 Matt Hasselbeck .30 .75
82 Brad Johnson .25 .60
83 Warrick Dunn .30 .75
84 Mike Alstott .25 .60
85 Kevin Dyson .20 .50
86 Eddie George .30 .75
87 Steve McNair .30 .75
88 Champ Bailey .30 .75
89 Michael Westbrook .20 .50
90 Stephen Davis .25 .60
91 Michael Vick JSY AU RC 700.00 1,000.00
92 Rod Gardner JSY AU RC 10.00 25.00
93 Freddie Mitchell JSY AU RC 8.00 20.00
94 Koren Robinson JSY/500 RC 6.00 15.00
95 David Terrell JSY/500 RC 6.00 15.00
96 Michael Bennett JSY RC 8.00 20.00
97 Robert Ferguson JSY RC 10.00 25.00
98 Deuce McAllister JSY RC 10.00 25.00
99 Travis Henry JSY RC 8.00 20.00
100 Andre Carter JSY RC 8.00 20.00
101 Drew Brees JSY RC 200.00 350.00
102 Santana Moss JSY/500 RC 10.00 25.00
103 Chris Weinke JSY/390 RC 8.00 20.00
104 Chad Johnson JSY/160 RC 75.00 150.00
105 Reggie Wayne JSY RC 40.00 80.00
106 Kevan Barlow JSY/500 RC 6.00 15.00
107 Chris Chambers JSY/500 RC 12.00 30.00
108 Todd Heap JSY/500 RC 12.00 30.00
109 Anthony Thomas JSY/500 RC 8.00 20.00
110 James Jackson JSY/500 RC 5.00 12.00
111 Rudi Johnson JSY/500 RC 8.00 20.00
112 Mike McMahon JSY RC 8.00 20.00
113 Josh Heupel JSY RC 10.00 25.00
114 Travis Minor JSY/500 RC 6.00 15.00
115 Quincy Morgan JSY/500 RC 6.00 15.00
116 Dan Morgan JSY/500 RC 6.00 15.00
117 Jesse Palmer JSY/500 RC 6.00 15.00
118 Sage Rosenfels JSY/300 RC 15.00 40.00
119 Marques Tuiasosopo JSY RC 6.00 15.00
120 LaDainian Tomlinson JSY/500 RC 125.00 250.00
123 Alge Crumpler AU RC 8.00 20.00
124 Arnold Jackson AU RC 5.00 12.00
125 Bobby Newcombe AU RC 6.00 15.00
126 Brand Manumaleuna AU RC 6.00 15.00
127 Cedrick Wilson AU RC 6.00 15.00
128 Brian Allen AU RC 5.00 12.00
129 Dee Brown AU RC 5.00 12.00
130 Darnerien McCants AU RC 6.00 15.00
131 Dave Dickenson AU RC 6.00 15.00
132 Derrick Blaylock AU RC 6.00 15.00
133 Eddie Berlin AU RC 5.00 12.00
134 Francis St.Paul AU RC 5.00 12.00
135 Jamar Fletcher AU RC 5.00 12.00
136 Josh Booty AU RC 6.00 15.00
137 Scotty Anderson AU RC 5.00 12.00
138 Ken-Yon Rambo AU RC 5.00 12.00
139 Kenyatta Walker AU RC 5.00 12.00
140 Kevin Kasper AU RC 5.00 12.00
141 Snoop Minnis AU RC 5.00 12.00
142 T.J. Houshmandzadeh AU RC 15.00 40.00
143 Quincy Carter AU RC 6.00 15.00
144 Ronney Daniels AU RC 5.00 12.00
145 Sedrick Hodge AU RC 5.00 12.00
146 Steve Smith AU RC 40.00 80.00
147 Tim Hasselbeck AU RC 6.00 15.00
148 Vinny Sutherland AU RC 5.00 12.00
149 Richard Seymour AU RC 8.00 20.00
150 Jamie Winborn AU 6.00 15.00
151 Gerard Warren RC 2.50 6.00
152 Justin Smith RC 3.00 8.00
153 David Martin RC 2.00 5.00
154 Jamal Reynolds RC 2.00 5.00
155 Dominic Rhodes RC 3.00 8.00
156 Nate Clements RC 2.50 6.00
157 Michael Lewis RC 3.00 8.00
158 Andre King RC 2.00 5.00
159 Benjamin Gay RC 2.50 6.00
160 Correll Buckhalter RC 3.00 8.00
161 Roderick Robinson RC 2.00 5.00
162 Moran Norris RC 2.00 5.00
163 Onome Ojo RC 2.00 5.00
164 Will Allen RC 3.00 8.00
165 Jonathan Carter RC 2.00 5.00
166 LaMont Jordan RC 3.00 8.00
167 DeLawrence Grant RC 2.00 5.00
168 Derrick Gibson RC 2.00 5.00
169 A.J. Feeley RC 2.50 6.00
170 Tim Baker RC 2.00 5.00
171 Kendrell Bell RC 3.00 8.00
172 Zeke Moreno RC 2.50 6.00
173 Carlos Polk RC 2.00 5.00
174 Ken Lucas RC 2.50 6.00
175 Heath Evans RC 2.50 6.00
176 Elvis Joseph RC 2.00 5.00
177 Damione Lewis RC 2.50 6.00
178 Tommy Polley RC 2.00 5.00
179 Fred Smoot RC 3.00 8.00
180 Jason Brookins RC 3.00 8.00
181 Nick Goings RC 3.00 8.00
182 Drew Bennett RC 3.00 8.00
183 Justin McCareins RC 2.50 6.00
184 Kabeer Gbaja-Biamila RC 3.00 8.00
185 Edgerton Hartwell RC 2.00 5.00
186 Robert Carswell RC 2.00 5.00
187 Aaron Schobel RC 3.00 8.00
188 Dan Alexander RC 2.50 6.00
189 Jamie Winborn RC 2.50 6.00
190 Karon Riley RC 2.00 5.00
EG Eddie George SAMPLE 1.50 3.00

2001 SP Authentic Rookie Gold 100

STATED PRINT RUN 100 SER.#'d SETS
91 Michael Vick 80.00 200.00
92 Rod Gardner 15.00 40.00
93 Freddie Mitchell 12.00 30.00
94 Koren Robinson 15.00 40.00
95 David Terrell 15.00 40.00
96 Michael Bennett 15.00 40.00
97 Robert Ferguson 20.00 50.00
98 Deuce McAllister 20.00 50.00
99 Travis Henry 15.00 40.00
100 Andre Carter 15.00 40.00
101 Drew Brees 150.00 250.00
102 Santana Moss 25.00 60.00
103 Chris Weinke 15.00 40.00
104 Chad Johnson 30.00 80.00
105 Reggie Wayne 40.00 100.00
106 Kevan Barlow 15.00 40.00
107 Chris Chambers 20.00 50.00
108 Todd Heap 20.00 50.00
109 Anthony Thomas 20.00 50.00
110 James Jackson 12.00 30.00
111 Rudi Johnson 20.00 50.00
112 Mike McMahon 15.00 40.00
113 Josh Heupel 20.00 50.00
114 Travis Minor 15.00 40.00
115 Quincy Morgan 15.00 40.00
116 Dan Morgan 15.00 40.00
117 Jesse Palmer 15.00 40.00
118 Sage Rosenfels 25.00 60.00
119 Marques Tuiasosopo 15.00 40.00
120 LaDainian Tomlinson 100.00 200.00
121 Adam Archuleta 15.00 40.00
122 Alex Bannister 12.00 30.00
123 Alge Crumpler 20.00 50.00
124 Arnold Jackson 12.00 30.00
125 Bobby Newcombe 15.00 40.00
126 Brandon Manumaleuna 15.00 40.00
127 Cedrick Wilson 15.00 40.00
128 Brian Allen 12.00 30.00
129 Dee Brown 12.00 30.00
130 Darnerien McCants 15.00 40.00
131 Dave Dickenson 15.00 40.00
132 Derrick Blaylock 15.00 40.00
133 Eddie Berlin 12.00 30.00
134 Francis St.Paul 12.00 30.00
135 Jamar Fletcher 12.00 30.00
136 Josh Booty 15.00 40.00
137 Scotty Anderson 12.00 30.00
138 Ken-Yon Rambo 12.00 30.00
139 Kenyatta Walker 12.00 30.00
140 Kevin Kasper 12.00 30.00
141 Snoop Minnis 12.00 30.00
142 T.J. Houshmandzadeh 25.00 60.00
143 Quincy Carter 15.00 40.00
144 Ronney Daniels 12.00 30.00
145 Sedrick Hodge 12.00 30.00
146 Steve Smith 40.00 100.00
147 Tim Hasselbeck 15.00 40.00
148 Vinny Sutherland 12.00 30.00
149 Richard Seymour 20.00 50.00
150 Jamie Winborn 15.00 40.00
151 Gerard Warren 15.00 40.00
152 Justin Smith 20.00 50.00
153 David Martin 12.00 30.00
154 Jamal Reynolds 12.00 30.00
155 Dominic Rhodes 20.00 50.00
156 Nate Clements 15.00 40.00
157 Michael Lewis 20.00 50.00
158 Andre King 12.00 30.00
159 Benjamin Gay 15.00 40.00
160 Correll Buckhalter 20.00 50.00
161 Roderick Robinson 12.00 30.00
162 Moran Norris 12.00 30.00
163 Onome Ojo 12.00 30.00
164 Will Allen 20.00 50.00
165 Jonathan Carter 12.00 30.00
166 LaMont Jordan 20.00 50.00
167 DeLawrence Grant 12.00 30.00
168 Derrick Gibson 12.00 30.00
169 A.J. Feeley 15.00 40.00
170 Tim Baker 12.00 30.00
171 Kendrell Bell 20.00 50.00
172 Zeke Moreno 15.00 40.00
173 Carlos Polk 12.00 30.00
174 Ken Lucas 15.00 40.00
175 Heath Evans 15.00 40.00
176 Elvis Joseph 12.00 30.00
177 Damione Lewis 15.00 40.00
178 Tommy Polley 12.00 30.00
179 Fred Smoot 20.00 50.00
180 Jason Brookins 20.00 50.00
181 Nick Goings 20.00 50.00
182 Drew Bennett 20.00 50.00
183 Justin McCareins 15.00 40.00
184 Kabeer Gbaja-Biamila 20.00 50.00
185 Edgerton Hartwell 12.00 30.00
186 Robert Carswell 12.00 30.00
187 Aaron Schobel 20.00 50.00
188 Dan Alexander 15.00 40.00
189 Jamie Winborn 15.00 40.00
190 Karon Riley 12.00 30.00

2001 SP Authentic Sign of the Times

STATED ODDS 1:47
*GOLD/25: .8X TO 2X BASIC AUTO
GOLD PRINT RUN 25 SER.#'d SETS
BJ Brad Johnson 8.00 20.00
CB Charlie Batch 8.00 20.00
CT Charley Taylor 8.00 20.00
DB Drew Bledsoe 12.00 30.00
DBR Drew Brees 100.00 175.00
DC Daunte Culpepper 8.00 20.00
DF Doug Flutie 12.00 30.00
DM Dan Marino 75.00 150.00
EJ Ed Too Tall Jones SP 6.00 15.00
HL Howie Long 30.00 50.00
JBL Jeff Blake 8.00 20.00
JBR Jim Brown 40.00 80.00
JGA Jeff Garcia 8.00 20.00
JK Jim Kelly 20.00 40.00
JM Joe Montana 60.00 120.00
JN Joe Namath 40.00 100.00
JP Jim Plunkett 8.00 20.00
JPL Jake Plummer 8.00 20.00
JR John Riggins 20.00 50.00
JS Junior Seau 25.00 50.00
JU Johnny Unitas 250.00 400.00
JY Jack Youngblood 6.00 15.00
KW Kurt Warner 25.00 50.00
MA Marcus Allen 20.00 35.00
PH Paul Hornung 20.00 50.00
PM Peyton Manning DP 60.00 120.00
PW Peter Warrick 8.00 20.00
RM Randy Moss SP 60.00 100.00
RS Roger Staubach 50.00 100.00
RW Ricky Williams 10.00 25.00
SD Stephen Davis 8.00 20.00
SY Steve Young 40.00 80.00
TB Terry Bradshaw 50.00 100.00
TDA Terrell Davis 15.00 40.00
TDI Trent Dilfer 8.00 20.00
TH Torry Holt 8.00 20.00
TO Terrell Owens 20.00 40.00
VT Vinny Testaverde SP 8.00 20.00

2001 SP Authentic Stat Jerseys

STAT JERSEY/13-1681 ODDS 1:23
#'d/23 or LESS NOT PRICED DUE TO SCARCITY
SPAF Antonio Freeman/1424 3.00 8.00
SPAT Amani Toomer/1094 2.50 6.00
SPBF1 Brett Favre/255 15.00 40.00
SPBF2 Brett Favre/260 15.00 40.00
SPBG1 Brian Griese/102 5.00 12.00
SPBG2 Brian Griese/327 3.00 8.00
SPBS1 Barry Sanders/99 15.00 40.00
SPBS2 Barry Sanders/1000 8.00 20.00
SPCM Curtis Martin/1204 3.00 8.00
SPCW2 Chris Weinke/223 4.00 10.00
SPDB1 Drew Brees/194 15.00 40.00
SPDB2 Drew Brees/349 12.00 30.00
SPDC1 Daunte Culpepper/40 6.00 15.00
SPDC2 Daunte Culpepper/470 3.00 8.00
SPDF Doug Flutie/129 6.00 15.00
SPDM2 Dan Marino/48 20.00 50.00
SPDM3 Dan Marino/420 10.00 25.00
SPES1 Emmitt Smith/156 15.00 40.00
SPFT Fred Taylor/1399 3.00 8.00
SPIB Isaac Bruce/1471 3.00 8.00
SPIH Ike Hilliard/787 2.50 6.00
SPJA Jesse Armstead/529 2.50 6.00
SPJE John Elway/300 10.00 25.00
SPJF1 Jay Fiedler/225 4.00 10.00
SPJF2 Jay Fiedler/1173 2.50 6.00
SPJK1 Jim Kelly/237 6.00 15.00
SPJK2 Jim Kelly/403 5.00 12.00
SPJR Jerry Rice/1281 6.00 15.00
SPJS Junior Seau/1058 3.00 8.00
SPJSM Jimmy Smith/1213 2.50 6.00
SPLT1 LaDainian Tomlinson/113 10.00 25.00
SPLT2 LaDainian Tomlinson/196 8.00 20.00
SPMA Mike Alstott/1219 2.50 6.00
SPMBR Mark Brunell/236 4.00 10.00
SPMB1 Michael Bennett/55 6.00 15.00
SPMB2 Michael Bennett/1681 2.50 6.00
SPMF1 Marshall Faulk/26 12.00 30.00
SPMF2 Marshall Faulk/1359 3.00 8.00
SPMV1 Michael Vick/32 40.00 100.00
SPMV2 Michael Vick/1234 10.00 25.00
SPPM1 Peyton Manning/33 25.00 60.00
SPPM2 Peyton Manning/87 15.00 40.00
SPPM3 Peyton Manning/94 15.00 40.00
SPPM4 Peyton Manning/231 12.00 30.00
SPPM5 Peyton Manning/440 10.00 25.00
SPRD Ron Dayne/770 2.50 6.00
SPRL Ray Lewis/137 6.00 15.00
SPRM1 Randy Moss/43 8.00 20.00
SPRM2 Randy Moss/226 5.00 12.00
SPSD Stephen Davis/1318 2.50 6.00
SPSE1 Jason Sehorn/260 4.00 10.00
SPSE2 Jason Sehorn/995 2.50 6.00
SPTA1 Troy Aikman/23 20.00 50.00
SPTA2 Troy Aikman/165 10.00 25.00
SPTC Tim Couch/1483 2.00 5.00
SPWD1 Warrick Dunn/422 4.00 10.00
SPWD2 Warrick Dunn/1133 3.00 8.00
SPWS1 Warren Sapp/58 6.00 15.00
SPWS2 Warren Sapp/1066 2.50 6.00

2002 SP Authentic

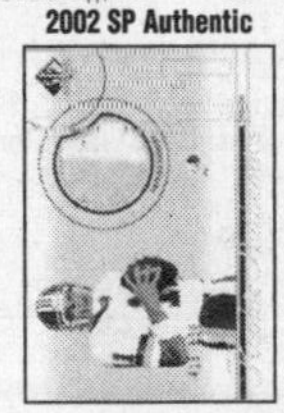

Released in late-December 2002, this set contains 94 veterans and 150 rookies. In addition, four base cards, 91-94, were only available autographed. Stated odds for these cards is 1:300. Subset cards 95-124 were #'d to 2000 and cards 125-154 were #'d to 1150. Rookie cards 155-184 were also #'d to 1150. Rookie cards 185-214 were all signed and #'d to 1150. Cards 215-234 all featured jersey swatches and were #'d to either 850 or 350. Cards 235-244 features autographs and jersey swatches and were #'d to 250. Some cards were issued as redemption cards with an expiration date of 12/13/2005. Note that #236 was intended to be Ashley Lelie but he never signed cards for the set.

COMP.SET w/o SP's (90) 10.00 25.00
155-184 ROOKIE PRINT RUN 1150
185-214 ROOKIE AU PRINT RUN 1150
ROOKIE JSY PRINT RUN 850
235-244 RC JSY AU PRINT RUN 250
1 Tom Brady 1.00 2.50
2 Antowain Smith .30 .75
3 Troy Brown .30 .75
4 Kurt Warner .40 1.00
5 Marshall Faulk .40 1.00
6 Isaac Bruce .40 1.00
7 Kordell Stewart .30 .75
8 Jerome Bettis .40 1.00
9 Plaxico Burress .30 .75
10 Hines Ward .40 1.00
11 Donovan McNabb .40 1.00
12 Duce Staley .30 .75
13 Dorsey Levens .30 .75
14 Antonio Freeman .40 1.00
15 Jerry Rice .75 2.00
16 Rich Gannon .30 .75
17 Tim Brown .40 1.00
18 Jim Miller .25 .60
19 Marty Booker .30 .75
20 Brian Urlacher .40 1.00
21 Jamal Lewis .30 .75
22 Chris Redman .25 .60
23 Ray Lewis .40 1.00
24 Brett Favre 1.00 2.50
25 Ahman Green .30 .75
26 Terry Glenn .30 .75
27 Keyshawn Johnson .30 .75
28 Keenan McCardell .30 .75
29 Michael Pittman .30 .75
30 Curtis Martin .40 1.00
31 Vinny Testaverde .30 .75
32 Chad Pennington .40 1.00
33 Wayne Chrebet .30 .75
34 Terrell Owens .40 1.00
35 Garrison Hearst .30 .75
36 Jay Fiedler .30 .75
37 Ricky Williams .30 .75
38 Chris Chambers .30 .75
39 Shaun Alexander .30 .75
40 Darrell Jackson .30 .75
41 Drew Bledsoe .40 1.00
42 Travis Henry .25 .60
43 Eric Moulds .30 .75
44 Stephen Davis .30 .75
45 Rod Gardner .25 .60
46 Brian Griese .30 .75
47 Olandis Gary .30 .75
48 Shannon Sharpe .40 1.00
49 Tim Couch .25 .60
50 Kevin Johnson .25 .60
51 Steve McNair .40 1.00
52 Eddie George .30 .75
53 Aaron Brooks .30 .75
54 Deuce McAllister .30 .75
55 Joe Horn .30 .75
56 Michael Vick .60 1.50
57 Warrick Dunn .30 .75
58 Kerry Collins .30 .75
59 Tiki Barber .40 1.00
60 Amani Toomer .30 .75
61 Jake Plummer .30 .75
62 David Boston .25 .60
63 Thomas Jones .40 1.00
64 Edgerrin James .30 .75
65 Marvin Harrison .40 1.00
66 Mark Brunell .30 .75
67 Jimmy Smith .30 .75
68 Fred Taylor .30 .75
69 Corey Dillon .30 .75
70 Jon Kitna .30 .75
71 Michael Westbrook .25 .60
72 Trent Green .30 .75
73 Priest Holmes .40 1.00
74 Tony Gonzalez .40 1.00
75 Daunte Culpepper .30 .75
76 Michael Bennett .30 .75
77 Randy Moss .40 1.00
78 Drew Brees .60 1.50
79 Curtis Conway .30 .75
80 Junior Seau .40 1.00
81 Quincy Carter .25 .60
82 Emmitt Smith 1.00 2.50
83 Joey Galloway .30 .75
84 Cory Schlesinger .25 .60
85 James Stewart .25 .60
86 Az-Zahir Hakim .25 .60
87 Rodney Peete .30 .75
88 Lamar Smith .30 .75
89 Corey Bradford .25 .60
90 Jermaine Lewis .25 .60
91 Peyton Manning AU 50.00 100.00
92 Anthony Thomas AU 10.00 25.00
93 LaDainian Tomlinson AU 25.00 50.00
94 Jeff Garcia AU 10.00 25.00
95 Kurt Warner SC 1.25 3.00
96 Brett Favre SC 3.00 8.00
97 Michael Vick SC 2.00 5.00
98 Donovan McNabb SC 1.25 3.00
99 Daunte Culpepper SC 1.00 2.50
100 Tom Brady SC 3.00 8.00
101 Drew Brees SC 2.00 5.00
102 Kordell Stewart SC 1.00 2.50
103 Steve McNair SC 1.25 3.00
104 Peyton Manning SC 2.50 6.00
105 Mark Brunell SC 1.00 2.50
106 Jeff Garcia SC 1.00 2.50
107 Aaron Brooks SC 1.00 2.50
108 Rich Gannon SC 1.00 2.50
109 Tim Couch SC .75 2.00
110 Jake Plummer SC 1.00 2.50
111 Drew Bledsoe SC 1.25 3.00
112 Brian Griese SC 1.00 2.50
113 Quincy Carter SC .75 2.00
114 Vinny Testaverde SC 1.00 2.50
115 Chad Pennington SC 1.25 3.00
116 Brad Johnson SC 1.00 2.50
117 Trent Dilfer SC 1.00 2.50
118 Jim Miller SC .75 2.00
119 Tommy Maddox SC 1.00 2.50
120 Trent Green SC 1.00 2.50
121 Rodney Peete SC 1.00 2.50
122 Jay Fiedler SC 1.00 2.50
123 Kerry Collins SC 1.00 2.50
124 Chris Redman SC .75 2.00
125 Marshall Faulk SS 1.50 4.00
126 Donovan McNabb SS 1.50 4.00
127 Michael Vick SS 2.50 6.00
128 Brett Favre SS 4.00 10.00
129 Peyton Manning SS 3.00 8.00
130 Kurt Warner SS 1.50 4.00
131 Curtis Martin SS 1.50 4.00
132 Randy Moss SS 1.50 4.00
133 Edgerrin James SS 1.25 3.00
134 Jerome Bettis SS 1.50 4.00
135 Emmitt Smith SS 4.00 10.00
136 LaDainian Tomlinson SS 2.00 5.00
137 Jeff Garcia SS 1.25 3.00
138 Kordell Stewart SS 1.25 3.00
139 Anthony Thomas SS 1.25 3.00
140 Tom Brady SS 4.00 10.00
141 Daunte Culpepper SS 1.25 3.00
142 Drew Bledsoe SS 1.50 4.00
143 Ricky Williams SS 1.25 3.00
144 Warrick Dunn SS 1.25 3.00
145 Steve McNair SS 1.50 4.00
146 Rich Gannon SS 1.25 3.00
147 Jake Plummer SS 1.25 3.00
148 Jerry Rice SS 3.00 8.00
149 Mark Brunell SS 1.25 3.00
150 Brian Griese SS 1.25 3.00
151 Eddie George SS 1.25 3.00
152 Tim Couch SS 1.00 2.50
153 Keyshawn Johnson SS 1.25 3.00
154 Shannon Sharpe SS 1.50 4.00
155 Phillip Buchanon RC 2.50 6.00
156 Brian Allen RC 2.00 5.00
157 Brian Westbrook RC 15.00 30.00
158 Lito Sheppard RC 2.50 6.00
159 Daryl Jones RC 1.50 4.00
160 Javin Hunter RC 1.50 4.00
161 Derrick Lewis RC 1.50 4.00
162 Javon Walker RC 2.50 6.00
163 Tank Williams RC 2.00 5.00
164 Shaun Hill RC 5.00 12.00

165 Napoleon Harris RC 2.00 5.00
166 Herb Haygood RC 1.50 4.00
167 Jake Schifino RC 1.50 4.00
168 Quentin Jammer RC 2.50 6.00
169 Jason McAddley RC 2.00 5.00
170 Jerramy Stevens RC 2.50 6.00
171 Jesse Chatman RC 1.50 4.00
172 Larry Ned RC 1.50 4.00
173 Najeh Davenport RC 2.50 6.00
174 Lamont Thompson RC 2.00 5.00
175 Darrell Hill RC 1.50 4.00
176 Ryan Sims RC 2.50 6.00
177 Ryan Denney RC 1.50 4.00
178 Jamin Elliott RC 1.50 4.00
179 Sam Simmons RC 1.50 4.00
180 Seth Burford RC 1.50 4.00
181 Tellis Redmon RC 1.50 4.00
182 Ben Leber RC 1.50 4.00
183 Kendall Newson RC 1.50 4.00
184 Marques Anderson RC 2.00 5.00
185 Adrian Peterson AU RC 8.00 20.00
187 Antwoine Womack AU RC 5.00 12.00
188 Brandon Doman AU RC 5.00 12.00
189 Craig Nall AU RC 6.00 15.00
190 Chad Hutchinson AU RC 5.00 12.00
191 Chester Taylor AU RC 8.00 20.00
192 Damien Anderson AU RC 5.00 12.00
193 Deion Branch AU RC 12.50 25.00
194 Dusty Bonner AU RC 5.00 12.00
195 Ed Reed AU RC 30.00 60.00
196 Eric McCoo AU RC 5.00 12.00
197 J.T. O'Sullivan AU RC 6.00 15.00
198 Kalimba Edwards AU RC 6.00 15.00
199 Jonathan Wells AU RC 8.00 20.00
200 Josh Scobey AU RC 6.00 15.00
201 Kelly Campbell AU RC 6.00 15.00
202 Kurt Kittner AU RC 5.00 12.00
203 Lamar Gordon AU RC 6.00 15.00
204 Lee Mays AU RC 5.00 12.00
205 Leonard Henry AU RC 5.00 12.00
206 Luke Staley AU RC 5.00 12.00
207 Justin Peelle AU RC 5.00 12.00
208 Randy Fasani AU RC 6.00 15.00
209 Ricky Williams AU RC 6.00 15.00
210 Ronald Curry AU RC 6.00 15.00
211 Travis Stephens AU RC 5.00 12.00
212 Wendell Bryant AU RC 5.00 12.00
213 Woody Dantzler AU RC 6.00 15.00
214 Kahlil Hill AU RC 5.00 12.00
215 Donte Stallworth JSY RC 6.00 15.00
216 Joey Harrington AU/280 RC 10.00 25.00
217 Cliff Russell JSY RC 4.00 10.00
218 Clinton Portis JSY RC 8.00 20.00
219 Daniel Graham JSY RC 5.00 12.00
220 David Garrard JSY RC 8.00 20.00
221 DeShaun Foster JSY RC 6.00 15.00
222 Julius Peppers JSY RC 12.00 30.00
223 Jeremy Shockey JSY RC 10.00 25.00
224 Patrick Ramsey JSY RC 6.00 15.00
225 Josh Reed JSY RC 5.00 12.00
226 LaDell Betts JSY RC 6.00 15.00
227 Mike Williams JSY/350 RC 4.00 10.00
228 Reche Caldwell JSY RC 6.00 15.00
229 Rohan Davey JSY RC 6.00 15.00
230 Ron Johnson JSY RC 5.00 12.00
231 Roy Williams JSY/350 RC 8.00 20.00
232 T.J. Duckett JSY RC 6.00 15.00
233 Tim Carter JSY RC 5.00 12.00
234 William Green JSY RC 5.00 12.00
235 Antwaan Randle El JSY AU RC 15.00 40.00
237 David Carr JSY AU RC 15.00 40.00
238 Andre Davis JSY AU RC 12.00 30.00
239 Eric Crouch JSY AU RC 15.00 40.00
240 Antonio Bryant JSY AU RC 15.00 40.00
241 Jabar Gaffney JSY AU RC 15.00 40.00
242 Marquise Walker JSY AU RC 10.00 25.00
243 Maurice Morris JSY AU RC 12.00 30.00
244 Josh McCown JSY AU RC 15.00 40.00
AP1 Walter Payton AU/34 500.00 750.00
SW1 Walter Payton Gold JSY/34 100.00 200.00
SW1 Walter Payton JSY/150 50.00 120.00
SCPS Walter Payton JSY/250 40.00 100.00
Emmitt Smith
SCPSG Walter Payton 175.00 300.00
Emmitt Smith
Gold JSY/34

2002 SP Authentic Gold

*VETS 1-90: 10X TO 25X BASIC CARDS
1-90 VETERAN PRINT RUN 50
91-94 VET AUTO PRINT RUN 25
*ROOKIE JSY 215-234: 1X TO 2.5X
215-234 ROOKIE JSY PRINT RUN 25
235-244 JSY AU PRINT RUN 25
91 Peyton Manning AU 75.00 150.00
92 Anthony Thomas AU 15.00 40.00
93 LaDainian Tomlinson AU 40.00 80.00
94 Jeff Garcia AU 15.00 40.00

2002 SP Authentic Sign of the Times

STATED ODDS 1:96
*GOLD/25: .8X TO 2X BASIC AU
GOLD/25: .5X TO 1.2X BASIC AU/63-150
*GOLD/25: .4X TO 1X BASIC AU/25
STAB Aaron Brooks SP 6.00 15.00
STAG Ahman Green SP/76 * 10.00 25.00
STAS Antowain Smith 6.00 15.00
STBJ Brad Johnson SP 6.00 15.00
STBR Drew Brees SP 40.00 80.00
STBT Antonio Bryant SP/75 * 8.00 20.00
STCA David Carr SP/25 * 20.00 50.00
STCH Chad Hutchinson 5.00 12.00
STDB Drew Bledsoe SP/75 * 12.00 30.00
STDC Daunte Culpepper SP 15.00 30.00
STDG David Garrard 10.00 25.00
STER Antwaan Randle El/235 * 8.00 20.00
STES Emmitt Smith SP/77 * 150.00 250.00
STFM Freddie Mitchell SP 5.00 12.00
STJG Jabar Gaffney SP 8.00 20.00
STJP Jake Plummer 6.00 15.00
STJR John Riggins 25.00 50.00
STLT LaDainian Tomlinson 25.00 60.00
STMB Marty Booker 6.00 15.00
STMM Maurice Morris SP 6.00 15.00
STMV Michael Vick 25.00 60.00
STPE Julius Peppers/150 * 60.00 100.00
STPM Peyton Manning 60.00 120.00
STRC Rosevelt Colvin 10.00 25.00
STRG Rich Gannon SP/63 * 10.00 25.00
STTC Tim Couch SP 5.00 12.00
STTG Tony Gonzalez SP 8.00 20.00

2002 SP Authentic Threads

STATED ODDS 1:52
*GOLD/25: 1X TO 2.5X BASIC JSY
GOLD PRINT RUN 25 SER.#'d SETS
AT1AB Antonio Bryant 5.00 12.00
AT1AL Ashley Lelie 4.00 10.00
AT1DC David Carr 5.00 12.00
AT1DF DeShaun Foster 5.00 12.00
AT1DS Donte Stallworth 5.00 12.00
AT1EC Eric Crouch 5.00 12.00
AT1JH Joey Harrington 5.00 12.00
AT1JP Julius Peppers 10.00 25.00
AT1JW Javon Walker 5.00 12.00
AT1MM Maurice Morris 4.00 10.00
AT1MW Marquise Walker 3.00 8.00
AT1PR Patrick Ramsey 5.00 12.00

2002 SP Authentic Threads Doubles

STATED ODDS 1:70
*GOLD/25: 1.2X TO 3X BASIC DUAL
GOLD PRINT RUN 25 SER.#'d SETS
AT2CB Reche Caldwell 8.00 20.00
Drew Brees
AT2CC David Carr 5.00 12.00
Tim Couch
AT2CW David Carr 5.00 12.00
Kurt Warner
AT2HC Joey Harrington 5.00 12.00
Daunte Culpepper
AT2HM Joey Harrington 5.00 12.00
Donovan McNabb
AT2MF Maurice Morris 4.00 10.00
Marshall Faulk
AT2RB Patrick Ramsey 12.00 30.00
Tom Brady
AT2SM Donte Stallworth 10.00 25.00
Peyton Manning

2002 SP Authentic Threads Triples

STATED PRINT RUN 250 SER.#'d SETS
UNPRICED TRIPLE GOLD PRINT RUN 10
AT3BP Drew Bledsoe 8.00 20.00
Peerless Price
Andre Reed
AT3CC David Carr 15.00 40.00
Eric Crouch
Peyton Manning
AT3CD Eric Crouch 8.00 20.00
Ron Dayne
Ricky Williams
AT3CH David Carr 8.00 20.00
Joey Harrington
Patrick Ramsey
AT3CM Daunte Culpepper 12.00 30.00
Donovan McNabb
Michael Vick
AT3CW Eric Crouch 8.00 20.00
Kurt Warner
Marshall Faulk
AT3FM Deshaun Foster 8.00 20.00
Freddie Mitchell
J.J. Stokes
AT3FW Brett Favre 20.00 50.00
Kurt Warner
Peyton Manning
AT3PB Jake Plummer 8.00 20.00
David Boston
Josh McCown
AT3PL Clinton Portis 10.00 25.00
Ray Lewis
Santana Moss
AT3SS Donte Stallworth 15.00 40.00
Travis Stephens
Peyton Manning
AT3WG Marquise Walker 6.00 15.00
Brian Griese
Desmond Howard

2002 SP Authentic Threads Quads

STATED PRINT RUN 100 SER.#'d SETS
*GOLD/25: .8X TO 2X BASIC QUAD
GOLD PRINT RUN 25 SER.#'d SETS
CB Eric Crouch 10.00 25.00
Tim Brown
Eddie George
Charles Woodson
CH David Carr 10.00 25.00
Joey Harrington
Patrick Ramsey
Rohan Davey
CW Eric Crouch 10.00 25.00
Kurt Warner
Marshall Faulk
Isaac Bruce
SL Jeremy Shockey 15.00 40.00
Ray Lws
Santana Moss
Warren Sapp
SS Donte Stallworth 20.00 50.00
Travis Stephens
Peyton Manning
Jamal Lewis
WG Kurt Warner 10.00 25.00
Brian Griese
Rich Gannon
Quincy Carter

2002 SP Authentic Sign of the Times Hawaii Trade Conference

This card, featuring HOFer John Riggins, was distributed by Upper Deck to attendees of the Hawaii Trade Conference in 2001. Each card was serial numbered to 500.

JR John Riggins/500 15.00 40.00

2003 SP Authentic

Released in January of 2004, this set consists of 269 cards, including 90 veterans and 179 rookies. Rookies 91-120 are serial numbered to 2200. Cards 121-150 make up the Star Status (SS) subset and are serial numbered to 1200. Rookies 151-211 are serial numbered to 1200. Rookies 212-240 are serial numbered to 1200 and feature authentic player autographs on the card. Please note that Chris Simms (#212) is serial numbered to 250. Rookies 241-270 feature event worn patch swatches. The patch cards of Bryant Johnson, Kyle Boller, Seneca Wallace, Byron Leftwich, and Carson Palmer also feature an authentic player autograph on the card. Non-autographed patch cards are serial numbered to 850, while autographed patches are serial numbered to 250. Several players were issued as exchange cards in packs with an expiration date of 12/29/2006. Please note that card number 267 was not released due to a production error. Boxes contained 24 packs of 5 cards. SRP was $4.99.

COMP.SET w/o SP's (90) 7.50 20.00
91-120 ROOKIE PRINT RUN 2200
151-211 ROOKIE PRINT RUN 1200
213-240 AU RC PRINT RUN 1200
1 Donovan McNabb .40 1.00
2 Tim Couch .25 .60
3 Joey Harrington .25 .60
4 Brett Favre 1.00 2.50
5 Jeff Garcia .30 .75
6 Kerry Collins .30 .75
7 Michael Vick .50 1.25
8 David Carr .30 .75
9 Steve McNair .40 1.00
10 Chad Pennington .40 1.00
11 Patrick Ramsey .30 .75
12 Rich Gannon .30 .75
13 Kurt Warner .40 1.00
14 Brad Johnson .30 .75
15 Jay Fiedler .25 .60
16 Jake Plummer .30 .75
17 Mark Brunell .30 .75
18 Peyton Manning .75 2.00
19 Brian Griese .30 .75
20 Kordell Stewart .30 .75
21 Kelly Holcomb .25 .60
22 Josh McCown .30 .75
23 Matt Hasselbeck .30 .75
24 Marc Bulger .40 1.00
25 Chris Redman .25 .60
26 Rodney Peete .25 .60
27 Jake Delhomme .40 1.00
28 Jon Kitna .30 .75
29 Trent Green .30 .75
30 Quincy Carter .25 .60
31 Chad Hutchinson .25 .60
32 Edgerrin James .40 1.00
33 Deuce McAllister .30 .75
34 Ricky Williams .30 .75
35 Priest Holmes .40 1.00
36 Curtis Martin .40 1.00
37 Shaun Alexander .30 .75
38 Eddie George .30 .75
39 Marshall Faulk .40 1.00
40 Garrison Hearst .30 .75
41 Ahman Green .30 .75
42 Corey Dillon .30 .75
43 Jamal Lewis .30 .75
44 William Green .25 .60
45 Travis Henry .25 .60
46 Mike Alstott .40 1.00
47 Amos Zereoue .25 .60
48 Stephen Davis .30 .75
49 Duce Staley .30 .75
50 Fred Taylor .30 .75
51 Anthony Thomas .30 .75
52 Charlie Garner .30 .75
53 Kevan Barlow .25 .60
54 Brian Urlacher .40 1.00
55 Junior Seau .40 1.00
56 Zach Thomas .40 1.00
57 Ray Lewis .40 1.00
58 Jerry Porter .25 .60
59 Marty Booker .30 .75
60 Javon Walker .30 .75
61 Donald Driver .40 1.00
62 Amani Toomer .30 .75
63 Peerless Price .25 .60
64 Santana Moss .30 .75
65 Laveranues Coles .25 .60
66 Troy Brown .30 .75
67 Chris Chambers .30 .75
68 Rod Smith .30 .75
69 Ashley Lelie .25 .60
70 Plaxico Burress .30 .75
71 Keyshawn Johnson .40 1.00
72 Isaac Bruce .40 1.00
73 Torry Holt .40 1.00
74 Koren Robinson .30 .75
75 Derrick Mason .30 .75
76 Kevin Johnson .25 .60
77 Andre' Davis .25 .60
78 Antonio Bryant .25 .60
79 Eric Moulds .30 .75
80 Jerry Rice .75 2.00
81 Tim Brown .40 1.00
82 Antwaan Randle El .30 .75
83 Donte Stallworth .25 .60
84 Randy Moss .40 1.00
85 Chad Johnson .40 1.00
86 Hines Ward .40 1.00
87 Rod Gardner .25 .60
88 Marvin Harrison .40 1.00
89 David Boston .25 .60
90 Julius Peppers .40 1.00
91 Dewayne White RC 1.00 2.50
92 Casey Fitzsimmons RC 1.25 3.00
93 Aaron Moorehead RC 1.25 3.00
94 Jimmy Farris RC 1.00 2.50
95 Eric Parker RC 1.50 4.00
96 Michael Haynes RC 1.00 2.50
97 J.J. Moses RC 1.00 2.50
98 Ken Hamlin RC 1.50 4.00
99 William Joseph RC 1.00 2.50
100 Alonzo Jackson RC 1.00 2.50
101 Tyler Brayton RC 1.25 3.00
102 Eddie Moore RC 1.00 2.50
103 Cleo Lemon RC 1.50 4.00
104 Arlen Harris RC 1.00 2.50
105 Cortez Hankton RC 1.25 3.00
106 Angelo Crowell RC 1.25 3.00
107 Johnathan Sullivan RC 1.00 2.50
108 Pisa Tinoisamoa RC 1.50 4.00
109 Boss Bailey RC 1.25 3.00
110 Tommy Jones RC 1.00 2.50
111 E.J. Henderson RC 1.25 3.00
112 Jimmy Kennedy RC 1.25 3.00
113 Nnamdi Asomugha RC 10.00 20.00
114 Hanik Milligan RC 1.00 2.50
115 Sammy Davis RC 1.25 3.00
116 Drayton Florence RC 1.50 4.00
117 Andre Woolfolk RC 1.25 3.00
118 Dennis Weathersby RC 1.00 2.50
119 Mike Doss RC 1.50 4.00
120 Troy Polamalu RC 25.00 50.00
121 Clinton Portis SS 1.25 3.00
122 Daunte Culpepper SS 1.25 3.00
123 Jeremy Shockey SS 1.50 4.00
124 Drew Brees SS 1.50 4.00
125 Marshall Faulk SS 1.50 4.00
126 Emmitt Smith SS 4.00 10.00
127 Terrell Owens SS 1.50 4.00
128 Ricky Williams SS 1.25 3.00
129 Deuce McAllister SS 1.25 3.00
130 Ahman Green SS 1.25 3.00
131 Chad Pennington SS 1.50 4.00
132 Plaxico Burress SS 1.25 3.00
133 Steve McNair SS 1.50 4.00
134 Keyshawn Johnson SS 1.50 4.00
135 Jeff Garcia SS 1.25 3.00
136 Drew Bledsoe SS 1.50 4.00
137 Jerry Rice SS 3.00 8.00
138 Randy Moss SS 1.50 4.00
139 David Carr SS 1.25 3.00
140 Joey Harrington SS 1.00 2.50
141 Michael Vick SS 2.00 5.00
142 Tom Brady SS 4.00 10.00
143 Brian Urlacher SS 1.50 4.00
144 Brett Favre SS 4.00 10.00
145 Kurt Warner SS 1.50 4.00
146 LaDainian Tomlinson SS 1.50 4.00
147 Aaron Brooks SS 1.25 3.00
148 Edgerrin James SS 1.50 4.00
149 Peyton Manning SS 3.00 8.00
150 Donovan McNabb SS 1.50 4.00
151 Jason Gesser RC 1.50 4.00
152 Ken Dorsey RC 1.50 4.00
153 Jason Johnson RC 1.25 3.00
154 Avon Cobourne RC 1.25 3.00
155 Andrew Pinnock RC 1.50 4.00
156 Kirk Farmer RC 1.50 4.00
157 Reno Mahe RC 1.50 4.00
158 Lon Sheriff RC 1.25 3.00
159 Marquel Blackwell RC 1.25 3.00
160 Quentin Griffin RC 1.50 4.00
161 Rashean Mathis RC 1.50 4.00
162 Lee Suggs RC 1.50 4.00
163 Jeremi Johnson RC 1.25 3.00
164 Ovie Mughelli RC 1.50 4.00
165 Nick Barnett RC 2.00 5.00
166 Brock Forsey RC 1.50 4.00
167 Malaefou MacKenzie RC 1.25 3.00
168 Ahmaad Galloway RC 1.50 4.00
169 Cecil Sapp RC 1.25 3.00
170 Kerry Carter RC 1.25 3.00
171A Terrence Edwards RC 1.25 3.00
should be card 177
171B Dahrran Diedrick RC 1.25 3.00
172 Joffrey Reynolds RC 1.25 3.00
173 Sultan McCullough RC 1.25 3.00
174 Brandon Drumm RC 1.25 3.00
175 Casey Moore RC 1.25 3.00
176 Gerald Hayes RC 1.50 4.00
178 Jamal Burke RC 1.25 3.00
179 Antonio Chatman RC 2.00 5.00
180 Reggie Newhouse RC 1.25 3.00
181 Chris Horn RC 1.50 4.00
182 Denero Marriott RC 1.25 3.00
183 DeAndrew Rubin RC 1.25 3.00
184 Taco Wallace RC 1.25 3.00
185 Doug Gabriel RC 1.50 4.00
186 Willie Ponder RC 1.25 3.00
187 David Tyree RC 2.00 5.00
188 Kevin Walter RC 3.00 8.00
189 Zuriel Smith RC 1.25 3.00
190 Keenan Howry RC 1.25 3.00
191 C.J. Jones RC 1.25 3.00
192 Arnaz Battle RC 2.00 5.00
193 Walter Young RC 1.25 3.00
194 Anthony Adams RC 1.50 4.00
195 Jerome McDougle RC 1.25 3.00
196 Will Heller RC 1.50 4.00
197 Cecil Moore RC 1.25 3.00
198 Mike Seidman RC 1.25 3.00
199 Jason Witten RC 15.00 40.00
200 L.J. Smith RC 2.00 5.00
201 Bennie Joppru RC 1.25 3.00
202 Donald Lee RC 1.50 4.00
203 Aaron Walker RC 1.50 4.00
204 Antonio Brown RC 1.25 3.00
205 George Wrighster RC 1.25 3.00
206 Danny Curley RC 1.25 3.00
207 Mike Banks RC 1.25 3.00
208 Mike Pinkard RC 1.25 3.00
209 Ryan Hoag RC 1.25 3.00
210 Brad Pyatt RC 1.25 3.00
211 Charles Rogers RC 1.50 4.00
212 Chris Simms AU/250 RC 12.00 30.00
213 Nate Hybl AU RC 4.00 10.00
214 Brandon Lloyd AU RC 8.00 20.00
215 ReShard Lee AU RC 5.00 12.00
216 Dwone Hicks AU RC 3.00 8.00
217 Tony Romo AU RC 150.00 300.00
218 Brett Engemann AU RC 3.00 8.00
219 Nick Maddox AU RC 3.00 8.00
220 James MacPherson AU RC 4.00 10.00
221 Juston Wood AU RC 3.00 8.00
222 Adrian Madise AU RC 3.00 8.00
223 Shaun McDonald AU RC 4.00 10.00
224 Carl Ford AU RC 3.00 8.00
225 Vishante Shiancoe AU RC 8.00 20.00
226 Gibran Hamdan AU RC 3.00 8.00
227 Brooks Bollinger AU RC 4.00 10.00
228 B.J. Askew AU RC 4.00 10.00
229 Domanick Davis AU RC 4.00 10.00
230 LaBrandon Toefield AU RC 4.00 10.00
231 Bobby Wade AU RC 4.00 10.00
232 Justin Gage AU RC 4.00 10.00
233 Billy McMullen AU RC 3.00 8.00
234 David Kircus AU RC 5.00 12.00
235 J.R. Tolver AU RC 4.00 10.00
236 Sam Aiken AU RC 4.00 10.00
237 LaTarence Dunbar AU RC 3.00 8.00
238 Kassim Osgood AU RC 5.00 12.00
239 Tony Hollings AU RC 4.00 10.00
240 Justin Griffith AU RC 4.00 10.00
241 Brian St.Pierre JSY RC 5.00 12.00
242 Kevin Curtis JSY RC 6.00 15.00
243 Dallas Clark JSY RC 15.00 30.00
244 Willis McGahee JSY RC 8.00 20.00
245 Terence Newman JSY RC 5.00 12.00
246 Justin Fargas JSY AU/250 RC 12.00 30.00
247 Artose Pinner JSY RC 4.00 10.00
248 Kelley Washington JSY RC 4.00 10.00
249 DeWayne Robertson JSY RC 5.00 12.00
250 Nate Burleson JSY RC 5.00 12.00
251 Kliff Kingsbury JSY RC 5.00 12.00
252 Bethel Johnson JSY RC 4.00 10.00
253 Anquan Boldin JSY RC 10.00 25.00
254 Bryant Johnson JSY AU/250 RC 12.00 30.00
255 Terrell Suggs JSY AU/250 RC 25.00 50.00
256 Musa Smith JSY RC 4.00 10.00
257 Chris Brown JSY RC 4.00 10.00
258 Marcus Trufant JSY RC 5.00 12.00
259 Teyo Johnson JSY RC 5.00 12.00
260 Tyrone Calico JSY RC 5.00 12.00
261 Dave Ragone JSY AU/250 RC 8.00 20.00
262 Kyle Boller JSY AU/250 RC 12.00 30.00
263 Onterrio Smith JSY AU/250 RC 8.00 20.00
264 Rex Grossman JSY RC 6.00 15.00
265 Larry Johnson JSY RC 6.00 15.00
266 Seneca Wallace JSY AU/250 RC 12.00 30.00
268 Taylor Jacobs JSY AU/250 RC 8.00 20.00
269 Byron Leftwich JSY AU/250 RC 12.00 30.00
270 Carson Palmer JSY AU/250 RC 75.00 150.00

2003 SP Authentic Gold

*VETS 1-90: 12X TO 30X BASIC CARDS
*ROOKIES 91-120: 2.5X TO 6X
*SS 121-150: 3X TO 8X BASIC CARDS
*ROOKIES 151-211: 2X TO 5X
*ROOKIE AU: .6X TO 1.5X BASE AU/250
*ROOKIE AU: 1.5X TO 4X BASE AU/1200
*ROOKIE JSY: 1X TO 2.5X BASIC JSY
*ROOK.JSY AUs: 1.2X TO 3X BASE CARD HI
STATED PRINT RUN 25 SERIAL #'d SETS
120 Troy Polamalu 175.00 300.00
217 Tony Romo AU 750.00 1,500.00
265 Larry Johnson JSY 40.00 100.00
270 Carson Palmer JSY AU 300.00 600.00

2003 SP Authentic Buy Back Autographs

NOT PRICED DUE TO SCARCITY

2003 SP Authentic Sign of the Times

STATED PRINT RUN 12-900
SERIAL #'d UNDER 20 NOT PRICED
AB Aaron Brooks/250 10.00 25.00
AL Mike Alstott/275 12.00 30.00
BA Barry Sanders/43 100.00 200.00
BJ Bryant Johnson/475 10.00 25.00
BL Byron Leftwich/75 15.00 40.00
BR Troy Brown/600 8.00 20.00
BS Bart Starr/120 90.00 150.00
BU Brian Urlacher/250 12.00 30.00
CP Chad Pennington/141 12.00 30.00
DA David Boston/250 8.00 20.00
DB Drew Brees/250 40.00 80.00
DC David Carr/250 10.00 25.00
DM Deuce McAllister/250 10.00 25.00
DO Donovan McNabb/75 40.00 80.00
DR Drew Bledsoe/250 12.00 30.00
JB Jim Brown/75 50.00 100.00
JE Jerry Porter/600 6.00 15.00
JF Justin Fargas/475 10.00 25.00
JG Jeff Garcia/50 15.00 40.00
JL Jamal Lewis/400 8.00 20.00
JM Joe Montana/21 125.00 250.00
JN Joe Namath/35 75.00 150.00
JW Javon Walker/600 8.00 20.00
KH Kelly Holcomb/475 6.00 15.00
KR Koren Robinson/530 8.00 20.00
LS Lynn Swann/125 100.00 200.00
MA Marcus Allen/21 40.00 80.00
MH Matt Hasselbeck/275 12.00 30.00
PH Priest Holmes/75 20.00 50.00
PM Peyton Manning/900 60.00 100.00
PO Clinton Portis/520 8.00 20.00
PP Peerless Price/350 6.00 15.00
RG Rod Gardner/215 8.00 20.00
RI John Riggins/105 20.00 50.00
RW Ricky Williams/50 15.00 40.00
SA Shaun Alexander/250 10.00 25.00
SU Lee Suggs/375 8.00 20.00
TA Troy Aikman/97 50.00 120.00
TB Tim Brown/246 20.00 40.00
TC Tyrone Calico/200 10.00 25.00
TE Teyo Johnson/250 10.00 25.00
TG Trent Green/200 10.00 25.00
TM Tommy Maddox/592 8.00 20.00
TO Terrell Owens/286 15.00 40.00
TS Terrell Suggs/475 12.00 30.00
ZT Zach Thomas/350 10.00 25.00

2003 SP Authentic Sign of the Times Gold

PRINT RUN 25 SERIAL #'d SETS
AB Aaron Brooks 20.00 50.00
AL Mike Alstott 25.00 60.00
BA Barry Sanders 75.00 150.00
BJ Bryant Johnson 20.00 50.00
BL Byron Leftwich 20.00 50.00
BR Troy Brown 20.00 50.00
BS Bart Starr 125.00 200.00
BU Brian Urlacher 25.00 60.00
CP Chad Pennington 25.00 60.00
DA David Boston 15.00 40.00
DB Drew Brees 60.00 120.00
DC David Carr 20.00 50.00
DM Deuce McAllister 20.00 50.00
DO Donovan McNabb 25.00 60.00
DR Drew Bledsoe 25.00 60.00
JB Jim Brown 60.00 120.00
JE Jerry Porter 15.00 40.00
JF Justin Fargas 20.00 50.00
JG Jeff Garcia 20.00 50.00
JL Jamal Lewis 20.00 50.00
JM Joe Montana 100.00 200.00
JN Joe Namath 60.00 120.00
JW Javon Walker 20.00 50.00
KH Kelly Holcomb 15.00 40.00
KR Koren Robinson 20.00 50.00
LS Lynn Swann 100.00 175.00
MA Marcus Allen 40.00 80.00
MH Matt Hasselbeck 20.00 50.00
PH Priest Holmes 25.00 60.00
PM Peyton Manning 75.00 150.00
PO Clinton Portis 20.00 50.00
PP Peerless Price 15.00 40.00
RG Rod Gardner 15.00 40.00
RI John Riggins 30.00 80.00
RW Ricky Williams 20.00 50.00
SA Shaun Alexander 20.00 50.00
SU Lee Suggs 15.00 40.00
TA Troy Aikman 50.00 100.00
TB Tim Brown 25.00 60.00
TC Tyrone Calico 15.00 40.00
TE Teyo Johnson 15.00 40.00
TG Trent Green 20.00 50.00
TM Tommy Maddox 20.00 50.00
TO Terrell Owens 25.00 60.00
TS Terrell Suggs 25.00 60.00
ZT Zach Thomas 25.00 60.00

2003 SP Authentic Threads

OVERALL THREADS STATED ODDS 1:24
ANNOUNCED PRINT RUN 450
*GOLD/25: 1X TO 2.5X BASIC JSY/450
GOLD STATED PRINT RUN 25 SER.#'d SETS
JCAB Anquan Boldin 6.00 15.00
JCAG Ahman Green 4.00 10.00
JCAJ Andre Johnson 10.00 25.00
JCBF Brett Favre 12.00 30.00
JCBJ Bethel Johnson 3.00 8.00
JCBR Bryant Johnson 4.00 10.00
JCCL Dallas Clark 6.00 15.00
JCCP Chad Pennington 5.00 12.00
JCCU Daunte Culpepper 4.00 10.00
JCDC David Carr 4.00 10.00
JCDR Dave Ragone 3.00 8.00
JCEJ Edgerrin James 5.00 12.00
JCES Emmitt Smith 12.00 30.00
JCHO Torry Holt 5.00 12.00
JCJP Jake Plummer 4.00 10.00
JCJR Jerry Rice 10.00 25.00
JCKB Kyle Boller 4.00 10.00
JCKC Kevin Curtis 4.00 10.00
JCKE Kelley Washington 2.50 6.00
JCKK Kliff Kingsbury 3.00 8.00
JCKW Kurt Warner 5.00 12.00
JCLJ Larry Johnson 4.00 10.00
JCMC Donovan McNabb 5.00 12.00
JCMH Marvin Harrison 5.00 12.00
JCMS Musa Smith 2.50 6.00
JCMV Michael Vick 6.00 15.00
JCNB Nate Burleson 3.00 8.00
JCOS Onterrio Smith 2.50 6.00
JCPA Carson Palmer 12.00 30.00
JCPH Priest Holmes 5.00 12.00
JCPM Peyton Manning 10.00 25.00
JCPO Clinton Portis 4.00 10.00
JCPP Peerless Price 3.00 8.00
JCRG Rich Gannon 4.00 10.00
JCRS Rod Smith 4.00 10.00
JCSM Santana Moss 4.00 10.00
JCST Steve McNair 5.00 12.00
JCTB Tom Brady 12.00 30.00
JCTC Tyrone Calico 3.00 8.00
JCTH Travis Henry 3.00 8.00
JCTJ Teyo Johnson 3.00 8.00
JCWM Willis McGahee 5.00 12.00

2003 SP Authentic Threads Doubles

DOUBLE STATED PRINT RUN 345
*GOLD/25: 1X TO 2.5X DUAL/345
GOLD PRINT RUN 25 SER.#'d SETS
ABBJ Anquan Boldin 6.00 15.00
Bryant Johnson
BFAG Brett Favre 12.00 30.00
Ahman Green
CPKW Carson Palmer 12.00 30.00
Kelley Washington
CPSM Chad Pennington 5.00 12.00
Santana Moss
DCAJ David Carr 10.00 25.00
Andre Johnson
DCDR David Carr 4.00 10.00
Dave Ragone
DCNB Daunte Culpepper 4.00 10.00
Nate Burleson
DCOS Daunte Culpepper 3.00 8.00
Onterrio Smith
DMMV Donovan McNabb 6.00 15.00
Michael Vick
EJCP Edgerrin James 5.00 12.00
Clinton Portis
ESCP Emmitt Smith 12.00 30.00
Clinton Portis
JFTJ Justin Fargas 5.00 12.00
Teyo Johnson
JPCP Jake Plummer 4.00 10.00
Clinton Portis
JPRS Jake Plummer 4.00 10.00
Rod Smith
JRRG Jerry Rice 10.00 25.00
Rich Gannon
KBMS Kyle Boller 5.00 12.00
Musa Smith
KKBJ Kliff Kingsbury 3.00 8.00
Bethel Johnson
KWKC Kurt Warner 4.00 10.00
Kevin Curtis
KWTH Kurt Warner 5.00 12.00
Torry Holt
LJPH Larry Johnson 4.00 10.00
Priest Holmes
MVPP Michael Vick 6.00 15.00
Peerless Price
OSNB Onterrio Smith 3.00 8.00
Nate Burleson
PMCP Peyton Manning 12.00 30.00
Carson Palmer
PMDC Peyton Manning 10.00 25.00
Dallas Clark
PMMH Peyton Manning 10.00 25.00
Marvin Harrison
RGTJ Rich Gannon 4.00 10.00
Teyo Johnson
SMTC Steve McNair 5.00 12.00
Tyrone Calico
TBBJ Tom Brady 3.00 8.00
Bethel Johnson
TBKK Tom Brady 12.00 30.00
Kliff Kingsbury
THWM Travis Henry 5.00 12.00
Willis McGahee

2003 SP Authentic Threads Triples

TRIPLE PRINT RUN 175 SER.#'d SETS
*GOLD/25: .8X TO 2X TRIPLE/175
GOLD STATED PRINT RUN 25 SER.#'d SETS
HMJ Marvin Harrison 12.00 30.00
Peyton Manning
Edgerrin James
HWC Torry Holt 6.00 15.00
Kurt Warner
Kevin Curtis
JBK Bethel Johnson 4.00 10.00
Tom Brady
Kliff Kingsbury
JCR Andre Johnson 10.00 25.00
David Carr
Dave Ragone
MCB Randy Moss 6.00 15.00
Daunte Culpepper
Nate Burleson
MPJ Willis McGahee 5.00 12.00
Clinton Portis
Edgerrin James
MPM Santana Moss 6.00 15.00
Chad Pennington
Curtis Martin
PPS Clinton Portis 5.00 12.00
Jake Plummer
Rod Smith
RGJ Jerry Rice 12.00 30.00
Rich Gannon
Teyo Johnson
VCP Michael Vick 8.00 20.00
David Carr
Carson Palmer

2003 SP Authentic Promo Strips

These three-card strips were issued by Upper Deck to promote the 2003 SP Authentic card release. Each was serial numbered on the front to 1000 and released primarily at the 2004 Super Bowl XXXVIII Card Show in Houston. We've numbered them below according to alphabetical order starting with the player to the far left on the strip.

1 Plaxico Burress .75 2.00
Travis Henry
Kelly Holcomb
2 Trent Green 1.25 3.00
Ray Lewis
Donte Stallworth
3 Edgerrin James 1.50 4.00
Zach Thomas
Tim Brown
4 Santana Moss 1.50 4.00
Donovan McNabb
Rodney Peete

2004 SP Authentic

SP Authentic initially released in late-December 2004 and was one of the most popular releases of the year. The base set consists of 216-cards including 60-rookies serial numbered to 1199, 35-rookie autographs serial numbered to 990 and 31-rookie jersey autographs numbered between 299 and 799. Hobby boxes contained 24-packs of 5-cards and carried an S.R.P. of $4.99 per pack. Two parallel sets and a variety of inserts can be found seeded in packs highlighted by the Scripts for Success and Sign of the Times autograph inserts.

COMP.SET w/o SP's (90) 10.00 25.00
91-150 ROOKIE PRINT RUN 1199
151-185 ROOKIE AU PRINT RUN 990
186-200 JSY AU RC PRINT RUN 799
201-206 JSY AU RC PRINT RUN 499
207-216 JSY AU RC PRINT RUN 299
1 Josh McCown .30 .75
2 Anquan Boldin .40 1.00
3 Michael Vick .50 1.25
4 Peerless Price .25 .60
5 Todd Heap .30 .75
6 Kyle Boller .30 .75
7 Jamal Lewis .30 .75
8 Drew Bledsoe .40 1.00
9 Travis Henry .25 .60
10 Eric Moulds .30 .75
11 Steve Smith .40 1.00
12 Stephen Davis .30 .75
13 Jake Delhomme .30 .75
14 Rex Grossman .30 .75
15 Brian Urlacher .40 1.00
16 Thomas Jones .40 1.00
17 Chad Johnson .40 1.00
18 Rudi Johnson .30 .75
19 Carson Palmer .40 1.00
20 William Green .25 .60
21 Andre Davis .25 .60
22 Jeff Garcia .30 .75
23 Roy Williams S .30 .75
24 Eddie George .30 .75
25 Keyshawn Johnson .30 .75
26 Ashley Lelie .25 .60
27 Jake Plummer .30 .75
28 Champ Bailey .30 .75
29 Charles Rogers .25 .60
30 Joey Harrington .30 .75
31 Ahman Green .30 .75
32 Brett Favre 1.00 2.50
33 Javon Walker .25 .60
34 David Carr .25 .60
35 Domanick Davis .25 .60
36 Andre Johnson .40 1.00
37 Marvin Harrison .40 1.00
38 Edgerrin James .30 .75
39 Peyton Manning .75 2.00
40 Byron Leftwich .30 .75
41 Fred Taylor .30 .75
42 Trent Green .30 .75
43 Tony Gonzalez .40 1.00
44 Priest Holmes .40 1.00
45 Ricky Williams .30 .75
46 Chris Chambers .30 .75
47 Jay Fiedler .25 .60
48 Daunte Culpepper .30 .75
49 Randy Moss .40 1.00
50 Onterrio Smith .25 .60
51 Tom Brady .75 2.00
52 Troy Brown .30 .75
53 Corey Dillon .30 .75
54 Deuce McAllister .30 .75
55 Aaron Brooks .30 .75
56 Joe Horn .30 .75
57 Amani Toomer .30 .75
58 Kurt Warner .40 1.00
59 Jeremy Shockey .30 .75
60 Chad Pennington .40 1.00
61 Santana Moss .30 .75
62 Curtis Martin .40 1.00
63 Rich Gannon .30 .75
64 Jerry Rice .75 2.00

65 Jerry Porter .25 .60
66 Terrell Owens .40 1.00
67 Jevon Kearse .30 .75
68 Donovan McNabb .40 1.00
69 Hines Ward .40 1.00
70 Plaxico Burress .30 .75
71 Tommy Maddox .30 .75
72 Drew Brees .40 1.00
73 LaDainian Tomlinson .40 1.00
74 Tim Rattay .25 .60
75 Brandon Lloyd .30 .75
76 Kevan Barlow .25 .60
77 Shaun Alexander .30 .75
78 Koren Robinson .25 .60
79 Matt Hasselbeck .30 .75
80 Marshall Faulk .40 1.00
81 Torry Holt .30 .75
82 Marc Bulger .30 .75
83 Brad Johnson .30 .75
84 Joey Galloway .30 .75
85 Steve McNair .40 1.00
86 Derrick Mason .30 .75
87 Chris Brown .25 .60
88 Mark Brunell .30 .75
89 Laveranues Coles .25 .60
90 Clinton Portis .40 1.00
91 Triandos Luke RC 1.50 4.00
92 Keith Smith RC 1.50 4.00
93 Shaun Phillips RC 2.50 6.00
94 D.J. Williams RC 2.50 6.00
95 Keiwan Ratliff RC 1.50 4.00
96 Madieu Williams RC 1.50 4.00
97 Chris Cooley RC 2.50 6.00
98 Stuart Schweigert RC 2.00 5.00
99 Sloan Thomas RC 2.00 5.00
100 Chad Lavalais RC 1.50 4.00
101 Jared Allen RC 8.00 20.00
102 Brian Jones RC 1.50 4.00
103 Matt Ware RC 2.50 6.00
104 Daryl Smith RC 1.50 4.00
105 J.R. Reed RC 1.50 4.00
106 D.J. Hackett RC 2.00 5.00
107 Jeris McIntyre RC 1.50 4.00
108 Dexter Reid RC 1.50 4.00
109 Courtney Anderson RC 1.50 4.00
110 Courtney Watson RC 1.50 4.00
111 Larry Croom RC 1.50 4.00
112 Jonathan Smith RC 1.50 4.00
113 Vernon Carey RC 1.50 4.00
114 Michael Gaines RC 1.50 4.00
115 Chris Snee RC 2.00 5.00
116 Nathan Vasher RC 2.50 6.00
117 Teddy Lehman RC 1.50 4.00
118 Marcus Tubbs RC 1.50 4.00
119 Ben Utecht RC 2.00 5.00
120 Maurice Mann RC 1.50 4.00
121 Thomas Tapeh RC 2.00 5.00
122 Will Allen RC 2.00 5.00
123 Demorrio Williams RC 2.50 6.00
124 Ran Carthon RC 1.50 4.00
125 Tim Euhus RC 1.50 4.00
126 Bradlee Van Pelt RC 2.00 5.00
127 Patrick Crayton RC 2.50 6.00
128 Ryan Krause RC 1.50 4.00
129 Joey Thomas RC 1.50 4.00
130 Antwan Odom RC 2.00 5.00
131 Karlos Dansby RC 2.50 6.00
132 Junior Siavii RC 1.50 4.00
133 Jamaar Taylor RC 1.50 4.00
134 Kendrick Starling RC 1.50 4.00
135 Wes Welker RC 10.00 25.00
136 Igor Olshansky RC 2.00 5.00
137 Mark Jones RC 1.50 4.00
138 Bruce Thornton RC 1.50 4.00
139 Michael Boulware RC 2.50 6.00
140 Matt Mauck RC 1.50 4.00
141 Clarence Moore RC 1.50 4.00
142 Derrick Strait RC 1.50 4.00
143 Jarrett Payton RC 2.00 5.00
144 Dontarrious Thomas RC 2.00 5.00
145 Shawntae Spencer RC 1.50 4.00
146 Bob Sanders RC 8.00 20.00
147 Darnell Dockett RC 1.50 4.00
148 Sean Taylor RC 5.00 12.00
149 Jason Babin RC 2.50 6.00
150 Ricardo Colclough RC 2.00 5.00
151 Brandon Chillar AU RC 4.00 10.00
152 Clarence Farmer AU RC 3.00 8.00
153 B.J. Symons AU RC 3.00 8.00
154 John Navarre AU RC 3.00 8.00
155 P.K. Sam AU RC 3.00 8.00
156 Casey Clausen AU RC 4.00 10.00
157 Drew Henson AU RC 3.00 8.00
158 Kris Wilson AU RC 4.00 10.00
159 Vince Wilfork AU RC 8.00 20.00
160 Michael Turner AU RC 25.00 50.00
161 Jonathan Vilma AU RC 5.00 12.00
162 Samie Parker AU RC 3.00 8.00
163 B.J. Sams AU RC 3.00 8.00
164 Adimchinobe Echemandu AU RC 4.00 10.00
165 Ernest Wilford AU RC 4.00 10.00
166 Troy Fleming AU RC 3.00 8.00
167 Tommie Harris AU RC 5.00 12.00
168 Jammal Lord AU RC 3.00 8.00
169 Kenechi Udeze AU RC 4.00 10.00
170 Chris Gamble AU RC 4.00 10.00
171 Carlos Francis AU RC 3.00 8.00
172 Mewelde Moore AU RC 4.00 10.00
173 Jared Lorenzen AU RC 4.00 10.00
174 Jeff Smoker AU RC 4.00 10.00
175 Ben Hartsock AU RC 3.00 8.00
176 Jerricho Cotchery AU RC 4.00 10.00
177 Josh Harris AU RC 3.00 8.00
178 Cody Pickett AU RC 4.00 10.00
179 Quincy Wilson AU RC 4.00 10.00
180 Will Smith AU RC 4.00 10.00
181 Ahmad Carroll AU RC 3.00 8.00
182 B.J. Johnson AU RC 3.00 8.00
183 Dunta Robinson AU RC 3.00 8.00
184 Craig Krenzel AU RC 4.00 10.00
185 Johnnie Morant AU RC 3.00 8.00
186 Cedric Cobbs JSY AU RC 8.00 20.00
187 Matt Schaub JSY AU RC 75.00 135.00
188 Bernard Berrian JSY AU RC 12.00 30.00
189 Devard Darling JSY AU RC 8.00 20.00
190 Ben Watson JSY AU RC 12.00 30.00
191 Darius Watts JSY AU RC 8.00 20.00
192 DeAngelo Hall JSY AU RC 12.00 30.00
193 Ben Troupe JSY AU RC 10.00 25.00
194 Michael Jenkins JSY AU RC 12.00 30.00
195 Keary Colbert JSY AU RC 8.00 20.00
196 Robert Gallery JSY AU RC 12.00 30.00
197 Greg Jones JSY AU RC 8.00 20.00
198 Michael Clayton JSY AU RC 10.00 25.00
199 Luke McCown JSY AU RC 10.00 25.00
200 Derrick Hamilton JSY AU RC 8.00 20.00
201 Rashaun Woods JSY AU RC 10.00 25.00
202 Chris Perry JSY AU RC 10.00 25.00
203 Devery Henderson JSY AU RC 15.00 40.00
204 Tatum Bell JSY AU RC 12.00 30.00
205 Lee Evans JSY AU RC 15.00 40.00
206 J.P. Losman JSY AU RC 12.00 30.00
207 Kellen Winslow JSY AU RC 20.00 50.00
208 Reggie Williams JSY AU RC 15.00 40.00
209 Julius Jones JSY AU RC 15.00 40.00
210 Steven Jackson JSY AU RC 60.00 120.00
211 Kevin Jones JSY AU RC 15.00 40.00
212 Roy Williams JSY AU RC 20.00 50.00
213 Ben Roethlisberger JSY AU RC 500.00 700.00
214 Philip Rivers JSY AU RC 250.00 500.00
215 Larry Fitzgerald JSY AU RC 150.00 300.00
216 Eli Manning JSY AU RC 450.00 700.00

2004 SP Authentic Black

UNPRICED BLACK PRINT RUN 10

2004 SP Authentic Gold

*VETS: 6X TO 15X BASIC CARDS
*ROOKIES 91-150: 1.5X TO 4X
1-150 STATED PRINT RUN 50
*ROOKIE JSY AU 186-200: 1.2X TO 3X
*ROOK.JSY AU 201-206: 1X TO 2.5X
*ROOK.JSY AU 207-216: .8X TO 2X
186-216 JSY AU PRINT RUN 25
101 Jared Allen 60.00 120.00
135 Wes Welker 60.00 120.00
187 Matt Schaub JSY AU 250.00 400.00
210 Steven Jackson JSY AU 150.00 300.00
213 Ben Roethlisberger JSY AU 1,000.00 1,500.00
214 Philip Rivers JSY AU 500.00 800.00
215 Larry Fitzgerald JSY AU 400.00 800.00
216 Eli Manning JSY AU 1,200.00 1,800.00

2004 SP Authentic Artifacts Jerseys

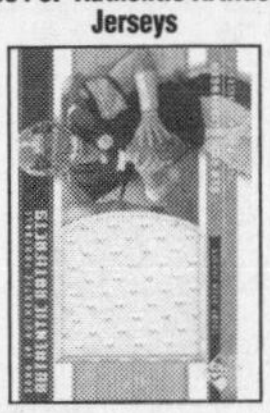

STATED PRINT RUN 75 SER.#'d SETS
AABF Brett Favre 15.00 40.00
AABL Byron Leftwich 5.00 12.00
AABR Ben Roethlisberger 25.00 60.00
AACH Chad Pennington 6.00 15.00
AACL Clinton Portis 6.00 15.00
AACP Chris Perry 5.00 12.00
AADB Drew Bledsoe 6.00 15.00
AADC David Carr 4.00 10.00
AADE Deuce McAllister 5.00 12.00
AADH Devery Henderson 6.00 15.00
AADM Donovan McNabb 6.00 15.00
AAEJ Edgerrin James 5.00 12.00
AAEM Eli Manning 25.00 60.00
AAGJ Greg Jones 4.00 10.00
AAJJ Julius Jones 5.00 12.00
AAJP J.P. Losman 5.00 12.00
AAJR Jerry Rice 12.00 30.00
AAJS Jeremy Shockey 5.00 12.00
AAKC Keary Colbert 4.00 10.00
AAKJ Kevin Jones 5.00 12.00
AAKU Kurt Warner 6.00 15.00
AAKW Kellen Winslow Jr. 6.00 15.00
AALE Lee Evans 6.00 15.00
AALF Larry Fitzgerald 10.00 25.00
AALT LaDainian Tomlinson 6.00 15.00
AAMC Michael Clayton 5.00 12.00
AAMF Marshall Faulk 6.00 15.00
AAMJ Michael Jenkins 6.00 15.00
AAPH Priest Holmes 6.00 15.00
AAPM Peyton Manning 12.00 30.00
AAPR Philip Rivers 15.00 40.00
AARE Reggie Williams 5.00 12.00
AARG Robert Gallery 6.00 15.00
AARI Ricky Williams 5.00 12.00
AARM Randy Moss 6.00 15.00
AARO Roy Williams WR 8.00 15.00
AAHW Rashaun Woods 4.00 10.00
AASJ Steven Jackson 6.00 15.00
AASM Steve McNair 6.00 15.00
AATB Tatum Bell 5.00 12.00
AATO Tom Brady 12.00 30.00

2004 SP Authentic Scripts for Success Autographs

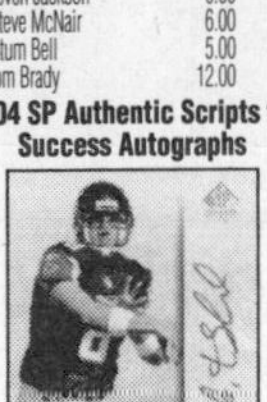

STATED ODDS 1:24
SSAG Ahman Green/100* 10.00 25.00
SSAR Antwaan Randle El 8.00 20.00
SSBF Brett Favre SP 100.00 200.00
SSBH Ben Hartsock 4.00 10.00
SSBJ B.J. Sams 4.00 10.00
SSBS B.J. Symons 4.00 10.00
SSBT Ben Troupe 5.00 12.00
SSBW Ben Watson 6.00 15.00
SSCA Carlos Francis 4.00 10.00
SSCG Chris Gamble 5.00 12.00
SSCJ Chad Johnson 10.00 25.00
SSGP Cody Pickett 5.00 12.00
SSDA Dante Hall 8.00 20.00
SSDB Drew Bledsoe SP 15.00 40.00
SSDH Derrick Hamilton 4.00 10.00
SSDM Derrick Mason 8.00 20.00
SSDR Dunta Robinson 4.00 10.00
SSDV Devery Henderson 6.00 15.00
SSDW Darius Watts 4.00 10.00
SSEW Ernest Wilford 5.00 12.00
SSHE Todd Heap 8.00 20.00
SSHO Joe Horn 6.00 15.00
SSJC Jerricho Cotchery 5.00 12.00
SSJM Johnnie Morant 4.00 10.00
SSJN John Navarre 4.00 10.00
SSJO Josh McCown 8.00 20.00
SSJP Jesse Palmer 6.00 15.00
SSJS Jeff Smoker 5.00 12.00
SSJV Jonathan Vilma 6.00 15.00
SSKC Keary Colbert 4.00 10.00
SSKU Kenechi Udeze 5.00 12.00
SSLE Lee Evans 6.00 15.00
SSLM Luke McCown 5.00 12.00
SSMJ Michael Jenkins 6.00 15.00
SSMM Mewelde Moore 5.00 12.00
SSMS Matt Schaub 10.00 25.00
SSMT Michael Turner 8.00 20.00
SSMV Michael Vick SP 30.00 60.00
SSPK P.K. Sam 4.00 10.00
SSRA Rashaun Woods 4.00 10.00
SSRJ Rudi Johnson 8.00 20.00
SSRW Roy Williams S 8.00 20.00
SSSP Samie Parker 4.00 10.00
SSTG Tony Gonzalez 10.00 25.00
SSTH Tommie Harris 6.00 15.00
SSTR Travis Henry 6.00 15.00
SSVW Vince Wilfork 6.00 15.00
SSWS Will Smith 5.00 12.00
SSZT Zach Thomas 10.00 25.00

2004 SP Authentic Sign of the Times

STATED ODDS 1:72
SOTAM Archie Manning 12.00 30.00
SOTAR Andy Reid 8.00 20.00
SOTBE Tatum Bell 6.00 15.00
SOTBF Brett Favre SP 125.00 200.00
SOTBL Byron Leftwich 8.00 20.00
SOTBP Bill Parcells 25.00 50.00
SOTBR Ben Roethlisberger 75.00 150.00
SOTBS Barry Sanders SP 60.00 120.00
SOTCH Chris Perry 6.00 15.00
SOTCJ Chad Johnson 10.00 25.00
SOTCP Chad Pennington 10.00 25.00
SOTDA David Carr 6.00 15.00
SOTDC Daunte Culpepper 8.00 20.00
SOTDE Deuce McAllister 8.00 20.00
SOTDH Dante Hall 8.00 20.00
SOTDM Donovan McNabb/50* 25.00 60.00
SOTDR Drew Henson 6.00 15.00
SOTEM Eli Manning 90.00 150.00
SOTGJ Greg Jones 5.00 12.00
SOTHL Howie Long 20.00 50.00
SOTJE John Elway SP 75.00 150.00
SOTJF John Fox 6.00 15.00
SOTJG Jon Gruden 8.00 20.00
SOTJJ Julius Jones 6.00 15.00
SOTJM Josh McCown 8.00 20.00
SOTJO Joe Montana SP 60.00 120.00
SOTJP J.P. Losman 6.00 15.00
SOTKB Kyle Boller 8.00 20.00
SOTKE Kellen Winslow Jr. 8.00 20.00
SOTKJ Kevin Jones 6.00 15.00
SOTKW Kellen Winslow Sr. 10.00 25.00
SOTLT LaDainian Tomlinson/50* 60.00 120.00
SOTMA Derrick Mason 8.00 20.00
SOTMB Mark Brunell 8.00 20.00
SOTMV Michael Vick/50 * 30.00 60.00
SOTPM Peyton Manning 60.00 120.00
SOTPR Philip Rivers 40.00 80.00
SOTRE Reggie Williams 6.00 15.00
SOTRG Rex Grossman 8.00 20.00
SOTRO Robert Gallery 8.00 20.00
SOTRS Roger Staubach SP 35.00 60.00
SOTRW Roy Williams S 8.00 20.00
SOTSJ Steven Jackson 12.00 30.00
SOTSM Steve McNair SP 20.00 40.00
SOTTA Troy Aikman 40.00 80.00
SOTTG Tony Gonzalez 10.00 25.00
SOTTH Travis Henry 6.00 15.00
SOTWI Roy Williams WR 8.00 20.00

2004 SP Authentic Sign of the Times Dual

STATED PRINT RUN 50 SER.#'d SETS
AE Archie Manning 250.00 400.00
Eli Manning
JG Jimmy Johnson 20.00 50.00
Jon Gruden
LE J.P. Losman 20.00 50.00
Lee Evans
LG Howie Long 40.00 75.00
Robert Gallery
MM Eli Manning 250.00 500.00
Peyton Manning
PJ Chris Perry 25.00 60.00
Steven Jackson
PR Bill Parcells 25.00 60.00
Andy Reid
RR Philip Rivers 200.00 350.00
Ben Roethlisberger
SJ Barry Sanders 100.00 200.00
Kevin Jones
WW Kellen Winslow Sr. 30.00 60.00
Kellen Winslow Jr.

2004 SP Authentic Sign of the Times Gold

*GOLD/25: .8X TO 2X BASIC AUTO
GOLD PRINT RUN 25 SER.#'d SETS
SOTBF Brett Favre 175.00 300.00
SOTBR Ben Roethlisberger 175.00 350.00
SOTBS Barry Sanders 100.00 200.00
SOTEM Eli Manning 200.00 350.00
SOTJE John Elway 125.00 250.00
SOTJO Joe Montana 125.00 250.00
SOTLT LaDainian Tomlinson 100.00 200.00
SOTPM Peyton Manning 100.00 200.00
SOTPR Philip Rivers 75.00 150.00
SOTSJ Steven Jackson 25.00 60.00

2004 SP Authentic Sign of the Times Triple

UNPRICED TRIPLE PRINT RUN 10 SETS

2005 SP Authentic

This 257-card set was released in December, 2005. The set was issued through the hobby in five-card packs with a $4.99 SRP which came 24 packs to a box. The first 90 cards of the set feature veterans in alphabetical order by team while the rest of the set features rookies. Cards numbered 91-180 were issued to a stated print run of 750 serial nuimbered sets while cards numbered 181-220 and 254-257 were issued to a stated print run of 850 serial numbered sets. The set also had a subset of rookies which were both signed and have a player-worn swatch and those cards were issued to stated print runs between 99 and 899 serial numbered copies. A few players did not return their signatures in time for pack out and those cards could be redeemed until December 20, 2008.

COMP.SET w/o RC's (90) 10.00 25.00
91-180 PRINT RUN 750 SER.#'d SETS
181-220/254-257 PRINT RUN 850 SETS
221-253 PRINT RUN 99-899 SER.#'d SETS
UNPRICED NFL LOGO PATCHES #'d TO 1
1 Kurt Warner .40 1.00
2 Larry Fitzgerald .40 1.00
3 Anquan Boldin .30 .75
4 Michael Vick .40 1.00
5 Alge Crumpler .30 .75
6 Warrick Dunn .30 .75
7 Kyle Boller .30 .75
8 Jamal Lewis .30 .75
9 J.P. Losman .25 .60
10 Willis McGahee .40 1.00
11 Lee Evans .30 .75
12 Jake Delhomme .30 .75
13 DeShaun Foster .30 .75
14 Muhsin Muhammad .30 .75
15 Walter Payton 1.00 2.50
16 Brian Urlacher .40 1.00
17 Carson Palmer .40 1.00
18 Rudi Johnson .30 .75
19 Chad Johnson .30 .75
20 Lee Suggs .25 .60
21 Antonio Bryant .25 .60
22 Julius Jones .25 .60
23 Drew Bledsoe .40 1.00
24 Keyshawn Johnson .30 .75
25 Tatum Bell .25 .60
26 Jake Plummer .30 .75
27 Roy Williams WR .30 .75
28 Kevin Jones .25 .60
29 Jeff Garcia .30 .75
30 Brett Favre 1.00 2.50
31 Ahman Green .30 .75
32 Javon Walker .25 .60
33 David Carr .25 .60
34 Andre Johnson .40 1.00
35 Domanick Davis .25 .60
36 Peyton Manning .75 2.00
37 Edgerrin James .30 .75
38 Reggie Wayne .40 1.00
39 Byron Leftwich .30 .75
40 Fred Taylor .30 .75
41 Jimmy Smith .30 .75
42 Priest Holmes .30 .75
43 Larry Johnson .30 .75
44 Trent Green .30 .75
45 Randy McMichael .25 .60
46 Chris Chambers .30 .75
47 Ricky Williams .30 .75
48 Daunte Culpepper .30 .75
49 Nate Burleson .25 .60
50 Tom Brady .75 2.00
51 Corey Dillon .30 .75
52 David Givens .25 .60
53 Aaron Brooks .25 .60
54 Deuce McAllister .30 .75
55 Joe Horn .30 .75
56 Eli Manning .60 1.50
57 Jeremy Shockey .40 1.00
58 Tiki Barber .40 1.00
59 Chad Pennington .40 1.00
60 Santana Moss .30 .75
61 Curtis Martin .40 1.00
62 Randy Moss .40 1.00
63 LaMont Jordan .30 .75
64 Kerry Collins .30 .75
65 Donovan McNabb .40 1.00
66 Brian Westbrook .30 .75
67 Terrell Owens .40 1.00
68 Ben Roethlisberger .60 1.50
69 Hines Ward .40 1.00
70 Jerome Bettis .40 1.00
71 Drew Brees .40 1.00
72 Antonio Gates .40 1.00
73 LaDainian Tomlinson .40 1.00
74 Kevan Barlow .25 .60
75 Brandon Lloyd .25 .60
76 Matt Hasselbeck .30 .75
77 Shaun Alexander .30 .75
78 Darrell Jackson .25 .60
79 Marc Bulger .30 .75
80 Steven Jackson .40 1.00
81 Torry Holt .30 .75
82 Brian Griese .30 .75
83 Michael Clayton .25 .60
84 Michael Pittman .25 .60
85 Steve McNair .40 1.00
86 Drew Bennett .30 .75
87 Chris Brown .25 .60
88 Clinton Portis .30 .75
89 Patrick Ramsey .30 .75
90 Laveranues Coles .25 .60
91 Nehemiah Broughton RC 2.00 5.00
92 Madison Hedgecock RC 2.50 6.00
93 Damien Nash RC 2.00 5.00
94 Michael Boley RC 2.50 6.00
95 Lionel Gates RC 1.50 4.00
96 Noah Herron RC 1.50 4.00
97 Bo Scaife RC 2.00 5.00
98 Joel Dreessen RC 2.00 5.00
99 Rasheed Marshall RC 2.00 5.00
100 Andre Maddox RC 1.50 4.00
101 Tab Perry RC 1.50 4.00
102 Dante Ridgeway RC 1.50 4.00
103 Patrick Estes RC 1.50 4.00
104 Billy Bajema RC 1.50 4.00
105 Paris Warren RC 2.00 5.00
106 LeRon McCoy RC 1.50 4.00
107 Adam Bergen RC 1.50 4.00
108 Manuel White RC 2.00 5.00
109 Stephen Spach RC 1.50 4.00
110 Dante Nicholson RC 1.50 4.00
111 Brodney Pool RC 2.00 5.00
112 Stanford Routt RC 2.00 5.00
113 Josh Bullocks RC 2.00 5.00
114 Ronald Bartell RC 2.00 5.00
115 Nick Collins RC 3.00 8.00
116 Darrent Williams RC 2.50 6.00
117 Justin Miller RC 2.00 5.00
118 Kelvin Hayden RC 2.00 5.00
119 Bryant McFadden RC 2.00 5.00
120 Oshiomogho Atogwe RC 2.50 6.00
121 Stanley Wilson RC 2.00 5.00
122 Eric Green RC 1.50 4.00
123 Michael Hawkins RC 1.50 4.00
124 Marcus Spears RC 2.00 5.00
125 Ellis Hobbs RC 2.50 6.00
126 Scott Starks RC 2.00 5.00
127 Domonique Foxworth RC 2.00 5.00
128 Sean Considine RC 1.50 4.00
129 James Sanders RC 1.50 4.00
130 Travis Daniels RC 2.00 5.00
131 Vincent Fuller RC 2.00 5.00
132 Marviel Underwood RC 2.00 5.00
133 Jerome Carter RC 1.50 4.00
134 Kerry Rhodes RC 2.00 5.00
135 Fred Amey RC 1.50 4.00
136 Eric King RC 1.50 4.00
137 Derrick Johnson CB RC 1.50 4.00
138 Luis Castillo RC 2.00 5.00
139 Shaun Cody RC 2.00 5.00
140 Matt Roth RC 2.00 5.00
141 Jonathan Babineaux RC 2.00 5.00
142 Justin Tuck RC 7.50 15.00
143 Sione Pouha RC 1.50 4.00
144 Daven Holly RC 1.50 4.00
145 Vincent Burns RC 1.50 4.00
146 Derrick Johnson RC 2.00 5.00
147 Lofa Tatupu RC 2.50 6.00
148 Odell Thurman RC 2.50 6.00
149 Rick Razzano RC 1.50 4.00
150 Channing Crowder RC 2.00 5.00
151 Kirk Morrison RC 2.50 6.00
152 Alfred Fincher RC 2.00 5.00
153 Jordan Beck RC 2.00 5.00
154 Darryl Blackstock RC 1.50 4.00
155 Leroy Hill RC 2.50 6.00
156 Jammal Brown RC 2.50 6.00
157 Alex Barron RC 1.50 4.00
158 Chris Spencer RC 2.50 6.00
159 Logan Mankins RC 2.50 6.00
160 David Baas RC 1.50 4.00
161 Michael Roos RC 1.50 4.00
162 Kurt Campbell RC 1.50 4.00
163 Khalif Barnes RC 1.50 4.00
164 Antonio Perkins RC 2.00 5.00
165 Vonta Leach RC 2.00 5.00
166 Brady Poppinga RC 2.50 6.00
167 Trent Cole RC 2.50 6.00
168 Dave Rayner RC 1.50 4.00
169 Bill Swancutt RC 1.50 4.00
170 Eric Moore RC 1.50 4.00
171 Justin Green RC 2.50 6.00
172 Shaun Suisham RC 1.50 4.00
173 C.J. Mosley RC 1.50 4.00
174 Ryan Riddle RC 1.50 4.00
175 Darrell Shropshire RC 1.50 4.00
176 Boomer Grigsby RC 2.50 6.00
177 Rian Wallace RC 2.00 5.00
178 Lance Mitchell RC 2.00 5.00
179 Nick Speegle RC 1.50 4.00
180 Tyson Thompson RC 1.50 4.00
181 Dan Orlovsky AU RC 6.00 15.00
182 Anthony Davis AU RC 4.00 10.00
183 Kay-Jay Harris AU RC 4.00 10.00
184 Walter Reyes AU RC 4.00 10.00
185 Darren Sproles AU RC 15.00 40.00
186 Marlin Jackson AU RC 4.00 10.00
187 Corey Webster AU RC 5.00 12.00
188 Marion Barber AU RC 6.00 15.00
189 Chris Henry AU RC 6.00 15.00
190 Derek Anderson AU RC 5.00 12.00
191 David Pollack AU RC 5.00 12.00
192 Anttaj Hawthorne AU RC 4.00 10.00
193 David Greene AU RC 4.00 10.00
194 Erasmus James AU RC 5.00 12.00
195 Ryan Fitzpatrick AU RC 25.00 60.00
196 Derrick Johnson AU 5.00 12.00
197 Barrett Ruud AU RC 6.00 15.00
198 Kevin Burnett AU RC 5.00 12.00
200 J.R. Russell AU RC 4.00 10.00
201 Larry Brackins AU RC 4.00 10.00
202 Thomas Davis AU RC 4.00 10.00
203 Fred Gibson AU RC 5.00 12.00
204 Craphonso Thorpe AU RC 4.00 10.00
205 Brandon Jacobs AU RC 12.00 30.00
206 Taylor Stubblefield AU RC 4.00 10.00
207 Shawne Merriman AU RC 12.00 30.00
208 Travis Johnson AU RC 4.00 10.00
209 Adrian McPherson AU RC 4.00 10.00
210 Brandon Jones AU RC 5.00 12.00
211 Jerome Mathis AU RC 6.00 15.00
212 Alex Smith TE AU RC 4.00 10.00
213 Fabian Washington AU RC 5.00 12.00
214 Mike Nugent AU RC 5.00 12.00
215 Chase Lyman AU RC 4.00 10.00
216 Roydell Williams AU RC 5.00 12.00
217 Matt Cassel AU RC 15.00 40.00
218 Alvin Pearman AU RC 4.00 10.00
219 DeMarcus Ware AU RC 25.00 50.00
220 Mike Patterson AU RC 4.00 10.00
221 Courtney Roby/ JSY/899 AU RC 8.00 20.00
222 Eric Shelton JSY/899 AU RC 6.00 15.00
223 Stefan LeFors JSY/899 AU RC 6.00 15.00
224 Frank Gore JSY/899 AU RC 40.00 80.00
225 Ryan Moats JSY/899 AU RC 6.00 15.00
226 Andrew Walter JSY/899 AU RC 8.00 20.00
227 Adam Jones JSY/899 AU RC 6.00 15.00
228 Carlos Rogers JSY/699 AU RC 10.00 25.00
229 Terrence Murphy/ JSY/899 AU RC 6.00 15.00
230 Kyle Orton JSY/699 AU RC 20.00 40.00
231 Ciatrick Fason/ JSY/699 AU RC 6.00 15.00
232 Vernand Morency/ JSY/699 AU RC 6.00 15.00
233 Roscoe Parrish JSY/699 AU RC 6.00 15.00
234 Vincent Jackson/ JSY/699 AU RC 20.00 50.00
235 Mark Bradley JSY/699 AU RC 6.00 15.00
236 Reggie Brown JSY/599 AU RC 6.00 15.00
237 Roddy White JSY/499 AU RC 25.00 60.00
238 Mark Clayton JSY/499 AU RC 8.00 20.00
239 Antrel Rolle JSY/499 AU RC 10.00 25.00
240 Maurice Clarett JSY/499 AU 10.00 25.00
241 J.J. Arrington JSY/699 AU RC 8.00 20.00
242 Matt Jones JSY/399 AU RC 8.00 20.00
243 Ronnie Brown/ JSY/299 AU RC 20.00 50.00
244 Charlie Frye JSY/499 AU RC 10.00 25.00
245 Jason Campbell JSY/299 AU RC 25.00 60.00
246 Troy Williamson JSY/299 AU RC 10.00 25.00
247 Braylon Edwards/ JSY/299 AU RC 20.00 50.00
248 Alex Smith QB/ JSY/299 AU RC 100.00 200.00
249 Cadillac Williams/ JSY/299 AU RC 12.00 30.00
250 Heath Miller JSY/299 AU RC 30.00 60.00
251 Cedric Benson/ JSY/99 AU RC 50.00 100.00
252 Aaron Rodgers/ JSY/99 AU RC 1,500.00 2,500.00
253 Mike Williams JSY/99 AU 50.00 100.00
254 Chris Carr AU RC 4.00 10.00
255 Deandra Cobb AU RC 4.00 10.00
256 James Kilian AU RC 4.00 10.00
257 Airese Currie AU RC 4.00 10.00

2005 SP Authentic Gold

*VETS 1-90: 8X TO 20X BASIC CARDS
*ROOK.91-180: 1.5X TO 4X BASIC CARDS
*ROOKIE JSY AU 221-253 : 1.5X TO 4X
STATED PRINT RUN 25 SER.#'d SETS
224 Frank Gore JSY AU 150.00 250.00
230 Kyle Orton JSY AU 60.00 150.00
237 Roddy White JSY AU 125.00 250.00
243 Ronnie Brown JSY AU 150.00 300.00
245 Jason Campbell JSY AU 100.00 200.00
247 Braylon Edwards JSY AU 75.00 150.00
248 Alex Smith QB JSY AU 250.00 400.00
249 Cadillac Williams JSY AU 60.00 120.00
250 Heath Miller JSY AU 100.00 200.00
251 Cedric Benson JSY AU 125.00 250.00
252 Aaron Rodgers JSY AU 4,500.00 5,500.00

2005 SP Authentic Rookie Gold 100

*GOLD 100: .6X TO 1.5X BASIC CARDS

2005 SP Authentic Rookie Fabrics Bronze

STATED PRINT RUN 100 SER.#'d SETS
*GOLD TRIPLES: .6X TO 1.5X BASIC INSERTS
GOLD TRIPLE PRINT RUN 50 SER.#'d SETS
*SILVER DOUBLE: .5X TO 1.2X BASE INSERT
SILVER DOUBLE PRINT RUN 75 SER.#'d SETS
RFAN Antrel Rolle 4.00 10.00
RFAR Aaron Rodgers 50.00 100.00
RFAS Alex Smith QB 6.00 15.00
RFBE Braylon Edwards 5.00 12.00
RFCA Carlos Rogers 4.00 10.00
RFCB Cedric Benson 4.00 10.00
RFCF Charlie Frye 4.00 10.00
RFCI Ciatrick Fason 2.50 6.00
RFCR Courtney Roby 3.00 8.00
RFCW Cadillac Williams 4.00 10.00
RFES Eric Shelton 2.50 6.00
RFFG Frank Gore 6.00 15.00
RFJA J.J. Arrington 3.00 8.00
RFJC Jason Campbell 5.00 12.00
RFKO Kyle Orton 4.00 10.00
RFMB Mark Bradley 2.50 6.00
RFMC Mark Clayton 3.00 8.00
RFMJ Matt Jones 3.00 8.00
RFMO Maurice Clarett 2.50 6.00
RFMW Mike Williams 4.00 10.00
RFRB Ronnie Brown 5.00 12.00
RFRE Reggie Brown 2.50 6.00
RFRM Ryan Moats 2.50 6.00
RFRP Roscoe Parrish 2.50 6.00
RFRW Roddy White 5.00 12.00
RFSL Stefan LeFors 2.50 6.00
RFTM Terrence Murphy 2.50 6.00
RFTW Troy Williamson 3.00 8.00
RFVJ Vincent Jackson 5.00 12.00
RFVM Vernand Morency 3.00 8.00

2005 SP Authentic Rookie Fabrics Autographs

STATED PRINT RUN 15 SER.#'d SETS
RFAN Antrel Rolle 40.00 100.00
RFAR Aaron Rodgers 500.00 800.00
RFAS Alex Smith QB 90.00 150.00
RFBE Braylon Edwards 75.00 150.00
RFCB Cedric Benson 40.00 100.00
RFCF Charlie Frye 40.00 100.00
RFCI Ciatrick Fason 25.00 60.00
RFCR Courtney Roby 30.00 80.00
RFCW Cadillac Williams 40.00 100.00
RFES Eric Shelton 25.00 60.00
RFFG Frank Gore 60.00 150.00
RFJA J.J. Arrington 30.00 80.00
RFJC Jason Campbell 75.00 150.00
RFKO Kyle Orton 100.00 200.00
RFMB Mark Bradley 25.00 60.00
RFMC Mark Clayton 30.00 80.00
RFMJ Matt Jones 30.00 80.00
RFMO Maurice Clarett 25.00 60.00
RFMW Mike Williams 50.00 125.00
RFRB Ronnie Brown 100.00 200.00
RFRE Reggie Brown 25.00 60.00
RFRM Ryan Moats 25.00 60.00
RFRP Roscoe Parrish 25.00 60.00
RFRW Roddy White 50.00 125.00
RFSL Stefan LeFors 25.00 60.00
RFTM Terrence Murphy 25.00 60.00
RFTW Troy Williamson 30.00 80.00
RFVJ Vincent Jackson 50.00 125.00
RFVM Vernand Morency 25.00 60.00

2005 SP Authentic Scripts for Success Autographs

STATED ODDS 1:24
SSAB Anquan Boldin 6.00 15.00
SSAC Airese Currie 4.00 10.00
SSAG Alge Crumpler 6.00 15.00
SSAH Ahman Green SP 10.00 25.00
SSAJ Adam Jones 6.00 15.00
SSAM Adrian McPherson 6.00 15.00
SSAR Antrel Rolle 6.00 15.00
SSAW Andrew Walter 6.00 15.00
SSCH Chad Owens 6.00 15.00
SSCJ Chad Johnson 10.00 25.00
SSCO Courtney Roby 4.00 10.00
SSDB Drew Bennett 4.00 10.00
SSDD Domanick Davis 4.00 10.00
SSDG David Greene 6.00 15.00
SSDM Donovan McNabb SP 20.00 50.00
SSDO Dan Orlovsky 6.00 15.00
SSEJ Edgerrin James SP 12.00 30.00
SSES Eric Shelton 4.00 10.00
SSFG Frank Gore 12.00 30.00
SSJH Joe Horn 4.00 10.00
SSJK James Kilian 4.00 10.00
SSJL J.P. Losman 6.00 15.00
SSKC Keary Colbert 6.00 15.00
SSKO Kyle Orton 10.00 25.00
SSLE Lee Evans 4.00 10.00
SSLJ Larry Johnson 10.00 25.00
SSLT LaDainian Tomlinson 25.00 60.00
SSMA Marion Barber 8.00 20.00
SSMB Mark Bradley 6.00 15.00
SSMB Marc Bulger 6.00 15.00
SSMC Michael Clayton 4.00 10.00
SSMM Muhsin Muhammad 6.00 15.00
SSMN Mike Nugent 4.00 10.00
SSMO Maurice Clarett 4.00 10.00
SSNB Nate Burleson 6.00 15.00
SSPM Peyton Manning SP 60.00 100.00
SSRB Reggie Brown 6.00 15.00
SSRJ Rudi Johnson 6.00 15.00
SSRM Ryan Moats 6.00 15.00
SSRP Roscoe Parrish 6.00 15.00
SSRW Roddy White 10.00 25.00
SSSL Stefan LeFors 4.00 10.00
SSTD Thomas Davis 4.00 10.00
SSTG Trent Green 6.00 15.00
SSTM Terrence Murphy 4.00 10.00
SSVJ Vincent Jackson 10.00 25.00
SSVM Vernand Morency 6.00 15.00

2005 SP Authentic Sign of the Times

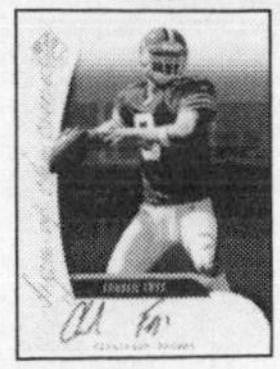

SOTAD Andre Reed 10.00 25.00
SOTAG Antonio Gates 10.00 25.00
SOTAH Ahman Green SP 8.00 20.00
SOTAR Aaron Rodgers SP 175.00 300.00
SOTAS Alex Smith QB SP 25.00 50.00
SOTBD Brian Dawkins 10.00 25.00
SOTBE Braylon Edwards 15.00 40.00
SOTBF Brett Favre SP 125.00 200.00
SOTBK Bernie Kosar 10.00 25.00
SOTBL Byron Leftwich 8.00 20.00
SOTBO Bo Jackson 40.00 80.00
SOTBR Ben Roethlisberger SP 60.00 120.00
SOTBS Barry Sanders SP 100.00 175.00
SOTBT Drew Bennett 8.00 20.00
SOTCB Cedric Benson 10.00 25.00
SOTCF Charlie Frye 10.00 25.00
SOTCP Carson Palmer SP 15.00 40.00
SOTCW Cadillac Williams SP 12.00 30.00
SOTDA Dan Marino SP 100.00 200.00
SOTDE Deuce McAllister SP 8.00 20.00
SOTDM Donovan McNabb SP 25.00 50.00
SOTEJ Edgerrin James SP 12.00 30.00
SOTEM Eli Manning SP 60.00 100.00
SOTJA J.J. Arrington 8.00 20.00
SOTJC Jason Campbell 12.00 30.00
SOTJE John Elway SP 100.00 200.00
SOTJK Jim Kelly SP 20.00 40.00
SOTLJ LaMont Jordan 8.00 20.00
SOTMA Marcus Allen 20.00 40.00
SOTMJ Matt Jones SP 10.00 25.00
SOTMM Muhsin Muhammad 8.00 20.00
SOTMV Michael Vick SP 30.00 60.00
SOTMW Mike Williams SP 10.00 25.00
SOTPM Peyton Manning SP 60.00 120.00
SOTRB Ronnie Brown SP 20.00 50.00
SOTRE Reggie Brown 6.00 15.00
SOTRG Reggie Wayne 15.00 30.00
SOTRW Roddy White 12.00 30.00
SOTRY Roy Williams WR SP 8.00 20.00
SOTSJ Steven Jackson 10.00 25.00
SOTTA Troy Aikman SP 30.00 60.00
SOTTB Tiki Barber 15.00 30.00
SOTTG Trent Green 8.00 20.00
SOTTW Troy Williamson 8.00 20.00

2005 SP Authentic Sign of the Times Gold

*GOLD: .8X TO 2X BASIC AUTOS
GOLD PRINT RUN 25 SER.#'d SETS
SOTAR Aaron Rodgers 400.00 600.00
SOTBF Brett Favre 150.00 300.00
SOTBO Bo Jackson 75.00 150.00
SOTBR Ben Roethlisberger 60.00 150.00
SOTBS Barry Sanders 125.00 250.00
SOTDA Dan Marino 125.00 250.00
SOTEM Eli Manning 90.00 150.00
SOTJE John Elway 100.00 200.00
SOTMV Michael Vick 40.00 80.00
SOTPM Peyton Manning 125.00 200.00

2005 SP Authentic Sign of the Times Dual

DUAL PRINT RUN 50 SER.#'d SETS
UNPRICED TRIPLE PRINT RUN 15 SETS
UNPRICED QUAD PRINT RUN 5 SETS
BJ Marc Bulger 15.00 40.00
Steven Jackson
BO Cedric Benson 20.00 50.00
Kyle Orton
BR Drew Bennett 12.00 30.00
Courtney Roby
BW Ronnie Brown 30.00 80.00
Cadillac Williams
CG Jason Campbell 20.00 50.00
David Greene
DM Domanick Davis 10.00 25.00
Vernand Morency
EF Braylon Edwards 30.00 80.00
Charlie Fyre
EP Lee Evans 12.00 30.00
Roscoe Parrish
GJ Antonio Gates 30.00 60.00
Vincent Jackson
JB Julius Jones 15.00 40.00
Marion Barber
LJ Byron Leftwich 15.00 40.00
Matt Jones
LS Stefan LeFors 10.00 25.00
Eric Shelton
NT Nate Burleson 12.00 30.00
Troy Williamson
RF Ben Roethlisbeger 40.00 100.00
Charlie Frye
RM Reggie Brown 15.00 40.00
Ryan Moats
SG Alex Smith QB 40.00 100.00
Frank Gore
SR Alex Smith QB 250.00 400.00
Aaron Rodgers
VW Michael Vick 40.00 80.00
Roddy White
WW Roy Williams WR 20.00 50.00
Mike Williams

2005 SP Authentic UD Promo

*SINGLES: .8X TO 2X BASIC CARDS

2006 SP Authentic

This 260-card set was released in January, 2007. The set was issued into the hobby in five-card packs, with a $5 SRP, which came 24 packs to a box. Cards numbered 1-90 feature players in alphabetical team order and cards numbered 91-260 feature 2006 rookies. The rookies are broken down into the following groupings: Cards numbered 91-120 and 251 were issued to a stated print run of 750 serial numbered sets, Cards numbered 121-180 were issued to a stated print run of 1399 serial numbered sets, cards numbered 181-226 were issued to a stated print run of 1175 serial numbered copies unless noted in our checklist. The set concludes with cards containing both player-worn jersey swatches and signatures from cards numbered 227-260. Those cards, with the exception of card numbered 251, have stated print runs of between 99 and 999 serial numbered copies.

COMP.SET w/o RC's (90) 8.00 20.00
91-120/251 PRINT RUN 750 SER.#'d SETS
121-180 PRINT RUN 1399 SER.#'d SETS
181-226 AU PRINT RUN 1175 UNLESS NOTED
227-260 JSY AU PRINT RUN 99-999
1 Edgerrin James .30 .75
2 Larry Fitzgerald .40 1.00
3 Anquan Boldin .30 .75
4 Michael Vick .40 1.00
5 Warrick Dunn .30 .75
6 Alge Crumpler .30 .75
7 Steve McNair .30 .75
8 Jamal Lewis .30 .75
9 Derrick Mason .30 .75
10 Willis McGahee .30 .75
11 Lee Evans .30 .75
12 Jake Delhomme .30 .75
13 Steve Smith .40 1.00
14 DeShaun Foster .30 .75
15 Rex Grossman .30 .75
16 Thomas Jones .30 .75
17 Brian Urlacher .40 1.00
18 Carson Palmer .40 1.00
19 Chad Johnson .30 .75
20 Rudi Johnson .30 .75
21 Charlie Frye .30 .75
22 Braylon Edwards .30 .75
23 Reuben Droughns .30 .75
24 Drew Bledsoe .40 1.00
25 Terrell Owens .40 1.00
26 Julius Jones .25 .60
27 Jake Plummer .30 .75
28 Tatum Bell .25 .60
29 Javon Walker .30 .75
30 Kevin Jones .25 .60
31 Roy Williams WR .30 .75
32 Brett Favre .75 2.00
33 Donald Driver .40 1.00
34 David Carr .25 .60
35 Ron Dayne .30 .75
36 Andre Johnson .40 1.00
37 Peyton Manning .60 1.50
38 Marvin Harrison .40 1.00
39 Reggie Wayne .30 .75
40 Byron Leftwich .30 .75
41 Fred Taylor .30 .75
42 Matt Jones .25 .60
43 Trent Green .30 .75
44 Larry Johnson .30 .75
45 Tony Gonzalez .30 .75
46 Daunte Culpepper .30 .75
47 Ronnie Brown .40 1.00
48 Chris Chambers .30 .75
49 Chester Taylor .30 .75
50 Troy Williamson .25 .60
51 Tom Brady .60 1.50
52 Corey Dillon .30 .75
53 Troy Brown .25 .60
54 Drew Brees .40 1.00
55 Deuce McAllister .30 .75
56 Joe Horn .30 .75
57 Eli Manning .50 1.25
58 Tiki Barber .40 1.00
59 Plaxico Burress .30 .75
60 Laveranues Coles .25 .60
61 Chad Pennington .30 .75
62 Aaron Brooks .30 .75
63 Randy Moss .40 1.00
64 LaMont Jordan .30 .75
65 Donovan McNabb .40 1.00
66 Brian Westbrook .30 .75
67 Ben Roethlisberger .50 1.25
68 Willie Parker .30 .75
69 Hines Ward .40 1.00
70 Philip Rivers .40 1.00
71 LaDainian Tomlinson .40 1.00
72 Antonio Gates .40 1.00
73 Alex Smith QB .40 1.00
74 Frank Gore .40 1.00
75 Antonio Bryant .25 .60
76 Matt Hasselbeck .30 .75
77 Shaun Alexander .30 .75
78 Darrell Jackson .30 .75
79 Marc Bulger .30 .75
80 Steven Jackson .40 1.00
81 Torry Holt .30 .75
82 Chris Simms .30 .75
83 Cadillac Williams .30 .75
84 Joey Galloway .30 .75
85 Travis Henry .25 .60
86 Drew Bennett .30 .75
87 David Givens .30 .75
88 Mark Brunell .30 .75
89 Clinton Portis .40 1.00
90 Santana Moss .30 .75
91 Bernard Pollard RC 4.00 10.00
92 Brodie Croyle RC 5.00 12.00
93 Cedric Griffin RC 4.00 10.00
94 Marques Colston RC 10.00 25.00
95 Daniel Bullocks RC 5.00 12.00
96 Darryl Tapp RC 4.00 10.00
97 David Thomas RC 4.00 10.00
98 Montell Owens RC 4.00 10.00
99 DeMeco Ryans RC 5.00 12.00
100 Devin Hester RC 10.00 25.00
101 Donte Whitner RC 5.00 12.00
102 D'Qwell Jackson RC 4.00 10.00
103 Patrick Cobbs RC 4.00 10.00
104 Haloti Ngata RC 5.00 12.00
105 Lawrence Vickers RC 4.00 10.00
106 Jeff King RC 4.00 10.00
107 Jeremy Bloom RC 4.00 10.00
108 Johnathan Joseph RC 4.00 10.00
109 DeDe Dorsey RC 4.00 10.00
110 Marcus Vick RC 3.00 8.00
111 Bobby Carpenter RC 3.00 8.00
112 Manny Lawson RC 4.00 10.00
113 Nick Mangold RC 4.00 10.00
114 Quinn Sypniewski RC 4.00 10.00
115 Richard Marshall RC 4.00 10.00
116 Rocky McIntosh RC 4.00 10.00
117 Roman Harper RC 4.00 10.00
118 Tamba Hali RC 5.00 12.00
119 Tony Scheffler RC 5.00 12.00
120 Wali Lundy RC 4.00 10.00
121 A.J. Nicholson RC 2.50 6.00
122 Abdul Hodge RC 2.50 6.00
123 Adam Jennings RC 3.00 8.00
124 Alan Zemaitis RC 4.00 10.00
125 Andrew Whitworth RC 2.50 6.00
126 Anthony Schlegel RC 3.00 8.00
127 Anthony Smith RC 4.00 10.00
128 Antoine Bethea RC 5.00 12.00
129 Barry Cofield RC 4.00 10.00
130 Brandon Johnson RC 3.00 8.00
131 Calvin Lowry RC 4.00 10.00
132 Shaun Bodiford RC 3.00 8.00
133 Charlie Peprah RC 3.00 8.00
134 Claude Wroten RC 2.50 6.00
135 Clint Ingram RC 4.00 10.00
136 Cortland Finnegan RC 4.00 10.00
137 Daryn Colledge RC 4.00 10.00
138 David Anderson RC 3.00 8.00
139 David Kirtman RC 3.00 8.00
140 Boone Stutz RC 3.00 8.00
141 Delanie Walker RC 4.00 10.00
142 Sam Hurd RC 2.50 6.00
143 Derrick Martin RC 3.00 8.00
144 Willie Andrews RC 3.00 8.00
145 Dusty Dvoracek RC 4.00 10.00
146 Elvis Dumervil RC 4.00 10.00
147 Eric Smith RC 3.00 8.00
148 Freddie Keiaho RC 3.00 8.00
149 Gabe Watson RC 2.50 6.00
150 Gerris Wilkinson RC 2.50 6.00
151 Greg Blue RC 3.00 8.00
152 Guy Whimper RC 2.50 6.00
153 Jamar Williams RC 3.00 8.00
154 James Anderson RC 2.50 6.00
155 Jason Spitz RC 4.00 10.00
156 Jeff Webb RC 3.00 8.00
157 Jeremy Mincey RC 3.00 8.00
158 Jeremy Trueblood RC 3.00 8.00
159 Omar Gaither RC 3.00 8.00
160 Jon Alston RC 2.50 6.00
161 Julian Jenkins RC 3.00 8.00
162 Keith Ellison RC 3.00 8.00
163 Kevin McMahan RC 3.00 8.00
164 Kyle Williams RC 4.00 10.00
165 Leon Williams RC 3.00 8.00
166 Mark Anderson RC 6.00 15.00
167 LaJuan Ramsey RC 4.00 10.00
168 Nate Salley RC 3.00 8.00
169 Rob Ninkovich RC 3.00 8.00
170 Parys Haralson RC 3.00 8.00
171 Pat Watkins RC 3.00 8.00
172 Paul McQuistan RC 2.50 6.00
173 Rashad Butler RC 2.50 6.00
174 Ray Edwards RC 4.00 10.00
175 Reed Doughty RC 3.00 8.00
176 Ronnie Prude RC 3.00 8.00
177 Stephen Tulloch RC 3.00 8.00
178 Tim Jennings RC 3.00 8.00
179 Jarrad Page RC 4.00 10.00
180 Victor Adeyanju RC 3.00 8.00
181 Andre Hall AU RC 5.00 12.00
182 Anthony Fasano AU RC 6.00 15.00
183 Antonio Cromartie AU RC 10.00 20.00
184 Ashton Youboty AU RC 4.00 10.00
185 Kamerion Wimbley AU RC 6.00 15.00
186 Brad Smith AU RC 6.00 15.00
187 Brodrick Bunkley AU RC 5.00 12.00
188 Bruce Gradkowski AU RC 8.00 20.00
189 Chad Greenway AU RC 8.00 20.00
190 Cory Rodgers AU RC 5.00 12.00
191 D.J. Shockley AU RC 5.00 12.00
192 Danieal Manning AU RC 6.00 15.00
193 Darnell Bing AU RC 5.00 12.00
194 Darrell Hackney AU RC 5.00 12.00
195 D'Brickashaw Ferguson AU RC 6.00 15.00
196 Dominique Byrd AU RC 5.00 12.00
197 Drew Olson AU RC 4.00 10.00
198 Ernie Sims AU RC 5.00 12.00
199 Garrett Mills AU/99 RC 20.00 50.00
200 Gerald Riggs AU RC 5.00 12.00
201 Greg Jennings AU RC 15.00 30.00
202 Greg Lee AU RC 4.00 10.00
203 Hank Baskett AU RC 6.00 15.00
204 Ingle Martin AU RC 5.00 12.00
205 Jason Allen AU RC 5.00 12.00
206 Jerome Harrison AU RC 8.00 20.00
207 Jimmy Williams AU RC 6.00 15.00
208 John McCargo AU RC 4.00 10.00
209 Josh Betts AU RC 5.00 12.00
210 Leonard Pope AU RC 6.00 15.00
211 Marques Hagans AU RC 4.00 10.00
212 Martin Nance AU RC 5.00 12.00
213 Mathias Kiwanuka AU RC 6.00 15.00
214 Mike Bell AU RC 6.00 15.00
215 Mike Hass AU RC 5.00 12.00
216 Owen Daniels AU RC 6.00 15.00
217 P.J. Daniels AU RC 4.00 10.00
218 Reggie McNeal AU RC 5.00 12.00
219 Skyler Green AU RC 4.00 10.00
220 Terrence Whitehead AU RC 5.00 12.00
221 Thomas Howard AU RC 5.00 12.00
222 Tye Hill AU RC 4.00 10.00
223 Will Blackmon AU RC 5.00 12.00
224 Willie Reid AU RC 5.00 12.00
225 Winston Justice AU RC 5.00 12.00
226 Jay Cutler AU/99 RC 400.00 800.00
227 Joseph Addai AU/99 RC 20.00 50.00
228 Brandon Williams JSY/999 AU RC 6.00 15.00
229 Brian Calhoun JSY/999 AU RC 6.00 15.00
230 Chad Jackson JSY/699 AU RC 6.00 15.00
231 Charlie Whitehurst JSY/999 AU RC 10.00 25.00
232 DeAngelo Williams JSY/175 AU RC 75.00 150.00
233 Demetrius Williams JSY/999 AU RC 8.00 20.00
234 Derek Hagan JSY/999 AU RC 8.00 20.00
235 Jason Avant JSY/999 AU RC 6.00 15.00
236 Jerious Norwood JSY/999 AU RC 8.00 20.00
237 Joe Klopfenstein JSY/999 AU RC 6.00 15.00
238 Kellen Clemens JSY/999 AU RC 8.00 20.00
239 Kelly Jennings JSY/199 AU RC 12.00 30.00
240 Laurence Maroney JSY/999 AU RC 8.00 20.00
241 LenDale White JSY/999 AU RC 8.00 20.00
242 Leon Washington JSY/999 AU RC 8.00 20.00
243 Marcedes Lewis JSY/999 AU RC 10.00 25.00
244 Marcus McNeill JSY/260 AU RC 12.00 30.00
245 Mario Williams JSY/699 AU RC 15.00 40.00
246 Matt Leinart JSY/299 AU RC 25.00 60.00
247 Maurice Drew JSY/999 AU RC 30.00 60.00
248 Maurice Stovall JSY/999 AU RC 6.00 15.00
249 Michael Huff JSY/999 AU RC 8.00 20.00
250 Michael Robinson JSY/999 AU RC 8.00 20.00
251 Omar Jacobs/750 RC 3.00 8.00
252 Reggie Bush JSY/299 AU RC 75.00 150.00
253 Santonio Holmes JSY/399 AU RC 15.00 40.00
254 Sinorice Moss JSY/99 AU RC 30.00 60.00
255 Tarvaris Jackson JSY/999 AU RC 12.00 30.00
256 Travis Wilson JSY/999 AU RC 6.00 15.00
257 Vernon Davis JSY/699 AU RC 35.00 60.00
258 Vince Young JSY/270 AU RC 40.00 80.00
259 A.J. Hawk JSY/399 AU RC 25.00 60.00
260 Brandon Marshall JSY/999 AU RC 25.00 60.00

2006 SP Authentic Gold

*VETS 1-90: 8X TO 20X BASIC CARDS
*ROOKIE 91-120/251: 1X TO 2.5X
*ROOKIE 121-180: 1.2X TO 3X BASIC CARDS
*ROOK.181-225: 1.2X TO 3X BASE AU/1175
*ROOK.228-260: 1.5X TO 3X JSY AU/699-999
STATED PRINT RUN 25 SER.#'d SETS
MULTI-COLORED PATCHES: .6X TO 1.2X
199 Garrett Mills AU 20.00 50.00
201 Greg Jennings AU 100.00 200.00
232 DeAngelo Williams JSY AU 100.00 200.00
246 Matt Leinart JSY AU 100.00 200.00
247 Maurice Drew JSY AU 150.00 300.00
252 Reggie Bush JSY AU 150.00 300.00
253 Santonio Holmes JSY AU 60.00 120.00
257 Vernon Davis JSY AU 90.00 150.00
258 Vince Young JSY AU 100.00 200.00
259 A.J. Hawk JSY AU 60.00 150.00

2006 SP Authentic Rookie Autographed NFL Logo Patches

UNPRICED NFL LOGO PRINT RUN 1

2006 SP Authentic Rookie Autographed Patches

UNPRICED PATCH EXCH PRINT RUN 5
ISSUED VIA MIAL EXCHANGE CARDS

2006 SP Authentic Autographs

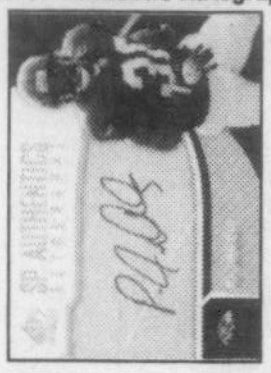

SPAC Alge Crumpler 5.00 12.00
SPAF Anthony Fasano 6.00 15.00
SPAG Antonio Gates 6.00 15.00
SPAV Jason Avant 4.00 10.00
SPBF Brett Favre SP 125.00 200.00
SPBG Bruce Gradkowski 6.00 15.00
SPBR Ben Roethlisberger SP 60.00 120.00
SPBU Marc Bulger SP 8.00 20.00
SPBW Brandon Williams 4.00 10.00
SPCG Chad Greenway 6.00 15.00
SPCR Cory Rodgers 5.00 12.00
SPCW Charlie Whitehurst 6.00 15.00
SPDB Darnell Bing 5.00 12.00
SPDG David Givens 5.00 12.00
SPDH Derek Hagan 5.00 12.00
SPDM Danieal Manning 6.00 15.00
SPDO Drew Olson 4.00 10.00
SPDS D.J. Shockley 5.00 12.00
SPDW Demetrius Williams 5.00 12.00
SPEM Eli Manning SP 40.00 80.00
SPFT Fran Tarkenton 20.00 40.00
SPGJ Greg Jennings 12.00 30.00
SPHA Mike Hass 5.00 12.00
SPHI Tye Hill 4.00 10.00
SPIM Ingle Martin 5.00 12.00
SPJA Jason Allen 5.00 12.00
SPJK Joe Klopfenstein 4.00 10.00
SPJM John McCargo 4.00 10.00
SPJN Jerious Norwood 8.00 20.00
SPJW Jimmy Williams 6.00 15.00
SPKC Kevin Curtis 5.00 12.00
SPKJ Keyshawn Johnson 5.00 12.00
SPLJ Larry Johnson SP 8.00 25.00
SPLP Leonard Pope 6.00 15.00
SPLW Leon Washington 8.00 20.00
SPMB Mike Bell 6.00 15.00
SPMH Marques Hagans 4.00 10.00
SPMO Joe Montana SP 100.00 200.00
SPMR Michael Robinson 5.00 12.00
SPMS Maurice Stovall 4.00 10.00
SPPD P.J. Daniels 4.00 10.00
SPPR Philip Rivers 15.00 40.00
SPRB Ronde Barber 5.00 12.00
SPRJ Rudi Johnson 5.00 12.00
SPRW Reggie Wayne 12.50 30.00
SPSG Skyler Green 4.00 10.00
SPTA Lofa Tatupu 6.00 15.00
SPTD Tony Dorsett SP 25.00 50.00
SPTH T.J. Houshmandzadeh 5.00 12.00
SPTJ Tarvaris Jackson 8.00 20.00
SPTW Travis Wilson 4.00 10.00
SPWR Willie Reid 5.00 12.00

2006 SP Authentic Chirography

CHAH A.J. Hawk 20.00 40.00
CHAY Ashton Youboty 3.00 8.00
CHBB Brodrick Bunkley 4.00 10.00
CHBC Brian Calhoun 3.00 8.00
CHBE Drew Bennett 4.00 10.00
CHBG Bob Griese SP
CHBL Brandon Lloyd 3.00 8.00
CHBM Brandon Marshall 8.00 20.00
CHBS Brad Smith 5.00 12.00
CHBU Reggie Bush SP 50.00 120.00
CHBW Brandon Williams 3.00 8.00
CHCB Cedric Benson 8.00 20.00
CHCJ Chad Jackson 3.00 8.00
CHCL Mark Clayton 4.00 10.00
CHDB Dominique Byrd 4.00 10.00
CHDC Dwight Clark 8.00 20.00
CHDF D'Brickashaw Ferguson 5.00 12.00
CHDM Dan Marino SP 100.00 200.00
CHDS D.J. Shockley 4.00 10.00
CHDW DeAngelo Williams SP 25.00 50.00
CHES Ernie Sims 4.00 10.00
CHFO DeShaun Foster 4.00 10.00
CHGM Garrett Mills 5.00 12.00
CHGR Gerald Riggs 4.00 10.00
CHJA Joseph Addai SP 12.00 30.00
CHJB Josh Betts 4.00 10.00
CHJC Jay Cutler 30.00 80.00
CHJE John Elway SP 100.00 200.00
CHJH Jerome Harrison 5.00 12.00
CHJJ Julius Jones 6.00 15.00
CHJT Joe Theismann 15.00 30.00
CHJW Jason Witten 20.00 40.00
CHKC Kellen Clemens 6.00 15.00
CHKO Kyle Orton 5.00 12.00
CHKS Ken Stabler SP 30.00 60.00
CHLE Byron Leftwich 4.00 10.00
CHLG L.C. Greenwood SP 40.00 80.00
CHLM Laurence Maroney 4.00 10.00
CHLT Lofa Tatupu 8.00 20.00
CHMA Matt Leinart SP
CHMB Marc Bulger 4.00 10.00
CHMC Deuce McAllister 4.00 10.00
CHMH Michael Huff 4.00 10.00
CHMI Michael Clayton 3.00 8.00
CHML Marcedes Lewis 5.00 12.00
CHMM Muhsin Muhammad 4.00 10.00
CHMW Mario Williams 5.00 12.00
CHNB Nate Burleson 3.00 8.00
CHOD Owen Daniels 5.00 12.00
CHPM Peyton Manning 60.00 100.00
CHRB Reggie Brown 3.00 8.00
CHTA Troy Aikman 40.00 100.00
CHTG Trent Green 4.00 10.00
CHTJ Thomas Jones 4.00 10.00
CHVY Vince Young SP 30.00 80.00
CHWB Will Blackmon 4.00 10.00
CHWP Willie Parker 6.00 15.00

2006 SP Authentic Chirography Gold

*GOLD/25: .6X TO 1.5X BASIC AUTO
GOLD STATED PRINT RUN 10-25
CHBU Reggie Bush 60.00 120.00
CHDM Dan Marino 125.00 250.00
CHJE John Elway 150.00 250.00
CHKS Ken Stabler 30.00 60.00
CHLM Laurence Maroney 6.00 15.00
CHMA Matt Leinart 25.00 60.00
CHPM Peyton Manning 75.00 150.00
CHTA Troy Aikman 60.00 120.00
CHVY Vince Young 40.00 100.00

2006 SP Authentic Chirography Duals

STATED PRINT RUN 10-50
SERIAL #'d UNDER 25 NOT PRICED
BB Nate Burleson/50 10.00 25.00
Reggie Brown
BL Reggie Bush/50 40.00 100.00
Matt Leinart
CJ Kellen Clemens/50 12.00 30.00
Tarvaris Jackson
DC Maurice Drew/50 20.00 50.00
Brian Calhoun
DL Vernon Davis/50 15.00 40.00
Marcedes Lewis
DM Tony Dorsett/25 30.00 80.00
Laurence Maroney
HB Michael Huff/50 12.00 30.00
Darnell Bing
HH Santonio Holmes/50 30.00 60.00
A.J. Hawk
JG Larry Johnson/50 12.00 30.00
Trent Green
JM Chad Jackson/50 12.00 30.00
Sinorice Moss
JS Omar Jacobs/50 10.00 25.00
D.J. Shockley
JW Julius Jones/25 25.00 50.00
Jason Witten
MA Peyton Manning/50 75.00 150.00
Joseph Addai
MD Garrett Mills/50 10.00 25.00
Owen Daniels
MJ Thomas Jones/50 12.00 30.00
Muhsin Muhammad
MR Eli Manning/50 40.00 80.00
Philip Rivers
MW Laurence Maroney/50 20.00 50.00
DeAngelo Williams
PH Carson Palmer/50
T.J. Houshmandzadeh
RP Ben Roethlisberger/50 40.00 80.00
Willie Parker
TS Lofa Tatupu/50 12.00 30.00
Ernie Sims
WF Mario Williams/50 12.00 30.00
D'Brickashaw Ferguson
WR Brandon Williams/50 10.00 25.00
Michael Robinson
YW Vince Young/50 30.00 80.00
LenDale White

2006 SP Authentic Chirography Triples

TRIPLE STATED PRINT RUN 20
BJG Drew Bledsoe 30.00 60.00
Julius Jones
Skyler Green
CCJ Jay Cutler 100.00 200.00
Kellen Clemens
Tarvaris Jackson
HMS Derek Hagan 20.00 50.00
Brandon Marshall
Maurice Stovall
MMM Dan Marino 300.00 500.00
Peyton Manning
Joe Montana
MWA Laurence Maroney 25.00 60.00
DeAngelo Williams
Joseph Addai
TJW LaDainian Tomlinson 60.00 120.00
Larry Johnson
Cadillac Williams
WDC LenDale White 25.00 60.00
Maurice Drew
Brian Calhoun
WHH Mario Williams 40.00 80.00
A.J. Hawk
Michael Huff
WJM Charlie Whitehurst 20.00 50.00
Omar Jacobs
Ingle Martin
WWA Travis Wilson
Demetrius Williams
Jason Avant

2006 SP Authentic Chirography Quads

UNPRICED QUAD PRINT RUN 5 SER.#'d SETS

2006 SP Authentic Rookie Exclusives Autographs

STATED PRINT RUN 100 UNLESS NOTED
REAAC Antonio Cromartie/75 12.50 30.00
REAAD Joseph Addai 8.00 20.00
REAAH A.J. Hawk 8.00 20.00
REAAV Jason Avant 5.00 12.00
REABM Brandon Marshall 8.00 20.00
REABS Brad Smith 8.00 20.00
REABW Brandon Williams 5.00 12.00
REACA Brian Calhoun 5.00 12.00
REACJ Chad Jackson 5.00 12.00
REACW Charlie Whitehurst 8.00 20.00
READB Dominique Byrd 6.00 15.00
READF D'Brickashaw Ferguson 8.00 20.00
READH Derek Hagan 6.00 15.00
READS D.J. Shockley 6.00 15.00
READW DeAngelo Williams 20.00 50.00
REAES Ernie Sims 6.00 15.00
REAGJ Greg Jennings 30.00 60.00
REAHA Mike Hass 6.00 15.00
REAIM Ingle Martin 6.00 15.00
REAJA Jason Allen 6.00 15.00
REAJC Jay Cutler 40.00 100.00
REAJK Joe Klopfenstein 5.00 12.00
REAJN Jerious Norwood 6.00 15.00
REAJW Jimmy Williams 8.00 20.00
REAKC Kellen Clemens 6.00 15.00
REALM Laurence Maroney 6.00 15.00
REALP Leonard Pope 8.00 20.00
REALW LenDale White 6.00 15.00
REAMD Maurice Drew/85 30.00 80.00
REAMH Michael Huff 6.00 15.00
REAML Marcedes Lewis 8.00 20.00
REAMR Michael Robinson 6.00 15.00
REAMS Maurice Stovall 5.00 12.00
REAMW Mario Williams 8.00 20.00
REAPD P.J. Daniels 5.00 12.00
REARB Reggie Bush 40.00 80.00
REASG Skyler Green 5.00 12.00
REASH Santonio Holmes 10.00 25.00
REASM Sinorice Moss/25 10.00 25.00
REATJ Tarvaris Jackson 8.00 20.00
REATW Travis Wilson 5.00 12.00
REAVD Vernon Davis 10.00 25.00
REAVY Vince Young 20.00 50.00
REAWA Leon Washington 6.00 15.00
REAWI Demetrius Williams 6.00 15.00

2006 SP Authentic Rookie Exclusives Jerseys

STATED PRINT RUN 150 SER.#'d SETS
REJAH A.J. Hawk 6.00 15.00
REJBC Brian Calhoun 4.00 10.00
REJBM Brandon Marshall 6.00 15.00
REJBW Brandon Williams 4.00 10.00
REJCJ Chad Jackson 4.00 10.00
REJCW Charlie Whitehurst 6.00 15.00
REJDH Derek Hagan 5.00 12.00
REJDW DeAngelo Williams 8.00 20.00
REJJA Jason Avant 4.00 10.00
REJJC Jay Cutler 12.00 30.00
REJJK Joe Klopfenstein 4.00 10.00
REJJN Jerious Norwood 5.00 12.00
REJKC Kellen Clemens 5.00 12.00
REJLE Matt Leinart 6.00 15.00
REJLM Laurence Maroney 5.00 12.00
REJLW LenDale White 5.00 12.00
REJMD Maurice Drew 10.00 25.00
REJMH Michael Huff 5.00 12.00
REJML Marcedes Lewis 6.00 15.00
REJMR Michael Robinson 5.00 12.00
REJMS Maurice Stovall 4.00 10.00
REJMW Mario Williams 6.00 15.00
REJOJ Omar Jacobs 4.00 10.00
REJRB Reggie Bush 12.00 30.00
REJSH Santonio Holmes 8.00 20.00
REJSM Sinorice Moss 6.00 15.00
REJTJ Tarvaris Jackson 6.00 15.00
REJTW Travis Wilson 4.00 10.00
REJVD Vernon Davis 8.00 20.00
REJVY Vince Young 8.00 20.00
REJWA Leon Washington 5.00 12.00
REJWI Demetrius Williams 5.00 12.00

2007 SP Authentic

This 298-card set was released in February, 2008. The set was issued into the hobby in five-card packs with an $4.99 SRP which came 24 packs to a box. Cards numbered 1-100 feature veterans in first name alphabetical order (with a couple of exceptions) while cards numbered 101-298 feature 2007 NFL rookies. Within the rookies, cards numbered 201-265 are signed by the player and cards numbered 266-298 have both signatures and a game-worn player swatch.

COMP.SET w/o RC's (100) 8.00 20.00
101-160 ROOKIE PRINT RUN 1399
161-200 ROOKIE PRINT RUN 999
201-230 AU RC PRINT RUN 1199
231-250 AU RC PRINT RUN 999
251-265 AU RC PRINT RUN 399
266-288 JSY AU RC PRINT RUN 725
289-298 JSY AU RC PRINT RUN 399
1 Ahman Green .25 .60
2 A.J. Hawk .25 .60
3 Alex Smith QB .30 .75
4 Andre Johnson .25 .60
5 Antonio Gates .30 .75
6 Ben Roethlisberger .30 .75
7 Bernard Berrian .20 .50
8 Brandon Jacobs .25 .60
9 Braylon Edwards .25 .60
10 Brett Favre .60 1.50
11 Brian Urlacher .30 .75
12 Brian Westbrook .25 .60
13 Brodie Croyle .25 .60
14 Byron Leftwich .25 .60
15 Cadillac Williams .25 .60
16 Carson Palmer .25 .60
17 Cedric Benson .25 .60
18 Chad Johnson .25 .60
19 Chad Pennington .25 .60
20 Champ Bailey .25 .60
21 Derek Anderson .20 .50
22 Chester Taylor .20 .50
23 Chris Brown .20 .50
24 Chris Chambers .25 .60
25 Clinton Portis .25 .60
26 Darrell Jackson .20 .50
27 Deuce McAllister .25 .60
28 Dominic Rhodes .25 .60
29 Donald Driver .30 .75
30 Donovan McNabb .30 .75
31 Donte Stallworth .25 .60
32 Drew Brees .30 .75
33 Edgerrin James .25 .60
34 Eli Manning .30 .75
35 Frank Gore .30 .75
36 Fred Taylor .25 .60
37 Greg Jennings .30 .75
38 Hines Ward .30 .75
39 Jake Delhomme .25 .60
40 Jamal Lewis .25 .60
41 Jason Campbell .25 .60
42 Jason Taylor .25 .60
43 Jason Witten .30 .75
44 Javon Walker .25 .60
45 Jay Cutler .30 .75
46 Jerious Norwood .25 .60
47 Jerry Porter .25 .60
48 Jon Kitna .20 .50
49 Joseph Addai .25 .60
50 Julius Jones .20 .50
51 LaDainian Tomlinson .30 .75
52 Larry Johnson .20 .50
53 Larry Fitzgerald .30 .75
54 Laurence Maroney .25 .60
55 Marc Bulger .25 .60
56 Marion Barber .25 .60
57 Mark Clayton .25 .60
58 Marques Colston .30 .75
59 Marvin Harrison .30 .75
60 Matt Hasselbeck .25 .60
61 Matt Jones .25 .60
62 Matt Leinart .25 .60
63 Matt Schaub .25 .60
64 Maurice Jones-Drew .30 .75
65 Jeff Garcia .25 .60
66 Mike Alstott .25 .60
67 David Garrard .25 .60
68 Peyton Manning .50 1.25
69 Philip Rivers .30 .75
70 Plaxico Burress .25 .60
71 Randy Moss .30 .75
72 Reggie Brown .20 .50
73 Reggie Bush .30 .75
74 Reggie Wayne .25 .60
75 Rex Grossman .25 .60
76 Ronnie Brown .25 .60
77 Roy Williams S .25 .60
78 Roy Williams WR .25 .60
79 Rudi Johnson .25 .60
80 Shaun Alexander .25 .60
81 Shawne Merriman .25 .60
82 Steven Jackson .30 .75
83 Steve McNair .25 .60
84 Steve Smith .25 .60
85 T.J. Houshmandzadeh .25 .60
86 Tarvaris Jackson .20 .50
87 Tedy Bruschi .30 .75
88 Terrell Owens .30 .75
89 Thomas Jones .25 .60
90 Tom Brady .50 1.25
91 Torry Holt .25 .60
92 Travis Henry .25 .60
93 Trent Green .25 .60
94 Vince Young .25 .60
95 Vincent Jackson .25 .60
96 Walter Jones .20 .50
97 Warrick Dunn .25 .60
98 Willie Parker .25 .60
99 Willis McGahee .25 .60
100 Tony Romo .40 1.00
101 Deon Anderson RC 3.00 8.00
102 Ben Patrick RC 3.00 8.00
103 Reagan Mauia RC 2.50 6.00
104 Derek Schouman RC 3.00 8.00
105 Keyunta Dawson RC 3.00 8.00
106 Usama Young RC 3.00 8.00
107 Syndric Steptoe RC 3.00 8.00
108 Martrez Milner RC 2.50 6.00
109 Brandon McDonald RC 2.50 6.00
110 Jason Snelling RC 4.00 10.00
111 Derek Stanley RC 3.00 8.00
112 Ed Johnson RC 3.00 8.00
113 Jacob Bender RC 2.50 6.00
114 Charles Ali RC 3.00 8.00
115 Tanard Jackson RC 2.50 6.00
116 Paul Soliai RC 2.50 6.00
117 Marvin White RC 2.50 6.00
118 Jared Gaither RC 2.50 6.00
119 Baraka Atkins RC 2.50 6.00
120 Marcus Thomas RC 3.00 8.00
121 Fred Bennett RC 2.50 6.00
122 Dashon Goldson RC 4.00 10.00
123 Kareem Brown RC 3.00 8.00
124 Courtney Bryan RC 2.50 6.00
125 Joe Cohen RC 2.50 6.00
126 Jay Richardson RC 3.00 8.00
127 Greg Peterson RC 3.00 8.00
128 Dallas Sartz RC 3.00 8.00
129 Brandon Harrison RC 2.50 6.00
130 Tarell Brown RC 4.00 10.00
131 Matt Gutierrez RC 4.00 10.00
132 Edmond Miles RC 3.00 8.00
133 Clifton Ryan RC 3.00 8.00
134 Antwan Barnes RC 4.00 10.00
135 Tim Shaw RC 3.00 8.00
136 Eric Frampton RC 3.00 8.00
137 William Gay RC 3.00 8.00
138 Nick Graham RC 3.00 8.00
139 Matt Toeaina RC 3.00 8.00
140 John Wendling RC 3.00 8.00
141 Mason Crosby RC 3.00 8.00
142 C.J. Wallace RC 3.00 8.00
143 Prescott Burgess RC 3.00 8.00
144 Oscar Lua RC 3.00 8.00
145 Chase Pittman RC 3.00 8.00
146 Zachary Diles RC 3.00 8.00
147 Kelvin Smith RC 3.00 8.00
148 Marvin Mitchell RC 3.00 8.00
149 Trumaine McBride RC 3.00 8.00
150 Edgar Jones RC 3.00 8.00
151 Abraham Wright RC 2.50 6.00
152 Nick Folk RC 4.00 10.00
153 Brandon Siler RC 2.50 6.00
154 Clint Session RC 3.00 8.00
155 Nedu Ndukwe RC 4.00 10.00
156 C.J. Wilson RC 3.00 8.00
157 Desmond Bishop RC 4.00 10.00
158 Melvin Bullitt RC 3.00 8.00
159 Courtney Brown RC 3.00 8.00
160 Troy Smith RC 4.00 10.00
161 Levi Brown RC 4.00 10.00
162 Justin Harrell RC 3.00 8.00
163 Jarvis Moss RC 3.00 8.00
164 Aaron Ross RC 4.00 10.00
165 Jon Beason RC 3.00 8.00
166 Anthony Spencer RC 4.00 10.00
167 Joe Staley RC 3.00 8.00
168 Ben Grubbs RC 3.00 8.00
169 Arron Sears RC 3.00 8.00
170 Eric Weddle RC 4.00 10.00
171 Justin Blalock RC 2.50 6.00
172 Chris Houston RC 3.00 8.00
173 David Harris RC 3.00 8.00
174 Justin Durant RC 3.00 8.00
175 Turk McBride RC 3.00 8.00
176 Josh Wilson RC 3.00 8.00
177 Tim Crowder RC 4.00 10.00
178 Victor Abiamiri RC 4.00 10.00
179 Ikaika Alama-Francis RC 4.00 10.00
180 Ryan Kalil RC 3.00 8.00
181 Samson Satele RC 3.00 8.00
182 Gerald Alexander RC 2.50 6.00
183 Corey Graham RC 2.50 6.00
184 Sabby Piscitelli RC 4.00 10.00
185 Quincy Black RC 4.00 10.00
186 Daniel Coats RC 3.00 8.00
187 Tony Ugoh RC 3.00 8.00
188 David Jones RC 2.50 6.00
189 DeMarcus Tank Tyler RC 2.50 6.00
190 Chad Nkang RC 2.50 6.00
191 Jonathan Wade RC 3.00 8.00
192 Brandon Mebane RC 3.00 8.00
193 Stewart Bradley RC 3.00 8.00
194 Aaron Rouse RC 3.00 8.00
195 Michael Okwo RC 3.00 8.00
196 Anthony Waters RC 3.00 8.00
197 Ray McDonald RC 3.00 8.00
198 Clifton Dawson RC 4.00 10.00
199 Brian Robison RC 4.00 10.00
200 Jay Moore RC 3.00 8.00
201 Dante Rosario AU RC 6.00 15.00
202 Ahmad Bradshaw AU RC 15.00 30.00
203 Roy Hall AU RC UER 6.00 15.00
(name misspelled Hali)
204 Aundrae Allison AU RC 4.00 10.00
205 Brent Celek AU RC 12.50 25.00
206 Chansi Stuckey AU RC 6.00 15.00
207 Courtney Taylor AU RC 5.00 12.00
208 Dallas Baker AU RC 4.00 10.00
209 Darius Walker AU RC 4.00 10.00
210 David Ball AU RC 5.00 12.00
211 David Clowney AU RC 5.00 12.00
212 David Irons AU RC 4.00 10.00
213 Daymeion Hughes AU RC 5.00 12.00
214 DeShawn Wynn AU RC 5.00 12.00
215 Jordan Kent AU RC 5.00 12.00
216 Dwayne Wright AU RC 5.00 12.00
217 Eric Wright AU RC 6.00 15.00
218 Gary Russell AU RC 5.00 12.00
219 Mike Walker AU RC 8.00 20.00
220 Isaiah Stanback AU RC 4.00 10.00
221 Jamaal Anderson AU RC 5.00 12.00
222 Jared Zabransky AU RC 5.00 12.00
223 Jeff Rowe AU RC 4.00 10.00
224 Joel Filani AU RC 5.00 12.00
225 Jordan Palmer AU RC 5.00 12.00
226 Kenneth Darby AU RC 5.00 12.00
227 Kolby Smith AU RC 5.00 12.00
228 Thomas Clayton AU RC 5.00 12.00
229 Steve Breaston AU RC 10.00 25.00
230 James Jones AU RC 6.00 15.00
231 Marcus McCauley AU RC 5.00 12.00
232 Alan Branch AU RC 5.00 12.00
233 Michael Griffin AU RC 6.00 15.00
234 Paul Posluszny AU RC 6.00 15.00
235 Quentin Moses AU RC 5.00 12.00
236 Lawrence Timmons AU RC 8.00 20.00
237 Scott Chandler AU RC 8.00 20.00
238 Jacoby Jones AU RC 6.00 15.00
239 Tyler Thigpen AU RC 6.00 15.00
240 Laurent Robinson AU RC 10.00 20.00
241 John Broussard AU RC 5.00 12.00
242 Zach Miller AU RC 6.00 15.00
243 Matt Spaeth AU RC 6.00 15.00
244 Ryne Robinson AU RC 5.00 12.00
245 Danny Ware AU RC 6.00 15.00
246 Legedu Naanee AU RC 8.00 20.00
247 Le'Ron McClain AU RC 6.00 15.00
248 Kevin Boss AU RC 12.00 30.00
249 Orenthal O'Neal AU RC 4.00 10.00
250 Amobi Okoye AU RC 6.00 15.00
251 Darrelle Revis AU RC 20.00 50.00
252 LaRon Landry AU RC 10.00 25.00
253 Chris Leak AU RC 8.00 20.00
254 Craig Davis AU RC 8.00 20.00
255 Leon Hall AU RC 8.00 20.00
256 Reggie Nelson AU RC 8.00 20.00
257 Adam Carriker AU RC 8.00 20.00
258 H.B. Blades AU RC 6.00 15.00
259 LaMarr Woodley AU RC 20.00 40.00
260 Korey Hall AU RC 8.00 20.00
261 Rhema McKnight AU RC 6.00 15.00
262 Brandon Meriweather AU RC 10.00 25.00
263 Matt Moore AU RC 12.00 30.00
264 Selvin Young AU RC 8.00 20.00
265 Tyler Palko AU RC 15.00 30.00
266 Anthony Gonzalez JSY AU RC 10.00 25.00
267 Antonio Pittman JSY AU RC 6.00 15.00
268 Brandon Jackson JSY AU RC 8.00 20.00
269 Brian Leonard JSY AU RC 8.00 20.00
270 Chris Henry JSY AU RC 6.00 15.00
271 Drew Stanton JSY AU RC 6.00 15.00
273 Garrett Wolfe JSY AU RC 6.00 15.00
274 Greg Olsen JSY AU RC 8.00 20.00
275 Jason Hill JSY AU RC 10.00 25.00
276 Joe Thomas JSY AU RC 10.00 25.00
277 John Beck JSY AU RC 12.00 30.00
278 Johnnie Lee Higgins JSY AU RC 8.00 20.00
279 Kenny Irons JSY AU RC 6.00 15.00
280 Kevin Kolb JSY AU RC 25.00 60.00
281 Lorenzo Booker JSY AU RC 8.00 20.00
282 Michael Bush JSY AU RC 10.00 25.00
283 Patrick Willis JSY AU RC 30.00 60.00
284 Paul Williams JSY AU RC 6.00 15.00
285 Steve Smith JSY AU RC 10.00 25.00
286 Tony Hunt JSY AU RC 6.00 15.00
287 Trent Edwards JSY AU RC 10.00 25.00
288 Yamon Figurs JSY AU RC 6.00 15.00
289 Adrian Peterson JSY AU RC 250.00 500.00
290 Brady Quinn JSY AU RC 15.00 40.00
291 Calvin Johnson JSY AU RC 175.00 300.00
292 JaMarcus Russell JSY AU RC 10.00 25.00
293 Marshawn Lynch JSY AU RC 25.00 50.00
294 Dwayne Bowe JSY AU RC 40.00 80.00
295 Sidney Rice JSY AU RC 20.00 50.00
296 Robert Meachem JSY AU RC 15.00 40.00
297 Dwayne Jarrett JSY AU RC 12.00 30.00
298 Ted Ginn JSY AU RC 12.00 30.00

2007 SP Authentic Gold

*VETS 1-100: 8X TO 20X BASIC CARDS
*ROOK 101-160: 1.2X TO 3X BASE RC/1399
*ROOKIE 161-200: 1.2X TO 3X BASE RC/999
*RK 201-230: 1.2X TO 3X BASE AU RC/1199
*RK 231-250: 1.2X TO 3X BASE AU RC/999
*ROOK 251-265: .8X TO 2X BASE AU RC/399
*RK.JSY AU 266-288: 1.2X TO 3X JSY AU/725
*RK.JSY AU 289-298: .6X TO 1.5X JSY AU/399
GOLD PRINT RUN 25 SER.#'d SETS
280 Kevin Kolb JSY AU 150.00 300.00
289 Adrian Peterson JSY AU 900.00 1,500.00
291 Calvin Johnson JSY AU 500.00 800.00

2007 SP Authentic Autographs

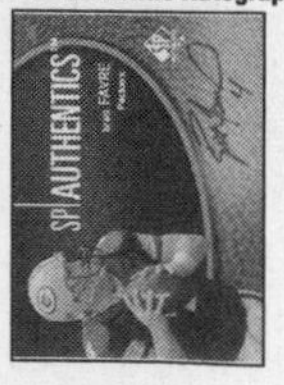

SPAAAP Adrian Peterson	150.00	250.00
SPAABF Brett Favre SP	125.00	200.00
SPAABJ Brandon Jackson	5.00	12.00
SPAACD Craig Buster Davis	5.00	12.00
SPAACH Chris Henry RB	4.00	10.00
SPAACJ Chad Johnson SP	10.00	25.00
SPAADB Drew Brees	30.00	60.00
SPAADJ Dwayne Jarrett	5.00	12.00
SPAAGO Greg Olsen	5.00	12.00
SPAAJC Jerricho Cotchery	10.00	25.00
SPAAJN Jerious Norwood	10.00	25.00
SPAAJP Jordan Palmer	5.00	12.00
SPAAJT Joe Thomas	6.00	15.00
SPAALB Lorenzo Booker	5.00	12.00
SPAALJ Larry Johnson SP	8.00	20.00
SPAALL LaRon Landry	6.00	15.00
SPAAMB Marc Bulger SP	10.00	25.00
SPAAMG Michael Griffin	6.00	15.00
SPAAML Matt Leinart	10.00	25.00
SPAAPW Paul Williams	4.00	10.00
SPAASC Scott Chandler	6.00	15.00
SPAATG Ted Ginn SP	5.00	12.00
SPAATH T.J. Houshmandzadeh SP	10.00	25.00
SPAAZM Zach Miller	6.00	15.00

2007 SP Authentic Autographs Gold

*GOLD/25: .8X TO 2X BASIC INSERTS
GOLD PRINT RUN 25 SER.#'d SETS

SPAAAP Adrian Peterson	200.00	400.00
SPAABF Brett Favre	150.00	250.00

2007 SP Authentic By The Letter Autographs

SERIAL NUMBERING BETWEEN 10-99
OVERALL PRINT RUNS ARE HIGHER

BTLAB Anquan Boldin/10	20.00	50.00
BTLAS1 Aaron Schobel/25	12.00	30.00
BTLAS2 Aaron Schobel/75	12.00	30.00
BTLBF Brett Favre/25	150.00	300.00
BTLBJ Bo Jackson/15	50.00	120.00
BTLBR Reggie Brown/75	12.00	30.00
BTLBS Barry Sanders/15	100.00	200.00
BTLCB Champ Bailey/75	25.00	50.00
BTLCC1 Chris Cooley/25	15.00	40.00
BTLCC2 Chris Cooley/75	12.00	30.00
BTLCR Roger Craig/99	15.00	40.00
BTLCW Cadillac Williams/25	15.00	40.00
BTLDB Drew Brees/15	60.00	120.00
BTLDM Dan Marino/15	125.00	250.00
BTLDP Drew Pearson/99	12.00	30.00
BTLDW1 DeMarcus Ware/60	20.00	50.00
BTLDW2 DeMarcus Ware/75	20.00	50.00
BTLES Emmitt Smith/15	100.00	200.00
BTLFG Frank Gore/25	15.00	40.00
BTLHE1 Heath Evans/50	10.00	25.00
BTLHE2 Heath Evans/70	10.00	25.00
BTLHN Haloti Ngata/70	10.00	25.00
BTLJA Joseph Addai/25	12.00	50.00
BTLJC Jason Campbell/35	12.00	30.00
BTLJM Joe Montana/15	125.00	250.00
BTLJN Joe Namath/15	75.00	150.00
BTLJT1 Jeremiah Trotter/40	10.00	25.00
BTLJT2 Jeremiah Trotter/45	10.00	25.00
BTLJT3 Jeremiah Trotter/70	10.00	25.00
BTLKB Keith Brooking/50	10.00	25.00
BTLLE Lee Evans/25	12.00	30.00
BTLLJ Larry Johnson/20	10.00	25.00
BTLLT LaDainian Tomlinson/10	40.00	100.00
BTLMA Matt Leinart/15	12.00	30.00
BTLMB Marc Bulger/25	12.00	30.00
BTLMC Marques Colston/50	15.00	40.00
BTLML1 Matt Light/25	12.00	30.00
BTLML2 Matt Light/50	10.00	25.00
BTLML3 Matt Light/70	10.00	25.00
BTLML4 Matt Light/75	10.00	25.00
BTLMS Mike Singletary/15	50.00	100.00
BTLNB1 Nick Barnett/35	12.00	30.00
BTLNB2 Nick Barnett/50	12.00	30.00
BTLNB3 Nick Barnett/70	12.00	30.00
BTLNM1 Nick Mangold/65	8.00	20.00
BTLNM2 Nick Mangold/70	8.00	20.00
BTLPC1 Patrick Crayton/50	12.00	30.00
BTLPC2 Patrick Crayton/55	12.00	30.00
BTLPC3 Patrick Crayton/60	12.00	30.00
BTLPH Paul Hornung/50	25.00	50.00
BTLQJ1 Quentin Jammer/50	8.00	20.00
BTLQJ2 Quentin Jammer/55	8.00	20.00
BTLRB Reggie Bush/15	40.00	100.00
BTLRC1 Ronald Curry/45	10.00	25.00
BTLRC2 Ronald Curry/65	10.00	25.00
BTLRC3 Ronald Curry/75	10.00	25.00
BTLRG Roberto Garza/75	12.00	30.00
BTLRO Ronnie Brown/25	25.00	60.00
BTLSA1 Bob Sanders/40	20.00	50.00
BTLSA2 Bob Sanders/70	20.00	50.00
BTLSH1 Steve Hutchinson/90	10.00	25.00
BTLSH2 Steve Hutchinson/25	10.00	25.00
BTLST1 Mack Strong/25	12.00	30.00
BTLST2 Mack Strong/65	12.00	30.00
BTLST3 Mack Strong/75	12.00	30.00
BTLTR Tony Romo/25	40.00	100.00
BTLTW1 Ty Warren/35	10.00	25.00
BTLTW2 Ty Warren/70	10.00	25.00
BTLTW3 Ty Warren/75	10.00	25.00
BTLWP Willie Parker/25	15.00	40.00

2007 SP Authentic Chirography

*GOLD/25: .8X TO 2X BASIC INSERTS
GOLD PRINT RUN 25 SER.#'d SETS

CAAC Adam Carriker	5.00	12.00
CAAG Anthony Gonzalez SP	6.00	15.00
CAAS Alex Smith QB SP	15.00	40.00
CABM Brandon Meriweather	6.00	15.00
CABQ Brady Quinn SP	30.00	80.00
CABR Ronnie Brown SP	15.00	30.00
CACB Champ Bailey SP	20.00	40.00
CACH Korey Hall	5.00	12.00
CACL Chris Leak	5.00	12.00
CACW Cadillac Williams SP	10.00	25.00
CADD Donald Driver		
CADR Darrelle Revis	10.00	25.00
CADS Drew Stanton SP	8.00	20.00
CAEM Eli Manning SP	40.00	80.00
CAIS Isaiah Stanback	4.00	10.00
CAJA Joseph Addai	10.00	25.00
CAJB John Beck	10.00	25.00
CAJC Jason Campbell	10.00	25.00
CAJH Jason Hill	6.00	15.00
CAKI Kenny Irons	4.00	10.00
CALE Lee Evans	10.00	25.00
CALT Lawrence Timmons	6.00	15.00
CAMB Marion Barber	10.00	25.00
CAMC Marques Colston	12.00	30.00
CAML Marshawn Lynch	10.00	25.00
CAMM Matt Moore	6.00	15.00
CAPR Philip Rivers	15.00	30.00
CAPW Patrick Willis	12.00	30.00
CARB Reggie Bush	25.00	60.00
CARN Reggie Nelson	5.00	12.00
CASR Sidney Rice	8.00	20.00
CATH Tony Hunt	4.00	10.00
CATO LaDainian Tomlinson SP	30.00	60.00
CATP Tyler Palko	5.00	12.00
CAVY Vince Young	20.00	50.00

2007 SP Authentic Chirography Duals

STATED PRINT RUN 50 SER.#'d SETS

AH Johnnie Lee Higgins	8.00	20.00
Aundrae Allison		
CW Adam Carriker	15.00	30.00
LaMarr Woodley		
FN Legedu Naanee	8.00	20.00
Joel Filani		
GA Michael Griffin	10.00	25.00
Jamaal Anderson		
HW Jason Hill	15.00	30.00
Paul Williams		
JB Brandon Jackson	8.00	20.00
Lorenzo Booker		
KE Kevin Kolb	25.00	60.00
Trent Edwards		
LB Chris Leak	10.00	25.00
John Beck		
LC Scott Chandler	10.00	25.00
Brian Leonard		
MB Dwayne Bowe	20.00	50.00
Robert Meachem		
NL LaRon Landry	10.00	25.00
Reggie Nelson		
OM Greg Olsen	10.00	25.00
Zach Miller		
PB Michael Bush	12.00	30.00
Antonio Pittman		
PS Isaiah Stanback	8.00	20.00
Jordan Palmer		
SF Steve Smith USC	10.00	25.00
Yamon Figurs		
WB Patrick Willis	15.00	40.00
H.B. Blades		
WH Tony Hunt	6.00	15.00
Garrett Wolfe		
WS Dwayne Wright	8.00	20.00
Kolby Smith		

2007 SP Authentic Chirography Triples

STATED PRINT RUN 25 SER.#'d SETS

JGB Calvin Johnson	100.00	200.00
Ted Ginn Jr.		
Dwayne Bowe		
LMP Chris Leak	15.00	40.00
Matt Moore		
Tyler Palko		
OMC Greg Olsen	15.00	40.00
Zach Miller		
Scott Chandler		
PLI Adrian Peterson	125.00	250.00
Marshawn Lynch		
Kenny Irons		
QRS JaMarcus Russell	30.00	80.00
Brady Quinn		
Drew Stanton		
WDH Tony Hunt	20.00	50.00
Garrett Wolfe		
Michael Bush		

2007 SP Authentic Chirography Quads

UNPRICED QUAD PRINT RUN 10
BOWM Quentin Moses
Amobi Okoye
Alan Branch
Patrick Willis
GACW Michael Griffin
Jamaal Anderson
Adam Carriker
LaMarr Woodley
JWDH Brandon Jackson
Lorenzo Booker
Tony Hunt
Garrett Wolfe
LOMC Brian Leonard
Greg Olsen
Zach Miller
Scott Chandler
PHLI Adrian Peterson
Marshawn Lynch
Kenny Irons
Chris Henry RB
QRBK JaMarcus Russell
Brady Quinn
Kevin Kolb
John Beck
SPES Drew Stanton
Trent Edwards
Isaiah Stanback
Jordan Palmer

2007 SP Authentic Sign of the Times

SOTTAB Anquan Boldin	10.00	25.00
SOTTAO Amobi Okoye	6.00	15.00
SOTTAP Antonio Pittman	4.00	10.00
SOTTBA Dallas Baker	4.00	10.00
SOTTBE Drew Bennett SP	8.00	20.00
SOTTBL Brian Leonard	5.00	12.00
SOTTBR Alan Branch	5.00	12.00
SOTTCJ Calvin Johnson SP	40.00	80.00
SOTTCT Chester Taylor SP	8.00	20.00
SOTTDB Dwayne Bowe SP	10.00	25.00
SOTTDC David Clowney	5.00	12.00
SOTTFG Frank Gore	12.00	30.00
SOTTGW Garrett Wolfe	4.00	10.00
SOTTJA Jamaal Anderson	5.00	12.00
SOTTJH Johnnie Lee Higgins	5.00	12.00
SOTTJL John Lynch	10.00	25.00
SOTTJR Jeff Rowe	4.00	10.00
SOTTJT Jason Taylor		
SOTTKK Kevin Kolb	10.00	25.00
SOTTLF Larry Fitzgerald	12.00	30.00
SOTTLH Leon Hall	5.00	12.00
SOTTMB Michael Bush	6.00	15.00
SOTTMJ Maurice Jones-Drew		
SOTTPM Peyton Manning SP	60.00	120.00
SOTTPP Paul Posluszny	6.00	15.00
SOTTRB Reggie Brown	8.00	20.00
SOTTRM Robert Meachem	6.00	15.00
SOTTRW Roy Williams S		
SOTTSJ Steven Jackson		
SOTTSS Steve Smith USC	6.00	15.00
SOTTTE Trent Edwards	6.00	15.00
SOTTTR Tony Romo SP	75.00	150.00
SOTTWP Willie Parker SP	10.00	25.00
SOTTYF Yamon Figurs	4.00	10.00

2007 SP Authentic Sign of the Times Gold

*GOLD/25: .8X TO 2X BASIC AUTOS
GOLD PRINT RUN 25 SER.#'d SETS

SOTTTR Tony Romo	100.00	200.00

2007 SP Authentic Sign of the Times Duals

STATED PRINT RUN 75 SER.#'d SETS

BT Lawrence Timmons	15.00	30.00
Lorenzo Booker		
DB Craig Buster Davis	20.00	50.00
Dwayne Bowe		
GG Ted Ginn Jr.	15.00	40.00
Anthony Gonzalez		
GP Anthony Gonzalez	20.00	50.00
Antonio Pittman		
HB Leon Hall	8.00	20.00
Alan Branch		
HM Chris Henry RB	10.00	25.00
Zach Miller		
HP Paul Posluszny	10.00	25.00
Tony Hunt		
HS Korey Hall	8.00	20.00
Chansi Stuckey		
II Kenny Irons	10.00	25.00
David Irons		
JC Brandon Jackson	12.00	30.00
Adam Carriker		
JS Dwayne Jarrett	10.00	25.00
Steve Smith USC		
LD Craig Buster Davis	10.00	25.00
LaRon Landry		
NW DeShawn Wynn	10.00	25.00
Reggie Nelson		
OM Brandon Meriweather	12.00	30.00
Greg Olsen		
PH Jordan Palmer	10.00	25.00
Johnnie Lee Higgins		
RB Darrelle Revis	15.00	30.00
H.B. Blades		
WW Paul Williams	10.00	25.00
Dwayne Wright		
ZN Jared Zabransky	10.00	25.00
Legedu Naanee		

2007 SP Authentic Sign of the Times Triples

STATED PRINT RUN 25

BJS Reggie Bush	40.00	100.00
Dwayne Jarrett		
Steve Smith USC		
LDB Dwayne Bowe	30.00	80.00
Craig Buster Davis		
LaRon Landry		
LWB Chris Leak	25.00	60.00
Dallas Baker		
DeShawn Wynn		
MOM Brandon Meriweather	20.00	50.00
Greg Olsen		
Tyrone Moss		
QWM Brady Quinn	50.00	120.00
Darius Walker		
Rhema McKnight		
SBO Michael Bush		
Amobi Okoye		
Kolby Smith		
WMW Marcus McCauley	20.00	50.00
Paul Williams		
Dwayne Wright		

2007 SP Authentic Sign of the Times Quads

UNPRICED QUAD PRINT RUN 15

2008 SP Authentic

This set was released on January 30, 2009. The base set consists of 303 cards. Cards 1-100 feature veterans, and cards 101-200 are rookies serial numbered of 999-1399. Cards 201-270 are autographed rookies serial numbered of 399-999, and cards 271-305 are autographed jersey rookies serial numbered of 499-999. This product was released with 5 cards per pack and 24 packs per hobby box. A retail version was also produced with a simple "SP" logo on the cardfronts for the first 100 veteran players instead of "SP Authentic." The Retail base rookies (101-140) were created with a new design and include no brand logos on the fronts while the Retail rookie autographs (141-175) have the simple "SP" logo on the fronts along with a unique design.

COMP.SET w/o RC's (100)	8.00	20.00
101-160 ROOKIE PRINT RUN 1399		
161-200 ROOKIE PRINT RUN 999		
201-230 AU RC PRINT RUN 1199		
231-250 AU RC PRINT RUN 999		
251-270 AU RC PRINT RUN 399-499		
271-298 JSY AU RC PRINT RUN 999		
299-305 JSY AU RC PRINT RUN 499		
UNPRICED NFL LOGO AU PRINT RUN 1		
1 Marshawn Lynch	.25	.60
2 Trent Edwards	.20	.50
3 Roscoe Parrish	.20	.50
4 Jason Taylor	.25	.60
5 Ronnie Brown	.25	.60
6 Chad Pennington	.25	.60
7 Tom Brady	.50	1.25
8 Laurence Maroney	.25	.60
9 Randy Moss	.30	.75
10 Darrelle Revis	.25	.60
11 Jerricho Cotchery	.25	.60
12 Thomas Jones	.25	.60
13 Ray Lewis	.30	.75
14 Ed Reed	.25	.60
15 Willis McGahee	.25	.60
16 Carson Palmer	.30	.75
17 T.J. Houshmandzadeh	.25	.60
18 Chad Johnson	.25	.60
19 Kellen Winslow	.25	.60
20 Derek Anderson	.20	.50
21 Braylon Edwards	.25	.60
22 Ben Roethlisberger	.30	.75
23 Willie Parker	.25	.60
24 Matt Schaub	.25	.60
25 DeMeco Ryans	.25	.60
26 Andre Johnson	.25	.60
27 Darius Walker	.20	.50
28 Peyton Manning	.50	1.25
29 Reggie Wayne	.25	.60
30 Joseph Addai	.25	.60
31 David Garrard	.25	.60
32 Maurice Jones-Drew	.25	.60
33 Fred Taylor	.25	.60
34 Vince Young	.25	.60
35 LenDale White	.25	.60
36 Alge Crumpler	.25	.60
37 Jay Cutler	.30	.75
38 Brandon Marshall	.25	.60
39 Jason Witten	.30	.75
40 Brodie Croyle	.25	.60
41 Larry Johnson	.25	.60
42 Derrick Johnson	.20	.50
43 JaMarcus Russell	.25	.60
44 Ronald Curry	.25	.60
45 Jeremy Shockey	.25	.60
46 Antonio Gates	.30	.75
47 LaDainian Tomlinson	.30	.75
48 Antonio Cromartie	.20	.50
49 Philip Rivers	.30	.75
50 Tony Romo	.40	1.00
51 Terrell Owens	.30	.75
52 DeMarcus Ware	.25	.60
53 Marion Barber	.25	.60
54 Eli Manning	.30	.75
55 Brandon Jacobs	.25	.60
56 Plaxico Burress	.25	.60
57 Antonio Pierce	.20	.50
58 Donovan McNabb	.30	.75
59 Brian Dawkins	.25	.60
60 Brian Westbrook	.25	.60
61 Chris Cooley	.25	.60
62 Jason Campbell	.25	.60
63 Clinton Portis	.25	.60
64 Brian Urlacher	.30	.75
65 Lance Briggs	.20	.50
66 Devin Hester	.30	.75
67 Roy Williams WR	.25	.60
68 Calvin Johnson	.30	.75
69 Brett Favre	.75	2.00
70 Aaron Rodgers	.60	1.50
71 Ryan Grant	.30	.75
72 Greg Jennings	.30	.75
73 Tarvaris Jackson	.25	.60
74 Adrian Peterson	.50	1.25
75 Sidney Rice	.30	.75
76 Michael Turner	.30	.75
77 Jerious Norwood	.25	.60
78 Jake Delhomme	.25	.60
79 DeAngelo Williams	.25	.60
80 Steve Smith	.25	.60
81 Julius Peppers	.25	.60
82 Drew Brees	.30	.75
83 Reggie Bush	.30	.75
84 Marques Colston	.25	.60
85 Jonathan Vilma	.25	.60
86 Joey Galloway	.25	.60
87 Jeff Garcia	.25	.60
88 Earnest Graham	.20	.50
89 Kurt Warner	.30	.75
90 Edgerrin James	.25	.60
91 Larry Fitzgerald	.30	.75
92 Anquan Boldin	.25	.60
93 Marc Bulger	.25	.60
94 Steven Jackson	.30	.75
95 Torry Holt	.25	.60
96 J.T. O'Sullivan	.20	.50
97 Frank Gore	.25	.60
98 Nate Clements	.20	.50
99 Matt Hasselbeck	.25	.60
100 Deion Branch	.25	.60
101 Kregg Lumpkin RC	3.00	8.00
102 Donovan Woods RC	2.50	6.00
103 Joe Mays RC	2.00	5.00
104 Anthony Alridge RC	2.50	6.00
105 Beau Bell RC	2.50	6.00
106 Brad Cottam RC	2.50	6.00
107 Brandon Flowers RC	3.00	8.00
108 Darrell Strong RC	2.50	6.00
109 Mike Tolbert RC	4.00	10.00
110 Bryan Kehl RC	2.50	6.00
111 Andy Studebaker RC	2.50	6.00
112 Duane Brown RC	2.50	6.00
113 Mike Humpal RC	3.00	8.00
114 Corey Clark RC	2.00	5.00
115 Josh Sitton RC	2.50	6.00
116 Curtis Lofton RC	2.50	6.00
117 Lance Leggett RC	3.00	8.00
118 Gary Barnidge RC	2.00	5.00
119 Marcus Dixon RC	2.00	5.00
120 Dominique Barber RC	2.00	5.00
121 Reggie Smith RC	2.50	6.00
122 John Sullivan RC	2.50	6.00
123 Jabari Arthur RC	2.50	6.00
124 Maurice Leggett RC	2.50	6.00
125 Jehuu Caulcrick RC	2.50	6.00
126 Philip Wheeler RC	2.50	6.00
127 Jo-Lonn Dunbar RC	2.50	6.00
128 Josh Barrett RC	2.00	5.00
129 Danny Amendola RC	8.00	20.00
130 Kenny Iwebema RC	2.00	5.00
131 Lance Ball RC	2.00	5.00
132 Caleb Hanie RC	10.00	20.00
133 Chris Chamberlain RC	2.00	5.00
134 Marcus Howard RC	3.00	8.00
135 Shaheer McBride RC	2.00	5.00
136 Orlando Scandrick RC	3.00	8.00
137 Quentin Groves RC	2.50	6.00
138 Quintin Demps RC	3.00	8.00
139 John Greco RC	2.50	6.00
140 Jamey Richard RC	2.00	5.00
141 Corey Lynch RC	2.00	5.00
142 Orlando Scandrick RC	3.00	8.00
143 Lex Hilliard RC	3.00	8.00
144 Tyrell Johnson RC	3.00	8.00
145 Martellus Bennett RC	2.50	6.00
146 Simeon Castille RC	2.50	6.00
147 Steve Johnson RC	6.00	15.00
148 Steve Justice RC	2.00	5.00
149 Terrell Thomas RC	2.50	6.00
150 Thomas Brown RC	2.50	6.00
151 Thomas DeCoud RC	2.00	5.00
152 Matt Slater RC	3.00	8.00
153 Tom Zbikowski RC	3.00	8.00
154 Jaymar Johnson RC	2.00	5.00
155 Brian Johnston RC	2.00	5.00
156 Trevor Laws RC	3.00	8.00
157 Will Franklin RC	2.50	6.00
158 Xavier Adibi RC	2.00	5.00
159 Chaz Schilens RC	3.00	8.00
160 Zack Bowman RC	2.50	6.00
161 Tim Hightower RC	3.00	8.00
162 Barry Richardson RC	2.00	5.00
163 Pierre Garcon RC	10.00	25.00
164 Tyvon Branch RC	2.50	6.00
165 Marcus Henry RC	2.50	6.00
166 Carl Nicks RC	2.50	6.00
167 Chauncey Washington RC	2.50	6.00
168 Chilo Rachal RC	2.00	5.00
169 Chris Williams RC	2.50	6.00
170 Craig Stevens RC	2.00	5.00
171 Jordan Dizon RC	3.00	8.00
172 Dantrell Savage RC	2.50	6.00
173 Clifton Smith RC	3.00	8.00
174 Drew Radovich RC	2.50	6.00
175 Jerome Felton RC	2.00	5.00
176 Haruki Nakamura RC	2.00	5.00
177 Olaniyi Sobomehin RC	2.00	5.00
178 Jamie Silva RC	2.50	6.00
179 Brandon Carr RC	2.50	6.00
180 Jeff Otah RC	2.50	6.00
181 William Hayes RC	2.00	5.00
182 Jerome Simpson RC	3.00	8.00
183 Anthony Collins RC	2.00	5.00
184 Alex Hall RC	2.50	6.00
185 Branden Albert RC	3.00	8.00
186 Jalen Parmele RC	2.50	6.00
187 Stanford Keglar RC	2.00	5.00
188 Louis Rankin RC	2.50	6.00
189 Maurice Purify RC	3.00	8.00
190 Darnell Jenkins RC	2.50	6.00
191 Pat Sims RC	2.50	6.00
192 Patrick Lee RC	2.50	6.00
193 Roy Schuening RC	2.00	5.00
194 Lynell Hamilton RC	5.00	12.00
195 Joey LaRocque RC	2.00	5.00
196 Terrence Wheatley RC	2.00	5.00
197 Tracy Porter RC	3.00	8.00
198 Brett Swain RC	2.50	6.00
199 Wesley Woodyard RC	2.50	6.00
200 Xavier Omon RC	3.00	8.00
201 Allen Patrick AU RC	4.00	10.00
202 Marcus Monk AU RC	4.00	10.00
203 Anthony Morelli AU RC	4.00	10.00
204 Antoine Cason AU RC	5.00	12.00
205 Aqib Talib AU RC	5.00	12.00
206 Ben Moffitt AU RC	3.00	8.00
207 Chris Long AU RC	20.00	40.00
208 Bruce Davis AU RC	4.00	10.00
209 Calais Campbell AU RC	4.00	10.00
210 Mario Urrutia AU RC	3.00	8.00
211 Chevis Jackson AU RC	3.00	8.00
212 Chris Ellis AU RC	3.00	8.00
213 Josh Morgan AU RC	5.00	12.00
214 Craig Steltz AU RC	4.00	10.00
215 DJ Hall AU RC	4.00	10.00
216 Dan Connor AU RC	5.00	12.00
217 Darius Reynaud AU RC	3.00	8.00
218 DeJuan Tribble AU RC	3.00	8.00
219 DeMario Pressley AU RC	4.00	10.00
220 Dennis Keyes AU RC	3.00	8.00
221 Derrick Harvey AU RC	3.00	8.00
222 Owen Schmitt AU RC	5.00	12.00
223 Dwight Lowery AU RC	12.50	25.00
224 Erik Ainge AU RC	5.00	12.00
225 Erin Henderson AU RC	5.00	12.00
226 DaJuan Morgan AU RC	4.00	10.00
227 Frank Okam AU RC	3.00	8.00
228 Matt Flynn AU RC	30.00	80.00
229 Phillip Merling AU RC SP	15.00	30.00
230 Ryan Clady AU RC	5.00	12.00
231 Davone Bess AU RC	5.00	12.00
232 Fred Davis AU RC	5.00	12.00
234 Gosder Cherilus AU RC	4.00	10.00
235 Tashard Choice AU RC	6.00	15.00
236 J Leman AU RC	3.00	8.00
237 Jack Ikegwuonu AU RC	3.00	8.00
238 Jacob Hester AU RC	5.00	12.00
239 Jacob Tamme AU RC	6.00	15.00
240 Sedrick Ellis AU RC	5.00	12.00
241 Jermichael Finley AU RC	25.00	50.00
242 John Carlson AU RC	8.00	20.00
243 Jonathan Goff AU RC	3.00	8.00
245 Shawn Crable AU RC	3.00	8.00
246 Josh Johnson AU RC	6.00	15.00
247 Justin Forsett AU RC	7.50	15.00
248 Justin King AU RC	4.00	10.00
249 Keenan Burton AU RC	3.00	8.00
250 Sam Baker AU RC	3.00	8.00
251 Colt Brennan AU/399 RC	12.00	30.00
252 Adrian Arrington AU/399 RC	6.00	15.00
253 Alex Brink AU/399 RC	8.00	20.00
254 Ali Highsmith AU/399 RC	5.00	12.00
255 Keith Rivers AU/499 RC	8.00	20.00
256 Kellen Davis AU/399 RC	5.00	12.00
257 Kenny Phillips AU/399 RC	8.00	20.00
258 Geno Hayes AU/399 RC	5.00	12.00
259 Paul Smith AU/399 RC	8.00	20.00
260 Lavelle Hawkins AU/499 RC	5.00	12.00
261 Lawrence Jackson AU/399 RC	6.00	15.00
262 Leodis McKelvin AU/399 RC	6.00	15.00
263 Andre Woodson AU/399 RC	8.00	20.00
264 Mike Hart AU/499 RC	8.00	20.00
265 Martin Rucker AU/399 RC	6.00	15.00
266 Dennis Dixon AU/399 RC	15.00	30.00
267 Paul Hubbard AU/399 RC	6.00	15.00
268 Peyton Hillis AU/399 RC	40.00	80.00
269 Ryan Grice Mullins AU/399 RC	5.00	12.00
270 Vernon Gholston AU/399 RC	6.00	15.00
271 Jerome Simpson JSY AU RC	10.00	25.00
272 Dexter Jackson JSY AU RC	8.00	20.00
273 Donnie Avery JSY AU RC	8.00	20.00
275 Jake Long JSY AU RC	10.00	25.00
276 Dustin Keller JSY AU RC	12.00	30.00
277 James Hardy JSY AU RC	8.00	20.00
278 Andre Caldwell JSY AU RC	8.00	20.00
279 Jordy Nelson JSY AU RC	30.00	60.00
280 Kevin Smith JSY AU RC	10.00	25.00
281 Eddie Royal JSY AU RC	10.00	25.00
282 Mario Manningham JSY AU RC	15.00	40.00
283 Earl Bennett JSY AU RC	10.00	25.00
284 Harry Douglas JSY AU RC	8.00	20.00
285 Ray Rice JSY AU RC	50.00	100.00
286 Steve Slaton JSY AU RC	10.00	25.00
288 Chris Johnson JSY AU RC	60.00	150.00
289 Kevin O'Connell JSY AU RC	8.00	20.00
290 DeSean Jackson JSY AU RC	50.00	100.00
291 Early Doucet JSY AU RC	8.00	20.00
292 Felix Jones JSY AU RC	20.00	50.00
293 Jamaal Charles JSY AU RC	30.00	60.00
294 John David Booty JSY AU RC	8.00	20.00
295 Joe Flacco JSY AU RC	90.00	175.00
297 Malcolm Kelly JSY AU RC	8.00	20.00
298 Matt Forte JSY AU RC	40.00	80.00
299 Darren McFadden JSY AU/499 RC	60.00	120.00
300 Matt Ryan JSY AU/499 RC	150.00	300.00
301 Brian Brohm JSY AU/499 RC	15.00	40.00
302 Chad Henne JSY AU/499 RC	30.00	80.00
303 Devin Thomas JSY AU/499 RC	12.00	30.00
304 Rashard Mendenhall JSY AU/499 RC	50.00	100.00
305 Jonathan Stewart JSY AU/499 RC	30.00	60.00

2008 SP Authentic Gold

*JSY AU 271-298: 1.2X TO 3X BASE JSY AU/999
*JSY AU 299-305: 1X TO 2.5X BASE JSY AU/499
STATED PRINT RUN 25 SER.#'d SETS

285 Ray Rice JSY AU	200.00	400.00
288 Chris Johnson JSY AU	500.00	
290 DeSean Jackson JSY AU	150.00	300.00
292 Felix Jones JSY AU	125.00	250.00
293 Jamaal Charles JSY AU	150.00	250.00
295 Joe Flacco JSY AU	300.00	600.00
298 Matt Forte JSY AU	200.00	350.00
299 Darren McFadden JSY AU	300.00	500.00
300 Matt Ryan JSY AU	500.00	800.00
302 Chad Henne JSY AU	200.00	400.00
304 Rashard Mendenhall JSY AU	200.00	400.00
305 Jonathan Stewart JSY AU	125.00	250.00

2008 SP Authentic Retail

COMP.SET w/o RC's (100)	8.00	20.00
*1-100 RETAIL VETS: .4X TO 1X HOBBY		
1-100 VETS HAVE SP BRAND LOGO ON FRONT		
101-140 RCs HAVE NO BRAND LOGO		
141-175 AU RC's HAVE SP BRAND LOGO ON FRONT		
101 Adrian Arrington RC	1.25	3.00
102 Anthony Morelli RC	1.25	3.00
103 Calais Campbell RC	1.25	3.00
104 Colt Brennan RC	1.50	4.00
105 Chevis Jackson RC	1.00	2.50
106 Chris Williams RC	1.25	3.00
107 Craig Stevens RC	1.00	2.50
108 Curtis Lofton RC	1.25	3.00
109 Dan Connor RC	1.50	4.00
110 Davone Bess RC	1.50	4.00
111 Dennis Dixon RC	1.50	4.00
112 Derrick Harvey RC	1.00	2.50
113 Dominique Rodgers-Cromartie RC	1.50	4.00
114 Dre Moore RC	1.25	3.00
115 Erik Ainge RC	1.50	4.00
116 Erin Henderson RC	1.50	4.00
117 Frank Okam RC	1.00	2.50
118 Haruki Nakamura RC	1.00	2.50
119 Jack Ikegwuonu RC	1.00	2.50
120 Jeff Otah RC	1.25	3.00
121 Jerod Mayo RC	1.50	4.00
122 Jonathan Goff RC	1.00	2.50
123 Jordon Dizon RC	1.50	4.00
124 Justin King RC	1.25	3.00
125 Kenny Phillips RC	1.50	4.00
126 Kentwan Balmer RC	1.25	3.00
127 King Dunlap RC	1.00	2.50
128 Leodis McKelvin RC	1.25	3.00
129 Mike Jenkins RC	1.50	4.00
130 Owen Schmitt RC	1.50	4.00
131 Patrick Lee RC	1.25	3.00
132 Peyton Hillis RC	2.00	5.00
133 Quentin Groves RC	1.25	3.00
134 Ryan Clady RC	1.50	4.00
135 Sam Baker RC	1.00	2.50
136 Josh Morgan RC	1.50	4.00
137 Tracy Porter RC	1.50	4.00
138 Vernon Gholston RC	1.25	3.00
139 Will Franklin RC	1.25	3.00
140 Xavier Omon RC	1.50	4.00
141 Andre Caldwell AU RC	6.00	15.00
142 Chad Henne AU RC	8.00	20.00
143 DeSean Jackson AU RC	25.00	50.00
144 Chris Johnson AU RC	30.00	60.00
145 Felix Jones AU RC		
146 Chris Long AU RC	8.00	20.00
147 Darren McFadden AU RC		
148 Joe Flacco AU RC	40.00	80.00
149 Ray Rice AU RC	30.00	60.00
150 Matt Ryan AU RC	50.00	100.00
152 Alex Brink AU RC	8.00	20.00
153 Thomas Brown AU RC	6.00	15.00
154 Mike Jenkins AU	8.00	20.00
155 Kellen Davis AU RC	5.00	12.00
156 Andre Woodson AU RC	8.00	20.00
157 Quintin Demps AU RC	8.00	20.00
158 Aqib Talib AU RC	8.00	20.00
159 Matt Flynn AU RC	25.00	60.00
160 Xavier Adibi AU RC	5.00	12.00
161 Shawn Crable AU RC	5.00	12.00
162 Trevor Laws AU RC	8.00	20.00
163 Tom Zbikowski AU RC	8.00	20.00
164 Erik Ainge AU	8.00	20.00
165 Josh Johnson AU RC	8.00	20.00
166 Terrell Thomas AU RC	6.00	15.00
167 Malcolm Kelly AU RC	6.00	15.00
168 Davone Bess AU	8.00	20.00
169 John David Booty AU RC	6.00	15.00
170 Lawrence Jackson AU RC	6.00	15.00
171 DeMario Pressley AU RC	6.00	15.00
172 Brian Brohm AU RC	8.00	20.00
173 Calais Campbell AU	6.00	15.00
174 Ryan Torain AU RC	8.00	20.00
175 Mario Urrutia AU RC	5.00	12.00

2008 SP Authentic Autographs

*GOLD VETS/25: .5X TO 1.2X BASIC AU
*GOLD ROOKIES/25: .8X TO 2X BASIC AU
GOLD PRINT RUN 25 SER.#'d SETS

SPAM Anthony Morelli	4.00	10.00
SPAP Adrian Peterson SP	60.00	120.00
SPBD Bruce Davis	4.00	10.00
SPBF Brett Favre SP	100.00	200.00
SPCE Chris Ellis	3.00	8.00
SPCJ Chris Johnson	30.00	60.00
SPCL Chris Long	5.00	12.00
SPCP Clinton Portis	10.00	25.00
SPCS Craig Steltz	4.00	10.00
SPDD Dennis Dixon	8.00	20.00
SPDM Darren McFadden SP	30.00	60.00
SPDR Dominique Rodgers-Cromartie	5.00	12.00
SPDT Devin Thomas	4.00	10.00
SPER Erin Henderson	5.00	12.00
SPFJ Felix Jones	15.00	40.00
SPGC Gosder Cherilus	4.00	10.00
SPGR Bob Griese	12.00	30.00
SPHD Harry Douglas	4.00	10.00
SPJL Jamal Lewis	10.00	25.00
SPJS Jonathan Stewart	15.00	40.00
SPMK Malcolm Kelly	4.00	10.00
SPMR Matt Ryan SP	100.00	200.00
SPOS Owen Schmitt	5.00	12.00
SPPM Peyton Manning	60.00	120.00
SPPW Patrick Willis	10.00	25.00
SPRT Rashard Mendenhall	10.00	25.00
SPSY Steve Young SP	30.00	60.00
SPVG Vernon Gholston	4.00	10.00
SPYT Y.A. Tittle	12.00	30.00

2008 SP Authentic By the Letter Autographs

SER.#'d 4-56, TOTAL PRINT RUNS 30-224

BLAH A.J. Hawk G/25	15.00	40.00
(Letters spell last name		
Total print run 100)		
BLAM Archie Manning/14	20.00	50.00
(Letters spell last name		
Total print run 98)		
BLAS Aaron Schobel/25	10.00	25.00
(Letters spell last name		
Total print run 175)		
BLBA Marion Barber/16	20.00	50.00
(Letters spell last name		
Total print run 96)		
BLBB Brian Bosworth/12	15.00	40.00
(Letters spell last name		
Total print run 96)		
BLBC Brodie Croyle/14	12.00	30.00
(Letters spell last name		
Total print run 84)		
BLBJ Bert Jones/20	12.00	30.00
(Letters spell last name		
Total print run 100)		
BLBR Ben Roethlisberger/4	100.00	200.00
(Letters spell last name		
Total print run 56)		
BLBW Ben Watson/16	10.00	25.00
(Letters spell last name		
Total print run 96)		
BLCB Chuck Bednarik/12	12.00	30.00
(Letters spell last name		
Total print run 96)		
BLCP Clinton Portis/17	12.00	30.00
(Letters spell last name		
Total print run 102)		
BLDA Derek Anderson/12	12.00	30.00
(Letters spell last name		
Total print run 96)		
BLDB Dwayne Bowe/24	15.00	40.00
(Letters spell last name		
Total print run 96)		
BLDG David Garrard/14	15.00	40.00
(Letters spell last name		
Total print run 98)		
BLDJ Daryl Johnston/21	30.00	60.00
(Letters spell last name		
Total print run 168)		
BLDM Don Maynard/14	12.00	30.00
(Letters spell last name		
Total print run 98)		
BLEM Eli Manning/14	50.00	120.00
(Letters spell last name		
Total print run 98)		
BLFT Fran Tarkenton/11	25.00	50.00
(Letters spell last name		
Total print run 99)		
BLHA A.J Hawk W/15	15.00	40.00
(Letters spell PACKERS		
Total print run 105)		
BLJK Jerry Kramer/16	20.00	50.00
(Letters spell last name		
Total print run 96)		
BLJT Joe Theismann/9	40.00	80.00
(Letters spell last name		
Total print run 72)		
BLKW Kellen Winslow Sr./14	15.00	40.00
(Letters spell last name		
Total print run 98)		
BLLJ Larry Johnson/10	12.00	30.00
(Letters spell last name		
Total print run 70)		
BLMF Marshall Faulk/10	30.00	60.00
(Letters spell last name		
Total print run 50)		
BLML Marshawn Lynch/16	15.00	40.00
(Letters spell last name		
Total print run 80)		
BLOA Ottis Anderson/14	15.00	40.00
(Letters spell last name		
Total print run 112)		
BLPH Paul Hornung/17	15.00	40.00
(Letters spell last name		
Total print run 119)		
BLPW Patrick Willis/23	30.00	60.00
(Letters spell last name		
Total print run 138)		
BLRA Tom Rathman/15	15.00	40.00
(Letters spell HUSKERS		
Total print run 105)		
BLRC Roger Craig/20	12.00	30.00
(Letters spell last name		
Total print run 100)		
BLRO Tony Romo/25	50.00	100.00
(Letters spell last name		
Total print run 100)		
BLRW Rod Woodson/14	30.00	80.00
(Letters spell last name		
Total print run 98)		
BLSI Billy Sims/56	12.00	30.00
(Letters spell last name		
Total print run 224)		
BLSY Steve Young/10	60.00	120.00
(Letters spell last name		
Total print run 50)		
BLTA Troy Aikman/5	75.00	150.00
(Letters spell last name		
Total print run 30)		
BLTR Tom Rathman/15	15.00	40.00
(Letters spell last name		
Total print run 105)		
BLWI Roy Williams WR/8	12.00	30.00
(Letters spell last name		
Total print run 64)		
BLYT Y.A. Tittle/17	25.00	50.00
(Letters spell last name		
Total print run 102)		

2008 SP Authentic Chirography

*GOLD VETS/25: .5X TO 1.2X BASIC AU
*GOLD ROOKIES/25: .8X TO 2X BASIC AU
GOLD PRINT RUN 25 SER.#'d SETS
UNPRICED QUAD AUTO PRIINT RUN 10

CHAT Aqib Talib	5.00	12.00
CHBB Brian Brohm	5.00	12.00
CHBD Bruce Davis	4.00	10.00
CHBR Ben Roethlisberger SP	60.00	120.00
CHCE Chris Ellis	3.00	8.00
CHCH Chad Henne	8.00	20.00
CHCJ Chris Johnson	15.00	40.00
CHCN Chad Johnson SP	10.00	25.00
CHCS Craig Steltz	4.00	10.00
CHDJ DeSean Jackson	10.00	25.00
CHDM Don Maynard	10.00	25.00
CHDT Devin Thomas	4.00	10.00
CHEH Erin Henderson	5.00	12.00
CHFJ Felix Jones	12.00	30.00
CHFT Fran Tarkenton	20.00	40.00
CHGC Gosder Cherilus	4.00	10.00
CHJA Joseph Addai SP	10.00	25.00
CHJF Joe Flacco	20.00	50.00
CHJK Jim Kelly SP		
CHJL Jamal Lewis	10.00	25.00
CHKA Anthony Morelli	4.00	10.00
CHKS Kevin Smith	5.00	12.00
CHKW Kellen Winslow Sr. SP	15.00	40.00
CHLH Lester Hayes	10.00	25.00
CHLJ Larry Johnson SP EXCH		
CHLO Jake Long	5.00	12.00
CHMB Marc Bulger	10.00	25.00
CHMF Matt Forte	12.00	30.00
CHMK Malcolm Kelly	4.00	10.00
CHOS Owen Schmitt	5.00	12.00
CHPM Peyton Manning SP	60.00	120.00
CHRM Rashard Mendenhall	10.00	25.00
CHSY Steve Young SP	40.00	80.00
CHTR Tony Romo	40.00	80.00
CHWP Emmitt Smith SP	100.00	175.00

2008 SP Authentic Chirography Duals

STATED PRINT RUN 10-100
DK Fred Davis/100 8.00 20.00
Dustin Keller
JM Lawrence Jackson/90 10.00 25.00
Phillip Merling
WD Kurt Warner/100 15.00 40.00
Early Doucet
BG Roman Gabriel/50 12.00 30.00
Marc Bulger
GF Gale Sayers/15 50.00 120.00
Darren McFadden
GH Bob Griese/20 30.00 60.00
Chad Henne
HC Jacob Hester/80 8.00 20.00
Antoine Cason
HF Chad Henne/50 50.00 100.00
Joe Flacco
JC Jamaal Charles/20 25.00 50.00
Larry Johnson
KE Jim Kelly/20 50.00 80.00
Trent Edwards
LC Jake Long/80 10.00 25.00
Gosder Cherilus
MA Peyton Manning/20 75.00 150.00
Joseph Addai
MT Y.A. Tittle/30 50.00 100.00
Eli Manning
MW Patrick Willis/30 50.00 100.00
Eli Manning
PW Kenny Phillips/80 25.00 60.00
Rod Woodson
RH Mike Hart/85 20.00 40.00
Ray Rice
SS Billy Sims/80 15.00 40.00
Kevin Smith
ST Gale Sayers/20 60.00 120.00
LaDainian Tomlinson
TK Devin Thomas/100 8.00 20.00
Malcolm Kelly
WW DeMarcus Ware/50 25.00 50.00
Patrick Willis

2008 SP Authentic Chirography Triples

STATED PRINT RUN 25 SER.#'d SETS
BFS Dick Butkus/25 125.00 200.00
Matt Forte
Gale Sayers
FRB Brett Favre
Aaron Rodgers
Brian Brohm

2008 SP Authentic Immortals Autographs

STATED PRINT RUN 15-55
UNPRICED QUAD AUTO PRINT RUN 5
UNPRICED TRIPLE AUTO PRINT RUN 5-10
SPIBG Bob Griese/35 15.00 40.00
SPIBJ Bo Jackson/35 50.00 100.00
SPIBS Barry Sanders/15 125.00 200.00
SPIFH Franco Harris/35 EXCH
SPIFT Fran Tarkenton/35 EXCH
SPIJK Jerry Kramer/50 15.00 40.00
SPIJR Jerry Rice/15 125.00 200.00
SPIJT Joe Theismann/55 15.00 40.00
SPIKA Ken Anderson/55 15.00 40.00
SPIPH Paul Hornung/35 15.00 40.00
SPIRG Roman Gabriel/55 15.00 40.00
SPISI Billy Sims/35 15.00 40.00
SPISY Steve Young/35 40.00 80.00
SPIYT Y.A. Tittle/35 EXCH

2008 SP Authentic Immortals Autographs Dual

STATED PRINT RUN 5-20
AT Ottis Anderson/40 20.00 40.00
Y.A. Tittle
JB Brian Bosworth/20 60.00 120.00
Bo Jackson

2008 SP Authentic Retail Pro Bowl Performers

ONE PER RETAIL PACK
PBP1 Aaron Kampman .40 1.00
PBP2 Adrian Peterson .75 2.00
PBP3 Andre Johnson .40 1.00
PBP4 Antonio Cromartie .30 .75
PBP5 Ben Roethlisberger .50 1.25
PBP6 Bob Sanders .40 1.00
PBP7 Braylon Edwards .40 1.00
PBP8 Carson Palmer .50 1.25
PBP9 Steve Smith .40 1.00
PBP10 Chad Johnson .40 1.00
PBP11 Champ Bailey .40 1.00
PBP12 Chris Chambers .40 1.00
PBP13 Deuce McAllister .40 1.00
PBP14 DeMarcus Ware .40 1.00
PBP15 Derrick Burgess .30 .75
PBP16 Devin Hester .50 1.25
PBP17 Drew Brees .50 1.25
PBP18 Dwight Freeney .40 1.00
PBP19 Ed Reed .40 1.00
PBP20 Edgerrin James .40 1.00
PBP21 Steven Jackson .50 1.25
PBP22 Fred Taylor .40 1.00
PBP23 Hines Ward .40 1.00
PBP24 Roy Williams WR .40 1.00
PBP25 Jason Taylor .40 1.00
PBP26 Jason Witten .50 1.25
PBP27 John Lynch .50 1.25
PBP28 LaDainian Tomlinson .50 1.25
PBP29 Larry Fitzgerald .50 1.25
PBP30 Larry Johnson .40 1.00
PBP31 Lofa Tatupu .40 1.00
PBP32 Marvin Harrison .50 1.25
PBP33 Peyton Manning .75 2.00
PBP34 Randy Moss .50 1.25
PBP35 Ray Lewis .50 1.25
PBP36 Reggie Wayne .40 1.00
PBP37 Shawne Merriman .40 1.00
PBP38 Terrell Owens .50 1.25
PBP39 T.J. Houshmandzadeh .40 1.00
PBP40 Tom Brady .75 2.00
PBP41 Tony Gonzalez .40 1.00
PBP42 Troy Polamalu .50 1.25
PBP43 Tony Romo .60 1.50
PBP44 Torry Holt .40 1.00
PBP45 Matt Hasselbeck .40 1.00

2008 SP Authentic Retail Rookie Authentics Jerseys

RA1 John David Booty 2.50 6.00
RA2 Brian Brohm 3.00 8.00
RA3 Andre Caldwell 2.50 6.00
RA4 Jamaal Charles 5.00 12.00
RA5 Glenn Dorsey 3.00 8.00
RA6 Early Doucet 2.50 6.00
RA7 Harry Douglas 2.50 6.00
RA8 Joe Flacco 10.00 25.00
RA9 Matt Forte 5.00 12.00
RA10 James Hardy 2.50 6.00
RA11 Chad Henne 3.00 8.00
RA12 DeSean Jackson 6.00 15.00
RA13 Chris Johnson 8.00 20.00
RA14 Felix Jones 5.00 12.00
RA15 Dustin Keller 5.00 12.00
RA16 Malcolm Kelly 2.50 6.00
RA17 Jake Long 3.00 8.00
RA18 Mario Manningham 3.00 8.00
RA19 Darren McFadden 8.00 20.00
RA20 Rashard Mendenhall 6.00 15.00
RA21 Jordy Nelson 4.00 10.00
RA22 Kevin O'Connell 2.50 6.00
RA23 Ray Rice 6.00 15.00
RA24 Matt Ryan 12.00 30.00
RA25 Jerome Simpson 3.00 8.00
RA26 Steve Slaton 3.00 8.00
RA27 Kevin Smith 3.00 8.00
RA28 Jonathan Stewart 5.00 12.00
RA29 Limas Sweed 3.00 8.00
RA30 Devin Thomas 2.50 6.00

2008 SP Authentic Retro Rookie Jerseys Autographs

STATED PRINT RUN 75 SER.#'d SETS
RRAS Aaron Schobel 10.00 25.00
RRBA Marion Barber 15.00 40.00
RRBB Brian Bosworth 20.00 50.00
RRBC Brodie Croyle 12.00 30.00
RRBF Brett Favre 125.00 200.00
RRBS Barry Sanders 75.00 150.00
RRDA Derek Anderson 10.00 25.00
RRDB Dick Butkus 40.00 80.00
RRDC Dallas Clark 15.00 40.00
RRDW DeMarcus Ware 12.00 30.00
RRFH Franco Harris 20.00 50.00
RRFT Fran Tarkenton 20.00 50.00
RRGS Gale Sayers 25.00 60.00
RRHW Herschel Walker
RRJA Joseph Addai 12.00 30.00
RRJE John Elway 75.00 150.00
RRJG Jeff Garcia 12.00 30.00
RRJN Joe Namath 60.00 120.00
RRJT Joe Theismann 20.00 50.00
RRKA Ken Anderson 15.00 40.00
RRKU Kurt Warner 40.00 80.00
RRKW Kellen Winslow Sr. 15.00 40.00
RRMB Marc Bulger 12.00 30.00
RRPH Paul Hornung 20.00 50.00
RRPM Peyton Manning 75.00 150.00
RRRC Roger Craig 15.00 40.00
RRRM Rod Woodson
RRSI Billy Sims 15.00 40.00
RRTM Tom Rathman
RRTR Tony Romo 50.00 100.00
RRWW Wes Welker 25.00 50.00

2008 SP Authentic Rookie Leatherheads Autographs

STATED PRINT RUN 50-150
LHAC Andre Caldwell/99 8.00 20.00
LHBB Brian Brohm/75 10.00 25.00
LHCH Chad Henne/150 10.00 25.00
LHCJ Chris Johnson/150 40.00 80.00
LHDA Donnie Avery/99 8.00 20.00
LHDJ DeSean Jackson/150 20.00 50.00
LHDK Dustin Keller/150 10.00 25.00
LHDM Darren McFadden/125 25.00 60.00
LHDT Devin Thomas/150 8.00 20.00
LHEB Earl Bennett/150 10.00 25.00
LHED Early Doucet/150 8.00 20.00
LHER Eddie Royal/150 10.00 25.00
LHFJ Felix Jones/150 15.00 40.00
LHHD Harry Douglas/150 8.00 20.00
LHJA Dexter Jackson/150 8.00 20.00
LHJB John David Booty/99 8.00 20.00
LHJC Jamaal Charles/150 15.00 40.00
LHJF Joe Flacco/150 40.00 80.00
LHJH James Hardy/150 8.00 20.00
LHJL Jake Long/150 10.00 25.00
LHJN Jordy Nelson/150 20.00 40.00
LHJS Jerome Simpson/150 10.00 25.00
LHKO Kevin O'Connell/99 8.00 20.00
LHKS Kevin Smith/150 10.00 25.00
LHMF Matt Forte/150 15.00 40.00
LHMK Malcolm Kelly/99 8.00 20.00
LHMM Mario Manningham/99 12.00 30.00
LHMR Matt Ryan/50 75.00 150.00
LHRM Rashard Mendenhall/99 25.00 60.00
LHRR Ray Rice/150 20.00 50.00
LHSS Steve Slaton/150 10.00 25.00
LHST Jonathan Stewart/99 15.00 40.00

2008 SP Authentic Sign of the Times

*GOLD VETS/25: .5X TO 1.2X BASIC AUTO
*GOLD ROOKIES/25: .8X TO 2X BASIC AUTO
GOLD PRINT RUN 25 SER.#'d SETS
UNPRICED QUAD PRINT RUN 10
SOTAB Alex Brink 5.00 12.00
SOTAC Andre Caldwell 4.00 10.00
SOTAM Anthony Morelli 4.00 10.00
SOTAP Adrian Peterson SP 50.00 100.00
SOTBB Brian Bosworth 20.00 40.00
SOTBD Bruce Davis 4.00 10.00
SOTBJ Bert Jones 5.00 12.00
SOTBS Barry Sanders 60.00 120.00
SOTCA Antoine Cason 5.00 12.00
SOTCC Calais Campbell 4.00 10.00
SOTCJ Chad Johnson SP 15.00 30.00
SOTDA Donnie Avery 4.00 10.00
SOTDT DeJuan Tribble 4.00 10.00
SOTEA Erik Ainge 5.00 12.00
SOTEM Eli Manning 30.00 60.00
SOTFD Fred Davis 5.00 12.00
SOTFH Franco Harris SP 20.00 40.00
SOTFO Frank Okam 3.00 8.00
SOTJH James Hardy 4.00 10.00
SOTJL Jack Lambert
SOTJT Joe Theismann 12.00 30.00
SOTLM Leodis McKelvin 4.00 10.00
SOTLT LaDainian Tomlinson 50.00 100.00
SOTMC Darren McFadden 20.00 40.00
SOTMF Marshall Faulk 20.00 40.00
SOTPH Paul Hornung 15.00 30.00
SOTPM Peyton Manning 60.00 120.00
SOTRW Roy Williams WR 10.00 25.00
SOTSA Bob Sanders
SOTSI Billy Sims 10.00 25.00
SOTST Bart Starr SP 75.00 150.00
SOTSY Steve Young SP 40.00 80.00
SOTTA Troy Aikman SP 50.00 100.00
SOTWO Rod Woodson 50.00 100.00
SOTWW Wes Welker

2008 SP Authentic Sign of the Times Duals

STATED PRINT RUN 20-100
AL Derek Anderson/50 12.00 30.00
Jamal Lewis
AM Ottis Anderson/20 50.00 100.00
Eli Manning
BG Davone Bess
Ryan Grice-Mullen
BP John David Booty/20 60.00 120.00
Adrian Peterson
CD Dominique Rodgers-Cromartie/99 20.00 40.00
Early Doucet
CH Dan Connor/80 12.00 30.00
A.J. Hawk
CK Andre Caldwell/99 10.00 25.00
Malcolm Kelly
DC Fred Davis/90 10.00 25.00
John Carlson
GH Bob Griese/50 15.00 40.00
Chad Henne
GW Frank Gore/50 30.00 60.00
Patrick Willis
HH Chad Henne/50 20.00 40.00
Mike Hart
JC Felix Jones/75 30.00 60.00
Jamaal Charles
JR Daryl Johnston/100 30.00 60.00
Tom Rathman
MD Kellen Davis/80 10.00 25.00
Marcus Monk
MJ Darren McFadden/20 40.00 100.00
Felix Jones
MM Peyton Manning/20 125.00 200.00
Eli Manning
MP DaJuan Morgan/50 8.00 20.00
Kenny Phillips
MS Rashard Mendenhall/50 30.00 60.00
Jonathan Stewart
RD JaMarcus Russell
Early Doucet
RM Ben Roethlisberger/20 60.00 120.00
Rashard Mendenhall
SB Barry Sanders/20 75.00 150.00
Kevin Smith
SF Gale Sayers/50 30.00 80.00
Matt Forte
TC Joe Theismann/50 EXCH 20.00 50.00
Jason Campbell
TF LaDainian Tomlinson/50 40.00 80.00
Marshall Faulk
TM LaDainian Tomlinson/20 40.00 100.00
Darren McFadden
WC Calais Campbell/80 12.00 30.00
DeMarcus Ware

2008 SP Authentic Sign of the Times Triples

STATED PRINT RUN 25-50
RJM Leodis McKelvin 10.00 25.00
Dominique Rodgers-Cromartie
Mike Jenkins
CBM Marion Barber EXCH 30.00 60.00
Rashard Mendenhall
Roger Craig
LJH DeSean Jackson EXCH 30.00 60.00
Marshawn Lynch
Lavelle Hawkins
MTP Y.A. Tittle 50.00 100.00
Eli Manning
Kenny Phillips
SSS Kevin Smith 75.00 150.00
Barry Sanders
Billy Sims

2008 SP Authentic SP Numbers Signatures

STATED PRINT RUN 15-150
NPAP Adrian Peterson/15 125.00 200.00
NPBB Brian Brohm/35 12.00 30.00
NPBG Bob Griese/35 15.00 40.00
NPBJ Bo Jackson/15 60.00 120.00
NPBO Brian Bosworth/150 15.00 40.00
NPCB Chuck Bednarik/150 12.00 30.00
NPCH Chad Henne/150 20.00 50.00
NPCL Chris Long/150 10.00 25.00
NPDB Dick Butkus/45 40.00 80.00
NPDM Don Maynard/150 12.00 30.00
NPDT Devin Thomas/150 8.00 20.00
NPEM Eli Manning/99 50.00 100.00
NPFA Marshall Faulk/35 25.00 50.00
NPFJ Felix Jones/150 20.00 50.00
NPFT Fran Tarkenton/35 30.00 60.00
NPJF Joe Flacco/150 40.00 100.00
NPJK Jim Kelly/15 40.00 80.00
NPJS Jeremy Shockey/35 12.00 30.00
NPJT Joe Theismann/150 15.00 40.00
NPKA Ken Anderson/150 12.00 30.00
NPKR Jerry Kramer/135 12.00 30.00
NPKS Kevin Smith/150 10.00 25.00
NPLH Lester Hayes/150 12.00 30.00
NPLT LaDainian Tomlinson/15 40.00 80.00
NPMB Marion Barber/35 15.00 40.00
NPMC Darren McFadden
NPMF Matt Forte/150 20.00 50.00
NPMR Matt Ryan/75 40.00 100.00
NPOA Ottis Anderson/150 10.00 25.00
NPPH Paul Hornung/135 15.00 40.00
NPPM Peyton Manning/99 75.00 150.00
NPPW Patrick Willis/150 10.00 25.00
NPRG Roman Gabriel/150 15.00 40.00
NPRM Rashard Mendenhall/150 25.00 50.00
NPRW Rod Woodson/135 40.00 100.00
NPSY Steve Young
NPTR Tony Romo/99 50.00 100.00
NPWI Roy Williams WR/15 20.00 40.00
NPYT Y.A. Tittle/135 15.00 40.00

2008 SP Authentic SP Star Signatures

SPSS1 Patrick Willis 10.00 25.00
SPSS2 Kenny Irons 8.00 20.00
SPSS3 Aaron Ross 8.00 20.00
SPSS4 Craig Davis 8.00 20.00
SPSS5 Chris Henry RB 10.00 25.00
SPSS6 Jerious Norwood 10.00 25.00
SPSS7 Kevin Boss 10.00 25.00
SPSS8 Yamon Figurs 8.00 20.00
SPSS9 Garrett Wolfe 10.00 25.00
SPSS10 Ahmad Bradshaw 10.00 25.00
SPSS11 Bernard Berrian 10.00 25.00
SPSS12 John Lynch 10.00 25.00
SPSS13 Greg Jennings 12.00 30.00
SPSS14 Anquan Boldin 10.00 25.00
SPSS15 Marques Colston 10.00 25.00
SPSS16 Willie Parker 12.00 30.00
SPSS17 Ted Ginn Jr. 10.00 25.00
SPSS18 Brandon Jacobs 12.00 30.00
SPSS19 Mark Clayton 10.00 25.00
SPSS20 Jerricho Cotchery 10.00 25.00
SPSS21 Champ Bailey 10.00 25.00
SPSS22 Darrell Jackson 8.00 20.00
SPSS23 Brady Quinn 10.00 25.00
SPSS24 John Beck 8.00 20.00
SPSS25 Derek Anderson 8.00 20.00

2009 SP Authentic

COMP.SET w/o RC's (100) 8.00 20.00
101-200 SP STATED ODDS 1:6
201-300 ROOKIE PRINT RUN 999
301-370 ROOKIE AU PRINT RUN 299-999
371-400 JSY AU RC PRINT RUN 475-999
EXCH EXPIRATION: 1/26/2012
1 Tony Romo .50 1.25
2 Marion Barber .25 .60
3 Roy Williams WR .25 .60
4 Jason Witten .30 .75
5 Eli Manning .30 .75
6 Brandon Jacobs .25 .60
7 Ahmad Bradshaw .25 .60
8 Steve Smith USC .25 .60
9 Donovan McNabb .30 .75
10 Brian Westbrook .25 .60
11 DeSean Jackson .25 .60
12 Jason Campbell .20 .50
13 Clinton Portis .25 .60
14 Santana Moss .25 .60
15 Trent Edwards .20 .50
16 Marshawn Lynch .25 .60
17 Terrell Owens .30 .75
18 Chad Pennington .25 .60
19 Ronnie Brown .25 .60
20 Ted Ginn .25 .60
21 Tom Brady .50 1.25
22 Randy Moss .30 .75
23 Wes Welker .30 .75
24 Jerod Mayo .25 .60
25 Kellen Clemens .20 .50
26 Thomas Jones .25 .60
27 Jerricho Cotchery .25 .60
28 Bart Scott .20 .50
29 Kurt Warner .30 .75
30 Anquan Boldin .25 .60
31 Larry Fitzgerald .30 .75
32 Shaun Hill .20 .50
33 Frank Gore .25 .60
34 Patrick Willis .25 .60
35 Matt Hasselbeck .25 .60
36 T.J. Houshmandzadeh .25 .60
37 Lofa Tatupu .25 .60
38 Marc Bulger .25 .60
39 Steven Jackson .25 .60
40 Donnie Avery .25 .60
41 Kyle Orton .25 .60
42 Eddie Royal .25 .60
43 Brian Dawkins .25 .60
44 Matt Cassel .25 .60
45 Larry Johnson .25 .60
46 Dwayne Bowe .25 .60
47 JaMarcus Russell .20 .50
48 Darren McFadden .30 .75
49 Nnamdi Asomugha .25 .60
50 Philip Rivers .30 .75
51 LaDainian Tomlinson .30 .75
52 Shawne Merriman .25 .60
53 Jay Cutler .30 .75
54 Matt Forte .30 .75
55 Brian Urlacher .30 .75
56 Daunte Culpepper .25 .60
57 Kevin Smith .25 .60
58 Calvin Johnson .30 .75
59 Aaron Rodgers .60 1.50
60 Ryan Grant .25 .60
61 Greg Jennings .30 .75
62 Brett Favre 2.50 6.00
63 Adrian Peterson .50 1.25
64 Bernard Berrian .25 .60
65 Joe Flacco .30 .75
66 Ray Lewis .30 .75
67 Ed Reed .25 .60
68 Carson Palmer .30 .75
69 Chad Ochocinco .25 .60
70 Laveranues Coles .20 .50
71 Brady Quinn .25 .60
72 Jamal Lewis .25 .60
73 Braylon Edwards .25 .60
74 Ben Roethlisberger .30 .75
75 James Harrison .30 .75
76 Troy Polamalu .30 .75
77 Matt Ryan .30 .75
78 Michael Turner .25 .60
79 Roddy White .25 .60
80 Jake Delhomme .25 .60
81 DeAngelo Williams .30 .75
82 Jonathan Stewart .25 .60
83 Drew Brees .30 .75
84 Reggie Bush .30 .75
85 Marques Colston .25 .60
86 Luke McCown .20 .50
87 Derrick Ward .20 .50
88 Antonio Bryant .20 .50
89 Matt Schaub .25 .60
90 Steve Slaton .25 .60
91 Andre Johnson .25 .60
92 Peyton Manning .50 1.25
93 Joseph Addai .30 .75
94 Reggie Wayne .25 .60
95 David Garrard .25 .60
96 Maurice Jones-Drew .25 .60
97 John Henderson .20 .50
98 Kerry Collins .25 .60
99 Chris Johnson .30 .75
100 LenDale White .25 .60
101 Archie Manning 2.00 5.00
102 Lem Barney 1.25 3.00
103 Steve Young 2.50 6.00
104 Dan Marino 4.00 10.00
105 Drew Bledsoe 1.50 4.00
106 Jim Kelly 2.00 5.00
107 Joe Theismann 2.00 5.00
108 Ken Anderson 1.50 4.00
109 Randall Cunningham 2.00 5.00
110 Mike Singletary 2.00 5.00
111 Terry Bradshaw 2.50 6.00
112 Warren Moon 2.00 5.00
113 Y.A. Tittle 2.00 5.00
114 Barry Sanders 3.00 8.00
115 Billy Sims 1.50 4.00
116 Christian Okoye 1.25 3.00
117 Earl Campbell 2.00 5.00
118 Franco Harris 2.00 5.00
119 Alan Page 1.50 4.00
120 Paul Hornung 2.00 5.00
121 Bob Griese 2.00 5.00
122 Doug Flutie 1.50 4.00
123 Thurman Thomas 2.00 5.00
124 Andre Reed 1.50 4.00
125 Phil Simms 1.50 4.00
126 Don Maynard 1.50 4.00
127 Herman Moore 1.25 3.00
128 Jerry Rice 3.00 8.00
129 Tim Brown 2.00 5.00
130 Steve Largent 2.00 5.00
131 Tony Romo 3.00 8.00
Jason Witten
132 Marion Barber 2.00 5.00
Felix Jones
133 Eli Manning 2.00 5.00
Brandon Jacobs
134 Donovan McNabb 2.00 5.00
Brian Westbrook
135 Jason Campbell 1.50 4.00
Clinton Portis
136 Marshawn Lynch 1.50 4.00
Trent Edwards
137 Ricky Williams 1.50 4.00
Ronnie Brown
138 Randy Moss 3.00 8.00
Tom Brady
139 Thomas Jones 1.50 4.00
Leon Washington
140 Anquan Boldin 2.00 5.00
Larry Fitzgerald
141 Takeo Spikes 1.50 4.00
Patrick Willis
142 Matt Hasselbeck 1.50 4.00
T.J. Houshmandzadeh
143 Donnie Avery 1.50 4.00
Steven Jackson
144 Eddie Royal 1.50 4.00
Brandon Marshall
145 Dwayne Bowe 1.50 4.00
Matt Cassel
146 JaMarcus Russell 2.00 5.00
Darren McFadden
147 Vincent Jackson 2.00 5.00
Philip Rivers
148 Darren Sproles 2.00 5.00
LaDainian Tomlinson
149 Jay Cutler 2.00 5.00
Matt Forte
150 Lance Briggs 2.00 5.00
Brian Urlacher
151 Calvin Johnson 2.00 5.00
Kevin Smith
152 Aaron Rodgers 4.00 10.00
Greg Jennings
153 Jared Allen 3.00 8.00
Adrian Peterson
154 Ed Reed 2.00 5.00
Ray Lewis
155 Chad Ochocinco 2.00 5.00
Carson Palmer
156 Brady Quinn 1.50 4.00
Braylon Edwards
157 Santonio Holmes 2.00 5.00
Ben Roethlisberger
158 Michael Turner 2.00 5.00
Matt Ryan
159 Jonathan Stewart 2.00 5.00
DeAngelo Williams
160 Drew Brees 2.50 6.00
Reggie Bush
161 Ronde Barber 1.25 3.00
Barrett Ruud
162 Andre Johnson 1.50 4.00
Steve Slaton
163 Peyton Manning 3.00 8.00
Reggie Wayne
164 David Garrard 1.50 4.00
Maurice Jones-Drew
165 Chris Johnson 2.00 5.00
LenDale White
166 Marion Barber 3.00 8.00
Jason Witten
Tony Romo
167 Brandon Jacobs 2.00 5.00
Eli Manning
Steve Smith USC
168 Brian Westbrook 2.00 5.00
Donovan McNabb
DeSean Jackson
169 Clinton Portis 1.50 4.00
Santana Moss
Jason Campbell
170 Terrell Owens 2.00 5.00
Lee Evans
Marshawn Lynch
171 Chad Pennington 1.50 4.00
Joey Porter
Ronnie Brown
172 Tom Brady 3.00 8.00
Randy Moss
Wes Welker
173 Dustin Keller 1.50 4.00
Thomas Jones
Jerricho Cotchery
174 Anquan Boldin 2.00 5.00
Larry Fitzgerald
Kurt Warner
175 Isaac Bruce 1.50 4.00
Frank Gore
Josh Morgan
176 Matt Hasselbeck 1.50 4.00
T.J. Houshmandzadeh
Julius Jones
177 Donnie Avery 1.50 4.00
Steven Jackson
Marc Bulger
178 Eddie Royal 1.50 4.00
Brandon Marshall
Kyle Orton
179 Larry Johnson 1.50 4.00
Matt Cassel
Dwayne Bowe
180 JaMarcus Russell 2.00 5.00
Michael Bush
Darren McFadden
181 LaDainian Tomlinson 2.00 5.00
Antonio Gates
Philip Rivers
182 Shawne Merriman 1.50 4.00
Antonio Cromartie
Quentin Jammer
183 Jay Cutler 2.00 5.00
Greg Olsen
Matt Forte
184 Brian Urlacher 2.00 5.00
Alex Brown
Lance Briggs
185 Kevin Smith 2.00 5.00
Calvin Johnson
Julian Peterson
186 Ryan Grant 4.00 10.00
Aaron Rodgers
Greg Jennings
187 Bernard Berrian 3.00 8.00
Adrian Peterson
Chester Taylor
188 Ed Reed 2.00 5.00
Ray Lewis
Dawan Landry
189 Chad Ochocinco 2.00 5.00
Laveranues Coles
Carson Palmer
190 Jamal Lewis 1.50 4.00
Braylon Edwards
Brady Quinn
191 Hines Ward 2.00 5.00
Willie Parker
Ben Roethlisberger
192 Troy Polamalu 2.00 5.00
James Harrison
LaMarr Woodley
193 Michael Turner 2.00 5.00
Roddy White
Matt Ryan
194 Steve Smith 2.00 5.00
DeAngelo Williams
Jonathan Stewart
195 Drew Brees 2.00 5.00
Reggie Bush
Marques Colston
196 Derrick Ward 1.50 4.00
Antonio Bryant
Kellen Winslow
197 Steve Slaton 1.50 4.00
Andre Johnson
Matt Schaub
198 Peyton Manning 3.00 8.00
Reggie Wayne
Dallas Clark
199 Maurice Jones-Drew 1.50 4.00
David Garrard
Marcedes Lewis
200 Kyle Vanden-Bosch 1.25 3.00
Cortland Finnegan
Keith Bulluck
201 Greg Toler RC 2.00 5.00
202 Herman Johnson RC 2.50 6.00
203 LaRod Stephens-Howling RC 4.00 10.00
204 Christopher Owens RC 2.50 6.00
205 Lawrence Sidbury RC 2.00 5.00
206 William Middleton RC 2.00 5.00
207 Paul Kruger RC 2.50 6.00
208 Lardarius Webb RC 3.00 8.00
209 Jason Phillips RC 2.50 6.00
210 Aaron Maybin RC 2.50 6.00
211 Andy Levitre RC 2.50 6.00
212 Nic Harris RC 2.50 6.00
213 Sherrod Martin RC 2.50 6.00
214 Corvey Irvin RC 2.00 5.00
215 Duke Robinson RC 2.00 5.00
216 Captain Munnerlyn RC 2.50 6.00
217 Henry Melton RC 2.00 5.00
218 Derek Kinder RC 2.00 5.00
219 D.J. Moore RC 2.50 6.00
220 Marcus Freeman RC 3.00 8.00
221 Jonathan Luigs RC 2.00 5.00
222 Morgan Trent RC 2.50 6.00
223 Kevin Huber RC 2.00 5.00
224 Fui Vakapuna RC 2.50 6.00
225 Freddie Brown RC 2.50 6.00
226 Ricky Jean-Francois RC 3.00 8.00
227 David Veikune RC 2.50 6.00
228 Coye Francies RC 2.00 5.00
229 Victor Butler RC 2.50 6.00
230 Jason Williams RC 3.00 8.00
231 Curtis Taylor RC 2.50 6.00
232 Clinton McDonald RC 2.00 5.00
233 Manuel Johnson RC 2.50 6.00
234 Ellis Lankster RC 2.00 5.00
235 Darcel McBath RC 2.50 6.00
236 David Bruton RC 2.50 6.00
237 Kareem Huggins RC 3.00 8.00
238 DeAndre Levy RC 3.00 8.00
239 Will Davis RC 2.00 5.00
240 Aaron Brown RC 3.00 8.00
241 T.J. Lang RC 2.50 6.00
242 Jamon Meredith RC 2.50 6.00
243 Jarius Wynn RC 3.00 8.00
244 Antoine Caldwell RC 2.00 5.00
245 Glover Quin RC 2.50 6.00
246 James Casey RC 2.50 6.00
247 Brice McCain RC 2.00 5.00
248 Jerraud Powers RC 2.50 6.00
249 Louis Murphy RC 3.00 8.00
250 Jaimie Thomas RC 2.00 5.00
251 Tiquan Underwood RC 2.50 6.00
252 Eben Britton RC 2.50 6.00
253 Terrance Knighton RC 2.50 6.00
254 Derek Cox RC 3.00 8.00
255 Zach Miller RC 2.50 6.00
256 Alex Magee RC 2.50 6.00
257 Donald Washington RC 2.50 6.00
258 Colin Brown RC 2.50 6.00
259 Javarris Williams RC 2.50 6.00
260 Jake O'Connell RC 2.00 5.00
261 John Matthews RC 2.50 6.00
262 John Parker Wilson RC 3.00 8.00
263 Spencer Adkins RC 2.00 5.00
264 Phil Loadholt RC 2.50 6.00
265 Jasper Brinkley RC 2.50 6.00
266 Jamarca Sanford RC 2.50 6.00
267 Ron Brace RC 2.50 6.00
268 Sebastian Vollmer RC 2.50 6.00
269 Brian Hoyer RC 3.00 8.00
270 Connor Barwin RC 3.00 8.00
271 Chip Vaughn RC 2.00 5.00
272 DeAndre Wright RC 2.00 5.00
273 Clint Sintim RC 3.00 8.00
274 William Beatty RC 2.00 5.00
275 Matt Slauson RC 3.00 8.00
276 Mike Mitchell RC 2.50 6.00
277 Matt Shaughnessy RC 2.50 6.00
278 Slade Norris RC 2.00 5.00
279 Fenuki Tupou RC 2.00 5.00
280 Brandon Gibson RC 3.00 8.00
281 Kraig Urbik RC 2.50 6.00
282 Joe Burnett RC 3.00 8.00
283 Evander Hood RC 4.00 10.00
284 Brandon Underwood RC 3.00 8.00
285 Louis Vasquez RC 2.50 6.00
286 Vaughn Martin RC 2.00 5.00
287 Kevin Ellison RC 2.50 6.00
288 Brandon Hughes RC 2.00 5.00
289 Ronald Talley RC 2.50 6.00
290 Scott McKillop RC 2.50 6.00
291 Bear Pascoe RC 2.50 6.00
292 Courtney Greene RC 2.00 5.00
293 Bradley Fletcher RC 2.50 6.00
294 Darell Scott RC 2.00 5.00
295 Shawn Nelson RC 2.50 6.00
296 Sammie Stroughter RC 3.00 8.00
297 Kyle Moore RC 2.50 6.00
298 Dominique Edison RC 2.00 5.00
299 David Johnson RC 2.50 6.00
300 Marko Mitchell RC 2.50 6.00
301 Asher Allen AU RC 4.00 10.00
302 Anthony Hill AU RC 3.00 8.00
303 Alex Mack AU RC 4.00 10.00
304 Bernard Scott AU RC 5.00 12.00
305 Julian Edelman AU RC 5.00 12.00
306 Cornelius Ingram AU RC 3.00 8.00
307 Cody Brown AU RC 3.00 8.00
308 DeAngelo Smith AU RC 5.00 12.00
309 Eric Wood AU RC 4.00 10.00
310 Gerald McRath AU RC 4.00 10.00
311 Jairus Byrd AU RC 8.00 20.00
312 Jarett Dillard AU RC 5.00 12.00
313 Malcolm Jenkins AU RC 5.00 12.00
314 Jarron Gilbert AU RC 4.00 10.00
315 Johnny Knox AU RC 10.00 25.00
316 Rashad Johnson AU RC 4.00 10.00
317 Kevin Barnes AU RC 4.00 10.00
318 Keenan Lewis AU RC 5.00 12.00
319 Kenny McKinley AU RC 6.00 15.00
320 Keith Null AU RC 4.00 10.00
321 Roy Miller AU RC 4.00 10.00
322 Mike Teel AU RC 6.00 15.00
323 Max Unger AU RC 4.00 10.00
324 Quinn Johnson AU RC 4.00 10.00
325 Quinten Lawrence AU RC 3.00 8.00
326 Mike Mickens AU RC 4.00 10.00
327 Richard Quinn AU RC 4.00 10.00
328 Ryan Mouton AU RC 4.00 10.00
329 Sean Smith AU RC 5.00 12.00
330 Tony Fiammetta AU RC 4.00 10.00
331 Austin Collie AU/799 RC 6.00 15.00
332 Andre Smith AU/799 RC 4.00 10.00
333 Travis Beckum AU/799 RC 4.00 10.00
334 Brooks Foster AU/799 RC 3.00 8.00
335 Cedric Peerman AU/799 RC 4.00 10.00
336 Darius Butler AU/799 RC 5.00 12.00
337 Eugene Monroe AU/799 RC 3.00 8.00
338 Fili Moala AU/799 RC 4.00 10.00
339 Frank Summers AU/799 RC 5.00 12.00
340 Gartrell Johnson AU/799 RC 3.00 8.00
341 Louis Delmas AU/799 RC 8.00 20.00
342 Mike Goodson AU/799 RC 5.00 12.00
343 Michael Johnson AU/799 RC 3.00 8.00
344 Curtis Painter AU/799 RC 8.00 20.00
345 Patrick Chung AU/799 RC 5.00 12.00
346 Chris Ogbonnaya AU/999 RC 4.00 10.00
347 Rashad Jennings AU/799 RC 6.00 15.00
348 Alphonso Smith AU/799 RC 4.00 10.00
349 Victor Harris AU/799 RC 5.00 12.00
350 William Moore AU/799 RC 5.00 12.00
351 Brian Cushing AU/299 RC 10.00 25.00
352 Brian Hartline AU/299 RC 10.00 25.00
354 B.J. Raji AU/299 RC 12.50 25.00
355 Brandon Tate AU/299 RC 10.00 25.00
356 Chase Coffman AU/299 RC 6.00 15.00
357 Clay Matthews AU/299 RC 40.00 80.00
359 Everette Brown AU/299 RC 6.00 15.00
360 Graham Harrell AU/299 RC 20.00 40.00
362 James Laurinaitis AU/299 RC 10.00 25.00
363 Larry English AU/299 RC 8.00 20.00
364 Terrance Taylor AU/999 RC 4.00 10.00
365 Michael Oher AU/299 RC 40.00 80.00
366 Rudy Carpenter AU/299 RC 6.00 15.00
367 Rey Maualuga AU/299 RC 8.00 20.00
368 Kaluka Maiava AU/999 RC 5.00 12.00
370 Vontae Davis AU/299 RC 8.00 20.00
371 Andre Brown JSY AU/999 RC 8.00 20.00
372 Aaron Curry JSY AU/999 RC 12.00 30.00
373 Rhett Bomar JSY AU/999 RC 10.00 25.00
374 Brandon Pettigrew JSY AU/999 RC 12.00 30.00
375 Brian Robiskie JSY AU/999 RC 12.00 30.00
376 Deon Butler JSY AU/999 RC 10.00 25.00
377 Chris Wells JSY AU/499 RC 20.00 50.00
378 Donald Brown JSY AU/499 RC 12.00 30.00
379 Darrius Heyward-Bey JSY AU/499 RC 12.0030.00
380 Derrick Williams JSY AU/999 RC 10.00 25.00
381 Glen Coffee JSY AU/999 RC 10.00 25.00
382 Hakeem Nicks JSY AU/999 RC 25.00 50.00
383 Josh Freeman JSY AU/999 RC 40.00 80.00
384 Juaquin Iglesias JSY AU/999 RC 10.00 25.00
385 Jeremy Maclin JSY AU/999 RC 25.00 50.00
386 Javon Ringer JSY AU/999 RC 12.00 30.00
387 Jason Smith JSY AU/999 RC 10.00 25.00
388 Kenny Britt JSY AU/999 RC 15.00 40.00
389 Knowshon Moreno JSY AU/499 RC 20.00 50.00
390 LeSean McCoy JSY AU/999 RC 50.00 100.00
391 Michael Crabtree JSY AU/499 RC 40.00 100.00
392 Mohamed Massaquoi JSY AU/999 RC 10.00 25.00
393 Mark Sanchez JSY AU/499 RC 75.00 150.00
394 Mike Thomas JSY AU/999 RC 12.00 30.00
395 Mike Wallace JSY AU/999 RC 40.00 80.00
396 Nate Davis JSY AU/999 RC 10.00 25.00
397 Percy Harvin JSY AU/999 RC 30.00 60.00
398 Patrick Turner JSY AU/999 RC 10.00 25.00
399 Pat White JSY AU/999 RC 12.00 30.00
400 Ramses Barden JSY AU/999 RC 8.00 20.00
401 Shonn Greene JSY AU/999 RC 15.00 40.00
402 Stephen McGee JSY AU/999 RC 12.00 30.00
403 Matthew Stafford JSY AU/499 RC 250.00 400.00
404 Tyson Jackson JSY AU/999 RC 10.00 25.00

2009 SP Authentic Bronze

*ROOKIES: .5X TO 1.2X BASIC CARDS
STATED PRINT RUN 150 SER.#'d SETS

2009 SP Authentic Gold

*201-300 ROOK/50: .8X TO 2X BASIC RC/999
201-300 ROOKIE PRINT RUN 50
*ROOKIE JSY AU/25: 1.2X TO 3X BASIC RC
371-404 ROOKIE JSY AU PRINT RUN 25
383 Josh Freeman JSY AU 250.00 500.00
390 LeSean McCoy JSY AU 175.00 300.00
393 Mark Sanchez JSY AU 350.00 600.00
397 Percy Harvin JSY AU 125.00 250.00
403 Matthew Stafford JSY AU 700.00 1,000.00

2009 SP Authentic Autographs

OVERALL AUTO ODDS 1:8 HOB
*GOLD/25: .6X TO 1.5X BASIC INSERTS
GOLD PRINT RUN 25 SER.#'d SETS
SPAB Andre Brown 3.00 8.00
SPAN Shawn Andrews 4.00 10.00
SPBC Brian Cushing 5.00 12.00
SPBO Brian Orakpo 8.00 20.00
SPBP Brandon Pettigrew 5.00 12.00
SPBU Deon Butler 4.00 10.00
SPCM Clay Matthews 30.00 60.00
SPCO Christian Okoye 6.00 15.00
SPDB Donald Brown 8.00 20.00
SPDW Derrick Williams 4.00 10.00
SPEC Earl Campbell 20.00 50.00
SPGC Greg Camarillo 5.00 12.00
SPHC Harry Carson 10.00 25.00
SPJF Josh Freeman 15.00 40.00
SPJP Joey Porter 6.00 15.00
SPJS Jason Smith 4.00 10.00
SPJY Jack Youngblood 10.00 25.00
SPLB Lem Barney 8.00 20.00
SPMW Mike Wallace 12.00 30.00
SPPT Patrick Turner 4.00 10.00
SPPW Pat White
SPQJ Quentin Jammer 6.00 15.00
SPRB Ramses Barden 3.00 8.00

SPSA Stacy Andrews	4.00	10.00
SPSG Shonn Greene	12.00	30.00
SPTJ Tyson Jackson	4.00	10.00
SPWA DeMarcus Ware	10.00	25.00
SPWM Warren Moon	20.00	50.00

2009 SP Authentic By the Letter Autographs

SER.#'d 3-90, TOTAL PRINT RUNS 21-98
EXCH EXPIRATION: 1/26/2012
LETTERS SPELL THE PLAYER'S TEAM NAME

BLSAH Albert Haynesworth/40*	15.00	40.00
BLSAK Alex Karras/72*	12.00	30.00
BLSAP Alan Page/42*	25.00	50.00
BLSBR Derrick Brooks/90*	25.00	50.00
BLSBW Brian Westbrook/24*	15.00	40.00
BLSCM Craig Morton/98*	10.00	25.00
BLSCO Christian Okoye/96*	12.00	30.00
BLSCP Clinton Portis/24*	15.00	40.00
BLSDB Drew Bledsoe/24*	30.00	60.00
BLSDE DeSean Jackson/45*	15.00	40.00
BLSDJ Deacon Jones/68*	12.00	30.00
BLSDR Drew Brees/24*	75.00	135.00
BLSDS Donnie Shell/64*	15.00	40.00
BLSDW DeMarcus Ware/35*	15.00	40.00
BLSGA Roman Gabriel/68*	12.00	30.00
BLSGC Greg Camarillo/96*	10.00	25.00
BLSHC Harry Carson/96*	15.00	40.00
BLSJA Jared Allen/98*	40.00	80.00
BLSJP Joey Porter/56*	15.00	40.00
BLSLB Lance Briggs/50*	25.00	50.00
BLSLE Lem Barney/95*	10.00	25.00
BLSLM Lance Moore/72*	40.00	80.00
BLSMC Matt Cassel/36*	15.00	40.00
BLSMD Maurice Jones-Drew/35*	15.00	40.00
BLSMF Matt Forte/30*	25.00	60.00
BLSMT Michael Turner/21*	25.00	50.00
BLSMW Mario Williams/50*	12.00	30.00
BLSPH Paul Hornung/63*	15.00	40.00
BLSPM Peyton Manning/60*	100.00	200.00
BLSPS Phil Simms/20*	15.00	40.00
BLSPW Patrick Willis/40*	30.00	60.00
BLSRB Rocky Bleier/64*	25.00	50.00
BLSRC Randall Cunningham/24*	40.00	80.00
BLSRL Ray Lewis/24*	125.00	200.00
BLSRW Reggie Wayne/35*	15.00	40.00
BLSSI Billy Sims/95*	12.00	30.00
BLSWO Rod Woodson/20* EXCH	40.00	80.00
BLSWP William Perry/70*	15.00	40.00

2009 SP Authentic Chirography

OVERALL AUTO ODDS 1:8 HOB
EXCH EXPIRATION: 1/26/2012
*GOLD/25: .6X TO 1.5X BASIC AUTO

CHAM Anthony Munoz	10.00	25.00
CHBC Brian Cushing	5.00	12.00
CHBP Brandon Pettigrew	5.00	12.00
CHBR Brian Robiskie	5.00	12.00
CHCF Glen Coffee	4.00	10.00
CHCM Clay Matthews	30.00	60.00
CHCP Clinton Portis	12.00	30.00
CHDB Drew Bledsoe	15.00	30.00
CHDQ D'Qwell Jackson	4.00	10.00
CHEM Eli Manning	30.00	60.00
CHFG Frank Gore	6.00	15.00
CHGC Greg Camarillo	5.00	12.00
CHJC Jason Campbell	6.00	15.00
CHJM Jerod Mayo	5.00	12.00
CHJP Joey Porter	6.00	15.00
CHJR Javon Ringer	5.00	12.00
CHJS Jason Smith	4.00	10.00
CHJY Jack Youngblood	10.00	25.00
CHKW Kurt Warner	40.00	80.00
CHMC Matt Cassel	10.00	25.00
CHML Marshawn Lynch	6.00	15.00
CHNA Nnamdi Asomugha	15.00	40.00
CHND Nate Davis	5.00	12.00
CHPH Percy Harvin	25.00	60.00
CHPM Peyton Manning	60.00	120.00
CHPW Pat White	8.00	20.00
CHRB Ronnie Brown	8.00	20.00
CHRM Rey Maualuga	6.00	15.00
CHSG Shonn Greene	15.00	40.00
CHSM Stephen McGee	6.00	15.00
CHST Matthew Stafford	60.00	120.00
CHSZ Mark Sanchez	30.00	80.00
CHTR Tony Romo	30.00	60.00

2009 SP Authentic Chirography Duals

STATED PRINT RUN 25-75

AJ Jared Allen/50	25.00	50.00
Tyson Jackson		
AP Aaron Curry/50	12.00	30.00
Patrick Willis		
BC Aaron Curry/75	12.00	30.00
Deon Butler		
BJ Joey Porter/75	12.00	30.00
Ronnie Brown		
BK Kurt Warner/50	25.00	50.00
Anquan Boldin		
BN Hakeem Nicks/75	12.00	30.00
Andre Brown		
CH Graham Harrell/50		
Michael Crabtree		
CS Mark Sanchez/50	50.00	100.00
Matt Cassel		
FD Nate Davis/50	15.00	40.00
Josh Freeman		
GC Frank Gore/50	15.00	40.00
Glen Coffee		
GS Glen Coffee/75	40.00	100.00
Shonn Greene		
JC Chris Wells/50	15.00	40.00
Javon Ringer		
JL Maurice Jones-Drew/50	12.00	30.00
Marshawn Lynch		
JS Jason Smith/75	10.00	25.00
James Laurinaitis		
MY Anthony Munoz/50	15.00	40.00
Ron Yary		
PC Clinton Portis/25	15.00	40.00
Jason Campbell		
RR Ramses Barden/75	10.00	25.00
Rhett Bomar		
RW Chris Wells/50	15.00	40.00
Brian Robiskie		
SC Matt Schaub/25	20.00	50.00
Steve Slaton		
SP Matthew Stafford/50	50.00	100.00
Brandon Pettigrew		
SW Steve Slaton/50	15.00	40.00
Pat White		
TC Fran Tarkenton/25	40.00	80.00
Randall Cunningham		
WC Aaron Curry/50	12.00	30.00
DeMarcus Ware		
WP Brandon Pettigrew/75	10.00	25.00
Derrick Williams		
WS Mark Sanchez/25	50.00	100.00
Pat White		
YO Merlin Olsen/35	30.00	60.00
Jack Youngblood		
XLIII Ben Roethlisberger/50	125.00	200.00
Kurt Warner		

2009 SP Authentic Chirography Triples

STATED PRINT RUN 10-35

BMD Rhett Bomar/35	12.00	30.00
Nate Davis		
Stephen McGee		
CLE Larry English/35	15.00	40.00
James Laurinaitis		
Aaron Curry		
CNB Michael Crabtree/25	40.00	80.00
Hakeem Nicks		
Kenny Britt		
OSU James Laurinaitis/25	30.00	60.00
Brian Robiskie		
Chris Wells		
PIT Evander Hood/25	50.00	100.00
Frank Summers		
Mike Wallace		
SDC Demetrius Byrd/35	12.00	30.00
Larry English		
Gartrell Johnson		
SSF Josh Freeman/25	125.00	250.00
Mark Sanchez		
Matthew Stafford		
USC Rey Maualuga/25	40.00	80.00
Clay Matthews		
Brian Cushing		

2009 SP Authentic Dynasties Autographs

STATED PRINT RUN 20 SER.#'d SETS

SADES Emmitt Smith	175.00	300.00
SADFH Franco Harris		
SADJH Jack Ham	40.00	80.00
SADJK Jerry Kramer	25.00	50.00
SADJR Jerry Rice	100.00	175.00
SADLG L.C. Greenwood	30.00	60.00
SADPH Paul Hornung	30.00	60.00
SADRB Rocky Bleier	40.00	80.00
SADRC Roger Craig	30.00	60.00
SADRL Ronnie Lott	50.00	100.00
SADSH Donnie Shell	30.00	60.00
SADSY Steve Young	50.00	100.00
SADTA Troy Aikman	60.00	120.00
SADTB Terry Bradshaw		
SADTR Tom Rathman	30.00	60.00

2009 SP Authentic Immortals Autographs

STATED PRINT RUN 25 SER.#'d SETS
EXCH EXPIRATION: 1/26/2012

ISBS Barry Sanders	75.00	150.00
ISFH Franco Harris		
ISJH Jack Ham	25.00	50.00
ISJT Joe Theismann	25.00	50.00
ISJY Jack Youngblood	25.00	50.00
ISKW Kellen Winslow Sr.	15.00	30.00
ISLB Lem Barney	15.00	30.00
ISLG L.C. Greenwood	25.00	50.00
ISLT Lawrence Taylor	30.00	60.00
ISMO Merlin Olsen	20.00	40.00
ISPS Phil Simms	25.00	50.00
ISRB Rocky Bleier	25.00	50.00
ISRC Randall Cunningham	25.00	50.00
ISRL Ronnie Lott	30.00	60.00
ISRY Ron Yary	15.00	30.00
ISSL Steve Largent	20.00	40.00
ISSY Steve Young	40.00	80.00
ISTA Troy Aikman	50.00	100.00
ISTT Thurman Thomas	25.00	50.00

2009 SP Authentic Immortals Autographs Duals

STATED PRINT RUN 15 SER.#'d SETS
EXCH EXPIRATION: 1/26/2012

SBS Lem Barney	25.00	50.00
Donnie Shell		
SHC Franco Harris	40.00	80.00
Earl Campbell		
SJO Merlin Olsen	30.00	60.00
Deacon Jones		
SMB Don Maynard	30.00	60.00
Fred Biletnikoff		
SSK Alex Karras	25.00	50.00
Bubba Smith		
SSS Barry Sanders	125.00	200.00
Gale Sayers		
STC Lawrence Taylor EXCH	40.00	80.00
Harry Carson		

2009 SP Authentic Rookie Super Patch Autographs

STATED PRINT RUN 99 SER.#'d SETS
EXCH EXPIRATION: 1/26/2012

RSPAC Aaron Curry	15.00	40.00
RSPBP Brandon Pettigrew	15.00	40.00
RSPBR Donald Brown	15.00	40.00
RSPCW Chris Wells	25.00	60.00
RSPDB Deon Butler	12.00	30.00
RSPDH Darrius Heyward-Bey	15.00	40.00
RSPDW Derrick Williams	12.00	30.00
RSPGC Glen Coffee	12.00	30.00
RSPHN Hakeem Nicks	30.00	80.00
RSPJF Josh Freeman	40.00	100.00
RSPJI Juaquin Iglesias	12.00	30.00
RSPJM Jeremy Maclin	25.00	60.00
RSPJR Javon Ringer	15.00	40.00
RSPJS Jason Smith	12.00	30.00
RSPKB Kenny Britt	20.00	50.00
RSPKM Knowshon Moreno	15.00	40.00
RSPLM LeSean McCoy	60.00	120.00
RSPMC Michael Crabtree	30.00	80.00
RSPMM Mohamed Massaquoi	12.00	30.00
RSPMS Matthew Stafford	125.00	200.00
RSPMW Mike Wallace	40.00	100.00
RSPND Nate Davis	12.00	30.00
RSPPH Percy Harvin	25.00	60.00
RSPPT Patrick Turner	12.00	30.00
RSPPW Pat White	15.00	40.00
RSPRB Ramses Barden	10.00	25.00
RSPSA Mark Sanchez	75.00	150.00
RSPSG Shonn Greene	25.00	60.00
RSPSM Stephen McGee	15.00	40.00
RSPTJ Tyson Jackson	12.00	30.00

2009 SP Authentic Sign of the Times

OVERALL AUTO ODDS 1:8 HOB
*GOLD/25: .6X TO 1.5X BASIC AUTO
EXCH EXPIRATION: 1/26/2012

STAB Anquan Boldin	8.00	20.00
STAC Aaron Curry	5.00	12.00
STAN Shawn Andrews	4.00	10.00
STBA Lem Barney	8.00	20.00
STBM Brandon Marshall	8.00	20.00
STDW DeMarcus Ware	10.00	25.00
STEV Lee Evans	5.00	12.00
STHN Hakeem Nicks	8.00	20.00
STJA Jared Allen	20.00	50.00
STJF Josh Freeman	12.00	30.00
STJR Javon Ringer	5.00	12.00
STKB Kenny Britt	6.00	15.00
STKM Knowshon Moreno	25.00	50.00
STKW Kurt Warner	40.00	80.00
STLB Lance Briggs	12.50	25.00
STLS LeSean McCoy	12.00	30.00
STMA Mark Sanchez	50.00	100.00
STMC Matt Cassel	10.00	25.00
STMF Matt Forte	8.00	20.00
STMJ Maurice Jones-Drew	8.00	20.00
STMS Matthew Stafford	50.00	100.00
STMW Mario Williams	5.00	12.00
STND Nate Davis	5.00	12.00
STPT Patrick Turner	4.00	10.00
STRB Ramses Barden	3.00	8.00
STRW Reggie Wayne	15.00	30.00
STRY Ron Yary	12.00	30.00
STSA Stacy Andrews	4.00	10.00
STSM Stephen McGee	6.00	15.00
STSS Steve Slaton	6.00	15.00
STTH Mike Thomas EXCH	5.00	12.00
STTJ Tyson Jackson	4.00	10.00
STTR Tony Romo	30.00	60.00

2009 SP Authentic Sign of the Times Duals

STATED PRINT RUN 10-100
EXCH EXPIRATION: 1/26/2012

AA Stacy Andrews/100	12.00	30.00
Shawn Andrews		
AW Jared Allen/50	40.00	80.00
Mario Williams		
BH Bernard Berrian/50	30.00	60.00
Percy Harvin		
BO Drew Brees/50	40.00	80.00
Kyle Orton		
CB Matt Cassel/50	15.00	40.00
Dwayne Bowe		
CM Randall Cunningham/25	40.00	80.00
Warren Moon		
DD Derrick Williams/100	10.00	25.00
Deon Butler		
FI Juaquin Iglesias/50	12.00	30.00
Matt Forte		
JC Aaron Curry/100	10.00	25.00
Tyson Jackson		
JM Jeremy Maclin/50	25.00	50.00
DeSean Jackson		
KK Alex Karras/50	30.00	60.00
Jerry Kramer		
LP Joey Porter/50	40.00	80.00
Ray Lewis		
LW Patrick Willis/50	50.00	100.00
Ronnie Lott		
MA Knowshon Moreno//75 EXCH	30.00	60.00
Robert Ayers		
MB Knowshon Moreno/50	30.00	60.00
Donald Brown		
NT Hakeem Nicks/100	15.00	40.00
Brandon Tate		
RS Matt Schaub/50	40.00	80.00
Tony Romo		
SG Shonn Greene/50	75.00	150.00
Mark Sanchez		
SS Mark Sanchez/25	100.00	200.00
Matthew Stafford		
SW Steve Slaton/50	15.00	40.00
Pat White		
TT Michael Turner/25	40.00	80.00
LaDainian Tomlinson		
WB Donald Brown/50	30.00	60.00
Chris Wells		
WC Dallas Clark/50	30.00	60.00
Reggie Wayne		
WF Matt Forte/50	15.00	40.00
Brian Westbrook		
WR Brian Robiskie/100	10.00	25.00
Brian Hartline		
NYG Harry Carson/25 EXCH	30.00	60.00
Lawrence Taylor		

2009 SP Authentic Sign of the Times Quads

STATED PRINT RUN 10-25

OLINE Ron Yary/25	20.00	40.00
Stacy Andrews		
Anthony Munoz		
Shawn Andrews		

2009 SP Authentic Sign of the Times Triples

STATED PRINT RUN 10-50
EXCH EXPIRATION: 1/26/2012

CMH Jeremy Maclin/25		
Percy Harvin		
Michael Crabtree		
HBN Kenny Britt/50	25.00	50.00
Darrius Heyward-Bey		
Hakeem Nicks		
SSF Matthew Stafford/25	175.00	350.00
Josh Freeman		
Mark Sanchez		
USC Brian Cushing/50	40.00	80.00
Rey Maualuga		
Clay Matthews		
WBM Donald Brown/25	40.00	80.00
Chris Wells		
LeSean McCoy		
49ER Michael Crabtree/25	60.00	120.00
Nate Davis		
Glen Coffee		
SBQB Peyton Manning/25	150.00	250.00
Ben Roethlisberger		
Eli Manning		

2009 SP Authentic Retail

COMP.SET w/o RC's (100)	8.00	20.00
1 Jason Campbell	.15	.40
2 Clinton Portis	.20	.50
3 Santana Moss	.20	.50
4 Kerry Collins	.20	.50
5 Chris Johnson	.25	.60
6 LenDale White	.20	.50
7 Luke McCown	.15	.40
8 Derrick Ward	.15	.40
9 Antonio Bryant	.15	.40
10 Marc Bulger	.20	.50
11 Steven Jackson	.20	.50
12 Donnie Avery	.20	.50
13 Matt Hasselbeck	.20	.50
14 T.J. Houshmandzadeh	.20	.50
15 Kyle Williams	.15	.40
16 Alex Smith QB	.20	.50
17 Frank Gore	.20	.50
18 Patrick Willis	.20	.50
19 Philip Rivers	.25	.60
20 LaDainian Tomlinson	.25	.60
21 Shawne Merriman	.20	.50
22 Ben Roethlisberger	.25	.60
23 James Harrison	.25	.60
24 Troy Polamalu	.25	.60
25 DeSean Jackson	.20	.50
26 Donovan McNabb	.25	.60
27 Brian Westbrook	.20	.50
28 JaMarcus Russell	.15	.40
29 Darren McFadden	.25	.60
30 Nnamdi Asomugha	.20	.50
31 Kellen Clemens	.15	.40
32 Thomas Jones	.20	.50
33 Jerricho Cotchery	.20	.50
34 Bart Scott	.15	.40
35 Eli Manning	.25	.60
36 Brandon Jacobs	.20	.50
37 Ahmad Bradshaw	.20	.50
38 Steve Smith USC	.20	.50
39 Drew Brees	.25	.60
40 Reggie Bush	.25	.60
41 Marques Colston	.20	.50
42 Tom Brady	.40	1.00
43 Randy Moss	.25	.60
44 Wes Welker	.25	.60
45 Jerod Mayo	.20	.50
46 Tarvaris Jackson	.20	.50
47 Adrian Peterson	.40	1.00
48 Bernard Berrian	.20	.50
49 Chad Pennington	.20	.50
50 Ronnie Brown	.20	.50
51 Ted Ginn Jr.	.20	.50
52 Matt Cassel	.20	.50
53 Larry Johnson	.20	.50
54 Dwayne Bowe	.20	.50
55 David Garrard	.20	.50
56 Maurice Jones-Drew	.20	.50
57 John Henderson	.15	.40
58 Peyton Manning	.40	1.00
59 Joseph Addai	.25	.60
60 Reggie Wayne	.20	.50
61 Matt Schaub	.20	.50
62 Steve Slaton	.20	.50
63 Andre Johnson	.20	.50
64 Aaron Rodgers	.50	1.25
65 Ryan Grant	.20	.50
66 Greg Jennings	.25	.60
67 Daunte Culpepper	.20	.50
68 Kevin Smith	.20	.50
69 Calvin Johnson	.25	.60
70 Kyle Orton	.20	.50
71 Eddie Royal	.20	.50
72 Brian Dawkins	.20	.50
73 Tony Romo	.40	1.00
74 Marion Barber	.20	.50
75 Roy Williams WR	.20	.50
76 Jason Witten	.25	.60
77 Brady Quinn	.20	.50
78 Jamal Lewis	.20	.50
79 Braylon Edwards	.20	.50
80 Carson Palmer	.25	.60
81 Chad Johnson	.20	.50
82 Laveranues Coles	.15	.40
83 Jay Cutler	.25	.60
84 Matt Forte	.25	.60
85 Brian Urlacher	.25	.60
86 Jake Delhomme	.20	.50
87 DeAngelo Williams	.25	.60
88 Jonathan Stewart	.20	.50
89 Trent Edwards	.15	.40
90 Marshawn Lynch	.20	.50
91 Terrell Owens	.25	.60
92 Joe Flacco	.25	.60
93 Ray Lewis	.25	.60
94 Ed Reed	.20	.50
95 Matt Ryan	.25	.60
96 Michael Turner	.20	.50
97 Roddy White	.20	.50
98 Kurt Warner	.25	.60
99 Anquan Boldin	.20	.50
100 Larry Fitzgerald	.25	.60
101 Aaron Maybin RC	1.00	2.50
102 Aaron Curry RC	1.25	3.00
103 Rhett Bomar RC	1.00	2.50
104 Brandon Pettigrew RC	1.25	3.00
105 Brian Robiskie RC	1.25	3.00
106 Deon Butler RC	1.00	2.50
107 Chris Wells RC	2.00	5.00
108 Donald Brown RC	1.25	3.00
109 Darrius Heyward-Bey RC	1.25	3.00
110 Derrick Williams RC	1.00	2.50
111 Kevin Ellison RC	1.00	2.50
112 Hakeem Nicks RC	2.00	5.00
113 Josh Freeman RC	2.50	6.00
114 Juaquin Iglesias RC	1.00	2.50
115 Jeremy Maclin RC	2.00	5.00
116 Javon Ringer RC	1.25	3.00
117 Jason Smith RC	1.00	2.50
118 Kenny Britt RC	1.50	4.00
119 Knowshon Moreno RC	1.25	3.00
120 LeSean McCoy RC	2.50	6.00
121 Michael Crabtree RC	2.50	6.00
122 Mohamed Massaquoi RC	1.00	2.50
123 Mark Sanchez RC	4.00	10.00
124 Mike Thomas RC	1.25	3.00
125 Sherrod Martin RC	2.50	6.00
126 Nate Davis RC	1.00	2.50
127 Percy Harvin RC	2.00	5.00
128 Patrick Turner RC	1.00	2.50
129 Pat White RC	1.25	3.00
130 Ramses Barden RC	.75	2.00
131 Shonn Greene RC	2.00	5.00
132 Louis Murphy RC	1.25	3.00
133 Matthew Stafford RC	6.00	15.00
134 Tyson Jackson RC	1.00	2.50
135 Andre Brown RC	.75	2.00
136 Antoine Caldwell RC	.75	2.00
137 Asher Allen RC	1.00	2.50
138 Austin Collie RC	1.25	3.00
139 Bear Pascoe RC	1.00	2.50
140 Bernard Scott RC	1.25	3.00
141 Bradley Fletcher RC	1.00	2.50
142 Brandon Gibson RC	1.25	3.00
143 Brian Hartline RC	1.25	3.00
144 Brooks Foster RC	.75	2.00
145 Cedric Peerman RC	1.00	2.50
146 Christopher Owens RC	1.00	2.50
147 Connor Barwin RC	1.25	3.00
148 Cornelius Ingram RC	.75	2.00
149 Tony Fiammetta RC	1.00	2.50
150 Curtis Painter RC	1.25	3.00
151 Darius Butler RC	1.25	3.00
152 David Veikune RC	1.00	2.50
153 DeAngelo Smith RC	1.00	2.50
154 Johnny Knox RC	2.00	5.00
155 Donald Washington RC	1.00	2.50
156 Eben Britton RC	1.00	2.50
157 Eric Wood RC	1.00	2.50
158 Evander Hood RC	1.50	4.00
159 Fili Moala RC	1.00	2.50
160 Gartrell Johnson RC	.75	2.00
161 Glen Coffee RC	1.00	2.50
162 Greg Toler RC	.75	2.00
163 Jairus Byrd RC	1.25	3.00
164 James Casey RC	1.00	2.50
165 Brandon Hughes RC	.75	2.00
166 Jamon Meredith RC	1.00	2.50
167 Jared Cook RC	1.25	3.00
168 Jarron Gilbert RC	1.00	2.50
169 Jason Phillips RC	1.00	2.50
170 Jason Williams RC	1.25	3.00
171 Jasper Brinkley RC	1.00	2.50
172 Jonathan Luigs RC	.75	2.00
173 Kaluka Maiava RC	1.25	3.00
174 Keenan Lewis RC	1.25	3.00
175 Kevin Barnes RC	1.00	2.50
176 Kraig Urbik RC	1.00	2.50
177 Larry English RC	1.25	3.00
178 Lawrence Sidbury RC	.75	2.00
179 Louis Delmas RC	1.25	3.00
180 Louis Vasquez RC	1.00	2.50
181 Marcus Freeman RC	1.25	3.00
182 Matt Shaughnessy RC	1.00	2.50
183 Max Unger RC	1.00	2.50
184 Mike Goodson RC	1.25	3.00
185 Mike Teel RC	1.25	3.00
186 Everette Brown RC	1.25	3.00
187 Mike Wallace RC	2.50	6.00
188 Nic Harris RC	1.00	2.50
189 Patrick Chung RC	1.25	3.00
190 Brian Orakpo RC	1.25	3.00
191 Paul Kruger RC	1.00	2.50
192 Phil Loadholt RC	1.00	2.50
193 Spencer Adkins RC	.75	2.00
194 Rashad Johnson RC	1.00	2.50
195 Robert Ayers RC	1.25	3.00
196 Sen'Derrick Marks RC	.75	2.00
197 Stephen McGee RC	1.25	3.00
198 Tom Brandstater RC	1.25	3.00
199 Travis Beckum RC	1.00	2.50
200 Victor Harris RC	1.25	3.00

2009 SP Authentic Retail Rookie Signatures

RANDOM INSERTS IN SP RETAIL PACKS

RSAB Alex Boone	5.00	12.00
RSAC Austin Collie	5.00	12.00
RSAM Alex Mack	4.00	10.00
RSBF Brooks Foster	3.00	8.00
RSBG Brandon Gibson	5.00	12.00
RSBH Brian Hartline	8.00	20.00
RSBR Brian Robiskie	5.00	12.00
RSBT Brandon Tate	5.00	12.00
RSCC Chase Coffman	4.00	10.00
RSCH Cullen Harper	5.00	12.00
RSDB Demetrius Byrd	4.00	10.00
RSEM Eugene Monroe	3.00	8.00
RSGH Graham Harrell	8.00	20.00
RSGJ Gartrell Johnson	3.00	8.00
RSHC Hunter Cantwell	5.00	12.00
RSJD Jarett Dillard	5.00	12.00
RSJE Malcolm Jenkins	5.00	12.00
RSJM Jeremy Maclin		
RSJR Javon Ringer	5.00	12.00
RSJW Jaison Williams	4.00	10.00
RSKL Keenan Lewis	5.00	12.00
RSKM Knowshon Moreno	30.00	60.00
RSMC Michael Crabtree		
RSMS Matthew Stafford		
RSQC Quan Cosby	4.00	10.00
RSRB Rhett Bomar	4.00	10.00
RSRJ Rashad Jennings	5.00	12.00
RSSA Mark Sanchez		
RSSG Shonn Greene	20.00	40.00
RSSM Stephen McGee	5.00	12.00
RSSS Sean Smith	5.00	12.00
RSTB Travis Beckum	4.00	10.00
RSTJ Tyson Jackson	4.00	10.00
RSVD Vontae Davis	5.00	12.00
RSVH Victor Harris	5.00	12.00
RSWM William Moore	5.00	12.00

2009 SP Authentic Retail Star Signatures

RANDOM INSERTS IN SP RETAIL PACKS

SRAB Alan Branch		
SRAH Ali Highsmith		
SRAT Aqib Talib		
SRAW Andre Woodson		
SRCB Cedric Benson		
SRCJ Chad Jackson		
SRCL Chris Long		
SRCS Chansi Stuckey		
SRDA Derek Anderson		
SRDC David Clowney		
SRDJ D'Qwell Jackson		
SRDL Donald Lee		
SRDM Darren McFadden		
SRDR Darrelle Revis		
SRDS DeSean Jackson		
SRDV Kellen Davis	5.00	12.00
SRER Eddie Royal	6.00	15.00
SRES Ernie Sims		
SRFT Fred Taylor		
SRGC Gosder Cherilus		
SRGO Greg Olsen		
SRGW Garrett Wolfe	5.00	12.00
SRJF Joe Flacco		
SRJH Justise Hairston		
SRJK Jordan Kent		
SRJM Jerod Mayo		
SRJO Calvin Johnson		
SRJS Jonathan Stewart		
SRKP Kenny Phillips		
SRLE Lee Evans		
SRLO Jake Long		
SRMB Marc Bulger		
SRML Matt Leinart		
SRMM Mario Manningham		
SRMR Matt Ryan		
SRMS Matt Schaub		
SROS Owen Schmitt		
SRPM Phillip Merling		
SRRB Reggie Bush		
SRRM Rashard Mendenhall	8.00	20.00
SRRU Martin Rucker		
SRSC Scott Chandler		
SRSH Jeremy Shockey		
SRSJ Jerome Simpson		
SRSK Sam Keller		
SRTG Ted Ginn Jr.		

2010 SP Authentic

COMP.SET w/o RC's (100) 8.00 20.00
101-134 RC JSY AU PRINT RUN 199-499
135-184 ROOKIE AU PRINT RUN 599
185-233 ROOKIE PRINT RUN 999
EXCH EXPIRATION: 2/17/2013

1 A.J. Hawk	.25	.60
2 Aaron Rodgers	.60	1.50
3 Adrian Peterson	.50	1.25
4 Ahmad Bradshaw	.25	.60
5 Alex Smith QB	.25	.60
6 Andre Johnson	.25	.60
7 Anquan Boldin	.25	.60
8 Ben Roethlisberger	.30	.75
9 Brady Quinn	.25	.60
10 Brandon Jacobs	.25	.60
11 Brandon Marshall	.25	.60
12 Braylon Edwards	.25	.60
13 Brent Celek	.25	.60
14 Brett Favre	.75	2.00
15 Calvin Johnson	.30	.75
16 Cadillac Williams	.25	.60
17 Carson Palmer	.25	.60
18 Cedric Benson	.25	.60
19 Chad Henne	.25	.60
20 Chad Johnson	.25	.60
21 Charles Woodson	.30	.75
22 Chris Johnson	.30	.75
23 Chris Wells	.25	.60
24 Dallas Clark	.25	.60
25 Darren McFadden	.25	.60
26 David Garrard	.25	.60
27 DeAngelo Williams	.25	.60
28 DeSean Jackson	.25	.60
29 Devery Henderson	.20	.50
30 Devin Hester	.30	.75
31 Donovan McNabb	.30	.75
32 Drew Brees	.30	.75
33 Eli Manning	.30	.75
34 Felix Jones	.25	.60
35 Frank Gore	.25	.60
36 Greg Jennings	.25	.60
37 Hines Ward	.25	.60
38 Peyton Hillis	.30	.75
39 Jamaal Charles	.25	.60
40 Jason Campbell	.25	.60
41 Jason Witten	.30	.75
42 Jay Cutler	.30	.75
43 Jerome Harrison	.20	.50
44 Joe Flacco	.30	.75
45 Jonathan Stewart	.25	.60
46 Joseph Addai	.25	.60
47 Josh Freeman	.30	.75
48 Hakeem Nicks	.25	.60
49 Kellen Winslow	.25	.60
50 Kevin Kolb	.25	.60
51 Knowshon Moreno	.25	.60
52 Kyle Orton	.25	.60
53 LaDainian Tomlinson	.30	.75
54 Larry Fitzgerald	.30	.75
55 Mario Manningham	.25	.60
56 Marion Barber	.25	.60
57 Mark Sanchez	.30	.75
58 Marques Colston	.25	.60
59 Matt Cassel	.25	.60
60 Matt Forte	.25	.60
61 Matt Hasselbeck	.20	.50
62 LeSean McCoy	.25	.60
63 Michael Vick	.40	1.00
64 Matt Ryan	.30	.75
65 Matt Schaub	.25	.60
66 Matthew Stafford	.30	.75
67 Maurice Jones-Drew	.25	.60
68 Michael Crabtree	.30	.75
69 Michael Turner	.20	.50
70 Miles Austin	.30	.75
71 Patrick Willis	.25	.60
72 Percy Harvin	.30	.75
73 Peyton Manning	.50	1.25
74 Philip Rivers	.30	.75
75 Pierre Thomas	.25	.60
76 Randy Moss	.30	.75
77 Rashard Mendenhall	.25	.60
78 Arian Foster	.25	.60
79 Ray Rice	.25	.60
80 Reggie Wayne	.25	.60
81 Ricky Williams	.25	.60
82 Roddy White	.25	.60
83 Ronnie Brown	.25	.60
84 Ryan Grant	.25	.60
85 Santana Moss	.25	.60
86 Santonio Holmes	.25	.60
87 Shonn Greene	.25	.60
88 Sidney Rice	.25	.60
89 Steve Smith USC	.25	.60
90 Austin Collie	.25	.60
91 Steven Jackson	.25	.60
92 Terrell Owens	.30	.75
93 Thomas Jones	.25	.60
94 Tom Brady	.50	1.25
95 Tony Romo	.40	1.00
96 Troy Polamalu	.30	.75
97 Vernon Davis	.25	.60
98 Vince Young	.20	.50
99 Vincent Jackson	.20	.50
100 Wes Welker	.30	.75
101 C.J. Spiller JSY AU/299 RC	30.00	80.00
102 Colt McCoy JSY AU/299 RC	30.00	80.00
103 Dez Bryant JSY AU/299 RC	60.00	120.00
104 Jahvid Best JSY AU/199 RC	40.00	80.00
105 Jimmy Clausen JSY AU/299 RC	12.00	30.00
106 Ryan Mathews JSY AU/299 RC	50.00	100.00
107 Sam Bradford JSY AU/299 RC	125.00	250.00
108 Tim Tebow JSY AU/299 RC	125.00	250.00
109 Demaryius Thomas JSY AU/199 RC	35.00	60.00
110 Ndamukong Suh JSY AU/299 RC	60.00	120.00
111 Gerald McCoy JSY AU/299 RC	12.00	30.00
112 Eric Berry JSY AU/299 RC	30.00	60.00
113 Damian Williams JSY AU/499 RC	10.00	25.00
114 Eric Decker JSY AU/199 RC	25.00	50.00
115 Armanti Edwards JSY AU/499 RC	10.00	25.00
116 Taylor Price JSY AU/499 RC	10.00	25.00
117 Mike Williams JSY AU/499 RC	25.00	60.00
118 Mike Kafka JSY AU/199 RC	25.00	50.00
119 Jonathan Dwyer JSY AU/499 RC	10.00	25.00
120 Rolando McClain JSY AU/499 RC	10.00	25.00
121 Dexter McCluster JSY AU/499 RC	10.00	25.00
122 Emmanuel Sanders JSY AU/199 RC	30.00	60.00
123 Jordan Shipley JSY AU/499 RC	10.00	25.00
124 Mardy Gilyard JSY AU/399 RC	10.00	25.00
125 Joe McKnight JSY AU/499 RC	12.00	30.00
126 Jermaine Gresham JSY AU/199 RC	15.00	40.00
127 Arrelious Benn JSY AU/399 RC	12.00	30.00
128 Rob Gronkowski JSY AU/499 RC	60.00	100.00
129 Toby Gerhart JSY AU/399 RC	10.00	25.00
130 Ben Tate JSY AU/499 RC	20.00	40.00
131 Montario Hardesty JSY AU/499 RC	15.00	40.00
132 Golden Tate JSY AU/499 RC	10.00	25.00
133 Marcus Easley JSY AU/499 RC	8.00	20.00
134 Andre Roberts JSY AU/499 RC	10.00	25.00
135 Carlos Dunlap AU RC EXCH	6.00	15.00
136 Russell Okung AU RC EXCH	8.00	20.00
137 Tyson Alualu AU RC	4.00	10.00
138 Brandon Graham AU RC	4.00	10.00
139 Earl Thomas AU RC EXCH	5.00	12.00
140 Jason Pierre-Paul AU RC	15.00	30.00
141 Derrick Morgan AU RC	4.00	10.00
142 Bryan Bulaga AU RC	6.00	15.00
143 Sean Weatherspoon AU RC	5.00	12.00
144 Kareem Jackson AU RC	5.00	12.00
145 Dan Williams AU RC	4.00	10.00
146 Jermaine Cunningham AU RC	5.00	12.00
147 Jared Odrick AU RC	6.00	15.00
148 David Nelson AU RC	10.00	20.00
149 Jerry Hughes AU RC	5.00	12.00
150 Sergio Kindle AU RC	5.00	12.00
151 Taylor Mays AU RC	5.00	12.00
152 Rennie Curran AU RC	4.00	10.00
153 Brian Price AU RC	6.00	15.00
154 John Skelton AU RC	8.00	20.00
155 Jonathan Crompton AU RC	4.00	10.00
156 Dan LeFevour AU RC	5.00	12.00
157 Joe Webb AU RC	8.00	20.00
158 Tony Pike AU RC	5.00	12.00
159 Sean Canfield AU RC	4.00	10.00
160 Zac Robinson AU RC	4.00	10.00
161 NaVorro Bowman AU RC	6.00	15.00
162 Lamarr Houston AU RC	4.00	10.00
163 Trent Williams AU RC	8.00	20.00
164 Sean Lee AU RC	7.50	15.00
165 Jarrett Brown AU RC	4.00	10.00
166 James Starks AU RC	15.00	30.00
167 Charles Scott AU RC	4.00	10.00
168 LeGarrette Blount AU RC	12.00	30.00
169 Koa Misi AU RC	4.00	10.00
170 Stafon Johnson AU RC	4.00	10.00
171 Jimmy Graham AU RC EXCH	25.00	50.00
172 Jacoby Ford AU RC	10.00	25.00
173 David Reed AU RC	4.00	10.00
174 Riley Cooper AU RC	6.00	15.00
175 Kerry Meier AU RC	4.00	10.00
176 Carlton Mitchell AU RC	4.00	10.00
177 Dezmon Briscoe AU RC	5.00	12.00
178 Antonio Brown AU RC	15.00	30.00
179 Patrick Robinson AU RC	5.00	12.00
180 Rusty Smith AU RC	6.00	15.00
181 Levi Brown AU RC	6.00	15.00
182 Anthony Dixon AU RC	8.00	20.00
183 Aaron Hernandez AU RC	20.00	40.00
184 Joe Haden AU RC	6.00	15.00
185 Brandon Spikes RC	3.00	8.00
186 Donald Butler RC	2.00	5.00
187 Phillip Dillard RC	2.00	5.00
188 Terrence Austin RC	2.50	6.00
189 Ed Wang RC	3.00	8.00
190 Stevenson Sylvester RC	3.00	8.00
191 Charles Brown RC	2.50	6.00
192 Anthony Davis RC	2.50	6.00
193 Mike Iupati RC	3.00	8.00
194 Maurkice Pouncey RC	5.00	12.00
195 Rodger Saffold RC	2.00	5.00
196 Chris Cook RC	3.00	8.00
197 Terrence Cody RC	2.50	6.00
198 Nate Allen RC	3.00	8.00
199 T.J. Ward RC	3.00	8.00
200 Morgan Burnett RC	3.00	8.00
201 Torell Troup RC	2.50	6.00
202 Ed Dickson RC	3.00	8.00
203 Linval Joseph RC	2.50	6.00
204 Daryl Washington RC	2.50	6.00
205 Javier Arenas RC	3.00	8.00
206 Jason Worilds RC	3.00	8.00
207 Brody Eldridge RC	3.00	8.00
208 Tony Moeaki RC	3.00	8.00
209 Mike Neal RC	3.00	8.00
210 Devin McCourty RC	3.00	8.00
211 Pat Angerer RC	3.00	8.00
212 Roddrick Muckelroy RC	2.50	6.00
213 Perry Riley RC	3.00	8.00
214 Kyle Wilson RC	3.00	8.00
215 Everson Griffen RC	3.00	8.00
216 Darryl Sharpton RC	2.00	5.00
217 Dennis Pitta RC	3.00	8.00
218 Thaddeus Gibson RC	2.50	6.00
219 Garrett Graham RC	2.50	6.00
220 Michael Hoomanawanui RC	3.00	8.00
221 John Conner RC	3.00	8.00
222 Deji Karim RC	3.00	8.00
223 Anthony McCoy RC	2.50	6.00
224 Trindon Holliday RC	3.00	8.00
225 David Gettis RC	3.00	8.00
226 Kyle Williams RC	3.00	8.00
227 Jevan Snead RC	3.00	8.00
228 Dorin Dickerson RC	2.00	5.00
229 Brandon LaFell RC	3.00	8.00
230 Major Wright RC	3.00	8.00
231 Andrew Quarless RC	3.00	8.00
232 Daniel Te'o-Nesheim RC	2.50	6.00
233 Nate Byham RC	2.50	6.00

2010 SP Authentic Gold

*ROOK JSY AU: 1X TO 2.5X RC JSY AU/399-499
*ROOK JSY AU: .8X TO 2X RC JSY AU/299
*ROOK JSY AU: .6X TO 1.5X RC JSY AU/199
*ROOKIE AU: 1.2X TO 3X BASE RC AU/599
*ROOKIE 185-233: 1X TO 2.5X BASE RC/999
GOLD PRINT RUN 25 SER.#'d SETS
EXCH EXPIRATION: 2/17/2013

102 Colt McCoy JSY AU	100.00	200.00
103 Dez Bryant JSY AU	200.00	400.00
106 Ryan Mathews JSY AU	100.00	200.00
107 Sam Bradford JSY AU	300.00	600.00
108 Tim Tebow JSY AU	350.00	600.00
109 Demaryius Thomas JSY AU	75.00	125.00
110 Ndamukong Suh JSY AU	150.00	300.00
112 Eric Berry JSY AU EXCH	125.00	250.00
128 Rob Gronkowski JSY AU	150.00	250.00

2010 SP Authentic Championship Patch Autographs

EXCH EXPIRATION: 2/17/2013

AH Aaron Hernandez	20.00	40.00
CM Colt McCoy	60.00	120.00
DM Derrick Morgan	6.00	15.00
DN David Nelson	12.00	30.00
DT Demaryius Thomas	10.00	25.00
ET Earl Thomas	20.00	40.00
HU Jerry Hughes	8.00	20.00
JC Jermaine Cunningham	8.00	20.00
JD Jonathan Dwyer EXCH	8.00	20.00
JH Joe Haden	15.00	40.00
JS Jordan Shipley	8.00	20.00
KJ Karoom Jackson	12.00	30.00
LB LeGarrette Blount	20.00	40.00
MG Mardy Gilyard EXCH	8.00	20.00
RC Riley Cooper	8.00	20.00
RM Rolando McClain	15.00	40.00
SK Sergio Kindle	8.00	20.00
TP Tony Pike	8.00	20.00
TT Tim Tebow	75.00	150.00
TW T.J. Ward	8.00	20.00

2010 SP Authentic Chirography

AB Anquan Boldin	10.00	25.00
AM Archie Manning	20.00	40.00
AP Adrian Peterson	60.00	120.00
BC Brent Celek	6.00	15.00
BM Brandon Marshall	8.00	20.00
BO Brian Orakpo	5.00	12.00
BR Ben Roethlisberger	50.00	100.00

BS Brandon Spikes 6.00 15.00
DB Drew Brees 30.00 60.00
DE Derrick Morgan 5.00 12.00
DF Doug Flutie 10.00 25.00
DM Dan Marino 75.00 150.00
DW Damian Williams 6.00 15.00
DX Dexter McCluster 6.00 15.00
ED Eric Decker 8.00 20.00
GJ Greg Jennings 15.00 30.00
GT Golden Tate 6.00 15.00
HE Herman Moore 5.00 12.00
HM Heath Miller 8.00 20.00
JA James Starks 10.00 25.00
JB Jahvid Best 10.00 25.00
JD Jonathan Dwyer 6.00 15.00
JF Joe Flacco 15.00 30.00
JG Jermaine Gresham 8.00 20.00
JM Joe McKnight 6.00 15.00
JO Josh Freeman 8.00 20.00
JS Jordan Shipley 6.00 15.00
KJ Kareem Jackson 6.00 15.00
KM Knowshon Moreno 6.00 15.00
MB Marion Barber 8.00 20.00
MF Matt Forte 6.00 15.00
MH Montario Hardesty 8.00 20.00
MJ Maurice Jones-Drew 8.00 20.00
MK Mike Kafka 5.00 12.00
MR Matt Ryan 25.00 50.00
MT Michael Turner 5.00 12.00
MW Mike Wallace 10.00 25.00
NA Nnamdi Asomugha 25.00 50.00
PW Patrick Willis 6.00 15.00
RC Rennie Curran 4.00 10.00
RM Ryan Mathews 12.00 30.00
RW Reggie Wayne 10.00 25.00
SG Shonn Greene 8.00 20.00
SK Sergio Kindle 5.00 12.00
TO Tony Pike 6.00 15.00
TP Taylor Price 6.00 15.00
TT Tim Tebow SP 125.00 200.00
WI DeAngelo Williams 8.00 20.00
YT Y.A. Tittle 12.00 30.00

2010 SP Authentic Chirography Duals

DUAL AUTO STATED PRINT RUN 5-15
BM Jahvid Best/15 40.00 80.00
Ryan Mathews
BW Lance Briggs/15 15.00 40.00
Patrick Willis
CR Roger Craig/15 15.00 40.00
Tom Rathman
GG Jermaine Gresham/15 30.00 60.00
Rob Gronkowski
HB Paul Hornung/15 40.00 80.00
Rocky Bleier
HG A.J. Hawk/15 20.00 50.00
Vernon Gholston
HM Clay Matthews/15 50.00 100.00
A.J. Hawk
HT Joe Theismann/15 40.00 80.00
Paul Hornung
JG Chris Johnson/15 20.00 50.00
David Garrard
JH T.J. Houshmandzadeh/15 20.00 50.00
Chad Johnson
KT Sergio Kindle/15 12.00 30.00
Earl Thomas
MB Steve Breaston/15 15.00 40.00
Mario Manningham
MH Heath Miller/15 30.00 60.00
Matt Schaub
MS Gerald McCoy/15 40.00 80.00
Ndamukong Suh
RC Brian Cushing/15 15.00 40.00
DeMeco Ryans
SR Dante Rosario/15 15.00 40.00
Jonathan Stewart
WB Mike Williams/15 30.00 60.00
Arrelious Benn
WS Jeremy Shockey/15 20.00 50.00
Reggie Wayne

2010 SP Authentic College Pride Patch Autographs

EXCH EXPIRATION: 2/17/2013
AB Arrelious Benn 10.00 25.00
AM Archie Manning
AP Adrian Peterson 60.00 120.00
BS Barry Sanders 75.00 150.00
BT Ben Tate 12.00 30.00
CH Chad Henne
CM Colt McCoy 60.00 120.00
CS C.J. Spiller 15.00 40.00
DF Doug Flutie
DT Demaryius Thomas 12.00 30.00
DW Damian Williams
EC Earl Campbell
EM Eli Manning 40.00 80.00
GT Golden Tate 10.00 25.00
JB Jahvid Best 15.00 40.00
JD Jonathan Dwyer 10.00 25.00
JM Joe McKnight 10.00 25.00
JS Jordan Shipley 10.00 25.00
MH Montario Hardesty 10.00 25.00
MK Mike Kafka 8.00 20.00
MO Craig Morton 12.00 30.00
MR Matt Ryan 25.00 50.00
MS Matt Schaub
PM Peyton Manning 125.00 200.00
RM Ryan Mathews
SB Sam Bradford 75.00 150.00
SI Billy Sims 10.00 25.00
TG Toby Gerhart 10.00 25.00
TT Tim Tebow 90.00 150.00

2010 SP Authentic Retro Rookie Patch Autographs

STATED PRINT RUN 5-25
EXCH EXPIRATION: 2/18/2013
AP Adrian Peterson/5
BB Brian Bosworth/15 40.00 80.00
BJ Bo Jackson/5
BS Barry Sanders/5
DB Drew Bledsoe/15
DS DeSean Jackson/15 30.00 60.00
EM Eli Manning/5
FG Frank Gore/35 EXCH 25.00 50.00
GJ Greg Jennings/15 40.00 80.00
HM Heath Miller/35 25.00 50.00
JE John Elway/5
KW Kellen Winslow Sr/15 30.00 60.00
MR Matt Ryan/5
PM Peyton Manning/5
PW Patrick Willis/35 30.00 60.00
RB Ronnie Brown/35 40.00 80.00
SI Billy Sims/15 30.00 60.00
SY Steve Young/15

2010 SP Authentic Rookie Super Jersey Autographs

STATED PRINT RUN 25 SER.#'d SETS
EXCH EXPIRATION: 2/17/2013
AB Arrelious Benn 15.00 40.00
AR Andre Roberts 15.00 40.00
BT Ben Tate 20.00 50.00
CM Colt McCoy 60.00 120.00
CS C.J. Spiller 25.00 60.00
DM Dexter McCluster 15.00 40.00
DT Demaryius Thomas 20.00 50.00
DW Damian Williams 15.00 40.00
ED Eric Decker 25.00 50.00
ES Emmanuel Sanders 15.00 40.00
GT Golden Tate 15.00 40.00
JB Jahvid Best 25.00 60.00
JC Jimmy Clausen 15.00 40.00
JD Jonathan Dwyer 15.00 40.00
JG Jermaine Gresham 20.00 50.00
JM Joe McKnight 15.00 40.00
JS Jordan Shipley 15.00 40.00
MC Rolando McClain 15.00 40.00
ME Marcus Easley 12.00 30.00
MG Mardy Gilyard 15.00 40.00
MH Montario Hardesty 20.00 50.00
MK Mike Kafka 15.00 40.00
MW Mike Williams EXCH 40.00 80.00
NS Ndamukong Suh 75.00 150.00
RG Rob Gronkowski 40.00 80.00
RM Ryan Mathews 30.00 80.00
SB Sam Bradford 150.00 300.00
TG Toby Gerhart 15.00 40.00
TP Taylor Price 15.00 40.00
TT Tim Tebow 200.00 350.00

2010 SP Authentic Sign of the Times

AB Arrelious Benn 6.00 15.00
AH Aaron Hernandez 10.00 25.00
AP Adrian Peterson 60.00 120.00
AR Andre Roberts 5.00 12.00
BC Brian Cushing 5.00 12.00
BG Brandon Graham 5.00 12.00
BS Billy Sims 8.00 20.00
CJ Chris Johnson 10.00 25.00
CS C.J. Spiller 10.00 25.00
DM Donovan McNabb 15.00 30.00
DT Demaryius Thomas 8.00 20.00
EB Eric Berry 15.00 30.00
EC Earl Campbell 15.00 30.00
EM Eli Manning 40.00 80.00
ES Emmanuel Sanders 6.00 15.00
ET Earl Thomas 5.00 12.00
FG Frank Gore 6.00 15.00
GT Golden Tate 6.00 15.00
JC Jason Campbell 6.00 15.00
JF Jacoby Ford 6.00 15.00
JH Jerry Hughes 5.00 12.00
JI Jimmy Clausen 6.00 15.00
JL James Laurinaitis 6.00 15.00
JO Joe Haden 6.00 15.00
JP Jason Pierre-Paul 8.00 20.00
JS John Skelton 5.00 12.00
KB Kenny Britt 5.00 12.00
KK Kevin Kolb 8.00 20.00
LB Lance Briggs 6.00 15.00
LE Lee Evans 6.00 15.00
LT LaDainian Tomlinson 15.00 30.00
ME Marcus Easley 5.00 12.00
MG Mardy Gilyard 5.00 12.00
MI Mike Williams 10.00 25.00
MM Mario Manningham 6.00 15.00
MO Michael Oher 10.00 25.00
MS Mark Sanchez
MW Mike Sims-Walker 5.00 12.00
PM Peyton Manning 100.00 175.00
RC Riley Cooper 5.00 12.00
RG Rob Gronkowski 20.00 40.00
RO Rolando McClain 6.00 15.00
SB Sam Bradford 75.00 150.00
SL Steve Largent 15.00 30.00
SW Sean Weatherspoon 5.00 12.00
TG Toby Gerhart 6.00 15.00
TM Taylor Mays 6.00 15.00
TR Tony Romo 25.00 50.00
VJ Vincent Jackson 5.00 12.00
WM Warren Moon 30.00 60.00

2010 SP Authentic Sign of the Times Duals

DUAL AUTO PRINT RUN 5-15
BH Paul Hornung/15 40.00 80.00
Tim Brown
BL Marshawn Lynch/15 20.00 50.00
Jahvid Best
BM Jahvid Best/15 40.00 80.00
Ryan Mathews
CM Clay Matthews/15 50.00 100.00
Brian Cushing
CS Mark Sanchez/15 30.00 60.00
Matt Cassel
DJ Damian Williams/15 15.00 40.00
Joe McKnight
GH Rob Gronkowski/15 50.00 100.00
Aaron Hernandez
GL James Laurinaitis/15 20.00 50.00
Vernon Gholston
HG Santonio Holmes/15 20.00 50.00
Ted Ginn
HL A.J. Hawk/15 30.00 60.00
James Laurinaitis
JM DeSean Jackson/15 20.00 50.00
Jeremy Maclin
KJ DeSean Jackson/15 20.00 50.00
Kevin Kolb
ME Mike Wallace/15 30.00 60.00
Emmanuel Sanders
MS Brandon Marshall/15 15.00 40.00
Mike Sims-Walker
RS Sean Weatherspoon/15 15.00 40.00
Rolando McClain
SC Earl Campbell/15 125.00 200.00
Barry Sanders
SJ Bo Jackson/15 60.00 120.00
Billy Sims
SL Steve Smith USC/15 20.00 50.00
Matt Leinart
TB Arrelious Benn/15 20.00 50.00
Golden Tate
WC Wes Welker/15 60.00 120.00
Michael Crabtree
WG Frank Gore/15 20.00 50.00
Reggie Wayne
WT Damian Williams/15 15.00 40.00
Golden Tate

2011 SP Authentic

COMP.SET w/o SP's (100) 8.00 20.00
101-200 FUTURE WATCH ODDS 1:4
201-234 JSY AU PRINT RUN 299-699
1 Tyrod Taylor .50 1.25
2 Anthony Castonzo .30 .75
3 Mark Herzlich .40 1.00
4 Da'Quan Bowers .50 1.25
5 Colin McCarthy .40 1.00
6 Dwayne Harris .50 1.25
7 Jeremy Kerley .50 1.25
8 Nick Fairley .60 1.50
9 Jamie Harper .50 1.25
10 Greg Little .50 1.25
11 Lester Jean .40 1.00
12 Bruce Carter .50 1.25
13 Ras-I Dowling .50 1.25
14 Aaron Williams .40 1.00
15 Austin Pettis .40 1.00
16 Anthony Allen .30 .75
17 Ryan Kerrigan .50 1.25
18 D.J. Williams .50 1.25
19 Pat Devlin .50 1.25
20 Drake Nevis .50 1.25
21 Andy Dalton 1.25 3.00
22 Nate Solder .50 1.25
23 Brandon Saine .50 1.25
24 Ronald Johnson .40 1.00
25 Allen Bailey .40 1.00
26 Cameron Jordan .40 1.00
27 Prince Amukamara .50 1.25
28 Ryan Whalen .40 1.00
29 Dane Sanzenbacher .50 1.25
30 Von Miller .60 1.50
31 Terrence Toliver .40 1.00
32 Kelvin Sheppard .50 1.25
33 Armon Binns .40 1.00
34 DeMarco Murray 1.00 2.50
35 Damien Berry .40 1.00
36 Stevan Ridley .50 1.25
37 Virgil Green .40 1.00
38 Vai Taua .40 1.00
39 Edmond Gates .40 1.00
40 Aldon Smith .75 2.00
41 Noel Devine .50 1.25
42 Akeem Ayers .40 1.00
43 Leonard Hankerson .50 1.25
44 Bilal Powell .30 .75
45 Ricky Stanzi .60 1.50
46 Jarvis Jenkins .30 .75
47 Greg Salas .50 1.25
48 Jerrel Jernigan .40 1.00
49 Mike Pouncey .50 1.25
50 Jeremy Beal .40 1.00
51 Cecil Shorts .40 1.00
52 T.J. Yates .60 1.50
53 Mason Foster .50 1.25
54 Derrick Locke .40 1.00
55 Jimmy Smith .50 1.25
56 Nathan Enderle .50 1.25
57 J.J. Watt .60 1.50
58 Titus Young .60 1.50
59 Vincent Brown .50 1.25
60 Luke Stocker .40 1.00
61 Quan Sturdivant .50 1.25
62 Evan Royster .50 1.25
63 Jake Locker 1.25 3.00
64 Christian Ponder 1.00 2.50
65 Jock Sanders .40 1.00
66 Ross Homan .50 1.25
67 Cameron Heyward .50 1.25
68 Lance Kendricks .40 1.00
69 Jeff Maehl .50 1.25
70 Roy Helu 1.00 2.50
71 Graig Cooper .40 1.00
72 Colin Kaepernick .60 1.50
73 Dion Lewis .50 1.25
74 Niles Paul .50 1.25
75 Delone Carter .40 1.00
76 Tyron Smith .60 1.50
77 Adrian Clayborn .50 1.25
78 Marvin Austin .40 1.00
79 Kendall Hunter .50 1.25
80 Daniel Thomas .50 1.25
81 Marcell Dareus .50 1.25
82 Greg Jones .40 1.00
83 Stephen Paea .50 1.25
84 Jordan Todman .30 .75
85 Mikel Leshoure .50 1.25
86 Shane Vereen .50 1.25
87 Jacquizz Rodgers .50 1.25
88 Tandon Doss .40 1.00
89 A.J. Green 1.00 2.50
90 Kyle Rudolph .50 1.25
91 Torrey Smith .60 1.50
92 Ryan Mallett 1.00 2.50
93 John Clay .50 1.25
94 Cam Newton 3.00 8.00
95 Mark Ingram 1.00 2.50
96 Jonathan Baldwin .50 1.25
97 Ryan Williams .60 1.50
98 Blaine Gabbert .75 2.00
99 Randall Cobb .60 1.50
100 Julio Jones 1.00 2.50
101 Austin Pettis FW .60 1.50
102 Lance Kendricks FW .60 1.50
103 Andy Dalton FW 2.00 5.00
104 Mikel Leshoure FW .75 2.00
105 Daniel Thomas FW .75 2.00
106 Marcell Dareus FW .75 2.00
107 D.J. Williams FW .75 2.00
108 Colin Kaepernick FW 1.00 2.50
109 Stevan Ridley FW .75 2.00
110 Cameron Heyward FW .75 2.00
111 Noel Devine FW .75 2.00
112 Evan Royster FW .75 2.00
113 John Clay FW .75 2.00
114 Kelvin Sheppard FW .75 2.00
115 Jake Locker FW 2.00 5.00
116 Delone Carter FW .60 1.50
117 Tyrod Taylor FW .75 2.00
118 Von Miller FW 1.00 2.50
119 Christian Ponder FW 1.50 4.00
120 Anthony Castonzo FW .50 1.25
121 Dane Sanzenbacher FW .75 2.00
122 J.J. Watt FW 1.00 2.50
123 Dwayne Harris FW .75 2.00
124 Kendall Hunter FW .75 2.00
125 Virgil Green FW .60 1.50
126 Luke Stocker FW .60 1.50
127 Terrence Toliver FW .60 1.50
128 Greg Little FW .75 2.00
129 Greg Jones FW .60 1.50
130 Quan Sturdivant FW .75 2.00
131 Derrick Locke FW .60 1.50
132 Vincent Brown FW .75 2.00
133 Adrian Clayborn FW .75 2.00
134 Ras-I Dowling FW .75 2.00
135 Greg Salas FW .75 2.00
136 Jerrel Jernigan FW .60 1.50
137 Niles Paul FW .75 2.00
138 Prince Amukamara FW .75 2.00
139 Leonard Hankerson FW .75 2.00
140 Pat Devlin FW .75 2.00
141 Roy Helu FW 1.50 4.00
142 Jeremy Kerley FW .75 2.00
143 Ronald Johnson FW .60 1.50
144 Titus Young FW 1.00 2.50
145 Ricky Stanzi FW 1.00 2.50
146 DeMarco Murray FW 1.50 4.00
147 Tyron Smith FW 1.00 2.50
148 Cameron Jordan FW .60 1.50
149 A.J. Green FW 1.50 4.00
150 Julio Jones FW 1.50 4.00
151 Cam Newton FW 4.00 10.00
152 Ryan Mallett FW 1.50 4.00
153 Shane Vereen FW .75 2.00
154 Mark Ingram FW 1.50 4.00
155 Cecil Shorts FW .60 1.50
156 Jonathan Baldwin FW .75 2.00
157 Randall Cobb FW 1.00 2.50
158 Tandon Doss FW .60 1.50
159 Torrey Smith FW 1.00 2.50
160 Kyle Rudolph FW .75 2.00
161 Blaine Gabbert FW 1.25 3.00
162 Ryan Williams FW 1.00 2.50
163 Nick Fairley FW 1.00 2.50
164 Jordan Todman FW .50 1.25
165 Dion Lewis FW .75 2.00
166 Jacquizz Rodgers FW .75 2.00
167 Edmond Gates FW .60 1.50
168 Da'Quan Bowers FW .75 2.00
169 Drew Brees FW 1.25 3.00
170 Steven Jackson FW 1.00 2.50
171 Aaron Rodgers FW 2.00 5.00
172 Rocket Ismail FW 1.00 2.50
173 Troy Aikman FW 1.50 4.00
174 Bob Griese FW 1.25 3.00
175 Tony Dorsett FW 1.25 3.00
176 Roman Gabriel FW 1.00 2.50
177 Bo Jackson FW 1.50 4.00
178 John Elway FW 2.00 5.00
179 Paul Hornung FW 1.25 3.00
180 Warren Moon FW 1.00 2.50
181 Jerry Rice FW 2.00 5.00
182 Gale Sayers FW 1.25 3.00
183 George Rogers FW .75 2.00
184 Tim Brown FW 1.25 3.00
185 Thurman Thomas FW 1.25 3.00
186 Doug Flutie FW 1.00 2.50
187 John Cappelletti FW .75 2.00
188 Bernie Kosar FW 1.00 2.50
189 Kellen Winslow Sr. FW 1.00 2.50
190 Jim Kelly FW 1.25 3.00
191 Barry Sanders FW 2.00 5.00
192 Steve Young FW 1.50 4.00
193 Floyd Little FW .75 2.00
194 Dan Marino FW 2.50 6.00
195 Charles White FW .75 2.00
196 Brian Bosworth FW 1.00 2.50
197 Earl Campbell FW 1.25 3.00
198 Drew Bledsoe FW 1.00 2.50
199 Mike Singletary FW 1.25 3.00
200 Billy Sims FW 1.00 2.50
201 Jake Locker JSY AU/299 75.00 150.00
202 Mark Ingram JSY AU/299 40.00 80.00
203 A.J. Green JSY AU/299 50.00 100.00
204 Cam Newton JSY AU/299 250.00 500.00
205 Blaine Gabbert JSY AU/299 50.00 100.00
206 Ryan Williams JSY AU/299 30.00 60.00
207 Julio Jones JSY AU/299 50.00 100.00
208 Ryan Mallett JSY AU/299 50.00 120.00
209 Randall Cobb JSY AU/699 15.00 40.00
210 Greg Salas JSY AU/699 10.00 25.00
211 Jerrel Jernigan JSY AU/699 8.00 20.00
212 Leonard Hankerson JSY AU/699 10.00 25.00
213 Kendall Hunter JSY AU/699 15.00 40.00
214 Niles Paul JSY AU/699 8.00 20.00
215 Terrence Toliver JSY AU/699 8.00 20.00
216 DeMarco Murray JSY AU/699 40.00 80.00
217 Tandon Doss JSY AU/699 8.00 20.00
218 Ronald Johnson JSY AU/699 8.00 20.00
219 Greg Little JSY AU/699 12.00 30.00
220 Titus Young JSY AU/699 15.00 40.00
221 Vincent Brown JSY AU/699 12.00 30.00
222 Mikel Leshoure JSY AU/699 15.00 40.00
223 Jacquizz Rodgers JSY AU/699 12.00 30.00
224 Jonathan Baldwin JSY AU/699 12.00 30.00
225 Jordan Todman JSY AU/699 8.00 20.00
226 Shane Vereen JSY AU/699 10.00 25.00
227 Torrey Smith JSY AU/699 15.00 40.00
228 Austin Pettis JSY AU/699 10.00 25.00
229 Christian Ponder JSY AU/699 30.00 80.00
230 Kyle Rudolph JSY AU/699 12.00 30.00
231 Daniel Thomas JSY AU/699 12.00 30.00
232 Andy Dalton JSY AU/699 75.00 150.00
233 Colin Kaepernick JSY AU/699 20.00 40.00
234 Delone Carter JSY AU/699 10.00 25.00
MCPATCH Marques Colston Patch/4

2011 SP Authentic Autographs Gold

*1-100 ROOKIE/15: 1.2X TO 3X BASIC AU
1-100 ROOKIE PRINT RUN 15
101-200 FUTURE WATCH PRINT RUN 5-25
OVERALL AUTO STATED ODDS 1:12
21 Andy Dalton/15 150.00 250.00
34 DeMarco Murray/15 150.00 250.00
63 Jake Locker/15 175.00 300.00
64 Christian Ponder/15 125.00 200.00
72 Colin Kaepernick/15 60.00 120.00
89 A.J. Green/15 125.00 200.00
92 Ryan Mallett/15 60.00 120.00
94 Cam Newton/15 600.00 800.00
95 Mark Ingram/15 125.00 200.00
98 Blaine Gabbert/15 75.00 150.00
100 Julio Jones/15 125.00 200.00
101 Austin Pettis FW/35 12.00 30.00
102 Lance Kendricks FW/35 10.00 25.00
103 Andy Dalton FW/35 125.00 200.00
104 Mikel Leshoure FW/5
105 Daniel Thomas FW/35 25.00 50.00
106 Marcell Dareus FW/35 20.00 40.00
107 D.J. Williams FW/35 12.00 30.00
108 Colin Kaepernick FW/35 60.00 120.00
109 Stevan Ridley FW/35 20.00 50.00
110 Cameron Heyward FW/35 12.00 30.00
111 Noel Devine FW/35 12.00 30.00
112 Evan Royster FW/35 15.00 40.00
113 John Clay FW/35 12.00 30.00
114 Kelvin Sheppard FW/35 12.00 30.00
115 Jake Locker FW/5
116 Delone Carter FW/35 15.00 40.00
117 Tyrod Taylor FW/35 25.00 60.00
118 Von Miller FW/35 40.00 80.00
119 Christian Ponder FW/5
120 Anthony Castonzo FW/35 8.00 20.00
121 Dane Sanzenbacher FW/35 30.00 60.00
122 J.J. Watt FW/35 30.00 60.00
123 Dwayne Harris FW/35 12.00 30.00
124 Kendall Hunter FW/5
125 Virgil Green FW/5
126 Luke Stocker FW/35 10.00 25.00
127 Terrence Toliver FW/35 10.00 25.00
128 Greg Little FW/35 12.00 30.00
129 Greg Jones FW/35 10.00 25.00
130 Quan Sturdivant FW/35 12.00 30.00
131 Derrick Locke FW/5
132 Vincent Brown FW/35 15.00 40.00
133 Adrian Clayborn FW/35 25.00 50.00
134 Ras-I Dowling FW/35 12.00 30.00
135 Greg Salas FW/35 15.00 40.00
136 Jerrel Jernigan FW/35 10.00 25.00
137 Niles Paul FW/35 12.00 30.00
138 Prince Amukamara FW/35 20.00 50.00
139 Leonard Hankerson FW/5
140 Pat Devlin FW/35 20.00 50.00
141 Roy Helu FW/35 50.00 100.00
142 Jeremy Kerley FW/35 12.00 30.00
143 Ronald Johnson FW/35 10.00 25.00
144 Titus Young FW/5
145 Ricky Stanzi FW/5
146 DeMarco Murray FW/35 125.00 250.00
147 Tyron Smith FW/35
148 Cameron Jordan FW/35 10.00 25.00
149 A.J. Green FW/5
150 Julio Jones FW/35 100.00 200.00
151 Cam Newton FW/5
152 Ryan Mallett FW/5
153 Shane Vereen FW/5
154 Mark Ingram FW/5
155 Cecil Shorts FW/5
156 Jonathan Baldwin FW/5
157 Randall Cobb FW/5
158 Tandon Doss FW/5
159 Torrey Smith FW/5
160 Kyle Rudolph FW/5
161 Blaine Gabbert FW/5
162 Ryan Williams FW/5
163 Nick Fairley FW/5
164 Jordan Todman FW/5
165 Dion Lewis FW/35 12.00 30.00
166 Jacquizz Rodgers FW/5
167 Edmond Gates FW/35
168 Da'Quan Bowers FW/35 20.00 50.00
169 Drew Brees FW/5
170 Steven Jackson FW/5
171 Aaron Rodgers FW/5
172 Rocket Ismail FW/5
173 Troy Aikman FW/5
174 Bob Griese FW/5
175 Tony Dorsett FW/5
176 Roman Gabriel FW/5
177 Bo Jackson FW/5
178 John Elway FW/5
179 Paul Hornung FW/5
180 Warren Moon FW/5
181 Jerry Rice FW/5
182 Gale Sayers FW/5
183 George Rogers FW/35 20.00 40.00
184 Tim Brown FW/5
185 Thurman Thomas FW/5
187 John Cappelletti FW/35 20.00 40.00
188 Bernie Kosar FW/5
189 Kellen Winslow Sr. FW/5
190 Jim Kelly FW/5
191 Barry Sanders FW/5
192 Steve Young FW/5
193 Floyd Little FW/35
194 Dan Marino FW/5
195 Charles White FW/35 15.00 30.00
196 Brian Bosworth FW/5
197 Earl Campbell FW/5
198 Drew Bledsoe FW/5
199 Mike Singletary FW/5
200 Billy Sims FW/35 25.00 50.00

2011 SP Authentic Autographs

OVERALL AUTO STATED ODDS 1:12
GROUP A ANNC'D ODDS 1:818
GROUP B ANNC'D ODDS 1:552
GROUP C ANNC'D ODDS 1:236
GROUP D ANNC'D ODDS 1:145
GROUP E ANNC'D ODDS 1:47
EXCH EXPIRATION: 1/12/2014
1 Tyrod Taylor E 8.00 20.00
2 Anthony Castonzo E 2.50 6.00
3 Mark Herzlich B 6.00 15.00
4 Da'Quan Bowers B 20.00 40.00
5 Colin McCarthy D 3.00 8.00
6 Dwayne Harris D 4.00 10.00
7 Jeremy Kerley C 4.00 10.00
8 Nick Fairley A EXCH 10.00 20.00
9 Jamie Harper A 8.00 20.00
10 Greg Little C 6.00 15.00
11 Lester Jean A EXCH 20.00 40.00
12 Bruce Carter A 8.00 20.00
13 Ras-I Dowling E 4.00 10.00
14 Aaron Williams A 8.00 20.00
15 Austin Pettis D 4.00 10.00
16 Anthony Allen E 2.50 6.00
17 Ryan Kerrigan C 5.00 12.00
18 D.J. Williams E 4.00 10.00
19 Pat Devlin E 5.00 12.00
20 Drake Nevis D 4.00 10.00
21 Andy Dalton C 50.00 100.00
22 Nate Solder E 4.00 10.00
23 Brandon Saine E 8.00 20.00
24 Ronald Johnson C 3.00 8.00
25 Allen Bailey E 3.00 8.00
26 Cameron Jordan D 3.00 8.00
27 Prince Amukamara E 6.00 15.00
28 Ryan Whalen E 3.00 8.00
29 Dane Sanzenbacher D 6.00 15.00
30 Von Miller E 15.00 30.00
31 Terrence Toliver D 3.00 8.00
32 Kelvin Sheppard E 4.00 10.00
33 Armon Binns E 3.00 8.00
34 DeMarco Murray D 30.00 60.00
35 Damien Berry D 3.00 8.00
36 Stevan Ridley A 20.00 40.00
37 Virgil Green C 4.00 10.00
38 Vai Taua E EXCH 3.00 8.00
39 Edmond Gates D EXCH 3.00 8.00
40 Aldon Smith B 20.00 40.00
41 Noel Devine E 5.00 12.00
42 Akeem Ayers C 5.00 12.00
43 Leonard Hankerson A 12.00 30.00
44 Bilal Powell D 2.50 6.00
45 Ricky Stanzi A 12.00 30.00
46 Jarvis Jenkins C 6.00 15.00
47 Greg Salas B 6.00 15.00
48 Jerrel Jernigan E 3.00 8.00
49 Mike Pouncey E 5.00 12.00
50 Jeremy Beal B 3.00 8.00
51 Cecil Shorts E 3.00 8.00
52 T.J. Yates A EXCH 15.00 30.00
53 Mason Foster E 5.00 12.00
54 Derrick Locke E 3.00 8.00
55 Jimmy Smith D 6.00 15.00
56 Nathan Enderle C 5.00 12.00
57 J.J. Watt C 8.00 20.00
58 Titus Young A 20.00 40.00
59 Vincent Brown E 5.00 12.00
60 Luke Stocker E 5.00 12.00
61 Quan Sturdivant E 4.00 10.00
62 Evan Royster E 6.00 15.00
63 Jake Locker B 75.00 150.00
64 Christian Ponder B 30.00 60.00
65 Jock Sanders E 4.00 10.00
66 Ross Homan D 6.00 15.00
67 Cameron Heyward E 5.00 12.00
68 Lance Kendricks E 3.00 8.00
69 Jeff Maehl D EXCH 6.00 15.00
70 Roy Helu E 12.50 25.00
71 Graig Cooper E 3.00 8.00
73 Dion Lewis D 4.00 10.00
74 Niles Paul C 6.00 15.00
75 Delone Carter E 4.00 10.00
76 Tyron Smith B EXCH 12.00 30.00
77 Adrian Clayborn C 8.00 20.00
79 Kendall Hunter C 8.00 20.00
80 Daniel Thomas B 10.00 25.00
81 Marcell Dareus A 15.00 30.00
82 Greg Jones E 3.00 8.00
83 Stephen Paea D 4.00 10.00
84 Jordan Todman A 8.00 20.00
85 Mikel Leshoure B 25.00 50.00
86 Shane Vereen A 8.00 20.00
87 Jacquizz Rodgers B EXCH 8.00 20.00
88 Tandon Doss A 20.00 40.00
89 A.J. Green A 40.00 80.00
90 Kyle Rudolph A 8.00 20.00
91 Torrey Smith C 15.00 30.00
92 Ryan Mallett A 40.00 80.00
93 John Clay C 4.00 10.00
94 Cam Newton A 400.00 600.00
95 Mark Ingram B 30.00 60.00
96 Jonathan Baldwin A 12.00 30.00
97 Ryan Williams A 25.00 50.00
98 Blaine Gabbert B 25.00 50.00
99 Randall Cobb A 15.00 30.00
100 Julio Jones B 40.00 80.00

2011 SP Authentic Sign of the Times

OVERALL AUTO STATED ODDS 1:12
GROUP A ANNC'D ODDS 1:1021
GROUP B ANNC'D ODDS 1:677
GROUP C ANNC'D ODDS 1:252
GROUP D ANNC'D ODDS 1:45
STAB Allen Bailey D 3.00 8.00
STAC Adrian Clayborn D 6.00 15.00
STAD Andy Dalton C 25.00 50.00
STAG A.J. Green A 25.00 50.00
STAI Troy Aikman A 30.00 60.00
STAM Mike Alstott A 12.00 30.00
STAP Alan Page A 10.00 25.00
STAR Aaron Rodgers A 150.00 225.00
STAU Austin Pettis D 3.00 8.00
STBB Brian Bosworth A 20.00 40.00
STBC Bruce Carter D 4.00 10.00
STBG Blaine Gabbert A 20.00 40.00
STBI Armon Binns D 3.00 8.00
STBJ Bo Jackson A 60.00 120.00
STBK Bernie Kosar A 15.00 30.00
STBO Bob Griese A 20.00 40.00
STBR Tim Brown A 25.00 50.00
STBS Barry Sanders A 60.00 120.00
STCA John Cappelletti B 8.00 20.00
STCH Cameron Heyward D 4.00 10.00
STCJ Cameron Jordan D 3.00 8.00
STCK Colin Kaepernick D 8.00 20.00
STCL John Clay C 4.00 10.00
STCM Colin McCarthy D 3.00 8.00
STCN Cam Newton A 125.00 200.00
STCP Christian Ponder C 15.00 40.00
STCS Cecil Shorts A 6.00 15.00
STCW Charles White B 6.00 15.00
STDB Da'Quan Bowers B 8.00 20.00
STDC Delone Carter B 5.00 12.00
STDH Dwayne Harris D 4.00 10.00
STDL Derrick Locke D 3.00 8.00
STDM DeMarco Murray C 20.00 40.00
STDN Drake Nevis C 4.00 10.00
STDS Dane Sanzenbacher B 8.00 20.00
STDT Daniel Thomas C 6.00 15.00
STDW D.J. Williams D 4.00 10.00
STEC Earl Campbell A 20.00 40.00
STEG Edmond Gates B 3.00 8.00
STER Evan Royster D 4.00 10.00
STFL Floyd Little B 10.00 25.00
STGJ Greg Jones D 5.00 12.00
STGL Greg Little D 4.00 10.00
STGP Greg Pruitt C 8.00 20.00
STGR George Rogers B 8.00 20.00
STGS Greg Salas D 4.00 10.00
STHE Roy Helu D 8.00 20.00
STJB Jonathan Baldwin A 6.00 15.00
STJE John Elway A 75.00 150.00
STJJ Jerrel Jernigan D 3.00 8.00
STJK Jeremy Kerley D 4.00 10.00
STJL Jake Locker A 40.00 80.00
STJO Julio Jones A 25.00 50.00
STJR Jerry Rice A 125.00 200.00
STJS Jimmy Smith B 4.00 10.00
STKE Jim Kelly A 25.00 50.00
STKH Kendall Hunter D 5.00 12.00
STKJ Keith Jackson B 12.50 25.00
STKS Kelvin Sheppard D 4.00 10.00
STLE Dion Lewis B 4.00 10.00
STLH Leonard Hankerson B 6.00 15.00
STLK Lance Kendricks D 3.00 8.00
STLR Lee Roy Jordan B 8.00 20.00
STLS Lee Roy Selmon B 25.00 50.00
STMD Marcell Dareus B 8.00 20.00
STMH Mark Herzlich D 3.00 8.00
STMI Mark Ingram A 30.00 60.00
STML Mikel Leshoure A 6.00 15.00
STMO Craig Morton B 6.00 15.00
STND Noel Devine D 6.00 15.00
STNE Nathan Enderle C 4.00 10.00
STNF Nick Fairley A 6.00 15.00
STNP Niles Paul D 5.00 12.00
STPA Prince Amukamara D 6.00 15.00
STPD Pat Devlin C 6.00 15.00
STPH Paul Hornung A 20.00 40.00
STRC Roger Craig A 8.00 20.00
STRD Ras-I Dowling D 4.00 10.00
STRG Roman Gabriel A 8.00 20.00
STRH Ross Homan D 5.00 12.00
STRJ Ronald Johnson D 3.00 8.00
STRK Ryan Kerrigan D 5.00 12.00
STRM Ryan Mallett A 25.00 50.00
STRS Ricky Stanzi A 8.00 20.00
STRW Ryan Whalen D 3.00 8.00
STRY Ron Yary B 6.00 15.00
STSI Billy Sims B 8.00 20.00
STSM Tyron Smith C 6.00 15.00
STSP Stephen Paea D 4.00 10.00
STST Luke Stocker B 5.00 12.00
STSY Steve Young A 25.00 50.00
STTA Tyrod Taylor D 15.00 30.00
STTH Thurman Thomas A 15.00 40.00
STTS Torrey Smith B 8.00 20.00
STTT Terrence Toliver D 3.00 8.00
STTY Titus Young C 6.00 15.00
STVB Vincent Brown D 4.00 10.00
STVM Von Miller C 8.00 20.00
STWI Ryan Williams A 15.00 30.00

2011 SP Authentic Sign of the Times Duals

STATED PRINT RUN 15 SER.#'d SETS
ST2AY Steve Young 50.00 100.00
Troy Aikman
ST2BH Tim Brown 30.00 60.00
Paul Hornung
ST2CS Billy Sims 40.00 80.00
Earl Campbell
ST2DR Evan Royster 12.00 30.00
Noel Devine
ST2FD Marcell Dareus 15.00 40.00
Nick Fairley
ST2GJ Julio Jones 60.00 120.00
A.J. Green
ST2GL Blaine Gabbert 50.00 120.00
Jake Locker
ST2GN Blaine Gabbert 100.00 200.00
Cam Newton
ST2HP Roy Helu 40.00 80.00
Niles Paul
ST2IJ Mark Ingram 60.00 120.00
Julio Jones
ST2JH Leonard Hankerson 15.00 40.00
Ronald Johnson
ST2JL Julio Jones 50.00 100.00
Greg Little
ST2KK Bernie Kosar 50.00 100.00
Jim Kelly
ST2MH DeMarco Murray 60.00 120.00
Kendall Hunter
ST2ML Jake Locker 50.00 120.00
Ryan Mallett
ST2MT Daniel Thomas 50.00 100.00
DeMarco Murray
ST2RW George Rogers 15.00 40.00
Charles White
ST2SL Greg Little 15.00 40.00
Torrey Smith
ST2SW Charles White 15.00 40.00
Billy Sims
ST2YP Austin Pettis 15.00 40.00
Titus Young

2011 SP Authentic Signature Threads

STATED PRINT RUN 25-99
THAD Andy Dalton/25 150.00 250.00
THAG A.J. Green/25 100.00 200.00
THAP Austin Pettis/99 12.00 30.00
THBG Blaine Gabbert/25 40.00 80.00
THCN Cam Newton/25 400.00 700.00
THCP Christian Ponder/25 60.00 120.00
THDC Delone Carter/99 15.00 40.00
THDM DeMarco Murray/25 125.00 200.00
THDT Daniel Thomas/25 20.00 50.00
THGL Greg Little/99 15.00 40.00
THGS Greg Salas/99 15.00 40.00
THJB Jonathan Baldwin/25 20.00 50.00
THJE Jerrel Jernigan/99 12.00 30.00
THJJ Julio Jones/25 125.00 200.00
THJL Jake Locker/25 125.00 250.00
THJR Jacquizz Rodgers/25 25.00 60.00
THJT Jordan Todman/25 12.00 30.00
THKH Kendall Hunter/99 15.00 40.00
THKR Kyle Rudolph/99 15.00 40.00
THLH Leonard Hankerson/25 20.00 50.00
THMI Mark Ingram/25 75.00 150.00
THML Mikel Leshoure/25 25.00 60.00
THNP Niles Paul/99 15.00 40.00
THRC Randall Cobb/99 20.00 50.00
THRJ Ronald Johnson/99 12.00 30.00
THRM Ryan Mallett/25 75.00 150.00
THRW Ryan Williams/25 30.00 80.00
THSV Shane Vereen/25 20.00 50.00
THTD Tandon Doss/25 15.00 40.00
THTS Torrey Smith/25 30.00 80.00
THTT Terrence Toliver/99 12.00 30.00
THTY Titus Young/99 20.00 50.00
THVB Vincent Brown/99 15.00 40.00

2007 SP Chirography

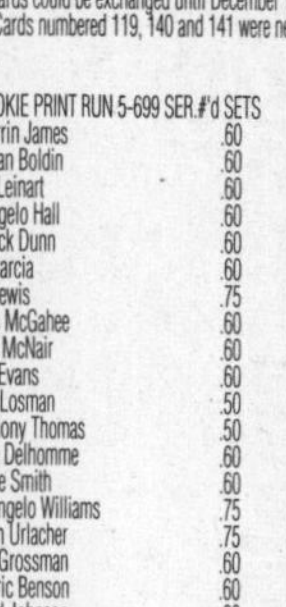

This 147-card set was released in December, 2007. The set was issued in three-card packs with an $50 SRP which came eight packs to a box. The first 100 cards in this set feature veterans in team alphabetical order while the final 47 cards in this set feature signed Rookie Cards. Those cards were signed in quantities between 75 and 699 cards and we have notated that information in our checklist. In addition, a few players did not return their signatures in time for pack out and those cards could be exchanged until December 10, 2009. Cards numbered 119, 140 and 141 were never issued.

AU ROOKIE PRINT RUN 5-699 SER.#'d SETS
1 Edgerrin James .60 1.50
2 Anquan Boldin .60 1.50
3 Matt Leinart .60 1.50
4 DeAngelo Hall .60 1.50
5 Warrick Dunn .60 1.50
6 Jeff Garcia .60 1.50
7 Ray Lewis .75 2.00
8 Willis McGahee .60 1.50
9 Steve McNair .60 1.50
10 Lee Evans .60 1.50
11 J.P. Losman .50 1.25
12 Anthony Thomas .50 1.25
13 Jake Delhomme .60 1.50
14 Steve Smith .60 1.50
15 DeAngelo Williams .75 2.00
16 Brian Urlacher .75 2.00
17 Rex Grossman .60 1.50
18 Cedric Benson .60 1.50
19 Chad Johnson .60 1.50
20 Carson Palmer .60 1.50
21 Rudi Johnson .60 1.50
22 Jamal Lewis .60 1.50
23 Derek Anderson .50 1.25
24 Braylon Edwards .60 1.50
25 Julius Jones .50 1.25
26 Tony Romo 1.00 2.50
27 Terrell Owens .75 2.00
28 Marion Barber .60 1.50
29 Jay Cutler .75 2.00
30 Travis Henry .60 1.50
31 Javon Walker .60 1.50
32 Tatum Bell .50 1.25
33 Jon Kitna .50 1.25
34 Roy Williams WR .60 1.50
35 Brett Favre 1.50 4.00
36 A.J. Hawk .60 1.50
37 Greg Jennings .75 2.00
38 Ahman Green .60 1.50
39 Andre Johnson .60 1.50

40 Matt Schaub	.60	1.50
41 Peyton Manning	1.25	3.00
42 Reggie Wayne	.60	1.50
43 Joseph Addai	.60	1.50
44 Marvin Harrison	.75	2.00
45 David Garrard	.60	1.50
46 Fred Taylor	.60	1.50
47 Maurice Jones-Drew	.75	2.00
48 Larry Johnson	.50	1.25
49 Tony Gonzalez	.60	1.50
50 Damon Huard	.60	1.50
51 Ronnie Brown	.60	1.50
52 Zach Thomas	.60	1.50
53 Chris Chambers	.60	1.50
54 Troy Williamson	.50	1.25
55 Tarvaris Jackson	.50	1.25
56 Chester Taylor	.50	1.25
57 Tom Brady	1.25	3.00
58 Randy Moss	.75	2.00
59 Laurence Maroney	.60	1.50
60 Reggie Bush	.75	2.00
61 Drew Brees	.75	2.00
62 Deuce McAllister	.60	1.50
63 Marques Colston	.75	2.00
64 Eli Manning	.75	2.00
65 Brandon Jacobs	.60	1.50
66 Plaxico Burress	.60	1.50
67 Chad Pennington	.60	1.50
68 Thomas Jones	.60	1.50
69 Laveranues Coles	.50	1.25
70 LaMont Jordan	.60	1.50
71 Josh McCown	.50	1.25
72 Ronald Curry	.60	1.50
73 Donovan McNabb	.75	2.00
74 Reggie Brown	.50	1.25
75 Brian Westbrook	.60	1.50
76 Ben Roethlisberger	.75	2.00
77 Willie Parker	.60	1.50
78 Hines Ward	.75	2.00
79 LaDainian Tomlinson	.75	2.00
80 Philip Rivers	.75	2.00
81 Antonio Gates	.75	2.00
82 Shawne Merriman	.60	1.50
83 Alex Smith QB	.75	2.00
84 Frank Gore	.75	2.00
85 Ashley Lelie	.60	1.50
86 Matt Hasselbeck	.60	1.50
87 Shaun Alexander	.60	1.50
88 Deion Branch	.60	1.50
89 Torry Holt	.60	1.50
90 Marc Bulger	.60	1.50
91 Steven Jackson	.75	2.00
92 Cadillac Williams	.60	1.50
93 Chris Brown	.50	1.25
94 Joey Galloway	.60	1.50
95 Vince Young	.60	1.50
96 David Givens	.50	1.25
97 LenDale White	.60	1.50
98 Clinton Portis	.60	1.50
99 Santana Moss	.60	1.50
100 Jason Campbell	.60	1.50
101 Adrian Peterson AU/199 RC	100.00	200.00
102 Brady Quinn AU/199 RC	10.00	25.00
103 Calvin Johnson AU/149 RC	75.00	125.00
104 Dwayne Bowe AU/199 RC	20.00	40.00
105 JaMarcus Russell AU/199 RC	6.00	15.00
106 Marshawn Lynch AU/199 RC	15.00	40.00
107 Ted Ginn Jr. AU/199 RC	8.00	20.00
108 Anthony Gonzalez AU/399 RC	6.00	15.00
109 Brian Leonard AU/399 RC	5.00	12.00
110 Darrelle Revis AU/399 RC	15.00	30.00
111 Drew Stanton AU/399 RC	4.00	10.00
112 Dwayne Jarrett AU/399 RC	5.00	12.00
113 Kevin Kolb AU/399 RC	10.00	25.00
114 LaRon Landry AU/399 RC	6.00	15.00
115 Leon Hall AU/399 RC	5.00	12.00
116 Robert Meachem AU/349 RC	10.00	20.00
117 Sidney Rice AU/99 RC	20.00	40.00
118 Antonio Pittman AU/699 RC	3.00	8.00
120 Chris Henry RB AU/699 RC	3.00	8.00
121 Garrett Wolfe AU/699 RC	3.00	8.00
122 Isaiah Stanback AU/699 RC	3.00	8.00
123 Jamaal Anderson AU/79 RC	7.50	20.00
124 Jason Hill AU/699 RC	5.00	12.00
125 Jeff Rowe AU/699 RC	3.00	8.00
126 John Beck AU/699 RC	5.00	12.00
127 Jordan Palmer AU/699 RC	4.00	10.00
128 Lawrence Timmons AU/699 RC	5.00	12.00
129 Lorenzo Booker AU/699 RC	4.00	10.00
130 Michael Bush AU/699 RC	5.00	12.00
131 Michael Griffin AU/699 RC	5.00	12.00
132 Patrick Willis AU/15 RC	60.00	120.00
133 Paul Posluszny AU/699 RC	5.00	12.00
134 Steve Smith AU/699 RC	8.00	20.00
135 Tony Hunt AU/109 RC	3.00	8.00
136 Trent Edwards AU/299 RC	5.00	12.00
137 Yamon Figurs AU/699 RC	3.00	8.00
138 Zach Miller AU/699 RC	5.00	12.00
139 Chris Leak AU/699 RC	4.00	10.00
142 Greg Olsen AU/699 RC	4.00	10.00
143 Kenny Irons AU/75 RC	7.50	20.00
144 Reggie Nelson AU/699 RC	4.00	10.00
145 David Clowney AU/699 RC	4.00	10.00
146 DeShawn Wynn AU/699 RC	4.00	10.00
147 Joe Thomas AU/699 RC	5.00	12.00
148 Johnnie Lee Higgins AU/699 RC	4.00	10.00
149 Paul Williams AU/699 RC	3.00	8.00

2007 SP Chirography Biography of a Rookie Autographs Gold

GOLD AU PRINT RUN 1-99
*SILVER/75: .4X TO 1X GOLD AU/99
*SILVER/50: .5X TO 1.2X GOLD AU/99
SILVER PRINT RUN 50-75
*EMERALD/50: .5X TO 1.2X GOLD AU/99
*EMERALD/25: .6X TO 1.5X GOLD AU/99
EMERALD PRINT RUN 25-50
UNPRICED SAPPHIRE PRINT RUN 1
UNPRICED BRONZE PRINT RUN 1

BORAP Antonio Pittman	3.00	8.00
BORBR John Broussard	4.00	10.00
BORCD Chris Davis	3.00	8.00
BORCH Chris Henry RB	3.00	8.00
BORDW DeShawn Wynn	4.00	10.00
BORGW Garrett Wolfe	3.00	8.00
BORHI Johnnie Lee Higgins	4.00	10.00
BORIS Isaiah Stanback	3.00	8.00
BORJB John Beck	5.00	12.00
BORJH Jason Hill	5.00	12.00
BORJP Jordan Palmer	4.00	10.00
BORMB Michael Bush	5.00	12.00
BORPP Paul Posluszny	5.00	12.00
BORSC Scott Chandler	5.00	12.00
BORTH Tony Hunt	3.00	8.00
BORWI Paul Williams	3.00	8.00
BORYF Yamon Figurs	3.00	8.00
BORZM Zach Miller	5.00	12.00

2007 SP Chirography Dual Autographs Gold

GOLD PRINT RUN 1-25
UNPRICED SILVER PRINT RUN 1
UNPRICED EMERALD PRINT RUN 1

CDHB Leon Hall		
Alan Branch/25		
CDOM Brandon Meriweather	12.00	30.00
Greg Olsen/25		

2007 SP Chirography First Signs Gold

GOLD PRINT RUN 99 SER.#'d SETS
*SILVER/75: .4X TO 1X GOLD AU/99
*SILVER/50: .5X TO 1.2X GOLD AU/99
SILVER PRINT RUN 50-75
*EMERALD/50: .5X TO 1.2X GOLD AU/99
*EMERALD/25: .6X TO 1.5X GOLD AU/99
EMERALD PRINT RUN 10-50
UNPRICED SAPPHIRE PRINT RUN 1
UNPRICED BRONZE PRINT RUN 1

FSAP Antonio Pittman	3.00	8.00
FSBR John Broussard	4.00	10.00
FSCH Chris Henry RB	3.00	8.00
FSCL Chris Leak	4.00	10.00
FSDW DeShawn Wynn	4.00	10.00
FSGO Greg Olsen	4.00	10.00
FSGW Garrett Wolfe	3.00	8.00
FSIS Isaiah Stanback	3.00	8.00
FSJA Jamaal Anderson	4.00	10.00
FSJB John Beck	5.00	12.00
FSJH Jason Hill	5.00	12.00
FSJP Jordan Palmer	4.00	10.00
FSJR Jeff Rowe	3.00	8.00
FSMB Michael Bush	5.00	12.00
FSMG Michael Griffin	5.00	12.00
FSPP Paul Posluszny	5.00	12.00
FSRN Reggie Nelson	4.00	10.00
FSSS Steve Smith USC	5.00	12.00
FSTH Tony Hunt	3.00	8.00
FSTT Tyler Thigpen	5.00	12.00
FSYF Yamon Figurs	3.00	8.00
FSZM Zach Miller	5.00	12.00

2007 SP Chirography Football Heroes Autographs Gold

GOLD PRINT RUN 4-99
*EMERALD/50: .5X TO 1.2X GOLD AU/99
*EMERALD/25: .6X TO 1.5X GOLD AU/99
*EMERALD/25: .6X TO 1.5X GOLD AU/75
EMERALD PRINT RUN 5-50
UNPRICED SAPPHIRE PRINT RUN 1
UNPRICED BRONZE PRINT RUN 1
SERIAL #'d UNDER 25 NOT PRICED

FHAD Joseph Addai/50	10.00	25.00
FHAG Anthony Gonzalez/50	6.00	15.00
FHCL Chris Leak/99	4.00	10.00
FHCW Cadillac Williams/50	10.00	25.00
FHDB Dwayne Bowe/50	15.00	40.00
FHDS Drew Stanton/99	3.00	8.00
FHGO Greg Olsen/99	4.00	10.00
FHGW Garrett Wolfe/99	3.00	8.00
FHJA Brandon Jacobs/99	8.00	20.00
FHJB John Beck/99	5.00	12.00
FHJJ Julius Jones/75	6.00	15.00
FHJT Joe Theismann/99	10.00	25.00
FHKK Kevin Kolb/75	8.00	20.00
FHLL LaRon Landry/99	5.00	12.00
FHMB Michael Bush/99	5.00	12.00
FHML Marshawn Lynch/25	12.00	30.00
FHPH Paul Hornung/75	10.00	25.00
FHPI Antonio Pittman/99	3.00	8.00
FHRC Roger Craig/50	10.00	25.00
FHSS Steve Smith USC/99	5.00	12.00
FHTH Tony Hunt/99	3.00	8.00

2007 SP Chirography Football Heroes Autographs Silver

*SILVER/75: .4X TO 1X GOLD AU/99
*SILVER/50: .5X TO 1.2X GOLD AU/99
*SILVER/50: .5X TO 1.2X GOLD AU/75
*SILVER/25: .5X TO 1.2X GOLD AU/50
SILVER PRINT RUN 10-75

FHMA Marcus Allen/50	15.00	40.00

2007 SP Chirography NFL Imagery Autographs Gold

GOLD PRINT RUN 1-99
*SILVER/75: .4X TO 1X GOLD AU/99
*SILVER/50: .5X TO 1.2X GOLD AU/99
*SILVER/25: .5X TO 1.2X GOLD AU/50
SILVER PRINT RUN 10-75
*EMERALD/50: .5X TO 1.2X GOLD AU/99
EMERALD PRINT RUN 5-50
UNPRICED SAPPHIRE PRINT RUN 1
UNPRICED BRONZE PRINT RUN 1

NFLIAG Anthony Gonzalez/50	6.00	15.00
NFLIBL Brian Leonard/99	4.00	10.00
NFLICH Chris Henry RB/99	3.00	8.00
NFLICL Chris Leak/99	4.00	10.00
NFLIDJ Dwayne Jarrett/99	4.00	10.00
NFLIDS Drew Stanton/99	3.00	8.00
NFLIDW DeShawn Wynn/99	4.00	10.00
NFLIGO Greg Olsen/99	4.00	10.00
NFLIGW Garrett Wolfe/99	3.00	8.00
NFLIHI Johnnie Lee Higgins/99	4.00	10.00
NFLIIS Isaiah Stanback/99	3.00	8.00
NFLIJA Joseph Addai/50	10.00	25.00
NFLIJB John Beck/99	5.00	12.00
NFLIJB John Broussard/99	4.00	10.00
NFLIJH Jason Hill/99	5.00	12.00
NFLIJT Joe Thomas/99	5.00	12.00
NFLILL LaRon Landry/99	5.00	12.00
NFLIPP Paul Posluszny/99	5.00	12.00
NFLIRM Robert Meachem/50	8.00	20.00
NFLISS Steve Smith USC/99	5.00	12.00
NFLIYF Yamon Figurs/99	3.00	8.00

2007 SP Chirography Notable Notations Autographs Gold

GOLD PRINT RUN 5-50
UNPRICED SILVER PRINT RUN 1

NNJB John Beck/50	6.00	15.00
NNJT Joe Thomas/50	6.00	15.00
NNRC Roger Craig/25	12.00	30.00

2007 SP Chirography Rookie Signatures Gold

GOLD PRINT RUN 1-25
UNPRICED SAPPHIRE AU PRINT RUN 1

101 Adrian Peterson	150.00	300.00
103 Calvin Johnson	75.00	150.00
104 Dwayne Bowe	25.00	60.00
106 Marshawn Lynch	25.00	60.00
110 Darrelle Revis	25.00	50.00
113 Kevin Kolb	12.00	30.00
117 Sidney Rice	40.00	100.00
134 Steve Smith USC	12.00	30.00

2007 SP Chirography Signature Running Backs Gold

STATED PRINT RUN 15-99 SER.#'d SETS
*SILVER/75: .4X TO 1X GOLD AU/99
*SILVER/50: .5X TO 1.2X GOLD AU/99
*SILVER/50: .5X TO 1.2X GOLD AU/75
SILVER PRINT RUN 10-75
*EMERALD/50: .5X TO 1.2X GOLD AU/99
*EMERALD/25: .6X TO 1.5X GOLD AU/99
EMERALD PRINT RUN 5-50
UNPRICED SAPPHIRE PRINT RUN 1
UNPRICED BRONZE PRINT RUN 1

SBDW DeShawn Wynn/99	4.00	10.00
SBFG Frank Gore/75	10.00	25.00
SBML Marshawn Lynch/25	12.00	30.00
SBRC Roger Craig/99	8.00	20.00
SBTH Tony Hunt/99	3.00	8.00

2007 SP Chirography Signature Numbers Gold

GOLD PRINT RUN 4-99
*SILVER/75: .4X TO 1X GOLD AU/99
*SILVER/50: .5X TO 1.2X GOLD AU/99
*SILVER/25: .5X TO 1.2X GOLD AU/50
SILVER PRINT RUN 10-75
*EMERALD/50: .5X TO 1.2X GOLD AU/99
*EMERALD/25: .6X TO 1.5X GOLD AU/99
EMERALD PRINT RUN 5-50
UNPRICED SAPPHIRE PRINT RUN 1
UNPRICED BRONZE PRINT RUN 1
SERIAL #'d UNDER 25 NOT PRICED

SNAG Anthony Gonzalez/99	5.00	12.00
SNCL Chris Leak/99	4.00	10.00
SNCW Cadillac Williams/50	10.00	25.00
SNDJ Dwayne Jarrett/99	4.00	10.00
SNGO Greg Olsen/99	4.00	10.00
SNJB John Beck/99	5.00	12.00
SNLD Len Dawson/35	15.00	40.00
SNRC Roger Craig/50	10.00	25.00
SNRN Reggie Nelson/99	4.00	10.00
SNTH Tony Hunt/99	3.00	8.00

2007 SP Chirography Signature Quarterbacks Gold

GOLD PRINT RUN 15-99
*SILVER/75: .4X TO 1X GOLD AU/99
SILVER PRINT RUN 10-75
*EMERALD/50: .5X TO 1.2X GOLD AU/99
EMERALD PRINT RUN 5-50
UNPRICED SAPPHIRE PRINT RUN 1
UNPRICED BRONZE PRINT RUN 1

SQCL Chris Leak/99	4.00	10.00
SQDS Drew Stanton/99	3.00	8.00
SQJB John Beck/99	5.00	12.00
SQJP Jordan Palmer/99	4.00	10.00
SQTR Tony Romo/25	90.00	150.00

2007 SP Chirography Signature Receivers Gold

GOLD PRINT RUN 50-99
*SILVER/75: .4X TO 1X GOLD AU/99
*SILVER/50: .5X TO 1.2X GOLD AU/75
*SILVER/50: .4X TO 1X GOLD AU/50
SILVER PRINT RUN 50-75
*EMERALD/50: .5X TO 1.2X GOLD AU/99
*EMERALD/25: .6X TO 1.5X GOLD AU/75
*EMERALD/25: .5X TO 1.2X GOLD AU/50
EMERALD PRINT RUN 25-50
UNPRICED SAPPHIRE PRINT RUN 1
UNPRICED BRONZE PRINT RUN 1

SRAG Anthony Gonzalez/99	5.00	12.00
SRBB Bernard Berrian/75	6.00	15.00
SRCJ Chad Johnson/75	8.00	20.00
SRDB Dwayne Bowe/75	12.00	30.00
SRDP Drew Pearson/99	8.00	20.00
SRJB John Broussard/99	4.00	10.00
SRRB Reggie Brown/75	6.00	15.00
SRRM Robert Meachem/50	8.00	20.00

2007 SP Chirography Signatures Gold

GOLD PRINT RUN 15-99
*SILVER/75: .4X TO 1X GOLD AU/99
*SILVER/50: .5X TO 1.2X GOLD AU/99
*SILVER/50: .5X TO 1.2X GOLD AU/75
SILVER PRINT RUN 10-75
*EMERALD/50: .5X TO 1.2X GOLD AU/99
*EMERALD/50: .4X TO 1X GOLD AU/50
*EMERALD/25: .6X TO 1.5X GOLD AU/99
*EMERALD/25: .6X TO 1.5X GOLD AU/75
EMERALD PRINT RUN 5-50
UNPRICED SAPPHIRE PRINT RUN 1
UNPRICED BRONZE PRINT RUN 1
SERIAL #'d UNDER 25 NOT PRICED

CSCD Chris Davis/99	3.00	8.00
CSCH Chris Henry RB/99	3.00	8.00
CSDJ Dwayne Jarrett/50	5.00	12.00
CSDP Drew Pearson/99	8.00	20.00
CSDS Drew Stanton/99	3.00	8.00
CSGJ Greg Jennings/99	10.00	25.00
CSGO Greg Olsen/99	4.00	10.00
CSGW Garrett Wolfe/99	3.00	8.00
CSJB John Beck/99	5.00	12.00
CSJJ Julius Jones/75	6.00	15.00
CSJM Jim McMahon/30	20.00	50.00
CSKK Kevin Kolb/75	8.00	20.00
CSLL LaRon Landry/99	5.00	12.00
CSML Marshawn Lynch/25	12.00	30.00
CSRC Roger Craig/50	10.00	25.00
CSSS Steve Smith USC/99	5.00	12.00
CSTH Tony Hunt/99	3.00	8.00

2007 SP Chirography Signs of Defense Gold

GOLD PRINT RUN 99 SER.#'d SETS
*SILVER/75: .4X TO 1X GOLD AU/99
*SILVER/50: .5X TO 1.2X GOLD AU/99
SILVER PRINT RUN 50-75
*EMERALD/50: .5X TO 1.2X GOLD AU/99
*EMERALD/25: .6X TO 1.5X GOLD AU/99
EMERALD PRINT RUN 25-50
UNPRICED SAPPHIRE PRINT RUN 1
UNPRICED BRONZE PRINT RUN 1

SODAC Adam Carriker	4.00	10.00
SODBM Brandon Meriweather	5.00	12.00
SODJA Jamaal Anderson	4.00	10.00
SODJL John Lynch	12.00	30.00
SODLW LaMarr Woodley	8.00	20.00
SODMG Michael Griffin	5.00	12.00
SODPP Paul Posluszny	5.00	12.00
SODRN Reggie Nelson	4.00	10.00

2007 SP Chirography Signs of September Dual Autographs Gold

GOLD PRINT RUN 2-50
UNPRICED SILVER PRINT RUN 1
UNPRICED EMERALD PRINT RUN 1
SERIAL #'d UNDER 50 NOT PRICED

AC Adam Carriker	6.00	15.00
Jamaal Anderson		
AM Jamaal Anderson	8.00	20.00
Brandon Meriweather		
BK Kevin Kolb	12.00	30.00
John Beck		
BW Alan Branch	12.00	30.00
LaMarr Woodley		
DN Craig Buster Davis	8.00	20.00
Legedu Naanee		
DR Darius Walker	5.00	12.00
Rhema McKnight		
GD Garrett Wolfe	6.00	15.00
David Ball		
GM Brandon Meriweather	8.00	20.00
Michael Griffin		
HP Paul Posluszny	8.00	20.00
Tony Hunt		
II Kenny Irons	5.00	12.00
David Irons		
LS Chris Leak	6.00	15.00
Drew Stanton		
MP Tyler Palko	8.00	20.00
Matt Moore		
NL Reggie Nelson	8.00	20.00
LaRon Landry		
OM Greg Olsen	8.00	20.00
Zach Miller		
PB Paul Posluszny	8.00	20.00
H.B. Blades		
PI Kenny Irons	5.00	12.00
Antonio Pittman		
PP Tyler Palko	5.00	12.00
Antonio Pittman		
RB Gary Russell	6.00	15.00
Dallas Baker		
SB Michael Bush	8.00	20.00
Kolby Smith		
WB Lorenzo Booker	6.00	15.00
DeShawn Wynn		
WM Dwayne Wright	6.00	15.00
Marcus McCauley		

2007 SP Chirography Triple Signatures Gold

GOLD PRINT RUN 1-25
UNPRICED SILVER PRINT RUN 1
UNPRICED EMERALD PRINT RUN 1

HWH Chris Henry RB	6.00	15.00
Tony Hunt		
Garrett Wolfe		
LWB Chris Leak	8.00	20.00
Dallas Baker		
DeShawn Wynn		
OMC Greg Olsen	10.00	25.00
Zach Miller		
Scott Chandler		

2001 SP Game Used Edition

Upper Deck released SP Game Used Edition in mid July of 2001. The packs contained 3 cards per pack and 1 of which was a jersey card. The base set design had a black and white photo in the background with a color photo on top of that. The cardbacks contained the featured players statistics and a quick summary about the player, along with the Upper Deck hologram.

COMP.SET w/o SP's (90)	50.00	100.00
ROOKIE PRINT RUN 500 SER.#'d SETS		
1 Jake Plummer	.75	2.00
2 David Boston	.60	1.50
3 Frank Sanders	.60	1.50
4 Jamal Anderson	.75	2.00
5 Doug Johnson	.60	1.50
6 Shawn Jefferson	.60	1.50
7 Jamal Lewis	1.00	2.50
8 Shannon Sharpe	1.00	2.50
9 Qadry Ismail	.75	2.00
10 Shawn Bryson	.60	1.50
11 Rob Johnson	.75	2.00
12 Eric Moulds	.75	2.00
13 Muhsin Muhammad	.75	2.00
14 Brad Hoover	.75	2.00
15 Tim Biakabutuka	.60	1.50
16 Cade McNown	.75	2.00
17 Marcus Robinson	.75	2.00
18 Brian Urlacher	1.25	3.00
19 Akili Smith	.60	1.50
20 Peter Warrick	.75	2.00
21 Corey Dillon	.75	2.00
22 Kevin Johnson	.60	1.50
23 Rickey Dudley	.60	1.50
24 Tim Couch	.60	1.50
25 Tony Banks	.60	1.50
26 Emmitt Smith	2.50	6.00
27 Carl Pickens	.75	2.00
28 Terrell Davis	1.00	2.50
29 Mike Anderson	.75	2.00
30 Brian Griese	.75	2.00
31 Ed McCaffrey	.75	2.00
32 Charlie Batch	.75	2.00
33 Germane Crowell	.60	1.50
34 James O. Stewart	.60	1.50
35 Brett Favre	3.00	8.00
36 Antonio Freeman	1.00	2.50
37 Ahman Green	1.00	2.50
38 Peyton Manning	2.50	6.00
39 Edgerrin James	1.00	2.50
40 Marvin Harrison	1.00	2.50
41 Mark Brunell	.75	2.00
42 Fred Taylor	1.00	2.50
43 Jimmy Smith	.75	2.00
44 Tony Gonzalez	1.00	2.50
45 Derrick Alexander	.60	1.50
46 Oronde Gadsden	.60	1.50
47 Ray Lucas	.60	1.50
48 Lamar Smith	.75	2.00
49 Randy Moss	1.00	2.50
50 Cris Carter	1.00	2.50
51 Daunte Culpepper	.75	2.00
52 Drew Bledsoe	1.00	2.50
53 Terry Glenn	.75	2.00
54 Ricky Williams	1.00	2.50
55 Jeff Blake	.75	2.00
56 Joe Horn	.75	2.00
57 Aaron Brooks	.75	2.00
58 Kerry Collins	.75	2.00
59 Tiki Barber	1.00	2.50
60 Ron Dayne	.75	2.00
61 Vinny Testaverde	.75	2.00
62 Wayne Chrebet	.75	2.00
63 Curtis Martin	1.00	2.50
64 Tim Brown	1.00	2.50
65 Rich Gannon	.75	2.00
66 Tyrone Wheatley	.75	2.00
67 Duce Staley	.75	2.00
68 Donovan McNabb	1.00	2.50
69 Kordell Stewart	.75	2.00
70 Jerome Bettis	1.00	2.50
71 Marshall Faulk	1.00	2.50
72 Kurt Warner	1.50	4.00
73 Isaac Bruce	1.00	2.50
74 Doug Flutie	1.00	2.50
75 Curtis Conway	.75	2.00
76 Jeff Garcia	.75	2.00
77 Jerry Rice	2.00	5.00
78 Charlie Garner	.75	2.00
79 Terrell Owens	1.00	2.50
80 Ricky Watters	.75	2.00
81 Matt Hasselbeck	1.00	2.50
82 Levon Kirkland	.60	1.50
83 Keyshawn Johnson	.75	2.00
84 Brad Johnson	.75	2.00
85 Mike Alstott	.75	2.00
86 Eddie George	1.00	2.50
87 Steve McNair	1.00	2.50
88 Jeff George	.75	2.00
89 Michael Westbrook	.60	1.50
90 Stephen Davis	.75	2.00
91 Michael Vick JSY RC	15.00	40.00
92 Chris Weinke JSY RC	3.00	8.00
93 Drew Brees JSY RC	30.00	60.00
94 Deuce McAllister JSY RC	4.00	10.00
95 Michael Bennett JSY RC	3.00	8.00
96 LaDainian Tomlinson JSY RC	15.00	40.00
97 Kevan Barlow JSY RC	3.00	8.00
98 Travis Minor JSY RC	3.00	8.00
99 Rudi Johnson JSY RC	4.00	10.00
100 Todd Heap JSY RC	4.00	10.00
101 Freddie Mitchell JSY RC	2.50	6.00
102 Santana Moss JSY RC	5.00	12.00
103 Reggie Wayne JSY RC	8.00	20.00
104 Koren Robinson JSY RC	3.00	8.00
105 Josh Heupel JSY RC	4.00	10.00
106 Rod Gardner JSY RC	3.00	8.00
107 Quincy Morgan JSY RC	3.00	8.00
108 Chad Johnson JSY RC	6.00	15.00
109 Dan Morgan JSY RC	3.00	8.00
110 Gerard Warren JSY RC	3.00	8.00
111 Chris Chambers JSY RC	4.00	10.00
112 James Jackson JSY RC	2.50	6.00
113 Jesse Palmer JSY RC	3.00	8.00
114 Sage Rosenfels JSY RC	4.00	10.00
115 Mike McMahon JSY RC	3.00	8.00
116 Marques Tuiasosopo JSY RC	3.00	8.00
117 Robert Ferguson JSY RC	4.00	10.00
118 Travis Henry JSY RC	3.00	8.00
119 Richard Seymour JSY RC	4.00	10.00
120 Andre Carter JSY RC	3.00	8.00
121 LaMont Jordan RC	2.50	6.00
122 Vinny Sutherland RC	1.50	4.00
123 Nate Clements RC	2.00	5.00
124 David Terrell RC	2.00	5.00
125 A.J. Feeley RC	2.00	5.00
126 David Rivers RC	1.50	4.00
127 Snoop Minnis RC	1.50	4.00
128 Josh Booty RC	2.00	5.00
129 Correll Buckhalter RC	2.50	6.00
130 Will Allen RC	2.50	6.00
131 Dan Alexander RC	2.00	5.00
132 Leonard Davis RC	2.50	6.00
133 Anthony Thomas RC	2.50	6.00
134 Alge Crumpler RC	2.50	6.00
135 Jamal Reynolds RC	1.50	4.00
136 Ken-Yon Rambo RC	1.50	4.00
137 Bobby Newcombe RC	2.00	5.00
138 Alex Bannister RC	1.50	4.00
139 Jabari Holloway RC	1.50	4.00
140 Jamar Fletcher RC	1.50	4.00
141 Adam Archuleta RC	2.00	5.00
142 Heath Evans RC	2.00	5.00
143 Scotty Anderson RC	1.50	4.00
144 Moran Norris RC	1.50	4.00
145 Justin Smith RC	2.50	6.00
146 Quincy Carter RC	2.00	5.00
147 Ronney Daniels RC	1.50	4.00
148 Ben Leard RC	1.50	4.00
149 Fred Smoot RC	2.50	6.00
150 Milton Wynn RC	1.50	4.00

2001 SP Game Used Edition Authentic Fabric

STATED ODDS ONE PER PACK
*GOLD/25: 1.5X TO 4X BASIC JSY
*GOLD/25: 1X TO 2.5X BASIC JSY SP
GOLD STATED PRINT RUN 25 SER.#'d SETS

AF Antonio Freeman	5.00	12.00
AG Ahman Green	5.00	12.00
AL Mike Alstott	4.00	10.00
AS Akili Smith	3.00	8.00
AT Amani Toomer	4.00	10.00
AZ Az Zahir Hakim	3.00	8.00
BA Tiki Barber	5.00	12.00
BF Brett Favre	15.00	40.00
BG Brian Griese	4.00	10.00
BJ Brad Johnson	4.00	10.00
BO David Boston	3.00	8.00
BR Drew Brees	20.00	50.00
BS Bart Starr SP	25.00	60.00
CB Champ Bailey	5.00	12.00
CC Chris Chambers	5.00	12.00
CD Corey Dillon	4.00	10.00
CH Chris Chandler	4.00	10.00
CO Curtis Conway	4.00	10.00
CW Charles Woodson	5.00	12.00
DB Drew Bledsoe	5.00	12.00
DC Daunte Culpepper SP	6.00	15.00
DF Bubba Franks	4.00	10.00
DL Dorsey Levens SP	12.00	30.00
DM Deuce McAllister	5.00	12.00
EJ Edgerrin James SP	8.00	20.00
EM Eric Moulds	4.00	10.00
FM Freddie Mitchell	3.00	8.00
FS Frank Sanders	3.00	8.00
FT Fran Tarkenton SP	12.00	30.00
IB Isaac Bruce	5.00	12.00
IH Ike Hilliard	4.00	10.00
JA Jamal Anderson	4.00	10.00
JB Jerome Bettis	6.00	15.00
JE John Elway SP	25.00	60.00
JG Jeff Garcia	4.00	10.00
JJ J.J. Stokes	3.00	8.00
JL Jamal Lewis SP	12.00	30.00
JM Joe Montana	20.00	50.00
JP Jake Plummer	4.00	10.00
JR Jerry Rice	10.00	25.00
JS Junior Seau	5.00	12.00
JU Johnny Unitas SP	25.00	60.00
KC Kerry Collins	4.00	10.00
KS Kordell Stewart	4.00	10.00
KW Kurt Warner	8.00	20.00
LT LaDainian Tomlinson SP	15.00	40.00
MA Marcus Allen SP	10.00	25.00
MB Mark Brunell	4.00	10.00
MC Ed McCaffrey	4.00	10.00
MF Marshall Faulk	5.00	12.00
MP Michael Pittman	4.00	10.00
MT Marques Tuiasosopo	4.00	10.00
MV Michael Vick	12.00	30.00
MW Michael Westbrook	3.00	8.00
PB Plaxico Burress	4.00	10.00
PM Peyton Manning	12.00	30.00
PW Peter Warrick	4.00	10.00
RD Ron Dayne	4.00	10.00
RL Ray Lewis	5.00	12.00
RM Randy Moss SP	8.00	20.00
RS Rod Smith	4.00	10.00
SD Stephen Davis	4.00	10.00
SE Jason Sehorn	4.00	10.00
SK Shaun King	3.00	8.00
SM Justin Smith	5.00	12.00
TA Troy Aikman SP	15.00	40.00
TB Terry Bradshaw SP	20.00	50.00
TC Tim Couch	3.00	8.00
TD Terrell Davis	5.00	12.00
TG Terry Glenn	4.00	10.00
TH Torry Holt	4.00	10.00
TJ Thomas Jones	4.00	10.00
TO Terrell Owens	5.00	12.00
WD Warrick Dunn	5.00	12.00
WE Chris Weinke	4.00	10.00
WP Walter Payton SP	25.00	60.00
WS Warren Sapp	4.00	10.00
FTA Fred Taylor	5.00	12.00

2001 SP Game Used Edition Authentic Fabric Autographs

STATED PRINT RUN 25 SER.#'d SETS

AZA Az Zahir Hakim	20.00	50.00
BJA Brad Johnson	25.00	60.00
BRA Drew Brees	150.00	300.00
BSA Bart Starr	125.00	250.00
CDA Corey Dillon	25.00	60.00
DCA Daunte Culpepper	25.00	60.00
DMA Deuce McAllister	30.00	80.00
EJA Edgerrin James	75.00	150.00
FTA Fran Tarkenton	40.00	100.00
JEA John Elway	150.00	250.00
JGA Jeff Garcia	25.00	60.00
JMA Joe Montana	100.00	175.00
JPA Jake Plummer	25.00	60.00
JRA Jerry Rice	150.00	250.00
JUA Johnny Unitas	250.00	400.00
KWA Kurt Warner	50.00	125.00
MBA Mark Brunell	25.00	60.00
MFA Marshall Faulk	30.00	80.00
PMA Peyton Manning	150.00	250.00
RDA Ron Dayne	25.00	60.00
RMA Randy Moss	75.00	150.00
TAA Troy Aikman	75.00	150.00
TBA Terry Bradshaw	100.00	200.00
TCA Tim Couch	20.00	50.00

2001 SP Game Used Edition Authentic Fabric Duals

STATED PRINT RUN 50 SER.#'d SETS

2CAD Mike Alstott	20.00	50.00
Warrick Dunn		
2CAS Troy Aikman	75.00	150.00
Emmitt Smith		
2CBM Mark Brunell	15.00	40.00
Keenan McCardell		
2CBS Frank Sanders	12.00	30.00
David Boston		
2CCM Cris Carter	30.00	80.00
Randy Moss		
2CCS Doug Chapman	15.00	40.00
Robert Smith		
2CDC Ron Dayne	15.00	40.00
Kerry Collins		
2CFF Brett Favre	50.00	120.00
Antonio Freeman		
2CJS Keyshawn Johnson	15.00	40.00
Warren Sapp		
2CMJ Peyton Manning	60.00	150.00
Edgerrin James		
2COG Terrell Owens	20.00	50.00
Jeff Garcia		
2CSB Kordell Stewart	20.00	50.00
Jerome Bettis		
2CWB Charles Woodson	20.00	50.00
Tim Brown		
2CWD Peter Warrick	15.00	40.00
Corey Dillon		
2CWH Kurt Warner	50.00	120.00
Torry Holt		

2001 SP Game Used Edition Authentic Fabric Triples

STATED PRINT RUN 25 SER.#'d SETS

3CCMC Cris Carter	30.00	80.00
Randy Moss		
Daunte Culpepper		
3CDCB Ron Dayne	30.00	80.00
Kerry Collins		
Tiki Barber		
3CDGJ Terrell Davis/Eddie George/Edgerrin James		
30.00	80.00	
3CFWM Brett Favre	100.00	200.00
Kurt Warner		
Peyton Manning		
3CHHB Torry Holt	30.00	80.00
Az Zahir Hakim		
Isaac Bruce		
3CLLD Jamal Lewis	30.00	80.00
Ray Lewis		
Trent Dilfer		

2003 SP Game Used Edition

Released in July of 2003, this set consists of 181 cards, including 90 veterans, 50 rookies, and 41 memorabilia cards featuring game worn jersey swatches. The rookies are serial numbered to 600. Boxes contained 6 packs of 3 cards, with a jersey or autograph card in each pack. SRP was $29.99.

COMP.SET w/o SP's (90)	30.00	60.00
1 Chad Hutchinson	.60	1.50
2 Quincy Carter	.60	1.50
3 Joey Galloway	.75	2.00
4 Kerry Collins	.75	2.00
5 Jeremy Shockey	1.00	2.50
6 Amani Toomer	.75	2.00
7 A.J. Feeley	.60	1.50
8 Duce Staley	.75	2.00
9 Dorsey Levens	.75	2.00
10 Ladell Betts	.60	1.50
11 Patrick Ramsey	.75	2.00
12 Anthony Thomas	.75	2.00
13 Marty Booker	.75	2.00
14 Brian Urlacher	1.00	2.50
15 Joey Harrington	.60	1.50
16 James Stewart	.60	1.50
17 Az-Zahir Hakim	.60	1.50
18 Donald Driver	1.00	2.50
19 Javon Walker	.75	2.00
20 Kordell Stewart	.75	2.00
21 Randy Moss	1.00	2.50
22 Shaun Hill	1.00	2.50
23 Brian Finneran	.60	1.50
24 T.J. Duckett	.75	2.00
25 Warrick Dunn	.75	2.00
26 Rodney Peete	.60	1.50
27 Stephen Davis	.75	2.00
28 Muhsin Muhammad	.75	2.00
29 Aaron Brooks	.75	2.00
30 Deuce McAllister	.75	2.00
31 Joe Horn	.75	2.00
32 Keyshawn Johnson	1.00	2.50
33 Brad Johnson	.75	2.00
34 Keenan McCardell	.75	2.00
35 Jake Plummer	.75	2.00
36 Josh McCown	.75	2.00
37 Thomas Jones	1.00	2.50
38 Tai Streets	.60	1.50
39 Kevan Barlow	.60	1.50
40 Garrison Hearst	.75	2.00
41 Maurice Morris	.60	1.50
42 Matt Hasselbeck	.75	2.00
43 Koren Robinson	.75	2.00
44 Marc Bulger	1.00	2.50
45 Trung Canidate	.60	1.50
46 Emmitt Smith	2.50	6.00
47 Alex Van Pelt	.60	1.50
48 Travis Henry	.60	1.50
49 Eric Moulds	.75	2.00
50 Jason Taylor	.75	2.00
51 Jay Fiedler	.60	1.50
52 Randy McMichael	.60	1.50
53 Tom Brady	2.50	6.00
54 Antowain Smith	.75	2.00
55 Troy Brown	.75	2.00
56 Curtis Martin	1.00	2.50
57 Vinny Testaverde	.75	2.00
58 Santana Moss	.75	2.00
59 Jamal Lewis	.75	2.00
60 Chris Redman	.60	1.50
61 Ray Lewis	1.00	2.50
62 Jon Kitna	.75	2.00
63 Peter Warrick	.75	2.00
64 Kelly Holcomb	.60	1.50
65 William Green	.60	1.50
66 Kevin Johnson	.60	1.50
67 Amos Zereoue	.60	1.50
68 Tommy Maddox	.75	2.00
69 Hines Ward	1.00	2.50
70 Corey Bradford	.60	1.50
71 Jonathan Wells	.60	1.50
72 Jabar Gaffney	.60	1.50
73 Edgerrin James	1.00	2.50
74 David Garrard	1.00	2.50
75 Mark Brunell	.75	2.00
76 Jimmy Smith	.75	2.00
77 Steve McNair	1.00	2.50
78 Kevin Dyson	.60	1.50
79 Terrell Davis	1.00	2.50
80 Shannon Sharpe	1.00	2.50
81 Rod Smith	.75	2.00
82 Trent Green	.75	2.00
83 Priest Holmes	1.00	2.50
84 Tony Gonzalez	1.00	2.50
85 Jerry Rice	2.00	5.00
86 Charlie Garner	.75	2.00
87 Jerry Porter	.60	1.50
88 Reche Caldwell	.60	1.50
89 Tim Dwight	.60	1.50
90 Junior Seau	1.00	2.50
91 Carson Palmer RC	8.00	20.00
92 Byron Leftwich RC	4.00	10.00
93 Dave Ragone RC	2.50	6.00
94 Kyle Boller RC	4.00	10.00
95 Rex Grossman RC	4.00	10.00
96 Chris Simms RC	4.00	10.00
97 Kliff Kingsbury RC	3.00	8.00
98 Jason Gesser RC	3.00	8.00
99 Brad Banks RC	3.00	8.00
100 Ken Dorsey RC	3.00	8.00
101 Juston Wood RC	2.50	6.00
102 Brian St.Pierre RC	3.00	8.00
103 Domanick Davis RC	3.00	8.00
104 Quentin Griffin RC	3.00	8.00
105 B.J. Askew RC	3.00	8.00
106 Onterrio Smith RC	2.50	6.00
107 Seneca Wallace RC	4.00	10.00
108 Artose Pinner RC	2.50	6.00
109 Justin Fargas RC	4.00	10.00
110 Chris Brown RC	2.50	6.00
111 Willis McGahee RC	5.00	12.00
112 Larry Johnson RC	4.00	10.00
113 Lee Suggs RC	3.00	8.00

114 Billy McMullen RC 2.50 6.00
115 Sultan McCullough RC 2.50 6.00
116 Musa Smith RC 2.50 6.00
117 Earnest Graham RC 4.00 10.00
118 Antwone Savage RC 2.50 6.00
119 Kirk Farmer RC 3.00 8.00
120 Kareem Kelly RC 2.50 6.00
121 J.R. Tolver RC 3.00 8.00
122 Tyrone Calico RC 3.00 8.00
123 Kevin Curtis RC 4.00 10.00
124 Bobby Wade RC 3.00 8.00
125 Justin Gage RC 3.00 8.00
126 Bryant Johnson RC 4.00 10.00
127 Doug Gabriel RC 3.00 8.00
128 Teyo Johnson RC 3.00 8.00
129 Brandon Lloyd RC 6.00 15.00
130 Kelley Washington RC 2.50 6.00
131 Talman Gardner RC 2.50 6.00
132 Anquan Boldin RC 6.00 15.00
133 Taylor Jacobs RC 2.50 6.00
134 Andre Johnson RC 10.00 25.00
135 Charles Rogers RC 3.00 8.00
136 Antonio Bryant JSY 3.00 8.00
137 Donovan McNabb JSY/99 8.00 20.00
138 Rod Gardner JSY 3.00 8.00
139 Ahman Green JSY 4.00 10.00
140 Brett Favre JSY/99 20.00 50.00
141 Daunte Culpepper JSY 4.00 10.00
142 Michael Bennett JSY 4.00 10.00
143 Michael Vick JSY/99 10.00 25.00
144 Jeff Garcia JSY 4.00 10.00
145 Terrell Owens JSY 5.00 12.00
146 Shaun Alexander JSY 4.00 10.00
147 Torry Holt JSY 5.00 12.00
148 Isaac Bruce JSY 5.00 12.00
149 Marshall Faulk JSY/99 8.00 20.00
150 Kurt Warner JSY/99 8.00 20.00
151 Drew Bledsoe JSY 5.00 12.00
152 Josh Reed JSY 3.00 8.00
153 Peerless Price JSY 3.00 8.00
154 David Boston JSY 3.00 8.00
155 Ricky Williams JSY/99 6.00 15.00
156 Chris Chambers JSY 4.00 10.00
157 Wayne Chrebet JSY 4.00 10.00
158 Chad Pennington JSY/99 8.00 20.00
159 Laveranues Coles JSY 3.00 8.00
160 Corey Dillon JSY 4.00 10.00
161 Tim Couch JSY 3.00 8.00
162 Jerome Bettis JSY 5.00 12.00
163 Plaxico Burress JSY 4.00 10.00
164 Antwaan Randle El JSY 4.00 10.00
165 David Carr JSY/99 6.00 15.00
166 Marvin Harrison JSY 5.00 12.00
167 Peyton Manning JSY 10.00 25.00
168 Fred Taylor JSY 4.00 10.00
169 Eddie George JSY 4.00 10.00
170 Clinton Portis JSY/99 6.00 15.00
171 Ashley Lelie JSY 3.00 8.00
172 Rich Gannon JSY 4.00 10.00
173 Phillip Buchanon JSY 3.00 8.00
174 Tim Brown JSY 5.00 12.00
175 LaDainian Tomlinson JSY 5.00 12.00
176 Drew Brees JSY/99 8.00 20.00
177 Jason Johnson RC 2.50 6.00
178 Sam Aiken RC 3.00 8.00
179 Nate Burleson RC 3.00 8.00
180 Tony Romo RC 20.00 50.00
181 Arnaz Battle RC 4.00 10.00

2003 SP Game Used Edition Gold Rookies

*GOLD/50: .8X TO 2X BASIC CARDS
GOLD PRINT RUN 50 SER.#'d SETS
180 Tony Romo 60.00 150.00

2003 SP Game Used Edition Field Fabrics

ANNOUNCED AVERAGE PRINT RUN 800
*GOLD/75: .8X TO 2X JSY/800
GOLD PRINT RUN 75 SER.#'d SETS
BF Brett Favre 10.00 25.00
BJ Brad Johnson 3.00 8.00
BU Brian Urlacher 4.00 10.00
DM Deuce McAllister 3.00 8.00
EM Eric Moulds 3.00 8.00
ES Emmitt Smith 10.00 25.00
JL Jamal Lewis 3.00 8.00
JR Jerry Rice 8.00 20.00
KJ Keyshawn Johnson 4.00 10.00
PM Peyton Manning 8.00 20.00
PP Peerless Price 2.50 6.00
RM Randy Moss 4.00 10.00
RW Ricky Williams 3.00 8.00
TG Tony Gonzalez 4.00 10.00
TO Terrell Owens 4.00 10.00

2003 SP Game Used Edition Field Fabrics Autographs

STATED PRINT RUN 100 SER.#'d SETS
SDM Deuce McAllister 15.00 40.00
SPM Peyton Manning 60.00 120.00
STG Tony Gonzalez 20.00 50.00
STH Travis Henry 12.00 30.00

2003 SP Game Used Edition Formations Four Wide

STATED PRINT RUN 25 SER.#'d SETS
UNPRICED GOLD PRINT RUN 10
FBBH Brett Favre
Mark Brunell
Aaron Brooks
Matt Hasselbeck
FPSM Marshall Faulk 50.00 120.00
Clinton Portis
Emmitt Smith
Deuce McAllister
GRBG Rich Gannon
Jerry Rice
Tim Brown
Charlie Garner
JETS Chad Pennington
Curtis Martin
Santana Moss
Wayne Chrebet
MCCV Peyton Manning 60.00 150.00
Tim Couch
David Carr
Michael Vick
MFCH Donovan McNabb 60.00 150.00
Brett Favre
Daunte Culpepper
Joey Harrington
RHOJ Jerry Rice
Marvin Harrison
Terrell Owens
Keyshawn Johnson
WFBH Kurt Warner
Marshall Faulk
Isaac Bruce
Torry Holt
WGAB Ricky Williams 25.00 60.00
Ahman Green
Shaun Alexander
Jerome Bettis

2003 SP Game Used Edition Formations Trips

STATED PRINT RUN 35 SER.#'d SETS
*GOLD/15: 5X TO 1.2X BASIC TRIO/35
BHM Drew Bledsoe 20.00 50.00
Travis Henry
Eric Moulds
CVM Daunte Culpepper 25.00 60.00
Michael Vick
Donovan McNabb
FBV Brett Favre 25.00 60.00
Drew Bledsoe
Michael Vick
FSG Marshall Faulk 40.00 100.00
Emmitt Smith
Ahman Green
GRB Rich Gannon 40.00 100.00
Jerry Rice
Tim Brown
MJH Peyton Manning 40.00 100.00
Edgerrin James
Marvin Harrison
OHG Terrell Owens 20.00 50.00
Garrison Hearst
Jeff Garcia
PCH Chad Pennington 15.00 40.00
David Carr
Joey Harrington
RHO Jerry Rice 40.00 100.00
Marvin Harrison
Terrell Owens
WCG Kurt Warner 20.00 50.00
Tim Couch
Rich Gannon

2003 SP Game Used Edition Formations Twins

PRINT RUN 50 SER. #'d SETS
*GOLD: .6X TO 1.5X TWIN JSY/50
GOLD STATED PRINT RUN 25
BM Drew Bledsoe 12.00 30.00
Eric Moulds
BT Drew Brees 12.00 30.00
LaDainian Tomlinson
CM Daunte Culpepper 12.00 30.00
Randy Moss
FG Brett Favre 30.00 80.00
Ahman Green
FS Marshall Faulk 30.00 80.00
Emmitt Smith
GO Jeff Garcia 12.00 30.00
Terrell Owens
MH Peyton Manning 25.00 60.00
Marvin Harrison
PM Chad Pennington 12.00 30.00
Santana Moss
VM Michael Vick 15.00 40.00
Donovan McNabb
WH Kurt Warner 12.00 30.00
Torry Holt

2003 SP Game Used Edition Formations Wing

ANNOUNCED PRINT RUN 99-750
*GOLD/50: .8X TO 2X JSY/750
*GOLD/25: .8X TO 2X JSY/99
GOLD STATED PRINT RUN 25-50
AT Anthony Thomas/750* 2.50 6.00
BU Brian Urlacher/750* 3.00 8.00
CM Curtis Martin/750* 3.00 8.00
CP1 Clinton Portis/750* 2.50 6.00
CP2 Chad Pennington/99 6.00 15.00
DB1 Drew Brees/750* 3.00 8.00
DB2 Drew Bledsoe/99 6.00 15.00
DC David Carr/750* 2.50 6.00
DM Donovan McNabb/99 6.00 15.00
ES Emmitt Smith/99 15.00 40.00
GH Garrison Hearst/750* 2.50 6.00
JG Jeff Garcia/99 5.00 12.00
JH Joey Harrington/750* 2.00 5.00
JL Jamal Lewis/750* 2.50 6.00
JR Jerry Rice/99 12.00 30.00
KJ Keyshawn Johnson/750* 3.00 8.00
KW Kurt Warner/750* 3.00 8.00
LT LaDainian Tomlinson/99 6.00 15.00
MF Marshall Faulk/99 6.00 15.00
MV Michael Vick/750* 4.00 10.00
PH Priest Holmes/99 6.00 15.00
PM Peyton Manning/99 12.00 30.00
RM Randy Moss/99 6.00 15.00
SM Santana Moss/750* 2.50 6.00
TG Trent Green/750* 2.50 6.00
TH Travis Henry/750* 2.00 5.00
TO Terrell Owens/99 6.00 15.00

2003 SP Game Used Edition Patch Singles

STATED PRINT RUN 99 SER. #'d SETS
AG Ahman Green 8.00 20.00
AR Antwaan Randle El 8.00 20.00
AT Anthony Thomas 8.00 20.00
BF Brett Favre 25.00 60.00
BO David Boston 6.00 15.00
BR Drew Brees 10.00 25.00
BU Brian Urlacher 10.00 25.00
CD Corey Dillon 8.00 20.00
CP Chad Pennington 10.00 25.00
DB Drew Bledsoe 10.00 25.00
DC Daunte Culpepper 8.00 20.00
DC David Carr 8.00 20.00
DM Deuce McAllister 8.00 20.00
DN Donovan McNabb 10.00 25.00
EG Eddie George 8.00 20.00
EJ Edgerrin James 10.00 25.00
ES Emmitt Smith 25.00 60.00
FT Fred Taylor 8.00 20.00
GH Garrison Hearst 8.00 20.00
JB Jerome Bettis 10.00 25.00
JG Jeff Garcia 8.00 20.00
JR Jerry Rice 20.00 50.00
KJ Keyshawn Johnson 10.00 25.00
KW Kurt Warner 10.00 25.00
LT LaDainian Tomlinson 10.00 25.00
MF Marshall Faulk 10.00 25.00
MV Michael Vick 12.00 30.00
PB Plaxico Burress 8.00 20.00
PH Priest Holmes 10.00 25.00
PM Peyton Manning 20.00 50.00
RM Randy Moss 10.00 25.00
RW Ricky Williams 8.00 20.00
SA Shaun Alexander 8.00 20.00
SM Steve McNair 10.00 25.00
TB Tom Brady 25.00 60.00
TC Tim Couch 6.00 15.00
TG Trent Green 8.00 20.00
TH Torry Holt 10.00 25.00
TO Terrell Owens 10.00 25.00
CPO Clinton Portis 8.00 20.00

2003 SP Game Used Edition Patch Doubles

STATED PRINT RUN 50 SER.#'d SETS
BE Drew Bledsoe 12.00 30.00
Eric Moulds
BF Drew Brees 12.00 30.00
LaDainian Tomlinson
BP Tom Brady 30.00 80.00
Chad Pennington
BR Plaxico Burress 10.00 25.00
Antwaan Randle El
BT Mark Brunell 10.00 25.00
Fred Taylor
CM Tim Couch 25.00 60.00
Peyton Manning
DM Daunte Culpepper 12.00 30.00
Randy Moss
DT Corey Dillon 10.00 25.00
Anthony Thomas
FG Brett Favre 30.00 80.00
Ahman Green
GD Clinton Portis 10.00 25.00
Ashley Lelie
GH Trent Green 12.00 30.00
Priest Holmes
GO Jeff Garcia 12.00 30.00
Terrell Owens
JM Keyshawn Johnson 12.00 30.00
Randy Moss
JP Edgerrin James 12.00 30.00
Clinton Portis
JW Edgerrin James 12.00 30.00
Ricky Williams
MC Steve McNair 12.00 30.00
Daunte Culpepper
MG Steve McNair 12.00 30.00
Eddie George
MH Peyton Manning 25.00 60.00
Marvin Harrison
MP Curtis Martin 12.00 30.00
Chad Pennington
RB Jerry Rice 25.00 60.00
Tim Brown
RG Jerry Rice 25.00 60.00
Rich Gannon
VM Michael Vick 15.00 40.00
Donovan McNabb
WF Kurt Warner 12.00 30.00
Marshall Faulk
WM Ricky Williams 10.00 25.00
Deuce McAllister

2003 SP Game Used Edition Patch Triples

STATED PRINT RUN 25 SER.#'d SETS
AMC Aaron Brooks 15.00 40.00
Donovan McNabb
Daunte Culpepper
BFB Aaron Brooks 15.00 40.00
Brett Favre
Mark Brunell
BPM Drew Bledsoe 20.00 50.00
Chad Pennington
Peyton Manning
CCV David Carr 25.00 60.00
Tim Couch
Michael Vick
CCW Kurt Warner 50.00 120.00
David Carr
Brett Favre
CVM Daunte Culpepper 25.00 60.00
Michael Vick
Donovan McNabb
FTB Doug Flutie 20.00 50.00
LaDainian Tomlinson
Drew Brees
GBC Jeff Garcia 20.00 50.00
Drew Brees
David Carr
GMC Jeff Garcia 40.00 100.00
Peyton Manning
Tim Couch
MJR Randy Moss 40.00 100.00
Keyshawn Johnson
Jerry Rice
MMP Santana Moss 20.00 50.00
Curtis Martin
Chad Pennington
MVD Steve McNair 25.00 60.00
Michael Vick
Aaron Brooks
OHG Terrell Owens 20.00 50.00
Garrison Hearst
Jeff Garcia
WFB Kurt Warner 50.00 120.00
Brett Favre
Tom Brady

2003 SP Game Used Edition Patch Autographs

STATED PRINT RUN 25-75
AB Aaron Brooks/50 15.00 40.00
BR Mark Brunell/40 15.00 40.00
CP Chad Pennington/25 30.00 80.00
DB Drew Brees/50 40.00 80.00
JF Jay Fiedler/50 12.00 30.00
JG Jeff Garcia/25 25.00 60.00
LT LaDainian Tomlinson/25 75.00 150.00
MB Michael Bennett/75 15.00 40.00
PM Peyton Manning/75 75.00 150.00
SA Shaun Alexander/50 15.00 40.00
SC Carson Palmer/25 150.00 300.00
TC Tim Couch/40 12.00 30.00
TG Trent Green/50 15.00 40.00
TR Travis Henry/50 12.00 30.00

2003 SP Game Used Edition Significant Signatures

STATED PRINT RUN 25-99
UNPRICED DUAL AUTOs #'d TO 10
AB Aaron Brooks/99 10.00 25.00
AT Anthony Thomas/99 10.00 25.00
BB Brad Banks/99 10.00 25.00
BE Michael Bennett/99 10.00 25.00
BF Brett Favre/25 150.00 250.00
BL Byron Leftwich/25 20.00 50.00
CB Chris Brown/99 8.00 20.00
CP Chad Pennington/50 15.00 40.00
CS Chris Simms/99 12.00 30.00
DB Drew Brees/50 40.00 80.00
DC David Carr/25 20.00 50.00
DE Deuce McAllister/25 20.00 50.00
EG Earnest Graham/99 12.00 30.00
GR Trent Green/99 10.00 25.00
JF1 Justin Fargas/99 12.00 30.00
JF2 Jay Fiedler/99 8.00 20.00
JG Jeff Garcia/25 20.00 50.00
JR Jerry Rice/25 100.00 200.00
KD Ken Dorsey/99 10.00 25.00
KK1 Kareem Kelly/99 8.00 20.00
KK2 Kliff Kingsbury/99 10.00 25.00
KW Kelley Washington/99 8.00 20.00
LJ Larry Johnson/99 12.00 30.00
LT LaDainian Tomlinson/25 75.00 135.00
MB Mark Brunell/99 10.00 25.00
PM1 Peyton Manning/50 60.00 120.00
(white jersey)
PM2 Peyton Manning/99 50.00 100.00
(blue jersey)
QG Quentin Griffin/99 10.00 25.00
RG Rod Gardner/99 8.00 20.00
SA Shaun Alexander/40 12.00 30.00
SC Carson Palmer/25 150.00 250.00
SW Seneca Wallace/99 12.00 30.00
TC Tim Couch/40 10.00 25.00
TG Tony Gonzalez/50 15.00 40.00
TJ Taylor Jacobs/99 8.00 20.00
TS Terrell Suggs/99 15.00 40.00
WM Willis McGahee/50 15.00 40.00

2003 SP Game Used Edition Significant Signatures Duals

STATED PRINT RUN 10 SER.#'d SETS

2004 SP Game Used Edition

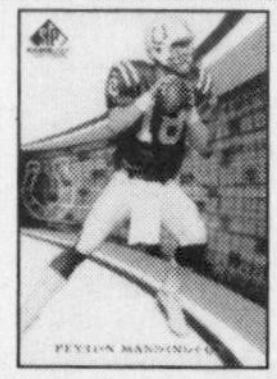

SP Game Used Edition initially released in mid-July 2004. The base set consists of 200-cards including 100-rookies serial numbered to 425. Hobby boxes contained 6-packs of 3-cards and carried an S.R.P. of $29.99 per pack. One parallel set and a variety of game jersey and autographed inserts can be found seeded in packs highlighted by the Rookie Exclusives Autographs, the Authentic Fabric Autograph Duals and the Legendary Fabric Autograph inserts.

1 Anquan Boldin 1.00 2.50
2 Marcel Shipp .60 1.50
3 Josh McCown .75 2.00
4 Michael Vick 1.25 3.00
5 T.J. Duckett .75 2.00
6 Peerless Price .60 1.50
7 Jamal Lewis .75 2.00
8 Todd Heap .75 2.00
9 Kyle Boller .75 2.00
10 Drew Bledsoe 1.00 2.50
11 Travis Henry .60 1.50
12 Eric Moulds .75 2.00
13 Jake Delhomme .75 2.00
14 Stephen Davis .75 2.00
15 Julius Peppers .75 2.00
16 Anthony Thomas .75 2.00
17 Rex Grossman .75 2.00
18 Brian Urlacher 1.00 2.50
19 Carson Palmer 1.00 2.50
20 Chad Johnson 1.00 2.50
21 Rudi Johnson .75 2.00
22 Jeff Garcia .75 2.00
23 Dennis Northcutt .60 1.50
24 Andre Davis .60 1.50
25 Quincy Carter .60 1.50
26 Roy Williams S .75 2.00
27 Keyshawn Johnson .75 2.00
28 Quentin Griffin .60 1.50
29 Jake Plummer .75 2.00
30 Ashley Lelie .60 1.50
31 Shannon Sharpe 1.00 2.50
32 Joey Harrington .75 2.00
33 Charles Rogers .60 1.50
34 Az-Zahir Hakim .60 1.50
35 Brett Favre 2.50 6.00
36 Javon Walker .60 1.50
37 Ahman Green .75 2.00
38 Andre Johnson 1.00 2.50
39 David Carr .60 1.50
40 Domanick Davis .60 1.50
41 Peyton Manning 2.00 5.00
42 Edgerrin James .75 2.00
43 Marvin Harrison 1.00 2.50
44 Byron Leftwich .75 2.00
45 Fred Taylor .75 2.00
46 Jimmy Smith .75 2.00
47 Priest Holmes 1.00 2.50
48 Trent Green .75 2.00
49 Dante Hall .75 2.00
50 Tony Gonzalez 1.00 2.50
51 Ricky Williams .75 2.00
52 Jay Fiedler .60 1.50
53 Chris Chambers .75 2.00
54 Randy Moss 1.00 2.50
55 Daunte Culpepper .75 2.00
56 Moe Williams .60 1.50
57 Tom Brady 2.00 5.00
58 Deion Branch .75 2.00
59 Corey Dillon .75 2.00
60 Deuce McAllister .75 2.00
61 Aaron Brooks .75 2.00
62 Joe Horn .75 2.00
63 Jeremy Shockey .75 2.00
64 Amani Toomer .75 2.00
65 Michael Strahan 1.00 2.50
66 Curtis Martin 1.00 2.50
67 Chad Pennington 1.00 2.50
68 Santana Moss .75 2.00
69 Jerry Rice 2.00 5.00
70 Tim Brown 1.00 2.50
71 Jerry Porter .60 1.50
72 Donovan McNabb 1.00 2.50
73 Brian Westbrook 1.00 2.50
74 Terrell Owens 1.00 2.50
75 Hines Ward 1.00 2.50
76 Plaxico Burress .75 2.00
77 Duce Staley .75 2.00
78 LaDainian Tomlinson 1.00 2.50
79 Quentin Jammer .60 1.50
80 Drew Brees 1.00 2.50
81 Brandon Lloyd .75 2.00
82 Kevan Barlow .60 1.50
83 Tim Rattay .60 1.50
84 Matt Hasselbeck .75 2.00
85 Shaun Alexander .75 2.00
86 Darrell Jackson .75 2.00
87 Marc Bulger .75 2.00
88 Torry Holt .75 2.00
89 Marshall Faulk 1.00 2.50
90 Isaac Bruce .75 2.00
91 Brad Johnson .75 2.00
92 Derrick Brooks .75 2.00
93 Warren Sapp .75 2.00
94 Steve McNair 1.00 2.50
95 Derrick Mason .75 2.00
96 Eddie George .75 2.00
97 Clinton Portis 1.00 2.50
98 Mark Brunell .75 2.00
99 Laveranues Coles .60 1.50
100 LaVar Arrington .75 2.00
101 Ben Troupe RC 4.00 10.00
102 Chris Gamble RC 4.00 10.00
103 DeAngelo Hall RC 5.00 12.00
104 Dunta Robinson RC 3.00 8.00
105 Jason Shivers RC 3.00 8.00
106 Keary Colbert RC 3.00 8.00
107 Craig Krenzel RC 4.00 10.00
108 Philip Rivers RC 20.00 50.00
109 Roy Williams RC 5.00 12.00
110 Will Allen RC 4.00 10.00
111 Bob Sanders RC 12.00 30.00
112 Kris Wilson RC 4.00 10.00
113 D.J. Williams RC 5.00 12.00
114 Devery Henderson RC 5.00 12.00
115 Carlos Francis RC 3.00 8.00
116 Jonathan Vilma RC 5.00 12.00
117 Luke McCown RC 4.00 10.00
118 Michael Turner RC 6.00 15.00
119 Richard Seigler RC 3.00 8.00
120 Jared Lorenzen RC 4.00 10.00
121 P.K. Sam RC 3.00 8.00
122 Justin Smiley RC 4.00 10.00
123 Marquise Hill RC 3.00 8.00
124 Ernest Wilford RC 4.00 10.00
125 Jerricho Cotchery RC 4.00 10.00
126 Kevin Jones RC 4.00 10.00
127 Michael Boulware RC 5.00 12.00
128 Jarrett Payton RC 4.00 10.00
129 Sean Taylor RC 10.00 25.00
130 Will Smith RC 4.00 10.00
131 Bernard Berrian RC 5.00 12.00
132 Ahmad Carroll RC 3.00 8.00
133 Derrick Hamilton RC 3.00 8.00
134 Dwan Edwards RC 3.00 8.00
135 Jeff Smoker RC 4.00 10.00
136 Kenechi Udeze RC 4.00 10.00
137 Mewelde Moore RC 4.00 10.00
138 Joey Thomas RC 3.00 8.00
139 Sean Jones RC 4.00 10.00
140 Will Poole RC 5.00 12.00
141 Casey Clausen RC 4.00 10.00
142 Stuart Schweigert RC 4.00 10.00
143 Cody Pickett RC 4.00 10.00
144 Derrick Strait RC 3.00 8.00
145 Greg Jones RC 3.00 8.00
146 John Navarre RC 3.00 8.00
147 Larry Fitzgerald RC 12.00 30.00
148 Michael Clayton RC 4.00 10.00
149 Rashaun Woods RC 3.00 8.00
150 Shawn Andrews RC 4.00 10.00
151 B.J. Symons RC 3.00 8.00
152 Cedric Cobbs RC 3.00 8.00
153 Darius Watts RC 3.00 8.00
154 B.J. Johnson RC 3.00 8.00
155 Max Starks RC 4.00 10.00
156 Josh Harris RC 3.00 8.00
157 Kendrick Starling RC 3.00 8.00
158 Brandon Miree RC 3.00 8.00
159 Robert Gallery RC 5.00 12.00
160 Tatum Bell RC 4.00 10.00
161 Ben Hartsock RC 3.00 8.00
162 Derek Abney RC 3.00 8.00
163 Ricardo Colclough RC 4.00 10.00
164 Justin Jenkins RC 3.00 8.00
165 Chris Cooley RC 5.00 12.00
166 Julius Jones RC 4.00 10.00
167 Matt Mauck RC 3.00 8.00
168 Vernon Carey RC 3.00 8.00
169 John Standeford RC 3.00 8.00
170 Teddy Lehman RC 3.00 8.00
171 Ben Roethlisberger RC 25.00 60.00
172 Ben Utecht RC 4.00 10.00
173 D.J. Hackett RC 4.00 10.00
174 Drew Henson RC 3.00 8.00
175 Rich Gardner RC 4.00 10.00
176 Karlos Dansby RC 5.00 12.00
177 Matt Schaub RC 10.00 25.00
178 Darrion Scott RC 4.00 10.00
179 Keyaron Fox RC 4.00 10.00
180 Tommie Harris RC 5.00 12.00
181 Ben Watson RC 5.00 12.00
182 Chris Perry RC 4.00 10.00
183 Travelle Wharton RC 3.00 8.00
184 Eli Manning RC 30.00 60.00
185 Demorrio Williams RC 5.00 12.00
186 Kellen Winslow RC 5.00 12.00
187 Jason Babin RC 5.00 12.00
188 Quincy Wilson RC 4.00 10.00
189 Samie Parker RC 3.00 8.00
190 Vince Wilfork RC 5.00 12.00
191 Antwan Odom RC 4.00 10.00
192 Josh Davis RC 4.00 10.00
193 Courtney Watson RC 3.00 8.00
194 Devard Darling RC 3.00 8.00
195 J.P. Losman RC 4.00 10.00
196 Johnnie Morant RC 3.00 8.00
197 Lee Evans RC 5.00 12.00
198 Michael Jenkins RC 5.00 12.00
199 Reggie Williams RC 4.00 10.00
200 Steven Jackson RC 8.00 20.00

2004 SP Game Used Edition Gold

*1-100 VETS: 1.2X TO 3X BASIC CARDS
1-100 VETERAN/100 ODDS 1:7
VETERAN PRINT RUN 100 SER.#'d SETS
*101-200 ROOKIES: .8X TO 2X
101-200 ROOKIES PRINT RUN 50

2004 SP Game Used Edition Authentic All-Pro Fabric

RANDOM INSERTS IN PACKS
AG Ahman Green 3.00 8.00
BF Brett Favre 10.00 25.00
CJ Chad Johnson 4.00 10.00
CP Clinton Portis 4.00 10.00
DC Daunte Culpepper 3.00 8.00
DM Donovan McNabb 4.00 10.00
JL Jamal Lewis 3.00 8.00
PH Priest Holmes 4.00 10.00
PM Peyton Manning 8.00 20.00
RM Randy Moss 4.00 10.00
SD Stephen Davis 3.00 8.00
SM Steve McNair 4.00 10.00

2004 SP Game Used Edition Authentic Fabric

ONE GAME USED OR AUTO CARD PER PACK
*GOLD/100: .8X TO 2X BASIC JSY
GOLD PRINT RUN 100 SER.#'d SETS
AFAB Anquan Boldin 3.00 8.00
AFAG Ahman Green 2.50 6.00
AFAJ Andre Johnson 3.00 8.00
AFBF Brett Favre 8.00 20.00
AFBL Byron Leftwich 2.50 6.00
AFBR Aaron Brooks 2.50 6.00
AFBU Brian Urlacher 3.00 8.00
AFCA Carson Palmer 3.00 8.00
AFCD Corey Dillon 2.50 6.00
AFCJ Chad Johnson 3.00 8.00
AFCL Clinton Portis 3.00 8.00
AFCP Chad Pennington 3.00 8.00
AFCR Charles Rogers 2.00 5.00
AFDA David Carr 2.00 5.00
AFDB Derrick Brooks 2.50 6.00
AFDC Daunte Culpepper 2.50 6.00
AFDD Domanick Davis 2.00 5.00
AFDE Deuce McAllister 2.50 6.00
AFDH Dante Hall 2.50 6.00
AFDK Derrick Mason 2.50 6.00
AFDM Donovan McNabb 3.00 8.00
AFDR Drew Bledsoe 3.00 8.00
AFDS Duce Staley 2.50 6.00
AFEJ Edgerrin James 2.50 6.00
AFEM Eric Moulds 2.50 6.00
AFES Emmitt Smith 8.00 20.00
AFFT Fred Taylor 2.50 6.00
AFHA Matt Hasselbeck 2.50 6.00
AFHW Hines Ward 3.00 8.00
AFIB Isaac Bruce 2.50 6.00
AFJB Jerome Bettis 3.00 8.00
AFJK Jevon Kearse 2.50 6.00
AFJL Jamal Lewis 2.50 6.00
AFJP Jake Plummer SP 2.50 6.00
AFJR Jerry Rice 6.00 15.00
AFJS Jeremy Shockey 2.50 6.00
AFJU Junior Seau 3.00 8.00
AFKB Kyle Boller 2.50 6.00
AFKM Keenan McCardell 2.00 5.00
AFKW Kurt Warner 3.00 8.00
AFLA LaVar Arrington 2.50 6.00
AFLC Laveranues Coles 2.00 5.00
AFLT LaDainian Tomlinson 3.00 8.00
AFLY John Lynch 2.50 6.00
AFMA Mark Brunell 2.50 6.00
AFMB Marc Bulger 2.50 6.00
AFMF Marshall Faulk 3.00 8.00
AFMH Marvin Harrison 3.00 8.00
AFMS Michael Strahan 3.00 8.00
AFMV Michael Vick 4.00 10.00
AFPH Priest Holmes 3.00 8.00
AFPM Peyton Manning 6.00 15.00
AFPP Peerless Price 2.00 5.00
AFRG Rex Grossman 2.50 6.00
AFRL Ray Lewis 3.00 8.00
AFRM Randy Moss 3.00 8.00
AFRO Roy Williams S 2.50 6.00
AFRW Ricky Williams 2.50 6.00
AFSA Shaun Alexander 2.50 6.00
AFSD Stephen Davis 2.50 6.00
AFSM Steve McNair 3.00 8.00
AFSS Shannon Sharpe SP 3.00 8.00
AFTB Tom Brady 6.00 15.00
AFTG Tony Gonzalez 3.00 8.00
AFTH Torry Holt 2.50 6.00
AFTJ Thomas Jones 3.00 8.00
AFTL Ty Law 2.50 6.00
AFTO Terrell Owens 3.00 8.00
AFTR Trent Green 2.50 6.00
AFTS Terrell Suggs 2.50 6.00
AFTY Troy Brown 2.50 6.00
AFWM Willis McGahee 3.00 8.00
AFWS Warren Sapp 2.50 6.00

2004 SP Game Used Edition Authentic Fabric Autographs

ONE GAME USED OR AUTO CARD PER PACK
STATED PRINT RUN 100 SER.#'d SETS
AG Ahman Green 10.00 25.00
BF Brett Favre 125.00 200.00
BL Byron Leftwich 10.00 25.00
CJ Chad Johnson 12.00 30.00
CP Chad Pennington 12.00 30.00
DA David Carr 8.00 20.00
DB Drew Bledsoe 12.00 30.00
DC Daunte Culpepper 10.00 25.00
DD Domanick Davis 8.00 20.00
DE Deuce McAllister 10.00 25.00
DH Dante Hall 10.00 25.00
DM Donovan McNabb 35.00 60.00
JH Joe Horn 10.00 25.00
JP Jesse Palmer 8.00 20.00
KB Kyle Boller 10.00 25.00
KS Ken Stabler 40.00 75.00
LT LaDainian Tomlinson 30.00 80.00
MA Mark Brunell 10.00 25.00
PM Peyton Manning 60.00 100.00
RW Ricky Williams 10.00 25.00
SM Steve McNair 12.00 30.00
TA Troy Aikman 60.00 100.00
TB Tom Brady 125.00 250.00
TG Tony Gonzalez 12.00 30.00
WM Willis McGahee 12.00 30.00
ZT Zach Thomas 12.00 30.00

2004 SP Game Used Edition Authentic Fabric Autographs Dual

STATED PRINT RUN 15-50
BB Mark Brunell/50 20.00 50.00
Drew Bledsoe
CD David Carr/50 12.00 30.00
Domanick Davis
CM Daunte Culpepper 40.00 100.00
Donovan McNabb/15
DK Drew Bledsoe/50 20.00 50.00
Kyle Boller
DS Daunte Culpepper 20.00 50.00
Steve McNair/50
DT Drew Bledsoe/50 100.00 200.00
Tom Brady
EF John Elway 200.00 350.00
Brett Favre/15
FG Brett Favre/15 150.00 250.00
Ahman Green
GH Tony Gonzalez/50 20.00 50.00
Dante Hall
HM Travis Henry/50 20.00 50.00
Willis McGahee
JJ Chad Johnson/50 20.00 50.00
Rudi Johnson
LC Byron Leftwich 20.00 50.00
Daunte Culpepper/50
LP Byron Leftwich 20.00 50.00
Chad Pennington/50
MB Willis McGahee/50 20.00 50.00
Drew Bledsoe
MH Deuce McAllister/50 15.00 40.00
Joe Horn
ML Steve McNair 50.00 100.00
Byron Leftwich/50
MM Steve McNair 125.00 200.00
Peyton Manning/15
MW Donovan McNabb/50 20.00 50.00
Brian Westbrook
PD Peyton Manning 60.00 120.00
Drew Bledsoe/50
PK Peyton Manning 50.00 100.00
Kyle Boller/50
PT Peyton Manning 250.00 400.00
Tom Brady/15
RZ Ricky Williams/50 20.00 50.00
Zach Thomas
ST Ken Stabler/50 40.00 100.00
Fran Tarkenton
TB Joe Theismann/50 20.00 50.00
Mark Brunell
TK Tom Brady/50 100.00 200.00
Kyle Boller
WT Ricky Williams 30.00 80.00
Ladainian Tomlinson/50

2004 SP Game Used Edition Authentic Fabric Duals

STATED PRINT RUN 100 SER.#'d SETS
BA Derrick Brooks 8.00 20.00
LaVar Arrington
BF Marc Bulger 8.00 20.00
Marshall Faulk
BH Isaac Bruce 6.00 15.00
Torry Holt
BL Tom Brady 15.00 40.00
Ty Law
BM Aaron Brooks 6.00 15.00
Deuce McAllister
BP Mark Brunell 8.00 20.00
Clinton Portis
BW Jerome Bettis 8.00 20.00
Hines Ward
CB Laveranues Coles 6.00 15.00
Mark Brunell
CD David Carr 5.00 12.00
Domanick Davis
CM Daunte Culpepper 8.00 20.00
Randy Moss
DD Jake Delhomme 6.00 15.00
Stephen Davis
DF Donovan McNabb 8.00 20.00
Freddie Mitchell
FG Brett Favre 20.00 50.00
Ahman Green
FM Brett Favre 20.00 50.00
Peyton Manning
GG Trent Green 8.00 20.00
Tony Gonzalez
GU Rex Grossman 8.00 20.00
Brian Urlacher
HA Matt Hasselbeck 6.00 15.00
Shaun Alexander
HH Priest Holmes 8.00 20.00
Dante Hall
HP Priest Holmes 8.00 20.00
Clinton Portis
JJ Chad Johnson 8.00 20.00
Rudi Johnson
LL Jamal Lewis 8.00 20.00
Ray Lewis
LP Byron Leftwich 8.00 20.00
Chad Pennington
LS Byron Leftwich 6.00 15.00
Jimmy Smith
MB Willis McGahee 8.00 20.00
Drew Bledsoe
MG Steve McNair 8.00 20.00
Eddie George
MH Peyton Manning 15.00 40.00
Marvin Harrison
MM Steve McNair 15.00 40.00
Peyton Manning
MW Donovan McNabb 8.00 20.00
Brian Westbrook
PM Chad Pennington 8.00 20.00
Santana Moss
RJ Jerry Rice 15.00 40.00
Keyshawn Johnson
SB Emmitt Smith 20.00 50.00
Anquan Boldin
VP Michael Vick 12.00 30.00
Peerless Price
WC Ricky Williams 6.00 15.00
Chris Chambers
WN Roy Williams S 6.00 15.00
Terence Newman

2004 SP Game Used Edition Authentic Fabric Quads

UNPRICED QUAD PRINT RUN 10 SETS

2004 SP Game Used Edition Authentic Fabric Triples

STATED PRINT RUN 25 SER.#'d SETS
BHF Marc Bulger 20.00 50.00
Torry Holt
Marshall Faulk
CDJ David Carr 20.00 50.00
Domanick Davis
Andre Johnson
CMS Daunte Culpepper 20.00 50.00
Randy Moss
Onterrio Smith
FGW Brett Favre 40.00 100.00
Ahman Green
Javon Walker
GHH Trent Green 20.00 50.00
Priest Holmes
Dante Hall
MHJ Peyton Manning 30.00 80.00
Marvin Harrison
Edgerrin James

MWM Donovan McNabb	20.00	50.00
Brian Westbrook		
Freddie Mitchell		
PBL Jake Plummer	15.00	40.00
Champ Bailey		
Ashley Lelie		
PMM Chad Pennington	20.00	50.00
Curtis Martin		
Santana Moss		
VPD Michael Vick	25.00	60.00
Peerless Price		
Warrick Dunn		

2004 SP Game Used Edition Authentic Patches

STATED PRINT RUN 100 SER.#'d SETS
UNPRICED TRIPLE PRINT RUN 10

APAB Anquan Boldin	6.00	15.00
APCJ Chad Johnson	6.00	15.00
APCP Chad Pennington	6.00	15.00
APDD Domanick Davis	4.00	10.00
APDH Dante Hall	5.00	12.00
APDN Donovan McNabb	6.00	15.00
APEJ Edgerrin James	5.00	12.00
APGO Tony Gonzalez	6.00	15.00
APJH Joey Harrington	5.00	12.00
APJN Joe Namath	10.00	25.00
APJO Joe Horn	5.00	12.00
APJP Jake Plummer	5.00	12.00
APJS Jeremy Shockey	5.00	12.00
APLC Laveranues Coles	4.00	10.00
APLT LaDainian Tomlinson	6.00	15.00
APMA Mark Brunell	5.00	12.00
APMV Michael Vick	8.00	20.00
APPH Priest Holmes	6.00	15.00
APPM Peyton Manning	12.00	30.00
APRG Rex Grossman	5.00	12.00
APRW Roy Williams S	5.00	12.00
APTB Tom Brady	12.00	30.00
APTG Trent Green	5.00	12.00
APTH Torry Holt	5.00	12.00

2004 SP Game Used Edition Authentic Patches Autographs

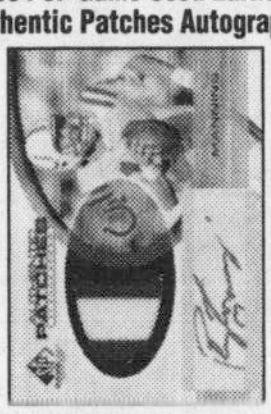

STATED PRINT RUN 25 SER.#'d SETS
UNPRICED DUAL AU PRINT RUN 5

AG Ahman Green	15.00	40.00
BL Byron Leftwich	15.00	40.00
CJ Chad Johnson	20.00	50.00
CP0 Chad Pennington	20.00	50.00
DB Drew Bledsoe	20.00	50.00
DD Domanick Davis	12.00	30.00
DH Dante Hall	15.00	40.00
DN Donovan McNabb	40.00	80.00
IB Isaac Bruce	15.00	40.00
JN Joe Namath	100.00	200.00
JO Joe Horn	15.00	40.00
KB Kyle Boller	15.00	40.00
LT LaDainian Tomlinson	40.00	80.00
MA Mark Brunell	15.00	40.00
PM Peyton Manning	100.00	200.00
RW Roy Williams S	15.00	40.00
SM Steve McNair	40.00	80.00
TB Tom Brady	175.00	300.00
TG Tony Gonzalez	30.00	60.00
TH Todd Heap	15.00	40.00
WM Willis McGahee	20.00	50.00
ZT Zach Thomas	20.00	50.00

2004 SP Game Used Edition Authentic Patches Dual

STATED PRINT RUN 25 SER.#'d SETS

BD Brett Favre	50.00	120.00
Daunte Culpepper		
BP Tom Brady	40.00	100.00
Chad Pennington		
FC Brett Favre	50.00	120.00
David Carr		
MH Randy Moss	20.00	50.00
Marvin Harrison		
MM Peyton Manning	40.00	100.00
Steve McNair		
MV Donovan McNabb	30.00	80.00
Michael Vick		
PJ Clinton Portis	20.00	50.00
Edgerrin James		

2004 SP Game Used Edition Awesome Authentics

STATED PRINT RUN 100 SER.#'d SETS

AAAB Anquan Boldin	6.00	15.00
AAAG Ahman Green	5.00	12.00
AABF Brett Favre	15.00	40.00
AABL Byron Leftwich	5.00	12.00
AACH Chad Pennington	6.00	15.00
AACJ Chad Johnson	6.00	15.00
AACP Clinton Portis	6.00	15.00
AADA David Carr	4.00	10.00
AADC Daunte Culpepper	5.00	12.00
AADE Deuce McAllister	5.00	12.00
AADH Dante Hall	5.00	12.00
AADM Donovan McNabb	6.00	15.00
AAEJ Edgerrin James	5.00	12.00
AAHE Todd Heap	5.00	12.00
AAJH Joey Harrington	5.00	12.00
AAJL Jamal Lewis	5.00	12.00
AAJP Jake Plummer	5.00	12.00
AAJS Jeremy Shockey	5.00	12.00
AALC Laveranues Coles	4.00	10.00
AALT LaDainian Tomlinson	6.00	15.00
AAMA Mark Brunell	5.00	12.00
AAMB Marc Bulger	5.00	12.00
AAMF Marshall Faulk	6.00	15.00
AAMH Marvin Harrison	6.00	15.00
AAMV Michael Vick	10.00	25.00
AAPH Priest Holmes	6.00	15.00
AAPM Peyton Manning	12.00	30.00
AARM Randy Moss	6.00	15.00
AARO Roy Williams S	5.00	12.00
AARW Ricky Williams	5.00	12.00
AASM Steve McNair	6.00	15.00
AATB Tom Brady	12.00	30.00
AATH Torry Holt	5.00	12.00

2004 SP Game Used Edition Legendary Fabric Autographs

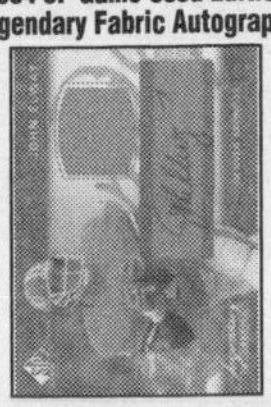

STATED PRINT RUN 50 SER.#'d SETS

AM Archie Manning	20.00	50.00
BS Barry Sanders	100.00	200.00
FT Fran Tarkenton	20.00	50.00
HL Howie Long	50.00	100.00
JE John Elway	100.00	200.00
JM Joe Montana	125.00	250.00
JN Joe Namath	75.00	150.00
JT Joe Theismann	20.00	50.00
KS Ken Stabler	25.00	60.00
KW Kellen Winslow	20.00	50.00
RS Roger Staubach	60.00	120.00
TA Troy Aikman	60.00	100.00

2004 SP Game Used Edition Rookie Exclusives Autographs

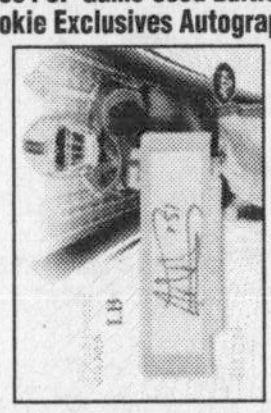

STATED PRINT RUN 100 SER.#'d SETS

REBB Bernard Berrian	20.00	50.00
REBC Brandon Chillar	15.00	40.00
REBJ B.J. Symons	12.00	30.00
REBR Ben Roethlisberger	150.00	300.00
REBT Ben Troupe	15.00	40.00
REBW Ben Watson	20.00	50.00
RECC Cedric Cobbs	12.00	30.00
RECH Chris Perry	15.00	40.00
RECP Cody Pickett	15.00	40.00
REDD Devard Darling	12.00	30.00
REDH DeAngelo Hall	20.00	50.00
REDR Drew Henson	12.00	30.00
REEM Eli Manning	175.00	300.00
REEW Ernest Wilford	15.00	40.00
REGJ Greg Jones	12.00	30.00
REJC Jerricho Cotchery	15.00	40.00
REJM Johnnie Morant	12.00	30.00
REJN John Navarre	12.00	30.00
REJP J.P. Losman	15.00	40.00
REJV Jonathan Vilma	20.00	50.00
REKC Keary Colbert	12.00	30.00
REKJ Kevin Jones	15.00	40.00
REKU Kenechi Udeze	15.00	40.00
REKW Kellen Winslow Jr.	20.00	50.00
RELE Lee Evans	20.00	50.00
RELF Larry Fitzgerald	60.00	120.00
RELM Luke McCown	15.00	40.00
REMC Michael Clayton	15.00	40.00
REMJ Michael Jenkins	20.00	50.00
REMS Matt Schaub	30.00	80.00
REPR Philip Rivers	75.00	150.00
RERA Rashaun Woods	12.00	30.00
RERE Reggie Williams	15.00	40.00
RERG Robert Gallery	20.00	50.00
RERW Roy Williams WR	20.00	50.00
RESJ Steven Jackson	50.00	100.00
RESP Samie Parker	12.00	30.00
RETH Tommie Harris	20.00	50.00
REVW Vince Wilfork	20.00	50.00
REWS Will Smith	15.00	40.00

2004 SP Game Used Edition SIGnificance

STATED PRINT RUN 100 SER.#'d SETS
*GOLD/10: .8X TO 2X BASIC AU
GOLD STATED PRINT RUN 10
UNPRICED NUMBERS PRINT RUN 4-12

AG Ahman Green	10.00	25.00
AM Archie Manning	15.00	40.00
BL Brandon Lloyd	10.00	25.00
BP Bill Parcells	30.00	60.00
BY Byron Leftwich	10.00	25.00
CJ Chad Johnson	12.00	30.00
DC Daunte Culpepper	10.00	25.00
DD Domanick Davis	8.00	20.00
DE Deuce McAllister	10.00	25.00
DH Dante Hall	10.00	25.00
DM Derrick Mason	10.00	25.00
GO Tony Gonzalez	12.00	30.00
GR Jon Gruden	10.00	25.00
HE Todd Heap	10.00	25.00
HL Howie Long	30.00	60.00
JF John Fox	8.00	20.00
JH Joe Horn	10.00	25.00
JJ Jimmy Johnson	12.00	30.00
JO Joey Galloway	10.00	25.00
JP Jesse Palmer	8.00	20.00
JT Joe Theismann	12.00	30.00
KB Kyle Boller	10.00	25.00
KS Ken Stabler	20.00	50.00
MA Mark Brunell	10.00	25.00
RE Andy Reid	10.00	25.00
TH Travis Henry	8.00	20.00
TS Tony Siragusa	10.00	25.00
WM Willis McGahee	12.00	30.00

2004 SP Game Used Edition SIGnificance Extra

EXTRA PRINT RUN 25 SETS
UNPRICED GOLD PRINT RUN 5

BT Mark Brunell	30.00	80.00
Joe Theismann		
JA Jimmy Johnson CO	60.00	120.00
Troy Aikman		
LS Howie Long	60.00	120.00
Ken Stabler		
MB Joe Montana	250.00	400.00
Tom Brady		
ME Joe Montana	125.00	250.00
John Elway		
MM Archie Manning	90.00	150.00
Peyton Manning		
PF Chad Pennington	125.00	250.00
Brett Favre		
SA Roger Staubach	100.00	200.00
Troy Aikman		
ST Barry Sanders	125.00	250.00
LaDainian Tomlinson		
TS Fran Tarkenton	40.00	100.00
Ken Stabler		

2004 SP Game Used Edition SIGnificant Numbers

UNPRICED NUMBERS PRINT RUN 4-12

2004 SP Game Used Hawaii Trade Conference

Given out by Upper Deck at the 2004 Hawaii Trade Conference, this set was sealed in one-card packages and distributed one-per to all paid attendees. Each card came sealed in a one-screw case where the screw was replaced with an un-tamperable piece of metal. Unless specified below, each card was serial numbered to 10. Due to market scarcity, no pricing is provided.

UNPRICED JSY AUTO's ISSUED
PP3 Brett Favre
PP4 Clinton Portis
PP9 Jamal Lewis
PP15 LaDainian Tomlinson
PP20 Marshall Faulk
PP25 Peyton Manning
PP26 Randy Moss
PP27 Ricky Williams

2002 SP Legendary Cuts

Released in late-December, this set contains 210 cards including 90 veterans, 30 veterans short-prints, and 90 rookies. Cards 91-100 were #'d to 2500, cards 101-110 were #'d to 1500, and cards 111-120 were #'d to 800. Rookies 121-150 were #'d to 500 and rookies 151-210 were #'d to 1100. Boxes contained 12 packs of 4 cards, and carried an SRP of $9.99

COMP.SET w/o SP's (90)	15.00	40.00
151-210 ROOKIE PRINT RUN 1100		
1 Tom Brady	1.25	3.00
2 Antowain Smith	.40	1.00
3 Troy Brown	.40	1.00
4 Drew Bledsoe	.50	1.25
5 Travis Henry	.30	.75
6 Eric Moulds	.40	1.00
7 Ricky Williams	.40	1.00
8 Jay Fiedler	.40	1.00
9 Chris Chambers	.40	1.00
10 Curtis Martin	.50	1.25
11 Chad Pennington	.50	1.25
12 Wayne Chrebet	.40	1.00
13 Jerome Bettis	.50	1.25
14 Tommy Maddox	.40	1.00
15 Hines Ward	.50	1.25
16 Tim Couch	.30	.75
17 Kevin Johnson	.30	.75
18 Jamal Lewis	.40	1.00
19 Chris Redman	.30	.75
20 Corey Dillon	.40	1.00
21 Michael Westbrook	.30	.75
22 Peyton Manning	1.00	2.50
23 Edgerrin James	.40	1.00
24 Marvin Harrison	.50	1.25
25 Qadry Ismail	.40	1.00
26 Mark Brunell	.40	1.00
27 Jimmy Smith	.40	1.00
28 Stacey Mack	.30	.75
29 Fred Taylor	.40	1.00
30 Steve McNair	.50	1.25
31 Eddie George	.40	1.00
32 Kevin Dyson	.40	1.00
33 James Allen	.30	.75
34 Corey Bradford	.30	.75
35 Shannon Sharpe	.50	1.25
36 Brian Griese	.40	1.00
37 Ed McCaffrey	.40	1.00
38 Jerry Rice	1.00	2.50
39 Rich Gannon	.40	1.00
40 Tim Brown	.50	1.25
41 Trent Green	.40	1.00
42 Priest Holmes	.50	1.25
43 Tony Gonzalez	.50	1.25
44 LaDainian Tomlinson	.60	1.50
45 Drew Brees	.75	2.00
46 Curtis Conway	.40	1.00
47 Donovan McNabb	.50	1.25
48 Duce Staley	.40	1.00
49 Antonio Freeman	.50	1.25
50 James Thrash	.40	1.00
51 Kerry Collins	.40	1.00
52 Tiki Barber	.50	1.25
53 Amani Toomer	.40	1.00
54 Emmitt Smith	1.25	3.00
55 Quincy Carter	.30	.75
56 Joey Galloway	.40	1.00
57 Stephen Davis	.40	1.00
58 Champ Bailey	.50	1.25
59 Anthony Thomas	.40	1.00
60 Jim Miller	.30	.75
61 Brian Urlacher	.50	1.25
62 Brett Favre	1.25	3.00
63 Ahman Green	.40	1.00
64 Robert Ferguson	.40	1.00
65 Randy Moss	.50	1.25
66 Daunte Culpepper	.40	1.00
67 Moe Williams	.30	.75
68 James Stewart	.30	.75
69 Az-Zahir Hakim	.30	.75
70 Keyshawn Johnson	.40	1.00
71 Brad Johnson	.40	1.00
72 Mike Alstott	.40	1.00
73 Michael Vick	.75	2.00
74 Warrick Dunn	.40	1.00
75 Shawn Jefferson	.30	.75
76 Aaron Brooks	.40	1.00
77 Deuce McAllister	.40	1.00
78 Joe Horn	.40	1.00
79 Rodney Peete	.40	1.00
80 Steve Smith	.50	1.25
81 Terrell Owens	.50	1.25
82 Jeff Garcia	.40	1.00
83 Garrison Hearst	.40	1.00
84 Kurt Warner	.50	1.25
85 Marshall Faulk	.50	1.25
86 Torry Holt	.50	1.25
87 Jake Plummer	.40	1.00
88 David Boston	.30	.75
89 Shaun Alexander	.40	1.00
90 Trent Dilfer	.40	1.00
91 Tom Brady VM	2.00	5.00
92 Michael Vick VM	1.25	3.00
93 LaDainian Tomlinson VM	1.00	2.50
94 Rich Gannon VM	.60	1.50
95 Randy Moss VM	.75	2.00
96 Aaron Brooks VM	.60	1.50
97 Mark Brunell VM	.60	1.50
98 Jeff Garcia VM	.60	1.50
99 Ahman Green VM	.60	1.50
100 Shaun Alexander VM	.60	1.50
101 Ricky Williams TG	.75	2.00
102 Bruce Smith TG	1.00	2.50
103 Curtis Martin TG	1.00	2.50
104 Brian Urlacher TG	1.00	2.50
105 Jerome Bettis TG	1.00	2.50
106 Ray Lewis TG	1.00	2.50
107 Edgerrin James TG	.75	2.00
108 Junior Seau TG	1.00	2.50
109 Priest Holmes TG	1.00	2.50
110 Warren Sapp TG	.75	2.00
111 Emmitt Smith RI	3.00	8.00
112 Jerry Rice RI	2.50	6.00
113 Brett Favre RI	3.00	8.00
114 Marshall Faulk RI	1.25	3.00
115 Drew Bledsoe RI	1.25	3.00
116 Tim Brown RI	1.25	3.00
117 Donovan McNabb RI	1.25	3.00
118 Peyton Manning RI	2.50	6.00
119 Kurt Warner RI	1.25	3.00
120 Shannon Sharpe RI	1.25	3.00
121 Andre Davis RC	2.00	5.00
122 Antonio Bryant RC	2.50	6.00
123 Antwaan Randle El RC	2.50	6.00
124 Ashley Lelie RC	2.00	5.00
125 Ben Leber RC	1.50	4.00
126 Chad Hutchinson RC	1.50	4.00
127 Clinton Portis RC	3.00	8.00
128 David Carr RC	2.50	6.00
129 Deion Branch RC	2.50	6.00
130 DeShaun Foster RC	2.50	6.00
131 Donte Stallworth RC	2.50	6.00
132 Jabar Gaffney RC	2.50	6.00
133 Javon Walker RC	2.50	6.00
134 Jeremy Shockey RC	4.00	10.00
135 Joey Harrington RC	2.50	6.00
136 Josh McCown RC	2.50	6.00
137 Josh Reed RC	2.00	5.00
138 Julius Peppers RC	5.00	12.00
139 Marquise Walker RC	1.50	4.00
140 Maurice Morris RC	2.00	5.00
141 Patrick Ramsey RC	2.50	6.00
142 Quentin Jammer RC	2.50	6.00
143 Randy Fasani RC	2.00	5.00
144 Reche Caldwell RC	2.50	6.00
145 Rohan Davey RC	2.50	6.00
146 Ron Johnson RC	2.00	5.00
147 Roy Williams RC	2.50	6.00
148 T.J. Duckett RC	2.50	6.00
149 Travis Stephens RC	1.50	4.00
150 William Green RC	2.00	5.00
151 Albert Haynesworth RC	2.00	5.00
152 Alex Brown RC	2.00	5.00
153 Andra Davis RC	1.25	3.00
154 Andre Gurode RC	3.00	8.00
155 Anthony Weaver RC	1.25	3.00
156 Brandon Doman RC	1.25	3.00
157 Brian Westbrook RC	3.00	8.00
158 Brian Williams RC	1.25	3.00
159 Lamont Brightful RC	1.25	3.00
160 Charles Grant RC	2.00	5.00
161 Chester Taylor RC	2.00	5.00
162 Cliff Russell RC	1.25	3.00
163 Daniel Graham RC	1.50	4.00
164 David Garrard RC	2.50	6.00
165 James Mungro RC	2.00	5.00
166 Dennis Johnson RC	1.25	3.00
167 Derek Ross RC	1.50	4.00
168 Dwight Freeney RC	2.50	6.00
169 Ed Reed RC	8.00	20.00
170 Carlos Hall RC	1.25	3.00
171 Jarrod Baxter RC	1.25	3.00
172 Jason McAddley RC	1.50	4.00
173 Jerramy Stevens RC	2.00	5.00
174 Jesse Chatman RC	1.25	3.00
175 John Henderson RC	1.50	4.00
176 Jon McGraw RC	1.25	3.00
177 Jonathan Wells RC	2.00	5.00
178 Justin Peelle RC	1.25	3.00
179 Kalimba Edwards RC	1.50	4.00
180 Keyou Craver RC	1.25	3.00
181 Kurt Kittner RC	1.25	3.00
182 LaDell Betts RC	2.00	5.00
183 Lamar Gordon RC	1.50	4.00
184 Lamont Thompson RC	1.50	4.00
185 Larry Tripplett RC	1.25	3.00
186 Randy McMichael RC	2.00	5.00
187 Lito Sheppard RC	2.00	5.00
188 Marques Anderson RC	1.50	4.00
189 Michael Lewis RC	2.00	5.00
190 Mike Pearson RC	1.25	3.00
191 Mike Rumph RC	1.25	3.00
192 Najeh Davenport RC	2.00	5.00
193 Napoleon Harris RC	1.50	4.00
194 Phillip Buchanon RC	2.00	5.00
195 Quinn Gray RC	1.50	4.00
196 Raonall Smith RC	1.25	3.00
197 Ricky Williams RC	1.50	4.00
198 Robert Thomas RC	1.25	3.00
199 Rocky Calmus RC	1.50	4.00
200 Ryan Denney RC	1.25	3.00
201 Ryan Sims RC	2.00	5.00
202 Jamal Robertson RC	1.25	3.00
203 Shaun Hill RC	2.50	6.00
204 Tank Williams RC	1.50	4.00
205 Tellis Redmon RC	1.25	3.00
206 Tim Carter RC	1.50	4.00
207 Tony Fisher RC	1.50	4.00
208 Travis Fisher RC	1.50	4.00
209 Verron Haynes RC	1.25	3.00
210 Wendell Bryant RC	1.25	3.00

2002 SP Legendary Cuts Autographs

STATED ODDS 1:192
PRINT RUN UNDER 20 NOT PRICED

LCAH Arnie Herber/25*	500.00	800.00
LCAW Alex Wojciechowicz/28*	125.00	250.00
LCBG Bill George/8*		
LCBL Bobby Layne/4*		
LCBN Bronko Nagurski/75*	300.00	550.00
LCBU Buck Buchanan/8*		
LCBW Bob Waterfield/12*		
LCCN Jack Christiansen/3*		
LCDF Dan Fortmann/30*	60.00	150.00
LCJU Johnny Unitas/29*	350.00	600.00
LCKS Ken Strong/120*	60.00	150.00
LCLF Len Ford/4*		
LCLG Lou Groza/20*	60.00	150.00
LCLL Link Lyman/11*		
LCMM Mike Michalske/7*		
LCMO Marion Motley/12*		
LCMU Johnny Unitas		
Peyton Manning/1*		
LCPS Emmitt Smith		
Walter Payton/1*		
LCPW Pop Warner/1*		
LCRB Red Badgro/57*	60.00	150.00
LCRF Ray Flaherty/25*	125.00	200.00
LCRG Red Grange/9*		
LCRN Ray Nitschke/115*	175.00	300.00
LCSL Sid Luckman/22*	175.00	300.00
LCSO Steve Owen/5*		
LCTE Turk Edwards/12*		
LCTF Tom Fears/9*		
LCTL Tom Landry/20*	350.00	600.00
LCVB Norm Van Brocklin/3*		
LCVL Vince Lombardi/240*	450.00	700.00
LCWP Walter Payton/65*	350.00	600.00

2002 SP Legendary Cuts Rookie Recruits Jerseys

STATED ODDS 1:17
*GOLD/75: .6X TO 1.5X BASIC JSY
GOLD PRINT RUN 75 SER.#'d SETS

RRAB Antonio Bryant	4.00	10.00
RRAD Andre Davis	3.00	8.00
RRAL Ashley Lelie	3.00	8.00
RRCP Clinton Portis	4.00	10.00
RRCR Cliff Russell	2.50	6.00
RRDC David Carr	4.00	10.00
RRDG Daniel Graham	3.00	8.00
RRDS Donte Stallworth	4.00	10.00
RREC Eric Crouch	3.00	8.00
RREL Antwaan Randle El	4.00	10.00
RRFO DeShaun Foster	4.00	10.00
RRJG Jabar Gaffney	4.00	10.00
RRJH Joey Harrington	4.00	10.00
RRJM Josh McCown	4.00	10.00
RRJP Julius Peppers	8.00	20.00
RRJR Josh Reed	3.00	8.00
RRJS Jeremy Shockey	6.00	15.00
RRJW Javon Walker	4.00	10.00
RRLB LaDell Betts	4.00	10.00
RRMM Maurice Morris	3.00	8.00
RRPR Patrick Ramsey	4.00	10.00
RRRC Reche Caldwell	4.00	10.00
RRRD Rohan Davey	4.00	10.00
RRRJ Ron Johnson	3.00	8.00
RRRO Roy Williams	4.00	10.00
RRTC Tim Carter	3.00	8.00
RRTJ T.J. Duckett	4.00	10.00
RRTS Travis Stephens	2.50	6.00
RRWA Marquise Walker	2.50	6.00
RRWG William Green	3.00	8.00

2002 SP Legendary Cuts SP Classic Threads

STATED PRINT RUN 350 SER.#'d SETS
*GOLD/75: .6X TO 1.5X BASIC JSY
GOLD PRINT RUN 75 SER.#'d SETS

CCAB Aaron Brooks	3.00	8.00
CCAG Ahman Green	3.00	8.00
CCAT Anthony Thomas	3.00	8.00
CCBF Brett Favre	10.00	25.00
CCBG Brian Griese	3.00	8.00
CCBO David Boston	2.50	6.00
CCBR Drew Brees	6.00	15.00
CCBY Tom Brady	10.00	25.00
CCCD Corey Dillon	3.00	8.00
CCCM Curtis Martin	4.00	10.00
CCCW Chris Weinke	2.50	6.00
CCDB Drew Bledsoe	4.00	10.00
CCDC Daunte Culpepper	3.00	8.00
CCDM Dan Marino	12.00	30.00
CCEG Eddie George	3.00	8.00
CCEJ Edgerrin James	3.00	8.00
CCES Emmitt Smith	12.00	30.00
CCGH Garrison Hearst	3.00	8.00
CCJB Jerome Bettis	4.00	10.00
CCJE John Elway	10.00	25.00
CCJG Jeff Garcia	3.00	8.00
CCJK Jim Kelly	6.00	15.00
CCJL Jamal Lewis	3.00	8.00
CCJR Jerry Rice	8.00	20.00
CCKC Kerry Collins	3.00	8.00
CCKJ Keyshawn Johnson	3.00	8.00
CCKW Kurt Warner	4.00	10.00
CCLT LaDainian Tomlinson	5.00	12.00
CCMA Marcus Allen	4.00	10.00
CCMC Donovan McNabb	4.00	10.00
CCMF Marshall Faulk	4.00	10.00
CCMH Marvin Harrison	4.00	10.00
CCMV Michael Vick	6.00	15.00
CCPH Priest Holmes	4.00	10.00
CCPM Peyton Manning	8.00	20.00
CCRG Rich Gannon	3.00	8.00
CCRM Randy Moss	4.00	10.00
CCRW Ricky Williams	3.00	8.00
CCSM Steve McNair	4.00	10.00
CCTB Tim Brown	4.00	10.00
CCTC Tim Couch	2.50	6.00
CCWP Walter Payton	20.00	50.00

2008 SP Legendary Cuts Mystery Cut Signatures

EXCHANGE DEADLINE 12/31/2010

2008 SP Rookie Edition

This set was released on November 26, 2008. The base set consists of 413 cards. Cards 1-100 are veterans, while cards 101-150 are rookies. Cards 151-200 are short printed rookies produced to look like cards from 1993 SP, cards 201-250 are rookies printed to look like cards from 1994 SP, cards 251-300 are rookies printed to look like cards from 1995 SP, and cards 301-350 are rookies printed to look like cards from 1996 SP. Cards 352-392 are legends printed to look like cards from 1996 SP, and cards 394-434 are legends printed to look like cards from 1993 SP.

COMP.SET w/o SP's (150)	25.00	50.00
ROOKIE STATED ODDS 4:1		
LEGENDS STATED ODDS 1:3.5		
1 Marshawn Lynch	.25	.60
2 Trent Edwards	.20	.50
3 Roscoe Parrish	.20	.50
4 Jason Taylor	.25	.60
5 Ronnie Brown	.25	.60
6 Hines Ward	.25	.60
7 Tom Brady	.50	1.25
8 Laurence Maroney	.25	.60
9 Randy Moss	.30	.75
10 Thomas Jones	.25	.60
11 Jerricho Cotchery	.25	.60
12 Brett Favre	1.50	4.00
13 Ray Lewis	.30	.75
14 Ed Reed	.25	.60
15 Willis McGahee	.25	.60
16 Carson Palmer	.30	.75
17 T.J. Houshmandzadeh	.25	.60
18 Dwayne Bowe	.25	.60
19 Kellen Winslow	.25	.60
20 Derek Anderson	.20	.50
21 Braylon Edwards	.25	.60
22 Ben Roethlisberger	.30	.75
23 Willie Parker	.25	.60
24 Wes Welker	.30	.75
25 DeMeco Ryans	.25	.60
26 Andre Johnson	.25	.60
27 Darius Walker	.20	.50
28 Peyton Manning	.50	1.25
29 Reggie Wayne	.25	.60
30 Joseph Addai	.25	.60
31 David Garrard	.25	.60
32 Maurice Jones-Drew	.25	.60
33 Fred Taylor	.25	.60
34 Vince Young	.25	.60
35 LenDale White	.25	.60
36 Alge Crumpler	.25	.60
37 Jay Cutler	.30	.75
38 Brandon Marshall	.25	.60
39 John Lynch	.25	.60
40 Brodie Croyle	.25	.60
41 Larry Johnson	.25	.60
42 Derrick Johnson	.20	.50
43 JaMarcus Russell	.25	.60
44 Ronald Curry	.25	.60
45 Jake Delhomme	.25	.60
46 Antonio Gates	.30	.75
47 LaDainian Tomlinson	.30	.75
48 Antonio Cromartie	.20	.50
49 Philip Rivers	.30	.75
50 Tony Romo	.40	1.00
51 Terrell Owens	.30	.75
52 DeMarcus Ware	.25	.60
53 Marion Barber	.25	.60
54 Eli Manning	.30	.75
55 Brandon Jacobs	.25	.60
56 Plaxico Burress	.25	.60
57 Antonio Pierce	.20	.50
58 Donovan McNabb	.30	.75
59 Brian Dawkins	.25	.60
60 Brian Westbrook	.25	.60
61 Chris Cooley	.25	.60
62 Jason Campbell	.25	.60
63 Clinton Portis	.25	.60
64 Brian Urlacher	.30	.75
65 Lance Briggs	.20	.50
66 Devin Hester	.30	.75
67 Roy Williams WR	.25	.60
68 Calvin Johnson	.30	.75
69 Ernie Sims	.20	.50
70 Aaron Rodgers	.60	1.50
71 Ryan Grant	.30	.75
72 Greg Jennings	.30	.75
73 Tarvaris Jackson	.25	.60
74 Adrian Peterson	.50	1.25
75 Sidney Rice	.30	.75
76 Michael Turner	.30	.75
77 Roddy White	.25	.60
78 Jason Witten	.30	.75
79 DeAngelo Williams	.25	.60
80 Steve Smith	.25	.60
81 Julius Peppers	.25	.60
82 Drew Brees	.30	.75
83 Reggie Bush	.30	.75
84 Marques Colston	.25	.60
85 Jonathan Vilma	.25	.60
86 Joey Galloway	.25	.60
87 Jeff Garcia	.25	.60
88 Cadillac Williams	.25	.60
89 Kurt Warner	.30	.75
90 Edgerrin James	.25	.60
91 Larry Fitzgerald	.30	.75
92 Anquan Boldin	.25	.60
93 Marc Bulger	.25	.60
94 Steven Jackson	.30	.75
95 Torry Holt	.25	.60
96 J.T. O'Sullivan	.20	.50
97 Frank Gore	.25	.60
98 Nate Clements	.20	.50
99 Matt Hasselbeck	.25	.60
100 Deion Branch	.25	.60
101 Alex Brink RC	.60	1.50
102 Andre Woodson RC	.60	1.50
103 Brian Brohm RC	.60	1.50
104 Dorien Bryant RC	.50	1.25
105 Colt Brennan RC	.60	1.50
106 Calais Campbell RC	.50	1.25
107 Chad Henne RC	.60	1.50
108 Chris Johnson RC	1.50	4.00
109 Chris Long RC	.60	1.50
110 Jacob Tamme RC	.60	1.50
111 Dan Connor RC	.60	1.50
112 Dennis Dixon RC	.60	1.50
113 DeSean Jackson RC	1.25	3.00
114 Dennis Keyes RC	.40	1.00
115 Darren McFadden RC	1.50	4.00
116 Dominique Rodgers-Cromartie RC	.60	1.50
117 Devin Thomas RC	.50	1.25
118 Erik Ainge RC	.60	1.50
119 Early Doucet RC	.50	1.25
120 Erin Henderson RC	.60	1.50
121 Fred Davis RC	.60	1.50
122 Felix Jones RC	1.00	2.50
123 Matt Forte RC	1.00	2.50
124 Glenn Dorsey RC	.60	1.50
125 John David Booty RC	.50	1.25
126 Jamaal Charles RC	1.00	2.50
127 Joe Flacco RC	2.00	5.00
128 Jonathan Goff RC	.40	1.00
129 Jake Long RC	.60	1.50
130 Jordy Nelson RC	.75	2.00
131 Jonathan Stewart RC	1.00	2.50
132 Davone Bess RC	.60	1.50
133 Kalvin McRae RC	.40	1.00
134 Kenny Phillips RC	.60	1.50
135 Kevin Smith RC	.60	1.50
136 Leodis McKelvin RC	.50	1.25
137 Limas Sweed RC	.60	1.50
138 Matt Flynn RC	1.25	3.00
139 Mike Hart RC	.60	1.50
140 Aqib Talib RC	.60	1.50
141 Malcolm Kelly RC	.50	1.25
142 Mario Manningham RC	.60	1.50
143 Matt Ryan RC	2.50	6.00
144 Paul Smith RC	.60	1.50
145 Rashard Mendenhall RC	1.25	3.00
146 Ray Rice RC	1.25	3.00
147 Sedrick Ellis RC	.60	1.50
148 Donnie Avery RC	.50	1.25
149 Tashard Choice RC	.50	1.25
150 Vernon Gholston RC	.50	1.25
151 Alex Brink 93	1.00	2.50
152 Andre Caldwell 93	.75	2.00
153 Allen Patrick 93	.75	2.00
154 Andre Woodson 93	1.00	2.50
155 Brian Brohm 93	1.00	2.50
156 Dorien Bryant 93	.75	2.00
157 Colt Brennan 93	1.00	2.50
158 Chris Ellis 93	.60	1.50
159 Chad Henne 93	1.00	2.50
160 Chris Johnson 93	2.50	6.00
161 Chris Long 93	1.00	2.50
162 Donnie Avery 93	.75	2.00
163 Davone Bess 93	1.00	2.50
164 Dan Connor 93	1.00	2.50
165 Dennis Dixon 93	1.00	2.50
166 DeSean Jackson 93	2.00	5.00
167 Darren McFadden 93	2.50	6.00
168 Erik Ainge 93	1.00	2.50
169 Early Doucet 93	.75	2.00
170 Fred Davis 93	1.00	2.50
171 Felix Jones 93	1.50	4.00
172 Matt Forte 93	1.50	4.00
173 Geno Hayes 93	.60	1.50
174 Chevis Jackson 93	.60	1.50
175 John David Booty 93	.75	2.00
176 Jamaal Charles 93	1.50	4.00
177 Joe Flacco 93	3.00	8.00
178 Peyton Hillis 93	1.25	3.00
179 Jake Long 93	1.00	2.50
180 Jordy Nelson 93	1.25	3.00
181 Jonathan Stewart 93	1.50	4.00
182 Justin Forsett 93	1.00	2.50
183 Kevin O'Connell 93	.75	2.00
184 Kenny Phillips 93	1.00	2.50
185 Kevin Smith 93	1.00	2.50
186 Lance Ball 93	.60	1.50
187 Leodis McKelvin 93	.75	2.00
188 Limas Sweed 93	1.00	2.50
189 Marcus Monk 93	.75	2.00
190 Matt Flynn 93	2.00	5.00
191 Mike Hart 93	1.00	2.50
192 Mike Jenkins 93	1.00	2.50
193 Malcolm Kelly 93	.75	2.00
194 Mario Manningham 93	1.00	2.50
195 Dre Moore 93	.75	2.00
196 Matt Ryan 93	4.00	10.00
197 Ryan Clady 93	1.00	2.50
198 Rashard Mendenhall 93	2.00	5.00
199 Ray Rice 93	2.00	5.00
200 Tashard Choice 93	.75	2.00
201 Alex Brink 94	1.25	3.00
202 Aqib Talib 94	1.25	3.00
203 Andre Woodson 94	1.25	3.00
204 Brian Brohm 94	1.25	3.00
205 Dorien Bryant 94	1.00	2.50
206 Colt Brennan 94	1.25	3.00
207 Calais Campbell 94	1.00	2.50
208 Chad Henne 94	1.25	3.00
209 Chris Johnson 94	3.00	8.00
210 Chris Long 94	1.25	3.00
211 Donnie Avery 94	1.00	2.50
212 Davone Bess 94	1.25	3.00
213 Dennis Dixon 94	1.25	3.00
214 DeSean Jackson 94	2.50	6.00
215 Darren McFadden 94	3.00	8.00
216 Dominique Rodgers-Cromartie 94	1.25	3.00
217 Erik Ainge 94	1.25	3.00
218 Early Doucet 94	1.00	2.50
219 Fred Davis 94	1.25	3.00
220 Felix Jones 94	2.00	5.00
221 Matt Forte 94	2.00	5.00
222 Harry Douglas 94	1.00	2.50
223 John David Booty 94	1.00	2.50
224 Jamaal Charles 94	2.00	5.00
225 Joe Flacco 94	4.00	10.00
226 James Hardy 94	1.00	2.50
227 Josh Johnson 94	1.25	3.00
228 Jordy Nelson 94	1.50	4.00
229 Jonathan Stewart 94	2.00	5.00
230 Keenan Burton 94	.75	2.00
231 Kenny Phillips 94	1.25	3.00
232 Keith Rivers 94	1.25	3.00
233 Kevin Smith 94	1.25	3.00
234 Lavelle Hawkins 94	.75	2.00
235 Leodis McKelvin 94	1.00	2.50
236 Limas Sweed 94	1.25	3.00
237 Matt Flynn 94	2.50	6.00
238 Mike Hart 94	1.25	3.00
239 Adrian Arrington 94	1.00	2.50
240 Malcolm Kelly 94	1.00	2.50
241 Mario Manningham 94	1.25	3.00
242 Matt Ryan 94	5.00	12.00
243 Phillip Merling 94	1.00	2.50
244 Darius Reynaud 94	.75	2.00
245 Rashard Mendenhall 94	2.50	6.00
246 Ray Rice 94	2.50	6.00
247 Ryan Torain 94	1.25	3.00
248 Thomas Brown 94	1.00	2.50
249 Tashard Choice 94	1.00	2.50
250 Vernon Gholston 94	1.00	2.50
251 Alex Brink 95	1.50	4.00
252 Allen Patrick 95	1.25	3.00
253 Aqib Talib 95	1.50	4.00
254 Andre Woodson 95	1.50	4.00
255 Brian Brohm 95	1.50	4.00
256 Dorien Bryant 95	1.25	3.00
257 Colt Brennan 95	1.50	4.00

258 Chad Henne 95	1.50	4.00
259 Chris Johnson 95	4.00	10.00
260 Chris Long 95	1.50	4.00
261 Davone Bess 95	1.50	4.00
262 Dennis Dixon 95	1.50	4.00
263 DeSean Jackson 95	3.00	8.00
264 Darren McFadden 95	4.00	10.00
265 Erik Ainge 95	1.50	4.00
266 Early Doucet 95	1.25	3.00
267 Fred Davis 95	1.50	4.00
268 Felix Jones 95	2.50	6.00
269 Matt Forte 95	2.50	6.00
270 Geno Hayes 95	1.00	2.50
271 Harry Douglas 95	1.25	3.00
272 John David Booty 95	1.25	3.00
273 Jamaal Charles 95	2.50	6.00
274 Joe Flacco 95	5.00	12.00
275 Peyton Hillis 95	2.00	5.00
276 Jacob Hester 95	1.50	4.00
277 Josh Johnson 95	1.50	4.00
278 Jordy Nelson 95	2.00	5.00
279 Jonathan Stewart 95	2.50	6.00
280 Keenan Burton 95	1.00	2.50
281 Kenny Phillips 95	1.50	4.00
282 Kevin Smith 95	1.50	4.00
283 Lance Ball 95	1.00	2.50
284 Lavelle Hawkins 95	1.00	2.50
285 Limas Sweed 95	1.50	4.00
286 Matt Flynn 95	3.00	8.00
287 Mike Hart 95	1.50	4.00
288 Adrian Arrington 95	1.25	3.00
289 Malcolm Kelly 95	1.25	3.00
290 Mario Manningham 95	1.50	4.00
291 Marcus Monk 95	1.25	3.00
292 Matt Ryan 95	6.00	15.00
293 Mario Urrutia 95	1.00	2.50
294 Paul Hubbard 95	1.25	3.00
295 Rashard Mendenhall 95	3.00	8.00
296 Ray Rice 95	3.00	8.00
297 Ryan Torain 95	1.50	4.00
298 Thomas Brown 95	1.25	3.00
299 Tashard Choice 95	1.25	3.00
300 Yvenson Bernard 95	1.50	4.00
301 Alex Brink 96	1.50	4.00
302 Chevis Jackson 96	1.00	2.50
303 Andre Caldwell 96	1.25	3.00
304 Allen Patrick 96	1.25	3.00
305 Kevin O'Connell 96	1.25	3.00
306 Andre Woodson 96	1.50	4.00
307 Brian Brohm 96	1.50	4.00
308 Mike Jenkins 96	1.50	4.00
309 Tom Zbikowski 96	1.50	4.00
310 Dorien Bryant 96	1.25	3.00
311 Colt Brennan 96	1.50	4.00
312 Chad Henne 96	1.50	4.00
313 Chris Johnson 96	4.00	10.00
314 Chris Long 96	1.50	4.00
315 Donnie Avery 96	1.25	3.00
316 Davone Bess 96	1.50	4.00
317 Dennis Dixon 96	1.50	4.00
318 DeSean Jackson 96	3.00	8.00
319 Darren McFadden 96	4.00	10.00
320 DeMario Pressley 96	1.25	3.00
321 Dre Moore 96	1.25	3.00
322 Erik Ainge 96	1.50	4.00
323 Early Doucet 96	1.25	3.00
324 Fred Davis 96	1.50	4.00
325 Felix Jones 96	2.50	6.00
326 Matt Forte 96	2.50	6.00
327 Harry Douglas 96	1.25	3.00
328 John David Booty 96	1.25	3.00
329 Jamaal Charles 96	2.50	6.00
330 Joe Flacco 96	5.00	12.00
331 Jordy Nelson 96	2.00	5.00
332 Jonathan Stewart 96	2.50	6.00
333 Kalvin McRae 96	1.00	2.50
334 Kenny Phillips 96	1.50	4.00
335 Kevin Smith 96	1.50	4.00
336 Lavelle Hawkins 96	1.00	2.50
337 Limas Sweed 96	1.50	4.00
338 Marcus Monk 96	1.25	3.00
339 Matt Flynn 96	3.00	8.00
340 Mike Hart 96	1.50	4.00
341 Adrian Arrington 96	1.25	3.00
342 Malcolm Kelly 96	1.25	3.00
343 Mario Manningham 96	1.50	4.00
344 Ben Moffitt 96	1.00	2.50
345 Matt Ryan 96	6.00	15.00
346 Mario Urrutia 96	1.00	2.50
347 Rashard Mendenhall 96	3.00	8.00
348 Ray Rice 96	3.00	8.00
349 Ryan Torain 96	1.50	4.00
350 Tashard Choice 96	1.25	3.00
352 Bob Griese 96	1.25	3.00
353 Bert Jones 96	.75	2.00
354 Bruce Smith 96	.75	2.00
355 Barry Sanders 96	2.00	5.00
356 Dick Butkus 96	1.50	4.00
357 Daryl Johnston 96	1.25	3.00
359 Franco Harris 96	1.25	3.00
360 Fran Tarkenton 96	1.25	3.00
363 Bo Jackson 96	1.50	4.00
365 John Elway 96	2.00	5.00
366 Joe Greene 96	1.25	3.00
367 Jack Ham 96	1.00	2.50
368 Jerry Kramer 96	1.00	2.50
369 Jim Kelly 96	1.25	3.00
372 Joe Theismann 96	1.25	3.00
373 Ken Anderson 96	1.00	2.50
376 Jerry Rice 96	2.00	5.00
377 Emmitt Smith 96	2.50	6.00
379 Ottis Anderson 96	.75	2.00
380 Paul Hornung 96	1.25	3.00
381 Roger Craig 96	1.00	2.50
382 Roman Gabriel 96	1.00	2.50
383 Chuck Bednarik 96	1.00	2.50
384 Rod Woodson 96	1.25	3.00
385 Billy Sims 96	1.00	2.50
386 Archie Manning 96	1.25	3.00
387 Bart Starr 96	2.00	5.00
388 Steve Young 96	1.50	4.00
389 Troy Aikman 96	1.50	4.00
391 Tom Rathman 96	1.00	2.50
392 Y.A. Tittle 96	1.25	3.00
394 Bob Griese 93	1.25	3.00
395 Bert Jones 93	.75	2.00
396 Bruce Smith 93	.75	2.00
397 Barry Sanders 93	2.00	5.00
398 Dick Butkus 93	1.50	4.00
399 Daryl Johnston 93	1.25	3.00
401 Franco Harris 93	1.25	3.00
402 Fran Tarkenton 93	1.25	3.00
405 Bo Jackson 93	1.50	4.00
407 John Elway 93	2.00	5.00
408 Joe Greene 93	1.25	3.00
409 Jack Ham 93	1.00	2.50
410 Jim Kelly 93	1.25	3.00
411 Jerry Kramer 93	1.00	2.50
414 Joe Theismann 93	1.25	3.00
415 Ken Anderson 93	1.00	2.50
418 Roger Staubach 93	1.50	4.00
419 Chuck Bednarik 93	1.00	2.50
421 Ottis Anderson 93	.75	2.00
422 Paul Hornung 93	1.25	3.00
423 Roger Craig 93	1.00	2.50
424 Roman Gabriel 93	1.00	2.50
426 Rod Woodson 93	1.25	3.00
427 Billy Sims 93	1.00	2.50
428 Archie Manning 93	1.25	3.00
429 Bart Starr 93	2.00	5.00
430 Steve Young 93	1.50	4.00
431 Troy Aikman 93	1.50	4.00
433 Tom Rathman 93	1.00	2.50
434 Y.A. Tittle 93	1.25	3.00

2008 SP Rookie Edition Autographs

STATED ODDS 1:7

152 Andre Caldwell 93	4.00	10.00
153 Allen Patrick 93	4.00	10.00
154 Andre Woodson 93	5.00	12.00
155 Brian Brohm 93	5.00	12.00
156 Dorien Bryant 93	4.00	10.00
157 Colt Brennan 93	5.00	12.00
158 Chris Ellis 93	3.00	8.00
159 Chad Henne 93	12.00	30.00
160 Chris Johnson 93	20.00	50.00
161 Chris Long 93	5.00	12.00
162 Donnie Avery 93	4.00	10.00
163 Davone Bess 93	5.00	12.00
164 Dan Connor 93	5.00	12.00
165 Dennis Dixon 93	10.00	20.00
166 DeSean Jackson 93	12.00	30.00
167 Darren McFadden 93	25.00	60.00
168 Erik Ainge 93	5.00	12.00
169 Early Doucet 93	4.00	10.00
170 Fred Davis 93	5.00	12.00
171 Felix Jones 93	15.00	40.00
172 Matt Forte 93	12.00	30.00
173 Geno Hayes 93	3.00	8.00
174 Chevis Jackson 93	3.00	8.00
175 John David Booty 93	4.00	10.00
176 Jamaal Charles 93	8.00	20.00
177 Joe Flacco 93	40.00	80.00
178 Peyton Hillis 93	10.00	25.00
179 Jake Long 93	5.00	12.00
180 Jordy Nelson 93	10.00	25.00
181 Jonathan Stewart 93	8.00	20.00
182 Justin Forsett 93	5.00	12.00
183 Kevin O'Connell 93	4.00	10.00
184 Kenny Phillips 93	5.00	12.00
185 Kevin Smith 93	5.00	12.00
186 Lance Ball 93	3.00	8.00
187 Leodis McKelvin 93	4.00	10.00
188 Limas Sweed 93	5.00	12.00
189 Marcus Monk 93	4.00	10.00
190 Matt Flynn 93	25.00	50.00
191 Mike Hart 93	5.00	12.00
192 Mike Jenkins 93	5.00	12.00
193 Malcolm Kelly 93	4.00	10.00
194 Mario Manningham 93	6.00	15.00
195 Dre Moore 93	4.00	10.00
196 Matt Ryan 93	40.00	100.00
197 Ryan Clady 93	5.00	12.00
198 Rashard Mendenhall 93	12.00	30.00
199 Ray Rice 93	15.00	40.00
200 Tashard Choice 93	4.00	10.00
201 Alex Brink 94	5.00	12.00
202 Aqib Talib 94	5.00	12.00
203 Andre Woodson 94	5.00	12.00
204 Brian Brohm 94	5.00	12.00
205 Dorien Bryant 94	4.00	10.00
206 Colt Brennan 94	5.00	12.00
207 Calais Campbell 94		
208 Chad Henne 94	12.00	30.00
209 Chris Johnson 94	20.00	50.00
210 Chris Long 94	5.00	12.00
211 Donnie Avery 94	4.00	10.00
212 Davone Bess 94	5.00	12.00
213 Dennis Dixon 94	10.00	20.00
214 DeSean Jackson 94	12.00	30.00
215 Darren McFadden 94	25.00	60.00
216 Dominique Rodgers-Cromartie 94	5.00	12.00
217 Erik Ainge 94	5.00	12.00
218 Early Doucet 94	4.00	10.00
220 Felix Jones 94	15.00	40.00
221 Matt Forte 94	12.00	30.00
222 Harry Douglas 94	4.00	10.00
223 John David Booty 94	4.00	10.00
224 Jamaal Charles 94	8.00	20.00
225 Joe Flacco 94	40.00	80.00
226 James Hardy 94	4.00	10.00
227 Josh Johnson 94	5.00	12.00
228 Jordy Nelson 94	10.00	25.00
229 Jonathan Stewart 94	8.00	20.00
230 Keenan Burton 94	3.00	8.00
231 Kenny Phillips 94	5.00	12.00
232 Keith Rivers 94	5.00	12.00
233 Kevin Smith 94	5.00	12.00
234 Lavelle Hawkins 94	3.00	8.00
235 Leodis McKelvin 94	4.00	10.00
236 Limas Sweed 94	5.00	12.00
237 Matt Flynn 94	25.00	50.00
238 Mike Hart 94	5.00	12.00
239 Adrian Arrington 94	4.00	10.00
240 Malcolm Kelly 94	4.00	10.00
241 Mario Manningham 94	6.00	15.00
242 Matt Ryan 94	40.00	100.00
243 Phillip Merling 94	4.00	10.00
244 Darius Reynaud 94	3.00	8.00
246 Ray Rice 94	15.00	40.00
247 Ryan Torain 94	5.00	12.00
248 Thomas Brown 94	4.00	10.00
249 Tashard Choice 94	4.00	10.00
250 Vernon Gholston 94	4.00	10.00
252 Allen Patrick 95	5.00	12.00
253 Aqib Talib 95	6.00	15.00
254 Andre Woodson 95	6.00	15.00
255 Brian Brohm 95	5.00	12.00
256 Dorien Bryant 95	5.00	12.00
257 Colt Brennan 95	5.00	12.00
258 Chad Henne 95	15.00	40.00
259 Chris Johnson 95	25.00	60.00
260 Chris Long 95	5.00	12.00
261 Davone Bess 95	5.00	12.00
263 DeSean Jackson 95	12.00	30.00
264 Darren McFadden 95	25.00	60.00
265 Erik Ainge 95	6.00	15.00
268 Felix Jones 95	15.00	40.00
269 Matt Forte 95	15.00	40.00
271 Harry Douglas 95	5.00	12.00
272 John David Booty 95	4.00	10.00
273 Jamaal Charles 95	10.00	25.00
274 Joe Flacco 95	40.00	100.00
275 Peyton Hillis 95	10.00	25.00
277 Josh Johnson 95	6.00	15.00
278 Jordy Nelson 95	12.00	30.00
279 Jonathan Stewart 95	10.00	25.00
280 Keenan Burton 95	4.00	10.00
281 Kenny Phillips 95	6.00	15.00
282 Kevin Smith 95	6.00	15.00
283 Lance Ball 95	4.00	10.00
284 Lavelle Hawkins 95	4.00	10.00
285 Limas Sweed 95	6.00	15.00
286 Matt Flynn 95	25.00	50.00
287 Mike Hart 95	6.00	15.00
288 Adrian Arrington 95	5.00	12.00
289 Malcolm Kelly 95	5.00	12.00
291 Marcus Monk 95	5.00	12.00
292 Matt Ryan 95	50.00	120.00
293 Mario Urrutia 95		
294 Paul Hubbard 95		
297 Ryan Torain 95	6.00	15.00
298 Thomas Brown 95	5.00	12.00
299 Tashard Choice 95	4.00	10.00
302 Chevis Jackson 96		
303 Andre Caldwell 96	5.00	12.00
304 Allen Patrick 96		
306 Andre Woodson 96		
307 Brian Brohm 96		
308 Mike Jenkins 96	6.00	15.00
309 Tom Zbikowski 96	6.00	15.00
310 Dorien Bryant 96		
311 Colt Brennan 96		
312 Chad Henne 96		
313 Chris Johnson 96	25.00	60.00
314 Chris Long 96	8.00	20.00
315 Donnie Avery 96	5.00	12.00
316 Davone Bess 96	6.00	15.00
318 DeSean Jackson 96	15.00	40.00
319 Darren McFadden 96		
320 DeMario Pressley 96	5.00	12.00
321 Dre Moore 96		
322 Erik Ainge 96		
325 Felix Jones 96	15.00	40.00
326 Matt Forte 96	15.00	40.00
327 Harry Douglas 96		
328 John David Booty 96	5.00	12.00
329 Jamaal Charles 96	10.00	25.00
330 Joe Flacco 96	40.00	100.00
331 Jordy Nelson 96	12.00	30.00
332 Jonathan Stewart 96	30.00	80.00
334 Kenny Phillips 96	6.00	15.00
335 Kevin Smith 96	6.00	15.00
337 Limas Sweed 96	6.00	15.00
338 Marcus Monk 96	5.00	12.00
339 Matt Flynn 96	25.00	50.00
340 Mike Hart 96	6.00	15.00
341 Adrian Arrington 96	5.00	12.00
342 Malcolm Kelly 96		
344 Ben Moffitt 96	4.00	10.00
345 Matt Ryan 96	50.00	120.00
346 Mario Urrutia 96		
349 Ryan Torain 96	8.00	20.00
350 Tashard Choice 96		
353 Bert Jones 96	15.00	30.00
354 Bruce Smith 96	30.00	60.00
355 Barry Sanders 96		
356 Dick Butkus 96	50.00	100.00
357 Daryl Johnston 96	25.00	50.00
359 Franco Harris 96	40.00	80.00
363 Bo Jackson 96	40.00	80.00
365 John Elway 96	50.00	100.00
367 Jack Ham 96		
368 Jerry Kramer 96		
372 Joe Theismann 96	20.00	40.00
376 Jerry Rice 96	100.00	175.00
377 Emmitt Smith 96		
379 Ottis Anderson 96	10.00	25.00
380 Paul Hornung 96	20.00	40.00
381 Roger Craig 96	15.00	30.00
382 Roman Gabriel 96	20.00	40.00
385 Billy Sims 96		
388 Steve Young 96	40.00	80.00
391 Tom Rathman 96	20.00	40.00
392 Y.A. Tittle 96	25.00	50.00
395 Bert Jones 93	15.00	30.00
396 Bruce Smith 93	30.00	60.00
397 Barry Sanders 93		
398 Dick Butkus 93	50.00	100.00
399 Daryl Johnston 93	20.00	40.00
401 Franco Harris 93		
405 Bo Jackson 93		
407 John Elway 93		
409 Jack Ham 93	30.00	60.00
411 Jerry Kramer 93	15.00	30.00
414 Joe Theismann 93		
418 Roger Staubach 93	75.00	125.00
421 Ottis Anderson 93		
422 Paul Hornung 93	20.00	40.00
423 Roger Craig 93	15.00	30.00
424 Roman Gabriel 93	20.00	40.00
427 Billy Sims 93	15.00	30.00
428 Archie Manning 93		
430 Steve Young 93	50.00	80.00
433 Tom Rathman 93		
434 Y.A. Tittle 93		

2007 SP Rookie Threads

This 160-card set was released in September, 2007. The set was issued into the hobby in five-card packs, with a $50 SRP, which came six packs to a box. Cards numbered 1-100 feature veterans while cards 101-160 feature 2007 NFL rookies, all of whom signed the cards. Those cards were issued to stated print runs of between 150 and 250 serial numbered sets. For those players who signed 150 cards we have notated that information in our checklist.

COMP.SET w/o RC's (100)	25.00	50.00
AU ROOKIE PRINT RUN 150-250		
1 Matt Leinart	.60	1.50
2 Anquan Boldin	.60	1.50
3 Larry Fitzgerald	.75	2.00
4 Edgerrin James	.60	1.50
5 Michael Vick	.75	2.00
6 Warrick Dunn	.60	1.50
7 Alge Crumpler	.60	1.50
8 Steve McNair	.60	1.50
9 Mark Clayton	.60	1.50
10 Ray Lewis	.75	2.00
11 J.P. Losman	.50	1.25
12 Lee Evans	.60	1.50
13 Anthony Thomas	.50	1.25
14 Jake Delhomme	.60	1.50
15 Steve Smith	.60	1.50
16 DeShaun Foster	.60	1.50
17 Brian Urlacher	.75	2.00
18 Cedric Benson	.60	1.50
19 Rex Grossman	.60	1.50
20 Bernard Berrian	.50	1.25
21 Chad Johnson	.60	1.50
22 Rudi Johnson	.60	1.50
23 Carson Palmer	.60	1.50
24 T.J. Houshmandzadeh	.60	1.50
25 Jamal Lewis	.60	1.50
26 Braylon Edwards	.60	1.50
27 Kellen Winslow	.60	1.50
28 Julius Jones	.50	1.25
29 Tony Romo	1.00	2.50
30 Terrell Owens	.75	2.00
31 Javon Walker	.60	1.50
32 Travis Henry	.60	1.50
33 Jay Cutler	.75	2.00
34 Champ Bailey	.60	1.50
35 Tatum Bell	.50	1.25
36 Roy Williams WR	.60	1.50
37 Jon Kitna	.50	1.25
38 Donald Driver	.75	2.00
39 Brett Favre	1.50	4.00
40 A.J. Hawk	.60	1.50
41 Ahman Green	.60	1.50
42 Matt Schaub	.60	1.50
43 Andre Johnson	.60	1.50
44 Reggie Wayne	.60	1.50
45 Joseph Addai	.60	1.50
46 Marvin Harrison	.75	2.00
47 Peyton Manning	1.25	3.00
48 Byron Leftwich	.60	1.50
49 Fred Taylor	.60	1.50
50 Maurice Jones-Drew	.75	2.00
51 Tony Gonzalez	.60	1.50
52 Larry Johnson	.50	1.25
53 Damon Huard	.60	1.50
54 Chris Chambers	.60	1.50
55 Ronnie Brown	.60	1.50
56 Chester Taylor	.50	1.25
57 Troy Williamson	.50	1.25
58 Tarvaris Jackson	.50	1.25
59 Tedy Bruschi	.75	2.00
60 Laurence Maroney	.60	1.50
61 Tom Brady	1.25	3.00
62 Reggie Bush	.75	2.00
63 Drew Brees	.75	2.00
64 Deuce McAllister	.60	1.50
65 Eli Manning	.75	2.00
66 Plaxico Burress	.60	1.50
67 Brandon Jacobs	.60	1.50
68 Chad Pennington	.60	1.50
69 Leon Washington	.60	1.50
70 Laveranues Coles	.50	1.25
71 Jerricho Cotchery	.60	1.50
72 Ronald Curry	.60	1.50
73 Dominic Rhodes	.60	1.50
74 Donovan McNabb	.75	2.00
75 Brian Westbrook	.60	1.50
76 Reggie Brown	.50	1.25
77 Ben Roethlisberger	.75	2.00
78 Hines Ward	.75	2.00
79 Willie Parker	.60	1.50
80 Santonio Holmes	.60	1.50
81 Philip Rivers	.75	2.00
82 Antonio Gates	.75	2.00
83 Shawne Merriman	.60	1.50
84 LaDainian Tomlinson	.75	2.00
85 Alex Smith QB	.75	2.00
86 Frank Gore	.75	2.00
87 Shaun Alexander	.60	1.50
88 Matt Hasselbeck	.60	1.50
89 Deion Branch	.60	1.50
90 Torry Holt	.60	1.50
91 Steven Jackson	.75	2.00
92 Marc Bulger	.60	1.50
93 Chris Simms	.50	1.25
94 Cadillac Williams	.60	1.50
95 Joey Galloway	.60	1.50
96 Keith Bulluck	.50	1.25
97 Vince Young	.60	1.50
98 Jason Campbell	.60	1.50
99 Santana Moss	.60	1.50
100 Clinton Portis	.60	1.50
101 Daymeion Hughes AU RC	10.00	25.00
102 Eric Wright AU RC	12.00	30.00
103 Leon Hall AU RC	10.00	25.00
104 Gaines Adams AU RC	12.00	30.00
105 LaMarr Woodley AU RC	20.00	40.00
106 Quentin Moses AU RC	10.00	25.00
107 Amobi Okoye AU RC	12.00	30.00
108 Lawrence Timmons AU RC	12.00	30.00
109 Joe Thomas AU RC	12.00	30.00
110 Brady Quinn AU/150 RC	20.00	50.00
111 Chris Leak AU RC	10.00	25.00
112 Drew Stanton AU RC	8.00	20.00
113 JaMarcus Russell AU/150 RC	10.00	25.00
114 Jeff Rowe AU RC	8.00	20.00
115 John Beck AU RC	12.00	30.00
116 Jordan Palmer AU RC	10.00	25.00
117 Kevin Kolb AU RC	20.00	50.00
118 Matt Moore AU RC	12.00	30.00
119 Trent Edwards AU RC	12.00	30.00
120 Jamaal Anderson AU RC	10.00	25.00
121 Tyler Palko AU RC	10.00	25.00
122 Adrian Peterson AU/150 RC	100.00	200.00
123 Antonio Pittman AU RC	8.00	20.00
124 Brandon Jackson AU RC	10.00	25.00
125 Brian Leonard AU RC	10.00	25.00
126 Chris Henry RB AU RC	8.00	20.00
127 Darius Walker AU RC	8.00	20.00
128 Dwayne Wright AU RC	10.00	25.00
129 Garrett Wolfe AU RC	8.00	20.00
130 Kenneth Darby AU RC	10.00	25.00
131 Kenny Irons AU RC	8.00	20.00
132 Kolby Smith AU RC	10.00	25.00
133 Lorenzo Booker AU RC	10.00	25.00
134 Marshawn Lynch AU RC	5.00	40.00
135 Michael Bush AU RC	12.00	30.00
136 Selvin Young AU RC	10.00	25.00
137 Tony Hunt AU RC	8.00	20.00
138 LaRon Landry AU RC	12.00	30.00
139 Scott Chandler AU RC	12.00	30.00
140 Greg Olsen AU RC	10.00	25.00
141 Zach Miller AU RC	12.00	30.00
142 Anthony Gonzalez AU RC	12.00	30.00
143 Aundrae Allison AU RC	8.00	20.00
144 Calvin Johnson AU/150 RC	40.00	100.00
145 Chansi Stuckey AU RC	12.00	30.00
146 Craig Buster Davis AU RC	10.00	25.00
147 Dallas Baker AU RC	8.00	20.00
148 David Ball AU RC	10.00	25.00
149 David Clowney AU RC	10.00	25.00
150 Dwayne Bowe AU RC	15.00	40.00
151 Dwayne Jarrett AU RC	10.00	25.00
152 Jason Hill AU RC	12.00	30.00
153 Johnnie Lee Higgins AU RC	10.00	25.00
154 Rhema McKnight AU RC	8.00	20.00
155 Robert Meachem AU RC	12.00	30.00
156 Sidney Rice AU RC	15.00	40.00
157 Steve Smith USC AU RC	12.00	30.00
158 Syvelle Newton AU RC	10.00	25.00
159 Ted Ginn Jr. AU RC	10.00	25.00
160 Legedu Naanee AU RC	12.00	30.00

2007 SP Rookie Threads Rookie Lettermen Black

*BLACK/25: .6X TO 1.5X BASIC AU/250
STATED PRINT RUN 5-25
SERIAL #'d UNDER 25 NOT PRICED

2007 SP Rookie Threads Rookie Lettermen Gold

*GOLD/75-99: .5X TO 1.2X BASIC AU/250
STATED PRINT RUN 25-99

122 Adrian Peterson AU/25	150.00	300.00

2007 SP Rookie Threads Rookie Lettermen Silver

*SILVER/150-199: .4X TO 1X BASIC AU/250
STATED PRINT RUN 75-199

122 Adrian Peterson AU/75	100.00	200.00

2007 SP Rookie Threads Double Coverage

COMMON CARD	4.00	10.00
SEMISTARS	5.00	12.00
UNLISTED STARS	6.00	15.00
DCAC Alge Crumpler	5.00	12.00
DCAG Antonio Gates	6.00	15.00
DCAP Adrian Peterson	15.00	40.00
DCAR Aaron Rodgers	20.00	50.00
DCBE Tatum Bell	4.00	10.00
DCBF Brett Favre	12.00	30.00
DCBL Byron Leftwich	5.00	12.00
DCBQ Brady Quinn	4.00	10.00
DCBR Ben Roethlisberger	6.00	15.00
DCBU Brian Urlacher	6.00	15.00
DCBW Brian Westbrook	5.00	12.00
DCCB Cedric Benson	5.00	12.00
DCCJ Calvin Johnson	12.00	30.00
DCCM Curtis Martin	6.00	15.00
DCCP Chad Pennington	5.00	12.00
DCCS Chris Simms	4.00	10.00
DCCW Cadillac Williams	5.00	12.00
DCDB Drew Brees	6.00	15.00
DCDC Daunte Culpepper	5.00	12.00
DCDM Donovan McNabb	6.00	15.00
DCEM Eli Manning	6.00	15.00
DCGI Ted Ginn Jr.	3.00	8.00
DCGO Tony Gonzalez	5.00	12.00
DCJA Joseph Addai	5.00	12.00
DCJH Joe Horn	5.00	12.00
DCJN Jerious Norwood	5.00	12.00
DCJO Chad Johnson	5.00	12.00
DCJP Julius Peppers	5.00	12.00
DCJR JaMarcus Russell	2.50	6.00
DCJS Jeremy Shockey	5.00	12.00
DCLJ Larry Johnson	4.00	10.00
DCLM Laurence Maroney	5.00	12.00
DCLT LaDainian Tomlinson	6.00	15.00
DCMB Marc Bulger	5.00	12.00
DCMC Deuce McAllister	5.00	12.00
DCMF Marshall Faulk	10.00	25.00
DCMH Marvin Harrison	6.00	15.00
DCML Matt Leinart	5.00	12.00
DCMM Muhsin Muhammad	5.00	12.00
DCMS Michael Strahan	5.00	12.00
DCMV Michael Vick	6.00	15.00
DCPA Carson Palmer	5.00	12.00
DCPB Plaxico Burress	5.00	12.00
DCPH Priest Holmes	5.00	12.00
DCPM Peyton Manning	15.00	30.00
DCRB Ronnie Brown	5.00	12.00
DCRL Ray Lewis	6.00	15.00
DCRS Rod Smith	5.00	12.00
DCRW Reggie Wayne	5.00	12.00
DCSJ Steven Jackson	6.00	15.00
DCSM Steve McNair	5.00	12.00
DCTB Tom Brady	15.00	30.00
DCTE Tedy Bruschi	10.00	25.00
DCTG Trent Green	5.00	12.00
DCTH T.J. Houshmandzadeh	5.00	12.00
DCTR Tony Romo	8.00	20.00
DCTW Troy Williamson	4.00	10.00
DCWI Roy Williams WR	5.00	12.00
DCWM Willis McGahee	5.00	12.00
DCWP Willie Parker	5.00	12.00

2007 SP Rookie Threads Draft Day Ink

DDIAA Aundrae Allison	3.00	8.00
DDIAB Alan Branch	4.00	10.00
DDIAG Anthony Gonzalez	5.00	12.00
DDIAP Adrian Peterson		
DDIBM Brandon Meriweather	5.00	12.00
DDIBQ Brady Quinn		
DDICD Craig Buster Davis	4.00	10.00
DDICH Chris Henry RB	3.00	8.00
DDICJ Calvin Johnson		
DDIDI David Irons	3.00	8.00
DDIDJ Dwayne Jarrett	4.00	10.00
DDIDS Drew Stanton	3.00	8.00
DDIDW Dwayne Wright	4.00	10.00
DDIGO Greg Olsen	4.00	10.00
DDIGW Garrett Wolfe	3.00	8.00
DDIHI Johnnie Lee Higgins	4.00	10.00
DDIIS Isaiah Stanback	3.00	8.00
DDIJA Jamaal Anderson	4.00	10.00
DDIJH Jason Hill	5.00	12.00
DDIJR JaMarcus Russell		
DDIJT Joe Thomas	5.00	12.00
DDIKI Kenny Irons	3.00	8.00
DDILL LaRon Landry		
DDIMG Michael Griffin	5.00	12.00
DDIML Marshawn Lynch	15.00	40.00
DDIMM Marcus McCauley	4.00	10.00
DDIPI Antonio Pittman	3.00	8.00
DDIPW Paul Williams	3.00	8.00
DDIRM Robert Meachem	5.00	12.00
DDISN Syvelle Newton	4.00	10.00
DDISS Steve Smith USC	5.00	12.00
DDITE Trent Edwards	12.00	30.00
DDITG Ted Ginn Jr.	4.00	10.00
DDIWI Patrick Willis	10.00	25.00
DDIYF Yamon Figurs	3.00	8.00

2007 SP Rookie Threads Maximum Threads

STATED PRINT RUN 50 SER.#'d SETS

MTAG Ahman Green	6.00	15.00
MTAJ Andre Johnson	6.00	15.00
MTAN Anthony Gonzalez	5.00	12.00
MTAP Adrian Peterson	20.00	50.00
MTAS Alex Smith QB	8.00	20.00
MTBF Brett Favre	15.00	40.00
MTBL Byron Leftwich	6.00	15.00
MTBQ Brady Quinn	5.00	12.00
MTBR Ben Roethlisberger	8.00	20.00
MTBW Brian Westbrook	6.00	15.00
MTCB Champ Bailey	6.00	15.00
MTCJ Calvin Johnson	15.00	40.00
MTCP Clinton Portis	6.00	15.00
MTCS Chris Simms	5.00	12.00
MTCT Chester Taylor	5.00	12.00
MTCU Jay Cutler	8.00	20.00
MTDB Dwayne Bowe	6.00	15.00
MTDD Donald Driver	8.00	20.00
MTDM Donovan McNabb	8.00	20.00
MTDR Drew Brees	8.00	20.00
MTEJ Edgerrin James	6.00	15.00
MTEM Eli Manning	8.00	20.00
MTEV Lee Evans	6.00	15.00
MTFG Frank Gore	8.00	20.00
MTFT Fred Taylor	6.00	15.00
MTGA Gaines Adams	5.00	12.00
MTGO Greg Olsen	4.00	10.00
MTHO T.J. Houshmandzadeh	6.00	15.00
MTHW Hines Ward	8.00	20.00
MTIB Isaac Bruce	6.00	15.00
MTJJ Julius Jones	5.00	12.00
MTJL J.P. Losman	5.00	12.00
MTJR JaMarcus Russell	3.00	8.00
MTJS Jeremy Shockey	6.00	15.00
MTJS2 Jeremy Shockey	6.00	15.00
MTJT Joe Thomas	5.00	12.00
MTLE Matt Leinart	6.00	15.00
MTLF Larry Fitzgerald	8.00	20.00
MTLJ Larry Johnson	5.00	12.00
MTLM Laurence Maroney	6.00	15.00
MTLT LaDainian Tomlinson	8.00	20.00
MTMB Marc Bulger	6.00	15.00
MTMC Marques Colston	8.00	20.00
MTMH Matt Hasselbeck	6.00	15.00
MTML Marshawn Lynch	5.00	12.00
MTPE Chad Pennington	6.00	15.00
MTPM Peyton Manning	15.00	40.00
MTPR Philip Rivers	8.00	20.00
MTRB Ronnie Brown	6.00	15.00
MTRJ Rudi Johnson	6.00	15.00
MTRM Robert Meachem	5.00	12.00
MTRW Roy Williams WR	6.00	15.00
MTSA Shaun Alexander	6.00	15.00
MTSM Shawne Merriman	6.00	15.00
MTST Steve McNair	6.00	15.00
MTTA Jason Taylor	6.00	15.00
MTTB Tom Brady	15.00	40.00
MTTG Ted Ginn Jr.	4.00	10.00
MTTH Todd Heap	5.00	12.00
MTTO Terrell Owens	8.00	20.00
MTTR Tony Romo	10.00	25.00
MTVY Vince Young	6.00	15.00
MTWD Warrick Dunn	6.00	15.00
MTWM Willis McGahee	6.00	15.00
MTWP Willie Parker	6.00	15.00

2007 SP Rookie Threads Phenom Flashbacks Jerseys

PHFAH A.J. Hawk	2.50	6.00
PHFDW DeAngelo Williams	3.00	8.00
PHFLM Laurence Maroney	2.50	6.00
PHFLW Leon Washington	2.50	6.00
PHFMJ Maurice Jones-Drew	3.00	8.00
PHFML Matt Leinart	2.50	6.00
PHFRB Reggie Bush	3.00	8.00
PHFSH Santonio Holmes	2.50	6.00
PHFVY Vince Young	2.50	6.00
PHFWH LenDale White	2.50	6.00

2007 SP Rookie Threads Rookie Exclusive Autographs

STATED PRINT RUN 89-100

REAG Anthony Gonzalez	8.00	20.00
REAP Adrian Peterson	150.00	250.00
REBA Dallas Baker	5.00	12.00
REBM Brandon Meriweather	8.00	20.00
REBQ Brady Quinn	20.00	50.00
RECD Craig Buster Davis	6.00	15.00
RECH Chris Henry RB	5.00	12.00
RECJ Calvin Johnson	60.00	120.00
RECS Chansi Stuckey	8.00	20.00
REDA David Ball	6.00	15.00
REDB Dwayne Bowe	10.00	25.00
REDH Daymeion Hughes	6.00	15.00
REDI David Irons	5.00	12.00
REDJ Dwayne Jarrett	6.00	15.00
REDR Darrelle Revis	12.00	30.00
REDW Darius Walker	5.00	12.00
REEW Eric Wright	8.00	20.00
REGA Gaines Adams	8.00	20.00
REGR Gary Russell	6.00	15.00
REHB H.B. Blades/89	5.00	12.00
REIS Isaiah Stanback	5.00	12.00
REJB John Beck	8.00	20.00
REJF Joel Filani	6.00	15.00
REJH Jason Hill	8.00	20.00
REJR JaMarcus Russell	5.00	12.00
REJT Joe Thomas	8.00	20.00
REKI Kenny Irons	5.00	12.00
REKK Kevin Kolb	12.00	30.00
RELH Leon Hall	6.00	15.00
RELL LaRon Landry	8.00	20.00
RELT Lawrence Timmons	8.00	20.00
REMG Michael Griffin	8.00	20.00
REML Marshawn Lynch	15.00	30.00
REMM Marcus McCauley	6.00	15.00
REPI Antonio Pittman	5.00	12.00
REPW Patrick Willis	15.00	40.00
RERM Robert Meachem	8.00	20.00
RERO Jeff Rowe	5.00	12.00
RESB Steve Breaston	8.00	20.00
RESC Scott Chandler	8.00	20.00
RESR Sidney Rice	10.00	25.00
RESS Steve Smith USC	8.00	20.00
RESY Selvin Young	6.00	15.00
RETG Ted Ginn Jr.	6.00	15.00
RETH Tony Hunt	5.00	12.00
RETM Tyrone Moss	5.00	12.00
RETP Tyler Palko	6.00	15.00
REWI Paul Williams	5.00	12.00
REYF Yamon Figurs	5.00	12.00
REZM Zach Miller	8.00	20.00

2007 SP Rookie Threads Rookie STATure

STATED PRINT RUN 9-45
SERIAL #'d UNDER 15 NOT PRICED

RSTAG Anthony Gonzalez/13		
RSTBJ Brandon Jackson/10		
RSTBL Brian Leonard/45	6.00	15.00
RSTBQ Brady Quinn/37	20.00	50.00
RSTCJ Calvin Johnson/15	30.00	80.00
RSTDB Dwayne Bowe/12		
RSTDJ Dwayne Jarrett/12		
RSTDS Drew Stanton/12		
RSTGW Garrett Wolfe/19	8.00	20.00
RSTHI Jason Hill/13		
RSTJB John Beck/32	8.00	20.00
RSTJH Johnnie Lee Higgins/13		
RSTJR JaMarcus Russell/28	10.00	25.00
RSTJT Joe Thomas/39	6.00	15.00
RSTKK Kevin Kolb/30	10.00	25.00
RSTPW Patrick Willis/11		
RSTSS Steve Smith USC/9		
RSTTE Trent Edwards/17	10.00	25.00
RSTTH Tony Hunt/14		
RSTTS Troy Smith/30	8.00	20.00
RSTWI Paul Williams/17	8.00	20.00

2007 SP Rookie Threads Rookie Threads Silver

*BRONZE/225: .5X TO 1.2X BASIC INSERTS
BRONZE PRINT RUN 225 SER.#'d SETS
*GOLD/150: .5X TO 1.2X BASIC INSERTS
GOLD PRINT RUN 150 SER.#'d SETS
*GOLD HOLO/99: .6X TO 1.5X BASIC INSERTS
GOLD HOLO.PRINT RUN 99 SER.#'d SETS
*GOLD PATCH: .6X TO 1.5X BASIC INSERTS
GOLD PATCH CARDS NOT SERIAL #'d

RTAG Anthony Gonzalez	2.50	6.00
RTAP Adrian Peterson	10.00	25.00
RTAP2 Adrian Peterson	10.00	25.00
RTBJ Brandon Jackson	2.00	5.00
RTBL Brian Leonard	2.00	5.00
RTBQ Brady Quinn	2.50	6.00
RTBQ2 Brady Quinn	2.50	6.00
RTCH Chris Henry RB	1.50	4.00
RTCJ Calvin Johnson	8.00	20.00
RTCJ2 Calvin Johnson	8.00	20.00
RTDB Dwayne Bowe	3.00	8.00
RTDB2 Dwayne Bowe	3.00	8.00
RTDJ Dwayne Jarrett	2.00	5.00
RTDS Drew Stanton	1.50	4.00
RTGA Gaines Adams	2.50	6.00
RTGO Greg Olsen	2.00	5.00
RTGW Garrett Wolfe	1.50	4.00
RTHI Johnnie Lee Higgins	2.00	5.00
RTJB John Beck	2.50	6.00
RTJH Jason Hill	2.50	6.00
RTJR JaMarcus Russell	1.50	4.00
RTJR2 JaMarcus Russell	1.50	4.00
RTJT Joe Thomas	2.50	6.00
RTKI Kenny Irons	1.50	4.00
RTKK Kevin Kolb	4.00	10.00
RTLB Lorenzo Booker	2.00	5.00
RTMB Michael Bush	2.50	6.00
RTML Marshawn Lynch	2.50	6.00
RTML2 Marshawn Lynch	2.50	6.00
RTPI Antonio Pittman	1.50	4.00
RTPW Patrick Willis	5.00	12.00
RTRM Robert Meachem	2.50	6.00
RTRM2 Robert Meachem	2.50	6.00
RTSR Sidney Rice	3.00	8.00
RTSS Steve Smith USC	2.50	6.00
RTTE Trent Edwards	2.50	6.00
RTTG Ted Ginn Jr.	2.00	5.00
RTTG2 Ted Ginn Jr.	2.00	5.00
RTTH Tony Hunt	1.50	4.00
RTTS Troy Smith	2.50	6.00
RTWI Paul Williams	1.50	4.00
RTYF Yamon Figurs	1.50	4.00

2007 SP Rookie Threads Rookie Threads Autographs

STATED PRINT RUN 25 SER.#'d SETS
UNPRICED HOLOFOIL PRINT RUN 10

RTAG Anthony Gonzalez	12.00	30.00
RTAP Adrian Peterson	150.00	300.00
RTAP2 Adrian Peterson	150.00	300.00
RTBJ Brandon Jackson	10.00	25.00
RTBL Brian Leonard	10.00	25.00
RTBQ Brady Quinn	30.00	80.00
RTBQ2 Brady Quinn	30.00	80.00
RTCJ Calvin Johnson	60.00	120.00
RTCJ2 Calvin Johnson	60.00	120.00
RTDB Dwayne Bowe	15.00	40.00
RTDB2 Dwayne Bowe	15.00	40.00
RTDJ Dwayne Jarrett	10.00	25.00
RTGO Greg Olsen	10.00	25.00
RTGW Garrett Wolfe	8.00	20.00
RTHI Johnnie Lee Higgins	10.00	25.00
RTJH Jason Hill	12.00	30.00
RTJR JaMarcus Russell	8.00	20.00
RTJR2 JaMarcus Russell	8.00	20.00
RTJT Joe Thomas	12.00	30.00
RTKI Kenny Irons	8.00	20.00
RTKK Kevin Kolb	20.00	50.00
RTMB Michael Bush	12.00	30.00
RTML Marshawn Lynch	15.00	40.00
RTML2 Marshawn Lynch	15.00	40.00
RTPI Antonio Pittman	8.00	20.00
RTPW Patrick Willis	25.00	60.00
RTRM Robert Meachem	12.00	30.00
RTRM2 Robert Meachem	12.00	30.00
RTSR Sidney Rice	15.00	40.00
RTSS Steve Smith USC	12.00	30.00
RTTE Trent Edwards	12.00	30.00
RTTG Ted Ginn Jr.	10.00	25.00
RTTG2 Ted Ginn Jr.	10.00	25.00
RTTH Tony Hunt	8.00	20.00
RTWI Paul Williams	8.00	20.00
RTYF Yamon Figurs	8.00	20.00

2007 SP Rookie Threads Rookie Threads Dual

UNPRICED BRONZE PATCH SER.#'d TO 10
UNPRICED GOLD PATCH SER.#'d TO 1

AW Gaines Adams / Patrick Willis	5.00	12.00
BE John Beck / Trent Edwards	2.50	6.00
BR JaMarcus Russell / Dwayne Bowe	6.00	15.00
EL Trent Edwards / Marshawn Lynch	2.50	6.00
GB Ted Ginn Jr. / John Beck	3.00	8.00
GG Ted Ginn Jr. / Anthony Gonzalez	4.00	10.00
HB Chris Henry RB / Lorenzo Booker	3.00	8.00
HF Johnnie Lee Higgins / Yamon Figurs	3.00	8.00
HL Chris Henry RB / Marshawn Lynch	2.50	6.00
HW Jason Hill / Paul Williams	3.00	8.00
IH Kenny Irons / Tony Hunt	3.00	8.00
JR Calvin Johnson / JaMarcus Russell	8.00	20.00
JS Calvin Johnson / Drew Stanton	8.00	20.00
LB Brian Leonard / Michael Bush	3.00	8.00
MB Robert Meachem / Dwayne Bowe	3.00	8.00
PJ Adrian Peterson / Brandon Jackson	10.00	25.00
PL Adrian Peterson / Marshawn Lynch	10.00	25.00
PR Adrian Peterson / Sidney Rice	10.00	25.00
QR Brady Quinn / JaMarcus Russell	8.00	20.00
QT Brady Quinn / Joe Thomas	8.00	20.00
RB JaMarcus Russell / Michael Bush	5.00	12.00

SD Dwayne Jarrett 3.00 8.00
Steve Smith USC
SK Drew Stanton 4.00 10.00
Kevin Kolb
SP Troy Smith 3.00 8.00
Antonio Pittman
WO Garrett Wolfe 5.00 12.00
Greg Olsen

2007 SP Rookie Threads Rookie Threads Triple

UNPRICED BRONZE PATCH SER.#'d TO 5
UNPRICED GOLD PATCH SER.#'d TO 1
ATW Gaines Adams 6.00 15.00
Joe Thomas
Patrick Willis
ODD Ted Ginn Jr. 6.00 15.00
John Beck
Lorenzo Booker
GGR Ted Ginn Jr. 8.00 20.00
Anthony Gonzalez
Sidney Rice
GSG Ted Ginn Jr. 8.00 20.00
Troy Smith
Anthony Gonzalez
JHS Dwayne Jarrett 4.00 10.00
Jason Hill
Steve Smith USC
JIH Brandon Jackson 8.00 20.00
Kenny Irons
Tony Hunt
JJS Calvin Johnson 10.00 25.00
Dwayne Jarrett
Steve Smith USC
JMB Calvin Johnson 10.00 25.00
Robert Meachem
Dwayne Bowe
JRP Calvin Johnson 15.00 40.00
JaMarcus Russell
Adrian Peterson
JTR Calvin Johnson 10.00 25.00
Joe Thomas
JaMarcus Russell
PHL Adrian Peterson 12.00 30.00
Chris Henry RB
Marshawn Lynch
PLB Antonio Pittman 5.00 12.00
Brian Leonard
Lorenzo Booker
QRS Brady Quinn 10.00 25.00
JaMarcus Russell
Troy Smith
QSE Brady Quinn 4.00 10.00
Drew Stanton
Trent Edwards
RBH JaMarcus Russell 6.00 15.00
Michael Bush
Johnnie Lee Higgins
RWF Sidney Rice 6.00 15.00
Paul Williams
Yamon Figurs
SBK Drew Stanton 8.00 20.00
John Beck
Kevin Kolb

2007 SP Rookie Threads Scripted in Time Autographs

STATED PRINT RUN 99-100
SITAB Anquan Boldin 8.00 20.00
SITAS Alex Smith QB 10.00 25.00
SITBA Marion Barber 8.00 20.00
SITBB Bernard Berrian 6.00 15.00
SITBF Brett Favre 125.00 200.00
SITBJ Bo Jackson 30.00 60.00
SITBM Brandon Marshall 8.00 20.00
SITBR Ronnie Brown 8.00 20.00
SITCA Jason Campbell 8.00 20.00
SITCJ Chad Johnson 8.00 20.00
SITCL Mark Clayton 8.00 20.00
SITCT Chester Taylor 6.00 15.00
SITCW Cadillac Williams 8.00 20.00
SITDB Drew Bennett 6.00 15.00
SITDD Donald Driver 15.00 30.00
SITDJ Darrell Jackson GRN 6.00 15.00
SITDJ2 Darrell Jackson WHT 6.00 15.00
SITDP Drew Pearson 8.00 20.00
SITDR Drew Brees 40.00 80.00
SITEM Eli Manning 40.00 80.00
SITFG Frank Gore 10.00 25.00
SITGJ Greg Jennings 10.00 25.00
SITJA Joseph Addai 8.00 20.00
SITJB Brandon Jacobs 8.00 20.00
SITJC Jerricho Cotchery 8.00 20.00
SITJT Joe Theismann 10.00 25.00
SITLE Lee Evans 8.00 20.00
SITLF Larry Fitzgerald 10.00 25.00
SITMA Marcus Allen 15.00 30.00
SITMB Marc Bulger/99 8.00 20.00
SITMC Marques Colston 10.00 25.00
SITML Matt Leinart 8.00 20.00
SITMS Matt Schaub 8.00 20.00
SITPH Paul Hornung 15.00 40.00
SITPM Peyton Manning 75.00 150.00
SITPM2 Peyton Manning 75.00 150.00
SITPR Philip Rivers 10.00 25.00
SITRB Reggie Brown 6.00 15.00
SITRC Roger Craig 8.00 20.00
SITTH T.J. Houshmandzadeh 8.00 20.00
SITVJ Vincent Jackson 8.00 20.00
SITWP Willie Parker 8.00 20.00

2007 SP Rookie Threads Signing Day Autographs

SDAAA Aundrae Allison 3.00 8.00
SDAAB Alan Branch 4.00 10.00
SDAAC Adam Carriker 4.00 10.00
SDAAO Amobi Okoye 5.00 12.00
SDAAP Antonio Pittman 3.00 8.00
SDABA David Ball 4.00 10.00
SDABJ Brandon Jackson 4.00 10.00
SDABL Brian Leonard 4.00 10.00
SDABM Brandon Meriweather 5.00 12.00
SDABO Dwayne Bowe 6.00 15.00
SDACD Craig Buster Davis 4.00 10.00
SDACH Chris Houston 4.00 10.00
SDACL Chris Leak 4.00 10.00
SDACS Chansi Stuckey 5.00 12.00
SDACT Courtney Taylor 4.00 10.00
SDADB Dallas Baker 3.00 8.00
SDADC David Clowney 4.00 10.00
SDADH Daymeion Hughes 4.00 10.00
SDADI David Irons 3.00 8.00
SDADR Darrelle Revis 8.00 20.00
SDADS Drew Stanton 3.00 8.00
SDADT Drew Tate 4.00 10.00
SDADW Darius Walker 3.00 8.00
SDAEW Eric Wright 5.00 12.00
SDAGA Gaines Adams 5.00 12.00
SDAGO Greg Olsen 4.00 10.00
SDAGR Gary Russell 4.00 10.00
SDAGW Garrett Wolfe 3.00 8.00
SDAHB H.B. Blades 3.00 8.00
SDAIS Isaiah Stanback 3.00 8.00
SDAJA Jamaal Anderson 4.00 10.00
SDAJF Joel Filani 4.00 10.00
SDAJH Jason Hill 5.00 12.00
SDAJP Jordan Palmer 4.00 10.00
SDAJR Jeff Rowe 3.00 8.00
SDAJT Joe Thomas 5.00 12.00
SDAJZ Jared Zabransky 4.00 10.00
SDAKD Kenneth Darby 4.00 10.00
SDAKS Kolby Smith 4.00 10.00
SDALB Lorenzo Booker 4.00 10.00
SDALH Leon Hall 4.00 10.00
SDALL LaRon Landry 5.00 12.00
SDALN Legedu Naanee 5.00 12.00
SDALT Lawrence Timmons 5.00 12.00
SDALW LaMarr Woodley 8.00 20.00
SDAMA Marcus McCauley 4.00 10.00
SDAMB Michael Bush 5.00 12.00
SDAMG Michael Griffin 5.00 12.00
SDAMM Matt Moore 5.00 12.00
SDAPP Paul Posluszny 5.00 12.00
SDAPW Patrick Willis 10.00 25.00
SDAQM Quentin Moses 4.00 10.00
SDARM Rhema McKnight 3.00 8.00
SDARN Reggie Nelson 4.00 10.00
SDASC Scott Chandler 5.00 12.00
SDASN Syvelle Newton 4.00 10.00
SDASY Selvin Young 8.00 20.00
SDATE Trent Edwards 15.00 40.00
SDATH Tony Hunt 3.00 8.00
SDATM Tyrone Moss 3.00 8.00
SDATP Tyler Palko 4.00 10.00
SDAWR Dwayne Wright 4.00 10.00
SDAWY DeShawn Wynn 4.00 10.00
SDAYF Yamon Figurs 3.00 8.00
SDAZM Zach Miller 5.00 12.00

2007 SP Rookie Threads SP Multi Marks Autographs Dual

STATED PRINT RUN 75 SER.#'d SETS
AR Joseph Addai 10.00 25.00
JaMarcus Russell
AS Sidney Rice 12.00 30.00
Aundrae Allison
BB Champ Bailey 8.00 20.00
Reggie Brown
BE Marc Bulger 10.00 25.00
Trent Edwards
BH Drew Bennett 10.00 25.00
Jason Hill
BL Matt Leinart 50.00 100.00
Reggie Bush
BM Brandon Jacobs 15.00 40.00
Marion Barber
BR Darrelle Revis 15.00 40.00
H.B. Blades
BS Alex Smith QB 10.00 25.00
John Beck
BW Bernard Berrian 6.00 15.00
Paul Williams
CO Greg Olsen 10.00 25.00
Scott Chandler
DB Craig Buster Davis 12.00 30.00
Dwayne Bowe
DD Drew Brees 30.00 60.00
Drew Stanton
DJ Donald Driver 25.00 50.00
Greg Jennings
DM Robert Meachem 10.00 25.00
Craig Buster Davis
EL Matt Leinart 10.00 25.00
Trent Edwards
FH T.J. Houshmandzadeh 8.00 20.00
Yamon Figurs
FJ Vincent Jackson 8.00 20.00
Yamon Figurs
FM Frank Gore 10.00 25.00
Michael Bush
GF Lee Evans 10.00 25.00
Anthony Gonzalez
GP Ted Ginn Jr. 6.00 15.00
Antonio Pittman
GY Selvin Young 10.00 25.00
Michael Griffin
HH Leon Hall 8.00 20.00
Daymeion Hughes
HJ Vincent Jackson 8.00 20.00
Johnnie Lee Higgins
HL Marshawn Lynch 12.00 30.00
Daymeion Hughes
HP Jordan Palmer 8.00 20.00
Johnnie Lee Higgins
HW Leon Hall 10.00 25.00
LaMarr Woodley
JB Darrell Jackson 6.00 15.00
Dallas Baker
JC Brandon Jackson 8.00 20.00
Adam Carriker
JJ Chad Johnson 60.00 120.00
Calvin Johnson
JM Calvin Johnson 40.00 100.00
Robert Meachem
JT Chester Taylor 8.00 20.00
Brandon Jackson
LB LaRon Landry 10.00 25.00
Dwayne Bowe
LC Jason Campbell 8.00 20.00
Chris Leak
LH Leon Hall 10.00 25.00
LaRon Landry
RB JaMarcus Russell 12.00 30.00
Dwayne Bowe
RC Jerricho Cotchery 15.00 40.00
Philip Rivers
RP Antonio Pittman 6.00 15.00
Gary Russell
SK Matt Schaub 20.00 50.00
Kevin Kolb
WJ DeAngelo Williams 10.00 25.00
Dwayne Jarrett
WW Darius Walker 6.00 15.00
Garrett Wolfe

2007 SP Rookie Threads SP Multi Marks Autographs Triple

STATED PRINT RUN 25 SER.#'d SETS
AAC Jamaal Anderson
Gaines Adams
Adam Carriker
ARD Joseph Addai 25.00 60.00
JaMarcus Russell
Craig Buster Davis
BHL Chris Henry RB 20.00 50.00
Brian Leonard
Lorenzo Booker
CBW Ronnie Brown 25.00 60.00
Cadillac Williams
Jason Campbell
ESQ Brady Quinn 20.00 50.00
Drew Stanton
Trent Edwards
FSQ Brett Favre 150.00 250.00
Alex Smith QB
Brady Quinn
GGP Ted Ginn Jr. 40.00 80.00
Antonio Pittman
Anthony Gonzalez
HWB Leon Hall 20.00 50.00
Alan Branch
LaMarr Woodley
JBC Anquan Boldin
Jerricho Cotchery
Calvin Johnson
JSC Calvin Johnson
David Clowney
Chansi Stuckey
JTA Calvin Johnson
Gaines Adams
Joe Thomas
LNB Chris Leak 15.00 40.00
Reggie Nelson
Dallas Baker
MOC Greg Olsen 20.00 50.00
Zach Miller
Scott Chandler
NML Reggie Nelson 15.00 40.00
LaRon Landry
Brandon Meriweather
PBR John Beck 20.00 50.00
Jordan Palmer
Jeff Rowe
RHW Leon Hall 25.00 60.00
Darrelle Revis
Eric Wright
RLB JaMarcus Russell 30.00 80.00
LaRon Landry
Dwayne Bowe
SHB Drew Bennett 20.00 50.00
Jason Hill
Steve Smith USC
TAO Gaines Adams
Joe Thomas
Greg Olsen
WBL Marshawn Lynch 30.00 80.00
Garrett Wolfe
Michael Bush
WTB Patrick Willis 20.00 50.00
Lawrence Timmons
H.B. Blades
WWM Dwayne Wright 20.00 50.00
Marcus McCauley
Paul Williams
YRC Jason Campbell 20.00 50.00
Vince Young
JaMarcus Russell

2008 SP Rookie Threads

This set was released on October 2, 2008. The base set consists of 160 cards. Cards 1-100 feature veterans, and cards 101-160 are rookies serial numbered of various quantities ranging from 152-402 that feature autographs and jersey swatches.

COMP.SET w/o RC's (100) 25.00 50.00
ROOKIE AU ANNOUNCED PRINT RUN 152-402
ACTUAL ROOKIE AU SERIAL #'s 18-87
1 Matt Leinart .60 1.50
2 Anquan Boldin .50 1.25
3 Larry Fitzgerald .60 1.50
4 Edgerrin James .50 1.25
5 Warrick Dunn .50 1.25
6 DeAngelo Hall .40 1.00
7 Todd Heap .40 1.00
8 Ray Lewis .60 1.50
9 Ed Reed .50 1.25
10 Trent Edwards .40 1.00
11 Marshawn Lynch .50 1.25
12 Lee Evans .50 1.25
13 Steve Smith .50 1.25
14 DeAngelo Williams .50 1.25
15 Julius Peppers .50 1.25
16 Brian Urlacher .60 1.50
17 Devin Hester .60 1.50
18 Rex Grossman .50 1.25
19 Carson Palmer .60 1.50
20 T.J. Houshmandzadeh .50 1.25
21 Rudi Johnson .50 1.25
22 Braylon Edwards .50 1.25
23 Kellen Winslow Jr. .50 1.25
24 Jamal Lewis .50 1.25
25 Terrell Owens .60 1.50
26 Tony Romo .75 2.00
27 Marion Barber .50 1.25
28 Jay Cutler .60 1.50
29 Brandon Marshall .50 1.25
30 Champ Bailey .50 1.25
31 Willis McGahee .50 1.25
32 Jon Kitna .50 1.25
33 Calvin Johnson .60 1.50
34 Brett Favre 1.50 4.00
35 Greg Jennings .60 1.50
36 Ryan Grant .60 1.50
37 A.J. Hawk .50 1.25
38 DeMeco Ryans .50 1.25
39 Andre Johnson .50 1.25
40 Matt Schaub .50 1.25
41 Peyton Manning 1.00 2.50
42 Reggie Wayne .50 1.25
43 Bob Sanders .50 1.25
44 David Garrard .50 1.25
45 Maurice Jones-Drew .50 1.25
46 Fred Taylor .50 1.25
47 Brodie Croyle .50 1.25
48 Larry Johnson .50 1.25
49 Derrick Johnson .40 1.00
50 Chad Johnson .50 1.25
51 Jason Taylor .50 1.25
52 John Beck .40 1.00
53 Tarvaris Jackson .50 1.25
54 Adrian Peterson 1.00 2.50
55 Darren Sharper .50 1.25
56 Tom Brady 1.00 2.50
57 Laurence Maroney .50 1.25
58 Randy Moss .60 1.50
59 Wes Welker .60 1.50
60 Drew Brees .60 1.50
61 Marques Colston .50 1.25
62 Reggie Bush .60 1.50
63 Eli Manning .60 1.50
64 Antonio Pierce .40 1.00
65 Aaron Ross .40 1.00
66 Brandon Jacobs .50 1.25
67 Thomas Jones .50 1.25
68 Kellen Clemens .50 1.25
69 Jerricho Cotchery .50 1.25
70 JaMarcus Russell .50 1.25
71 Kirk Morrison .40 1.00
72 Ronald Curry .50 1.25
73 Donovan McNabb .60 1.50
74 Brian Dawkins .50 1.25
75 Brian Westbrook .50 1.25
76 Ben Roethlisberger .60 1.50
77 Willie Parker .50 1.25
78 Santonio Holmes .50 1.25
79 LaDainian Tomlinson .60 1.50
80 Antonio Cromartie .40 1.00
81 Shawne Merriman .50 1.25
82 Antonio Gates .60 1.50
83 Frank Gore .50 1.25
84 Alex Smith QB .60 1.50
85 Patrick Willis .50 1.25
86 Matt Hasselbeck .50 1.25
87 Clinton Portis .50 1.25
88 Deion Branch .50 1.25
89 Marc Bulger .50 1.25
90 Torry Holt .50 1.25
91 Steven Jackson .60 1.50
92 Jeff Garcia .50 1.25
93 Cadillac Williams .50 1.25
94 Joey Galloway .50 1.25
95 Vince Young .50 1.25
96 LenDale White .50 1.25
97 Alge Crumpler .50 1.25
98 Jason Campbell .50 1.25
99 Chris Cooley .50 1.25
100 LaRon Landry .50 1.25
AA59 Adrian Arrington AU/252* RC 6.00 15.00
(each letter serial #'d to 28)
AH12 Ali Highsmith AU/252* RC 5.00 12.00
(each letter serial #'d to 39)
AT14 Aqib Talib AU/250* RC 8.00 20.00
(each letter serial #'d to 50)
AW43 Andre Woodson AU/252* RC 8.00 20.00
(each letter serial #'d to 36)
BB39 Brian Brohm AU/250* RC 8.00 20.00
(each letter serial #'d to 30)
BD13 Bruce Davis AU/250* RC 6.00 15.00
(each letter serial #'d to 50)
BE46 Davone Bess AU/352* RC 8.00 20.00
(each letter serial #'d to 87)
CB41 Colt Brennan AU/252* RC 12.00 30.00
(each letter serial #'d to 36)
CC15 Calais Campbell AU/248* RC 6.00 15.00
(each letter serial #'d to 32)
CH38 Chad Henne AU/250* RC 20.00 50.00
(each letter serial #'d to 50)
CJ44 Chris Johnson AU/252* RC 60.00 100.00
(each letter serial #'d to 35)
CL45 Chris Long AU/252* RC 8.00 20.00
(each letter serial #'d to 61)
DA17 Donnie Avery AU/250* RC 6.00 15.00
(each letter serial #'d to 50)
DB10 Dorien Bryant AU/348* RC UER 6.00 15.00
(each letter serial #'d to 58)/(name misspelled Dorian)
DC16 Dan Connor AU/252* RC 8.00 20.00
(each letter serial #'d to 42)
DD47 Dennis Dixon AU/250* RC 12.50 25.00
(each letter serial #'d to 50)
DJ37 DeSean Jackson AU/154* RC 25.00 60.00
(each letter serial #'d to 21)
DM1 Darren McFadden AU/152* RC 40.00 80.00
(each letter serial #'d to 19)
EA49 Erik Ainge AU/250* RC 8.00 20.00
(each letter serial #'d to 49)
ED48 Early Doucet AU/252* RC 6.00 15.00
(each letter serial #'d to 42)
FD51 Fred Davis AU/250* RC 8.00 20.00
(each letter serial #'d to 50)
FJ50 Felix Jones AU/250* RC 25.00 50.00
(each letter serial #'d to 50)
FO5 Matt Forte AU/250* RC 5.00 50.00
(each letter serial #'d to 50)
JB54 John David Booty AU/250* RC 6.00 15.00
(each letter serial #'d to 50)
JC52 Jamaal Charles AU/245* RC 20.00 50.00
(each letter serial #'d to 35)
JF53 Joe Flacco AU/252* RC 50.00 100.00
(each letter serial #'d to 41)
JH19 Jacob Hester AU/252* RC 8.00 20.00
(each letter serial #'d to 41)
JJ22 Josh Johnson AU/245* RC 8.00 20.00
(each letter serial #'d to 50)
JK23 Justin King AU/252* RC 6.00 15.00
(each letter serial #'d to 63)
JL20 Jake Long AU/248* RC 8.00 20.00
(each letter serial #'d to 62)
JL21 J Leman AU/250* RC 5.00 12.00
(each letter serial #'d to 50)
JN55 Jordy Nelson AU/252* RC 20.00 40.00
(each letter serial #d to 42)
JS2 Jonathan Stewart AU/245* RC 20.00 50.00
(each letter serial #'d to 22)
KO26 Kevin O'Connell AU/248* RC 6.00 15.00
(each letter serial #'d to 31)
KP25 Kenny Phillips AU/256* RC 8.00 20.00
(each letter serial #'d to 32)
KR24 Keith Rivers AU/252* RC 8.00 20.00
(each letter serial #'d to 42)
KS57 Kevin Smith AU/250* RC 8.00 20.00
(each letter serial #'d to 49)
LH27 Lavelle Hawkins AU/252* RC 5.00 12.00
(each letter serial #'d to 36)
LJ28 Lawrence Jackson AU/259* RC 6.00 15.00
(each letter serial #'d to 37)
LM30 Leodis McKelvin AU/248* RC 6.00 15.00
(each letter serial #'d to 32)
LS58 Limas Sweed AU/250* RC 8.00 20.00
(each letter serial #'d to 50)
MF4 Matt Flynn AU/250* RC 30.00 60.00
(each letter serial #'d to 70)
MH6 Mike Hart AU/248* RC 15.00 30.00
(each letter serial #'d to 62)
MJ7 Mike Jenkins AU/252* RC 10.00 25.00
(each letter serial #'d to 35)
MK60 Malcolm Kelly AU/250* RC 6.00 15.00
(each letter serial #'d to 50)
MR40 Matt Ryan AU/152* RC 50.00 100.00
(each letter serial #'d to 38)
PH56 Philip Wheeler AU/252* RC 6.00 15.00
(each letter serial #'d to 36)
PS29 Paul Smith AU/250* RC 8.00 20.00
(each letter serial #'d to 50)
QG31 Quentin Groves AU/252* RC 6.00 15.00
(each letter serial #'d to 41)
RM42 Rashard Mendenhall AU/250* RC 25.00 60.00
(each letter serial #'d to 25)
RR8 Ray Rice AU/252* RC 30.00 60.00
(each letter serial #'d to 63)
SB32 Sam Baker AU/250* RC 5.00 12.00
(each letter serial #'d to 50)
SC33 Shawn Crable AU/402* RC 5.00 12.00
(each letter serial #'d to 66)
SS9 Steve Slaton AU/252* RC 8.00 20.00
(each letter serial #'d to 42)
TC11 Tashard Choice AU/252* RC 6.00 15.00
(each letter serial #'d to 42)
TZ35 Tom Zbikowski AU/252* RC 8.00 20.00
(each letter serial #'d to 28)
VG34 Vernon Gholston AU/248* RC 6.00 15.00
(each letter serial #'d to 31)
XA36 Xavier Adibi AU/250* RC 8.00 20.00
(each letter serial #'d to 50)

2008 SP Rookie Threads Flashback Fabrics 175-200

FF DIE CUT PRINT RUN 175-200
*SQUARE/99-115: .4X TO 1X JSY/175-200
SQUARE DIE CUT PRINT RUN 99-115
*DIAMOND/85: .4X TO 1X JSY/175-200
DIAMOND DIE CUT PRINT RUN 85
*TRAPEZOID/50-60: .4X TO 1X JSY/175-200
TRAPEZOID DIE CUT PRINT RUN 50-60
*UD LOGO/25-30: .5X TO 1.2X JSY/175-200
UD LOGO DIE CUT PRINT RUN 25-30
*SHIELD/15-20: .5X TO 1.2X JSY/175-200
SHIELD DIE CUT PRINT RUN 15-20
SERIAL #'d 1/1 TOO SCARCE TO PRICE
FFAG Anthony Gonzalez 2.00 5.00
FFAH A.J. Hawk 2.50 6.00
FFAP Adrian Peterson 5.00 12.00
FFAS Alex Smith QB 3.00 8.00
FFAV Jason Avant 2.00 5.00
FFBE Braylon Edwards 2.50 6.00
FFBM Brandon Marshall 2.50 6.00
FFBQ Brady Quinn 2.50 6.00
FFBR Ben Roethlisberger 3.00 8.00
FFCF Charlie Frye 2.00 5.00
FFCH Chris Henry RB 2.50 6.00
FFCJ Calvin Johnson 3.00 8.00
FFCP Carson Palmer/175 3.00 8.00
FFCW Cadillac Williams 2.50 6.00
FFDB Dwayne Bowe 2.50 6.00
FFDS Drew Stanton 2.00 5.00
FFEM Eli Manning 3.00 8.00
FFFG Frank Gore 2.50 6.00
FFGA Gaines Adams 2.00 5.00
FFGO Greg Olsen 2.50 6.00
FFGW Garrett Wolfe 2.50 6.00
FFJA Chad Jackson 2.50 6.00
FFJB John Beck 2.00 5.00
FFJC Jason Campbell 2.50 6.00
FFJK Joe Klopfenstein 2.00 5.00
FFJR JaMarcus Russell 2.50 6.00
FFJT Joe Thomas 2.50 6.00
FFKI Kenny Irons 2.00 5.00
FFKK Kevin Kolb 2.50 6.00
FFLE Matt Leinart 3.00 8.00
FFLF Larry Fitzgerald 3.00 8.00
FFLM Laurence Maroney 2.50 6.00
FFLW LenDale White/175 2.50 6.00
FFLY Marshawn Lynch 2.50 6.00
FFMC Mark Clayton 2.50 6.00
FFMH Michael Huff 2.00 5.00
FFMJ Maurice Jones-Drew 2.50 6.00
FFML Marcedes Lewis 2.00 5.00
FFPW Patrick Willis 2.50 6.00
FFRB Reggie Bush 3.00 8.00
FFRM Robert Meachem 2.50 6.00
FFRO Ronnie Brown 2.50 6.00
FFSH Santonio Holmes 2.50 6.00
FFSJ Steven Jackson 3.00 8.00
FFSM Sinorice Moss 2.50 6.00
FFSR Sidney Rice 3.00 8.00
FFSS Steve Smith USC 2.50 6.00
FFTE Trent Edwards 2.00 5.00
FFTJ Tarvaris Jackson 2.50 6.00
FFTS Troy Smith 2.50 6.00
FFTW Travis Wilson 2.00 5.00
FFVY Vince Young/175 2.50 6.00
FFWI Troy Williamson/175 2.00 5.00

2008 SP Rookie Threads Legendary Numbers 99

STARS PRINT RUN 99 SER.#'d SETS
*INTIALS/50: .5X TO 1.2X STARS/99
PLAYER INITIALS PRINT RUN 50
*BADGE/15: .6X TO 1.5X BASIC JSY/99
BADGE DIE CUT PRINT RUN 15
JERSEY 1/1 TOO SCARCE TO PRICE
*JSY NUM/80: .4X TO 1X BASIC JSY/99
*JSY NUM/20-40: .5X TO 1.2X BASIC JSY/99
JERSEY NUMBER PRINT RUN 7-40
LNBJ Bo Jackson 8.00 20.00
LNBS Barry Sanders 8.00 20.00
LNDM Dan Marino 10.00 25.00
LNGS Gale Sayers 8.00 20.00
LNHW Herschel Walker 4.00 10.00
LNJE John Elway 8.00 20.00
LNJM Jim McMahon 5.00 12.00
LNJR Jerry Rice 8.00 20.00
LNJT Joe Theismann 5.00 12.00
LNKA Ken Anderson 4.00 10.00
LNKS Ken Stabler 5.00 12.00
LNMO Joe Montana 10.00 25.00
LNRC Roger Craig 4.00 10.00
LNTB Terry Bradshaw 8.00 20.00

2008 SP Rookie Threads Multi Marks Dual

DUAL PRINT RUN 15-399
UNPRICED SIX PRINT RUN 6
UNPRICED EIGHT PRINT RUN 8
MMD1 Jonathan Stewart 25.00 50.00
Rashard Mendenhall
MMD2 Limas Sweed 8.00 20.00
James Hardy
MMD3 Limas Sweed 25.00 50.00
Rashard Mendenhall
MMD4 Brian Brohm 12.00 30.00
Chad Henne
MMD5 Jake Long 8.00 20.00
Chris Long
MMD6 Brian Brohm 50.00 100.00
Matt Ryan
MMD7 John David Booty 12.00 30.00
Chad Henne
MMD8 Jamaal Charles 20.00 40.00
Matt Forte
MMD10 Donnie Avery 15.00 40.00
DeSean Jackson
MMD11 Kevin Smith 10.00 25.00
Steve Slaton
MMD12 Gale Sayers 60.00 120.00
Adrian Peterson
MMD13 Andre Woodson 6.00 15.00
Erik Ainge
MMD14 Dennis Dixon 10.00 25.00
John David Booty
MMD15 Darren McFadden 40.00 80.00
Felix Jones
MMD16 Jamaal Charles 6.00 15.00
Jacob Hester
MMD17 Chris Johnson 50.00 80.00
Rashard Mendenhall
MMD18 Jonathan Stewart 20.00 40.00
Dennis Dixon
MMD19 Tashard Choice 10.00 25.00
Jamaal Charles
MMD20 Gale Sayers 40.00 80.00
Matt Forte
MMD21 Donnie Avery 6.00 15.00
Early Doucet
MMD22 Matt Ryan 25.00 60.00
Harry Douglas
MMD23 Andre Woodson 6.00 15.00
Kevin O'Connell
MMD24 Lavelle Hawkins 15.00 40.00
DeSean Jackson
MMD25 Brian Brohm 25.00 50.00
Jordy Nelson
MMD26 Andre Woodson 8.00 20.00
Brian Brohm
MMD27 Keith Rivers 6.00 15.00
Sedrick Ellis
MMD28 Calvin Johnson 30.00 60.00
Marques Colston
MMD30 Tom Rathman 25.00 50.00
Daryl Johnston
MMD31 Tom Rathman 35.00 60.00
Roger Craig
MMD32 Craig Stellz 5.00 12.00
Chevis Jackson
MMD33 Marion Barber 50.00 100.00
Felix Jones
MMD34 Ray Rice 15.00 30.00
Mike Hart
MMD35 Tashard Choice 15.00 40.00
Felix Jones
MMD36 Vernon Gholston 8.00 20.00
Chris Long
MMD38 Brodie Croyle 8.00 20.00
Dwayne Bowe
MMD39 David Garrard 12.00 30.00
Jason Campbell
MMD40 Y. A. Tittle 20.00 40.00
Paul Hornung
MMD41 Paul Hornung 20.00 40.00
Jerry Kramer
MMD43 Bert Jones 15.00 30.00
Ken Anderson
MMD45 Tom Zbikowski 6.00 15.00
Mike Jenkins
MMD46 Marc Bulger 35.00 60.00
Roman Gabriel
MMD47 Jason Campbell 20.00 40.00
Joe Theismann
MMD48 Dustin Keller 6.00 15.00
John Carlson
MMD49 Aaron Ross 8.00 20.00
Ahmad Bradshaw
MMD50 Andre Woodson 8.00 20.00
John David Booty

2008 SP Rookie Threads Multi Marks Triple

STATED PRINT RUN 15-75
MMT1 Ray Rice/25 60.00 120.00
Matt Forte
Chris Johnson
MMT2 Aaron Rodgers
Brian Brohm
Matt Flynn
MMT3 Matt Ryan/15 125.00 200.00
Brian Brohm
Joe Flacco
MMT4 Malcolm Kelly
Limas Sweed
DeSean Jackson
MMT5 Dustin Keller/55 10.00 25.00
John Carlson
Fred Davis
MMT6 Limas Sweed
Eddie Royal
James Hardy
MMT7 Kevin Smith/35 30.00 60.00
Matt Forte
Mike Hart
MMT8 Chad Henne/55 20.00 40.00
Kevin O'Connell
Andre Woodson
MMT9 Steve Slaton/35 60.00 120.00
Ray Rice
Chris Johnson
MMT10 Earl Bennett
Dexter Jackson
Donnie Avery
MMT11 Eddie Royal
Earl Bennett
Early Doucet
MMT12 Darren McFadden/15 75.00 150.00
Felix Jones
Jonathan Stewart
MMT13 Matt Flynn
Early Doucet
Jacob Hester
MMT14 Leodis McKelvin/55 10.00 25.00
Dominque Rodgers-Cromartie
Mike Jenkins
MMT15 Chris Long/55 10.00 25.00
Vernon Gholston
Derrick Harvey
MMT16 Jordy Nelson/75 20.00 40.00
Harry Douglas
Andre Caldwell
MMT17 John David Booty/35 20.00 40.00
Dennis Dixon
Erik Ainge
MMT18 Jacob Hester/55 15.00 30.00
Peyton Hillis
Owen Schmitt
MMT19 Peyton Manning/15
Dallas Clark
Joseph Addai EXCH
MMT20 Derek Anderson
Trent Edwards
Brian Brohm
MMT21 Adrian Peterson/15 125.00 200.00
Marshawn Lynch
Clinton Portis
MMT22 DeMarcus Ware/15 40.00 100.00
Marion Barber
Felix Jones
MMT23 Jack Lambert
Jack Ham
Mel Blount
MMT24 Devin Thomas
Fred Davis
Malcolm Kelly
MMT25 Joe Flacco/55 50.00 100.00
Ray Rice
Tom Zbikowski

2008 SP Rookie Threads Multi Marks Quad

STATED PRINT RUN 5-45
SERIAL #'d UNDER 15 NOT PRICED
MMQ1 Darren McFadden
Felix Jones
Jonathan Stewart
Rashard Mendenhall
MMQ3 Limas Sweed/25 25.00 60.00
Earl Bennett
DeSean Jackson
Donnie Avery
MMQ4 Matt Forte/40 35.00 60.00
Ray Rice
Jacob Hester
Kevin Smith
MMQ5 Kevin O'Connell/25 20.00 50.00
John David Booty
Andre Woodson
Colt Brennan
MMQ6 Chris Long/40 10.00 25.00
Vernon Gholston
Derrick Harvey
Lawrence Jackson
MMQ7 Leodis McKelvin/45 12.00 30.00
Dominique Rodgers-Cromartie
Mike Jenkins
Antoine Cason
MMQ9 Early Doucet
Eddie Royal
Harry Douglas
Andre Caldwell
MMQ10 Dustin Keller/15 12.00 30.00
Fred Davis
John Carlson
Martellus Bennett
MMQ11 Dan Connor/45 12.00 30.00
Keith Rivers
Xavier Adibi
Bruce Davis
MMQ12 Y. A. Tittle
Fran Tarkenton
Roman Gabriel
Bob Griese
MMQ13 Jeff Garcia
David Garrard
Jason Campbell
Marc Bulger
MMQ14 Joe Theismann
Ken Anderson
Bert Jones
Ken Stabler

2008 SP Rookie Threads Rookie Lettermen College Autographs

*SINGLES: .4X TO 1X BASE AU RC
ANNOUNCED PRINT RUN 72-126
ACTUAL CARD SERIAL NUMBERING
DM1 Darren McFadden JSY AU/72* 30.00 60.00
(each letter serial #'d to 9)
FO5 Matt Forte JSY AU/120* 20.00 50.00
(each letter serial #'d to 20)
JS2 Jonathan Stewart JSY AU/120* 20.00 50.00
(each letter serial #'d to 13)
MF4 Matt Flynn JSY AU/120* 30.00 60.00
(each letter serial #'d to 35)
MH6 Mike Hart JSY AU/120* 8.00 20.00
(each letter serial #'d to 16)
MJ7 Mike Jenkins JSY AU/120* 10.00 25.00
(each letter serial #'d to 41)
RR8 Ray Rice JSY AU/126* 30.00 60.00
(each letter serial #'d to 18)
SS9 Steve Slaton JSY AU/120* 15.00 40.00
(each letter serial #'d to 10)
AA59 Adrian Arrington JSY AU/120* 6.00 15.00
(each letter serial #'d to 15)
AH12 Ali Highsmith JSY AU/120* 5.00 12.00
(each letter serial #'d to 58)
AT14 Aqib Talib JSY AU/126* 8.00 20.00
(each letter serial #'d to 21)
AW43 Andre Woodson JSY AU/120* 8.00 20.00
(each letter serial #'d to 16)
BB39 Brian Brohm JSY AU/120* 8.00 20.00
(each letter serial #'d to 8)
BD13 Bruce Davis JSY AU/124* 6.00 15.00
(each letter serial #'d to 31)
BE46 Davone Bess JSY AU/126* 8.00 20.00
(each letter serial #'d to 29)
CB41 Colt Brennan JSY AU/120* 12.00 30.00
(each letter serial #'d to 21)
CC15 Calais Campbell JSY AU/120* 6.00 15.00
(each letter serial #'d to 25)
CH38 Chad Henne JSY AU/120* 25.00 60.00
(each letter serial #'d to 16)
CJ44 Chris Johnson JSY AU/120* 50.00 100.00
(each letter serial #'d to 10)
CL45 Chris Long JSY AU/120* 10.00 25.00
(each letter serial #'d to 16)
DA17 Donnie Avery JSY AU/126* 6.00 15.00
(each letter serial #'d to 18)
DB10 Dorien Bryant JSY AU/126* 6.00 15.00
(each letter serial #'d to 29)
DC16 Dan Connor JSY AU/117* 8.00 20.00
(each letter serial #'d to 14)
DD47 Dennis Dixon JSY AU/126* 12.50 25.00
(each letter serial #'d to 21)
DJ37 DeSean Jackson JSY AU/120* 30.00 60.00
(each letter serial #'d to 25)
EA49 Erik Ainge JSY AU/126* 8.00 20.00
(each letter serial #'d to 14)
ED48 Early Doucet JSY AU/120* 6.00 15.00
(each letter serial #'d to 42)
FD51 Fred Davis JSY AU/120* 8.00 20.00
(each letter serial #'d to 42)
FJ50 Felix Jones JSY AU/120* 20.00 50.00
(each letter serial #'d to 16)
JB54 John David Booty JSY AU/120* 6.00 15.00
(each letter serial #'d to 42)
JC52 Jamaal Charles JSY AU/120* 20.00 50.00
(each letter serial #'d to 25)
JF53 Joe Flacco JSY AU/120* 40.00 100.00
(each letter serial #'d to 16)
JH19 Jacob Hester JSY AU/120* 8.00 20.00
(each letter serial #'d to 42)
JJ22 Josh Johnson JSY AU/120* 8.00 20.00
(each letter serial #'d to 58)
JK23 Justin King JSY AU/126* 6.00 15.00
(each letter serial #'d to 14)
JL20 Jake Long JSY AU/120* 8.00 20.00
(each letter serial #'d to 10)
JL21 J Leman JSY AU/120* 5.00 12.00
(each letter serial #'d to 16)
JN55 Jordy Nelson JSY AU/121* 20.00 40.00
(each letter serial #'d to 11)
KO26 Kevin O'Connell JSY AU/117* 6.00 15.00
(each letter serial #'d to 10)
KP25 Kenny Phillips JSY AU/120* 8.00 20.00
(each letter serial #'d to 25)
KR24 Keith Rivers JSY AU/120* 8.00 20.00
(each letter serial #'d to 41)
KS57 Kevin Smith JSY AU/120* 8.00 20.00
(each letter serial #'d to 41)
LH27 Lavelle Hawkins JSY AU/120* 5.00 12.00
(each letter serial #'d to 41)
LJ28 Lawrence Jackson JSY AU/120* 6.00 15.00
(each letter serial #'d to 42)

LM30 Leodis McKelvin JSY AU/116*	6.00	15.00
(each letter serial #'d to 31)		
LS58 Limas Sweed JSY AU/120*	8.00	20.00
(each letter serial #'d to 25)		
MK60 Malcolm Kelly JSY AU/120*	6.00	15.00
(each letter serial #'d to 16)		
MR40 Matt Ryan JSY AU/78*	50.00	120.00
(each letter serial #'d to 6)		
PH56 Philip Wheeler JSY AU/121*	6.00	15.00
(each letter serial #'d to 11)		
PS29 Paul Smith JSY AU/120*	8.00	20.00
(each letter serial #'d to 25)		
QG31 Quentin Groves JSY AU/120*	6.00	15.00
(each letter serial #'d to 21)		
RM42 Rashard Mendenhall JSY AU/120*	25.00	50.00
(each letter serial #'d to 16)		
SB32 Sam Baker JSY AU/120*	5.00	12.00
(each letter serial #'d to 42)		
SC33 Shawn Crable JSY AU/120*	5.00	12.00
(each letter serial #'d to 16)		
TC11 Tashard Choice JSY AU/121*	6.00	15.00
(each letter serial #'d to 11)		
TZ35 Tom Zbikowski JSY AU/126*	8.00	20.00
(each letter serial #'d to 14)		
VG34 Vernon Gholston JSY AU/126*	6.00	15.00
(each letter serial #'d to 14)		
XA36 Xavier Adibi JSY AU/120*	5.00	12.00
(each letter serial #'d to 16)		

2008 SP Rookie Threads Rookie Lettermen College Nickname Autographs

*SINGLES: .5X TO 1.2X BASE AU RC
ANNOUNCED PRINT RUN 45-60
ACTUAL CARD SERIAL NUMBERING

DM1 Darren McFadden JSY AU/48*	30.00	60.00
(each letter serial #'d to 12)		
FO5 Matt Forte JSY AU/54*	20.00	50.00
(each letter serial #'d to 6)		
JS2 Jonathan Stewart JSY AU/50*	20.00	50.00
(each letter serial #'d to 10)		
MF4 Matt Flynn JSY AU/48*	30.00	80.00
(each letter serial #'d to 8)		
MH6 Mike Hart JSY AU/50*	10.00	25.00
(each letter serial #'d to 5)		
MJ7 Mike Jenkins JSY AU/50*	12.00	30.00
(each letter serial #'d to 4)		
RR8 Ray Rice JSY AU/56*	30.00	80.00
(each letter serial #'d to 4)		
SS9 Steve Slaton JSY AU/48*	25.00	50.00
(each letter serial #'d to 4)		
AA59 Adrian Arrington JSY AU/50*	8.00	20.00
(each letter serial #'d to 5)		
AH12 Ali Highsmith JSY AU/48*	6.00	15.00
(each letter serial #'d to 8)		
AT14 Aqib Talib JSY AU/56*	10.00	25.00
(each letter serial #'d to 7)		
AW43 Andre Woodson JSY AU/48*	10.00	25.00
(each letter serial #'d to 6)		
BB39 Brian Brohm JSY AU/54*	10.00	25.00
(each letter serial #'d to 5)		
BD13 Bruce Davis JSY AU/54*	8.00	20.00
(each letter serial #'d to 9)		
BE46 Davone Bess JSY AU/48*	10.00	25.00
(each letter serial #'d to 7)		
CB41 Colt Brennan JSY AU/48*	15.00	40.00
(each letter serial #'d to 6)		
CC15 Calais Campbell JSY AU/50*	8.00	20.00
(each letter serial #'d to 10)		
CH38 Chad Henne JSY AU/50*	40.00	80.00
(each letter serial #'d to 5)		
CJ44 Chris Johnson JSY AU/49*	60.00	120.00
(each letter serial #'d to 7)		
CL45 Chris Long JSY AU/54*	12.00	30.00
(each letter serial #'d to 6)		
DA17 Donnie Avery JSY AU/49*	8.00	20.00
(each letter serial #'d to 7)		
DB10 Dorien Bryant JSY AU/60*	8.00	20.00
(each letter serial #'d to 5)		
DC16 Dan Connor JSY AU/48*	10.00	25.00
(each letter serial #'d to 4)		
DD47 Dennis Dixon JSY AU/50*	15.00	30.00
(each letter serial #'d to 10)		
DJ37 DeSean Jackson JSY AU/50*	30.00	60.00
(each letter serial #'d to 10)		
EA49 Erik Ainge JSY AU/52*	10.00	25.00
(each letter serial #'d to 13)		
ED48 Early Doucet JSY AU/48*	8.00	20.00
(each letter serial #'d to 8)		
FD51 Fred Davis JSY AU/49*	10.00	25.00
(each letter serial #'d to 7)		
FJ50 Felix Jones JSY AU/48*	25.00	60.00
(each letter serial #'d to 12)		
JB54 John David Booty JSY AU/49*	8.00	20.00
(each letter serial #'d to 7)		
JC52 Jamaal Charles JSY AU/54*	25.00	60.00
(each letter serial #'d to 6)		
JF53 Joe Flacco JSY AU/56*	50.00	120.00
(each letter serial #'d to 7)		
JH19 Jacob Hester JSY AU/48*	10.00	25.00
(each letter serial #'d to 8)		
JJ22 Josh Johnson JSY AU/49*	10.00	25.00
(each letter serial #'d to 6)		
JK23 Justin King JSY AU/48*	8.00	20.00
(each letter serial #'d to 4)		
JL20 Jake Long JSY AU/50*	10.00	25.00
(each letter serial #'d to 5)		
JL21 J Leman JSY AU/56*	6.00	15.00
(each letter serial #'d to 4)		
JN55 Jordy Nelson JSY AU/56*	25.00	50.00
(each letter serial #'d to 7)		
KO26 Kevin O'Connell JSY AU/48*	8.00	20.00
(each letter serial #'d to 8)		
KP25 Kenny Phillips JSY AU/50*	10.00	25.00
(each letter serial #'d to 10)		
KR24 Keith Rivers JSY AU/49*	10.00	25.00
(each letter serial #'d to 7)		
KS57 Kevin Smith JSY AU/49*	10.00	25.00
(each letter serial #'d to 4)		
LH27 Lavelle Hawkins JSY AU/50*	6.00	15.00
(each letter serial #'d to 10)		
LJ28 Lawrence Jackson JSY AU/49*	8.00	20.00
(each letter serial #'d to 7)		
LM30 Leodis McKelvin JSY AU/49*	8.00	20.00
(each letter serial #'d to 7)		
LS58 Limas Sweed JSY AU/54*	10.00	25.00
(each letter serial #'d to 6)		
MK60 Malcolm Kelly JSY AU/49*	8.00	20.00
(each letter serial #'d to 8)		
MR40 Matt Ryan JSY AU/48*	60.00	120.00
(each letter serial #'d to 8)		
PH56 Philip Wheeler JSY AU/52*	8.00	20.00
(each letter serial #'d to 4)		
PS29 Paul Smith JSY AU/45*	10.00	25.00
(each letter serial #'d to 3)		
QG31 Quentin Groves JSY AU/48*	8.00	20.00
(each letter serial #'d to 8)		
RM42 Rashard Mendenhall JSY AU/56*	25.00	60.00
(each letter serial #'d to 4)		
SB32 Sam Baker JSY AU/49*	6.00	15.00
(each letter serial #'d to 7)		
SC33 Shawn Crable JSY AU/50*	6.00	15.00
(each letter serial #'d to 5)		
TC11 Tashard Choice JSY AU/52*	8.00	20.00
(each letter serial #'d to 4)		
TZ35 Tom Zbikowski JSY AU/52*	10.00	25.00
(each letter serial #'d to 4)		
VG34 Vernon Gholston JSY AU/48*	8.00	20.00
(each letter serial #'d to 7)		
XA36 Xavier Adibi JSY AU/48*	6.00	15.00
(each letter serial #'d to 8)		

2008 SP Rookie Threads Rookie Numbers Silver 135

SILVER PRINT RUN 135
*HOLOFOIL/30: .5X TO 1.2X SILVER/135
HOLOFOIL PRINT RUN 30
*GOLD/72-87: .4X TO 1X SILVER JSY
*GOLD/17-39: .5X TO 1.2X SILVER JSY
GOLD PRINT RUN 1-87
*HOLO.PATCH/75: .6X TO 1.5X SLVR/135
HOLOFOIL PATCH PRINT RUN 75

RNAC Andre Caldwell	2.00	5.00
RNBB Brian Brohm	2.50	6.00
RNCH Chad Henne	2.50	6.00
RNCJ Chris Johnson	6.00	15.00
RNDA Donnie Avery	2.00	5.00
RNDJ DeSean Jackson	5.00	12.00
RNDK Dustin Keller	2.50	6.00
RNDM Darren McFadden	6.00	15.00
RNDT Devin Thomas	2.00	5.00
RNDX Dexter Jackson	2.00	5.00
RNEB Earl Bennett	2.50	6.00
RNED Early Doucet	2.00	5.00
RNER Eddie Royal	2.50	6.00
RNFJ Felix Jones	4.00	10.00
RNFO Matt Forte	4.00	10.00
RNGD Glenn Dorsey	2.50	6.00
RNHD Harry Douglas	2.00	5.00
RNJB John David Booty	2.00	5.00
RNJC Jamaal Charles	4.00	10.00
RNJF Joe Flacco	8.00	20.00
RNJH James Hardy	2.00	5.00
RNJL Jake Long	2.50	6.00
RNJN Jordy Nelson	3.00	8.00
RNJS Jonathan Stewart	4.00	10.00
RNKO Kevin O'Connell	2.00	5.00
RNKS Kevin Smith	2.50	6.00
RNLS Limas Sweed	2.50	6.00
RNMK Malcolm Kelly	2.00	5.00
RNMM Mario Manningham	2.50	6.00
RNMR Matt Ryan	8.00	20.00
RNRM Rashard Mendenhall	5.00	12.00
RNRR Ray Rice	5.00	12.00
RNSI Jerome Simpson	2.50	6.00
RNSS Steve Slaton	2.50	6.00

2008 SP Rookie Threads Rookie Super Swatch Blue 175

BLUE PRINT RUN 175 SER.#'d SETS
*GREEN/99: .4X TO 1X BLUE/175
GREEN PRINT RUN 99 SER.#'d SETS
*SILVER HOLO/55: .4X TO 1X BLUE/175
SILVER HOLOFOIL PRINT RUN 55
*GOLD HOLO/25: .5X TO 1.2X BLUE/175
GOLD HOLOFOIL PRINT RUN 25
*GOLD PATCH/25: .6X TO 1.5X BLUE/175
GOLD PATCH PRINT RUN 25
UNPRICED AUTO PRINT RUN 5-15

RSSAC Andre Caldwell	2.00	5.00
RSSBB Brian Brohm	2.50	6.00
RSSBE Earl Bennett	2.50	6.00
RSSCH Chad Henne	2.50	6.00
RSSCJ Chris Johnson	6.00	15.00
RSSDA Donnie Avery	2.00	5.00
RSSDJ DeSean Jackson	5.00	12.00
RSSDK Dustin Keller	2.50	6.00
RSSDM Darren McFadden	6.00	15.00
RSSDT Devin Thomas	2.00	5.00
RSSDX Dexter Jackson	2.00	5.00
RSSED Early Doucet	2.00	5.00
RSSER Eddie Royal	2.50	6.00
RSSFJ Felix Jones	4.00	10.00
RSSGD Glenn Dorsey	2.50	6.00
RSSHD Harry Douglas	2.00	5.00
RSSJB John David Booty	2.00	5.00
RSSJC Jamaal Charles	4.00	10.00
RSSJF Joe Flacco	8.00	20.00
RSSJH James Hardy	2.00	5.00
RSSJL Jake Long	2.50	6.00
RSSJN Jordy Nelson	3.00	8.00
RSSJS Jonathan Stewart	4.00	10.00
RSSKO Kevin O'Connell	2.00	5.00
RSSKS Kevin Smith	2.50	6.00
RSSLS Limas Sweed	2.50	6.00
RSSMF Matt Forte	4.00	10.00
RSSMK Malcolm Kelly	2.00	5.00
RSSMM Mario Manningham	2.50	6.00
RSSMR Matt Ryan	8.00	20.00
RSSRM Rashard Mendenhall	5.00	12.00
RSSRR Ray Rice	5.00	12.00
RSSSI Jerome Simpson	2.50	6.00
RSSSS Steve Slaton	2.50	6.00

2008 SP Rookie Threads Rookie Super Swatch Autographs

UNPRICED AUTO PRINT RUN 5-15

2008 SP Rookie Threads Rookie Threads 250

STATED PRINT RUN 250 SER.#'d SETS
*199: .4X TO 1X BASIC JSY/250
*125: .5X TO 1.2X BASIC JSY/250
*99: .5X TO 1.2X BASIC JSY/250
*75: .5X TO 1.2X BASIC JSY/250
*50: .5X TO 1.2X BASIC JSY/250
*25: .6X TO 1.5X BASIC JSY/250
*JSY NUM/72-87: .5X TO 1.2X JSY/250
*JSY NUM/17-39: .6X TO 1.5X JSY/250
*PATCH/99: .6X TO 1.5X JSY/250
*PATCH/75: .6X TO 1.5X JSY/250
*PATCH/25: .8X TO 2X JSY/250
*PATCH/15: .8X TO 2X JSY/250
*PATCH JSY #/72-87: .6X TO 1.5X JSY/250
*PATCH JSY #/17-39: .8X TO 2X JSY/250

RTAC Andre Caldwell	1.50	4.00
RTBB Brian Brohm	2.00	5.00
RTCH Chad Henne	2.00	5.00
RTCJ Chris Johnson	5.00	12.00
RTDA Donnie Avery	1.50	4.00
RTDJ DeSean Jackson	4.00	10.00
RTDK Dustin Keller	2.00	5.00
RTDM Darren McFadden	5.00	12.00
RTDT Devin Thomas	1.50	4.00
RTDX Dexter Jackson	1.50	4.00
RTEB Earl Bennett	2.00	5.00
RTED Early Doucet	1.50	4.00
RTER Eddie Royal	2.00	5.00
RTFJ Felix Jones	3.00	8.00
RTFO Matt Forte	3.00	8.00
RTGD Glenn Dorsey	2.00	5.00
RTHD Harry Douglas	1.50	4.00
RTJB John David Booty	1.50	4.00
RTJC Jamaal Charles	3.00	8.00
RTJF Joe Flacco	6.00	15.00
RTJH James Hardy	1.50	4.00
RTJL Jake Long	2.00	5.00
RTJN Jordy Nelson	2.50	6.00
RTJS Jonathan Stewart	3.00	8.00
RTKO Kevin O'Connell	1.50	4.00
RTKS Kevin Smith	2.00	5.00
RTLS Limas Sweed	2.00	5.00
RTMK Malcolm Kelly	1.50	4.00
RTMM Mario Manningham	2.00	5.00
RTMR Matt Ryan	6.00	15.00
RTRM Rashard Mendenhall	4.00	10.00
RTRR Ray Rice	4.00	10.00
RTSI Jerome Simpson	2.00	5.00
RTSS Steve Slaton	2.00	5.00

2008 SP Rookie Threads Rookie Threads Autographs 50

AUTO PRINT RUN 50 SER.#'d SETS
*AUTO POSIT/24-25: .5X TO 1.2X AU/50
AUTO POSITION PRINT RUN 24-25
AUTO/1 TOO SCARCE TO PRICE
*PATCH AU/24-25: .6X TO 1.5X AU/50
PATCH AUTO/1 TOO SCARCE TO PRICE

RTAC Andre Caldwell	6.00	15.00
RTBB Brian Brohm	8.00	20.00
RTCH Chad Henne	8.00	20.00
RTCJ Chris Johnson	30.00	80.00
RTDA Donnie Avery	6.00	15.00
RTDJ DeSean Jackson	25.00	50.00
RTDK Dustin Keller	8.00	20.00
RTDM Darren McFadden	30.00	60.00
RTDT Devin Thomas	6.00	15.00
RTDX Dexter Jackson	6.00	15.00
RTEB Earl Bennett	8.00	20.00
RTED Early Doucet	6.00	15.00
RTER Eddie Royal	8.00	20.00
RTFJ Felix Jones	20.00	50.00
RTFO Matt Forte	20.00	50.00
RTHD Harry Douglas	6.00	15.00
RTJB John David Booty	6.00	15.00
RTJC Jamaal Charles	20.00	50.00
RTJF Joe Flacco	30.00	80.00
RTJH James Hardy	6.00	15.00
RTJL Jake Long	8.00	20.00
RTJN Jordy Nelson	15.00	40.00
RTJS Jonathan Stewart	12.00	30.00
RTKO Kevin O'Connell	6.00	15.00
RTKS Kevin Smith	8.00	20.00
RTLS Limas Sweed	8.00	20.00
RTMK Malcolm Kelly	6.00	15.00
RTMM Mario Manningham	12.00	30.00
RTMR Matt Ryan	50.00	100.00
RTRM Rashard Mendenhall	15.00	40.00
RTRR Ray Rice	25.00	50.00
RTSI Jerome Simpson	8.00	20.00
RTSS Steve Slaton	8.00	20.00

2008 SP Rookie Threads Dual Threads 160

DUAL PRINT RUN 160 SER.#'d SETS
*DUAL/99: .5X TO 1.2X DUAL JSY/160
*DUAL/75: .5X TO 1.2X DUAL JSY/160
*DUAL/50: .5X TO 1.2X DUAL JSY/160
*DUAL PATCH/35: .8X TO 2X DUAL JSY/160
*DUAL/25: .6X TO 1.5X DUAL JSY/160
*DUAL/15: .6X TO 1.5X DUAL JSY/160
DUAL/2 TOO SCARCE TO PRICE

DTBR Brian Brohm	6.00	15.00
Matt Ryan		
DTBS Steve Slaton	2.00	5.00
Brian Brohm		
DTCM Jake Long	2.00	5.00
Chad Henne		
DTDD Glenn Dorsey	2.00	5.00
Early Doucet		
DTDF Darren McFadden	6.00	15.00
Felix Jones		
DTDR Early Doucet	6.00	15.00
Matt Ryan		
DTFC Jamaal Charles	3.00	8.00
Matt Forte		
DTFO Joe Flacco	6.00	15.00
Kevin O'Connell		
DTHF Chad Henne	6.00	15.00
Joe Flacco		
DTHK James Hardy	1.50	4.00
Malcolm Kelly		
DTJJ Jonathan Stewart	1.50	4.00
John David Booty		
DTJS Chris Johnson	5.00	12.00
Kevin Smith		
DTKT Malcolm Kelly	1.50	4.00
Devin Thomas		
DTMJ Darren McFadden	6.00	15.00
DeSean Jackson		
DTMM Rashard Mendenhall	6.00	15.00
Darren McFadden		
DTMR Eddie Royal	2.00	5.00
Mario Manningham		
DTNB Jordy Nelson	2.50	6.00
Earl Bennett		
DTOB Kevin O'Connell	1.50	4.00
John David Booty		
DTRJ Chris Johnson	5.00	12.00
Ray Rice		
DTSJ Dexter Jackson	2.00	5.00
Jerome Simpson		

2008 SP Rookie Threads Trio Threads 100

TRIPLE PRINT RUN 100 SER.#'d SETS
*TRIPLE/60: .4X TO 1X TRIPLE/100
*TRIPLE/45: .4X TO 1X TRIPLE/100
*TRIPLE/25: .5X TO 1.2X TRIPLE/100
*TRIPLE/15: .5X TO 1.2X TRIPLE/100
*TRIPLE PATCH/20: .6X TO 1.5X TRIPLE/100
TRIPLE/5 TOO SCARCE TO PRICE
TRIPLE 1/1 TOO SCARCE TO PRICE

ABR Donnie Avery	2.50	6.00
Earl Bennett		
Eddie Royal		
BHB Brian Brohm	2.00	5.00
Chad Henne		
John David Booty		
BRO Brian Brohm	8.00	20.00
Matt Ryan		
Kevin O'Connell		
DMC Glenn Dorsey	8.00	20.00
Darren McFadden		
Jamaal Charles		
DTS Harry Douglas	2.50	6.00
Devin Thomas		
Jerome Simpson		
FBO Joe Flacco	2.00	5.00
John David Booty		
Kevin O'Connell		
JJS DeSean Jackson	5.00	12.00
Jerome Simpson		
Dexter Jackson		
JKS Malcolm Kelly	2.50	6.00
Jerome Simpson		
Dexter Jackson		
JNT Jordy Nelson	3.00	8.00
Devin Thomas		
Dexter Jackson		
KDK Dustin Keller	2.50	6.00
Early Doucet		
Malcolm Kelly		
LMR Darren McFadden	8.00	20.00
Jake Long		
Matt Ryan		
MFC Darren McFadden	8.00	20.00
Matt Forte		
Jamaal Charles		
MJM Darren McFadden	8.00	20.00
Felix Jones		
Rashard Mendenhall		
RJS Ray Rice	8.00	20.00
Chris Johnson		
Kevin Smith		
RRM Darren McFadden	10.00	25.00
Eddie Royal		
Matt Ryan		

2008 SP Rookie Threads Rookie Threads Foursome 75

QUAD PRINT RUN 75 SER.#'d SETS
*QUAD/50: .4X TO 1X QUAD JSY/75
*QUAD PATCH/15: .8X TO 2X QUAD JSY/75
QUAD 1/1 TOO SCARCE TO PRICE

AKFR Donnie Avery	10.00	25.00
Dustin Keller		
Joe Flacco		
Ray Rice		
BHBO Brian Brohm	2.50	6.00
Chad Henne		
John David Booty		
Kevin O'Connell		
FBRO Joe Flacco	10.00	25.00
John David Booty		
Matt Ryan		
Kevin O'Connell		
JCRK Andre Caldwell	3.00	8.00
Eddie Royal		
Malcolm Kelly		
Dexter Jackson		
JSTS Chris Johnson	8.00	20.00
Kevin Smith		
Devin Thomas		
Jerome Simpson		
MJRM Darren McFadden	8.00	20.00
Felix Jones		
Ray Rice		
Rashard Mendenhall		
MLRT Darren McFadden	12.00	30.00
Jake Long		
Matt Ryan		
Devin Thomas		

2008 SP Rookie Threads Scripted in Time

STATED PRINT RUN 5-304
SERIAL #'d UNDER 20 NOT PRICED

STAO Amobi Okoye/304	5.00	12.00
STBJ Bo Jackson/34	30.00	60.00
STBR Brian Brohm/120	5.00	12.00
STBS Barry Sanders/20	90.00	150.00
STBS Bob Sanders/21		
STCA Calvin Johnson/304	25.00	50.00
STCH Chad Henne/304	10.00	25.00
STCJ Chad Johnson/60	8.00	20.00
STCP Clinton Portis/80	8.00	20.00
STDB Dwayne Bowe/82	6.00	15.00
STDM Darren McFadden/41		
STEM Eli Manning/90	30.00	60.00
STFJ Felix Jones/255	8.00	20.00
STJS Jonathan Stewart/41	8.00	20.00
STKS Kevin Smith/304	5.00	12.00
STLH Lavelle Hawkins/230	3.00	8.00
STLJ Larry Johnson/41	10.00	25.00
STMB Marion Barber/41	15.00	40.00
STMH Mike Hart/204	5.00	12.00
STML Marshawn Lynch/46	8.00	20.00
STMR Matt Ryan/50	40.00	100.00
STPH Paul Hornung/101	15.00	40.00
STPM Peyton Manning/50	50.00	100.00
STRM Rashard Mendenhall/230	10.00	25.00
STRR Ray Rice/230	15.00	30.00
STSS Steve Slaton/154	6.00	15.00
STTC Tashard Choice/255	4.00	10.00
STTM Tom Brady/25	125.00	200.00
STYT Y.A. Tittle/80	12.00	30.00

2008 SP Rookie Threads Signature Draft Choice

STATED PRINT RUN 50-280

SDCAW Andre Woodson/241	5.00	12.00
SDCBB Brian Brohm/71	5.00	12.00
SDCCC Calais Campbell/224	4.00	10.00
SDCCH Chad Henne/210	5.00	12.00
SDCCL Chris Long/114	5.00	12.00
SDCDA Donnie Avery/280	4.00	10.00
SDCDC Dan Connor/136	5.00	12.00
SDCDD Dennis Dixon/116	6.00	15.00
SDCDJ DeSean Jackson/141	10.00	25.00
SDCDM Darren McFadden/55	15.00	40.00
SDCED Early Doucet/280	4.00	10.00
SDCFD Fred Davis/229	5.00	12.00
SDCFJ Felix Jones/280	8.00	20.00
SDCHD Harry Douglas/280	4.00	10.00
SDCJL Jake Long/229	5.00	12.00
SDCJN Jordy Nelson/180	12.50	25.00
SDCJS Jonathan Stewart/61	8.00	20.00
SDCKP Kenny Phillips/254	5.00	12.00
SDCKS Kevin Smith/121	5.00	12.00
SDCLS Limas Sweed/199	5.00	12.00
SDCMJ Mike Jenkins/99	5.00	12.00
SDCMK Malcolm Kelly/149	4.00	10.00
SDCMR Matt Ryan/50	40.00	100.00
SDCRC Ryan Clady/99	5.00	12.00
SDCRM Rashard Mendenhall/50	12.00	30.00

2008 SP Rookie Threads Signing Day

STATED PRINT RUN 20-329

SDAA Adrian Arrington/280	4.00	10.00
SDAM Anthony Morelli/254	4.00	10.00
SDAT Aqib Talib/231	5.00	12.00
SDAW Andre Woodson/120	5.00	12.00
SDBB Brian Brohm/71	5.00	12.00
SDCB Colt Brennan/96	12.00	30.00
SDCC Calais Campbell/329	4.00	10.00
SDCH Chad Henne/180	10.00	25.00
SDCL Chris Long/116	5.00	12.00
SDDA Donnie Avery/111	4.00	10.00
SDDB Davone Bess/116	5.00	12.00
SDDD Dennis Dixon/128	6.00	15.00
SDDJ DeSean Jackson/181	12.00	30.00
SDDK Dustin Keller/280	5.00	12.00
SDDM Darren McFadden/51	15.00	40.00
SDEA Erik Ainge/131	5.00	12.00
SDED Early Doucet/201	4.00	10.00
SDFD Fred Davis/249	5.00	12.00
SDFJ Felix Jones/280	8.00	20.00
SDFO Matt Forte/280	15.00	40.00
SDJB John David Booty/116	4.00	10.00
SDJC Jamaal Charles/131	10.00	25.00
SDJF Joe Flacco/20	50.00	100.00
SDJL Jake Long/180	5.00	12.00
SDJN Jordy Nelson/180	12.50	25.00
SDJS Jonathan Stewart/71	8.00	20.00
SDKP Kenny Phillips/180	5.00	12.00
SDKS Kevin Smith/131	5.00	12.00
SDLS Limas Sweed/280	5.00	12.00
SDMH Mike Hart/116	5.00	12.00
SDMJ Mike Jenkins/231	5.00	12.00
SDMR Matt Ryan/51	50.00	100.00
SDRM Rashard Mendenhall/65	12.00	30.00
SDRR Ray Rice/254	10.00	25.00
SDSS Steve Slaton/136	5.00	12.00
SDTC Tashard Choice/181	4.00	10.00

2008 SP Rookie Threads SP Authentics

STATED PRINT RUN 10-284
SERIAL #'d UNDER 20 NOT PRICED

SPAA Adrian Arrington/244	4.00	10.00
SPAB Ahmad Bradshaw/244	6.00	15.00
SPAC Antoine Cason/244	5.00	12.00
SPAH A.J. Hawk/60	8.00	20.00
SPAO Amobi Okoye/240	5.00	12.00
SPAP Adrian Peterson/25	75.00	150.00
SPAT Aqib Talib/234	5.00	12.00
SPAW Andre Woodson/100	5.00	12.00
SPBB Brian Brohm/45	10.00	25.00
SPBC Brodie Croyle/20	8.00	20.00
SPBK Bo Jackson/35	30.00	60.00
SPBO Dwayne Bowe/60	6.00	15.00
SPBR Bert Jones/80	8.00	20.00
SPBS Bob Sanders/40	25.00	50.00
SPBU Dick Butkus/35	30.00	60.00
SPBW Ben Watson/80	5.00	12.00
SPCA Jason Campbell/60	8.00	20.00
SPCB Colt Brennan/60	10.00	25.00
SPCC Calais Campbell/184	4.00	10.00
SPCH Chad Henne/184	5.00	12.00
SPCJ Chris Johnson/244	30.00	60.00
SPCL Chris Long/60	5.00	12.00
SPCP Clinton Portis/120	8.00	20.00
SPCR Roger Craig/60	10.00	25.00
SPDB Davone Bess/80	5.00	12.00
SPDC Dan Connor/195	5.00	12.00
SPDD Dennis Dixon/80	6.00	15.00
SPDM Don Maynard/30	12.00	30.00
SPDT DeJuan Tribble/217	3.00	8.00
SPEA Erik Ainge/80	5.00	12.00
SPED Early Doucet/244	4.00	10.00
SPFD Fred Davis/249	5.00	12.00
SPFG Frank Gore/60	8.00	20.00
SPFJ Felix Jones/244	15.00	30.00
SPFO Matt Forte/159	20.00	40.00
SPHD Harry Douglas/284	4.00	10.00
SPJA Joseph Addai/25		
SPJB John David Booty/80	4.00	10.00
SPJC Jamaal Charles/80	8.00	20.00
SPJD Daryl Johnston/60	20.00	40.00
SPJM Jim Kelly/20	50.00	80.00
SPJN Jordy Nelson/244	15.00	30.00
SPJS Jonathan Stewart/50	8.00	20.00
SPJT Joe Theismann/60	12.00	30.00
SPJW Jerious Norwood/244	6.00	15.00
SPJX DeSean Jackson/80	15.00	40.00
SPKB Kevin Boss/155	8.00	20.00
SPKO Kevin O'Connell/80	4.00	10.00
SPKP Kenny Phillips/244	5.00	12.00
SPKR Keith Rivers/224	5.00	12.00
SPKS Kevin Smith/80	5.00	12.00
SPLG L.C. Greenwood/99	15.00	40.00
SPLO Jake Long/244	5.00	12.00
SPLS Limas Sweed/182	5.00	12.00
SPMB Marc Bulger/60	8.00	20.00
SPMC Darren McFadden/35	15.00	40.00
SPMH Mike Hart/80	5.00	12.00
SPMJ Mike Jenkins/144	5.00	12.00
SPML Marshawn Lynch/35	8.00	20.00
SPMO DaJuan Morgan/209	4.00	10.00
SPMR Matt Ryan/35	40.00	100.00
SPPH Paul Hornung/60	12.00	30.00
SPPL Phillip Merling/259	4.00	10.00
SPPM Peyton Manning/75	50.00	100.00
SPPS Paul Smith/259	5.00	12.00
SPPW Patrick Willis/284	6.00	15.00
SPRC Ryan Clady/244	5.00	12.00
SPRM Rashard Mendenhall/60	12.00	30.00
SPRR Ray Rice/259	12.50	25.00
SPSB Sam Baker/244	3.00	8.00
SPSC Shawn Crable/244	3.00	8.00
SPSM Billy Sims/80	10.00	25.00
SPSS Steve Slaton/80	5.00	12.00
SPTC Tashard Choice/120	4.00	10.00
SPTR Tony Romo/175	40.00	80.00

2008 SP Rookie Threads Stitch in Time 99

STATED PRINT RUN 99 SER.#'d SETS
*JSY/50: .5X TO 1.2X JSY/99
*JSY/15: .6X TO 1.5X JSY/99
JERSEY 1/1 TOO SCARCE TO PRICE
*JSY NUMBER/72-82: .4X TO 1X JSY/99
*JSY NUMBER/20-50: .5X TO 1.2X JSY/99
JERSEY NUMBER PRINT RUN 1-82

STAH A.J. Hawk	2.00	5.00
STBS Barry Sanders	8.00	20.00
STDA Derek Anderson	1.50	4.00
STDJ DeSean Jackson	4.00	10.00
STDK Dustin Keller	2.00	5.00
STDM Darren McFadden	5.00	12.00
STED Early Doucet	1.50	4.00
STER Ed Reed	2.00	5.00
STGD Glenn Dorsey	2.00	5.00
STJS Jonathan Stewart	3.00	8.00
STLT LaDainian Tomlinson	2.50	6.00
STMA Dan Marino	10.00	25.00
STMJ Maurice Jones-Drew	2.00	5.00
STMR Matt Ryan	6.00	15.00
STRC Roger Craig	4.00	10.00
STRM Rashard Mendenhall	4.00	10.00

2008 SP Rookie Threads Super Swatch 25

STATED PRINT RUN 25 SER.#'d SETS
*SUPER SWATCH/15: .5X TO 1.2X JSY/25
SUPER SWATCH/5 TOO SCARCE TO PRICE
SS PATCH/10 TOO SCARCE TO PRICE
UNPRICED AUTO PRINT RUN 5
SUPER SWATCH 1/1 TOO SCARCE TO PRICE

SSAP Adrian Peterson	10.00	25.00
SSBF Brett Favre	15.00	40.00
SSBR Ben Roethlisberger	6.00	15.00
SSBW Ben Watson	4.00	10.00
SSCU Jay Cutler	6.00	15.00
SSDA Derek Anderson	4.00	10.00
SSDH Devin Hester	6.00	15.00
SSER Ed Reed	5.00	12.00
SSFG Frank Gore	5.00	12.00
SSLJ Larry Johnson	5.00	12.00
SSML Marshawn Lynch	5.00	12.00
SSPW Patrick Willis	5.00	12.00
SSRY Roy Williams WR	5.00	12.00
SSTB Tom Brady	10.00	25.00
SSTG Tony Gonzalez	5.00	12.00
SSTR Tony Romo	8.00	20.00
SSVY Vince Young	5.00	12.00

1999 SP Signature

This set was released in one series initially with a total of 170-cards. The cards feature current NFL stars as well as a group (#131-170) of past football greats and were released 3-cards per pack. Ten rookies slated to be included in the initial print run missed the product pack-out. These cards were distributed roughly 4-months later directly through the Upper Deck dealer/distributor network in 2-card generic packs. The ten rookie cards can often be found missing the gold foil on the cardfronts.

COMPLETE SET (180)	200.00	400.00
COMP.SET w/o SP's (170)	50.00	100.00
1 Jake Plummer	.30	.75
2 Mario Bates	.25	.60
3 Adrian Murrell	.30	.75
4 Jamal Anderson	.30	.75
5 Chris Chandler	.30	.75
6 Bob Christian	.25	.60
7 O.J. Santiago	.25	.60
8 Jim Harbaugh	.30	.75
9 Priest Holmes	.40	1.00
10 Ray Lewis	.40	1.00
11 Michael Jackson	.25	.60
12 Tony Siragusa	.40	1.00
13 Doug Flutie	.40	1.00
14 Antowain Smith	.25	.60
15 Eric Moulds	.30	.75
16 William Floyd	.30	.75
17 Fred Lane	.25	.60
18 Muhsin Muhammad	.30	.75
19 Bobby Engram	.30	.75
20 Curtis Enis	.25	.60
21 Curtis Conway	.30	.75
22 Corey Dillon	.30	.75
23 Carl Pickens	.30	.75
24 Ashley Ambrose	.25	.60
25 Darnay Scott	.25	.60
26 Troy Aikman	.60	1.50
27 Jason Garrett	.40	1.00
28 Emmitt Smith	1.00	2.50
29 Deion Sanders	.40	1.00
30 John Elway	1.25	3.00
31 Terrell Davis	.40	1.00
32 Ed McCaffrey	.30	.75
33 John Mobley	.25	.60
34 Maa Tanuvasa	.25	.60
35 Ray Crockett	.25	.60
36 Barry Sanders	1.00	2.50
37 Herman Moore	.30	.75
38 Charlie Batch	.30	.75
39 Robert Porcher	.25	.60
40 Tommy Vardell	.30	.75
41 Brett Favre	1.25	3.00
42 Antonio Freeman	.30	.75
43 Darick Holmes	.25	.60
44 Robert Brooks	.30	.75
45 Peyton Manning	1.25	3.00
46 Marshall Faulk	.40	1.00
47 Torrance Small	.25	.60
48 Lamont Warren	.30	.75
49 Zack Crockett	.25	.60
50 Mark Brunell	.30	.75
51 Pete Mitchell	.25	.60
52 Fred Taylor	.30	.75
53 Jimmy Smith	.30	.75
54 Andre Rison	.30	.75
55 Rich Gannon	.30	.75
56 Donnell Bennett	.25	.60
57 Dan Marino	1.25	3.00
58 Karim Abdul-Jabbar	.30	.75
59 Troy Drayton	.25	.60
60 Jason Taylor	.30	.75
61 Cris Carter	.40	1.00
62 Randy Moss	.40	1.00
63 Robert Smith	.30	.75
64 Leroy Hoard	.25	.60
65 Randall Cunningham	.40	1.00
66 Derrick Alexander DE	.25	.60
67 Drew Bledsoe	.40	1.00
68 Robert Edwards	.25	.60
69 Willie McGinest	.30	.75
70 Chris Slade	.25	.60
71 Terry Glenn	.30	.75
72 Ty Law	.30	.75
73 Kerry Collins	.30	.75
74 Sean Dawkins	.25	.60
75 Cam Cleeland	.25	.60
76 Sammy Knight	.25	.60
77 Danny Kanell	.25	.60
78 Gary Brown	.25	.60
79 Chris Calloway	.25	.60
80 Curtis Martin	.40	1.00
81 Keyshawn Johnson	.30	.75
82 Vinny Testaverde	.30	.75
83 Leon Johnson	.25	.60
84 Kyle Brady	.25	.60
85 Tim Brown	.40	1.00
86 Jeff George	.25	.60
87 Rickey Dudley	.25	.60
88 Napoleon Kaufman	.25	.60
89 James Jett	.25	.60
90 Harvey Williams	.25	.60
91 Koy Detmer	.25	.60
92 Duce Staley	.30	.75
93 Charlie Garner	.30	.75
94 Jerome Bettis	.40	1.00
95 Kordell Stewart	.30	.75
96 Courtney Hawkins	.25	.60
97 Hines Ward	.40	1.00
98 Isaac Bruce	.40	1.00
99 Tony Banks	.30	.75
100 Greg Hill	.25	.60
101 Keith Lyle	.25	.60
102 Ryan Leaf	.30	.75
103 Craig Whelihan	.25	.60
104 Charlie Jones	.25	.60
105 Junior Seau	.40	1.00
106 Natrone Means	.30	.75
107 Rodney Harrison	.30	.75
108 Steve Young	.50	1.25
109 Garrison Hearst	.30	.75
110 Jerry Rice	.75	2.00
111 Chris Doleman	.25	.60
112 Roy Barker	.25	.60
113 Ricky Watters	.30	.75
114 Jon Kitna	.30	.75
115 Joey Galloway	.30	.75
116 Chad Brown	.25	.60
117 Michael Sinclair	.25	.60
118 Warrick Dunn	.30	.75
119 Mike Alstott	.40	1.00
120 Bert Emanuel	.30	.75
121 Hardy Nickerson	.25	.60
122 Eddie George	.30	.75
123 Steve McNair	.40	1.00
124 Yancey Thigpen	.25	.60
125 Frank Wycheck	.30	.75
126 Jackie Harris	.30	.75
127 Terry Allen	.30	.75
128 Trent Green	.30	.75
129 Jamie Asher	.25	.60
130 Brian Mitchell	.30	.75
131 Lance Alworth	.50	1.25
132 Fred Biletnikoff	.50	1.25
133 Mel Blount	.40	1.00
134 Cliff Branch	.40	1.00
135 Harold Carmichael	.30	.75
136 Larry Csonka	.50	1.25
137 Eric Dickerson	.40	1.00
138 Randy Gradishar	.30	.75
139 Joe Greene	.50	1.25
140 Jack Ham	.50	1.25
141 Ted Hendricks	.30	.75
142 Charlie Joiner	.30	.75
143 Ed Jones	.30	.75
144 Billy Kilmer	.40	1.00
145 Paul Krause	.30	.75
146 James Lofton	.30	.75
147 Archie Manning	.40	1.00
148 Don Maynard	.40	1.00
149 Ozzie Newsome	.30	.75
150 Jim Otto	.30	.75
151 Lee Roy Selmon	.30	.75
152 Billy Sims	.40	1.00
153 Mike Singletary	.50	1.25
154 Ken Stabler	.60	1.50
155 John Stallworth	.40	1.00
156 Roger Staubach	1.00	2.50
157 Charley Taylor	.40	1.00
158 Paul Warfield	.50	1.25
159 Kellen Winslow	.40	1.00
160 Jack Youngblood	.30	.75
161 Bill Bergey	.30	.75
162 Raymond Berry	.40	1.00
163 Chuck Howley	.30	.75
164 Rocky Bleier	.40	1.00
165 Russ Francis	.30	.75
166 Drew Pearson	.40	1.00
167 Mercury Morris	.30	.75
168 Dick Anderson	.30	.75
169 Earl Morrall	.30	.75
170 Jim Hart	.30	.75
171 Ricky Williams RC	3.00	8.00
172 Cade McNown RC	1.50	4.00
173 Tim Couch RC	2.00	5.00
174 Daunte Culpepper RC	2.00	5.00
175 Akili Smith RC	1.50	4.00
176 Brock Huard RC	1.50	4.00
177 Donovan McNabb RC	5.00	12.00
178 Michael Bishop RC	1.50	4.00
179 Shaun King RC	1.50	4.00
180 Torry Holt RC	3.00	8.00

1999 SP Signature Autographs

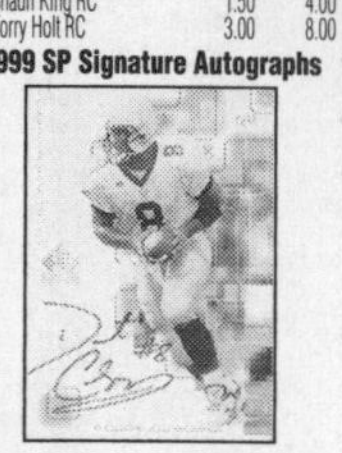

ONE AUTOGRAPH PER PACK

AA Ashley Ambrose	4.00	10.00
AF Antonio Freeman	25.00	60.00
AK Akili Smith	8.00	20.00
AM Adrian Murrell	4.00	10.00
AN Dick Anderson	6.00	15.00
AS Antowain Smith	6.00	15.00
BB Bill Bergey	6.00	15.00
BC Bob Christian	4.00	10.00
BE Bobby Engram	6.00	15.00
BH Brock Huard	15.00	40.00
BT Bert Emanuel	4.00	10.00
CB Charlie Batch	6.00	15.00
CC Chris Chandler	6.00	15.00
CD Corey Dillon	8.00	20.00
CE Curtis Enis	6.00	15.00
CG Charlie Garner	6.00	15.00
CJ Charlie Joiner	8.00	20.00
CK Ray Crockett	4.00	10.00
CL Cameron Cleeland	4.00	10.00
CP Mike Singletary	15.00	30.00
CS Chris Slade	4.00	10.00
CT Charley Taylor	6.00	15.00
CW Curtis Conway	6.00	15.00
CY Chris Calloway	4.00	10.00
DA Derrick Alexander DE	4.00	10.00
DB Donnell Bennett	4.00	10.00
DC Daunte Culpepper	50.00	120.00
DE Roy Barker	4.00	10.00
DH Darick Holmes	4.00	10.00
DM Dan Marino	125.00	250.00
DP Drew Pearson	8.00	20.00
EG Eddie George	25.00	50.00
EJ Ed Too Tall Jones	12.50	30.00
EM Eric Moulds	6.00	15.00
ES Emmitt Smith	150.00	300.00
FL Fred Lane	8.00	20.00
FW Frank Wycheck	6.00	15.00
GA Joey Galloway	10.00	25.00
GB Gary Brown	4.00	10.00
GE Jeff George	15.00	40.00
GH Garrison Hearst	6.00	15.00
GN Trent Green	8.00	20.00
GR Randy Gradishar	6.00	15.00
HC Harold Carmichael	6.00	15.00
HL Greg Hill	4.00	10.00
HM Herman Moore	6.00	15.00
HN Hardy Nickerson	6.00	15.00
HT Jim Hart	6.00	15.00
HV Harvey Williams	4.00	10.00
HW Hines Ward	35.00	60.00
HY Chuck Howley	8.00	20.00
IB Isaac Bruce	8.00	20.00
JG Jason Garrett	10.00	25.00

JH Jack Ham	15.00	40.00
JJ James Jett	4.00	10.00
JK Jackie Harris	4.00	10.00
JL James Lofton	8.00	20.00
JM John Mobley	4.00	10.00
JP Jake Plummer	40.00	80.00
JR Junior Seau	75.00	150.00
JS Jimmy Smith	6.00	15.00
JT Jason Taylor	15.00	40.00
JY Jack Youngblood	6.00	15.00
KA Karim Abdul-Jabbar	4.00	10.00
KB Kyle Brady	4.00	10.00
KD Koy Detmer	6.00	15.00
KI Jon Kitna	8.00	20.00
KJ Keyshawn Johnson	10.00	25.00
KL Keith Lyle	4.00	10.00
KR Brian Mitchell	6.00	15.00
KS Ken Stabler	20.00	40.00
KW Kellen Winslow	8.00	20.00
LB Chad Brown	4.00	10.00
LH Leroy Hoard	4.00	10.00
LJ Leon Johnson	4.00	10.00
LS Lee Roy Selmon	15.00	40.00
LW Lamont Warren	4.00	10.00
MA Mike Alstott	30.00	60.00
MB Mario Bates	4.00	10.00
MF Marshall Faulk	25.00	60.00
MG Archie Manning	12.50	30.00
MI Michael Bishop	30.00	60.00
MJ Michael Jackson	4.00	10.00
MK Mark Brunell	15.00	40.00
ML Mel Blount	15.00	30.00
MM Muhsin Muhammad	6.00	15.00
MN Donovan McNabb	60.00	150.00
MO Earl Morrall	8.00	20.00
MS Michael Sinclair	4.00	10.00
MT Maa Tanuvasa	4.00	10.00
MY Mercury Morris	8.00	20.00
ND Ricky Watters	6.00	15.00
NM Natrone Means	6.00	15.00
NO Sean Dawkins	4.00	10.00
NY Don Maynard	8.00	20.00
OJ O.J. Santiago	4.00	10.00
OZ Ozzie Newsome	8.00	20.00
PH Priest Holmes	10.00	25.00
PK Paul Krause	8.00	20.00
PT Pete Mitchell	4.00	10.00
PW Paul Warfield	8.00	20.00
QB Cade McNown	8.00	20.00
RB Robert Brooks	12.00	30.00
RD Rickey Dudley	4.00	10.00
RE Robert Edwards	6.00	15.00
RF Russ Francis	8.00	20.00
RH Rodney Harrison	8.00	20.00
RL Ray Lewis	40.00	80.00
RM Randy Moss	75.00	150.00
RP Robert Porcher	4.00	10.00
RW Ricky Williams	40.00	100.00
RY Raymond Berry	8.00	20.00
SD Charlie Jones	4.00	10.00
SH Shaun King	8.00	20.00
SK Sammy Knight	4.00	10.00
ST Duce Staley	8.00	20.00
SW John Stallworth	15.00	30.00
TA Troy Aikman	60.00	120.00
TB Tim Brown	40.00	100.00
TC Tim Couch	20.00	50.00
TE Jamie Asher	4.00	10.00
TH Ted Hendricks	8.00	20.00
TL Ty Law	8.00	20.00
TO Torrance Small	4.00	10.00
TR Troy Drayton	4.00	10.00
TS Tony Siragusa	8.00	20.00
TV Tommy Vardell	4.00	10.00
WF William Floyd	4.00	10.00
WH Craig Whelihan	4.00	10.00
WM Willie McGinest	6.00	15.00
WP Torry Holt	75.00	150.00
ZC Zack Crockett	4.00	10.00

1999 SP Signature Autographs Gold

*UNLISTED GOLDS: .8X TO 2X BASIC INSERTS		
AK Akili Smith	60.00	150.00
BH Brock Huard	60.00	150.00
DC Daunte Culpepper	125.00	250.00
JR Junior Seau	200.00	400.00
MI Michael Bishop	60.00	150.00
MN Donovan McNabb	150.00	300.00
QB Cade McNown	60.00	150.00
RW Ricky Williams	125.00	250.00
SH Shaun King	60.00	150.00
TC Tim Couch	60.00	150.00
WP Torry Holt	100.00	250.00

1999 SP Signature Montana Great Performances

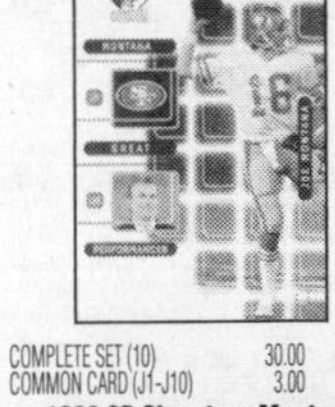

COMPLETE SET (10)	30.00	60.00
COMMON CARD (J1-J10)	3.00	8.00

1999 SP Signature Montana Signature Performances

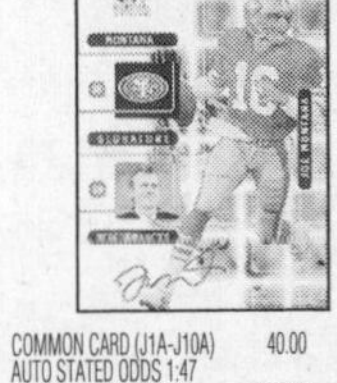

COMMON CARD (J1A-J10A)	40.00	100.00
AUTO STATED ODDS 1:47		
COMMON GOLD AUTO	125.00	250.00
GOLD STATED ODDS 1:880		
J1A Joe Montana	40.00	100.00
J2A Joe Montana	40.00	100.00
J3A Joe Montana	40.00	100.00
J4A Joe Montana	40.00	100.00
J5A Joe Montana	40.00	100.00
J6A Joe Montana	40.00	100.00
J7A Joe Montana	40.00	100.00
J8A Joe Montana	40.00	100.00
J9A Joe Montana	40.00	100.00
J10A Joe Montana	40.00	100.00

1999 SP Signature UD Authentics

TD Terrell Davis	15.00	30.00

2003 SP Signature

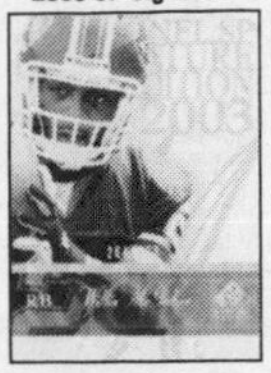

Released in November of 2003, this set contains 200 cards, including 100 veterans and 100 rookies. Rookies 101-170 are serial numbered to 750. Rookies 171-200 are serial numbered to 250. Each 3-card pack contained an authentic player autograph card, and had an SRP of $49.99. Boxes contained 5 packs.

101-170 ROOKIE PRINT RUN 750		
171-200 ROOKIE PRINT RUN 250		
1 Michael Vick	2.00	5.00
2 Aaron Brooks	1.25	3.00
3 Jim Brown	3.00	8.00
4 Steve Young	2.50	6.00
5 Jeff Garcia	1.25	3.00
6 Warren Moon	1.50	4.00
7 John Elway	5.00	12.00
8 Troy Aikman	2.50	6.00
9 Drew Brees	1.50	4.00
10 Chad Pennington	1.50	4.00
11 Fran Tarkenton	2.00	5.00
12 Joe Namath	3.00	8.00
13 Dan Marino	5.00	12.00
14 Terry Bradshaw	3.00	8.00
15 Edgerrin James	1.50	4.00
16 Joe Montana	5.00	12.00
17 Ken Stabler	2.50	6.00
18 Peyton Manning	3.00	8.00
19 Johnny Unitas	4.00	10.00
20 Barry Sanders	4.00	10.00
21 Jim Kelly	2.50	6.00
22 Michael Bennett	1.25	3.00
23 Phil Simms	2.00	5.00
24 David Carr	1.25	3.00
25 Deuce McAllister	1.25	3.00
26 Clinton Portis	1.25	3.00
27 Brad Johnson	1.25	3.00
28 Tim Couch	1.00	2.50
29 Archie Manning	2.00	5.00
30 Ahman Green	1.25	3.00
31 Priest Holmes	1.50	4.00
32 Marcus Allen	2.00	5.00
33 Ricky Williams	1.25	3.00
34 Walter Payton	6.00	15.00
35 Anthony Thomas	1.25	3.00
36 Eddie George	1.25	3.00
37 Shaun Alexander	1.25	3.00
38 Rich Gannon	1.25	3.00
39 Jay Fiedler	1.00	2.50
40 Travis Henry	1.00	2.50
41 Chad Johnson	1.50	4.00
42 Eric Moulds	1.25	3.00
43 Julius Peppers	1.50	4.00
44 John Riggins	2.00	5.00
45 Antonio Bryant	1.00	2.50
46 Laveranues Coles	1.00	2.50
47 Josh McCown	1.25	3.00
48 Matt Hasselbeck	1.25	3.00
49 William Green	1.00	2.50
50 Peerless Price	1.00	2.50
51 Kerry Collins	1.25	3.00
52 Zach Thomas	1.50	4.00
53 Bruiser Kinard	1.50	4.00
54 Brian Urlacher	1.50	4.00
55 Junior Seau	1.50	4.00
56 Jamal Lewis	1.25	3.00
57 Duce Staley	1.25	3.00
58 Chris Redman	1.00	2.50
59 Kordell Stewart	1.25	3.00
60 Chad Hutchinson	1.00	2.50
61 Kevan Barlow	1.00	2.50
62 Charlie Garner	1.25	3.00
63 Fred Taylor	1.25	3.00
64 Jerome Bettis	1.50	4.00
65 Donte Stallworth	1.00	2.50
66 Rod Smith	1.25	3.00
67 Antwaan Randle El	1.25	3.00
68 Brian Griese	1.25	3.00
69 Corey Dillon	1.25	3.00
70 Chris Chambers	1.25	3.00
71 Steve McNair	1.50	4.00
72 Jake Plummer	1.25	3.00
73 Keyshawn Johnson	1.50	4.00
74 Marvin Harrison	1.50	4.00
75 Plaxico Burress	1.25	3.00
76 Tim Brown	1.50	4.00
77 Mark Brunell	1.25	3.00
78 Curtis Martin	1.50	4.00
79 Cal Hubbard	1.50	4.00
80 Isaac Bruce	1.50	4.00
81 Terrell Owens	1.50	4.00
82 Santana Moss	1.25	3.00
83 Tommy Maddox	1.25	3.00
84 Randy Moss	1.50	4.00
85 Drew Bledsoe	1.50	4.00
86 Az-Zahir Hakim	1.00	2.50
87 Rod Gardner	1.00	2.50
88 Tom Brady	4.00	10.00
89 David Boston	1.00	2.50
90 Trent Green	1.25	3.00
91 Jeremy Shockey	1.50	4.00
92 Daunte Culpepper	1.25	3.00
93 Emmitt Smith	4.00	10.00
94 Jerry Rice	3.00	8.00
95 LaDainian Tomlinson	1.50	4.00
96 Marshall Faulk	1.50	4.00
97 Kurt Warner	1.50	4.00
98 Brett Favre	4.00	10.00
99 Doak Walker	2.00	5.00
100 Donovan McNabb	1.50	4.00
101 Ken Dorsey RC	2.00	5.00
102 Kirk Farmer RC	2.00	5.00
103 Nate Hybl RC	2.00	5.00
104 Marquel Blackwell RC	1.50	4.00
105 Brett Engemann RC	1.50	4.00
106 Tony Romo RC	20.00	50.00
107 Derick Armstrong RC	2.00	5.00
108 Lon Sheriff RC	1.50	4.00
109 Casey Moore RC	1.50	4.00
110 Jason Gesser RC	2.00	5.00
111 Brock Forsey RC	2.00	5.00
112 Willis McGahee RC	3.00	8.00
113 Nick Maddox RC	1.50	4.00
114 LaBrandon Toefield RC	2.00	5.00
115 Kareem Kelly RC	1.50	4.00
116 Malaefou MacKenzie RC	1.50	4.00
117 Troy Polamalu RC	15.00	30.00
118 Terence Newman RC	2.00	5.00
119 Marcus Trufant RC	2.00	5.00
120 Terrell Suggs RC	2.50	6.00
121 DeWayne Robertson RC	2.00	5.00
122 Justin Griffith RC	2.00	5.00
123 Lee Suggs RC	2.00	5.00
124 Bryant Johnson RC	2.50	6.00
125 Andre Woolfolk RC	2.00	5.00
126 Cedric Henry RC	1.50	4.00
127 Billy McMullen RC	1.50	4.00
128 Charles Rogers RC	2.00	5.00
129 David Kircus RC	2.50	6.00
130 Jerome McDougle RC	1.50	4.00
131 Ryan Hoag RC	1.50	4.00
132 Mike Pinkard RC	1.50	4.00
133 Shaun McDonald RC	2.00	5.00
134 Bobby Wade RC	2.00	5.00
135 Kassim Osgood RC	2.50	6.00
136 Ovie Mughelli RC	2.00	5.00
137 Doug Gabriel RC	2.00	5.00
138 Aaron Walker RC	2.00	5.00
139 Brandon Lloyd RC	4.00	10.00
140 Donald Lee RC	2.00	5.00
141 George Wrighster RC	1.50	4.00
142 Antwone Savage RC	1.50	4.00
143 Keenan Howry RC	1.50	4.00
144 Kevin Walter RC	4.00	10.00
145 Gerald Hayes RC	2.00	5.00
146 Walter Young RC	1.50	4.00
147 Casey Fitzsimmons RC	2.00	5.00
148 Vishante Shiancoe RC	2.50	6.00
149 Lance Briggs RC	6.00	15.00
150 Zuriel Smith RC	1.50	4.00
151 Terrence Edwards RC	1.50	4.00
152 Arnaz Battle RC	2.50	6.00
153 DeAndrew Rubin RC	1.50	4.00
154 Pisa Tinoisamoa RC	2.50	6.00
155 David Tyree RC	2.50	6.00
156 Bradie James RC	2.50	6.00
157 Anquan Boldin RC	4.00	10.00
158 Kevin Curtis RC	2.50	6.00
159 Taylor Jacobs RC	1.50	4.00
160 Cato June RC	3.00	8.00
161 Jason Witten RC	6.00	15.00
162 Mike Seidman RC	1.50	4.00
163 Dallas Clark RC	4.00	10.00
164 Gibran Hamdan RC	1.50	4.00
165 Kliff Kingsbury RC	2.00	5.00
166 Brooks Bollinger RC	2.00	5.00
167 Nick Barnett RC	2.50	6.00
168 Rex Grossman RC	2.50	6.00
169 Byron Leftwich RC	2.50	6.00
170 Kyle Boller RC	2.50	6.00
171 Chris Brown RC	2.50	6.00
172 Carl Ford RC	2.50	6.00
173 Kelley Washington RC	2.50	6.00
174 Charles Tillman RC	5.00	12.00
175 Ken Hamlin RC	4.00	10.00
176 Bennie Joppru RC	2.50	6.00
177 Nate Burleson RC	3.00	8.00
178 Boss Bailey RC	3.00	8.00
179 LaTarence Dunbar RC	2.50	6.00
180 Adrian Madise RC	2.50	6.00
181 J.R. Tolver RC	3.00	8.00
182 Tyrone Calico RC	3.00	8.00
183 Justin Gage RC	3.00	8.00
184 Teyo Johnson RC	3.00	8.00
185 B.J. Askew RC	3.00	8.00
186 Sam Aiken RC	3.00	8.00
187 Andre Johnson RC	10.00	25.00
188 Bethel Johnson RC	2.50	6.00
189 Artose Pinner RC	2.50	6.00
190 Quentin Griffin RC	3.00	8.00
191 Musa Smith RC	2.50	6.00
192 Larry Johnson RC	4.00	10.00
193 Onterrio Smith RC	2.50	6.00
194 Justin Fargas RC	4.00	10.00
195 Dwone Hicks RC	2.50	6.00
196 Brian St.Pierre RC	3.00	8.00
197 Dave Ragone RC	2.50	6.00
198 Seneca Wallace RC	4.00	10.00
199 Chris Simms RC	4.00	10.00
200 Carson Palmer RC	8.00	20.00

2003 SP Signature Autographs Black Ink

COMMON CARD	6.00	15.00
SEMISTARS	8.00	20.00
UNLISTED STARS	10.00	25.00
AB Anquan Boldin	15.00	40.00
AJ Andre Johnson	20.00	50.00
AM Archie Manning	15.00	40.00
BY Byron Leftwich	12.00	30.00
CP Chad Pennington	12.00	30.00
DA David Boston SP/25*	15.00	40.00
DB Drew Brees SP/20*	40.00	80.00
DM Dan Marino SP	75.00	150.00
FT Fran Tarkenton SP	20.00	50.00
JM Joe Montana	60.00	120.00
JN Joe Namath SP	60.00	120.00
KS Ken Stabler SP	25.00	50.00
LJ Larry Johnson	10.00	25.00
PH Priest Holmes SP/25*	30.00	80.00
PM Peyton Manning	60.00	120.00
SC Carson Palmer	25.00	60.00
TM Tommy Maddox SP/25*	15.00	40.00

2003 SP Signature Autographs Blue Ink

OVERALL AUTOGRAPH ODDS ONE PER PACK		
SERIAL #'d UNDER 25 NOT PRICED		
AA Aaron Brooks	6.00	15.00
AB Anquan Boldin	12.00	30.00
AH Az-Zahir Hakim	4.00	10.00
AJ Andre Johnson	20.00	50.00
AM Archie Manning SP/25*	30.00	60.00
AP Artose Pinner	6.00	15.00
AR Arnaz Battle	6.00	15.00
AT Anthony Thomas	6.00	15.00
BB Brad Banks	5.00	12.00
BJ Brad Johnson SP/25*	15.00	40.00
BL Brandon Lloyd	8.00	20.00
BO Brooks Bollinger	6.00	15.00
BR Bryant Johnson	6.00	15.00
BY Byron Leftwich	10.00	25.00
CA Tyrone Calico	6.00	15.00
CB Chris Brown	6.00	15.00
CP Chad Pennington SP	12.00	30.00
CS Chris Simms SP	15.00	40.00
DB Drew Brees SP	30.00	60.00
DC David Carr	6.00	15.00
DO Donovan McNabb SP/19*		
DR DeWayne Robertson	5.00	12.00
EG Earnest Graham	6.00	15.00
FA Justin Fargas	6.00	15.00
IB Isaac Bruce	6.00	15.00
JB Jim Brown SP	50.00	100.00
JF Jay Fiedler	6.00	15.00
JG Jeff Garcia SP/24*		
JO Teyo Johnson	6.00	15.00
KA Kareem Kelly	4.00	10.00
KB Kyle Boller	6.00	15.00
KC Kevin Curtis	6.00	15.00
KD Ken Dorsey	6.00	15.00
KK Kliff Kingsbury	5.00	12.00
KW Kelley Washington	6.00	15.00
LJ Larry Johnson	6.00	15.00
LS Lee Suggs	6.00	15.00
MB Michael Bennett	6.00	15.00
MM Malaefou MacKenzie	4.00	10.00
MO Warren Moon	20.00	40.00
MS Musa Smith	6.00	15.00
MT Marcus Trufant	6.00	15.00
NB Nate Burleson	6.00	15.00
OS Onterrio Smith	6.00	15.00
PM Peyton Manning	50.00	100.00
PO Clinton Portis SP/25*	25.00	60.00
QG Quentin Griffin	6.00	15.00
RA Dave Ragone	6.00	15.00
RE Rex Grossman	8.00	20.00
RG Rod Gardner	5.00	12.00
RM Randy Moss SP/10*		
RW Ricky Williams SP/25*	25.00	60.00
SA Shaun Alexander	6.00	15.00
SC Carson Palmer	20.00	50.00
SM Santana Moss	8.00	20.00
SP Brian St.Pierre	6.00	15.00
SW Seneca Wallace	6.00	15.00
TC Tim Couch	4.00	10.00
TJ Taylor Jacobs	6.00	15.00
TN Terence Newman	6.00	15.00
TS Terrell Suggs	8.00	20.00
WM Willis McGahee SP	12.00	30.00

2003 SP Signature Autographs Blue Ink Numbered

STATED PRINT RUN 100 SER.#'d SETS		
AA Aaron Brooks	10.00	25.00
AB Anquan Boldin	20.00	50.00
AH Az-Zahir Hakim	8.00	20.00
AJ Andre Johnson	25.00	60.00
AM Archie Manning	20.00	50.00
AP Artose Pinner	10.00	25.00
AR Arnaz Battle	10.00	25.00
AT Anthony Thomas	12.00	30.00
BB Brad Banks	8.00	20.00
BL Brandon Lloyd	12.50	30.00
BO Brooks Bollinger	10.00	25.00
BR Bryant Johnson	10.00	25.00
BY Byron Leftwich	12.00	30.00
CA Tyrone Calico	12.00	30.00
CB Chris Brown	10.00	25.00
CP Chad Pennington	12.00	30.00
CS Chris Simms	12.00	30.00
DR DeWayne Robertson	8.00	20.00
EG Earnest Graham	12.00	30.00
FA Justin Fargas	10.00	25.00
IB Isaac Bruce	10.00	25.00
JB Jim Brown	30.00	80.00
JF Jay Fiedler	10.00	25.00
JO Teyo Johnson	10.00	25.00
KA Kareem Kelly	8.00	20.00
KB Kyle Boller	10.00	25.00
KC Kevin Curtis	10.00	25.00
KD Ken Dorsey	10.00	25.00
KK Kliff Kingsbury	8.00	20.00
KW Kelley Washington	12.00	30.00
LJ Larry Johnson	12.00	30.00
LS Lee Suggs	10.00	25.00
MB Michael Bennett	10.00	25.00
MM Malaefou MacKenzie	8.00	20.00
MS Musa Smith	10.00	25.00
MT Marcus Trufant	10.00	25.00
NB Nate Burleson	10.00	25.00
OS Onterrio Smith	10.00	25.00
PM Peyton Manning	60.00	120.00
QG Quentin Griffin	10.00	25.00
RA Dave Ragone	10.00	25.00
RE Rex Grossman	15.00	40.00
RG Rod Gardner	8.00	20.00
SA Shaun Alexander	12.00	30.00
SC Carson Palmer	25.00	60.00
SM Santana Moss	12.00	30.00
SP Brian St.Pierre	10.00	25.00
SW Seneca Wallace	10.00	25.00
TC Tim Couch	8.00	20.00
TG Trent Green	10.00	25.00
TJ Taylor Jacobs	12.00	30.00
TN Terence Newman	12.00	30.00
TS Terrell Suggs	12.00	30.00

2003 SP Signature Autographs Green Ink

COMMON CARD	10.00	25.00
SEMISTARS	12.50	30.00
UNLISTED STARS	15.00	40.00
STATED PRINT RUN 50 SER.#'d SETS		
AB Anquan Boldin	25.00	60.00
AJ Andre Johnson	40.00	100.00
AM Archie Manning	30.00	80.00
BA Barry Sanders	60.00	120.00
BY Byron Leftwich	20.00	50.00
CP Chad Pennington	15.00	40.00
DB Drew Brees	30.00	60.00
DC David Carr	15.00	40.00
DM Dan Marino	75.00	150.00
EG Earnest Graham	15.00	40.00
FT Fran Tarkenton	30.00	60.00
JB Jim Brown	50.00	100.00
JE John Elway	75.00	150.00
JK Jim Kelly	40.00	80.00
JM Joe Montana	75.00	150.00
JN Joe Namath	60.00	120.00
JR John Riggins	25.00	60.00
KS Ken Stabler	30.00	60.00
LJ Larry Johnson	15.00	40.00
MA Marcus Allen	25.00	50.00
MO Warren Moon	40.00	80.00
PH Priest Holmes	20.00	50.00
PM Peyton Manning	75.00	150.00
SC Carson Palmer	40.00	100.00
SM Santana Moss	20.00	50.00
SY Steve Young	40.00	80.00
TB Terry Bradshaw	40.00	100.00
TO Terrell Owens	35.00	60.00
WM Willis McGahee	25.00	60.00

2003 SP Signature Autographs Red Ink

COMMON CARD	6.00	15.00
SEMISTARS	8.00	20.00
UNLISTED STARS	10.00	26.00
STATED PRINT RUN 100 SER. #'d SETS		
AB Anquan Boldin	20.00	50.00
AJ Andre Johnson	25.00	60.00
AM Archie Manning	20.00	50.00
BA Barry Sanders	60.00	100.00
BY Byron Leftwich	12.00	30.00
CP Chad Pennington	12.00	30.00
DB Drew Brees	30.00	60.00
FT Fran Tarkenton	15.00	40.00
JB Jim Brown	40.00	100.00
JE John Elway	75.00	125.00
JK Jim Kelly		
JM Joe Montana	75.00	150.00
JN Joe Namath	50.00	100.00
JR John Riggins	20.00	40.00
KS Ken Stabler	25.00	50.00
LJ Larry Johnson	12.00	30.00
MA Marcus Allen	25.00	50.00
MO Warren Moon Purple	25.00	60.00
PH Priest Holmes	15.00	40.00
PM Peyton Manning	75.00	150.00
RE Rex Grossman	12.00	30.00
SA Shaun Alexander	10.00	25.00
SC Carson Palmer	25.00	60.00
SY Steve-Young	35.00	60.00
TB Terry Bradshaw	40.00	80.00
TO Terrell Owens	30.00	60.00
WM Willis McGahee	15.00	40.00

2003 SP Signature Dual Autographs

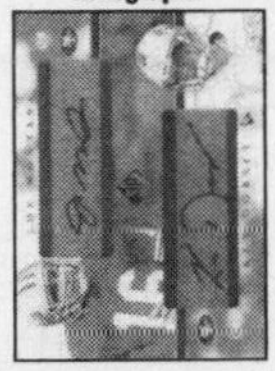

STATED PRINT RUN 75 SER.#'d SETS		
ABKK Aaron Brooks	12.00	30.00
Kareem Kelly		
BJAB Bryant Johnson	15.00	40.00
Anquan Boldin		
CPKW Carson Palmer	30.00	80.00
Kelley Washington		
CPSM Chad Pennington	15.00	40.00
Santana Moss		
CPVT Chad Pennington	15.00	40.00
Vinny Testaverde		
DBDB Drew Brees	30.00	60.00
David Boston		
DCAJ David Carr	30.00	60.00
Andre Johnson		
JMKD Joe Montana	60.00	150.00
Ken Dorsey		
JNCP Joe Namath	40.00	100.00
Chad Pennington		
KDTO Ken Dorsey	15.00	40.00
Terrell Owens		
MBOS Michael Bennett	10.00	25.00
Onterrio Smith		
PHLJ Priest Holmes	15.00	40.00
Larry Johnson		
PMAM Peyton Manning	75.00	150.00
Archie Manning		
PSCS Phil Simms	20.00	50.00
Chris Simms		
RGAT Rex Grossman	12.00	30.00
Anthony Thomas		
TMBS Tommy Maddox	12.00	30.00
Brian St. Pierre		

2003 SP Signature SP Legendary Cuts

STATED PRINT RUN 11-45		
SER.#'d UNDER 20 NOT PRICED		
LCBK Bruiser Kinard/22	200.00	400.00
LCCH Cal Hubbard/22	200.00	400.00
LCWP Walter Payton/45	500.00	750.00

2009 SP Signature

COMP.SET w/o RC's (200)	40.00	80.00
OVERALL AUTO STATED ODDS 1.5:1		
EXCH EXPIRATION: 11/19/2011		
1 John Abraham	.25	.60
2 Joseph Addai	.40	1.00
3 Jared Allen	.40	1.00
4 Derek Anderson	.25	.60
5 Oshiomogho Atogwe	.25	.60
6 Donnie Avery	.30	.75
7 Champ Bailey	.30	.75
8 Ronde Barber	.25	.60
9 Marion Barber	.30	.75
10 Jon Beason	.25	.60
11 Cedric Benson	.30	.75
12 Bernard Berrian	.30	.75
13 Anquan Boldin	.30	.75
14 Dwayne Bowe	.30	.75
15 Ahmad Bradshaw	.30	.75
16 Tom Brady	.60	1.50
17 Deion Branch	.30	.75
18 Steve Breaston	.30	.75
19 Drew Brees	.40	1.00
20 Lance Briggs	.30	.75
21 Keith Brooking	.25	.60
22 Ronnie Brown	.30	.75
23 Isaac Bruce	.30	.75
24 Antonio Bryant	.25	.60
25 Marc Bulger	.30	.75
26 Reggie Bush	.40	1.00
27 Greg Camarillo	.30	.75
28 Jason Campbell	.25	.60
29 John Carlson	.30	.75
30 Matt Cassel	.30	.75
31 Jamaal Charles	.40	1.00
32 Tashard Choice	.25	.60
33 Dallas Clark	.30	.75
34 Michael Clayton	.25	.60
35 Kellen Clemens	.25	.60
36 Laveranues Coles	.25	.60
37 Kerry Collins	.30	.75
38 Marques Colston	.30	.75
39 Chris Cooley	.30	.75
40 Jerricho Cotchery	.30	.75
41 Daunte Culpepper	.30	.75
42 Kevin Curtis	.25	.60
43 Jay Cutler	.40	1.00
44 Owen Daniels	.25	.60
45 Karlos Dansby	.25	.60
46 Brian Dawkins	.30	.75
47 Jake Delhomme	.30	.75
48 Quintin Demps	.25	.60
49 Donald Driver	.30	.75
50 Braylon Edwards	.30	.75
51 Trent Edwards	.25	.60
52 Shaun Ellis	.25	.60
53 Lee Evans	.30	.75
54 Justin Fargas	.25	.60
55 James Farrior	.25	.60
56 Kevin Faulk	.25	.60
57 Miles Austin	.60	1.50
58 Larry Fitzgerald	.40	1.00
59 Joe Flacco	.40	1.00
60 Matt Forte	.40	1.00
61 Dwight Freeney	.30	.75
62 Justin Gage	.25	.60
63 David Garrard	.30	.75
64 Antonio Gates	.30	.75
65 Ted Ginn	.30	.75
66 Anthony Gonzalez	.25	.60
67 Tony Gonzalez	.30	.75
68 Frank Gore	.30	.75
69 Earnest Graham	.25	.60
70 Ryan Grant	.30	.75
71 Chad Greenway	.25	.60
72 Brian Griese	.25	.60
73 Michael Griffin	.25	.60
74 Jason Hanson	.25	.60
75 James Harrison	.40	1.00
76 Rodney Harrison	.25	.60
77 Matt Hasselbeck	.30	.75
78 A.J. Hawk	.30	.75
79 Albert Haynesworth	.25	.60
80 Chad Henne	.30	.75
81 Devin Hester	.40	1.00
82 Johnnie Lee Higgins	.25	.60
83 Tim Hightower	.25	.60
84 Shaun Hill	.25	.60
85 Peyton Hillis	.40	1.00
86 Domenik Hixon	.25	.60
87 Torry Holt	.30	.75
88 T.J. Houshmandzadeh	.30	.75
89 DeSean Jackson	.30	.75
90 D'Qwell Jackson	.25	.60
91 Steven Jackson	.30	.75
92 Tarvaris Jackson	.30	.75
93 Vincent Jackson	.30	.75
94 Brandon Jacobs	.30	.75
95 Bradie James	.25	.60
96 Greg Jennings	.40	1.00
97 Andre Johnson	.30	.75
98 Calvin Johnson	.40	1.00
99 Chad Ochocinco	.30	.75
100 Chris Johnson	.40	1.00
101 Larry Johnson	.30	.75
102 Dhani Jones	.25	.60
103 Julius Jones	.25	.60
104 Brett Favre Vikings	6.00	15.00
105 Thomas Jones	.30	.75
106 Maurice Jones-Drew	.30	.75
107 Dustin Keller	.25	.60
108 Jamal Lewis	.30	.75
109 Ray Lewis	.40	1.00
110 Marshawn Lynch	.30	.75
111 Eli Manning	.40	1.00
112 Peyton Manning	.60	1.50
113 Brandon Marshall	.30	.75
114 Derrick Mason	.30	.75
115 Jerod Mayo	.30	.75
116 Le'Ron McClain	.30	.75
117 Darren McFadden	.40	1.00
118 Willis McGahee	.30	.75
119 Donovan McNabb	.40	1.00
120 Rashard Mendenhall	.30	.75
121 Shawne Merriman	.30	.75
122 Zach Miller	.25	.60
123 Lance Moore	.30	.75
124 Mewelde Moore	.25	.60
125 Maurice Morris	.25	.60
126 Kirk Morrison	.25	.60
127 Randy Moss	.40	1.00
128 Santana Moss	.30	.75
129 Muhsin Muhammad	.30	.75
130 Jerious Norwood	.30	.75
131 Kyle Orton	.30	.75
132 Terrell Owens	.40	1.00
133 Carson Palmer	.40	1.00
134 Willie Parker	.25	.60
135 Julius Peppers	.30	.75
136 Julian Peterson	.25	.60
137 Mike Peterson	.25	.60
138 Adrian Peterson	.60	1.50
139 Antonio Pierce	.25	.60
140 Troy Polamalu	.40	1.00
141 Joey Porter	.30	.75
142 Clinton Portis	.30	.75
143 Brady Quinn	.30	.75
144 Ed Reed	.30	.75
145 Darrelle Revis	.30	.75
146 Dominic Rhodes	.25	.60
147 Philip Rivers	.40	1.00
148 Aaron Rodgers	.75	2.00
149 Dominique Rodgers-Cromartie	.25	.60
150 Ben Roethlisberger	.40	1.00
151 Tony Romo	.60	1.50
152 Eddie Royal	.30	.75
153 JaMarcus Russell	.25	.60
154 Barrett Ruud	.25	.60
155 Matt Ryan	.40	1.00
156 DeMeco Ryans	.30	.75
157 Bob Sanders	.30	.75
158 Matt Schaub	.30	.75
159 Tony Scheffler	.25	.60
160 Richard Seymour	.25	.60
161 Ernie Sims	.25	.60
162 Steve Slaton	.30	.75
163 Alex Smith QB	.30	.75
164 Kevin Smith	.30	.75
165 Kolby Smith	.25	.60
166 Steve Smith USC	.30	.75
167 Steve Smith	.30	.75
168 Darren Sproles	.30	.75
169 Jonathan Stewart	.30	.75
170 Chester Taylor	.25	.60
171 Fred Taylor	.30	.75
172 Tyler Thigpen	.25	.60
173 Pierre Thomas	.30	.75
174 LaDainian Tomlinson	.40	1.00
175 Justin Tuck	.30	.75
176 Michael Turner	.30	.75
177 Brian Urlacher	.40	1.00
178 Jonathan Vilma	.25	.60
179 Kevin Walter	.30	.75
180 Derrick Ward	.25	.60
181 Hines Ward	.30	.75
182 DeMarcus Ware	.30	.75
183 Kurt Warner	.40	1.00
184 Leon Washington	.30	.75
185 Reggie Wayne	.30	.75
186 Eric Weddle	.25	.60
187 Wes Welker	.40	1.00
188 Brian Westbrook	.30	.75
189 LenDale White	.30	.75
190 Roddy White	.30	.75
191 Cadillac Williams	.30	.75
192 DeAngelo Williams	.40	1.00
193 Mario Williams	.30	.75
194 Ricky Williams	.30	.75
195 Roy Williams WR	.30	.75
196 Patrick Willis	.30	.75
197 Adrian Wilson	.25	.60
198 Kellen Winslow	.30	.75
199 Jason Witten	.40	1.00
200 Charles Woodson	.40	1.00
201 Ramses Barden AU RC	6.00	15.00
202 Rhett Bomar AU RC	8.00	20.00
203 Tom Brandstater AU RC	10.00	25.00
204 Kenny Britt AU RC	12.00	30.00
205 Aaron Brown AU RC	10.00	25.00
206 Andre Brown AU RC	6.00	15.00
207 Donald Brown AU RC	10.00	25.00
208 Deon Butler AU RC	8.00	20.00
209 Patrick Chung AU RC	10.00	25.00
210 Glen Coffee AU RC	8.00	20.00
211 Austin Collie AU RC	12.00	30.00
212 Michael Crabtree AU RC	60.00	120.00
213 Aaron Curry AU RC EXCH	10.00	25.00
214 Brian Cushing AU RC	10.00	25.00
215 James Davis AU RC	10.00	25.00
216 Nate Davis AU RC	8.00	20.00
217 Vontae Davis AU RC	10.00	25.00
218 Louis Delmas AU RC	10.00	25.00
219 Josh Freeman AU RC	20.00	50.00
220 Mike Goodson AU RC	10.00	25.00
221 Shonn Greene AU RC	15.00	40.00
222 Brian Hartline AU RC	12.00	30.00
223 Percy Harvin AU RC	60.00	120.00
224 Darrius Heyward-Bey AU RC	10.00	25.00
225 Juaquin Iglesias AU RC	8.00	20.00
226 Tyson Jackson AU RC	8.00	20.00
227 Malcolm Jenkins AU RC	10.00	25.00
228 Gartrell Johnson AU RC	6.00	15.00
229 Manuel Johnson AU RC	8.00	20.00
230 Johnny Knox AU RC	15.00	40.00
231 Jeremy Maclin AU RC	30.00	60.00
232 Mohamed Massaquoi AU RC	8.00	20.00
233 Clay Matthews AU RC	25.00	50.00
234 LeSean McCoy AU RC	40.00	80.00
235 Stephen McGee AU RC	10.00	25.00
236 Kenny McKinley AU RC EXCH	10.00	25.00
237 Knowshon Moreno AU RC	20.00	50.00
238 Louis Murphy AU RC		
239 Hakeem Nicks AU RC	15.00	40.00
240 Keith Null AU RC EXCH	8.00	20.00
241 Brian Orakpo AU RC	10.00	25.00
242 Curtis Painter AU RC	10.00	25.00
243 Cedric Peerman AU RC	8.00	20.00
244 Brandon Pettigrew AU RC	10.00	25.00
245 Richard Quinn AU RC	8.00	20.00
246 B.J. Raji AU RC	10.00	25.00
247 Javon Ringer AU RC	10.00	25.00
248 Mark Sanchez AU SP RC	75.00	150.00
249 Bernard Scott AU RC EXCH	10.00	25.00
250 Jason Smith AU RC	8.00	20.00
251 Matthew Stafford AU RC	100.00	200.00
252 Frank Summers AU RC	10.00	25.00
253 Brandon Tate AU RC	10.00	25.00
254 Mike Teel AU RC	10.00	25.00
255 Mike Thomas AU RC	10.00	25.00
256 Patrick Turner AU RC	8.00	20.00
257 Mike Wallace AU RC	30.00	60.00
258 Chris Wells AU RC	50.00	100.00
259 Pat White AU RC	40.00	80.00
260 Derrick Williams AU RC	8.00	20.00

2009 SP Signature Draft Years Autographs

STATED PRINT RUN 20-199		
AW Patrick Willis/20	12.00	30.00
Jamaal Anderson		
BR Laurent Robinson/99	6.00	15.00
Steve Breaston		
CJ Vincent Jackson/99	6.00	15.00
Mark Clayton		
DH Korey Hall/199	5.00	12.00
Buster Davis		
FJ Matt Flynn/115	8.00	20.00
Josh Johnson		
FR Matt Ryan/50	40.00	80.00
Joe Flacco		
HH Korey Hall/199	5.00	12.00
Justise Hairston		
HM Santonio Holmes/35	10.00	25.00
Brandon Marshall		
JC Dallas Clark/15	12.00	30.00
Larry Johnson		
MO Oren O'Neal/199	5.00	12.00
Quentin Moses		
NA Joseph Addai/50	12.00	30.00
Marques Colston		
PT Allen Patrick/199	5.00	12.00
Ryan Torain		
SF Jonathan Stewart/50	12.00	30.00
Matt Forte		
SM Rashard Mendenhall/50	12.00	30.00
Steve Slaton		
ST Jeremy Shockey/35	8.00	20.00
Chester Taylor		
TB Thomas Brown/199	5.00	12.00
Ryan Torain		
WC Mark Clayton/30	8.00	20.00
Mike Williams		

2009 SP Signature Party of Four Autographs

STATED PRINT RUN 10-99		
AHIB Thomas Brown/35	10.00	25.00
Jerious Norwood		
Chris Houston		
Jamaal Anderson		
ALBY Matt Leinart/15	60.00	100.00
Reggie Bush		
Joseph Addai		
Vince Young		
ARIB Laurent Robinson/45	8.00	20.00
Keenan Burton		
Jamaal Anderson		
Thomas Brown		
BCME Alan Branch/60	6.00	15.00
Adam Carriker		
Ray McDonald		
Sedrick Ellis		
CBDF Jermichael Finley/50	12.00	30.00
Martellus Bennett		
Scott Chandler		
Kellen Davis		
CCSK Jerricho Cotchery/35	10.00	25.00
Chansi Stuckey		
David Clowney		
Dustin Keller		
CHBH David Clowney/50	8.00	20.00
Paul Hubbard		
John Broussard		
Roy Hall		
CLAK Adam Carriker/35	10.00	25.00
Donnie Avery		
Keenan Burton		
Chris Long		
CMBM Kentwan Balmer/15	12.00	30.00
Ray McDonald		
Alex Smith		
Josh Morgan		
CMFF Joe Flacco/35	50.00	80.00
Michael Oher		
Yamon Figurs		
Le'Ron McClain		

CRKA Adrian Arrington/75 6.00 15.00
Laurent Robinson
David Clowney
Jordan Kent
DBJK Steve Breaston/35 10.00 25.00
Malcolm Kelly
Chris Davis
Jacoby Jones
DHAH Xavier Adibi/40 8.00 20.00
Geno Hayes
Buster Davis
Korey Hall
DRFR Aaron Rodgers/20 125.00 200.00
Joe Flacco
Matt Ryan
Jake Delhomme
FTMS Jonathan Stewart/25 25.00 50.00
Kevin Smith
Matt Forte
Rashard Mendenhall
GNWG Reggie Nelson/25 12.00 30.00
David Garrard
Quentin Groves
Mike Sims-Walker
HIKD Dennis Keyes/15 10.00 25.00
David Irons
Chris Houston
Quintin Demps
ILPM Dwight Lowery/50 8.00 20.00
Kenny Phillips
Eric Weddle
DaJuan Morgan
JJFM Larry Johnson/20 25.00 50.00
Rashard Mendenhall
Matt Forte
Julius Jones
JJSF Julius Jones/20 15.00 40.00
Matt Forte
Larry Johnson
Jonathan Stewart
JYFT Selvin Young/15 10.00 25.00
Ryan Torain
Julius Jones
Justin Forsett
KHAJ Malcolm Kelly/35 8.00 20.00
Dexter Jackson
Adrian Arrington
Lavelle Hawkins
MFSR Jonathan Stewart/15 75.00 125.00
Joe Flacco
Darren McFadden
Matt Ryan
MGBS Steve Smith/35 10.00 25.00
Steve Breaston
Brandon Marshall
Ted Ginn Jr.
MHRM Rashard Mendenhall/35 20.00 40.00
Gary Russell
Mike Reilly
Heath Miller
MOPB Keon Lattimore/99 5.00 12.00
Oren O'Neal
Thomas Brown
Allen Patrick
OPFB Allen Patrick/35 8.00 20.00
Thomas Brown
Justin Forsett
Oren O'Neal
OPFS Oren O'Neal/35 8.00 20.00
Justin Forsett
Owen Schmitt
Allen Patrick
RHFJ JaMarcus Russell/15 15.00 40.00
Jacob Hester
Matt Flynn
Bert Jones
SBRM John Beck/40 10.00 25.00
Matt Moore
Mike Reilly
Jordan Palmer
SJBJ Anthony Spencer/15 25.00 50.00
Keon Lattimore
Felix Jones
Roy Williams WR
SKAJ Josh Johnson/35 10.00 25.00
Kevin Kolb
Erik Ainge
Drew Stanton
SRKF Jeremy Shockey/25 12.00 30.00
Matt Spaeth
Jermichael Finley
Dante Rosario
TRHB Ryne Robinson/75 6.00 15.00
John Broussard
Roy Hall
Courtney Taylor
WJJK Darrelle Revis/35 10.00 25.00
Justin King
Eric Weddle
Mike Jenkins
WJJM Mike Jenkins/35 10.00 25.00
Eric Weddle
Darrelle Revis
DaJuan Morgan
WWHH Lavelle Hawkins/50 10.00 25.00
Mike Sims-Walker
Paul Williams
Paul Hubbard
YRTC Selvin Young/15 12.00 30.00
Ryan Torain
Ryan Clady
Eddie Royal

2009 SP Signature Reflections Dual Autographs

STATED PRINT RUN 5-99
RAJ Alex Brink/30 10.00 25.00
Jacoby Jones
RBB Hunter Cantwell/25 15.00 40.00
Brian Brohm
RBC Thomas Clayton/50 8.00 20.00
Thomas Brown
RBD Kellen Davis/50 10.00 25.00
Richard Quinn
RBG Quentin Groves/99 5.00 12.00
Kentwan Balmer
RBL John Broussard/50 8.00 20.00
Donald Lee
RBM Mario Manningham/50 10.00 25.00
Reggie Brown
RBR Laurent Robinson/50 8.00 20.00
Keenan Burton
RCB Martellus Bennett/50 10.00 25.00
Brent Celek
RCP Thomas Clayton/50 8.00 20.00
Allen Patrick
RCR Martin Rucker/50 8.00 20.00
Scott Chandler
RCT Keenan Burton/50 8.00 20.00
David Clowney
RCW David Clowney/50 10.00 25.00
Mike Sims-Walker
RDB Keith Null/50 12.00 30.00
Nate Davis
RDH Chris Davis/50 8.00 20.00
Lavelle Hawkins
RDK Korey Hall/99 5.00 12.00
Keon Lattimore
RDM Kellen Davis/99 5.00 12.00
Marcus Monk
RDW Buster Davis/50 8.00 20.00
Philip Wheeler
REN Josh Johnson/50 8.00 20.00
Dre Moore
RFB Keon Lattimore/99 5.00 12.00
Justise Hairston
RFM Darren McFadden/25 20.00 50.00
Jonathan Stewart
RHB Alex Mack/50 8.00 15.00
Andre Smith
RHC Korey Hall/99 5.00 12.00
Shawn Crable
RHF Chad Henne/50 12.00 30.00
Matt Flynn
RHL Korey Hall/50 8.00 20.00
Donald Lee
RIJ Jim Leonhard/50 12.00 30.00
William Moore
RIM William Moore/50 8.00 20.00
DaJuan Morgan
RJB Thomas Brown/50 8.00 20.00
Julius Jones
RJC Kellen Davis/50 8.00 20.00
Scott Chandler
RKA Adrian Arrington/25 10.00 25.00
Jordan Kent
RKB Travis Beckum/50 10.00 25.00
Martellus Bennett
RKC Keenan Burton/50 8.00 20.00
Jordan Kent
RKM Justin King/99 5.00 12.00
Craig Steltz
RLG Chris Long/50 8.00 20.00
Quentin Groves
RLP Lavelle Hawkins/50 8.00 20.00
Paul Williams
RLW Darius Walker/99 5.00 12.00
Keon Lattimore
RMB Kentwan Balmer/99 5.00 12.00
Ray McDonald
RMD Quintin Demps/99 5.00 12.00
DaJuan Morgan
RME Quentin Moses/50 8.00 20.00
Michael Johnson
RMK Heath Miller/25 12.00 30.00
Dustin Keller
RNE Matt Moore/50 10.00 25.00
Ryne Robinson
RNK Jordy Nelson/45 12.00 30.00
Malcolm Kelly
ROE Sedrick Ellis/40 8.00 20.00
Frank Okam
ROP Oren O'Neal/50 8.00 20.00
Allen Patrick
RPJ Mike Jenkins/50 8.00 20.00
Kenny Phillips
RPT Keon Lattimore/99 5.00 12.00
Ryan Torain
RRB Mario Manningham/50 10.00 25.00
John Broussard
RRC Brandon Pettigrew/50 12.00 30.00
Brent Celek
RRJ Malcolm Jenkins/20 10.00 25.00
Sean Smith
RRM Matt Moore/50 10.00 25.00
Dante Rosario
RRW Keenan Burton/50 8.00 20.00
Ryne Robinson
RSC Matt Spaeth/50 10.00 25.00
Brent Celek
RTM Rashard Mendenhall/50 12.00 30.00
Ryan Torain
RTY Ryan Torain/25 10.00 25.00
Keon Lattimore
RWH Austin Collie/20 20.00 50.00
Reggie Wayne
RWR Laurent Robinson/50 8.00 20.00
Paul Williams

2009 SP Signature Rivalries Autographs

STATED PRINT RUN 10-35
AS Bruce Smith/25 25.00 50.00
Ottis Anderson
BH A.J. Hawk/20 12.00 30.00
Lance Briggs
BJ Brandon Jacobs/25 12.00 30.00
Marion Barber
FB Matt Forte/25 15.00 40.00
Nick Barnett
HB Anquan Boldin/35 10.00 25.00
Santonio Holmes
LB Tiki Barber/25 40.00 80.00
Ray Lewis
TG Joe Theismann/25 25.00 50.00
Bob Griese

2009 SP Signature Signature Duals

STATED PRINT RUN 10-99
AF Joseph Addai/25 20.00 50.00
Curtis Painter
AP Keon Lattimore/99 5.00 12.00
Allen Patrick
AR Donnie Avery/25 12.00 30.00
Eddie Royal
BD Brent Celek/99 6.00 15.00
Kellen Davis
BF Alex Brink/90 5.00 12.00
Ben Moffitt
BG Eugene Monroe/50 8.00 20.00
Lawrence Jackson
BJ Keenan Burton/25 12.00 30.00
Vincent Jackson
BW Keenan Burton/99 6.00 15.00
Mike Sims-Walker
CB Brandon Pettigrew/25 10.00 25.00
Shawn Nelson
CC David Clowney/50 12.00 30.00
Shonn Greene
CK David Clowney/99 5.00 12.00
Dustin Keller
CL Chris Long/25 10.00 25.00
Adam Carriker
CN Quan Cosby/50 10.00 25.00
Chase Coffman
CR David Clowney/99 5.00 12.00
Keenan Burton
CS Scott Chandler/99 5.00 12.00
Matt Spaeth
CT Tyler Thigpen/25 12.00 30.00
Matt Cassel
DB Thomas Brown/70 6.00 15.00
Harry Douglas
DI Victor Harris/75 10.00 25.00
Jack Ikegwuonu
DW Paul Williams/99 5.00 12.00
Chris Davis
EG Shawn Nelson/99 6.00 15.00
Chris Ellis
ET Jordan Kent/99 5.00 12.00
Jeff Rowe
EY Jeff Rowe/99 6.00 15.00
Mike Reilly
FB Matt Flynn/25 25.00 50.00
Brian Brohm
FG Jeff Garcia/25 25.00 60.00
Joe Flacco
FH Justin Forsett/99 5.00 12.00
Lavelle Hawkins
FR Matt Ryan/15 50.00 100.00
Joe Flacco
FS Matt Forte/25 15.00 40.00
Steve Slaton
HF Matt Flynn/30 25.00 50.00
Hunter Cantwell
HG Jack Ham/25 30.00 60.00
Joe Greene
HH Korey Hall/25 12.00 30.00
A.J. Hawk
HL Donald Lee/25 10.00 25.00
Korey Hall
JB Marion Barber/25 15.00 50.00
Brandon Jacobs
JC Scott Chandler/50 8.00 20.00
Gartrell Johnson
JJ Vincent Jackson/25 12.00 30.00
Chad Ochocinco
JM Felix Jones/25 20.00 50.00
Rashard Mendenhall
JS Kevin Smith/25 15.00 40.00
Chris Johnson
KD Marcus Monk/99 5.00 12.00
John Broussard
KM Matt Flynn/99 15.00 30.00
Korey Hall
KP Malcolm Kelly/25 10.00 25.00
Aundrae Allison
KR Dominique Rodgers-Cromartie/50 8.00 20.00
Dennis Keyes
LB Steve Breaston/15 12.00 30.00
Matt Leinart
LK Chris Long/25 10.00 25.00
Justin King
MB Kentwan Balmer/99 5.00 12.00
Ray McDonald
MC Ray McDonald/99 5.00 12.00
Ezra Butler-Beaton
MJ Fili Moala/50 10.00 25.00
Tyson Jackson
MK Keenan Burton/99 6.00 15.00
Mario Manningham
MM Martellus Bennett/99 6.00 15.00
Matt Spaeth
MR Dante Rosario/99 6.00 15.00
Matt Moore
MS Heath Miller/25 10.00 25.00
Brandon Pettigrew
MT Richard Quinn/25 12.00 30.00
Brandon Marshall
NK Marcus Monk/99 5.00 12.00
Keenan Burton
OB Oren O'Neal/99 5.00 12.00
Thomas Brown
OF Joe Flacco/25 50.00 100.00
Michael Oher
PB Thomas Brown/99 5.00 12.00
Allen Patrick
PH Allen Patrick/99 5.00 12.00
Paul Hubbard
PK Allen Patrick/25 10.00 25.00
Malcolm Kelly
RF Matt Ryan/15 50.00 100.00
Joe Flacco
RJ Mike Jenkins/25 10.00 25.00
Victor Harris
RK Victor Harris/25 10.00 25.00
Leon Hall
RM Keon Lattimore/99 5.00 12.00
Justise Hairston
RR Ryne Robinson/99 5.00 12.00
Keenan Burton
RT Thomas Clayton/99 5.00 12.00
Ryan Torain
SA Steve Slaton/25 12.00 30.00
Alex Brink
SO Mario Manningham/99 6.00 15.00
Marcus Monk
SS Kevin Smith/25 10.00 25.00
Drew Stanton
TB Thomas Brown/99 5.00 12.00
Darius Walker
TC Ryan Torain/99 5.00 12.00
Ryan Clady
TO Oren O'Neal/99 5.00 12.00
Ryan Torain
WC Darius Walker/99 5.00 12.00
Thomas Clayton
WH Brian Hartline/25 15.00 40.00
Greg Camarillo
WO Michael Oher/25 40.00 80.00
Patrick Willis
WR Mike Sims-Walker/30 10.00 25.00
Jarett Dillard
WS Patrick Willis/25 10.00 25.00
Aaron Curry
WT Darius Walker/99 5.00 12.00
Ryan Torain
WW Patrick Willis/25 15.00 40.00
DeMarcus Ware
YH Mario Manningham/99 6.00 15.00
Lavelle Hawkins

2009 SP Signature Signature Eight

EIGHT AUTO PRINT RUN 5-50
EBCMLBG Anthony Spencer/20 25.00 50.00
Chris Long
Adam Carriker
Kentwan Balmer
Ray McDonald
Alan Branch
Quentin Groves
Ben Moffitt
EBMBSAK Brandon Marshall/20 25.00 50.00
Steve Breaston
Steve Smith USC
Malcolm Kelly
Lee Evans
Darius Reynaud
Donnie Avery
Drew Bennett
EBWSJHG Ronnie Lott/20 150.00 250.00
Jack Ham
L.C. Greenwood
Joe Greene
Rod Woodson
Mike Singletary
Dick Butkus
Deacon Jones
ECOPFTB Jamaal Charles/20 30.00 60.00
Justise Hairston
Oren O'Neal
Justin Forsett
Thomas Brown
Allen Patrick
Thomas Clayton
Jacob Hester
ECSBRDF Scott Chandler/50 25.00 50.00
Martellus Bennett
Jermichael Finley
Matt Spaeth
Martin Rucker
Shawn Nelson
Kellen Davis
Dante Rosario
ECWWRHH Ryne Robinson/20
Lavelle Hawkins
Mike Sims-Walker
James Hardy
Marko Mitchell
David Clowney
Roy Hall
Brooks Foster
EDBRCFR Marc Bulger/20 100.00 200.00
Joe Flacco
Tony Romo
Matt Ryan
Jason Campbell
Jake Delhomme
Matt Schaub
Vince Young
EHIKJDM DaJuan Morgan/20 30.00 60.00
LaRon Landry
Dominique Rodgers-Cromartie
Dennis Keyes
Chris Houston
Quintin Demps
Mike Jenkins
Malcolm Jenkins
EMPRBSM Mike Reilly/20 50.00 100.00
Willie Parker
Bruce Davis
Heath Miller
Dallas Baker
Matt Spaeth
Limas Sweed
Rashard Mendenhall
ESMRBFJ Matt Moore/50 30.00 60.00
Alex Brink
Jordan Palmer
Jeff Rowe
Josh Johnson
Mike Reilly
Brian Brohm
Matt Flynn
ESRCKBF Shawn Nelson/30 25.00 50.00
Brent Celek
Dustin Keller
Matt Spaeth
Scott Chandler
Martellus Bennett
Jermichael Finley
Dante Rosario
ETRKBHA Ryne Robinson/20
Keenan Burton
Adrian Arrington
Jordan Kent
Courtney Taylor
Paul Hubbard
Laurent Robinson
John Broussard
EWSHHHW Geno Hayes/25 25.00 50.00
Patrick Willis
Kentwan Balmer
Philip Wheeler
Korey Hall
Anthony Spencer
Erin Henderson
Ali Highsmith

2009 SP Signature Signature Fours

STATED PRINT RUN 5-85
AKHA Lavelle Hawkins/35 10.00 25.00
Malcolm Kelly
Donnie Avery
Adrian Arrington
APRH Alex Mack/25 12.00 30.00
Derek Anderson
Allen Patrick
Martin Rucker
AWRH Darius Reynaud/35 8.00 20.00
Aundrae Allison
Lavelle Hawkins
Paul Williams
BBFD Matt Forte/25 20.00 50.00
Kellen Davis
John Broussard
Earl Bennett
BCLK Justin King/15 12.00 30.00
Adam Carriker
Marc Bulger
Chris Long
BCSW Keenan Burton/25 12.00 30.00
Steve Smith USC
Jericho Cotchery
Mike Sims-Walker
BEMS Steve Smith USC/25 12.00 30.00
Lee Evans
Keenan Burton
Robert Meachem
BFFJ Josh Johnson/35 30.00 60.00
Matt Flynn
Joe Flacco
Alex Brink
BFFR Joe Flacco/15 60.00 100.00
Matt Flynn
Brian Brohm
Matt Ryan
BHHA James Hardy/35 10.00 25.00
Earl Bennett
Adrian Arrington
Lavelle Hawkins
BJFM Rashard Mendenhall/15 30.00 60.00
Felix Jones
Marion Barber
Matt Forte
BMOE Frank Okam/35 8.00 20.00
Sedrick Ellis
Ray McDonald
Alan Branch
BWFJ Andre' Woodson/35 12.00 30.00
Josh Johnson
Matt Flynn
Alex Brink
BWHA Mike Sims-Walker/35 12.00 30.00
Brian Hartline
Adrian Arrington
Steve Breaston
CABH Andre Caldwell/35 10.00 25.00
Earl Bennett
Donnie Avery
Lavelle Hawkins
CBDF Jermichael Finley/60 8.00 20.00
Martellus Bennett
Scott Chandler
Kellen Davis
CBHA Earl Bennett/40 10.00 25.00
David Clowney
Adrian Arrington
Lavelle Hawkins
CDWH Lavelle Hawkins/35 8.00 20.00
Chris Davis
Paul Williams
Alge Crumpler
CPMJ Brandon Marshall/15 25.00 50.00
Drew Pearson
Anquan Boldin
Calvin Johnson
CSCF Brent Celek/35 12.00 30.00
Scott Chandler
Jermichael Finley
Matt Spaeth
CSCM Heath Miller/15 12.00 30.00
Dallas Clark
Jeremy Shockey
Alge Crumpler
CSKA David Clowney/45 10.00 25.00
Erik Ainge
Chansi Stuckey
Dustin Keller
CWMK Jeremy Shockey/15 12.00 30.00
Heath Miller
Alge Crumpler
Ben Watson
CWWH Mike Sims-Walker/50 10.00 25.00
Lavelle Hawkins
Keenan Burton
David Clowney
DBCF Jason Campbell/15 25.00 60.00
Marc Bulger
Joe Flacco
Jake Delhomme
DBFR Jake Delhomme/15 60.00 100.00
Joe Flacco
Marc Bulger
Matt Ryan
DHHH Ali Highsmith/50 8.00 20.00
Korey Hall
Buster Davis
Geno Hayes
GFAJ Ken Anderson/15 30.00 60.00
Vince Ferragamo
Bob Griese
Bert Jones
HIJD Chris Houston/85 8.00 20.00
Quintin Demps
Mike Jenkins
Eric Weddle
HIJM Mike Jenkins/35 8.00 20.00
Chris Houston
Kenny Phillips
DaJuan Morgan
HWIJ Dominique Rodgers-Cromartie/35 8.00 20.00
Chris Houston
Mike Jenkins
Eric Weddle
JFTC Felix Jones/15 30.00 60.00
Matt Forte
Jamaal Charles
Jonathan Stewart
JJAL Julius Jones/15 25.00 50.00
Marshawn Lynch
Joseph Addai
Larry Johnson
JJFM Larry Johnson/15 25.00 50.00
Rashard Mendenhall
Matt Forte
Julius Jones
KCDI Kevin Kolb/35 10.00 25.00
Brent Celek
Jack Ikegwuonu
Quintin Demps
MLJG Lawrence Jackson/35 10.00 25.00
Chris Long
Quentin Groves
Quentin Moses
MRSM Rashard Mendenhall/15 15.00 40.00
Dorian Bryant
Bruce Davis
Gary Russell
MSFM Darren McFadden/15 40.00 80.00
Matt Forte
Rashard Mendenhall
Jonathan Stewart
NHIJ Reggie Nelson/35 8.00 20.00
Mike Jenkins
Jack Ikegwuonu
Chris Houston
NWIJ Dominique Rodgers-Cromartie/35 10.00 25.00
Mike Jenkins
Eric Weddle
Reggie Nelson
OPFT Justin Forsett/15 10.00 25.00
Oren O'Neal
Keon Lattimore
Ryan Torain
RBRD Dante Rosario/70 10.00 25.00
Jared Cook
Kellen Davis
Martin Rucker
RBSM Rashard Mendenhall/35 15.00 40.00
Bruce Davis
Dallas Baker
Gary Russell
RCOB Thomas Clayton/55 6.00 15.00
Keon Lattimore
Thomas Brown
Oren O'Neal
RRHB John Broussard/35 8.00 20.00
Laurent Robinson
Roy Hall
Ryne Robinson
SBFJ Alex Brink/35 20.00 50.00
Josh Johnson
Matt Flynn
Drew Stanton
SBRF Martin Rucker/35 12.00 30.00
Jermichael Finley
Martellus Bennett
Matt Spaeth
SDHA Buster Davis/35 8.00 20.00
Korey Hall
Ernie Sims
Xavier Adibi
SEBG Quentin Groves/75 6.00 15.00
Chris Ellis
Anthony Spencer
Kentwan Balmer
SHSW Patrick Willis/20 30.00 60.00
A.J. Hawk
Ernie Sims
Mike Singletary
SSMS Rashard Mendenhall/15 25.00 60.00
Kevin Smith
Jonathan Stewart
Steve Slaton
TRKF Jeff Rowe/45 8.00 20.00
Courtney Taylor
Justin Forsett
Jordan Kent
WSSJ Bruce Smith No AU/15 30.00 80.00
Mike Singletary
Rod Woodson
Deacon Jones
WWMC Ben Watson/25 30.00 60.00
Jerod Mayo
Laurence Maroney
Wes Welker
YCFT Ryan Torain/15 10.00 25.00
Selvin Young
Thomas Clayton
Justin Forsett
YCTB Thomas Brown/15 10.00 25.00
Thomas Clayton
Selvin Young
Ryan Torain

2009 SP Signature Signature Six

STATED PRINT RUN 10-50
DB1 Jack Ikegwuonu/30 15.00 40.00
Quintin Demps
Chris Houston
LaRon Landry
Eric Weddle
Mike Jenkins
DB2 Mike Jenkins/30 15.00 40.00
Malcolm Jenkins
Antrel Rolle
Dominique Rodgers-Cromartie
Chris Houston
Reggie Nelson
LB1 DeMeco Ryans/15 50.00 80.00
Mike Singletary
Ernie Sims
Patrick Willis
DeMarcus Ware
A.J. Hawk
LB2 Korey Hall/30 15.00 40.00
Anthony Spencer
Philip Wheeler
Buster Davis
Ali Highsmith
Xavier Adibi
LB3 Xavier Adibi/30 15.00 40.00
Ernie Sims
Buster Davis
Philip Wheeler
Geno Hayes
Korey Hall
QB1 Aaron Rodgers/30 125.00 200.00
Marc Bulger
Joe Flacco
Derek Anderson
Jason Campbell
Jake Delhomme
QB2 Alex Brink/30 40.00 80.00
Erik Ainge
Joe Flacco
Brian Brohm
Matt Flynn
Josh Johnson
QB3 Josh Johnson/30 40.00 80.00
Brian Brohm
Joe Flacco
Matt Flynn
Alex Brink
Chad Henne
QB4 John Beck/20 20.00 50.00
Matt Moore
Tyler Thigpen
Jeff Rowe
Kevin Kolb
Drew Stanton
QB5 Jordan Palmer/30 20.00 50.00
Jeff Rowe
Erik Ainge
Josh Johnson
Matt Moore
Alex Brink
RB1 Oren O'Neal/30 15.00 40.00
Thomas Brown
Allen Patrick
Justin Forsett
Jacob Hester
Thomas Clayton
RB2 Frank Gore/15 100.00 200.00
Joseph Addai
Julius Jones
Adrian Peterson
Jonathan Stewart
Larry Johnson
RB3 Larry Johnson/15 100.00 200.00
Adrian Peterson
Matt Forte
Joseph Addai
Willie Parker
Reggie Bush
RB6 DeShawn Wynn/30 20.00 50.00
Rashard Mendenhall
Carnell Williams
Justin Forsett
Allen Patrick
Thomas Brown
TE1 Jeremy Shockey/15 25.00 60.00
Dallas Clark
Heath Miller
Jermichael Finley
Dante Rosario
Alge Crumpler
TE2 Jermichael Finley/30 15.00 40.00
Martellus Bennett
Matt Spaeth
Brent Celek
Martin Rucker
Kellen Davis
WR1 Earl Bennett/30 15.00 40.00
Malcolm Kelly
Andre Caldwell
Adrian Arrington
Donnie Avery
Eddie Royal
WR2 Ryne Robinson/30 15.00 40.00
Lavelle Hawkins
Paul Williams
John Broussard
Jordan Kent
Darius Reynaud
WR4 Mike Sims-Walker/30 15.00 40.00
Adrian Arrington
Paul Hubbard
Courtney Taylor
David Clowney
Earl Bennett
WR5 David Clowney/30 15.00 40.00
Jordan Kent
Laurent Robinson
Roy Hall
Lavelle Hawkins
Paul Williams
DEF1 DaJuan Morgan/40 15.00 40.00
Chris Houston
Quintin Demps
Erin Henderson
Craig Steltz
Darnell Bing
DEF2 Alan Branch/30 15.00 40.00
Lawrence Jackson
Kentwan Balmer
Adam Carriker
Chris Long
Quentin Groves
DEF3 Quentin Moses/30 15.00 40.00
Chris Long
Ray McDonald
Terrance Taylor
Jamaal Anderson
Alan Branch
DEF4 Terrance Taylor/30 15.00 40.00
Ray McDonald
Kentwan Balmer
Quentin Moses
Quentin Groves
Tyson Jackson
DEF5 DaJuan Morgan/30 15.00 40.00
Justin King
Malcolm Jenkins
Mike Jenkins
Quentin Jammer
Vernon Gholston
RBX2 Matt Forte/30 40.00 80.00
Gale Sayers
Billy Sims
Kevin Smith
Frank Gore
Roger Craig
DSTR Lofa Tatupu/15 50.00 100.00
Mike Singletary
Chuck Bednarik
Rod Woodson
Jack Ham
Patrick Willis
PITT Mike Reilly/30 25.00 60.00
Dallas Baker
Heath Miller
Bruce Davis
Rashard Mendenhall
Limas Sweed
JET1 Jerricho Cotchery/30 15.00 40.00
Dustin Keller
David Clowney
Lavelle Hawkins
Paul Williams
Alge Crumpler
JET2 David Clowney/30 15.00 40.00
Darrelle Revis
Chansi Stuckey
Erik Ainge
Dustin Keller
Jerricho Cotchery
PACK Matt Flynn/50 30.00 60.00
Jermichael Finley
Donald Lee
A.J. Hawk
Brian Brohm
Korey Hall
QBLG Y.A. Tittle/15 50.00 100.00
Ken Anderson
Joe Theismann
Bert Jones
Roman Gabriel
Bob Griese
RBLG Bo Jackson/15 175.00 300.00
Gale Sayers
Paul Hornung
Emmitt Smith
Franco Harris
Roger Craig

2009 SP Signature Signature Trios

STATED PRINT RUN 5-109
ABM Josh Morgan/49 10.00 25.00
Keenan Burton
Donnie Avery
AFH Keon Lattimore/99 5.00 12.00
Justin Forsett
Lavelle Hawkins
AHR Lavelle Hawkins/99 5.00 12.00
Darius Reynaud
Adrian Arrington
APH Paul Hubbard/25 10.00 25.00
Allen Patrick
Derek Anderson
ARN Donnie Avery/25 15.00 40.00
Jordy Nelson
Eddie Royal
BBD John Broussard/99 6.00 15.00
Earl Bennett
Kellen Davis
BBF Brian Brohm/25 15.00 40.00
Donald Lee
Matt Flynn
BDF Martellus Bennett/99 6.00 15.00
Jermichael Finley
Kellen Davis
BFF Donald Lee/25 10.00 25.00
Brian Brohm
Korey Hall
BFJ Matt Flynn/20 15.00 40.00
Josh Johnson
Hunter Cantwell
BFR Joe Flacco/15 60.00 100.00
Colt Brennan
Matt Ryan
BGE Alan Branch/49 8.00 20.00
Sedrick Ellis
Quentin Groves
BJD Jacoby Jones/99 6.00 15.00
Quintin Demps
Steve Breaston
BKA Keenan Burton/49 10.00 25.00
Earl Bennett
Malcolm Kelly
BMB Alex Brink/70 8.00 20.00
Matt Moore
John Beck
BOS Alex Brink/25 12.00 30.00
Frank Okam
Steve Slaton
BSM Keenan Lewis/20 15.00 40.00
Rashard Mendenhall
Bruce Davis
BSS Dick Butkus/15 60.00 120.00
Gale Sayers
Mike Singletary
BWW Paul Williams/99 6.00 15.00
Mike Sims-Walker
Ryne Robinson
CBA Earl Bennett/49 10.00 25.00
Andre Caldwell
Adrian Arrington

CBS Steve Breaston/25	12.00	30.00
Steve Smith USC		
Jerricho Cotchery		
CKS Dustin Keller/25	12.00	30.00
Jeremy Shockey		
Dallas Clark		
CLA Keenan Burton/49	10.00	25.00
Chris Long		
Adam Carriker		
COB Thomas Clayton/99	5.00	12.00
Thomas Brown		
Oren O'Neal		
CSK David Clowney/49	8.00	20.00
Dustin Keller		
Chansi Stuckey		
COR Chase Coffman/20	10.00	25.00
Scott Chandler		
Matt Spaeth		
CWH Lavelle Hawkins/25	10.00	25.00
Paul Williams		
Alge Crumpler		
DBC Jake Delhomme/25	12.00	30.00
Marc Bulger		
Jason Campbell		
DCH Keith Rivers/70	6.00	15.00
Geno Hayes		
Shawn Crable		
DHW Jerod Mayo/25	12.00	30.00
Keith Rivers		
Erin Henderson		
DRS Jake Delhomme/25	12.00	30.00
Jonathan Stewart		
Dante Rosario		
FAJ Bob Griese/20	25.00	60.00
Ken Anderson		
Archie Manning		
FSH Mike Hart/60	8.00	20.00
Owen Schmitt		
Justin Forsett		
FSJ Matt Forte/25	30.00	60.00
Chris Johnson		
Steve Slaton		
FSM Steve Slaton/25	25.00	50.00
Matt Forte		
Rashard Mendenhall		
GJW Frank Gore/20	12.00	30.00
Brandon Jacobs		
Clinton Portis		
HBK Ali Highsmith/109	5.00	12.00
Dennis Keyes		
Anthony Morelli		
HFF Korey Hall/49	12.00	30.00
Donald Lee		
Jermichael Finley		
HMT Archie Manning/25	25.00	60.00
Y.A. Tittle		
Bob Griese		
HSW Rey Maualuga/20	15.00	40.00
A.J. Hawk		
Patrick Willis		
JAK Jerome Simpson/25	12.00	30.00
Vincent Jackson		
Donnie Avery		
JBJ Manuel Johnson/20	12.00	30.00
Martellus Bennett		
Keon Lattimore		
JDM William Moore/40	12.00	30.00
Quintin Demps		
DaJuan Morgan		
JEB Larry English/20	12.00	30.00
Gartrell Johnson		
Demetrius Byrd		
JJA Steven Jackson/25	15.00	40.00
Joseph Addai		
Larry Johnson		
JJG Larry Johnson/25	12.00	30.00
Frank Gore		
Julius Jones		
JRF Julius Jones/25	10.00	25.00
Justin Forsett		
Jeff Rowe		
LMS Marshawn Lynch/25	15.00	40.00
Jonathan Stewart		
Le'Ron McClain		
MCT Ryan Clady/25	12.00	30.00
Ryan Torain		
Brandon Marshall		
MFS Matt Forte/25	25.00	50.00
Rashard Mendenhall		
Steve Slaton		
MJG Brandon Marshall/15	15.00	40.00
Ted Ginn Jr.		
Calvin Johnson		
MRM Rashard Mendenhall/49	15.00	40.00
Heath Miller		
Gary Russell		
MRR Dante Rosario/20	10.00	25.00
Mike Goodson		
Ryne Robinson		
MTC Brandon Marshall/20	15.00	40.00
Kenny McKinley		
Ryan Clady		
NRB Laurent Robinson/25	12.00	30.00
Jerious Norwood		
Thomas Brown		
OBD Greg Olsen/55	10.00	25.00
Earl Bennett		
Kellen Davis		
PCK Jaison Williams/20	12.00	30.00
Clinton Portis		
Jason Campbell		
PRH Alex Mack/99	6.00	15.00
Martin Rucker		
Allen Patrick		
RBF Travis Beckum/20	15.00	40.00
Martellus Bennett		
Jermichael Finley		
RBS Gary Russell/65	8.00	20.00
Dallas Baker		
Matt Spaeth		
RFR Tony Romo/15	75.00	135.00
Matt Ryan		
Joe Flacco		
RHA Paul Hubbard/99	5.00	12.00
Keenan Burton		
Adrian Arrington		
SBM Jeff Rowe/99	6.00	15.00
Drew Stanton		
Matt Moore		
SCK Jeremy Shockey/25	15.00	40.00
Dallas Clark		
Dustin Keller		
SFM Matt Forte/25	25.00	50.00
Rashard Mendenhall		
Jonathan Stewart		
SHW Ernie Sims/49	8.00	20.00
Korey Hall		
Philip Wheeler		
SJE Sedrick Ellis/99	6.00	15.00
Anthony Spencer		
Lawrence Jackson		
SMR Jeff Rowe/99	6.00	15.00
Drew Stanton		
Matt Moore		
TJJ Larry Johnson/25	12.00	30.00
Fred Taylor		
Julius Jones		
TKB Jordan Kent/99	5.00	12.00
Courtney Taylor		
John Broussard		
WJR Paul Williams/99	5.00	12.00
Jacoby Jones		
Ryne Robinson		
WMB Patrick Willis/25	15.00	40.00
Alex Smith		
Ray McDonald		
WRK Jordan Kent/99	5.00	12.00
Laurent Robinson		
Paul Williams		
WSO Mike Singletary/25	40.00	80.00
Bruce Smith		
Rod Woodson		
WWR Patrick Willis/25	12.00	30.00
DeMarcus Ware		
Darrelle Revis		
YTR Justise Hairston/99	5.00	12.00
Thomas Brown		
Keon Lattimore		

2009 SP Signature Triple Scripts

STATED PRINT RUN 10-99

ABK Keenan Burton/50	10.00	25.00
Earl Bennett		
Malcolm Kelly		
AHA Keenan Burton/99	5.00	12.00
Adrian Arrington		
Lavelle Hawkins		
AHB Jamaal Anderson/50	8.00	20.00
Chris Houston		
Sam Baker		
BCM Alan Branch/75	6.00	15.00
Adam Carriker		
Quentin Moses		
BDF Jermichael Finley/75	10.00	25.00
Martellus Bennett		
Kellen Davis		
BFF Matt Flynn/50	20.00	50.00
Joe Flacco		
Alex Brink		
BFJ Alex Brink/99	8.00	20.00
Matt Flynn		
Josh Johnson		
BHK Alan Branch/99	5.00	12.00
Ali Highsmith		
Dennis Keyes		
BMC Thomas Clayton/99	5.00	12.00
Ray McDonald		
Kentwan Balmer		
BNR Laurent Robinson/25	15.00	40.00
Thomas Brown		
William Moore		
BSH Steve Smith USC/99	6.00	15.00
Keenan Burton		
Lavelle Hawkins		
BSS Dick Butkus/25	60.00	120.00
Gale Sayers		
Mike Singletary		
CAW Dallas Clark/25	15.00	40.00
Philip Wheeler		
Joseph Addai		
CGR Roger Craig/25	20.00	40.00
Frank Gore		
Tom Rathman		
CJB John Broussard/99	5.00	12.00
David Clowney		
Jacoby Jones		
CLK Justin King/50	10.00	25.00
Chris Long		
Adam Carriker		
CMB Adam Carriker/99	5.00	12.00
Kentwan Balmer		
Ray McDonald		
COP Thomas Clayton/99	5.00	12.00
Keon Lattimore		
Oren O'Neal		
CRF Jermichael Finley/50	12.00	30.00
Alge Crumpler		
Dante Rosario		
CSC Scott Chandler/99	6.00	15.00
Matt Spaeth		
Brent Celek		
CSK Chase Coffman/50	8.00	20.00
Matt Spaeth		
Scott Chandler		
CWR David Clowney/99	6.00	15.00
Ryne Robinson		
Mike Sims-Walker		
DBC Jake Delhomme/25	12.00	30.00
Jason Campbell		
Marc Bulger		
DHH Korey Hall/50	8.00	20.00
Buster Davis		
Geno Hayes		
DHM Buster Davis/25	10.00	25.00
Korey Hall		
Rey Maualuga		
DKA Jordan Kent/99	5.00	12.00
Adrian Arrington		
Chris Davis		
DMR Jake Delhomme/99	10.00	25.00
Matt Moore		
Ryne Robinson		
DMS Jonathan Stewart/25	15.00	40.00
Jake Delhomme		
Mike Goodson		
FBJ Alex Brink/99	12.00	30.00
Josh Johnson		
Matt Flynn		
HCH Shawn Crable/50	8.00	20.00
Korey Hall		
Geno Hayes		
HFF Matt Flynn/50	25.00	50.00
Korey Hall		
Jermichael Finley		
HGG Joe Greene/25	60.00	120.00
L.C. Greenwood		
Jack Ham		
HJH Chris Houston/50	8.00	20.00
Victor Harris		
Mike Jenkins		
HJM Vincent Jackson/25	12.00	30.00
Santonio Holmes		
Brandon Marshall		
HKM DaJuan Morgan/50	8.00	20.00
Victor Harris		
Dennis Keyes		
HLF Donald Lee/75	10.00	25.00
Korey Hall		
Matt Flynn		
HWB Philip Wheeler/25	10.00	25.00
Donald Brown		
Mike Hart		
JBF Reggie Bush/25	25.00	50.00
Matt Forte		
Julius Jones		
JBJ Martellus Bennett/99	8.00	20.00
Mike Jenkins		
Keon Lattimore		
JCW Vincent Jackson/50	10.00	25.00
David Clowney		
Mike Sims-Walker		
JDM DaJuan Morgan/99	5.00	12.00
Quintin Demps		
Mike Jenkins		
JFS Julius Jones/25	10.00	25.00
Owen Schmitt		
Justin Forsett		
JMS Rashard Mendenhall/25	20.00	50.00
Larry Johnson		
Jonathan Stewart		
JSM Rashard Mendenhall/25	25.00	50.00
Felix Jones		
Jonathan Stewart		
KHA Malcolm Kelly/50	8.00	20.00
Adrian Arrington		
Lavelle Hawkins		
LBG Quentin Groves/50	10.00	25.00
Kentwan Balmer		
Chris Long		
LJE Lawrence Jackson/50	10.00	25.00
Sedrick Ellis		
Chris Long		
MHA Mario Manningham/75	8.00	20.00
Adrian Arrington		
Lavelle Hawkins		
MLB Keenan Burton/99	6.00	15.00
Donald Lee		
Mario Manningham		
MRA Erik Ainge/75	8.00	20.00
Jeff Rowe		
Matt Moore		
MRR Mike Goodson/75	8.00	20.00
Ryne Robinson		
Dante Rosario		
OPB Oren O'Neal/99	5.00	12.00
Allen Patrick		
Thomas Brown		
PRH Martin Rucker/99	6.00	15.00
Allen Patrick		
Alex Mack		
RBF Martellus Bennett/50	12.00	30.00
Jermichael Finley		
Dante Rosario		
RBS Buster Davis/25	10.00	25.00
Dallas Baker		
Gary Russell		
RCJ Jerricho Cotchery/25	12.00	30.00
Vincent Jackson		
Eddie Royal		
RCW Mike Sims-Walker/99	6.00	15.00
Darius Reynaud		
David Clowney		
RFS Justin Forsett/75	6.00	15.00
Owen Schmitt		
Jeff Rowe		
RHN Legedu Naanee/99	5.00	12.00
Laurent Robinson		
Lavelle Hawkins		
RPJ Mike Jenkins/50	8.00	20.00
Kenny Phillips		
Dominique Rodgers-Cromartie		
RTC Eddie Royal/25	12.00	30.00
Ryan Clady		
Ryan Torain		
RWC Paul Williams/99	5.00	12.00
David Clowney		
Laurent Robinson		
SBJ Anthony Spencer/50	10.00	25.00
Mike Jenkins		
Keon Lattimore		
SBM Jeff Rowe/50	10.00	25.00
Jordan Palmer		
Matt Moore		
SCM Heath Miller/25	15.00	40.00
Dallas Clark		
Jeremy Shockey		
SFF Joe Flacco/25	25.00	60.00
Matt Flynn		
Drew Stanton		
SGW Mike Singletary/25	40.00	80.00
Patrick Willis		
Joe Greene		
SHH Geno Hayes/50	8.00	20.00
Korey Hall		
Ernie Sims		
SJE Steve Smith USC/99	6.00	15.00
Lawrence Jackson		
Sedrick Ellis		
SJK Jordan Kent/99	6.00	15.00
Steve Smith USC		
Jacoby Jones		
SJM Steve Slaton/25	25.00	50.00
Rashard Mendenhall		
Felix Jones		
SMJ Felix Jones/25	25.00	50.00
Rashard Mendenhall		
Jonathan Stewart		
SMR Matt Moore/99	10.00	25.00
Drew Stanton		
Jeff Rowe		
STS Kevin Smith/25	15.00	40.00
Jonathan Stewart		
Ryan Torain		
TJL Marshawn Lynch/25	12.00	30.00
Larry Johnson		
Fred Taylor		
TMA Ken Anderson/25	30.00	60.00
Y.A. Tittle		
Archie Manning		
TWH Paul Hubbard/99	6.00	15.00
Courtney Taylor		
Mike Sims-Walker		
WHA Xavier Adibi/25	12.00	30.00
Patrick Willis		
Korey Hall		
WRJ Mike Jenkins/50	8.00	20.00
Eric Weddle		
Dominique Rodgers-Cromartie		
WST Alphonso Smith/25	12.00	30.00
Darius Walker		
Ryan Torain		
WTC Ryan Torain/99	5.00	12.00
Ryan Clady		
Darius Walker		

1963-66 Spalding Advisory Staff Photos

Spalding released a number of player photos during the 1960s. Each measures roughly 8" by 10" and carries a black and white photo of the player surrounding by a white border. Included below the photo is a note that the player is a member of Spalding's advisory staff. Some include the Spalding logo while other do not. The photos are blankbacked and unnumbered and checklisted below in alphabetical order. Since many of the photos differ in type style and design, it is thought that they were released over a number of years. Any additions to the list below are appreciated.

1 Jon Arnett	7.50	15.00
2 Ronnie Bull	7.50	15.00
3 Gail Cogdill	7.50	15.00
4 John David Crow	7.50	15.00
5 Len Dawson	12.50	25.00
6 Sonny Gibbs	7.50	15.00
7 Pete Retzlaff	7.50	15.00
8 Fran Tarkenton	15.00	30.00
9 Norm Van Brocklin	15.00	30.00
10 Bill Wade	7.50	15.00

1966 Spalding Brown Frame Photos

These photos are similar to other Spalding photos of the era except for the brown wood grain frame border that surrounds the picture. Spalding released a number of player photos during the 1960s. Each measures roughly 8" by 10" and carries a black and white photo of the player. The photos are blankbacked and unnumbered and checklisted below in alphabetical order. Any additions to the list below are appreciated.

1 Roman Gabriel	10.00	20.00
2 Johnny Unitas	30.00	50.00

1967 Spalding Red Border Photos

This group of photos is similar to other Spalding photos of the era except for the red border that surrounds the picture. Spalding released a number of player photos during the 1960s. Each measures roughly 8" by 10" and carries a black and white photo of the player. The photos are blankbacked and unnumbered and checklisted below in alphabetical order. Any additions to the list below are appreciated.

1 Norm Snead	10.00	15.00
2 Johnny Unitas	30.00	50.00

1968 Spalding Green Frame Photos

This group of photos is similar to other Spalding photos of the era except for the green frame border that surrounds the picture. Spalding released a number of player photos during the 1960s. Each measures roughly 8" by 10" and carries a black and white photo of the player. The photos are blankbacked and unnumbered and checklisted below in alphabetical order. Any additions to the list below are appreciated.

COMPLETE SET (5)	60.00	120.00
1 Len Dawson	10.00	20.00
2 Bobby Mitchell	10.00	20.00
3 Fran Tarkenton	15.00	30.00
4 Charley Taylor	10.00	20.00
5 Johnny Unitas	20.00	40.00

1993 Spectrum QB Club Tribute Sheet Promos

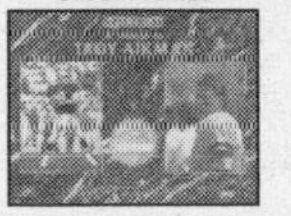

These two 8 1/2" by 11" blank-backed sheets were issued to herald the release of the 1993 Spectrum Quarterback Club Tribute Sheets, which honor NFL quarterbacks. Five thousand of each sheet were produced. They feature color player photos on a black marbleized background. Each sheet has two color photos of the featured player. The photo on the left is an action shot; the one on the right is a closeup. The gold foil stamped player's name is shown near the top, and the gold foil stamped set title rests at the bottom. The sheets are unnumbered and checklisted below in alphabetical order.

COMPLETE SET (2)	4.00	10.00
1 Troy Aikman	1.60	4.00
2 Dan Marino	2.40	6.00

1993 Spectrum QB Club Tribute Sheets

These twelve 8 1/2" by 11" blank-backed sheets pay tribute to NFL quarterbacks and feature color player photos and 24-karat gold player signature reproductions, all on a black marbleized background. Each sheet (except numbers 11 and 12 below) has two color photos of the honored player. The photo on the left is an action shot; the one on the right is a closeup. The player's 24K gold facsimile autograph, and the sheet's production number out of a total of 5,000 produced, appear between the two photos. The gold foil stamped player's name is shown near the top, and the gold foil stamped set title rests at the bottom. The sheets are unnumbered and checklisted below in alphabetical order.

COMPLETE SET (12)	16.00	40.00
1 Troy Aikman	2.00	5.00
2 Randall Cunningham	1.00	2.50
3 John Elway	4.00	10.00
4 Boomer Esiason	.60	1.50
5 Brett Favre	4.00	10.00
6 Jim Kelly	1.00	2.50
7 Dan Marino	4.00	10.00
8 Warren Moon	.60	1.50
9 Phil Simms	.60	1.50
10 Steve Young	1.60	4.00
11 AFC Stars	.60	1.50
Jeff Hostetler		
Dave Klingler		
Bernie Kosar		
Neil O'Donnell		
12 NFC Stars	.60	1.50
Jim Everett		
Jim Harbaugh		
Chris Miller		
Mark Rypien		

1926 Sport Company of America

This 151-card set encompasses athletes from a multitude of different sports. There are 49-cards representing baseball and 14-cards for football. Each includes a black-and-white player photo within a fancy frame border. The player's name and sport are printed at the bottom. The backs carry a short player biography and statistics. The cards originally came in a small glassine envelope along with a coupon that could be redeemed for sporting equipment and are often still found in this form. The cards are unnumbered and have been checklisted below in alphabetical order within sport. We've assigned prefixes to the card numbers which serves to group the cards by sport (BB- baseball, FB- football).

FB1 Peggy Flournoy	100.00	200.00
FB1B Peggy Flournoy AD	125.00	250.00
FB2 Benny Friedman	175.00	300.00
FB3 Ed Garbisch	100.00	200.00
FB4 Red Grango Promo	1,500.00	2,500.00
FB5 Homer Hazel	100.00	200.00
FB6 Walter Koppisch	125.00	250.00
FB6B Walter Koppisch AD	150.00	300.00
FB7 Edward McGinley	100.00	200.00
FB8 Edward McMillan	125.00	250.00
FB8B Edward McMillan AD	150.00	300.00
FB9 Harry Stuhldreher	250.00	500.00
FB9B Harry Stuhldreher AD	300.00	600.00
FB10 Brick Muller	100.00	200.00
FB11 Ernie Nevers	1,000.00	1,500.00
FB12 Swede Oberlander	100.00	200.00
FB12B Swede Oberlander AD	125.00	250.00
FB13 Edward Tryon	125.00	250.00
FB14 Ed Weir	100.00	200.00
FB15 George Wilson	125.00	250.00
FB15B George Wilson AD	150.00	300.00

1992 Sport Decks Promo Aces

Produced by Junior Card and Toy Inc. and given away at the 1992 National Sports Collectors Convention in Atlanta, this four-card standard-size set was produced to promote the premier edition of Sport Decks NFL playing cards. One card was given away on each of the four days of the convention. The color action player cut-outs on the fronts stand out against a full-bleed background that has a metallic sheen to it. A metallic bar overlays the photo at the top and bottom; the top bar carries the card's number, suit, and the Team NFL logo, while the bottom bar has the team helmet, player's name and position, and the Sport Decks logo. All cards come in two varieties, with either gold or silver metallic bars on their fronts. The production figures for the silver were reportedly approximately 6,000, and for the gold, approximately 1,000. On a white background with hot pink and black lettering, the backs carry an advertisement, logos, and a list of players featured in the different card sets. All these cards are Aces, and this is indicated below by the number one followed by a letter indicating the suit. The silver versions are valued individually below.

COMPLETE SET (4)	12.00	30.00
*GOLD CARDS: 1.5X TO 3X SILVERS		
1C Emmitt Smith	6.00	15.00
1D Thurman Thomas	.80	2.00
1H Dan Marino	6.00	15.00
1S Mark Rypien	.40	1.00

1992 Sport Decks

This 55-card standard-size set was issued in a box as if it were a playing card deck. According to Sport Decks, 294,632 decks were produced and 7,500 certified uncut sheets. The design of these cards differ from the promo deck in that a Team NFL logo appears in the ghosted top stripe (promo issue has a NFL logo) and TM (trademark) is printed by the helmet. The back differs from the promo issue in that the Team NFL logo appears again, which slightly alters the back design. Since the set is similar to a playing card set, the set is arranged just like a card deck and checklisted below accordingly. In the checklist below S means Spades, D means Diamonds, C means Clubs, H means Hearts, and JK means Joker. The cards are checklisted below in playing card order by suits and numbers are assigned to Aces (1), Jacks (11), Queens (12), and Kings (13). The jokers are unnumbered and listed at the end.

COMP.FACT SET (55)	3.20	8.00
1C Troy Aikman	.40	1.00
1D Jim Kelly	.10	.30
1H Dan Marino	.80	2.00
1S Mark Rypien	.01	.05
2C Rodney Peete	.01	.05
2D John Friesz	.01	.05
2H Anthony Munoz	.02	.10
2S Phil Simms	.02	.10
3C Cris Carter	.07	.20
3D Gaston Green	.01	.05
3H Nick Bell	.01	.05
3S Pat Swilling	.01	.05
4C Randal Hill	.01	.05
4D Hugh Millen	.01	.05
4H Michael Dean Perry	.02	.10
4S Jim Harbaugh	.02	.10
5C Jeff Hostetler	.02	.10
5D Dan McGwire	.01	.05
5H Haywood Jeffires	.01	.05
5S Mike Singletary	.02	.10
6C Flipper Anderson	.01	.05
6D Eric Green	.01	.05
6H Bubby Brister	.01	.05
6S Lawrence Taylor	.02	.10
7C Chris Miller	.01	.05
7D Christian Okoye	.01	.05
7H Andre Reed	.02	.10
7S John Taylor	.01	.05
8C Anthony Carter	.02	.10
8D Ronnie Lott	.02	.10
8H Anthony Miller	.02	.10
8S Keith Jackson	.02	.10
9C Timm Rosenbach	.01	.05
9D Rob Moore	.02	.10
9H Ken O'Brien	.01	.05
9S Vinny Testaverde	.02	.10
10C Sterling Sharpe	.02	.10
10D Mark Clayton	.01	.05
10H Bernie Kosar	.02	.10
10S Andre Rison	.02	.10
11C Ricky Ervins	.01	.05
11D Thurman Thomas	.02	.10
11H Derrick Thomas	.07	.20
11S Michael Irvin	.07	.20
12C Jerry Rice	.40	1.00
12D John Elway	.80	2.00
12H Jeff George	.02	.10
12S Earnest Byner	.01	.05
13C Emmitt Smith	.80	2.00
13D Warren Moon	.07	.20
13H Boomer Esiason	.02	.10
13S Randall Cunningham	.07	.20
JK1 Eric Dickerson	.02	.10
JK2 Jim Everett	.02	.10
NNO Title Card	.01	.05

1994 Sportflics Samples

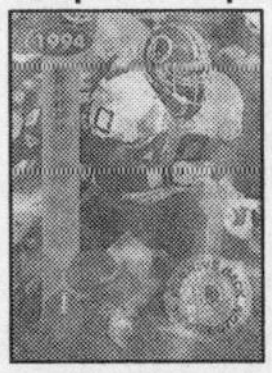

This seven-card standard-size set was issued to preview the 1994 Sportflics series. When tilted, the full-bleed fronts show two different action photos of the same player. The backs carry another player photo as well as statistics and/or player profile. The cards are very similar to the regular issue Sportflics cards with only slight differences as noted below, usually on the cardback. The upper right corner of each card is cut off to indicate that these are samples.

COMPLETE SET (7)	3.00	7.50
3 Flipper Anderson	.25	.60
yellow Anderson name		
on back missing shadow		
50 Reggie Brooks	.25	.60
yellow 'Brooks' name		
on back missing shadow		
70 Herman Moore	.40	1.00
name on front 1/4-inch		
away from year logo		
145 Chuck Levy	.25	.60
back photo black and white		
180 Jerome Bettis	.80	2.00
('TM' by Starflics logo on front)		
HH1 Dante Jones	1.60	4.00
Barry Sanders		
Head-to-Head		
production number box		
on back missing		
NNO Sportflics Ad Card	.10	.30
corners intact		

1994 Sportflics

This set consists of 184 standard size motion cards which offer a different photo depending on how they are held. The set closes with Rookies (143-175) and Starflics (176-184) subsets. The fronts have the player's name in a yellow banner up the left side with three footballs at the bottom. At bottom right, the team helmet and logo can be viewed. Horizontal backs have two player photos, statistics and highlights. Rookie Cards include Marshall Faulk, William Floyd, Errict Rhett, Darnay Scott and Heath Shuler.

COMPLETE SET (184)	10.00	25.00
1 Deion Sanders	.25	.60
2 Leslie O'Neal	.02	.10
3 Flipper Anderson	.02	.10
4 Anthony Carter	.07	.20
5 Thurman Thomas	.10	.30
6 Johnny Mitchell	.02	.10
7 Jeff Hostetler	.07	.20
8 Renaldo Turnbull	.02	.10
9 Chris Warren	.07	.20
10 Darrell Green	.02	.10
11 Randall Cunningham	.10	.30
12 Barry Sanders	.75	2.00
13 Jeff Cross	.02	.10
14 Glyn Milburn	.07	.20
15 Willie Davis	.07	.20
16 Tony McGee	.02	.10
17 Gary Clark	.07	.20
18 Michael Jackson	.07	.20
19 Alvin Harper	.07	.20
20 Tim Worley	.02	.10
21 Quentin Coryatt	.07	.20
22 Michael Brooks	.02	.10
23 Boomer Esiason	.07	.20
24 Ricky Watters	.07	.20
25 Craig Erickson	.02	.10
26 Willie Green	.02	.10
27 Brett Favre	1.00	2.50
28 John Elway	1.00	2.50
29 Steve Beuerlein	.07	.20
30 Emmitt Smith	.75	2.00
31 Troy Aikman	.50	1.25
32 Cody Carlson	.02	.10
33 Brian Mitchell	.02	.10
34 Herschel Walker	.07	.20
35 Bruce Smith	.07	.20
36 Harold Green	.02	.10
37 Eric Pegram	.02	.10
38 Ronnie Harmon	.02	.10
39 Brian Blades	.07	.20
40 Sterling Sharpe	.07	.20
41 Leonard Russell	.02	.10
42 Cleveland Gary	.02	.10
43 Tom Waddle	.02	.10
44 Lawrence Dawsey	.02	.10
45 Jerry Rice	.50	1.25
46 Terry Allen	.07	.20
47 Reggie Langhorne	.02	.10
48 Derek Brown RBK	.02	.10
49 Terry Kirby	.07	.20
50 Reggie Brooks	.07	.20
51 Calvin Williams	.07	.20
52 Cornelius Bennett	.07	.20
53 Russell Maryland	.02	.10
54 Rob Moore	.07	.20
55 Dana Stubblefield	.07	.20
56 Rod Woodson	.07	.20
57 Rodney Hampton	.07	.20
58 Neil Smith	.07	.20
59 Anthony Smith	.02	.10
60 Neal Anderson	.02	.10
61 Drew Bledsoe	.40	1.00
62 John Copeland	.02	.10
63 David Klingler	.02	.10
64 Phil Simms	.07	.20
65 Vincent Brisby	.07	.20
66 Richard Dent	.07	.20
67 Eric Metcalf	.07	.20
68 Eric Curry	.02	.10
69 Victor Bailey	.02	.10
70 Herman Moore	.10	.30
71 Steve Jordan	.02	.10
72 Jerome Bettis	.25	.60
73 Natrone Means	.10	.30
74 Webster Slaughter	.02	.10
75 Jackie Harris	.02	.10
76 Michael Irvin	.10	.30
77 Steve Emtman	.02	.10
78 Eugene Robinson	.02	.10
79 Tim Brown	.10	.30
80 Derrick Thomas	.10	.30
81 Vinny Testaverde	.07	.20
82 Mark Jackson	.02	.10
83 Ricky Proehl	.02	.10
84 Stan Humphries	.07	.20
85 Garrison Hearst	.10	.30
86 Jim Kelly	.10	.30
87 Brent Jones	.07	.20
88 Eric Martin	.02	.10
89 Wilber Marshall	.02	.10
90 Chris Spielman	.07	.20
91 Eric Green	.02	.10
92 Andre Rison	.07	.20
93 Andre Reed	.07	.20
94 Carl Pickens	.07	.20
95 Junior Seau	.10	.30
96 Dwight Stone	.02	.10
97 Mike Sherrard	.02	.10
98 Vincent Brown	.02	.10
99 Cris Carter	.25	.60
100 Mark Higgs	.02	.10
101 Steve Young	.30	.75
102 Mark Carrier WR	.07	.20
103 Barry Foster	.02	.10
104 Tommy Vardell	.02	.10
105 Shannon Sharpe	.07	.20
106 Reggie White	.10	.30
107 Ernest Givins	.07	.20
108 Marcus Allen	.10	.30
109 James Jett	.02	.10
110 Keith Jackson	.02	.10
111 Irving Fryar	.07	.20
112 Ronnie Lott	.07	.20
113 Cortez Kennedy	.07	.20
114 Ronald Moore	.02	.10
115 Rick Mirer	.07	.20
116 Neil O'Donnell	.07	.20
117 Courtney Hawkins	.02	.10
118 Johnny Johnson	.02	.10
119 Ben Coates	.07	.20
120 Dan Marino	1.00	2.50
121 Sean Gilbert	.02	.10
122 Rocket Ismail	.07	.20
123 Joe Montana	1.00	2.50
124 Roosevelt Potts	.02	.10
125 Gary Brown	.02	.10
126 Reggie Cobb	.02	.10
127 Marion Butts	.02	.10
128 Scott Mitchell	.07	.20
129 John L. Williams	.02	.10
130 Jeff George	.07	.20
131 Bobby Hebert	.02	.10
132 John Friesz	.07	.20
133 Anthony Miller	.07	.20
134 Jim Harbaugh	.07	.20
135 Erik Kramer	.07	.20
136 Jim Everett	.07	.20
137 Michael Haynes	.07	.20
138 Rod Bernstine	.02	.10
139 Chris Miller	.02	.10
140 Henry Ellard	.07	.20
141 William Fuller	.02	.10
142 Warren Moon	.10	.30
143 Lamar Smith RC	.50	1.25
144 Charlie Garner RC	.40	1.00
145 Chuck Levy RC	.02	.10
146 Dan Wilkinson RC	.07	.20
147 Perry Klein RC	.02	.10
148 William Floyd RC	.07	.20
149 Lake Dawson RC	.07	.20
150 David Palmer RC	.10	.30
151 James Bostic RC	.07	.20
152 Marshall Faulk RC	2.00	5.00
153 Greg Hill RC	.10	.30
154 Heath Shuler RC	.10	.30
155 Errict Rhett RC	.10	.30
156 Sam Adams RC	.07	.20
157 Charles Johnson RC	.10	.30
158 Ryan Yarborough RC	.02	.10
159 Thomas Lewis RC	.07	.20
160 Willie McGinest RC	.10	.30
161 Jamir Miller RC	.07	.20
162 Calvin Jones RC	.02	.10
163 Donnell Bennett RC	.10	.30
164 Trev Alberts RC	.07	.20
165 LeShon Johnson RC	.07	.20
166 Johnnie Morton RC	.25	.60
167 Derrick Alexander WR RC	.10	.30
168 Jeff Cothran RC	.02	.10
169 Bucky Brooks RC	.02	.10
170 Bert Emanuel RC	.10	.30
171 Darnay Scott RC	.25	.60
172 Kevin Lee RC	.02	.10
173 Mario Bates RC	.07	.20
174 Bryant Young RC	.20	.50
175 Trent Dilfer RC	.40	1.00
176 Joe Montana SF	.50	1.25
177 Emmitt Smith SF	.40	1.00
178 Troy Aikman SF	.25	.60
179 Steve Young SF	.10	.30
180 Jerome Bettis SF	.10	.30
181 John Elway SF	.50	1.25
182 Dan Marino SF	.50	1.25
183 Brett Favre SF	.50	1.25
184 Barry Sanders SF	.40	1.00
FTF1 Terry Kirby	1.50	4.00
Leonard Russell		

1994 Sportflics Artist's Proofs

COMPLETE SET (184)	125.00	300.00
*STARS: 5X TO 12X BASIC CARDS		
*RCs: 3X TO 8X BASIC CARDS		
STATED ODDS 1:24		

1994 Sportflics Head-To-Head
COMPLETE SET (10) 20.00 50.00
STATED ODDS 1:72
HH1 Barry Sanders 5.00 12.00
Dante Jones
HH2 Emmit Smith 5.00 12.00
Carlton Bailey
HH3 Rod Woodson 6.00 15.00
Dan Marino
HH4 Jerry Rice 3.00 8.00
Deion Sanders
HH5 Vaughan Johnson 1.50 4.00
Jerome Bettis
HH6 Reggie White 3.00 8.00
Troy Aikman
HH7 Steve Young 2.00 5.00
Renaldo Turnbull
HH8 Sterling Sharpe .50 1.25
Eric Allen
HH9 Joe Montana 6.00 15.00
Anthony Smith
HH10 John Elway 6.00 15.00
Neil Smith

1994 Sportflics Rookie Rivalry
COMPLETE SET (10) 10.00 25.00
STATED ODDS 1:18
RR1 William Floyd 4.00 10.00
Marshall Faulk
RR2 Dan Wilkinson .40 1.00
Sam Adams
RR3 Trent Dilfer 1.00 2.50
Heath Shuler
RR4 Jamir Miller .40 1.00
Trev Alberts
RR5 Johnnie Morton .60 1.50
Charles Johnson
RR6 Chuck Levy 1.00 2.50
Charlie Garner
RR7 Thomas Lewis .60 1.50
Derrick Alexander WR
RR8 Darnay Scott 4.00 10.00
Isaac Bruce
RR9 David Palmer .40 1.00
Ryan Yarborough
RR10 LeShon Johnson .60 1.50
Donnell Bennett

1994 Sportflics Pride of Texas
COMPLETE SET (4) 6.00 15.00
N1 Alvin Harper 1.50 4.00
N2 Gary Brown 1.50 4.00

1995 Sportflix

This 175 card set was issued through both hobby and retail outlets for the first time and breaks down into 118 regular cards, 30 rookie cards, 20 Game Winners cards and seven checklists. Rookie Cards include Kerry Collins, Terrell Davis, Joey Galloway, Steve McNair, Rashaan Salaam, Kordell Stewart, J.J. Stokes and Michael Westbrook. . Three Promo cards were produced and priced at the end of our checklist.

COMPLETE SET (175) 10.00 25.00
1 Troy Aikman .40 1.00
2 Rodney Hampton .07 .20
3 Jerry Rice .40 1.00
4 Reggie White .10 .30
5 Mark Ingram .02 .10
6 Chris Spielman .07 .20
7 Curtis Conway .10 .30
8 Erik Kramer .02 .10
9 Emmitt Smith .60 1.50
10 Alvin Harper .02 .10
11 Junior Seau .10 .30
12 Mike Pritchard .02 .10
13 Ricky Ervins .02 .10
14 Jim Harbaugh .07 .20
15 Dan Marino .75 2.00
16 Marshall Faulk .50 1.25
17 Lorenzo White .02 .10
18 Cortez Kennedy .07 .20
19 Rocket Ismail .07 .20
20 Eric Metcalf .07 .20
21 Chris Chandler .07 .20
22 John Elway .75 2.00
23 Boomer Esiason .07 .20
24 Herman Moore .10 .30
25 Deion Sanders .25 .60
26 Charles Johnson .07 .20
27 Daryl Johnston .07 .20
28 Dave Krieg .02 .10
29 Jim Kelly .10 .30
30 Warren Moon .07 .20
31 Lewis Tillman .02 .10
32 Bruce Smith .10 .30
33 Jake Reed .07 .20
34 Craig Heyward .07 .20
35 Frank Reich .02 .10
36 Stan Humphries .07 .20
37 Charles Haley .07 .20
38 Andre Rison .07 .20
39 James Jett .07 .20
40 Jay Novacek .07 .20
41 Gary Brown .02 .10
42 Steve Bono .07 .20
43 Cris Carter .10 .30
44 Steve Atwater .02 .10
45 Andre Reed .07 .20
46 Greg Lloyd .07 .20
47 Mark Seay .07 .20
48 Dave Meggett .02 .10
49 Steve Beuerlein .07 .20
50 Jeff Graham .02 .10
51 Barry Sanders .60 1.50
52 Willie Davis .07 .20
53 Robert Smith .10 .30
54 Steve Walsh .02 .10
55 Michael Irvin .10 .30
56 Natrone Means .07 .20
57 Chris Warren .07 .20
58 Tim Brown .10 .30
59 Steve Young .30 .75
60 Jerome Bettis .10 .30
61 Shannon Sharpe .07 .20
62 Errict Rhett .07 .20
63 Scott Mitchell .07 .20
64 Leroy Hoard .02 .10
65 Garrison Hearst .10 .30
66 Terance Mathis .07 .20
67 Sean Gilbert .07 .20
68 Fred Barnett .07 .20
69 Hardy Nickerson .02 .10
70 Jim Everett .02 .10
71 Randall Cunningham .10 .30
72 Carl Pickens .07 .20
73 Jeff Hostetler .07 .20
74 Marcus Allen .10 .30
75 Jeff George .07 .20
76 Brett Favre .75 2.00
77 Chris Miller .02 .10
78 Craig Erickson .02 .10
79 Herschel Walker .07 .20
80 Bert Emanuel .10 .30
81 Leonard Russell .02 .10
82 Ricky Watters .07 .20
83 Robert Brooks .10 .30
84 Dave Brown .07 .20
85 Henry Ellard .07 .20
86 Barry Foster .07 .20
87 Johnny Mitchell .02 .10
88 Eric Allen .02 .10
89 Darnay Scott .07 .20
90 Harvey Williams .02 .10
91 Neil O'Donnell .07 .20
92 Drew Bledsoe .25 .60
93 Ken Harvey .02 .10
94 Irving Fryar .07 .20
95 Rod Woodson .07 .20
96 Anthony Miller .07 .20
97 Mario Bates .07 .20
98 Jeff Blake RC .30 .75
99 Rick Mirer .07 .20
100 William Floyd .07 .20
101 Michael Haynes .07 .20
102 Flipper Anderson .02 .10
103 Greg Hill .07 .20
104 Mark Brunell .25 .60
105 Vinny Testaverde .07 .20
106 Heath Shuler .07 .20
107 Ronald Moore .02 .10
108 Ernest Givins .02 .10
109 Mike Sherrard .02 .10
110 Charlie Garner .10 .30
111 Trent Dilfer .10 .30
112 Byron Bam Morris .02 .10
113 Lake Dawson .07 .20
114 Brian Blades .07 .20
115 Brent Jones .02 .10
116 Ronnie Harmon .02 .10
117 Eric Green .02 .10
118 Ben Coates .07 .20
119 Ki-Jana Carter RC .10 .30
120 Steve McNair RC 1.25 3.00
121 Michael Westbrook RC .10 .30
122 Kerry Collins RC .75 2.00
123 Joey Galloway RC .60 1.50
124 Kyle Brady RC .10 .30
125 J.J. Stokes RC .10 .30
126 Tyrone Wheatley RC .50 1.25
127 Rashaan Salaam RC .07 .20
128 Napoleon Kaufman RC .50 1.25
129 Frank Sanders RC .10 .30
130 Stoney Case RC .02 .10
131 Todd Collins RC .50 1.25
132 Lovell Pinkney RC .02 .10
133 Sherman Williams RC .02 .10
134 Rob Johnson RC .40 1.00
135 Mark Bruener RC .07 .20
136 Lee DeRamus RC .02 .10
137 Chad May RC .02 .10
138 James A.Stewart RC .02 .10
139 Ray Zellars RC .07 .20
140 Dave Barr RC .02 .10
141 Kordell Stewart RC .60 1.50
142 Jimmy Oliver RC .02 .10
143 Terrell Fletcher RC .02 .10
144 James O. Stewart RC .50 1.25
145 Terrell Davis RC 1.00 2.50
146 Joe Aska RC .02 .10
147 John Walsh RC .02 .10
148 Tyrone Davis RC .02 .10
149 Emmitt Smith GW .30 .75
150 Barry Sanders GW .30 .75
151 Jerry Rice GW .20 .50
152 Steve Young GW .15 .40
153 Dan Marino GW .40 1.00
154 Troy Aikman GW .20 .50
155 Drew Bledsoe GW .10 .30
156 John Elway GW .40 1.00
157 Brett Favre GW .40 1.00
158 Michael Irvin GW .07 .20
159 Heath Shuler GW .07 .20
160 Warren Moon GW .02 .10
161 Jim Kelly GW .10 .30
162 Randall Cunningham GW .07 .20
163 Jeff Hostetler GW .07 .20
164 Dave Brown GW .07 .20
165 Neil O'Donnell GW .07 .20
166 Rick Mirer GW .07 .20
167 Jim Everett GW .02 .10
168 Boomer Esiason GW .07 .20
169 Dan Marino CL .20 .50
170 Drew Bledsoe CL .10 .30
171 John Elway CL .10 .30
172 Emmitt Smith CL .15 .40
173 Steve Young CL .10 .30
174 Barry Sanders CL .10 .30
175 Jerry Rice CL .10 .30
Junior Seau CL
P1 Troy Aikman Promo .50 1.25
P6 J.J. Stokes Lightning Promo .30 .75
P92 Drew Bledsoe Promo .40 1.00

1995 Sportflix Artist's Proofs
COMPLETE SET (175) 250.00 500.00
*STARS: 6X TO 15X BASIC CARDS
*RCs: 4X TO 10X BASIC CARDS
STATED ODDS 1:36

1995 Sportflix Man 2 Man
COMPLETE SET (12) 20.00 50.00
RANDOM INSERTS IN JUMBO PACKS
1 Dan Marino 5.00 12.00
Troy Aikman
2 Emmitt Smith 4.00 10.00
Marshall Faulk
3 Drew Bledsoe 1.50 4.00
Kerry Collins
4 Steve Young 3.00 8.00
Steve McNair
5 Barry Sanders 4.00 10.00
Ki-Jana Carter
6 John Elway 5.00 12.00
Heath Shuler
7 Byron Bam Morris .20 .50
Rashaan Salaam
8 Natrone Means .50 1.25
Ricky Watters
9 Jerry Rice 2.50 6.00
J.J.Stokes
10 Kordell Stewart 1.50 4.00
Warren Moon
11 Brett Favre 5.00 12.00
Jeff Blake
12 Joey Galloway 1.50 4.00
Michael Wetsbrook

1995 Sportflix ProMotion
COMPLETE SET (12) 30.00 80.00
PM1 Steve Young 3.00 8.00
PM2 Troy Aikman 4.00 10.00
PM3 Dan Marino 8.00 20.00
PM4 Drew Bledsoe 2.50 6.00
PM5 John Elway 8.00 20.00
PM6 Jim Kelly 1.25 3.00
PM7 Jerry Rice 4.00 10.00
PM8 Michael Irvin 1.25 3.00
PM9 Emmitt Smith 6.00 15.00
PM10 Marshall Faulk 5.00 12.00
PM11 Natrone Means .75 2.00
PM12 Ki-Jana Carter 1.25 3.00

1995 Sportflix Rolling Thunder
COMPLETE SET (12) 12.50 30.00
1 Emmitt Smith 4.00 10.00
2 Barry Sanders 4.00 10.00
3 Marshall Faulk 3.00 8.00
4 Ki-Jana Carter .75 2.00
5 Rashaan Salaam .50 1.25
6 Tyrone Wheatley 3.00 8.00
7 Natrone Means .50 1.25
8 Jerome Bettis .75 2.00
9 Errict Rhett .50 1.25
10 Byron Bam Morris .25 .60
11 William Floyd .50 1.25
12 Mario Bates .50 1.25

1995 Sportflix Rookie Lightning
COMPLETE SET (12) 15.00 40.00
1 Ki-Jana Carter .50 1.25
2 Steve McNair 5.00 12.00
3 Michael Westbrook .50 1.25
4 Kerry Collins 2.50 6.00
5 Joey Galloway 2.50 6.00
6 J.J. Stokes .50 1.25
7 Tyrone Wheatley 2.00 5.00
8 Rashaan Salaam .30 .75
9 Napoleon Kaufman 2.00 5.00
10 Kordell Stewart 2.50 6.00
11 James O. Stewart 2.00 5.00
12 Todd Collins 2.00 5.00

1933 Sport Kings
The cards in this 48-card set measure 2 3/8" by 2 7/8". The 1933 Sport Kings set, issued by the Goudey Gum Company, contains cards for the most famous athletic heroes of the times. No less than 18 different sports are represented in the set. The baseball cards of Cobb, Hubbell, and Ruth, and the football cards of Rockne, Grange and Thorpe command premium prices. The cards were issued in one-card penny packs which came 100 packs to a box along with a piece of gum. The catalog designation for this set is R338.

COMPLETE SET 10,000.00 16,000.00
4 Red Grange RC 500.00 800.00
(football)
6 Jim Thorpe RC 600.00 1,000.00
(football)
35 Knute Rockne RC 350.00 600.00
(football)

1934 Sport Kings Varsity Game
Goudey Gum Co. produced this 24-card set in wax packs under the Sport Kings Gum label. The year of issue is thought to be 1934, one year after the first set of Sport Kings. Each 2 3/8" by 2 7/8" card features the same front, but a slightly different back. The backs contain a card number followed by play results under the headings of kick off, rush, forward pass, punt, place kick, and goal after touchdown. The play results were designed to be used in a football card game played with the set. The first few words, when available, of the top line of text are included below to help identify each card.

1 Game Card 12.50 25.00
(A 62 yd.kick landing)
2 Game Card 12.50 25.00
(25 yds. L.H.B. signals)
3 Game Card 12.50 25.00
(Only 30 yds. -- to the)
4 Game Card 12.50 25.00
(30 yds. taken)
5 Game Card 12.50 25.00
(Out of bounds)
6 Game Card 12.50 25.00
(25 yds. R. H. B.)
7 Game Card 12.50 25.00
(To the 37 yd. line)
8 Game Card 12.50 25.00
(39 yds. To 21 yd. line)
9 Game Card 12.50 25.00
(50 yds. to 10 yd. line)
10 Game Card 12.50 25.00
(Out of bounds)
11 Game Card 12.50 25.00
(A long high kick)
12 Game Card 12.50 25.00
13 Game Card SP 125.00 200.00
14 Game Card 12.50 25.00
15 Game Card 12.50 25.00
16 Game Card 12.50 25.00
17 Game Card 12.50 25.00
18 Game Card 12.50 25.00
19 Game Card SP 75.00 150.00
20 Game Card 12.50 25.00
21 Game Card SP 75.00 150.00
22 Game Card 12.50 25.00
23 Game Card 12.50 25.00
24 Game Card SP 75.00 150.00

2007 Sportkings
COMPLETE SET (48) 600.00 900.00
THREE PER PACK
1 Troy Aikman 5.00 12.00
8 Tony Dorsett 4.00 10.00
38 Bart Starr 8.00 20.00
41 Thurman Thomas 4.00 10.00
42 Sammy Baugh 6.00 15.00
43 Reggie White 5.00 12.00
48 Steve Young 4.00 10.00

2007 Sportkings Mini
*MINIS: 1X TO 2X BASIC
ONE PER PACK
ANNOUNCED PRINT RUN 93 SETS

2007 Sportkings Autograph Gold
*GOLD: 1.2X TO 2X BASIC
RANDOM INSERTS IN PACKS
ANNOUNCED PRINT RUN 10 SETS
ABS Bart Starr 90.00 150.00

2007 Sportkings Autograph Silver
RANDOM INSERTS IN PACKS
ANNOUNCED PRINT RUN B/WN 95-99 PER
ABS Bart Starr 60.00 100.00
ASY Steve Young 20.00 40.00
ATA Troy Aikman 35.00 60.00
ATD Tony Dorsett 20.00 40.00
ATT Thurman Thomas 15.00 30.00

2007 Sportkings Autograph Memorabilia Gold
*GOLD/10: 1.2X TO 2X SILVER/40
ANNOUNCED PRINT RUN 10 SETS

2007 Sportkings Autograph Memorabilia Silver
RANDOM INSERTS IN PACKS
ANNOUNCED PRINT RUN 40 SETS
AMRB Reggie Bush Jsy 25.00 50.00
AMSY Steve Young Jsy 25.00 50.00
AMTA Troy Aikman Jsy 50.00 80.00
AMTD Tony Dorsett Jsy 25.00 50.00
AMTT Thurman Thomas Jsy 20.00 40.00

2007 Sportkings Cityscapes Silver
ANNOUNCED PRINT RUN 20 SETS
*GOLD: .5X TO 1.2X BASIC
GOLD ANNOUNCED PRINT RUN 10 SETS
RANDOM INSERTS IN PACKS
CS01 Tony Dorsett Jsy 20.00 40.00
Troy Aikman Jsy
Dallas

2007 Sportkings Decades Silver
ANNOUNCED PRINT RUN 20 SETS
*GOLD: .5X TO 1.2X BASIC
GOLD ANNOUNCED PRINT RUN 10 SETS
RANDOM INSERTS IN PACKS
D06 Troy Aikman Jsy 40.00 80.00
Patrick Roy Jsy
Roger Clemens Jsy/1990s
D07 Freddy Adu Jsy 40.00 80.00
Quinton Jackson Shirt
Reggie Bush Jsy/2000s

2007 Sportkings Double Memorabilia Silver
RANDOM INSERTS IN PACKS
ANNOUNCED PRINT RUN 4-40 SETS
DM15, DM16 ANNOUNCED PRINT RUN 4 PER
NO DM15, DM16 PRICING DUE TO SCARCITY
DM9 Reggie Bush Cleats-Jsy 10.00 25.00
DM10 Reggie White Cleats-Jsy 15.00 40.00
DM14 Troy Aikman Jsy-Pants 15.00 40.00

2007 Sportkings Double Memorabilia Gold
*GOLD: .6X TO 1.5X BASIC
RANDOM INSERTS IN PACKS
ANNOUNCED PRINT RUN 10 SETS
DM15, DM16 ANNOUNCED PRINT RUN 1 PER
NO DM15, DM16 PRICING DUE TO SCARCITY

2007 Sportkings Future Sportkings Autograph
COMMON CARD 10.00 25.00
ANNOUNCED PRINT RUN B/WN 95-99 PER
*GOLD: 1.2X TO 2X BASIC
GOLD ANNOUNCED PRINT RUN 10 SETS
RANDOM INSERTS IN PACKS
FSARB Reggie Bush 20.00 40.00

2007 Sportkings Papercuts
RANDOM INSERTS IN PACKS
ANNOUNCED PRINT RUNS B/WN 1-10 PER
NO PRICING DUE TO SCARCITY
PCSB Sammy Baugh/10 *

2007 Sportkings Patch Silver
ANNOUNCED PRINT RUN 20 SETS
P28-P30 ANNOUNCED PRINT RUN 4 PER
NO P28-P30 PRICING DUE TO SCARCITY
*GOLD: .6X TO 1.2X BASIC
GOLD ANNOUNCED PRINT RUN 10 SETS
GOLD P28-P30 ANCD. PRINT RUN 1 PER
GOLD P28-P30 NO PRICING AVAILABLE
RANDOM INSERTS IN PACKS
P13 Troy Aikman Jsy 15.00 40.00
P20 Reggie Bush Jsy 10.00 30.00
P21 Reggie White Jsy 15.00 40.00
P24 Steve Young Jsy 15.00 40.00
P25 Tony Dorsett Jsy 12.50 30.00
P27 Thurman Thomas Jsy 10.00 30.00

2007 Sportkings Single Memorabilia Silver
RANDOM INSERTS IN PACKS
ANNOUNCED PRINT RUN 90 SETS
SM3, SM13 ANNOUNCED PRINT RUN 4 PER
NO SM3, SM13 PRICING DUE TO SCARCITY
SM20 Reggie Bush Jsy 4.00 15.00
SM21 Reggie White Jsy 8.00 20.00
SM26 Steve Young Jsy 4.00 15.00
SM28 Thurman Thomas Jsy 4.00 15.00
SM29 Tony Dorsett Jsy 4.00 15.00
SM30 Troy Aikman Pants 8.00 20.00
SM31 Troy Aikman Jsy 8.00 20.00
SM43 Reggie White Cleats 8.00 20.00

2007 Sportkings Triple Memorabilia Silver
ANNOUNCED PRINT RUN 10 SETS
TM7, TM8 ANNOUNCED PRINT RUN 4 PER
NO TM7, TM8 PRICING DUE TO SCARCITY
GOLD ANNOUNCED PRINT RUN 1 SET
NO GOLD PRICING DUE TO SCARCITY
RANDOM INSERTS IN PACKS
TM06 Reggie Bush 15.00 40.00
Cleats-Glove-Jsy
TM10 Troy Aikman Jsy 40.00 80.00
Steve Young Jsy
Tony Dorsett Jsy
TM13 Quinton Jackson Shirt 20.00 50.00
Freddy Adu Jsy
Reggie Bush Jsy

2007 Sportkings National Convention Preview
1 Troy Aikman 1.00 2.50

2008 Sportkings
FIVE CARDS PER BOX
50 Jim Brown 6.00 12.00
51 Barry Sanders 7.50 15.00
52 Michael Irvin 4.00 8.00
58 John Elway 7.50 15.00
66 Vince Lombardi 10.00 20.00
74 Deion Sanders 6.00 12.00
86 Drew Pearson 4.00 8.00
96 Dan Marino 6.00 12.00
101 Bo Jackson 6.00 12.00
106 Joe Montana 15.00 30.00

2008 Sportkings Mini
*MINI: 1X TO 2X BASIC
ONE PER BOX
106 Joe Montana 15.00 30.00

2008 Sportkings 1933 Redemption
UNPRICED ANNOUNCED PRINT RUN 1

2008 Sportkings 1933 The Year
UNPRICED PRINT RUN 1

2008 Sportkings Admit One Redemptions
RANDOM INSERTS IN PACKS
ANNOUNCED PRINT RUN 1 SET
NO PRICING DUE TO SCARCITY

2008 Sportkings At the Movies
RANDOM INSERTS IN PACKS
STATED PRINT RUN 1 SERIAL #'d SET
NO PRICING DUE TO SCARCITY

2008 Sportkings Autograph Silver
ANNOUNCED PRINT RUN B/WN 20-90 PER
RANDOM INSERTS IN PACKS
MI Michael Irvin/40 * 20.00 40.00
BJ1 Bo Jackson/30 * 30.00 60.00
BJ2 Bo Jackson/30 * 30.00 60.00
BSA Barry Sanders/40 * 50.00 100.00
DP1 Drew Pearson/40 * 10.00 25.00
DP2 Drew Pearson/40 * 10.00 25.00
JE1 John Elway/30 * 40.00 80.00
JE2 John Elway/30 * 40.00 80.00
JE3 John Elway/30 * 40.00 80.00
MI2 Michael Irvin/40 * 20.00 40.00
BSA2 Barry Sanders/40 * 50.00 100.00
DMA1 Dan Marino/40 * 60.00 120.00
DMA2 Dan Marino/40 * 60.00 120.00
DSA1 Deion Sanders/20 * 40.00 80.00
DSA2 Deion Sanders/20 * 40.00 80.00
DSA3 Deion Sanders/20 * 40.00 80.00
JBR1 Jim Brown/90 * 30.00 60.00
JBR2 Jim Brown/90 * 30.00 60.00
JMO1 Joe Montana/40 * 50.00 100.00
JMO2 Joe Montana/40 * 50.00 100.00
JMO3 Joe Montana/40 * 50.00 100.00

2008 Sportkings Autograph Memorabilia Silver
ANNOUNCED PRINT RUN B/WN 15-50 PER
NO GOLD PRICING DUE TO SCARCITY
RANDOM INSERTS IN PACKS
BJ1 Bo Jackson/25 * 40.00 80.00
BJ2 Bo Jackson/25 * 40.00 80.00
BS Barry Sanders/40 * 50.00 100.00
DMA1 Dan Marino/40 * 100.00 150.00
DMA2 Dan Marino/40 * 100.00 150.00
DP1 Drew Pearson/40 * 15.00 30.00
DP2 Drew Pearson/40 * 15.00 30.00
DSA1 Deion Sanders/15 * 50.00 100.00
DSA2 Deion Sanders/15 * 50.00 100.00
DSA3 Deion Sanders/15 * 50.00 100.00
JE John Elway/20 * 50.00 100.00
JMO1 Joe Montana/40 * 75.00 125.00
JMO2 Joe Montana/40 * 75.00 125.00
MI Michael Irvin/40 * 25.00 50.00

2008 Sportkings Cityscapes Double Silver
RANDOM INSERTS IN PACKS
1 Patrick Roy 30.00 60.00
John Elway
Denver
2 Deion Sanders 15.00 40.00
Dominique Wilkins
Atlanta
4 Brett Hull 15.00 40.00
Michael Irvin
Dallas
9 Joe Montana 20.00 50.00
Juan Marichal
San Francisco
10 Barry Sanders 20.00 50.00
Brett Hull
Detroit

2008 Sportkings Cityscapes Triple Silver
RANDOM INSERTS IN PACKS
2 Michael Irvin 20.00 50.00
Troy Aikman
Brett Hull
Dallas
4 Joe Montana 40.00 80.00
Steve Young
Juan Marichal
San Francisco

2008 Sportkings Decades Silver
RANDOM INSERTS IN PACKS
2 Jim Brown 20.00 50.00
Jacque Plante
Juan Marichal
3 Ron Turcotte 75.00 125.00
Joe Montana
Pel??
4 Dan Marino 30.00 60.00
Mark Messier
Robert Parish
5 Brett Hull 20.00 50.00
Michael Irvin
Hakeem Olajuwon

2008 Sportkings Double Memorabilia Silver
RANDOM INSERTS IN PACKS
1 Michael Irvin 10.00 25.00
Tony Dorsett
5 Troy Aikman 10.00 25.00
Michael Irvin
6 Barry Sanders 15.00 40.00
Deion Sanders
11 Joe Montana 30.00 60.00
Steve Young
13 Bo Jackson BB-FB 20.00 50.00
14 Deion Sanders BB-FB 15.00 40.00

2008 Sportkings Numerology Silver
STATED PRINT RUN 9 SERIAL #'d SETS
GOLD PRINT RUN 1 SERIAL #'d SET
RANDOM INSERTS IN PACKS
NO PRICING DUE TO SCARCITY

2008 Sportkings Papercuts
RANDOM INSERTS IN PACKS
ANNOUNCED PRINT RUN B/WN 1-10 PER
NO PRICING DUE TO SCARCITY
VL Vince Lombardi/3 *

2008 Sportkings Passing the Torch Silver
RANDOM INSERTS IN PACKS
3 Joe Montana 30.00 60.00
Steve Young
10 Jim Brown 30.00 60.00
Barry Sanders
13 Barry Sanders 10.00 25.00
Reggie Bush
14 Drew Pearson 10.00 25.00
Michael Irvin

2008 Sportkings Patch Silver
RANDOM INSERTS IN PACKS
2 Barry Sanders 20.00 50.00
3 Bo Jackson 20.00 50.00
6 Dan Marino 40.00 80.00
7 Drew Pearson 12.50 30.00
13 Deion Sanders 15.00 40.00
14 John Elway 15.00 40.00
20 Michael Irvin 12.50 30.00
22 Joe Montana 40.00 80.00

2008 Sportkings Single Memorabilia Silver
RANDOM INSERTS IN PACKS
3 Barry Sanders 10.00 25.00
4 Bart Starr SP/4 *
7 Bo Jackson 8.00 20.00
12 Drew Pearson 6.00 15.00
20 Jim Brown 10.00 25.00
22 Joe Montana 10.00 25.00
24 John Elway 10.00 25.00
30 Michael Irvin 6.00 15.00
43 Dan Marino 15.00 40.00
44 Deion Sanders 10.00 25.00

2008 Sportkings Triple Memorabilia Silver
RANDOM INSERTS IN PACKS
4 John Elway 50.00 100.00
Joe Montana
Dan Marino
12 Troy Aikman 10.00 25.00
Tony Dorsett
Michael Irvin
13 Bo Jackson 30.00 60.00
Barry Sanders
Jim Brown

2008 Sportkings Vintage Memorabilia
RANDOM INSERTS IN PACKS
STATED PRINT RUN 1 SERIAL #'d SET
NO PRICING DUE TO SCARCITY

2008 Sportkings Vintage Papercuts
RANDOM INSERTS IN PACKS
STATED PRINT RUN 1 SERIAL #'d SET
NO PRICING DUE TO SCARCITY

2008 Sportkings National Convention VIP Promo
5 Jim Brown 4.00 10.00
Red Grange
15 Vince Lombardi 5.00 12.00
Knute Rockne

2008 Sportkings Post Card Redemption Dual Memorabilia
ANNOUNCED PRINT RUN 1 SET
NO PRICING DUE TO SCARCITY

2009 Sportkings
COMPLETE SET (52) 250.00 450.00
COMMON CARD (109-160) 5.00 12.00
SEMISTARS 6.00 15.00
UNLISTED STARS 8.00 20.00
114 Doug Flutie 6.00 15.00
125 Joe Namath 8.00 20.00
126 Jerry Rice 8.00 20.00
135 Bronko Nagurski 8.00 20.00
156 Kurt Warner 6.00 15.00
158 Lawrence Taylor 8.00 20.00

2009 Sportkings Mini
*MINI: .6X TO 1.5X BASIC CARDS
STATED ODDS ONE PER BOX
UNPRICED SILVER PRINT RUN 7 SETS
UNPRICED GOLD PRINT RUN 3 SETS

2009 Sportkings Admit One Redemptions
ANNOUNCED PRINT RUN 1 SET
NO PRICING DUE TO SCARCITY
2 Super Bowl XXV/1/27/91
3 Super Bowl XLIII/2/1/09

2009 Sportkings Autograph Silver
ANNOUNCED PRINT RUN B/WN 15-70 PER
UNPRICED GOLD PRINT RUN 10
DF1 Doug Flutie/30* 30.00 60.00
DF2 Doug Flutie/30* 30.00 60.00
JN1 Joe Namath/25* 60.00 120.00
JN2 Joe Namath/25* 60.00 120.00
JR1 Jerry Rice/20* 75.00 150.00
JR2 Jerry Rice/20* 75.00 150.00
KW1 Kurt Warner/25* 25.00 50.00
KW2 Kurt Warner/25* 25.00 50.00
KW3 Kurt Warner/25* 25.00 50.00
LT1 Lawrence Taylor/40* 30.00 60.00
LT2 Lawrence Taylor/40* 30.00 60.00

2009 Sportkings Autograph Memorabilia Silver
ANNOUNCED PRINT RUN B/WN 15-40 PER
UNPRICED GOLD PRINT RUN 10
RANDOM INSERTS IN PACKS
DF1 Doug Flutie Jsy/30* 20.00 40.00
DF2 Doug Flutie Jsy/30* 20.00 40.00
JN1 Joe Namath Jsy/25* 60.00 120.00
JN2 Joe Namath Jsy/25* 60.00 120.00
JR1 Jerry Rice Jsy/20* 75.00 150.00
JR2 Jerry Rice Jsy/20* 75.00 150.00
KW1 Kurt Warner Jsy/25* 30.00 60.00
KW2 Kurt Warner Jsy/25* 30.00 60.00
LT1 Lawrence Taylor Jsy/40* 30.00 60.00
LT2 Lawrence Taylor Jsy/40* 30.00 60.00

2009 Sportkings Cityscapes Double Silver
ANNOUNCED PRINT RUN 19 SETS
UNPRICED GOLD PRINT RUN 1
RANDOM INSERTS IN PACKS
1 Reggie Jackson Jsy 25.00 50.00
Joe Namath Jsy
2 Jerry Rice Jsy 40.00 80.00
Joe Montana Jsy
3 Doug Flutie Jsy 15.00 30.00
Thurman Thomas Jsy
6 Lawrence Taylor Jsy 20.00 40.00
Joe Namath Jsy
7 Doug Flutie Jsy 20.00 40.00
Bobby Hull Jsy

2009 Sportkings Cityscapes Triple Silver
ANNOUNCED PRINT RUN 19 SETS
UNPRICED GOLD PRINT RUN 1
RANDOM INSERTS IN PACKS
1 Reggie Jackson Jsy 50.00 100.00
Joe Namath Jsy
Pele Jsy
2 Jerry Rice Jsy 60.00 120.00
Joe Montana Jsy
Orlando Cepeda Jsy
3 Lawrence Taylor Jsy 25.00 50.00
Reggie Jackson Jsy
Phil Esposito Jsy
4 Doug Flutie Jsy 20.00 40.00
Bobby Hull Jsy
Tony Esposito Jsy

2009 Sportkings Decades Silver
ANNOUNCED PRINT RUN 19 SETS
UNPRICED GOLD PRINT RUN 1
RANDOM INSERTS IN PACKS
1 Pele Jsy 50.00 100.00
Joe Namath Jsy
Orlando Cepeda Jsy
3 Lawrence Taylor Jsy 40.00 80.00
Rusty Wallace Jsy
Mike Schmidt Jsy
4 Jerry Rice Jsy 40.00 80.00
Lennox Lewis Shorts
Jackie Joyner-Kersee Shirt

2009 Sportkings Double Memorabilia Silver
ANNOUNCED PRINT RUN B/WN 1-19
UNPRICED GOLD PRINT RUN 1
RANDOM INSERTS IN PACKS
1 Kurt Warner Jsy/19* 20.00 40.00
Lawrence Taylor Jsy
2 Jerry Rice Jsy/19* 40.00 80.00
Joe Montana Jsy
5 Joe Namath Jsy/19* 30.00 60.00
Joe Montana Jsy
13 Doug Flutie Jsy/19* 15.00 30.00

2009 Sportkings Numerology Silver
ANNOUNCED PRINT RUN B/WN 4-9 PER
GOLD PRINT RUN 1 SET
NO PRICING DUE TO SCARCITY
RANDOM INSERTS IN PACKS

2009 Sportkings Owner's Box Cut Autographs
RANDOM INSERTS IN PACKS
ANNOUNCED PRINT RUN 1 SET
NO PRICING DUE TO SCARCITY

2009 Sportkings Papercuts
RANDOM INSERTS IN PACKS
ANNOUNCED PRINT RUN 1 SET
NO PRICING DUE TO SCARCITY

2009 Sportkings Patch Silver
ANNOUNCED PRINT RUN B/WN 4-19
UNPRICED GOLD PRINT RUN 1 SET
RANDOM INSERTS IN PACKS
14 Lawrence Taylor/19* 15.00 30.00
15 Joe Namath/4*
16 Jerry Rice/19* 40.00 80.00
17 Doug Flutie/19* 20.00 40.00

2009 Sportkings Single Memorabilia Silver
ANNOUNCED PRINT RUN B/WN 4-29
UNPRICED GOLD PRINT RUN B/WN 1-4
RANDOM INSERTS IN PACKS
2 Doug Flutie Jsy/29* 12.00 30.00
5 Jerry Rice Jsy/29* 30.00 60.00
6 Lawrence Taylor Jsy/29* 10.00 25.00
7 Joe Namath Jsy/29* 20.00 50.00

2009 Sportkings Triple Memorabilia Silver
ANNOUNCED PRINT RUN B/WN 3-19
UNPRICED GOLD PRINT RUN 1 SET
RANDOM INSERTS IN PACKS
1 Doug Flutie Jsy/19* 40.00 80.00
Joe Namath Jsy
Joe Montana Jsy
2 Jerry Rice Jsy/19* 60.00 120.00
Steve Young Jsy
Joe Montana Jsy
4 Lawrence Taylor Jsy/19* 40.00 80.00
Barry Sanders Jsy
Jerry Rice Jsy

2009 Sportkings Vintage Memorabilia
RANDOM INSERTS IN PACKS
ANNOUNCED PRINT RUN 1 SET
NO PRICING DUE TO SCARCITY
1 Knute Rockne Jkt

2009 Sportkings National Convention VIP Promo
COMPLETE SET (7)
2 Lisa Lèslie 5.00 12.00
Joe Namath
Doug Flutie
Vladislav Tretiak
Tony Oliva
Akebono Taro
4 Jerry West 5.00 12.00
Byron Nelson
Fred Perry
Mark Martin
Minnesota Fats
Jerry Rice
5 Lennox Lewis 5.00 12.00
Reggie Jackson
Ian Thorpe
Kurt Warner
Seabiscuit
Jackie Joyner-Kersee
6 Lawrence Taylor 4.00 10.00
Giorgio Chinaglia
Dezso Gyarmati
Bela Karolyi
Wilma Rudolph
Cecil Smith
7 Howie Morenz 5.00 12.00
Red Pollard
Rafer Johnson
Bronko Nagurski
Stan Smith
Pele

2010 Sportkings
COMPLETE SET (48) 150.00 300.00
COMP.SET w/o ALI SP (47) 100.00 200.00
175 Warren Sapp 4.00 10.00
189 Johnny Unitas 6.00 15.00
190 Joe Greene 5.00 12.00
201 Raymond Berry 5.00 12.00
203 Bob Lilly 5.00 12.00

2010 Sportkings Mini
COMPLETE SET (48) 175.00 350.00
*MINI: .5X TO 1.2X BASIC CARDS
STATED ODDS 1:2

2010 Sportkings Mini Gold
OVERALL GOLD/SILVER ODDS 1:19
UNPRICED GOLD PRINT RUN 3

2010 Sportkings Mini Silver
OVERALL GOLD/SILVER ODDS 1:19
UNPRICED SILVER PRINT RUN 7

2010 Sportkings Autograph Silver
ANNOUNCED PRINT RUN 10-50
UNPRICED GOLD PRINT RUN 5-10
ABL1 Bob Lilly/40* 12.00 25.00
ABL2 Bob Lilly/40* 12.00 25.00
AJG1 Joe Greene/40* 15.00 30.00
AJG2 Joe Greene/40* 15.00 30.00
AWS1 Warren Sapp/40* 12.00 25.00
AWS2 Warren Sapp/40* 12.00 25.00
ARBE1 Raymond Berry/25* 20.00 40.00

ARBE2 Raymond Berry/25* 20.00 40.00
ARBE3 Raymond Berry/25* 20.00 40.00

2010 Sportkings Autograph Memorabilia Silver
ANNOUNCED PRINT RUN 10-40
UNPRICED GOLD PRINT RUN 5-10
AMBL1 Bob Lilly Jsy/40* 15.00 30.00
AMBL2 Bob Lilly Jsy/40* 15.00 30.00
AMJG1 Joe Greene Jsy/40* 25.00 50.00
AMJG2 Joe Greene Jsy/40* 25.00 50.00
AMWS1 Warren Sapp Jsy/40* 15.00 30.00
AMWS2 Warren Sapp Jsy/40* 15.00 30.00
AMRBE1 Raymond Berry Jsy/25* 20.00 40.00
AMRBE2 Raymond Berry Jsy/25* 20.00 40.00
AMRBE3 Raymond Berry Jsy/25* 20.00 40.00

2010 Sportkings Cityscapes Double Silver
UNPRICED SILVER PRINT RUN 19
UNPRICED GOLD PRINT RUN 1

2010 Sportkings Coaches Corner Cut Autographs
STATED PRINT RUN 1
UNPRICED DUE TO SCARCITY

2010 Sportkings Commissioner's Office Cut Autographs
STATED PRINT RUN 1
UNPRICED DUE TO SCARCITY

2010 Sportkings Decades Silver
UNPRICED SILVER PRINT RUN 19
UNPRICED GOLD PRINT RUN 1

2010 Sportkings Double Memorabilia Silver
STATED PRINT RUN 20 UNLESS NOTED
DM8 Warren Sapp 15.00 40.00
Lawrence Taylor

2010 Sportkings Four Horsemen Cut Autographs
STATED PRINT RUN 1
UNPRICED DUE TO SCARCITY

2010 Sportkings Heisman Winners Cut Autographs
STATED PRINT RUN 1
UNPRICED DUE TO SCARCITY

2010 Sportkings King-Sized Memorabilia
UNPRICED PRINT RUN 1

2010 Sportkings Logos
UNPRICED LOGO PRINT RUN 1

2010 Sportkings Numerology Silver
UNPRICED SILVER PRINT RUN 9
UNPRICED GOLD PRINT RUN 1

2010 Sportkings Papercuts
UNPRICED PAPERCUT PRINT RUN 1

2010 Sportkings Patch Silver
STATED PRINT RUN 20
UNPRICED GOLD PRINT RUN 10
P6 Warren Sapp 10.00 25.00
P8 Lawrence Taylor 10.00 25.00

2010 Sportkings Quad Memorabilia Silver
UNPRICED SILVER PRINT RUN 4-9
UNPRICED GOLD PRINT RUN 1

2010 Sportkings Single Memorabilia Gold
STATED PRINT RUN 10
UNPRICED DUE TO SCARCITY

2010 Sportkings Single Memorabilia Silver
STATED PRINT RUN 26 UNLESS NOTED
SM17 Joe Greene 12.00 25.00
SM20 Raymond Berry 6.00 12.00
SM29 Warren Sapp 6.00 12.00

2010 Sportkings Triple Memorabilia Silver
SILVER PRINT RUN 4-20
UNPRICED GOLD PRINT RUN 1-10
TM5 Warren Sapp 15.00 30.00
Lawrence Taylor
Joe Greene

2010 Sportkings Vintage Memorabilia
UNPRICED PRINT RUN 1

2010 Sportkings Vintage Papercuts
UNPRICED PAPERCUT PRINT RUN 1

2010 Sportkings National Convention VIP Promo
9 Warren Sapp 1.25 3.00
18 Joe Greene 1.50 4.00
22 Bob Lilly 1.25 3.00

2012 Sportkings
229 Gale Sayers 4.00 10.00
230 Franco Harris 4.00 10.00
231 Bob Waterfield 4.00 10.00
232 Roosevelt Brown 4.00 10.00
233 Paul Hornung 5.00 12.00

2012 Sportkings Mini
*MINI: .5X TO 1.2X BASIC CARDS
RANDOM INSERT IN PACKS

2012 Sportkings Premium Back
*SINGLES: .5X TO 1.2X BASIC CARDS
STATED ODDS ONE PER PACK

2012 Sportkings Autograph Memorabilia Silver
ANNOUNCED PRINT RUN 15-50
AMFH1 Franco Harris/40* 25.00 50.00
AMFH2 Franco Harris/40* 25.00 50.00
AMGS1 Gale Sayers/30* 30.00 60.00
AMGS2 Gale Sayers/30* 30.00 60.00

2012 Sportkings Autographs Silver
ANNOUNCED PRINT RUN 15-130
AFH1 Franco Harris/40* 20.00 40.00
AFH2 Franco Harris/40* 20.00 40.00
AGS1 Gale Sayers/30* 25.00 50.00
AGS2 Gale Sayers/30* 25.00 50.00
AGS3 Gale Sayers/30* 25.00 50.00
APHO1 Paul Hornung/40* 20.00 40.00
APHO2 Paul Hornung/40* 20.00 40.00

2012 Sportkings Cityscapes Double Silver
ANNOUNCED PRINT RUN 30
CS4 Franco Harris 10.00 20.00
Dave Parker
CS12 Gale Sayers 20.00 40.00
Ryne Sandberg

2012 Sportkings Cityscapes Double Gold
ANNOUNCED PRINT RUN 10
UNPRICED DUE TO SCARCITY

2012 Sportkings Decades Silver
ANNOUNCED PRINT RUN 40
D1 Franco Harris 20.00 40.00
Bill Walton
Guy Lafleur
Bjorn Borg

2012 Sportkings Decades Gold
ANNOUNCED PRINT RUN 10
UNPRICED DUE TO SCARCITY
D1 Franco Harris
Bill Walton
Guy Lafleur
Bjorn Borg

2012 Sportkings Numerology Gold
ANNOUNCED PRINT RUN 1
UNPRICED DUE TO SCARCITY

2012 Sportkings Numerology Silver
ANNOUNCED PRINT RUN 4
UNPRICED DUE TO SCARCITY
N15 Gale Sayers

2012 Sportkings Papercuts
STATED PRINT RUN 1
UNPRICED DUE TO SCARCITY
PCBW Bob Waterfield
PCRB Roosevelt Brown
PCRW Reggie White

2012 Sportkings Patch Silver
ANNOUNCED PRINT RUN 4
UNPRICED DUE TO SCARCITY
P9 Gale Sayers

2012 Sportkings Patch Gold
ANNOUNCED PRINT RUN 1
UNPRICED DUE TO SCARCITY

2012 Sportkings Single Memorabilia Silver
ANNOUNCED PRINT RUN 90
SM14 Franco Harris 7.50 15.00

2012 Sportkings Single Memorabilia Number Gold
STATED PRINT RUN 1
UNPRICED DUE TO SCARCITY

2012 Sportkings Single Memorabilia Number Silver
ANNOUNCED PRINT RUN 9
UNPRICED DUE TO SCARCITY

2012 Sportkings Single Memorabilia Patch Gold
STATED PRINT RUN 1
UNPRICED DUE TO SCARCITY

2012 Sportkings Single Memorabilia Patch Silver
ANNOUNCED PRINT RUN 9
UNPRICED DUE TO SCARCITY

2012 Sportkings Top 50 Broadcasters Cut Autographs
STATED PRINT RUN 1
UNPRICED DUE TO SCARCITY
TBCJMA John Madden

2012 Sportkings Triple Memorabilia Silver
ANNOUNCED PRINT RUN 30
TM5 David Robinson 15.00 30.00
Kyle Petty
Gale Sayers

1953 Sport Magazine Premiums
This 10-card set features 5 1/2" by 7" color portraits and was issued as a subscription premium by Sport Magazine. These photos were taken by noted sports photographer Ozzie Sweet. Each features a top player from a number of different sports. The photo backs are blank and unnumbered. We've checklisted the set below in alphabetical order.

COMPLETE SET (10) 30.00 60.00
3 Elroy Hirsch FB 7.50 15.00
7 John Olszewski FB 4.00 8.00

1968-73 Sport Pix
These 8" by 10" blank-backed photos feature black and white photos with the players name and the words "Sport Pix" on the bottom. The address for Sport Pix is also on the bottom. Since the cards are not numbered, we have sequenced them in alphabetical order.

COMPLETE SET (22) 150.00 300.00
1 Sammy Baugh 7.50 15.00
2 Jim Brown 10.00 20.00
3 Billy Cannon 5.00 10.00
4 Red Grange 7.50 15.00
6 Paul Hornung 7.50 15.00
7 Sam Huff 6.00 12.00
13 Bobby Mitchell 5.00 10.00
15 Bronko Nagurski 6.00 12.00
Not in football uniform
17 Jim Taylor 6.00 12.00
18 Jim Thorpe 7.50 15.00
19 Y.A. Tittle 6.00 12.00
20 Johnny Unitas 10.00 20.00

1996 Sportscall Phone Cards

This set of phone cards was released in 1996 in pack form with 36 packs to a box and 4-cards per pack. Each card includes a color player photo (with airbrushed helmet logos) surrounded by a black border on the cardfronts. The cardbacks contain instructions on the use of the card which expired in late 1996. The cards measure standard size and have square corners.

COMPLETE SET (400) 30.00 80.00
1 Michael Irvin .40 1.00
2 Cory Fleming .08 .25
3 Daryl Johnston .20 .50
4 Larry Brown .08 .25
5 Emmitt Smith 1.60 4.00
6 Sherman Williams .08 .25
7 Chris Boniol .08 .25
8 Jason Garrett .30 .75
9 Wade Wilson .08 .25
10 Troy Aikman 1.00 2.50
11 Dana Stubblefield .20 .50
12 Rickey Jackson .08 .25
13 John Taylor .08 .25
14 J.J. Stokes .40 1.00
15 Brent Jones .08 .25
16 Jerry Rice 1.00 2.50
17 Ricky Ervins .08 .25
18 William Floyd .20 .50
19 Elvis Grbac .20 .50
20 Steve Young .80 2.00
21 Michael Zordich .08 .25
22 Ricky Watters .20 .50
23 Kelvin Martin .08 .25
24 Randall Cunningham .40 1.00
25 Rodney Peete .08 .25
26 Toi Cook .08 .25
27 Eric Davis .08 .25
28 Tim McDonald .08 .25
29 Merton Hanks .08 .25
30 Ken Norton .08 .25
31 Brett Favre 2.00 5.00
32 George Teague .08 .25
33 Charlie Garner .20 .50
34 Gary Anderson K .08 .25
35 William Fuller .08 .25
36 Calvin Williams .08 .25
37 Fred Barnett .08 .25
38 Antone Davis .08 .25
39 Mike Mamula .08 .25
40 Greg Jackson .08 .25
41 Kevin Butler .08 .25
42 Craig Newsome .08 .25
43 Chris Jacke .08 .25
44 John Jurkovic .08 .25
45 Sean Jones .08 .25
46 Reggie White .40 1.00
47 Robert Brooks .20 .50
48 Mark Ingram .08 .25
49 Edgar Bennett .20 .50
50 Ty Detmer .20 .50
51 Rob Moore .20 .50
52 Dave Krieg .08 .25
53 Robert Green .08 .25
54 Donnell Woolford .08 .25
55 Chris Zorich .08 .25
56 Michael Timpson .08 .25
57 Curtis Conway .20 .50
58 Rashaan Salaam .20 .50
59 Lewis Tillman .08 .25
60 Erik Kramer .08 .25
61 Ken Harvey .08 .25
62 Scott Galbraith .08 .25
63 Michael Westbrook .40 1.00
64 Henry Ellard .08 .25
65 Reggie Brooks .08 .25
66 Brian Mitchell .08 .25
67 Terry Allen .20 .50
68 Gus Frerotte .20 .50
69 Clyde Simmons .08 .25
70 Frank Sanders .40 1.00
71 Pete Metzelaars .08 .25
72 Eric Guliford .08 .25
73 Mark Carrier .08 .25
74 Derrick Moore .08 .25
75 Jack Trudeau .08 .25
76 Frank Reich .08 .25
77 Kerry Collins .40 1.00
78 James Washington .08 .25
79 Stanley Richard .20 .50
80 Darrell Green .08 .25
81 Rodney Holman .08 .25
82 Brett Perriman .08 .25
83 Herman Moore .20 .50
84 Scott Mitchell .20 .50
85 Tyrone Poole .08 .25
86 Carlton Bailey .08 .25
87 Sam Mills .08 .25
88 Lamar Lathon .08 .25
89 Lawyer Tillman .08 .25
90 Don Beebe .08 .25
91 Chris Spielman .08 .25
92 Tracy Scroggins .08 .25
93 Jason Hanson .08 .25
94 Aubrey Matthews .08 .25
95 Darryl Talley .08 .25
96 J.J. Birden .08 .25
97 Craig Heyward .08 .25
98 Eric Metcalf .08 .25
99 Bobby Hebert .08 .25
P1 Troy Aikman Prototype .80 2.00
100 Jeff George .20 .50
101 Ed McCaffrey .20 .50
102 Anthony Miller .20 .50
103 Shannon Sharpe .20 .50
104 Glyn Milburn .08 .25
105 Aaron Craver .08 .25
106 Terrell Davis 2.00 5.00
107 Bill Musgrave .08 .25
108 Hugh Millen .08 .25
109 John Elway 2.00 5.00
110 Bennie Blades .08 .25
111 Keith Byars .08 .25
112 Terry Kirby .20 .50
113 Bernie Parmalee .08 .25
114 Bernie Kosar .08 .25
115 Dan Marino 2.00 5.00
116 Steve Atwater .08 .25
117 Simon Fletcher .08 .25
118 Michael Perry .08 .25
119 Jason Elam .20 .50
120 Mike Pritchard .08 .25
121 Troy Vincent .08 .25
122 Chris Singleton .08 .25
123 Steve Emtman .08 .25
124 Trace Armstrong .08 .25
125 Pete Stoyanovich .08 .25
126 Randal Hill .08 .25
127 Gary Clark .08 .25
128 Eric Green .08 .25
129 O.J. McDuffie .20 .50
130 Irving Fryar .08 .25
131 Ray Childress .08 .25
132 Haywood Jeffires .08 .25
133 Todd McNair .08 .25
134 Gary Brown .08 .25
135 Rodney Thomas .08 .25
136 Will Furrer .08 .25
137 Steve McNair .80 2.00
138 Chris Chandler .20 .50
139 Aubrey Beavers .08 .25
140 Gene Atkins .08 .25
141 Rocket Ismail .08 .25
142 Tim Brown .40 1.00
143 Derrick Fenner .08 .25
144 Napoleon Kaufman .40 1.00
145 Harvey Williams .08 .25
146 Billy Joe Hobert .08 .25
147 Vince Evans .08 .25
148 Jeff Hostetler .08 .25
149 Mel Gray .08 .25
150 Chris Dishman .08 .25
151 Quinn Early .08 .25
152 Derek Brown RB .08 .25
153 Jim Everett .08 .25
154 Albert Lewis .08 .25
155 Jeff Gossett .08 .25
156 Terry McDaniel .08 .25
157 Aundray Bruce .08 .25
158 Chester McGlockton .08 .25
159 Pat Swilling .08 .25
160 James Jett .08 .25
161 Kimble Anders .20 .50
162 Greg Hill .20 .50
163 Steve Bono .08 .25
164 J.J. McCleskey .08 .25
165 Eric Allen .08 .25
166 Renaldo Turnbull .08 .25
167 Wayne Martin .08 .25
168 Torrance Small .08 .25
169 Michael Haynes .08 .25
170 Irv Smith .08 .25
171 Dan Saleaumua .08 .25
172 Neil Smith .20 .50
173 Lin Elliott .08 .25
174 Tamarick Vanover .20 .50
175 Derrick Walker .08 .25
176 Willie Davis .08 .25
177 Webster Slaughter .08 .25
178 Lake Dawson .08 .25
179 Keith Cash .08 .25
180 Leroy Thompson .08 .25
181 Leslie O'Neal .08 .25
182 John Carney .08 .25
183 Alfred Pupunu .08 .25
184 Mark Seay .08 .25
185 Shawn Jefferson .08 .25
186 Tony Martin .20 .50
187 Louie Aguiar .08 .25
188 Marcus Allen .40 1.00
189 Mark Collins .08 .25
190 Dale Carter .08 .25
191 Kelvin Pritchett .08 .25
192 Joel Smeenge .08 .25
193 Mike Hollis .08 .25
194 Desmond Howard .20 .50
195 Ernest Givins .08 .25
196 Reggie Cobb .08 .25
197 James O.Stewart .50 1.25
198 Steve Beuerlein .20 .50
199 Mark Brunell .80 2.00
200 Junior Seau .20 .50
201 Mark Higgs .08 .25
202 Kevin Smith .08 .25
203 John Elliott .08 .25
204 Doug Riesenberg .08 .25
205 Chad Hennings .08 .25
206 Charles Haley .20 .50
207 Tony Tolbert .08 .25
208 Scott Case .08 .25
209 Russell Maryland .08 .25
210 Robert Jones .08 .25
211 Mark Stepnoski .08 .25
212 Richmond Webb .08 .25
213 Broderick Thompson .08 .25
214 Bart Oates .08 .25
215 Jesse Sapolu .08 .25
216 Luther Elliss .08 .25
217 Kent Graham .08 .25
218 Lomas Brown .08 .25
219 Browning Nagle .08 .25
220 Blake Brockermeyer .08 .25
221 Kent Hull .08 .25
222 Todd Steussie .08 .25
223 Chad May .08 .25
224 Robert Young .08 .25
225 Brock Marion .08 .25
226 Darren Woodson .20 .50
227 Tony Boselli .08 .25
228 Derek Brown .08 .25
229 Jeff Novak .08 .25
230 Bruce Matthews .08 .25
231 Alvin Harper .08 .25
232 Jackie Harris .08 .25
233 Lawrence Dawsey .08 .25
234 Hardy Nickerson .08 .25
235 Errict Rhett .20 .50
236 Trent Dilfer .40 1.00
237 Reggie Roby .08 .25
238 Thomas Everett .08 .25
239 Kevin Greene .20 .50
240 Kordell Stewart .50 1.25
241 Corey Miller .08 .25
242 Mike Croel .08 .25
243 Herschel Walker .20 .50
244 Tyrone Wheatley .20 .50
245 Rodney Hampton .20 .50
246 Phillippi Sparks .08 .25
247 Dave Brown .08 .25
248 Derrick Brooks .40 1.00
249 Warren Sapp .08 .25
250 Horace Copeland .08 .25
251 Craig Erickson .08 .25
252 Dave Meggett .08 .25
253 Scott Zolak .08 .25
254 Chris Calloway .08 .25
255 Michael Brooks .08 .25
256 Mike Sherrard .08 .25
257 Howard Cross .08 .25
258 Thomas Lewis .08 .25
259 Bill Bates .08 .25
260 Deion Sanders .60 1.50
261 Kevin Williams .08 .25
262 Jay Novacek .08 .25
263 Derek Loville .08 .25
264 Randy Baldwin .08 .25
265 Ronnie Harmon .08 .25
266 Natrone Means .20 .50
267 Stan Humphries .20 .50
268 Ray Buchanan .08 .25
269 Trev Alberts .08 .25
270 Roosevelt Potts .08 .25
271 Dixon Edwards .08 .25
272 Lorenzo White .08 .25
273 Derek Kennard .08 .25
274 Morten Andersen .08 .25
275 Terance Mathis .20 .50
276 Barry Sanders 2.00 5.00
277 Seth Joyner .08 .25
278 Larry Centers .20 .50
279 Garrison Hearst .20 .50
280 Raymont Harris UER .08 .25
(Raymond on front)
281 Mario Bates .20 .50
282 Darren Smith .08 .25
283 Godfrey Myles .08 .25
284 Clayton Holmes .08 .25
285 Erik Williams .08 .25
286 Leon Lett .08 .25
287 Larry Allen .08 .25
288 Mark Tuinei .08 .25
289 Ron Stone .08 .25
290 Nate Newton .08 .25
291 Sean Landeta .08 .25
292 Mark Carrier DB .08 .25
293 Jim Kelly .40 1.00
294 Todd Collins QB .20 .50
295 Steve Walsh .08 .25
296 Tony Casillas .08 .25
297 Nick Lowery .08 .25
298 Kyle Brady .08 .25
299 Ronald Moore .08 .25
300 Boomer Esiason .20 .50
301 Robert Smith .20 .50
302 Warren Moon .40 1.00
303 Shane Conlan UER .08 .25
(Conlen on front)
304 Todd Lyght .08 .25
305 Sean Gilbert .08 .25
306 Alex Wright .08 .25
307 Isaac Bruce .40 1.00
308 Leonard Russell .08 .25
309 Jerome Bettis .40 1.00
310 Chris Miller .08 .25
311 James Harris DE .08 .25
312 Jack Del Rio .08 .25
313 Esera Tuaolo .08 .25
314 Jeff Brady .08 .25
315 Fuad Reveiz .08 .25
316 David Palmer .08 .25
317 Adrian Cooper .08 .25
318 Andrew Jordan .08 .25
319 Jake Reed .20 .50
320 Amp Lee .08 .25
321 Doug Pelfrey .08 .25
322 Derek Ware .08 .25
323 Darnay Scott .20 .50
324 Tony McGee .08 .25
325 Carl Pickens .20 .50
326 Eric Bieniemy .08 .25
327 Harold Green .08 .25
328 David Klingel .08 .25
329 Jeff Blake .40 1.00
330 Mike Saxon .08 .25
331 Cortez Kennedy .08 .25
332 Ricky Proehl .08 .25
333 Joey Galloway .40 1.00
334 Brian Blades .08 .25
335 Steve Broussard .08 .25
336 Chris Warren .20 .50
337 John Friesz .08 .25
338 Rick Mirer .20 .50
339 Keith Rucker .08 .25
340 Dan Wilkinson .08 .25
341 Yancy Thigpen .20 .50
342 Carnell Lake .08 .25
343 Byron Bam Morris .08 .25
344 Rod Woodson .08 .25
345 John L. Williams .08 .25
346 Deon Figures .08 .25
347 Erric Pegram .08 .25
348 Mike Tomczak .08 .25
349 Neil O'Donnell .20 .50
350 Sam Adams .08 .25
351 Todd Collins .08 .25
352 Jim Kelly .40 1.00
353 Carl Banks .08 .25
354 Derrick Alexander WR .08 .25
355 Michael Jackson .20 .50
356 Andre Rison .08 .25
357 Earnest Byner .08 .25
358 Eric Zeier .08 .25
359 Vinny Testaverde .20 .50
360 Greg Lloyd .20 .50
361 Mark Pike .08 .25
362 Cornelius Bennett .08 .25
363 Bruce Smith .20 .50
364 Steve Christie .08 .25
365 Steve Tasker .08 .25
366 Andre Reed .08 .25
367 Russell Copeland .08 .25
368 Bill Brooks .08 .25
369 Carwell Gardner .08 .25
370 Alex Van Pelt .40 1.00
371 Ben Coates .20 .50
372 Curtis Martin .60 1.50
373 Drew Bledsoe .80 2.00
374 Jeff Herrod .08 .25
375 Freddie Joe Nunn .08 .25
376 Sean Dawkins .08 .25
377 Tony Bennett .08 .25
378 Quentin Coryatt .08 .25
379 Marshall Faulk .40 1.00
380 Jim Harbaugh .20 .50
381 Myron Guyton UER .08 .25
(Guxton on front)
382 Darren Carrington .08 .25
383 Irv Eatman .08 .25
384 Blaine Bishop .08 .25
385 Rickey Sanders .08 .25
386 Tim Bowens .08 .25
387 Vincent Brown .08 .25
388 Willie McGinest .08 .25
389 Matt Bahr .08 .25
390 Vincent Brisby .08 .25
391 Darren Smith .08 .25
392 John Copeland .08 .25
393 Bryce Paup .08 .25
394 Phil Hansen .08 .25
395 Romon Phifer .08 .25
396 J.T. Thomas .08 .25
397 Jeff Criswell .08 .25
398 Mo Lewis .08 .25
399 Anthony Smith .08 .25
400 Steve Wisniewski .08 .25

1977-79 Sportscaster Series 1
COMPLETE SET (24) 17.50 35.00
115 Johnny Unitas FB 2.00 4.00
120 Jets vs. Colts .75 1.50
Football

1977-79 Sportscaster Series 2
COMPLETE SET (24) 30.00 60.00
204 George Blanda FB 1.00 2.00

1977-79 Sportscaster Series 3
COMPLETE SET (24) 15.00 30.00
307 O.J. Simpson FB 1.50 4.00
320 Joe Namath FB 2.50 6.00

1977-79 Sportscaster Series 5
COMPLETE SET (24) 12.50 25.00
523 Gale Sayers FB 2.00 4.00

1977-79 Sportscaster Series 6
COMPLETE SET (24) 12.50 25.00
613 Red Grange FB 2.00 4.00
618 Jim Brown FB 2.50 5.00

1977-79 Sportscaster Series 7
COMPLETE SET (24) 15.00 30.00
715 The 1967 Green Bay .75 2.00
Packers
Football

1977-79 Sportscaster Series 8
COMPLETE SET (24) 12.50 25.00
806 Fran Tarkenton FB 1.25 2.50

1977-79 Sportscaster Series 9
COMPLETE SET (24) 15.00 30.00
922 The Rose Bowl .75 1.50
Football

1977-79 Sportscaster Series 10
COMPLETE SET (24) 17.50 35.00
1024 Tony Dorsett FB 2.00 4.00

1977-79 Sportscaster Series 11
COMPLETE SET (25) 20.00 40.00
1113 Larry Csonka 1.50 3.00
Jim Kiick FB

1977-79 Sportscaster Series 12
COMPLETE SET (24) 12.50 25.00
1206 A Very Warlike Game .75 1.50
Football Action
Football
1209 Joe Greene 2.00 4.00
Steelers
Vikings
Football

1977-79 Sportscaster Series 13
COMPLETE SET (24) 12.50 25.00
1306 Archie Griffin FB 1.00 2.50
1321 Miami Dolphins vs. 1.00 2.00
Kansas City
Garo Yepremian
Football

1977-79 Sportscaster Series 16
COMPLETE SET (24) 15.00 30.00
1612 Paul Hornung 1.50 3.00
Packers
Browns
Football

1977-79 Sportscaster Series 17
COMPLETE SET (24) 10.00 20.00
1701 Jim Taylor FB 1.25 2.50
1715 Ken Stabler FB 2.00 4.00

1977-79 Sportscaster Series 20
COMPLETE SET (24) 7.50 15.00
2020 Ken Anderson FB 1.25 2.50

1977-79 Sportscaster Series 21
COMPLETE SET (24) 15.00 30.00
2118 College AS Game 1.00 2.00
All-Stars vs. Steelers
Football

1977-79 Sportscaster Series 22
COMPLETE SET (24) 15.00 30.00
2216 Lingo 1.50 4.00
(Fran Tarkenton being chased, by Chris Hanburger)

1977-79 Sportscaster Series 23
COMPLETE SET (24) 20.00 40.00
2311 Super Bowl Show .75 1.50
Football

1977-79 Sportscaster Series 24
COMPLETE SET (24) 10.00 20.00
2405 Bert Jones .75 1.50
Football

1977-79 Sportscaster Series 25
COMPLETE SET (24) 10.00 20.00
2523 Charley Taylor FB .75 1.50

1977-79 Sportscaster Series 26
COMPLETE SET (24) 15.00 30.00
2611 Presidents In 5.00 10.00
Sport
Gerald Ford
Beyond Sports
2614 Walter Payton FB 4.00 8.00

1977-79 Sportscaster Series 27
COMPLETE SET (24) 12.50 25.00
2706 Packers vs. Bears .50 1.00
(Wally Chambers)
Football

1977-79 Sportscaster Series 29
COMPLETE SET (24) 17.50 35.00
2907 Defensive Formations 3.00 6.00
Harry Carson
Roger Staubach
Football
2916 NFL History .75 1.50
Packers
Browns
Football

1977-79 Sportscaster Series 31
COMPLETE SET (24) 12.50 25.00
3102 Trick Plays .75 1.50
Russ Francis
Football

1977-79 Sportscaster Series 32
COMPLETE SET (24) 17.50 35.00
3203 Offensive .75 1.50
Alignments
UCLA In Action
Football

1977-79 Sportscaster Series 33
COMPLETE SET (24) 10.00 20.00
3301 Holding .75 1.50
Patriots
Raiders
Football
3314 Chuck Foreman FB .75 1.50
3322 Gene Upshaw 1.00 2.00
Raiders vs Colts
Football

1977-79 Sportscaster Series 34
COMPLETE SET (24) 15.00 30.00
3418 Preston Pearson FB .75 2.00

1977-79 Sportscaster Series 35
COMPLETE SET (24) 15.00 30.00
3518 Jim Bakken FB .50 1.00

1977-79 Sportscaster Series 36
COMPLETE SET (26) 15.00 30.00
3617 Goal Line Defense .75 1.50
Bills vs Colts
Football
3620 Two-Minute Offense 1.50 3.00
Ken Stabler
Football

1977-79 Sportscaster Series 37
Please note that cards number 4 and 17 are not listed. Any information on the two missing cards is very appreciated.

COMPLETE SET (24) 12.50 25.00
3715 Legal and Illegal .25 .50
Blocks: Blocking Action
Football
3717 Lynn Swann 2.00 5.00
Football

1977-79 Sportscaster Series 38
COMPLETE SET (24) 20.00 40.00
3822 Jack Youngblood FB 1.00 2.00

1977-79 Sportscaster Series 39
COMPLETE SET (24) 7.50 15.00
3917 Ball Control .75 1.50
Packers vs Chiefs
Football
3921 Grab Face Mask .75 1.50
Colts vs Bills
Football
3922 Harvey Martin FB 1.00 2.00

1977-79 Sportscaster Series 40
COMPLETE SET (24) 10.00 20.00
4004 Pass Interference .75 1.50
Bob Chandler
Football
4010 Rick Upchurch FB .50 1.00

1977-79 Sportscaster Series 42
COMPLETE SET (24) 15.00 30.00
4213 Curley Culp FB .50 1.00
4224 Cheerleading .75 1.50
USC Cheerleaders
Football

1977-79 Sportscaster Series 43
COMPLETE SET (24) 12.50 25.00
4312 Holding the Ball .75 1.50
For Placement
Roger Wehrli
Jim Bakken
Football

1977-79 Sportscaster Series 44
COMPLETE SET (24) 12.50 25.00
4422 Punting 1.25 2.50
Ray Guy
Football
4424 Special Team .50 1.00
Defense
Kick Return
Football

1977-79 Sportscaster Series 45
Card number 11 is not in our checklist. Any information on this missing card is greatly appreciated.

COMPLETE SET (24) 20.00 40.00
4504 Throwing the Ball 1.50 3.00
Bob Griese
Football
4509 Punt Returns 1.00 2.00
Lem Barney
Football

1977-79 Sportscaster Series 46
COMPLETE SET (24) 12.50 25.00
4601 NFL Draft 1.25 2.50
Bubba Smith
Football
4613 Kickoff Returns 2.00 4.00
Gale Sayers
Football

1977-79 Sportscaster Series 47
COMPLETE SET (24) 17.50 35.00
4721 Tom Jackson 2.00 4.00
O.J.Simpson
Football

1977-79 Sportscaster Series 50
COMPLETE SET (24) 15.00 30.00
5001 Equipment .75 1.50
S.D. Chargers
Football
5020 Ernie Nevers FB 1.00 2.00

1977-79 Sportscaster Series 53
COMPLETE SET (24) 15.00 30.00
5310 The Sidelines .75 1.50
S.D. Chargers
Football
5317 Great Moments 1.50 4.00
Joe Namath
Football

1977-79 Sportscaster Series 54
COMPLETE SET (24) 15.00 30.00
5414 Joe Kapp 1.00 2.00
Vikings
Colts
Football
5420 Jim Thorpe FB 4.00 8.00

1977-79 Sportscaster Series 55
COMPLETE SET (24) 12.50 25.00
5501 Dave Casper FB 1.00 2.00

1977-79 Sportscaster Series 56
COMPLETE SET (24) 37.50 75.00
5615 Ray Guy FB 2.50 5.00
5618 Great Moments 7.50 15.00
Joe Namath
Football

1977-79 Sportscaster Series 57
COMPLETE SET (24) 40.00 80.00
5701 Willie Lanier FB 2.50 5.00

1977-79 Sportscaster Series 59
COMPLETE SET (24) 50.00 100.00
5902 Roger Staubach 5.00 10.00
Cowboys
Giants
Football

1977-79 Sportscaster Series 60
COMPLETE SET (24) 37.50 75.00
6004 Whizzer White 4.00 8.00
Beyond Sports

1977-79 Sportscaster Series 61
COMPLETE SET (24) 50.00 100.00
6120 Heisman Trophy 5.00 10.00
Earl Campbell
Football

1977-79 Sportscaster Series 62
COMPLETE SET (24) 40.00 80.00
6214 Eddie Lee Ivery FB 2.00 4.00

1977-79 Sportscaster Series 63
COMPLETE SET (24) 30.00 60.00
6302 17-0 Dolphins 5.00 10.00
Bob Griese
Larry Csonka
Football
6316 Outland Award 1.00 2.00
Brad Shearer
Football

1977-79 Sportscaster Series 64
COMPLETE SET (24) 25.00 50.00
6411 Harvard Stadium 2.00 4.00
Football
6419 Floyd Little FB 2.50 5.00

1977-79 Sportscaster Series 65
COMPLETE SET (24) 40.00 80.00
6524 Franco Harris FB 3.00 8.00

1977-79 Sportscaster Series 66
COMPLETE SET (24) 37.50 75.00
6607 The Four Horsemen 7.50 15.00
Horsemen
Knute Rockne
Football

1977-79 Sportscaster Series 67
COMPLETE SET (24) 40.00 80.00
6705 The Bahr Family 2.50 5.00
Chris, Matt and Dad
Soccer-Football

1977-79 Sportscaster Series 68
COMPLETE SET (24) 40.00 80.00
6806 Incredible Playoff 2.00 4.00
Bill Osmanski
Football
6820 John Cappelletti 2.50 5.00
Rams
Falcons
Football

1977-79 Sportscaster Series 69
COMPLETE SET (24) 40.00 80.00
6902 Terry Bradshaw FB 5.00 10.00
6912 First Televised 1.00 2.00
Football Games
Skip Walz
Beyond Sports
6915 Indian HOF 4.00 8.00
Sonny Sixkiller
Beyond Sports

1977-79 Sportscaster Series 70
COMPLETE SET (24) 30.00 60.00
7010 Pro Bowl 2.50 5.00
Jan Stenerud
Football

1977-79 Sportscaster Series 71
COMPLETE SET (24) 40.00 80.00
7101 Dave Jennings FB 2.00 4.00
7123 Chuck Noll 6.00 12.00
Terry Bradshaw FB

1977-79 Sportscaster Series 72
COMPLETE SET (24) 50.00 100.00
7217 Joe Paterno 10.00 20.00
Jeff Hostetler
Football
7221 Greg Pruitt 2.50 5.00
Beyond Sports

1977-79 Sportscaster Series 73
COMPLETE SET (24) 40.00 80.00
7306 Bear Bryant FB 10.00 20.00

1977-79 Sportscaster Series 75
COMPLETE SET (24) 30.00 60.00
7502 Nick Buoniconti 2.50 5.00
Football

1977-79 Sportscaster Series 76
COMPLETE SET (24) 30.00 60.00
7605 NFL Hall of Fame 2.00 4.00
Canton, Ohio HOF
Football
7624 Walter Camp All- 2.00 4.00
America Team
Walter Camp
Football

1977-79 Sportscaster Series 78
COMPLETE SET (24) 150.00 300.00
7809 Tom Landry FB 7.50 15.00
7820 Rating Passers 5.00 10.00
Dan Fouts
Football

1977-79 Sportscaster Series 79
COMPLETE SET (24) 60.00 120.00
7922 College Football 10.00 20.00
Hall of Fame
Ronald Reagan
Football

1977-79 Sportscaster Series 80
COMPLETE SET (24) 62.50 125.00
8019 Jim Marshall 4.00 8.00
Larry Csonka FB

1977-79 Sportscaster Series 81
COMPLETE SET (24) 62.50 125.00
8118 Dan Pastorini FB 3.00 6.00
8122 Billy Sims FB 4.00 8.00

1977-79 Sportscaster Series 82
COMPLETE SET (24) 50.00 100.00
8203 Jerome Holland 2.00 4.00
Brud Holland
Joe Holland
Beyond Sports
8221 Tom Cousineau FB 2.50 5.00

1977-79 Sportscaster Series 83
COMPLETE SET (24) 62.50 125.00
8310 Ed Too Tall Jones 4.00 8.00
At Football
Boxing

1977-79 Sportscaster Series 85
COMPLETE SET (24) 62.50 125.00
8502 Barefoot Athletes 3.00 6.00
Tony Franklin
Football
8510 Protecting the 3.00 6.00
Quarterback
Craig Morton
Football
8520 Lou Holtz FB 10.00 20.00

1977-79 Sportscaster Series 86
COMPLETE SET (24) 50.00 100.00
8601 Grambling 3.00 6.00
Doug Williams
Football

1977-79 Sportscaster Series 88
COMPLETE SET (24) 50.00 100.00
8811 Ernie Davis FB 7.50 15.00

1977-79 Sportscaster Series 101
COMPLETE SET (24) 62.50 125.00
10117 Pat Haden 2.00 5.00
Beyond Sports, Football

1977-79 Sportscaster Series 102
COMPLETE SET (24) 75.00 150.00
10220 NCAA Records 4.00 8.00
Steve Owens
Football

1977-79 Sportscaster Series 103
COMPLETE SET (24) 87.50 175.00
10301 Jim Turner FB 4.00 8.00
10316 Longest Runs 4.00 8.00
Jack Tatum
Football

1978 Sports Challenge
2 Roman Gabriel 2.00 4.00
6 Jim O'Brien 1.50 3.00

1987 Sports Cube Game
3 1/2" by 5 3/8" cards with nine black and white portrait shots on front and questions on the back

COMPLETE SET (3) 8.00 20.00
1 James Naismith 6.00 15.00
Babe Ruth
America's Cup
Knute Rockne
Vince Lombardi
Herb Brooks
Jack Johnson
Bobby Jones
Jim Thorpe
3 Joe Louis 3.20 8.00
Bill Klem
Ken Anderson
Thurman Munson
Earl Averill
Elston Howard
Arky Vaughan
Miller Huggins
Eddie Cicotte

1977 Sports Illustrated Ad Cards
This set is a multi-sport set and features cards with action player photos from various sports as they appeared on different covers of Sports Illustrated Magazine. The cards measure approximately 3 1/2" by 4 3/4" with the backs displaying the player's name and team name and information on how to subscribe to the magazine at a special rate. It was issued by Mrs. Carter Breads.

COMPLETE SET 12.50 25.00
4 Oakland Raiders 2.50 5.00
5 Michigan Wolverines FB 2.50 5.00

1999 Sports Illustrated

The 1999 Sports Illustrated set was issued in one series totalling 150 cards and was distributed in seven-card packs with a suggested retail price of $15. The fronts feature color action player photos printed on 20 pt. card stock. The backs carry another player photo with biographical information and career statistics. The set includes the following two subsets: Super Bowl MVPs (1-30) and Fresh Faces (126-150).

COMPLETE SET (150) 30.00 60.00
1 Bart Starr MVP .75 2.00
2 Bart Starr MVP .75 2.00
3 Joe Namath MVP .60 1.50
4 Len Dawson MVP .30 .75
5 Chuck Howley MVP .20 .50
6 Roger Staubach MVP .60 1.50
7 Jake Scott MVP .20 .50
8 Larry Csonka MVP .30 .75
9 Franco Harris MVP .30 .75
10 Fred Biletnikoff MVP .30 .75
11 Harvey Martin MVP .25 .60
Randy White MVP
12 Terry Bradshaw MVP .75 2.00
13 Terry Bradshaw MVP .75 2.00
14 Jim Plunkett MVP .25 .60
15 Joe Montana MVP 1.00 2.50
16 Marcus Allen MVP .30 .75
17 Joe Montana MVP 1.00 2.50
18 Richard Dent MVP .20 .50
19 Phil Simms MVP .30 .75
20 Doug Williams MVP .25 .60
21 Jerry Rice MVP .60 1.50
22 Joe Montana MVP 1.00 2.50
23 Ottis Anderson MVP .20 .50
24 Mark Rypien MVP .20 .50
25 Troy Aikman MVP .50 1.25
26 Emmitt Smith MVP .75 2.00
27 Steve Young MVP .40 1.00
28 Larry Brown MVP .20 .50
29 Desmond Howard MVP .25 .60
30 Terrell Davis MVP .30 .75
31 Y.A. Tittle .25 .60
32 Paul Hornung .30 .75
33 Gale Sayers .50 1.25
34 Garo Yepremian .20 .50
35 Bert Jones .20 .50
36 Joe Washington .20 .50
37 Joe Theismann .30 .75
38 Roger Craig .25 .60
39 Mike Singletary .30 .75
40 Bobby Bell .20 .50
41 Ken Houston .20 .50
42 Lenny Moore .25 .60
43 Mark Moseley .20 .50
44 Chuck Bednarik .25 .60
45 Ted Hendricks .20 .50
46 Steve Largent .30 .75
47 Bob Lilly .25 .60
48 Don Maynard .25 .60
49 John Mackey .20 .50
50 Anthony Munoz .25 .60
51 Bobby Mitchell .25 .60
52 Jim Brown .50 1.25
53 Otto Graham .25 .60
54 Earl Morrall .20 .50
55 Danny White .25 .60
56 Karim Abdul-Jabbar .25 .60
57 Charlie Garner .25 .60
58 Jeff Blake .25 .60
59 Reggie White .30 .75
60 Derrick Thomas .30 .75
61 Duce Staley .25 .60
62 Tim Brown .30 .75
63 Elvis Grbac .20 .50
64 Tony Banks .25 .60
65 Rob Johnson .25 .60
66 Danny Kanell .20 .50
67 Marshall Faulk .30 .75
68 Warrick Dunn .25 .60
69 Dan Marino 1.00 2.50
70 Jimmy Smith .25 .60
71 John Elway 1.00 2.50
72 Charles Way .20 .50
73 Ricky Watters .25 .60
74 Terry Glenn .25 .60
75 Bobby Hoying .20 .50
76 Curtis Martin .30 .75
77 Trent Dilfer .25 .60
78 Emmitt Smith .75 2.00
79 Irving Fryar .25 .60
80 Troy Aikman .50 1.25
81 Barry Sanders .75 2.00
82 Brett Favre 1.00 2.50
83 Robert Smith .25 .60
84 Dorsey Levens .25 .60
85 Cris Carter .30 .75
86 Jeff George .20 .50
87 Jerome Bettis .30 .75
88 Warren Moon .30 .75
89 Steve Young .40 1.00
90 Fred Lane .20 .50
91 Jerry Rice .60 1.50
92 Natrone Means .25 .60
93 Mike Alstott .30 .75
94 Kordell Stewart .25 .60
95 Jake Plummer .25 .60
96 Jamal Anderson .25 .60
97 Corey Dillon .25 .60
98 Deion Sanders .30 .75
99 Mark Brunell .25 .60
100 Garrison Hearst .25 .60
101 Andre Rison .25 .60
102 Antowain Smith .20 .50
103 Drew Bledsoe .30 .75
104 Eddie George .25 .60
105 Keyshawn Johnson .25 .60
106 Isaac Bruce .30 .75
107 Rob Moore .20 .50
108 Steve McNair .30 .75
109 Terrell Davis .30 .75
110 Carl Pickens .25 .60
111 Wayne Chrebet .25 .60
112 Kerry Collins .25 .60
113 Eric Metcalf .20 .50
114 Joey Galloway .25 .60
115 Shannon Sharpe .30 .75
116 Robert Brooks .25 .60
117 Glenn Foley .20 .50
118 Yancey Thigpen .20 .50
119 Frank Sanders .20 .50
120 Herman Moore .25 .60
121 Antonio Freeman .25 .60
122 Michael Irvin .30 .75
123 Brad Johnson .25 .60
124 James Stewart .20 .50
125 Jim Harbaugh .25 .60
126 Peyton Manning FF 2.50 6.00
127 Ryan Leaf FF .30 .75
128 Curtis Enis FF .25 .60
129 Fred Taylor FF .30 .75
130 Randy Moss FF .75 2.00
131 John Avery FF .25 .60
132 Charles Woodson FF .40 1.00
133 Robert Edwards FF .25 .60
134 Charlie Batch FF .30 .75
135 Brian Griese FF .30 .75
136 Skip Hicks FF .25 .60
137 Jacquez Green FF .25 .60
138 Robert Holcombe FF .25 .60
139 Kevin Dyson FF .25 .60
140 Rodney Williams FF .25 .60
141 Ahman Green FF .30 .75
142 Tavian Banks FF .25 .60
143 Donald Hayes FF .25 .60
144 Tony Simmons FF .25 .60
145 Pat Johnson FF .25 .60
146 Marcus Nash FF .25 .60
147 Germane Crowell FF .25 .60
148 R.W. McQuarters FF .25 .60
149 Jonathan Quinn FF .25 .60
150 Andre Wadsworth FF .25 .60
P35 Gale Sayers Promo 1.25 3.00

1999 Sports Illustrated Autographs

ONE PER PACK
1 Ottis Anderson 6.00 15.00
2 Chuck Bednarik 8.00 20.00
3 Bobby Bell 8.00 20.00
4 Terry Bradshaw 125.00 250.00
5 Jim Brown 50.00 100.00
6 Roger Craig 8.00 20.00
7 Len Dawson 60.00 120.00
8 Otto Graham 20.00 50.00
9 Franco Harris 40.00 100.00
10 Ted Hendricks 6.00 15.00
11 Paul Hornung SP 100.00 200.00
12 Ken Houston 6.00 15.00
13 Bert Jones 6.00 15.00
14 Steve Largent 12.50 30.00
15 Bob Lilly 8.00 20.00
16 John Mackey 8.00 20.00
17 Don Maynard 8.00 20.00
18 Bobby Mitchell 8.00 20.00
19 Joe Montana 125.00 250.00
20 Lenny Moore 10.00 25.00
21 Earl Morrall 6.00 15.00
22 Mark Moseley 6.00 15.00
23 Anthony Munoz 8.00 20.00
24 Joe Namath 125.00 250.00
25 Jim Plunkett 8.00 20.00
26 Gale Sayers 20.00 40.00
27 Mike Singletary 30.00 60.00
28 Bart Starr 125.00 250.00
29 Roger Staubach 150.00 250.00
30 Joe Theismann 20.00 50.00
31 Y.A. Tittle 50.00 100.00
32 Joe Washington 6.00 15.00
33 Danny White 10.00 25.00
34 Doug Williams 12.00 30.00
35 Garo Yepremian 6.00 15.00

1999 Sports Illustrated Canton Calling
COMPLETE SET (8) 30.00 60.00
STATED ODDS 1:12 HOBBY
*GOLDS: 1.5X TO 4X BASIC INSERTS
GOLD STATED ODDS 1:120
1 Warren Moon 1.50 4.00
2 Emmitt Smith 5.00 12.00
3 Jerry Rice 3.00 8.00
4 Brett Favre 6.00 15.00
5 Barry Sanders 5.00 12.00
6 Dan Marino 6.00 15.00
7 John Elway 6.00 15.00
8 Troy Aikman 3.00 8.00

1999 Sports Illustrated Covers
COMPLETE SET (60) 10.00 25.00
ONE PER PACK
1 Jim Brown .30 .75
2 Y.A. Tittle .20 .50
3 Dallas Cowboys .10 .30
4 Joe Namath .30 .75
5 Bart Starr .30 .75
6 Earl Morrall .10 .30
7 Minnesota Vikings .10 .30
8 Kansas City Chiefs .10 .30
9 Len Dawson .20 .50
10 Monday Night Football .10 .30
11 Jim Plunkett .20 .50
12 Garo Yepremian .10 .30
13 Larry Csonka .20 .50
14 Terry Bradshaw .30 .75
15 Franco Harris .20 .50
16 Bert Jones .10 .30
17 Harvey Martin .10 .30
Randy White
18 Roger Staubach .30 .75
19 Marcus Allen .30 .75
20 Joe Washington .10 .30
21 Dan Marino 1.25 3.00
22 Joe Theismann .20 .50
23 Roger Craig .20 .50
24 Mike Singletary .20 .50
25 Chicago Bears .10 .30
Dan Hampton
26 Phil Simms .20 .50
27 Vinny Testaverde .20 .50
28 Doug Williams .10 .30
29 Jerry Rice .60 1.50
30 Herschel Walker .20 .50
31 Joe Montana .60 1.50
32 Ottis Anderson .10 .30
33 Rocket Ismail .20 .50
34 Bruce Smith .20 .50
35 Thurman Thomas .20 .50
36 Mark Rypien .10 .30
37 Jim Harbaugh .20 .50
38 Randall Cunningham .30 .75
39 Troy Aikman .60 1.50
40 Reggie White .30 .75
41 Junior Seau .30 .75
42 Emmitt Smith 1.00 2.50
43 Natrone Means .20 .50
44 Ricky Watters .20 .50
45 Pittsburgh Steelers .10 .30
46 Steve Young .40 1.00
Troy Aikman
47 Steve Young .40 1.00
48 Deion Sanders .30 .75
49 Elvis Grbac .20 .50
50 Packers vs. Chiefs .10 .30
Brett Favre
Reggie White
Robert Brooks
Marcus Allen
Neil Smith
Steve Bono
51 Brett Favre 1.25 3.00
52 Mark Brunell .30 .75
Kerry Collins
53 Antonio Freeman .30 .75
54 Desmond Howard .20 .50
55 AFC Central QB's .20 .50
56 Warrick Dunn .30 .75
57 Jerome Bettis .30 .75
58 John Elway 1.25 3.00
59 Brent Jones .10 .30
60 Terrell Davis .30 .75

1989 Sports Illustrated for Kids I
Since its debut issue in January 1989, SI for Kids has included a perforated sheet of nine standard-size cards bound into each magazine. The cards were consecutively numbered 1-324 through December 1991. The athletes featured represent an extremely wide spectrum of sports. Each card features color photos with variously colored borders. The borders are as follows: aqua (1-108), green (109-207), woodgrain (208-216), red (217-315), marble (316-324). The player's name is printed in a white bar at the top, while his or her sport appears at the bottom. The backs carry biographical information, career highlights, and a trivia question with answer. The cards' magazine issue date appears on the back in very small type. Although originally distributed in sheet form, the cards are frequently traded as singles. Thus, they are priced individually. The value of an intact sheet is equal to the sum of the nine cards plus a premium of up to 20%.

3 Howie Long FB .40 1.00
7 Doug Williams FB .40 1.00
17 Herschel Walker FB .40 1.00
59 Jerry Rice FB 2.50 6.00
65 Al Toon FB .40 1.00
76 Boomer Esiason FB .40 1.00
78 Mike Singletary FB .40 1.00
84 Dan Marino FB 4.00 10.00
86 Eric Dickerson FB .40 1.00
94 Reggie Roby FB .40 1.00
98 Bobby Hebert FB .40 1.00
103 John Elway FB 4.00 10.00
105 Mike Rozier FB .40 1.00

1990 Sports Illustrated for Kids I
110 Randall Cunningham FB .30 .75
168 Joe Montana FB 4.00 10.00
180 Bobby Humphrey FB .10 .30
185 Ronnie Lott FB .30 .75
194 Bernie Kosar FB .20 .50
198 Bo Jackson FB .30 .75
202 Barry Sanders FB 3.00 8.00
206 Flipper Anderson FB .10 .30

1991 Sports Illustrated for Kids I
218 Don Majkowski FB .10 .30
225 Lawrence Taylor FB .40 1.00
232 Warren Moon FB .30 .75
234 Karl Mecklenburg FB .10 .30
277 Ottis Anderson FB .15 .40
284 Thurman Thomas FB 1.00 2.50
291 Derrick Thomas FB .30 .75
295 Emmitt Smith FB 3.00 8.00
298 Art Monk FB .20 .50
306 Mark Carrier FB .10 .30
311 Keith Jackson FB .10 .30
315 Morten Andersen FB .10 .30
320 Jim Thorpe .60 1.50
Track and Field
Football

Baseball
322 Red Grange FB .60 1.50

1992 Sports Illustrated for Kids II
Since its debut issue in January 1989, SI for Kids has included a perforated sheet of nine standard-size cards bound into each magazine. In January 1992, the card numbers started over again at 1. This listing comprises the cards contained from that magazine through the last 2000 issue. The athletes featured represent an extremely wide spectrum of sports. Each card features color photos with borders of various designs and colors. The borders are as follows: navy (1-9, 19-99), clouds (10-18, 55-63, 226-234), marble (100-108, 208-216, 316-324), pink (109-207), purple (217-225), blue (235-315), gold/silver (325-486), clouds (487-495) and gold/silver (496-621). The athlete's name is printed at the top while his or her sport appears at the bottom. The backs carry biographical information, career highlights, and a trivia question with answer. The cards' magazine issue date appears on the back in very small type. Although originally distributed in sheet form, the cards are frequently traded as singles. Thus, they are priced individually. The value of an intact sheet is equal to the sum of the nine cards plus a premium of up to 20 percent. The cards labeled as "MC" were issued in SI for Kids as part of a milk promotion.

3 Jim Kelly FB .40 1.00
5 Christian Okoye FB .10 .30
23 Mark Rypien FB .10 .30
69 Deion Sanders FB 1.00 2.50
74 Troy Aikman FB 2.50 6.00
76 Marcus Allen FB .40 1.00
82 Leonard Russell FB .10 .30
89 Anthony Carter FB .10 .30
94 Haywood Jeffires FB .10 .30
99 Bruce Smith FB .20 .50
106 Jim Brown FB 1.00 2.50

1993 Sports Illustrated for Kids II
113 Dan Marino FB 4.00 10.00
115 Anthony Munoz FB .20 .50
119 Steve Young FB 2.00 5.00
123 Andre Rison FB .20 .50
133 Rod Woodson FB .20 .50
138 Junior Seau FB .30 .75
180 Sterling Sharpe FB .20 .50
183 Nick Lowery FB .10 .30
188 Randall Cunningham FB .30 .75
192 Cortez Kennedy FB .10 .30
194 Barry Foster FB .10 .30
203 Brett Favre FB 3.00 8.00
205 Clyde Simmons .10 .30
Football
210 Johnny Unitas FB 1.25 3.00

1994 Sports Illustrated for Kids II
240 Phil Simms FB .20 .50
248 Tim Brown FB .30 .75
256 Emmitt Smith FB 2.00 5.00
263 Ricky Watters FB .20 .50
272 Jerome Bettis FB .40 1.00
283 Reggie White FB .30 .75
291 Drew Bledsoe FB .75 2.00
296 John Taylor FB .20 .50
302 Joe Montana FB 4.00 10.00
304 Renaldo Turnbull FB .10 .30
310 Eric Metcalf FB .20 .50
315 Seth Joyner FB .10 .30
321 Walter Payton FB 1.00 2.50

1996 Sports Illustrated for Kids II
437 John Elway FB 2.00 5.00
441 Terance Mathis FB .20 .50
445 Deion Sanders FB .60 1.50
450 Brett Favre FB 2.00 5.00
454 Barry Sanders FB .75 2.00
kid photo
459 Troy Aikman FB .40 1.00
kid photo
467 Kordell Stewart FB .40 1.00
476 Jim Harbaugh FB .20 .50
483 Darrell Green FB .20 .50
501 Herman Moore FB .20 .50
502 Danny Wuerffel FB .20 .50
510 Bryce Paup FB .10 .30
511 Ricky Watters FB .20 .50
517 Willie Roaf FB .10 .30
521 Jeff George FB .20 .50
526 Neil O'Donnell FB .10 .30
531 Darren Bennett FB .10 .30
532 Curtis Martin FB .40 1.00
538 Doug Flutie FB .60 1.50

1997 Sports Illustrated for Kids II
548 Brian Mitchell FB .10 .30
554 Terrell Davis FB 1.50 4.00
558 Stan Humphries FB .10 .30
592 Jerome Bettis FB .40 1.00
604 Drew Bledsoe FB .50 1.25
610 Mark Chmura FB .20 .50
615 Simeon Rice FB .20 .50
620 Mark Brunell FB .40 1.00
625 Troy Aikman FB .60 1.50
cartoon
632 Jerry Rice FB .60 1.50
636 Vinny Testaverde FB .20 .50
640 Rod Woodson FB .20 .50
644 Dan Marino FB 1.25 3.00

1998 Sports Illustrated for Kids II
649 Tim Brown FB .30 .75
671 Barry Sanders FB 2.00 5.00
687 Rob Moore FB .10 .30
694 Brett Favre FB 1.25 3.00
704 Warrick Dunn FB .40 1.00
719 Jason Sehorn FB .10 .30
723 Eddie George FB .40 1.00
724 Bruce Smith FB .20 .50
733 Barry Sanders FB 1.25 3.00
740 Cris Carter FB .30 .75
747 Mike Alstott FB .20 .50
750 Dana Stubblefield FB .10 .30
752 Steve Young FB .50 1.25

1999 Sports Illustrated for Kids II
757 Ricky Watters FB .10 .30
761 Deion Sanders FB .40 1.00
766 Randall Cunningham FB .30 .75
774 Kevin Greene FB .10 .30
788 John Elway FB 1.25 3.00
791 Jerry Rice FB .60 1.50
797 Emmitt Smith FB .75 2.00
806 Jamal Anderson FB .20 .50
812 Randy Moss FB 2.00 5.00
822 O.J. McDuffie FB .10 .30
824 Terrell Davis FB .75 2.00
829 Vinny Testaverde FB .20 .50
834 Gary Anderson FB .10 .30
843 Brett Favre FB 1.25 3.00
844 Shannon Sharpe FB .20 .50
848 Antonio Freeman FB .30 .75
855 Ray Lewis FB .30 .75
858 Jake Plummer FB .40 1.00
862 Ty Law FB .10 .30

2000 Sports Illustrated for Kids II
867 Jim Thorpe .40 1.00
Football
874 Peyton Manning FB 2.00 5.00
887 Kurt Warner FB 1.00 2.50
902 Jimmy Smith FB .20 .50
915 Edgerrin James FB .75 2.00
917 Kevin Carter FB .10 .30
932 Steve Beuerlein FB .20 .50
938 Marvin Harrison FB .30 .75
943 Jevon Kearse FB .20 .50
947 Randy Moss FB 1.25 3.00
949 Tim Dwight FB .20 .50
959 Stephen Davis FB .20 .50
963 Warren Sapp FB .20 .50

2001 Sports Illustrated for Kids
Since its debut issue in January 1989, SI for Kids has included a perforated sheet of nine standard-size cards bound into each magazine. In December 2000, for the second time, the card numbers started over again at 1. The athletes featured represent an extremely wide spectrum of sports. The athlete's name is printed at the top while his or her sport appears at the bottom. The backs carry biographical information, career highlights, and a trivia question with answer. The cards' magazine issue date appears on the back in very small type. Although originally distributed in sheet form, the cards are frequently traded as singles. Thus, they are priced individually. The value of an intact sheet is equal to the sum of the nine cards plus a premium of up to 20 percent.

COMPLETE SET (108) 25.00 50.00
3 Junior Seau FB .10 .30
5 Mark Brunell FB .15 .40
14 Daunte Culpepper FB .20 .50
10 Keyshawn Johnson FB .15 .40
21 Isaac Bruce FB .15 .40
26 Wayne Chrebet FB .15 .40
32 Brian Mitchell FB .08 .25
44 Aaron Brooks FB .15 .40
48 Jamal Lewis FB .20 .50
56 Donovan McNabb FB .20 .50
64 La'Roi Glover FB .08 .25
81 Eddie George FB .15 .40
86 Marshall Faulk FB .40 1.00
95 Jeff Garcia FB .10 .30
100 Champ Bailey FB .10 .30
104 Randy Moss FB .40 1.00

2002 Sports Illustrated for Kids
112 Matt Stover FB .08 .25
114 Courtney Brown FB .08 .25
118 Corey Dillon FB .15 .40
123 Michael Strahan FB .10 .30
129 Brett Favre FB 1.00 2.50
133 Curtis Martin FB .15 .40
140 Jerome Bettis FB .15 .40
145 Eric Crouch FB .40 1.00
153 Anthony Thomas FB .20 .50
158 Kurt Warner FB .20 .50
165 LaDainian Tomlinson FB .60 1.50
170 Tom Brady FB .40 1.00
172 Emmitt Smith FB .40 1.00
177 Marvin Harrison FB .15 .40
181 Andre Johnson FB .30 .75
189 Tim Couch FB .10 .30
194 Ty Law FB .10 .30
201 Terrell Owens FB .15 .40
203 Kordell Stewart FB .10 .30
208 Steve McNair FB .15 .40
213 Ahman Green FB .15 .40
218 Ronde Barber FB .10 .30
222 Brian Urlacher FB .25 .60

2003 Sports Illustrated for Kids
Since its debut issue in January 1989, SI for Kids has included a perforated sheet of nine standard-size cards bound into each magazine. In January 2001, for the second time, the card numbers started over at 1. Listed below are the cards issued in magazines that carry 2003 cover dates. The athletes featured represent an extremely wide spectrum of sports. Although originally distributed in sheet form, the cards are frequently traded as singles. Thus, they are priced individually. The value of an intact sheet is equal to the sum of the nine cards plus a premium of up to 20 percent.

230 Rich Gannon FB .10 .30
234 LaVar Arrington FB .20 .50
235 Mike Brown S FB .08 .25
239 Drew Bledsoe FB .15 .40
245 Deuce McAllister FB .15 .40
252 Peerless Price FB .07 .20
253 Willis McGahee FB .50 1.25
258 Joe Horn FB .10 .30
263 Brad Johnson FB .10 .30
270 Clinton Portis FB .60 1.50
272 Plaxico Burress FB .25 .60
281 Donald Driver FB .20 .50
285 Jason Taylor FB .10 .30
290 Chad Pennington FB .25 .60
294 Priest Holmes FB .20 .50
302 Tommy Maddox FB .10 .30
304 Shaun Alexander FB .20 .50
308 Charlie Garner FB .10 .30
312 Eli Manning FB 2.00 5.00
314 Torry Holt FB .10 .30
318 Tony Gonzalez FB .10 .30
320 Tiki Barber FB .10 .30
327 Kellen Winslow Jr. FB .50 1.25
329 Trent Green FB .10 .30
333 Takeo Spikes FB .07 .20

2004 Sports Illustrated for Kids
ONE NINE-CARD SHEET PER MAGAZINE
341 Emmitt Smith FB .50 1.25
345 Stephen Davis FB .15 .40
351 Simeon Rice FB .10 .30
353 Jason White FB .40 1.00
357 Chad Johnson FB .10 .30
365 Marc Bulger FB .15 .40
369 Mike Vanderjagt FB .07 .20
375 Steve Smith FB .15 .40
379 Dwight Freeney FB .10 .30
394 Tony Parrish FB .07 .20
399 Steve McNair FB .15 .40
409 Santana Moss FB .10 .30
411 Daunte Culpepper FB .15 .40
420 David Greene FB .07 .20
421 Derrick Mason FB .10 .30
426 Michael Strahan FB .07 .20
431 Darren Sproles .20 .50
438 Darrell Jackson FB .10 .30
440 Patrick Kerney FB .07 .20

2005 Sports Illustrated for Kids
444 Andre Johnson FB .10 .30
446 Tiki Barber FB .10 .30
452 Ben Roethlisberger FB 1.50 4.00
454 Adrian Peterson FB 2.50 6.00
461 Javon Walker FB .10 .30
465 Curtis Martin FB .15 .40
474 Ed Reed FB .10 .30
480 Tedy Bruschi FB .15 .40
484 Jake Plummer FB .08 .25
492 Bert Berry FB .08 .25
494 Joe Horn FB .10 .30
498 Drew Brees FB .15 .40
503 Willis McGahee FB .15 .40
506 Keith Brooking FB .07 .20
513 Brian Westbrook FB .10 .30
516 Kabeer Gbaja-Biamila FB .07 .20
518 Matt Leinart FB 1.00 2.50
524 Keith Bulluck FB .07 .20
528 Antonio Gates FB .20 .50
532 Vince Young FB 2.00 5.00
537 Shaun Alexander FB .20 .50

2006 Sports Illustrated for Kids
3 Jimmy Smith FB .07 .20
4 Carson Palmer FB .20 .50
12 Warrick Dunn FB .10 .30
17 Torry Holt FB .10 .30
21 Santana Moss FB .08 .25
26 Edgerrin James FB .10 .30
32 Michael Vick FB .15 .40
36 Robert Mathis FB .07 .20
42 Larry Johnson FB .20 .50
44 Anquan Boldin FB .08 .25
50 Tom Brady FB .60 1.50
52 Osi Umenyiora FB .08 .25
57 LaDainian Tomlinson FB .30 .75
65 Eli Manning FB .30 .75
70 Nathan Vasher FB .08 .25
75 Jake Delhomme FB .08 .25
76 DeAngelo Hall FB .08 .25
86 Willie Parker FB .10 .30
88 Larry Fitzgerald FB .10 .30
92 Reggie Wayne FB .10 .30
98 Matt Hasselbeck FB .08 .25
102 Cadillac Williams FB .25 .60
108 Champ Bailey FB .08 .25

2007 Sports Illustrated for Kids
ONE NINE-CARD SHEET PER MAGAZINE
111 Tom Brady FB .60 1.50
120 Jimmy Clausen HS FB .75 2.00
124 Marvin Austin HS FB .60 1.50
127 Frank Gore FB .10 .30
131 Philip Rivers FB .15 .40
140 Reggie Bush FB .75 2.00
146 Devin Hester FB .40 1.00
158 Vince Young FB .60 1.50
168 Tony Romo FB 1.00 2.50
173 Maurice Jones-Drew FB .40 1.00
183 Brian Urlacher FB .10 .30
187 Darren McFadden FB 2.00 5.00
192 Steven Jackson FB .10 .30
198 Jonathan Vilma FB .08 .25
201 Jason Taylor FB .08 .25
203 Drew Brees FB .10 .30
210 Joseph Addai FB .40 1.00
211 Julius Peppers FB .10 .30

2008 Sports Illustrated for Kids
217 Reggie White FB .10 .30
218 Jerry Rice FB .40 1.00
219 Walter Payton FB .75 2.00
220 Jim Brown FB .30 .75
221 Johnny Unitas FB .50 1.25
222 Deion Sanders FB .20 .50
223 Anthony Munoz FB .10 .30
224 Joe Greene FB .10 .30
225 John Elway FB .50 1.25
227 Derek Anderson FB .20 .50
231 Terrell Owens FB .20 .50
239 Brett Favre FB .75 2.00
252 Ryan Grant FB .10 .30
258 T.J. Houshmandzadeh FB .08 .25
266 Randy Moss FB .10 .30
275 Adrian Peterson FB .20 .50
277 Chase Daniel FB .15 .40
280 Antonio Cromartie FB .08 .25
288 Fred Taylor FB .08 .25
291 Knowshon Moreno FB .08 .25
296 Marques Colston FB .10 .30
300 Clinton Portis FB .08 .25
301 Mario Williams FB .08 .25
307 Peyton Manning FB .25 .60
311 Brett Favre FB .40 1.00
318 Justin Tuck FB .08 .25
322 Sam Bradford FB .10 .30
325 Adrian Peterson ART FB .20 .50
326 Reggie Bush ART FB .10 .30
327 Devin Hester ART FB .10 .30
328 Marion Barber ART FB .10 .30
329 Aaron Rodgers ART FB .30 .75
330 LaDainian Tomlinson ART FB .10 .30
331 Chris Chambers ART FB .08 .25
332 Brian Westbrook ART FB .08 .25
333 Frank Gore ART FB .08 .25

1976 Sportstix

These ten blank-backed irregularly shaped stickers measure approximately 3 1/2" in diameter and feature borderless color player action photos. Team markings were crudely obliterated from the players' helmets. The numbering is a continuation from other non-football Sportstix. The stickers came in packs of five, with stickers 31-35 in packs marked "Series 3B" and stickers 36-40 in packs marked "Series 4B." The player's name, along with the sticker's number& appears in black lettering (except the Drew Pearson and Gary Huff stickers have white lettering). The stickers are numbered on the front.

COMPLETE SET (11) 100.00 175.00
31 Carl Eller 6.00 15.00
32 Fred Biletnikoff UER 10.00 25.00
(Misspelled
Belitnikoff)
33 Terry Metcalf 5.00 12.00
34 Gary Huff 4.00 10.00
35 Steve Bartkowski 6.00 15.00
36 Dan Pastorini 5.00 12.00
37 Drew Pearson UER 7.50 20.00
(Photo is of
Gloster Richardson)
38 Bert Jones 5.00 12.00
39 Otis Armstrong 5.00 12.00
40 Don Woods 4.00 10.00
C Dick Butkus 15.00 40.00

1997 Sprint Phone Cards

This set of 4-phone cards was produced for Sprint. Each unnumbered card carries 15-minutes worth of phone time with an expiration date of 10/03/98. A color player portrait was included on the cardfronts with instructions on the use of the card on back. Each was also numbered of 27,800 sets made. Although the phone cards measure roughly 2 1/8" by 3 3/8" loose, we've included pricing below for cards still mounted on their paper backers which measure 3 1/2" by 7." The backers include more detailed cardlike player information on the backs and a description of the set on the fronts.

COMPLETE SET (4) 8.00 20.00
1 Marcus Allen .80 2.00
2 Brett Favre 3.20 8.00
3 Dan Marino 3.20 8.00
4 Steve Young 1.20 3.00

2009 SP Threads

COMP.SET w/o RC's (100) 15.00 40.00
ROOKIE AU ANNOUNCED PRINT RUNS 120-126
ACTUAL ROOKIE AUTO SERIAL #'s 11-30
EXCH EXPIRATION: 10/7/2011
1 Aaron Rodgers .75 2.00
2 Adrian Peterson .60 1.50
3 Andre Johnson .30 .75
4 Anquan Boldin .30 .75
5 Antonio Bryant .25 .60
6 Ben Roethlisberger .40 1.00
7 Bernard Berrian .30 .75
8 Bob Sanders .30 .75
9 Brady Quinn .30 .75
10 Brandon Jacobs .30 .75
11 Brandon Marshall .30 .75
12 Braylon Edwards .30 .75
13 Brian Urlacher .40 1.00
14 Brian Westbrook .30 .75
15 Calvin Johnson .40 1.00
16 Carson Palmer .40 1.00
17 Chad Ochocinco .30 .75
18 Chad Pennington .30 .75
19 Champ Bailey .30 .75
20 Chris Johnson .40 1.00
21 Chris Long .30 .75
22 Clinton Portis .30 .75
23 Darren McFadden .40 1.00
24 Darren Sproles .30 .75
25 David Garrard .30 .75
26 DeAngelo Williams .40 1.00
27 DeMarcus Ware .30 .75
28 DeMeco Ryans .30 .75
29 Derrick Johnson .25 .60
30 Donnie Avery .30 .75
31 Donovan McNabb .40 1.00
32 D'Qwell Jackson .25 .60
33 Drew Brees .40 1.00
34 Dwayne Bowe .30 .75
35 Ed Reed .30 .75
36 Eddie Royal .30 .75
37 Eli Manning .40 1.00
38 Frank Gore .30 .75
39 Greg Jennings .40 1.00
40 Hines Ward .30 .75
41 Jamal Lewis .30 .75
42 JaMarcus Russell .25 .60
43 James Harrison .40 1.00
44 Jared Allen .40 1.00
45 Jason Campbell .25 .60
46 Jay Cutler .40 1.00
47 Jeremy Shockey .25 .60
48 Jerod Mayo .30 .75
49 Jerricho Cotchery .30 .75
50 Joe Flacco .40 1.00
51 Joey Porter .30 .75
52 John Abraham .25 .60
53 Julius Peppers .30 .75
54 Justin Tuck .30 .75
55 Kellen Winslow .30 .75
56 Kevin Smith .30 .75
57 Kurt Warner .40 1.00
58 LaDainian Tomlinson .40 1.00
59 Lance Briggs .30 .75
60 Larry Fitzgerald .40 1.00
61 Larry Johnson .30 .75
62 Laveranues Coles .25 .60
63 Lee Evans .30 .75
64 LenDale White .30 .75
65 Lofa Tatupu .30 .75
66 Marc Bulger .30 .75
67 Marion Barber .30 .75
68 Marques Colston .30 .75
69 Marshawn Lynch .30 .75
70 Matt Forte .40 1.00
71 Matt Hasselbeck .30 .75
72 Matt Ryan .40 1.00
73 Maurice Jones-Drew .30 .75
74 Michael Turner .30 .75
75 Patrick Willis .30 .75
76 Peyton Manning .60 1.50
77 Philip Rivers .40 1.00
78 Randy Moss .40 1.00
79 Ray Lewis .40 1.00
80 Reggie Bush .40 1.00
81 Reggie Wayne .30 .75
82 Roddy White .30 .75
83 Ryan Grant .30 .75
84 Santana Moss .30 .75
85 Stephen Cooper RC .30 .75
86 Steve Breaston .30 .75
87 Steve Slaton .30 .75
88 Steve Smith .30 .75
89 Steven Jackson .30 .75
90 T.J. Houshmandzadeh .30 .75
91 Terrell Owens .40 1.00
92 Thomas Jones .30 .75
93 Tom Brady .60 1.50
94 Tony Gonzalez .30 .75
95 Tony Romo .60 1.50
96 Vincent Jackson .30 .75
97 Warrick Dunn .30 .75
98 Wes Welker .40 1.00
99 Willie Parker .25 .60
100 Willis McGahee .30 .75
101 Aaron Brown RC 2.00 5.00
102 Alex Magee RC 1.50 4.00
103 Andre Brown RC 1.25 3.00
104 Andy Levitre RC 1.50 4.00
105 Antoine Caldwell RC 1.25 3.00
106 Asher Allen RC 1.50 4.00
107 Austin Collie RC 2.00 5.00
108 Bear Pascoe RC 1.50 4.00
109 Bernard Scott RC 2.00 5.00
110 Bradley Fletcher RC 1.50 4.00
111 Brandon Gibson RC 2.00 5.00
112 Brian Hartline RC 2.00 5.00
113 Brooks Foster RC 1.25 3.00
114 Cedric Peerman RC 1.50 4.00
115 Chip Vaughn RC 1.25 3.00
116 Chris Owens RC 1.50 4.00
117 Cody Brown RC 1.25 3.00
118 Cody Glenn RC 1.50 4.00
119 Connor Barwin RC 2.00 5.00
120 Cornelius Ingram RC 1.25 3.00
121 Corvey Irvin RC 1.25 3.00
122 Curtis Painter RC 2.00 5.00
123 Darcel McBath RC 1.50 4.00
124 Darius Butler RC 2.00 5.00
125 David Veikune RC 1.50 4.00
126 DeAndre Levy RC 2.00 5.00
127 DeAngelo Smith RC 1.50 4.00
128 Deon Butler RC 1.50 4.00
129 Derek Cox RC 2.00 5.00
130 Donald Washington RC 1.50 4.00
131 Darell Scott RC 1.25 3.00
132 Eben Britton RC 1.50 4.00
133 Eric Wood RC 1.50 4.00
134 Evander Hood RC 2.50 6.00
135 Fenuki Tupou RC 1.25 3.00
136 Fili Moala RC 1.50 4.00
137 Gartrell Johnson RC 1.25 3.00
138 Gerald McRath RC 1.50 4.00
139 Glen Coffee RC 1.50 4.00
140 Greg Toler RC 1.25 3.00
141 Henry Melton RC 1.25 3.00
142 Jairus Byrd RC 2.00 5.00
143 James Casey RC 1.50 4.00
144 Brandon Hughes RC 2.00 5.00
145 Jamon Meredith RC 1.50 4.00
146 Jared Cook RC 2.00 5.00
147 Jarron Gilbert RC 1.50 4.00
148 Jason Phillips RC 1.50 4.00
149 Jason Williams RC 2.00 5.00
150 Jasper Brinkley RC 1.50 4.00
151 Jerraud Powers RC 1.50 4.00
152 Jonathan Luigs RC 1.25 3.00
153 Kaluka Maiava RC 2.00 5.00
154 Keenan Lewis RC 2.00 5.00
155 Kevin Barnes RC 1.50 4.00
156 Kraig Urbik RC 1.50 4.00
157 Kyle Moore RC 1.50 4.00
158 Lardarius Webb RC 2.00 5.00
159 Larry English RC 2.00 5.00
160 Lawrence Sidbury RC 1.25 3.00
161 Louis Delmas RC 2.00 5.00
162 Louis Vasquez RC 1.50 4.00
163 Marcus Freeman RC 2.00 5.00
164 Matt Shaughnessy RC 1.50 4.00
165 Max Unger RC 1.50 4.00
166 Michael Hamlin RC 1.50 4.00
167 Mike Goodson RC 2.00 5.00
168 Mike Mitchell RC 1.50 4.00
169 Mike Teel RC 2.00 5.00
170 Mike Thomas RC 2.00 5.00
171 Mike Wallace RC 4.00 10.00
172 Morgan Trent RC 1.50 4.00
173 Nic Harris RC 1.50 4.00
174 Patrick Chung RC 2.00 5.00
175 Patrick Turner RC 1.50 4.00
176 Paul Kruger RC 1.50 4.00
177 Phil Loadholt RC 1.50 4.00
178 Ramses Barden RC 1.25 3.00
179 Rashad Johnson RC 1.50 4.00
180 Richard Quinn RC 1.50 4.00
181 Robert Ayers RC 2.00 5.00
182 Robert Brewster RC 1.25 3.00
183 Ron Brace RC 1.50 4.00
184 Roy Miller RC 1.50 4.00
185 Ryan Mouton RC 1.50 4.00
186 Scott McKillop RC 1.50 4.00
187 Sebastian Vollmer RC 1.50 4.00
188 Sen'Derrick Marks RC 1.25 3.00
189 Sherrod Martin RC 1.50 4.00
190 Stanley Arnoux RC 1.50 4.00
191 Stephen McGee RC 2.00 5.00
192 T.J. Lang RC 1.50 4.00
193 Terrance Knighton RC 1.50 4.00
194 Terrance Taylor RC 1.50 4.00
195 Tom Brandstater RC 2.00 5.00
196 Travis Beckum RC 1.50 4.00
197 Tyrone Mckenzie RC 1.50 4.00
198 Victor Harris RC 2.00 5.00
199 William Beatty RC 1.25 3.00
200 William Middleton RC 1.25 3.00
201 Mohamed Massaquoi AU/126* RC 6.00 15.00
(cards serial numbered of 14)
203 Alex Mack/120* AU RC 6.00 15.00
(cards serial numbered of 30)
204 Andre Smith AU/120* RC 6.00 15.00
(cards serial numbered of 24)
205 B.J. Raji AU/120* RC 8.00 20.00
(cards serial numbered of 30)
207 Brandon Pettigrew AU/126* RC 8.00 20.00
(cards serial numbered of 14)
208 Brian Cushing AU/126* RC 8.00 20.00
(cards serial numbered of 18)
209 Brian Robiskie AU/120* RC 8.00 20.00
(cards serial numbered of 15)
210 Rhett Bomar AU/120* RC 6.00 15.00
(cards serial numbered of 24)
211 Chase Coffman AU/126* RC 6.00 15.00
(cards serial numbered of 18)
213 Chris Wells AU/120* RC 12.00 30.00
(cards serial numbered of 24)
214 Hunter Cantwell AU/120* RC 8.00 20.00
(cards serial numbered of 15)
215 D.J. Moore AU/120* RC 6.00 15.00
(cards serial numbered of 24)
216 Darrius Heyward-Bey AU/120* RC 8.00 20.00
(cards serial numbered of 12)
217 Sean Smith AU/120* RC EXCH 8.00 20.00
(cards serial numbered of 24)
218 Demetrius Byrd AU/120* RC 6.00 15.00
(cards serial numbered of 30)
219 Derrick Williams AU/120* RC 10.00 25.00
(cards serial numbered of 15)
220 Duke Robinson AU/120* RC 8.00 20.00
(cards serial numbered of 15)
221 Eugene Monroe AU/120* RC 5.00 12.00
(cards serial numbered of 20)
223 Clint Sintim AU/120* RC 8.00 20.00
(cards serial numbered of 20)
224 Rashad Jennings AU/120* RC 8.00 20.00
(cards serial numbered of 15)
225 Aaron Curry AU/120* RC 8.00 20.00
(cards serial numbered of 24)
226 Hakeem Nicks AU/120* RC 15.00 40.00
(cards serial numbered of 24)
227 Juaquin Iglesias AU/120* RC 6.00 15.00
(cards serial numbered of 15)
228 Brian Orakpo AU/120* RC 8.00 20.00
(cards serial numbered of 20)
229 James Laurinaitis AU/121* RC 12.00 30.00
(cards serial numbered of 11)
230 Jason Smith AU/120* RC 6.00 15.00
(cards serial numbered of 24)
231 Javon Ringer AU/120* RC 10.00 25.00
(cards serial numbered of 20)
232 Jeremy Maclin AU/120* RC 12.00 30.00
(cards serial numbered of 20)
233 Nate Davis AU/120* RC 6.00 15.00
(cards serial numbered of 24)
234 Josh Freeman AU/126* RC 30.00 60.00
(cards serial numbered of 18)
235 Kenny Britt AU/120* RC 12.00 30.00
(cards serial numbered of 24)
236 Knowshon Moreno AU/120* RC 30.00 60.00
(cards serial numbered of 20)
237 Louis Murphy AU/120* RC 12.00 30.00
(cards serial numbered of 20)
238 Malcolm Jenkins AU/126* RC 8.00 20.00
(cards serial numbered of 18)
239 James Davis AU/120* RC 8.00 20.00
(cards serial numbered of 24)
240 Mark Sanchez AU/126* RC 50.00 100.00
(cards serial numbered of 18)
241 Matthew Stafford AU/120* RC 50.00 100.00
(cards serial numbered of 15)
242 Michael Crabtree AU/120* RC 40.00 80.00
(cards serial numbered of 15)
243 Michael Johnson AU/126* RC 5.00 12.00
(cards serial numbered of 18)
244 Michael Oher AU/120* RC 30.00 60.00
(cards serial numbered of 30)
245 Donald Brown AU/120* RC 8.00 20.00
(cards serial numbered of 24)
246 Pat White AU/120* RC 12.00 30.00
(cards serial numbered of 24)
247 Jarett Dillard AU/126* RC 8.00 20.00
(cards serial numbered of 18)
248 Percy Harvin AU/120* RC 40.00 80.00
(cards serial numbered of 20)
249 Peria Jerry AU/120* RC 6.00 15.00
(cards serial numbered of 24)
250 Rey Maualuga AU/120* RC 8.00 20.00
(cards serial numbered of 15)
251 Brandon Tate AU/120* RC 8.00 20.00
(cards serial numbered of 30)
252 Alphonso Smith AU/120* RC 6.00 15.00
(cards serial numbered of 24)
253 Shonn Greene AU/120* RC 12.00 30.00
(cards serial numbered of 20)
254 Clay Matthews AU/120* RC 60.00 120.00
(cards serial numbered of 15)
255 Devin Moore AU/120* RC 6.00 15.00
(cards serial numbered of 24)
256 LeSean McCoy AU/120* RC 15.00 40.00
(cards serial numbered of 24)
257 Travis Beckum AU/120* RC 10.00 25.00
(cards serial numbered of 20)
258 Tyson Jackson AU/126* RC 6.00 15.00
(cards serial numbered of 18)
259 Vontae Davis AU/120* RC 8.00 20.00
(cards serial numbered of 24)
260 William Moore AU/120* RC 8.00 20.00
(cards serial numbered of 24)

2009 SP Threads Rookie Lettermen Autographs Gold

*GOLD: .5X TO 1.2X BASE AUTO
GOLD AU ANNCD PRINT RUNS 33-42
ACTUAL GOLD AUTO SERIAL #'s 3-9
EXCH EXPIRATION: 10/7/2011

2009 SP Threads Rookie Lettermen College Autographs

*COLLEGE: .4X TO 1X BASE AUTO
COLLEGE AU ANNCD PRINT RUNS 72-126
ACTUAL COLLEGE AUTO SER.#'s 7-28
EXCH EXPIRATION: 10/7/2011

2009 SP Threads Rookie Lettermen College Nickname Autographs

*COLL.NICKNAME: .4X TO 1X BASE AUTO
COLL.NICKNAME ANNCD PRINT RUNS 63-72
ACTUAL NICKNAME AUTO SER.#'s 5-17
EXCH EXPIRATION: 10/7/2011

2009 SP Threads Die Cut

AP1 Michael Crabtree 2.50 6.00
AP2 Matt Ryan 1.50 4.00
AP3 JaMarcus Russell 1.00 2.50
AP4 Brett Favre 4.00 10.00
AP5 Paul Hornung 2.00 5.00
AP6 Terry Bradshaw 2.50 6.00
AP7 David Garrard 1.25 3.00
AP8 Steve Young 2.50 6.00
AP9 Tony Romo 2.50 6.00
AP10 Eli Manning 1.50 4.00
AP11 Roy Williams WR 1.25 3.00
AP12 Don Maynard 2.50 6.00
AP13 Brady Quinn 1.25 3.00
AP14 Bernard Berrian 1.50 4.00
AP15 Brandon Marshall 1.25 3.00
AP16 Marques Colston 1.25 3.00
AP17 Braylon Edwards 1.25 3.00
AP18 Peyton Manning 2.50 6.00
AP19 Felix Jones 1.50 4.00
AP20 Barry Sanders 3.00 8.00
AP21 Bob Sanders 1.25 3.00
AP22 Emmitt Smith 3.00 8.00
AP23 Quentin Jammer 1.00 2.50
AP24 Champ Bailey 1.25 3.00
AP25 Reggie Bush 1.50 4.00
AP26 Rod Woodson 1.50 4.00
AP27 Brandon Jacobs 1.25 3.00
AP28 Adrian Peterson 2.50 6.00
AP29 Donald Brown 1.25 3.00
AP30 Wes Welker 1.50 4.00
AP31 Chris Johnson 1.50 4.00
AP32 Franco Harris 2.00 5.00
AP33 Roger Craig 1.50 4.00
AP34 Bo Jackson 2.50 6.00
AP35 Brian Orakpo 1.25 3.00
AP36 Chris Wells 2.00 5.00
AP37 Ernie Sims 1.00 2.50
AP38 Greg Jennings 1.50 4.00
AP39 Willie Parker 1.00 2.50
AP40 Gale Sayers 2.50 6.00
AP41 James Laurinaitis 1.25 3.00
AP42 Jake Delhomme 1.25 3.00
AP43 Joe Flacco 1.50 4.00
AP44 Tom Rathman 1.25 3.00
AP45 Jeremy Maclin 2.00 5.00
AP46 Jonathan Stewart 1.25 3.00
AP47 Chris Cooley 1.25 3.00
AP48 Knowshon Moreno 1.25 3.00
AP49 Le'Ron McClain 1.25 3.00
AP50 Calvin Johnson 1.50 4.00
AP51 Marc Bulger 1.25 3.00
AP52 Patrick Willis 1.25 3.00
AP53 LeSean McCoy 2.50 6.00
AP54 Marion Barber 1.25 3.00
AP55 Mark Sanchez 4.00 10.00
AP56 Rashard Mendenhall 1.25 3.00
AP57 Jack Youngblood 2.50 6.00
AP58 Reggie Brown 1.00 2.50
AP59 Jack Ham 1.50 4.00
AP60 Steve Breaston 1.25 3.00
AP61 Santonio Holmes 1.25 3.00
AP62 Steve Slaton 1.25 3.00
AP63 Matthew Stafford 6.00 15.00
AP64 Vince Young 1.25 3.00
AP65 Darren McFadden 1.50 4.00
AP66 Joseph Addai 1.50 4.00
AP67 Chad Pennington 1.25 3.00
AP68 Eddie Royal 1.25 3.00
AP69 Josh Freeman 2.50 6.00
AP70 Kevin Smith 1.25 3.00
AP71 Frank Gore 1.25 3.00
AP72 Ed Jones 1.25 3.00
AP73 Ronde Barber 1.00 2.50
AP74 Jim Kelly 2.00 5.00
AP75 Deacon Jones 1.50 4.00
AP76 DeSean Jackson 1.25 3.00
AP77 Malcolm Jenkins 1.25 3.00
AP78 Marshawn Lynch 1.25 3.00
AP79 Jeff Garcia 1.25 3.00
AP80 Jerry Rice 3.00 8.00
AP81 Dustin Keller 1.00 2.50
AP82 Dwayne Bowe 1.25 3.00
AP83 Vincent Jackson 1.25 3.00
AP84 T.J. Houshmandzadeh 1.25 3.00
AP85 Chad Ochocinco 1.25 3.00
AP86 Roger Staubach 2.50 6.00
AP87 Reggie Wayne 1.25 3.00
AP88 Larry Johnson 1.25 3.00
AP89 Jerricho Cotchery 1.25 3.00
AP90 Matt Forte 1.50 4.00
AP91 A.J. Hawk 1.25 3.00
AP92 Aaron Curry 1.25 3.00
AP93 Donald Driver 1.25 3.00
AP94 Laurence Maroney 1.25 3.00
AP95 Nate Davis 1.00 2.50
AP96 Hakeem Nicks 2.00 5.00
AP97 Donnie Avery 1.25 3.00
AP98 Rey Maualuga 1.25 3.00
AP99 Kellen Winslow Sr. 1.50 4.00
AP100 Percy Harvin 2.00 5.00

2009 SP Threads Die Cut Autographs

STATED PRINT RUN 5-25
SERIAL #'d UNDER 25 NOT PRICED
AP19 Felix Jones/25 20.00 40.00
AP25 Reggie Bush/25 20.00 40.00
AP37 Ernie Sims/25 6.00 15.00
AP41 James Laurinaitis/25 10.00 25.00
AP44 Tom Rathman/25 15.00 30.00
AP49 Le'Ron McClain/25 8.00 20.00
AP60 Steve Breaston/25 8.00 20.00
AP75 Deacon Jones/25 15.00 40.00
AP79 Jeff Garcia/25 8.00 20.00
AP81 Dustin Keller/25 6.00 15.00
AP88 Larry Johnson/15 8.00 20.00
AP89 Jerricho Cotchery/25 8.00 20.00
AP90 Matt Forte/25 20.00 40.00

2009 SP Threads Dual Threads

STATED PRINT RUN 199 SER.#'d SETS
AR Donnie Avery 3.00 8.00
Eddie Royal
BB Drew Brees 4.00 10.00
Reggie Bush
BR Dwayne Bowe 3.00 8.00
Eddie Royal
CK Jerricho Cotchery 3.00 8.00
Dustin Keller
CM Marques Colston 3.00 8.00
Robert Meachem
EB Eli Manning 4.00 10.00
Brandon Jacobs
EC Champ Bailey 3.00 8.00
Eddie Royal
EE Trent Edwards 3.00 8.00
Lee Evans
EL Trent Edwards 3.00 8.00
Marshawn Lynch
EP Eli Manning 4.00 10.00
Plaxico Burress
FR Joe Flacco 4.00 10.00
Ray Rice
GJ David Garrard 3.00 8.00
Maurice Jones-Drew
GM Frank Gore 4.00 10.00
Darren McFadden
HF A.J. Hawk 4.00 10.00
Matt Forte
HH Matt Hasselbeck 3.00 8.00
T.J. Houshmandzadeh
JA DeSean Jackson 3.00 8.00
Donnie Avery
JB Tarvaris Jackson 3.00 8.00
John David Booty
JF Edgerrin James 4.00 10.00
Larry Fitzgerald
JP Adrian Peterson 6.00 15.00
Tarvaris Jackson
KC Kevin Smith 4.00 10.00
Calvin Johnson
KJ Kevin Kolb 3.00 8.00
DeSean Jackson
KR Dustin Keller 3.00 8.00
Antonio Gates
LB Matt Leinart 4.00 10.00
Reggie Bush
LE Marshawn Lynch 3.00 8.00
Lee Evans
LF Larry Fitzgerald 4.00 10.00
Matt Leinart
LG Marshawn Lynch 3.00 8.00
Frank Gore
LR Ray Lewis 8.00 20.00
Ed Reed
MA Peyton Manning 6.00 15.00
Joseph Addai
MC Donovan McNabb 4.00 10.00
Jason Campbell
MF Rashard Mendenhall 4.00 10.00
Matt Forte
MH Kirk Morrison 2.50 6.00
Michael Huff
MJ Donovan McNabb 4.00 10.00
DeSean Jackson
ML Shawne Merriman 4.00 10.00
Ray Lewis
MM Randy Moss 4.00 10.00
Laurence Maroney
MP Rashard Mendenhall 4.00 10.00
Willie Parker
MS Steve Slaton 4.00 10.00
Darren McFadden
MY Vince Young 4.00 10.00
Donovan McNabb
OE Trent Edwards 4.00 10.00
Terrell Owens
PB Chad Pennington 3.00 8.00
Ronnie Brown
PC Jason Campbell 3.00 8.00
Clinton Portis
PR Peyton Manning 6.00 15.00
Reggie Wayne
QE Brady Quinn 3.00 8.00
Braylon Edwards
QP Brady Quinn 4.00 10.00
Carson Palmer
RF Matt Ryan 4.00 10.00
Matt Forte
RM JaMarcus Russell 4.00 10.00
Darren McFadden
RR Ray Lewis 5.00 12.00
Ray Rice
RS Matt Ryan 4.00 10.00
Jonathan Stewart
RY JaMarcus Russell 3.00 8.00
Vince Young
SE Limas Sweed 3.00 8.00
Braylon Edwards
SJ Jonathan Stewart 3.00 8.00
Dwayne Jarrett
SM Limas Sweed 4.00 10.00
Rashard Mendenhall
SP Julius Peppers 3.00 8.00
Jonathan Stewart
SS Matt Schaub 3.00 8.00
Steve Slaton
TJ Maurice Jones-Drew 3.00 8.00
Fred Taylor
WH A.J. Hawk 5.00 12.00
Charles Woodson
WQ Brady Quinn 3.00 8.00
Kellen Winslow
WW Wes Welker 4.00 10.00
Ben Watson
YJ Chris Johnson 4.00 10.00
Vince Young

2009 SP Threads Foursome Fabrics

STATED PRINT RUN 25 SER.#'d SETS
2008 Matt Ryan 10.00 25.00
Joe Flacco
Darren McFadden
Matt Forte
AUB1 Jason Campbell 8.00 20.00
Ronnie Brown
Carnell Williams
Rudi Johnson
BOLT Shawne Merriman 10.00 25.00
LaDainian Tomlinson
Antonio Gates
Vincent Jackson
CANE Ray Lewis 10.00 25.00
Andre Johnson
Frank Gore
Edgerrin James
DENV Jay Cutler 10.00 25.00
Brandon Marshall
Eddie Royal
Champ Bailey
LSU1 JaMarcus Russell 10.00 25.00
Joseph Addai
Dwayne Bowe
Michael Clayton
MICH Tom Brady 15.00 40.00
Charles Woodson
Mario Manningham
Jake Long
NYG1 Eli Manning 10.00 25.00
Brandon Jacobs
Mario Manningham
Plaxico Burress
OSU1 Santonio Holmes 8.00 20.00
A.J. Hawk
Anthony Gonzalez
Mike Vrabel
PATS Tom Brady 15.00 40.00
Randy Moss
Laurence Maroney
Mike Vrabel
PHIL Donovan McNabb 10.00 25.00
Brian Westbrook
DeSean Jackson
Kevin Kolb
PITT Ben Roethlisberger 10.00 25.00
Santonio Holmes
Willie Parker
Limas Sweed
SBQB Peyton Manning 20.00 50.00
Tom Brady
Ben Roethlisberger
Eli Manning
TEX1 Vince Young 10.00 25.00
Limas Sweed
Aaron Ross
Jamaal Charles
USC1 Carson Palmer 10.00 25.00
Reggie Bush
Matt Leinart
John David Booty
VOLS Peyton Manning 15.00 40.00
Jamal Lewis
Jason Witten
Robert Meachem

2009 SP Threads Multi Marks Dual

STATED PRINT RUN 5-75
SERIAL #'d UNDER 25 NOT PRICED
BG Donald Brown/50 25.00 50.00
Shonn Greene
BJ Marion Barber/25 30.00 60.00
Felix Jones
BT Demetrius Byrd/50 12.00 30.00
Brandon Tate
DS Jake Delhomme/25 15.00 40.00
Jonathan Stewart
FB Matt Forte/25 20.00 50.00
Lance Briggs
JM Michael Johnson/40 6.00 15.00
Alex Mack
JR DeSean Jackson/50 12.00 30.00
Eddie Royal
ML Rey Maualuga/75 10.00 25.00
James Laurinaitis
MW Knowshon Moreno/25 50.00 100.00
Chris Wells
NH Hakeem Nicks/25 20.00 40.00
Darrius Heyward-Bey
SW Matt Schaub/50 12.00 30.00
Mario Williams
WS DeAngelo Williams/25 15.00 40.00
Jonathan Stewart
WW Patrick Willis/50 8.00 20.00
Mario Williams

2009 SP Threads Multi Marks Quad

HOGS Darren McFadden/20
Felix Jones
Peyton Hillis
Marcus Monk

2009 SP Threads Multi Marks Triple

STATED PRINT RUN 5-50
BGR Donald Brown/50 30.00 60.00
Shonn Greene
Javon Ringer
CMH Michael Crabtree/25 40.00 100.00
Jeremy Maclin
Percy Harvin
JMM Michael Johnson/50
Alex Mack
Eugene Monroe
MJS Eli Manning/25 60.00 120.00
Brandon Jacobs
Steve Smith
MWM Knowshon Moreno/50 50.00 100.00
Chris Wells
LeSean McCoy
PHI DeSean Jackson/25
Kevin Kolb
Jeremy Maclin

2009 SP Threads Rookie Threads Dual Swatch

STATED PRINT RUN 299 SER.#'d SETS
*PATCH/50: .6X TO 1.5X DUAL JSY/299
*TRIPLE/199: .5X TO 1.2X DUAL JSY/299
RTAB Andre Brown 1.50 4.00
RTAC Aaron Curry 2.50 6.00
RTBO Rhett Bomar 2.00 5.00
RTBP Brandon Pettigrew 2.50 6.00
RTBR Brian Robiskie 2.50 6.00
RTBU Deon Butler 2.00 5.00
RTCW Chris Wells 5.00 12.00
RTDB Donald Brown 2.50 6.00
RTDH Darrius Heyward-Bey 2.50 6.00
RTDW Derrick Williams 2.00 5.00
RTGC Glen Coffee 2.00 5.00
RTHN Hakeem Nicks 4.00 10.00
RTJF Josh Freeman 5.00 12.00
RTJI Juaquin Iglesias 2.00 5.00
RTJM Jeremy Maclin 4.00 10.00
RTJR Javon Ringer 2.50 6.00
RTJS Jason Smith 2.00 5.00
RTKB Kenny Britt 3.00 8.00
RTKM Knowshon Moreno 2.50 6.00
RTLM LeSean McCoy 4.00 10.00
RTMC Michael Crabtree 5.00 12.00
RTMM Mohamed Massaquoi 2.00 5.00
RTMS Mark Sanchez 8.00 20.00
RTMT Mike Thomas 2.50 6.00
RTMW Mike Wallace 5.00 12.00
RTND Nate Davis 2.00 5.00
RTPH Percy Harvin 4.00 10.00
RTPT Patrick Turner 2.00 5.00
RTPW Pat White 2.50 6.00
RTRB Ramses Barden 1.50 4.00
RTSG Shonn Greene 4.00 10.00
RTSM Stephen McGee 2.50 6.00
RTST Matthew Stafford 6.00 15.00
RTTJ Tyson Jackson 2.00 5.00

2009 SP Threads Rookie Threads Dual Swatch Autographs

STATED PRINT RUN 10-30
RTAB Andre Brown 5.00 12.00
RTBO Rhett Bomar 6.00 15.00
RTBP Brandon Pettigrew 8.00 20.00
RTBU Deon Butler 6.00 15.00
RTDW Derrick Williams 6.00 15.00
RTGC Glen Coffee 6.00 15.00
RTHN Hakeem Nicks 12.00 30.00
RTJF Josh Freeman
RTJI Juaquin Iglesias 6.00 15.00
RTJM Jeremy Maclin/10 12.00 30.00
RTJR Javon Ringer 8.00 20.00
RTKB Kenny Britt 10.00 25.00
RTKM Knowshon Moreno/10 0.00 20.00
RTLM LeSean McCoy 15.00 40.00
RTMC Michael Crabtree/10 15.00 40.00
RTMM Mohamed Massaquoi 6.00 15.00
RTMS Mark Sanchez/10 60.00 120.00
RTMT Mike Thomas 8.00 20.00
RTMW Mike Wallace 25.00 50.00
RTND Nate Davis 6.00 15.00
RTPH Percy Harvin 40.00 80.00
RTPT Patrick Turner 6.00 15.00
RTPW Pat White 8.00 20.00
RTSM Stephen McGee 8.00 20.00
RTST Matthew Stafford 60.00 120.00
RTTJ Tyson Jackson 6.00 15.00

2009 SP Threads SP Threads Patch

PATCH PRINT RUN 25 SER.#'d SETS
TAB Anquan Boldin 6.00 15.00
TAC Alge Crumpler 5.00 12.00
TAG Anthony Gonzalez 5.00 12.00
TAH A.J. Hawk 6.00 15.00
TAJ Andre Johnson 6.00 15.00
TAP Adrian Peterson 12.00 30.00
TAS Alex Smith QB 6.00 15.00
TBD Brian Dawkins 6.00 15.00
TBE Braylon Edwards 6.00 15.00
TBF Brett Favre 20.00 50.00
TBJ Bo Jackson 15.00 40.00
TBO Dwayne Bowe 6.00 15.00
TBQ Brady Quinn 6.00 15.00
TBS Barry Sanders 20.00 50.00
TBU Brian Urlacher 8.00 20.00
TCH Jamaal Charles 8.00 20.00
TCJ Calvin Johnson 8.00 20.00
TCP Carson Palmer 8.00 20.00
TCW Charles Woodson 8.00 20.00
TDA Donnie Avery 6.00 15.00
TDB Drew Brees
TDG David Garrard 6.00 15.00
TDJ DeSean Jackson 6.00 15.00
TDK Derrick Brooks 6.00 15.00
TDM Darren McFadden 8.00 20.00
TDO Donovan McNabb 8.00 20.00
TDW DeAngelo Williams 8.00 20.00
TEJ Edgerrin James 6.00 15.00
TEM Eli Manning 8.00 20.00
TER Ed Reed 6.00 15.00
TES Emmitt Smith 15.00 40.00
TFG Frank Gore 6.00 15.00
TFJ Felix Jones 8.00 20.00
TFR Fred Taylor 6.00 15.00
TGJ Greg Jennings 8.00 20.00
THA Marvin Harrison 8.00 20.00
THC Chad Henne 6.00 15.00
THD Harry Douglas 5.00 12.00
THJ James Hardy 6.00 15.00
THU Michael Huff 5.00 12.00
THW Hines Ward 6.00 15.00
TJA Jamal Lewis 6.00 15.00
TJB John David Booty 6.00 15.00
TJC Jason Campbell 5.00 12.00
TJF Joe Flacco 8.00 20.00
TJH Jack Ham
TJL Jake Long 5.00 12.00
TJO Chad Ochocinco 6.00 15.00
TJP Julius Peppers 6.00 15.00
TJR JaMarcus Russell 5.00 12.00
TJS Jonathan Stewart 6.00 15.00
TJT Joe Theismann 12.00 30.00
TKS Kevin Smith 6.00 15.00
TKW Kellen Winslow 8.00 20.00
TLE Lee Evans 6.00 15.00
TLF Larry Fitzgerald 8.00 20.00
TLM Laurence Maroney 6.00 15.00
TLS Limas Sweed 6.00 15.00
TLT LaDainian Tomlinson 8.00 20.00
TLW LenDale White 6.00 15.00
TLY Marshawn Lynch 6.00 15.00
TMA Marc Bulger 6.00 15.00
TMC Marques Colston 6.00 15.00
TMF Matt Forte 8.00 20.00
TMH Matt Hasselbeck 6.00 15.00
TMJ Maurice Jones-Drew 6.00 15.00
TML Matt Leinart 6.00 15.00
TMM Mario Manningham 6.00 15.00
TMO Randy Moss 8.00 20.00
TMR Matt Ryan 8.00 20.00
TMV Mike Vrabel 6.00 15.00
TNE Jordy Nelson 8.00 20.00
TPI Antonio Pierce 5.00 12.00
TPM Peyton Manning 12.00 30.00
TPO Clinton Portis 6.00 15.00
TPW Patrick Willis 6.00 15.00
TRB Reggie Bush 8.00 20.00
TRE Eddie Royal 6.00 15.00
TRL Ray Lewis 8.00 20.00
TRM Rashard Mendenhall 8.00 20.00
TRO Ronnie Brown 8.00 20.00
TRR Ray Rice 10.00 25.00
TSH Santonio Holmes 6.00 15.00
TSI Ernie Sims 5.00 12.00
TSL Steve Largent 12.00 30.00
TSS Steve Smith 6.00 15.00
TST Steve Slaton 6.00 15.00
TTA Troy Aikman 15.00 40.00
TTB Tom Brady 12.00 30.00
TTE Trent Edwards 5.00 12.00
TTJ Tarvaris Jackson 6.00 15.00
TTO Terrell Owens 8.00 20.00
TTR Tony Romo 12.00 30.00
TVJ Vincent Jackson 6.00 15.00
TVY Vince Young 6.00 15.00
TWP Willie Parker 5.00 12.00
TWW Wes Welker 8.00 20.00

2009 SP Threads Stitch in Time Autographs

SITAB Anquan Boldin 6.00 15.00
SITAS Anthony Spencer 4.00 10.00
SITBA Dallas Baker 4.00 10.00
SITBB Brian Brohm 4.00 10.00
SITBC Brent Celek 5.00 12.00
SITBE Martellus Bennett 4.00 10.00
SITBU Marc Bulger 5.00 12.00
SITCJ Chris Johnson 8.00 20.00
SITCL Chris Long 5.00 12.00
SITCS Chansi Stuckey 4.00 10.00
SITCW Chris Wells
SITDA Donnie Avery 5.00 12.00
SITDB Dwayne Bowe 5.00 12.00
SITDC Dan Connor 4.00 10.00
SITDJ D'Qwell Jackson 4.00 10.00
SITDM Devin Moore 5.00 12.00
SITDR Darrelle Revis 8.00 20.00
SITDW Darius Walker 4.00 10.00
SITEM Eli Manning 40.00 80.00
SITER Eddie Royal 6.00 15.00
SITES Ernie Sims 4.00 10.00
SITEW Eric Weddle 4.00 10.00
SITGJ Greg Jennings 6.00 15.00
SITHM Heath Miller 6.00 15.00
SITJD Jake Delhomme 5.00 12.00
SITJF Joe Flacco
SITJJ James Jones 4.00 10.00
SITJM Jeremy Maclin 10.00 25.00
SITJN Jordy Nelson 6.00 15.00
SITJS Jonathan Stewart 6.00 15.00
SITKM Knowshon Moreno
SITLE Le'Ron McClain 5.00 12.00
SITLL LaRon Landry 4.00 10.00
SITLM LeSean McCoy 12.00 30.00
SITLN Legedu Naanee 4.00 10.00
SITLS Limas Sweed 5.00 12.00
SITMB Marion Barber
SITMC Michael Crabtree 30.00 60.00
SITMJ Mike Jenkins 4.00 10.00
SITML Matt Leinart
SITMM Marcus Monk 4.00 10.00
SITMR Matt Ryan 25.00 50.00
SITMS Mark Sanchez 75.00 150.00
SITMY Jerod Mayo 5.00 12.00
SITPH Percy Harvin 25.00 50.00
SITQM Quentin Moses 4.00 10.00
SITRE Mike Reilly 5.00 12.00
SITRM Rashard Mendenhall 6.00 15.00
SITRO Dominique Rodgers-Cromartie 4.00 10.00
SITRR Ray Rice 6.00 15.00
SITRT Ryan Torain 6.00 15.00
SITSB Steve Breaston 5.00 12.00
SITSH Santonio Holmes
SITSS Steve Slaton
SITSY Selvin Young 4.00 10.00
SITTA Terrance Taylor 5.00 12.00
SITTT Tyler Thigpen 4.00 10.00
SITVG Vernon Gholston 4.00 10.00
SITVJ Vincent Jackson 5.00 12.00

2009 SP Threads Tri Threads

STATED PRINT RUN 99 SER.#'d SETS
AFR Brett Favre 15.00 40.00
Matt Ryan
Troy Aikman
BFR Matt Ryan 6.00 15.00
Joe Flacco
Brian Brohm
BHH Terry Bradshaw 12.00 30.00
Franco Harris
Jack Ham
BLG Ronnie Brown 5.00 12.00
Frank Gore
Marshawn Lynch
DPS Tony Dorsett 15.00 40.00
Adrian Peterson
Barry Sanders
FSM Steve Slaton 6.00 15.00
Matt Forte
Darren McFadden
GWR Anthony Gonzalez 6.00 15.00
Wes Welker
Eddie Royal
JFR Larry Fitzgerald 6.00 15.00
DeSean Jackson
Eddie Royal
JJM DeSean Jackson 6.00 15.00
Felix Jones
Mario Manningham
JRS Eddie Royal 5.00 12.00
DeSean Jackson
Limas Sweed
LBM Matt Leinart 6.00 15.00
Drew Brees
Eli Manning
MOB Terrell Owens 6.00 15.00
Randy Moss
Plaxico Burress

MRM Ben Roethlisberger	6.00	15.00
Eli Manning		
Donovan McNabb		
PML Adrian Peterson	10.00	25.00
Darren McFadden		
Marshawn Lynch		
RYC Jerry Rice	15.00	40.00
Roger Craig		
Steve Young		
SAT Roger Staubach	12.00	30.00
Joe Theismann		
Troy Aikman		

1996 SPx

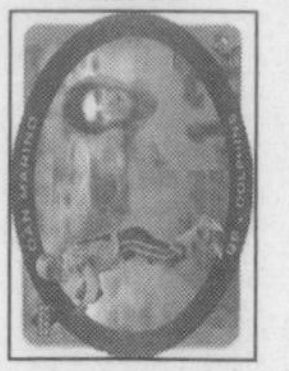

The Upper Deck SPx was issued in one series totalling 50 cards. The 1-card packs originally retailed for $2.99. The 50-card set features limited, state-of-the art holoview printed on 32 point card stock. The cards all feature a die-cut design and have two photos on the front. The backs have a color player photo, vital statistics, recent season as well as career totals as well as some text. There are no Rookie Cards in this set. Two promo cards were produced and distributed by Upper Deck in various ways, including card show give-aways. Special cards inserted into these packs included Joe Montana tribute and Dan Marino record breaker cards as well as autographed cards of these players. The Montana tribute was inserted one every 95 packs, the Marino record breaker was one every 81 packs while the autographed cards were each inserted one every 433 packs.

COMPLETE SET (50)	10.00	25.00
1 Frank Sanders	.40	1.00
2 Terance Mathis	.20	.50
3 Todd Collins	.40	1.00
4 Kerry Collins	.75	2.00
5 Carl Pickens	.40	1.00
6 Darnay Scott	.40	1.00
7 Ki-Jana Carter	.40	1.00
8 Eric Zeier	.20	.50
9 Andre Rison	.40	1.00
10 Sherman Williams	.20	.50
11 Troy Aikman	1.50	4.00
12 Michael Irvin	.75	2.00
13 Emmitt Smith	2.50	6.00
14 Shannon Sharpe	.40	1.00
15 John Elway	3.00	8.00
16 Barry Sanders	2.50	6.00
17 Brett Favre	3.00	8.00
18 Rodney Thomas	.20	.50
19 Marshall Faulk	1.00	2.50
20 James O.Stewart	.40	1.00
21 Greg Hill	.40	1.00
22 Tamarick Vanover	.40	1.00
23 Dan Marino	3.00	8.00
24 Cris Carter	.75	2.00
25 Warren Moon	.40	1.00
26 Drew Bledsoe	1.00	2.50
27 Ben Coates	.40	1.00
28 Curtis Martin	1.25	3.00
29 Mario Bates	.40	1.00
30 Tyrone Wheatley	.40	1.00
31 Rodney Hampton	.40	1.00
32 Kyle Brady	.20	.50
33 Jeff Hostetler	.20	.50
34 Napoleon Kaufman	.75	2.00
35 Tim Brown	.75	2.00
36 Charles Johnson	.20	.50
37 Rod Woodson UER	.40	1.00
Incorrect birth year		
38 Natrone Means	.40	1.00
39 J.J. Stokes	.75	2.00
40 Steve Young	1.50	4.00
41 Brent Jones	.20	.50
42 Jerry Rice	1.50	4.00
43 Joe Montana	3.00	8.00
44 Rick Mirer	.40	1.00
45 Chris Warren	.40	1.00
46 Joey Galloway	.75	2.00
47 Isaac Bruce	.75	2.00
48 Jerome Bettis	.75	2.00
49 Errict Rhett	.40	1.00
50 Michael Westbrook	.75	2.00
UDT13 Dan Marino	6.00	15.00
Record Breaker		
UDT13A Dan Marino AUTO	50.00	120.00
Record Breaker signed		
UDT19 Joe Montana Tribute	6.00	15.00
UDT19A Joe Montana AUTO	40.00	100.00
Tribute card signed		
P1 Dan Marino Promo	2.00	5.00
P2 Joe Montana Promo	2.00	5.00

1996 SPx Gold

COMPLETE SET (50)	25.00	60.00
*GOLDS: 1X TO 2.5X BASIC CARDS		
STATED ODDS 1:7		

1996 SPx HoloFame

COMPLETE SET (10)	25.00	60.00
STATED ODDS 1:24		
HM1 Troy Aikman	2.50	6.00
HM2 Emmitt Smith	4.00	10.00
HM3 Barry Sanders	4.00	10.00
HM4 Steve Young	2.50	6.00
HM5 Jerry Rice	2.50	6.00
HM6 John Elway	5.00	12.00
HM7 Marshall Faulk	1.50	4.00
HM8 Dan Marino	5.00	12.00
HM9 Drew Bledsoe	1.50	4.00
HM10 Natrone Means	.60	1.50

1997 SPx

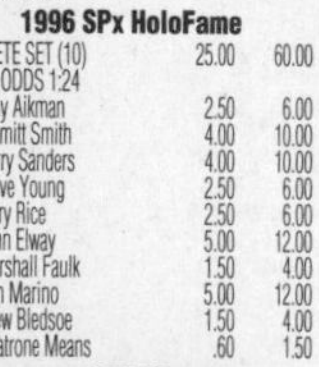

The 1997 SPx set was issued in one series totaling 50 cards and was distributed in one card packs with a suggested retail of $3.49. The 50-card set features color player photos of the best players and rookies of the NFL in an all new Holoview, Hologram and Light F/X design. A lenticular player portrait appears on the right side of the card front. The backs carry player information and statistics.

COMPLETE SET (50)	12.50	30.00
1 Jerry Rice	1.50	4.00
2 Steve Young	1.00	2.50
3 Karim Abdul-Jabbar	.75	2.00
4 Dan Marino	3.00	8.00
5 Bobby Engram	.50	1.25
6 Rashaan Salaam	.30	.75
7 Marvin Harrison	.75	2.00
8 Jim Harbaugh	.50	1.25
9 Marshall Faulk	1.00	2.50
10 Eric Moulds	.75	2.00
11 Thurman Thomas	.75	2.00
12 Tamarick Vanover	.50	1.25
13 Steve Bono	.50	1.25
14 Warren Moon	.75	2.00
15 Cris Carter	.75	2.00
16 Carl Pickens	.50	1.25
17 Ki-Jana Carter	.30	.75
18 Jeff Blake	.50	1.25
19 Tim Biakabutuka	.50	1.25
20 Kerry Collins	.75	2.00
21 Leeland McElroy	.30	.75
22 Simeon Rice	.50	1.25
23 John Elway	3.00	8.00
24 Terrell Davis	1.00	2.50
25 Jeff Lewis	.30	.75
26 Terry Glenn	.75	2.00
27 Curtis Martin	1.00	2.50
28 Drew Bledsoe	1.00	2.50
29 Lawrence Phillips	.30	.75
30 Isaac Bruce	.75	2.00
31 Eddie Kennison	.50	1.25
32 Keyshawn Johnson	.75	2.00
33 Stepfret Williams	.30	.75
34 Emmitt Smith	2.50	6.00
35 Troy Aikman	1.50	4.00
36 Deion Sanders	.75	2.00
37 Joey Galloway	.50	1.25
38 Rick Mirer	.30	.75
39 Rickey Dudley	.50	1.25
40 Jeff Hostetler	.30	.75
41 Junior Seau	.75	2.00
42 Derrick Mayes	.50	1.25
43 Brett Favre	3.00	8.00
44 Edgar Bennett	.50	1.25
45 Barry Sanders	2.50	6.00
46 Herman Moore	.50	1.25
47 Kordell Stewart	.75	2.00
48 Jerome Bettis	.75	2.00
49 Eddie George	.75	2.00
50 Steve McNair	1.00	2.50
P80 Jerry Rice Promo	1.25	3.00
numbered SPX80		
(1996 on copyright line)		

1997 SPx Gold

COMPLETE SET (50)	60.00	120.00
*GOLD STARS: 1.5X TO 3X BASIC CARDS		

1997 SPx HoloFame

COMPLETE SET (20)	100.00	200.00
STATED ODDS 1:75		
HX1 Jerry Rice	6.00	15.00
HX2 Emmitt Smith	10.00	25.00
HX3 Karim Abdul-Jabbar	3.00	8.00
HX4 Brett Favre	12.50	30.00
HX5 Curtis Martin	4.00	10.00
HX6 Eddie Kennison	2.00	5.00
HX7 Troy Aikman	6.00	15.00
HX8 Steve Young	4.00	10.00
HX9 Tim Biakabutuka	2.00	5.00
HX10 Reggie White	3.00	8.00
HX11 Terry Glenn	3.00	8.00
HX12 Lawrence Phillips	1.25	3.00
HX13 Dan Marino	12.50	30.00
HX14 Deion Sanders	3.00	8.00
HX15 Terrell Davis	4.00	10.00
HX16 Marvin Harrison	3.00	8.00
HX17 Eddie George	3.00	8.00
HX18 Marshall Faulk	4.00	10.00
HX19 Keyshawn Johnson	3.00	8.00
HX20 Barry Sanders	10.00	25.00

1997 SPx ProMotion

COMPLETE SET (6)	60.00	150.00
STATED ODDS 1:433		
1 Dan Marino	20.00	50.00
2 Joe Montana	20.00	50.00
3 Troy Aikman	10.00	25.00
4 Barry Sanders	15.00	40.00
5 Karim Abdul-Jabbar	5.00	12.00
6 Eddie George	5.00	12.00

1997 SPx ProMotion Autographs

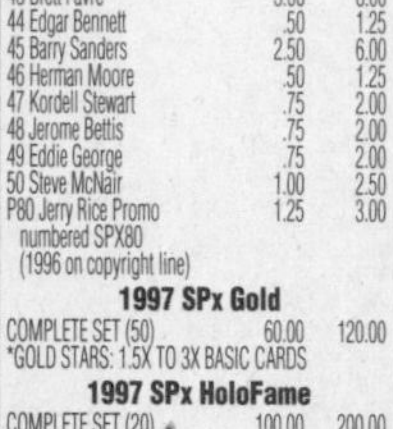

AUTO/100 STATED ODDS 1:4331		
STATED PRINT RUN 100 SETS		
1 Dan Marino	125.00	250.00
2 Joe Montana	125.00	250.00
3 Troy Aikman	75.00	150.00
4 Barry Sanders	100.00	200.00
5 Karim Abdul-Jabbar	25.00	60.00
6 Eddie George	30.00	80.00

1998 SPx

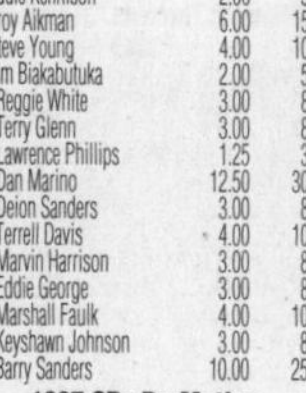

The 1998 SPx set was issued in one series totalling 50-cards and distributed in three-card packs with a suggested retail price of $5.99. These holoview die-cut cards feature color player photos on 32 pt. card stock with decorative foil and Light F/X highlights. Five additional parallel sets were inserted with the overall ratio of one per pack. The Piece of History trade program included trade insert cards that could be reedemed for game used NFL equipment (1:892 packs). The redemption program expired on 12/1/1998.

COMPLETE SET (50)	30.00	80.00
1 Jake Plummer	.75	2.00
2 Byron Hanspard	.30	.75
3 Vinny Testaverde	.50	1.25
4 Antowain Smith	.75	2.00
5 Kerry Collins	.50	1.25
6 Rae Carruth	.30	.75
7 Darnell Autry	.30	.75
8 Rick Mirer	.30	.75
9 Jeff Blake	.50	1.25
10 Carl Pickens	.50	1.25
11 Troy Aikman	1.50	4.00
12 Emmitt Smith	3.00	6.00
13 Deion Sanders	.75	2.00
14 John Elway	3.00	8.00
15 Terrell Davis	.75	2.00
16 Herman Moore	.50	1.25
17 Barry Sanders	2.50	6.00
18 Brett Favre	3.00	8.00
19 Reggie White	.75	2.00
20 Marshall Faulk	1.00	2.50
21 Mark Brunell	.75	2.00
22 Elvis Grbac	.50	1.25
23 Marcus Allen	.75	2.00
24 Karim Abdul-Jabbar	.75	2.00
25 Dan Marino	3.00	8.00
26 Cris Carter	.75	2.00
27 Drew Bledsoe	1.25	3.00
28 Curtis Martin	.75	2.00
29 Heath Shuler	.30	.75
30 Ike Hilliard	.50	1.25
31 Keyshawn Johnson	.75	2.00
32 Jeff George	.50	1.25
33 Napoleon Kaufman	.75	2.00
34 Darrell Russell	.30	.75
35 Ricky Watters	.50	1.25
36 Kordell Stewart	.75	2.00
37 Jerome Bettis	.75	2.00
38 Junior Seau	.75	2.00
39 Steve Young	1.00	2.50
40 Jerry Rice	2.00	4.00
41 Joey Galloway	.50	1.25
42 Chris Warren	.50	1.25
43 Orlando Pace	.30	.75
44 Isaac Bruce	.75	2.00
45 Tony Banks	.50	1.25
46 Trent Dilfer	.75	2.00
47 Warrick Dunn	.75	2.00
48 Steve McNair	.75	2.00
49 Eddie George	.75	2.00
50 Terry Allen	.75	2.00

1998 SPx Bronze

COMP.BRONZE SET (50)	75.00	150.00
*BRONZE STARS: .8X TO 2X BASIC CARDS		
STATED ODDS 1:3 HOBBY		

1998 SPx Gold

COMP.GOLD SET (50)	250.00	500.00
*GOLD STARS: 2X TO 5X BASIC CARDS		
STATED ODDS 1:17		

1998 SPx Grand Finale

GRAND FINALE/50: 12X TO 30X
ANNOUNCED PRINT RUN 50

1998 SPx Silver

COMP.SILVER SET (50)	125.00	250.00
*SILVER STARS: 1.2X TO 3X BASIC CARDS		
STATED ODDS 1:6 HOBBY		

1998 SPx Steel

COMP.STEEL SET (50)	50.00	100.00
*STEEL STARS: .6X TO 1.2X BASIC CARDS		
STATED ODDS 1:1 HOBBY		

1998 SPx HoloFame

COMPLETE SET (20)	75.00	200.00
STATED ODDS 1:54		
HF1 Troy Aikman	8.00	20.00
HF2 Emmitt Smith	12.50	30.00
HF3 John Elway	15.00	40.00
HF4 Terrell Davis	4.00	10.00
HF5 Herman Moore	2.50	6.00
HF6 Reggie White	4.00	10.00
HF7 Brett Favre	15.00	40.00
HF8 Napoleon Kaufman	4.00	10.00
HF9 Dan Marino	15.00	40.00
HF10 Karim Abdul-Jabbar	4.00	10.00
HF11 Cris Carter	4.00	10.00
HF12 Drew Bledsoe	6.00	15.00
HF13 Curtis Martin	4.00	10.00
HF14 Kordell Stewart	4.00	10.00
HF15 Junior Seau	4.00	10.00
HF16 Steve Young	5.00	12.00
HF17 Jerry Rice	8.00	20.00
HF18 Marshall Faulk	5.00	12.00
HF19 Eddie George	4.00	10.00
HF20 Terry Allen	4.00	10.00

1998 SPx ProMotion

COMPLETE SET (10)	150.00	400.00
STATED ODDS 1:252		
P1 Troy Aikman	20.00	50.00
P2 Emmitt Smith	30.00	80.00
P3 Terrell Davis	10.00	25.00
P4 Brett Favre	40.00	100.00
P5 Marcus Allen	10.00	25.00
P6 Dan Marino	40.00	100.00
P7 Drew Bledsoe	15.00	40.00
P8 Ike Hilliard	6.00	15.00
P9 Warrick Dunn	10.00	25.00
P10 Eddie George	10.00	25.00

1998 SPx Finite

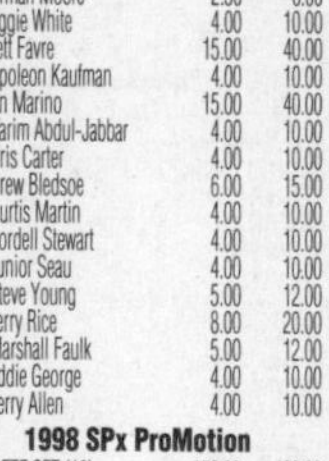

The SPx Finite set was issued in two series for a totoal of 370-cards. Series one was issued with a total of 190-cards and Series two with a total of 180-cards. Each card was individually serial numbered. Series One contains: base cards (#1-90; 7600-sets), Playmakers (#91-120; 5500-sets), Youth Movement (#121-150; 3000-sets), Pure Energy (#151-170; 2500-sets), and Heroes of the Game (#171-180; 1250-sets). Series Two contains: base cards (#191-280; 10,100-sets, #218/221/239; 1998-sets), Extreme Talent (#281-310; 7200-sets), the New School (311-340; 4000-sets, #321/338/339; 1700-sets), Sixth Sense (#341-360; 2700-sets), and Uncommon Valor (#361-370; 1620-sets). Each card was printed with two parallel color variations.

COMP.SERIES 1 (190)	400.00	750.00
COMP.SERIES 2 (180)	400.00	750.00
1 Jake Plummer	1.00	2.50
2 Eric Swann	.40	1.00
3 Rob Moore	.60	1.50
4 Jamal Anderson	1.00	2.50
5 Byron Hanspard	.40	1.00
6 Cornelius Bennett	.40	1.00
7 Michael Jackson	.40	1.00
8 Peter Boulware	.40	1.00
9 Jermaine Lewis	.60	1.50
10 Antowain Smith	1.00	2.50
11 Bruce Smith	.60	1.50
12 Bryce Paup	.40	1.00
13 Rae Carruth	.40	1.00
14 Michael Bates	.40	1.00
15 Fred Lane	.40	1.00
16 Darnell Autry	.60	1.50
17 Curtis Conway	.60	1.50
18 Erik Kramer	.40	1.00
19 Corey Dillon	1.00	2.50
20 Darnay Scott	.60	1.50
21 Reinard Wilson	.40	1.00
22 Troy Aikman	2.00	5.00
23 David LaFleur	.40	1.00
24 Emmitt Smith	3.00	8.00
25 John Elway	4.00	10.00
26 John Mobley	.40	1.00
27 Terrell Davis	1.00	2.50
28 Rod Smith	.60	1.50
29 Bryant Westbrook	.40	1.00
30 Scott Mitchell	.60	1.50
31 Barry Sanders	3.00	8.00
32 Dorsey Levens	1.00	2.50
33 Antonio Freeman	1.00	2.50
34 Reggie White	1.00	2.50
35 Marshall Faulk	1.25	3.00
36 Marvin Harrison	1.00	2.50
37 Ken Dilger	.40	1.00
38 Mark Brunell	1.00	2.50
39 Keenan McCardell	.60	1.50
40 Renaldo Wynn	.40	1.00
41 Marcus Allen	1.00	2.50
42 Elvis Grbac	.60	1.50
43 Andre Rison	.60	1.50
44 Yatil Green	.40	1.00
45 Zach Thomas	1.00	2.50
46 Karim Abdul-Jabbar	1.00	2.50
UER Karim Abdul front and back		
47 John Randle	.60	1.50
48 Brad Johnson	1.00	2.50
49 Jake Reed	.60	1.50
50 Danny Wuerffel	.60	1.50
51 Andre Hastings	.40	1.00
52 Drew Bledsoe	1.50	4.00
53 Terry Glenn	1.00	2.50
54 Ty Law	.60	1.50
55 Danny Kanell	.60	1.50
56 Tiki Barber	1.00	2.50
57 Jessie Armstead	.40	1.00
58 Glenn Foley	.60	1.50
59 James Farrior	.40	1.00
60 Wayne Chrebet	1.00	2.50
61 Tim Brown	1.00	2.50
62 Napoleon Kaufman	1.00	2.50
63 Darrell Russell	.40	1.00
64 Bobby Hoying	.60	1.50
65 Irving Fryar	.60	1.50
66 Charlie Garner	.60	1.50
67 Will Blackwell	.40	1.00
68 Kordell Stewart	1.00	2.50
69 Levon Kirkland	.40	1.00
70 Tony Banks	.60	1.50
71 Ryan McNeil	.40	1.00
72 Isaac Bruce	1.00	2.50
73 Tony Martin	.60	1.50
74 Junior Seau	1.00	2.50
75 Natrone Means	.60	1.50
76 Jerry Rice	2.00	5.00
77 Garrison Hearst	1.00	2.50
78 Terrell Owens	1.00	2.50
79 Warren Moon	1.00	2.50
80 Joey Galloway	.60	1.50
81 Chad Brown	.40	1.00
82 Warrick Dunn	1.00	2.50
83 Mike Alstott	1.00	2.50
84 Hardy Nickerson	.40	1.00
85 Steve McNair	1.00	2.50
86 Chris Sanders	.40	1.00
87 Darryll Lewis	.40	1.00
88 Gus Frerotte	.40	1.00
89 Terry Allen	1.00	2.50
90 Chris Dishman	.40	1.00
91 Kordell Stewart PM	1.25	3.00
92 Jerry Rice PM	2.50	6.00
93 Michael Irvin PM	1.25	3.00
94 Brett Favre PM	5.00	12.00
95 Jeff George PM	.75	2.00
96 Joey Galloway PM	.75	2.00
97 John Elway PM	5.00	12.00
98 Troy Aikman PM	2.50	6.00
99 Steve Young PM	1.50	4.00
100 Andre Rison PM	.75	2.00
101 Ben Coates PM	.75	2.00
102 Robert Brooks PM	.75	2.00
103 Dan Marino PM	5.00	12.00
104 Isaac Bruce PM	1.25	3.00
105 Junior Seau PM	1.25	3.00
106 Jake Plummer PM	1.25	3.00
107 Curtis Conway PM	.75	2.00
108 Jeff Blake PM	.75	2.00
109 Rod Smith PM	.75	2.00
110 Barry Sanders PM	4.00	10.00
111 Deion Sanders PM	1.25	3.00
112 Drew Bledsoe PM	2.00	5.00
113 Emmitt Smith PM	4.00	10.00
114 Herman Moore PM	.75	2.00
115 Dorsey Levens PM	1.25	3.00
116 Jimmy Smith PM	.75	2.00
117 Tony Martin PM	.50	1.25
118 Carl Pickens PM	.75	2.00
119 Keyshawn Johnson PM	1.25	3.00
120 Cris Carter PM	1.25	3.00
121 Warrick Dunn YM	2.00	5.00
122 Marshall Faulk YM	2.50	6.00
123 Trent Dilfer YM	2.00	5.00
124 Napoleon Kaufman YM	2.00	5.00
125 Corey Dillon YM	2.00	5.00
126 Darrell Russell YM	.75	2.00
127 Danny Kanell YM	1.25	3.00
128 Reidel Anthony YM	1.25	3.00
129 Steve McNair YM	2.00	5.00
130 Ike Hilliard YM	1.25	3.00
131 Tony Banks YM	1.25	3.00
132 Yatil Green YM	.75	2.00
133 J.J. Stokes YM	1.25	3.00
134 Fred Lane YM	.75	2.00
135 Bryant Westbrook YM	.75	2.00
136 Jake Plummer YM	2.00	5.00
137 Byron Hanspard YM	.75	2.00
138 Rae Carruth YM	.75	2.00
139 Keyshawn Johnson YM	2.00	5.00
140 Jim Druckenmiller YM	.75	2.00
141 Amani Toomer YM	1.25	3.00
142 Troy Davis YM	.75	2.00
143 Antowain Smith YM	2.00	5.00
144 Shawn Springs YM	.75	2.00
145 Rickey Dudley YM	.75	2.00
146 Terry Glenn YM	2.00	5.00
147 Johnnie Morton YM	1.25	3.00
148 David LaFleur YM	.75	2.00
149 Eddie Kennison YM	1.25	3.00
150 Bobby Hoying YM	1.25	3.00
151 Junior Seau PE	2.50	6.00
152 Shannon Sharpe PE	1.50	4.00
153 Bruce Smith PE	1.50	4.00
154 Brett Favre PE	7.50	20.00
155 Emmitt Smith PE	6.00	15.00
156 Keenan McCardell PE	1.00	2.50
157 Kordell Stewart PE	2.50	6.00
158 Troy Aikman PE	4.00	10.00
159 Steve Young PE	2.50	6.00
160 Tim Brown PE	2.50	6.00
161 Eddie George PE	2.50	6.00
162 Herman Moore PE	1.50	4.00
163 Dan Marino PE	7.50	20.00
164 Dorsey Levens PE	2.50	6.00
165 Jerry Rice PE	4.00	10.00
166 Warren Sapp PE	1.50	4.00
167 Robert Smith PE	2.50	6.00
168 Mark Brunell PE	2.50	6.00
169 Terrell Davis PE	2.50	6.00
170 Jerome Bettis PE	2.50	6.00
171 Dan Marino HG	12.50	30.00
172 Barry Sanders HG	10.00	25.00
173 Marcus Allen HG	3.00	8.00
174 Brett Favre HG	12.50	30.00
175 Warrick Dunn HG	3.00	8.00
176 Eddie George HG	3.00	8.00
177 John Elway HG	12.50	30.00
178 Troy Aikman HG	6.00	15.00
179 Cris Carter HG	3.00	8.00
180 Terrell Davis HG	3.00	8.00
181 Peyton Manning RC	75.00	150.00
182 Ryan Leaf RC	12.50	25.00
183 Andre Wadsworth RC	10.00	20.00
184 Charles Woodson RC	15.00	30.00
185 Curtis Enis RC	7.50	15.00
186 Grant Wistrom RC	10.00	20.00
187 Fred Taylor RC	20.00	40.00
188 Takeo Spikes RC	12.50	25.00
189 Kevin Dyson RC	12.50	25.00
190 Robert Edwards RC	10.00	20.00
191 Adrian Murrell	.40	1.00
192 Simeon Rice	.40	1.00
193 Frank Sanders	.40	1.00
194 Chris Chandler	.40	1.00
195 Terance Mathis	.40	1.00
196 Keith Brooking RC	.60	1.50
197 Jim Harbaugh	.40	1.00
198 Errict Rhett	.40	1.00
199 Pat Johnson RC	1.00	2.50
200 Rob Johnson	.40	1.00
201 Andre Reed	.40	1.00
202 Thurman Thomas	.60	1.50
203 Kerry Collins	.40	1.00
204 William Floyd	.25	.60
205 Sean Gilbert	.25	.60
206 Bobby Engram	.40	1.00
207 Edgar Bennett	.40	1.00
208 Walt Harris	.40	1.00
209 Carl Pickens	.40	1.00
210 Neil O'Donnell	.40	1.00
211 Tony McGee	.25	.60
212 Deion Sanders	.60	1.50
213 Michael Irvin	.60	1.50
214 Greg Ellis RC	.50	1.25
215 Shannon Sharpe	.40	1.00
216 Neil Smith	.40	1.00
217 Marcus Nash RC	.50	1.25
218 Brian Griese RC	10.00	25.00
219 Johnnie Morton	.40	1.00
220 Herman Moore	.60	1.50
221 Charlie Batch RC	6.00	15.00
222 Robert Brooks	.40	1.00
223 Mark Chmura	.40	1.00
224 Brett Favre	2.50	6.00
225 Jerome Pathon RC	2.00	5.00
226 Zack Crockett	.25	.60
227 Dan Footman	.25	.60
228 Jimmy Smith	.40	1.00
229 Bryce Paup	.25	.60
230 James Stewart	.40	1.00
231 Derrick Thomas	.60	1.50
232 Derrick Alexander	.40	1.00
233 Tony Gonzalez	.60	1.50
234 Dan Marino	2.50	6.00
235 O.J. McDuffie	.40	1.00
236 Troy Drayton	.25	.60
237 Cris Carter	.60	1.50
238 Robert Smith	.60	1.50
239 Randy Moss RC	25.00	60.00
240 Lamar Smith	.40	1.00
241 Sean Dawkins	.25	.60
242 Alex Molden	.25	.60
243 Ben Coates	.40	1.00
244 Ted Johnson	.25	.60
245 Sedrick Shaw	.25	.60
246 Ike Hilliard	.40	1.00
247 Jason Sehorn	.40	1.00
248 Michael Strahan	.40	1.00
249 Keyshawn Johnson	.60	1.50
250 Curtis Martin	.60	1.50
251 Jeff George	.40	1.00
252 Rickey Dudley	.25	.60
253 James Jett	.40	1.00
254 Bobby Taylor UER	.40	1.00
(photo on back is William Thomas)		
255 Rodney Peete	.40	1.00
256 William Thomas	.40	1.00
257 Jerome Bettis	.60	1.50
258 Charles Johnson	.25	.60
259 C.Fuamatu-Ma'afala RC	1.00	2.50
260 Eddie Kennison	.40	1.00
261 Az-Zahir Hakim RC	2.00	5.00
262 Robert Holcombe RC	1.00	2.50
263 Bryan Still	.25	.60
264 Mikhael Ricks RC	1.00	2.50
265 Charlie Jones	.25	.60
266 J.J. Stokes	.40	1.00
267 Marc Edwards	.25	.60
268 Steve Young	.75	2.00
269 Ricky Watters	.40	1.00
270 Cortez Kennedy	.25	.60
271 Shawn Springs	.25	.60
272 Trent Dilfer	.60	1.50
273 Warren Sapp	.40	1.00
274 Reidel Anthony	.40	1.00
275 Yancey Thigpen	.25	.60
276 Chris Sanders	.25	.60
277 Eddie George	.60	1.50
278 Leslie Shepherd	.25	.60
279 Skip Hicks RC	1.00	2.50
280 Dana Stubblefield	.25	.60
281 John Elway ET	3.00	8.00
282 Brett Favre ET	3.00	8.00
283 Junior Seau ET	.75	2.00
284 Barry Sanders ET	2.50	6.00
285 Jerry Rice ET	1.50	4.00
286 Antonio Freeman ET	.75	2.00
287 Peyton Manning ET	15.00	30.00
288 Warrick Dunn ET	.75	2.00
289 Steve Young ET	1.00	2.50
290 Dan Marino ET	3.00	8.00
291 Jerome Bettis ET	.75	2.00
292 Ryan Leaf ET	.75	2.00
293 Deion Sanders ET	.75	2.00
294 Eddie George ET	.75	2.00
295 Joey Galloway ET	.50	1.25
296 Troy Aikman ET	1.50	4.00
297 Andre Wadsworth ET	.50	1.25
298 Terrell Davis ET	.75	2.00
299 Steve McNair ET	.75	2.00
300 Jake Plummer ET	.75	2.00
301 Emmitt Smith ET	2.50	6.00
302 Isaac Bruce ET	.75	2.00
303 Kordell Stewart ET	.75	2.00
304 Dorsey Levens ET	.75	2.00
305 Antowain Smith ET	.75	2.00
306 Drew Bledsoe ET	1.25	3.00
307 Marshall Faulk ET	1.00	2.50
308 Herman Moore ET	.50	1.25
309 Mark Brunell ET	.75	2.00
310 Charles Woodson ET	2.00	5.00
311 Peyton Manning NS	15.00	30.00
312 Curtis Enis NS	.60	1.50
313 Terry Fair NS RC	1.00	2.50
314 Andre Wadsworth NS	1.00	2.50
315 A.Simmons NS RC	1.00	2.50
316 Jacquez Green NS RC	3.00	8.00
317 Takeo Spikes NS	2.00	5.00
318 Vonnie Holliday NS RC	3.00	8.00
319 Kyle Turley NS RC	2.00	5.00
320 Keith Brooking NS	2.00	5.00
321 Randy Moss NS	12.50	25.00
322 Shaun Williams NS RC	1.00	2.50
323 Greg Ellis NS	.60	1.50
324 Mikhael Ricks NS	1.00	2.50
325 Charles Woodson NS	5.00	12.00
326 Corey Chavous NS RC	2.00	5.00
327 S.Alexander NS RC	2.00	5.00
328 Marcus Nash NS	.60	1.50
329 Tra Thomas NS RC	1.00	2.50
330 Duane Starks NS RC	2.00	5.00
331 John Avery NS RC	1.00	2.50
332 Kevin Dyson NS	2.00	5.00
333 Fred Taylor NS	3.00	8.00
334 Grant Wistrom NS	1.00	2.50
335 Ryan Leaf NS	2.00	5.00
336 Robert Edwards NS	1.00	2.50
337 Jason Peter NS RC	1.00	2.50
338 Brian Griese NS	5.00	12.00
339 Charlie Batch NS	2.00	5.00
340 Pat Johnson NS	1.00	2.50
341 John Elway SS	6.00	15.00
342 Curtis Enis SS	.60	1.50
343 Antonio Freeman SS	1.50	4.00
344 Mark Brunell SS	1.50	4.00
345 Robert Edwards SS	1.00	2.50
346 Ryan Leaf SS	1.50	4.00
347 Steve Young SS	2.00	5.00
348 Jerome Bettis SS	1.50	4.00
349 Antowain Smith SS	1.50	4.00
350 Tim Brown SS	1.50	4.00
351 Peyton Manning SS	15.00	30.00
352 Troy Aikman SS	3.00	8.00
353 Natrone Means SS	1.00	2.50
354 Dan Marino SS	6.00	15.00
355 Junior Seau SS	.60	1.50
356 Brad Johnson SS	1.50	4.00
357 Jerry Rice SS	3.00	8.00
358 Drew Bledsoe SS	2.50	6.00
359 Fred Taylor SS	3.00	8.00
360 Emmitt Smith SS	5.00	12.00
361 Terrell Davis UV	3.00	8.00
362 Kordell Stewart UV	2.50	6.00
363 Barry Sanders UV	7.50	20.00
364 Jake Plummer UV	2.50	6.00
365 Brett Favre UV	10.00	25.00
366 Curtis Enis UV	2.50	6.00
367 Eddie George UV	2.50	6.00
368 Napoleon Kaufman UV	2.50	6.00
369 Randy Moss UV	20.00	40.00
370 Warrick Dunn UV	2.50	6.00
S8 Troy Aikman Sample	.40	1.00
S234 Dan Marino Sample	.75	2.00

1998 SPx Finite Radiance

*1-90 RADIANCE STARS: .6X TO 1.5X HI		
1-90 PRINT RUN 3800 SERIAL #'d SETS		
*91-120 RADIANCE STARS: .6X TO 1.5X HI		
91-120 PM PRINT RUN 2750 SERIAL #'d SETS		
*121-150 RADIANCE STARS: .6X TO 1.5X HI		
121-150 YM PRINT RUN 1500 SERIAL #'d SETS		
*151-170 RADIANCE STARS: .8X TO 2X HI		
151-170 PE PRINT RUN 1000 SERIAL #'d SETS		
*171-180 RADIANCE STARS: 2X TO 5X		
171-180 HG PRINT RUN 100 SERIAL #'d SETS		
181-190 PRINT RUN 50 SERIAL #'d SETS		
*191-280 RADIANCE STARS: .6X TO 1.5X HI		
*191-280 RADIANCE RCs: .4X TO 1X		
191-280 PRINT RUN 5050 SERIAL #'d SETS		
218/221/239 PRINT RUN 1700 SER.#'d SETS		
*281-310 RADIANCE STARS: .6X TO 1.5X		
281-310 ET PRINT RUN 3600 SER.#'d SETS		
*311-340 RADIANCE STARS: .6X TO 1.5X		
311-340 NS PRINT RUN 2000 SER.#'d SETS		
321/338/339 PRINT RUN 850 SER.#'d SETS		
*341-360 RADIANCE STARS: .8X TO 2X		
341-360 SS PRINT RUN 900 SER.#'d SETS		
*361-370 RADIANCE STARS: .8X TO 2X		
*361-370 RAD.ROOKIES: .6X TO 1.5X		
361-370 UV PRINT RUN 540 SER.#'d SETS		
181 Peyton Manning	500.00	750.00
182 Ryan Leaf	25.00	60.00
183 Andre Wadsworth	20.00	50.00
184 Charles Woodson	40.00	80.00
185 Curtis Enis	15.00	40.00
186 Grant Wistrom	20.00	50.00
187 Fred Taylor	25.00	60.00
188 Takeo Spikes	25.00	60.00
189 Kevin Dyson	25.00	60.00
190 Robert Edwards	15.00	40.00
221 Charlie Batch	10.00	25.00
239 Randy Moss	30.00	80.00

1998 SPx Finite Spectrum

*1-90 SPECTRUM STARS: 1.2X TO 3X HI
1-90 PRINT RUN 1900 SERIAL #'d SETS
*91-120 SPECTRUM PM STARS: 1.2X TO 3X
91-120 PM PRINT RUN 1375 SERIAL #'d SETS
*121-150 SPECTRUM YM STARS: 1.2X TO 3X
121-150 YM PRINT RUN 750 SERIAL #'d SETS
*151-170 SPECTRUM PE STARS: 6X TO 15X
151-170 PE PRINT RUN 50 SERIAL #'d SETS
171-180 HG PRINT RUN 1 SERIAL #'d SET
181-190 PRINT RUN 1 SERIAL #'d SET
*191-280 SPECTRUM STARS: 3X TO 8X
*191-280 SPECTRUM RCs: 1.2X TO 3X
*218/221/239 SPECTRUM RCs: .5X TO 1.2X
191-280 PRINT RUN 325 SERIAL #'d SETS
*281-310 SPECTRUM ET STARS: 4X TO 10X
*281-310 SPECTRUM ROOKIES: 1.2X TO 3X
281-310 ET PRINT RUN 150 SERIAL #'d SETS
*311-340 SPECTRUM NS: 3X TO 8X
*321/338/339 SPECTRUM NS: 1.5X TO 4X
311-340 NS PRINT RUN 50 SERIAL #'d SETS
*341-360 SPECTRUM SS STARS: 8X TO 20X
*341-360 SPECTRUM SS ROOKIES: 3X TO 8X
341-360 SS PRINT RUN 25 SERIAL #'d SETS

1998 SPx Finite UD Authentics

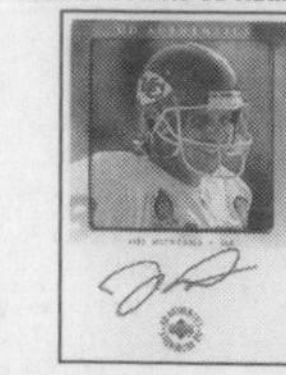

COMP.BLUE INK SET (4)	125.00	300.00
DM1 Dan Marino/400	50.00	120.00
JM1 Joe Montana/1984	40.00	100.00
(Chiefs photo)		
RS1 Roger Staubach/463	30.00	80.00
TA1 Troy Aikman/1992	40.00	80.00

1999 SPx

Released as a 135-card set, 1999 SPx football features 90 veteran player cards and 45 rookies sequentially numbered to 1999 where 26 of the rookie cards are acutally autographed. Card numbers 130-135 are signed and numbered out of 500. Packaged in 18 pack boxes with three cards per pack, SPx carried a suggested retail price of $5.99.

COMPLETE SET (135)	1,000.00	2,000.00
COMP.SET w/o RCs (90)	12.50	25.00
*HAND NUMBERED RCs: .5X TO .8X		
1 Jake Plummer	.30	.75
2 Adrian Murrell	.30	.75
3 Frank Sanders	.25	.60
4 Jamal Anderson	.30	.75
5 Chris Chandler	.30	.75
6 Terance Mathis	.25	.60
7 Tony Banks	.30	.75
8 Priest Holmes	.40	1.00
9 Jermaine Lewis	.25	.60
10 Antowain Smith	.25	.60
11 Doug Flutie	.40	1.00
12 Eric Moulds	.30	.75
13 Tim Biakabutuka	.30	.75
14 Steve Beuerlein	.30	.75
15 Muhsin Muhammad	.30	.75
16 Bobby Engram	.30	.75
17 Curtis Conway	.30	.75
18 Curtis Enis	.25	.60
19 Corey Dillon	.30	.75
20 Jeff Blake	.30	.75
21 Carl Pickens	.30	.75
22 Ty Detmer	.30	.75
23 Terry Kirby	.25	.60
24 Leslie Shepherd	.25	.60
25 Troy Aikman	.60	1.50
26 Emmitt Smith	1.00	2.50
27 Deion Sanders	.40	1.00
28 Terrell Davis	.40	1.00
29 Rod Smith	.30	.75
30 Bubby Brister	.25	.60
31 Barry Sanders	1.00	2.50
32 Herman Moore	.30	.75
33 Charlie Batch	.30	.75
34 Brett Favre	1.25	3.00
35 Antonio Freeman	.30	.75
36 Dorsey Levens	.30	.75
37 Peyton Manning	1.25	3.00
38 Marvin Harrison	.40	1.00
39 Jerome Pathon	.25	.60
40 Mark Brunell	.30	.75
41 Jimmy Smith	.30	.75
42 Fred Taylor	.30	.75
43 Elvis Grbac	.25	.60
44 Andre Rison	.30	.75
45 Warren Moon	.40	1.00
46 Dan Marino	1.25	3.00
47 Karim Abdul-Jabbar	.30	.75
48 O.J. McDuffie	.30	.75
49 Randall Cunningham	.40	1.00
50 Robert Smith	.30	.75
51 Randy Moss	.40	1.00
52 Drew Bledsoe	.40	1.00
53 Terry Glenn	.30	.75
54 Tony Simmons	.25	.60
55 Danny Wuerffel	.30	.75
56 Cam Cleeland	.25	.60
57 Kerry Collins	.30	.75
58 Gary Brown	.25	.60
59 Ike Hilliard	.30	.75
60 Vinny Testaverde	.30	.75
61 Curtis Martin	.40	1.00
62 Keyshawn Johnson	.30	.75
63 Rich Gannon	.30	.75
64 Napoleon Kaufman	.25	.60
65 Tim Brown	.40	1.00
66 Duce Staley	.30	.75
67 Doug Pederson	.25	.60
68 Charles Johnson	.25	.60
69 Kordell Stewart	.30	.75
70 Jerome Bettis	.40	1.00
71 Trent Green	.30	.75
72 Marshall Faulk	.40	1.00
73 Ryan Leaf	.30	.75
74 Natrone Means	.30	.75
75 Jim Harbaugh	.30	.75
76 Steve Young	.50	1.25
77 Garrison Hearst	.30	.75
78 Jerry Rice	.75	2.00
79 Terrell Owens	.40	1.00
80 Ricky Watters	.30	.75
81 Joey Galloway	.30	.75
82 Jon Kitna	.30	.75
83 Warrick Dunn	.30	.75
84 Trent Dilfer	.30	.75

85 Mike Alstott	.40	1.00
86 Steve McNair	.40	1.00
87 Eddie George	.30	.75
88 Yancey Thigpen	.25	.60
89 Skip Hicks	.25	.60
90 Michael Westbrook	.25	.60
91 Amos Zereoue RC	4.00	10.00
92 Chris Claiborne AU RC	5.00	12.00
93 Scott Covington RC	3.00	8.00
94 Jeff Paulk RC	3.00	8.00
95 Brandon Stokley AUTO RC	8.00	20.00
96 Antoine Winfield RC	3.00	8.00
97 Reginald Kelly RC	3.00	8.00
98 Jermaine Fazande AUTO RC	5.00	12.00
99 Andy Katzenmoyer RC	4.00	10.00
100 Craig Yeast RC	3.00	8.00
101 Joe Montgomery RC	3.00	8.00
102 Darrin Chiaverini RC	3.00	8.00
103 Travis McGriff RC	3.00	8.00
104 Jevon Kearse RC	5.00	12.00
105 Joel Makovicka AUTO RC	5.00	12.00
106 Aaron Brooks RC	5.00	12.00
107 Chris McAlister RC	4.00	10.00
108 Jim Kleinsasser RC	5.00	12.00
109 Ebenezer Ekuban RC	3.00	8.00
110 Karsten Bailey RC	3.00	8.00
111 Sedrick Irvin AU RC	5.00	12.00
112 D'Wayne Bates AUTO RC	5.00	12.00
113 Joe Germaine AU RC	6.00	15.00
114 Cecil Collins AU RC	5.00	12.00
115 Mike Cloud RC	3.00	8.00
116 James Johnson RC	3.00	8.00
117 Champ Bailey AU RC	15.00	40.00
118 Rob Konrad RC	3.00	8.00
119 Peerless Price AU RC	6.00	15.00
120 Kevin Faulk AU RC	8.00	20.00
121 Dameane Douglas RC	3.00	8.00
122 Kevin Johnson AU RC	6.00	15.00
123 Troy Edwards AU RC	6.00	15.00
124 Edgerrin James AU RC	10.00	25.00
125 David Boston AU RC	6.00	15.00
126 Michael Bishop AU RC	6.00	15.00
127 Shaun King AU SP RC (thought to be far less than 1999 issued)	20.00	40.00
127X Shaun King EXCH	3.00	8.00
128 Brock Huard AU RC	6.00	15.00
129 Torry Holt AU RC	15.00	40.00
130 Cade McNown AU/500 RC	10.00	25.00
131 Tim Couch AU/500 RC	12.00	30.00
132 Donovan McNabb AUTO RC	30.00	60.00
132X Donovan McNabb EXCH	2.00	5.00
133 Akili Smith AU/500 RC	10.00	25.00
134 Daunte Culpepper AUTO/500 RC	15.00	40.00
134X Daunte Culpepper EXCH	2.00	5.00
135 Ricky Williams AUTO/500 RC	30.00	60.00
S8 Troy Aikman Sample	.75	2.00

1999 SPx Radiance

*RADIANCE VETS: 6X TO 15X BASIC CARD
RADIANCE PRINT RUN 100 SER.#'d SETS

8 Priest Holmes	15.00	40.00
91 Amos Zereoue	10.00	25.00
92 Chris Claiborne	8.00	20.00
93 Scott Covington	8.00	20.00
94 Jeff Paulk	8.00	20.00
95 Brandon Stokley	12.00	30.00
96 Antoine Winfield	8.00	20.00
97 Reginald Kelly	8.00	20.00
98 Jermaine Fazande	8.00	20.00
99 Andy Katzenmoyer	10.00	25.00
100 Craig Yeast	8.00	20.00
101 Joe Montgomery	8.00	20.00
102 Darrin Chiaverini	8.00	20.00
103 Travis McGriff	8.00	20.00
104 Jevon Kearse	12.00	30.00
105 Joel Makovicka	8.00	20.00
106 Aaron Brooks	12.00	30.00
107 Chris McAlister	10.00	25.00
108 Jim Kleinsasser	12.00	30.00
109 Ebenezer Ekuban	8.00	20.00
110 Karsten Bailey	8.00	20.00
111 Sedrick Irvin	8.00	20.00
112 D'Wayne Bates	8.00	20.00
113 Joe Germaine	10.00	25.00
114 Cecil Collins	8.00	20.00
115 Mike Cloud	8.00	20.00
116 James Johnson	8.00	20.00
117 Champ Bailey	25.00	60.00
118 Rob Konrad	8.00	20.00
119 Peerless Price	10.00	25.00
120 Kevin Faulk	12.00	30.00
121 Dameane Douglas	8.00	20.00
122 Kevin Johnson	10.00	25.00
123 Troy Edwards	10.00	25.00
124 Edgerrin James	15.00	40.00
125 David Boston	10.00	25.00
126 Michael Bishop	10.00	25.00
127 Shaun King	10.00	25.00
128 Brock Huard	10.00	25.00
129 Torry Holt	20.00	50.00
130 Cade McNown	10.00	25.00
131 Tim Couch	12.00	30.00
132 Donovan McNabb	30.00	80.00
133 Akili Smith	10.00	25.00
134 Daunte Culpepper	12.00	30.00
135 Ricky Williams	20.00	50.00

1999 SPx Highlight Heroes

COMPLETE SET (10)	10.00	25.00
STATED ODDS 1:9		
H1 Jake Plummer	.75	2.00
H2 Doug Flutie	1.25	3.00
H3 Garrison Hearst	.75	2.00
H4 Fred Taylor	1.25	3.00
H5 Dorsey Levens	1.25	3.00
H6 Kordell Stewart	.75	2.00
H7 Marshall Faulk	1.50	4.00
H8 Steve Young	1.50	4.00
H9 Troy Aikman	2.50	6.00
H10 Jerome Bettis	1.25	3.00

1999 SPx Masters

COMPLETE SET (15)	35.00	80.00
STATED ODDS 1:17		
M1 Dan Marino	5.00	12.00
M2 Barry Sanders	5.00	12.00
M3 Peyton Manning	5.00	12.00
M4 Joey Galloway	1.00	2.50
M5 Steve Young	2.00	5.00
M6 Warrick Dunn	1.50	4.00
M7 Deion Sanders	1.50	4.00
M8 Fred Taylor	1.50	4.00
M9 Charlie Batch	1.50	4.00
M10 Jamal Anderson	1.50	4.00
M11 Jake Plummer	1.00	2.50
M12 Terrell Davis	1.50	4.00
M13 Eddie George	1.50	4.00
M14 Mark Brunell	1.50	4.00
M15 Randy Moss	4.00	10.00

1999 SPx Prolifics

COMPLETE SET (15)	25.00	60.00
STATED ODDS 1:17		
P1 John Elway	5.00	12.00
P2 Barry Sanders	5.00	12.00
P3 Jamal Anderson	1.50	4.00
P4 Terrell Owens	1.50	4.00
P5 Marshall Faulk	2.00	5.00
P6 Napoleon Kaufman	1.50	4.00
P7 Antonio Freeman	1.50	4.00
P8 Doug Flutie	1.50	4.00
P9 Vinny Testaverde	1.00	2.50
P10 Jerry Rice	3.00	8.00
P11 Eric Moulds	1.50	4.00
P12 Emmitt Smith	3.00	8.00
P13 Brett Favre	5.00	12.00
P14 Randall Cunningham	1.50	4.00
P15 Keyshawn Johnson	1.50	4.00

1999 SPx Spxcitement

COMPLETE SET (20)	12.50	30.00
STATED ODDS 1:3		
S1 Troy Aikman	1.25	3.00
S2 Edgerrin James	2.50	6.00
S3 Jerry Rice	1.25	3.00
S4 Daunte Culpepper	2.50	6.00
S5 Antowain Smith	.60	1.50
S6 Kevin Faulk	.60	1.50
S7 Steve McNair	.60	1.50
S8 Antonio Freeman	.60	1.50
S9 Torry Holt	1.25	3.00
S10 Napoleon Kaufman	.60	1.50
S11 Curtis Martin	.60	1.50
S12 Randall Cunningham	.60	1.50
S13 Eric Moulds	.60	1.50
S14 Priest Holmes	1.00	2.50
S15 David Boston	.60	1.50
S16 Herman Moore	.40	1.00
S17 Champ Bailey	.60	1.50
S18 Vinny Testaverde	.40	1.00
S19 Garrison Hearst	.40	1.00
S20 Jon Kitna	.60	1.50

1999 SPx Spxtreme

COMPLETE SET (20)	15.00	40.00
STATED ODDS 1:6		
X1 Emmitt Smith	2.00	5.00
X2 Brock Huard	.60	1.50
X3 David Boston	1.00	2.50
X4 Edgerrin James	3.00	8.00
X5 Kevin Faulk	1.00	2.50
X6 Daunte Culpepper	3.00	8.00
X7 Charlie Batch	1.00	2.50
X8 Torry Holt	1.50	4.00
X9 Andre Rison	.60	1.50
X10 Karim Abdul-Jabbar	.60	1.50
X11 Kordell Stewart	.60	1.50
X12 Curtis Enis	.40	1.00
X13 Terrell Owens	1.00	2.50
X14 Curtis Martin	1.00	2.50
X15 Ricky Watters	.60	1.50
X16 Corey Dillon	1.00	2.50
X17 Tim Brown	1.00	2.50
X18 Warrick Dunn	1.00	2.50
X19 Drew Bledsoe	1.25	3.00
X20 Eddie George	1.00	2.50

1999 SPx Starscape

COMPLETE SET (10)	7.50	20.00
STATED ODDS 1:9		
ST1 Randy Moss	2.50	6.00
ST2 Keyshawn Johnson	1.00	2.50
ST3 Curtis Enis	.40	1.00
ST4 Jerome Bettis	1.00	2.50
ST5 Mark Brunell	1.00	2.50
ST6 Antowain Smith	1.00	2.50
ST7 Joey Galloway	.60	1.50
ST8 Drew Bledsoe	1.25	3.00
ST9 Corey Dillon	1.00	2.50
ST10 Steve McNair	1.00	2.50

1999 SPx Winning Materials

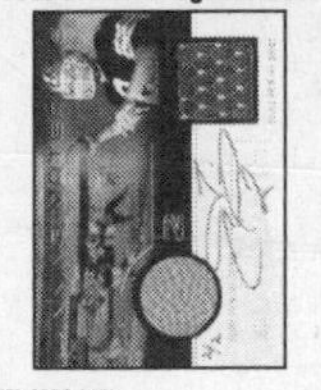

STATED ODDS 1:252		
BFS Brett Favre	30.00	80.00
CMS Cade McNown	10.00	25.00
DBS David Boston	10.00	25.00
DCS Daunte Culpepper	15.00	40.00
DMS Dan Marino	30.00	80.00
JRA Jerry Rice AUTO/80	150.00	300.00
JRS Jerry Rice	25.00	60.00
MCS Donovan McNabb	20.00	50.00
RWS Ricky Williams	12.50	30.00
TCS Tim Couch	10.00	25.00
THS Torry Holt	12.50	30.00

2000 SPx

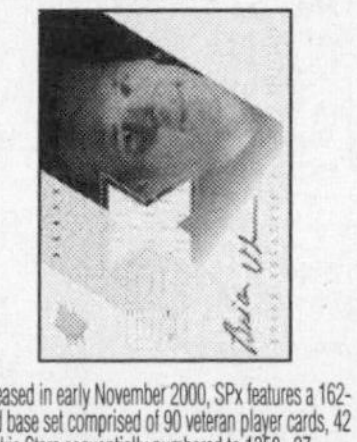

Released in early November 2000, SPx features a 162-card base set comprised of 90 veteran player cards, 42 Rookie Stars sequentially numbered to 1350, 27 Signed Rookie Jersey cards sequentially numbered to 2000, and three Signed Rookie Jersey Stars sequentially numbered to 500. Several rookies were issued via redemption cards which carried an expiration date of 7/20/2001. Thomas Jones was one of these players and ultimately signed a small number of cards to be mailed out. Although they are serial numbered to 2000, it is commonly believed that far fewer actually exist as live cards. Base cards feature action photography and foil highlights. SPx was packaged in 18-pack boxes with packs containing four cards and carried a suggested retail price of $6.99.

COMP.SET w/o SP's (90)	7.50	20.00
91-132 ROOKIE PRINT RUN 1350		
160-162 JSY AU ROOKIE PRINT RUN 500		
1 Jake Plummer	.30	.75
2 David Boston	.25	.60
3 Frank Sanders	.25	.60
4 Chris Chandler	.30	.75
5 Jamal Anderson	.30	.75
6 Shawn Jefferson	.25	.60
7 Qadry Ismail	.30	.75
8 Tony Banks	.25	.60
9 Shannon Sharpe	.40	1.00
10 Rob Johnson	.30	.75
11 Eric Moulds	.30	.75
12 Muhsin Muhammad	.30	.75
13 Steve Beuerlein	.30	.75
14 Cade McNown	.25	.60
15 Marcus Robinson	.30	.75
16 Akili Smith	.25	.60
17 Corey Dillon	.30	.75
18 Darnay Scott	.30	.75
19 Tim Couch	.30	.75
20 Kevin Johnson	.25	.60
21 Errict Rhett	.30	.75
22 Troy Aikman	.60	1.50
23 Emmitt Smith	1.00	2.50
24 Joey Galloway	.30	.75
25 Terrell Davis	.40	1.00
26 Olandis Gary	.30	.75
27 Brian Griese	.30	.75
28 Charlie Batch	.30	.75
29 Germane Crowell	.25	.60
30 James Stewart	.25	.60
31 Brett Favre	1.25	3.00
32 Antonio Freeman	.30	.75
33 Dorsey Levens	.30	.75
34 Peyton Manning	1.00	2.50
35 Edgerrin James	.40	1.00
36 Marvin Harrison	.40	1.00
37 Mark Brunell	.30	.75
38 Fred Taylor	.40	1.00
39 Jimmy Smith	.30	.75
40 Keenan McCardell	.30	.75
41 Elvis Grbac	.25	.60
42 Tony Gonzalez	.40	1.00
43 Tony Martin	.30	.75
44 Jay Fiedler	.30	.75
45 Damon Huard	.30	.75
46 Randy Moss	.40	1.00
47 Robert Smith	.30	.75
48 Cris Carter	.40	1.00
49 Daunte Culpepper	.30	.75
50 Drew Bledsoe	.40	1.00
51 Terry Glenn	.30	.75
52 Ricky Williams	.40	1.00
53 Jeff Blake	.30	.75
54 Keith Poole	.25	.60
55 Kerry Collins	.30	.75
56 Amani Toomer	.30	.75
57 Ike Hilliard	.30	.75
58 Ray Lucas	.25	.60
59 Curtis Martin	.40	1.00
60 Vinny Testaverde	.30	.75
61 Tim Brown	.40	1.00
62 Rich Gannon	.30	.75
63 Tyrone Wheatley	.25	.60
64 Napoleon Kaufman	.30	.75
65 Duce Staley	.30	.75
66 Donovan McNabb	.40	1.00
67 Troy Edwards	.25	.60
68 Jerome Bettis	.40	1.00
69 Kordell Stewart	.30	.75
70 Marshall Faulk	.40	1.00
71 Kurt Warner	.60	1.50
72 Isaac Bruce	.40	1.00
73 Torry Holt	.40	1.00
74 Ryan Leaf	.30	.75
75 Jim Harbaugh	.30	.75
76 Jerry Rice	.75	2.00
77 Terrell Owens	.40	1.00
78 Jeff Garcia	.30	.75
79 Ricky Watters	.30	.75
80 Jon Kitna	.30	.75
81 Derrick Mayes	.25	.60
82 Shaun King	.25	.60
83 Mike Alstott	.40	1.00
84 Keyshawn Johnson	.30	.75
85 Eddie George	.30	.75
86 Steve McNair	.40	1.00
87 Jevon Kearse	.30	.75
88 Brad Johnson	.30	.75
89 Stephen Davis	.30	.75
90 Michael Westbrook	.25	.60
91 Anthony Lucas RC	2.50	6.00
92 Avion Black RC	2.50	6.00
93 Corey Moore RC	2.50	6.00
94 Chris Cole RC	3.00	8.00
95 Chris Hovan RC	3.00	8.00
96 Dante Hall RC	4.00	10.00
97 Darrell Jackson RC	3.00	8.00
98 Deltha O'Neal RC	3.00	8.00
99 Doug Chapman RC	2.50	6.00
100 Doug Johnson RC	3.00	8.00
101 Erron Kinney RC	2.50	6.00
102 Frank Moreau RC	2.50	6.00
103 Patrick Pass RC	3.00	8.00
104 Gari Scott RC	2.50	6.00
105 Giovanni Carmazzi RC	2.50	6.00
106 JaJuan Dawson RC	2.50	6.00
107 James Williams RC	2.50	6.00
108 Jarious Jackson RC	3.00	8.00
109 John Abraham RC	4.00	10.00
110 Keith Bulluck RC	3.00	8.00
111 Jonas Lewis RC	2.50	6.00
112 Mike Green RC	4.00	10.00
113 Ronney Jenkins RC	2.50	6.00
114 Michael Wiley RC	2.50	6.00
115 Mike Anderson RC	4.00	10.00
116 Mareno Philyaw RC	2.50	6.00
117 Muneer Moore RC	2.50	6.00
118 Paul Smith RC	2.50	6.00
119 Raynoch Thompson RC	2.50	6.00
120 Rob Morris RC	3.00	8.00
121 Ron Dixon RC	2.50	6.00
122 Rondell Mealey RC	2.50	6.00
123 Sebastian Janikowski RC	4.00	10.00
124 Shaun Ellis RC	4.00	10.00
125 Charles Lee RC	2.50	6.00
126 Shyrone Stith RC	2.50	6.00
127 Thomas Hamner RC	2.50	6.00
128 Tim Rattay RC	3.00	8.00
129 Todd Husak RC	2.50	6.00
130 Tom Brady RC	250.00	400.00
131 Trevor Gaylor RC	2.50	6.00
132 Windrell Hayes RC	2.50	6.00
133 Anthony Becht JSY AU RC	8.00	20.00
134 Brian Urlacher JSY AU RC	50.00	100.00
135 Bubba Franks JSY AU RC	10.00	25.00
136 Chad Pennington JSY AU RC	15.00	40.00
137 Chris Redman JSY AU RC	8.00	20.00
138 Corey Simon JSY AU RC	8.00	20.00
139 Curtis Keaton JSY AU RC	6.00	15.00
140 Danny Farmer JSY AU RC	6.00	15.00
141 Dennis Northcutt JSY AU RC	8.00	20.00
142 Dez White JSY AU RC	8.00	20.00
143 J.R. Redmond JSY AU SP RC	6.00	15.00
144 Jamal Lewis JSY AU RC	10.00	25.00
145 Jerry Porter JSY AU RC	10.00	25.00
146 Joe Hamilton EXCH	1.25	3.00
147 Laveranues Coles JSY AU RC	10.00	25.00
148 R.Jay Soward JSY AU RC	6.00	15.00
149 Reuben Droughns JSY AU RC	10.00	25.00
150 Ron Dayne JSY AU RC	10.00	25.00
151 Ron Dugans JSY AU RC	6.00	15.00
152 Shaun Alexander JSY AU RC	12.00	30.00
153 Sylvester Morris JSY AU RC	6.00	15.00
154 Tee Martin JSY AU RC	10.00	25.00
155 Thomas Jones JSY AU RC SP	75.00	150.00
156 Todd Pinkston JSY AU RC	6.00	15.00
157 Travis Prentice JSY AU RC	8.00	20.00
158 Travis Taylor JSY AU SP RC	8.00	20.00
159 Trung Canidate JSY AU RC	8.00	20.00
160 Courtney Brown JSY AU RC	12.00	30.00
161 Peter Warrick JSY AU RC/500	15.00	40.00
162 Plaxico Burress JSY AU RC	50.00	80.00
S1 Peyton Manning Sample	1.50	4.00

2000 SPx Spectrum

*VETS 1-90: 12X TO 30X BASIC CARDS
*ROOKIES 91-132: 1.2X TO 3X
*ROOKIE JSY AU 133-159: 1.2X TO 3X
*ROOKIE JSY AU 160-162: .8X TO 2X
SPECTRUM PRINT RUN 25 SER.#'d SETS

130 Tom Brady	1,000.00	1,500.00
134 Brian Urlacher JSY AU	200.00	400.00
146 Joe Hamilton JSY AU EXCH	.75	2.00
1$\bar{6}$5 Thomas Jones JSY AU	150.00	300.00

2000 SPx Highlight Heroes

COMPLETE SET (12)	6.00	15.00
STATED ODDS 1:8		
HH1 Fred Taylor	.60	1.50
HH2 Eddie George	.50	1.25
HH3 Marshall Faulk	.60	1.50
HH4 Shaun King	.40	1.00
HH5 Cris Carter	.60	1.50
HH6 Emmitt Smith	1.50	4.00
HH7 Jerry Rice	1.25	3.00
HH8 Tim Couch	.50	1.25
HH9 Keyshawn Johnson	.50	1.25
HH10 Troy Aikman	1.00	2.50
HH11 Terrell Davis	.60	1.50
HH12 Ricky Williams	.60	1.50

2000 SPx Powerhouse

STATED ODDS 1:9		
PH1 Akili Smith	.30	.75
PH2 Kevin Johnson	.30	.75
PH3 Olandis Gary	.40	1.00
PH4 Jeff Garcia	.40	1.00
PH5 Germane Crowell	.30	.75
PH6 Donovan McNabb	.50	1.25
PH7 Rob Johnson	.40	1.00
PH8 Marcus Robinson	.40	1.00
PH9 Shaun King	.30	.75
PH10 Troy Edwards	.30	.75

2000 SPx Prolifics

COMPLETE SET (12)	10.00	25.00
STATED ODDS 1:18		
P1 Stephen Davis	.75	2.00
P2 Terrell Davis	1.00	2.50
P3 Jamal Anderson	.75	2.00
P4 Jerry Rice	2.00	5.00
P5 Emmitt Smith	2.50	6.00
P6 Troy Aikman	1.50	4.00
P7 Cris Carter	1.00	2.50
P8 Brett Favre	3.00	8.00
P9 Mark Brunell	.75	2.00
P10 Tim Couch	.75	2.00
P11 Eddie George	.75	2.00
P12 Marshall Faulk	1.00	2.50

2000 SPx Rookie Starscape

COMPLETE SET (12)	12.50	30.00
STATED ODDS 1:18		
RS1 Thomas Jones	1.00	2.50
RS2 Courtney Brown	.60	1.50
RS3 Peter Warrick	.75	2.00
RS4 Jamal Lewis	.75	2.00
RS5 Sylvester Morris	.50	1.25
RS6 Plaxico Burress	.75	2.00
RS7 Travis Taylor	.60	1.50
RS8 Chad Pennington	1.25	3.00
RS9 Ron Dayne	.75	2.00
RS10 Shaun Alexander	1.00	2.50
RS11 Giovanni Carmazzi	.50	1.25
RS12 Ron Dugans	.50	1.25

2000 SPx Spxcitement

COMPLETE SET (10)	3.00	8.00
STATED ODDS 1:5		
XC1 Plaxico Burress	.30	.75
XC2 Peter Warrick	.30	.75
XC3 Travis Taylor	.25	.60
XC4 Ron Dayne	.30	.75
XC5 Thomas Jones	.40	1.00
XC6 Danny Farmer	.20	.50
XC7 Bubba Franks	.30	.75
XC8 Laveranues Coles	.30	.75
XC9 Chad Pennington	.50	1.25
XC10 J.R. Redmond	.20	.50

2000 SPx Spxtreme

COMPLETE SET (18)	15.00	40.00
STATED ODDS 1:12		
X1 Isaac Bruce	1.00	2.50
X2 Cade McNown	.60	1.50
X3 Daunte Culpepper	.75	2.00
X4 Donovan McNabb	1.00	2.50
X5 Brett Favre	3.00	8.00
X6 Peyton Manning	2.50	6.00
X7 Edgerrin James	1.00	2.50
X8 Jon Kitna	.75	2.00
X9 Mark Brunell	.75	2.00
X10 Brad Johnson	.75	2.00
X11 Jevon Kearse	.75	2.00
X12 Curtis Martin	1.00	2.50
X13 Steve McNair	1.00	2.50
X14 Ricky Williams	1.00	2.50
X15 Stephen Davis	.75	2.00
X16 Kurt Warner	1.50	4.00
X17 Marvin Harrison	1.00	2.50
X18 Randy Moss	1.00	2.50

2000 SPx Winning Materials

STATED ODDS 1:83		
WMBF Brett Favre	25.00	60.00
WMBG Brian Griese	6.00	15.00
WMCB Courtney Brown	6.00	15.00
WMCM Cade McNown	5.00	12.00
WMCP Chad Pennington	10.00	40.00
WMCR Chris Redman	5.00	12.00
WMDF Bubba Franks	6.00	15.00
WMDW Dez White	5.00	12.00
WMEG Eddie George	6.00	15.00
WMEJ Edgerrin James	8.00	20.00
WMJJ J.J. Stokes	6.00	15.00
WMJL Jamal Lewis	6.00	15.00
WMJP Jerry Porter	6.00	15.00
WMJR Jerry Rice	15.00	40.00
WMKJ Keyshawn Johnson	6.00	15.00
WMKW Kurt Warner	12.00	30.00
WMMC Steve McNair	8.00	20.00
WMMF Marshall Faulk	8.00	20.00
WMNE J.R. Redmond	5.00	12.00
WMPB Plaxico Burress	6.00	15.00
WMPM Peyton Manning	20.00	50.00
WMPW Peter Warrick	6.00	15.00
WMRD Ron Dayne	6.00	15.00
WMRD Reuben Droughns	6.00	15.00
WMRJ R.Jay Coward	5.00	12.00
WMRM Randy Moss	8.00	20.00
WMSA Shaun Alexander	8.00	20.00
WMSK Shaun King	5.00	12.00
WMSM Sylvester Morris	5.00	12.00
WMTC Trung Canidate	5.00	12.00
WMTD Terrell Davis	8.00	20.00
WMTH Torry Holt	8.00	20.00
WMTJ Thomas Jones	8.00	20.00
WMTM Tee Martin	6.00	15.00
WMTO Terrell Owens	8.00	20.00
WMWD Warrick Dunn	6.00	15.00

2000 SPx Winning Materials Autographs

STATED PRINT RUN 225 SER.#'d SETS		
AWMCP Chad Pennington	30.00	80.00
AWMEG Eddie George	12.00	30.00
AWMEJ Edgerrin James	15.00	40.00
AWMJL Jamal Lewis	25.00	60.00
AWMKJ Keyshawn Johnson	12.00	30.00
AWMKW Kurt Warner	25.00	60.00
AWMPM Peyton Manning	100.00	200.00
AWMPW Peter Warrick	15.00	40.00
AWMRD Ron Dayne	15.00	40.00
AWMRM Randy Moss	50.00	100.00
AWMSA Shaun Alexander	20.00	50.00
AWMTC Tim Couch	12.00	30.00
AWMTD Terrell Davis	25.00	60.00
AWMTM Tee Martin	15.00	40.00
AWMTT Travis Taylor	12.00	30.00

2001 SPx

Released in late December, SPx features 90 veterans along with 66 rookies. Each rookie player has two versions of their card, one featuring platinum blue foil and the other featuring gold foil on the front. Josh Heupel originally was only available in packs as an exchange card and is considered a short-print.

COMP.SET w/o SP's (90)	7.50	20.00
1 Jake Plummer	.25	.60
2 David Boston	.20	.50
3 Jamal Anderson	.25	.60
4 Chris Chandler	.25	.60
5 Tony Martin	.25	.60
6 Elvis Grbac	.25	.60
7 Qadry Ismail	.25	.60
8 Ray Lewis	.30	.75
9 Rob Johnson	.25	.60
10 Shawn Bryson	.20	.50
11 Eric Moulds	.25	.60
12 Tim Biakabutuka	.20	.50
13 Jeff Lewis	.20	.50
14 Muhsin Muhammad	.25	.60
15 Shane Matthews	.20	.50
16 Marcus Robinson	.25	.60
17 Brian Urlacher	.40	1.00
18 Jon Kitna	.25	.60
19 Peter Warrick	.25	.60
20 Corey Dillon	.25	.60
21 Tim Couch	.20	.50
22 Travis Prentice	.20	.50
23 Kevin Johnson	.20	.50
24 Rocket Ismail	.25	.60
25 Emmitt Smith	.75	2.00
26 Joey Galloway	.25	.60
27 Terrell Davis	.30	.75
28 Brian Griese	.25	.60
29 Rod Smith	.25	.60
30 Ed McCaffrey	.25	.60
31 Charlie Batch	.25	.60
32 Germane Crowell	.20	.50
33 James O. Stewart	.20	.50
34 Brett Favre	1.00	2.50
35 Antonio Freeman	.30	.75
36 Ahman Green	.30	.75
37 Peyton Manning	.75	2.00
38 Edgerrin James	.30	.75
39 Marvin Harrison	.30	.75
40 Mark Brunell	.25	.60
41 Fred Taylor	.30	.75
42 Jimmy Smith	.25	.60
43 Tony Gonzalez	.30	.75
44 Trent Green	.30	.75
45 Priest Holmes	.30	.75
46 Lamar Smith	.25	.60
47 Jay Fiedler	.25	.60
48 Oronde Gadsden	.20	.50
49 Daunte Culpepper	.25	.60
50 Randy Moss	.30	.75
51 Cris Carter	.30	.75
52 Drew Bledsoe	.30	.75
53 Troy Brown	.25	.60
54 Ricky Williams	.30	.75
55 Joe Horn	.25	.60
56 Aaron Brooks	.25	.60
57 Albert Connell	.20	.50
58 Kerry Collins	.25	.60
59 Tiki Barber	.30	.75
60 Ron Dayne	.25	.60
61 Vinny Testaverde	.25	.60
62 Wayne Chrebet	.25	.60
63 Curtis Martin	.30	.75
64 Tim Brown	.30	.75
65 Jerry Rice	.60	1.50
66 Rich Gannon	.25	.60
67 Duce Staley	.25	.60
68 Donovan McNabb	.30	.75
69 Kordell Stewart	.25	.60
70 Jerome Bettis	.30	.75
71 Marshall Faulk	.30	.75
72 Kurt Warner	.50	1.25
73 Isaac Bruce	.30	.75
74 Torry Holt	.25	.60
75 Doug Flutie	.30	.75
76 Junior Seau	.30	.75
77 Jeff Garcia	.25	.60
78 Garrison Hearst	.25	.60
79 Terrell Owens	.30	.75
80 Ricky Watters	.25	.60
81 Matt Hasselbeck	.30	.75
82 Brad Johnson	.25	.60
83 Keyshawn Johnson	.25	.60
84 Warrick Dunn	.30	.75
85 Mike Alstott	.25	.60
86 Kevin Dyson	.20	.50
87 Eddie George	.30	.75
88 Steve McNair	.30	.75
89 Michael Westbrook	.20	.50
90 Stephen Davis	.25	.60
91B Deuce McAllister JSY AU/250 RC	15.00	40.00
91G Deuce McAllister JSY AU/250 RC	15.00	40.00
92B Freddie Mitchell JSY AU/250 RC	10.00	25.00
92G Freddie Mitchell JSY AU/250 RC	10.00	25.00
93B Koren Robinson/999 RC	2.00	5.00
93G Koren Robinson/999 RC	2.00	5.00
94B David Terrell/999 RC	2.00	5.00
94G David Terrell/999 RC	2.00	5.00
95B Michael Vick JSY AU/250 RC	125.00	250.00
95G Michael Vick JSY AU/250 RC	125.00	250.00
96B Michael Bennett JSY AU/550 RC	8.00	20.00
96G Michael Bennett JSY AU/550 RC	8.00	20.00
07B Robert Ferguson/999 RC	2.50	6.00
97G Robert Ferguson/999 RC	2.50	6.00
98B Rod Gardner/999 RC	2.00	5.00
98G Rod Gardner/999 RC	2.00	5.00
99B Travis Henry JSY AU/550 RC	8.00	20.00
99G Travis Henry JSY AU/550 RC	8.00	20.00
100B Chad Johnson JSY AU/550 RC	15.00	40.00
100G Chad Johnson JSY AU/550 RC	15.00	40.00
101B Drew Brees JSY AU/250 RC	200.00	400.00
101G Drew Brees JSY AU/250 RC	200.00	400.00
102B Santana Moss JSY AU/550 RC	12.00	30.00
102G Santana Moss JSY AU/550 RC	12.00	30.00
103B Chris Weinke JSY AU/550 RC	8.00	20.00
103G Chris Weinke JSY AU/550 RC	8.00	20.00
104B Richard Seymour JSY AU/900 RC	10.00	25.00
104G Richard Seymour JSY AU/900 RC	10.00	25.00
105B Reggie Wayne/999 RC	5.00	12.00
105G Reggie Wayne/999 RC	5.00	12.00
106B Kevan Barlow JSY AU/550 RC	8.00	20.00
106G Kevan Barlow JSY AU/550 RC	8.00	20.00
107B Chris Chambers JSY AU/900 RC	10.00	25.00
107G Chris Chambers JSY AU/900 RC	10.00	25.00
108B Todd Heap JSY AU/900 RC	12.00	30.00
108G Todd Heap JSY AU/900 RC	12.00	30.00
109B Anthony Thomas JSY AU/550 RC	10.00	25.00
109G Anthony Thomas JSY AU/550 RC	10.00	25.00
110B James Jackson JSY AU/550 RC	6.00	15.00
110G James Jackson JSY AU/550 RC	6.00	15.00
111B Rudi Johnson JSY AU/900 RC	10.00	25.00
111G Rudi Johnson JSY AU/900 RC	10.00	25.00
112B Mike McMahon JSY AU RC/900	8.00	20.00
112G Mike McMahon JSY AU RC/900	8.00	20.00
113B Josh Heupel JSY AU/900 RC	10.00	25.00
113G Josh Heupel JSY AU/900 RC	10.00	25.00
114B Travis Minor JSY AU/900 RC	8.00	20.00
114G Travis Minor JSY AU/900 RC	8.00	20.00
115B Quincy Morgan/999 RC	2.00	5.00
115G Quincy Morgan/999 RC	2.00	5.00
116B Dan Morgan JSY AU/900 RC	8.00	20.00
116G Dan Morgan JSY AU/900 RC	8.00	20.00
117B Jesse Palmer JSY AU/900 RC	8.00	20.00
117G Jesse Palmer JSY AU/900 RC	8.00	20.00
118B Sage Rosenfels JSY AU/900 RC	10.00	25.00
118G Sage Rosenfels JSY AU/900 RC	10.00	25.00
119B Marques Tuiasosopo JSY AU/900 RC	8.00	20.00
119G Marques Tuiasosopo JSY AU/900 RC	8.00	20.00
120B Darnerien McCants/999 RC	2.00	5.00
120G Darnerien McCants/999 RC	2.00	5.00
121B Snoop Minnis/999 RC	1.50	4.00
121G Snoop Minnis/999 RC	1.50	4.00
122B LaDainian Tomlinson JSY/250 RC	40.00	100.00
122G LaDainian Tomlinson JSY/250 RC	40.00	100.00
123B Quincy Carter/999 RC	2.00	5.00
123G Quincy Carter/999 RC	2.00	5.00
124B Arnold Jackson/999 RC	1.50	4.00
124G Arnold Jackson/999 RC	1.50	4.00
125B Justin McCareins/999 RC	2.00	5.00
125G Justin McCareins/999 RC	2.00	5.00
126B Eddie Berlin/999 RC	1.50	4.00
126G Eddie Berlin/999 RC	1.50	4.00
127B Quentin McCord/999 RC	2.00	5.00
127G Quentin McCord/999 RC	2.00	5.00
128B Vinny Sutherland/999 RC	1.50	4.00
128G Vinny Sutherland/999 RC	1.50	4.00
129B Willie Middlebrooks/999 RC	2.00	5.00
129G Willie Middlebrooks/999 RC	2.00	5.00
130B Dan Alexander/999 RC	2.00	5.00
130G Dan Alexander/999 RC	2.00	5.00
131B Dee Brown/999 RC	1.50	4.00
131G Dee Brown/999 RC	1.50	4.00
132B Andre Carter/999 RC	2.00	5.00
132G Andre Carter/999 RC	2.00	5.00
133B Justin Smith/999 RC	2.50	6.00
133G Justin Smith/999 RC	2.50	6.00
134B T.J. Houshmandzadeh/999 RC	3.00	8.00
134G T.J. Houshmandzadeh/999 RC	3.00	8.00
135B Andre King/999 RC	1.50	4.00
135G Andre King/999 RC	1.50	4.00
136B Nick Goings/999 RC	2.50	6.00
136G Nick Goings/999 RC	2.50	6.00
137B Scotty Anderson/999 RC	1.50	4.00
137G Scotty Anderson/999 RC	1.50	4.00
138B David Martin/999 RC	1.50	4.00
138G David Martin/999 RC	1.50	4.00
139B Derrick Blaylock/999 RC	2.00	5.00
139G Derrick Blaylock/999 RC	2.00	5.00
140B Onome Ojo/999 RC	1.50	4.00
140G Onome Ojo/999 RC	1.50	4.00
141B Jonathan Carter/999 RC	1.50	4.00
141G Jonathan Carter/999 RC	1.50	4.00
142B LaMont Jordan/999 RC	2.50	6.00
142G LaMont Jordan/999 RC	2.50	6.00
143B Dominic Rhodes/999 RC	2.50	6.00
143G Dominic Rhodes/999 RC	2.50	6.00
145B A.J. Feeley/999 RC	2.00	5.00
145G A.J. Feeley/999 RC	2.00	5.00
146B Correll Buckhalter/999 RC	2.50	6.00
146G Correll Buckhalter/999 RC	2.50	6.00
147B Steve Smith/999 RC	5.00	12.00
147G Steve Smith/999 RC	5.00	12.00
148B Dave Dickenson/999 RC	2.00	5.00
148G Dave Dickenson/999 RC	2.00	5.00
149B Cedrick Wilson/999 RC	2.00	5.00
149G Cedrick Wilson/999 RC	2.00	5.00
150B Jamie Winborn/999 RC	2.00	5.00
150G Jamie Winborn/999 RC	2.00	5.00
151B Alex Bannister/999 RC	1.50	4.00
151G Alex Bannister/999 RC	1.50	4.00
152B Heath Evans/999 RC	2.00	5.00
152G Heath Evans/999 RC	2.00	5.00
153B Josh Booty/999 RC	2.00	5.00
153G Josh Booty/999 RC	2.00	5.00
154B Adam Archuleta/999 RC	2.00	5.00
154G Adam Archuleta/999 RC	2.00	5.00
155B Francis St.Paul/999 RC	1.50	4.00
155G Francis St.Paul/999 RC	1.50	4.00
156B Andre Dyson/999 RC	1.50	4.00
156G Andre Dyson/999 RC	1.50	4.00
RM Randy Moss SAMPLE	.75	2.00

2001 SPx Winning Materials

WIN MATERIAL/20-750 ODDS 1:18		
WMAC1 Andre Carter/750	3.00	8.00
WMAC2 Andre Carter/250	4.00	10.00
WMAS1 Akili Smith/300	3.00	8.00
WMAS2 Akili Smith/20	8.00	20.00
WMAT1 Anthony Thomas/500	4.00	10.00
WMAT2 Anthony Thomas/100	6.00	15.00
WMBE1 Michael Bennett/500	3.00	8.00
WMBE2 Michael Bennett/100	5.00	12.00
WMBF1 Brett Favre/300	15.00	40.00
WMBF2 Brett Favre/20	40.00	100.00
WMBO1 David Boston/300	3.00	8.00
WMBO2 David Boston/20	8.00	20.00
WMCG1 Charlie Garner/500	3.00	8.00
WMCG2 Charlie Garner/100	5.00	12.00
WMCH1 Chris Chambers/500	4.00	10.00
WMCH2 Chris Chambers/100	6.00	15.00
WMCW1 Chris Weinke/750	3.00	8.00
WMCW2 Chris Weinke/250	4.00	10.00
WMDB1 Drew Brees/500	12.00	30.00
WMDB2 Drew Brees/100	25.00	60.00
WMDB3 Drew Brees/250	15.00	40.00
WMDB4 Drew Brees/750	12.00	30.00
WMDF1 Doug Flutie/750	4.00	10.00
WMDF2 Doug Flutie/250	5.00	12.00
WMDT1 David Terrell/750	3.00	8.00
WMDT2 David Terrell/250	4.00	10.00
WMDU1 Deuce McAllister/750	4.00	10.00
WMDU2 Deuce McAllister/250	5.00	12.00
WMEG1 Elvis Grbac/500	3.00	8.00
WMEG2 Elvis Grbac/100	5.00	12.00
WMEJ1 Edgerrin James/300	5.00	12.00
WMEJ2 Edgerrin James/20	12.00	30.00
WMFM1 Freddie Mitchell/500	2.50	6.00
WMFM2 Freddie Mitchell/100	4.00	10.00
WMGA1 Rod Gardner/750	3.00	8.00
WMGA2 Rod Gardner/250	4.00	10.00
WMHE1 Travis Henry/300	4.00	10.00
WMHE2 Travis Henry/20	10.00	25.00
WMJF1 Jay Fiedler/750	3.00	8.00
WMJF2 Jay Fiedler/250	4.00	10.00
WMJJ1 James Jackson/300	3.00	8.00
WMJJ2 James Jackson/20	8.00	20.00
WMJP1 Jake Plummer/300	4.00	10.00
WMJP2 Jake Plummer/20	10.00	25.00
WMJR1 Jerry Rice/750	8.00	20.00
WMJR2 Jerry Rice/250	10.00	25.00
WMJS1 Junior Seau/750	4.00	10.00
WMJS2 Junior Seau/250	5.00	12.00
WMKB1 Kevan Barlow/500	3.00	8.00
WMKB2 Kevan Barlow/100	5.00	12.00
WMKR1 Koren Robinson/750	3.00	8.00
WMKR2 Koren Robinson/250	4.00	10.00
WMKW1 Kurt Warner/300	8.00	20.00
WMKW2 Kurt Warner/20	20.00	50.00
WMLT1 LaDainian Tomlinson/300	10.00	25.00
WMLT2 LaDainian Tomlinson/20	25.00	60.00
WMMA1 Mike Alstott/750	3.00	8.00
WMMA2 Mike Alstott/250	4.00	10.00
WMMB1 Mark Brunell/300	4.00	10.00
WMMB2 Mark Brunell/20	10.00	25.00
WMMF1 Marshall Faulk/300	5.00	12.00
WMMF2 Marshall Faulk/20	12.00	30.00
WMMO1 Dan Morgan/500	3.00	8.00
WMMO2 Dan Morgan/100	5.00	12.00
WMMT1 Marques Tuiasosopo/750	3.00	8.00
WMMT2 Marques Tuiasosopo/250	4.00	10.00
WMMV1 Michael Vick/750	12.00	30.00
WMMV2 Michael Vick/250	20.00	50.00
WMPA1 Jesse Palmer/500	3.00	8.00
WMPA2 Jesse Palmer/100	5.00	12.00
WMPM1 Peyton Manning/750	10.00	25.00
WMPM2 Peyton Manning/250	12.00	30.00
WMPW1 Peter Warrick/300	4.00	10.00
WMPW2 Peter Warrick/20	10.00	25.00
WMQM1 Quincy Morgan/750	3.00	8.00
WMQM2 Quincy Morgan/250	4.00	10.00
WMRD1 Ron Dayne/500	3.00	8.00
WMRD2 Ron Dayne/100	5.00	12.00
WMRF1 Robert Ferguson/750	4.00	10.00
WMRF2 Robert Ferguson/250	5.00	12.00
WMRG1 Rich Gannon/300	4.00	10.00
WMRG2 Rich Gannon/20	10.00	25.00
WMSE1 Jason Sehorn/500	3.00	8.00
WMSE2 Jason Sehorn/100	5.00	12.00
WMSM1 Santana Moss/750	5.00	12.00
WMSM2 Santana Moss/250	6.00	15.00
WMTA1 Troy Aikman/300	8.00	20.00
WMTA2 Troy Aikman/20	20.00	50.00
WMTB1 Tiki Barber/750	4.00	10.00
WMTB2 Tiki Barber/250	5.00	12.00
WMTC1 Tim Couch/750	2.50	6.00
WMTC2 Tim Couch/250	3.00	8.00
WMTJ1 Thomas Jones/500	3.00	8.00
WMTJ2 Thomas Jones/100	5.00	12.00
WMTO1 Terrell Owens/300	5.00	12.00
WMTO2 Terrell Owens/20	12.00	30.00
WMWA1 Reggie Wayne/750	8.00	20.00
WMWA2 Reggie Wayne/250	10.00	25.00

2002 SPx

Released in December 2002, this product features 90 veterans and 88 rookies. Cards 91-150 were serial #'d to 1500, cards 151-175 featured jersey swatches and autographs (if noted below) and were #'d to either 999, 650, or 250. Some cards were issued only as exchange cards with an expiration date of 11/26/2005. Boxes contained 18 packs of 4 cards.

COMP.SET w/o SP's (90)	7.50	20.00
91-150 ROOKIE PRINT RUN 1500		
151-175 ROOKIE JSY PRINT RUN 250-999		
1 Drew Bledsoe	.30	.75
2 Peerless Price	.20	.50
3 Travis Henry	.20	.50
4 Ricky Williams	.25	.60
5 Jay Fiedler	.25	.60
6 Tom Brady	.75	2.00
7 Troy Brown	.25	.60
8 Antowain Smith	.25	.60

9 Santana Moss	.25	.60
10 Curtis Martin	.30	.75
11 Vinny Testaverde	.25	.60
12 Jamal Lewis	.25	.60
13 Chris Redman	.20	.50
14 Travis Taylor	.20	.50
15 Corey Dillon	.25	.60
16 T.J. Houshmandzadeh	.30	.75
17 Peter Warrick	.25	.60
18 Courtney Brown	.20	.50
19 Kevin Johnson	.20	.50
20 Tim Couch	.20	.50
21 Hines Ward	.30	.75
22 Jerome Bettis	.30	.75
23 Kordell Stewart	.25	.60
24 Corey Bradford	.20	.50
25 Jermaine Lewis	.20	.50
26 Edgerrin James	.25	.60
27 Marvin Harrison	.30	.75
28 Peyton Manning	.60	1.50
29 Jimmy Smith	.25	.60
30 Mark Brunell	.25	.60
31 Fred Taylor	.25	.60
32 Eddie George	.25	.60
33 Steve McNair	.30	.75
34 Brian Griese	.25	.60
35 Shannon Sharpe	.30	.75
36 Rod Smith	.25	.60
37 Trent Green	.25	.60
38 Johnnie Morton	.25	.60
39 Priest Holmes	.30	.75
40 Jerry Rice	.60	1.50
41 Rich Gannon	.25	.60
42 Tim Brown	.30	.75
43 Drew Brees	.50	1.25
44 Junior Seau	.30	.75
45 LaDainian Tomlinson	.40	1.00
46 Emmitt Smith	.75	2.00
47 Quincy Carter	.20	.50
48 Rocket Ismail	.25	.60
49 Amani Toomer	.25	.60
50 Kerry Collins	.25	.60
51 Ron Dayne	.25	.60
52 Donovan McNabb	.30	.75
53 Duce Staley	.25	.60
54 Antonio Freeman	.30	.75
55 Rod Gardner	.20	.50
56 Stephen Davis	.25	.60
57 Brian Urlacher	.30	.75
58 Anthony Thomas	.25	.60
59 Jim Miller	.20	.50
60 Marty Booker	.25	.60
61 Az-Zahir Hakim	.20	.50
62 James Stewart	.20	.50
63 Ahman Green	.25	.60
64 Brett Favre	.75	2.00
65 Robert Ferguson	.25	.60
66 Terry Glenn	.25	.60
67 Randy Moss	.30	.75
68 Daunte Culpepper	.25	.60
69 Michael Bennett	.25	.60
70 Michael Vick	.50	1.25
71 Warrick Dunn	.25	.60
72 Rodney Peete	.25	.60
73 Muhsin Muhammad	.25	.60
74 Aaron Brooks	.25	.60
75 Deuce McAllister	.25	.60
76 Keyshawn Johnson	.25	.60
77 Michael Pittman	.25	.60
78 Brad Johnson	.25	.60
79 Thomas Jones	.30	.75
80 David Boston	.20	.50
81 Jake Plummer	.25	.60
82 Terrell Owens	.30	.75
83 Garrison Hearst	.25	.60
84 Jeff Garcia	.25	.60
85 Darrell Jackson	.25	.60
86 Shaun Alexander	.25	.60
87 Trent Dilfer	.25	.60
88 Isaac Bruce	.30	.75
89 Kurt Warner	.30	.75
90 Marshall Faulk	.30	.75
91 Saleem Rasheed RC	1.50	4.00
92 Jason McAddley RC	2.00	5.00
93 Brandon Doman RC	1.50	4.00
94 Mike Rumph RC	1.50	4.00
95 Wendell Bryant RC	1.50	4.00
96 Bryan Thomas RC	1.50	4.00
97 Anthony Weaver RC	1.50	4.00
98 Chester Taylor RC	2.50	6.00
99 Ed Reed RC	8.00	20.00
100 Lamar Gordon RC	2.00	5.00
101 Tellis Redmon RC	1.50	4.00
102 Ben Leber RC	1.50	4.00
103 Javin Hunter RC	1.50	4.00
104 Javon Walker RC	2.50	6.00
105 Shaun Hill RC	3.00	8.00
106 Raonall Smith RC	1.50	4.00
107 Darrell Hill RC	1.50	4.00
108 Kalimba Edwards RC	2.00	5.00
109 Robert Thomas RC	1.50	4.00
110 Craig Nall RC	2.00	5.00
111 Marques Anderson RC	2.00	5.00
112 Najeh Davenport RC	2.50	6.00
113 Jonathan Wells RC	2.50	6.00
114 Dwight Freeney RC	3.00	8.00
115 Larry Tripplett RC	1.50	4.00
116 T.J. Duckett RC	2.50	6.00
117 John Henderson RC	2.00	5.00
118 Albert Haynesworth RC	2.50	6.00
119 Tank Williams RC	2.00	5.00
120 Ryan Sims RC	2.50	6.00
121 Leonard Henry RC	1.50	4.00
122 Clinton Portis RC	3.00	8.00
123 Josh Reed RC	2.00	5.00
124 Chad Hutchinson RC	1.50	4.00
125 Deion Branch RC	2.50	6.00
126 Rocky Calmus RC	2.00	5.00
127 Donte Stallworth RC	2.50	6.00
128 Daryl Jones RC	1.50	4.00
129 Joey Harrington RC	2.50	6.00
130 Napoleon Harris RC	2.00	5.00
131 Phillip Buchanon RC	2.50	6.00
132 Patrick Ramsey RC	2.50	6.00
133 Brian Westbrook RC	4.00	10.00
134 Freddie Milons RC	1.50	4.00
135 Lito Sheppard RC	2.50	6.00
136 Michael Lewis RC	2.50	6.00
137 Jamin Elliott RC	1.50	4.00
138 Lee Mays RC	1.50	4.00
139 Verron Haynes RC	1.50	4.00
140 Jesse Chatman RC	1.50	4.00
141 Quentin Jammer RC	2.50	6.00
142 Seth Burford RC	1.50	4.00
143 Julius Peppers RC	5.00	12.00
144 William Green RC	2.00	5.00
145 DeShaun Foster RC	2.50	6.00
146 Daniel Graham RC	2.00	5.00
147 David Garrard RC	3.00	8.00
148 Reche Caldwell RC	2.50	6.00
149 Randy Fasani RC	2.00	5.00
150 J.T. O'Sullivan RC	2.00	5.00
151 Josh McCown JSY AU RC	8.00	20.00
152 Kurt Kittner JSY AU RC	5.00	12.00
153 Kahlil Hill JSY AU RC	5.00	12.00
154 Ladell Betts JSY AU RC	8.00	20.00
155 Ron Johnson JSY AU RC	6.00	15.00
156 Maurice Morris JSY AU RC	6.00	15.00
157 Andre Davis JSY AU RC	6.00	15.00
158 Antonio Bryant JSY AU RC	8.00	20.00
159 Roy Williams JSY AU RC	8.00	20.00
160 Lamont Thompson JSY AU RC	6.00	15.00
161 Cliff Russell JSY AU RC	5.00	12.00
162 Woody Dantzler JSY AU RC	6.00	15.00
163 Travis Stephens JSY AU RC	5.00	12.00
164 Tony Fisher JSY AU RC	6.00	15.00
165 Eric McCoo JSY AU RC	5.00	12.00
166 Eric Crouch JSY AU RC	8.00	20.00
167 Rohan Davey JSY AU RC	8.00	20.00
168 Marquise Walker JSY AU RC	5.00	12.00
169 Jeremy Shockey JSY RC	8.00	20.00
170 Tim Carter JSY AU RC	6.00	15.00
171 Atrews Bell JSY AU RC	5.00	12.00
172 Antwaan Randle El JSY AU RC	8.00	20.00
173 Ricky Williams JSY AU RC	6.00	15.00
174 Mike Williams JSY AU	5.00	12.00
175 Adrian Peterson JSY AU RC	8.00	20.00
176 Jabar Gaffney JSY AU/650 RC	8.00	20.00
177 Ashley Lelie JSY AU/250 RC	8.00	20.00
178 David Carr JSY AU/250 RC	10.00	25.00

2002 SPx Supreme Signatures

STATED ODDS 1:36

SSAG Ahman Green	8.00	20.00
SSAM Archie Manning	25.00	50.00
SSAT Anthony Thomas	6.00	15.00
SSBE Michael Bennett	6.00	15.00
SSBJ Brad Johnson	6.00	15.00
SSBO David Boston	5.00	12.00
SSCC Chris Chambers	6.00	15.00
SSCW Chris Weinke	5.00	12.00
SSDB Drew Brees	40.00	80.00
SSFM Freddie Mitchell	5.00	12.00
SSJB Jim Brown	40.00	80.00
SSJE John Elway/52*	60.00	120.00
SSJG Jeff Garcia/62*	15.00	40.00
SSJL Jamal Lewis	6.00	15.00
SSJR John Riggins	25.00	50.00
SSKJ Kevin Johnson	5.00	12.00
SSKS Kordell Stewart	6.00	15.00
SSMM Mike McMahon	5.00	12.00
SSMO Dan Morgan	5.00	12.00
SSMT Marques Tuiasosopo	5.00	12.00
SSMV Michael Vick	30.00	60.00
SSPH Priest Holmes	12.00	30.00
SSPM Peyton Manning	50.00	100.00
SSQM Quincy Morgan	5.00	12.00
SSSM Santana Moss	6.00	15.00
SSSR Sage Rosenfels	6.00	15.00
SSTC Tim Couch	5.00	12.00

2002 SPx Winning Materials

VETERAN STATED ODDS 1:28
ROOKIE STATED ODDS 1:85
*GOLD VETS/250: .5X TO 1.2X BASE JSY
*GOLD VETS/250: .4X TO 1X BASE SP
*GOLD ROOKIES/50: .8X TO 2X BASE JSY
*GOLD ROOKIES/50: .6X TO 1.5X BASE SP
UNPRICED NFL LOGO PRINT RUN 1-5

WMAT Anthony Thomas	4.00	10.00
WMBF Brett Favre	12.00	30.00
WMBL Mark Brunell	4.00	10.00
WMBO David Boston	3.00	8.00
WMBR Tom Brady SP	12.00	30.00
WMCW Chris Weinke	3.00	8.00
WMDB Drew Bledsoe	5.00	12.00
WMDM Donovan McNabb	5.00	12.00
WMDT David Terrell	3.00	8.00
WMDW Drew Brees	8.00	20.00
WMEJ Edgerrin James	4.00	10.00
WMES Emmitt Smith	12.00	30.00
WMJB Jerome Bettis	8.00	20.00
WMJG Jeff Garcia	4.00	10.00
WMJR Jerry Rice	10.00	25.00
WMKC Kerry Collins	4.00	10.00
WMKW Kurt Warner SP	6.00	15.00
WMLT LaDainian Tomlinson	6.00	15.00
WMMA Mike Anderson	4.00	10.00
WMMF Marshall Faulk SP	6.00	15.00
WMMV Michael Vick	8.00	20.00
WMPM Peyton Manning	10.00	25.00
WMRAB Antonio Bryant SP	4.00	10.00
WMRAL Ashley Lelie	4.00	10.00
WMRCP Clinton Portis	5.00	12.00
WMRDC David Carr	5.00	12.00
WMRDF DeShaun Foster	5.00	12.00
WMRDS Donte Stallworth SP	4.00	10.00
WMRJG Jabar Gaffney	5.00	12.00
WMRJH Joey Harrington	5.00	12.00
WMRJM Josh McCown SP	4.00	10.00
WMRJP Julius Peppers	8.00	20.00
WMRJR Josh Reed	4.00	10.00
WMRM Randy Moss	5.00	12.00
WMRMW Marquise Walker	3.00	8.00
WMRPR Patrick Ramsey SP	4.00	10.00
WMRW Ricky Williams	4.00	10.00
WMRWG William Green	4.00	10.00
WMSM Steve McNair	5.00	12.00
WMTO Terrell Owens	5.00	12.00
WMVT Vinny Testaverde	4.00	10.00

2003 SPx

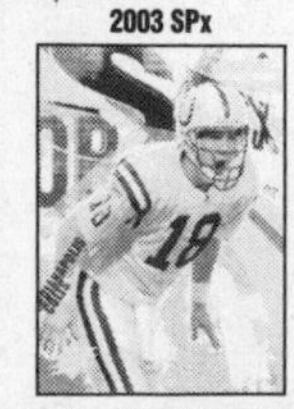

Released in October of 2003, this set consists of 218 cards, including 110 veterans and 108 rookies. Rookies 111-190 were serial numbered to 1500 and were inserted at a rate of 1:6. Rookies 191-220 feature jersey swatches and autographs and were inserted at a rate of 1:18. Each rookie jersey autograph was serial numbered to 1100 with the exceptions noted below. Please note that cards 209 and 214 were not released. Boxes contained 18 packs of 4 cards. Pack SRP was $6.99.

COMP.SET w/o SP's (110)	10.00	25.00
111-190 ROOKIE/1500 ODDS 1:6		
1 Peyton Manning	.75	2.00
2 Aaron Brooks	.30	.75
3 Joey Harrington	.25	.60
4 Tim Couch	.25	.60
5 Jeff Garcia	.30	.75
6 Jay Fiedler	.25	.60
7 Chad Hutchinson	.25	.60
8 Tommy Maddox	.30	.75
9 Drew Brees	.40	1.00
10 Trent Green	.30	.75
11 Patrick Ramsey	.30	.75
12 Daunte Culpepper	.30	.75
13 Kurt Warner	.40	1.00
14 Brad Johnson	.30	.75
15 Rich Gannon	.30	.75
16 Jake Plummer	.30	.75
17 Steve McNair	.40	1.00
18 Mark Brunell	.30	.75
19 Drew Bledsoe	.40	1.00
20 Kordell Stewart	.30	.75
21 Kelly Holcomb	.25	.60
22 Josh McCown	.30	.75
23 Matt Hasselbeck	.30	.75
24 Marc Bulger	.40	1.00
25 Chris Redman	.25	.60
26 Rodney Peete	.25	.60
27 Jake Delhomme	.40	1.00
28 Jon Kitna	.30	.75
29 Kerry Collins	.30	.75
30 Quincy Carter	.25	.60
31 Ricky Williams	.30	.75
32 Clinton Portis	.30	.75
33 Deuce McAllister	.30	.75
34 Ahman Green	.30	.75
35 Priest Holmes	.40	1.00
36 Curtis Martin	.40	1.00
37 Michael Bennett	.30	.75
38 Eddie George	.30	.75
39 Marshall Faulk	.40	1.00
40 Garrison Hearst	.30	.75
41 Shaun Alexander	.30	.75
42 Corey Dillon	.30	.75
43 Jamal Lewis	.30	.75
44 William Green	.25	.60
45 Travis Henry	.25	.60
46 Randy Moss	.40	1.00
47 Terrell Owens	.40	1.00
48 Peerless Price	.25	.60
49 David Boston	.25	.60
50 Eric Moulds	.30	.75
51 Marvin Harrison	.40	1.00
52 Laveranues Coles	.25	.60
53 Santana Moss	.30	.75
54 Troy Brown	.30	.75
55 Chris Chambers	.30	.75
56 Tim Brown	.40	1.00
57 Rod Smith	.30	.75
58 Hines Ward	.40	1.00
59 Keyshawn Johnson	.40	1.00
60 Isaac Bruce	.40	1.00
61 Torry Holt	.40	1.00
62 Koren Robinson	.30	.75
63 Chad Johnson	.40	1.00
64 Derrick Mason	.30	.75
65 Antonio Bryant	.25	.60
66 Kevin Johnson	.25	.60
67 Todd Heap	.30	.75
68 Tony Gonzalez	.40	1.00
69 Jeremy Shockey	.40	1.00
70 Brian Urlacher	.40	1.00
71 Emmitt Smith/500	6.00	15.00
72 Edgerrin James/500	2.50	6.00
73 LaDainian Tomlinson/500	2.50	6.00
74 Brett Favre/500	6.00	15.00
75 Donovan McNabb/500	2.50	6.00
76 Tom Brady/500	6.00	15.00
77 Michael Vick/500	3.00	8.00
78 David Carr/500	2.00	5.00
79 Jerry Rice/500	5.00	12.00
80 Chad Pennington/500	2.50	6.00
81 Joey Harrington XCT	.25	.60
82 Clinton Portis XCT	.30	.75
83 Jeremy Shockey XCT	.40	1.00
84 David Boston XCT	.25	.60
85 Marshall Faulk XCT	.40	1.00
86 Emmitt Smith XCT	1.00	2.50
87 Terrell Owens XCT	.40	1.00
88 Randy Moss XCT	.40	1.00
89 Deuce McAllister XCT	.30	.75
90 Ahman Green XCT	.30	.75
91 Peerless Price XCT	.25	.60
92 Plaxico Burress XCT	.30	.75
93 Marvin Harrison XCT	.40	1.00
94 Keyshawn Johnson XCT	.40	1.00
95 Laveranues Coles XCT	.25	.60
96 Drew Bledsoe XCT	.40	1.00
97 Eric Moulds XCT	.30	.75
98 Chad Pennington XCT	.40	1.00
99 Jerry Rice XCT	.75	2.00
100 David Carr XCT	.30	.75
101 Michael Vick XCT	.50	1.25
102 Tom Brady XCT	1.00	2.50
103 Donovan McNabb XCT	.40	1.00
104 Brett Favre XCT	1.00	2.50
105 Kurt Warner XCT	.40	1.00
106 LaDainian Tomlinson XCT	.40	1.00
107 Drew Brees XCT	.40	1.00
108 Edgerrin James XCT	.40	1.00
109 Peyton Manning XCT	.75	2.00
110 Ricky Williams XCT	.30	.75
111 Brooks Bollinger RC	2.00	5.00
112 Gibran Hamden RC	1.50	4.00
113 Jason Johnson RC	1.50	4.00
114 Tony Romo RC	20.00	50.00
115 Juston Wood RC	1.50	4.00
116 Kirk Farmer RC	2.00	5.00
117 Kliff Kingsbury RC	2.00	5.00
118 Jason Gesser RC	2.00	5.00
119 Brad Banks RC	2.00	5.00
120 Rob Adamson RC	1.50	4.00
121 Ken Dorsey RC	2.00	5.00
122 Curt Anes RC	1.50	4.00
123 George Wrighster RC	1.50	4.00
124 Brett Engemann RC	1.50	4.00
125 Aaron Walker RC	2.00	5.00
126 Nate Hybl RC	2.00	5.00
127 Chris Simms RC	2.50	6.00
128 Marquel Blackwell RC	1.50	4.00
129 Domanick Davis RC	2.00	5.00
130 Quentin Griffin RC	2.00	5.00
131 B.J. Askew RC	2.00	5.00
132 Earnest Graham RC	2.50	6.00
133 Sultan McCullough RC	1.50	4.00
134 Dahrran Diedrick RC	1.50	4.00
135 Cecil Sapp RC	1.50	4.00
136 LaBrandon Toefield RC	2.00	5.00
137 ReShard Lee RC	2.50	6.00
138 Dwone Hicks RC	1.50	4.00
139 Brock Forsey RC	2.00	5.00
140 Bethel Johnson RC	1.50	4.00
141 Andrew Pinnock RC	2.00	5.00
142 Ahmaad Galloway RC	2.00	5.00
143 J.T. Wall RC	1.50	4.00
144 Tom Lopienski RC	1.50	4.00
145 Justin Griffith RC	2.00	5.00
146 Lee Suggs RC	2.00	5.00
147 Nick Maddox RC	1.50	4.00
148 Jeremi Johnson RC	1.50	4.00
149 Doug Gabriel RC	2.00	5.00
150 Bobby Wade RC	2.00	5.00
151 Justin Gage RC	2.00	5.00
152 Arnaz Battle RC	2.50	6.00
153 Brandon Lloyd RC	4.00	10.00
154 Talman Gardner RC	1.50	4.00
155 Kareem Kelly RC	1.50	4.00
156 Billy McMullen RC	1.50	4.00
157 Antwone Savage RC	1.50	4.00
158 J.R. Tolver RC	2.00	5.00
159 Kassim Osgood RC	2.50	6.00
160 Shaun McDonald RC	2.00	5.00
161 Sam Aiken RC	2.00	5.00
162 Adrian Madise RC	1.50	4.00
163 Charles Rogers RC	2.00	5.00
164 David Kircus RC	2.50	6.00
165 Zuriel Smith RC	1.50	4.00
166 LaTarence Dunbar RC	1.50	4.00
167 Willie Ponder RC	1.50	4.00
168 David Tyree RC	2.50	6.00
169 Kevin Walter RC	4.00	10.00
170 Keenan Howry RC	1.50	4.00
171 Walter Young RC	1.50	4.00
172 DeAndrew Rubin RC	1.50	4.00
173 Carl Ford RC	1.50	4.00
174 Taco Wallace RC	1.50	4.00
175 Travis Anglin RC	1.50	4.00
176 Ryan Hoag RC	1.50	4.00
177 Ronald Bellamy RC	2.00	5.00
178 Terrence Edwards RC	1.50	4.00
179 Jerel Myers RC	1.50	4.00
180 Mike Bush RC	1.50	4.00
181 Dan Curley RC	1.50	4.00
182 Carl Morris RC	1.50	4.00
183 Reggie Newhouse RC	1.50	4.00
184 Troy Polamalu RC	25.00	50.00
185 Cecil Moore RC	1.50	4.00
186 Bennie Joppru RC	1.50	4.00
187 Donald Lee RC	2.00	5.00
188 Jason Witten RC	6.00	15.00
189 Mike Seidman RC	1.50	4.00
190 Vishante Shiancoe RC	2.50	6.00
191 Anquan Boldin JSY AU RC	15.00	40.00
192 Kyle Boller JSY AU/450 RC	12.00	30.00
193 Chris Brown JSY AU RC	6.00	15.00
194 Nate Burleson JSY AU RC	8.00	20.00
195 Tyrone Calico JSY AU/450 RC	10.00	25.00
196 Dallas Clark JSY AU RC	12.00	30.00
197 Kevin Curtis JSY AU RC	10.00	25.00
198 Kliff Kingsbury JSY AU RC	8.00	20.00
199 Justin Fargas JSY AU RC	10.00	25.00
200 Rex Grossman JSY AU/450 RC	12.00	30.00
201 Taylor Jacobs JSY AU RC	6.00	15.00
202 Andre Johnson JSY AU/250 RC	90.00	150.00
203 Malaefou MacKenzie JSY AU RC	6.00	15.00
204 Bryant Johnson JSY AU RC	10.00	25.00
205 Larry Johnson JSY AU RC	10.00	25.00
206 Teyo Johnson JSY AU/450 RC	10.00	25.00
207 Byron Leftwich JSY AU/250 RC	15.00	40.00
208 Willis McGahee JSY AU/450 RC	15.00	40.00
210 Carson Palmer JSY AU/250 RC	50.00	100.00
211 Artose Pinner JSY AU RC	6.00	15.00
212 Dave Ragone JSY AU RC	6.00	15.00
213 Terrell Suggs JSY AU RC	15.00	40.00
215 Onterio Smith JSY AU RC	6.00	15.00
216 Musa Smith JSY AU RC	6.00	15.00
217 Brian St.Pierre JSY AU RC	8.00	20.00
218 Marcus Trufant JSY AU RC	8.00	20.00
219 Seneca Wallace JSY AU RC	10.00	25.00
220 Kelley Washington JSY AU RC	6.00	15.00

2003 SPx Spectrum

*VETS 1-70/81-110: 8X TO 20X
*VETS 71-80: 1.2X TO 3X
*ROOKIES 111-190: 1.2X TO 3X
1-190 STATED PRINT RUN 50
*ROOK.JSY AU: 1.2X TO 3X JSY AU/1100
*ROOK.JSY AU: 1X TO 2.5X JSY AU/450
*ROOK.JSY AU: .8X TO 2X JSY AU/250
191-218 JSY AU PRINT RUN 25

114 Tony Romo	60.00	150.00
184 Troy Polamalu	75.00	135.00

2003 SPx Supreme Signatures

SSAB Aaron Brooks	8.00	20.00
SSAH Az-Zahir Hakim	6.00	15.00
SSAM Archie Manning	10.00	25.00
SSBB Brad Banks	8.00	20.00
SSBJ Bryant Johnson	10.00	25.00
SSBL Byron Leftwich	10.00	25.00
SSBR Brad Johnson	8.00	20.00
SSBS Brian St.Pierre	8.00	20.00
SSCH Chad Pennington	10.00	25.00
SSCP Carson Palmer	50.00	100.00
SSCS Chris Simms	10.00	25.00
SSDC David Carr SP	10.00	25.00
SSDR Dave Ragone	6.00	15.00
SSEG Earnest Graham	10.00	25.00
SSIB Isaac Bruce	10.00	25.00
SSJG Jeff Garcia	8.00	20.00
SSJK Jim Kelly SP	30.00	60.00
SSKB Kevan Barlow	6.00	15.00
SSKB Kyle Boller	10.00	25.00
SSKK Kareem Kelly	6.00	15.00
SSKL Kliff Kingsbury	8.00	20.00
SSKW Kelley Washington	6.00	15.00
SSLS Lee Suggs	8.00	20.00
SSMB Mark Brunell	8.00	20.00
SSMH Matt Hasselbeck SP	25.00	60.00
SSMI Michael Bennett SP	8.00	20.00
SSMV Michael Vick	25.00	50.00
SSOS Onterrio Smith	6.00	15.00
SSPM Peyton Manning	60.00	100.00
SSPO Clinton Portis	12.00	30.00
SSQG Quentin Griffin	8.00	20.00
SSRG Rod Gardner	6.00	15.00
SSRS Rod Smith SP	8.00	20.00
SSTB Tom Brady SP	125.00	250.00
SSTC Tim Couch	6.00	15.00
SSTG Trent Green	8.00	20.00
SSTH Travis Henry	6.00	15.00
SSTJ Taylor Jacobs	6.00	15.00
SSTS Terrell Suggs	12.00	30.00

2003 SPx Supreme Signatures Spectrum

*SPECTRUM: .6X TO 1.5X BASIC INSERTS
PRINT RUN 50 SERIAL #'d SETS

SSJK Jim Kelly	30.00	60.00
SSMH Matt Hasselbeck	20.00	50.00
SSTB Tom Brady	125.00	250.00

2003 SPx Winning Materials

STATED PRINT RUN 220-350
*TEAM LOGO/147-250: .5X TO 1.2X BASE JSY
*TEAM LOGO/50-99: .6X TO 1.5X BASE JSY
TEAM LOGO PRINT RUN 50-250
*TL SPECTRUM/50: .6X TO 1.5X BASE JSY
TEAM LOGO SPECTRUM PRINT RUN 50
*USA FLAGS/25: 1X TO 2.5X BASE JSY
USA FLAG PRINT RUN 25

AB Aaron Brooks	4.00	10.00
AJ Andre Johnson	10.00	25.00
AN Anquan Boldin	6.00	15.00
AP Artose Pinner	3.00	8.00
BJ Bryant Johnson	5.00	12.00
BL Byron Leftwich	4.00	10.00
BR Tim Brown	5.00	12.00
CC Chris Chambers/300	4.00	10.00
CD Corey Dillon/266	4.00	10.00
CJ Chad Johnson/220	5.00	12.00
CM Curtis Martin	5.00	12.00
CP Chad Pennington	5.00	12.00
DC David Carr	4.00	10.00
DM Donovan McNabb	5.00	12.00
EJ Edgerrin James	5.00	12.00
EM Eric Moulds/264	4.00	10.00
ES Emmitt Smith	12.00	30.00
JH Joey Harrington	3.00	8.00
JP Julius Peppers	5.00	12.00
JR Jerry Rice/300	10.00	25.00
KC Kevin Curtis	5.00	12.00
KJ Keyshawn Johnson/268	5.00	12.00
KW Kurt Warner	5.00	12.00
LJ Larry Johnson	4.00	10.00
MB Mark Brunell	4.00	10.00
MF Marshall Faulk	5.00	12.00
MH Marvin Harrison/278	5.00	12.00
MT Marcus Trufant	4.00	10.00
PM Peyton Manning	10.00	25.00
PO Clinton Portis	4.00	10.00
PR Priest Holmes	5.00	12.00
RS Rod Smith/300	4.00	10.00
RW Ricky Williams	4.00	10.00
SC Carson Palmer	8.00	20.00
SH Jeremy Shockey	5.00	12.00
SW Seneca Wallace	5.00	12.00
TB Tom Brady	20.00	50.00
TJ Taylor Jacobs	3.00	8.00
TN Terence Newman	3.00	8.00
WG William Green	3.00	8.00
WM Willis McGahee	5.00	12.00

2003 SPx Winning Materials Patches

STATED PRINT RUN 15-75

BF Brett Favre	50.00	120.00
BJ Bryant Johnson	20.00	50.00
CP Chad Pennington	25.00	60.00
DC David Carr	15.00	40.00
DM Donovan McNabb	25.00	60.00
JR Jerry Rice	40.00	100.00
LT LaDainian Tomlinson	30.00	60.00
MV Michael Vick	25.00	60.00
PM Peyton Manning	30.00	80.00
PO Clinton Portis	25.00	60.00
RM Randy Moss	25.00	60.00
RW Ricky Williams	15.00	40.00
SM Santana Moss/47	20.00	50.00
SW Seneca Wallace	20.00	50.00
TC Tim Couch	12.00	30.00

2003 SPx Winning Materials Patches Autographs

STATED PRINT RUN 25-50

BL Byron Leftwich/25	25.00	60.00
CP Chad Pennington/50	30.00	80.00
DB Drew Brees/50	50.00	100.00
JG Jeff Garcia/50	25.00	60.00
JR Jerry Rice/25	150.00	300.00
LT LaDainian Tomlinson/50	40.00	100.00
MVO Michael Vick/25	60.00	100.00
PM Peyton Manning/50	100.00	175.00
RM Randy Moss/50	50.00	100.00
SA Shaun Alexander/50	30.00	80.00
SC Carson Palmer/25	100.00	200.00
TC Tim Couch/50	20.00	50.00
TO Terrell Owens/50	30.00	80.00

2004 SPx

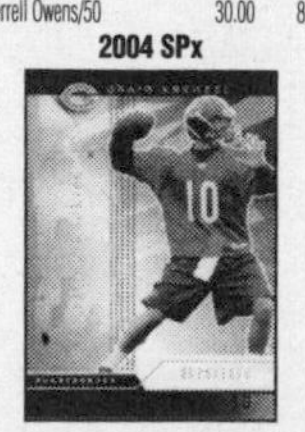

SPx initially released in early-November 2004. The base set consists of 221-cards including 65-rookies serial numbered to 1650, 25-rookies serial numbered to 799, and 30-rookie jersey autographs numbered between 375 and 1499. Finally, the Larry Fitzgerald JSY AU card #219 was serial numbered to just 100-copies. Hobby boxes contained 18-packs of 5-cards and carried an S.R.P. of $6.99 per pack. One basic parallel set and four Player Printing Plate 1/1 parallels can be found seeded in packs. The balance of the inserts consists of jersey memorabilia cards and autographed cards.

COMP.SET w/o SP's (100)	15.00	30.00
101-165 RC PRINT RUN 1650 SER.#'d SETS		
166-190 RC PRINT RUN 799 SER.#'d SETS		
191-221 JSY AU RC #'d TO 1499 UNLESS NOTED		
UNPRICED PRINT.PLATE #'d TO 1		
1 Anquan Boldin	.40	1.00
2 Marcel Shipp	.25	.60
3 Josh McCown	.30	.75
4 Peerless Price	.25	.60
5 Michael Vick	.50	1.25
6 T.J. Duckett	.30	.75
7 Kyle Boller	.30	.75
8 Todd Heap	.30	.75
9 Jamal Lewis	.30	.75
10 Travis Henry	.25	.60
11 Drew Bledsoe	.40	1.00
12 Eric Moulds	.30	.75
13 Jake Delhomme	.30	.75
14 Steve Smith	.40	1.00
15 Stephen Davis	.30	.75
16 Brian Urlacher	.40	1.00
17 Rex Grossman	.30	.75
18 Thomas Jones	.40	1.00
19 Chad Johnson	.40	1.00
20 Carson Palmer	.40	1.00
21 Rudi Johnson	.30	.75
22 William Green	.25	.60
23 Jeff Garcia	.30	.75
24 Andre Davis	.25	.60
25 Roy Williams S	.30	.75
26 Eddie George	.30	.75
27 Keyshawn Johnson	.30	.75
28 Jake Plummer	.30	.75
29 Ashley Lelie	.25	.60
30 Quentin Griffin	.25	.60
31 Charles Rogers	.25	.60
32 Olandis Gary	.25	.60
33 Joey Harrington	.30	.75
34 Brett Favre	1.00	2.50
35 Javon Walker	.25	.60
36 Ahman Green	.30	.75
37 Andre Johnson	.40	1.00
38 Domanick Davis	.25	.60
39 David Carr	.25	.60
40 Peyton Manning	.75	2.00
41 Edgerrin James	.30	.75
42 Marvin Harrison	.40	1.00
43 Byron Leftwich	.30	.75
44 Jimmy Smith	.30	.75
45 Fred Taylor	.30	.75
46 Trent Green	.30	.75
47 Priest Holmes	.40	1.00
48 Dante Hall	.30	.75
49 Tony Gonzalez	.40	1.00
50 A.J. Feeley	.25	.60
51 Marty Booker	.30	.75
52 Chris Chambers	.30	.75
53 Zach Thomas	.40	1.00
54 Randy Moss	.40	1.00
55 Daunte Culpepper	.30	.75
56 Onterrio Smith	.25	.60
57 Troy Brown	.30	.75
58 Corey Dillon	.30	.75
59 Tom Brady	.75	2.00
60 Deuce McAllister	.30	.75
61 Joe Horn	.30	.75
62 Aaron Brooks	.30	.75
63 Jeremy Shockey	.30	.75
64 Kurt Warner	.40	1.00
65 Tiki Barber	.40	1.00
66 Chad Pennington	.40	1.00
67 Curtis Martin	.40	1.00
68 Santana Moss	.30	.75
69 Rich Gannon	.30	.75
70 Jerry Rice	.75	2.00
71 Warren Sapp	.30	.75
72 Donovan McNabb	.40	1.00
73 Terrell Owens	.40	1.00
74 Jevon Kearse	.30	.75
75 Brian Westbrook	.40	1.00
76 Hines Ward	.40	1.00
77 Duce Staley	.30	.75
78 Tommy Maddox	.30	.75
79 LaDainian Tomlinson	.40	1.00
80 Drew Brees	.40	1.00
81 Tim Rattay	.25	.60
82 Kevan Barlow	.25	.60
83 Brandon Lloyd	.30	.75
84 Shaun Alexander	.30	.75
85 Matt Hasselbeck	.30	.75
86 Koren Robinson	.25	.60
87 Marc Bulger	.30	.75
88 Marshall Faulk	.40	1.00
89 Torry Holt	.30	.75
90 Isaac Bruce	.30	.75
91 Brad Johnson	.30	.75
92 Keenan McCardell	.25	.60
93 Derrick Brooks	.30	.75
94 Steve McNair	.40	1.00
95 Chris Brown	.25	.60
96 Derrick Mason	.30	.75
97 Clinton Portis	.40	1.00
98 Mark Brunell	.30	.75
99 Laveranues Coles	.25	.60
100 LaVar Arrington	.30	.75
101 B.J. Johnson RC	1.25	3.00
102 Craig Krenzel RC	1.50	4.00
103 Will Smith RC	1.50	4.00
104 Jamaar Taylor RC	1.25	3.00
105 Tommie Harris RC	2.00	5.00
106 Shawn Andrews RC	1.50	4.00
107 Kendrick Starling RC	1.25	3.00
108 Jeris McIntyre RC	1.25	3.00
109 Jason Babin RC	2.00	5.00
110 Marcus Tubbs RC	1.25	3.00
111 Triandos Luke RC	1.25	3.00
112 Karlos Dansby RC	2.00	5.00
113 Vernon Carey RC	1.25	3.00
114 Ryan Krause RC	1.25	3.00
115 Daryl Smith RC	1.25	3.00
116 Ricardo Colclough RC	1.50	4.00
117 Michael Boulware RC	2.00	5.00
118 Chris Cooley RC	2.00	5.00
119 Tank Johnson RC	1.25	3.00
120 Marquise Hill RC	1.25	3.00
121 Teddy Lehman RC	1.25	3.00
122 Antwan Odom RC	1.50	4.00
123 Sean Jones RC	1.50	4.00
124 Junior Siavii RC	1.25	3.00
125 Joey Thomas RC	1.25	3.00
126 Shawntae Spencer RC	1.25	3.00
127 Dontarrious Thomas RC	1.50	4.00
128 Travis LaBoy RC	1.50	4.00
129 Justin Jenkins RC	1.25	3.00
130 Dwan Edwards RC	1.25	3.00
131 Derrick Strait RC	1.25	3.00
132 Matt Ware RC	2.00	5.00
133 Jared Lorenzen RC	1.50	4.00
134 Demorrio Williams RC	2.00	5.00
135 Bob Sanders RC	5.00	12.00
136 Justin Smiley RC	1.50	4.00
137 Casey Bramlet RC	1.25	3.00
138 Jake Grove RC	1.25	3.00
139 Thomas Tapeh RC	1.50	4.00
140 Igor Olshansky RC	1.50	4.00
141 Stuart Schweigert RC	1.50	4.00
142 Cody Pickett RC	1.50	4.00
143 Derrick Ward RC	2.00	5.00
144 Gilbert Gardner RC	1.25	3.00
145 D.J. Hackett RC	1.50	4.00
146 Marquis Cooper RC	1.25	3.00
147 Courtney Watson RC	1.25	3.00
148 Jim Sorgi RC	1.50	4.00
149 Caleb Miller RC	1.25	3.00
150 Casey Clausen RC	1.50	4.00
151 Jammal Lord RC	1.25	3.00
152 Sloan Thomas RC	1.50	4.00
153 Keyaron Fox RC	1.50	4.00
154 Adimchinobe Echemandu RC	1.50	4.00
155 Ryan Dinwiddie RC	1.25	3.00
156 Kris Wilson RC	1.50	4.00
157 D.J. Williams RC	2.00	5.00
158 Tim Euhus RC	1.25	3.00
159 Bradlee Van Pelt RC	1.50	4.00
160 Keiwan Ratliff RC	1.25	3.00
161 Darnell Dockett RC	1.25	3.00
162 Troy Fleming RC	1.25	3.00
163 Tramon Douglas RC	1.25	3.00
164 Jeremy LeSueur RC	1.25	3.00
165 Matt Mauck RC	1.25	3.00
166 Sean Taylor RC	8.00	20.00
167 B.J. Symons RC	2.50	6.00
168 Quincy Wilson RC	3.00	8.00
169 Ernest Wilford RC	3.00	8.00
170 Jerricho Cotchery RC	3.00	8.00
171 Michael Turner RC	5.00	12.00
172 Samie Parker RC	2.50	6.00
173 Andy Hall RC	2.50	6.00
174 Keith Smith RC	2.50	6.00
175 Josh Harris RC	2.50	6.00
176 Maurice Mann RC	2.50	6.00
177 Jonathan Vilma RC	4.00	10.00
178 Jeff Smoker RC	3.00	8.00
179 Ben Hartsock RC	2.50	6.00
180 Chris Gamble RC	3.00	8.00
181 Derrick Hamilton RC	2.50	6.00
182 John Navarre RC	2.50	6.00
183 P.K. Sam RC	2.50	6.00
184 Kenechi Udeze RC	3.00	8.00
185 Mewelde Moore RC	3.00	8.00
186 Carlos Francis RC	2.50	6.00
187 Dunta Robinson RC	2.50	6.00
188 Johnnie Morant RC	2.50	6.00
189 Ahmad Carroll RC	2.50	6.00
190 Vince Wilfork RC	4.00	10.00
191 Tatum Bell JSY AU RC	6.00	15.00
192 Cedric Cobbs JSY AU RC	5.00	12.00
193 Darius Watts JSY AU RC	5.00	12.00
194 Julius Jones JSY AU/375 RC	10.00	25.00
195 Robert Gallery JSY AU RC	8.00	20.00
196 DeAngelo Hall JSY AU RC	8.00	20.00
197 Ben Watson JSY AU RC	6.00	15.00
198 Ben Troupe JSY AU RC	6.00	15.00
199 Matt Schaub JSY AU RC	15.00	40.00
200 Michael Jenkins JSY AU RC	8.00	20.00
201 Luke McCown JSY AU RC	6.00	15.00
202 Devery Henderson JSY AU RC	8.00	20.00
203 Bernard Berrian JSY AU RC	8.00	20.00
204 Keary Colbert JSY AU RC	5.00	12.00
205 Devard Darling JSY AU RC	5.00	12.00
206 Lee Evans JSY AU RC	8.00	20.00
207 Greg Jones JSY AU RC	5.00	12.00
208 Michael Clayton JSY AU RC	6.00	15.00
209 Reggie Williams JSY AU RC	6.00	15.00
210 Chris Perry JSY AU/799 RC	6.00	15.00
211 Rashaun Woods JSY AU RC	5.00	12.00
212 J.P. Losman JSY AU RC	6.00	15.00
213 Kevin Jones JSY AU RC	6.00	15.00
214 Kellen Winslow JSY AU/375 RC	12.00	30.00
215 Steven Jackson JSY AU/375 RC	20.00	50.00
216 Joe Hamilton JSY AU RC	5.00	12.00
217 Roy Williams JSY AU/375 RC	12.00	30.00
218 Philip Rivers JSY AU/375 RC	40.00	100.00
219 Larry Fitzgerald JSY AU/100 RC	100.00	200.00
220 Ben Roethlisberger JSY AU/375 RC	125.00	200.00
221 Eli Manning JSY AU/375 RC	100.00	200.00

2004 SPx Spectrum Gold

*VETS 1-100: 8X TO 20X BASIC CARDS
*ROOKIES 101-165: 1.2X TO 3X
*ROOKIES 166-190: 1X TO 2.5X
*ROOK.AU: 1.5X TO 4X AU/799-1499
*ROOKIE AU: 1X TO 2.5X AU/375
STATED PRINT RUN 25 SER.#'d SETS

199 Matt Schaub JSY AU	75.00	150.00
218 Philip Rivers JSY AU	200.00	400.00
219 Larry Fitzgerald JSY AU	150.00	300.00
220 Ben Roethlisberger JSY AU	300.00	600.00
221 Eli Manning JSY AU	400.00	600.00

2004 SPx Rookie Swatch Supremacy

STATED ODDS 1:18

SWRBB Bernard Berrian	3.00	8.00
SWRBR Ben Roethlisberger	15.00	40.00
SWRBT Ben Troupe	2.50	6.00
SWRBW Ben Watson	3.00	8.00
SWRCC Cedric Cobbs	2.00	5.00
SWRCP Chris Perry	2.50	6.00
SWRDD Devard Darling	2.00	5.00
SWRDE Devery Henderson	3.00	8.00
SWRDH DeAngelo Hall	3.00	8.00
SWRDW Darius Watts	2.00	5.00
SWREM Eli Manning	15.00	40.00
SWRGJ Greg Jones	2.00	5.00
SWRHA Derrick Hamilton	2.00	5.00
SWRJJ Julius Jones	2.50	6.00
SWRJP J.P. Losman	2.50	6.00
SWRKC Keary Colbert	2.00	5.00
SWRKJ Kevin Jones	2.50	6.00
SWRKW Kellen Winslow Jr.	3.00	8.00
SWRLE Lee Evans	3.00	8.00
SWRLF Larry Fitzgerald	8.00	20.00
SWRLM Luke McCown	2.50	6.00
SWRMC Michael Clayton	2.50	6.00
SWRMJ Michael Jenkins	3.00	8.00
SWRPR Philip Rivers	10.00	25.00
SWRRA Rashaun Woods	2.00	5.00
SWRRG Robert Gallery	3.00	8.00
SWRRO Roy Williams WR	3.00	8.00
SWRRW Reggie Williams	2.50	6.00
SWRSJ Steven Jackson	5.00	12.00
SWRTB Tatum Bell	2.50	6.00

2004 SPx Rookie Winning Materials

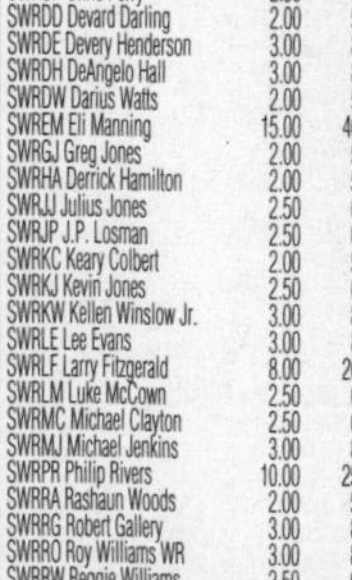

STATED ODDS 1:126

WMRBB Bernard Berrian	4.00	10.00
WMRBR Ben Roethlisberger	15.00	40.00

WMRBT Ben Troupe	3.00	8.00
WMRBW Ben Watson	4.00	10.00
WMRCC Cedric Cobbs	2.50	6.00
WMRCP Chris Perry	3.00	8.00
WMRDD Devard Darling	2.50	6.00
WMRDE Devery Henderson	4.00	10.00
WMRDH DeAngelo Hall	4.00	10.00
WMRDW Darius Watts	2.50	6.00
WMREM Eli Manning	15.00	40.00
WMRGJ Greg Jones	2.50	6.00
WMRHA Derrick Hamilton	2.50	6.00
WMRJJ Julius Jones	3.00	8.00
WMRJP J.P. Losman	0.00	8.00
WMRKC Keary Colbert	2.50	6.00
WMRKJ Kevin Jones	3.00	8.00
WMRKW Kellen Winslow Jr.	4.00	10.00
WMRLE Lee Evans	4.00	10.00
WMRLF Larry Fitzgerald	10.00	25.00
WMRLM Luke McCown	3.00	8.00
WMRMC Michael Clayton	3.00	8.00
WMRMJ Michael Jenkins	4.00	10.00
WMRPR Philip Rivers	15.00	40.00
WMRRA Rashaun Woods	2.50	6.00
WMRRG Robert Gallery	4.00	10.00
WMRRO Roy Williams WR	4.00	10.00
WMRRW Reggie Williams	3.00	8.00
WMRSJ Steven Jackson	6.00	15.00
WMRTB Tatum Bell	3.00	8.00

2004 SPx Super Scripts Autographs

STATED ODDS 1:54

SSAG Ahman Green	6.00	15.00
SSAR Andy Reid CO	6.00	15.00
SSBC Brandon Chillar	6.00	15.00
SSBF Brett Favre SP	100.00	200.00
SSBH Ben Hartsock	5.00	12.00
SSBL Brandon Lloyd	6.00	15.00
SSBW Brian Westbrook	8.00	20.00
SSBY Byron Leftwich	6.00	15.00
SSCC Chris Chambers	6.00	15.00
SSCF Clarence Farmer	5.00	12.00
SSCJ Chad Johnson	8.00	20.00
SSCP Chad Pennington	8.00	20.00
SSDB Drew Bledsoe	8.00	20.00
SSDC David Carr	5.00	12.00
SSDD Domanick Davis	5.00	12.00
SSDE Deuce McAllister	6.00	15.00
SSDH Dante Hall	6.00	15.00
SSDM Derrick Mason	6.00	15.00
SSDO Donovan McNabb SP	25.00	60.00
SSEL Antwaan Randle El	6.00	15.00
SSHE Todd Heap	6.00	15.00
SSJF Justin Fargas	6.00	15.00
SSJG Jon Gruden CO	6.00	15.00
SSJH Joe Horn	6.00	15.00
SSJJ Jimmy Johnson CO	6.00	15.00
SSJO Joey Galloway	6.00	15.00
SSJP Jesse Palmer	5.00	12.00
SSKB Kyle Boller	6.00	15.00
SSKD Ken Dorsey	5.00	12.00
SSKW Kelley Washington	5.00	12.00
SSLT LaDainian Tomlinson	25.00	50.00
SSMB Mark Brunell	6.00	15.00
SSMV Michael Vick SP	25.00	50.00
SSPM Peyton Manning	40.00	80.00
SSRG Rex Grossman	6.00	15.00
SSRJ Rudi Johnson	6.00	15.00
SSRW Roy Williams S	8.00	15.00
SSSM Steve McNair	15.00	30.00
SSTB Tom Brady SP	125.00	200.00
SSTG Tony Gonzalez	8.00	20.00
SSTH Travis Henry	5.00	12.00
SSWM Willis McGahee	8.00	20.00
SSZT Zach Thomas	10.00	25.00

2004 SPx Super Scripts Triple Autographs

STATED PRINT RUN 10-25
SERIAL #'d TO 10 NOT PRICED

GBL Rex Grossman	30.00	80.00
Kyle Boller		
Byron Leftwich/25		
GSL Robert Gallery	75.00	150.00
Ken Stabler		
Howie Long/25		
JGR Jimmy Johnson	40.00	100.00
Jon Gruden		
Andy Reid/25		
JJJ Steven Jackson	50.00	120.00
Julius Jones		
Kevin Jones/25		
MBM Steve McNair	75.00	150.00
Chris Brown		
Derrick Mason/25		
RRM Philip Rivers	350.00	600.00
Ben Roethlisberger		
Eli Manning/25		
SEA Barry Sanders	200.00	400.00
John Elway		
Troy Aikman/25		
TMG LaDainian Tomlinson	50.00	120.00
Deuce McAllister		
Ahman Green/25		
TST Joe Theismann	100.00	200.00
Ken Stabler		
Fran Tarkenton/25		
WWE Roy Williams	50.00	120.00
(Reggie Williams		
Lee Evans/25 ERR		

2004 SPx Swatch Supremacy

STATED ODDS 1:18

SWAG Ahman Green	3.00	8.00
SWAR Antwaan Randle El	3.00	8.00
SWBL Byron Leftwich	3.00	8.00
SWBW Brian Westbrook	4.00	10.00
SWCB Chris Brown	2.50	6.00
SWCC Chris Chambers	3.00	8.00
SWCJ Chad Johnson	4.00	10.00
SWCP Chad Pennington	4.00	10.00
SWDC Daunte Culpepper	3.00	8.00
SWDD Domanick Davis	2.50	6.00
SWDE Derrick Mason	3.00	8.00
SWDH Dante Hall	3.00	8.00
SWDM Deuce McAllister	3.00	8.00
SWDO Donovan McNabb	4.00	10.00
SWHE Todd Heap	3.00	8.00
SWJG Joey Galloway	3.00	8.00
SWJH Joe Horn	3.00	8.00
SWJW Javon Walker	2.50	6.00
SWKB Kyle Boller	3.00	8.00
SWLT LaDainian Tomlinson	4.00	10.00
SWMB Mark Brunell	3.00	8.00
SWMV Michael Vick	6.00	15.00
SWPM Peyton Manning	8.00	20.00
SWRG Rex Grossman	3.00	8.00
SWRJ Rudi Johnson	3.00	8.00
SWRW Roy Williams S	3.00	8.00
SWTB Tom Brady	8.00	20.00
SWTG Tony Gonzalez	4.00	10.00
SWTH Travis Henry	2.50	6.00
CWZT Zach Thomas	4.00	10.00

2004 SPx Swatch Supremacy Autographs

STATED PRINT RUN 100 SER.#'d SETS

SWAAG Ahman Green	10.00	25.00
SWAAR Antwaan Randle El	10.00	25.00
SWABL Byron Leftwich	10.00	25.00
SWABW Brian Westbrook	12.00	30.00
SWACB Chris Brown	8.00	20.00
SWACC Chris Chambers	10.00	25.00
SWACJ Chad Johnson	12.00	30.00
SWACP Chad Pennington	12.00	30.00
SWADC Daunte Culpepper	10.00	25.00
SWADD Domanick Davis	8.00	20.00
SWADE Derrick Mason	10.00	25.00
SWADH Dante Hall	10.00	25.00
SWADM Deuce McAllister	10.00	25.00
SWADO Donovan McNabb	20.00	50.00
SWAHE Todd Heap	10.00	25.00
SWAJG Joey Galloway	10.00	25.00
SWAJH Joe Horn	10.00	25.00
SWAKB Kyle Boller	10.00	25.00
SWALT LaDainian Tomlinson	30.00	60.00
SWAMB Mark Brunell	10.00	25.00
SWAMV Michael Vick	30.00	60.00
SWAPM Peyton Manning	60.00	120.00
SWARG Rex Grossman	10.00	25.00
SWARJ Rudi Johnson	10.00	25.00
SWARW Roy Williams S	10.00	25.00
SWATB Tom Brady	125.00	260.00
SWATG Tony Gonzalez	12.00	30.00
SWATH Travis Henry	8.00	20.00
SWAZT Zach Thomas	12.00	30.00

2004 SPx Winning Materials

STATED ODDS 1:72

WMAC LaVar Arrington	5.00	12.00
Laveranues Coles		
WMBD Tom Brady	12.00	30.00
Corey Dillon		
WMBM Aaron Brooks	5.00	12.00
Deuce McAllister		
WMBP Mark Brunell	6.00	15.00
Clinton Portis		
WMCJ David Carr	6.00	15.00
Andre Johnson		
WMCM Daunte Culpepper	6.00	15.00
Randy Moss		
WMDF Stephen Davis	5.00	12.00
DeShaun Foster		
WMDT Drew Bledsoe	6.00	15.00
Travis Henry		
WMFG Brett Favre	15.00	40.00
Ahman Green		
WMFH Marshall Faulk	6.00	15.00
Torry Holt		
WMFM Brett Favre	15.00	40.00
Donovan McNabb		
WMGG Trent Green	6.00	15.00
Tony Gonzalez		
WMHA Matt Hasselbeck	5.00	12.00
Shaun Alexander		
WMHR Joey Harrington	5.00	12.00
Charles Rogers		
WMHW Priest Holmes	6.00	15.00
Ricky Williams		
WMMJ Peyton Manning	12.00	30.00
Edgerrin James		
WMMM Curtis Martin	6.00	15.00
Santana Moss		
WMMO Donovan McNabb	6.00	15.00
Terrell Owens		
WMMR Randy Moss	12.00	30.00
Jerry Rice		
WMMV Steve McNair	8.00	20.00
Michael Vick		
WMPG Jake Plummer	5.00	12.00
Quentin Griffin		
WMPJ Carson Palmer	6.00	15.00
Rudi Johnson		
WMPL Chad Pennington	6.00	15.00
Byron Leftwich		
WMPS Peyton Manning	12.00	30.00
Steve McNair		
WMRG Jerry Rice	12.00	30.00
Rich Gannon		
WMSK Michael Strahan	6.00	15.00
Jevon Kearse		
WMSU Junior Seau	6.00	15.00
Brian Urlacher		
WMSW Jeremy Shockey	6.00	15.00
Kurt Warner		
WMTH LaDainian Tomlinson	6.00	15.00
Priest Holmes		
WMVB Michael Vick	12.00	30.00
Tom Brady		

2004 SPx Winning Materials Autographs

STATED PRINT RUN 25 SER.#'d SETS

BF Tom Brady	300.00	500.00
Brett Favre		
BH Larry Fitzgerald	75.00	150.00
Reggie Williams		
JJ Kevin Jones	40.00	100.00
Steven Jackson		
MG Deuce McAllister	30.00	60.00
Ahman Green		
MM Peyton Manning	100.00	200.00
Steve McNair		
PE Peyton Manning	200.00	350.00
Eli Manning		
PL Chad Pennington	30.00	80.00
Byron Leftwich		
RR Philip Rivers	200.00	350.00
Ben Roethlisberger		
SA Roger Staubach	100.00	200.00
Troy Aikman		
TB Joe Theismann	30.00	80.00
Mark Brunell		
TC Fran Tarkenton	30.00	80.00
Daunte Culpepper		
TM LaDainian Tomlinson	30.00	80.00
Deuce McAllister		
VM Michael Vick	60.00	120.00
Donovan McNabb		
WJ Roy Williams WR	25.00	60.00
Kevin Jones		
WW Kellen Winslow Jr.	30.00	80.00
Kellen Winslow Sr.		

2005 SPx

This 232-card set was released in September, 2005. The set was issued in four-card packs with an $6.99 SRP which came 18 packs to a box. Cards numbered 1-100 feature veteran players in team alphabetical order while cards numbered 101-223 are all 2005 rookies. Cards numbered 191-200 have two different players pictured (both regular rookie and rookies with both signatures and player-worn jersey swatches). Cards numbered 101-170 was issued to a stated print run of 1199 serial numbered sets. Cards numbered 171-190 and the non-signed no jersey swatch 191-200 cards were issued to a stated print run of 499 serial numbered sets. The signed jersey cards 191-200 and all the cards 201-223 were issued to a stated print run of 1275 serial numbered sets.

COMP.SET w/o SP's (100)	15.00	30.00

101-170 RC PRINT RUN 1199 SER.#'d SETS
171-200 RC PRINT RUN 499 SER.#'d SETS
JSY AU RC PRINT RUN 150-1275
UNPRICED NFL LOGO AUTOS #'d OF 1

1 Larry Fitzgerald	.40	1.00
2 Anquan Boldin	.30	.75
3 Josh McCown	.30	.75
4 Michael Vick	.40	1.00
5 Alge Crumpler	.30	.75
6 Peerless Price	.25	.60
7 Ray Lewis	.40	1.00
8 Jamal Lewis	.30	.75
9 Kyle Boller	.30	.75
10 J.P. Losman	.25	.60
11 Willis McGahee	.40	1.00
12 Eric Moulds	.25	.60
13 Jake Delhomme	.30	.75
14 DeShaun Foster	.30	.75
15 Steve Smith	.40	1.00
16 Brian Urlacher	.40	1.00
17 Rex Grossman	.30	.75
18 Muhsin Muhammad	.30	.75
19 Carson Palmer	.40	1.00
20 Rudi Johnson	.30	.75
21 Chad Johnson	.30	.75
22 Julius Jones	.25	.60
23 Keyshawn Johnson	.30	.75
24 Roy Williams S	.25	.60
25 Tatum Bell	.25	.60
26 Jake Plummer	.30	.75
27 Ashley Lelie	.25	.60
28 Roy Williams WR	.30	.75
29 Kevin Jones	.25	.60
30 Joey Harrington	.30	.75
31 Brett Favre	1.00	2.50
32 Ahman Green	.30	.75
33 Javon Walker	.25	.60
34 David Carr	.25	.60
35 Andre Johnson	.40	1.00
36 Domanick Davis	.25	.60
37 Peyton Manning	.75	2.00
38 Reggie Wayne	.40	1.00
39 Edgerrin James	.30	.75
40 Marvin Harrison	.40	1.00
41 Byron Leftwich	.30	.75
42 Fred Taylor	.30	.75
43 Jimmy Smith	.30	.75
44 Priest Holmes	.30	.75
45 Larry Johnson	.30	.75
46 Trent Green	.30	.75
47 A.J. Feeley	.25	.60
48 Chris Chambers	.30	.75
49 Randy McMichael	.25	.60
50 Daunte Culpepper	.30	.75
51 Nate Burleson	.25	.60
52 Michael Bennett	.30	.75
53 Tom Brady	.75	2.00
54 Corey Dillon	.30	.75
55 Deion Branch	.25	.60
56 David Givens	.25	.60
57 Aaron Brooks	.25	.60
58 Deuce McAllister	.30	.75
59 Joe Horn	.30	.75
60 Eli Manning	.60	1.50
61 Jeremy Shockey	.40	1.00
62 Tiki Barber	.40	1.00
63 Chad Pennington	.40	1.00
64 Curtis Martin	.40	1.00
65 Laveranues Coles	.25	.60
66 Kerry Collins	.30	.75
67 Jerry Porter	.25	.60
68 Randy Moss	.40	1.00
69 Donovan McNabb	.40	1.00
70 Terrell Owens	.40	1.00
71 Brian Dawkins	.30	.75
72 Brian Westbrook	.30	.75
73 Ben Roethlisberger	.60	1.50
74 Jerome Bettis	.40	1.00
75 Hines Ward	.40	1.00
76 Duce Staley	.30	.75
77 Drew Brees	.40	1.00
78 LaDainian Tomlinson	.40	1.00
79 Antonio Gates	.40	1.00
80 Eric Parker	.25	.60
81 Tim Rattay	.25	.60
82 Kevan Barlow	.25	.60
83 Eric Johnson	.25	.60
84 Shaun Alexander	.30	.75
85 Darrell Jackson	.25	.60
86 Matt Hasselbeck	.30	.75
87 Marc Bulger	.30	.75
88 Steven Jackson	.40	1.00
89 Marshall Faulk	.40	1.00
90 Torry Holt	.30	.75
91 Michael Pittman	.25	.60
92 Brian Griese	.30	.75
93 Michael Clayton	.25	.60
94 Steve McNair	.40	1.00
95 Drew Bennett	.30	.75
96 Billy Volek	.25	.60
97 Chris Brown	.25	.60
98 Clinton Portis	.30	.75
99 Patrick Ramsey	.30	.75
100 Santana Moss	.30	.75
101 Matt Jones RC	1.50	4.00
102 Jonathan Babineaux RC	1.50	4.00
103 Darrent Williams RC	2.00	5.00
104 Timmy Chang RC	1.50	4.00
105 Kelvin Hayden RC	1.50	4.00
106 Paris Warren RC	1.50	4.00
107 Stanley Wilson RC	1.50	4.00
108 Walter Reyes RC	1.25	3.00
109 Roydell Williams RC	1.50	4.00
110 Chase Lyman RC	1.25	3.00
111 Anthony Davis RC	1.25	3.00
112 Rasheed Marshall RC	1.50	4.00
113 Jerome Carter RC	1.25	3.00
114 Mike Nugent RC	1.50	4.00
115 Brodney Pool RC	1.50	4.00
116 Sean Considine RC	1.25	3.00
117 Chris Rix RC	1.50	4.00
118 Donte Nicholson RC	1.25	3.00
119 Dustin Fox RC	1.50	4.00
120 Oshiomogho Atogwe RC	2.00	5.00
121 Vincent Fuller RC	1.50	4.00
122 Josh Bullocks RC	1.50	4.00
123 Ronald Bartell RC	1.50	4.00
124 Brock Berlin RC	1.50	4.00
125 Fabian Washington RC	1.50	4.00
126 Domonique Foxworth RC	1.50	4.00
127 Bryant McFadden RC	1.50	4.00
128 Marlin Jackson RC	1.25	3.00
129 Eric Green RC	1.25	3.00
130 Justin Miller RC	1.50	4.00
131 Lofa Tatupu RC	2.00	5.00
132 Justin Tuck RC	2.50	6.00
133 Kurt Campbell RC	1.25	3.00
134 Darryl Blackstock RC	1.25	3.00
135 Kevin Burnett RC	1.50	4.00
136 Marviel Underwood RC	1.50	4.00
137 Kirk Morrison RC	2.00	5.00
138 Alfred Fincher RC	1.50	4.00
139 Lance Mitchell RC	1.50	4.00
140 Barrett Ruud RC	2.00	5.00
141 David Pollack RC	1.50	4.00
142 Bill Swancutt RC	1.25	3.00
143 DeMarcus Ware RC	4.00	10.00
144 Steve Savoy RC	1.25	3.00
145 Matt Roth RC	1.50	4.00
146 Shaun Cody RC	1.50	4.00
147 Dan Cody RC	1.50	4.00
148 Jordan Beck RC	1.50	4.00
149 Kevin Everett RC	2.00	5.00
150 Anttaj Hawthorne RC	1.25	3.00
151 Mike Patterson RC	1.25	3.00
152 Jerome Collins RC	1.50	4.00
153 Dante Ridgeway RC	1.25	3.00
154 Bryan Randall RC	1.50	4.00
155 Marcus Maxwell RC	1.25	3.00
156 Airese Currie RC	1.25	3.00
157 Chad Owens RC	1.50	4.00
158 Brandon Jacobs RC	2.50	6.00
159 Manuel White RC	1.50	4.00
160 Ellis Hobbs RC	2.00	5.00
161 Lionel Gates RC	1.25	3.00
162 Ryan Fitzpatrick RC	3.00	8.00
163 Noah Herron RC	1.25	3.00
164 Kay-Jay Harris RC	1.25	3.00
165 T.A. McLendon RC	1.25	3.00
166 Kerry Rhodes RC	1.50	4.00
167 Nick Collins RC	2.00	5.00
168 Eric Moore RC	1.25	3.00
169 Harry Williams RC	1.50	4.00
170 Luis Castillo RC	1.50	4.00
171 James Kilian RC	2.00	5.00
172 Matt Cassel RC	6.00	15.00
173 Alvin Pearman RC	2.00	5.00
174 Dan Orlovsky RC	3.00	8.00
175 Damien Nash RC	2.50	6.00
176 Jason White RC	3.00	8.00
177 Craig Bragg RC	2.00	5.00
178 Craphonso Thorpe RC	2.00	5.00
179 Derrick Johnson RC	2.50	6.00
180 Derek Anderson RC	2.50	6.00
181 Darren Sproles RC	3.00	8.00
182 Cedric Houston RC	3.00	8.00
183 Jerome Mathis RC	3.00	8.00
184 Larry Brackins RC	2.00	5.00
185 Fred Gibson RC	2.50	6.00
186 J.R. Russell RC	2.00	5.00
187 Alex Smith TE RC	2.00	5.00
188 Deandra Cobb RC	2.00	5.00
189 Tab Perry RC	2.00	5.00
190 Travis Johnson RC	2.00	5.00
191A Marion Barber RC	3.00	8.00
191B Andrew Walter JSY AU RC	6.00	15.00
192A Erasmus James RC	2.50	6.00
192B Vernand Morency/ JSY AU RC	5.00	12.00
193A Marcus Spears RC	2.50	6.00
193B Antrel Rolle JSY AU RC	8.00	20.00
194A Channing Crowder RC	2.50	6.00
194B Adam Jones JSY AU RC	5.00	12.00
195A Odell Thurman RC	3.00	8.00
195B Maurice Clarett JSY AU/250	5.00	12.00
196A Shawne Merriman RC	3.00	8.00
196B Mark Bradley JSY AU RC	5.00	12.00
197A Adrian McPherson RC	2.00	5.00
197B Eric Shelton JSY AU RC	5.00	12.00
198A Chris Henry RC	3.00	8.00
198B Kyle Orton JSY AU RC	10.00	25.00
199A Thomas Davis RC	2.00	5.00
199B Ryan Moats JSY AU RC	5.00	12.00
200A Corey Webster RC	2.50	6.00
200B Frank Gore JSY AU RC	15.00	40.00
201 J.J. Arrington JSY AU RC	6.00	15.00
202 Mike Williams JSY AU/250	20.00	40.00
203 Vincent Jackson JSY AU RC	12.00	30.00
204 Stefan LeFors JSY AU RC	5.00	12.00
206 Terrence Murphy/ JSY AU RC	5.00	12.00
207 Courtney Roby JSY AU RC	6.00	15.00
208 Carlos Rogers JSY AU RC	8.00	20.00
209 Charlie Frye JSY AU RC	8.00	20.00
210 Mark Clayton JSY AU RC	6.00	15.00
211 Roddy White JSY AU RC	12.00	30.00
212 Jason Campbell JSY AU RC	10.00	25.00
213 Roscoe Parrish JSY AU RC	5.00	12.00
214 Reggie Brown JSY AU RC	5.00	12.00
215 Heath Miller JSY AU RC	10.00	25.00
216 Troy Williamson/ JSY AU/250 RC	12.00	30.00
217 Ciatrick Fason JSY AU RC	5.00	12.00
218 Cedric Benson/ JSY AU/150 RC	30.00	60.00
219 Braylon Edwards/ JSY AU/250 RC	15.00	40.00
220 Ronnie Brown/ JSY AU/250 RC	25.00	50.00
221 Cadillac Williams/ JSY AU/250 RC	15.00	40.00
222 Alex Smith QB/ JSY AU/250 RC	50.00	100.00
223 Aaron Rodgers/ JSY AU/250 RC	400.00	750.00

2005 SPx Spectrum

*VETERANS: 6X TO 15X BASIC CARDS
*ROOKIES 101-170: 2X TO 5X BASE/1199
*ROOKIES 171-200: 1.2X TO 3X BASE/499
*ROOK.JSY AU: 1.2X TO 3X BASE JSY AU/250
*ROOK.JSY AU: 1.5X TO 4X BASE JSY AU/499
*ROOK.JSY AU: 2X TO 5X BASE JSY AU/1275
STATED PRINT RUN 25 SER.#'d SETS

220 Ronnie Brown JSY AU	125.00	250.00
221 Cadillac Williams JSY AU	60.00	150.00
222 Alex Smith QB JSY AU	175.00	300.00
223 Aaron Rodgers JSY AU	1,500.00	2,000.00

2005 SPx Holoview

COMPLETE SET (29)	40.00	100.00

STATED ODDS 1:126
UNPRICED DIE CUT PRINT RUN 10 SETS

1 Adam Jones	2.00	5.00
2 Antrel Rolle	2.50	6.00
3 Mark Bradley	1.60	4.00
4 Alex Smith QB	4.00	10.00
5 Andrew Walter	2.00	5.00
6 Braylon Edwards	3.00	8.00
7 J.J. Arrington	2.00	5.00
8 Charlie Frye	2.50	6.00
9 Carlos Rogers	2.50	6.00
10 Ciatrick Fason	1.50	4.00
11 Maurice Clarett	2.00	5.00
12 Cadillac Williams	2.50	6.00
13 Matt Jones	2.50	6.00
14 Courtney Roby	2.00	5.00
15 Frank Gore	4.00	10.00
16 Kyle Orton	2.50	6.00
17 Eric Shelton	1.50	4.00
18 Stefan LeFors	1.50	4.00
19 Ryan Moats	2.00	5.00
20 Jason Campbell	3.00	8.00
21 Mark Clayton	2.50	6.00
22 Ronnie Brown	3.00	8.00
23 Reggie Brown	1.50	4.00
24 Roscoe Parrish	1.50	4.00
25 Roddy White	3.00	8.00
26 Terrence Murphy	1.50	4.00
27 Vincent Jackson	3.00	8.00
28 Troy Williamson	2.00	5.00
29 Vernand Morency	2.00	5.00

2005 SPx Rookie Swatch Supremacy

STATED ODDS 1:18

RSAJ Adam Jones	2.50	6.00
RSAN Antrel Rolle	3.00	8.00
RSAR Aaron Rodgers	30.00	60.00
RSAS Alex Smith QB	6.00	15.00
RSAW Andrew Walter	2.50	6.00
RSBE Braylon Edwards	6.00	15.00
RSCA Carlos Rogers	3.00	8.00
RSCF Charlie Frye	3.00	8.00
RSCI Ciatrick Fason	2.00	5.00
RSCR Courtney Roby	2.50	6.00
RSCW Cadillac Williams	6.00	15.00
RSES Eric Shelton	2.00	5.00
RSFG Frank Gore	6.00	15.00
RSJA J.J. Arrington	2.50	6.00
RSJC Jason Campbell	4.00	10.00
RSKO Kyle Orton	3.00	8.00
RSMB Mark Bradley	2.00	5.00
RSMC Mark Clayton	3.00	8.00
RSMO Maurice Clarett	2.50	6.00
RSRB Ronnie Brown	8.00	20.00
RSRE Reggie Brown	2.00	5.00
RSRM Ryan Moats	2.50	6.00
RSRP Roscoe Parrish	2.00	5.00
RSRW Roddy White	4.00	10.00
RSTW Troy Williamson	2.50	6.00
RSVJ Vincent Jackson	4.00	10.00
RSVM Vernand Morency	2.50	6.00

2005 SPx Rookie Winning Materials

STATED ODDS 1:126

RWMAJ Adam Jones	3.00	8.00
RWMAN Antrel Rolle SP	4.00	10.00
RWMAR Aaron Rodgers SP	40.00	80.00
RWMAS Alex Smith QB	10.00	25.00
RWMAW Andrew Walter	3.00	8.00
RWMBE Braylon Edwards	10.00	25.00
RWMCA Carlos Rogers	4.00	10.00
RWMCF Charlie Frye	4.00	10.00
RWMCI Ciatrick Fason	2.50	6.00
RWMCR Courtney Roby	3.00	8.00
RWMCW Cadillac Williams	8.00	20.00
RWMES Eric Shelton	2.50	6.00
RWMFG Frank Gore	8.00	20.00
RWMJA J.J. Arrington	3.00	8.00
RWMJC Jason Campbell	5.00	12.00
RWMKO Kyle Orton	4.00	10.00
RWMMB Mark Bradley	2.50	6.00
RWMMC Mark Clayton	4.00	10.00
RWMMO Maurice Clarett	3.00	8.00
RWMRB Ronnie Brown	12.50	30.00
RWMRE Reggie Brown	2.50	6.00
RWMRM Ryan Moats	3.00	8.00
RWMRP Roscoe Parrish	2.50	6.00
RWMRW Roddy White	5.00	12.00
RWMTW Troy Williamson	3.00	8.00
RWMVJ Vincent Jackson	5.00	12.00
RWMVM Vernand Morency	3.00	8.00

2005 SPx Rookie Winning Materials Autographs

STATED PRINT RUN 25 SER.#'d SETS

AJ Adam Jones	15.00	40.00
AN Antrel Rolle	25.00	60.00
AR Aaron Rodgers	350.00	500.00
AS Alex Smith QB	50.00	100.00
AW Andrew Walter	20.00	50.00
BE Braylon Edwards	75.00	150.00
CA Carlos Rogers	25.00	60.00
CB Cedric Benson	25.00	60.00
CF Charlie Frye	25.00	60.00
CI Ciatrick Fason	15.00	40.00
CR Courtney Roby	20.00	50.00
CW Cadillac Williams	40.00	100.00
ES Eric Shelton	15.00	40.00
FG Frank Gore	75.00	150.00
HM Heath Miller	30.00	80.00
JA J.J. Arrington	20.00	50.00
JC Jason Campbell	40.00	100.00
KO Kyle Orton	30.00	80.00
MB Mark Bradley	15.00	40.00
MC Mark Clayton	20.00	50.00
MO Maurice Clarett	15.00	40.00
MW Mike Williams	25.00	60.00
RB Ronnie Brown	125.00	250.00
RE Reggie Brown	15.00	40.00
RM Ryan Moats	15.00	40.00
RP Roscoe Parrish	15.00	40.00
RW Roddy White	40.00	80.00
TW Troy Williamson	20.00	50.00
VJ Vincent Jackson	30.00	80.00
VM Vernand Morency	15.00	40.00

2005 SPx Super Scripts Autographs

STATED ODDS 1:126

SSAR Aaron Brooks	5.00	12.00
SSAG Antonio Gates	12.00	30.00
SSAN Anquan Boldin	5.00	12.00
SSBF Brett Favre SP	125.00	200.00
SSCB Chris Brown	5.00	12.00
SSCE Chris Berman SP	60.00	100.00
SSDD Domanick Davis	5.00	12.00
SSDP Dan Patrick SP		
SSDT Drew Bennett	7.50	20.00
SSEJ Edgerrin James	12.00	30.00
SSEM Eli Manning	50.00	100.00
SSFT Fred Taylor	5.00	12.00
SSJJ Julius Jones SP	60.00	100.00
SSKC Keary Colbert	5.00	12.00
SSKM Kenny Mayne SP		
SSLA LaMont Jordan	12.00	30.00
SSLC Linda Cohn SP	15.00	40.00
SSLE Lee Evans	5.00	12.00
SSLJ Larry Johnson	12.00	30.00
SSMB Marc Bulger	7.50	20.00
SSMC Michael Clayton	7.50	20.00
SSMV Michael Vick SP	40.00	80.00
SSNB Nate Burleson	7.50	20.00
SSPM Peyton Manning	50.00	100.00
SSSJ Steven Jackson		
SSSS Stuart Scott SP	25.00	50.00
SSTG Trent Green	7.50	20.00
SSTI Tiki Barber	12.00	30.00

2005 SPx Super Scripts Quad Autographs

STATED PRINT RUN 25 SER.#'d SETS

BJD Anquan Boldin	50.00	120.00
Larry Johnson RBK		
Domanick Davis		
Chris Brown		
BWB Cedric Benson	75.00	150.00
Cadillac Williams		
Ronnie Brown		
J.J. Arrington		
EWW Braylon Edwards	50.00	120.00
Mike Williams		
Troy Williamson		
Roddy White		
MMA Dan Marino	350.00	600.00
Joe Montana		
Troy Aikman		
Roger Staubach		
RFM Ben Roethlisberger	450.00	700.00
Brett Favre		
Eli Manning		
Peyton Manning		
RSF Aaron Rodgers	175.00	300.00
Alex Smith QB		
Charlie Frye		
Jason Campbell		
SSA Barry Sanders	350.00	500.00
Gale Sayers		
Marcus Allen		
Tony Dorsett		
VJT Michael Vick	75.00	150.00
Chad Johnson		
LaDainian Tomlinson		
LaMont Jordan		
VMB Michael Vick	100.00	200.00
Donovan McNabb		
Ben Roethlisberger		
Byron Leftwich		
WBW Reggie Wayne	50.00	120.00
Anquan Boldin		
Roy Williams WR		
Michael Clayton		

2005 SPx Swatch Supremacy

STATED ODDS 1:18

SWAB Anquan Boldin	2.50	6.00
SWAG Antonio Gates	3.00	8.00
SWAH Ahman Green	2.50	6.00
SWAM Archie Manning SP	5.00	12.00
SWBD Brian Dawkins	2.50	6.00
SWBF Brett Favre	8.00	20.00
SWBL Byron Leftwich	2.50	6.00
SWBR Ben Roethlisberger SP	6.00	15.00
SWCB Chris Brown	2.00	5.00
SWCJ Chad Johnson	2.50	6.00
SWCP Carson Palmer	3.00	8.00
SWDB Drew Bledsoe	3.00	8.00
SWDD Domanick Davis	2.00	5.00
SWDE Deuce McAllister	2.50	6.00
SWDM Donovan McNabb	3.00	8.00
SWDW Drew Bennett	2.50	6.00
SWEM Eli Manning	5.00	12.00
SWFT Fred Taylor	2.50	6.00
SWJH Joe Horn	2.50	6.00
SWJJ Julius Jones	2.00	5.00
SWJL J.P. Losman	2.00	5.00
SWKC Keary Colbert	2.00	5.00
SWKS Ken Stabler	6.00	15.00
SWLA LaMont Jordan	2.50	6.00
SWLE Lee Evans	2.50	6.00
SWLJ Larry Johnson	2.50	6.00
SWLT LaDainian Tomlinson	3.00	8.00
SWMB Marc Bulger	2.50	6.00
SWMC Michael Clayton	2.00	5.00
SWMM Muhsin Muhammad	2.50	6.00
SWMO Merlin Olsen SP	5.00	12.00
SWMV Michael Vick SP	4.00	10.00
SWNB Nate Burleson	2.00	5.00
SWPM Peyton Manning	6.00	15.00
SWRE Reggie Wayne	3.00	8.00
SWRJ Rudi Johnson	2.50	6.00
SWRS Roger Staubach SP	10.00	25.00
SWRW Roy Williams WR	2.50	6.00
SWSJ Steven Jackson	3.00	8.00
SWTG Trent Green	2.50	6.00
SWTI Tiki Barber	3.00	8.00

2005 SPx Swatch Supremacy Autographs

STATED PRINT RUN 50 SER.#'d SETS

AB Anquan Boldin	12.50	30.00
AG Antonio Gates	20.00	50.00
AH Ahman Green	20.00	50.00
AM Archie Manning	20.00	50.00
BD Brian Dawkins	30.00	60.00
BF Brett Favre	125.00	250.00
BL Byron Leftwich	20.00	50.00
BR Ben Roethlisberger	75.00	150.00
CB Chris Brown	12.50	30.00
CJ Chad Johnson	20.00	50.00
CP Carson Palmer	40.00	80.00
DB Drew Bledsoe	30.00	60.00
DD Domanick Davis	12.50	30.00
DE Deuce McAllister	20.00	50.00
DW Drew Bennett	15.00	40.00
EM Eli Manning	75.00	135.00
FT Fred Taylor	12.50	30.00
JH Joe Horn	12.50	30.00
JJ Julius Jones	20.00	50.00
JL J.P. Losman	15.00	40.00
KC Keary Colbert	12.50	30.00
KS Ken Stabler	40.00	80.00
LA LaMont Jordan	20.00	50.00
LE Lee Evans	12.50	30.00
LJ Larry Johnson	20.00	50.00
LT LaDainian Tomlinson	50.00	100.00
MB Marc Bulger	15.00	40.00
MC Michael Clayton	15.00	40.00
MM Muhsin Muhammad	12.50	30.00
MO Merlin Olsen	20.00	50.00
MV Michael Vick	40.00	80.00
NB Nate Burleson	15.00	40.00
PM Peyton Manning	60.00	120.00
RE Reggie Wayne	20.00	50.00
RJ Rudi Johnson	12.50	30.00
RS Roger Staubach	60.00	120.00
RW Roy Williams WR	15.00	40.00
TG Trent Green	15.00	40.00
TI Tiki Barber	30.00	60.00

2005 SPx Winning Materials

STATED ODDS 1:72

AL Ahman Green	6.00	15.00
LaDainian Tomlinson		
BA Drew Bennett	5.00	12.00
Anquan Boldin		
BB Chris Brown	5.00	12.00
Drew Bennett		
BJ Chris Brown	5.00	12.00
LaMont Jordan		
CC Michael Clayton	4.00	10.00
Keary Colbert		
DH Deuce McAllister	5.00	12.00
Joe Horn		
DM Brian Dawkins	6.00	15.00
Donovan McNabb		
ET John Elway	15.00	40.00
Joe Theismann		
EW Lee Evans	5.00	12.00
Roy Williams WR		
FM Brett Favre	15.00	40.00
Peyton Manning		
FR Brett Favre	15.00	40.00
Ben Roethlisberger		
GT Antonio Gates	6.00	15.00
LaDainian Tomlinson		
JB Steven Jackson	6.00	15.00
Marc Bulger		
JD Julius Jones	6.00	15.00
Drew Bledsoe		
JJ Rudi Johnson	5.00	12.00
Chad Johnson		
LE J.P. Losman	5.00	12.00
Lee Evans		
LT Byron Leftwich	5.00	12.00
Fred Taylor		
MJ Deuce McAllister	5.00	12.00
LaMont Jordan		
MM Donovan McNabb	12.00	30.00
Peyton Manning		
MT Eli Manning	10.00	25.00
Tiki Barber		
PL Carson Palmer	6.00	15.00
Byron Leftwich		
RM Ben Roethlisberger	10.00	25.00
Eli Manning		
SS Gale Sayers	10.00	25.00
Mike Singletary		
TS Joe Theismann SP	10.00	25.00
Roger Staubach		
VG Michael Vick	6.00	15.00
Trent Green		
VT Michael Vick	6.00	15.00
LaDainian Tomlinson		
WB Reggie Wayne	6.00	15.00
Anquan Boldin		
WM Reggie Wayne	12.00	30.00
Peyton Manning		

2005 SPx Winning Materials Autographs

STATED PRINT RUN 25 SER.#'d SETS
AL Ahman Green 60.00 120.00
LaDainian Tomlinson
BA Drew Bennett 25.00 60.00
Anquan Boldin
BB Chris Brown 25.00 60.00
Drew Bennett
BJ Chris Brown 25.00 60.00
LaMont Jordan
CC Michael Clayton 25.00 60.00
Keary Colbert
DH Deuce McAllister 25.00 60.00
Joe Horn
ET John Elway 125.00 250.00
Joe Theismann
EW Lee Evans 25.00 60.00
Roy Williams WR
FM Brett Favre 250.00 400.00
Peyton Manning
FR Brett Favre 250.00 400.00
Ben Roethlisberger
GB Trent Green 25.00 60.00
Marc Bulger
GT Antonio Gates 60.00 120.00
LaDainian Tomlinson
JB Steven Jackson 30.00 80.00
Marc Bulger
JD Julius Jones 50.00 120.00
Drew Bledsoe
JG Larry Johnson 25.00 60.00
Trent Green
JJ Rudi Johnson 25.00 60.00
Chad Johnson
LE J.P. Losman 25.00 60.00
Lee Evans
LT Byron Leftwich 25.00 60.00
Fred Taylor
MJ Deuce McAllister 25.00 60.00
LaMont Jordan
MM Donovan McNabb 100.00 200.00
Peyton Manning
MT Eli Manning 125.00 200.00
Tiki Barber
PL Carson Palmer 30.00 80.00
Byron Leftwich
RM Ben Roethlisberger 150.00 300.00
Eli Manning
SS Gale Sayers 90.00 150.00
Mike Singletary
TS Joe Theismann 75.00 150.00
Roger Staubach
VG Michael Vick 60.00 120.00
Trent Green
VT Michael Vick 75.00 150.00
LaDainian Tomlinson
WB Reggie Wayne 30.00 80.00
Anquan Boldin
WM Reggie Wayne 100.00 175.00
Peyton Manning

2005 SPx Winning Materials Patches

*PATCHES: 1X TO 2.5X BASIC JERSEYS
PATCH PRINT RUN 25 SER.#'d SETS
GB Trent Green 12.00 30.00
Marc Bulger
JG Larry Johnson 12.00 30.00
Trent Green

2006 SPx

This 213-card set was released in September, 2006. The set was issued in four-card packs with an $6.99 SRP which came 18 packs to a box. Cards numbered 1-90 feature veteran players in team alphabetical order while cards 91-213 feature 2006 rookies. Withiin the rookie subset, cards numbered 181-213 feature both player-worn swatches and signatures. Cards numbered 91-180 were issued to a stated print run of 1299 serial numbered cards, while cards 181-187 were issued to a stated print run of 399 serial numbered copies and cards numbered 188-213 were issued to a stated print run of 1650 serial numbered sets.

COMP.SET w/o RC's (90) 12.50 30.00
91-180 ROOKIE PRINT RUN 1299
181-187 RC JSY AU PRINT RUN 399
188-213 RC JSY AU PRINT RUN 1650
1 Edgerrin James .30 .75
2 Kurt Warner .40 1.00
3 Larry Fitzgerald .40 1.00
4 Michael Vick .40 1.00
5 Warrick Dunn .30 .75
6 Michael Jenkins .30 .75
7 Jamal Lewis .30 .75
8 Kyle Boller .30 .75
9 Derrick Mason .30 .75
10 Willis McGahee .30 .75
11 Lee Evans .30 .75
12 Jake Delhomme .30 .75
13 Steve Smith .40 1.00
14 DeShaun Foster .30 .75
15 Rex Grossman .30 .75
16 Muhsin Muhammad .30 .75
17 Thomas Jones .30 .75
18 Carson Palmer .40 1.00
19 Chad Johnson .30 .75
20 Rudi Johnson .30 .75
21 Charlie Frye .30 .75
22 Reuben Droughns .30 .75
23 Braylon Edwards .30 .75
24 Drew Bledsoe .40 1.00
25 Terrell Owens .40 1.00
26 Julius Jones .25 .60
27 Jake Plummer .30 .75
28 Tatum Bell .25 .60
29 Rod Smith .30 .75
30 Kevin Jones .25 .60
31 Roy Williams WR .30 .75
32 Brett Favre .75 2.00
33 Ahman Green .30 .75
34 Donald Driver .40 1.00
35 David Carr .25 .60
36 Andre Johnson .40 1.00
37 Peyton Manning .60 1.50
38 Marvin Harrison .40 1.00
39 Reggie Wayne .30 .75
40 Byron Leftwich .30 .75
41 Fred Taylor .30 .75
42 Ernest Wilford .25 .60
43 Larry Johnson .30 .75
44 Trent Green .30 .75
45 Tony Gonzalez .30 .75
46 Daunte Culpepper .30 .75
47 Ronnie Brown .40 1.00
48 Chris Chambers .30 .75
49 Troy Williamson .25 .60
50 Chester Taylor .30 .75
51 Brad Johnson .30 .75
52 Tom Brady .60 1.50
53 Deion Branch .30 .75
54 Corey Dillon .30 .75
55 Drew Brees .40 1.00
56 Deuce McAllister .30 .75
57 Donte Stallworth .25 .60
58 Eli Manning .50 1.25
59 Tiki Barber .40 1.00
60 Plaxico Burress .30 .75
61 Chad Pennington .30 .75
62 Curtis Martin .40 1.00
63 Randy Moss .40 1.00
64 LaMont Jordan .30 .75
65 Aaron Brooks .30 .75
66 Donovan McNabb .40 1.00
67 Brian Westbrook .30 .75
68 Ben Roethlisberger .50 1.25
69 Hines Ward .40 1.00
70 Willie Parker .30 .75
71 LaDainian Tomlinson .40 1.00
72 Philip Rivers .40 1.00
73 Antonio Gates .40 1.00
74 Alex Smith QB .40 1.00
75 Antonio Bryant .25 .60
76 Frank Gore .40 1.00
77 Shaun Alexander .30 .75
78 Matt Hasselbeck .30 .75
79 Nate Burleson .25 .60
80 Marc Bulger .30 .75
81 Steven Jackson .40 1.00
82 Torry Holt .30 .75
83 Cadillac Williams .30 .75
84 Joey Galloway .30 .75
85 Chris Simms .30 .75
86 Billy Volek .25 .60
87 Drew Bennett .30 .75
88 Clinton Portis .40 1.00
89 Santana Moss .30 .75
90 Mark Brunell .30 .75
91 Haloti Ngata RC 4.00 10.00
92 Willie Reid RC 3.00 8.00
93 Kamerion Wimbley RC 4.00 10.00
94 Donte Whitner RC 4.00 10.00
95 Ethan Kilmer RC 3.00 8.00
96 Johnathan Joseph RC 3.00 8.00
97 Brodie Croyle RC 4.00 10.00
98 Bobby Carpenter RC 2.50 6.00
99 Antonio Cromartie RC 4.00 10.00
100 Eric Winston RC 2.50 6.00
101 Nick Mangold RC 3.00 8.00
102 Manny Lawson RC 3.00 8.00
103 Claude Wroten RC 2.50 6.00
104 D'Qwell Jackson RC 3.00 8.00
105 Richard Marshall RC 3.00 8.00
106 Tamba Hali RC 4.00 10.00
107 Ko Simpson RC 3.00 8.00
108 Danieal Manning RC 4.00 10.00
109 Gabe Watson RC 2.50 6.00
110 Kevin McMahan RC 3.00 8.00
111 Jai Lewis RC 3.00 8.00
112 Darryl Tapp RC 3.00 8.00
113 John McCargo RC 2.50 6.00
114 Jeff King RC 3.00 8.00
115 Charles Davis RC 3.00 8.00
116 Calvin Lowry RC 4.00 10.00
117 Delanie Walker RC 4.00 10.00
118 Roman Harper RC 3.00 8.00
119 Nate Salley RC 3.00 8.00
120 Cooper Wallace RC 3.00 8.00
121 Bernard Pollard RC 3.00 8.00
122 Derrick Ross RC 3.00 8.00
123 Ingle Martin RC 3.00 8.00
124 Wali Lundy RC 3.00 8.00
125 Marcus Vick RC 2.50 6.00
126 Cedric Humes RC 2.50 6.00
127 Marques Hagans RC 2.50 6.00
128 Taurean Henderson RC 4.00 10.00
129 Marques Colston RC 8.00 20.00
130 Devin Aromashodu RC 4.00 10.00
131 Jonathan Orr RC 3.00 8.00
132 Skyler Green RC 2.50 6.00
133 Jeff Webb RC 3.00 8.00
134 Jon Alston RC 2.50 6.00
135 Daniel Bullocks RC 4.00 10.00
136 Anthony Schlegel RC 3.00 8.00
137 Adam Jennings RC 3.00 8.00
138 Gerris Wilkinson RC 2.50 6.00
139 James Anderson RC 2.50 6.00
140 Owen Daniels RC 4.00 10.00
141 Ray Edwards RC 4.00 10.00
142 Chris Gocong RC 3.00 8.00
143 Babatunde Oshinowo RC 3.00 8.00
144 Marvin Philip RC 4.00 10.00
145 Stanley McClover RC 3.00 8.00
146 DeMeco Ryans RC 4.00 10.00
147 Tony Scheffler RC 4.00 10.00
148 T.J. Williams RC 4.00 10.00
149 P.J. Daniels RC 2.50 6.00
150 Bennie Brazell RC 3.00 8.00
151 Will Blackmon RC 3.00 8.00
152 Bruce Gradkowski RC 4.00 10.00
153 Drew Olson RC 2.50 6.00
154 Darnell Bing RC 3.00 8.00
155 Darrell Hackney RC 3.00 8.00
156 Cory Rodgers RC 3.00 8.00
157 DonTrell Moore RC 3.00 8.00
158 Ernie Sims RC 3.00 8.00
159 Jay Cutler RC 8.00 20.00
160 D.J. Shockley RC 3.00 8.00
161 Martin Nance RC 3.00 8.00
162 Joseph Addai RC 4.00 10.00
163 Leonard Pope RC 4.00 10.00
164 Anthony Fasano RC 4.00 10.00
165 Mathias Kiwanuka RC 4.00 10.00
166 Greg Jennings RC 10.00 20.00
167 Greg Lee RC 2.50 6.00
168 Jerome Harrison RC 4.00 10.00
169 Jimmy Williams RC 4.00 10.00
170 Josh Betts RC 3.00 8.00
171 Ashton Youboty RC 2.50 6.00
172 Terrence Whitehead RC 3.00 8.00
173 Brad Smith RC 4.00 10.00
174 D'Brickashaw Ferguson RC 4.00 10.00
175 Mike Hass RC 3.00 8.00
176 Reggie McNeal RC 3.00 8.00
177 Dominique Byrd RC 3.00 8.00
178 Winston Justice RC 3.00 8.00
179 Chad Greenway RC 4.00 10.00
180 Tye Hill RC 2.50 6.00
181 Chad Jackson JSY AU RC 8.00 20.00
182 DeAngelo Williams JSY AU RC 15.00 40.00
183 Vince Young JSY AU RC 15.00 40.00
184 Santonio Holmes JSY AU RC 15.00 40.00
185 Sinorice Moss JSY AU RC 12.00 30.00
186 Matt Leinart JSY AU RC 12.00 30.00
187 Reggie Bush JSY AU RC 30.00 80.00
188 LenDale White JSY AU RC 6.00 15.00
189 Vernon Davis JSY AU RC 12.50 25.00
190 Laurence Maroney JSY AU RC 6.00 15.00
191 A.J. Hawk JSY AU RC 10.00 25.00
192 Marcus McNeill JSY AU RC 6.00 15.00
193 Kelly Jennings JSY AU RC 6.00 15.00
194 Brandon Williams JSY AU RC 5.00 12.00
195 Brian Calhoun JSY AU RC 5.00 12.00
196 Travis Wilson JSY AU RC 5.00 12.00
197 Charlie Whitehurst JSY AU RC 8.00 20.00
198 Omar Jacobs JSY AU RC 5.00 12.00
199 Joe Klopfenstein JSY AU RC 5.00 12.00
200 Derek Hagan JSY AU RC 6.00 15.00
201 Michael Huff JSY AU RC 6.00 15.00
202 Maurice Stovall JSY AU RC 5.00 12.00
203 Maurice Drew JSY AU RC 15.00 40.00
204 Jason Avant JSY AU RC 5.00 12.00
205 Kellen Clemens JSY AU RC 6.00 15.00
206 Jerious Norwood JSY AU RC 6.00 15.00
207 Tarvaris Jackson JSY AU RC 8.00 20.00
208 Brandon Marshall JSY AU RC 10.00 25.00
209 Demetrius Williams JSY AU RC 6.00 15.00
210 Leon Washington JSY AU RC 6.00 15.00
211 Michael Robinson JSY AU RC 6.00 15.00
212 Marcedes Lewis JSY AU RC 8.00 20.00
213 Mario Williams JSY AU RC 8.00 20.00

2006 SPx Spectrum

*VETS 1-90: 5X TO 12X BASIC CARDS
*ROOKIES 91-150: 1X TO 2.5X BASIC CARDS
COMMON ROOK.AU (151-180) 12.00 30.00
ROOKIE AU SEMISTARS 15.00 40.00
ROOKIE AU UNL.STARS 20.00 50.00
*ROOKIE JSY AU: 1X TO 2.5X JSY AU/399
*ROOKIE JSY AU: 1.5X TO 4X JSY AU/1650
STATED PRINT RUN 25 SER.#'d SETS
159 Jay Cutler AU 200.00 400.00
166 Greg Jennings AU 100.00 200.00
183 Vince Young JSY AU 100.00 250.00
184 Santonio Holmes JSY AU 100.00 200.00
187 Reggie Bush JSY AU 175.00 350.00
203 Maurice Drew JSY AU 100.00 250.00
208 Brandon Marshall JSY AU 75.00 150.00

2006 SPx Rookie Autographed Jerseys Gold

*GOLD/99: .5X TO 1.2X JSY AU/399
*GOLD/350: .5X TO 1.2X JSY AU/1650
GOLD STATED PRINT RUN 99-350
UNPRICED NFL LOGO SER.#'d TO 1

2006 SPx Rookie Autographs Gold

ANNOUNCED PRINT RUN 299 SETS
151 Will Blackmon 6.00 15.00
152 Bruce Gradkowski 8.00 20.00
153 Drew Olson 5.00 12.00
154 Darnell Bing 6.00 15.00
155 Darrell Hackney 6.00 15.00
156 Cory Rodgers 6.00 15.00
157 DonTrell Moore 6.00 15.00
158 Ernie Sims 6.00 15.00
159 Jay Cutler 40.00 100.00
160 D.J. Shockley 6.00 15.00
161 Martin Nance 6.00 15.00
162 Joseph Addai 8.00 20.00
163 Leonard Pope 8.00 20.00
164 Anthony Fasano 8.00 20.00
165 Mathias Kiwanuka 8.00 20.00
166 Greg Jennings 40.00 80.00
167 Greg Lee 5.00 12.00
168 Jerome Harrison 8.00 20.00
169 Jimmy Williams 8.00 20.00
170 Josh Betts 6.00 15.00
171 Ashton Youboty 5.00 12.00
172 Terrence Whitehead 6.00 15.00
173 Brad Smith 8.00 20.00
174 D'Brickashaw Ferguson 8.00 20.00
175 Mike Hass 6.00 15.00
176 Reggie McNeal 6.00 15.00
177 Dominique Byrd 6.00 15.00
178 Winston Justice 6.00 15.00
179 Chad Greenway 8.00 20.00
180 Tye Hill 5.00 12.00

2006 SPx Rookie Swatch Supremacy

STATED ODDS 1:50
SWAH A.J. Hawk 6.00 15.00
SWBC Brian Calhoun 2.50 6.00
SWBU Reggie Bush 6.00 15.00
SWCH Chad Jackson 2.50 6.00
SWDW DeAngelo Williams 4.00 10.00
SWKC Kellen Clemens 3.00 8.00
SWLE Matt Leinart 3.00 8.00
SWLM Laurence Maroney 2.50 6.00
SWLW LenDale White 3.00 8.00
SWMD Maurice Drew 5.00 12.00
SWMH Michael Huff 3.00 8.00
SWML Marcedes Lewis 2.50 6.00
SWMR Michael Robinson 2.50 6.00
SWMS Maurice Stovall 2.50 6.00
SWMW Mario Williams 4.00 10.00
SWOJ Omar Jacobs 2.50 6.00
SWSH Santonio Holmes 4.00 10.00
SWSM Sinorice Moss 2.50 6.00
SWVD Vernon Davis 4.00 10.00
SWVY Vince Young 4.00 10.00

2006 SPx Rookie Winning Materials

STATED ODDS 1:126
WMRAH A.J. Hawk 4.00 10.00
WMRBM Brandon Marshall 4.00 10.00
WMRBU Reggie Bush 8.00 20.00
WMRBW Brandon Williams 2.50 6.00
WMRCA Brian Calhoun 2.50 6.00
WMRCJ Chad Jackson 2.50 6.00
WMRDH Derek Hagan 3.00 8.00
WMRDW DeAngelo Williams 5.00 12.00
WMRJA Jason Avant 2.50 6.00
WMRJK Joe Klopfenstein 2.50 6.00
WMRJN Jerious Norwood 3.00 8.00
WMRKC Kellen Clemens 3.00 8.00
WMRLE Matt Leinart 4.00 10.00
WMRLM Laurence Maroney 3.00 8.00
WMRLW LenDale White 3.00 8.00
WMRMD Maurice Drew 6.00 15.00
WMRMH Michael Huff 3.00 8.00
WMRML Marcedes Lewis 4.00 10.00
WMRMR Michael Robinson 3.00 8.00
WMRMS Maurice Stovall 2.50 6.00
WMRMW Mario Williams 4.00 10.00
WMROJ Omar Jacobs 2.50 6.00
WMRSH Santonio Holmes 5.00 12.00
WMRSM Sinorice Moss 4.00 10.00
WMRTJ Tarvaris Jackson 4.00 10.00
WMRTR Travis Wilson 2.50 6.00
WMRVD Vernon Davis 5.00 12.00
WMRVY Vince Young 5.00 12.00
WMRWA Leon Washington 3.00 8.00
WMRWH Charlie Whitehurst 4.00 10.00
WMRWI Demetrius Williams 3.00 8.00

2006 SPx Rookie Winning Materials Autographs

STATED PRINT RUN 25 SER.#'d SETS
WMRAH A.J. Hawk 30.00 80.00
WMRBM Brandon Marshall 30.00 60.00
WMRBU Reggie Bush 60.00 120.00
WMRBW Brandon Williams 12.00 30.00
WMRCA Brian Calhoun 12.00 30.00
WMRCJ Chad Jackson 12.00 30.00
WMRDH Derek Hagan 15.00 40.00
WMRDW DeAngelo Williams 40.00 100.00
WMRJA Jason Avant 12.00 30.00
WMRJK Joe Klopfenstein 12.00 30.00
WMRJN Jerious Norwood 15.00 40.00
WMRKC Kellen Clemens 15.00 40.00
WMRLE Matt Leinart 20.00 50.00
WMRLM Laurence Maroney 15.00 40.00
WMRLW LenDale White 15.00 40.00
WMRMD Maurice Drew 30.00 80.00
WMRMH Michael Huff 15.00 40.00
WMRML Marcedes Lewis 20.00 50.00
WMRMR Michael Robinson 15.00 40.00
WMRMS Maurice Stovall 12.00 30.00
WMRMW Mario Williams 20.00 50.00
WMROJ Omar Jacobs 12.00 30.00
WMRSH Santonio Holmes 25.00 60.00
WMRSM Sinorice Moss 20.00 50.00
WMRTJ Tarvaris Jackson 20.00 50.00
WMRTR Travis Wilson 12.00 30.00
WMRVD Vernon Davis 25.00 60.00
WMRVY Vince Young 30.00 80.00
WMRWA Leon Washington 15.00 40.00
WMRWH Charlie Whitehurst 20.00 50.00
WMRWI Demetrius Williams 15.00 40.00

2006 SPx SPxcellence

STATED PRINT RUN 650 SER.#'d SETS
UNPRICED AUTO PRINT RUN 10
SPAC Alge Crumpler 2.50 6.00
SPAD Joseph Addai 2.00 5.00
SPAH A.J. Hawk 2.00 5.00
SPAV Jason Avant 1.25 3.00
SPBL Drew Bledsoe 3.00 8.00
SPBM Brandon Marshall 2.00 5.00
SPBR Ben Roethlisberger 4.00 10.00
SPCG Chad Greenway 2.00 5.00
SPCL Mark Clayton 2.50 6.00
SPCP Carson Palmer 3.00 8.00
SPCS Chris Simms 2.50 6.00
SPCW Charlie Whitehurst 2.00 5.00
SPDB Dominique Byrd 1.50 4.00
SPDG David Givens 2.50 6.00
SPDR DeMeco Ryans 2.00 5.00
SPDW Demetrius Williams 1.50 4.00
SPEM Eli Manning 4.00 10.00
SPHI Tye Hill 1.25 3.00
SPJA Tarvaris Jackson 2.00 5.00
SPJC Jay Cutler 4.00 10.00
SPJH Jerome Harrison 2.00 5.00
SPKC Kellen Clemens 1.50 4.00
SPKO Kyle Orton 3.00 8.00
SPLE Matt Leinart 2.00 5.00
SPLJ Larry Johnson 2.50 6.00
SPLM Laurence Maroney 1.50 4.00
SPLP Leonard Pope 2.00 5.00
SPLW LenDale White 1.50 4.00
SPMC Michael Clayton 2.00 5.00
SPMD Maurice Drew 3.00 8.00
SPMH Michael Huff 1.50 4.00
SPML Marcedes Lewis 2.00 5.00
SPMR Michael Robinson 1.50 4.00
SPMS Maurice Stovall 1.25 3.00
SPMW Mario Williams 2.00 5.00
SPOJ Omar Jacobs 1.25 3.00
SPPM Peyton Manning 5.00 12.00
SPRB Reggie Bush 5.00 12.00
SPRJ Rudi Johnson 2.50 6.00
SPRM Reggie McNeal 1.50 4.00
SPRO Ronnie Brown 3.00 8.00
SPSM Sinorice Moss 2.00 5.00
SPSS Steve Smith 3.00 8.00
SPTB Tedy Bruschi 3.00 8.00
SPTH T.J. Houshmandzadeh 2.50 6.00
SPTJ Thomas Jones 2.50 6.00
SPVD Vernon Davis 2.50 6.00
SPVY Vince Young 2.50 6.00
SPWA Leon Washington 1.50 4.00
SPWP Willie Parker 2.50 6.00

2006 SPx SPxclusives

STATED PRINT RUN 650 SER.#'d SETS
UNPRICED AUTO PRINT RUN 10
EXAG Antonio Gates 3.00 8.00
EXBC Brian Calhoun 2.50 6.00
EXBE Braylon Edwards 3.00 8.00
EXBF Brett Favre 6.00 15.00
EXBL Byron Leftwich 2.00 5.00
EXBU Reggie Bush 5.00 12.00
EXCB Cedric Benson 3.00 8.00
EXCJ Chad Jackson 2.50 6.00
EXCW Cadillac Williams 3.00 8.00
EXDB Drew Bledsoe 3.00 8.00
EXDF DeShaun Foster 2.00 5.00
EXDM Deuce McAllister 2.00 5.00
EXDR Drew Bennett 1.50 4.00
EXDW DeAngelo Williams 3.00 8.00
EXES Ernie Sims 2.50 6.00
EXFE D'Brickashaw Ferguson 2.50 6.00
EXGJ Greg Jones 1.50 4.00
EXJA Joseph Addai 2.50 6.00
EXJC Jay Cutler 5.00 12.00
EXJJ Julius Jones 3.00 8.00
EXJO LaMont Jordan 2.00 5.00
EXJW Jason Witten 2.00 5.00
EXKC Kevin Curtis 1.50 4.00
EXKJ Keyshawn Johnson 2.00 5.00
EXLJ Larry Johnson 3.00 8.00
EXLT LaDainian Tomlinson 3.00 8.00
EXML Matt Leinart 2.50 6.00
EXMW Mike Williams 3.00 8.00
EXPM Peyton Manning 5.00 12.00
EXPR Philip Rivers 3.00 8.00
EXRB Ronde Barber 1.50 4.00
EXRW Reggie Wayne 2.00 5.00
EXSH Santonio Holmes 4.00 10.00
EXSS Steve Smith 3.00 8.00
EXTA Lofa Tatupu 2.50 6.00
EXTB Tiki Barber 3.00 8.00
EXTG Trent Green 2.00 5.00
EXVD Vernon Davis 4.00 10.00
EXVY Vince Young 3.00 8.00
EXWI Jimmy Williams 2.50 6.00

2006 SPx SPxclusives Autographs

UNPRICED AUTO PRINT RUN 10

2006 SPx Super Scripts Autographs

STATED ODDS 1:252
SSAG Antonio Gates 10.00 25.00
SSAH A.J. Hawk SP 25.00 50.00
SSBE Braylon Edwards 8.00 20.00
SSBL Byron Leftwich 8.00 20.00
SSBR Ben Roethlisberger SP 50.00 100.00
SSBU Reggie Bush SP 60.00 120.00
SSCJ Chad Jackson SP 15.00 30.00
SSCS Chris Simms 8.00 20.00
SSDB Drew Bennett 8.00 20.00
SSDF DeShaun Foster 8.00 20.00
SSDG David Givens 8.00 20.00
SSDH Derek Hagan 5.00 12.00
SSDW DeAngelo Williams SP
SSFE D'Brickashaw Ferguson 6.00 15.00
SSGL Greg Lee 6.00 15.00
SSHA Andre Hall 5.00 12.00
SSJC Jay Cutler SP 75.00 150.00
SSJH Jerome Harrison 6.00 15.00
SSJW Jason Witten 20.00 40.00
SSKC Kevin Curtis 8.00 20.00
SSKO Kyle Orton 10.00 25.00
SSLJ LaMont Jordan 8.00 20.00
SSLL Brandon Lloyd 6.00 15.00
SSLM Laurence Maroney SP 12.00 30.00
SSLT LaDainian Tomlinson 40.00 80.00
SSLW LenDale White SP 15.00 30.00
SSMC Reggie McNeal 5.00 12.00
SSML Matt Leinart SP 25.00 60.00
SSMM Muhsin Muhammad 8.00 20.00
SSMW Mario Williams 12.50 30.00
SSPM Peyton Manning 50.00 100.00
SSPR Philip Rivers 12.00 30.00
SSRB Ronde Barber 8.00 20.00
SSRM Ryan Moats 4.00 10.00
SSRW Reggie Wayne 12.50 30.00
SSSH Santonio Holmes 15.00 40.00
SSSM Sinorice Moss SP 8.00 20.00
SSSS Steve Smith SP 10.00 25.00
SSTA Lofa Tatupu 8.00 20.00
SSVD Vernon Davis 8.00 20.00
SSVY Vince Young SP
SSWP Willie Parker SP

2006 SPx Swatch Supremacy

STATED ODDS 1:26
SWBE Braylon Edwards 4.00 10.00
SWBF Brett Favre 8.00 20.00
SWBL Byron Leftwich 3.00 8.00
SWBR Ben Roethlisberger 8.00 20.00
SWBT Tom Brady 6.00 15.00
SWCB Champ Bailey 3.00 8.00
SWCF Charlie Frye 4.00 10.00
SWCP Carson Palmer 4.00 10.00
SWCW Cadillac Williams 4.00 10.00
SWDB Drew Bledsoe 4.00 10.00
SWDC Daunte Culpepper 4.00 10.00
SWDM Deuce McAllister 3.00 8.00
SWDR Drew Brees SP 3.00 8.00
SWEJ Edgerrin James 4.00 10.00
SWGR Trent Green 3.00 8.00
SWHW Hines Ward 5.00 12.00
SWJJ Julius Jones 4.00 10.00
SWJO Larry Johnson 4.00 10.00
SWJT Jason Taylor 3.00 8.00
SWKO Kyle Orton 3.00 8.00
SWKW Kurt Warner 3.00 8.00
SWLJ LaMont Jordan 3.00 8.00
SWLT LaDainian Tomlinson 4.00 10.00
SWMC Donovan McNabb 4.00 10.00
SWMV Michael Vick 4.00 10.00
SWPH Priest Holmes 3.00 8.00
SWPM Peyton Manning 6.00 15.00
SWRB Ronnie Brown 4.00 10.00
SWRE Reggie Brown 3.00 8.00
SWRM Randy Moss 4.00 10.00
SWRW Roy Williams S 3.00 8.00
SWSA Shaun Alexander 4.00 10.00
SWSJ Steven Jackson 4.00 10.00
SWTB Tatum Bell 3.00 8.00
SWTG Tony Gonzalez 3.00 8.00
SWWA Reggie Wayne 3.00 8.00
SWWP Willie Parker 4.00 10.00

2006 SPx Winning Combo Autographs

STATED PRINT RUN 50 SER.#'d SETS
WCBA Reggie Brown 12.00 30.00
Jason Avant
WCBB Tiki Barber 40.00 80.00
Ronde Barber
WCBC Marc Bulger 20.00 40.00
Kevin Curtis
WCBH Darnell Bing 12.00 30.00
Michael Huff
WCBJ Brodrick Bunkley 12.00 30.00
Winston Justice
WCBL Dominique Byrd 12.00 30.00
Marcedes Lewis
WCBT LaDainian Tomlinson 60.00 120.00
Reggie Bush
WCBW LenDale White 40.00 100.00
Reggie Bush
WCCW Demetrius Williams 12.00 30.00
Kellen Clemens
WCEA Braylon Edwards 12.00 30.00
Jason Avant
WCEW Braylon Edwards 20.00 50.00
Travis Wilson
WCFD DeShaun Foster 25.00 60.00
Maurice Drew
WCFJ D'Brickashaw Ferguson 12.00 30.00
Winston Justice
WCFS Anthony Fasano 20.00 40.00
Maurice Stovall
WCGD Antonio Gates 25.00 50.00
Vernon Davis
WCGJ Chad Greenway 20.00 50.00
Tarvaris Jackson
WCHH T.J. Houshmandzadeh 12.00 30.00
Mike Hass
WCHJ Omar Jacobs 20.00 50.00
Santonio Holmes
WCHW A.J. Hawk 30.00 60.00
Mario Williams
WCIW Travis Wilson 20.00 40.00
Clint Ingram
WCJH Kelly Jennings 12.00 30.00
Tye Hill
WCJM Thomas Jones 15.00 40.00
Laurence Maroney
WCJW Larry Johnson 25.00 60.00
DeAngelo Williams
WCKB Dominique Byrd 12.00 30.00
Joe Klopfenstein
WCKL Kellen Clemens 15.00 40.00
Leon Washington
WCLB Matt Leinart 40.00 100.00
Reggie Bush
WCMJ Chad Jackson 12.00 30.00
Sinorice Moss
WCML Peyton Manning 75.00 150.00
Matt Leinart
WCMW Derrick Mason 12.00 30.00
Demetrius Williams
WCOD Drew Olson 30.00 60.00
Maurice Drew
WCOJ Kyle Orton 15.00 40.00
Tarvaris Jackson
WCPJ Willie Parker 20.00 50.00
Omar Jacobs
WCRW Philip Rivers 40.00 80.00
Charlie Whitehurst
WCSH Santonio Holmes 30.00 60.00
Steve Smith
WCSP D.J. Shockley 20.00 40.00
Leonard Pope
WCSR DeMeco Ryans 15.00 40.00
Ernie Sims
WCTB Lofa Tatupu 20.00 50.00
Darnell Bing
WCVY Michael Vick 40.00 80.00
Vince Young
WCWB Ronnie Brown 20.00 50.00
Cadillac Williams
WCWC Brandon Williams 12.00 30.00
Brian Calhoun
WCWF Jason Witten 30.00 60.00
Anthony Fasano
WCWH Jimmy Williams 12.00 30.00
Michael Huff
WCWS Ernie Sims 15.00 40.00
Leon Washington
WCYC Jay Cutler 75.00 150.00
Vince Young

2006 SPx Winning Materials

STATED ODDS 1:18
WMVAC Alge Crumpler SP 3.00 8.00
WMVAG Antonio Gates 4.00 10.00
WMVAR Aaron Rodgers 12.00 30.00
WMVBA Ronde Barber 3.00 8.00
WMVBD Brian Dawkins 3.00 8.00
WMVBE Braylon Edwards 4.00 10.00
WMVBF Brett Favre 8.00 20.00
WMVBL Byron Leftwich 3.00 8.00
WMVBR Ben Roethlisberger 8.00 20.00
WMVBU Brian Urlacher SP 4.00 10.00
WMVCF Charlie Frye 4.00 10.00
WMVCL Michael Clayton 3.00 8.00
WMVCP Carson Palmer 4.00 10.00
WMVCS Chris Simms 3.00 8.00
WMVCW Cadillac Williams 4.00 10.00
WMVDB Drew Bledsoe 4.00 10.00
WMVDF DeShaun Foster 3.00 8.00
WMVDG David Givens 3.00 8.00
WMVDM Deuce McAllister 3.00 8.00
WMVEM Eli Manning 5.00 12.00
WMVGJ Greg Jones 2.50 6.00
WMVJJ Julius Jones 4.00 10.00
WMVJO LaMont Jordan 3.00 8.00
WMVJW Jason Witten 3.00 8.00
WMVKC Kevin Curtis 2.50 6.00
WMVKJ Keyshawn Johnson 3.00 8.00
WMVKO Kyle Orton 3.00 8.00
WMVLJ Larry Johnson 4.00 10.00
WMVLT LaDainian Tomlinson 4.00 10.00
WMVMC Mark Clayton 3.00 8.00
WMVMM Muhsin Muhammad 3.00 8.00
WMVMV Michael Vick 4.00 10.00
WMVNB Nate Burleson 3.00 8.00
WMVPM Peyton Manning 6.00 15.00
WMVPR Philip Rivers 4.00 10.00
WMVRB Reggie Brown 3.00 8.00
WMVRJ Rudi Johnson 3.00 8.00
WMVRM Ryan Moats 2.50 6.00
WMVRO Ronnie Brown 4.00 10.00
WMVRW Reggie Wayne 3.00 8.00
WMVSS Steve Smith 4.00 10.00
WMVTB Tiki Barber 4.00 10.00
WMVTE Tedy Bruschi 4.00 10.00
WMVTG Trent Green 3.00 8.00
WMVTH T.J. Houshmandzadeh SP 3.00 8.00
WMVTJ Thomas Jones 3.00 8.00
WMVTP Troy Polamalu 6.00 15.00
WMVTW Troy Williamson 3.00 8.00
WMVWP Willie Parker 3.00 8.00

2006 SPx Winning Materials Autographs

STATED PRINT RUN 25 SER.#'d SETS
WMVAC Alge Crumpler 15.00 40.00
WMVBA Ronde Barber 15.00 40.00
WMVBD Brian Dawkins
WMVBE Braylon Edwards 15.00 40.00
WMVBF Brett Favre 125.00 200.00
WMVBL Byron Leftwich 15.00 40.00
WMVBR Ben Roethlisberger 75.00 150.00
WMVCF Charlie Frye 15.00 40.00
WMVCL Michael Clayton 12.00 30.00
WMVCP Carson Palmer 30.00 80.00
WMVCS Chris Simms 15.00 40.00
WMVCW Cadillac Williams
WMVDB Drew Bledsoe
WMVDF DeShaun Foster 15.00 40.00
WMVDG David Givens 15.00 40.00
WMVDM Deuce McAllister 15.00 40.00
WMVEM Eli Manning 90.00 150.00
WMVGJ Greg Jones 12.00 30.00
WMVJJ Julius Jones 12.00 30.00
WMVJO LaMont Jordan 15.00 40.00
WMVJW Jason Witten 40.00 80.00
WMVKC Kevin Curtis 15.00 40.00
WMVKJ Keyshawn Johnson
WMVKO Kyle Orton 20.00 50.00
WMVLJ Larry Johnson 15.00 40.00
WMVLT LaDainian Tomlinson 60.00 120.00
WMVMC Mark Clayton 15.00 40.00
WMVMM Muhsin Muhammad 15.00 40.00
WMVMV Michael Vick 40.00 80.00
WMVNB Nate Burleson 12.00 30.00
WMVPM Peyton Manning 125.00 200.00
WMVPR Philip Rivers 25.00 60.00
WMVRB Reggie Brown 12.00 30.00
WMVRJ Rudi Johnson 15.00 40.00
WMVRM Ryan Moats 12.00 30.00
WMVRO Ronnie Brown 25.00 60.00
WMVRW Reggie Wayne 15.00 40.00
WMVSS Steve Smith 20.00 50.00
WMVTB Tiki Barber 35.00 60.00
WMVTG Trent Green 15.00 40.00
WMVTH T.J. Houshmandzadeh 15.00 40.00
WMVTJ Thomas Jones 15.00 40.00
WMVWP Willie Parker 20.00 50.00

2007 SPx

This 223-card set was released in August, 2007. The set was issued into the hobby in three-card packs, with an $19.99 SRP, which came 10 packs to a box. Cards numbered 1-100 feature veterans in team alphabetical order while cards 101-224 feature 2007 NFL rookies. The Rookie Cards are broken down like this: Cards numbered 101-160 were issued to a stated print run of 899 serial numbered cards; cards numbered 161-190 were signed by the player and those cards were issued to a stated print run of 499 serial numbered cards; and the set concludes with cards with both player-worn jersey swatches and autographs which were issued to stated print runs between 299 and 599 serial numbered copies.

COMP.SET w/o RC's (100) 20.00 40.00
101-160 ROOKIE PRINT RUN 899
161-190 AU ROOKIE PRINT RUN 499
191-224 JSY AU ROOKIE PRINT RUN 299-599
UNPRICED NFL LOGO AUs #'d TO 1
1 Matt Leinart .40 1.00
2 Anquan Boldin .40 1.00
3 Larry Fitzgerald .50 1.25
4 Edgerrin James .40 1.00
5 Michael Vick .50 1.25
6 Warrick Dunn .40 1.00
7 DeAngelo Hall .40 1.00
8 Steve McNair .40 1.00
9 Willis McGahee .40 1.00
10 Ray Lewis .50 1.25
11 J.P. Losman .30 .75
12 Lee Evans .40 1.00
13 Anthony Thomas .30 .75
14 Jake Delhomme .40 1.00
15 Steve Smith .40 1.00
16 DeAngelo Williams .50 1.25
17 Brian Urlacher .50 1.25
18 Cedric Benson .40 1.00
19 Rex Grossman .40 1.00
20 Carson Palmer .40 1.00
21 Chad Johnson .40 1.00
22 Rudi Johnson .40 1.00
23 Charlie Frye .40 1.00
24 Braylon Edwards .40 1.00
25 Jamal Lewis .40 1.00
26 Tony Romo .60 1.50
27 Terrell Owens .50 1.25
28 Julius Jones .30 .75
29 Marion Barber .40 1.00
30 Jay Cutler .50 1.25
31 Javon Walker .40 1.00
32 Travis Henry .40 1.00
33 Roy Williams WR .40 1.00
34 Mike Furrey .40 1.00
35 Tatum Bell .30 .75
36 Greg Jennings .50 1.25
37 Brett Favre 1.00 2.50
38 A.J. Hawk .40 1.00
39 Matt Schaub .40 1.00
40 Andre Johnson .40 1.00
41 Ahman Green .40 1.00
42 Peyton Manning .75 2.00
43 Marvin Harrison .50 1.25
44 Reggie Wayne .40 1.00
45 Joseph Addai .40 1.00
46 Fred Taylor .40 1.00
47 Maurice Jones-Drew .50 1.25
48 Byron Leftwich .40 1.00
49 Damon Huard .40 1.00
50 Larry Johnson .30 .75
51 Tony Gonzalez .40 1.00
52 Zach Thomas .40 1.00
53 Ronnie Brown .40 1.00
54 Chris Chambers .40 1.00
55 Tarvaris Jackson .30 .75
56 Chester Taylor .30 .75
57 Troy Williamson .30 .75
58 Tom Brady .75 2.00
59 Donte Stallworth .40 1.00
60 Laurence Maroney .40 1.00
61 Reggie Bush .50 1.25
62 Deuce McAllister .40 1.00
63 Drew Brees .50 1.25
64 Marques Colston .50 1.25
65 Eli Manning .50 1.25
66 Plaxico Burress .40 1.00
67 Brandon Jacobs .40 1.00
68 Chad Pennington .40 1.00
69 Thomas Jones .40 1.00
70 Laveranues Coles .30 .75
71 LaMont Jordan .40 1.00
72 Randy Moss .50 1.25
73 Nnamdi Asomugha .50 1.25
74 Donovan McNabb .50 1.25
75 Brian Westbrook .40 1.00
76 Reggie Brown .30 .75
77 Ben Roethlisberger .50 1.25
78 Hines Ward .50 1.25
79 Willie Parker .40 1.00
80 LaDainian Tomlinson .50 1.25
81 Philip Rivers .50 1.25
82 Antonio Gates .50 1.25
83 Frank Gore .50 1.25
84 Alex Smith QB .50 1.25
85 Ashley Lelie .40 1.00
86 Matt Hasselbeck .40 1.00
87 Shaun Alexander .40 1.00

88 Deion Branch .40 1.00
89 Marc Bulger .40 1.00
90 Torry Holt .40 1.00
91 Steven Jackson .50 1.25
92 Cadillac Williams .40 1.00
93 Chris Simms .30 .75
94 Joey Galloway .40 1.00
95 Vince Young .40 1.00
96 David Givens .30 .75
97 LenDale White .40 1.00
98 Jason Campbell .40 1.00
99 Santana Moss .40 1.00
100 Clinton Portis .40 1.00
101 Levi Brown RC 4.00 10.00
102 Adam Carriker RC 3.00 8.00
103 Jarvis Moss RC 3.00 8.00
104 Aaron Ross RC 4.00 10.00
105 Chris Houston RC 3.00 8.00
106 Michael Griffin RC 4.00 10.00
107 Justin Harrell RC 3.00 8.00
108 Joe Staley RC 3.00 8.00
109 Jon Beason RC 3.00 8.00
110 Anthony Spencer RC 4.00 10.00
111 Ben Grubbs RC 3.00 8.00
112 Charles Johnson RC 2.50 6.00
113 Marcus McCauley RC 3.00 8.00
114 Justin Blalock RC 2.50 6.00
115 Tim Crowder RC 4.00 10.00
116 Brandon Meriweather RC 4.00 10.00
117 Arron Sears RC 3.00 8.00
118 Zach Miller RC 4.00 10.00
119 Turk McBride RC 3.00 8.00
120 Ryan Kalil RC 3.00 8.00
121 Tony Ugoh RC 3.00 8.00
122 David Harris RC 3.00 8.00
123 Jonathan Wade RC 3.00 8.00
124 Josh Wilson RC 3.00 8.00
125 Demarcus Tank Tyler RC 2.50 6.00
126 Tanard Jackson RC 2.50 6.00
127 Jordan Kent RC 3.00 8.00
128 Ray McDonald RC 3.00 8.00
129 Quentin Moses RC 3.00 8.00
130 Eric Weddle RC 4.00 10.00
131 Victor Abiamiri RC 4.00 10.00
132 Josh Beekman RC 2.50 6.00
133 Brandon Siler RC 2.50 6.00
134 Aundrae Allison RC 2.50 6.00
135 Ben Patrick RC 3.00 8.00
136 Chris Davis RC 2.50 6.00
137 A.J. Davis RC 2.50 6.00
138 Scott Chandler RC 4.00 10.00
139 Mason Crosby RC 3.00 8.00
140 Zak DeOssie RC 3.00 8.00
141 Matt Spaeth RC 4.00 10.00
142 James Jones RC 4.00 10.00
143 Mike Walker RC 4.00 10.00
144 Martrez Milner RC 2.50 6.00
145 Michael Okwo RC 3.00 8.00
146 Steve Breaston RC 4.00 10.00
147 Isaiah Stanback RC 2.50 6.00
148 Laurent Robinson RC 4.00 10.00
149 Brandon Mebane RC 3.00 8.00
150 Quinn Pitcock RC 3.00 8.00
151 Roy Hall RC 4.00 10.00
152 Buster Davis RC 3.00 8.00
153 Alan Branch RC 3.00 8.00
154 Josh Gattis RC 2.50 6.00
155 Aaron Rouse RC 3.00 8.00
156 Tim Shaw RC 3.00 8.00
157 Sabby Piscitelli RC 4.00 10.00
158 Rufus Alexander RC 3.00 8.00
159 Marcus Thomas RC 3.00 8.00
160 Tarell Brown RC 4.00 10.00
161 Chris Leak AU RC 6.00 15.00
162 Amobi Okoye AU RC 8.00 20.00
163 Tyler Palko AU RC 6.00 15.00
164 Craig Buster Davis AU RC 6.00 15.00
165 Courtney Taylor AU RC 6.00 15.00
166 Tyrone Moss AU RC 5.00 12.00
167 Darrelle Revis AU RC 12.00 30.00
168 David Ball AU RC 6.00 15.00
169 David Clowney AU RC 6.00 15.00
170 Daymeion Hughes AU RC 6.00 15.00
171 DeShawn Wynn AU RC 6.00 15.00
172 Drew Tate AU RC 6.00 15.00
173 Dwayne Wright AU RC 6.00 15.00
174 Eric Wright AU RC 8.00 20.00
175 Kenneth Darby AU RC 6.00 15.00
176 H.B. Blades AU RC 5.00 12.00
177 Jamaal Anderson AU RC 6.00 15.00
178 Jared Zabransky AU RC 6.00 15.00
179 Rhema McKnight AU RC 5.00 12.00
180 Jeff Rowe AU RC 5.00 12.00
181 LaRon Landry AU RC 8.00 20.00
182 Jordan Palmer AU RC 6.00 15.00
183 Kolby Smith AU RC 6.00 15.00
184 LaMarr Woodley AU RC 10.00 25.00
185 Lawrence Timmons AU RC 8.00 20.00
186 Leon Hall AU RC 6.00 15.00
187 Matt Moore AU RC 8.00 20.00
188 Gary Russell AU RC 6.00 15.00
189 Paul Posluszny AU RC 8.00 20.00
190 Reggie Nelson AU RC 6.00 15.00
191 Antonio Pittman JSY AU RC 6.00 15.00
192 Anthony Gonzalez JSY AU/399 RC 12.00 30.00
193 Gaines Adams JSY AU RC 10.00 25.00
194 Brandon Jackson JSY AU RC 8.00 20.00
195 Brian Leonard JSY AU RC 8.00 20.00
196 Johnnie Lee Higgins JSY AU RC 8.00 20.00
197 Chris Henry RB JSY AU RC 6.00 15.00
198 Patrick Willis JSY AU RC 20.00 50.00
199 Drew Stanton JSY AU RC 6.00 15.00
200 Dwayne Bowe JSY AU/399 RC 15.00 40.00
201 Greg Olsen JSY AU RC 8.00 20.00
202 John Beck JSY AU RC 10.00 25.00
203 Jason Hill JSY AU RC 10.00 25.00
204 Paul Williams JSY AU RC 6.00 15.00
205 Joe Thomas JSY AU RC 10.00 25.00
206 Lorenzo Booker JSY AU RC 8.00 20.00
207 Yamon Figurs JSY AU RC 6.00 15.00
208 Kenny Irons JSY AU RC 6.00 15.00
209 Kevin Kolb JSY AU/399 RC 15.00 40.00
210 Garrett Wolfe JSY AU RC 6.00 15.00
211 Michael Bush JSY AU RC 10.00 25.00
212 Robert Meachem JSY AU/399 RC 12.00 30.00
213 Sidney Rice JSY AU/399 RC 15.00 40.00
214 Steve Smith JSY AU RC 12.00 30.00
215 Tony Hunt JSY AU RC 6.00 15.00
217 Trent Edwards JSY AU/399 RC 12.00 30.00
218 Adrian Peterson JSY AU/299 RC 125.00 250.00
219 Brady Quinn JSY AU/299 RC 15.00 40.00
220 Calvin Johnson JSY AU/299 RC 60.00 120.00
221 Dwayne Jarrett JSY AU/299 RC 12.00 30.00
222 JaMarcus Russell JSY AU/299 RC 10.00 25.00
223 Marshawn Lynch JSY AU/299 RC 25.00 50.00
224 Ted Ginn JSY AU/299 RC 12.00 30.00

2007 SPx Gold Rookies

*ROOKIES 101-160: .5X TO 1.2X BASIC RC/899
101-160 PRINT RUN 699 SER.#'d SETS
*ROOKIE AU: .5X TO 1.2X BASIC RC/499
*ROOKIE JSY AU: .6X TO 1.5X BASIC RC/599
*ROOKIE JSY AU: .6X TO 1.5X BASIC RC/399
161-217 PRINT RUN 199 SER.#'d SETS
218 Adrian Peterson JSY AU/99 150.00 300.00

2007 SPx Gold Holofoil Rookies

*ROOKIES 101-160: 1X TO 2.5X BASIC RC/899
*ROOK.AU 161-190: 1X TO 2.5X BASE RC/499
*ROOKIE JSY AU: 1.2X TO 3X BASIC RC/599
STATED PRINT RUN 25 SER.#'d SETS
218 Adrian Peterson JSY/FB AU 300.00 600.00

2007 SPx Silver Holofoil Rookies

*ROOKIES 101-160: .6X TO 1.5X BASIC RC/899
101-160 PRINT RUN 299 SER.#'d SETS
*ROOK.AU 161-190: .6X TO 1.5X BASE RC/499
161-190 PRINT RUN 99 SER.#'d SETS

2007 SPx Endorsements Autographs

ENAB Anquan Boldin 6.00 15.00
ENAO Amobi Okoye 5.00 12.00
ENAP Adrian Peterson SP 150.00 250.00
ENBE Drew Bennett 4.00 10.00
ENBL Brian Leonard SP 8.00 20.00
ENBO Dwayne Bowe SP 10.00 25.00
ENBQ Brady Quinn SP 40.00 100.00
ENBR Reggie Brown 4.00 10.00
ENCD Craig Buster Davis 6.00 15.00
ENCJ Calvin Johnson SP 75.00 150.00
ENCL Chris Leak 6.00 15.00
ENCO Jerricho Cotchery 5.00 12.00
ENCT Chester Taylor 4.00 10.00
ENDB Drew Brees SP 30.00 60.00
ENDJ Dwayne Jarrett 6.00 15.00
ENDP Drew Pearson 8.00 20.00
ENDS Drew Stanton SP 6.00 15.00
ENES Emmitt Smith SP 125.00 200.00
ENGO Greg Olsen 6.00 15.00
ENHB H.B. Blades 5.00 12.00
ENHO T.J. Houshmandzadeh 6.00 15.00
ENJC Jason Campbell 6.00 15.00
ENJR JaMarcus Russell SP 20.00 50.00
ENJT Joe Thomas 6.00 15.00
ENLE Lee Evans 5.00 12.00
ENLJ Larry Johnson SP 20.00 40.00
ENLL LaRon Landry 6.00 15.00
ENLN Legedu Naanee 5.00 12.00
ENLT Lawrence Timmons 6.00 15.00
ENLW LaMarr Woodley 8.00 20.00
ENMB Michael Bush 6.00 15.00
ENML Marshawn Lynch SP 15.00 40.00
ENNA Joe Namath SP 40.00 80.00
ENPM Peyton Manning 50.00 100.00
ENPP Paul Posluszny 8.00 20.00
ENRB Reggie Bush SP 90.00 150.00
ENRM Robert Meachem SP 10.00 25.00
ENRN Reggie Nelson 5.00 12.00
ENSC Scott Chandler 6.00 15.00
ENSM Matt Schaub 6.00 15.00
ENSY Selvin Young 6.00 15.00
ENTG Ted Ginn Jr. SP 15.00 40.00
ENTH Joe Theismann SP 15.00 30.00
ENWP Willie Parker 8.00 20.00

2007 SPx Freshman Tandems Dual Jerseys

FT2AO Gaines Adams 4.00 10.00
Greg Olsen
FT2AT Gaines Adams 4.00 10.00
Joe Thomas
FT2AW Gaines Adams 8.00 20.00
Patrick Willis
FT2BH Michael Bush 4.00 10.00
Tony Hunt
FT2ES Trent Edwards 4.00 10.00
Troy Smith
FT2GG Ted Ginn Jr. 4.00 10.00
Anthony Gonzalez
FT2HL Chris Henry 4.00 10.00
Marshawn Lynch
FT2HW Johnnie Lee Higgins 2.50 6.00
Paul Williams
FT2IW Kenny Irons 2.50 6.00
Garrett Wolfe
FT2JG Calvin Johnson 10.00 25.00
Ted Ginn Jr.
FT2JJ Calvin Johnson 10.00 25.00
Drew Stanton
FT2JS Dwayne Jarrett 4.00 10.00
Steve Smith USC
FT2KS Kevin Kolb 6.00 15.00
Drew Stanton
FT2LB Brian Leonard 3.00 8.00
Lorenzo Booker
FT2LH Brian Leonard 3.00 8.00
Tony Hunt
FT2MB Robert Meachem 5.00 12.00
Dwayne Bowe
FT2MR Robert Meachem 5.00 12.00
Sidney Rice
FT2PG Antonio Pittman 4.00 10.00
Anthony Gonzalez
FT2PJ Adrian Peterson 12.00 30.00
Brandon Jackson
FT2PL Adrian Peterson 12.00 30.00
Marshawn Lynch
FT2QB Brady Quinn 4.00 10.00
John Beck
FT2QR Brady Quinn 4.00 10.00
JaMarcus Russell
FT2QT Brady Quinn 4.00 10.00
Joe Thomas
FT2QW JaMarcus Russell 10.00 25.00
Calvin Johnson
FT2RB JaMarcus Russell 5.00 12.00
Dwayne Bowe
FT2SB Drew Stanton 4.00 10.00
John Beck
FT2SF Troy Smith 4.00 10.00
Yamon Figurs
FT2SH Steve Smith USC 4.00 10.00
Jason Hill
FT2SP Troy Smith 4.00 10.00
Antonio Pittman
FT2WH Patrick Willis 8.00 20.00
Jason Hill

2007 SPx Freshman Tandems Dual Jerseys Autographs

STATED PRINT RUN 25 SER.#'d SETS
FT2AO Gaines Adams 20.00 50.00
Greg Olsen
FT2AT Gaines Adams 20.00 50.00
Joe Thomas
FT2AW Gaines Adams 30.00 80.00
Patrick Willis
FT2BH Michael Bush 20.00 50.00
Tony Hunt
FT2GG Ted Ginn Jr. 20.00 50.00
Anthony Gonzalez
FT2HL Chris Henry 20.00 50.00
Marshawn Lynch
FT2HW Johnnie Lee Higgins 12.00 30.00
Paul Williams
FT2IW Garrett Wolfe 12.00 30.00
Kenny Irons
FT2JG Calvin Johnson 60.00 150.00
Ted Ginn Jr.
FT2JJ Calvin Johnson 60.00 150.00
Drew Stanton
FT2JS Dwayne Jarrett 20.00 50.00
Steve Smith USC
FT2KS Drew Stanton 30.00 80.00
Kevin Kolb
FT2LB Brian Leonard 15.00 40.00
Lorenzo Booker
FT2LH Brian Leonard 15.00 40.00
Tony Hunt
FT2MB Robert Meachem 20.00 50.00
Dwayne Bowe
FT2MR Robert Meachem 20.00 50.00
Sidney Rice
FT2PG Antonio Pittman 12.00 30.00
Anthony Gonzalez
FT2PJ Adrian Peterson 200.00 400.00
Brandon Jackson
FT2PL Adrian Peterson 200.00 400.00
Marshawn Lynch
FT2QB Brady Quinn 20.00 50.00
John Beck
FT2QR Brady Quinn 20.00 50.00
JaMarcus Russell
FT2QT Brady Quinn 20.00 50.00
Joe Thomas
FT2QW Calvin Johnson 60.00 150.00
JaMarcus Russell
FT2RB JaMarcus Russell 25.00 60.00
Dwayne Bowe
FT2SB Drew Stanton 20.00 50.00
John Beck
FT2SH Jason Hill 20.00 50.00
Steve Smith USC
FT2WH Jason Hill 40.00 100.00
Patrick Willis

2007 SPx Freshman Tandems Triple Jerseys

UNPRICED AUTO STATED PRINT RUN 10
ATW Gaines Adams 5.00 12.00
Joe Thomas
Patrick Willis
RHL Lorenzo Booker 4.00 10.00
Tony Hunt
Brian Leonard
BHR Michael Bush 5.00 12.00
Johnnie Lee Higgins
JaMarcus Russell
BKS John Beck 8.00 20.00
Kevin Kolb
Drew Stanton
GGS Ted Ginn Jr. 5.00 12.00
Anthony Gonzalez
Troy Smith
GSJ Anthony Gonzalez 5.00 12.00
Steve Smith USC
Dwayne Jarrett
HJS Jason Hill 5.00 12.00
Dwayne Jarrett
Steve Smith USC
HLJ Tony Hunt 4.00 10.00
Brian Leonard
Brandon Jackson
IWB Kenny Irons 4.00 10.00
Garrett Wolfe
Lorenzo Booker
JMG Calvin Johnson 12.00 30.00
Robert Meachem
Ted Ginn Jr.
LPD Marshawn Lynch 4.00 10.00
Antonio Pittman
Brandon Jackson
PJB Adrian Peterson 15.00 40.00
Brandon Jackson
Michael Bush
PLI Adrian Peterson 15.00 40.00
Marshawn Lynch
Kenny Irons
QES Brady Quinn 5.00 12.00
Trent Edwards
Drew Stanton
RJB JaMarcus Russell 12.00 30.00
Calvin Johnson
Dwayne Bowe
RJP JaMarcus Russell 20.00 50.00
Calvin Johnson
Adrian Peterson
RJT JaMarcus Russell 12.00 30.00
Calvin Johnson
Joe Thomas
RMB Sidney Rice 5.00 12.00
Robert Meachem
Dwayne Bowe
RQK JaMarcus Russell 8.00 20.00
Brady Quinn
Kevin Kolb
SPG Troy Smith 3.00 8.00
Antonio Pittman
Anthony Gonzalez

2007 SPx Freshman Tandems Quad Jerseys

GRJS Anthony Gonzalez 8.00 20.00
Sidney Rice
Dwayne Jarrett
Steve Smith USC
HBLJ Tony Hunt 6.00 15.00
Lorenzo Booker
Brian Leonard
Brandon Jackson
JGJR Calvin Johnson 12.00 30.00
Ted Ginn Jr.
Robert Meachem
Jason Hill
LLPH Marshawn Lynch 15.00 40.00
Brian Leonard
Adrian Peterson
Tony Hunt
MBSJ Robert Meachem 10.00 25.00
Dwayne Bowe
Steve Smith USC
Dwayne Jarrett
PLIB Adrian Peterson 15.00 40.00
Marshawn Lynch
Kenny Irons
Michael Bush
QKEB Brady Quinn 10.00 25.00
Kevin Kolb
Trent Edwards
John Beck
QRSK Brady Quinn 10.00 25.00
JaMarcus Russell
Troy Smith
Kevin Kolb
RQPL JaMarcus Russell 12.00 30.00
Brady Quinn
Adrian Peterson
Marshawn Lynch
SGGP Troy Smith 10.00 25.00
Ted Ginn Jr.
Anthony Gonzalez
Antonio Pittman

2007 SPx Super Scripts Autographs

SSAP Adrian Peterson SP 125.00 250.00
SSAS Alex Smith QB SP 10.00 25.00
SSBF Brett Favre SP 125.00 200.00
SSBJ Bo Jackson SP 40.00 80.00
SSBM Brandon Meriweather 8.00 20.00
SSBQ Brady Quinn SP 20.00 50.00
SSBU Michael Bush 8.00 20.00
SSCB Champ Bailey 15.00 40.00
SSCD Craig Buster Davis 6.00 15.00
SSCJ Calvin Johnson SP 60.00 120.00
SSCW Cadillac Williams SP 8.00 20.00
SSDB Dwayne Bowe SP 20.00 40.00
SSDH Daymeion Hughes 6.00 15.00
SSDJ Dwayne Jarrett 6.00 15.00
SSDM Dan Marino SP 125.00 250.00
SSDR Darrelle Revis 12.00 30.00
SSDS Drew Stanton SP 6.00 15.00
SSDW Darius Walker 5.00 12.00
SSEW Eric Wright 8.00 20.00
SSFG Frank Gore SP 20.00 40.00
SSGA Gaines Adams SP
SSIS Isaiah Stanback 5.00 12.00
SSJA Joseph Addai SP 8.00 20.00
SSJF Joel Filani 6.00 15.00
SSJM Joe Montana SP 100.00 200.00
SSJR JaMarcus Russell SP 6.00 15.00
SSKI Kenny Irons 5.00 12.00
SSLB Lorenzo Booker 6.00 15.00
SSLF Larry Fitzgerald SP 15.00 40.00
SSLG L.C. Greenwood 15.00 30.00
SSLL LaRon Landry 8.00 20.00
SSLY Marshawn Lynch SP 10.00 25.00
SSMB Marc Bulger SP 8.00 20.00
SSMC Marques Colston 8.00 20.00
SSMG Michael Griffin 8.00 20.00
SSML Matt Leinart SP 8.00 20.00
SSPR Philip Rivers SP 25.00 50.00
SSRB Ronnie Brown SP 15.00 30.00
SSRC Roger Craig 10.00 25.00
SSRN Reggie Nelson 6.00 15.00
SSSS Steve Smith USC SP 12.00 30.00
SSTG Ted Ginn Jr. 6.00 15.00
SSTH T.J. Houshmandzadeh 6.00 15.00
SSVY Vince Young SP 20.00 50.00

2007 SPx Winning Materials Jersey Number

*DUAL: .5X TO 1.2X BASIC JSYs
*PATCH/10: 1.5X TO 4X BASIC JSYs
*DUAL PATCH/10: 2X TO 5X BASIC JSYs
PATCH PRINT RUN 10 SER.#'d SETS
WMAG Anthony Gonzalez 2.50 6.00
WMAP Adrian Peterson 10.00 25.00
WMAR Aaron Rodgers 10.00 25.00
WMBE Cedric Benson 4.00 10.00
WMBF1 Brett Favre 8.00 20.00
WMBF2 Brett Favre 8.00 20.00
WMBJ Brad Johnson 3.00 8.00
WMBL1 Byron Leftwich 3.00 8.00
WMBL2 Byron Leftwich 3.00 8.00
WMBO Anquan Boldin 3.00 8.00
WMBQ Brady Quinn 2.50 6.00
WMBR1 Ben Roethlisberger 6.00 15.00
WMBR2 Ben Roethlisberger 6.00 15.00
WMBU Michael Bush 4.00 10.00
WMCB1 Champ Bailey 3.00 8.00
WMCB2 Champ Bailey 3.00 8.00
WMCF Charlie Frye 3.00 8.00
WMCH Chris Brown 2.50 6.00
WMCJ Calvin Johnson 8.00 20.00
WMCP Carson Palmer 4.00 10.00
WMCS1 Chris Simms 2.50 6.00
WMCS2 Chris Simms 2.50 6.00
WMCU1 Daunte Culpepper 3.00 8.00
WMCU2 Daunte Culpepper 3.00 8.00
WMCW Cadillac Williams 3.00 8.00
WMDB Drew Brees 3.00 8.00
WMDC David Carr 3.00 8.00
WMDE Derrick Mason 2.50 6.00
WMDF DeShaun Foster 3.00 8.00
WMDJ Dwayne Jarrett 4.00 10.00
WMDM Dan Marino 10.00 25.00
WMDO1 Donovan McNabb 4.00 10.00
WMDO2 Donovan McNabb 4.00 10.00
WMDR1 Drew Bledsoe 4.00 10.00
WMDR2 Drew Bledsoe 4.00 10.00
WMDS Drew Stanton 4.00 10.00
WMDW Dwayne Bowe 3.00 8.00
WMEJ Edgerrin James 4.00 10.00
WMEM Eli Manning 4.00 10.00
WMGA Gaines Adams 3.00 8.00
WMGO Tony Gonzalez 3.00 8.00
WMGR Trent Green 3.00 8.00
WMHM Heath Miller 2.50 6.00
WMHW Hines Ward 4.00 10.00
WMIB Isaac Bruce 3.00 8.00
WMJA Brandon Jackson 2.00 5.00
WMJB John Beck 4.00 10.00
WMJD1 Jake Delhomme 3.00 8.00
WMJD2 Jake Delhomme 3.00 8.00
WMJH Joe Horn 3.00 8.00
WMJJ Julius Jones 3.00 8.00
WMJL Jamal Lewis 3.00 8.00
WMJO1 Chad Johnson 3.00 8.00
WMJO2 Chad Johnson 3.00 8.00
WMJP1 Jake Plummer 3.00 8.00
WMJP2 Jake Plummer 3.00 8.00
WMJR JaMarcus Russell 1.50 4.00
WMJS Jeremy Shockey 3.00 8.00
WMJT Joe Thomas 3.00 8.00
WMJU Julius Peppers 3.00 8.00
WMJV Jonathan Vilma 3.00 8.00
WMKI Kenny Irons 2.50 6.00
WMKJ Kevin Jones 2.50 6.00
WMKK Kevin Kolb 4.00 10.00
WMLT LaDainian Tomlinson 4.00 10.00
WMMA Mark Brunell 3.00 8.00
WMMB Marc Bulger 3.00 8.00
WMMC1 Deuce McAllister 3.00 8.00
WMMC2 Deuce McAllister 3.00 8.00
WMME Robert Meachem 4.00 10.00
WMMH Marvin Harrison 4.00 10.00
WMML Marshawn Lynch 2.50 6.00
WMMV Michael Vick 4.00 10.00
WMMW Mike Williams 2.50 6.00
WMOL Greg Olsen 2.00 5.00
WMOW Terrell Owens 4.00 10.00
WMPH Priest Holmes 3.00 8.00
WMPI Antonio Pittman 2.50 6.00
WMPM Peyton Manning 6.00 15.00
WMRE Antwaan Randle El 2.50 6.00
WMRM Randy Moss 4.00 10.00
WMRO Ronnie Brown 3.00 8.00
WMSA Shaun Alexander 4.00 10.00
WMSJ Steven Jackson 4.00 10.00
WMSR Sidney Rice 3.00 8.00
WMSS Steve Smith USC 2.50 6.00
WMST Donte Stallworth 3.00 8.00
WMTB Tatum Bell 3.00 8.00
WMTG Ted Ginn Jr. 4.00 10.00
WMTH Torry Holt 3.00 8.00
WMTO Tom Brady 5.00 12.00
WMTS Troy Smith 2.50 6.00
WMUR Brian Urlacher 4.00 10.00
WMWM Willis McGahee 3.00 8.00

2007 SPx Winning Materials Jersey Number Dual Autographs

STATED PRINT RUN 10-25
SERIAL #'d UNDER 25 NOT PRICED
WMBO Anquan Boldin/25 15.00 30.00
WMBR1 Ben Roethlisberger/25
WMBR2 Ben Roethlisberger/25
WMCB1 Champ Bailey/25 25.00 50.00
WMCB2 Champ Bailey/25 25.00 50.00
WMDB Drew Brees/25 40.00 80.00
WMEM Eli Manning/25 50.00 80.00
WMLT LaDainian Tomlinson/25 60.00 120.00
WMMB Marc Bulger/25 25.00 50.00
WMPM Peyton Manning/25 100.00 175.00
WMRO Ronnie Brown/25 25.00 50.00

2007 SPx Winning Materials Stat

*DUAL: .5X TO 1.2X BASIC JSYs
*PATCH/10: 1.5X TO 4X BASIC JSYs
*DUAL PATCH/10: 2X TO 5X BASIC JSYs
PATCH PRINT RUN 10 SER.#'d SETS
WMSAG Anthony Gonzalez 2.50 6.00
WMSAH Ahman Green 3.00 8.00
WMSAP1 Adrian Peterson 10.00 25.00
WMSAP2 Adrian Peterson 10.00 25.00
WMSAR Aaron Rodgers 12.00 30.00
WMSBA Ronde Barber 2.50 6.00
WMSBF1 Brett Favre 8.00 20.00
WMSBF2 Brett Favre 8.00 20.00
WMSBL1 Byron Leftwich 3.00 8.00
WMSBL2 Byron Leftwich 3.00 8.00
WMSBO Anquan Boldin 3.00 8.00
WMSBQ1 Brady Quinn 2.50 6.00
WMSBQ2 Brady Quinn 2.50 6.00
WMSBR Ben Roethlisberger 6.00 15.00
WMSBU Michael Bush 4.00 10.00
WMSCB Champ Bailey 3.00 8.00
WMSCJ1 Calvin Johnson 8.00 20.00
WMSCJ2 Calvin Johnson 8.00 20.00
WMSCP Carson Palmer 4.00 10.00
WMSCU Daunte Culpepper 3.00 8.00
WMSD02 Donovan McNabb 4.00 10.00
WMSDB Drew Brees 3.00 8.00
WMSDC David Carr 3.00 8.00
WMSDJ Dwayne Jarrett 4.00 10.00
WMSD01 Donovan McNabb 4.00 10.00
WMSDR Drew Bledsoe 4.00 10.00
WMSDW Dwayne Bowe 4.00 10.00
WMSEM Eli Manning 4.00 10.00
WMSGA Gaines Adams 3.00 8.00
WMSGO Tony Gonzalez 3.00 8.00
WMSGR Trent Green 3.00 8.00
WMSHA Matt Hasselbeck 3.00 8.00
WMSHO Torry Holt 3.00 8.00
WMSHU Tony Hunt 4.00 10.00
WMSHW Hines Ward 4.00 10.00
WMSJA Javon Walker 3.00 8.00
WMSJB John Beck 4.00 10.00
WMSJD Jake Delhomme 3.00 8.00
WMSJH Joe Horn 3.00 8.00
WMSJJ Julius Jones 3.00 8.00
WMSJL Jamal Lewis 3.00 8.00
WMSJM Joe Montana 10.00 25.00
WMSJO Joe Theismann 4.00 10.00
WMSJP1 Jake Plummer 3.00 8.00
WMSJP2 Jake Plummer 3.00 8.00
WMSJR1 JaMarcus Russell 2.50 6.00
WMSJR2 JaMarcus Russell 2.50 6.00
WMSJS1 Jeremy Shockey 3.00 8.00
WMSJS2 Jeremy Shockey 3.00 8.00
WMSJT Joe Thomas 3.00 8.00
WMSKB Kyle Boller 2.50 6.00
WMSKC Keary Colbert 2.50 6.00
WMSKI Kenny Irons 2.50 6.00
WMSKJ Keyshawn Johnson 3.00 8.00
WMSKK Kevin Kolb 4.00 10.00
WMSKO Kyle Orton 2.50 6.00
WMSLE Matt Leinart 5.00 12.00
WMSLT1 LaDainian Tomlinson 4.00 10.00
WMSLT2 LaDainian Tomlinson 4.00 10.00
WMSLT3 LaDainian Tomlinson 4.00 10.00
WMSMB Marc Bulger 3.00 8.00
WMSMC Deuce McAllister 3.00 8.00
WMSME Robert Meachem 4.00 10.00
WMSMH Marvin Harrison 4.00 10.00
WMSML Marshawn Lynch 2.50 6.00
WMSMM Muhsin Muhammad 3.00 8.00
WMSMV1 Michael Vick 4.00 10.00
WMSMV2 Michael Vick 4.00 10.00
WMSOW Terrell Owens 4.00 10.00
WMSPH Priest Holmes 3.00 8.00
WMSPI Antonio Pittman 1.50 4.00
WMSPM1 Peyton Manning 6.00 15.00
WMSPM2 Peyton Manning 6.00 15.00
WMSPO Clinton Portis 3.00 8.00
WMSPR Philip Rivers 4.00 10.00
WMSRB Reggie Bush 8.00 20.00
WMSRM Randy Moss 4.00 10.00
WMSRO Ronnie Brown 3.00 8.00
WMSRS Rod Smith 3.00 8.00
WMSRW1 Reggie Wayne 3.00 8.00
WMSRW2 Reggie Wayne 3.00 8.00
WMSRW3 Reggie Wayne 3.00 8.00
WMSSA Shaun Alexander 4.00 10.00
WMSSJ Steven Jackson 4.00 10.00
WMSSR Sidney Rice 3.00 8.00
WMSSS Steve Smith USC 2.50 6.00
WMSTB Tatum Bell 3.00 8.00
WMSTE Tedy Bruschi 4.00 10.00
WMSTG Ted Ginn Jr. 4.00 10.00
WMSTH T.J. Houshmandzadeh 3.00 8.00
WMSTJ Thomas Jones 3.00 8.00
WMSTO1 Tom Brady 5.00 12.00
WMSTO2 Tom Brady 5.00 12.00
WMSTS Troy Smith 4.00 10.00
WMSTW Troy Williamson 2.50 6.00
WMSUR Brian Urlacher 4.00 10.00
WMSWM1 Willis McGahee 3.00 8.00
WMSWM2 Willis McGahee 3.00 8.00
WMSWP Willie Parker 4.00 10.00

2007 SPx Winning Trios Jerseys

BHS Marc Bulger 6.00 15.00
Torry Holt
Steven Jackson
BMB Tom Brady 10.00 25.00
Laurence Maroney
Tedy Bruschi
BMC Reggie Bush 12.00 30.00
Deuce McAllister
Marques Colston
BWS Tatum Bell 5.00 12.00
Javon Walker
Rod Smith
CBS Daunte Culpepper 5.00 12.00
Ronnie Brown
Junior Seau
CWM Kevin Curtis 5.00 12.00
Troy Williamson
Muhsin Muhammad
FBL Brett Favre 15.00 40.00
Tom Brady
Matt Leinart
FSM Charlie Frye 5.00 12.00
Alex Smith
Eli Manning
GHH Trent Green 5.00 12.00
Priest Holmes
Dante Hall
JOB Julius Jones 6.00 15.00
Terrell Owens
Drew Bledsoe
JTJ Thomas Jones 5.00 12.00
Fred Taylor
Steven Jackson
LDR Laurence Maroney 10.00 25.00
DeAngelo Williams
Reggie Bush
LEB Matt Leinart 6.00 15.00
Edgerrin James
Anquan Boldin
LTD Byron Leftwich 5.00 12.00
Fred Taylor
Maurice Jones-Drew
MBB Peyton Manning 12.00 30.00
Tom Brady
Drew Brees
MHW Peyton Manning 10.00 25.00
Marvin Harrison
Reggie Wayne
MWB Donovan McNabb 6.00 15.00
Brian Westbrook
Reggie Brown
MWF Peyton Manning 10.00 25.00
Reggie Wayne
Dwight Freeney
OBM Kyle Orton 6.00 15.00
Cedric Benson
Muhsin Muhammad
PJH Carson Palmer 6.00 15.00
Chad Johnson
T.J. Houshmandzadeh
PRF Carson Palmer 8.00 20.00
Ben Roethlisberger
Charlie Frye
PWB Troy Polamalu 6.00 15.00
Roy Williams S
Ronde Barber
RPW Ben Roethlisberger 8.00 20.00
Willie Parker
Hines Ward
RTG Philip Rivers 8.00 20.00
LaDainian Tomlinson
Antonio Gates
SBS Michael Strahan 5.00 12.00
Plaxico Burress
Jeremy Shockey
TJA LaDainian Tomlinson 8.00 20.00
Larry Johnson
Shaun Alexander
WMF Cadillac Williams 5.00 12.00
Willis McGahee
DeShaun Foster
YLC Vince Young 15.00 40.00
Matt Leinart
Reggie Bush
YWG Vince Young 8.00 20.00
Chris Brown
David Givens

2008 SPx

COMP.SET w/o RC's (90) 25.00 50.00
91-150 ROOKIE PRINT RUN 999
151-177 JSY AU RC PRINT RUN 599
179-185 JSY AU RC PRINT RUN 325
186-225 AU RC PRINT RUN 399
UNPRICED NFL LOGO AU PRINT RUN 1
1 A.J. Hawk .40 1.00
2 Adrian Peterson .75 2.00
3 Alex Smith QB .50 1.25
4 Andre Johnson .40 1.00
5 Antonio Cromartie .30 .75
6 Antonio Gates .50 1.25
7 Fran Tarkenton .60 1.50
8 Ben Roethlisberger .50 1.25
9 Brandon Jacobs .40 1.00
10 Donovan McNabb .50 1.25
11 Braylon Edwards .40 1.00
12 Brett Favre 1.25 3.00
13 Brian Dawkins .40 1.00
14 Brian Urlacher .50 1.25
15 Brian Westbrook .40 1.00
16 Brodie Croyle .40 1.00
17 Calvin Johnson .50 1.25
18 Cadillac Williams .40 1.00
19 Carson Palmer .50 1.25
20 Chad Johnson .40 1.00
21 Champ Bailey .40 1.00
22 Charles Woodson .50 1.25
23 Marc Bulger .40 1.00
24 Clinton Portis .40 1.00
25 Dallas Clark .40 1.00
26 David Garrard .40 1.00
27 DeAngelo Williams .40 1.00
28 Deion Branch .40 1.00
29 DeMarcus Ware .40 1.00
30 Matt Leinart .50 1.25
31 Derek Anderson .30 .75
32 Devin Hester .50 1.25
33 Donte Stallworth .30 .75
34 Drew Brees .50 1.25
35 Dwayne Bowe .40 1.00
36 Ed Reed .40 1.00
37 Edgerrin James .40 1.00
38 Eli Manning .50 1.25
39 Gale Sayers .75 2.00
40 Frank Gore .40 1.00
41 Fred Taylor .40 1.00
42 Barry Sanders 1.00 2.50
43 Greg Jennings .50 1.25
44 JaMarcus Russell .40 1.00
45 Jason Campbell .40 1.00
46 Jason Taylor .40 1.00
47 Jay Cutler .50 1.25
48 Jeff Garcia .40 1.00
49 Y.A. Tittle .60 1.50
50 Joseph Addai .40 1.00
51 Kellen Winslow Jr. .40 1.00
52 Joe Montana 1.25 3.00
53 LaDainian Tomlinson .50 1.25
54 Larry Fitzgerald .50 1.25
55 Larry Johnson .40 1.00
56 Laurence Maroney .40 1.00
57 Jerry Rice 1.00 2.50
58 Paul Hornung .60 1.50
59 Lofa Tatupu .40 1.00
60 Kurt Warner .50 1.25
61 Marshawn Lynch .40 1.00
62 Marvin Harrison .50 1.25
63 Matt Hasselbeck .40 1.00
64 Maurice Jones-Drew .40 1.00
65 Michael Strahan .40 1.00
66 Hines Ward .40 1.00
67 Reggie Wayne .40 1.00
68 Peyton Manning .75 2.00
69 Plaxico Burress .40 1.00
70 Randy Moss .50 1.25
71 Reggie Bush .50 1.25
72 Bob Griese .60 1.50
73 Ronnie Brown .40 1.00
74 Jim Brown .75 2.00
75 Shawne Merriman .40 1.00
76 Jamal Lewis .40 1.00
77 Steve Smith .40 1.00
78 Steven Jackson .50 1.25
79 Terrell Owens .50 1.25
80 Joey Galloway .40 1.00
81 Tom Brady .75 2.00
82 Tony Gonzalez .40 1.00
83 Tony Romo .60 1.50
84 Torry Holt .40 1.00
85 Troy Polamalu .50 1.25
86 Vince Young .40 1.00
87 Warrick Dunn .40 1.00
88 Wes Welker .50 1.25
89 Willie Parker .40 1.00
90 Willis McGahee .40 1.00
91 Marcus Thomas RC 2.00 5.00
92 Caleb Campbell RC 2.50 6.00
93 Xavier Omon RC 2.50 6.00
94 Spencer Larsen RC 1.50 4.00
95 Barry Richardson RC 1.50 4.00
96 Beau Bell RC 2.00 5.00
97 Brandon Flowers RC 2.50 6.00
98 Chauncey Washington RC 2.00 5.00
99 Cory Boyd RC 1.50 4.00
100 Chris Williams RC 2.00 5.00
101 Craig Stevens RC 1.50 4.00
102 Darius Reynaud RC 1.50 4.00
103 DeJuan Tribble RC 1.50 4.00
104 Dennis Keyes RC 1.50 4.00
105 Erin Henderson RC 2.50 6.00
106 Brad Cottam RC 2.00 5.00
107 Jamie Silva RC 2.00 5.00
108 Gosder Cherilus RC 2.00 5.00
109 Jacob Hester RC 2.50 6.00
110 Jehuu Caulcrick RC 2.00 5.00
111 Trae Williams RC 1.50 4.00
112 Jonathan Goff RC 1.50 4.00
113 Jonathan Hefney RC 2.00 5.00
114 Jordon Dizon RC 2.50 6.00
115 Josh Barrett RC 1.50 4.00
116 Josh Johnson RC 2.50 6.00
117 Justin Forsett RC 2.50 6.00
118 Justin King RC 2.00 5.00
119 Kalvin McRae RC 1.50 4.00
120 Keenan Burton RC 1.50 4.00
121 Kellen Davis RC 1.50 4.00
122 Keon Lattimore RC 2.00 5.00
123 Lance Leggett RC 2.50 6.00
124 Lavelle Hawkins RC 1.50 4.00
125 Marcus Monk RC 2.00 5.00
126 Mario Urrutia RC 1.50 4.00
127 Curtis Lofton RC 2.00 5.00
128 Martin Rucker RC 2.00 5.00
129 Will Franklin RC 2.00 5.00
130 Phillip Merling RC 2.00 5.00
131 Wesley Woodyard RC 2.00 5.00
132 Josh Morgan RC 2.50 6.00
133 Owen Schmitt RC 2.50 6.00
134 Paul Hubbard RC 2.00 5.00
135 Paul Smith RC 2.50 6.00
136 Philip Wheeler RC 2.00 5.00
137 Quentin Groves RC 2.00 5.00
138 Quintin Demps RC 2.50 6.00
139 Roy Schuening RC 1.50 4.00
140 Ryan Torain RC 2.50 6.00
141 Simeon Castille RC 2.00 5.00
142 T.C. Ostrander RC 2.00 5.00
143 Jerod Mayo RC 2.50 6.00
144 Tom Zbikowski RC 2.50 6.00
145 Thomas DeCoud RC 1.50 4.00
146 Tracy Porter RC 2.50 6.00
147 Trevor Laws RC 2.50 6.00
148 Trevor Scott RC 2.00 5.00
149 Vince Hall RC 1.50 4.00
150 Xavier Adibi RC 1.50 4.00
151 Donnie Avery JSY AU RC 6.00 15.00
152 Chad Henne JSY AU RC 8.00 20.00
153 Chris Johnson JSY AU RC 25.00 60.00
154 Earl Bennett JSY AU RC 8.00 20.00
155 Glenn Dorsey JSY AU RC 8.00 20.00
156 Harry Douglas JSY AU RC 6.00 15.00
157 Early Doucet JSY AU RC 6.00 15.00
158 Andre Caldwell JSY AU RC 6.00 15.00
159 Felix Jones JSY AU RC 12.00 30.00
160 Dustin Keller JSY AU RC 8.00 20.00
161 Jake Long JSY AU RC 8.00 20.00
162 Joe Flacco JSY AU RC 30.00 80.00
163 John David Booty JSY AU RC 6.00 15.00
164 Jordy Nelson JSY AU RC 15.00 30.00
165 Jerome Simpson JSY AU RC 8.00 20.00
166 Kevin Smith JSY AU RC 8.00 20.00

167 Limas Sweed JSY AU RC 8.00 20.00
168 Malcolm Kelly JSY AU RC 6.00 15.00
169 Mario Manningham JSY AU RC 12.50 25.00
170 James Hardy JSY AU RC 6.00 15.00
171 Matt Forte JSY AU RC 15.00 40.00
172 Dexter Jackson JSY AU RC 6.00 15.00
173 Eddie Royal JSY AU RC 8.00 20.00
174 Rashard Mendenhall JSY AU RC 15.00 40.00
175 Ray Rice JSY AU RC 15.00 40.00
176 Steve Slaton JSY AU RC 8.00 20.00
177 Kevin O'Connell JSY AU RC 6.00 15.00
179 Jamaal Charles JSY AU RC 15.00 40.00
180 Brian Brohm JSY AU RC 10.00 25.00
181 Devin Thomas JSY AU RC 8.00 20.00
182 Darren McFadden JSY AU RC 25.00 50.00
183 DeSean Jackson JSY AU RC 15.00 40.00
184 Jonathan Stewart JSY AU RC 15.00 40.00
185 Matt Ryan JSY AU RC 40.00 100.00
186 Yvenson Bernard AU RC 5.00 12.00
187 Alex Brink AU RC 5.00 12.00
188 Ali Highsmith AU RC 3.00 8.00
189 Allen Patrick AU RC 4.00 10.00
190 Antoine Cason AU RC 5.00 12.00
191 Aqib Talib AU RC 6.00 15.00
192 Ben Moffitt AU RC 3.00 8.00
193 Anthony Morelli AU RC 4.00 10.00
194 Bruce Davis AU RC 4.00 10.00
195 Calais Campbell AU RC 4.00 10.00
196 Chevis Jackson AU RC 3.00 8.00
197 Chris Ellis AU RC 3.00 8.00
198 Craig Steltz AU RC 4.00 10.00
199 DJ Hall AU RC 4.00 10.00
200 Dan Connor AU RC 5.00 12.00
201 DeMario Pressley AU RC 4.00 10.00
202 Derrick Harvey AU RC 3.00 8.00
203 Dominique Rodgers-Cromartie AU RC 5.00 12.00
204 Chris Long AU RC 5.00 12.00
205 Dre Moore AU RC 4.00 10.00
206 Fred Davis AU RC 5.00 12.00
207 Dwight Lowery AU RC 5.00 12.00
208 Davone Bess AU RC 5.00 12.00
209 Frank Okam AU RC 3.00 8.00
210 Dennis Dixon AU RC 10.00 20.00
211 Leodis McKelvin AU RC 4.00 10.00
212 Jack Ikegwuonu AU RC 3.00 8.00
213 Jacob Tamme AU RC 5.00 12.00
214 J Leman AU RC 3.00 8.00
215 John Carlson AU RC 5.00 12.00
216 Keith Rivers AU RC 5.00 12.00
217 Geno Hayes AU RC 3.00 8.00
218 Lawrence Jackson AU RC 4.00 10.00
219 Martellus Bennett AU RC 4.00 10.00
220 Ryan Clady AU RC 5.00 12.00
221 Sam Baker AU RC 3.00 8.00
222 Sedrick Ellis AU RC 5.00 12.00
223 Shawn Crable AU RC 3.00 8.00
224 Terrell Thomas AU RC 4.00 10.00
225 Vernon Gholston AU RC 4.00 10.00

2008 SPx Gold Holofoil Rookies

*ROOKIES 91-150: 1.2X TO 3X BASIC CARDS
*ROOKIE JSY AU 151-177: 1.2X TO 3X
*ROOKIE JSY AU 179-185: 1.2X TO 3X
*ROOKIE AU 186-225: 1X TO 2.5X
STATED PRINT RUN 25 SER.#'d SETS
153 Chris Johnson JSY AU 125.00 250.00
162 Joe Flacco JSY AU 150.00 300.00
182 Darren McFadden JSY AU 125.00 200.00
183 DeSean Jackson JSY AU 100.00 200.00
185 Matt Ryan JSY AU 175.00 350.00

2008 SPx Green Holofoil Rookies

*ROOKIES/499: .5X TO 1.2X BASIC CARDS
91-150 ROOKIE PRINT RUN 499
*ROOK.JSY AU/199: .6X TO 1.5X BASIC CARDS
151-177 JSY AU PRINT RUN 199
*ROOK.JSY AU/99: .6X TO 1.5X BASIC CARDS
179-185 JSY AU PRINT RUN 99
*ROOKIE AU/199: .6X TO 1.5X BASIC CARDS
186-225 ROOKIE AU PRINT RUN 199
153 Chris Johnson JSY AU 40.00 80.00
162 Joe Flacco JSY AU 40.00 100.00
182 Darren McFadden JSY AU/99 50.00 100.00
183 DeSean Jackson JSY AU/99 40.00 100.00
185 Matt Ryan JSY AU/99 75.00 150.00

2008 SPx Platinum

UNPRICED PLATINUM PRINT RUN 1
EACH PLAYER HAS MULTIPLE 1/1 PLAT.
WITH DIFFERING STAT LINES ON FRONT

2008 SPx Silver Holofoil Rookies

*SILVER HOLO/299: .6X TO 1.5X BASIC RC
*SILVER HOLO AU/99: .6X TO 1.5X BASIC RC
STATED PRINT RUN 99-299

2008 SPx Rookie Materials Autographs SPX Triple

STATED PRINT RUN 25 SER.#'d SETS
RMAC Andre Caldwell 10.00 25.00
RMBB Brian Brohm 12.00 30.00
RMCH Chad Henne 25.00 60.00
RMCJ Chris Johnson 40.00 100.00
RMCL Chris Long 12.00 30.00
RMDA Donnie Avery 10.00 25.00
RMDJ DeSean Jackson 30.00 80.00
RMDK Dustin Keller 12.00 30.00
RMDM Darren McFadden 40.00 80.00
RMDT Devin Thomas 10.00 25.00
RMEB Earl Bennett 12.00 30.00
RMED Early Doucet 10.00 25.00
RMER Eddie Royal 12.00 30.00
RMFJ Felix Jones 25.00 60.00
RMFO Matt Forte 25.00 60.00
RMGD Glenn Dorsey 12.00 30.00
RMHD Harry Douglas 10.00 25.00
RMJA Dexter Jackson 10.00 25.00
RMJB John David Booty 10.00 25.00
RMJC Jamaal Charles 20.00 50.00
RMJF Joe Flacco 50.00 120.00
RMJH James Hardy 10.00 25.00
RMJL Jake Long 12.00 30.00
RMJN Jordy Nelson 30.00 60.00
RMJS Jonathan Stewart 20.00 50.00
RMKO Kevin O'Connell 10.00 25.00
RMKS Kevin Smith 12.00 30.00
RMLS Limas Sweed 12.00 30.00
RMMK Malcolm Kelly 10.00 25.00
RMMM Mario Manningham 20.00 40.00
RMMR Matt Ryan 75.00 150.00
RMRM Rashard Mendenhall 30.00 80.00
RMRR Ray Rice 30.00 80.00
RMSI Jerome Simpson 12.00 30.00
RMSS Steve Slaton 12.00 30.00

2008 SPx Rookie Materials SPX Dual 199

SPX DUAL PRINT RUN 199
*NFL DUAL/199: .4X TO 1X SPX DUAL/199
*JER.# DUAL/175: .4X TO 1X SPX DUAL/199
*POSIT.DUAL/149: .4X TO 1X SPX DUAL/199
*FOOTBALL/119: .4X TO 1X SPX DUAL/199
*AFC/NFC DUAL/99: .4X TO 1X SPX DUAL/199
*NFL SHIELD/99: .4X TO 1X SPX DUAL/199
*SPX PATCH/99: .5X TO 1.2X SPX DUAL/199
*SPX TRIPLE/99: .4X TO 1X SPX DUAL/199
*SPX NEW DUAL/75: .5X TO 1.2X SPX/199
*LOGO X LOGO/75: .5X TO 1.2X SPX DUAL/199
*AFC/NFC TRIPLE/50: .5X TO 1.2X
*NFL PATCH DUAL/50: .5X TO 1.2X
*UNIQUE SHAPE/50: .5X TO 1.2X SPX/199
*FOOTBALL/35: .6X TO 1.5X SPX DUAL/199
*LOGO X LOGO/35: .6X TO 1.5X SPX DUAL/199
*JER.# DUAL/25: .6X TO 1.5X SPX DUAL/199
*SPX TRIP PATCH/25: .8X TO 2X SPX DUAL/199
*POSIT.DUAL/25: .6X TO 1.5X SPX DUAL/199
*AFC/NFC PATCH/15: 1X TO 2.5X DUAL/199
*NFL PATCH TRIPLE/15: 1X TO 2.5X DUAL/199
*UNIQUE SHAPE/15: .8X TO 2X SPX DUAL/199
*NFL SHIELD/5: 1.2X TO 3X SPX DUAL/199
UNPRICED NFL LOGO PATCH #'d TO 1
UNPRICED SPX NEW LOGO TRIPLE #'d TO 1
RMAC Andre Caldwell 2.00 5.00
RMBB Brian Brohm 2.50 6.00
RMCH Chad Henne 2.50 6.00
RMCJ Chris Johnson 6.00 15.00
RMCL Chris Long 2.50 6.00
RMDA Donnie Avery 2.00 5.00
RMDJ DeSean Jackson 5.00 12.00
RMDK Dustin Keller 2.50 6.00
RMDM Darren McFadden 6.00 15.00
RMDT Devin Thomas 2.00 5.00
RMEB Earl Bennett 2.50 6.00
RMED Early Doucet 2.00 5.00
RMER Eddie Royal 2.50 6.00
RMFJ Felix Jones 4.00 10.00
RMFO Matt Forte 4.00 10.00
RMGD Glenn Dorsey 2.50 6.00
RMHD Harry Douglas 2.00 5.00
RMJA Dexter Jackson 2.00 5.00
RMJB John David Booty 2.00 5.00
RMJC Jamaal Charles 4.00 10.00
RMJF Joe Flacco 8.00 20.00
RMJH James Hardy 2.00 5.00
RMJL Jake Long 2.50 6.00
RMJN Jordy Nelson 3.00 8.00
RMJS Jonathan Stewart 5.00 12.00
RMKO Kevin O'Connell 2.00 5.00
RMKS Kevin Smith 2.50 6.00
RMLS Limas Sweed 2.50 6.00
RMMK Malcolm Kelly 2.00 5.00
RMMM Mario Manningham 2.50 6.00
RMMR Matt Ryan 6.00 15.00
RMRM Rashard Mendenhall 5.00 12.00
RMRR Ray Rice 5.00 12.00
RMSI Jerome Simpson 2.50 6.00
RMSS Steve Slaton 2.50 6.00

2008 SPx Signature Supremacy

SSAA Adrian Arrington 3.00 8.00
SSAC Andre Caldwell 3.00 8.00
SSAS Aaron Schobel 4.00 10.00
SSAV Donnie Avery 3.00 8.00
SSBD Bruce Davis 3.00 8.00
SSBM Ben Moffitt 3.00 8.00
SSBS Bob Sanders 25.00 50.00
SSBW Ben Watson 4.00 10.00
SSCC Calais Campbell 3.00 8.00
SSCJ Chris Johnson 15.00 40.00
SSCL Chris Long 4.00 10.00
SSCW Cadillac Williams 6.00 15.00
SSDA Derek Anderson 4.00 10.00
SSDB Dorien Bryant 3.00 8.00
SSDD Dennis Dixon 6.00 15.00
SSDJ Dexter Jackson 3.00 8.00
SSDK Dustin Keller 5.00 12.00
SSDL Donald Lee 5.00 12.00
SSDT Devin Thomas 3.00 8.00
SSES Emmitt Smith 75.00 150.00
SSFD Fred Davis 4.00 10.00
SSFO Matt Forte 15.00 30.00
SSGJ Frank Gore 8.00 20.00
SSHA Mike Hart 4.00 10.00
SSJB Jacob Hester 4.00 10.00
SSJC Jerricho Cotchery 5.00 12.00
SSJF Joe Flacco 20.00 50.00
SSJG Jeff Garcia EXCH
SSJH James Hardy 3.00 8.00
SSJL Jamal Lewis EXCH
SSLH Lavelle Hawkins 2.50 6.00
SSLT LaDainian Tomlinson 15.00 30.00
SSMB Marion Barber 15.00 30.00
SSME Rashard Mendenhall 15.00 40.00
SSMF Matt Flynn 15.00 40.00
SSMH Michael Huff 4.00 10.00
SSMK Malcolm Kelly 3.00 8.00
SSMS Matt Schaub 6.00 15.00
SSPW Patrick Willis 6.00 15.00
SSRR Ray Rice 8.00 20.00
SSSS Steve Slaton 6.00 15.00
SSTB Tom Brady 90.00 150.00
SSTR Tony Romo 40.00 100.00
SSTT Terrell Thomas 3.00 8.00
SSTZ Tom Zbikowski 4.00 10.00
SSWH Philip Wheeler 3.00 8.00
SSWW Wes Welker 15.00 30.00
SSXA Xavier Adibi 2.50 6.00
SSYT Y.A. Tittle 10.00 25.00

2008 SPx Super Scripts Autographs

UNPRICED TRIPLE AU PRINT RUN 20
UNPRICED QUAD AU PRINT RUN 15
UNPRICED SIX AU PRINT RUN 6
UNPRICED EIGHT AU PRINT RUN 8
SSS1 A.J. Hawk 10.00 25.00
SSS2 Aaron Schobel 4.00 10.00
SSS3 Adrian Arrington 3.00 8.00
SSS4 Andre Caldwell 3.00 8.00
SSS5 Patrick Willis 8.00 20.00
SSS6 Kevin O'Connell 3.00 8.00
SSS7 Devin Thomas 3.00 8.00
SSS8 Steve Young 20.00 40.00
SSS9 Dexter Jackson 3.00 8.00
SSS10 Ben Moffitt 2.50 6.00
SSS12 Bruce Davis 3.00 8.00
SSS13 Calais Campbell 3.00 8.00
SSS15 Chad Henne 12.00 30.00
SSS16 Cadillac Williams 5.00 12.00
SSS17 Chris Long 4.00 10.00
SSS18 Derek Anderson 4.00 10.00
SSS19 Derrick Harvey 2.50 6.00
SSS20 Daryl Johnston 12.50 25.00
SSS21 DeMarcus Ware 8.00 20.00
SSS22 Dennis Dixon 5.00 12.00
SSS23 Early Doucet 3.00 8.00
SSS24 Erin Henderson 4.00 10.00
SSS25 Eli Manning 40.00 80.00
SSS26 Fred Davis 4.00 10.00
SSS27 Frank Gore 8.00 20.00
SSS28 Jacob Hester 4.00 10.00
SSS29 James Hardy 3.00 8.00
SSS30 Jacob Tamme 4.00 10.00
SSS31 Joe Flacco 20.00 50.00
SSS32 Joe Namath
SSS33 Jonathan Stewart 6.00 15.00
SSS34 Jordy Nelson 15.00 30.00
SSS35 Keith Rivers 4.00 10.00
SSS36 Kenny Phillips 4.00 10.00
SSS37 Lawrence Jackson 3.00 8.00
SSS38 LaDainian Tomlinson 25.00 50.00
SSS39 Lavelle Hawkins 2.50 6.00
SSS40 Limas Sweed 4.00 10.00
SSS41 Jerome Simpson 4.00 10.00
SSS42 Malcolm Kelly 3.00 8.00
SSS43 Mario Urrutia 2.50 6.00
SSS44 Martin Rucker 3.00 8.00
SSS45 Matt Flynn 15.00 30.00
SSS46 Marc Bulger 5.00 12.00
SSS47 Michael Huff 4.00 10.00
SSS48 Rashard Mendenhall 15.00 40.00
SSS49 Y.A. Tittle 10.00 25.00
SSS50 Xavier Adibi 2.50 6.00
SSS53 Aaron Ross 4.00 10.00
SSS54 Buster Davis 4.00 10.00
SSS55 Quentin Groves 3.00 8.00
SSS57 Mike Hart 5.00 12.00
SSS58 Antoine Cason 4.00 10.00
SSS59 Peyton Hillis 12.00 30.00

2008 SPx Super Scripts Autographs Dual

STATED PRINT RUN 75-99
SSD1 A.J. Hawk
Ernie Sims
SSD2 Sam Baker 5.00 12.00
Jake Long
SSD3 Matt Schaub 8.00 20.00
Derek Anderson
SSD4 Chad Henne 20.00 50.00
Mike Hart
SSD5 Joe Flacco 25.00 50.00
Matt Schaub
SSD6 Ahmad Bradshaw 20.00 50.00
Felix Jones
SSD7 Calais Campbell/99 4.00 10.00
Bruce Davis
SSD8 Cadillac Williams 25.00 50.00
Chris Johnson
SSD9 Aqib Talib
Mike Jenkins
SSD10 Sedrick Ellis 6.00 15.00
Lawrence Jackson
SSD11 David Garrard 20.00 50.00
Joe Flacco
SSD12 Devin Thomas 12.00 30.00
DeSean Jackson
SSD13 James Hardy 12.50 25.00
Jordy Nelson
SSD14 Matt Forte 20.00 40.00
Earl Bennett
SSD15 Frank Gore 8.00 20.00
Jerious Norwood
SSD16 Glenn Dorsey 8.00 20.00
Jacob Hester
SSD17 Brodie Croyle 10.00 25.00
DJ Hall
SSD18 John David Booty 4.00 10.00
Fred Davis
SSD19 Jason Campbell 12.50 25.00
Andre Woodson
SSD20 Leodis McKelvin 5.00 12.00
Dwight Lowery
SSD21 Colt Brennan 8.00 20.00
Davone Bess
SSD22 Steve Slaton 8.00 20.00
Alex Brink
SSD23 John David Booty/99 4.00 10.00
Sedrick Ellis
SSD24 Jonathan Stewart 20.00 50.00
Marion Barber
SSD25 Joseph Addai 8.00 20.00
Steve Slaton
SSD26 Antoine Cason 5.00 12.00
Mike Jenkins
SSD27 Kenny Phillips
Mel Blount
SSD28 Rashard Mendenhall 25.00 50.00
Matt Forte
SSD29 Limas Sweed 5.00 12.00
Darrell Jackson
SSD30 DeMarcus Ware 8.00 20.00
Dan Connor
SSD31 Malcolm Kelly 10.00 25.00
DeSean Jackson
SSD32 Marc Bulger 8.00 20.00
Erik Ainge
SSD33 Adrian Arrington 5.00 12.00
Chad Henne
SSD34 Devin Thomas 8.00 20.00
Jerricho Cotchery
SSD35 Dan Connor 8.00 20.00
Justin King
SSD36 Chris Johnson 30.00 80.00
Felix Jones
SSD37 Antoine Cason 5.00 12.00
Jack Ikegwuonu
SSD38 Wes Welker 125.00 250.00
Tom Brady
SSD39 Kevin Boss 8.00 20.00
Martin Rucker
SSD40 Josh Johnson 10.00 25.00
Dennis Dixon

2008 SPx Super Scripts Autographs Triple

SUPER SCRIPTS TRIPLE AU PRINT RUN 20
SST2 Chris Long 20.00 40.00
Glenn Dorsey
Lawrence Jackson
SST3 Derek Anderson 25.00 50.00
Marc Bulger
Colt Brennan
SST6 Frank Gore 50.00 100.00
Kevin Smith
Chris Johnson
SST8 Joe Flacco 60.00 120.00
Ben Roethlisberger
David Garrard
SST10 LaDainian Tomlinson 125.00 200.00
Gale Sayers
Barry Sanders
SST11 Marc Bulger 40.00 80.00
Matt Schaub
Eli Manning
SST12 Marion Barber 50.00 100.00
Tony Romo
Tashard Choice
SST14 Ray Rice 40.00 80.00
Darren McFadden
Rashard Mendenhall
SST15 Sedrick Ellis 20.00 40.00
Terrell Thomas
John David Booty
SST16 Andre Woodson 40.00 80.00
Joe Flacco
Kevin O'Connell
SST18 Matt Ryan 60.00 120.00
Brian Brohm
Chad Henne
SST20 DeMarcus Ware 40.00 80.00
Dan Connor
Dick Butkus

2008 SPx Winning Combos 99

STATED PRINT RUN 99 SER.#'d SETS
*COMBOS/49: .5X TO 1.2X COMBO/99
*COMBOS/25: .6X TO 1.5X COMBO/99
*COMBOS/5: 1.2X TO 3X COMBO/99
*COMBOS PATCH/15: 1X TO 2.5X COMBO/99
WC1 DeMarcus Ware 3.00 8.00
A.J. Hawk
WC2 Adrian Peterson 8.00 20.00
Chris Johnson
WC3 Brodie Croyle 5.00 12.00
Glenn Dorsey
WC4 Bob Sanders 3.00 8.00
Asante Samuel
WC5 Derek Anderson 3.00 8.00
Kevin O'Connell
WC6 Tony Gonzalez 3.00 8.00
Ben Watson
WC7 Deion Sanders 6.00 15.00
Bob Sanders
WC8 Jay Cutler 5.00 12.00
Brandon Marshall
WC9 Braylon Edwards 5.00 12.00
Mario Manningham
WC10 Edgerrin James 4.00 10.00
Anquan Boldin
WC11 Dan Marino 10.00 25.00
Brian Brohm
WC12 Donovan McNabb 5.00 12.00
Brian Westbrook
WC13 Calvin Johnson 4.00 10.00
Limas Sweed
WC14 Ben Roethlisberger 6.00 15.00
Chad Henne
WC15 Champ Bailey 5.00 12.00
Mario Manningham
WC16 Marvin Harrison 4.00 10.00
Reggie Wayne
WC17 Clinton Portis 3.00 8.00
Devin Thomas
WC18 Franco Harris 10.00 25.00
Bo Jackson
WC19 Peyton Manning 6.00 15.00
Dallas Clark
WC20 Darrell Jackson 2.50 6.00
Chester Taylor
WC21 Barry Sanders 15.00 40.00
Darren McFadden
WC22 Matt Hasselbeck 3.00 8.00
Deion Branch
WC23 Fred Taylor 3.00 8.00
David Garrard
WC24 Michael Clayton 4.00 10.00
Earl Bennett
WC25 DeAngelo Williams 3.00 8.00
DeShaun Foster
WC26 Ray Lewis 4.00 10.00
Shawne Merriman
WC27 Larry Fitzgerald 5.00 12.00
DeSean Jackson
WC28 Brian Urlacher 6.00 15.00
Devin Hester
WC29 Steve Smith 4.00 10.00
Eddie Royal
WC30 Antonio Gates 4.00 10.00
Darren Sproles
WC31 Drew Brees 5.00 12.00
Reggie Bush
WC32 Edgerrin James 4.00 10.00
Willis McGahee
WC33 Emmitt Smith 10.00 25.00
Fred Taylor
WC34 Jeremy Shockey 4.00 10.00
Dustin Keller
WC35 JaMarcus Russell 5.00 12.00
Glenn Dorsey
WC36 Greg Jennings 4.00 10.00
Early Doucet
WC37 Marques Colston 3.00 8.00
Dwayne Bowe
WC38 Bernard Berrian 3.00 8.00
Greg Olsen
WC39 Hines Ward 5.00 12.00
Santonio Holmes
WC40 Chris Cooley 5.00 12.00
Jason Campbell
WC41 Jason Witten 5.00 12.00
Heath Miller
WC42 Jeff Garcia 3.00 8.00
Joey Galloway
WC43 Michael Strahan 3.00 8.00
Jeremy Shockey
WC44 Fred Taylor 3.00 8.00
Frank Gore
WC45 Joey Galloway 3.00 8.00
Malcolm Kelly
WC46 Roy Williams 4.00 10.00
Calvin Johnson
WC47 Jonathan Stewart 6.00 15.00
Rashard Mendenhall
WC48 Dwayne Bowe 5.00 12.00
Jordy Nelson
WC49 Joseph Addai 4.00 10.00
Kevin Smith
WC50 Kellen Winslow Jr. 4.00 10.00
Jeremy Shockey
WC51 Aaron Schobel 3.00 8.00
Julius Peppers
WC52 Dre Bly 4.00 10.00
Champ Bailey
WC53 Jerome Simpson 4.00 10.00
Dexter Jackson
WC54 Roy Williams 3.00 8.00
Ernie Sims
WC55 Brett Favre 12.00 30.00
Aaron Rodgers
WC56 LaDainian Tomlinson 8.00 20.00
Gale Sayers
WC57 LaDainian Tomlinson 4.00 10.00
Kevin Smith
WC58 Larry Johnson 5.00 12.00
Jonathan Stewart
WC59 LenDale White 6.00 15.00
Felix Jones
WC60 Lofa Tatupu 3.00 8.00
Antonio Pierce
WC61 Vincent Jackson 3.00 8.00
Malcolm Kelly
WC62 Chad Pennington 3.00 8.00
Marc Bulger
WC63 Trent Edwards 4.00 10.00
Marshawn Lynch
WC64 Brandon Jacobs 6.00 15.00
Matt Forte
WC65 Anquan Boldin 4.00 10.00
Matt Leinart
WC66 Carson Palmer 8.00 20.00
Matt Ryan
WC67 Michael Strahan 5.00 12.00
Dwight Freeney
WC68 Steve Slaton 4.00 10.00
Maurice Jones-Drew
WC69 Glenn Dorsey 4.00 10.00
Jake Long
WC70 Eli Manning 5.00 12.00
Philip Rivers
WC71 Plaxico Burress 5.00 12.00
Eli Manning
WC72 Plaxico Burress 3.00 8.00
Brandon Jacobs
WC73 Cadillac Williams 5.00 12.00
Rashard Mendenhall
WC74 Peyton Manning 8.00 20.00
Reggie Wayne
WC75 Ronald Curry 3.00 8.00
Kirk Morrison
WC76 Tiki Barber 2.50 6.00
Ronde Barber
WC77 Ronnie Brown 3.00 8.00
Cadillac Williams
WC78 Rudi Johnson 3.00 8.00
Chad Johnson
WC79 Greg Jones 5.00 12.00
Ryan Grant
WC80 Shaun Alexander 3.00 8.00
Matt Hasselbeck
WC81 Steve Young 5.00 12.00
Steve McNair
WC82 Cedric Benson 4.00 10.00
Steve Slaton
WC83 Brian Westbrook 4.00 10.00
Steven Jackson
WC84 Terry Glenn 5.00 12.00
Terrell Owens
WC85 Vincent Jackson 4.00 10.00
Darren Sproles
WC86 John Elway 10.00 25.00
Tom Brady
WC87 Randy Moss 10.00 25.00
Tom Brady
WC88 Brodie Croyle 4.00 10.00
Tony Gonzalez
WC89 Tony Romo 8.00 20.00
Matt Ryan
WC90 Torry Holt 4.00 10.00
Isaac Bruce
WC91 Troy Polamalu 6.00 15.00
John David Booty
WC92 Fran Tarkenton 4.00 10.00
Sidney Rice
WC93 Frank Gore 3.00 8.00
Vernon Davis
WC94 Vince Young 5.00 12.00
Glenn Dorsey
WC95 Walter Payton 12.00 30.00
Cedric Benson
WC96 Michael Jenkins 3.00 8.00
Warrick Dunn
WC97 Wes Welker 4.00 10.00
Laurence Maroney
WC98 Willie Parker 5.00 12.00
Ray Rice
WC99 Ray Lewis 4.00 10.00
Willis McGahee
WC100 Jason Taylor 3.00 8.00
Ronnie Brown

2008 SPx Winning Materials SPX 149

SPX STATED PRINT RUN 149
*AFC/NFC/5: 1.2X TO 3X SPX/149
*AFC/NFC DUAL/75: .4X TO 1X SPX/149
*AFC/NFC DUAL PAT/25: .8X TO 2X SPX/149
*FOOTBALLS/39: .5X TO 1.2X SPX/149
*JERSEY #/75: .4X TO 1X SPX/149
*JSY # DUAL/25: .6X TO 1.5X SPX/149
*NFL/99: .4X TO 1X SPX/149
*NFL DUAL/50: .5X TO 1.2X SPX/149
*NFL PATCH/25: .8X TO 2X SPX/149
*SPX PATCH/50: .5X TO 1.2X SPX/149
*SPX DUAL/99: .4X TO 1X SPX/149
*SPX DUAL PAT/15: 1.2X TO 3X SPX/149
*TEAM LOGO/25: .6X TO 1.5X SPX/149
*UD LOGOS/99: .4X TO 1X SPX/149
*UNIQUE SHAPE/50: .5X TO 1.2X SPX/149
UNPRICED FOOTBALL SHAPE DUAL #'d TO 1
WMAB Anquan Boldin 2.50 6.00
WMAC Andre Caldwell 2.00 5.00
WMAH A.J. Hawk 2.50 6.00
WMAN Derek Anderson 2.00 5.00
WMAP Adrian Peterson 5.00 12.00
WMAS Aaron Schobel 2.00 5.00
WMBA Brandon Jacobs 2.50 6.00
WMBB Brian Brohm 2.50 6.00
WMBC Brodie Croyle 2.50 6.00
WMBE Braylon Edwards 2.50 6.00
WMBF Brett Favre 8.00 20.00
WMBJ Bo Jackson 5.00 12.00
WMBO Dwayne Bowe 2.50 6.00
WMBQ Brady Quinn 2.50 6.00
WMBR Ben Roethlisberger 3.00 8.00
WMBS Bob Sanders 2.50 6.00
WMBU Marc Bulger 2.50 6.00
WMBW Brian Westbrook 2.50 6.00
WMBZ Brian Bosworth 4.00 10.00
WMCA Jason Campbell 2.50 6.00
WMCB Champ Bailey 2.50 6.00
WMCH Chad Henne 2.50 6.00
WMCJ Calvin Johnson 3.00 8.00
WMCO Chris Johnson 6.00 15.00
WMCP Clinton Portis 2.50 6.00
WMCU Jay Cutler 3.00 8.00
WMCW Cadillac Williams 2.50 6.00
WMDA Donnie Avery 2.00 5.00
WMDE Dexter Jackson 2.00 5.00
WMDG David Garrard 2.50 6.00
WMDH Devin Hester 3.00 8.00
WMDJ DeSean Jackson 5.00 12.00
WMDK Dustin Keller 2.50 6.00
WMDL Donald Lee 2.50 6.00
WMDM Darren McFadden 6.00 15.00
WMDR Darrell Jackson 2.00 5.00
WMDT Devin Thomas 2.00 5.00
WMDW DeMarcus Ware 2.50 6.00
WMEB Earl Bennett 2.50 6.00
WMED Early Doucet 2.00 5.00
WMEM Eli Manning 3.00 8.00
WMER Ed Reed 2.50 6.00
WMES Ernie Sims 2.00 5.00
WMFG Frank Gore 2.50 6.00
WMFJ Felix Jones 4.00 10.00
WMFO Matt Forte 4.00 10.00
WMGD Glenn Dorsey 2.50 6.00
WMGJ Greg Jennings 3.00 8.00
WMGO Tony Gonzalez 2.50 6.00
WMGS Gale Sayers 5.00 12.00
WMHD Harry Douglas 2.00 5.00
WMJA Joseph Addai 2.50 6.00
WMJB John David Booty 2.00 5.00
WMJC Jamaal Charles 4.00 10.00
WMJE Jerricho Cotchery 2.50 6.00
WMJF Joe Flacco 8.00 20.00
WMJH James Hardy 2.00 5.00
WMJL Jake Long 2.50 6.00
WMJN Jordy Nelson 3.00 8.00
WMJO Chad Johnson 2.50 6.00
WMJR JaMarcus Russell 2.50 6.00
WMJS Jonathan Stewart 5.00 12.00
WMKO Kevin O'Connell 2.00 5.00
WMKS Kevin Smith 2.50 6.00
WMLE Matt Leinart 3.00 8.00
WMLJ Larry Johnson 2.50 6.00
WMLS Limas Sweed 2.50 6.00
WMLT LaDainian Tomlinson 3.00 8.00
WMMB Marion Barber 2.50 6.00
WMMC Mark Clayton 2.50 6.00
WMME Rashard Mendenhall 5.00 12.00
WMMK Malcolm Kelly 2.00 5.00
WMML Marshawn Lynch 2.50 6.00
WMMM Mario Manningham 2.50 6.00
WMMR Matt Ryan 6.00 15.00
WMMS Matt Schaub 2.50 6.00
WMMV Mike Vrabel 2.00 5.00
WMNO Jerious Norwood 2.50 6.00
WMPM Peyton Manning 5.00 12.00
WMPR Philip Rivers 3.00 8.00
WMPW Patrick Willis 2.50 6.00
WMRC Roger Craig 3.00 8.00
WMRM Randy Moss 3.00 8.00
WMRO Eddie Royal 2.50 6.00
WMRR Ray Rice 5.00 12.00
WMRW Roy Williams WR 2.50 6.00
WMSA Asante Samuel 2.00 5.00
WMSH Jeremy Shockey 2.50 6.00
WMSI Jerome Simpson 2.50 6.00
WMSS Steve Slaton 2.50 6.00
WMTO Tom Brady 5.00 12.00
WMTP Troy Polamalu 4.00 10.00
WMTR Tony Romo 4.00 10.00
WMVY Vince Young 2.50 6.00
WMWA Ben Watson 2.00 5.00
WMWH Michael Huff 2.00 5.00
WMWP Willie Parker 2.50 6.00
WMWW1 Wes Welker 3.00 8.00
WMWW2 Wes Welker 3.00 8.00

2008 SPx Winning Materials Autographs SPX Triple

UNPRICED AUTO PRINT RUN 10

2008 SPx Winning Trios Autographs

UNPRICED TRIO AU PRINT RUN 10

2008 SPx Winning Trios 99

UNPRICED TRIO AU PRINT RUN 10
*TRIOS/49: .5X TO 1.2X TRIOS/99
*TRIOS/25: .6X TO 1.5X TRIOS/99
*TRIOS/5: 1.2X TO 3X TRIOS/99
*TRIOS PATCH/5: 1.5X TO 4X TRIOS/99
WT1 Gale Sayers 10.00 25.00
Adrian Peterson
Rashard Mendenhall
WT2 Marc Bulger 10.00 25.00
Chad Henne
Kevin O'Connell
WT3 DeSean Jackson 6.00 15.00
Jerome Simpson
Dexter Jackson
WT4 Clinton Portis 6.00 15.00
Ben Roethlisberger
DeSean Jackson
WT5 Clinton Portis 6.00 15.00
Jason Campbell
Malcolm Kelly
WT6 Brian Brohm 8.00 20.00
Chad Henne
Matt Ryan
WT7 Eddie Royal 4.00 10.00
Jerome Simpson
Dexter Jackson
WT8 Limas Sweed 5.00 12.00
Jordy Nelson
Devin Thomas
WT9 Chad Johnson 4.00 10.00
Darrell Jackson
Derek Anderson
WT10 Barry Sanders 20.00 50.00
LaDainian Tomlinson
Darren McFadden
WT11 Derek Anderson 4.00 10.00
Brady Quinn
Brian Brohm
WT12 DeSean Jackson 6.00 15.00
Early Doucet
Dexter Jackson
WT13 Cadillac Williams 10.00 25.00
Chris Johnson
Emmitt Smith
WT14 Derek Anderson 8.00 20.00
Braylon Edwards
Jonathan Stewart
WT15 Herschel Walker 10.00 25.00
Jonathan Stewart
Matt Forte
WT16 LaDainian Tomlinson 10.00 25.00
Adrian Peterson
Jamaal Charles
WT17 JaMarcus Russell 10.00 25.00
Joe Flacco
Matt Ryan
WT18 Jeremy Shockey 4.00 10.00
Kellen Winslow Sr.
Dustin Keller
WT19 Frank Gore 6.00 15.00
Jerious Norwood
Steve Slaton
WT20 Marc Bulger 8.00 20.00
Joe Flacco
Kevin O'Connell
WT21 Felix Jones 8.00 20.00
Joe Flacco
Jordy Nelson
WT22 Marshawn Lynch 8.00 20.00
Jonathan Stewart
Matt Forte
WT23 Andre Caldwell 4.00 10.00
Jerome Simpson
Dexter Jackson
WT24 Darren McFadden 12.00 30.00
Jake Long
Matt Ryan
WT25 Ernie Sims 4.00 10.00
Kevin Smith
Roy Williams
WT26 Felix Jones 12.00 30.00
Chris Johnson
Kevin Smith
WT27 Tony Romo 15.00 40.00
Marion Barber
Terrell Owens
WT28 Mark Clayton 8.00 20.00
Brodie Croyle
Matt Forte
WT29 Jerious Norwood 6.00 15.00
Marshawn Lynch
Chris Johnson
WT30 Brian Brohm 3.00 8.00
John David Booty
Kevin O'Connell
WT31 Matt Schaub 15.00 40.00
Matt Ryan
Ken Anderson
WT32 Chad Henne 6.00 15.00
Jake Long
Mario Manningham
WT33 Peyton Manning 10.00 25.00
Matt Schaub
Joe Flacco
WT34 Eli Manning 8.00 20.00
Ben Roethlisberger
Philip Rivers
WT35 Ray Rice 8.00 20.00
Steve Slaton
Kevin Smith
WT36 Brett Favre 20.00 50.00
Peyton Manning
Tom Brady
WT37 Kevin O'Connell 6.00 15.00
Ben Watson
Wes Welker
WT38 Larry Johnson 5.00 12.00
Brodie Croyle
Jamaal Charles
WT39 Eli Manning 10.00 25.00
Brian Brohm
Tony Romo
WT40 Ben Roethlisberger 10.00 25.00
Limas Sweed
Rashard Mendenhall
WT41 Ray Rice 8.00 20.00
Rashard Mendenhall
Kevin Smith
WT42 Jerricho Cotchery 6.00 15.00
Wes Welker
Earl Bennett

2009 SPx

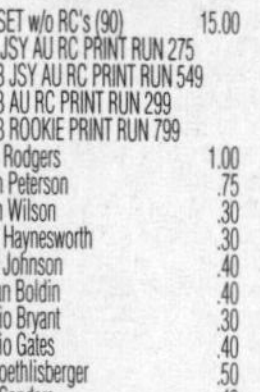

COMP.SET w/o RC's (90) 15.00 40.00
91-100 JSY AU RC PRINT RUN 275
101-123 JSY AU RC PRINT RUN 549
124-163 AU RC PRINT RUN 299
164-223 ROOKIE PRINT RUN 799
1 Aaron Rodgers 1.00 2.50
2 Adrian Peterson .75 2.00
3 Adrian Wilson .30 .75
4 Albert Haynesworth .30 .75
5 Andre Johnson .40 1.00
6 Anquan Boldin .40 1.00
7 Antonio Bryant .30 .75
8 Antonio Gates .40 1.00
9 Ben Roethlisberger .50 1.25
10 Bob Sanders .40 1.00
11 Brady Quinn .40 1.00
12 Brandon Jacobs .40 1.00
13 Brandon Marshall .40 1.00
14 Braylon Edwards .40 1.00
15 Brian Westbrook .40 1.00
16 Calvin Johnson .50 1.25
17 Carson Palmer .50 1.25
18 Chad Pennington .40 1.00
19 Charles Woodson .50 1.25
20 Chris Johnson .50 1.25
21 Clinton Portis .40 1.00
22 Darren McFadden .50 1.25
23 Darren Sproles .40 1.00
24 David Garrard .40 1.00
25 DeAngelo Williams .50 1.25
26 DeMarcus Ware .40 1.00
27 DeSean Jackson .40 1.00
28 Donnie Avery .40 1.00
29 Donovan McNabb .50 1.25
30 Drew Brees .50 1.25
31 Dwayne Bowe .40 1.00
32 Ed Reed .40 1.00
33 Eddie Royal .40 1.00
34 Eli Manning .50 1.25
35 Frank Gore .40 1.00
36 Greg Jennings .50 1.25
37 Hines Ward .40 1.00
38 Jake Delhomme .40 1.00
39 Jamal Lewis .40 1.00
40 James Farrior .30 .75
41 James Harrison .50 1.25
42 Jason Witten .50 1.25

43 Jay Cutler .50 1.25
44 Joe Flacco .50 1.25
45 Joey Porter .40 1.00
46 Jonathan Stewart .40 1.00
47 Julius Peppers .40 1.00
48 Justin Tuck .40 1.00
49 Kevin Smith .40 1.00
50 Kevin Williams .30 .75
51 Kurt Warner .50 1.25
52 LaDainian Tomlinson .50 1.25
53 Lance Briggs .40 1.00
54 Lance Moore .40 1.00
55 Larry Fitzgerald .50 1.25
56 Lee Evans .40 1.00
57 Le'Ron McClain .40 1.00
58 Mario Williams .40 1.00
59 Marion Barber .40 1.00
60 Marshawn Lynch .40 1.00
61 Matt Cassel .40 1.00
62 Matt Forte .50 1.25
63 Matt Ryan .50 1.25
64 Matt Schaub .40 1.00
65 Maurice Jones-Drew .40 1.00
66 Michael Turner .40 1.00
67 Nnamdi Asomugha .40 1.00
68 Patrick Willis .40 1.00
69 Peyton Manning .75 2.00
70 Philip Rivers .50 1.25
71 Randy Moss .50 1.25
72 Ray Lewis .50 1.25
73 Reggie Wayne .40 1.00
74 Roddy White .40 1.00
75 Ronde Barber .30 .75
76 Ronnie Brown .40 1.00
77 Ryan Grant .40 1.00
78 Santana Moss .40 1.00
79 Steve Slaton .40 1.00
80 Steve Smith .40 1.00
81 Steven Jackson .40 1.00
82 T.J. Houshmandzadeh .40 1.00
83 Terrell Owens .50 1.25
84 Thomas Jones .40 1.00
85 Tom Brady .75 2.00
86 Tony Gonzalez .40 1.00
87 Tony Romo .75 2.00
88 Troy Polamalu .50 1.25
89 Walter Jones .40 1.00
90 Wes Welker .50 1.25
91 Matthew Stafford JSY AU/275 RC 75.00 135.00
92 Michael Crabtree JSY AU/275 RC 20.00 50.00
93 Mark Sanchez JSY AU/275 RC 30.00 80.00
94 Chris Wells JSY AU/275 RC 15.00 40.00
95 Knowshon Moreno JSY AU/275 RC 10.00 25.00
96 Donald Brown JSY AU/275 RC 10.00 25.00
97 Josh Freeman JSY AU/275 RC 25.00 60.00
98 Darrius Heyward-Bey JSY AU/275 RC 10.00 25.00
99 Jeremy Maclin JSY AU/275 RC 15.00 40.00
100 Pat White JSY AU/275 RC 10.00 25.00
101 Brian Robiskie JSY AU RC 8.00 20.00
102 Aaron Curry JSY AU/546 RC 8.00 20.00
103 Derrick Williams JSY AU RC 6.00 15.00
104 LeSean McCoy JSY AU RC 20.00 40.00
105 Stephen McGee JSY AU RC 8.00 20.00
106 Rhett Bomar JSY AU RC 6.00 15.00
107 Ramses Barden JSY AU RC 5.00 12.00
108 Javon Ringer JSY AU RC 8.00 20.00
109 Andre Brown JSY AU RC 5.00 12.00
110 Juaquin Iglesias JSY AU RC 6.00 15.00
111 Patrick Turner JSY AU RC 5.00 12.00
112 Tyson Jackson JSY AU RC 6.00 15.00
113 Nate Davis JSY AU RC 6.00 15.00
114 Glen Coffee JSY AU RC 6.00 15.00
115 Percy Harvin JSY AU RC 12.00 30.00
116 Mohamed Massaquoi JSY AU RC 6.00 15.00
117 Shonn Greene JSY AU RC 15.00 40.00
118 Mike Thomas JSY AU RC 8.00 20.00
119 Kenny Britt JSY AU RC 10.00 25.00
120 Mike Wallace JSY AU RC 20.00 40.00
121 Brandon Pettigrew JSY AU RC 8.00 20.00
122 Hakeem Nicks JSY AU RC 15.00 30.00
123 Jason Smith JSY AU RC 6.00 15.00
124 Brian Orakpo AU RC 6.00 15.00
125 Frank Summers AU RC 6.00 15.00
126 Tom Brandstater AU RC 6.00 15.00
127 Gartrell Johnson AU RC 4.00 10.00
128 Eugene Monroe AU RC 6.00 15.00
129 B.J. Raji AU RC 10.00 20.00
130 Vontae Davis AU RC 6.00 15.00
131 Mike Goodson AU RC 6.00 15.00
132 Clay Matthews AU RC 40.00 80.00
133 Michael Johnson AU RC 4.00 10.00
134 Peria Jerry AU RC 5.00 12.00
135 Brian Cushing AU RC 8.00 20.00
136 Brandon Tate AU RC 6.00 15.00
137 Louis Delmas AU RC 6.00 15.00
138 Malcolm Jenkins AU RC 6.00 15.00
139 Cedric Peerman AU RC 5.00 12.00
140 Bear Pascoe AU RC 5.00 12.00
141 Curtis Painter AU RC 6.00 15.00
142 James Laurinaitis AU RC 6.00 15.00
143 Travis Beckum AU RC 5.00 12.00
144 Clint Sintim AU RC 5.00 12.00
145 Patrick Chung AU RC 6.00 15.00
146 Marko Mitchell AU RC 5.00 12.00
147 Austin Collie AU RC 8.00 20.00
148 Chase Coffman AU RC 5.00 12.00
149 Andre Smith AU RC 5.00 12.00
150 Demetrius Byrd AU RC 5.00 12.00
151 Deon Butler AU RC 5.00 12.00
152 Alphonso Smith AU RC 5.00 12.00
153 Brandon Gibson AU RC 6.00 15.00
154 Brian Hartline AU RC 10.00 20.00
155 James Davis AU RC 6.00 15.00
156 Alex Mack AU RC 5.00 12.00
157 Rey Maualuga AU RC 8.00 20.00
158 Jarett Dillard AU RC 6.00 15.00
159 Robert Ayers AU RC 8.00 20.00
160 Jared Cook AU RC 6.00 15.00
161 Brooks Foster AU RC 4.00 10.00
162 Larry English AU RC 6.00 15.00
163 Rashad Jennings AU RC 6.00 15.00
164 Aaron Brown RC 2.50 6.00
165 Connor Barwin RC 2.50 6.00
166 Evander Hood RC 3.00 8.00
167 David Veikune RC 2.00 5.00
168 Bernard Scott RC 2.50 6.00
169 Darcel McBath RC 2.00 5.00
170 Keith Null RC 2.00 5.00
171 Andy Levitre RC 2.00 5.00
172 Louis Murphy RC 2.50 6.00
173 Eric Wood RC 2.00 5.00
174 Freddie Brown RC 2.00 5.00
175 Cody Brown RC 1.50 4.00
176 Kenny McKinley RC 2.50 6.00
177 Paul Kruger RC 2.00 5.00
178 Johnny Knox RC 4.00 10.00
179 Sebastian Vollmer RC 2.00 5.00
180 Shawn Nelson RC 2.00 5.00
181 Jairus Byrd RC 2.50 6.00
182 Anthony Hill RC 1.50 4.00
183 Eben Britton RC 2.00 5.00
184 Max Unger RC 2.00 5.00
185 Ron Brace RC 2.00 5.00
186 Mike Teel RC 2.50 6.00
187 Sherrod Martin RC 2.00 5.00
188 Fili Moala RC 2.00 5.00
189 Aaron Maybin RC 2.00 5.00
190 Chris Ogbonnaya RC 2.00 5.00
191 Louis Vasquez RC 2.00 5.00
192 Javarris Williams RC 2.00 5.00
193 D.J. Moore RC 2.00 5.00
194 Sean Smith RC 2.50 6.00
195 Brandon Williams RC 2.50 6.00
196 William Beatty RC 1.50 4.00
197 Fui Vakapuna RC 2.00 5.00
198 David Bruton RC 2.00 5.00
199 Quinn Johnson RC 2.00 5.00
200 Kraig Urbik RC 2.00 5.00
201 LaRod Stephens-Howling RC 6.00 12.00
202 Tony Fiammetta RC 2.00 5.00
203 William Moore RC 2.50 6.00
204 Eddie Williams RC 2.00 5.00
205 Manuel Johnson RC 2.50 6.00
206 Tiquan Underwood RC 2.00 5.00
207 Marlon Lucky RC 2.00 5.00
208 Julian Edelman RC 6.00 15.00
209 Dominique Edison RC 1.50 4.00
210 Michael Oher RC 4.00 10.00
211 Sen'Derrick Marks RC 1.50 4.00
212 Mike Mitchell RC 2.00 5.00
213 DeAndre Levy RC 2.50 6.00
214 Sammie Stroughter RC 2.50 6.00
215 Derek Kinder RC 1.50 4.00
216 Richard Quinn RC 2.00 5.00
217 Kaluka Maiava RC 2.50 6.00
218 Keenan Lewis RC 2.50 6.00
219 Kyle Moore RC 2.00 5.00
220 Victor Butler RC 2.00 5.00
221 Everette Brown RC 2.50 6.00
222 Phil Loadholt RC 2.00 5.00
223 Darius Butler RC 2.50 6.00

2009 SPx Rookies Silver

*RK JSY AU 91-99: 1X TO 2.5X JSY AU/275
*RK JSY AU 101-123: 1.2X TO 3X JSY AU/549
91-123 JSY AU PRINT RUN 25
*ROOK AU 124-163: .5X TO 1.2X AU/299
124-163 ROOKIE AU PRINT RUN 99
*ROOKIE 164-223: .5X TO 1.2X RC/799
164-223 ROOKIE PRINT RUN 399
91 Matthew Stafford JSY AU 300.00 500.00
93 Mark Sanchez JSY AU 200.00 400.00

2009 SPx Rookies Gold Holofoil

*ROOK AU 124-163: .6X TO 1.5X AU/299
*ROOKIE 164-223: 1X TO 2.5X RC/799
124-163 ROOKIE AU PRINT RUN 25

2009 SPx Rookie Materials

STATED PRINT RUN 249 SER.#'d SETS
*DUAL PATCH/99: .8X TO 2X BASIC JSY/299
*GOLD DUAL/99: .6X TO 1.5X BASIC JSY/299
*GREEN DUAL/149: .5X TO 1.2X BASIC JSY/299
RMAB Andre Brown 1.25 3.00
RMAC Aaron Curry 2.00 5.00
RMBO Rhett Bomar 1.50 4.00
RMBP Brandon Pettigrew 2.00 5.00
RMBR Brian Robiskie 2.00 5.00
RMCW Chris Wells 3.00 8.00
RMDB Donald Brown 2.00 5.00
RMDH Darrius Heyward-Bey 2.00 5.00
RMDW Derrick Williams 1.50 4.00
RMGC Glen Coffee 1.50 4.00
RMHN Hakeem Nicks 3.00 8.00
RMJF Josh Freeman 4.00 10.00
RMJI Juaquin Iglesias 1.50 4.00
RMJM Jeremy Maclin 3.00 8.00
RMJR Javon Ringer 2.00 5.00
RMJS Jason Smith 1.50 4.00
RMKB Kenny Britt 2.50 6.00
RMKM Knowshon Moreno 3.00 8.00
RMLM LeSean McCoy 4.00 10.00
RMMC Michael Crabtree 4.00 10.00
RMMM Mohamed Massaquoi 1.50 4.00
RMMS Mark Sanchez 6.00 15.00
RMMT Mike Thomas 2.00 5.00
RMMW Mike Wallace 4.00 10.00
RMND Nate Davis 1.50 4.00
RMPH Percy Harvin 3.00 8.00
RMPT Patrick Turner 1.25 3.00
RMPW Pat White 2.00 5.00
RMRB Ramses Barden 1.25 3.00
RMSG Shonn Greene 2.50 6.00
RMSM Stephen McGee 2.00 5.00
RMST Matthew Stafford 6.00 15.00
RMTJ Tyson Jackson 1.50 4.00

2009 SPx Rookie Materials Autographs

STATED PRINT RUN 25-50
RMAB Andre Brown 6.00 15.00
RMAC Aaron Curry 10.00 25.00
RMBO Rhett Bomar 8.00 20.00
RMBP Brandon Pettigrew 10.00 25.00
RMBR Brian Robiskie 10.00 25.00
RMCW Chris Wells 15.00 40.00
RMDB Donald Brown 10.00 25.00
RMDH Darrius Heyward-Bey 10.00 25.00
RMDW Derrick Williams 8.00 20.00
RMGC Glen Coffee 8.00 20.00
RMHN Hakeem Nicks 15.00 40.00
RMJF Josh Freeman 30.00 80.00
RMJI Juaquin Iglesias 8.00 20.00
RMJM Jeremy Maclin 15.00 40.00
RMJR Javon Ringer 10.00 25.00
RMJS Jason Smith 8.00 20.00
RMKB Kenny Britt 12.00 30.00
RMKM Knowshon Moreno 15.00 40.00
RMLM LeSean McCoy 30.00 60.00
RMMC Michael Crabtree 30.00 60.00
RMMM Mohamed Massaquoi 8.00 20.00
RMMS Mark Sanchez/25 75.00 150.00
RMMT Mike Thomas 10.00 25.00
RMMW Mike Wallace 25.00 60.00
RMND Nate Davis
RMPH Percy Harvin 30.00 80.00
RMPT Patrick Turner 8.00 20.00
RMPW Pat White 10.00 25.00
RMRB Ramses Barden 6.00 15.00
RMSG Shonn Greene 15.00 40.00
RMSM Stephen McGee 10.00 25.00
RMST Matthew Stafford/25 100.00 200.00
RMTJ Tyson Jackson 8.00 20.00

2009 SPx Shadow Box

ANNOUNCED PRINT RUN 10-100
ANNC'D PRINT RUN OF 10 NOT PRICED
SAJ Andre Johnson/50* 10.00 25.00
SAM Archie Manning/50* 15.00 40.00
SAP Adrian Peterson/10*
SBF Brett Favre/10*
SBR Ben Roethlisberger/10*
SBS Barry Sanders/10*
SBW Brian Westbrook/50* 10.00 25.00
SCJ Chris Johnson/100* 15.00 40.00
SCW Chris Wells/25* 15.00 40.00
SDB Donald Brown/25* 20.00 50.00
SDG Darrell Green/75* 10.00 25.00
SDH Devin Hester/75* 12.00 30.00
SDJ Daryl Johnston/75*
SDW DeAngelo Williams/75* 10.00 25.00
SEM Eli Manning/10*
SER Ed Reed/100* 15.00 40.00
SGJ Greg Jennings/100* 10.00 25.00
SGS Gale Sayers/25* 15.00 40.00
SJF Joe Flacco/25* 20.00 50.00
SJH James Harrison/100* 12.00 30.00
SJO Calvin Johnson/25* 15.00 40.00
SJR Jerry Rice/10*
SJS Jonathan Stewart/75* 10.00 25.00
SJV Javon Ringer/25*
SKM Knowshon Moreno/25* 30.00 60.00
SKS Kevin Smith/100* 8.00 20.00
SKW Kurt Warner/10*
SLF Larry Fitzgerald/25* 20.00 50.00
SMC Michael Crabtree/10*
SMR Matt Ryan/10*
SMS Mike Singletary/50* 15.00 40.00
SMT Michael Turner/75* 8.00 20.00
SPM Peyton Manning/10*
SRA Tom Rathman/100* 12.00 30.00
SRC Roger Craig/100* 10.00 25.00
SSI Billy Sims/100* 10.00 25.00
SSS Steve Slaton/100* 12.00 30.00
SST Matthew Stafford/10*
SSZ Mark Sanchez/10*
STB Tom Brady/10*
STP Troy Polamalu/100* 15.00 40.00
STR Tony Romo/10*
STT Thurman Thomas 15.00 40.00

2009 SPx Shadow Box Autographs

COMMON CARD 25.00 50.00
UNLISTED STARS 30.00 60.00
SBW Brian Westbrook 30.00 60.00
SCJ Chris Johnson 40.00 80.00
SDB Donald Brown 50.00 100.00
SDG Darrell Green 30.00 60.00
SGJ Greg Jennings 25.00 50.00
SJS Jonathan Stewart 30.00 60.00
SJV Javon Ringer 40.00 80.00
SKM Knowshon Moreno 125.00 200.00
SKS Kevin Smith 20.00 50.00
SMT Michael Turner 25.00 50.00
SRC Roger Craig 25.00 50.00
SSS Steve Slaton 25.00 50.00

2009 SPx Super Scripts Autographs

SAB Anquan Boldin 7.50 15.00
SAC Adam Carriker 3.00 8.00
SAS Alex Smith QB 8.00 20.00
SBC Brent Celek 7.50 15.00
SBE Braylon Edwards
SBM Brandon Marshall 7.50 15.00
SBR Thomas Brown 3.00 8.00
SCB Colt Brennan 5.00 12.00
SCH Chad Henne 5.00 12.00
SCJ Chris Johnson 10.00 20.00
SCL Chris Long 4.00 10.00
SCR Alge Crumpler 3.00 8.00
SCS Chansi Stuckey 3.00 8.00
SDB Dwayne Bowe 5.00 12.00
SDK Dustin Keller 3.00 8.00
SDL Donald Lee 3.00 8.00
SDR Dominique Rodgers-Cromartie 3.00 8.00
SDR Darrelle Revis 8.00 20.00
SDW Darius Walker 3.00 8.00
SEM Eli Manning 40.00 80.00
SEW Eric Weddle 3.00 8.00
SFG Frank Gore 7.50 15.00
SHM Heath Miller 7.50 15.00
SHO Chris Houston 3.00 8.00
SJA Joseph Addai 5.00 12.00
SJD Jake Delhomme 7.50 15.00
SJF Joe Flacco 15.00 30.00
SJJ James Jones 3.00 8.00
SJN Jordy Nelson 7.50 15.00
SJO Larry Johnson 7.50 15.00
SJS Jonathan Stewart
SJU Julius Jones 6.00 15.00
SKR Kevin Boss 5.00 12.00
SKP Kenny Phillips 3.00 8.00
SKS Kevin Smith 4.00 10.00
SLB Lance Ball 3.00 8.00
SLJ Lawrence Jackson 3.00 8.00
SLL LaRon Landry 7.50 15.00
SLM Leodis McKelvin 3.00 8.00
SMC Le'Ron McClain 5.00 12.00
SMM Mario Manningham 7.50 15.00
SPW Patrick Willis 5.00 12.00
SRB Reggie Brown 3.00 8.00
SRC Ryan Clady 3.00 8.00
SRW Reggie Wayne 7.50 15.00
STH Tyler Thigpen 3.00 8.00
STT Terrell Thomas 3.00 8.00
SVJ Vincent Jackson 4.00 10.00
SVY Vince Young
SWI DeAngelo Williams

2009 SPx Super Scripts Autographs Dual

DUAL STATED PRINT RUN 25-99
DAR Eddie Royal 8.00 20.00
Donnie Avery
DBF Matt Flynn 25.00 50.00
Brian Brohm
DBJ Steve Breaston 6.00 15.00
James Jones
DBW Deon Butler 15.00 30.00
Mike Wallace
DCF Joe Flacco 20.00 40.00
Mark Clayton
DCJ David Clowney 5.00 12.00
James Jones
DCS David Clowney 5.00 12.00
Chansi Stuckey
DDB Thomas Brown 6.00 15.00
Harry Douglas
DDH Lavelle Hawkins/99 5.00 12.00
Chris Davis
DDJ James Jones 20.00 35.00
Donald Driver
DFF Matt Flynn 40.00 80.00
Jermichael Finley
DFR Joe Flacco/25 50.00 100.00
Matt Ryan
DFS Matt Forte/25 20.00 40.00
Steve Slaton
DGB Mike Goodson/99 8.00 20.00
Andre Brown
DJB Brandon Jacobs/25 15.00 40.00
Marion Barber
DJC Scott Chandler 6.00 15.00
Vincent Jackson
DJD Malcolm Jenkins 6.00 15.00
Vontae Davis
DJH Korey Hall/45 8.00 20.00
Brandon Jackson
DJM Felix Jones 20.00 40.00
Rashard Mendenhall
DJS Chris Johnson 12.00 30.00
Kevin Smith
DJT Tyler Thigpen 8.00 20.00
Larry Johnson
DKP Korey Hall 25.00 50.00
Peyton Hillis
DLM Le'Ron McClain 10.00 25.00
Marshawn Lynch
DMA Adrian Arrington 8.00 20.00
Mario Manningham
DMB Stephen McGee 6.00 15.00
Rhett Bomar
DMF Joe Flacco 20.00 40.00
Le'Ron McClain
DMH Matt Spaeth 15.00 30.00
Heath Miller
DMS Eugene Monroe 6.00 15.00
Jason Smith
DNB Thomas Brown 6.00 15.00
Jerious Norwood
DOC Scott Chandler 6.00 15.00
Greg Olsen
DPH Allen Patrick/99 6.00 15.00
Paul Hubbard
DRD Roy Hall 5.00 12.00
Dante Hughes
DRR Matt Ryan/25 50.00 100.00
JaMarcus Russell
DRT Ryan Torain 8.00 20.00
Eddie Royal
DSM Darren McFadden/25 10.00 25.00
Jonathan Stewart
DTB Thomas Brown/99 6.00 15.00
Ryan Torain
DTC Tyler Thigpen 10.00 25.00
Jamaal Charles
DTH Ryan Torain 25.00 50.00
Peyton Hillis
DWT Derrick Williams 15.00 40.00
Brandon Tate
DYT Ryan Torain 6.00 15.00
Selvin Young

2009 SPx Super Scripts Autographs Triple

TRIPLE STATED PRINT RUN 10-25
TOL Eugene Monroe 20.00 40.00
Jason Smith
Andre Smith
TARI Anquan Boldin 20.00 40.00
Matt Leinart
Steve Breaston
TDEF DeMarcus Ware 30.00 60.00
Patrick Willis
Darrelle Revis
TOSU Malcolm Jenkins 20.00 50.00
Chris Wells
James Laurinaitis
TQB1 Matt Ryan 50.00 120.00
Joe Flacco
Colt Brennan
TTB1 Steve Slaton 30.00 60.00
Matt Forte
Chris Johnson
TRB2 Jonathan Stewart 20.00 40.00
Kevin Smith
Darren McFadden
TRBT Le'Ron McClain 20.00 40.00
Jonathan Stewart
Marshawn Lynch
TRBY DeAngelo Williams 20.00 40.00
Brandon Jacobs
Frank Gore
TREC Wes Welker 30.00 60.00
Brandon Marshall
T.J. Houshmandzadeh
TRET Quintin Demps 10.00 25.00
Steve Breaston
Jacoby Jones
TRLB Brian Cushing 40.00 80.00
Aaron Curry
Clay Matthews
TRQB Matthew Stafford 100.00 200.00
Mark Sanchez
Josh Freeman
TRRB Chris Wells 30.00 80.00
Knowshon Moreno
LeSean McCoy
TRTD Martellus Bennett 15.00 30.00
James Hardy
Dustin Keller
TRWR Michael Crabtree 60.00 120.00
Jeremy Maclin
Percy Harvin
TWR1 Eddie Royal 15.00 30.00
Donnie Avery
Jordy Nelson
TWR2 Keenan Burton 10.00 25.00
Josh Morgan
Donnie Avery

2009 SPx Winning Combos

STATED PRINT RUN 99 SER.#'d SETS
*GOLD/35: .5X TO 1.2X BASIC COMBOS
*GREEN/59: .5X TO 1.2X BASIC INSERTS
*PATCH/25: .8X TO 2X BASIC JSY
AR Donnie Avery 4.00 10.00
Eddie Royal
AW Brady Quinn 4.00 10.00
Derek Anderson
BR Tom Brady 8.00 20.00
Ben Roethlisberger
CH Michael Crabtree 5.00 12.00
Darrius Heyward-Bey
CJ Aaron Curry 2.50 6.00
Tyson Jackson
EA John Elway 12.00 30.00
Troy Aikman
FJ Calvin Johnson 5.00 12.00
Larry Fitzgerald
FR Matt Ryan 8.00 20.00
Joe Flacco
FW Josh Freeman 5.00 12.00
Pat White
JJ Greg Jennings 5.00 12.00
DeSean Jackson
JL Jeremy Maclin 4.00 10.00
LeSean McCoy
JS Kevin Smith 5.00 12.00
Felix Jones
LK Donald Lee 3.00 8.00
Dustin Keller
MM Darren McFadden 5.00 12.00
Rashard Mendenhall
MP Carson Palmer 5.00 12.00
Donovan McNabb
MR Aaron Rodgers 10.00 25.00
Eli Manning
MW Knowshon Moreno 4.00 10.00
Chris Wells
NB Hakeem Nicks 5.00 12.00
Ramses Barden
PP Adrian Peterson 8.00 20.00
Clinton Portis
RM Brian Robiskie 4.00 10.00
Mohamed Massaquoi
SG Mark Sanchez 10.00 25.00
Shonn Greene
SJ Chris Johnson 5.00 12.00
Steve Slaton
SP Matthew Stafford 8.00 20.00
Brandon Pettigrew
SS Matthew Stafford 12.00 30.00
Mark Sanchez
WF Matt Forte 5.00 12.00
Brian Westbrook
WH Charles Woodson 5.00 12.00
A.J. Hawk
WO Terrell Owens 5.00 12.00
Hines Ward
WS Jonathan Stewart 5.00 12.00
DeAngelo Williams

2009 SPx Fantastic Foursome

STATED PRINT RUN 20 SER.#'d SETS
QBS Jay Cutler 12.00 30.00
Drew Brees
Tony Romo
Matt Schaub
RBS Marshawn Lynch 8.00 20.00
Frank Gore
Jamal Lewis
Reggie Bush
RQB Matthew Stafford 25.00 60.00
Mark Sanchez
Josh Freeman
Stephen McGee
RRB Knowshon Moreno 10.00 25.00
Donald Brown
Chris Wells
LeSean McCoy
RWR Darrius Heyward-Bey 8.00 20.00
Michael Crabtree
Jeremy Maclin
Percy Harvin
WRS T.J. Houshmandzadeh 8.00 20.00
Marques Colston
Lee Evans
Devin Hester
EAGL Donovan McNabb 8.00 20.00
Brian Westbrook
DeSean Jackson
Kevin Kolb
FISH Ronnie Brown 5.00 12.00
Chad Henne
Pat White
Chad Pennington
GNTS Antonio Pierce 8.00 20.00
Eli Manning
Lawrence Taylor
Phil Simms
PATS Tom Brady 12.00 30.00
Randy Moss
Wes Welker
Ben Watson
PTHR DeAngelo Williams 8.00 20.00
Jonathan Stewart
Julius Peppers
Steve Smith
RAVN Joe Flacco 8.00 20.00
Ray Rice
Mark Clayton
Willis McGahee
STLR Ben Roethlisberger 8.00 20.00
Hines Ward
Troy Polamalu
Santonio Holmes
TITN Chris Johnson 10.00 25.00
LenDale White
Vince Young
Kenny Britt
VIKN Adrian Peterson 12.00 30.00
Sidney Rice
Tarvaris Jackson
John David Booty

2009 SPx Winning Materials

STATED PRINT RUN 65-349
*BLUE DUAL/50: .6X TO 1.5X BASIC JSY
*BRONZE DUAL/99: .5X TO 1.2X BASIC JSY
*BRONZE DUAL/24: .8X TO 2X BASIC JSY
*GREEN DUAL/149: .5X TO 1.2X BASIC JSY
*PATCH/99: .6X TO 1.5X BASIC JSY
*PATCH/35: .8X TO 2X BASIC JSY
*PATCH PLAT/15-25: 1X TO 2.5X BASIC JSY
WAC Aaron Curry/349 2.00 5.00
WAJ Andre Johnson/99 3.00 8.00
WAK Aaron Kampman/99 5.00 12.00
WAN Derek Anderson/159 2.50 6.00
WAP Antonio Pierce/249 3.00 8.00
WAV Donnie Avery/249 3.00 8.00
WBA Marion Barber/149 3.00 8.00
WBR Tom Brady/249 6.00 15.00
WBS Barry Sanders/249 8.00 20.00
WBU Deon Butler/349 1.50 4.00
WCC Chris Cooley/249 3.00 8.00
WCD Craig Davis/249 2.50 6.00
WCH Jamaal Charles/349 4.00 10.00
WCJ Calvin Johnson/349 4.00 10.00
WCO Jerricho Cotchery/249 3.00 8.00
WCP Carson Palmer/249 4.00 10.00
WCR Michael Crabtree/349 4.00 10.00
WCW Charles Woodson/249 4.00 10.00
WDA Daryl Johnston/249 6.00 15.00
WDB Drew Brees/249 4.00 10.00
WDE Derrick Brooks/249 3.00 8.00
WDG David Garrard/249 3.00 8.00
WDH Devin Hester/249 4.00 10.00
WDJ DeSean Jackson/349 3.00 8.00
WDK Dustin Keller/249 2.50 6.00
WDM Donovan McNabb/249 4.00 10.00
WDO Donald Brown/349 2.00 5.00
WDW DeAngelo Williams/249 4.00 10.00
WEC Earl Campbell/249 4.00 10.00
WEJ Edgerrin James/349 3.00 8.00
WEM Eli Manning/249 4.00 10.00
WER Eddie Royal/349 3.00 8.00
WES Ernie Sims/249 2.50 6.00
WFG Frank Gore/349 3.00 8.00
WFH Franco Harris/249 6.00 15.00
WFJ Felix Jones/349 4.00 10.00
WFT Fred Taylor/175 3.00 8.00
WGD Glenn Dorsey/249 2.50 6.00
WGJ Greg Jennings/249 3.00 8.00
WHE Chad Henne/349 3.00 8.00
WHW Hines Ward/125 5.00 12.00
WIB Isaac Bruce/249 3.00 8.00
WIE Brian Robiskie/349 2.00 5.00
WJC Jay Cutler/349 4.00 10.00
WJE John Elway/249 8.00 20.00
WJF Joe Flacco/349 4.00 10.00
WJK Jim Kelly/249 5.00 12.00
WJL Jamal Lewis/249 3.00 8.00
WJN Joe Namath/249 6.00 15.00
WJO Chris Johnson/349 4.00 10.00
WJP Julius Peppers/125 3.00 8.00
WJR Jerry Rice/249 8.00 20.00
WJS Jonathan Stewart/349 3.00 8.00
WJT Joe Theismann/249 5.00 12.00
WJW Jason Witten/225 4.00 10.00
WKM Knowshon Moreno/349 2.00 5.00
WKS Kevin Smith/349 3.00 8.00
WKW Kellen Winslow Jr./249 3.00 8.00
WLE Lee Evans/349 3.00 8.00
WLF Larry Fitzgerald/249 4.00 10.00
WLT Lawrence Taylor/249 6.00 15.00
WMB Marc Bulger/249 3.00 8.00
WMC Darren McFadden/349 4.00 10.00
WME Rashard Mendenhall/349 3.00 8.00
WMF Matt Forte/349 4.00 10.00
WMH Marvin Harrison/249 4.00 10.00
WML Marshawn Lynch/349 3.00 8.00
WMO Merlin Olsen/249 4.00 10.00
WMR Matt Ryan/349 4.00 10.00
WMS Mike Singletary/249 5.00 12.00
WMV Mike Vrabel/249 3.00 8.00
WNE Jordy Nelson/249 4.00 10.00
WOA Ottis Anderson/249 4.00 10.00
WPB Plaxico Burress/349 3.00 8.00
WPE Adrian Peterson/349 6.00 15.00
WPM Peyton Manning/249 6.00 15.00
WPS Phil Simms/249 4.00 10.00
WPW Patrick Willis/349 3.00 8.00
WRA Ray Lewis/249 4.00 10.00
WRB Ronnie Brown/349 3.00 8.00
WRC Roger Craig/249 4.00 10.00
WRL Ronnie Lott/249 5.00 12.00
WRM Randy Moss/249 4.00 10.00
WRO Ben Roethlisberger/249 4.00 10.00
WSA Mark Sanchez/349 6.00 15.00
WSC Matt Schaub/249 3.00 8.00
WSH Santonio Holmes/249 3.00 8.00
WSI Billy Sims/249 4.00 10.00
WSL Steve Largent/249 5.00 12.00
WSS Steve Slaton/349 3.00 8.00
WST Matthew Stafford/349 6.00 15.00
WTB Terry Bradshaw/249 6.00 15.00
WTH T.J. Houshmandzadeh/249 3.00 8.00
WLW LenDale White/65 4.00 10.00
WVJ Vincent Jackson/249 3.00 8.00
WWA Javon Walker/249 2.50 6.00
WWE Chris Wells/349 3.00 8.00
WWI Kellen Winslow Sr./249 4.00 10.00

2009 SPx Winning Trios

STATED PRINT RUN 50 SER.#'d SETS
*GREEN/15: .6X TO 1.5X BASIC TRIO/50
*PATCH/25: .6X TO 1.5X BASIC TRIO/50
ARI Larry Fitzgerald 6.00 15.00
Anquan Boldin
Kurt Warner
BAL Joe Flacco 6.00 15.00
Ray Lewis
Ed Reed
DB1 Ed Reed 10.00 25.00
Troy Polamalu
Charles Woodson
PHI Donovan McNabb 10.00 25.00
Brian Westbrook
DeSean Jackson
PIT Ben Roethlisberger 6.00 15.00
Willie Parker
Santonio Holmes
QB1 Peyton Manning 10.00 25.00
Drew Brees
Kurt Warner
RC1 Aaron Curry 4.00 10.00
Tyson Jackson
Jason Smith
RCR Percy Harvin 6.00 15.00
Brandon Pettigrew
Hakeem Nicks
REC Brandon Marshall 5.00 12.00
Anquan Boldin
T.J. Houshmandzadeh
RQB Matthew Stafford 15.00 40.00
Mark Sanchez
Josh Freeman
RRB Knowshon Moreno 6.00 15.00
Chris Wells
Donald Brown
RWR Michael Crabtree 6.00 15.00
Darrius Heyward-Bey
Jeremy Maclin
SQB Eli Manning 20.00 50.00
Peyton Manning
Aaron Rodgers
WR1 Andre Johnson 6.00 15.00
Larry Fitzgerald
Calvin Johnson
YRD Calvin Johnson 6.00 15.00
Greg Jennings
Reggie Wayne

2009 SPx X-Factor Autographs

XAA Aundrae Allison 3.00 8.00
XAS Anthony Spencer 3.00 8.00
XAV Donnie Avery 4.00 10.00
XBA Sam Baker 3.00 8.00
XBB Brian Brohm 3.00 8.00
XBD Buster Davis 3.00 8.00
XBU Keenan Burton 3.00 8.00
XCD Craig Davis 3.00 8.00
XCH Chris Henry RB 3.00 8.00
XCJ Calvin Johnson 15.00 40.00
XCT Courtney Taylor 3.00 8.00
XDA Chris Davis 3.00 8.00
XDB Drew Bennett 3.00 8.00
XDC David Clowney 3.00 8.00
XDI David Irons 3.00 8.00
XDJ DeSean Jackson 7.50 15.00
XDM Darren McFadden 7.50 20.00
XDR Dante Rosario 3.00 8.00
XDS Drew Stanton 3.00 8.00
XJA Chevis Jackson 3.00 8.00
XJB John David Booty 4.00 10.00
XJF Justin Forsett 3.00 8.00
XJJ Josh Johnson 3.00 8.00
XJK Jordan Kent 3.00 8.00
XJO Jacoby Jones 3.00 8.00
XJS Jerome Simpson 3.00 8.00
XJT Jacob Tamme 3.00 8.00
XKB Kentwan Balmer 3.00 8.00
XKH Korey Hall 3.00 8.00
XKW Kelley Washington 3.00 8.00
XLH Lavelle Hawkins 3.00 8.00
XLR Laurent Robinson 3.00 8.00
XMF Matt Flynn 6.00 15.00
XMK Malcolm Kelly 3.00 8.00
XMM Matt Moore 4.00 10.00
XMR Matt Ryan 25.00 50.00
XMS Matt Spaeth 3.00 8.00
XPH Paul Hubbard 3.00 8.00
XQD Quintin Demps 3.00 8.00
XQG Quintin Groves 3.00 8.00
XQM Quentin Moses 3.00 8.00
XRB Reggie Bush 10.00 25.00
XRM Rashard Mendenhall 7.50 20.00
XRT Ryan Torain 3.00 8.00
XSB Steve Breaston 4.00 10.00
XSJ Steven Jackson 7.50 15.00
XSS Steve Smith USC 7.50 15.00
XSY Selvin Young 3.00 8.00

2010 SPx

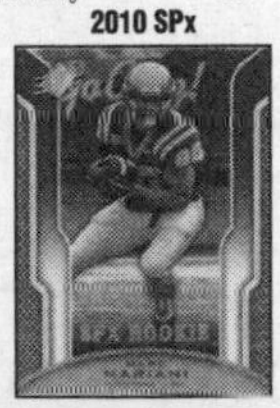

COMP.SET w/o RC's (100) 8.00 20.00
101-112 ROOK.JSY AU PRINT RUN 99
113-135 ROOK.JSY AU PRINT RUN 375
136-184 ROOKIE AU PRINT RUN 140
186-234 ROOKIE PRINT RUN 599
UNPRICED ROOK.PATCH AU GOLD #'d TO 1
UNPRICED ROOK.PATCH AU SLVR #'d TO 10
1 Devin Hester .40 1.00
2 Aaron Rodgers .75 2.00
3 Vincent Jackson .25 .60
4 Larry Fitzgerald .40 1.00
5 Jeremy Maclin .30 .75
6 Adrian Peterson .60 1.50
7 Jamaal Charles .30 .75
8 Matt Forte .30 .75
9 Calvin Johnson .40 1.00
10 Philip Rivers .40 1.00
11 Matt Cassel .30 .75
12 Mario Manningham .30 .75
13 Kyle Orton .30 .75
14 Joseph Addai .30 .75
15 Jay Cutler .40 1.00
16 Percy Harvin .40 1.00
17 Jason Witten .40 1.00
18 Thomas Jones .30 .75
19 Tony Romo .50 1.25
20 Chad Henne .30 .75
21 Pierre Thomas .30 .75
22 Carson Palmer .30 .75
23 Cadillac Williams .30 .75
24 Andre Johnson .30 .75
25 Roddy White .30 .75
26 Rashard Mendenhall .30 .75
27 Brady Quinn .30 .75
28 Ryan Grant .30 .75
29 Drew Brees .40 1.00
30 Sidney Rice .30 .75
31 Matthew Stafford .40 1.00
32 Ricky Williams .30 .75
33 DeSean Jackson .30 .75
34 Cedric Benson .30 .75
35 Lee Evans .30 .75
36 Santana Moss .30 .75
37 Steven Jackson .30 .75
38 Matt Hasselbeck .25 .60
39 Darren McFadden .30 .75
40 Ben Roethlisberger .40 1.00
41 Steve Smith USC .30 .75
42 Chad Johnson .30 .75
43 Brent Celek .30 .75
44 Vince Young .25 .60
45 Shonn Greene .30 .75
46 Ray Rice .30 .75
47 Wes Welker .40 1.00
48 Dallas Clark .30 .75
49 Josh Freeman .40 1.00
50 Miles Austin .40 1.00
51 Michael Crabtree .40 1.00
52 Marion Barber .30 .75
53 DeAngelo Williams .30 .75
54 Chris Wells .30 .75
55 Brett Favre 1.00 2.50
56 Mike Sims-Walker .30 .75
57 Frank Gore .30 .75
58 Jerricho Cotchery .30 .75
59 Felix Jones .30 .75
60 Michael Turner .25 .60
61 Peyton Manning .60 1.50
62 Patrick Willis .30 .75
63 Joe Flacco .40 1.00
64 Anquan Boldin .30 .75
65 Santonio Holmes .30 .75
66 Knowshon Moreno .40 1.00
67 Hines Ward .30 .75
68 Kevin Kolb .30 .75
69 Vernon Davis .30 .75
70 LaDainian Tomlinson .40 1.00
71 David Garrard .30 .75
72 Maurice Jones-Drew .30 .75
73 Randy Moss .40 1.00
74 Matt Leinart .30 .75
75 Troy Polamalu .40 1.00
76 Matt Moore .30 .75
77 Jonathan Stewart .30 .75
78 Matt Ryan .40 1.00
79 Donovan McNabb .40 1.00
80 Eli Manning .40 1.00
81 Greg Jennings .30 .75
82 Brandon Marshall .30 .75
83 Jerome Harrison .25 .60
84 Reggie Wayne .30 .75
85 Ronnie Brown .30 .75
86 Tom Brady .60 1.50
87 Jason Campbell .30 .75
88 Matt Schaub .30 .75
89 Braylon Edwards .30 .75
90 Brandon Jacobs .30 .75
91 Marques Colston .30 .75
92 Mark Sanchez .40 1.00
93 Chris Johnson .40 1.00
94 Alex Smith QB .30 .75
95 Steve Johnson .30 .75
96 T.J. Houshmandzadeh .30 .75
97 Mike Wallace .30 .75
98 Kellen Winslow .30 .75
99 Clinton Portis .30 .75
100 Terrell Owens .40 1.00
101 Sam Bradford JSY AU RC 250.00 400.00
102 Tim Tebow JSY AU RC 200.00 400.00
103 C.J. Spiller JSY AU RC 40.00 80.00
104 Ryan Mathews JSY AU RC 40.00 80.00
105 Jahvid Best JSY AU RC 20.00 50.00
106 Jimmy Clausen JSY AU RC 20.00 50.00
107 Colt McCoy JSY AU RC 50.00 120.00
108 Demaryius Thomas JSY AU RC 20.00 40.00
109 Dez Bryant JSY AU RC 60.00 120.00

110 Ndamukong Suh JSY AU RC 60.00 120.00
111 Brandon LaFell JSY AU RC 12.00 30.00
112 Gerald McCoy JSY AU RC 12.00 30.00
113 Dexter McCluster JSY AU RC 8.00 20.00
114 Arrelious Benn JSY AU RC 10.00 25.00
115 Toby Gerhart JSY AU RC 8.00 20.00
116 Eric Berry JSY AU RC 20.00 40.00
117 Rolando McClain JSY AU RC 8.00 20.00
118 Jermaine Gresham JSY AU RC 10.00 25.00
119 Ben Tate JSY AU RC 12.50 25.00
120 Montario Hardesty JSY AU RC 15.00 30.00
121 Rob Gronkowski JSY AU RC 35.00 60.00
122 Golden Tate JSY AU RC 8.00 20.00
123 Mike Kafka JSY AU RC 6.00 15.00
124 Damian Williams JSY AU RC 8.00 20.00
125 Emmanuel Sanders JSY AU RC 8.00 20.00
126 Jordan Shipley JSY AU RC 8.00 20.00
127 Eric Decker JSY AU RC 10.00 25.00
128 Andre Roberts JSY AU RC 12.00 30.00
129 Armanti Edwards JSY AU RC 8.00 20.00
130 Taylor Price JSY AU RC 8.00 20.00
131 Mardy Gilyard JSY AU RC 8.00 20.00
132 Mike Williams JSY AU RC 20.00 40.00
133 Marcus Easley JSY AU RC 6.00 15.00
134 Joe McKnight JSY AU RC 8.00 20.00
135 Jonathan Dwyer JSY AU RC 8.00 20.00
136 Carlos Dunlap AU RC 8.00 20.00
137 Russell Okung AU RC 8.00 20.00
138 Tyson Alualu AU RC 6.00 15.00
139 Brandon Graham AU RC 10.00 25.00
140 Earl Thomas AU RC 8.00 20.00
141 Jason Pierre-Paul AU RC 12.00 30.00
142 Derrick Morgan AU RC 6.00 15.00
143 Bryan Bulaga AU RC 8.00 20.00
144 Sean Weatherspoon AU RC 8.00 20.00
145 Kareem Jackson AU RC 8.00 20.00
146 Dan Williams AU RC 10.00 25.00
147 Jermaine Cunningham AU RC 15.00 30.00
148 Jared Odrick AU RC 12.50 25.00
149 Sean Lee AU RC 12.50 25.00
150 Jerry Hughes AU RC 8.00 20.00
151 Sergio Kindle AU RC 8.00 20.00
152 Taylor Mays AU RC 8.00 20.00
153 Rennie Curran AU RC 6.00 15.00
154 Brandon Spikes AU RC 8.00 20.00
155 John Skelton AU RC 12.00 30.00
156 Jonathan Crompton AU RC 6.00 15.00
157 Dan LeFevour AU RC 8.00 20.00
158 Joe Webb AU RC 15.00 30.00
159 Tony Pike AU RC 8.00 20.00
160 Sean Canfield AU RC 6.00 15.00
161 Zac Robinson AU RC 6.00 15.00
162 Trent Williams AU RC 8.00 20.00
163 Ed Dickson AU RC 8.00 20.00
164 NaVorro Bowman AU RC 8.00 20.00
165 Koa Misi AU RC 8.00 20.00
166 Jarrett Brown AU RC 6.00 15.00
167 James Starks AU RC 15.00 40.00
168 Charles Scott AU RC 6.00 15.00
169 LeGarrette Blount AU RC 30.00 60.00
170 Brian Price AU RC 8.00 20.00
171 Stafon Johnson AU RC 8.00 20.00
173 Jacoby Ford AU RC 10.00 25.00
174 David Reed AU RC 6.00 15.00
175 Riley Cooper AU RC 8.00 20.00
176 Kerry Meier AU RC 10.00 25.00
177 Carlton Mitchell AU RC 6.00 15.00
178 Dezmon Briscoe AU RC 8.00 20.00
179 Antonio Brown AU RC 15.00 30.00
180 Patrick Robinson AU RC 8.00 20.00
181 Rusty Smith AU RC 12.00 30.00
182 Levi Brown AU RC 6.00 15.00
183 Anthony Dixon AU RC 8.00 20.00
184 Aaron Hernandez AU RC 12.00 30.00
186 Andrew Quarless RC 2.50 6.00
187 Donald Butler RC 1.50 4.00
188 Anthony Davis RC 2.00 5.00
189 Mike Iupati RC 2.50 6.00
190 Maurkice Pouncey RC 2.50 6.00
191 Rodger Saffold RC 1.50 4.00
192 Chris Cook RC 2.50 6.00
193 Phillip Dillard RC 1.50 4.00
194 Nate Allen RC 2.50 6.00
195 T.J. Ward RC 2.50 6.00
196 Tony Moeaki RC 2.50 6.00
197 Victor Cruz RC 12.50 25.00
198 Lamarr Houston RC 2.50 6.00
199 Linval Joseph RC 2.00 5.00
200 Daryl Washington RC 2.00 5.00
201 Javier Arenas RC 2.50 6.00
202 Jason Worilds RC 2.50 6.00
203 Devin McCourty RC 2.50 6.00
204 Jevan Snead RC 2.50 6.00
205 Mike Neal RC 2.50 6.00
206 Clay Harbor RC 2.50 6.00
207 Pat Angerer RC 4.00 10.00
208 Charles Brown RC 2.00 5.00
209 Terrence Cody RC 2.00 5.00
210 Corey Wootton RC 2.00 5.00
211 Kyle Wilson RC 2.50 6.00
212 Everson Griffen RC 2.50 6.00
213 Darryl Sharpton RC 1.50 4.00
214 Perry Riley RC 2.50 6.00
215 Dennis Pitta RC 2.50 6.00
216 Thaddeus Gibson RC 2.00 5.00
217 Garrett Graham RC 2.00 5.00
218 Roddrick Muckelroy RC 2.00 5.00
219 Michael Hoomanawanui RC 2.50 6.00
220 John Conner RC 2.50 6.00
221 Deji Karim RC 2.50 6.00
222 Nate Byham RC 2.00 5.00
223 Anthony McCoy RC 2.00 5.00
224 Trindon Holliday RC 2.50 6.00
225 David Gettis RC 2.50 6.00
226 Kyle Williams RC 2.50 6.00
227 Myron Rolle RC 2.00 5.00
228 Terrence Austin RC 2.00 5.00
229 Marc Mariani RC 2.50 6.00
230 Dorin Dickerson RC 1.50 4.00
231 Jameson Konz RC 2.00 5.00
232 Tim Toone RC 2.00 5.00
233 Major Wright RC 2.50 6.00
234 Daniel Te'o-Nesheim RC 2.00 5.00

2010 SPx Fantastic Foursome Jerseys

STATED PRINT RUN 25 SER.#'d SETS
BBSM Sam Bradford 25.00 50.00
Dez Bryant
C.J. Spiller
Ryan Mathews
BTBT Dez Bryant
Demaryius Thomas
Arrelious Benn
Golden Tate
BTCM Sam Bradford 25.00 60.00
Tim Tebow
Jimmy Clausen
Colt McCoy
MKTM Dan Marino
Jim Kelly
Fran Tarkenton
Warren Moon
MWCB Peyton Manning 25.00 50.00
Reggie Wayne
Dallas Clark
Donald Brown
PTJG Adrian Peterson 15.00 40.00
LaDainian Tomlinson
Chris Johnson
Frank Gore
RBSP Tony Romo 15.00 40.00
Tom Brady
Mark Sanchez
Carson Palmer
RJBB Tony Romo 15.00 30.00
Felix Jones
Marion Barber
Dez Bryant
SMBT C.J. Spiller 8.00 20.00
Ryan Mathews
Jahvid Best
Ben Tate
SWPB Barry Sanders
Ricky Williams
Carson Palmer
Tim Brown

2010 SPx Rookie Materials

STATED PRINT RUN 375 SER.#'d SETS
RMAB Arrelious Benn 3.00 8.00
RMAE Armanti Edwards 2.50 6.00
RMAR Andre Roberts 2.50 6.00
RMBL Brandon LaFell 2.50 6.00
RMBT Ben Tate 3.00 8.00
RMCM Colt McCoy 5.00 12.00
RMCS C.J. Spiller 4.00 10.00
RMDB Dez Bryant 8.00 20.00
RMDM Dexter McCluster 2.50 6.00
RMDT Demaryius Thomas 3.00 8.00
RMDW Damian Williams 2.50 6.00
RMEB Eric Berry 6.00 15.00
RMED Eric Decker 3.00 8.00
RMES Emmanuel Sanders 2.50 6.00
RMGM Gerald McCoy 2.50 6.00
RMGT Golden Tate 2.50 6.00
RMJB Jahvid Best 5.00 12.00
RMJC Jimmy Clausen 2.50 6.00
RMJD Jonathan Dwyer 2.50 6.00
RMJG Jermaine Gresham 3.00 8.00
RMJM Joe McKnight 2.50 6.00
RMJS Jordan Shipley 2.50 6.00
RMMA Ryan Mathews 5.00 12.00
RMME Marcus Easley 2.00 5.00
RMMG Mardy Gilyard 2.50 6.00
RMMH Montario Hardesty 5.00 12.00
RMMK Mike Kafka 2.50 6.00
RMMW Mike Williams 5.00 12.00
RMNS Ndamukong Suh 10.00 25.00
RMRG Rob Gronkowski 6.00 15.00
RMRM Rolando McClain 4.00 10.00
RMSB Sam Bradford 10.00 25.00
RMTG Toby Gerhart 4.00 10.00
RMTP Taylor Price 2.50 6.00
RMTT Tim Tebow 15.00 30.00

2010 SPx Rookie Materials Autographs

STATED PRINT RUN 3-20
RMAB Arrelious Benn/20 15.00 40.00
RMAE Armanti Edwards/20 15.00 40.00
RMAR Andre Roberts/20 15.00 40.00
RMBL Brandon LaFell/20 15.00 40.00
RMBT Ben Tate/20 20.00 50.00
RMCM Colt McCoy/3
RMCS C.J. Spiller/3
RMDM Dexter McCluster/20 15.00 40.00
RMDT Demaryius Thomas/3
RMDW Damian Williams/20 15.00 40.00
RMEB Eric Berry/20 15.00 40.00
RMED Eric Decker/20 20.00 50.00
RMES Emmanuel Sanders/20 15.00 40.00
RMGM Gerald McCoy/20 15.00 40.00
RMGT Golden Tate/20 15.00 40.00
RMJB Jahvid Best/3
RMJC Jimmy Clausen/3
RMJD Jonathan Dwyer/20 15.00 40.00
RMJG Jermaine Gresham/20 20.00 50.00
RMJM Joe McKnight/20 15.00 40.00
RMJS Jordan Shipley/20 15.00 40.00
RMMA Ryan Mathews/3
RMME Marcus Easley/20 12.00 30.00
RMMG Mardy Gilyard/20 15.00 40.00
RMMH Montario Hardesty/20 15.00 40.00
RMMK Mike Kafka/3
RMMW Mike Williams/20
RMNS Ndamukong Suh/3
RMRG Rob Gronkowski/20 40.00 80.00
RMRM Rolando McClain/20 15.00 40.00
RMSB Sam Bradford/3
RMTG Toby Gerhart/20 15.00 40.00
RMTP Taylor Price/20 15.00 40.00
RMTT Tim Tebow/3

2010 SPx Shadow Box

AUTOS TOO SCARCE TO PRICE
SBAB Arrelious Benn 15.00 40.00
SBAM Archie Manning 15.00 40.00
SBAP Adrian Peterson 50.00 100.00
SBAR Aaron Rodgers 40.00 80.00
SBBF Brett Favre 90.00 150.00
SBBL Drew Bledsoe 15.00 40.00
SBBR Drew Brees 40.00 80.00
SBBS Barry Sanders 40.00 80.00
SBBT Ben Tate
SBCM Colt McCoy
SBCP Carson Palmer 15.00 40.00
SBCS C.J. Spiller 30.00 80.00
SBDB Dez Bryant 50.00 100.00
SBDM Dexter McCluster 20.00 50.00
SBDT Demaryius Thomas 20.00 50.00
SBDW Damian Williams 15.00 40.00
SBEC Earl Campbell
SBEM Eli Manning 30.00 60.00
SBFG Frank Gore 15.00 40.00
SBGT Golden Tate 12.00 30.00
SBJB Jahvid Best 30.00 60.00
SBJC Jimmy Clausen 20.00 50.00
SBJD Jonathan Dwyer
SBJM Joe McKnight 15.00 40.00
SBJO Chris Johnson 30.00 60.00
SBJS Jordan Shipley 25.00 60.00
SBLT LaDainian Tomlinson 20.00 50.00
SBMC Donovan McNabb 30.00 60.00
SBMR Matt Ryan 20.00 50.00
SBPM Peyton Manning 50.00 100.00
SBPR Philip Rivers 15.00 40.00
SBRC Randall Cunningham 15.00 40.00
SBRM Ryan Mathews 40.00 80.00
SBSB Sam Bradford 75.00 150.00
SBSI Billy Sims 15.00 40.00
SBTB Tom Brady 40.00 80.00
SBTG Toby Gerhart 15.00 40.00
SBTH Thurman Thomas 20.00 50.00
SBTI Tim Brown 20.00 50.00
SBTR Tony Romo 20.00 50.00
SBTT Tim Tebow 75.00 150.00
SBWM Warren Moon

2010 SPx Super Scripts Autographs

SSAC Austin Collie 8.00 20.00
SSAP Adrian Peterson
SSBC Brent Celek 5.00 12.00
SSBF Brett Favre 125.00 250.00
SSBH Brian Hartline 8.00 20.00
SSBM Brandon Marshall
SSBO Brian Orakpo 6.00 15.00
SSCA Matt Cassel 10.00 25.00
SSCH Chad Henne 5.00 12.00
SSCJ Chad Johnson
SSCM Clay Matthews 20.00 40.00
SSCO Marques Colston
SSDB Drew Brees 50.00 100.00
SSDJ DeSean Jackson
SSDK Dustin Keller 5.00 12.00
SSDR Dominique Rodgers-Cromartie 5.00 12.00
SSDW DeMarcus Ware
SSEM Eli Manning 40.00 80.00
SSFG Frank Gore
SSFJ Felix Jones
SSHM Heath Miller 8.00 20.00
SSJA Joseph Addai 5.00 12.00
SSJC Jason Campbell
SSJF Joe Flacco 20.00 40.00
SSJM Josh Morgan 5.00 12.00
SSKO Kyle Orton 6.00 15.00
SSLC LeSean McCoy 8.00 20.00
SSLE Larry English 5.00 12.00
SSLM Le'Ron McClain 8.00 20.00
SSMA Rey Maualuga 12.50 25.00
SSMC Donovan McNabb
SSMF Matt Forte
SSMJ Maurice Jones-Drew 8.00 20.00
SSMM Mario Manningham 8.00 20.00
SSMO Matt Moore 6.00 15.00
SSMR Matt Ryan
SSMS Mark Sanchez
SSMW Mike Wallace 8.00 20.00
SSNA Nnamdi Asomugha 25.00 50.00
SSOH Michael Oher 15.00 30.00
SSPH Percy Harvin 6.00 15.00
SSPM Peyton Manning 100.00 200.00
SSPW Patrick Willis
SSRM Rashard Mendenhall 8.00 20.00
SSRR Ray Rice 8.00 20.00
SSSB Steve Breaston 5.00 12.00
SSSG Shonn Greene 8.00 20.00
SSTR Tony Romo
SSVJ Vincent Jackson
SSWW Wes Welker 20.00 40.00

2010 SPx Winning Combos Dual Jerseys

STATED PRINT RUN 99 SER.#'d SETS
WCAL A.J. Hawk 4.00 10.00
Lance Briggs
WCBB Fred Biletnikoff 6.00 15.00
Anquan Boldin
WCBH Tom Brady 10.00 25.00
Chad Henne
WCBJ Marion Barber 5.00 12.00
Felix Jones
WCBT Dez Bryant 6.00 15.00
Demaryius Thomas
WCCM Jimmy Clausen 8.00 20.00
Colt McCoy
WCCS Jamaal Charles 5.00 12.00
Jordan Shipley
WCCT Jimmy Clausen 5.00 12.00
Joe Theismann
WCFR Matt Ryan 6.00 15.00
Doug Flutie
WCGJ David Garrard 5.00 12.00
Chris Johnson
WCGS Ndamukong Suh 10.00 25.00
Gerald McCoy
WCHP Paul Hornung 6.00 15.00
Alan Page
WCHW A.J. Hawk 4.00 10.00
DeMarcus Ware
WCMM Matt Ryan 6.00 15.00
Mark Sanchez
WCMS Mark Sanchez 6.00 15.00
Eli Manning
WCPJ Adrian Peterson 8.00 20.00
Chris Johnson
WCQB Sam Bradford 20.00 40.00
Tim Tebow
WCRJ Ryan Mathews 6.00 15.00
Jahvid Best
WCRS Tony Romo 6.00 15.00
Mark Sanchez
WCSM C.J. Spiller 6.00 15.00
Ryan Mathews
WCTB Arrelious Benn 3.00 8.00
Golden Tate
WCTD Demaryius Thomas 6.00 15.00
Jonathan Dwyer
WCTS Fran Tarkenton 8.00 20.00
Matthew Stafford
WCWG Frank Gore 5.00 12.00
Reggie Wayne
WCWM Damian Williams 4.00 10.00
Joe McKnight
WCWO Mario Williams 4.00 10.00
Brian Orakpo

2010 SPx Winning Combos Dual Jerseys Patch

*PATCH/25: .6X TO 1.5X BASIC DUAL/99
PATCH PRINT RUN 25 SER.#'d SETS
WCJW Bo Jackson 12.00 30.00
Cadillac Williams
WCMB Peyton Manning 20.00 50.00
Drew Brees

2010 SPx Winning Materials Patch

STATED PRINT RUN 25-125
WMPAB Anquan Boldin/125 5.00 12.00
WMPAH A.J. Hawk/25
WMPAL Mike Alstott/125 8.00 20.00
WMPAP Adrian Peterson/125 10.00 25.00
WMPAR Aaron Rodgers/125 10.00 25.00
WMPBJ Brandon Jacobs/125 5.00 12.00
WMPBM Brandon Marshall/125 5.00 12.00
WMPBN Donald Brown/125 5.00 12.00
WMPBO Brian Orakpo/125 4.00 10.00
WMPBP Brandon Pettigrew/125 4.00 10.00
WMPBR Ronnie Brown/125 5.00 12.00
WMPBS Barry Sanders/125 12.00 30.00
WMPBU Brian Urlacher/125 6.00 15.00
WMPCA Jason Campbell/125 5.00 12.00
WMPCB Champ Bailey/125 5.00 12.00
WMPCC Chris Cooley/125 8.00 20.00
WMPCH Chad Henne/125 8.00 20.00
WMPCJ Calvin Johnson/125 6.00 15.00
WMPCO Jerricho Cotchery/125 5.00 12.00
WMPCR Michael Crabtree/125 6.00 15.00
WMPCW Cadillac Williams/125 5.00 12.00
WMPDB Drew Brees/25 8.00 20.00
WMPDH Darrius Heyward-Bey/125 5.00 12.00
WMPDJ DeSean Jackson/125 5.00 12.00
WMPDM Dan Marino/125 15.00 40.00
WMPDO Donovan McNabb/125 6.00 15.00
WMPDW DeAngelo Williams/125 5.00 12.00
WMPEM Eli Manning/25 8.00 20.00
WMPFG Frank Gore/125 5.00 12.00
WMPFR Josh Freeman/125 6.00 15.00
WMPHA Albert Haynesworth/125 4.00 10.00
WMPHM Heath Miller/25 6.00 15.00
WMPHN Hakeem Nicks/125 5.00 12.00
WMPJA Jamaal Charles/125 5.00 12.00
WMPJF Joe Flacco/125 6.00 15.00
WMPJM Jeremy Maclin/125 5.00 12.00
WMPJN Chris Johnson/125 6.00 15.00
WMPJO Chad Johnson/125 5.00 12.00
WMPJP Julius Peppers/125 5.00 12.00
WMPJR Jerry Rice/125 10.00 25.00
WMPJS Jonathan Stewart/125 5.00 12.00
WMPJW Jason Witten/125 6.00 15.00
WMPKB Kenny Britt/125 5.00 12.00
WMPKM Knowshon Moreno/125 5.00 12.00
WMPLB Lance Briggs/125 5.00 12.00
WMPLE Lee Evans/125 5.00 12.00
WMPLF Larry Fitzgerald/25 8.00 20.00
WMPLM LeSean McCoy/125 5.00 12.00
WMPLT LaDainian Tomlinson/125 5.00 12.00
WMPMB Marc Bulger/125 4.00 10.00
WMPMC Darren McFadden/125 5.00 12.00
WMPMI Mike Wallace/125 5.00 12.00
WMPMM Mohamed Massaquoi/125 5.00 12.00
WMPMR Matt Ryan/125 6.00 15.00
WMPMS Mark Sanchez/125 6.00 15.00
WMPMT Michael Turner/125 4.00 10.00
WMPMW Mario Williams/125 5.00 12.00
WMPPA Alan Page/125 6.00 15.00
WMPPM Peyton Manning/25 15.00 40.00
WMPPO Clinton Portis/125 5.00 12.00
WMPPR Philip Rivers/25 8.00 20.00
WMPRC Roger Craig/125 6.00 15.00
WMPRL Ray Lewis/125 8.00 20.00
WMPRM Rashard Mendenhall/125 5.00 12.00
WMPRW Reggie Wayne/125 5.00 12.00
WMPSA Bob Sanders/125 5.00 12.00
WMPSI Mike Singletary/125 8.00 20.00
WMPSL Steve Largent/125 6.00 15.00
WMPSM Shawne Merriman/125 5.00 12.00
WMPSS Steve Smith/125 5.00 12.00
WMPST Matthew Stafford/125 6.00 15.00
WMPTB Tim Brown/125 8.00 20.00
WMPTH Todd Heap/125 4.00 10.00
WMPTO Tom Brady/125 10.00 25.00
WMPVY Vince Young/25
WMPWE Chris Wells/125 5.00 12.00
WMPWI Ricky Williams/25 6.00 15.00
WMPWO Charles Woodson/125 12.50 25.00

2010 SPx Winning Trios Jerseys

STATED PRINT RUN 50 SER.#'d SETS
*PATCH/15: .6X TO 1.5X BASIC TRIO/50
WTBTB Dez Bryant 12.00 30.00
Demaryius Thomas
Arrelious Benn
WTBTC Sam Bradford 15.00 40.00
Tim Tebow
Jimmy Clausen
WTGCS Frank Gore 6.00 15.00
Michael Crabtree
Alex Smith QB
WTHWB Chad Henne 8.00 20.00
Ricky Williams
Ronnie Brown
WTMJM Jeremy Maclin 6.00 15.00
DeSean Jackson
LeSean McCoy
WTMKM Dan Marino 25.00 50.00
Jim Kelly
Warren Moon
WTPJS Adrian Peterson 8.00 20.00
Chris Johnson
Jonathan Stewart
WTRFH Matt Ryan 8.00 20.00
Doug Flutie
Matt Hasselbeck
WTRRP Matt Ryan 10.00 25.00
Tony Romo
Carson Palmer
WTRSS Matt Ryan 10.00 25.00
Mark Sanchez
Matthew Stafford
WTSBF Barry Sanders 20.00 40.00
Tim Brown
Doug Flutie
WTSBJ Barry Sanders 15.00 40.00
Adrian Peterson
Chris Johnson
WTSMB C.J. Spiller 10.00 25.00
Ryan Mathews
Jahvid Best
WTWHW Patrick Willis 6.00 15.00
A.J. Hawk
DeMarcus Ware

2011 SPx

1-42 STATED PRINT RUN 350
43-72 JSY AU PRINT RUN 150-225
ONE SPx PACK PER 1:6 SP AUTH. BOXES
1 Earl Campbell 1.50 4.00
2 Bernie Kosar 1.25 3.00
3 Jim Kelly 1.50 4.00
4 Barry Sanders 2.50 6.00
5 Tim Brown 1.50 4.00
6 Thurman Thomas 1.50 4.00
7 Doug Flutie 1.25 3.00
8 Dan Marino 3.00 8.00
9 Jerry Rice 2.50 6.00
10 Paul Hornung 1.50 4.00
11 John Elway 2.50 6.00
12 Bo Jackson 2.00 5.00
13 Troy Aikman 2.00 5.00
14 Steve Young 2.00 5.00
15 Tony Dorsett 1.50 4.00
16 Herschel Walker 1.25 3.00
17 Warren Moon 1.25 3.00
18 Archie Griffin 1.25 3.00
19 Eddie George 1.25 3.00
20 Cris Carter 1.50 4.00
21 Drew Brees 1.50 4.00
22 Aaron Rodgers 2.50 6.00
23 Dion Lewis 2.00 5.00
24 Dwayne Harris 2.00 5.00
25 Kris Durham 1.50 4.00
26 Edmond Gates 1.50 4.00
27 Aldon Smith 3.00 8.00
28 Evan Royster 2.00 5.00
29 Jamie Harper 2.00 5.00
30 Bilal Powell 1.25 3.00
31 Marcell Dareus 2.00 5.00
32 Roy Helu 4.00 10.00
33 Prince Amukamara 2.00 5.00
34 Ronald Johnson 1.50 4.00
35 Jeremy Kerley 2.00 5.00
36 Cecil Shorts 1.50 4.00
37 Tyrod Taylor 2.00 5.00
38 Ricky Stanzi 2.50 6.00
39 Jordan Todman 1.25 3.00
40 Kyle Rudolph 2.00 5.00
41 Von Miller 2.50 6.00
42 Stevan Ridley 2.00 5.00
43 Ryan Williams JSY AU/150 15.00 40.00
44 Austin Pettis JSY AU/225 8.00 20.00
45 Christian Ponder JSY AU/225 25.00 60.00
46 Colin Kaepernick JSY AU/150 15.00 40.00
47 Daniel Thomas JSY AU/225 10.00 25.00
48 DeMarco Murray JSY AU/225 40.00 80.00
49 Tandon Doss JSY AU/225 6.00 15.00
50 Greg Little JSY AU/225 12.00 30.00
51 Jonathan Baldwin JSY AU/150 12.00 30.00
52 Greg Salas JSY AU/225 10.00 25.00
53 Jerrel Jernigan JSY AU/225 6.00 15.00
54 Leonard Hankerson JSY AU/225 10.00 25.00
55 Kendall Hunter JSY AU/225 15.00 30.00
56 Niles Paul JSY AU/225 8.00 20.00
57 Mikel Leshoure JSY AU/225 15.00 30.00
58 Torrey Smith JSY AU/225 20.00 40.00
59 Shane Vereen JSY AU/225 10.00 25.00
60 Andy Dalton JSY AU/225 40.00 100.00
61 Randall Cobb JSY AU/225 12.00 30.00
62 Titus Young JSY AU/225 12.00 30.00
63 Vincent Brown JSY AU/225 10.00 25.00
64 Julio Jones JSY AU/150 30.00 80.00
65 Jake Locker JSY AU/150 50.00 120.00
66 Mark Ingram JSY AU/150 30.00 80.00
67 A.J. Green JSY AU/150 40.00 80.00
68 Cam Newton JSY AU/150 175.00 300.00
69 Blaine Gabbert JSY AU/150 30.00 60.00
70 Jacquizz Rodgers JSY AU/225 EXCH 10.00 25.00
71 Delone Carter JSY AU/225 8.00 20.00
72 Ryan Mallett JSY AU/150 25.00 60.00

2011 SPx Jersey Autographs Gold

GOLD/30: .8X TO 2X BASIC JSY AU/225
GOLD/30: .6X TO 1.5X BASIC JSY AU/150
STATED PRINT RUN 30 SER.#'d SETS
48 DeMarco Murray 100.00 200.00
60 Andy Dalton 100.00 200.00
64 Julio Jones 75.00 150.00
65 Jake Locker 125.00 250.00
67 A.J. Green 75.00 150.00
68 Cam Newton 500.00 800.00
72 Ryan Mallett 60.00 120.00

2012 SPx

COMP.SET w/o RC's (50) 6.00 15.00
51-77 JSY AUTO PRINT RUN 399
78-85 JSY AUTO PRINT RUN 199
86-145 AUTO PRINT RUN 225
146-205 ROOKIE PRINT RUN 750
AUTO EXCH EXPIRATION: 6/7/2014
QB DRAFT EXPIRATION: 6/1/2015
1 Aaron Rodgers .60 1.50
2 Bernie Kosar .30 .75
3 Billy Cannon .25 .60
4 Billy Sims .30 .75
5 Bo Jackson .50 1.25
6 Bob Lilly .30 .75
7 Charles White .25 .60
8 Chris Spielman .25 .60
9 Cornelius Bennett .25 .60
10 Danny Wuerffel .25 .60
11 Daryl Johnston .30 .75
12 Dave Casper .25 .60
13 Drew Brees .40 1.00
14 Dwight Stephenson .25 .60
15 Earl Campbell .40 1.00
16 Eric Metcalf .25 .60
17 Floyd Little .25 .60
18 Gale Sayers .40 1.00
19 Gary Beban .25 .60
20 George Rogers .25 .60
21 Gino Torretta .25 .60
22 Harry Carson .25 .60
23 Herman Moore .25 .60
24 Herschel Walker .30 .75
25 Jason White .30 .75
26 Jerry Rice .60 1.50
27 Jim Plunkett .30 .75
28 Joe Washington .25 .60
29 John Cappelletti .25 .60
30 Johnny Rodgers .25 .60
31 Keith Jackson .25 .60
32 Kellen Winslow Sr. .30 .75
33 Lawrence Taylor .30 .75
34 Lee Roy Jordan .25 .60
35 Marques Colston .30 .75
36 Mike Alstott .25 .60
37 Ozzie Newsome .30 .75
38 Rocket Ismail .30 .75
39 Randy White .30 .75
40 Roger Staubach .50 1.25
41 Roman Gabriel .30 .75
42 Ron Dayne .25 .60
43 Ron Yary .25 .60
44 Steve Young .50 1.25
45 Thurman Thomas .40 1.00
46 Todd Marinovich .25 .60
47 Tony Dorsett .40 1.00
48 Troy Aikman .50 1.25
49 Ty Detmer .25 .60
50 Warren Moon .40 1.00
51 Nick Foles JSY AU 8.00 20.00
52 Juron Criner JSY AU 6.00 15.00
53 Kendall Wright JSY AU 10.00 25.00
54 Kellen Moore JSY AU 12.00 30.00
55 Doug Martin JSY AU 15.00 30.00
56 Case Keenum JSY AU 10.00 25.00
57 Coby Fleener JSY AU 10.00 25.00
58 Isaiah Pead JSY AU 8.00 20.00
59 Kirk Cousins JSY AU 12.00 30.00
60 Jarius Wright JSY AU 8.00 20.00
61 B.J. Cunningham JSY AU 8.00 20.00
62 Dwight Jones JSY AU 6.00 15.00
63 Marquis Maze JSY AU 8.00 20.00
64 Mohamed Sanu JSY AU 10.00 25.00
65 Dan Herron JSY AU 8.00 20.00
66 DeVier Posey JSY AU 8.00 20.00
67 Ryan Broyles JSY AU 8.00 20.00
68 Brandon Weeden JSY AU 30.00 60.00
69 Dwayne Allen JSY AU 8.00 20.00
70 Cyrus Gray JSY AU 8.00 20.00
71 Jeff Fuller JSY AU 10.00 25.00
72 Ryan Tannehill JSY AU 30.00 60.00
73 Bernard Pierce JSY AU 8.00 20.00
74 Melvin Ingram JSY AU 10.00 25.00
75 Russell Wilson JSY AU 20.00 40.00
76 Nick Toon JSY AU 10.00 25.00
77 Rueben Randle JSY AU 8.00 20.00
78 Trent Richardson JSY AU/199 EXCH 60.00 120.00
79 Robert Griffin III JSY AU/199 175.00 300.00
80 LaMichael James JSY AU/199 40.00 80.00
81 Justin Blackmon JSY AU/199 40.00 80.00
82 Brock Osweiler JSY AU/199 15.00 40.00
83 Alshon Jeffery JSY AU/199 20.00 50.00
84 Michael Floyd JSY AU/199 25.00 60.00
85 Stephen Hill JSY AU/199 15.00 40.00
86 Mark Barron AU EXCH 10.00 25.00
87 Dre Kirkpatrick AU 8.00 20.00
88 Stephen Garcia AU 5.00 12.00
89 Courtney Upshaw AU 6.00 15.00
90 Brian Quick AU 6.00 15.00
91 Gerell Robinson AU 5.00 12.00
92 Ladarius Green AU 5.00 12.00
93 Greg Childs AU 6.00 15.00
94 Joe Adams AU 6.00 15.00
95 Keshawn Martin AU 5.00 12.00
96 Luke Kuechly AU 8.00 20.00
97 Audie Cole AU 4.00 10.00
98 Alameda Ta'amu AU EXCH 6.00 15.00
99 Edwin Baker AU 6.00 15.00
100 Brandon Thompson AU 4.00 10.00
101 Stephon Gilmore AU 6.00 15.00
102 Dominique Davis AU 4.00 10.00
104 Eric Page AU 4.00 10.00
105 Shea McClellin AU 10.00 25.00
106 Quinton Coples AU 5.00 12.00
107 Orson Charles AU 5.00 12.00
108 Pat Edwards AU 5.00 12.00
109 A.J. Jenkins AU 6.00 15.00
110 Riley Reiff AU 8.00 20.00
111 Marvin McNutt AU 6.00 15.00
112 Bobby Wagner AU 5.00 12.00
113 Davin Meggett AU 4.00 10.00
114 Mike Willie AU 5.00 12.00
115 Travis Benjamin AU 6.00 15.00
116 Tyler Hansen AU 4.00 10.00
117 Dontari Poe AU EXCH 5.00 12.00
118 Brandon Bolden AU 5.00 12.00
119 Jason Ford AU 4.00 10.00
120 Marvin Jones AU 4.00 10.00
121 Alfred Morris AU 4.00 10.00
122 Andre Branch AU 5.00 12.00
123 Alfonzo Dennard AU 5.00 12.00
124 Janoris Jenkins AU 5.00 12.00
125 Rodney Stewart AU 4.00 10.00
126 Michael Brockers AU 5.00 12.00
127 Jermaine Kearse AU 5.00 12.00
128 Ronnell Lewis AU 8.00 20.00
129 T.J. Graham AU 5.00 12.00
130 Bobby Rainey AU 5.00 12.00
131 Derek Moye AU 5.00 12.00
132 Aaron Corp AU 4.00 10.00
133 Rishard Matthews AU 5.00 12.00
134 Ryan Lindley AU 5.00 12.00
135 Da'Jon McKnight AU 4.00 10.00
136 Jonathan Martin AU 4.00 10.00
137 David DeCastro AU 8.00 20.00
138 Dont'a Hightower AU 20.00 40.00
139 Tauren Poole AU 4.00 10.00
140 Marc Tyler AU 5.00 12.00
141 Matt Kalil AU EXCH 6.00 15.00
142 Jarrett Boykin AU 5.00 12.00
143 Ronnie Hillman AU 6.00 15.00
144 Whitney Mercilus AU 5.00 12.00
145 Jordan White AU 4.00 10.00
146 Josh Chapman 2.00 5.00
147 Darius Hanks 2.00 5.00
148 Vontaze Burfict 1.50 4.00
149 Tyler Shoemaker 1.50 4.00
150 Michael Egnew 1.50 4.00
151 Billy Winn 2.00 5.00
152 Mychal Kendricks 2.00 5.00
153 Tank Carder 2.00 5.00
154 Stephfon Green 2.00 5.00
155 Casey Hayward 2.00 5.00
156 Nigel Bradham 1.50 4.00
157 Kendall Reyes 1.50 4.00
158 Shaun Prater 2.00 5.00
159 Donnie Fletcher 1.25 3.00
160 Josh Norman 1.25 3.00
161 Leonard Johnson 1.50 4.00
162 Bryce Beall 1.25 3.00
163 Jordan Jefferson 2.00 5.00
164 Lennon Creer 1.50 4.00
165 Jarrett Lee 2.00 5.00
166 Evan Rodriguez 1.50 4.00
167 Jermaine Thomas 1.50 4.00
168 Kevin Koger 2.00 5.00
169 Laron Byrd 1.50 4.00
170 Brian Linthicum 1.50 4.00
171 Junior Hemingway 2.00 5.00
172 Duane Bennett 1.50 4.00
173 Cliff Harris 2.00 5.00
174 Lavonte David 2.50 6.00
175 James-Michael Johnson 1.50 4.00
176 Marshall Lobbestael 1.50 4.00
177 Jeremy Ebert 1.50 4.00
178 Bradie Ewing 1.50 4.00
179 Harrison Smith 2.00 5.00
180 Trenton Robinson 1.50 4.00
181 Levy Adcock 1.50 4.00
182 Markelle Martin 1.50 4.00
183 Lavasier Tuinei 1.50 4.00
184 Bobby Massie 1.25 3.00
185 Cody Johnson 1.50 4.00
186 Thomas Mayo 1.25 3.00
187 Jamell Fleming 2.00 5.00
188 Dan Persa 1.50 4.00
189 Trevor Guyton 1.50 4.00
190 Brian Reader 1.50 4.00
191 Antwon Bailey 1.50 4.00
192 David Paulson 2.50 6.00
193 Coryell Judie 1.50 4.00
194 Keenan Robinson 1.50 4.00
195 Jared Crick 2.00 5.00
196 Foswhitt Whittaker 2.00 5.00
197 Travis Lewis 1.50 4.00
198 Nelson Rosario 1.50 4.00
199 Rhett Ellison 1.50 4.00
200 Cam Johnson 2.00 5.00
201 Jayron Hosley 2.00 5.00
202 Devon Wylie 2.00 5.00
203 George Iloka 1.50 4.00
204 Tim Benford 1.25 3.00
205 Brandon Carswell 1.50 4.00
NNO QB Draft Trade 150.00 225.00

2012 SPx Rookie Patch Autographs Spectrum

*51-77 PATCH/25: 1.2X TO 3X
*78-85 PATCH/25: .8X TO 2X
STATED PRINT RUN 25 SER.#'d SETS
68 Brandon Weeden 125.00 200.00
72 Ryan Tannehill 125.00 200.00
78 Trent Richardson 150.00 250.00
79 Robert Griffin III 400.00 700.00
80 LaMichael James 100.00 175.00

2012 SPx Finite Rookies

STATED PRINT RUN 99-499
*RADIANCE/99: .8X TO 2X BASIC INSERT/499
*RADIANCE/50: .8X TO 2X BASIC INSERT/199
OVERALL STATED ODDS 1:9
FAB Andre Branch/499 1.25 3.00
FAJ A.J. Jenkins/499 2.00 5.00
FBA Mark Barron/299 3.00 8.00
FBB Brandon Bolden/499 1.50 4.00
FBC B.J. Cunningham/499 1.25 3.00
FBO Jarrett Boykin/499 1.50 4.00
FBP Bernard Pierce/499 1.50 4.00
FBQ Brian Quick/499 2.00 5.00
FBW Brandon Weeden/299 5.00 12.00
FCF Coby Fleener/499 2.00 5.00
FCG Cyrus Gray/499 1.50 4.00
FCH Chandler Harnish/499 1.50 4.00
FCK Case Keenum/299 2.50 6.00
FCU Courtney Upshaw/299 2.50 6.00
FDA Dwayne Allen/499 1.50 4.00
FDH Dan Herron/299 2.00 5.00
FDJ Dwight Jones/299 1.50 4.00
FDK Dre Kirkpatrick/499 2.50 6.00
FDM Doug Martin/299 3.00 8.00
FDP DeVier Posey/499 1.50 4.00
FGC Greg Childs/499 1.50 4.00
FGR Gerell Robinson/499 1.50 4.00
FIP Isaiah Pead/499 1.50 4.00
FJA Joe Adams/499 1.50 4.00
FJB Justin Blackmon/99 6.00 15.00
FJC Juron Criner/299 1.50 4.00
FJE Alshon Jeffery/99 5.00 12.00
FJF Jeff Fuller/299 2.50 6.00
FJK Jermaine Kearse/499 1.50 4.00
FJW Jarius Wright/499 1.50 4.00
FKC Kirk Cousins/499 2.50 6.00
FKM Keshawn Martin/499 1.50 4.00
FKW Kendall Wright/99 4.00 10.00
FLJ LaMichael James/99 10.00 25.00
FLK Luke Kuechly/299 2.50 6.00
FMA Marquis Maze/499 1.50 4.00
FMB Michael Brockers/299 2.00 5.00
FMF Michael Floyd/99 6.00 15.00
FMI Melvin Ingram/499 2.00 5.00
FMJ Marvin Jones/499 1.25 3.00
FMK Matt Kalil/299 2.50 6.00
FMM Marvin McNutt/499 1.50 4.00
FMO Kellen Moore/299 3.00 8.00
FMS Mohamed Sanu/299 2.00 5.00
FMT Marc Tyler/499 1.50 4.00
FNF Nick Foles/299 3.00 8.00
FNT Nick Toon/299 2.50 6.00
FOS Brock Osweiler/99 4.00 10.00
FQC Quinton Coples/299 2.00 5.00
FRB Ryan Broyles/299 2.00 5.00
FRG Robert Griffin III/99 40.00 80.00
FRH Ronnie Hillman/299 2.50 6.00
FRL Ryan Lindley/499 1.50 4.00
FRR Rueben Randle/499 1.50 4.00
FRT Ryan Tannehill/99 8.00 20.00
FRW Russell Wilson/499 2.50 6.00
FSH Stephen Hill/99 3.00 8.00
FTJ T.J. Graham/499 1.50 4.00
FTP Tauren Poole/299 1.50 4.00
FTR Trent Richardson/99 20.00 40.00

2012 SPx Shadow Box

AR Aaron Rodgers 40.00 80.00
BJ Bo Jackson 15.00 40.00
BK Bernie Kosar 12.00 30.00
BS Barry Sanders 30.00 60.00
CW Charles White 8.00 20.00
DB Drew Brees 25.00 60.00
DM Dan Marino 25.00 60.00
EC Earl Campbell 12.00 30.00
GR George Rogers 8.00 20.00
HW Herschel Walker 8.00 20.00
JB Justin Blackmon 12.00 30.00
JE John Elway 20.00 50.00
JK Jim Kelly 12.00 30.00
JP Jim Plunkett 10.00 25.00
JR Johnny Rodgers 8.00 20.00
LJ LaMichael James 25.00 50.00
MF Michael Floyd 20.00 40.00
RG Robert Griffin III 40.00 80.00
SY Steve Young 12.00 30.00
TA Troy Aikman 12.00 30.00
TR Trent Richardson 25.00 60.00

2012 SPx Shadow Slots Pose 1

OVERALL STATED ODDS 1:6
*POSE TWO: .4X TO 1X POSE ONE
*POSE THREE: .5X TO 1.2X POSE ONE
*POSE FOUR: .5X TO 1.2X POSE ONE
AR1 Aaron Rodgers 3.00 8.00
BJ1 Bo Jackson 2.50 6.00
BK1 Bernie Kosar 1.50 4.00
BS1 Barry Sanders 3.00 8.00
CW1 Charles White 1.25 3.00
DB1 Drew Brees 2.00 5.00
DM1 Dan Marino 5.00 12.00
EC1 Earl Campbell 2.00 5.00
GR1 George Rogers 1.25 3.00
HW1 Herschel Walker 1.50 4.00
JB1 Justin Blackmon 2.50 6.00
JE1 John Elway 3.00 8.00
JK1 Jim Kelly 2.00 5.00
JP1 Jim Plunkett 1.50 4.00
JR1 Johnny Rodgers 1.25 3.00
LJ1 LaMichael James 2.50 6.00
MF1 Michael Floyd 2.50 6.00
RG1 Robert Griffin III 6.00 15.00
SY1 Steve Young 2.50 6.00
TA1 Troy Aikman 2.50 6.00
TR1 Trent Richardson 4.00 10.00

2012 SPx Signature Supremacy

OVERALL STATED ODDS 1:9
SUPAC Aaron Corp 3.00 8.00
SUPAD Alfonzo Dennard 4.00 10.00
SUPAF Antonio Freeman 8.00 20.00
SUPAR Aaron Rodgers
SUPBK Bernie Kosar
SUPBP Bernard Pierce 4.00 10.00
SUPBS Billy Sims 6.00 15.00
SUPBW Brandon Weeden
SUPCF Coby Fleener
SUPCG Cyrus Gray 4.00 10.00
SUPDH Dan Herron 6.00 15.00
SUPDJ Dwight Jones 4.00 10.00
SUPDP DeVier Posey 5.00 12.00
SUPDS Dwight Stephenson 8.00 20.00
SUPDW Devon Wylie 4.00 10.00
SUPEC Earl Campbell
SUPEL John Elway
SUPFW Foswhitt Whittaker 4.00 10.00
SUPGC Greg Childs 6.00 15.00
SUPGT Gino Torretta
SUPIP Isaiah Pead 5.00 12.00
SUPJB Justin Blackmon 15.00 30.00
SUPJC Juron Criner 4.00 10.00
SUPJJ Jordan Jefferson 4.00 10.00
SUPJK Jermaine Kearse 4.00 10.00
SUPJO Daryl Johnston
SUPKM Keshawn Martin 4.00 10.00
SUPKW Kendall Wright 6.00 15.00
SUPLJ LaMichael James 20.00 40.00
SUPLK Luke Kuechly 5.00 12.00

SUPMC Marvin McNutt	6.00	15.00
SUPME Michael Egnew	3.00	8.00
SUPMI Melvin Ingram	5.00	12.00
SUPMM Marquis Maze	6.00	15.00
SUPMO Kellen Moore	12.50	25.00
SUPNT Nick Toon	8.00	20.00
SUPON Ozzie Newsome		
SUPQC Quinton Coples	6.00	15.00
SUPRG Robert Griffin III		
SUPRI Rocket Ismail		
SUPRL Ryan Lindley	4.00	10.00
SUPRO Johnny Rodgers	5.00	12.00
SUPRW Russell Wilson		
SUPSA Shaun Alexander		
SUPSH Stephen Hill	4.00	10.00
SUPTA Troy Aikman		
SUPTD Tony Dorsett		
SUPTG T.J. Graham	4.00	10.00
SUPWA Joe Washington	8.00	20.00
SUPWM Warren Moon	15.00	30.00

2012 SPx Super Scripts Autographs

OVERALL AUTO STATED ODDS 1:9
EXCH EXPIRATION: 6/6/2014

SSAB Andre Branch	4.00	10.00
SSAJ A.J. Jenkins	6.00	15.00
SSAL Mike Alstott	15.00	30.00
SSBB Brandon Bolden	5.00	12.00
SSBJ B.J. Cunningham	4.00	10.00
SSBO Jarrett Boykin	5.00	12.00
SSBQ Brian Quick	6.00	15.00
SSCH Chandler Harnish	5.00	12.00
SSCK Case Keenum	6.00	15.00
SSCS Chris Spielman		
SSCU Courtney Upshaw	6.00	15.00
SSDA Dwayne Allen	5.00	12.00
SSDB Drew Brees	25.00	50.00
SSDC Dave Casper	8.00	20.00
SSDD David DeCastro	6.00	15.00
SSDK Dre Kirkpatrick	8.00	20.00
SSDM Doug Martin	8.00	20.00
SSDW Danny Wuerffel		
SSFL Floyd Little		
SSGA Roman Gabriel	10.00	25.00
SSGL Cordy Glenn	4.00	10.00
SSHW Herschel Walker	25.00	50.00
SSJA Joe Adams	5.00	12.00
SSJE Alshon Jeffery	15.00	30.00
SSJF Jeff Fuller	6.00	15.00
SSJP Jim Plunkett	10.00	25.00
SSJR Jerry Rice	75.00	150.00
SSJW Jarius Wright	6.00	15.00
SSKC Kirk Cousins	8.00	20.00
SSKE Jim Kelly		
SSLT Lawrence Taylor	10.00	25.00
SSMA Dan Marino	100.00	200.00
SSMB Michael Brockers	5.00	12.00
SSMF Michael Floyd	15.00	30.00
SSMK Matt Kalil EXCH	8.00	20.00
SSMS Mohamed Sanu	6.00	15.00
SSNF Nick Foles	8.00	20.00
SSOS Brock Osweiler	8.00	20.00
SSRB Ryan Broyles	5.00	12.00
SSRH Ronnie Hillman	8.00	15.00
SSRR Rueben Randle	6.00	15.00
SSRS Roger Staubach	40.00	80.00
SSRT Ryan Tannehill	20.00	40.00
SSSY Steve Young	30.00	60.00
SSTM Todd Marinovich EXCH	15.00	30.00
SSTP Tauren Poole	4.00	10.00
SSTR Trent Richardson EXCH	40.00	80.00
SSTT Thurman Thomas		
SSVB Vontaze Burfict	4.00	10.00
SSWH Jason White EXCH	10.00	25.00

2012 SPx Winning Big Materials

STATED PRINT RUN 199 SER.#'d SETS
UNPRICED PATCH PRINT RUN 10

WM1 Alshon Jeffery	5.00	12.00
WM2 Brock Osweiler	4.00	10.00
WM3 Brandon Weeden	6.00	15.00
WM4 Case Keenum	4.00	10.00
WM5 Isaiah Pead	3.00	8.00
WM6 Dan Herron	3.00	8.00
WM7 Dwayne Allen	3.00	8.00
WM8 DeVier Posey	3.00	8.00
WM9 Doug Martin	5.00	12.00
WM10 Dwight Jones	2.50	6.00
WM11 Jeff Fuller	4.00	10.00
WM12 B.J. Cunningham	2.50	6.00
WM13 Justin Blackmon	10.00	25.00
WM14 Kellen Moore	5.00	12.00
WM15 Kirk Cousins	5.00	12.00
WM16 Coby Fleener	4.00	10.00
WM17 LaMichael James	8.00	20.00
WM18 Rueben Randle	3.00	8.00
WM19 Mohamed Sanu	4.00	10.00
WM20 Michael Floyd	6.00	15.00
WM21 Juron Criner	2.50	6.00
WM22 Kendall Wright	4.00	10.00
WM23 Nick Foles	5.00	12.00
WM24 Nick Toon	4.00	10.00
WM25 Jarius Wright	3.00	8.00
WM26 Robert Griffin III	15.00	40.00
WM27 Russell Wilson	5.00	12.00
WM28 Ryan Broyles	3.00	8.00
WM29 Ryan Tannehill	8.00	20.00
WM30 Trent Richardson	12.00	30.00

2012 SPx Winning Combos Dual Jerseys

STATED PRINT RUN 299 SER.#'d SETS
*PATCH/25: 1X TO 2.5X BASIC DUAL/299

WM21 Case Keenum	5.00	12.00
Kellen Moore		
WM22 Dan Herron	4.00	10.00
DeVier Posey		
WM23 Rueben Randle	3.00	8.00
Stephen Hill		
WM24 Kirk Cousins	5.00	12.00
B.J. Cunningham		
WM25 Nick Foles	5.00	12.00
Brock Osweiler		
WM26 Michael Floyd	6.00	15.00
Kendall Wright		
WM27 Justin Blackmon	6.00	15.00
Brandon Weeden		
WM28 LaMichael James	6.00	15.00
Doug Martin		
WM29 Ryan Tannehill	6.00	15.00
Jeff Fuller		
WM210 Robert Griffin III	15.00	40.00
Trent Richardson		
WM211 Alshon Jeffery	5.00	12.00
Mohamed Sanu		
WM212 Coby Fleener	4.00	10.00
Dwayne Allen		
WM213 Russell Wilson	5.00	12.00
Nick Toon		
WM214 Ryan Broyles	4.00	10.00
Juron Criner		
WM215 Bernard Pierce	3.00	8.00
Isaiah Pead		

2012 SPx Winning Quad Jerseys

STATED PRINT RUN 75 SER.#'d SETS

WM41 Robert Griffin III	25.00	60.00
Ryan Tannehill		
Brock Osweiler		
Nick Foles		
WM42 Brandon Weeden	12.00	30.00
Kirk Cousins		
Russell Wilson		
Case Keenum		
WM43 Justin Blackmon	12.00	30.00
Michael Floyd		
Kendall Wright		
Alshon Jeffery		
WM44 Mohamed Sanu	8.00	20.00
Stephen Hill		
Nick Toon		
Juron Criner		
WM45 Trent Richardson	20.00	50.00
LaMichael James		
Doug Martin		
Isaiah Pead		

2012 SPx Winning Trios Triple Jerseys

STATED PRINT RUN 99 SER.#'d SETS

WM31 Robert Griffin III	25.00	60.00
Trent Richardson		
Justin Blackmon		
WM32 Trent Richardson	15.00	40.00
LaMichael James		
Doug Martin		
WM33 Mohamed Sanu	5.00	12.00
Jarius Wright		
DeVier Posey		
WM34 Isaiah Pead	5.00	12.00
Bernard Pierce		
Dan Herron		
WM35 Russell Wilson	8.00	20.00
Kellen Moore		
Case Keenum		
WM36 Michael Floyd	10.00	25.00
Kendall Wright		
Alshon Jeffery		
WM37 Brandon Weeden	10.00	25.00
Nick Foles		
Kirk Cousins		
WM38 Michael Floyd	10.00	25.00
Rueben Randle		
Stephen Hill		
WM39 Nick Toon	6.00	15.00
Ryan Broyles		
B.J. Cunningham		
WM310 Ryan Tannehill	12.00	30.00
Jeff Fuller		
Cyrus Gray		

1991 Stadium Club

The 1991 Stadium Club set contains 500 standard-size cards. Cards were issued in 12-card packs. . Rookie Cards include Mike Croel, Ricky Ervins, Brett Favre, Jeff Graham, Randal Hill, Russell Maryland, Leonard Russell, Ricky Watters and Harvey Williams. In conjunction with Super Bowl XXVI in Minneapolis, Topps issued cellophane packs containing Stadium Club cards. These cards differ from the basic issue in that an embossed Super Bowl XXVI logo appears at the top right or left corner of the card front.

COMPLETE SET (500)	30.00	60.00
1 Pepper Johnson	.07	.20
2 Emmitt Smith	2.00	5.00
3 Deion Sanders	.60	1.50
4 Andre Collins	.07	.20
5 Eric Metcalf	.15	.40
6 Richard Dent	.15	.40
7 Eric Martin	.07	.20
8 Marcus Allen	.30	.75
9 Gary Anderson K	.07	.20
10 Joey Browner	.07	.20
11 Lorenzo White	.07	.20
12 Bruce Smith	.30	.75
13 Mark Boyer	.07	.20
14 Mike Piel	.07	.20
15 Albert Bentley	.07	.20
16 Bennie Blades	.07	.20
17 Jason Staurovsky	.07	.20
18 Anthony Toney	.07	.20
19 Dave Krieg	.15	.40
20 Harvey Williams RC	.30	.75
21 Bubba Paris	.07	.20
22 Tim McGee	.07	.20
23 Brian Noble	.07	.20
24 Vinny Testaverde	.15	.40
25 Doug Widell	.07	.20
26 John Jackson RC	.07	.20
27 Marion Butts	.15	.40
28 Deron Cherry	.07	.20
29 Don Warren	.07	.20
30 Rod Woodson	.30	.75
31 Mike Baab	.07	.20
32 Greg Jackson RC	.07	.20
33 Jerry Robinson	.07	.20
34 Dalton Hilliard	.07	.20
35 Brian Jordan	.15	.40
36 James Thornton UER (Misspelled Thorton on card back)	.07	.20
37 Michael Irvin	.30	.75
38 Billy Joe Tolliver	.07	.20
39 Jeff Herrod	.07	.20
40 Scott Norwood	.07	.20
41 Ferrell Edmunds	.07	.20
42 Andre Waters	.07	.20
43 Kevin Glover	.07	.20
44 Ray Berry	.07	.20
45 Timm Rosenbach	.07	.20
46 Reuben Davis	.07	.20
47 Charles Wilson	.07	.20
48 Todd Marinovich RC	.07	.20
49 Harris Barton	.07	.20
50 Jim Breech	.07	.20
51 Ron Holmes	.07	.20
52 Chris Singleton	.07	.20
53 Pat Leahy	.07	.20
54 Tom Newberry	.07	.20
55 Greg Montgomery	.07	.20
56 Robert Blackmon	.07	.20
57 Jay Hilgenberg	.07	.20
58 Rodney Hampton	.30	.75
59 Brett Perriman	.30	.75
60 Ricky Watters RC	2.00	5.00
61 Howie Long	.30	.75
62 Frank Cornish	.07	.20
63 Chris Miller	.15	.40
64 Keith Taylor	.07	.20
65 Tony Paige	.07	.20
66 Gary Zimmerman	.07	.20
67 Mark Royals RC	.07	.20
68 Ernie Jones	.07	.20
69 David Grant	.07	.20
70 Shane Conlan	.07	.20
71 Jerry Rice	1.00	2.50
72 Christian Okoye	.07	.20
73 Eddie Murray	.07	.20
74 Reggie White	.30	.75
75 Jeff Graham RC	.30	.75
76 Mark Jackson	.07	.20
77 David Grayson	.07	.20
78 Dan Stryzinski	.07	.20
79 Sterling Sharpe	.30	.75
80 Cleveland Gary	.07	.20
81 Johnny Meads	.07	.20
82 Howard Cross	.07	.20
83 Ken O'Brien	.07	.20
84 Brian Blades	.15	.40
85 Ethan Horton	.07	.20
86 Bruce Armstrong	.07	.20
87 James Washington RC	.07	.20
88 Eugene Daniel	.07	.20
89 James Lofton	.15	.40
90 Louis Oliver	.07	.20
91 Boomer Esiason	.15	.40
92 Seth Joyner	.15	.40
93 Mark Carrier WR	.30	.75
94 Brett Favre UER RC (Favre misspelled as Farve)	15.00	40.00
95 Lee Williams	.07	.20
96 Neal Anderson	.15	.40
97 Brent Jones	.30	.75
98 John Alt	.07	.20
99 Rodney Peete	.15	.40
100 Steve Broussard	.07	.20
101 Cedric Mack	.07	.20
102 Pat Swilling	.15	.40
103 Stan Humphries	.30	.75
104 Darrell Thompson	.07	.20
105 Reggie Langhorne	.07	.20
106 Kenny Davidson	.07	.20
107 Jim Everett	.15	.40
108 Keith Millard	.07	.20
109 Garry Lewis	.07	.20
110 Jeff Hostetler	.15	.40
111 Lamar Lathon	.07	.20
112 Johnny Bailey	.07	.20
113 Cornelius Bennett	.15	.40
114 Travis McNeal	.07	.20
115 Jeff Lageman	.07	.20
116 Nick Bell RC	.07	.20
117 Calvin Williams	.15	.40
118 Shawn Lee RC	.07	.20
119 Anthony Munoz	.15	.40
120 Jay Novacek	.30	.75
121 Kevin Fagan	.07	.20
122 Leo Goeas	.07	.20
123 Vance Johnson	.07	.20
124 Brent Williams	.07	.20
125 Clarence Verdin	.07	.20
126 Luis Sharpe	.07	.20
127 Darrell Green	.07	.20
128 Barry Word	.07	.20
129 Steve Walsh	.07	.20
130 Bryan Hinkle	.07	.20
131 Ed West	.07	.20
132 Jeff Campbell	.07	.20
133 Dennis Byrd	.07	.20
134 Nate Odomes	.07	.20
135 Trace Armstrong	.07	.20
136 Jarvis Williams	.07	.20
137 Warren Moon	.30	.75
138 Eric Moten RC	.07	.20
139 Tony Woods	.07	.20
140 Phil Simms	.15	.40
141 Ricky Reynolds	.07	.20
142 Frank Stams	.07	.20
143 Kevin Mack	.07	.20
144 Wade Wilson	.15	.40
145 Shawn Collins	.07	.20
146 Roger Craig	.15	.40
147 Jeff Feagles RC	.07	.20
148 Norm Johnson	.07	.20
149 Terance Mathis	.15	.40
150 Reggie Cobb	.07	.20
151 Chip Banks	.07	.20
152 Darryl Pollard	.07	.20
153 Karl Mecklenburg	.07	.20
154 Ricky Proehl	.07	.20
155 Pete Stoyanovich	.07	.20
156 John Stephens	.07	.20
157 Ron Morris	.07	.20
158 Steve DeBerg	.07	.20
159 Mike Munchak	.15	.40
160 Brett Maxie	.07	.20
161 Don Beebe	.07	.20
162 Martin Mayhew	.07	.20
163 Merril Hoge	.07	.20
164 Kelvin Pritchett RC	.15	.40
165 Jim Jeffcoat	.07	.20
166 Myron Guyton	.07	.20
167 Ickey Woods	.07	.20
168 Andre Ware	.15	.40
169 Gary Plummer	.07	.20
170 Henry Ellard	.15	.40
171 Scott Davis	.07	.20
172 Randall McDaniel	.07	.20
173 Randal Hill RC	.15	.40
174 Anthony Bell	.07	.20
175 Gary Anderson RB	.07	.20
176 Byron Evans	.07	.20
177 Tony Mandarich	.07	.20
178 Jeff George	.40	1.00
179 Art Monk	.15	.40
180 Mike Kenn	.07	.20
181 Sean Landeta	.07	.20
182 Shaun Gayle	.07	.20
183 Michael Carter	.07	.20
184 Robb Thomas	.07	.20
185 Richmond Webb	.07	.20
186 Carnell Lake	.07	.20
187 Rueben Mayes	.07	.20
188 Issiac Holt	.07	.20
189 Leon Seals	.07	.20
190 Al Smith	.07	.20
191 Steve Atwater	.07	.20
192 Greg McMurtry	.07	.20
193 Al Toon	.15	.40
194 Cortez Kennedy	.30	.75
195 Gill Byrd	.07	.20
196 Carl Zander	.07	.20
197 Robert Brown	.07	.20
198 Buford McGee	.07	.20
199 Mervyn Fernandez	.07	.20
200 Mike Dumas RC	.07	.20
201 Rob Burnett RC	.15	.40
202 Brian Mitchell	.15	.40
203 Randall Cunningham	.30	.75
204 Sammie Smith	.07	.20
205 Ken Clarke	.07	.20
206 Floyd Dixon	.07	.20
207 Ken Norton	.15	.40
208 Tony Siragusa RC	.60	1.50
209 Louis Lipps	.07	.20
210 Chris Martin	.07	.20
211 Jamie Mueller	.07	.20
212 Dave Waymer	.07	.20
213 Donnell Woolford	.07	.20
214 Paul Gruber	.07	.20
215 Ken Harvey	.15	.40
216 Henry Jones RC	.15	.40
217 Tommy Barnhardt RC	.07	.20
218 Arthur Cox	.07	.20
219 Pat Terrell	.07	.20
220 Curtis Duncan	.07	.20
221 Jeff Jaeger	.07	.20
222 Scott Stephen RC	.07	.20
223 Rob Moore	.40	1.00
224 Chris Hinton	.07	.20
225 Marv Cook	.07	.20
226 Patrick Hunter RC	.07	.20
227 Earnest Byner	.07	.20
228 Troy Aikman	1.25	3.00
229 Kevin Walker RC	.07	.20
230 Keith Jackson	.15	.40
231 Russell Maryland RC (UER, Card back says Dallas Cowboy)	.30	.75
232 Charles Haley	.15	.40
233 Nick Lowery	.07	.20
234 Erik Howard	.07	.20
235 Leonard Smith	.07	.20
236 Tim Irwin	.07	.20
237 Simon Fletcher	.07	.20
238 Thomas Everett	.07	.20
239 Reggie Roby	.07	.20
240 Leroy Hoard	.15	.40
241 Wayne Haddix	.07	.20
242 Gary Clark	.30	.75
243 Eric Andolsek	.07	.20
244 Jim Wahler RC	.07	.20
245 Vaughan Johnson	.07	.20
246 Kevin Butler	.07	.20
247 Steve Tasker	.15	.40
248 LeRoy Butler	.15	.40
249 Darion Conner	.07	.20
250 Eric Turner RC	.15	.40
251 Kevin Ross	.07	.20
252 Stephen Baker	.07	.20
253 Harold Green	.15	.40
254 Rohn Stark	.07	.20
255 Joe Nash	.07	.20
256 Jesse Sapolu	.07	.20
257 Willie Gault	.15	.40
258 Jerome Brown	.07	.20
259 Ken Willis	.07	.20
260 Courtney Hall	.07	.20
261 Hart Lee Dykes	.07	.20
262 William Fuller	.15	.40
263 Stan Thomas	.07	.20
264 Dan Marino	1.50	4.00
265 Ron Cox	.07	.20
266 Eric Green	.07	.20
267 Anthony Carter	.15	.40
268 Jerry Ball	.07	.20
269 Ron Hall	.07	.20
270 Dennis Smith	.07	.20
271 Eric Hill	.07	.20
272 Dan McGwire RC	.07	.20
273 Lewis Billups UER Louis on back	.07	.20
274 Rickey Jackson	.07	.20
275 Jim Sweeney	.07	.20
276 Pat Beach	.07	.20
277 Kevin Porter	.07	.20
278 Mike Sherrard	.07	.20
279 Andy Heck	.07	.20
280 Ron Brown	.07	.20
281 Lawrence Taylor	.30	.75
282 Anthony Pleasant	.07	.20
283 Wes Hopkins	.07	.20
284 Jim Lachey	.07	.20
285 Tim Harris	.07	.20
286 Tory Epps	.07	.20
287 Wendell Davis	.07	.20
288 Bubba McDowell	.07	.20
289 Bubby Brister	.07	.20
290 Chris Zorich RC	.30	.75
291 Mike Merriweather	.07	.20
292 Burt Grossman	.07	.20
293 Erik McMillan	.07	.20
294 John Elway	1.50	4.00
295 Toi Cook RC	.07	.20
296 Tom Rathman	.07	.20
297 Matt Bahr	.07	.20
298 Chris Spielman	.15	.40
299 Freddie Joe Nunn (Troy Aikman and Emmitt Smith shown in background)	.15	.40
300 Jim C. Jensen	.07	.20
301 David Fulcher UER (Rookie card should be '88, not '89)	.07	.20
302 Tommy Hodson	.07	.20
303 Stephone Paige	.07	.20
304 Greg Townsend	.07	.20
305 Dean Biasucci	.07	.20
306 Jimmie Jones	.07	.20
307 Eugene Marve	.07	.20
308 Flipper Anderson	.07	.20
309 Darryl Talley	.07	.20
310 Mike Croel RC	.07	.20
311 Thane Gash	.07	.20
312 Perry Kemp	.07	.20
313 Heath Sherman	.07	.20
314 Mike Singletary	.15	.40
315 Chip Lohmiller	.07	.20
316 Tunch Ilkin	.07	.20
317 Junior Seau	.50	1.25
318 Mike Gann	.07	.20
319 Tim McDonald	.07	.20
320 Kyle Clifton	.07	.20
321 Dan Owens	.07	.20
322 Tim Grunhard	.07	.20
323 Stan Brock	.07	.20
324 Rodney Holman	.07	.20
325 Mark Ingram	.15	.40
326 Browning Nagle RC	.07	.20
327 Joe Montana	2.00	5.00
328 Carl Lee	.07	.20
329 John L. Williams	.07	.20
330 David Griggs	.07	.20
331 Clarence Kay	.07	.20
332 Irving Fryar	.15	.40
333 Doug Smith DT RC	.15	.40
334 Kent Hull	.07	.20
335 Mike Wilcher	.07	.20
336 Ray Donaldson	.07	.20
337 Mark Carrier DB UER (Rookie card should be '90, not '89)	.07	.20
338 Kelvin Martin	.07	.20
339 Keith Byars	.07	.20
340 Wilber Marshall	.07	.20
341 Ronnie Lott	.15	.40
342 Blair Thomas	.07	.20
343 Ronnie Harmon	.07	.20
344 Brian Brennan	.07	.20
345 Charles McRae RC	.07	.20
346 Michael Cofer	.07	.20
347 Keith Willis	.07	.20
348 Bruce Kozerski	.07	.20
349 Dave Meggett	.15	.40
350 John Taylor	.15	.40
351 Johnny Holland	.07	.20
352 Steve Christie	.07	.20
353 Ricky Ervins RC	.15	.40
354 Robert Massey	.07	.20
355 Derrick Thomas	.30	.75
356 Tommy Kane	.07	.20
357 Melvin Bratton	.07	.20
358 Bruce Matthews	.15	.40
359 Mark Duper	.15	.40
360 Jeff Wright RC	.07	.20
361 Barry Sanders	1.50	4.00
362 Chuck Webb RC	.07	.20
363 Darryl Grant	.07	.20
364 William Roberts	.07	.20
365 Reggie Rutland	.07	.20
366 Clay Matthews	.15	.40
367 Anthony Miller	.15	.40
368 Mike Prior	.07	.20
369 Jessie Tuggle	.07	.20
370 Brad Muster	.07	.20
371 Jay Schroeder	.07	.20
372 Greg Lloyd	.30	.75
373 Mike Cofer	.07	.20
374 James Brooks	.15	.40
375 Danny Noonan UER (Misspelled Noonen on card back)	.07	.20
376 Latin Berry RC	.07	.20
377 Brad Baxter	.07	.20
378 Godfrey Myles RC	.07	.20
379 Morten Andersen	.07	.20
380 Keith Woodside	.07	.20
381 Bobby Humphrey	.07	.20
382 Mike Golic	.07	.20
383 Keith McCants	.07	.20
384 Anthony Thompson	.07	.20
385 Mark Clayton	.15	.40
386 Neil Smith	.30	.75
387 Bryan Millard	.07	.20
388 Mel Gray UER (Wrong Mel Gray pictured on card back)	.15	.40
389 Ernest Givins	.15	.40
390 Reyna Thompson	.07	.20
391 Eric Bieniemy RC	.07	.20
392 Jon Hand	.07	.20
393 Mark Rypien	.15	.40
394 Bill Romanowski	.07	.20
395 Thurman Thomas	.30	.75
396 Jim Harbaugh	.30	.75
397 Don Mosebar	.07	.20
398 Andre Rison	.15	.40
399 Mike Johnson	.07	.20
400 Dermontti Dawson	.07	.20
401 Herschel Walker	.15	.40
402 Joe Prokop	.07	.20
403 Eddie Brown	.07	.20
404 Nate Newton	.15	.40
405 Damone Johnson RC	.07	.20
406 Jessie Hester	.07	.20
407 Jim Arnold	.07	.20
408 Ray Agnew	.07	.20
409 Michael Brooks	.07	.20
410 Keith Sims	.07	.20
411 Carl Banks	.07	.20
412 Jonathan Hayes	.07	.20
413 Richard Johnson RC	.07	.20
414 Darryll Lewis RC	.15	.40
415 Jeff Bryant	.07	.20
416 Leslie O'Neal	.15	.40
417 Andre Reed	.15	.40
418 Charles Mann	.07	.20
419 Keith DeLong	.07	.20
420 Bruce Hill	.07	.20
421 Matt Brock RC	.07	.20
422 Johnny Johnson	.07	.20
423 Mark Bortz	.07	.20
424 Ben Smith	.07	.20
425 Jeff Cross	.07	.20
426 Irv Pankey	.07	.20
427 Hassan Jones	.07	.20
428 Andre Tippett	.07	.20
429 Tim Worley	.07	.20
430 Daniel Stubbs	.07	.20
431 Max Montoya	.07	.20
432 Jumbo Elliott	.07	.20
433 Duane Bickett	.07	.20
434 Nate Lewis RC	.07	.20
435 Leonard Russell RC	.30	.75
436 Hoby Brenner	.07	.20
437 Ricky Sanders	.07	.20
438 Pierce Holt	.07	.20
439 Derrick Fenner	.07	.20
440 Drew Hill	.07	.20
441 Will Wolford	.07	.20
442 Albert Lewis	.07	.20
443 James Francis	.07	.20
444 Chris Jacke	.07	.20
445 Mike Farr	.07	.20
446 Stephen Braggs	.07	.20
447 Michael Haynes	.30	.75
448 Freeman McNeil UER (2,008 Pounds for weight)	.07	.20
449 Kevin Donnalley RC	.07	.20
450 John Offerdahl	.07	.20
451 Eric Allen	.07	.20
452 Keith McKeller	.07	.20
453 Kevin Greene	.15	.40
454 Ronnie Lippett	.07	.20
455 Ray Childress	.07	.20
456 Mike Saxon	.07	.20
457 Mark Robinson	.07	.20
458 Greg Kragen	.07	.20
459 Steve Jordan	.07	.20
460 John Johnson RC	.07	.20
461 Sam Mills	.07	.20
462 Bo Jackson	.40	1.00
463 Mark Collins	.07	.20
464 Percy Snow	.07	.20
465 Jeff Bostic	.07	.20
466 Jacob Green	.07	.20
467 Dexter Carter	.07	.20
468 Rich Camarillo	.07	.20
469 Bill Brooks	.07	.20
470 John Carney	.07	.20
471 Don Majkowski	.07	.20
472 Ralph Tamm RC	.07	.20
473 Fred Barnett	.30	.75
474 Jim Covert	.07	.20
475 Kenneth Davis	.07	.20
476 Jerry Gray	.07	.20
477 Broderick Thomas	.07	.20
478 Chris Doleman	.07	.20
479 Haywood Jeffires	.15	.40
480 Craig Heyward	.15	.40
481 Markus Koch	.07	.20
482 Tim Krumrie	.07	.20
483 Robert Clark	.07	.20
484 Mike Rozier	.07	.20
485 Danny Villa	.07	.20
486 Gerald Williams	.07	.20
487 Steve Wisniewski	.07	.20
488 J.B. Brown	.07	.20
489 Eugene Robinson	.07	.20
490 Ottis Anderson	.15	.40
491 Tony Stargell	.07	.20
492 Jack Del Rio	.15	.40
493 Lamar Rogers RC	.07	.20
494 Ricky Nattiel	.07	.20
495 Dan Saleaumua	.07	.20
496 Checklist 1-100	.07	.20
497 Checklist 101-200	.07	.20
498 Checklist 201-300	.07	.20
499 Checklist 301-400	.07	.20
500 Checklist 401-500	.07	.20

1991 Stadium Club Super Bowl XXVI

COMPLETE SET (300)	560.00	1,400.00
*STARS: 6X TO 12X BASIC CARDS		
*ROOKIES: 2.5X TO 6X BASIC CARDS		
94 Brett Favre UER	150.00	300.00

1992 Stadium Club

The 1992 Stadium Club football set was issued in three series and totaled 700 standard-size cards. The first two series consisted of 300 cards followed by a less abundant 100-card high series. The set includes 30 Members Choice (291-310, 601-610) cards. Rookie Cards include Edgar Bennett, Steve Bono, Robert Brooks, Terrell Buckley, Quentin Coryatt, Amp Lee, Dale Carter, Steve Emtman, Johnny Mitchell and Darren Woodson. Members of both NFL Properties and the NFL Players Association were included in the third series. Two different 9-card promo sheets were distributed at the 1992 National Sports Collector's Convention. They are differentiated by the card show date printed on the sheet backs.

COMPLETE SET (700)	75.00	150.00
COMP.SERIES 1 (300)	6.00	16.00
COMP.SERIES 2 (300)	6.00	15.00
COMP.HIGH SER.(100)	60.00	120.00
1 Mark Rypien	.02	.10
2 Carlton Bailey RC	.02	.10
3 Kevin Glover	.02	.10
4 Vance Johnson	.02	.10
5 Jim Jeffcoat	.02	.10
6 Dan Saleaumua	.02	.10
7 Darion Conner	.02	.10
8 Don Maggs	.02	.10
9 Richard Dent	.05	.15
10 Mark Murphy	.02	.10
11 Wesley Carroll	.02	.10
12 Chris Burkett	.02	.10
13 Steve Wallace	.02	.10
14 Jacob Green	.02	.10
15 Roger Ruzek	.02	.10
16 J.B. Brown	.02	.10
17 Dave Meggett	.05	.15
18 D.J. Johnson	.02	.10
19 Rich Gannon	.10	.30
20 Kevin Mack	.02	.10
21A Reggie Cobb ERR	.02	.10
21B Reggie Cobb COR	.02	.10
22 Nate Lewis	.02	.10
23 Doug Smith	.02	.10
24 Irving Fryar	.05	.15
25 Anthony Thompson	.02	.10
26 Duane Bickett	.02	.10
27 Don Majkowski	.02	.10
28 Mark Schlereth RC	.02	.10
29 Melvin Jenkins	.02	.10
30 Michael Haynes	.05	.15
31 Greg Lewis	.02	.10
32 Kenneth Davis	.02	.10
33 Derrick Thomas	.10	.30
34 David Williams	.02	.10
35 Neal Anderson	.02	.10
36 Andre Collins	.02	.10
37 Jesse Solomon	.02	.10
38 Barry Sanders	1.00	2.50
39 Jeff Gossett	.02	.10
40 Rickey Jackson	.02	.10
41 Ray Berry	.02	.10
42 Leroy Hoard	.05	.15
43 Eric Thomas	.02	.10
44 Brian Washington	.02	.10
45 Pat Terrell	.02	.10
46 Eugene Robinson	.02	.10
47 Luis Sharpe	.02	.10
48 Jerome Brown	.02	.10
49 Mark Collins	.02	.10
50 Johnny Holland	.02	.10
51 Tony Paige	.02	.10
52 Willie Green	.02	.10
53 Steve Atwater	.02	.10
54 Brad Muster	.02	.10
55 Cris Dishman	.02	.10
56 Eddie Anderson	.02	.10
57 Sam Mills	.02	.10
58 Donald Evans	.02	.10
59 Jon Vaughn	.02	.10
60 Marion Butts	.02	.10
61 Rodney Holman	.02	.10
62 Dwayne White RC	.02	.10
63 Martin Mayhew	.02	.10
64 Jonathan Hayes	.02	.10
65 Andre Rison	.05	.15
66 Calvin Williams	.05	.15
67 James Washington	.02	.10
68 Tim Harris	.02	.10
69 Jim Ritcher	.02	.10
70 Johnny Johnson	.02	.10
71 John Offerdahl	.02	.10
72 Herschel Walker	.05	.15
73 Perry Kemp	.02	.10
74 Erik Howard	.02	.10
75 Lamar Lathon	.02	.10
76 Greg Kragen	.02	.10
77 Jay Schroeder	.02	.10
78 Jim Arnold	.02	.10
79 Chris Miller	.05	.15
80 Deron Cherry	.02	.10
81 Jim Harbaugh	.10	.30
82 Gill Fenerty	.02	.10
83 Fred Stokes	.02	.10
84 Roman Phifer	.02	.10
85 Clyde Simmons	.02	.10
86 Vince Newsome	.02	.10
87 Lawrence Dawsey	.05	.15
88 Eddie Brown	.02	.10
89 Greg Montgomery	.02	.10
90 Jeff Lageman	.02	.10
91 Terry Wooden	.02	.10
92 Nate Newton	.02	.10
93 David Richards	.02	.10
94 Derek Russell	.02	.10
95 Steve Jordan	.02	.10
96 Hugh Millen	.02	.10
97 Mark Duper	.02	.10
98 Sean Landeta	.02	.10
99 James Thornton	.02	.10
100 Darrell Green	.02	.10
101 Harris Barton	.02	.10
102 John Alt	.02	.10
103 Mike Farr	.02	.10
104 Bob Golic	.02	.10
105 Gene Atkins	.02	.10
106 Gary Anderson K	.02	.10
107 Norm Johnson	.02	.10
108 Eugene Daniel	.02	.10
109 Kent Hull	.02	.10
110 John Elway	1.00	2.50
111 Rich Camarillo	.02	.10
112 Charles Wilson	.02	.10
113 Matt Bahr	.02	.10
114 Mark Carrier WR	.05	.15
115 Richmond Webb	.02	.10
116 Charles Mann	.02	.10
117 Tim McGee	.02	.10
118 Wes Hopkins	.02	.10
119 Mo Lewis	.02	.10
120 Warren Moon	.10	.30
121 Damone Johnson	.02	.10
122 Kevin Gogan	.02	.10
123 Joey Browner	.02	.10
124 Tommy Kane	.02	.10
125 Vincent Brown	.02	.10
126 Barry Word	.02	.10
127 Michael Brooks	.02	.10
128 Jumbo Elliott	.02	.10
129 Marcus Allen	.10	.30
130 Tom Waddle	.02	.10
131 Jim Dombrowski	.02	.10
132 Aeneas Williams	.05	.15
133 Clay Matthews	.05	.15
134 Thurman Thomas	.10	.30
135 Dean Biasucci	.02	.10
136 Moe Gardner	.02	.10
137 James Campen	.02	.10
138 Tim Johnson	.02	.10
139 Erik Kramer	.05	.15
140 Keith McCants	.02	.10
141 John Carney	.02	.10
142 Tunch Ilkin	.02	.10
143 Louis Oliver	.02	.10
144 Bill Maas	.02	.10
145 Wendell Davis	.02	.10
146 Pepper Johnson	.02	.10
147 Howie Long	.10	.30
148 Brett Maxie	.02	.10
149 Tony Casillas	.02	.10
150 Michael Carter	.02	.10
151 Byron Evans	.02	.10
152 Lorenzo White	.02	.10
153 Larry Kelm	.02	.10
154 Andy Heck	.02	.10
155 Harry Newsome	.02	.10
156 Chris Singleton	.02	.10
157 Mike Kenn	.02	.10
158 Jeff Faulkner	.02	.10
159 Ken Lanier	.02	.10
160 Darryl Talley	.02	.10
161 Louie Aguiar RC	.02	.10
162 Danny Copeland	.02	.10
163 Kevin Porter	.02	.10
164 Trace Armstrong	.02	.10
165 Dermontti Dawson	.02	.10
166 Fred McAfee RC	.02	.10
167 Ronnie Lott	.05	.15
168 Tony Mandarich	.02	.10
169 Howard Cross	.02	.10
170 Vestee Jackson	.02	.10
171 Jeff Herrod	.02	.10
172 Randy Hilliard RC	.02	.10
173 Robert Wilson	.02	.10
174 Joe Walter RC	.02	.10
175 Chris Spielman	.05	.15
176 Darryl Henley	.02	.10
177 Jay Hilgenberg	.02	.10
178 John Kidd	.02	.10
179 Doug Widell	.02	.10
180 Seth Joyner	.02	.10
181 Nick Bell	.02	.10
182 Don Griffin	.02	.10
183 Johnny Meads	.02	.10
184 Jeff Bostic	.02	.10
185 Johnny Hector	.02	.10
186 Jessie Tuggle	.02	.10
187 Robb Thomas	.02	.10
188 Shane Conlan	.02	.10
189 Michael Zordich RC	.02	.10
190 Emmitt Smith	1.50	3.00
191 Robert Blackmon	.02	.10
192 Carl Lee	.02	.10
193 Harry Galbreath	.02	.10
194 Ed King	.02	.10
195 Stan Thomas	.02	.10
196 Andre Waters	.02	.10
197 Pat Harlow	.02	.10
198 Zefross Moss	.02	.10
199 Bobby Hebert	.02	.10
200 Doug Riesenberg	.02	.10
201 Mike Croel	.02	.10
202 Jeff Jaeger	.02	.10
203 Gary Plummer	.02	.10
204 Chris Jacke	.02	.10
205 Neil O'Donnell	.05	.15
206 Mark Bortz	.02	.10
207 Tim Barnett	.02	.10
208 Jerry Ball	.02	.10
209 Chip Lohmiller	.02	.10
210 Jim Everett	.05	.15
211 Tim McKyer	.02	.10
212 Aaron Craver	.02	.10
213 John L. Williams	.02	.10
214 Simon Fletcher	.02	.10
215 Walter Reeves	.02	.10
216 Terance Mathis	.05	.15
217 Mike Pitts	.02	.10
218 Bruce Matthews	.02	.10

219 Howard Ballard	.02	.10
220 Leonard Russell	.05	.15
221 Michael Stewart	.02	.10
222 Mike Merriweather	.02	.10
223 Ricky Sanders	.02	.10
224 Ray Horton	.02	.10
225 Michael Jackson	.05	.15
226 Bill Romanowski	.02	.10
227 Steve McMichael UER	.05	.15
228 Chris Martin	.02	.10
229 Tim Green	.02	.10
230 Karl Mecklenburg	.02	.10
231 Felix Wright	.02	.10
232 Charles McRae	.02	.10
233 Pete Stoyanovich	.02	.10
234 Stephen Baker	.02	.10
235 Herman Moore	.10	.30
236 Terry McDaniel	.02	.10
237 Dalton Hilliard	.02	.10
238 Gill Byrd	.02	.10
239 Leon Seals	.02	.10
240 Rod Woodson	.10	.30
241 Curtis Duncan	.02	.10
242 Keith Jackson	.05	.15
243 Mark Stepnoski	.05	.15
244 Art Monk	.05	.15
245 Matt Stover	.02	.10
246 John Roper	.02	.10
247 Rodney Hampton	.05	.15
248 Steve Wisniewski	.02	.10
249 Bryan Millard	.02	.10
250 Todd Lyght	.02	.10
251 Marvin Washington	.02	.10
252 Eric Swann	.05	.15
253 Bruce Kozerski	.02	.10
254 Jon Hand	.02	.10
255 Scott Fulhage	.02	.10
256 Chuck Cecil	.02	.10
257 Eric Martin	.02	.10
258 Eric Metcalf	.05	.15
259 T.J. Turner	.02	.10
260 Kirk Lowdermilk	.02	.10
261 Keith McKeller	.02	.10
262 Wymon Henderson	.02	.10
263 David Alexander	.02	.10
264 George Jamison	.02	.10
265 Ken Norton Jr.	.05	.15
266 Jim Lachey	.02	.10
267 Bo Orlando RC	.02	.10
268 Nick Lowery	.02	.10
269 Keith Van Horne	.02	.10
270 Dwight Stone	.02	.10
271 Keith DeLong	.02	.10
272 James Francis	.02	.10
273 Greg McMurtry	.02	.10
274 Ethan Horton	.02	.10
275 Stan Brock	.02	.10
276 Ken Harvey	.02	.10
277 Ronnie Harmon	.02	.10
278 Mike Pritchard	.05	.15
279 Kyle Clifton	.02	.10
280 Anthony Johnson	.05	.15
281 Esera Tuaolo	.02	.10
282 Vernon Turner	.02	.10
283 David Griggs	.02	.10
284 Dino Hackett	.02	.10
285 Carwell Gardner	.02	.10
286 Ron Hall	.02	.10
287 Reggie White	.10	.30
288 Checklist 1-100	.02	.10
289 Checklist 101-200	.02	.10
290 Checklist 201-300	.02	.10
291 Mark Clayton MC	.02	.10
292 Pat Swilling MC	.02	.10
293 Ernest Givins MC	.02	.10
294 Broderick Thomas MC	.02	.10
295 John Friesz MC	.02	.10
296 Cornelius Bennett MC	.02	.10
297 Anthony Carter MC	.05	.15
298 Earnest Byner MC	.02	.10
299 Michael Irvin MC	.10	.30
300 Cortez Kennedy MC	.02	.10
301 Barry Sanders MC	.60	1.50
302 Mike Croel MC	.02	.10
303 Emmitt Smith MC	.75	2.00
304 Leonard Russell MC	.02	.10
305 Neal Anderson MC	.02	.10
306 Derrick Thomas MC	.05	.15
307 Mark Rypien MC	.02	.10
308 Reggie White MC	.05	.15
309 Rod Woodson MC	.05	.15
310 Rodney Hampton MC	.05	.15
311 Carnell Lake	.02	.10
312 Robert Delpino	.02	.10
313 Brian Blades	.05	.15
314 Marc Spindler	.02	.10
315 Scott Norwood	.02	.10
316 Frank Warren	.02	.10
317 David Treadwell	.02	.10
318 Steve Broussard	.02	.10
319 Lorenzo Lynch	.02	.10
320 Ray Agnew	.02	.10
321 Derrick Walker	.02	.10
322 Vinson Smith RC	.02	.10
323 Gary Clark	.10	.30
324 Charles Haley	.05	.15
325 Keith Byars	.02	.10
326 Winston Moss	.02	.10
327 Paul McJulien RC UER	.02	.10
(Has Brett Perriman		
card back; see also 453)		
328 Tony Covington	.02	.10
329 Mark Carrier DB	.02	.10
330 Mark Tuinei	.02	.10
331 Tracy Simien RC	.02	.10
332 Jeff Wright	.02	.10
333 Bryan Cox	.05	.15
334 Lonnie Young	.02	.10
335 Clarence Verdin	.02	.10
336 Dan Fike	.02	.10
337 Steve Sewell	.02	.10
338 Gary Zimmerman	.02	.10
339 Barney Bussey	.02	.10
340 William Perry	.05	.15
341 Jeff Hostetler	.05	.15
342 Doug Smith	.02	.10
343 Cleveland Gary	.02	.10
344 Todd Marinovich	.02	.10
345 Rich Moran	.02	.10
346 Tony Woods	.02	.10
347 Vaughan Johnson	.02	.10
348 Marv Cook	.02	.10
349 Pierce Holt	.02	.10
350 Gerald Williams	.02	.10
351 Kevin Butler	.02	.10
352 William White	.02	.10
353 Henry Rolling	.02	.10
354 James Joseph	.02	.10
355 Vinny Testaverde	.05	.15
356 Scott Radecic	.02	.10
357 Lee Johnson	.02	.10
358 Steve Tasker	.05	.15
359 David Lutz	.02	.10
360 Audray McMillian UER	.02	.10
361 Brad Baxter	.02	.10
362 Mark Dennis	.02	.10
363 Erric Pegram	.05	.15
364 Sean Jones	.02	.10
365 William Roberts	.02	.10
366 Steve Young	.40	1.00
367 Joe Jacoby	.02	.10
368 Richard Brown RC	.02	.10
369 Keith Kartz	.02	.10
370 Freddie Joe Nunn	.02	.10
371 Darren Comeaux	.02	.10
372 Larry Brown DB	.02	.10
373 Haywood Jeffires	.05	.15
374 Tom Newberry	.02	.10
375 Steve Bono RC	.10	.30
376 Kevin Ross	.02	.10
377 Kelvin Pritchett	.02	.10
378 Jessie Hester	.02	.10
379 Mitchell Price	.02	.10
380 Barry Foster	.05	.15
381 Reyna Thompson	.02	.10
382 Cris Carter	.30	.75
383 Lemuel Stinson	.02	.10
384 Rod Bernstine	.02	.10
385 James Lofton	.05	.15
386 Kevin Murphy	.02	.10
387 Greg Townsend	.02	.10
388 Edgar Bennett RC	.10	.30
389 Rob Moore	.05	.15
390 Eugene Lockhart	.02	.10
391 Bern Brostek	.02	.10
392 Craig Heyward	.05	.15
393 Ferrell Edmunds	.02	.10
394 John Kasay	.02	.10
395 Jesse Sapolu	.02	.10
396 Jim Breech	.02	.10
397 Neil Smith	.10	.30
398 Bryce Paup	.10	.30
399 Tony Tolbert	.02	.10
400 Bubby Brister	.02	.10
401 Dennis Smith	.02	.10
402 Dan Owens	.02	.10
403 Steve Beuerlein	.05	.15
404 Rick Tuten	.02	.10
405 Eric Allen	.02	.10
406 Eric Hill	.02	.10
407 Don Warren	.02	.10
408 Greg Jackson	.02	.10
409 Chris Doleman	.02	.10
410 Anthony Munoz	.05	.15
411 Michael Young	.02	.10
412 Cornelius Bennett	.05	.15
413 Ray Childress	.02	.10
414 Kevin Call	.02	.10
415 Burt Grossman	.02	.10
416 Scott Miller	.02	.10
417 Tim Newton	.02	.10
418 Robert Young	.02	.10
419 Tommy Vardell RC	.02	.10
420 Michael Walter	.02	.10
421 Chris Port RC	.02	.10
422 Carlton Haselrig RC	.02	.10
423 Rodney Peete	.05	.15
424 Scott Stephen	.02	.10
425 Chris Warren	.10	.30
426 Scott Galbraith RC	.02	.10
427 Fuad Reveiz UER	.02	.10
428 Irv Eatman	.02	.10
429 David Szott	.02	.10
430 Brent Williams	.02	.10
431 Mike Horan	.02	.10
432 Brent Jones	.05	.15
433 Paul Gruber	.02	.10
434 Carlos Huerta	.02	.10
435 Scott Case	.02	.10
436 Greg Davis	.02	.10
437 Ken Clarke	.02	.10
438 Alfred Williams	.02	.10
439 Jim C. Jensen	.02	.10
440 Louis Lipps	.02	.10
441 Larry Roberts	.02	.10
442 James Jones DT	.02	.10
443 Don Mosebar	.02	.10
444 Quinn Early	.05	.15
445 Robert Brown	.02	.10
446 Tom Thayer	.02	.10
447 Michael Irvin	.10	.30
448 Jarrod Bunch	.02	.10
449 Riki Ellison	.02	.10
450 Joe Phillips	.02	.10
451 Ernest Givins	.05	.15
452 Glenn Parker	.02	.10
453 Brett Perriman UER	.10	.30
(Has Paul McJulien		
card back; see also 327)		
454 Jayice Pearson RC	.02	.10
455 Mark Jackson	.02	.10
456 Siran Stacy RC	.02	.10
457 Rufus Porter	.02	.10
458 Michael Ball	.02	.10
459 Craig Taylor	.02	.10
460 George Thomas RC	.02	.10
461 Alvin Wright	.02	.10
462 Ron Hallstrom	.02	.10
463 Mike Mooney RC	.02	.10
464 Dexter Carter	.02	.10
465 Marty Carter RC	.02	.10
466 Pat Swilling	.02	.10
467 Mike Golic	.02	.10
468 Reggie Roby	.02	.10
469 Randall McDaniel	.05	.15
470 John Stephens	.02	.10
471 Ricardo McDonald RC	.02	.10
472 Wilber Marshall	.02	.10
473 Jim Sweeney	.02	.10
474 Ernie Jones	.02	.10
475 Bennie Blades	.02	.10
476 Don Beebe	.02	.10
477 Grant Feasel	.02	.10
478 Ernie Mills	.02	.10
479 Tony Jones T	.02	.10
480 Jeff Uhlenhake	.02	.10
481 Gaston Green	.02	.10
482 John Taylor	.05	.15
483 Anthony Smith	.02	.10
484 Tony Bennett	.02	.10
485 David Brandon RC	.02	.10
486 Shawn Jefferson	.02	.10
487 Christian Okoye	.02	.10
488 Leonard Marshall	.02	.10
489 Jay Novacek	.05	.15
490 Harold Green	.02	.10
491 Bubba McDowell	.02	.10
492 Gary Anderson RB	.02	.10
493 Terrell Buckley RC	.02	.10
494 Jamie Dukes RC	.02	.10
495 Morten Andersen	.02	.10
496 Henry Thomas	.02	.10
497 Bill Lewis	.02	.10
498 Jeff Cross	.02	.10
499 Hardy Nickerson	.05	.15
500 Henry Ellard	.05	.15
501 Joe Bowden RC	.02	.10
502 Brian Noble	.02	.10
503 Mike Cofer	.02	.10
504 Jeff Bryant	.02	.10
505 Lomas Brown	.02	.10
506 Chip Banks	.02	.10
507 Keith Traylor	.02	.10
508 Mark Kelso	.02	.10
509 Dexter McNabb RC	.02	.10
510 Gene Chilton RC	.02	.10
511 George Thornton	.02	.10
512 Jeff Criswell	.02	.10
513 Brad Edwards	.02	.10
514 Ron Heller	.02	.10
515 Tim Brown	.10	.30
516 Keith Hamilton RC	.05	.15
517 Mark Higgs	.02	.10
518 Tommy Barnhardt	.02	.10
519 Brian Jordan	.05	.15
520 Ray Crockett	.02	.10
521 Karl Wilson	.02	.10
522 Ricky Reynolds	.02	.10
523 Max Montoya	.02	.10
524 David Little	.02	.10
525 Alonzo Mitz RC	.02	.10
526 Darryll Lewis	.02	.10
527 Keith Henderson	.02	.10
528 LeRoy Butler	.02	.10
529 Rob Burnett	.02	.10
530 Chris Chandler	.10	.30
531 Maury Buford	.02	.10
532 Mark Ingram	.02	.10
533 Mike Saxon	.02	.10
534 Bill Fralic	.02	.10
535 Craig Patterson RC	.02	.10
536 John Randle	.05	.15
537 Dwayne Harper	.02	.10
538 Chris Hakel RC	.02	.10
539 Maurice Hurst	.02	.10
540 Warren Powers UER	.02	.10
541 Will Wolford	.02	.10
542 Dennis Gibson	.02	.10
543 Jackie Slater	.02	.10
544 Floyd Turner	.02	.10
545 Guy McIntyre	.02	.10
546 Eric Green	.02	.10
547 Rohn Stark	.02	.10
548 William Fuller	.02	.10
549 Alvin Harper	.05	.15
550 Mark Clayton	.05	.15
551 Natu Tuatagaloa RC	.02	.10
552 Fred Barnett	.10	.30
553 Bob Whitfield RC	.02	.10
554 Courtney Hall	.02	.10
555 Brian Mitchell	.05	.15
556 Patrick Hunter	.02	.10
557 Rick Bryan	.02	.10
558 Anthony Carter	.05	.15
559 Jim Wahler	.02	.10
560 Joe Morris	.02	.10
561 Tony Zendejas	.02	.10
562 Mervyn Fernandez	.02	.10
563 Jamie Williams	.02	.10
564 Darrell Thompson	.02	.10
565 Adrian Cooper	.02	.10
566 Chris Goode	.02	.10
567 Jeff Davidson RC	.02	.10
568 James Hasty	.02	.10
569 Chris Mims RC	.02	.10
570 Ray Seals RC	.02	.10
571 Myron Guyton	.02	.10
572 Todd McNair	.02	.10
573 Andre Tippett	.02	.10
574 Kirby Jackson	.02	.10
575 Mel Gray	.05	.15
576 Stephone Paige	.02	.10
577 Scott Davis	.02	.10
578 John Gesek	.02	.10
579 Earnest Byner	.02	.10
580 John Friesz	.05	.15
581 Al Smith	.02	.10
582 Flipper Anderson	.02	.10
583 Amp Lee RC	.02	.10
584 Greg Lloyd	.05	.15
585 Cortez Kennedy	.05	.15
586 Keith Sims	.02	.10
587 Terry Allen	.10	.30
588 David Fulcher	.02	.10
589 Chris Hinton	.02	.10
590 Tim McDonald	.02	.10
591 Bruce Armstrong	.02	.10
592 Sterling Sharpe	.10	.30
593 Tom Rathman	.02	.10
594 Bill Brooks	.02	.10
595 Broderick Thomas	.02	.10
596 Jim Wilks	.02	.10
597 Tyrone Braxton UER	.02	.10
598 Checklist 301-400 UER	.02	.10
599 Checklist 401-500	.02	.10
600 Checklist 501-600	.02	.10
601 Andre Reed MC	.30	.75
602 Troy Aikman MC	2.00	4.00
603 Dan Marino MC	2.50	6.00
604 Randall Cunningham MC	.30	.75
605 Jim Kelly MC	.60	1.50
606 Deion Sanders MC	.75	2.00
607 Junior Seau MC	.60	1.50
608 Jerry Rice MC	2.00	4.00
609 Bruce Smith MC	.30	.75
610 Lawrence Taylor MC	.60	1.50
611 Todd Collins RC	.20	.50
612 Ty Detmer	.60	1.50
613 Browning Nagle	.20	.50
614 Tony Sacca RC UER	.20	.50
(Reverse negative		
photo on back)		
615 Boomer Esiason	.30	.75
616 Billy Joe Tolliver	.20	.50
617 Leslie O'Neal	.30	.75
618 Mark Wheeler RC	.20	.50
619 Eric Dickerson	.30	.75
620 Phil Simms	.30	.75
621 Troy Vincent RC	.20	.50
622 Jason Hanson RC	.30	.75
623 Andre Reed	.30	.75
624 Russell Maryland	.20	.50
625 Steve Emtman RC	.20	.50
626 Sean Gilbert RC	.30	.75
627 Dana Hall RC	.20	.50
628 Dan McGwire	.20	.50
629 Lewis Billups	.20	.50
630 Darryl Williams RC	.20	.50
631 Dwayne Sabb RC	.20	.50
632 Mark Royals	.20	.50
633 Cary Conklin	.20	.50
634 Al Toon	.30	.75
635 Junior Seau	.60	1.50
636 Greg Skrepenak RC UER	.20	.50
(Card misnumbered 686)		
637 Deion Sanders	1.50	3.00
638 Steve DeOssie	.20	.50
639 Randall Cunningham	.60	1.50
640 Jim Kelly	.60	1.50
641 Michael Brandon RC	.20	.50
642 Clayton Holmes RC	.20	.50
643 Webster Slaughter	.20	.50
644 Ricky Proehl	.20	.50
645 Jerry Rice	2.50	5.00
646 Carl Banks	.20	.50
647 J.J.Birden	.20	.50
648 Tracy Scroggins RC	.20	.50
649 Alonzo Spellman RC	.30	.75
650 Joe Montana	3.00	8.00
651 Courtney Hawkins RC	.30	.75
652 Corey Widmer RC	.20	.50
653 Robert Brooks RC	1.50	4.00
654 Darren Woodson RC	.60	1.50
655 Derrick Fenner	.20	.50
656 Steve Christie	.20	.50
657 Chester McGlockton RC	.30	.75
658 Steve Israel RC	.20	.50
659 Robert Harris RC	.20	.50
660 Dan Marino	3.00	8.00
661 Ed McCaffrey	2.00	5.00
662 Johnny Mitchell RC	.20	.50
663 Timm Rosenbach	.20	.50
664 Anthony Miller	.30	.75
665 Merril Hoge	.20	.50
666 Eugene Chung RC	.20	.50
667 Rueben Mayes	.20	.50
668 Martin Bayless	.20	.50
669 Ashley Ambrose RC	.60	1.50
670 Michael Cofer UER	.20	.50
(Back shows card for		
Mike Cofer, the kicker)		
671 Shane Dronett RC	.20	.50
672 Bernie Kosar	.30	.75
673 Mike Singletary	.30	.75
674 Mike Lodish RC	.20	.50
675 Phillippi Sparks RC	.20	.50
676 Joel Steed RC	.20	.50
677 Kevin Fagan	.20	.50
678 Randal Hill	.20	.50
679 Ken O'Brien	.20	.50
680 Lawrence Taylor	.60	1.50
681 Harvey Williams	.60	1.50
682 Quentin Coryatt RC	.20	.50
683 Brett Favre	40.00	100.00
684 Robert Jones RC	.20	.50
685 Michael Dean Perry	.30	.75
686 Bruce Smith	.60	1.50
687 Troy Auzenne RC	.20	.50
688 Thomas McLemore RC	.20	.50
689 Dale Carter RC	.30	.75
690 Marc Boutte RC	.20	.50
691 Jeff George	.60	1.50
692 Dion Lambert RC UER	.20	.50
(Birthdate is 2/12/19; should		
be 2/12/69)		
693 Vaughn Dunbar RC	.20	.50
694 Derek Brown TE RC	.20	.50
695 Troy Aikman	2.50	5.00
696 John Fina RC	.20	.50
697 Kevin Smith RC	.20	.50
698 Corey Miller RC	.20	.50
699 Lance Olberding RC	.20	.50
700 Checklist 601-700 UER	.20	.50
(Numbering sequence		
off from 616 to 636)		
P1 Promo Sheet Natl.	4.00	10.00
P2 Promo Sheet Diam.Day	5.00	12.00

1992 Stadium Club No.1 Draft Picks

COMPLETE SET (4)	17.50	35.00
RANDOM INSERTS IN HIGH SERIES		
1 Jeff George	6.00	12.00
2 Russell Maryland	4.00	8.00
3 Steve Emtman	4.00	8.00
4 Rocket Ismail	5.00	10.00

1992 Stadium Club QB Legends

COMPLETE SET (6)	8.00	20.00
RANDOM INSERTS IN SER.2 PACKS		
1 Y.A. Tittle	1.25	2.50
2 Bart Starr	1.75	3.50
3 Johnny Unitas	1.75	3.50
4 George Blanda	1.25	2.50
5A Roger Staubach ERR	2.50	6.00
(Terry Bradshaw's '71 Topps		
card on back)		
5B Roger Staubach COR	2.50	6.00
6 Terry Bradshaw	2.50	6.00

1993 Stadium Club

The 1993 Stadium Club football set was issued in two series of 250 cards each and a third 50-card series for a total of 550 standard-size cards. The cards were distributed in 14 and 23-card packs. The third, or high series, was also packaged as a 51-card factory set that included one First Day Issue. Cards from the Members Choice subsets are numbered 241-250 and 491-500. Rookie Cards include Reggie Brooks, Jerome Bettis, Drew Bledsoe, Garrison Hearst, Terry Kirby, O.J. McDuffie, Natrone Means, Glyn Milburn, Rick Mirer and Kevin Williams. The nine-card promo sheet was distributed at the 1993 National Sports Collector's Convention. It is not considered part of the complete set.

COMPLETE SET (550)	15.00	40.00
COMP.SERIES 1 (250)	10.00	25.00
COMP.SERIES 2 (250)	6.00	15.00
COMP.HIGH SERIES (50)	4.00	8.00
COMP.HIGH FACT.SET (51)	5.00	12.00
1 Sterling Sharpe	.07	.20
2 Chris Burkett	.02	.10
3 Santana Dotson	.07	.20
4 Michael Jackson	.07	.20
5 Neal Anderson	.02	.10
6 Bryan Cox	.02	.10
7 Dennis Gibson	.02	.10
8 Jeff Graham	.07	.20
9 Roger Ruzek	.02	.10
10 Duane Bickett	.02	.10
11 Charles Mann	.02	.10
12 Tommy Maddox	.15	.40
13 Vaughn Dunbar	.02	.10
14 Gary Plummer	.02	.10
15 Chris Miller	.07	.20
16 Chris Warren	.07	.20
17 Alvin Harper	.07	.20
18 Eric Dickerson	.07	.20
19 Mike Jones	.02	.10
20 Ernest Givins	.07	.20
21 Natrone Means RC	.15	.40
22 Doug Riesenberg	.02	.10
23 Barry Word	.02	.10
24 Sean Salisbury	.02	.10
25 Derrick Fenner	.02	.10
26 David Howard	.02	.10
27 Mark Kelso	.02	.10
28 Todd Lyght	.02	.10
29 Dana Hall	.02	.10
30 Eric Metcalf	.07	.20
31 Jason Hanson	.02	.10
32 Dwight Stone	.02	.10
33 Johnny Mitchell	.02	.10
34 Reggie Roby	.02	.10
35 Terrell Buckley	.02	.10
36 Steve McMichael	.07	.20
37 Marty Carter	.02	.10
38 Seth Joyner	.02	.10
39 Rohn Stark	.02	.10
40 Eric Curry RC	.02	.10
41 Tommy Barnhardt	.02	.10
42 Karl Mecklenburg	.02	.10
43 Darion Conner	.02	.10
44 Ronnie Harmon	.02	.10
45 Cortez Kennedy	.07	.20
46 Tim Brown	.15	.40
47 Bill Lewis	.02	.10
48 Randall McDaniel	.05	.15
49 Curtis Duncan	.02	.10
50 Troy Aikman	.60	1.50
51 David Klingler	.02	.10
52 Brent Jones	.07	.20
53 Dave Krieg	.07	.20
54 Bruce Smith	.15	.40
55 Vincent Brown	.02	.10
56 O.J. McDuffie RC	.15	.40
57 Cleveland Gary	.02	.10
58 Larry Centers RC	.15	.40
59 Pepper Johnson	.02	.10
60 Dan Marino	1.25	3.00
61 Robert Porcher	.02	.10
62 Jim Harbaugh	.15	.40
63 Sam Mills	.02	.10
64 Gary Anderson RB	.02	.10
65 Neil O'Donnell	.07	.20
66 Keith Byars	.02	.10
67 Jeff Herrod	.02	.10
68 Marion Butts	.02	.10
69 Terry McDaniel	.02	.10
70 John Elway	1.25	3.00
71 Steve Broussard	.02	.10
72 Kelvin Martin	.02	.10
73 Tom Carter RC	.07	.20
74 Bryce Paup	.07	.20
75 Jim Kelly UER	.07	.20
back shows 1992		
Topps card as RC		
76 Bill Romanowski	.02	.10
77 Andre Collins	.02	.10
78 Mike Farr	.02	.10
79 Henry Ellard	.07	.20
80 Dale Carter	.02	.10
81 Johnny Bailey	.02	.10
82 Garrison Hearst RC	.60	1.50
83 Brent Williams	.02	.10
84 Ricardo McDonald	.02	.10
85 Emmitt Smith	1.50	3.00
86 Vai Sikahema	.02	.10
87 Jackie Harris	.02	.10
88 Alonzo Spellman	.02	.10
89 Mark Wheeler	.02	.10
90 Dalton Hilliard	.02	.10
91 Mark Higgs	.02	.10
92 Aaron Wallace	.02	.10
93 Earnest Byner	.02	.10
94 Stanley Richard	.02	.10
95 Cris Carter	.15	.40
96 Bobby Houston RC	.02	.10
97 Craig Heyward	.07	.20
98 Bernie Kosar	.07	.20
99 Mike Croel	.02	.10
100 Deion Sanders	.40	1.00
101 Warren Moon	.07	.20
102 Christian Okoye	.02	.10
103 Ricky Watters	.15	.40
104 Eric Swann	.07	.20
105 Rodney Hampton	.07	.20
106 Daryl Johnston	.07	.20
107 Andre Reed	.07	.20
108 Jerome Bettis RC	4.00	8.00
109 Eugene Daniel	.02	.10
110 Leonard Russell	.07	.20
111 Darryl Williams	.02	.10
112 Rod Woodson	.15	.40
113 Boomer Esiason	.07	.20
114 James Hasty	.02	.10
115 Marc Boutte	.02	.10
116 Tom Waddle	.02	.10
117 Lawrence Dawsey	.02	.10
118 Mark Collins	.02	.10
119 Willie Gault	.02	.10
120 Barry Sanders	1.00	2.50
121 Leroy Hoard	.07	.20
122 Anthony Munoz	.07	.20
123 Jesse Sapolu	.02	.10
124 Art Monk	.07	.20
125 Randal Hill	.02	.10
126 John Offerdahl	.02	.10
127 Carlos Jenkins	.02	.10
128 Al Smith	.02	.10
129 Michael Irvin	.15	.40
130 Kenneth Davis	.02	.10
131 Curtis Conway RC	.30	.75
132 Steve Atwater	.02	.10
133 Neil Smith	.15	.40
134 Steve Everitt RC	.02	.10
135 Chris Mims	.02	.10
136 Rickey Jackson	.02	.10
137 Edgar Bennett	.15	.40
138 Mike Pritchard	.07	.20
139 Richard Dent	.07	.20
140 Barry Foster	.07	.20
141 Eugene Robinson	.02	.10
142 Jackie Slater	.02	.10
143 Paul Gruber	.02	.10
144 Rob Moore	.07	.20
145 Robert Smith RC	1.00	2.50
146 Lorenzo White	.02	.10
147 Tommy Vardell	.02	.10
148 Dave Meggett	.02	.10
149 Vince Workman	.02	.10
150 Terry Allen	.15	.40
151 Howie Long	.15	.40
152 Charles Haley	.07	.20
153 Pete Metzelaars	.02	.10
154 John Copeland RC	.07	.20
155 Aeneas Williams	.02	.10
156 Ricky Sanders	.02	.10
157 Andre Ware	.02	.10
158 Tony Paige	.02	.10
159 Jerome Henderson	.02	.10
160 Harold Green	.02	.10
161 Wymon Henderson	.02	.10
162 Andre Rison	.07	.20
163 Donald Evans	.02	.10
164 Todd Scott	.02	.10
165 Steve Emtman	.02	.10
166 William Fuller	.02	.10
167 Michael Dean Perry	.07	.20
168 Randall Cunningham	.15	.40
169 Toi Cook	.02	.10
170 Browning Nagle	.02	.10
171 Darryl Henley	.02	.10
172 George Teague RC	.07	.20
173 Derrick Thomas	.15	.40
174 Jay Novacek	.07	.20
175 Mark Carrier DB	.02	.10
176 Kevin Fagan	.02	.10
177 Nate Lewis	.02	.10
178 Courtney Hawkins	.02	.10
179 Robert Blackmon	.02	.10
180 Rick Mirer RC	.15	.40
181 Mike Lodish	.02	.10
182 Jarrod Bunch	.02	.10
183 Anthony Smith	.02	.10
184 Brian Noble	.02	.10
185 Eric Bieniemy	.02	.10
186 Keith Jackson	.07	.20
187 Eric Martin	.02	.10
188 Vance Johnson	.02	.10
189 Kevin Mack	.02	.10
190 Rich Camarillo	.02	.10
191 Ashley Ambrose	.02	.10
192 Ray Childress	.02	.10
193 Jim Arnold	.02	.10
194 Ricky Ervins	.02	.10
195 Gary Anderson K	.02	.10
196 Eric Allen	.02	.10
197 Roger Craig	.07	.20
198 Jon Vaughn	.02	.10
199 Tim McDonald	.02	.10
200 Broderick Thomas	.02	.10
201 Jessie Tuggle	.02	.10
202 Alonzo Mitz	.02	.10
203 Harvey Williams	.07	.20
204 Russell Maryland	.02	.10
205 Marvin Washington	.02	.10
206 Jim Everett	.07	.20
207 Trace Armstrong	.02	.10
208 Steve Young	.60	1.50
209 Tony Woods	.02	.10
210 Brett Favre	2.00	4.00
211 Nate Odomes	.02	.10
212 Ricky Proehl	.02	.10
213 Jim Dombrowski	.02	.10
214 Anthony Carter	.07	.20
215 Tracy Simien	.02	.10
216 Clay Matthews	.07	.20
217 Patrick Bates RC	.02	.10
218 Jeff George	.15	.40
219 David Fulcher	.02	.10
220 Phil Simms	.07	.20
221 Eugene Chung	.02	.10
222 Reggie Cobb	.02	.10
223 Jim Sweeney	.02	.10
224 Greg Lloyd	.07	.20
225 Sean Jones	.02	.10
226 Marvin Jones RC	.02	.10
227 Bill Brooks	.02	.10
228 Moe Gardner	.02	.10
229 Louis Oliver	.02	.10
230 Flipper Anderson	.02	.10
231 Marc Spindler	.02	.10
232 Jerry Rice	.75	2.00
233 Chip Lohmiller	.02	.10
234 Nolan Harrison	.02	.10
235 Heath Sherman	.02	.10
236 Reyna Thompson	.02	.10
237 Derrick Walker	.02	.10
238 Rufus Porter	.02	.10
239 Checklist 1-125	.02	.10
240 Checklist 126-250	.02	.10
241 John Elway MC	.60	1.50
242 Troy Aikman MC	.30	.75
243 Steve Emtman MC	.02	.10
244 Ricky Watters MC	.07	.20
245 Barry Foster MC	.02	.10
246 Dan Marino MC	.60	1.50
247 Reggie White MC	.07	.20
248 Thurman Thomas MC	.07	.20
249 Broderick Thomas MC	.02	.10
250 Joe Montana MC	.60	1.50
251 Tim Goad	.02	.10
252 Joe Nash	.02	.10
253 Anthony Johnson	.07	.20
254 Carl Pickens	.07	.20
255 Steve Beuerlein	.07	.20
256 Anthony Newman	.02	.10
257 Corey Miller	.02	.10
258 Steve DeBerg	.02	.10
259 Johnny Holland	.02	.10
260 Jerry Ball	.02	.10
261 Siupeli Malamala RC	.02	.10
262 Steve Wisniewski	.02	.10
263 Kelvin Pritchett	.02	.10
264 Chris Gardocki	.02	.10
265 Henry Thomas	.02	.10
266 Arthur Marshall RC	.02	.10
267 Quinn Early	.07	.20
268 Jonathan Hayes	.02	.10
269 Eric Pegram	.07	.20
270 Clyde Simmons	.02	.10
271 Eric Moten	.02	.10
272 Brian Mitchell	.07	.20
273 Adrian Cooper	.02	.10
274 Gaston Green	.02	.10
275 John Taylor	.07	.20
276 Jeff Uhlenhake	.02	.10
277 Phil Hansen	.02	.10
278A K.Williams RC WR ERR	.15	.40
missing draft pick logo on front		
278B K.Williams RC WR COR	.15	.40
with draft pick logo		
279 Robert Massey	.02	.10
280A Drew Bledsoe RC ERR	3.00	8.00
missing draft pick logo on front		
280B Drew Bledsoe RC COR	2.00	5.00
(draft pick logo on front)		
281 Walter Reeves	.02	.10
282A Carlton Gray ERR RC	.08	.25
282B Carlton Gray COR RC	.05	.15
283 Derek Brown TE	.02	.10
284 Martin Mayhew	.02	.10
285 Sean Gilbert	.07	.20
286 Jessie Hester	.02	.10
287 Mark Clayton	.02	.10
288 Blair Thomas	.02	.10
289 J.J. Birden	.02	.10
290 Shannon Sharpe	.15	.40
291 Richard Fain RC	.02	.10
292 Gene Atkins	.02	.10
293 Burt Grossman	.02	.10
294 Chris Doleman	.02	.10
295 Pat Swilling	.02	.10
296 Mike Kenn	.02	.10
297 Merril Hoge	.02	.10
298 Don Mosebar	.02	.10
299 Kevin Smith	.07	.20
300 Darrell Green	.02	.10
301A Dan Footman RC ERR	.08	.25
(missing draft pick logo on front)		
301B Dan Footman RC COR	.05	.15
draft pick logo on front)		
302 Vestee Jackson	.02	.10
303 Carwell Gardner	.02	.10
304 Amp Lee	.02	.10
305 Bruce Matthews	.02	.10
306 Antone Davis	.02	.10
307 Dean Biasucci	.02	.10
308 Maurice Hurst	.02	.10
309 John Kasay	.02	.10
310 Lawrence Taylor	.07	.20
311 Ken Harvey	.02	.10
312 Willie Davis	.07	.20
313 Tony Bennett	.02	.10
314 Jay Schroeder	.02	.10
315 Darren Perry	.02	.10
316A Troy Drayton RC ERR	.08	.25
(missing draft pick logo on front)		
316B Troy Drayton RC COR	.05	.15
(draft pick logo on front)		
317A Dan Williams RC ERR	.08	.25
(missing draft pick logo on front)		
317B Dan Williams RC COR	.05	.15
(draft pick logo on front)		
318 Michael Haynes	.07	.20
319 Renaldo Turnbull	.02	.10
320 Junior Seau	.15	.40
321 Ray Crockett	.02	.10
322 Will Furrer	.02	.10
323 Byron Evans	.02	.10
324 Jim McMahon	.07	.20
325 Robert Jones	.02	.10
326 Eric Davis	.02	.10
327 Jeff Cross	.02	.10
328 Kyle Clifton	.02	.10
329 Haywood Jeffires	.07	.20
330 Jeff Hostetler	.07	.20
331 Darryl Talley	.02	.10
332 Keith McCants	.02	.10
333 Mo Lewis	.02	.10
334 Matt Stover	.02	.10
335 Ferrell Edmunds	.02	.10
336 Matt Brock	.02	.10
337 Ernie Mills	.02	.10
338 Shane Dronett	.02	.10
339 Brad Muster	.02	.10
340 Jesse Solomon	.02	.10
341 John Randle	.07	.20
342 Chris Spielman	.07	.20
343 David Whitmore	.02	.10
344 Glenn Parker	.02	.10
345 Marco Coleman	.02	.10
346 Kenneth Gant	.02	.10
347 Cris Dishman	.02	.10
348 Kenny Walker	.02	.10
349A R.Potts RC ERR	.08	.25
missing draft pick logo on front		
349B R.Potts RC COR	.05	.15
draft pick logo on front		
350 Reggie White	.15	.40
351 Gerald Robinson	.02	.10
352 Mark Rypien	.02	.10
353 Stan Humphries	.07	.20
354 Chris Singleton	.02	.10
355 Herschel Walker	.07	.20
356 Ron Hall	.02	.10
357 Ethan Horton	.02	.10
358 Anthony Pleasant	.02	.10
359A Thomas Smith RC ERR	.08	.25
(missing draft pick logo on front)		
359B Thomas Smith RC COR	.05	.15
(draft pick logo on front)		
360 Audray McMillian	.02	.10
361 D.J. Johnson	.02	.10
362 Ron Heller	.02	.10
363 Bern Brostek	.02	.10
364 Ronnie Lott	.07	.20
365 Reggie Johnson	.02	.10
366 Lin Elliott	.02	.10
367 Lemuel Stinson	.02	.10
368 William White	.02	.10
369 Ernie Jones	.02	.10
370 Tom Rathman	.02	.10
371 Tommy Kane	.02	.10
372 David Brandon	.02	.10
373 Lee Johnson	.02	.10
374 Wade Wilson	.02	.10
375 Nick Lowery	.02	.10
376 Bubba McDowell	.02	.10
377A W.Simmons RC ERR	.08	.25
missing draft pick logo on front		
377B W.Simmons RC COR	.05	.15
draft pick logo on front		
378 Calvin Williams	.07	.20
379 Courtney Hall	.02	.10
380 Troy Vincent	.02	.10
381 Tim McGee	.02	.10
382 Russell Freeman RC	.02	.10
383 Steve Tasker	.07	.20
384A M.Strahan RC ERR	1.25	3.00
(missing draft pick logo on front)		
384B Michael Strahan RC COR	1.00	2.50
(draft pick logo on front)		

385 Greg Skrepenak .02 .10
386 Jake Reed .07 .20
387 Pete Stoyanovich .02 .10
388 Levon Kirkland .02 .10
389 Mel Gray .07 .20
390 Brian Washington .02 .10
391 Don Griffin .02 .10
392 Desmond Howard .07 .20
393 Luis Sharpe .02 .10
394 Mike Johnson .02 .10
395 Andre Tippett .02 .10
396 Donnell Woolford .02 .10
397A D.DuBose RC ERR .08 .25
missing draft pick logo on front
397B D.DuBose RC COR .05 .15
(draft pick logo on front)
398 Pat Terrell .02 .10
399 Todd McNair .02 .10
400 Ken Norton .07 .20
401 Keith Hamilton .02 .10
402 Andy Heck .02 .10
403 Jeff Gossett .02 .10
404 Dexter McNabb .02 .10
405 Richmond Webb .02 .10
406 Irving Fryar .07 .20
407 Brian Hansen .02 .10
408 David Little .02 .10
409A Glyn Milburn RC ERR .15 .40
(missing draft pick logo on front)
409B Glyn Milburn RC COR .07 .20
(draft pick logo on front)
410 Doug Dawson .02 .10
411 Scott Mersereau .02 .10
412 Don Beebe .02 .10
413 Vaughan Johnson .02 .10
414 Jack Del Rio .02 .10
415A D.Gordon RC ERR .08 .25
missing draft pick logo on front
415B Darrien Gordon COR RC .05 .15
416 Mark Schlereth .02 .10
417 Lomas Brown .02 .10
418 William Thomas .02 .10
419 James Francis .02 .10
420 Quentin Coryatt .07 .20
421 Tyji Armstrong .02 .10
422 Hugh Millen .02 .10
423 Adrian White RC .02 .10
424 Eddie Anderson .02 .10
425 Mark Ingram .02 .10
426 Ken O'Brien .02 .10
427 Simon Fletcher .02 .10
428 Tim McKyer .02 .10
429 Leonard Marshall .02 .10
430 Eric Green .02 .10
431 Leonard Harris .02 .10
432 Darin Jordan RC .02 .10
433 Erik Howard .02 .10
434 David Lang .02 .10
435 Eric Turner .02 .10
436 Michael Cofer .02 .10
437 Jeff Bryant .02 .10
438 Charles McRae .02 .10
439 Henry Jones .02 .10
440 Joe Montana 1.25 3.00
441 Morten Andersen .02 .10
442 Jeff Jaeger .02 .10
443 Leslie O'Neal .07 .20
444 LeRoy Butler .02 .10
445 Steve Jordan .02 .10
446 Brad Edwards .02 .10
447 J.R. Brown .02 .10
448 Kerry Cash .02 .10
449 Mark Tuinei .02 .10
450 Rodney Peete .02 .10
451 Sheldon White .02 .10
452 Wesley Carroll .02 .10
453 Brad Baxter .02 .10
454 Mike Pitts .02 .10
455 Greg Montgomery .02 .10
456 Kenny Davidson .02 .10
457 Scott Fulhage .02 .10
458 Greg Townsend .02 .10
459 Rod Bernstine .02 .10
460 Gary Clark .07 .20
461 Hardy Nickerson .07 .20
462 Sean Landeta .02 .10
463 Rob Burnett .02 .10
464 Fred Barnett .07 .20
465 John L. Williams .02 .10
466 Anthony Miller .07 .20
467 Roman Phifer .02 .10
468 Rich Moran .02 .10
469A Willie Roaf RC ERR .08 .25
(missing draft pick logo on front)
469B Willie Roaf RC COR .05 .15
(draft pick logo on front)
470 William Perry .07 .20
471 Marcus Allen .15 .40
472 Carl Lee .02 .10
473 Kurt Gouveia .02 .10
474 Jarvis Williams .02 .10
475 Alfred Williams .02 .10
476 Mark Stepnoski .02 .10
477 Steve Wallace .02 .10
478 Pat Harlow .02 .10
479 Chip Banks .02 .10
480 Cornelius Bennett .07 .20
481A Ryan McNeil RC ERR .05 .15
(missing draft pick logo on front)
481B Ryan McNeil RC COR .15 .40
(draft pick logo on front)
482 Norm Johnson .02 .10
483 Dermontti Dawson .02 .10
484 Dwayne White .02 .10
485 Derek Russell .02 .10
486 Lionel Washington .02 .10
487 Eric Hill .02 .10
488 Micheal Barrow RC .15 .40
489 Checklist 251-375 UER .02 .10
(No. 277 Hansen misspelled Hanson)
490 Checklist 376-500 UER .02 .10
(No. 488 Micheal Barrow misspelled Michael)
491 Emmitt Smith MC .60 1.50
492 Derrick Thomas MC .07 .20
493 Deion Sanders MC .15 .40
494 Randall Cunningham MC .07 .20
495 Sterling Sharpe MC .07 .20
496 Barry Sanders MC .50 1.25
497 Thurman Thomas MC .07 .20
498 Brett Favre MC .75 2.00
499 Vaughan Johnson MC .02 .10
500 Steve Young MC .30 .75
501 Marvin Jones MC .02 .10
502 Reggie Brooks MC RC .07 .20
503 Eric Curry MC .02 .10
504 Drew Bledsoe MC .75 2.00
505 Glyn Milburn MC .07 .20
506 Jerome Bettis MC 1.50 4.00
507 Robert Smith MC .40 1.00
508 Dana Stubblefield MC RC .15 .40
509 Tom Carter MC .07 .20
510 Rick Mirer MC .15 .40
511 Russell Copeland RC .07 .20
512 Deon Figures RC .07 .20
513 Tony McGee RC .07 .20
514 Derrick Lassic RC .02 .10
515 Everett Lindsay RC .02 .10
516 Derek Brown RBK RC .02 .10
517 Harold Alexander RC .02 .10
518 Tom Scott RC .02 .10
519 Elvis Grbac RC 1.25 3.00
520 Terry Kirby RC .15 .40
521 Doug Pelfrey RC .02 .10
522 Horace Copeland RC .07 .20
523 Irv Smith RC .02 .10
524 Lincoln Kennedy RC .02 .10
525 Jason Elam RC .15 .40
526 Qadry Ismail RC .15 .40
527 Artie Smith RC .02 .10
528 Tyrone Hughes RC .07 .20
529 Lance Gunn RC .02 .10
530 Vincent Brisby RC .15 .40
531 Patrick Robinson RC .02 .10
532 Rocket Ismail .07 .20
533 Willie Beamon RC .02 .10
534 Vaughn Hebron RC .02 .10
535 Darren Drozdov RC .15 .40
536 James Jett RC .15 .40
537 Michael Bates RC .02 .10
538 Tom Rouen RC .02 .10
539 Michael Husted RC .02 .10
540 Greg Robinson RC .02 .10
541 Carl Banks .02 .10
542 Kevin Greene .07 .20
543 Scott Mitchell .15 .40
544 Michael Brooks .02 .10
545 Shane Conlan .02 .10
546 Vinny Testaverde .07 .20
547 Robert Delpino .02 .10
548 Bill Fralic .02 .10
549 Carlton Bailey .02 .10
550 Johnny Johnson .02 .10
NNO Jerry Rice RB UER 4.00 10.00
(Wrong date for record touchdown)
P1 Promo Sheet 2.00 5.00
Johnny Bailey
Vai Sikahema
Richard Dent
Sterling Sharpe
Tommy Barnhardt
Cris Carter
Cortez Kennedy
Christian Okoye
Reggie Cobb

1993 Stadium Club First Day

COMPLETE SET (550) 400.00 800.00
*STARS: 5X TO 12X BASE CARD HI
*RCs: 2.5X TO 6X BASE CARD HI
STATED ODDS 1:24

1993 Stadium Club Master Photos I

COMPLETE SET (12) 6.00 15.00
ONE PER SERIES 1 HOBBY BOX
*TRADE CARD: .3X to .8X MASTER PHOTO
PRICES ARE PER SINGLE LARGE CARD
1 Barry Foster .30 .75
2 Barry Sanders 2.00 5.00
3 Reggie Cobb .30 .75
4 Cortez Kennedy .30 .75
5 Steve Young 1.25 3.00
6 Ricky Watters .40 1.00
7 Rob Moore .30 .75
8 Derrick Thomas .50 1.25
9 Jeff George .40 1.00
10 Sterling Sharpe .40 1.00
11 Bruce Smith .50 1.25
12 Deion Sanders .75 2.00

1993 Stadium Club Master Photos II

COMPLETE SET (12) 4.00 8.00
ONE PER SERIES 2 HOBBY BOX
*TRADE CARD: .3X TO .8X MASTER PHOTOHI
PRICES ARE PER SINGLE LARGE CARD
1 Morten Andersen .40 1.00
2 Ken Norton Jr. .30 .75
3 Clyde Simmons .30 .75
4 Roman Phifer .30 .75
5 Greg Townsend .30 .75
6 Darryl Talley .30 .75
7 Herschel Walker .40 1.00
8 Reggie White .60 1.50
9 Jesse Solomon .30 .75
10 Joe Montana 2.50 6.00
11 John Taylor .40 1.00
12 Cornelius Bennett .50 1.25

1993 Stadium Club Super Teams

COMPLETE SET (28) 40.00 75.00
STATED ODDS 1:24 H/R, 1:15 JUM
1 Bears 1.00 2.50
Jim Harbaugh
2 Bengals .60 1.50
David Klingler
3 Bills WIN 2.00 4.00
Jim Kelly
4 Broncos 5.00 12.00
John Elway
5 Browns .60 1.50
Bernie Kosar
6 Buccaneers .60 1.50
Reggie Cobb
7 Cardinals .60 1.50
Eric Swann
8 Chargers .60 1.50
Stan Humphries
9 Chiefs WIN 2.00 4.00
Derrick Thomas
10 Colts .60 1.50
Steve Emtman
11 Cowboys WIN 6.00 15.00
Emmitt Smith
12 Dolphins 5.00 12.00
Dan Marino
13 Eagles 1.25 3.00
Randall Cunningham
14 Falcons 2.00 4.00
Deion Sanders
15 49ers WIN 4.00 8.00
Steve Young
16 Giants 1.00 2.50
Lawrence Taylor
17 Jets .60 1.50
Brad Baxter
18 Lions WIN 5.00 12.00
Barry Sanders
19 Oilers WIN 2.00 4.00
Warren Moon
20 Packers 8.00 20.00
Brett Favre
21 Patriots .60 1.50
Brent Williams
22 Raiders 1.25 3.00
Howie Long
23 Rams .60 1.50
Cleveland Gary
24 Redskins .60 1.50
Mark Rypien
25 Saints .60 1.50
Sam Mills
26 Seahawks .60 1.50
Cortez Kennedy
27 Steelers .60 1.50
Barry Foster
28 Vikings 1.00 2.50
Terry Allen

1993 Stadium Club Super Teams Division Winners

Collectors who redeemed a Super Team card of a division winner received a Super Team card redemption set. If the team also won the conference championship, collectors were entitled to receive a master photo set of the team. Finally, if the team was the Super Bowl XXVIII champion, they received additionally a factory set of 1993 Stadium Club cards with official gold foil embossed Super Bowl logo. The cards are similar in design to the basic Stadium Club issue except the words "Division Winner" are gold foil-stamped on the front.

COMPLETE BAG BILLS (13) 2.80 7.00
COMPLETE BAG CHIEFS (13) 4.00 10.00
COMPLETE BAG COWBOYS (13) 6.00 15.00
COMPLETE BAG 49ERS (13) 4.80 12.00
COMPLETE BAG LIONS (13) 3.20 8.00
COMPLETE BAG OILERS (13) 2.80 7.00
B27 Mark Kelso .20 .50
B54 Bruce Smith .40 1.00
B75 Jim Kelly .40 1.00
B107 Andre Reed .40 1.00
B153 Pete Metzelaars .20 .50
B211 Nate Odomes .20 .50
B227 Bill Brooks .20 .50
B331 Darryl Talley .20 .50
B383 Steve Tasker .20 .50
B412 Don Beebe .20 .50
B439 Henry Jones .20 .50
B480 Cornelius Bennett .30 .75
F29 Dana Hall .20 .50
F52 Brent Jones .30 .75
F76 Bill Romanowski .20 .50
F103 Ricky Watters .40 1.00
F123 Jesse Sapolu .20 .50
F176 Kevin Fagan .20 .50
F199 Tim McDonald .20 .50
F208 Steve Young 1.00 2.50
F232 Jerry Rice 1.20 3.00
F275 John Taylor .30 .75
F326 Eric Davis .20 .50
F370 Tom Rathman .20 .50
L7 Dennis Gibson .20 .50
L31 Jason Hanson .20 .50
L61 Robert Porcher .20 .50
L120 Barry Sanders 2.00 5.00
L231 Marc Spindler .20 .50
L263 Kelvin Pritchett .20 .50
L295 Pat Swilling .30 .75
L321 Ray Crockett .20 .50
L342 Chris Spielman .20 .50
L368 William White .20 .50
L389 Mel Gray .30 .75
L450 Rodney Peete .20 .50
O20 Ernest Givins .30 .75
O101 Warren Moon .40 1.00
O128 Al Smith .20 .50
O146 Lorenzo White .30 .75
O166 William Fuller .20 .50
O192 Ray Childress .20 .50
O225 Sean Jones .20 .50
O305 Bruce Matthews .20 .50
O329 Haywood Jeffires .30 .75
O347 Cris Dishman .20 .50
O376 Bubba McDowell .20 .50
O455 Greg Montgomery .20 .50
CH80 Dale Carter .20 .50
CH133 Neil Smith .30 .75
CH173 Derrick Thomas .40 1.00
CH203 Harvey Williams .30 .75
CH215 Tracy Simien .20 .50
CH268 Jonathan Hayes .20 .50
CH289 J.J. Birden .20 .50
CH312 Willie Davis .30 .75
CH375 Nick Lowery .20 .50
CH399 Todd McNair .20 .50
CH440 Joe Montana 1.20 3.00
CH471 Marcus Allen .40 1.00
C017 Alvin Harper .30 .75
C050 Troy Aikman 1.20 3.00
C085 Emmitt Smith 2.00 5.00
C0106 Daryl Johnston .30 .75
C0129 Michael Irvin .40 1.00
C0152 Charles Haley .30 .75
C0174 Jay Novacek .30 .75
C0204 Russell Maryland .20 .50
C0278 Kevin Williams WR .30 .75
C0299 Kevin Smith .20 .50
C0325 Robert Jones .20 .50
C0400 Ken Norton Jr. .30 .75
DW3 Bills Super Team DW .40 1.00
Jim Kelly
DW9 Chiefs Super Team DW .40 1.00
Derrick Thomas
DW11 Cowboys 1.20 3.00
Emmitt Smith Stamped
DW15 49ers Super Team DW .60 1.50
Steve Young
DW18 Detroit Lions .70 1.75
Barry Sanders Stamped
DW19 Oilers Super Team DW .40 1.00
Warren Moon

1993 Stadium Club Super Teams Conference Winners

Collectors who redeemed a Super Team card of a conference winner received a master photo team set stamped with the conference logo along with the Super Team card featuring the conference logo.

COMP.BAG BILLS (13) 2.80 7.00
COMP.BAG COWBOYS (13) 6.00 15.00
CW3 Cowboys 1.00 2.50
E.Smith
CW11 Bills Super Team CW .40 1.00
Jim Kelly

1993 Stadium Club Super Teams Master Photos

Featuring either the NFC Champion Dallas Cowboys or the AFC Champion Buffalo Bills, these 12 Master Photos measure approximately 5" by 7" each. Collectors who redeemed the conference winner's Super Team card received that teams' Master Photo as well as a Super Team card featuring the conference logo. Carrying uncropped versions of regular Stadium Club cards, the fronts give 17 percent more photo area than a regular card. A gold-foil "N" for NFC or "A" for AFC edged by stars appears beneath each picture. The backs are blank except for Team NFL, NFLPA, and Topps logos. The cards are unnumbered and checklisted below in alphabetical order by team.

COMP.BAG BILLS (12) 4.00 10.00
COMP.BAG COWBOYS (12) 8.00 20.00
B1 Don Beebe .30 .75
B2 Cornelius Bennett .40 1.00
B3 Bill Brooks .30 .75
B4 Henry Jones .30 .75
B5 Jim Kelly .60 1.50
B6 Mark Kelso .30 .75
B7 Pete Metzelaars .30 .75
B8 Nate Odomes .30 .75
B9 Andre Reed .40 1.00
B10 Bruce Smith .40 1.00
B11 Darryl Talley .30 .75
B12 Steve Tasker .30 .75
C01 Troy Aikman 1.50 4.00
C02 Charles Haley .40 1.00
C03 Alvin Harper .40 1.00
C04 Michael Irvin .60 1.50
C05 Daryl Johnston .40 1.00
C06 Robert Jones .30 .75
C07 Russell Maryland .30 .75
C08 Ken Norton Jr. .30 .75
C09 Jay Novacek .40 1.00
C010 Emmitt Smith 3.00 8.00
C011 Kevin Smith .30 .75
C012 Kevin Williams WR .40 1.00

1993 Stadium Club Super Teams Super Bowl

COMPLETE SB SET (501) 30.00 75.00
*STARS: 1X to 2.5X BASIC CARDS
*ROOKIES: .6X to 1.5X BASIC CARDS
SB3 Cowboys 1.50 4.00
Emmitt Smith

1993 Stadium Club Members Only Parallel

COMP.FACT.SET (603) 80.00 200.00
*1-550 VETS: 1.2X TO 3X BASIC CARDS
*1-550 ROOKIES: .8X TO 2X BASIC CARDS
*SUPER TEAMS: .2X TO .5X BASIC INSERTS
*MASTER PHOTOS: .4X TO 1X BASIC INSERT
NNO Jerry Rice RB AUTO 25.00 50.00

1993 Stadium Club Pre-Production Samples

COMPLETE SET (9) 6.00 15.00
1 Sterling Sharpe 1.00 2.50
41 Tommy Barnhardt .60 1.50
45 Cortez Kennedy .60 1.50
81 Johnny Bailey .60 1.50
86 Vai Sikahema .60 1.50
95 Cris Carter 1.25 3.00
102 Christian Okoye .75 2.00
139 Richard Dent .75 2.00
222 Reggie Cobb .60 1.50

1994 Stadium Club

This 630 standard size set was released in three series. Foil packs contained 12 player cards plus one info card or unnumbered checklist card. In the first two series, one in every eight packs contained a special insert card as opposed to an information card. Frequent Scorer Point cards were randomly packed one in every three packs. For 30 frequent scorer points of his favorite player, the collector received a Finest quality upgrade card of that player. Topical subsets included in this set are Chalk Talk (371-374), Best Defense (435-445), and Red Zone (511-525). Collectors who attended the Super Bowl show XXIX in Miami could trade five wrappers for a cellophane pack of '94 Stadium Club cards embossed with the Super Bowl XXIX logo. Rookie Cards in this set include Mario Bates, Bert Emanuel, Marshall Faulk, William Floyd, Bernie Parmalee, Errict Rhett, Darnay Scott and Heath Shuler.

COMPLETE SET (630) 25.00 60.00
COMP.SERIES 1 (270) 10.00 25.00
COMP.SERIES 2 (270) 10.00 25.00
COMP.HIGH SERIES (90) 5.00 10.00
1 Dan Wilkinson RC .07 .20
2 Chip Lohmiller .02 .10
3 Roosevelt Potts .02 .10
4 Martin Mayhew .02 .10
5 Shane Conlan .02 .10
6 Sam Adams RC .07 .20
7 Mike Kenn .02 .10
8 Tim Goad .02 .10
9 Tony Jones T .02 .10
10 Ronald Moore .02 .10
11 Mark Bortz .02 .10
12 Darren Carrington .02 .10
13 Eric Martin .02 .10
14 Eric Allen .02 .10
15 Aaron Glenn RC .15 .40
16 Bryan Cox .02 .10
17 Levon Kirkland .02 .10
18 Qadry Ismail .15 .40
19 Shane Dronett .02 .10
20 Chris Spielman .07 .20
21 Rob Fredrickson RC .07 .20
22 Wayne Simmons .02 .10
23 Glenn Montgomery .02 .10
24 Jason Sehorn RC .25 .60
25 Nick Lowery .02 .10
26 Dennis Brown .02 .10
27 Kenneth Davis .02 .10
28 Shante Carver RC .02 .10
29 Ryan Yarborough RC .02 .10
30 Cortez Kennedy .07 .20
31 Anthony Pleasant .02 .10
32 Jessie Tuggle .02 .10
33 Herschel Walker .07 .20
34 Andre Collins .02 .10
35 William Floyd RC .15 .40
36 Harold Green .02 .10
37 Courtney Hawkins .02 .10
38 Curtis Conway .15 .40
39 Ben Coates .07 .20
40 Natrone Means .15 .40
41 Eric Hill .02 .10
42 Keith Kartz .02 .10
43 Alexander Wright .02 .10
44 Willie Roaf .02 .10
45 Vencie Glenn .02 .10
46 Ronnie Lott .07 .20
47 George Koonce .02 .10
48 Rod Woodson .07 .20
49 Tim Grunhard .02 .10
50 Cody Carlson .02 .10
51 Bryant Young RC .25 .60
52 Jay Novacek .07 .20
53 Darryl Talley .02 .10
54 Harry Colon .02 .10
55 Dave Meggett .02 .10
56 Aubrey Beavers RC .02 .10
57 James Folston .02 .10
58 Willie Davis .07 .20
59 Jason Elam .07 .20
60 Eric Metcalf .07 .20
61 Bruce Armstrong .02 .10
62 Ron Heller .02 .10
63 LeRoy Butler .02 .10
64 Terry Obee .02 .10
65 Kurt Gouveia .02 .10
66 Pierce Holt .02 .10
67 David Alexander .02 .10
68 Deral Boykin .02 .10
69 Carl Pickens .07 .20
70 Broderick Thomas .02 .10
71 Barry Sanders CT .50 1.25
72 Qadry Ismail CT .15 .40
73 Thurman Thomas CT .15 .40
74 Junior Seau .15 .40
75 Vinny Testaverde .07 .20
76 Tyrone Hughes .07 .20
77 Nate Newton .02 .10
78 Eric Swann .07 .20
79 Brad Baxter .02 .10
80 Dana Stubblefield .07 .20
81 Jumbo Elliott .02 .10
82 Steve Wisniewski .02 .10
83 Eddie Robinson .02 .10
84 Isaac Davis .02 .10
85 Cris Carter .25 .60
86 Mel Gray .02 .10
87 Cornelius Bennett .07 .20
88 Neil O'Donnell .15 .40
89 Jon Hand .02 .10
90 John Elway 1.25 3.00
91 Bill Hitchcock .02 .10
92 Neil Smith .07 .20
93 Joe Johnson RC .02 .10
94 Edgar Bennett .15 .40
95 Vincent Brown .02 .10
96 Tommy Vardell .02 .10
97 Donnell Woolford .02 .10
98 Lincoln Kennedy .02 .10
99 O.J. McDuffie .15 .40
100 Heath Shuler RC .15 .40
101 Jerry Rice BO .30 .75
102 Erik Williams BO .02 .10
103 Randall McDaniel BO .05 .15
104 Dermontti Dawson BO .02 .10
105 Nate Newton BO .02 .10
106 Harris Barton BO .02 .10
107 Shannon Sharpe BO .07 .20
108 Sterling Sharpe BO .07 .20
109 Steve Young BO .25 .60
110 Emmitt Smith BO .50 1.25
111 Thurman Thomas BO .15 .40
112 Kyle Clifton .02 .10
113 Desmond Howard .07 .20
114 Quinn Early .07 .20
115 David Klingler .02 .10
116 Bern Brostek .02 .10
117 Gary Clark .07 .20
118 Courtney Hall .02 .10
119 Joe King .02 .10
120 Quentin Coryatt .02 .10
121 Johnnie Morton RC .75 2.00
122 Andre Reed .07 .20
123 Eric Davis .02 .10
124 Jack Del Rio .02 .10
125 Greg Lloyd .07 .20
126 Bubba McDowell .02 .10
127 Mark Jackson .02 .10
128 Jeff Jaeger .02 .10
129 Chris Warren .07 .20
130 Tom Waddle .02 .10
131 Tony Smith RB .02 .10
132 Todd Collins .02 .10
133 Mark Bavaro .02 .10
134 Joe Phillips .02 .10
135 Chris Jacke .02 .10
136 Glyn Milburn .07 .20
137 Keith Jackson .02 .10
138 Steve Tovar .02 .10
139 Tim Johnson .02 .10
140 Brian Washington .02 .10
141 Troy Drayton .02 .10
142 Dewayne Washington RC .07 .20
143 Erik Williams .02 .10
144 Eric Turner .02 .10
145 John Taylor .07 .20
146 Richard Cooper .02 .10
147 Van Malone .02 .10
148 Tim Ruddy RC .02 .10
149 Henry Jones .02 .10
150 Tim Brown .15 .40
151 Stan Humphries .07 .20
152 Harry Newsome .02 .10
153 Craig Erickson .02 .10
154 Gary Anderson K .02 .10
155 Ray Childress .02 .10
156 Howard Cross .02 .10
157 Heath Sherman .02 .10
158 Terrell Buckley .02 .10
159 J.B. Brown .02 .10
160 Joe Montana 1.25 3.00
161 David Wyman .02 .10
162 Norm Johnson .02 .10
163 Rod Stephens .02 .10
164 Willie McGinest RC .15 .40
165 Barry Sanders 1.00 2.50
166 Marc Logan .02 .10
167 Anthony Newman .02 .10
168 Russell Maryland .02 .10
169 Luis Sharpe .02 .10
170 Jim Kelly .15 .40
171 Tre Johnson RC .02 .10
172 Johnny Mitchell .02 .10
173 David Palmer RC .15 .40
174 Bob Dahl .02 .10
175 Aaron Wallace .02 .10
176 Chris Gardocki .02 .10
177 Hardy Nickerson .07 .20
178 Jeff Query .02 .10
179 Leslie O'Neal .02 .10
180 Kevin Greene .07 .20
181 Alonzo Spellman .02 .10
182 Reggie Brooks .07 .20
183 Dana Stubblefield .07 .20
184 Tyrone Hughes .07 .20
185 Drew Bledsoe GE .15 .40
186 Ronald Moore GE .02 .10
187 Jason Elam GE .02 .10
188 Rick Mirer GE .15 .40
189 Willie Roaf GE .02 .10
190 Jerome Bettis GE .15 .40
191 Brad Hopkins .02 .10
192 Derek Brown RBK .02 .10
193 Nolan Harrison .02 .10
194 John Randle .07 .20
195 Carlton Bailey .02 .10
196 Kevin Williams WR .07 .20
197 Greg Hill RC .15 .40
198 Mark McMillian .02 .10
199 Brad Edwards .02 .10
200 Dan Marino 1.25 3.00
201 Ricky Watters .07 .20
202 George Teague .02 .10
203 Steve Beuerlein .07 .20
204 Jeff Burris RC .07 .20
205 Steve Atwater .02 .10
206 John Thierry RC .02 .10
207 Patrick Hunter .02 .10
208 Wayne Gandy .02 .10
209 Derrick Moore .02 .10
210 Phil Simms .07 .20
211 Kirk Lowdermilk .02 .10
212 Patrick Robinson .02 .10
213 Kevin Mitchell .02 .10
214 Jonathan Hayes .02 .10
215 Michael Dean Perry .07 .20
216 John Fina .02 .10
217 Anthony Smith .02 .10
218 Paul Gruber .02 .10
219 Carnell Lake .02 .10
220 Carl Lee .02 .10
221 Steve Christie .02 .10
222 Greg Montgomery .02 .10
223 Reggie Brooks .07 .20
224 Derrick Thomas .15 .40
225 Eric Metcalf .07 .20
226 Michael Haynes .07 .20
227 Bobby Hebert .02 .10
228 Tyrone Hughes .07 .20
229 Donald Frank .02 .10
230 Vaughan Johnson .02 .10
231 Eric Thomas .02 .10
232 Ernest Givins .07 .20
233 Charles Haley .07 .20
234 Darrell Green .02 .10
235 Harold Alexander .02 .10
236 Dwayne Sabb .02 .10
237 Harris Barton .02 .10
238 Randall Cunningham .15 .40
239 Ray Buchanan .02 .10
240 Sterling Sharpe .07 .20
241 Chris Mims .02 .10
242 Mark Carrier DB .02 .10
243 Ricky Proehl .02 .10
244 Michael Brooks .02 .10
245 Sean Gilbert .02 .10
246 David Lutz .02 .10
247 Kelvin Martin .02 .10
248 Scottie Graham RC .07 .20
249 Irving Fryar .07 .20
250 Ricardo McDonald .02 .10
251 Marvcus Patton .02 .10
252 Errict Rhett RC .15 .40
253 Winston Moss .02 .10
254 Rod Bernstine .02 .10
255 Terry Wooden .02 .10
256 Antonio Langham RC .07 .20
257 Tommy Barnhardt .02 .10
258 Marvin Washington .02 .10
259 Bo Orlando .02 .10
260 Marcus Allen .15 .40
261 Mario Bates RC .15 .40
262 Marco Coleman .02 .10
263 Doug Riesenberg .02 .10
264 Jesse Sapolu .02 .10
265 Dermontti Dawson .02 .10
266 Fernando Smith RC .02 .10
267 David Szott .02 .10
268 Steve Christie .02 .10
269 Bruce Matthews .02 .10
270 Michael Irvin .15 .40
271 Seth Joyner .02 .10
272 Santana Dotson .07 .20
273 Vincent Brisby .07 .20
274 Rohn Stark .02 .10
275 John Copeland .02 .10
276 Toby Wright .02 .10
277 David Griggs .02 .10
278 Aaron Taylor .02 .10
279 Chris Doleman .02 .10
280 Reggie Brooks .07 .20
281 Flipper Anderson .02 .10
282 Alvin Harper .07 .20
283 Chris Hinton .02 .10
284 Kelvin Pritchett .02 .10
285 Russell Copeland .02 .10
286 Dwight Stone .02 .10
287 Jeff Gossett .02 .10
288 Larry Allen RC .15 .40
289 Kevin Mawae RC .15 .40
290 Mark Collins .02 .10
291 Chris Zorich .02 .10
292 Vince Buck .02 .10
293 Gene Atkins .02 .10
294 Webster Slaughter .02 .10
295 Steve Young .50 1.25
296 Dan Williams .02 .10
297 Jessie Armstead .02 .10
298 Victor Bailey .02 .10
299 John Carney .02 .10
300 Emmitt Smith 1.00 2.50
301 Bucky Brooks RC .02 .10
302 Mo Lewis .02 .10
303 Eugene Daniel .02 .10
304 Tyji Armstrong .02 .10
305 Eugene Chung .02 .10
306 Rocket Ismail .07 .20
307 Sean Jones .02 .10
308 Rick Cunningham .02 .10
309 Ken Harvey .02 .10
310 Jeff George .15 .40
311 Jon Vaughn .02 .10
312 Roy Barker RC .02 .10
313 Micheal Barrow .02 .10
314 Ryan McNeil .02 .10
315 Pete Stoyanovich .02 .10
316 Darryl Williams .02 .10
317 Renaldo Turnbull .02 .10
318 Eric Green .02 .10
319 Nate Lewis .02 .10
320 Mike Flores .02 .10
321 Derek Russell .02 .10
322 Marcus Spears RC .02 .10
323 Corey Miller .02 .10
324 Derrick Thomas .15 .40
325 Steve Everitt .02 .10
326 Brent Jones .07 .20
327 Marshall Faulk RC 2.50 6.00
328 Don Beebe .02 .10
329 Harry Swayne .02 .10
330 Boomer Esiason .07 .20
331 Don Mosebar .02 .10
332 Isaac Bruce RC 2.00 5.00
333 Rickey Jackson .02 .10
334 Daryl Johnston .07 .20
335 Lorenzo Lynch .02 .10
336 Brian Blades .07 .20
337 Michael Timpson .02 .10
338 Reggie Cobb .02 .10
339 Joe Walter .02 .10
340 Barry Foster .02 .10
341 Richmond Webb .02 .10
342 Pat Swilling .02 .10
343 Shaun Gayle .02 .10
344 Reggie Roby .02 .10
345 Chris Calloway .02 .10
346 Doug Dawson .02 .10
347 Rob Burnett .02 .10
348 Dana Hall .02 .10
349 Horace Copeland .02 .10
350 Shannon Sharpe .07 .20
351 Rich Miano .02 .10
352 Henry Thomas .02 .10
353 Dan Saleaumua .02 .10
354 Kevin Ross .02 .10
355 Morten Andersen .02 .10
356 Anthony Blaylock .02 .10
357 Stanley Richard .02 .10
358 Albert Lewis .02 .10
359 Darren Woodson .07 .20
360 Drew Bledsoe .40 1.00
361 Eric Mahlum .02 .10
362 Trent Dilfer RC .60 1.50
363 William Roberts .02 .10
364 Robert Brooks .15 .40
365 Jason Hanson .02 .10
366 Troy Vincent .02 .10
367 William Thomas .02 .10
368 Lonnie Johnson RC .02 .10
369 Jamir Miller RC .07 .20
370 Michael Jackson .07 .20
371 Charlie Ward CT RC .15 .40
372 Shannon Sharpe CT .07 .20
373 Jackie Slater CT .02 .10
374 Steve Young CT .25 .60
375 Bobby Wilson .02 .10
376 Paul Frase .02 .10
377 Dale Carter .02 .10
378 Robert Delpino .02 .10
379 Bert Emanuel RC .15 .40
380 Rick Mirer .15 .40
381 Carlos Jenkins .02 .10
382 Gary Brown .02 .10
383 Doug Pelfrey .02 .10
384 Dexter Carter .02 .10
385 Chris Miller .02 .10
386 Charles Johnson RC .15 .40
387 James Joseph .02 .10
388 Darrin Smith .02 .10
389 James Jett .02 .10
390 Junior Seau .15 .40
391 Chris Slade .02 .10
392 Jim Harbaugh .15 .40
393 Herman Moore .15 .40
394 Thomas Randolph RC .02 .10
395 Lamar Thomas .02 .10
396 Reggie Rivers .02 .10
397 Larry Centers .15 .40
398 Chad Brown .02 .10
399 Terry Kirby .15 .40
400 Bruce Smith .15 .40
401 Keenan McCardell RC .75 2.00
402 Tim McDonald .02 .10
403 Robert Smith .15 .40
404 Matt Brock .02 .10
405 Tony McGee .02 .10
406 Ethan Horton .02 .10
407 Michael Haynes .07 .20
408 Steve Jackson .02 .10
409 Erik Kramer .07 .20
410 Jerome Bettis .25 .60
411 D.J. Johnson .02 .10
412 John Alt .02 .10
413 Jeff Lageman .02 .10
414 Rick Tuten .02 .10
415 Jeff Robinson .02 .10
416 Kevin Lee RC .02 .10
417 Thomas Lewis RC .07 .20
418 Kerry Cash .02 .10
419 Chuck Levy RC .02 .10
420 Mark Ingram .02 .10
421 Dennis Gibson .02 .10
422 Tyronne Drakeford .02 .10
423 James Washington .02 .10
424 Dante Jones .02 .10
425 Eugene Robinson .02 .10
426 Johnny Johnson .02 .10
427 Brian Mitchell .02 .10

428 Charles Mincy .02 .10
429 Mark Carrier WR .07 .20
430 Vince Workman .02 .10
431 James Francis .02 .10
432 Clay Matthews .02 .10
433 Randall McDaniel .05 .15
434 Brad Ottis .02 .10
435 Bruce Smith .15 .40
436 Cortez Kennedy BD .02 .10
437 John Randle BD .07 .20
438 Neil Smith BD .07 .20
439 Cornelius Bennett BD .07 .20
440 Junior Seau BD .07 .20
441 Derrick Thomas BD .07 .20
442 Rod Woodson BD .07 .20
443 Terry McDaniel BD .02 .10
444 Tim McDonald BD .02 .10
445 Mark Carrier DB BD .02 .10
446 Irv Smith .02 .10
447 Steve Wallace .02 .10
448 Cris Dishman .02 .10
449 Bill Brooks .02 .10
450 Jeff Hostetler .07 .20
451 Brentson Buckner RC .02 .10
452 Ken Ruettgers .02 .10
453 Marc Boutte .02 .10
454 John Offerdahl .02 .10
455 Allen Aldridge .02 .10
456 Steve Emtman .02 .10
457 Andre Rison .07 .20
458 Shawn Jefferson .02 .10
459 Todd Steussie RC .07 .20
460 Scott Mitchell .07 .20
461 Tom Carter .02 .10
462 Donnell Bennett RC .15 .40
463 James Jones DT .02 .10
464 Antone Davis .02 .10
465 Jim Everett .07 .20
466 Tony Tolbert .02 .10
467 Merril Hoge .02 .10
468 Michael Bates .02 .10
469 Phil Hansen .02 .10
470 Rodney Hampton .07 .20
471 Aeneas Williams .02 .10
472 Al Del Greco .02 .10
473 Todd Lyght .02 .10
474 Joel Steed .02 .10
475 Merton Hanks .07 .20
476 Tony Stargell .02 .10
477 Greg Robinson .02 .10
478 Roger Duffy .02 .10
479 Simon Fletcher .02 .10
480 Reggie White .15 .40
481 Lee Johnson .02 .10
482 Wayne Martin .02 .10
483 Thurman Thomas .15 .40
484 Warren Moon .15 .40
485 Sam Rogers RC .02 .10
486 Eric Pegram .02 .10
487 Will Wolford .02 .10
488 Duane Young .02 .10
489 Keith Hamilton .02 .10
490 Haywood Jeffires .07 .20
491 Trace Armstrong .02 .10
492 J.J. Birden .02 .10
493 Ricky Ervins .02 .10
494 Robert Blackmon .02 .10
495 William Perry .07 .20
496 Robert Massey .02 .10
497 Jim Jeffcoat .02 .10
498 Pat Harlow .02 .10
499 Jeff Cross .02 .10
500 Jerry Rice .60 1.50
501 Darnay Scott RC .40 1.00
502 Clyde Simmons .02 .10
503 Henry Rolling .02 .10
504 James Hasty .02 .10
505 Leroy Thompson .02 .10
506 Darrell Thompson .02 .10
507 Tim Bowens RC .07 .20
508 Gerald Perry .02 .10
509 Mike Croel .02 .10
510 Sam Mills .02 .10
511 Steve Young RZ .25 .60
512 Hardy Nickerson RZ .07 .20
513 Cris Carter RZ .07 .20
514 Boomer Esiason RZ .07 .20
515 Bruce Smith RZ .07 .20
516 Emmitt Smith RZ .50 1.25
517 Eugene Robinson RZ .02 .10
518 Gary Brown RZ .02 .10
519 Jerry Rice RZ .30 .75
520 Troy Aikman RZ .30 .75
521 Marcus Allen RZ .07 .20
522 Junior Seau RZ .07 .20
523 Sterling Sharpe RZ .07 .20
524 Dana Stubblefield RZ .07 .20
525 Tom Carter RZ .02 .10
526 Pete Metzelaars .02 .10
527 Russell Freeman .02 .10
528 Keith Cash .02 .10
529 Willie Drewrey .02 .10
530 Randal Hill .02 .10
531 Pepper Johnson .02 .10
532 Rob Moore .07 .20
533 Todd Kelly .02 .10
534 Keith Byars .02 .10
535 Mike Fox .02 .10
536 Brett Favre 1.25 3.00
537 Terry McDaniel .02 .10
538 Darren Perry .02 .10
539 Maurice Hurst .02 .10
540 Troy Aikman .60 1.50
541 Junior Seau .15 .40
542 Steve Broussard .02 .10
543 Lorenzo White .02 .10
544 Terry McDaniel .02 .10
545 Henry Thomas .02 .10
546 Tyrone Hughes .07 .20
547 Mark Collins .02 .10
548 Gary Anderson K .02 .10
549 Darrell Green .02 .10
550 Jerry Rice .50 1.25
551 Cornelius Bennett .07 .20
552 Aeneas Williams .02 .10
553 Eric Metcalf .07 .20
554 Jumbo Elliott .02 .10
555 Mo Lewis .02 .10
556 Darren Carrington .02 .10
557 Kevin Greene .07 .20
558 John Elway 1.00 2.50
559 Eugene Robinson .02 .10
560 Drew Bledsoe .30 .75
561 Fred Barnett .07 .20
562 Bernie Parmalee RC .15 .40
563 Bryce Paup .07 .20
564 Donnell Woolford .02 .10
565 Terance Mathis .07 .20
566 Santana Dotson .07 .20
567 Randall McDaniel .05 .15
568 Stanley Richard .02 .10
569 Brian Blades .07 .20
570 Jerome Bettis .20 .50
571 Neil Smith .07 .20
572 Andre Reed .07 .20
573 Michael Bankston .02 .10
574 Dana Stubblefield .07 .20
575 Rod Woodson .07 .20
576 Ken Harvey .02 .10
577 Andre Rison .02 .10
578 Darion Conner .02 .10
579 Michael Strahan .15 .40
580 Barry Sanders .75 2.00
581 Pepper Johnson .02 .10
582 Lewis Tillman .02 .10
583 Jeff George .15 .40
584 Michael Haynes .07 .20
585 Herschel Walker .07 .20
586 Tim Brown .15 .40
587 Jim Kelly .15 .40
588 Ricky Watters .15 .40
589 Randall Cunningham .15 .40
590 Troy Aikman UER .50 1.25
Threw for 56
TD's in 93 season
591 Ken Norton Jr. .07 .20
592 Cortez Kennedy .07 .20
593 Ricky Ervins .02 .10
594 Cris Carter .20 .50
595 Sterling Sharpe .07 .20
596 John Randle .07 .20
597 Shannon Sharpe .07 .20
598 Ray Crittenden RC .02 .10
599 Barry Foster .02 .10
600 Deion Sanders .25 .60
601 Seth Joyner .02 .10
602 Chris Warren .07 .20
603 Tom Rathman .02 .10
604 Brett Favre 1.00 2.50
605 Marshall Faulk .75 2.00
606 Terry Allen .07 .20
607 Ben Coates .07 .20
608 Brian Washington .02 .10
609 Henry Ellard .07 .20
610 Dave Meggett .02 .10
611 Stan Humphries .07 .20
612 Warren Moon .15 .40
613 Marcus Allen .15 .40
614 Ed McDaniel .02 .10
615 Joe Montana 1.00 2.50
616 Jeff Hostetler .07 .20
617 Johnny Johnson .02 .10
618 Andre Coleman RC .02 .10
619 Willie Davis .07 .20
620 Rick Mirer .15 .40
621 Dan Marino 1.00 2.50
622 Rob Moore .07 .20
623 Byron Bam Morris RC .07 .20
624 Natrone Means .15 .40
625 Steve Young .30 .75
626 Jim Everett .07 .20
627 Michael Brooks .02 .10
628 Dermontti Dawson .02 .10
629 Reggie White .15 .40
630 Emmitt Smith .60 1.50
0 Micheal Barrow TSC 2.00 4.00
NNO Checklist Card 3 .02 .10
NNO Checklist Card 1 .02 .10
NNO Checklist Card 2 .02 .10

1994 Stadium Club First Day

COMPLETE SET (630) 300.00 600.00
COMP.SERIES 1 (270) 125.00 250.00
COMP.SERIES 2 (270) 125.00 250.00
COMP.HI SERIES (90) 50.00 100.00
*STARS: 3X TO 8X BASIC CARDS
*RCs: 1.5X TO 4X BASIC CARDS
STATED ODDS 1:12

1994 Stadium Club Super Bowl XXIX

COMPLETE SET (540) 320.00 800.00
*STARS: 3X TO 8X BASIC CARDS
*RCs: 2X TO 5X BASIC CARDS

1994 Stadium Club Bowman's Best

COMPLETE SET (45) 20.00 50.00
STATED ODDS 1:3 SER.3
*REFRACT: 1X TO 2.5X BASIC INSERTS
REFRACTOR STATED ODDS 1:12 SER.3
BK1 Jerry Rice 1.25 3.00
BK2 Deion Sanders .50 1.25
BK3 Reggie White .30 .75
BK4 Dan Marino 2.50 6.00
BK5 Natrone Means .30 .75
BK6 Rick Mirer .30 .75
BK7 Michael Irvin .30 .75
BK8 John Elway 2.50 6.00
BK9 Junior Seau .30 .75
BK10 Drew Bledsoe .75 2.00
BK11 Sterling Sharpe .15 .40
BK12 Brett Favre 2.50 6.00
BK13 Troy Aikman 1.25 3.00
BK14 Barry Sanders 2.00 5.00
BK15 Steve Young 1.00 2.50
BK16 Emmitt Smith 2.00 5.00
BK17 Joe Montana 2.50 6.00
BU1 Marshall Faulk 3.00 8.00
BU2 Derrick Alexander WR .15 .40
BU3 Darnay Scott .40 1.00
BU4 Gus Frerotte .50 1.25
BU5 Jeff Blake 1.00 2.50
BU6 Charles Johnson .15 .40
BU7 Thomas Lewis .07 .20
BU8 Charlie Garner .50 1.25
BU9 Aaron Glenn .15 .40
BU10 William Floyd .15 .40
BU11 Antonio Langham .07 .20
BU12 Errict Rhett .15 .40
BU13 Heath Shuler .15 .40
BU14 Jeff Burris .07 .20
BU15 Dan Wilkinson .07 .20
BU16 Rob Fredrickson .07 .20
BU17 Tim Bowens .07 .20
18 Deion Sanders .75 2.00
Aaron Glenn
19 Barry Sanders 2.50 6.00
Marshall Faulk
20 William Floyd .07 .20
Daryl Johnston UER
21 Reggie White .15 .40
Tim Bowens
22 Troy Aikman 1.25 3.00
Heath Shuler
23 Antonio Langham .15 .40
Donnell Woolford
24 Errict Rhett .15 .40
Rodney Hampton
25 Jeff Burris .15 .40
Tyrone Hughes
26 Henry Thomas .15 .40
Dan Wilkinson
27 Jerry Rice 1.25 3.00
Derrick Alexander WR
28 Emmitt Smith 1.50 4.00
Byron Bam Morris

1994 Stadium Club Dynasty and Destiny

COMPLETE SET (6) 10.00 20.00
COMP.SERIES 1 (3) 6.00 12.00
COMP.SERIES 2 (3) 4.00 8.00
STATED ODDS 1:24 H/R, 1:15J
1 Emmitt Smith 3.00 8.00
Walter Payton
2 Steve Largent .75 2.00
Tom Waddle
3 Randy White .75 2.00
Cortez Kennedy
4 Troy Aikman 1.50 4.00
Dan Fouts
5 Junior Seau 1.25 3.00
Mike Singletary
6 Shannon Sharpe .75 2.00
Ozzie Newsome

1994 Stadium Club Expansion Team Redemption

JAGUARS PRIZE SET (22) 10.00 20.00
PANTHERS PRIZE SET (22) 10.00 20.00
J1 James O. Stewart 1.50 4.00
J2 Kelvin Pritchett .40 1.00
J3 Mike Dumas .40 1.00
J4 Brian DeMarco .40 1.00
J5 James Williams LB .40 1.00
J6 Ernest Givins .40 1.00
J7 Harry Colon .40 1.00
J8 Derek Brown TE .40 1.00
J9 Santo Stephens .40 1.00
J10 Jeff Lageman .40 1.00
J11 Bryan Barker .40 1.00
J12 Dave Widell .40 1.00
J13 Willie Jackson .60 1.50
J14 Vinnie Clark .40 1.00
J15 Mickey Washington .40 1.00
J16 Le'Shai Maston .40 1.00
J17 Darren Carrington .40 1.00
J18 Steve Beuerlein .50 1.25
J19 Mark Williams .40 1.00
J20 Keith Goganious .40 1.00
J21 Shawn Bouwens .40 1.00
J22 Chris Hudson .40 1.00
P1 Kerry Collins 4.00 10.00
P2 Rod Smith .40 1.00
P3 Willie Green .40 1.00
P4 Greg Kragen .40 1.00
P5 Blake Brockermeyer .40 1.00
P6 Bob Christian .40 1.00
P7 Carlton Bailey .40 1.00
P8 Bubba McDowell .40 1.00
P9 Matt Elliott .40 1.00
P10 Tyrone Poole .60 1.50
P11 John Kasay .50 1.25
P12 Gerald Williams .40 1.00
P13 Derrick Moore .40 1.00
P14 Don Beebe .40 1.00
P15 Sam Mills .50 1.25
P16 Darion Conner .40 1.00
P17 Eric Guliford .40 1.00
P18 Mike Fox .40 1.00
P19 Pete Metzelaars .40 1.00
P20 Frank Reich .50 1.25
P21 Mark Carrier WR .60 1.50
P22 Vince Workman .40 1.00
NNO Jacksonville Jaguars .20 .50
Defense Redemption
NNO Jacksonville Jaguars .20 .50
Offense Redemption
NNO Jacksonville Jaguars .20 .50
Special Teams Redemption
NNO Carolina Panthers .20 .50
Defense Redemption
NNO Carolina Panthers .20 .50
Offense Redemption
NNO Carolina Panthers .20 .50
Special Teams Redemption
NNO Carolina Panthers .20 .50
Jacksonville Jaguars
Complete Set Redemption

1994 Stadium Club Frequent Scorer Points Upgrades

COMPLETE SET (10) 15.00 40.00
ONE CARD VIA MAIL PER 30 FS POINTS
55 Dave Meggett .30 .75
75 Vinny Testaverde .75 1.50
129 Chris Warren .75 1.50
151 Stan Humphries .75 1.50
200 Dan Marino 10.00 20.00
310 Jeff George 1.50 3.00
327 Marshall Faulk 8.00 15.00
360 Drew Bledsoe 4.00 8.00
374 Steve Young 4.00 8.00
380 Rick Mirer 1.50 3.00

1994 Stadium Club Ring Leaders

COMPLETE SET (12) 15.00 40.00
STATED ODDS 1:24 SERIES 2
1 Emmitt Smith 5.00 12.00
2 Steve Young 2.50 6.00
3 Deion Sanders 1.25 3.00
4 Warren Moon .75 2.00
5 Thurman Thomas .75 2.00
6 Jerry Rice 3.00 8.00
7 Sterling Sharpe .40 1.00
8 Barry Sanders 5.00 12.00
9 Reggie White .75 2.00
10 Michael Irvin .75 2.00
11 Ronnie Lott .40 1.00
12 Herschel Walker .40 1.00

1994 Stadium Club Super Teams

COMPLETE SET (28) 30.00 80.00
STATED ODDS 1:24 HOB/RET, 1:15JUM
1 Cardinals 1.25 3.00
Steve Beuerlein
2 Falcons .75 2.00
Drew Hill
3 Bills 1.25 3.00
Jim Kelly
4 Bears .75 2.00
Joe Cain
5 Bengals .75 2.00
Derrick Fenner
6 Browns .75 2.00
Tommy Vardell
7 Cowboys WIN 5.00 12.00
Emmitt Smith
8 Broncos 4.00 10.00
John Elway
9 Lions 4.00 10.00
Barry Sanders
10 Packers 8.00 20.00
Brett Favre
11 Oilers .75 2.00
Gary Brown
12 Colts .75 2.00
Zefross Moss
13 Chiefs 2.50 6.00
Joe Montana
14 Raiders .75 2.00
Howie Long
15 Rams 1.25 3.00
Jerome Bettis
16 Dolphins WIN 1.50 4.00
Irving Fryar
17 Vikings WIN 1.50 4.00
Cris Carter
18 Patriots 2.50 6.00
Drew Bledsoe
19 Saints .75 2.00
Rickey Jackson
20 Giants .75 2.00
Phil Simms
21 Jets .75 2.00
Boomer Esiason
22 Eagles .75 2.00
Herschel Walker
23 Steelers WIN 1.50 4.00
Neil O'Donnell
24 Chargers WIN 1.50 4.00
Natrone Means
25 49ers WIN 5.00 12.00
Jerry Rice
Steve Young
26 Seahawks .75 2.00
Rick Mirer
27 Buccaneers .75 2.00
Craig Erickson
28 Redskins .75 2.00
Reggie Brooks

1994 Stadium Club Super Teams Division Winners

COMPLETE BAG CHARGERS (11) 2.00 5.00
COMPLETE BAG COWBOYS (11) 4.00 10.00
COMPLETE BAG DOLPHINS (11) 3.20 8.00
COMPLETE BAG 49ERS (11) 4.00 10.00
COMPLETE BAG VIKINGS (11) 2.00 5.00
COMPLETE BAG STEELERS (11) 2.00 5.00
7DW Cowboys Super 1.00 2.50
Team DW
Emmitt Smith
Troy Aikman
16DW Dolphins Super .25 .60
Team DW
Irving Fryar
17DW Vikings Super .25 .60
Team DW
Cris Carter
23DW Steelers Super .15 .40
Team DW
Neil O'Donnell
24DW Chargers Super .25 .60
Team DW
Natrone Means
25DW 49ers Super .50 1.25
Team DW
Jerry Rice
Steve Young
Ricky Watters
D16 Bryan Cox .15 .40
D56 Aubrey Beavers .15 .40
D99 O.J. McDuffie .40 1.00
D200 Dan Marino 1.60 4.00
D249 Irving Fryar .25 .60
D262 Marco Coleman .15 .40
D341 Richmond Webb .15 .40
D399 Terry Kirby .40 1.00
D507 Tim Bowens .25 .60
D562 Bernie Parmalee .40 1.00
F35 William Floyd .40 1.00
F51 Bryant Young .60 1.50
F80 Dana Stubblefield .25 .60
F201 Ricky Watters .25 .60
F295 Steve Young .60 1.50
F326 Brent Jones .25 .60
F402 Tim McDonald .15 .40
F475 Merton Hanks .15 .40
F500 Jerry Rice .80 2.00
F600 Deion Sanders .50 1.25
V18 Qadry Ismail .40 1.00
V85 Cris Carter .40 1.00
V124 Jack Del Rio .15 .40
V142 Dewayne Washington .25 .60
V173 David Palmer .25 .60
V194 John Randle .25 .60
V352 Henry Thomas .15 .40
V433 Randall McDaniel .15 .40
V459 Todd Steussie .25 .60
V484 Warren Moon .25 .60
CH12 Darren Carrington .15 .40
CH40 Natrone Means .40 1.00
CH84 Isaac Davis .15 .40
CH151 Stan Humphries .25 .60
CH179 Leslie O'Neal .25 .60
CH299 John Carney .15 .40
CH357 Stanley Richard .15 .40
CH390 Junior Seau .40 1.00
CH421 Dennis Gibson .15 .40
CH458 Shawn Jefferson .25 .60
C052 Jay Novacek .25 .60
C0168 Russell Maryland .25 .60
C0233 Charles Haley .25 .60
C0270 Michael Irvin .40 1.00
C0282 Alvin Harper .25 .60
C0300 Emmitt Smith 1.60 4.00
C0334 Daryl Johnston .25 .60
C0359 Darren Woodson .15 .40
C0423 James Washington .15 .40
C0540 Troy Aikman .80 2.00

1994 Stadium Club Super Teams Master Photos

COMPLETE BAG CHARGERS (11) 3.00 7.50
COMPLETE BAG 49ERS (11) 6.40 16.00
24CW Chargers Super .30 .75
Team CW
Natrone Means
25CW 49ers Super .60 1.50
Team CW
Jerry Rice
Steve Young
Ricky Watters
F35 William Floyd .40 1.00
F51 Bryant Young .50 1.25
F80 Dana Stubblefield .30 .75
F201 Ricky Watters .30 .75
F295 Steve Young 1.20 3.00
F326 Brent Jones .30 .75
F402 Tim McDonald .20 .50
F475 Merton Hanks .20 .50
F500 Jerry Rice 1.60 4.00
F600 Deion Sanders .60 1.50
CH12 Darren Carrington .20 .50
CH40 Natrone Means .40 1.00
CH84 Isaac Davis .20 .50
CH151 Stan Humphries .30 .75
CH179 Leslie O'Neal .20 .50
CH299 John Carney .20 .50
CH357 Stanley Richard .20 .50
CH390 Junior Seau .40 1.00
CH421 Dennis Gibson .20 .50
CH458 Shawn Jefferson .20 .50

1994 Stadium Club Super Teams Super Bowl

COMPLETE SET (541) 24.00 60.00
*STARS: 1X TO 2.5X BASIC CARDS
*ROOKIES: .6X TO 1.5X BASIC CARDS
SB25 49ers Super Team SB 1.50 4.00
Jerry Rice
Steve Young
Ricky Watters

1994 Stadium Club Members Only Parallel

COMP.FACT.SET (722) 100.00 200.00
*VETS 1-630: 1.5X TO 4X BASIC CARDS
*ROOKIES 1-630: 1X TO 2.5X BASIC CARDS
*BOW.BEST: .8X TO 2X BASIC INSERTS
*DYN-DESTINY: .3X TO .8X BASIC INSERTS
*RING LEADERS: .3X TO .8X BASIC INSERTS
*SUPER TEAMS: .2X TO .5X BASIC INSERTS

1994 Stadium Club Members Only 50

COMP. FACT SET (50) 6.00 15.00
1 Jerry Rice 1.25 3.00
2 Erik Williams .08 .25
3 Nate Newton .08 .25
4 Jesse Sapolu .08 .25
5 Randall McDaniel .08 .25
6 Harris Barton .08 .25
7 Jay Novacek .15 .40
8 Michael Irvin .30 .75
9 Steve Young 1.00 2.50
10 Jerome Bettis .60 1.50
11 Daryl Johnston .15 .40
12 Neil Smith .15 .40
13 Cortez Kennedy .15 .40
14 Ray Childress .08 .25
15 Leslie O'Neal .08 .25
16 Derrick Thomas .15 .40
17 Junior Seau .30 .75
18 Greg Lloyd .15 .40
19 Rod Woodson .15 .40
20 Nate Odomes .08 .25
21 Dennis Smith .08 .25
22 Steve Atwater .08 .25
23 Reggie White .30 .75
24 John Randle .15 .40
25 Sean Gilbert .08 .25
26 Richard Dent .15 .40
27 Rickey Jackson .08 .25
28 Hardy Nickerson .08 .25
29 Renaldo Turnbull .08 .25
30 Deion Sanders .60 1.50
31 Eric Allen .08 .25
32 Tim McDonald .08 .25
33 Mark Carrier DB .08 .25
34 Tim Brown .30 .75
35 Richmond Webb .08 .25
36 Keith Sims .08 .25
37 Bruce Matthews .08 .25
38 Steve Wisniewski .08 .25
39 Howard Ballard .08 .25
40 Shannon Sharpe .15 .40
41 Anthony Miller .15 .40
42 John Elway 2.40 6.00
43 Thurman Thomas .30 .75
44 Marcus Allen .30 .75
45 Andre Rison .15 .40
46 Drew Bledsoe 1.25 3.00
47 Willie Roaf .08 .25
48 Reggie Brooks .08 .25
49 Dana Stubblefield .15 .40
50 Rick Mirer .30 .75

1995 Stadium Club

This 450-card standard-size set was issued in two series in both 12-card foil packs and 26-card jumbo packs. Subsets include Extreme Corps/Expansion Teams (181-210/406-435) and Draft Picks (211-225/436-450), which were seeded at a rate of one per pack, thus making them slightly tougher to find (per card) than the regular cards. Each of those subset cards was printed in a Diffraction parallel version with series one Diffraction featuring text in solid red foil against silver holofoil and series two with solid green foil against gold.

COMPLETE SET (450) 25.00 60.00
COMP.SERIES 1 (225) 12.50 30.00
COMP.SERIES 2 (225) 12.50 30.00
1 Steve Young .50 1.25
2 Stan Humphries .07 .20
3 Chris Boniol RC .02 .10
4 Darren Perry .02 .10
5 Vinny Testaverde .07 .20
6 Aubrey Beavers .02 .10
7 Dewayne Washington .07 .20
8 Marion Butts .02 .10
9 George Koonce .02 .10
10 Joe Cain .02 .10
11 Mike Johnson .02 .10
12 Dale Carter .07 .20
13 Greg Biekert .02 .10
14 Aaron Pierce .02 .10
15 Aeneas Williams .02 .10
16 Stephen Grant RC .02 .10
17 Henry Jones .02 .10
18 James Williams .02 .10
19 Andy Harmon .02 .10
20 Anthony Miller .07 .20
21 Kevin Ross .02 .10
22 Erik Howard .02 .10
23 Brian Blades .07 .20
24 Trent Dilfer .15 .40
25 Bernard Williams .02 .10
26 Bruce Kozerski .02 .10
27 Henry Ellard .07 .20
28 Rich Camarillo .02 .10
29 Richmond Webb .02 .10
30 George Teague .02 .10
31 Antonio Langham .02 .10
32 Barry Foster .07 .20
33 Bruce Armstrong .02 .10
34 Tim McDonald .02 .10
35 James Harris DE .02 .10
36 Lomas Brown .02 .10
37 Jay Novacek .07 .20
38 John Thierry .02 .10
39 John Elliott .02 .10
40 Terry McDaniel .02 .10
41 Shawn Lee .02 .10
42 Shane Dronett .02 .10
43 Cornelius Bennett .07 .20
44 Steve Bono .07 .20
45 Byron Evans .02 .10
46 Eugene Robinson .02 .10
47 Tony Bennett .02 .10
48 Michael Bankston .02 .10
49 Willie Roaf .02 .10
50 Bobby Houston .02 .10
51 Ken Harvey .02 .10
52 Bruce Matthews .02 .10
53 Lincoln Kennedy .02 .10
54 Todd Lyght .02 .10
55 Paul Gruber .02 .10
56 Corey Sawyer .02 .10
57 Myron Guyton .02 .10
58 John Jackson .02 .10
59 Sean Jones .02 .10
60 Pepper Johnson .02 .10
61 Steve Walsh .02 .10
62 Corey Miller .02 .10
63 Fuad Reveiz .02 .10
64 Rickey Jackson .02 .10
65 Scott Mitchell .07 .20
66 Michael Irvin .15 .40
67 Andre Reed .07 .20
68 Mark Seay .07 .20
69 Keith Byars .02 .10
70 Marcus Allen .15 .40
71 Shannon Sharpe .07 .20
72 Eric Hill .02 .10
73 James Washington .02 .10
74 Greg Jackson .02 .10
75 Chris Warren .07 .20
76 Will Wolford .02 .10
77 Anthony Smith .02 .10
78 Cris Dishman .02 .10
79 Carl Pickens .07 .20
80 Tyrone Hughes .07 .20
81 Chris Miller .02 .10
82 Clay Matthews .02 .10
83 Lonnie Marts .02 .10
84 Jerome Henderson .02 .10
85 Ben Coates .07 .20
86 Deon Figures .02 .10
87 Anthony Pleasant .02 .10
88 Guy McIntyre .02 .10
89 Jake Reed .07 .20
90 Rodney Hampton .07 .20
91 Santana Dotson .02 .10
92 Jeff Blackshear RC .02 .10
93 Willie Clay .02 .10
94 Nate Newton .07 .20
95 Bucky Brooks .02 .10
96 Lamar Lathon .02 .10
97 Tim Grunhard .02 .10
98 Harris Barton .02 .10
99 Brian Mitchell .02 .10
100 Natrone Means .07 .20
101 Sean Dawkins .07 .20
102 Chris Slade .07 .20
103 Tom Rathman .02 .10
104 Fred Barnett .07 .20
105 Gary Brown .02 .10
106 Leonard Russell .02 .10
107 Alfred Williams .02 .10
108 Keith Hamilton .02 .10
109 Alexander Wright .02 .10
110 O.J. McDuffie .15 .40
111 Mario Bates .07 .20
112 Tony Casillas .02 .10
113 Michael Timpson .02 .10
114 Robert Brooks .15 .40
115 Rob Burnett .02 .10
116 Mark Collins .02 .10
117 Chris Calloway .02 .10
118 Courtney Hawkins .02 .10
119 Marcus Patton .02 .10
120 Greg Lloyd .07 .20
121 Ryan McNeil .02 .10
122 Gary Plummer .02 .10
123 Dwayne Sabb .02 .10
124 Jessie Hester .02 .10
125 Terance Mathis .07 .20
126 Steve Atwater .02 .10
127 Lorenzo Lynch .02 .10
128 James Francis .02 .10
129 John Fina .02 .10
130 Emmitt Smith 1.25 2.50
131 Bryan Cox .02 .10
132 Robert Blackmon .02 .10
133 Kenny Davidson .02 .10
134 Eugene Daniel .02 .10
135 Vince Buck .02 .10
136 Leslie O'Neal .07 .20
137 James Jett .07 .20
138 Johnny Johnson .02 .10
139 Michael Zordich .02 .10
140 Warren Moon .07 .20
141 William White .02 .10
142 Carl Banks .02 .10
143 Marty Carter .02 .10
144 Keith Hamilton .02 .10
145 Alvin Harper .02 .10
146 Corey Harris .02 .10
147 Elijah Alexander RC .02 .10
148 Darrell Green .02 .10
149 Yancey Thigpen RC .07 .20
150 Deion Sanders .40 1.00
151 Burt Grossman .02 .10
152 J.B. Brown .02 .10
153 Johnny Bailey .02 .10
154 Harvey Williams .02 .10
155 Jeff Blake RC .40 1.00
156 Al Smith .02 .10
157 Chris Doleman .02 .10
158 Garrison Hearst .15 .40
159 Bryce Paup .07 .20
160 Herman Moore .15 .40
161 Cortez Kennedy .07 .20
162 Marquez Pope .02 .10
163 Quinn Early .07 .20
164 Broderick Thomas .02 .10
165 Jeff Herrod .02 .10
166 Robert Jones .02 .10
167 Mo Lewis .02 .10
168 Ray Crittenden .02 .10
169 Raymont Harris .02 .10
170 Bruce Smith .15 .40
171 Dana Stubblefield .07 .20
172 Charles Haley .07 .20
173 Charles Johnson .07 .20
174 Shawn Jefferson .02 .10
175 Leroy Hoard .02 .10
176 Bernie Parmalee .07 .20
177 Scottie Graham .07 .20
178 Edgar Bennett .07 .20
179 Aubrey Matthews .02 .10
180 Don Beebe .02 .10
181 Eric Swann EC SP .10 .30
182 Jeff George EC SP .10 .30
183 Jim Kelly EC SP .25 .60
184 Sam Mills EC SP .10 .30
185 Mark Carrier DB EC SP .07 .20
186 Dan Wilkinson EC SP .10 .30
187 Eric Turner EC SP .07 .20
188 Troy Aikman EC SP .75 2.00
189 John Elway EC SP 1.50 4.00
190 Barry Sanders EC SP 1.25 3.00
191 Brett Favre EC SP 2.00 4.00
192 Micheal Barrow EC SP .07 .20
193 Marshall Faulk EC SP 1.00 2.50
194 Steve Beuerlein EC SP .10 .30
195 Neil Smith EC SP .10 .30
196 Jeff Hostetler EC SP .10 .30
197 Jerome Bettis EC SP .25 .60
198 Dan Marino EC SP 1.50 4.00
199 Cris Carter EC SP .25 .60
200 Drew Bledsoe EC SP .40 1.00
201 Jim Everett EC SP .07 .20
202 Dave Brown EC SP .10 .30
203 Boomer Esiason EC SP .10 .30
204 R.Cunningham EC SP .10 .30
205 Rod Woodson EC SP .10 .30
206 Junior Seau EC SP .25 .60
207 Jerry Rice EC SP .75 2.00
208 Rick Mirer EC SP .10 .30
209 Errict Rhett EC SP .10 .30
210 Heath Shuler EC SP .10 .30
211 Bobby Taylor SP RC .25 .60
212 Jesse James SP RC .07 .20
213 Devin Bush DP SP RC .07 .20
214 Luther Elliss DP SP RC .07 .20
215 Kerry Collins SP RC 1.00 2.50
216 Derrick Alexander SP RC .07 .20
217 Rashaan Salaam SP RC .10 .30
218 J.J. Stokes SP RC .25 .60
219 Todd Collins SP RC .75 2.00
220 Ki-Jana Carter SP RC .25 .60
221 Kyle Brady SP RC .25 .60
222 Kevin Carter SP RC .25 .60
223 Tony Boselli SP RC .25 .60
224 Scott Gragg SP RC .07 .20
225 Warren Sapp SP RC .75 2.00
226 Ricky Reynolds .02 .10
227 Roosevelt Potts .02 .10
228 Jessie Tuggle .02 .10
229 Anthony Newman .02 .10
230 Randall Cunningham .15 .40
231 Jason Elam .07 .20
232 Darnay Scott .07 .20
233 Tom Carter .02 .10
234 Micheal Barrow .02 .10
235 Steve Tasker .07 .20
236 Howard Cross .02 .10
237 Charles Wilson .02 .10
238 Rob Fredrickson .02 .10
239 Russell Maryland .02 .10
240 Dan Marino 1.25 3.00
241 Rafael Robinson .02 .10
242 Ed McDaniel .02 .10
243 Brett Perriman .07 .20
244 Chuck Levy .02 .10
245 Errict Rhett .07 .20
246 Tracy Simien .02 .10
247 Steve Everitt .02 .10
248 John Jurkovic .02 .10
249 Johnny Mitchell .02 .10
250 Mark Carrier .02 .10
251 Merton Hanks .02 .10
252 Joe Johnson .02 .10
253 Andre Coleman .02 .10
254 Ray Buchanan .02 .10
255 Jeff George .07 .20
256 Shane Conlan .02 .10
257 Gus Frerotte .07 .20
258 Doug Pelfrey .02 .10
259 Glenn Montgomery .02 .10
260 John Elway 1.25 3.00
261 Larry Centers .07 .20
262 Calvin Williams .07 .20
263 Gene Atkins .02 .10
264 Tim Brown .15 .40
265 Leon Lett .02 .10
266 Martin Mayhew .02 .10
267 Arthur Marshall .02 .10
268 Maurice Hurst .02 .10
269 Greg Hill .07 .20
270 Junior Seau .15 .40
271 Rick Mirer .07 .20
272 Jack Del Rio .02 .10
273 Lewis Tillman .02 .10
274 Renaldo Turnbull .02 .10
275 Dan Footman .02 .10
276 John Taylor .02 .10
277 Russell Copeland .07 .20
278 Tracy Scroggins .02 .10
279 Lou Benfatti .02 .10
280 Rod Woodson .07 .20
281 Troy Drayton .02 .10
282 Quentin Coryatt .07 .20
283 Craig Heyward .07 .20
284 Jeff Cross .02 .10
285 Hardy Nickerson .02 .10
286 Dorsey Levens .30 .75
287 Derek Russell .02 .10
288 Seth Joyner .02 .10
289 Kimble Anders .07 .20
290 Drew Bledsoe .30 .75
291 Bryant Young .07 .20
292 Chris Zorich .02 .10

293 Michael Strahan .15 .40
294 Kevin Greene .07 .20
295 Aaron Glenn .02 .10
296 Jimmy Spencer RC .02 .10
297 Eric Turner .02 .10
298 William Thomas .02 .10
299 Dan Wilkinson .07 .20
300 Troy Aikman .60 1.50
301 Terry Wooden .02 .10
302 Heath Shuler .07 .20
303 Jeff Burris .02 .10
304 Mark Stepnoski .02 .10
305 Chris Mims .02 .10
306 Todd Steussie .02 .10
307 Johnnie Morton .07 .20
308 Darryl Talley .02 .10
309 Nolan Harrison .02 .10
310 Dave Brown .07 .20
311 Brent Jones .02 .10
312 Curtis Conway .15 .40
313 Ronald Humphrey .02 .10
314 Richie Anderson RC .20 .50
315 Jim Everett .02 .10
316 Willie Davis .07 .20
317 Ed Cunningham .02 .10
318 Willie McGinest .07 .20
319 Sean Gilbert .07 .20
320 Brett Favre 1.50 3.00
321 Bennie Thompson .02 .10
322 Neil O'Donnell .07 .20
323 Vince Workman .02 .10
324 Terry Kirby .07 .20
325 Simon Fletcher .02 .10
326 Ricardo McDonald .02 .10
327 Duane Young .02 .10
328 Jim Harbaugh .07 .20
329 D.J. Johnson .02 .10
330 Boomer Esiason .07 .20
331 Donnell Woolford .02 .10
332 Mike Sherrard .02 .10
333 Tyrone Legette .02 .10
334 Larry Brown DB .02 .10
335 William Floyd .07 .20
336 Reggie Brooks .07 .20
337 Patrick Bates .02 .10
338 Jim Jeffcoat .02 .10
339 Ray Childress .02 .10
340 Cris Carter .15 .40
341 Charlie Garner .15 .40
342 Bill Hitchcock .02 .10
343 Levon Kirkland .02 .10
344 Robert Porcher .02 .10
345 Darryl Williams .02 .10
346 Vincent Brisby .02 .10
347 Kenyon Rasheed RC .02 .10
348 Floyd Turner .02 .10
349 Bob Whitfield .02 .10
350 Jerome Bettis .15 .40
351 Brad Baxter .02 .10
352 Darrin Smith .02 .10
353 Lamar Thomas .02 .10
354 Lorenzo Noal .02 .10
355 Erik Kramer .02 .10
356 Dwayne Harper .02 .10
357 Doug Evans RC .15 .40
358 Jeff Feagles .02 .10
359 Ray Crockett .02 .10
360 Neil Smith .07 .20
361 Troy Vincent .02 .10
362 Don Griffin .02 .10
363 Michael Brooks .02 .10
364 Carlton Gray .02 .10
365 Thomas Smith .02 .10
366 Ken Norton .07 .20
367 Tony McGee .02 .10
368 Eric Metcalf .07 .20
369 Mel Gray .02 .10
370 Barry Sanders 1.00 2.50
371 Rocket Ismail .07 .20
372 Chad Brown .07 .20
373 Qadry Ismail .07 .20
374 Anthony Prior .02 .10
375 Kevin Lee .02 .10
376 Robert Young .02 .10
377 Kevin Williams WR .07 .20
378 Tydus Winans .02 .10
379 Ricky Watters .07 .20
380 Jim Kelly .15 .40
381 Eric Swann .07 .20
382 Mike Pritchard .02 .10
383 Derek Brown RBK .02 .10
384 Dennis Gibson .02 .10
385 Byron Bam Morris .02 .10
386 Reggie White .15 .40
387 Jeff Graham .02 .10
388 Marshall Faulk .75 2.00
389 Joe Phillips .02 .10
390 Jeff Hostetler .07 .20
391 Irving Fryar .07 .20
392 Stevon Moore .02 .10
393 Bert Emanuel .15 .40
394 Leon Searcy .02 .10
395 Robert Smith .15 .40
396 Michael Bates .02 .10
397 Thomas Lewis .07 .20
398 Joe Bowden .02 .10
399 Steve Tovar .02 .10
400 Jerry Rice .60 1.50
401 Toby Wright .02 .10
402 Daryl Johnston .07 .20
403 Vincent Brown .02 .10
404 Marvin Washington .02 .10
405 Chris Spielman .07 .20
406 Willie Jackson ET SP .10 .30
407 Harry Boatswain ET SP .07 .20
408 Kelvin Pritchett ET SP .07 .20
409 Dave Widell ET SP .07 .20
410 Frank Reich ET SP .07 .20
411 Corey Mayfield ET SP RC .07 .20
412 Pete Metzelaars ET SP .07 .20
413 Keith Goganious ET SP .07 .20
414 John Kasay ET SP .07 .20
415 Ernest Givins ET SP .07 .20
416 Randy Baldwin ET SP .07 .20
417 Shawn Bouwens ET SP .07 .20
418 Mike Fox ET SP .07 .20
419 Mark Carrier WR ET SP .10 .30
420 Steve Beuerlein ET SP .10 .30
421 Steve Lofton ET SP .07 .20
422 Jeff Lageman ET SP .07 .20
423 Paul Butcher ET SP .07 .20
424 Mark Brunell ET SP .40 1.00
425 Vernon Turner ET SP .07 .20
426 Tim McKyer ET SP .07 .20
427 James Williams ET SP .07 .20
428 Tommy Barnhardt ET SP .07 .20
429 Rogerick Green ET SP .07 .20
430 Desmond Howard ET SP .10 .30
431 Darion Conner ET SP .07 .20
432 Reggie Clark ET SP .07 .20
433 Eric Guliford ET SP .07 .20
434 Rob Johnson SP RC .50 1.25
435 Sam Mills ET SP .10 .30
436 Kordell Stewart SP RC .75 2.00
437 James O. Stewart SP RC .60 1.50
438 Zach Wiegert SP .07 .20
439 Ellis Johnson SP RC .07 .20
440 Matt O'Dwyer SP RC .07 .20
441 Anthony Cook SP RC .07 .20
442 Ron Davis SP RC .07 .20
443 Chris Hudson SP RC .07 .20
444 Hugh Douglas SP RC .25 .60
445 Tyrone Poole RC SP .25 .60
446 Korey Stringer SP RC .20 .50
447 Ruben Brown SP RC .25 .60
448 Brian DeMarco SP RC .07 .20
449 Michael Westbrook SP RC .25 .60
450 Steve McNair SP RC 1.50 4.00

1995 Stadium Club Diffraction

*DIFFRACTION: .5X TO 1.2X BASIC CARDS
RANDOM INSERTS IN ALL PACKS
SERIES ONE PRINTED WITH RED FOIL
SERIES TWO PRINTED WITH GREEN FOIL
*MEMBERS ONLY: .4X TO 1X BASIC INSERTS

1995 Stadium Club Members Only Parallel

COMPLETE SET (550) 80.00 200.00
COMP.SERIES 1 (275) 40.00 100.00
COMP.SERIES 2 (275) 40.00 100.00
*VETS 1-450: 1.5X TO 4X BASIC CARDS
*ROOKIES 1-450: .6X TO 1.5X BASIC CARDS
*POWER SURGE: .2X TO .5X BASIC INSERTS
*GRND ATTACK: .2X TO .5X BASIC INSERTS
*METALISTS: .2X TO .5X BASIC INSERTS
*MVPs: .3X TO .8X BASIC INSERTS
*NEMESES: .2X TO .5X BASIC INSERTS
*NIGHTMARES: .2X TO .5X BASIC INSERTS

1995 Stadium Club Ground Attack

COMPLETE SET (15) 15.00 40.00
RANDOM INSERTS IN PACKS
STATED ODDS 1:16 SPEC.RET SER.2
G1 Emmitt Smith 3.00 8.00
Daryl Johnston
G2 Brett Favre 5.00 12.00
Edgar Bennett
G3 Bernie Parmalee .60 1.50
Irving Spikes
G4 John Elway 5.00 12.00
Glen Milburn
G5 Rick Mirer .75 2.00
Chris Warren
G6 Greg Hill .75 2.00
Marcus Allen
G7 Errict Rhett .75 2.00
Vince Workman
G8 Byron Bam Morris .60 1.50
Erric Pegram
G9 Derek Brown RBK .60 1.50
Mario Bates
G10 Steve Young 2.00 5.00
William Floyd
G11 Charlie Garner 1.25 3.00
Randall Cunningham
G12 Lewis Tillman .60 1.50
Raymont Harris
G13 Harvey Williams .60 1.50
Jeff Hostetler
G14 Garrison Hearst .75 2.00
Larry Centers
G15 Marshall Faulk 2.50 6.00
Roosevelt Potts

1995 Stadium Club Metalists

COMPLETE SET (8) 12.50 30.00
STATED ODDS 1:24H, 1:9J, 1:28R SER.1
STATED ODDS 1:21 SPEC.RET SER.1
M1 Jerry Rice 2.50 6.00
M2 Barry Sanders 3.00 8.00
M3 John Elway 4.00 10.00
M4 Dana Stubblefield .30 .75
M5 Emmitt Smith 3.00 8.00
M6 Deion Sanders 1.25 3.00
M7 Marshall Faulk 1.25 3.00
M8 Steve Young 1.50 4.00

1995 Stadium Club MVPs

COMPLETE SET (8) 10.00 25.00
STATED ODDS 1:24H, 1:9J, 1:24R SER.2
STATED ODDS 1:28 SPEC.RET SER.2
MVP1 Jerry Rice 2.00 4.00
MVP2 Boomer Esiason .30 .75
MVP3 Randall Cunningham .40 1.00
MVP4 Marcus Allen .40 1.00
MVP5 John Elway 4.00 8.00
MVP6 Dan Marino 4.00 8.00
MVP7 Emmitt Smith 3.00 6.00
MVP8 Steve Young 1.50 3.00

1995 Stadium Club Nemeses

COMPLETE SET (15) 25.00 60.00
STATED ODDS 1:24H, 1:9J, 1:16SP.RET SER.1
N1 Barry Sanders 5.00 12.00
Jack Del Rio
N2 Reggie White 1.50 4.00
Lomas Brown
N3 Terry McDaniel 1.00 2.50
Anthony Miller
N4 Brett Favre 5.00 12.00
Chris Spielman
N5 Junior Seau 2.00 5.00
Chris Warren
N6 Cortez Kennedy 1.00 2.50
Steve Wisniewski
N7 Rod Woodson 2.00 5.00
Tim Brown
N8 Troy Aikman 3.00 8.00
Michael Brooks
N9 Bruce Smith 1.50 4.00
Bruce Armstrong
N10 Jerry Rice 3.00 8.00
Donnell Woolford
N11 Emmitt Smith 4.00 10.00
Seth Joyner
N12 Dan Marino 5.00 12.00
Cornelius Bennett
N13 Marshall Faulk 3.00 8.00
Bryan Cox
N14 Stan Humphries 1.50 4.00
Greg Lloyd
N15 Michael Irvin 2.00 5.00
Deion Sanders

1995 Stadium Club Nightmares

COMPLETE SET (30) 40.00 100.00
COMP.SERIES 1 (15) 30.00 70.00
COMP.SERIES 2 (15) 12.00 30.00
NM1-NM15 ODDS 1:24H, 1:9J SER.1
NM16-NM30 ODDS 1:18H, 1:6J SER.2
NM1 Drew Bledsoe .75 2.00
NM2 Barry Sanders 4.00 10.00
NM3 Reggie White .75 2.00
NM4 Michael Irvin .75 2.00
NM5 Jerry Rice 3.00 8.00
NM6 Jerome Bettis .75 2.00
NM7 Dan Marino 6.00 15.00
NM8 Bruce Smith .75 2.00
NM9 Steve Young 2.00 5.00
NM10 Junior Seau .75 2.00
NM11 Emmitt Smith 4.00 10.00
NM12 Deion Sanders 1.50 4.00
NM13 Rod Woodson .50 1.25
NM14 Marshall Faulk 1.50 4.00
NM15 Troy Aikman 2.50 6.00
NM16 Stan Humphries .50 1.25
NM17 Chris Warren .50 1.25
NM18 Jack Del Rio .30 .75
NM19 Randall Cunningham .75 2.00
NM20 Natrone Means .50 1.25
NM21 Dana Stubblefield .50 1.25
NM22 Jim Kelly .75 2.00
NM23 Cris Carter .75 2.00
NM24 Cornelius Bennett .50 1.25
NM25 Errict Rhett .50 1.25
NM26 Terry McDaniel .30 .75
NM27 Rodney Hampton .50 1.25
NM28 Brett Favre 6.00 15.00
NM29 Bryan Cox .30 .75
NM30 John Elway 6.00 15.00

1995 Stadium Club Power Surge

COMPLETE SET (24) 30.00 80.00
COMP.SERIES 1 (12) 20.00 50.00
COMP.SERIES 2 (12) 12.50 30.00
P1-P12 ODDS 1:18H, 1:28R SER.1
PS1-PS12 ODDS 1:36H, 1:28R SER.2
P1 Steve Young 2.50 6.00
P2 Natrone Means .40 1.00
P3 Cris Carter .75 2.00
P4 Junior Seau .75 2.00
P5 Barry Sanders 5.00 12.00
P6 Michael Irvin .75 2.00
P7 John Elway 6.00 15.00
P8 Emmitt Smith 5.00 12.00
P9 Greg Lloyd .40 1.00
P10 Jerry Rice 3.00 8.00
P11 Marshall Faulk 4.00 10.00
P12 Drew Bledsoe 1.50 4.00
PS1 Dan Marino 6.00 15.00
PS2 Ken Harvey .20 .50
PS3 Chris Warren .40 1.00
PS4 Henry Ellard .40 1.00
PS5 Marshall Faulk 1.25 3.00
PS6 Irving Fryar .40 1.00
PS7 Kevin Ross .20 .50
PS8 Vince Workman .20 .50
PS9 Ray Buchanan .20 .50
PS10 Tony Martin .40 1.00
PS11 D.J.Johnson .20 .50
PS12 Steve Young 2.50 6.00

1995 Stadium Club Members Only 50

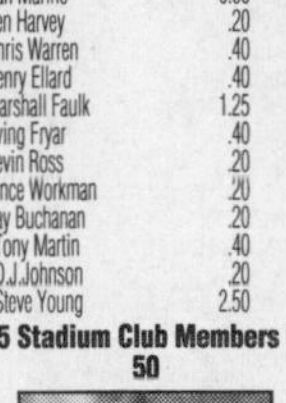

Topps produced a 50-card boxed set for each of the four major sports. With their club membership, members received one set of their choice and had the option of purchasing additional sets for $10.00 each. The set consists of 45 Stadium Club cards (reflecting the 44 starting players from the 1995 Pro Bowl and a special card of Jerry Rice and Emmitt Smith who were both elected to the starting team but did not play due to injuries) and five Finest cards (representing Topps' selection of the Top Rookies of 1994). The fronts carry the distinctive Topps Stadium Club Members Only gold foil seal.

COMP.FACT SET (50) 6.00 15.00
1 Tim Brown .30 .75
2 Richmond Webb .07 .20
3 Keith Sims .07 .20
4 Dermontti Dawson .07 .20
5 Duval Love .07 .20
6 Bruce Armstrong .07 .20
7 Ben Coates .15 .40
8 Andre Reed .15 .40
9 John Elway 1.60 4.00
10 Marshall Faulk .80 2.00
11 Natrone Means .15 .40
12 Charles Haley .07 .20
13 John Randle .15 .40
14 Leon Lett .07 .20
15 William Fuller .07 .20
16 Ken Harvey .07 .20
17 Chris Spielman .07 .20
18 Bryce Paup .07 .20
19 Deion Sanders .60 1.50
20 Aeneas Williams .07 .20
21 Darren Woodson .07 .20
22 Merton Hanks .07 .20
23 Michael Irvin .30 .75
24 William Roaf .07 .20
25 Nate Newton .07 .20
26 Mark Stepnoski .07 .20
27 Randall McDaniel .07 .20
28 Lomas Brown .07 .20
29 Brent Jones .07 .20
30 Cris Carter .30 .75
31 Steve Young .80 2.00
32 Barry Sanders 1.60 4.00
Detroit Lions
33 Jerome Bettis .30 .75
34 Bruce Smith .15 .40
35 Michael Dean Perry .07 .20
36 Cortez Kennedy .07 .20
37 Leslie O'Neal .07 .20
38 Derrick Thomas .15 .40
39 Junior Seau .15 .40
40 Greg Lloyd .07 .20
41 Rod Woodson .15 .40
42 Terry McDaniel .07 .20
43 Eric Turner .07 .20
44 Carnell Lake .07 .20
45 Jerry Rice 1.60 4.00
Emmitt Smith
46 William Floyd .15 .40
47 Tim Bowens .07 .20
48 Heath Shuler .15 .40
49 Bryant Young .15 .40
50 Marshall Faulk .80 2.00

1996 Stadium Club

This 360-card set was issued in two series totalling 180 cards each. The set was distributed in 10-card packs with a suggested retail price of $2.50. Each pack of both Series I and Series II cards contained eight regular cards and two foil subset cards. Series I contains 135 regular cards with textured foil stamping and 45 double foil stamped subset cards from the following categories: Draft Picks (136-153), Shining Moments (154-171, highlights milestones or great plays from the '95 season), and Golden Moments (172-180, features record-breaking performances from the '95 season). Series 2 contained 135 regular cards stamped with etched gold foil and UV coated and 45-subset cards of rookies, free agents and traded veterans showcased in their new uniforms. Several Protoype cards were produced that look nearly exactly like base cards. The only difference is found is the base cards have a white ghosting on the team name printed on the cardbacks. There were likely more prototype cards printed than listed below.

COMPLETE SET (360) 30.00 60.00
COMP.SERIES 1 (180) 15.00 30.00
COMP.SERIES 2 (180) 15.00 30.00
1 Kyle Brady .02 .10
2 Mickey Washington .02 .10
3 Seth Joyner .02 .10
4 Vinny Testaverde .08 .25
5 Thomas Randolph .02 .10
6 Heath Shuler .08 .25
7 Ty Law .20 .50
8 Blake Brockermeyer .02 .10
9 Darryll Lewis .02 .10
10 Jeff Blake .20 .50
11 Tyrone Hughes .02 .10
12 Horaco Copeland .02 .10
13 Roman Phifer .02 .10
14 Eugene Robinson .02 .10
15 Anthony Miller .08 .25
16 Robert Smith .08 .25
17 Chester McGlockton .02 .10
18 Marty Carter .02 .10
19 Scott Mitchell .08 .25
20 O.J. McDuffie .08 .25
21 Stan Humphries .08 .25
22 Eugene Daniel .02 .10
23 Devin Bush .02 .10
24 Darick Holmes .02 .10
25 Ricky Watters .08 .25
26 J.J. Stokes .20 .50
27 George Koonce .02 .10
28 Tamarick Vanover .08 .25
29 Yancey Thigpen .08 .25
30 Troy Aikman .50 1.25
31 Rashaan Salaam .08 .25
32 Anthony Cook .02 .10
33 Tim McKyer .02 .10
34 Dale Carter .02 .10
35 Marvin Washington .02 .10
36 Terry Allen .08 .25
37 Keith Goganious .02 .10
38 Pepper Johnson .02 .10
39 Dave Brown .02 .10
40 Levon Kirkland .02 .10
41 Ken Dilger .08 .25
42 Harvey Williams .02 .10
43 Robert Blackmon .02 .10
44 Kevin Carter .02 .10
45 Warren Moon .08 .25
46 Allen Aldridge .02 .10
47 Terance Mathis .02 .10
48 Junior Seau .20 .50
49 William Fuller .02 .10
50 Lee Woodall .02 .10
51 Aeneas Williams .02 .10
52 Thomas Smith .02 .10
53 Chris Slade .02 .10
54 Eric Allen .02 .10
55 David Sloan .02 .10
56 Hardy Nickerson .02 .10
57 Michael Irvin .20 .50
58 Corey Sawyer .02 .10
59 Eric Green .02 .10
60 Reggie White .20 .50
61 Isaac Bruce .20 .50
62 Darrell Green .02 .10
63 Aaron Glenn .02 .10
64 Mark Brunell .30 .75
65 Mark Carrier WR .02 .10
66 Mel Gray .02 .10
67 Phillippi Sparks .02 .10
68 Ernie Mills .02 .10
69 Rick Mirer .08 .25
70 Neil Smith .08 .25
71 Terry McDaniel .02 .10
72 Terrell Davis .40 1.00
73 Alonzo Spellman .02 .10
74 Jessie Tuggle .02 .10
75 Terry Kirby .08 .25
76 David Palmer .02 .10
77 Calvin Williams .02 .10
78 Shaun Gayle .02 .10
79 Bryant Young .08 .25
80 Jim Harbaugh .08 .25
81 Michael Jackson .08 .25
82 Dave Meggett .02 .10
83 Henry Thomas .02 .10
84 Jim Kelly .20 .50
85 Frank Sanders .08 .25
86 Daryl Johnston .08 .25
87 Alvin Harper .02 .10
88 John Copeland .02 .10
89 Mark Chmura .08 .25
90 Jim Everett .02 .10
91 Bobby Houston .02 .10
92 Willie Jackson .08 .25
93 Carlton Bailey .02 .10
94 Todd Lyght .02 .10
95 Ken Harvey .02 .10
96 Erric Pegram .02 .10
97 Anthony Smith .02 .10
98 Kimble Anders .08 .25
99 Steve McNair .40 1.00
100 Jeff George .08 .25
101 Michael Timpson .02 .10
102 Brent Jones .02 .10
103 Mike Mamula .02 .10
104 Jeff Cross .02 .10
105 Craig Newsome .02 .10
106 Howard Cross .02 .10
107 Terry Wooden .02 .10
108 Randall McDaniel .05 .15
109 Andre Reed .08 .25
110 Steve Atwater .02 .10
111 Larry Centers .08 .25
112 Tony Bennett .02 .10
113 Drew Bledsoe .30 .75
114 Terrell Fletcher .02 .10
115 Warren Sapp .02 .10
116 Deion Sanders .30 .75
117 Bryce Paup .02 .10
118 Mario Bates .08 .25
119 Steve Tovar .02 .10
120 Barry Sanders .75 2.00
121 Tony Boselli .02 .10
122 Micheal Barrow .02 .10
123 Sam Mills .02 .10
124 Tim Brown .20 .50
125 Darren Perry .02 .10
126 Brian Blades .02 .10
127 Tyrone Wheatley .08 .25
128 Derrick Thomas .20 .50
129 Edgar Bennett .08 .25
130 Cris Carter .20 .50
131 Stephen Grant .02 .10
132 Kevin Williams .02 .10
133 Darnay Scott .08 .25
134 Rod Stephens .02 .10
135 Ken Norton .02 .10
136 Tim Biakabutuka SP RC .20 .50
137 Willie Anderson SP RC .02 .10
138 Lawrence Phillips SP RC .20 .50
139 Jonathan Ogden SP RC .20 .50
140 Simeon Rice RC .50 1.25
141 Alex Van Dyke SP RC .08 .25
142 Jerome Woods RC .02 .10
143 Eric Moulds RC .75 2.00
144 Mike Alstott SP RC .60 1.50
145 Marvin Harrison SP RC 1.50 4.00
146 Duane Clemons RC .02 .10
147 Regan Upshaw RC .02 .10
148 Eddie Kennison RC .20 .50
149 John Mobley SP RC .02 .10
150 Keyshawn Johnson SP RC .60 1.50
151 Marco Battaglia SP RC .02 .10
152 Rickey Dudley SP RC .20 .50
153 Kevin Hardy SP RC .20 .50
154 Curtis Martin SM .40 1.00
155 Dan Marino SM 1.00 2.50
156 Rashaan Salaam SM .08 .25
157 Joey Galloway SM .20 .50
158 John Elway SM 1.00 2.50
159 Marshall Faulk SM .25 .60
160 Jerry Rice SM .50 1.25
161 Darren Bennett SM .02 .10
162 Tamarick Vanover SM .08 .25
163 Orlando Thomas SM .02 .10
164 Jim Kelly SM .20 .50
165 Larry Brown SM .02 .10
166 Errict Rhett SM .08 .25
167 Warren Moon SM .02 .10
168 Hugh Douglas SM .02 .10
169 Jim Everett SM .02 .10
170 AFC Champ. Game .02 .10
Colts vs. Steelers
Hail Mary Pass
171 Larry Centers SM .08 .25
172 Marcus Allen GM .20 .50
173 Morten Andersen GM .02 .10
174 Brett Favre GM SP 1.00 2.50
175 Jerry Rice GM .50 1.25
176 Glyn Milburn GM .02 .10
177 Thurman Thomas GM .08 .25
178 Michael Irvin GM .08 .25
179 Barry Sanders GM SP .75 2.00
180 Dan Marino GM 1.00 2.50
181 Joey Galloway .20 .50
182 Dwayne Harper .02 .10
183 Antonio Langham .02 .10
184 Chris Zorich .02 .10
185 Willie McGinest .02 .10
186 Wayne Chrebet .30 .75
187 Dermontti Dawson .02 .10
188 Charlie Garner .08 .25
189 Quentin Coryatt .02 .10
190 Rodney Hampton .08 .25
191 Kelvin Pritchett .02 .10
192 Willie Green .02 .10
193 Garrison Hearst .08 .25
194 Tracy Scroggins .02 .10
195 Rocket Ismail .02 .10
196 Michael Westbrook .20 .50
197 Troy Drayton .02 .10
198 Rob Fredrickson .02 .10
199 Sean Lumpkin .02 .10
200 John Elway 1.00 2.50
201 Bernie Parmalee .02 .10
202 Chris Chandler .08 .25
203 Lake Dawson .02 .10
204 Orlando Thomas .02 .10
205 Carl Pickens .08 .25
206 Kurt Schulz .02 .10
207 Clay Matthews .02 .10
208 Winston Moss .02 .10
209 Sean Dawkins .02 .10
210 Emmitt Smith .75 2.00
211 Mark Carrier DB .02 .10
212 Clyde Simmons .02 .10
213 Derrick Brooks .20 .50
214 William Floyd .08 .25
215 Aaron Hayden .02 .10
216 Brian DeMarco .02 .10
217 Ben Coates .08 .25
218 Renaldo Turnbull .02 .10
219 Adrian Murrell .08 .25
220 Marcus Allen .20 .50
221 Brett Maxie .02 .10
222 Trev Alberts .02 .10
223 Darren Woodson .08 .25
224 Brian Mitchell .02 .10
225 Michael Haynes .02 .10
226 Sean Jones .02 .10
227 Eric Zeier .02 .10
228 Herman Moore .08 .25
229 Shane Conlan .02 .10
230 Chris Warren .08 .25
231 Dana Stubblefield .08 .25
232 Andre Coleman .02 .10
233 Kordell Stewart UER .20 .50
card actually numbered 223
234 Ray Crockett .02 .10
235 Craig Heyward .02 .10
236 Mike Fox .02 .10
237 Derek Brown RBK .02 .10
238 Thomas Lewis .02 .10
239 Hugh Douglas .08 .25
240 Tom Carter .02 .10
241 Toby Wright .02 .10
242 Jason Belser .02 .10
243 Rodney Peete .02 .10
244 Napoleon Kaufman .20 .50
245 Merton Hanks .02 .10
246 Harry Colon .02 .10
247 Greg Hill .08 .25
248 Vincent Brisby .02 .10
249 Eric Hill .02 .10
250 Brett Favre 1.00 2.50
251 Leroy Hoard .02 .10
252 Eric Guliford .02 .10
253 Stanley Richard .08 .25
254 Carlos Jenkins .02 .10
255 D'Marco Farr .02 .10
256 Carlton Gray .02 .10
257 Derek Loville .02 .10
258 Ray Buchanan .02 .10
259 Jake Reed .08 .25
260 Dan Marino 1.00 2.50
261 Brad Baxter .02 .10
262 Pat Swilling .02 .10
263 Andy Harmon .02 .10
264 Harold Green .02 .10
265 Shannon Sharpe .08 .25
266 Erik Kramer .02 .10
267 Lamar Lathon .02 .10
268 Stevon Moore .02 .10
269 Tony Martin .08 .25
270 Bruce Smith .08 .25
271 James Washington .02 .10
272 Tyrone Poole .02 .10
273 Eric Swann .02 .10
274 Dexter Carter .02 .10
275 Greg Lloyd .08 .25
276 Michael Zordich .02 .10
277 Steve Wisniewski .02 .10
278 Chris Calloway .02 .10
279 Irv Smith .02 .10
280 Steve Young .40 1.00
281 James O.Stewart .08 .25
282 Blaine Bishop .02 .10
283 Rob Moore .08 .25
284 Eric Metcalf .02 .10
285 Kerry Collins .20 .50
286 Dan Wilkinson .02 .10
287 Curtis Conway .20 .50
288 Jay Novacek .02 .10
289 Henry Ellard .02 .10
290 Curtis Martin .40 1.00
291 Brett Perriman .02 .10
292 Jeff Lageman .02 .10
293 Trent Dilfer .20 .50
294 Cortez Kennedy .02 .10
295 Jeff Hostetler .02 .10
296 Mark Fields .02 .10
297 Qadry Ismail .08 .25
298 Steve Bono .02 .10
299 Tony Tolbert .02 .10
300 Jerry Rice .50 1.25
301 Marvcus Patton .02 .10
302 Robert Brooks .20 .50
303 Terry Ray RC .02 .10
304 John Thierry .02 .10
305 Errict Rhett .08 .25
306 Ricardo McDonald .02 .10
307 Antonio London .02 .10
308 Lonnie Johnson .02 .10
309 Mark Collins .02 .10
310 Marshall Faulk .25 .60
311 Anthony Pleasant .02 .10
312 Howard Griffith .02 .10
313 Roosevelt Potts .02 .10
314 Jim Flanigan .02 .10
315 Omar Ellison RC .02 .10
316 Boomer Esiason SP .08 .25
317 Leslie O'Neal SP .02 .10
318 Jerome Bettis SP .20 .50
319 Larry Brown SP .02 .10
320 Neil O'Donnell SP .08 .25
321 Andre Rison SP .08 .25
322 Cornelius Bennett SP .02 .10
323 Quinn Early SP .02 .10
324 Bryan Cox SP .02 .10
325 Irving Fryar SP .08 .25
326 Eddie Robinson SP .02 .10
327 Chris Doleman SP .02 .10
328 Sean Gilbert SP .02 .10
329 Steve Walsh SP .02 .10
330 Kevin Greene SP .08 .25
331 Chris Spielman SP .02 .10
332 Jeff Graham SP .02 .10
333 Anthony Dorsett SP RC .02 .10
334 Amani Toomer SP RC .60 1.50
335 Walt Harris SP RC .02 .10
336 Ray Mickens SP RC .02 .10
337 Danny Kanell SP RC .20 .50
338 Daryl Gardener SP RC .02 .10
339 Jonathan Ogden SP .08 .25
340 Eddie George SP RC .75 2.00
341 Jeff Lewis SP RC .08 .25
342 Terrell Owens SP RC 1.50 4.00
343 Brian Dawkins SP RC .75 2.00
344 Tim Biakabutuka SP .20 .50
345 Marvin Harrison SP .60 1.50
346 Lawyer Milloy SP RC .25 .60
347 Eric Moulds SP .30 .75
348 Alex Van Dyke SP .08 .25
349 John Mobley SP .02 .10
350 Kevin Hardy SP .20 .50
351 Ray Lewis SP RC 2.00 5.00
352 Lawrence Phillips SP .20 .50
353 Stepfret Williams SP RC .08 .25
354 Bobby Engram SP RC .20 .50
355 Leeland McElroy SP RC .08 .25
356 Marco Battaglia SP .02 .10
357 Rickey Dudley SP .20 .50
358 Bobby Hoying SP RC .20 .50
359 Cedric Jones SP RC .02 .10
360 Keyshawn Johnson SP .20 .50
P19 Scott Mitchell Proto .20 .50
team name on back
not ghosted in white
P31 R.Salaam Proto .30 .75
team name on back
not ghosted in white
P56 H.Nickerson Proto .20 .50
team name on back
not ghosted in white
NNO Checklist Card .02 .10

1996 Stadium Club Dot Matrix

*DOT MATRIX: 4X TO 10X BASIC CARDS
D.MAT STATED ODDS 1:12H/R, 1:4J SER.1
STATED ODDS 1:12H, 1:16R SER.2

1996 Stadium Club Match Proofs

*MATCH PROOFS: 15X TO 40X BASIC CARDS
STATED ODDS 1:240 SER.1
STATED ODDS 1:150H, 1:200R SER.2

1996 Stadium Club Brace Yourself

COMPLETE SET (10) 25.00 60.00
STATED ODDS 1:24 HOB, 1:32 RET SER.2
BY1 Dan Marino 10.00 20.00
BY2 Marshall Faulk 2.50 5.00
BY3 Greg Lloyd 1.00 2.00
BY4 Steve Young 4.00 8.00
BY5 Emmitt Smith 8.00 15.00
BY6 Junior Seau 2.00 4.00
BY7 Chris Warren 1.00 2.00
BY8 Jerry Rice 5.00 10.00
BY9 Troy Aikman 5.00 10.00
BY10 Barry Sanders 8.00 15.00

1996 Stadium Club Contact Prints

COMPLETE SET (10) 6.00 15.00
SER.1 STATED ODDS 1:12HOB/RET, 1:4 JUM
CP1 Ken Norton 1.50 4.00
vs. Drew Bledsoe
CP2 Chris Zorich 1.50 4.00
vs. Barry Sanders
CP3 Corey Harris .60 1.50
vs. Harvey Williams
CP4 Sam Mills .75 2.00
vs. Thurman Thomas
CP5 Bryce Paup .60 1.50
vs. Derrick Moore
CP6 Rob Fredrickson .60 1.50
vs. Chris Warren
CP7 Darnell Walker .60 1.50
vs. Bernie Parmalee
CP8 Derrick Thomas .75 2.00
vs. Gus Frerotte
CP9 Hardy Nickerson .60 1.50
vs. Robert Smith
CP10 Reggie White .75 2.00
vs. Dave Brown

1996 Stadium Club Cut Backs

COMPLETE SET (8) 15.00 40.00
STATED ODDS 1:36 HOB, 1:12 JUM SER.1
C1 Emmitt Smith 6.00 15.00
C2 Barry Sanders 6.00 15.00
C3 Curtis Martin 3.00 8.00
C4 Chris Warren 1.00 2.50
C5 Errict Rhett 1.00 2.50
C6 Rodney Hampton 1.00 2.50
C7 Ricky Watters 1.00 2.50
C8 Terry Allen 1.00 2.50

1996 Stadium Club Fusion

COMPLETE SET (16) 35.00 80.00
STATED ODDS 1:24 SER.2 HOBBY
F1A Steve Young 3.00 8.00
F1B Jerry Rice 4.00 10.00
F2A Drew Bledsoe 2.50 6.00
F2B Curtis Martin 3.00 8.00
F3A Trent Dilfer 1.50 4.00
F3B Errict Rhett .75 2.00
F4A Jeff Hostetler .30 .75
F4B Tim Brown 1.50 4.00
F5A Brett Favre 8.00 20.00
F5B Robert Brooks 1.50 4.00
F6A Jim Harbaugh .75 2.00
F6B Marshall Faulk 2.00 5.00
F7A Rashaan Salaam .75 2.00
F7B Erik Kramer .30 .75
F8A Scott Mitchell .75 2.00
F8B Barry Sanders 6.00 15.00

1996 Stadium Club Laser Sites

COMPLETE SET (8) 15.00 40.00
STATED ODDS 1:36 HOB, 1:12 JUM SER.1
LS1 Brett Favre 8.00 20.00
LS2 Dan Marino 8.00 20.00
LS3 Steve Young 3.00 8.00
LS4 Troy Aikman 4.00 10.00
LS5 Jim Harbaugh .75 2.00
LS6 Scott Mitchell .75 2.00
LS7 Erik Kramer .30 .75
LS8 Warren Moon .75 2.00

1996 Stadium Club Namath Finest

COMPLETE SET (10) 40.00 80.00
COMMON CARD (1-10) 4.00 10.00
STATED ODDS 1:24 HOB/RET, 1:8 JUM SER.1
*REFRACTORS: .8X TO 2X BASIC INSERTS
REF.STAT.ODDS 1:96 H/R, 1:32 JUM SER.1
1 Joe Namath 1965 5.00 12.00

1996 Stadium Club New Age

COMPLETE SET (20) 50.00 100.00
STATED ODDS 1:24 HOB, 1:32 RET SER.2
NA1 Alex Van Dyke .75 2.00
NA2 Lawrence Phillips 1.50 4.00
NA3 Tim Biakabutuka 1.50 4.00
NA4 Reggie Brown .30 .75
NA5 Duane Clemons .30 .75
NA6 Marco Battaglia .30 .75
NA7 Cedric Jones .30 .75
NA8 Jerome Woods .30 .75
NA9 Eric Moulds 6.00 15.00
NA10 Kevin Hardy 1.50 4.00
NA11 Rickey Dudley 1.50 4.00
NA12 Regan Upshaw .30 .75
NA13 Eddie Kennison 1.50 4.00
NA14 Jonathan Ogden 1.50 4.00
NA15 John Mobley .30 .75
NA16 Mike Alstott 5.00 12.00
NA17 Alex Molden .30 .75
NA18 Marvin Harrison 12.50 30.00
NA19 Simeon Rice 4.00 10.00
NA20 Keyshawn Johnson 5.00 12.00

1996 Stadium Club Photo Gallery

COMPLETE SET (21) 100.00 200.00
STATED ODDS 1:18 HOB, 1:24 RET SER.2
PG1 Emmitt Smith 5.00 12.00
PG2 Jeff Blake 1.25 3.00
PG3 Junior Seau 1.25 3.00
PG4 Robert Brooks 1.25 3.00
PG5 Barry Sanders 5.00 12.00
PG6 Drew Bledsoe 2.00 5.00
PG7 Joey Galloway 1.25 3.00

PG8 Marshall Faulk 1.50 4.00
PG9 Mark Brunell 2.00 5.00
PG10 Jerry Rice 3.00 8.00
PG11 Rashaan Salaam .60 1.50
PG12 Troy Aikman 3.00 8.00
PG13 Steve Young 2.50 6.00
PG14 Tim Brown 1.25 3.00
PG15 Brett Favre 6.00 15.00
PG16 Kerry Collins 1.25 3.00
PG17 John Elway 6.00 15.00
PG18 Curtis Martin 2.50 6.00
PG19 Deion Sanders 2.00 5.00
PG20 Dan Marino 6.00 15.00
PG21 Chris Warren .60 1.50

1996 Stadium Club Pro Bowl

COMPLETE SET (20) 75.00 150.00
STATED ODDS 1:24 RET. SER.1
PB1 Brett Favre 12.50 30.00
PB2 Bruce Smith 1.25 3.00
PB3 Ricky Watters 1.25 3.00
PB4 Yancey Thigpen 1.25 3.00
PB5 Barry Sanders 10.00 25.00
PB6 Jim Harbaugh 1.25 3.00
PB7 Michael Irvin 2.50 6.00
PB8 Chris Warren 1.25 3.00
PB9 Dana Stubblefield 1.25 3.00
PB10 Jeff Blake 2.50 6.00
PB11 Emmitt Smith 10.00 25.00
PB12 Bryce Paup .50 1.25
PB13 Steve Young 5.00 12.00
PB14 Kevin Greene .50 1.25
PB15 Jerry Rice 6.00 15.00
PB16 Curtis Martin 5.00 12.00
PB17 Reggie White 2.50 6.00
PB18 Derrick Thomas 2.50 6.00
PB19 Cris Carter 2.50 6.00
PB20 Greg Lloyd 1.25 3.00

1996 Stadium Club Members Only Parallel

COMPLETE SET (476) 120.00 300.00
*STARS 1-360: 1.2X TO 3X BASIC CARDS
*ROOKIES 1-360: .5X TO 1.2X BASIC CARDS
C1 Emmitt Smith 2.00 5.00
C2 Barry Sanders 2.40 6.00
C3 Curtis Martin .80 2.00
C4 Chris Warren .14 .35
C5 Errict Rhett .14 .35
C6 Rodney Hampton .14 .35
C7 Ricky Watters .20 .50
C8 Terry Allen .20 .50
F1A Steve Young 1.00 2.50
F1B Jerry Rice 1.20 3.00
F2A Drew Bledsoe 1.20 3.00
F2B Curtis Martin .80 2.00
F3A Trent Dilfer .40 1.00
F3B Errict Rhett .14 .35
F4A Jeff Hostetler .14 .35
F4B Tim Brown .30 .75
F5A Brett Favre 2.40 6.00
F5B Robert Brooks .20 .50
F6A Jim Harbaugh .20 .50
F6B Marshall Faulk .30 .75
F7A Rashaan Salaam .20 .50
F7B Erik Kramer .14 .35
F8A Scott Mitchell .14 .35
F8B Barry Sanders 2.40 6.00
N1 Joe Namath 1965 .40 1.00
N2 Joe Namath 1966 .40 1.00
N3 Joe Namath 1967 .40 1.00
N4 Joe Namath 1968 .40 1.00
N5 Joe Namath 1969 .40 1.00
N6 Joe Namath 1970 .40 1.00
N7 Joe Namath 1971 .40 1.00
N8 Joe Namath 1972 .40 1.00
N9 Joe Namath 1972 .40 1.00
N10 Joe Namath 1973 .40 1.00
BY1 Dan Marino 2.40 6.00
BY2 Marshall Faulk .30 .75
BY3 Greg Lloyd .14 .35
BY4 Steve Young 1.00 2.50
BY5 Emmitt Smith 2.00 5.00
BY6 Junior Seau .20 .50
BY7 Chris Warren .14 .35
BY8 Jerry Rice 1.20 3.00
BY9 Troy Aikman 1.20 3.00
BY10 Barry Sanders 2.40 6.00
CP1 Ken Norton 1.20 3.00
vs. Drew Bledsoe
CP2 Chris Zorich 2.40 6.00
vs. Barry Sanders
CP3 Corey Harris .14 .35
vs. Harvey Williams
CP4 Sam Mills .20 .50
vs. Thurman Thomas
CP5 Bryce Paup .14 .35
vs. Derrick Moore
CP6 Rob Fredrickson .14 .35
vs. Chris Warren
CP7 Darnell Walker .14 .35
vs. Bernie Parmalee
CP8 Derrick Thomas .20 .50
vs. Gus Frerotte
CP9 Hardy Nickerson .14 .35
vs. Robert Smith
CP10 Reggie White .30 .75
vs. Dave Brown
NA1 Alex Van Dyke .14 .35
NA2 Lawrence Phillips .40 1.00
NA3 Tim Biakabutuka .40 1.00
NA4 Reggie Brown .14 .35
NA5 Duane Clemons .14 .35
NA6 Marco Battaglia .14 .35
NA7 Cedric Jones .14 .35
NA8 Jerome Woods .14 .35
NA9 Eric Moulds 1.20 3.00
NA10 Kevin Hardy .14 .35
NA11 Rickey Dudley .20 .50
NA12 Regan Upshaw .14 .35
NA13 Eddie Kennison .50 1.25
NA14 Jonathan Ogden
NA15 John Mobley .14 .35
NA16 Mike Alstott .80 2.00
NA17 Alex Molden .14 .35
NA18 Marvin Harrison .50 1.25
NA19 Simeon Rice .20 .50
NA20 Keyshawn Johnson 1.20 3.00
PB1 Brett Favre 2.40 6.00
PB2 Bruce Smith .20 .50
PB3 Ricky Watters .20 .50
PB4 Yancey Thigpen .20 .50
PB5 Barry Sanders 2.40 6.00
PB6 Jim Harbaugh .20 .50
PB7 Michael Irvin .30 .75
PB8 Chris Warren .14 .35
PB9 Dana Stubblefield .14 .35
PB10 Jeff Blake .20 .50
PB11 Emmitt Smith 2.00 5.00
PB12 Bryce Paup .14 .35
PB13 Steve Young 1.20 3.00
PB14 Kevin Greene .14 .35
PB15 Jerry Rice 1.20 3.00
PB16 Curtis Martin .80 2.00
PB17 Reggie White .30 .75
PB18 Derrick Thomas .20 .50
PB19 Cris Carter .30 .75
PB20 Greg Lloyd .14 .35
PG1 Emmitt Smith 2.00 5.00
PG2 Jeff Blake .20 .50
PG3 Junior Seau .20 .50
PG4 Robert Brooks .20 .50
PG5 Barry Sanders 2.40 6.00
PG6 Drew Bledsoe 1.20 3.00
PG7 Joey Galloway .80 2.00
PG8 Marshall Faulk .30 .75
PG9 Mark Brunell 1.20 3.00
PG10 Jerry Rice 1.20 3.00
PG11 Rashaan Salaam .20 .50
PG12 Troy Aikman 1.20 3.00
PG13 Steve Young 1.00 2.50
PG14 Tim Brown .30 .75
PG15 Brett Favre 2.40 6.00
PG16 Kerry Collins .20 .50
PG17 John Elway 2.40 6.00
PG18 Curtis Martin .80 2.00
PG19 Deion Sanders .80 2.00
PG20 Dan Marino 2.40 6.00
PG21 Chris Warren .20 .50

1996 Stadium Club Members Only 50

Topps produced a 50-card boxed set for each of the four major sports again in 1996. With their club membership, members received one set of their choice and had the option of purchasing additional sets for $10.00 each. The set consists of 45 Stadium Club cards and five Finest styled cards. The fronts carry the distinctive Topps Stadium Club Members Only gold foil seal.

COMP.FACT SET (50) 6.00 15.00
1 Bruce Smith .10 .30
2 Chester McGlockton .07 .20
3 Dan Saleaumua .07 .20
4 Neil Smith .07 .20
5 Bryce Paup .07 .20
6 Junior Seau .20 .50
7 Greg Lloyd .07 .20
8 Dale Carter .07 .20
9 Terry McDaniel .07 .20
10 Carnell Lake .07 .20
11 Steve Atwater .07 .20
12 Jerry Rice .60 1.50
13 Lomas Brown .07 .20
14 Nate Newton .07 .20
15 Kevin Glover .07 .20
16 Randall McDaniel .07 .20
17 William Roaf .07 .20
18 Mark Chmura .07 .20
19 Herman Moore .10 .30
20 Brett Favre 1.20 3.00
21 Emmitt Smith 1.00 2.50
22 Barry Sanders 1.20 3.00
23 Carl Pickens .10 .30
24 Richmond Webb .07 .20
25 Keith Sims .07 .20
26 Dermontti Dawson .07 .20
27 Steve Wisniewski .07 .20
28 Bruce Armstrong .07 .20
29 Ben Coates .10 .30
30 Tim Brown .20 .50
31 Jeff Blake .20 .50
32 Marshall Faulk .20 .50
33 Chris Warren .10 .30
34 Reggie White .20 .50
35 John Randle .10 .30
36 Eric Swann .07 .20
37 Charles Haley .07 .20
38 Ken Harvey .07 .20
39 Jessie Tuggle .07 .20
40 Lee Woodall .07 .20
41 Aeneas Williams .07 .20
42 Eric Davis .07 .20
43 Darren Woodson .07 .20
44 Merton Hanks .07 .20
45 Dan Marino 1.20 3.00
46 Kordell Stewart MC F .80 2.00
47 Rashaan Salaam MC F .10 .30
48 Joey Galloway MC F .80 2.00
49 Kerry Collins MC F .60 1.50
50 Curtis Martin MC F 1.00 2.50

1996 Stadium Club Sunday Night Redemption

Topps inserted Sunday Night Redemption cards randomly in 1996 Stadium Club series 1 packs (1:24 hobby and retail, 1:20 jumbo). Each card featured two numbers that were to be compared to the final scores of each week's NFL Sunday Night football game. Matching numbers (winning cards) were redeemable for two special jumbo (roughly 4" by 6") Finest cards featuring players that participated in that NFL game. The cards are arranged below in the order in which they were awarded each week. Note that there was no Sunday Night Football game in NFL Week 8. The contest expired 3/3/1997 and only the prize cards are listed below.

COMPLETE SET (32) 120.00 300.00
1A Rodney Hampton 1.60 4.00
1B Jim Kelly 3.20 8.00
2A Dan Marino 12.00 30.00
2B Frank Sanders 3.20 8.00
3A Trent Dilfer 2.40 6.00
3B John Elway 12.00 30.00
4A Eric Metcalf 1.60 4.00
4B Ricky Watters 2.40 6.00
5A Terry Allen 2.40 6.00
5B Keyshawn Johnson 8.00 20.00
6A Jeff Blake 3.20 8.00
6B Steve McNair 6.00 15.00
7A Marshall Faulk 4.00 10.00
7B Eric Zeier 1.60 4.00
9A Drew Bledsoe 6.00 15.00
9B Bruce Smith 2.40 6.00
10A Jim Everett 1.60 4.00
10B Steve Young 4.80 12.00
11A Dave Brown 1.60 4.00
11B Kerry Collins 4.00 10.00
12A Tim Brown 3.20 8.00
12B Cris Carter 3.20 8.00
13A Isaac Bruce 3.20 8.00
13B Brett Favre 12.00 30.00
14A Curtis Martin 6.00 15.00
14B Junior Seau 2.40 6.00
15A Warren Moon 3.20 8.00
15B Barry Sanders 12.00 30.00
16A Mark Brunell 6.00 15.00
16B Chris Warren 1.60 4.00
17A Terrell Davis 12.00 30.00
17B Stan Humphries 1.60 4.00

1997 Stadium Club

The 1997 Stadium Club was issued in two series of 170 cards each and was distributed in six-card retail packs with a suggested price of $2. Hobby packs contained nine cards with a price of $3.00. The Series 1 set consists of only the odd numbered cards while Series 2 consists of the even numbered ones. Six prototype cards were released for Series 1. These cards contain only very subtle differences versus the regular base cards. Most noteably they can be differentiated by the white line of text below the copyrights and licensing logos instead of above. Included in eight of every nine Series 2 packs was a Pro Bowl ballot which offered collectors a chance to win a grand prize of a trip to the Pro Bowl in Hawaii. One hundred runners up could win an uncut sheet of Stadium Club Football Series 2 with the official Pro Bowl logo stamped on it. A checklist for Stadium Club Series 2 was included in every ninth pack.

COMPLETE SET (340) 25.00 60.00
COMP.SERIES 1 (170) 15.00 30.00
COMP.SERIES 2 (170) 15.00 30.00
1 Junior Seau .30 .75
2 Michael Irvin .30 .75
3 Marcus Allen .30 .75
4 Dale Carter .10 .30
5 Darnell Autry RC .20 .50
6 Isaac Bruce .30 .75
7 Darrell Green .20 .50
8 Joey Galloway .20 .50
9 Steve Atwater .10 .30
10 Kordell Stewart .30 .75
11 Tony Brackens .10 .30
12 Gus Frerotte .10 .30
13 Henry Ellard .10 .30
14 Charles Way .20 .50
15 Jim Druckenmiller RC .20 .50
16 Orlando Thomas .10 .30
17 Terrell Davis .40 1.00
18 Jim Schwantz .10 .30
19 Derrick Thomas .30 .75
20 Curtis Martin .40 1.00
21 Deion Sanders .30 .75
22 Bruce Smith .20 .50
23 Jake Reed .20 .50
24 Leeland McElroy .10 .30
25 Jerome Bettis .30 .75
26 Neil Smith .20 .50
27 Terry Allen .30 .75
28 Gilbert Brown .20 .50
29 Steve McNair .40 1.00
30 Kerry Collins .30 .75
31 Thurman Thomas .30 .75
32 Kenny Holmes RC .30 .75
33 Karim Abdul-Jabbar .30 .75
34 Steve Young .40 1.00
35 Jerry Rice .60 1.50
36 Jeff George .20 .50
37 Errict Rhett .10 .30
38 Mike Alstott .30 .75
39 Tim Brown .30 .75
40 Keyshawn Johnson .30 .75
41 Jim Harbaugh .20 .50
42 Kevin Hardy .10 .30
43 Kevin Greene .20 .50
44 Eric Metcalf .20 .50
45 Troy Aikman .60 1.50
46 Marshall Faulk .40 1.00
47 Shannon Sharpe .20 .50
48 Warren Moon .30 .75
49 Mark Brunell .40 1.00
50 Dan Marino 1.25 3.00
51 Byron Hanspard RC .20 .50
52 Chris Chandler .20 .50
53 Wayne Chrebet .30 .75
54 Antonio Langham .10 .30
55 Barry Sanders 1.00 2.50
56 Curtis Conway .20 .50
57 Ricky Watters .20 .50
58 William Thomas .10 .30
59 Chris Warren .20 .50
60 Terry Glenn .30 .75
61 Peter Boulware RC .30 .75
62 Chad Cota .10 .30
63 Eddie Kennison .20 .50
64 Lamar Smith .30 .75
65 Brett Favre 1.50 3.00
66 Michael Westbrook .20 .50
67 Larry Centers .20 .50
68 Trent Dilfer .30 .75
69 Stevon Moore .10 .30
70 John Elway 1.25 3.00
71 Bryce Paup .10 .30
72 Quentin Coryatt .10 .30
73 Rashaan Salaam .10 .30
74 Thomas Lewis .10 .30
75 Drew Bledsoe .40 1.00
76 Cris Carter .30 .75
77 Joe Bowden .10 .30
78 Allen Aldridge .10 .30
79 Zach Thomas .30 .75
80 Emmitt Smith 1.00 2.50
81 Daryl Johnston .20 .50
82 Vinny Testaverde .20 .50
83 James O.Stewart .20 .50
84 Edgar Bennett .20 .50
85 Shawn Springs RC .20 .50
86 Elvis Grbac .20 .50
87 Levon Kirkland .10 .30
88 Jeff Graham .10 .30
89 Terrell Fletcher .10 .30
90 Eddie George .30 .75
91 Jessie Tuggle .10 .30
92 Terrell Owens .40 1.00
93 Wayne Martin .10 .30
94 Dwayne Harper .10 .30
95 Mark Collins .10 .30
96 Marvcus Patton .10 .30
97 Napoleon Kaufman .30 .75
98 Keenan McCardell .20 .50
99 Ty Detmer .20 .50
100 Reggie White .30 .75
101 William Floyd .20 .50
102 Scott Mitchell .20 .50
103 Robert Blackmon .10 .30
104 Dan Wilkinson .10 .30
105 Warren Sapp .20 .50
106 Dave Meggett .10 .30
107 Brian Mitchell .10 .30
108 Tyrone Poole .10 .30
109 Derrick Alexander WR .20 .50
110 David Palmer .10 .30
111 James Farrior RC .30 .75
112 Chad Brown .10 .30
113 Marty Carter .10 .30
114 Lawrence Phillips .10 .30
115 Wesley Walls .20 .50
116 John Friesz .10 .30
117 Roman Phifer .10 .30
118 Jason Sehorn .20 .50
119 Henry Thomas .10 .30
120 Natrone Means .20 .50
121 Ty Law .20 .50
122 Tony Gonzalez RC 1.50 4.00
123 Kevin Williams .10 .30
124 Regan Upshaw .10 .30
125 Antonio Freeman .30 .75
126 Jessie Armstead .10 .30
127 Pat Barnes RC .30 .75
128 Charlie Garner .20 .50
129 Irving Fryar .20 .50
130 Rickey Dudley .20 .50
131 Rodney Harrison RC .60 1.50
132 Brent Jones .20 .50
133 Neil O'Donnell .20 .50
134 Darryll Lewis .10 .30
135 Jason Belser .10 .30
136 Mark Chmura .20 .50
137 Seth Joyner .10 .30
138 Herschel Walker .20 .50
139 Santana Dotson .10 .30
140 Carl Pickens .20 .50
141 Terance Mathis .20 .50
142 Walt Harris .10 .30
143 John Mobley .10 .30
144 Gabe Northern .10 .30
145 Herman Moore .20 .50
146 Michael Jackson .20 .50
147 Chris Sanders .10 .30
148 LeShon Johnson .10 .30
149 Darrell Russell RC .10 .30
150 Winslow Oliver .10 .30
151 Tamarick Vanover .20 .50
152 Tony Martin .20 .50
153 Lamar Lathon .10 .30
154 Ray Mickens .10 .30
155 Derrick Brooks .30 .75
156 Warrick Dunn RC 1.25 3.00
157 Tim McDonald .10 .30
158 Keith Lyle .10 .30
159 Terry McDaniel .10 .30
160 Andre Hastings .10 .30
161 Phillippi Sparks .10 .30
162 Tedy Bruschi .60 1.50
163 Bryant Westbrook RC .10 .30
164 Victor Green .10 .30
165 Jimmy Smith .20 .50
166 Greg Biekert .10 .30
167 Frank Sanders .20 .50
168 Chris Doleman .10 .30
169 Phil Hansen .10 .30
170 Walter Jones RC .30 .75
171 Mark Carrier WR .10 .30
172 Greg Hill .10 .30
173 Erik Kramer .10 .30
174 Chris Spielman .10 .30
175 Tom Knight RC .10 .30
176 Sam Mills .10 .30
177 Robert Smith .20 .50
178 Dorsey Levens .30 .75
179 Chris Slade .10 .30
180 Troy Vincent .10 .30
181 Mario Bates .10 .30
182 Ed McCaffrey .20 .50
183 Mike Mamula .10 .30
184 Chad Hennings .10 .30
185 Stan Humphries .20 .50
186 Reinard Wilson RC .20 .50
187 Kevin Carter .10 .30
188 Qadry Ismail .20 .50
189 Cortez Kennedy .10 .30
190 Eric Swann .10 .30
191 Corey Dillon RC 1.50 4.00
192 Renaldo Wynn .10 .30
193 Bobby Hebert .10 .30
194 Fred Barnett .10 .30
195 Ray Lewis .50 1.25
196 Robert Jones .10 .30
197 Brian Williams .10 .30
198 Willie McGinest .10 .30
199 Jake Plummer RC 1.50 4.00
200 Aeneas Williams .10 .30
201 Ashley Ambrose .10 .30
202 Cornelius Bennett .10 .30
203 Mo Lewis .10 .30
204 James Hasty .10 .30
205 Carnell Lake .10 .30
206 Heath Shuler .10 .30
207 Dana Stubblefield .10 .30
208 Corey Miller .10 .30
209 Ike Hilliard RC .50 1.25
210 Bryant Young .10 .30
211 Hardy Nickerson .10 .30
212 Blaine Bishop .10 .30
213 Marcus Robertson .10 .30
214 Tony Bennett .10 .30
215 Kent Graham .10 .30
216 Steve Bono .20 .50
217 Will Blackwell RC .20 .50
218 Tyrone Braxton .10 .30
219 Eric Moulds .30 .75
220 Rod Woodson .20 .50
221 Anthony Johnson .10 .30
222 Willie Davis .10 .30
223 Darrin Smith .10 .30
224 Rick Mirer .10 .30
225 Marvin Harrison .30 .75
226 Terrell Buckley .10 .30
227 Joe Aska .10 .30
228 Yatil Green RC .20 .50
229 William Fuller .10 .30
230 Eddie Robinson .10 .30
231 Brian Blades .10 .30
232 Michael Sinclair .10 .30
233 Ken Harvey .10 .30
234 Harvey Williams .10 .30
235 Simeon Rice .20 .50
236 Chris T. Jones .10 .30
237 Bert Emanuel .20 .50
238 Corey Sawyer .10 .30
239 Chris Calloway .10 .30
240 Jeff Blake .20 .50
241 Alonzo Spellman .10 .30
242 Bryan Cox .10 .30
243 Antowain Smith RC 1.00 2.50
244 Tim Biakabutuka .20 .50
245 Ray Crockett .10 .30
246 Dwayne Rudd .10 .30
247 Glyn Milburn .10 .30
248 Gary Plummer .10 .30
249 O.J. McDuffie .20 .50
250 Willie Clay .10 .30
251 Jim Everett .10 .30
252 Eugene Daniel .10 .30
253 Corey Widmer .10 .30
254 Mel Gray .10 .30
255 Ken Norton .10 .30
256 Johnnie Morton .20 .50
257 Courtney Hawkins .10 .30
258 Ricardo McDonald .10 .30
259 Todd Lyght .10 .30
260 Micheal Barrow .10 .30
261 Aaron Glenn .10 .30
262 Jeff Herrod .10 .30
263 Troy Davis RC .20 .50
264 Eric Hill .10 .30
265 Darrien Gordon .10 .30
266 Lake Dawson .10 .30
267 John Randle .20 .50
268 Henry Jones .10 .30
269 Mickey Washington .10 .30
270 Amani Toomer .20 .50
271 Steve Grant .10 .30
272 Adrian Murrell .20 .50
273 Derrick Witherspoon .10 .30
274 Albert Lewis .10 .30
275 Ben Coates .20 .50
276 Reidel Anthony RC .30 .75
277 Jim Schwantz .10 .30
278 Aaron Hayden .10 .30
279 Ryan McNeil .10 .30
280 LeRoy Butler .10 .30
281 Craig Newsome .10 .30
282 Bill Romanowski .10 .30
283 Michael Bankston .10 .30
284 Kevin Smith .10 .30
285 Byron Bam Morris .10 .30
286 Darnay Scott .20 .50
287 David LaFleur RC .10 .30
288 Randall Cunningham .30 .75
289 Eric Davis .10 .30
290 Todd Collins .10 .30
291 Steve Tovar .10 .30
292 Jermaine Lewis .30 .75
293 Alfred Williams .10 .30
294 Brad Johnson .30 .75
295 Charles Johnson .20 .50
296 Ted Johnson .10 .30
297 Merton Hanks .10 .30
298 Andre Coleman .10 .30
299 Keith Jackson .10 .30
300 Terry Kirby .20 .50
301 Tony Banks .20 .50
302 Terrance Shaw .10 .30
303 Bobby Engram .20 .50
304 Hugh Douglas .10 .30
305 Lawyer Milloy .20 .50
306 James Jett .20 .50
307 Joey Kent RC .30 .75
308 Rodney Hampton .20 .50
309 Dewayne Washington .10 .30
310 Kevin Lockett RC .20 .50
311 Ki-Jana Carter .10 .30
312 Jeff Lageman .10 .30
313 Don Beebe .10 .30
314 Willie Williams .10 .30
315 Tyrone Wheatley .20 .50
316 Leslie O'Neal .10 .30
317 Quinn Early .10 .30
318 Sean Gilbert .10 .30
319 Tim Bowens .10 .30
320 Sean Dawkins .10 .30
321 Ken Dilger .10 .30
322 George Koonce .10 .30
323 Jevon Langford .10 .30
324 Mike Caldwell .10 .30
325 Orlando Pace RC .30 .75
326 Garrison Hearst .20 .50
327 Mike Tomczak .10 .30
328 Rob Moore .20 .50
329 Andre Reed .20 .50
330 Kimble Anders .20 .50
331 Qadry Ismail .20 .50
332 Eric Allen .10 .30
333 Dave Brown .10 .30
334 Bennie Blades .10 .30
335 Jamal Anderson .30 .75
336 John Lynch .20 .50
337 Tyrone Hughes .10 .30
338 Ronnie Harmon .10 .30
339 Rae Carruth RC .10 .30
340 Robert Brooks .20 .50
P1 Junior Seau Prototype .20 .50
(line of text below copyrights)
P20 Curtis Martin Prototype .40 1.00
(line of text below copyrights)
P21 Deion Sanders Prototype .20 .50
(line of text below copyrights)
P30 Kerry Collins Prototype .30 .75
(line of text below copyrights)
P47 Sh.Sharpe Prototype .20 .50
line of text below copyrights
P84 Edgar Bennett Prototype .20 .50
(line of text below copyrights)

1997 Stadium Club First Day

*STARS: 6X TO 15X BASIC CARDS
*RCs: 3X TO 8X BASIC CARDS
STATED ODDS 1:24 RETAIL

1997 Stadium Club One of a Kind

*VETS: 12X TO 30X BASIC CARDS
*ROOKIE STARS: 8X TO 20X BASIC RC
STATED ODDS 1:48 HOB/RET, 1:30 JUM

1997 Stadium Club Aerial Assault

COMPLETE SET (10) 20.00 50.00
STATED ODDS 1:12 HOB/RET, 1:4 JUM
AA1 Dan Marino 5.00 12.00
AA2 Mark Brunell 1.50 4.00
AA3 Troy Aikman 2.50 6.00
AA4 Ty Detmer .75 2.00
AA5 John Elway 5.00 12.00
AA6 Drew Bledsoe 1.50 4.00
AA7 Steve Young 1.50 4.00
AA8 Vinny Testaverde .75 2.00
AA9 Kerry Collins 1.25 3.00
AA10 Brett Favre 5.00 12.00

1997 Stadium Club Bowman's Best Previews

COMPLETE SET (15) 40.00 80.00
STATED ODDS 1:24 HOB/RET, 1:8 JUM
*REFRACTOR: 1X TO 2.5X BASIC INSERT
REFRACTOR STATED ODDS 1:96
*ATOMIC REF: 1.5X TO 4X BASIC INSERT
ATOMIC REFRACTOR ODDS 1:192
BBP1 Dan Marino 6.00 15.00
BBP2 Terry Allen 1.50 4.00
BBP3 Jerome Bettis 2.00 5.00
BBP4 Kevin Greene 1.50 4.00
BBP5 Junior Seau 2.00 5.00
BBP6 Brett Favre 6.00 15.00
BBP7 Isaac Bruce 2.00 5.00
BBP8 Michael Irvin 2.00 5.00
BBP9 Kerry Collins 2.00 5.00
BBP10 Karim Abdul-Jabbar 1.50 4.00
BBP11 Keenan McCardell 1.50 4.00
BBP12 Ricky Watters 1.50 4.00
BBP13 Mark Brunell 2.00 5.00
BBP14 Jerry Rice 4.00 10.00
BBP15 Drew Bledsoe 2.00 5.00

1997 Stadium Club Bowman's Best Rookie Previews

COMPLETE SET (15) 20.00 40.00
STATED ODDS 1:24
*REFRACTOR: 1X TO 2.5X BASIC INSERT
REFRACTOR STATED ODDS 1:96
*ATOMIC REF: 2X TO 5X BASIC INSERT
ATOMIC REFRACTOR ODDS 1:192
BBP1 Orlando Pace 1.50 4.00
BBP2 David LaFleur .60 2.50
BBP3 James Farrior 1.50 4.00
BBP4 Tony Gonzalez 5.00 12.00
BBP5 Ike Hilliard 1.50 4.00
BBP6 Antowain Smith 2.50 6.00
BBP7 Tom Knight .60 2.50
BBP8 Troy Davis 1.00 3.00
BBP9 Yatil Green 1.00 3.00
BBP10 Jim Druckenmiller 1.00 3.00
BBP11 Bryant Westbrook .60 2.50
BBP12 Darrell Russell .60 2.50
BBP13 Rae Carruth .60 2.50
BBP14 Shawn Springs 1.00 3.00
BBP15 Peter Boulware 1.50 4.00

1997 Stadium Club Co-Signers

SERIES 1 OVERALL STATED ODDS 1:63
SERIES 2 OVERALL STATED ODDS 1:68
CO1 Karim Abdul-Jabbar 100.00 200.00
Eddie George
CO2 Trace Armstrong 12.50 30.00
Alonzo Spellman
CO3 Steve Atwater 12.50 30.00
Kevin Hardy
CO4 Fred Barnett 15.00 40.00
Lake Dawson
CO5 Blaine Bishop 20.00 50.00
Darrell Green
CO6 Jeff Blake 50.00 100.00
Gus Frerotte
CO7 Steve Bono 50.00 100.00
Cris Carter
CO8 Tim Brown 50.00 100.00
Isaac Bruce
CO9 Wayne Chrebet 12.50 30.00
Mickey Washington
CO10 Curtis Conway 12.50 30.00
Eddie Kennison
CO11 Eric Davis 15.00 40.00
Jason Sehorn
CO12 Terrell Davis 50.00 100.00
Thurman Thomas
CO13 Ken Dilger 15.00 40.00
Kent Graham
CO14 Stephen Grant 12.50 30.00
Marvcus Patton
CO15 Keith Hamilton 12.50 30.00
Mike Tomczak
CO16 Rodney Hampton 20.00 50.00
Dave Meggett
CO17 Merton Hanks 12.50 30.00
Aeneas Williams
CO19 Brent Jones 12.50 30.00
Wesley Walls
CO20 Carnell Lake 12.50 30.00
Tim McDonald
CO21 Thomas Lewis 12.50 30.00
Keith Lyle
CO22 Leeland McElroy 12.50 30.00
Jeff Lageman
CO23 Ray Mickens 12.50 30.00
Willie Davis
CO24 Herman Moore 12.50 30.00
Desmond Howard
CO25 Stevon Moore 12.50 30.00
William Thomas
CO26 Adrian Murrell 12.50 30.00
Levon Kirkland
CO27 Simeon Rice 15.00 40.00
Winslow Oliver
CO28 Bill Romanowski 12.50 30.00
Gary Plummer
CO29 Junior Seau 30.00 60.00
Chris Spielman
CO30 Chris Slade 12.50 30.00
Kevin Greene
CO31 Derrick Thomas 60.00 100.00
Chris T. Jones
CO32 Orlando Thomas 15.00 40.00
Bobby Engram
CO33 Amani Toomer 20.00 50.00
Thomas Randolph
CO34 Steve Tovar 12.50 30.00
Ellis Johnson LB
CO35 Herschel Walker 20.00 50.00
Anthony Johnson
CO36 Darren Woodson 20.00 50.00
Aaron Glenn
CO37 Karim Abdul-Jabbar 40.00 80.00
Thurman Thomas
CO38 Blaine Bishop 12.50 30.00
Tim McDonald
CO39 Jeff Blake 60.00 120.00
Derrick Thomas
CO41 Cris Carter 60.00 120.00
Marvin Harrison
CO42 Curtis Conway 12.50 30.00
Wesley Walls
CO43 Willie Davis 15.00 40.00
Amani Toomer
CO44 Lake Dawson 10.00 25.00
Ray Mickens
CO45 Ken Dilger 12.50 30.00
Ellis Johnson LB
CO46 Bobby Engram 12.50 30.00
Thomas Lewis
CO47 Gus Frerotte 20.00 50.00
Chris T. Jones
CO48 Eddie George 30.00 80.00
Terrell Davis
CO49 Aaron Glenn 12.50 30.00
Eric Davis
CO50 Kent Graham 10.00 25.00
Steve Tovar
CO51 Darrell Green 25.00 50.00
Carnell Lake
CO52 Kevin Greene 12.50 30.00
Steve Atwater
CO53 Rodney Hampton 15.00 40.00
Anthony Johnson
CO54 Kevin Hardy 12.50 30.00
Merton Hanks
CO55 Desmond Howard 40.00 80.00
Tim Brown
CO56 Eddie Kennison 12.50 20.00
Brent Jones
CO57 Levon Kirkland 12.50 30.00
Simeon Rice
CO58 Jeff Lageman 10.00 25.00
Adrian Murrell
CO59 Keith Lyle 15.00 40.00
Wayne Chrebet
CO60 Dave Meggett 15.00 40.00
Herschel Walker
CO61 Herman Moore 40.00 80.00
Isaac Bruce
CO62 Winslow Oliver 10.00 25.00
Leeland McElroy
CO63 Marvcus Patton 10.00 25.00
Keith Hamilton
CO64 Gary Plummer 30.00 60.00
Junior Seau
CO65 Thomas Randolph 10.00 25.00
Fred Barnett
CO66 Alonzo Spellman 10.00 25.00
Stephen Grant
CO67 Chris Spielman 10.00 25.00
Stevon Moore
CO68 William Thomas 12.50 30.00
Bill Romanowski
CO69 Mike Tomczak 10.00 25.00
Trace Armstrong
CO70 Mickey Washington 10.00 25.00
Orlando Thomas
CO71 Aeneas Williams 12.50 30.00
Chris Slade
CO72 Darren Woodson 15.00 40.00
Jason Sehorn
CO73 Trace Armstrong 6.00 15.00
Keith Hamilton
CO74 Steve Atwater 6.00 15.00
Chris Slade
CO75 Fred Barnett 10.00 25.00
Amani Toomer
CO76 Tim Brown 25.00 60.00
Herman Moore
CO77 Isaac Bruce 25.00 60.00
Desmond Howard
CO78 Wayne Chrebet 10.00 25.00
Thomas Lewis
CO79 Eric Davis 8.00 20.00
Darren Woodson
CO80 Terrell Davis 15.00 40.00
Karim Abdul-Jabbar
CO81 Willie Davis 8.00 20.00
Lake Dawson
CO82 Bobby Engram 6.00 15.00
Marvin Washington
CO83 Stephen Grant 6.00 15.00
Mike Tomczak
CO84 Merton Hanks 8.00 20.00
Kevin Greene
CO85 Marvin Harrison 15.00 40.00
Steve Bono
CO86 Anthony Johnson 6.00 15.00
Dave Meggett
CO87 Ellis Johnson LB 6.00 15.00
Kent Graham
CO88 Brent Jones 10.00 25.00
Curtis Conway
CO89 Chris T. Jones 10.00 25.00
Jeff Blake
CO90 Carnell Lake 6.00 15.00
Blaine Bishop
CO91 Tim McDonald 25.00 50.00
Darrell Green
CO92 Ray Mickens 6.00 15.00
Thomas Randolph
CO93 Stevon Moore 6.00 15.00
Gary Plummer
CO94 Adrian Murrell 6.00 15.00
Leeland McElroy
CO95 Winslow Oliver 6.00 15.00
Levon Kirkland
CO96 Marvcus Patton 6.00 15.00
Alonzo Spellman
CO98 Simeon Rice 10.00 25.00
Jeff Lageman
CO99 Junior Seau 30.00 60.00
Bill Romanowski
CO100 Jason Sehorn 8.00 20.00
Aaron Glenn
CO101 Derrick Thomas 60.00 120.00
Gus Frerotte
CO102 Orlando Thomas 6.00 15.00
Keith Lyle
CO103 Thurman Thomas 30.00 80.00
Eddie George
CO104 William Thomas 6.00 15.00
Chris Spielman
CO105 Steve Tovar 6.00 15.00
Ken Dilger
CO106 Herschel Walker 12.00 30.00
Rodney Hampton

CO107 Wesley Walls 15.00 30.00
Eddie Kennison
CO108 Aeneas Williams 6.00 15.00
Kevin Hardy

1997 Stadium Club Grid Kids

COMPLETE SET (20) 30.00 60.00
STATED ODDS 1:36 HOB/RET, 1:12 JUM
GK1 Orlando Pace 1.25 3.00
GK2 Darrell Russell .50 1.25
GK3 Shawn Springs .75 2.00
GK4 Peter Boulware 1.25 3.00
GK5 Bryant Westbrook .50 1.25
GK6 Darnell Autry .75 2.00
GK7 Ike Hilliard 2.00 5.00
GK8 James Farrior 1.25 3.00
GK9 Jake Plummer 6.00 15.00
GK10 Tony Gonzalez 6.00 15.00
GK11 Yatil Green .75 2.00
GK12 Corey Dillon 6.00 15.00
GK13 Dwayne Rudd .50 1.25
GK14 Renaldo Wynn .50 1.25
GK15 David LaFleur .50 1.25
GK16 Antowain Smith 4.00 10.00
GK17 Jim Druckenmiller .75 2.00
GK18 Rae Carruth .50 1.25
GK19 Tom Knight .50 1.25
GK20 Byron Hanspard .75 2.00

1997 Stadium Club Never Compromise

COMPLETE SET (40) 60.00 150.00
STATED ODDS 1:12 SERIES 2
NC1 Orlando Pace 1.50 4.00
NC2 Corey Dillon 2.50 6.00
NC3 Tony Gonzalez 3.00 8.00
NC4 Tom Knight .75 2.00
NC5 Deion Sanders 2.00 5.00
NC6 Dwayne Rudd 1.25 3.00
NC7 Warrick Dunn 2.50 6.00
NC8 Kenny Holmes 1.25 3.00
NC9 Will Blackwell 1.25 3.00
NC10 Shawn Springs 1.25 3.00
NC11 Rae Carruth .75 2.00
NC12 Edgar Bennett 1.50 4.00
NC13 Walter Jones 1.25 3.00
NC14 Reidel Anthony 1.25 3.00
NC15 Troy Davis 1.25 3.00
NC16 Mark Brunell 1.50 4.00
NC17 Pat Barnes 1.25 3.00
NC18 Reggie White 1.50 4.00
NC19 Darrell Russell .75 2.00
NC20 Ike Hilliard 1.50 4.00
NC21 Emmitt Smith 4.00 10.00
NC22 David LaFleur .75 2.00
NC23 Yatil Green .75 2.00
NC24 Barry Sanders 4.00 10.00
NC25 Bryant Westbrook .75 2.00
NC26 Lawrence Phillips 1.25 3.00
NC27 Peter Boulware 1.50 4.00
NC28 Joey Kent .75 2.00
NC29 Kevin Lockett .75 2.00
NC30 Derrick Thomas 1.50 4.00
NC31 Antowain Smith 2.00 5.00
NC32 James Farrior 1.50 4.00
NC33 Kordell Stewart 1.50 4.00
NC34 Byron Hanspard 1.25 3.00
NC35 Jim Druckenmiller 1.25 3.00
NC36 Reinard Wilson 1.25 3.00
NC37 Darnell Autry 1.25 3.00
NC38 Steve Young 2.50 6.00
NC39 Renaldo Wynn .75 2.00
NC40 Jake Plummer 2.50 6.00

1997 Stadium Club Offensive Strikes

COMPLETE SET (10) 10.00 25.00
STATED ODDS 1:12 HOBY/RET, 1:4 JUM
AF1 Jerry Rice 2.00 5.00
AF2 Carl Pickens UER .60 1.50
(Perkins on back)
AF3 Shannon Sharpe .60 1.50
AF4 Herman Moore .60 1.50
AF5 Terry Glenn 1.00 2.50
GC1 Barry Sanders 3.00 8.00
GC2 Curtis Martin 1.25 3.00
GC3 Emmitt Smith 3.00 8.00
GC4 Terrell Davis 1.25 3.00
GC5 Eddie George 1.00 2.50

1997 Stadium Club Triumvirate I

COMP.SERIES 1 SET (18) 60.00 120.00
STATED ODDS 1:36 SER.1 RETAIL
*REFRACTORS: .8X TO 2X BASIC INSERTS
REFRACTOR STATED ODDS 1:144
*ATOMIC REF: 1.2X TO 3X BASIC INSERTS
ATOMIC REF.STATED ODDS 1:288
T1A Emmitt Smith 6.00 15.00
T1B Troy Aikman 4.00 10.00
T1C Michael Irvin 2.00 5.00
T2A Curtis Martin 2.50 6.00
T2B Drew Bledsoe 2.50 6.00
T2C Terry Glenn 2.00 5.00
T3A Barry Sanders 6.00 15.00
T3B Scott Mitchell 1.25 3.00
T3C Herman Moore 1.25 3.00
T4A William Floyd 1.25 3.00
T4B Steve Young 2.50 6.00
T4C Jerry Rice 4.00 10.00
T5A Terrell Davis 2.50 6.00
T5B John Elway 8.00 20.00
T5C Shannon Sharpe 1.25 3.00
T6A Edgar Bennett 1.25 3.00
T6B Brett Favre 8.00 20.00
T6C Antonio Freeman 2.00 5.00

1997 Stadium Club Triumvirate II

COMP.SERIES 2 SET (18) 75.00 150.00
STATED ODDS 1:36 SER.2 RETAIL
*REFRACTOR: .8X TO 2X BASIC INSERTS
REFRACTOR STATED ODDS 1:144
*ATOMIC REF: 1.2X TO 3X BASIC INSERTS
ATOMIC REF.STATED ODDS 1:288
T1A John Elway 8.00 20.00
T1B Drew Bledsoe 2.50 6.00
T1C Dan Marino 8.00 20.00
T2A Troy Aikman 4.00 10.00
T2B Brett Favre 8.00 20.00
T2C Steve Young 2.50 6.00
T3A Terrell Davis 2.50 6.00
T3B Eddie George 2.00 5.00
T3C Curtis Martin 2.50 6.00
T4A Emmitt Smith 6.00 15.00
T4B Ricky Watters 1.25 3.00
T4C Barry Sanders 6.00 15.00
T5A Peter Boulware .75 2.00
T5B Shawn Springs .75 2.00
T5C Tony Gonzalez 2.50 6.00
T6A Jake Plummer 2.50 6.00
T6B Orlando Pace .75 2.00
T6C Jim Druckenmiller .75 2.00

1997 Stadium Club Members Only Parallel

COMPLETE SET (486) 125.00 250.00
*1-340 VETS: 1.2X TO 3X BASIC CARDS
*1-340 ROOKIE STARS: .8X TO 2X
*TRIUMVIRATE 1: .2X TO .5X BASIC INSERTS
*TRIUMVIRATE 2: .2X TO .5X BASIC INSERTS
*AERIAL ASSAULT: .3X TO .8X BASIC INSERTS
*OFFEN.STRIKES: .4X TO 1X BASIC INSERTS
*GRID KIDS: .3X TO .8X BASIC INSERTS
*NEVER COMPROM: .3X TO .8X BASIC INSERTS
*BOW.BEST: .25X TO .6X BASIC INSERTS
*BOW.BEST ROOKIES: .25X TO .6X BASIC INSERTS

1997 Stadium Club Members Only 55

This 55-card 1997 Stadium Club Members Only set feflects Topps' selection of the 50 top NFL players. The five Finest-quality cards (51-55) represent Topps' selection of the top rookies from 1996. The fronts feature color action player photos with gold foil highlights including the "Members Only" seal. The backs carry player information.

COMP.FACT SET (55) 6.00 15.00
1 Brett Favre 1.20 3.00
2 Lamar Lathon .07 .20
3 Derrick Thomas .10 .30
4 Rod Woodson .10 .30
5 Dan Marino 1.20 3.00
6 Ashley Ambrose .07 .20
7 Herman Moore .10 .30
8 Larry Centers .10 .30
9 Cris Carter .20 .50
10 Jerry Rice .60 1.50
11 Hardy Nickerson .07 .20
12 Darrell Green .07 .20
13 Tim Brown .20 .50
14 Terrell Davis 1.00 2.50
15 Curtis Martin .40 1.00
16 Carl Pickens .10 .30
17 Darren Woodson .07 .20
18 Wesley Walls .10 .30
19 David Meggett .07 .20
20 Juhior Seau .10 .30
21 Merton Hanks .07 .20
22 Terry Allen .10 .30
23 Keenan McCardell .10 .30
24 Shannon Sharpe .10 .30
25 Reggie White .20 .50
26 Chad Brown .07 .20
27 Aeneas Williams .07 .20
28 Vinny Testaverde .10 .30
29 Rickey Watters .07 .20
30 Drew Bledsoe .50 1.25
31 Kevin Greene .10 .30
32 Tony Martin .10 .30
33 Ben Coates .10 .30
34 Isaac Bruce .20 .50
35 Troy Aikman .60 1.50
36 LeRoy Butler .07 .20
37 Kimble Anders .10 .30
38 Levon Kirkland .07 .20
39 Willie McGinest .07 .20
40 Barry Sanders 1.20 3.00
41 Eric Davis .07 .20
42 Gus Frerotte .10 .30
43 Jerome Bettis .20 .50
44 Steve Young .50 1.25
45 Emmitt Smith 1.00 2.50
46 Sam Mills .07 .20
47 Mark Brunell .50 1.25
48 Kerry Collins .20 .50
49 Deion Sanders .40 1.00
50 John Elway 1.20 3.00
51 Keyshawn Johnson FIN .40 1.00
52 Terry Glenn FIN .20 .50
53 Eddie Kennison FIN .20 .50
54 Karim Abdul-Jabbar FIN .10 .30
55 Eddie George FIN .60 1.50

1998 Stadium Club Promos

COMPLETE SET (5) 3.00 8.00
PP2 Michael Jackson .40 1.00
PP3 John Elway 2.00 4.00
PP4 Warrick Dunn .50 1.25
PP5 Chris Slade .40 1.00
PP6 Darrell Green .60 1.50

1998 Stadium Club

The 1998 Stadium Club Set was issued with a total of 195-standard size cards and distributed in nine-card packs with a suggested retail price of $3. The fronts feature color action player photos printed on embossed, thick 20 pt. stock with a holographic foil logo. The set contains the subset: Draft Picks (181-210).

COMPLETE SET (195) 25.00 60.00
1 Barry Sanders 1.00 2.50
2 Tony Martin .20 .50
3 Fred Lane .10 .30
4 Darren Woodson .10 .30
5 Andre Reed .20 .50
6 Blaine Bishop .10 .30
7 Robert Brooks .20 .50
8 Tony Banks .20 .50
9 Charles Way .10 .30
10 Mark Brunell .30 .75
11 Darrell Green .20 .50
12 Aeneas Williams .10 .30
13 Rob Johnson .20 .50
14 Deion Sanders .30 .75
15 Marshall Faulk .40 1.00
16 Stephen Boyd .10 .30
17 Adrian Murrell .20 .50
18 Wayne Chrebet .30 .75
19 Michael Sinclair .10 .30
20 Dan Marino 1.25 3.00
21 Willie Davis .10 .30
22 Chris Warren .20 .50
23 John Mobley .10 .30
24 Shannon Sharpe .20 .50
25 Thurman Thomas .30 .75
26 Corey Dillon .30 .75
27 Zach Thomas .30 .75
28 James Jett .20 .50
29 Eric Metcalf .10 .30
30 Drew Bledsoe .50 1.25
31 Scott Greene .10 .30
32 Simeon Rice .20 .50
33 Robert Smith .30 .75
34 Keenan McCardell .20 .50
35 Jessie Armstead .10 .30
36 Jerry Rice .60 1.50
37 Eric Green .10 .30
38 Terrell Owens .30 .75
39 Tim Brown .30 .75
40 Vinny Testaverde .20 .50
41 Brian Stablein .10 .30
42 Bert Emanuel .20 .50
43 Terry Glenn .30 .75
44 Chad Cota .10 .30
45 Jermaine Lewis .20 .50
46 Derrick Thomas .30 .75
47 O.J. McDuffie .20 .50
48 Frank Wycheck .10 .30
49 Steve Broussard .10 .30
50 Terrell Davis .30 .75
51 Eric Allen .10 .30
52 Napoleon Kaufman .30 .75
53 Dan Wilkinson .10 .30
54 Kerry Collins .20 .50
55 Frank Sanders .20 .50
56 Jeff Burris .10 .30
57 Michael Westbrook .20 .50
58 Michael McCrary .10 .30
59 Bobby Hoying .20 .50
60 Jerome Bettis .30 .75
61 Amp Lee .10 .30
62 Levon Kirkland .10 .30
63 Dana Stubblefield .10 .30
64 Terance Mathis .20 .50
65 Mark Chmura .20 .50
66 Bryant Westbrook .10 .30
67 Rod Smith .20 .50
68 Derrick Alexander .20 .50
69 Jason Taylor .20 .50
70 Eddie George .30 .75
71 Elvis Grbac .20 .50
72 Junior Seau .30 .75
73 Marvin Harrison .30 .75
74 Neil O'Donnell .20 .50
75 Johnnie Morton .20 .50
76 John Randle .20 .50
77 Danny Kanell .20 .50
78 Charlie Garner .20 .50
79 J.J. Stokes .20 .50
80 Troy Aikman .60 1.50
81 Gus Frerotte .10 .30
82 Jake Plummer .30 .75
83 Andre Hastings .10 .30
84 Steve Atwater .10 .30
85 Larry Centers .10 .30
86 Kevin Hardy .10 .30
87 Willie McGinest .10 .30
88 Joey Galloway .20 .50
89 Charles Johnson .10 .30
90 Warrick Dunn .30 .75
91 Derrick Rodgers .10 .30
92 Aaron Glenn .10 .30
93 Shawn Jefferson .10 .30
94 Antonio Freeman .30 .75
95 Jake Reed .20 .50
96 Reidel Anthony .20 .50
97 Cris Dishman .10 .30
98 Jason Sehorn .20 .50
99 Herman Moore .20 .50
100 John Elway 1.25 3.00
101 Brad Johnson .30 .75
102 Jeff George .20 .50
103 Emmitt Smith 1.00 2.50
104 Steve McNair .30 .75
105 Ed McCaffrey .20 .50
106 Errict Rhett .20 .50
107 Dorsey Levens .30 .75
108 Michael Jackson .10 .30
109 Carl Pickens .20 .50
110 James Stewart .20 .50
111 Karim Abdul-Jabbar .30 .75
112 Jim Harbaugh .20 .50
113 Yancey Thigpen .10 .30
114 Chad Brown .10 .30
115 Chris Sanders .10 .30
116 Cris Carter .30 .75
117 Glenn Foley .20 .50
118 Ben Coates .20 .50
119 Jamal Anderson .30 .75
120 Steve Young .40 1.00
121 Scott Mitchell .20 .50
122 Rob Moore .20 .50
123 Bobby Engram .20 .50
124 Rod Woodson .20 .50
125 Terry Allen .30 .75
126 Warren Sapp .20 .50
127 Irving Fryar .20 .50
128 Isaac Bruce .30 .75
129 Rae Carruth .10 .30
130 Sean Dawkins .10 .30
131 Andre Rison .20 .50
132 Kevin Greene .20 .50
133 Warren Moon .30 .75
134 Keyshawn Johnson .30 .75
135 Jay Graham .10 .30
136 Mike Alstott .30 .75
137 Peter Boulware .10 .30
138 Doug Evans .10 .30
139 Jimmy Smith .20 .50
140 Kordell Stewart .30 .75
141 Tamarick Vanover .10 .30
142 Chris Slade .10 .30
143 Freddie Jones .10 .30
144 Erik Kramer .10 .30
145 Ricky Watters .20 .50
146 Chris Chandler .20 .50
147 Garrison Hearst .30 .75
148 Trent Dilfer .30 .75
149 Bruce Smith .20 .50
150 Brett Favre 1.25 3.00
151 Will Blackwell .10 .30
152 Rickey Dudley .10 .30
153 Natrone Means .20 .50
154 Curtis Conway .20 .50
155 Tony Gonzalez .30 .75
156 Jeff Blake .20 .50
157 Michael Irvin .30 .75
158 Curtis Martin .30 .75
159 Tim McDonald .10 .30
160 Wesley Walls .20 .50
161 Michael Strahan .20 .50
162 Reggie White .30 .75
163 Jeff Graham .10 .30
164 Ray Lewis .30 .75
165 Antowain Smith .30 .75
166 Ryan Leaf RC 1.00 2.50
167 Jerome Pathon RC 1.00 2.50
168 Duane Starks RC .50 1.25
169 Brian Simmons RC .75 2.00
170 Pat Johnson RC .75 2.00
171 Keith Brooking RC 1.00 2.50
172 Kevin Dyson RC 1.00 2.50
173 Robert Edwards RC .75 2.00
174 Grant Wistrom RC .75 2.00
175 Curtis Enis RC .50 1.25
176 John Avery RC .75 2.00
177 Jason Peter RC .50 1.25
178 Brian Griese RC 2.00 5.00
179 Tavian Banks RC .75 2.00
180 Andre Wadsworth RC .75 2.00
181 Skip Hicks RC .75 2.00
182 Hines Ward RC 5.00 10.00
183 Greg Ellis RC .50 1.25
184 Robert Holcombe RC .75 2.00
185 Joe Jurevicius RC 1.00 2.50
186 Takeo Spikes RC 1.00 2.50
187 Ahman Green RC 2.50 6.00
188 Jacquez Green RC .75 2.00
189 Randy Moss RC 5.00 12.00
190 Charles Woodson RC 1.25 3.00
191 Fred Taylor RC 1.50 4.00
192 Marcus Nash RC .50 1.25
193 Germane Crowell RC .75 2.00
194 Tim Dwight RC 1.00 2.50
195 Peyton Manning RC 10.00 25.00

1998 Stadium Club First Day

*FIRST DAY STARS: 3X TO 8X BASIC CARDS
*FIRST DAY RCs: 1.5X TO 4X BASIC CARDS
STATED ODDS 1:47 RETAIL
STATED PRINT RUN 200 SER.#'d SETS

1998 Stadium Club One of a Kind

*ONE OF KIND STARS: 6X TO 12X BASIC CARDS
*ONE OF KIND RC'S: 2X TO 5X BASIC CARDS
STATED ODDS 1:32 HOBBY
STATED PRINT RUN 150 SER.#'d SETS

1998 Stadium Club Chrome

COMPLETE SET (20) 60.00 120.00
STATED ODDS 1:12 H/R, 1:6 JUM
*REFRACTORS: 1X TO 2X BASIC INSERTS
REFRACTOR ODDS 1:48 H/R, 1:24 JUM
*JUMBOS: .4X TO 1X BASIC INSERTS
JUMBO ODDS ONE PER BOX
*JUMBO REFRACT: 2X TO 5X BASIC INSERTS
JUMBO REFRACTOR ODDS 1:12 HTA BOXES
SCC1 John Elway 6.00 15.00
SCC2 Mark Brunell 1.50 4.00
SCC3 Jerome Bettis 1.50 4.00
SCC4 Steve Young 2.00 5.00
SCC5 Herman Moore 1.00 2.50
SCC6 Emmitt Smith 5.00 12.00
SCC7 Warrick Dunn 1.50 4.00
SCC8 Dan Marino 6.00 15.00
SCC9 Kordell Stewart 1.50 4.00
SCC10 Barry Sanders 5.00 12.00
SCC11 Tim Brown 1.50 4.00
SCC12 Dorsey Levens 1.50 4.00
SCC13 Eddie George 1.50 4.00
SCC14 Jerry Rice 3.00 8.00
SCC15 Terrell Davis 1.50 4.00
SCC16 Napoleon Kaufman 1.50 4.00
SCC17 Troy Aikman 3.00 8.00
SCC18 Drew Bledsoe 2.50 6.00
SCC19 Antonio Freeman 1.50 4.00
SCC20 Brett Favre 6.00 15.00

1998 Stadium Club Co-Signers

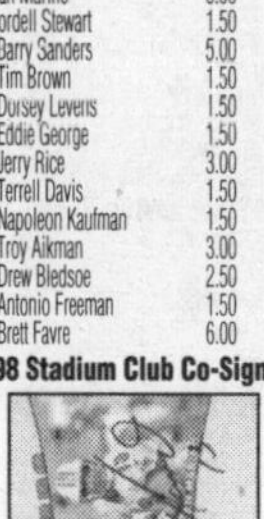

CO1-CO4: STATED ODDS 1:9400H, 1:5640J
CO5-CO8: STATED ODDS 1:3133H, 1:1880J
CO9-CO12: STATED ODDS 1:261H, 1:157J
OVERALL STATED ODDS 1:235H, 1:141J
CO1 Peyton Manning 250.00 400.00
Ryan Leaf
CO2 Dan Marino 125.00 250.00
Kordell Stewart
CO3 Eddie George 20.00 50.00
Corey Dillon
CO4 Dorsey Levens 30.00 80.00
Mike Alstott
CO5 Ryan Leaf 75.00 200.00
Dan Marino
CO6 Peyton Manning 200.00 350.00
Kordell Stewart
CO7 Eddie George 25.00 60.00
Mike Alstott
CO8 Dorsey Levens 20.00 50.00
Corey Dillon
CO9 Peyton Manning 250.00 500.00
Dan Marino
CO10 Ryan Leaf 12.00 30.00
Kordell Stewart
CO11 Eddie George 20.00 50.00
Dorsey Levens
CO12 Mike Alstott 20.00 50.00
Corey Dillon

1998 Stadium Club Double Threat

COMPLETE SET (10) 15.00 40.00
STATED ODDS 1:8 H/R, 1:4 JUM
DT1 Marshall Faulk 6.00 15.00
Peyton Manning
DT2 Curtis Conway 1.00 2.50
Curtis Enis
DT3 Drew Bledsoe 2.00 5.00
Robert Edwards
DT4 Warrrick Dunn 1.00 2.50
Jacquez Green
DT5 John Elway 4.00 10.00
Marcus Nash
DT6 Mark Brunell 1.00 2.50
Fred Taylor
DT7 Eddie George 1.00 2.50
Kevin Dyson
DT8 Michael Jackson 1.00 2.50
Pat Johnson
DT9 Terry Glenn 1.00 2.50
Tony Simmons
DT10 Natrone Means 1.00 2.50
Ryan Leaf

1998 Stadium Club Leading Legends

COMPLETE SET (10) 20.00 40.00
STATED ODDS 1:12 RETAIL
1 John Elway 4.00 10.00
2 Brett Favre 4.00 10.00
3 Dan Marino 4.00 10.00
4 Warren Moon 1.00 2.50
5 Jerry Rice 2.00 5.00
6 Barry Sanders 3.00 8.00
7 Bruce Smith .60 1.50
8 Emmitt Smith 3.00 8.00
9 Reggie White 1.00 2.50
10 Steve Young 1.25 3.00

1998 Stadium Club Prime Rookies

COMPLETE SET (10) 15.00 40.00
STATED ODDS 1:8 H/R, 1:4 JUM
PR1 Ryan Leaf .60 1.50
PR2 Andre Wadsworth .40 1.00
PR3 Fred Taylor 1.00 2.50
PR4 Kevin Dyson .60 1.50
PR5 Charles Woodson .75 2.00
PR6 Robert Edwards .30 .75
PR7 Grant Wistrom .40 1.00
PR8 Curtis Enis .30 .75
PR9 Randy Moss 4.00 10.00
PR10 Peyton Manning 7.50 15.00

1998 Stadium Club Triumvirate Luminous

COMPLETE SET (15) 35.00 80.00
STATED ODDS 1:24 H, 1:12 JUM HOB
*LUMINESCENTS: 1X TO 2X BASIC INSERTS
LUMINESCENT ODDS 1:96 H, 1:48 JUM HOB
*ILLUMINATORS: 1.5X TO 3X BASIC INSERTS
ILLUMINATOR ODDS 1:192 H, 1:96 JUM HOB
T1A Terrell Davis 2.00 5.00
T1B John Elway 8.00 20.00
T1C Shannon Sharpe 1.25 3.00
T2A Barry Sanders 6.00 15.00
T2B Scott Mitchell 1.25 3.00
T2C Herman Moore 1.25 3.00
T3A Dorsey Levens 2.00 5.00
T3B Brett Favre 8.00 20.00
T3C Antonio Freeman 2.00 5.00
T4A Emmitt Smith 6.00 15.00
T4B Troy Aikman 4.00 10.00
T4C Michael Irvin 2.00 5.00
T5A Napoleon Kaufman 2.00 5.00
T5B Jeff George 1.25 3.00
T5C Tim Brown 2.00 5.00

1999 Stadium Club Promos

COMPLETE SET (6) 2.50 6.00
PP1 Antowain Smith .40 1.00
PP2 Warren Sapp .50 1.25
PP3 Ty Law .40 1.00
PP4 Emmitt Smith 1.25 3.00
PP5 Randall Cunningham .50 1.25
PP6 Tim Dwight .30 .75

1999 Stadium Club

Released as a 200-card set, 1999 Stadium Club features 150 base veterans, 25 Transactions cards, and 25 Draft Picks seeded at one in three packs. Base cards are full-bleed color on a 20-point card stock. Stadium Club was packaged in 24-pack boxes with six cards per pack and carried a suggested retail price of $2.00 per pack.

COMPLETE SET (200) 25.00 60.00
COMP.SET w/o SP's (175) 7.50 20.00
UNPRICED PRINT.PLATES #'d TO 1
1 Dan Marino 1.00 2.50
2 Andre Reed .30 .75
3 Michael Westbrook .20 .50
4 Isaac Bruce .30 .75
5 Curtis Martin .30 .75
6 Courtney Hawkins .20 .50
7 Charles Way .20 .50
8 Terrell Owens .30 .75
9 Warrick Dunn .25 .60
10 Jake Plummer .25 .60
11 Chad Brown .20 .50
12 Yancey Thigpen .20 .50
13 Lamar Thomas .20 .50
14 Keenan McCardell .25 .60
15 Shannon Sharpe .30 .75
16 Robert Brooks .25 .60
17 Cameron Cleeland .20 .50
18 Derrick Thomas .30 .75
19 Mark Brunell .25 .60
20 Jamal Anderson .25 .60
21 Germane Crowell .20 .50
22 Rod Smith .25 .60
23 Ty Law .25 .60
24 Cris Carter .30 .75
25 Terrell Davis .30 .75
26 Takeo Spikes .20 .50
27 Tim Biakabutuka .25 .60
28 Jermaine Lewis .20 .50
29 Adrian Murrell .25 .60
30 Doug Flutie .30 .75
31 Curtis Enis .20 .50
32 Skip Hicks .20 .50
33 Steve McNair .30 .75
34 Charles Woodson .30 .75
35 Jessie Armstead .25 .60
36 Shawn Springs .20 .50
37 Levon Kirkland .20 .50
38 Freddie Jones .20 .50
39 Warren Sapp .25 .60
40 Emmitt Smith .75 2.00
41 Reidel Anthony .20 .50
42 Tony Simmons .20 .50
43 Andre Hastings .20 .50
44 Byron Bam Morris .20 .50
45 Jimmy Smith .25 .60
46 Antonio Freeman .25 .60
47 Herman Moore .25 .60
48 Muhsin Muhammad .25 .60
49 Chris Chandler .25 .60
50 John Elway 1.00 2.50
51 Aeneas Williams .20 .50
52 Bobby Engram .25 .60
53 Keith Poole .20 .50
54 Zach Thomas .30 .75
55 Mike Alstott .30 .75
56 Junior Seau .30 .75
57 Aaron Glenn .20 .50
58 Darrell Green .30 .75
59 Thurman Thomas .30 .75
60 Troy Aikman .50 1.25
61 Bill Romanowski .25 .60
62 Wesley Walls .25 .60
63 Andre Wadsworth .20 .50
64 Robert Smith .25 .60
65 Elvis Grbac .20 .50
66 Terry Fair .20 .50
67 Ben Coates .25 .60
68 Bert Emanuel .25 .60
69 Jacquez Green .20 .50
70 Barry Sanders .75 2.00
71 James Jett .20 .50
72 Gary Brown .20 .50
73 Stephen Alexander .20 .50
74 Wayne Chrebet .25 .60
75 Drew Bledsoe .30 .75
76 John Lynch .25 .60
77 Jake Reed .25 .60
78 Marvin Harrison .30 .75
79 Johnnie Morton .25 .60
80 Brett Favre 1.00 2.50
81 Charlie Batch .25 .60
82 Antowain Smith .20 .50
83 Mikhael Ricks .20 .50
84 Derrick Mayes .20 .50
85 John Mobley .20 .50
86 Ernie Mills .20 .50
87 Jeff Blake .25 .60
88 Curtis Conway .25 .60
89 Bruce Smith .30 .75
90 Peyton Manning 1.00 2.50
91 Tyrone Davis .20 .50
92 Ray Buchanan .20 .50
93 Tim Dwight .25 .60
94 O.J. McDuffie .25 .60
95 Vonnie Holliday .20 .50
96 Jon Kitna .25 .60
97 Trent Dilfer .25 .60
98 Jerome Bettis .30 .75
99 Dedric Ward .20 .50
100 Fred Taylor .25 .60
101 Ike Hilliard .25 .60
102 Frank Wycheck .25 .60
103 Eric Moulds .25 .60
104 Rob Moore .20 .50
105 Ed McCaffrey .25 .60
106 Carl Pickens .25 .60
107 Priest Holmes .30 .75
108 Kevin Hardy .20 .50
109 Terry Glenn .25 .60
110 Keyshawn Johnson .25 .60
111 Karim Abdul-Jabbar .25 .60
112 Stephen Boyd .20 .50
113 Ahman Green .25 .60
114 Duce Staley .25 .60
115 Vinny Testaverde .25 .60
116 Napoleon Kaufman .20 .50
117 Frank Sanders .20 .50
118 Peter Boulware .20 .50
119 Kevin Greene .25 .60
120 Steve Young .40 1.00
121 Darnay Scott .20 .50
122 Deion Sanders .30 .75
123 Corey Dillon .25 .60
124 Randall Cunningham .30 .75
125 Eddie George .25 .60
126 Derrick Alexander .20 .50
127 Mark Chmura .20 .50
128 Michael Sinclair .20 .50
129 Rickey Dudley .20 .50
130 Joey Galloway .25 .60
131 Michael Strahan .25 .60
132 Ricky Proehl .20 .50
133 Natrone Means .25 .60
134 Dorsey Levens .25 .60
135 Andre Rison .25 .60
136 Alonzo Mayes .20 .50
137 John Randle .25 .60
138 Terance Mathis .20 .50
139 Rae Carruth .20 .50
140 Jerry Rice .60 1.50
141 Michael Irvin .30 .75
142 Oronde Gadsden .20 .50
143 Jerome Pathon .20 .50
144 Ricky Watters .25 .60
145 J.J. Stokes .20 .50
146 Kordell Stewart .25 .60
147 Tim Brown .30 .75
148 Garrison Hearst .25 .60
149 Tony Gonzalez .30 .75
150 Randy Moss .30 .75
151 Daunte Culpepper RC .50 1.25
152 Amos Zereoue RC .40 1.00
153 Champ Bailey RC 1.00 2.50
154 Peerless Price RC .40 1.00
155 Edgerrin James RC .60 1.50
156 Joe Germaine RC .40 1.00
157 David Boston RC .40 1.00
158 Kevin Faulk RC .50 1.25
159 Troy Edwards RC .40 1.00
160 Akili Smith RC .40 1.00
161 Kevin Johnson RC .40 1.00
162 Rob Konrad RC .30 .75
163 Shaun King RC .40 1.00
164 James Johnson RC .30 .75
165 Donovan McNabb RC 1.25 3.00
166 Torry Holt RC .75 2.00
167 Mike Cloud RC .30 .75
168 Sedrick Irvin RC .30 .75
169 Cade McNown RC .40 1.00
170 Ricky Williams RC .75 2.00
171 Karsten Bailey RC .30 .75
172 Cecil Collins RC .30 .75
173 Brock Huard RC .40 1.00
174 D'Wayne Bates RC .30 .75
175 Tim Couch RC .50 1.25
176 Torrance Small .20 .50
177 Warren Moon .30 .75
178 Rocket Ismail .25 .60
179 Marshall Faulk .30 .75
180 Trent Green .25 .60
181 Sean Dawkins .20 .50
182 Pete Mitchell .20 .50
183 Jeff Graham .20 .50
184 Eddie Kennison .25 .60
185 Kerry Collins .25 .60
186 Eric Green .20 .50
187 Kyle Brady .20 .50
188 Tony Martin .25 .60
189 Jim Harbaugh .25 .60
190 Erik Kramer .25 .60
191 Steve Atwater .25 .60
192 Chad Bratzke .20 .50
193 Charles Johnson .20 .50
194 Damon Gibson .20 .50
195 Jeff George .20 .50
196 Scott Mitchell .20 .50
197 Terry Kirby .20 .50
198 Rich Gannon .25 .60
199 Chris Spielman .25 .60
200 Brad Johnson .25 .60

1999 Stadium Club First Day

COMPLETE SET (200) 300.00 600.00
*STARS: 6X TO 15X HI COL.
*RCs: 1.5X TO 4X
STATED PRINT RUN 150 SER.#'d SETS
STATED ODDS 1:38 RETAIL

1999 Stadium Club One of a Kind

COMPLETE SET (200) 300.00 600.00
*STARS: 6X TO 15X HI COL.
*RCs: 1.5X TO 4X
STATED PRINT RUN 150 SER.#'d SETS
STATED ODDS 1:48 HOBBY

1999 Stadium Club 3X3 Luminous

COMPLETE SET (15) 25.00 60.00
STATED ODDS 1:36 HOB/RET, 1:18 HTA
*LUMINESCENT: .8X TO 2X BASIC INSERTS
LUMINESCENT ODDS 1:144 H/R,1:72 HTA
*ILLUMINATOR: 1.2X TO 3X BASIC INSERTS
ILLUMINATOR ODDS 1:288 H/R,1:144 HTA
T1A Brett Favre 5.00 12.00
T1B Troy Aikman 3.00 8.00
T1C Jake Plummer 1.00 2.50
T2A Jamal Anderson 1.50 4.00
T2B Emmitt Smith 3.00 8.00
T2C Barry Sanders 5.00 12.00
T3A Antonio Freeman 1.50 4.00
T3B Randy Moss 4.00 10.00
T3C Jerry Rice 3.00 8.00
T4A Peyton Manning 5.00 12.00
T4B John Elway 5.00 12.00
T4C Dan Marino 5.00 12.00
T5A Fred Taylor 1.50 4.00
T5B Terrell Davis 1.50 4.00
T5C Curtis Martin 1.50 4.00

1999 Stadium Club Chrome Previews

COMPLETE SET (20) 50.00 100.00
STATED ODDS 1:24 HOB/RET, 1:6 HTA
*REFRACTORS: .8X TO 2X BASIC INSERTS
REFRACTOR STATED ODDS 1:96H/R,1:24HTA
*JUMBOS: .3X TO .8X BASIC INSERTS
JUMBOS STATED ODDS 1.96H/R,1.24HTA
*JUMBO REF.: 1X TO 2.5X BASIC INSERTS
JUMBO REF.ODDS 1:12 HOBBY BOXES
C1 Randy Moss 3.00 8.00
C2 Terrell Davis 1.25 3.00
C3 Peyton Manning 4.00 10.00
C4 Fred Taylor 1.25 3.00
C5 John Elway 4.00 10.00
C6 Steve Young 1.50 4.00
C7 Brett Favre 4.00 10.00
C8 Jamal Anderson 1.25 3.00
C9 Barry Sanders 4.00 10.00
C10 Dan Marino 4.00 10.00
C11 Jerry Rice 2.50 6.00
C12 Emmitt Smith 2.50 6.00
C13 Randall Cunningham 1.25 3.00
C14 Troy Aikman 2.50 6.00
C15 Akili Smith .75 2.00
C16 Donovan McNabb 4.00 10.00
C17 Edgerrin James 3.00 8.00
C18 Torry Holt 2.00 5.00
C19 Ricky Williams 1.50 4.00
C20 Tim Couch 1.00 2.50

1999 Stadium Club Co-Signers

CS1/CS2 STATED ODDS 1:2854H,1:1142HTA
CS3-CS6 STATED ODDS 1:1189H,1:476HTA
OVERALL STATED ODDS 1:840 HOB
CS1 Terrell Davis 25.00 60.00
Ricky Williams
CS2 Terrell Davis 25.00 60.00
Edgerrin James
CS3 Dan Marino 60.00 120.00
Tim Couch
CS4 Peyton Manning 60.00 120.00
Tim Couch
CS5 Randy Moss 150.00 250.00
Jerry Rice
CS6 Dan Marino 60.00 120.00
Vinny Testaverde

1999 Stadium Club Emperors of the Zone

COMPLETE SET (10) 12.50 30.00
STATED ODDS 1:12 HOB/RET, 1:4 HTA
E1 Ricky Williams .75 2.00
E2 Brett Favre 2.00 5.00
E3 Donovan McNabb 2.00 5.00
E4 Peyton Manning 2.00 5.00
E5 Terrell Davis .60 1.50
E6 Jamal Anderson .60 1.50
E7 Edgerrin James 1.50 4.00
E8 Fred Taylor .60 1.50
E9 Tim Couch .50 1.25
E10 Randy Moss 1.50 4.00

1999 Stadium Club Lone Star Signatures

OVERALL STATED ODDS 1:697

LS1 Randy Moss	40.00	80.00
LS2 Jerry Rice	60.00	120.00
LS3 Peyton Manning	60.00	120.00
LS4 Vinny Testaverde	10.00	25.00
LS5 Tim Couch	12.50	30.00
LS6 Dan Marino	75.00	150.00
LS7 Edgerrin James	15.00	40.00
LS8 Fred Taylor	12.50	30.00
LS9 Garrison Hearst	10.00	25.00
LS10 Antonio Freeman	15.00	40.00
LS11 Torry Holt	15.00	40.00

1999 Stadium Club Never Compromise

COMPLETE SET (30)	30.00	60.00
STATED ODDS 1:12 HOB/RET, 1:4 HTA		
NC1 Tim Couch	.75	2.00
NC2 David Boston	.60	1.50
NC3 Daunte Culpepper	.75	2.00
NC4 Donovan McNabb	2.00	5.00
NC5 Ricky Williams	1.25	3.00
NC6 Troy Edwards	.60	1.50
NC7 Akili Smith	.60	1.50
NC8 Torry Holt	1.25	3.00
NC9 Cade McNown	.60	1.50
NC10 Edgerrin James	1.00	2.50
NC11 Randy Moss	.75	2.00
NC12 Peyton Manning	2.50	6.00
NC13 Eddie George	.60	1.50
NC14 Fred Taylor	.60	1.50
NC15 Jamal Anderson	.60	1.50
NC16 Joey Galloway	.60	1.50
NC17 Terrell Davis	.75	2.00
NC18 Keyshawn Johnson	.60	1.50
NC19 Antonio Freeman	.60	1.50
NC20 Jake Plummer	.60	1.50
NC21 Steve Young	1.00	2.50
NC22 Barry Sanders	2.00	5.00
NC23 Dan Marino	2.50	6.00
NC24 Emmitt Smith	2.00	5.00
NC25 Brett Favre	2.50	6.00
NC26 Randall Cunningham	.75	2.00
NC27 John Elway	2.50	6.00
NC28 Drew Bledsoe	.75	2.00
NC29 Jerry Rice	1.50	4.00
NC30 Troy Aikman	1.25	3.00

2000 Stadium Club Promos

This 6-card set was released at various Topps sponsored events and through its dealer network to promote the 2000 football release. The cards look very similar to the base set except for the card numbering scheme.

COMPLETE SET (6)	2.00	5.00
PP1 Peyton Manning	1.00	2.50
PP2 Antonio Freeman	.30	.75
PP3 O.J. McDuffie	.30	.75
PP4 Junior Seau	.40	1.00
PP5 Mark Brunell	.30	.75
PP6 Ed McCaffrey	.30	.75

2000 Stadium Club

Released as a 175-card set, Stadium Club is composed of 150 base cards and 25 short printed Rookie cards inserted at one in four, and one in one HTA. Base cards feature full color crystal clear action photography and highlight some of the key moments and plays from the 1999 season. Stadium Club HTA was packaged in 12-pack boxes with each pack containing 18 cards including one rookie card and carried a suggested retail price of $6.00. Regular packing was 24-pack boxes with packs containing seven cards and carried a suggested retail price of $2.50.

COMPLETE SET (175)	20.00	50.00
COMP.SET w/o RC's (150)	7.50	20.00
151-175 ROOKIE STATED ODDS 1:4		
1 Peyton Manning	.60	1.50
2 Pete Mitchell	.15	.40
3 Napoleon Kaufman	.20	.50
4 Mikhael Ricks	.15	.40
5 Mike Alstott	.25	.60
6 Brad Johnson	.20	.50
7 Tony Gonzalez	.25	.60
8 Germane Crowell	.15	.40
9 Marcus Robinson	.20	.50
10 Stephen Davis	.20	.50
11 Terance Mathis	.15	.40
12 Jake Plummer	.20	.50
13 Qadry Ismail	.20	.50
14 Cade McNown	.15	.40
15 Zach Thomas	.25	.60
16 Curtis Martin	.25	.60
17 Torrance Small	.15	.40
18 Steve McNair	.25	.60
19 Jim Harbaugh	.20	.50
20 Keyshawn Johnson	.20	.50
21 Antonio Freeman	.20	.50
22 Ed McCaffrey	.20	.50
23 Elvis Grbac	.15	.40
24 Peerless Price	.20	.50
25 Jerome Bettis	.25	.60
26 Yancey Thigpen	.15	.40
27 Jake Delhomme RC	.60	1.50
28 Keith Poole	.15	.40
29 Carl Pickens	.20	.50
30 Jerry Rice	.50	1.25
31 Rob Moore	.15	.40
32 Reidel Anthony	.15	.40
33 Jimmy Smith	.20	.50
34 Ray Lucas	.15	.40
35 Troy Aikman	.40	1.00
36 Steve Beuerlein	.20	.50
37 Charlie Batch	.20	.50
38 Derrick Mayes	.15	.40
39 Tim Brown	.25	.60
40 Eddie George	.20	.50
41 O.J. McDuffie	.20	.50
42 Ike Hilliard	.20	.50
43 Bill Schroeder	.20	.50
44 Jim Miller	.15	.40
45 Chris Chandler	.20	.50
46 Fred Taylor	.25	.60
47 Ricky Watters	.20	.50
48 Tyrone Wheatley	.15	.40
49 Bruce Smith	.25	.60
50 Marshall Faulk	.25	.60
51 Kevin Carter	.15	.40
52 Champ Bailey	.20	.50
53 Troy Edwards	.15	.40
54 Doug Flutie	.25	.60
55 Charles Johnson	.15	.40
56 Michael Westbrook	.15	.40
57 Frank Wycheck	.20	.50
58 Drew Bledsoe	.25	.60
59 Terrence Wilkins	.15	.40
60 Ricky Williams	.25	.60
61 Rod Smith	.20	.50
62 Errict Rhett	.20	.50
63 Vinny Testaverde	.20	.50
64 Jacquez Green	.15	.40
65 Curtis Conway	.20	.50
66 Wayne Chrebet	.20	.50
67 Albert Connell	.15	.40
68 Kordell Stewart	.20	.50
69 Bert Emanuel	.15	.40
70 Randy Moss	.25	.60
71 Akili Smith	.15	.40
72 Brian Griese	.20	.50
73 Frank Sanders	.15	.40
74 Wesley Walls	.15	.40
75 Michael Pittman	.15	.40
76 Steve Young	.30	.75
77 Jevon Kearse	.20	.50
78 Az-Zahir Hakim	.15	.40
79 James Stewart	.15	.40
80 Brett Favre	.75	2.00
81 Dan Marino	.75	2.00
82 Joe Horn	.20	.50
83 Mark Brunell	.20	.50
84 Eddie Kennison	.15	.40
85 Deion Sanders	.25	.60
86 Priest Holmes	.25	.60
87 Terry Glenn	.20	.50
88 Olandis Gary	.20	.50
89 Patrick Jeffers	.20	.50
90 Emmitt Smith	.60	1.50
91 J.J. Stokes	.20	.50
92 Warrick Dunn	.20	.50
93 Damon Huard	.20	.50
94 Herman Moore	.20	.50
95 Corey Dillon	.20	.50
96 Joey Galloway	.20	.50
97 Jamal Anderson	.20	.50
98 Junior Seau	.25	.60
99 Robert Smith	.20	.50
100 Edgerrin James	.25	.60
101 Derrick Alexander	.15	.40
102 Johnnie Morton	.20	.50
103 Sean Dawkins	.15	.40
104 Derrick Brooks	.25	.60
105 Rickey Dudley	.15	.40
106 Keenan McCardell	.20	.50
107 Kerry Collins	.20	.50
108 Kevin Johnson	.15	.40
109 Eric Moulds	.20	.50
110 Terrell Davis	.25	.60
111 Shawn Jefferson	.15	.40
112 Donovan McNabb	.25	.60
113 Torry Holt	.25	.60
114 Marvin Harrison	.25	.60
115 Amani Toomer	.20	.50
116 Tony Martin	.20	.50
117 Curtis Enis	.15	.40
118 Tiki Barber	.25	.60
119 Freddie Jones	.15	.40
120 Muhsin Muhammad	.20	.50
121 Shaun King	.15	.40
122 Isaac Bruce	.25	.60
123 Duce Staley	.20	.50
124 Hardy Nickerson	.15	.40
125 Corey Bradford	.15	.40
126 Kevin Hardy	.15	.40
127 Hines Ward	.25	.60
128 Charlie Garner	.20	.50
129 Warren Sapp	.20	.50
130 Tim Couch	.20	.50
131 Kevin Dyson	.20	.50
132 Rocket Ismail	.20	.50
133 Tim Dwight	.20	.50
134 Darnay Scott	.20	.50
135 Jeff George	.20	.50
136 Dorsey Levens	.20	.50
137 Jeff Blake	.20	.50
138 Jon Kitna	.20	.50
139 Rich Gannon	.20	.50
140 Cris Carter	.25	.60
141 Jeff Graham	.15	.40
142 James Johnson	.15	.40
143 Tim Biakabutuka	.20	.50
144 Bobby Engram	.20	.50
145 Tony Banks	.15	.40
146 Shannon Sharpe	.25	.60
147 Antowain Smith	.20	.50
148 Terrell Owens	.25	.60
149 Rob Johnson	.20	.50
150 Kurt Warner	.40	1.00
151 Thomas Jones RC	1.00	2.50
152 Chad Pennington RC	1.25	3.00
153 Ron Dayne RC	.75	2.00
154 Tee Martin RC	.75	2.00
155 Reuben Droughns RC	.75	2.00
156 Jerry Porter RC	.75	2.00
157 R.Jay Soward RC	.50	1.25
158 Sylvester Morris RC	.50	1.25
159 Todd Pinkston RC	.50	1.25
160 Courtney Brown RC	.60	1.50
161 Travis Taylor RC	.60	1.50
162 Ron Dugans RC	.50	1.25
163 Laveranues Coles RC	.75	2.00
164 Joe Hamilton RC	.50	1.25
165 Curtis Keaton RC	.50	1.25
166 Bubba Franks RC	.75	2.00
167 Dennis Northcutt RC	.60	1.50
168 Chris Redman RC	.60	1.50
169 Travis Prentice RC	.60	1.50
170 Shaun Alexander RC	1.00	2.50
171 Jamal Lewis RC	.75	2.00
172 Peter Warrick RC	.75	2.00
173 J.R. Redmond RC	.50	1.25
174 Trung Canidate RC	.60	1.50
175 Plaxico Burress RC	.75	2.00

2000 Stadium Club Beam Team

COMPLETE SET (30)	75.00	150.00
BEAM TEAM/500 ODDS 1:171, 1:66 HTA		
STATED PRINT RUN 500 SER.#'d SETS		
BT1 Brett Favre	10.00	25.00
BT2 Stephen Davis	2.50	6.00
BT3 Germane Crowell	2.00	5.00
BT4 Jevon Kearse	2.50	6.00
BT5 Edgerrin James	3.00	8.00
BT6 Randy Moss	3.00	8.00
BT7 Isaac Bruce	3.00	8.00
BT8 Charlie Garner	2.50	6.00
BT9 Eddie George	2.50	6.00
BT10 Kurt Warner	5.00	12.00
BT11 Rocket Ismail	2.50	6.00
BT12 Doug Flutie	3.00	8.00
BT13 Jimmy Smith	2.50	6.00
BT14 Eric Moulds	2.50	6.00
BT15 Marvin Harrison	3.00	8.00
BT16 Ricky Watters	2.50	6.00
BT17 Marcus Robinson	2.50	6.00
BT18 Mark Brunell	2.50	6.00
BT19 Tim Dwight	2.50	6.00
BT20 Peyton Manning	8.00	20.00
BT21 Patrick Jeffers	2.50	6.00
BT22 Az-Zahir Hakim	2.00	5.00
BT23 Fred Taylor	3.00	8.00
BT24 Tim Biakabutuka	2.50	6.00
BT25 Marshall Faulk	3.00	8.00
BT26 Shannon Sharpe	3.00	8.00
BT27 Tony Gonzalez	3.00	8.00
BT28 Steve McNair	3.00	8.00
BT29 Antonio Freeman	2.50	6.00
BT30 Keyshawn Johnson	2.50	6.00

2000 Stadium Club Capture the Action

COMPLETE SET (30)	15.00	40.00
STATED ODDS 1:8, 1:2 HTA		
*GAME VIEW/100: 3X TO 8X BASIC INSERTS		
GAME VIEW/100 STATED ODDS 1:454		
GAME VIEW PRINT RUN 100 SER.#'d SETS		
CA1 Brett Favre	2.00	5.00
CA2 Drew Bledsoe	.60	1.50
CA3 Dan Marino	2.00	5.00
CA4 Peyton Manning	1.50	4.00
CA5 Kurt Warner	1.00	2.50
CA6 Brad Johnson	.50	1.25
CA7 Steve Beuerlein	.50	1.25
CA8 Troy Aikman	1.00	2.50
CA9 Edgerrin James	.60	1.50
CA10 Marshall Faulk	.60	1.50
CA11 Stephen Davis	.50	1.25
CA12 Eddie George	.50	1.25
CA13 Emmitt Smith	1.50	4.00
CA14 Curtis Martin	.60	1.50
CA15 Ricky Williams	.60	1.50
CA16 Jimmy Smith	.50	1.25
CA17 Marvin Harrison	.60	1.50
CA18 Muhsin Muhammad	.50	1.25
CA19 Keyshawn Johnson	.50	1.25
CA20 Marcus Robinson	.50	1.25
CA21 Antonio Freeman	.50	1.25
CA22 Randy Moss	.60	1.50
CA23 Tim Brown	.60	1.50
CA24 Cris Carter	.60	1.50
CA25 Isaac Bruce	.60	1.50
CA26 Zach Thomas	.60	1.50
CA27 Warren Sapp	.50	1.25
CA28 Jevon Kearse	.50	1.25
CA29 Junior Seau	.60	1.50
CA30 Kevin Carter	.40	1.00

2000 Stadium Club Co-Signers

STATED ODDS 1:2270 HOB, 1:880 HTA		
CS1 Peyton Manning	125.00	250.00
Kurt Warner		
CS2 Edgerrin James	50.00	100.00
Marshall Faulk		
CS3 Stephen Davis	20.00	50.00
Eddie George		
CS4 Jimmy Smith	20.00	50.00
Cris Carter		
CS5 Marvin Harrison	50.00	100.00
Isaac Bruce		
CS6 Jon Kitna	20.00	50.00
Cade McNown		

2000 Stadium Club Goal to Go

COMPLETE SET (16)	5.00	12.00
STATED ODDS 1:8, 1:3 HTA		
G1 Cris Carter	.40	1.00
G2 Stephen Davis	.30	.75
G3 Marvin Harrison	.40	1.00
G4 Edgerrin James	.40	1.00
G5 Zach Thomas	.40	1.00
G6 Terrell Davis	.40	1.00
G7 Leroy Hoard	.25	.60
G8 Kurt Warner	.60	1.50
G9 Tony Gonzalez	.40	1.00
G10 James Stewart	.25	.60
G11 Isaac Bruce	.40	1.00
G12 Emmitt Smith	1.00	2.50
G13 Dorsey Levens	.30	.75
G14 Jevon Kearse	.30	.75
G15 Eddie George	.30	.75
G16 Warren Sapp	.30	.75

2000 Stadium Club Lone Star Signatures

OVERALL STATED ODDS 1:202, 1:79 HTA		
ANNOUNCED PRINT RUNS 100-575		
LS1 Edgerrin James	12.00	30.00
LS2 Stephen Davis	6.00	15.00
LS3 Marshall Faulk	12.00	30.00
LS4 Eddie George	8.00	20.00
LS5 Isaac Bruce	8.00	20.00
LS6 Jimmy Smith	6.00	15.00
LS7 Cris Carter	15.00	40.00
LS8 Kurt Warner	25.00	50.00
LS9 Marvin Harrison	20.00	50.00
LS10 Kevin Carter	5.00	12.00
LS11 Ron Dayne	8.00	20.00
LS12 Chad Pennington	12.00	30.00
LS13 Sylvester Morris	5.00	12.00
LS14 Thomas Jones	10.00	25.00
LS15 Shaun Alexander	8.00	20.00
LS16 Chris Redman	6.00	15.00
LS18 Peter Warrick	8.00	20.00
LS19 Jon Kitna	6.00	15.00
LS20 Cade McNown	5.00	12.00
LS21 Az-Zahir Hakim	5.00	12.00
LS22 Amani Toomer	6.00	15.00
LS23 Wesley Walls	5.00	12.00
LS24 Marcus Robinson	6.00	15.00
LS25 Zach Thomas	8.00	20.00
LS26 Tony Gonzalez	10.00	25.00
LS27 Muhsin Muhammad	6.00	15.00
LS28 Ed McCaffrey	8.00	20.00
LS29 Eric Moulds	6.00	15.00
LS30 Peyton Manning	75.00	135.00
LS31 Joe Montana SP	75.00	150.00

2000 Stadium Club Pro Bowl Jerseys

OVERALL STATED ODDS 1:353, 1:137 HTA		
ANNOUNCED PRINT RUNS 300-900		
CCWR Cris Carter	10.00	25.00
EGRB Eddie George	8.00	20.00
EJRB Edgerrin James	10.00	25.00
FWTE Frank Wycheck	8.00	20.00
HNLB Hardy Nickerson	6.00	15.00
IBWR Isaac Bruce	10.00	25.00
JKDE Jevon Kearse	8.00	20.00
KHILB Kevin Hardy	6.00	15.00
KJWR Keyshawn Johnson	8.00	20.00
MFRB Marshall Faulk	10.00	25.00
MMWR Muhsin Muhammad	8.00	20.00
PBOLB Peter Boulware	6.00	15.00
RMWR Randy Moss	10.00	25.00
SBQB Steve Beuerlein	8.00	20.00
SDRB Stephen Davis	8.00	20.00
TLCB Todd Lyght	6.00	15.00
WSLM Warren Sapp	8.00	20.00
WWTE Wesley Walls	6.00	15.00

2000 Stadium Club Pro Bowl Jerseys Autographs

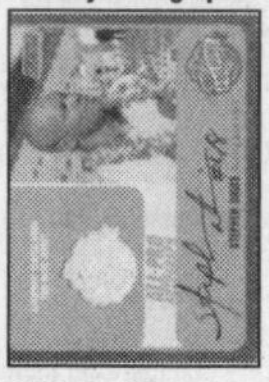

JSY AU/50 ODDS 1:5474 HOB, 1:2116 HTA		
STATED PRINT RUN 50 SETS		
APA1 Eddie George	50.00	100.00
APA2 Edgerrin James	60.00	120.00
APA3 Marshall Faulk	60.00	120.00
APA4 Stephen Davis	40.00	80.00
APA5 Isaac Bruce	50.00	100.00

2000 Stadium Club Pro Bowl Jerseys Combos

COMBO JSY/50 ODDS 1:523 HTA		
STATED PRINT RUN 50 SER.#'d SETS		
APC1 Jevon Kearse	20.00	50.00
Warren Sapp		
APC2 Marshall Faulk	25.00	60.00
Edgerrin James		
APC3 Keyshawn Johnson	25.00	60.00
Randy Moss		
APC4 Frank Wycheck	20.00	50.00
Wesley Walls		
APC5 Stephen Davis	20.00	50.00
Eddie George		
APC6 Cris Carter	25.00	60.00
Isaac Bruce		

2000 Stadium Club Tunnel Vision

COMPLETE SET (8)	5.00	12.00
ONE PER BOX		
TV1 Edgerrin James	.50	1.25
TV2 Brett Favre	1.50	4.00
TV3 Marshall Faulk	.50	1.25
TV4 Emmitt Smith	1.25	3.00
TV5 Peyton Manning	1.25	3.00
TV6 Eddie George	.40	1.00
TV7 Kurt Warner	.75	2.00
TV8 Fred Taylor	.50	1.25

2001 Stadium Club

Topps released Stadium Club in July of 2001. The set had 175 cards and 50 of those were short printed rookies. Cards 126-175 were all rookies that were available in packs at a rate of 1:4. The cardfronts featured a borderless action photo with a gold-foil bar for the player's name and position.

COMPLETE SET (175)	60.00	120.00
COMP.SET w/o SPs (125)	7.50	20.00
ROOKIE STATED ODDS 1:4		
1 Peyton Manning	.60	1.50
2 Akili Smith	.15	.40
3 Brian Griese	.20	.50
4 Wayne Chrebet	.20	.50
5 Oronde Gadsden	.15	.40
6 Marvin Harrison	.25	.60
7 Charles Johnson	.15	.40
8 Jay Fiedler	.20	.50
9 Kerry Collins	.20	.50
10 Troy Aikman	.40	1.00
11 Donovan McNabb	.25	.60
12 Ike Hilliard	.20	.50
13 Warrick Dunn	.25	.60
14 Derrick Alexander	.15	.40
15 Jake Plummer	.20	.50
16 Corey Dillon	.20	.50
17 Ahman Green	.25	.60
18 Keenan McCardell	.20	.50
19 Derrick Mason	.20	.50
20 Jerry Rice	.50	1.25
21 Emmitt Smith	.60	1.50
22 Dedric Ward	.15	.40
23 Jamal Anderson	.20	.50
24 Charlie Garner	.20	.50
25 Vinny Testaverde	.20	.50
26 Shaun Alexander	.25	.60
27 Terry Glenn	.20	.50
28 Cade McNown	.20	.50
29 Germane Crowell	.15	.40
30 Jeff Graham	.15	.40
31 Rich Gannon	.20	.50
32 Jevon Kearse	.20	.50
33 Shannon Sharpe	.25	.60
34 Marcus Robinson	.20	.50
35 Rod Smith	.20	.50
36 Curtis Martin	.25	.60
37 Robert Smith	.20	.50
38 Marshall Faulk	.25	.60
39 Tony Richardson	.15	.40
40 Travis Prentice	.15	.40
41 Edgerrin James	.25	.60
42 Duce Staley	.20	.50
43 Keyshawn Johnson	.20	.50
44 Joe Horn	.20	.50
45 Shawn Bryson	.15	.40
46 Ray Lewis	.25	.60
47 Fred Taylor	.25	.60
48 Jeff George	.20	.50
49 Sean Dawkins	.15	.40
50 Daunte Culpepper	.20	.50
51 Chris Chandler	.20	.50
52 Tim Couch	.15	.40
53 Trent Dilfer	.20	.50
54 Steve McNair	.25	.60
55 Kordell Stewart	.20	.50
56 Aaron Brooks	.20	.50
57 Michael Pittman	.20	.50
58 Bill Schroeder	.20	.50
59 Junior Seau	.25	.60
60 Kurt Warner	.40	1.00
61 Drew Bledsoe	.25	.60
62 Steve Beuerlein	.20	.50
63 Mike Anderson	.20	.50
64 Brad Johnson	.20	.50
65 Tim Brown	.25	.60
66 Qadry Ismail	.20	.50
67 Doug Flutie	.25	.60
68 Terrell Owens	.25	.60
69 Rocket Ismail	.20	.50
70 Charlie Batch	.20	.50
71 Jerome Pathon	.15	.40
72 Peter Warrick	.20	.50
73 Hines Ward	.25	.60
74 Ron Dayne	.20	.50
75 Lamar Smith	.20	.50
76 Amani Toomer	.20	.50
77 Joey Galloway	.20	.50
78 James Allen	.15	.40
79 Isaac Bruce	.25	.60
80 David Boston	.15	.40
81 James Thrash	.20	.50
82 Tony Gonzalez	.25	.60
83 Jason Taylor	.25	.60
84 Ricky Watters	.20	.50
85 Terance Mathis	.15	.40
86 Troy Brown	.20	.50
87 Mark Brunell	.20	.50
88 Rob Johnson	.20	.50
89 Freddie Jones	.15	.40
90 Eddie George	.25	.60
91 Tiki Barber	.25	.60
92 Donald Hayes	.15	.40
93 Muhsin Muhammad	.20	.50
94 Johnnie Morton	.20	.50
95 Warren Sapp	.20	.50
96 Bobby Shaw	.15	.40
97 Randy Moss	.25	.60
98 Jerome Bettis	.25	.60
99 Antonio Freeman	.25	.60
100 Jamal Lewis	.25	.60
101 Andre Rison	.20	.50
102 Kevin Faulk	.20	.50
103 Jon Kitna	.20	.50
104 Shawn Jefferson	.15	.40
105 Kevin Johnson	.15	.40
106 Torry Holt	.20	.50
107 Cris Carter	.25	.60
108 Chad Lewis	.15	.40
109 Stephen Davis	.20	.50
110 Jeff Blake	.20	.50
111 Elvis Grbac	.20	.50
112 Ed McCaffrey	.20	.50
113 Tim Biakabutuka	.15	.40
114 Trent Green	.25	.60
115 Jeff Garcia	.20	.50
116 Jacquez Green	.15	.40
117 Shaun King	.15	.40
118 Jimmy Smith	.20	.50
119 James Stewart	.15	.40
120 Brian Urlacher	.30	.75
121 Tyrone Wheatley	.20	.50
122 J.R. Redmond	.15	.40
123 Eric Moulds	.20	.50
124 Ricky Williams	.25	.60
125 Brett Favre	.75	2.00
126 Koren Robinson RC	.60	1.50
127 Richard Seymour RC	.75	2.00
128 Jamal Reynolds RC	.50	1.25
129 Kevin Kasper RC	.50	1.25
130 LaMont Jordan RC	.75	2.00
131 Reggie Wayne RC	1.50	4.00
132 Travis Henry RC	.60	1.50
133 Alge Crumpler RC	.75	2.00
134 Quincy Carter RC	.60	1.50
135 Michael Bennett RC	.60	1.50
136 Jamie Winborn RC	.60	1.50
137 Josh Heupel RC	.75	2.00
138 Will Allen RC	.75	2.00
139 Scotty Anderson RC	.50	1.25
140 LaDainian Tomlinson RC	2.50	6.00
141 Freddie Mitchell RC	.50	1.25
142 Gerard Warren RC	.60	1.50
143 Chad Johnson RC	1.25	3.00
144 Todd Heap RC	.75	2.00
145 Leonard Davis RC	.75	2.00
146 Kevan Barlow RC	.60	1.50
147 Correll Buckhalter RC	.75	2.00
148 Fred Smoot RC	.75	2.00
149 Steve Smith RC	1.50	4.00
150 David Terrell RC	.60	1.50
151 Chris Chambers RC	.75	2.00
152 Mike McMahon RC	.60	1.50
153 Rudi Johnson RC	.75	2.00
154 Marques Tuiasosopo RC	.60	1.50
155 Deuce McAllister RC	.75	2.00
156 Marcus Stroud RC	.60	1.50
157 Bobby Newcombe RC	.60	1.50
158 Rod Gardner RC	.60	1.50
159 Drew Brees RC	5.00	12.00
160 Jesse Palmer RC	.60	1.50
161 Derrick Gibson RC	.50	1.25
162 James Jackson RC	.50	1.25
163 Dan Morgan RC	.60	1.50
164 Michael Vick RC	3.00	8.00
165 Snoop Minnis RC	.50	1.25
166 Anthony Thomas RC	.75	2.00
167 Andre Carter RC	.60	1.50
168 Travis Minor RC	.60	1.50
169 Quincy Morgan RC	.60	1.50
170 Justin Smith RC	.75	2.00
171 Tay Cody RC	.50	1.25
172 Santana Moss RC	1.00	2.50
173 Sage Rosenfels RC	.75	2.00
174 Robert Ferguson RC	.75	2.00
175 Chris Weinke RC	.60	1.50

2001 Stadium Club Common Threads

RANDOM INSERTS IN HTA PACKS		
CTCR Daunte Culpepper	6.00	15.00
David Rivers		
CTDM Corey Dillon	6.00	15.00
Travis Minor		
CTGT Eddie George	15.00	40.00
LaDainian Tomlinson		
CTHW Marvin Harrison	15.00	40.00
Reggie Wayne		
CTJB Edgerrin James	8.00	20.00
Kevan Barlow		
CTMJ Eric Moulds	15.00	40.00
Chad Johnson		

2001 Stadium Club Common Threads Autographs

RANDOM INSERTS IN HTA PACKS		
CTACR Daunte Culpepper	30.00	80.00
David Rivers		
CTAHW Marvin Harrison	40.00	100.00
Reggie Wayne		
CTAJB Edgerrin James	30.00	80.00
Kevan Barlow		
CTMJ Eric Moulds	25.00	60.00
Chad Johnson		

2001 Stadium Club Co-Signers

COAL Mike Anderson	20.00	40.00
Jamal Lewis		
COCG Daunte Culpepper	25.00	50.00
Jeff Garcia		
COFB Brett Favre	100.00	200.00
Aaron Brooks		

2001 Stadium Club Highlight Reels

COMPLETE SET (5)	6.00	15.00
STATED ODDS 1:6 HOB/RET, 1:4 HTA		
HRAA Alan Ameche	.60	1.50
HRBG Bob Griese	1.00	2.50
HRBS Bart Starr	2.00	5.00
HRJE John Elway	2.50	6.00
HRJN Joe Namath	1.50	4.00

2001 Stadium Club In Focus

COMPLETE SET (15)	7.50	20.00
STATED ODDS 1:8 HOB/RET, 1:6 HTA		
IF1 Peyton Manning	1.25	3.00
IF2 Marshall Faulk	.50	1.25
IF3 Torry Holt	.40	1.00
IF4 Daunte Culpepper	.40	1.00
IF5 Edgerrin James	.50	1.25
IF6 Marvin Harrison	.50	1.25
IF7 Jeff Garcia	.40	1.00
IF8 Robert Smith	.40	1.00
IF9 Randy Moss	.50	1.25
IF10 Mike Anderson	.40	1.00
IF11 Corey Dillon	.40	1.00
IF12 Rod Smith	.40	1.00
IF13 Brett Favre	1.50	4.00
IF14 Eddie George	.50	1.25
IF15 Terrell Owens	.50	1.25

2001 Stadium Club Lone Star Signatures

GROUP 1 ODDS 1:13,802H, 1:14,515R		
GROUP 2 ODDS 1:8971H, 1:9117R		
GROUP 3 ODDS 1:1701H, 1:1698R		
GROUP 4 ODDS 1:2719H, 1:2707R		
GROUP 5 ODDS 1:4542H, 1:4559R		
GROUP 6 ODDS 1:3385H, 1:3456R		
GROUP 7 ODDS 1:451 HOB/RET		
GROUP 8 ODDS 1:451 HOB/RET		
GROUP 9 ODDS 1:693 HOB/RET		
GROUP 10 ODDS 1:225 HOB/RET		
OVERALL ODDS: 1:84 HOB/RET		
LSAT Anthony Thomas 8	8.00	20.00
LSDA Dan Alexander 7	6.00	15.00
LSDB Drew Brees 7	50.00	100.00
LSDC Daunte Culpepper 2	6.00	15.00
LSDM Deuce McAllister 1	10.00	25.00
LSDT David Terrell 3	6.00	15.00
LSEG Eddie George 3	8.00	20.00
LSEJ Edgerrin James 1	10.00	25.00
LSJB Josh Booty 10	6.00	15.00
LSJH Joe Horn 7	6.00	15.00
LSJP Jesse Palmer 10	6.00	15.00
LSKB Kevan Barlow 9	6.00	15.00
LSKW Kenyatta Walker 10	5.00	12.00
LSLT LaDainian Tomlinson 7	40.00	80.00
LSMA Mike Anderson 7	6.00	15.00
LSMF Marshall Faulk 3	15.00	30.00
LSMH Marvin Harrison 6	15.00	30.00
LSMV Michael Vick 4	60.00	120.00
LSQM Quincy Morgan 8	6.00	15.00
LSRW Reggie Wayne 3	25.00	50.00
LSSD Stephen Davis 4	6.00	15.00
LSTH Travis Henry 7	6.00	15.00
LSTO Terrell Owens 5	15.00	40.00

2001 Stadium Club Pro Bowl Jerseys

OVERALL STATED ODDS 1:44 HOB/RET		
SPBM Brock Marion	5.00	12.00
SPCB Champ Bailey	8.00	20.00
SPCC Cris Carter	8.00	20.00
SPDA Donnie Abraham	5.00	12.00
SPDC Daunte Culpepper	6.00	15.00
SPDH Desmond Howard	6.00	15.00
SPEGE Eddie George	8.00	20.00
SPEJ Edgerrin James	8.00	20.00
SPHD Hugh Douglas	5.00	12.00
SPJA Jessie Armstead	5.00	12.00
SPJC Jeff Christy	5.00	12.00
SPJK Jevon Kearse	6.00	15.00
SPJO Jonathan Ogden	6.00	15.00
SPJS Jimmy Smith	6.00	15.00
SPJT Jeremiah Trotter	5.00	12.00
SPKM Keith Mitchell	5.00	12.00
SPLA Larry Allen	6.00	15.00
SPLE Luther Elliss	5.00	12.00
SPLG La'Roi Glover	5.00	12.00
SPMC Marco Coleman	5.00	12.00
SPMG Martin Gramatica	5.00	12.00
SPMH Marvin Harrison	8.00	20.00
SPRA Richie Anderson	5.00	12.00
SPRB Ruben Brown	5.00	12.00
SPRG Robert Griffith	5.00	12.00
SPRS Rod Smith	6.00	15.00
SPRW Rod Woodson	8.00	20.00
SPSA Stephen Alexander	5.00	12.00
SPTA Trace Armstrong	5.00	12.00
SPTG Tony Gonzalez	8.00	20.00
SPTO Terrell Owens	8.00	20.00
SPTV Troy Vincent	6.00	15.00
SPWS Warren Sapp	6.00	15.00

2001 Stadium Club Pro Bowl Jerseys Autographs

RANDOM INSERTS IN HTA PACKS		
SPADC Daunte Culpepper	12.00	30.00
SPAEJ Edgerrin James	15.00	40.00
SPAMH Marvin Harrison	15.00	40.00

2001 Stadium Club Stepping Up

COMPLETE SET (15)	12.50	25.00
STATED ODDS 1:8 HOB/RET, 1:6 HTA		
SU1 David Terrell	.40	1.00
SU2 LaDainian Tomlinson	1.50	4.00
SU3 Michael Vick	2.00	5.00
SU4 Koren Robinson	.40	1.00
SU5 Michael Bennett	.40	1.00
SU6 Chad Johnson	.75	2.00
SU7 Drew Brees	3.00	8.00
SU8 Reggie Wayne	1.00	2.50
SU9 Freddie Mitchell	.30	.75
SU10 Chris Weinke	.40	1.00
SU11 Rod Gardner	.40	1.00
SU12 Chris Chambers	.50	1.25
SU13 Deuce McAllister	.50	1.25
SU14 Santana Moss	.60	1.50
SU15 Robert Ferguson	.50	1.25

2002 Stadium Club

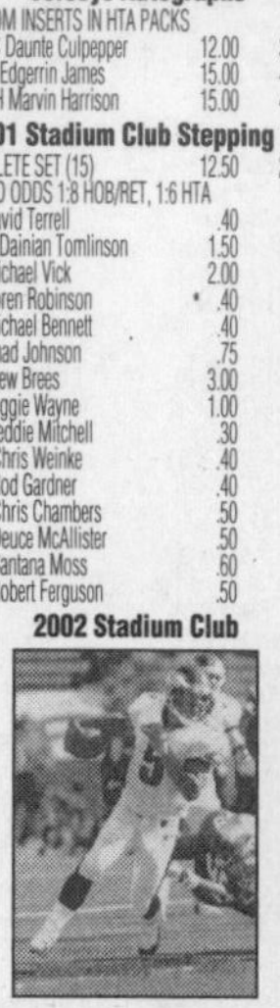

This 200-card base set includes 125 veterans and 75 rookies. The rookies were inserted at a rate of 1:4. Boxes contained 24 packs of six cards. HTA jumbo packs contained 15 cards. Hobby pack SRP was $2.99 and HTA jumbo pack SRP was $5.99.

COMPLETE SET (200)	40.00	80.00
COMP.SET w/o SP's (125)	10.00	25.00
126-200 ROOKIE STATED ODDS 1:4		
1 Randy Moss	.25	.60
2 Kordell Stewart	.20	.50
3 Marvin Harrison	.25	.60
4 Chris Weinke	.15	.40
5 James Allen	.15	.40
6 Michael Pittman	.20	.50
7 Quincy Carter	.15	.40
8 Mike Anderson	.20	.50
9 Mike McMahon	.15	.40
10 Chris Chambers	.20	.50
11 Laveranues Coles	.20	.50
12 Curtis Conway	.20	.50
13 Brad Johnson	.20	.50
14 Shaun Alexander	.20	.50
15 Jerry Rice	.50	1.25
16 Rod Gardner	.15	.40
17 Derrick Mason	.20	.50
18 Tom Brady	.60	1.50
19 Jimmy Smith	.20	.50
20 Tim Couch	.15	.40
21 Jim Miller	.15	.40
22 Eric Moulds	.20	.50
23 Michael Vick	.40	1.00
24 Jon Kitna	.20	.50
25 Johnnie Morton	.20	.50
26 Priest Holmes	.25	.60
27 Aaron Brooks	.20	.50
28 Duce Staley	.20	.50
29 LaDainian Tomlinson	.30	.75
30 Lamar Smith	.20	.50
31 Rod Smith	.20	.50
32 Richard Huntley	.15	.40
33 Antonio Freeman	.25	.60
34 Amani Toomer	.20	.50
35 Hines Ward	.25	.60
36 Marshall Faulk	.25	.60
37 Steve McNair	.25	.60
38 Tim Brown	.25	.60
39 Curtis Martin	.25	.60
40 Kevin Johnson	.15	.40
41 Rob Johnson	.20	.50
42 Qadry Ismail	.20	.50
43 Daunte Culpepper	.20	.50
44 Willie Jackson	.15	.40
45 Jeff Garcia	.20	.50
46 Matt Hasselbeck	.25	.60
47 Corey Bradford	.15	.40
48 Snoop Minnis	.15	.40
49 Ron Dayne	.20	.50
50 Peyton Manning	.50	1.25
51 Drew Bledsoe	.25	.60
52 Terry Glenn	.20	.50
53 Warrick Dunn	.20	.50
54 Mark Brunell	.20	.50
55 James Stewart	.15	.40
56 Muhsin Muhammad	.20	.50
57 Jake Plummer	.20	.50

58 Terance Mathis .15 .40
59 Rocket Ismail .20 .50
60 Joe Horn .20 .50
61 Wayne Chrebet .20 .50
62 James Thrash .20 .50
63 Stephen Davis .20 .50
64 Isaac Bruce .25 .60
65 Peter Warrick .20 .50
66 Anthony Thomas .20 .50
67 Maurice Smith .15 .40
68 Tony Gonzalez .25 .60
69 Michael Bennett .20 .50
70 Ike Hilliard .20 .50
71 Plaxico Burress .20 .50
72 Darrell Jackson .20 .50
73 Kevan Barlow .15 .40
74 Ray Lewis .25 .60
75 Emmitt Smith .60 1.50
76 Bill Schroeder .15 .40
77 Az-Zahir Hakim .15 .40
78 Troy Brown .20 .50
79 Keyshawn Johnson .20 .50
80 Tim Dwight .15 .40
81 Peerless Price .15 .40
82 Marty Booker .20 .50
83 Terrell Davis .25 .60
84 Dominic Rhodes .20 .50
85 Jay Fiedler .20 .50
86 Rich Gannon .20 .50
87 Terrell Owens .25 .60
88 Donald Hayes .15 .40
89 Thomas Jones .25 .60
90 Ricky Williams .20 .50
91 Donovan McNabb .25 .60
92 Eddie George .20 .50
93 Germane Crowell .15 .40
94 David Terrell .15 .40
95 Alex Van Pelt .15 .40
96 Antowain Smith .20 .50
97 Jerome Bettis .25 .60
98 Mike Alstott .20 .50
99 Doug Flutie .25 .60
100 Kurt Warner .25 .60
101 Cris Carter .25 .60
102 Oronde Gadsden .15 .40
103 Ahman Green .20 .50
104 Corey Dillon .20 .50
105 Marcus Robinson .20 .50
106 Shannon Sharpe .25 .60
107 Kerry Collins .20 .50
108 Garrison Hearst .20 .50
109 David Boston .15 .40
110 Travis Henry .15 .40
111 James Jackson .15 .40
112 Fred Taylor .20 .50
113 Edgerrin James .20 .50
114 Vinny Testaverde .20 .50
115 Todd Pinkston .15 .40
116 Koren Robinson .15 .40
117 Torry Holt .25 .60
118 Brian Griese .20 .50
119 Trent Green .20 .50
120 James McKnight .15 .40
121 Charlie Garner .20 .50
122 Tiki Barber .25 .60
123 Joey Galloway .20 .50
124 Quincy Morgan .15 .40
125 Brett Favre .60 1.50
126 Joey Harrington RC 1.00 2.50
127 Ashley Lelie RC .75 2.00
128 Terry Charles RC .60 1.50
129 Charles Grant RC 1.00 2.50
130 Levar Fisher RC .60 1.50
131 Larry Tripplett RC .60 1.50
132 Quentin Jammer RC 1.00 2.50
133 Ron Johnson RC .75 2.00
134 Maurice Morris RC .75 2.00
135 Roy Williams RC 1.00 2.50
136 Kurt Kittner RC .60 1.50
137 Dennis Johnson RC .60 1.50
138 Seth Burford RC .60 1.50
139 Michael Lewis RC 1.00 2.50
140 William Green RC .75 2.00
141 Rohan Davey RC 1.00 2.50
142 Rocky Calmus RC .75 2.00
143 Robert Thomas RC .60 1.50
144 Travis Stephens RC .60 1.50
145 Ladell Betts RC 1.00 2.50
146 Daniel Graham RC .75 2.00
147 Chester Taylor RC 1.00 2.50
148 Tim Carter RC .75 2.00
149 Lito Sheppard RC 1.00 2.50
150 David Carr RC 1.00 2.50
151 Alex Brown RC 1.00 2.50
152 John Henderson RC .75 2.00
153 Jamar Martin RC .75 2.00
154 Raonall Smith RC .60 1.50
155 Leonard Henry RC .60 1.50
156 T.J. Duckett RC 1.00 2.50
157 Patrick Ramsey RC 1.00 2.50
158 Antwaan Randle El RC 1.00 2.50
159 Luke Staley RC .60 1.50
160 Jon McGraw RC .60 1.50
161 Phillip Buchanon RC 1.00 2.50
162 Dwight Freeney RC 1.25 3.00
163 Mike Rumph RC .60 1.50
164 Albert Haynesworth RC 1.00 2.50
165 Antonio Bryant RC 1.00 2.50
166 Josh Reed RC .75 2.00
167 Eric Crouch RC 1.00 2.50
168 Reche Caldwell RC 1.00 2.50
169 Adrian Peterson RC 1.00 2.50
170 Jonathan Wells RC 1.00 2.50
171 Wendell Bryant RC .60 1.50
172 Tellis Redmon RC .60 1.50
173 Josh McCown RC 1.00 2.50
174 DeShaun Foster RC 1.00 2.50
175 Cliff Russell RC .60 1.50
176 David Garrard RC 1.25 3.00
177 Brian Westbrook RC 1.50 4.00
178 Anthony Weaver RC .60 1.50
179 Bryan Thomas RC .60 1.50
180 Kalimba Edwards RC .75 2.00
181 Javon Walker RC 1.00 2.50
182 Marquise Walker RC .60 1.50
183 Deion Branch RC 1.00 2.50
184 Lamar Gordon RC .75 2.00
185 Jeremy Shockey RC 1.50 4.00
186 Clinton Portis RC 1.25 3.00
187 Napoleon Harris RC .75 2.00
188 Freddie Milons RC .60 1.50
189 Julius Peppers RC 2.00 5.00
190 Andre Davis RC .75 2.00
191 Travis Fisher RC .75 2.00
192 Chad Hutchinson RC .60 1.50
193 Najeh Davenport RC 1.00 2.50
194 Ed Reed RC 4.00 10.00
195 Donte Stallworth RC 1.00 2.50
196 Brandon Doman RC .60 1.50
197 Zak Kustok RC .60 1.50
198 Randy Fasani RC .75 2.00
199 J.T. O'Sullivan RC .75 2.00
200 Jabar Gaffney RC 1.00 2.50

2002 Stadium Club Photographer's Proofs

*1-125 VETS: 6X TO 15X BASIC CARDS
*126-200 ROOKIES: 1.5X TO 4X
STATED ODDS 1:21
STATED PRINT RUN 199 SER.#'d SETS

2002 Stadium Club Super Bowl Predictor Red

*1-125 RED VETS: 20X TO 50X BASIC CARDS
*126-200 RED ROOKIES: 5X TO 12X BASIC RC
ANNOUNCED PRINT RUN 29 SETS

2002 Stadium Club Co-Signers

STATED ODDS 1:640
CSCH David Carr 25.00 60.00
  Joey Harrington
CSFW Brett Favre 125.00 250.00
  Kurt Warner
CSGF Willie Green 15.00 40.00
  DeShaun Foster
CSOB Terrell Owens 40.00 80.00
  David Boston
CSWB Kurt Warner 150.00 250.00
  Tom Brady

2002 Stadium Club Fabric of Champions

FABRIC/1499 STATED ODDS 1:87
STATED PRINT RUN 1499 SER.#'d SETS
*GOLD/25: 1X TO 2.5X BASIC JSY
GOLD/25 STATED ODDS 1:1581
GOLD PRINT RUN 25 SER.#'d SETS
FCAF Antonio Freeman 4.00 10.00
FCJK Jevon Kearse 3.00 8.00
FCPH Priest Holmes 4.00 10.00
FCRL Ray Lewis 4.00 10.00
FCRS Rod Smith 3.00 8.00
FCSY Steve Young 6.00 15.00
FCTD Terrell Davis 5.00 12.00
FCWD Warrick Dunn 3.00 8.00

2002 Stadium Club Highlight Material

STATED ODDS 1:31
*GOLD/25: 1X TO 2.5X BASIC JSY
GOLD/25 STATED ODDS 1:702
GOLD STATED PRINT RUN 25 SER.#'d SETS
HMAG Ahman Green 3.00 8.00
HMBU Brian Urlacher 4.00 10.00
HMDB David Boston 2.50 6.00
HMGH Garrison Hearst 3.00 8.00
HMHD Hugh Douglas 2.50 6.00
HMJA Jessie Armstead 2.50 6.00
HMJG Jeff Garcia 3.00 8.00
HMJR John Randle 3.00 8.00
HMJS Junior Seau 4.00 10.00
HMKS Kordell Stewart 3.00 8.00
HMKW Kurt Warner 4.00 10.00
HMMA Mike Alstott 3.00 8.00
HMMH Marvin Harrison 4.00 10.00
HMMS Michael Strahan 4.00 10.00
HMRG Rich Gannon 3.00 8.00
HMSS Steve Smith 4.00 10.00
HMTB Tim Brown 4.00 10.00
HMTO Terrell Owens 4.00 10.00

2002 Stadium Club Lone Star Signatures

OVERALL STATED ODDS 1:92
LSAP Adrian Peterson 8.00 20.00
LSAS Antowain Smith 6.00 15.00
LSBF Brett Favre 100.00 175.00
LSCC Chris Chambers 6.00 15.00
LSDB David Boston
LSDC David Carr 8.00 20.00
LSDF DeShaun Foster 8.00 20.00
LSJA John Abraham 6.00 15.00
LSJH Joey Harrington 8.00 20.00
LSJR Josh Reed 6.00 15.00
LSJT James Thrash 6.00 15.00
LSKK Kurt Kittner 5.00 12.00
LSKW Kurt Warner 25.00 60.00
LSMB Marty Booker 6.00 15.00
LSMP Mike Pearson 5.00 12.00
LSRW Roy Williams 8.00 20.00
LSTB Tom Brady 200.00 350.00
LSTO Terrell Owens 20.00 40.00
LSWG William Green 6.00 15.00

2002 Stadium Club Reel Time

COMPLETE SET (25) 25.00 60.00
STATED ODDS 1:12
RT1 Marshall Faulk 1.25 3.00
RT2 Peyton Manning 2.50 6.00
RT3 Randy Moss 1.25 3.00
RT4 Stephen Davis 1.00 2.50
RT5 Jeff Garcia 1.00 2.50
RT6 Donovan McNabb 1.25 3.00
RT7 Edgerrin James 1.00 2.50
RT8 Trent Green 1.00 2.50
RT9 Eddie George 1.00 2.50
RT10 Ahman Green 1.00 2.50
RT11 Plaxico Burress 1.00 2.50
RT12 David Boston .75 2.00
RT13 Tom Brady 3.00 8.00
RT14 Marvin Harrison 1.25 3.00
RT15 Brett Favre 3.00 8.00
RT16 Ricky Williams 1.00 2.50
RT17 Kordell Stewart 1.00 2.50
RT18 Curtis Martin 1.25 3.00
RT19 Anthony Thomas 1.00 2.50
RT20 Shaun Alexander 1.00 2.50
RT21 LaDainian Tomlinson 1.50 4.00
RT22 Kurt Warner 1.25 3.00
RT23 Jerome Bettis 1.25 3.00
RT24 Priest Holmes 1.25 3.00
RT25 Terrell Owens 1.25 3.00

2002 Stadium Club Touchdown Treasures

PYLON/75 STATED ODDS 1:516
STATED PRINT RUN 75 SER.#'d SETS
*GOLD/25: .6X TO 1.5X BASIC PYLON
GOLD/25 STATED ODDS 1:2067
GOLD PRINT RUN 25 SER.#'d SETS
TTDP David Patten 6.00 15.00
TTKW Kurt Warner 12.00 30.00
TTRP Ricky Proehl 8.00 20.00
TTTB Tom Brady 40.00 80.00
TTTL Ty Law 8.00 20.00

2008 Stadium Club

COMP.SET w/o RC's (100) 25.00 50.00
ROOKIE/1799 ODDS 1:2 HOB, 1:7 RET
UNPRICED 1-100 PRINT PLATE/1 ODDS 1:232 H
UNPRICED 101-200 PRNT PLTE/1 ODDS 1:777 H
1 Drew Brees .50 1.25
2 Tom Brady .75 2.00
3 Peyton Manning .75 2.00
4 Carson Palmer .50 1.25
5 Ben Roethlisberger .50 1.25
6 Eli Manning .50 1.25
7 Tony Romo .60 1.50
8 Tarvaris Jackson .40 1.00
9 Vince Young .40 1.00
10 Steven Jackson .50 1.25
11 Willie Parker .40 1.00
12 Clinton Portis .40 1.00
13 Adrian Peterson .75 2.00
14 LaDainian Tomlinson .50 1.25
15 Marion Barber .40 1.00
16 Brian Westbrook .40 1.00
17 Fred Taylor .40 1.00
18 Marshawn Lynch .40 1.00
19 Joseph Addai .40 1.00
20 Willis McGahee .40 1.00
21 Frank Gore .40 1.00
22 Reggie Wayne .40 1.00
23 Anquan Boldin .40 1.00
24 Randy Moss .50 1.25
25 Plaxico Burress .40 1.00
26 Terrell Owens .50 1.25
27 Andre Johnson .40 1.00
28 Larry Fitzgerald .50 1.25
29 Braylon Edwards .40 1.00
30 Steve Smith .40 1.00
31 Jon Kitna .40 1.00
32 Matt Hasselbeck .40 1.00
33 Derek Anderson .30 .75
34 Jay Cutler .50 1.25
35 Kurt Warner .50 1.25
36 Donovan McNabb .50 1.25
37 Philip Rivers .50 1.25
38 Jason Campbell .40 1.00
39 David Garrard .40 1.00
40 Jeff Garcia .40 1.00
41 Marc Bulger .40 1.00
42 Jamal Lewis .40 1.00
43 Edgerrin James .40 1.00
44 Thomas Jones .40 1.00
45 Lendale White .40 1.00
46 Justin Fargas .30 .75
47 Brandon Jacobs .40 1.00
48 Ryan Grant .50 1.25
49 Earnest Graham .30 .75
50 Chad Johnson .40 1.00
51 Brandon Marshall .40 1.00
52 Roddy White .40 1.00
53 Marques Colston .40 1.00
54 Torry Holt .40 1.00
55 Wes Welker .50 1.25
56 Bobby Engram .30 .75
57 T.J. Houshmandzadeh .40 1.00
58 Jerricho Cotchery .40 1.00
59 Kevin Curtis .30 .75
60 Derrick Mason .40 1.00
61 Donald Driver .40 1.00
62 Jason Witten .50 1.25
63 Tony Gonzalez .40 1.00
64 Kellen Winslow .40 1.00
65 Antonio Gates .50 1.25
66 Chris Cooley .40 1.00
67 Matt Schaub .40 1.00
68 Laurence Maroney .40 1.00
69 Joey Galloway .40 1.00
70 Jeremy Shockey .40 1.00
71 Dwayne Bowe .40 1.00
72 Dallas Clark .40 1.00
73 Maurice Jones-Drew .40 1.00
74 Ray Lewis .50 1.25
75 Michael Strahan .40 1.00
76 Derrick Brooks .40 1.00
77 Ed Reed .40 1.00
78 Brian Urlacher .50 1.25
79 Jason Taylor .40 1.00
80 Bob Sanders .40 1.00
81 Patrick Kerney .30 .75
82 Albert Haynesworth .30 .75
83 Antonio Cromartie .30 .75
84 Mike Vrabel .30 .75
85 DeMarcus Ware .40 1.00
86 Ronde Barber .30 .75
87 James Harrison RC 3.00 8.00
88 Patrick Willis .40 1.00
89 Mario Williams .40 1.00
90 Osi Umenyiora .40 1.00
91 Damon Huard .30 .75
92 Joey Harrington .30 .75
93 Roy Williams WR .40 1.00
94 Champ Bailey .40 1.00
95 Shawne Merriman .40 1.00
96 Chester Taylor .30 .75
97 Ron Dayne .30 .75
98 Santonio Holmes .40 1.00
99 Lee Evans .40 1.00
100 Chris Chambers .40 1.00
101 Matt Ryan RC 6.00 15.00
102 Brian Brohm RC 1.50 4.00
103 Chad Henne RC 1.50 4.00
104 Joe Flacco RC 5.00 12.00
105 Andre Woodson RC 1.50 4.00
106 John David Booty RC 1.25 3.00
107 Josh Johnson RC 1.50 4.00
108 Colt Brennan RC 1.50 4.00
109 Dennis Dixon RC 1.50 4.00
110 Erik Ainge RC 1.50 4.00
111 Darren McFadden RC 4.00 10.00
112 Rashard Mendenhall RC 3.00 8.00
113 Jonathan Stewart RC 2.50 6.00
114 Felix Jones RC 2.50 6.00
115 Jamaal Charles RC 2.50 6.00
116 Ray Rice RC 3.00 8.00
117 Chris Johnson RC 4.00 10.00
118 Mike Hart RC 1.50 4.00
119 Matt Forte RC 2.50 6.00
120 Kevin Smith RC 1.50 4.00
121 Steve Slaton RC 1.50 4.00
122 Malcolm Kelly RC 1.25 3.00
123 Limas Sweed RC 1.50 4.00
124 DeSean Jackson RC 3.00 8.00
125 James Hardy RC 1.25 3.00
126 Mario Manningham RC 1.50 4.00
127 Devin Thomas RC 1.25 3.00
128 Early Doucet RC 1.25 3.00
129 Andre Caldwell RC 1.25 3.00
130 Jordy Nelson RC 2.00 5.00
131 Eddie Royal RC 1.50 4.00
132 Earl Bennett RC 1.50 4.00
133 Fred Davis RC 1.50 4.00
134 Dustin Keller RC 1.50 4.00
135 John Carlson RC 1.50 4.00
136 Chris Long RC 1.50 4.00
137 Jake Long RC 1.50 4.00
138 Glenn Dorsey RC 1.50 4.00
139 Sedrick Ellis RC 1.50 4.00
140 Vernon Gholston RC 1.25 3.00
141 Kevin O'Connell RC 1.50 4.00
142 Leodis McKelvin RC 1.25 3.00
143 Keith Rivers RC 1.50 4.00
144 Mike Jenkins RC 1.50 4.00
145 Derrick Harvey RC 1.00 2.50
146 Phillip Merling RC 1.25 3.00
147 Kentwan Balmer RC 1.25 3.00
148 Dan Connor RC 1.50 4.00
149 Dominique Rodgers-Cromartie RC 1.50 4.00
150 Aqib Talib RC 1.50 4.00
151 Sam Baker RC 1.25 3.00
152 Adrian Arrington RC 1.25 3.00
153 Donnie Avery RC 1.25 3.00
154 Marcus Henry RC 1.50 4.00
155 Dexter Jackson RC 1.25 3.00
156 Jerome Simpson RC 1.50 4.00
157 Keenan Burton RC 1.00 2.50
158 Tashard Choice RC 1.25 3.00
159 Harry Douglas RC 1.25 3.00
160 Marcus Griffin RC 1.00 2.50
161 DJ Hall RC 1.25 3.00
162 Justin Forsett RC 1.50 4.00
163 Jaymar Johnson RC 2.50 6.00
164 Jacob Hester RC 1.50 4.00
165 Ali Highsmith RC 1.00 2.50
166 Sam Keller RC 1.25 3.00
167 Lance Leggett RC 1.50 4.00
168 Xavier Omon RC 1.50 4.00
169 Marcus Monk RC 1.25 3.00
170 Anthony Morelli RC 1.25 3.00
171 Marcus Smith RC 1.25 3.00
172 Allen Patrick RC 1.25 3.00
173 Kenny Phillips RC 1.50 4.00
174 Tyrell Johnson RC 1.50 4.00
175 Matt Flynn RC 3.00 8.00
176 Martin Rucker RC 1.25 3.00
177 Jordon Dizon RC 1.50 4.00
178 Owen Schmitt RC 1.50 4.00
179 Martellus Bennett RC 1.50 4.00
180 Terrence Wheatley RC 1.50 4.00
181 Terrell Thomas RC 1.25 3.00
182 Kyle Wright RC 1.25 3.00
183 Darius Reynaud RC 1.00 2.50
184 Chris Williams RC 1.25 3.00
185 Jeff Otah RC 1.25 3.00
186 Xavier Adibi RC 1.00 2.50
187 Jerod Mayo RC 1.50 4.00
188 Calais Campbell RC 1.25 3.00
189 Charles Godfrey RC 1.50 4.00
190 Reggie Smith RC 1.25 3.00
191 Pat Sims RC 1.25 3.00
192 Curtis Lofton RC 1.25 3.00
193 Tracy Porter RC 1.50 4.00
194 Patrick Lee RC 1.25 3.00
195 Cliff Avril RC 1.25 3.00
196 Trevor Laws RC 1.50 4.00
197 Lawrence Jackson RC 1.25 3.00
198 Antoine Cason RC 1.50 4.00
199 Chevis Jackson RC 1.25 3.00
200 Justin King RC 1.25 3.00

2008 Stadium Club First Day Issue

*VETS 1-100: 1X TO 2.5X BASIC CARDS
FIRST DAY/1499 ODDS 1:2 H, 1:7 R

2008 Stadium Club Photographer's Proofs Gold

*VETS 1-100: 3X TO 8X BASIC CARDS
*ROOKIES 101-200: .8X TO 2X BASIC CARDS
1-100 PP GOLD/50 ODDS 1:32H, 1:195R
101-200 PP GOLD/50 ODDS 1:32H, 1:335R

2008 Stadium Club Photographer's Proofs Platinum

UNPRICED PLATINUM 1/1 ODDS 1:940 HOB

2008 Stadium Club Photographer's Proofs Silver

*VETS 1-100: 2X TO 5X BASIC CARDS
*ROOKIES 101-200: .5X TO 1.2X BASIC CARDS
1-100 PP SLVR/199 ODDS 1:9H, 1:43R
101-200 PP SLVR/199 ODDS 1:9H, 1:75R

2008 Stadium Club Beam Team Autographs

GROUP A ODDS 1:452 H, 1:30,870 R
GROUP B ODDS 1:100 H, 1:6200 R
*GOLD/25: .5X TO 1.2X BASIC AUTO
GOLD/25 ODDS 1:141 H, 1:8500 R
UNPRICED PLATINUM/1 ODDS 1:3300 HOB
BTAAG Anthony Gonzalez A 10.00 25.00
BTAAK Aaron Kampman A 40.00 80.00
BTAAW Andre Woodson B 10.00 25.00
BTABB Bernard Berrian A 10.00 25.00
BTABBR Brian Brohm B 10.00 25.00
BTABE Braylon Edwards A 10.00 25.00
BTACB Colt Brennan B 12.00 30.00
BTACH Chad Henne B 20.00 50.00
BTACL Chris Long B 6.00 15.00
BTADJ DeSean Jackson B 12.00 30.00
BTADM Darren McFadden B 25.00 60.00
BTAEM Eli Manning A 40.00 80.00
BTAFJ Felix Jones B 25.00 60.00
BTAGD Glenn Dorsey B 10.00 25.00
BTAJA Joseph Addai A 12.00 30.00
BTAJC Jamaal Charles B 8.00 20.00
BTAJF Joe Flacco B 50.00 100.00
BTAJH James Hardy B 10.00 25.00
BTAJS Jonathan Stewart B 20.00 50.00
BTAKW Kellen Winslow A 12.00 30.00
BTALS Limas Sweed B 6.00 15.00
BTAMH Mike Hart B 10.00 25.00
BTAMK Malcolm Kelly B 10.00 25.00
BTAMR Matt Ryan B 60.00 120.00
BTARM Rashard Mendenhall B 15.00 40.00
BTARR Ray Rice B 12.00 30.00
BTARW Reggie Wayne A 10.00 25.00
BTASS Steve Slaton B 10.00 25.00
BTAVY Vince Young A 15.00 40.00

2008 Stadium Club Beam Team Jerseys

JERSEY/99 ODDS 1:52 H, 1:503 R
*RETAIL: .3X TO .8X HOBBY/99
ONE SILVER PER SPECIAL RETAIL BOX
BTRAP Adrian Peterson 10.00 25.00
BTRBB Brian Brohm 2.00 5.00
BTRBR Ben Roethlisberger 6.00 15.00
BTRBU Brian Urlacher 6.00 15.00
BTRBW Brian Westbrook 5.00 12.00
BTRCH Chad Henne 2.00 5.00
BTRCL Chris Long 2.00 5.00
BTRDA Donnie Avery 5.00 12.00
BTRDM Darren McFadden 5.00 12.00
BTREM Eli Manning 6.00 15.00
BTRFJ Felix Jones 3.00 8.00
BTRFT Fred Taylor 5.00 12.00
BTRGD Glenn Dorsey 2.00 5.00
BTRJB John David Booty 1.50 4.00
BTRJL Jake Long 2.00 5.00
BTRJS Jonathan Stewart 3.00 8.00
BTRKO Kevin O'Connell 1.50 4.00
BTRLT LaDainian Tomlinson 6.00 15.00
BTRMB Marion Barber 5.00 12.00
BTRMK Malcolm Kelly 1.50 4.00
BTRMR Matt Ryan 8.00 20.00
BTRMS Michael Strahan 5.00 12.00
BTRPM Peyton Manning 10.00 25.00
BTRPR Philip Rivers 6.00 15.00
BTRRM Rashard Mendenhall 4.00 10.00
BTRTR Tony Romo 10.00 25.00

2008 Stadium Club Impact Relics

GROUP A/549 ODDS 1:39H, 1:375R
GROUP B/1349 ODDS 1:3H, 1:30R
*GOLD/50: .6X TO 1.5X BASIC JSY/1349
*GOLD/50: .6X TO 1.5X BASIC JSY/549
GOLD/50 ODDS 1:52 HOB, 1:505 RET
IRAC Andre Caldwell 2.00 5.00
IRAH Al Harris/1399 4.00 10.00
IRAS Asante Samuel 2.50 6.00
IRBB Brian Brohm 2.50 6.00
IRCH Chad Henne 5.00 12.00
IRCIJ Chad Johnson 3.00 8.00
IRCJ Chris Johnson 6.00 15.00
IRCP Carson Palmer/549 4.00 10.00
IRDJ DeSean Jackson 5.00 12.00
IRDM Darren McFadden 6.00 15.00
IRDR DeMeco Ryans 3.00 8.00
IRED Early Doucet 2.00 5.00
IRER Ed Reed 3.00 8.00
IRFJ Felix Jones 4.00 10.00
IRHD Harry Douglas 2.50 6.00
IRGE Greg Ellis 2.50 6.00
IRJB John David Booty 2.00 5.00
IRJC Jamaal Charles 4.00 10.00
IRJF Joe Flacco 8.00 20.00
IRJG Jeff Garcia 3.00 8.00
IRJH James Hardy 2.00 5.00
IRJL John Lynch 3.00 8.00
IRJLO Jake Long 2.50 6.00
IRJN Jerious Norwood/549 2.50 6.00
IRJR JaMarcus Russell/549 3.00 8.00
IRJS Jonathan Stewart 4.00 10.00
IRKO Kevin O'Connell 2.00 5.00
IRKS Kevin Smith 3.00 8.00
IRKW Kevin Williams 2.50 6.00
IRKWI Kellen Winslow 3.00 8.00
IRLN Lorenzo Neal 2.50 6.00
IRLS Limas Sweed 2.50 6.00
IRLT Lofa Tatupu/1399 3.00 8.00
IRLW LenDale White/549 3.00 8.00
IRMF Matt Forte 4.00 10.00
IRMK Malcolm Kelly 3.00 8.00
IRML Marshawn Lynch/549 3.00 8.00
IRMM Mario Manningham 3.00 8.00
IRMR Matt Ryan 6.00 15.00
IRMT Marcus Trufant 2.50 6.00
IRRL Ray Lewis 4.00 10.00
IRRM Rashard Mendenhall 4.00 10.00
IRRR Ray Rice 2.50 6.00
IRRW Roy Williams S 3.00 8.00
IRSA Shaun Alexander 3.00 8.00
IRSS Steve Slaton 2.50 6.00
IRTO Terrell Owens/549 4.00 10.00
IRVY Vince Young 3.00 8.00
IRWD Warrick Dunn 3.00 8.00

2008 Stadium Club Impact Relics Dual

DUAL/50 ODDS 1:52 HOB, 1:505 RET
UNPRICED GOLD/10 ODDS 1:280 HOB
DRBA Ronnie Brown 5.00 12.00
  Joseph Addai
DRBB Champ Bailey 5.00 12.00
  Ronde Barber
DRBD Brian Brohm 3.00 8.00
  Harry Douglas
DRBDO Dwayne Bowe 2.50 6.00
  Early Doucet
DRBM Reggie Bush 3.00 8.00
  Deuce McAllister
DRBME Marion Barber 6.00 15.00
  Rashard Mendenhall
DRBP Ladell Betts 5.00 12.00
  Clinton Portis
DRCB Brodie Croyle 5.00 12.00
  Dwayne Bowe
DRCD Jamaal Charles 5.00 12.00
  Glenn Dorsey
DRCS Andre Caldwell 4.00 10.00
  Jerome Simpson
DRCSW Jamaal Charles 5.00 12.00
  Limas Sweed
DRGD David Garrard 5.00 12.00
  Maurice Jones-Drew
DRHA Matt Hasselbeck 5.00 12.00
  Shaun Alexander
DRHF Chad Henne 6.00 15.00
  Joe Flacco
DRHM Chad Henne 6.00 15.00
  Mario Manningham
DRHE Chad Henne 6.00 15.00
  Braylon Edwards
DRHW A.J. Hawk 5.00 12.00
  Patrick Willis
DRJD DeSean Jackson 6.00 15.00
  Early Doucet
DRJF Andre Johnson 6.00 15.00
  Larry Fitzgerald
DRJL DeSean Jackson 6.00 15.00
  Marshawn Lynch
DRJJ Rudi Johnson 5.00 12.00
  Chad Johnson
DRJJA Steven Jackson 6.00 15.00
  Brandon Jacobs
DRJS Chris Johnson 8.00 20.00
  Kevin Smith
DRJW Brandon Jackson 5.00 12.00
  DeShawn Wynn
DRJWA Thomas Jones 5.00 12.00
  Leon Washington
DRLB Matt Leinart 6.00 15.00
  John David Booty
DRLF J.P. Losman 5.00 12.00
  Matt Forte
DRLH Jake Long 3.00 8.00
  Chad Henne
DRMJ Darren McFadden 8.00 20.00
  Felix Jones
DRMM Eli Manning 12.00 30.00
  Peyton Manning
DRMS Rashard Mendenhall 6.00 15.00
  Jonathan Stewart
DROK Greg Olsen 4.00 10.00
  Dustin Keller
DRPE Roscoe Parrish 3.00 8.00
  Lee Evans
DRPM Adrian Peterson 8.00 20.00
  Darren McFadden
DRPW Troy Polamalu 8.00 20.00
  Roy Williams S
DRRB Matt Ryan 8.00 20.00
  Brian Brohm
DRRJ Ray Rice 6.00 15.00
  Felix Jones
DRRM Matt Ryan 12.00 30.00
  Darren McFadden
DRRQ JaMarcus Russell 5.00 12.00
  Brady Quinn
DRRS Aaron Rodgers 5.00 12.00
  Alex Smith QB
DRSR Steve Slaton 6.00 15.00
  Ray Rice
DRTM Devin Thomas 3.00 8.00
  Mario Manningham
DRTP LaDainian Tomlinson 10.00 25.00
  Adrian Peterson
DRWO Mario Williams 5.00 12.00
  Amobi Okoye
DRWS DeAngelo Williams 2.50 6.00
  Jonathan Stewart
DRHWA Santonio Holmes 8.00 20.00
  Hines Ward

2008 Stadium Club Impact Relics Triple

TRIPLE/50 ODDS 1:52 HOB, 1:505 RET
UNPRICED GOLD/10 ODDS 1:280 HOB
TRBHF Brian Brohm 6.00 15.00
  Chad Henne
  Joe Flacco
TRBMJ Brian Brohm 6.00 15.00
  Rashard Mendenhall
  DeSean Jackson
TRBMM Tom Brady 12.00 30.00
  Lawrence Maroney
  Randy Moss
TRBSS John David Booty 6.00 15.00
  Jonathan Stewart
  Limas Sweed
TRBST Plaxico Burress 6.00 15.00
  Steve Smith USC
  Amani Toomer
TRCCC Kellen Clemens 5.00 12.00
  Laveranues Coles
  Jerricho Cotchery
TRCSJ Jamaal Charles 6.00 15.00
  Jonathan Stewart
  Steven Jackson
TRDAW Glenn Dorsey 5.00 12.00
  Gaines Adams
  Mario Williams
TRDPW Brian Dawkins 8.00 20.00
  Troy Polamalu
  Roy Williams S
TREPE Trent Edwards 6.00 15.00
  Roscoe Parrish
  Lee Evans
TRFBB Larry Fitzgerald 5.00 12.00
  Anquan Boldin
  Steve Breaston
TRFHB Joe Flacco 6.00 15.00
  Chad Henne
  Brian Brohm
TRFME Larry Fitzgerald 8.00 20.00
  Randy Moss
  Braylon Edwards
TRHAT Matt Hasselbeck 5.00 12.00
  Shaun Alexander
  Marcus Trufant
TRHFB Chad Henne 6.00 15.00
  Joe Flacco
  John David Booty
TRHJH Chad Henne 8.00 20.00
  Felix Jones
  James Hardy
TRHLM Chad Henne 6.00 15.00
  Jake Long
  Mario Manningham
TRHMD James Hardy 5.00 12.00
  Mario Manningham
  Early Doucet
TRHWT David Harris 5.00 12.00
  Patrick Willis
  Lawrence Timmons
TRJCR Felix Jones 10.00 25.00
  Jamaal Charles
  Ray Rice
TRJGG Calvin Johnson 6.00 15.00
  Ted Ginn Jr.
  Anthony Gonzalez
TRJPR Tarvaris Jackson 12.00 30.00
  Adrian Peterson
  Sidney Rice
TRJRJ Felix Jones 10.00 25.00
  Ray Rice
  Chris Johnson
TRJSF Chris Johnson 8.00 20.00
  Kevin Smith
  Matt Forte
TRKBC Malcolm Kelly 5.00 12.00
  Mark Bradley
  Mark Clayton
TRKJH Malcolm Kelly 5.00 12.00
  Calvin Johnson
  Santonio Holmes
TRKJS Malcolm Kelly 6.00 15.00
  DeSean Jackson
  Limas Sweed
TRKOD Dustin Keller 5.00 12.00
  Greg Olsen
  Vernon Davis
TRKTJ Malcolm Kelly 6.00 15.00
  Devin Thomas
  DeSean Jackson
TRLTF Jake Long 5.00 12.00
  Joe Thomas
  D'Brickashaw Ferguson
TRLUB Ray Lewis 6.00 15.00
  Brian Urlacher
  Derrick Brooks
TRMBM Eli Manning 15.00 40.00
  Tom Brady
  Peyton Manning
TRMMS Rashard Mendenhall 12.00 30.00
  Darren McFadden
  Jonathan Stewart
TRMRR Eli Manning 8.00 20.00
  Philip Rivers
  Ben Roethlisberger
TRMWB Donovan McNabb 6.00 15.00
  Brian Westbrook
  Reggie Brown
TRPBM Clinton Portis 5.00 12.00
  Ladell Betts
  Santana Moss
TRPJH Carson Palmer 6.00 15.00
  Chad Johnson
  T.J. Houshmandzadeh
TRPLB Carson Palmer 8.00 20.00
  Matt Leinart
  John David Booty
TRPPM Clinton Portis 6.00 15.00
  Willie Parker
  Laurence Maroney
TRRBH Matt Ryan 12.00 30.00
  Brian Brohm
  Chad Henne
TRRBO Tony Romo 12.00 30.00
  Marion Barber
  Terrell Owens
TRRDA JaMarcus Russell 6.00 15.00
  Early Doucet
  Joseph Addai
TRRJJ Aaron Rodgers 12.00 30.00
  James Jones
  Greg Jennings
TRRLD Matt Ryan 10.00 25.00
  Jake Long
  Glenn Dorsey
TRRMK Matt Ryan 12.00 30.00
  Darren McFadden
  Malcolm Kelly
TRRPW Ben Roethlisberger 10.00 25.00
  Willie Parker
  Hines Ward
TRRRY Matt Ryan 10.00 25.00
  JaMarcus Russell
  Vince Young
TRSGG Jeremy Shockey 5.00 12.00
  Antonio Gates
  Tony Gonzalez
TRTPJ Chester Taylor 12.00 30.00
  Adrian Peterson
  Tarvaris Jackson
TRWSD DeAngelo Williams 5.00 12.00
  Steve Smith
  Jake Delhomme

2008 Stadium Club Rookie Autographs

T10 GROUP A ODDS 1:190 H, 1:36,000 R
T10 GROUP B ODDS 1:35 H, 1:6600 R
T10 GROUP C ODDS 1:18 H, 1:4500 R
GROUP A ODDS 1:66 H, 1:4000 R
GROUP B ODDS 1:40 H, 1:2375 R
GROUP C ODDS 1:14 H, 1:790 R
GROUP D ODDS 1:10 H, 1:197 R
GROUP E ODDS 1:9 H, 1:495 R
UNPRICED PLATINUM/1 ODDS 1:1625
UNPRICED T10 PLATINUM/1 ODDS 1:8868
UNPRICED PRINT PLATE PRINT RUN 1
101 Matt Ryan T10 A 40.00 100.00
102 Brian Brohm A 6.00 15.00
103 Chad Henne B 12.00 30.00
104 Joe Flacco A 30.00 60.00
105 Andre Woodson B 4.00 10.00
106 John David Booty D 4.00 10.00
107 Josh Johnson D 5.00 12.00
108 Colt Brennan A 10.00 25.00
109 Dennis Dixon B 8.00 20.00
110 Erik Ainge C 5.00 12.00
111 Darren McFadden T10 A 25.00 50.00
112 Rashard Mendenhall A 12.00 30.00
113 Jonathan Stewart A 12.00 30.00
114 Felix Jones B 12.00 30.00
115 Jamaal Charles C 10.00 25.00
116 Ray Rice B 12.00 30.00
117 Chris Johnson E 20.00 50.00
118 Mike Hart C 5.00 12.00
119 Matt Forte E 12.00 30.00
120 Kevin Smith E 5.00 12.00
121 Steve Slaton C 5.00 12.00
122 Malcolm Kelly C 4.00 10.00
123 Limas Sweed B 5.00 12.00
124 DeSean Jackson C 10.00 25.00
125 James Hardy C 4.00 10.00
126 Mario Manningham D 6.00 15.00
127 Devin Thomas C 6.00 15.00
128 Early Doucet C 4.00 10.00
129 Andre Caldwell E 4.00 10.00
130 Jordy Nelson C 12.50 25.00
131 Eddie Royal D 5.00 12.00
132 Earl Bennett D 5.00 12.00
133 Fred Davis D 5.00 12.00
134 Dustin Keller C 4.00 10.00
135 John Carlson D 5.00 12.00
136 Chris Long T10 B 6.00 15.00
137 Jake Long T10 B 6.00 15.00
138 Glenn Dorsey T10 B 5.00 12.00
139 Sedrick Ellis T10 C 5.00 12.00
140 Vernon Gholston T10 C 4.00 10.00
141 Kevin O'Connell C 4.00 10.00
143 Keith Rivers T10 C 5.00 12.00
145 Derrick Harvey T10 C 3.00 8.00

149 Dominique Rodgers-Cromartie D 5.00 12.00
151 Sam Baker E 3.00 8.00
152 Adrian Arrington E 4.00 10.00
153 Donnie Avery C 4.00 10.00
154 Marcus Henry E 4.00 10.00
155 Dexter Jackson C 4.00 10.00
156 Jerome Simpson C 5.00 12.00
157 Keenan Burton D 3.00 8.00
158 Tashard Choice D 4.00 10.00
159 Harry Douglas D 4.00 10.00
160 Marcus Griffin D 3.00 8.00
161 DJ Hall D 4.00 10.00
162 Justin Forsett D 5.00 12.00
164 Jacob Hester D 5.00 12.00
167 Lance Leggett E 5.00 12.00
168 Xavier Omon E 5.00 12.00
169 Marcus Monk E 4.00 10.00
170 Anthony Morelli E 4.00 10.00
171 Marcus Smith E 4.00 10.00
172 Allen Patrick E 4.00 10.00
173 Kenny Phillips D 5.00 12.00
175 Matt Flynn D 20.00 40.00
176 Martin Rucker D 4.00 10.00
178 Owen Schmitt E 5.00 12.00
182 Kyle Wright E 4.00 10.00
183 Darius Reynaud D 3.00 8.00
187 Jerod Mayo T10 C 6.00 15.00

2008 Stadium Club Rookie Autographs Gold

*GOLD/25: .8X TO 2X BASIC AUTO
GOLD/25 T10 ODDS 1:397H, 1:45,000R
GOLD/25 ODDS 1:69H, 1:4050R
101 Matt Ryan 50.00 120.00
104 Joe Flacco 40.00 100.00
111 Darren McFadden 30.00 80.00
112 Rashard Mendenhall 25.00 60.00
114 Felix Jones 30.00 80.00
117 Chris Johnson 40.00 100.00

2008 Stadium Club Rookie Autographs Silver Holofoil

*SILVER/50: .6X TO 1.5X BASIC AUTO
SLVR/50 T10 ODDS 1:191H, 1:75,000R
SLVR/50 ODDS 1:34H, 1:1950R
101 Matt Ryan 40.00 100.00
104 Joe Flacco 30.00 80.00
111 Darren McFadden 25.00 60.00
112 Rashard Mendenhall 20.00 50.00
114 Felix Jones 25.00 60.00
117 Chris Johnson 30.00 80.00

2008 Stadium Club Super Teams

STATED ODDS 1:58 HOB
WIN CARDS GOOD FOR ROOKIE SET
1 Buffalo Bills 3.00 8.00
2 Miami Dolphins 3.00 8.00
3 New England Patriots 5.00 12.00
Jabar Gaffney
Randy Moss
4 New York Jets 3.00 8.00
5 Baltimore Ravens WIN 10.00 25.00
6 Cincinnati Bengals 2.50 6.00
7 Cleveland Browns 2.50 6.00
Braylon Edwards
8 Pittsburgh Steelers 25.00 50.00
Ben Roethlisberger
9 Houston Texans 2.50 6.00
10 Indianapolis Colts 6.00 15.00
Peyton Manning
11 Jacksonville Jaguars 3.00 8.00
12 Tennessee Titans 3.00 8.00
Vince Young
LenDale White
13 Denver Broncos 3.00 8.00
14 Kansas City Chiefs 2.50 6.00
15 Oakland Raiders 3.00 8.00
16 San Diego Chargers 4.00 10.00
LaDainian Tomlinson
17 Dallas Cowboys 6.00 15.00
Tony Romo
18 New York Giants 4.00 10.00
Eli Manning
19 Philadelphia Eagles WIN 10.00 25.00
20 Washington Redskins 3.00 8.00
21 Chicago Bears 3.00 8.00
Rex Grosman
22 Detroit Lions 2.50 6.00
23 Green Bay Packers 4.00 10.00
24 Minnesota Vikings 3.00 8.00
25 Atlanta Falcons 3.00 8.00
26 Carolina Panthers 3.00 8.00
27 New Orleans Saints 3.00 8.00
Drew Brees
28 Tampa Bay Buccaneers 2.50 6.00
29 Arizona Cardinals WIN 10.00 25.00
30 San Francisco 49ers 2.50 6.00
31 Seattle Seahawks 3.00 8.00
Matt Hasselbeck
32 St. Louis Rams 2.50 6.00

1991 Stadium Club Charter Member

This 50-card multi-sport standard-size set was sent to charter members in the Topps Stadium Club. The sports represented in the set are baseball (1-32), football (33-41), and hockey (42-50). The cards feature on the fronts full-bleed posed and action glossy color player photos. The player's name is shown in the light blue stripe that intersects the Stadium Club logo near the bottom of the picture. The words "Charter Member" are printed in gold foil lettering immediately below the stripe. The back design features a newspaper-like masthead (The Stadium Club Herald) complete with a headline announcing a major event in the player's season with copy below providing more information about the event. The cards are unnumbered and arranged below alphabetically within sports. Topps apparently made two printings of this set, which are most easily identifiable by the small asterisks on the bottom left of the card backs. The first printing cards have one asterisk, the second printing cards have two. The display box that contained the cards also included a Nolan Ryan bronze metallic card and a key chain. Very early members of the Stadium Club received a large size bronze metallic Nolan Ryan 1990 Topps card. It is valued below as well as the normal size Ryan metallic card. A third varation on the Ryan medallion has been found. This is another version of the 1991 Stadium Club charter member bronze medallion, except this one has a 24K logo on it. It is suspected that this might be a Home Shopping Newtork variety. No pricing is provided at this time for this piece due to lack of market information.

COMP.FACT SET (50) 6.00 15.00
33 Ottis Anderson .07 .20
MVP of Super Bowl XXV
34 Ottis Anderson .07 .20
Reaches 10,000
35 Randall Cunningham .10 .30
36 Warren Moon .20 .50
37 Barry Sanders 1.00 2.50
38 Pete Stoyanovich .07 .20
39 Lawrence Taylor .20 .50
40 Derrick Thomas .20 .50
41 Richmond Webb .07 .20

1999 Stadium Club Chrome

Released as a 150-card set, the 1999 Stadium Club Chrome set parallels the earlier issue 1999 Stadium Club set in chrome version with updated rookie photography and traded information. The set was packaged in 24-pack boxes containing five cards each and carried a suggested retail price of $4.00.

COMPLETE SET (150) 25.00 60.00
1 Dan Marino 1.25 3.00
2 Andre Reed .40 1.00
3 Michael Westbrook .25 .60
4 Isaac Bruce .40 1.00
5 Curtis Martin .40 1.00
6 Terrell Owens .40 1.00
7 Warrick Dunn .30 .75
8 Jake Plummer .30 .75
9 Chad Brown .25 .60
10 Yancey Thigpen .25 .60
11 Keenan McCardell .30 .75
12 Shannon Sharpe .40 1.00
13 Cameron Cleeland .25 .60
14 Mark Brunell .30 .75
15 Jamal Anderson .30 .75
16 Germane Crowell .25 .60
17 Rod Smith .30 .75
18 Cris Carter .40 1.00
19 Terrell Davis .40 1.00
20 Tim Biakabutuka .30 .75
21 Jermaine Lewis .25 .60
22 Adrian Murrell .30 .75
23 Doug Flutie .40 1.00
24 Curtis Enis .25 .60
25 Skip Hicks .25 .60
26 Steve McNair .40 1.00
27 Charles Woodson .40 1.00
28 Freddie Jones .25 .60
29 Warren Sapp .30 .75
30 Emmitt Smith 1.00 2.50
31 Reidel Anthony .25 .60
32 Tony Simmons .25 .60
33 Andre Hastings .25 .60
34 Byron Bam Morris .25 .60
35 Jimmy Smith .30 .75
36 Antonio Freeman .30 .75
37 Herman Moore .30 .75
38 Muhsin Muhammad .30 .75
39 Chris Chandler .30 .75
40 John Elway 1.25 3.00
41 Bobby Engram .30 .75
42 Keith Poole .25 .60
43 Mike Alstott .40 1.00
44 Junior Seau .40 1.00
45 Thurman Thomas .40 1.00
46 Troy Aikman .60 1.50
47 Wesley Walls .30 .75
48 Robert Smith .30 .75
49 Elvis Grbac .25 .60
50 Ben Coates .30 .75
51 Bert Emanuel .30 .75
52 Jacquez Green .25 .60
53 Barry Sanders 1.00 2.50
54 James Jett .25 .60
55 Gary Brown .25 .60
56 Stephen Alexander .25 .60
57 Wayne Chrebet .30 .75
58 Drew Bledsoe .40 1.00
59 Jake Reed .30 .75
60 Marvin Harrison .40 1.00
61 Johnnie Morton .30 .75
62 Brett Favre 1.25 3.00
63 Charlie Batch .30 .75
64 Antowain Smith .25 .60
65 Ernie Mills .25 .60
66 Jeff Blake .30 .75
67 Curtis Conway .30 .75
68 Bruce Smith .40 1.00
69 Peyton Manning 1.25 3.00
70 Tim Dwight .30 .75
71 O.J. McDuffie .30 .75
72 Jon Kitna .30 .75
73 Trent Dilfer .30 .75
74 Jerome Bettis .40 1.00
75 Dedric Ward .25 .60
76 Fred Taylor .30 .75
77 Ike Hilliard .30 .75
78 Frank Wycheck .30 .75
79 Eric Moulds .30 .75
80 Rob Moore .25 .60
81 Ed McCaffrey .30 .75
82 Carl Pickens .30 .75
83 Priest Holmes .40 1.00
84 Terry Glenn .30 .75
85 Keyshawn Johnson .30 .75
86 Karim Abdul-Jabbar .30 .75
87 Ahman Green .30 .75
88 Duce Staley .30 .75
89 Vinny Testaverde .30 .75
90 Napoleon Kaufman .25 .60
91 Frank Sanders .25 .60
92 Steve Young .50 1.25
93 Darnay Scott .25 .60
94 Deion Sanders .40 1.00
95 Corey Dillon .30 .75
96 Randall Cunningham .40 1.00
97 Eddie George .30 .75
98 Derrick Alexander .25 .60
99 Mark Chmura .25 .60
100 Rickey Dudley .25 .60
101 Joey Galloway .30 .75
102 Ricky Proehl .25 .60
103 Natrone Means .30 .75
104 Dorsey Levens .30 .75
105 Andre Rison .30 .75
106 John Randle .30 .75
107 Terance Mathis .25 .60
108 Rae Carruth .25 .60
109 Jerry Rice .75 2.00
110 Michael Irvin .40 1.00
111 Oronde Gadsden .25 .60
112 Jerome Pathon .25 .60
113 Ricky Watters .30 .75
114 J.J. Stokes .25 .60
115 Kordell Stewart .30 .75
116 Tim Brown .40 1.00
117 Tony Gonzalez .40 1.00
118 Randy Moss .40 1.00
119 Daunte Culpepper RC .60 1.50
120 Amos Zereoue RC .50 1.25
121 Champ Bailey RC 1.25 3.00
122 Peerless Price RC .50 1.25
123 Edgerrin James RC .75 2.00
124 Joe Germaine RC .50 1.25
125 David Boston RC .50 1.25
126 Kevin Faulk RC .60 1.50
127 Troy Edwards RC .50 1.25
128 Akili Smith RC .50 1.25
129 Kevin Johnson RC .50 1.25
130 Rob Konrad RC .40 1.00
131 Shaun King RC .50 1.25
132 James Johnson RC .40 1.00
133 Donovan McNabb RC 2.50 6.00
134 Torry Holt RC 1.00 2.50
135 Mike Cloud RC .40 1.00
136 Sedrick Irvin RC .40 1.00
137 Cade McNown RC .50 1.25
138 Ricky Williams RC 1.00 2.50
139 Karsten Bailey RC .40 1.00
140 Cecil Collins RC .40 1.00
141 Brock Huard RC .50 1.25
142 D'Wayne Bates RC .40 1.00
143 Tim Couch RC .60 1.50
144 Rocket Ismail .30 .75
145 Marshall Faulk .40 1.00
146 Trent Green .30 .75
147 Tony Martin .30 .75
148 Jim Harbaugh .30 .75
149 Rich Gannon .30 .75
150 Brad Johnson .30 .75

1999 Stadium Club Chrome First Day

*STARS: 8X TO 20X BASIC CARDS
*RCs: 3X TO 8X
STATED ODDS 1:59
STATED PRINT RUN 100 SER.#'d SETS

1999 Stadium Club Chrome First Day Refractors

*STARS: 15X TO 40X BASIC CARDS
*ROOKIES: 5X TO 12X
STATED ODDS 1:235
STATED PRINT RUN 25 SER.#'d SETS

1999 Stadium Club Chrome Refractors

COMPLETE SET (150) 150.00 300.00
*STARS: 2.5X TO 6X BASIC CARDS
*RCs: .8X TO 2X
STATED ODDS 1:12

1999 Stadium Club Chrome Clear Shots

COMPLETE SET (9) 15.00 40.00
STATED ODDS 1:22
*REFRACTORS: 1X TO 2.5X BASIC INSERTS
REFRACTOR STATED ODDS 1:110
1 David Boston 1.50 4.00
2 Edgerrin James 5.00 12.00
3 Chris Claiborne 1.25 3.00
4 Torry Holt 3.00 8.00
5 Tim Couch 1.50 4.00
6 Donovan McNabb 6.00 15.00
7 Akili Smith 1.25 3.00
8 Champ Bailey 2.00 5.00
9 Troy Edwards 1.25 3.00

1999 Stadium Club Chrome Eyes of the Game

COMPLETE SET (7) 20.00 50.00
STATED ODDS 1:20
*REFRACTORS: 1X TO 2.5X BASIC INSERTS
REFRACTOR STATED ODDS 1:100
20 Tim Couch 1.00 2.50
21 Ricky Williams 1.50 4.00
22 Barry Sanders 6.00 15.00
23 Brett Favre 6.00 15.00
24 Terrell Davis 2.00 5.00
25 Peyton Manning 6.00 15.00
26 Randy Moss 5.00 12.00

1999 Stadium Club Chrome Never Compromise

COMPLETE SET (40) 75.00 150.00
STATED ODDS 1:6
*REFRACTORS: 1X TO 2.5X BASIC INSERTS
REFRACTOR STATED ODDS 1:30
NC1 Tim Couch 1.00 2.50
NC2 David Boston 1.00 2.50
NC3 Daunte Culpepper 4.00 10.00
NC4 Donovan McNabb 5.00 12.00
NC5 Ricky Williams 3.00 8.00
NC6 Troy Edwards 1.00 2.50
NC7 Akili Smith 1.00 2.50
NC8 Torry Holt 2.50 6.00
NC9 Cade McNown 1.00 2.50
NC10 Edgerrin James 4.00 10.00
NC11 Cecil Collins 1.00 2.50
NC12 Peerless Price 1.00 2.50
NC13 Kevin Johnson 1.00 2.50
NC14 Champ Bailey 1.50 4.00
NC15 Kevin Faulk 1.00 2.50
NC16 D'Wayne Bates 1.00 2.50
NC17 Shaun King 1.00 2.50
NC18 Sedrick Irvin 1.00 2.50
NC19 James Johnson 1.00 2.50
NC20 Rob Konrad 1.00 2.50
NC21 Randy Moss 6.00 15.00
NC22 Peyton Manning 8.00 20.00
NC23 Eddie George 1.50 4.00
NC24 Fred Taylor 2.50 6.00
NC25 Jamal Anderson 2.50 6.00
NC26 Joey Galloway 1.50 4.00
NC27 Terrell Davis 2.50 6.00
NC28 Keyshawn Johnson 1.50 4.00
NC29 Antonio Freeman 1.50 4.00
NC30 Jake Plummer 1.50 4.00
NC31 Steve Young 3.00 8.00
NC32 Barry Sanders 8.00 20.00
NC33 Dan Marino 8.00 20.00
NC34 Emmitt Smith 5.00 12.00
NC35 Brett Favre 8.00 20.00
NC36 Randall Cunningham 2.50 6.00
NC37 John Elway 8.00 20.00
NC38 Drew Bledsoe 3.00 8.00
NC39 Jerry Rice 5.00 12.00
NC40 Troy Aikman 5.00 12.00

1999 Stadium Club Chrome True Colors

COMPLETE SET (10) 25.00 60.00
STATED ODDS 1:24
*REFRACTORS: 1X TO 2.5X BASIC INSERTS
REFRACTOR STATED ODDS 1:120
10 Doug Flutie 1.50 4.00
11 Steve Young 2.00 5.00
12 Jake Plummer 1.00 2.50
13 Jerry Rice 3.00 8.00
14 Randy Moss 4.00 10.00
15 Fred Taylor 1.50 4.00
16 Peyton Manning 5.00 12.00
17 Dan Marino 5.00 12.00
18 Brett Favre 5.00 12.00
19 Emmitt Smith 3.00 8.00

1991 Stadium Club Members Only

This 50-card multi-sport standard-size set was sent in three installments to members in the Topps Stadium Club. The first and second installments featured baseball players (card numbers 1-10 and 11-30), while the third spotlighted football (31-37) and hockey (38-50) players. The cards feature on the fronts full-bleed posed and action glossy color player photos. The player's name is shown in the light blue stripe that intersects the Stadium Club logo near the bottom of the picture. The words "Members Only" are printed in gold foil lettering immediately below the stripe. The back design features a newspaper-like masthead (The Stadium Club Herald) complete with a headline announcing a major event in the player's season with copy below providing more information about the event. The cards are unnumbered and arranged below alphabetically according to and within installments.

COMPLETE SET (50) 6.00 15.00
31 Art Monk .08 .25
32 Warren Moon .15 .40
33 Leonard Russell .07 .20
34 Mark Rypien .07 .20
35 Barry Sanders 1.00 2.50
36 Emmitt Smith 1.00 2.50
37 Tony Zendejas .07 .20

1992 Stadium Club Members Only

This 50-card standard-size set was sent to 1992 Stadium Club members in four installments. In addition to the Stadium Club cards, the first installment included one "Top Draft Picks of the '90s" card (as a bonus) and a randomly chosen "Master Photo" printed on 5" by 7" white card stock. The third and fourth installments included hockey and football players in addition to baseball players. The cards feature full-bleed glossy color player photos. The fronts of the regular cards have the words "Members Only" printed in gold foil at the bottom along with the player's name and the Stadium Club logo. The backs feature a stadium scene with the scoreboard displaying, in yellow neon, a career highlight. The cards are unnumbered and checklisted below alphabetically, with the two-player cards listed at the end.

COMPLETE SET (50) 12.00 30.00
37 Troy Aikman .50 1.25
38 Dale Carter .07 .20
39 Art Monk .07 .20
40 Frank Reich .07 .20
41 Emmitt Smith .75 2.00
42 Steve Young .40 1.00

1993 Stadium Club Members Only

This 59-card standard-size set was mailed out to Stadium Club Members in four separate mailings. Each box contained several sports. The fronts have full-bleed color action player photos with the words "Members Only" printed in gold foil at the bottom along with the player's name and the Stadium Club logo. On a multi-colored background, the horizontal backs carry player information and a computer generated drawing of a baseball player. The cards are unnumbered and checklisted below alphabetically according to sport as follows: baseball (1-28), basketball (29-44), football (45-53), and hockey (54-59).

COMPLETE SET (59) 10.00 20.00
45 Morten Andersen .07 .20
46 Jerome Bettis .30 .75
47 Steve Christie .07 .20
48 Jim Kelly .15 .40
49 Dan Marino 1.00 2.50
50 Sterling Sharpe .08 .25
51 Emmitt Smith .75 2.00
52 Dana Stubblefield .08 .25
53 Steve Young .40 1.00

1984 Stallions Team Sheets

This set was issued in one series totalling 6-different sheets of the USFL Birmingham Stallions. Each sheet includes black and white photos of eight or nine players and measure 8" by 10" with a white border.

COMPLETE SET (6) 10.00 25.00
1 Greg Anderson 2.00 5.00
Buddy Aydelette
Tom Banks
Mark Battaglia
Dario Casarino
Billy Cesare
Jackie Cline
Reggie Collier
2 Lester Dickey 2.00 5.00
Ron Frederick
Earl Gant
Charles GrandJean
Mike Hatchett
Dallas Hickman
Mike Hirn
Tim James
3 Johnny Dirden 2.00 5.00
Mark Goodspeed
Lonnie Johnson
Sylvester Moy
Cornelius Quarles
Herbie Spencer
Mike Turner
Brett Williams
Melvin Williams
4 Michael Kincaid 2.00 5.00
Bob Lane
Reggie Lewis
Charles Martin
Darryl Mason
Carl McGee
Larry McPherson
Kevin Miller
5 Mike Murphy 2.00 5.00
Scott Norwood
Pat Phenix
Mike Raines
Wendell Ray
Frank Reed
Pat Saindon
John Skibinski
6 Steve Stephens 2.00 5.00
Ken Talton
Michael Thomas
Emmuel Thompson
Charlie Trotman
Jimmy Walker
Billy White
Robert Woods

1963 Stancraft Playing Cards

This 54-card set, subtitled "Official NFL All-Time Greats," commemorates outstanding NFL players and was issued in conjunction with the opening of the Pro Football Hall of Fame in Canton, Ohio. It should be noted that several of the players in the set are not in the Pro Football Hall of Fame. The back of the cards was produced two different ways. One style has a checkerboard pattern, with the NFL logo in the middle and logos for the 14 NFL teams surrounding it against a red background; the other style has the 14 NFL team helmets floating on a green background. The set was issued in a plastic box which fit into a cardboard outer slip-case box. Apart from the aces and two jokers (featuring the NFL logo), the fronts of the other cards have a skillfully drawn picture (in brown ink) of the player, with his name, position, year(s), and team below the drawing. The set was also reportedly made in a pinochle format. We have checklisted this set in playing card order by suits and assigned numbers to Aces (1), Jacks (11), Queens (12), and Kings (13). Each card measures approximately 2 1/4" by 3 1/2" with rounded corners.

COMP. FACT SET (54) 125.00 250.00
*GREEN BACKS: SAME PRICE
1C NFL Logo 1.50 3.00
1D NFL Logo 1.50 3.00
1H NFL Logo 1.50 3.00
1S NFL Logo 1.50 3.00
2C Johnny Blood McNally 2.00 4.00
2D Frankie Albert 1.50 3.00
2H Paul Hornung 5.00 10.00
2S Eddie LeBaron 2.00 4.00
3C Bobby Mitchell 3.00 6.00
3D Del Shofner 1.50 3.00
3H Johnny Unitas 7.50 15.00
3S Don Hutson 3.00 6.00
4C Billy Howton 1.50 3.00
4D Ollie Matson 3.00 6.00
4H Doak Walker 3.00 6.00
4S Clarke Hinkle 2.00 4.00
5C Fats Henry 2.00 4.00
5D Mike Ditka 6.00 12.00
5H Tom Fears 3.00 6.00
5S Charley Conerly 3.00 6.00
6C Tony Canadeo 2.50 5.00
6D Otto Graham 5.00 10.00
6H Jim Thorpe 7.50 15.00
6S Earl(Curly) Lambeau 1.50 3.00
7C Bulldog Turner 3.00 6.00
7D Chuck Bednarik 4.00 8.00
7H Gino Marchetti 3.00 6.00
7S Sid Luckman 4.00 8.00
8C Charley Trippi 3.00 6.00
8D Jim Taylor 4.00 8.00
8H Buddy Young 1.50 3.00
8S Pete Pihos 2.50 5.00
9C Tommy Mason 1.50 3.00
9D Mel Hein 2.00 4.00
9H Jim Benton 1.50 3.00
9S Dante Lavelli 3.00 6.00
10C Dutch Clark 2.50 5.00
10D Eddie Price 1.50 3.00
10H Jim Brown 10.00 20.00
10S Norm Van Brocklin 4.00 8.00
11C Y.A. Tittle 4.00 8.00
11D Sonny Randle 1.50 3.00
11H George Halas 5.00 10.00
11S Clyde Box 1.50 3.00
12C Lou Groza 3.00 6.00
12D Joe Perry 3.00 6.00
12H Sammy Baugh 5.00 10.00
12S Joe Schmidt 3.00 6.00
13C Bobby Layne 4.00 8.00
13D Bob Waterfield 4.00 8.00
13H Bill Dudley 2.50 5.00
13S Elroy Hirsch 3.00 6.00
NNO Joker (NFL Logo) 1.50 3.00
NNO Joker (NFL Logo) 1.50 3.00

1989 Star-Cal Decals

These decals were licensed by the NFL and NFL Players' Association. The first series features players from six NFL teams. The decals measure approximately 3" by 4 1/2" with rounded corners and a full-color action photo of the player. In the upper left corner, a silver logo with the words "First Edition 1989" distinguishes this series from future releases. As a bonus, each decal comes with a pennant-shaped miniature team banner decal in the player's team colors, with the team helmet and nickname on the banner. The decals are unnumbered and checklisted below alphabetically by player.

COMPLETE SET (54) 50.00 100.00
1 Raul Allegre .75 2.00
2 Carl Banks 1.25 3.00
3 Cornelius Bennett 1.25 3.00
4 Brian Blades 1.00 2.50
5 Kevin Butler .75 2.00
6 Harry Carson 1.25 3.00
7 Anthony Carter 1.25 3.00
8 Michael Carter .75 2.00
9 Shane Conlan .75 2.00
10 Roger Craig 1.50 4.00
11 Richard Dent 1.50 4.00
12 Chris Doleman 1.00 2.50
13 Tony Dorsett 2.50 6.00
14 Dave Duerson .75 2.00
15 Charles Haley 1.25 3.00
16 Dan Hampton 1.25 3.00
17 Al Harris .75 2.00
18 Mark Jackson 1.00 2.50
19 Vance Johnson 1.00 2.50
20 Steve Jordan 1.00 2.50
21 Clarence Kay .75 2.00
22 Jim Kelly 4.00 10.00
23 Tommy Kramer 1.25 3.00
24 Ronnie Lott 1.50 4.00
25 Lionel Manuel 1.00 2.50
26 Guy McIntyre .75 2.00
27 Steve McMichael 1.00 2.50
28 Karl Mecklenburg 1.25 3.00
29 Orson Mobley .75 2.00
30 Joe Montana 10.00 25.00
31 Joe Morris .75 2.00
32 Joe Nash .75 2.00
33 Ricky Nattiel .75 2.00
34 Chuck Nelson .75 2.00
35 Darrin Nelson .75 2.00
36 Karl Nelson .75 2.00
37 Scott Norwood .75 2.00
38 Bart Oates .75 2.00
39 Rufus Porter .75 2.00
40 Andre Reed 2.00 5.00
41 Phil Simms 1.50 4.00
42 Mike Singletary 1.50 4.00
43 Fred Smerlas .75 2.00
44 Bruce Smith 2.50 6.00
45 Kelly Stouffer .75 2.00
46 Scott Studwell .75 2.00
47 Matt Suhey .75 2.00
48 Steve Tasker 1.25 3.00
49 Keena Turner .75 2.00
50 John L. Williams 1.00 2.50
51 Wade Wilson 1.00 2.50
52 Sammy Winder .75 2.00
53 Tony Woods .75 2.00
54 Eric Wright 1.00 2.50

1990 Star-Cal Decals Prototypes

These prototype cards are unnumbered and are checklisted alphabetically. They were issued to promote the 1990 Star-Cal Decal set in their second year of issue.

COMPLETE SET (4) 2.00 5.00
1 Jeff Hostetler .30 .75
2 Mike Kenn .30 .75
3 Freeman McNeil .30 .75
4 Steve Young 1.20 3.00

1990 Star-Cal Decals

The 1990 Star-Cal decal set features six players from 12 of the most popular NFL teams and 36 NFL stars (most also represented in the team sets). The player decals measure approximately 3" by 4 1/2" and have on the fronts full-bleed color action player photos with rounded corners and a facsimile autograph. The player's name is printed on the lower left corner of the decal. The backs have instructions for applying the decals. Each player decal was issued with a pennant-shaped miniature team banner (3 1/2" by 2"), which displayed the team's helmet and name in the team's colors. The player decals are unnumbered and checklisted below according to player's name. The set is also known as the Grid-Star decal set. A few player decals (e.g., Steve Young) are known to exist in a variation with a serial number on their fronts. Also some decals vary slightly in autograph placement and the printing of his name in black or white at the lower left corner. Complete set price includes all variations.

COMPLETE SET (94) 75.00 150.00
1 Eric Allen .60 1.50
2A Marcus Allen 2.00 5.00
printed name in black letters
2B Marcus Allen 2.00 5.00
printed name in white letters
3 Flipper Anderson .60 1.50
4A Neal Anderson .60 1.50
printed name in black letters
4B Neal Anderson .60 1.50
printed name in white letters
5A Carl Banks .60 1.50
printed name in black letters
5B Carl Banks .60 1.50
printed name in white letters
6 Mark Bavaro .60 1.50
7 Cornelius Bennett .75 2.00
8 Brian Blades .60 1.50
9 Joey Browner .50 1.25
10 Keith Byars .60 1.50
11A Anthony Carter .60 1.50
printed name in black letters
11B Anthony Carter .60 1.50
printed name in white letters
12 Cris Carter 2.50 6.00
13 Michael Carter .50 1.25
14 Gary Clark .75 2.00
15 Mark Collins .50 1.25
16 Shane Conlan .50 1.25
17 Jim Covert .60 1.50
18A Roger Craig 1.00 2.50
printed name black letters
18B Roger Craig 1.00 2.50
printed name white letters
19 Richard Dent 1.00 2.50
20 Chris Doleman .60 1.50
21 Dave Duerson .50 1.25
22 Henry Ellard .75 2.00
23A John Elway 8.00 20.00
printed name in black letters
23B John Elway 10.00 25.00
printed name in white letters
24 Jim Everett .75 2.00
25 Mervyn Fernandez .50 1.25
26 Willie Gault .60 1.50
27 Bob Golic .60 1.50
28 Darrell Green 1.00 2.50
29 Kevin Greene .60 1.50
30 Charles Haley 1.00 2.50
31 Jay Hilgenberg .60 1.50
32 Pete Holohan .50 1.25
33 Kent Hull .50 1.25
34 Bobby Humphrey .60 1.50
35A Bo Jackson 1.50 4.00
printed name in black letters
35B Bo Jackson 1.50 4.00
printed name in white letters
36 Keith Jackson .75 2.00
37 Mark Jackson .60 1.50
38 Joe Jacoby .60 1.50
39 Vance Johnson .60 1.50
40 Jim Kelly 2.50 6.00
41 Bernie Kosar 1.00 2.50
42 Greg Kragen .50 1.25
43 Jeff Lageman .50 1.25
44 Pat Leahy .50 1.25
45 Howie Long 1.50 4.00
46A Ronnie Lott 1.25 3.00
serial numbered 11419
46B Ronnie Lott 1.25 3.00
serial numbered 11414
47 Kevin Mack .50 1.25
48 Charles Mann .50 1.25
49 Leonard Marshall .60 1.50
50 Clay Matthews .75 2.00
51 Erik McMillan .50 1.25
52 Karl Mecklenburg .60 1.50
53 Dave Meggett UER .60 1.50
name misspelled Megget
54A Eric Metcalf .60 1.50
serial numbered 11414
54B Eric Metcalf .60 1.50
serial numbered 11424
55 Keith Millard .50 1.25
56 Frank Minnifield .50 1.25
57A Joe Montana 8.00 20.00
printed name in black letters
autograph covers only left leg
57B Joe Montana 10.00 25.00
printed name in black letters
autograph covers both legs
57C Joe Montana 8.00 20.00
printed name in white letters
autograph covers only left leg
58 Joe Nash .50 1.25
59 Ken O'Brien .60 1.50
60 Rufus Porter .50 1.25
61 Andre Reed 1.25 3.00
62 Mark Rypien .75 2.00
63 Gerald Riggs .60 1.50
64 Mickey Shuler .50 1.25
65 Clyde Simmons .60 1.50
66A Phil Simms 1.00 2.50
printed name in black letters
66B Phil Simms 1.00 2.50
printed name in white letters
67A Mike Singletary 1.25 3.00
67B Mike Singletary 1.25 3.00
68 Jackie Slater .60 1.50
69 Bruce Smith 1.25 3.00
70A Kelly Stouffer .50 1.25
serial numbered 11414
70B Kelly Stouffer .50 1.25
serial numbered 11427
71 John Taylor .75 2.00
72 Lawyer Tillman .50 1.25
73 Al Toon .60 1.50
74A Herschel Walker .75 2.00
printed name in black letters
74B Herschel Walker .75 2.00
printed name in white letters
75 Reggie White 2.00 5.00
76A John L. Williams .60 1.50
printed name in black letters
autograph below knees
76B John L. Williams .60 1.50
printed name in black letters
autograph above knees
76C John L. Williams .60 1.50
printed name in white letters
autograph below knees
77 Tony Woods .50 1.25
78 Gary Zimmerman .75 2.00

1988 Starline Prototypes

Issued as a prototype set for a release that never made it to market, these 4-cards carry a colored border and color player photo. Reportedly, just 300 complete sets were produced.

COMPLETE SET (4) 300.00 600.00
1 John Elway 75.00 150.00
2 Bernie Kosar 25.00 50.00
3 Joe Montana 100.00 200.00
4 Phil Simms 30.00 60.00

1928 Star Player Candy

This recently discovered set of cards is thought to have been issued by Dockman and Son's candy company since it closely resembles the 1928 Star Player Candy baseball card set. Based upon the players in the set, the year of issue is thought to be 1928 so it is possible that both the football and baseball players were packaged together. Red Grange is listed as Illinois instead of Professional so the true year of issue often comes under question. Each card is blankbacked and features a sepia colored photo of the player on the cardfront along with his name and either name of his university or the word "professional" (noted below) for those few players in the pros at the time. Each card measures roughly 2" by 3."

1 Russell Avery 150.00 300.00
2 Bullet Baker 150.00 300.00
3 Richard Black 150.00 300.00
4 E.J. Burke 150.00 300.00
5 Jack Chevigney 200.00 400.00
6 Fred Collins 200.00 400.00
7 A.C. Cornsweet 150.00 300.00
8 Jus Dart 150.00 300.00
9 Paddy Driscoll 1,200.00 2,000.00
(Professional)
10A Bruce Dumont 150.00 300.00
10B Bruce Dumont ERR 150.00 300.00
(name misspelled Dumon)
11 Fred Ellis 150.00 300.00
12 Benny Friedman 1,200.00 2,000.00
13 Gene Fritz 150.00 300.00
14 Walter Gebert 150.00 300.00
15 Louis Gilbert 150.00 300.00

16 Red Grange	1,500.00	2,500.00
17 Glen Harmeson	150.00	300.00
18 John Hazen	150.00	300.00
19 Gibson Holliday	150.00	300.00
20 Walt Holmer	150.00	300.00
21 John Karcis	150.00	300.00
22 Harry Lindblom	150.00	300.00
23 Jim McMillen UER	150.00	300.00
misspelled McMillan)		
24 Hugh Mendenhall	150.00	300.00
25 Fred Miller	150.00	300.00
26 John Murrell	150.00	300.00
27 John Niemiec	150.00	300.00
28 A.J. Nowak	150.00	300.00
29 Irvine Phillips	150.00	300.00
30 E.H. Rose	150.00	300.00
31 Stanley Rosen	150.00	300.00
32 Paul Scull	150.00	300.00
33 J.W. Slagle	150.00	300.00
34 John Smith Ford.	150.00	300.00
35 John Smith Penn.	150.00	300.00
36 Euil Snitz Snider	150.00	300.00
37 M.E. Bud Sprague	150.00	300.00
38 Joe Sternaman	600.00	1,000.00
(Professional)		
39 Eddie Tryon	250.00	500.00
40 Rube Wagner	150.00	300.00
41 Saul Weislow	150.00	300.00
42 Ralph Welch	150.00	300.00
43 George Wilson	250.00	500.00

1959 Steelers San Giorgio Flipbooks

This set features members of the Pittsburgh Steelers printed on velum type paper stock created in a multi-image action sequence. The set is commonly referenced as the San Giorgio Macaroni Football Flipbooks. Members of the Philadelphia Eagles, Pittsburgh Steelers, and Washington Redskins were produced regionally with 15-players, reportedly, issued per team. Some players were produced in more than one sequence of poses with different captions and/or slightly different photos used. When the flipbooks are still in uncut form (which is most desirable), they measure approximately 5 3/4" by 3 9/16". The sheets are blank backed, in black and white, and provide 14-small numbered pages when cut apart. Collectors were encouraged to cut out each photo and stack them in such a way as to create a moving image of the player when flipped with the fingers. Any additions to this list are appreciated.

1 Darrel Brewster	90.00	150.00
2 Jack Butler	90.00	150.00
3 Gern Nagler	90.00	150.00
4 Tom Tracy	100.00	175.00

1961 Steelers Jay Publishing

This 12-card set features (approximately) 5" by 7" black-and-white player photos. The photos show players in traditional poses with the quarterback preparing to throw, the runner heading downfield, and the defenseman ready for the tackle. These cards were packaged 12 to a packet and originally sold for 25 cents. The backs are blank. The cards are unnumbered and checklisted below in alphabetical order.

COMPLETE SET (12)	75.00	150.00
1 Preston Carpenter	5.00	10.00
2 Dean Derby	5.00	10.00
3 Duddy Dial	5.00	10.00
4 John Henry Johnson	10.00	20.00
5 Bobby Layne	15.00	30.00
6 Gene Lipscomb	6.00	12.00
7 Bill Mack	5.00	10.00
8 Fred Mautino	5.00	10.00
9 Lou Michaels	5.00	10.00
10 Buddy Parker CO	5.00	10.00
11 Myron Pottios	5.00	10.00
12 Tom Tracy	5.00	10.00

1963 Steelers IDL

This unnumbered black and white card set (featuring the Pittsburgh Steelers) is complete at 26 cards. The cards feature an identifying logo of IDL Drug Store on the front left corner of the card. The cards measure approximately 4" by 5". Cards are blank backed and unnumbered and hence are ordered alphabetically in the checklist below.

COMPLETE SET (26)	125.00	250.00
1 Frank Atkinson	6.00	12.00
2 Jim Bradshaw	6.00	12.00
3 Ed Brown	6.00	12.00
4 John Burrell	6.00	12.00
5 Preston Carpenter	6.00	12.00
6 Lou Cordileone	6.00	12.00
7 Buddy Dial	6.00	12.00
8 Bob Ferguson	6.00	12.00
9 Glenn Glass	6.00	12.00
10 Dick Haley	6.00	12.00
11 Dick Hoak	7.50	15.00
12 John Henry Johnson	10.00	25.00
13 Brady Keys	6.00	12.00
14 Joe Krupa	6.00	12.00
15 Ray Lemek	6.00	12.00
16 Bill(Red) Mack	6.00	12.00
17 Lou Michaels	6.00	12.00
18 Bill Nelsen	6.00	12.00
19 Buzz Nutter	6.00	12.00
20 Myron Pottios	6.00	12.00
21 John Reger	6.00	12.00
22 Mike Sandusky	6.00	12.00
23 Ernie Stautner	10.00	25.00
24 George Tarasovic	6.00	12.00
25 Clendon Thomas	6.00	12.00
26 Tom Tracy	7.50	15.00

1963 Steelers McCarthy Postcards

This set of the Pittsburgh Steelers features posed player photos printed on postcard-size cards. Each was produced from photos taken by photographer J.D. McCarthy and likely distributed over a number of years. The cards are unnumbered and checklisted below in alphabetical order. Any additions to the checklist below are appreciated.

COMPLETE SET (3)	15.00	30.00
1 John Henry Johnson	7.50	15.00
2 Brady Keys	4.00	8.00
3 Buzz Nutter	4.00	8.00

1964 Steelers Emenee Electric Football

These sepia toned photos were sponsored by Emenee Electric Pro Football Game and KDKA TV and radio. Each includes a large photo of a Steelers player with an advertisement for the Emenee Football Game below the photo, as well as a mail in contest offer for fans to guess Steelers game yardage totals. The backs are blank and the photos have been arranged alphabetically below.

COMPLETE SET (9)	800.00	1,400.00
1 Frank Atkinson	75.00	125.00
2 Gary Ballman	75.00	125.00
3 Ed Brown	90.00	150.00
4 Dick Hoak	75.00	125.00
5 Dan James	75.00	125.00
6 John Henry Johnson	100.00	175.00
7 Jim Kelly	75.00	125.00
8 Ray Lemek	75.00	125.00
9 Paul Martha	75.00	125.00
10 Buzz Nutter	75.00	125.00
11 Mike Sandusky	75.00	125.00

1965 Steelers Program Inserts

The Steelers issued these black and white player photos bound into game programs during the 1965-68 seasons. The 1965 version includes a large player photo along with bio information below the image on the front and another page of the program on the back.

1 Gary Ballman	3.00	8.00
2 Jim Bradshaw	3.00	8.00
3 Dan James	3.00	8.00
4 Ray Lemek	3.00	8.00

1966 Steelers Program Inserts

The Steelers issued these black and white player photos bound into home game programs during the 1965-68 seasons. The 1966 set was issued in two different styles. Version 1 follows the 1965 fomat and includes a large player photo along with bio information below the image on the front. Version two features a large player photo and bio as well as three circles intended to direct the collector to punch them out and insert the photos into a binder. Both versions have another page of the program on the back.

COMPLETE SET (12)	40.00	100.00
1 Gary Ballman 2	3.00	8.00
2 Charlie Bradshaw 1	3.00	8.00
3 John Campbell 1	3.00	8.00
4 Riley Gunnels 1	3.00	8.00
5 Chuck Hinton 1	3.00	8.00
6 Dick Hoak 2	3.00	8.00
7 Brady Keys 2	3.00	8.00
8 Ken Kortas 2	3.00	8.00
9 Ben McGee 1	3.00	8.00
10 Andy Russell 2	4.00	10.00
11 Bill Saul 1	3.00	8.00
12 Marv Woodson 2	3.00	8.00

1966 Steelers Team Issue

These photos were issued in the mid-1960s by the Pittsburgh Steelers. Each measures roughly 8" by 10", contains a black and white photo and was printed on glossy stock. The photos look nearly identical to the 1969 Team Issue set. The photo backs are blank and unnumbered.

COMPLETE SET (24)	100.00	200.00
1 Mike Clark	5.00	10.00
2 Dick Compton	5.00	10.00
3 Sam Davis G	5.00	10.00
4 Mike Haggerty	5.00	10.00
5 John Hilton	5.00	10.00
6 Chuck Hinton	5.00	10.00
7 Dick Hoak	5.00	10.00
8 Bob Hohn	5.00	10.00
9 Roy Jefferson	6.00	12.00
10 Ken Kortas	5.00	10.00
11 Ray Mansfield	5.00	10.00
12 Paul Martha	5.00	10.00
13 Ray May	5.00	10.00
14 Ben McGee	5.00	10.00
15 Bill Nelsen	6.00	12.00
16 Andy Russell	6.00	12.00
17 Bill Saul	5.00	10.00
18 Don Shy	5.00	10.00
19 Clendon Thomas	5.00	10.00
20 Bruce Van Dyke	5.00	10.00
21 Lloyd Voss	5.00	10.00
22 J.R. Wilburn	5.00	10.00
23 Marv Woodson	5.00	10.00
24 Coaching Staff	5.00	10.00
Bill Austin		
Don Heinrich		
Leon McLaughlin		
Hugh Taylor		
Tom Fletcher		
Torgy Torgeson		

1967 Steelers Program Inserts

The Steelers issued these black and white player photos bound into home game programs during the 1965-68 seasons. The 1967 set was issued one, two or three per program and includes a large player photo along with bio information below the image on the front as well as three circles intended to direct the collector to punch them out and insert the photos into a binder. Each has another page of the program on the back.

COMPLETE SET (10)	40.00	80.00
1 John Baker	3.00	8.00
2 Jim Butler	3.00	8.00
3 Dick Compton	3.00	8.00
4 Larry Gagner	3.00	8.00
5 John Hilton	3.00	8.00
6 Ray Mansfield	3.00	8.00
7 Bill Saul	3.00	8.00
8 Clendon Thomas	3.00	8.00
9 J.R. Wilburn	3.00	8.00
10 Marv Woodson	3.00	8.00

1968 Steelers KDKA

The 1968 KDKA Pittsburgh Steelers card set contains 15 cards with horizontal poses of several players per card. The cards measure approximately 2 3/8" by 4 1/8". Each card depicts players of a particular position (defensive backs, tight ends, linebackers). The backs are essentially advertisements for radio station KDKA, the sponsor of the card set. The cards are unnumbered and hence are listed below alphabetically by position name for convenience.

COMPLETE SET (15)	75.00	150.00
1 John Knight	5.00	10.00
Ray Mansfield		
2 Bill Austin HCO	6.00	12.00
Fletcher Torgeson CO		
Leon McLaughlin CO		
Hugh Taylor CO		
Don Heinrich CO		
Carl DePasqua CO		
Berlin TR		
3 Bob Hohn	5.00	10.00
Paul Martha		
Marv Woodson		
4 John Foruria	5.00	10.00
Clendon Thomas		
Bob Morgan		
5 Ben McGee	5.00	10.00
Chuck Hinton		
Dick Arndt		
Ken Kortas		
Lloyd Voss		
6 Roy Jefferson	5.00	10.00
End-Kicker:		
Ken Hebert		
7 Earl Gros	5.00	10.00
Bill Asbury		
8 Larry Gagner	5.00	10.00
Sam Davis		
Bruce Van Dyke		
9 Andy Russell	6.00	12.00
Bill Saul		
John Campbell		
Ray May		
10 Dick Shiner	5.00	10.00
Kent Nix		
11 Ken Hebert	5.00	10.00
Ernie Ruple		
Mike Taylor		
12 Dick Hoak	5.00	10.00
Don Shy		
Jim Butler		
13 J.R. Wilburn	5.00	10.00
Dick Compton		
14 Fran O'Brien	5.00	10.00
Mike Haggerty		
John Brown		
15 John Hilton	5.00	10.00
Chet Anderson		

1968 Steelers Program Inserts

The Steelers issued these black and white player photos bound into home game programs during the 1965-68 seasons. The 1968 set was issued one per program and includes a large player photo along with bio information below the image on the front as well as three circles intended to direct the collector to punch them out and insert the photos into a binder. Each has another page of the program on the back.

1 Roy Jefferson	3.00	8.00
2 Ben McGee	3.00	8.00

1968 Steelers Team Issue

These photos were issued around 1968 by the Pittsburgh Steelers. Each measures roughly 5" by 7" and contains a black and white photo printed on paper stock. The photo backs are blank and unnumbered.

COMPLETE SET (5)	25.00	50.00
1 Earl Gros	5.00	10.00
2 Paul Martha	5.00	10.00
3 Kent Nix	5.00	10.00
4 Andy Russell	6.00	12.00
5 Marv Woodson	5.00	10.00

1969 Steelers Team Issue

These photos were issued around 1969 by the Pittsburgh Steelers. Each measures roughly 8" by 10", contains a black and white photo and was printed on glossy stock. The photos look nearly identical to the 1966 Team Issue set. The photo backs are blank and unnumbered.

COMPLETE SET (6)	25.00	50.00
1 Earl Gros	5.00	10.00
2 Jerry Hillebrand	5.00	10.00
3 Gene Mingo	5.00	10.00
4 Dick Shiner	5.00	10.00
5 Bobby Walden	5.00	10.00
6 Erwin Williams	5.00	10.00

1972 Steelers Team Sheets

This set consists of eight 8" by 10" sheets that display eight glossy black-and-white player photos each. Each individual photo measures approximately 2" by 3". The player's name, number, and position are printed below the photo. A Steelers helmet icon appears in the lower left corner of the sheet. The backs are blank. The sheets are unnumbered and checklisted below alphabetically according to the player featured in the upper left corner.

COMPLETE SET (8)	75.00	150.00
1 Ralph Anderson	6.00	15.00
Jim Clack		
Bob Maples		
Henry Davis		
Jon Kolb		
Ray Mansfield		
Sam Davis		
Chuck Allen		
2 Jim Brumfield	7.50	20.00
Chuck Beatty		
Bobby Walden		
Frank Lewis		
Lee Calland		
Warren Bankston		
Mel Blount		
John Rowser		
3 Bud Carson CO	7.50	20.00
Bob Fry CO		
Dick Hoak CO		
Babe Parilli CO		
George Perles CO		
Lou Riecke CO		
Charlie Sumner CO		
Lionel Taylor CO		
4 Jack Ham	7.50	20.00
Ben McGee		
Brian Stenger		
Lloyd Voss		
Bruce Van Dyke		
L.C. Greenwood		
Gerry Mullins		
John Brown		
5 Joe Greene	10.00	25.00
Bert Askson UER		
(Misspelled Burt)		
Mel Holmes		
Dwight White		
Bob Adams		
Larry Brown		
Dave Smith		
John McMakin		
6 Chuck Noll CO	15.00	30.00
Jon Staggers		
Terry Hanratty		
Roy Gerela		
Terry Bradshaw		
Bob Leahy		
Joe Gilliam		
Rocky Bleier		
7 Dick Post	10.00	25.00
Franco Harris		
Dennis Meyer		
Lorenzo Brinkley		
Steve Furness		
Gordon Gravelle		
Rick Sharp		
Dave Kalina		
8 Mike Wagner	6.00	15.00
Ron Shanklin		
Preston Pearson		
Glen Edwards		
Al Young		
John Fuqua		
Andy Russell		
Steve Davis		

1973 Steelers Team Issue

The NFLPA worked with many teams in 1973 to issued photo packs to be sold at stadium concession stands. Each measures approximately 7" by 8-5/8" and features a color player photo with a blank back. A small sheet with a player checklist was included in each 6-photo pack which was also assigned a series number as follows: A (cards #1-6), B (cards #7-12), and C (cards #13-18).

COMPLETE SET (18)	60.00	120.00
1 Jim Clack	4.00	8.00
2 Henry Davis	4.00	8.00
3 Franco Harris	7.50	15.00
4 Ron Shanklin	4.00	8.00
5 Bruce Van Dyke	4.00	8.00
6 Dwight White	5.00	10.00
7 Terry Bradshaw	12.50	25.00
8 Larry Brown	4.00	8.00
9 Roy Gerela	4.00	8.00
10 L.C. Greenwood	6.00	12.00
11 Frank Lewis	4.00	8.00
12 Andy Russell	5.00	10.00
13 John Fuqua	5.00	10.00
14 Joe Greene	6.00	12.00
15 Jack Ham	6.00	12.00
16 Terry Hanratty	4.00	8.00
17 Ray Mansfield	4.00	8.00
18 Preston Pearson	5.00	10.00

1973 Steelers Team Issue Color

The NFLPA worked with many teams in 1973 to issued photo packs to be sold at stadium concession stands. Each measures approximately 7" by 8-5/8" and features a color player photo with a blank back. A small sheet with a player checklist was included in each 6-photo pack.

COMPLETE SET (6)	25.00	50.00
1 Jim Clack	4.00	8.00
2 Henry Davis	4.00	8.00
3 Franco Harris	7.50	15.00
4 Ron Shanklin	4.00	8.00
5 Bruce Van Dyke	4.00	8.00
6 Dwight White	5.00	10.00

1973 Steelers Team Sheets

This set consists of eight 8" by 10" sheets that display eight glossy black-and-white player photos each. Each individual photo on the sheets measures approximately 2" by 3". A Steelers helmet icon appears in the lower left corner of the sheet. The backs are blank. The sheets are unnumbered and checklisted below alphabetically according to the player featured in the upper left corner.

COMPLETE SET (8)	50.00	100.00
1 Ralph Anderson	6.00	12.00
Jim Clack		
Henry Davis		
Jon Kolb		
Ray Mansfield		
Sam Davis		
Jack Ham		
Roger Bernhardt		
2 Glen Edwards	7.50	15.00
Stahle Vincent		
John Dockery		
Al Young		
Franco Harris		
John Fuqua		
Andy Russell		
Steve Davis		
3 Terry Hanratty	12.50	25.00
Roy Gerela		
Terry Bradshaw		
Joe Gilliam		
Rocky Bleier		
Mike Wagner		
Ron Shanklin		
Preston Pearson		
4 Gerry Mullins	6.00	12.00
Joe Greene		
Mel Holmes		
Dwight White		
Barry Pearson		
Larry Brown		
John McMakin		
George Webster		
5 Coaches	6.00	12.00
Chuck Noll		
Bud Carson		
Bob Fry		
Dick Hoak		
Babe Parilli		
George Perles		
Lou Riecke		
Lionel Taylor		
Paul Uram		
Woody Widenhofer		
6 Ken Phares	6.00	12.00
Ed Bradley		
Bobby Walden		
Dennis Meyer		
Frank Lewis		
Warren Bankston		
Mel Blount		
John Rowser		
7 Glenn Scolnik	5.00	10.00
James Thomas		
Loren Toews		
Gail Clark		
Lee Nystrom		
Nate Dorsey		
Bracey Bonham		
Tom Keating		
8 Brian Stenger	6.00	12.00
Ernie Holmes		
Steve Furness		
Bruce Van Dyke		
Craig Henneman		
L.C. Greenwood		
Ron Curl		
Gordon Gravelle		

1974 Steelers Tribune-Review Posters

These posters (measuring roughly 14" by 21 1/2") were issued one per Greensburg Tribune-Review newspaper in 1974. Each includes a black and white photo of a Steelers' player on one side and another page from the newspaper on the back. We've listed them below in alphabetical order.

1 Mel Blount	7.50	15.00
2 Roy Gerela	5.00	10.00
3 Joe Greene	7.50	15.00
4 Jack Ham	7.50	15.00
5 Andy Russell	5.00	10.00
6 Ron Shanklin	5.00	10.00
7 Dwight White	6.00	12.00

1974 Steelers WTAE

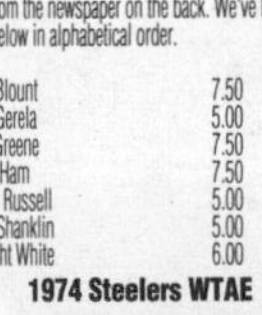

These color 8" X 10" photos feature players of the Pittsburgh Steelers. The cards were sponsored by radio station WTAE and the cardbacks include player bio information. The cards may have been distributed by Arby's Restaurants as well. The set is thought to contain 14-different photos. Any additions to this checklist are appreciated.

1 Terry Bradshaw	75.00	125.00
2 Sam Davis	15.00	30.00
3 Glen Edwards	15.00	30.00
4 John Fuqua	25.00	40.00
5 Roy Gerela	15.00	30.00
6 Joe Gilliam	15.00	30.00
7 Joe Greene	35.00	60.00
8 Jack Ham	35.00	60.00
9 Terry Hanratty	25.00	40.00
10 Franco Harris	40.00	75.00
11 Ray Mansfield	15.00	30.00
12 Ron Shanklin	15.00	30.00
13 Mike Wagner	15.00	30.00

1976 Steelers Glasses

This set of glasses was issued for the Pittsburgh Steelers in 1976, licensed through MSA and sponsored by WTAE. Each features a black and white photo of a Steelers' player along with a gold and black stripe running above and below the photo. Any additions to the list below are appreciated. These glasses were available at the Isaly or Sweet William restaurants.

COMPLETE SET (7)	50.00	100.00
1 Rocky Bleier	6.00	12.00
2 Terry Bradshaw	15.00	30.00
3 Mel Blount	6.00	12.00
4 Joe Greene	7.50	15.00
5 Jack Ham	6.00	12.00
6 Jack Lambert	7.50	15.00
7 Andy Russell	5.00	10.00

1976 Steelers MSA Cups

This set of plastic cups was issued for the Pittsburgh Steelers in 1976 and licensed through MSA. Each features an artist's rendering of a Steelers' player wearing a black jersey. Some players also appeared in the nationally issued 1976 MSA Cups set with only slight differences in each. The unnumbered cups are listed below alphabetically.

COMPLETE SET (23)	100.00	200.00
1 Rocky Bleier	5.00	10.00
2 Mel Blount	5.00	10.00
3 Terry Bradshaw	10.00	20.00
(black uniform)		
4 Jim Clack	4.00	8.00
5 Sam Davis	4.00	8.00
6 Roy Gerela	4.00	8.00
7 Gordon Gravelle	4.00	8.00
8 Joe Greene	6.00	12.00
9 L.C. Greenwood	5.00	10.00
10 Randy Grossman	4.00	8.00
11 Jack Ham	5.00	10.00
12 Franco Harris	7.50	15.00
13 Marv Kellum	4.00	8.00
14 Jon Kolb	4.00	8.00
15 Jack Lambert	7.50	15.00
16 Ray Mansfield	4.00	8.00
17 Andy Russell	4.00	8.00
18 John Stallworth	6.00	12.00
19 Lynn Swann	7.50	15.00
20 J.T. Thomas	4.00	8.00
21 Loren Toews	4.00	8.00
22 Mike Wagner	4.00	8.00
23 Bobby Walden	4.00	8.00

1978 Steelers Team Issue

This set consists of 5" by 7" glossy black-and-white player photos. The player's jersey number, name, position (initials), and team name are printed in all caps below the photo. Each is blankbacked, unnumbered and checklisted below alphabetically.

1 Rocky Bleier	6.00	12.00
2 Mel Blount	6.00	12.00
3 Terry Bradshaw	12.50	25.00
4 Joe Greene	7.50	15.00
5 L.C. Greenwood	6.00	12.00
6 Jack Ham	7.50	15.00

1978 Steelers Team Sheets

This set consists of eight 10" by 8" sheets that display eight glossy black-and-white player photos each. Each photo measures approximately 2" by 3". The player's name, number, and position are printed below the photo. The sheets are blankbacked, unnumbered and checklisted below alphabetically according to the player featured in the upper left corner.

COMPLETE SET (8)	40.00	80.00
1 B Carr	6.00	12.00
Reggie Harrison RB		
Mel Blount		
Doug Becker		
Tom Brzoza		
Loren Toews		
Mike Webster		
Dennis Winston		
2 Jack Deloplaine	5.00	10.00
Wentford Gains		
Sidney Thornton		
Rick Moser		
Randy Reutershan		
Nat Terry		
Frank Lewis		
Brad Wagner		
3 Willie Fry	6.00	12.00
Steve Furness		
Tom Beasley		
Ted Petersen		
Gary Dunn		
L.C. Greenwood		
Fred Anderson		
Lance Reynolds		
4 Dave LaCrosse	6.00	12.00
Jon Kolb		
Robin Cole		
Sam Davis G		
Jack Lambert		
Jack Ham		
Brad Cousina		
John Hicks		
5 Gerry Mullins	6.00	12.00
Dave Pureifory		
Ray Pinney		
Joe Greene		
John Banaszak		
Steve Courson		
Dwight White		
Larry Brown		
6 Chuck Noll CO	10.00	20.00
Craig Colquitt		
Roy Gerela		
Terry Bradshaw		
Mike Kruczek		
Cliff Stoudt		
Rocky Bleier		
Tony Dungy		
7 John Stallworth	7.50	15.00
Theo Bell		
Randy Grossman		
Andre Keys		
Jim Smith		
L McCarthey		
Lynn Swann		
Bennie Cunningham		
8 Mike Wagner	6.00	12.00
R Scott		
Glen Edwards		
Alvin Maxson		
Ron Johnson DB		
Larry Anderson		
Donnie Shell		
Franco Harris		

1979 Steelers McDonald's Glasses

McDonald's stores issued this set of glasses in the Pittsburgh area in 1979 following Super Bowl XIII. Each features a black and white photo of three different Steelers players with the McDonald's logo circling the bottom of the glass.

COMPLETE SET (4)	30.00	60.00
1 John Banaszak	7.50	15.00
Sam Davis		
Jack Lambert		
2 Rocky Bleier	7.50	15.00
Jack Ham		
Donnie Shell		
3 Terry Bradshaw	12.50	25.00
L.C. Greenwood		
Mike Webster		
4 Joe Greene	7.50	15.00
John Stallworth		
Mike Wagner		

1979 Steelers Notebook Pittsburgh Press

These small posters measure roughly 5 1/2" by 8" when properly cut. Each was issued in Pittsburgh Press newspapers in 1979 and includes a black and white photo of a Steelers' player or coach with extensive bio information on the front. The backs feature another page from the newspaper. We've listed them below in alphabetical order.

COMPLETE SET (56)	125.00	250.00
1 Anthony Anderson	3.00	6.00
2 Larry Anderson	3.00	6.00
3 Matt Bahr	3.00	6.00
4 John Banaszak	3.00	6.00
5 Tom Beasley	3.00	6.00
6 Theo Bell	3.00	6.00
7 Rocky Bleier	4.00	8.00
8 Mel Blount	5.00	10.00
9 Terry Bradshaw	10.00	20.00
10 Larry Brown	3.00	6.00
11 Robin Cole	3.00	6.00
12 Craig Colquitt	3.00	6.00
13 Steve Courson	3.00	6.00
14 Bennie Cunningham	3.00	6.00
15 Sam Davis	3.00	6.00
16 Tom Dornbrook	3.00	6.00
17 Rollie Dotsch CO	3.00	6.00
18 Gary Dunn	3.00	6.00
19 Steve Furness	3.00	6.00
20 Roy Gerela	3.00	6.00
21 Joe Greene	6.00	12.00
22 L.C. Greenwood	5.00	10.00
23 Randy Grossman	4.00	8.00
24 Jack Ham	5.00	10.00
25 Franco Harris	6.00	12.00
26 Greg Hawthorne	3.00	6.00
27 Dick Hoak CO	3.00	6.00
28 Ron Johnson	3.00	6.00
29 Jon Kolb	3.00	6.00
30 Mike Kruczek	3.00	6.00
31 Jack Lambert	6.00	12.00
32 Tom Moore CO	3.00	6.00
33 Rick Moser	3.00	6.00
34 Gerry Mullins	3.00	6.00
35 Chuck Noll CO	7.50	15.00
36 George Perles CO	3.00	6.00
37 Ted Peterson	3.00	6.00
38 Ray Pinney	3.00	6.00
39 Lou Riecke CO	3.00	6.00
40 Donnie Shell	4.00	8.00
41 Jim Smith	4.00	8.00
42 John Stallworth	6.00	12.00
43 Cliff Stoudt	4.00	8.00
44 Lynn Swann	7.50	15.00
45 Loren Toews	3.00	6.00
46 J.T. Thomas	3.00	6.00
47 Sidney Thornton	3.00	6.00
48 Paul Uram CO	3.00	6.00
49 Zack Valentine CO	3.00	6.00
50 Mike Wagner	3.00	6.00
51 Dick Walker CO	3.00	6.00
52 Mike Webster	5.00	10.00
53 Dwight White	4.00	8.00
54 Woody Widenhofer CO	3.00	6.00
55 Dennis Winston	3.00	6.00
56 Dwayne Woodruff	3.00	6.00

1979-80 Steelers Postcards

The Steelers released these postcards presumably in the late 1970s. The Bradshaw and Greene cards were printed by Coastal Printing and include a typical postcard format on the back with a color player photo on the front. The Swann card was printed by Ellie's and is slightly different in back design. Each measures roughly 6" by 9." The checklist below is thought to be incomplete.

COMPLETE SET (3)	20.00	40.00
1 Terry Bradshaw	10.00	20.00
2 Joe Greene	5.00	10.00
3 Lynn Swann	6.00	12.00

1980 Steelers McDonald's Glasses

McDonald's stores issued this set of glasses in the Pittsburgh area in 1980 following Super Bowl XIV. Each features a black and white photo of three different Steelers players with the McDonald's logo circling the bottom of the glass. The logos for the NFL Player's Association and MSA also appear.

COMPLETE SET (4)	17.50	35.00
1 Rocky Bleier	4.00	8.00
John Stallworth		
Roy Winston		
2 Mel Blount	4.00	8.00
Jon Kolb		
Jack Lambert		
3 Terry Bradshaw	7.50	15.00
Sam Davis		
Jack Ham		
4 Matt Bahr	4.00	8.00
Joe Greene		
Sidney Thornton		

1980 Steelers Pittsburgh Press Posters

These small posters (measuring roughly 13 1/2" by 21") were issued one per Pittsburgh Press newspaper in 1980. Each includes a color artist's rendering of a Steelers' player with a facsimile autograph below the image along with a copyright line and date. The backs feature a comics page from the newspaper. We've listed them below in alphabetical order.

COMPLETE SET (12)	50.00	100.00
1 Chris Bahr	3.00	6.00
2 Mel Blount	5.00	10.00
(December 7, 1980)		
3 Terry Bradshaw	10.00	20.00
(September 7, 1980)		
4 Sam Davis	3.00	6.00
(October 26, 1980)		
5 Jack Ham	5.00	10.00
6 Franco Harris	6.00	12.00
(September 21, 1980)		
7 Jon Kolb	3.00	6.00
(November 30, 1980)		
8 Chuck Noll CO	5.00	10.00
(December 21, 1980)		
9 Donnie Shell	4.00	8.00
(December 14, 1980)		
10 John Stallworth	5.00	10.00
(October 12, 1980)		
11 Lynn Swann	6.00	12.00
(October 5, 1980)		
12 Mike Webster	4.00	8.00
(November 9, 1980)		

1980-82 Steelers Boy Scouts

These standard sized cards were issued for the Boy Scouts and used as membership cards. Each was printed on thin stock and features a Steelers player on the front and Boy Scouts membership information on the back.

1 Rocky Bleier	20.00	40.00
2 Terry Bradshaw 1982	40.00	75.00
3 Franco Harris	25.00	50.00
4 John Stallworth 1981	20.00	40.00
5 Cliff Stoudt 1981	15.00	30.00
6 Lynn Swann	25.00	50.00
7 Mike Webster 1981	20.00	40.00

1981 Steelers Police

The 1981 Pittsburgh Steelers police set consists of 16 unnumbered cards which have been listed in the checklist below by the uniform number appearing on the fronts of the cards. The cards measure approximately 2 5/8" by 4 1/8". The set is sponsored by the local police department, the Pittsburgh Steelers, the Kiwanis Club, and Coca-Cola, the last three of which have their logos appearing on the backs of the cards. In addition, "Steelers' Tips" are featured on the back. Card backs have black printing with gold accent on white card stock. This set is very similar to the 1982 Police Steelers set; differences are noted parenthetically in the list below. The set also contains the only trading card of popular Steeler John Banaszak.

COMPLETE SET (16)	20.00	35.00
9 Matt Bahr	.40	1.00
12 Terry Bradshaw	3.00	8.00
(Passing)		
31 Donnie Shell	.50	1.25
(Referee back)		
32 Franco Harris	2.00	5.00
(Running with ball)		
47 Mel Blount	1.00	2.50
(Running without ball)		
52 Mike Webster	.60	1.50
(Standing)		
57 Sam Davis	.40	1.00
58 Jack Lambert	1.25	3.00
(Facing left)		
59 Jack Ham	1.00	2.50
(Sportsmanship back)		
64 Steve Furness	.40	1.00
68 L.C. Greenwood	.75	2.00
75 Joe Greene	1.25	3.00
76 John Banaszak	1.25	3.00
79 Larry Brown	.40	1.00
(Chin 7/16– from bottom)		
82 John Stallworth	1.00	2.50
(Running with ball)		
88 Lynn Swann	2.50	6.00
(Double coverage back)		

1982 Steelers McDonald's Glasses

McDonald's issued this set of four glasses as part of the Steelers' "50 Seasons" celebration. Each glass includes six current or former Steelers greats featured in a black and white photo. The glasses measure roughly 4 3/4" tall.

COMPLETE SET (4)	12.00	30.00
1 Gerry Mullins	3.00	8.00
Larry Brown		
Jack Lambert		
Franco Harris		
Pat Brady		
Dwight White		
2 Joe Greene	2.00	8.00
Elbie Nickel		
Jon Kolb		
Rocky Bleier		
Donnie Shell		
Jack Ham		
3 Roy Gerela	3.00	8.00
Sam Davis		
Mike Wagner		
L.C. Greenwood		
Mike Webster		
Lynn Swann		
4 Mel Blount	5.00	12.00
Ernie Stautner		
Terry Bradshaw		
Andy Russell		
John Stallworth		
Jack Butler		

1982 Steelers Police

The 16-card, 1982 Pittsburgh Steelers set is unnumbered, but has been listed in the checklist below by the player's uniform number which appears on the fronts of the cards. The cards measure 2 5/8" by 4 1/8". The backs of the cards feature Steelers' Tips, the Kiwanis logo, the Coca-Cola logo, and a Steelers helmet logo. The local police department sponsored this set, in addition to the organizations whose logos appear on the back. Card backs feature black print with gold trim. This set is very similar to the 1981 Police Steelers set; differences are noted parenthetically in the list below.

COMPLETE SET (16)	10.00	20.00
12 Terry Bradshaw	2.00	5.00
(Portrait)		
31 Donnie Shell	.30	.75
(Double Coverage back)		
32 Franco Harris	1.00	2.50
(Portrait)		
44 Frank Pollard	.25	.60
47 Mel Blount	.50	1.25
(Running with ball)		
52 Mike Webster	.40	1.00
(Portrait)		
58 Jack Lambert	.75	2.00
(Facing forward)		
59 Jack Ham	.50	1.25
(Teamwork back)		
65 Tom Beasley	1.00	2.50
(Joe Montana in background)		
67 Gary Dunn	.25	.60
74 Ray Pinney	.25	.60
79 Larry Brown	.25	.60
(Chin 5/16– from bottom)		
82 John Stallworth	.50	1.25
(Posed shot)		
88 Lynn Swann	1.25	3.00
(Sportsmanship back)		
89 Bennie Cunningham	.25	.60
90 Bob Kohrs	.25	.60

1982 Steelers Nu-Maid Butter Tubs

This set of butter cups or tubs was released by Nu-Maid and Miami Margarine in 1982 in the Pittsburgh area. Each tub includes color illustrations of the featured player and measures roughly 3 3/4" tall and 3" in diameter.

COMPLETE SET (6)	25.00	50.00
1 Mel Blount	3.00	8.00
2 L.C. Greenwood	3.00	8.00
3 Jack Ham	4.00	10.00
4 Franco Harris	6.00	15.00
5 John Stallworth	4.00	10.00
6 Mike Webster	2.50	6.00

1983 Steelers Police

This 17-card set features the Pittsburgh Steelers. Cards measure approximately 2 5/8" by 4 1/8" and read "1983" on the card backs. There was an error on the Chuck Noll ("Knoll") card, which was corrected. The set is considered complete with either one of the Noll variations. The set is unnumbered and hence is listed below ordered (and numbered) alphabetically by subject.

COMPLETE SET (16)	7.50	15.00
1 Walter Abercrombie	.20	.50
2 Gary Anderson K	.60	1.50
3 Mel Blount	.40	1.00
4 Terry Bradshaw	1.50	4.00
5 Robin Cole	.20	.50
6 Steve Courson	.20	.50
7 Bennie Cunningham	.20	.50
8 Franco Harris	.75	2.00
9 Greg Hawthorne	.20	.50
10 Jack Lambert	.60	1.50
11A Chuck Noll CO ERR	1.50	4.00
(Misspelled Knoll)		
11B Chuck Noll CO COR	.40	1.00
12 Donnie Shell	.25	.60
13 John Stallworth	.50	1.25
14 Mike Webster	.30	.75
15 Dwayne Woodruff	.20	.50
16 Rick Woods	.20	.50

1983 Steelers Team Issue

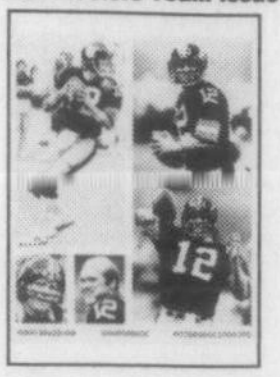

This set consists of team issued photos released in 1983. Each measures roughly 8" by 10" and includes black and white photos of the featured player or players printed on glossy stock. The top superstars on the team were given an entire sheet of photos for themselves, while the other players were grouped in traditional team sheet fashion with eight players to a page.

COMPLETE SET (5)	20.00	50.00
1 Walter Abercrombie	3.00	6.00
Gary Anderson K		
Bennie Cunningham		
Greg Hawthorne		
Mel Blount		
Dwayne Woodruff		
Rick Woods		
Gabe Rivera		
2 Terry Bradshaw	10.00	20.00
(includes five photos)		
3 Franco Harris	5.00	10.00
(includes six photos)		
4 Jack Lambert	6.00	12.00
(includes six photos)		
5 John Stallworth	4.00	8.00
(includes six photos)		

1984 Steelers Police

This unnumbered set of 16 cards features players from the Pittsburgh Steelers. Cards measure 2 5/8" by 4 1/8". Card backs feature black printing on thin white card stock. The set was sponsored by McDonald's, Kiwanis, and local police departments. The players are listed below by uniform number. The set can be differentiated from other similar Steelers police sets by the presence of the Kiwanis logo on the card fronts.

COMPLETE SET (16)	5.00	10.00
1 Gary Anderson K	.40	1.00
16 Mark Malone	.25	.60
19 David Woodley	.25	.60
30 Frank Pollard	.20	.50
32 Franco Harris	.75	2.00
34 Walter Abercrombie	.20	.50
49 Dwayne Woodruff	.20	.50
52 Mike Webster	.40	1.00
57 Mike Merriweather	.20	.50
58 Jack Lambert	.50	1.25
67 Gary Dunn	.20	.50
73 Craig Wolfley	.20	.50
82 John Stallworth	.50	1.25
83 Louis Lipps	.25	.60
92 Keith Gary	.20	.50
92 Keith Willis	.20	.50

1985 Steelers Pittsburgh Press Pin-Ups

These small posters (measuring roughly 10" by 13") were issued one per Pittsburgh Press newspaper in 1985. Each includes a color artist's rendering of two member of the Steelers' with facsimile autographs of both. Each is numbered on the front and the backs feature another page from the newspaper.

COMPLETE SET (12)	50.00	100.00
1 Mark Malone	5.00	10.00
David Woodley		
2 John Stallworth	6.00	12.00
Louis Lipps		
3 Weegie Thompson	4.00	8.00
Rich Erenberg		
4 Donnie Shell	5.00	10.00
Dwayne Woodruff		
5 Frank Pollard	5.00	10.00
Walter Abercrombie		
6 Mike Webster	5.00	10.00
Bennie Cunningham		
7 Gary Dunn	4.00	8.00
Darryl Sims		
8 John Goodman	4.00	8.00
Ed Nelson		
9 Robin Cole	4.00	8.00
David Little		
10 Bryan Hinkle	4.00	8.00
Mike Merriweather		
11 Scott Campbell	4.00	8.00
Gary Anderson		
12 Chuck Noll CO	6.00	12.00
Dan Rooney Pres.		

1985 Steelers Police

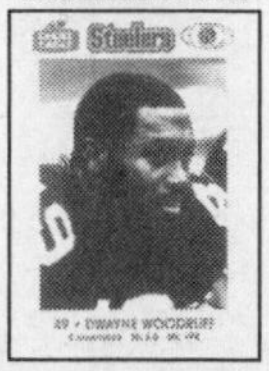

This 16-card set of Pittsburgh Steelers is unnumbered except for uniform number. Cards measure approximately 2 5/8" by 4 1/8". The backs contain "Steeler Tips". The set was sponsored by Kiwanis, Giant Eagle, local Police Departments, and the Steelers. Card backs are written in black on white card stock. The 1985, 1986, and 1987 Police Steelers sets are identical except for the individual card differences noted parenthetically below.

COMPLETE SET (16)	5.00	10.00
1 Gary Anderson K	.30	.75
(Kickoff back)		
16 Mark Malone	.25	.60
(Playbook back)		
21 Eric Williams	.20	.50
30 Frank Pollard	.20	.50
(Second Effort back)		
31 Donnie Shell	.30	.75
(Zone back)		
34 Walter Abercrombie	.20	.50
(Teamwork back)		
49 Dwayne Woodruff	.20	.50
(Turnover back)		
50 David Little	.20	.50
52 Mike Webster	.40	1.00
(Offside back)		
53 Bryan Hinkle	.20	.50
(Blindside back)		
56 Robin Cole	.20	.50
(Timeout back)		
57 Mike Merriweather	.20	.50
(Blitz back)		
82 John Stallworth	.60	1.50
(Captains back)		
83 Louis Lipps	.25	.60
(Pride back)		
93 Keith Willis	.20	.50
(QB Sack back)		
NNO Chuck Noll CO	.60	1.50
(Coach back)		

1985 Steelers Stop'N'Go Cups

This set of 32-ounce cups was sponsored and distributed by Stop-n-Go stores in the Pittsburgh area. Each includes a picture of two-Steelers players and is numbered by both the series and cup number. Any additions to the list below are appreciated.

1-Jan Jack Lambert	2.50	6.00
Louis Lipps		
2-Jan John Stallworth	2.50	6.00
Mike Webster		

1986 Steelers Police

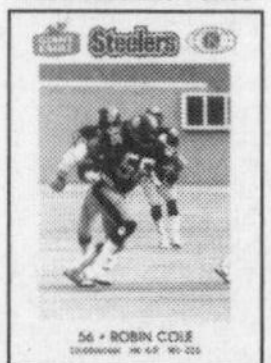

This 15-card set of Pittsburgh Steelers is unnumbered except for uniform number. Cards measure approximately 2 5/8" by 4 1/8". The backs contain "Steeler Tips". The set was sponsored by Kiwanis, Giant Eagle, local Police Departments, and the Steelers. Card backs are written in black on white card stock. The 1985, 1986, and 1987 Police Steelers sets are identical except for the individual card differences noted parenthetically below.

COMPLETE SET (15)	4.00	8.00
1 Gary Anderson K	.30	.75
(Field Goal back)		
16 Mark Malone	.25	.60
(Quarterback back)		
24 Rich Erenberg	.20	.50
30 Frank Pollard	.20	.50
(Running Back back)		
31 Donnie Shell	.30	.75
(Interception back)		
34 Walter Abercrombie	.20	.50
(Penalty back)		
49 Dwayne Woodruff	.20	.50
(Practice back)		
52 Mike Webster	.30	.75
(Possession back)		
53 Bryan Hinkle	.20	.50
(Prevent back)		
56 Robin Cole	.20	.50
(Equipment back)		
57 Mike Merriweather	.20	.50
(Linebacker back)		
62 Tunch Ilkin	.20	.50
64 Edmund Nelson	.20	.50
67 Gary Dunn	.20	.50
(Defensive Holding back)		
82 John Stallworth	.50	1.25
(Victory back)		
83 Louis Lipps	.25	.60
(Receiver back)		

1987 Steelers Police

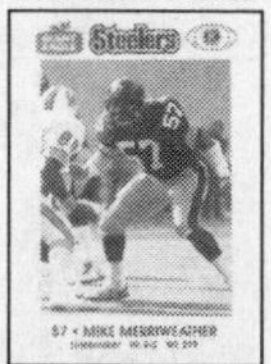

This 16-card set of Pittsburgh Steelers is unnumbered except for uniform number. Cards measure approximately 2 5/8" by 4 1/8". The backs contain "Steeler Tips". The set was sponsored by Kiwanis, Giant Eagle, local Police Departments, and the Steelers. The cards were given out by Pittsburgh area police officers one card per week. Card backs are written in black on white card stock. The 1985, 1986, and 1987 Police Steelers sets are identical except for the individual card differences noted parenthetically below.

COMPLETE SET (16)	4.00	8.00
1 Walter Abercrombie	.20	.50
(Option Pass back)		
2 Gary Anderson K	.25	.60
(Extra Point back)		
3 Bubby Brister	.30	.75
4 Gary Dunn	.20	.50
(Neutral Zone back)		
5 Preston Gothard	.20	.50
6 Bryan Hinkle	.20	.50
(Outside Linebackers back)		
7 Earnest Jackson	.25	.60
8 Louis Lipps	.25	.60
(Corner Pattern back)		
9 Mark Malone	.25	.60
(Adverse Conditions back)		
10 Mike Merriweather	.20	.50
(Instant Replay back)		
11 Chuck Noll CO	.40	1.00
(Referee back)		
12 John Rienstra	.20	.50
13 Donnie Shell	.30	.75
(Defense back)		
14 John Stallworth	.50	1.25
(Crackback Block back)		
15 Mike Webster	.30	.75
(Sportsmanship back)		
16 Keith Willis	.20	.50
(Down back)		

1988 Steelers Police

The 1988 Police Pittsburgh Steelers set contains 16 player cards measuring approximately 2 5/8" by 4 1/8". The fronts show the players in uniform but not wearing helmets. The backs have definitions of football terms and safety tips. This unnumbered set is listed alphabetically below for convenience. The 1988 Police Steelers set is distinguishable from the 1985-87 Police Steelers sets by the Steelers helmet on back having three white diamonds instead of one white and two black diamonds.

COMPLETE SET (16)	4.00	8.00
1 Gary Anderson K	.25	.60
2 Bubby Brister	.30	.75
3 Thomas Everett	.20	.50
4 Delton Hall	.20	.50
5 Bryan Hinkle	.20	.50
6 Tunch Ilkin	.20	.50
7 Earnest Jackson	.20	.50
8 Louis Lipps	.25	.60
9 David Little	.20	.50
10 Mike Merriweather	.20	.50
11 Frank Pollard	.20	.50
12 John Rienstra	.20	.50
13 Mike Webster	.40	1.00
14 Keith Willis	.20	.50
15 Craig Wolfley	.20	.50
16 Rod Woodson	.75	2.00

1989 Steelers Police

The 1989 Police Pittsburgh Steelers set contains 16 cards measuring approximately 2 5/8" by 4 1/8". The fronts have white borders and color action photos; the vertically-oriented backs have safety tips. These cards were printed on very thin stock. The cards are unnumbered, so therefore are listed below according to uniform number. The card backs are subtitled "Steelers Tips '89". It has been reported that 175,000 cards of each player were given away by police officers in Western Pennsylvania.

COMPLETE SET (16)	4.00	8.00
1 Gary Anderson K	.20	.50
6 Bubby Brister	.20	.50
18 Harry Newsome	.15	.40
24 Rodney Carter	.15	.40
26 Rod Woodson	.50	1.25
27 Thomas Everett	.15	.40
33 Merril Hoge	.15	.40
53 Bryan Hinkle	.15	.40
54 Hardy Nickerson	.30	.75
62 Tunch Ilkin	.15	.40
63 Dermontti Dawson	.20	.50
74 Terry Long	.15	.40
78 Tim Johnson	.15	.40
83 Louis Lipps	.20	.50
97 Aaron Jones	.15	.40
98 Gerald Williams	.15	.40

1990 Steelers McDonald's Glasses

McDonald's issued this set of four glasses to commemorate Steelers players in the Pro Football Hall of Fame. Each glass includes former Steelers greats featured in a black and white photo. The glasses measure roughly 6 3/8" tall and include sponsors logos by McDonald's, Diet Coke, and WPXI-TV.

COMPLETE SET (4)	8.00	20.00
1 Mel Blount	2.00	5.00
Jack Ham		
Bobby Layne		
2 Terry Bradshaw	3.20	8.00
Bill Dudley		
John Henry Johnson		
3 Joe Greene	2.00	5.00
Franco Harris		
Johnny Blood McNally		
4 Jack Lambert	2.00	5.00
Art Rooney		
Ernie Stautner		

1990 Steelers Police

This 16-card set, which measures approximately 2 5/8" by 4 1/8", was issued to promote safety in the Pittsburgh Area using members of the Pittsburgh Steelers to make safety tips. The fronts of the cards feature color portrait shots of the players surrounded by white borders. There are advertisements for the Giant Eagle shopping chain and the Kiwanis Club on the front along with the Steelers name on top of the photo and underneath the photo is the player's name and position. The back of the card features a safety tip. The back says the cards were sponsored by the local Kiwanis club, Giant Eagle, the local police departments, and the Pittsburgh Steelers. The set is checklisted below alphabetically.

COMPLETE SET (16)	4.00	8.00
1 Gary Anderson K	.15	.40
2 Bubby Brister	.30	.75
3 Thomas Everett	.15	.40
4 Merril Hoge	.15	.40
5 Tunch Ilkin	.15	.40
6 Carnell Lake	.20	.50
7 Louis Lipps	.20	.50
8 David Little	.15	.40
9 Greg Lloyd	.40	1.00
10 Mike Mularkey	.15	.40
11 Hardy Nickerson	.20	.50
12 Chuck Noll CO	.40	1.00
13 John Rienstra	.15	.40
14 Keith Willis	.15	.40
15 Rod Woodson	.30	.75
16 Tim Worley	.15	.40

1991 Steelers Police

This 16-card set was sponsored by the Kiwanis and Giant Eagle. The cards measure approximately 2 5/8" by 4 1/8". They were distributed by participating Pennsylvania police departments. The fronts feature color action player photos, with the team name at the top sandwiched between the two sponsor logos. Player information appears below the picture. On the card backs below a Steelers helmet, the backs have "Steelers Tips '91," which consist of anti-crime or anti-drug messages. The cards are unnumbered and checklisted below in alphabetical order.

COMPLETE SET (16)	4.00	8.00
1 Gary Anderson K	.15	.40
2 Bubby Brister	.20	.50
3 Dermontti Dawson	.15	.40
4 Eric Green	.20	.50
5 Bryan Hinkle	.15	.40
6 Merril Hoge	.20	.50
7 John Jackson	.15	.40
8 D.J. Johnson	.15	.40
9 Carnell Lake	.20	.50
10 Louis Lipps	.20	.50
11 Greg Lloyd	.30	.75
12 Mike Mularkey	.15	.40
13 Chuck Noll CO	.40	1.00
14 Dan Stryzinski	.15	.40
15 Gerald Williams	.15	.40
16 Rod Woodson	.40	1.00

1992 Steelers Police

This 16-card set was sponsored by the Kiwanis Club and Giant Eagle, and it was distributed by local police departments. The cards measure approximately 2 5/8" by 4 3/16" and feature still color player photos on white card stock. Beneath the picture are the player's name, number, position, height, and weight. The team name and sponsor logos appear at the top. The backs are plain white with public service "Steelers Tips '92" printed within a black outline. The cards are unnumbered and checklisted below in alphabetical order.

COMPLETE SET (16)	4.00	8.00
1 Gary Anderson K	.15	.40
2 Bubby Brister	.20	.50
3 Bill Cowher CO	1.25	3.00
4 Dermontti Dawson	.15	.40
5 Eric Green	.20	.50
6 Carlton Haselrig	.15	.40
7 Merril Hoge	.15	.40
8 John Jackson	.15	.40
9 Carnell Lake	.20	.50
10 Louis Lipps	.20	.50
11 Greg Lloyd	.30	.75
12 Neil O'Donnell	.30	.75
13 Tom Ricketts	.15	.40
14 Gerald Williams	.15	.40
15 Jerrol Williams	.15	.40
16 Rod Woodson	.30	.75

1993 Steelers Police

Sponsored by the Pittsburgh Police Department, Kiwanis Club, and Giant Eagle, these 16 cards, when cut from the sheet, measure approximately 2 1/2" by 4". The fronts feature white-bordered color player action shots, with the player's name, uniform number, position, height, and weight appearing in black lettering within the bottom white margin. The team name appears in team color-coded lettering within the white margin above the photo, along with the Kiwanis and Giant Eagle logos. The white back has a large Steeler helmet logo at the top, followed below by the words "Steelers Tips '93," then the player's name, position, and highlight. The tip then appears, which contains a stay-in-school, anti-drug, or safety message. The Giant Eagle and Kiwanis logos at the bottom round out the card. The cards are unnumbered and checklisted below in alphabetical order.

COMPLETE SET (16)	3.00	6.00
1 Gary Anderson K	.15	.40
2 Adrian Cooper	.15	.40
3 Bill Cowher CO	.40	1.00
4 Dermontti Dawson	.15	.40
5 Donald Evans	.15	.40
6 Eric Green	.20	.50
7 Bryan Hinkle	.15	.40
8 Merril Hoge	.15	.40
9 Garry Howe	.15	.40
10 Greg Lloyd	.30	.75
11 Neil O'Donnell	.20	.50
12 Jerry Olsavsky	.15	.40
13 Leon Searcy	.15	.40
14 Dwight Stone	.15	.40
15 Gerald Williams	.15	.40
16 Rod Woodson	.30	.75

1995 Steelers Eat'n Park

This set of the Pittsburgh Steelers was issued in four strips of three peel-off player cards. Each sold for $.99 per strip. One strip was issued each week by Eat'n Park stores for four weeks. The fronts feature color action player cut-outs on a silver background with the player's name and position printed vertically on one side. The backs are blank. The cards are unnumbered and checklisted below according to the week number of the strip. A poster to house the set was also available for 99-cents.

COMPLETE SET (4)	4.00	10.00
1 Darren Perry	.80	2.00
Rod Woodson		
Greg Lloyd		
2 Ray Seals	.80	2.00
Carnell Lake		
Kevin Greene		
3 Dermontti Dawson	.50	1.25
Erric Pegram		
Mark Bruener		
4 Kordell Stewart	2.40	6.00
Yancey Thigpen		
Neil O'Donnell		

1995 Steelers Giant Eagle Proline/Coins

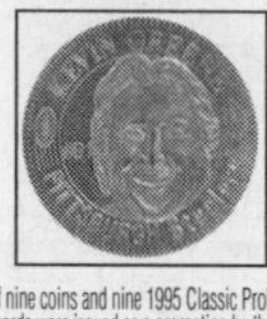

A set of nine coins and nine 1995 Classic ProLine series cards were issued as a promotion by the Pittsburgh Steelers and Giant Eagle Supermarkets in Pittsburgh. Each coin and card combo pack could be acquired for approximately $1.89 each at Giant Eagle Supermarkets in Pittsburgh. The program launch date was September 3, the duration was nine weeks, and the offer was valid while supplies lasted. The coin fronts display the player's face along with the player's name and team name. The backs carry the Steelers logo and the year '95-96. The coins are unnumbered and listed below alphabetically with a "CO" prefix. A colorful cardboard display featuring the Steelers defense was also produced to house the coins. The card fronts display full-bleed color action photos, with the player's name in a team color-coded diagonal stripe across the bottom. The back of every card carries a checklist for the set. We've numbered them below using a "CA" prefix on the card numbers.

COMP.CARD/COIN SET (18)	9.60	24.00
COMPLETE CARD SET (9)	4.80	12.00
COMPLETE COIN SET (9)	4.80	12.00
CA1 Kevin Greene	.50	1.25
CA2 Franco Harris	.60	1.50
CA3 Greg Lloyd	.60	1.50
GA4 Joe Greene	.60	1.50
CA5 Byron Bam Morris	.50	1.25
CA6 Jack Lambert	.60	1.50
CA7 Rod Woodson	.60	1.50
CA8 Mel Blount	.50	1.25
CA9 Bill Cowher CO	.50	1.25
CO1 Mel Blount	.50	1.25
CO2 Bill Cowher CO	.50	1.25
CO3 Joe Greene	.60	1.50
CO4 Kevin Greene	.50	1.25
CO5 Franco Harris	.60	1.50
CO6 Jack Lambert	.60	1.50
CO7 Greg Lloyd	.60	1.50
CO8 Byron Bam Morris	.50	1.25
CO9 Rod Woodson	.60	1.50
NNO Set Display Holder	.80	2.00
Steelers Defense		

1996 Steelers Kids Club

The Steelers sponsored this set featuring three top players and the head coach. Each card measures the standard size, is unnumbered, and features a black and yellow border.

COMPLETE SET (4)	2.00	5.00
1 Bill Cowher CO	.40	1.00
2 Greg Lloyd	.40	1.00
3 Kordell Stewart	1.20	3.00
4 Rod Woodson	.40	1.00

1996 Steelers Team Issue

The Steelers issued these player photos in 1996. Each measures roughly 5" by 7" and features a black and white photo of a Steelers player with his uniform number, name, and position below the photo. The backs are blank and unnumbered. The 1996 release closely resembles the 1997 photos and are differentiated as noted below for like players.

1 Jerome Bettis 4.00 8.00
(NFL Logo fully visible)
2 Chad Brown 2.50 5.00
3 Mark Bruener 2.00 4.00
(NFL Logo partially hidden)
4 Brentson Buckner 2.00 4.00
5 Dermontti Dawson 2.00 4.00
(NFL Logo fully visible)
6 Deon Figures 2.00 4.00
7 Jason Gildon 2.50 5.00
8 Norm Johnson 2.00 4.00
9 Carnell Lake 2.50 5.00
(NFL Logo fully visible)
10 Greg Lloyd 2.00 4.00
(NFL Logo partially hidden)
11 Jim Miller 2.50 5.00
12 Ernie Mills 2.00 4.00
13 Jerry Olsavsky 2.00 4.00
(NFL Logo partially hidden)
14 Erric Pegram 2.00 4.00
15 Ray Seals 2.00 4.00
16 Joel Steed 2.00 4.00
17 Kordell Stewart 4.00 8.00
(NFL Logo fully visible)
18 Yancey Thigpen 2.00 4.00
(NFL Logo partially hidden)
19 Mike Tomczak 2.00 4.00
(1/3 of NFL Logo visible)
20 Willie Williams 2.00 4.00
21 Rod Woodson 2.50 5.00
22 Will Wolford 2.00 4.00
(NFL Logo fully visible)

1997 Steelers Collector's Choice

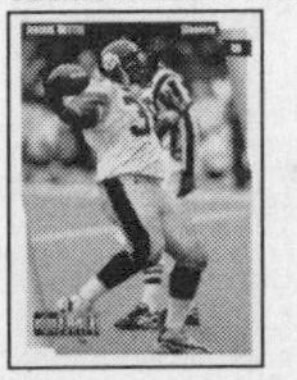

Upper Deck released several team sets in 1997 in a blister pack wrapper. Each of the 14-cards in this set are very similar to the base Collector's Choice cards except for the card numbering on the cardback. A cover/checklist card was added featuring the team helmet.

COMPLETE SET (14) 1.20 3.00
PI1 Jerome Bettis .15 .40
PI2 Charles Johnson .08 .25
PI3 Mike Tomczak .05 .15
PI4 Levon Kirkland .05 .15
PI5 Carnell Lake .05 .15
PI6 Donnell Woolford .05 .15
PI7 Kordell Stewart .40 1.00
PI8 Greg Lloyd .08 .25
PI9 Will Blackwell .08 .25
PI10 George Jones .08 .25
PI11 J.B. Brown .05 .15
PI12 Darren Perry .05 .15
PI13 Mark Bruener .05 .15
PI14 Steelers Logo .05 .15
Checklist

1997 Steelers Eat'n Park Glasses

These set of glasses was released by Eat'n Park stores in 1997. Each glass features an artist's rendering of a member of the Steelers on one side with a short write-up of the player on the other side.

COMPLETE SET (4) 4.80 12.00
1 Jerome Bettis 2.00 5.00
2 Bill Cowher 1.20 3.00
3 Carnell Lake 1.20 3.00
4 Greg Lloyd 1.20 3.00

1997 Steelers Team Issue

The Steelers issued these player photos in 1997. Each measures roughly 5" by 7" and features a black and white photo of a Steelers player with his uniform number, name, and position below the photo. The backs are blank and unnumbered. The 1997 release closely resembles the 1996 photos and are differentiated as noted below for like players.

COMPLETE SET (20) 30.00 60.00
1 Jerome Bettis 4.00 8.00
(NFL Logo partially hidden)
2 Mark Bruener 2.00 4.00
(NFL Logo is hidden)
3 Bill Cowher CO 2.00 4.00
4 Dermontti Dawson 2.00 4.00
(NFL Logo is hidden)
5 delete 2.00 4.00
6 John Jackson 2.00 4.00
7 Charles Johnson 2.00 4.00
8 Donta Jones 2.00 4.00
9 Levon Kirkland 2.00 4.00
10 Carnell Lake 2.50 5.00
(NFL Logo is hidden)
11 Greg Lloyd 2.00 4.00
12 Fred McAfee 2.00 4.00
13 Jerry Olsavsky 2.00 4.00
(NFL Logo is hidden)
14 Darren Perry 2.00 4.00
15 Kordell Stewart 4.00 8.00
(NFL Logo is hidden)
16 Justin Strzelczyk 2.00 4.00
17 Yancey Thigpen 2.00 4.00
18 Mike Tomczak 2.00 4.00
(only tip of NFL Logo showing)
19 Jon Witman 2.00 4.00
20 Will Wolford 2.00 4.00
(NFL Logo partially hidden)

1999 Steelers Tribune-Review Posters

These posters (measuring roughly 14" by 21 1/2") were issued one per Greensburg Tribune-Review newspaper in 1999. Each includes a color photo of a current or retired Steelers' player on one side and another page from the newspaper on the back. We've listed them below in alphabetical order.

1 Lethon Flowers 3.00 6.00
2 Donnie Shell 4.00 8.00

2000 Steelers Giant Eagle

This set was issued one card at a time to attendees of home game at Three Rivers Stadium during the 2000 Steelers regular season. Each card hightlights one "Three Rivers Greatest Moment" using a color action photo from a famous Steeler's event at the stadium. A Pin version of each cardfront was also produced and collectors would need to redeem one card at a Giant Eagle Store to get a pin. Reportedly, cards and pins #9 and #10 were short printed.

COMPLETE SET 12.50 25.00
*PINS: 1X TO 2X CARDS
1 23-Dec-72 2.00 4.00
(Franco Harris;
Immaculate Reception)
2 30-Dec-78 3.00 5.00
(Lynn Swann 38-yard TD catch)
3 14-Jan-96 1.25 3.00
(Bill Cowher lifting
AFC Championship trophy)
4 6-Jan-80 2.00 4.00
(Joe Greene making
tackle in AFC Championship)
5 24-Sep-78 1.25 3.00
Bennie Cunningham/37-yard flea flicker)
6 6-Jan-80 2.00 4.00
(Rocky Bleier
AFC Championship)
7 27-Dec-75 1.25 3.00
(Andy Russell 93-yard fumble return)
8 26-Oct-97 3.00 5.00
(Jerome Bettis 17-yard TD on OT)
9 30-Dec-78 4.00 8.00
(Terry Bradshaw
John Stallworth/48-yard TD)
10 7-Jan-79 3.00 5.00
(Jack Lambert and rest of defense)

2002 Steelers Post-Gazette

This set of oversized cards (roughly 4 1/2" by 6") was issued one card at a time for the Steelers 8-home games during the 2002 season. Each unnumbered card features a Steelers star on the front along with two small color photos of the player on the back, a brief bio, and the Pittsburgh Post-Gazette sponsor logo.

COMPLETE SET (6) 15.00 30.00
1 Jerome Bettis 2.50 6.00
2 Mark Bruener 1.25 3.00
3 Plaxico Burress 2.50 6.00
4 Jason Gildon 1.25 3.00
5 Joey Porter 1.50 4.00
6 Antwaan Randle El 4.00 10.00
7 Kordell Stewart 1.50 4.00
8 Hines Ward 2.50 6.00

2004 Steelers Beaver County Times Posters

These posters (measuring roughly 13 1/2" by 19") were issued one per Beaver County Times newspaper in 2004. Each includes a color photo of a Steeler's player on one side and another page from the newspaper on the back. We've listed them below in alphabetical order.

1 Jerome Bettis 5.00 10.00
2 Ben Roethlisberger 6.00 12.00
3 Joey Porter 3.00 6.00
4 Kimo Von Oelhoffen 3.00 6.00
5 Willie Williams 3.00 6.00

2005 Steelers Activa Medallions

COMPLETE SET (25) 30.00 80.00
1 Jerome Bettis 2.00 5.00
2 Alan Faneca 1.25 3.00
3 James Farrior 1.25 3.00
4 Larry Foote 1.25 3.00
5 Clark Haggans 1.25 3.00
6 Casey Hampton 1.25 3.00
7 Jeff Hartings 1.25 3.00
8 Chris Hope 1.25 3.00
9 Dan Kreider 1.25 3.00
10 Troy Polamalu 1.50 4.00
11 Joey Porter 1.25 3.00
12 Antwaan Randle El 1.50 4.00
13 Jeff Reed 1.25 3.00
14 Ben Roethlisberger 2.50 6.00
15 Kendall Simmons 1.25 3.00
16 Aaron Smith 1.25 3.00
17 Marvel Smith 1.25 3.00
18 Duce Staley 1.25 3.00
19 Max Starks 1.25 3.00
20 Deshea Townsend 1.25 3.00
21 Jerame Tuman 1.25 3.00
22 Kimo Von Oelhoffen 1.25 3.00
23 Hines Ward 1.50 4.00
24 Willie Williams 1.25 3.00
25 Steelers Logo 1.25 3.00

2006 Steelers Merrick Mint Quarters

COMPLETE SET (11) 60.00 100.00
1 Jerome Bettis 6.00 12.00
2 Tommy Maddox 5.00 10.00
3 Troy Polamalu 6.00 12.00
4 Joey Porter 5.00 10.00
5 Antwaan Randle El 5.00 10.00
6 Ben Roethlisberger 6.00 12.00
7 Duce Staley 5.00 10.00
8 DeShea Townsend 5.00 10.00
9 Hines Ward 5.00 10.00
10 Steelers black logo 5.00 10.00
11 Steelers throwback logo 5.00 10.00

2006 Steelers Topps

COMPLETE SET (12) 3.00 6.00
PIT1 Troy Polamalu .40 1.00
PIT2 Willie Parker .25 .60
PIT3 Heath Miller .25 .60
PIT4 Jerome Bettis .30 .75
PIT5 Hines Ward .30 .75
PIT6 Ben Roethlisberger .40 1.00
PIT7 James Farrior .20 .50
PIT8 Cedrick Wilson .20 .50
PIT9 Joey Porter .20 .50
PIT10 Larry Foote .20 .50
PIT11 Santonio Holmes .40 1.00
PIT12 Omar Jacobs .20 .50

2006 Steelers Topps Super Bowl XL

This boxed factory set was offered by Topps shortly after the Steelers Super Bowl victory in February 2006. Nearly every member of the team was featured in the set which carried an initial SRP of $19.95. One bonus jumbo (3 1/2" by 5") card was also included in every sealed set.

COMPLETE SET (55) 15.00 25.00
1 Jerome Bettis .50 1.25
2 Hines Ward .40 1.00
3 Heath Miller .40 1.00
4 James Farrior .30 .75
5 Ben Roethlisberger 2.00 5.00
6 Troy Polamalu .60 1.50
7 Willie Parker .60 1.50
8 Clark Haggans .30 .75
9 Antwaan Randle El .40 1.00
10 Charlie Batch .30 .75
11 Aaron Smith .30 .75
12 Casey Hampton .30 .75
13 Cedrick Wilson .30 .75
14 Ike Taylor .30 .75
15 Jeff Hartings .30 .75
16 Chris Hope .30 .75
17 Quincy Morgan .30 .75
18 Kimo von Oelhoffen .30 .75
19 Kendall Simmons .30 .75
20 DeShea Townsend .30 .75
21 Ricardo Colclough .30 .75
22 Jeff Reed .30 .75
23 Marvel Smith .30 .75
24 Larry Foote .30 .75
25 Joey Porter .30 .75
26 Tommy Maddox .30 .75
27 Chris Gardocki .30 .75
28 Verron Haynes .30 .75
29 Dan Kreider .30 .75
30 Tyrone Carter .30 .75
31 Duce Staley .40 1.00
32 Mike Logan .30 .75
33 Bryant McFadden .30 .75
34 Clint Kriewaldt .30 .75
35 Chris Hoke .30 .75
36 Jerame Tuman .30 .75
37 Chidi Iwuoma .30 .75
38 Brett Keisel .40 1.00
39 Pittsburgh Steelers Team .40 1.00
40 Willie Parker HL .50 1.25
41 Troy Polamalu HL .50 1.25
42 Ben Roethlisberger HL 1.00 2.50
43 Hines Ward HL .40 1.00
44 Jerome Bettis HL .50 1.25
45 Hines Ward HL .40 1.00
46 Cedrick Wilson HL .30 .75
47 Ben Roethlisberger HL 1.00 2.50
48 Joey Porter HL .30 .75
49 Ben Roethlisberger HL 1.00 2.50
50 Hines Ward HL .40 1.00
51 Ben Roethlisberger HL 1.00 2.50
52 Willie Parker HL .50 1.25
53 Antwaan Randle El HL .30 .75
54 Jerome Bettis HL .50 1.25
Hines Ward
55 Hines Ward MVP .40 1.00
JUM Pittsburgh Steelers Team Jumbo .75 2.00

2006 Steelers Upper Deck Super Bowl XL

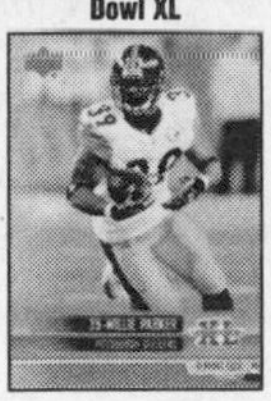

This boxed factory set was offered by Upper Deck shortly after the Steelers Super Bowl victory in February 2006. Nearly every member of the team was featured in the set which carried an initial SRP of $19.95. One bonus jumbo (3 1/2" by 5") card was also included in every sealed set.

COMPLETE SET (51) 15.00 25.00
1 Charlie Batch .30 .75
2 Jerome Bettis .50 1.25
3 Tyrone Carter .30 .75
4 Ricardo Colclough .30 .75
5 Alan Faneca .30 .75
6 James Farrior .30 .75
7 Larry Foote .30 .75
8 Andre Frazier .30 .75
9 Chris Gardocki .30 .75
10 Clark Haggans .30 .75
11 Casey Hampton .30 .75
12 Chris Hope .30 .75
13 Jeff Hartings .30 .75
14 Verron Haynes .30 .75
15 Brett Keisel .40 1.00
16 Travis Kirschke .30 .75
17 Dan Kreider .30 .75
18 Clint Kriewaldt .30 .75
19 Mike Logan .30 .75
20 Tommy Maddox .30 .75
21 Bryant McFadden .30 .75
22 Heath Miller .40 1.00
23 Quincy Morgan .30 .75
24 Kimo von Oelhoffen .30 .75
25 Willie Parker .60 1.50
26 Troy Polamalu .60 1.50
27 Joey Porter .30 .75
28 Antwaan Randle El .40 1.00
29 Jeff Reed .30 .75
30 Ben Roethlisberger 2.00 5.00
31 Kendall Simmons .30 .75
32 Aaron Smith .30 .75
33 Marvel Smith .30 .75
34 Duce Staley .40 1.00
35 Max Starks .30 .75
36 Ike Taylor .30 .75
37 Deshea Townsend .30 .75
38 Hines Ward .40 1.00
39 Greg Warren .30 .75
40 Cedrick Wilson .30 .75
MM1 Ben Roethlisberger MM 1.00 2.50
MM2 Willie Parker MM .50 1.25
MM3 Antwaan Randle El MM .30 .75
MM4 Jerome Bettis MM .50 1.25
SH1 Willie Parker SH .50 1.25
SH2 Ben Roethlisberger SH 1.00 2.50
SH3 Troy Polamalu SH .50 1.25
SH4 Antwaan Randle El SH .30 .75
SH5 Jerome Bettis SH .50 1.25
MVP1 Hines Ward MVP .40 1.00
SBCC Super Bowl Champs .75 2.00
(jumbo card)
Hines Ward
Antwaan Randle EL
Ben Roethlisberger

2007 Steelers Playoff Promos

COMPLETE SET (6) 3.00 6.00
P1 Ben Roethlisberger .50 1.25
P2 Willie Parker .40 1.00
P3 Hines Ward .50 1.25
P4 Santonio Holmes .40 1.00
P5 Troy Polamalu .50 1.25
P6 Matt Spaeth .50 1.25

2007 Steelers Topps

COMPLETE SET (12) 3.00 6.00
1 Willie Parker .25 .60
2 Santonio Holmes .25 .60
3 Heath Miller .20 .50
4 Ben Roethlisberger .30 .75
5 Hines Ward .30 .75
6 Troy Polamalu .30 .75
7 Nate Washington .20 .50
8 James Farrior .20 .50
9 Jeff Reed .20 .50
10 Clark Haggans .20 .50
11 Najeh Davenport .20 .50
12 Lawrence Timmons .30 .75

2008 Steelers Topps

COMPLETE SET (12) 4.00 8.00
1 Heath Miller .20 .50
2 Willie Parker .25 .60
3 Ben Roethlisberger .30 .75
4 Santonio Holmes .25 .60
5 Najeh Davenport .20 .50
6 Hines Ward .25 .60
7 Casey Hampton .20 .50
8 Troy Polamalu .30 .75
9 James Harrison 1.25 3.00
10 James Farrior .20 .50
11 Rashard Mendenhall .60 1.50
12 Limas Sweed .30 .75

2009 Steelers Breast Cancer Awareness

This three card set was issued at a Steelers game in 2009. Each unnumbered card was created by one of the three NFL licensed manufacturers and features the pink ribbon breast cancer awareness logo on the fronts.

COMPLETE SET (3) 2.50 6.00
1 Troy Polamalu Upper Deck 1.00 2.50
2 Ben Roethlisberger Topps 1.00 2.50
3 Hines Ward Panini .75 2.00

2009 Steelers Donruss Super Bowl XLIII

This set was issued at the Donruss/Playoff booth during the 2009 Super Bowl Card Show in Tampa, Florida. A complete set of Steelers and Cardinals was given to any collector that purchased a Score Super Bowl XLIII factory set at the booth during the show.

COMPLETE SET (9) 4.00 8.00
1 Ben Roethlisberger .60 1.50
2 Willie Parker .40 1.00
3 Mewelde Moore .40 1.00
4 Hines Ward .50 1.25
5 Santonio Holmes .50 1.25
6 Heath Miller .50 1.25
7 Limas Sweed .50 1.25
8 Troy Polamalu .60 1.50
9 James Harrison .60 1.50

2009 Steelers Public Opinion Posters

These large posters (measuring roughly 11 1/2" by 22 3/4") were issued one per Public Opinion newspaper in February 2009 the day of the Super Bowl and the day after. Each includes a color photo of a Steeler's player on one side and another page from the newspaper on the back. We've listed them below in alphabetical order.

2 Ben Roethlisberger 4.00 8.00
(February 1, 2009)
1 Santonio Holmes 2.50 5.00
Super Bowl Champions
(February 2, 2009)

2009 Steelers Upper Deck Super Bowl XLIII

COMP.FACT.SET (51) 7.50 15.00
1 Aaron Smith .25 .60
2 Ben Roethlisberger .40 1.00
3 Brett Keisel .30 .75
4 Bruce Davis .25 .60
5 Bryant McFadden .25 .60
6 Byron Leftwich .30 .75
7 Carey Davis .25 .60
8 Casey Hampton .25 .60
9 Chris Hoke .25 .60
10 Chris Kemoeatu .25 .60
11 Darnell Stapleton .25 .60
12 Deshea Townsend .25 .60
13 Gary Russell .25 .60
14 Hines Ward .30 .75
15 Ike Taylor .25 .60
16 James Farrior .25 .60
17 James Harrison .40 1.00
18 Jeff Reed .25 .60
19 Justin Hartwig .25 .60
20 Keyaron Fox .25 .60
21 LaMarr Woodley .25 .60
22 Larry Foote .25 .60
23 Lawrence Timmons .25 .60
24 Limas Sweed .30 .75
25 Matt Spaeth .25 .60
26 Max Starks .25 .60
27 Mewelde Moore .25 .60
28 Mitch Berger .25 .60
29 Nate Washington .25 .60
30 Nick Eason .25 .60
31 Orpheus Roye .25 .60
32 Ryan Clark .25 .60
33 Santonio Holmes .30 .75
34 Trai Essex .25 .60
35 Travis Kirschke .25 .60
36 Troy Polamalu .40 1.00
37 Tyrone Carter .25 .60
38 William Gay .25 .60
39 Willie Colon .25 .60
40 Willie Parker .25 .60
41 Troy Polamalu SH .40 1.00
42 Ben Roethlisberger SH .40 1.00
43 Willie Parker SH .25 .60
44 Mewelde Moore SH .25 .60
45 James Harrison SH .40 1.00
46 Santonio Holmes MM .30 .75
47 Ben Roethlisberger MM .40 1.00
48 James Harrison MM .40 1.00
49 Santonio Holmes MM .30 .75
50 Santonio Holmes SB MVP .30 .75
51 Pittsburgh Steelers Jumbo .75 2.00
Ben Roethlisberger
Willie Parker
Byron Leftwich
Carey Davis
Limas Sweed

2011 Steelers Panini Super Bowl XLV

This set was sold exclusively at the 2011 Super Bowl Card Show in Dallas. The cards feature the Super Bowl XLV logo on the fronts and the backs are numbered.

COMPLETE SET (9) 8.00 20.00
1 Troy Polamalu 1.25 3.00
2 Ben Roethlisberger 1.25 3.00
3 Hines Ward 1.00 2.50
4 James Harrison 1.25 3.00
5 LaMarr Woodley .75 2.00
6 Lawrence Timmons .75 2.00
7 Mike Wallace 1.25 3.00
8 Rashard Mendenhall 1.00 2.50
9 Emmanuel Sanders .75 2.00

1979 Stop'N'Go

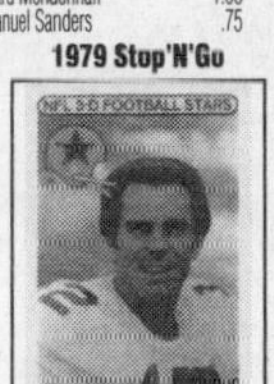

The 1979 Stop 'N' Go Markets set contains 18 3-D cards. The cards measure approximately 2 1/8" by 3 1/4". They are numbered and contain both a 1979 National Football League Players Association copyright date and a Xograph (predecessor of Sportflics and Score) trademark registration on the back. The set shows a heavy emphasis on players from the two Texas teams, the Dallas Cowboys and Houston Oilers, as they were issued primarily in the south.

COMPLETE SET (18) 40.00 75.00
1 Gregg Bingham .60 1.50
2 Ken Burrough .75 2.00
3 Preston Pearson .75 2.00
4 Sam Cunningham .75 2.00
5 Robert Newhouse .75 2.00
6 Walter Payton 15.00 30.00
7 Robert Brazile .60 1.50
8 Rocky Bleier 2.00 4.00
9 Toni Fritsch .60 1.50
10 Jack Ham 2.00 4.00
11 Jay Saldi .60 1.50
12 Roger Staubach 12.00 20.00
13 Franco Harris 4.00 8.00
14 Otis Armstrong 1.50 3.00
15 Lyle Alzado 1.50 3.00
16 Billy Johnson .75 2.00
17 Elvin Bethea 1.50 3.00
18 Joe Greene 3.00 6.00

1980 Stop'N'Go

The 1980 Stop 'N' Go Markets football card set contains 48 3-D cards. The cards measure approximately 2 1/8" by 3 1/4". Although similar to the 1979 issue, the cards can easily be distinguished by the two stars surrounding the name plaque on the front of the 1980 set and the obvious copyright date on the respective backs. One card was given out with each soda fountain drink purchased through September at participating Stop'N'Go and Doty stores. While players from National Football League teams, other than those in Texas, are indeed contained in the set, the emphasis remains on the Cowboys and Oilers. Cards with a "Doty" logo on back are more difficult to find than the base Stop'N'Go.

COMPLETE SET (48) 25.00 40.00
*DOTY BACKS: 2.5X TO 6X
1 John Jefferson .40 1.00
2 Herb Scott .25 .60
3 Pat Donovan .25 .60
4 William Andrews .40 1.00
5 Frank Corral .25 .60
6 Fred Dryer .40 1.00
7 Franco Harris 3.00 6.00
8 Leon Gray .25 .60
9 Gregg Bingham .25 .60
10 Louie Kelcher .25 .60
11 Robert Newhouse .30 .75
12 Preston Pearson .40 1.00
13 Wallace Francis .30 .75
14 Pat Haden .40 1.00
15 Jim Youngblood .25 .60
16 Rocky Bleier UER .75 2.00
Name spelled Blier on front
17 Gifford Nielsen .25 .60
18 Elvin Bethea .40 1.00
19 Charlie Joiner .75 2.00
20 Tony Hill .40 1.00
21 Drew Pearson .75 2.00
22 Alfred Jenkins .30 .75
23 Dave Elmendorf .25 .60
24 Jack Reynolds .30 .75
25 Joe Greene UER 2.00 4.00
Name spelled Green on front
26 Robert Brazile .25 .60
27 Mike Reinfeldt .25 .60
28 Bob Griese 3.00 6.00
29 Harold Carmichael .60 1.50
30 Ottis Anderson 1.50 3.00
31 Ahmad Rashad .75 2.00
32 Archie Manning .60 1.50
33 Ricky Bell .40 1.00
34 Jay Saldi .25 .60
35 Ken Burrough .30 .75
36 Don Woods .25 .60
37 Henry Childs .25 .60
38 Wilbur Jackson .25 .60
39 Steve DeBerg .40 1.00
40 Ron Jessie .30 .75
41 Mel Blount .75 2.00
42 Cliff Branch .75 2.00
43 Chuck Muncie .30 .75
44 Ken MacAfee .25 .60
45 Charle Young .30 .75
46 Cody Jones .25 .60
47 Jack Ham 1.00 2.50
48 Ray Guy .40 1.00

1997 Studio

The 1997 Studio football set was released in two-card packs with most cards being jumbo sized (roughly 8' by 10"). Only Quarterback Club members were included in the release. A 12-card Class of Distinction subset was included as well as three parallel and two insert sets.

COMPLETE SET (36) 7.50 20.00
1 Troy Aikman .75 2.00
2 Tony Banks .25 .60
3 Jeff Blake .25 .60
4 Drew Bledsoe .50 1.25
5 Mark Brunell .50 1.25
6 Kerry Collins .40 1.00
7 Trent Dilfer .40 1.00
8 John Elway 1.50 4.00
9 Brett Favre 1.50 4.00
10 Gus Frerotte .25 .60
11 Jeff George .25 .60
12 Neil O'Donnell .15 .40
13 Jim Harbaugh .25 .60
14 Michael Irvin .40 1.00
15 Dan Marino 1.50 4.00
16 Steve McNair .50 1.25
17 Rick Mirer .15 .40
18 Jerry Rice .75 2.00
19 Barry Sanders 1.25 3.00
20 Junior Seau .40 1.00
21 Heath Shuler .15 .40
22 Emmitt Smith 1.25 3.00
23 Kordell Stewart .40 1.00
24 Steve Young .50 1.25
25 Troy Aikman CD .40 1.00
26 Drew Bledsoe CD .25 .60
27 Mark Brunell CD .40 1.00
28 Kerry Collins CD .25 .60
29 John Elway CD .75 2.00
30 Brett Favre CD .75 2.00
31 Dan Marino CD .75 2.00
32 Jerry Rice CD .40 1.00
33 Barry Sanders CD .60 1.50
34 Emmitt Smith CD .60 1.50
35 Kordell Stewart CD .25 .60
36 Steve Young CD .40 1.00

1997 Studio Postcard Portraits

COMPLETE SET (36) 20.00 50.00
*PC PORTRAITS: .8X TO 2X BASIC CARDS

1997 Studio Press Proofs Gold

COMPLETE SET (36) 60.00 150.00
*GOLD STARS: 2.5X TO 6X BASIC CARDS
STATED PRINT RUN 1000 SERIAL #'d SETS

1997 Studio Press Proofs Silver

COMPLETE SET (36) 40.00 80.00
*SILVER STARS: 1.2X TO 3X BASIC CARDS
STATED PRINT RUN 4000 SETS

1997 Studio Red Zone Masterpieces

COMPLETE SET (24) 50.00 120.00
STATED PRINT RUN 3500 SERIAL #'d SETS
1 Troy Aikman 4.00 10.00
2 Tony Banks 1.25 3.00
3 Jeff Blake 1.25 3.00
4 Drew Bledsoe 2.50 6.00
5 Mark Brunell 2.50 6.00
6 Kerry Collins 2.00 5.00
7 Trent Dilfer 2.00 5.00
8 John Elway 8.00 20.00
9 Brett Favre 8.00 20.00
10 Gus Frerotte 1.25 3.00
11 Jeff George 1.25 3.00
12 Elvis Grbac 1.25 3.00
13 Neil O'Donnell .75 2.00
14 Michael Irvin 2.00 5.00
15 Dan Marino 8.00 20.00
16 Steve McNair 2.50 6.00
17 Rick Mirer .75 2.00
18 Jerry Rice 4.00 10.00
19 Barry Sanders 6.00 15.00
20 Warren Moon 2.00 5.00
21 Heath Shuler .75 2.00
22 Emmitt Smith 6.00 15.00
23 Kordell Stewart 2.00 5.00
24 Steve Young 2.50 6.00

1997 Studio Stained Glass Stars

COMPLETE SET (24) 125.00 250.00
STATED PRINT RUN 1000 SERIAL #'d SETS
1 Troy Aikman 12.50 30.00
2 Tony Banks 4.00 10.00
3 Jeff Blake 4.00 10.00
4 Drew Bledsoe 8.00 20.00
5 Mark Brunell 8.00 20.00
6 Kerry Collins 6.00 15.00
7 Trent Dilfer 6.00 15.00
8 John Elway 25.00 60.00
9 Brett Favre 25.00 60.00
10 Gus Frerotte 4.00 10.00
11 Jeff George 4.00 10.00
12 Elvis Grbac 4.00 10.00
13 Jim Harbaugh 4.00 10.00
14 Michael Irvin 6.00 15.00
15 Dan Marino 25.00 60.00
16 Steve McNair 8.00 20.00
17 Rick Mirer 2.50 6.00
18 Jerry Rice 12.50 30.00
19 Barry Sanders 20.00 50.00
20 Junior Seau 6.00 15.00
21 Vinny Testaverde 4.00 10.00
22 Emmitt Smith 20.00 50.00
23 Kordell Stewart 6.00 15.00
24 Steve Young 8.00 20.00

1995 Summit

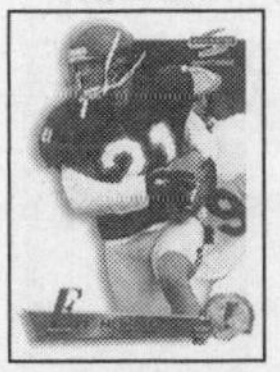

This is the first year of release for Summit and the 200 card set is billed as the series two Score set. The set came seven cards per pack with a suggested retail price of $1.99. Card fronts have a 24 paint white stock background with the player's name and helmet logo in gold foil at the bottom. Rookie Cards include Ki-Jana Carter, Kerry Collins, Joey Galloway, Curtis Martin, Steve McNair, Rashaan Salaam, Kordell Stewart, J.J. Stokes, Tamarick Vanover and Michael Westbrook. Three Promo cards were produced and listed at the end of our checklist.

COMPLETE SET (200) 7.50 20.00
1 Neil O'Donnell .07 .20
2 Jim Everett .02 .10
3 Craig Heyward .07 .20
4 Jeff Blake RC .40 1.00
5 Alvin Harper .02 .10
6 Heath Shuler .07 .20
7 Rodney Hampton .07 .20
8 Dave Krieg .02 .10
9 Mark Brunell .25 .60
10 Rob Moore .07 .20
11 Daryl Johnston .07 .20
12 Marcus Allen .15 .40
13 Terance Mathis .07 .20
14 Frank Reich .02 .10
15 Gus Frerotte .07 .20
16 John Elway .75 2.00
17 Amp Lee .02 .10
18 Chris Miller .02 .10
19 Leroy Hoard .02 .10
20 Stan Humphries .07 .20
21 Charlie Garner .15 .40
22 Jim Kelly .15 .40
23 Gary Brown .02 .10
24 Byron Bam Morris .02 .10
25 Edgar Bennett .07 .20
26 Erik Kramer .02 .10
27 Dan Marino .75 2.00
28 Michael Haynes .07 .20
29 Lake Dawson .07 .20
30 Ben Coates .07 .20
31 Michael Jackson .07 .20
32 Brett Favre .75 2.00
33 Calvin Williams .07 .20
34 Steve Young .30 .75
35 Troy Aikman .30 .75
36 Greg Hill .07 .20
37 Leonard Russell .02 .10
38 Jeff George .07 .20
39 Herschel Walker .07 .20
40 Eric Green .02 .10
41 Haywood Jeffires .02 .10
42 Terry Kirby .07 .20
43 Darnay Scott .07 .20
44 Tim Brown .15 .40
45 Brian Mitchell .02 .10
46 Desmond Howard .07 .20
47 Warren Moon .07 .20
48 Andre Reed .07 .20
49 Adrian Murrell .07 .20
50 Marshall Faulk .50 1.25
51 Lewis Tillman .02 .10
52 Don Beebe .02 .10
53 Jerome Bettis .15 .40
54 Brett Perriman .07 .20
55 Mario Bates .07 .20
56 Ronnie Harmon .02 .10
57 Isaac Bruce .25 .60
58 Jackie Harris .02 .10
59 Dexter Carter .02 .10
60 Charles Johnson .07 .20
61 Herman Moore .15 .40
62 Craig Erickson .02 .10
63 Tony Martin .07 .20
64 Emmitt Smith .60 1.50
65 Brent Jones .02 .10
66 Ricky Watters .07 .20
67 Henry Ellard .07 .20
68 Vinny Testaverde .07 .20
69 Mark Pike .02 .10
70 Curtis Conway .15 .40
71 Michael Irvin .15 .40
72 Jay Novacek .07 .20
73 Howard Cross .02 .10
74 Drew Bledsoe .25 .60
75 Steve Beuerlein .07 .20
76 Andre Rison .07 .20
77 Morten Andersen .02 .10
78 Trent Dilfer .15 .40
79 Cris Carter .15 .40
80 Natrone Means .07 .20
81 Bernie Parmalee .07 .20
82 Randall Cunningham .15 .40
83 Eric Metcalf .07 .20
84 Rick Mirer .07 .20
85 Mark Ingram .02 .10
86 David Klingler .07 .20
87 Kevin Williams .07 .20
88 Erric Pegram .07 .20
89 Keith Byars .02 .10
90 Sean Dawkins .07 .20
91 Chris Warren .07 .20
92 William Floyd .07 .20
93 Jeff Hostetler .07 .20
94 Carl Pickens .07 .20
95 Flipper Anderson .02 .10
96 Johnny Mitchell .02 .10
97 Larry Centers .07 .20

98 Shannon Sharpe .07 .20
99 Errict Rhett .07 .20
100 Fred Barnett .07 .20
101 Harold Green .02 .10
102 Scott Mitchell .07 .20
103 Jerry Rice .40 1.00
104 Shawn Jefferson .02 .10
105 Glyn Milburn .02 .10
106 Garrison Hearst .15 .40
107 John Taylor .02 .10
108 Keith Cash .02 .10
109 Robert Brooks .15 .40
110 Barry Sanders .60 1.50
111 Ernest Givins .02 .10
112 Steve Tasker .07 .20
113 Jeff Graham .02 .10
114 Chris Chandler .07 .20
115 Lorenzo Neal .02 .10
116 Bert Emanuel .15 .40
117 Mike Sherrard .02 .10
118 Harvey Williams .02 .10
119 Reggie Brooks .07 .20
120 Steve Walsh .02 .10
121 Leroy Thompson .02 .10
122 Dave Brown .07 .20
123 Lorenzo White .02 .10
124 Steve Bono .07 .20
125 Irving Fryar .07 .20
126 Jake Reed .07 .20
127 Boomer Esiason .07 .20
128 Rocket Ismail .07 .20
129 Vincent Brisby .02 .10
130 Robert Smith .15 .40
131 Anthony Miller .07 .20
132 Roosevelt Potts .02 .10
133 Dave Meggett .02 .10
134 Junior Seau CC .15 .40
135 Neil Smith CC .07 .20
136 Charles Haley CC .07 .20
137 Rod Woodson CC .07 .20
138 Deion Sanders CC .25 .60
139 Reggie White CC .15 .40
140 John Randle CC .07 .20
141 Greg Lloyd CC .07 .20
142 Cortez Kennedy CC .07 .20
143 Bruce Smith CC .15 .40
144 J.J. Stokes RC .15 .40
145 Kyle Brady RC .15 .40
146 Frank Sanders RC .15 .40
147 Michael Westbrook RC .15 .40
148 Rob Johnson RC .50 1.25
149 Tyrone Poole RC .15 .40
150 Lovell Pinkney RC .02 .10
151 Tyrone Wheatley RC .60 1.50
152 Steve McNair RC 1.50 4.00
153 Napoleon Kaufman RC .60 1.50
154 Tamarick Vanover RC .15 .40
155 Todd Collins RC .50 1.25
156 Kevin Carter RC .15 .40
157 Rodney Thomas RC .07 .20
158 Stoney Case RC .02 .10
159 Kordell Stewart RC .75 2.00
160 Tony Boselli RC .15 .40
161 Sherman Williams RC .02 .10
162 Christian Fauria RC .07 .20
163 Ray Zellars RC .07 .20
164 Ki-Jana Carter RC .15 .40
165 Terrell Fletcher RC .02 .10
166 Curtis Martin RC 1.50 4.00
167 Eric Zeier RC .15 .40
168 Joey Galloway RC .75 2.00
169 Warren Sapp RC .75 2.00
170 Kerry Collins RC .75 2.00
171 Mark Bruener RC .07 .20
172 Chris Sanders RC .07 .20
173 Rashaan Salaam RC .07 .20
174 Jerry Rice OW .20 .50
175 Marshall Faulk OW .25 .60
176 Drew Bledsoe OW .15 .40
177 Emmitt Smith OW .30 .75
178 Tim Brown OW .07 .20
179 Steve Young OW .15 .40
180 Barry Sanders OW .30 .75
181 Michael Irvin OW .07 .20
182 Dan Marino OW .40 1.00
183 Jeff George OW .07 .20
184 Chris Warren OW .07 .20
185 Herman Moore OW .15 .40
186 Andre Rison OW .07 .20
187 Byron Bam Morris OW .02 .10
188 Troy Aikman OW .20 .50
189 Jim Kelly OW .15 .40
190 John Elway OW .40 1.00
191 Cris Carter OW .15 .40
192 Shannon Sharpe OW .02 .10
193 Brett Favre OW .40 1.00
194 Drew Bledsoe CL .15 .40
195 John Elway CL .25 .60
196 Dan Marino CL .25 .60
197 Brett Favre CL .25 .60
198 Troy Aikman CL .15 .40
199 Steve Young CL .15 .40
200 Rick Mirer CL .07 .20
P1 Emmitt Smith Promo .75 2.00
Backfield Stars
P34 Steve Young Promo .40 1.00
P74 Drew Bledsoe Promo .50 1.25

1995 Summit Ground Zero

COMPLETE SET (200) 60.00 120.00
*STARS: 3X TO 8X BASIC CARDS
*RCs: 1.5X TO 4X BASIC CARDS
STATED ODDS 1:7

1995 Summit Backfield Stars

COMPLETE SET (20) 25.00 60.00
STATED ODDS 1:37
1 Emmitt Smith 5.00 12.00
2 Marshall Faulk 4.00 10.00
3 Barry Sanders 5.00 12.00
4 Ricky Watters .60 1.50
5 Rodney Hampton .60 1.50
6 Chris Warren .60 1.50
7 Garrison Hearst 1.25 3.00
8 Tyrone Wheatley 3.00 6.00
9 Rashaan Salaam .30 .75
10 Natrone Means .60 1.50
11 Byron Bam Morris .30 .75
12 Jerome Bettis 1.25 3.00
13 Errict Rhett .60 1.50
14 William Floyd .60 1.50
15 Edgar Bennett .60 1.50
16 Marcus Allen 1.25 3.00
17 Mario Bates .60 1.50
18 Lorenzo White .30 .75
19 Gary Brown .30 .75
20 Craig Heyward .60 1.50

1995 Summit Rookie Summit

COMPLETE SET (18) 40.00 80.00
STATED ODDS 1:23
1 Kevin Carter 1.50 4.00
2 Sherman Williams .75 2.00
3 Kordell Stewart 2.00 5.00
4 Christian Fauria .75 2.00
5 J.J. Stokes 1.25 3.00
6 Joey Galloway 2.00 5.00
7 Michael Westbrook 1.50 4.00
8 James O. Stewart 1.50 4.00
9 Stoney Case .75 2.00
10 Kyle Brady .75 2.00
11 Terrell Fletcher .75 2.00
12 Todd Collins 3.00 8.00
13 Jimmy Oliver .75 2.00
14 Napoleon Kaufman 1.50 4.00
15 John Walsh .75 2.00
16 Kerry Collins 2.00 5.00
17 Ki-Jana Carter 1.25 3.00
18 Terrell Davis 3.00 8.00

1995 Summit Team Summit

COMPLETE SET (12) 50.00 100.00
STATED ODDS 1:91
1 Dan Marino 8.00 20.00
2 Emmitt Smith 6.00 15.00
3 Drew Bledsoe 2.50 6.00
4 Troy Aikman 3.00 8.00
5 Byron Bam Morris .40 1.00
6 Steve Young 3.00 8.00
7 Randall Cunningham 1.50 4.00
8 Natrone Means .75 2.00
9 Barry Sanders 6.00 15.00
10 Brett Favre 8.00 20.00
11 Errict Rhett .75 2.00
12 Jerry Rice 4.00 10.00

1996 Summit

This standard-sized set of 200 cards was issued in seven-card packs. The cards have a picture of the player inside of a jagged oval with a black gridiron edging. There is gold foil stamping on the bottom which gives the players name and a gold foil helmet of his team. The backs have a picture of the player within a helmet, the card number, and a group of 1995 statistics.

COMPLETE SET (200) 12.00 30.00
1 Troy Aikman .50 1.25
2 Marshall Faulk .25 .60
3 Bruce Smith .08 .25
4 Jerome Bettis .20 .50
5 Bryan Cox .02 .10
6 Robert Brooks .20 .50
7 Dan Marino 1.00 2.50
8 Irving Fryar .08 .25
9 Jerry Rice .50 1.25
10 Ki-Jana Carter .08 .25
11 Herman Moore .08 .25
12 Derrick Thomas .20 .50
13 Curtis Martin .40 1.00
14 Jeff Hostetler .02 .10
15 Errict Rhett .08 .25
16 Emmitt Smith .75 2.00
17 Aaron Craver .02 .10
18 Kyle Brady .02 .10
19 Tony Martin .08 .25
20 Vinny Testaverde .08 .25
21 Charles Haley .08 .25
22 Rodney Thomas .02 .10
23 Jim Everett .02 .10
24 Brian Blades .02 .10
25 Frank Sanders .08 .25
26 Bryce Paup .02 .10
27 Anthony Miller .08 .25
28 Ken Dilger .08 .25
29 Orlando Thomas .02 .10
30 Rodney Hampton .08 .25
31 Ken Norton Jr. .02 .10
32 Darren Woodson .08 .25
33 Antonio Freeman .20 .50
34 Steve Bono .02 .10
35 Ben Coates .08 .25
36 Jeff George .08 .25
37 Curtis Conway .20 .50
38 Steve Atwater .02 .10
39 Fred Barnett .02 .10
40 Joey Galloway .20 .50
41 Jim Kelly .20 .50
42 Michael Irvin .20 .50
43 Steve Tasker .02 .10
44 Warren Moon .08 .25
45 Hugh Douglas .08 .25
46 Steve Walsh .02 .10
47 Kerry Collins .20 .50
48 Barry Sanders .75 2.00
49 Steve Young .40 1.00
50 Jim Harbaugh .08 .25
51 Tyrone Wheatley .08 .25
52 Boomer Esiason .08 .25
53 Deion Sanders .30 .75
54 Steve McNair .40 1.00
55 Willie McGinest .02 .10
56 Adrian Murrell .08 .25
57 Thurman Thomas .20 .50
58 John Elway 1.00 2.50
59 William Floyd .08 .25
60 Eric Zeier .02 .10
61 Dave Krieg .02 .10
62 Eric Bjornson .02 .10
63 Brett Favre 1.00 2.50
64 Derrick Alexander DE .02 .10
65 Charlie Garner .08 .25
66 Stan Humphries .08 .25
67 Bert Emanuel .08 .25
68 Scott Mitchell .08 .25
69 Quentin Coryatt .02 .10
70 Eric Green .02 .10
71 Jeff Graham .02 .10
72 Ernie Mills .02 .10
73 Trent Dilfer .20 .50
74 Sherman Williams .02 .10
75 Tamarick Vanover .08 .25
76 Drew Bledsoe .30 .75
77 Jay Novacek .02 .10
78 Edgar Bennett .08 .25
79 Tim Brown .20 .50
80 Greg Lloyd .08 .25
81 Darick Holmes .02 .10
82 Carl Pickens .08 .25
83 Flipper Anderson .02 .10
84 Bernie Kosar .02 .10
85 Dave Brown .02 .10
86 Calvin Williams .02 .10
87 Michael Westbrook .20 .50
88 Kevin Williams .02 .10
89 Chris Sanders .08 .25
90 Robert Smith .08 .25
91 Cris Carter .20 .50
92 Gus Frerotte .08 .25
93 Larry Centers .08 .25
94 Eric Metcalf .02 .10
95 Isaac Bruce .20 .50
96 Kordell Stewart .20 .50
97 Ricky Watters .08 .25
98 Terrell Fletcher .02 .10
99 Bernie Parmalee .02 .10
100 Harvey Williams .02 .10
101 Hardy Nickerson .02 .10
102 Jeff Blake .20 .50
103 Terry Allen .08 .25
104 Yancey Thigpen .08 .25
105 Greg Hill .08 .25
106 Chris Warren .08 .25
107 Terrell Davis .40 1.00
108 Mark Brunell .30 .75
109 Alvin Harper .02 .10
110 Marcus Allen .20 .50
111 Garrison Hearst .08 .25
112 Derek Loville .02 .10
113 Craig Heyward .02 .10
114 Kimble Anders .08 .25
115 O.J. McDuffie .08 .25
116 Junior Seau .20 .50
117 Terry Kirby .08 .25
118 Erric Pegram .02 .10
119 Rick Mirer .08 .25
120 Erik Kramer .02 .10
121 Brett Perriman .02 .10
122 Shawn Jefferson .02 .10
123 J.J. Stokes .20 .50
124 Kevin Greene .08 .25
125 Daryl Johnston .08 .25
126 Mark Chmura .08 .25
127 James O.Stewart .08 .25
128 Mario Bates .08 .25
129 Rodney Peete .02 .10
130 Quinn Early .02 .10
131 Shannon Sharpe .08 .25
132 Neil Smith .08 .25
133 Herschel Walker .08 .25
134 Aaron Bailey .02 .10
135 Rashaan Salaam .08 .25
136 Kevin Smith .02 .10
137 Sean Dawkins .02 .10
138 Jake Reed .08 .25
139 Neil O'Donnell .08 .25
140 Reggie White .20 .50
141 Vincent Brisby .02 .10
142 Napoleon Kaufman .20 .50
143 Brent Jones .02 .10
144 Mark Seay .02 .10
145 Heath Shuler .08 .25
146 Wayne Chrebet .30 .75
147 Leeland McElroy RC .08 .25
148 Tim Biakabutuka RC .20 .50
149 John Mobley RC .02 .10
150 Tony Brackens RC .20 .50
151 Danny Kanell RC .20 .50
152 Eddie Kennison RC .20 .50
153 Jonathan Ogden RC .20 .50
154 Bobby Engram RC .20 .50
155 Chris Darkins RC .02 .10
156 Daryl Gardener RC .02 .10
157 Keyshawn Johnson RC .50 1.25
158 Mike Alstott RC .50 1.25
159 Simeon Rice RC .50 1.25
160 Eric Moulds RC .60 1.50
161 Stepfret Williams RC .08 .25
162 Eddie George RC .60 1.50
163 Duane Clemons RC .02 .10
164 Amani Toomer RC .50 1.25
165 Rickey Dudley RC .20 .50
166 Bobby Hoying RC .20 .50
167 Lawrence Phillips RC .20 .50
168 Willie Anderson RC .02 .10
169 Derrick Mayes RC .20 .50
170 Kevin Hardy RC .20 .50
171 Terry Glenn RC .50 1.25
172 Stephen Davis RC .75 2.00
173 Walt Harris RC .02 .10
174 Marvin Harrison RC 1.25 3.00
175 Karim Abdul-Jabbar RC .20 .50
176 Alex Molden RC .02 .10
177 Regan Upshaw RC .02 .10
178 Jerald Moore RC .08 .25
179 Alex Van Dyke RC .08 .25
180 Jeff Lewis RC .08 .25
181 Cedric Jones RC .02 .10
182 Jim Kelly QH .20 .50
183 Troy Aikman QH .25 .60
184 Jim Harbaugh QH .08 .25
185 Neil O'Donnell QH .08 .25
186 Steve Young QH .20 .50
187 Kerry Collins QH .20 .50
188 Scott Mitchell QH .02 .10
189 Drew Bledsoe QH .20 .50
190 Kordell Stewart QH .20 .50
191 Erik Kramer QH .02 .10
192 Brett Favre QH .50 1.25
193 Warren Moon QH .02 .10
194 Jeff Blake QH .08 .25
195 Mark Brunell QH .20 .50
196 John Elway QH .50 1.25
197 Emmitt Smith .20 .50
Checklist back
198 Dan Marino .25 .60
Checklist back
199 Brett Favre CL .25 .60
200 Jim Harbaugh .08 .25
Checklist back

1996 Summit Artist's Proofs

*AP STARS: 6X TO 15X BASIC CARDS
*AP RCs: 3X TO 8X BASIC CARDS

1996 Summit Ground Zero

COMPLETE SET (200) 125.00 250.00
*STARS: 3X TO 8X BASIC CARDS
*RCs: 1.5X TO 4X BASIC CARDS

1996 Summit Premium Stock

COMPLETE SET (200) 12.00 30.00
*PREMIUM STOCK: SAME PRICE AS BASIC CARDS

1996 Summit Hit The Hole

COMPLETE SET (16) 60.00 150.00
RANDOM INSERTS IN MAGAZINE PACKS
1 Rashaan Salaam 1.25 3.00
2 Marshall Faulk 5.00 12.00
3 Ricky Watters 2.00 5.00
4 Leeland McElroy 1.25 3.00
5 Emmitt Smith 15.00 40.00
6 Eddie George 8.00 20.00
7 Curtis Martin 8.00 20.00
8 Lawrence Phillips 2.50 6.00
9 Darick Holmes .75 2.00
10 Barry Sanders 15.00 40.00
11 Karim Abdul-Jabbar 4.00 10.00
12 Errict Rhett 2.00 5.00
13 Terrell Davis 8.00 20.00
14 Chris Warren 2.00 5.00
15 Rodney Thomas .75 2.00
16 Tim Biakabutuka 2.50 6.00

1996 Summit Silver Foil

COMP.SILVER FOIL SET (200) 12.00 30.00
*SILVER FOILS: .4X TO 1X BASIC CARDS

1996 Summit Inspirations

COMPLETE SET (18) 25.00 60.00
STATED ODDS 1:17
STATED PRINT RUN 8000 SERIAL #'d SETS
1 Jim Harbaugh .75 2.00
2 Alex Van Dyke .30 .75
3 Mike Alstott 1.50 4.00
4 Jonathan Ogden .60 1.50
5 Brett Favre 8.00 20.00
6 Tony Brackens .60 1.50
7 Drew Bledsoe 2.50 6.00
8 Danny Kanell .60 1.50
9 Eric Moulds 2.00 5.00
10 John Elway 8.00 20.00
11 Eddie George 2.00 5.00
12 Karim Abdul-Jabbar .60 1.50
13 Tim Biakabutuka .60 1.50
14 Jeff Lewis .30 .75
15 Terry Glenn 1.50 4.00
16 Jeff Blake 1.50 4.00
17 Kevin Hardy .60 1.50
18 Bobby Engram .60 1.50

1996 Summit Third and Long

COMPLETE SET (18) 60.00 150.00
STATED PRINT RUN 2000
*MIRAGE REDEMPTIONS: .05X TO .1X
*MIRAGE PRIZE/600: .6X TO 1.5X
*PROMOS: .2X TO .5X BASIC INSERTS
1 Michael Irvin 2.00 5.00
2 Dan Marino 10.00 25.00
3 Keyshawn Johnson 2.50 6.00
4 Chris Warren 1.00 2.50
5 Rashaan Salaam 1.00 2.50
6 Brett Favre 10.00 25.00
7 Terry Glenn 2.50 6.00
8 Steve Young 4.00 10.00
9 Kerry Collins 2.00 5.00
10 Emmitt Smith 8.00 20.00
11 Marvin Harrison 6.00 15.00
12 Jerry Rice 5.00 12.00
13 John Elway 10.00 25.00
14 Drew Bledsoe 3.00 8.00
15 Eddie Kennison 1.00 2.50
16 Troy Aikman 5.00 12.00
17 Barry Sanders 8.00 20.00
18 Terrell Davis 4.00 10.00

1996 Summit Turf Team

COMPLETE SET (16) 50.00 125.00
STATED PRINT RUN 4000 SER.#'d SETS
*FOILS: 1X TO 2X BASIC INSERTS
FOILS: RAND.INS.IN PREMIUM STOCK
1 Emmitt Smith 6.00 15.00
2 Brett Favre 8.00 20.00
3 Curtis Martin 3.00 8.00
4 Steve Young 3.00 8.00
5 Kerry Collins 1.50 4.00
6 Barry Sanders 6.00 15.00
7 Dan Marino 8.00 20.00
8 Isaac Bruce 1.50 4.00
9 Troy Aikman 4.00 10.00
10 Marshall Faulk 2.00 5.00
11 Joey Galloway 1.50 4.00
12 Jeff Blake 1.50 4.00
13 Drew Bledsoe 2.50 6.00
14 John Elway 8.00 20.00
15 Jerry Rice 4.00 10.00
16 Michael Irvin 1.50 4.00

1976 Sunbeam NFL Die Cuts

This 28-card set features standard size cards. The cards are die-cut so that they can stand up when the perforation is popped. The team's helmet, team nickname, and a generic player drawing are pictured on each card front. The card back features a narrative about the team and the Sunbeam logo. The cards were printed on white or gray card stock. The cards are unnumbered and may be found with or without the Sunbeam logo on the white stock version. A header card was produced announcing the 1976 season. There was also a card saver book issued. All the prices below are for unpunched cards.

COMPLETE SET (29) 137.50 275.00
1 Atlanta Falcons 6.00 12.00
2 Baltimore Colts 6.00 12.00
3 Buffalo Bills 6.00 12.00
4 Chicago Bears 7.50 15.00
5 Cincinnati Bengals 6.00 12.00
6 Cleveland Browns 6.00 12.00
7 Dallas Cowboys 7.50 15.00
8 Denver Broncos 6.00 12.00
9 Detroit Lions 6.00 12.00
10 Green Bay Packers 7.50 15.00
11 Houston Oilers 6.00 12.00
12 Kansas City Chiefs 6.00 12.00
13 Los Angeles Rams 6.00 12.00
14 Miami Dolphins 7.50 15.00
15 Minnesota Vikings 7.50 15.00
16 New England Patriots 6.00 12.00
17 New Orleans Saints 6.00 12.00
18 New York Giants 6.00 12.00
19 New York Jets 6.00 12.00
20 Oakland Raiders 7.50 15.00
21 Philadelphia Eagles 6.00 12.00
22 Pittsburgh Steelers 7.50 15.00
23 St. Louis Cardinals 6.00 12.00
24 San Diego Chargers 6.00 12.00
25 San Francisco 49ers 7.50 15.00
26 Seattle Seahawks 6.00 12.00
27 Tampa Bay Buccaneers 6.00 12.00
28 Washington Redskins 7.50 15.00
NNO NFL Logo 7.50 15.00
Blankbacked
NNO Saver Book 12.50 25.00

1976 Sunbeam NFL Pennant Stickers

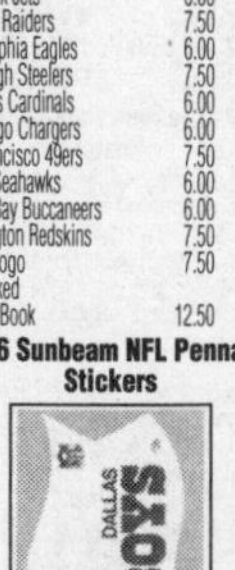

This set of stickers was issued along with the logo cards and was intended to be pasted into the saver album. Each measures roughly 1 3/4" by 2 7/8" and includes the team's logo and name within a pennant shaped design. The backs feature the team's all-time record along with a Sunbeam ad.

COMPLETE SET (28) 137.50 275.00
1 Atlanta Falcons 6.00 12.00
2 Baltimore Colts 6.00 12.00
3 Buffalo Bills 6.00 12.00
4 Chicago Bears 7.50 15.00
5 Cincinnati Bengals 6.00 12.00
6 Cleveland Browns 7.50 15.00
7 Dallas Cowboys 7.50 15.00
8 Denver Broncos 6.00 12.00
9 Detroit Lions 6.00 12.00
10 Green Bay Packers 7.50 15.00
11 Houston Oilers 6.00 12.00
12 Kansas City Chiefs 6.00 12.00
13 Los Angeles Rams 6.00 12.00
14 Miami Dolphins 7.50 15.00
15 Minnesota Vikings 7.50 15.00
16 New England Patriots 6.00 12.00
17 New Orleans Saints 6.00 12.00
18 New York Giants 7.50 15.00
19 New York Jets 6.00 12.00
20 Oakland Raiders 7.50 15.00
21 Philadelphia Eagles 6.00 12.00
22 Pittsburgh Steelers 7.50 15.00
23 St. Louis Cardinals 6.00 12.00
24 San Diego Chargers 6.00 12.00
25 San Francisco 49ers 7.50 15.00
26 Seattle Seahawks 6.00 12.00
27 Tampa Bay Buccaneers 6.00 12.00
28 Washington Redskins 7.50 15.00

1972 Sunoco Stamps

In 1972, the Sun Oil Company issued a stamp set and two types of albums. Each stamp measures approximately 1 5/8" by 2 3/8" whereas the albums are approximately 10 3/8" by 10 15/16". The logo on the cover of the 56-page stamp album indicates "NFL Action '72". The other "deluxe" album contains 128 pages. Each team was represented with 12 offensive and 12 defensive player stamps. There are a total of 624 unnumbered stamps in the set, which made this stamp set the largest football set to date at that time. The albums indicate where each stamp is to be placed. The square for each player's stamp was marked by the player's number, name, position, height, weight, age, and college attended. When the album was issued, the back of the book included perforated sheets of stamps comprising more than one fourth of the set. The album also had sheets of tabs which were to be used for putting the stamps in the book, rather than licking the entire stamp. Each week of the promotion a purchase of gasoline yielded an additional nine-player perforated stamp sheet. The stamps and the album positions are unnumbered so the stamps are ordered and numbered below according to the team order in which they appear in the book. The team order is alphabetical. Since the same 144 stamps were included as an insert with each album; these 144 stamps are easier to find and are marked as DP's in the checklist below. The stamp set is considered in very good condition at best when glued in the album. There are a number of players appearing in this set in (or before) their Rookie Card year: Lyle Alzado, Mel Blount, Harold Carmichael, Dan Dierdorf, L.C. Greenwood, Jack Ham, Cliff Harris, Ted Hendricks, Charlie Joiner, Bob Kuechenberg, Larry Little, Archie Manning, Ray Perkins, Jim Plunkett, John Riggins, Art Shell, Steve Spurrier, Roger Staubach, Gene Upshaw, Jeff Van Note, and Jack Youngblood.

COMPLETE SET (624) 75.00 150.00
1 Ken Burrow .10 .20
2 Bill Sandeman .10 .20
3 Andy Maurer DP .08 .15
4 Jeff Van Note DP .13 .25
5 Malcolm Snider .10 .20
6 George Kunz .10 .20
7 Jim Mitchell .10 .20
8 Wes Chesson .10 .20
9 Bob Berry .10 .20
10 Dick Shiner .10 .20
11 Jim Butler .10 .20
12 Art Malone .10 .20
13 Claude Humphrey DP .13 .25
14 John Small DP .08 .15
15 Glen Condren .10 .20
16 John Zook .10 .20
17 Don Hansen .10 .20
18 Tommy Nobis .30 .60
19 Greg Brezina .10 .20
20 Ken Reaves .10 .20
21 Tom Hayes .10 .20
22 Tom McCauley DP .08 .15
23 Bill Bell DP .08 .15
24 Billy Lothridge .10 .20
25 Eddie Hinton .10 .20
26 Bob Vogel DP .08 .15
27 Glenn Ressler .10 .20
28 Bill Curry DP .08 .15
29 John Williams G .10 .20
30 Dan Sullivan .10 .20
31 Tom Mitchell .10 .20
32 John Mackey .50 1.00
33 Ray Perkins .25 .50
34 Johnny Unitas 2.50 5.00
35 Tom Matte .15 .30
36 Norm Bulaich .10 .20
37 Bubba Smith DP .38 .75
38 Billy Newsome .10 .20
39 Fred Miller DP .08 .15
40 Roy Hilton .10 .20
41 Ray May DP .08 .15
42 Ted Hendricks .50 1.00
43 Charlie Stukes .10 .20
44 Rex Kern .10 .20
45 Jerry Logan .10 .20
46 Rick Volk .10 .20
47 David Lee .10 .20
48 Jim O'Brien .15 .30
49 J.D. Hill .15 .30
50 Willie Young .10 .20
51 Jim Reilly .10 .20
52 Bruce Jarvis DP .08 .15
53 Levert Carr .10 .20
54 Donnie Green DP .08 .15
55 Jan White DP .08 .15
56 Marlin Briscoe .10 .20
57 Dennis Shaw .15 .30
58 O.J. Simpson 2.00 4.00
59 Wayne Patrick .10 .20
60 John Leypoldt .10 .20
61 Al Cowlings .15 .30
62 Jim Dunaway DP .08 .15
63 Bob Tatarek .10 .20
64 Cal Snowden .10 .20
65 Paul Guidry .10 .20
66 Edgar Chandler .10 .20
67 Al Andrews DP .08 .15
68 Robert James .10 .20
69 Alvin Wyatt .10 .20
70 John Pitts DP .08 .15
71 Pete Richardson .10 .20
72 Spike Jones .10 .20
73 Dick Gordon .10 .20
74 Randy Jackson DP .08 .15
75 Glen Holloway .10 .20
76 Rich Coady DP .08 .15
77 Jim Cadile DP .08 .15
78 Steve Wright .10 .20
79 Bob Wallace .10 .20
80 George Farmer .10 .20
81 Bobby Douglass .15 .30
82 Don Shy .10 .20
83 Cyril Pinder .10 .20
84 Mac Percival .10 .20
85 Willie Holman .10 .20
86 George Seals DP .08 .15
87 Bill Staley .10 .20
88 Ed O'Bradovich DP .08 .15
89 Doug Buffone DP .08 .15
90 Dick Butkus 2.00 4.00
91 Ross Brupbacher .10 .20
92 Charlie Ford .10 .20
93 Joe Taylor .10 .20
94 Ron Smith .15 .30
95 Jerry Moore .10 .20
96 Bobby Joe Green .10 .20
97 Chip Myers .10 .20
98 Rufus Mayes DP .08 .15
99 Howard Fest .10 .20
100 Bob Johnson .15 .30
101 Pat Matson DP .08 .15
102 Vern Holland .10 .20
103 Bruce Coslet .15 .30
104 Bob Trumpy .20 .40
105 Virgil Carter .10 .20
106 Fred Willis .10 .20
107 Jess Phillips .10 .20
108 Horst Muhlmann .10 .20
109 Royce Berry .10 .20
110 Mike Reid DP .25 .50
111 Steve Chomyszak DP .08 .15
112 Ron Carpenter .10 .20
113 Al Beauchamp DP .08 .15
114 Bill Bergey .15 .30
115 Ken Avery .10 .20
116 Lemar Parrish .15 .30
117 Ken Riley .15 .30
118 Sandy Durko DP .08 .15
119 Dave Lewis .10 .20
120 Paul Robinson .10 .20
121 Fair Hooker .10 .20
122 Doug Dieken DP .08 .15
123 John Demarie .10 .20
124 Jim Copeland .10 .20
125 Gene Hickerson DP .10 .25
126 Bob McKay .10 .20
127 Milt Morin .10 .20
128 Frank Pitts .10 .20
129 Mike Phipps .15 .30
130 Leroy Kelly .50 1.00
131 Bo Scott .15 .30
132 Don Cockroft .10 .20
133 Ron Snidow .10 .20
134 Walter Johnson DP .08 .15
135 Jerry Sherk .15 .30
136 Jack Gregory .10 .20
137 Jim Houston DP .08 .15
138 Dale Lindsey .10 .20
139 Bill Andrews .10 .20
140 Clarence Scott .10 .20
141 Ernie Kellerman .10 .20
142 Walt Sumner .10 .20
143 Mike Howell DP .08 .15
144 Reece Morrison .10 .20
145 Bob Hayes .50 1.00
146 Ralph Neely .10 .20
147 John Niland DP .08 .15
148 Dave Manders .10 .20
149 Blaine Nye .10 .20
150 Rayfield Wright .10 .20
151 Billy Truax .10 .20
152 Lance Alworth 1.00 2.00
153 Roger Staubach 4.00 8.00
154 Duane Thomas .25 .50
155 Walt Garrison .15 .30
156 Mike Clark .10 .20
157 Larry Cole DP .08 .15
158 Jethro Pugh .10 .20
159 Bob Lilly .75 1.50
160 George Andrie .10 .20
161 Dave Edwards DP .08 .15
162 Lee Roy Jordan .38 .75
163 Chuck Howley .15 .30
164 Herb Adderley DP .38 .75
165 Mel Renfro .50 1.00
166 Cornell Green .15 .30
167 Cliff Harris DP .20 .40
168 Ron Widby .10 .20
169 Jerry Simmons .10 .20
170 Roger Shoals .10 .20
171 Larron Jackson .10 .20
172 George Goeddeke DP .08 .15
173 Mike Schnitker .10 .20
174 Mike Current .10 .20
175 Billy Masters .10 .20
176 Jack Gehrke .10 .20
177 Don Horn .10 .20
178 Floyd Little .30 .60
179 Bob Anderson .10 .20
180 Jim Turner DP .13 .25
181 Rich Jackson .10 .20
182 Paul Smith DP .08 .15
183 Dave Costa .10 .20
184 Lyle Alzado DP .38 .75
185 Olen Underwood .10 .20
186 Fred Forsberg DP .08 .15
187 Chip Myrtle .10 .20
188 Leroy Mitchell .10 .20
189 Bill Thompson DP .08 .15
190 Charlie Greer .10 .20
191 George Saimes .10 .20
192 Billy Van Heusen .10 .20
193 Earl McCullouch .15 .30
194 Jim Yarbrough .10 .20
195 Chuck Walton .10 .20
196 Ed Flanagan .10 .20
197 Frank Gallagher .10 .20
198 Rockne Freitas .10 .20
199 Charlie Sanders DP .10 .25
200 Larry Walton .10 .20
201 Greg Landry .20 .40
202 Altie Taylor .10 .20
203 Steve Owens .20 .40
204 Errol Mann DP .08 .15
205 Joe Robb .10 .20
206 Dick Evey .10 .20
207 Jerry Rush .10 .20
208 Larry Hand DP .08 .15
209 Paul Naumoff .10 .20
210 Mike Lucci .15 .30
211 Wayne Walker DP .13 .25
212 Lem Barney DP .38 .75
213 Dick LeBeau DP .08 .15
214 Mike Weger .10 .20
215 Wayne Rasmussen .10 .20
216 Herman Weaver .10 .20
217 John Spilis .10 .20
218 Francis Peay DP .08 .15
219 Bill Lueck .10 .20
220 Ken Bowman DP .08 .15
221 Gale Gillingham DP .08 .15
222 Dick Himes DP .08 .15
223 Rich McGeorge .10 .20
224 Carroll Dale .15 .30
225 Bart Starr 2.00 4.00
226 Scott Hunter .15 .30
227 John Brockington .15 .30
228 Dave Hampton .10 .20
229 Clarence Williams .10 .20
230 Mike McCoy .10 .20
231 Bob Brown DT .10 .20
232 Alden Roche .10 .20
233 Dave Robinson DP .13 .25
234 Jim Carter .10 .20
235 Fred Carr .10 .20
236 Ken Ellis .10 .20
237 Doug Hart .10 .20
238 Al Randolph .10 .20
239 Al Matthews .10 .20
240 Tim Webster .10 .20
241 Jim Beirne DP .08 .15
242 Bob Young .10 .20
243 Elbert Drungo .10 .20
244 Sam Walton .10 .20
245 Alvin Reed .10 .20
246 Charlie Joiner .75 1.50
247 Dan Pastorini .20 .40
248 Charley Johnson .15 .30
249 Lynn Dickey .15 .30
250 Woody Campbell .10 .20
251 Robert Holmes .10 .20
252 Mark Moseley .15 .30
253 Pat Holmes .10 .20
254 Mike Tilleman DP .08 .15
255 Leo Brooks .10 .20
256 Elvin Bethea .15 .30
257 George Webster .15 .30
258 Garland Boyette .10 .20
259 Ron Pritchard .10 .20
260 Zeke Moore DP .13 .25
261 Willie Alexander .10 .20
262 Ken Houston .50 1.00
263 John Charles DP .08 .15
264 Linzy Cole DP .08 .15
265 Elmo Wright .10 .20
266 Jim Tyrer DP .13 .25
267 Ed Budde .10 .20
268 Jack Rudnay DP .08 .15
269 Mo Moorman .10 .20
270 Dave Hill .10 .20
271 Morris Stroud .10 .20
272 Otis Taylor .20 .40
273 Len Dawson 1.00 2.00
274 Ed Podolak .15 .30
275 Wendell Hayes .15 .30
276 Jan Stenerud .38 .75
277 Marvin Upshaw DP .08 .15
278 Curley Culp .15 .30
279 Buck Buchanan .50 1.00
280 Aaron Brown .10 .20
281 Bobby Bell .50 1.00
282 Willie Lanier .50 1.00
283 Jim Lynch .10 .20
284 Jim Marsalis DP .08 .15
285 Emmitt Thomas .30 .75
286 Jim Kearney DP .08 .15
287 Johnny Robinson .15 .30
288 Jerrel Wilson DP .08 .15
289 Jack Snow .15 .30
290 Charlie Cowan .10 .20
291 Tom Mack DP .13 .25
292 Ken Iman .10 .20
293 Joe Scibelli .10 .20
294 Harry Schuh DP .08 .15
295 Bob Klein .10 .20
296 Lance Rentzel .15 .30
297 Roman Gabriel .25 .50
298 Les Josephson .15 .30
299 Willie Ellison .10 .20
300 David Ray .10 .20
301 Jack Youngblood .50 1.00
302 Merlin Olsen .50 1.00
303 Phil Olsen .15 .30
304 Coy Bacon .15 .30
305 Jim Purnell DP .08 .15
306 Marlin McKeever .10 .20
307 Isiah Robertson .15 .30
308 Jim Nettles DP .08 .15
309 Gene Howard DP .08 .15
310 Kermit Alexander .15 .30
311 Dave Elmendorf DP .08 .15
312 Pat Studstill .10 .20
313 Paul Warfield 1.00 2.00
314 Doug Crusan .10 .20
315 Bob Kuechenberg .15 .30
316 Bob DeMarco DP .08 .15
317 Larry Little .50 1.00
318 Norm Evans DP .13 .25
319 Marv Fleming DP .13 .25
320 Howard Twilley .15 .30
321 Bob Griese 1.25 2.50
322 Jim Kiick .20 .40
323 Larry Csonka 1.00 2.00
324 Garo Yepremian .15 .30
325 Jim Riley DP .08 .15
326 Manny Fernandez .15 .30
327 Bob Heinz DP .08 .15
328 Bill Stanfill .15 .30
329 Doug Swift .10 .20
330 Nick Buoniconti .38 .75
331 Mike Kolen .10 .20
332 Tim Foley .15 .30
333 Curtis Johnson .10 .20
334 Dick Anderson .15 .30
335 Jake Scott .20 .40
336 Larry Seiple .10 .20
337 Gene Washington Vik .15 .30
338 Grady Alderman .10 .20
339 Ed White DP .13 .25
340 Mick Tingelhoff DP .13 .25
341 Milt Sunde DP .08 .15
342 Ron Yary .15 .30
343 John Beasley .10 .20
344 John Henderson .10 .20
345 Fran Tarkenton 1.25 2.50
346 Clint Jones .10 .20

347 Dave Osborn	.15	.30
348 Fred Cox	.15	.30
349 Carl Eller DP	.25	.50
350 Gary Larsen DP	.08	.15
351 Alan Page	.50	1.00
352 Jim Marshall	.38	.75
353 Roy Winston	.10	.20
354 Lonnie Warwick	.10	.20
355 Wally Hilgenberg	.10	.20
356 Bobby Bryant	.10	.20
357 Ed Sharockman	.10	.20
358 Charlie West	.10	.20
359 Paul Krause	.25	.50
360 Bob Lee	.10	.20
361 Randy Vataha	.10	.20
362 Mike Montler DP	.08	.15
363 Halvor Hagen	.10	.20
364 Jon Morris DP	.08	.15
365 Len St. Jean	.10	.20
366 Tom Neville	.10	.20
367 Tom Beer	.10	.20
368 Ron Sellers	.10	.20
369 Jim Plunkett	.63	1.25
370 Carl Garrett	.15	.30
371 Jim Nance	.15	.30
372 Charlie Gogolak	.10	.20
373 Ike Lassiter DP	.08	.15
374 Dave Rowe	.10	.20
375 Julius Adams	.10	.20
376 Dennis Wirgowski	.10	.20
377 Ed Weisacosky	.10	.20
378 Jim Cheyunski DP	.08	.15
379 Steve Kiner	.10	.20
380 Larry Carwell DP	.08	.15
381 John Outlaw	.10	.20
382 Rickie Harris	.10	.20
383 Don Webb DP	.08	.15
384 Tom Janik	.10	.20
385 Al Dodd DP	.08	.15
386 Don Morrison	.10	.20
387 Jake Kupp	.10	.20
388 John Didion	.10	.20
389 Del Williams	.10	.20
390 Glen Ray Hines	.10	.20
391 Dave Parks DP	.08	.15
392 Dan Abramowicz	.15	.30
393 Archie Manning	.63	1.25
394 Bob Gresham	.10	.20
395 Virgil Robinson	.10	.20
396 Charlie Durkee	.10	.20
397 Richard Neal	.10	.20
398 Bob Pollard DP	.08	.15
399 Dave Long DP	.08	.15
400 Joe Owens	.10	.20
401 Carl Cunningham	.10	.20
402 Jim Flanigan	.10	.20
403 Wayne Colman	.10	.20
404 D'Artagnan Martin DP	.08	.15
405 Delles Howell	.10	.20
406 Hugo Hollas	.10	.20
407 Doug Wyatt DP	.08	.15
408 Julian Fagan	.10	.20
409 Don Hormann	.10	.20
410 Willie Young	.10	.20
411 Bob Hyland	.10	.20
412 Greg Larson DP	.08	.15
413 Doug Van Horn	.10	.20
414 Charlie Harper DP	.08	.15
415 Bob Tucker	.15	.30
416 Joe Morrison	.15	.30
417 Randy Johnson	.15	.30
418 Tucker Frederickson	.15	.30
419 Ron Johnson	.15	.30
420 Pete Gogolak	.15	.30
421 Henry Reed	.10	.20
422 Jim Kanicki DP	.08	.15
423 Roland Lakes	.10	.20
424 John Douglas DP	.08	.15
425 Ron Hornsby DP	.08	.15
426 Jim Files	.10	.20
427 Willie Williams DP	.08	.15
428 Otto Brown	.10	.20
429 Scott Eaton	.10	.20
430 Spider Lockhart	.15	.30
431 Tom Blanchard	.10	.20
432 Rocky Thompson	.10	.20
433 Richard Caster	.15	.30
434 Randy Rasmussen	.10	.20
435 John Schmitt	.10	.20
436 Dave Herman DP	.08	.15
437 Winston Hill DP	.08	.15
438 Pete Lammons	.10	.20
439 Don Maynard	1.00	2.00
440 Joe Namath	4.00	8.00
441 Emerson Boozer	.15	.30
442 John Riggins	1.25	2.50
443 George Nock	.10	.20
444 Bobby Howfield	.10	.20
445 Gerry Philbin	.10	.20
446 John Little DP	.08	.15
447 Chuck Hinton	.10	.20
448 Mark Lomas	.10	.20
449 Ralph Baker	.10	.20
450 Al Atkinson DP	.08	.15
451 Larry Grantham DP	.08	.15
452 John Dockery	.10	.20
453 Earlie Thomas DP	.08	.15
454 Phil Wise	.10	.20
455 W.K. Hicks	.10	.20
456 Steve O'Neal	.10	.20
457 Drew Buie	.10	.20
458 Art Shell	.50	1.00
459 Gene Upshaw	.38	.75
460 Jim Otto DP	.38	.75
461 George Buehler	.10	.20
462 Bob Brown OT	.15	.30
463 Raymond Chester	.15	.30
464 Fred Biletnikoff	1.00	2.00
465 Daryle Lamonica	.30	.60
466 Marv Hubbard	.15	.30
467 Clarence Davis	.10	.20
468 George Blanda	1.00	2.00
469 Tony Cline	.10	.20
470 Art Thoms	.10	.20
471 Tom Keating DP	.08	.15
472 Ben Davidson	.25	.50
473 Phil Villapiano	.15	.30
474 Dan Conners DP	.08	.15
475 Duane Benson DP	.08	.15
476 Nemiah Wilson DP	.08	.15
477 Willie Brown DP	.38	.75
478 George Atkinson	.10	.20
479 Jack Tatum	.20	.40
480 Jerry DePoyster	.10	.20
481 Harold Jackson	.20	.40
482 Wade Key DP	.08	.15
483 Henry Allison DP	.08	.15
484 Mike Evans DP	.08	.15
485 Steve Smith	.10	.20
486 Harold Carmichael	.50	1.00
487 Ben Hawkins	.10	.20
488 Pete Liske	.15	.30
489 Rick Arrington	.10	.20
490 Lee Bouggess	.10	.20
491 Tom Woodeshick	.10	.20
492 Tom Dempsey	.15	.30
493 Richard Harris	.10	.20
494 Don Hultz	.10	.20
495 Ernie Calloway	.10	.20
496 Mel Tom DP	.08	.15
497 Steve Zabel	.10	.20
498 Tim Rossovich DP	.08	.15
499 Ron Porter	.10	.20
500 Al Nelson	.10	.20
501 Nate Ramsey	.10	.20
502 Leroy Keyes	.15	.30
503 Bill Bradley	.15	.30
504 Tom McNeill	.10	.20
505 Dave Smith	.10	.20
506 Jon Kolb	.08	.15
507 Gerry Mullins	.10	.20
508 Ray Mansfield DP	.08	.15
509 Bruce Van Dyke DP	.08	.15
510 John Brown DP	.08	.15
511 Ron Shanklin	.10	.20
512 Terry Bradshaw	3.00	6.00
513 Terry Hanratty	.15	.30
514 Preston Pearson	.20	.40
515 John Fuqua	.15	.30
516 Roy Gerela	.10	.20
517 L.C. Greenwood	.38	.75
518 Joe Greene	1.00	2.00
519 Lloyd Voss DP	.08	.15
520 Dwight White DP	.13	.25
521 Jack Ham	1.25	2.50
522 Chuck Allen	.10	.20
523 Brian Stenger	.10	.20
524 Andy Russell	.15	.30
525 John Rowser	.10	.20
526 Mel Blount	1.00	2.00
527 Mike Wagner	.15	.30
528 Bobby Walden	.10	.20
529 Mel Gray	.20	.40
530 Bob Reynolds	.10	.20
531 Dan Dierdorf DP	.38	.75
532 Wayne Mulligan	.10	.20
533 Clyde Williams	.10	.20
534 Ernie McMillan	.10	.20
535 Jackie Smith	.38	.75
536 John Gilliam DP	.13	.25
537 Jim Hart	.25	.50
538 Pete Beathard	.15	.30
539 Johnny Roland	.15	.30
540 Jim Bakken	.15	.30
541 Ron Yankowski DP	.08	.15
542 Fred Heron	.10	.20
543 Bob Rowe	.10	.20
544 Chuck Walker	.10	.20
545 Larry Stallings	.10	.20
546 Jamie Rivers DP	.08	.15
547 Mike McGill	.10	.20
548 Miller Farr	.10	.20
549 Roger Wehrli	.15	.30
550 Larry Willingham DP	.08	.15
551 Larry Wilson	.50	1.00
552 Chuck Latourette	.10	.20
553 Billy Parks	.10	.20
554 Terry Owens	.15	.30
555 Doug Wilkerson	.10	.20
556 Carl Mauck DP	.08	.15
557 Walt Sweeney	.10	.20
558 Russ Washington DP	.08	.15
559 Pettis Norman	.10	.20
560 Gary Garrison	.15	.30
561 John Hadl	.25	.50
562 Mike Montgomery	.10	.20
563 Mike Garrett	.15	.30
564 Dennis Partee DP	.08	.15
565 Deacon Jones	.50	1.00
566 Ron East DP	.08	.15
567 Kevin Hardy	.10	.20
568 Steve DeLong	.10	.20
569 Rick Redman DP	.08	.15
570 Bob Babich	.10	.20
571 Pete Barnes	.10	.20
572 Bob Howard	.10	.20
573 Joe Beauchamp	.10	.20
574 Bryant Salter	.10	.20
575 Chris Fletcher	.10	.20
576 Jerry LeVias	.15	.30
577 Dick Witcher	.10	.20
578 Len Rohde	.10	.20
579 Randy Beisler	.10	.20
580 Forrest Blue	.10	.20
581 Woody Peoples	.10	.20
582 Cas Banaszek	.10	.20
583 Ted Kwalick	.15	.30
584 Gene Washington 49er	.15	.30
585 John Brodie	.50	1.00
586 Ken Willard	.15	.30
587 Vic Washington	.10	.20
588 Bruce Gossett DP	.08	.15
589 Tommy Hart	.10	.20
590 Charlie Krueger	.10	.20
591 Earl Edwards	.10	.20
592 Cedrick Hardman DP	.08	.15
593 Dave Wilcox DP	.13	.25
594 Frank Nunley	.10	.20
595 Skip Vanderbundt DP	.08	.15
596 Jim Johnson DP	.38	.75
597 Bruce Taylor	.10	.20
598 Mel Phillips	.10	.20
599 Roosevelt Taylor	.15	.30
600 Steve Spurrier	2.00	4.00
601 Charley Taylor	.50	1.00
602 Jim Snowden DP	.08	.15
603 Ray Schoenke	.10	.20
604 Len Hauss DP	.08	.15
605 John Wilbur	.10	.20
606 Walter Rock DP	.08	.15
607 Jerry Smith	.15	.30
608 Roy Jefferson	.15	.30
609 Billy Kilmer	.30	.60
610 Larry Brown	.38	.75
611 Charlie Harraway	.10	.20
612 Curt Knight	.10	.20
613 Ron McDole	.10	.20
614 Manny Sistrunk DP	.13	.25
615 Diron Talbert	.10	.20
616 Verlon Biggs DP	.08	.15
617 Jack Pardee	.20	.40
618 Myron Pottios	.10	.20
619 Chris Hanburger	.15	.30
620 Pat Fischer	.15	.30
621 Mike Bass	.10	.20
622 Richie Petitbon DP	.13	.25
623 Brig Owens	.10	.20
624 Mike Bragg	.10	.20
NNO Album (64 pages)	5.00	10.00
NNO Deluxe Album (128 pages)	7.50	15.00

1972 Sunoco Stamps Update

The players listed below are those who are not explicitly listed in the 1972 Sunoco stamp album. They are otherwise indistinguishable from the 1972 Sunoco stamps listed immediately above. These unnumbered stamps are ordered below in team order and alphabetically within team. The stamps measure approximately 1 5/8" by 2 3/8" and were issued later in the year as part of complete team sheets. Uncut team sheets typically sell for $15-50 per team, except for the Bears and Raiders sheets which are the toughest to find. There are a number of players appearing in this set before their Rookie Card year: Cliff Branch, Jim Langer, and Bobby Moore (later known as Ahmad Rashad).

COMPLETE SET (82)	125.00	200.00
1 Clarence Ellis	1.50	4.00
2 Dave Hampton	1.50	4.00
3 Dennis Havig	1.25	3.00
4 John James	1.25	3.00
5 Joe Profit	1.25	3.00
6 Lonnie Hepburn	1.25	3.00
7 Dennis Nelson	1.25	3.00
8 Mike McBath	1.25	3.00
9 Walt Patulski	1.25	3.00
10 Bob Asher	10.00	20.00
11 Steve DeLong	10.00	20.00
12 Tony McGee	10.00	20.00
13 Jim Osborne	10.00	20.00
14 Jim Seymour	10.00	20.00
15 Tommy Casanova	1.50	4.00
16 Neal Craig	1.25	3.00
17 Essex Johnson	1.25	3.00
18 Sherman White	1.25	3.00
19 Bob Briggs	1.25	3.00
20 Thom Darden	1.25	3.00
21 Marv Bateman	1.25	3.00
22 Toni Fritsch	1.25	3.00
23 Calvin Hill	2.00	5.00
24 Pat Toomay	1.25	3.00
25 Pete Duranko	1.25	3.00
26 Marv Montgomery	1.25	3.00
27 Rod Sherman	1.25	3.00
28 Bob Kowalkowski	1.25	3.00
29 Jim Mitchell	1.25	3.00
30 Larry Woods	1.25	3.00
31 Willie Buchanon	1.50	4.00
32 Leland Glass	1.25	3.00
33 MacArthur Lane	1.50	4.00
34 Chester Marcol	1.25	3.00
35 Ron Widby	1.25	3.00
36 Ken Burrough	1.50	4.00
37 Calvin Hunt	1.25	3.00
38 Ron Saul	1.25	3.00
39 Greg Simpson	1.25	3.00
40 Mike Sensibaugh	1.50	4.00
41 Dave Chapple	1.25	3.00
42 Jim Langer	2.50	6.00
43 Mike Eischeid	1.25	3.00
44 John Gilliam	1.50	4.00
45 Ron Acks	1.25	3.00
46 Bob Gladieux	1.25	3.00
47 Honor Jackson	1.25	3.00
48 Reggie Rucker	1.50	4.00
49 Pat Studstill	1.25	3.00
50 Bob Windsor	1.25	3.00
51 Joe Federspiel	1.25	3.00
52 Bob Newland	1.25	3.00
53 Pete Athas	1.25	3.00
54 Charlie Evans	1.25	3.00
55 Jack Gregory	1.25	3.00
56 John Mendenhall	1.25	3.00
57 Ed Bell	1.25	3.00
58 John Elliott	1.25	3.00
59 Chris Farasopoulos	1.25	3.00
60 Bob Svihus	1.25	3.00
61 Steve Tannen	1.25	3.00
62 Cliff Branch	12.50	25.00
63 Gus Otto	10.00	20.00
64 Otis Sistrunk	10.00	20.00
65 Charlie Smith	10.00	20.00
66 John Reaves	1.25	3.00
67 Larry Watkins	1.25	3.00
68 Henry Davis	1.25	3.00
69 Ben McGee	1.25	3.00
70 Donny Anderson	2.00	5.00
71 Walker Gillette	1.25	3.00
72 Martin Imhoff	1.25	3.00
73 Bobby Moore (aka Ahmad Rashad)	5.00	10.00
74 Norm Thompson	1.25	3.00
75 Lionel Aldridge	1.50	4.00
76 Dave Costa	1.25	3.00
77 Cid Edwards	1.25	3.00
78 Tim Rossovich	1.25	3.00
79 Dave Williams	1.25	3.00
80 Johnny Fuller	1.25	3.00
81 Terry Hermeling	1.25	3.00
82 Paul Laaveg	1.25	3.00

2001 Super Bowl XXXV Marino

This 5-card set was issued one card at a time at the 2001 NFL Experience Super Bowl Card Show in Tampa Florida. Each major card company produced one card as a wrapper redemption (for 5-wrappers) to be exchanged at their booth at the card show. Collector's Edge did not issue a card for the set. The Topps card was issued in a cello pack with one stick of gum.

COMPLETE SET (5)	35.00	50.00
COMMON MARINO (1-6)	6.00	10.00
1 Dan Marino Topps	8.00	12.00

2002 Super Bowl XXXVI Aikman

These five cards were issued at the 2002 Super Bowl Card Show in New Orleans as part of a wrapper redemption program. Each of the five NFL card manufacturers in attendance gave away one card of Troy Aikman in exchange for a number of card packs opened at their booths.

COMPLETE SET (5)	6.00	15.00
COMMON AIKMAN (1-5)	1.25	3.00

2003 Super Bowl XXXVII Chargers

These 12-cards were issued at the 2003 Super Bowl Card Show in San Diego as part of a wrapper redemption program. Each of the five NFL card manufacturers in attendance gave away two cards in exchange for a number of card packs opened at their booths. Two additional cards were produced and given away by Sports Collector's Digest and Tuff Stuff magazines.

COMPLETE SET (12)	12.50	25.00
1 Drew Brees	1.50	4.00
2 LaDainian Tomlinson	1.50	4.00
3 Curtis Conway Pacific	.60	1.50
4 Junior Seau Playoff	1.00	2.50
5 Quentin Jammer Upper Deck	.40	1.00
6 Tim Dwight Tuff Stuff	.60	1.50
7 Quentin Jammer SCD	.40	1.00
8 Drew Brees	1.50	4.00
9 Tim Dwight Playoff	.60	1.50
10 Junior Seau Pacific	1.00	2.50
11 Curtis Conway (Fleer	.60	1.50
12 LaDainian Tomlinson	1.50	4.00

1992 Super Silhouettes

This 14-card set features plastic silhouettes of top players made from a material that clings to any smooth surface without adhesive and can be used over and over again. The image can be rolled up or folded in half essentially without destroying its original form. The silhouettes were distributed one to a package with the player's name, postion, and statistics printed on the back.

COMPLETE SET (14)	12.00	30.00
1 Dan Marino	2.40	6.00
2 Jim Kelly	.80	2.00
3 John Elway	2.00	5.00
4 Lawrence Taylor	.60	1.50
5 Bernie Kosar	.40	1.00
6 Troy Aikman	1.20	3.00
7 Randall Cunningham	.80	2.00
8 Mark Rypien	.40	1.00
9 Chris Miller	.40	1.00
10 Boomer Esiason	.60	1.50
11 Warren Moon	.60	1.50
12 Ronnie Lott	.60	1.50
13 Jim Harbaugh	.40	1.00
14 Barry Sanders	2.40	6.00

2005 Superstars Road to Forty Activa Medallions

COMPLETE SET (30)	30.00	60.00
1 Tom Brady	1.50	4.00
2 Randy Moss	1.25	3.00
3 Curtis Martin	1.25	3.00
4 Clinton Portis	1.25	3.00
5 Carson Palmer	1.25	3.00
6 Peyton Manning	1.50	4.00
7 Torry Holt	1.25	3.00
8 Ben Roethlisberger	2.00	5.00
9 Tiki Barber	1.25	3.00
10 Daunte Culpepper	1.25	3.00
11 Brett Favre	2.00	5.00
12 Roy Williams S	1.25	3.00
13 Tony Gonzalez	1.25	3.00
14 Terrell Owens	1.25	3.00
15 LaDainian Tomlinson	1.25	3.00
16 Michael Vick	1.50	4.00
17 Marvin Harrison	1.25	3.00
18 Takeo Spikes	1.00	2.50
19 Andre Johnson	1.00	2.50
20 Julius Peppers	1.00	2.50
21 Donovan McNabb	1.25	3.00
22 Priest Holmes	1.25	3.00
23 Ed Reed	1.00	2.50
24 Champ Bailey	1.00	2.50
25 Deuce Mcallister	1.00	2.50
26 Brian Urlacher	1.25	3.00
27 Hines Ward	1.25	3.00
28 Shaun Alexander	1.25	3.00
29 Jason Taylor	1.00	2.50
30 Ray Lewis	1.25	3.00

2002 Sweet Spot

Released in December 2002, this set features 90 veterans and 76 rookies. Rookies 91-150 were serial #'d to 1050, while rookies 151-166 were serial #'d to 550 or 125, and were also autographed. Please note some players were issed as redemption cards which expired 12/6/2005. Boxes contained 12 packs of 4 cards along with one oversized patch card box topper.

COMP.SET w/o SP's (90)	12.50	30.00
91-150 ROOKIE PRINT RUN 1050		
1 Aaron Brooks	.40	1.00
2 Tim Couch	.30	.75
3 Jon Kitna	.40	1.00
4 Brett Favre	1.25	3.00
5 Donovan McNabb	.50	1.25
6 Jeff Garcia	.40	1.00
7 Michael Vick	.75	2.00
8 Mark Brunell	.40	1.00
9 Steve McNair	.50	1.25
10 Kordell Stewart	.40	1.00
11 Drew Bledsoe	.50	1.25
12 Tom Brady	1.25	3.00
13 Kurt Warner	.50	1.25
14 Brian Griese	.40	1.00
15 Jim Miller	.30	.75
16 Jake Plummer	.40	1.00
17 Quincy Carter	.30	.75
18 Peyton Manning	1.00	2.50
19 Keyshawn Johnson	.40	1.00
20 Travis Henry	.30	.75
21 LaDainian Tomlinson	.60	1.50
22 Emmitt Smith	1.25	3.00
23 Michael Bennett	.40	1.00
24 Duce Staley	.40	1.00
25 Thomas Jones	.50	1.25
26 Deuce McAllister	.40	1.00
27 Eddie George	.40	1.00
28 Marshall Faulk	.50	1.25
29 Curtis Martin	.50	1.25
30 Ahman Green	.40	1.00
31 Priest Holmes	.50	1.25
32 Edgerrin James	.40	1.00
33 Antowain Smith	.40	1.00
34 Ricky Williams	.40	1.00
35 Anthony Thomas	.40	1.00
36 Jerome Bettis	.50	1.25
37 Shaun Alexander	.40	1.00
38 Kerry Collins	.40	1.00
39 Drew Brees	.75	2.00
40 Chris Redman	.30	.75
41 Marc Bulger	.40	1.00
42 Jay Fiedler	.40	1.00
43 Trent Green	.40	1.00
44 Daunte Culpepper	.40	1.00
45 Rich Gannon	.40	1.00
46 Rodney Peete	.40	1.00
47 Vinny Testaverde	.40	1.00
48 Stephen Davis	.40	1.00
49 James Allen	.30	.75
50 Tiki Barber	.50	1.25
51 Ron Dayne	.40	1.00
52 Ray Lewis	.50	1.25
53 Corey Dillon	.40	1.00
54 Brian Urlacher	.50	1.25
55 Junior Seau	.50	1.25
56 Warrick Dunn	.40	1.00
57 Fred Taylor	.40	1.00
58 Jamal Lewis	.40	1.00
59 Trent Dilfer	.40	1.00
60 James Stewart	.30	.75
61 David Patten	.30	.75
62 Eric Moulds	.40	1.00
63 Isaac Bruce	.50	1.25
64 Troy Brown	.40	1.00
65 Terrell Owens	.50	1.25
66 Moe Williams	.30	.75
67 Joe Horn	.40	1.00
68 Az-Zahir Hakim	.30	.75
69 Jimmy Smith	.40	1.00
70 Michael Westbrook	.30	.75
71 Olandis Gary	.40	1.00
72 Chris Chambers	.40	1.00
73 Kevin Johnson	.30	.75
74 Joey Galloway	.40	1.00
75 Hines Ward	.50	1.25
76 Garrison Hearst	.40	1.00
77 Wayne Chrebet	.40	1.00
78 Muhsin Muhammad	.40	1.00
79 Rod Gardner	.30	.75
80 Jerry Rice	1.00	2.50
81 Tim Brown	.50	1.25
82 Shannon Sharpe	.50	1.25
83 Terry Glenn	.40	1.00
84 Randy Moss	.50	1.25
85 Corey Bradford	.30	.75
86 Marty Booker	.40	1.00
87 Keenan McCardell	.40	1.00
88 Marvin Harrison	.50	1.25
89 David Boston	.30	.75
90 Eddie Kennison	.40	1.00
91 Tim Carter RC	1.50	4.00
92 Joey Harrington RC	2.00	5.00
93 Patrick Ramsey RC	2.00	5.00
94 David Garrard RC	2.50	6.00
95 Donte Stallworth RC	2.00	5.00
96 Reche Caldwell RC	2.00	5.00
97 William Green RC	1.50	4.00
98 Josh Reed RC	1.50	4.00
99 DeShaun Foster RC	2.00	5.00
100 Jeremy Shockey RC	3.00	8.00
101 Mike Williams RC	1.25	3.00
102 Daniel Graham RC	1.50	4.00
103 Josh McCown RC	2.00	5.00
104 Javon Walker RC	2.00	5.00
105 Travis Stephens RC	1.25	3.00
106 Marquise Walker RC	1.25	3.00
107 T.J. Duckett RC	2.00	5.00
108 Damien Anderson RC	1.25	3.00
109 Quentin Jammer RC	2.00	5.00
110 Bryan Thomas RC	1.25	3.00
111 Chad Hutchinson RC	1.25	3.00
112 Brian Westbrook RC	3.00	8.00
113 Lamar Gordon RC	1.50	4.00
114 Deion Branch RC	2.00	5.00
115 Ed Reed RC	8.00	20.00
116 Jonathan Wells RC	2.00	5.00
117 Phillip Buchanon RC	2.00	5.00
118 Wendell Bryant RC	1.25	3.00
119 Kurt Kittner RC	1.25	3.00
120 Randy McMichael RC	2.00	5.00
121 Brandon Doman RC	1.25	3.00
122 Adrian Peterson RC	2.00	5.00
123 Ricky Williams RC	1.50	4.00
124 Seth Burford RC	1.25	3.00
125 Shaun Hill RC	2.50	6.00
126 Anthony Weaver RC	1.25	3.00
127 Freddie Milons RC	1.25	3.00
128 Darrell Hill RC	1.25	3.00
129 Daryl Jones RC	1.25	3.00
130 Chester Taylor RC	2.00	5.00
131 Najeh Davenport RC	2.00	5.00
132 Jason McAddley RC	1.50	4.00
133 Preston Parsons RC	1.25	3.00
134 Michael Lewis RC	2.00	5.00
135 Mike Rumph RC	1.25	3.00
136 Lamont Thompson RC	1.50	4.00
137 Dwight Freeney RC	2.50	6.00
138 Napoleon Harris RC	1.50	4.00
139 Tank Williams RC	1.50	4.00
140 Lee Mays RC	1.25	3.00
141 Robert Thomas RC	1.25	3.00
142 Tellis Redmon RC	1.25	3.00
143 Alex Brown RC	2.00	5.00
144 Ryan Sims RC	2.00	5.00
145 Larry Tripplett RC	1.25	3.00
146 Quinn Gray RC	1.50	4.00
147 Jesse Chatman RC	1.25	3.00
148 Jamin Elliott RC	1.25	3.00
149 Ben Leber RC	1.25	3.00
150 Lito Sheppard RC	2.00	5.00
151 Antonio Bryant AU/550 RC	8.00	20.00
152 Rohan Davey AU/550 RC	8.00	20.00
153 Randy Fasani AU/550 RC	6.00	15.00
154 J.T. O'Sullivan AU/550 RC	6.00	15.00
155 Ron Johnson AU/550 RC	6.00	15.00
156 Maurice Morris AU/550 RC	6.00	15.00
157 Kahlil Hill AU/550 RC	5.00	12.00
158 Antwaan Randle El AU/550 RC	8.00	20.00
159 Cliff Russell AU/550 RC	5.00	12.00
160 Ladell Betts AU/550 RC	8.00	20.00
161 David Carr AU/125 RC	12.00	30.00
162 Andre Davis AU/125 RC	10.00	25.00
163 Julius Peppers AU/125	75.00	125.00
164 Ashley Lelie AU/125 RC	10.00	25.00
165 Jabar Gaffney AU/125 RC	12.00	30.00
166 Clinton Portis AU/125 RC	15.00	40.00

2002 Sweet Spot Gold Rookie Autographs

STATED PRINT RUN 25 SER.#'d SETS		
151 Antonio Bryant	12.00	30.00
152 Rohan Davey	12.00	30.00
153 Randy Fasani	10.00	25.00
154 J.T. O'Sullivan	10.00	25.00
155 Ron Johnson		
156 Maurice Morris	10.00	25.00
157 Kahlil Hill	8.00	20.00
158 Antwaan Randle El	15.00	40.00
159 Cliff Russell	8.00	20.00
160 Ladell Betts	12.00	30.00
161 David Carr	15.00	40.00
162 Andre Davis	10.00	25.00
163 Julius Peppers	60.00	120.00
164 Ashley Lelie	10.00	25.00
165 Jabar Gaffney	12.00	30.00
166 Clinton Portis	75.00	150.00

2002 Sweet Spot Hot Spots Football

STATED PRINT RUN 9 74		
SERIAL #'d UNDER 20 NOT PRICED		
UNPRICED OFFICIAL PRINT RUN 3-24		
HSAG Ahman Green/21	10.00	25.00
HSBU Brian Urlacher/41	10.00	25.00
HSCP Chad Pennington/23	12.00	30.00
HSCR Chris Redman/32	6.00	15.00
HSCS Corey Simon/58	5.00	12.00
HSDB Drew Brees/41	20.00	50.00
HSDC Daunte Culpepper/44	8.00	20.00
HSDM Donovan McNabb/41	10.00	25.00
HSEJ Edgerrin James/44	8.00	20.00
HSLT LaDainian Tomlinson/32	12.00	30.00
HSMC Deuce McAllister/35	8.00	20.00
HSMV Michael Vick/21	20.00	50.00
HSPM Peyton Manning/74	30.00	80.00
HSPW Peter Warrick/23	10.00	25.00
HSQC Quincy Carter/29	8.00	20.00
HSRD Ron Dayne/21	10.00	25.00
HSRM Randy Moss/23	12.00	30.00
HSSA Shaun Alexander/44	8.00	20.00
HSSM Santana Moss/23	10.00	25.00
HSTJ Thomas Jones/21	12.00	30.00

2002 Sweet Spot Patches

STATED ODDS ONE PER BOX		
SWPAB Aaron Brooks	3.00	8.00
SWPAF Antonio Freeman	4.00	10.00
SWPAG Ahman Green	3.00	8.00
SWPAT Anthony Thomas	3.00	8.00
SWPBF Brett Favre	10.00	25.00
SWPBG Brian Griese	3.00	8.00
SWPBJ Brad Johnson	3.00	8.00
SWPBO David Boston	2.50	6.00
SWPBR Tom Brady	10.00	25.00
SWPBU Brian Urlacher	4.00	10.00
SWPCA David Carr SP	4.00	10.00
SWPCD Corey Dillon	3.00	8.00
SWPCM Curtis Martin	4.00	10.00
SWPDB Drew Bledsoe	4.00	10.00
SWPDC Daunte Culpepper	3.00	8.00
SWPDE Deuce McAllister	3.00	8.00
SWPDM Donovan McNabb	4.00	10.00
SWPDR Drew Brees	6.00	15.00
SWPEG Eddie George	3.00	8.00
SWPEJ Edgerrin James	3.00	8.00
SWPES Emmitt Smith	10.00	25.00
SWPJB Jerome Bettis	4.00	10.00
SWPJG Jeff Garcia	3.00	8.00
SWPJH Joey Harrington SP	4.00	10.00
SWPJP Jake Plummer	3.00	8.00
SWPJR Jerry Rice	8.00	20.00
SWPJS Jeremy Shockey SP	6.00	15.00
SWPKJ Keyshawn Johnson	3.00	8.00
SWPKS Kordell Stewart	3.00	8.00
SWPKW Kurt Warner	4.00	10.00
SWPLT LaDainian Tomlinson	5.00	12.00
SWPMB Mark Brunell	3.00	8.00
SWPMF Marshall Faulk	4.00	10.00
SWPMV Michael Vick	6.00	15.00
SWPPE Julius Peppers SP	8.00	20.00
SWPPM Peyton Manning	8.00	20.00
SWPPR Patrick Ramsey SP	4.00	10.00
SWPRG Rich Gannon	3.00	8.00
SWPRM Randy Moss	4.00	10.00
SWPRW Ricky Williams	3.00	8.00
SWPSA Shaun Alexander	3.00	8.00
SWPSD Stephen Davis	3.00	8.00
SWPSM Steve McNair	4.00	10.00
SWPSS Shannon Sharpe	4.00	10.00
SWPTB Tiki Barber	4.00	10.00
SWPTC Tim Couch	2.50	6.00
SWPTO Terrell Owens	4.00	10.00
SWPVT Vinny Testaverde	3.00	8.00
SWPWD Warrick Dunn	3.00	8.00
SWPWG William Green SP	3.00	8.00

2002 Sweet Spot Rookie Gallery Jersey

STATED ODDS 1:8		
*GOLD/100: .6X TO 1.5X		
*GOLD/50: .8X TO 2X		
GOLD PRINT RUN 50-100		
RGAB Antonio Bryant	3.00	8.00
RGAL Ashley Lelie	2.50	6.00
RGCP Clinton Portis	4.00	10.00
RGDC David Carr/350	3.00	8.00
RGDF DeShaun Foster	3.00	8.00
RGDS Donte Stallworth/350	3.00	8.00
RGEC Eric Crouch	3.00	8.00
RGEL Antwaan Randle El	3.00	8.00
RGJG Jabar Gaffney/350	3.00	8.00
RGJH Joey Harrington/350	3.00	8.00
RGJM Josh McCown	3.00	8.00
RGJR Josh Reed	2.50	6.00
RGJW Javon Walker	3.00	8.00
RGMM Maurice Morris	2.50	6.00
RGMW Marquise Walker	2.00	5.00
RGPR Patrick Ramsey/350	3.00	8.00
RGRC Reche Caldwell	3.00	8.00
RGRD Rohan Davey	3.00	8.00
RGTC Tim Carter	2.50	6.00
RGTJ T.J. Duckett	3.00	8.00
RGTS Travis Stephens	2.00	5.00
RGWG William Green	2.50	6.00

2002 Sweet Spot Sunday Stars Jerseys

STATED PRINT RUN 150-250		
*GOLD/25: 1X TO 2.5X BASIC JSY		
GOLD PRINT RUN 10-25		
SSAG Ahman Green/250	4.00	10.00
SSAT Anthony Thomas/250	4.00	10.00
SSBF Brett Favre/150	12.00	30.00
SSDC Daunte Culpepper/150	4.00	10.00
SSDM Donovan McNabb/150	5.00	12.00
SSEJ Edgerrin James/150	4.00	10.00
SSES Emmitt Smith/150	12.00	30.00
SSJB Jerome Bettis/250	5.00	12.00
SSJP Jake Plummer/250	4.00	10.00
SSJR Jerry Rice/150	10.00	25.00
SSKJ Keyshawn Johnson/250	4.00	10.00
SSKW Kurt Warner/150	5.00	12.00
SSLT LaDainian Tomlinson/250	6.00	15.00
SSMF Marshall Faulk/150	5.00	12.00
SSMV Michael Vick/150	8.00	20.00
SSPM Peyton Manning/250	10.00	25.00
SSRM Randy Moss/150	5.00	12.00
SSRW Ricky Williams/250	4.00	10.00
SSTB Tom Brady/250	12.00	30.00
SSTC Tim Couch/250	3.00	8.00

2002 Sweet Spot Sweet Impressions Autographs

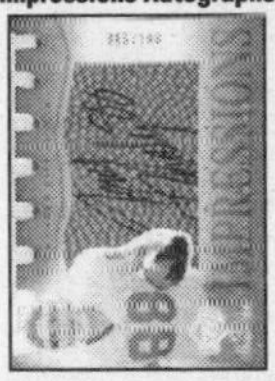

STATED PRINT RUN 50-450		
*GOLD/25: .8X TO 2X BASIC AU/450		
*GOLD/25: .6X TO 1.5X BASIC AU/50-100		
SIAB Aaron Brooks/75	10.00	25.00
SIAS Antowain Smith/100	10.00	25.00
SIBR Drew Brees/50	40.00	80.00
SIDB Drew Bledsoe/450	12.00	30.00
SIDC Daunte Culpepper/50	12.00	30.00
SIER Ed Reed/450	25.00	50.00
SIFM Freddie Mitchell/450	6.00	15.00
SIGH Garrison Hearst/450	8.00	20.00
SIJB Jerome Bettis/450	30.00	60.00
SIJM Jim Miller/450	6.00	15.00
SIJP Jake Plummer/75	10.00	25.00
SIMB Michael Bennett/450	10.00	25.00
SIPM1 Peyton Manning/450	40.00	80.00
SIPM2 Peyton Manning/450	40.00	80.00
SIPM3 Peyton Manning/450	40.00	80.00
SIPM4 Peyton Manning/450	40.00	80.00
SISM Santana Moss/450	8.00	20.00
SISR Sage Rosenfels/450	8.00	20.00
SITC Tim Carter/450	8.00	20.00
SITG Tony Gonzalez/100	12.00	30.00

2003 Sweet Spot

Released in December of 2003, this set features 231 cards, consisting of 90 veterans, 126 rookies, and 15 Sunday Stars subset cards. Rookies 91-120 are serial numbered to 1500. The Sunday Stars subset (121-135) were inserted at a rate of 1:6, and are serial numbered to 100. Tier 1 rookies (136-185) are serial numbered to 675, Tier 2 rookies (186-210) are serial numbered to 300, and Tier 3 rookies (211-225) are serial numbered to 100. Rookies 226-231 are serial numbered to 250, and feature authentic player autographs on plastic helmet pieces embedded in card front. Please note that Byron Leftwich was issued as an exchange card in packs. The exchange deadline is 3/19/2007.

COMP.SET w/o SP's (90)	12.50	30.00
226-231 AU RC PRINT RUN 250		
1 Chad Pennington	.40	1.00

2 Aaron Brooks	.30	.75
3 Joey Harrington	.25	.60
4 Brett Favre	1.00	2.50
5 Donovan McNabb	.40	1.00
6 Jeff Garcia	.30	.75
7 Michael Vick	.50	1.25
8 David Carr	.30	.75
9 Drew Brees	.40	1.00
10 Trent Green	.30	.75
11 Patrick Ramsey	.30	.75
12 Tom Brady	1.00	2.50
13 Kurt Warner	.40	1.00
14 Brad Johnson	.30	.75
15 Brian Griese	.30	.75
16 Jake Plummer	.30	.75
17 Drew Bledsoe	.40	1.00
18 Peyton Manning	.75	2.00
19 Tim Couch	.25	.60
20 Kordell Stewart	.30	.75
21 Jay Fiedler	.25	.60
22 Rich Gannon	.30	.75
23 Josh McCown	.30	.75
24 Matt Hasselbeck	.30	.75
25 Tommy Maddox	.30	.75
26 Rodney Peete	.25	.60
27 Jake Delhomme	.40	1.00
28 Chris Redman	.25	.60
29 Mark Brunell	.30	.75
30 Marc Bulger	.40	1.00
31 Kelly Holcomb	.25	.60
32 Chad Hutchinson	.25	.60
33 Quincy Carter	.25	.60
34 Steve McNair	.40	1.00
35 Marshall Faulk	.40	1.00
36 Deuce McAllister	.30	.75
37 Emmitt Smith	1.00	2.50
38 LaDainian Tomlinson	.40	1.00
39 Kevan Barlow	.25	.60
40 Michael Bennett	.30	.75
41 Shaun Alexander	.30	.75
42 Edgerrin James	.40	1.00
43 Ricky Williams	.30	.75
44 Priest Holmes	.40	1.00
45 Ahman Green	.30	.75
46 Curtis Martin	.40	1.00
47 Anthony Thomas	.30	.75
48 Travis Henry	.25	.60
49 Jerome Bettis	.40	1.00
50 Fred Taylor	.30	.75
51 Corey Dillon	.30	.75
52 Jamal Lewis	.30	.75
53 William Green	.25	.60
54 Brian Urlacher	.40	1.00
55 Junior Seau	.40	1.00
56 Ray Lewis	.40	1.00
57 Julius Peppers	.40	1.00
58 Terrell Owens	.40	1.00
59 David Boston	.25	.60
60 Isaac Bruce	.40	1.00
61 Marvin Harrison	.40	1.00
62 Chris Chambers	.30	.75
63 Chad Johnson	.40	1.00
64 Peter Warrick	.30	.75
65 Peerless Price	.25	.60
66 Antonio Bryant	.25	.60
67 Laveranues Coles	.25	.60
68 Rod Gardner	.25	.60
69 Hines Ward	.40	1.00
70 Plaxico Burress	.30	.75
71 Keyshawn Johnson	.40	1.00
72 Jabar Gaffney	.25	.60
73 Eric Moulds	.30	.75
74 Santana Moss	.30	.75
75 Koren Robinson	.30	.75
76 Jimmy Smith	.30	.75
77 Donte Stallworth	.25	.60
78 Kevin Johnson	.25	.60
79 Quincy Morgan	.25	.60
80 Jerry Rice	.75	2.00
81 Tim Brown	.40	1.00
82 Rod Smith	.30	.75
83 Ashley Lelie	.25	.60
84 Randy Moss	.40	1.00
85 Torry Holt	.40	1.00
86 Troy Brown	.30	.75
87 Donald Driver	.40	1.00
88 Todd Heap	.30	.75
89 Tony Gonzalez	.40	1.00
90 Jeremy Shockey	.40	1.00
91 Casey Moore RC	1.50	4.00
92 Chris Crocker RC	2.00	5.00
93 Pisa Tinoisamoa RC	2.50	6.00
94 Nnamdi Asomugha RC	5.00	12.00
95 Tyler Brayton RC	2.00	5.00
96 Eddie Moore RC	1.50	4.00
97 Terrence Kiel RC	2.00	5.00
98 Casey Fitzsimmons RC	2.00	5.00
99 George Foster RC	1.50	4.00
100 J.J. Moses RC	1.50	4.00
101 Dan Klecko RC	2.00	5.00
102 Terry Pierce RC	1.50	4.00
103 Brad Pyatt RC	1.50	4.00
104 Boss Bailey RC	2.00	5.00
105 Michael Haynes RC	1.50	4.00
106 Jimmy Kennedy RC	2.00	5.00
107 Jerome McDougle RC	1.50	4.00
108 William Joseph RC	1.50	4.00
109 Visanthe Shiancoe RC	2.50	6.00
110 L.J. Smith RC	2.50	6.00
111 Avon Cobourne RC	1.50	4.00
112 Bennie Joppru RC	1.50	4.00
113 Ken Hamlin RC	2.50	6.00
114 Jeremi Johnson RC	1.50	4.00
115 Justin Griffith RC	2.00	5.00
116 Joffrey Reynolds RC	1.50	4.00
117 Kassim Osgood RC	2.50	6.00
118 Donald Lee RC	2.00	5.00
119 Denero Marriott RC	1.50	4.00
120 Jamal Burke RC	1.50	4.00
121 Michael Vick SS	5.00	12.00
122 Donovan McNabb SS	4.00	10.00
123 Jerry Rice SS	8.00	20.00
124 Brett Favre SS	10.00	25.00
125 Kurt Warner SS	4.00	10.00
126 Marshall Faulk SS	4.00	10.00
127 Ricky Williams SS	3.00	8.00
128 Emmitt Smith SS	10.00	25.00
129 Tom Brady SS	10.00	25.00
130 Randy Moss SS	4.00	10.00
131 LaDainian Tomlinson SS	4.00	10.00
132 Jeff Garcia SS	3.00	8.00
133 Brian Urlacher SS	4.00	10.00
134 Drew Bledsoe SS	4.00	10.00
135 Peyton Manning SS	8.00	20.00
136 Dave Ragone RC	2.00	5.00
137 Brian St.Pierre RC	2.50	6.00
138 Kliff Kingsbury RC	2.50	6.00
139 Marquel Blackwell RC	2.00	5.00
140 Brett Engemann RC	2.00	5.00
141 Kirk Farmer RC	2.50	6.00
142 Andrew Pinnock RC	2.50	6.00
143 Tony Romo RC	25.00	60.00
144 Nate Hybl RC	2.50	6.00
145 Ken Dorsey RC	2.50	6.00
146 Brock Forsey RC	2.50	6.00
147 Musa Smith RC	2.00	5.00
148 Domanick Davis RC	2.50	6.00
149 LaBrandon Toefield RC	2.50	6.00
150 B.J. Askew RC	2.50	6.00
151 Quentin Griffin RC	2.50	6.00
152 Ahmaad Galloway RC	2.50	6.00
153 Cecil Sapp RC	2.00	5.00
154 Justin Fargas RC	3.00	8.00
155 Sultan McCullough RC	2.00	5.00
156 Malaefou MacKenzie RC	2.00	5.00
157 Tom Lopienski RC	2.00	5.00
158 Lee Suggs RC	2.50	6.00
159 Richard Angulo RC	2.00	5.00
160 Dwone Hicks RC	2.00	5.00
161 Nate Burleson RC	2.50	6.00
162 Billy McMullen RC	2.00	5.00
163 David Tyree RC	3.00	8.00
164 Gerald Hayes RC	2.50	6.00
165 Anthony Adams RC	2.50	6.00
166 George Wrighster RC	2.00	5.00
167 Tyrone Calico RC	2.50	6.00
168 Shaun McDonald RC	2.50	6.00
169 Bobby Wade RC	2.50	6.00
170 Larry Johnson RC	3.00	8.00
171 Ryan Hoag RC	2.00	5.00
172 Doug Gabriel RC	2.50	6.00
173 Antonio Gates RC	25.00	50.00
174 Brandon Lloyd RC	5.00	12.00
175 Arnaz Battle RC	3.00	8.00
176 Kelley Washington RC	2.00	5.00
177 Antwone Savage RC	2.00	5.00
178 Keenan Howry RC	2.00	5.00
179 Adrian Madise RC	2.00	5.00
180 LaTarence Dunbar RC	2.00	5.00
181 Walter Young RC	2.00	5.00
182 Travaris Robinson RC	2.00	5.00
183 DeAndrew Rubin RC	2.00	5.00
184 Carl Ford RC	2.00	5.00
185 Zuriel Smith RC	2.00	5.00
186 Willie Ponder RC	2.50	6.00
187 Gibran Hamdan RC	2.50	6.00
188 Aaron Moorehead RC	3.00	8.00
189 Nick Barnett RC	4.00	10.00
190 Chris Brown RC	2.50	6.00
191 ReShard Lee RC	4.00	10.00
192 Anquan Boldin RC	6.00	15.00
193 Kevin Curtis RC	4.00	10.00
194 Taylor Jacobs RC	2.50	6.00
195 Sam Aiken RC	3.00	8.00
196 Aaron Walker RC	3.00	8.00
197 Mike Seidman RC	2.50	6.00
198 Jason Witten RC	10.00	25.00
199 Dallas Clark RC	6.00	15.00
200 Rashean Mathis RC	3.00	8.00
201 DeWayne Robertson RC	3.00	8.00
202 Johnathan Sullivan RC	2.50	6.00
203 Drayton Florence RC	4.00	10.00
204 Sammy Davis RC	3.00	8.00
205 Andre Woolfolk RC	3.00	8.00
206 Terence Newman RC	3.00	8.00
207 Mike Doss RC	4.00	10.00
208 Troy Polamalu RC	30.00	60.00
209 Terrell Suggs RC	4.00	10.00
210 Marcus Trufant RC	3.00	8.00
211 Seneca Wallace RC	5.00	12.00
212 Brooks Bollinger RC	4.00	10.00
213 Jason Gesser RC	4.00	10.00
214 Onterrio Smith RC	3.00	8.00
215 Artose Pinner RC	3.00	8.00
216 J.R. Tolver RC	4.00	10.00
217 Kerry Carter RC	3.00	8.00
218 Tony Hollings RC	4.00	10.00
219 Teyo Johnson RC	4.00	10.00
220 Bethel Johnson RC	3.00	8.00
221 Rex Grossman RC	5.00	12.00
222 Andre Johnson RC	15.00	40.00
223 Terrence Edwards RC	3.00	8.00
224 Willis McGahee RC	6.00	15.00
225 Charles Rogers RC	4.00	10.00
226 Chris Simms AU RC	10.00	25.00
227 Bryant Johnson AU RC	10.00	25.00
228 Byron Leftwich AU RC	10.00	25.00
229 Carson Palmer AU RC	30.00	80.00
230 Justin Gage AU RC	8.00	20.00
231 Kyle Boller AU RC	10.00	25.00

2003 Sweet Spot Gold

*ROOKIES 136-185: 1.5X TO 4X BASIC CARDS
*ROOKIES 186-210: 1.2X TO 3X BASIC CARDS
*ROOKIES 211-225: 1X TO 2.5X BASIC CARDS
*ROOK.AU 226-231: .8X TO 2X BASIC CARDS
STATED PRINT RUN 25 SER.#'d SETS

143 Tony Romo	125.00	250.00
173 Antonio Gates	125.00	200.00
208 Troy Polamalu	125.00	200.00
229 Carson Palmer AU	125.00	250.00

2003 Sweet Spot By the Letters Autographed 10x12

STATED PRINT RUN 5-49
UNPRICED GOLD PRINT RUN 1-5
SERIAL #'d UNDER 20 NOT PRICED

AB Anquan Boldin/43	40.00	100.00
AJ Andre Johnson/49	60.00	120.00
AP Artose Pinner/43	15.00	40.00
BJ Bethel Johnson/43	15.00	40.00
BL Byron Leftwich/43	25.00	60.00
BR Bryant Johnson/43	25.00	60.00
CB Chris Brown/43		
CP Carson Palmer/43	100.00	200.00
DC Dallas Clark/43	40.00	100.00
DR Dave Ragone/43	15.00	40.00
JF Justin Fargas/42	25.00	60.00
KB Kyle Boller/40	25.00	60.00
KC Kevin Curtis/43	25.00	60.00
KK Kliff Kingsbury/43	20.00	50.00
KW Kelley Washington/44	15.00	40.00
LJ Larry Johnson/47	20.00	50.00
MS Musa Smith/43		
MT Marcus Trufant/43	20.00	50.00
NB Nate Burleson/43	20.00	50.00
OS Onterrio Smith/43	15.00	40.00
RG Rex Grossman/43	25.00	60.00
RO DeWayne Robertson/24	20.00	50.00
SP Brian St.Pierre/45	20.00	50.00
SW Seneca Wallace/43	25.00	60.00
TC Tyrone Calico/44	20.00	50.00
TE Teyo Johnson/43	20.00	50.00
TJ Taylor Jacobs/43	15.00	40.00
TN Terence Newman/43	20.00	50.00
TS Terrell Suggs/43	30.00	80.00
WM Willis McGahee/43	75.00	150.00

2003 Sweet Spot Classics

OVERALL CLASSICS ODDS 1:4
*NUMBER/100: .8X TO 2X BASIC INSERT
NUMBERS PRINT RUN 100 SER.#'d SETS
*GOLD/25: 1.2X TO 3X BASIC INSERT
GOLD PRINT RUN 25 SER.#'d SETS

PAB Aaron Brooks	3.00	8.00
PAG Ahman Green	3.00	8.00
PAJ Andre Johnson	6.00	15.00
PBE Bethel Johnson	2.50	6.00
PBF Brett Favre	10.00	25.00
PBJ Brad Johnson	3.00	8.00
PBL Byron Leftwich	2.50	6.00
PBR Drew Brees	4.00	10.00
PBU Brian Urlacher	4.00	10.00
PCP Chad Pennington	4.00	10.00
PCR Charles Rogers	2.50	6.00
PCS Chris Simms	4.00	10.00
PCU Daunte Culpepper	3.00	8.00
PDD Drew Bledsoe	4.00	10.00
PDC David Carr	3.00	8.00
PDM Donovan McNabb	4.00	10.00
PDU Deuce McAllister	3.00	8.00
PEG Eddie George	3.00	8.00
PEJ Edgerrin James	4.00	10.00
PES Emmitt Smith	10.00	25.00
PJG Jeff Garcia	3.00	8.00
PJH Joey Harrington	2.50	6.00
PJO Bryant Johnson	2.50	6.00
PJR Jerry Rice	8.00	20.00
PJS Jeremy Shockey	4.00	10.00
PKB Kyle Boller	4.00	10.00
PKW Kurt Warner	4.00	10.00
PLJ Larry Johnson	2.50	6.00
PLT LaDainian Tomlinson	4.00	10.00
PMF Marshall Faulk	4.00	10.00
PMV Michael Vick	5.00	12.00
PPH Priest Holmes	4.00	10.00
PPM Peyton Manning	8.00	20.00
PPO Clinton Portis	3.00	8.00
PRG Rex Grossman	2.50	6.00
PRM Randy Moss	4.00	10.00
PRW Ricky Williams	3.00	8.00
PSC Carson Palmer	5.00	12.00
PTB Tom Brady	10.00	25.00
PTJ Taylor Jacobs	2.50	6.00
PTO Terrell Owens	4.00	10.00
PWM Willis McGahee	3.00	8.00

2003 Sweet Spot Jerseys

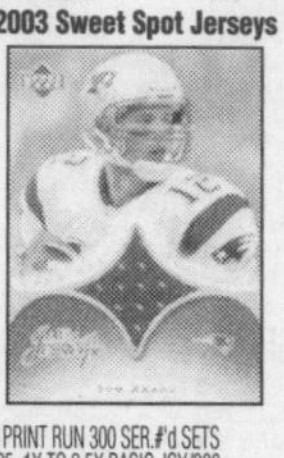

STATED PRINT RUN 300 SER.#'d SETS
*GOLD/25: 1X TO 2.5X BASIC JSY/300
GOLD PRINT RUN 25 SER.#'d SETS
OVERALL JSY ODDS 1:12

JCAB Aaron Brooks	3.00	8.00
JCBF Brett Favre	10.00	25.00
JCBG Brian Griese	3.00	8.00
JCBO David Boston	2.50	6.00
JCBU Brian Urlacher	4.00	10.00
JCCP Chad Pennington	4.00	10.00
JCDB Drew Brees	4.00	10.00
JCDC David Carr	3.00	8.00
JCDM Donovan McNabb	4.00	10.00
JCEG Eddie George	3.00	8.00
JCEJ Edgerrin James	4.00	10.00
JCES Emmitt Smith	10.00	25.00
JCJF Jay Fiedler	2.50	6.00
JCJG Jeff Garcia	3.00	8.00
JCJP Jake Plummer	3.00	8.00
JCJR Jerry Rice	8.00	20.00
JCJS Jeremy Shockey	4.00	10.00
JCKC Kerry Collins	3.00	8.00
JCKS Kordell Stewart	3.00	8.00
JCKW Kurt Warner	4.00	10.00
JCLC Laveranues Coles	2.50	6.00
JCLT LaDainian Tomlinson	4.00	10.00
JCMV Michael Vick	5.00	12.00
JCPM Peyton Manning	8.00	20.00
JCPO Clinton Portis	3.00	8.00
JCRG Rich Gannon	3.00	8.00
JCRL Ray Lewis	4.00	10.00
JCRM Randy Moss	4.00	10.00
JCSM Steve McNair	4.00	10.00
JCTB Tom Brady	10.00	25.00
JCTI Tim Brown	4.00	10.00
JCTO Terrell Owens	4.00	10.00
JCWD Warrick Dunn	3.00	8.00

2003 Sweet Spot Rookie Gallery Jersey

PRINT RUN 300 SERIAL #'d SETS
OVERALL JSY ODDS 1:12

RGAB Anquan Boldin	6.00	15.00
RGAJ Andre Johnson	8.00	20.00
RGAP Artose Pinner	2.00	5.00
RGBE Bethel Johnson	2.00	5.00
RGBJ Bryant Johnson	3.00	8.00
RGBL Byron Leftwich	3.00	8.00
RGCA Curt Anes	2.00	5.00
RGCB Chris Brown	2.00	5.00
RGCM Carl Morris	2.00	5.00
RGCP Carson Palmer	10.00	25.00
RGDC Dallas Clark	5.00	12.00
RGDR Dave Ragone	2.00	5.00
RGJF Justin Fargas	3.00	8.00
RGJG Justin Gage	2.50	6.00
RGKB Kyle Boller	3.00	8.00
RGKC Kevin Curtis	3.00	8.00
RGKK Kliff Kingsbury	2.50	6.00
RGKO Kassim Osgood	3.00	8.00
RGKW Kelley Washington	2.00	5.00
RGLJ Larry Johnson	3.00	8.00
RGMS Musa Smith	2.00	5.00
RGMT Marcus Trufant	2.50	6.00
RGNB Nate Burleson	2.50	6.00
RGOS Onterrio Smith	2.00	5.00
RGRG Rex Grossman	3.00	8.00
RGRO DeWayne Robertson	2.50	6.00
RGSP Brian St.Pierre	2.50	6.00
RGSW Seneca Wallace	3.00	8.00
RGTC Tyrone Calico	2.50	6.00
RGTE Teyo Johnson	2.50	6.00
RGTN Terence Newman	2.50	6.00
RGTP Troy Polamalu	40.00	80.00
RGTS Terrell Suggs	3.00	8.00
RGWM Willis McGahee	6.00	15.00
RGWY Walter Young	2.00	5.00

2003 Sweet Spot Rookie Gallery Jersey Gold

*GOLD/25: 1.2X TO 3X BASIC JSY
GOLD PRINT RUN 25 SER.#'d SETS

RGTP Troy Polamalu	75.00	150.00

2003 Sweet Spot Signatures

OVERALL SIGNATURES ODDS 1:24
*GOLD/25: .8X TO 2X BASIC AUTO
*GOLD/25: .5X TO 1.2X AUTO/60-100
*GOLD/25: .4X TO 1X AUTO/20
GOLD PRINT RUN 25 SER.#'d SETS

SSAB Aaron Brooks	12.00	30.00
SSAN Anquan Boldin/100*	25.00	60.00
SSBB Boss Bailey	12.00	30.00
SSBL Drew Bledsoe	25.00	50.00
SSBU Brian Urlacher	40.00	80.00
SSCJ Chad Johnson	15.00	40.00
SSCP Chad Pennington	15.00	40.00
SSDB Drew Brees	30.00	60.00
SSDC David Carr	12.00	30.00
SSDE Deuce McAllister/75*	20.00	50.00
SSDH Dwone Hicks	10.00	25.00
SSDM Donovan McNabb/99*	30.00	60.00
SSJB Jim Brown/75	75.00	135.00
SSJG Jeff Garcia	12.00	30.00
SSJM Joe Montana/60*	100.00	200.00
SSJR Jerry Rice/20*	150.00	300.00
SSLD LaTarence Dunbar	10.00	25.00
SSLS Lynn Swann	100.00	175.00
SSMH Matt Hasselbeck	12.00	30.00
SSMS Musa Smith	10.00	25.00
SSOS Onterrio Smith	10.00	25.00
SSPH Priest Holmes/450	15.00	40.00
SSPM Peyton Manning	60.00	120.00
SSPO Clinton Portis	12.00	30.00
SSRI John Riggins/75*	40.00	80.00
SSRW Ricky Williams/75*	30.00	60.00
SSSW Seneca Wallace	15.00	40.00
SSTA Troy Aikman	50.00	100.00
SSTB Tim Brown/75*	40.00	80.00
SSTB Terry Bradshaw/65*	60.00	120.00
SSTC Tyrone Calico	12.00	30.00
SSTG Trent Green	12.00	30.00
SSTO Terrell Owens	25.00	50.00

2004 Sweet Spot

Sweet Spot initially released in late-January 2005. The base set consists of 289-cards including 12-Legends serial numbered to 2499, 63-rookies numbered to 1299, 35-rookies numbered to 999, and 20-rookies numbered to 499. Additionally, 59-rookies were issued as autograph cards serial numbered between 125 and 699. Hobby boxes contained 12-packs of 4-cards and carried an S.R.P. of $9.99 per pack. Two parallel sets and a variety of autographed and jersey memorabilia inserts can be found seeded in packs.

COMP.SET w/o SP's (100)	15.00	30.00
176-210 ROOKIE PRINT RUN 999		
211-230 ROOKIE PRINT RUN 499		
1 Anquan Boldin	.50	1.25
2 Emmitt Smith	1.25	3.00
3 Josh McCown	.40	1.00
4 Michael Vick	.60	1.50
5 Warrick Dunn	.40	1.00
6 Peerless Price	.30	.75
7 Jamal Lewis	.40	1.00
8 Deion Sanders	.50	1.25
9 Kyle Boller	.40	1.00
10 Drew Bledsoe	.50	1.25
11 Travis Henry	.30	.75
12 Eric Moulds	.40	1.00
13 Jake Delhomme	.40	1.00
14 Stephen Davis	.40	1.00
15 Julius Peppers	.40	1.00
16 Thomas Jones	.50	1.25
17 Rex Grossman	.40	1.00
18 Brian Urlacher	.50	1.25
19 Carson Palmer	.50	1.25
20 Chad Johnson	.50	1.25
21 Rudi Johnson	.40	1.00
22 Jeff Garcia	.40	1.00
23 William Green	.30	.75
24 Andre Davis	.30	.75
25 Vinny Testaverde	.40	1.00
26 Eddie George	.40	1.00
27 Keyshawn Johnson	.40	1.00
28 Reuben Droughns	.40	1.00
29 Jake Plummer	.40	1.00
30 Ashley Lelie	.30	.75
31 Rod Smith	.40	1.00
32 Joey Harrington	.40	1.00
33 Artose Pinner	.30	.75
34 Az-Zahir Hakim	.30	.75
35 Brett Favre	1.25	3.00
36 Javon Walker	.30	.75
37 Ahman Green	.40	1.00
38 Andre Johnson	.50	1.25
39 David Carr	.30	.75
40 Domanick Davis	.30	.75
41 Peyton Manning	1.00	2.50
42 Edgerrin James	.40	1.00
43 Marvin Harrison	.50	1.25
44 Byron Leftwich	.40	1.00
45 Fred Taylor	.40	1.00
46 Jimmy Smith	.40	1.00
47 Priest Holmes	.50	1.25
48 Trent Green	.40	1.00
49 Dante Hall	.40	1.00
50 Tony Gonzalez	.50	1.25
51 Randy McMichael	.30	.75
52 Jay Fiedler	.30	.75
53 Chris Chambers	.40	1.00
54 Randy Moss	.50	1.25
55 Daunte Culpepper	.40	1.00
56 Onterrio Smith	.30	.75
57 Tom Brady	1.00	2.50
58 Deion Branch	.40	1.00
59 Corey Dillon	.40	1.00
60 Deuce McAllister	.40	1.00
61 Aaron Brooks	.40	1.00
62 Joe Horn	.40	1.00
63 Jeremy Shockey	.40	1.00
64 Tiki Barber	.50	1.25
65 Michael Strahan	.50	1.25
66 Curtis Martin	.50	1.25
67 Chad Pennington	.50	1.25
68 Santana Moss	.40	1.00
69 Charles Woodson	.50	1.25
70 Kerry Collins	.40	1.00
71 Warren Sapp	.40	1.00
72 Donovan McNabb	.50	1.25
73 Brian Westbrook	.50	1.25
74 Terrell Owens	.50	1.25
75 Hines Ward	.50	1.25
76 Plaxico Burress	.40	1.00
77 Duce Staley	.40	1.00
78 LaDainian Tomlinson	.50	1.25
79 Antonio Gates	.50	1.25
80 Drew Brees	.50	1.25
81 Eric Johnson	.30	.75
82 Kevan Barlow	.30	.75
83 Tim Rattay	.30	.75
84 Matt Hasselbeck	.40	1.00
85 Shaun Alexander	.40	1.00
86 Jerry Rice	1.00	2.50
87 Marc Bulger	.40	1.00
88 Torry Holt	.40	1.00
89 Marshall Faulk	.50	1.25
90 Isaac Bruce	.40	1.00
91 Brad Johnson	.40	1.00
92 Derrick Brooks	.40	1.00
93 Joey Galloway	.40	1.00
94 Steve McNair	.50	1.25
95 Derrick Mason	.40	1.00
96 Chris Brown	.30	.75
97 Clinton Portis	.50	1.25
98 Mark Brunell	.40	1.00
99 Laveranues Coles	.30	.75
100 LaVar Arrington	.40	1.00
101 Roger Staubach	2.50	6.00
102 Troy Aikman	2.50	6.00
103 John Elway	4.00	10.00
104 Barry Sanders	3.00	8.00
105 Fran Tarkenton	1.50	4.00
106 Archie Manning	1.50	4.00
107 Joe Namath	2.50	6.00
108 Ken Stabler	2.00	5.00
109 Howie Long	1.50	4.00
110 Kellen Winslow Sr.	1.50	4.00
111 Joe Montana	4.00	10.00
112 Joe Theismann	1.50	4.00
113 Darnell Dockett RC	2.00	5.00
114 Randy Starks RC	2.00	5.00
115 Rashad Baker RC	2.50	6.00
116 Tim Anderson RC	2.50	6.00
117 Darrion Scott RC	2.50	6.00
118 Courtney Watson RC	2.00	5.00
119 Gilbert Gardner RC	2.00	5.00
120 Marquis Cooper RC	2.00	5.00
121 Caleb Miller RC	2.00	5.00
122 Jeff Shoate RC	2.00	5.00
123 Keyaron Fox RC	2.50	6.00
124 Landon Johnson RC	2.00	5.00
125 Reggie Torbor RC	2.00	5.00
126 Demorrio Williams RC	3.00	8.00
127 Niko Koutouvides RC	2.00	5.00
128 Richard Seigler RC	2.00	5.00
129 Brandon Chillar RC	2.50	6.00
130 Nate Kaeding RC	3.00	8.00
131 Dave Ball RC	2.50	6.00
132 Josh Thomas RC	2.00	5.00
133 Josh Scobee RC	2.50	6.00
134 Wes Welker RC	12.00	30.00
135 Darrell McClover RC	2.00	5.00
136 Ben Utecht RC	2.50	6.00
137 Chris Snee RC	2.50	6.00
138 Jake Grove RC	2.00	5.00
139 Justin Smiley RC	2.50	6.00
140 Max Starks RC	2.50	6.00
141 Randall Gay RC	3.00	8.00
142 Charlie Anderson RC	2.00	5.00
143 Alain Kashama RC	2.00	5.00
144 Eric Edwards RC	2.00	5.00
145 Jacques Reeves RC	2.50	6.00
146 Jarrett Payton RC	2.50	6.00
147 Curtis Deloatch RC	2.00	5.00
148 Michael Gaines RC	2.00	5.00
149 Erik Jensen RC	2.00	5.00
150 Courtney Anderson RC	2.00	5.00
151 Bruce Thornton RC	2.00	5.00
152 Glenn Earl RC	2.00	5.00
153 Michael Waddell RC	2.00	5.00
154 J.R. Reed RC	2.00	5.00
155 Dwight Anderson RC	2.50	6.00
156 Von Hutchins RC	2.00	5.00
157 Travis LaBoy RC	2.50	6.00
158 Terry Johnson RC	2.00	5.00
159 Dwan Edwards RC	2.00	5.00
160 Colby Bockwoldt RC	2.00	5.00
161 Madieu Williams RC	2.00	5.00
162 Will Poole RC	3.00	8.00
163 Igor Olshansky RC	2.50	6.00
164 Michael Boulware RC	3.00	8.00
165 Shaun Phillips RC	3.00	8.00
166 Keith Smith RC	2.00	5.00
167 Will Smith RC	2.50	6.00
168 D.J. Williams RC	3.00	8.00
169 Derrick Strait RC	2.00	5.00
170 Karlos Dansby RC	3.00	8.00
171 Ricardo Colclough RC	2.50	6.00
172 Chad Lavalais RC	2.00	5.00
173 Teddy Lehman RC	2.00	5.00
174 Jim Sorgi RC	2.50	6.00
175 Bob Sanders RC	8.00	20.00
176 Sean Taylor RC	8.00	20.00
177 Marcus Tubbs RC	2.50	6.00
178 Daryl Smith RC	2.50	6.00
179 Bradlee Van Pelt RC	3.00	8.00
180 Shawntae Spencer RC	2.50	6.00
181 Nathan Vasher RC	4.00	10.00
182 Jared Allen RC	10.00	25.00
183 Rod Davis RC	2.50	6.00
184 Brian Jones RC	2.50	6.00
185 Will Allen RC	3.00	8.00
186 Antwan Odom RC	3.00	8.00
187 Vernon Carey RC	2.50	6.00
188 Mike Karney RC	3.00	8.00
189 Joey Thomas RC	2.50	6.00
190 Casey Bramlet RC	2.50	6.00
191 Keiwan Ratliff RC	2.50	6.00
192 Rich Gardner RC	3.00	8.00
193 Jason Babin RC	4.00	10.00
194 Dontarrious Thomas RC	3.00	8.00
195 Dexter Reid RC	2.50	6.00
196 Marquise Hill RC	2.50	6.00
197 Jonathan Smith RC	2.50	6.00
198 Larry Croom RC	2.50	6.00
199 Gibril Wilson RC	4.00	10.00
200 Erik Coleman RC	3.00	8.00
201 B.J. Sams RC	2.50	6.00
202 Bruce Perry RC	2.50	6.00
203 Brock Lesnar RC	10.00	25.00
204 Brandon Miree RC	2.50	6.00
205 Clarence Moore RC	2.50	6.00
206 Mark Jones RC	2.50	6.00
207 Patrick Crayton RC	4.00	10.00
208 Jeff Dugan RC	2.50	6.00
209 Sean Ryan RC	2.50	6.00
210 Sloan Thomas RC	3.00	8.00
211 Triandos Luke RC	3.00	8.00
212 Dexter Wynn RC	3.00	8.00
213 Matt Kranchick RC	4.00	10.00
214 Tim Euhus RC	3.00	8.00
215 Ryan Krause RC	3.00	8.00
216 Junior Siavii RC	3.00	8.00
217 Ran Carthon RC	3.00	8.00
218 Derrick Pope RC	4.00	10.00
219 Alex Lewis RC	3.00	8.00
220 Chris Cooley RC	5.00	12.00
221 Jamaar Taylor RC	3.00	8.00
222 Stuart Schweigert RC	4.00	10.00
223 Jason David RC	3.00	8.00
224 Maurice Mann RC	3.00	8.00
225 Robert Geathers RC	3.00	8.00
226 Matt Mauck RC	3.00	8.00
227 Jammal Lord RC	3.00	8.00
228 Travelle Wharton RC	3.00	8.00
229 D.J. Hackett RC	4.00	10.00
230 Thomas Tapeh RC	4.00	10.00
232 Ahmad Carroll AU/699 RC	6.00	15.00
233 Kenechi Udeze AU/699 RC	8.00	20.00
234 Tommie Harris AU/699 RC	10.00	25.00
235 Jonathan Vilma AU/699 RC	10.00	25.00
236 Vince Wilfork AU/699 RC	15.00	30.00
237 B.J. Symons AU/699 RC	6.00	15.00
238 B.J. Johnson AU/699 RC	6.00	15.00
239 Kris Wilson AU/699 RC	8.00	20.00
240 Josh Harris AU/699 RC	6.00	15.00
241 Troy Fleming AU/699 RC	6.00	15.00
242 Johnnie Morant AU/699 RC	6.00	15.00
243 Craig Krenzel AU/699 RC	8.00	20.00
244 Quincy Wilson AU/699 RC	8.00	20.00
245 P.K. Sam AU/699 RC	6.00	15.00
246 Michael Turner AU/699 RC	12.00	30.00
247 Carlos Francis AU/699 RC	6.00	15.00
248 Jared Lorenzen AU/699 RC	8.00	20.00
249 John Navarre AU/675 RC	6.00	15.00
250 Jeff Smoker AU/699 RC	8.00	20.00
251 Ernest Wilford AU/559 RC	8.00	20.00
252 Mewelde Moore AU/699 RC	8.00	20.00
253 Chris Gamble AU/699 RC	8.00	20.00
254 Jerricho Cotchery AU/699 RC	8.00	20.00
255 Derrick Hamilton AU/699 RC	6.00	15.00
256 Samie Parker AU/699 RC	6.00	15.00
257 Cody Pickett AU/699 RC	8.00	20.00
259 Ben Hartsock AU/699 RC	6.00	15.00
260 Cedric Cobbs AU/699 RC	6.00	15.00
261 Matt Schaub AU/699 RC	20.00	50.00
262 Bernard Berrian AU/699 RC	10.00	25.00
263 Devard Darling AU/699 RC	6.00	15.00
264 Ben Watson AU/699 RC	10.00	25.00
265 Darius Watts AU/699 RC	6.00	15.00
266 DeAngelo Hall AU/399 RC	12.00	30.00
267 Ben Troupe AU/699 RC	8.00	20.00
268 Michael Jenkins AU/399 RC	12.00	30.00
269 Keary Colbert AU/699 RC	6.00	15.00
270 Robert Gallery AU/699 RC	10.00	25.00
271 Greg Jones AU/650 RC	6.00	15.00
272 Michael Clayton AU/699 RC	8.00	20.00
273 Luke McCown AU/699 RC	8.00	20.00
274 Rashaun Woods AU/699 RC	6.00	15.00
275 Reggie Williams AU/699 RC	8.00	20.00
276 Devery Henderson AU/699 RC	10.00	25.00
277 Tatum Bell AU/699 RC	8.00	20.00
278 Lee Evans AU/350 RC	12.00	30.00
279 J.P. Losman AU/199 RC	12.00	30.00
280 Drew Henson AU/199 RC	12.00	30.00
281 Kellen Winslow AU/125 RC	15.00	40.00
282 Chris Perry AU/199 RC	12.00	30.00
283 Julius Jones AU/199 RC	12.00	30.00
284 Steven Jackson AU/199 RC	25.00	60.00
285 Kevin Jones AU/199 RC	12.00	30.00
286 Roy Williams AU/149 RC	15.00	40.00
287 Ben Roethlisberger AU/199 RC	75.00	150.00
288 Philip Rivers AU/199 RC	50.00	100.00
289 Larry Fitzgerald AU/150 RC	50.00	120.00
290 Eli Manning AU/150 RC	100.00	175.00

2004 Sweet Spot Gold

*VETS: 4X TO 10X BASIC CARDS
*LEGENDS: 1X TO 2.5X BASIC CARDS
*ROOKIES 113-175: 1X TO 2.5X
*ROOKIES 176-210: .8X TO 2X
*ROOKIES 211-230: .6X TO 1.5X
STATED PRINT RUN 50 SER.#'d SETS

2004 Sweet Spot Silver

*VETS: 2.5X TO 6X BASIC CARDS
*LEGENDS: .6X TO 1.5X BASIC CARDS
*ROOKIES 113-175: .6X TO 1.5X
*ROOKIES 176-210: .5X TO 1.2X
*ROOKIES 211-230: .4X TO 1X BASE CARD HI
STATED PRINT RUN 100 SER.#'d SETS

2004 Sweet Spot Gold Rookie Autographs

STATED PRINT RUN 35-100

232 Ahmad Carroll	8.00	20.00
233 Kenechi Udeze	10.00	25.00
234 Tommie Harris	12.00	30.00
235 Jonathan Vilma	12.00	30.00
236 Vince Wilfork	20.00	40.00
237 B.J. Symons	8.00	20.00
238 B.J. Johnson	8.00	20.00
239 Kris Wilson	10.00	25.00
240 Josh Harris	8.00	20.00
241 Troy Fleming	8.00	20.00
242 Johnnie Morant	8.00	20.00
243 Craig Krenzel	10.00	25.00
244 Quincy Wilson	10.00	25.00
245 P.K. Sam	8.00	20.00
246 Michael Turner	15.00	40.00
247 Carlos Francis	8.00	20.00
248 Jared Lorenzen	10.00	25.00
249 John Navarre	8.00	20.00
250 Jeff Smoker	10.00	25.00
251 Ernest Wilford	10.00	25.00
252 Mewelde Moore	10.00	25.00
253 Chris Gamble	10.00	25.00
254 Jerricho Cotchery	10.00	25.00
255 Derrick Hamilton	8.00	20.00
256 Samie Parker	8.00	20.00
257 Cody Pickett	10.00	25.00
259 Ben Hartsock	8.00	20.00
260 Cedric Cobbs	8.00	20.00
261 Matt Schaub	25.00	60.00
262 Bernard Berrian	12.00	30.00
263 Devard Darling	8.00	20.00
264 Ben Watson	12.00	30.00
265 Darius Watts	8.00	20.00
266 DeAngelo Hall	12.00	30.00
267 Ben Troupe	10.00	25.00
268 Michael Jenkins	12.00	30.00
269 Keary Colbert	8.00	20.00
270 Robert Gallery	12.00	30.00
271 Greg Jones	8.00	20.00
272 Michael Clayton	10.00	25.00
273 Luke McCown	10.00	25.00
274 Rashaun Woods	8.00	20.00
275 Reggie Williams	10.00	25.00
276 Devery Henderson	12.00	30.00
277 Tatum Bell	10.00	25.00
278 Lee Evans	12.00	30.00
279 J.P. Losman	10.00	25.00
280 Drew Henson	8.00	20.00
281 Kellen Winslow/50	15.00	40.00
282 Chris Perry	10.00	25.00
283 Julius Jones	10.00	25.00
284 Steven Jackson	25.00	60.00
285 Kevin Jones	10.00	25.00
286 Roy Williams WR	12.00	30.00
287 Ben Roethlisberger	75.00	150.00
288 Philip Rivers	50.00	120.00
289 Larry Fitzgerald/35	75.00	150.00
290 Eli Manning/50	125.00	200.00

2004 Sweet Spot Signatures

STATED ODDS 1:24
*GOLD/100: .5X TO 1.2X BASIC AU
*GOLD/100: .4X TO 1X BASIC AU SP
GOLD PRINT RUN 100 SER.#'d SETS

SSAG Ahman Green	12.00	30.00
SSAP Alan Page	12.00	30.00
SSBF Brett Favre	150.00	250.00
SSBG Bob Griese	15.00	40.00
SSBP Bill Parcells	25.00	60.00
SSBS Barry Sanders SP	75.00	150.00
SSBW Brian Westbrook	15.00	40.00
SSCB Chris Brown	10.00	25.00
SSCH Charlie Joiner	10.00	25.00
SSCJ Chad Johnson	12.00	30.00
SSCP Chad Pennington	15.00	40.00
SSDA Dave Casper	12.00	30.00
SSDD Domanick Davis	10.00	25.00
SSDF Dan Fouts	20.00	50.00
SSDM Donovan McNabb	30.00	80.00
SSDP Drew Pearson	12.00	30.00
SSFT Fran Tarkenton	25.00	60.00
SSHL Howie Long	25.00	50.00
SSJA Jack Ham	15.00	40.00
SSJE John Elway SP	75.00	150.00
SSJG Jon Gruden	12.00	30.00
SSJJ Jimmy Johnson	15.00	40.00
SSJN Joe Namath SP	75.00	150.00
SSJO Joe Montana SP	100.00	200.00
SSJT Joe Theismann SP	25.00	50.00
SSKA Ken Anderson	10.00	25.00
SSKE Kellen Winslow Sr.	15.00	40.00
SSKS Ken Stabler	25.00	60.00
SSLD Len Dawson	15.00	40.00
SSLT LaDainian Tomlinson	40.00	80.00
SSMA Dan Marino SP	125.00	250.00
SSMC Mark Clayton	10.00	25.00
SSMV Michael Vick SP	30.00	60.00
SSPH Paul Hornung SP	30.00	60.00
SSPM Peyton Manning SP	75.00	125.00
SSRG Rex Grossman	12.00	30.00
SSRJ Rudi Johnson	12.00	30.00
SSRO Roy Williams S	12.00	30.00
SSRS Roger Staubach SP	75.00	150.00
SSRW Randy White	12.00	30.00
SSTA Troy Aikman	40.00	100.00

2004 Sweet Spot Sweet Panel Signatures

STATED PRINT RUN 80-100
*GOLD/25: .6X TO 1.5X BASIC AU
GOLD PRINT RUN 25 SER.#'d SETS

SPBL Byron Leftwich	12.00	30.00
SPBR Ben Roethlisberger	75.00	135.00
SPBS Bart Starr/80	75.00	150.00
SPCH Chris Perry	12.00	30.00
SPCP Chad Pennington	15.00	40.00
SPDD Domanick Davis	10.00	25.00
SPEM Eli Manning	90.00	150.00
SPFT Fran Tarkenton	20.00	50.00
SPHL Howie Long	30.00	60.00
SPJP J.P. Losman	12.00	30.00
SPJT Joe Theismann	25.00	60.00
SPKJ Kevin Jones	12.00	30.00
SPKW Kellen Winslow Jr.	15.00	40.00
SPMV Michael Vick	30.00	60.00
SPPH Paul Hornung	25.00	60.00
SPPM Peyton Manning	60.00	120.00
SPPR Philip Rivers	40.00	80.00
SPRJ Rudi Johnson	12.00	30.00
SPRO-Roman Gabriel	12.00	30.00
SPTA Tatum Bell	12.00	30.00
SPZT Zach Thomas	15.00	40.00

2004 Sweet Spot Sweet Swatches

STATED ODDS 1:12
SWBR Ben Roethlisberger 12.00 30.00
SWBT Ben Troupe 2.50 6.00
SWBW Ben Watson 3.00 8.00
SWCC Cedric Cobbs 2.00 5.00
SWCP Chris Perry 2.50 6.00
SWDD Devard Darling 2.00 5.00
SWDE Devery Henderson 3.00 8.00
SWDH DeAngelo Hall 3.00 8.00
SWDW Darius Watts 2.00 5.00
SWEM Eli Manning 12.00 30.00
SWGJ Greg Jones 2.00 5.00
SWHA Derrick Hamilton 2.00 5.00
SWJJ Julius Jones 2.50 6.00
SWJP J.P. Losman 2.50 6.00
SWKC Keary Colbert 2.00 5.00
SWKJ Kevin Jones SP 2.50 6.00
SWKW Kellen Winslow Jr. 3.00 8.00
SWLE Lee Evans 3.00 8.00
SWLF Larry Fitzgerald 8.00 20.00
SWLM Luke McCown 2.50 6.00
SWMC Michael Clayton 2.50 6.00
SWMJ Michael Jenkins 3.00 8.00
SWMS Matt Schaub 6.00 15.00
SWPR Philip Rivers 8.00 20.00
SWRA Rashaun Woods 2.00 5.00
SWRG Robert Gallery 3.00 8.00
SWRO Roy Williams WR 3.00 8.00
SWRW Reggie Williams SP 2.50 6.00
SWSJ Steven Jackson 5.00 12.00
SWTB Tatum Bell 2.50 6.00

2005 Sweet Spot

This 302-card set was released in December, 2005. The set was issued in the hobby through four-card packs with an $9.99 SRP which came 12 packs to a box. Cards numbered 1-99 feature veterans in sequential order by team while the rest of the set features rookies. Cards numbered 243-284 were all signed by the player and those cards have stated print runs between 175 and 650 serial numbered sets. The other rookies have the following print runs: Cards numbered 101-142 was issued to a stated print run of 899 serial numbered sets while cards numbered 143-182 were issued to a stated print run of 699 serial nuimbered sets, cards numbered 183-222 was issued to a stated print run of 499 serial numbered sets, cards numbered 223-242 was issued to a stated print run of 299 serial numbered sets and cards numbered 285-302 were issued to a stated print run of 899 serial numbered sets. Some players did not return their signatures in time for pack out and those cards could be redeemed until December 9, 2008.

COMP.SET w/o RCs (100) 15.00 30.00
101-142 PRINT RUN 899 SER.#'d SETS
143-182 PRINT RUN 699 SER.#'d SETS
183-222 PRINT RUN 499 SER.#'d SETS
223-242 PRINT RUN 299 SER.#'d SETS
285-302 PRINT RUN 899 SER.#'d SETS
1 Larry Fitzgerald .40 1.00
2 Anquan Boldin .30 .75
3 Kurt Warner .40 1.00
4 Michael Vick .40 1.00
5 T.J. Duckett .25 .60
6 Peerless Price .25 .60
7 Todd Heap .30 .75
8 Jamal Lewis .30 .75
9 Kyle Boller .30 .75
10 Derrick Mason .30 .75
11 J.P. Losman .25 .60
12 Willis McGahee .40 1.00
13 Lee Evans .30 .75
14 Eric Moulds .25 .60
15 Jake Delhomme .30 .75
16 Keary Colbert .25 .60
17 DeShaun Foster .30 .75
18 Brian Urlacher .40 1.00
19 Rex Grossman .30 .75
20 Muhsin Muhammad .30 .75
21 Carson Palmer .40 1.00
22 Rudi Johnson .30 .75
23 Chad Johnson .30 .75
24 Julius Jones .25 .60
25 Keyshawn Johnson .30 .75
26 Drew Bledsoe .40 1.00
27 Tatum Bell .25 .60
28 Jake Plummer .30 .75
29 Ashley Lelie .25 .60
30 Roy Williams WR .30 .75
31 Kevin Jones .25 .60
32 Joey Harrington .30 .75
33 Brett Favre 1.00 2.50
34 Ahman Green .30 .75
35 Javon Walker .25 .60
36 David Carr .25 .60
37 Andre Johnson .40 1.00
38 Domanick Davis .25 .60
39 Peyton Manning .75 2.00
40 Reggie Wayne .40 1.00
41 Edgerrin James .30 .75
42 Marvin Harrison .40 1.00
43 Byron Leftwich .30 .75
44 Fred Taylor .30 .75
45 Jimmy Smith .30 .75
46 Priest Holmes .30 .75
47 Tony Gonzalez .30 .75
48 Trent Green .30 .75
49 A.J. Feeley .25 .60
50 Chris Chambers .30 .75
51 Randy McMichael .25 .60
52 Daunte Culpepper .30 .75
53 Michael Bennett .30 .75
54 Nate Burleson .25 .60
55 Tom Brady .75 2.00
56 Corey Dillon .30 .75
57 Deion Branch .25 .60
58 Richard Seymour .25 .60
59 Aaron Brooks .25 .60
60 Deuce McAllister .30 .75
61 Joe Horn .30 .75
62 Eli Manning .60 1.50
63 Jeremy Shockey .40 1.00
64 Tiki Barber .40 1.00
65 Chad Pennington .40 1.00
66 Curtis Martin .40 1.00
67 Laveranues Coles .25 .60
68 Kerry Collins .30 .75
69 LaMont Jordan .30 .75
70 Randy Moss .40 1.00
71 Donovan McNabb .40 1.00
72 Terrell Owens .40 1.00
73 Jeremiah Trotter .25 .60
74 Brian Westbrook .30 .75
75 Ben Roethlisberger .60 1.50
76 Willie Parker .30 .75
77 Hines Ward .40 1.00
78 Antwaan Randle El .30 .75
79 Drew Brees .40 1.00
80 LaDainian Tomlinson .40 1.00
81 Antonio Gates .40 1.00
82 Tim Rattay .25 .60
83 Brandon Lloyd .25 .60
84 Eric Johnson .25 .60
85 Shaun Alexander .30 .75
86 Darrell Jackson .25 .60
87 Matt Hasselbeck .30 .75
88 Marc Bulger .30 .75
89 Steven Jackson .40 1.00
90 Marshall Faulk .40 1.00
91 Torry Holt .30 .75
92 Joey Galloway .30 .75
93 Brian Griese .30 .75
94 Michael Clayton .25 .60
95 Steve McNair .40 1.00
96 Drew Bennett .30 .75
97 Chris Brown .25 .60
98 Clinton Portis .30 .75
99 Patrick Ramsey .30 .75
100 Santana Moss .30 .75
101 Antonio Perkins RC 2.00 5.00
102 James Sanders RC 1.50 4.00
103 Justin Green RC 2.50 6.00
104 Andre Maddox RC 1.50 4.00
105 C.C. Brown RC 1.50 4.00
106 Michael Hawkins RC 1.50 4.00
107 Deandra Cobb RC 1.50 4.00
108 Nehemiah Broughton RC 2.00 5.00
109 Madison Hedgecock RC 2.50 6.00
110 Paris Warren RC 2.00 5.00
111 Chris Harris RC 2.00 5.00
112 Matt Cassel RC 5.00 12.00
113 Justin Beriault RC 1.50 4.00
114 Roydell Williams RC 2.00 5.00
115 Alex Barron RC 1.50 4.00
116 Jammal Brown RC 2.50 6.00
117 Bo Scaife RC 2.00 5.00
118 Patrick Estes RC 1.50 4.00
119 Elton Brown RC 1.50 4.00
120 Rasheed Marshall RC 2.00 5.00
121 Jovan Haye RC 1.50 4.00
122 Nick Collins RC 2.50 6.00
123 Travis Daniels RC 2.00 5.00
124 Reynaldo Hill RC 2.00 5.00
125 Billy Bajema RC 1.50 4.00
126 Jim Leonhard RC 2.00 5.00
127 Boomer Grigsby RC 2.50 6.00
128 Chauncey Davis RC 1.50 4.00
129 David McMillan RC 2.50 6.00
130 Alfred Fincher RC 2.00 5.00
131 Kelvin Hayden RC 2.00 5.00
132 Kevin Burnett RC 2.00 5.00
133 Jonathan Welsh RC 1.50 4.00
134 Stanley Wilson RC 2.00 5.00
135 Stanford Routt RC 2.00 5.00
136 Korry Rhodes RC 2.00 5.00
137 Ellis Hobbs RC 2.50 6.00
138 Darrent Williams RC 2.50 6.00
139 Eric King RC 1.50 4.00
140 Domonique Foxworth RC 2.00 5.00
141 Anthony Bryant RC 2.00 5.00
142 Scott Starks RC 2.00 5.00
143 Marviel Underwood RC 2.00 5.00
144 Mike Montgomery RC 2.50 6.00
145 Kevin Vickerson RC 2.50 6.00
146 Jerome Carter RC 1.50 4.00
147 Jay Ratliff RC 6.00 15.00
148 Damien Nash RC 2.00 5.00
149 Noah Herron RC 1.50 4.00
150 Jonathan Fanene RC 2.50 6.00
151 Chase Lyman RC 1.50 4.00
152 Adam Seward RC 2.00 5.00
153 Michael Boley RC 2.50 6.00
154 Pat Thomas RC 1.50 4.00
155 Evan Mathis RC 1.50 4.00
156 Derrick Johnson CB RC 1.50 4.00
157 Tab Perry RC 1.50 4.00
158 Joel Dreessen RC 2.00 5.00
159 Daven Holly RC 1.50 4.00
160 Brandon Jones RC 2.00 5.00
161 Dan Buenning RC 2.50 6.00
162 Kurt Campbell RC 1.50 4.00
163 Kerry Wright RC 2.00 5.00
164 Matt McCoy RC 2.00 5.00
165 Dave Rayner RC 1.50 4.00
166 Kirk Morrison RC 2.50 6.00
167 Lofa Tatupu RC 2.50 6.00
168 Bryant McFadden RC 2.00 5.00
169 Corey Webster RC 2.00 5.00
170 Eric Green RC 1.50 4.00
171 Fabian Washington RC 2.00 5.00
172 Donte Nicholson RC 1.50 4.00
173 Vonta Leach RC 2.00 5.00
174 Ronald Bartell RC 2.00 5.00
175 Sean Considine RC 1.50 4.00
176 Oshiomogho Atogwe RC 2.50 6.00
177 Ryan Grant RC 20.00 50.00
178 James Butler RC 2.00 5.00
179 Paul Ernster RC 1.50 4.00
180 Duke Preston RC 2.00 5.00
181 Mike Nugent RC 2.00 5.00
182 Sione Pouha RC 1.50 4.00
183 Geoff Hangartner RC 3.00 8.00
184 Justin Geisinger RC 3.00 8.00
185 Chris Kemoeatu RC 3.00 8.00
186 Ryan Fitzpatrick RC 5.00 12.00
187 Lionel Gates RC 2.00 5.00
188 Brandon Jacobs RC 4.00 10.00
189 Alvin Pearman RC 2.00 5.00
190 J.R. Russell RC 2.00 5.00
191 Manuel White RC 2.50 6.00
192 Tyson Thompson RC 2.00 5.00
193 Chad Owens RC 2.50 6.00
194 Dante Ridgeway RC 2.00 5.00
195 Stephen Spach RC 2.00 5.00
196 Scott Mruczkowski RC 3.00 8.00
197 Chris Carr RC 2.00 5.00
198 Jonathan Babineaux RC 2.50 6.00
199 Will Whitticker RC 3.00 8.00
200 Luis Castillo RC 2.50 6.00
201 Matt Roth RC 2.50 6.00
202 Shaun Cody RC 2.50 6.00
203 Justin Tuck RC 4.00 10.00
204 Vincent Burns RC 2.00 5.00
205 DeMarcus Ware RC 6.00 15.00
206 Bill Swancutt RC 2.00 5.00
207 Darryl Blackstock RC 2.00 5.00
208 Brady Poppinga RC 3.00 8.00
209 Leroy Hill RC 3.00 8.00
210 Ryan Claridge RC 2.00 5.00
211 Odell Thurman RC 3.00 8.00
212 Barrett Ruud RC 3.00 8.00
213 Lance Mitchell RC 2.50 6.00
214 Trent Cole RC 3.00 8.00
215 Jerome Mathis RC 3.00 8.00
216 Brandon Browner RC 3.00 8.00
217 Justin Miller RC 2.50 6.00
218 Thomas Davis RC 2.00 5.00
219 Brodney Pool RC 2.50 6.00
220 Dylan Gandy RC 2.00 5.00
221 Josh Bullocks RC 2.50 6.00
222 Vincent Fuller RC 2.50 6.00
223 Jordan Beck RC 2.50 6.00
224 Claude Terrell RC 3.00 8.00
225 Adrian McPherson RC 2.00 5.00
226 Jerome Collins RC 2.50 6.00
227 Cedric Houston RC 3.00 8.00
228 Daniel Loper RC 3.00 8.00
229 Adam Bergen RC 2.00 5.00
230 Jeb Huckeba RC 2.50 6.00
231 Eric Moore RC 2.00 5.00
232 Dan Cody RC 2.50 6.00
233 Alex Smith TE RC 2.00 5.00
234 Travis Johnson RC 2.00 5.00
235 Ryan Riddle RC 2.00 5.00
236 Mike Patterson RC 2.00 5.00
237 Darrell Shropshire RC 2.00 5.00
238 David Pollack RC 2.50 6.00
239 Marcus Spears RC 2.50 6.00
240 Shawne Merriman RC 3.00 8.00
241 Channing Crowder RC 2.50 6.00
242 Derrick Johnson RC 2.50 6.00
243 Kyle Orton AU/199 RC 15.00 40.00
244 David Greene AU/650 RC 5.00 12.00
245 Derek Anderson AU/650 RC 6.00 15.00
246 Dan Orlovsky AU/650 RC 8.00 20.00
247 Eric Shelton AU/650 RC 5.00 12.00
248 Stefan LeFors AU/650 RC 5.00 12.00
249 Reggie Brown AU/650 RC 5.00 12.00
250 Andrew Walter AU/650 RC 6.00 15.00
251 Mark Bradley AU/650 RC 5.00 12.00
252 Courtney Roby AU/650 RC 6.00 15.00
253 Vincent Jackson AU/650 RC 10.00 25.00
254 Terrence Murphy AU/650 RC 5.00 12.00
255 Marion Barber AU/650 RC 8.00 20.00
256 Frank Gore AU/650 RC 15.00 40.00
257 Chris Henry AU/650 RC 8.00 20.00
258 Heath Miller AU/650 RC 12.00 30.00
259 J.J.Arrington AU/650 RC 6.00 15.00
260 Antrell Rolle AU/650 RC 8.00 20.00
261 Fred Gibson AU/650 RC 6.00 15.00
262 Charlie Frye AU/650 RC 8.00 20.00
263 Adam Jones AU/650 RC 5.00 12.00
264 Ciatrick Fason AU/650 RC 5.00 12.00
265 Roscoe Parrish AU/650 RC 5.00 12.00
266 Erasmus James AU/650 RC 6.00 15.00
267 Carlos Rogers AU/650 RC 8.00 20.00
268 Ryan Moats AU/650 RC 5.00 12.00
269 Marlin Jackson AU/650 RC 5.00 12.00
270 Darren Sproles AU/650 RC 8.00 20.00
271 Maurice Clarett AU/199 RC 6.00 15.00
272 Jason Campbell AU/199 RC 12.00 30.00
273 Vernand Morency AU/199 RC 6.00 15.00
274 Mark Clayton AU/199 RC 8.00 20.00
275 Roddy White AU/650 RC 10.00 25.00
276 T.Williamson AU/199 RC 8.00 20.00
277 Mike Williams AU/199 10.00 25.00
278 Braylon Edwards AU/199 RC 12.00 30.00
279 Cedric Benson AU/199 RC 10.00 25.00
280 Cadillac Williams AU/199 RC 10.00 25.00
281 Ronnie Brown AU/199 RC 12.00 30.00
282 Matt Jones AU/199 RC 8.00 20.00
283 Alex Smith QB AU/175 RC 30.00 60.00
284 Aaron Rodgers AU/199 RC 250.00 400.00
285 Rian Wallace RC 2.00 5.00
286 Nick Speegle RC 1.50 4.00
287 Chris Spencer RC 2.50 6.00
288 Logan Mankins RC 2.50 6.00
289 David Baas RC 1.50 4.00
290 Michael Roos RC 1.50 4.00
291 Khalif Barnes RC 1.50 4.00
292 Matt Giordano RC 2.00 5.00
293 Rick Razzano RC 1.50 4.00
294 Trai Essex RC 2.50 6.00
295 Roy Manning RC 2.50 6.00
296 Gerald Sensabaugh RC 2.50 6.00
297 Nick Kaczur RC 3.00 8.00
298 Ray Willis RC 1.50 4.00
299 Jason Brown RC 2.00 5.00
300 Frank Omiyale RC 1.50 4.00
301 Fred Amey RC 1.50 4.00
302 Reggie Hodges RC 1.50 4.00

2005 Sweet Spot Gold Rookie Autographs

*SINGLES: .5X TO 1.2X BASIC AUTO/650
*SINGLES: .4X TO 1X BASIC AUTO/175/199
STATED PRINT RUN 100 SER.#'d SETS
284 Aaron Rodgers 350.00 500.00

2005 Sweet Spot Rookie Sweet Swatches

STATED ODDS 1:12
SRAJ Adam Jones 2.00 5.00
SRAN Antrel Rolle 2.50 6.00
SRAR Aaron Rodgers 30.00 60.00
SRAS Alex Smith QB 5.00 12.00
SRAW Andrew Walter 2.00 5.00
SRBE Braylon Edwards 5.00 12.00
SRCB Cedric Benson 2.50 6.00
SRCF Charlie Frye 2.50 6.00
SRCI Ciatrick Fason 1.50 4.00
SRCR Carlos Rogers 2.50 6.00
SRCW Cadillac Williams 4.00 10.00
SRES Eric Shelton 1.50 4.00
SRFG Frank Gore 5.00 12.00
SRJA J.J. Arrington 2.00 5.00
SRJC Jason Campbell 3.00 8.00
SRKO Kyle Orton 2.50 6.00
SRMB Mark Bradley 1.50 4.00
SRMC Mark Clayton 2.50 6.00
SRMJ Matt Jones 2.50 6.00
SRMO Maurice Clarett 2.00 5.00
SRMW Mike Williams 2.50 6.00
SRRB Ronnie Brown 6.00 15.00
SRRE Reggie Brown 1.50 4.00
SRRP Roscoe Parrish 1.50 4.00
SRRW Roddy White 3.00 8.00
SRSL Stefan LeFors 1.50 4.00
SRTM Terrence Murphy 2.00 5.00
SRTW Troy Williamson 2.00 5.00
SRVJ Vincent Jackson 3.00 8.00
SRVM Vernand Morency 2.00 5.00

2005 Sweet Spot Signatures

OVERALL AUTO ODDS 1:12
SSAB Anquan Boldin 12.00 30.00
SSAG Ahman Green SP 12.00 30.00
SSAM Adrian McPherson 6.00 15.00
SSAN Antonio Gates 12.00 30.00
SSAS Alex Smith TE 7.50 20.00
SSBF Brett Favre SP 125.00 200.00
SSBI Billy Kilmer 12.00 30.00
SSBJ Bo Jackson SP 50.00 100.00
SSBK Bernie Kosar 12.00 30.00
SSBR Ben Roethlisberger SP 75.00 150.00
SSBS Barry Sanders SP 75.00 150.00
SSCP Carson Palmer SP 30.00 60.00
SSDB Drew Bennett 6.00 15.00
SSDD Domanick Davis 6.00 15.00
SSDM Donovan McNabb SP 30.00 60.00
SSDO Don Maynard 7.50 20.00
SSDP David Pollack 6.00 15.00
SSDR Drew Bledsoe SP 30.00 60.00
SSEM Eli Manning SP 75.00 135.00
SSHA Herb Adderley 7.50 20.00
SSJF Joe Ferguson 7.50 20.00
SSJJ Julius Jones SP 12.00 30.00
SSJM Joe Montana 100.00 200.00
SSJP Jim Plunkett 12.00 30.00
SSKC Keary Colbert 6.00 15.00
SSLE Lee Evans 7.50 20.00
SSLJ Larry Johnson 12.00 30.00
SSMA Marcus Allen SP 20.00 40.00
SSMB Marc Bulger 12.00 30.00
SSMM Muhsin Muhammad 7.50 20.00
SSMV Michael Vick SP 30.00 60.00
SSNB Nate Burleson 6.00 15.00
SSPH Paul Hornung 25.00 50.00
SSPM Peyton Manning SP 75.00 125.00
SSRJ Rudi Johnson 7.50 20.00
SSRW Reggie Wayne 15.00 40.00
SSSJ Steven Jackson SP 15.00 40.00
SSTA Troy Aikman SP 50.00 80.00

2005 Sweet Spot Signatures Gold

*GOLD: .6X TO 1.6X BASIC AUTOS
*GOLD: .6X TO 1.5X SP AUTOS
GOLD PRINT RUN 50 SER.#'d SETS
SSBF Brett Favre 150.00 250.00
SSBJ Bo Jackson 75.00 150.00
SSBR Ben Roethlisberger/40 90.00 150.00
SSBS Barry Sanders 75.00 150.00
SSCP Carson Palmer 40.00 80.00
SSEM Eli Manning 90.00 150.00
SSJM Joe Montana 125.00 200.00
SSPM Peyton Manning 75.00 150.00
SSSJ Steven Jackson 25.00 50.00

2005 Sweet Spot Sweet Panel Dual Signatures

UNPRICED PRINT RUN 10 SER.#'d SETS

2005 Sweet Spot Sweet Panel Signatures

STATED PRINT RUN 50 SER.#'d SETS
UNPRICED GOLD PRINT RUN 15 SETS
SPAB Anquan Boldin 10.00 25.00
SPAD Anthony Davis 6.00 15.00
SPAJ Adam Jones 8.00 20.00
SPAN Antrel Rolle
SPAR Aaron Rodgers 350.00 500.00
SPAS Alex Smith QB 30.00 60.00
SPAW Andrew Walter 8.00 20.00
SPBE Braylon Edwards 12.00 30.00
SPCF Charlie Frye 10.00 25.00
SPCI Ciatrick Fason 6.00 15.00
SPCR Carlos Rogers 10.00 25.00
SPCW Cadillac Williams 10.00 25.00
SPDA Derek Anderson 8.00 20.00
SPDB Drew Bledsoe 12.00 30.00
SPDD Domanick Davis 8.00 20.00
SPDG David Greene 6.00 15.00
SPDO Dan Orlovsky 10.00 25.00
SPEJ Erasmus James 8.00 20.00
SPFG Fred Gibson 8.00 20.00
SPFR Frank Gore 15.00 40.00
SPHA Herb Adderley 12.00 30.00
SPJC Jason Campbell 12.00 30.00
SPJH Joe Horn 10.00 25.00
SPJJ Julius Jones 8.00 20.00
SPKO Kyle Orton 10.00 25.00
SPMA Mark Clayton 10.00 25.00
SPMC Maurice Clarett 8.00 20.00
SPMI Michael Clayton 6.00 15.00
SPMW Mike Williams 10.00 25.00
SPNB Nate Burleson 6.00 15.00
SPPM Peyton Manning 75.00 135.00
SPRB Ronnie Brown 12.00 30.00
SPRE Reggie Brown 6.00 15.00
SPRM Ryan Moats 8.00 20.00
SPRO Roddy White 12.00 30.00
SPRP Roscoe Parrish 6.00 15.00
SPRW Reggie Wayne 15.00 40.00
SPTW Troy Williamson 8.00 20.00
SPVJ Vincent Jackson 12.00 30.00
SPVM Vernand Morency 8.00 20.00

2005 Sweet Spot Sweet Swatches

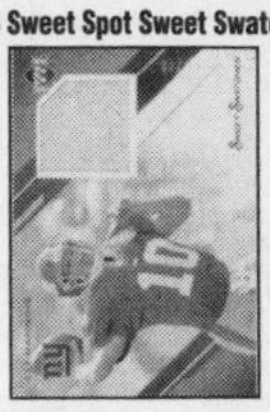

STATED PRINT RUN 40 SER.#'d SETS
SWAB Anquan Boldin 4.00 10.00
SWAG Ahman Green 4.00 10.00
SWAL Ashley Lelie 3.00 8.00
SWAR Antwaan Randle El 4.00 10.00
SWBF Brett Favre 12.00 30.00
SWBL Byron Leftwich 4.00 10.00
SWBR Ben Roethlisberger 8.00 20.00
SWBU Brian Urlacher 5.00 12.00
SWBW Brian Westbrook 4.00 10.00
SWCL Clinton Portis 4.00 10.00
SWCM Curtis Martin 5.00 12.00
SWCP Carson Palmer 5.00 12.00
SWCW Charles Woodson 5.00 12.00
SWDB Drew Bledsoe 5.00 12.00
SWDC David Carr 3.00 8.00
SWDM Deuce McAllister 4.00 10.00
SWDO Donovan McNabb 5.00 12.00
SWDR Drew Brees 5.00 12.00
SWDU Daunte Culpepper 4.00 10.00
SWEJ Edgerrin James 4.00 10.00
SWEM Eli Manning 8.00 20.00
SWJB Jerome Bettis 5.00 12.00
SWJJ Julius Jones 3.00 8.00
SWJP Jerry Porter 3.00 8.00
SWJS Jeremy Shockey 5.00 12.00
SWLA Lavar Arrington 4.00 10.00
SWLC Laveranues Coles 3.00 8.00
SWLT LaDainian Tomlinson 5.00 12.00
SWMA Matt Hasselbeck 4.00 10.00
SWMB Marc Bulger 4.00 10.00
SWMF Marshall Faulk 5.00 12.00
SWMH Marvin Harrison 5.00 12.00
SWMV Michael Vick 5.00 12.00
SWPH Priest Holmes 4.00 10.00
SWPM Peyton Manning 10.00 25.00
SWRG Rex Grossman 4.00 10.00
SWRJ Rudi Johnson 4.00 10.00
SWRL Ray Lewis 5.00 12.00
SWRM Randy Moss 5.00 12.00
SWRW Roy Williams S 3.00 8.00
SWSA Shaun Alexander 4.00 10.00
SWSM Steve McNair 5.00 12.00

2006 Sweet Spot

This 242-card set was released in December, 2006. The set was issued into the hobby in four-card packs, with an $9.99 SRP, which came 12 packs to a box. Cards numbered 1-100 are veterans in team alphabetical order while cards numbered 101-242 feature rookies. In the rookie groupings; cards numbered 101-200 were issued to a stated print run of 699 serial numbered sets while cards 201-242 were signed by the player to stated print runs of between 199 and 899 serial numbered copies. We have notated the specific print run for those signed cards in our checklist.

COMP.SET w/o RC's (100) 15.00 40.00
101-200 ROOKIE PRINT RUN 699
101-200 AU ROOKIE PRINT RUN 199-899
1 Larry Fitzgerald .40 1.00
2 Anquan Boldin .30 .75
3 Edgerrin James .30 .75
4 Kurt Warner .40 1.00
5 Michael Vick .40 1.00
6 Warrick Dunn .30 .75
7 Alge Crumpler .30 .75
8 Steve McNair .30 .75
9 Jamal Lewis .30 .75
10 Mark Clayton .30 .75
11 Willis McGahee .30 .75
12 Lee Evans .30 .75
13 J.P. Losman .30 .75
14 Jake Delhomme .30 .75
15 Steve Smith .40 1.00
16 DeShaun Foster .30 .75
17 Keyshawn Johnson .30 .75
18 Cedric Benson .30 .75
19 Brian Urlacher .40 1.00
20 Rex Grossman .30 .75
21 Carson Palmer .40 1.00
22 Chad Johnson .30 .75
23 Rudi Johnson .30 .75
24 Charlie Frye .30 .75
25 Reuben Droughns .30 .75
26 Braylon Edwards .30 .75
27 Drew Bledsoe .40 1.00
28 Julius Jones .25 .60
29 Terrell Owens .40 1.00
30 Jake Plummer .30 .75
31 Tatum Bell .25 .60
32 Rod Smith .30 .75
33 Kevin Jones .25 .60
34 Roy Williams WR .30 .75
35 Jon Kitna .30 .75
36 Brett Favre .75 2.00
37 Donald Driver .40 1.00
38 Ahman Green .30 .75
39 David Carr .25 .60
40 Ron Dayne .30 .75
41 Andre Johnson .40 1.00
42 Peyton Manning .60 1.50
43 Dominic Rhodes .30 .75
44 Reggie Wayne .30 .75
45 Marvin Harrison .40 1.00
46 Byron Leftwich .30 .75
47 Greg Jones .25 .60
48 Matt Jones .25 .60
49 Trent Green .30 .75
50 Larry Johnson .30 .75
51 Tony Gonzalez .30 .75
52 Daunte Culpepper .30 .75
53 Ronnie Brown .40 1.00
54 Chris Chambers .30 .75
55 Brad Johnson .30 .75
56 Chester Taylor .30 .75
57 Travis Taylor .25 .60
58 Tom Brady .60 1.50
59 Corey Dillon .30 .75
60 Doug Gabriel .25 .60
61 Drew Brees .40 1.00
62 Deuce McAllister .30 .75
63 Joe Horn .30 .75
64 Eli Manning .50 1.25
65 Tiki Barber .40 1.00
66 Plaxico Burress .30 .75
67 Jeremy Shockey .40 1.00
68 Chad Pennington .30 .75
69 Laveranues Coles .25 .60
70 Justin McCareins .25 .60
71 Andrew Walter .25 .60
72 Randy Moss .40 1.00
73 LaMont Jordan .30 .75
74 Donovan McNabb .40 1.00
75 Brian Westbrook .30 .75
76 Reggie Brown .25 .60
77 Ben Roethlisberger .50 1.25
78 Willie Parker .30 .75
79 Hines Ward .40 1.00
80 Philip Rivers .40 1.00
81 LaDainian Tomlinson .40 1.00
82 Antonio Gates .40 1.00
83 Alex Smith QB .40 1.00
84 Frank Gore .40 1.00
85 Antonio Bryant .25 .60
86 Matt Hasselbeck .30 .75
87 Shaun Alexander .30 .75
88 Nate Burleson .25 .60
89 Marc Bulger .30 .75
90 Steven Jackson .40 1.00
91 Torry Holt .30 .75
92 Chris Simms .30 .75
93 Cadillac Williams .30 .75
94 Joey Galloway .30 .75
95 Kerry Collins .30 .75
96 Drew Bennett .30 .75
97 Chris Brown .25 .60
98 Mark Brunell .30 .75
99 Clinton Portis .40 1.00
100 Santana Moss .30 .75
101 Abdul Hodge RC 2.00 5.00
102 Adam Jennings RC 2.50 6.00
103 Anthony Fasano RC 3.00 8.00
104 Anthony Schlegel RC 2.50 6.00
105 Anthony Smith RC 3.00 8.00
106 Antoine Bethea RC 4.00 10.00
107 Cortland Finnegan RC 3.00 8.00
108 Ben Obomanu RC 3.00 8.00
109 Bennie Brazell RC 2.50 6.00
110 Bernard Pollard RC 2.50 6.00
111 Bobby Carpenter RC 2.00 5.00
112 Brandon Marshall RC 3.00 8.00
113 Brodie Croyle RC 3.00 8.00
114 Brodrick Dunkley RC 2.50 6.00
115 Bruce Gradkowski RC 3.00 8.00
116 Calvin Lowry RC 3.00 8.00
117 Cedric Griffin RC 2.50 6.00
118 Dawan Landry RC 3.00 8.00
119 Chad Greenway RC 3.00 8.00
120 Charles Davis RC 2.50 6.00
121 Chris Gocong RC 2.50 6.00
122 Claude Wroten RC 2.00 5.00
123 Clint Ingram RC 3.00 8.00
124 Corey Bramlet RC 2.50 6.00
125 Cory Rodgers RC 2.50 6.00
126 D.J. Shockley RC 2.50 6.00
127 Danieal Manning RC 3.00 8.00
128 Daniel Bullocks RC 3.00 8.00
129 Darrell Bing RC 2.50 6.00
130 Darryl Tapp RC 2.50 6.00
131 David Anderson RC 2.50 6.00
132 David Kirtman RC 2.50 6.00
133 David Pittman RC 2.50 6.00
134 David Thomas RC 2.50 6.00
135 Davin Joseph RC 2.50 6.00
136 Delanie Walker RC 3.00 8.00
137 DeMeco Ryans RC 3.00 8.00
138 Devin Aromashodu RC 3.00 8.00
139 John Madsen RC 3.00 8.00
140 Donte Whitner RC 3.00 8.00
141 D'Qwell Jackson RC 2.50 6.00
142 Dusty Dvoracek RC 3.00 8.00
143 Elvis Dumervil RC 3.00 8.00
144 Eric Smith RC 2.50 6.00
145 Ernie Sims RC 2.50 6.00
146 Ethan Kilmer RC 2.50 6.00
147 Freddie Keiaho RC 2.50 6.00
148 Frostee Rucker RC 2.50 6.00
149 Gabe Watson RC 2.00 5.00
150 Garrett Mills RC 3.00 8.00
151 Gerris Wilkinson RC 2.00 5.00
152 Greg Lee RC 2.00 5.00
153 Haloti Ngata RC 3.00 8.00
154 Hank Baskett RC 3.00 8.00
155 Ingle Martin RC 2.50 6.00
156 Jamar Williams RC 2.50 6.00
157 James Anderson RC 2.00 5.00
158 Jason Allen RC 2.50 6.00
159 Jason Avant RC 2.00 5.00
160 Jason Pociask RC 2.50 6.00
161 Jeff King RC 2.50 6.00
162 Jeff Webb RC 2.50 6.00
163 Jeremy Bloom RC 2.50 6.00
164 Jimmy Williams RC 3.00 8.00
165 Joe Klopfenstein RC 2.00 5.00
166 John McCargo RC 2.00 5.00
167 Johnathan Joseph RC 2.50 6.00
168 Jon Alston RC 2.00 5.00
169 Jonathan Orr RC 2.50 6.00
170 Kamerion Wimbley RC 3.00 8.00
171 Kelly Jennings RC 2.50 6.00
172 Kevin McMahan RC 2.50 6.00
173 Ko Simpson RC 2.50 6.00
174 Lawrence Vickers RC 2.50 6.00
175 Leon Williams RC 2.50 6.00
176 Manny Lawson RC 2.50 6.00
177 Marcus Vick RC 2.00 5.00
178 Marques Colston RC 6.00 15.00
179 Marques Hagans RC 2.00 5.00
180 Mathias Kiwanuka RC 3.00 8.00
181 Mike Bell RC 3.00 8.00
182 Mike Hass RC 2.50 6.00
183 Nick Mangold RC 2.50 6.00
184 Owen Daniels RC 3.00 8.00
185 Quinn Sypniewski RC 2.50 6.00
186 Quinton Ganther RC 2.00 5.00
187 Richard Marshall RC 2.00 5.00
188 Rocky McIntosh RC 2.50 6.00
189 Roman Harper RC 2.50 6.00
190 Stephen Tulloch RC 2.50 6.00
191 Keith Ellison RC 2.50 6.00
192 Tamba Hali RC 3.00 8.00
193 Thomas Howard RC 2.50 6.00
194 Todd Watkins RC 2.00 5.00
195 Tony Scheffler RC 3.00 8.00
196 Troy Bergeron RC 2.50 6.00
197 Tye Hill RC 2.00 5.00
198 Wali Lundy RC 2.50 6.00
199 Willie Reid RC 2.50 6.00
200 Winston Justice RC 2.50 6.00
201 Jay Cutler AU/299 RC 40.00 80.00
202 Matt Leinart AU/199 RC 15.00 40.00
203 A.J. Hawk AU/299 RC 15.00 40.00
204 DeAngelo Williams AU/299 RC 20.00 50.00
205 Reggie Bush AU/199 RC 40.00 80.00
206 Santonio Holmes AU/299 RC 20.00 50.00
207 Vince Young AU/199 RC 20.00 50.00
208 Vernon Davis AU/499 RC 12.00 30.00
209 Joseph Addai AU/499 RC 10.00 25.00
210 Sinorice Moss AU/499 RC 10.00 25.00
211 Chad Jackson AU/899 RC 5.00 12.00
212 Laurence Maroney AU/499 RC 8.00 20.00
213 Michael Huff AU/499 RC 8.00 20.00
214 Mario Williams AU/499 RC 10.00 25.00
215 Brandon Williams AU/899 RC 5.00 12.00
216 Michael Robinson AU/899 RC 6.00 15.00
217 Devin Hester AU/899 RC 30.00 60.00
218 Reggie McNeal AU/899 RC 6.00 15.00
219 Travis Wilson AU/899 RC 5.00 12.00
220 Jerome Harrison AU/899 RC 8.00 20.00
221 Maurice Stovall AU/899 RC 5.00 12.00
222 Leonard Pope AU/899 RC 8.00 20.00
223 Antonio Cromartie AU/899 RC 8.00 20.00
224 Charlie Whitehurst AU/899 RC 8.00 20.00
225 Skyler Green AU/899 RC 5.00 12.00
226 Derek Hagan AU/899 RC 6.00 15.00
227 Jerious Norwood AU/899 RC 6.00 15.00
228 Maurice Drew AU/899 RC 25.00 50.00
229 Marcedes Lewis AU/899 RC 8.00 20.00
230 D'Brickashaw Ferguson AU/899 RC 8.00 20.00
231 Kellen Clemens AU/899 RC 6.00 15.00
232 Leon Washington AU/899 RC 6.00 15.00
233 Brad Smith AU/899 RC 8.00 20.00
234 Brian Calhoun AU/899 RC 5.00 12.00
235 Greg Jennings AU/899 RC 20.00 40.00
236 Will Blackmon AU/899 RC 6.00 15.00
237 Dominique Byrd AU/899 RC 6.00 15.00
238 Demetrius Williams AU/899 RC 6.00 15.00
239 P.J. Daniels AU/899 RC 5.00 12.00
240 Omar Jacobs AU/899 RC 5.00 12.00
241 LenDale White AU/899 RC 6.00 15.00
242 Tarvaris Jackson AU/899 RC 10.00 25.00

2006 Sweet Spot Gold Rookie Autographs

*GOLD/100: .5X TO 1.2X BASIC AU/899
*GOLD/50: .5X TO 1.2X BASIC AU/499
*GOLD/50: .4X TO 1X BASIC AU/199-299
GOLD STATED PRINT RUN 50-100

2006 Sweet Spot Signatures

AB Aaron Brooks 8.00 20.00
AF Anthony Fasano 8.00 20.00
AG Antonio Gates 10.00 25.00
BA Ronde Barber 10.00 25.00
BF Brett Favre SP 100.00 200.00
BG Bruce Gradkowski 8.00 20.00
BM Brandon Marshall 0.00 20.00
BR Ben Roethlisberger SP 60.00 120.00
CR Cory Rodgers 6.00 15.00
CW Cadillac Williams SP 10.00 25.00
DB Drew Bledsoe SP 15.00 30.00
DF DeShaun Foster 8.00 20.00
DG David Givens 8.00 20.00
DM Dan Marino SP 125.00 200.00
DS D.J. Shockley 6.00 15.00
DW Donte Whitner 8.00 20.00
EM Eli Manning SP 40.00 80.00
GM Garrett Mills 8.00 20.00
HA Mike Hass 6.00 15.00
IM Ingle Martin 6.00 15.00
JA Jason Avant 5.00 12.00
JE John Elway SP 75.00 150.00
JM Joe Montana SP 100.00 175.00
JO LaMont Jordan 8.00 20.00
JW Jeff Webb 6.00 15.00
LJ Larry Johnson SP 12.00 30.00
LT LaDainian Tomlinson SP 30.00 80.00
MH Marques Hagans 5.00 12.00
MV Michael Vick SP 30.00 60.00
NM Nat Moore 8.00 20.00
OR Jonathan Orr 6.00 15.00
PH Paul Hornung 20.00 40.00
PM Peyton Manning 60.00 120.00
RB Reggie Brown 5.00 12.00
RW Reggie Wayne 10.00 25.00
SM Stanley Morgan 10.00 25.00
SS Steve Smith SP 12.00 30.00
TA Lofa Tatupu 8.00 20.00
TH Tye Hill 5.00 12.00

2006 Sweet Spot Signatures Gold

*GOLD/100: .5X TO 1.2X BASIC AUTOS
*GOLD/50: .5X TO 1.2X BASIC AUTOS
GOLD PRINT RUN 50-100
BF Brett Favre 100.00 200.00
BR Ben Roethlisberger 60.00 100.00
DM Dan Marino 125.00 200.00
EM Eli Manning 50.00 100.00
JE John Elway 75.00 150.00
JM Joe Montana/50 100.00 200.00
LT LaDainian Tomlinson 60.00 120.00
PM Peyton Manning 60.00 120.00

2006 Sweet Spot Sweet Images 5x7

ONE PER BOX
SIAC Alge Crumpler 2.50 6.00
SIBD Brian Dawkins 2.50 6.00
SIBE Braylon Edwards 2.50 6.00
SIBF Brett Favre 6.00 15.00
SIBG Bob Griese 3.00 8.00
SIBR Ben Roethlisberger 4.00 10.00
SICB Cedric Benson 2.50 6.00

SICF Charlie Frye 2.50 6.00
SICP Carson Palmer 3.00 8.00
SICW Cadillac Williams 2.50 6.00
SIDB Drew Bledsoe 3.00 8.00
SIDM Deuce McAllister 2.50 6.00
SIEM Eli Manning 4.00 10.00
SIJJ Julius Jones 2.00 5.00
SIJT Joe Theismann 3.00 8.00
SIKO Kyle Orton 3.00 8.00
SIMB Marc Bulger 2.50 6.00
SIMC Mark Clayton 2.50 6.00
SIMV Michael Vick 3.00 8.00
SIMW Mike Williams 2.00 5.00
SIPM Peyton Manning 5.00 12.00
SIRB Reggie Brown 2.00 5.00
SIRO Ronnie Brown 3.00 8.00
SIRW Reggie Wayne 2.50 6.00
SITB Tiki Barber 3.00 8.00

2006 Sweet Spot Sweet Images 5x7 Autographs

SIAC Alge Crumpler SP
SIBD Brian Dawkins SP
SIBE Braylon Edwards 10.00 25.00
SIBF Brett Favre SP 125.00 200.00
SIBG Bob Griese 15.00 30.00
SIBR Ben Roethlisberger 50.00 100.00
SICB Cedric Benson 10.00 25.00
SICF Charlie Frye 10.00 25.00
SICP Carson Palmer SP
SICW Cadillac Williams SP 15.00 40.00
SIDB Drew Bledsoe 20.00 40.00
SIDM Deuce McAllister SP
SIEM Eli Manning SP
SIJJ Julius Jones SP 12.00 30.00
SIJT Joe Theismann 25.00 50.00
SIKO Kyle Orton 8.00 20.00
SIMB Marc Bulger SP 10.00 25.00
SIMC Mark Clayton 10.00 25.00
SIMV Michael Vick SP 30.00 60.00
SIMW Mike Williams 8.00 20.00
SIPM Peyton Manning 60.00 120.00
SIRB Reggie Brown 8.00 20.00
SIRO Ronnie Brown 15.00 30.00
SIRW Reggie Wayne SP 15.00 30.00
SITB Tiki Barber 20.00 40.00

2006 Sweet Spot Sweet Leather Signatures

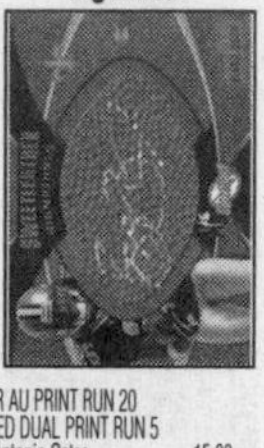

LEATHER AU PRINT RUN 20
UNPRICED DUAL PRINT RUN 5
SLSAG Antonio Gates 15.00 40.00
SLSBC Brian Calhoun 8.00 20.00
SLSBE Braylon Edwards 12.00 30.00
SLSBL Byron Leftwich 12.00 30.00
SLSBU Reggie Bush 25.00 60.00
SLSCB Cedric Benson 12.00 30.00
SLSCS Chris Simms 12.00 30.00
SLSDB Drew Bennett 12.00 30.00
SLSDF DeShaun Foster 10.00 25.00
SLSDM Derrick Mason 12.00 30.00
SLSEM Eli Manning 30.00 60.00
SLSGM Garrett Mills 12.00 30.00
SLSJC Jay Cutler 40.00 80.00
SLSJJ Julius Jones 10.00 25.00
SLSJN Jerious Norwood 10.00 25.00
SLSJO LaMont Jordan 12.00 30.00
SLSKC Kevin Curtis 12.00 30.00
SLSLJ Larry Johnson 12.00 30.00
SLSLM Laurence Maroney 10.00 25.00
SLSLT LaDainian Tomlinson 30.00 60.00
SLSMB Marc Bulger 12.00 30.00
SLSML Matt Leinart 12.00 30.00
SLSMM Muhsin Muhammad 12.00 30.00
SLSMR Michael Robinson 10.00 25.00
SLSMW Mario Williams 12.00 30.00
SLSNB Nate Burleson 10.00 25.00
SLSPM Peyton Manning 60.00 120.00
SLSPR Philip Rivers 30.00 60.00
SLSRB Reggie Brown 10.00 25.00
SLSRW Reggie Wayne 12.00 30.00
SLSSH Santonio Holmes 15.00 40.00
SLSSS Steve Smith 15.00 40.00
SLSTA Lofa Tatupu 12.00 30.00
SLSTH T.J. Houshmandzadeh 12.00 30.00
SLSTJ Thomas Jones 12.00 30.00
SLSTW Travis Wilson 8.00 20.00
SLSVD Vernon Davis 15.00 40.00
SLSVY Vince Young 15.00 40.00
SLSWI Mike Williams 12.00 30.00
SLSWP Willie Parker 12.00 30.00
SLSWR Willie Reid 10.00 25.00

2006 Sweet Spot Sweet Pairings Jerseys Dual

SPDAM Jason Avant 5.00 12.00
Sinorice Moss
SPDAS Jason Avant 4.00 10.00
Maurice Stovall
SPDBL Reggie Bush 15.00 40.00
Matt Leinart
SPDBW Reggie Bush 12.00 30.00
LenDale White
SPDCD Brian Calhoun 6.00 15.00
Maurice Drew
SPDCM Jay Cutler 10.00 25.00
Brandon Marshall
SPDCW Kellen Clemens 6.00 15.00
Leon Washington
SPDDC Derek Hagan 5.00 12.00
Chad Jackson
SPDDD Demetrius Williams 4.00 10.00
Derek Hagan
SPDDK Demetrius Williams 4.00 10.00
Kellen Clemens
SPDDL Vernon Davis 6.00 15.00
Marcedes Lewis
SPDDN Maurice Drew 6.00 15.00
Jerious Norwood
SPDDR Vernon Davis 6.00 15.00
Michael Robinson
SPDHH A.J. Hawk 8.00 20.00
Michael Huff
SPDHJ Santonio Holmes 6.00 15.00
Omar Jacobs
SPDHW Santonio Holmes 6.00 15.00
Travis Wilson
SPDHY Michael Huff 12.00 30.00
Vince Young
SPDJC Tarvaris Jackson 5.00 12.00
Kellen Clemens
SPDJH Chad Jackson 6.00 15.00
Santonio Holmes
SPDJJ Tarvaris Jackson 5.00 12.00
Omar Jacobs
SPDJM Chad Jackson 5.00 12.00
Sinorice Moss
SPDJW Omar Jacobs 4.00 10.00
Charlie Whitehurst
SPDKD Joe Klopfenstein 6.00 15.00
Vernon Davis
SPDLD Marcedes Lewis 6.00 15.00
Maurice Drew
SPDLL Laurence Maroney 6.00 15.00
LenDale White
SPDLW Matt Leinart 8.00 20.00
LenDale White
SPDLY Matt Leinart 10.00 25.00
Vince Young
SPDMM Laurence Maroney 6.00 15.00
Sinorice Moss
SPDMW Brandon Marshall 4.00 10.00
Brandon Williams
SPDNW Jerious Norwood 6.00 15.00
Leon Washington
SPDRS Michael Robinson 5.00 12.00
Maurice Stovall
SPDRW Michael Robinson 5.00 12.00
Brandon Williams
SPDTB Travis Wilson 4.00 10.00
Brandon Marshall
SPDWB Mario Williams 12.00 30.00
Reggie Bush
SPDWC Brandon Williams 4.00 10.00
Brian Calhoun
SPDWH Mario Williams 8.00 20.00
A.J. Hawk
SPDWJ Charlie Whitehurst 5.00 12.00
Tarvaris Jackson
SPDWM DeAngelo Williams 10.00 25.00
Laurence Maroney
SPDWN DeAngelo Williams 10.00 25.00
Jerious Norwood
SPDWS Travis Wilson 4.00 10.00
Maurice Stovall
SPDYC Vince Young 15.00 30.00
Jay Cutler
SPDYW Vince Young 12.00 30.00
LenDale White

2006 Sweet Spot Update Spokesmen Signatures

OVERALL AUTO ODDS 1:6
UNPRICED AU PRINT RUN 5-20

2007 Sweet Spot

This 141-card set was released in December, 2007. The set was issued into the hobby in six-card pack (boxes) with an $120 SRP. Cards numbered 1-100 feature veterans in alphabetical order by team with a stated print run of 625 serial numbered sets. Cards 101-142 feature signed Rookie Cards. Cards numbered 101-130 were issued to stated print runs between 755 and 799 serial numbered sets and cards 131-142 were issued to stated print runs between 299 and 399 serial numbered sets. A few players did not return their signatures in time for pack out and those cards could be exchanged until November 26, 2009. Card number 127 was never issued.

1-100 STATED PRINT RUN 625
101-130 AU RC PRINT RUN 755-799
131-142 AU RC PRINT RUN 299-399
1 Matt Leinart 2.00 5.00
2 Edgerrin James 2.00 5.00
3 Larry Fitzgerald 2.50 6.00
4 Anquan Boldin 2.00 5.00
5 Joey Galloway 2.00 5.00
6 Warrick Dunn 2.00 5.00
7 Alge Crumpler 2.00 5.00
8 Steve McNair 2.00 5.00
9 Willis McGahee 2.00 5.00
10 Mark Clayton 2.00 5.00
11 J.P. Losman 1.50 4.00
12 Aaron Schobel 1.50 4.00
13 Lee Evans 2.00 5.00
14 Jake Delhomme 2.00 5.00
15 DeAngelo Williams 2.50 6.00
16 Steve Smith 2.00 5.00
17 Rex Grossman 2.00 5.00
18 Cedric Benson 2.00 5.00
19 Brian Urlacher 2.50 6.00
20 Carson Palmer 2.00 5.00
21 Rudi Johnson 2.00 5.00
22 Chad Johnson 2.00 5.00
23 T.J. Houshmandzadeh 2.00 5.00
24 Charlie Frye 2.00 5.00
25 Kellen Winslow 2.00 5.00
26 Braylon Edwards 2.00 5.00
27 Tony Romo 3.00 8.00
28 Marion Barber 2.00 5.00
29 Terrell Owens 2.50 6.00
30 Jay Cutler 2.50 6.00
31 Travis Henry 2.00 5.00
32 Javon Walker 2.00 5.00
33 Jon Kitna 1.50 4.00
34 Roy Williams WR 2.00 5.00
35 Mike Furrey 2.00 5.00
36 Brett Favre 5.00 12.00
37 Donald Driver 2.50 6.00
38 Greg Jennings 2.50 6.00
39 Matt Schaub 2.00 5.00
40 Ahman Green 2.00 5.00
41 Andre Johnson 2.00 5.00
42 Peyton Manning 4.00 10.00
43 Joseph Addai 2.00 5.00
44 Marvin Harrison 2.50 6.00
45 Reggie Wayne 2.00 5.00
46 David Garrard 2.00 5.00
47 Maurice Jones-Drew 2.50 6.00
48 Fred Taylor 2.00 5.00
49 Brodie Croyle 2.00 5.00
50 Larry Johnson 1.50 4.00
51 Tony Gonzalez 2.00 5.00
52 Trent Green 2.00 5.00
53 Ronnie Brown 2.00 5.00
54 Chris Chambers 2.00 5.00
55 Tarvaris Jackson 1.50 4.00
56 Chester Taylor 1.50 4.00
57 Bobby Wade 1.50 4.00
58 Tom Brady 4.00 10.00
59 Laurence Maroney 2.00 5.00
60 Randy Moss 2.50 6.00
61 Drew Brees 2.50 6.00
62 Reggie Bush 2.50 6.00
63 Deuce McAllister 2.00 5.00
64 Marques Colston 2.50 6.00
65 Eli Manning 2.50 6.00
66 Brandon Jacobs 2.00 5.00
67 Plaxico Burress 2.00 5.00
68 Chad Pennington 2.00 5.00
69 Thomas Jones 2.00 5.00
70 Jerricho Cotchery 2.00 5.00
71 LaMont Jordan 2.00 5.00
72 Dominic Rhodes 2.00 5.00
73 Ronald Curry 2.00 5.00
74 Donovan McNabb 2.50 6.00
75 Brian Westbrook 2.00 5.00
76 Reggie Brown 1.50 4.00
77 Ben Roethlisberger 2.50 6.00
78 Willie Parker 2.00 5.00
79 Hines Ward 2.50 6.00
80 Philip Rivers 2.50 6.00
81 LaDainian Tomlinson 2.50 6.00
82 Antonio Gates 2.50 6.00
83 Alex Smith QB 2.50 6.00
84 Frank Gore 2.50 6.00
85 Darrell Jackson 1.50 4.00
86 Matt Hasselbeck 2.00 5.00
87 Shaun Alexander 2.00 5.00
88 Deion Branch 2.00 5.00
89 Marc Bulger 2.00 5.00
90 Steven Jackson 2.50 6.00
91 Torry Holt 2.00 5.00
92 Jeff Garcia 2.00 5.00
93 Cadillac Williams 2.00 5.00
94 Josh Bidwell 1.50 4.00
95 Vince Young 2.00 5.00
96 LenDale White 2.00 5.00
97 Brandon Jones 1.50 4.00
98 Jason Campbell 2.00 5.00
99 Clinton Portis 2.00 5.00
100 Santana Moss 2.00 5.00
101 Laurent Robinson AU RC 8.00 20.00
102 Trent Edwards AU RC 8.00 20.00
103 Dwayne Wright AU RC 6.00 15.00
104 Chris Leak AU RC 6.00 15.00
105 Garrett Wolfe AU RC 5.00 12.00
106 Greg Olsen AU/755 RC 6.00 15.00
107 Leon Hall AU RC 6.00 15.00
108 Kenny Irons AU RC 5.00 12.00
109 Joe Thomas AU RC 8.00 20.00
110 Isaiah Stanback AU RC 5.00 12.00
111 Drew Stanton AU RC 5.00 12.00
112 Brandon Jackson AU RC 6.00 15.00
113 Amobi Okoye AU RC 8.00 20.00
114 John Beck AU RC 8.00 20.00
115 Lorenzo Booker AU RC 6.00 15.00
116 Antonio Pittman AU RC 5.00 12.00
117 Steve Smith USC AU RC 8.00 20.00
118 Michael Bush AU RC 8.00 20.00
119 Zach Miller AU RC 8.00 20.00
120 Johnnie Lee Higgins AU RC 6.00 15.00
121 Tony Hunt AU RC 5.00 12.00
122 Gary Russell AU RC 6.00 15.00
123 Craig Buster Davis AU RC 6.00 15.00
124 Patrick Willis AU RC 15.00 40.00
125 Courtney Taylor AU RC 6.00 15.00
126 Brian Leonard AU RC 6.00 15.00
128 Paul Williams AU RC 5.00 12.00
129 Jordan Palmer AU RC 6.00 15.00
130 LaRon Landry AU RC 8.00 20.00
131 Marshawn Lynch AU/399 RC 12.50 30.00
132 Dwayne Jarrett AU/399 RC 8.00 20.00
133 Adrian Peterson AU/299 RC 75.00 200.00
134 Brady Quinn AU/399 RC 15.00 40.00
135 Calvin Johnson AU/299 RC 40.00 80.00
136 Anthony Gonzalez AU/399 RC 10.00 25.00
137 Dwayne Bowe AU/399 RC 12.00 30.00
138 Ted Ginn AU/399 RC 8.00 20.00
139 Sidney Rice AU/315 RC 12.00 30.00
140 Robert Meachem AU/399 RC 10.00 25.00
141 JaMarcus Russell AU/399 RC 6.00 15.00
142 Kevin Kolb AU/399 RC 25.00 50.00

2007 Sweet Spot Pigskin Signatures Dual

STATED PRINT RUN 50 SER.#'d SETS
AA Anthony Gonzalez 15.00 40.00
Antonio Pittman
AL Alan Branch 10.00 25.00
Leon Hall
BB Reggie Brown 10.00 25.00
Drew Bennett
BH Champ Bailey 12.00 30.00
Daymeion Hughes
BV Brandon Marshall 10.00 25.00
Vincent Jackson
CM Scott Chandler 12.00 30.00
Zach Miller
CS Jason Campbell 15.00 40.00
Drew Stanton
DB Craig Buster Davis 15.00 40.00
Dwayne Bowe
DE Daymeion Hughes 12.00 30.00
Eric Wright
DY Kenneth Darby 12.00 30.00
Selvin Young
GW Michael Griffin 12.00 30.00
Eric Weddle
HF T.J. Houshmandzadeh 12.00 30.00
Joel Filani
HT Paul Hornung 40.00 100.00
Joe Theismann
II Kenny Irons 12.00 30.00
David Irons
JE Darrell Jackson 12.00 30.00
Lee Evans
KS Kevin Kolb 20.00 50.00
Drew Stanton
LL LaRon Landry 12.00 30.00
John Lynch
LZ Chris Leak 12.00 30.00
Jared Zabransky
MC Rhema McKnight 12.00 30.00
David Clowney
MG Brandon Meriweather 12.00 30.00
Michael Griffin
MW Marcus McCauley 12.00 30.00
Eric Wright
PL Adrian Peterson 75.00 150.00
Marshawn Lynch
QR Brady Quinn 20.00 50.00
JaMarcus Russell
RJ Sidney Rice 20.00 50.00
Chad Johnson
SA Chansi Stuckey 10.00 25.00
Aundrae Allison
TP Lawrence Timmons 12.00 30.00
Paul Posluszny
WC Paul Williams 12.00 30.00
David Clowney
WM Reggie Wayne 60.00 120.00
Peyton Manning
ZN Jared Zabransky 12.00 30.00
Legedu Naanee

2007 Sweet Spot Pigskin Signatures Bronze 49

BRONZE 49 PRINT RUN 49 SER.#'d SETS
*BRONZE/25: .5X TO 1.2X BRONZE/49
GOLD 1/1 TOO SCARCE TO PRICE
*RED 15: .6X TO 1.5X BRONZE/49
RED/5 TOO SCARCE TO PRICE
AA2 Aundrae Allison 6.00 15.00
AN Jamaal Anderson 8.00 20.00
AO Amobi Okoye 10.00 25.00
AP Antonio Pittman 6.00 15.00
BA2 Marion Barber 12.00 30.00
BE2 Drew Bennett 8.00 20.00
BN Brandon Jacobs 10.00 25.00
CB Champ Bailey 12.00 30.00
CD2 Craig Buster Davis 8.00 20.00
CJ Chad Johnson 10.00 25.00
CS2 Chansi Stuckey 10.00 25.00
DC David Clowney 8.00 20.00
DJ2 Dwayne Jarrett 8.00 20.00
DS2 Drew Stanton 6.00 15.00
FG Frank Gore 12.00 30.00
GO2 Greg Olsen 8.00 20.00
GW2 Garrett Wolfe 6.00 15.00
HO2 T.J. Houshmandzadeh 10.00 25.00
HU Tony Hunt 6.00 15.00
JB2 John Beck 10.00 25.00
JC Jerricho Cotchery 10.00 25.00
JH Johnnie Lee Higgins 8.00 20.00
JL2 John Lynch 12.00 30.00
JP2 Jordan Palmer 8.00 20.00
JT2 Joe Thomas 10.00 25.00
LE2 Lee Evans 10.00 25.00
LW LaMarr Woodley 12.00 30.00
MB2 Michael Bush 10.00 25.00
MC Marques Colston 12.00 30.00
MS Matt Schaub 10.00 25.00
PM2 Peyton Manning 60.00 120.00
PW Patrick Willis 20.00 50.00
RB Ronnie Brown 10.00 25.00
RN Reggie Nelson 8.00 20.00
RW2 Reggie Wayne 12.00 30.00
SI Mike Singletary 15.00 40.00
SS2 Steve Smith USC 10.00 25.00
TA Chester Taylor 8.00 20.00
TH Joe Theismann 15.00 40.00
WI Paul Williams 6.00 15.00
WP2 Willie Parker 10.00 25.00

2007 Sweet Spot Pigskin Signatures Green 99

GREEN 99 PRINT RUN 99 SER.#'d SETS
*GREEN 75: .4X TO 1X GREEN/99
GREEN 75 PRINT RUN 75 SER.#'d SETS
*GREEN 50: .5X TO 1.2X GREEN/99
GREEN 50 PRINT RUN 50 SER.#'d SETS
*BLUE 20: .6X TO 1.5X GREEN/99
BLUE 20 PRINT RUN 20 SER.#'d SETS
GREEN 1/1 TOO SCARCE TO PRICE
AA Aundrae Allison 5.00 12.00
BA Marion Barber 10.00 25.00
BB Bernard Berrian 6.00 15.00
BE Drew Bennett 6.00 15.00
BL Brian Leonard 6.00 15.00
BM Brandon Marshall 8.00 20.00
BR Reggie Brown 6.00 15.00
CD Craig Buster Davis 6.00 15.00
CH Chris Henry RB 5.00 12.00
CL Mark Clayton 8.00 20.00
CS Chansi Stuckey 8.00 20.00
DJ Dwayne Jarrett 6.00 15.00
DS Drew Stanton 5.00 12.00
DW Darius Walker 5.00 12.00
GJ Greg Jennings 10.00 25.00
GO Greg Olsen 6.00 15.00
GW Garrett Wolfe 5.00 12.00
HI Jason Hill 8.00 20.00
HO T.J. Houshmandzadeh 8.00 20.00
JA Darrell Jackson 6.00 15.00
JB John Beck 8.00 20.00
JJ Jacoby Jones 8.00 20.00
JL John Lynch 10.00 25.00
JO James Jones 8.00 20.00
JP Jordan Palmer 6.00 15.00
JT Joe Thomas 8.00 20.00
KI Kenny Irons 5.00 12.00
KS Kolby Smith 6.00 15.00
LB Lorenzo Booker 6.00 15.00
LE Lee Evans 8.00 20.00
LL LaRon Landry 8.00 20.00
MB Michael Bush 8.00 20.00
ME Brandon Meriweather 8.00 20.00
PM Peyton Manning 50.00 100.00
QM Quentin Moses 6.00 15.00
RO Jeff Rowe 5.00 12.00
RW Reggie Wayne 10.00 25.00
SS Steve Smith USC 8.00 20.00
WP Willie Parker 8.00 20.00
YF Yamon Figurs 5.00 12.00

2007 Sweet Spot Rookie Signatures Gold 15

*GOLD/29: 1X TO 2.5X BASE AU/755-799
*GOLD/29: .8X TO 2X BASE AU/315-399
GOLD 15 PRINT RUN 15 SER.#'d SETS
133 Adrian Peterson 200.00 400.00
135 Calvin Johnson 60.00 150.00

2007 Sweet Spot Rookie Signatures Gold 29

*GOLD/29: .8X TO 2X BASE AU/755-799
*GOLD/29: .6X TO 1.5X BASE AU/315-399
GOLD 29 PRINT RUN 29 SER.#'d SETS
GOLD/5 TOO SCARCE TO PRICE
GOLD 1/1 TOO SCARCE TO PRICE
133 Adrian Peterson 150.00 300.00
135 Calvin Johnson 50.00 120.00

2007 Sweet Spot Signatures Silver 25

SILVER 25 PRINT RUN 25 SER.#'d SETS
*SILVER/49: .3X TO .8X SILVER/25
SILVER 49 PRINT RUN 49 SER.#'d SETS
*SILVER/15: .5X TO 1.2X SILVER/25
SILVER 15 PRINT RUN 15 SER.#'d SETS
*GOLD 15: .5X TO 1.2X SILVER/25
GOLD 15 PRINT RUN 15 SER.#'d SETS
GOLD/5 TOO SCARCE TO PRICE
AP Adrian Peterson 175.00 300.00
BF Brett Favre 150.00 250.00
BQ Brady Quinn 50.00 120.00
BR2 Ronnie Brown 15.00 40.00
BU2 Michael Bush 15.00 40.00
CD2 Craig Buster Davis 12.00 30.00
CL2 Chris Leak 12.00 30.00
CT2 Chester Taylor 12.00 30.00
CW2 Cadillac Williams 15.00 40.00
DB Drew Brees 40.00 80.00
ES Emmitt Smith 175.00 300.00
GO2 Greg Olsen 12.00 30.00
GW2 Garrett Wolfe 10.00 25.00
JA2 Joseph Addai 15.00 40.00
JB2 John Beck 15.00 40.00
JC2 Jason Campbell 15.00 40.00
JJ2 Jacoby Jones 15.00 40.00
JN2 Jerious Norwood 15.00 40.00
JO2 James Jones 15.00 40.00
JR JaMarcus Russell 10.00 25.00
JT2 Joe Thomas 15.00 40.00
KI2 Kenny Irons 10.00 25.00
LE2 Lee Evans [illegible]
LJ Larry Johnson 12.00 30.00
LL2 LaRon Landry 15.00 40.00
LR2 Laurent Robinson 15.00 40.00
MB2 Marion Barber 25.00 60.00
MG2 Michael Griffin 15.00 40.00
ML Matt Leinart 25.00 60.00
MS2 Matt Schaub 15.00 40.00
NA Joe Namath
PM2 Peyton Manning 100.00 200.00
RB Reggie Bush 40.00 100.00
RN2 Reggie Nelson 12.00 30.00
RO2 Jeff Rowe 10.00 25.00
RW2 Reggie Wayne 20.00 50.00
SS2 Steve Smith USC 20.00 50.00
TH2 T.J. Houshmandzadeh 15.00 40.00
TN2 Joe Theismann 25.00 60.00
VY Vince Young 40.00 100.00
WP2 Willie Parker 15.00 40.00

2007 Sweet Spot Signatures Silver 99

SILVER 99 PRINT RUN 99 SER.#'d SETS
*SILVER/75: .4X TO 1X SILVER/99
SILVER 75 PRINT RUN 75 SER.#'d SETS
*SILVER/50: .5X TO 1.2X SILVER/99
SILVER 50 PRINT RUN 50 SER.#'d SETS
*GOLD/20: .6X TO 1.5X SILVER/99
GOLD 20 PRINT RUN 20 SER.#'d SETS
GOLD/10 TOO SCARCE TO PRICE
SILVER 1/1 TOO SCARCE TO PRICE
AB Anquan Boldin 10.00 25.00
AG Anthony Gonzalez 10.00 25.00
BB Bernard Berrian 8.00 20.00
BM Brandon Meriweather 10.00 25.00
BR Ronnie Brown 10.00 25.00
BU Michael Bush 10.00 25.00
CD Craig Buster Davis 8.00 20.00
CT Chester Taylor 8.00 20.00
CW Cadillac Williams 10.00 25.00
DJ Dwayne Jarrett 8.00 20.00
FG Frank Gore 12.00 30.00
GO Greg Olsen 8.00 20.00
GW Garrett Wolfe 6.00 15.00
HU Daymeion Hughes 8.00 20.00
JA Joseph Addai 10.00 25.00
JB John Beck 10.00 25.00
JC Jason Campbell 10.00 25.00
JJ Jacoby Jones 10.00 25.00
JN Jerious Norwood 10.00 25.00
JO James Jones 10.00 25.00
JP Jordan Palmer 10.00 25.00
JT Joe Thomas 10.00 25.00
KI Kenny Irons 6.00 15.00
LE Lee Evans 10.00 25.00
LF Larry Fitzgerald 20.00 50.00
LL LaRon Landry 10.00 25.00
LN Legedu Naanee 10.00 25.00
LR Laurent Robinson 10.00 25.00
MB Marion Barber 15.00 40.00
MC Marques Colston 12.00 30.00
MG Michael Griffin 10.00 25.00
MS Matt Schaub 10.00 25.00
PM Peyton Manning 60.00 120.00
RN Reggie Nelson 8.00 20.00
RO Jeff Rowe 6.00 15.00
RW Reggie Wayne 12.00 30.00
SS Steve Smith USC 12.00 30.00
TH T.J. Houshmandzadeh 10.00 25.00
TN Joe Theismann 15.00 40.00
WP Willie Parker 10.00 25.00

2007 Sweet Spot Sweet Swatch Jersey

*PATCH/50: .8X TO 2X BASIC JSYs
PATCH PRINT RUN 50 SER.#'d SETS
SSAB Anquan Boldin 3.00 8.00
SSAC Alge Crumpler 3.00 8.00
SSAD Gaines Adams 2.50 6.00
SSAG Anthony Gonzalez 2.00 5.00
SSAG2 Anthony Gonzalez 2.00 5.00
SSAP Adrian Peterson 10.00 25.00
SSAP2 Adrian Peterson 10.00 25.00
SSAV Adam Vinatieri 4.00 10.00
SSBA Champ Bailey 4.00 10.00
SSBD Brian Dawkins 3.00 8.00
SSBE Drew Bennett 2.50 6.00
SSBF Brett Favre 8.00 20.00
SSBJ Brandon Jackson 1.50 4.00
SSBL Brian Leonard 2.50 6.00
SSBO Dwayne Bowe 2.50 6.00
SSBO2 Dwayne Bowe 2.50 6.00
SSBQ Brady Quinn 5.00 12.00
SSBQ2 Brady Quinn 5.00 12.00
SSBR Ronnie Brown 3.00 8.00
SSBU Brian Urlacher 4.00 10.00
SSCB Cedric Benson 3.00 8.00
SSCH Chris Henry RB 2.50 6.00
SSCJ Calvin Johnson 5.00 12.00
SSCJ2 Calvin Johnson 5.00 12.00
SSCL Michael Clayton 2.50 6.00
SSCP Carson Palmer 3.00 8.00
SSCT Chester Taylor 2.50 6.00
SSDB Deion Branch 3.00 8.00
SSDC Daunte Culpepper 3.00 8.00
SSDJ Dwayne Jarrett 1.50 4.00
SSDJ2 Dwayne Jarrett 1.50 4.00
SSDM Donovan McNabb 4.00 10.00
SSDS Drew Stanton 1.25 3.00
SSDS2 Drew Stanton 1.25 3.00
SSEM Eli Manning 4.00 10.00
SSGA Antonio Gates 4.00 10.00
SSGJ Greg Jennings 4.00 10.00
SSGL Terry Glenn 3.00 8.00
SSGR Trent Green 3.00 8.00
SSGW Garrett Wolfe 1.25 3.00
SSHE Todd Heap 2.50 6.00
SSHI Johnnie Lee Higgins 2.50 6.00
SSHO Joe Horn 3.00 8.00
SSHU Tony Hunt 2.50 6.00
SSHW Hines Ward 4.00 10.00
SSJA Brandon Jacobs 3.00 8.00
SSJB John Beck 2.00 5.00
SSJB2 John Beck 2.00 5.00
SSJH Jason Hill 2.50 6.00
SSJL Jamal Lewis 3.00 8.00
SSJN Jerious Norwood 3.00 8.00
SSJO Thomas Jones 3.00 8.00
SSJP Jerry Porter 3.00 8.00
SSJR JaMarcus Russell 1.25 3.00
SSJR2 JaMarcus Russell 1.25 3.00
SSJS Jeremy Shockey 3.00 8.00
SSJT Jason Taylor 3.00 8.00
SSJW Javon Walker 3.00 8.00
SSKI Kenny Irons 2.50 6.00
SSKK Kevin Kolb 3.00 8.00
SSKK2 Kevin Kolb 3.00 8.00
SSKW Kellen Winslow 3.00 8.00
SSLB Lorenzo Booker 2.50 6.00
SSLE Byron Leftwich 3.00 8.00
SSLJ Larry Johnson 2.50 6.00
SSLM Laurence Maroney 3.00 8.00
SSMA Marion Barber 5.00 12.00
SSMB Michael Bush 2.00 5.00
SSMC Mark Clayton 3.00 8.00
SSMJ Maurice Jones-Drew [illegible] 10.00
SSML Marshawn Lynch 2.00 5.00
SSML2 Marshawn Lynch 2.00 5.00
SSOL Greg Olsen 1.50 4.00
SSPE Julius Peppers 3.00 8.00
SSPI Antonio Pittman 2.50 6.00
SSPM Peyton Manning 6.00 15.00
SSPW Patrick Willis 4.00 10.00
SSRB Reggie Bush 4.00 10.00
SSRG Rex Grossman 3.00 8.00
SSRM Robert Meachem 2.50 6.00
SSRM2 Robert Meachem 2.50 6.00
SSRO Roy Williams WR 3.00 8.00
SSRW Reggie Wayne 3.00 8.00
SSSR Sidney Rice 2.50 6.00
SSSS Steve Smith USC 2.50 6.00
SSSS2 Steve Smith USC 2.50 6.00
SSTB Tedy Bruschi 4.00 10.00
SSTE Trent Edwards 2.00 5.00
SSTE2 Trent Edwards 2.00 5.00
SSTG Ted Ginn Jr. 1.50 4.00
SSTG2 Ted Ginn Jr. 1.50 4.00
SSTH Joe Thomas 2.50 6.00
SSTJ T.J. Houshmandzadeh 3.00 8.00
SSTO Tom Brady 6.00 15.00
SSTS Troy Smith 2.00 5.00
SSTS2 Troy Smith 2.00 5.00
SSWD Warrick Dunn 3.00 8.00
SSWI Paul Williams 2.50 6.00
SSWM Willis McGahee 3.00 8.00
SSYF Yamon Figurs 2.50 6.00

2010 Sweet Spot

COMP.SET w/o AU's (100) 12.00 30.00
ROOKIE AUTO PRINT RUN 100-400
1 Peyton Manning .50 1.25
2 Tom Brady .50 1.25
3 Ben Roethlisberger .30 .75
4 Matt Ryan .30 .75
5 Matthew Stafford .30 .75
6 Mark Sanchez .30 .75
7 Chris Johnson .30 .75
8 Chad Henne .25 .60
9 LaDainian Tomlinson .30 .75
10 Eli Manning .30 .75
11 Rashard Mendenhall .25 .60
12 Knowshon Moreno .25 .60
13 Brandon Marshall .25 .60
14 Philip Rivers .30 .75
15 Vincent Jackson .20 .50
16 Percy Harvin .30 .75
17 Sidney Rice .25 .60
18 Mike Wallace .25 .60
19 Kevin Kolb .25 .60
20 Carson Palmer .25 .60
21 Cedric Benson .25 .60
22 Chad Johnson .25 .60
23 A.J. Hawk .25 .60
24 Tony Romo .40 1.00
25 Josh Freeman .30 .75
26 Donovan McNabb .30 .75
27 Adrian Peterson .50 1.25
28 Brett Favre 1.25 3.00
29 Santonio Holmes .25 .60
30 Steven Jackson .25 .60
31 Larry Fitzgerald .30 .75
32 Marion Barber .25 .60
33 DeAngelo Williams .25 .60
34 Alex Smith QB .25 .60
35 Aaron Rodgers .60 1.50
36 Elvis Dumervil .20 .50
37 Matt Schaub .25 .60
38 Frank Gore .25 .60
39 Steve Smith USC .25 .60
40 Troy Polamalu .30 .75
41 Joseph Addai .25 .60
42 Ronnie Brown .25 .60
43 Ricky Williams .25 .60
44 Ray Rice .25 .60
45 Matt Cassel .25 .60
46 Ryan Grant .25 .60
47 DeSean Jackson .25 .60
48 Josh Cribbs .30 .75
49 Jeremy Maclin .25 .60
50 Anquan Boldin .25 .60
51 Joe Flacco .30 .75
52 Matt Moore .25 .60
53 Andre Johnson .25 .60
54 Jonathan Stewart .25 .60
55 Felix Jones .25 .60
56 Jason Campbell .25 .60
57 Jamaal Charles .25 .60
58 Jay Cutler .30 .75
59 Darren McFadden .25 .60
60 Mario Manningham .25 .60
61 Devin Hester .30 .75
62 Drew Brees .30 .75
63 Wes Welker .30 .75
64 Hines Ward .25 .60
65 Maurice Jones-Drew .25 .60
66 Calvin Johnson .30 .75
67 Randy Moss .30 .75
68 Thomas Jones .25 .60
69 Michael Turner .20 .50
70 Vince Young .20 .50
71 Sean Weatherspoon RC 1.00 2.50
72 Taylor Price RC 1.00 2.50
73 Levi Brown RC .75 2.00
74 Zac Robinson RC .75 2.00
75 Jonathan Crompton RC .75 2.00
76 Joe Webb RC 1.00 2.50
77 Riley Cooper RC 1.00 2.50
78 Carlos Dunlap RC 1.00 2.50
79 Earl Thomas RC 1.00 2.50
80 Jevan Snead RC 1.00 2.50
81 Antonio Brown RC 1.50 4.00
82 Rob Gronkowski RC 2.50 6.00
83 Taylor Mays RC 1.00 2.50
84 David Reed RC .75 2.00
85 James Starks RC 1.50 4.00
86 Marcus Easley RC .75 2.00
87 Carlton Mitchell RC .75 2.00
88 Rusty Smith RC 1.00 2.50
89 Sean Lee RC 1.00 2.50
90 Mike Kafka RC 1.00 2.50
91 Jimmy Graham RC 2.00 5.00
92 John Skelton RC 1.00 2.50
93 Kareem Jackson RC 1.00 2.50
94 Emmanuel Sanders RC 1.00 2.50
95 Kerry Meier RC .75 2.00
96 Bryan Bulaga RC 1.00 2.50
97 Rolando McClain RC 1.00 [illegible]
98 Armanti Edwards RC 1.00 2.50
99 Jason Pierre-Paul RC 1.50 4.00
100 Jerry Hughes RC 1.00 2.50
101 Joe Haden AU/400 RC 8.00 20.00
102 Blair White AU/400 RC 8.00 20.00
103 Demaryius Thomas AU/100 RC 15.00 40.00
105 Jimmy Clausen AU/100 RC 15.00 40.00
106 Keiland Williams AU/400 RC 8.00 20.00
107 Jahvid Best AU/100 RC 25.00 60.00
108 Jonathan Dwyer AU/300 RC 8.00 20.00
109 Eric Berry AU/400 RC 20.00 50.00
110 Golden Tate AU/100 RC 12.00 30.00
111 Arrelious Benn AU/150 RC 12.00 30.00
112 Damian Williams AU/300 RC 8.00 20.00
113 Gerald McCoy AU/400 RC 8.00 20.00
115 Ndamukong Suh AU/400 RC 25.00 50.00
116 Brandon Spikes AU/400 RC 8.00 20.00
117 Bill Stull AU/350 RC 6.00 15.00
118 Ryan Mathews AU/300 RC 15.00 40.00
119 Sergio Kindle AU/400 RC 8.00 20.00
120 Russell Okung AU/350 RC 8.00 20.00
121 Daryll Clark AU/400 RC 8.00 20.00
122 Dezmon Briscoe AU/350 RC 6.00 15.00
123 Max Hall AU/400 RC 8.00 20.00
124 Colt McCoy AU/100 RC 40.00 80.00
125 Dan LeFevour AU/150 RC 12.00 30.00
126 Jarrett Brown AU/150 RC 12.00 30.00
127 Sam Bradford AU/100 RC 75.00 150.00
128 Sean Canfield AU/100 RC 10.00 25.00
129 Tim Tebow AU/100 RC 90.00 150.00
130 Tony Pike AU/100 RC 12.00 30.00
131 Derrick Morgan AU/300 RC 6.00 15.00
132 Chris McGaha AU/400 RC 5.00 12.00
133 Brandon Minor AU/400 RC 8.00 20.00
134 Anthony Dixon AU/400 RC 8.00 20.00
135 Ben Tate AU/350 RC 10.00 25.00
136 Charles Scott AU/400 RC 6.00 15.00
137 Chris Brown AU/400 RC 8.00 20.00
138 C.J. Spiller AU/100 RC 25.00 60.00
139 Javarris James AU/300 RC 8.00 20.00
140 Andre Roberts AU/350 RC 8.00 20.00
141 Montario Hardesty AU/400 RC 8.00 20.00
142 Toby Gerhart AU/300 RC 8.00 20.00
143 Joe McKnight AU/300 RC 8.00 20.00
144 Dennis Pitta AU/400 RC 8.00 20.00
145 Garrett Graham AU/350 RC 6.00 15.00
146 Anthony McCoy AU/300 RC 6.00 15.00
147 Ed Dickson AU/350 RC 8.00 20.00
148 Jermaine Gresham AU/300 RC 12.00 30.00
149 Brandon LaFell AU/100 RC 12.00 30.00
150 Jeremy Williams AU/300 RC 5.00 12.00
151 Dez Bryant AU/100 RC 40.00 100.00
152 Eric Decker AU/400 RC 10.00 25.00
153 Jacoby Ford AU/300 RC 10.00 25.00
154 Jordan Shipley AU/300 RC 12.00 30.00
155 Mardy Gilyard AU/250 RC 8.00 20.00
156 Mike Williams AU/300 RC 12.00 30.00
157 LeGarrette Blount AU/300 RC 15.00 40.00
158 Aaron Hernandez AU/400 RC 12.00 30.00
159 Dexter McCluster AU/300 RC 8.00 20.00
160 Brandon Graham AU/400 RC 6.00 15.00

2010 Sweet Spot Rookie Signatures Variations

*VAR AU/350: .4X TO 1X BASE AU/400
*VAR AU/200-250: .5X TO 1.2X BASE/250-400
*VAR AU/100-150: .6X TO 1.5X BASE/250-400
*VAR AU/50-75: .5X TO 1.2X BASE/100-150
*VAR AU/50: .8X TO 2X BASIC AU/300
*VAR AU/25: .6X TO 1.5X BASIC AU/100-150
VARIATION PRINT RUN 25-350
127A Sam Bradford/50 100.00 200.00
127B Sam Bradford/25 125.00 250.00
129A Tim Tebow/50 125.00 200.00
129B Tim Tebow/25 150.00 250.00

2010 Sweet Spot Signatures

STATED PRINT RUN 10-400
SERIAL #'d UNDER 30 NOT PRICED
AM Archie Manning/75 40.00 80.00
CM Craig Morton/300 8.00 20.00
CO Christian Okoye/400 8.00 20.00
DJ Daryl Johnston/100 15.00 40.00
DS Donnie Shell/125 10.00 25.00
FG Frank Gore/75 20.00 50.00
GJ Greg Jennings/125 15.00 40.00
HC Harry Carson/125 10.00 25.00
JT Joe Theismann/100 15.00 40.00
JY Jack Youngblood/100 15.00 40.00
MA Mike Alstott/150 15.00 40.00
MO Herman Moore/200 10.00 25.00
MS Mike Singletary/125 20.00 50.00
PA Alan Page/100 15.00 40.00
PH Paul Hornung/75 25.00 60.00
RC Roger Craig/100 15.00 40.00
RG Roman Gabriel/125 12.00 30.00
RI Rocket Ismail/100 15.00 40.00
RO Antrel Rolle/100 10.00 25.00
RW Ricky Williams/75 25.00 60.00
RY Ron Yary/300 8.00 20.00
SI Billy Sims/300 12.00 30.00
SM Bubba Smith/100 12.00 30.00
SR Sidney Rice/150 12.00 30.00
SS Steve Smith USC/100 10.00 25.00
SY Steve Young/30 90.00 150.00
TR Tom Rathman/75 15.00 40.00

2010 Sweet Spot Signatures Variations

STATED PRINT RUN 3-125
SERIAL #'d UNDER 25 NOT PRICED
AM1 Archie Manning/50 40.00 80.00
AM2 Archie Manning/25 40.00 100.00
CM1 Craig Morton/100 10.00 25.00
CM2 Craig Morton/50 12.00 30.00
DJ1 Daryl Johnston/50 20.00 50.00
DJ2 Daryl Johnston/25 25.00 60.00
DS1 Donnie Shell/25 15.00 40.00
FG1 Frank Gore/50 20.00 50.00
FG2 Frank Gore/25 25.00 60.00
GJ1 Greg Jennings/25 25.00 60.00
HC1 Harry Carson/25 15.00 40.00
JT1 Joe Theismann/50 20.00 50.00
JT2 Joe Theismann/25 25.00 60.00
JY1 Jack Youngblood/50 20.00 50.00
JY2 Jack Youngblood/25 25.00 60.00
MA1 Mike Alstott/100 15.00 40.00
MO1 Herman Moore/125 10.00 25.00
MO2 Herman Moore/125 10.00 25.00
MS1 Mike Singletary/25 NCAA 20.00 50.00
PA1 Alan Page/50 20.00 50.00
PA2 Alan Page/25 25.00 60.00

PH1 Paul Hornung/50	25.00	60.00
PH2 Paul Hornung/25	30.00	80.00
RC1 Roger Craig/50	20.00	50.00
RC2 Roger Craig/25	25.00	60.00
RG1 Roman Gabriel/25 NCAA	15.00	40.00
RI1 Rocket Ismail/50	20.00	50.00
RI2 Rocket Ismail/25	25.00	60.00
RO1 Antrel Rolle/50	12.00	30.00
RO2 Antrel Rolle/25		
RW1 Ricky Williams/50	25.00	60.00
RW2 Ricky Williams/25	30.00	80.00
RY1 Ron Yary/100	10.00	25.00
RY2 Ron Yary/50	12.00	30.00
SI1 Billy Sims/100	20.00	50.00
SI2 Billy Sims/50	25.00	60.00
SM1 Bubba Smith/50	15.00	40.00
SR1 Sidney Rice/25 NCAA	15.00	40.00
SS1 Steve Smith USC/50	12.00	30.00
SS2 Steve Smith USC/25	15.00	40.00
TR1 Tom Rathman/50	15.00	40.00
TR2 Tom Rathman/25	25.00	60.00

2010 Sweet Spot Sweet Swatches

ONE AUTO OR JSY CARD PER PACK

SSW1 A.J. Hawk	3.00	8.00
SSW2 Gale Sayers	8.00	20.00
SSW3 Albert Haynesworth	2.50	6.00
SSW4 Ben Roethlisberger	5.00	12.00
SSW5 Bo Jackson	8.00	20.00
SSW6 Brandon Pettigrew	2.50	6.00
SSW7 Brett Favre	10.00	25.00
SSW8 Tom Brady	15.00	40.00
SSW9 Calvin Johnson	4.00	10.00
SSW10 Carson Palmer	3.00	8.00
SSW11 Chad Henne	3.00	8.00
SSW12 Chad Pennington	3.00	8.00
SSW13 Chris Johnson	4.00	10.00
SSW14 Chris Wells	3.00	8.00
SSW15 Chris Wells	3.00	8.00
SSW16 Dan Marino	10.00	25.00
SSW17 Darren McFadden	3.00	8.00
SSW18 Darrius Heyward-Bey	3.00	8.00
SSW19 DeSean Jackson	3.00	8.00
SSW20 Donald Brown	3.00	8.00
SSW21 Donald Brown	3.00	8.00
SSW22 Donnie Avery	3.00	8.00
SSW23 Donovan McNabb	4.00	10.00
SSW24 Drew Brees	4.00	10.00
SSW25 Dwayne Bowe	3.00	8.00
SSW26 Felix Jones	3.00	8.00
SSW27 Frank Gore	3.00	8.00
SSW28 Fran Tarkenton	6.00	15.00
SSW29 Hakeem Nicks	3.00	8.00
SSW30 Hakeem Nicks	3.00	8.00
SSW31 Mike Singletary	5.00	12.00
SSW32 Randall Cunningham	5.00	12.00
SSW33 Jamaal Charles	3.00	8.00
SSW34 Peyton Manning	15.00	40.00
SSW35 Jay Cutler	4.00	10.00
SSW36 Jeremy Maclin	3.00	8.00
SSW37 Jeremy Maclin	3.00	8.00
SSW38 Jim Kelly	6.00	15.00
SSW39 John Elway	8.00	20.00
SSW40 Jonathan Stewart	3.00	8.00
SSW41 Josh Freeman	4.00	10.00
SSW42 Josh Freeman	4.00	10.00
SSW43 Kenny Britt	3.00	8.00
SSW44 Kevin Smith	3.00	8.00
SSW45 Knowshon Moreno	3.00	8.00
SSW46 Knowshon Moreno	3.00	8.00
SSW47 Michael Crabtree	4.00	10.00
SSW48 Adrian Peterson	6.00	15.00
SSW49 LeSean McCoy	3.00	8.00
SSW50 LeSean McCoy	3.00	8.00
SSW51 Mario Manningham	3.00	8.00
SSW52 Marion Barber	3.00	8.00
SSW53 Mark Sanchez	4.00	10.00
SSW54 Mark Sanchez	4.00	10.00
SSW55 Aaron Rodgers	8.00	20.00
SSW56 Matt Forte	3.00	8.00
SSW57 Matt Leinart	2.50	6.00
SSW58 Matt Ryan	4.00	10.00
SSW59 Matthew Stafford	4.00	10.00
SSW60 Matthew Stafford	4.00	10.00
SSW61 Michael Crabtree	4.00	10.00
SSW62 Mike Wallace	3.00	8.00
SSW63 Mike Wallace	3.00	8.00
SSW64 Mohamed Massaquoi	3.00	8.00
SSW65 Percy Harvin	4.00	10.00
SSW66 Rashard Mendenhall	3.00	8.00
SSW67 Rashard Mendenhall	3.00	8.00
SSW68 Mario Williams	3.00	8.00
SSW69 Ricky Williams	3.00	8.00
SSW70 Ronnie Brown	3.00	8.00
SSW71 Steve Young	8.00	20.00
SSW72 Troy Aikman	8.00	20.00
SSW73 Warren Moon	6.00	15.00
SSW74 Paul Hornung	6.00	15.00
SSW75 Patrick Willis	3.00	8.00
SSW76 Drew Bledsoe	5.00	12.00
SSW77 Joe Flacco	4.00	10.00

2011 Sweet Spot

1 Tyron Smith	1.00	2.50
2 Daniel Thomas	.75	2.00
3 Greg Salas	.75	2.00
4 Vai Taua	.60	1.50
5 DeMarco Murray	1.50	4.00
6 Stevan Ridley	.75	2.00
7 Bilal Powell	.50	1.25
8 Colin McCarthy	.60	1.50
9 Da'Quan Bowers	.75	2.00
10 Mark Herzlich	.60	1.50
11 Edmond Gates	.60	1.50
12 Courtney Smith	.60	1.50
13 Niles Paul	.75	2.00
14 Stefen Wisniewski	.75	2.00
15 Stephen Paea	.75	2.00
16 Ras-I Dowling	.75	2.00
17 Cameron Jordan	.60	1.50
18 Allen Bailey	.60	1.50
19 Nate Solder	.75	2.00
20 Christian Ponder	1.50	4.00
21 Kendall Hunter	.75	2.00
22 Dwayne Harris	.75	2.00
23 Akeem Ayers	.60	1.50
24 Bruce Carter	.75	2.00
25 Tyrod Taylor	.75	2.00
26 Prince Amukamara	.75	2.00
27 Mario Fannin	.75	2.00
28 Jordan Todman	.50	1.25
29 Ronald Johnson	.60	1.50
30 Greg Little	.75	2.00
31 Cecil Shorts	.60	1.50
32 Von Miller	1.00	2.50
33 Matt Szczur	1.50	4.00
34 Greg Jones	.60	1.50
35 J.J. Watt	1.00	2.50
36 Noel Devine	.75	2.00
37 Armon Binns	.60	1.50
38 James Cleveland	.50	1.25
39 Nick Fairley	1.00	2.50
40 Austin Pettis	.60	1.50
41 Dane Sanzenbacher	.75	2.00
42 Armando Allen	.75	2.00
43 Brandon Saine	.75	2.00
44 Ryan Kerrigan	.75	2.00
45 John Clay	.75	2.00
46 Kelvin Sheppard	.75	2.00
47 Ryan Whalen	.60	1.50
48 Lance Kendricks	.60	1.50
49 Colin Kaepernick	1.00	2.50
50 Anthony Allen	.50	1.25
51 Mike Pouncey	.75	2.00
52 Pat Devlin	.75	2.00
53 Nathan Enderle	.75	2.00
54 Leonard Hankerson	.75	2.00
55 Delone Carter	.60	1.50
56 Marvin Austin	.60	1.50
57 Jeff Maehl	.75	2.00
58 Jerrel Jernigan	.60	1.50
59 Vincent Brown	.75	2.00
60 Andy Dalton	2.00	5.00
61 Roy Helu	1.50	4.00
62 Adrian Clayborn	.75	2.00
63 Luke Stocker	.60	1.50
64 Terrence Toliver	.60	1.50
65 Anthony Castonzo	.50	1.25
66 Jeremy Beal	.60	1.50
67 Ross Homan	.75	2.00
68 DeAndre McDaniel	.60	1.50
69 Evan Royster	.75	2.00
70 Tandon Doss	.60	1.50
71 Aldon Smith	1.25	3.00
72 Cameron Heyward	.75	2.00
73 Drake Nevis	.75	2.00
74 Quan Sturdivant	.75	2.00
75 Jamie Harper	.75	2.00
76 Jeremy Kerley	.75	2.00
77 Jake Locker	2.00	5.00
78 Ricky Stanzi	1.00	2.50
79 Titus Young	1.00	2.50
80 D.J. Williams	.75	2.00
81 Benjamin Ijalana	.60	1.50
82 Graig Cooper	.60	1.50
83 Derrick Locke	.60	1.50
84 Randall Cobb	1.00	2.50
85 Cam Newton	4.00	10.00
86 Mikel Leshoure	.75	2.00
87 Justin Houston	.75	2.00
88 Jacquizz Rodgers	.75	2.00
89 Mark Ingram	1.50	4.00
90 Blaine Gabbert	1.25	3.00
91 Ryan Mallett	1.50	4.00
92 Kyle Rudolph	.75	2.00
93 Julio Jones	1.50	4.00
94 Shane Vereen	.75	2.00
95 Dion Lewis	.75	2.00
96 Torrey Smith	1.00	2.50
97 A.J. Green	1.50	4.00
98 Jonathan Baldwin	.75	2.00
99 Marcell Dareus	.75	2.00
100 Ryan Williams	1.00	2.50
101 Terrelle Pryor	5.00	12.00

2011 Sweet Spot Autographs

1 Tyron Smith	10.00	25.00
2 Daniel Thomas	12.50	30.00
3 Greg Salas	6.00	15.00
4 Vai Taua	5.00	12.00
5 DeMarco Murray	25.00	60.00
6 Stevan Ridley	6.00	15.00
7 Bilal Powell	4.00	10.00
8 Colin McCarthy	5.00	12.00
9 Da'Quan Bowers	6.00	15.00
10 Mark Herzlich	5.00	12.00
11 Edmond Gates	5.00	12.00
12 Courtney Smith	5.00	12.00
13 Niles Paul	6.00	15.00
14 Stefen Wisniewski	6.00	15.00
15 Stephen Paea	6.00	15.00
16 Ras-I Dowling	6.00	15.00
17 Cameron Jordan	5.00	12.00
18 Allen Bailey	5.00	12.00
19 Nate Solder	6.00	15.00
20 Christian Ponder	20.00	50.00
21 Kendall Hunter	6.00	15.00
22 Dwayne Harris	6.00	15.00
23 Akeem Ayers	5.00	12.00
24 Bruce Carter	8.00	20.00
25 Tyrod Taylor	6.00	15.00
26 Prince Amukamara	8.00	20.00
27 Mario Fannin	6.00	15.00
28 Jordan Todman	4.00	10.00
29 Ronald Johnson	5.00	12.00
30 Greg Little	6.00	15.00
31 Cecil Shorts	5.00	12.00
32 Von Miller	12.50	25.00
33 Matt Szczur	12.00	30.00
34 Greg Jones	5.00	12.00
35 J.J. Watt	8.00	20.00
36 Noel Devine	6.00	15.00
37 Armon Binns	5.00	12.00
38 James Cleveland	5.00	12.00
40 Austin Pettis	5.00	12.00
41 Dane Sanzenbacher	8.00	20.00
42 Armando Allen	6.00	15.00
43 Brandon Saine	8.00	20.00
44 Ryan Kerrigan	6.00	15.00
45 John Clay	6.00	15.00
46 Kelvin Sheppard	6.00	15.00
47 Ryan Whalen	5.00	12.00
48 Lance Kendricks	5.00	12.00
49 Colin Kaepernick	15.00	30.00
50 Anthony Allen	4.00	10.00
51 Mike Pouncey	8.00	20.00
52 Pat Devlin	6.00	15.00
53 Nathan Enderle	6.00	15.00
54 Leonard Hankerson	6.00	15.00
55 Delone Carter	5.00	12.00
57 Jeff Maehl	6.00	15.00
58 Jerrel Jernigan	5.00	12.00
59 Vincent Brown	8.00	20.00
60 Andy Dalton	30.00	60.00
61 Roy Helu	12.00	30.00
62 Adrian Clayborn	15.00	30.00
63 Luke Stocker	5.00	12.00
64 Terrence Toliver	5.00	12.00
65 Anthony Castonzo	4.00	10.00
66 Jeremy Beal	5.00	12.00
67 Ross Homan	6.00	15.00
68 DeAndre McDaniel	5.00	12.00
69 Evan Royster	6.00	15.00
70 Tandon Doss	5.00	12.00
71 Aldon Smith	10.00	25.00
72 Cameron Heyward	6.00	15.00
73 Drake Nevis	6.00	15.00
74 Quan Sturdivant	6.00	15.00
75 Jamie Harper	6.00	15.00
76 Jeremy Kerley	6.00	15.00
77 Jake Locker	50.00	100.00
78 Ricky Stanzi	20.00	50.00
79 Titus Young	8.00	20.00
80 D.J. Williams	6.00	15.00
81 Benjamin Ijalana	5.00	12.00
82 Graig Cooper	5.00	12.00
83 Derrick Locke	5.00	12.00
84 Randall Cobb	8.00	20.00
85 Cam Newton	90.00	150.00
86 Mikel Leshoure	6.00	15.00
87 Justin Houston	6.00	15.00
88 Jacquizz Rodgers	15.00	30.00
89 Mark Ingram	25.00	60.00
90 Blaine Gabbert	20.00	50.00
91 Ryan Mallett	30.00	60.00
92 Kyle Rudolph	6.00	15.00
93 Julio Jones	30.00	60.00
94 Shane Vereen	6.00	15.00
95 Dion Lewis	6.00	15.00
96 Torrey Smith	8.00	20.00
97 A.J. Green	40.00	80.00
98 Jonathan Baldwin	10.00	25.00
99 Marcell Dareus	15.00	30.00
100 Ryan Williams	20.00	40.00
101 Terrelle Pryor	40.00	80.00

2011 Sweet Spot Chris Mortensen Retro Report

AVERAGE ODDS 1:2
AUTOS TOO SCARCE TO PRICE

MR1 Charles White	1.00	2.50
MR2 Troy Aikman	2.00	5.00
MR3 Steve Largent	1.50	4.00
MR4 Earl Campbell	1.50	4.00
MR5 Floyd Little	1.00	2.50
MR6 John Elway	2.50	6.00
MR7 Bob Griese	1.50	4.00
MR8 Jack Ham	1.25	3.00
MR9 Barry Sanders	2.50	6.00
MR10 Thurman Thomas	1.50	4.00
MR11 Brian Bosworth	1.25	3.00
MR12 Greg Pruitt	1.00	2.50
MR13 Alan Page	1.25	3.00
MR14 Paul Hornung	1.50	4.00
MR15 Rocket Ismail	1.25	3.00
MR16 Tim Brown	1.50	4.00
MR17 Roman Gabriel	1.25	3.00
MR18 Kellen Winslow Sr.	1.25	3.00
MR19 Jerry Rice	2.50	6.00
MR20 Bernie Kosar	1.25	3.00
MR21 Jim Kelly	1.50	4.00
MR22 Steve Young	2.00	5.00
MR23 Doug Flutie	1.25	3.00
MR24 Bo Jackson	2.00	5.00
MR25 Chris Mortensen	1.00	2.50

2011 Sweet Spot Rivalries Dual Autographs

STATED PRINT RUN 5-99
EXCH EXPIRATION: 7/14/2013

RBC Tim Brown/25 EXCH Anthony Carter	30.00	60.00
RBM Drew Bledsoe/25 EXCH Warren Moon	40.00	80.00
RCD Ras-I Dowling/99 Bruce Carter	12.00	30.00
RCS Billy Sims/99 Roger Craig	25.00	50.00
RGC Archie Griffin/25 EXCH Anthony Carter	25.00	50.00
HGK Kellen Winslow Sr./25 Gale Sayers		
RHM DeMarco Murray/99 EXCH Kendall Hunter	50.00	100.00
HMP Eric Metcalf/75 Greg Pruitt	25.00	50.00
RPH Christian Ponder/75 Leonard Hankerson	30.00	60.00
RPS Alan Page/99 EXCH Bubba Smith		
RPY Ron Yary/99 Alan Page	20.00	40.00
RRJ Greg Jones/99 Evan Royster	20.00	40.00
RRS Brandon Saine/99 Evan Royster	20.00	40.00
RSC Anthony Carter/25 Chris Spielman		
RSW Kellen Winslow Sr./75 Billy Sims	20.00	40.00
RTS Billy Sims/25 EXCH Thurman Thomas	30.00	60.00
RTW Charles White/99 Joe Theismann	25.00	50.00
RWJ Herschel Walker/25 EXCH Bo Jackson	60.00	120.00
RYD Ron Yary/25 Gary Beban	30.00	60.00

2011 Sweet Spot Rookie Signatures

STATED PRINT RUN 199-599
EXCH EXPIRATION: 7/14/2013

RSAB Allen Bailey/599	5.00	12.00
RSAC Adrian Clayborn/599	12.50	25.00
RSAD Andy Dalton/199	30.00	60.00
RSAG A.J. Green/199	40.00	80.00
RSAP Austin Pettis/599	8.00	20.00
RSBA Jonathan Baldwin/199	12.00	30.00
RSBC Bruce Carter/599	8.00	20.00
RSBG Blaine Gabbert/275	25.00	50.00
RSBI Armon Binns/599	5.00	12.00
RSBS Brandon Saine/599	10.00	25.00
RSCH Cameron Heyward/599	6.00	15.00
RSCK Colin Kaepernick/599	15.00	30.00
RSCN Cam Newton/199	90.00	150.00
RSCP Christian Ponder/199	30.00	60.00
RSDH Dwayne Harris/599	8.00	20.00
RSDM DeMarco Murray/199	30.00	60.00
RSDS Dane Sanzenbacher/599	8.00	20.00
RSDT Daniel Thomas/199	15.00	30.00
RSER Evan Royster/199	10.00	25.00
RSGC Graig Cooper/599	5.00	12.00
RSGJ Greg Jones/599	5.00	12.00
RSGL Greg Little/199	10.00	25.00
RSGS Greg Salas/599	12.50	25.00
RSHE Roy Helu/599	12.00	30.00
RSJB Jeremy Beal/599	5.00	12.00
RSJC James Cleveland/599	5.00	12.00
RSJK Jeremy Kerley/599	6.00	15.00
RSJL Jake Locker/275	40.00	80.00
RSJO Julio Jones/199	30.00	60.00
RSKH Kendall Hunter/599	6.00	15.00
RSKS Kelvin Sheppard/599	6.00	15.00
RSLH Leonard Hankerson/599	6.00	15.00
RSMH Mark Herzlich/599	5.00	12.00
RSMI Mark Ingram/199	30.00	80.00
RSND Noel Devine/599	8.00	20.00
RSNE Nathan Enderle/599 EXCH	8.00	20.00
RSNP Niles Paul/599	6.00	15.00
RSPA Prince Amukamara/199	15.00	30.00
RSPD Pat Devlin/199	10.00	25.00
RSQS Quan Sturdivant/599	6.00	15.00
RSRD Ras-I Dowling/599	6.00	15.00
RSRH Ross Homan/599	6.00	15.00
RSRJ Ronald Johnson/599	5.00	12.00
RSRK Ryan Kerrigan/599	6.00	15.00
RSRM Ryan Mallett/199	30.00	60.00
RSRS Ricky Stanzi/599	15.00	40.00
RSRW Ryan Williams/199	15.00	40.00
RSSP Stephen Paea/599	6.00	15.00
RSTA Tyrod Taylor/599	6.00	15.00
RSTT Terrence Toliver/599	5.00	12.00
RSTY Titus Young/599	8.00	20.00
RSVB Vincent Brown/599	8.00	20.00
RSVM Von Miller/599	12.50	25.00

2011 Sweet Spot Rookie Signatures Variations

*VARIATION/299: .5X TO 1.2X BASIC AU/599
*VARIATION/75: .5X TO 1.2X BASIC AU/199-275
STATED PRINT RUN 75-299

RSCN Cam Newton/75	100.00	200.00

2011 Sweet Spot Todd McShay Scouting Report

AVERAGE ODDS 1:2
AUTOS TOO SCARCE TO PRICE

TM1 Jordan Todman	.40	1.00
TM2 Jonathan Baldwin	.60	1.50
TM3 Ryan Williams	.75	2.00
TM4 Mikel Leshoure	.60	1.50
TM5 Torrey Smith	.75	2.00
TM6 Christian Ponder	1.25	3.00
TM7 Jake Locker	1.50	4.00
TM8 Kendall Hunter	.60	1.50
TM9 Tandon Doss	.50	1.25
TM10 Jacquizz Rodgers	.60	1.50
TM11 DeMarco Murray	1.25	3.00
TM12 Daniel Thomas	.60	1.50
TM13 Leonard Hankerson	.60	1.50
TM14 Randall Cobb	.75	2.00
TM15 Kyle Rudolph	.60	1.50
TM16 Titus Young	.75	2.00
TM17 Cam Newton	3.00	8.00
TM18 Shane Vereen	.60	1.50
TM19 Greg Little	.60	1.50
TM20 Ryan Mallett	1.25	3.00
TM21 A.J. Green	1.25	3.00
TM22 Blaine Gabbert	1.00	2.50
TM23 Julio Jones	1.25	3.00
TM24 Mark Ingram	1.25	3.00
TM25 Todd McShay	.40	1.00

2011 Sweet Spot Ultimate Rookie Signatures

STATED ODDS 1:360

21 Ras-I Dowling	12.00	30.00
22 Prince Amukamara	12.00	30.00
23 Adrian Clayborn	12.00	30.00
24 Greg Jones	10.00	25.00
25 Jeremy Beal	10.00	25.00
26 Bruce Carter	12.00	30.00
27 Colin Kaepernick	40.00	80.00
28 Ricky Stanzi		
29 Andy Dalton		
30 Roy Helu	25.00	60.00
31 Cameron Jordan	10.00	25.00
32 Tyrod Taylor	12.00	30.00
33 James Cleveland	8.00	20.00
34 Ryan Kerrigan	12.00	30.00
35 Greg Salas	12.00	30.00
36 Jeremy Kerley	12.00	30.00
37 Leonard Hankerson	12.00	30.00
38 Dwayne Harris	12.00	30.00
39 Vincent Brown	12.00	30.00
40 Jerrel Jernigan	10.00	25.00

2011 Sweet Spot Veteran Signatures

STATED PRINT RUN 15-80
*VARIATION/30: .5X TO 1.2X BASIC AU/50
EXCH EXPIRATION: 7/14/2013

SSAC Anthony Carter/80	15.00	40.00
SSAG Archie Griffin/15 EXCH	30.00	60.00
SSAP Adrian Peterson/15		
SSBB Brian Bosworth/50	20.00	50.00
SSBC Billy Cannon/50	20.00	50.00
SSBG Bob Griese/15		
SSBJ Bo Jackson/15		
SSBK Bernie Kosar/50	15.00	40.00
SSBS Barry Sanders/15 EXCH	125.00	250.00
SSCS Chris Spielman/50 EXCH	12.00	30.00
SSCW Charles White/50	12.00	30.00
SSDB Drew Brees/15		
SSDC Dave Casper/50	15.00	40.00
SSDL Daryle Lamonica/50	15.00	40.00
SSDM Dan Marino/15	125.00	250.00
SSDW Danny Wuerffel/50	30.00	60.00
SSEC Earl Campbell/50	30.00	60.00
SSEG Eddie George/15		
SSEM Eric Metcalf/50	20.00	50.00
SSGB Gary Beban/80	12.00	30.00
SSGP Greg Pruitt/50	12.00	30.00
SSGS Gale Sayers/15		
SSHW Herschel Walker/50 EXCH	30.00	60.00
SSJC John Cappelletti/50	12.00	30.00
SSJE John Elway/15 EXCH		
SSJH Jack Ham/15		
SSJK Jim Kelly/15	40.00	80.00
SSJM Jim McMahon/80	30.00	60.00
SSJP Jim Plunkett/50 EXCH	30.00	60.00
SSJT Joe Theismann/50	12.00	30.00
SSJW Jason White/50	12.00	30.00
SSKW Kellen Winslow Sr./80	15.00	40.00
SSLS Lee Roy Selmon/50	20.00	50.00
SSMO Chris Mortensen/80	15.00	40.00
SSPA Alan Page/50	15.00	40.00
SSPH Paul Hornung/50	20.00	50.00
SSRB Rocky Bleier/50	15.00	40.00
SSRD Ron Dayne/80	12.00	30.00
SSSI Billy Sims/50	20.00	50.00
SSSJ Steven Jackson/15		
SSSM Bubba Smith/80 EXCH	15.00	40.00
SSSY Steve Young/25		
SSTA Troy Aikman/15 EXCH	50.00	100.00
SSTB Tim Brown/15		
SSTD Tony Dorsett/15		
SSTM Todd McShay/80	15.00	40.00
SSTR Tom Rathman/50	12.00	30.00
SSTT Thurman Thomas/15		
SSWM Warren Moon/50	25.00	50.00

1988 Swell Greats

The 1988 Swell Football Greats set contains 144 standard size cards. This set was issued in 10-card packs. Each card depicts a member of the Pro Football Hall of Fame. The fronts have blue borders and color photos. The backs are baby blue and contain each player's career highlights. This issue was distributed in wax packs of ten cards and also as a complete set. The factory-collated complete set cards are sometimes found with slight notches along the upper border; this does not seem to be the case with the cards taken from wax packs. After each player's name below is listed his year of induction into the Hall of Fame. The set includes the 1988 Pro Football Hall of Fame inductees.

COMPLETE SET (144)	12.50	25.00
1 Pete Rozelle 85	.05	.15
2 Joe Namath 85	.50	1.25
3 Frank Gatski 85	.02	.10
4 O.J. Simpson 85	.15	.40
5 Roger Staubach 85	.30	.75
6 Herb Adderley 80	.05	.15
7 Lance Alworth 78	.10	.30
8 Doug Atkins 82	.05	.15
9 Red Badgro 81	.02	.10
10 Cliff Battles 68	.02	.10
11 Sammy Baugh 63	.25	.60
12 Raymond Berry 73	.10	.30
13 Charles W. Bidwill 67	.02	.10
14 Chuck Bednarik 67	.10	.30
15 Bert Bell 63	.02	.10
16 Bobby Bell 83	.05	.15
17 George Blanda 81	.10	.30
18 Jim Brown 71	.40	1.00
19 Paul Brown 67	.08	.25
20 Roosevelt Brown 75	.05	.15
21 Ray Flaherty 76	.02	.10
22 Len Ford 76	.05	.15
23 Dan Fortmann 65	.02	.10
24 Bill George 74	.05	.15
25 Art Donovan 68	.08	.25
26 Paddy Driscoll 65	.02	.10
27 Jimmy Conzelman 64	.02	.10
28 Willie Davis 81	.05	.15
29 Dutch Clark 63	.05	.15
30 George Connor 75	.05	.15
31 Guy Chamberlin 65	.02	.10
32 Jack Christiansen 70	.05	.15
33 Tony Canadeo 74	.05	.15
34 Joe Carr 63	.02	.10
35 Willie Brown 84	.05	.15
36 Dick Butkus 79	.25	.60
37 Bill Dudley 66	.05	.15
38 Turk Edwards 69	.02	.10
39 Weeb Ewbank 78	.02	.10
40 Tom Fears 70	.05	.15
41 Otto Graham 65	.25	.60
42 Red Grange 63	.20	.50
43 Frank Gifford 77	.20	.50
44 Sid Gillman 83	.02	.10
45 Forrest Gregg 77	.05	.15
46 Lou Groza 74	.08	.25
47 Joe Guyon 66	.02	.10
48 George Halas 63	.10	.30
49 Ed Healey 64	.02	.10
50 Mel Hein 63	.02	.10
51 Fats Henry 63	.02	.10
52 Arnie Herber 66	.02	.10
53 Bill Hewitt 71	.02	.10
54 Clarke Hinkle 64	.02	.10
55 Elroy Hirsch 68 (Crazy Legs)	.08	.25
56 Robert(Cal) Hubbard 63	.02	.10
57 Sam Huff 82	.08	.25
58 Lamar Hunt 72	.02	.10
59 Don Hutson 63	.08	.25
60 Deacon Jones 80	.08	.25
61 Sonny Jurgensen 83	.08	.25
62 Walt Kiesling 66	.02	.10
63 Frank(Bruiser) Kinard 71	.02	.10
64 Curly Lambeau 62	.02	.10
65 Dick Lane 74	.05	.15
66 Yale Lary 79	.05	.15
67 Dante Lavelli 75	.05	.15
68 Bobby Layne 67	.20	.50
69 Tuffy Leemans 78	.02	.10
70 Bob Lilly 80	.10	.30
71 Vince Lombardi 71	.20	.50
72 Sid Luckman 65	.10	.30
73 Link Lyman 64	.02	.10
74 Tim Mara 63	.02	.10
75 Gino Marchetti 72	.05	.15
76 Geo.Preston Marshall 63	.02	.10
77 Ollie Matson 72	.08	.25
78 George McAfee 66	.05	.15
79 Mike McCormack 84	.05	.15
80 Hugh McElhenny 70	.08	.25
81 Johnny Blood McNally 63	.02	.10
82 Mike Michalske 64	.02	.10
83 Wayne Millner 68	.02	.10
84 Bobby Mitchell 83	.08	.25
85 Ron Mix 79	.05	.15
86 Lenny Moore 75	.10	.30
87 Marion Motley 68	.08	.25
88 George Musso 82	.02	.10
89 Bronko Nagurski 63	.10	.30
90 Greasy Neale 69	.02	.10
91 Ernie Nevers 63	.05	.15
92 Ray Nitschke 78	.10	.30
93 Leo Nomellini 69	.05	.15
94 Merlin Olsen 82	.08	.25
95 Jim Otto 80	.08	.25
96 Steve Owen 66	.02	.10
97 Clarence(Ace) Parker 72	.02	.10
98 Jim Parker 73	.05	.15
99 Joe Perry 69	.08	.25
100 Pete Pihos 70	.05	.15
101 Hugh(Shorty) Ray 66	.02	.10
102 Dan Reeves 67	.02	.10
103 Jim Ringo 81	.05	.15
104 Andy Robustelli 71	.05	.15
105 Art Rooney 64 UER (Misspelled Janurary on card back)	.02	.10
106 Gale Sayers 77	.20	.50
107 Joe Schmidt 73	.05	.15
108 Bart Starr 77	.30	.75
109 Ernie Stautner 69	.08	.25
110 Ken Strong 67	.05	.15
111 Joe Stydahar 67	.02	.10
112 Charley Taylor 84	.05	.15
113 Jim Taylor 76	.08	.25
114 Jim Thorpe 63	.20	.50
115 Y.A. Tittle 71	.15	.40
116 George Trafton 64	.02	.10
117 Charley Trippi 68	.05	.15
118 Emlen Tunnell 67	.05	.15
119 Bulldog Turner 66	.08	.25
120 Johnny Unitas 79	.30	.75
121 Norm Van Brocklin 71	.08	.25
122 Steve Van Buren 65 UER (Misspelled Lousianna and Decemer on back)	.08	.25
123 Paul Warfield 83	.08	.25
124 Bob Waterfield 65	.08	.25
125 Arnie Weinmeister 84	.02	.10
126 Bill Willis 77	.05	.15
127 Larry Wilson 78	.05	.15
128 Alex Wojciechowicz 68	.02	.10
129 Doak Walker 86	.08	.25
130 Willie Lanier 86	.05	.15
131 Paul Hornung 86	.15	.40
132 Ken Houston 86	.05	.15
133 Fran Tarkenton 86	.15	.40
134 Don Maynard 87	.08	.25
135 Larry Csonka 87	.10	.30
136 Joe Greene 87	.10	.30
137 Len Dawson 87	.10	.30
138 Gene Upshaw 87	.05	.15
139 Jim Langer 87	.05	.15
140 John Henry Johnson 87	.05	.15
141 Fred Biletnikoff 88	.10	.30
142 Mike Ditka 88	.25	.60
143 Jack Ham 88	.10	.30
144 Alan Page 88	.05	.15

1989 Swell Greats

The 1989 Swell Football Greats set contains 150 standard-size cards, depicting all Pro Football Hall of Famers. The fronts have white borders and vintage photos; the vertically oriented backs feature player profiles. The cards were available in ten-card wax packs.

COMPLETE SET (150)	12.50	25.00
1 Terry Bradshaw	.30	.75
2 Bert Bell	.02	.10
3 Joe Carr	.02	.10
4 Dutch Clark	.05	.15
5 Red Grange	.20	.50
6 Fats Henry	.02	.10
7 Mel Hein	.02	.10
8 Robert(Cal) Hubbard	.02	.10
9 George Halas	.10	.30
10 Don Hutson	.08	.25
11 Curly Lambeau	.02	.10
12 Tim Mara	.02	.10
13 Geo.Preston Marshall	.02	.10
14 Johnny Blood McNally	.02	.10
15 Bronko Nagurski	.10	.30
16 Ernie Nevers	.05	.15
17 Jim Thorpe	.20	.50
18 Ed Healey	.02	.10
19 Clarke Hinkle	.02	.10
20 Link Lyman	.02	.10
21 Mike Michalske	.02	.10
22 George Trafton	.02	.10
23 Guy Chamberlin	.02	.10
24 Paddy Driscoll	.02	.10
25 Dan Fortmann	.02	.10
26 Otto Graham	.25	.60
27A Sid Luckman ERR (First name and first part of Chicago showing in upper left corner)	.10	.30
27B Sid Luckman COR	.40	1.00
28 Steve Van Buren	.08	.25
29 Bob Waterfield	.08	.25
30 Bill Dudley	.05	.15
31 Joe Guyon	.02	.10
32 Arnie Herber	.02	.10
33 Walt Kiesling	.02	.10
34 Jimmy Conzelman	.02	.10
35 Art Rooney	.05	.15
36 Willie Wood	.05	.15
37 Art Shell	.08	.25
38 Sammy Baugh	.25	.60
39 Mel Blount	.08	.25
40 Lamar Hunt	.02	.10
41 Norm Van Brocklin	.08	.25
42 Y.A. Tittle	.15	.40
43 Andy Robustelli	.05	.15
44 Vince Lombardi	.20	.50
45 Frank(Bruiser) Kinard	.02	.10
46 Bill Hewitt	.02	.10
47 Jim Brown	.40	1.00
48 Pete Pihos	.05	.15
49 Hugh McElhenny	.08	.25
50 Tom Fears	.05	.15
51 Jack Christiansen	.05	.15
52 Ernie Stautner	.08	.25
53 Joe Perry	.08	.25
54 Leo Nomellini	.05	.15
55 Greasy Neale	.02	.10
56 Turk Edwards	.02	.10
57 Alex Wojciechowicz	.02	.10
58 Charley Trippi	.05	.15
59 Marion Motley	.08	.25
60 Wayne Millner	.02	.10
61 Elroy Hirsch	.08	.25
62 Art Donovan	.08	.25
63 Cliff Battles	.02	.10
64 Emlen Tunnell	.05	.15
65 Joe Stydahar	.02	.10
66 Ken Strong	.05	.15
67 Dan Reeves OWN	.02	.10
68 Bobby Layne	.20	.50
69 Paul Brown	.08	.25
70 Charles W. Bidwill UER (Name misspelled Biowill on front)	.02	.10
71 Chuck Bednarik	.10	.30
72 Bulldog Turner	.08	.25
73 Hugh(Shorty) Ray	.02	.10
74 Steve Owen	.02	.10
75 George McAfee	.05	.15
76 Forrest Gregg	.05	.15
77 Frank Gifford	.20	.50
78 Jim Taylor	.08	.25
79 Len Ford	.05	.15
80 Ray Flaherty	.02	.10
81 Lenny Moore	.10	.30
82 Dante Lavelli	.05	.15
83 George Connor	.05	.15
84 Roosevelt Brown	.05	.15
85 Dick Lane	.05	.15
86 Lou Groza	.08	.25
87 Bill George	.05	.15
88 Tony Canadeo	.05	.15
89 Joe Schmidt	.05	.15
90 Jim Parker	.05	.15
91 Raymond Berry	.10	.30
92 Clarence(Ace) Parker	.02	.10
93 Ollie Matson	.08	.25
94 Gino Marchetti	.05	.15
95 Larry Wilson	.05	.15
96 Ray Nitschke	.10	.30
97 Tuffy Leemans	.02	.10
98 Weeb Ewbank UER (Misspelled Uwbank on card front)	.02	.10
99 Lance Alworth	.10	.30
100 Bill Willis	.05	.15
101 Bart Starr	.30	.75
102 Gale Sayers	.20	.50
103 Herb Adderley	.05	.15
104 Johnny Unitas	.30	.75
105 Ron Mix	.05	.15
106 Yale Lary	.05	.15
107 Red Badgro	.02	.10
108 Jim Otto	.08	.25
109 Bob Lilly	.10	.30
110 Deacon Jones	.08	.25
111 Doug Atkins	.05	.15
112 Jim Ringo	.05	.15
113 Willie Davis	.05	.15
114 George Blanda	.10	.30
115 Bobby Bell	.05	.15
116 Merlin Olsen	.08	.25
117 George Musso	.02	.10
118 Sam Huff	.08	.25
119 Paul Warfield	.08	.25
120 Bobby Mitchell	.08	.25
121 Sonny Jurgensen	.08	.25
122 Sid Gillman UER (Misspelled Gilman on card back)	.02	.10
123 Arnie Weinmeister	.02	.10
124 Charley Taylor	.05	.15
125 Mike McCormack	.05	.15
126 Willie Brown	.05	.15
127 O.J. Simpson	.20	.50
128 Pete Rozelle	.05	.15
129 Joe Namath	.50	1.25
130 Frank Gatski	.02	.10
131 Willie Lanier	.05	.15
132 Ken Houston	.05	.15
133 Paul Hornung	.15	.40
134 Roger Staubach	.30	.75
135 Len Dawson	.10	.30
136 Larry Csonka	.10	.30
137 Doak Walker	.08	.25
138 Fran Tarkenton	.15	.40
139 Don Maynard	.08	.25
140 Jim Langer	.05	.15
141 John Henry Johnson	.05	.15
142 Joe Greene	.10	.30
143 Jack Ham	.10	.30
144 Mike Ditka	.25	.60
145 Alan Page	.05	.15
146 Fred Biletnikoff	.10	.30
147 Gene Upshaw	.05	.15
148 Dick Butkus	.25	.60
149 Checklist Card	.02	.10
150 Checklist Card	.02	.10

1990 Swell Greats

The 1990 Swell Greats set contains 160 standard size cards, depicting all Pro Football Hall of Famers. The fronts have color photos, with a white border and blue and yellow lines. As in previous sets, some cards of the older players are sepia-toned. In fact, in several cases the same photos were reused from the previous two years of Swell sets. The vertically-oriented backs feature player profiles. The cards were primarily available in the form of ten-card wax packs.

COMPLETE SET (160)	12.50	25.00
1 Terry Bradshaw	.30	.75
2 Bert Bell	.02	.10
3 Joe Carr	.02	.10
4 Dutch Clark	.05	.15
5 Red Grange	.20	.50
6 Fats Henry	.02	.10
7 Mel Hein	.02	.10
8 Robert(Cal) Hubbard	.02	.10
9 George Halas	.10	.30
10 Don Hutson	.08	.25
11 Curly Lambeau	.02	.10
12 Tim Mara	.02	.10
13 Geo.Preston Marshall	.02	.10
14 Johnny Blood McNally	.02	.10
15 Bronko Nagurski	.10	.30
16 Ernie Nevers	.05	.15
17 Jim Thorpe	.20	.50
18 Ed Healey	.02	.10
19 Clarke Hinkle	.02	.10
20 Link Lyman	.02	.10
21 Mike Michalske	.02	.10
22 George Trafton	.02	.10
23 Guy Chamberlin	.02	.10
24 Paddy Discoll	.02	.10
25 Dan Fortmann	.02	.10
26 Otto Graham	.25	.60
27 Sid Luckman	.10	.30
28 Steve Van Buren	.08	.25
29 Bob Waterfield	.08	.25
30 Bill Dudley	.05	.15
31 Joe Guyon	.02	.10
32 Arnie Herber	.02	.10
33 Walt Kiesling	.02	.10
34 Jimmy Conzelman	.02	.10
35 Art Rooney	.05	.15
36 Willie Wood	.05	.15
37 Art Shell	.08	.25
38 Sammy Baugh	.25	.60
39 Mel Blount	.08	.25
40 Lamar Hunt	.02	.10
41 Norm Van Brocklin	.08	.25
42 Y.A. Tittle	.15	.40
43 Andy Robustelli	.05	.15
44 Vince Lombardi	.20	.50
45 Frank(Bruiser) Kinard	.02	.10
46 Bill Hewitt	.02	.10
47 Jim Brown	.40	1.00
48 Pete Pihos	.05	.15
49 Hugh McElhenny	.08	.25
50 Tom Fears	.05	.15
51 Jack Christiansen	.05	.15
52 Ernie Stautner	.08	.25
53 Joe Perry	.08	.25
54 Leo Nomellini	.05	.15
55 Greasy Neale	.02	.10
56 Turk Edwards	.02	.10
57 Alex Wojciechowicz	.02	.10
58 Charley Trippi	.05	.15
59 Marion Motley	.08	.25
60 Wayne Millner	.02	.10
61 Elroy Hirsch	.08	.25
62 Art Donovan	.08	.25
63 Cliff Battles	.02	.10
64 Emlen Tunnell	.05	.15

65 Joe Stydahar .02 .10
66 Ken Strong .05 .15
67 Dan Reeves OWN .02 .10
68 Bobby Layne .20 .50
69 Paul Brown .08 .25
70 Charles W. Bidwill .02 .10
71 Chuck Bednarik .10 .30
72 Bulldog Turner .08 .25
73 Hugh(Shorty) Ray .02 .10
74 Steve Owen .02 .10
75 George McAfee .05 .15
76 Forrest Gregg .05 .15
77 Frank Gifford .20 .50
78 Jim Taylor .08 .25
79 Len Ford .05 .15
80 Ray Flaherty .02 .10
81 Lenny Moore .10 .30
82 Dante Lavelli .05 .15
83 George Connor .05 .15
84 Roosevelt Brown .05 .15
85 Dick Lane .05 .15
86 Lou Groza .08 .25
87 Bill George .05 .15
88 Tony Canadeo .05 .15
89 Joe Schmidt .05 .15
90 Jim Parker .05 .15
91 Raymond Berry .10 .30
92 Clarence(Ace) Parker .02 .10
93 Ollie Matson .08 .25
94 Gino Marchetti .05 .15
95 Larry Wilson .05 .15
96 Ray Nitschke .10 .30
97 Tuffy Leemans .02 .10
98 Weeb Ewbank .02 .10
99 Lance Alworth .10 .30
100 Bill Willis .05 .15
101 Bart Starr .30 .75
102 Gale Sayers .20 .50
103 Herb Adderley .05 .15
104 Johnny Unitas .30 .75
105 Ron Mix .05 .15
106 Yale Lary .05 .15
107 Red Badgro .02 .10
108 Jim Otto .08 .25
109 Bob Lilly .10 .30
110 Deacon Jones .08 .25
111 Doug Atkins .05 .15
112 Jim Ringo .05 .15
113 Willie Davis .05 .15
114 George Blanda .10 .30
115 Bobby Bell .05 .15
116 Merlin Olsen .08 .25
117 George Musso .02 .10
118 Sam Huff .08 .25
119 Paul Warfield .08 .25
120 Bobby Mitchell .08 .25
121 Sonny Jurgensen .08 .25
122 Sid Gillman .02 .10
123 Arnie Weinmeister .02 .10
124 Charley Taylor .05 .15
125 Mike McCormack .05 .15
126 Willie Brown .05 .15
127 O.J. Simpson .20 .50
128 Pete Rozelle .05 .15
129 Joe Namath .50 1.25
130 Frank Gatski .02 .10
131 Willie Lanier .05 .15
132 Ken Houston .05 .15
133 Paul Hornung .15 .40
134 Roger Staubach .30 .75
135 Len Dawson .10 .30
136 Larry Csonka .10 .30
137 Doak Walker .08 .25
138 Fran Tarkenton .15 .40
139 Don Maynard .08 .25
140 Jim Langer .05 .15
141 John Henry Johnson .05 .15
142 Joe Greene .10 .30
143 Jack Ham .10 .30
144 Mike Ditka .25 .60
145 Alan Page .05 .15
146 Fred Biletnikoff .10 .30
147 Gene Upshaw .05 .15
148 Dick Butkus .25 .60
149 Buck Buchanan .05 .15
150 Franco Harris .15 .40
151 Tom Landry .10 .30
152 Ted Hendricks .05 .15
153 Bob St. Clair .05 .15
154 Jack Lambert .15 .40
155 Bob Griese .10 .30
156 Admission coupon .02 .10
157 Enshrinement Day .02 .10
158 Hall of Fame .02 .10
159 Checklist 1/2 .02 .10
160 Checklist 3/4 .02 .10

2001 Tallahassee Thunder AF2

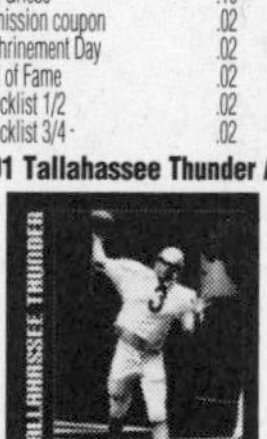

COMPLETE SET (26) 6.00 12.00
1 Andrae Brooks .20 .50
2 Monk Bonasorte GM .20 .50
3 Ernest Certain .20 .50
4 Kevin Cleveland .20 .50
5 James Dickerson .20 .50
6 Paul Ficaro .20 .50
7 Chris Hixson .20 .50
8 Lamonte Jackson .20 .50
9 Demarco Johnson .20 .50
10 Canary Knight .20 .50
11 Billy Luckie .20 .50
12 Gene McDowell CO .20 .50
13 Michael McKee .20 .50
14 Salofi Nua .20 .50
15 Mesiah Porter .20 .50
16 Kenton Rickerson .20 .50
17 Terrence Samuel .20 .50
18 Phil Setterquist .20 .50
19 Marvin Taylor .20 .50
20 Kerry Ware .20 .50
21 Larry Williams DS .20 .50
22 Asssitant Coaches .30 .75
Ricky Bell
Michael McClinton
23 Support Staff .20 .50
24 Lightning Girls .20 .50
25 Team Card .20 .50

1998 Tampa Bay Storm AFL

COMPLETE SET (27) 7.50 15.00
1 Stevie Thomas .30 .75
2 Ron Adams .30 .75
3 Les Barley .30 .75
4 Mel Agee .40 1.00
5 Terry Beauford .30 .75
6 Sylvester Bembery .30 .75
7 Andre Bowden .30 .75
8 Johnnie Harris .30 .75
9 Steve Roughton .30 .75
10 George LaFrance .30 .75
11 Tony Jones .30 .75
12 Cornell Parker .30 .75
13 Tracey Perkins .30 .75
14 Lynn Rowland .30 .75
15 Lawrence Samuels .30 .75
16 Tracy Sanders .30 .75
17 Bjorn Nittmo .30 .75
18 Wayne Williams .30 .75
19 Peter Tom Willis .40 1.00
20 Tony Woods .30 .75
21 Antoine Worthman .30 .75
22 Willie Wyatt .30 .75
23 Keo Coleman .30 .75
24 Robert Goff .30 .75
25 Alvoid Mays .30 .75
26 Nyle Wiren .30 .75
27 Tim Marcum CO .30 .75

1962 Tang Team Photos

Each team in the NFL is represented in this set of 10" by 8" white-bordered color team photos. The team logo is superimposed over the picture at the lower right, and all the players and team personnel are identified by rows in wider white border. The backs are completely blank and the paper stock is thin. While Tang is not specifically identified as the sponsor on the photos, advertising pieces exist to verify this fact. Originally, complete sets were available via mail for 50-cents each with one innerseal from a Tang drink mix jar. The team photos are listed below in alphabetical order. Beware reprints.

COMPLETE SET (14) 150.00 250.00
1 Baltimore Colts 12.00 20.00
2 Chicago Bears 15.00 25.00
3 Cleveland Browns 20.00 35.00
4 Dallas Cowboys 20.00 35.00
5 Detroit Lions 12.00 20.00
6 Green Bay Packers 25.00 40.00
7 Los Angeles Rams 12.00 20.00
8 Minnesota Vikings 15.00 25.00
9 New York Giants 12.00 20.00
10 Philadelphia Eagles 12.00 20.00
11 Pittsburgh Steelers 12.00 20.00
12 St. Louis Cardinals 12.00 20.00
13 San Francisco 49ers 15.00 25.00
14 Washington Redskins 20.00 35.00

1981 TCMA Greats

This 78-card standard-size set was put out by TCMA in 1981. The set features retired football players from the '50s and '60s. The cards are in the popular "pure card" format where there is nothing on the card front except the color photo of the subject inside a simple white border. The card backs provide a short narrative printed in black ink on white card stock. The TCMA copyright is located in the lower right corner. The cards are numbered on the back at the top inside a football; however, some cards can also be found without the card number inside the football.

COMPLETE SET (78) 25.00 50.00
*UNNUMBERED: 2X TO 5X BASIC CARDS
1 Alex Karras .40 1.00
2 Fran Tarkenton .75 2.00
3 Johnny Unitas 2.50 6.00
4 Bobby Layne .75 2.00
5 Roger Staubach 1.50 4.00
6 Joe Namath 2.50 6.00
7 1954 New York Giants .25 .60
Offense
8 Jim Brown 2.00 5.00
9 Ray Wietecha .20 .50
10 R.C. Owens .20 .50
11 Alex Webster .20 .50
12 Jim Otto UER .30 .75
(College was Miami, not Minnesota)
13 Jim Taylor .60 1.50
14 Kyle Rote .25 .60
15 Roger Ellis .20 .50
16 Nick Pietrosante .20 .50
17 Milt Plum .20 .50
18 Eddie LeBaron .25 .60
19 Jimmy Patton .20 .50
20 Yale Lary .25 .60
21 Leo Nomellini .30 .75
22 John Olszewski .20 .50
23 Ernie Koy .20 .50
24 Bill Wade .20 .50
25 Billy Wells .20 .50
26 Ron Waller .20 .50
27 Pat Summerall .30 .75
28 Joe Schmidt .30 .75
29 Bob St.Clair .25 .60
30 Dick Lynch .20 .50
31 Tommy McDonald .30 .75
32 Earl Morrall .20 .50
33 Jim Martin .20 .50
34 Dick Modzelewski .20 .50
35 Dick LeBeau .20 .50
36 Dick Post .20 .50
37 Les Richter .20 .50
38 Andy Robustelli .30 .75
39 Pete Retzlaff .20 .50
40 Fred Biletnikoff .60 1.50
41 Timmy Brown .20 .50
42 Babe Parilli .20 .50
43 Lance Alworth .60 1.50
44 Sammy Baugh .75 2.00
45 Paul(Tank) Younger .20 .50
46 Chuck Bednarik .50 1.25
47 Art Donovan .50 1.25
48 Len Dawson .75 2.00
49 Don Maynard .50 1.25
50 Joe Morrison .20 .50
51 John Elliott .20 .50
52 Jim Ringo .30 .75
53 Max McGee .20 .50
54 Art Powell .20 .50
55 Galen Fiss .20 .50
56 Jack Stroud .20 .50
57 Bake Turner .20 .50
58 Mike McCormack .25 .60
59 L.G. Dupre .20 .50
60 Bill McPeak .20 .50
61 Art Spinney .20 .50
62 Fran Rogel .20 .50
63 Ollie Matson .40 1.00
64 Doak Walker .40 1.00
65 Lenny Moore .50 1.25
66 George Shaw .20 .50
Bert Rechichar
67 Kyle Rote .25 .60
Jim Lee Howell
Ray Krouse UER
(name misspelled Krause)
68 Andy Robustelli .30 .75
Roosevelt Grier
Dick Modzelewski
Jim Katcavage
69 Tucker Frederickson .20 .50
Ernie Koy
70 Gino Marchetti .30 .75
71 Earl Morrall .20 .50
Allie Sherman
72 Roosevelt Brown .25 .60
73 Howard Cassady .20 .50
74 Don Chandler .20 .50
75 Joe Childress .20 .50
76 Rick Casares .20 .50
77 Charley Conerly .40 1.00
78 1958 Giants QB's .25 .60
(Don Heinrich
Tom Dublinski
Charley Conerly)

1987 TCMA Update CMC

In 1987 CMC (the successor to TCMA) produced this 12-card standard-size set updating the 1981 TCMA issue. In fact the first 78 numbered cards were reissued at this time as part of a 90-card set; only the new-issue cards are listed below. Instead of copyright TCMA 1981, these 12 cards indicate copyright CMC 1987.

COMPLETE SET (12) 75.00 125.00
79 Fred Dryer 5.00 10.00
80 Ed Marinaro 6.00 12.00
81 O.J. Simpson 12.50 25.00
82 Joe Theismann 10.00 20.00
83 Roman Gabriel 5.00 10.00
84 Terry Metcalf 5.00 10.00
85 Lyle Alzado 5.00 10.00
86 Jake Scott 5.00 10.00
87 Cliff Branch 7.50 15.00
88 Rocky Bleier 10.00 20.00
89 Cliff Harris 5.00 10.00
90 Archie Manning 7.50 15.00

1994 Ted Williams

The 1994 Ted Williams Roger Staubach's NFL Football Preview Edition consists of 90 standard-size cards. Only 5,000 twelve box cases were produced. The cards are checklisted according to teams. The series closes with three topical subsets: Chalkboard Legends (64-72), Golden Arms (73-81), and Dawning of a Legacy (82-90). Randomly inserted in foil packs were three special chase cards: Charles Barkley, Fred Dryer, and Ted Williams. Two promo cards were produced and are listed below. They carry different photos than the regular issue cards.

COMPLETE SET (90) 4.00 10.00
1 Roger Staubach .30 .75
2 Tony Dorsett .15 .40
3 Bob Lilly .07 .20
4 Art Donovan .07 .20
5 Bert Jones UER .02 .10
(Text states he was 1985 HOF inductee. Jones is not in HOF)
6 Johnny Unitas .20 .50
7 Jack Kemp .07 .20
8 O.J. Simpson .20 .50
9 Dick Butkus .20 .50
10 Gale Sayers .20 .50
11 Mike Singletary .02 .10
12 Bronko Nagurski .08 .20
13 Ken Anderson .02 .10
14 Otto Graham .16 .40
15 Lou Groza .07 .20
16 Marion Motley .02 .10
17 Floyd Little .02 .10
18 Haven Moses .02 .10
19 Lem Barney .02 .10
20 Dick(Night Train) Lane .02 .10
21 Bobby Layne .16 .40
22 Ray Nitschke .08 .20
23 Willie Wood .02 .10
24 Billy(White Shoes) .02 .10
Johnson
25 Mike Bell .02 .10
26 Buck Buchanan .02 .10
27 Len Dawson .08 .20
28 Roman Gabriel .02 .10
29 LeRoy Irvin .02 .10
30 Deacon Jones .02 .10
31 Bob Waterfield .07 .20
32 Bob Griese .16 .40
33 Carl Eller .02 .10
34 Fran Tarkenton .16 .40
35 John Hannah .02 .10
36 Jim Plunkett .02 .10
37 Tom Dempsey .02 .10
38 Archie Manning .04 .10
39 Sam Huff .07 .20
40 Andy Robustelli .02 .10
41 Charley Conerly .02 .10
42 Don Maynard .07 .20
43 Matt Snell .02 .10
44 Wesley Walker .02 .10
45 George Blanda .07 .20
46 Ben Davidson .02 .10
47 Jim Otto .02 .10
48 Norm Van Brocklin .07 .20
49 Harold Carmichael .02 .10
50 Joe Greene .08 .20
51 L.C. Greenwood .07 .20
52 Jack Lambert .08 .20
53 Lance Alworth .08 .20
54 Dan Fouts .07 .20
55 John Brodie .07 .20
56 Steve Largent .16 .40
57 Jim Zorn .02 .10
58 Jim Hart .02 .10
59 Mel Gray .02 .10
60 Lee Roy Selmon .02 .05
61 Sonny Jurgensen .07 .20
62 Sammy Baugh .16 .40
63 Checklist UER .02 .10
(Players on card nos./61 and 62 reversed)
64 George Allen CO .07 .20
65 George Halas CO .16 .40
66 Tom Landry CO .16 .40
67 Vince Lombardi CO .20 .50
68 John Madden CO .16 .40
69 Chuck Noll CO .07 .20
70 Don Shula CO .12 .30
71 Hank Stram CO .02 .10
72 Checklist .02 .10
73 Terry Bradshaw .30 .75
74 Len Dawson .08 .20
75 Dan Fouts .07 .20
76 Bart Starr .20 .50
77 Roger Staubach .30 .75
78 Fran Tarkenton .16 .40
79 Y.A. Tittle .16 .40
80 Johnny Unitas .20 .50
81 Checklist .02 .10
82 Brett Favre .60 1.50
83 Brett Favre .60 1.50
84 Brett Favre .60 1.50
85 Brett Favre .60 1.50
86 Neil O'Donnell/1991 .02 .10
87 Neil O'Donnell .02 .10
College
88 Neil O'Donnell .02 .10
High Notes
89 Neil O'Donnell/1992 .02 .10
90 Checklist Card .02 .10
P1 Roger Staubach Promo .40 1.00
P73 Terry Bradshaw Promo .40 1.00
S32 O.J. Simpson AU/500 20.00 50.00
(signed and issued while in jail)
CB1 Charles Barkley .30 .75
CB1AU Charles Barkley AU 60.00 150.00
(Certified autograph)
AU/34
HM1 Fred Dryer .30 .75
Hollywood Makeovers
TF1 Ted Williams .80 2.00
Teddy Football
TF1AU Ted Williams AU/54 200.00 500.00
(Certified autograph)

1994 Ted Williams Auckland Collection

COMPLETE SET (9) 10.00 25.00
AC1 Brett Favre 3.20 8.00
AC2 Vince Lombardi 1.60 4.00
AC3 Walter Payton 3.20 8.00
AC4 Phil Simms .80 2.00
AC5 Bart Starr 1.60 4.00
AC6 Roger Staubach 2.00 5.00
AC7 Jim Thorpe 1.20 3.00
AC8 Johnny Unitas 1.60 4.00
AC9 Checklist .60 1.50
AC6A Roger Staubach AU/500 40.00 80.00

1994 Ted Williams Etched In Stone Unitas

COMPLETE SET (9) 4.00 10.00
COMMON CARD (ES1-ES9) .50 1.25

1994 Ted Williams Instant Replays

COMPLETE SET (17) 8.00 20.00
IR1 Phil Simms .40 1.00
IR2 Y.A. Tittle .50 1.25
IR3 Sam Huff .50 1.25
IR4 Brad Van Pelt .30 .75
IR5 Brett Favre 2.40 6.00
IR6 Bart Starr 1.00 2.50
IR7 Paul Hornung .60 1.50
IR8 Ray Nitschke .50 1.25
IR9 Neil O'Donnell .40 1.00
IR10 Terry Bradshaw 1.00 2.50
IR11 Joe Greene .50 1.25
IR12 Jack Lambert .50 1.25
IR13 Jeff Hostetler .30 .75
IR14 Lyle Alzado .30 .75
IR15 Dave Casper .30 .75
IR16 Ken Stabler .60 1.50
IR17 Checklist Card .30 .75

1994 Ted Williams Path to Greatness

COMPLETE SET (9) 4.80 12.00
PG1 Tony Dorsett .80 2.00
PG2 Red Grange .80 2.00
PG3 Bob Griese .50 1.25
PG4 Jeff Hostetler .20 .50
PG5 Neil O'Donnell .20 .50
PG6 Jim Plunkett .30 .75
PG7 O.J. Simpson .80 2.00
PG8 Roger Staubach 1.20 3.00
PG9 Checklist Card .20 .50
PG7A O.J. Simpson AU/500 30.00 60.00
(features Ted Williams embossing)

1994 Ted Williams Walter Payton

COMPLETE SET (9) 4.80 12.00
COMMON CARD (WP1-WP9) .60 1.50

1994 Ted Williams POG Cards

COMPLETE SET (18) 2.50 6.00
1 Roger Staubach .75 2.00
Brett Favre
2 Roman Gabriel .07 .20
Lee Roy Jordan
3 Dan Fouts .08 .25
John Brodie
4 Terry Bradshaw .40 1.00
Bart Starr
5 O.J. Simpson .15 .40
Floyd Little
6 Pete Pihos .08 .25
Steve Largent
7 Dick Lane .07 .20
Carl Eller
8 Sam Huff .07 .20
Ben Davidson
9 Jack Lambert .08 .25
Jethro Pugh
10 Mike Singletary .10 .30
Harold Carmichael
11 Chuck Noll CO .10 .30
Bud Grant CO
12 John Madden CO .20 .50
Lyle Alzado
13 Walter Payton .50 1.25
Gale Sayers
14 Fred Dryer .07 .20
Ron Mix
15 Bob Griese .08 .25
Doug Williams
16 Tony Dorsett .30 .75
Red Grange
17 Sonny Jurgensen .07 .20
Jeff Hostetler
18 Checklist Card .07 .20

1994 Ted Williams Trade for Staubach

COMPLETE SET (10) 4.80 12.00
COMMON CARD (TR1-TR9) .50 1.25
NNO Trade for Roger .50 1.25
Redemption Card

2004 Tennessee Valley AFL

COMPLETE SET (30) 7.50 15.00
1 John Bradley .30 .75
2 Corl Bucknor .30 .75
3 Michael Caraway .30 .75
4 Ronney Daniels .40 1.00
5 Kelly Fields .30 .75
6 Marquis Floyd .30 .75
7 Henry Freeman .30 .75
8 Andy Fuller .30 .75
9 Calvin Hall .30 .75
10 Kyle Henderson .30 .75
11 Jerrian James .30 .75
12 Curtis Jeter .30 .75
13 Josh Kellett .30 .75
14 Tracy Kendall .30 .75
15 Dedric Maffett .30 .75
16 Travis McAlpine .30 .75
17 Joe Minucci .30 .75
18 Dave Morrill .30 .75
19 Chris Royle .30 .75
20 Matt Sauk .30 .75
21 Tanaka Scott .30 .75
22 Bryan Snyder .30 .75
23 Wes Stephens .30 .75
24 Alex Walls .30 .75
25 Deon White .30 .75
26 Ron Wilson .30 .75
27 Kevin Guy CO .30 .75
28 Dance Team .30 .75
29 Team Mascot .30 .75
30 Cover Card CL .30 .75

2007 Tennessee Valley Vipers AF2

COMPLETE SET (28) 6.00 12.00
1 Farouk Adelekan .20 .50
2 Anthony Andriano .20 .50
3 Joel Babb .20 .50
4 Travis Blanchard .20 .50
5 John Bradley .20 .50
6 Quentin Burrell .20 .50
7 Carlos Campbell .20 .50
8 Tony Colston .20 .50
9 John Cousins .20 .50
10 Gary Elliott .20 .50
11 Henry Freeman .20 .50
12 James Gibson .20 .50
13 Troy Graham .20 .50
14 Chris Gunn .20 .50
15 Victor Horn .20 .50
16 Lewis Howes .20 .50
17 Brandon Isaiah .20 .50
18 Matt Jirges .20 .50
19 Steven Lee .20 .50
20 Marcus Lindsey .20 .50
21 Chad Motte .20 .50
22 Frisner Nelson .20 .50
23 Calvin Ousby .20 .50
24 Shaheed Richardson .20 .50
25 Milt Theodosatos CO .20 .50
26 Jon Williams .20 .50
27 Vinnie The Viper (Mascot) .20 .50
28 Dream Team Dancers .20 .50

2008 Tennessee Valley Vipers AF2

COMPLETE SET (16) 5.00 10.00
1 Travis Blanchard .30 .75
2 Maurice Brown .30 .75
3 Demetrius Derico .30 .75
4 Kevin Eakin .30 .75
5 Gary Elliott .30 .75
6 Kelly Fields .30 .75
7 Terrance Ford .30 .75
8 Andy Fuller .30 .75
9 Andy Hall .30 .75
10 Jerrian James .30 .75
11 Rajohn Myles .30 .75
12 Alonzo Nix .30 .75
13 Eric Scott .30 .75
14 John Simmons .30 .75
15 Wes Stephens .30 .75
16 Matt Weber .30 .75

1960 Texans 7-Eleven

This set was issued by 7-11 convenience stores in the Dallas area in 1960. Each card measures the standard size 2 1/2" by 3 1/2" and was unnumbered. The fronts include a posed sepia toned photo of the player with no border. The player's name, position, and school are listed below the picture in small print. The font size used on three of the cards is about 50% larger: Boydston, Burford, and Haynes. On all cards but two, the team name is printed from bottom to top along the right or left hand sides. The exceptions are Ray Collins, which is missing the team altogether, and Cotton Davidson which was printed with the team name along the top. The backs include biographical information running the length of the card in typewriter style print. A Paul Miller card is rumored to exist and was once cataloged. We've removed the card from the checklist after years of research trying to verify its existence. Since the cards are unnumbered, they are listed below alphabetically.

COMPLETE SET (11) 2,000.00 3,000.00
1 Max Boydston 175.00 300.00
2 Mel Branch 175.00 300.00
3 Chris Burford 175.00 300.00
4 Ray Collins UER 175.00 300.00
(No team name on front)
5 Cotton Davidson 175.00 300.00
6 Abner Haynes 200.00 350.00
7 Sherrill Headrick 175.00 300.00
8 Bill Krisher 175.00 300.00
9 Johnny Robinson 175.00 300.00
10 Jack Spikes 175.00 300.00

1960 Texans Team Issue

These photos were issued around 1960 by the Dallas Texans. Each features a black and white player photo with the player's position, name and team name printed below the picture. They measure approximately 8" by 10 1/4" and include a brief player bio on the unnumbered cardbacks. Any additions to this list are welcomed.

COMPLETE SET (12) 75.00 150.00
1 Max Boydston 6.00 12.00
2 Mel Branch 6.00 12.00
3 Chris Burford 6.00 12.00
4 Cotton Davidson 6.00 12.00
5 Abner Haynes 10.00 20.00
6 Charlie Jackson 6.00 12.00
7 Curley Johnson 6.00 12.00
8 Paul Miller 6.00 12.00
9 Johnny Robinson 7.50 15.00
10 Jack Spikes 6.00 12.00
11 Hank Stram CO 12.50 25.00
12 Jim Swink 6.00 12.00

1962 Texans Team Issue

These photos were issued in 1962 by the Dallas Texans. Each features a black and white player photo with the player's facsimile autograph printed within the picture. They measure approximately 5" by 7" and were printed on thick blankbacked paper stock.

1 Chris Burford 6.00 12.00
2 Walt Corey 6.00 12.00
3 Bobby Hunt 6.00 12.00
4 Curtis McClinton 7.50 15.00
5 Curt Merz 6.00 12.00
6 Al Reynolds 6.00 12.00
7 Smokey Stover 6.00 12.00
8 Jim Tyrer 6.00 12.00

2002 Texans Upper Deck

This set was issued by Upper Deck to commemorate the Houston Texans first season. The 20-cards and jumbo Houston Texans Logo card were issued in a factory set box and sold through Texan's souvenir outlets.

COMPLETE SET (21) 15.00 30.00
HT1 Jermaine Lewis .75 2.00
HT2 Jabar Gaffney 1.25 3.00
HT3 Corey Bradford .75 2.00
HT4 James Allen .75 2.00
HT6 Jonathan Wells .75 2.00
HT6 David Carr 1.50 4.00
HT7 Rod Rutledge .50 1.25
HT8 Steve McKinney .50 1.25
HT9 Ryan Young .50 1.25
HT10 Tony Boselli .50 1.25
HT11 Gary Walker .50 1.25
HT12 Seth Payne .50 1.25
HT13 Kailee Wong .50 1.25
HT14 Charles Hill .50 1.25
HT15 Jamie Sharper .50 1.25
HT16 Jay Foreman .50 1.25
HT17 Aaron Glenn .50 1.25
HT18 Marcus Coleman .50 1.25
HT19 Matt Stevens .50 1.25
HT20 Kevin Williams .50 1.25
HT21 Houston Texans Jumbo .50 1.25

2004 Texans Super Bowl XXXVIII Promos

This set of 8-cards was released at the 2004 Super Bowl XXXVIII Card Show in Houston. Each card was released in exchange for a group of wrappers from card packs opened at the featured manufacturer's booth at the show. Four different cards were issued the weekend before the game and four others the weekend of the game. Each card was printed in a style unique to the card company, but all are numbered of 8-cards in the set on the backs.

COMPLETE SET (8) 10.00 20.00
1 Aaron Glenn Topps .75 2.00
2 Corey Bradford Playoff .75 2.00
3 Billy Miller Fleer .75 2.00
4 Dave Ragone Upper Deck 1.00 2.50
5 Andre Johnson Upper Deck 1.50 4.00
6 Jabar Gaffney Fleer 1.00 2.50
7 Domanick Davis Playoff 1.50 4.00
8 David Carr Topps 1.50 4.00

2006 Texans Topps

COMPLETE SET (12) 3.00 6.00
HOU1 Jerome Mathis .20 .50
HOU2 Andre Johnson .30 .75
HOU3 David Carr .20 .50
HOU4 Domanick Davis .20 .50
HOU5 Dunta Robinson .20 .50
HOU6 Vernand Morency .20 .50
HOU7 Jeb Putzier .20 .50
HOU8 Kris Brown .20 .50
HOU9 Jason Babin .20 .50
HOU10 Eric Moulds .20 .50
HOU11 Mario Williams .30 .75
HOU12 DeMeco Ryans .30 .75

2007 Texans Topps

COMPLETE SET (12) 2.50 5.00
1 Andre Johnson .25 .60
2 Owen Daniels .20 .50
3 Ron Dayne .25 .60
4 Ahman Green .25 .60
5 Matt Schaub .25 .60
6 Kevin Walter .25 .60
7 Wali Lundy .20 .50
8 Mario Williams .25 .60
9 Dunta Robinson .20 .50
10 DeMeco Ryans .25 .60
11 Kris Brown .20 .50
12 Amobi Okoye .30 .75

2008 Texans Topps

COMPLETE SET (12) 2.50 5.00
1 Matt Schaub .25 .60
2 Sage Rosenfels .20 .50
3 Andre Johnson .25 .60
4 Ron Dayne .20 .50
5 Owen Daniels .20 .50
6 Mario Williams .25 .60
7 Chris Brown .20 .50
8 Kevin Walter .25 .60
9 Amobi Okoye .20 .50
10 DeMeco Ryans .25 .60
11 Steve Slaton .40 1.00
12 Xavier Adibi .25 .60

2009-10 The Cup Sidney Crosby Tribute Autographs

STATED PRINT RUN 10 SER.#'d SETS
NOT PRICED DUE TO SCARCITY
180BS Barry Sanders
180DM Dan Marino

1937 Thrilling Moments

Doughnut Company of America produced these cards and distributed them on the outside of doughnut boxes twelve per box. The cards were to be cut from the boxes and affixed to an album that housed the set. The set's full name is Thrilling Moments in the Lives of Famous Americans. Only seven athletes were included among 65-other famous non-sport American figures. Each blankbacked card measures roughly 1 7/8" by 2 7/8" when neatly trimmed. The set was produced in four different colored backgrounds: blue, green, orange, and yellow with each subject being printed in only one background color.

28 Red Grange FB 800.00 1,200.00
55 Knute Rockne FB 800.00 1,200.00

2005 Throwback Threads

This 229-card set was released in September, 2005. The set was issued in five-card packs with an $4 SRP which came 24 packs to a box. Cards numbered 1-150 feature veterans sequenced in team alphabetical order while cards numbered 151-229 featured members of the 2005 rookie class. Cards numbered 201-229 were issued with player-worn jersey swatches. Cards numbered 151-200 were issued to a stated print run of 999 serial numbered sets while cards numbered 201-229 were issued to stated odds of one in 15 hobby packs and one in 1337 retail packs.

COMP.SET w/o SP's (150)	10.00	25.00
151-200 ROOK.PRINT RUN 999 SER.#'d SETS		
ROOKIE JSY ODDS 1:15 HOB, 1:1337 RET		
1 Anquan Boldin	.25	.60
2 Bryant Johnson	.20	.50
3 Josh McCown	.25	.60
4 Larry Fitzgerald	.30	.75
5 Michael Vick	.30	.75
6 Warrick Dunn	.25	.60
7 Peerless Price	.20	.50
8 T.J. Duckett	.20	.50
9 Alge Crumpler	.25	.60
10 Jamal Lewis	.25	.60
11 Kyle Boller	.25	.60
12 Todd Heap	.25	.60
13 Ray Lewis	.30	.75
14 J.P. Losman	.20	.50
15 Eric Moulds	.20	.50
16 Josh Reed	.20	.50
17 Lee Evans	.25	.60
18 Willis McGahee	.30	.75
19 DeShaun Foster	.25	.60
20 Jake Delhomme	.25	.60
21 Julius Peppers	.25	.60
22 Muhsin Muhammad	.25	.60
23 Stephen Davis	.25	.60
24 Steve Smith	.30	.75
25 Brian Urlacher	.30	.75
26 David Terrell	.20	.50
27 Rex Grossman	.25	.60
28 Thomas Jones	.30	.75
29 Carson Palmer	.30	.75
30 Chad Johnson	.25	.60
31 Peter Warrick	.20	.50
32 Rudi Johnson	.25	.60
33 Jeff Garcia	.25	.60
34 Kelly Holcomb	.20	.50
35 Kellen Winslow Jr.	.25	.60
36 Lee Suggs	.20	.50
37 William Green	.20	.50
38 Julius Jones	.20	.50
39 Drew Bledsoe	.30	.75
40 Roy Williams S	.20	.50
41 Keyshawn Johnson	.25	.60
42 Terence Newman	.20	.50
43 Ashley Lelie	.20	.50
44 Rod Smith	.25	.60
45 Tatum Bell	.20	.50
46 Champ Bailey	.25	.60
47 Darius Watts	.20	.50
48 Jake Plummer	.25	.60
49 Quentin Griffin	.20	.50
50 Charles Rogers	.20	.50
51 Joey Harrington	.25	.60
52 Kevin Jones	.20	.50
53 Roy Williams WR	.25	.60
54 Ahman Green	.25	.60
55 Brett Favre	.75	2.00
56 Javon Walker	.20	.50
57 Nick Barnett	.25	.60
58 Robert Ferguson	.20	.50
59 Andre Johnson	.30	.75
60 David Carr	.20	.50
61 Domanick Davis	.20	.50
62 Dallas Clark	.25	.60
63 Edgerrin James	.25	.60
64 Marvin Harrison	.30	.75
65 Peyton Manning	.60	1.50
66 Reggie Wayne	.30	.75
67 Byron Leftwich	.25	.60
68 Jimmy Smith	.25	.60
69 Fred Taylor	.25	.60
70 Reggie Williams	.20	.50
71 Dante Hall	.20	.50
72 Priest Holmes	.25	.60
73 Tony Gonzalez	.25	.60
74 Trent Green	.25	.60
75 Eddie Kennison	.20	.50
76 Chris Chambers	.25	.60
77 Junior Seau	.30	.75
78 Randy McMichael	.20	.50
79 Zach Thomas	.30	.75
80 A.J. Feeley	.20	.50
81 Daunte Culpepper	.25	.60
82 Michael Bennett	.25	.60
83 Nate Burleson	.20	.50
84 Onterrio Smith	.20	.50
85 Corey Dillon	.25	.60
86 Bethel Johnson	.20	.50
87 Deion Branch	.20	.50
88 Tom Brady	.60	1.50
89 Ty Law	.25	.60
90 Aaron Brooks	.20	.50
91 Deuce McAllister	.25	.60
92 Joe Horn	.25	.60
93 Donte Stallworth	.20	.50
94 Eli Manning	.50	1.25
95 Ike Hilliard	.20	.50
96 Jeremy Shockey	.30	.75
97 Michael Strahan	.30	.75
98 Tiki Barber	.30	.75
99 Anthony Becht	.20	.50
100 Chad Pennington	.30	.75
101 Curtis Martin	.30	.75
102 John Abraham	.20	.50
103 Justin McCareins	.20	.50
104 Santana Moss	.25	.60
105 Shaun Ellis	.20	.50
106 Kerry Collins	.25	.60
107 Randy Moss	.30	.75
108 Jerry Porter	.20	.50
109 Chad Lewis	.20	.50
110 Donovan McNabb	.30	.75
111 Freddie Mitchell	.20	.50
112 Jevon Kearse	.25	.60
113 Terrell Owens	.30	.75
114 Brian Westbrook	.25	.60
115 Antwaan Randle El	.25	.60
116 Ben Roethlisberger	.50	1.25
117 Duce Staley	.25	.60
118 Hines Ward	.30	.75
119 Jerome Bettis	.30	.75
120 Plaxico Burress	.25	.60
121 Antonio Gates	.30	.75
122 Drew Brees	.30	.75
123 LaDainian Tomlinson	.30	.75
124 Kevan Barlow	.20	.50
125 Brandon Lloyd	.20	.50
126 Darrell Jackson	.20	.50
127 Koren Robinson	.20	.50
128 Matt Hasselbeck	.25	.60
129 Shaun Alexander	.25	.60
130 Marc Bulger	.25	.60
131 Isaac Bruce	.25	.60
132 Marshall Faulk	.30	.75
133 Steven Jackson	.30	.75
134 Torry Holt	.25	.60
135 Michael Clayton	.20	.50
136 Brian Griese	.25	.60
137 Derrick Brooks	.25	.60
138 Mike Alstott	.20	.50
139 Chris Brown	.25	.60
140 Derrick Mason	.20	.50
141 Keith Bullock	.20	.50
142 Steve McNair	.30	.75
143 Tyrone Calico	.20	.50
144 Drew Bennett	.25	.60
145 Clinton Portis	.25	.60
146 LaVar Arrington	.25	.60
147 Sean Taylor	.30	.75
148 Patrick Ramsey	.25	.60
149 Laveranues Coles	.20	.50
150 Rod Gardner	.20	.50
151 Cedric Benson RC	2.00	5.00
152 DeMarcus Ware RC	4.00	10.00
153 Shawne Merriman RC	2.00	5.00
154 Thomas Davis RC	1.25	3.00
155 Derrick Johnson RC	1.50	4.00
156 Travis Johnson RC	1.25	3.00
157 David Pollack RC	1.50	4.00
158 Erasmus James RC	1.50	4.00
159 Marcus Spears RC	1.50	4.00
160 Fabian Washington RC	1.50	4.00
161 Marlin Jackson RC	1.25	3.00
162 Heath Miller RC	2.50	6.00
163 Shaun Cody RC	1.50	4.00
164 Dan Cody RC	1.50	4.00
165 Justin Miller RC	1.50	4.00
166 Chris Henry RC	2.00	5.00
167 David Greene RC	1.25	3.00
168 Brandon Jones RC	1.50	4.00
169 Marion Barber RC	2.00	5.00
170 Brandon Jacobs RC	2.50	6.00
171 Jerome Mathis RC	2.00	5.00
172 Craphonso Thorpe RC	1.25	3.00
173 Alvin Pearman RC	1.25	3.00
174 Darren Sproles RC	2.00	5.00
175 Fred Gibson RC	1.50	4.00
176 Roydell Williams RC	1.50	4.00
177 Airese Currie RC	1.25	3.00
178 Damien Nash RC	1.50	4.00
179 Dan Orlovsky RC	2.00	5.00
180 Adrian McPherson RC	1.25	3.00
181 Larry Brackins RC	1.25	3.00
182 Rasheed Marshall RC	1.50	4.00
183 Cedric Houston RC	2.00	5.00
184 Chad Owens RC	1.50	4.00
185 Tab Perry RC	1.25	3.00
186 Dante Ridgeway RC	1.25	3.00
187 Craig Bragg RC	1.25	3.00
188 Deandra Cobb RC	1.25	3.00
189 Derek Anderson RC	1.50	4.00
190 Marcus Maxwell RC	1.25	3.00
191 Paris Warren RC	1.50	4.00
192 Aaron Rodgers RC	20.00	40.00
193 James Kilian RC	1.25	3.00
194 Matt Cassel RC	4.00	10.00
195 Mike Williams	2.00	5.00
196 Lionel Gates RC	1.25	3.00
197 Anthony Davis RC	1.25	3.00
198 Noah Herron RC	1.25	3.00
199 Ryan Fitzpatrick RC	3.00	8.00
200 J.R. Russell RC	1.25	3.00
201 Adam Jones JSY RC	2.50	6.00
202 Alex Smith QB JSY RC	8.00	20.00
203 Antrel Rolle JSY RC	3.00	8.00
204 Andrew Walter JSY RC	2.50	6.00
205 Braylon Edwards JSY RC	6.00	15.00
206 Cadillac Williams JSY RC	5.00	12.00
207 Carlos Rogers JSY RC	3.00	8.00
208 Charlie Frye JSY RC	3.00	8.00
209 Ciatrick Fason JSY RC	2.00	5.00
210 Courtney Roby JSY RC	2.50	6.00
211 Eric Shelton JSY RC	2.00	5.00
212 Frank Gore JSY RC	5.00	12.00
213 J.J. Arrington JSY RC	2.50	6.00
214 Kyle Orton JSY RC	3.00	8.00
215 Jason Campbell JSY RC	4.00	10.00
216 Mark Bradley JSY RC	2.00	5.00
217 Mark Clayton JSY RC	3.00	8.00
218 Matt Jones JSY RC	3.00	8.00
219 Maurice Clarett JSY	2.50	6.00
220 Reggie Brown JSY RC	2.00	5.00
221 Ronnie Brown JSY RC	8.00	20.00
222 Roddy White JSY RC	4.00	10.00
223 Ryan Moats JSY RC	2.50	6.00
224 Roscoe Parrish JSY RC	2.00	5.00
225 Stefan LeFors JSY RC	2.00	5.00
226 Terrence Murphy JSY RC	2.00	5.00
227 Troy Williamson JSY RC	2.50	6.00
228 Vernand Morency JSY RC	2.50	6.00
229 Vincent Jackson JSY RC	4.00	10.00

2005 Throwback Threads Bronze Holofoil

*VETERANS: 2X TO 5X BASIC CARDS
BRONZE VETS PRINT RUN 250 SER.#'d SETS
*ROOKIES: .6X TO 1.5X BASIC CARDS
BRONZE ROOKIE PRINT RUN 150 SER.#'d SETS

2005 Throwback Threads Gold Holofoil

*VETERANS: 4X TO 10X BASIC CARDS
GOLD VET PRINT RUN 99 SER.#'d SETS
*ROOKIES: 1.2X TO 3X BASIC CARDS
GOLD ROOKIE PRINT RUN 50 SER.#'d SETS

2005 Throwback Threads Green

*VETERANS: 3X TO 8X BASIC CARDS
ATOMIC GREEN VET PRINT RUN 175 SETS
*ROOKIES: .8X TO 2X BASIC CARDS
ATOMIC GREEN ROOKIE PRINT RUN 75 SETS
ATOMIC GREENS IN SPECIAL RETAIL BOXES

2005 Throwback Threads Platinum Holofoil

*VETERANS: 6X TO 15X BASIC CARDS
PLAT.VET PRINT RUN 50 SER.#'d SETS
*ROOKIES: 2X TO 5X BASIC CARDS
PLAT.ROOKIE PRINT RUN 25 SER.#'d SETS

2005 Throwback Threads Red

*VETERANS: 4X TO 10X BASIC CARDS
RED VETERAN PRINT RUN 150 SETS
*ROOKIES: X TO X BASIC CARDS
RED ROOKIES SER.#'d TO 10
REDS INSERTED IN SPECIAL RETAIL BOXES

2005 Throwback Threads Retail Foil Rookies

*ROOKIES: .4X TO 1X BASIC CARDS
FOIL RETAIL ROOKIES SER.#'d OF 999

2005 Throwback Threads Silver Holofoil

*VETERANS: 3X TO 8X BASIC CARDS
SILVER VET PRINT RUN 150 SER.#'d SETS
*ROOKIES: .8X TO 2X BASIC CARDS
SILVER ROOKIE PRINT RUN 99 SER.#'d SETS

2005 Throwback Threads Century Stars

STATED ODDS 1:24 HOB/RET
*BLUE: .8X TO 2X BASIC INSERTS
BLUE PRINT RUN 100 SER.#'d SETS

1 Brett Favre	3.00	8.00
2 Carson Palmer	1.25	3.00
3 Corey Dillon	1.00	2.50
4 Dan Marino	3.00	8.00
5 Deion Sanders	1.50	4.00
6 Donovan McNabb	1.25	3.00
7 Edgerrin James	1.00	2.50
8 Jeremy Shockey	1.25	3.00
9 Jerry Rice	2.50	6.00
10 Joe Montana	3.00	8.00
11 Joe Namath	2.00	5.00
12 Marc Bulger	1.00	2.50
13 Marcus Allen	1.25	3.00
14 Michael Irvin	1.25	3.00
15 Michael Strahan	1.25	3.00
16 Michael Vick	1.25	3.00
17 Peyton Manning	2.50	6.00
18 Priest Holmes	1.00	2.50
19 Randy Moss	1.25	3.00
20 Shaun Alexander	1.00	2.50
21 Steve Young	1.50	4.00
22 Terrell Owens	1.25	3.00
23 Tom Brady	2.50	6.00
24 Troy Aikman	1.50	4.00
25 Walter Payton	3.00	8.00

2005 Throwback Threads Century Stars Material

STATED PRINT RUN 100 SER.#'d SETS
*PRIME: 1X TO 2.5X BASIC JERSEYS
PRIME PRINT RUN 25 SER.#'d SETS

1 Brett Favre	10.00	25.00
2 Carson Palmer	4.00	10.00
3 Corey Dillon	3.00	8.00
4 Dan Marino	12.00	30.00
5 Deion Sanders	6.00	15.00
6 Donovan McNabb	4.00	10.00
7 Edgerrin James	3.00	8.00
8 Jeremy Shockey	4.00	10.00
9 Jerry Rice	8.00	20.00
10 Joe Montana	12.00	30.00
11 Joe Namath	8.00	20.00
12 Marc Bulger	3.00	8.00
13 Marcus Allen	5.00	12.00
14 Michael Irvin	5.00	12.00
15 Michael Strahan	4.00	10.00
16 Michael Vick	4.00	10.00
17 Peyton Manning	8.00	20.00
18 Priest Holmes	3.00	8.00
19 Randy Moss	4.00	10.00
20 Shaun Alexander	3.00	8.00
21 Steve Young	6.00	15.00
22 Terrell Owens	4.00	10.00
23 Tom Brady	8.00	20.00
24 Troy Aikman	6.00	15.00
25 Walter Payton	12.00	30.00

2005 Throwback Threads Dynasty

STATED ODDS 1:54 HOB/RET
*BLUE: 1X TO 2.5X BASIC INSERTS
BLUE PRINT RUN 100 SER.#'d SETS

1 Jamal Lewis	1.25	3.00
Ray Lewis		
Priest Holmes		
2 Walter Payton	4.00	10.00
Mike Singletary		
Richard Dent		
3 Deion Sanders	2.00	5.00
Troy Aikman		
Michael Irvin		
4 John Elway	2.50	6.00
Terrell Davis		
Rod Smith		
5 Marcus Allen	1.50	4.00
Ken Stabler		
Gene Upshaw		
6 Tom Brady	2.00	5.00
Corey Dillon		
Troy Brown		
7 Terry Bradshaw	2.50	6.00
Franco Harris		
Joe Greene		
8 Joe Montana	3.00	8.00
Jerry Rice		
Roger Craig		
9 Kurt Warner	1.00	2.50
Marshall Faulk		
Torry Holt		
10 Brad Johnson	1.00	2.50
Mike Alstott		
Keyshawn Johnson		

2005 Throwback Threads Dynasty Material

STATED PRINT RUN 50 SER.#'d SETS
UNPRICED PRIME PRINT RUN 5 SETS

1 Jamal Lewis	7.50	20.00
Ray Lewis		
Priest Holmes		
2 Walter Payton	40.00	80.00
Mike Singletary		
Richard Dent		
3 Deion Sanders	15.00	40.00
Troy Aikman		
Michael Irvin		
4 John Elway	15.00	40.00
Terrell Davis		
Rod Smith		
5 Marcus Allen	15.00	40.00
Ken Stabler		
Gene Upshaw		
6 Tom Brady	15.00	40.00
Corey Dillon		
Troy Brown		
7 Terry Bradshaw	20.00	50.00
Franco Harris		
Joe Greene		
8 Joe Montana	30.00	80.00
Jerry Rice		
Roger Craig		
9 Kurt Warner	6.00	15.00
Marshall Faulk		
Torry Holt		
10 Brad Johnson	6.00	15.00
Mike Alstott		
Keyshawn Johnson		

2005 Throwback Threads Footballs

STATED PRINT RUN 275 SER.#'d SETS

1 Anquan Boldin	3.00	8.00
6 Warrick Dunn	3.00	8.00
7 Peerless Price	2.50	6.00
9 Alge Crumpler	3.00	8.00
10 Jamal Lewis	3.00	8.00
13 Ray Lewis	4.00	10.00
15 Eric Moulds	2.50	6.00
22 Muhsin Muhammad	3.00	8.00
23 Stephen Davis	3.00	8.00
25 Brian Urlacher	4.00	10.00
26 David Terrell	2.50	6.00
28 Thomas Jones	4.00	10.00
31 Peter Warrick	2.50	6.00
32 Rudi Johnson	3.00	8.00
33 Jeff Garcia	3.00	8.00
39 Drew Bledsoe	4.00	10.00
41 Keyshawn Johnson	3.00	8.00
44 Rod Smith	3.00	8.00
46 Champ Bailey	3.00	8.00
48 Jake Plummer	3.00	8.00
60 David Carr	2.50	6.00
63 Edgerrin James	3.00	8.00
64 Marvin Harrison	4.00	10.00
65 Peyton Manning	8.00	20.00
68 Jimmy Smith	3.00	8.00
72 Priest Holmes	3.00	8.00
76 Chris Chambers	3.00	8.00
77 Junior Seau	4.00	10.00
79 Zach Thomas	4.00	10.00
81 Daunte Culpepper	3.00	8.00
85 Corey Dillon	3.00	8.00
88 Tom Brady	8.00	20.00
89 Ty Law	3.00	8.00
90 Aaron Brooks	2.50	6.00
92 Joe Horn	3.00	8.00
97 Michael Strahan	4.00	10.00
98 Tiki Barber	4.00	10.00
100 Chad Pennington	4.00	10.00
101 Curtis Martin	4.00	10.00
102 John Abraham	2.50	6.00
104 Santana Moss	3.00	8.00
106 Kerry Collins	3.00	8.00
107 Randy Moss	4.00	10.00
108 Jerry Porter	2.50	6.00
109 Chad Lewis	2.50	6.00
110 Donovan McNabb	4.00	10.00
111 Freddie Mitchell	2.50	6.00
113 Terrell Owens	4.00	10.00
117 Duce Staley	3.00	8.00
123 LaDainian Tomlinson	4.00	10.00
124 Kevan Barlow	2.50	6.00
128 Matt Hasselbeck	3.00	8.00
129 Shaun Alexander	3.00	8.00
132 Marshall Faulk	4.00	10.00
134 Torry Holt	3.00	8.00
136 Brian Griese	3.00	8.00
137 Derrick Brooks	3.00	8.00
138 Mike Alstott	3.00	8.00
140 Derrick Mason	3.00	8.00
142 Steve McNair	4.00	10.00
145 Clinton Portis	3.00	8.00
146 LaVar Arrington	3.00	8.00
149 Laveranues Coles	2.50	6.00
150 Rod Gardner	2.50	6.00

2005 Throwback Threads Generations

STATED ODDS 1:24 HOB/RET
*BLUE: .8X TO 2X BASIC INSERTS
BLUE PRINT RUN 100 SER.#'d SETS

1 Terrell Owens	1.25	3.00
Andre Johnson		
2 Terry Bradshaw	4.00	10.00
Ben Roethlisberger		
3 Barry Sanders	2.50	6.00
Kevin Jones		
4 John Elway	3.00	8.00
Brett Favre		
5 Bo Jackson	1.50	4.00
Jamal Lewis		
6 Joe Namath	1.50	4.00
Chad Pennington		
7 Ickey Woods	1.25	3.00
Rudi Johnson		
8 Joe Montana	4.00	10.00
Tom Brady		
9 Jerry Rice	2.00	5.00
Marvin Harrison		
10 Dan Marino	3.00	8.00
Peyton Manning		
11 Fran Tarkenton	1.25	3.00
Daunte Culpepper		
12 Deion Sanders	1.25	3.00
Champ Bailey		
13 John Riggins	1.25	3.00
Clinton Portis		
14 Gale Sayers	1.50	4.00
Julius Jones		
15 Walter Payton	4.00	10.00
LaDainian Tomlinson		
16 Marcus Allen	1.25	3.00
Priest Holmes		
17 Randall Cunningham	1.50	4.00
Donovan McNabb		
18 Steve Young	2.00	5.00
Michael Vick		
19 Randy Moss	1.25	3.00
Javon Walker		
20 Troy Aikman	2.50	6.00
Eli Manning		
21 Steve McNair	1.25	3.00
Byron Leftwich		
22 Earl Campbell	1.25	3.00
Steven Jackson		
23 Edgerrin James	1.50	4.00
Shaun Alexander		
24 Lee Evans	1.00	2.50
Eric Moulds		
25 Thurman Thomas	1.25	3.00
Willis McGahee		

2005 Throwback Threads Generations Material

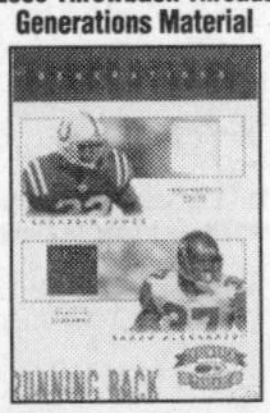

STATED PRINT RUN 50 SER.#'d SETS
UNPRICED PRIME PRINT RUN 10 SETS

1 Terrell Owens	7.50	20.00
Andre Johnson		
2 Terry Bradshaw	20.00	50.00
Ben Roethlisberger		
3 Barry Sanders	20.00	50.00
Kevin Jones		
4 John Elway	20.00	50.00
Brett Favre		
5 Bo Jackson	12.50	30.00
Jamal Lewis		
6 Joe Namath	12.50	30.00
Chad Pennington		
7 Ickey Woods	6.00	15.00
Rudi Johnson		
8 Joe Montana	40.00	80.00
Tom Brady		
9 Jerry Rice	12.50	30.00
Marvin Harrison		
10 Dan Marino	20.00	50.00
Peyton Manning		
11 Fran Tarkenton	10.00	25.00
Daunte Culpepper		
12 Deion Sanders	7.50	20.00
Champ Bailey		
13 John Riggins	7.50	20.00
Clinton Portis		
14 Gale Sayers	12.50	30.00
Julius Jones		
15 Walter Payton	25.00	60.00
LaDainian Tomlinson		
16 Marcus Allen	10.00	25.00
Priest Holmes		
17 Randall Cunningham	10.00	25.00
Donovan McNabb		
18 Steve Young	15.00	40.00
Michael Vick		
19 Randy Moss	7.50	20.00
Javon Walker		
20 Troy Aikman	15.00	30.00
Eli Manning		
21 Steve McNair	7.50	20.00
Byron Leftwich		
22 Earl Campbell	10.00	25.00
Steven Jackson		
23 Edgerrin James	10.00	25.00
Shaun Alexander		
24 Lee Evans	6.00	15.00
Eric Moulds		
25 Thurman Thomas	7.50	20.00
Willis McGahee		

2005 Throwback Threads Gridiron Kings

STATED ODDS 1:12
*BRONZE/500: .5X TO 1.2X BASIC INSERTS
BRONZE PRINT RUN 500 SER.#'d SETS
*FRAMED BLK/25: 2.5X TO 6X BASIC INSERTS
FRAMED BLACK PRINT RUN 25 SER.#'d SETS
*FRAMED BLU/100: .8X TO 2X BASIC INSERTS
FRAMED BLUE PRINT RUN 100 SER.#'d SETS
*FRAMED GRN/50: 1.2X TO 3X BASIC INSERTS
FRAMED GREEN PRINT RUN 50 SER.#'d SETS
*FRAMED PLAT/10: 4X TO 10X BASIC INSERTS
UNPRICED FRAMED PLATINUM #'d TO 10
*FRAMED RED: .5X TO 1.2X BASIC INSERTS
*GOLD/100: .8X TO 2X BASIC INSERTS
GOLD PRINT RUN 100 SER.#'d SETS
*PLATINUM/20: 4X TO 10X BASIC INSERTS
PLATINUM PRINT RUN 10 SER.#'d SETS
*SILVER/250: .6X TO 1.5X BASIC INSERTS
SILVER PRINT RUN 250 SER.#'d SETS

1 Ben Roethlisberger	1.50	4.00
2 Brett Favre	2.50	6.00
3 Brian Urlacher	1.00	2.50
4 Byron Leftwich	.75	2.00
5 Carson Palmer	1.00	2.50
6 Chad Pennington	1.00	2.50
7 Clinton Portis	.75	2.00
8 Corey Dillon	.75	2.00
9 Daunte Culpepper	.75	2.00
10 David Carr	.60	1.50
11 Donovan McNabb	1.00	2.50
12 Edgerrin James	.75	2.00
13 Eli Manning	1.50	4.00
14 Jerry Rice	2.00	5.00
15 Julius Jones	.60	1.50
16 Kevin Jones	.60	1.50
17 LaDainian Tomlinson	1.00	2.50
18 LaVar Arrington	.75	2.00
19 Michael Vick	1.00	2.50
20 Peyton Manning	2.00	5.00
21 Priest Holmes	.75	2.00
22 Randy Moss	1.00	2.50
23 Shaun Alexander	.75	2.00
24 Terrell Owens	1.00	2.50
25 Tom Brady	2.00	5.00

2005 Throwback Threads Gridiron Kings Dual Material

STATED PRINT RUN 75 SER.#'d SETS
*PRIME: 1X TO 2.5X BASIC JERSEYS
PRIME PRINT RUN 25 SER.#'d SETS

1 Ben Roethlisberger	8.00	20.00
2 Brett Favre	12.00	30.00
3 Brian Urlacher	5.00	12.00
4 Byron Leftwich	4.00	10.00
5 Carson Palmer	5.00	12.00
6 Chad Pennington	5.00	12.00
7 Clinton Portis	4.00	10.00
8 Corey Dillon	4.00	10.00
9 Daunte Culpepper	4.00	10.00
10 David Carr	3.00	8.00
11 Donovan McNabb	5.00	12.00
12 Edgerrin James	4.00	10.00
13 Eli Manning	8.00	20.00
14 Jerry Rice	10.00	25.00
15 Julius Jones	3.00	8.00
16 Kevin Jones	3.00	8.00
17 LaDainian Tomlinson	5.00	12.00
18 LaVar Arrington	4.00	10.00
19 Michael Vick	5.00	12.00
20 Peyton Manning	10.00	25.00
21 Priest Holmes	4.00	10.00
22 Randy Moss	5.00	12.00
23 Shaun Alexander	4.00	10.00
24 Terrell Owens	5.00	12.00
25 Tom Brady	10.00	25.00

2005 Throwback Threads Jerseys

1 Anquan Boldin	2.50	6.00
2 Bryant Johnson	2.00	5.00
3 Josh McCown	2.50	6.00
4 Larry Fitzgerald	3.00	8.00
5 Michael Vick	3.00	8.00
7 Peerless Price	2.00	5.00
8 T.J. Duckett	2.00	5.00
10 Jamal Lewis	2.50	6.00
11 Kyle Boller	2.50	6.00
12 Todd Heap	2.50	6.00
15 Eric Moulds	2.00	5.00
16 Josh Reed	2.00	5.00
17 Lee Evans	2.50	6.00
18 Willis McGahee	3.00	8.00
19 DeShaun Foster	2.50	6.00
20 Jake Delhomme	2.50	6.00
21 Julius Peppers	2.50	6.00
22 Muhsin Muhammad	2.50	6.00
23 Stephen Davis	2.50	6.00
25 Brian Urlacher	3.00	8.00
26 David Terrell	2.00	5.00
27 Rex Grossman	2.50	6.00
28 Thomas Jones	3.00	8.00
29 Carson Palmer	3.00	8.00
30 Chad Johnson	2.50	6.00
31 Peter Warrick	2.00	5.00
33 Jeff Garcia	2.50	6.00
34 Kelly Holcomb	2.00	5.00
36 Lee Suggs	2.00	5.00
37 William Green	2.00	5.00
38 Julius Jones	2.00	5.00
39 Drew Bledsoe	3.00	8.00
40 Roy Williams S	2.00	5.00
42 Terence Newman	2.00	5.00
43 Ashley Lelie	2.00	5.00
46 Champ Bailey	2.50	6.00
47 Darius Watts	2.00	5.00
48 Jake Plummer	2.50	6.00
49 Quentin Griffin	2.00	5.00
50 Charles Rogers	2.00	5.00
51 Joey Harrington	2.50	6.00
52 Kevin Jones	2.00	5.00
53 Roy Williams WR	2.50	6.00
54 Ahman Green	2.50	6.00
55 Brett Favre	8.00	20.00
56 Javon Walker	2.00	5.00
57 Nick Barnett	2.50	6.00
58 Robert Ferguson	2.00	5.00
59 Andre Johnson	3.00	8.00
60 David Carr	2.00	5.00
61 Domanick Davis	2.00	5.00
62 Dallas Clark	2.50	6.00
63 Edgerrin James	2.50	6.00
64 Marvin Harrison	3.00	8.00
65 Peyton Manning	6.00	15.00
66 Reggie Wayne	3.00	8.00
67 Byron Leftwich	2.50	6.00
68 Jimmy Smith	2.50	6.00
69 Fred Taylor	2.50	6.00
70 Reggie Williams	2.00	5.00
71 Dante Hall	2.00	5.00
72 Priest Holmes	2.50	6.00
73 Tony Gonzalez	2.50	6.00
74 Trent Green	2.50	6.00
76 Chris Chambers	2.50	6.00
77 Junior Seau	3.00	8.00
78 Randy McMichael	2.00	5.00
79 Zach Thomas	3.00	8.00
81 Daunte Culpepper	2.50	6.00
82 Michael Bennett	2.50	6.00
85 Corey Dillon	2.50	6.00
86 Bethel Johnson	2.00	5.00
88 Tom Brady	6.00	15.00
89 Ty Law	2.50	6.00
90 Aaron Brooks	2.00	5.00
91 Deuce McAllister	2.50	6.00
93 Donte Stallworth	2.00	5.00
94 Eli Manning	5.00	12.00
95 Ike Hilliard	2.00	5.00
96 Jeremy Shockey	3.00	8.00
97 Michael Strahan	3.00	8.00
98 Tiki Barber	3.00	8.00
99 Anthony Becht	2.00	5.00
100 Chad Pennington	3.00	8.00
101 Curtis Martin	3.00	8.00
102 John Abraham	2.00	5.00
103 Justin McCareins	2.00	5.00
104 Santana Moss	2.50	6.00
105 Shaun Ellis	2.00	5.00
107 Randy Moss	3.00	8.00
108 Jerry Porter	2.00	5.00
109 Chad Lewis	2.00	5.00
110 Donovan McNabb	3.00	8.00
111 Freddie Mitchell	2.00	5.00
112 Jevon Kearse	2.50	6.00
113 Terrell Owens	3.00	8.00
115 Antwaan Randle El	2.50	6.00
116 Ben Roethlisberger	5.00	12.00
117 Duce Staley	2.50	6.00
118 Hines Ward	3.00	8.00
119 Jerome Bettis	3.00	8.00
120 Plaxico Burress	2.50	6.00
121 Antonio Gates	3.00	8.00
122 Drew Brees	3.00	8.00
123 LaDainian Tomlinson	3.00	8.00
124 Kevan Barlow	2.00	5.00
126 Darrell Jackson	2.00	5.00
127 Koren Robinson	2.00	5.00
128 Matt Hasselbeck	2.50	6.00
129 Shaun Alexander	2.50	6.00
130 Marc Bulger	2.50	6.00
131 Isaac Bruce	2.50	6.00
132 Marshall Faulk	3.00	8.00
133 Steven Jackson	3.00	8.00
134 Torry Holt	2.50	6.00
138 Mike Alstott	2.50	6.00
139 Chris Brown	2.00	5.00
140 Derrick Mason	2.50	6.00
141 Keith Bulluck	2.00	5.00
142 Steve McNair	3.00	8.00
143 Tyrone Calico	2.00	5.00
144 Drew Bennett	2.50	6.00
147 Sean Taylor	10.00	25.00
148 Patrick Ramsey	2.50	6.00
149 Laveranues Coles	2.00	5.00
150 Rod Gardner	2.00	5.00

2005 Throwback Threads Jerseys Prime

*PRIME: 1.2X TO 3X BASIC JERSEYS
PRIME PRINT RUN 25 SER.#'d SETS

6 Warrick Dunn	8.00	20.00
13 Ray Lewis	10.00	25.00
24 Steve Smith	10.00	25.00
32 Rudi Johnson	8.00	20.00
41 Keyshawn Johnson	8.00	20.00
44 Rod Smith	8.00	20.00
114 Brian Westbrook	8.00	20.00
145 Clinton Portis	8.00	20.00
146 LaVar Arrington	8.00	20.00

2005 Throwback Threads Pig Pens Autographs

2 Ahman Green/50	12.50	30.00
3 Antonio Gates/150	7.50	20.00
4 Chris Brown/150	7.50	20.00
6 Domanick Davis/150	7.50	20.00
7 Michael Vick/50	30.00	60.00
8 Christian Okoye/200	7.50	20.00
9 Deacon Jones/100	10.00	25.00
10 Herschel Walker/200	10.00	25.00
11 Ickey Woods/200	6.00	15.00
12 Jim Brown/50	40.00	80.00
13 Joe Montana/50	75.00	150.00
14 Joe Namath/50	50.00	100.00
15 John Taylor/100	7.50	20.00

2005 Throwback Threads Player Timelines

STATED ODDS 1:24 HOB/RET
*BLUE: .8X TO 2X BASIC INSERTS
BLUE PRINT RUN 100 SER.#'d SETS

1 Ahman Green	1.00	2.50
2 Andre Johnson	1.25	3.00
3 Anquan Boldin	1.00	2.50
4 Barry Sanders	2.00	5.00
5 Carson Palmer	1.25	3.00
6 Clinton Portis	1.00	2.50
7 Corey Dillon	1.00	2.50
8 Curtis Martin	1.25	3.00
9 Drew Bledsoe	1.25	3.00
10 Duce Staley	1.00	2.50
11 Edgerrin James	1.00	2.50
12 Jeremy Shockey	1.25	3.00
13 Jerry Rice	2.50	6.00
14 Jevon Kearse	1.00	2.50
15 Joe Montana	3.00	8.00
16 Jake Plummer	1.00	2.50
17 Kellen Winslow Jr.	1.00	2.50
18 Keyshawn Johnson	1.00	2.50
19 Michael Vick	1.25	3.00
20 Priest Holmes	1.00	2.50
21 Reggie Wayne	1.25	3.00
22 Steven Jackson	1.25	3.00
23 Thomas Jones	1.25	3.00
24 Thurman Thomas	1.25	3.00
25 Trent Green	1.00	2.50

2005 Throwback Threads Player Timelines Dual Material

STATED PRINT RUN 250 SER.#'d SETS
*PRIME: 1X TO 2.5X BASIC JERSEYS
PRIME PRINT RUN 25 SER.#'d SETS

1 Ahman Green	3.00	8.00
2 Andre Johnson	4.00	10.00
3 Anquan Boldin	3.00	8.00
4 Barry Sanders	6.00	15.00
5 Carson Palmer	4.00	10.00
6 Clinton Portis	3.00	8.00
7 Corey Dillon	3.00	8.00
8 Curtis Martin	4.00	10.00
9 Drew Bledsoe	4.00	10.00
10 Duce Staley	3.00	8.00
11 Edgerrin James	3.00	8.00
12 Jeremy Shockey	4.00	10.00
13 Jerry Rice	8.00	20.00
14 Jevon Kearse	3.00	8.00
15 Joe Montana	10.00	25.00
16 Jake Plummer	3.00	8.00
17 Kellen Winslow Jr.	3.00	8.00
18 Keyshawn Johnson	3.00	8.00
19 Michael Vick	4.00	10.00
20 Priest Holmes	3.00	8.00
21 Reggie Wayne	4.00	10.00
22 Steven Jackson	4.00	10.00
23 Thomas Jones	4.00	10.00
24 Thurman Thomas	4.00	10.00
25 Trent Green	3.00	8.00

2005 Throwback Threads Rookie Hoggs

STATED PRINT RUN 750 SER.#'d SETS
*GOLD HOLO: .8X TO 2X BASIC INSERTS
GOLD HOLOFOIL PRINT RUN 100 SETS

1 Alex Smith QB	2.00	5.00
2 Ronnie Brown	1.50	4.00
3 Braylon Edwards	1.50	4.00
4 Cedric Benson	1.25	3.00
5 Cadillac Williams	1.25	3.00
6 Adam Jones	1.00	2.50
7 Troy Williamson	1.00	2.50
8 Carlos Rogers	1.25	3.00
9 Antrel Rolle	1.25	3.00
10 Mike Williams	1.25	3.00
11 DeMarcus Ware	2.50	6.00
12 Erasmus James	1.00	2.50
13 Matt Jones	1.25	3.00
14 Mark Clayton	1.25	3.00
15 Aaron Rodgers	10.00	25.00
16 Jason Campbell	1.50	4.00
17 Roddy White	1.50	4.00
18 Heath Miller	1.50	4.00
19 Reggie Brown	.75	2.00
20 Mark Bradley	.75	2.00
21 J.J. Arrington	1.00	2.50
22 Eric Shelton	.75	2.00
23 Roscoe Parrish	.75	2.00
24 Terrence Murphy	.75	2.00
25 Vincent Jackson	1.50	4.00
26 Frank Gore	2.00	5.00
27 Charlie Frye	1.25	3.00
28 Courtney Roby	1.00	2.50
29 Andrew Walter	1.00	2.50
30 Vernand Morency	1.00	2.50
31 Ryan Moats	1.00	2.50
32 Maurice Clarett	1.00	2.50
33 Kyle Orton	1.25	3.00
34 Ciatrick Fason	.75	2.00
35 Stefan LeFors	.75	2.00

2005 Throwback Threads Rookie Hoggs Autographs

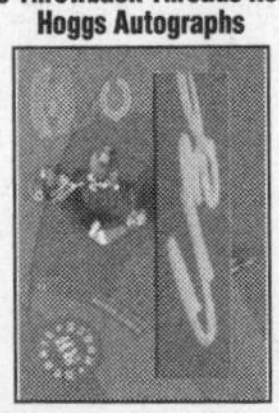

STATED PRINT RUN 150 SER.#'d SETS

1 Alex Smith QB	30.00	60.00
2 Ronnie Brown	25.00	60.00
3 Braylon Edwards	20.00	50.00
4 Cedric Benson	10.00	25.00
5 Cadillac Williams	15.00	40.00
6 Adam Jones	5.00	12.00
7 Troy Williamson	6.00	15.00
8 Carlos Rogers	8.00	20.00
9 Antrel Rolle	8.00	20.00
13 Matt Jones	6.00	15.00
14 Mark Clayton	6.00	15.00
15 Aaron Rodgers	200.00	350.00
16 Jason Campbell	10.00	25.00
17 Roddy White	10.00	25.00
19 Reggie Brown	5.00	12.00
20 Mark Bradley	5.00	12.00
21 J.J. Arrington	6.00	15.00
22 Eric Shelton	5.00	12.00
23 Roscoe Parrish	5.00	12.00
24 Terrence Murphy	5.00	12.00
25 Vincent Jackson	10.00	25.00
26 Frank Gore	15.00	40.00
27 Charlie Frye	8.00	20.00
28 Courtney Roby	6.00	15.00

29 Andrew Walter 6.00 15.00
30 Vernand Morency 5.00 12.00
31 Ryan Moats 5.00 12.00
32 Maurice Clarett 5.00 12.00
33 Kyle Orton 8.00 20.00
34 Ciatrick Fason 5.00 12.00
35 Stefan LeFors 5.00 12.00

2005 Throwback Threads Rookie Hoggs Autographs Hawaii

HAWAII/12 TOO SCARCE TO PRICE

2005 Throwback Threads Throwback Collection

STATED ODDS 1:24 HOB/RET
*BLUE: .8X TO 2X BASIC INSERTS
BLUE PRINT RUN 100 SER.#'d SETS
1 Jason Campbell / Alex Smith QB 2.00 5.00
2 Charlie Frye / Andrew Walter 1.25 3.00
3 Kyle Orton / Stefan LeFors 1.25 3.00
4 Cadillac Williams / Ronnie Brown 1.50 4.00
5 Eric Shelton / J.J. Arrington 1.00 2.50
6 Frank Gore / Vernand Morency 2.00 5.00
7 Maurice Clarett / Ryan Moats .75 2.00
8 Ciatrick Fason / Braylon Edwards 1.50 4.00
9 Matt Jones / Troy Williamson 1.00 2.50
10 Mark Clayton / Roddy White 1.50 4.00
11 Reggie Brown / Mark Bradley .75 2.00
12 Terrence Murphy / Roscoe Parrish .75 2.00
13 Braylon Edwards / Vincent Jackson 1.50 4.00
14 Adam Jones / Courtney Roby 1.00 2.50
15 Antrel Rolle / Carlos Rogers 1.25 3.00
16 Charlie Frye / Jason Campbell / Alex Smith QB 2.50 6.00
17 Kyle Orton / Andrew Walter / Stefan LeFors 1.50 4.00
18 Cadillac Williams / J.J. Arrington / Ronnie Brown 2.00 5.00
19 Frank Gore / Eric Shelton / Vernand Morency 2.50 6.00
20 Maurice Clarett / Ciatrick Fason / Ryan Moats 1.00 2.50
21 Troy Williamson / Braylon Edwards / Matt Jones 2.00 5.00
22 Reggie Brown / Mark Clayton / Roddy White 2.00 5.00
23 Terrence Murphy / Mark Bradley / Roscoe Parrish 1.00 2.50
24 Braylon Edwards / Vincent Jackson / Courtney Roby 2.00 5.00
25 Antrel Rolle / Adam Jones / Carlos Rogers 1.50 4.00

2005 Throwback Threads Throwback Collection Material

1-15 DUAL PRINT RUN 150 SER.#'d SETS
16-25 TRIPLE PRINT RUN 100 SER.#'d SETS
*PRIME: 1X TO 2.5X BASIC JSY DUALS
*PRIME: .8X TO 2X BASIC JSY TRIPLES
PRIME PRINT RUN 25 SER.#'d SETS
1 Jason Campbell / Alex Smith QB 10.00 25.00
2 Charlie Frye / Andrew Walter 3.00 8.00
3 Kyle Orton / Stefan LeFors 3.00 8.00
4 Cadillac Williams / Ronnie Brown 10.00 25.00
5 Eric Shelton / J.J. Arrington 2.50 6.00
6 Frank Gore / Vernand Morency 5.00 12.00
7 Maurice Clarett / Ryan Moats 2.00 5.00
8 Ciatrick Fason / Braylon Edwards 8.00 20.00
9 Matt Jones / Troy Williamson 2.50 6.00
10 Mark Clayton / Roddy White 4.00 10.00
11 Reggie Brown / Mark Bradley 2.00 5.00
12 Terrence Murphy / Roscoe Parrish 2.00 5.00
13 Braylon Edwards / Vincent Jackson 8.00 20.00
14 Adam Jones / Courtney Roby 2.50 6.00
15 Antrel Rolle / Carlos Rogers 3.00 8.00
16 Charlie Frye / Jason Campbell / Alex Smith QB 12.00 30.00
17 Kyle Orton / Andrew Walter / Stefan LeFors 4.00 10.00
18 Cadillac Williams / J.J. Arrington / Ronnie Brown 10.00 25.00
19 Frank Gore / Eric Shelton / Vernand Morency 6.00 15.00
20 Maurice Clarett / Ciatrick Fason / Ryan Moats 2.50 6.00
21 Troy Williamson / Braylon Edwards / Matt Jones 5.00 12.00
22 Reggie Brown / Mark Clayton / Roddy White 5.00 12.00
23 Terrence Murphy / Mark Bradley / Roscoe Parrish 2.50 6.00
24 Braylon Edwards / Vincent Jackson / Courtney Roby 10.00 25.00
25 Antrel Rolle / Adam Jones / Carlos Rogers 4.00 10.00

1988 Time Capsule John Reaves

This set of five-cards was produced by Time Capsule for John Reaves during his run for Florida House of Representatives in 1988. Each card features a red border, a black and white photo, and the exact same card back except for the card number.

COMPLETE SET (5) 3.00 6.00
COMMON REAVES (1-5) .60 1.50

2011 Timeless Treasures

1-125 STATED PRINT RUN 499
ROOKIE AU PRINT RUN 99-499
EXCH EXPIRATION: 3/21/2013
1 Aaron Rodgers 3.00 8.00
2 Adrian Peterson 2.00 5.00
3 Ahmad Bradshaw 1.25 3.00
4 Andre Johnson 1.25 3.00
5 Anquan Boldin 1.25 3.00
6 Antonio Gates 1.25 3.00
7 Arian Foster 1.25 3.00
8 Beanie Wells 1.25 3.00
9 Ben Roethlisberger 1.50 4.00
10 Brandon Lloyd 1.25 3.00
11 Braylon Edwards 1.25 3.00
12 Calvin Johnson 1.50 4.00
13 Jordan Shipley 1.25 3.00
14 Cedric Benson 1.25 3.00
15 Chad Henne 1.25 3.00
16 Chad Ochocinco 1.25 3.00
17 Chris Cooley 1.25 3.00
18 Chris Johnson 1.25 3.00
19 Colt McCoy 1.25 3.00
20 Danny Amendola 1.25 3.00
21 Danny Woodhead 1.50 4.00
22 Darren McFadden 1.25 3.00
23 David Garrard 1.25 3.00
24 Davone Bess 1.00 2.50
25 DeAngelo Williams 1.25 3.00
26 DeSean Jackson 1.25 3.00
27 Devin Hester 1.50 4.00
28 Donald Driver 1.25 3.00
29 Donovan McNabb 1.50 4.00
30 Drew Brees 1.50 4.00
31 Dwayne Bowe 1.25 3.00
32 Eli Manning 1.50 4.00
33 Felix Jones 1.25 3.00
34 Frank Gore 1.25 3.00
35 Fred Jackson 1.50 4.00
36 Greg Jennings 1.25 3.00
37 Hakeem Nicks 1.25 3.00
38 Jahvid Best 1.25 3.00
39 Jamaal Charles 1.25 3.00
40 Jason Campbell 1.25 3.00
41 Jason Witten 1.50 4.00
42 Jay Cutler 1.25 3.00
43 Jeremy Maclin 1.25 3.00
44 Joe Flacco 1.50 4.00
45 John Carlson 1.00 2.50
46 Johnny Knox 1.25 3.00
47 Jonathan Stewart 1.25 3.00
48 Josh Cribbs 1.25 3.00
49 Josh Freeman 1.50 4.00
50 Justin Forsett 1.25 3.00
51 Kenny Britt 1.25 3.00
52 Knowshon Moreno 1.25 3.00
53 LaDainian Tomlinson 1.50 4.00
54 Larry Fitzgerald 1.25 3.00
55 LeGarrette Blount 1.25 3.00
56 LeSean McCoy 1.25 3.00
57 Marcedes Lewis 1.00 2.50
58 Mario Manningham 1.25 3.00
59 Mark Sanchez 1.50 4.00
60 Marques Colston 1.25 3.00
61 Matt Cassel 1.25 3.00
62 Matt Forte 1.25 3.00
63 Matt Ryan 1.50 4.00
64 Matt Schaub 1.25 3.00
65 Matthew Stafford 1.50 4.00
66 Maurice Jones-Drew 1.25 3.00
67 Michael Crabtree 1.25 3.00
68 Michael Turner 1.25 3.00
69 Michael Vick 1.50 4.00
70 Mike Tolbert 1.25 3.00
71 Mike Wallace 1.50 4.00
72 Mike Williams 1.25 3.00
73 Mike Williams USC 1.25 3.00
74 Miles Austin 1.25 3.00
75 Nate Washington 1.00 2.50
76 Percy Harvin 1.25 3.00
77 Peyton Hillis 1.25 3.00
78 Peyton Manning 2.50 6.00
79 Philip Rivers 1.50 4.00
80 Pierre Garcon 1.25 3.00
81 Rashard Mendenhall 1.25 3.00
82 Ray Rice 1.25 3.00
83 Reggie Bush 1.25 3.00
84 Reggie Wayne 1.25 3.00
85 Roddy White 1.25 3.00
86 Ronnie Brown 1.25 3.00
87 Ryan Fitzpatrick 1.25 3.00
88 Ryan Torain 1.00 2.50
89 Sam Bradford 1.50 4.00
90 Sidney Rice 1.25 3.00
91 Steve Breaston 1.00 2.50
92 Steve Johnson 1.25 3.00
93 Steve Smith 1.25 3.00
94 Steven Jackson 1.25 3.00
95 Tim Tebow 4.00 10.00
96 Tom Brady 2.50 6.00
97 Tony Romo 1.50 4.00
98 Vernon Davis 1.25 3.00
99 Wes Welker 1.50 4.00
100 Zach Miller 1.25 3.00
101 Barry Sanders 3.00 8.00
102 Bob Griese 2.00 5.00
103 Bob Hayes 2.00 5.00
104 Boomer Esiason 1.50 4.00
105 Brett Favre 4.00 10.00
106 Bruce Smith 1.50 4.00
107 Dan Fouts 2.00 5.00
108 Deion Sanders 2.00 5.00
109 Dick Butkus 2.50 6.00
110 Emmitt Smith 3.00 8.00
111 Forrest Gregg 1.25 3.00
112 Fran Tarkenton 2.00 5.00
113 Franco Harris 2.00 5.00
114 Jack Lambert 2.00 5.00
115 Joe Greene 2.00 5.00
116 Joe Montana 4.00 10.00
117 John Randle 1.25 3.00
118 Priest Holmes 1.25 3.00
119 Ron Mix 1.25 3.00
120 Shannon Sharpe 1.50 4.00
121 Steve Young 2.50 6.00
122 Thurman Thomas 2.00 5.00
123 Tony Dorsett 2.00 5.00
124 Walter Payton 4.00 10.00
125 Y.A. Tittle 2.00 5.00
126 A.J. Green AU/165 RC 15.00 40.00
127 Aaron Williams AU/163 RC EXCH 6.00 15.00
128 Adrian Clayborn AU/299 RC 6.00 15.00
129 Ahmad Black AU/463 RC 5.00 12.00
130 Akeem Ayers AU/297 RC 5.00 12.00
131 Aldon Smith AU/299 RC EXCH 10.00 25.00
132 Aldrick Robinson AU/297 RC 4.00 10.00
133 Alex Green AU/265 RC 6.00 15.00
134 Allen Bradford AU/299 RC 5.00 12.00
135 Andy Dalton AU/165 RC 25.00 50.00
136 Anthony Allen AU/299 RC 4.00 10.00
137 Anthony Castonzo AU/499 RC 4.00 10.00
138 Austin Pettis AU/265 RC 5.00 12.00
139 Bilal Powell AU/265 RC 4.00 10.00
140 Blaine Gabbert AU/165 RC 25.00 50.00
141 Brandon Harris AU/463 RC 4.00 10.00
142 Cam Newton AU/163 RC 100.00 175.00
143 Cameron Heyward AU/458 RC 6.00 15.00
144 Cameron Jordan AU/463 RC 5.00 12.00
145 Cecil Shorts AU/299 RC 5.00 12.00
146 Christian Ponder AU/163 RC 30.00 60.00
147 Clyde Gates AU/265 RC 5.00 12.00
148 Colin Kaepernick AU/165 RC 10.00 25.00
149 Corey Liuget AU/299 RC 4.00 10.00
150 D.J. Williams AU/299 RC 6.00 15.00
151 Daniel Thomas AU/265 RC 10.00 25.00
152 Da'Quan Bowers AU/463 RC 6.00 15.00
153 Da'Rel Scott AU/294 RC 5.00 12.00
154 Delone Carter AU/265 RC 5.00 12.00
155 DeMarco Murray AU/265 RC 25.00 50.00
156 Denarius Moore AU/264 RC 12.00 30.00
157 Dion Lewis AU/463 RC 6.00 15.00
158 Dwayne Harris AU/299 RC 6.00 15.00
159 Evan Royster AU/299 RC 6.00 15.00
160 Greg Jones AU/299 RC 5.00 12.00
161 Greg Little AU/165 RC 8.00 20.00
162 Greg McElroy AU/299 RC 6.00 15.00
163 Greg Salas AU/299 RC 6.00 15.00
164 J.J. Watt AU/299 RC 8.00 20.00
165 Jacquizz Rodgers AU/490 RC 6.00 15.00
166 Jake Locker AU/165 RC 30.00 60.00
167 Jamie Harper AU/265 RC 6.00 15.00
168 Jeremy Kerley AU/299 RC 6.00 15.00
169 Jerrel Jernigan AU/165 RC 6.00 15.00
170 Jimmy Smith AU/463 RC 6.00 15.00
171 Johnny White AU/463 RC 5.00 12.00
172 Jonathan Baldwin AU/265 RC 6.00 15.00
173 Jordan Cameron AU/299 RC 5.00 12.00
174 Jordan Todman AU/260 RC 4.00 10.00
175 Julio Jones AU/165 RC 25.00 50.00
176 Julius Thomas AU/298 RC 5.00 12.00
177 Justin Houston AU/463 RC 6.00 15.00
178 Kealoha Pilares AU/299 RC 6.00 15.00
179 Kendall Hunter AU/265 RC 6.00 15.00
180 Kris Durham AU/299 RC 5.00 12.00
181 Kyle Rudolph AU/265 RC 6.00 15.00
182 Lance Kendricks AU/299 RC 5.00 12.00
183 Leonard Hankerson AU/265 RC 6.00 15.00
184 Luke Stocker AU/463 RC 5.00 12.00
185 Marcell Dareus AU/265 RC 6.00 15.00
186 Marcus Cannon AU/490 RC 4.00 10.00
187 Mark Ingram AU/265 RC 25.00 50.00
188 Martez Wilson AU/299 RC 6.00 15.00
189 Mikel Leshoure AU/265 RC 6.00 15.00
190 Nathan Enderle AU/99 RC EXCH 8.00 20.00
191 Niles Paul AU/463 RC 6.00 15.00
192 Owen Marecic AU/99 RC EXCH 8.00 20.00
193 Phil Taylor AU/458 RC 5.00 12.00
194 Prince Amukamara AU/296 RC 6.00 15.00
195 Quinton Carter AU/299 RC 4.00 10.00
196 Rahim Moore AU/299 RC 5.00 12.00
197 Randall Cobb AU/265 RC 8.00 20.00
198 Ricky Stanzi AU/299 RC 8.00 20.00
199 Robert Housler AU/299 RC 5.00 12.00
200 Ronald Johnson AU/299 RC 5.00 12.00
201 Roy Helu AU/299 RC 12.00 30.00
202 Ryan Kerrigan AU/299 RC 8.00 20.00
203 Ryan Mallett AU/165 RC 15.00 40.00
204 Ryan Whalen AU/299 RC 5.00 12.00
205 Ryan Williams AU/165 RC 10.00 25.00
206 Scotty McKnight AU/299 RC 5.00 12.00
207 Shane Bannon AU/299 RC EXCH 4.00 10.00
208 Shane Vereen AU/265 RC 6.00 15.00
209 Stanley Havili AU/450 RC 4.00 10.00
210 Stephen Burton AU/297 RC 4.00 10.00
211 Stephen Paea AU/299 RC 8.00 20.00
212 Stevan Ridley AU/265 RC 6.00 15.00
213 T.J. Yates AU/299 RC 8.00 20.00
214 Taiwan Jones AU/265 RC 6.00 15.00
215 Tandon Doss AU/463 RC 5.00 12.00
216 Titus Young AU/265 RC 8.00 20.00
217 Torrey Smith AU/265 RC 8.00 20.00
218 Tyler Sash AU/290 RC 6.00 15.00
219 Tyrod Taylor AU/299 RC 6.00 15.00
220 Tyron Smith AU/299 RC 10.00 25.00
221 Vincent Brown AU/265 RC 6.00 15.00
222 Von Miller AU/265 RC 8.00 20.00

2011 Timeless Treasures Gold

*VETS 1-100: 1.2X TO 3X BASIC CARDS
*LEGENDS 101-125: 1X TO 2.5X BASIC CARDS
1-125 STATED PRINT RUN 49
UNPRICED ROOKIE AUTO PRINT RUN 10

2011 Timeless Treasures Silver

*VETS 1-100: .8X TO 2X BASIC CARDS
*LEGENDS 101-125: .6X TO 1.5X BASIC CARDS
1-125 STATED PRINT RUN 99
*ROOK.AU/25: .6X TO 1.5X BASIC AU/260-499
*ROOK.AU/25: .5X TO 1.2X BASIC AU/99-165
126-222 ROOKIE AU PRINT RUN 25
EXCH EXPIRATION: 3/21/2013
142 Cam Newton AU 125.00 200.00

2011 Timeless Treasures All Time Leaders Materials

STATED PRINT RUN 25 SER.#'d SETS
1 Brett Favre 20.00 50.00
2 Emmitt Smith 15.00 40.00
3 Jerry Rice 15.00 40.00
4 Bruce Smith 8.00 20.00
5 George Blanda 8.00 20.00

2011 Timeless Treasures Autographs Gold

STATED PRINT RUN 4-25
EXCH EXPIRATION: 3/21/2013
3 Ahmad Bradshaw/15 EXCH 15.00 40.00
4 Andre Johnson/15 EXCH
5 Anquan Boldin/15
6 Antonio Gates/15 EXCH
8 Beanie Wells/15
9 Ben Roethlisberger/15 50.00 100.00
11 Braylon Edwards/15 12.00 30.00
12 Calvin Johnson/15
15 Chad Henne/25
16 Chad Ochocinco/15
17 Chris Cooley/15 15.00 40.00
19 Colt McCoy/25 40.00 80.00
20 Danny Amendola/15 15.00 40.00
25 DeAngelo Williams/15
27 Devin Hester/15 EXCH 15.00 40.00
28 Donald Driver/15
29 Donovan McNabb/15 15.00 40.00
32 Eli Manning/15 40.00 80.00
34 Frank Gore/15
36 Greg Jennings/15
38 Jahvid Best/25
39 Jamaal Charles/15 EXCH
41 Jason Witten/20 15.00 40.00
42 Jay Cutler/15
43 Jeremy Maclin/15 EXCH
44 Joe Flacco/15 15.00 40.00
49 Josh Freeman/15 15.00 40.00
51 Kenny Britt/15 EXCH
52 Knowshon Moreno/15
53 LaDainian Tomlinson/15 15.00 40.00
54 Larry Fitzgerald/15 15.00 40.00
56 LeSean McCoy/15
60 Marques Colston/15 EXCH
62 Matt Forte/25
64 Matt Schaub/15
65 Matthew Stafford/25 30.00 60.00
66 Maurice Jones-Drew/15 12.00 30.00
67 Michael Crabtree/15 EXCH
68 Michael Turner/15
69 Michael Vick/15 40.00 80.00
70 Mike Tolbert/25 15.00 40.00
71 Mike Wallace/15
73 Mike Williams/15
76 Percy Harvin/25 15.00 40.00
77 Peyton Hillis/25 25.00 50.00
78 Peyton Manning/15
83 Reggie Bush/15 EXCH
84 Reggie Wayne/15 12.00 30.00
86 Ronnie Brown/15
88 Ryan Torain/25
90 Sidney Rice/25
93 Steve Smith/15
97 Tony Romo/15 30.00 60.00
101 Barry Sanders/25 60.00 120.00
102 Bob Griese/25
104 Boomer Esiason/25
106 Bruce Smith/25 EXCH
108 Deion Sanders/25 30.00 60.00
109 Dick Butkus/25 30.00 60.00
110 Emmitt Smith/22 100.00 175.00
111 Forrest Gregg/25 15.00 40.00
112 Fran Tarkenton/25 15.00 40.00
113 Franco Harris/25
114 Jack Lambert/25 30.00 60.00
115 Joe Greene/25
116 Joe Montana/25
117 John Randle/25
119 Ron Mix/25 12.00 30.00
120 Shannon Sharpe/25
122 Thurman Thomas/25 20.00 50.00
123 Tony Dorsett/25
125 Y.A. Tittle/19

2011 Timeless Treasures Championship Season Materials

STATED PRINT RUN 30-100
*PRIME/25: .8X TO 2X BASIC JSY/100
*PRIME/25: .6X TO 1.5X BASIC JSY/30
1 Troy Aikman/100 8.00 20.00
2 Steve Young/100 8.00 20.00
4 Terrell Davis/30 8.00 20.00
5 John Elway/100 10.00 25.00
7 Tom Brady/100 8.00 20.00
8 Peyton Manning/100 8.00 20.00
9 Aaron Rodgers/100 8.00 20.00

2011 Timeless Treasures Championship Season Materials Autographs

STATED PRINT RUN 5-20
UNPRICED PRIME AU PRINT RUN 1-10
1 Troy Aikman EXCH
2 Steve Young EXCH
4 Terrell Davis 20.00 50.00
5 John Elway 75.00 150.00

2011 Timeless Treasures Championship Season Materials Combos

1 Lou Groza/25 / Otto Graham 12.00 30.00

2011 Timeless Treasures Changing Stripes

STATED PRINT RUN 3-249
1 Anquan Boldin/149 5.00 12.00
2 Y.A. Tittle/20 15.00 40.00
3 Braylon Edwards/249 5.00 12.00
4 Brett Favre/249 15.00 40.00
5 Cedric Benson/100 6.00 15.00
6 Deion Sanders/65 12.00 30.00
7 Donovan McNabb/249 6.00 15.00
8 Eric Dickerson/249 6.00 15.00
9 Fran Tarkenton/99 10.00 25.00
10 Jay Cutler/249 5.00 12.00
12 Jerry Rice/249 12.00 30.00
13 Joe Montana/249 15.00 40.00
14 Joe Namath/249 10.00 25.00
15 John Riggins/3
16 Boomer Esiason/249 6.00 15.00
17 Kellen Winslow/249 6.00 15.00
18 Keyshawn Johnson/15 8.00 20.00
19 LaDainian Tomlinson/249 6.00 15.00
20 Marcus Allen/249 8.00 20.00
21 Michael Vick/249 6.00 15.00
22 Randall Cunningham/249 8.00 20.00
23 Randy Moss/220 5.00 12.00
24 Reggie White/35 12.00 30.00
25 Ricky Williams/249 5.00 12.00
26 Ronnie Lott/210 6.00 15.00
27 Santonio Holmes/40 8.00 20.00
28 Steve McNair/249 6.00 15.00
29 Thurman Thomas/125 8.00 20.00
30 Tony Dorsett/249 8.00 20.00
31 Tony Gonzalez/249 5.00 12.00

2011 Timeless Treasures Changing Stripes Prime

PRIME PRINT RUN 1-49
6 Deion Sanders/21 20.00 50.00
7 Donovan McNabb/49 12.00 30.00
8 Eric Dickerson/49 12.00 30.00
11 Jeremy Shockey/49 10.00 25.00
12 Jerry Rice/49 25.00 60.00
13 Joe Montana/49 30.00 80.00
16 Boomer Esiason/49 12.00 30.00
17 Kellen Winslow/49 12.00 30.00
18 Keyshawn Johnson/49 8.00 20.00
19 LaDainian Tomlinson/15 15.00 40.00
20 Marcus Allen/35 15.00 40.00
22 Randall Cunningham/49 15.00 40.00
23 Randy Moss/49 10.00 25.00
25 Ricky Williams/49 10.00 25.00
26 Ronnie Lott/40 12.00 30.00
27 Santonio Holmes/49 10.00 25.00
28 Steve McNair/49 12.00 30.00
29 Thurman Thomas/49 15.00 40.00
30 Tony Dorsett/49 15.00 40.00
31 Tony Gonzalez/49 10.00 25.00
32 Warren Moon/49 15.00 40.00

2011 Timeless Treasures Classic Cuts Materials

STATED PRINT RUN 1-25
2 Bulldog Turner/25
7 Johnny Unitas/25 250.00 400.00

2011 Timeless Treasures Game Day Souvenirs 1st Quarter

1ST QUARTER PRINT RUN 20-250
*1Q-4Q PRM/15-25: 1X TO 2.5X 1Q JSY/115-250
*1Q-4Q PRIME/15-25: .8X TO 2X 1Q JSY/80
*2ND-4TH QUARTER: .4X TO 1X 1ST QRTR
1 Felix Jones/190 3.00 8.00
2 Michael Vick/250 4.00 10.00
3 DeSean Jackson/250 3.00 8.00
4 Marques Colston/165 3.00 8.00
5 Eli Manning/185 4.00 10.00
6 Adrian Peterson/155 5.00 12.00
7 Matt Ryan/190 4.00 10.00
8 Roddy White/115 3.00 8.00
9 Ahmad Bradshaw/20 6.00 15.00
10 Sam Bradford/90 5.00 12.00
11 Steven Jackson/250 3.00 8.00
12 Mark Sanchez/200 4.00 10.00
13 Joe Flacco/250 4.00 10.00
14 Ray Rice/250 3.00 8.00
15 Brandon Lloyd/50 4.00 10.00
16 Maurice Jones-Drew/125 3.00 8.00
17 David Garrard/185 3.00 8.00
18 Chris Johnson/200 3.00 8.00
19 Knowshon Moreno/150 3.00 8.00
20 Matt Cassel/250 3.00 8.00
21 Jamaal Charles/164 3.00 8.00
22 Darren McFadden/180 3.00 8.00
23 Philip Rivers/190 4.00 10.00
24 Antonio Gates/170 3.00 8.00
25 Hakeem Nicks/80 4.00 10.00
26 Johnny Knox/50 4.00 10.00
27 Peyton Manning/250 6.00 15.00
28 Philip Rivers/75 5.00 12.00
29 Roddy White/99 4.00 10.00
30 Santonio Holmes/99 4.00 10.00
31 Jon Beason/75 3.00 8.00
32 Visanthe Shiancoe/99 4.00 10.00

2011 Timeless Treasures Game Day Souvenirs Combos

STATED PRINT RUN 50 SER.#'d SETS
*PRIME/25: .6X TO 1.5X BASIC COMBO/50
1 DeSean Jackson / Michael Vick 6.00 15.00
2 James Laurinaitis / Sam Bradford 6.00 15.00
3 Malcom Floyd / Philip Rivers 6.00 15.00
4 Mark Sanchez / Shonn Greene 6.00 15.00
5 David Garrard / Maurice Jones-Drew 5.00 12.00

2011 Timeless Treasures Hall of Fame

RANDOM INSERTS IN PACKS
8 Deion Sanders 2.00 5.00
9 Richard Dent 1.50 4.00
10 Marshall Faulk 2.00 5.00
11 Chris Hanburger 1.25 3.00
12 Les Richter 1.25 3.00
13 Shannon Sharpe 1.50 4.00
14 Ed Sabol 1.25 3.00

2011 Timeless Treasures Hall of Fame Autographs

RANDOM INSERTS IN PACKS
8 Deion Sanders 60.00 120.00
9 Richard Dent 40.00 80.00
10 Marshall Faulk
11 Chris Hanburger 20.00 40.00
13 Shannon Sharpe 40.00 80.00
14 Ed Sabol 50.00 100.00

2011 Timeless Treasures HOF Combo Materials

STATED PRINT RUN 25 SER.#'d SETS
1 Jim Brown / Y.A. Tittle 12.00 30.00
2 Dick Lane / Lou Groza 8.00 20.00
3 Otto Graham / Sid Luckman 12.00 30.00
4 Dan Fouts / Walter Payton
5 Deion Sanders / Marshall Faulk 12.00 30.00

2011 Timeless Treasures HOF Quad Materials

STATED PRINT RUN 5-25
2 Doak Walker/25 / Fran Tarkenton / Paul Hornung / Willie Lanier 40.00 80.00
3 Don Maynard/25 / Joe Greene / Larry Csonka / Len Dawson 15.00 40.00
4 Bob Griese/25 / Buck Buchanan / Franco Harris / Jack Lambert 15.00 40.00
5 Emmitt Smith/25 / Jerry Rice / John Randle / Rickey Jackson

2011 Timeless Treasures HOF Triple Materials

STATED PRINT RUN 10-25
1 Bart Starr/25 / Forrest Gregg / Gale Sayers
3 Bob Griese/25 / Buck Buchanan / Franco Harris
4 Barry Sanders/25 / Carl Eller / John Elway 15.00 40.00
5 Bob Hayes/25 / Bruce Smith / Rod Woodson

2011 Timeless Treasures Jerseys

STATED PRINT RUN 9-250
1 Aaron Rodgers/250 8.00 20.00
2 Adrian Peterson/250 5.00 12.00
3 Ahmad Bradshaw/99 4.00 10.00
4 Andre Johnson/199 3.00 8.00
5 Anquan Boldin/50 5.00 12.00
6 Antonio Gates/250 3.00 8.00
7 Arian Foster/250 4.00 10.00
8 Beanie Wells/250 3.00 8.00
9 Ben Roethlisberger/250 4.00 10.00
10 Brandon Lloyd/99 4.00 10.00
11 Braylon Edwards/250 3.00 8.00
12 Calvin Johnson/250 4.00 10.00
14 Cedric Benson/250 3.00 8.00
15 Chad Henne/50 5.00 12.00
16 Chad Ochocinco/99 4.00 10.00
17 Chris Cooley/250 3.00 8.00
18 Chris Johnson/250 3.00 8.00
19 Colt McCoy/99 4.00 10.00
21 Danny Woodhead/250 6.00 15.00
22 Darren McFadden/250 3.00 8.00
23 David Garrard/250 3.00 8.00
25 DeAngelo Williams/250 3.00 8.00
26 DeSean Jackson/250 3.00 8.00
27 Devin Hester/250 4.00 10.00
29 Donovan McNabb/250 4.00 10.00
30 Drew Brees/99 5.00 12.00
31 Dwayne Bowe/250 3.00 8.00
32 Eli Manning/250 4.00 10.00
33 Felix Jones/250 3.00 8.00
34 Frank Gore/250 3.00 8.00
35 Fred Jackson/250 6.00 15.00
37 Hakeem Nicks/35 5.00 12.00
38 Jahvid Best/250 3.00 8.00
39 Jamaal Charles/99 4.00 10.00
40 Jason Campbell/250 3.00 8.00
41 Jason Witten/250 4.00 10.00
42 Jay Cutler/250 3.00 8.00
43 Jeremy Maclin/250 3.00 8.00
44 Joe Flacco/250 4.00 10.00
46 Johnny Knox/250 3.00 8.00
47 Jonathan Stewart/99 4.00 10.00
48 Josh Cribbs/99 4.00 10.00
49 Josh Freeman/250 4.00 10.00
52 Knowshon Moreno/250 3.00 8.00
53 LaDainian Tomlinson/250 4.00 10.00
54 Larry Fitzgerald/99 4.00 10.00
56 LeSean McCoy/250 3.00 8.00
59 Mark Sanchez/250 4.00 10.00
60 Marques Colston/250 3.00 8.00
61 Matt Cassel/250 3.00 8.00
62 Matt Forte/250 3.00 8.00
63 Matt Ryan/250 4.00 10.00
64 Matt Schaub/250 3.00 8.00
65 Matthew Stafford/99 5.00 12.00
66 Maurice Jones-Drew/99 4.00 10.00
67 Michael Crabtree/250 3.00 8.00
68 Michael Turner/250 3.00 8.00
69 Michael Vick/250 4.00 10.00
71 Mike Wallace/250 4.00 10.00
74 Miles Austin/250 4.00 10.00
75 Nate Washington/250 2.50 6.00
76 Percy Harvin/250 3.00 8.00
77 Peyton Hillis/250 6.00 15.00
78 Peyton Manning/99 8.00 20.00
79 Philip Rivers/99 5.00 12.00
80 Pierre Garcon/250 3.00 8.00
81 Rashard Mendenhall/250 3.00 8.00
82 Ray Rice/250 3.00 8.00
83 Reggie Bush/250 3.00 8.00
84 Reggie Wayne/250 3.00 8.00
85 Roddy White/250 3.00 8.00
86 Ronnie Brown/250 3.00 8.00
87 Ryan Fitzpatrick/250 3.00 8.00
89 Sam Bradford/250 4.00 10.00
90 Sidney Rice/250 3.00 8.00
94 Steven Jackson/250 3.00 8.00
95 Tim Tebow/250 8.00 20.00
96 Tom Brady/250 8.00 20.00
97 Tony Romo/250 4.00 10.00
98 Vernon Davis/250 3.00 8.00
99 Wes Welker/250 4.00 10.00
101 Barry Sanders/99 12.00 30.00
102 Bob Griese/250 6.00 15.00
103 Bob Hayes/250 8.00 20.00
104 Boomer Esiason/250 5.00 12.00
105 Brett Favre/250 10.00 25.00
106 Bruce Smith/99 6.00 15.00
107 Dan Fouts/250 6.00 15.00
108 Deion Sanders/250 6.00 15.00
109 Dick Butkus/250 8.00 20.00
110 Emmitt Smith/250 10.00 25.00
111 Forrest Gregg/250 4.00 10.00
112 Fran Tarkenton/250 5.00 12.00
113 Franco Harris/250 6.00 15.00
114 Jack Lambert/250 6.00 15.00
115 Joe Greene/250 6.00 15.00
116 Joe Montana/250 12.00 30.00
117 John Randle/99 5.00 12.00
118 Priest Holmes/250 4.00 10.00
120 Shannon Sharpe/99 6.00 15.00
121 Steve Young/250 6.00 15.00
122 Thurman Thomas/250 6.00 15.00
123 Tony Dorsett/250 6.00 15.00
124 Walter Payton/250 12.00 30.00
125 Y.A. Tittle/99 8.00 20.00

2011 Timeless Treasures Jerseys Prime

*PRIME/25: 1X TO 2.5X BASIC JSY/199-250
*PRIME/20-25: .8X TO 2X BASIC JSY/99
*PRIME/25: .6X TO 1.5X BASIC JSY/35-50
STATED PRINT RUN 2-25
28 Donald Driver/18 8.00 20.00
93 Steve Smith/25 8.00 20.00

2011 Timeless Treasures Material Ink Jerseys

STATED PRINT RUN 15-35
*PRIME/25: .4X TO 1X BASIC AU/30-35
EXCH EXPIRATION: 3/21/2013
1 Darren McFadden/15
2 Tim Tebow/15 40.00 80.00
3 Ray Rice/15 EXCH
4 Rashard Mendenhall/15 EXCH
5 Percy Harvin/15
6 Jared Allen/35 30.00 80.00
7 DeSean Jackson/15 15.00 40.00
8 Hines Ward/15 30.00 60.00
9 Roddy White/15 12.00 30.00
10 Michael Vick/15
11 Josh Freeman/15 EXCH
12 Steven Jackson/15 15.00 40.00
13 Hakeem Nicks/15
14 Aaron Rodgers/15 175.00 300.00
15 Miles Austin/15 15.00 40.00
16 London Fletcher/30 25.00 60.00
17 Nnamdi Asomugha/30 20.00 40.00
18 Felix Jones/15 12.00 30.00
19 Philip Rivers/15
20 Jonathan Stewart/15 12.00 30.00

2011 Timeless Treasures MVP Materials

STATED PRINT RUN 99 SER.#'d SETS
1 Steve McNair 6.00 15.00
2 Steve Young 8.00 20.00
3 Walter Payton 15.00 40.00

2011 Timeless Treasures Rookie Recruits Materials

STATED PRINT RUN 250 SER.#'d SETS
*PRIME/25: .8X TO 2X BASIC INSERTS
1 Andy Dalton 6.00 15.00
2 A.J. Green 5.00 12.00
3 Cam Newton 12.00 30.00
4 Taiwan Jones 2.50 6.00
5 DeMarco Murray 5.00 12.00
6 Torrey Smith 3.00 8.00
7 Shane Vereen 2.50 6.00
8 Stevan Ridley 2.50 6.00
9 Ryan Mallett 5.00 12.00
10 Austin Pettis 2.00 5.00
11 Mikel Leshoure 2.50 6.00
12 Titus Young 3.00 8.00
13 Christian Ponder 5.00 12.00
14 Kyle Rudolph 2.50 6.00
15 Jordan Todman 1.50 4.00
16 Vincent Brown 2.50 6.00
17 Von Miller 3.00 8.00
18 Jonathan Baldwin 2.50 6.00
19 Jake Locker 6.00 15.00
20 Jamie Harper 2.50 6.00
21 Mark Ingram 5.00 12.00
22 Leonard Hankerson 2.50 6.00
23 Jerrel Jernigan 2.00 5.00
24 Delone Carter 2.00 5.00
25 Blaine Gabbert 4.00 10.00
26 Julio Jones 5.00 12.00
27 Marcell Dareus 2.50 6.00
28 Ryan Williams 3.00 8.00
29 Clyde Gates 2.00 5.00
30 Daniel Thomas 2.50 6.00
31 Greg Little 2.50 6.00
32 Colin Kaepernick 3.00 8.00
33 Kendall Hunter 2.50 6.00
34 Alex Green 2.50 6.00
35 Randall Cobb 3.00 8.00
36 Bilal Powell 1.50 4.00

2011 Timeless Treasures Rookie Recruits Materials Autographs

STATED PRINT RUN 30-100
*PRIME/25: .6X TO 1.5X BASIC AU/100
1 Andy Dalton/100 30.00 60.00
2 A.J. Green/100 30.00 60.00
3 Cam Newton/30 150.00 250.00
4 Taiwan Jones/50
5 DeMarco Murray/100 15.00 40.00
6 Torrey Smith/100 10.00 25.00
7 Shane Vereen/100 8.00 20.00
8 Stevan Ridley/50
9 Ryan Mallett/100 25.00 50.00
10 Austin Pettis/100 6.00 15.00
11 Mikel Leshoure/100 8.00 20.00
12 Titus Young/100 10.00 25.00
13 Christian Ponder/100 25.00 50.00
14 Kyle Rudolph/100 8.00 20.00
15 Jordan Todman/100 5.00 12.00
16 Vincent Brown/100 8.00 20.00
17 Von Miller/100 10.00 25.00
18 Jonathan Baldwin/100 8.00 20.00
19 Jake Locker/100 40.00 80.00
20 Jamie Harper/100 8.00 20.00
21 Mark Ingram/100 25.00 50.00
22 Leonard Hankerson/100 8.00 20.00
23 Jerrel Jernigan/100 6.00 15.00
24 Delone Carter/100 6.00 15.00
25 Blaine Gabbert/100 25.00 50.00
26 Julio Jones/100 30.00 60.00
27 Marcell Dareus/100 8.00 20.00
28 Ryan Williams/100 10.00 25.00
29 Clyde Gates/100 6.00 15.00
30 Daniel Thomas/100 12.00 30.00
31 Greg Little/100 8.00 20.00
32 Colin Kaepernick/100 15.00 40.00
33 Kendall Hunter/50 8.00 20.00
34 Alex Green/50
35 Randall Cobb/100 10.00 25.00
36 Bilal Powell/100 5.00 12.00

2011 Timeless Treasures Rookie Year Materials

STATED PRINT RUN 10-99
1 Troy Aikman/99 10.00 25.00
2 Don Meredith/99 10.00 25.00
3 Doak Walker/99 15.00 40.00
5 Darren McFadden/99 4.00 10.00
8 C.J. Spiller/99 4.00 10.00
10 Sam Bradford/99 5.00 12.00
11 Ryan Mathews/99 4.00 10.00
12 Tim Tebow/99 10.00 25.00

2011 Timeless Treasures Rookie Year Materials Prime

*PRIME/25: .8X TO 2X BASIC JSY/99
PRIME STATED PRINT RUN 25
6 Darren Sproles 8.00 20.00
7 Curtis Martin 15.00 40.00
9 Calvin Johnson 10.00 25.00

2011 Timeless Treasures Significant Signatures

STATED PRINT RUN 31-100
1 Bo Jackson/35 40.00 80.00
2 Boyd Dowler/100 12.00 30.00
3 Charlie Joiner/35 12.00 30.00
4 Dan Fouts/35 15.00 40.00
5 Dave Casper/35 15.00 40.00
6 Deacon Jones
7 Doug Williams
8 Gale Sayers
9 Jack Youngblood/33 10.00 25.00
10 Jim Otto/37 12.00 30.00
11 Joe Greene/38 15.00 40.00
12 Ken Stabler/37 25.00 50.00

13 Len Dawson/37	15.00	40.00
14 Leroy Kelly		
15 Marshall Faulk/35	25.00	50.00
16 Paul Hornung/31	15.00	40.00
17 Ronnie Lott/37	25.00	50.00
18 Steve Young/35	25.00	50.00
19 Warren Moon/37	15.00	40.00
20 Y.A. Tittle/37	15.00	40.00

2011 Timeless Treasures Statistical Champions Materials

STATED PRINT RUN 45-100

1 Walter Payton/100	12.00	30.00
2 Dan Fouts/100	6.00	15.00
3 John Riggins/100	6.00	15.00
4 Jerry Rice/100	10.00	25.00
5 Steve Young/100	8.00	20.00
7 Brett Favre/100	10.00	25.00
8 Peyton Manning/100	8.00	20.00
9 Marshall Faulk/100	5.00	12.00
11 Priest Holmes/100	4.00	10.00
13 Curtis Martin/45	8.00	20.00
14 Michael Vick/100	5.00	12.00
15 Tony Gonzalez/100	4.00	10.00
16 Drew Brees/100	5.00	12.00
17 Peyton Manning/100	8.00	20.00
19 Adrian Peterson/100	6.00	15.00
20 Vernon Davis/100	4.00	10.00
21 Philip Rivers/100	5.00	12.00
22 Roddy White/100	4.00	10.00
23 Dwayne Bowe/100	4.00	10.00
24 Brandon Lloyd/100	4.00	10.00
25 Arian Foster/100	4.00	10.00

2011 Timeless Treasures Statistical Champions Materials Prime

*PRIME/25: 1X TO 2.5X BASIC JSY/100
*PRIME/25: .8X TO 2X BASIC JSY/45
PRIME PRINT RUN 25 SER.#'d SETS

6 Terrell Davis	15.00	40.00
10 Ricky Williams	12.00	30.00
18 Terrell Owens	12.00	30.00

2011 Timeless Treasures Statistical Champions Materials Autographs

STATED PRINT RUN 10-15

2 Dan Fouts/15		
3 John Riggins/15		
4 Jerry Rice/15 EXCH		
5 Steve Young/15 EXCH		
7 Brett Favre/15		
8 Peyton Manning/15		
9 Marshall Faulk/15		
11 Priest Holmes/15	10.00	25.00
13 Curtis Martin/15	40.00	80.00
14 Michael Vick/15	50.00	100.00
16 Drew Brees/15	60.00	120.00
17 Peyton Manning/15	60.00	120.00
19 Adrian Peterson/15	60.00	120.00
20 Vernon Davis/15		
22 Roddy White/15	12.00	30.00
23 Dwayne Bowe/15 EXCH		
24 Brandon Lloyd/15	12.00	30.00
25 Arian Foster/15	40.00	80.00

2009 Time Warner Cable Posluszny

NNO Paul Posluszny	2.00	5.00

2005 Tinactin All-Madden Team 20th Anniversary

This set was distributed by Tinactin and features members of the 20th Anniversary of the All-Madden Team. The fronts feature the Tinactin logo and the backs were printed in black and white.

COMPLETE SET (3)	4.00	10.00
1 Troy Aikman	2.00	5.00
2 Marcus Allen	1.25	3.00
3 Jackie Slater	1.00	2.50

2001 Titanium

This 216 card set was issued in five card packs with a SRP of $19.99 per pack and were issued six packs to a box. Each pack contained one double sided jersey card. Cards numbered 145-216 feature rookies and were inserted at a stated rate of one in 31 and were also serial numbered to 75.

COMP.SET w/o SP's (144)	40.00	80.00
ROOKIE/75 ODDS 1:31 HOBBY		
1 David Boston	.30	.75
2 Thomas Jones	.40	1.00
3 Rob Moore	.30	.75
4 Michael Pittman	.40	1.00
5 Jake Plummer	.40	1.00
6 Jamal Anderson	.40	1.00
7 Chris Chandler	.40	1.00
8 Shawn Jefferson	.30	.75
9 Terance Mathis	.30	.75
10 Terry Allen	.40	1.00
11 Jason Brookins UER RC	.50	1.25
(Chad Pennington wrongback, card number on back is #93)		
12 Elvis Grbac	.40	1.00
13 Qadry Ismail	.40	1.00
14 Jamal Lewis	.50	1.25
15 Ray Lewis	.50	1.25
16 Shannon Sharpe	.50	1.25
17 Shawn Bryson	.30	.75
18 Rob Johnson	.40	1.00
19 Sammy Morris	.40	1.00
20 Eric Moulds	.40	1.00
21 Peerless Price	.30	.75
22 Tim Biakabutuka	.30	.75
23 Patrick Jeffers	.30	.75
24 Muhsin Muhammad	.40	1.00
25 James Allen	.30	.75
26 Shane Matthews	.30	.75
27 Marcus Robinson	.40	1.00
28 Brian Urlacher	.60	1.50
29 Corey Dillon	.40	1.00
30 Jon Kitna	.40	1.00
31 Akili Smith	.30	.75
32 Peter Warrick	.40	1.00
33 Tim Couch	.30	.75
34 Kevin Johnson	.30	.75
35 Dennis Northcutt	.30	.75
36 Joey Galloway	.40	1.00
37 Rocket Ismail	.40	1.00
38 Emmitt Smith	1.25	3.00
39 Mike Anderson	.40	1.00
40 Terrell Davis	.50	1.25
41 Brian Griese	.40	1.00
42 Ed McCaffrey	.40	1.00
43 Rod Smith	.40	1.00
44 Charlie Batch	.40	1.00
45 Germane Crowell	.30	.75
46 Herman Moore	.40	1.00
47 Johnnie Morton	.40	1.00
48 James Stewart	.30	.75
49 Brett Favre	1.50	4.00
50 Antonio Freeman	.50	1.25
51 Ahman Green	.50	1.25
52 Bill Schroeder	.40	1.00
53 Marvin Harrison	.50	1.25
54 Edgerrin James	.50	1.25
55 Peyton Manning	1.25	3.00
56 Jerome Pathon	.30	.75
57 Terrence Wilkins	.30	.75
58 Mark Brunell	.40	1.00
59 Keenan McCardell	.40	1.00
60 Jimmy Smith	.40	1.00
61 Fred Taylor	.50	1.25
62 Derrick Alexander	.30	.75
63 Tony Gonzalez	.50	1.25
64 Trent Green	.50	1.25
65 Priest Holmes	.50	1.25
66 Jay Fiedler	.40	1.00
67 Oronde Gadsden	.30	.75
68 James McKnight	.30	.75
69 Lamar Smith	.40	1.00
70 Zach Thomas	.50	1.25
71 Cris Carter	.50	1.25
72 Daunte Culpepper	.40	1.00
73 Randy Moss	.50	1.25
74 Drew Bledsoe	.50	1.25
75 Troy Brown	.40	1.00
76 Charles Johnson	.30	.75
77 J.R. Redmond	.30	.75
78 Antowain Smith	.40	1.00
79 Jeff Blake	.40	1.00
80 Aaron Brooks	.40	1.00
81 Albert Connell	.30	.75
82 Joe Horn	.40	1.00
83 Ricky Williams	.50	1.25
84 Tiki Barber	.50	1.25
85 Kerry Collins	.40	1.00
86 Ron Dayne	.40	1.00
87 Ike Hilliard	.40	1.00
88 Amani Toomer	.40	1.00
89 Richie Anderson	.30	.75
90 Wayne Chrebet	.40	1.00
91 Laveranues Coles	.40	1.00
92 Curtis Martin	.50	1.25
93 Chad Pennington UER	.50	1.25
(Jason Brookins wrongback, card number on back is #11)		
94 Vinny Testaverde	.40	1.00
95 Tim Brown	.50	1.25
96 Rich Gannon	.40	1.00
97 Charlie Garner	.40	1.00
98 Jerry Rice	1.00	2.50
99 Tyrone Wheatley	.40	1.00
100 Charles Woodson	.50	1.25
101 Donovan McNabb	.50	1.25
102 Todd Pinkston	.30	.75
103 Duce Staley	.40	1.00
104 James Thrash	.40	1.00
105 Jerome Bettis	.50	1.25
106 Plaxico Burress	.40	1.00
107 Tommy Maddox	.40	1.00
108 Bobby Shaw	.30	.75
109 Kordell Stewart	.40	1.00
110 Hines Ward	.50	1.25
111 Isaac Bruce	.50	1.25
112 Marshall Faulk	.50	1.25
113 Az-Zahir Hakim	.30	.75
114 Torry Holt	.40	1.00
115 Kurt Warner	.75	2.00
116 Curtis Conway	.40	1.00
117 Tim Dwight	.40	1.00
118 Doug Flutie	.50	1.25
119 Jeff Graham	.30	.75
120 Jeff Garcia	.40	1.00
121 Garrison Hearst	.40	1.00
122 Terrell Owens	.50	1.25
123 J.J. Stokes	.30	.75
124 Tai Streets	.30	.75
125 Shaun Alexander	.50	1.25
126 Matt Hasselbeck	.50	1.25
127 Darrell Jackson	.40	1.00
128 Ricky Watters	.40	1.00
129 Mike Alstott	.40	1.00
130 Warrick Dunn	.50	1.25
131 Jacquez Green	.30	.75
132 Brad Johnson	.40	1.00
133 Keyshawn Johnson	.40	1.00
134 Warren Sapp	.40	1.00
135 Kevin Dyson	.30	.75
136 Eddie George	.50	1.25
137 Mike Green	.30	.75
138 Jevon Kearse	.40	1.00
139 Derrick Mason	.40	1.00
140 Steve McNair	.50	1.25
141 Champ Bailey	.50	1.25
142 Tony Banks	.30	.75
143 Stephen Davis	.40	1.00
144 Michael Westbrook	.30	.75
145 Bill Gramatica JSY RC	5.00	12.00
146 Arnold Jackson JSY RC	5.00	12.00
147 Bobby Newcombe JSY RC	6.00	15.00
148 Marcel Shipp JSY RC	8.00	20.00
149 Quentin McCord JSY RC	6.00	15.00
150 Michael Vick JSY RC	30.00	80.00
151 Chris Barnes JSY RC	5.00	12.00
152 Todd Heap JSY RC	8.00	20.00
153 Reggie Germany JSY RC	5.00	12.00
154 Travis Henry JSY RC	6.00	15.00
155 Chris Taylor JSY RC	5.00	12.00
156 Dee Brown JSY RC	5.00	12.00
157 Dan Morgan JSY RC	6.00	15.00
158 Steve Smith JSY RC	15.00	40.00
159 Chris Weinke JSY RC	6.00	15.00
160 David Terrell JSY RC	6.00	15.00
161 Anthony Thomas JSY RC	8.00	20.00
162 T.J. Houshmandzadeh JSY RC	10.00	25.00
163 Chad Johnson JSY RC	12.00	30.00
164 Rudi Johnson JSY RC	8.00	20.00
165 James Jackson JSY RC	5.00	12.00
166 Andre King JSY RC	5.00	12.00
167 Quincy Morgan JSY RC	6.00	15.00
168 Quincy Carter JSY RC	6.00	15.00
169 Ken-Yon Rambo JSY RC	5.00	12.00
170 Kevin Kasper JSY RC	5.00	12.00
171 Scotty Anderson JSY RC	5.00	12.00
172 Mike McMahon JSY RC	6.00	15.00
173 Robert Ferguson JSY RC	8.00	20.00
174 David Martin JSY RC	5.00	12.00
175 Reggie Wayne JSY RC	15.00	40.00
176 Richmond Flowers JSY RC	5.00	12.00
177 Derrick Blaylock JSY RC	6.00	15.00
178 Snoop Minnis JSY RC	5.00	12.00
179 Chris Chambers JSY RC	8.00	20.00
180 Josh Heupel JSY RC	8.00	20.00
181 Travis Minor JSY RC	6.00	15.00
182 Michael Bennett JSY RC	6.00	15.00
183 Cedric James JSY RC	5.00	12.00
184 Deuce McAllister JSY RC	8.00	20.00
185 Onome Ojo JSY RC	5.00	12.00
186 Jonathan Carter JSY RC	5.00	12.00
187 Jesse Palmer JSY RC	6.00	15.00
188 LaMont Jordan JSY RC	8.00	20.00
189 Derek Combs JSY RC	5.00	12.00
190 Marques Tuiasosopo JSY RC	6.00	15.00
191 Correll Buckhalter JSY RC	8.00	20.00
192 Freddie Mitchell JSY RC	5.00	12.00
193 Adam Archuleta JSY RC	6.00	15.00
194 Francis St.Paul JSY RC	5.00	12.00
195 Drew Brees JSY RC	50.00	125.00
196 LaDainian Tomlinson JSY RC	50.00	100.00
197 Kevan Barlow JSY RC	6.00	15.00
199 Cedrick Wilson JSY RC	6.00	15.00
200 Alex Bannister JSY RC	5.00	12.00
201 Koren Robinson JSY RC	6.00	15.00
202 Milton Wynn JSY RC	5.00	12.00
203 Dan Alexander JSY RC	6.00	15.00
204 Eddie Berlin JSY RC	5.00	12.00
205 Justin McCareins JSY RC	6.00	15.00
206 Rod Gardner JSY RC	6.00	15.00
207 Damerien McCants JSY RC	6.00	15.00
208 Sage Rosenfels JSY RC	8.00	20.00
209 Nick Goings JSY RC	8.00	20.00
210 Josh Booty JSY RC	6.00	15.00
211 Benjamin Gay JSY RC	6.00	15.00
212 Gerard Warren JSY RC	6.00	15.00
213 Jamal Reynolds JSY RC	5.00	12.00
214 Will Allen JSY RC	8.00	20.00
215 Santana Moss JSY RC	10.00	25.00
216 Andre Carter JSY RC	6.00	15.00

2001 Titanium Premiere Date

*VETERANS: 4X TO 10X BASIC CARDS
PREMIERE DATE/99 ODDS 1:7 HOBBY
STATED PRINT RUN 99 SER.#'d SETS

2001 Titanium Red

*VETERANS: 5X TO 12X BASIC CARDS
RED/58 ODDS 1:13 HOBBY
STATED PRINT RUN 58 SER.#'d SETS

2001 Titanium Retail

*RETAIL VETS 1-144: .25X TO .6X HOBBY		
COMMON ROOKIE (145-216)	.75	2.00
ROOKIE SEMISTARS	1.00	2.50
ROOKIE UNL.STARS	1.25	3.00
ROOKIE STATED ODDS 2:25		
150 Michael Vick RC	5.00	12.00
158 Steve Smith RC	2.50	6.00
162 T.J. Houshmandzadeh RC	1.50	4.00
163 Chad Johnson RC	2.00	5.00
175 Reggie Wayne RC	2.50	6.00
179 Chris Chambers RC	1.25	3.00
184 Deuce McAllister RC	1.25	3.00
195 Drew Brees RC	8.00	20.00
196 LaDainian Tomlinson RC	4.00	10.00
215 Santana Moss RC	1.50	4.00

2001 Titanium Double Sided Jerseys

STATED ODDS ONE PER PACK		
1 Bobby Newcombe	5.00	12.00
Arnold Jackson		
2 Marcel Shipp	6.00	15.00
Bill Gramatica		
3 LaMont Jordan	6.00	15.00
Rod Gardner		
5 Michael Vick	15.00	40.00
Quincy Carter		
7 Reggie Germany	5.00	12.00
Travis Henry		
8 Dee Brown	8.00	20.00
Steve Smith		
10 Dan Morgan	5.00	12.00
Adam Archuleta		
11 David Terrell	6.00	15.00
Anthony Thomas		
13 Rudi Johnson	6.00	15.00
James Jackson		
14 Andre King	5.00	12.00
Quincy Morgan		
15 Kevin Kasper	4.00	10.00
Richmond Flowers		
16 Scotty Anderson	5.00	12.00
Mike McMahon		
17 Robert Ferguson	6.00	15.00
David Martin		
18 Reggie Wayne	8.00	20.00
Freddie Mitchell		
19 Derrick Blaylock	5.00	12.00
Snoop Minnis		
20 Chris Chambers	6.00	15.00
Travis Minor		
21 Michael Bennett	5.00	12.00
Cedric James		
22 Deuce McAllister	6.00	15.00
Onome Ojo		
23 Jonathan Carter	5.00	12.00
Jesse Palmer		
24 Derek Combs	4.00	10.00
Ken-Yon Rambo		
25 Marques Tuiasosopo	6.00	15.00
Sage Rosenfels		
26 Correll Buckhalter	6.00	15.00
Dan Alexander		
27 Chris Taylor	5.00	12.00
Damerien McCants		
28 Francis St. Paul	4.00	10.00
Milton Wynn		
29 Drew Brees	25.00	60.00
LaDainian Tomlinson		
30 Kevan Barlow	5.00	12.00
Cedric Wilson		
31 Alex Bannister	5.00	12.00
Koren Robinson		
32 Eddie Berlin	5.00	12.00
Justin McCareins		
33 Na Brown	4.00	10.00
Chad Lewis		
34 Terry Hardy	4.00	10.00
David Sloan		
35 Tywan Mitchell	4.00	10.00
Dennis McKinley		
36 Bryan Gilmore	4.00	10.00
Jermaine Lewis		
37 David Boston	5.00	12.00
Jimmy Smith		
38 Martay Jenkins	4.00	10.00
R.Jay Soward		
39 Thomas Jones	6.00	15.00
Fred Taylor		
40 Frank Sanders	6.00	15.00
Terrell Owens		
41 Chris Gedney	4.00	10.00
Frank Wycheck		
42 Chris Griesen	5.00	12.00
Neil O'Donnell		
43 Jammi German	4.00	10.00
Shawn Jefferson		
44 Reggie Kelly	4.00	10.00
Maurice Smith		
45 Tony Martin	5.00	12.00
Derrick Alexander		
46 Jamal Anderson	6.00	15.00
Curtis Martin		
47 Jamal Lewis	6.00	15.00
Mike Anderson		
48 Shannon Sharpe	6.00	15.00
Tony Gonzalez		
49 Ray Lewis	6.00	15.00
Bryan Cox		
50 Elvis Grbac	5.00	12.00
Kerry Collins		
51 Obafemi Ayanbadejo	4.00	10.00
Chris Fuamatu-Ma'afala		
52 Antowain Smith	5.00	12.00
Sammy Morris		
53 Thurman Thomas	6.00	15.00
J.J. Johnson		
54 Donald Hayes	4.00	10.00
Chris Hetherington		
55 Isaac Byrd	6.00	15.00
Reggie White		
56 Brad Hoover	5.00	12.00
Steve Beuerlein		
57 Tim Biakabutuka	4.00	10.00
William Floyd		
58 Shane Matthews	5.00	12.00
Jim Miller		
59 Marcus Robinson	5.00	12.00
Johnnie Morton		
60 Dez White	5.00	12.00
Sylvester Morris		
61 Brian Urlacher	12.00	30.00
Zach Thomas		
62 Clif Groce	4.00	10.00
Nick Williams		
63 Corey Dillon	5.00	12.00
Peter Warrick		
64 Damon Griffin	4.00	10.00
Tremain Mack		
05 Danny Farmer	4.00	10.00
Craig Yeast		
66 Marco Battaglia	4.00	10.00
Takeo Spikes		
67 Darnay Scott	5.00	12.00
Bill Schroeder		
68 Kevin Thompson	4.00	10.00
Jamel White		
69 Tim Couch	5.00	12.00
Jake Plummer		
70 Kevin Johnson	6.00	15.00
Antonio Freeman		
71 Dennis Northcutt	5.00	12.00
Keenan McCardell		
72 Aaron Shea	4.00	10.00
Marc Edwards		
73 Rocket Ismail	5.00	12.00
Jason Tucker		
74 Troy Hambrick	5.00	12.00
Darren Woodson		
75 Jeff Garcia	6.00	15.00
Warren Moon		
76 Wane McGarity	4.00	10.00
James McKnight		
77 Emmitt Smith	15.00	40.00
Eddie George		
78 Dwayne Carswell	4.00	10.00
Byron Chamberlain		
79 Terrell Davis	6.00	15.00
Brian Griese		
81 Ed McCaffrey	5.00	12.00
Torry Holt		
82 Germane Crowell	5.00	12.00
Herman Moore		
83 Larry Foster	4.00	10.00
Allen Rossum		
84 James Stewart	5.00	12.00
Robert Smith		
85 Charlie Batch	6.00	15.00
Steve McNair		
86 Herbert Goodman	4.00	10.00
De'Mond Parker		
87 Dorsey Levens	5.00	12.00
Lamar Smith		
88 Brett Favre	20.00	50.00
Kurt Warner		
89 E.G. Green	4.00	10.00
Jerome Pathon		
90 Edgerrin James	15.00	40.00
Peyton Manning		
91 Marvin Harrison	6.00	15.00
Amani Toomer		
92 Anthony Johnson	4.00	10.00
Stacey Mack		
93 Mark Brunell	5.00	12.00
Chris Chandler		
94 Sean Dawkins	4.00	10.00
Derrick Mayes		
95 Priest Holmes	6.00	15.00
Charlie Garner		
96 Kimble Anders	5.00	12.00
Mike Alstott		
97 Leslie Shepherd	4.00	10.00
Bert Emanuel		
98 O.J. McDuffie	4.00	10.00
J.J. Stokes		
99 Chris Walsh	4.00	10.00
Troy Walters		
100 Daunte Culpepper	6.00	15.00
Randy Moss		
101 Cris Carter	6.00	15.00
Wayne Chrebet		
102 Charles Johnson	4.00	10.00
Torrance Small		
103 Drew Bledsoe	6.00	15.00
Rich Gannon		
104 Damon Huard	5.00	12.00
Brock Huard		
105 Jeff Blake	5.00	12.00
Chad Morton		
106 Willie Jackson	4.00	10.00
Kevin Dyson		
107 Ron Dayne	6.00	15.00
Tiki Barber		
108 Jason Sehorn	6.00	15.00
Charles Woodson		
109 Ron Dixon	4.00	10.00
Az-Zahir Hakim		
110 Chad Pennington	6.00	15.00
Vinny Testaverde		
111 Tim Brown	12.00	30.00
Jerry Rice		
112 Andre Rison	5.00	12.00
Tai Streets		
113 Tyrone Wheatley	6.00	15.00
Shaun Alexander		
114 Donovan McNabb	6.00	15.00
Duce Staley		
115 Jerome Bettis	10.00	25.00
Kordell Stewart		
116 Orlando Pace	5.00	12.00
Justin Watson		
117 Curtis Conway	6.00	15.00
Doug Flutie		
118 Fred Beasley	4.00	10.00
Paul Smith		
119 Christian Fauria	4.00	10.00
Itula Mili		
120 Darrell Jackson	5.00	12.00
Ricky Watters		
121 Trent Dilfer	5.00	12.00
Tony Banks		
122 Rabih Abdullah	4.00	10.00
Aaron Stecker		
123 Dave Moore	4.00	10.00
Erron Kinney		
124 Yancey Thigpen	4.00	10.00
Rodney Thomas		
125 Deion Sanders	6.00	15.00
Champ Bailey		

2001 Titanium Double Sided Jerseys Patches

COMMON CARD	6.00	15.00
SEMISTARS	8.00	20.00
UNLISTED STARS	10.00	25.00
5 Michael Vick	25.00	60.00
Quincy Carter		
8 Dee Brown	12.00	30.00
Steve Smith		
18 Reggie Wayne	12.00	30.00
Freddie Mitchell		
55 Isaac Byrd	12.00	30.00
Reggie White		
77 Emmitt Smith	25.00	60.00
Eddie George		
111 Tim Brown	20.00	50.00
Jerry Rice		
114 Donovan McNabb	10.00	25.00
Duce Staley		

2001 Titanium Monday Knights

COMPLETE SET (25)	15.00	40.00
STATED ODDS 1:7		
1 Emmitt Smith	2.00	5.00
2 Mike Anderson	.60	1.50
3 Terrell Davis	.75	2.00
4 Brian Griese	.60	1.50
5 Rod Smith	.60	1.50
6 Brett Favre	2.50	6.00
7 Antonio Freeman	.75	2.00
8 Ahman Green	.75	2.00
9 Edgerrin James	.75	2.00
10 Peyton Manning	2.00	5.00
11 Mark Brunell	.60	1.50
12 Jimmy Smith	.60	1.50
13 Fred Taylor	.75	2.00
14 Cris Carter	.75	2.00
15 Daunte Culpepper	.60	1.50
16 Randy Moss	.75	2.00
17 Rich Gannon	.60	1.50
18 Jerry Rice	1.50	4.00
19 Donovan McNabb	.75	2.00
20 Duce Staley	.75	2.00
21 Isaac Bruce	.75	2.00
22 Marshall Faulk	.75	2.00
23 Kurt Warner	1.25	3.00
24 Eddie George	.75	2.00
25 Steve McNair	.75	2.00

2001 Titanium Players Fantasy

COMPLETE SET (25)	25.00	60.00
STATED ODDS 1:7		
*SILVER/2000: .2X TO .5X GOLD		
SILVER PRINT RUIN 2000 SER.#'d SETS		
1 Michael Vick	4.00	10.00
2 Travis Henry	.75	2.00
3 Chris Weinke	.75	2.00
4 David Terrell	.75	2.00
5 Anthony Thomas	1.00	2.50
6 Chad Johnson	1.50	4.00
7 James Jackson	.60	1.50
8 Quincy Morgan	.75	2.00
9 Quincy Carter	.75	2.00
10 Kevin Kasper	.60	1.50
11 Reggie Wayne	2.00	5.00
12 Snoop Minnis	.60	1.50
13 Chris Chambers	1.00	2.50
14 Travis Minor	.75	2.00
15 Michael Bennett	.75	2.00
16 Deuce McAllister	1.00	2.50
17 Santana Moss	1.25	3.00
18 Marques Tuiasosopo	.75	2.00
19 Correll Buckhalter	1.00	2.50
20 Freddie Mitchell	.60	1.50
21 Drew Brees	6.00	15.00
22 LaDainian Tomlinson	3.00	8.00
23 Kevan Barlow	.75	2.00
24 Koren Robinson	.75	2.00
25 Rod Gardner	.75	2.00

2001 Titanium Team

COMPLETE SET (25)	60.00	120.00
STATED ODDS 1:25		
1 Corey Dillon	1.25	3.00
2 Peter Warrick	1.25	3.00
3 Tim Couch	1.00	2.50
4 Emmitt Smith	4.00	10.00
5 Mike Anderson	1.25	3.00
6 Olandis Gary	1.00	2.50
7 Brian Griese	1.25	3.00
8 Brett Favre	5.00	12.00
9 Edgerrin James	1.50	4.00
10 Peyton Manning	4.00	10.00
11 Mark Brunell	1.25	3.00
12 Fred Taylor	1.50	4.00
13 Daunte Culpepper	1.25	3.00
14 Randy Moss	1.50	4.00
15 Drew Bledsoe	1.50	4.00
16 Aaron Brooks	1.25	3.00
17 Ricky Williams	1.50	4.00
18 Ron Dayne	1.25	3.00
19 Jerry Rice	3.00	8.00
20 Donovan McNabb	1.50	4.00
21 Marshall Faulk	1.50	4.00
22 Kurt Warner	2.50	6.00
23 Jeff Garcia	1.25	3.00
24 Eddie George	1.50	4.00
25 Steve McNair	1.50	4.00

2002 Titanium

Released in January, 2003, this set features 100 veterans and 75 rookies. The first 100-veteran player cards were printed with gold foil highlights. Each serial numbered rookie card includes two players; the rookie and a veteran player. Those cards also feature a jersey swatch of the veteran player and were inserted one per pack. Boxes contained 6 packs of 10 cards and cases contained 20 boxes.

COMP.SET w/o SP's (100)	30.00	60.00
1 David Boston	.25	.60
2 Thomas Jones	.40	1.00
3 Jake Plummer	.30	.75
4 Warrick Dunn	.30	.75
5 Shawn Jefferson	.25	.60
6 Michael Vick	.60	1.50
7 Jamal Lewis	.30	.75
8 Chris Redman	.25	.60
9 Travis Taylor	.25	.60
10 Drew Bledsoe	.40	1.00
11 Travis Henry	.25	.60
12 Eric Moulds	.30	.75
13 Peerless Price	.25	.60
14 Muhsin Muhammad	.30	.75
15 Rodney Peete	.30	.75
16 Lamar Smith	.30	.75
17 Chris Weinke	.25	.60
18 Marty Booker	.30	.75
19 Jim Miller	.25	.60
20 Anthony Thomas	.30	.75
21 Corey Dillon	.30	.75
22 Gus Frerotte	.30	.75
23 Peter Warrick	.30	.75
24 Tim Couch	.25	.60
25 Kevin Johnson	.25	.60
26 Jamel White	.25	.60
27 Quincy Carter	.25	.60
28 Joey Galloway	.30	.75
29 Emmitt Smith	1.00	2.50
30 Olandis Gary	.30	.75
31 Brian Griese	.30	.75
32 Ed McCaffrey	.30	.75
33 Rod Smith	.30	.75
34 Mike McMahon	.25	.60
35 Bill Schroeder	.25	.60
36 James Stewart	.25	.60
37 Brett Favre	1.00	2.50
38 Terry Glenn	.30	.75
39 Ahman Green	.30	.75
40 James Allen	.25	.60
41 Corey Bradford	.25	.60
42 Jermaine Lewis	.25	.60
43 Marvin Harrison	.40	1.00
44 Edgerrin James	.30	.75
45 Peyton Manning	.75	2.00
46 Mark Brunell	.30	.75
47 Jimmy Smith	.30	.75
48 Fred Taylor	.30	.75
49 Tony Gonzalez	.40	1.00
50 Trent Green	.30	.75
51 Priest Holmes	.40	1.00
52 Chris Chambers	.30	.75
53 Jay Fiedler	.30	.75
54 Ricky Williams	.30	.75
55 Michael Bennett	.30	.75
56 Daunte Culpepper	.30	.75
57 Randy Moss	.40	1.00
58 Tom Brady	1.00	2.50
59 Troy Brown	.30	.75
60 Antowain Smith	.30	.75
61 Aaron Brooks	.30	.75
62 Joe Horn	.30	.75
63 Deuce McAllister	.30	.75
64 Tiki Barber	.40	1.00
65 Kerry Collins	.30	.75
66 Amani Toomer	.30	.75
67 Laveranues Coles	.30	.75
68 Curtis Martin	.40	1.00
69 Vinny Testaverde	.30	.75
70 Tim Brown	.40	1.00
71 Rich Gannon	.30	.75
72 Jerry Rice	.75	2.00
73 Donovan McNabb	.40	1.00
74 Duce Staley	.30	.75
75 James Thrash	.30	.75
76 Jerome Bettis	.40	1.00
77 Kordell Stewart	.30	.75
78 Hines Ward	.40	1.00
79 Isaac Bruce	.40	1.00
80 Marshall Faulk	.40	1.00
81 Torry Holt	.40	1.00
82 Kurt Warner	.40	1.00
83 Drew Brees	.60	1.50
84 LaDainian Tomlinson	.50	1.25
85 Jeff Garcia	.30	.75
86 Garrison Hearst	.30	.75
87 Terrell Owens	.40	1.00
88 Shaun Alexander	.30	.75
89 Trent Dilfer	.30	.75
90 Koren Robinson	.25	.60
91 Brad Johnson	.30	.75
92 Keyshawn Johnson	.30	.75
93 Keenan McCardell	.30	.75
94 Eddie George	.30	.75
95 Derrick Mason	.30	.75
96 Steve McNair	.40	1.00
97 Stephen Davis	.30	.75
98 Rod Gardner	.25	.60
99 Shane Matthews	.25	.60
100 Derrius Thompson	.25	.60
101 Freddie Jones JSY/1000	2.50	6.00
Jason McAddley RC		
102 Jake Plummer JSY/250	4.00	10.00
Josh McCown RC		
103 Kyle Vanden Bosch JSY/1100	4.00	10.00
Wendell Bryant RC		
104 Thomas Jones JSY/1100	5.00	12.00
Chester Taylor RC		
105 Bryan Gilmore JSY/1100	2.50	6.00
Tim Carter RC		
106 Michael Vick JSY/300	6.00	15.00
Kurt Kittner RC		
107 Brandon Stokley JSY/150	4.00	10.00
Ron Johnson RC		
108 Chris Redman JSY/100	2.50	6.00
Javin Hunter RC		
109 Peerless Price JSY/250	3.00	8.00
Josh Reed RC		
110 Isaac Byrd JSY/250	4.00	10.00
Julius Peppers RC		
111 Dez White JSY/250	2.50	6.00
Jamin Elliott RC		
142 Rabih Abdullah JSY/1000	2.50	6.00
Adrian Peterson RC		
113 Brian Urlacher JSY/500	5.00	12.00
Napoleon Harris RC		
114 Michael Westbrook JSY/1100	3.00	8.00
Lamont Thompson RC		
115 Corey Dillon JSY/750	4.00	10.00
T.J. Duckett RC		
116 Takeo Spikes JSY/500	4.00	10.00
Roy Williams RC		
117 Akili Smith JSY/1000	3.00	8.00
Craig Nall RC		
118 Tim Couch JSY/250	4.00	10.00
Andr?? Davis RC		
119 Jamel White JSY/500	2.50	6.00
Tellis Redmon RC		
120 Quincy Carter JSY/100	4.00	10.00
Chad Hutchinson RC		
121 Troy Hambrick JSY/250	4.00	10.00
Antonio Bryant RC		
122 Emmitt Smith JSY/500	8.00	20.00
William Green RC		
123 La'Roi Glover JSY/1100	4.00	10.00
John Henderson RC		
124 Deltha O'Neal JSY/300	2.50	6.00
Mike Rumph RC		
125 Larry Foster JSY/1100	2.50	6.00
Eddie Drummond RC		
126 Ahman Green JSY/300	4.00	10.00
Najeh Davenport RC		
127 Donald Driver JSY/150	5.00	12.00
Javon Walker RC		
128 Brett Favre JSY/500	10.00	25.00
David Carr RC		
129 James Allen JSY/300	2.50	6.00
Jonathan Wells RC		
130 Jermaine Lewis JSY/200	2.50	6.00
Jabar Gaffney RC		
131 Edgerrin James JSY/250	5.00	12.00
Ricky Williams RC		
132 Peyton Manning JSY/750	8.00	20.00
Dwight Freeney RC		
133 Mark Brunell JSY/500	5.00	12.00
David Garrard RC		
134 Jimmy Smith JSY/500	2.50	6.00
Marquise Walker RC		
135 Curtis Jackson JSY/1100	3.00	8.00
Marc Boerigter RC		
136 Tony Richardson JSY/300	2.50	6.00
Omar Easy RC		
137 Desmond Clark JSY/1000	3.00	8.00
Randy McMichael RC		
138 Zach Thomas JSY/250	3.00	8.00
Robert Thomas RC		
139 Chris Walsh JSY/500	3.00	8.00
Shaun Hill RC		
140 Daunte Culpepper JSY/1000	4.00	10.00
Randy Fasani RC		
141 Jim Kleinsasser JSY/1100	4.00	10.00
Jarrod Baxter RC		
142 Randy Moss JSY/500	5.00	12.00
Donte Stallworth RC		
143 Corey Chavous JSY/1100	2.50	6.00
Phillip Buchanon RC		
144 Christian Fauria JSY/750	2.50	6.00
Daniel Graham RC		
145 Damon Huard JSY/300	4.00	10.00
Rohan Davey RC		
146 Donald Hayes JSY/500	4.00	10.00
Deion Branch RC		
147 Terrelle Smith JSY/300	2.50	6.00
J.T. O'Sullivan RC		
148 Jonathan Carter JSY/300	2.50	6.00
Daryl Jones RC		
149 Ron Dayne JSY/300	4.00	10.00
Jeremy Shockey RC		
150 Anthony Becht JSY/1100	2.50	6.00
Bryan Thomas RC		
151 Curtis Martin JSY/250	4.00	10.00
Dameon Hunter RC		
152 Jerry Rice JSY/750	8.00	20.00
Ashley Lelie RC		
153 Jon Ritchie JSY/1100	2.50	6.00
Ed Stansbury RC		
154 Cecil Martin JSY/1100	2.50	6.00
Freddie Milons RC		
155 Donovan McNabb JSY/1000	5.00	12.00
Lito Sheppard RC		
156 James Thrash JSY/1000	5.00	12.00
Brian Westbrook RC		
157 Jerome Bettis JSY/1000	5.00	12.00
Verron Haynes RC		
158 Kordell Stewart JSY/500	4.00	10.00
Antwaan Randle El RC		
159 Marshall Faulk JSY/300	4.00	10.00
Lamar Gordon RC		
160 Kurt Warner JSY/500	5.00	12.00
Joey Harrington RC		
161 Drew Brees JSY/500	6.00	15.00
Quentin Jammer RC		
162 Fred McCrary JSY/1100	2.50	6.00
Seth Burford RC		
163 Stephen Alexander JSY/1000	3.00	8.00
Reche Caldwell RC		
164 LaDainian Tomlinson JSY/500	6.00	15.00
Clinton Portis RC		
165 Jeff Garcia JSY/200	4.00	10.00
Brandon Doman RC		
166 Paul Smith JSY/250	2.50	6.00
Lee Mays RC		
167 Shaun Alexnder JSY/500	4.00	10.00
Maurice Morris RC		
168 Michael Pittman JSY/500	3.00	8.00
Travis Stephens RC		
169 Ken Dilger JSY/750	2.50	6.00
Jerramy Stevens RC		
170 Erron Kinney JSY/500	2.50	6.00
John Simon RC		
171 Steve McNair JSY/500	5.00	12.00
Albert Haynesworth RC		
172 Eddie George JSY/500	4.00	10.00
DeShaun Foster RC		
173 Jacquez Green JSY/250	6.00	15.00
Ladell Betts RC		
174 Rod Gardner JSY/200	2.50	6.00
Cliff Russell RC		
175 Shane Matthews JSY/250	3.00	8.00
Patrick Ramsey RC		

2002 Titanium Blue

*1-100 VETS: .8X TO 2X BASIC CARDS		
COMMON ROOKIE (101-175)	.50	1.25
ROOKIE SEMISTARS	.60	1.50
ROOKIE UNL.STARS	.75	2.00
STATED PRINT RUN 325 SERIAL #'d SETS		
104 Thomas Jones	.75	2.00
Chester Taylor		
110 Isaac Byrd	1.50	4.00
Julius Peppers		

113 Brian Urlacher	.75	2.00
Napoleon Harris		
116 Takeo Spikes	.75	2.00
Roy Williams		
121 Troy Hambrick	.75	2.00*
Antonio Bryant		
122 Emmitt Smith	2.00	5.00
William Green		
128 Brett Favre	2.00	5.00
David Carr		
132 Peyton Manning	1.50	4.00
Dwight Freeney		
133 Mark Brunell	1.00	2.50
David Garrard		
139 Chris Walsh	1.00	2.50
Shaun Hill		
149 Ron Dayne	1.25	3.00
Jeremy Shockey		
152 Jerry Rice	1.50	4.00
Ashley Lelie		
155 Donovan McNabb	.75	2.00
Lito Sheppard		
156 James Thrash	1.25	3.00
Brian Westbrook		
161 Drew Brees	1.25	3.00
Quentin Jammer		
164 LaDainian Tomlinson	1.00	2.50
Clinton Portis		

2002 Titanium Blue Jerseys

*BLUE/100-200: .8X TO 2X BASIC CARD
*BLUE/45-85: 1X TO 2.5X BASIC CARD
*BLUE/20: 1.5X TO 4X BASIC CARD
BLUE STATED PRINT RUN 20-200

2002 Titanium Red

*1-100 VETS: .8X TO 2X BASIC CARDS

COMMON ROOKIE (101-175)	.50	1.25
ROOKIE SEMISTARS	.60	1.50
ROOKIE UNL.STARS	.75	2.00
STATED PRINT RUN 275 SER.#'d SETS		
104 Thomas Jones	.75	2.00
Chester Taylor		
110 Isaac Byrd	1.50	4.00
Julius Peppers		
113 Brian Urlacher	.75	2.00
Napoleon Harris		
116 Takeo Spikes	.75	2.00
Roy Williams		
121 Troy Hambrick	.75	2.00
Antonio Bryant		
122 Emmitt Smith	2.00	5.00
William Green		
128 Brett Favre	2.00	5.00
David Carr		
132 Peyton Manning	1.50	4.00
Dwight Freeney		
133 Mark Brunell	1.00	2.50
David Garrard		
139 Chris Walsh	1.00	2.50
Shaun Hill		
149 Ron Dayne	1.25	3.00
Jeremy Shockey		
152 Jerry Rice	1.50	4.00
Ashley Lelie		
155 Donovan McNabb	.75	2.00
Lito Sheppard		
156 James Thrash	1.25	3.00
Brian Westbrook		
161 Drew Brees	1.25	3.00
Quentin Jammer		
164 LaDainian Tomlinson	1.00	2.50
Clinton Portis		

2002 Titanium Retail

*RETAIL SILVER: .4X TO 1X BASE CARDS

COMMON ROOKIE (101-175)	.25	.60
ROOKIE SEMISTARS	.30	.75
ROOKIE UNL.STARS	.40	1.00
RET.ROOKIES DO NOT CONTAIN JSYs		
104 Thomas Jones	.40	1.00
Chester Taylor RC		
110 Isaac Byrd	.75	2.00
Julius Peppers RC		
113 Brian Urlacher	.40	1.00
Napoleon Harris RC		
116 Takeo Spikes	.40	1.00
Roy Williams RC		
121 Troy Hambrick	.40	1.00
Antonio Bryant RC		
122 Emmitt Smith	1.00	2.50
William Green RC		
128 Brett Favre	1.00	2.50
David Carr RC		
132 Peyton Manning	.75	2.00
Dwight Freeney RC		
133 Mark Brunell	.50	1.25
David Garrard RC		
139 Chris Walsh	.50	1.25
Shaun Hill RC		
149 Ron Dayne	.60	1.50
Jeremy Shockey RC		
152 Jerry Rice	.75	2.00
Ashley Lelie RC		
155 Donovan McNabb	.40	1.00
Lito Sheppard RC		
156 James Thrash	.60	1.50
Brian Westbrook RC		
161 Drew Brees	.60	1.50
Quentin Jammer RC		
164 LaDainian Tomlinson	.50	1.25
Clinton Portis RC		

2002 Titanium High Capacity

COMPLETE SET (10)	12.00	30.00
STATED ODDS 1:7		
1 Michael Vick	1.50	4.00
2 Anthony Thomas	.75	2.00
3 Emmitt Smith	2.50	6.00
4 Brett Favre	2.50	6.00
5 Peyton Manning	2.00	5.00
6 Randy Moss	1.00	2.50
7 Tom Brady	2.50	6.00
8 Jerry Rice	2.00	5.00
9 Marshall Faulk	1.00	2.50
10 Kurt Warner	1.00	2.50

2002 Titanium Monday Knights

COMPLETE SET (21)	25.00	60.00
STATED ODDS 1:3		
1 Jamal Lewis	1.00	2.50
2 Anthony Thomas	1.00	2.50
3 Brian Griese	1.00	2.50
4 Ashley Lelie	.75	2.00
5 Clinton Portis	1.25	3.00
6 Brett Favre	3.00	8.00
7 Edgerrin James	1.00	2.50
8 Peyton Manning	2.50	6.00
9 Tom Brady	3.00	8.00
10 Curtis Martin	1.25	3.00
11 Jerry Rice	2.50	6.00
12 Donovan McNabb	1.25	3.00
13 Jerome Bettis	1.25	3.00
14 Antwaan Randle El	1.25	3.00
15 Marshall Faulk	1.25	3.00
16 Kurt Warner	1.25	3.00
17 Jeff Garcia	1.00	2.50
18 Terrell Owens	1.25	3.00
19 Shaun Alexander	.75	2.00
20 Eddie George	1.00	2.50
21 Steve McNair	1.25	3.00

2002 Titanium Rookie Team

COMPLETE SET (10)	15.00	40.00
STATED ODDS 1:13		
1 Josh Reed	1.25	3.00
2 DeShaun Foster	1.50	4.00
3 William Green	1.25	3.00
4 Antonio Bryant	1.50	4.00
5 Ashley Lelie	1.25	3.00
6 Clinton Portis	2.00	5.00
7 Joey Harrington	1.50	4.00
8 David Carr	1.50	4.00
9 Donte Stallworth	1.50	4.00
10 Antwaan Randle El	1.50	4.00

2002 Titanium Shadows

COMPLETE SET (9)	12.00	30.00
STATED ODDS 1:5		
1 Michael Vick	1.50	4.00
2 Emmitt Smith	2.50	6.00
3 Joey Harrington	1.00	2.50
4 Brett Favre	2.50	6.00
5 David Carr	1.00	2.50
6 Randy Moss	1.00	2.50
7 Tom Brady	2.50	6.00
8 Jerry Rice	2.00	5.00
9 Kurf Warner	1.00	2.50

2001 Titanium Post Season

This 100 card set was issued in February, 2002. The cards were issued in two card packs which came 10 packs to a box. The card stock is a reproduction of Pacific's Prism Atomic release with Post Season Edition writtten on the card front.Packs included one jersey card and one base card per pack. Rookies were serial numbered on card back to 750 of each made. A patch variation of the jerseys were also produced with limited quantatites of each player serial numbered on card front.

1 Arnold Jackson RC	.75	2.00
2 Marcel Shipp RC	1.25	3.00
3 Alge Crumpler RC	1.25	3.00
4 Quentin McCord RC	1.00	2.50
5 Michael Vick RC	5.00	12.00
6 Kenyon Hambrick RC	.75	2.00
7 Todd Heap RC	1.25	3.00
8 Nate Clements RC	1.00	2.50
9 Reggie Germany RC	.75	2.00
10 Travis Henry RC	1.00	2.50
11 Jarrod Cooper RC	1.00	2.50
12 Nick Goings RC	1.25	3.00
13 Dan Morgan RC	1.00	2.50
14 Steve Smith RC	2.50	6.00
15 Chris Weinke RC	1.00	2.50
16 David Terrell RC	1.00	2.50
17 Anthony Thomas RC	1.25	3.00
18 T.J. Houshmandzadeh RC	1.50	4.00
19 Chad Johnson RC	2.00	5.00
20 Rudi Johnson RC	1.25	3.00
21 Justin Smith RC	1.25	3.00
22 Josh Booty RC	1.00	2.50
23 Benjamin Gay RC	1.00	2.50
24 Anthony Henry RC	1.25	3.00
25 James Jackson RC	.75	2.00
26 Andre King RC	.75	2.00
27 Quincy Morgan RC	1.00	2.50
28 Gerrard Warren RC	1.00	2.50
29 Quincy Carter RC	1.00	2.50
30 Tony Dixon RC	.75	2.00
31 Ken-Yon Rambo RC	.75	2.00
32 Randal Williams RC	.75	2.00
33 Kevin Kasper RC	.75	2.00
34 Willie Middlebrooks RC	1.00	2.50
35 Scotty Anderson RC	.75	2.00
36 Mike McMahon RC	1.00	2.50
37 Shaun Rogers RC	1.25	3.00
38 Stephen Trejo RC	.75	2.00
39 Robert Ferguson RC	1.25	3.00
40 Bhawoh Jue RC	1.00	2.50
41 David Martin RC	.75	2.00
42 Idrees Bashir RC	.75	2.00
43 Dominic Rhodes RC	1.25	3.00
44 Reggie Wayne RC	2.50	6.00
45 Elvis Joseph RC	.75	2.00
46 Marcus Stroud RC	1.00	2.50
47 Derrick Blaylock RC	1.00	2.50
48 Snoop Minnis RC	.75	2.00
49 Chris Chambers RC	1.25	3.00
50 Travis Minor RC	1.00	2.50
51 Michael Bennett RC	1.00	2.50
52 Richard Seymour RC	1.25	3.00
53 Deuce McAllister RC	1.25	3.00
54 Onome Ojo RC	.75	2.00
55 Will Allen RC	1.25	3.00
56 Jesse Palmer RC	1.00	2.50
57 Will Peterson RC	1.00	2.50
58 Jamie Henderson RC	1.00	2.50
59 LaMont Jordan RC	1.25	3.00
60 Tory Woodbury RC	.75	2.00
61 Derrick Gibson RC	.75	2.00
62 Marques Tuiasosopo RC	1.00	2.50
63 Correll Buckhalter RC	1.25	3.00
64 A.J. Feeley RC	1.00	2.50
65 Freddie Mitchell RC	.75	2.00
66 Tim Baker RC	.75	2.00
67 Kendrell Bell RC	1.25	3.00
68 Casey Hampton RC	1.25	3.00
69 Adam Archuleta RC	1.00	2.50
70 Damione Lewis RC	1.00	2.50
71 Brandon Manumaleuna RC	1.00	2.50
72 Ryan Pickett RC	.75	2.00
73 Tommy Polley RC	.75	2.00
74 Drew Brees RC	8.00	20.00
75 Robert Carswell RC	.75	2.00
76 Tay Cody RC	.75	2.00
77 LaDainian Tomlinson RC	4.00	10.00
78 Nate Turner RC	.75	2.00
79 Kevan Barlow RC	1.00	2.50
80 Andre Carter RC	1.00	2.50
81 Vinny Sutherland RC	.75	2.00
82 Cedrick Wilson RC	1.00	2.50
83 Jamie Winborn RC	1.00	2.50
84 Alex Bannister RC	.75	2.00
85 Heath Evans RC	1.00	2.50
86 Ken Lucas RC	1.00	2.50
87 Koren Robinson RC	1.00	2.50
88 Jameel Cook RC	1.00	2.50
89 Dan Alexander RC	1.00	2.50
90 Drew Bennett RC	1.25	3.00
91 Eddie Berlin RC	.75	2.00
92 Andre Dyson RC	.75	2.00
93 Justin McCareins RC	1.00	2.50
94 Rod Gardner RC	1.00	2.50
95 Darnerien McCants RC	1.00	2.50
96 Sage Rosenfels RC	1.25	3.00
97 Justin Skaggs RC	.75	2.00
98 Fred Smoot RC	1.25	3.00
99 Stanley Stephens RC	.75	2.00
100 Kenny Watson RC	1.25	3.00

2001 Titanium Post Season Jerseys

ONE PER PACK		
1 David Boston	2.50	6.00
2 Chris Greisen	2.50	6.00
3 Thomas Jones	3.00	8.00
4 Rob Moore	2.50	6.00
5 Michael Pittman	3.00	8.00
6 Jake Plummer	3.00	8.00
7 Terance Mathis	2.50	6.00
8 Randall Cunningham	4.00	10.00
9 Jamal Lewis	4.00	10.00
10 Moe Williams	2.50	6.00
11 Kwame Cavil	2.50	6.00
12 Reggie Germany	2.50	6.00
13 Travis Henry	3.00	8.00
14 Rob Johnson	3.00	8.00
15 Eric Moulds	3.00	8.00
16 Dee Brown	2.50	6.00
17 Patrick Jeffers	2.50	6.00
18 Dan Morgan	3.00	8.00
19 Steve Smith	5.00	12.00
20 Chris Weinke	3.00	8.00
21 James Allen	2.50	6.00
22 Marlon Barnes	2.50	6.00
23 Macey Brooks	2.50	6.00
24 David Terrell	3.00	8.00
25 Anthony Thomas	4.00	10.00
26 Brian Urlacher	5.00	12.00
27 Corey Dillon	3.00	8.00
28 T.J. Houshmandzadeh	5.00	12.00
29 Chad Johnson	4.00	10.00
30 Curtis Keaton	2.50	6.00
31 Peter Warrick	3.00	8.00
32 Tim Couch	2.50	6.00
33 Rickey Dudley	2.50	6.00
34 Curtis Enis	2.50	6.00
35 James Jackson	2.50	6.00
36 Andre King	2.50	6.00
37 Quincy Morgan	3.00	8.00
38 Quincy Carter	3.00	8.00
39 Emmitt Smith	10.00	25.00
40 Mike Anderson	3.00	8.00
41 Olandis Gary	2.50	6.00
42 Brian Griese	3.00	8.00
43 Eddie Kennison	3.00	8.00
44 Ed McCaffrey	3.00	8.00
45 Brett Favre	12.00	30.00
46 Ahman Green	4.00	10.00
47 Marvin Harrison	4.00	10.00
48 Edgerrin James	4.00	10.00
49 Peyton Manning	10.00	25.00
50 Reggie Wayne	5.00	12.00
51 Mark Brunell	3.00	8.00
52 Fred Taylor	4.00	10.00
53 Trent Green	4.00	10.00
54 Chris Chambers	4.00	10.00
55 Josh Heupel	4.00	10.00
56 Ray Lucas	2.50	6.00
57 Travis Minor	3.00	8.00
58 Dedric Ward	2.50	6.00
59 Michael Bennett	3.00	8.00
60 Cris Carter	4.00	10.00
61 Daunte Culpepper	3.00	8.00
62 Randy Moss	4.00	10.00
63 Travis Prentice	2.50	6.00
64 David Patten	2.50	6.00
65 Deuce McAllister	4.00	10.00
66 Onome Ojo	2.50	6.00
67 Ricky Williams	4.00	10.00
68 Ron Dayne	3.00	8.00
69 Ike Hilliard	3.00	8.00
70 Wayne Chrebet	3.00	8.00
71 Curtis Martin	4.00	10.00
72 Tim Brown	4.00	10.00
73 Jerry Rice	8.00	20.00
74 Marques Tuiasosopo	3.00	8.00
75 Tyrone Wheatley	3.00	8.00
76 Donovan McNabb	4.00	10.00
77 Freddie Mitchell	2.50	6.00
78 Duce Staley	3.00	8.00
79 Adam Archuleta	3.00	8.00
80 Marshall Faulk	4.00	10.00
81 Kurt Warner	6.00	15.00
82 Aeneas Williams	3.00	8.00
83 Drew Brees	15.00	40.00
84 Tim Dwight	3.00	8.00
85 LaDainian Tomlinson	8.00	20.00
86 Jeff Garcia	3.00	8.00
87 Karsten Bailey	2.50	6.00
88 Alex Bannister	2.50	6.00
89 Bobby Engram	3.00	8.00
90 Matt Hasselbeck	4.00	10.00
91 Koren Robinson	3.00	8.00
92 Ricky Watters	3.00	8.00
93 Warrick Dunn	4.00	10.00
94 Keyshawn Johnson	3.00	8.00
95 Warren Sapp	3.00	8.00
96 Eddie George	4.00	10.00
97 Steve McNair	4.00	10.00
98 Michael Bates	2.50	6.00
99 Rod Gardner	3.00	8.00
100 Sage Rosenfels	4.00	10.00

2001 Titanium Post Season Jersey Patches

STATED PRINT RUN 8-386		
SERIAL #'d UNDER 15 NOT PRICED		
4 Rob Moore/28	8.00	20.00
5 Michael Pittman/45	8.00	20.00
6 Jake Plummer/30	10.00	25.00
7 Terance Mathis/60	6.00	15.00
8 Randall Cunningham/93	8.00	20.00
9 Jamal Lewis/62	10.00	25.00
10 Moe Williams/146	5.00	12.00
16 Dee Brown/203	4.00	10.00
17 Patrick Jeffers/77	5.00	12.00
18 Dan Morgan/50	8.00	20.00
19 Steve Smith/50	12.00	30.00
20 Chris Weinke/125	6.00	15.00
21 James Allen/129	5.00	12.00
22 Marlon Barnes/15	10.00	25.00
23 Macey Brooks/209	4.00	10.00
24 David Terrell/86	6.00	15.00
25 Anthony Thomas/75	8.00	20.00
27 Corey Dillon/161	5.00	12.00
28 T.J. Houshmandzadeh/116	10.00	25.00
29 Chad Johnson/111	8.00	20.00
30 Curtis Keaton/244	4.00	10.00
31 Peter Warrick/120	6.00	15.00
32 Tim Couch/113	5.00	12.00
33 Rickey Dudley/310	4.00	10.00
34 Curtis Enis/25	8.00	20.00
35 James Jackson/244	4.00	10.00
36 Andre King/224	4.00	10.00
37 Quincy Morgan/145	6.00	15.00
38 Quincy Carter/75	6.00	15.00
39 Emmitt Smith/75	20.00	50.00
40 Mike Anderson/116	6.00	15.00
41 Olandis Gary/75	5.00	12.00
42 Brian Griese/111	6.00	15.00
43 Eddie Kennison/50	8.00	20.00
44 Ed McCaffrey/23	10.00	25.00
45 Brett Favre/74	30.00	80.00
46 Ahman Green/41	10.00	25.00
47 Marvin Harrison/136	8.00	20.00
48 Edgerrin James/213	6.00	15.00
49 Peyton Manning/173	15.00	40.00
50 Reggie Wayne/75	10.00	25.00
51 Mark Brunell/50	8.00	20.00
52 Fred Taylor/24	12.00	30.00
53 Trent Green/50	10.00	25.00
54 Chris Chambers/75	8.00	20.00
55 Josh Heupel/117	8.00	20.00
57 Travis Minor/75	6.00	15.00
58 Dedric Ward/35	8.00	20.00
59 Michael Bennett/84	6.00	15.00
60 Cris Carter/100	8.00	20.00
61 Daunte Culpepper/71	8.00	20.00
62 Randy Moss/100	8.00	20.00
63 Travis Prentice/20	8.00	20.00
64 David Patten/69	6.00	15.00
65 Deuce McAllister/79	8.00	20.00
66 Onome Ojo/75	5.00	12.00
67 Ricky Williams/104	8.00	20.00
68 Ron Dayne/50	8.00	20.00
71 Curtis Martin/50	10.00	25.00
72 Tim Brown/50	10.00	25.00
73 Jerry Rice/50	20.00	50.00
74 Marques Tuiasosopo/158	5.00	12.00
76 Donovan McNabb/109	8.00	20.00
77 Freddie Mitchell/86	5.00	12.00
78 Duce Staley/173	5.00	12.00
79 Adam Archuleta/241	5.00	12.00
80 Marshall Faulk/84	8.00	20.00
81 Kurt Warner/115	12.00	30.00
82 Aeneas Williams/386	5.00	12.00
84 Tim Dwight/195	5.00	12.00
86 Jeff Garcia/210	5.00	12.00
87 Karsten Bailey/50	6.00	15.00
88 Alex Bannister/75	5.00	12.00
89 Bobby Engram/64	8.00	20.00
90 Matt Hasselbeck/15	15.00	40.00
91 Koren Robinson/87	6.00	15.00
93 Warrick Dunn/219	6.00	15.00
94 Keyshawn Johnson/50	8.00	20.00
95 Warren Sapp/219	5.00	12.00
96 Eddie George/87	8.00	20.00
97 Steve McNair/98	8.00	20.00
98 Michael Bates/127	5.00	12.00

2002 Titanium Post Season

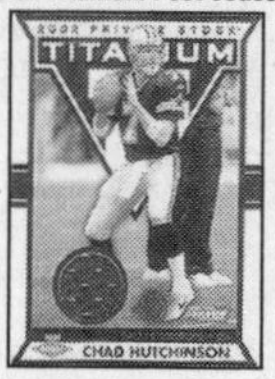

Released in late-January 2003, this set is composed of 50 rookies, 28 rookie jerseys, and 47 veteran jerseys. The jerseys were serial #'d to 435, and the rookies were serial #'d to 699.

1-50 ROOKIE PRINT RUN 699		
1 Damien Anderson RC	1.25	3.00
2 Preston Parsons RC	1.25	3.00
3 T.J. Duckett RC	2.00	5.00
4 Kurt Kittner RC	1.25	3.00
5 Javin Hunter RC	1.25	3.00
6 Ed Reed RC	8.00	20.00
7 Anthony Weaver RC	1.25	3.00
8 Coy Wire RC	1.50	4.00
9 Randy Fasani RC	1.50	4.00
10 Matt Schobel RC	2.00	5.00
11 Derek Ross RC	1.50	4.00
12 Chris Cash RC	1.25	3.00
13 Najeh Davenport RC	2.00	5.00
14 Tony Fisher RC	1.50	4.00
15 Craig Nall RC	1.50	4.00
16 Dwight Freeney RC	2.50	6.00
17 Larry Tripplett RC	1.25	3.00
18 Ricky Williams RC	1.50	4.00
19 Akin Ayodele RC	1.50	4.00
20 John Henderson RC	1.50	4.00
21 Randy McMichael RC	2.00	5.00
22 Shaun Hill RC	2.50	6.00
23 Deion Branch RC	2.00	5.00
24 Rohan Davey RC	2.00	5.00
25 David Givens RC	2.00	5.00
26 Daniel Graham RC	1.50	4.00
27 Charles Grant RC	2.00	5.00
28 J.T. O'Sullivan RC	1.50	4.00
29 Daryl Jones RC	1.25	3.00
30 Jeremy Shockey RC	3.00	8.00
31 Charles Stackhouse RC	1.25	3.00
32 Phillip Buchanon RC	2.00	5.00
33 Napoleon Harris RC	1.50	4.00
34 Larry Foote RC	3.00	8.00
35 Lee Mays RC	1.25	3.00
36 Travis Fisher RC	1.50	4.00
37 Robert Thomas RC	1.25	3.00
38 Seth Burford RC	1.25	3.00
39 Quentin Jammer RC	2.00	5.00
40 Ben Leber RC	1.25	3.00
41 Josh Norman RC	1.25	3.00
42 Brandon Doman RC	1.25	3.00
43 Jeff Kelly RC	1.25	3.00
44 Jerramy Stevens RC	2.00	5.00
45 Travis Stephens RC	1.25	3.00
46 Carlos Hall RC	1.25	3.00
47 Darrell Hill RC	1.25	3.00
48 John Simon RC	1.25	3.00
49 Tank Williams RC	1.50	4.00
50 Rock Cartwright RC	2.00	5.00
51 Josh McCown JSY RC	4.00	10.00
52 Ron Johnson JSY RC	3.00	8.00
53 Josh Reed JSY RC	3.00	8.00
54 DeShaun Foster JSY RC	4.00	10.00
55 Julius Peppers JSY RC	8.00	20.00
56 Andre Davis JSY RC	3.00	8.00
57 William Green JSY RC	3.00	8.00
58 Antonio Bryant JSY RC	4.00	10.00
59 Chad Hutchinson JSY RC	2.50	6.00
60 Roy Williams JSY RC	4.00	10.00
61 Ashley Lelie JSY RC	3.00	8.00
62 Clinton Portis JSY RC	5.00	12.00
63 Joey Harrington JSY RC	4.00	10.00
64 Javon Walker JSY RC	4.00	10.00
65 David Carr JSY RC	4.00	10.00
66 Jabar Gaffney JSY RC	4.00	10.00
67 Jonathan Wells JSY RC	4.00	10.00
68 David Garrard JSY RC	5.00	12.00
69 Donte Stallworth JSY RC	4.00	10.00
70 Tim Carter JSY RC	3.00	8.00
71 Brian Westbrook JSY RC	6.00	15.00
72 Antwaan Randle El JSY RC	4.00	10.00
73 Lamar Gordon JSY RC	3.00	8.00
74 Reche Caldwell JSY RC	4.00	10.00
75 Maurice Morris JSY RC	3.00	8.00
76 Ladell Betts JSY RC	4.00	10.00
77 Patrick Ramsey JSY RC	4.00	10.00
78 Cliff Russell JSY RC	2.50	6.00
79 David Boston JSY	3.00	8.00
80 Jamal Lewis JSY	4.00	10.00
81 Drew Bledsoe JSY	5.00	12.00
82 Eric Moulds JSY	4.00	10.00
83 Anthony Thomas JSY	4.00	10.00
84 Brian Urlacher JSY	5.00	12.00
85 Corey Dillon JSY	4.00	10.00
86 Tim Couch JSY	3.00	8.00
87 Quincy Carter JSY	3.00	8.00
88 Emmitt Smith JSY	12.00	30.00
89 Terrell Davis JSY	5.00	12.00
90 Brian Griese JSY	4.00	10.00
91 Ed McCaffrey JSY	4.00	10.00
92 Brett Favre JSY	12.00	30.00
93 Terry Glenn JSY	4.00	10.00
94 Ahman Green JSY	4.00	10.00
95 Corey Bradford JSY	3.00	8.00
96 Marvin Harrison JSY	5.00	12.00
97 Edgerrin James JSY	4.00	10.00
98 Peyton Manning JSY	10.00	25.00
99 Fred Taylor JSY	4.00	10.00
100 Trent Green JSY	4.00	10.00
101 Priest Holmes JSY	5.00	12.00
102 Chris Chambers JSY	4.00	10.00
103 Ricky Williams JSY	4.00	10.00
104 Derrick Alexander JSY	3.00	8.00
105 Michael Bennett JSY	4.00	10.00
106 Randy Moss JSY	5.00	12.00
107 Aaron Brooks JSY	4.00	10.00
108 Deuce McAllister JSY	4.00	10.00
109 Tiki Barber JSY	5.00	12.00
110 Curtis Martin JSY	5.00	12.00
111 Tim Brown JSY	5.00	12.00
112 Duce Staley JSY	4.00	10.00
113 Jerome Bettis JSY	5.00	12.00
114 Kordell Stewart JSY	4.00	10.00
115 Isaac Bruce JSY	5.00	12.00
116 Marshall Faulk JSY	5.00	12.00
117 Torry Holt JSY	5.00	12.00
118 Kurt Warner JSY	5.00	12.00
119 Drew Brees JSY	8.00	20.00
120 LaDainian Tomlinson JSY	6.00	15.00
121 Jeff Garcia JSY	4.00	10.00
122 Terrell Owens JSY	5.00	12.00
123 Shaun Alexander JSY	4.00	10.00
124 Eddie George JSY	4.00	10.00
125 Steve McNair JSY	5.00	12.00

1961 Titans Jay Publishing

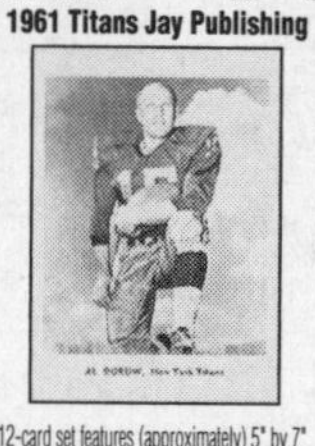

This 12-card set features (approximately) 5" by 7" black-and-white player photos of the New York Titans, one of the original AFL teams who later became the New York Jets. The photos show players in traditional poses with the quarterback preparing to throw, the runner heading downfield, and the defenseman ready for the tackle. The player's name and the team name appear in the wider bottom border. These cards were packaged 12 to a packet and originally sold for 25 cents through various Jay Publishing products. The backs are blank. The cards are unnumbered and checklisted below in alphabetical order.

COMPLETE SET (12)	60.00	120.00
1 Al Dorow	5.00	10.00
2 Larry Grantham	5.00	10.00
3 Mike Hagler	5.00	10.00
4 Mike Hudock	5.00	10.00
5 Bob Jewett	5.00	10.00
6 Jack Klotz	5.00	10.00
7 Don Maynard	15.00	30.00
8 John McMullan	5.00	10.00
9 Bob Mischak	5.00	10.00
10 Art Powell	6.00	12.00
11 Bob Reifsnyder	5.00	10.00
12 Sid Youngelman	5.00	10.00

1999 Titans Coca-Cola Kroger

This set was originally distributed as a perforated uncut sheet. Each card includes a color player photo on the cardfront with a brief player bio on the back. The cards were sponsored by Coca-Cola and Kroger. Each card is unnumbered and listed alphabetically below.

COMPLETE SET (16)	5.00	12.00
1 Blaine Bishop	.20	.50
2 Joe Bowden	.20	.50
3 Al Del Greco	.20	.50
4 Kevin Dyson	.40	1.00
5 Jeff Fisher CO	.20	.50
6 Eddie George	1.20	3.00
7 Craig Hentrich	.20	.50
8 Jevon Kearse	1.20	3.00
9 Bruce Matthews	.20	.50
10 Steve McNair	.80	2.00
11 Lorenzo Neal	.20	.50
12 Eddie Robinson	.20	.50
13 Samari Rolle	.20	.50
14 Yancey Thigpen	.30	.75
15 Denard Walker	.20	.50
16 Frank Wycheck	.30	.75

2006 Titans Topps

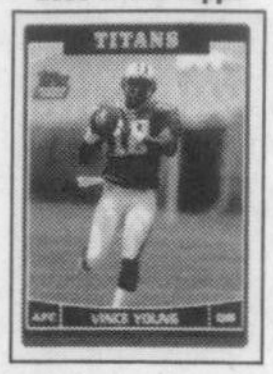

COMPLETE SET (12)	5.00	8.00
TEN1 Chris Brown	.20	.50
TEN2 Drew Bennett	.25	.60
TEN3 David Givens	.25	.60
TEN4 Courtney Roby	.20	.50
TEN5 Erron Kinney	.20	.50
TEN6 Adam Jones	.20	.50
TEN7 Steve McNair	.25	.60
TEN8 Billy Volek	.20	.50
TEN9 Kyle Vanden Bosch	.20	.50
TEN10 Travis Henry	.20	.50
TEN11 Vince Young	2.00	5.00
TEN12 LenDale White	.50	1.25

2007 Titans Topps

COMPLETE SET (12)	2.50	5.00
1 LenDale White	.25	.60
2 Vince Young	.25	.60
3 Bo Scaife	.20	.50
4 Brandon Jones	.20	.50
5 Michael Griffin	.30	.75
6 David Givens	.20	.50
7 Ben Troupe	.20	.50
8 Keith Bulluck	.20	.50
9 Kyle Vanden Bosch	.20	.50
10 Chris Hope	.20	.50
11 Rob Bironas	.20	.50
12 Chris Henry	.20	.50

2008 Titans Topps

COMPLETE SET (12)	3.00	6.00
1 LenDale White	.25	.60
2 Alge Crumpler	.25	.60
3 Vince Young	.25	.60
4 Albert Haynesworth	.20	.50
5 Kyle Vanden Bosch	.20	.50
6 Keith Bulluck	.20	.50
7 Rob Bironas	.20	.50
8 Bo Scaife	.20	.50
9 Justin Gage	.20	.50
10 Roydell Williams	.20	.50
11 Chris Johnson	1.00	2.50
12 Lavelle Hawkins	.25	.60

2009 Titans Tennessean

These cards feature members of the 2009 Titans and were sponsored by The Tennessean newspaper (noted at the top of the card). Each is standard size with the addition of a perforated coupon attached below the card for a discount off a purchase at the Titans Pro Shop.

COMPLETE SET (6)	4.00	8.00
1 Keith Bulluck	.40	1.00
2 Kerry Collins	.50	1.25
3 Chris Johnson	1.00	2.50
4 Kevin Mawae	.40	1.00
5 Kyle Vanden Bosch	.50	1.25
6 Vince Young	.60	1.50

1995 Tombstone Pizza

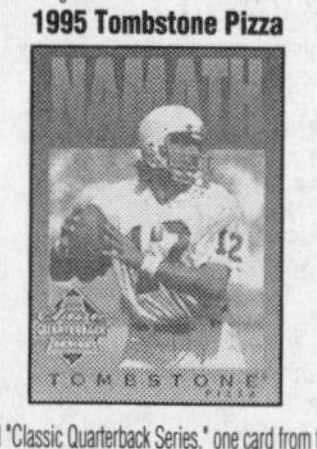

Titled "Classic Quarterback Series," one card from this 12-card standard-size set was inserted in specially-marked packages of Tombstone Pizza. Each of the quarterbacks autographed 10,000 cards for random insertion. The entire set was available through a mail-in offer for three Tombstone pizza logos plus 1.00. The fronts display color action cutouts framed by borders that fade from dark brown to orange. The player's last name is printed in large block lettering across the top. In addition to biography, career statistics, and a color headshot, the backs carry a "Classic Quarterback Quote."

COMPLETE SET (12)	10.00	25.00
1 Ken Anderson	.50	1.25
2 Terry Bradshaw	1.60	4.00
3 Len Dawson	.60	1.50
4 Dan Fouts	.60	1.50
5 Bob Griese	.80	2.00
6 Billy Kilmer	.50	1.25
7 Joe Namath	2.00	5.00
8 Jim Plunkett	.50	1.25
9 Ken Stabler	1.00	2.50
10 Bart Starr	1.20	3.00
11 Joe Theismann	.50	1.25
12 Johnny Unitas	1.20	3.00

1995 Tombstone Pizza Autographs

1 Ken Anderson	6.00	15.00
2 Terry Bradshaw	30.00	60.00
3 Len Dawson	10.00	25.00
4 Dan Fouts	12.00	30.00
5 Bob Griese	10.00	25.00
6 Billy Kilmer	6.00	15.00
7 Joe Namath	40.00	100.00
8 Jim Plunkett	6.00	15.00
9 Ken Stabler	15.00	40.00
10 Bart Starr	25.00	60.00
11 Joe Theismann	6.00	15.00
12 Johnny Unitas	100.00	175.00

1996 Tombstone Pizza Quarterback Club Caps

This "milk cap" set was produced for Tombstone Pizza by Pinnacle Brands. The caps were distributed as a complete player set of 14 in a punch-out type board measuring approximately 8-1/2" by 11" and as two-cap packs in selected Tombstone Pizza packages. The two-cap packs included one player cap and a team logo cap. Each cap has a 1-5/8" diameter and features a player in the Quarterback Club. A black plastic "slammer" was also included with the Player Board set.

COMP.PANEL SET (28)	8.80	22.00
COMP.PLAYER BOARD (14)	8.00	20.00
1 Steve Young	.50	1.25
2 Emmitt Smith	1.00	2.50
3 Junior Seau	.20	.50
4 Barry Sanders	1.20	3.00
5 Jerry Rice	.60	1.50
6 Dan Marino	1.20	3.00
7 Jim Kelly	.30	.75
8 Michael Irvin	.30	.75
9 Brett Favre	1.20	3.00
10 Marshall Faulk	.50	1.25
11 John Elway	1.20	3.00
12 Randall Cunningham	.30	.75
13 Drew Bledsoe	.60	1.50
14 Troy Aikman	.60	1.50
1T San Francisco 49ers	.07	.20
2T Dallas Cowboys	.07	.20
3T San Diego Chargers	.07	.20
4T Detroit Lions	.07	.20
5T San Francisco 49ers	.07	.20
6T Miami Dolphins	.07	.20
7T Buffalo Bills	.07	.20
8T Dallas Cowboys	.07	.20
9T Green Bay Packers	.07	.20
10T Indianapolis Colts	.07	.20
11T Denver Broncos	.07	.20
12T Philadelphia Eagles	.07	.20
13T New England Patriots	.07	.20
14T Dallas Cowboys	.07	.20

1983 Tonka Figurines

These small figurines were issued by Tonka in small blister packages as well as separate packaging with a Tonka die-cast truck. Each statue is a generic posable figure produced in the uniform of one of the 28-NFL teams with most being produced in a white and black player version. A sheet of numbers was also included with each statue so that any jersey number could be created.

1 Atlanta Falcons	25.00	40.00
2 Baltimore Colts	25.00	40.00
3 Buffalo Bills	30.00	50.00
4 Chicago Bears	30.00	50.00
5 Cincinnati Bengals	25.00	40.00
6 Cleveland Browns	30.00	50.00
7 Dallas Cowboys	40.00	75.00
8 Denver Broncos	30.00	50.00
9 Detroit Lions	25.00	40.00
10 Green Bay Packers	40.00	75.00
11 Houston Oilers	25.00	40.00
12 Kansas City Chiefs	30.00	50.00
13 Los Angeles Raiders	40.00	75.00
14 Los Angeles Rams	25.00	40.00
15 Miami Dolphins	30.00	50.00
16 Minnesota Vikings	25.00	40.00
17 New England Patriots	25.00	40.00
18 New Orleans Saints	25.00	40.00
19 New York Giants	30.00	50.00
20 New York Jets	30.00	50.00
21 Philadelphia Eagles	25.00	40.00
22 Pittsburgh Steelers	40.00	75.00
23 St. Louis Cardinals	25.00	40.00
24 San Diego Chargers	25.00	40.00
25 San Francisco 49ers	30.00	50.00
26 Seattle Seahawks	25.00	40.00
27 Tampa Bay Buccaneers	25.00	40.00
28 Washington Redskins	40.00	75.00

1994 Tony's Pizza QB Cubes

These "Cubes" were actually part of the backs of Tony's Pizza boxes. The collector was to to cut the cube from the box and fold it into a square. Each cube features one NFL QB Club member, an "In the Zone" moment from his career, and a small piece of a Troy Aikman picture. The full Aikman picture could be seen when all 6-cubes were used to complete the puzzle.

COMPLETE SET (6)	30.00	60.00
1 Troy Aikman	5.00	10.00
2 Randall Cunningham	2.50	5.00
3 John Elway	7.50	15.00
4 Jim Kelly	3.00	6.00
5 Dan Marino	10.00	20.00
6 Steve Young	4.00	8.00

1950 Topps Felt Backs

The 1950 Topps Felt Backs set contains 100-cards with each measuring approximately 7/8" by 1 7/16".

The cards are unnumbered and arranged in alphabetical order below. The cardbacks are made of felt and depict a college pennant. Twenty-five of the cards were produced with either a brown or yellow background on the cardfront. The yellow version is considered slightly more difficult to find. Sheets of 25 cards with the same color background are often found. It is also thought that there are two different versions of the wrapper with either the year 1949 or 1950 printed on them leading to the suggestion that the cards could have been issued over a 2-year period.

COMPLETE SET (100) 6,000.00 8,000.00
WRAPPER (1-CENT) 200.00 350.00
1 Lou Allen RC 35.00 60.00
2 Morris Bailey RC 35.00 60.00
3 George Bell RC 35.00 60.00
4 Lindy Berry HOR RC 35.00 60.00
5A Mike Boldin Brn RC 35.00 60.00
5B Mike Boldin Yel RC 50.00 80.00
6A Bernie Botula Brn RC 35.00 60.00
6B Bernie Botula Yel RC 50.00 80.00
7 Bob Bowlby RC 35.00 60.00
8 Bob Bucher RC 35.00 60.00
9A Al Burnett Brn RC 35.00 60.00
9B Al Burnett Yel RC 50.00 80.00
10 Don Burson RC 35.00 60.00
11 Paul Campbell 35.00 60.00
12 Herb Carey RC 35.00 60.00
13A Bimbo Cecconi Brn RC 35.00 60.00
13B Bimbo Cecconi Yel RC 50.00 80.00
14 Bill Chauncey RC 35.00 60.00
15 Dick Clark RC 35.00 60.00
16 Tom Coleman RC 35.00 60.00
17 Billy Conn RC 35.00 60.00
18 John Cox RC 35.00 60.00
19 Lou Creekmur RC 90.00 150.00
20 Richard Glen Davis RC 40.00 75.00
21 Warren Davis RC 35.00 60.00
22 Bob Deuber RC 35.00 60.00
23 Ray Dooney RC 35.00 60.00
24 Tom Dublinski RC 40.00 75.00
25 Jeff Fleischman RC 35.00 60.00
26 Jack Friedland RC 35.00 60.00
27 Bob Fuchs RC 35.00 60.00
28 Arnold Galiffa RC 40.00 75.00
29 Dick Gilman RC 35.00 60.00
30A Frank Gitschier Brn RC 35.00 60.00
30B Frank Gitschier Yel RC 50.00 80.00
31 Gene Glick 35.00 60.00
32 Bill Gregus RC 35.00 60.00
33 Harold Hagan RC 35.00 60.00
34 Charles Hall RC 35.00 60.00
35A Leon Hart Brown 75.00 125.00
35B Leon Hart Yellow 125.00 200.00
36A Bob Hester Brn RC 35.00 60.00
36B Bob Hester Yel RC 50.00 80.00
37 George Hughes RC 35.00 60.00
38 Levi Jackson 40.00 75.00
39A Jackie Jensen Brown 125.00 200.00
39B Jackie Jensen Yellow 150.00 250.00
40 Charlie Justice 90.00 150.00
41 Gary Kerkorian RC 35.00 60.00
42 Bernie Krueger RC 35.00 60.00
43 Bill Kuhn RC 35.00 60.00
44 Dean Laun RC 35.00 60.00
45 Chet Leach RC 35.00 60.00
46A Bobby Lee Brn RC 35.00 60.00
46B Bobby Lee Yel RC 50.00 80.00
47 Roger Lehew RC 35.00 60.00
48 Glenn Lippman RC 35.00 60.00
49 Melvin Lyle RC 35.00 60.00
50 Len Makowski RC 35.00 60.00
51A Al Malekoff Brn RC 35.00 60.00
51B Al Malekoff Yel RC 50.00 80.00
52A Jim Martin Brown 40.00 75.00
52B Jim Martin Yellow 60.00 100.00
53 Frank Mataya RC 35.00 60.00
54A Ray Mathews Brown RC 40.00 75.00
54B Ray Mathews Yellow RC 60.00 100.00
55A Dick McKissack Brn RC 35.00 60.00
55B Dick McKissack Yel RC 50.00 80.00
56 Frank Miller RC 35.00 60.00
57A John Miller Brn RC 35.00 60.00
57B John Miller Yel RC 50.00 80.00
58 Ed Modzelewski RC 40.00 75.00
59 Don Mouser RC 35.00 60.00
60 James Murphy RC 35.00 60.00
61A Ray Nagle Brn RC 35.00 60.00
61B Ray Nagle Yel RC 50.00 80.00
62 Leo Nomellini 200.00 350.00
63 James O'Day RC 35.00 60.00
64 Joe Paterno RC 1,200.00 2,000.00
65 Andy Pavich RC 35.00 60.00
66A Pete Perini Brn RC 35.00 60.00
66B Pete Perini Yellow 50.00 80.00
67 Jim Powers RC 35.00 60.00
68 Dave Rakestraw RC 35.00 60.00
69 Herb Rich RC 35.00 60.00
70 Fran Rogel RC 35.00 60.00
71A Darrell Royal Brown RC 250.00 400.00
71B Darrell Royal Yellow RC 300.00 500.00
72 Steve Sawle RC 35.00 60.00
73 Nick Sebek RC 35.00 60.00
74 Herb Seidell RC 35.00 60.00
75A Charles Shaw Brn RC 35.00 60.00
75B Charles Shaw Yel RC 50.00 80.00
76A Emil Sitko Brown RC 40.00 75.00
76B Emil Sitko Yellow RC 50.00 80.00
77 Butch Songin RC 40.00 75.00
78A Mariano Stalloni Brn RC 35.00 60.00
78B Mariano Stalloni Yel RC 50.00 80.00
79 Ernie Stautner RC 175.00 300.00
80 Don Stehley RC 35.00 60.00
81 Gil Stevenson RC 35.00 60.00
82 Bishop Strickland RC 35.00 60.00
83 Harry Szulborski 35.00 60.00
84A Wally Teninga Brn RC 35.00 60.00
84B Wally Teninga Yel RC 50.00 80.00
85 Clayton Tonnemaker 35.00 60.00
86A Deacon Dan Towler RC 100.00 175.00
Brown
86B Deacon Dan Towler RC 150.00 250.00
Yellow
87A Bert Turek Brn RC 35.00 60.00
87B Bert Turek Yel RC 50.00 80.00
88 Harry Ulinski 35.00 60.00
89 Leon Van Billingham RC 35.00 60.00
90 Langdon Viracola RC 35.00 60.00
91 Leo Wagner RC 35.00 60.00
92A Doak Walker Brown 250.00 400.00
92B Doak Walker Yellow 300.00 500.00
93 Jim Ward RC 35.00 60.00
94 Art Weiner 35.00 60.00
95 Dick Weiss RC 35.00 60.00
96 Froggie Williams RC 35.00 60.00
97 Robert Wilson RC 35.00 60.00
98 Roger Red Wilson RC 35.00 60.00
99 Carl Wren RC 35.00 60.00
100A Pete Zinaich Brn RC 35.00 60.00
100B Pete Zinaich Yel RC 50.00 80.00

1951 Topps Magic

The 1951 Topps Magic football set was Topps' second major college football issue and featured 75 different players. The cards measure approximately 2 1/16" by 2 15/16" and were produced with a perforated edge along the bottom. Two different distinct perforation configurations have been found - one with a very tight pattern of dimples and the other with the dimples roughly 3/16" apart. The tight pattern version are usually found slightly diamond cut. Despite the perforation, the cards were issued as single cards and not as pairs in 1951. The fronts contain color portraits with the player's name, position and team nickname in a black box at the bottom. The backs contain a brief write-up, a black and white photo of the player's college or university within a 'scratch-off' section (unscratched cards still show the silver substance) which gives the answer to a football quiz. Cards with the scratch-off back intact are valued at 50 percent more than the prices listed below. Rookie Cards in this set include Marion Campbell, Vic Janowicz, Babe Parilli, Bert Rechichar, Bill Wade and George Young.

COMPLETE SET (75) 800.00 1,200.00
*BACK UNSCRATCHED: 1.5X TO 2.5X
WRAPPER (1-CENT) 150.00 200.00
WRAPPER (5-CENT) 250.00 300.00
1 Jimmy Monahan RC 15.00 30.00
2 Bill Wade RC 30.00 50.00
3 Bill Reichardt RC 10.00 18.00
4 Babe Parilli RC 30.00 50.00
5 Billie Burkhalter RC 10.00 18.00
6 Ed Weber RC 10.00 18.00
7 Tom Scott RC 15.00 25.00
8 Frank Guthridge RC 10.00 18.00
9 John Karras 10.00 18.00
10 Vic Janowicz RC 100.00 175.00
11 Lloyd Hill RC 10.00 18.00
12 Jim Weatherall RC 15.00 25.00
13 Howard Hansen RC 10.00 18.00
14 Lou D'Achille RC 10.00 18.00
15 Johnny Turco RC 10.00 10.00
16 Jerrell Price RC 10.00 18.00
17 John Coatta RC 10.00 18.00
18 Bruce Patton RC 10.00 18.00
19 Marion Campbell RC 20.00 35.00
20 Blaine Earon RC 10.00 18.00
21 Dewey McConnell RC 10.00 18.00
22 Ray Beck RC 10.00 18.00
23 Jim Prewett RC 10.00 18.00
24 Bob Steele RC 10.00 18.00
25 Art Betts RC 10.00 18.00
26 Walt Trillhaase RC 10.00 10.00
27 Gil Bartosh RC 10.00 18.00
28 Bob Bestwick RC 10.00 18.00
29 Tom Rushing RC 10.00 18.00
30 Bert Rechichar RC 20.00 35.00
31 Bill Owens RC 10.00 18.00
32 Mike Goggins RC 10.00 18.00
33 John Petitbon RC 10.00 18.00
34 Byron Townsend RC 10.00 18.00
35 Ed Rotticci RC 10.00 18.00
36 Steve Wadiak RC 10.00 18.00
37 Bobby Marlow RC 15.00 25.00
38 Bill Fuchs RC 10.00 18.00
39 Ralph Staub RC 10.00 18.00
40 Bill Vesprini RC 10.00 18.00
41 Zack Jordan RC 10.00 18.00
42 Bob Smith RC 15.00 25.00
43 Charles Hanson RC 10.00 18.00
44 Glenn Smith RC 10.00 18.00
45 Armand Kitto RC 10.00 18.00
46 Vinnie Drake RC 10.00 18.00
47 Bill Putich RC 10.00 18.00
48 George Young RC 30.00 50.00
49 Don McRae RC 10.00 18.00
50 Frank Smith RC 10.00 18.00
51 Dick Hightower RC 10.00 18.00
52 Clyde Pickard RC 10.00 18.00
53 Bob Reynolds RC 15.00 25.00
54 Dick Gregory RC 10.00 18.00
55 Dale Samuels RC 10.00 18.00
56 Gale Galloway RC 10.00 18.00
57 Vic Pujo RC 10.00 18.00
58 Dave Waters RC 10.00 18.00
59 Joe Ernest RC 10.00 18.00
60 Elmer Costa RC 10.00 18.00
61 Nick Liotta RC 10.00 18.00
62 John Dottley RC 10.00 18.00
63 Hi Faubion RC 10.00 18.00
64 David Harr RC 10.00 18.00
65 Bill Matthews RC 10.00 18.00
66 Carroll McDonald RC 10.00 18.00
67 Dick Dewing RC 10.00 18.00
68 Joe Johnson RB RC 10.00 18.00
69 Arnold Burwitz RC 10.00 18.00
70 Ed Dobrowolski RC 10.00 18.00
71 Joe Dudeck RC 10.00 18.00
72 Johnny Bright RC 15.00 25.00
73 Harold Loehlein RC 10.00 18.00
74 Lawrence Hairston RC 10.00 18.00
75 Bob Carey RC 15.00 25.00

1955 Topps All American

Issued in one-card penny packs, nine-card nickel packs as well as 22-card cello packs, the 1955 Topps All-American set features 100-cards of college football greats from years past. The cards measure approximately 2 5/8" by 3 5/8". Card fronts contain a color player photo superimposed over a black and white action photo. The player's college logo is in one upper corner and an All-American logo is at the bottom with the player's name and position. The backs contain collegiate highlights and a cartoon. There are many numbers which were printed in lesser supply. These short-printed cards are denoted in the checklist below by SP. The key Rookie Cards in this set are Doc Blanchard, Tommy Harmon, Don Hutson, Ernie Nevers and Amos Alonzo Stagg. The Four Horsemen (Notre Dame backfield in 1924), Knute Rockne, Jim Thorpe, Red Grange and former Supreme Court Justice Whizzer White are also key cards. Wrongbacks can be found on some cards with the Amos A. Stagg card seemingly the most common of those wrongbacks. They are not cataloged below as error cards.

COMPLETE SET (100) 2,800.00 3,800.00
WRAPPER (1-CENT) 250.00 400.00
WRAPPER (5-CENT) 200.00 350.00
1 Herman Hickman RC 65.00 125.00
2 John Kimbrough RC 10.00 18.00
3 Ed Weir RC 10.00 18.00
4 Erny Pinckert RC 10.00 18.00
5 Bobby Grayson RC 10.00 18.00
6 Nile Kinnick UER RC 75.00 135.00
Spelled Niles
7 Andy Bershak RC 10.00 18.00
8 George Cafego RC 10.00 18.00
9 Tom Hamilton SP RC 20.00 30.00
10 Bill Dudley 25.00 40.00
11 Bobby Dodd SP RC 20.00 30.00
12 Otto Graham 100.00 200.00
13 Aaron Rosenberg 10.00 18.00
14A Gaynell Tinsley ERR RC 50.00 100.00
(with Whizzer White bio)
14B Gaynell Tinsley COR RC 15.00 25.00
(correct bio)
15 Ed Kaw SP 20.00 30.00
16 Knute Rockne 175.00 275.00
17 Bob Reynolds 10.00 18.00
18 Pudge Heffelfinger SP RC 25.00 40.00
19 Bruce Smith 25.00 40.00
20 Sammy Baugh 125.00 200.00
21A W.White RC SP ERR 150.00 250.00
with Gaynell Tinsley bio
21B W.White RC SP COR 60.00 100.00
correct bio
22 Brick Muller RC 10.00 18.00
23 Dick Kazmaier RC 15.00 25.00
24 Ken Strong 30.00 50.00
25 Casimir Myslinski SP RC 20.00 30.00
26 Larry Kelley SP RC 25.00 40.00
27 Red Grange UER 200.00 300.00
Card says he was QB
should say halfback
28 Mel Hein SP RC 60.00 100.00
29 Leo Nomellini SP 50.00 80.00
30 Wes Fesler RC 10.00 18.00
31 George Sauer Sr. RC 15.00 25.00
32 Hank Foldberg RC 10.00 10.00
33 Bob Higgins RC 10.00 18.00
34 Davey O'Brien RC 30.00 50.00
35 Tom Harmon SP RC 60.00 100.00
36 Turk Edwards SP 35.00 60.00
37 Jim Thorpe 275.00 400.00
38 Amos A. Stagg RC 40.00 75.00
39 Jerome Holland RC 15.00 25.00
40 Donn Moomaw RC 10.00 18.00
41 Joseph Alexander SP RC 20.00 30.00
42 Eddie Tryon SP RC 25.00 40.00
43 George Savitsky RC 10.00 10.00
44 Ed Garbisch RC 10.00 18.00
45 Elmer Oliphant RC 10.00 18.00
46 Arnold Lassman RC 10.00 18.00
47 Bo McMillin RC 15.00 25.00
48 Ed Widseth RC 10.00 18.00
49 Don Gordon Zimmerman RC 10.00 18.00
50 Ken Kavanaugh 15.00 25.00
51 Duane Purvis SP RC 20.00 30.00
52 Johnny Lujack 50.00 90.00
53 John F. Green RC 10.00 18.00
54 Edwin Dooley SP RC 20.00 30.00
55 Frank Merritt SP RC 20.00 30.00
56 Ernie Nevers RC 75.00 125.00
57 Vic Hanson SP RC 20.00 30.00
58 Ed Franco RC 10.00 18.00
59 Doc Blanchard RC 30.00 50.00
60 Dan Hill RC 10.00 18.00
61 Charles Brickley SP RC 20.00 30.00
62 Harry Newman RC 10.00 18.00
63 Charlie Justice 20.00 35.00
64 Benny Friedman RC 20.00 35.00
65 Joe Donchess SP RC 20.00 30.00
66 Bruiser Kinard RC 20.00 35.00
67 Frankie Albert 15.00 25.00
68 Four Horsemen SP RC 325.00 500.00
Jim Crowley
Elmer Layden
Don Miller
Harry Stuhldreher
69 Frank Sinkwich RC 15.00 25.00
70 Bill Daddio RC 10.00 18.00
71 Bobby Wilson 10.00 18.00
72 Chub Peabody RC 10.00 18.00
73 Paul Governali RC 15.00 25.00
74 Gene McEver RC 10.00 18.00
75 Hugh Gallarneau RC 10.00 18.00
76 Angelo Bertelli RC 15.00 25.00
77 Bowden Wyatt SP RC 20.00 30.00
78 Jay Berwanger RC 20.00 35.00
79 Pug Lund RC 10.00 18.00
80 Bennie Oosterbaan RC 10.00 18.00
81 Cotton Warburton RC 10.00 18.00
82 Alex Wojciechowicz 20.00 35.00
83 Ted Coy SP RC 20.00 30.00
84 Ace Parker SP RC 30.00 50.00
85 Sid Luckman 60.00 120.00
86 Albie Booth SP RC 20.00 30.00
87 Adolph Schultz SP 20.00 30.00
88 Ralph Kercheval 10.00 18.00
89 Marshall Goldberg 18.00 30.00
90 Charlie O'Rourke RC 10.00 18.00
91 Bob Odell UER RC 10.00 18.00
Photo actually
Howard Odell
92 Biggie Munn RC 10.00 18.00
93 Willie Heston SP RC 25.00 40.00
94 Joe Bernard SP RC 25.00 40.00
95 Chris Cagle SP RC 25.00 40.00
96 Bill Hollenback SP 25.00 40.00
97 Don Hutson SP RC 150.00 225.00
98 Beattie Feathers SP 60.00 100.00
99 Don Whitmire SP RC 25.00 40.00
100 Fats Henry SP RC 100.00 200.00

1956 Topps

The 1956 set of 120 player cards marks Topps' first standard NFL football card set since acquiring Bowman. The cards measure 2 5/8" by 3 5/8" and were issued in one-card penny packs, nickel packs and 15-card cello packs. The card fronts have a player photo superimposed over a solid color background. The team logo is an upper corner with the player's name, team name and position grouped in a box toward the bottom of the photo. The card backs were printed in red and black on gray card stock. Statistical information from the immediate past season and career totals are given at the bottom. Players from the Washington Redskins and the Chicago Cardinals were apparently produced in lesser quantities, as they are more difficult to find compared to the other teams. Some veteran collectors believe that cards of members of the Baltimore Colts, Chicago Bears, and Cleveland Browns may also be slightly more difficult to find as well. An unnumbered checklist card and six contest cards were also issued along with this set, although in much lesser quantities. The contest cards have advertisements on both sides for Bazooka Bubble Gum. Both sides have orange-red and blue type on an off-white background. The fronts of the contest cards feature an offer to win one of three prizes (basketball, football, or autographed baseball glove) in the Bazooka Bubble Gum football contest, and the rules governing the contest are listed on the back. Any eligible contestant (not over 15 years old) who mailed in (before November 19th) the correct scores to the two NFL football games listed on the front of that particular card and includes five one-cent Bazooka Bubble Gum wrappers or one nickel Bazooka wrapper with the entry received a choice of one of the three above-mentioned prizes. The cards are either numbered (1-3) or lettered (A-C). Some dealers have doubted the existence of Contest Card C. Any proof of this card would be greatly appreciated. There also exists a three-card advertising panel consis

COMPLETE SET (120) 1,200.00 1,800.00
WRAPPER (1-CENT) 200.00 250.00
WRAPPER (5-CENT) 60.00 100.00
1 Johnny Carson SP 40.00 80.00
2 Gordy Soltau 3.50 6.00
3 Frank Varrichione 3.50 6.00
4 Eddie Bell 3.50 6.00
5 Alex Webster RC 7.50 15.00
6 Norm Van Brocklin 18.00 30.00
7 Green Bay Packers 15.00 25.00
Team Card
8 Lou Creekmur 7.50 15.00
9 Lou Groza 15.00 25.00
10 Tom Bienemann SP RC 15.00 25.00
11 George Blanda 30.00 50.00
12 Alan Ameche 6.00 12.00
13 Vic Janowicz SP 25.00 45.00
14 Dick Moegle 4.00 8.00
15 Fran Rogel 3.50 6.00
16 Harold Giancanelli 3.50 6.00
17 Emlen Tunnell 7.50 15.00
18 Tank Younger 6.00 12.00
19 Billy Howton 4.00 8.00
20 Jack Christiansen 7.50 15.00
21 Darrel Brewster 3.50 6.00
22 Chicago Cardinals SP 60.00 100.00
Team Card
23 Ed Brown 4.00 8.00
24 Joe Campanella 3.50 6.00
25 Leon Heath SP 15.00 25.00
26 San Francisco 49ers 10.00 18.00
Team Card
27 Dick Flanagan RC 3.50 6.00
28 Chuck Bednarik 15.00 25.00
29 Kyle Rote 6.00 12.00
30 Les Richter 4.00 8.00
31 Howard Ferguson 3.50 6.00
32 Dorne Dibble 3.50 6.00
33 Kenny Konz 3.50 6.00
34 Dave Mann SP RC 15.00 25.00
35 Rick Casares 6.00 12.00
36 Art Donovan 18.00 30.00
37 Chuck Drazenovich SP 15.00 25.00
38 Joe Arenas 3.50 6.00
39 Lynn Chandnois 3.50 6.00
40 Philadelphia Eagles 10.00 18.00
Team Card
41 Roosevelt Brown RC 25.00 40.00
42 Tom Fears 15.00 25.00
43 Gary Knafelc RC 3.50 6.00
44 Joe Schmidt RC 35.00 60.00
45 Cleveland Browns 10.00 18.00
Team Card UER
(Card back does not
credit the Browns with
being Champs in 1955)
46 Len Teeuws SP RC 15.00 25.00
47 Bill George RC 25.00 40.00
48 Baltimore Colts 10.00 18.00
Team Card
49 Eddie LeBaron SP 25.00 50.00
50 Hugh McElhenny 18.00 30.00
51 Ted Marchibroda 6.00 12.00
52 Adrian Burk 3.50 6.00
53 Frank Gifford 35.00 60.00
54 Charley Toogood 3.50 6.00
55 Tobin Rote 4.00 8.00
56 Bill Stits 3.50 6.00
57 Don Colo 3.50 6.00
58 Ollie Matson SP 35.00 60.00
59 Harlon Hill 4.00 8.00
60 Lenny Moore RC 75.00 125.00
61 Washington Redskins SP 50.00 90.00
Team Card
62 Billy Wilson 3.50 6.00
63 Pittsburgh Steelers 10.00 18.00
Team Card
64 Bob Pellegrini RC 3.50 6.00
65 Ken MacAfee 3.50 6.00
66 Willard Sherman RC 3.50 6.00
67 Roger Zatkoff 3.50 6.00
68 Dave Middleton RC 3.50 6.00
69 Ray Renfro 4.00 8.00
70 Don Stonesifer SP 15.00 25.00
71 Stan Jones RC 25.00 40.00
72 Jim Mutscheller RC 3.50 6.00
73 Volney Peters SP 15.00 25.00
74 Leo Nomellini 12.00 20.00
75 Ray Mathews 3.50 6.00
76 Dick Bielski 3.50 6.00
77 Charley Conerly 15.00 25.00
78 Elroy Hirsch 18.00 30.00
79 Bill Forester RC 4.00 8.00
80 Jim Doran RC 3.50 6.00
81 Fred Morrison 3.50 6.00
82 Jack Simmons SP 15.00 25.00
83 Bill McColl 3.50 6.00
84 Bert Rechichar 3.50 6.00
85 Joe Scudero SP RC 15.00 25.00
86 Y.A. Tittle UER 30.00 50.00
(misspelled Yelverton on back)
87 Ernie Stautner 12.00 20.00
88 Norm Willey 3.50 6.00
89 Bob Schnelker RC 3.50 6.00
90 Dan Towler 6.00 12.00
91 John Martinkovic 3.50 6.00
92 Detroit Lions 10.00 18.00
Team Card
93 George Ratterman 4.00 8.00
94 Chuck Ulrich SP 15.00 25.00
95 Bobby Watkins 3.50 6.00
96 Buddy Young 6.00 12.00
97 Billy Wells SP RC 15.00 25.00
98 Bob Toneff 3.50 6.00
99 Bill McPeak 3.50 6.00
100 Bobby Thomason 3.50 6.00
101 Roosevelt Grier RC 30.00 50.00
102 Ron Waller RC 3.50 6.00
103 Bobby Dillon 3.50 6.00
104 Leon Hart 6.00 12.00
105 Mike McCormack 7.50 15.00
106 John Olszewski SP 15.00 25.00
107 Bill Wightkin 3.50 6.00
108 George Shaw RC 4.00 8.00
109 Dale Atkeson SP 15.00 25.00
110 Joe Perry 15.00 25.00
111 Dale Dodrill 3.50 6.00
112 Tom Scott 3.50 6.00
113 New York Giants 10.00 18.00
Team Card
114 Los Angeles Rams 10.00 18.00
Team Card UER
(back incorrect, Rams
were not 1955 champs)
115 Al Carmichael 3.50 6.00
116 Bobby Layne 30.00 50.00
117 Ed Modzelewski 3.50 6.00
118 Lamar McHan RC SP 15.00 25.00
119 Chicago Bears 10.00 18.00
Team Card
120 Billy Vessels RC 20.00 40.00
AD1 Advertising Panel 500.00 800.00
Lou Groza
Don Colo
Darrel Brewster
(no player on back)
NNO Checklist Card SP 250.00 400.00
(unnumbered)
C1 Contest Card 45.00 80.00
Sunday, October 14
Colts vs. Packers
Cards vs. Redskins
C2 Contest Card 45.00 80.00
Sunday, October 14
Rams vs. Lions
Giants vs. Browns
C3 Contest Card 45.00 80.00
Sunday, October 14
Eagles vs. Steelers/49ers vs. Bears
CA Contest Card 50.00 90.00
Sunday, November 25
Bears vs. Giants
Rams vs. Colts
CB Contest Card 70.00 110.00
Sunday, November 25
Steelers vs. Cards/49ers vs. Eagles

1957 Topps

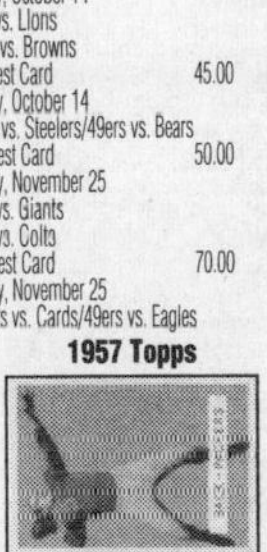

The 1957 Topps football set contains 154 standard-size cards of NFL players. Cards were issued in penny, nickel and cello packs. Horizontally designed fronts have a close-up photo (with player name) on the left and an in-action pose (with position and team name) to the right. Both have solid color backgrounds. The card backs were printed in red and black on gray card stock. Backs are also divided in two with statistical information on one side and a cartoon on the other. The Rookie Cards of Johnny Unitas, Bart Starr, and Paul Hornung are included in this set. Other notable Rookie Cards in this set are Raymond Berry, Dick "Night Train" Lane, Tommy McDonald and Earl Morrall. The second series (89-154) is generally more difficult to obtain than the first series. A number of cards (22) from the second series are much easier to find than the other 44, making those double prints (DP). It's thought that the John Unitas Rookie card is among the 22-DPs. An unnumbered checklist card was also issued with this set. The checklist card was printed in red, yellow, and blue or in red, white, and blue; neither variety currently is recognized as having any additional premium value above the price listed below. There also were produced several three-card advertising panels consisting of the card fronts of three players with ad copy on the reverse of the top two cards and a player's cardback at the bottom. The complete set price below refers to the 154 numbered cards minus the unnumbered checklist card.

COMPLETE SET (154) 1,600.00 2,200.00
WRAPPER (1-CENT) 30.00 50.00
WRAPPER (5-CENT) 50.00 75.00
1 Eddie LeBaron 30.00 50.00
2 Pete Retzlaff RC 7.50 15.00
3 Mike McCormack 6.00 12.00
4 Lou Baldacci RC 2.50 4.00
5 Gino Marchetti 10.00 20.00
6 Leo Nomellini 10.00 20.00
7 Bobby Watkins 2.50 4.00
8 Dave Middleton 2.50 4.00
9 Bobby Dillon 2.50 4.00
10 Les Richter 3.50 6.00
11 Roosevelt Brown 10.00 20.00
12 Lavern Torgeson RC 2.50 4.00
13 Dick Bielski 2.50 4.00
14 Pat Summerall 10.00 20.00
15 Jack Butler RC 6.00 15.00
16 John Henry Johnson 7.50 15.00
17 Art Spinney 2.50 4.00
18 Bob St. Clair 6.00 12.00
19 Perry Jeter RC 2.50 4.00
20 Lou Creekmur 6.00 12.00
21 Dave Hanner 3.50 6.00
22 Norm Van Brocklin 18.00 30.00
23 Don Chandler RC 5.00 10.00
24 Al Dorow 2.50 4.00
25 Tom Scott 2.50 4.00
26 Ollie Matson 12.00 20.00
27 Fran Rogel 2.50 4.00
28 Lou Groza 15.00 25.00
29 Billy Vessels 3.50 6.00
30 Y.A. Tittle 25.00 40.00
31 George Blanda 25.00 40.00
32 Bobby Layne 25.00 40.00
33 Billy Howton 3.50 6.00
34 Bill Wade 5.00 10.00
35 Emlen Tunnell 7.50 15.00
36 Leo Elter RC 2.50 4.00
37 Clarence Peaks RC 3.50 6.00
38 Don Stonesifer 2.50 4.00
39 George Tarasovic 2.50 4.00
40 Darrel Brewster 2.50 4.00
41 Bert Rechichar 2.50 4.00
42 Billy Wilson 2.50 4.00
43 Ed Brown 3.50 6.00
44 Gene Gedman RC 2.50 4.00
45 Gary Knafelc 2.50 4.00
46 Elroy Hirsch 18.00 30.00
47 Don Heinrich 3.50 6.00
48 Gene Brito 2.50 4.00
49 Chuck Bednarik 15.00 25.00
50 Dave Mann 2.50 4.00
51 Bill McPeak 2.50 4.00
52 Kenny Konz 2.50 4.00
53 Alan Ameche 5.00 10.00
54 Gordy Soltau 2.50 4.00
55 Rick Casares 3.50 6.00
56 Charlie Ane 2.50 4.00
57 Al Carmichael 2.50 4.00
58A Willard Sherman ERR 175.00 300.00
(no position or team on front)
58B Willard Sherman COR 2.50 4.00
58C Willard Sherman ERR 125.00 200.00
(no team on front)
59 Kyle Rote 5.00 10.00
60 Chuck Drazenovich 2.50 4.00
61 Bobby Walston 2.50 4.00
62 John Olszewski 2.50 4.00
63 Ray Mathews 2.50 4.00
64 Maurice Bassett 2.50 4.00
65 Art Donovan 15.00 25.00
66 Joe Arenas 2.50 4.00
67 Harlon Hill 3.50 6.00
68 Yale Lary 6.00 12.00
69 Bill Forester 3.50 6.00
70 Bob Boyd 2.50 4.00
71 Andy Robustelli 12.00 20.00
72 Sam Baker RC 3.50 6.00
73 Bob Pellegrini 2.50 4.00
74 Leo Sanford 2.50 4.00
75 Sid Watson RC 2.50 4.00
76 Ray Renfro 3.50 6.00
77 Carl Taseff 2.50 4.00
78 Clyde Conner RC 2.50 4.00
79 J.C. Caroline RC 2.50 4.00
80 Howard Cassady RC 7.50 15.00
81 Tobin Rote 3.50 6.00
82 Ron Waller 2.50 4.00
83 Jim Patton RC 3.50 6.00
84 Volney Peters 2.50 4.00
85 Dick Lane RC 35.00 60.00
86 Royce Womble 2.50 4.00
87 Duane Putnam RC 3.50 6.00
88 Frank Gifford 30.00 60.00
89 Steve Meilinger 5.00 10.00
90 Buck Lansford 5.00 10.00
91 Lindon Crow DP 4.00 8.00
92 Ernie Stautner DP 12.50 25.00
93 Preston Carpenter DP RC 4.00 8.00
94 Raymond Berry RC 75.00 150.00
95 Hugh McElhenny 18.00 30.00
96 Stan Jones 15.00 25.00
97 Dorne Dibble 5.00 10.00
98 Joe Scudero DP 4.00 8.00
99 Eddie Bell 5.00 10.00
100 Joe Childress DP RC 4.00 8.00
101 Elbert Nickel 6.00 12.00
102 Walt Michaels 6.00 12.00
103 Jim Mutscheller DP 4.00 8.00
104 Earl Morrall RC 35.00 60.00
105 Larry Strickland RC 5.00 10.00
106 Jack Christiansen 7.50 15.00
107 Fred Cone DP 4.00 8.00
108 Bud McFadin RC 6.00 12.00
109 Charley Conerly 18.00 30.00
110 Tom Runnels DP RC 4.00 8.00
111 Ken Keller DP RC 4.00 8.00
112 James Root RC 5.00 10.00
113 Ted Marchibroda DP 5.00 10.00
114 Don Paul 5.00 10.00
115 George Shaw 6.00 12.00
116 Dick Moegle 6.00 12.00
117 Don Bingham 5.00 10.00
118 Leon Hart 7.50 15.00
119 Bart Starr RC 350.00 500.00
120 Paul Miller DP RC 4.00 8.00
121 Alex Webster 6.00 12.00
122 Ray Wietecha DP 4.00 8.00
123 Johnny Carson 5.00 10.00
124 Tommy McDonald DP RC 18.00 30.00
125 Jerry Tubbs RC 6.00 12.00
126 Jack Scarbath 5.00 10.00
127 Ed Modzelewski DP 4.00 8.00
128 Lenny Moore 30.00 50.00
129 Joe Perry DP 15.00 25.00
130 Bill Wightkin 5.00 10.00
131 Jim Doran 5.00 10.00
132 Howard Ferguson UER 5.00 10.00
(Name misspelled Furgeson on front)
133 Tom Wilson RC 5.00 10.00
134 Dick James RC 5.00 10.00
135 Jimmy Harris RC 5.00 10.00
136 Chuck Ulrich 5.00 10.00
137 Lynn Chandnois 5.00 10.00
138 Johnny Unitas DP RC 300.00 450.00
139 Jim Ridlon DP RC 4.00 8.00
140 Zeke Bratkowski DP 5.00 10.00
141 Ray Krouse 5.00 10.00
142 John Martinkovic 5.00 10.00
143 Jim Cason DP RC 4.00 8.00
144 Ken MacAfee 5.00 10.00
145 Sid Youngelman RC 6.00 12.00
146 Paul Larson RC 5.00 10.00
147 Len Ford 18.00 30.00
148 Bob Toneff DP 4.00 8.00
149 Ronnie Knox DP RC 4.00 8.00
150 Jim David RC 6.00 12.00
151 Paul Hornung RC 250.00 400.00
152 Tank Younger 7.50 15.00
153 Bill Svoboda DP RC 4.00 8.00
154 Fred Morrison 35.00 70.00
AD1 Advertising Panel 400.00 700.00
Al Dorow
Harlon Hill
Bert Rechichar
(Ollie Matson back)
AD2 Advertising Panel 400.00 700.00
Bobby Watkins
Gino Marchetti
Clarence Peaks
(Ollie Matson back)
AD3 Advertising Panel 400.00 700.00
Mike McCormack
Leo Elter
J.C. Caroline
(Elroy Hirsch back)
CL1 Checklist Card SP 500.00 750.00
(Bazooka back)
CL2 Checklist Card SP 500.00 750.00
(Twin Blony back)

1958 Topps

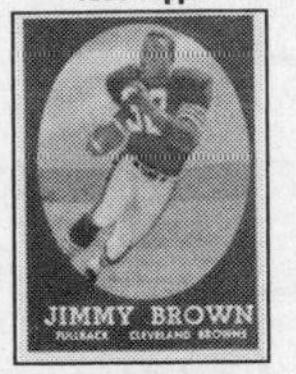

The 1958 Topps set of 132 standard-size cards contains NFL players. After a one-year interruption, team cards returned to the Topps lineup. The cards were issued in penny, nickel and cello packs. Card fronts have an oval player photo surrounded by a solid color that varies according to team. The player's name, position and team are at the bottom. The backs are easily distinguished from other years, as they are printed in bright red ink on white stock. The right-hand side has a trivia question with which the answer could be obtained by rubbing with a coin over the blank space. The left side has stats and highlights. The key Rookie Cards in this set are Jim Brown and Sonny Jurgensen. Topps also randomly inserted in packs a card with the words "Free Felt Initial" across the top. The horizontally oriented front pictures a boy in a red shirt and a girl in a blue shirt, with a large yellow "L" and "A" respectively on each of their shirts. The card back indicates an initial could be obtained by sending in three Bazooka or Blony wrappers and a self-addressed stamped envelope with the initial of choice printed on the front and back of the envelope. According to a note in the December 15th, 1958 issue of Sports Illustrated, 110 million cards were produced for this issue.

COMPLETE SET (132) 850.00 1,250.00
WRAPPER (1-CENT) 35.00 60.00
WRAPPER (5-CENT) 75.00 125.00
1 Gene Filipski RC 7.50 15.00
2 Bobby Layne 20.00 35.00
3 Joe Schmidt 6.00 12.00
4 Bill Barnes RC 2.00 4.00
5 Milt Plum RC 5.00 10.00
6 Billy Howton UER 2.50 5.00
(Misspelled Billie
on card front)
7 Howard Cassady 2.50 5.00
8 Jim Dooley 2.00 4.00
9 Cleveland Browns 3.00 6.00
Team Card
10 Lenny Moore 15.00 30.00
11 Darrel Brewster 2.00 4.00
12 Alan Ameche 4.00 8.00
13 Jim David 2.00 4.00
14 Jim Mutscheller 2.00 4.00
15 Andy Robustelli UER 5.00 10.00
(Never played for
San Francisco)
16 Gino Marchetti 6.00 12.00
17 Ray Renfro 2.50 5.00
18 Yale Lary 4.00 8.00
19 Gary Glick RC 2.00 4.00
20 Jon Arnett RC 4.00 8.00
21 Bob Boyd 2.00 4.00
22 John Unitas UER 75.00 135.00
(College: Pittsburgh
should be Louisville)
23 Zeke Bratkowski 2.50 5.00
24 Sid Youngelman UER 2.00 4.00
(Misspelled Youngleman
on card back)
25 Leo Elter 2.00 4.00
26 Kenny Konz 2.00 4.00
27 Washington Redskins 3.00 6.00
Team Card
28 Carl Brettschneider UER RC 2.00 4.00
(Misspelled on back
as Brettschnieder)
29 Chicago Bears 3.00 6.00
Team Card
30 Alex Webster 2.50 5.00
31 Al Carmichael 2.00 4.00
32 Bobby Dillon 2.00 4.00
33 Steve Meilinger 2.00 4.00
34 Sam Baker 2.00 4.00
35 Chuck Bednarik UER 7.50 15.00
(Misspelled Bednarick
on card back)
36 Bert Vic Zucco RC 2.00 4.00
37 George Tarasovic 2.00 4.00
38 Bill Wade 4.00 8.00
39 Dick Stanfel 2.50 5.00
40 Jerry Norton 2.00 4.00
41 San Francisco 49ers 3.00 6.00
Team Card
42 Emlen Tunnell 5.00 10.00
43 Jim Doran 2.00 4.00
44 Ted Marchibroda 4.00 8.00
45 Chet Hanulak 2.00 4.00
46 Dale Dodrill 2.00 4.00
47 Johnny Carson 2.00 4.00
48 Dick Deschaine RC 2.00 4.00
49 Billy Wells UER 2.00 4.00
(College should be
Michigan State)
50 Larry Morris RC 2.00 4.00
51 Jack McClairen RC 2.00 4.00
52 Lou Groza 7.50 15.00
53 Rick Casares 2.50 5.00
54 Don Chandler 2.50 5.00
55 Duane Putnam 2.00 4.00
56 Gary Knafelc 2.00 4.00
57 Earl Morrall UER 5.00 10.00
(Misspelled Morall
on card back)
58 Ron Kramer RC 2.50 5.00
59 Mike McCormack 4.00 8.00
60 Gern Nagler 2.00 4.00

61 New York Giants 3.00 6.00
Team Card
62 Jim Brown RC 350.00 500.00
63 Joe Marconi RC UER 2.00 4.00
(Avg. gain should be 4.4)
64 R.C. Owens RC UER 2.50 5.00
(Photo actually Don Owens)
65 Jimmy Carr RC 2.50 5.00
66 Bart Starr UER 90.00 150.00
(Life and year
stats reversed)
67 Tom Wilson 2.00 4.00
68 Lamar McHan 2.00 4.00
69 Chicago Cardinals 3.00 6.00
Team Card
70 Jack Christiansen 4.00 8.00
71 Don McIlhenny RC 2.00 4.00
72 Ron Waller 2.00 4.00
73 Frank Gifford 25.00 50.00
74 Bert Rechichar 2.00 4.00
75 John Henry Johnson 5.00 10.00
76 Jack Butler 4.00 8.00
77 Frank Varrichione 2.00 4.00
78 Ray Mathews 2.00 4.00
79 Marv Matuszak UER RC 2.00 4.00
(Misspelled Matuzsak
on card front)
80 Harlon Hill UER 2.00 4.00
(Lifetime yards and
Avg. gain incorrect)
81 Lou Creekmur 4.00 8.00
82 Woodley Lewis UER 2.00 4.00
(misspelled Woodly on
front; end on front
and halfback on back)
83 Don Heinrich 2.00 4.00
84 Charley Conerly UER 7.50 15.00
(Misspelled Charlie
on card back)
85 Los Angeles Rams 3.00 6.00
Team Card
86 Y.A. Tittle 18.00 30.00
87 Bobby Walston 2.00 4.00
88 Earl Putman RC 2.00 4.00
89 Leo Nomellini 7.50 15.00
90 Sonny Jurgensen RC 60.00 100.00
91 Don Paul 2.00 4.00
92 Paige Cothren RC 2.00 4.00
93 Joe Perry 7.50 15.00
94 Tobin Rote 2.50 5.00
95 Billy Wilson 2.00 4.00
96 Green Bay Packers 7.50 15.00
Team Card
97 Lavern Torgeson 2.00 4.00
98 Milt Davis RC 2.00 4.00
99 Larry Strickland 2.00 4.00
100 Matt Hazeltine RC 2.50 5.00
101 Walt Yowarsky RC 2.00 4.00
102 Roosevelt Brown 4.00 8.00
103 Jim Ringo 5.00 10.00
104 Joe Krupa RC 2.00 4.00
105 Les Richter 2.50 5.00
106 Art Donovan 12.00 20.00
107 John Olszewski 2.00 4.00
108 Ken Keller 2.00 4.00
109 Philadelphia Eagles 3.00 6.00
Team Card
110 Baltimore Colts 3.00 6.00
Team Card
111 Dick Bielski 2.00 4.00
112 Eddie LeBaron 4.00 8.00
113 Gene Brito 2.00 4.00
114 Willie Galimore RC 5.00 10.00
115 Detroit Lions 3.00 6.00
Team Card
116 Pittsburgh Steelers 3.00 6.00
Team Card
117 L.G. Dupre 2.50 5.00
118 Babe Parilli 2.50 5.00
119 Bill George 5.00 10.00
120 Raymond Berry 25.00 40.00
121 Jim Podoley UER 2.00 4.00
(Photo actually
Volney Peters;
Podoly in cartoon)
122 Hugh McElhenny 7.50 15.00
123 Ed Brown 2.50 5.00
124 Dick Moegle 2.50 5.00
125 Tom Scott 2.00 4.00
126 Tommy McDonald 6.00 12.00
127 Ollie Matson 10.00 20.00
128 Preston Carpenter 2.00 4.00
129 George Blanda 18.00 30.00
130 Gordy Soltau 2.00 4.00
131 Dick Nolan RC 2.50 5.00
132 Don Bosseler RC 10.00 20.00
NNO Free Felt Initial Card 15.00 25.00

1959 Topps

The 1959 Topps football set contains 176 standard-size cards which were issued in two series of 88. The cards were issued in penny, nickel and cello packs. The cello packs contained 12 cards at a cost of 10 cents per and were packed 36 to a box. Card fronts contain a player photo over a solid background. Beneath the photo, is the player's name in red and blue letters. Beneath the name are the player's position and team. The card backs were printed in gray on white card stock. Statistical information from the immediate past season and career totals are given on the reverse. Card backs include a scratch-off quiz. Team cards (with checklist backs) as well as team pennant cards are included in the set. The key Rookie Cards in this set are Sam Huff, Alex Karras, Jerry Kramer, Bobby Mitchell, Jim Parker and Jim Taylor. The Taylor card was supposed to portray the great Packers running back. Instead, the card depicts the Cardinals linebacker.

COMPLETE SET (176) 600.00 900.00
WRAPPER (1-CENT) 50.00 90.00
WRAPPER (1-CENT, REP) 50.00 80.00
WRAPPER (5-CENT) 75.00 125.00
1 Johnny Unitas 90.00 150.00
2 Gene Brito 1.50 3.00
3 Detroit Lions 3.00 6.00
Team Card
(checklist back)
4 Max McGee RC 15.00 30.00
5 Hugh McElhenny 7.50 15.00
6 Joe Schmidt 4.00 8.00
7 Kyle Rote 3.00 6.00
8 Clarence Peaks 1.50 3.00
9 Pittsburgh Steelers 1.75 3.50
Pennant Card
10 Jim Brown 90.00 150.00
11 Ray Mathews 1.50 3.00
12 Bobby Dillon 1.50 3.00
13 Joe Childress 1.50 3.00
14 Terry Barr RC 1.50 3.00
15 Del Shofner RC 2.00 4.00
16 Bob Pellegrini UER 1.50 3.00
(Misspelled Pellagrini
on card back)
17 Baltimore Colts 3.00 6.00
Team Card
(checklist back)
18 Preston Carpenter 1.50 3.00
19 Leo Nomellini 5.00 10.00
20 Frank Gifford 25.00 40.00
21 Charlie Ane 1.50 3.00
22 Jack Butler 2.50 6.00
23 Bart Starr 35.00 60.00
24 Chicago Cardinals 1.75 3.50
Pennant Card
25 Bill Barnes 1.50 3.00
26 Walt Michaels 2.00 4.00
27 Clyde Conner UER 1.50 3.00
(Misspelled Connor
on card back)
28 Paige Cothren 1.50 3.00
29 Roosevelt Grier 3.00 6.00
30 Alan Ameche 3.00 6.00
31 Philadelphia Eagles 3.00 6.00
Team Card
(checklist back)
32 Dick Nolan 2.00 4.00
33 R.C. Owens 2.00 4.00
34 Dale Dodrill 1.50 3.00
35 Gene Gedman 1.50 3.00
36 Gene Lipscomb RC 5.00 10.00
37 Ray Renfro 2.00 4.00
38 Cleveland Browns 1.75 3.50
Pennant Card
39 Bill Forester 2.00 4.00
40 Bobby Layne 15.00 25.00
41 Pat Summerall 5.00 10.00
42 Jerry Mertens RC 1.50 3.00
43 Steve Myhra RC 1.50 3.00
44 John Henry Johnson 4.00 8.00
45 Woodley Lewis UER 1.50 3.00
(misspelled Woody)
46 Green Bay Packers 5.00 10.00
Team Card
(checklist back)
47 Don Owens UER RC 1.50 3.00
48 Ed Beatty RC 1.50 3.00
49 Don Chandler 1.50 3.00
50 Ollie Matson 6.00 12.00
51 Sam Huff RC 30.00 50.00
52 Tom Miner RC 1.50 3.00
53 New York Giants 1.75 3.50
Pennant Card
54 Kenny Konz 1.50 3.00
55 Raymond Berry 10.00 20.00
56 Howard Ferguson UER 1.50 3.00
(Misspelled Fergeson
on card back)
57 Chuck Ulrich 1.50 3.00
58 Bob St. Clair 3.00 6.00
59 Don Burroughs RC 1.50 3.00
60 Lou Groza 7.50 15.00
61 San Francisco 49ers 3.00 6.00
Team Card
(checklist back)
62 Andy Nelson RC 1.50 3.00
63 Harold Bradley RC 1.50 3.00
64 Dave Hanner 2.00 4.00
65 Charley Conerly 6.00 12.00
66 Gene Cronin RC 1.50 3.00
67 Duane Putnam 1.50 3.00
68 Baltimore Colts 1.75 3.50
Pennant Card
69 Ernie Stautner 4.00 8.00
70 Jon Arnett 2.00 4.00
71 Ken Panfil RC 1.50 3.00
72 Matt Hazeltine 1.50 3.00
73 Harley Sewell 1.50 3.00
74 Mike McCormack 3.00 6.00
75 Jim Ringo 4.00 8.00
76 Los Angeles Rams 3.00 6.00
Team Card
(checklist back)
77 Bob Gain RC 1.50 3.00
78 Buzz Nutter RC 1.50 3.00
79 Jerry Norton 1.50 3.00
80 Joe Perry 6.00 12.00
81 Carl Brettschneider 1.50 3.00
82 Paul Hornung 30.00 60.00
83 Philadelphia Eagles 1.75 3.50
Pennant Card
84 Les Richter 2.00 4.00
85 Howard Cassady 2.00 4.00
86 Art Donovan 7.50 15.00
87 Jim Patton 2.00 4.00
88 Pete Retzlaff 2.00 4.00
89 Jim Mutscheller 1.00 2.00
90 Zeke Bratkowski 1.50 3.00
91 Washington Redskins 2.00 4.00
Team Card
(Checklist back)
92 Art Hunter 1.00 2.00
93 Gern Nagler 1.00 2.00
94 Chuck Weber RC 1.00 2.00
95 Lew Carpenter RC 1.50 3.00
96 Stan Jones 2.50 5.00
97 Ralph Guglielmi UER 1.50 3.00
(Misspelled Gugliemi
on card front)
98 Green Bay Packers 2.00 4.00
Pennant Card
99 Ray Wietecha 1.00 2.00
100 Lenny Moore 6.00 12.00
101 Jim Ray Smith UER RC 1.50 3.00
(Lions logo on front)
102 Abe Woodson RC 1.50 3.00
103 Alex Karras RC 25.00 40.00
104 Chicago Bears 2.00 4.00
Team Card
(checklist back)
105 John David Crow RC 6.00 12.00
106 Joe Fortunato RC 1.00 2.00
107 Babe Parilli 1.50 3.00
108 Proverb Jacobs RC 1.00 2.00
109 Gino Marchetti 4.00 8.00
110 Bill Wade 1.50 3.00
111 San Francisco 49ers 1.50 3.00
Pennant Card
112 Karl Rubke RC 1.00 2.00
113 Dave Middleton UER 1.00 2.00
(Browns logo in
upper left corner)
114 Roosevelt Brown 2.50 5.00
115 John Olszewski 1.00 2.00
116 Jerry Kramer RC 18.00 30.00
117 King Hill RC 1.50 3.00
118 Chicago Cardinals 2.00 4.00
Team Card
(Checklist back)
119 Frank Varrichione 1.00 2.00
120 Rick Casares 1.50 3.00
121 George Strugar RC 1.00 2.00
122 Bill Glass RC UER 1.50 3.00
(Center on front,
tackle on back)
123 Don Bosseler 1.00 2.00
124 John Reger RC 1.00 2.00
125 Jim Ninowski RC 1.00 2.00
126 Los Angeles Rams 1.50 3.00
Pennant Card
127 Willard Sherman 1.00 2.00
128 Bob Schnelker 1.00 2.00
129 Ollie Spencer RC 1.00 2.00
130 Y.A. Tittle 15.00 25.00
131 Yale Lary 2.50 5.00
132 Jim Parker RC 15.00 30.00
133 New York Giants 2.00 4.00
Team Card
(Checklist back)
134 Jim Schrader RC 1.00 2.00
135 M.C. Reynolds RC 1.00 2.00
136 Mike Sandusky RC 1.00 2.00
137 Ed Brown 1.50 3.00
138 Al Barry RC 1.00 2.00
139 Detroit Lions 1.50 3.00
Pennant Card
140 Bobby Mitchell RC 20.00 35.00
141 Larry Morris 1.00 2.00
142 Jim Phillips RC 1.50 3.00
143 Jim David 1.00 2.00
144 Joe Krupa 1.00 2.00
145 Willie Galimore 1.50 3.00
146 Pittsburgh Steelers 2.00 4.00
Team Card
(Checklist back)
147 Andy Robustelli 4.00 8.00
148 Billy Wilson 1.00 2.00
149 Leo Sanford 1.00 2.00
150 Eddie LeBaron 2.50 5.00
151 Bill McColl 1.00 2.00
152 Buck Lansford UER 1.00 2.00
(Tackle on front&
guard on back)
153 Chicago Bears 1.50 3.00
Pennant Card
154 Leo Sugar RC 1.00 2.00
155 Jim Taylor RC UER 20.00 35.00
(Photo actually
other Jim Taylor,
Cardinal LB)
156 Lindon Crow 1.00 2.00
157 Jack McClairen 1.00 2.00
158 Vince Costello RC UER 1.00 2.00
(Linebacker on front,
Guard on back)
159 Stan Wallace RC 1.00 2.00
160 Mel Triplett RC 1.00 2.00
161 Cleveland Browns 2.00 4.00
Team Card
(Checklist back)
162 Dan Currie RC 2.00 4.00
163 L.G. Dupre UER 1.50 3.00
(Misspelled DuPre
on back)
164 John Morrow UER RC 1.00 2.00
165 Jim Podoley 1.00 2.00
166 Bruce Bosley RC 1.00 2.00
167 Harlon Hill 1.00 2.00
168 Washington Redskins 1.50 3.00
Pennant Card
169 Junior Wren RC 1.00 2.00
170 Tobin Rote 1.50 3.00
171 Art Spinney 1.00 2.00
172 Chuck Drazenovich UER 1.00 2.00
(Linebacker on front,
Defensive Back on back)
173 Bobby Joe Conrad RC 1.50 3.00
174 Jesse Richardson RC 1.00 2.00
175 Sam Baker 1.00 2.00
176 Tom Tracy RC 4.00 8.00

1960 Topps

The 1960 Topps football set contains 132 standard-size cards. Card fronts have a "pure card" effect in that the player photo dominates the card. The only design on front is the player's name, team name and position within a football-shaped icon toward the bottom of the file. The card backs are printed in green on white card stock. Statistical information from the immediate past season and career totals are given on the reverse. The set marks the debut of the Dallas Cowboys into the NFL. The backs feature a "Football Funnies" scratch-off quiz; answer was revealed by rubbing with an edge of a coin. The team cards feature numerical checklist backs. The team cards that have the 67-132 checklist backs (card Nos. 60, 102, 112, 122, 132) all misspell 124 Don Bosseler as Bossler along with a number of other like errors. Several 3-card panel advertisement sheets were released to promote the set. Each features the cardfronts of three base cards with the sheet back including a Gene Cronin mock cardback and several Topps ads.

COMPLETE SET (132) 400.00 600.00
WRAPPER (1-CENT) 60.00 100.00
WRAPPER (1-CENT, REP) 250.00 400.00
WRAPPER (5-CENT) 50.00 80.00
1 John Unitas 40.00 80.00
2 Alan Ameche 2.00 4.00
3 Lenny Moore 5.00 10.00
4 Raymond Berry 6.00 12.00
5 Jim Parker 4.00 8.00
6 George Preas RC 1.25 2.50
7 Art Spinney 1.25 2.50
8 Bill Pellington RC 1.50 3.00
9 John Sample RC 1.50 3.00
10 Gene Lipscomb UER 1.50 3.00
(Def. Tackle on front,
Tackle on back)
11 Baltimore Colts 1.50 3.00
Team Card
(Checklist 67-132)
12 Ed Brown 1.50 3.00
13 Rick Casares 1.50 3.00
14 Willie Galimore 1.50 3.00
15 Jim Dooley 1.25 2.50
16 Harlon Hill UER 1.25 2.50
(Lifetime yards and
Avg. gain incorrect)
17 Stan Jones UER 2.00 4.00
(Defensive ... All-Star
Team, should be
Offensive)
18 Bill George 2.00 4.00
19 Erich Barnes RC 1.50 3.00
20 Doug Atkins UER 3.00 6.00
(reversed negative)
21 Chicago Bears 1.50 3.00
Team Card
(Checklist 1-66)
22 Milt Plum 1.50 3.00
23 Jim Brown 60.00 100.00
24 Sam Baker 1.25 2.50
25 Bobby Mitchell 5.00 10.00
26 Ray Renfro 1.50 3.00
27 Billy Howton 1.50 3.00
28 Jim Ray Smith 1.25 2.50
29 Jim Shofner RC 1.50 3.00
30 Bob Gain 1.25 2.50
31 Cleveland Browns 1.50 3.00
Team Card
(Checklist 1-66)
32 Don Heinrich 1.25 2.50
33 Ed Modzelewski UER 1.25 2.50
(Lifetime yards and
Avg. gain incorrect)
34 Fred Cone 1.25 2.50
35 L.G. Dupre 1.50 3.00
36 Dick Bielski 1.25 2.50
37 Charlie Ane UER 1.25 2.50
(Misspelled Charley)
38 Jerry Tubbs 1.50 3.00
39 Doyle Nix RC 1.25 2.50
40 Ray Krouse 1.25 2.50
41 Earl Morrall 2.00 4.00
42 Howard Cassady 1.50 3.00
43 Dave Middleton 1.25 2.50
44 Jim Gibbons RC 1.50 3.00
45 Darris McCord RC 1.25 2.50
46 Joe Schmidt 3.00 6.00
47 Terry Barr 1.25 2.50
48 Yale Lary UER 2.00 4.00
(Def.back on front,
halfback on back)
49 Gil Mains RC 1.25 2.50
50 Detroit Lions 1.50 3.00
Team Card
(Checklist 1-66)
51 Bart Starr 30.00 50.00
52 Jim Taylor UER 4.00 8.00
(photo actually
Jim Taylor,
Cardinal LB)
53 Lew Carpenter 1.50 3.00
54 Paul Hornung UER 30.00 45.00
(Halfback on front,
fullback on back)
55 Max McGee 2.00 4.00
56 Forrest Gregg RC 25.00 40.00
57 Jim Ringo 2.50 5.00
58 Bill Forester 1.50 3.00
59 Dave Hanner 1.50 3.00
60 Green Bay Packers 4.00 8.00
Team Card
(Checklist 67-132)
61 Bill Wade 1.50 3.00
62 Frank Ryan RC 2.50 5.00
63 Ollie Matson 5.00 10.00
64 Jon Arnett 1.50 3.00
65 Del Shofner 1.50 3.00
66 Jim Phillips 1.25 2.50
67 Art Hunter 1.25 2.50
68 Les Richter 1.50 3.00
69 Lou Michaels RC 1.50 3.00
70 John Baker RC 1.25 2.50
71 Los Angeles Rams 1.50 3.00
Team Card
(Checklist 1-66)
72 Charley Conerly 4.00 8.00
73 Mel Triplett 1.25 2.50
74 Frank Gifford 20.00 35.00
75 Alex Webster 1.50 3.00
76 Bob Schnelker 1.25 2.50
77 Pat Summerall 4.00 8.00
78 Roosevelt Brown 2.00 4.00
79 Jim Patton 1.25 2.50
80 Sam Huff UER 10.00 20.00
(Def.tackle on front,
linebacker on back)
81 Andy Robustelli 3.00 6.00
82 New York Giants 1.50 3.00
Team Card
(Checklist 1-66)
83 Clarence Peaks 1.25 2.50
84 Bill Barnes 1.25 2.50
85 Pete Retzlaff 1.50 3.00
86 Bobby Walston 1.25 2.50
87 Chuck Bednarik UER 4.00 8.00
(Misspelled Bednarick
on both sides of card)
88 Bob Pellegrini 1.25 2.50
(Misspelled Pellagrini
on both sides)
89 Tom Brookshier RC 1.50 3.00
90 Marion Campbell 1.50 3.00
91 Jesse Richardson 1.25 2.50
92 Philadelphia Eagles 1.50 3.00
Team Card
(Checklist 1-66)
93 Bobby Layne 18.00 30.00
94 John Henry Johnson 3.00 6.00
95 Tom Tracy UER 1.50 3.00
(Halfback on front,
fullback on back)
96 Preston Carpenter 1.25 2.50
97 Frank Varrichione UER 1.25 2.50
(Reversed negative)
98 John Nisby RC 1.25 2.50
99 Dean Derby RC 1.25 2.50
100 George Tarasovic 1.25 2.50
101 Ernie Stautner 2.50 5.00
102 Pittsburgh Steelers 1.50 3.00
Team Card
(Checklist 67-132)
103 King Hill 1.25 2.50
104 Mal Hammack RC 1.25 2.50
105 John David Crow 1.50 3.00
106 Bobby Joe Conrad 1.50 3.00
107 Woodley Lewis 1.25 2.50
108 Don Gillis RC 1.25 2.50
109 Carl Brettschneider 1.25 2.50
110 Leo Sugar 1.25 2.50
111 Frank Fuller RC 1.25 2.50
112 St. Louis Cardinals 1.50 3.00
Team Card
(Checklist 67-132)
113 Y.A. Tittle 18.00 30.00
114 Joe Perry 4.00 8.00
115 J.D. Smith RC 1.50 3.00
116 Hugh McElhenny 4.00 8.00
117 Billy Wilson 1.25 2.50
118 Bob St. Clair 2.00 4.00
119 Matt Hazeltine 1.25 2.50
120 Abe Woodson 1.25 2.50
121 Leo Nomellini 2.50 5.00
122 San Francisco 49ers 1.50 3.00
Team Card
(Checklist 67-132)
123 Ralph Guglielmi UER 1.25 2.50
(Misspelled Gugliemi
on card front)
124 Don Bosseler 1.25 2.50
125 John Olszewski 1.25 2.50
126 Bill Anderson UER RC 1.25 2.50
(Walt on back)
127 Joe Walton RC 1.50 3.00
128 Jim Schrader 1.25 2.50
129 Ralph Felton RC 1.25 2.50
130 Gary Glick 1.25 2.50
131 Bob Toneff 1.25 2.50
132 Washington Redskins 18.00 30.00
Team Card
(Checklist 67-132)
AD1 Advertising Panel 200.00 350.00
Alan Ameche
Paul Hornung
Tom Tracy
(Gene Cronin back)
AD2 Advertising Panel 125.00 200.00
Del Shofner
Milt Plum
Jim Patton
(Gene Cronin back)
AD3 Advertising Panel 125.00 200.00
Bob St.Clair
Jim Shofner
Gil Mains
(Gene Cronin back)
AD4 Advertising Panel 125.00 200.00
Tom Brookshier
Packers Team
George Preas
(Gene Cronin back)

1960 Topps Metallic Stickers Inserts

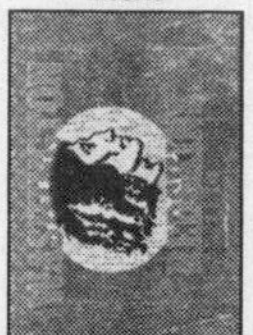

This set of 33 metallic team emblem stickers was inserted with the 1960 Topps regular issue football set. The stickers are unnumbered and are ordered below alphabetically within type. NFL teams are listed first (1-13) followed by college teams (14-33). The stickers measure approximately 2 1/8" by 3 1/16". The sticker fronts are either silver, gold, or blue with a black border.

COMPLETE SET (33) 200.00 400.00
1 Baltimore Colts 7.50 15.00
2 Chicago Bears 12.50 25.00
3 Cleveland Browns 12.50 25.00
4 Dallas Cowboys 12.50 25.00
5 Detroit Lions 7.50 15.00
6 Green Bay Packers 15.00 30.00
7 Los Angeles Rams 7.50 15.00
8 New York Giants 7.50 15.00
9 Philadelphia Eagles 7.50 15.00
10 Pittsburgh Steelers 7.50 15.00
11 St. Louis Cardinals 7.50 15.00
12 San Francisco 49ers 12.50 25.00
13 Washington Redskins 12.50 25.00
14 Air Force Falcons 5.00 10.00
15 Army Cadets 5.00 10.00
16 California Golden Bears 5.00 10.00
17 Dartmouth Indians 5.00 10.00
18 Duke Blue Devils 5.00 10.00
19 LSU Tigers 7.50 15.00
20 Michigan Wolverines 10.00 20.00
21 Minnesota Golden Gophers 5.00 10.00
22 Mississippi Rebels 5.00 10.00
23 Navy Midshipmen 5.00 10.00
24 Notre Dame Fighting Irish 12.50 25.00
25 SMU Mustangs 5.00 10.00
26 USC Trojans 7.50 15.00
27 Syracuse Orangemen 5.00 10.00
28 Tennessee Volunteers 7.50 15.00
29 Texas Longhorns 7.50 15.00
30 UCLA Bruins 7.50 15.00
31 Washington Huskies 5.00 10.00
32 Wisconsin Badgers 5.00 10.00
33 Yale Bulldogs 5.00 10.00

1960 Topps Tattoos

This set was thought to have been distributed in 1960 like the corresponding baseball issue. It appears they were issued as a separate set by both Topps and O-Pee-Chee in Canada. Each is actually the inside surface of the outer wrapper (measuring roughly 1 9/16" by 3 1/2") in which the collector would apply the tatoo by moistening the skin and then pressing the tattoo to the moistened spot. The tattoos are unnumbered and where produced in color. Any additions to the list below are appreciated.

1 Bill Anderson 125.00 250.00
2 Jim Brown 350.00 600.00
3 Rick Casares 125.00 250.00
4 Howard Cassady 125.00 250.00
5 Frank Gifford 200.00 350.00
6 Paul Hornung 250.00 400.00
7 Bobby Layne 200.00 350.00
8 Y.A. Tittle 200.00 350.00
9 Johnny Unitas 350.00 600.00
10 Bill Wade 125.00 250.00
11 Chicago Bears 50.00 100.00
12 Cleveland Browns 40.00 80.00
13 Dallas Cowboys 125.00 200.00
14 Detroit Lions 40.00 80.00
15 Green Bay Packers 125.00 200.00
16 New York Giants 40.00 80.00
17 Pittsburgh Steelers 60.00 120.00
18 St.Louis Cardinals 40.00 80.00
19 San Francisco 49ers 40.00 80.00
20 Washington Redskins 90.00 150.00
21 Air Force 30.00 60.00
22 Army 30.00 60.00
23 Baylor 30.00 60.00
24 Boston College 30.00 60.00
25 California 30.00 60.00
26 Duke 30.00 60.00
27 Illinois 30.00 60.00
28 Indiana 30.00 60.00
29 Iowa 30.00 60.00
30 Kentucky 40.00 80.00
31 Michigan 50.00 100.00
32 Michigan State 30.00 60.00
33 Minnesota 30.00 60.00
34 Mississippi 30.00 60.00
35 Navy 30.00 60.00
36 Nebraska 40.00 80.00
37 Northwestern 30.00 60.00
38 Notre Dame 75.00 150.00
39 Oklahoma 40.00 80.00
40 Oregon 30.00 60.00
41 Oregon State 30.00 60.00
42 Penn State 50.00 100.00
43 Pennsylvania 30.00 60.00
44 Pittsburgh 30.00 60.00
45 Princeton 30.00 60.00
46 Rice 30.00 60.00
47 Rutgers 30.00 60.00
48 SMU 30.00 60.00
49 South Carolina 30.00 60.00
50 Stanford 30.00 60.00
51 TCU 30.00 60.00
52 Tennessee 40.00 80.00
53 Texas 40.00 80.00
54 UCLA 40.00 80.00
55 USC 40.00 80.00
56 Washington State 30.00 60.00
57 Wisconsin 30.00 60.00
58 Wyoming 30.00 50.00
59 Generic 15.00 30.00
Actual Kicking of Football
60 Generic 15.00 30.00
Catching a Pass
61 Generic 15.00 30.00
Chasing a fumble
62 Generic 15.00 30.00
Defender is grabbing shirt
63 Generic 15.00 30.00
Defender trying to block kick
64 Generic 15.00 30.00
Kicking Follow Through
65 Generic 15.00 30.00
Lateral
66 Generic 15.00 30.00
Passer ready to throw
67 Generic 15.00 30.00
Player #8 is charging
68 Generic 15.00 30.00
Player yelling at Referee
69 Generic 15.00 30.00
Profile view of Passer
70 Generic 15.00 30.00
Receiver and Defender
71 Generic 15.00 30.00
Runner being tackled
72 Generic 15.00 30.00
Runner is falling down
73 Generic 15.00 30.00
Runner is Fumbling
74 Generic 15.00 30.00
Runner using stiff arm
75 Generic 15.00 30.00
Runner with football
76 Generic 15.00 30.00
Taking a snap on one knee

1961 Topps

The 1961 Topps football set of 198 standard-size cards contains NFL players (1-132) and AFL players (133-197). The fronts are very similar to the Topps 1961 baseball issue with the player's name, team and position at beneath posed player photos. The card backs are printed in light blue on white card stock. Statistical information from the immediate past season and career totals are given on the reverse. A "coin-rub" picture was featured on the right of the reverse. Cards are essentially numbered in team order by league. There are three checklist cards in the set, numbers 67, 122, and 198. The key Rookie Cards in this set are John Brodie, Tom Flores, Henry Jordan, Don Maynard, and Jim Otto. A 3-card advertising panel was issued as well.

COMPLETE SET (198) 650.00 1,000.00
WRAPPER (1-CENT) 250.00 400.00
WRAPPER (1-CENT, REP) 125.00 200.00
WRAPPER (5-CENT) 60.00 100.00
1 Johnny Unitas 50.00 100.00
2 Lenny Moore 6.00 12.00
3 Alan Ameche 2.00 4.00
4 Raymond Berry 6.00 12.00
5 Jim Mutscheller 1.25 2.50
6 Jim Parker 2.50 5.00
7 Gino Marchetti 3.00 6.00
8 Gene Lipscomb 2.00 4.00
9 Baltimore Colts 1.50 3.00
Team Card
10 Bill Wade 1.50 3.00
11 Johnny Morris RC UER 3.00 6.00
(Years pro and return
averages wrong)
12 Rick Casares 1.50 3.00
13 Harlon Hill 1.25 2.50
14 Stan Jones 2.00 4.00
15 Doug Atkins 2.50 5.00
16 Bill George 2.00 4.00
17 J.C. Caroline 1.25 2.50
18 Chicago Bears 1.50 3.00
Team Card
19 Big Time Football 1.50 3.00
Comes to Texas
(Eddie LeBaron)
20 Eddie LeBaron 1.50 3.00
21 Don McIlhenny 1.25 2.50
22 L.G. Dupre 1.50 3.00
23 Jim Doran 1.25 2.50
24 Billy Howton 1.50 3.00
25 Buzz Guy RC 1.25 2.50
26 Jack Patera RC 1.25 2.50
27 Tom Franckhauser RC UER 1.25 2.50
(misspelled Frankhauser)
28 Dallas Cowboys 7.50 15.00
Team Card
29 Jim Ninowski 1.25 2.50
30 Dan Lewis RC 1.25 2.50
31 Nick Pietrosante RC 1.50 3.00
32 Gail Cogdill RC 1.50 3.00
33 Jim Gibbons 1.25 2.50
34 Jim Martin 1.25 2.50
35 Alex Karras 7.50 15.00
36 Joe Schmidt 2.50 5.00
37 Detroit Lions 1.50 3.00
Team Card
38 Packers' Hornung 9.00 18.00
Sets NFL Scoring
Record
39 Bart Starr 25.00 40.00
40 Paul Hornung 25.00 40.00
41 Jim Taylor 20.00 35.00
42 Max McGee 2.00 4.00
43 Boyd Dowler RC 4.00 8.00
44 Jim Ringo 2.50 5.00
45 Hank Jordan RC 18.00 30.00
46 Bill Forester 1.50 3.00
47 Green Bay Packers 7.50 15.00
Team Card
48 Frank Ryan 1.50 3.00
49 Jon Arnett 1.50 3.00
50 Ollie Matson 4.00 8.00
51 Jim Phillips 1.25 2.50
52 Del Shofner 1.50 3.00
53 Art Hunter 1.25 2.50
54 Gene Brito 1.25 2.50
55 Lindon Crow 1.25 2.50
56 Los Angeles Rams 1.50 3.00
Team Card
57 Colts' Unitas/25 TD Passes 15.00 25.00
58 Y.A. Tittle 18.00 30.00
59 John Brodie RC 25.00 40.00
60 J.D. Smith 1.25 2.50
61 R.C. Owens 1.50 3.00
62 Clyde Conner 1.25 2.50
63 Bob St. Clair 2.00 4.00
64 Leo Nomellini 3.00 6.00
65 Abe Woodson 1.25 2.50
66 San Francisco 49ers 1.50 3.00
Team Card
67 Checklist Card 25.00 40.00
68 Milt Plum 1.50 3.00
69 Ray Renfro 1.50 3.00
70 Bobby Mitchell 4.00 8.00
71 Jim Brown 75.00 125.00
72 Mike McCormack 2.00 4.00
73 Jim Ray Smith 1.25 2.50
74 Sam Baker 1.25 2.50
75 Walt Michaels 1.50 3.00
76 Cleveland Browns 1.50 3.00
Team Card
77 Jimmy Brown Gains/1257 Yards 20.00 35.00
78 George Shaw 1.25 2.50
79 Hugh McElhenny 4.00 8.00
80 Clancy Osborne RC 1.25 2.50
81 Dave Middleton 1.25 2.50
82 Frank Youso RC 1.25 2.50
83 Don Joyce RC 1.25 2.50
84 Ed Culpepper RC 1.25 2.50
85 Charley Conerly 4.00 8.00
86 Mel Triplett 1.25 2.50
87 Kyle Rote 1.50 3.00
88 Roosevelt Brown 2.00 4.00
89 Ray Wietecha 1.25 2.50
90 Andy Robustelli 2.50 5.00
91 Sam Huff 4.00 8.00
92 Jim Patton 1.25 2.50
93 New York Giants 1.50 3.00
Team Card
94 Charley Conerly UER 3.00 6.00
Leads Giants for/13th Year
(Misspelled Charlie
on card)
95 Sonny Jurgensen 15.00 25.00
96 Tommy McDonald 2.50 5.00
97 Bill Barnes 1.25 2.50
98 Bobby Walston 1.25 2.50
99 Pete Retzlaff 1.50 3.00
100 Jim McCusker RC 1.25 2.50
101 Chuck Bednarik 4.00 8.00
102 Tom Brookshier 1.50 3.00
103 Philadelphia Eagles 1.50 3.00
Team Card
104 Bobby Layne 18.00 30.00
105 John Henry Johnson 2.00 4.00
106 Tom Tracy 1.50 3.00
107 Buddy Dial RC 1.25 2.50
108 Jimmy Orr RC 3.00 6.00
109 Mike Sandusky 1.25 2.50
110 John Reger 1.25 2.50
111 Junior Wren 1.25 2.50
112 Pittsburgh Steelers 1.50 3.00
Team Card
113 Bobby Layne Sets 5.00 10.00
New Passing Record
114 John Roach RC 1.25 2.50
115 Sam Etcheverry RC 1.50 3.00
116 John David Crow 1.50 3.00
117 Mal Hammack 1.25 2.50
118 Sonny Randle RC 1.50 3.00
119 Leo Sugar 1.25 2.50
120 Jerry Norton 1.25 2.50
121 St. Louis Cardinals 1.50 3.00
Team Card
122 Checklist Card 30.00 50.00
123 Ralph Guglielmi 1.25 2.50
124 Dick James 1.25 2.50
125 Don Bosseler 1.25 2.50
126 Joe Walton 1.25 2.50
127 Bill Anderson 1.25 2.50
128 Vince Promuto RC 1.25 2.50
129 Bob Toneff 1.25 2.50
130 John Paluck RC 1.25 2.50
131 Washington Redskins 1.50 3.00
Team Card
132 Browns' Plum Wins 1.25 2.50
NFL Passing Title
133 Abner Haynes 4.00 8.00
134 Mel Branch UER 2.00 4.00
(Def. Tackle on front&
Def. End on back)
135 Jerry Cornelison UER 1.50 3.00
(Misspelled Cornielson)
136 Bill Krisher 1.50 3.00
137 Paul Miller 1.50 3.00
138 Jack Spikes 2.00 4.00
139 Johnny Robinson RC 4.00 8.00
140 Cotton Davidson RC 2.00 4.00
141 Dave Smith 1.50 3.00
142 Bill Groman 1.50 3.00

143 Rich Michael RC	1.50	3.00
144 Mike Dukes RC	1.50	3.00
145 George Blanda	15.00	25.00
146 Billy Cannon	3.00	6.00
147 Dennit Morris RC	1.50	3.00
148 Jacky Lee UER (Misspelled Jackie on card back)	2.00	4.00
149 Al Dorow	1.50	3.00
150 Don Maynard RC	25.00	50.00
151 Art Powell RC	4.00	8.00
152 Sid Youngelman	1.50	3.00
153 Bob Mischak RC	1.50	3.00
154 Larry Grantham	1.50	3.00
155 Tom Saidock	1.50	3.00
156 Roger Donnahoo RC	1.50	3.00
157 Laverne Torczon RC	1.50	3.00
158 Archie Matsos RC	2.00	4.00
159 Elbert Dubenion	2.00	4.00
160 Wray Carlton RC	2.00	4.00
161 Rich McCabe RC	1.50	3.00
162 Ken Rice RC	1.50	3.00
163 Art Baker RC	1.50	3.00
164 Tom Rychlec	1.50	3.00
165 Mack Yoho	1.50	3.00
166 Jack Kemp	35.00	60.00
167 Paul Lowe	3.00	6.00
168 Ron Mix	5.00	10.00
169 Paul Maguire UER (name misspelled McGuire)	3.00	6.00
170 Volney Peters	1.50	3.00
171 Ernie Wright RC	2.00	4.00
172 Ron Nery RC	1.50	3.00
173 Dave Kocourek RC	2.00	4.00
174 Jim Colclough RC	1.50	3.00
175 Babe Parilli	2.00	4.00
176 Billy Lott	1.50	3.00
177 Fred Bruney	1.50	3.00
178 Ross O'Hanley RC	1.50	3.00
179 Walt Cudzik RC	1.50	3.00
180 Charley Leo	1.50	3.00
181 Bob Dee	1.50	3.00
182 Jim Otto RC	25.00	40.00
183 Eddie Macon RC	1.50	3.00
184 Dick Christy RC	1.50	3.00
185 Alan Miller RC	1.50	3.00
186 Tom Flores RC	10.00	20.00
187 Joe Cannavino RC	1.50	3.00
188 Don Manoukian	1.50	3.00
189 Bob Coolbaugh RC	1.50	3.00
190 Lionel Taylor RC	4.00	8.00
191 Bud McFadin	1.50	3.00
192 Goose Gonsoulin RC	3.00	6.00
193 Frank Tripucka	2.00	4.00
194 Gene Mingo RC	2.00	4.00
195 Eldon Danenhauer RC	1.50	3.00
196 Bob McNamara	1.50	3.00
197 Dave Rolle UER RC	1.50	3.00
198 Checklist Card UER (135 Cornielson)	40.00	80.00
AD1 Advertising Panel Jim Martin George Shaw Jim Ray Smith	125.00	200.00

1961 Topps Flocked Stickers Inserts

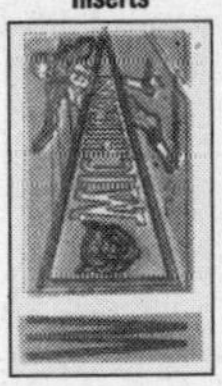

This set of 48 flocked stickers was inserted with the 1961 Topps regular issue football set. The stickers are unnumbered and are ordered below alphabetically within type. NFL teams are listed first (1-15), followed by AFL teams (16-24), and college teams (25-48). The capital letters in the listing below signify the letter on the detachable tab. The stickers measure approximately 2" by 2 3/4" without the letter tab and 2" by 3 3/8" with the letter tab. The prices below are for the stickers with tabs intact; stickers without tabs would be considered VG-E at best. There are letter tab variations on 12 of the stickers as noted by the double letters below. The complete set price below considers the set complete with the 48 different distinct teams, i.e., not including all 60 different tab combinations.

COMPLETE SET (48)	500.00	800.00
1 NFL Emblem N	10.00	20.00
2 Baltimore Colts U	10.00	20.00
3 Chicago Bears H	10.00	20.00
4 Cleveland Browns I	10.00	20.00
5 Dallas Cowboys K	25.00	40.00
6 Detroit Lions E	10.00	20.00
7 Green Bay Packers A	25.00	40.00
8 Los Angeles Rams M	10.00	20.00
9 Minnesota Vikings R	10.00	20.00
10 New York Giants D	10.00	20.00
11 Philadelphia Eagles O	10.00	20.00
12 Pittsburgh Steelers S	12.50	25.00
13 San Francisco 49ers P	10.00	20.00
14 St. Louis Cardinals L	10.00	20.00
15 Washington Redskins J	12.50	25.00
16 AFL Emblem A/G	10.00	20.00
17 Boston Patriots F/T	10.00	20.00
18 Buffalo Bills I/M	10.00	20.00
19 Dallas Texans P/R	12.50	25.00
20 Denver Broncos G/I	12.50	25.00
21 Houston Oilers A/H	10.00	20.00
22 Oakland Raiders B/O	18.00	30.00
23 San Diego Chargers E/K	10.00	20.00
24 New York Titans D/E	10.00	20.00
25 Air Force Falcons V	7.50	15.00
26 Alabama Crimson Tide L	10.00	20.00
27 Arkansas Razorbacks A	7.50	15.00
28 Army Cadets G	7.50	15.00
29 Baylor Bears E	7.50	15.00
30 California Golden Bears T	7.50	15.00
31 Georgia Tech F	7.50	15.00
32 Illinois Fighting Illini C	7.50	15.00
33 Kansas Jayhawks J	7.50	15.00
34 Kentucky Wildcats R	7.50	15.00
35 Miami Hurricanes H	7.50	15.00
36 Michigan Wolverines W	15.00	25.00
37 Missouri Tigers B	7.50	15.00
38 Navy Midshipmen J/S	7.50	15.00
39 Oregon Ducks C/N	7.50	15.00
40 Penn State Nittany Lions Z	10.00	20.00
41 Pittsburgh Panthers G	7.50	15.00
42 Purdue Boilermakers B	7.50	15.00
43 USC Trojans Y	7.50	15.00
44 Stanford Indians L/O	7.50	15.00
45 TCU Horned Frogs C	7.50	15.00
46 Virginia Cavaliers S	7.50	15.00
47 Washington Huskies D	7.50	15.00
48 Washington St.Cougers M UER (logo is Washington Huskies)	7.50	15.00

1962 Topps

The 1962 Topps football set contains 176 black bordered standard-size cards. In designing the 1962 set, Topps chose a horizontally oriented card front for the first time since 1957. Two photos include a small action photo to the left that is joined by the player's name, team name and position. An up-close photo to the right covers majority of the card. Black borders, which are prone to chipping, make it quite difficult to put together a set in top grades. The short-printed (SP) cards are indicated in the checklist below. The shortage is probably attributable to the fact that the set size is not the standard 132-card, single-sheet size; hence all cards were not printed in equal amounts. Cards are again organized numerically in team order. The last card within each team grouping was a "rookie prospect" for that team. Many of the black and white inset photos on the card fronts (especially those of the rookie prospects) are not the player pictured and described on the card. The key Rookie Cards in this set are Ernie Davis, Mike Ditka, Roman Gabriel, Bill Kilmer, Norm Snead and Fran Tarkenton.

COMPLETE SET (176)	1,200.00	2,000.00
WRAPPER (1-CENT)	175.00	250.00
WRAPPER (5-CENT,STARS)	25.00	50.00
WRAPPER (5-CENT, BUCKS)	25.00	40.00
1 Johnny Unitas	125.00	200.00
2 Lenny Moore	6.00	12.00
3 Alex Hawkins SP RC	5.00	10.00
4 Joe Perry	4.00	8.00
5 Raymond Berry SP	25.00	40.00
6 Steve Myhra	2.00	4.00
7 Tom Gilburg SP RC	4.00	8.00
8 Gino Marchetti	4.00	8.00
9 Bill Pellington	2.00	4.00
10 Andy Nelson	2.00	4.00
11 Wendell Harris SP RC	4.00	8.00
12 Baltimore Colts Team Card	3.00	6.00
13 Bill Wade SP	5.00	10.00
14 Willie Galimore	2.50	5.00
15 Johnny Morris SP	4.00	8.00
16 Rick Casares	2.50	5.00
17 Mike Ditka RC	175.00	300.00
18 Stan Jones	3.00	6.00
19 Roger LeClerc RC	2.00	4.00
20 Angelo Coia RC	2.00	4.00
21 Doug Atkins	4.00	8.00
22 Bill George	3.00	6.00
23 Richie Petitbon RC	2.50	5.00
24 Ronnie Bull SP RC	4.00	8.00
25 Chicago Bears Team Card	3.00	6.00
26 Howard Cassady	2.50	5.00
27 Ray Renfro SP	5.00	10.00
28 Jim Brown	100.00	175.00
29 Rich Kreitling RC	2.00	4.00
30 Jim Ray Smith	2.00	4.00
31 John Morrow	2.00	4.00
32 Lou Groza	7.50	15.00
33 Bob Gain	2.00	4.00
34 Bernie Parrish RC	2.00	4.00
35 Jim Shofner	2.00	4.00
36 Ernie Davis SP RC	90.00	150.00
37 Cleveland Browns Team Card	3.00	6.00
38 Eddie LeBaron	2.50	5.00
39 Don Meredith SP	60.00	100.00
40 J.W. Lockett SP RC	4.00	8.00
41 Don Perkins RC	7.50	15.00
42 Billy Howton	2.50	5.00
43 Dick Bielski	2.00	4.00
44 Mike Connelly RC	2.00	4.00
45 Jerry Tubbs SP	4.00	8.00
46 Don Bishop SP RC	4.00	8.00
47 Dick Moegle	2.00	4.00
48 Bobby Plummer SP RC	4.00	8.00
49 Dallas Cowboys Team Card	12.00	20.00
50 Milt Plum	2.50	5.00
51 Dan Lewis	2.00	4.00
52 Nick Pietrosante SP	4.00	8.00
53 Gail Cogdill	2.00	4.00
54 Jim Gibbons	2.00	4.00
55 Jim Martin	2.00	4.00
56 Yale Lary	3.00	6.00
57 Darris McCord	2.00	4.00
58 Alex Karras	15.00	25.00
59 Joe Schmidt	4.00	8.00
60 Dick Lane	3.00	6.00
61 John Lomakoski SP RC	4.00	8.00
62 Detroit Lions SP Team Card	10.00	18.00
63 Bart Starr SP	75.00	125.00
64 Paul Hornung SP	60.00	100.00
65 Tom Moore SP	6.00	12.00
66 Jim Taylor SP	30.00	50.00
67 Max McGee SP	6.00	12.00
68 Jim Ringo SP	7.50	15.00
69 Fuzzy Thurston RC SP	15.00	25.00
70 Forrest Gregg	4.00	8.00
71 Boyd Dowler	3.00	6.00
72 Hank Jordan SP	7.50	15.00
73 Bill Forester SP	5.00	10.00
74 Earl Gros SP RC	4.00	8.00
75 Green Bay Packers SP Team Card	25.00	40.00
76 Checklist SP	50.00	80.00
77 Zeke Bratkowski SP (Inset photo is Johnny Unitas)	5.00	10.00
78 Jon Arnett SP	5.00	10.00
79 Ollie Matson SP	20.00	35.00
80 Dick Bass SP	5.00	10.00
81 Jim Phillips	2.00	4.00
82 Carroll Dale RC	2.50	5.00
83 Frank Varrichione	2.00	4.00
84 Art Hunter	2.00	4.00
85 Danny Villanueva RC	2.00	4.00
86 Les Richter SP	4.00	8.00
87 Lindon Crow	2.00	4.00
88 Roman Gabriel RC SP (Inset photo is Y.A. Tittle)	35.00	60.00
89 Los Angeles Rams SP Team Card	10.00	18.00
90 F.Tarkenton SP RC UER Small photo actually Sonny Jurgensen with airbrushed jersey	125.00	225.00
91 Jerry Reichow SP RC	4.00	8.00
92 Hugh McElhenny SP	18.00	30.00
93 Mel Triplett SP	4.00	8.00
94 Tommy Mason SP RC	6.00	12.00
95 Dave Middleton SP	4.00	8.00
96 Frank Youso SP	4.00	8.00
97 Mike Mercer SP RC	4.00	8.00
98 Rip Hawkins SP	4.00	8.00
99 Cliff Livingston SP RC	4.00	8.00
100 Roy Winston SP RC	4.00	8.00
101 Minnesota Vikings SP Team Card	15.00	25.00
102 Y.A. Tittle	25.00	40.00
103 Joe Walton	2.00	4.00
104 Frank Gifford	30.00	50.00
105 Alex Webster	2.50	5.00
106 Del Shofner	2.50	5.00
107 Don Chandler	2.00	4.00
108 Andy Robustelli	4.00	8.00
109 Jim Katcavage RC	2.50	5.00
110 Sam Huff SP	25.00	40.00
111 Erich Barnes	2.00	4.00
112 Jim Patton	2.00	4.00
113 Jerry Hillebrand SP	4.00	8.00
114 New York Giants Team Card	3.00	6.00
115 Sonny Jurgensen	25.00	40.00
116 Tommy McDonald	4.00	8.00
117 Ted Dean SP	4.00	8.00
118 Clarence Peaks	2.00	4.00
119 Bobby Walston	2.00	4.00
120 Pete Retzlaff SP	5.00	10.00
121 Jim Schrader SP	4.00	8.00
122 J.D. Smith T RC	2.00	4.00
123 King Hill	2.00	4.00
124 Maxie Baughan	2.50	5.00
125 Pete Case SP RC	4.00	8.00
126 Philadelphia Eagles Team Card	3.00	6.00
127 Bobby Layne UER (Bears until 1958& should be Lions)	25.00	40.00
128 Tom Tracy	2.50	5.00
129 John Henry Johnson	3.00	6.00
130 Buddy Dial SP	5.00	10.00
131 Preston Carpenter	2.00	4.00
132 Lou Michaels SP	4.00	8.00
133 Gene Lipscomb SP	5.00	10.00
134 Ernie Stautner SP	12.00	20.00
135 John Reger SP	4.00	8.00
136 Myron Pottios RC	2.00	4.00
137 Bob Ferguson SP RC	4.00	8.00
138 Pittsburgh Steelers SP Team Card	10.00	18.00
139 Sam Etcheverry	2.50	5.00
140 John David Crow SP	5.00	10.00
141 Bobby Joe Conrad SP	5.00	10.00
142 Prentice Gautt SP RC	4.00	8.00
143 Frank Mestnik	2.00	4.00
144 Sonny Randle	2.50	5.00
145 Gerry Perry UER RC	2.00	4.00
146 Jerry Norton	2.00	4.00
147 Jimmy Hill RC	2.00	4.00
148 Bill Stacy	2.00	4.00
149 Fate Echols SP RC	4.00	8.00
150 St. Louis Cardinals Team Card	3.00	6.00
151 Bill Kilmer RC	25.00	40.00
152 John Brodie	10.00	18.00
153 J.D. Smith RB	2.50	5.00
154 C.R. Roberts SP RC	4.00	8.00
155 Monty Stickles	2.00	4.00
156 Clyde Conner UER (Misspelled Connor on card back)	2.00	4.00
157 Bob St. Clair	3.00	6.00
158 Tommy Davis RC	2.00	4.00
159 Leo Nomellini	4.00	8.00
160 Matt Hazeltine	2.00	4.00
161 Abe Woodson	2.00	4.00
162 Dave Baker	2.00	4.00
163 San Francisco 49ers Team Card	3.00	6.00
164 Norm Snead SP RC	18.00	30.00
165 Dick James RC	2.50	5.00
166 Bobby Mitchell	4.00	8.00
167 Sam Horner RC	2.00	4.00
168 Bill Barnes	2.00	4.00
169 Bill Anderson	2.00	4.00
170 Fred Dugan	2.00	4.00
171 John Aveni SP RC	4.00	8.00
172 Bob Toneff	2.00	4.00
173 Jim Kerr RC	2.00	4.00
174 Leroy Jackson SP RC	4.00	8.00
175 Washington Redskins Team Card	3.00	6.00
176 Checklist	60.00	100.00

1962 Topps Bucks Inserts

The 1962 Topps Football Bucks set contains 48 cards and was issued as an insert into wax packs of the 1962 Topps regular issue of football cards. Printing was done with black and green ink on off-white (very thin) paper stock. Bucks are typically found with a fold crease in the middle as they were inserted in packs in that manner. These "football bucks" measure approximately 1 1/4" by 4 1/4". Mike Ditka and Fran Tarkenton appear in their Rookie Card year.

COMPLETE SET (48)	350.00	450.00
1 J.D. Smith	2.00	4.00
2 Bart Starr	15.00	30.00
3 Dick James	2.00	4.00
4 Alex Webster	2.50	5.00
5 Paul Hornung	10.00	20.00
6 John David Crow	2.50	5.00
7 Jim Brown	30.00	50.00
8 Don Perkins	2.50	5.00
9 Bobby Walston	2.00	4.00
10 Jim Phillips	2.00	4.00
11 Y.A. Tittle	7.50	15.00
12 Sonny Randle	2.00	4.00
13 Jerry Reichow	2.00	4.00
14 Yale Lary	3.00	6.00
15 Buddy Dial	2.50	5.00
16 Ray Renfro	2.50	5.00
17 Norm Snead	3.00	6.00
18 Leo Nomellini	3.00	6.00
19 Hugh McElhenny	5.00	10.00
20 Eddie LeBaron	2.50	5.00
21 Billy Howton	2.50	5.00
22 Bobby Mitchell	4.00	8.00
23 Nick Pietrosante	2.00	4.00
24 Johnny Unitas	20.00	40.00
25 Raymond Berry	5.00	10.00
26 Billy Kilmer	4.00	8.00
27 Lenny Moore	5.00	10.00
28 Tommy McDonald	3.00	6.00
29 Del Shofner	2.50	5.00
30 Jim Taylor	7.50	15.00
31 Joe Schmidt	4.00	8.00
32 Bill George	3.00	6.00
33 Fran Tarkenton	30.00	50.00
34 Willie Galimore	2.50	5.00
35 Bobby Layne	7.50	15.00
36 Max McGee	2.50	5.00
37 Jon Arnett	2.50	5.00
38 Lou Groza	6.00	12.00
39 Frank Varrichione	2.00	4.00
40 Milt Plum	2.50	5.00
41 Prentice Gautt	2.00	4.00
42 Bill Wade	2.50	5.00
43 Gino Marchetti	4.00	8.00
44 John Brodie	5.00	10.00
45 Sonny Jurgensen UER (Misspelled Jurgenson)	7.50	15.00
46 Clarence Peaks	2.50	5.00
47 Mike Ditka	15.00	30.00
48 John Henry Johnson	4.00	8.00

1963 Topps

The 1963 Topps set contains 170 standard-size cards of NFL players grouped together by teams. The card backs are printed in light orange ink on white card stock. Statistical information from the immediate past season and career totals are given on the reverse. The illustrated trivia question on the reverse (of each card) could be answered by placing red cellophane paper (which was inserted into wax packs) over the card. The 76 cards indicated by SP below are in shorter supply than the others because the set size is not the standard 132-card, single-sheet size; hence, all cards were not printed in equal amounts. There also exists a three-card advertising panel consisting of card fronts of Charlie Johnson, John David Crow and Bobby Joe Conrad. The back of the latter two players contains ad copy and a Y.A. Tittle card back on Johnson. Interestingly, Y.A. Tittle was also used as the player featured on the full box of packs. Finally, most of the cards in the set were printed with color variations in the background of the player photo. This resulting in one version of the photo that appears to have a purple tinted background while the other is a color corrected blue background. This is most evident on cards with a large portion of sky in the background of the photo. We have not yet identified if one version is more difficult to find than the other, but have not been able to track any price differences thus far.

COMPLETE SET (170)	850.00	1,350.00
WRAPPER (1-CENT)	1,000.00	1,500.00
WRAPPER (5-CENT)	50.00	80.00
1 John Unitas	75.00	135.00
2 Lenny Moore	4.00	8.00
3 Jimmy Orr	1.50	3.00
4 Raymond Berry	4.00	8.00
5 Jim Parker	2.50	5.00
6 Alex Sandusky	1.25	2.50
7 Dick Szymanski RC	1.25	2.50
8 Gino Marchetti	3.00	6.00
9 Billy Ray Smith RC	1.50	3.00
10 Bill Pellington	1.25	2.50
11 Bob Boyd DB RC	1.25	2.50
12 Baltimore Colts SP Team Card	5.00	10.00
13 Frank Ryan SP	4.00	8.00
14 Jim Brown SP	100.00	200.00
15 Ray Renfro SP	4.00	8.00
16 Rich Kreitling SP	3.50	6.00
17 Mike McCormack SP	5.00	10.00
18 Jim Ray Smith SP	3.50	6.00
19 Lou Groza SP	15.00	25.00
20 Bill Glass SP	3.50	6.00
21 Galen Fiss SP	3.50	6.00
22 Don Fleming SP RC	4.00	8.00
23 Bob Gain SP	3.50	6.00
24 Cleveland Browns SP Team Card	5.00	10.00
25 Milt Plum	1.50	3.00
26 Dan Lewis	1.25	2.50
27 Nick Pietrosante	1.25	2.50
28 Gail Cogdill	1.25	2.50
29 Harley Sewell	1.25	2.50
30 Jim Gibbons	1.25	2.50
31 Carl Brettschneider	1.25	2.50
32 Dick Lane	2.50	5.00
33 Yale Lary	2.50	5.00
34 Roger Brown RC	1.50	3.00
35 Joe Schmidt	3.00	6.00
36 Detroit Lions SP Team Card	5.00	10.00
37 Roman Gabriel	4.00	8.00
38 Zeke Bratkowski	1.50	3.00
39 Dick Bass	1.50	3.00
40 Jon Arnett	1.50	3.00
41 Jim Phillips	1.25	2.50
42 Frank Varrichione	1.25	2.50
43 Danny Villanueva	1.25	2.50
44 Deacon Jones RC	30.00	50.00
45 Lindon Crow	1.25	2.50
46 Marlin McKeever RC	1.25	2.50
47 Ed Meador RC	1.25	2.50
48 Los Angeles Rams Team Card	2.00	4.00
49 Y.A. Tittle SP	30.00	50.00
50 Del Shofner SP	3.50	6.00
51 Alex Webster SP	4.00	8.00
52 Phil King SP RC	3.50	6.00
53 Jack Stroud SP	3.50	6.00
54 Darrell Dess SP	3.50	6.00
55 Jim Katcavage SP	3.50	6.00
56 Roosevelt Grier SP	5.00	10.00
57 Erich Barnes SP	3.50	6.00
58 Jim Patton SP	3.50	6.00
59 Sam Huff SP	12.00	20.00
60 New York Giants Team Card	2.00	4.00
61 Bill Wade	1.50	3.00
62 Mike Ditka	35.00	60.00
63 Johnny Morris	1.25	2.50
64 Roger LeClerc	1.25	2.50
65 Roger Davis RC	1.25	2.50
66 Joe Marconi	1.25	2.50
67 Herman Lee RC	1.25	2.50
68 Doug Atkins	3.00	6.00
69 Joe Fortunato	1.25	2.50
70 Bill George	2.50	5.00
71 Richie Petitbon	1.50	3.00
72 Chicago Bears SP Team Card	5.00	10.00
73 Eddie LeBaron SP	5.00	10.00
74 Don Meredith SP	35.00	60.00
75 Don Perkins SP	5.00	10.00
76 Amos Marsh SP RC	3.50	6.00
77 Billy Howton SP	4.00	8.00
78 Andy Cvercko SP RC	3.50	6.00
79 Sam Baker SP	3.50	6.00
80 Jerry Tubbs SP	3.50	6.00
81 Don Bishop SP	3.50	6.00
82 Bob Lilly SP RC	100.00	175.00
83 Jerry Norton SP UER (not a first round Cowboys pick)	3.50	6.00
84 Dallas Cowboys SP Team Card	12.00	20.00
85 Checklist 1	15.00	25.00
86 Bart Starr	40.00	75.00
87 Jim Taylor	18.00	30.00
88 Boyd Dowler	2.50	5.00
89 Forrest Gregg	3.00	6.00
90 Fuzzy Thurston	3.00	6.00
91 Jim Ringo	3.00	6.00
92 Ron Kramer	1.50	3.00
93 Hank Jordan	3.00	6.00
94 Bill Forester	1.50	3.00
95 Willie Wood RC	25.00	40.00
96 Ray Nitschke RC	90.00	150.00
97 Green Bay Packers Team Card	7.50	15.00
98 Fran Tarkenton	35.00	60.00
99 Tommy Mason	1.50	3.00
100 Mel Triplett	1.25	2.50
101 Jerry Reichow	1.25	2.50
102 Frank Youso	1.25	2.50
103 Hugh McElhenny	4.00	8.00
104 Gerald Huth RC	1.25	2.50
105 Ed Sharockman RC	1.25	2.50
106 Rip Hawkins	1.25	2.50
107 Jim Marshall RC	20.00	40.00
108 Jim Prestel RC	1.25	2.50
109 Minnesota Vikings Team Card	2.00	4.00
110 Sonny Jurgensen SP	15.00	25.00
111 Tim Brown SP RC	5.00	10.00
112 Tommy McDonald SP	7.50	15.00
113 Clarence Peaks SP	3.50	6.00
114 Pete Retzlaff SP	4.00	8.00
115 Jim Schrader SP	3.50	6.00
116 Jim McCusker SP	3.50	6.00
117 Don Burroughs SP	3.50	6.00
118 Maxie Baughan SP	3.50	6.00
119 Riley Gunnels SP RC	3.50	6.00
120 Jimmy Carr SP	3.50	6.00
121 Philadelphia Eagles SP Team Card	5.00	10.00
122 Ed Brown SP	4.00	8.00
123 John Henry Johnson SP	7.50	15.00
124 Buddy Dial SP	3.50	6.00
125 Bill Red Mack SP RC	3.50	6.00
126 Preston Carpenter SP	3.50	6.00
127 Ray Lemek SP RC	3.50	6.00
128 Buzz Nutter SP	3.50	6.00
129 Ernie Stautner SP	7.50	15.00
130 Lou Michaels SP	3.50	6.00
131 Clendon Thomas SP RC	3.50	6.00
132 Tom Bettis SP	3.50	6.00
133 Pittsburgh Steelers SP Team Card	5.00	10.00
134 John Brodie	4.00	8.00
135 J.D. Smith	1.25	2.50
136 Bill Kilmer UER (College listed as San Francisco 49ers)	2.50	5.00
137 Bernie Casey RC	1.50	3.00
138 Tommy Davis	1.25	2.50
139 Ted Connolly RC	1.25	2.50
140 Bob St. Clair	2.50	5.00
141 Abe Woodson	1.25	2.50
142 Matt Hazeltine	1.25	2.50
143 Leo Nomellini	3.00	6.00
144 Dan Colchico RC	1.25	2.50
145 San Francisco 49ers SP Team Card	5.00	10.00
146 Charley Johnson RC	4.00	8.00
147 John David Crow	1.50	3.00
148 Bobby Joe Conrad	1.50	3.00
149 Sonny Randle	1.25	2.50
150 Prentice Gautt	1.25	2.50
151 Taz Anderson RC	1.25	2.50
152 Ernie McMillan RC	1.50	3.00
153 Jimmy Hill	1.25	2.50
154 Bill Koman RC	1.25	2.50
155 Larry Wilson RC	12.00	20.00
156 Don Owens	1.25	2.50
157 St. Louis Cardinals SP Team Card	5.00	10.00
158 Norm Snead SP	5.00	10.00
159 Bobby Mitchell SP	7.50	15.00
160 Bill Barnes SP	3.50	6.00
161 Fred Dugan SP	3.50	6.00
162 Don Bosseler SP	3.50	6.00
163 John Nisby SP	3.50	6.00
164 Riley Mattson SP RC	3.50	6.00
165 Bob Toneff SP	3.50	6.00
166 Rod Breedlove SP RC	3.50	6.00
167 Dick James SP	3.50	6.00
168 Claude Crabb SP RC	3.50	6.00
169 Washington Redskins SP Team Card	5.00	10.00
170 Checklist Card UER (108 Jim Prestal)	30.00	50.00
AD1 Advertising Panel Charley Johnson John David Crow Bobby Joe Conrad (Y.A. Tittle back)	500.00	800.00

1964 Topps

The 1964 Topps football set begins a run of four straight years that Topps issued cards of American Football League (AFL) player cards. The cards in this 176-card set measure the standard size and are grouped by teams. Because the cards were not printed on a standard 132-card sheet, some cards are printed in lesser quantities than others. These cards are marked in the checklist with SP for short print. Cards fronts feature white boders with tiny red stars outlining the photo. The player's name, team and position are in a black box beneath the photo. The backs of the cards contain the card number, vital statistics, a short biography, the player's record for the past year and his career, and a cartoon-illustrated question and answer section. The cards are organized alphabetically within teams. The key Rookie Cards in this set are Bobby Bell, Buck Buchanan, John Hadl, and Daryle Lamonica.

COMPLETE SET (176)	1,000.00	1,500.00
WRAPPER (1-CENT)	60.00	100.00
WRAPPER (5-CENT, PENN)	75.00	125.00
WRAPPER (5-CENT, 8-CARD)	90.00	150.00
1 Tommy Addison SP	15.00	40.00
2 Houston Antwine RC	2.00	4.00
3 Nick Buoniconti	15.00	25.00
4 Ron Burton SP	5.00	10.00
5 Gino Cappelletti UER (Misspelled Cappalletti on card front)	2.50	5.00
6 Jim Colclough SP	3.00	6.00
7 Bob Dee SP	3.00	6.00
8 Larry Eisenhauer	2.00	4.00
9 Dick Felt SP	3.00	6.00
10 Larry Garron	2.00	4.00
11 Art Graham RC	2.00	4.00
12 Ron Hall DB RC	2.00	4.00
13 Charles Long	2.00	4.00
14 Don McKinnon RC	2.00	4.00
15 Don Oakes SP RC	3.00	6.00
16 Ross O'Hanley SP	3.00	6.00
17 Babe Parilli SP	5.00	10.00
18 Jesse Richardson SP	3.00	6.00
19 Jack Rudolph SP RC	3.00	6.00
20 Don Webb RC	2.00	4.00
21 Boston Patriots Team Card	3.00	6.00
22 Ray Abruzzese UER (photo is Ed Rutkowski)	2.00	4.00
23 Stew Barber RC	2.00	4.00
24 Dave Behrman RC	2.00	4.00
25 Al Bemiller RC	2.00	4.00
26 Elbert Dubenion SP	5.00	10.00
27 Jim Dunaway SP RC	3.00	6.00
28 Booker Edgerson SP	3.00	6.00
29 Cookie Gilchrist SP	15.00	25.00
30 Jack Kemp SP	50.00	100.00
31 Daryle Lamonica RC	35.00	60.00
32 Bill Miller	2.00	4.00
33 Herb Paterra RC	2.00	4.00
34 Ken Rice SP	3.00	6.00
35 Ed Rutkowski UER RC (photo is Ray Abruzzese)	2.00	4.00
36 George Saimes RC	2.00	4.00
37 Tom Sestak	2.00	4.00
38 Billy Shaw SP	7.50	15.00
39 Mike Stratton	2.50	5.00
40 Gene Sykes RC	2.00	4.00
41 John Tracey SP RC	3.00	6.00
42 Sid Youngelman SP	3.00	6.00
43 Buffalo Bills Team Card	3.00	6.00
44 Eldon Danenhauer SP	3.00	6.00
45 Jim Fraser SP	3.00	6.00
46 Chuck Gavin SP	3.00	6.00
47 Goose Gonsoulin SP	5.00	10.00
48 Ernie Barnes RC	2.00	4.00
49 Tom Janik RC	2.00	4.00
50 Billy Joe RC	2.50	5.00
51 Ike Lassiter RC	2.00	4.00
52 John McCormick SP RC	3.00	6.00
53 Bud McFadin SP	3.00	6.00
54 Gene Mingo SP	3.00	6.00
55 Charlie Mitchell RC	2.00	4.00
56 John Nocera SP RC	3.00	6.00
57 Tom Nomina RC	2.00	4.00
58 Harold Olson SP RC	3.00	6.00
59 Bob Scarpitto	2.00	4.00
60 John Sklopan RC	2.00	4.00
61 Mickey Slaughter RC	2.00	4.00
62 Don Stone	2.00	4.00
63 Jerry Sturm RC	2.00	4.00
64 Lionel Taylor SP	6.00	12.00
65 Denver Broncos SP Team Card	10.00	20.00
66 Scott Appleton RC	2.00	4.00
67 Tony Banfield SP	3.00	6.00
68 George Blanda SP	40.00	80.00
69 Billy Cannon	3.00	6.00
70 Doug Cline SP	3.00	6.00
71 Gary Cutsinger SP RC	3.00	6.00
72 Willard Dewveall SP RC	3.00	6.00
73 Don Floyd SP	3.00	6.00
74 Freddy Glick SP RC	3.00	6.00
75 Charlie Hennigan SP	5.00	10.00
76 Ed Husmann SP	3.00	6.00
77 Bobby Jancik SP RC	3.00	6.00
78 Jacky Lee SP	5.00	10.00
79 Bob McLeod SP RC	3.00	6.00
80 Rich Michael SP	3.00	6.00
81 Larry Onesti RC	2.00	4.00
82 Checklist Card UER (16 Ross O'Hanldy)	30.00	60.00
83 Bob Schmidt SP RC	3.00	6.00
84 Walt Suggs SP RC	3.00	6.00
85 Bob Talamini SP	3.00	6.00
86 Charley Tolar SP	3.00	6.00
87 Don Trull RC	2.00	4.00
88 Houston Oilers Team Card	3.00	6.00
89 Fred Arbanas	2.00	4.00
90 Bobby Bell RC	25.00	40.00
91 Mel Branch SP	5.00	10.00
92 Buck Buchanan RC	25.00	40.00
93 Ed Budde RC	2.00	4.00
94 Chris Burford SP	5.00	10.00
95 Walt Corey RC	2.50	5.00
96 Len Dawson SP	40.00	75.00
97 Dave Grayson RC	2.00	4.00
98 Abner Haynes	3.00	6.00
99 Sherrill Headrick SP	5.00	10.00
100 E.J. Holub	2.00	4.00
101 Bobby Hunt RC	2.00	4.00
102 Frank Jackson SP	3.00	6.00
103 Curtis McClinton	2.50	5.00
104 Jerry Mays SP	5.00	10.00
105 Johnny Robinson SP	6.00	12.00
106 Jack Spikes SP	3.00	6.00
107 Smokey Stover SP RC	3.00	6.00
108 Jim Tyrer RC	5.00	10.00
109 Duane Wood SP RC	3.00	6.00
110 Kansas City Chiefs Team Card	3.00	6.00
111 Dick Christy SP	3.00	6.00
112 Dan Ficca SP RC	3.00	6.00
113 Larry Grantham	2.00	4.00
114 Curley Johnson SP	3.00	6.00
115 Gene Heeter RC	2.00	4.00
116 Jack Klotz RC	2.00	4.00
117 Pete Liske RC	2.50	5.00
118 Bob McAdam RC	2.00	4.00
119 Dee Mackey SP RC	3.00	6.00
120 Bill Mathis SP	5.00	10.00
121 Don Maynard	20.00	35.00
122 Dainard Paulson SP	3.00	6.00
123 Gerry Philbin RC	2.50	5.00
124 Mark Smolinski SP RC	3.00	6.00
125 Matt Snell RC	10.00	20.00
126 Mike Taliaferro RC	2.00	4.00
127 Bake Turner SP RC	5.00	10.00
128 Jeff Ware RC	2.00	4.00
129 Clyde Washington RC	2.00	4.00
130 Dick Wood RC	2.00	4.00
131 New York Jets Team Card	3.00	6.00
132 Dalva Allen SP	3.00	6.00
133 Dan Birdwell RC	2.00	4.00
134 Dave Costa RC	2.00	4.00
135 Dobie Craig RC	2.00	4.00
136 Clem Daniels	2.50	5.00
137 Cotton Davidson SP	5.00	10.00
138 Claude Gibson RC	2.00	4.00
139 Tom Flores SP	7.50	15.00
140 Wayne Hawkins SP	3.00	6.00
141 Ken Herock RC	2.00	4.00
142 Jon Jelacic SP RC	3.00	6.00
143 Joe Krakoski RC	2.00	4.00
144 Archie Matsos SP	3.00	6.00
145 Mike Mercer	2.00	4.00
146 Alan Miller SP	3.00	6.00
147 Bob Mischak SP	3.00	6.00
148 Jim Otto SP	18.00	30.00
149 Clancy Osborne SP	3.00	6.00
150 Art Powell SP	6.00	12.00
151 Bo Roberson (Raider helmet placed over his foot)	2.00	4.00
152 Fred Williamson SP	18.00	30.00
153 Oakland Raiders Team Card	3.00	6.00
154 Chuck Allen RC SP	5.00	10.00
155 Lance Alworth	30.00	50.00
156 George Blair RC	2.00	4.00
157 Earl Faison	2.00	4.00
158 Sam Gruneisen RC	2.00	4.00
159 John Hadl RC	25.00	40.00
160 Dick Harris SP	3.00	6.00
161 Emil Karas SP RC	3.00	6.00
162 Dave Kocourek SP	3.00	6.00
163 Ernie Ladd	4.00	8.00
164 Keith Lincoln	3.00	6.00
165 Paul Lowe SP	6.00	12.00
166 Charlie McNeil	2.00	4.00
167 Jacque MacKinnon SP RC	3.00	6.00
168 Ron Mix SP	10.00	20.00
169 Don Norton SP	3.00	6.00
170 Don Rogers SP RC	3.00	6.00
171 Tobin Rote SP	5.00	10.00
172 Henry Schmidt SP RC	3.00	6.00
173 Bud Whitehead RC	2.00	4.00
174 Ernie Wright SP	5.00	10.00
175 San Diego Chargers Team Card	3.00	6.00
176 Checklist SP UER (155 Lance Allworth)	80.00	160.00

1964 Topps Pennant Stickers Inserts

This set of 24 pennant stickers was inserted into the 1964 Topps regular issue AFL set. These inserts are actually 2 1/8" by 4 1/2" glassine type peel-offs on gray backing. The pennants are unnumbered and are ordered below alphabetically within type. The stickers were folded in order to fit into the 1964 Topps wax packs, so they are virtually always found with a crease or fold.

COMPLETE SET (24)	750.00	1,500.00
1 Boston Patriots	50.00	100.00
2 Buffalo Bills	50.00	100.00
3 Denver Broncos	60.00	120.00
4 Houston Oilers	50.00	100.00
5 Kansas City Chiefs	50.00	100.00
6 New York Jets	50.00	100.00
7 Oakland Raiders	60.00	120.00
8 San Diego Chargers	50.00	100.00
9 Air Force Falcons	30.00	60.00
10 Army Cadets	30.00	60.00
11 Dartmouth Indians	30.00	60.00
12 Duke Blue Devils	30.00	60.00
13 Michigan Wolverines	37.50	75.00
14 Minnesota Golden Gophers	30.00	60.00
15 Mississippi Rebels	30.00	60.00
16 Navy Midshipmen	30.00	60.00
17 Notre Dame Fighting Irish	75.00	150.00
18 SMU Mustangs	30.00	60.00
19 USC Trojans	30.00	60.00
20 Syracuse Orangemen	30.00	60.00
21 Texas Longhorns	30.00	60.00
22 Washington Huskies	30.00	60.00
23 Wisconsin Badgers	30.00	60.00
24 Yale Bulldogs	30.00	60.00

1965 Topps

The 1965 Topps football card set contains 176 oversized (2 1/2" by 4 11/16") cards of American Football League players. Colorful card fronts have a player photo over a solid color background. The team name is at the top with the player's name and position at the bottom. Horizontal backs contain highlights and statistics to the left with a cartoon pertaining to the player to the right. The cards are grouped together and numbered in basic alphabetical order by teams. Since this set was not printed in the standard fashion, many of the cards were printed in lesser quantities than others. These cards are marked in the checklist with SP for short print. This set is somewhat significant in that it contains the Rookie Card of Joe Namath. Other notable Rookie Cards in this set of Oakland Raiders stars Fred Biletnikoff, Willie Brown and Ben Davidson.

COMPLETE SET (176)	2,500.00	4,000.00
WRAPPER (5-CENT)	90.00	150.00
1 Tommy Addison SP	20.00	35.00
2 Houston Antwine SP	7.00	12.00
3 Nick Buoniconti SP	18.00	30.00
4 Ron Burton SP	10.00	20.00
5 Gino Cappelletti SP	10.00	20.00
6 Jim Colclough	3.50	7.00
7 Bob Dee SP	7.00	12.00
8 Larry Eisenhauer	3.50	7.00
9 J.D. Garrett RC	3.50	7.00
10 Larry Garron	3.50	7.00
11 Art Graham SP	7.00	12.00
12 Ron Hall	3.50	7.00
13 Charles Long	3.50	7.00
14 Jon Morris RC	5.00	10.00
15 Billy Neighbors SP	7.00	12.00
16 Ross O'Hanley	3.50	7.00
17 Babe Parilli SP	10.00	20.00
18 Tony Romeo SP RC	7.00	12.00
19 Jack Rudolph SP	7.00	12.00
20 Bob Schmidt	3.50	7.00
21 Don Webb SP	7.00	12.00
22 Jim Whalen SP RC	7.00	12.00
23 Stew Barber	3.50	7.00
24 Glenn Bass SP RC	7.00	12.00
25 Al Bemiller SP	7.00	12.00
26 Wray Carlton SP	7.00	12.00
27 Tom Day RC	3.50	7.00
28 Elbert Dubenion SP	7.50	15.00
29 Jim Dunaway	3.50	7.00
30 Pete Gogolak SP RC	10.00	20.00
31 Dick Hudson SP	7.00	12.00
32 Harry Jacobs SP	7.00	12.00
33 Billy Joe SP	7.50	15.00
34 Tom Keating SP RC	7.00	12.00
35 Jack Kemp SP	75.00	150.00
36 Daryle Lamonica SP	30.00	50.00
37 Paul Maguire SP	10.00	20.00
38 Ron McDole SP RC	7.00	12.00
39 George Saimes SP	7.00	12.00
40 Tom Sestak SP	7.00	12.00
41 Billy Shaw SP	10.00	20.00
42 Mike Stratton SP	7.00	12.00
43 John Tracey SP	7.00	12.00
44 Ernie Warlick	3.50	7.00
45 Odell Barry RC	3.50	7.00
46 Willie Brown SP RC	75.00	135.00
47 Gerry Bussell SP RC	7.00	12.00
48 Eldon Danenhauer SP	7.00	12.00
49 Al Denson SP RC	7.00	12.00
50 Hewritt Dixon SP RC	7.50	15.00
51 Cookie Gilchrist SP	18.00	30.00
52 Goose Gonsoulin SP	7.50	15.00
53 Abner Haynes SP	10.00	20.00
54 Jerry Hopkins RC	3.50	7.00
55 Ray Jacobs SP	7.00	12.00
56 Jacky Lee SP	7.50	15.00
57 John McCormick	3.50	7.00
58 Bob McCullough SP	7.00	12.00
59 John McGeever RC	3.50	7.00
60 Charlie Mitchell SP	7.00	12.00
61 Jim Perkins SP RC	7.00	12.00
62 Bob Scarpitto SP	7.00	12.00
63 Mickey Slaughter SP	7.00	12.00
64 Jerry Sturm SP	7.00	12.00
65 Lionel Taylor SP	10.00	20.00
66 Scott Appleton SP	7.00	12.00
67 Johnny Baker SP RC	7.00	12.00
68 Sonny Bishop SP RC	7.00	12.00
69 George Blanda SP	75.00	125.00
70 Sid Blanks SP RC	7.00	12.00
71 Ode Burrell SP RC	7.00	12.00
72 Doug Cline SP	7.00	12.00
73 Willard Dewveall	3.50	7.00
74 Larry Elkins RC	3.50	7.00
75 Don Floyd SP	7.00	12.00
76 Freddy Glick	3.50	7.00
77 Tom Goode SP RC	7.00	12.00
78 Charlie Hennigan SP	10.00	20.00
79 Ed Husmann	3.50	7.00
80 Bobby Jancik SP	7.00	12.00
81 Bud McFadin SP	7.00	12.00
82 Bob McLeod SP	7.00	12.00
83 Jim Norton SP	7.00	12.00
84 Walt Suggs	3.50	7.00
85 Bob Talamini	3.50	7.00
86 Charley Tolar SP	7.00	12.00
87 Checklist SP	100.00	175.00
88 Don Trull SP	7.00	12.00
89 Fred Arbanas SP	7.00	12.00
90 Pete Beathard SP RC	7.00	12.00
91 Bobby Bell SP	25.00	40.00
92 Mel Branch SP	7.00	12.00
93 Tommy Brooker SP RC	7.00	12.00
94 Buck Buchanan SP	20.00	35.00
95 Ed Budde SP	7.00	12.00
96 Chris Burford SP	7.00	12.00
97 Walt Corey	3.50	7.00
98 Jerry Cornelison	3.50	7.00
99 Len Dawson SP	60.00	100.00
100 Jon Gilliam SP RC	7.00	12.00
101 Sherrill Headrick SP UER (Name spelled Sherill on front)	7.00	12.00
102 Dave Hill SP RC	7.00	12.00
103 E.J. Holub SP	7.00	12.00
104 Bobby Hunt SP	7.00	12.00
105 Frank Jackson SP	7.00	12.00
106 Jerry Mays	5.00	10.00
107 Curtis McClinton SP	7.50	15.00
108 Bobby Ply SP RC	7.00	12.00
109 Johnny Robinson SP	7.50	15.00
110 Jim Tyrer SP	7.00	12.00
111 Bill Baird SP RC	7.00	12.00
112 Ralph Baker SP RC	7.00	12.00
113 Sam DeLuca SP	7.00	12.00
114 Larry Grantham SP	7.50	15.00
115 Gene Heeter SP	7.00	12.00
116 Winston Hill SP RC	10.00	20.00
117 John Huarte SP RC	18.00	30.00
118 Cosmo Iacavazzi SP RC	7.00	12.00
119 Curley Johnson SP	7.00	12.00
120 Dee Mackey UER (College WVU, should be East Texas State)	3.50	7.00
121 Don Maynard	30.00	50.00
122 Joe Namath SP RC	1,200.00	1,800.00
123 Dainard Paulson	3.50	7.00
124 Gerry Philbin SP	7.00	12.00
125 Sherman Plunkett SP RC	7.50	15.00
126 Mark Smolinski	3.50	7.00
127 Matt Snell SP	18.00	30.00
128 Mike Taliaferro SP	7.00	12.00
129 Bake Turner SP	7.00	12.00
130 Clyde Washington SP	7.00	12.00
131 Verlon Biggs SP RC	7.00	12.00
132 Dalva Allen	3.50	7.00
133 Fred Biletnikoff SP RC	150.00	250.00
134 Billy Cannon SP	10.00	20.00
135 Dave Costa SP	7.00	12.00
136 Clem Daniels SP	7.50	15.00
137 Ben Davidson SP RC	35.00	60.00
138 Cotton Davidson SP	7.50	15.00
139 Tom Flores SP	10.00	20.00
140 Claude Gibson	3.50	7.00
141 Wayne Hawkins	3.50	7.00
142 Archie Matsos SP	7.00	12.00
143 Mike Mercer SP	7.00	12.00
144 Bob Mischak SP	7.00	12.00
145 Jim Otto	18.00	30.00
146 Art Powell UER (Photo actually Clem Daniels)	5.00	10.00
147 Warren Powers SP RC	7.00	12.00
148 Ken Rice SP	7.00	12.00
149 Bo Roberson SP	7.00	12.00
150 Harry Schuh RC	3.50	7.00
151 Larry Todd SP RC	7.00	12.00
152 Fred Williamson SP	15.00	30.00
153 J.R. Williamson RC	3.50	7.00
154 Chuck Allen	5.00	10.00
155 Lance Alworth	50.00	75.00
156 Frank Buncom RC	3.50	7.00
157 Steve DeLong SP RC	7.00	12.00
158 Earl Faison SP	7.50	15.00
159 Kenny Graham SP RC	7.00	12.00
160 George Gross SP RC	7.00	12.00
161 John Hadl SP	20.00	35.00
162 Emil Karas SP	7.00	12.00
163 Dave Kocourek SP	7.00	12.00
164 Ernie Ladd SP	10.00	20.00
165 Keith Lincoln SP	10.00	20.00
166 Paul Lowe SP	10.00	20.00
167 Jacque MacKinnon	3.50	7.00
168 Ron Mix	12.00	20.00
169 Don Norton SP	7.00	12.00
170 Bob Petrich RC	3.50	7.00
171 Rick Redman SP RC	7.00	12.00
172 Pat Shea RC	3.50	7.00
173 Walt Sweeney SP RC	7.50	15.00
174 Dick Westmoreland RC	3.50	7.00
175 Ernie Wright SP	10.00	20.00
176 Checklist SP	125.00	225.00

1965 Topps Magic Rub-Off Inserts

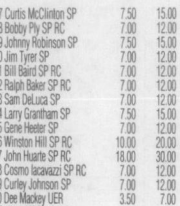

This set of 36 rub-off team emblems was inserted into packs of the 1965 Topps AFL regular football issue. They are very similar to the 1961 Topps Baseball Magic Rub-Offs. Each rub-off measures 2" by 3"; eight AFL teams and 28 college teams are featured. The rub-offs are unnumbered and, hence, are numbered below alphabetically within type, i.e., AFL teams 1-8 and college teams 9-36.

COMPLETE SET (36)	400.00	800.00
1 Boston Patriots	15.00	30.00
2 Buffalo Bills	15.00	30.00
3 Denver Broncos	20.00	40.00
4 Houston Oilers	15.00	30.00
5 Kansas City Chiefs	15.00	30.00
6 New York Jets	15.00	30.00
7 Oakland Raiders	20.00	40.00
8 San Diego Chargers	15.00	30.00
9 Alabama Crimson Tide	12.50	25.00
10 Air Force Falcons	10.00	20.00
11 Arkansas Razorbacks	10.00	20.00
12 Army Cadets	10.00	20.00
13 Boston College Eagles	10.00	20.00
14 Duke Blue Devils	10.00	20.00
15 Illinois Fighting Illini	10.00	20.00
16 Kansas Jayhawks	10.00	20.00
17 Kentucky Wildcats	10.00	20.00
18 Maryland Terrapins	10.00	20.00
19 Miami Hurricanes	10.00	20.00
20 Minnesota Golden Gophers	10.00	20.00
21 Mississippi Rebels	10.00	20.00
22 Navy Midshipmen	10.00	20.00
23 Nebraska Cornhuskers	10.00	20.00
24 Notre Dame Fighting Irish	20.00	40.00
25 Penn State Nittany Lions	12.50	25.00
26 Purdue Boilermakers	10.00	20.00
27 SMU Mustangs	10.00	20.00
28 USC Trojans	10.00	20.00
29 Stanford Indians	10.00	20.00
30 Syracuse Orangemen	10.00	20.00
31 TCU Horned Frogs	10.00	20.00
32 Texas Longhorns	10.00	20.00
33 Virginia Cavaliers	10.00	20.00
34 Washington Huskies	10.00	20.00
35 Wisconsin Badgers	10.00	20.00
36 Yale Bulldogs	10.00	20.00

1966 Topps

The 1966 Topps set of 132 standard-size cards contains AFL players grouped together and numbered alphabetically within teams. The set marks the debut into the AFL of the Miami Dolphins. Card fronts are horizontal with woodgrain borders. Such a border offers a challenge to locate cards in top grades. The player's name, team and position are within the border below the photo. The card backs are printed in black and pink on white card stock. In actuality, card number 15 is not a football card at all but a "Funny Ring" checklist card; nevertheless, it is considered part of the set and is now regarded as the toughest card in the set to find in mint condition. Funny Ring cards were inserted one per pack but measure only 2 1/2" by 3 3/8". Notable Rookie Cards in this set include Wendell Hayes, George Sauer Jr., Otis Taylor, and Jim Turner.

COMPLETE SET (132)	950.00	1,500.00
WRAPPER (5-CENT)	30.00	60.00
1 Tommy Addison	10.00	20.00
2 Houston Antwine	3.00	5.00
3 Nick Buoniconti	5.00	10.00
4 Gino Cappelletti	4.00	8.00
5 Bob Dee	3.00	5.00
6 Larry Garron	3.00	5.00
7 Art Graham	3.00	5.00
8 Ron Hall	3.00	5.00
9 Charles Long	3.00	5.00
10 Jon Morris	3.00	5.00
11 Don Oakes	3.00	5.00
12 Babe Parilli	4.00	8.00
13 Don Webb	3.00	5.00
14 Jim Whalen	3.00	5.00
15 Funny Ring Checklist	200.00	300.00
16 Stew Barber	3.00	5.00
17 Glenn Bass	3.00	5.00
18 Dave Behrman	3.00	5.00
19 Al Bemiller	3.00	5.00
20 George Butch Byrd RC	4.00	8.00
21 Wray Carlton	3.00	5.00
22 Tom Day	3.00	5.00
23 Elbert Dubenion	4.00	8.00
24 Jim Dunaway	3.00	5.00
25 Dick Hudson	3.00	5.00
26 Jack Kemp	60.00	120.00
27 Daryle Lamonica	12.00	20.00
28 Tom Sestak	3.00	5.00
29 Billy Shaw	5.00	10.00
30 Mike Stratton	3.00	5.00
31 Eldon Danenhauer	3.00	5.00
32 Cookie Gilchrist	5.00	10.00
33 Goose Gonsoulin	4.00	8.00
34 Wendell Hayes RC	5.00	10.00
35 Abner Haynes	5.00	10.00
36 Jerry Hopkins	3.00	5.00
37 Ray Jacobs	3.00	5.00
38 Charlie Janerette RC	3.00	5.00
39 Ray Kubala RC	3.00	5.00
40 John McCormick	3.00	5.00
41 Leroy Moore RC	3.00	5.00
42 Bob Scarpitto	3.00	5.00
43 Mickey Slaughter	3.00	5.00
44 Jerry Sturm	3.00	5.00
45 Lionel Taylor	5.00	10.00
46 Scott Appleton	3.00	5.00
47 Johnny Baker	3.00	5.00
48 George Blanda	20.00	35.00
49 Sid Blanks	3.00	5.00
50 Danny Brabham RC	3.00	5.00
51 Ode Burrell	3.00	5.00
52 Gary Cutsinger	3.00	5.00
53 Larry Elkins	3.00	5.00
54 Don Floyd	3.00	5.00
55 Willie Frazier RC	4.00	8.00
56 Freddy Glick	3.00	5.00
57 Charlie Hennigan	4.00	8.00
58 Bobby Jancik	3.00	5.00
59 Rich Michael	3.00	5.00
60 Don Trull	3.00	5.00
61 Checklist Card	30.00	55.00
62 Fred Arbanas	3.00	5.00
63 Pete Beathard	3.00	5.00
64 Bobby Bell	5.00	10.00
65 Ed Budde	3.00	5.00
66 Chris Burford	3.00	5.00
67 Len Dawson	25.00	40.00
68 Jon Gilliam	3.00	5.00
69 Sherrill Headrick	3.00	5.00
70 E.J. Holub UER (College: TCU, should be Texas Tech)	3.00	5.00
71 Bobby Hunt	3.00	5.00
72 Curtis McClinton	4.00	8.00
73 Jerry Mays	3.00	5.00
74 Johnny Robinson	4.00	8.00
75 Otis Taylor RC	15.00	25.00
76 Tom Erlandson RC	4.00	8.00
77 Norm Evans UER RC (Flanker on front, tackle on back)	5.00	10.00
78 Tom Goode	4.00	8.00
79 Mike Hudock	4.00	8.00
80 Frank Jackson	4.00	8.00
81 Billy Joe	4.00	8.00
82 Dave Kocourek	4.00	8.00
83 Bo Roberson	4.00	8.00
84 Jack Spikes	4.00	8.00
85 Jim Warren RC	4.00	8.00
86 Willie West RC	4.00	8.00
87 Dick Westmoreland	4.00	8.00
88 Eddie Wilson RC	4.00	8.00
89 Dick Wood	4.00	8.00
90 Verlon Biggs	4.00	8.00
91 Sam DeLuca	3.00	5.00
92 Winston Hill	3.00	5.00
93 Dee Mackey	3.00	5.00
94 Bill Mathis	3.00	5.00
95 Don Maynard	18.00	30.00
96 Joe Namath	150.00	250.00
97 Dainard Paulson	3.00	5.00
98 Gerry Philbin	4.00	8.00
99 Sherman Plunkett	3.00	5.00
100 Paul Rochester	3.00	5.00
101 George Sauer Jr. RC	7.50	15.00
102 Matt Snell	5.00	10.00
103 Jim Turner RC	4.00	8.00
104 Fred Biletnikoff UER (Misspelled on back as Bilentnikoff)	30.00	50.00
105 Bill Budness RC	3.00	5.00
106 Billy Cannon	5.00	10.00
107 Clem Daniels	4.00	8.00
108 Ben Davidson	7.50	15.00
109 Cotton Davidson	4.00	8.00
110 Claude Gibson	3.00	5.00
111 Wayne Hawkins	3.00	5.00
112 Ken Herock	3.00	5.00
113 Bob Mischak	3.00	5.00
114 Gus Otto RC	3.00	5.00
115 Jim Otto	12.00	20.00
116 Art Powell	5.00	10.00
117 Harry Schuh	3.00	5.00
118 Chuck Allen	3.00	5.00
119 Lance Alworth	25.00	40.00
120 Frank Buncom	3.00	5.00
121 Steve DeLong	3.00	5.00
122 John Farris RC	3.00	5.00
123 Kenny Graham	3.00	5.00
124 Sam Gruneisen	3.00	5.00
125 John Hadl	5.00	10.00
126 Walt Sweeney	3.00	5.00
127 Keith Lincoln	5.00	10.00
128 Ron Mix	5.00	10.00
129 Don Norton	3.00	5.00
130 Pat Shea	3.00	5.00
131 Ernie Wright	5.00	10.00
132 Checklist Card	50.00	100.00

1967 Topps

The 1967 Topps set of 132 standard-size cards contains AFL players only, with players grouped together and numbered by teams. The cardfronts include an oval design player photo surrounded by a team color. The cardbacks are printed in black text with a dark yellow or gold colored background on white card stock. A question (with upside-down answer) is given on the bottom of the cardbacks. Additionally, some cards were also issued along with the "Win-A-Card" board game from Milton Bradley that included cards from the 1965 Topps Hot Rods and 1968 Topps baseball card sets. This version of the cards is somewhat difficult to distinguish, but are often found with a slight touch of the 1968 baseball set border on the front top or bottom edge as well as a brighter yellow card back instead of the darker yellow or gold color. Known cards issued in this version include: #2, 12, 13, 18, 22, 28, 30, 31, 32, 48, 49, 51, 58, 60, 67, 68, 71, 84, 86, 87, 88, 92, 95, 98, 103, 106, 110, 116, 117, 121, 124, 125, and 130.

COMPLETE SET (132)	400.00	700.00
WRAPPER (5-CENT)	30.00	60.00
1 John Huarte	10.00	18.00
2 Babe Parilli	2.00	4.00
3 Gino Cappelletti	2.00	4.00
4 Larry Garron	1.50	3.00
5 Tommy Addison	1.50	3.00
6 Jon Morris	1.50	3.00
7 Houston Antwine	1.50	3.00
8 Don Oakes	1.50	3.00
9 Larry Eisenhauer	1.50	3.00
10 Jim Hunt RC	1.50	3.00
11 Jim Whalen	1.50	3.00
12 Art Graham	1.50	3.00
13 Nick Buoniconti	3.00	6.00
14 Bob Dee	1.50	3.00
15 Keith Lincoln	3.00	6.00
16 Tom Flores	2.00	4.00
17 Art Powell	2.00	4.00
18 Stew Barber	1.50	3.00
19 Wray Carlton	1.50	3.00
20 Elbert Dubenion	2.00	4.00
21 Jim Dunaway	1.50	3.00
22 Dick Hudson	1.50	3.00
23 Harry Jacobs	1.50	3.00
24 Jack Kemp	40.00	80.00
25 Ron McDole	1.50	3.00
26 George Saimes	1.50	3.00
27 Tom Sestak	1.50	3.00
28 Billy Shaw	3.00	6.00
29 Mike Stratton	1.50	3.00
30 Nemiah Wilson RC	1.50	3.00
31 John McCormick	1.50	3.00
32 Rex Mirich RC	1.50	3.00
33 Dave Costa	1.50	3.00
34 Goose Gonsoulin	2.00	4.00
35 Abner Haynes	3.00	6.00
36 Wendell Hayes	2.00	4.00
37 Archie Matsos	1.50	3.00
38 John Bramlett RC	1.50	3.00
39 Jerry Sturm	1.50	3.00
40 Max Leetzow RC	1.50	3.00
41 Bob Scarpitto	1.50	3.00
42 Lionel Taylor	3.00	6.00
43 Al Denson	1.50	3.00
44 Miller Farr RC	1.50	3.00
45 Don Trull	1.50	3.00
46 Jacky Lee	2.00	4.00
47 Bobby Jancik	1.50	3.00
48 Ode Burrell	1.50	3.00
49 Larry Elkins	1.50	3.00
50 W.K. Hicks RC	1.50	3.00
51 Sid Blanks	1.50	3.00
52 Jim Norton	1.50	3.00
53 Bobby Maples RC	1.50	3.00
54 Bob Talamini	1.50	3.00
55 Walt Suggs	1.50	3.00
56 Gary Cutsinger	1.50	3.00
57 Danny Brabham	1.50	3.00
58 Ernie Ladd	3.00	6.00
59 Checklist Card	25.00	50.00
60 Pete Beathard	1.50	3.00
61 Len Dawson	18.00	30.00
62 Bobby Hunt	1.50	3.00
63 Bert Coan RC	1.50	3.00
64 Curtis McClinton	2.00	4.00
65 Johnny Robinson	2.00	4.00
66 E.J. Holub	1.50	3.00
67 Jerry Mays	1.50	3.00
68 Jim Tyrer	2.00	4.00
69 Bobby Bell	3.00	6.00
70 Fred Arbanas	1.50	3.00
71 Buck Buchanan	3.00	6.00
72 Chris Burford	1.50	3.00
73 Otis Taylor	3.00	6.00
74 Cookie Gilchrist	4.00	8.00
75 Earl Faison	1.50	3.00
76 George Wilson Jr. RC	2.00	4.00
77 Rick Norton RC	1.50	3.00
78 Frank Jackson	2.00	4.00
79 Joe Auer RC	1.50	3.00
80 Willie West	1.50	3.00
81 Jim Warren	1.50	3.00
82 Wahoo McDaniel RC	30.00	50.00
83 Ernie Park RC	1.50	3.00
84 Billy Neighbors	1.50	3.00
85 Norm Evans	2.00	4.00
86 Tom Nomina	1.50	3.00
87 Rich Zecher RC	1.50	3.00
88 Dave Kocourek	1.50	3.00
89 Bill Baird	1.50	3.00
90 Ralph Baker	1.50	3.00
91 Verlon Biggs	1.50	3.00
92 Sam DeLuca	1.50	3.00
93 Larry Grantham	2.00	4.00
94 Jim Harris RC	1.50	3.00
95 Winston Hill	1.50	3.00
96 Bill Mathis	1.50	3.00
97 Don Maynard	12.00	20.00
98 Joe Namath	75.00	150.00
99 Gerry Philbin	2.00	4.00
100 Paul Rochester	1.50	3.00
101 George Sauer Jr.	2.00	4.00
102 Matt Snell	3.00	6.00
103 Daryle Lamonica	5.00	10.00
104 Glenn Bass	1.50	3.00
105 Jim Otto	3.00	6.00
106 Fred Biletnikoff	18.00	30.00
107 Cotton Davidson	2.00	4.00
108 Larry Todd	1.50	3.00
109 Billy Cannon	3.00	6.00
110 Clem Daniels	2.00	4.00
111 Dave Grayson	1.50	3.00
112 Kent McCloughan RC	1.50	3.00
113 Bob Svihus RC	1.50	3.00
114 Ike Lassiter	1.50	3.00
115 Harry Schuh	1.50	3.00
116 Ben Davidson	4.00	8.00
117 Tom Day	1.50	3.00
118 Scott Appleton	1.50	3.00
119 Steve Tensi RC	1.50	3.00
120 John Hadl	3.00	6.00
121 Paul Lowe	2.00	4.00
122 Jim Allison RC	1.50	3.00
123 Lance Alworth	20.00	35.00
124 Jacque MacKinnon	1.50	3.00
125 Ron Mix	3.00	6.00
126 Bob Petrich	1.50	3.00
127 Howard Kindig RC	1.50	3.00
128 Steve DeLong	1.50	3.00
129 Chuck Allen	1.50	3.00
130 Frank Buncom	1.50	3.00
131 Speedy Duncan RC	2.50	5.00
132 Checklist Card	35.00	70.00

1967 Topps Comic Pennants

This set was issued as an insert with the 1967 Topps regular issue football cards as well as being issued separately. The stickers are standard size, and the backs are blank. The set can also be found in adhesive form with the pennant merely printed on card stock. They are numbered in the upper right corner, although reportedly they can also occasionally be found without numbers. Many of the cards feature sayings or depictions that are in poor taste, i.e., sick humor. Perhaps they were discontinued or recalled before the end of the season, which would explain their relative scarcity.

COMPLETE SET (31)	300.00	600.00
1 Navel Academy	10.00	25.00
2 City College of Useless Knowledge	10.00	25.00
3 Notre Dame (Hunchback of)	20.00	40.00
4 Psychedelic State	10.00	25.00
5 Minneapolis Mini-skirts	10.00	25.00
6 School of Art Go& Van Gogh	10.00	25.00
7 Washington Is Dead	10.00	25.00
8 School of Hard Knocks	10.00	25.00
9 Alaska (If I See Her ...)	10.00	25.00
10 Confused State	10.00	25.00
11 Yale Locks Are Tough to Pick	10.00	25.00
12 University of Transylvania	10.00	25.00
13 Down With Teachers	10.00	25.00
14 Cornell Caught Me Cheating	10.00	25.00
15 Houston Oilers (You're a Fink)	10.00	25.00
16 Harvard (Flunked Out)	10.00	25.00
17 Diskotech	10.00	25.00
18 Dropout U.	10.00	25.00
19 Air Force (Gas Masks)	10.00	25.00
20 Nutstu U.	10.00	25.00
21 Michigan State Pen	10.00	25.00
22 Denver Broncos (Girls Look Like)	15.00	30.00
23 Buffalo Bills (Without Paying My)	12.50	30.00
24 Army of Dropouts	10.00	25.00
25 Miami Dolphins (Bitten by Two)	15.00	30.00
26 Kansas City (Has Too Few Workers And Too Many) Chiefs	10.00	25.00
27 Boston Patriots (Banned In)	10.00	25.00
28 (Fat People In) Oakland (Are Usually Icebox) Raiders	15.00	30.00
29 (I'd Go) West (If You'd Just) Point (In The Right Direction)	10.00	25.00
30 New York Jets (Skies Are Crowded With)	12.50	30.00
31 San Diego Chargers (Police Will Press)	10.00	25.00

1968 Topps

The 1968 set marks the beginning of a 21-year run of Topps being the only major producer of football cards. The two-series set of 219 standard-size cards is Topps' first set in seven years (since 1961) to contain players from both leagues. The set marks the AFL debut of the Cincinnati Bengals. Card fronts feature the player photo over a solid background. A team logo is in an upper corner. The player's name, team name and position are in a colored cicular box at the bottom. Cards for players from the previous year's Super Bowl teams, the Green Bay Packers and the Oakland Raiders, are the only cards to contain horizontally designed fronts. In addition, these cards also have color boders at top and bottom and the player photo is superimposed over yellow tinted game action artwork. The backs have statistics and highlights as well as a rub-off cartoon at the bottom. The cards in the second series have blue printing on the back whereas the cards in the first series had green printing on the back. Card backs of some of the cards in the second series can be used to form a ten-card puzzle of Bart Starr (141, 148, 153, 155, 168, 172, 186, 197, 201, and 213) or Len Dawson (145, 146, 151, 152, 163, 166, 170, 195, 199, and 200). The set features the Rookie Cards of quarterbacks Bob Griese, Jim Hart, and Craig Morton, and (ex-Syracuse) running backs Floyd Little and Jim Nance. The second series (132-219) is slightly more difficult to obtain than the first series. This set was issued in five card wax packs which cost five cents and came 24 packs to a box.

COMPLETE SET (219)	350.00	550.00
WRAPPER (5-CENT, SER.1)	10.00	20.00
WRAPPER (5-CENT, SER.2)	20.00	30.00
1 Bart Starr	25.00	40.00
2 Dick Bass	1.00	2.00
3 Grady Alderman	.75	1.50
4 Obert Logan	.75	1.50
5 Ernie Koy RC	1.00	2.00
6 Don Hultz RC	.75	1.50
7 Earl Gros	.75	1.50
8 Jim Bakken	.75	1.50
9 George Mira	1.00	2.00
10 Carl Kammerer RC	.75	1.50
11 Willie Frazier	.75	1.50
12 Kent McCloughan UER (McCloughlan on card back)	.75	1.50
13 George Sauer Jr.	1.00	2.00
14 Jack Clancy RC	.75	1.50
15 Jim Tyrer	1.00	2.00
16 Bobby Maples	.75	1.50
17 Bo Hickey RC	.75	1.50
18 Frank Buncom	.75	1.50
19 Keith Lincoln	1.00	2.00
20 Jim Whalen	.75	1.50
21 Junior Coffey	.75	1.50
22 Billy Ray Smith	.75	1.50
23 Johnny Morris	.75	1.50
24 Ernie Green	.75	1.50
25 Don Meredith	15.00	25.00
26 Wayne Walker	.75	1.50
27 Carroll Dale	1.00	2.00
28 Bernie Casey	1.00	2.00
29 Dave Osborn RC	1.00	2.00
30 Ray Poage	.75	1.50
31 Homer Jones	.75	1.50
32 Sam Baker	.75	1.50
33 Bill Saul RC	.75	1.50
34 Ken Willard	1.00	2.00
35 Bobby Mitchell	2.00	4.00
36 Gary Garrison RC	1.00	2.00
37 Billy Cannon	1.00	2.00
38 Ralph Baker	.75	1.50
39 Howard Twilley RC	2.00	4.00
40 Wendell Hayes	1.00	2.00
41 Jim Norton	.75	1.50
42 Tom Beer RC	.75	1.50
43 Chris Burford	.75	1.50
44 Stew Barber	.75	1.50
45 Leroy Mitchell UER RC (Lifetime Int. should be 3, not 2)	.75	1.50
46 Dan Grimm	.75	1.50
47 Jerry Logan	.75	1.50
48 Andy Livingston RC	.75	1.50
49 Paul Warfield	7.50	15.00
50 Don Perkins	1.50	3.00
51 Ron Kramer	.75	1.50
52 Bob Jeter RC	1.00	2.00
53 Les Josephson RC	1.00	2.00
54 Bobby Walden	.75	1.50
55 Checklist Card	7.50	15.00
56 Walter Roberts	.75	1.50
57 Henry Carr	.75	1.50
58 Gary Ballman	.75	1.50
59 J.R. Wilburn RC	.75	1.50
60 Jim Hart RC	5.00	10.00
61 Jim Johnson	1.50	3.00
62 Chris Hanburger	1.00	2.00
63 John Hadl	1.50	3.00
64 Hewritt Dixon	1.00	2.00
65 Joe Namath	50.00	80.00
66 Jim Warren	.75	1.50
67 Curtis McClinton	1.00	2.00
68 Bob Talamini	.75	1.50
69 Steve Tensi	.75	1.50
70 Dick Van Raaphorst UER RC	.75	1.50
71 Art Powell	1.00	2.00
72 Jim Nance RC	2.00	4.00
73 Bob Riggle RC	.75	1.50
74 John Mackey	2.50	5.00
75 Gale Sayers	25.00	40.00
76 Gene Hickerson	1.25	2.50
77 Dan Reeves	5.00	10.00
78 Tom Nowatzke	.75	1.50
79 Elijah Pitts	1.50	3.00
80 Lamar Lundy	1.00	2.00
81 Paul Flatley	.75	1.50
82 Dave Whitsell	.75	1.50
83 Spider Lockhart	1.00	2.00
84 Dave Lloyd	.75	1.50
85 Roy Jefferson	1.00	2.00
86 Jackie Smith	3.00	6.00
87 John David Crow	1.00	2.00
88 Sonny Jurgensen	3.00	6.00
89 Ron Mix	1.50	3.00
90 Clem Daniels	1.00	2.00
91 Cornell Gordon RC	.75	1.50
92 Tom Goode	.75	1.50
93 Bobby Bell	1.50	3.00
94 Walt Suggs	.75	1.50
95 Eric Crabtree RC	.75	1.50
96 Sherrill Headrick	.75	1.50
97 Wray Carlton	.75	1.50
98 Gino Cappelletti	1.00	2.00
99 Tommy McDonald	2.00	4.00
100 John Unitas	25.00	40.00
101 Richie Petitbon	.75	1.50
102 Erich Barnes	.75	1.50
103 Bob Hayes	5.00	10.00
104 Milt Plum	1.00	2.00
105 Boyd Dowler	1.00	2.00
106 Ed Meador	.75	1.50
107 Fred Cox	.75	1.50
108 Steve Stonebreaker RC	.75	1.50
109 Aaron Thomas	.75	1.50
110 Norm Snead	1.00	2.00
111 Paul Martha RC	.75	1.50
112 Jerry Stovall	.75	1.50
113 Kay McFarland RC	.75	1.50
114 Pat Richter	.75	1.50
115 Rick Redman	.75	1.50
116 Tom Keating	.75	1.50
117 Matt Snell	1.00	2.00
118 Dick Westmoreland	.75	1.50
119 Jerry Mays	.75	1.50
120 Sid Blanks	.75	1.50
121 Al Denson	.75	1.50
122 Bobby Hunt	.75	1.50
123 Mike Mercer	.75	1.50
124 Nick Buoniconti	1.50	3.00
125 Ron Vanderkelen RC	.75	1.50
126 Ordell Braase	.75	1.50
127 Dick Butkus	30.00	50.00
128 Gary Collins	1.00	2.00
129 Mel Renfro	3.00	6.00
130 Alex Karras	2.50	5.00
131 Herb Adderley	2.50	5.00
132 Roman Gabriel	2.00	4.00
133 Bill Brown	1.25	2.50
134 Kent Kramer RC	1.00	2.00
135 Tucker Frederickson	1.25	2.50
136 Nate Ramsey	1.00	2.00
137 Marv Woodson RC	1.00	2.00
138 Ken Gray	1.00	2.00
139 John Brodie	2.50	5.00
140 Jerry Smith	1.00	2.00
141 Brad Hubbert RC	1.00	2.00
142 George Blanda	10.00	20.00
143 Pete Lammons RC	1.00	2.00
144 Doug Moreau RC	1.00	2.00
145 E.J. Holub	1.00	2.00
146 Ode Burrell	1.00	2.00
147 Bob Scarpitto	1.00	2.00
148 Andre White RC	1.00	2.00
149 Jack Kemp	30.00	50.00
150 Art Graham	1.00	2.00
151 Tommy Nobis	3.00	6.00
152 Willie Richardson RC	1.25	2.50
153 Jack Concannon	1.00	2.00
154 Bill Glass	1.00	2.00
155 Craig Morton RC	5.00	10.00
156 Pat Studstill	1.00	2.00
157 Ray Nitschke	5.00	10.00
158 Roger Brown	1.00	2.00
159 Joe Kapp RC	2.50	5.00
160 Jim Taylor (Shown in uniform of Green Bay Packers)	7.50	15.00
161 Fran Tarkenton	10.00	20.00
162 Mike Ditka	18.00	30.00
163 Andy Russell RC	4.00	8.00
164 Larry Wilson	2.00	4.00
165 Tommy Davis	1.00	2.00
166 Paul Krause	2.00	4.00
167 Speedy Duncan	1.00	2.00
168 Fred Biletnikoff	7.50	15.00
169 Don Maynard	5.00	10.00
170 Frank Emanuel RC	1.00	2.00
171 Len Dawson	7.50	15.00
172 Miller Farr	1.00	2.00
173 Floyd Little RC	12.50	25.00
174 Lonnie Wright RC	1.00	2.00
175 Paul Costa RC	1.00	2.00
176 Don Trull	1.00	2.00
177 Jerry Simmons RC	1.00	2.00
178 Tom Matte	1.25	2.50
179 Bennie McRae	1.00	2.00
180 Jim Kanicki RC	1.00	2.00
181 Bob Lilly	7.50	15.00
182 Tom Watkins	1.00	2.00
183 Jim Grabowski RC	3.00	6.00
184 Jack Snow RC	2.00	4.00
185 Gary Cuozzo RC	1.25	2.50
186 Billy Kilmer	2.00	4.00
187 Jim Katcavage	1.00	2.00
188 Floyd Peters	1.00	2.00
189 Bill Nelsen	1.25	2.50
190 Bobby Joe Conrad	1.25	2.50
191 Kermit Alexander	1.00	2.00
192 Charley Taylor UER (Called Charley and Charlie on back)	3.00	6.00
193 Lance Alworth	10.00	20.00
194 Daryle Lamonica	2.50	5.00
195 Al Atkinson RC	1.00	2.00
196 Bob Griese RC	50.00	90.00
197 Buck Buchanan	2.00	4.00
198 Pete Beathard	1.00	2.00
199 Nemiah Wilson	1.00	2.00
200 Ernie Wright	1.00	2.00
201 George Saimes	1.00	2.00
202 John Charles RC	1.00	2.00
203 Randy Johnson	1.00	2.00
204 Tony Lorick	1.00	2.00
205 Dick Evey	1.00	2.00
206 Leroy Kelly	5.00	10.00
207 Lee Roy Jordan	3.00	6.00
208 Jim Gibbons	1.00	2.00
209 Donny Anderson RC	2.00	4.00
210 Maxie Baughan	1.00	2.00
211 Joe Morrison	1.00	2.00
212 Jim Snowden RC	1.00	2.00
213 Lenny Lyles	1.00	2.00
214 Bobby Joe Green	1.00	2.00
215 Frank Ryan	1.25	2.50
216 Cornell Green	1.25	2.50
217 Karl Sweetan	1.00	2.00
218 Dave Williams RC	1.00	2.00
219A Checklist 132-218 (green print on back)	10.00	18.00
219B Checklist 132-218 (blue print on back)	12.00	20.00

1968 Topps Posters Inserts

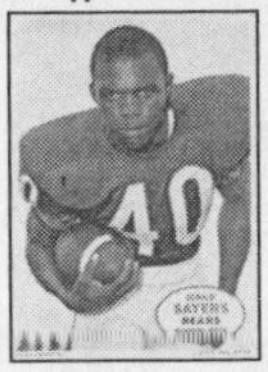

The 1968 Topps Football Posters set contains 16 NFL and AFL players on paper stock; the cards (posters) measure approximately 5" by 7". The posters, folded twice for insertion into first series wax packs, are numbered on the obverse at the lower left hand corner. The backs of these posters are blank. Fold marks are normal and do not detract from the poster's condition. These posters are the same style as the 1967 Topps baseball

COMPLETE SET (16)	40.00	80.00
1 Johnny Unitas	10.00	20.00
2 Leroy Kelly	2.50	5.00
3 Bob Hayes	3.00	6.00
4 Bart Starr	7.50	15.00
5 Charley Taylor	2.50	5.00
6 Fran Tarkenton	5.00	10.00
7 Jim Bakken	1.50	3.00
8 Gale Sayers	6.00	12.00
9 Gary Cuozzo	1.50	3.00
10 Les Josephson	1.50	3.00
11 Jim Nance	1.50	3.00
12 Brad Hubbert	1.50	3.00
13 Keith Lincoln	1.50	3.00
14 Don Maynard	3.00	6.00
15 Len Dawson	4.00	8.00
16 Jack Clancy	1.50	3.00

1968 Topps Stand-Ups Inserts

The 22-card 1968 Topps Football Stand-Ups standard-size set is unnumbered but has been numbered alphabetically in the checklist below for your convenience. Values listed below are for complete cards; the value is greatly reduced if the backs are detached, and such a card can be considered fair to good at best. The cards were issued as an insert in second series packs of 1968 Topps football cards, one per pack.

COMPLETE SET (22)	150.00	250.00
1 Sid Blanks	3.00	6.00
2 John Brodie	6.00	12.00
3 Jack Concannon	3.00	6.00
4 Roman Gabriel	4.00	8.00
5 Art Graham	3.00	6.00
6 Jim Grabowski	3.00	6.00
7 John Hadl	4.00	8.00
8 Jim Hart	4.00	8.00
9 Homer Jones	3.00	6.00
10 Sonny Jurgensen	6.00	12.00
11 Alex Karras	5.00	10.00
12 Billy Kilmer	4.00	8.00
13 Daryle Lamonica	4.00	8.00
14 Floyd Little	4.00	8.00
15 Curtis McClinton	3.00	6.00
16 Don Meredith	20.00	40.00
17 Joe Namath	40.00	80.00
18 Bill Nelsen	3.50	7.00
19 Dave Osborn	3.00	6.00
20 Willie Richardson	3.00	6.00
21 Frank Ryan	3.50	7.00
22 Norm Snead	3.50	7.00

1968 Topps Test Teams

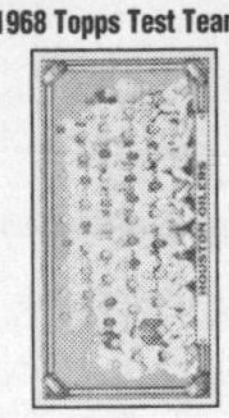

The 25-card set of team cards was issued as a stand alone wax pack (10-cents per pack) product with cloth patch/sticker inserts. The fronts provide a black and white picture of the team while the backs give the names of the players in the picture in red print on vanilla card stock. Due to their positioning within the pack, these test team cards are typically found with gum stains on the card backs. The cards measure approximately 2 1/2" by 4 11/16" and are numbered on the back.

COMPLETE SET (25)	1,800.00	3,000.00
WRAPPER (10-cent)	250.00	350.00
1 Green Bay Packers	87.50	175.00
2 New Orleans Saints	50.00	100.00
3 New York Jets	75.00	150.00
4 Miami Dolphins	87.50	175.00
5 Pittsburgh Steelers	62.50	125.00
6 Detroit Lions	50.00	100.00
7 Los Angeles Rams	50.00	100.00
8 Atlanta Falcons	50.00	100.00
9 New York Giants	62.50	125.00
10 Denver Broncos	175.00	300.00
11 Dallas Cowboys	175.00	300.00
12 Buffalo Bills	62.50	125.00
13 Cleveland Browns	62.50	125.00
14 San Francisco 49ers	62.50	125.00
15 Baltimore Colts	50.00	100.00
16 San Diego Chargers	50.00	100.00
17 Oakland Raiders	100.00	200.00
18 Houston Oilers	50.00	100.00
19 Minnesota Vikings	62.50	125.00
20 Washington Redskins	87.50	175.00
21 St. Louis Cardinals	50.00	100.00
22 Kansas City Chiefs	50.00	100.00
23 Boston Patriots	50.00	100.00
24 Chicago Bears	67.50	135.00
25 Philadelphia Eagles	50.00	100.00

1968 Topps Test Team Patches

These team emblem cloth patches/stickers were distributed as an insert with the 1968 Topps Test Teams: one sticker per 10 cent pack along with one test team. In fact according to the wrapper, these stickers were the featured item; however the hobby has deemed the team cards to be more collectible and hence more valuable than these rather bland, but scarce, logo stickers. The complete set of 44 patches consisted of team emblems, the letters A through Z, and the numbers 0 through 9. The letters and number patches contained two letters or numbers on each patch. The number patches are printed in black on a blue background, the letter patches are white on a red background, and the team emblems were done in the team colors. The stickers measure 2 1/2" by 3 1/2". The backs are blank.

COMPLETE SET (44)	1,000.00	2,000.00
1 1 and 2	6.00	12.00
2 3 and 4	6.00	12.00
3 5 and 6	6.00	12.00
4 7 and 8	6.00	12.00
5 9 and 0	6.00	12.00
6 A and B	6.00	12.00
7 C and D	6.00	12.00
8 E and F	6.00	12.00
9 G and H	6.00	12.00
10 I and W	6.00	12.00
11 J and X	6.00	12.00
12 Atlanta Falcons	30.00	60.00
13 Baltimore Colts	30.00	60.00
14 Chicago Bears	45.00	90.00
15 Cleveland Browns	30.00	60.00
16 Dallas Cowboys	100.00	175.00
17 Detroit Lions	30.00	60.00
18 Green Bay Packers	75.00	125.00
19 Los Angeles Rams	30.00	60.00
20 Minnesota Vikings	45.00	90.00
21 New Orleans Saints	30.00	60.00
22 New York Giants	45.00	90.00
23 K and L	6.00	12.00
24 M and O	6.00	12.00
25 N and P	6.00	12.00
26 Q and R	6.00	12.00
27 S and T	6.00	12.00
28 U and V	6.00	12.00
29 Y and Z	6.00	12.00
30 Philadelphia Eagles	30.00	60.00
31 Pittsburgh Steelers	45.00	90.00
32 St. Louis Cardinals	30.00	60.00
33 San Francisco 49ers	30.00	60.00
34 Washington Redskins	100.00	200.00
35 Boston Patriots	30.00	60.00
36 Buffalo Bills	30.00	60.00
37 Denver Broncos	67.50	135.00
38 Houston Oilers	30.00	60.00
39 Kansas City Chiefs	30.00	60.00
40 Miami Dolphins	75.00	150.00
41 New York Jets	30.00	60.00
42 Oakland Raiders	75.00	150.00
43 San Diego Chargers	30.00	60.00
44 Cincinnati Bengals	30.00	60.00

1969 Topps

The 1969 Topps set of 263 standard-size cards was issued in two series. First series cards (1-132) are borderless whereas the second series (133-263) cards have white borders. The lack of borders makes the first series especially difficult to find in mint condition. The checklist card (132) was obviously printed with each series as it is found in both styles (with and without borders). The set was issued in 12-card 10-cent packs. Though the borders differ, the fronts have otherwise consistent designs. A player photo is superimposed over a solid color background with the team logo, player's name, team name and position at the bottom. The backs of the cards are predominantly black, but with a green and white accent. Card backs of some of the cards in the second series can be used to form a ten-card puzzle of Fran Tarkenton (137, 145, 168, 174, 177, 194, 211, 219, 224, and 256). This set is distinctive in that it contains the late Brian Piccolo's only regular issue card. Another notable Rookie Card in this set is Larry Csonka.

COMPLETE SET (263)	350.00	550.00
WRAPPER (5-CENT)	15.00	30.00
1 Leroy Kelly	10.00	20.00
2 Paul Flatley	.75	1.50
3 Jim Cadile RC	.75	1.50
4 Erich Barnes	.75	1.50
5 Willie Richardson	.75	1.50
6 Bob Hayes	4.00	8.00
7 Bob Jeter	.75	1.50
8 Jim Colclough	.75	1.50
9 Sherrill Headrick	.75	1.50
10 Jim Dunaway	.75	1.50
11 Bill Munson	1.00	2.00
12 Jack Pardee	1.00	2.00
13 Jim Lindsey RC	.75	1.50
14 Dave Whitsell	.75	1.50
15 Tucker Frederickson	.75	1.50
16 Alvin Haymond	1.00	2.00
17 Andy Russell	1.00	2.00
18 Tom Beer	.75	1.50
19 Bobby Maples	.75	1.50
20 Len Dawson	4.00	8.00
21 Willis Crenshaw	.75	1.50
22 Tommy Davis	.75	1.50
23 Rickie Harris	.75	1.50
24 Jerry Simmons	.75	1.50
25 John Unitas	25.00	40.00
26 Brian Piccolo UER RC (Misspelled Bryon on front and Bryan on back)	50.00	80.00
27 Bob Matheson RC	.75	1.50
28 Howard Twilley	1.00	2.00
29 Jim Turner	1.00	2.00
30 Pete Banaszak RC	1.00	2.00
31 Lance Rentzel RC	1.00	2.00
32 Bill Triplett	.75	1.50
33 Boyd Dowler	1.00	2.00
34 Merlin Olsen	2.50	5.00
35 Joe Kapp	1.50	3.00
36 Dan Abramowicz RC	2.00	4.00
37 Spider Lockhart	1.00	2.00
38 Tom Day	.75	1.50
39 Art Graham	.75	1.50
40 Bob Cappadona RC	.75	1.50
41 Gary Ballman	.75	1.50
42 Clendon Thomas	.75	1.50
43 Jackie Smith	2.00	4.00
44 Dave Wilcox	1.50	3.00
45 Jerry Smith	.75	1.50
46 Dan Grimm	.75	1.50
47 Tom Matte	1.00	2.00
48 John Stofa RC	.75	1.50
49 Rex Mirich	.75	1.50
50 Miller Farr	.75	1.50
51 Gale Sayers	25.00	40.00
52 Bill Nelsen	1.00	2.00
53 Bob Lilly	3.00	6.00
54 Wayne Walker	.75	1.50
55 Ray Nitschke	2.50	5.00
56 Ed Meador	.75	1.50
57 Lonnie Warwick RC	.75	1.50
58 Wendell Hayes	.75	1.50
59 Dick Anderson RC	2.50	5.00
60 Don Maynard	3.00	6.00
61 Tony Lorick	.75	1.50
62 Pete Gogolak	.75	1.50
63 Nate Ramsey	.75	1.50
64 Dick Shiner RC	.75	1.50
65 Larry Wilson	1.50	3.00
66 Ken Willard	1.00	2.00
67 Charley Taylor UER (Led Redskins in pass interceptions)	2.50	5.00
68 Billy Cannon	1.00	2.00
69 Lance Alworth	4.00	8.00
70 Jim Nance	1.00	2.00
71 Nick Rassas RC	.75	1.50
72 Lenny Lyles	.75	1.50
73 Bennie McRae	.75	1.50
74 Bill Glass	.75	1.50
75 Don Meredith	15.00	25.00
76 Dick LeBeau	1.00	2.50
77 Carroll Dale	1.00	2.00
78 Ron McDole	.75	1.50
79 Charley King RC	.75	1.50
80 Checklist 1-132 UER (26 Bryon Piccolo)	7.50	15.00
81 Dick Bass	1.00	2.00
82 Roy Winston	.75	1.50
83 Don McCall RC	.75	1.50
84 Jim Katcavage	1.00	2.00
85 Norm Snead	1.00	2.00
86 Earl Gros	.75	1.50
87 Don Brumm RC	.75	1.50
88 Sonny Bishop	.75	1.50
89 Fred Arbanas	.75	1.50
90 Karl Noonan RC	.75	1.50
91 Dick Witcher RC	.75	1.50
92 Vince Promuto	.75	1.50
93 Tommy Nobis	2.00	4.00
94 Jerry Hill RC	.75	1.50
95 Ed O'Bradovich RC	.75	1.50
96 Ernie Kellerman RC	.75	1.50
97 Chuck Howley	1.00	2.00
98 Hewritt Dixon	.75	1.50
99 Ron Mix	1.50	3.00
100 Joe Namath	40.00	75.00
101 Billy Gambrell RC	.75	1.50
102 Elijah Pitts	1.00	2.00
103 Billy Truax RC	1.00	2.00
104 Ed Sharockman	.75	1.50
105 Doug Atkins	1.50	3.00
106 Greg Larson	.75	1.50
107 Israel Lang RC	.75	1.50
108 Houston Antwine	.75	1.50
109 Paul Guidry RC	.75	1.50
110 Al Denson	.75	1.50
111 Roy Jefferson	1.00	2.00
112 Chuck Latourette RC	.75	1.50
113 Jim Johnson	1.50	3.00
114 Bobby Mitchell	2.00	4.00
115 Randy Johnson	.75	1.50
116 Lou Michaels	.75	1.50
117 Rudy Kuechenberg RC	.75	1.50
118 Walt Suggs	.75	1.50
119 Goldie Sellers RC	.75	1.50
120 Larry Csonka RC	40.00	75.00
121 Jim Houston	.75	1.50
122 Craig Baynham RC	.75	1.50
123 Alex Karras	2.50	5.00
124 Jim Grabowski	1.00	2.00
125 Roman Gabriel	1.50	3.00
126 Larry Bowie	.75	1.50
127 Dave Parks	1.00	2.00
128 Ben Davidson	1.50	3.00
129 Steve DeLong	.75	1.50
130 Fred Hill RC	.75	1.50
131 Ernie Koy	1.00	2.00
132A Checklist 133-263 (no border)	7.50	15.00
132B Checklist 133-263 (thin white border like second series)	10.00	20.00
133 Dick Hoak	1.00	2.00
134 Larry Stallings RC	1.00	2.00
135 Clifton McNeil RC	1.00	2.00
136 Walter Rock	1.00	2.00
137 Billy Lothridge RC	1.00	2.00
138 Bob Vogel	1.00	2.00
139 Dick Butkus	25.00	40.00
140 Frank Ryan	1.25	2.50
141 Larry Garron	1.00	2.00
142 George Saimes	1.00	2.00
143 Frank Buncom	1.00	2.00
144 Don Perkins	1.25	2.50
145 Johnnie Robinson UER (Misspelled Johnny)	1.00	2.00
146 Lee Roy Caffey	1.25	2.50
147 Bernie Casey	1.25	2.50
148 Billy Martin E	1.00	2.00
149 Gene Howard RC	1.00	2.00
150 Fran Tarkenton	10.00	20.00
151 Eric Crabtree	1.00	2.00
152 W.K. Hicks	1.00	2.00
153 Bobby Bell	2.00	4.00
154 Sam Baker	1.00	2.00
155 Marv Woodson	1.00	2.00
156 Dave Williams	1.00	2.00
157 Bruce Bosley UER (Considered one of the three centers in all of pro football)	1.00	2.00
158 Carl Kammerer	1.00	2.00
159 Jim Burson RC	1.00	2.00
160 Roy Hilton RC	1.00	2.00
161 Bob Griese	15.00	25.00
162 Bob Talamini	1.00	2.00
163 Jim Otto	2.00	4.00
164 Ronnie Bull	1.00	2.00
165 Walter Johnson RC	1.00	2.00
166 Lee Roy Jordan	2.00	4.00
167 Mike Lucci	1.25	2.50
168 Willie Wood	2.00	4.00
169 Maxie Baughan	1.00	2.00
170 Bill Brown	1.25	2.50
171 John Hadl	2.00	4.00
172 Gino Cappelletti	1.25	2.50
173 George Butch Byrd	1.25	2.50
174 Steve Stonebreaker	1.00	2.00
175 Joe Morrison	1.00	2.00
176 Joe Scarpati	1.00	2.00
177 Bobby Walden	1.00	2.00
178 Roy Shivers	1.00	2.00
179 Kermit Alexander	1.00	2.00
180 Pat Richter	1.00	2.00
181 Pete Perreault RC	1.00	2.00
182 Pete Duranko RC	1.00	2.00
183 Leroy Mitchell	1.00	2.00
184 Jim Simon RC	1.00	2.00
185 Billy Ray Smith	1.00	2.00
186 Jack Concannon	1.00	2.00
187 Ben Davis RC	1.00	2.00
188 Mike Clark	1.00	2.00
189 Jim Gibbons	1.00	2.00
190 Dave Robinson	1.25	2.50
191 Otis Taylor	1.25	2.50
192 Nick Buoniconti	2.00	4.00
193 Matt Snell	1.25	2.50
194 Bruce Gossett	1.00	2.00
195 Mick Tingelhoff	1.25	2.50
196 Earl Leggett	1.00	2.00
197 Pete Case	1.00	2.00
198 Tom Woodeshick RC	1.00	2.00
199 Ken Kortas RC	1.00	2.00
200 Jim Hart	2.00	4.00
201 Fred Biletnikoff	5.00	10.00
202 Jacque MacKinnon	1.00	2.00
203 Jim Whalen	1.00	2.00
204 Matt Hazeltine	1.00	2.00
205 Charlie Gogolak	1.00	2.00
206 Ray Ogden RC	1.00	2.00
207 John Mackey	2.00	4.00
208 Roosevelt Taylor	1.00	2.00
209 Gene Hickerson	1.25	2.50
210 Dave Edwards RC	1.25	2.50
211 Tom Sestak	1.00	2.00
212 Ernie Wright	1.00	2.00
213 Dave Costa	1.00	2.00
214 Tom Vaughn RC	1.00	2.00
215 Bart Starr	25.00	40.00
216 Les Josephson	1.00	2.00
217 Fred Cox	1.00	2.00
218 Mike Tilleman RC	1.00	2.00
219 Darrell Dess	1.00	2.00
220 Dave Lloyd	1.00	2.00
221 Pete Beathard	1.00	2.00
222 Buck Buchanan	2.00	4.00
223 Frank Emanuel	1.00	2.00
224 Paul Martha	1.00	2.00
225 Johnny Roland	1.00	2.00
226 Gary Lewis	1.00	2.00
227 Sonny Jurgensen UER (Chiefs logo)	3.00	6.00
228 Jim Butler	1.00	2.00
229 Mike Curtis RC	4.00	8.00
230 Richie Petitbon	1.00	2.00
231 George Sauer Jr.	1.25	2.50
232 George Blanda	10.00	20.00
233 Gary Garrison	1.00	2.00
234 Gary Collins	1.25	2.50
235 Craig Morton	2.00	4.00
236 Tom Nowatzke	1.00	2.00
237 Donny Anderson	1.25	2.50
238 Deacon Jones	2.00	4.00
239 Grady Alderman	1.00	2.00
240 Bill Kilmer	2.00	4.00
241 Mike Taliaferro	1.00	2.00
242 Stew Barber	1.00	2.00
243 Bobby Hunt	1.00	2.00
244 Homer Jones	1.00	2.00
245 Bob Brown OT	2.00	4.00
246 Bill Asbury	1.00	2.00
247 Charley Johnson UER (Misspelled Charley on both sides)	1.25	2.50
248 Chris Hanburger	1.25	2.50
249 John Brodie	3.00	6.00
250 Earl Morrall	1.25	2.50
251 Floyd Little	2.50	5.00
252 Jerrel Wilson RC	1.00	2.00
253 Jim Keyes RC	1.00	2.00
254 Mel Renfro	2.00	4.00
255 Herb Adderley	2.00	4.00
256 Jack Snow	1.25	2.50
257 Charlie Durkee RC	1.00	2.00
258 Charlie Harper RC	1.00	2.00
259 J.R. Wilburn	1.00	2.00
260 Charlie Krueger	1.00	2.00
261 Pete Jacques RC	1.00	2.00
262 Gerry Philbin	1.00	2.00
263 Daryle Lamonica	5.00	10.00

1969 Topps Four-in-One Inserts

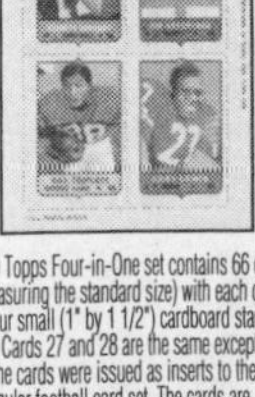

The 1969 Topps Four-in-One set contains 66 cards (each measuring the standard size) with each card having four small (1" by 1 1/2") cardboard stamps on the front. Cards 27 and 28 are the same except for colors. The cards were issued as inserts to the 1969 Topps regular football card set. The cards are unnumbered, but have been numbered in the checklist below for convenience in alphabetical order by the player in the northwest quadrant of the card. Prices below are for complete cards; individual stamps are not priced. An album exists to house the stamps on these cards (see 1969 Topps Mini Albums). It is interesting to note that not all the players appearing in this set also appear in the 1969 Topps regular issue set especially since there are almost the same number of players in each set. Jack Kemp is included in this set but not in the regular 1969 Topps set. Bryan Piccolo also appears in his only Topps appearance other than the 1969 Topps regular issue set. There are 19 players in this set who do not appear in the regular issue 1969 Topps set; they are marked by asterisks in the list below.

COMPLETE SET (66)	150.00	300.00
1 Grady Alderman	6.00	12.00
Jerry Smith		
Gale Sayers		
Dick LeBeau		
2 Jim Allison *	1.75	3.50
Frank Buncom		
Frank Emanuel		
George Sauer Jr.		
3 Lance Alworth	3.00	6.00
Don Maynard		
Ron McDole		
Billy Cannon		
4 Dick Anderson	3.00	6.00
Mike Taliaferro		
Fred Biletnikoff		
Otis Taylor		
5 Ralph Baker	2.50	5.00
Speedy Duncan		
Eric Crabtree		
Bobby Bell		
6 Gary Ballman	1.75	3.50
Jerry Hill		
Roy Jefferson		
Boyd Dowler		
7 Tom Beer	1.75	3.50
Miller Farr		
Jim Colclough		
Steve DeLong		
8 Sonny Bishop	1.75	3.50
Pete Banaszak		
Paul Guidry		
Tom Day		
9 Bruce Bosley	1.75	3.50
J.R. Wilburn		
Tom Nowatzke		
Jim Simon		
10 Larry Bowie	1.75	3.50
Willis Crenshaw		
Tommy Davis		
Paul Flatley		
11 Nick Buoniconti	2.50	5.00
George Saimes		
Jacque MacKinnon		
Pete Duranko		
12 Jim Burson	1.75	3.50
Dan Abramowicz		
Ed O'Bradovich		
Dick Witcher		
13 Reg Carolan *	1.75	3.50
Larry Garron		
W.K. Hicks		
Pete Jacques		
14 Bert Coan *	2.50	5.00
John Hadl		
Dan Birdwell *		
Sam Brunelli *		
15 Hewritt Dixon	15.00	30.00
Goldie Sellers		
Joe Namath		
Howard Twilley		
16 Charlie Durkee	5.00	10.00
Clifton McNeil		
Maxie Baughan		
Fran Tarkenton		
17 Pete Gogolak	1.75	3.50
Ronnie Bull		
Chuck Latourette		
Willie Richardson		
18 Bob Griese	5.00	10.00
Jim LeMoine *		
Dave Grayson		
Walt Sweeney		
19 Jim Hart	1.75	3.50
Darrell Dess		
Kermit Alexander		
Mick Tingelhoff		
20 Alvin Haymond	1.75	3.50
Elijah Pitts		
Billy Ray Smith		
Ken Willard		
21 Gene Hickerson	6.00	12.00
Donny Anderson		
Dick Butkus		
Mike Lucci		
22 Fred Hill	2.50	5.00
Ernie Koy		
Tommy Nobis		
Bennie McRae		
23 Dick Hoak	2.50	5.00
Roman Gabriel		
Ed Sharockman		
Dave Williams		
24 Jim Houston	1.75	3.50
Roy Shivers		
Carroll Dale		
Bill Asbury		
25 Gene Howard	1.75	3.50
Joe Morrison		
Billy Martin E		
Ben Davis		
26 Chuck Howley	12.50	25.00
Brian Piccolo UER		
Chris Hanburger		
Erich Barnes		
27 Charley Johnson (red)	1.75	3.50
Jim Katcavage		
Gary Lewis		
Bill Triplett (white)		
28 Charley Johnson (white)	1.75	3.50
Jim Katcavage		
Gary Lewis		
Bill Triplett (red)		
29 Walter Johnson	1.75	3.50
Tucker Frederickson		
Dave Lloyd		
Bobby Walden		
30 Sonny Jurgensen	4.00	8.00
Dick Bass		
Paul Martha		
Dave Parks		
31 Leroy Kelly	7.50	15.00
Ed Meador		
Bart Starr		
Ray Ogden		
32 Charley King	1.75	3.50
Bob Cappadona		
Fred Arbanas		
Ben Davidson		
33 Daryle Lamonica	2.50	5.00
Carl Cunningham *		
Bobby Hunt		
Stew Barber		
34 Israel Lang	3.00	6.00
Bob Lilly		
Jim Butler		
John Brodie		
35 Jim Lindsey	2.50	5.00
Ray Nitschke		
Rickie Harris		
Bob Vogel		
36 Billy Lothridge	2.50	5.00
Herb Adderley		
Charlie Gogolak		
John Mackey		
37 Bobby Maples	1.75	3.50
Karl Noonan		
Houston Antwine		
Wendell Hayes		
38 Don Meredith	6.00	12.00
Gary Collins		
Homer Jones		
Marv Woodson		
39 Rex Mirich	1.75	3.50
Art Graham		
Jim Turner		
John Stofa		
40 Leroy Mitchell	1.75	3.50
Sid Blanks *		
Paul Rochester *		
Pete Perreault		
41 Jim Nance	6.00	12.00
Jim Dunaway		
Larry Csonka		
Ron Mix		
42 Bill Nelsen	1.75	3.50
Bill Munson		
Nate Ramsey		
Mike Curtis		
43 Jim Otto	2.50	5.00
Dave Herman *		
Dave Costa		
Dennis Randall *		
44 Jack Pardee	1.75	3.50
Norm Snead		
Craig Baynham		
Bob Jeter		
45 Richie Petitbon	1.75	3.50
Johnny Robinson		
Mike Clark		
Jack Snow		
46 Nick Rassas	2.50	5.00
Tom Matte		
Lance Rentzel		
Bobby Mitchell		
47 Pat Richter	1.75	3.50
Dave Whitsell		
Joe Kapp		
Bill Glass		
48 Johnny Roland	1.75	3.50
Craig Morton		
Bill Brown		
Sam Baker		
49 Andy Russell	3.00	6.00
Randy Johnson		
Bob Matheson		
Alex Karras		
50 Joe Scarpati	1.75	3.50
Walter Rock		
Jack Concannon		
Bernie Casey		
51 Tom Sestak	1.75	3.50
Ernie Wright		
Doug Moreau *		
Matt Snell		
52 Jerry Simmons	2.50	5.00
Bob Hayes		
Doug Atkins		
Spider Lockhart		
53 Jackie Smith	3.00	6.00
Jim Grabowski		
Jim Johnson		
Charley Taylor		
54 Larry Stallings	2.50	5.00
Roosevelt Taylor		
Jim Gibbons		
Bob Brown OT		
55 Mike Stratton *	1.75	3.50
Marion Rushing *		
Solomon Brannan *		
Jim Keyes		
56 Walt Suggs	3.00	6.00
Len Dawson		
Sherrill Headrick		
Al Denson		
57 Bob Talamini	12.50	25.00
George Blanda		
Jim Whalen		
Jack Kemp *		
58 Clendon Thomas	1.75	3.50
Don McCall		
Earl Morrall		
Lonnie Warwick		
59 Don Trull *	2.50	5.00
Gerry Philbin		
Gary Garrison		
Buck Buchanan		
60 Johnny Unitas	7.50	15.00
Les Josephson		
Fred Cox		
Mel Renfro		
61 Wayne Walker	2.50	5.00
Tony Lorick		
Dave Wilcox		
Merlin Olsen		
62 Willie West *	1.75	3.50
Ken Herock *		
George Byrd		
Gino Cappelletti		
63 Jerrel Wilson	1.75	3.50
John Bramlett *		
Pete Beathard		
Floyd Little		
64 Larry Wilson	2.50	5.00
Lou Michaels		
Billy Gambrell		
Earl Gros		
65 Willie Wood	2.50	5.00
Steve Stonebreaker		
Vince Promuto		
Jim Cadile		
66 Tom Woodeshick	2.50	5.00
Greg Larson		
Billy Kilmer		
Don Perkins		

1969 Topps Mini-Albums Inserts

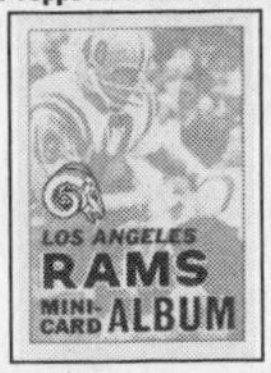

The 1969 Topps Mini Card Team Albums is a set of 26 small (2 1/2" by 3 1/2") booklets which were issued in conjunction with the 1969 Four-in-One inserts. Each of these booklets has eight pages and a game action photo on the front. Many of the cover photos were from games from the early 1960s. We've included the player's names when known. A picture of each player is contained in the album, over which the stamps from the Four-in-One inserts were to be pasted. In order to be mint, the album must have no stamps pasted in it. The booklets are printed in blue and black ink on thick white paper and are numbered on the last page of the album. The card numbering cooresponds to an alphabetical listing by team name within each league.

COMPLETE SET (26)	37.50	75.00
1 Atlanta Falcons	1.50	3.00
2 Baltimore Colts (John Unitas pictured on front)	3.00	6.00
3 Chicago Bears (Bob Gaiters pictured)	1.50	3.00
4 Cleveland Browns (Bill George and Bill Wade pictured)	2.00	4.00
5 Dallas Cowboys (Jimmy Patton and Joe Morrison pictured)	2.50	5.00
6 Detroit Lions (college teams pictured)	1.50	3.00
7 Green Bay Packers (Bart Starr pictured)	3.00	6.00
8 Los Angeles Rams (college teams pictured)	1.50	3.00
9 Minnesota Vikings (J.D.Smith pictured)	1.50	3.00
10 New Orleans Saints (Mel Triplett pictured)	1.50	3.00
11 New York Giants (Dick Modzelewski and Norm Snead pictured)	1.50	3.00
12 Philadelphia Eagles (Ray Nitschke pictured)	2.00	4.00
13 Pittsburgh Steelers (Kyle Rote pictured)	2.00	4.00
14 St. Louis Cardinals (Tom Brookshier pictured)	1.50	3.00
15 San Francisco 49ers (Joe Walton pictured)	1.50	3.00
16 Washington Redskins (Dick James pictured)	1.50	3.00
17 Boston Patriots (Jim Katcavage, Andy Robustelli and Timmy Brown pictured)	1.50	3.00
18 Buffalo Bills (Roosevelt Grier and Tom Scott pictured)	2.00	4.00
19 Cincinnati Bengals (Norm Van Brocklin and J.D.Smith pictured)	2.00	4.00
20 Denver Broncos (college teams pictured)	1.50	3.00
21 Houston Oilers (Billy Ray Smith Sr. and Carl Taseff pictured)	1.50	3.00
22 Kansas City Chiefs (Jim Brown and Bobby Freeman pictured)	3.00	6.00
23 Miami Dolphins (Roosevelt Grier and Frank Budd pictured)	2.00	4.00
24 New York Jets Bobby Layne pictured)	2.00	4.00
25 Oakland Raiders (Jim Taylor and Linden Crow pictured)	2.50	5.00
26 San Diego Chargers (Rich Kreitling and Steeler defender pictured)	1.50	3.00

1970 Topps

The 1970 Topps football set contains 263 standard-size cards that were issued in two series. The second series (133-263) was printed in slightly lesser quantities than the first series. This set was issued in 10 count, 10 cent packs which came 24 packs to a box. Card fronts have an oval photo surrounded by tan borders. At the bottom of photo is a color banner that contains the player's name and team. A football at bottom right contain the player's position. The card backs are done in orange, purple, and white and are horizontally designed. Statistics, highlights and a player cartoon adorn the backs. In the second series, card backs of offensive and defensive linemen have a coin rub-off cartoon rather than a printed cartoon as seen on all the other cards in the set. O.J. Simpson's Rookie Card appears in this set. Other notable Rookie Cards in this set are Lem Barney, Bill Bergey, Larry Brown, Fred Dryer, Mike Garrett, Calvin Hill, Harold Jackson, Tom Mack, Alan Page, Bubba Smith, Jan Stenerud, Bob Trumpy, and both Gene Washingtons.

COMPLETE SET (263)	300.00	475.00
WRAPPER (10-CENT)	8.00	12.00
1 Len Dawson UER (Cartoon caption says, 'AFL AN NFL')	12.00	20.00
2 Doug Hart RC	.40	1.00
3 Verlon Biggs	.40	1.00
4 Ralph Neely RC	.60	1.50
5 Harmon Wages RC	.40	1.00
6 Dan Conners RC	.40	1.00
7 Gino Cappelletti	.60	1.50
8 Erich Barnes	.40	1.00
9 Checklist 1-132	5.00	10.00

10 Bob Griese	7.50	15.00
11 Ed Flanagan RC	.40	1.00
12 George Seals RC	.40	1.00
13 Harry Jacobs	.40	1.00
14 Mike Haffner RC	.40	1.00
15 Bob Vogel	.40	1.00
16 Bill Peterson RC	.40	1.00
17 Spider Lockhart	.40	1.00
18 Billy Truax	.40	1.00
19 Jim Beirne RC	.40	1.00
20 Leroy Kelly	3.00	6.00
21 Dave Lloyd	.40	1.00
22 Mike Tilleman	.40	1.00
23 Gary Garrison	.40	1.00
24 Larry Brown RC	4.00	8.00
25 Jan Stenerud RC	6.00	12.00
26 Rolf Krueger RC	.40	1.00
27 Roland Lakes	.40	1.00
28 Dick Hoak	.40	1.00
29 Gene Washington Vik RC	1.25	2.50
30 Bart Starr	12.50	25.00
31 Dave Grayson	.40	1.00
32 Jerry Rush RC	.40	1.00
33 Len St. Jean RC	.40	1.00
34 Randy Edmunds RC	.40	1.00
35 Matt Snell	.60	1.50
36 Paul Costa	.40	1.00
37 Mike Pyle	.40	1.00
38 Roy Hilton	.40	1.00
39 Steve Tensi	.40	1.00
40 Tommy Nobis	1.25	2.50
41 Pete Case	.40	1.00
42 Andy Rice RC	.40	1.00
43 Elvin Bethea RC	4.00	8.00
44 Jack Snow	.60	1.50
45 Mel Renfro	1.25	2.50
46 Andy Livingston	.40	1.00
47 Gary Ballman	.40	1.00
48 Bob DeMarco	.40	1.00
49 Steve DeLong	.40	1.00
50 Daryle Lamonica	2.00	4.00
51 Jim Lynch RC	.40	1.00
52 Mel Farr RC	.40	1.00
53 Bob Long RC	.40	1.00
54 John Elliott RC	.40	1.00
55 Ray Nitschke	2.50	5.00
56 Jim Shorter	.40	1.00
57 Dave Wilcox	1.25	2.50
58 Eric Crabtree	.40	1.00
59 Alan Page RC	15.00	30.00
60 Jim Nance	.60	1.50
61 Glen Ray Hines RC	.40	1.00
62 John Mackey	1.25	2.50
63 Ron McDole	.40	1.00
64 Tom Beier RC	.40	1.00
65 Bill Nelsen	.60	1.50
66 Paul Flatley	.40	1.00
67 Sam Brunelli RC	.40	1.00
68 Jack Pardee	.60	1.50
69 Brig Owens	.40	1.00
70 Gale Sayers	12.50	25.00
71 Lee Roy Jordan	1.25	2.50
72 Harold Jackson RC	2.50	5.00
73 John Hadl	1.25	2.50
74 Dave Parks	.40	1.00
75 Lem Barney RC	7.50	15.00
76 Johnny Roland	.40	1.00
77 Ed Budde	.40	1.00
78 Ben McGee	.40	1.00
79 Ken Bowman RC	.40	1.00
80 Fran Tarkenton	7.50	15.00
81 Gene Washington 49er RC	2.50	5.00
82 Larry Grantham	.40	1.00
83 Bill Brown	.60	1.50
84 John Charles	.40	1.00
85 Fred Biletnikoff	3.50	7.00
86 Royce Berry RC	.40	1.00
87 Bob Lilly	2.50	5.00
88 Earl Morrall	.60	1.50
89 Jerry LeVias RC	.60	1.50
90 O.J. Simpson RC	40.00	80.00
91 Mike Howell RC	.40	1.00
92 Ken Gray	.40	1.00
93 Chris Hanburger	.40	1.00
94 Larry Seiple RC	.40	1.00
95 Rich Jackson RC	.40	1.00
96 Rockne Freitas RC	.40	1.00
97 Dick Post RC	.60	1.50
98 Ben Hawkins RC	.40	1.00
99 Ken Reaves RC	.40	1.00
100 Roman Gabriel	1.25	2.50
101 Dave Rowe RC	.40	1.00
102 Dave Robinson	.40	1.00
103 Otis Taylor	.60	1.50
104 Jim Turner	.40	1.00
105 Joe Morrison	.40	1.00
106 Dick Evey	.40	1.00
107 Ray Mansfield RC	.40	1.00
108 Grady Alderman	.40	1.00
109 Bruce Gossett	.40	1.00
110 Bob Trumpy RC	2.00	4.00
111 Jim Hunt	.40	1.00
112 Larry Stallings	.40	1.00
113A Lance Rentzel (name in red)	.60	1.50
113B Lance Rentzel (name in black)	.60	1.50
114 Bubba Smith RC	12.50	25.00
115 Norm Snead	.60	1.50
116 Jim Otto	1.25	2.50
117 Bo Scott RC	.40	1.00
118 Rick Redman	.40	1.00
119 George Butch Byrd	.40	1.00
120 George Webster RC	.60	1.50
121 Chuck Walton RC	.40	1.00
122 Dave Costa	.40	1.00
123 Al Dodd RC	.40	1.00
124 Len Hauss	.40	1.00
125 Deacon Jones	1.25	2.50
126 Randy Johnson	.40	1.00
127 Ralph Heck	.40	1.00
128 Emerson Boozer RC	.60	1.50
129 Johnny Robinson	.60	1.50
130 John Brodie	2.50	5.00
131 Gale Gillingham RC	.40	1.00
132 Checklist 133-263 DP UER (145 Charley Taylor misspelled Charlie)	3.00	6.00
133 Chuck Walker RC	.50	1.25
134 Bennie McRae	.50	1.25
135 Paul Warfield	3.50	7.00
136 Dan Darragh RC	.50	1.25
137 Paul Robinson RC	.50	1.25
138 Ed Philpott RC	.50	1.25
139 Craig Morton	1.50	3.00
140 Tom Dempsey RC	.75	2.00
141 Al Nelson RC	.50	1.25
142 Tom Matte	.75	2.00
143 Dick Schafrath	.50	1.25
144 Willie Brown	2.00	4.00
145 Charley Taylor UER (Misspelled Charlie on both sides)	2.50	5.00
146 John Huard RC	.50	1.25
147 Dave Osborn	.50	1.25
148 Gene Mingo	.50	1.25
149 Larry Hand RC	.50	1.25
150 Joe Namath	25.00	50.00
151 Tom Mack RC	5.00	10.00
152 Kenny Graham	.50	1.25
153 Don Herrmann RC	.50	1.25
154 Bobby Bell	1.50	3.00
155 Hoyle Granger RC	.50	1.25
156 Claude Humphrey RC	4.00	8.00
157 Clifton McNeil	.50	1.25
158 Mick Tingelhoff	.75	2.00
159 Don Horn RC	.50	1.25
160 Larry Wilson	1.50	3.00
161 Tom Neville RC	.50	1.25
162 Larry Csonka	10.00	20.00
163 Doug Buffone RC	.50	1.25
164 Cornell Green	.75	2.00
165 Haven Moses RC	.75	2.00
166 Bill Kilmer	1.50	3.00
167 Tim Rossovich RC	.50	1.25
168 Bill Bergey RC	2.00	4.00
169 Gary Collins	.75	2.00
170 Floyd Little	1.50	3.00
171 Tom Keating	.50	1.25
172 Pat Fischer	.50	1.25
173 Walt Sweeney	.50	1.25
174 Greg Larson	.50	1.25
175 Carl Eller	1.50	3.00
176 George Sauer Jr.	.75	2.00
177 Jim Hart	1.50	3.00
178 Bob Brown OT	1.50	3.00
179 Mike Garrett RC	.75	2.00
180 John Unitas	15.00	25.00
181 Tom Regner RC	.50	1.25
182 Bob Jeter	.50	1.25
183 Gail Cogdill	.50	1.25
184 Earl Gros	.50	1.25
185 Dennis Partee RC	.50	1.25
186 Charlie Krueger	.50	1.25
187 Martin Baccaglio RC	.50	1.25
188 Charles Long	.50	1.25
189 Bob Hayes	3.00	6.00
190 Dick Butkus	12.50	25.00
191 Al Bemiller	.50	1.25
192 Dick Westmoreland	.50	1.25
193 Joe Scarpati	.50	1.25
194 Ron Snidow RC	.50	1.25
195 Earl McCullouch RC	.50	1.25
196 Jake Kupp RC	.50	1.25
197 Bob Lurtsema RC	.50	1.25
198 Mike Current RC	.50	1.25
199 Charlie Smith RB RC	.50	1.25
200 Sonny Jurgensen	3.00	6.00
201 Mike Curtis	.75	2.00
202 Aaron Brown RC	.50	1.25
203 Richie Petitbon	.50	1.25
204 Walt Suggs	.50	1.25
205 Roy Jefferson	.50	1.25
206 Russ Washington RC	.50	1.25
207 Woody Peoples RC	.50	1.25
208 Dave Williams	.50	1.25
209 John Zook RC	.50	1.25
210 Tom Woodeshick	.50	1.25
211 Howard Fest RC	.50	1.25
212 Jack Concannon	.50	1.25
213 Jim Marshall	1.50	3.00
214 Jon Morris	.50	1.25
215 Dan Abramowicz	.75	2.00
216 Paul Martha	.50	1.25
217 Ken Willard	.50	1.25
218 Walter Rock	.50	1.25
219 Garland Boyette	.50	1.25
220 Buck Buchanan	1.50	3.00
221 Bill Munson	.75	2.00
222 David Lee RC	.50	1.25
223 Karl Noonan	.50	1.25
224 Harry Schuh	.50	1.25
225 Jackie Smith	1.50	3.00
226 Gerry Philbin	.50	1.25
227 Ernie Koy	.50	1.25
228 Chuck Howley	.75	2.00
229 Billy Shaw	1.50	3.00
230 Jerry Hillebrand	.50	1.25
231 Bill Thompson RC	.75	2.00
232 Carroll Dale	.75	2.00
233 Gene Hickerson	1.50	3.00
234 Jim Butler	.50	1.25
235 Greg Cook RC	.50	1.25
236 Lee Roy Caffey	.50	1.25
237 Merlin Olsen	2.00	4.00
238 Fred Cox	.50	1.25
239 Nate Ramsey	.50	1.25
240 Lance Alworth	3.50	7.00
241 Chuck Hinton RC	.50	1.25
242 Jerry Smith	.50	1.25
243 Tony Baker FB RC	.50	1.25
244 Nick Buoniconti	1.50	3.00
245 Jim Johnson	1.50	3.00
246 Willie Richardson	.50	1.25
247 Fred Dryer RC	5.00	10.00
248 Bobby Maples	.50	1.25
249 Alex Karras	2.00	4.00
250 Joe Kapp	.75	2.00
251 Ben Davidson	1.50	3.00
252 Mike Stratton	.50	1.25
253 Les Josephson	.50	1.25
254 Don Maynard	3.00	6.00
255 Houston Antwine	.50	1.25
256 Mac Percival RC	.50	1.25
257 George Goeddeke RC	.50	1.25
258 Homer Jones	.50	1.25
259 Bob Berry RC	.50	1.25
260A Calvin Hill RC (Name in red)	7.50	15.00
260B Calvin Hill RC (Name in black)	10.00	20.00
261 Willie Wood	1.50	3.00
262 Ed Weisacosky RC	.50	1.25
263 Jim Tyrer	1.50	3.00

1970 Topps Glossy Inserts

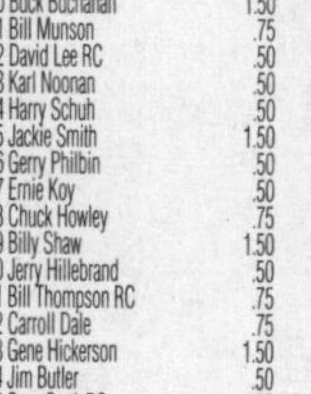

The 1970 Topps Super Glossy football set features 33 full-color, thick-stock, glossy cards each measuring 2 1/4" by 3 1/4". The corners are rounded and the backs contain only the player's name, his position, his team and the card number. The set numbering follows the player's team location within league (NFC 1-20 and AFC 21-33). The cards are quite attractive and a favorite with collectors. The cards were inserted in 1970 Topps first series football wax packs. The key cards in the set are Joe Namath and O.J. Simpson, appearing in his Rookie Card year.

COMPLETE SET (33)	150.00	250.00
1 Tommy Nobis	3.00	6.00
2 Johnny Unitas	20.00	40.00
3 Tom Matte	2.50	5.00
4 Mac Percival	2.00	4.00
5 Leroy Kelly	3.00	6.00
6 Mel Renfro	3.00	6.00
7 Bob Hayes	3.00	6.00
8 Earl McCullouch	2.00	4.00
9 Bart Starr	15.00	30.00
10 Willie Wood	3.00	6.00
11 Jack Snow	2.00	4.00
12 Joe Kapp	2.50	5.00
13 Dave Osborn	2.00	4.00
14 Dan Abramowicz	2.00	4.00
15 Fran Tarkenton	10.00	20.00
16 Tom Woodeshick	2.00	4.00
17 Roy Jefferson	2.00	4.00
18 Jackie Smith	2.50	5.00
19 Jim Johnson	2.50	5.00
20 Sonny Jurgensen	5.00	10.00
21 Houston Antwine	2.00	4.00
22 O.J. Simpson	10.00	20.00
23 Greg Cook	2.00	4.00
24 Floyd Little	2.50	5.00
25 Rich Jackson	2.00	4.00
26 George Webster	2.00	4.00
27 Len Dawson	5.00	10.00
28 Bob Griese	7.50	15.00
29 Joe Namath	20.00	40.00
30 Matt Snell	2.50	5.00
31 Daryle Lamonica	3.00	6.00
32 Fred Biletnikoff	5.00	10.00
33 Dick Post	2.00	4.00

1970 Topps Posters Inserts

This insert set of 24 folded thin paper posters was issued with the 1970 Topps regular football card issue. The posters are approximately 8" by 10" and were inserted in wax packs along with the 1970 Topps regular issue (second series) football cards. The posters are blank backed.

COMPLETE SET (24)	60.00	100.00
1 Gale Sayers	7.50	15.00
2 Bobby Bell	2.00	4.00
3 Roman Gabriel	1.50	3.00
4 Jim Tyrer	1.25	2.50
5 Willie Brown	2.00	4.00
6 Carl Eller	1.50	3.00
7 Tom Mack	1.50	3.00
8 Deacon Jones	2.00	4.00
9 Johnny Robinson	1.25	2.50
10 Jan Stenerud	1.50	3.00
11 Dick Butkus	7.50	15.00
12 Lem Barney	2.00	4.00
13 David Lee	1.25	2.50
14 Larry Wilson	1.50	3.00
15 Gene Hickerson	1.25	3.00
16 Lance Alworth	4.00	8.00
17 Merlin Olsen	2.50	5.00
18 Bob Trumpy	1.50	3.00
19 Bob Lilly	3.00	6.00
20 Mick Tingelhoff SP	3.00	6.00
21 Calvin Hill	1.50	3.00
22 Paul Warfield	4.00	8.00
23 Chuck Howley	1.50	3.00
24 Bob Brown OT	1.50	3.00

1970 Topps Super

The 1970 Topps Super set contains 35 cards. The cards measure approximately 3 1/8" by 5 1/4". The backs of the cards are identical in format to the regular football issue of 1970. The cards were sold in packs of three with a stick of gum for a dime and are on very thick card stock. The last seven cards in the set were printed in smaller quantities, i.e., short printed; these seven are designated SP in the checklist below. The cards were printed in sheets of seven rows and nine columns or 63 cards; thus 28 cards were double printed and seven cards were single printed. In more recent years wrongbacks and uncut sheets of the cards have been uncovered as well as some featuring square corners instead of rounded.

COMPLETE SET (35)	125.00	250.00
WRAPPER (10-CENT)	10.00	20.00
1 Fran Tarkenton	6.00	12.00
2 Floyd Little	1.50	4.00
3 Bart Starr	12.50	25.00
4 Len Dawson	4.00	8.00
5 Dick Post	1.25	3.00
6 Sonny Jurgensen	4.00	8.00
7 Deacon Jones	2.00	5.00
8 Leroy Kelly	2.00	5.00
9 Larry Wilson	1.50	4.00
10 Greg Cook	1.25	3.00
11 Carl Eller	1.50	4.00
12 Lem Barney	2.00	5.00
13 Lance Alworth	5.00	10.00
14 Dick Butkus	7.50	15.00
15 Johnny Unitas	15.00	30.00
16 Roy Jefferson	1.25	3.00
17 Bobby Bell	2.00	5.00
18 John Brodie	3.00	6.00
19 Dan Abramowicz	1.25	3.00
20 Matt Snell	1.50	4.00
21 Tom Matte	1.25	3.00
22 Gale Sayers	7.50	15.00
23 Tom Woodeshick	1.25	3.00
24 O.J. Simpson	7.50	15.00
25 Roman Gabriel	1.50	4.00
26 Jim Nance	1.25	3.00
27 Joe Morrison	1.25	3.00
28 Calvin Hill	1.50	4.00
29 Tommy Nobis SP	3.00	6.00
30 Bob Hayes SP	4.00	8.00
31 Joe Kapp SP	2.00	4.00
32 Daryle Lamonica SP	3.00	6.00
33 Joe Namath SP	25.00	50.00
34 George Webster SP	2.00	4.00
35 Bob Griese SP	10.00	20.00

1971 Topps

The 1971 Topps set contains 263 standard-size cards issued in two series. The second series (133-263) was printed in slightly lesser quantities than the first series. Card have a player photo surrounded by either a red (AFC), blue (NFC) or blue and red (All-Pros) border. The player's name, team name, position and conference are within the bottom border. An animated cartoon-like player icon appears by the position listing at the bottom. The card backs are printed in black ink with a gold accent on gray card stock. The content includes highlights and, a first for Topps football cards, yearly statistics. A player cartoon is at the top. The first cards of two Steeler greats, Terry Bradshaw and Mean Joe Greene, appear in this set. Other notable Rookie Cards in this set are Hall of Famers Ken Houston and Willie Lanier.

COMPLETE SET (263)	300.00	500.00
WRAPPER (10-CENT)	10.00	20.00
1 Johnny Unitas	15.00	30.00
2 Jim Butler	.40	1.00
3 Marty Schottenheimer RC	6.00	12.00
4 Joe O'Donnell RC	.40	1.00
5 Tom Dempsey	.50	1.25
6 Chuck Allen	.40	1.00
7 Ernie Kellerman	.40	1.00
8 Walt Garrison RC	.75	2.00
9 Bill Van Heusen RC	.40	1.00
10 Lance Alworth	4.00	8.00
11 Greg Landry RC	.75	2.00
12 Larry Krause RC	.40	1.00
13 Buck Buchanan	.75	2.00
14 Roy Gerela RC	.50	1.25
15 Clifton McNeil	.40	1.00
16 Bob Brown OT	.75	2.00
17 Lloyd Mumphord RC	.40	1.00
18 Gary Cuozzo	.40	1.00
19 Don Maynard	2.50	5.00
20 Larry Wilson	.75	2.00
21 Charlie Smith	.40	1.00
22 Ken Avery RC	.40	1.00
23 Billy Walik RC	.40	1.00
24 Jim Johnson	.75	2.00
25 Dick Butkus	12.50	25.00
26 Charley Taylor UER (Misspelled Charlie on both sides)	2.00	4.00
27 Checklist 1-132 UER (26 Charlie Taylor should be Charley)	4.00	8.00
28 Lionel Aldridge RC	.40	1.00
29 Billy Lothridge	.40	1.00
30 Terry Hanratty RC	.50	1.25
31 Lee Roy Jordan	.75	2.00
32 Rick Volk RC	.40	1.00
33 Howard Kindig	.40	1.00
34 Carl Garrett RC	.40	1.00
35 Bobby Bell	.75	2.00
36 Gene Hickerson	.75	2.00
37 Dave Parks	.40	1.00
38 Paul Martha	.40	1.00
39 George Blanda	7.50	15.00
40 Tom Woodeshick	.40	1.00
41 Alex Karras	1.50	3.00
42 Rick Redman	.40	1.00
43 Zeke Moore RC	.40	1.00
44 Jack Snow	.50	1.25
45 Larry Csonka	7.50	15.00
46 Karl Kassulke RC	.40	1.00
47 Jim Hart	.75	2.00
48 Al Atkinson	.40	1.00
49 Horst Muhlmann RC	.40	1.00
50 Sonny Jurgensen	2.50	5.00
51 Ron Johnson RC	.50	1.25
52 Cas Banaszek RC	.40	1.00
53 Bubba Smith	4.00	8.00
54 Bobby Douglass RC	.50	1.25
55 Willie Wood	.75	2.00
56 Bake Turner	.40	1.00
57 Mike Morgan LB RC	.40	1.00
58 George Butch Byrd	.50	1.25
59 Don Horn	.40	1.00
60 Tommy Nobis	.75	2.00
61 Jan Stenerud	2.00	4.00
62 Altie Taylor RC	.40	1.00
63 Gary Pettigrew RC	.40	1.00
64 Spike Jones RC	.40	1.00
65 Duane Thomas RC	.75	2.00
66 Marty Domres RC	.40	1.00
67 Dick Anderson	.50	1.25
68 Ken Iman RC	.40	1.00
69 Miller Farr	.40	1.00
70 Daryle Lamonica	1.50	3.00
71 Alan Page	6.00	12.00
72 Pat Matson RC	.40	1.00
73 Emerson Boozer	.40	1.00
74 Pat Fischer	.40	1.00
75 Gary Collins	.50	1.25
76 John Fuqua RC	.50	1.25
77 Bruce Gossett	.40	1.00
78 Ed O'Bradovich	.40	1.00
79 Bob Tucker RC	.50	1.25
80 Mike Curtis	.50	1.25
81 Rich Jackson	.40	1.00
82 Tom Janik	.40	1.00
83 Gale Gillingham	.40	1.00
84 Jim Mitchell TE RC	.40	1.00
85 Charley Johnson	.50	1.25
86 Edgar Chandler RC	.40	1.00
87 Cyril Pinder RC	.40	1.00
88 Johnny Robinson	.50	1.25
89 Ralph Neely	.40	1.00
90 Dan Abramowicz	.40	1.00
91 Mercury Morris RC	4.00	8.00
92 Steve DeLong	.40	1.00
93 Larry Stallings	.40	1.00
94 Tom Mack	.75	2.00
95 Hewritt Dixon	.40	1.00
96 Fred Cox	.40	1.00
97 Chris Hanburger	.40	1.00
98 Gerry Philbin	.40	1.00
99 Ernie Wright	.40	1.00
100 John Brodie	2.00	4.00
101 Tucker Frederickson	.40	1.00
102 Bobby Walden	.40	1.00
103 Dick Gordon	.40	1.00
104 Walter Johnson	.40	1.00
105 Mike Lucci	.50	1.25
106 Checklist 133-263 DP	3.00	6.00
107 Ron Berger RC	.40	1.00
108 Dan Sullivan RC	.40	1.00
109 George Kunz RC	.40	1.00
110 Floyd Little	.75	2.00
111 Zeke Bratkowski	.50	1.25
112 Haven Moses	.50	1.25
113 Ken Houston RC	7.50	15.00
114 Willie Lanier RC	7.50	15.00
115 Larry Brown	.75	2.00
116 Tim Rossovich	.40	1.00
117 Errol Linden RC	.40	1.00
118 Mel Renfro	.75	2.00
119 Mike Garrett	.40	1.00
120 Fran Tarkenton	7.50	15.00
121 Garo Yepremian RC	.75	2.00
122 Glen Condren RC	.40	1.00
123 Johnny Roland	.40	1.00
124 Dave Herman	.40	1.00
125 Merlin Olsen	1.50	3.00
126 Doug Buffone	.40	1.00
127 Earl McCullouch	.40	1.00
128 Spider Lockhart	.40	1.00
129 Ken Willard	.40	1.00
130 Gene Washington Vik	.40	1.00
131 Mike Phipps RC	.50	1.25
132 Andy Russell	.50	1.25
133 Ray Nitschke	2.00	4.00
134 Jerry Logan	.50	1.25
135 MacArthur Lane RC	.60	1.50
136 Jim Turner	.50	1.25
137 Kent McCloughan	.50	1.25
138 Paul Guidry	.50	1.25
139 Otis Taylor	.60	1.50
140 Virgil Carter RC	.50	1.25
141 Joe Dawkins RC	.50	1.25
142 Steve Preece RC	.50	1.25
143 Mike Bragg RC	.50	1.25
144 Bob Lilly	2.50	5.00
145 Joe Kapp	.60	1.50
146 Al Dodd	.50	1.25
147 Nick Buoniconti	1.25	2.50
148 Speedy Duncan (Back mentions his trade to Redskins)	.50	1.25
149 Cedrick Hardman RC	.50	1.25
150 Gale Sayers	12.50	25.00
151 Jim Otto	1.25	2.50
152 Billy Truax	.50	1.25
153 John Elliott	.50	1.25
154 Dick LeBeau	1.25	2.50
155 Bill Bergey	.60	1.50
156 Terry Bradshaw RC	125.00	200.00
157 Leroy Kelly	3.00	6.00
158 Paul Krause	1.25	2.50
159 Ted Vactor RC	.50	1.25
160 Bob Griese	7.50	15.00
161 Ernie McMillan	.50	1.25
162 Donny Anderson	.60	1.50
163 John Pitts RC	.50	1.25
164 Dave Costa	.50	1.25
165 Gene Washington 49er	.60	1.50
166 John Zook	.50	1.25
167 Pete Gogolak	.50	1.25
168 Erich Barnes	.50	1.25
169 Alvin Reed RC	.50	1.25
170 Jim Nance	.60	1.50
171 Craig Morton	1.25	2.50
172 Gary Garrison	.50	1.25
173 Joe Scarpati	.50	1.25
174 Adrian Young UER RC (Photo actually Rick Duncan)	.50	1.25
175 John Mackey	1.25	2.50
176 Mac Percival	.50	1.25
177 Preston Pearson RC	2.00	4.00
178 Fred Biletnikoff	4.00	8.00
179 Mike Battle RC	.50	1.25
180 Len Dawson	4.00	8.00
181 Les Josephson	.50	1.25
182 Royce Berry	.50	1.25
183 Herman Weaver RC	.50	1.25
184 Norm Snead	.60	1.50
185 Sam Brunelli	.50	1.25
186 Jim Kiick RC	2.50	5.00
187 Austin Denney RC	.50	1.25
188 Roger Wehrli RC	6.00	12.00
189 Dave Wilcox	1.25	2.50
190 Bob Hayes	2.00	4.00
191 Joe Morrison	.50	1.25
192 Manny Sistrunk RC	.50	1.25
193 Don Cockroft RC	.50	1.25
194 Lee Bouggess RC	.50	1.25
195 Bob Berry	.50	1.25
196 Ron Sellers RC	.50	1.25
197 George Webster	.50	1.25
198 Hoyle Granger	.50	1.25
199 Bob Vogel	.50	1.25
200 Bart Starr	10.00	20.00
201 Mike Mercer	.50	1.25
202 Dave Smith	.50	1.25
203 Lee Roy Caffey	.50	1.25
204 Mick Tingelhoff	.60	1.50
205 Matt Snell	.60	1.50
206 Jim Tyrer	.50	1.25
207 Willie Brown	1.25	2.50
208 Bob Johnson RC	.50	1.25
209 Deacon Jones	1.25	2.50
210 Charlie Sanders RC	6.00	12.00
211 Jake Scott RC	3.00	6.00
212 Bob Anderson RC	.50	1.25
213 Charlie Krueger	.50	1.25
214 Jim Bakken	.50	1.25
215 Harold Jackson	.60	1.50
216 Bill Brundige RC	.50	1.25
217 Calvin Hill	2.50	5.00
218 Claude Humphrey	.50	1.25
219 Glen Ray Hines	.50	1.25
220 Bill Nelsen	.60	1.50
221 Roy Hilton	.50	1.25
222 Don Herrmann	.50	1.25
223 John Bramlett	.50	1.25
224 Ken Ellis RC	.50	1.25
225 Dave Osborn	.60	1.50
226 Edd Hargett RC	.50	1.25
227 Gene Mingo	.50	1.25
228 Larry Grantham	.50	1.25
229 Dick Post	.50	1.25
230 Roman Gabriel	1.25	2.50
231 Mike Eischeid RC	.50	1.25
232 Jim Lynch	.50	1.25
233 Lemar Parrish RC	.60	1.50
234 Cecil Turner RC	.50	1.25
235 Dennis Shaw RC	.50	1.25
236 Mel Farr	.50	1.25
237 Curt Knight RC	.50	1.25
238 Chuck Howley	.60	1.50
239 Bruce Taylor RC	.50	1.25
240 Jerry LeVias	.50	1.25
241 Bob Lurtsema	.50	1.25
242 Earl Morrall	.60	1.50
243 Kermit Alexander	.50	1.25
244 Jackie Smith	1.25	2.50
245 Joe Greene RC	30.00	50.00
246 Harmon Wages	.50	1.25
247 Errol Mann	.50	1.25
248 Mike McCoy DT RC	.50	1.25
249 Milt Morin RC	.50	1.25
250 Joe Namath UER In 9th line, Joe is spelled in small letters	35.00	60.00
251 Jackie Burkett	.50	1.25
252 Steve Chomyszak RC	.50	1.25
253 Ed Sharockman	.50	1.25
254 Robert Holmes RC	.50	1.25
255 John Hadl	1.25	2.50
256 Cornell Gordon	.50	1.25
257 Mark Moseley RC	.60	1.50
258 Gus Otto	.50	1.25
259 Mike Taliaferro	.50	1.25
260 O.J. Simpson	12.50	25.00
261 Paul Warfield	4.00	8.00
262 Jack Concannon	.50	1.25
263 Tom Matte	1.25	2.50

1971 Topps Game Inserts

The 1971 Topps Game cards were issued as inserts with the 1971 regular issue football cards. The cards measure 2 1/4" by 3 1/4" with rounded corners. The cards can be used for a table game of football. The 52 player cards in the set are numbered and have light blue backs. The 53rd card (actually unnumbered) is a field position/first down marker which is used in the table game. Six of the cards in the set were double printed and are marked as DP in the checklist below. The key card in the set is Terry Bradshaw, appearing in his Rookie Card year.

COMPLETE SET (53)	75.00	125.00
1 Dick Butkus DP	3.00	6.00
2 Bob Berry DP	.30	.60
3 Joe Namath DP	6.00	12.00
4 Mike Curtis	.30	.60
5 Jim Nance	.30	.60
6 Ron Berger	.30	.60
7 O.J. Simpson	7.50	15.00
8 Haven Moses	.50	1.00
9 Tommy Nobis	.50	1.00
10 Gale Sayers	6.00	12.00
11 Virgil Carter	.30	.60
12 Andy Russell DP	.30	.60
13 Bill Nelsen	.30	.60
14 Gary Collins	.30	.60
15 Duane Thomas	.50	1.00
16 Bob Hayes	1.00	2.00
17 Floyd Little	.50	1.00
18 Sam Brunelli	.30	.60
19 Charlie Sanders	.40	1.00
20 Mike Lucci	.30	.60
21 Gene Washington 49er	.50	1.00
22 Willie Wood	1.00	2.00
23 Jerry LeVias	.30	.60
24 Charley Johnson	.50	1.00
25 Len Dawson	2.00	4.00
26 Bobby Bell	1.00	2.00
27 Merlin Olsen	1.50	3.00
28 Roman Gabriel	1.00	2.00
29 Bob Griese	3.00	6.00
30 Larry Csonka	3.00	6.00
31 Dave Osborn	.30	.60
32 Gene Washington Vik	.30	.60
33 Dan Abramowicz	.30	.60
34 Tom Dempsey	.30	.60
35 Fran Tarkenton	4.00	8.00
36 Clifton McNeil	.30	.60
37 Johnny Unitas	7.50	15.00
38 Matt Snell	.50	1.00
39 Daryle Lamonica	1.00	2.00
40 Hewritt Dixon	.30	.60
41 Tom Woodeshick DP	.30	.60
42 Harold Jackson	.50	1.00
43 Terry Bradshaw	12.50	25.00
44 Ken Avery	.30	.60
45 MacArthur Lane	.30	.60
46 Larry Wilson	.50	1.00
47 John Hadl	.50	1.00
48 Lance Alworth	2.00	4.00
49 John Brodie	1.50	3.00
50 Bart Starr DP	4.00	8.00
51 Sonny Jurgensen	2.50	5.00
52 Larry Brown	.50	1.00
NNO Field Marker	.30	.60

1971 Topps Posters Inserts

The 1971 Topps Football pin-up posters are a set of 32 paper inserts each folded twice for insertion into gum packs. The cards (small posters) measure 4 7/8" by 6 7/8". The lower left hand corner of the obverse contains the pin-up number while the back features a green simulated football field upon which a football card game could be played as well as the instructions to accompany the card insert game. Inexplicably the second half of the set seems to be somewhat more difficult to find.

COMPLETE SET (32)	50.00	100.00
1 Gene Washington 49er	.75	1.50
2 Andy Russell	.75	1.50
3 Harold Jackson	.75	1.50
4 Joe Namath	7.50	15.00
5 Fran Tarkenton	2.00	4.00
6 Dave Osborn	.50	1.00
7 Bob Griese	2.50	5.00
8 Roman Gabriel	1.00	2.00
9 Jerry LeVias	.50	1.00
10 Bart Starr	6.00	12.00
11 Bob Hayes	1.50	3.00
12 Gale Sayers	4.00	8.00
13 O.J. Simpson	4.00	8.00
14 Sam Brunelli	.50	1.00
15 Jim Nance	.75	1.50
16 Bill Nelsen	.50	1.00
17 Sonny Jurgensen	2.00	4.00
18 John Brodie	2.00	4.00
19 Lance Alworth	2.50	5.00
20 Larry Wilson	1.50	3.00
21 Daryle Lamonica	1.50	3.00
22 Dan Abramowicz	1.00	2.00
23 Gene Washington Vik	1.00	2.00
24 Bobby Bell	2.00	4.00
25 Merlin Olsen	2.00	4.00
26 Charlie Sanders	1.25	2.50
27 Virgil Carter	1.00	2.00
28 Dick Butkus	4.00	8.00
29 Johnny Unitas	7.50	15.00
30 Tommy Nobis	1.50	3.00
31 Floyd Little	1.50	3.00
32 Larry Brown	1.00	2.00

1972 Topps

The 1972 Topps set contains 351 standard size cards that were issued in three series. The third series (264-351) is considerably more difficult to obtain than cards in the first two series. Card fronts are either horizontal and vertical and contain player photos that are bordered by a color that, for the most part, is part of the player's team color scheme. Vertical photos have team names at the top and horizontal photos have team names to the left. In either case, the player's name and position are at the bottom of the photo. The card backs are printed in blue and green on gray card stock. The backs have yearly statistics and a cartoon. Subsets include league leaders (1-8), In-Action cards (119-132, 250-263, 338-351), 1971 Playoffs (133-139) and All-Pro (264-287). The key Rookie Cards in this set are Lyle Alzado, L.C. Greenwood, Ted Hendricks, Charlie Joiner, Larry Little, Archie Manning, Jim Plunkett, John Riggins, Steve Spurrier, Roger Staubach, and Gene Upshaw. The cards were isssued in 10 cents wax packs.

COMPLETE SET (351)	1,500.00	2,500.00
WRAPPER (10-CENT)	6.00	10.00
WRAPPER SER.3 (10-CENT)	15.00	20.00
1 AFC Rushing Leaders Floyd Little Larry Csonka Marv Hubbard	2.00	4.00
2 NFC Rushing Leaders John Brockington Steve Owens Willie Ellison	.25	.60
3 AFC Passing Leaders Bob Griese Len Dawson Virgil Carter	.75	2.00
4 NFC Passing Leaders Roger Staubach Greg Landry Bill Kilmer	2.50	5.00
5 AFC Receiving Leaders Fred Biletnikoff Otis Taylor Randy Vataha	.50	1.25
6 NFC Receiving Leaders Bob Tucker Ted Kwalick Harold Jackson Roy Jefferson	.25	.60
7 AFC Scoring Leaders Garo Yepremian Jan Stenerud Jim O'Brien	.25	.60
8 NFC Scoring Leaders Curt Knight Errol Mann Bruce Gossett	.25	.60
9 Jim Kiick	.75	2.00
10 Otis Taylor	.50	1.25
11 Bobby Joe Green	.25	.60
12 Ken Ellis	.25	.60
13 John Riggins RC	10.00	20.00
14 Dave Parks	.25	.60
15 John Hadl	.75	2.00
16 Ron Hornsby RC	.25	.60
17 Chip Myers RC	.25	.60
18 Bill Kilmer	.75	2.00
19 Fred Hoaglin RC	.25	.60
20 Carl Eller	.75	2.00
21 Steve Zabel RC	.25	.60
22 Vic Washington RC	.25	.60
23 Len St. Jean	.25	.60
24 Bill Thompson	.25	.60
25 Steve Owens RC	1.25	3.00
26 Ken Burrough RC	.50	1.25
27 Mike Clark	.25	.60
28 Willie Brown	.75	2.00
29 Checklist 1-132	3.00	6.00
30 Marlin Briscoe RC	.25	.60
31 Jerry Logan	.25	.60
32 Donny Anderson	.50	1.25
33 Rich McGeorge RC	.25	.60
34 Charlie Durkee	.25	.60
35 Willie Lanier	2.00	4.00
36 Chris Farasopoulos RC	.25	.60
37 Ron Shanklin RC	.25	.60
38 Forrest Blue RC	.25	.60
39 Ken Reaves	.25	.60
40 Roman Gabriel	.75	2.00
41 Mac Percival	.25	.60
42 Lem Barney	1.50	3.00
43 Nick Buoniconti	.75	2.00
44 Charlie Gogolak	.25	.60
45 Bill Bradley RC	.50	1.25
46 Joe Jones DE RC	.25	.60
47 Dave Williams	.25	.60
48 Pete Athas RC	.25	.60
49 Virgil Carter	.25	.60
50 Floyd Little	.75	2.00
51 Curt Knight	.25	.60

52 Bobby Maples .25 .60
53 Charlie West RC .25 .60
54 Marv Hubbard RC .50 1.25
55 Archie Manning RC 10.00 20.00
56 Jim O'Brien RC .50 1.25
57 Wayne Patrick RC .25 .60
58 Ken Bowman .25 .60
59 Roger Wehrli .50 1.25
60 Charlie Sanders UER .50 1.25
(Front WR, back TE)
61 Jan Stenerud .75 2.00
62 Willie Ellison RC .25 .60
63 Walt Sweeney .25 .60
64 Ron Smith .25 .60
65 Jim Plunkett RC 10.00 20.00
66 Herb Adderley UER .75 2.00
(misspelled Adderly)
67 Mike Reid RC .75 2.00
68 Richard Caster RC .50 1.25
69 Dave Wilcox .75 2.00
70 Leroy Kelly 1.50 3.00
71 Bob Lee RC .25 .60
72 Verlon Biggs .25 .60
73 Henry Allison RC .25 .60
74 Steve Ramsey RC .25 .60
75 Claude Humphrey .50 1.25
76 Bob Grim RC .25 .60
77 John Fuqua .50 1.25
78 Ken Houston 2.00 4.00
79 Checklist 133-263 DP 2.50 5.00
80 Bob Griese 4.00 8.00
81 Lance Rentzel .50 1.25
82 Ed Podolak RC .50 1.25
83 Ike Hill RC .25 .60
84 George Farmer RC .25 .60
85 John Brockington RC .75 2.00
86 Jim Otto .75 2.00
87 Richard Neal RC .25 .60
88 Jim Hart .75 2.00
89 Bob Babich RC .25 .60
90 Gene Washington 49er .50 1.25
91 John Zook .25 .60
92 Bobby Duhon RC .25 .60
93 Ted Hendricks RC 7.50 15.00
94 Rockne Freitas .25 .60
95 Larry Brown .75 2.00
96 Mike Phipps .50 1.25
97 Julius Adams RC .25 .60
98 Dick Anderson .50 1.25
99 Fred Willis RC .25 .60
100 Joe Namath 20.00 35.00
101 L.C. Greenwood RC 7.50 15.00
102 Mark Nordquist RC .25 .60
103 Robert Holmes .25 .60
104 Ron Yary RC 2.00 5.00
105 Bob Hayes 1.00 2.50
106 Lyle Alzado RC 7.50 15.00
107 Bob Berry .25 .60
108 Phil Villapiano RC .50 1.25
109 Dave Elmendorf RC .25 .60
110 Gale Sayers 10.00 20.00
111 Jim Tyrer .25 .60
112 Mel Gray RC .75 2.00
113 Gerry Philbin .25 .60
114 Bob James RC .25 .60
115 Garo Yepremian .50 1.25
116 Dave Robinson .50 1.25
117 Jeff Queen RC .25 .60
118 Norm Snead .50 1.25
119 Jim Nance IA .50 1.25
120 Terry Bradshaw IA 7.50 15.00
121 Jim Kiick IA .50 1.25
122 Roger Staubach IA 12.00 20.00
123 Bo Scott IA .25 .60
124 John Brodie IA .75 2.00
125 Rick Volk IA .25 .60
126 John Riggins IA 3.00 6.00
127 Bubba Smith IA .75 2.00
128 Roman Gabriel IA .50 1.25
129 Calvin Hill IA .50* 1.25
130 Bill Nelsen IA .25 .60
131 Tom Matte IA .50 1.25
132 Bob Griese IA 2.00 4.00
133 AFC Semi-Final .50 1.25
Dolphins 27,
Chiefs 24
134 NFC Semi-Final .50 1.25
Cowboys 20,
Vikings 12
(Duane Thomas
getting tackled)
135 AFC Semi-Final .50 1.25
Colts 20,
Browns 3
(Don Nottingham)
136 NFC Semi-Final/49ers 24, .50 1.25
Redskins 20
137 AFC Title Game 1.50 3.00
Dolphins 21,
Colts 0
(Johnny Unitas
getting tackled)
138 NFC Title Game .75 2.00
Cowboys 14,/49ers 3
(Bob Lilly
making tackle)
139 Super Bowl 2.50 5.00
Cowboys 24,
Dolphins 3
(Roger Staubach
rolling out)
140 Larry Csonka 4.00 8.00
141 Rick Volk .30 .75
142 Roy Jefferson .50 1.25
143 Raymond Chester RC .50 1.25
144 Bobby Douglass .30 .75
145 Bob Lilly 2.50 5.00
146 Harold Jackson .50 1.25
147 Pete Gogolak .30 .75
148 Art Malone RC .30 .75
149 Ed Flanagan .30 .75
150 Terry Bradshaw 25.00 40.00
151 MacArthur Lane .50 1.25
152 Jack Snow .50 1.25
153 Al Beauchamp RC .30 .75
154 Bob Anderson .30 .75
155 Ted Kwalick RC .30 .75
156 Dan Pastorini RC 1.00 2.50
157 Emmitt Thomas RC 10.00 20.00
158 Randy Vataha RC .30 .75
159 Al Atkinson .30 .75
160 O.J. Simpson 7.50 15.00
161 Jackie Smith .75 2.00
162 Ernie Kellerman .30 .75
163 Dennis Partee .30 .75
164 Jake Kupp .30 .75
165 John Unitas 10.00 20.00
166 Clint Jones RC .30 .75
167 Paul Warfield 3.00 6.00
168 Roland McDole RC .30 .75
169 Daryle Lamonica .75 2.00
170 Dick Butkus 7.50 15.00
171 Jim Butler .30 .75
172 Mike McCoy .30 .75
173 Dave Smith .30 .75
174 Greg Landry .50 1.25
175 Tom Dempsey .50 1.25
176 John Charles .30 .75
177 Bobby Bell .75 2.00
178 Don Horn .30 .75
179 Bob Trumpy .75 2.00
180 Duane Thomas .50 1.25
181 Merlin Olsen 1.50 3.00
182 Dave Herman .30 .75
183 Jim Nance .50 1.25
184 Pete Beathard .30 .75
185 Bob Tucker .30 .75
186 Gene Upshaw RC 7.50 15.00
187 Bo Scott .30 .75
188 J.D. Hill RC .30 .75
189 Bruce Gossett .30 .75
190 Bubba Smith 2.00 4.00
191 Edd Hargett .30 .75
192 Gary Garrison .30 .75
193 Jake Scott .50 1.25
194 Fred Cox .30 .75
195 Sonny Jurgensen 2.00 4.00
196 Greg Brezina RC .30 .75
197 Ed O'Bradovich .30 .75
198 John Rowser RC .30 .75
199 Altie Taylor UER .30 .75
(Taylor misspelled as
Tayor on front)
200 Roger Staubach RC 100.00 175.00
201 Leroy Keyes RC .30 .75
202 Garland Boyette .30 .75
203 Tom Beer .30 .75
204 Buck Buchanan .75 2.00
205 Larry Wilson .75 2.00
206 Scott Hunter RC .30 .75
207 Ron Johnson .30 .75
208 Sam Brunelli .30 .75
209 Deacon Jones .75 2.00
210 Fred Biletnikoff 3.00 6.00
211 Bill Nelsen .50 1.25
212 George Nock RC .30 .75
213 Dan Abramowicz .50 1.25
214 Irv Goode .30 .75
215 Isiah Robertson RC .50 1.25
216 Tom Matte .50 1.25
217 Pat Fischer .30 .75
218 Gene Washington Vik .30 .75
219 Paul Robinson .30 .75
220 John Brodie 2.00 4.00
221 Manny Fernandez RC .50 1.25
222 Errol Mann .30 .75
223 Dick Gordon .30 .75
224 Calvin Hill .75 2.00
225 Fran Tarkenton UER 6.00 12.00
(Plays in the Masters
each spring)
226 Jim Turner .30 .75
227 Jim Mitchell .30 .75
228 Pete Liske .30 .75
229 Carl Garrett .30 .75
230 Joe Greene 10.00 20.00
231 Gale Gillingham .30 .75
232 Norm Bulaich RC .50 1.25
233 Spider Lockhart .30 .75
234 Ken Willard .30 .75
235 George Blanda 6.00 12.00
236 Wayne Mulligan RC .30 .75
237 Dave Lewis RC .30 .75
238 Dennis Shaw .30 .75
239 Fair Hooker RC .30 .75
240 Larry Little RC 7.50 15.00
241 Mike Garrett .30 .75
242 Glen Ray Hines .30 .75
243 Myron Pottios .30 .75
244 Charlie Joiner RC 10.00 20.00
245 Len Dawson 3.00 6.00
246 W.K. Hicks .30 .75
247 Les Josephson .30 .75
248 Lance Alworth UER 3.00 6.00
(Front TE, back WR)
249 Frank Nunley RC .30 .75
250 Mel Farr IA .30 .75
251 Johnny Unitas IA 4.00 8.00
252 George Farmer IA .30 .75
253 Duane Thomas IA .50 1.25
254 John Hadl IA .75 2.00
255 Vic Washington IA .30 .75
256 Don Horn IA .30 .75
257 L.C. Greenwood IA .75 2.00
258 Bob Lee IA .30 .75
259 Larry Csonka IA 2.00 4.00
260 Mike McCoy IA .30 .75
261 Greg Landry IA .50 1.25
262 Ray May IA .30 .75
263 Bobby Douglass IA .30 .75
264 Charlie Sanders AP 15.00 30.00
265 Ron Yary AP 15.00 30.00
266 Rayfield Wright AP 20.00 40.00
267 Larry Little AP 20.00 35.00
268 John Niland AP 15.00 30.00
269 Forrest Blue AP 15.00 30.00
270 Otis Taylor AP 15.00 30.00
271 Paul Warfield AP 30.00 50.00
272 Bob Griese AP 40.00 70.00
273 John Brockington AP 15.00 30.00
274 Floyd Little AP 15.00 30.00
275 Garo Yepremian AP 15.00 30.00
276 Jerrel Wilson AP 10.00 18.00
277 Carl Eller AP 15.00 30.00
278 Bubba Smith AP 25.00 40.00
279 Alan Page AP 25.00 40.00
280 Bob Lilly AP 30.00 60.00
281 Ted Hendricks AP 30.00 50.00
282 Dave Wilcox AP 15.00 30.00
283 Willie Lanier AP 20.00 35.00
284 Jim Johnson AP 15.00 30.00
285 Willie Brown AP 20.00 35.00
286 Bill Bradley AP 15.00 30.00
287 Ken Houston AP 20.00 35.00
288 Mel Farr 10.00 18.00
289 Kermit Alexander 10.00 18.00
290 John Gilliam RC 15.00 30.00
291 Steve Spurrier RC 50.00 100.00
292 Walter Johnson 10.00 18.00
293 Jack Pardee 12.50 25.00
294 Checklist 264-351 UER 50.00 80.00
(334 Charlie Taylor
should be Charley)
295 Winston Hill 10.00 18.00
296 Hugo Hollas RC 10.00 18.00
297 Ray May RC 10.00 18.00
298 Jim Bakken 10.00 18.00
299 Larry Carwell RC 10.00 18.00
300 Alan Page 30.00 50.00
301 Walt Garrison 12.50 25.00
302 Mike Lucci 12.50 25.00
303 Nemiah Wilson 10.00 18.00
304 Carroll Dale 12.50 25.00
305 Jim Kanicki 10.00 18.00
306 Preston Pearson 15.00 30.00
307 Lemar Parrish 12.50 25.00
308 Earl Morrall 12.50 25.00
309 Tommy Nobis 12.50 25.00
310 Rich Jackson 10.00 18.00
311 Doug Cunningham RC 10.00 18.00
312 Jim Marsalis RC 10.00 18.00
313 Jim Beirne 10.00 18.00
314 Tom McNeill RC 10.00 18.00
315 Milt Morin 10.00 18.00
316 Rayfield Wright RC 30.00 50.00
317 Jerry LeVias 12.50 25.00
318 Travis Williams RC 12.50 25.00
319 Edgar Chandler 10.00 18.00
320 Bob Wallace RC 10.00 18.00
321 Delles Howell RC 10.00 18.00
322 Emerson Boozer 12.50 25.00
323 George Atkinson RC 12.50 25.00
324 Mike Montler RC 10.00 18.00
325 Randy Johnson 10.00 18.00
326 Mike Curtis UER 12.50 25.00
(Text on back states he was
named Super Bowl MVP in 1972.
Chuck Howley won the award)
327 Miller Farr 10.00 18.00
328 Horst Muhlmann 10.00 18.00
329 John Niland RC 12.50 25.00
330 Andy Russell 15.00 30.00
331 Mercury Morris 25.00 40.00
332 Jim Johnson 15.00 30.00
333 Jerrel Wilson 10.00 18.00
334 Charley Taylor UER 25.00 40.00
(Misspelled Charlie
on both sides)
335 Dick LeBeau 10.00 18.00
336 Jim Marshall 15.00 30.00
337 Tom Mack 15.00 30.00
338 Steve Spurrier IA 30.00 60.00
339 Floyd Little IA 12.50 25.00
340 Len Dawson IA 25.00 40.00
341 Dick Butkus IA 40.00 70.00
342 Larry Brown IA 12.50 25.00
343 Joe Namath IA 75.00 150.00
344 Jim Turner IA 10.00 18.00
345 Doug Cunningham IA 10.00 18.00
346 Edd Hargett IA 10.00 18.00
347 Steve Owens IA 10.00 18.00
348 George Blanda IA 30.00 50.00
349 Ed Podolak IA 10.00 18.00
350 Rich Jackson IA 10.00 18.00
351 Ken Willard IA 25.00 40.00

1973 Topps

The 1973 set marks the first of ten years in a row that Topps produced a 528-card football standard-size set issued in a single series. The fronts have the players name at the top and position and team name at the bottom. The player's first name and team name are in a color that corresponds to one of the colors in a small banner-like design that emanates from the photo. The card backs are printed in blue ink with a red background on gray card stock. Highlights and statistics are accompanied by a cartoon and trivia question and answer. The first six cards in the set are statistical league leader cards. Cards 133-139 show the results of the previous season's playoff games. Cards 265-267 are Kid Pictures (KP) showing the player in a boyhood photo. Rookie Cards include this set are Ken Anderson, Al Cowlings, Dan Dierdorf, Jack Ham, Franco Harris, Jim Langer, Art Shell, Ken Stabler, and Jack Youngblood. An uncut sheet of team checklist cards was also available via a mail-in offer on wax pack wrappers.

COMPLETE SET (528) 200.00 400.00
1 Rushing Leaders 3.00 8.00
Larry Brown
O.J. Simpson
2 Passing Leaders .40 1.00
Norm Snead
Earl Morrall
3 Receiving Leaders UER .60 1.50
Harold Jackson
Fred Biletnikoff
(Charley Taylor mis-
spelled as Charlie)
4 Scoring Leaders .25 .60
Chester Marcol
Bobby Howfield
5 Interception Leaders .25 .60
Bill Bradley
Mike Sensibaugh
6 Punting Leaders .25 .60
Dave Chapple
Jerrel Wilson
7 Bob Trumpy .60 1.50
8 Mel Tom RC .25 .60
9 Clarence Ellis RC .25 .60
10 John Niland .25 .60
11 Randy Jackson RC .25 .60
12 Greg Landry .60 1.50
13 Cid Edwards RC .25 .60
14 Phil Olsen RC .25 .60
15 Terry Bradshaw 15.00 25.00
16 Al Cowlings RC .60 1.50
17 Walker Gillette RC .25 .60
18 Bob Atkins RC .25 .60
19 Diron Talbert RC .25 .60
20 Jim Johnson .60 1.50
21 Howard Twilley .40 1.00
22 Dick Enderle RC .25 .60
23 Wayne Colman RC .25 .60
24 John Schmitt RC .25 .60
25 George Blanda 5.00 10.00
26 Milt Morin .25 .60
27 Mike Current .25 .60
28 Rex Kern RC .25 .60
29 MacArthur Lane .40 1.00
30 Alan Page 1.50 3.00
31 Randy Vataha .25 .60
32 Jim Kearney RC .25 .60
33 Steve Smith T RC .25 .60
34 Ken Anderson RC 7.50 15.00
35 Calvin Hill .60 1.50
36 Andy Maurer RC .25 .60
37 Joe Taylor RC .25 .60
38 Deacon Jones .60 1.50
39 Mike Weger RC .25 .60
40 Roy Gerela .40 1.00
41 Les Josephson .25 .60
42 Dave Washington RC .25 .60
43 Bill Curry RC .40 1.00
44 Fred Heron RC .25 .60
45 John Brodie 1.50 3.00
46 Roy Winston .25 .60
47 Mike Bragg .25 .60
48 Mercury Morris .60 1.50
49 Jim Files RC .25 .60
50 Gene Upshaw 1.50 3.00
51 Hugo Hollas .25 .60
52 Rod Sherman RC .25 .60
53 Ron Snidow .25 .60
54 Steve Tannen RC .25 .60
55 Jim Carter RC .25 .60
56 Lydell Mitchell RC .60 1.50
57 Jack Rudnay RC .25 .60
58 Halvor Hagen RC .25 .60
59 Tom Dempsey .40 1.00
60 Fran Tarkenton 5.00 10.00
61 Lance Alworth 2.50 5.00
62 Vern Holland RC .25 .60
63 Steve DeLong .25 .60
64 Art Malone .25 .60
65 Isiah Robertson .40 1.00
66 Jerry Rush .25 .60
67 Bryant Salter RC .25 .60
68 Checklist 1-132 2.50 .5.00
69 J.D. Hill .25 .60
70 Forrest Blue .25 .60
71 Myron Pottios .25 .60
72 Norm Thompson RC .25 .60
73 Paul Robinson .25 .60
74 Larry Grantham .25 .60
75 Manny Fernandez .40 1.00
76 Kent Nix RC .25 .60
77 Art Shell RC 7.50 15.00
78 George Saimes .25 .60
79 Don Cockroft .25 .60
80 Bob Tucker .40 1.00
81 Don McCauley RC .25 .60
82 Bob Brown DT RC .25 .60
83 Larry Carwell .25 .60
84 Mo Moorman RC .25 .60
85 John Gilliam .40 1.00
86 Wade Key RC .25 .60
87 Ross Brupbacher RC .25 .60
88 Dave Lewis .25 .60
89 Franco Harris RC 25.00 50.00
90 Tom Mack .60 1.50
91 Mike Tilleman .25 .60
92 Carl Mauck RC .25 .60
93 Larry Hand .25 .60
94 Dave Foley RC .25 .60
95 Frank Nunley .25 .60
96 John Charles .25 .60
97 Jim Bakken .25 .60
98 Pat Fischer .40 1.00
99 Randy Rasmussen RC .25 .60
100 Larry Csonka 3.00 6.00
101 Mike Siani RC .25 .60
102 Tom Roussel RC .25 .60
103 Clarence Scott RC .40 1.00
104 Charley Johnson .40 1.00
105 Rick Volk .25 .60
106 Willie Young RC .25 .60
107 Emmitt Thomas .60 1.50
108 Jon Morris .25 .60
109 Clarence Williams RC .25 .60
110 Rayfield Wright .40 1.00
111 Norm Bulaich .25 .60
112 Mike Eischeid .25 .60
113 Speedy Thomas RC .25 .60
114 Glen Holloway RC .25 .60
115 Jack Ham RC 15.00 30.00
116 Jim Nettles RC .25 .60
117 Errol Mann .25 .60
118 John Mackey .60 1.50
119 George Kunz .25 .60
120 Bob James .25 .60
121 Garland Boyette .25 .60
122 Mel Phillips RC .25 .60
123 Johnny Roland .25 .60
124 Doug Swift RC .25 .60
125 Archie Manning 2.00 4.00
126 Dave Herman .25 .60
127 Carleton Oats RC .25 .60
128 Bill Van Heusen .25 .60
129 Rich Jackson .25 .60
130 Lon Hauss .40 1.00
131 Billy Parks RC .25 .60
132 Ray May .25 .60
133 NFC Semi-Final 2.00 5.00
(Cowboys 30, 49ers 28:
Roger Staubach dropping back)
134 AFC Semi-Final 1.00 2.50
(Steelers 13, Raiders 7:
Immaculate Reception Game)
135 NFC Semi-Final .40 1.00
(Redskins 16, Packers 3:
Redskins defense)
136 AFC Semi-Final .75 2.00
(Dolphins 20, Browns 14:
Bob Griese handing
off to Larry Csonka)
137 NFC Title Game .60 1.50
(Redskins 26, Cowboys 3:
Billy Kilmer handing
off to Larry Brown)
138 AFC Title Game .40 1.00
(Dolphins 21, Steelers 17:
Miami stops John Fuqua)
139 Super Bowl .60 1.50
(Dolphins 14, Redskins 7:
Miami defense)
140 Dwight White RC UER 2.00 5.00
(College North Texas
State, should be
East Texas State)
141 Jim Marsalis .25 .60
142 Doug Van Horn RC .25 .60
143 Al Matthews RC .25 .60
144 Bob Windsor RC .25 .60
145 Dave Hampton RC .25 .60
146 Horst Muhlmann .25 .60
147 Wally Hilgenberg RC .25 .60
148 Ron Smith .25 .60
149 Coy Bacon RC .40 1.00
150 Winston Hill .25 .60
151 Ron Jessie RC .40 1.00
152 Ken Iman .25 .60
153 Ron Saul RC .25 .60
154 Jim Braxton RC .40 1.00
155 Bubba Smith 1.25 2.50
156 Gary Cuozzo .40 1.00
157 Charlie Krueger .40 1.00
158 Tim Foley RC .40 1.00
159 Lee Roy Jordan .60 1.50
160 Bob Brown OT .60 1.50
161 Margene Adkins RC .25 .60
162 Ron Widby RC .25 .60
163 Jim Houston .25 .60
164 Joe Dawkins .25 .60
165 L.C. Greenwood 2.00 4.00
166 Richmond Flowers RC .25 .60
167 Curley Culp RC .60 1.50
168 Len St. Jean .25 .60
169 Walter Rock .25 .60
170 Bill Bradley .40 1.00
171 Ken Riley RC .60 1.50
172 Rich Coady RC .25 .60
173 Don Hansen RC .25 .60
174 Lionel Aldridge .25 .60
175 Don Maynard 2.00 4.00
176 Dave Osborn .40 1.00
177 Jim Bailey .25 .60
178 John Pitts .25 .60
179 Dave Parks .25 .60
180 Chester Marcol RC .25 .60
181 Len Rohde RC .25 .60
182 Jeff Staggs RC .25 .60
183 Gene Hickerson .60 1.25
184 Charlie Evans RC .25 .60
185 Mel Renfro .60 1.50
186 Marvin Upshaw RC .25 .60
187 George Atkinson .40 1.00
188 Norm Evans .40 1.00
189 Steve Ramsey .25 .60
190 Dave Chapple RC .25 .60
191 Gerry Mullins RC .25 .60
192 John Didion RC .25 .60
193 Bob Gladieux RC .25 .60
194 Don Hultz .25 .60
195 Mike Lucci .25 .60
196 John Wilbur RC .25 .60
197 George Farmer .25 .60
198 Tommy Casanova RC .40 1.00
199 Russ Washington .25 .60
200 Claude Humphrey .60 1.50
Tackling Roger Staubach
201 Pat Hughes RC .25 .60
202 Zeke Moore .25 .60
203 Chip Glass RC .25 .60
204 Glenn Ressler RC .25 .60
205 Willie Ellison .40 1.00
206 John Leypoldt RC .25 .60
207 Johnny Fuller RC .25 .60
208 Bill Hayhoe RC .25 .60
209 Ed Bell RC .25 .60
210 Willie Brown .60 1.50
211 Carl Eller .60 1.50
212 Mark Nordquist .25 .60
213 Larry Willingham RC .25 .60
214 Nick Buoniconti .60 1.50
215 John Hadl .60 1.50
216 Jethro Pugh RC .60 1.50
217 Leroy Mitchell .25 .60
218 Billy Newsome RC .25 .60
219 John McMakin RC .25 .60
220 Larry Brown .60 1.50
221 Clarence Scott RC .25 .60
222 Paul Naumoff RC .25 .60
223 Ted Fritsch Jr. RC .25 .60
224 Checklist 133-264 2.50 5.00
225 Dan Pastorini .60 1.50
226 Joe Beauchamp UER RC .25 .60
227 Pat Matson .25 .60
228 Tony McGee DT RC .25 .60
229 Mike Phipps .40 1.00
230 Harold Jackson .60 1.50
231 Willie Williams RC .25 .60
232 Spike Jones .25 .60
233 Jim Tyrer .25 .60
234 Roy Hilton .25 .60
235 Phil Villapiano .40 1.00
236 Charley Taylor UER 1.50 3.00
(Misspelled Charlie
on both sides)
237 Malcolm Snider RC .25 .60
238 Vic Washington .25 .60
239 Grady Alderman .25 .60
240 Dick Anderson .40 1.00
241 Ron Yankowski RC .25 .60
242 Billy Masters RC .25 .60
243 Herb Adderley .60 1.50
244 David Ray RC .25 .60
245 John Riggins 4.00 8.00
246 Mike Wagner RC 1.25 3.00
247 Don Morrison RC .25 .60
248 Earl McCullouch .25 .60
249 Dennis Wirgowski RC .25 .60
250 Chris Hanburger .40 1.00
251 Pat Sullivan RC .60 1.50
252 Walt Sweeney .25 .60
253 Willie Alexander RC .25 .60
254 Doug Dressler RC .25 .60
255 Walter Johnson .25 .60
256 Ron Hornsby .25 .60
257 Ben Hawkins .25 .60
258 Donnie Green RC .25 .60
259 Fred Hoaglin .25 .60
260 Jerrel Wilson .25 .60
261 Horace Jones .25 .60
262 Woody Peoples .25 .60
263 Jim Hill RC .25 .60
264 John Fuqua .25 .60
265 Donny Anderson KP .40 1.00
266 Roman Gabriel KP .60 1.50
267 Mike Garrett KP .40 1.00
268 Rufus Mayes RC .25 .60
269 Chip Myrtle RC .25 .60
270 Bill Stanfill RC .40 1.00
271 Clint Jones .25 .60
272 Miller Farr .25 .60
273 Harry Schuh .25 .60
274 Bob Hayes .75 2.00
275 Bobby Douglass .40 1.00
276 Gus Hollomon RC .25 .60
277 Del Williams RC .25 .60
278 Julius Adams .25 .60
279 Herman Weaver .25 .60
280 Joe Greene 4.00 8.00
281 Wes Chesson RC .25 .60
282 Charlie Harraway RC .25 .60
283 Paul Guidry .25 .60
284 Terry Owens RC .25 .60
285 Jan Stenerud .60 1.50
286 Pete Athas .25 .60
287 Dale Lindsey RC .25 .60
288 Jack Tatum RC 6.00 15.00
289 Floyd Little .60 1.50
290 Bob Johnson .25 .60
291 Tommy Hart RC .25 .60
292 Tom Mitchell RC .25 .60
293 Walt Patulski RC .25 .60
294 Jim Skaggs .25 .60
295 Bob Griese 3.00 6.00
296 Mike McCoy .25 .60
297 Mel Gray .40 1.00
298 Bobby Bryant RC .25 .60
299 Blaine Nye RC .25 .60
300 Dick Butkus 6.00 12.00
301 Charlie Cowan RC .25 .60
302 Mark Lomas RC .25 .60
303 Josh Ashton RC .25 .60
304 Happy Feller RC .25 .60
305 Ron Shanklin .25 .60
306 Wayne Rasmussen .25 .60
307 Jerry Smith .25 .60
308 Ken Reaves .25 .60
309 Ron East RC .25 .60
310 Otis Taylor .60 1.50
311 John Garlington RC .25 .60
312 Lyle Alzado 2.00 4.00
313 Remi Prudhomme RC .25 .60
314 Cornelius Johnson RC .25 .60
315 Lemar Parrish .40 1.00
316 Jim Kiick .60 1.50
317 Steve Zabel .25 .60
318 Alden Roche RC .25 .60
319 Tom Blanchard RC .25 .60
320 Fred Biletnikoff 2.00 4.00
321 Ralph Neely .40 1.00
322 Dan Dierdorf RC 7.50 20.00
323 Richard Caster .40 1.00
324 Gene Howard .25 .60
325 Elvin Bethea .60 1.50
326 Carl Garrett .40 1.00
327 Ron Billingsley RC .25 .60
328 Charlie West .25 .60
329 Tom Neville .25 .60
330 Ted Kwalick .40 1.00
331 Rudy Redmond RC .25 .60
332 Henry Davis RC .25 .60
333 John Zook .25 .60
334 Jim Turner .25 .60
335 Len Dawson 2.50 5.00
336 Bob Chandler RC .40 1.00
337 Al Beauchamp .25 .60
338 Tom Matte .40 1.00
339 Paul Laaveg RC .25 .60
340 Ken Ellis .25 .60
341 Jim Langer RC 6.00 12.00
342 Ron Porter .25 .60
343 Jack Youngblood RC 7.50 15.00
344 Cornell Green .60 1.50
345 Marv Hubbard .40 1.00
346 Bruce Taylor .25 .60
347 Sam Havrilak RC .25 .60
348 Walt Sumner RC .25 .60
349 Steve O'Neal RC .25 .60
350 Ron Johnson .40 1.00
351 Rockne Freitas .25 .60
352 Larry Stallings .25 .60
353 Jim Cadile .25 .60
354 Ken Burrough .40 1.00
355 Jim Plunkett 2.00 4.00
356 Dave Long RC .25 .60
357 Ralph Anderson RC .25 .60
358 Checklist 265-396 2.50 5.00
359 Gene Washington Vik .40 1.00
360 Dave Wilcox .60 1.50
361 Paul Smith RC .25 .60
362 Alvin Wyatt RC .25 .60
363 Charlie Smith .25 .60
364 Royce Berry .25 .60
365 Dave Elmendorf .25 .60
366 Scott Hunter .40 1.00
367 Bob Kuechenberg RC 1.25 3.00
368 Pete Gogolak .25 .60
369 Dave Edwards .25 .60
370 Lem Barney 1.25 2.50
371 Verlon Biggs .25 .60
372 John Reaves RC .25 .60
373 Ed Podolak .40 1.00
374 Chris Farasopoulos .25 .60
375 Gary Garrison .25 .60
376 Tom Funchess RC .25 .60
377 Bobby Joe Green .25 .60
378 Don Brumm .25 .60
379 Jim O'Brien .25 .60
380 Paul Krause .60 1.50
381 Leroy Kelly 1.25 2.50
382 Ray Mansfield .25 .60
383 Dan Abramowicz .40 1.00
384 John Outlaw RC .25 .60
385 Tommy Nobis .60 1.50
386 Tom Domres RC .25 .60
387 Ken Willard .25 .60
388 Mike Stratton .25 .60
389 Fred Dryer 1.25 2.50
390 Jake Scott .60 1.50
391 Rich Houston RC .25 .60
392 Virgil Carter .25 .60
393 Tody Smith RC .25 .60
394 Ernie Calloway RC .25 .60
395 Charlie Sanders .60 1.50
396 Fred Willis .25 .60
397 Curt Knight .25 .60
398 Nemiah Wilson .25 .60
399 Carroll Dale .40 1.00
400 Joe Namath 15.00 30.00
401 Wayne Mulligan .25 .60
402 Jim Harrison RC .25 .60
403 Tim Rossovich .25 .60
404 David Lee .25 .60
405 Frank Pitts RC .25 .60
406 Jim Marshall .60 1.50
407 Bob Brown TE .25 .60
408 John Rowser .25 .60
409 Mike Montler .25 .60
410 Willie Lanier .60 1.50
411 Bill Bell K RC .25 .60
412 Cedrick Hardman .25 .60
413 Bob Anderson .25 .60
414 Earl Morrall .60 1.50
415 Ken Houston .60 1.50
416 Jack Snow .40 1.00
417 Dick Cunningham RC .25 .60
418 Greg Larson .25 .60
419 Mike Bass RC .40 1.00
420 Mike Reid .60 1.50
421 Walt Garrison .60 1.50
422 Pete Liske .25 .60
423 Jim Yarbrough RC .25 .60
424 Rich McGeorge .25 .60
425 Bobby Howfield RC .25 .60
426 Pete Banaszak .25 .60
427 Willie Holman RC .25 .60
428 Dale Hackbart .25 .60
429 Fair Hooker .25 .60
430 Ted Hendricks 2.50 5.00
431 Mike Garrett .40 1.00
432 Glen Ray Hines .25 .60
433 Fred Cox .25 .60
434 Bobby Walden .25 .60
435 Bobby Bell .60 1.50
436 Dave Rowe .25 .60
437 Bob Berry .25 .60
438 Bill Thompson .25 .60
439 Jim Beirne .25 .60
440 Larry Little 1.50 3.00
441 Rocky Thompson RC .25 .60
442 Brig Owens .25 .60
443 Richard Neal .25 .60
444 Al Nelson .25 .60
445 Chip Myers .25 .60
446 Ken Bowman .25 .60
447 Jim Purnell RC .25 .60
448 Altie Taylor .25 .60
449 Linzy Cole .25 .60
450 Bob Lilly 2.50 5.00
451 Charlie Ford RC .25 .60
452 Milt Sunde .25 .60
453 Doug Wyatt RC .25 .60
454 Don Nottingham RC .40 1.00
455 John Unitas 7.50 15.00
456 Frank Lewis RC .40 1.00
457 Roger Wehrli .40 1.00
458 Jim Cheyunski RC .25 .60
459 Jerry Sherk RC .40 1.00
460 Gene Washington 49er .40 1.00
461 Jim Otto .60 1.50
462 Ed Budde .25 .60
463 Jim Mitchell .40 1.00
464 Emerson Boozer .40 1.00
465 Garo Yepremian .60 1.50
466 Pete Duranko .25 .60
467 Charlie Joiner 4.00 8.00
468 Spider Lockhart .40 1.00
469 Marty Domres .25 .60
470 John Brockington .60 1.50
471 Ed Flanagan .25 .60
472 Roy Jefferson .40 1.00
473 Julian Fagan RC .25 .60
474 Bill Brown .40 1.00
475 Roger Staubach 15.00 30.00
476 Jan White RC .25 .60
477 Pat Holmes RC .25 .60
478 Bob DeMarco .25 .60
479 Merlin Olsen 1.25 2.50
480 Andy Russell .60 1.50
481 Steve Spurrier 10.00 20.00
482 Nate Ramsey .25 .60
483 Dennis Partee .25 .60
484 Jerry Simmons .25 .60
485 Donny Anderson .60 1.50
486 Ralph Baker .25 .60
487 Ken Stabler RC 35.00 60.00
488 Ernie McMillan .25 .60
489 Ken Burrow RC .25 .60
490 Jack Gregory RC .25 .60
491 Larry Seiple .40 1.00
492 Mick Tingelhoff .40 1.00
493 Craig Morton .60 1.50
494 Cecil Turner .25 .60
495 Steve Owens .60 1.50
496 Rickie Harris .25 .60
497 Buck Buchanan .60 1.50
498 Checklist 397-528 2.50 5.00
499 Billy Kilmer .60 1.50
500 O.J. Simpson 7.50 15.00
501 Bruce Gossett .25 .60
502 Art Thoms RC .25 .60
503 Larry Kaminski RC .25 .60
504 Larry Smith RB RC .25 .60
505 Bruce Van Dyke RC .25 .60
506 Alvin Reed .25 .60
507 Delles Howell .25 .60
508 Leroy Keyes .25 .60
509 Bo Scott .40 1.00
510 Ron Yary .60 1.50
511 Paul Warfield 2.50 5.00
512 Mac Percival .25 .60
513 Essex Johnson RC .25 .60
514 Jackie Smith .60 1.50
515 Norm Snead .60 1.50
516 Charlie Stukes RC .25 .60
517 Reggie Rucker RC .40 1.00
518 Bill Sandeman UER RC .25 .60
(Should be a period
between run and he
instead of a comma)
519 Mel Farr .40 1.00
520 Raymond Chester .40 1.00
521 Fred Carr RC .40 1.00
522 Jerry LeVias .40 1.00
523 Jim Strong RC .25 .60
524 Roland McDole .25 .60
525 Dennis Shaw .25 .60
526 Dave Manders .25 .60
527 Skip Vanderbundt RC .25 .60
528 Mike Sensibaugh RC .60 1.50

1973 Topps Team Checklists

The 1973 Topps Team Checklist set contains 26 checklist cards, one for each of the 26 NFL teams. The cards measure 2-1/2" by 3 1/2" and were inserted into regular issue 1973 Topps football wax packs. The fronts show action scenes at the top of the card and a Topps helmet with the team name at its immediate right. The bottom portion of the card contains the checklist, complete with boxes in which to place check marks. Uniform numbers and positions are also given with the player's name. The backs of the cards form puzzles of Joe Namath and Larry Brown. These unnumbered cards are numbered below for convenience in alphabetical order by team name. The cards can all be found with one or two asterisks on the front and in a blank backed version.

COMPLETE SET (26) 50.00 100.00
1 Atlanta Falcons 2.00 4.00
2 Baltimore Colts 2.00 4.00
3 Buffalo Bills 2.00 4.00
4 Chicago Bears 2.50 5.00
5 Cincinnati Bengals 2.00 4.00
6 Cleveland Browns 2.50 5.00
7 Dallas Cowboys 3.00 6.00
8 Denver Broncos 2.00 4.00
9 Detroit Lions 2.00 4.00
10 Green Bay Packers 2.50 5.00
11 Houston Oilers 2.00 4.00
12 Kansas City Chiefs 2.00 4.00
13 Los Angeles Rams 2.00 4.00
14 Miami Dolphins 2.50 5.00
15 Minnesota Vikings 2.50 5.00
16 New England Patriots 2.00 4.00
17 New Orleans Saints 2.00 4.00
18 New York Giants 2.00 4.00
19 New York Jets 2.00 4.00
20 Oakland Raiders 3.00 6.00
21 Philadelphia Eagles 2.00 4.00
22 Pittsburgh Steelers 2.50 5.00
23 St. Louis Cardinals 2.00 4.00
24 San Diego Chargers 2.00 4.00
25 San Francisco 49ers 2.50 5.00
26 Washington Redskins 2.50 5.00

1974 Topps

The 1974 Topps set contains 528 standard-size cards. Card fronts have photos that are bordered on either side by uprights of a goal post. The goal post has a different color depending upon the player's team. The team name is in a color bar at the bottom. The player's name and position are beneath the crossbar. The card backs are printed in blue and yellow on gray card stock and include statistics and highlights. The bottom of the back provides part of a simulated football game which could be played by drawing cards. Subsets inlcude All-Pro (121-144), league leaders (328-333) and post-season action (460-463). This set contains the Rookie Cards of Harold Carmichael, Chuck Foreman, Ray Guy, John Hannah, Bert Jones, Ed Marinaro, John Matuszak and Ahmad Rashad. An uncut sheet of team checklist cards was also available via a mail-in offer on wax pack wrappers. There are a number of cards with copyright variations. On cards 26, 129, 130, 156, 162, 219, 265-364, 367-422, and 424-528, there are two asterisks with the copyright line. The rest of the cards have one asterisk. Topps also printed a very similar (and very confusing) 50-card set for Parker Brothers in early 1974 as part of its Pro Draft football board game. The only players in this set (game) were offensive players (with an emphasis on the skill positions) that were among the first 132 cards in the 1974 Topps set. There are several notable differences between these Parker Brothers Pro Draft cards and the basic issue. Those cards ending with 1972 statistics on the back (unlike the basic issue which go through 1973) are Parker Brothers cards. Parker Brothers game cards can also be distinguished by the presence of two asterisks rather than one on the copyright line. However, as noted above, there are cards in the regular 1974 Topps set that do have two asterisks but are not Parker Brothers Pro Draft cards. In fact, variations 23A, 49A, 116A, 124A, 126A, and 127A listed in the checklist below were issued with a later

COMPLETE SET (528)	175.00	300.00
1 O.J. Simpson RB UER	10.00	20.00
(Text on back says/100 years, should say/100 yards)		
2 Blaine Nye	.25	.60
3 Don Hansen	.25	.60
4 Ken Bowman	.25	.60
5 Carl Eller	.60	1.50
6 Jerry Smith	.25	.60
7 Ed Podolak	.25	.60
8 Mel Gray	.60	1.50
9 Pat Matson	.25	.60
10 Floyd Little	.60	1.50
11 Frank Pitts	.25	.60
12 Vern Den Herder RC	.40	1.00
13 John Fuqua	.40	1.00
14 Jack Tatum	.75	2.00
15 Winston Hill	.25	.60
16 John Beasley RC	.25	.60
17 David Lee	.25	.60
18 Rich Coady	.25	.60
19 Ken Willard	.25	.60
20 Coy Bacon	.40	1.00
21 Ben Hawkins	.25	.60
22 Paul Guidry	.25	.60
23 Norm Snead	.40	1.00
(Horizontal pose)		
24 Jim Yarbrough	.25	.60
25 Jack Reynolds RC	1.25	3.00
26 Josh Ashton	.25	.60
27 Donnie Green	.25	.60
28 Bob Hayes	.75	2.00
29 John Zook	.25	.60
30 Bobby Bryant	.25	.60
31 Scott Hunter	.40	1.00
32 Dan Dierdorf	3.00	6.00
33 Curt Knight	.25	.60
34 Elmo Wright RC	.25	.60
35 Essex Johnson	.25	.60
36 Walt Sumner	.25	.60
37 Marv Montgomery RC	.25	.60
38 Tim Foley	.40	1.00
39 Mike Siani	.25	.60
40 Joe Greene	3.00	6.00
41 Bobby Howfield	.25	.60
42 Del Williams	.25	.60
43 Don McCauley	.25	.60
44 Randy Jackson	.25	.60
45 Ron Smith	.25	.60
46 Gene Washington 49er	.40	1.00
47 Po James RC	.25	.60
48 Solomon Freelon RC	.25	.60
49 Bob Windsor	.25	.60
(Horizontal pose)		
50 John Hadl	.60	1.50
51 Greg Larson	.25	.60
52 Steve Owens	.40	1.00
53 Jim Cheyunski	.25	.60
54 Rayfield Wright	.40	1.00
55 Dave Hampton	.25	.60
56 Ron Widby	.25	.60
57 Milt Sunde	.25	.60
58 Billy Kilmer	.60	1.50
59 Bobby Bell	.60	1.50
60 Jim Bakken	.25	.60
61 Rufus Mayes	.25	.60
62 Vic Washington	.25	.60
63 Gene Washington Vik	.40	1.00
64 Clarence Scott	.25	.60
65 Gene Upshaw	.75	2.00
66 Larry Seiple	.40	1.00
67 John McMakin	.25	.60
68 Ralph Baker	.25	.60
69 Lydell Mitchell	.40	1.00
70 Archie Manning	1.25	2.50
71 George Farmer	.25	.60
72 Ron East	.25	.60
73 Al Nelson	.25	.60
74 Pat Hughes	.25	.60
75 Fred Willis	.25	.60
76 Larry Walton RC	.25	.60
77 Tom Neville	.25	.60
78 Ted Kwalick	.25	.60
79 Walt Patulski	.25	.60
80 John Niland	.25	.60
81 Ted Fritsch Jr.	.25	.60
82 Paul Krause	.60	1.50
83 Jack Snow	.40	1.00
84 Mike Bass	.25	.60
85 Jim Tyrer	.25	.60
86 Ron Yankowski	.25	.60
87 Mike Phipps	.40	1.00
88 Al Beauchamp	.25	.60
89 Riley Odoms RC	.60	1.50
90 MacArthur Lane	.25	.60
91 Art Thoms	.25	.60
92 Marlin Briscoe	.25	.60
93 Bruce Van Dyke	.25	.60
94 Tom Myers RC	.25	.60
95 Calvin Hill	.60	1.50
96 Bruce Laird RC	.25	.60
97 Tony McGee	.25	.60
98 Len Rohde	.25	.60
99 Tom McNeill	.25	.60
100 Delles Howell	.25	.60
101 Gary Garrison	.25	.60
102 Dan Goich RC	.25	.60
103 Len St. Jean	.25	.60
104 Zeke Moore	.25	.60
105 Ahmad Rashad RC	10.00	20.00
106 Mel Renfro	.60	1.50
107 Jim Mitchell	.25	.60
108 Ed Budde	.25	.60
109 Harry Schuh	.25	.60
110 Greg Pruitt RC	2.00	4.00
111 Ed Flanagan	.25	.60
112 Larry Stallings	.25	.60
113 Chuck Foreman RC	2.50	5.00
114 Royce Berry	.25	.60
115 Gale Gillingham	.25	.60
116 Charley Johnson	.60	1.50
(Horizontal pose)		
117 Checklist 1-132 UER	2.00	4.00
(345 Hamburger)		
118 Bill Butler RC	.25	.60
119 Roy Jefferson	.40	1.00
120 Bobby Douglass	.40	1.00
121 Harold Carmichael RC	6.00	12.00
122 George Kunz AP	.25	.60
123 Larry Little AP	.75	2.00
124 Forrest Blue AP	.25	.60
125 Ron Yary AP	.60	1.50
126 Tom Mack AP	.60	1.50
127 Bob Tucker AP	.40	1.00
128 Paul Warfield AP	2.00	4.00
129 Fran Tarkenton AP	5.00	10.00
130 O.J. Simpson AP	6.00	12.00
131 Larry Csonka AP	3.00	6.00
132 Bruce Gossett AP	.25	.60
133 Bill Stanfill AP	.40	1.00
134 Alan Page AP	1.25	2.50
135 Paul Smith AP	.25	.60
136 Claude Humphrey AP	.40	1.00
137 Jack Ham AP	5.00	10.00
138 Lee Roy Jordan AP	.60	1.50
139 Phil Villapiano AP	.40	1.00
140 Ken Ellis AP	.25	.60
141 Willie Brown AP	.60	1.50
142 Dick Anderson AP	.40	1.00
143 Bill Bradley AP	.40	1.00
144 Jerrel Wilson AP	.25	.60
145 Reggie Rucker	.40	1.00
146 Marty Domres	.25	.60
147 Bob Kowalkowski RC	.25	.60
148 John Matuszak RC	2.50	6.00
149 Mike Adamle RC	.40	1.00
150 John Unitas	7.50	15.00
151 Charlie Ford	.25	.60
152 Bob Klein RC	.25	.60
153 Jim Merlo RC	.25	.60
154 Willie Young	.25	.60
155 Donny Anderson	.40	1.00
156 Brig Owens	.25	.60
157 Bruce Jarvis RC	.25	.60
158 Ron Carpenter RC	.25	.60
159 Don Cockroft	.25	.60
160 Tommy Nobis	.60	1.50
161 Craig Morton	.60	1.50
162 Jon Staggers RC	.25	.60
163 Mike Eischeid	.25	.60
164 Jerry Sisemore RC	.25	.60
165 Cedrick Hardman	.25	.60
166 Bill Thompson	.40	1.00
167 Jim Lynch	.40	1.00
168 Bob Moore RC	.25	.60
169 Glen Edwards RC	.25	.60
170 Mercury Morris	.60	1.50
171 Julius Adams	.25	.60
172 Cotton Speyrer RC	.25	.60
173 Bill Munson	.40	1.00
174 Benny Johnson	.25	.60
175 Burgess Owens RC	.25	.60
176 Cid Edwards	.25	.60
177 Doug Buffone	.25	.60
178 Charlie Cowan	.25	.60
179 Bob Newland RC	.25	.60
180 Ron Johnson	.40	1.00
181 Bob Rowe RC	.25	.60
182 Len Hauss	.25	.60
183 Joe DeLamielleure RC	6.00	12.00
184 Sherman White RC	.25	.60
185 Fair Hooker	.25	.60
186 Nick Mike-Mayer RC	.25	.60
187 Ralph Neely	.25	.60
188 Rich McGeorge	.25	.60
189 Ed Marinaro RC	1.50	4.00
190 Dave Wilcox	.60	1.50
191 Joe Owens RC	.25	.60
192 Bill Van Heusen	.25	.60
193 Jim Kearney	.25	.60
194 Otis Sistrunk RC	.60	1.50
195 Ron Shanklin	.25	.60
196 Bill Lenkaitis RC	.25	.60
197 Tom Drougas RC	.25	.60
198 Larry Hand	.25	.60
199 Mack Alston RC	.25	.60
200 Bob Griese	3.00	6.00
201 Earlie Thomas RC	.25	.60
202 Carl Gersbach RC	.25	.60
203 Jim Harrison	.25	.60
204 Jake Kupp	.25	.60
205 Merlin Olsen	.75	2.00
206 Spider Lockhart	.40	1.00
207 Walker Gillette	.25	.60
208 Verlon Biggs	.25	.60
209 Bob James	.25	.60
210 Bob Trumpy	.60	1.50
211 Jerry Sherk	.25	.60
212 Andy Maurer	.25	.60
213 Fred Carr	.25	.60
214 Mick Tingelhoff	.40	1.00
215 Steve Spurrier	7.50	15.00
216 Richard Harris RC	.25	.60
217 Charlie Greer RC	.25	.60
218 Buck Buchanan	.60	1.50
219 Ray Guy RC	6.00	12.00
220 Franco Harris	6.00	12.00
221 Darryl Stingley RC	.60	1.50
222 Rex Kern	.25	.60
223 Toni Fritsch RC	.40	1.00
224 Levi Johnson RC	.25	.60
225 Bob Kuechenberg	.40	1.00
226 Elvin Bethea	.60	1.50
227 Al Woodall RC	.40	1.00
228 Terry Owens	.25	.60
229 Bivian Lee RC	.25	.60
230 Dick Butkus	5.00	10.00
231 Jim Bertelsen RC	.40	1.00
232 John Mendenhall RC	.25	.60
233 Conrad Dobler RC	.60	1.50
234 J.D. Hill	.40	1.00
235 Ken Houston	.60	1.50
236 Dave Lewis	.25	.60
237 John Garlington	.25	.60
238 Bill Sandeman	.25	.60
239 Alden Roche	.25	.60
240 John Gilliam	.40	1.00
241 Bruce Taylor	.25	.60
242 Vern Winfield RC	.25	.60
243 Bobby Maples	.25	.60
244 Wendell Hayes	.25	.60
245 George Blanda	4.00	8.00
246 Dwight White	.40	1.00
247 Sandy Durko RC	.25	.60
248 Tom Mitchell	.25	.60
249 Chuck Walton	.25	.60
250 Bob Lilly	2.00	4.00
251 Doug Swift	.25	.60
252 Lynn Dickey RC	.60	1.50
253 Jerome Barkum RC	.25	.60
254 Clint Jones	.25	.60
255 Billy Newsome	.25	.60
256 Bob Asher RC	.25	.60
257 Joe Scibelli RC	.25	.60
258 Tom Blanchard	.25	.60
259 Norm Thompson	.25	.60
260 Larry Brown	.60	1.50
261 Paul Seymour RC	.25	.60
262 Checklist 133-264	2.00	4.00
263 Doug Dieken RC	.25	.60
264 Lemar Parrish	.40	1.00
265 Bob Lee UER	.25	.60
(listed as Atlanta		
Hawks on card back)		
266 Bob Brown DT	.25	.60
267 Roy Winston	.25	.60
268 Randy Beisler RC	.25	.60
269 Joe Dawkins	.25	.60
270 Tom Dempsey	.40	1.00
271 Jack Rudnay	.25	.60
272 Art Shell	2.50	5.00
273 Mike Wagner	.40	1.00
274 Rick Cash RC	.25	.60
275 Greg Landry	.60	1.50
276 Glenn Ressler	.25	.60
277 Billy Joe DuPree RC	1.25	3.00
278 Norm Evans	.25	.60
279 Billy Parks	.25	.60
280 John Riggins	3.00	6.00
281 Lionel Aldridge	.25	.60
282 Steve O'Neal	.25	.60
283 Craig Clemons RC	.25	.60
284 Willie Williams	.25	.60
285 Isiah Robertson	.40	1.00
286 Dennis Shaw	.25	.60
287 Bill Brundige	.25	.60
288 John Leypoldt	.25	.60
289 John DeMarie RC	.25	.60
290 Mike Reid	.60	1.50
291 Greg Brezina	.25	.60
292 Willie Buchanon RC	.25	.60
293 Dave Osborn	.40	1.00
294 Mel Phillips	.25	.60
295 Haven Moses	.40	1.00
296 Wade Key	.25	.60
297 Marvin Upshaw	.25	.60
298 Ray Mansfield	.25	.60
299 Edgar Chandler	.25	.60
300 Marv Hubbard	.40	1.00
301 Herman Weaver	.25	.60
302 Jim Bailey	.25	.60
303 D.D. Lewis RC	.60	1.50
304 Ken Burrough	.40	1.00
305 Jake Scott	.60	1.50
306 Randy Rasmussen	.25	.60
307 Pettis Norman	.25	.60
308 Carl Johnson RC	.25	.60
309 Joe Taylor	.25	.60
310 Pete Gogolak	.25	.60
311 Tony Baker	.25	.60
312 John Richardson RC	.25	.60
313 Dave Robinson	.40	1.00
314 Reggie McKenzie RC	.60	1.50
315 Isaac Curtis RC	.60	1.50
316 Thom Darden RC	.25	.60
317 Ken Reaves	.25	.60
318 Malcolm Snider	.25	.60
319 Jeff Siemon RC	.40	1.00
320 Dan Abramowicz	.40	1.00
321 Lyle Alzado	.75	2.00
322 John Reaves	.25	.60
323 Morris Stroud RC	.25	.60
324 Bobby Walden	.25	.60
325 Randy Vataha	.25	.60
326 Nemiah Wilson	.25	.60
327 Paul Naumoff	.25	.60
328 Rushing Leaders	1.50	3.00
O.J. Simpson		
John Brockington		
329 Passing Leaders	2.50	5.00
Ken Stabler		
Roger Staubach		
330 Receiving Leaders	.60	1.50
Fred Willis		
Harold Carmichael		
331 Scoring Leaders	.40	1.00
Roy Gerela		
David Ray		
332 Interception Leaders	.40	1.00
Dick Anderson		
Mike Wagner		
Bobby Bryant		
333 Punting Leaders	.40	1.00
Jerrel Wilson		
Tom Wittum		
334 Dennis Nelson RC	.25	.60
335 Walt Garrison	.40	1.00
336 Tody Smith	.25	.60
337 Ed Bell	.25	.60
338 Bryant Salter	.25	.60
339 Wayne Colman	.25	.60
340 Garo Yepremian	.40	1.00
341 Bob Newton RC	.25	.60
342 Vince Clements RC	.25	.60
343 Ken Iman	.25	.60
344 Jim Tolbert RC	.25	.60
345 Chris Hanburger	.40	1.00
346 Dave Foley	.25	.60
347 Tommy Casanova	.40	1.00
348 John James RC	.25	.60
349 Clarence Williams	.25	.60
350 Leroy Kelly	.60	1.50
351 Stu Voigt RC	.40	1.00
352 Skip Vanderbundt	.25	.60
353 Pete Duranko	.25	.60
354 John Outlaw	.25	.60
355 Jan Stenerud	.60	1.50
356 Barry Pearson RC	.25	.60
357 Brian Dowling RC	.25	.60
358 Dan Conners	.25	.60
359 Bob Bell RC	.25	.60
360 Rick Volk	.25	.60
361 Pat Toomay RC	.40	1.00
362 Bob Gresham RC	.25	.60
363 John Schmitt	.25	.60
364 Mel Rogers RC	.25	.60
365 Manny Fernandez	.40	1.00
366 Ernie Jackson RC	.25	.60
367 Gary Huff RC	.40	1.00
368 Bob Grim	.25	.60
369 Ernie McMillan	.25	.60
370 Dave Elmendorf	.25	.60
371 Mike Bragg	.25	.60
372 John Skorupan RC	.25	.60
373 Howard Fest	.25	.60
374 Jerry Tagge RC	.40	1.00
375 Art Malone	.25	.60
376 Bob Babich	.25	.60
377 Jim Marshall	.60	1.50
378 Bob Hoskins RC	.25	.60
379 Don Zimmerman RC	.25	.60
380 Ray May	.25	.60
381 Emmitt Thomas	.40	1.00
382 Terry Hanratty	.40	1.00
383 John Hannah RC	7.50	15.00
384 George Atkinson	.25	.60
385 Ted Hendricks	1.50	3.00
386 Jim O'Brien	.25	.60
387 Jethro Pugh	.40	1.00
388 Elbert Drungo RC	.25	.60
389 Richard Caster	.40	1.00
390 Deacon Jones	.60	1.50
391 Checklist 265-396	2.00	4.00
392 Jess Phillips RC	.25	.60
393 Garry Lyle UER	.25	.60
(Misspelled Gary		
on card front)		
394 Jim Files	.25	.60
395 Jim Hart	.60	1.50
396 Dave Chapple	.25	.60
397 Jim Langer	.75	2.00
398 John Wilbur	.25	.60
399 Dwight Harrison RC	.25	.60
400 John Brockington	.40	1.00
401 Ken Anderson	3.00	6.00
402 Mike Tilleman	.25	.60
403 Charlie Hall RC	.25	.60
404 Tommy Hart	.25	.60
405 Norm Bulaich	.40	1.00
406 Jim Turner	.25	.60
407 Mo Moorman	.25	.60
408 Ralph Anderson	.25	.60
409 Jim Otto	.60	1.50
410 Andy Russell	.60	1.50
411 Glenn Doughty RC	.25	.60
412 Altie Taylor	.25	.60
413 Marv Bateman RC	.25	.60
414 Willie Alexander	.25	.60
415 Bill Zapalac RC	.25	.60
416 Russ Washington	.25	.60
417 Joe Federspiel RC	.25	.60
418 Craig Cotton RC	.25	.60
419 Randy Johnson	.25	.60
420 Harold Jackson	.60	1.50
421 Roger Wehrli	.40	1.00
422 Charlie Harraway	.25	.60
423 Spike Jones	.25	.60
424 Bob Johnson	.25	.60
425 Mike McCoy	.25	.60
426 Dennis Havig RC	.25	.60
427 Bob McKay RC	.25	.60
428 Steve Zabel	.25	.60
429 Horace Jones	.25	.60
430 Jim Johnson	.60	1.50
431 Roy Gerela	.40	1.00
432 Tom Graham RC	.25	.60
433 Curley Culp	.40	1.00
434 Ken Mendenhall RC	.25	.60
435 Jim Plunkett	1.25	2.50
436 Julian Fagan	.25	.60
437 Mike Garrett	.40	1.00
438 Bobby Joe Green	.25	.60
439 Jack Gregory	.25	.60
440 Charlie Sanders	.40	1.00
441 Bill Curry	.40	1.00
442 Bob Pollard RC	.25	.60
443 David Ray	.25	.60
444 Terry Metcalf RC	1.50	3.00
445 Pat Fischer	.40	1.00
446 Bob Chandler	.40	1.00
447 Bill Bergey	.40	1.00
448 Walter Johnson	.25	.60
449 Charle Young RC	.60	1.50
450 Chester Marcol	.25	.60
451 Ken Stabler	10.00	20.00
452 Preston Pearson	.60	1.50
453 Mike Current	.25	.60
454 Ron Bolton RC	.25	.60
455 Mark Lomas	.25	.60
456 Raymond Chester	.40	1.00
457 Jerry LeVias	.40	1.00
458 Skip Butler RC	.25	.60
459 Mike Livingston RC	.25	.60
460 AFC Semi-Finals	.40	1.00
Raiders 33;		
Steelers 14		
Dolphins 34;		
Bengals 16		
461 NFC Semi-Finals	2.00	4.00
Vikings 27;		
Redskins 20		
Cowboys 27;		
Rams 16		
(Staubach)		
462 Playoff Championship	1.50	3.00
Dolphins 27;		
Raiders 10		
Vikings 27;		
Cowboys 10		
(Ken Stabler and		
Fran Tarkenton)		
463 Super Bowl	.75	2.00
Dolphins 24;		
Vikings 7		
(Larry Csonka pictured)		
464 Wayne Mulligan	.25	.60
465 Horst Muhlmann	.25	.60
466 Milt Morin	.25	.60
467 Don Parish RC	.25	.60
468 Richard Neal	.25	.60
469 Ron Jessie	.40	1.00
470 Terry Bradshaw	12.50	25.00
471 Fred Dryer	.60	1.50
472 Jim Carter	.25	.60
473 Ken Burrow	.25	.60
474 Wally Chambers RC	.40	1.00
475 Dan Pastorini	.60	1.50
476 Don Morrison	.25	.60
477 Carl Mauck	.25	.60
478 Larry Cole RC	.40	1.00
479 Jim Kiick	.60	1.50
480 Willie Lanier	.60	1.50
481 Don Herrmann	.40	1.00
482 George Hunt RC	.25	.60
483 Bob Howard RC	.25	.60
484 Myron Pottios	.25	.60
485 Jackie Smith	.60	1.50
486 Vern Holland	.25	.60
487 Jim Braxton	.25	.60
488 Joe Reed RC	.25	.60
489 Wally Hilgenberg	.25	.60
490 Fred Biletnikoff	2.00	4.00
491 Bob DeMarco	.25	.60
492 Mark Nordquist	.25	.60
493 Larry Brooks RC	.25	.60
494 Pete Athas	.25	.60
495 Emerson Boozer	.40	1.00
496 L.C. Greenwood	.75	2.00
497 Rockne Freitas	.25	.60
498 Checklist 397-528 UER	2.00	4.00
(510 Charlie Taylor		
should be Charley)		
499 Joe Schmiesing RC	.25	.60
500 Roger Staubach	12.50	25.00
501 Al Cowlings UER	.40	1.00
(Def. tackle on front,		
Def. End on back)		
502 Sam Cunningham RC	.60	1.50
503 Dennis Partee	.25	.60
504 John Didion	.25	.60
505 Nick Buoniconti	.60	1.50
506 Carl Garrett	.40	1.00
507 Doug Van Horn	.25	.60
508 Jamie Rivers RC	.25	.60
509 Jack Youngblood	2.00	4.00
510 Charley Taylor UER	1.25	2.50
(Misspelled Charlie		
on both sides)		
511 Ken Riley	.60	1.50
512 Joe Ferguson RC	1.25	3.00
513 Bill Lueck RC	.25	.60
514 Ray Brown RC	.25	.60
515 Fred Cox	.25	.60
516 Joe Jones	.25	.60
517 Larry Schreiber RC	.25	.60
518 Dennis Wirgowski	.25	.60
519 Leroy Mitchell	.25	.60
520 Otis Taylor	.60	1.50
521 Henry Davis	.25	.60
522 Bruce Barnes RC	.25	.60
523 Charlie Smith	.25	.60
524 Bert Jones RC	3.00	6.00
525 Lem Barney	.75	2.00
526 John Fitzgerald RC	.25	.60
527 Tom Funchess	.25	.60
528 Steve Tannen	.60	1.50

1974 Topps Parker Brothers Pro Draft

This 50-card standard-size set was printed by Topps for distribution by Parker Brothers in early 1974 as part of a football board game. The only players in this set (game) are offensive players (with an emphasis on the skill positions) and all come from the first 132 cards in the 1974 Topps football card set. The cards are very similar and often confused with the 1974 Topps regular issue football cards. There are several notable differences between these cards and the 1974 Topps regular issue; those cards with 1972 statistics on the back (unlike the 1974 Topps regular issue) are indicated in the checklist below with an asterisk. Those cards with pose variations (different from the 1974 Topps) are noted as well parenthetically; these six pose variations are numbers 23, 49, 116, 124, 126, and 127. Parker Brothers game cards can also be distinguished by the presence of two asterisks rather than one on the copyright line. However, there are cards in the regular 1974 Topps set that do have two asterisks but are not Parker Brothers Pro Draft cards. Cards in the 1974 Topps regular set with two asterisks include 26, 129, 130, 156, 162, 219, 265-364, 367-422, and 424-528; the rest have only one asterisk. The Parker Brothers cards are skip-numbered with the number on the back corresponding to that player's number in the Topps regular issue.

COMPLETE SET (50)	62.50	125.00
4 Ken Bowman	.50	1.00
6 Jerry Smith *	1.00	2.00
7 Ed Podolak *	1.00	2.00
9 Pat Matson	.50	1.00
11 Frank Pitts *	1.00	2.00
15 Winston Hill	.50	1.00
18 Rich Coady *	1.00	2.00
19 Ken Willard *	1.25	2.50
21 Ben Hawkins *	1.00	2.00
23A Norm Snead *	2.00	5.00
(Vertical pose; 1972		
stats; two asterisks		
before TCG on back)		
23B Norm Snead *	2.00	5.00
(Vertical pose; 1973		
stats; one asterisk		
before TCG on back)		
24 Jim Yarbrough *	1.00	2.00
28 Bob Hayes *	2.50	5.00
32 Dan Dierdorf *	3.00	6.00
35 Essex Johnson *	1.00	2.00
39 Mike Siani	.50	1.00
42 Del Williams	.50	1.00
43 Don McCauley *	1.00	2.00
44 Randy Jackson *	1.00	2.00
46 Gene Washington 49er *	1.50	3.00
49A Bob Windsor *	1.50	3.00
(Vertical pose; 1972		
stats; two asterisks		
before TCG on back)		
49B Bob Windsor *	1.50	3.00
(Vertical pose; 1973		
stats; one asterisk		
before TCG on back)		
50 John Hadl *	2.00	4.00
52 Steve Owens *	2.00	4.00
54 Rayfield Wright *	1.00	2.00
57 Milt Sunde *	1.00	2.00
58 Billy Kilmer *	2.00	4.00
61 Rufus Mayes *	1.00	2.00
63 Gene Washington Vik *	1.25	2.50
65 Gene Upshaw	2.50	5.00
75 Fred Willis *	1.00	2.00
77 Tom Neville	.50	1.00
78 Ted Kwalick *	1.25	2.50
80 John Niland *	1.00	2.00
81 Ted Fritsch Jr.	.50	1.00
83 Jack Snow *	1.50	3.00
87 Mike Phipps *	1.50	3.00
90 MacArthur Lane *	1.50	3.00
95 Calvin Hill *	1.00	2.00
98 Len Rohde	.50	1.00
101 Gary Garrison *	1.00	2.00
103 Len St. Jean	.50	1.00
107 Jim Mitchell *	1.00	2.00
109 Harry Schuh	.50	1.00
110 Greg Pruitt *	2.00	4.00
111 Ed Flanagan	.50	1.00
113 Chuck Foreman *	2.00	4.00
116A Charley Johnson *	2.00	5.00
(Vertical pose; 1972		
stats; two asterisks		
before TCG on back)		
116B Charley Johnson *	2.00	5.00
(Vertical pose; 1973		
stats; one asterisk		
before TCG on back)		
119 Roy Jefferson *	1.25	2.50
124A Forrest Blue *	1.50	3.00
(Not All-Pro style; 1972		
stats; two asterisks		
before TCG on back)		
124B Forrest Blue	1.50	3.00
(Not All-Pro style; 1973		
stats; one asterisk		
before TCG on back)		
126A Tom Mack *	4.00	8.00
(Not All-Pro style; 1972		
stats; two asterisks		
before TCG on back)		
126B Tom Mack	4.00	8.00
(Not All-Pro style; 1973		
stats; one asterisk		
before TCG on back)		
127B Bob Tucker *	1.50	3.00
(Not All-Pro style; 1973		
stats; one asterisk		
before TCG on back)		
127A Bob Tucker *	1.50	3.00
(Not All-Pro style; 1972		
stats; two asterisks		
before TCG on back)		

1974 Topps Team Checklists

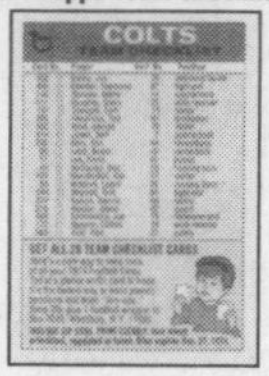

The 1974 Topps Team Checklist set contains 26 standard-size cards. The cards were inserted into regular issue 1974 Topps football wax packs. The Topps logo and team name appear at the top of the card, while the mid-portion of the card contains the actual checklist giving each player's card number, check-off box, name, uniform number, and position. The lower portion of the card contains an ad to obtain all 26 team checklists. A picture of a boy collector is shown in the lower right corner. The back of the card contains rules for a football game to be played with the 1974 Topps football cards. These unnumbered cards are numbered below for convenience in alphabetical order by team name. Twenty of the 26 checklist cards show players out of alphabetical order on the card front. The cards can all be found with one or two asterisks on the front. The set was also available directly from Topps as a mail-away offer as a pair of unperforated uncut sheets, which had blank backs. Measuring approximately 13 1/2" by 10 1/2", each sheet featured thirteen team checklist cards and an offer for a football action poster.

COMPLETE SET (26)	37.50	75.00
*BLANKBACKS: 2X TO 4X BASIC CARDS		
1 Atlanta Falcons	1.50	3.00
2 Baltimore Colts	1.50	3.00
3 Buffalo Bills	1.50	3.00
4 Chicago Bears	2.00	4.00
5 Cincinnati Bengals	1.50	3.00
6 Cleveland Browns UER	1.50	3.00
(Reggie Rucher)		
7 Dallas Cowboys	2.50	5.00
8 Denver Broncos	1.50	3.00
9 Detroit Lions	1.50	3.00
10 Green Bay Packers	2.00	4.00
11 Houston Oilers	1.50	3.00
12 Kansas City Chiefs	1.50	3.00
13 Los Angeles Rams	1.50	3.00
14 Miami Dolphins	2.00	4.00
15 Minnesota Vikings	2.00	4.00
16 New England Patriots	1.50	3.00
17 New Orleans Saints	1.50	3.00
18 New York Giants	2.00	4.00
19 New York Jets	1.50	3.00
20 Oakland Raiders	2.50	5.00
21 Philadelphia Eagles	1.50	3.00
22 Pittsburgh Steelers	2.00	4.00
23 St. Louis Cardinals	1.50	3.00
24 San Diego Chargers	1.50	3.00
25 San Francisco 49ers	2.00	4.00
26 Washington Redskins UER	2.00	4.00
(Charley Taylor mis-		
spelled as Charlie)		

1975 Topps

The 1975 Topps football set contains 528 standard-size cards. Beneath a color photo, card fronts contain a banner with the team name. Both were done in a team color. To the right of the banner is a football helmet the includes the player's position. The player's name is at the bottom. Subsets include leaders (1-6), All-Pro (201-225), Record Breakers (351-356), Highlights (452-460) and playoffs (526-528). The card backs are printed in black ink with a green background on gray card stock and contain statistics and highlights. The key Rookie Cards in this set are Otis Armstrong, Rocky Bleier, Mel Blount, Cliff Branch, Dan Fouts, Cliff Harris, Drew Pearson, Lynn Swann and Charlie Waters. The set also includes Joe Theismann's first NFL card after having performed in the Canadian Football League. An uncut sheet of team checklist cards was also available via a mail-in offer wax pack wrappers.

COMPLETE SET (528)	175.00	300.00
1 Rushing Leaders	.60	1.50
Lawrence McCutcheon		
Otis Armstrong		
2 Passing Leaders	.60	1.50
Sonny Jurgensen		
Ken Anderson		
3 Receiving Leaders	.60	1.50
Charle Young		
Lydell Mitchell		
4 Scoring Leaders	.30	.75
Chester Marcol		
Roy Gerela		
5 Interception Leaders	.30	.75
Ray Brown		
Emmitt Thomas		
6 Punting Leaders	.60	1.50
Tom Blanchard		
Ray Guy		
7 George Blanda	2.50	5.00
(Black jersey;		
highlights on back)		
8 George Blanda	2.50	5.00
(White jersey;		
career record on back)		
9 Ralph Baker	.20	.50
10 Don Woods RC	.20	.50
11 Bob Asher	.20	.50
12 Mel Blount RC	10.00	20.00
13 Sam Cunningham	.30	.75
14 Jackie Smith	.60	1.50
15 Greg Landry	.30	.75
16 Buck Buchanan	.60	1.50
17 Haven Moses	.30	.75
18 Clarence Ellis	.20	.50
19 Jim Carter	.20	.50
20 Charley Taylor UER	.75	2.00
(Misspelled Charlie		
on card front)		
21 Jess Phillips	.20	.50
22 Larry Seiple	.20	.50
23 Doug Dieken	.20	.50
24 Ron Saul	.20	.50
25 Isaac Curtis UER	.60	1.50
(Misspelled Issac		
on card front)		
26 Gary Larsen RC	.20	.50
27 Bruce Jarvis	.20	.50
28 Steve Zabel	.20	.50
29 John Mendenhall	.20	.50
30 Rick Volk	.20	.50
31 Checklist 1-132	2.00	4.00
32 Dan Abramowicz	.30	.75
33 Bubba Smith	.60	1.50
34 David Ray	.20	.50
35 Dan Dierdorf	2.00	4.00
36 Randy Rasmussen	.20	.50
37 Bob Howard	.20	.50
38 Gary Huff	.30	.75
39 Rocky Bleier RC	10.00	20.00
40 Mel Gray	.30	.75
41 Tony McGee	.20	.50
42 Larry Hand	.20	.50
43 Wendell Hayes	.20	.50
44 Doug Wilkerson RC	.20	.50
45 Paul Smith	.20	.50
46 Dave Robinson	.30	.75
47 Bivian Lee	.20	.50
48 Jim Mandich RC	.30	.75
49 Greg Pruitt	.60	1.50
50 Dan Pastorini UER	.60	1.50
(5/26/39 birthdate		
incorrect)		
51 Ron Pritchard RC	.20	.50
52 Dan Conners	.20	.50
53 Fred Cox	.20	.50
54 Tony Greene RC	.20	.50
55 Craig Morton	.60	1.50
56 Jerry Sisemore	.20	.50
57 Glenn Doughty	.20	.50
58 Larry Schreiber	.20	.50
59 Charlie Waters RC	2.00	4.00
60 Jack Youngblood	.60	1.50
61 Bill Lenkaitis	.20	.50
62 Greg Brezina	.20	.50
63 Bob Pollard	.20	.50
64 Mack Alston	.20	.50
65 Drew Pearson RC	10.00	20.00
66 Charlie Stukes	.20	.50
67 Emerson Boozer	.30	.75
68 Dennis Partee	.20	.50
69 Bob Newton	.20	.50
70 Jack Tatum	.60	1.50
71 Frank Lewis	.20	.50
72 Bob Young RC	.20	.50
73 Julius Adams	.20	.50
74 Paul Naumoff	.20	.50
75 Otis Taylor	.60	1.50
76 Dave Hampton	.20	.50
77 Mike Current	.20	.50
78 Brig Owens	.20	.50
79 Bobby Scott RC	.20	.50
80 Harold Carmichael	1.50	3.00
81 Bill Stanfill	.20	.50
82 Bob Babich	.20	.50
83 Vic Washington	.20	.50
84 Mick Tingelhoff	.30	.75
85 Bob Trumpy	.60	1.50
86 Earl Edwards RC	.20	.50
87 Ron Hornsby	.20	.50
88 Don McCauley	.20	.50
89 Jim Johnson	.60	1.50
90 Andy Russell	.30	.75
91 Cornell Green	.60	1.50
92 Charlie Cowan	.20	.50
93 Jon Staggers	.20	.50
94 Billy Newsome	.20	.50
95 Willie Brown	.60	1.50
96 Carl Mauck	.20	.50
97 Doug Buffone	.20	.50
98 Preston Pearson	.30	.75
99 Jim Bakken	.20	.50
100 Bob Griese	2.50	5.00
101 Bob Windsor	.20	.50
102 Rockne Freitas	.20	.50
103 Jim Marsalis	.20	.50
104 Bill Thompson	.30	.75
105 Ken Burrow	.20	.50
106 Diron Talbert	.20	.50
107 Joe Federspiel	.20	.50
108 Norm Bulaich	.30	.75
109 Bob DeMarco	.20	.50
110 Tom Wittum RC	.20	.50
111 Larry Hefner RC	.20	.50
112 Tody Smith	.20	.50
113 Stu Voigt	.20	.50
114 Horst Muhlmann	.20	.50
115 Ahmad Rashad	3.00	6.00
116 Joe Dawkins	.20	.50
117 George Kunz	.20	.50
118 D.D. Lewis	.30	.75
119 Levi Johnson	.20	.50
120 Len Dawson	2.00	4.00
121 Jim Bertelsen	.20	.50
122 Ed Bell	.20	.50
123 Art Thoms	.20	.50
124 Joe Beauchamp	.20	.50
125 Jack Ham	3.00	6.00
126 Carl Garrett	.20	.50
127 Roger Finnie RC	.20	.50
128 Howard Twilley	.30	.75
129 Bruce Barnes	.20	.50
130 Nate Wright RC	.20	.50
131 Jerry Tagge	.20	.50
132 Floyd Little	.60	1.50
133 John Zook	.20	.50
134 Len Hauss	.20	.50
135 Archie Manning	.60	1.50
136 Po James	.20	.50

137 Walt Sumner .20 .50
138 Randy Beisler .20 .50
139 Willie Alexander .20 .50
140 Garo Yepremian .30 .75
141 Chip Myers .20 .50
142 Jim Braxton .20 .50
143 Doug Van Horn .20 .50
144 Stan White RC .20 .50
145 Roger Staubach 10.00 20.00
146 Herman Weaver .20 .50
147 Marvin Upshaw .20 .50
148 Bob Klein .20 .50
149 Earlie Thomas .20 .50
150 John Brockington .30 .75
151 Mike Siani .20 .50
152 Sam Davis RC .20 .50
153 Mike Wagner .30 .75
154 Larry Stallings .20 .50
155 Wally Chambers .20 .50
156 Randy Vataha .20 .50
157 Jim Marshall .60 1.50
158 Jim Turner .20 .50
159 Walt Sweeney .20 .50
160 Ken Anderson 2.00 4.00
161 Ray Brown .20 .50
162 John Didion .20 .50
163 Tom Dempsey .20 .50
164 Clarence Scott .20 .50
165 Gene Washington 49er .30 .75
166 Willie Rodgers RC .20 .50
167 Doug Swift .20 .50
168 Rufus Mayes .20 .50
169 Marv Bateman .20 .50
170 Lydell Mitchell .30 .75
171 Ron Smith .20 .50
172 Bill Munson .30 .75
173 Bob Grim .20 .50
174 Ed Budde .20 .50
175 Bob Lilly UER 2.00 4.00
(Was first draft,
not first player)
176 Jim Youngblood RC .60 1.50
177 Steve Tannen .20 .50
178 Rich McGeorge .20 .50
179 Jim Tyrer .20 .50
180 Forrest Blue .20 .50
181 Jerry LeVias .30 .75
182 Joe Gilliam RC .60 1.50
183 Jim Otis RC .30 .75
184 Mel Tom .20 .50
185 Paul Seymour .20 .50
186 George Webster .20 .50
187 Pete Duranko .20 .50
188 Essex Johnson .20 .50
189 Bob Lee .30 .75
190 Gene Upshaw .60 1.50
191 Tom Myers .20 .50
192 Don Zimmerman .20 .50
193 John Garlington .20 .50
194 Skip Butler .20 .50
195 Tom Mitchell .20 .50
196 Jim Langer .60 1.50
197 Ron Carpenter .20 .50
198 Dave Foley .20 .50
199 Bert Jones .60 1.50
200 Larry Brown .30 .75
201 All Pro Receivers .75 2.00
Charley Taylor
Fred Biletnikoff
202 All Pro Tackles .20 .50
Rayfield Wright
Russ Washington
203 All Pro Guards .60 1.50
Tom Mack
Larry Little
204 All Pro Centers .20 .50
Jeff Van Note
Jack Rudnay
205 All Pro Guards .60 1.50
Gale Gillingham
John Hannah
206 All Pro Tackles .60 1.50
Dan Dierdorf
Winston Hill
207 All Pro Tight Ends .30 .75
Charle Young
Riley Odoms
208 All Pro Quarterbacks 2.00 4.00
Fran Tarkenton
Ken Stabler
209 All Pro Backs 1.50 3.00
Lawrence McCutcheon
O.J. Simpson
210 All Pro Backs .30 .75
Terry Metcalf
Otis Armstrong
211 All Pro Receivers .30 .75
Mel Gray
Isaac Curtis
212 All Pro Kickers .20 .50
Chester Marcol
Roy Gerela
213 All Pro Ends .60 1.50
Jack Youngblood
Elvin Bethea
214 All Pro Tackles .30 .75
Alan Page
Otis Sistrunk
215 All Pro Tackles .60 1.50
Merlin Olsen
Mike Reid
216 All Pro Ends .60 1.50
Carl Eller
Lyle Alzado
217 All Pro Linebackers .60 1.50
Ted Hendricks
Phil Villapiano
218 All Pro Linebackers .60 1.50
Lee Roy Jordan
Willie Lanier
219 All Pro Linebackers .30 .75
Isiah Robertson
Andy Russell
220 All Pro Cornerbacks .20 .50
Nate Wright
Emmitt Thomas
221 All Pro Cornerbacks .20 .50
Willie Buchanon
Lemar Parrish
222 All Pro Safeties .30 .75
Ken Houston
Dick Anderson
223 All Pro Safeties .60 1.50
Cliff Harris
Jack Tatum
224 All Pro Punters .30 .75
Tom Wittum
Ray Guy
225 All Pro Returners .30 .75
Terry Metcalf
Greg Pruitt
226 Ted Kwalick .20 .50
227 Spider Lockhart .30 .75
228 Mike Livingston .20 .50
229 Larry Cole .20 .50
230 Gary Garrison .20 .50
231 Larry Brooks .20 .50
232 Bobby Howfield .20 .50
233 Fred Carr .20 .50
234 Norm Evans .20 .50
235 Dwight White .30 .75
236 Conrad Dobler .30 .75
237 Garry Lyle .20 .50
238 Darryl Stingley .60 1.50
239 Tom Graham .20 .50
240 Chuck Foreman .60 1.50
241 Ken Riley .30 .75
242 Don Morrison .20 .50
243 Lynn Dickey .30 .75
244 Don Cockroft .20 .50
245 Claude Humphrey .30 .75
246 John Skorupan .20 .50
247 Raymond Chester .30 .75
248 Cas Banaszek .20 .50
249 Art Malone .20 .50
250 Ed Flanagan .20 .50
251 Checklist 133-264 2.00 4.00
252 Nemiah Wilson .20 .50
253 Ron Jessie .20 .50
254 Jim Lynch .20 .50
255 Bob Tucker .30 .75
256 Terry Owens .20 .50
257 John Fitzgerald .20 .50
258 Jack Snow .30 .75
259 Garry Puetz RC .20 .50
260 Mike Phipps .30 .75
261 Al Matthews .20 .50
262 Bob Kuechenberg .20 .50
263 Ron Yankowski .20 .50
264 Ron Shanklin .20 .50
265 Bobby Douglass .30 .75
266 Josh Ashton .20 .50
267 Bill Van Heusen .20 .50
268 Jeff Siemon .20 .50
269 Bob Newland .20 .50
270 Gale Gillingham .20 .50
271 Zeke Moore .20 .50
272 Mike Tilleman .20 .50
273 John Leypoldt .20 .50
274 Ken Mendenhall .20 .50
275 Norm Snead .30 .75
276 Bill Bradley .30 .75
277 Jerry Smith .20 .50
278 Clarence Davis RC .20 .50
279 Jim Yarbrough .20 .50
280 Lemar Parrish .20 .50
281 Bobby Bell .60 1.50
282 Lynn Swann UER RC 30.00 60.00
(Wide Reciever on front)
283 John Hicks RC .20 .50
284 Coy Bacon .30 .75
285 Lee Roy Jordan .60 1.50
286 Willie Buchanon .20 .50
287 Al Woodall .20 .50
288 Reggie Rucker .30 .75
289 John Schmitt .20 .50
290 Carl Eller .60 1.50
291 Jake Scott .30 .75
292 Donny Anderson .30 .75
293 Charley Wade RC .20 .50
294 John Tanner RC .20 .50
295 Charley Johnson .30 .75
(Misspelled Charley
on both sides)
296 Tom Blanchard .20 .50
297 Curley Culp .30 .75
298 Jeff Van Note RC .30 .75
299 Bob James .20 .50
300 Franco Harris 4.00 0.00
301 Tim Berra RC .30 .75
302 Bruce Gossett .20 .50
303 Verlon Biggs .20 .50
304 Bob Kowalkowski .20 .50
305 Marv Hubbard .20 .50
306 Ken Avery .20 .50
307 Mike Adamle .20 .50
308 Don Herrmann .20 .50
309 Chris Fletcherv RC .20 .50
310 Roman Gabriel .60 1.50
311 Billy Joe DuPree .60 1.50
312 Fred Dryer .60 1.50
313 John Riggins 2.50 5.00
314 Bob McKay .20 .50
315 Ted Hendricks .60 1.50
316 Bobby Bryant .20 .50
317 Don Nottingham .20 .50
318 John Hannah 2.00 4.00
319 Rich Coady .20 .50
320 Phil Villapiano .30 .75
321 Jim Plunkett .60 1.50
322 Lyle Alzado .60 1.50
323 Ernie Jackson .20 .50
324 Billy Parks .20 .50
325 Willie Lanier .60 1.50
326 John James .20 .50
327 Joe Ferguson .30 .75
328 Ernie Holmes RC 2.00 4.00
329 Bruce Laird .20 .50
330 Chester Marcol .20 .50
331 Dave Wilcox .60 1.50
332 Pat Fischer .30 .75
333 Steve Owens .30 .75
334 Royce Berry .20 .50
335 Russ Washington .20 .50
336 Walker Gillette .20 .50
337 Mark Nordquist .20 .50
338 James Harris RC 1.00 2.50
339 Warren Koegel RC .20 .50
340 Emmitt Thomas .30 .75
341 Walt Garrison .30 .75
342 Thom Darden .20 .50
343 Mike Eischeid .20 .50
344 Ernie McMillan .20 .50
345 Nick Buoniconti .60 1.50
346 George Farmer .20 .50
347 Sam Adams .20 .50
348 Larry Cipa RC .20 .50
349 Bob Moore .20 .50
350 Otis Armstrong RC .60 1.50
351 George Blanda RB 1.50 3.00
All Time Scoring
Leader
352 Fred Cox RB/151 Straight PAT's .30 .75
353 Tom Dempsey RB/63 Yard FG .30 .75
354 Ken Houston RB/9th Int. for TD .60 1.50
(Shown as Oiler,
should be Redskin)
355 O.J. Simpson RB/2003 Yard Season 2.50 5.00
356 Ron Smith RB .30 .75
All Time Return
Yardage Mark
357 Bob Atkins .20 .50
358 Pat Sullivan .30 .75
359 Joe DeLamielleure 1.00 2.50
360 Lawrence McCutcheon RC .60 1.50
361 David Lee .20 .50
362 Mike McCoy .20 .50
363 Skip Vanderbundt .20 .50
364 Mark Moseley .30 .75
365 Lem Barney .60 1.50
366 Doug Dressler .20 .50
367 Dan Fouts RC 20.00 40.00
368 Bob Hyland RC .20 .50
369 John Outlaw .20 .50
370 Roy Gerela .20 .50
371 Isiah Robertson .30 .75
372 Jerome Barkum .20 .50
373 Ed Podolak .20 .50
374 Milt Morin .20 .50
375 John Niland .20 .50
376 Checklist 265-396 UER 2.00 4.00
(295 Charlie Johnson
misspelled as Charley)
377 Ken Iman .20 .50
378 Manny Fernandez .30 .75
379 Dave Gallagher RC .20 .50
380 Ken Stabler 7.50 15.00
381 Mack Herron RC .20 .50
382 Bill McClard RC .20 .50
383 Ray May .20 .50
384 Don Hansen .20 .50
385 Elvin Bethea .60 1.50
386 Joe Scibelli .20 .50
387 Neal Craig RC .20 .50
388 Marty Domres .20 .50
389 Ken Ellis .20 .50
390 Charle Young .30 .75
391 Tommy Hart .20 .50
392 Moses Denson RC .20 .50
393 Larry Walton .20 .50
394 Dave Green RC .20 .50
395 Ron Johnson .30 .75
396 Ed Bradley RC .20 .50
397 J.T. Thomas RC .20 .50
398 Jim Bailey .20 .50
399 Barry Pearson .20 .50
400 Fran Tarkenton 4.00 8.00
401 Jack Rudnay .20 .50
402 Rayfield Wright .30 .75
403 Roger Wehrli .40 1.00
404 Vern Den Herder .20 .50
405 Fred Biletnikoff 1.50 3.00
406 Ken Grandberry RC .20 .50
407 Bob Adams RC .20 .50
408 Jim Merlo .20 .50
409 John Pitts .20 .50
410 Dave Osborn .30 .75
411 Dennis Havig .20 .50
412 Bob Johnson .20 .50
413 Ken Burrough UER .30 .75
(Misspelled Burrow
on card front)
414 Jim Cheyunski .20 .50
415 MacArthur Lane .20 .50
416 Joe Theismann RC 12.50 25.00
417 Mike Boryla RC .20 .50
418 Bruce Taylor .20 .50
419 Chris Hanburger .30 .75
420 Tom Mack .60 1.50
421 Errol Mann .20 .50
422 Jack Gregory .20 .50
423 Harrison Davis RC .20 .50
424 Burgess Owens .20 .50
425 Joe Greene 2.50 5.00
426 Morris Stroud .20 .50
427 John DeMarie .20 .50
428 Mel Renfro .60 1.50
429 Cid Edwards .20 .50
430 Mike Reid .60 1.50
431 Jack Mildren RC .20 .50
432 Jerry Simmons .20 .50
433 Ron Yary .60 1.50
434 Howard Stevens RC .20 .50
435 Ray Guy .75 2.00
436 Tommy Nobis .60 1.50
437 Solomon Freelon .20 .50
438 J.D. Hill .30 .75
439 Toni Linhart RC .20 .50
440 Dick Anderson .30 .75
441 Guy Morriss RC .20 .50
442 Bob Hoskins .20 .50
443 John Hadl .60 1.50
444 Roy Jefferson .20 .50
445 Charlie Sanders .40 1.00
446 Pat Curran RC .20 .50
447 David Knight RC .20 .50
448 Bob Brown DT .20 .50
449 Pete Gogolak .20 .50
450 Terry Metcalf .60 1.50
451 Bill Bergey .60 1.50
452 Dan Abramowicz HL/105 Straight Games .30
.75
453 Otis Armstrong HL/183 Yard Game.30 .75
454 Cliff Branch HL/13 TD Passes .60 1.50
455 John James HL .20 .50
Record 96 Punts
456 Lydell Mitchell HL/13 Passes in Game .30
.75
457 Lemar Parrish HL/3 TD Punt Returns.30 .75
458 Ken Stabler HL/26 TD Passes 2.50 5.00
in One Season
459 Lynn Swann HL/577 Yards in 4.00 8.00
Punt Returns
460 Emmitt Thomas HL/73 Yd. Interception .20
.50
461 Terry Bradshaw 10.00 20.00
462 Jerrel Wilson .20 .50
463 Walter Johnson .20 .50
464 Golden Richards RC .30 .75
465 Tommy Casanova .30 .75
466 Randy Jackson .20 .50
467 Ron Bolton .20 .50
468 Joe Owens .20 .50
469 Wally Hilgenberg .20 .50
470 Riley Odoms .30 .75
471 Otis Sistrunk .30 .75
472 Eddie Ray RC .20 .50
473 Reggie McKenzie .30 .75
474 Elbert Drungo .20 .50
475 Mercury Morris .60 1.50
476 Dan Dickel RC .20 .50
477 Merritt Kersey RC .20 .50
478 Mike Holmes RC .20 .50
479 Clarence Williams .20 .50
480 Billy Kilmer .60 1.50
481 Altie Taylor .20 .50
482 Dave Elmendorf .20 .50
483 Bob Rowe .20 .50
484 Pete Athas .20 .50
485 Winston Hill .20 .50
486 Bo Matthews RC .20 .50
487 Earl Thomas RC .20 .50
488 Jan Stenerud .60 1.50
489 Steve Holden RC .20 .50
490 Cliff Harris RC 3.00 6.00
491 Boobie Clark RC .30 .75
492 Joe Taylor .20 .50
493 Tom Neville .20 .50
494 Wayne Colman .20 .50
495 Jim Mitchell .20 .50
496 Paul Krause .60 1.50
497 Jim Otto .60 1.50
498 John Rowser .20 .50
499 Larry Little .60 1.50
500 O.J. Simpson 5.00 10.00
501 John Dutton RC .60 1.50
502 Pat Hughes .20 .50
503 Malcolm Snider .20 .50
504 Fred Willis .20 .50
505 Harold Jackson .60 1.50
506 Mike Bragg .20 .50
507 Jerry Sherk .30 .75
508 Mirro Roder RC .20 .50
509 Tom Sullivan RC .20 .50
510 Jim Hart .60 1.50
511 Cedrick Hardman .20 .50
512 Blaine Nye .20 .50
513 Elmo Wright .20 .50
514 Herb Orvis RC .20 .50
515 Richard Caster .30 .75
516 Doug Kotar RC .20 .50
517 Checklist 397-528 2.00 4.00
518 Jesse Freitas RC .20 .50
519 Ken Houston .60 1.50
520 Alan Page .60 1.50
521 Tim Foley .30 .75
522 Bill Olds RC .20 .50
523 Bobby Maples .20 .50
524 Cliff Branch RC 7.50 15.00
525 Merlin Olsen .60 1.50
526 AFC Champs 2.00 4.00
Pittsburgh 24,
Oakland 13
(Bradshaw and
Franco Harris)
527 NFC Champs .60 1.50
Minnesota 14;
Los Angeles 10
(Chuck Foreman tackled)
528 Super Bowl IX 2.50 5.00
Steelers 16;
Vikings 6
(Bradshaw watching
pass)

1975 Topps Team Checklists

The 1975 Topps Team Checklist set contains 26 standard-size cards, one for each of the 26 NFL teams. The front of the card has the 1975 schedule, while the back of the card contains the checklist, complete with boxes in which to place check marks. The player's position is also listed with his name. The set was only available directly from Topps as a send-off offer as an uncut sheet; the prices below apply equally to uncut sheets as they are frequently found in their original uncut condition. As for individual cards, thin card stock mkaes it a challenge to find these cards in top grades. These unnumbered cards are numbered below for convenience in alphabetical order by team name.

COMPLETE SET (26) 125.00 250.00
1 Atlanta Falcons 5.00 10.00
2 Baltimore Colts 5.00 10.00
3 Buffalo Bills 5.00 10.00
4 Chicago Bears 7.50 15.00
5 Cincinnati Bengals 5.00 10.00
6 Cleveland Browns 7.50 15.00
7 Dallas Cowboys 10.00 20.00
8 Denver Broncos 5.00 10.00
9 Detroit Lions 5.00 10.00
10 Green Bay Packers 7.50 15.00
11 Houston Oilers 5.00 10.00
12 Kansas City Chiefs 5.00 10.00
13 Los Angeles Rams 5.00 10.00
14 Miami Dolphins 7.50 15.00
15 Minnesota Vikings 7.50 15.00
16 New England Patriots 5.00 10.00
17 New York Giants 7.50 15.00
18 New York Jets 5.00 10.00
19 New Orleans Saints 5.00 10.00
20 Oakland Raiders 10.00 20.00
21 Philadelphia Eagles 5.00 10.00
22 Pittsburgh Steelers 7.50 15.00
23 St. Louis Cardinals 5.00 10.00
24 San Diego Chargers 5.00 10.00
25 San Francisco 49ers 7.50 15.00
26 Washington Redskins 7.50 15.00

1976 Topps

The 1976 Topps football set contains 528 standard-size cards including the first year cards of Seattle Seahawks and Tampa Bay Buccaneers. Underneath photos that are bordered by a team color, card fronts contain a team colored football at bottom left with the team name within. The player's name and position are also at the bottom. The card backs are printed in orange and blue on gray card stock and are horizontally designed. The content includes statistics, highlights and a trivia question with answer. Subsets include Record Breakers (1-8), league leaders (201-206), playoffs (331-333) and team checklist (451-478) cards. The key Rookie Card belongs to all-time rushing leader Walter Payton. Other Rookie Cards include Randy Gradishar, Ed Too Tall Jones, Jack Lambert, Harvey Martin, and Randy White. An uncut sheet of team checklist cards was also available via a mail-in offer on wax packs.

COMPLETE SET (528) 200.00 350.00
1 George Blanda RB 2.50 5.00
First to Score/2000 Points
2 Neal Colzie RB .30 .75
Punt Returns
3 Chuck Foreman RB .30 .75
Catches 73 Passes
4 Jim Marshall RB/26th Fumble Recovery.30 .75
5 Terry Metcalf RB .30 .75
Most all-purpose yards;
season
6 O.J. Simpson RB/23 Touchdowns 1.50 3.00
7 Fran Tarkenton RB 1.50 3.00
Most Attempts;Season
8 Charley Taylor RB .60 1.50
Career Receptions
9 Ernie Holmes .30 .75
10 Ken Anderson AP .60 1.50
11 Bobby Bryant .20 .50
12 Jerry Smith .30 .75
13 David Lee .20 .50
14 Robert Newhouse RC .60 1.50
15 Vern Den Herder .20 .50
16 John Hannah .60 1.50
17 J.D. Hill .30 .75
18 James Harris .30 .75
19 Willie Buchanon .20 .50
20 Charle Young .30 .75
21 Jim Yarbrough .20 .50
22 Ronnie Coleman RC .20 .50
23 Don Cockroft .20 .50
24 Willie Lanier .60 1.50
25 Fred Biletnikoff 1.50 3.00
26 Ron Yankowski .20 .50
27 Spider Lockhart .20 .50
28 Bob Johnson .20 .50
29 J.T. Thomas .20 .50
30 Ron Yary .60 1.50
31 Brad Dusek RC .20 .50
32 Raymond Chester .30 .75
33 Larry Little .60 1.50
34 Pat Leahy RC .60 1.50
35 Steve Bartkowski RC 2.00 4.00
36 Tom Myers .20 .50
37 Bill Van Heusen .20 .50
38 Russ Washington .20 .50
39 Tom Sullivan .20 .50
40 Curley Culp .30 .75
41 Johnnie Gray RC .20 .50
42 Bob Klein .20 .50
43 Lem Barney .60 1.50
44 Harvey Martin RC 3.00 6.00
45 Reggie Rucker .30 .75
46 Neil Clabo RC .20 .50
47 Ray Hamilton RC .20 .50
48 Joe Ferguson .30 .75
49 Ed Podolak .20 .50
50 Ray Guy AP .60 1.50
51 Glen Edwards .20 .50
52 Jim LeClair RC .20 .50
53 Mike Barnes RC .20 .50
54 Nat Moore RC .60 1.50
55 Billy Kilmer .60 1.50
56 Larry Stallings .20 .50
57 Jack Gregory .20 .50
58 Steve Mike-Mayer RC .20 .50
59 Virgil Livers RC .20 .50
60 Jerry Sherk .30 .75
61 Guy Morriss .20 .50
62 Barty Smith .20 .50
63 Jerome Barkum .20 .50
64 Ira Gordon RC .20 .50
65 Paul Krause .60 1.50
66 John McMakin .20 .50
67 Checklist 1-132 1.50 3.00
68 Charley Johnson UER .30 .75
(Misspelled Charley
on both sides)
69 Tommy Nobis .60 1.50
70 Lydell Mitchell .30 .75
71 Vern Holland .20 .50
72 Tim Foley .30 .75
73 Golden Richards .30 .75
74 Bryant Salter .20 .50
75 Terry Bradshaw 10.00 20.00
76 Ted Hendricks .60 1.50
77 Rich Saul RC .20 .50
78 John Smith RC .20 .50
79 Altie Taylor .20 .50
80 Cedrick Hardman .20 .50
81 Ken Payne RC .20 .50
82 Zeke Moore .20 .50
83 Alvin Maxson RC .20 .50
84 Wally Hilgenberg .20 .50
85 John Niland .20 .50
86 Mike Sensibaugh .20 .50
87 Ron Johnson .30 .75
88 Winston Hill .20 .50
89 Charlie Joiner 2.00 4.00
90 Roger Wehrli .30 .75
91 Mike Bragg .20 .50
92 Dan Dickel .20 .50
93 Earl Morrall .30 .75
94 Pat Toomay .20 .50
95 Gary Garrison .20 .50
96 Ken Geddes RC .20 .50
97 Mike Current .20 .50
98 Bob Avellini RC .30 .75
99 Dave Pureifory RC .20 .50
100 Franco Harris AP 4.00 8.00
101 Randy Logan RC .20 .50
102 John Fitzgerald .20 .50
103 Gregg Bingham RC .30 .75
104 Jim Plunkett .60 1.50
105 Carl Eller .60 1.50
106 Larry Walton .20 .50
107 Clarence Scott .20 .50
108 Skip Vanderbundt .20 .50
109 Boobie Clark .30 .75
110 Tom Mack .60 1.50
111 Bruce Laird .20 .50
112 Dave Dalby RC .20 .50
113 John Leypoldt .20 .50
114 Barry Pearson .20 .50
115 Larry Brown .30 .75
116 Jackie Smith .60 1.50
117 Pat Hughes .20 .50
118 Al Woodall .20 .50
119 John Zook .20 .50
120 Jake Scott .30 .75
121 Rich Glover RC .20 .50
122 Ernie Jackson .20 .50
123 Otis Armstrong .60 1.50
124 Bob Grim .20 .50
125 Jeff Siemon .30 .75
126 Harold Hart RC .20 .50
127 John DeMarie .20 .50
128 Dan Fouts 6.00 12.00
129 Jim Kearney .20 .50
130 John Dutton AP .30 .75
131 Calvin Hill .60 1.50
132 Toni Fritsch .20 .50
133 Ron Jessie .20 .50
134 Don Nottingham .20 .50
135 Lemar Parrish .20 .50
136 Russ Francis RC .60 1.50
137 Joe Reed .20 .50
138 C.L. Whittington RC .20 .50
139 Otis Sistrunk .30 .75
140 Lynn Swann AP 10.00 20.00
141 Jim Carter .20 .50
142 Mike Montler .20 .50
143 Walter Johnson .20 .50
144 Doug Kotar .20 .50
145 Roman Gabriel .60 1.50
146 Billy Newsome .20 .50
147 Ed Bradley .20 .50
148 Walter Payton RC 125.00 250.00
149 Johnny Fuller .20 .50
150 Alan Page AP .60 1.50
151 Frank Grant RC .20 .50
152 Dave Green .20 .50
153 Nelson Munsey RC .20 .50
154 Jim Mandich .20 .50
155 Lawrence McCutcheon .60 1.50
156 Steve Ramsey .20 .50
157 Ed Flanagan .20 .50
158 Randy White RC 10.00 20.00
159 Gerry Mullins .20 .50
160 Jan Stenerud AP .60 1.50
161 Steve Odom RC .20 .50
162 Roger Finnie .20 .50
163 Norm Snead .30 .75
164 Jeff Van Note .30 .75
165 Bill Bergey .60 1.50
166 Allen Carter RC .20 .50
167 Steve Holden .20 .50
168 Sherman White .20 .50
169 Bob Berry .20 .50
170 Ken Houston AP .60 1.50
171 Bill Olds .20 .50
172 Larry Seiple .20 .50
173 Cliff Branch 2.00 4.00
174 Reggie McKenzie .30 .75
175 Dan Pastorini .60 1.50
176 Paul Naumoff .20 .50
177 Checklist 133-264 1.50 3.00
178 Durwood Keeton RC .20 .50
179 Earl Thomas .20 .50
180 L.C. Greenwood AP .60 1.50
181 John Outlaw .20 .50
182 Frank Nunley .20 .50
183 Dave Jennings RC .30 .75
184 MacArthur Lane .20 .50
185 Chester Marcol .20 .50
186 J.J. Jones RC .20 .50
187 Tom DeLeone RC .20 .50
188 Steve Zabel .20 .50
189 Ken Johnson DT RC .20 .50
190 Rayfield Wright .30 .75
191 Brent McClanahan RC .20 .50
192 Pat Fischer .30 .75
193 Roger Carr RC .30 .75
194 Manny Fernandez .30 .75
195 Roy Gerela .20 .50
196 Dave Elmendorf .20 .50
197 Bob Kowalkowski .20 .50
198 Phil Villapiano .30 .75
199 Will Wynn RC .20 .50
200 Terry Metcalf .60 1.50
201 Passing Leaders .75 2.00
Ken Anderson
Fran Tarkenton
202 Receiving Leaders .30 .75
Reggie Rucker
Lydell Mitchell
Chuck Foreman
203 Rushing Leaders 1.25 2.50
O.J. Simpson
Jim Otis
204 Scoring Leaders 1.25 2.50
O.J. Simpson
Chuck Foreman
205 Interception Leaders .60 1.50
Mel Blount
Paul Krause
206 Punting Leaders .30 .75
Ray Guy
Herman Weaver
207 Ken Ellis .20 .50
208 Ron Saul .20 .50
209 Toni Linhart .20 .50
210 Jim Langer AP .60 1.50
211 Jeff Wright S RC .20 .50
212 Moses Denson .20 .50
213 Earl Edwards .20 .50
214 Walker Gillette .20 .50
215 Bob Trumpy .30 .75
216 Emmitt Thomas .30 .75
217 Lyle Alzado .60 1.50
218 Carl Garrett .30 .75
219 Van Green RC .20 .50
220 Jack Lambert AP RC 20.00 35.00
221 Spike Jones .20 .50
222 John Hadl .60 1.50
223 Billy Johnson RC .60 1.50
224 Tony McGee .20 .50
225 Preston Pearson .30 .75
226 Isiah Robertson .30 .75
227 Errol Mann .20 .50
228 Paul Seal RC .20 .50
229 Roland Harper RC .20 .50
230 Ed White RC .30 .75
231 Joe Theismann 3.00 6.00
232 Jim Cheyunski .20 .50
233 Bill Stanfill .30 .75
234 Marv Hubbard .20 .50
235 Tommy Casanova .30 .75
236 Bob Hyland .20 .50
237 Jesse Freitas .20 .50
238 Norm Thompson .20 .50
239 Charlie Smith .20 .50
240 John James .20 .50
241 Alden Roche .20 .50
242 Gordon Jolley RC .20 .50
243 Larry Ely RC .20 .50
244 Richard Caster .20 .50
245 Joe Greene 2.00 5.00
246 Larry Schreiber .20 .50
247 Terry Schmidt RC .20 .50
248 Jerrel Wilson .20 .50
249 Marty Domres .20 .50
250 Isaac Curtis .30 .75
251 Harold McLinton RC .20 .50
252 Fred Dryer .60 1.50
253 Bill Lenkaitis .20 .50
254 Don Hardeman RC .20 .50
255 Bob Griese 2.00 4.00
256 Oscar Roan RC .20 .50
257 Randy Gradishar RC 2.00 5.00
258 Bob Thomas RC .20 .50
259 Joe Owens .20 .50
260 Cliff Harris AP .60 1.50
261 Frank Lewis .20 .50
262 Mike McCoy .20 .50
263 Rickey Young RC .20 .50
264 Brian Kelley RC .20 .50
265 Charlie Sanders .30 .75
266 Jim Hart .60 1.50
267 Greg Gantt RC .20 .50
268 John Ward RC .20 .50
269 Al Beauchamp .20 .50
270 Jack Tatum .60 1.50
271 Jim Lash RC .20 .50
272 Diron Talbert .20 .50
273 Checklist 265-396 1.50 3.00
274 Steve Spurrier 3.00 8.00
275 Greg Pruitt .60 1.50
276 Jim Mitchell .20 .50
277 Jack Rudnay .20 .50
278 Freddie Solomon RC .30 .75
279 Frank LeMaster RC .20 .50
280 Wally Chambers .20 .50
281 Mike Collier RC .20 .50
282 Clarence Williams .20 .50
283 Mitch Hoopes RC .20 .50
284 Ron Bolton .20 .50
285 Harold Jackson .60 1.50
286 Greg Landry .30 .75
287 Tony Greene .20 .50
288 Howard Stevens .20 .50
289 Roy Jefferson .20 .50
290 Jim Bakken .20 .50
291 Doug Sutherland RC .20 .50
292 Marvin Cobb RC .20 .50
293 Mack Alston .20 .50
294 Rod McNeill RC .20 .50
295 Gene Upshaw .60 1.50
296 Dave Gallagher .20 .50
297 Larry Ball RC .20 .50
298 Ron Howard RC .20 .50
299 Don Strock RC .60 1.50
300 O.J. Simpson AP 4.00 8.00
301 Ray Mansfield .20 .50
302 Larry Marshall RC .20 .50
303 Dick Himes RC .20 .50
304 Ray Wersching RC .20 .50
305 John Riggins 2.00 4.00
306 Bob Parsons RC .20 .50
307 Ray Brown .20 .50
308 Len Dawson 1.50 3.00
309 Andy Maurer .20 .50
310 Jack Youngblood AP .60 1.50
311 Essex Johnson .20 .50
312 Stan White .20 .50
313 Drew Pearson 2.00 5.00
314 Rockne Freitas .20 .50
315 Mercury Morris .60 1.50
316 Willie Alexander .20 .50
317 Paul Warfield 1.50 3.00
318 Bob Chandler .30 .75
319 Bobby Walden .20 .50
320 Riley Odoms .30 .75
321 Mike Boryla .20 .50
322 Bruce Van Dyke .20 .50
323 Pete Banaszak .20 .50
324 Darryl Stingley .60 1.50
325 John Mendenhall .20 .50
326 Dan Dierdorf .75 2.00
327 Bruce Taylor .20 .50
328 Don McCauley .20 .50
329 John Reaves UER .20 .50
(24 attempts in '72; should be 224)
330 Chris Hanburger .30 .75
331 NFC Champions 1.50 3.00
Cowboys 37;
Rams 7
(Roger Staubach)
332 AFC Champions .75 2.00
Steelers 16;
Raiders 10
(Franco Harris)
333 Super Bowl X 1.25 2.50
Steelers 21,
Cowboys 17
(Terry Bradshaw)
334 Godwin Turk RC .20 .50
335 Dick Anderson .30 .75
336 Woody Green RC .20 .50
337 Pat Curran .20 .50
338 Council Rudolph RC .20 .50
339 Joe Lavender RC .20 .50
340 John Gilliam .30 .75
341 Steve Furness RC .30 .75
342 D.D. Lewis .30 .75
343 Duane Carrell RC .20 .50
344 Jon Morris .20 .50
345 John Brockington .30 .75
346 Mike Phipps .30 .75
347 Lyle Blackwood RC .20 .50
348 Julius Adams .20 .50
349 Terry Hermeling RC .20 .50
350 R.Lawrence AP RC .20 .50
351 Glenn Doughty .20 .50
352 Doug Swift .20 .50
353 Mike Strachan RC .20 .50
354 Craig Morton .60 1.50
355 George Blanda 2.50 5.00
356 Garry Puetz .20 .50
357 Carl Mauck .20 .50
358 Walt Patulski .20 .50
359 Stu Voigt .20 .50
360 Fred Carr .20 .50
361 Po James .20 .50
362 Otis Taylor .60 1.50
363 Jeff West RC .20 .50
364 Gary Huff .30 .75
365 Dwight White .30 .75
366 Dan Ryczek RC .20 .50
367 Jon Keyworth RC .20 .50
368 Mel Renfro .60 1.50
369 Bruce Coslet RC .60 1.50
370 Len Hauss .20 .50
371 Rick Volk .20 .50
372 Howard Twilley .30 .75
373 Cullen Bryant RC .30 .75
374 Bob Babich .20 .50
375 Herman Weaver .20 .50
376 Steve Grogan RC 1.25 3.00
377 Bubba Smith .60 1.50
378 Burgess Owens .20 .50
379 Al Matthews .20 .50
380 Art Shell .60 1.50
381 Larry Brown .20 .50
382 Horst Muhlmann .20 .50
383 Ahmad Rashad 1.25 2.50
384 Bobby Maples .20 .50
385 Jim Marshall .60 1.50
386 Joe Dawkins .20 .50
387 Dennis Partee .20 .50
388 Eddie McMillan RC .20 .50
389 Randy Johnson .20 .50
390 Bob Kuechenberg .20 .50
391 Rufus Mayes .20 .50
392 Lloyd Mumphord .20 .50
393 Ike Harris RC .20 .50
394 Dave Hampton .20 .50
395 Roger Staubach 10.00 20.00
396 Doug Buffone .20 .50
397 Howard Fest .20 .50
398 Wayne Mulligan .20 .50
399 Bill Bradley .30 .75
400 Chuck Foreman AP .60 1.50
401 Jack Snow .30 .75
402 Bob Howard .20 .50
403 John Matuszak .60 1.50
404 Bill Munson .30 .75
405 Andy Russell .30 .75
406 Skip Butler .20 .50
407 Hugh McKinnis RC .20 .50

408 Bob Penchion RC	.20	.50
409 Mike Bass	.20	.50
410 George Kunz	.20	.50
411 Ron Pritchard	.20	.50
412 Barry Smith RC	.20	.50
413 Norm Bulaich	.20	.50
414 Marv Bateman	.20	.50
415 Ken Stabler	6.00	12.00
416 Conrad Dobler	.30	.75
417 Bob Tucker	.30	.75
418 Gene Washington 49er	.30	.75
419 Ed Marinaro	.60	1.50
420 Jack Ham AP	2.00	4.00
421 Jim Turner	.20	.50
422 Chris Fletcher	.20	.50
423 Carl Barzilauskas RC	.20	.50
424 Robert Brazile RC	.60	1.50
425 Harold Carmichael	.75	2.00
426 Ron Jaworski RC	3.00	6.00
427 Ed Too Tall Jones RC	10.00	20.00
428 Larry McCarren RC	.20	.50
429 Mike Thomas RC	.20	.50
430 Joe DeLamielleure	.60	1.50
431 Tom Blanchard	.20	.50
432 Ron Carpenter	.20	.50
433 Levi Johnson	.20	.50
434 Sam Cunningham	.30	.75
435 Garo Yepremian	.30	.75
436 Mike Livingston	.20	.50
437 Larry Csonka	2.00	4.00
438 Doug Dieken	.30	.75
439 Bill Lueck	.20	.50
440 Tom MacLeod RC	.20	.50
441 Mick Tingelhoff	.30	.75
442 Terry Hanratty	.30	.75
443 Mike Siani	.20	.50
444 Dwight Harrison	.20	.50
445 Jim Otis	.30	.75
446 Jack Reynolds	.30	.75
447 Jean Fugett RC	.30	.75
448 Dave Beverly RC	.20	.50
449 Bernard Jackson RC	.20	.50
450 Charley Taylor	.75	2.00
451 Atlanta Falcons	.75	2.00
Team Checklist		
452 Baltimore Colts	.75	2.00
Team Checklist		
453 Buffalo Bills	.75	2.00
Team Checklist		
454 Chicago Bears	.75	2.00
Team Checklist		
455 Cincinnati Bengals	.75	2.00
Team Checklist		
456 Cleveland Browns	.75	2.00
Team Checklist		
457 Dallas Cowboys	.75	2.00
Team Checklist		
458 Denver Broncos UER	.75	2.00
Team Checklist		
(Charlie Johnson		
spelled Charley)		
459 Detroit Lions	.75	2.00
Team Checklist		
460 Green Bay Packers	.75	2.00
Team Checklist		
461 Houston Oilers	.75	2.00
Team Checklist		
462 Kansas City Chiefs	.75	2.00
Team Checklist		
463 Los Angeles Rams	.75	2.00
Team Checklist		
464 Miami Dolphins	.75	2.00
Team Checklist		
465 Minnesota Vikings	.75	2.00
Team Checklist		
466 New England Patriots	.75	2.00
Team Checklist		
467 New Orleans Saints	.75	2.00
Team Checklist		
468 New York Giants	.75	2.00
Team Checklist		
469 New York Jets	.75	2.00
Team Checklist		
470 Oakland Raiders	.75	2.00
Team Checklist		
471 Philadelphia Eagles	.75	2.00
Team Checklist		
472 Pittsburgh Steelers	.75	2.00
Team Checklist		
473 St. Louis Cardinals	.75	2.00
Team Checklist		
474 San Diego Chargers	.75	2.00
Team Checklist		
475 San Francisco 49ers	.75	2.00
Team Checklist		
476 Seattle Seahawks	.75	2.00
Team Checklist		
477 Tampa Bay Buccaneers	.75	2.00
Team Checklist		
478 Washington Redskins	.75	2.00
Team Checklist		
479 Fred Cox	.20	.50
480 Mel Blount AP	3.00	6.00
481 John Bunting RC	.30	.75
482 Ken Mendenhall	.20	.50
483 Will Harrell RC	.20	.50
484 Marlin Briscoe	.20	.50
485 Archie Manning	.60	1.50
486 Tody Smith	.20	.50
487 George Hunt	.20	.50
488 Roscoe Word RC	.20	.50
489 Paul Seymour	.20	.50
490 Lee Roy Jordan AP	.60	1.50
491 Chip Myers	.20	.50
492 Norm Evans	.20	.50
493 Jim Bertelsen	.20	.50
494 Mark Moseley	.30	.75
495 George Buehler RC	.20	.50
496 Charlie Hall	.20	.50
497 Marvin Upshaw	.20	.50
498 Tom Banks RC	.20	.50
499 Randy Vataha	.20	.50
500 Fran Tarkenton AP	3.00	6.00
501 Mike Wagner	.30	.75
502 Art Malone	.20	.50
503 Fred Cook RC	.20	.50
504 Rich McGeorge	.20	.50
505 Ken Burrough	.30	.75
506 Nick Mike-Mayer	.20	.50
507 Checklist 397-528	1.50	3.00
508 Steve Owens	.30	.75
509 Brad Van Pelt RC	.20	.50
510 Ken Riley	.30	.75
511 Art Thoms	.20	.50
512 Ed Bell	.20	.50
513 Tom Wittum	.20	.50
514 Jim Braxton	.20	.50
515 Nick Buoniconti	.60	1.50
516 Brian Sipe RC	2.50	6.00
517 Jim Lynch	.20	.50
518 Prentice McCray RC	.20	.50
519 Tom Dempsey	.20	.50
520 Mel Gray	.30	.75
521 Nate Wright	.20	.50
522 Rocky Bleier	3.00	6.00
523 Dennis Johnson RC	.20	.50
524 Jerry Sisemore	.20	.50
525 Bert Jones	.20	.50
526 Perry Smith RC	.20	.50
527 Blaine Nye	.20	.50
528 Bob Moore	.60	1.50

1976 Topps Team Checklists

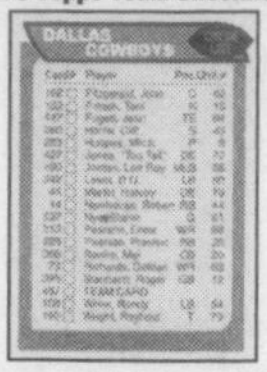

The 1976 Topps Team Checklist set contains 30 standard-size cards, one for each of the 28 NFL teams plus two checklist cards. The front of the card has the 1976 Topps checklist for that particular team, complete with boxes in which to place check marks. The set was only available directly from Topps as a send-off offer as an uncut sheet; the prices below apply equally to uncut sheets as they are frequently found in their original uncut condition. As for individual cards, thin card stock makes it a challenge to obtain singles in top grades. These unnumbered cards are numbered below for convenience in alphabetical order by team name.

COMPLETE SET (30)	62.50	125.00
1 Atlanta Falcons	2.50	5.00
2 Baltimore Colts	2.50	5.00
3 Buffalo Bills	2.50	5.00
4 Chicago Bears	2.50	5.00
5 Cincinnati Bengals	2.50	5.00
6 Cleveland Browns	2.50	5.00
7 Dallas Cowboys	5.00	10.00
8 Denver Broncos	2.50	5.00
9 Detroit Lions	2.50	5.00
10 Green Bay Packers	3.75	7.50
11 Houston Oilers	2.50	5.00
12 Kansas City Chiefs	2.50	5.00
13 Los Angeles Rams	2.50	5.00
14 Miami Dolphins	3.75	7.50
15 Minnesota Vikings	2.50	5.00
16 New England Patriots	2.50	5.00
17 New York Giants	2.50	5.00
18 New York Jets	2.50	5.00
19 New Orleans Saints	2.50	5.00
20 Oakland Raiders	5.00	10.00
21 Philadelphia Eagles	2.50	5.00
22 Pittsburgh Steelers	3.75	7.50
23 St. Louis Cardinals	2.50	5.00
24 San Diego Chargers	2.50	5.00
25 San Francisco 49ers	3.75	7.50
26 Seattle Seahawks	2.50	5.00
27 Tampa Bay Buccaneers	2.50	5.00
28 Washington Redskins	3.75	7.50
29 Checklist 1-132	2.50	5.00
30 Checklist 133-264	2.50	5.00

1977 Topps

The 1977 Topps football set contains 528 standard-size cards. Card fronts have a banner (with team name), the player's name and position at the top. Backs that rushed for 1,000 yards have a "1,000 Yarder" football logo on front. The card backs are printed in purple and black on gray card stock. The backs contain yearly statistics, highlights and a note on the player's college career. Subsets include league leaders (1-6), team checklist cards (201-208), Record Breakers (451-455) and playoffs (526-528). The key Rookie Card is Steve Largent. Other Rookie Cards include Harry Carson, Dave Casper, Archie Griffin, Mike Haynes, Ray Rhodes, Lee Roy Selmon, Mike Webster, Danny White and Jim Zorn. An uncut sheet of team checklist cards was also available via a mail-in offer on wax pack wrappers. A Mexican version of this set was produced. All text is in Spanish (front and back) and is quite a bit tougher to find than the basic issue.

COMPLETE SET (528)	125.00	250.00
1 Passing Leaders	1.25	2.50
James Harris		
Ken Stabler		
2 Receiving Leaders	.40	1.00
Drew Pearson		
MacArthur Lane		
3 W.Payton	5.00	10.00
Simpson LL		
4 Scoring Leaders	.25	.60
Mark Moseley		
Toni Linhart		
5 Interception Leaders	.25	.60
Monte Jackson		
Ken Riley		
6 Punting Leaders	.15	.40
John James		
Marv Bateman		
7 Mike Phipps	.25	.60
8 Rick Volk	.15	.40
9 Steve Furness	.25	.60
10 Isaac Curtis	.25	.60
11 Nate Wright	.25	.60
12 Jean Fugett	.15	.40
13 Ken Mendenhall	.15	.40
14 Sam Adams	.15	.40
15 Charlie Waters	.40	1.00
16 Bill Stanfill	.15	.40
17 John Holland RC	.15	.40
18 Pat Haden RC	.75	2.00
19 Bob Young	.15	.40
20 Wally Chambers	.15	.40
21 Lawrence Gaines RC	.15	.40
22 Larry McCarren	.15	.40
23 Horst Muhlmann	.15	.40
24 Phil Villapiano	.25	.60
25 Greg Pruitt	.25	.60
26 Ron Howard	.15	.40
27 Craig Morton	.40	1.00
28 Rufus Mayes	.15	.40
29 Lee Roy Selmon RC UER	6.00	12.00
Misspelled Leroy		
30 Ed White	.25	.60
31 Harold McLinton	.15	.40
32 Glenn Doughty	.15	.40
33 Bob Kuechenberg	.40	1.00
34 Duane Carrell	.15	.40
35 Riley Odoms	.15	.40
36 Bobby Scott	.15	.40
37 Nick Mike-Mayer	.15	.40
38 Bill Lenkaitis	.15	.40
39 Roland Harper	.25	.60
40 Tommy Hart	.15	.40
41 Mike Sensibaugh	.15	.40
42 Rusty Jackson RC	.15	.40
43 Levi Johnson	.15	.40
44 Mike McCoy	.15	.40
45 Roger Staubach	10.00	20.00
46 Fred Cox	.15	.40
47 Bob Babich	.15	.40
48 Reggie McKenzie	.25	.60
49 Dave Jennings	.15	.40
50 Mike Haynes RC	4.00	10.00
51 Larry Brown	.25	.60
52 Marvin Cobb	.15	.40
53 Fred Cook	.15	.40
54 Freddie Solomon	.25	.60
55 John Riggins	1.25	2.50
56 John Bunting	.25	.60
57 Ray Wersching	.25	.60
58 Mike Livingston	.15	.40
59 Billy Johnson	.25	.60
60 Mike Wagner	.15	.40
61 Waymond Bryant RC	.15	.40
62 Jim Otis	.25	.60
63 Ed Galigher RC	.15	.40
64 Randy Vataha	.15	.40
65 Jim Zorn RC	2.00	5.00
66 Jon Keyworth	.15	.40
67 Checklist 1-132	.75	2.00
68 Henry Childs RC	.15	.40
69 Thom Darden	.15	.40
70 George Kunz	.15	.40
71 Lenvil Elliott RC	.15	.40
72 Curtis Johnson RC	.15	.40
73 Doug Van Horn	.15	.40
74 Joe Theismann	2.00	4.00
75 Dwight White	.25	.60
76 Scott Laidlaw RC	.15	.40
77 Monte Johnson RC	.15	.40
78 Dave Beverly	.15	.40
79 Jim Mitchell	.15	.40
80 Jack Youngblood AP	.40	1.00
81 Mel Gray	.25	.60
82 Dwight Harrison	.15	.40
83 John Hadl	.25	.60
84 Matt Blair RC	.40	1.00
85 Charlie Sanders	.25	.60
86 Noah Jackson RC	.15	.40
87 Ed Marinaro	.25	.60
88 Bob Howard	.15	.40
89 John McDaniel RC	.15	.40
90 Dan Dierdorf AP	.60	1.50
91 Mark Moseley	.25	.60
92 Cleo Miller RC	.15	.40
93 Andre Tillman RC	.15	.40
94 Bruce Taylor	.15	.40
95 Bert Jones	.40	1.00
96 Anthony Davis RC	.40	1.00
97 Don Goode RC	.15	.40
98 Ray Rhodes RC	2.00	6.00
99 Mike Webster RC	6.00	12.00
100 O.J. Simpson AP	3.00	6.00
101 Doug Plank RC	.15	.40
102 Efren Herrera RC	.25	.60
103 Charlie Smith	.15	.40
104 Carlos Brown RC	.40	1.00
105 Jim Marshall	.40	1.00
106 Paul Naumoff	.15	.40
107 Walter White RC	.15	.40
108 John Cappelletti RC	1.25	3.00
109 Chip Myers	.15	.40
110 Ken Stabler AP	5.00	10.00
111 Joe Ehrmann RC	.15	.40
112 Rick Engles RC	.15	.40
113 Jack Dolbin RC	.15	.40
114 Ron Bolton	.15	.40
115 Mike Thomas	.15	.40
116 Mike Fuller RC	.15	.40
117 John Hill RC	.15	.40
118 Richard Todd RC	.40	1.00
119 Duriel Harris RC	.40	1.00
120 John James	.15	.40
121 Lionel Antoine RC	.15	.40
122 John Skorupan	.15	.40
123 Skip Butler	.15	.40
124 Bob Tucker	.15	.40
125 Paul Krause	.40	1.00
126 Dave Hampton	.15	.40
127 Tom Wittum	.15	.40
128 Gary Huff	.25	.60
129 Emmitt Thomas	.25	.60
130 Drew Pearson AP	.75	2.00
131 Ron Saul	.15	.40
132 Steve Niehaus RC	.15	.40
133 Fred Carr	.40	1.00
134 Norm Bulaich	.15	.40
135 Bob Trumpy	.25	.60
136 Greg Landry	.25	.60
137 George Buehler	.15	.40
138 Reggie Rucker	.25	.60
139 Julius Adams	.15	.40
140 Jack Ham AP	1.25	2.50
141 Wayne Morris RC	.15	.40
142 Marv Bateman	.15	.40
143 Bobby Maples	.15	.40
144 Harold Carmichael	.40	1.00
145 Bob Avellini	.25	.60
146 Harry Carson RC	2.50	5.00
147 Lawrence Pillers RC	.15	.40
148 Ed Williams RC	.15	.40
149 Dan Pastorini	.25	.60
150 Ron Yary	.40	1.00
151 Joe Lavender	.15	.40
152 Pat McInally RC	.25	.60
153 Lloyd Mumphord	.15	.40
154 Cullen Bryant	.25	.60
155 Willie Lanier	.40	1.00
156 Gene Washington 49er	.25	.60
157 Scott Hunter	.15	.40
158 Jim Merlo	.15	.40
159 Randy Grossman RC	.25	.60
160 Blaine Nye	.15	.40
161 Ike Harris	.15	.40
162 Doug Dieken	.15	.40
163 Guy Morriss	.15	.40
164 Bob Parsons	.15	.40
165 Steve Grogan	.40	1.00
166 John Brockington	.25	.60
167 Charlie Joiner	1.25	2.50
168 Ron Carpenter	.15	.40
169 Jeff Wright	.15	.40
170 Chris Hanburger	.15	.40
171 Roosevelt Leaks RC	.25	.60
172 Larry Little	.40	1.00
173 John Matuszak	.25	.60
174 Joe Ferguson	.25	.60
175 Brad Van Pelt	.25	.60
176 Dexter Bussey RC	.25	.60
177 Steve Largent RC	20.00	40.00
178 Dewey Selmon RC	.25	.60
179 Randy Gradishar	.40	1.00
180 Mel Blount AP	1.50	3.00
181 Dan Neal RC	.15	.40
182 Rich Szaro RC	.15	.40
183 Mike Boryla	.15	.40
184 Steve Jones RC	.15	.40
185 Paul Warfield	1.25	2.50
186 Greg Buttle RC	.15	.40
187 Rich McGeorge	.15	.40
188 Leon Gray RC	.25	.60
189 John Shinners RC	.15	.40
190 Toni Linhart	.15	.40
191 Robert Miller RC	.15	.40
192 Jake Scott	.15	.40
193 Jon Morris	.15	.40
194 Randy Crowder RC	.15	.40
195 Lynn Swann UER	10.00	18.00
(Interception Record		
on card back)		
196 Marsh White RC	.15	.40
197 Rod Perry RC	.40	1.00
198 Willie Hall RC	.15	.40
199 Mike Hartenstine RC	.15	.40
200 Jim Bakken	.15	.40
201 Atlanta Falcons UER	.50	1.25
Team Checklist		
(79 Jim Mitchell		
is not listed)		
202 Baltimore Colts	.50	1.25
Team Checklist		
203 Buffalo Bills	.50	1.25
Team Checklist		
204 Chicago Bears	.50	1.25
Team Checklist		
205 Cincinnati Bengals	.50	1.25
Team Checklist		
206 Cleveland Browns	.50	1.25
Team Checklist		
207 Dallas Cowboys	.50	1.25
Team Checklist		
208 Denver Broncos	.50	1.25
Team Checklist		
209 Detroit Lions	.50	1.25
Team Checklist		
210 Green Bay Packers	.50	1.25
Team Checklist		
211 Houston Oilers	.50	1.25
Team Checklist		
212 Kansas City Chiefs	.50	1.25
Team Checklist		
213 Los Angeles Rams	.50	1.25
Team Checklist		
214 Miami Dolphins	.50	1.25
Team Checklist		
215 Minnesota Vikings	.50	1.25
Team Checklist		
216 New England Patriots	.50	1.25
Team Checklist		
217 New Orleans Saints	.50	1.25
Team Checklist		
218 New York Giants	.50	1.25
Team Checklist		
219 New York Jets	.50	1.25
Team Checklist		
220 Oakland Raiders	.50	1.25
Team Checklist		
221 Philadelphia Eagles	.50	1.25
Team Checklist		
222 Pittsburgh Steelers	.50	1.25
Team Checklist		
223 St. Louis Cardinals	.50	1.25
Team Checklist		
224 San Diego Chargers	.50	1.25
Team Checklist		
225 San Francisco 49ers	.50	1.25
Team Checklist		
226 Seattle Seahawks	.50	1.25
Team Checklist		
227 Tampa Bay Buccaneers	.50	1.25
Team Checklist UER		
(Lee Roy Selmon mis-		
spelled as Leroy)		
228 Washington Redskins	.50	1.25
Team Checklist		
229 Sam Cunningham	.25	.60
230 Alan Page AP	.40	1.00
231 Eddie Brown S RC	.15	.40
232 Stan White	.15	.40
233 Vern Den Herder	.15	.40
234 Clarence Davis	.15	.40
235 Ken Anderson	.40	1.00
236 Karl Chandler RC	.15	.40
237 Will Harrell	.15	.40
238 Clarence Scott	.15	.40
239 Bo Rather RC	.15	.40
240 Robert Brazile AP	.25	.60
241 Bob Bell	.15	.40
242 Rolland Lawrence	.15	.40
243 Tom Sullivan	.15	.40
244 Larry Brunson RC	.15	.40
245 Terry Bradshaw	10.00	20.00
246 Rich Saul	.15	.40
247 Cleveland Elam RC	.15	.40
248 Don Woods	.15	.40
249 Bruce Laird	.15	.40
250 Coy Bacon	.25	.60
251 Russ Francis	.40	1.00
252 Jim Braxton	.15	.40
253 Perry Smith	.15	.40
254 Jerome Barkum	.15	.40
255 Garo Yepremian	.25	.60
256 Checklist 133-264	.75	2.00
257 Tony Galbreath RC	.25	.60
258 Troy Archer RC	.15	.40
259 Brian Sipe	.40	1.00
260 Billy Joe DuPree AP	.25	.60
261 Bobby Walden	.15	.40
262 Larry Marshall	.15	.40
263 Ted Fritsch Jr.	.15	.40
264 Larry Hand	.15	.40
265 Tom Mack	.40	1.00
266 Ed Bradley	.15	.40
267 Pat Leahy	.25	.60
268 Louis Carter RC	.15	.40
269 Archie Griffin RC	3.00	6.00
270 Art Shell AP	.40	1.00
271 Stu Voigt	.15	.40
272 Prentice McCray	.15	.40
273 MacArthur Lane	.15	.40
274 Dan Fouts	3.00	6.00
275 Charle Young	.25	.60
276 Wilbur Jackson RC	.15	.40
277 John Hicks	.15	.40
278 Nat Moore	.40	1.00
279 Virgil Livers	.15	.40
280 Curley Culp	.25	.60
281 Rocky Bleier	1.25	2.50
282 John Zook	.15	.40
283 Tom DeLeone	.15	.40
284 Danny White RC	6.00	12.00
285 Otis Armstrong	.25	.60
286 Larry Walton	.15	.40
287 Jim Carter	.15	.40
288 Don McCauley	.15	.40
289 Frank Grant	.15	.40
290 Roger Wehrli	.25	.60
291 Mick Tingelhoff	.25	.60
292 Bernard Jackson	.15	.40
293 Tom Owen RC	.15	.40
294 Mike Esposito RC	.15	.40
295 Fred Biletnikoff	1.25	2.50
296 Revie Sorey RC	.15	.40
297 John McMakin	.15	.40
298 Dan Ryczek	.15	.40
299 Wayne Moore RC	.15	.40
300 Franco Harris AP	2.00	4.00
301 Rick Upchurch RC	.40	1.00
302 Jim Stienke RC	.15	.40
303 Charlie Davis RC	.15	.40
304 Don Cockroft	.15	.40
305 Ken Burrough	.25	.60
306 Clark Gaines RC	.15	.40
307 Bobby Douglass	.15	.40
308 Ralph Perretta RC	.15	.40
309 Wally Hilgenberg	.15	.40
310 Monte Jackson AP RC	.25	.60
311 Chris Bahr RC	.25	.60
312 Jim Cheyunski	.15	.40
313 Mike Patrick RC	.15	.40
314 Ed Too Tall Jones	2.50	5.00
315 Bill Bradley	.15	.40
316 Benny Malone RC	.15	.40
317 Paul Seymour	.15	.40
318 Jim Laslavic RC	.15	.40
319 Frank Lewis	.25	.60
320 Ray Guy AP	.40	1.00
321 Allan Ellis RC	.15	.40
322 Conrad Dobler	.25	.60
323 Chester Marcol	.15	.40
324 Doug Kotar	.15	.40
325 Lemar Parrish	.25	.60
326 Steve Holden	.15	.40
327 Jeff Van Note	.25	.60
328 Howard Stevens	.15	.40
329 Brad Dusek	.25	.60
330 Joe DeLamielleure	.40	1.00
331 Jim Plunkett	.40	1.00
332 Checklist 265-396	.75	2.00
333 Lou Piccone RC	.15	.40
334 Ray Hamilton	.15	.40
335 Jan Stenerud	.40	1.00
336 Jeris White RC	.15	.40
337 Sherman Smith RC	.15	.40
338 Dave Green	.15	.40
339 Terry Schmidt	.15	.40
340 Sammie White RC	.50	1.25
341 Jon Kolb RC	.15	.40
342 Randy White	4.00	8.00
343 Bob Klein	.15	.40
344 Bob Kowalkowski	.15	.40
345 Terry Metcalf	.25	.60
346 Joe Danelo RC	.15	.40
347 Ken Payne	.15	.40
348 Neal Craig	.15	.40
349 Dennis Johnson	.15	.40
350 Bill Bergey AP	.25	.60
351 Raymond Chester	.15	.40
352 Bob Matheson	.15	.40
353 Mike Kadish RC	.15	.40
354 Mark Van Eeghen RC	.60	1.50
355 L.C. Greenwood	.40	1.00
356 Sam Hunt RC	.15	.40
357 Darrell Austin RC	.15	.40
358 Jim Turner	.15	.40
359 Ahmad Rashad	.75	2.00
360 Walter Payton AP	15.00	40.00
361 Mark Arneson RC	.15	.40
362 Jerrel Wilson	.15	.40
363 Steve Bartkowski	.40	1.00
364 John Watson RC	.15	.40
365 Ken Riley	.25	.60
366 Gregg Bingham	.15	.40
367 Golden Richards	.25	.60
368 Clyde Powers RC	.15	.40
369 Diron Talbert	.15	.40
370 Lydell Mitchell	.25	.60
371 Bob Jackson RC	.15	.40
372 Jim Mandich	.15	.40
373 Frank LeMaster	.15	.40
374 Benny Ricardo RC	.15	.40
375 Lawrence McCutcheon	.25	.60
376 Lynn Dickey	.25	.60
377 Phil Wise RC	.15	.40
378 Tony McGee	.15	.40
379 Norm Thompson	.15	.40
380 Dave Casper RC	2.00	5.00
381 Glen Edwards	.15	.40
382 Bob Thomas	.15	.40
383 Bob Chandler	.25	.60
384 Rickey Young	.25	.60
385 Carl Eller	.40	1.00
386 Lyle Alzado	.40	1.00
387 John Leypoldt	.15	.40
388 Gordon Bell RC	.15	.40
389 Mike Bragg	.15	.40
390 Jim Langer AP	.40	1.00
391 Vern Holland	.15	.40
392 Nelson Munsey	.15	.40
393 Mack Mitchell RC	.15	.40
394 Tony Adams RC	.15	.40
395 Preston Pearson	.25	.60
396 Emanuel Zanders RC	.15	.40
397 Vince Papale RC	8.00	20.00
398 Joe Fields RC	.25	.60
399 Craig Clemons	.15	.40
400 Fran Tarkenton AP	2.50	5.00
401 Andy Johnson RC	.15	.40
402 Willie Buchanon	.15	.40
403 Pat Curran	.15	.40
404 Ray Jarvis RC	.15	.40
405 Joe Greene	1.25	2.50
406 Bill Simpson RC	.15	.40
407 Ronnie Coleman	.15	.40
408 J.K. McKay RC	.25	.60
409 Pat Fischer	.25	.60
410 John Dutton	.25	.60
411 Boobie Clark	.15	.40
412 Pat Tilley RC	.40	1.00
413 Don Strock	.25	.60
414 Brian Kelley	.15	.40
415 Gene Upshaw	.40	1.00
416 Mike Montler	.15	.40
417 Checklist 397-528	.75	2.00
418 John Gilliam	.15	.40
419 Brent McClanahan	.15	.40
420 Jerry Sherk	.15	.40
421 Roy Gerela	.15	.40
422 Tim Fox RC	.25	.60
423 John Ebersole RC	.15	.40
424 James Scott RC	.15	.40
425 Delvin Williams RC	.25	.60
426 Spike Jones	.15	.40
427 Harvey Martin	.40	1.00
428 Don Herrmann	.15	.40
429 Calvin Hill	.25	.60
430 Isiah Robertson	.15	.40
431 Tony Greene	.15	.40
432 Bob Johnson	.15	.40
433 Lem Barney	.40	1.00
434 Eric Torkelson RC	.15	.40
435 John Mendenhall	.15	.40
436 Larry Seiple	.25	.60
437 Art Kuehn RC	.15	.40
438 John Vella RC	.15	.40
439 Greg Latta RC	.15	.40
440 Roger Carr	.25	.60
441 Doug Sutherland	.15	.40
442 Mike Kruczek RC	.15	.40
443 Steve Zabel	.15	.40
444 Mike Pruitt RC	.40	1.00
445 Harold Jackson	.25	.60
446 George Jakowenko RC	.15	.40
447 John Fitzgerald	.15	.40
448 Carey Joyce RC	.15	.40
449 Jim LeClair	.15	.40
450 Ken Houston AP	.40	1.00
451 Steve Grogan RB	.25	.60
Most TDs Rushing		
by QB in a Season		
452 Jim Marshall RB	.25	.60
Most Games		
Played: Lifetime		
453 O.J. Simpson RB	1.25	2.50
Most Yardage,		
Rushing: Game		
454 Fran Tarkenton RB	1.50	3.00
Most Yardage,		
Passing: Lifetime		
455 Jim Zorn RB	.40	1.00
Most Passing Yards		
Season& Rookie		
456 Robert Pratt RC	.15	.40
457 Walker Gillette	.15	.40
458 Charlie Hall	.15	.40
459 Robert Newhouse	.25	.60
460 John Hannah AP	.40	1.00
461 Ken Reaves	.15	.40
462 Herman Weaver	.15	.40
463 James Harris	.25	.60
464 Howard Twilley	.25	.60
465 Jeff Siemon	.25	.60
466 John Outlaw	.15	.40
467 Chuck Muncie RC	.40	1.00
468 Bob Moore	.15	.40
469 Robert Woods RC	.15	.40
470 Cliff Branch AP	.75	2.00
471 Johnnie Gray	.15	.40
472 Don Hardeman	.15	.40
473 Steve Ramsey	.15	.40
474 Steve Mike-Mayer	.15	.40
475 Gary Garrison	.15	.40
476 Walter Johnson	.15	.40
477 Neil Clabo	.15	.40
478 Len Hauss	.15	.40
479 Darryl Stingley	.25	.60
480 Jack Lambert AP	4.00	8.00
481 Mike Adamle	.25	.60
482 David Lee	.15	.40
483 Tom Mullen RC	.15	.40
484 Claude Humphrey	.15	.40
485 Jim Hart	.40	1.00
486 Bobby Thompson RC	.15	.40
487 Jack Rudnay	.15	.40
488 Rich Sowells RC	.15	.40
489 Reuben Gant RC	.15	.40
490 Cliff Harris AP	.40	1.00
491 Bob Brown DT	.15	.40
492 Don Nottingham	.15	.40
493 Ron Jessie	.15	.40
494 Otis Sistrunk	.25	.60
495 Billy Kilmer	.25	.60
496 Oscar Roan	.15	.40
497 Bill Van Heusen	.15	.40
498 Randy Logan	.15	.40
499 John Smith	.15	.40
500 Chuck Foreman AP	.25	.60
501 J.T. Thomas	.15	.40
502 Steve Schubert RC	.15	.40
503 Mike Barnes	.15	.40
504 J.V. Cain RC	.15	.40
505 Larry Csonka	1.50	3.00
506 Elvin Bethea	.40	1.00
507 Ray Easterling RC	.15	.40
508 Joe Reed	.15	.40
509 Steve Odom	.15	.40
510 Tommy Casanova	.15	.40
511 Dave Dalby	.15	.40
512 Richard Caster	.15	.40
513 Fred Dryer	.40	1.00
514 Jeff Kinney RC	.15	.40
515 Bob Griese	1.50	3.00
516 Butch Johnson RC	.40	1.00
517 Gerald Irons RC	.15	.40
518 Don Calhoun RC	.15	.40
519 Jack Gregory	.15	.40
520 Tom Banks	.15	.40
521 Bobby Bryant	.15	.40
522 Reggie Harrison RC	.15	.40
523 Terry Hermeling	.15	.40
524 David Taylor RC	.15	.40
525 Brian Baschnagel RC	.25	.60
526 AFC Championship	.40	1.00
Raiders 24;		
Steelers 7		
(Ken Stabler)		
527 NFC Championship	.25	.60
Vikings 24;		
Rams 13		
528 Super Bowl XI	.60	1.50
Raiders 32;		
Vikings 14		
(line play)		

1977 Topps Holsum Packers/Vikings

In 1977 Topps produced a set of 11 Green Bay Packers (1-11) and 11 Minnesota Vikings (12-22) for Holsum Bread for distribution in the general area of those teams. One card was packed inside each loaf of bread. Unfortunately, nowhere on the card is Holsum mentioned leading to frequent misclassification of this set. The cards are in color and are standard size. An uncut production sheet was offered in the 1989 Topps Archives auction. The personal data on the card back is printed in brown and orange.

COMPLETE SET (22)	25.00	50.00
1 Lynn Dickey	1.25	3.00
2 John Brockington	1.00	2.50
3 Will Harrell	.75	2.00
4 Ken Payne	.75	2.00
5 Rich McGeorge	.75	2.00
6 Steve Odom	.75	2.00
7 Jim Carter	.75	2.00
8 Fred Carr	.75	2.00
9 Willie Buchanon	1.00	2.50
10 Mike McCoy	.75	2.00
11 Chester Marcol	.75	2.00
12 Chuck Foreman	2.00	4.00
13 Ahmad Rashad	3.00	6.00
14 Sammie White	1.25	3.00
15 Stu Voigt	.75	2.00
16 Fred Cox	.75	2.00
17 Carl Eller	2.00	4.00
18 Alan Page	3.00	6.00
19 Jeff Siemon	.75	2.00
20 Bobby Bryant	.75	2.00
21 Paul Krause	1.25	3.00
22 Ron Yary	1.25	3.00

1977 Topps Mexican

The Mexican version of the 1977 Topps football series contains the same 528 players as the American issue. The cards were issued in 2-card packs with a stick of gum, or in scarcer four-card packs without gum. All text is in Spanish (front and back). Several cases of cards made their way into the organized hobby in the early 1990s. Since then, all cards have been discovered. However, some cards are considered to be tougher to obtain and are priced below at higher levels than otherwise might be expected. Some collectors also pursue the wrappers, which feature various NFL stars on them.

COMPLETE SET (528)	5,000.00	10,000.00
1 Passing Leaders SP	75.00	125.00
James Harris		
Ken Stabler		
2 Receiving Leaders SP	200.00	400.00
Drew Pearson		
MacArthur Lane		
3 Rushing Leaders SP	300.00	600.00
Walter Payton		
O.J. Simpson		
4 Scoring Leaders SP	200.00	400.00
Mark Moseley		
Toni Linhart		
5 Interception Leaders SP	200.00	400.00
Monte Jackson		
Ken Riley		
6 Punting Leaders SP	125.00	250.00
John James		
Marv Bateman		
7 Mike Phipps	4.00	8.00
8 Rick Volk SP	150.00	300.00
9 Steve Furness	4.00	8.00
10 Isaac Curtis	4.00	8.00
11 Nate Wright	4.00	8.00
12 Jean Fugett	6.00	12.00
13 Ken Mendenhall	3.00	6.00
14 Sam Adams	3.00	6.00
15 Charlie Waters	5.00	10.00
16 Bill Stanfill SP	50.00	100.00
17 John Holland	3.00	6.00
18 Pat Haden	20.00	40.00
19 Bob Young	3.00	6.00
20 Wally Chambers SP	100.00	200.00
21 Lawrence Gaines SP	125.00	250.00
22 Larry McCarren	3.00	6.00
23 Horst Muhlmann	3.00	6.00
24 Phil Villapiano	4.00	8.00
25 Greg Pruitt SP	40.00	80.00
26 Ron Howard	6.00	12.00
27 Craig Morton	5.00	10.00
28 Rufus Mayes	3.00	6.00
29 Lee Roy Selmon UER SP	100.00	200.00
Misspelled Leroy		
30 Ed White SP	75.00	150.00
31 Harold McLinton SP	50.00	100.00
32 Glenn Doughty	3.00	6.00
33 Bob Kuechenberg	3.00	6.00
34 Duane Carrell	3.00	6.00
35 Riley Odoms	3.00	6.00
36 Bobby Scott	3.00	6.00
37 Nick Mike-Mayer	3.00	6.00
38 Bill Lenkaitis	3.00	6.00
39 Roland Harper	3.00	6.00
40 Tommy Hart SP	100.00	200.00
41 Mike Sensibaugh	3.00	6.00
42 Rusty Jackson	3.00	6.00
43 Levi Johnson	3.00	6.00
44 Mike McCoy	6.00	12.00
45 Roger Staubach	75.00	150.00
46 Fred Cox	3.00	6.00
47 Bob Babich	3.00	6.00
48 Reggie McKenzie	3.00	6.00
49 Dave Jennings SP	50.00	100.00
50 Mike Haynes	12.50	25.00
51 Larry Brown	4.00	8.00
52 Marvin Cobb	3.00	6.00
53 Fred Cook	3.00	6.00
54 Freddie Solomon	6.00	12.00
55 John Riggins	25.00	50.00
56 John Bunting	3.00	6.00
57 Ray Wersching	3.00	6.00
58 Mike Livingston	3.00	6.00
59 Billy Johnson	40.00	80.00
60 Mike Wagner	6.00	12.00
61 Waymond Bryant	3.00	6.00
62 Jim Otis	3.00	6.00
63 Ed Galigher SP	50.00	100.00
64 Randy Vataha	3.00	6.00
65 Jim Zorn	15.00	30.00
66 Jon Keyworth SP	50.00	100.00
67 Checklist 1-132	4.00	8.00
68 Henry Childs	3.00	6.00
69 Thom Darden	3.00	6.00
70 George Kunz	3.00	6.00
71 Lenvil Elliott	3.00	6.00
72 Curtis Johnson	3.00	6.00
73 Doug Van Horn	3.00	6.00
74 Joe Theismann	20.00	40.00
75 Dwight White	4.00	8.00

76 Scott Laidlaw 3.00 6.00
77 Monte Johnson 3.00 6.00
78 Dave Beverly 3.00 6.00
79 Jim Mitchell SP 40.00 80.00
80 Jack Youngblood 7.50 15.00
81 Mel Gray 3.00 6.00
82 Dwight Harrison 3.00 6.00
83 John Hadl 4.00 8.00
84 Matt Blair 4.00 8.00
85 Charlie Sanders 4.00 8.00
86 Noah Jackson 3.00 6.00
87 Ed Marinaro 5.00 10.00
88 Bob Howard 3.00 6.00
89 John McDaniel SP 150.00 300.00
90 Dan Dierdorf 6.00 12.00
91 Mark Moseley 3.00 6.00
92 Cleo Miller 3.00 6.00
93 Andre Tillman 3.00 6.00
94 Bruce Taylor 3.00 6.00
95 Bert Jones 5.00 10.00
96 Anthony Davis SP 50.00 100.00
97 Don Goode 3.00 6.00
98 Ray Rhodes SP 150.00 300.00
99 Mike Webster SP 60.00 120.00
100 O.J. Simpson 50.00 100.00
101 Doug Plank 3.00 6.00
102 Efren Herrera 3.00 6.00
103 Charlie Smith WR SP 75.00 150.00
104 Carlos Brown SP 40.00 80.00
105 Jim Marshall 5.00 10.00
106 Paul Naumoff 6.00 12.00
107 Walter White 6.00 12.00
108 John Cappelletti 7.50 15.00
109 Chip Myers 3.00 6.00
110 Ken Stabler 100.00 200.00
111 Joe Ehrmann 3.00 6.00
112 Rick Engles 3.00 6.00
113 Jack Dolbin 3.00 6.00
114 Ron Bolton 3.00 6.00
115 Mike Thomas 3.00 6.00
116 Mike Fuller 3.00 6.00
117 John Hill 3.00 6.00
118 Richard Todd SP 60.00 120.00
119 Duriel Harris 3.00 6.00
120 John James 3.00 6.00
121 Lionel Antoine 3.00 6.00
122 John Skorupan 3.00 6.00
123 Skip Butler 3.00 6.00
124 Bob Tucker 3.00 6.00
125 Paul Krause 3.00 6.00
126 Dave Hampton SP 75.00 150.00
127 Tom Wittum 3.00 6.00
128 Gary Huff 3.00 6.00
129 Emmitt Thomas 3.00 6.00
130 Drew Pearson 12.50 25.00
131 Ron Saul 6.00 12.00
132 Steve Niehaus 3.00 6.00
133 Fred Carr 3.00 6.00
134 Norm Bulaich 3.00 6.00
135 Bob Trumpy 5.00 10.00
136 Greg Landry 4.00 8.00
137 George Buehler 3.00 6.00
138 Reggie Rucker 3.00 6.00
139 Julius Adams 3.00 6.00
140 Jack Ham 15.00 30.00
141 Wayne Morris 3.00 6.00
142 Marv Bateman 6.00 12.00
143 Bobby Maples 3.00 6.00
144 Harold Carmichael 5.00 10.00
145 Bob Avellini 3.00 6.00
146 Harry Carson 20.00 40.00
147 Lawrence Pillers SP 75.00 150.00
148 Ed Williams 3.00 6.00
149 Dan Pastorini 3.00 6.00
150 Ron Yary 5.00 10.00
151 Joe Lavender 3.00 6.00
152 Pat McInally 3.00 6.00
153 Lloyd Mumphord 3.00 6.00
154 Cullen Bryant 3.00 6.00
155 Willie Lanier SP 30.00 60.00
156 Gene Washington 49er 4.00 8.00
157 Scott Hunter 3.00 6.00
158 Jim Merlo 3.00 6.00
159 Randy Grossman 3.00 6.00
160 Blaine Nye 3.00 6.00
161 Ike Harris 3.00 6.00
162 Doug Dieken 3.00 6.00
163 Guy Morriss SP 50.00 100.00
164 Bob Parsons SP 50.00 100.00
165 Steve Grogan SP 40.00 80.00
166 John Brockington 3.00 6.00
167 Charlie Joiner 7.50 15.00
168 Ron Carpenter SP 40.00 80.00
169 Jeff Wright SP 40.00 80.00
170 Chris Hanburger 4.00 8.00
171 Roosevelt Leaks 3.00 6.00
172 Larry Little 4.00 8.00
173 John Matuszak 7.50 15.00
174 Joe Ferguson 3.00 6.00
175 Brad Van Pelt SP 40.00 80.00
176 Dexter Bussey SP 150.00 300.00
177 Steve Largent 300.00 500.00
178 Dewey Selmon 4.00 8.00
179 Randy Gradishar 5.00 10.00
180 Mel Blount 20.00 35.00
181 Dan Neal SP 40.00 80.00
182 Rich Szaro SP 75.00 150.00
183 Mike Boryla 6.00 12.00
184 Steve Jones 3.00 6.00
185 Paul Warfield 20.00 35.00
186 Greg Buttle SP 75.00 150.00
187 Rich McGeorge 3.00 6.00
188 Leon Gray SP 75.00 150.00
189 John Shinners 3.00 6.00
190 Toni Linhart 3.00 6.00
191 Robert Miller 3.00 6.00
192 Jake Scott 3.00 6.00
193 Jon Morris 40.00 80.00
194 Randy Crowder 3.00 6.00
195 Lynn Swann 60.00 120.00
196 Marsh White 3.00 6.00
197 Rod Perry 3.00 6.00
198 Willie Hall 3.00 6.00
199 Mike Hartenstine 3.00 6.00
200 Jim Bakken AP 3.00 6.00
201 Atlanta Falcons UER SP 50.00 100.00
(79 Jim Mitchell
is not listed)
Team Checklist
202 Baltimore Colts 4.00 8.00
Team Checklist
203 Buffalo Bills 10.00 20.00
Team Checklist
204 Chicago Bears 4.00 8.00
Team Checklist
205 Cincinnati Bengals 4.00 8.00
Team Checklist
206 Cleveland Browns 4.00 8.00
Team Checklist
207 Dallas Cowboys SP 75.00 150.00
Team Checklist
208 Denver Broncos 4.00 8.00
Team Checklist
209 Detroit Lions 4.00 8.00
Team Checklist
210 Green Bay Packers 4.00 8.00
Team Checklist
211 Houston Oilers 4.00 8.00
Team Checklist
212 Kansas City Chiefs 4.00 8.00
Team Checklist
213 Los Angeles Rams SP 50.00 100.00
Team Checklist
214 Miami Dolphins 4.00 8.00
Team Checklist
215 Minnesota Vikings 4.00 8.00
Team Checklist
216 New England Patriots 4.00 8.00
Team Checklist
217 New Orleans Saints 10.00 20.00
Team Checklist
218 New York Giants 4.00 8.00
Team Checklist
219 New York Jets 4.00 8.00
Team Checklist
220 Oakland Raiders 4.00 8.00
Team Checklist
221 Philadelphia Eagles 4.00 8.00
Team Checklist
222 Pittsburgh Steelers 4.00 8.00
Team Checklist
223 St. Louis Cardinals 4.00 8.00
Team Checklist
224 San Diego Chargers 4.00 8.00
Team Checklist
225 San Francisco 49ers 4.00 8.00
Team Checklist
226 Seattle Seahawks SP 50.00 100.00
Team Checklist
227 Tampa Bay Buccaneers 4.00 8.00
Team Checklist UER
(Lee Roy Selmon mis-
spelled as Leroy)
228 Washington Redskins SP 75.00 150.00
Team Checklist
229 Sam Cunningham 4.00 8.00
230 Alan Page AP 7.50 15.00
231 Eddie Brown S SP 125.00 250.00
232 Stan White 3.00 6.00
233 Vern Den Herder 3.00 6.00
234 Clarence Davis 3.00 6.00
235 Ken Anderson 10.00 20.00
236 Karl Chandler 6.00 12.00
237 Will Harrell SP 100.00 200.00
238 Clarence Scott 3.00 6.00
239 Bo Rather 3.00 6.00
240 Robert Brazile AP 3.00 6.00
241 Bob Bell 3.00 6.00
242 Rolland Lawrence 3.00 6.00
243 Tom Sullivan SP 50.00 100.00
244 Larry Brunson 3.00 6.00
245 Terry Bradshaw 65.00 125.00
246 Rich Saul 3.00 6.00
247 Cleveland Elam 3.00 6.00
248 Don Woods 3.00 6.00
249 Bruce Laird 3.00 6.00
250 Coy Bacon 3.00 6.00
251 Russ Francis 5.00 10.00
252 Jim Braxton 3.00 6.00
253 Perry Smith SP 30.00 60.00
254 Jerome Barkum 3.00 6.00
255 Garo Yepremian 3.00 6.00
256 Checklist 133-264 4.00 8.00
257 Tony Galbreath 3.00 6.00
258 Troy Archer 3.00 6.00
259 Brian Sipe 5.00 10.00
260 Billy Joe DuPree 10.00 20.00
261 Bobby Walden 3.00 6.00
262 Larry Marshall 3.00 6.00
263 Ted Fritsch Jr. 3.00 6.00
264 Larry Hand 3.00 6.00
265 Tom Mack SP 50.00 100.00
266 Ed Bradley 3.00 6.00
267 Pat Leahy 3.00 6.00
268 Louis Carter SP 50.00 100.00
269 Archie Griffin SP 150.00 300.00
270 Art Shell 6.00 12.00
271 Stu Voigt 3.00 6.00
272 Prentice McCray 3.00 6.00
273 MacArthur Lane 7.50 15.00
274 Dan Fouts 25.00 50.00
275 Charle Young 3.00 6.00
276 Wilbur Jackson SP 125.00 250.00
277 John Hicks 3.00 6.00
278 Nat Moore 3.00 6.00
279 Virgil Livers 3.00 6.00
280 Curley Culp 3.00 6.00
281 Rocky Bleier 15.00 30.00
282 John Zook 7.50 15.00
283 Tom DeLeone 3.00 6.00
284 Danny White SP 150.00 300.00
285 Otis Armstrong 4.00 8.00
286 Larry Walton 3.00 6.00
287 Jim Carter 3.00 6.00
288 Don McCauley 3.00 6.00
289 Frank Grant 7.50 15.00
290 Roger Wehrli 4.00 8.00
291 Mick Tingelhoff 10.00 20.00
292 Bernard Jackson 7.50 15.00
293 Tom Owen 6.00 12.00
294 Mike Esposito 3.00 6.00
295 Fred Biletnikoff SP 200.00 400.00
296 Revie Sorey 3.00 6.00
297 John McMakin 3.00 6.00
298 Dan Ryczek 3.00 6.00
299 Wayne Moore 7.50 15.00
300 Franco Harris 60.00 120.00
301 Rick Upchurch 4.00 8.00
302 Jim Stienke 3.00 6.00
303 Charlie Davis 3.00 6.00
304 Don Cockroft 3.00 6.00
305 Ken Burrough 3.00 6.00
306 Clark Gaines SP 75.00 150.00
307 Bobby Douglass 4.00 8.00
308 Ralph Perretta 3.00 6.00
309 Wally Hilgenberg 3.00 6.00
310 Monte Jackson 3.00 6.00
311 Chris Bahr 3.00 6.00
312 Jim Cheyunski 3.00 6.00
313 Mike Patrick 3.00 6.00
314 Ed Too Tall Jones SP 75.00 150.00
315 Bill Bradley 3.00 6.00
316 Benny Malone 3.00 6.00
317 Paul Seymour 3.00 6.00
318 Jim Laslavic 3.00 6.00
319 Frank Lewis 3.00 6.00
320 Ray Guy SP 40.00 80.00
321 Allan Ellis 3.00 6.00
322 Conrad Dobler 3.00 6.00
323 Chester Marcol 3.00 6.00
324 Doug Kotar 3.00 6.00
325 Lemar Parrish 3.00 6.00
326 Steve Holden 3.00 6.00
327 Jeff Van Note 4.00 8.00
328 Howard Stevens 3.00 6.00
329 Brad Dusek 3.00 6.00
330 Joe DeLamielleure 5.00 10.00
331 Jim Plunkett SP 100.00 200.00
332 Checklist 265-396 SP 100.00 200.00
333 Lou Piccone 3.00 6.00
334 Ray Hamilton 3.00 6.00
335 Jan Stenerud 5.00 10.00
336 Jeris White 3.00 6.00
337 Sherman Smith 4.00 8.00
338 Dave Green 3.00 6.00
339 Terry Schmidt 3.00 6.00
340 Sammie White RC 4.00 8.00
341 Jon Kolb 7.50 15.00
342 Randy White 25.00 50.00
343 Bob Klein 3.00 6.00
344 Bob Kowalkowski 6.00 12.00
345 Terry Metcalf 4.00 8.00
346 Joe Danelo 3.00 6.00
347 Ken Payne 3.00 6.00
348 Neal Craig 3.00 6.00
349 Dennis Johnson 3.00 6.00
350 Bill Bergey 7.50 15.00
351 Raymond Chester SP 75.00 150.00
352 Bob Matheson 4.00 8.00
353 Mike Kadish 3.00 6.00
354 Mark Van Eeghen 5.00 10.00
355 L.C. Greenwood 6.00 12.00
356 Sam Hunt 3.00 6.00
357 Darrell Austin 3.00 6.00
358 Jim Turner 3.00 6.00
359 Ahmad Rashad 10.00 20.00
360 Walter Payton 250.00 400.00
361 Mark Arneson 3.00 6.00
362 Jerrel Wilson 3.00 6.00
363 Steve Bartkowski 5.00 10.00
364 John Watson 3.00 6.00
365 Ken Riley 3.00 6.00
366 Gregg Bingham SP 30.00 60.00
367 Golden Richards 4.00 8.00
368 Clyde Powers 3.00 6.00
369 Diron Talbert 7.50 15.00
370 Lydell Mitchell 20.00 40.00
371 Bob Jackson 3.00 6.00
372 Jim Mandich SP 75.00 150.00
373 Frank LeMaster SP 30.00 60.00
374 Benny Ricardo SP 125.00 250.00
375 Lawrence McCutcheon 3.00 6.00
376 Lynn Dickey 4.00 8.00
377 Phil Wise 3.00 6.00
378 Tony McGee 3.00 6.00
379 Norm Thompson 3.00 6.00
380 Dave Casper 20.00 40.00
381 Glen Edwards 3.00 6.00
382 Bob Thomas 3.00 6.00
383 Bob Chandler 3.00 6.00
384 Rickey Young 3.00 6.00
385 Carl Eller 5.00 10.00
386 Lyle Alzado 5.00 10.00
387 John Leypoldt 3.00 6.00
388 Gordon Bell SP 125.00 250.00
389 Mike Bragg 3.00 6.00
390 Jim Langer 4.00 8.00
391 Vern Holland 3.00 6.00
392 Nelson Munsey 3.00 6.00
393 Mack Mitchell 3.00 6.00
394 Tony Adams 3.00 6.00
395 Preston Pearson 4.00 8.00
396 Emanuel Zanders 3.00 6.00
397 Vince Papale 12.50 25.00
398 Joe Fields 3.00 6.00
399 Craig Clemons 3.00 6.00
400 Fran Tarkenton 30.00 60.00
401 Andy Johnson 3.00 6.00
402 Willie Buchanon 7.50 15.00
403 Pat Curran 3.00 6.00
404 Ray Jarvis SP 125.00 250.00
405 Joe Greene 20.00 35.00
406 Bill Simpson 3.00 6.00
407 Ronnie Coleman 3.00 6.00
408 J.K. McKay 3.00 6.00
409 Pat Fischer 10.00 20.00
410 John Dutton 3.00 6.00
411 Boobie Clark 3.00 6.00
412 Pat Tilley 6.00 12.00
413 Don Strock SP 75.00 150.00
414 Brian Kelley 3.00 6.00
415 Gene Upshaw 7.50 15.00
416 Mike Montler 3.00 6.00
417 Checklist 397-528 SP 100.00 200.00
418 John Gilliam 3.00 6.00
419 Brent McClanahan 3.00 6.00
420 Jerry Sherk 3.00 6.00
421 Roy Gerela 3.00 6.00
422 Tim Fox 3.00 6.00
423 John Ebersole SP 75.00 150.00
424 James Scott SP 75.00 150.00
425 Delvin Williams SP 30.00 60.00
426 Spike Jones SP 30.00 60.00
427 Harvey Martin SP 50.00 100.00
428 Don Herrmann 3.00 6.00
429 Calvin Hill 5.00 10.00
430 Isiah Robertson SP 30.00 60.00
431 Tony Greene 3.00 6.00
432 Bob Johnson 3.00 6.00
433 Lem Barney SP 100.00 200.00
434 Eric Torkelson SP 125.00 250.00
435 John Mendenhall 3.00 6.00
436 Larry Seiple 3.00 6.00
437 Art Kuehn 3.00 6.00
438 John Vella 3.00 6.00
439 Greg Latta 3.00 6.00
440 Roger Carr 3.00 6.00
441 Doug Sutherland 3.00 6.00
442 Mike Kruczek 6.00 12.00
443 Steve Zabel 3.00 6.00
444 Mike Pruitt SP 125.00 250.00
445 Harold Jackson SP 75.00 150.00
446 George Jakowenko 3.00 6.00
447 John Fitzgerald 3.00 6.00
448 Carey Joyce 3.00 6.00
449 Jim LeClair 4.00 8.00
450 Ken Houston 5.00 10.00
451 Steve Grogan RB 5.00 10.00
Most TDs Rushing
by QB in a Season
452 Jim Marshall RB 5.00 10.00
Most Games
Played: Lifetime
453 O.J. Simpson RB SP 75.00 150.00
454 Fran Tarkenton RB 20.00 40.00
Most Yardage;
Passing: Lifetime
455 Jim Zorn RB 25.00 50.00
Most Passing Yards
Season: Rookie
456 Robert Pratt 3.00 6.00
457 Walker Gillette 6.00 12.00
458 Charlie Hall 3.00 6.00
459 Robert Newhouse 4.00 8.00
460 John Hannah 5.00 10.00
461 Ken Reaves 3.00 6.00
462 Herman Weaver 3.00 6.00
463 James Harris 3.00 6.00
464 Howard Twilley 3.00 6.00
465 Jeff Siemon SP 75.00 150.00
466 John Outlaw 3.00 6.00
467 Chuck Muncie 5.00 10.00
468 Bob Moore 3.00 6.00
469 Robert Woods 3.00 6.00
470 Cliff Branch SP 125.00 250.00
471 Johnnie Gray 3.00 6.00
472 Don Hardeman 3.00 6.00
473 Steve Ramsey 3.00 6.00
474 Steve Mike-Mayer SP 75.00 150.00
475 Gary Garrison 4.00 8.00
476 Walter Johnson 3.00 6.00
477 Neil Clabo 6.00 12.00
478 Len Hauss 3.00 6.00
479 Darryl Stingley 4.00 8.00
480 Jack Lambert 40.00 80.00
481 Mike Adamle 4.00 8.00
482 David Lee 3.00 6.00
483 Tom Mullen 3.00 6.00
484 Claude Humphrey 3.00 6.00
485 Jim Hart 3.00 6.00
486 Bobby Thompson SP 100.00 200.00
487 Jack Rudnay 3.00 6.00
488 Rich Sowells SP 125.00 250.00
489 Reuben Gant SP 100.00 200.00
490 Cliff Harris 5.00 10.00
491 Bob Brown DT 3.00 6.00
492 Don Nottingham 6.00 12.00
493 Ron Jessie SP 75.00 150.00
494 Otis Sistrunk 12.50 25.00
495 Billy Kilmer 4.00 8.00
496 Oscar Roan 3.00 6.00
497 Bill Van Heusen 3.00 6.00
498 Randy Logan SP 30.00 60.00
499 John Smith 3.00 6.00
500 Chuck Foreman SP 60.00 120.00
501 J.T. Thomas 3.00 6.00
502 Steve Schubert 3.00 6.00
503 Mike Barnes 3.00 6.00
504 J.V. Cain 3.00 6.00
505 Larry Csonka 30.00 60.00
506 Elvin Bethea 5.00 10.00
507 Ray Easterling 3.00 6.00
508 Joe Reed 6.00 12.00
509 Steve Odom 3.00 6.00
510 Tommy Casanova 4.00 8.00
511 Dave Dalby 3.00 6.00
512 Richard Caster 3.00 6.00
513 Fred Dryer SP 100.00 200.00
514 Jeff Kinney 6.00 12.00
515 Bob Griese 25.00 50.00
516 Butch Johnson 3.00 6.00
517 Gerald Irons 3.00 6.00
518 Don Calhoun 3.00 6.00
519 Jack Gregory 3.00 6.00
520 Tom Banks 3.00 6.00
521 Bobby Bryant 3.00 6.00
522 Reggie Harrison 3.00 6.00
523 Terry Hermeling 3.00 6.00
524 David Taylor 3.00 6.00
525 Brian Baschnagel 3.00 6.00
526 AFC Championship 30.00 60.00
(Ken Stabler)
527 NFC Championship 30.00 60.00
528 Super Bowl XI SP 500.00 800.00

1977 Topps Team Checklists

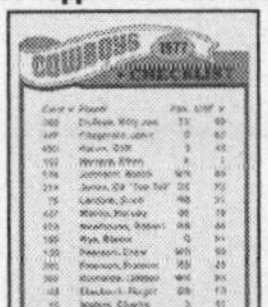

The 1977 Topps Team Checklist set contains 30 standard-size cards. The 28 NFL teams as well as 2 regular checklists were printed in this set. The front of the card has the 1977 Topps checklist for that particular team, complete with boxes in which to place check marks. The set was only available directly from Topps as a send-off offer as an uncut sheet; the prices below apply equally to uncut sheets as they are frequently found in their original uncut condition. As for individual cards, thin white card (almost paper-thin) stock makes it a challenge to find singles in top grades. These unnumbered cards are numbered below for convenience in alphabetical order by team name.

COMPLETE SET (30) 55.00 110.00
1 Atlanta Falcons 2.50 5.00
2 Baltimore Colts 2.50 5.00
3 Buffalo Bills 2.50 5.00
4 Chicago Bears 3.75 7.50
5 Cincinnati Bengals 2.50 5.00
6 Cleveland Browns 2.50 5.00
7 Dallas Cowboys 5.00 10.00
8 Denver Broncos 2.50 5.00
9 Detroit Lions 2.50 5.00
10 Green Bay Packers 5.00 10.00
11 Houston Oilers 2.50 5.00
12 Kansas City Chiefs 2.50 5.00
13 Los Angeles Rams 2.50 5.00
14 Miami Dolphins 3.75 7.50
15 Minnesota Vikings 2.50 5.00
16 New England Patriots 2.50 5.00
17 New York Giants 2.50 5.00
18 New York Jets 2.50 5.00
19 New Orleans Saints 2.50 5.00
20 Oakland Raiders 3.75 7.50
21 Philadelphia Eagles 2.50 5.00
22 Pittsburgh Steelers 3.75 7.50
23 St. Louis Cardinals 2.50 5.00
24 San Diego Chargers 2.50 5.00
25 San Francisco 49ers 3.75 7.50
26 Seattle Seahawks 2.50 5.00
27 Tampa Bay Buccaneers 2.50 5.00
28 Washington Redskins 3.75 7.50
NNO1 Checklist 1-132 2.50 5.00
NNO2 Checklist 133-264 2.50 5.00

1978 Topps

The 1978 Topps football set contains 528 standard-size cards. Card fronts have a color border that runs up the left side and contains the team name. The player's name is at the top and his position is within a football at the bottom right of the photo. The card backs are printed in black and green on gray card stock and are horizontally designed. Statistics, highlights and a player fact cartton are inlcuded. Subsets include Highlights (1-6), playoffs (166-168), league leaders (331-336) and team leaders (501-528). Rookie Cards include Tony Dorsett, Randy Cross, Tom Jackson, Joe Klecko, Stanley Morgan, John Stallworth, Wesley Walker and Reggie Williams.

COMPLETE SET (528) 80.00 150.00
1 Gary Huff HL .40 1.00
Huff Leads Bucs
to First Win
2 Craig Morton HL .40 1.00
Morton Passes Broncos
to Super Bowl
3 Walter Payton HL 3.00 8.00
Rushes for 275 Yards
4 O.J. Simpson HL .75 2.00
Reaches 10,000 Yards
5 Fran Tarkenton HL .75 2.00
Completes 17 of 18
6 Bob Thomas HL .10 .30
Thomas' FG Sends
Bears to Playoffs
7 Joe Pisarcik RC .20 .50
8 Skip Thomas RC .10 .30
9 Roosevelt Leaks .10 .30
10 Ken Houston AP .40 1.00
11 Tom Blanchard .10 .30
12 Jim Turner .10 .30
13 Tom DeLeone .10 .30
14 Jim LeClair .10 .30
15 Bob Avellini .20 .50
16 Tony McGee .10 .30
17 James Harris .20 .50
18 Terry Nelson RC .10 .30
19 Rocky Bleier .75 2.00
20 Joe DeLamielleure .40 1.00
21 Richard Caster .10 .30
22 A.J. Duhe RC .40 1.00
23 John Outlaw .10 .30
24 Danny White .50 1.25
25 Larry Csonka 1.00 2.50
26 David Hill RC .20 .50
27 Mark Arneson .10 .30
28 Jack Tatum .20 .50
29 Norm Thompson .10 .30
30 Sammie White .20 .50
31 Dennis Johnson .10 .30
32 Robin Earl RC .10 .30
33 Don Cockroft .10 .30
34 Bob Johnson .10 .30
35 John Hannah .40 1.00
36 Scott Hunter .10 .30
37 Ken Burrough .20 .50
38 Wilbur Jackson .20 .50
39 Rich McGeorge .10 .30
40 Lyle Alzado AP .40 1.00
41 John Ebersole .10 .30
42 Gary Green RC .10 .30
43 Art Kuehn .10 .30
44 Glen Edwards .20 .50
45 Lawrence McCutcheon .20 .50
46 Duriel Harris .10 .30
47 Rich Szaro .10 .30
48 Mike Washington RC .10 .30
49 Stan White .10 .30
50 Dave Casper AP .40 1.00
51 Len Hauss .10 .30
52 James Scott .10 .30
53 Brian Sipe .40 1.00
54 Gary Shirk RC .10 .30
55 Archie Griffin .40 1.00
56 Mike Patrick .10 .30
57 Mario Clark RC .10 .30
58 Jeff Siemon .10 .30
59 Steve Mike-Mayer .10 .30
60 Randy White AP 2.00 4.00
61 Darrell Austin .10 .30
62 Tom Sullivan .10 .30
63 Johnny Rodgers RC .40 1.00
64 Ken Reaves .10 .30
65 Terry Bradshaw 6.00 12.00
66 Fred Steinfort RC .10 .30
67 Curley Culp .20 .50
68 Ted Hendricks .40 1.00
69 Raymond Chester .10 .30
70 Jim Langer AP .40 1.00
71 Calvin Hill .20 .50
72 Mike Hartenstine .10 .30
73 Gerald Irons .10 .30
74 Billy Brooks RC .20 .50
75 John Mendenhall .10 .30
76 Andy Johnson .10 .30
77 Tom Wittum .10 .30
78 Lynn Dickey .20 .50
79 Carl Eller .40 1.00
80 Tom Mack .40 1.00
81 Clark Gaines .10 .30
82 Lem Barney .40 1.00
83 Mike Montler .10 .30
84 Jon Kolb .10 .30
85 Bob Chandler .20 .50
86 Robert Newhouse .20 .50
87 Frank LeMaster .10 .30
88 Jeff West .10 .30
89 Lyle Blackwood .20 .50
90 Gene Upshaw AP .40 1.00
91 Frank Grant .10 .30
92 Tom Hicks RC .10 .30
93 Mike Pruitt .20 .50
94 Chris Bahr .10 .30
95 Russ Francis .20 .50
96 Norris Thomas RC .10 .30
97 Gary Barbaro RC .20 .50
98 Jim Merlo .10 .30
99 Karl Chandler .10 .30
100 Fran Tarkenton 1.50 4.00
101 Abdul Salaam RC .10 .30
102 Marv Kellum RC .10 .30
103 Herman Weaver .10 .30
104 Roy Gerela .10 .30
105 Harold Jackson .20 .50
106 Dewey Selmon .20 .50
107 Checklist 1-132 .40 1.00
108 Clarence Davis .10 .30
109 Robert Pratt .10 .30
110 Harvey Martin AP .40 1.00
111 Brad Dusek .10 .30
112 Greg Latta .10 .30
113 Tony Peters RC .10 .30
114 Jim Braxton .10 .30
115 Ken Riley .20 .50
116 Steve Nelson RC .10 .30
117 Rick Upchurch .20 .50
118 Spike Jones .10 .30
119 Doug Kotar .10 .30
120 Bob Griese AP 1.00 2.50
121 Burgess Owens .10 .30
122 Rolf Benirschke RC .20 .50
123 Haskel Stanback RC .10 .30
124 J.T. Thomas .10 .30
125 Ahmad Rashad .60 1.50
126 Rick Kane RC .10 .30
127 Elvin Bethea .40 1.00
128 Dave Dalby .10 .30
129 Mike Barnes .10 .30
130 Isiah Robertson .10 .30
131 Jim Plunkett .40 1.00
132 Allan Ellis .10 .30
133 Mike Bragg .10 .30
134 Bob Jackson .10 .30
135 Coy Bacon .10 .30
136 John Smith .10 .30
137 Chuck Muncie .20 .50
138 Johnnie Gray .10 .30
139 Jimmy Robinson RC .10 .30
140 Tom Banks .10 .30
141 Marvin Powell RC .10 .30
142 Jerrel Wilson .10 .30
143 Ron Howard .10 .30
144 Rob Lytle RC .20 .50
145 L.C. Greenwood .40 1.00
146 Morris Owens RC .10 .30
147 Joe Reed .10 .30
148 Mike Kadish .10 .30
149 Phil Villapiano .20 .50
150 Lydell Mitchell .20 .50
151 Randy Logan .10 .30
152 Mike Williams RC .10 .30
153 Jeff Van Note .20 .50
154 Steve Schubert .10 .30
155 Billy Kilmer .20 .50
156 Boobie Clark .10 .30
157 Charlie Hall .10 .30
158 Raymond Clayborn RC .40 1.00
159 Jack Gregory .10 .30
160 Cliff Harris AP .40 1.00
161 Joe Fields .10 .30
162 Don Nottingham .10 .30
163 Ed White .20 .50
164 Toni Fritsch .10 .30
165 Jack Lambert 2.00 4.00
166 NFC Champions .60 1.50
Cowboys 23;
Vikings 6
(Roger Staubach)
167 AFC Champions .20 .50
Broncos 20;
Raiders 17
(Lytle running)
168 Super Bowl XII 1.50 3.00
Cowboys 27;
Broncos 10
(Tony Dorsett)
169 Neal Colzie RC .10 .30
170 Cleveland Elam .10 .30
171 David Lee .10 .30
172 Jim Otis .10 .30
173 Archie Manning .40 1.00
174 Jim Carter .10 .30
175 Jean Fugett .10 .30
176 Willie Parker RC .10 .30
177 Haven Moses .20 .50
178 Horace King RC .10 .30
179 Bob Thomas .10 .30
180 Monte Jackson .10 .30
181 Steve Zabel .10 .30
182 John Fitzgerald .10 .30
183 Mike Livingston .10 .30
184 Larry Poole RC .10 .30
185 Isaac Curtis .20 .50
186 Chuck Ramsey RC .10 .30
187 Bob Klein .10 .30
188 Ray Rhodes .40 1.00
189 Otis Sistrunk .20 .50
190 Bill Bergey .20 .50
191 Sherman Smith .20 .50
192 Dave Green .10 .30
193 Carl Mauck .10 .30
194 Reggie Harrison .10 .30
195 Roger Carr .20 .50
196 Steve Bartkowski .40 1.00
197 Ray Wersching .10 .30
198 Willie Buchanon .10 .30
199 Neil Clabo .10 .30
200 Walter Payton AP 12.50 26.00
UER (Born 7/5/54;
should be 7/25/54)
201 Sam Adams .10 .30
202 Larry Gordon RC .10 .30
203 Pat Tilley .20 .50
204 Mack Mitchell .10 .30
205 Ken Anderson .40 1.00
206 Scott Dierking RC .10 .30
207 Jack Rudnay .10 .30
208 Jim Stienke .10 .30
209 Bill Simpson .10 .30
210 Errol Mann .10 .30
211 Bucky Dilts RC .10 .30
212 Reuben Gant .10 .30
213 Thomas Henderson RC .60 1.50
214 Steve Furness .20 .50
215 John Riggins .75 2.00
216 Keith Krepfle RC .10 .30
217 Fred Dean RC 6.00 12.00
218 Emanuel Zanders .10 .30
219 Don Testerman RC .10 .30
220 George Kunz .10 .30
221 Darryl Stingley .20 .50
222 Ken Sanders RC .10 .30
223 Gary Huff .10 .30
224 Gregg Bingham .10 .30
225 Jerry Sherk .10 .30
226 Doug Plank .10 .30
227 Ed Taylor RC .10 .30
228 Emery Moorehead RC .10 .30
229 Reggie Williams RC .40 1.00
230 Claude Humphrey .10 .30
231 Randy Cross RC 1.25 3.00
232 Jim Hart .40 1.00
233 Bobby Bryant .10 .30
234 Larry Brown .10 .30
235 Mark Van Eeghen .20 .50
236 Terry Hermeling .10 .30
237 Steve Odom .10 .30
238 Jan Stenerud .40 1.00
239 Andre Tillman .10 .30
240 Tom Jackson RC 2.00 5.00
241 Ken Mendenhall .10 .30
242 Tim Fox .10 .30
243 Don Herrmann .10 .30
244 Eddie McMillan .10 .30
245 Greg Pruitt .20 .50
246 J.K. McKay .10 .30
247 Larry Keller RC .10 .30
248 Dave Jennings .20 .50
249 Bo Harris RC .10 .30
250 Revie Sorey .10 .30
251 Tony Greene .10 .30
252 Butch Johnson .20 .50
253 Paul Naumoff .10 .30
254 Rickey Young .20 .50
255 Dwight White .20 .50
256 Joe Lavender .10 .30
257 Checklist 133-264 .40 1.00
258 Ronnie Coleman .10 .30
259 Charlie Smith .10 .30
260 Ray Guy AP .40 1.00
261 David Taylor .10 .30
262 Bill Lenkaitis .10 .30
263 Jim Mitchell .10 .30
264 Delvin Williams .10 .30
265 Jack Youngblood .40 1.00
266 Chuck Crist RC .10 .30
267 Richard Todd .20 .50
268 Dave Logan RC .40 1.00
269 Rufus Mayes .10 .30
270 Brad Van Pelt .10 .30
271 Chester Marcol .10 .30
272 J.V. Cain .10 .30
273 Larry Seiple .10 .30
274 Brent McClanahan .10 .30
275 Mike Wagner .10 .30
276 Diron Talbert .10 .30
277 Brian Baschnagel .10 .30
278 Ed Podolak .10 .30
279 Don Goode .10 .30
280 John Dutton .20 .50
281 Don Calhoun .10 .30
282 Monte Johnson .10 .30
283 Ron Jessie .10 .30
284 Jon Morris .10 .30
285 Riley Odoms .10 .30
286 Marv Bateman .10 .30
287 Joe Klecko RC .40 1.00
288 Oliver Davis RC .10 .30
289 John McDaniel .10 .30
290 Roger Staubach 6.00 12.00
291 Brian Kelley .10 .30
292 Mike Hogan RC .10 .30
293 John Leypoldt .10 .30
294 Jack Novak RC .10 .30
295 Joe Greene .75 2.00
296 John Hill .10 .30
297 Danny Buggs RC .10 .30
298 Ted Albrecht RC .10 .30
299 Nelson Munsey .10 .30
300 Chuck Foreman .20 .50
301 Dan Pastorini .20 .50
302 Tommy Hart .10 .30
303 Dave Beverly .10 .30
304 Tony Reed RC .20 .50
305 Cliff Branch .60 1.50
306 Clarence Duren RC .10 .30
307 Randy Rasmussen .10 .30
308 Oscar Roan .10 .30
309 Lenvil Elliott .10 .30
310 Dan Dierdorf AP .40 1.00
311 Johnny Perkins RC .10 .30
312 Rafael Septien RC .20 .50
313 Terry Beeson RC .10 .30
314 Lee Roy Selmon .75 2.00
315 Tony Dorsett RC 25.00 40.00
316 Greg Landry .20 .50
317 Jake Scott .10 .30
318 Dan Peiffer RC .10 .30
319 John Bunting .20 .50
320 John Stallworth RC 10.00 20.00
321 Bob Howard .10 .30
322 Larry Little .40 1.00
323 Reggie McKenzie .20 .50
324 Duane Carrell .10 .30
325 Ed Simonini RC .10 .30
326 John Vella .10 .30
327 Wesley Walker RC 1.50 3.00
328 Jon Keyworth .10 .30
329 Ron Bolton .10 .30
330 Tommy Casanova .10 .30
331 Passing Leaders 2.00 4.00
Bob Griese
Roger Staubach
332 Receiving Leaders .40 1.00
Lydell Mitchell
Ahmad Rashad
333 W.Payton 1.25 3.00
VanEeghenLL
334 W.Payton 1.25 3.00
E.Mann LL
335 Interception Leaders .10 .30
Lylo Blackwood
Rolland Lawrence
336 Punting Leaders .20 .50
Ray Guy
Tom Blanchard
337 Robert Brazile .20 .50
338 Charlie Joiner .60 1.50
339 Joe Ferguson .20 .50
340 Bill Thompson .10 .30
341 Sam Cunningham .20 .50
342 Curtis Johnson .10 .30
343 Jim Marshall .40 1.00
344 Charlie Sanders .20 .50
345 Willie Hall .10 .30
346 Pat Haden .40 1.00
347 Jim Bakken .10 .30
348 Bruce Taylor .10 .30
349 Barty Smith .10 .30
350 Drew Pearson AP .60 1.50
351 Mike Webster 1.00 2.50
352 Bobby Hammond RC .10 .30
353 Dave Mays RC .10 .30
354 Pat McInally .10 .30
355 Toni Linhart .10 .30
356 Larry Hand .10 .30
357 Ted Fritsch Jr. .10 .30
358 Larry Marshall .10 .30
359 Waymond Bryant .10 .30
360 Louie Kelcher RC .20 .50
361 Stanley Morgan RC .75 2.00
362 Bruce Harper RC .20 .50
363 Bernard Jackson .10 .30
364 Walter White .10 .30
365 Ken Stabler 4.00 8.00
366 Fred Dryer .40 1.00
367 Ike Harris .10 .30
368 Norm Bulaich .10 .30
369 Merv Krakau RC .10 .30
370 John James .10 .30
371 Bennie Cunningham RC .10 .30
372 Doug Van Horn .10 .30
373 Thom Darden .10 .30
374 Eddie Edwards RC .10 .30
375 Mike Thomas .10 .30
376 Fred Cook .10 .30
377 Mike Phipps .20 .50
378 Paul Krause .40 1.00
379 Harold Carmichael .40 1.00
380 Mike Haynes AP .40 1.00
381 Wayne Morris .10 .30
382 Greg Buttle .10 .30
383 Jim Zorn .40 1.00
384 Jack Dolbin .10 .30
385 Charlie Waters .20 .50
386 Dan Ryczek .10 .30
387 Joe Washington RC .40 1.00
388 Checklist 265-396 .40 1.00
389 James Hunter RC .10 .30
390 Billy Johnson .20 .50
391 Jim Allen RC .10 .30

392 George Buehler	.10	.30
393 Harry Carson	.40	1.00
394 Cleo Miller	.10	.30
395 Gary Burley RC	.10	.30
396 Mark Moseley	.20	.50
397 Virgil Livers	.10	.30
398 Joe Ehrmann	.10	.30
399 Freddie Solomon	.10	.30
400 O.J. Simpson	2.00	4.00
401 Julius Adams	.10	.30
402 Artimus Parker RC	.10	.30
403 Gene Washington 49er	.20	.50
404 Herman Edwards RC	.20	.50
405 Craig Morton	.40	1.00
406 Alan Page	.40	1.00
407 Larry McCarren	.10	.30
408 Tony Galbreath	.20	.50
409 Roman Gabriel	.40	1.00
410 Efren Herrera	.10	.30
411 Jim Smith RC	.40	1.00
412 Bill Bryant RC	.10	.30
413 Doug Dieken	.10	.30
414 Marvin Cobb	.10	.30
415 Fred Biletnikoff	.75	2.00
416 Joe Theismann	1.00	2.50
417 Roland Harper	.10	.30
418 Derrel Luce RC	.10	.30
419 Ralph Perretta	.10	.30
420 Louis Wright RC	.40	1.00
421 Prentice McCray	.10	.30
422 Garry Puetz	.10	.30
423 Alfred Jenkins RC	.40	1.00
424 Paul Seymour	.10	.30
425 Garo Yepremian	.20	.50
426 Emmitt Thomas	.20	.50
427 Dexter Bussey	.10	.30
428 John Sanders RC	.10	.30
429 Ed Too Tall Jones	.75	2.00
430 Ron Yary	.40	1.00
431 Frank Lewis	.20	.50
432 Jerry Golsteyn RC	.10	.30
433 Clarence Scott	.10	.30
434 Pete Johnson RC	.40	1.00
435 Charle Young	.20	.50
436 Harold McLinton	.10	.30
437 Noah Jackson	.10	.30
438 Bruce Laird	.10	.30
439 John Matuszak	.20	.50
440 Nat Moore AP	.20	.50
441 Leon Gray	.10	.30
442 Jerome Barkum	.10	.30
443 Steve Largent	6.00	12.00
444 John Zook	.10	.30
445 Preston Pearson	.20	.50
446 Conrad Dobler	.20	.50
447 Wilbur Summers RC	.10	.30
448 Lou Piccone	.10	.30
449 Ron Jaworski	.40	1.00
450 Jack Ham AP	.60	1.50
451 Mick Tingelhoff	.20	.50
452 Clyde Powers	.10	.30
453 John Cappelletti	.40	1.00
454 Dick Ambrose RC	.10	.30
455 Lemar Parrish	.10	.30
456 Ron Saul	.10	.30
457 Bob Parsons	.10	.30
458 Glenn Doughty	.10	.30
459 Don Woods	.10	.30
460 Art Shell AP	.40	1.00
461 Sam Hunt	.10	.30
462 Lawrence Pillers	.10	.30
463 Henry Childs	.10	.30
464 Roger Wehrli	.20	.50
465 Otis Armstrong	.20	.50
466 Bob Baumhower RC	.75	2.00
467 Ray Jarvis	.10	.30
468 Guy Morriss	.10	.30
469 Matt Blair	.20	.50
470 Billy Joe DuPree	.20	.50
471 Roland Hooks RC	.10	.30
472 Joe Danelo	.10	.30
473 Reggie Rucker	.20	.50
474 Vern Holland	.10	.30
475 Mel Blount	.60	1.50
476 Eddie Brown	.10	.30
477 Bo Rather	.10	.30
478 Don McCauley	.10	.30
479 Glen Walker RC	.10	.30
480 Randy Gradishar AP	.40	1.00
481 Dave Rowe	.10	.30
482 Pat Leahy	.20	.50
483 Mike Fuller	.10	.30
484 David Lewis RC	.10	.30
485 Steve Grogan	.40	1.00
486 Mel Gray	.20	.50
487 Eddie Payton RC	.20	.50
488 Checklist 397-528	.40	1.00
489 Stu Voigt	.10	.30
490 Rolland Lawrence	.10	.30
491 Nick Mike-Mayer	.10	.30
492 Troy Archer	.10	.30
493 Benny Malone	.10	.30
494 Golden Richards	.20	.50
495 Chris Hanburger	.10	.30
496 Dwight Harrison	.10	.30
497 Gary Fencik RC	.40	1.00
498 Rich Saul	.10	.30
499 Dan Fouts	2.00	4.00
500 Franco Harris AP	2.00	4.00
501 Atlanta Falcons TL	.30	.75
Haskel Stanback		
Alfred Jenkins		
Claude Humphrey		
Jeff Merrow		
Rolland Lawrence		
(checklist back)		
502 Baltimore Colts TL	.30	.75
Lydell Mitchell		
Lydell Mitchell		
Lyle Blackwood		
Fred Cook		
(checklist back)		
503 Buffalo Bills TL	.60	1.50
O.J. Simpson		
Bob Chandler		
Tony Greene		
Sherman White		
(checklist back)		
504 Chicago Bears TL	.75	2.00
Walter Payton		
James Scott		
Allan Ellis		
Ron Rydalch		
(checklist back)		
505 Cincinnati Bengals TL	.30	.75
Pete Johnson		
Billy Brooks		
Lemar Parrish		
Reggie Williams		
Gary Burley		
(checklist back)		
506 Cleveland Browns TL	.30	.75
Greg Pruitt		
Reggie Rucker		
Thom Darden		
Mack Mitchell		
(checklist back)		
507 Dallas Cowboys TL	1.00	2.50
Tony Dorsett		
Drew Pearson		
Cliff Harris		
Harvey Martin		
(checklist back)		
508 Denver Broncos TL	.40	1.00
Otis Armstrong		
Haven Moses		
Bill Thompson		
Rick Upchurch		
(checklist back)		
509 Detroit Lions TL	.30	.75
Horace King		
David Hill		
James Hunter		
Ken Sanders		
(checklist back)		
510 Green Bay Packers TL	.40	1.00
Barty Smith		
Steve Odom		
Steve Luke		
Mike C. McCoy		
Dave Pureifory		
Dave Roller		
(checklist back)		
511 Houston Oilers TL	.30	.75
Ronnie Coleman		
Ken Burrough		
Mike Reinfeldt		
James Young		
(checklist back)		
512 Kansas City Chiefs TL	.30	.75
Ed Podolak		
Walter White		
Gary Barbaro		
Wilbur Young		
(checklist back)		
513 Los Angeles Rams TL	.30	.75
Lawrence McCutcheon		
Harold Jackson		
Bill Simpson		
Jack Youngblood		
(checklist back)		
514 Miami Dolphins TL	.40	1.00
Benny Malone		
Nat Moore		
Curtis Johnson		
A.J. Duhe		
(checklist back)		
515 Minnesota Vikings TL	.30	.75
Chuck Foreman		
Sammie White		
Bobby Bryant		
Carl Eller		
(checklist back)		
516 New England Patriots TL	.30	.75
Sam Cunningham		
Darryl Stingley		
Mike Haynes		
Tony McGee		
(checklist back)		
517 New Orleans Saints TL	.30	.75
Chuck Muncie		
Don Herrmann		
Chuck Crist		
Elois Grooms		
(checklist back)		
518 New York Giants TL	.30	.75
Bobby Hammond		
Jimmy Robinson		
Bill Bryant		
John Mendenhall		
(checklist back)		
519 New York Jets TL	.30	.75
Clark Gaines		
Wesley Walker		
Burgess Owens		
Joe Klecko		
(checklist back)		
520 Oakland Raiders TL	.40	1.00
Mark Van Eeghen		
Dave Casper		
Jack Tatum		
Neal Colzie		
(checklist back)		
521 Philadelphia Eagles TL	.30	.75
Mike Hogan		
Harold Carmichael		
Herman Edwards		
John Sanders		
Lem Burnham		
(checklist back)		
522 Pittsburgh Steelers TL	.40	1.00
Franco Harris		
Jim Smith		
Mel Blount		
Steve Furness		
(checklist back)		
523 St.Louis Cardinals TL	.30	.75
Terry Metcalf		
Mel Gray		
Roger Wehrli		
Mike Dawson		
(checklist back)		
524 San Diego Chargers TL	.40	1.00
Rickey Young		
Charlie Joiner		
Mike Fuller		
Gary Johnson		
(checklist back)		
525 San Francisco 49ers TL	.30	.75
Delvin Williams		
Gene Washington		
Mel Phillips		
Dave Washington		
Cleveland Elam		
(checklist back)		
526 Seattle Seahawks TL	.60	1.50
Sherman Smith		
Steve Largent		
Autry Beamon		
Walter Packer		
(checklist back)		
527 Tampa Bay Bucs TL	.30	.75
Morris Owens		
Isaac Hagins		
Mike Washington		
Lee Roy Selmon		
(checklist back)		
528 Wash. Redskins TL	.40	1.00
Mike Thomas		
Jean Fugett		
Ken Houston		
Dennis Johnson		
(checklist back)		

1978 Topps Holsum

In 1978, Topps produced a set of 33 NFL full-color standard-size cards for Holsum Bread. One card was packed inside each loaf of bread. Unfortunately, nowhere on the card is Holsum mentioned, leading to frequent misclassification of this set. An uncut production sheet was offered in the 1989 Topps Archives auction. The personal data on the card back is printed in yellow and green. Each card can be found with either one or two asterisks on the copyright line.

COMPLETE SET (33)	150.00	300.00
1 Rolland Lawrence	2.00	4.00
2 Walter Payton	60.00	120.00
3 Lydell Mitchell	2.50	5.00
4 Joe DeLamielleure	3.50	6.00
5 Ken Anderson	5.00	10.00
6 Greg Pruitt	2.50	5.00
7 Harvey Martin	3.00	6.00
8 Tom Jackson	3.00	6.00
9 Chester Marcol	2.00	4.00
10 Jim Carter	2.00	4.00
11 Will Harrell	2.00	4.00
12 Greg Landry	2.50	5.00
13 Billy Johnson	2.50	5.00
14 Jan Stenerud	3.00	6.00
15 Lawrence McCutcheon	2.50	5.00
16 Bob Griese	12.50	25.00
17 Chuck Foreman	2.50	5.00
18 Sammie White	2.50	5.00
19 Jeff Siemon	2.00	4.00
20 Mike Haynes	4.00	8.00
21 Archie Manning	7.50	15.00
22 Brad Van Pelt	2.00	4.00
23 Richard Todd	2.50	5.00
24 Dave Casper	4.00	8.00
25 Bill Bergey	2.50	5.00
26 Franco Harris	12.50	25.00
27 Mel Gray	2.50	5.00
28 Louie Kelcher	2.00	4.00
29 O.J. Simpson	15.00	30.00
30 Jim Zorn	2.50	5.00
31 Lee Roy Selmon	4.00	8.00
32 Ken Houston	3.00	6.00
33 Checklist Card	10.00	20.00

1978 Topps Team Checklists

These cards are essentially a parallel to the base 1978 Topps team checklist subset cards. The set was only available directly from Topps as a send-off offer in uncut sheet form. The prices below apply equally to uncut sheets as they are frequently found in their original uncut condition. As for individual cards, thin white card (almost paper-thin) stock makes it a challenge to find singles in top grades.

COMPLETE SET (28)	62.50	125.00
501 Atlanta Falcons TL	2.00	4.00
Haskel Stanback		
Alfred Jenkins		
Claude Humphrey		
Jeff Merrow		
Rolland Lawrence		
(checklist back)		
502 Baltimore Colts TL	2.00	4.00
Lydell Mitchell		
Lydell Mitchell		
Lyle Blackwood		
Fred Cook		
(checklist back)		
503 Buffalo Bills TL	4.00	8.00
O.J. Simpson		
Bob Chandler		
Tony Greene		
Sherman White		
(checklist back)		
504 Chicago Bears TL	7.50	15.00
Walter Payton		
James Scott		
Allan Ellis		
Ron Rydalch		
(checklist back)		
505 Cincinnati Bengals TL	2.00	4.00
Pete Johnson		
Billy Brooks		
Lemar Parrish		
Reggie Williams		
Gary Burley		
(checklist back)		
506 Cleveland Browns TL	2.00	4.00
Greg Pruitt		
Reggie Rucker		
Thom Darden		
Mack Mitchell		
(checklist back)		
507 Dallas Cowboys TL	5.00	10.00
Tony Dorsett		
Drew Pearson		
Cliff Harris		
Harvey Martin		
(checklist back)		
508 Denver Broncos TL	3.00	6.00
Otis Armstrong		
Haven Moses		
Bill Thompson		
Rick Upchurch		
(checklist back)		
509 Detroit Lions TL	2.00	4.00
Horace King		
David Hill		
James Hunter		
Ken Sanders		
(checklist back)		
510 Green Bay Packers TL	3.00	6.00
Barty Smith		
Steve Odom		
Steve Luke		
Mike C. McCoy		
Dave Pureifory		
Dave Roller		
(checklist back)		
511 Houston Oilers TL	2.00	4.00
Ronnie Coleman		
Ken Burrough		
Mike Reinfeldt		
James Young		
(checklist back)		
512 Kansas City Chiefs TL	2.00	4.00
Ed Podolak		
Walter White		
Gary Barbaro		
Wilbur Young		
(checklist back)		
513 Los Angeles Rams TL	2.00	4.00
Lawrence McCutcheon		
Harold Jackson		
Bill Simpson		
Jack Youngblood		
(checklist back)		
514 Miami Dolphins TL	3.00	6.00
Benny Malone		
Nat Moore		
Curtis Johnson		
A.J. Duhe		
(checklist back)		
515 Minnesota Vikings TL	3.00	6.00
Chuck Foreman		
Sammie White		
Bobby Bryant		
Carl Eller		
(checklist back)		
516 New England Patriots TL	2.00	4.00
Sam Cunningham		
Darryl Stingley		
Mike Haynes		
Tony McGee		
(checklist back)		
517 New Orleans Saints TL	2.00	4.00
Chuck Muncie		
Don Herrmann		
Chuck Crist		
Elois Grooms		
(checklist back)		
518 New York Giants TL	2.00	4.00
Bobby Hammond		
Jimmy Robinson		
Bill Bryant		
John Mendenhall		
(checklist back)		
519 New York Jets TL	2.00	4.00
Clark Gaines		
Wesley Walker		
Burgess Owens		
Joe Klecko		
(checklist back)		
520 Oakland Raiders TL	3.00	6.00
Mark Van Eeghen		
Dave Casper		
Jack Tatum		
Neal Colzie		
(checklist back)		
521 Philadelphia Eagles TL	3.00	6.00
Mike Hogan		
Harold Carmichael		
Herman Edwards		
John Sanders		
Lem Burnham		
(checklist back)		
522 Pittsburgh Steelers TL	4.00	8.00
Franco Harris		
Jim Smith		
Mel Blount		
Steve Furness		
(checklist back)		
523 St.Louis Cardinals TL	2.00	4.00
Terry Metcalf		
Mel Gray		
Roger Wehrli		
Mike Dawson		
(checklist back)		
524 San Diego Chargers TL	3.00	6.00
Rickey Young		
Charlie Joiner		
Mike Fuller		
Gary Johnson		
(checklist back)		
525 San Francisco 49ers TL	3.00	6.00
Delvin Williams		
Gene Washington		
Mel Phillips		
Dave Washington		
Cleveland Elam		
(checklist back)		
526 Seattle Seahawks TL	4.00	8.00
Sherman Smith		
Steve Largent		
Autry Beamon		
Walter Packer		
(checklist back)		
527 Tampa Bay Bucs TL	3.00	6.00
Morris Owens		
Isaac Hagins		
Mike Washington		
Lee Roy Selmon		
(checklist back)		
528 Wash. Redskins TL	3.00	6.00
Mike Thomas		
Jean Fugett		
Ken Houston		
Dennis Johnson		
(checklist back)		

1979 Topps

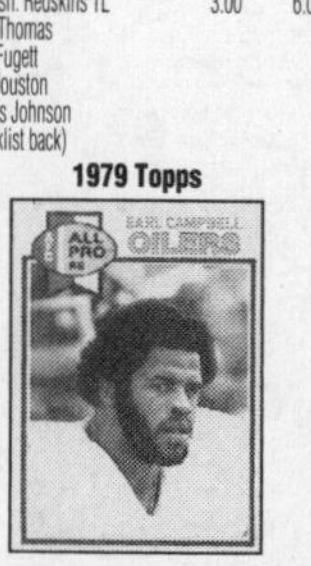

The 1979 Topps football set contains 528 standard-size cards. The cardfronts have the player's name, team name and position at the top and the position is within a football that is part of a banner-like design. The backs contain yearly statistics, highlights and a player cartoon. Subsets include League Leaders (1-6), Playoffs (166-168) and Record Breakers (331-336). Team Leaders (TL) depict team leaders in various categories on front and a team checklist on back. An uncut sheet of the 28-Team Leaders cards along with two checklists was available via a wrapper mail order offer. The set features the first and only major issue cards of Earl Campbell. Other Rookie Cards include Steve DeBerg, James Lofton, Ozzie Newsome and Doug Williams. Finally, every card was printed on the standard dark colored gray card stock as well as a thinner cream colored card stock that is slightly more difficult to find.

COMPLETE SET (528)	75.00	150.00
*CREAM BACK: .4X TO 1X GRAY BACK		
1 Passing Leaders	4.00	8.00
Roger Staubach		
Terry Bradshaw		
2 Receiving Leaders	.40	1.00
Rickey Young		
Steve Largent		
3 Rushing Leaders	4.00	8.00
Earl Campbell		
Walter Payton		
4 Scoring Leaders	.10	.30
Frank Corral		
Pat Leahy		
5 Interception Leaders	.10	.30
Willie Buchanon		
Ken Stone		
Thom Darden		
6 Punting Leaders	.10	.30
Tom Skladany		
Pat McInally		
7 Johnny Perkins	.10	.30
8 Charles Phillips RC	.10	.30
9 Derrel Luce	.10	.30
10 John Riggins	.50	1.25
11 Chester Marcol	.10	.30
12 Bernard Jackson	.10	.30
13 Dave Logan	.10	.30
14 Bo Harris	.10	.30
15 Alan Page	.40	1.00
16 John Smith	.10	.30
17 Dwight McDonald RC	.10	.30
18 John Cappelletti	.20	.50
19 Pittsburgh Steelers TL	5.00	12.00
Franco Harris		
Larry Anderson		
Tony Dungy		
L.C. Greenwood		
(checklist back)		
20 Bill Bergey AP	.20	.50
21 Jerome Barkum	.10	.30
22 Larry Csonka	1.00	2.50
23 Joe Ferguson	.20	.50
24 Ed Too Tall Jones	.50	1.25
25 Dave Jennings	.20	.50
26 Horace King	.10	.30
27 Steve Little RC	.20	.50
28 Morris Bradshaw RC	.10	.30
29 Joe Ehrmann	.10	.30
30 Ahmad Rashad AP	.40	1.00
31 Joe Lavender	.10	.30
32 Dan Neal	.10	.30
33 Johnny Evans RC	.10	.30
34 Pete Johnson	.20	.50
35 Mike Haynes AP	.40	1.00
36 Tim Mazzetti RC	.10	.30
37 Mike Barber RC	.10	.30
38 San Francisco 49ers TL	.60	1.50
O.J. Simpson		
Freddie Solomon		
Chuck Crist		
Cedrick Hardman		
(checklist back)		
39 Bill Gregory RC	.10	.30
40 Randy Gradishar AP	.40	1.00
41 Richard Todd	.20	.50
42 Henry Marshall	.10	.30
43 John Hill	.10	.30
44 Sidney Thornton RC	.10	.30
45 Ron Jessie	.10	.30
46 Bob Baumhower	.20	.50
47 Johnnie Gray	.10	.30
48 Doug Williams RC	3.00	6.00
49 Don McCauley	.10	.30
50 Ray Guy AP	.20	.50
51 Bob Klein	.10	.30
52 Golden Richards	.10	.30
53 Mark Miller QB RC	.10	.30
54 John Sanders	.10	.30
55 Gary Burley	.10	.30
56 Steve Nelson	.10	.30
57 Buffalo Bills TL	.30	.75
Terry Miller		
Frank Lewis		
Mario Clark		
Lucius Sanford		
(checklist back)		
58 Bobby Bryant	.10	.30
59 Rick Kane	.10	.30
60 Larry Little	.40	1.00
61 Ted Fritsch Jr.	.10	.30
62 Larry Mallory RC	.10	.30
63 Marvin Powell	.10	.30
64 Jim Hart	.40	1.00
65 Joe Greene AP	.60	1.50
66 Walter White	.10	.30
67 Gregg Bingham	.10	.30
68 Errol Mann	.10	.30
69 Bruce Laird	.10	.30
70 Drew Pearson	.40	1.00
71 Steve Bartkowski	.40	1.00
72 Ted Albrecht	.10	.30
73 Charlie Hall	.10	.30
74 Pat McInally	.10	.30
75 Bubba Baker RC	.40	1.00
76 New England Pats TL	.30	.75
Sam Cunningham		
Stanley Morgan		
Mike Haynes		
Tony McGee		
(checklist back)		
77 Steve DeBerg RC	.75	2.00
78 John Yarno RC	.10	.30
79 Stu Voigt	.10	.30
80 Frank Corral AP RC	.10	.30
81 Troy Archer	.10	.30
82 Bruce Harper	.10	.30
83 Tom Jackson	.60	1.50
84 Larry Brown	.20	.50
85 Wilbert Montgomery AP RC	.40	1.00
86 Butch Johnson	.20	.50
87 Mike Kadish	.10	.30
88 Ralph Perretta	.10	.30
89 David Lee	.10	.30
90 Mark Van Eeghen	.20	.50
91 John McDaniel	.10	.30
92 Gary Fencik	.20	.50
93 Mack Mitchell	.10	.30
94 Cincinnati Bengals TL	.40	1.00
Pete Johnson		
Isaac Curtis		
Dick Jauron		
Ross Browner		
(checklist back)		
95 Steve Grogan	.40	1.00
96 Garo Yepremian	.20	.50
97 Barty Smith	.10	.30
98 Frank Reed RC	.10	.30
99 Jim Clack RC	.10	.30
100 Chuck Foreman	.20	.50
101 Joe Klecko	.40	1.00
102 Pat Tilley	.20	.50
103 Conrad Dobler	.20	.50
104 Craig Colquitt RC	.10	.30
105 Dan Pastorini	.20	.50
106 Rod Perry AP	.10	.30
107 Nick Mike-Mayer	.10	.30
108 John Matuszak	.20	.50
109 David Taylor	.10	.30
110 Billy Joe DuPree AP	.20	.50
111 Harold McLinton	.10	.30
112 Virgil Livers	.10	.30
113 Cleveland Browns TL	.30	.75
Greg Pruitt		
Reggie Rucker		
Thom Darden		
Mack Mitchell		
(checklist back)		
114 Checklist 1-132	.40	1.00
115 Ken Anderson	.40	1.00
116 Bill Lenkaitis	.10	.30
117 Bucky Dilts	.10	.30
118 Tony Greene	.10	.30
119 Bobby Hammond	.10	.30
120 Nat Moore	.20	.50
121 Pat Leahy AP	.20	.50
122 James Harris	.20	.50
123 Lee Roy Selmon	.50	1.25
124 Bennie Cunningham	.20	.50
125 Matt Blair AP	.20	.50
126 Jim Allen	.10	.30
127 Alfred Jenkins	.20	.50
128 Arthur Whittington RC	.10	.30
129 Norm Thompson	.10	.30
130 Pat Haden	.40	1.00
131 Freddie Solomon	.10	.30
132 Chicago Bears TL	.75	2.00
Walter Payton		
James Scott		
Gary Fencik		
Alan Page		
(checklist back)		
133 Mark Moseley	.10	.30
134 Cleo Miller	.10	.30
135 Ross Browner RC	.20	.50
136 Don Calhoun	.10	.30
137 David Whitehurst RC	.10	.30
138 Terry Beeson	.10	.30
139 Ken Stone RC	.10	.30
140 Brad Van Pelt AP	.10	.30
141 Wesley Walker AP	.40	1.00
142 Jan Stenerud	.40	1.00
143 Henry Childs	.10	.30
144 Otis Armstrong	.40	1.00
145 Dwight White	.20	.50
146 Steve Wilson RC	.10	.30
147 Tom Skladany RC	.10	.30
148 Lou Piccone	.10	.30
149 Monte Johnson	.10	.30
150 Joe Washington	.20	.50
151 Philadelphia Eagles TL	.30	.75
Wilbert Montgomery		
Harold Carmichael		
Herman Edwards		
Dennis Harrison		
(checklist back)		
152 Fred Dean	.40	1.00
153 Rolland Lawrence	.10	.30
154 Brian Baschnagel	.10	.30
155 Joe Theismann	.75	2.00
156 Marvin Cobb	.10	.30
157 Dick Ambrose	.10	.30
158 Mike Patrick	.10	.30
159 Gary Shirk	.10	.30
160 Tony Dorsett	6.00	12.00
161 Greg Buttle	.10	.30
162 A.J. Duhe	.20	.50
163 Mick Tingelhoff	.20	.50
164 Ken Burrough	.20	.50
165 Mike Wagner	.10	.30
166 AFC Championship	.40	1.00
Steelers 34;		
Oilers 5		
(Franco Harris)		
167 NFC Championship	.20	.50
Cowboys 28;		
Rams 0		
(line of scrimmage)		
168 Super Bowl XIII	.50	1.25
Steelers 35;		
Cowboys 31		
(Franco Harris)		
169 Oakland Raiders TL	.40	1.00
Mark Van Eeghen		
Dave Casper		
Charles Phillips		
Ted Hendricks		
(checklist back)		
170 O.J. Simpson	1.50	4.00
171 Doug Nettles RC	.10	.30
172 Dan Dierdorf AP	.40	1.00
173 Dave Beverly	.10	.30
174 Jim Zorn	.40	1.00
175 Mike Thomas	.10	.30
176 John Outlaw	.10	.30
177 Jim Turner	.10	.30
178 Freddie Scott RC	.10	.30
179 Mike Phipps	.20	.50
180 Jack Youngblood AP	.40	1.00
181 Sam Hunt	.10	.30
182 Tony Hill RC	.40	1.00
183 Gary Barbaro	.10	.30
184 Archie Griffin	.20	.50
185 Jerry Sherk	.10	.30
186 Bobby Jackson RC	.10	.30
187 Don Woods	.10	.30
188 New York Giants TL	.30	.75
Doug Kotar		
Jimmy Robinson		
Terry Jackson		
George Martin		
(checklist back)		
189 Raymond Chester	.10	.30
190 Joe DeLamielleure AP	.40	1.00
191 Tony Galbreath	.20	.50
192 Robert Brazile AP	.20	.50
193 Neil O'Donoghue RC	.10	.30
194 Mike Webster AP	.40	1.00
195 Ed Simonini	.10	.30
196 Benny Malone	.10	.30
197 Tom Wittum	.10	.30
198 Steve Largent AP	4.00	8.00
199 Tommy Hart	.10	.30
200 Fran Tarkenton	1.50	3.00
201 Leon Gray AP	.10	.30
202 Leroy Harris RC	.10	.30
203 Eric Williams LB RC	.10	.30
204 Thom Darden AP	.10	.30
205 Ken Riley	.20	.50
206 Clark Gaines	.10	.30
207 Kansas City.Chiefs TL	.30	.75
Tony Reed		
Tony Reed		
Tim Gray		
Art Still		
(checklist back)		
208 Joe Danelo	.10	.30
209 Glen Walker	.10	.30
210 Art Shell	.40	1.00
211 Jon Keyworth	.10	.30
212 Herman Edwards	.10	.30
213 John Fitzgerald	.10	.30
214 Jim Smith	.20	.50
215 Coy Bacon	.20	.50
216 Dennis Johnson RBK RC	.10	.30
217 John Jefferson RC	1.50	3.00
(Charlie Joiner		
in background)		
218 Gary Weaver RC	.10	.30
219 Tom Blanchard	.10	.30
220 Bert Jones	.40	1.00
221 Stanley Morgan	.40	1.00
222 James Hunter	.10	.30
223 Jim O'Bradovich	.10	.30
224 Carl Mauck	.10	.30
225 Chris Bahr	.10	.30
226 New York Jets TL	.30	.75
Kevin Long		
Wesley Walker		
Bobby Jackson		
Burgess Owens		
Joe Klecko		
(checklist back)		
227 Roland Harper	.10	.30
228 Randy Dean RC	.10	.30
229 Bob Jackson	.10	.30
230 Sammie White	.20	.50
231 Mike Dawson RC	.10	.30
232 Checklist 133-264	.40	1.00
233 Ken MacAfee RC	.10	.30
234 Jon Kolb AP	.10	.30
235 Willie Hall	.10	.30
236 Ron Saul AP	.10	.30
237 Haskel Stanback	.10	.30
238 Zenon Andrusyshyn RC	.10	.30
239 Norris Thomas	.10	.30
240 Rick Upchurch	.20	.50
241 Robert Pratt	.10	.30
242 Julius Adams	.10	.30
243 Rich McGeorge	.10	.30
244 Seattle Seahawks TL	.50	1.25
Sherman Smith		
Steve Largent		
Cornell Webster		
Bill Gregory		
(checklist back)		
245 Blair Bush RC	.10	.30
246 Billy Johnson	.20	.50
247 Randy Rasmussen	.10	.30
248 Brian Kelley	.10	.30
249 Mike Pruitt	.20	.50
250 Harold Carmichael AP	.40	1.00
251 Mike Hartenstine	.10	.30
252 Robert Newhouse	.20	.50
253 Gary Danielson RC	.40	1.00
254 Mike Fuller	.10	.30
255 L.C. Greenwood AP	.40	1.00
256 Lemar Parrish	.10	.30
257 Ike Harris	.10	.30
258 Ricky Bell RC	.40	1.00
259 Willie Parker	.10	.30
260 Gene Upshaw	.40	1.00
261 Glenn Doughty	.10	.30
262 Steve Zabel	.10	.30
263 Atlanta Falcons TL	.30	.75
Bubba Bean		
Wallace Francis		
Rolland Lawrence		
Greg Brezina		
(checklist back)		
264 Ray Wersching	.10	.30
265 Lawrence McCutcheon	.20	.50
266 Willie Buchanon AP	.10	.30
267 Matt Robinson RC	.10	.30
268 Reggie Rucker	.20	.50
269 Doug Van Horn	.10	.30
270 Lydell Mitchell	.20	.50
271 Vern Holland	.10	.30
272 Eason Ramson RC	.10	.30
273 Steve Towle RC	.10	.30
274 Jim Marshall	.40	1.00
275 Mel Blount	.50	1.25
276 Bob Kuziel RC	.10	.30
277 James Scott	.10	.30
278 Tony Reed	.10	.30
279 Dave Green	.10	.30
280 Toni Linhart	.10	.30
281 Andy Johnson	.10	.30
282 Los Angeles Rams TL	.30	.75
Cullen Bryant		
Willie Miller		
Rod Perry		
Pat Thomas		
Larry Brooks		
(checklist back)		
283 Phil Villapiano	.20	.50
284 Dexter Bussey	.10	.30
285 Craig Morton	.40	1.00
286 Guy Morriss	.10	.30
287 Lawrence Pillers	.10	.30
288 Gerald Irons	.10	.30
289 Scott Perry RC	.10	.30
290 Randy White AP	.75	2.00
291 Jack Gregory	.10	.30
292 Bob Chandler	.10	.30
293 Rich Szaro	.10	.30
294 Sherman Smith	.10	.30
295 Tom Banks AP	.10	.30
296 Revie Sorey AP	.10	.30
297 Ricky Thompson RC	.10	.30
298 Ron Yary	.40	1.00
299 Lyle Blackwood	.10	.30
300 Franco Harris	1.25	2.50
301 Houston Oilers TL	1.50	3.00
Earl Campbell		
Ken Burrough		
Willie Alexander		
Elvin Bethea		
(checklist back)		
302 Scott Bull RC	.10	.30
303 Dewey Selmon	.20	.50
304 Jack Rudnay	.10	.30
305 Fred Biletnikoff	.75	2.00
306 Jeff West	.10	.30
307 Shafer Suggs RC	.10	.30
308 Ozzie Newsome RC	6.00	12.00
309 Boobie Clark	.10	.30
310 James Lofton RC	6.00	12.00
311 Joe Pisarcik	.10	.30
312 Bill Simpson AP	.10	.30
313 Haven Moses	.20	.50
314 Jim Merlo	.10	.30
315 Preston Pearson	.20	.50
316 Larry Tearry RC	.10	.30
317 Tom Dempsey	.10	.30
318 Greg Latta	.10	.30
319 Wash. Redskins TL	.60	1.50
John Riggins		
John McDaniel		
Jake Scott		
Coy Bacon		
(checklist back)		
320 Jack Ham AP	.50	1.25
321 Harold Jackson	.20	.50

322 George Roberts RC .10 .30
323 Ron Jaworski .40 1.00
324 Jim Otis .10 .30
325 Roger Carr .20 .50
326 Jack Tatum .20 .50
327 Derrick Gaffney RC .10 .30
328 Reggie Williams .40 1.00
329 Doug Dieken .10 .30
330 Efren Herrera .10 .30
331 Earl Campbell RB 3.00 6.00
Most Yards
Rushing& Rookie
332 Tony Galbreath RB .10 .30
Most Receptions&
Running Back& Game
333 Bruce Harper RB .10 .30
Most Combined Kick
Return Yards& Season
334 John James RB .10 .30
Most Punts& Season
335 Walter Payton RB 1.50 4.00
Most Combined
Attempts& Season
336 Rickey Young RB .10 .30
Most Receptions&
Running Back& Season
337 Jeff Van Note .20 .50
338 San Diego Chargers TL .40 1.00
Lydell Mitchell
John Jefferson
Mike Fuller
Fred Dean
(checklist back)
339 Stan Walters RC .10 .30
340 Louis Wright AP .20 .50
341 Horace Ivory RC .10 .30
342 Andre Tillman .10 .30
343 Greg Coleman RC .10 .30
344 Doug English AP RC .40 1.00
345 Ted Hendricks .40 1.00
346 Rich Saul .10 .30
347 Mel Gray .20 .50
348 Toni Fritsch .10 .30
349 Cornell Webster RC .10 .30
350 Ken Houston .40 1.00
351 Ron Johnson DB RC .20 .50
352 Doug Kotar .10 .30
353 Brian Sipe .40 1.00
354 Billy Brooks .10 .30
355 John Dutton .20 .50
356 Don Goode .10 .30
357 Detroit Lions TL .30 .75
Dexter Bussey
David Hill
Jim Allen
Al(Bubba) Baker
(checklist back)
358 Reuben Gant .10 .30
359 Bob Parsons .10 .30
360 Cliff Harris AP .40 1.00
361 Raymond Clayborn .20 .50
362 Scott Dierking .10 .30
363 Bill Bryan RC .10 .30
364 Mike Livingston .10 .30
365 Otis Sistrunk .20 .50
366 Charle Young .20 .50
367 Keith Wortman RC .10 .30
368 Checklist 265-396 .40 1.00
369 Mike Michel RC .10 .30
370 Delvin Williams AP .10 .30
371 Steve Furness .20 .50
372 Emery Moorehead .10 .30
373 Clarence Scott .10 .30
374 Rufus Mayes .10 .30
375 Chris Hanburger .10 .30
376 Baltimore Colts TL .30 .75
Joe Washington
Roger Carr
Norm Thompson
John Dutton
(checklist back)
377 Bob Avellini .20 .50
378 Jeff Siemon .10 .30
379 Holand Hooks .10 .30
380 Russ Francis .20 .50
381 Roger Wehrli .20 .50
382 Joe Fields .10 .30
383 Archie Manning .40 1.00
384 Rob Lytle .10 .30
385 Thomas Henderson .20 .50
386 Morris Owens .10 .30
387 Dan Fouts 1.50 3.00
388 Chuck Crist .10 .30
389 Ed O'Neil RC .10 .30
390 Earl Campbell RC 15.00 30.00
391 Randy Grossman .10 .30
392 Monte Jackson .10 .30
393 John Mendenhall .10 .30
394 Miami Dolphins TL .40 1.00
Delvin Williams
Duriel Harris
Tim Foley
Vern Den Herder
(checklist back)
395 Isaac Curtis .20 .50
396 Mike Bragg .10 .30
397 Doug Plank .10 .30
398 Mike Barnes .10 .30
399 Calvin Hill .20 .50
400 Roger Staubach AP 5.00 10.00
401 Doug Beaudoin RC .10 .30
402 Chuck Ramsey .10 .30
403 Mike Hogan .10 .30
404 Mario Clark .10 .30
405 Riley Odoms .10 .30
406 Carl Eller .40 1.00
407 Green Bay Packers TL .60 1.50
Terdell Middleton
James Lofton
Willie Buchanon
Ezra Johnson
(checklist back)
408 Mark Arneson .10 .30
409 Vince Ferragamo RC .40 1.00
410 Cleveland Flam .10 .30
411 Donnie Shell RC 1.50 4.00
412 Ray Rhodes .40 1.00
413 Don Cockroft .10 .30
414 Don Bass RC .20 .50
415 Cliff Branch .40 1.00
416 Diron Talbert .10 .30
417 Tom Hicks .10 .30
418 Roosevelt Leaks .10 .30
419 Charlie Joiner .40 1.00
420 Lyle Alzado AP .40 1.00
421 Sam Cunningham .20 .50
422 Larry Keller .10 .30
423 Jim Mitchell .10 .30
424 Randy Logan .10 .30
425 Jim Langer .40 1.00
426 Gary Green .10 .30
427 Luther Blue RC .10 .30
428 Dennis Johnson .10 .30
429 Danny White .40 1.00
430 Roy Gerela .10 .30
431 Jimmy Robinson .10 .30
432 Minnesota Vikings TL .30 .75
Chuck Foreman
Ahmad Rashad
Bobby Bryant
Mark Mullaney
(checklist back)
433 Oliver Davis .10 .30
434 Lenvil Elliott .10 .30
435 Willie Miller RC .10 .30
436 Brad Dusek .10 .30
437 Bob Thomas .10 .30
438 Ken Mendenhall .10 .30
439 Clarence Davis .10 .00
440 Bob Griese 1.00 2.50
441 Tony McGee .10 .30
442 Ed Taylor .10 .30
443 Ron Howard .10 .30
444 Wayne Morris .10 .30
445 Charlie Waters .20 .50
446 Rick Danmeier RC .10 .30
447 Paul Naumoff .10 .30
448 Keith Krepfle .10 .30
449 Rusty Jackson .10 .30
450 John Stallworth 2.00 4.00
451 New Orleans Saints TL .30 .75
Tony Galbreath
Henry Childs
Tom Myers
Elex Price
(checklist back)
452 Ron Mikolajczyk RC .10 .30
453 Fred Dryer .40 1.00
454 Jim LeClair .10 .30
455 Greg Pruitt .20 .50
456 Jake Scott .10 .30
457 Steve Schubert .10 .30
458 George Kunz .10 .30
459 Mike Williams .10 .30
460 Dave Casper AP .40 1.00
461 Sam Adams .10 .30
462 Abdul Salaam .10 .30
463 Terdell Middleton RC .20 .50
464 Mike Wood RC .10 .30
465 Bill Thompson AP .10 .30
466 Larry Gordon .10 .30
467 Benny Ricardo .10 .30
468 Reggie McKenzie .20 .50
469 Dallas Cowboys TL .60 1.50
Tony Dorsett
Tony Hill
Benny Barnes
Harvey Martin
Randy White
(checklist back)
470 Rickey Young .20 .50
471 Charlie Smith .10 .30
472 Al Dixon RC .10 .30
473 Tom DeLeone .10 .30
474 Louis Breeden RC .20 .50
475 Jack Lambert .75 2.00
476 Terry Hermeling .10 .30
477 J.K. McKay .10 .30
478 Stan White .10 .30
479 Terry Nelson .10 .30
480 Walter Payton AP 10.00 20.00
481 Dave Dalby .10 .30
482 Burgess Owens .10 .30
483 Rolf Benirschke .10 .30
484 Jack Dolbin .10 .30
485 John Hannah AP .40 1.00
486 Checklist 397-528 .40 1.00
487 Greg Landry .20 .50
488 St. Louis Cardinals TL .30 .75
Jim Otis
Pat Tilley
Ken Stone
Mike Dawson
(checklist back)
489 Paul Krause .40 1.00
490 John James .10 .30
401 Morv Krakau .10 .30
492 Dan Doornink RC .10 .30
493 Curtis Johnson .10 .30
494 Rafael Septien .10 .30
495 Jean Fugett .10 .30
496 Frank LeMaster .10 .30
497 Allan Ellis .10 .30
498 Billy Waddy RC .20 .50
499 Hank Bauer RC .10 .30
500 Terry Bradshaw AP UER 5.00 10.00
(Stat headers on back
are for a runner)
501 Larry McCarren .10 .30
502 Fred Cook .10 .30
503 Chuck Muncie .20 .50
504 Herman Weaver .10 .30
505 Eddie Edwards .10 .30
506 Tony Peters .10 .30
507 Denver Broncos TL .30 .75
Lonnie Perrin
Riley Odoms
Steve Foley
Bernard Jackson
Lyle Alzado
(checklist back)
508 Jimbo Elrod RC .10 .30
509 David Hill .10 .30
510 Harvey Martin .20 .50
511 Terry Miller RC .20 .50
512 June Jones RC .20 .50
513 Randy Cross .40 1.00
514 Duriel Harris .10 .30
515 Harry Carson .40 1.00
516 Tim Fox .10 .30
517 John Zook .10 .30
518 Bob Tucker .10 .30
519 Kevin Long RC .10 .30
520 Ken Stabler 3.00 6.00
521 John Bunting .20 .50
522 Rocky Bleier .50 1.25
523 Noah Jackson .10 .30
524 Cliff Parsley RC .10 .30
525 Louie Kelcher AP .20 .50
526 Tampa Bay Bucs TL .30 .75
Ricky Bell
Morris Owens
Cedric Brown
Lee Roy Selmon
(checklist back)
527 Bob Brudzinski RC .10 .30
528 Danny Buggs .10 .30

1979 Topps Team Checklists

These cards are essentially a parallel to the base 1979 Topps team checklist subset cards. The set was only available directly from Topps as a send-off offer in uncut sheet form. The prices below apply equally to uncut sheets as they are frequently found in their original uncut condition. As for individual cards, thin white card (almost paper-thin) stock makes it a challenge to find singles in top grades.

COMPLETE SET (28) 62.50 125.00
19 Pittsburgh Steelers TL 5.00 10.00
Franco Harris
Larry Anderson
Tony Dungy
L.C. Greenwood
(checklist back)
38 San Francisco 49ers TL 4.00 8.00
O.J. Simpson
Freddie Solomon
Chuck Crist
Cedrick Hardman
(checklist back)
57 Buffalo Bills TL 2.00 4.00
Terry Miller
Frank Lewis
Mario Clark
Lucius Sanford
(checklist back)
76 New England Pats TL 2.00 4.00
Sam Cunningham
Stanley Morgan
Mike Haynes
Tony McGee
(checklist back)
94 Cincinnati Bengals TL 4.00 8.00
Pete Johnson
Isaac Curtis
Dick Jauron
Ross Browner
(checklist back)
113 Cleveland Browns TL 2.00 4.00
Greg Pruitt
Reggie Rucker
Thom Darden
Mack Mitchell
(checklist back)
132 Chicago Bears TL 6.00 12.00
Walter Payton
James Scott
Gary Fencik
Alan Page
(checklist back)
151 Philadelphia Eagles TL 3.00 6.00
Wilbert Montgomery
Harold Carmichael
Herman Edwards
Dennis Harrison
(checklist back)
169 Oakland Raiders TL 4.00 8.00
Mark Van Eeghen
Dave Casper
Charles Phillips
Ted Hendricks
(checklist back)
188 New York Giants TL 2.00 4.00
Doug Kotar
Jimmy Robinson
Terry Jackson
George Martin
(checklist back)
207 Kansas City Chiefs TL 2.00 4.00
Tony Reed
Tony Reed
Tim Gray
Art Still
(checklist back)
226 New York Jets TL 2.00 4.00
Kevin Long
Wesley Walker
Bobby Jackson
Burgess Owens
Joe Klecko
(checklist back)
244 Seattle Seahawks TL 4.00 8.00
Sherman Smith
Steve Largent
Cornell Webster
Bill Gregory
(checklist back)
263 Atlanta Falcons TL 2.00 4.00
Bubba Bean
Wallace Francis
Rolland Lawrence
Greg Brezina
(checklist back)
282 Los Angeles Rams TL 2.00 4.00
Cullen Bryant
Willie Miller
Rod Perry
Pat Thomas
Larry Brooks
(checklist back)
301 Houston Oilers TL 6.00 12.00
Earl Campbell
Ken Burrough
Willie Alexander
Elvin Bethea
(checklist back)
319 Wash. Redskins TL 4.00 8.00
John Riggins
John McDaniel
Jake Scott
Coy Bacon
(checklist back)
338 San Diego Chargers TL 3.00 6.00
Lydell Mitchell
John Jefferson
Mike Fuller
Fred Dean
(checklist back)
357 Detroit Lions TL 2.00 4.00
Dexter Bussey
David Hill
Jim Allen
Al(Bubba) Baker
(checklist back)
376 Baltimore Colts TL 2.00 4.00
Joe Washington
Roger Carr
Norm Thompson
John Dutton
(checklist back)
394 Miami Dolphins TL 2.00 4.00
Delvin Williams
Duriel Harris
Tim Foley
Vern Den Herder
(checklist back)
407 Green Bay Packers TL 5.00 10.00
Terdell Middleton
James Lofton
Willie Buchanon
Ezra Johnson
(checklist back)
432 Minnesota Vikings TL 3.00 6.00
Chuck Foreman
Ahmad Rashad
Bobby Bryant
Mark Mullaney
(checklist back)
451 New Orleans Saints TL 2.00 4.00
Tony Galbreath
Henry Childs
Tom Myers
Elex Price
(checklist back)
469 Dallas Cowboys TL 5.00 10.00
Tony Dorsett
Tony Hill
Benny Barnes
Harvey Martin
Randy White
(checklist back)
488 St. Louis Cardinals TL 2.00 4.00
Jim Otis
Pat Tilley
Ken Stone
Mike Dawson
(checklist back)
507 Denver Broncos TL 3.00 6.00
Lonnie Perrin
Riley Odoms
Steve Foley
Bernard Jackson
Lyle Alzado
(checklist back)
526 Tampa Bay Bucs TL 3.00 6.00
Ricky Bell
Morris Owens
Cedric Brown
Lee Roy Selmon
(checklist back)

1980 Topps

The 1980 Topps football card set contains 528 standard-size cards of NFL players. The set was issued in 12-card packs along with a bubble gum slab. The fronts feature a football at the bottom of the photo. Within the football is the player's team and position. A bar with the player's name runs through the center of the football. The backs of the cards contain year-by-year and career statistics and a cartoon-illustrated fact section. Subsets include Record-Breakers (1-6), league leaders (331-336) and playoffs (492-494). Team Leader (TL) cards depict team statistical leaders on the front and a team checklist on the back. The key Rookie Cards in this set are Ottis Anderson, Clay Matthews, and Phil Simms.

COMPLETE SET (528) 40.00 75.00
1 Ottis Anderson RB .40 1.00
Most Yardage
Rushing: Rookie
2 Harold Carmichael RB .40 1.00
Most Consec. Games
One or More Receptions
3 Dan Fouts RB .40 1.00
Most Yardage
Passing: Season
4 Paul Krause RB .20 .50
Most Interceptions
Lifetime
5 Rick Upchurch RB .20 .50
Most Punt Return
Yards: Lifetime
6 Garo Yepremian RB .08 .25
7 Harold Jackson .20 .50
8 Mike Williams .08 .25
9 Calvin Hill .20 .50
10 Jack Ham AP .40 1.00
11 Dan Melville .08 .25
12 Matt Robinson .08 .25
13 Billy Campfield .08 .25
14 Phil Tabor RC .08 .25
15 Randy Hughes UER RC .08 .25
(Cowboys didn't play
in SB VII)
16 Andre Tillman .08 .25
17 Isaac Curtis .20 .50
18 Charley Hannah .08 .25
19 Wash. Redskins TL .40 1.00
John Riggins
Danny Buggs
Joe Lavender
Coy Bacon
(checklist back)
20 Jim Zorn .20 .50
21 Brian Baschnagel .08 .25
22 Jon Keyworth .08 .25
23 Phil Villapiano .08 .25
24 Richard Osborne .08 .25
25 Rich Saul AP .08 .25
26 Doug Beaudoin .08 .25
27 Cleveland Elam .08 .25
28 Charlie Joiner .40 1.00
29 Dick Ambrose .08 .25
30 Mike Reinfeldt RC .08 .25
31 Matt Bahr RC .40 1.00
32 Keith Krepfle .08 .25
33 Herb Scott .08 .25
34 Doug Kotar .08 .25
35 Bob Griese .60 1.50
36 Jerry Butler RC .40 1.00
37 Rolland Lawrence .08 .25
38 Gary Weaver .08 .25
39 Kansas City Chiefs TL .20 .50
Ted McKnight
J.T. Smith
Gary Barbaro
Art Still
(checklist back)
40 Chuck Muncie .20 .50
41 Mike Hartenstine .08 .25
42 Sammie White .20 .50
43 Ken Clark .08 .25
44 Clarence Harmon .08 .25
45 Bert Jones .40 1.00
46 Mike Washington .08 .25
47 Joe Fields .08 .25
48 Mike Wood .08 .25
49 Oliver Davis .08 .25
50 Stan Walters AP .08 .25
51 Riley Odoms .08 .25
52 Steve Pisarkiewicz .08 .25
53 Tony Hill .40 1.00
54 Scott Perry .08 .25
55 George Martin RC .08 .25
56 George Roberts .08 .25
57 Seattle Seahawks TL .40 1.00
Sherman Smith
Steve Largent
Dave Brown
Manu Tuiasosopo
(checklist back)
58 Billy Johnson .20 .50
59 Reuben Gant .08 .25
60 Dennis Harrah RC .08 .25
61 Rocky Bleier .40 1.00
62 Sam Hunt .08 .25
63 Allan Ellis .08 .25
64 Ricky Thompson .08 .25
65 Ken Stabler 2.00 4.00
66 Dexter Bussey .08 .25
67 Ken Mendenhall .08 .25
68 Woodrow Lowe .08 .25
69 Thom Darden .08 .25
70 Randy White AP .60 1.50
71 Ken MacAfee .00 .25
72 Ron Jaworski .40 1.00
73 William Andrews RC .40 1.00
74 Jimmy Robinson .08 .25
75 Roger Wehrli AP .20 .50
76 Miami Dolphins TL .40 1.00
Larry Csonka
Nat Moore
Neal Colzie
Gerald Small
Vern Den Herder
(checklist back)
77 Jack Rudnay .08 .25
78 James Lofton .75 2.00
79 Robert Brazile .20 .50
80 Russ Francis .20 .50
81 Ricky Bell .40 1.00
82 Bob Avellini .20 .50
83 Bobby Jackson .08 .25
84 Mike Bragg .08 .25
85 Cliff Branch .40 1.00
86 Blair Bush .08 .25
87 Sherman Smith .08 .25
88 Glen Edwards .08 .25
89 Don Cockroft .08 .25
90 Louis Wright AP .20 .50
91 Randy Grossman .08 .25
92 Carl Hairston RC .40 1.00
93 Archie Manning .40 1.00
94 New York Giants TL .20 .50
Billy Taylor
Earnest Gray
George Martin
(checklist back)
95 Preston Pearson .20 .50
96 Rusty Chambers .08 .25
97 Greg Coleman .08 .25
98 Charle Young .08 .25
99 Matt Cavanaugh RC .20 .50
100 Jesse Baker .08 .25
101 Doug Plank .08 .25
102 Checklist 1-132 .30 .75
103 Luther Bradley RC .08 .25
104 Bob Kuziel .08 .25
105 Craig Morton .20 .50
106 Sherman White .08 .25
107 Jim Breech RC .20 .50
108 Hank Bauer .08 .25
109 Tom Blanchard .08 .25
110 Ozzie Newsome AP .75 2.00
111 Steve Furness .08 .25
112 Frank LeMaster .08 .25
113 Dallas Cowboys TL .40 1.00
Tony Dorsett
Tony Hill
Harvey Martin
(checklist back)
114 Doug Van Horn .08 .25
115 Delvin Williams .08 .25
116 Lyle Blackwood .08 .25
117 Derrick Gaffney .08 .25
118 Cornell Webster .08 .25
119 Sam Cunningham .20 .50
120 Jim Youngblood AP .20 .50
121 Bob Thomas .08 .25
122 Jack Thompson RC .20 .50
123 Randy Cross .40 1.00
124 Karl Lorch RC .08 .25
125 Mel Gray .08 .25
126 John James .08 .25
127 Terdell Middleton .08 .25
128 Leroy Jones .08 .25
129 Tom DeLeone .08 .25
130 John Stallworth AP .60 1.50
131 Jimmie Giles RC .20 .50
132 Philadelphia Eagles TL .40 1.00
Wilbert Montgomery
Harold Carmichael
Brenard Wilson
Carl Hairston
(checklist back)
133 Gary Green .08 .25
134 John Dutton .20 .50
135 Harry Carson AP .40 1.00
136 Bob Kuechenberg .20 .50
137 Ike Harris .08 .25
138 Tommy Kramer RC .40 1.00
139 Sam Adams OL .08 .25
140 Doug English AP .20 .50
141 Steve Schubert .08 .25
142 Rusty Jackson .08 .25
143 Reese McCall .08 .25
144 Scott Dierking .08 .25
145 Ken Houston AP .40 1.00
146 Bob Martin .08 .25
147 Sam McCullum .08 .25
148 Tom Banks .08 .25
149 Willie Buchanon .08 .25
150 Greg Pruitt .20 .50
151 Denver Broncos TL .40 1.00
Otis Armstrong
Rick Upchurch
Steve Foley
Brison Manor
(checklist back)
152 Don Smith RC .08 .25
153 Pete Johnson .20 .50
154 Charlie Smith WR .08 .25
155 Mel Blount .40 1.00
156 John Mendenhall .08 .25
157 Danny White .40 1.00
158 Jimmy Cefalo RC .20 .50
159 Richard Bishop AP .08 .25
160 Walter Payton AP 6.00 12.00
161 Dave Dalby .08 .25
162 Preston Dennard .08 .25
163 Johnnie Gray .08 .25
164 Russell Erxleben .08 .25
165 Toni Fritsch AP .08 .25
166 Terry Hermeling .08 .25
167 Roland Hooks .08 .25
168 Roger Carr .08 .25
169 San Diego Chargers TL .40 1.00
Clarence Williams
John Jefferson
Woodrow Lowe
Ray Preston
Wilbur Young
(checklist back)
170 Ottis Anderson RC 1.50 4.00
171 Brian Sipe .40 1.00
172 Leonard Thompson .08 .25
173 Tony Reed .08 .25
174 Bob Tucker .08 .25
175 Joe Greene .40 1.00
176 Jack Dolbin .08 .25
177 Chuck Ramsey .08 .25
178 Paul Hofer .08 .25
179 Randy Logan .08 .25
180 David Lewis AP .08 .25
181 Duriel Harris .08 .25
182 June Jones .20 .50
183 Larry McCarren .08 .25
184 Ken Johnson RB .08 .25
185 Charlie Waters .20 .50
186 Noah Jackson .08 .25
187 Reggie Williams .20 .50
188 New England Patriots TL .20 .50
Sam Cunningham
Harold Jackson
Raymond Clayborn
Tony McGee
(checklist back)
189 Carl Eller .40 1.00
190 Ed White AP .08 .25
191 Mario Clark .08 .25
192 Roosevelt Leaks .08 .25
193 Ted McKnight .08 .25
194 Danny Buggs .08 .25
195 Lester Hayes RC 1.50 4.00
196 Clarence Scott .08 .25
197 New Orleans Saints TL .20 .50
Chuck Muncie
Wes Chandler
Tom Myers
Elois Grooms
Don Reese
(checklist back)
198 Richard Caster .08 .25
199 Louie Giammona .08 .25
200 Terry Bradshaw 3.00 8.00
201 Ed Newman .08 .25
202 Fred Dryer .40 1.00
203 Dennis Franks .08 .25
204 Bob Breunig RC .20 .50
205 Alan Page .40 1.00
206 Earnest Gray RC .08 .25
207 Minnesota Vikings TL .40 1.00
Rickey Young
Ahmad Rashad
Tom Hannon
Nate Wright
Mark Mullaney
(checklist back)
208 Horace Ivory .08 .25
209 Isaac Hagins .08 .25
210 Gary Johnson AP .08 .25
211 Kevin Long .08 .25
212 Bill Thompson .08 .25
213 Don Bass .08 .25
214 George Starke RC .08 .25
215 Efren Herrera .08 .25
210 Theo Bell .08 .25
217 Monte Jackson .08 .25
218 Reggie McKenzie .08 .25
219 Bucky Dilts .08 .25
220 Lyle Alzado .40 1.00
221 Tim Foley .08 .25
222 Mark Arneson .08 .25
223 Fred Quillan .08 .25
224 Benny Ricardo .08 .25
225 Phil Simms RC 4.00 10.00
226 Chicago Bears TL .50 1.25
Walter Payton
Brian Baschnagel
Gary Fencik
Terry Schmidt
Jim Osborne
(checklist back)
227 Max Runager .08 .25
228 Barty Smith .08 .25
229 Jay Saldi .20 .50
230 John Hannah AP .40 1.00
231 Tim Wilson .08 .25
232 Jeff Van Note .08 .25
233 Henry Marshall .08 .25
234 Diron Talbert .08 .25
235 Garo Yepremian .20 .50
236 Larry Brown .08 .25
237 Clarence Williams RB .08 .25
238 Burgess Owens .08 .25
239 Vince Ferragamo .20 .50
240 Rickey Young .08 .25
241 Dave Logan .08 .25
242 Larry Gordon .08 .25
243 Terry Miller .08 .25
244 Baltimore Colts TL .40 1.00
Joe Washington
Joe Washington
Fred Cook
(checklist back)
245 Steve DeBerg .40 1.00
246 Checklist 133-264 .30 .75
247 Greg Latta .08 .25
248 Raymond Clayborn .20 .50
249 Jim Clack .08 .25
250 Drew Pearson .40 1.00
251 John Bunting .20 .50
252 Rob Lytle .08 .25
253 Jim Hart .40 1.00
254 John McDaniel .08 .25
255 Dave Pear AP .08 .25
256 Donnie Shell .40 1.00
257 Dan Doornink .08 .25
258 Wallace Francis RC .40 1.00
259 Dave Beverly .08 .25
260 Lee Roy Selmon AP .40 1.00
261 Doug Dieken .08 .25
262 Gary Davis .08 .25
263 Bob Rush .08 .25
264 Buffalo Bills TL .20 .50
Curtis Brown
Frank Lewis
Keith Moody
Sherman White
(checklist back)
265 Greg Landry .20 .50
266 Jan Stenerud .40 1.00
267 Tom Hicks .08 .25
268 Pat McInally .08 .25
269 Tim Fox .08 .25
270 Harvey Martin .20 .50
271 Dan Lloyd .08 .25
272 Mike Barber .08 .25
273 Wendell Tyler RC .40 1.00
274 Jeff Komlo .08 .25
275 Wes Chandler RC .40 1.00
276 Brad Dusek .08 .25
277 Charlie Johnson NT .08 .25
278 Dennis Swilley .08 .25
279 Johnny Evans .08 .25
280 Jack Lambert AP .60 1.50
281 Vern Den Herder .08 .25
282 Tampa Bay Bucs TL .40 1.00
Ricky Bell
Isaac Hagins
Lee Roy Selmon
(checklist back)
283 Bob Klein .08 .25
284 Jim Turner .08 .25
285 Marvin Powell AP .20 .50
286 Aaron Kyle .08 .25
287 Dan Neal .08 .25
288 Wayne Morris .08 .25
289 Steve Bartkowski .20 .50
290 Dave Jennings AP .20 .50
291 John Smith .08 .25
292 Bill Gregory .08 .25
293 Frank Lewis .08 .25
294 Fred Cook .08 .25
295 David Hill AP .08 .25
296 Wade Key .08 .25
297 Sidney Thornton .08 .25
298 Charlie Hall .08 .25
299 Joe Lavender .08 .25
300 Tom Rafferty RC .08 .25
301 Mike Renfro RC .20 .50
302 Wilbur Jackson .20 .50
303 Green Bay Packers TL .40 1.00
Terdell Middleton
James Lofton
Johnnie Gray
Robert Barber
Ezra Johnson
(checklist back)
304 Henry Childs .08 .25
305 Russ Washington AP .08 .25
306 Jim LeClair .08 .25
307 Tommy Hart .08 .25
308 Gary Barbaro .08 .25
309 Billy Taylor .08 .25
310 Ray Guy .20 .50
311 Don Hasselbeck RC .20 .50
312 Doug Williams .40 1.00
313 Nick Mike-Mayer .08 .25
314 Don McCauley .08 .25
315 Wesley Walker .40 1.00
316 Dan Dierdorf .40 1.00
317 Dave Brown RC .20 .50
318 Leroy Harris .08 .25
319 Pittsburgh Steelers TL .40 1.00
Franco Harris
John Stallworth
Jack Lambert
Steve Furness
L.C. Greenwood
(checklist back)
320 Mark Moseley AP UER .08 .25
321 Mark Dennard .08 .25
322 Terry Nelson .08 .25
323 Tom Jackson .40 1.00
324 Rick Kane .08 .25
325 Jerry Sherk .08 .25
326 Ray Preston .08 .25
327 Golden Richards .08 .25
328 Randy Dean .08 .25
329 Rick Danmeier .08 .25
330 Tony Dorsett 3.00 6.00
331 Passing Leaders 1.50 3.00
Dan Fouts
Roger Staubach
332 Receiving Leaders .20 .50
Joe Washington
Ahmad Rashad
333 Sacks Leaders .40 1.00
Jesse Baker
Al(Bubba) Baker
Jack Youngblood
334 Scoring Leaders .40 1.00
John Smith
Mark Moseley
335 Interception Leaders .40 1.00
Mike Reinfeldt
Lemar Parrish
336 Punting Leaders .40 1.00
Bob Grupp
Dave Jennings
337 Freddie Solomon .08 .25
338 Cincinnati Bengals TL .40 1.00
Pete Johnson
Don Bass
Dick Jauron
Gary Burley
(checklist back)
339 Ken Stone .08 .25
340 Greg Buttle AP .08 .25
341 Bob Baumhower .20 .50
342 Billy Waddy .08 .25
343 Cliff Parsley .08 .25
344 Walter White .08 .25
345 Mike Thomas .08 .25
346 Neil O'Donoghue .08 .25
347 Freddie Scott .08 .25
348 Joe Ferguson .20 .50
349 Doug Nettles .08 .25
350 Mike Webster AP .40 1.00
351 Ron Saul .08 .25
352 Julius Adams .08 .25
353 Rafael Septien .08 .25
354 Cleo Miller .08 .25
355 Keith Simpson AP .08 .25
356 Johnny Perkins .08 .25
357 Jerry Sisemore .08 .25
358 Arthur Whittington .08 .25
359 St. Louis Cardinals TL .40 1.00
Ottis Anderson
Pat Tilley
Ken Stone
Bob Pollard
(checklist back)
360 Rick Upchurch .20 .50
361 Kim Bokamper RC .08 .25
362 Roland Harper .08 .25
363 Pat Leahy .08 .25
364 Louis Breeden .08 .25
365 John Jefferson .40 1.00
366 Jerry Eckwood .08 .25
367 David Whitehurst .08 .25
368 Willie Parker C .08 .25
369 Ed Simonini .08 .25
370 Jack Youngblood AP .40 1.00
371 Don Warren RC .40 1.00
372 Andy Johnson .08 .25
373 D.D. Lewis .20 .50
374A Beasley Reece ERR RC .40 1.00
(No S in position
on front of card)
374B Beasley Reece COR RC .20 .50
375 L.C. Greenwood .40 1.00
376 Cleveland Browns TL .20 .50
377 Herman Edwards .08 .25
378 Rob Carpenter RC .08 .25
379 Herman Weaver .08 .25
380 Gary Fencik .08 .25
381 Don Strock .20 .50
382 Art Shell .40 1.00
383 Tim Mazzetti .08 .25

384 Bruce Harper .08 .25
385 Al (Bubba) Baker .20 .50
386 Conrad Dobler .08 .25
387 Stu Voigt .08 .25
388 Ken Anderson .40 1.00
389 Pat Tilley .08 .25
390 John Riggins .40 1.00
391 Checklist 265-396 .30 .75
392 Fred Dean .20 .50
393 Benny Barnes RC .08 .25
394 Los Angeles Rams TL .20 .50
395 Brad Van Pelt .08 .25
396 Eddie Hare .08 .25
397 John Sciarra RC .08 .25
398 Bob Jackson .08 .25
399 John Yarno .08 .25
400 Franco Harris AP .75 2.00
401 Ray Wersching .08 .25
402 Virgil Livers .08 .25
403 Raymond Chester .08 .25
404 Leon Gray .08 .25
405 Richard Todd .20 .50
406 Larry Little .40 1.00
407 Ted Fritsch Jr. .08 .25
408 Larry Mucker .08 .25
409 Jim Allen .08 .25
410 Randy Gradishar .40 1.00
411 Atlanta Falcons TL .40 1.00
William Andrews
Wallace Francis
Rolland Lawrence
Don Smith
(checklist back)
412 Louie Kelcher .20 .50
413 Robert Newhouse .20 .50
414 Gary Shirk .08 .25
415 Mike Haynes AP .40 1.00
416 Craig Colquitt .08 .25
417 Lou Piccone .08 .25
418 Clay Matthews RC 1.00 2.50
419 Marvin Cobb .08 .25
420 Harold Carmichael AP .40 1.00
421 Uwe Von Schamann RC .20 .50
422 Mike Phipps .20 .50
423 Nolan Cromwell RC .40 1.00
424 Glenn Doughty .08 .25
425 Bob Young AP .08 .25
426 Tony Galbreath .08 .25
427 Luke Prestridge RC .08 .25
428 Terry Beeson .08 .25
429 Jack Tatum .20 .50
430 Lemar Parrish AP .08 .25
431 Chester Marcol .08 .25
432 Houston Oilers TL .40 1.00
Dan Pastorini
Ken Burrough
Mike Reinfeldt
Jesse Baker
(checklist back)
433 John Fitzgerald .08 .25
434 Gary Jeter RC .20 .50
435 Steve Grogan .40 1.00
436 Jon Kolb UER .08 .25
437 Jim O'Bradovich UER .08 .25
438 Gerald Irons .08 .25
439 Jeff West .08 .25
440 Wilbert Montgomery .20 .50
441 Norris Thomas .08 .25
442 James Scott .08 .25
443 Curtis Brown .08 .25
444 Ken Fantetti .08 .25
445 Pat Haden .40 1.00
446 Carl Mauck .08 .25
447 Bruce Laird .08 .25
448 Otis Armstrong .08 .25
449 Gene Upshaw .40 1.00
450 Steve Largent AP 3.00 6.00
451 Benny Malone .08 .25
452 Steve Nelson .08 .25
453 Mark Cotney .08 .25
454 Joe Danelo .08 .25
455 Billy Joe DuPree .20 .50
456 Ron Johnson DB .08 .25
457 Archie Griffin .20 .50
458 Reggie Rucker .08 .25
459 Claude Humphrey .08 .25
460 Lydell Mitchell .20 .50
461 Steve Towle .08 .25
462 Revie Sorey .08 .25
463 Tom Skladany .08 .25
464 Clark Gaines .08 .25
465 Frank Corral .08 .25
466 Steve Fuller RC .20 .50
467 Ahmad Rashad AP .40 1.00
468 Oakland Raiders TL .40 1.00
Mark Van Eeghen
Cliff Branch
Lester Hayes
Willie Jones
(checklist back)
469 Brian Peets .08 .25
470 Pat Donovan RC .20 .50
471 Ken Burrough .08 .25
472 Don Calhoun .08 .25
473 Bill Bryan .08 .25
474 Terry Jackson .08 .25
475 Joe Theismann .50 1.25
476 Jim Smith .20 .50
477 Joe DeLamielleure .40 1.00
478 Mike Pruitt AP .20 .50
479 Steve Mike-Mayer .08 .25
480 Bill Bergey .20 .50
481 Mike Fuller .08 .25
482 Bob Parsons .08 .25
483 Billy Brooks .08 .25
484 Jerome Barkum .08 .25
485 Larry Csonka .60 1.50
486 John Hill .08 .25
487 Mike Dawson .08 .25
488 Detroit Lions TL .20 .50
Dexter Bussey
Freddie Scott
Jim Allen
Luther Bradley
Al(Bubba) Baker
(checklist back)
489 Ted Hendricks .40 1.00
490 Dan Pastorini .20 .50
491 Stanley Morgan .40 1.00
492 AFC Championship .40 1.00
Steelers 27,
Oilers 13
(Rocky Bleier running)
493 NFC Championship .20 .50
Rams 9,
Buccaneers 0
(Vince Ferragamo)
494 Super Bowl XIV .40 1.00
Steelers 31,
Rams 19
(line play)
495 Dwight White .20 .50
496 Haven Moses .08 .25
497 Guy Morriss .08 .25
498 Dewey Selmon .20 .50
499 Dave Butz RC .40 1.00
500 Chuck Foreman .20 .50
501 Chris Bahr .08 .25
502 Mark Miller QB .08 .25
503 Tony Greene .08 .25
504 Brian Kelley .08 .25
505 Joe Washington .20 .50
506 Butch Johnson .20 .50
507 New York Jets TL .20 .50
Clark Gaines
Wesley Walker
Burgess Owens
Joe Klecko
(checklist back0
508 Steve Little .08 .25
509 Checklist 397-528 .30 .75
510 Mark Van Eeghen .08 .25
511 Gary Danielson .20 .50
512 Manu Tuiasosopo .08 .25
513 Paul Coffman RC .20 .50
514 Cullen Bryant .08 .25
515 Nat Moore .20 .50
516 Bill Lenkaitis .08 .25
517 Lynn Cain RC .08 .25
518 Gregg Bingham .08 .25
519 Ted Albrecht .08 .25
520 Dan Fouts AP .75 2.00
521 Bernard Jackson .08 .25
522 Coy Bacon .08 .25
523 Tony Franklin RC .20 .50
524 Bo Harris .08 .25
525 Bob Grupp AP .08 .25
526 San Francisco 49ers TL .40 1.00
Paul Hofer
Freddie Solomon
James Owens
Dwaine Board
(checklist back)
527 Steve Wilson .08 .25
528 Bennie Cunningham .20 .50

1980 Topps Super

The 1980 Topps Superstar Photo Football set features 30 large (approximately 4 7/8" by 6 7/8") and very colorful cards. This set, a football counterpart to Topps' Superstar Photo Baseball set of the same year, is numbered and is printed on white stock. The cards in this set, sold over the counter without gum at retail establishments, could be individually chosen by the buyer.

COMPLETE SET (30) 7.50 15.00
1 Franco Harris .75 2.00
2 Bob Griese .75 2.00
3 Archie Manning .20 .50
4 Harold Carmichael .20 .50
5 Wesley Walker .20 .50
6 Richard Todd .15 .40
7 Dan Fouts .60 1.50
8 Ken Stabler 1.50 3.00
9 Jack Youngblood .20 .50
10 Jim Zorn .20 .50
11 Tony Dorsett 1.50 3.00
12 Lee Roy Selmon .30 .75
13 Russ Francis .15 .40
14 John Stallworth .30 .75
15 Terry Bradshaw 2.00 4.00
16 Joe Theismann .50 1.25
17 Ottis Anderson .30 .75
18 John Jefferson .30 .75
19 Jack Ham .30 .75
20 Joe Greene .40 1.00
21 Chuck Muncie .15 .40
22 Ron Jaworski .20 .50
23 John Hannah .20 .50
24 Randy Gradishar .15 .40
25 Jack Lambert .40 1.00
26 Ricky Bell .15 .40
27 Drew Pearson .30 .75
28 Rick Upchurch .15 .40
29 Brad Van Pelt .15 .40
30 Walter Payton 3.00 6.00

1980 Topps Team Checklists

These cards are essentially a parallel to the base 1980 Topps team checklist subset cards. The set was only available directly from Topps as a send-off offer in uncut sheet form. The prices below apply equally to uncut sheets as they are frequently found in their original uncut condition. As for individual cards, thin white card (almost paper-thin) stock makes it a challenge to find singles in top grades. We've cataloged the cards below for convenience in alphabetical order by team name.

COMPLETE SET (28) 50.00 100.00
19 Wash. Redskins TL 3.00 6.00
John Riggins
Danny Buggs
Joe Lavender
Coy Bacon
(checklist back)
39 Kansas City Chiefs TL 1.50 3.00
Ted McKnight
J.T. Smith
Gary Barbaro
Art Still
(checklist back)
57 Seattle Seahawks TL 3.00 6.00
Sherman Smith
Steve Largent
Dave Brown
Manu Tuiasosopo
(checklist back)
76 Miami Dolphins TL 3.00 6.00
Larry Csonka
Nat Moore
Neal Colzie
Gerald Small
Vern Den Herder
(checklist back)
94 New York Giants TL 1.50 3.00
Billy Taylor
Earnest Gray
George Martin
(checklist back)
113 Dallas Cowboys TL 4.00 8.00
Tony Dorsett
Tony Hill
Harvey Martin
(checklist back)
132 Philadelphia Eagles TL 2.00 4.00
Wilbert Montgomery
Harold Carmichael
Brenard Wilson
Carl Hairston
(checklist back)
151 Denver Broncos TL 2.00 4.00
Otis Armstrong
Rick Upchurch
Steve Foley
Brison Manor
(checklist back)
169 San Diego Chargers TL 2.00 4.00
Clarence Williams
John Jefferson
Woodrow Lowe
Ray Preston
Wilbur Young
(checklist back)
188 New England Patriots TL 1.50 3.00
Sam Cunningham
Harold Jackson
Raymond Clayborn
Tony McGee
(checklist back)
197 New Orleans Saints TL 1.50 3.00
Chuck Muncie
Wes Chandler
Tom Myers
Elois Grooms
Don Reese
(checklist back)
207 Minnesota Vikings TL 2.00 4.00
Rickey Young
Ahmad Rashad
Tom Hannon
Nate Wright
Mark Mullaney
(checklist back)
226 Chicago Bears TL 5.00 10.00
Walter Payton
Brian Baschnagel
Gary Fencik
Terry Schmidt
Jim Osborne
(checklist back)
244 Baltimore Colts TL 1.50 3.00
Joe Washington
Joe Washington
Fred Cook
(checklist back)
264 Buffalo Bills TL 1.50 3.00
Curtis Brown
Frank Lewis
Keith Moody
Sherman White
(checklist back)
282 Tampa Bay Bucs TL 2.00 4.00
Ricky Bell
Isaac Hagins
Lee Roy Selmon
(checklist back)
303 Green Bay Packers TL 2.00 4.00
Terdell Middleton
James Lofton
Johnnie Gray
Robert Barber
Ezra Johnson
(checklist back)
319 Pittsburgh Steelers TL 3.00 6.00
Franco Harris
John Stallworth
Jack Lambert
Steve Furness
L.C. Greenwood
(checklist back)
338 Cincinnati Bengals TL 3.00 6.00
Pete Johnson
Don Bass
Dick Jauron
Gary Burley
(checklist back)
359 St. Louis Cardinals TL 3.00 6.00
Ottis Anderson
Pat Tilley
Ken Stone
Bob Pollard
(checklist back)
376 Cleveland Browns TL 1.50 3.00
Mike Pruitt
Dave Logan
Thom Darden
Jerry Sherk
(checklist back)
394 Los Angeles Rams TL 2.00 4.00
Wendell Tyler
Preston Dennard
Nolan Cromwell
Jim Youngblood
Jack Youngblood
(checklist back)
411 Atlanta Falcons TL 2.00 4.00
William Andrews
Wallace Francis
Rolland Lawrence
Don Smith
(checklist back)
432 Houston Oilers TL 2.00 4.00
Dan Pastorini
Ken Burrough
Mike Reinfeldt
Jesse Baker
(checklist back)
468 Oakland Raiders TL 2.00 4.00
Mark Van Eeghen
Cliff Branch
Lester Hayes
Willie Jones
(checklist back)
488 Detroit Lions TL 1.50 3.00
Dexter Bussey
Freddie Scott
Jim Allen
Luther Bradley
Al(Bubba) Baker
(checklist back)
507 New York Jets TL 1.50 3.00
Clark Gaines
Wesley Walker
Burgess Owens
Joe Klecko
(checklist back0
526 San Francisco 49ers TL 2.00 4.00
Paul Hofer
Freddie Solomon
James Owens
Dwaine Board
(checklist back)

1981 Topps

The 1981 Topps football card set contains 528 standard-size cards. This set was issued in 15-card wax packs as well as rack packs and cello packs. The fronts have a pennant-like design at the bottom. This design includes the team name and the player's name. The player's position is also at the bottom. Horizontally designed backs contain year-by-year records, highlights and a cartoon. Super Action (SA) cards of top players are scattered throughout the set. Subsets include league leaders (1-6), Record Breakers (331-336) and playoffs (492-494). Team Leader (TL) cards feature statistical leaders on the front and a team checklist on the back. The key Rookie Card in this set is Joe Montana. Other Rookie Cards include Dwight Clark, Vince Evans, Dan Hampton, Art Monk, Eddie Murray, Billy Sims and Kellen Winslow.

COMPLETE SET (528) 100.00 200.00
1 Passing Leaders .40 1.00
Ron Jaworski
Brian Sipe
2 Receiving Leaders .40 1.00
Earl Cooper
Kellen Winslow
3 Sack Leaders .20 .50
Al(Bubba) Baker
Gary Johnson
4 Scoring Leaders .08 .25
Eddie Murray
John Smith
5 Interception Leaders .20 .50
Nolan Cromwell
Lester Hayes
6 Punting Leaders .08 .25
Dave Jennings
Luke Prestridge
7 Don Calhoun .08 .25
8 Jack Tatum .20 .50
9 Reggie Rucker .08 .25
10 Mike Webster AP .40 1.00
11 Vince Evans RC .40 1.00
12 Ottis Anderson SA .40 1.00
13 Leroy Harris .08 .25
14 Gordon King .08 .25
15 Harvey Martin .20 .50
16 Johnny Lam Jones RC .20 .50
17 Ken Greene .08 .25
18 Frank Lewis .08 .25
19 Seattle Seahawks TL .40 1.00
Jim Jodat
Dave Brown
John Harris
Steve Largent
Jacob Green
(checklist back)
20 Lester Hayes AP .40 1.00
21 Uwe Von Schamann .08 .25
22 Joe Washington .08 .25
23 Louie Kelcher .08 .25
24 Willie Miller .08 .25
25 Steve Grogan .40 1.00
26 John Hill .08 .25
27 Stan White .08 .25
28 William Andrews SA .20 .50
29 Clarence Scott .08 .25
30 Leon Gray AP .08 .25
31 Craig Colquitt .08 .25
32 Doug Williams .40 1.00
33 Bob Breunig .20 .50
34 Billy Taylor .08 .25
35 Harold Carmichael .40 1.00
36 Ray Wersching .08 .25
37 Dennis Johnson LB RC .08 .25
38 Archie Griffin .20 .50
39 Los Angeles Rams TL .20 .50
Cullen Bryant
Billy Waddy
Nolan Cromwell
Jack Youngblood
(checklist back)
40 Gary Fencik .20 .50
41 Lynn Dickey .08 .25
42 Steve Bartkowski SA .20 .50
43 Art Shell .40 1.00
44 Wilbur Jackson .08 .25
45 Frank Corral .08 .25
46 Ted McKnight .08 .25
47 Joe Klecko .20 .50
48 Dan Doornink .08 .25
49 Doug Dieken .08 .25
50 Jerry Robinson RC .20 .50
51 Wallace Francis .08 .25
52 Dave Preston RC .08 .25
53 Jay Saldi .08 .25
54 Rush Brown .08 .25
55 Phil Simms 1.00 2.50
56 Nick Mike-Mayer .08 .25
57 Wash. Redskins TL .75 ·2.00
Wilbur Jackson
Art Monk
Lemar Parrish
Coy Bacon
(checklist back)
58 Mike Renfro .08 .25
59 Ted Brown SA .08 .25
60 Steve Nelson .08 .25
61 Sidney Thornton .08 .25
62 Kent Hill .08 .25
63 Don Bessillieu .08 .25
64 Fred Cook .08 .25
65 Raymond Chester .08 .25
66 Rick Kane .08 .25
67 Mike Fuller .08 .25
68 Dewey Selmon .20 .50
69 Charles White RC .40 1.00
70 Jeff Van Note .08 .25
71 Robert Newhouse .20 .50
72 Roynell Young RC .08 .25
73 Lynn Cain SA .08 .25
74 Mike Friede .08 .25
75 Earl Cooper RC .08 .25
76 New Orleans Saints TL .20 .50
Jimmy Rogers
Wes Chandler
Tom Myers
Elois Grooms
Derland Moore
(checklist back)
77 Rick Danmeier .08 .25
78 Darrol Ray RC .08 .25
79 Gregg Bingham .08 .25
80 John Hannah AP .40 1.00
81 Jack Thompson .20 .50
82 Rick Upchurch .20 .50
83 Mike Butler .08 .25
84 Don Warren .08 .25
85 Mark Van Eeghen .08 .25
86 J.T. Smith RC .40 1.00
87 Herman Weaver .08 .25
88 Terry Bradshaw SA 1.00 2.50
89 Charlie Hall .08 .25
90 Donnie Shell .40 1.00
91 Ike Harris .08 .25
92 Charlie Johnson .08 .25
93 Rickey Watts .08 .25
94 New England Patriots TL .40 1.00
Vagas Ferguson
Stanley Morgan
Raymond Clayborn
Julius Adams
(checklist back)
95 Drew Pearson .40 1.00
96 Neil O'Donoghue .08 .25
97 Conrad Dobler .08 .25
98 Jewerl Thomas RC .08 .25
99 Mike Barber .08 .25
100 Billy Sims AP RC 1.25 3.00
101 Vern Den Herder .08 .25
102 Greg Landry .20 .50
103 Joe Cribbs SA .20 .50
104 Mark Murphy RC .08 .25
105 Chuck Muncie .20 .50
106 Alfred Jackson .20 .50
107 Chris Bahr .08 .25
108 Gordon Jones .08 .25
109 Willie Harper RC .08 .25
110 Dave Jennings .08 .25
111 Bennie Cunningham .08 .25
112 Jerry Sisemore .08 .25
113 Cleveland Browns TL .40 1.00
Mike Pruitt
Dave Logan
Ron Bolton
Lyle Alzado
(checklist back)
114 Rickey Young .08 .25
115 Ken Anderson .40 1.00
116 Randy Gradishar .40 1.00
117 Eddie Lee Ivery RC .08 .25
118 Wesley Walker .40 1.00
119 Chuck Foreman .20 .50
120 Nolan Cromwell AP .20 .50
UER (Rushing TD's
added wrong)
121 Curtis Dickey SA .08 .25
122 Wayne Morris .08 .25
123 Greg Stemrick .08 .25
124 Coy Bacon .08 .25
125 Jim Zorn .20 .50
(Steve Largent
in background)
126 Henry Childs .08 .25
127 Checklist 1-132 .40 1.00
128 Len Walterscheid .08 .25
129 Johnny Evans .08 .25
130 Gary Barbaro .08 .25
131 Jim Smith .08 .25
132 New York Jets TL .20 .50
Scott Dierking
Bruce Harper
Ken Schroy
Mark Gastineau
(checklist back)
133 Curtis Brown .08 .25
134 D.D. Lewis .08 .25
135 Jim Plunkett .40 1.00
136 Nat Moore .20 .50
137 Don McCauley .08 .25
138 Tony Dorsett SA .40 1.00
139 Julius Adams .08 .25
140 Ahmad Rashad AP .40 1.00
141 Rich Saul .08 .25
142 Ken Fantetti .08 .25
143 Kenny Johnson .08 .25
144 Clark Gaines .08 .25
145 Mark Moseley .08 .25
146 Vernon Perry RC .08 .25
147 Jerry Eckwood .08 .25
148 Freddie Solomon .08 .25
149 Jerry Sherk .08 .25
150 Kellen Winslow RC 4.00 8.00
151 Green Bay Packers TL .40 1.00
Eddie Lee Ivery
James Lofton
Johnnie Gray
Mike Butler
(checklist back)
152 Ross Browner .08 .25
153 Dan Fouts SA .40 1.00
154 Woody Peoples .08 .25
155 Jack Lambert .50 1.25
156 Mike Dennis .08 .25
157 Rafael Septien .08 .25
158 Archie Manning .40 1.00
159 Don Hasselbeck .08 .25
160 Alan Page AP .40 1.00
161 Arthur Whittington .08 .25
162 Billy Waddy .08 .25
163 Horace Belton .08 .25
164 Luke Prestridge .08 .25
165 Joe Theismann .50 1.25
166 Morris Towns .08 .25
167 Dave Brown .08 .25
168 Ezra Johnson .08 .25
169 Tampa Bay Bucs TL .08 .25
Ricky Bell
Gordon Jones
Mike Washington
Lee Roy Selmon
(checklist back)
170 Joe DeLamielleure .40 1.00
171 Earnest Gray SA .08 .25
172 Mike Thomas .08 .25
173 Jim Haslett RC .75 2.00
174 David Woodley RC .20 .50
175 Al(Bubba) Baker .20 .50
176 Nesby Glasgow RC .08 .25
177 Pat Leahy .08 .25
178 Tom Brahaney RC .08 .25
179 Herman Edwards .08 .25
180 Junior Miller AP RC .08 .25
181 Richard Wood RC .08 .25
182 Lenvil Elliott .08 .25
183 Sammie White .20 .50
184 Russell Erxleben .08 .25
185 Ed Too Tall Jones .50 1.25
186 Ray Guy SA .20 .50
187 Haven Moses .08 .25
188 New York Giants TL .20 .50
Billy Taylor
Earnest Gray
Mike Dennis
Gary Jeter
(checklist back)
189 David Whitehurst .08 .25
190 John Jefferson AP .40 1.00
191 Terry Beeson .08 .25
192 Dan Ross RC .20 .50
193 Dave Williams RB RC .08 .25
194 Art Monk RC 7.50 15.00
195 Roger Wehrli .20 .50
196 Ricky Feacher .08 .25
197 Miami Dolphins TL .40 1.00
Delvin Williams
Tony Nathan
Gerald Small
Kim Bokamper
A.J. Duhe
(checklist back)
198 Carl Roaches RC .08 .25
199 Billy Campfield .08 .25
200 Ted Hendricks AP .40 1.00
201 Fred Smerlas RC .40 1.00
202 Walter Payton SA 1.25 3.00
203 Luther Bradley .08 .25
204 Herb Scott .08 .25
205 Jack Youngblood .40 1.00
206 Danny Pittman .08 .25
207 Houston Oilers TL .20 .50
Carl Roaches
Mike Barber
Jack Tatum
Jesse Baker
Robert Brazile
(checklist back)
208 Vagas Ferguson RC .20 .50
209 Mark Dennard .08 .25
210 Lemar Parrish .08 .25
211 Bruce Harper .08 .25
212 Ed Simonini .08 .25
213 Nick Lowery RC .40 1.00
214 Kevin House RC .20 .50
215 Mike Kenn RC .40 1.00
216 Joe Montana RC 50.00 100.00
217 Joe Senser .08 .25
218 Lester Hayes SA .20 .50
219 Gene Upshaw .40 1.00
220 Franco Harris .60 1.50
221 Ron Bolton .08 .25
222 Charles Alexander RC .20 .50
223 Matt Robinson .08 .25
224 Ray Oldham .08 .25
225 George Martin .08 .25
226 Buffalo Bills TL .40 1.00
Joe Cribbs
Jerry Butler
Steve Freeman
Ben Williams
(checklist back)
227 Tony Franklin .08 .25
228 George Cumby .08 .25
229 Butch Johnson .20 .50
230 Mike Haynes .40 1.00
231 Rob Carpenter .20 .50
232 Steve Fuller .20 .50
233 John Sawyer .08 .25
234 Kenny King SA .08 .25
235 Jack Ham .50 1.25
236 Jimmy Rogers RC .08 .25
237 Bob Parsons .08 .25
238 Marty Lyons RC .40 1.00
239 Pat Tilley .08 .25
240 Dennis Harrah .08 .25
241 Thom Darden .08 .25
242 Rolf Benirschke .08 .25
243 Gerald Small .08 .25
244 Atlanta Falcons TL .40 1.00
William Andrews
Alfred Jenkins
Al Richardson
Joel Williams
(checklist back)
245 Roger Carr .08 .25
246 Sherman White .08 .25
247 Ted Brown .08 .25
248 Matt Cavanaugh .20 .50
249 John Dutton .08 .25
250 Bill Bergey AP .20 .50
251 Jim Allen .08 .25
252 Mike Nelms SA .08 .25
253 Tom Blanchard .08 .25
254 Ricky Thompson .08 .25
255 John Matuszak .20 .50
256 Randy Grossman .08 .25
257 Ray Griffin RC .08 .25
258 Lynn Cain .08 .25
259 Checklist 133-264 .40 1.00
260 Mike Pruitt .20 .50
261 Chris Ward RC .08 .25
262 Fred Steinfort .08 .25
263 James Owens .08 .25
264 Chicago Bears TL .60 1.50
Walter Payton
James Scott
Len Walterscheid
Dan Hampton
(checklist back)
265 Dan Fouts .60 1.50
266 Arnold Morgado .08 .25
267 John Jefferson SA .40 1.00
268 Bill Lenkaitis .08 .25
269 James Jones .08 .25
270 Brad Van Pelt .08 .25
271 Steve Largent 1.25 2.50
272 Elvin Bethea .40 1.00
273 Cullen Bryant .08 .25
274 Gary Danielson .20 .50
275 Tony Galbreath .08 .25
276 Dave Butz .08 .25
277 Steve Mike-Mayer .08 .25
278 Ron Johnson .08 .25
279 Tom DeLeone .08 .25
280 Ron Jaworski .40 1.00
281 Mel Gray .08 .25
282 San Diego Chargers TL .40 1.00
Chuck Muncie
John Jefferson
Glen Edwards
Gary Johnson
(checklist back)
283 Mark Brammer RC .08 .25
284 Alfred Jenkins SA .20 .50
285 Greg Buttle .08 .25
286 Randy Hughes .08 .25
287 Delvin Williams .08 .25
288 Brian Baschnagel .08 .25
289 Gary Jeter .08 .25
290 Stanley Morgan AP .40 1.00
291 Gerry Ellis .08 .25
292 Al Richardson .08 .25
293 Jimmie Giles .20 .50
294 Dave Jennings SA .08 .25
295 Wilbert Montgomery .20 .50
296 Dave Pureifory .08 .25
297 Greg Hawthorne .08 .25
298 Dick Ambrose .08 .25
299 Terry Hermeling .08 .25
300 Danny White .40 1.00
301 Ken Burrough .08 .25
302 Paul Hofer .08 .25
303 Denver Broncos TL .40 1.00
Jim Jensen
Haven Moses
Steve Foley
Rulon Jones
(checklist back)
304 Eddie Payton .20 .50
305 Isaac Curtis .20 .50
306 Benny Ricardo .08 .25
307 Riley Odoms .08 .25
308 Bob Chandler .08 .25
309 Larry Heater .08 .25
310 Art Still AP RC .40 1.00
311 Harold Jackson .20 .50
312 Charlie Joiner SA .40 1.00
313 Jeff Nixon .08 .25
314 Aundra Thompson .08 .25
315 Richard Todd .20 .50
316 Dan Hampton RC 1.25 3.00
317 Doug Marsh .08 .25
318 Louie Giammona .08 .25
319 San Francisco 49ers TL .40 1.00
Earl Cooper
Dwight Clark
Ricky Churchman
Dwight Hicks
Jim Stuckey
(checklist back)
320 Manu Tuiasosopo .08 .25
321 Rich Milot .08 .25
322 Mike Guman RC .08 .25
323 Bob Kuechenberg .20 .50
324 Tom Skladany .08 .25
325 Dave Logan .08 .25
326 Bruce Laird .08 .25
327 James Jones SA .08 .25
328 Joe Danelo .08 .25
329 Kenny King RC .20 .50
330 Pat Donovan .08 .25
331 Earl Cooper RB .20 .50
Most Receptions
Running Back;
Season: Rookie
332 John Jefferson RB .40 1.00
Most Consec. Seasons,/1000 Yards Receiving,
Start of Career
333 Kenny King RB .20 .50
Longest Pass Caught,
Super Bowl History
334 Rod Martin RB .20 .50
Most Interceptions
Super Bowl Game
335 Jim Plunkett RB .40 1.00
Longest Pass,
Super Bowl History
336 Bill Thompson RB .20 .50
Most Touchdowns,
Fumble Recoveries:
Lifetime
337 John Cappelletti .20 .50
338 Detroit Lions TL .40 1.00
Billy Sims
Freddie Scott
Jim Allen
James Hunter
Al(Bubba) Baker
(checklist back)
339 Don Smith .08 .25
340 Rod Perry .08 .25
341 David Lewis .08 .25
342 Mark Gastineau RC .50 1.25
343 Steve Largent SA .40 1.00
344 Charle Young .08 .25
345 Toni Fritsch .08 .25
346 Matt Blair .20 .50
347 Don Bass .08 .25
348 Jim Jensen RC .20 .50
349 Karl Lorch .08 .25
350 Brian Sipe AP .20 .50
351 Theo Bell .08 .25
352 Sam Adams .08 .25
353 Paul Coffman .08 .25
354 Eric Harris .08 .25
355 Tony Hill .20 .50
356 J.T. Turner .08 .25
357 Frank LeMaster .08 .25
358 Jim Jodat .08 .25
359 Oakland Raiders TL .40 1.00
Mark Van Eeghen
Cliff Branch
Lester Hayes
Cedrick Hardman
Ted Hendricks
(checklist back)
360 Joe Cribbs AP RC .40 1.00
361 James Lofton SA .40 1.00
362 Dexter Bussey .08 .25
363 Bobby Jackson .08 .25
364 Steve DeBerg .40 1.00
365 Ottis Anderson .40 1.00
366 Tom Myers .08 .25
367 John James .08 .25
368 Reese McCall .08 .25
369 Jack Reynolds .20 .50
370 Gary Johnson .08 .25
371 Jimmy Cefalo .08 .25
372 Horace Ivory .08 .25
373 Garo Yepremian .08 .25
374 Brian Kelley .08 .25
375 Terry Bradshaw 3.00 8.00
376 Dallas Cowboys TL .40 1.00
Tony Dorsett
Tony Hill
Dennis Thurman
Charlie Waters
Harvey Martin
(checklist back)
377 Randy Logan .08 .25
378 Tim Wilson .08 .25
379 Archie Manning SA .40 1.00
380 Revie Sorey .08 .25
381 Randy Holloway .08 .25
382 Henry Lawrence .08 .25
383 Pat McInally .08 .25
384 Kevin Long .08 .25
385 Louis Wright .20 .50
386 Leonard Thompson .08 .25
387 Jan Stenerud .20 .50
388 Raymond Butler RC .08 .25
389 Checklist 265-396 .40 1.00
390 Steve Bartkowski AP .20 .50
391 Clarence Harmon .08 .25
392 Wilbert Montgomery SA .20 .50
393 Billy Joe DuPree .20 .50
394 Kansas City Chiefs TL .20 .50
Ted McKnight
Henry Marshall
Gary Barbaro
Art Still
(checklist back)

395 Earnest Gray .08 .25
396 Ray Hamilton .08 .25
397 Brenard Wilson .08 .25
398 Calvin Hill .20 .50
399 Robin Cole .08 .25
400 Walter Payton 6.00 12.00
401 Jim Hart .40 1.00
402 Ron Yary .20 .50
403 Cliff Branch .40 1.00
404 Roland Hooks .08 .25
405 Ken Stabler 1.50 3.00
406 Chuck Ramsey .08 .25
407 Mike Nelms RC .08 .25
408 Ron Jaworski SA .20 .50
409 James Hunter .08 .25
410 Lee Roy Selmon AP .40 1.00
411 Baltimore Colts TL .20 .50
Curtis Dickey
Roger Carr
Bruce Laird
Mike Barnes
(checklist back)
412 Henry Marshall .08 .25
413 Preston Pearson .20 .50
414 Richard Bishop .08 .25
415 Greg Pruitt .20 .50
416 Matt Bahr .20 .50
417 Tom Mullady .08 .25
418 Glen Edwards .08 .25
419 Sam McCullum .08 .25
420 Stan Walters .08 .25
421 George Roberts .08 .25
422 Dwight Clark RC 2.00 5.00
423 Pat Thomas RC .08 .25
424 Bruce Harper SA .08 .25
425 Craig Morton .20 .50
426 Derrick Gaffney .08 .25
427 Pete Johnson .08 .25
428 Wes Chandler .40 1.00
429 Burgess Owens .08 .25
430 James Lofton AP .75 2.00
431 Tony Reed .08 .25
432 Minnesota Vikings TL .40 1.00
Ted Brown
Ahmad Rashad
John Turner
Doug Sutherland
(checklist back)
433 Ron Springs RC .20 .50
434 Tim Fox .08 .25
435 Ozzie Newsome .75 2.00
436 Steve Furness .08 .25
437 Will Lewis .08 .25
438 Mike Hartenstine .08 .25
439 John Bunting .08 .25
440 Eddie Murray RC .40 1.00
441 Mike Pruitt SA .20 .50
442 Larry Swider .08 .25
443 Steve Freeman .08 .25
444 Bruce Hardy RC .08 .25
445 Pat Haden .20 .50
446 Curtis Dickey RC .08 .25
447 Doug Wilkerson .08 .25
448 Alfred Jenkins .20 .50
449 Dave Dalby .08 .25
450 Robert Brazile .08 .25
451 Bobby Hammond .08 .25
452 Raymond Clayborn .08 .25
453 Jim Miller P RC .08 .25
454 Roy Simmons .08 .25
455 Charlie Waters .20 .50
456 Ricky Bell .40 1.00
457 Ahmad Rashad SA .40 1.00
458 Don Cockroft .08 .25
459 Keith Krepfle .08 .25
460 Marvin Powell .08 .25
461 Tommy Kramer .40 1.00
462 Jim LeClair .08 .25
463 Freddie Scott .08 .25
464 Rob Lytle .08 .25
465 Johnnie Gray .08 .25
466 Doug France RC .08 .25
467 Carlos Carson RC .20 .50
468 St. Louis Cardinals TL .40 1.00
Ottis Anderson
Pat Tilley
Ken Stone
Curtis Greer
Steve Neils
(checklist back)
469 Efren Herrera .08 .25
470 Randy White AP .50 1.25
471 Richard Caster .08 .25
472 Andy Johnson .08 .25
473 Billy Sims SA .40 1.00
474 Joe Lavender .08 .25
475 Harry Carson .20 .50
476 John Stallworth .50 1.25
477 Bob Thomas .08 .25
478 Keith Wright RC .08 .25
479 Ken Stone .08 .25
480 Carl Hairston .20 .50
481 Reggie McKenzie .08 .25
482 Bob Griese .60 1.50
483 Mike Bragg .08 .25
484 Scott Dierking .08 .25
485 David Hill .08 .25
486 Brian Sipe SA .20 .50
487 Rod Martin RC .20 .50
488 Cincinnati Bengals TL .20 .50
Pete Johnson
Dan Ross
Louis Breeden
Eddie Edwards
(checklist back)
489 Preston Dennard .08 .25
490 John Smith .08 .25
491 Mike Reinfeldt .08 .25
492 1980 NFC Champions .40 1.00
Eagles 20,
Cowboys 7
(Ron Jaworski)
493 1980 AFC Champions .40 1.00
Raiders 34,
Chargers 27
(Jim Plunkett)
494 Super Bowl XV .40 1.00
Raiders 27,
Eagles 10
(Plunkett handing
off to Kenny King)
495 Joe Greene .50 1.25
496 Charlie Joiner .40 1.00
497 Rolland Lawrence .08 .25
498 Al(Bubba) Baker SA .20 .50
499 Brad Dusek .08 .25
500 Tony Dorsett 2.00 4.00
501 Robin Earl .08 .25
502 Theotis Brown RC .08 .25
503 Joe Ferguson .20 .50
504 Beasley Reece .08 .25
505 Lyle Alzado .40 1.00
506 Tony Nathan RC .40 1.00
507 Philadelphia Eagles TL .20 .50
Wilbert Montgomery
Charlie Smith
Brenard Wilson
Claude Humphrey
(checklist back)
508 Herb Orvis .08 .25
509 Clarence Williams .08 .25
510 Ray Guy AP .20 .50
511 Jeff Komlo .08 .25
512 Freddie Solomon SA .08 .25
513 Tim Mazzetti .08 .25
514 Elvis Peacock RC .08 .25
515 Russ Francis .20 .50
516 Roland Harper .08 .25
517 Checklist 397-528 .40 1.00
518 Billy Johnson .20 .50
519 Dan Dierdorf .40 1.00
520 Fred Dean .20 .50
521 Jerry Butler .08 .25
522 Ron Saul .08 .25
523 Charlie Smith .08 .25
524 Kellen Winslow SA 1.50 3.00
525 Bert Jones .40 1.00
526 Pittsburgh Steelers TL .40 1.00
Franco Harris
Theo Bell
Donnie Shell
L.C. Greenwood
(checklist back)
527 Duriel Harris .08 .25
528 William Andrews .40 1.00

1981 Topps Team Checklists

These cards are essentially a parallel to the base 1981 Topps team checklist subset cards. The set was only available directly from Topps as a send-off offer in uncut sheet form. The prices below apply equally to uncut sheets as they are frequently found in their original uncut condition. As for individual cards, thin white card (almost paper-thin) stock makes it a challenge to find singles in top grades. We've cataloged the cards below for convenience in alphabetical order by team name.

COMPLETE SET (28) 40.00 100.00
19 Seattle Seahawks TL 2.00 5.00
Jim Jodat
Dave Brown
John Harris
Steve Largent
Jacob Green
(checklist back)
39 Los Angeles Rams TL 1.50 4.00
Cullen Bryant
Billy Waddy
Nolan Cromwell
Jack Youngblood
(checklist back)
57 Wash. Redskins TL 2.00 5.00
Wilbur Jackson
Art Monk
Lemar Parrish
Coy Bacon
(checklist back)
76 New Orleans Saints TL 1.50 4.00
Jimmy Rogers
Wes Chandler
Tom Myers
Elois Grooms
Derland Moore
(checklist back)
94 New England Patriots TL 1.25 3.00
Vagas Ferguson
Stanley Morgan
Raymond Clayborn
Julius Adams
(checklist back)
113 Cleveland Browns TL 1.50 4.00
Mike Pruitt
Dave Logan
Ron Bolton
Lyle Alzado
(checklist back)
132 New York Jets TL 1.25 3.00
Scott Dierking
Bruce Harper
Ken Schroy
Mark Gastineau
(checklist back)
151 Green Bay Packers TL 2.00 5.00
Eddie Lee Ivery
James Lofton
Johnnie Gray
Mike Butler
(checklist back)
169 Tampa Bay Buccaneers TL 1.50 4.00
Ricky Bell
Gordon Jones
Mike Washington
Lee Roy Selmon
(checklist back)
188 New York Giants TL 1.25 3.00
Billy Taylor
Earnest Gray
Mike Dennis
Gary Jeter
(checklist back)
197 Miami Dolphins TL 1.50 4.00
Delvin Williams
Tony Nathan
Gerald Small
Kim Bokamper
A.J. Duhe
(checklist back)
207 Houston Oilers TL 1.25 3.00
Carl Roaches
Mike Barber
Jack Tatum
Jesse Baker
Robert Brazile
(checklist back)
226 Buffalo Bills TL 1.50 4.00
Joe Cribbs
Jerry Butler
Steve Freeman
Ben Williams
(checklist back)
244 Atlanta Falcons TL 1.50 4.00
William Andrews
Alfred Jenkins
Al Richardson
Joel Williams
(checklist back)
264 Chicago Bears TL 3.00 8.00
Walter Payton
James Scott
Len Walterscheid
Dan Hampton
(checklist back)
282 San Diego Chargers TL 1.50 4.00
Chuck Muncie
John Jefferson
Glen Edwards
Gary Johnson
(checklist back)
303 Denver Broncos TL 1.50 4.00
Jim Jensen
Haven Moses
Steve Foley
Rulon Jones
(checklist back)
319 San Francisco 49ers TL 1.50 4.00
Earl Cooper
Dwight Clark
Ricky Churchman
Dwight Hicks
Jim Stuckey
(checklist back)
338 Detroit Lions TL 1.50 4.00
Billy Sims
Freddie Scott
Jim Allen
James Hunter
Al(Bubba) Baker
(checklist back)
359 Oakland Raiders TL 2.00 5.00
Mark Van Eeghen
Cliff Branch
Lester Hayes
Cedrick Hardman
Ted Hendricks
(checklist back)
376 Dallas Cowboys TL 2.50 6.00
Tony Dorsett
Tony Hill
Dennis Thurman
Charlie Waters
Harvey Martin
(checklist back)
394 Kansas City Chiefs TL 1.25 3.00
Ted McKnight
Henry Marshall
Gary Barbaro
Art Still
(checklist back)
411 Baltimore Colts TL 1.25 3.00
Curtis Dickey
Roger Carr
Bruce Laird
Mike Barnes
(checklist back)
432 Minnesota Vikings TL 1.50 4.00
Ted Brown
Ahmad Rashad
John Turner
Doug Sutherland
(checklist back)
468 St. Louis Cardinals TL 1.50 4.00
Ottis Anderson
Pat Tilley
Ken Stone
Curtis Greer
Steve Neils
(checklist back)
488 Cincinnati Bengals TL 1.25 3.00
Pete Johnson
Dan Ross
Louis Breeden
Eddie Edwards
(checklist back)
507 Philadelphia Eagles TL 1.25 3.00
Wilbert Montgomery
Charlie Smith
Brenard Wilson
Claude Humphrey
(checklist back)
526 Pittsburgh Steelers TL 2.00 5.00
Franco Harris
Theo Bell
Donnie Shell
L.C. Greenwood
(checklist back)

1981 Topps Thirst Break

This 56-card set is actually a set of gum wrappers. These wrappers were issued in Thirst Break Orange Gum, which was reportedly only distributed in Pennsylvania and Ohio. Each of these small gum wrappers has a cartoon-type image of a particular great moment in sports. As the checklist below shows, many different sports are represented in this set. The wrappers each measure approximately 2 9/16" by 1 5/8". The wrappers are numbered in small print at the top. The backs of the wrappers are blank. The "1981 Topps" copyright is at the bottom of each card.

COMPLETE SET (56) 60.00 150.00
29 Garo Yepremian .40 1.00
30 Bert Jones .75 2.00
31 Norm Van Brocklin 1.00 2.50
32 Fran Tarkenton 2.00 5.00
33 Johnny Unitas 2.00 5.00
36 Bart Starr 2.00 5.00
37 O.J. Simpson .75 2.00
38 Jim Brown 2.00 5.00
Football Fact
39 Jim Marshall 1.00 2.50
40 George Blanda 1.00 2.50
41 Jack Tatum 1.00 2.50
42 Jim Brown UER 2.00 5.00
Touchdown Record
(Tim Brown on card)
48 Tom Dempsey .60 1.50
49 Gale Sayers 1.60 4.00

1982 Topps

The 1982 Topps football set features 528 standard-size cards and marked a breakthrough of sorts. Wax packs contained 15 cards. Licensed by NFL Properties for the first time, Topps was able to use team logos within its photos. Previously, logos on helmets were airbrushed. Card fronts contained a team helmet at bottom left and the player's name and position within a color banner at bottom right. Horizontally designed backs featured yearly statistics and highlights. Subsets include Record Breakers (1-6), playoffs (7-9), league leaders (257-262) and brothers (263-270). In-Action (IA) cards of top players are scattered throughout the set. Team Leader (TL) cards feature statistical leaders on the front as well as a team checklist on the back. The set is organized in team order alphabetically by team within conference (and with players within teams in alphabetical order). Rookie Cards include James Brooks, Cris Collinsworth, Drew Hill, Ronnie Lott, Freeman McNeil, Anthony Munoz and Lawrence Taylor.

COMPLETE SET (528) 40.00 80.00
1 Ken Anderson RB .40 1.00
Most Completions
Super Bowl Game
2 Dan Fouts RB .40 1.00
Most Passing Yards
Playoff Game
3 LeRoy Irvin RB .08 .25
Most Punt Return
Yardage: Game
4 Stump Mitchell RB .08 .25
Most Return
Yardage: Season
5 George Rogers RB .40 1.00
Most Rushing Yards:
Rookie Season
6 Dan Ross RB .08 .25
Most Receptions:
Super Bowl Game
7 AFC Championship .40 1.00
Bengals 27,
Chargers 7
(Ken Anderson
handing off to
Pete Johnson)
8 NFC Championship/49ers 28, .40 1.00
Cowboys 27
(Earl Cooper)
9 Super Bowl XVI/49ers 26, .40 1.00
Bengals 7
(Anthony Munoz
blocking)
10 Baltimore Colts TL .08 .25
Curtis Dickey
Raymond Butler
Larry Braziel
Bruce Laird
11 Raymond Butler .08 .25
12 Roger Carr .08 .25
13 Curtis Dickey .20 .50
14 Zachary Dixon .08 .25
15 Nesby Glasgow .08 .25
16 Bert Jones .40 1.00
17 Bruce Laird .08 .25
18 Reese McCall .08 .25
19 Randy McMillan .08 .25
20 Ed Simonini .08 .25
21 Buffalo Bills TL .20 .50
Joe Cribbs
Frank Lewis
Mario Clark
Fred Smerlas
22 Mark Brammer .08 .25
23 Curtis Brown .08 .25
24 Jerry Butler .08 .25
25 Mario Clark .08 .25
26 Joe Cribbs .20 .50
27 Joe Cribbs IA .20 .50
28 Joe Ferguson .20 .50
29 Jim Haslett .40 1.00
30 Frank Lewis .08 .25
31 Frank Lewis IA .08 .25
32 Shane Nelson .08 .25
33 Charles Romes .08 .25
34 Bill Simpson .08 .25
35 Fred Smerlas .08 .25
36 Cincinnati Bengals TL .20 .50
Pete Johnson
Cris Collinsworth
Ken Riley
Reggie Williams
37 Charles Alexander .08 .25
38 Ken Anderson AP .40 1.00
39 Ken Anderson IA .40 1.00
40 Jim Breech .08 .25
41 Jim Breech IA .08 .25
42 Louis Breeden .08 .25
43 Ross Browner .08 .25
44 Cris Collinsworth RC .75 2.00
45 Cris Collinsworth IA .40 1.00
46 Isaac Curtis .08 .25
47 Pete Johnson .08 .25
48 Pete Johnson IA .08 .25
49 Steve Kreider .08 .25
50 Pat McInally .08 .25
51 Anthony Munoz RC 4.00 8.00
52 Dan Ross .08 .25
53 David Verser RC .08 .25
54 Reggie Williams .08 .25
55 Cleveland Browns TL .20 .50
Mike Pruitt
Ozzie Newsome
Clarence Scott
Lyle Alzado
56 Lyle Alzado .40 1.00
57 Dick Ambrose .08 .25
58 Ron Bolton .08 .25
59 Steve Cox .08 .25
60 Joe DeLamielleure .40 1.00
61 Tom DeLeone .08 .25
62 Doug Dieken .08 .25
63 Ricky Feacher .08 .25
64 Don Goode .08 .25
65 Robert L. Jackson RC .08 .25
66 Dave Logan .08 .25
67 Ozzie Newsome .50 1.25
68 Ozzie Newsome IA .40 1.00
69 Greg Pruitt .20 .50
70 Mike Pruitt .20 .50
71 Mike Pruitt IA .20 .50
72 Reggie Rucker .08 .25
73 Clarence Scott .08 .25
74 Brian Sipe .20 .50
75 Charles White .20 .50
76 Denver Broncos TL .20 .50
Rick Parros
Steve Watson
Steve Foley
Rulon Jones
77 Rubin Carter .08 .25
78 Steve Foley .08 .25
79 Randy Gradishar .20 .50
80 Tom Jackson .40 1.00
81 Craig Morton .20 .50
82 Craig Morton IA .20 .50
83 Riley Odoms .08 .25
84 Rick Parros .08 .25
85 Dave Preston .08 .25
86 Tony Reed .08 .25
87 Bob Swenson RC .08 .25
88 Bill Thompson .08 .25
89 Rick Upchurch .20 .50
90 Steve Watson RC .20 .50
91 Steve Watson IA .08 .25
92 Houston Oilers TL .08 .25
Carl Roaches
Ken Burrough
Carter Hartwig
Greg Stemrick
Jesse Baker
93 Mike Barber .08 .25
94 Elvin Bethea .40 1.00
95 Gregg Bingham .08 .25
96 Robert Brazile .08 .25
97 Ken Burrough .08 .25
98 Toni Fritsch .08 .25
99 Leon Gray .08 .25
100 Gifford Nielsen RC .20 .50
101 Vernon Perry .08 .25
102 Mike Reinfeldt .08 .25
103 Mike Renfro .08 .25
104 Carl Roaches .08 .25
105 Ken Stabler .75 2.00
106 Greg Stemrick .08 .25
107 J.C. Wilson .08 .25
108 Tim Wilson .08 .25
109 Kansas City Chiefs TL .08 .25
Joe Delaney
J.T. Smith
Eric Harris
Ken Kremer
110 Gary Barbaro .08 .25
111 Brad Budde RC .08 .25
112 Joe Delaney AP RC .40 1.00
113 Joe Delaney IA .20 .50
114 Steve Fuller .20 .50
115 Gary Green .08 .25
116 James Hadnot .08 .25
117 Eric Harris .08 .25
118 Billy Jackson .08 .25
119 Bill Kenney RC .20 .50
120 Nick Lowery AP .40 1.00
121 Nick Lowery IA .20 .50
122 Henry Marshall .08 .25
123 J.T. Smith .20 .50
124 Art Still .08 .25
125 Miami Dolphins TL .20 .50
Tony Nathan
Duriel Harris
Glenn Blackwood
Bob Baumhower
126 Bob Baumhower .20 .50
127 Glenn Blackwood RC .08 .25
128 Jimmy Cefalo .08 .25
129 A.J. Duhe .20 .50
130 Andra Franklin RC .08 .25
131 Duriel Harris .08 .25
132 Nat Moore .20 .50
133 Tony Nathan .20 .50
134 Ed Newman .08 .25
135 Earnie Rhone .08 .25
136 Don Strock .08 .25
137 Tommy Vigorito .08 .25
138 Uwe Von Schamann .08 .25
139 Uwe Von Schamann IA .08 .25
140 David Woodley .20 .50
141 New England Pats TL .20 .50
Tony Collins
Stanley Morgan
Tim Fox
Rick Sanford
Tony McGee
142 Julius Adams .08 .25
143 Richard Bishop .08 .25
144 Matt Cavanaugh .08 .25
145 Raymond Clayborn .08 .25
146 Tony Collins RC .08 .25
147 Vagas Ferguson .08 .25
148 Tim Fox .08 .25
149 Steve Grogan .20 .50
150 John Hannah AP .40 1.00
151 John Hannah IA .20 .50
152 Don Hasselbeck .08 .25
153 Mike Haynes .20 .50
154 Harold Jackson .20 .50
155 Andy Johnson .08 .25
156 Stanley Morgan .20 .50
157 Stanley Morgan IA .20 .50
158 Steve Nelson .08 .25
159 Rod Shoate RC .08 .25
160 New York Jets TL .20 .50
Freeman McNeil
Wesley Walker
Darrol Ray
Joe Klecko
161 Dan Alexander RC .08 .25
162 Mike Augustyniak .08 .25
163 Jerome Barkum .08 .25
164 Greg Buttle .08 .25
165 Scott Dierking .08 .25
166 Joe Fields .08 .25
167 Mark Gastineau AP .20 .50
168 Mark Gastineau IA .20 .50
169 Bruce Harper .08 .25
170 Johnny Lam Jones .08 .25
171 Joe Klecko AP .20 .50
172 Joe Klecko IA .20 .50
173 Pat Leahy .20 .50
174 Pat Leahy IA .08 .25
175 Marty Lyons .20 .50
176 Freeman McNeil RC .40 1.00
177 Marvin Powell .08 .25
178 Chuck Ramsey .08 .25
179 Darrol Ray .08 .25
180 Abdul Salaam .08 .25
181 Richard Todd .20 .50
182 Richard Todd IA .20 .50
183 Wesley Walker .20 .50
184 Chris Ward .08 .25
185 Oakland Raiders TL .20 .50
Kenny King
Derrick Ramsey
Lester Hayes
Odis McKinney
Rod Martin
186 Cliff Branch .40 1.00
187 Bob Chandler .08 .25
188 Ray Guy .20 .50
189 Lester Hayes .20 .50
190 Ted Hendricks AP .40 1.00
191 Monte Jackson .08 .25
192 Derrick Jensen .08 .25
193 Kenny King .08 .25
194 Rod Martin .08 .25
195 John Matuszak .08 .25
196 Matt Millen RC .60 1.50
197 Derrick Ramsey .08 .25
198 Art Shell .40 1.00
199 Mark Van Eeghen .08 .25
200 Arthur Whittington .08 .25
201 Marc Wilson RC .20 .50
202 Pittsburgh Steelers TL .40 1.00
Franco Harris
John Stallworth
Mel Blount
Jack Lambert
Gary Dunn
203 Mel Blount AP .40 1.00
204 Terry Bradshaw 2.00 5.00
205 Terry Bradshaw IA .75 2.00
206 Craig Colquitt .08 .25
207 Bennie Cunningham .08 .25
208 Russell Davis RC .08 .25
209 Gary Dunn .08 .25
210 Jack Ham .40 1.00
211 Franco Harris .50 1.25
212 Franco Harris IA .40 1.00
213 Jack Lambert AP .40 1.00
214 Jack Lambert IA .40 1.00
215 Mark Malone RC .40 1.00
216 Frank Pollard RC .08 .25
217 Donnie Shell AP .40 1.00
218 Jim Smith .08 .25
219 John Stallworth .40 1.00
220 John Stallworth IA .40 1.00
221 David Trout .08 .25
222 Mike Webster AP .40 1.00
223 San Diego Chargers TL .40 1.00
Chuck Muncie
Charlie Joiner
Willie Buchanon
Gary Johnson
224 Rolf Benirschke .08 .25
225 Rolf Benirschke IA .08 .25
226 James Brooks RC .40 1.00
227 Willie Buchanon .08 .25
228 Wes Chandler .40 1.00
229 Wes Chandler IA .20 .50
230 Dan Fouts .50 1.25
231 Dan Fouts IA .40 1.00
232 Gary Johnson .08 .25
233 Charlie Joiner .40 1.00
234 Charlie Joiner IA .40 1.00
235 Louie Kelcher .08 .25
236 Chuck Muncie .20 .50
237 Chuck Muncie IA .08 .25
238 George Roberts .08 .25
239 Ed White .08 .25
240 Doug Wilkerson .08 .25
241 Kellen Winslow AP .75 2.00
242 Kellen Winslow IA .40 1.00
243 Seattle Seahawks TL .40 1.00
Theotis Brown
Steve Largent
John Harris
Jacob Green
244 Theotis Brown .08 .25
245 Dan Doornink .08 .25
246 John Harris .08 .25
247 Efren Herrera .08 .25
248 David Hughes .08 .25
249 Steve Largent .75 2.00
250 Steve Largent IA .40 1.00
251 Sam McCullum .08 .25
252 Sherman Smith .08 .25
253 Manu Tuiasosopo .08 .25
254 John Yarno .08 .25
255 Jim Zorn .20 .50
(Sitting with Dave Krieg)
256 Jim Zorn IA .20 .50
257 Passing Leaders 2.00 4.00
Ken Anderson
Joe Montana
258 Receiving Leaders .40 1.00
Kellen Winslow
Dwight Clark
259 QB Sack Leaders .08 .25
Joe Klecko
Curtis Greer
260 Scoring Leaders .20 .50
Jim Breech
Nick Lowery
Eddie Murray
Rafael Septien
261 Interception Leaders .20 .50
John Harris
Everson Walls
262 Punting Leaders .08 .25
Pat McInally
Tom Skladany
263 Brothers: Bahr .08 .25
Chris and Matt
264 Brothers: Blackwood .20 .50
Lyle and Glenn
265 Brothers: Brock .08 .25
Pete and Stan
266 Brothers: Griffin .20 .50
Archie and Ray
267 Brothers: Hannah .40 1.00
John and Charley
268 Brothers: Jackson .08 .25
Monte and Terry
269 Walter .50 1.25
Eddie Payton
270 Brothers: Selmon .40 1.00
Dewey and Lee Roy
271 Atlanta Falcons TL .20 .50
William Andrews
Alfred Jenkins
Tom Pridemore
Al Richardson
272 William Andrews .20 .50
273 William Andrews IA .20 .50
274 Steve Bartkowski .20 .50
275 Steve Bartkowski IA .20 .50
276 Bobby Butler RC .08 .25
277 Lynn Cain .08 .25
278 Wallace Francis .08 .25
279 Alfred Jackson .08 .25
280 John James .08 .25
281 Alfred Jenkins .08 .25
282 Alfred Jenkins IA .08 .25
283 Kenny Johnson .08 .25
284 Mike Kenn AP .40 1.00
285 Fulton Kuykendall .08 .25
286 Mick Luckhurst RC .08 .25
287 Mick Luckhurst IA .08 .25
288 Junior Miller .08 .25
289 Al Richardson .08 .25
290 R.C. Thielemann RC .08 .25
291 Jeff Van Note .08 .25
292 Chicago Bears TL .40 1.00
Walter Payton
Ken Margerum
Gary Fencik
Dan Hampton
Alan Page
293 Brian Baschnagel .08 .25
294 Robin Earl .08 .25
295 Vince Evans .20 .50
296 Gary Fencik .08 .25
297 Dan Hampton .40 1.00
298 Noah Jackson .08 .25
299 Ken Margerum .08 .25
300 Jim Osborne .08 .25
301 Bob Parsons .08 .25
302 Walter Payton 4.00 10.00
303 Walter Payton IA 1.50 4.00
304 Revie Sorey .08 .25
305 Matt Suhey RC .60 1.50
(Walter Payton
in background)
306 Rickey Watts .08 .25
307 Dallas Cowboys TL .40 1.00
Tony Dorsett
Tony Hill
Everson Walls
Harvey Martin
308 Bob Breunig .08 .25
309 Doug Cosbie RC .08 .25
310 Pat Donovan .08 .25
311 Tony Dorsett AP .75 2.00
312 Tony Dorsett IA .40 1.00
313 Michael Downs RC .08 .25
314 Billy Joe DuPree .20 .50
315 John Dutton .08 .25
316 Tony Hill .20 .50
317 Butch Johnson .20 .50
318 Ed Too Tall Jones AP .40 1.00
319 James Jones .08 .25
320 Harvey Martin .20 .50
321 Drew Pearson .40 1.00
322 Herb Scott AP .08 .25
323 Rafael Septien .08 .25
324 Rafael Septien IA .08 .25
325 Ron Springs .20 .50
326 Dennis Thurman RC .08 .25
327 Everson Walls RC .40 1.00
328 Everson Walls IA .40 1.00
329 Danny White .40 1.00
330 Danny White IA .20 .50
331 Randy White AP .40 1.00
332 Randy White IA .40 1.00
333 Detroit Lions TL .20 .50
Billy Sims
Freddie Scott
Jim Allen
Dave Pureifory
334 Jim Allen .08 .25
335 Al(Bubba) Baker .20 .50
336 Dexter Bussey .08 .25
337 Doug English .20 .50
338 Ken Fantetti .08 .25
339 William Gay .08 .25
340 David Hill .08 .25
341 Eric Hipple RC .08 .25
342 Rick Kane .08 .25
343 Ed Murray .40 1.00
344 Ed Murray IA .20 .50
345 Ray Oldham .08 .25
346 Dave Pureifory .08 .25
347 Freddie Scott .08 .25
348 Freddie Scott IA .08 .25
349 Billy Sims AP .40 1.00
350 Billy Sims IA .40 1.00
351 Tom Skladany .08 .25
352 Leonard Thompson .08 .25
353 Stan White .08 .25
354 Green Bay Packers TL .40 1.00
Gerry Ellis
James Lofton
Maurice Harvey
Mark Lee
Mike Butler
355 Paul Coffman .08 .25
356 George Cumby .08 .25
357 Lynn Dickey .08 .25
358 Lynn Dickey IA .08 .25
359 Gerry Ellis .08 .25
360 Maurice Harvey .08 .25
361 Harlan Huckleby .08 .25
362 John Jefferson .40 1.00
363 Mark Lee RC .08 .25
364 James Lofton AP .50 1.25
365 James Lofton IA .40 1.00
366 Jan Stenerud .20 .50
367 Jan Stenerud IA .20 .50
368 Rich Wingo .08 .25
369 Los Angeles Rams TL .20 .50
Wendell Tyler
Preston Dennard
Nolan Cromwell
Jack Youngblood
370 Frank Corral .08 .25
371 Nolan Cromwell AP .20 .50
372 Nolan Cromwell IA .20 .50
373 Preston Dennard .08 .25
374 Mike Fanning .08 .25
375 Doug France .08 .25
376 Mike Guman .08 .25
377 Pat Haden .20 .50
378 Dennis Harrah .08 .25
379 Drew Hill RC .40 1.00
380 LeRoy Irvin RC .20 .50
381 Cody Jones .08 .25
382 Rod Perry .08 .25
383 Rich Saul .08 .25
384 Pat Thomas .08 .25
385 Wendell Tyler .20 .50
386 Wendell Tyler IA .20 .50
387 Billy Waddy .08 .25
388 Jack Youngblood .40 1.00
389 Minnesota Vikings TL .08 .25
Ted Brown
Joe Senser
Tom Hannon
Willie Teal
Matt Blair
390 Matt Blair .08 .25
391 Ted Brown .08 .25
392 Ted Brown IA .08 .25
393 Rick Danmeier .08 .25
394 Tommy Kramer .20 .50
395 Mark Mullaney .08 .25
396 Eddie Payton .08 .25
397 Ahmad Rashad .40 1.00
398 Joe Senser .08 .25
399 Joe Senser IA .08 .25
400 Sammie White .20 .50
401 Sammie White IA .20 .50
402 Ron Yary .40 1.00
403 Rickey Young .08 .25
404 New Orleans Saints TL .30 .75
George Rogers
Guido Merkens
Dave Waymer
Rickey Jackson
405 Russell Erxleben .08 .25
406 Elois Grooms .08 .25
407 Jack Holmes .08 .25
408 Archie Manning .40 1.00
409 Derland Moore RC .08 .25
410 George Rogers RC .40 1.00
411 George Rogers IA .40 1.00
412 Toussaint Tyler .08 .25
413 Dave Waymer RC .08 .25
414 Wayne Wilson .08 .25
415 New York Giants TL .08 .25
Rob Carpenter
Johnny Perkins
Beasley Reece
George Martin
416 Scott Brunner RC .08 .25
417 Rob Carpenter .08 .25
418 Harry Carson AP .20 .50
419 Bill Currier .08 .25
420 Joe Danelo .08 .25
421 Joe Danelo IA .08 .25
422 Mark Haynes RC .08 .25
423 Terry Jackson .08 .25
424 Dave Jennings .08 .25
425 Gary Jeter .08 .25

426 Brian Kelley .08 .25
427 George Martin .08 .25
428 Curtis McGriff .08 .25
429 Bill Neill .08 .25
430 Johnny Perkins .08 .25
431 Beasley Reece .08 .25
432 Gary Shirk .08 .25
433 Phil Simms 1.00 1.50
434 Lawrence Taylor RC 7.50 20.00
435 Lawrence Taylor IA 4.00 10.00
436 Brad Van Pelt .08 .25
437 Philadelphia Eagles TL .20 .50
Wilbert Montgomery
Harold Carmichael
Brenard Wilson
Carl Hairston
438 John Bunting .08 .25
439 Billy Campfield .08 .25
440 Harold Carmichael .40 1.00
441 Harold Carmichael IA .40 1.00
442 Herman Edwards .08 .25
443 Tony Franklin .08 .25
444 Tony Franklin IA .08 .25
445 Carl Hairston .08 .25
446 Dennis Harrison .08 .25
447 Ron Jaworski .40 1.00
448 Charlie Johnson .08 .25
449 Keith Krepfle .08 .25
450 Frank LeMaster .08 .25
451 Randy Logan .08 .25
452 Wilbert Montgomery .20 .50
453 Wilbert Montgomery IA .20 .50
454 Hubie Oliver .08 .25
455 Jerry Robinson .08 .25
456 Jerry Robinson IA .08 .25
457 Jerry Sisemore .08 .25
458 Charlie Smith .08 .25
459 Stan Walters .08 .25
460 Brenard Wilson .08 .25
461 Roynell Young .08 .25
462 St. Louis Cardinals TL .20 .50
Ottis Anderson
Pat Tilley
Ken Greene
Curtis Greer
463 Ottis Anderson .40 1.00
464 Ottis Anderson IA .40 1.00
465 Carl Birdsong .08 .25
466 Rush Brown .08 .25
467 Mel Gray .20 .50
468 Ken Greene .08 .25
469 Jim Hart .40 1.00
470 E.J. Junior RC .20 .50
471 Neil Lomax RC .40 1.00
472 Stump Mitchell RC .40 1.00
473 Wayne Morris .08 .25
474 Neil O'Donoghue .08 .25
475 Pat Tilley .08 .25
476 Pat Tilley IA .08 .25
477 San Francisco 49ers TL .20 .50
Ricky Patton
Dwight Clark
Dwight Hicks
Fred Dean
478 Dwight Clark .40 1.00
479 Dwight Clark IA .40 1.00
480 Earl Cooper .08 .25
481 Randy Cross .20 .50
482 Johnny Davis RC .08 .25
483 Fred Dean .20 .50
484 Fred Dean IA .08 .25
485 Dwight Hicks RC .40 1.00
486 Ronnie Lott RC 7.50 20.00
487 Ronnie Lott IA 3.00 6.00
488 Joe Montana AP 7.50 20.00
489 Joe Montana IA 5.00 12.00
490 Ricky Patton .08 .25
491 Jack Reynolds .20 .50
492 Freddie Solomon .08 .25
493 Ray Wersching .08 .25
494 Charle Young .08 .25
495 Tampa Bay Bucs TL .20 .50
Jerry Eckwood
Kevin House
Cedric Brown
Lee Roy Selmon
496 Cedric Brown .08 .25
497 Neal Colzie .08 .25
498 Jerry Eckwood .08 .25
499 Jimmie Giles .20 .50
500 Hugh Green RC .40 1.00
501 Kevin House .08 .25
502 Kevin House IA .08 .25
503 Cecil Johnson .08 .25
504 James Owens .08 .25
505 Lee Roy Selmon AP .40 1.00
506 Mike Washington .08 .25
507 James Wilder RC .20 .50
508 Doug Williams .20 .50
509 Wash. Redskins TL .40 1.00
Joe Washington
Art Monk
Mark Murphy
Perry Brooks
510 Perry Brooks .08 .25
511 Dave Butz .20 .50
512 Wilbur Jackson .08 .25
513 Joe Lavender .08 .25
514 Terry Metcalf .20 .50
515 Art Monk 1.25 3.00
516 Mark Moseley .08 .25
517 Mark Murphy .08 .25
518 Mike Nelms .08 .25
519 Lemar Parrish .08 .25
520 John Riggins .40 1.00
521 Joe Theismann .40 1.00
522 Ricky Thompson .08 .25
523 Don Warren UER .08 .25
(photo actually
Ricky Thompson)
524 Joe Washington .20 .50
525 Checklist 1-132 .40 1.00
526 Checklist 133-264 .40 1.00
527 Checklist 265-396 .40 1.00
528 Checklist 397-528 .40 1.00

1982 Topps Team Checklists

These cards are essentially a parallel to the base 1982 Topps team checklist subset cards. The set was only available directly from Topps as a send-off offer in uncut sheet form. The prices below apply equally to uncut sheets as they are frequently found in their original uncut condition. As for individual cards, thin white card (almost paper-thin) stock makes it a challenge to find singles in top grades. We've cataloged the cards below for convenience in alphabetical order by team name.

COMPLETE SET (28) 40.00 100.00
10 Baltimore Colts TL 1.25 3.00
Curtis Dickey
Raymond Butler
Larry Braziel
Bruce Laird
21 Buffalo Bills TL 1.50 4.00
Joe Cribbs
Frank Lewis
Mario Clark
Fred Smerlas
36 Cincinnati Bengals TL 1.50 4.00
Pete Johnson
Cris Collinsworth
Ken Riley
Reggie Williams
55 Cleveland Browns TL 1.50 4.00
Mike Pruitt
Ozzie Newsome
Clarence Scott
Lyle Alzado
76 Denver Broncos TL 1.50 4.00
Rick Parros
Steve Watson
Steve Foley
Rulon Jones
92 Houston Oilers TL 1.25 3.00
Carl Roaches
Ken Burrough
Carter Hartwig
Greg Stemrick
Jesse Baker
109 Kansas City Chiefs TL 1.25 3.00
Joe Delaney
J.T. Smith
Eric Harris
Ken Kremer
125 Miami Dolphins TL 1.50 4.00
Tony Nathan
Duriel Harris
Glenn Blackwood
Bob Baumhower
141 New England Pats TL 1.25 3.00
Tony Collins
Stanley Morgan
Tim Fox
Rick Sanford
Tony McGee
160 New York Jets TL 1.50 4.00
Freeman McNeil
Wesley Walker
Darrol Ray
Joe Klecko
185 Oakland Raiders TL 1.50 4.00
Kenny King
Derrick Ramsey
Lester Hayes
Odis McKinney
Rod Martin
202 Pittsburgh Steelers TL 2.00 5.00
Franco Harris
John Stallworth
Mel Blount
Jack Lambert
Gary Dunn
223 San Diego Chargers TL 1.50 4.00
Chuck Muncie
Charlie Joiner
Willie Buchanon
Gary Johnson
243 Seattle Seahawks TL 2.00 5.00
Theotis Brown
Steve Largent
John Harris
Jacob Green
271 Atlanta Falcons TL 1.50 4.00
William Andrews
Alfred Jenkins
Tom Pridemore
Al Richardson
292 Chicago Bears TL 3.00 8.00
Walter Payton
Ken Margerum
Gary Fencik
Dan Hampton
Alan Page
307 Dallas Cowboys TL 2.50 6.00
Tony Dorsett
Tony Hill
Everson Walls
Harvey Martin
333 Detroit Lions TL 1.50 4.00
Billy Sims
Freddie Scott
Jim Allen
Dave Pureifory
354 Green Bay Packers TL 2.00 5.00
Gerry Ellis
James Lofton
Maurice Harvey
Mark Lee
Mike Butler
369 Los Angeles Rams TL 1.50 4.00
Wendell Tyler
Preston Dennard
Nolan Cromwell
Jack Youngblood
389 Minnesota Vikings TL 1.25 3.00
Ted Brown
Joe Senser
Tom Hannon
Willie Teal
Matt Blair
404 New Orleans Saints TL 1.50 4.00
George Rogers
Guido Merkens
Dave Waymer
Rickey Jackson
415 New York Giants TL 1.25 3.00
Rob Carpenter
Johnny Perkins
Beasley Reece
George Martin
437 Philadelphia Eagles TL 1.50 4.00
Wilbert Montgomery
Harold Carmichael
Brenard Wilson
Carl Hairston
462 St. Louis Cardinals TL 1.50 4.00
Ottis Anderson
Pat Tilley
Ken Greene
Curtis Greer
477 San Francisco 49ers TL 1.50 4.00
Ricky Patton
Dwight Clark
Dwight Hicks
Fred Dean
495 Tampa Bay Bucs TL 1.50 4.00
Jerry Eckwood
Kevin House
Cedric Brown
Lee Roy Selmon
509 Wash. Redskins TL 2.00 5.00
Joe Washington
Art Monk
Mark Murphy
Perry Brooks

1983 Topps

After issuing 528-card sets since 1973, Topps dropped to 396 standard-size cards for 1983. The set was printed on four sheets. As a result, there are 132 double-printed cards which are noted in the checklist below by DP. The card fronts contain the player's name and position at the bottom in a rectangular area that differs in color according to team. Team names are in block letters at the top of the cards. The backs of the cards contain yearly statistics and a "Personal Facts" section. All the text is printed over a faint white team helmet. Subsets include Record Breakers (1-9), playoffs (10-12) and league leaders (202-207). The Team Leader (TL) cards are distributed throughout the set as the first card of the team sequence. The design of these cards differs from previous years in that only one leader (usually the team's rushing leader) is pictured. The backs contain team scoring information from the previous season. The team numbering is arranged alphabetically within each conference (with players ordered alphabetically within team). Rookie Cards include Marcus Allen, Gary Anderson (K), Todd Christensen, Roy Green, Jim McMahon, and Mike Singletary.

COMPLETE SET (396) 30.00 60.00
1 Ken Anderson RB/20 Consecutive .25 .60
Pass Completions
2 Tony Dorsett RB/99 Yard Run .25 .60
3 Dan Fouts RB/30 Games Over .25 .60
300 Yards Passing
4 Joe Montana RB 1.50 3.00
Five Straight/300 Yard Games
5 Mark Moseley RB/21 Straight .15 .40
Field Goals
6 Mike Nelms RB .08 .25
Most Yards
Punt Returns:
Super Bowl Game
7 Darrol Ray RB .08 .25
Longest Interception
Return: Playoff Game
8 John Riggins RB .25 .60
Most Yards Rushing:
Super Bowl Game
9 Fulton Walker RB .08 .25
Most Yards
Kickoff Returns:
Super Bowl Game
10 NFC Championship .25 .60
Redskins 31,
Cowboys 17
(John Riggins tackled)
11 AFC Championship .15 .40
Dolphins 14,
Jets 0
12 Super Bowl XVII .08 .25
Redskins 27,
Dolphins 17
(John Riggins running)
13 Atlanta Falcons TL .15 .40
William Andrews
14 William Andrews DP .15 .40
15 Steve Bartkowski .15 .40
16 Bobby Butler .08 .25
17 Buddy Curry .08 .25
18 Alfred Jackson DP .08 .25
19 Alfred Jenkins .08 .25
20 Kenny Johnson .08 .25
21 Mike Kenn .08 .25
22 Mick Luckhurst .08 .25
23 Junior Miller .08 .25
24 Al Richardson .08 .25
25 Gerald Riggs DP RC .15 .40
26 R.C. Thielemann .08 .25
27 Jeff Van Note .08 .25
28 Chicago Bears TL .40 1.00
Walter Payton
29 Brian Baschnagel .08 .25
30 Dan Hampton PB .25 .60
31 Mike Hartenstine .08 .25
32 Noah Jackson .08 .25
33 Jim McMahon RC 4.00 8.00
34 Emery Moorehead DP .08 .25
35 Bob Parsons .08 .25
36 Walter Payton 3.00 8.00
37 Terry Schmidt .08 .25
38 Mike Singletary RC 5.00 10.00
39 Matt Suhey DP .15 .40
40 Rickey Watts DP .08 .25
41 Otis Wilson DP RC .15 .40
42 Dallas Cowboys TL .25 .60
Tony Dorsett
43 Bob Breunig .15 .40
44 Doug Cosbie .08 .25
45 Pat Donovan .08 .25
46 Tony Dorsett DP PB .40 1.00
47 Tony Hill .15 .40
48 Butch Johnson DP .15 .40
49 Ed Jones DP PB .25 .60
50 Harvey Martin DP .15 .40
51 Drew Pearson .25 .60
52 Rafael Septien .08 .25
53 Ron Springs DP .08 .25
54 Dennis Thurman .08 .25
55 Everson Walls PB .15 .40
56 Danny White DP PB .25 .60
57 Randy White PB .25 .60
58 Detroit Lions TL .15 .40
Billy Sims
59 Al(Bubba) Baker DP .15 .40
60 Dexter Bussey DP .08 .25
61 Gary Danielson DP .08 .25
62 Keith Dorney DP .08 .25
63 Doug English .08 .25
64 Ken Fantetti DP .08 .25
65 Alvin Hall DP .08 .25
66 David Hill DP .08 .25
67 Eric Hipple .08 .25
68 Ed Murray DP .15 .40
69 Freddie Scott .08 .25
70 Billy Sims DP PB .15 .40
71 Tom Skladany DP .08 .25
72 Leonard Thompson DP .08 .25
73 Bobby Watkins .08 .25
74 Green Bay Packers TL .08 .25
Eddie Lee Ivery
75 John Anderson .08 .25
76 Paul Coffman .08 .25
77 Lynn Dickey .08 .25
78 Mike Douglass DP .08 .25
79 Eddie Lee Ivery .08 .25
80 John Jefferson DP PB .25 .60
81 Ezra Johnson .08 .25
82 Mark Lee .08 .25
83 James Lofton PB .25 .60
84 Larry McCarren .08 .25
85 Jan Stenerud DP .15 .40
86 Los Angeles Rams TL .08 .25
Wendell Tyler
87 Bill Bain DP .08 .25
88 Nolan Cromwell .15 .40
89 Preston Dennard .08 .25
90 Vince Ferragamo DP .15 .40
91 Mike Guman .08 .25
92 Kent Hill .08 .25
93 Mike Lansford DP RC .08 .25
94 Rod Perry .08 .25
95 Pat Thomas DP .08 .25
96 Jack Youngblood .25 .60
97 Minnesota Vikings TL .08 .25
Ted Brown
98 Matt Blair .08 .25
99 Ted Brown .08 .25
100 Greg Coleman .08 .25
101 Randy Holloway .08 .25
102 Tommy Kramer .15 .40
103 Doug Martin DP .08 .25
104 Mark Mullaney .08 .25
105 Joe Senser .08 .25
106 Willie Teal DP .08 .25
107 Sammie White .15 .40
108 Rickey Young .08 .25
109 New Orleans Saints TL .15 .40
George Rogers
110 Stan Brock RC .08 .25
111 Bruce Clark RC .08 .25
112 Russell Erxleben DP .08 .25
113 Russell Gary .08 .25
114 Jeff Groth DP .08 .25
115 John Hill DP .08 .25
116 Derland Moore .08 .25
117 George Rogers PB .15 .40
118 Ken Stabler .60 1.50
119 Wayne Wilson .08 .25
120 New York Giants TL .08 .25
Butch Woolfolk
121 Scott Brunner .08 .25
122 Rob Carpenter .08 .25
123 Harry Carson PB .15 .40
124 Joe Danelo DP .08 .25
125 Earnest Gray .08 .25
126 Mark Haynes DP .15 .40
127 Terry Jackson .08 .25
128 Dave Jennings .08 .25
129 Brian Kelley .08 .25
130 George Martin .08 .25
131 Tom Mullady .08 .25
132 Johnny Perkins .08 .25
133 Lawrence Taylor PB 2.00 5.00
134 Brad Van Pelt .08 .25
135 Butch Woolfolk DP RC .08 .25
136 Philadelphia Eagles TL .15 .40
Wilbert Montgomery
137 Harold Carmichael .25 .60
138 Herman Edwards .08 .25
139 Tony Franklin DP .08 .25
140 Carl Hairston DP .08 .25
141 Dennis Harrison DP .08 .25
142 Ron Jaworski DP .15 .40
143 Frank LeMaster .08 .25
144 Wilbert Montgomery DP .15 .40
145 Guy Morriss .08 .25
146 Jerry Robinson .08 .25
(TD stats don't match)
147 Max Runager .08 .25
148 Ron Smith DP RC .08 .25
149 John Spagnola .08 .25
150 Stan Walters DP .08 .25
151 Roynell Young DP .08 .25
152 St. Louis Cardinals TL .15 .40
Ottis Anderson
153 Ottis Anderson .25 .60
154 Carl Birdsong .08 .25
155 Dan Dierdorf DP .25 .60
156 Roy Green RC .25 .60
157 Elois Grooms .08 .25
158 Neil Lomax DP .15 .40
159 Wayne Morris .08 .25
160 Tootie Robbins RC .08 .25
161 Luis Sharpe RC .08 .25
162 Pat Tilley .08 .25
163 San Francisco 49ers TL .08 .25
Jeff Moore
164 Dwight Clark PB .25 .60
165 Randy Cross .15 .40
166 Russ Francis .15 .40
167 Dwight Hicks .08 .25
168 Ronnie Lott PB 1.25 2.50
169 Joe Montana DP 4.00 10.00
170 Jeff Moore .08 .25
171 R.Nehemiah DP RC .25 .60
172 Freddie Solomon .08 .25
173 Ray Wersching DP .08 .25
174 Tampa Bay Bucs TL .08 .25
James Wilder
175 Cedric Brown .08 .25
176 Bill Capece .08 .25
177 Neal Colzie .08 .25
178 Jimmie Giles .08 .25
179 Hugh Green PB .15 .40
180 Kevin House DP .08 .25
181 James Owens .08 .25
182 Lee Roy Selmon PB .25 .60
183 Mike Washington .08 .25
184 James Wilder .08 .25
185 Doug Williams DP .15 .40
186 Wash. Redskins TL .25 .60
John Riggins
187 Jeff Bostic DP RC .40 1.00
188 Charlie Brown PB RC .15 .40
189 Vernon Dean DP RC .08 .25
190 Joe Jacoby RC 1.25 3.00
191 Dexter Manley RC .15 .40
192 Rich Milot .08 .25
193 Art Monk DP .40 1.00
194 Mark Moseley DP .08 .25
195 Mike Nelms .08 .25
196 Neal Olkewicz DP .08 .25
197 Tony Peters .08 .25
198 John Riggins DP .25 .60
199 Joe Theismann PB .25 .60
200 Don Warren .08 .25
201 Jeris White DP .08 .25
202 Passing Leaders .25 .60
Joe Theismann
Ken Anderson
203 Receiving Leaders .15 .40
Dwight Clark
Kellen Winslow
204 Rushing Leaders .25 .60
Tony Dorsett
Freeman McNeil
205 Scoring Leaders .50 1.25
Wendell Tyler
Marcus Allen
206 Interception Leaders .15 .40
Everson Walls
AFC Tie (Four)
207 Punting Leaders .08 .25
Carl Birdsong
Luke Prestridge
208 Baltimore Colts TL .08 .25
Randy McMillan
209 Matt Bouza .08 .25
210 Johnie Cooks DP RC .08 .25
211 Curtis Dickey .08 .25
212 Nesby Glasgow DP .08 .25
213 Derrick Hatchett .08 .25
214 Randy McMillan .08 .25
215 Mike Pagel RC .15 .40
216 Rohn Stark DP RC .15 .40
217 Donnell Thompson DP RC .08 .25
218 Leo Wisniewski DP .08 .25
219 Buffalo Bills TL .15 .40
Joe Cribbs
220 Curtis Brown .08 .25
221 Jerry Butler .08 .25
222 Greg Cater DP .08 .25
223 Joe Cribbs .15 .40
224 Joe Ferguson .15 .40
225 Roosevelt Leaks .08 .25
226 Frank Lewis .08 .25
227 Eugene Marve RC .08 .25
228 Fred Smerlas DP PB .08 .25
229 Ben Williams DP .08 .25
230 Cincinnati Bengals TL .08 .25
Pete Johnson
231 Charles Alexander .08 .25
232 Ken Anderson DP PB .25 .60
233 Jim Breech DP .08 .25
234 Ross Browner .08 .25
235 Cris Collinsworth .25 .60
DP PB
236 Isaac Curtis .08 .25
237 Pete Johnson .08 .25
238 Steve Kreider DP .08 .25
239 Max Montoya DP RC .08 .25
240 Anthony Munoz PB .40 1.00
241 Ken Riley .08 .25
242 Dan Ross .08 .25
243 Reggie Williams .15 .40
244 Cleveland Browns TL .15 .40
Mike Pruitt
245 Chip Banks DP RC .15 .40
246 Tom Cousineau DP RC .15 .40
247 Joe DeLamielleure DP .15 .40
248 Doug Dieken DP .08 .25
249 Hanford Dixon RC .08 .25
250 Ricky Feacher DP .08 .25
251 Lawrence Johnson DP .08 .25
252 Dave Logan DP .08 .25
253 Paul McDonald DP .08 .25
254 Ozzie Newsome DP .25 .60
255 Mike Pruitt .15 .40
256 Clarence Scott DP .08 .25
257 Brian Sipe DP .15 .40
258 Dwight Walker DP .08 .25
259 Charles White .15 .40
260 Denver Broncos TL .08 .25
Gerald Willhite
261 Steve DeBerg DP .15 .40
262 Randy Gradishar DP PB .15 .40
263 Rulon Jones DP RC .08 .25
264 Rich Karlis DP .08 .25
265 Don Latimer .08 .25
266 Rick Parros DP .08 .25
267 Luke Prestridge .08 .25
268 Rick Upchurch .15 .40
269 Steve Watson DP .08 .25
270 Gerald Willhite DP .08 .25
271 Houston Oilers TL .08 .25
Gifford Nielsen
272 Harold Bailey .08 .25
273 Jesse Baker DP .08 .25
274 Gregg Bingham DP .08 .25
275 Robert Brazile DP .08 .25
276 Donnie Craft .08 .25
277 Daryl Hunt RC .08 .25
278 Archie Manning DP .15 .40
279 Gifford Nielsen .08 .25
280 Mike Renfro .08 .25
281 Carl Roaches DP .08 .25
282 Kansas City Chiefs TL .15 .40
Joe Delaney
283 Gary Barbaro .08 .25
284 Joe Delaney .08 .25
285 Jeff Gossett RC .25 .60
286 Gary Green DP .08 .25
287 Eric Harris DP .08 .25
288 Billy Jackson DP .08 .25
289 Bill Kenney DP .08 .25
290 Nick Lowery .25 .60
291 Henry Marshall .08 .25
292 Art Still DP .08 .25
293 Los Angeles Raiders TL .75 2.00
Marcus Allen
294 Marcus Allen DP RC 6.00 15.00
295 Lyle Alzado .25 .60
296 Chris Bahr DP .08 .25
297 Cliff Branch .25 .60
298 Todd Christensen RC .30 .75
299 Ray Guy .15 .40
300 Frank Hawkins DP .08 .25
301 Lester Hayes DP .08 .25
302 Ted Hendricks DP PB .25 .60
303 Kenny King DP .08 .25
304 Rod Martin .08 .25
305 Matt Millen DP .25 .60
306 Burgess Owens .08 .25
307 Jim Plunkett .25 .60
308 Miami Dolphins TL .15 .40
Andra Franklin
309 Bob Baumhower .08 .25
310 Glenn Blackwood .08 .25
311 Lyle Blackwood DP .08 .25
312 A.J. Duhe .08 .25
313 Andra Franklin .08 .25
314 Duriel Harris .08 .25
315 Bob Kuechenberg DP .15 .40
316 Don McNeal .08 .25
317 Tony Nathan .15 .40
318 Ed Newman .08 .25
319 Earnie Rhone DP .08 .25
320 Joe Rose DP .08 .25
321 Don Strock DP .08 .25
322 Uwe Von Schamann .08 .25
323 David Woodley DP .15 .40
324 New England Pats TL .08 .25
Tony Collins
325 Julius Adams .08 .25
326 Pete Brock .08 .25
327 Rich Camarillo DP RC .08 .25
328 Tony Collins DP .08 .25
329 Steve Grogan .15 .40
330 John Hannah PB .25 .60
331 Don Hasselbeck .08 .25
332 Mike Haynes .15 .40
333 Roland James RC .08 .25
334A Stanley Morgan ERR .25 .60
(Inside Linebacker is
printed upside down
on card back)
334B Stanley Morgan COR .15 .40
335 Steve Nelson .08 .25
336 Kenneth Sims DP .08 .25
337 Mark Van Eeghen .15 .40
338 New York Jets TL .15 .40
Freeman McNeil
339 Greg Buttle .08 .25
340 Joe Fields .08 .25
341 Mark Gastineau DP .15 .40
342 Bruce Harper .08 .25
343 Bobby Jackson .08 .25
344 Bobby Jones .08 .25
345 Johnny Lam Jones DP .08 .25
346 Joe Klecko .15 .40
347 Marty Lyons .08 .25
348 Freeman McNeil PB .25 .60
349 Lance Mehl RC .08 .25
350 Marvin Powell DP .08 .25
351 Darrol Ray DP .08 .25
352 Abdul Salaam .08 .25
353 Richard Todd .15 .40
354 Wesley Walker PB .15 .40
355 Pittsburgh Steelers TL .25 .60
Franco Harris
356 Gary Anderson DP RC 3.00 6.00
357 Mel Blount DP .25 .60
358 Terry Bradshaw DP .60 1.50
359 Larry Brown .08 .25
360 Bennie Cunningham .08 .25
361 Gary Dunn .08 .25
362 Franco Harris .30 .75
363 Jack Lambert PB .25 .60
364 Frank Pollard .08 .25
365 Donnie Shell .15 .40
366 John Stallworth PB .25 .60
367 Loren Toews .08 .25
368 Mike Webster DP PB .25 .60
369 Dwayne Woodruff RC .08 .25
370 San Diego Chargers TL .15 .40
Chuck Muncie
371 Rolf Benirschke DP .08 .25
372 James Brooks .25 .60
373 Wes Chandler .15 .40
374 Dan Fouts DP PB .25 .60
375 Tim Fox .08 .25
376 Gary Johnson .08 .25
377 Charlie Joiner DP .25 .60
378 Louie Kelcher .08 .25
379 Chuck Muncie .08 .25
380 Cliff Thrift .08 .25
381 Doug Wilkerson .08 .25
382 Kellen Winslow PB .30 .75
383 Seattle Seahawks TL .08 .25
Sherman Smith
384 Kenny Easley RC .25 .60
385 Jacob Green RC .15 .40
386 John Harris .08 .25
387 Michael Jackson .08 .25
388 Norm Johnson RC .08 .25
389 Steve Largent .50 1.25
390 Keith Simpson .08 .25
391 Sherman Smith .08 .25
392 Jeff West DP .08 .25
393 Jim Zorn DP .15 .40
394 Checklist 1-132 .25 .60
395 Checklist 133-264 .25 .60
396 Checklist 265-396 .25 .60

1983 Topps Sticker Inserts

COMPLETE SET (33) 6.00 15.00
1 Marcus Allen 1.25 3.00
(Completed red border
puzzle on back)
2 Ken Anderson .25 .60
(Completed red border
puzzle on back)
3 Ottis Anderson .15 .40
4 William Andrews .15 .40
5 Terry Bradshaw .60 1.50
6 Wes Chandler .08 .25
7 Dwight Clark .15 .40
8 Cris Collinsworth .15 .40
9 Joe Cribbs .08 .25
10 Nolan Cromwell .08 .25
11 Tony Dorsett .60 1.50
12 Dan Fouts .30 .75
13 Mark Gastineau .08 .25
14 Jimmie Giles .08 .25
15 Franco Harris .30 .75
(Completed green border
puzzle on back)
16 Ted Hendricks .15 .40
17 Tony Hill .08 .25
18 John Jefferson .15 .40
(Completed red border
puzzle on back)
19 James Lofton .25 .60
20 Freeman McNeil .08 .25
(Completed red border
puzzle on back)
21 Joe Montana 2.50 6.00
22 Mark Moseley .08 .25
23 Ozzie Newsome .25 .60
24 Walter Payton 1.50 4.00
25 John Riggins .30 .75
26 Billy Sims .15 .40
27 John Stallworth .25 .60
28 Lawrence Taylor .40 1.00
29 Joe Theismann .25 .60
30 Richard Todd .08 .25
(Completed green border
puzzle on back)
31 Wesley Walker .08 .25
32 Danny White .15 .40
33 Kellen Winslow .25 .60

1984 Topps

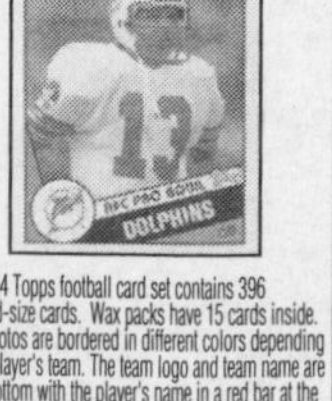

The 1984 Topps football card set contains 396 standard-size cards. Wax packs have 15 cards inside. Card photos are bordered in different colors depending on the player's team. The team logo and team name are at the bottom with the player's name in a red bar at the top. Horizontally designed green tinted backs have yearly statistics, highlights and a cartoon. Subsets include Record Breakers (1-6), playoffs (7-9) and league leaders (202-207). Team Leader (TL) cards primarily feature the team's rushing leader. The backs contain team scoring information from the previous year. Instant Replay (IR) cards of top players are scattered throughout the set. Cards are numbered and alphabetically arranged within teams except for the Colts which moved from Baltimore to Indianapolis. The set features the Rookie Cards of Morten Andersen, Roger Craig, Eric Dickerson, John Elway, Willie Gault, Darrell Green, Rickey Jackson, Dave Krieg, Howie Long, Dan Marino, Andre Tippett and Curt Warner.

COMPLETE SET (396) 75.00 150.00
COMP.FACT.SET (396) 250.00 400.00
1 Eric Dickerson RB .25 .60
Sets Rookie Mark
With 1808 Yards
2 Ali Haji-Sheikh RB .15 .40
Sets Field Goal
Mark as a Rookie
3 Franco Harris RB .25 .60
Records Eighth/1000 Yard Year
4 Mark Moseley RB/161 Points Sets .15 .40
Mark for Kickers
5 John Riggins RB/24 Rushing TD's .25 .60
6 Jan Stenerud RB/338th Career FG .15 .40
7 AFC Championship .25 .60
Raiders 30,
Seahawks 14
(Marcus Allen running)
8 NFC Championship .15 .40
Redskins 24,/49ers 21
(John Riggins running)
9 Super Bowl XVIII UER .25 .60
Raiders 38,
Redskins 9
(hand-off to Marcus
Allen; score wrong,/28-9 on card front)
10 Indianapolis Colts TL .08 .25
Curtis Dickey
11 Raul Allegre RC .08 .25
12 Curtis Dickey .15 .40
13 Ray Donaldson RC .15 .40
14 Nesby Glasgow .08 .25
15 Chris Hinton PB RC .25 .60
16 Vernon Maxwell RC .08 .25
17 Randy McMillan .08 .25
18 Mike Pagel .15 .40
19 Rohn Stark .15 .40
20 Leo Wisniewski .08 .25
21 Buffalo Bills TL .15 .40
Joe Cribbs
22 Jerry Butler .08 .25
23 Joe Danelo .08 .25
24 Joe Ferguson .15 .40
25 Steve Freeman .08 .25
26 Roosevelt Leaks .15 .40
27 Frank Lewis .08 .25
28 Eugene Marve .08 .25
29 Booker Moore .08 .25
30 Fred Smerlas .08 .25
31 Ben Williams .15 .40
32 Cincinnati Bengals TL .15 .40
Cris Collinsworth
33 Charles Alexander .08 .25
34 Ken Anderson .25 .60
35 Ken Anderson IR .25 .60
36 Jim Breech .08 .25
37 Cris Collinsworth PB .25 .60
38 Cris Collinsworth IR .25 .60
39 Isaac Curtis .15 .40
40 Eddie Edwards .08 .25
41 Ray Horton RC .08 .25
42 Pete Johnson .15 .40
43 Steve Kreider .08 .25
44 Max Montoya .08 .25
45 Anthony Munoz PB .25 .60
46 Reggie Williams .15 .40
47 Cleveland Browns TL .15 .40
Mike Pruitt
48 Matt Bahr .15 .40
49 Chip Banks PB .08 .25
50 Tom Cousineau .08 .25
51 Joe DeLamielleure .25 .60
52 Doug Dieken .08 .25
53 Bob Golic RC .25 .60
54 Bobby Jones .08 .25
55 Dave Logan .08 .25
56 Clay Matthews .25 .60
57 Paul McDonald .08 .25
58 Ozzie Newsome .25 .60
59 Ozzie Newsome IR .25 .60
60 Mike Pruitt .15 .40
61 Denver Broncos TL .15 .40
Steve Watson
62 Barney Chavous RC .08 .25
63 John Elway RC 25.00 50.00
64 Steve Foley .08 .25
65 Tom Jackson .25 .60
66 Rich Karlis .08 .25
67 Luke Prestridge .08 .25
68 Zach Thomas .08 .25
69 Rick Upchurch .15 .40
70 Steve Watson .15 .40
71 Sammy Winder RC .15 .40
72 Louis Wright .15 .40
73 Houston Oilers TL .08 .25
Tim Smith
74 Jesse Baker .08 .25
75 Gregg Bingham .08 .25
76 Robert Brazile .15 .40
77 Steve Brown RC .08 .25
78 Chris Dressel .08 .25
79 Doug France .08 .25
80 Florian Kempf .08 .25
81 Carl Roaches .15 .40
82 Tim Smith RC .15 .40
83 Willie Tullis .08 .25
84 Kansas City Chiefs TL .08 .25
Carlos Carson
85 Mike Bell RC .08 .25
86 Theotis Brown .08 .25
87 Carlos Carson PB .25 .60
88 Carlos Carson IR .15 .40
89 Deron Cherry PB RC .15 .40
90 Gary Green .08 .25
91 Billy Jackson .08 .25
92 Bill Kenney .15 .40
93 Bill Kenney IR .15 .40
94 Nick Lowery .25 .60
95 Henry Marshall .08 .25
96 Art Still .08 .25
97 Los Angeles Raiders TL .15 .40
Todd Christensen
98 Marcus Allen 2.50 5.00
99 Marcus Allen IR 1.00 2.50
100 Lyle Alzado .15 .40
101 Lyle Alzado IR .15 .40
102 Chris Bahr .08 .25
103 Malcolm Barnwell RC .08 .25
104 Cliff Branch .25 .60
105 Todd Christensen PB .25 .60
106 Todd Christensen IR .25 .60
107 Ray Guy .25 .60
108 Frank Hawkins .08 .25
109 Lester Hayes .15 .40
110 Ted Hendricks PB .25 .60
111 Howie Long PB RC 6.00 15.00
112 Rod Martin .15 .40

113 Vann McElroy RC	.08	.25
114 Jim Plunkett	.25	.60
115 Greg Pruitt PB	.15	.40
116 Miami Dolphins TL	.25	.60
Mark Duper		
117 Bob Baumhower	.08	.25
118 Doug Betters PB RC	.08	.25
119 A.J. Duhe	.08	.25
120 Mark Duper PB RC	.25	.60
121 Andra Franklin	.08	.25
122 William Judson	.08	.25
123 Dan Marino PB RC UER	25.00	50.00
(Quaterback on back)		
124 Dan Marino IR	5.00	12.00
125 Nat Moore	.15	.40
126 Ed Newman	.08	.25
127 Reggie Roby RC	.15	.40
128 Gerald Small	.08	.25
129 Dwight Stephenson RC	2.00	5.00
130 Uwe Von Schamann	.08	.25
131 New England Pats TL	.08	.25
Tony Collins		
132 Rich Camarillo	.15	.40
133 Tony Collins	.15	.40
134 Tony Collins IR	.08	.25
135 Bob Cryder	.08	.25
136 Steve Grogan	.15	.40
137 John Hannah PB	.25	.60
138 Brian Holloway RC	.08	.25
139 Roland James	.08	.25
140 Stanley Morgan	.15	.40
141 Rick Sanford	.08	.25
142 Mosi Tatupu RC	.08	.25
143 Andre Tippett RC	2.00	5.00
144 New York Jets TL	.15	.40
Wesley Walker		
145 Jerome Barkum	.08	.25
146 Mark Gastineau	.15	.40
147 Mark Gastineau IR	.15	.40
148 Bruce Harper	.08	.25
149 Johnny Lam Jones	.08	.25
150 Joe Klecko	.15	.40
151 Pat Leahy	.08	.25
152 Freeman McNeil	.15	.40
153 Lance Mehl	.08	.25
154 Marvin Powell	.15	.40
155 Darrol Ray UER	.08	.25
(card number printed in brown)		
156 Pat Ryan RC	.08	.25
157 Kirk Springs	.08	.25
158 Wesley Walker	.15	.40
159 Pittsburgh Steelers TL	.25	.60
Franco Harris		
160 Walter Abercrombie RC	.15	.40
161 Gary Anderson K	.25	.60
162 Terry Bradshaw	.75	2.00
163 Craig Colquitt	.08	.25
164 Bennie Cunningham	.08	.25
165 Franco Harris	.25	.60
166 Franco Harris IR	.25	.60
167 Jack Lambert PB	.25	.60
168 Jack Lambert IR	.25	.60
169 Frank Pollard	.08	.25
170 Donnie Shell	.15	.40
171 Mike Webster PB	.15	.40
172 Keith Willis RC	.08	.25
173 Rick Woods	.08	.25
174 San Diego Chargers TL	.25	.60
Kellen Winslow		
175 Rolf Benirschke	.08	.25
176 James Brooks	.15	.40
177 Maury Buford	.08	.25
178 Wes Chandler	.15	.40
179 Dan Fouts PB	.30	.75
180 Dan Fouts IR	.25	.60
181 Charlie Joiner	.25	.60
182 Linden King	.08	.25
183 Chuck Muncie	.15	.40
184 Billy Ray Smith RC	.25	.60
185 Danny Walters RC	.08	.25
186 Kellen Winslow PB	.30	.75
187 Kellen Winslow IR	.25	.60
188 Seattle Seahawks TL	.25	.60
Curt Warner		
189 Steve August	.08	.25
190 Dave Brown	.08	.25
191 Zachary Dixon	.08	.25
192 Kenny Easley	.15	.40
193 Jacob Green	.08	.25
194 Norm Johnson	.15	.40
195 Dave Krieg RC	.60	1.50
196 Steve Largent	.40	1.00
197 Steve Largent IR	.25	.60
198 Curt Warner PB RC	.25	.60
199 Curt Warner IR	.25	.60
200 Jeff West	.08	.25
201 Charle Young	.08	.25
202 Passing Leaders	2.50	6.00
Dan Marino		
Steve Bartkowski		
203 Receiving Leaders	.15	.40
Todd Christensen		
Charlie Brown		
Earnest Gray		
Roy Green		
204 Rushing Leaders	.25	.60
Curt Warner		
Eric Dickerson		
205 Scoring Leaders	.08	.25
Gary Anderson K		
Mark Moseley		
206 Interception Leaders	.08	.25
Vann McElroy		
Ken Riley		
Mark Murphy		
207 Punting Leaders	.08	.25
Rich Camarillo		
Greg Coleman		
208 Atlanta Falcons TL	.15	.40
William Andrews		
209 William Andrews	.15	.40
210 William Andrews IR	.15	.40
211 Stacey Bailey RC	.08	.25
212 Steve Bartkowski	.25	.60
213 Steve Bartkowski IR	.15	.40
214 Ralph Giacomarro	.08	.25
215 Billy Johnson	.15	.40
216 Mike Kenn	.15	.40
217 Mick Luckhurst	.08	.25
218 Gerald Riggs	.25	.60
219 R.C. Thielemann	.08	.25
220 Jeff Van Note	.15	.40
221 Chicago Bears TL	.30	.75
Walter Payton		
222 Jim Covert RC	.25	.60
223 Leslie Frazier	.08	.25
224 Willie Gault RC	.25	.60
225 Mike Hartenstine	.08	.25
226 Noah Jackson UER	.08	.25
(photo actually		
Jim Osborne)		
227 Jim McMahon	.50	1.25
228 Walter Payton PB	3.00	8.00
229 Walter Payton IR	.60	1.50
230 Mike Richardson RC	.08	.25
231 Terry Schmidt	.08	.25
232 Mike Singletary	.50	1.25
233 Matt Suhey	.15	.40
234 Bob Thomas	.08	.25
235 Dallas Cowboys TL	.25	.60
Tony Dorsett		
236 Bob Breunig	.08	.25
237 Doug Cosbie	.15	.40
238 Tony Dorsett PB	.40	1.00
239 Tony Dorsett IR	.25	.60
240 John Dutton	.08	.25
241 Tony Hill	.15	.40
242 Ed Jones PB	.25	.60
243 Drew Pearson	.25	.60
244 Rafael Septien	.08	.25
245 Ron Springs	.15	.40
246 Dennis Thurman	.08	.25
247 Everson Walls PB	.08	.25
248 Danny White	.25	.60
249 Randy White PB	.25	.60
250 Detroit Lions TL	.15	.40
Billy Sims		
251 Jeff Chadwick RC	.15	.40
252 Garry Cobb	.08	.25
253 Doug English	.15	.40
254 William Gay	.08	.25
255 Eric Hipple	.15	.40
256 James Jones RC	.15	.40
257 Bruce McNorton	.08	.25
258 Eddie Murray	.15	.40
259 Ulysses Norris	.08	.25
260 Billy Sims	.25	.60
261 Billy Sims IR	.15	.40
262 Leonard Thompson	.08	.25
263 Green Bay Packers TL	.25	.60
James Lofton		
264 John Anderson	.08	.25
265 Paul Coffman	.15	.40
266 Lynn Dickey	.15	.40
267 Gerry Ellis	.08	.25
268 John Jefferson	.25	.60
269 John Jefferson IR	.25	.60
270 Ezra Johnson	.08	.25
271 Tim Lewis RC	.08	.25
272 James Lofton PB	.25	.60
273 James Lofton IR	.25	.60
274 Larry McCarren	.08	.25
275 Jan Stenerud	.15	.40
276 Los Angeles Rams TL	.25	.60
Eric Dickerson		
277 Mike Barber	.08	.25
278 Jim Collins	.08	.25
279 Nolan Cromwell	.15	.40
280 Eric Dickerson RC	4.00	10.00
281 Eric Dickerson IR	.75	2.00
282 George Farmer	.08	.25
283 Vince Ferragamo	.15	.40
284 Kent Hill	.08	.25
285 John Misko	.08	.25
286 Jackie Slater PB RC	1.50	4.00
287 Jack Youngblood	.15	.40
288 Minnesota Vikings TL	.08	.25
Darrin Nelson		
289 Ted Brown	.15	.40
290 Greg Coleman	.08	.25
291 Steve Dils	.08	.25
292 Tony Galbreath	.08	.25
293 Tommy Kramer	.15	.40
294 Doug Martin	.08	.25
295 Darrin Nelson RC	.15	.40
296 Benny Ricardo	.08	.25
297 John Swain	.08	.25
298 John Turner	.08	.25
299 New Orleans Saints TL	.15	.40
George Rogers		
300 Morten Andersen RC	.60	1.50
301 Russell Erxleben	.08	.25
302 Jeff Groth	.08	.25
303 Rickey Jackson RC	.75	2.00
304 Johnnie Poe RC	.08	.25
305 George Rogers	.15	.40
306 Richard Todd	.15	.40
307 Jim Wilks RC	.08	.25
308 Dave Wilson RC	.08	.25
309 Wayne Wilson	.08	.25
310 New York Giants TL	.08	.25
Earnest Gray		
311 Leon Bright	.08	.25
312 Scott Brunner	.08	.25
313 Rob Carpenter	.08	.25
314 Harry Carson PB	.15	.40
315 Earnest Gray	.08	.25
316 Ali Haji-Sheikh RC	.08	.25
317 Mark Haynes	.15	.40
318 Dave Jennings	.08	.25
319 Brian Kelley	.08	.25
320 Phil Simms	.30	.75
321 Lawrence Taylor PB	1.50	3.00
322 Lawrence Taylor IR	.60	1.50
323 Brad Van Pelt	.08	.25
324 Butch Woolfolk	.08	.25
325 Philadelphia Eagles TL	.15	.40
Mike Quick		
326 Harold Carmichael	.15	.40
327 Herman Edwards	.08	.25
328 Michael Haddix RC	.08	.25
329 Dennis Harrison	.08	.25
330 Ron Jaworski	.15	.40
331 Wilbert Montgomery	.15	.40
332 Hubie Oliver	.08	.25
333 Mike Quick PB RC	.25	.60
334 Jerry Robinson	.08	.25
335 Max Runager	.08	.25
336 Michael Williams	.08	.25
337 St. Louis Cardinals TL	.15	.40
Ottis Anderson		
338 Ottis Anderson	.25	.60
339 Al (Bubba) Baker	.15	.40
340 Carl Birdsong	.08	.25
341 David Galloway	.08	.25
342 Roy Green PB	.15	.40
343 Roy Green IR	.15	.40
344 Curtis Greer RC	.08	.25
345 Neil Lomax	.15	.40
346 Doug Marsh	.08	.25
347 Stump Mitchell	.15	.40
348 Lionel Washington RC	.15	.40
349 San Francisco 49ers TL	.15	.40
Dwight Clark		
350 Dwaine Board	.08	.25
351 Dwight Clark	.25	.60
352 Dwight Clark IR	.15	.40
353 Roger Craig RC	1.50	4.00
354 Fred Dean	.15	.40
355 Fred Dean IR	.25	.60
Marino in background		
356 Dwight Hicks	.15	.40
357 Ronnie Lott PB	.60	1.50
358 Joe Montana PB	4.00	10.00
359 Joe Montana IR	1.50	3.00
360 Freddie Solomon	.08	.25
361 Wendell Tyler	.08	.25
362 Ray Wersching	.08	.25
363 Eric Wright RC	.15	.40
364 Tampa Bay Bucs TL	.08	.25
Kevin House		
365 Gerald Carter	.08	.25
366 Hugh Green	.15	.40
367 Kevin House	.15	.40
368 Michael Morton RC	.08	.25
369 James Owens	.08	.25
370 Booker Reese	.08	.25
371 Lee Roy Selmon	.25	.60
372 Jack Thompson	.15	.40
373 James Wilder	.15	.40
374 Steve Wilson	.08	.25
375 Wash. Redskins TL	.25	.60
John Riggins		
376 Jeff Bostic	.08	.25
377 Charlie Brown	.25	.60
378 Charlie Brown IR	.15	.40
379 Dave Butz	.15	.40
380 Darrell Green RC	6.00	12.00
381 Russ Grimm PB RC	1.50	4.00
382 Joe Jacoby PB	.15	.40
383 Dexter Manley	.15	.40
384 Art Monk	.40	1.00
385 Mark Moseley	.15	.40
386 Mark Murphy	.08	.25
387 Mike Nelms	.08	.25
388 John Riggins	.25	.60
389 John Riggins IR	.25	.60
390 Joe Theismann PB	.25	.60
391 Joe Theismann IR	.25	.60
392 Don Warren	.15	.40
393 Joe Washington	.15	.40
394 Checklist 1-132	.10	.60
395 Checklist 133-264	.10	.60
396 Checklist 265-396	.10	.60

1984 Topps Glossy Inserts

COMPLETE SET (11)	10.00	25.00
1 Curt Warner	.30	.75
2 Eric Dickerson	1.25	3.00
3 Dan Marino	10.00	20.00
4 Steve Bartkowski	.30	.75
5 Todd Christensen	.30	.75
6 Roy Green	.20	.50
7 Charlie Brown	.20	.50
8 Earnest Gray	.20	.50
9 Mark Gastineau	.20	.50
10 Fred Dean	.20	.50
11 Lawrence Taylor	.60	1.50

1984 Topps Play Cards

Inserted one per 1984 Topps pack, this 27-card set measures the standard size. On a yellow background, the fronts describe what collectors could win and how to play the game. A team name and a number of yards gained appears on the fronts. Collectors needed to accumulate a total of 25 yards to trade for a group of five 1984 Topps Glossy Send-In cards. The backs carry the official rules. The cards are numbered on the front as "Play x of 27".

COMPLETE SET (27)	8.00	20.00
1 Houston Oilers/2 yards gained	.30	.75
2 Houston Oilers/3 yards gained	.30	.75
3 Cleveland Browns/4 yards gained	.30	.75
4 Cleveland Browns/5 yards gained	.30	.75
5 Cincinnati Bengals/6 yards gained	.30	.75
6 Pittsburgh Steelers/7 yards gained	.40	1.00
7 New Orleans Saints/8 yards gained	.40	1.00
8 New York Giants/2 yards gained	.30	.75
9 Washington Redskins/3 yards gained	.40	1.00
10 Green Bay Packers/4 yards gained	.30	.75
11 Atlanta Falcons/5 yards gained	.30	.75
12 Detroit Lions/6 yards gained	.30	.75
13 New England Patriots/7 yards gained	.30	.75
14 New York Jets/8 yards gained	.40	1.00
15 Buffalo Bills/2 yards gained	.30	.75
16 Kansas City Chiefs/3 yards gained	.30	.75
17 Miami Dolphins/4 yards gained	.40	1.00
18 San Diego Chargers/5 yards gained	.30	.75
19 Seattle Seahawks/6 yards gained	.30	.75
20 Seattle Seahawks/7 yards gained	.30	.75
21 Dallas Cowboys/8 yards gained	.60	1.50
22 St. Louis Cardinals/2 yards gained	.30	.75
23 Chicago Bears/3 yards gained	.30	.75
24 San Francisco 49ers/4 yards gained	.60	1.50
25 Philadelphia Eagles/5 yards gained	.30	.75
26 Minnesota Vikings/6 yards gained	.30	.75
27 Los Angeles Rams/7 yards gained	.40	1.00

1984 Topps Glossy Send-In

COMPLETE SET (30)	10.00	25.00
1 Marcus Allen	.75	2.00
2 John Riggins	.30	.75
3 Walter Payton	3.00	8.00
4 Tony Dorsett	.75	2.00
5 Franco Harris	.30	.75
6 Curt Warner	.15	.40
7 Eric Dickerson	.30	.75
8 Mike Pruitt	.15	.40
9 Ken Anderson	.30	.75
10 Dan Fouts	.30	.75
11 Terry Bradshaw	1.25	3.00
12 Joe Theismann	.30	.75
13 Joe Montana	2.50	6.00
14 Danny White	.20	.50
15 Kellen Winslow	.30	.75
16 Wesley Walker	.15	.40
17 Drew Pearson	.30	.75
18 James Lofton	.30	.75
19 Cris Collinsworth	.15	.40
20 Dwight Clark	.20	.50
21 Mark Gastineau	.15	.40
22 Lawrence Taylor	.40	1.00
23 Randy White	.30	.75
24 Ed Too Tall Jones	.30	.75
25 Jack Lambert	.30	.75
26 Fred Dean	.15	.40
27 Jan Stenerud	.20	.50
28 Bruce Harper	.15	.40
29 Todd Christensen	.15	.40
30 Greg Pruitt	.15	.40

1984 Topps USFL

The 1984 Topps USFL set contains 132 standard-size cards, which were available as a complete set housed in its own specially made box. Card fronts have the "Premier USFL Edition" logo at the top border. Beneath the player photo is the team helmet and the player's name, team and position in a yellow box. The backs have NFL and USFL statistics (rookies have collecge stats) and a team fact. The cards in the set are numbered in alphabetical team order (with players arranged alphabetically within teams). Popular Extended Rookie Cards are quarterbacks Jim Kelly and Steve Young. Herschel Walker and Reggie White are other notable XRC's. More players making their first professional card appearence include Gary Anderson, Anthony Carter, Bobby Hebert, Craig James, Vaughan Johnson, Gary Plummer and Ricky Sanders.

COMP.FACT.SET (132)	150.00	300.00
COMPLETE SET (132)	150.00	300.00
1 Luther Bradley	.75	2.00
2 Frank Corral	.75	2.00
3 Trumaine Johnson	.75	2.00
4 Greg Landry	1.25	2.50
5 Kit Lathrop	.75	2.00
6 Kevin Long	.75	2.00
7 Tim Spencer	.75	2.00
8 Stan White	.75	2.00
9 Buddy Aydelette	.75	2.00
10 Tom Banks	.75	2.00
11 Fred Bohannon	.75	2.00
12 Joe Cribbs	2.00	4.00
13 Joey Jones	.75	2.00
14 Scott Norwood XRC	1.25	2.50
15 Jim Smith	1.25	2.50
16 Cliff Stoudt	2.00	4.00
17 Vince Evans	2.00	4.00
18 Vagas Ferguson	.75	2.00
19 John Gillen	.75	2.00
20 Kris Haines	.75	2.00
21 Glenn Hyde	.75	2.00
22 Mark Keel	.75	2.00
23 Gary Lewis XRC	.75	2.00
24 Doug Plank	.75	2.00
25 Neil Balholm	.75	2.00
26 David Dumars	.75	2.00
27 David Martin XRC	.75	2.00
28 Craig Penrose	.75	2.00
29 Dave Stalls	.75	2.00
30 Harry Sydney XRC	.75	2.00
31 Vincent White	.75	2.00
32 George Yarno	.75	2.00
33 Kiki DeAyala	.75	2.00
34 Sam Harrell	.75	2.00
35 Mike Hawkins	.75	2.00
36 Jim Kelly XRC	30.00	60.00
37 Mark Rush	.75	2.00
38 Ricky Sanders XRC	3.00	6.00
39 Paul Bergmann	.75	2.00
40 Tom Dinkel	.75	2.00
41 Wyatt Henderson	.75	2.00
42 Vaughan Johnson XRC	1.25	2.50
43 Willie McClendon	.75	2.00
44 Matt Robinson	.75	2.00
45 George Achica	.75	2.00
46 Mark Adickes XRC	.75	2.00
47 Howard Carson	.75	2.00
48 Kevin Nelson	.75	2.00
49 Jeff Partridge	.75	2.00
50 Jo Jo Townsell	1.25	2.50
51 Eddie Weaver	.75	2.00
52 Steve Young XRC	50.00	100.00
53 Derrick Crawford	.75	2.00
54 Walter Lewis	.75	2.00
55 Phil McKinnely	.75	2.00
56 Vic Minore	.75	2.00
57 Gary Shirk	.75	2.00
58 Reggie White XRC	30.00	60.00
59 Anthony Carter XRC	5.00	12.00
60 John Corker	.75	2.00
61 David Greenwood	.75	2.00
62 Bobby Hebert XRC	2.00	4.00
63 Derek Holloway	.75	2.00
64 Ken Lacy	.75	2.00
65 Tyrone McGriff	.75	2.00
66 Ray Pinney	.75	2.00
67 Gary Barbaro	.75	2.00
68 Sam Bowers	.75	2.00
69 Clarence Collins	.75	2.00
70 Willie Harper	.75	2.00
71 Jim LeClair	.75	2.00
72 Bobby Leopold XRC	.75	2.00
73 Brian Sipe	2.00	4.00
74 Herschel Walker XRC	12.50	25.00
75 Junior Ah You XRC	.75	2.00
76 Marcus Dupree XRC	10.00	20.00
77 Marcus Marek	.75	2.00
78 Tim Mazzetti	.75	2.00
79 Mike Robinson XRC	.75	2.00
80 Dan Ross	2.00	4.00
81 Mark Schellen	.75	2.00
82 Johnnie Walton	.75	2.00
83 Gordon Banks	.75	2.00
84 Fred Besana	.75	2.00
85 Dave Browning	.75	2.00
86 Eric Jordan	.75	2.00
87 Frank Manumaleuga	.75	2.00
88 Gary Plummer XRC	2.00	4.00
89 Stan Talley	.75	2.00
90 Arthur Whittington	.75	2.00
91 Terry Beeson	.75	2.00
92 Mel Gray	2.00	4.00
93 Mike Katolin	.75	2.00
94 Dewey McClain	.75	2.00
95 Sidney Thornton	.75	2.00
96 Doug Williams	2.00	4.00
97 Kelvin Bryant XRC	2.00	4.00
98 John Bunting	.75	2.00
99 Irv Eatman XRC	1.25	2.50
100 Scott Fitzkee	.75	2.00
101 Chuck Fusina	.75	2.00
102 Sean Landeta XRC	1.25	2.50
103 David Trout	.75	2.00
104 Scott Woerner	.75	2.00
105 Glenn Carano	.75	2.00
106 Ron Crosby	.75	2.00
107 Jerry Holmes	.75	2.00
108 Bruce Huther	.75	2.00
109 Mike Rozier XRC	2.00	4.00
110 Larry Swider	.75	2.00
111 Danny Buggs	.75	2.00
112 Putt Choate	.75	2.00
113 Rich Garza	.75	2.00
114 Joey Hackett	.75	2.00
115 Rick Neuheisel XRC	2.00	4.00
116 Mike St. Clair	.75	2.00
117 Gary Anderson XRC RB	2.00	4.00
118 Zenon Andrusyshyn	.75	2.00
119 Doug Beaudoin	.75	2.00
120 Mike Butler	.75	2.00
121 Willie Gillespie	.75	2.00
122 Fred Nordgren	.75	2.00
123 John Reaves	.75	2.00
124 Eric Truvillion	.75	2.00
125 Reggie Collier	.75	2.00
126 Mike Guess	.75	2.00
127 Mike Hohensee	.75	2.00
128 Craig James XRC	3.00	8.00
129 Eric Robinson	.75	2.00
130 Billy Taylor	.75	2.00
131 Joey Walters	.75	2.00
132 Checklist 1-132	1.25	2.50

1985 Topps

The 1985 Topps set contains 396 standard-size cards. Wax packs contained 15-cards. Horizontal card fronts have black borders that are prone to chipping. To the right is the player's name and team name. Vertical backs have highlights and statistics. Subsets include Record Breakers (1-6), playoffs (7-9) and league leaders (192-197). Team Leader (TL) cards feature an action photo on the front with a caption. The backs contain team scoring information from the previous year. The order of teams (alphabetically arranged by conference with players themselves alphabetically ordered within each team). The key Rookie Card in this set is Warren Moon (although he had already appeared in several JOGO CFL card issues). Other Rookie Cards include Carl Banks, Mark Clayton, Richard Dent, Henry Ellard, Irving Fryar, Louis Lipps, Steve McMichael, Mike Munchak and Darryl Talley.

COMPLETE SET (396)	30.00	60.00
COMP.FACT.SET (396)	40.00	75.00
1 Mark Clayton RB	.20	.50
Most Touchdown		
Receptions: Season		
2 Eric Dickerson RB	.20	.50
Most Yards		
Rushing: Season		
3 Charlie Joiner RB	.20	.50
Most Receptions:		
Career		
4 Dan Marino RB UER	3.00	6.00
Most Touchdown		
Passes: Season		
(Dolphins misspelled		
as Dophins)		
5 Art Monk RB	.20	.50
Most Receptions:		
Season		
6 Walter Payton RB	.40	1.00
Most Yards		
Rushing: Career		
7 NFC Championship/49ers 23, Bears 0	.10	.30
(Matt Suhey tackled)		
8 AFC Championship	.10	.30
Dolphins 45,		
Steelers 28		
(Woody Bennett over)		
9 Super Bowl XIX/49ers 38,	.10	.30
Dolphins 16		
(Wendell Tyler)		
10 Atlanta Falcons TL	.07	.20
Stretching For The		
First Down		
(Gerald Riggs)		
11 William Andrews	.10	.30
12 Stacey Bailey	.07	.20
13 Steve Bartkowski	.20	.50
14 Rick Bryan RC	.07	.20
15 Alfred Jackson	.07	.20
16 Kenny Johnson	.07	.20
17 Mike Kenn	.07	.20
18 Mike Pitts RC	.07	.20
19 Gerald Riggs	.10	.30
20 Sylvester Stamps	.07	.20
21 R.C. Thielemann	.07	.20
22 Chicago Bears TL	.30	.75
Sweetness Sets		
Record Straight		
(Walter Payton)		
23 Todd Bell RC	.07	.20
24 Richard Dent AP RC	1.50	4.00
25 Gary Fencik	.10	.30
26 Dave Finzer	.07	.20
27 Leslie Frazier	.07	.20
28 Steve Fuller	.10	.30
29 Willie Gault	.20	.50
30 Dan Hampton AP	.20	.50
31 Jim McMahon	.30	.75
32 Steve McMichael RC	.20	.50
33 Walter Payton AP	3.00	8.00
34 Mike Singletary	.30	.75
35 Matt Suhey	.07	.20
36 Bob Thomas	.07	.20
37 Dallas Cowboys TL	.20	.50
Busting Through		
The Defense		
(Tony Dorsett)		
38 Bill Bates RC	.40	1.00
39 Doug Cosbie	.10	.30
40 Tony Dorsett	.30	.75
41 Michael Downs	.07	.20
42 Mike Hegman RC UER	.07	.20
(reference to SB VIII,		
should be SB XIII)		
43 Tony Hill	.10	.30
44 Gary Hogeboom RC	.07	.20
45 Jim Jeffcoat RC	.20	.50
46 Ed Too Tall Jones	.20	.50
47 Mike Renfro	.07	.20
48 Rafael Septien	.07	.20
49 Dennis Thurman	.07	.20
50 Everson Walls	.10	.30
51 Danny White	.20	.50
52 Randy White	.20	.50
53 Detroit Lions TL	.07	.20
Popping One Loose		
(Lions' Defense)		
54 Jeff Chadwick	.07	.20
55 Mike Cofer RC	.07	.20
56 Gary Danielson	.07	.20
57 Keith Dorney	.07	.20
58 Doug English	.10	.30
59 William Gay	.07	.20
60 Ken Jenkins	.07	.20
61 James Jones	.10	.30
62 Eddie Murray	.10	.30
63 Billy Sims	.20	.50
64 Leonard Thompson	.07	.20
65 Bobby Watkins	.07	.20
66 Green Bay Packers TL	.10	.30
Spotting His		
Deep Receiver		
(Lynn Dickey)		
67 Paul Coffman	.07	.20
68 Lynn Dickey	.10	.30
69 Mike Douglass	.07	.20
70 Tom Flynn RC	.07	.20
71 Eddie Lee Ivery	.07	.20
72 Ezra Johnson	.07	.20
73 Mark Lee	.07	.20
74 Tim Lewis	.07	.20
75 James Lofton	.20	.50
76 Bucky Scribner	.07	.20
77 Los Angeles Rams TL	.20	.50
Record-Setting		
Ground Attack		
(Eric Dickerson)		
78 Nolan Cromwell	.10	.30
79 Eric Dickerson AP	.50	1.25
80 Henry Ellard RC	1.00	2.50
81 Kent Hill	.07	.20
82 LeRoy Irvin	.10	.30
83 Jeff Kemp RC	.10	.30
84 Mike Lansford	.07	.20
85 Barry Redden	.07	.20
86 Jackie Slater	.20	.50
87 Doug Smith C RC	.10	.30
88 Jack Youngblood	.10	.30
89 Minnesota Vikings TL	.07	.20
Smothering The		
Opposition		
(Vikings' Defense)		
90 Alfred Anderson RC	.07	.20
91 Ted Brown	.10	.30
92 Greg Coleman	.07	.20
93 Tommy Hannon	.07	.20
94 Tommy Kramer	.10	.30
95 Leo Lewis RC	.10	.30
96 Doug Martin	.07	.20
97 Darrin Nelson	.10	.30
98 Jan Stenerud AP	.10	.30
99 Sammie White	.10	.30
100 New Orleans Saints TL	.07	.20
Hurdling Over		
Front Line		
101 Morten Andersen	.20	.50
102 Hoby Brenner RC	.10	.30
103 Bruce Clark	.07	.20
104 Hokie Gajan	.07	.20
105 Brian Hansen RC	.07	.20
106 Rickey Jackson	.30	.75
107 George Rogers	.10	.30
108 Dave Wilson	.07	.20
109 Tyrone Young	.07	.20
110 New York Giants TL	.07	.20
Engulfing The		
Quarterback		
(Giants' Defense)		
111 Carl Banks RC	.40	1.00
112 Jim Burt RC	.20	.50
113 Rob Carpenter	.07	.20
114 Harry Carson	.10	.30
115 Earnest Gray	.07	.20
116 Ali Haji-Sheikh	.07	.20
117 Mark Haynes	.10	.30
118 Bobby Johnson	.07	.20
119 Lionel Manuel RC	.10	.30
120 Joe Morris RC	.20	.50
121 Zeke Mowatt RC	.10	.30
122 Jeff Rutledge RC	.07	.20
123 Phil Simms	.20	.50
124 Lawrence Taylor AP	.60	1.50
125 Philadelphia Eagles TL	.07	.20
Finding The Wide		
Open Spaces		
(Wilbert Montgomery)		
126 Greg Brown	.07	.20
127 Ray Ellis	.07	.20
128 Dennis Harrison	.07	.20
129 Wes Hopkins RC	.10	.30
130 Mike Horan RC	.07	.20
131 Kenny Jackson RC	.07	.20
132 Ron Jaworski	.10	.30
133 Paul McFadden	.07	.20
134 Wilbert Montgomery	.10	.30
135 Mike Quick	.20	.50
136 John Spagnola	.07	.20
137 St.Louis Cardinals TL	.07	.20
Exploiting The		
Air Route		
(Neil Lomax)		
138 Ottis Anderson	.20	.50
139 Al(Bubba) Baker	.10	.30
140 Roy Green	.10	.30
141 Curtis Greer	.07	.20
142 E.J. Junior AP	.07	.20
143 Neil Lomax	.10	.30
144 Stump Mitchell	.10	.30
145 Neil O'Donoghue	.07	.20
146 Pat Tilley	.07	.20
147 Lionel Washington	.07	.20
148 San Francisco 49ers TL	.50	1.25
The Road To		
Super Bowl XIX		
(Joe Montana)		
149 Dwaine Board	.07	.20
150 Dwight Clark	.20	.50
151 Roger Craig	.40	1.00
152 Randy Cross	.10	.30
153 Fred Dean	.10	.30
154 Keith Fahnhorst RC	.07	.20
155 Dwight Hicks	.07	.20
156 Ronnie Lott	.20	.50
157 Joe Montana	4.00	10.00
158 Renaldo Nehemiah	.10	.30
159 Fred Quillan	.07	.20
160 Jack Reynolds	.07	.20
161 Freddie Solomon	.07	.20
162 Keena Turner RC	.07	.20
163 Wendell Tyler	.07	.20
164 Ray Wersching	.07	.20
165 Carlton Williamson	.07	.20
166 Tampa Bay Bucs TL	.10	.30
Protecting The		
Quarterback		
(Steve DeBerg)		
167 Gerald Carter	.07	.20
168 Mark Cotney	.07	.20
169 Steve DeBerg	.20	.50
170 Sean Farrell RC	.07	.20
171 Hugh Green	.10	.30
172 Kevin House	.10	.30
173 David Logan	.07	.20
174 Michael Morton	.07	.20
175 Lee Roy Selmon	.20	.50
176 James Wilder	.07	.20
177 Wash. Redskins TL	.20	.50
Diesel Named Desire		
(John Riggins)		
178 Charlie Brown	.07	.20
179 Monte Coleman RC	.10	.30
180 Vernon Dean	.07	.20
181 Darrell Green	.20	.50
182 Russ Grimm	.30	.75
183 Joe Jacoby	.10	.30
184 Dexter Manley	.10	.30
185 Art Monk AP	.20	.50
186 Mark Moseley	.10	.30
187 Calvin Muhammad	.07	.20
188 Mike Nelms	.07	.20
189 John Riggins	.20	.50
190 Joe Theismann	.20	.50
191 Joe Washington	.10	.30
192 Passing Leaders	4.00	10.00
Dan Marino		
Joe Montana		
193 Receiving Leaders	.10	.30
Ozzie Newsome		
Art Monk		
194 Rushing Leaders	.20	.50
Earnest Jackson		
Eric Dickerson		
195 Scoring Leaders	.07	.20
Gary Anderson K		
Ray Wersching		
196 Interception Leaders	.07	.20
Kenny Easley		
Tom Flynn		
197 Punting Leaders	.07	.20
Jim Arnold		
Brian Hansen		
198 Buffalo Bills TL	.07	.20
Rushing Toward		
Rookie Stardom		
(Greg Bell)		
199 Greg Bell RC	.10	.30
200 Preston Dennard	.07	.20
201 Joe Ferguson	.10	.30
202 Byron Franklin	.07	.20
203 Steve Freeman	.07	.20
204 Jim Haslett	.10	.30
205 Charles Romes	.07	.20
206 Fred Smerlas	.07	.20
207 Darryl Talley RC	.20	.50
208 Van Williams	.07	.20
209 Cincinnati Bengals TL	.10	.30
Advancing The		
Ball Downfield		
(Ken Anderson and		
Larry Kinnebrew)		
210 Ken Anderson	.20	.50
211 Jim Breech	.07	.20
212 Louis Breeden	.07	.20
213 James Brooks	.10	.30
214 Ross Browner	.10	.30
215 Eddie Edwards	.07	.20
216 M.L. Harris	.07	.20
217 Bobby Kemp	.07	.20
218 Larry Kinnebrew RC	.07	.20
219 Anthony Munoz AP	.20	.50
220 Reggie Williams	.10	.30
221 Cleveland Browns TL	.07	.20
Evading The		
Defensive Pursuit		
(Boyce Green)		
222 Matt Bahr	.10	.30
223 Chip Banks	.07	.20
224 Reggie Camp	.07	.20
225 Tom Cousineau	.07	.20
226 Joe DeLamielleure	.20	.50
227 Ricky Feacher	.07	.20
228 Boyce Green RC	.07	.20
229 Al Gross	.07	.20
230 Clay Matthews	.20	.50
231 Paul McDonald	.07	.20
232 Ozzie Newsome AP	.20	.50
233 Mike Pruitt	.10	.30
234 Don Rogers	.07	.20
235 Denver Broncos TL	1.00	2.50
Thousand Yarder		
Gets The Ball		
(Sammy Winder and		
John Elway)		
236 Rubin Carter	.07	.20
237 Barney Chavous	.07	.20
238 John Elway	5.00	12.00
239 Steve Foley	.07	.20
240 Mike Harden RC	.07	.20
241 Tom Jackson	.20	.50
242 Butch Johnson	.07	.20
243 Rulon Jones	.07	.20
244 Rich Karlis	.07	.20
245 Steve Watson	.10	.30
246 Gerald Willhite	.07	.20
247 Sammy Winder	.10	.30
248 Houston Oilers TL	.07	.20
Eluding A		
Traffic Jam		
(Larry Moriarty)		
249 Jesse Baker	.07	.20
250 Carter Hartwig	.07	.20
251 Warren Moon RC	6.00	15.00
252 Larry Moriarty RC	.07	.20
253 Mike Munchak RC	1.25	3.00
254 Carl Roaches	.07	.20
255 Tim Smith	.10	.30
256 Willie Tullis	.07	.20
257 Jamie Williams RC	.07	.20
258 Indianapolis Colts TL	.07	.20
Start Of A		
Long Gainer		
(Art Schlichter)		
259 Raymond Butler	.07	.20
260 Johnie Cooks	.07	.20
261 Eugene Daniel RC	.07	.20
262 Curtis Dickey	.10	.30
263 Chris Hinton	.10	.30
264 Vernon Maxwell	.07	.20
265 Randy McMillan	.07	.20
266 Art Schlichter RC	.20	.50
267 Rohn Stark	.10	.30
268 Leo Wisniewski	.07	.20
269 Kansas City Chiefs TL	.07	.20
Pigskin About To		
Soar Upward		
(Bill Kenney)		
270 Jim Arnold	.07	.20
271 Mike Bell	.07	.20
272 Todd Blackledge RC	.10	.30
273 Carlos Carson	.10	.30
274 Deron Cherry	.10	.30
275 Herman Heard RC	.07	.20
276 Bill Kenney	.10	.30
277 Nick Lowery	.20	.50
278 Bill Maas RC	.07	.20
279 Henry Marshall	.07	.20
280 Art Still	.07	.20
281 Los Angeles Raiders TL	.20	.50
Diving For The		
Goal Line		
(Marcus Allen)		
282 Marcus Allen	1.00	2.50
283 Lyle Alzado	.10	.30
284 Chris Bahr	.07	.20
285 Malcolm Barnwell	.07	.20
286 Cliff Branch	.20	.50
287 Todd Christensen	.20	.50
288 Ray Guy	.20	.50
289 Lester Hayes	.10	.30
290 Mike Haynes	.10	.30
291 Henry Lawrence	.07	.20
292 Howie Long	.75	2.00
293 Rod Martin	.10	.30
294 Vann McElroy	.07	.20
295 Matt Millen	.10	.30
296 Bill Pickel RC	.07	.20
297 Jim Plunkett	.20	.50

298 Dokie Williams RC .07 .20
299 Marc Wilson .10 .30
300 Miami Dolphins TL .10 .30
Super Duper
Performance
(Mark Duper)
301 Bob Baumhower .07 .20
302 Doug Betters .07 .20
303 Glenn Blackwood .10 .30
304 Lyle Blackwood .10 .30
305 Kim Bokamper .07 .20
306 Charles Bowser RC .07 .20
307 Jimmy Cefalo .07 .20
308 Mark Clayton AP RC .50 1.25
309 A.J. Duhe .07 .20
310 Mark Duper .20 .50
311 Andra Franklin .07 .20
312 Bruce Hardy .07 .20
313 Pete Johnson .10 .30
314 Dan Marino AP UER 5.00 12.00
(Fouts 4802 yards in/1981, should be 4082)
315 Tony Nathan .10 .30
316 Ed Newman .07 .20
317 Reggie Roby AP .20 .50
318 Dwight Stephenson .40 1.00
319 Uwe Von Schamann .07 .20
320 New England Pats TL .07 .20
Refusing To
Be Denied
(Tony Collins)
321 Raymond Clayborn .10 .30
322 Tony Collins .10 .30
323 Tony Eason RC .20 .50
324 Tony Franklin .07 .20
325 Irving Fryar RC 2.00 5.00
326 John Hannah AP .20 .50
327 Brian Holloway .07 .20
328 Craig James RC .50 1.25
329 Stanley Morgan .10 .30
330 Steve Nelson .07 .20
331 Derrick Ramsey .07 .20
332 Stephen Starring RC .10 .30
333 Mosi Tatupu .07 .20
334 Andre Tippett .20 .50
335 New York Jets TL .10 .30
Thwarting The
Passing Game
(Mark Gastineau
and Joe Ferguson)
336 Russell Carter RC .07 .20
337 Mark Gastineau .10 .30
338 Bruce Harper .07 .20
339 Bobby Humphery RC .07 .20
340 Johnny Lam Jones .07 .20
341 Joe Klecko .10 .30
342 Pat Leahy .07 .20
343 Marty Lyons .10 .30
344 Freeman McNeil .10 .30
345 Lance Mehl .07 .20
346 Ken O'Brien RC .20 .50
347 Marvin Powell .07 .20
348 Pat Ryan .07 .20
349 Mickey Shuler RC .07 .20
350 Wesley Walker .10 .30
351 Pittsburgh Steelers TL .10 .30
Testing Defensive
Pass Coverage
(Mark Malone)
352 Walter Abercrombie .07 .20
353 Gary Anderson K .10 .30
354 Robin Cole .07 .20
355 Bennie Cunningham .07 .20
356 Rich Erenberg .07 .20
357 Jack Lambert .20 .50
358 Louis Lipps RC .20 .50
359 Mark Malone .10 .30
360 Mike Merriweather RC .07 .20
361 Frank Pollard .07 .20
362 Donnie Shell .10 .30
363 John Stallworth .20 .50
364 Sam Washington .07 .20
365 Mike Webster .10 .30
366 Dwayne Woodruff .07 .20
367 San Diego Chargers TL .07 .20
Jarring The
Ball Loose
(Chargers' Defense)
368 Rolf Benirschke .07 .20
369 Gill Byrd RC .20 .50
370 Wes Chandler .10 .30
371 Bobby Duckworth .07 .20
372 Dan Fouts .20 .50
373 Mike Green .07 .20
374 Pete Holohan RC .07 .20
375 Earnest Jackson RC .10 .30
376 Lionel James RC .10 .30
377 Charlie Joiner .20 .50
378 Billy Ray Smith .10 .30
379 Kellen Winslow .20 .50
380 Seattle Seahawks TL .10 .30
Setting Up For
The Air Attack
(Dave Krieg)
381 Dave Brown .07 .20
382 Jeff Bryant .07 .20
383 Dan Doornink .07 .20
384 Kenny Easley .10 .30
385 Jacob Green .10 .30
386 David Hughes .07 .20
387 Norm Johnson .07 .20
388 Dave Krieg .20 .50
389 Steve Largent .40 1.00
390 Joe Nash RC .07 .20
391 Daryl Turner RC .07 .20
392 Curt Warner .20 .50
393 Fredd Young RC .10 .30
394 Checklist 1-132 .20 .50
395 Checklist 133-264 .20 .50
396 Checklist 265-396 .20 .50

1985 Topps Box Bottoms

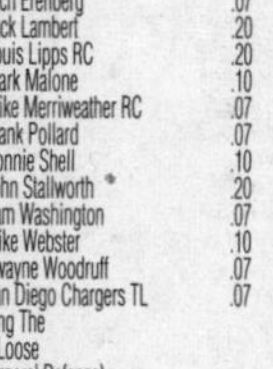

This 16-card set, which measures 2 1/2" by 3 1/2", was issued on the bottom of 1985 Topps wax pack boxes. The cards are in the same design as the 1985 Topps regular issues except they are bordered in red and have the words "Topps Superstars" printed in very small letters above the players' photos. Similar to the regular issue, these cards have a horizontal orientation. The backs of the cards are just like the regular card in that they have biographical and complete statistical information. The cards are arranged in alphabetical order and include such stars as Joe Montana and Walter Payton.

COMPLETE SET (16) 20.00 40.00
A Marcus Allen 1.25 3.00
B Ottis Anderson .60 1.50
C Mark Clayton .60 1.50
D Eric Dickerson .75 2.00
E Tony Dorsett 1.25 3.00
F Dan Fouts 1.00 2.50
G Mark Gastineau .60 1.50
H Charlie Joiner .75 2.00
I James Lofton .75 2.00
J Neil Lomax .60 1.50
K Dan Marino 5.00 10.00
L Art Monk .75 2.00
M Joe Montana 5.00 10.00
N Walter Payton 5.00 10.00
O John Stallworth 1.00 2.50
P Lawrence Taylor 1.00 2.50

1985 Topps Glossy Inserts

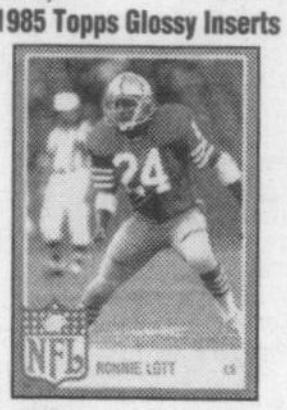

COMPLETE SET (11) 8.00 20.00
1 Mark Clayton .20 .50
2 Eric Dickerson .30 .75
3 John Elway 2.00 5.00
4 Mark Gastineau .20 .50
5 Ronnie Lott UER .30 .75
(Shown wearing 24)
6 Dan Marino 2.00 5.00
7 Joe Montana 2.50 6.00
8 Walter Payton 1.25 3.00
9 John Riggins .30 .75
10 John Stallworth .30 .75
11 Lawrence Taylor .40 1.00

1985 Topps USFL

The 1985 Topps USFL set contains 132 football standard-size cards, which were available as a complete set housed in its own specially made box. The card fronts have a red border with a blue and white stripe in the middle. The USFL logo is at the top of the photo with the team name in red block letters in a white box at the bottom of the photo. Also toward the bottom of the photo, is the player's name and position within a yellow football. The card backs are printed in red and blue on white card stock. Card backs describe each player's highlights of the previous USFL season and have NFL and USFL statistics. The cards in the set are ordered numerically by team with players within teams also ordered alphabetically. The key Extended Rookie Cards in this set are Gary Clark, Doug Flutie, William Fuller and Sam Mills. Other key cards in the set include the second USFL cards of Jim Kelly, Herschel Walker, Reggie White, and Steve Young.

COMP.FACT.SET (132) 60.00 120.00
COMPLETE SET (132) 60.00 120.00
1 Case DeBruijn .20 .50
2 Mike Katolin .20 .50
3 Bruce Laird .20 .50
4 Kit Lathrop .20 .50
5 Kevin Long .20 .50
6 Karl Lorch .20 .50
7 Dave Tipton .20 .50
8 Doug Williams .75 2.00
9 Luis Zendejas XRC .20 .50
10 Kelvin Bryant .40 1.00
11 Willie Collier .20 .50
12 Irv Eatman .20 .50
13 Scott Fitzkee .20 .50
14 William Fuller XRC 1.25 3.00
15 Chuck Fusina .20 .50
16 Pete Kugler .20 .50
17 Garcia Lane .20 .50
18 Mike Lush .20 .50
19 Sam Mills XRC 2.00 5.00
20 Buddy Aydelette .20 .50
21 Joe Cribbs .75 2.00
22 David Dumars .20 .50
23 Robin Earl .20 .50
24 Joey Jones .20 .50
25 Leon Perry .20 .50
26 Dave Pureifory .20 .50
27 Bill Roe .20 .50
28 Doug Smith DT XRC .75 2.00
29 Cliff Stoudt .40 1.00
30 Jeff Delaney .20 .50
31 Vince Evans .40 1.00
32 Leonard Harris XRC .20 .50
33 Bill Johnson .20 .50
34 Marc Lewis XRC .20 .50
35 David Martin .20 .50
36 Bruce Thornton .20 .50
37 Craig Walls .20 .50
38 Vincent White .20 .50
39 Luther Bradley .20 .50
40 Pete Catan .20 .50
41 Kiki DeAyala .20 .50
42 Toni Fritsch .20 .50
43 Sam Harrell .20 .50
44 Richard Johnson WR XRC .40 1.00
45 Jim Kelly 10.00 20.00
46 Gerald McNeil XRC .20 .50
47 Clarence Verdin XRC .75 2.00
48 Dale Walters .20 .50
49 Gary Clark XRC 2.50 6.00
50 Tom Dinkel .20 .50
51 Mike Edwards .20 .50
52 Brian Franco .20 .50
53 Bob Gruber .20 .50
54 Robbie Mahfouz .20 .50
55 Mike Rozier .75 2.00
56 Brian Sipe .40 1.00
57 J.T. Turner .20 .50
58 Howard Carson .20 .50
59 Wymon Henderson XRC .20 .50
60 Kevin Nelson .20 .50
61 Jeff Partridge .20 .50
62 Ben Rudolph .20 .50
63 Jo Jo Townsell .40 1.00
64 Eddie Weaver .20 .50
65 Steve Young 15.00 30.00
66 Tony Zendejas XRC .40 1.00
67 Mossy Cade .20 .50
68 Leonard Coleman XRC .20 .50
69 John Corker .20 .50
70 Derrick Crawford .20 .50
71 Art Kuehn .20 .50
72 Walter Lewis .20 .50
73 Tyrone McGriff .20 .50
74 Tim Spencer .40 1.00
75 Reggie White 10.00 20.00
76 Gizmo Williams XRC .75 2.00
77 Sam Bowers .20 .50
78 Maurice Carthon XRC .75 2.00
79 Clarence Collins .20 .50
80 Doug Flutie XRC 10.00 20.00
81 Freddie Gilbert .20 .50
82 Kerry Justin .20 .50
83 Dave Lapham .20 .50
84 Rick Partridge .20 .50
85 Roger Ruzek XRC .40 1.00
86 Herschel Walker 3.00 8.00
87 Gordon Banks .20 .50
88 Monte Bennett .20 .50
89 Albert Bentley XRC .40 1.00
90 Novo Bojovic .20 .50
91 Dave Browning .20 .50
92 Anthony Carter .75 2.00
93 Bobby Hebert .75 2.00
94 Ray Pinney .20 .50
95 Stan Talley .20 .50
96 Ruben Vaughan .20 .50
97 Curtis Bledsoe .20 .50
98 Reggie Collier .20 .50
99 Jerry Doerger .20 .50
100 Jerry Golsteyn .20 .50
101 Bob Niziolek .20 .50
102 Joel Patten .20 .50
103 Ricky Simmons .20 .50
104 Joey Walters .20 .50
105 Marcus Dupree 4.00 10.00
106 Jeff Gossett .40 1.00
107 Frank Lockett .20 .50
108 Marcus Marek .20 .50
109 Kenny Neil .20 .50
110 Robert Pennywell .20 .50
111 Matt Robinson .20 .50
112 Dan Ross .40 1.00
113 Doug Woodward .20 .50
114 Danny Buggs .20 .50
115 Putt Choate .20 .50
116 Greg Fields .20 .50
117 Ken Hartley .20 .50
118 Nick Mike-Mayer .20 .50
119 Rick Neuheisel .75 2.00
120 Peter Raeford .20 .50
121 Gary Worthy .20 .50
122 Gary Anderson RB .40 1.00
123 Zenon Andrusyshyn .20 .50
124 Greg Boone .20 .50
125 Mike Butler .20 .50
126 Mike Clark .20 .50
127 Willie Gillespie .20 .50
128 James Harrell .20 .50
129 Marvin Harvey .20 .50
130 John Reaves .40 1.00
131 Eric Truvillion .20 .50
132 Checklist 1-132 .40 1.00

1985 Topps USFL Generals

Topps produced this nine-card panel for the New Jersey Generals of the USFL. The entire panel measures approximately 7 1/2" by 10 1/2" and the individual cards, when cut, measure the standard size. Card backs are printed in yellow and red on gray card stock. The panels were supposedly distributed to members of the Generals' Infantry Club, which was a fan club for youngsters. The values below are applicable also for uncut sheets as that is the most common way this set is seen.

COMPLETE SET (9) .10.00 25.00
1 Walt Michaels CO .75 2.00
2 Sam Bowers .50 1.25
3 Clarence Collins .50 1.25
4 Doug Flutie 6.00 15.00
5 Gregory Johnson .50 1.25
6 Jim LeClair .50 1.25
7 Bobby Leopold .50 1.25
8 Herschel Walker 3.00 8.00
9 Membership card .50 1.25
(Schedule on back)

1986 Topps

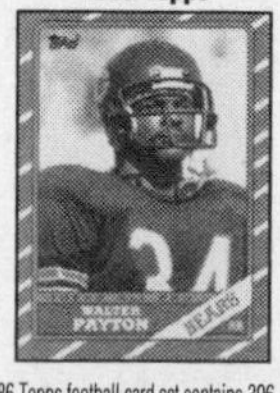

The 1986 Topps football card set contains 396 standard-size cards. As if to resemble a football field, player photos are surrounded by green borders with white lines. The player's name, team name and position are at the bottom. Horizontally designed backs have yearly statistics and highlights. The copyright line on the back also includes a letter (A, B, C, or D) to indicate which sheet the card was cut from. Note that each card in the set was produced on two different sheets. This resulted in each card including one of two different letter designations on the back, thus creating a variation on each card. Subsets include Record Breakers (1-7) and league leaders (225-229). Team cards feature a distinctive yellow border on the front with the team's results and leaders (from the previous season) listed on the back. The set numbering is in order of 1984 finish. Rookie Cards in this set include Mark Bavaro, Ray Childress, Boomer Esiason, Bernie Kosar, Wilber Marshall, Karl Mecklenburg, William Perry, Andre Reed, Jerry Rice, Bruce Smith and Al Toon. In addition, Anthony Carter, Gary Clark, Bobby Hebert, Reggie White and Steve Young are Rookie Cards, although they had each appeared in a previous Topps USFL set.

COMPLETE SET (396) 50.00 100.00
COMP.FACT.SET (396) 150.00 225.00
1 Marcus Allen RB .30 .75
Most Yards From
Scrimmage: Season
2 Eric Dickerson RB .20 .50
Most Yards Rushing:
Playoff Game
3 Lionel James RB .07 .20
Most All-Purpose
Yards: Season
4 Steve Largent RB .20 .50
Most Seasons 50 or
More Receptions
5 George Martin RB .07 .20
Most Touchdowns
Defensive Lineman: Career
6 Stephone Paige RB .07 .20
Most Yards
Receiving: Game
7 Walter Payton RB .30 .75
Most Consecutive
Games 100 or More
Yards Rushing
8 Super Bowl XX .10 .30
Bears 46, Patriots 10
(Jim McMahon
handing off)
9 Bears TL .25 .60
(Walter Payton in Motion)
10 Jim McMahon .20 .50
11 Walter Payton AP 3.00 8.00
12 Matt Suhey .07 .20
13 Willie Gault .10 .30
14 Dennis McKinnon RC .07 .20
15 Emery Moorehead .07 .20
16 Jim Covert AP .10 .30
17 Jay Hilgenberg RC .20 .50
18 Kevin Butler RC .10 .30
19 Richard Dent AP .30 .75
20 William Perry RC .60 1.50
21 Steve McMichael .20 .50
22 Dan Hampton .20 .50
23 Otis Wilson .07 .20
24 Mike Singletary .25 .60
25 Wilber Marshall RC .20 .50
26 Leslie Frazier .07 .20
27 Dave Duerson RC .07 .20
28 Gary Fencik .07 .20
29 Patriots TL .20 .50
(Craig James on the Run)
30 Tony Eason .07 .20
31 Steve Grogan .10 .30
32 Craig James .20 .50
33 Tony Collins .07 .20
34 Irving Fryar .50 1.25
35 Brian Holloway .07 .20
36 John Hannah AP .20 .50
37 Tony Franklin .07 .20
38 Garin Veris RC .07 .20
39 Andre Tippett AP .20 .50
40 Steve Nelson .07 .20
41 Raymond Clayborn .07 .20
42 Fred Marion RC .07 .20
43 Rich Camarillo .07 .20
44 Dolphins TL .75 2.00
(Dan Marino Sets Up)
45 Dan Marino AP 4.00 8.00
46 Tony Nathan .10 .30
47 Ron Davenport RC .07 .20
48 Mark Duper .20 .50
49 Mark Clayton .20 .50
50 Nat Moore .10 .30
51 Bruce Hardy .07 .20
52 Roy Foster .07 .20
53 Dwight Stephenson .30 .75
54 Fuad Reveiz RC .10 .30
55 Bob Baumhower .07 .20
56 Mike Charles .07 .20
57 Hugh Green .10 .30
58 Glenn Blackwood .07 .20
59 Reggie Roby .10 .30
60 Raiders TL .20 .50
(Marcus Allen Cuts Upfield)
61 Marc Wilson .07 .20
62 Marcus Allen AP .60 1.50
63 Dokie Williams .07 .20
64 Todd Christensen .20 .50
65 Chris Bahr .07 .20
66 Fulton Walker .07 .20
67 Howie Long .50 1.25
68 Bill Pickel .07 .20
69 Ray Guy .20 .50
70 Greg Townsend RC .20 .50
71 Rod Martin .10 .30
72 Matt Millen .10 .30
73 Mike Haynes .10 .30
74 Lester Hayes .10 .30
75 Vann McElroy .07 .20
76 Rams TL .20 .50
(Eric Dickerson Stiff-Arm)
77 Dieter Brock RC .10 .30
78 Eric Dickerson .30 .75
79 Henry Ellard .40 1.00
80 Ron Brown RC .10 .30
81 Tony Hunter RC .07 .20
82 Kent Hill AP .07 .20
83 Doug Smith .07 .20
84 Dennis Harrah .07 .20
85 Jackie Slater .20 .50
86 Mike Lansford .07 .20
87 Gary Jeter .07 .20
88 Mike Wilcher .07 .20
89 Jim Collins .07 .20
90 LeRoy Irvin .10 .30
91 Gary Green .07 .20
92 Nolan Cromwell .10 .30
93 Dale Hatcher RC .07 .20
94 Jets TL .10 .30
(Freeman McNeil Powers)
95 Ken O'Brien .20 .50
96 Freeman McNeil .10 .30
97 Tony Paige RC .07 .20
98 Johnny Lam Jones .07 .20
99 Wesley Walker .10 .30
100 Kurt Sohn .07 .20
101 Al Toon RC .20 .50
102 Mickey Shuler .07 .20
103 Marvin Powell .07 .20
104 Pat Leahy .07 .20
105 Mark Gastineau .10 .30
106 Joe Klecko .10 .30
107 Marty Lyons .07 .20
108 Lance Mehl .07 .20
109 Bobby Jackson .07 .20
110 Dave Jennings .07 .20
111 Broncos TL .10 .30
(Sammy Winder Up Middle)
112 John Elway 4.00 8.00
113 Sammy Winder .10 .30
114 Gerald Willhite .07 .20
115 Steve Watson .07 .20
116 Vance Johnson RC .20 .50
117 Rich Karlis .07 .20
118 Rulon Jones .07 .20
119 Karl Mecklenburg AP RC .20 .50
120 Louis Wright .07 .20
121 Mike Harden .07 .20
122 Dennis Smith RC .20 .50
123 Steve Foley .07 .20
124 Cowboys TL .10 .30
(Tony Hill Evades Defender)
125 Danny White .20 .50
126 Tony Dorsett .25 .60
127 Timmy Newsome .07 .20
128 Mike Renfro .07 .20
129 Tony Hill .10 .30
130 Doug Cosbie .10 .30
131 Rafael Septien .07 .20
132 Ed Too Tall Jones .20 .50
133 Randy White .20 .50
134 Jim Jeffcoat .20 .50
135 Everson Walls .10 .30
136 Dennis Thurman .07 .20
137 Giants TL .10 .30
(Joe Morris Opening)
138 Phil Simms .20 .50
139 Joe Morris .20 .50
140 George Adams RC .07 .20
141 Lionel Manuel .10 .30
142 Bobby Johnson .07 .20
143 Phil McConkey RC .10 .30
144 Mark Bavaro RC .20 .50
145 Zeke Mowatt .07 .20
146 Brad Benson RC .07 .20
147 Bart Oates RC .10 .30
148 Leonard Marshall RC .20 .50
149 Jim Burt .10 .30
150 George Martin .07 .20
151 Lawrence Taylor AP .50 1.25
152 Harry Carson AP .10 .30
153 Elvis Patterson RC .07 .20
154 Sean Landeta RC .10 .30
155 49ers TL .20 .50
(Roger Craig Scampers)
156 Joe Montana 4.00 8.00
157 Roger Craig .20 .50
158 Wendell Tyler .07 .20
159 Carl Monroe .07 .20
160 Dwight Clark .10 .30
161 Jerry Rice RC 30.00 60.00
162 Randy Cross .10 .30
163 Keith Fahnhorst .07 .20
164 Jeff Stover .07 .20
165 Michael Carter RC .07 .20
166 Dwaine Board .07 .20
167 Eric Wright .10 .30
168 Ronnie Lott .30 .75
169 Carlton Williamson .07 .20
170 Redskins TL .10 .30
(Dave Butz Gets His Man)
171 Joe Theismann .20 .50
172 Jay Schroeder RC .20 .50
173 George Rogers .10 .30
174 Ken Jenkins .07 .20
175 Art Monk AP .20 .50
176 Gary Clark RC .75 2.00
177 Joe Jacoby .10 .30
178 Russ Grimm .20 .50
179 Mark Moseley .07 .20
180 Dexter Manley .10 .30
181 Charles Mann RC .20 .50
182 Vernon Dean .07 .20
183 Raphel Cherry RC .07 .20
184 Curtis Jordan .07 .20
185 Browns TL .20 .50
(Bernie Kosar Fakes Handoff)
186 Gary Danielson .10 .30
187 Bernie Kosar RC 1.25 3.00
188 Kevin Mack RC .20 .50
189 Earnest Byner RC .30 .75
190 Glen Young .07 .20
191 Ozzie Newsome .20 .50
192 Mike Baab .07 .20
193 Cody Risien .10 .30
194 Bob Golic .10 .30
195 Reggie Camp .07 .20
196 Chip Banks .10 .30
197 Tom Cousineau .07 .20
198 Frank Minnifield RC .07 .20
199 Al Gross .07 .20
200 Seahawks TL .10 .30
(Curt Warner Breaks Free)
201 Dave Krieg .20 .50
202 Curt Warner .10 .30
203 Steve Largent AP .25 .60
204 Norm Johnson .07 .20
205 Daryl Turner .07 .20
206 Jacob Green .07 .20
207 Joe Nash .07 .20
208 Jeff Bryant .07 .20
209 Randy Edwards .07 .20
210 Fredd Young .07 .20
211 Kenny Easley .07 .20
212 John Harris .07 .20
213 Packers TL .07 .20
(Paul Coffman Conquers)
214 Lynn Dickey .10 .30
215 Gerry Ellis .07 .20
216 Eddie Lee Ivery .07 .20
217 Jessie Clark .07 .20
218 James Lofton .20 .50
219 Paul Coffman .07 .20
220 Alphonso Carreker .07 .20
221 Ezra Johnson .07 .20
222 Mike Douglass .07 .20
223 Tim Lewis .07 .20
224 Mark Murphy RC .07 .20
225 Passing Leaders: .40 1.00
Ken O'Brien AFC
Joe Montana NFC
226 Receiving Leaders: .10 .30
Lionel James AFC
Roger Craig NFC
227 Rushing Leaders: .20 .50
Marcus Allen AFC
Gerald Riggs NFC
228 Scoring Leaders: .10 .30
Gary Anderson K AFC
Kevin Butler NFC
229 Interception Leaders: .07 .20
Eugene Daniel AFC
Albert Lewis AFC
Everson Walls NFC
230 Chargers TL .20 .50
(Dan Fouts Over Top)
231 Dan Fouts .20 .50
232 Lionel James .07 .20
233 Gary Anderson RB RC .20 .50
234 Tim Spencer RC .10 .30
235 Wes Chandler .10 .30
236 Charlie Joiner .20 .50
237 Kellen Winslow .20 .50
238 Jim Lachey RC .20 .50
239 Bob Thomas .07 .20
240 Jeffery Dale .07 .20
241 Ralf Mojsiejenko .07 .20
242 Lions TL .07 .20
(Eric Hipple Spots Receiver)
243 Eric Hipple .07 .20
244 Billy Sims .10 .30
245 James Jones .07 .20
246 Pete Mandley RC .07 .20
247 Leonard Thompson .07 .20
248 Lomas Brown RC .10 .30
249 Eddie Murray .10 .30
250 Curtis Green .07 .20
251 William Gay .07 .20
252 Jimmy Williams .07 .20
253 Bobby Watkins .07 .20
254 Bengals TL .20 .50
(Boomer Esiason Zeroes In)
255 Boomer Esiason RC 2.50 6.00
256 James Brooks .10 .30
257 Larry Kinnebrew .07 .20
258 Cris Collinsworth .10 .30
259 Mike Martin .07 .20
260 Eddie Brown RC .20 .50
261 Anthony Munoz .20 .50
262 Jim Breech .07 .20
263 Ross Browner .10 .30
264 Carl Zander .07 .20
265 James Griffin .07 .20
266 Robert Jackson .07 .20
267 Pat McInally .07 .20
268 Eagles TL .20 .50
(Ron Jaworski Surveys)
269 Ron Jaworski .10 .30
270 Earnest Jackson .10 .30
271 Mike Quick .10 .30
272 John Spagnola .07 .20
273 Mark Dennard .07 .20
274 Paul McFadden .07 .20
275 Reggie White RC 7.50 15.00
276 Greg Brown .07 .20
277 Herman Edwards .07 .20
278 Roynell Young .07 .20
279 Wes Hopkins .07 .20
280 Steelers TL .10 .30
(Walter Abercrombie Inches)
281 Mark Malone .10 .30
282 Frank Pollard .07 .20
283 Walter Abercrombie .07 .20
284 Louis Lipps .20 .50
285 John Stallworth .20 .50
286 Mike Webster .10 .30
287 Gary Anderson K .10 .30
288 Keith Willis .07 .20
289 Mike Merriweather .07 .20
290 Dwayne Woodruff .07 .20
291 Donnie Shell .10 .30
292 Vikings TL .10 .30
(Tommy Kramer Audible)
293 Tommy Kramer .10 .30
294 Darrin Nelson .07 .20
295 Ted Brown .10 .30
296 Buster Rhymes RC .07 .20
297 Anthony Carter RC .40 1.00
298 Steve Jordan RC .20 .50
299 Keith Millard RC .20 .50
300 Joey Browner RC .20 .50
301 John Turner .07 .20
302 Greg Coleman .07 .20
303 Chiefs TL .07 .20
(Todd Blackledge)
304 Bill Kenney .07 .20
305 Herman Heard .07 .20
306 Stephone Paige RC .20 .50
307 Carlos Carson .10 .30
308 Nick Lowery .10 .30
309 Mike Bell .07 .20
310 Bill Maas .07 .20
311 Art Still .07 .20
312 Albert Lewis RC .20 .50
313 Deron Cherry AP .10 .30
314 Colts TL .07 .20
(Rohn Stark Booms It)
315 Mike Pagel .07 .20
316 Randy McMillan .07 .20
317 Albert Bentley RC .10 .30
318 George Wonsley RC .07 .20
319 Robbie Martin .07 .20
320 Pat Beach .07 .20
321 Chris Hinton .10 .30
322 Duane Bickett RC .20 .50
323 Eugene Daniel .07 .20
324 Cliff Odom RC .07 .20
325 Rohn Stark .10 .30
326 Cardinals TL .07 .20
(Stump Mitchell Outside)
327 Neil Lomax .10 .30
328 Stump Mitchell .10 .30
329 Ottis Anderson .20 .50
330 J.T. Smith .10 .30
331 Pat Tilley .07 .20
332 Roy Green .10 .30
333 Lance Smith RC .07 .20
334 Curtis Greer .07 .20
335 Freddie Joe Nunn RC .10 .30
336 E.J. Junior .10 .30
337 Lonnie Young RC .07 .20
338 Saints TL .07 .20
(Wayne Wilson running)
339 Bobby Hebert RC .20 .50
340 Dave Wilson .07 .20
341 Wayne Wilson .07 .20
342 Hoby Brenner .07 .20
343 Stan Brock .10 .30
344 Morten Andersen .20 .50
345 Bruce Clark .07 .20
346 Rickey Jackson .20 .50
347 Dave Waymer .07 .20
348 Brian Hansen .07 .20
349 Oilers TL .20 .50
(Warren Moon Throws Bomb)
350 Warren Moon 1.50 3.00
351 Mike Rozier RC .20 .50
352 Butch Woolfolk .07 .20
353 Drew Hill .20 .50
354 Willie Drewrey RC .07 .20
355 Tim Smith .10 .30
356 Mike Munchak .20 .50
357 Ray Childress RC .20 .50
358 Frank Bush .07 .20
359 Steve Brown .07 .20
360 Falcons TL .07 .20
(Gerald Riggs Around End)
361 David Archer RC .20 .50
362 Gerald Riggs .10 .30
363 William Andrews .10 .30
364 Billy Johnson .10 .30
365 Arthur Cox .07 .20
366 Mike Kenn .07 .20
367 Bill Fralic RC .10 .30
368 Mick Luckhurst .07 .20
369 Rick Bryan .07 .20
370 Bobby Butler .07 .20
371 Rick Donnelly RC .07 .20
372 Buccaneers TL .07 .20
(James Wilder Sweeps Left)
373 Steve DeBerg .20 .50
374 Steve Young RC 10.00 20.00
375 James Wilder .07 .20
376 Kevin House .07 .20
377 Gerald Carter .07 .20
378 Jimmie Giles .10 .30
379 Sean Farrell .07 .20
380 Donald Igwebuike .07 .20
381 David Logan .07 .20
382 Jeremiah Castille RC .07 .20
383 Bills TL .07 .20
(Greg Bell Sees Daylight)
384 Bruce Mathison RC .07 .20
385 Joe Cribbs .10 .30
386 Greg Bell .10 .30
387 Jerry Butler .07 .20
388 Andre Reed RC 3.00 8.00
389 Bruce Smith RC 4.00 8.00
390 Fred Smerlas .07 .20
391 Darryl Talley .20 .50
392 Jim Haslett .10 .30
393 Charles Romes .07 .20
394 Checklist 1-132 .10 .30
395 Checklist 133-264 .10 .30
396 Checklist 265-396 .10 .30

1986 Topps Box Bottoms

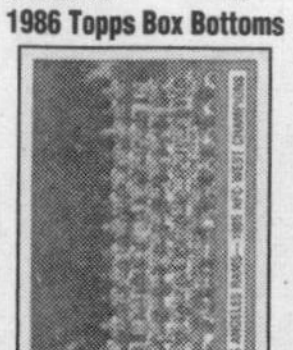

This four-card set, which measures 2 1/2" by 3 1/2", features the four teams which participated in the Super Bowl and in the Conference Championships. This set is arranged in order of how the teams finished, with the Super Bowl Champion Bears being the first team listed. The fronts of the card feature a team photo and identification of all those players is pictured on the back of the card. The cards were issued one per wax box as the side panel of the box, not on the box bottom as was typical of similar sets.

COMPLETE SET (4) 4.00 10.00
A Chicago Bears 1.00 2.50
NFL Champions
B New England Patriots .75 2.00
AFC Champions
C Los Angeles Rams .75 2.00
NFC West Champions
D Miami Dolphins 1.50 4.00
AFC East Champions

1986 Topps 1000 Yard Club

COMPLETE SET (26) 2.50 6.00
1 Marcus Allen .60 1.50
2 Gerald Riggs .08 .25
3 Walter Payton 1.00 2.50
4 Joe Morris .08 .25
5 Freeman McNeil .08 .25
6 Tony Dorsett .30 .75
7 James Wilder .08 .25
8 Steve Largent .40 1.00
9 Mike Quick .08 .25
10 Eric Dickerson .30 .75
11 Craig James .20 .50
12 Art Monk .20 .50
13 Wes Chandler .08 .25
14 Drew Hill .08 .25
15 James Lofton .20 .50
16 Louis Lipps .08 .25
17 Cris Collinsworth .08 .25
18 Tony Hill .08 .25
19 Kevin Mack .08 .25
20 Curt Warner .08 .25
21 George Rogers .08 .25
22 Roger Craig .20 .50
23 Earnest Jackson .08 .25
24 Lionel James .08 .25
25 Stump Mitchell .08 .25
26 Earnest Byner .08 .25

1987 Topps

The 1987 Topps set consists of 396 standard-size cards. Wax packs contained 15 cards as well as a 1,000 yard club card. For the first time, hobby factory sets were issued. Card fronts have the team and player name in banners at the top above the player photo. These banners are in the colors of the player's team.

The backs have highlights and statistics within an outline of the NFL shield. To the left is biographical information. Subsets include Record Breakers (2-8) and league leaders (227-231). The set numbering is ordered by teams. Team cards feature an action photo on the front with the team's statistical leaders and week-by-week game results from the previous season on back. The copyright line on the back also includes a letter (A, B, C, or D) to indicate which sheet the card was cut from. Note that each card in the set was produced on two different sheets. This resulted in each card including one of two different letter designations on the back, thus creating a variation on each card. Rookie Cards include Bill Brooks, Keith Byars, Randall Cunningham, Kenneth Davis, Jim Everett, Doug Flutie, Ernest Givins, Charles Haley, Sean Jones, Eric Martin and Jim Kelly. Kelly and Flutie previously appeared in a USFL set.

COMPLETE SET (396) 20.00 40.00
COMP.FACT.SET (396) 50.00 80.00
1 Super Bowl XXI .20 .50
Giants 39,
Broncos 20
(Line play shown)
2 Todd Christensen RB .08 .25
Most Seasons/80 or More Receptions
3 Dave Jennings RB .05 .15
Most Punts: Career
4 Charlie Joiner RB .20 .50
Most Receiving
Yards: Career
5 Steve Largent RB .20 .50
Most Consec. Games
With a Reception
6 Dan Marino RB .75 2.00
Most Consec. Seasons/30 or More TD Passes
7 Donnie Shell RB .08 .25
Most Interceptions&
Strong Safety: Career
8 Phil Simms RB .20 .50
Highest Completion
Percentage: Super Bowl
9 New York Giants TL .08 .25
(Mark Bavaro Pulls Free)
10 Phil Simms .20 .50
11 Joe Morris AP .08 .25
12 Maurice Carthon RC .20 .50
13 Lee Rouson .05 .15
14 Bobby Johnson .05 .15
15 Lionel Manuel .05 .15
16 Phil McConkey .05 .15
17 Mark Bavaro AP .20 .50
18 Zeke Mowatt .05 .15
19 Raul Allegre .05 .15
20 Sean Landeta .05 .15
21 Brad Benson .05 .15
22 Jim Burt .05 .15
23 Leonard Marshall .20 .50
24 Carl Banks .20 .50
25 Harry Carson .05 .15
26 Lawrence Taylor AP .30 .75
27 Terry Kinard RC .05 .15
28 Pepper Johnson RC .20 .50
29 Erik Howard RC .05 .15
30 Broncos TL .05 .15
(Gerald Willhite Dives)
31 John Elway 2.50 6.00
32 Gerald Willhite .05 .15
33 Sammy Winder .08 .25
34 Ken Bell .05 .15
35 Steve Watson .05 .15
36 Rich Karlis .05 .15
37 Keith Bishop .05 .15
38 Rulon Jones .05 .15
39 Karl Mecklenburg AP .20 .50
40 Louis Wright .05 .15
41 Mike Harden .05 .15
42 Dennis Smith .08 .25
43 Bears TL .20 .50
(Walter Payton Barrels)
44 Jim McMahon .20 .50
45 Doug Flutie RC 3.00 8.00
46 Walter Payton 2.00 5.00
47 Matt Suhey .05 .15
48 Willie Gault .08 .25
49 Dennis Gentry RC .05 .15
50 Kevin Butler .05 .15
51 Jim Covert .05 .15
52 Jay Hilgenberg .08 .25
53 Dan Hampton .20 .50
54 Steve McMichael .20 .50
55 William Perry .20 .50
56 Richard Dent .20 .50
57 Otis Wilson .05 .15
58 Mike Singletary .20 .50
59 Wilber Marshall .20 .50
60 Mike Richardson .05 .15
61 Dave Duerson .05 .15
62 Gary Fencik .05 .15
63 Redskins TL .08 .25
(George Rogers Plunges)
64 Jay Schroeder .08 .25
65 George Rogers .08 .25
66 Kelvin Bryant RC .08 .25
67 Ken Jenkins .05 .15
68 Gary Clark .60 1.50
69 Art Monk .20 .50
70 Clint Didier RC .05 .15
71 Steve Cox .05 .15
72 Joe Jacoby .05 .15
73 Russ Grimm .08 .25
74 Charles Mann .08 .25
75 Dave Butz .05 .15
76 Dexter Manley .08 .25
77 Darrell Green AP .20 .50
78 Curtis Jordan .05 .15
79 Browns TL .05 .15
(Harry Holt Sees Daylight)
80 Bernie Kosar .20 .50
81 Curtis Dickey .05 .15
82 Kevin Mack .08 .25
83 Herman Fontenot .05 .15
84 Brian Brennan RC .05 .15
85 Ozzie Newsome .20 .50
86 Jeff Gossett .08 .25
87 Cody Risien .05 .15
88 Reggie Camp .05 .15
89 Bob Golic .05 .15
90 Carl Hairston .05 .15
91 Chip Banks .05 .15
92 Frank Minnifield .05 .15
93 Hanford Dixon .05 .15
94 Gerald McNeil RC .05 .15
95 Dave Puzzuoli .05 .15
96 Patriots TL .05 .15
(Andre Tippett Gets
His Man (Marcus Allen))
97 Tony Eason .08 .25
98 Craig James .08 .25
99 Tony Collins .08 .25
100 Mosi Tatupu .05 .15
101 Stanley Morgan .08 .25
102 Irving Fryar .20 .50
103 Stephen Starring .05 .15
104 Tony Franklin .05 .15
105 Rich Camarillo .05 .15
106 Garin Veris .05 .15
107 Andre Tippett AP .08 .25
108 Don Blackmon .05 .15
109 Ronnie Lippett RC .05 .15
110 Raymond Clayborn .05 .15
111 49ers TL .08 .25
(Roger Craig Up the Middle)
112 Joe Montana 2.50 6.00
113 Roger Craig .20 .50
114 Joe Cribbs .08 .25
115 Jerry Rice AP 2.50 6.00
116 Dwight Clark .08 .25
117 Ray Wersching .05 .15
118 Max Runager .05 .15
119 Jeff Stover .05 .15
120 Dwaine Board .05 .15
121 Tim McKyer RC .08 .25
122 Don Griffin RC .08 .25
123 Ronnie Lott AP .20 .50
124 Tom Holmoe .05 .15
125 Charles Haley RC .75 2.00
126 Jets TL .05 .15
(Mark Gastineau Seeks)
127 Ken O'Brien .08 .25
128 Pat Ryan .05 .15
129 Freeman McNeil .08 .25
130 Johnny Hector RC .05 .15
131 Al Toon AP .20 .50
132 Wesley Walker .08 .25
133 Mickey Shuler .05 .15
134 Pat Leahy .05 .15
135 Mark Gastineau .08 .25
136 Joe Klecko .08 .25
137 Marty Lyons .05 .15
138 Bob Crable .05 .15
139 Lance Mehl .05 .15
140 Dave Jennings .05 .15
141 Harry Hamilton RC .05 .15
142 Lester Lyles .05 .15
143 Bobby Humphery UER .05 .15
(Misspelled Humphrey
on card front)
144 Rams TL .20 .50
(Eric Dickerson
Through the Line)
145 Jim Everett RC .50 1.25
146 Eric Dickerson AP .20 .50
147 Barry Redden .05 .15
148 Ron Brown .08 .25
149 Kevin House .05 .15
150 Henry Ellard .20 .50
151 Doug Smith .05 .15
152 Dennis Harrah .05 .15
153 Jackie Slater .08 .25
154 Gary Jeter .05 .15
155 Carl Ekern .05 .15
156 Mike Wilcher .05 .15
157 Jerry Gray RC .05 .15
158 LeRoy Irvin .05 .15
159 Nolan Cromwell .08 .25
160 Chiefs TL .05 .15
(Todd Blackledge Hands Off)
161 Bill Kenney .05 .15
162 Stephone Paige .08 .25
163 Henry Marshall .05 .15
164 Carlos Carson .05 .15
165 Nick Lowery .08 .25
166 Irv Eatman RC .05 .15
167 Brad Budde .05 .15
168 Art Still .05 .15
169 Bill Maas .05 .15
170 Lloyd Burruss RC .05 .15
171 Deron Cherry AP .05 .15
172 Seahawks TL .08 .25
(Curt Warner Finds Opening)
173 Dave Krieg .20 .50
174 Curt Warner .08 .25
175 John L. Williams RC .20 .50
176 Bobby Joe Edmonds RC .08 .25
177 Steve Largent .25 .60
178 Bruce Scholtz .05 .15
179 Norm Johnson .05 .15
180 Jacob Green .05 .15
181 Fredd Young .05 .15
182 Dave Brown .05 .15
183 Kenny Easley .05 .15
184 Bengals TL .08 .25
(James Brooks Stiff-Arm)
185 Boomer Esiason .20 .50
186 James Brooks .08 .25
187 Larry Kinnebrew .05 .15
188 Cris Collinsworth .08 .25
189 Eddie Brown .20 .50
190 Tim McGee RC .20 .50
191 Jim Breech .05 .15
192 Anthony Munoz .20 .50
193 Max Montoya .05 .15
194 Eddie Edwards .05 .15
195 Ross Browner .08 .25
196 Emanuel King .05 .15
197 Louis Breeden .05 .15
198 Vikings TL .05 .15
(Darrin Nelson In Motion)
199 Tommy Kramer .08 .25
200 Darrin Nelson .05 .15
201 Allen Rice .05 .15
202 Anthony Carter .20 .50
203 Leo Lewis .05 .15
204 Steve Jordan .20 .50
205 Chuck Nelson RC .05 .15
206 Greg Coleman .05 .15
207 Gary Zimmerman RC 1.00 2.50
208 Doug Martin .05 .15
209 Keith Millard .05 .15
210 Issiac Holt RC .05 .15
211 Joey Browner .08 .25
212 Rufus Bess .05 .15
213 Raiders TL .20 .50
(Marcus Allen Quick Feet)
214 Jim Plunkett .20 .50
215 Marcus Allen .40 1.00
216 Napoleon McCallum RC .08 .25
217 Dokie Williams .05 .15
218 Todd Christensen .08 .25
219 Chris Bahr .05 .15
220 Howie Long .25 .60
221 Bill Pickel .05 .15
222 Sean Jones RC .20 .50
223 Lester Hayes .08 .25
224 Mike Haynes .08 .25
225 Vann McElroy .05 .15
226 Fulton Walker .05 .15
227 Passing Leaders .50 1.25
Tommy Kramer
Dan Marino
228 Receiving Leaders .50 1.25
Jerry Rice
Todd Christensen
229 Rushing Leaders .20 .50
Eric Dickerson
Curt Warner
230 Scoring Leaders .05 .15
Kevin Butler
Tony Franklin
231 Interception Leaders .20 .50
Ronnie Lott
Deron Cherry
232 Dolphins TL .08 .25
(Reggie Roby Booms It)
233 Dan Marino AP 2.50 6.00
234 Lorenzo Hampton RC .05 .15
235 Tony Nathan .08 .25
236 Mark Duper .20 .50
237 Mark Clayton .20 .50
238 Nat Moore .08 .25
239 Bruce Hardy .05 .15
240 Reggie Roby .08 .25
241 Roy Foster .05 .15
242 Dwight Stephenson .20 .50
243 Hugh Green .05 .15
244 John Offerdahl RC .20 .50
245 Mark Brown .05 .15
246 Doug Betters .05 .15
247 Bob Baumhower .05 .15
248 Falcons TL .05 .15
(Gerald Riggs Uses Blockers)
249 David Archer .20 .50
250 Gerald Riggs .08 .25
251 William Andrews .08 .25
252 Charlie Brown .05 .15
253 Arthur Cox .05 .15
254 Rick Donnelly .05 .15
255 Bill Fralic AP .05 .15
256 Mike Gann RC .05 .15
257 Rick Bryan .05 .15
258 Bret Clark .05 .15
259 Mike Pitts .05 .15
260 Cowboys TL .20 .50
(Tony Dorsett Cuts)
261 Danny White .20 .50
262 Steve Pelluer RC .20 .50
263 Tony Dorsett .20 .50
264 Herschel Walker RC UER 1.00 2.50
(Stats show 12 TD's
in 1986, text says 14)
265 Timmy Newsome .05 .15
266 Tony Hill .08 .25
267 Mike Sherrard RC .20 .50
268 Jim Jeffcoat .20 .50
269 Ron Fellows .20 .50
270 Bill Bates .20 .50
271 Michael Downs .05 .15
272 Saints TL .08 .25
(Bobby Hebert Fakes)
273 Dave Wilson .05 .15
274 Rueben Mayes UER RC .05 .15
(Stats show 1353 comple-
tions, should be yards)
275 Hoby Brenner .05 .15
276 Eric Martin RC .20 .50
277 Morten Andersen .08 .25
278 Brian Hansen .05 .15
279 Rickey Jackson .20 .50
280 Dave Waymer .05 .15
281 Bruce Clark .05 .15
282 James Geathers RC .08 .25
283 Steelers TL .08 .25
(Walter Abercrombie Resists)
284 Mark Malone .08 .25
285 Earnest Jackson .05 .15
286 Walter Abercrombie .05 .15
287 Louis Lipps .08 .25
288 John Stallworth UER .20 .50
(Stats only go up
through 1981)
289 Gary Anderson K .05 .15
290 Keith Willis .05 .15
291 Mike Merriweather .05 .15
292 Lupe Sanchez .05 .15
293 Donnie Shell .08 .25
294 Eagles TL .20 .50
(Keith Byars Inches Ahead)
295 Mike Reichenbach .05 .15
296 Randall Cunningham RC 3.00 6.00
297 Keith Byars RC .30 .75
298 Mike Quick .08 .25
299 Kenny Jackson .05 .15
300 John Teltschik RC .05 .15
301 Reggie White AP 1.50 3.00
302 Ken Clarke .05 .15
303 Greg Brown .05 .15
304 Roynell Young .05 .15
305 Andre Waters RC .20 .50
306 Oilers TL .20 .50
(Warren Moon Plots Play)
307 Warren Moon .60 1.50
308 Mike Rozier .08 .25
309 Drew Hill .08 .25
310 Ernest Givins RC .20 .50
311 Lee Johnson RC .05 .15
312 Kent Hill .05 .15
313 Dean Steinkuhler RC .05 .15
314 Ray Childress .20 .50
315 John Grimsley RC .05 .15
316 Jesse Baker .05 .15
317 Lions TL .05 .15
(Eric Hipple Surveys)
318 Chuck Long RC .08 .25
319 James Jones .05 .15
320 Garry James .05 .15
321 Jeff Chadwick .05 .15
322 Leonard Thompson .05 .15
323 Pete Mandley .05 .15
324 Jimmie Giles .05 .15
325 Herman Hunter .05 .15
326 Keith Ferguson .05 .15
327 Devon Mitchell .05 .15
328 Cardinals TL .05 .15
(Neil Lomax Audible)
329 Neil Lomax .08 .25
330 Stump Mitchell .05 .15
331 Earl Ferrell .05 .15
332 Vai Sikahema RC .08 .25
333 Ron Wolfley RC .05 .15
334 J.T. Smith .05 .15
335 Roy Green .08 .25
336 Al(Bubba) Baker .05 .15
337 Freddie Joe Nunn .05 .15
338 Cedric Mack .05 .15
339 Chargers TL .08 .25
(Gary Anderson Evades)
340 Dan Fouts .20 .50
341 Gary Anderson UER .20 .50
(Two Topps logos
on card front)
342 Wes Chandler .08 .25
343 Kellen Winslow .20 .50
344 Ralf Mojsiejenko .05 .15
345 Rolf Benirschke .05 .15
346 Lee Williams RC .08 .25
347 Leslie O'Neal RC .40 1.00
348 Billy Ray Smith .08 .25
349 Gill Byrd .08 .25
350 Packers TL .05 .15
(Paul Ott Carruth Around End)
351 Randy Wright .05 .15
352 Kenneth Davis RC .20 .50
353 Gerry Ellis .05 .15
354 James Lofton .20 .50
355 Phillip Epps RC .05 .15
356 Walter Stanley RC .05 .15
357 Eddie Lee Ivery .05 .15
358 Tim Harris RC .20 .50
359 Mark Lee UER .05 .15
(Red flag, rest of
Packers have yellow)
360 Mossy Cade .05 .15
361 Bills TL .40 1.00
(Jim Kelly Works Ground)
362 Jim Kelly RC 4.00 10.00
363 Robb Riddick RC .05 .15
364 Greg Bell .05 .15
365 Andre Reed .50 1.25
366 Pete Metzelaars RC .05 .15
367 Sean McNanie .05 .15
368 Fred Smerlas .05 .15
369 Bruce Smith .75 2.00
370 Darryl Talley .08 .25
371 Charles Romes .05 .15
372 Colts TL .05 .15
(Rohn Stark High and Far)
373 Jack Trudeau RC .08 .25
374 Gary Hogeboom .05 .15
375 Randy McMillan .05 .15
376 Albert Bentley .05 .15
377 Matt Bouza .05 .15
378 Bill Brooks RC .30 .75
379 Rohn Stark .05 .15
380 Chris Hinton .05 .15
381 Ray Donaldson .05 .15
382 Jon Hand RC .05 .15
383 Buccaneers TL .05 .15
(James Wilder Braces)
384 Steve Young 2.00 5.00
385 James Wilder .05 .15
386 Frank Garcia .05 .15
387 Gerald Carter .05 .15
388 Phil Freeman .05 .15
389 Calvin Magee .05 .15
390 Donald Igwebuike .05 .15
391 David Logan .05 .15
392 Jeff Davis .05 .15
393 Chris Washington .05 .15
394 Checklist 1-132 .08 .25
395 Checklist 133-264 .08 .25
396 Checklist 265-396 .08 .25

1987 Topps Box Bottoms

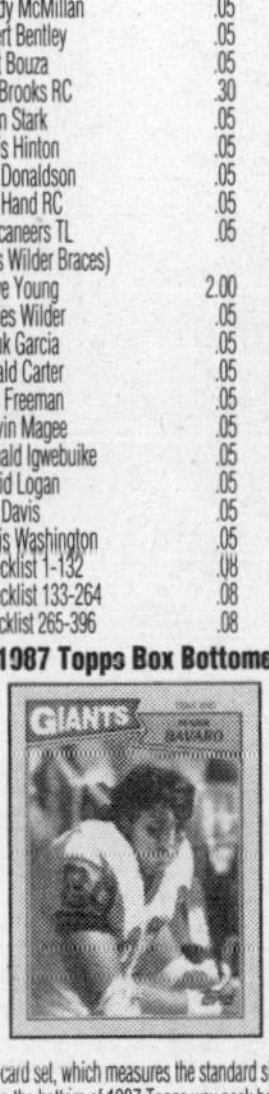

This 16-card set, which measures the standard size, was issued on the bottom of 1987 Topps wax pack boxes. The cards are in the same design as the 1987 Topps regular issues except they are bordered in yellow. The backs of the cards are just like the regular card in that they have biographical and complete statistical information. The cards are arranged in alphabetical order and include such stars as Joe Montana, Walter Payton, and Jerry Rice.

COMPLETE SET (16) 15.00 30.00
A Mark Bavaro .40 1.00
B Todd Christensen .30 .75
C Eric Dickerson .40 1.00
D John Elway 2.50 6.00
E Rulon Jones .30 .75
F Dan Marino 2.50 6.00
G Karl Mecklenburg .30 .75
H Joe Montana 2.50 6.00
I Joe Morris .30 .75
J Walter Payton 2.00 5.00
K Jerry Rice 2.00 5.00
L Phil Simms .50 1.25
M Lawrence Taylor .50 1.25
N Al Toon .40 1.00
O Curt Warner .40 1.00
P Reggie White .60 1.50

1987 Topps 1000 Yard Club

COMPLETE SET (24) 2.50 6.00
1 Eric Dickerson .30 .75
2 Jerry Rice 1.25 3.00
3 Joe Morris .08 .25
4 Stanley Morgan .08 .25
5 Curt Warner .08 .25
6 Rueben Mayes .08 .25
7 Walter Payton .75 2.00
8 Gerald Riggs .08 .25
9 Mark Duper .20 .50
10 Gary Clark .20 .50
11 George Rogers .08 .25
12 Al Toon .08 .25
13 Todd Christensen .08 .25
14 Mark Clayton .20 .50
15 Bill Brooks .08 .25
16 Drew Hill .08 .25
17 James Brooks .08 .25
18 Steve Largent .40 1.00
19 Art Monk .20 .50
20 Ernest Givins .08 .25
21 Cris Collinsworth .20 .50
22 Wesley Walker .08 .25
23 J.T. Smith .08 .25
24 Mark Bavaro .20 .50

1987 Topps American/UK

This mini-size version of 1987 football cards was distributed in the United Kingdom for British fans of American football. Cards measure only 2 1/8" by 3". The photos used are different from the regular issue Topps football cards, although the style is essentially the same. The card backs are colorful and feature a "Talking Football" section where a football term is explained. A collector box (with a complete set checklist on the side) is also available. The cards are arranged according to teams. Cards 76 through 87 are puzzle pieces, combining to show team action photos on their fronts and William "The Refrigerator" Perry on their backs.

COMPLETE SET (88) 25.00 60.00
1 Phil Simms .75 2.00
2 Joe Morris .30 .75
3 Mark Bavaro .30 .75
4 Sean Landeta .20 .50
5 Lawrence Taylor 1.00 2.50
6 John Elway 5.00 12.00
7 Sammy Winder .20 .50
8 Rulon Jones .20 .50
9 Karl Mecklenburg .30 .75
10 Walter Payton 5.00 10.00
11 Dennis Gentry .20 .50
12 Kevin Butler .20 .50
13 Jim Covert .20 .50
14 Richard Dent .40 1.00
15 Mike Singletary .75 2.00
16 Jay Schroeder .20 .50
17 George Rogers .30 .75
18 Gary Clark .40 1.00
19 Art Monk .75 2.00
20 Dexter Manley .20 .50
21 Darrell Green .50 1.25
22 Bernie Kosar .40 1.00
23 Cody Risien .20 .50
24 Hanford Dixon .20 .50
25 Tony Eason .30 .75
26 Stanley Morgan .30 .75
27 Tony Franklin .20 .50
28 Andre Tippett .30 .75
29 Joe Montana 6.00 12.00
30 Jerry Rice 5.00 10.00
31 Ronnie Lott .75 2.00
32 Ken O'Brien .30 .75
33 Freeman McNeil .30 .75
34 Al Toon .30 .75
35 Wesley Walker .30 .75
36 Eric Dickerson .60 1.50
37 Dennis Harrah .20 .50
38 Bill Maas .20 .50
39 Deron Cherry .20 .50
40 Curt Warner .30 .75
41 Bobby Joe Edmonds .20 .50
42 Steve Largent 1.25 3.00
43 Boomer Esiason 1.00 2.50
44 James Brooks .30 .75
45 Cris Collinsworth .40 1.00
46 Tim McGee .20 .50
47 Tommy Kramer .30 .75
48 Marcus Allen 1.50 4.00
49 Todd Christensen .30 .75
50 Sean Jones .20 .50
51 Dan Marino 5.00 12.00
52 Mark Duper .30 .75
53 Mark Clayton .30 .75
54 Dwight Stephenson .30 .75
55 Gerald Riggs .30 .75
56 Bill Fralic .20 .50
57 Tony Dorsett 1.25 3.00
58 Herschel Walker .60 1.50
59 Rueben Mayes .20 .50
60 Lupe Sanchez .20 .50
61 Reggie White 2.00 5.00
62 Warren Moon .75 2.00
63 Ernest Givins .40 1.00
64 Drew Hill .30 .75
65 Jeff Chadwick .20 .50
66 Herman Hunter .20 .50
67 Vai Sikahema .20 .50
68 J.T. Smith .20 .50
69 Dan Fouts .75 2.00
70 Lee Williams .20 .50
71 Randy Wright .20 .50
72 Jim Kelly 2.50 6.00
73 Bruce Smith 1.25 3.00
74 Bill Brooks .30 .75
75 Rohn Stark .20 .50
76 Team Action .20 .50
77 Team Action .20 .50
78 Team Action .20 .50
79 Team Action .20 .50
80 Team Action .20 .50
81 Team Action .20 .50
82 Team Action .20 .50
83 Team Action .20 .50
84 Team Action .20 .50
85 Team Action .20 .50
86 Team Action .20 .50
87 Team Action .20 .50
88 Checklist Card .20 .50

1988 Topps

This 396-card, standard-size set was issued in 15-card wax packs as well as in factory sets. The wax packs also included an 1,000 yard club card. Card fronts feature a team helmet, player's name and position beneath the player photo. The borders surrounding the photo are in the colors of the team. The backs have highlights and yearly statistics. The set is ordered by how the teams finished. The Team Leader (TL) cards show an action scene for each team. Potential young stars are also designated by Topps as "Super Rookies." Rookie Cards include Neal Anderson, Cornelius Bennett, Jerome Brown, Shane Conlan, Chris Doleman, Mel Gray, Kevin Greene, Bo Jackson, Mark Jackson, Seth Joyner, Tom Rathman, Clyde Simmons, Webster Slaughter, Pat Swilling and Vinny Testaverde.

COMPLETE SET (396) 7.50 20.00
COMP.FACT.SET (396) 15.00 30.00
1 Super Bowl XXII .07 .20
Redskins 42,
Broncos 10
(Redskins celebrating)
2 Vencie Glenn RB .05 .15
Longest Interception
Return
3 Steve Largent RB .15 .40
Most Receptions:
Career
4 Joe Montana RB .30 .75
Most Consecutive
Pass Completions
5 Walter Payton RB .15 .40
Most Rushing
Touchdowns: Career
6 Jerry Rice RB .30 .75
Most Touchdown
Receptions: Season
7 Redskins TL .07 .20
(Kelvin Bryant Sees Daylight)
8 Doug Williams .07 .20
9 George Rogers .07 .20
10 Kelvin Bryant .07 .20
11 Timmy Smith SR .07 .20
12 Art Monk .15 .40
13 Gary Clark .15 .40
14 Ricky Sanders RC .15 .40
15 Steve Cox .05 .15
16 Joe Jacoby .05 .15
17 Charles Mann .07 .20
18 Dave Butz .05 .15
19 Darrell Green AP .07 .20
20 Dexter Manley .05 .15
21 Barry Wilburn .05 .15
22 Broncos TL .05 .15
(Sammy Winder Winds
Through)
23 John Elway AP .75 2.00
24 Sammy Winder .05 .15
25 Vance Johnson .07 .20
26 Mark Jackson RC .15 .40
27 Ricky Nattiel SR RC .05 .15
28 Clarence Kay .05 .15
29 Rich Karlis .05 .15
30 Keith Bishop .05 .15
31 Mike Horan .05 .15
32 Rulon Jones .05 .15
33 Karl Mecklenburg .07 .20
34 Jim Ryan .05 .15
35 Mark Haynes .07 .20
36 Mike Harden .05 .15
37 49ers TL .15 .40
(Roger Craig Gallops
For Yardage)
38 Joe Montana .75 2.00
39 Steve Young .40 1.00
40 Roger Craig .07 .20
41 Tom Rathman RC .15 .40
42 Joe Cribbs .07 .20
43 Jerry Rice AP .75 2.00
44 Mike Wilson RC .05 .15
45 Ron Heller RC .05 .15
46 Ray Wersching .05 .15
47 Michael Carter .05 .15
48 Dwaine Board .05 .15
49 Michael Walter .05 .15
50 Don Griffin .05 .15
51 Ronnie Lott .15 .40
52 Charles Haley .15 .40
53 Dana McLemore .05 .15
54 Saints TL .07 .20
(Bobby Hebert Hands Off)
55 Bobby Hebert .07 .20
56 Rueben Mayes .05 .15
57 Dalton Hilliard RC .05 .15
58 Eric Martin .07 .20
59 John Tice RC .05 .15
60 Brad Edelman .05 .15
61 Morten Andersen AP .07 .20
62 Brian Hansen .05 .15
63 Mel Gray RC .15 .40
64 Rickey Jackson .07 .20
65 Sam Mills RC .30 .75
66 Pat Swilling RC .15 .40
67 Dave Waymer .05 .15
68 Bears TL .07 .20
(Willie Gault Powers
Forward)
69 Jim McMahon .15 .40
70 Mike Tomczak RC .05 .15
71 Neal Anderson RC .15 .40
72 Willie Gault .07 .20
73 Dennis Gentry .05 .15
74 Dennis McKinnon .05 .15
75 Kevin Butler .05 .15
76 Jim Covert .05 .15
77 Jay Hilgenberg .05 .15
78 Steve McMichael .07 .20
79 William Perry .07 .20
80 Richard Dent .15 .40
81 Ron Rivera RC .05 .15
82 Mike Singletary .15 .40
83 Dan Hampton .07 .20
84 Dave Duerson .05 .15
85 Browns TL .07 .20
(Bernie Kosar Lets it Go)
86 Bernie Kosar .15 .40
87 Earnest Byner .15 .40
88 Kevin Mack .07 .20
89 Webster Slaughter RC .15 .40
90 Gerald McNeil .05 .15
91 Brian Brennan .05 .15
92 Ozzie Newsome .15 .40
93 Cody Risien .05 .15
94 Bob Golic .05 .15
95 Carl Hairston .05 .15
96 Mike Johnson RC .05 .15
97 Clay Matthews .07 .20
98 Frank Minnifield .05 .15
99 Hanford Dixon .05 .15
100 Dave Puzzuoli .05 .15
101 Felix Wright RC .05 .15
102 Oilers TL .15 .40
(Warren Moon Over The Top)
103 Warren Moon .20 .50
104 Mike Rozier .05 .15
105 Alonzo Highsmith RC .07 .20
106 Drew Hill .07 .20
107 Ernest Givins .15 .40
108 Curtis Duncan RC .15 .40
109 Tony Zendejas RC .05 .15
110 Mike Munchak AP .15 .40
111 Kent Hill .05 .15
112 Ray Childress .07 .20
113 Al Smith RC .07 .20
114 Keith Bostic RC .05 .15
115 Jeff Donaldson .05 .15
116 Colts TL .15 .40
(Eric Dickerson Finds Opening)
117 Jack Trudeau .05 .15
118 Eric Dickerson AP .15 .40
119 Albert Bentley .05 .15
120 Matt Bouza .05 .15
121 Bill Brooks .15 .40
122 Dean Biasucci RC .05 .15
123 Chris Hinton .05 .15
124 Ray Donaldson .05 .15
125 Ron Solt RC .05 .15
126 Donnell Thompson .05 .15
127 Barry Krauss RC .05 .15
128 Duane Bickett .05 .15
129 Mike Prior RC .05 .15
130 Seahawks TL .07 .20
(Curt Warner Follows Blocking)
131 Dave Krieg .07 .20
132 Curt Warner .07 .20
133 John L. Williams .15 .40
134 Bobby Joe Edmonds .05 .15
135 Steve Largent .15 .40
136 Raymond Butler .05 .15
137 Norm Johnson .05 .15
138 Ruben Rodriguez .05 .15
139 Blair Bush .05 .15
140 Jacob Green .05 .15
141 Joe Nash .05 .15
142 Jeff Bryant .05 .15
143 Fredd Young .05 .15
144 Brian Bosworth SR RC .60 1.50
145 Kenny Easley .05 .15
146 Vikings TL .07 .20
(Tommy Kramer Spots His Man)
147 Wade Wilson RC .15 .40
148 Tommy Kramer .07 .20
149 Darrin Nelson .05 .15
150 D.J. Dozier SR RC .07 .20
151 Anthony Carter .07 .20
152 Leo Lewis .05 .15
153 Steve Jordan .07 .20
154 Gary Zimmerman .10 .30
155 Chuck Nelson .05 .15
156 Henry Thomas RC .15 .40
157 Chris Doleman RC .15 .40
158 Scott Studwell RC .05 .15
159 Jesse Solomon RC .05 .15
160 Joey Browner AP .05 .15
161 Neal Guggemos .05 .15
162 Steelers TL .07 .20
(Louis Lipps In a Crowd)
163 Mark Malone .05 .15
164 Walter Abercrombie .05 .15
165 Earnest Jackson .05 .15
166 Frank Pollard .05 .15
167 Dwight Stone RC .07 .20
168 Gary Anderson K .05 .15
169 Harry Newsome RC .05 .15
170 Keith Willis .05 .15
171 Keith Gary RC .05 .15
172 David Little RC .07 .20
173 Mike Merriweather .05 .15
174 Dwayne Woodruff .05 .15
175 Patriots TL .15 .40
(Irving Fryar One on One)
176 Steve Grogan .07 .20
177 Tony Eason .07 .20
178 Tony Collins .07 .20
179 Mosi Tatupu .05 .15
180 Stanley Morgan .07 .20
181 Irving Fryar .15 .40
182 Stephen Starring .05 .15
183 Tony Franklin .05 .15
184 Rich Camarillo .05 .15
185 Garin Veris .05 .15
186 Andre Tippett .07 .20
187 Ronnie Lippett .05 .15
188 Fred Marion .05 .15
189 Dolphins TL .30 .75
(Dan Marino Play-
Action Pass)
190 Dan Marino .75 2.00
191 Troy Stradford RC .07 .20
192 Lorenzo Hampton .05 .15
193 Mark Duper .07 .20
194 Mark Clayton .07 .20
195 Reggie Roby .07 .20
196 Dwight Stephenson .15 .40
197 T.J. Turner RC .05 .15
198 John Bosa RC .05 .15
199 Jackie Shipp RC .05 .15
200 John Offerdahl .07 .20
201 Mark Brown .05 .15
202 Paul Lankford .05 .15
203 Chargers TL .15 .40
(Kellen Winslow Sure Hands)
204 Tim Spencer .05 .15
205 Gary Anderson RB .07 .20
206 Curtis Adams .05 .15
207 Lionel James .05 .15
208 Chip Banks .05 .15
209 Kellen Winslow .15 .40
210 Ralf Mojsiejenko .05 .15
211 Jim Lachey .07 .20
212 Lee Williams .05 .15
213 Billy Ray Smith .05 .15
214 Vencie Glenn RC .05 .15
215 Passing Leaders .20 .50
Bernie Kosar
Joe Montana
216 Receiving Leaders .07 .20
Al Toon
J.T. Smith
217 Rushing Leaders .07 .20
Charles White
Eric Dickerson
218 Scoring Leaders .15 .40
Jim Breech
Jerry Rice
219 Interception Leaders .05 .15
Keith Bostic
Mark Kelso
Mike Prior
Barry Wilburn

1988 Topps

220 Bills TL .15 .40
(Jim Kelly Plots His Course)
221 Jim Kelly .30 .75
222 Ronnie Harmon RC .15 .40
223 Robb Riddick .05 .15
224 Andre Reed .15 .40
225 Chris Burkett RC .05 .15
226 Pete Metzelaars .15 .40
227 Bruce Smith AP .20 .50
228 Darryl Talley .07 .20
229 Eugene Marve .05 .15
230 Cornelius Bennett RC .30 .75
231 Mark Kelso RC .05 .15
232 Shane Conlan RC .15 .40
233 Eagles TL .15 .40
(Randall Cunningham
QB Keeper)
234 Randall Cunningham .40 1.00
235 Keith Byars .15 .40
236 Anthony Toney RC .05 .15
237 Mike Quick .07 .20
238 Kenny Jackson .05 .15
239 John Spagnola .05 .15
240 Paul McFadden .05 .15
241 Reggie White AP .25 .60
242 Ken Clarke .05 .15
243 Mike Pitts .05 .15
244 Clyde Simmons RC .15 .40
245 Seth Joyner RC .15 .40
246 Andre Waters .15 .40
247 Jerome Brown SR RC .15 .40
248 Cardinals TL .05 .15
(Stump Mitchell On the Run)
249 Neil Lomax .07 .20
250 Stump Mitchell .05 .15
251 Earl Ferrell .05 .15
252 Vai Sikahema .05 .15
253 J.T. Smith .07 .20
254 Roy Green .07 .20
255 Robert Awalt RC .07 .20
256 Freddie Joe Nunn .05 .15
257 Leonard Smith RC .05 .15
258 Travis Curtis .05 .15
259 Cowboys TL .15 .40
(Herschel Walker Around End)
260 Danny White .15 .40
261 Herschel Walker .15 .40
262 Tony Dorsett .15 .40
263 Doug Cosbie .05 .15
264 Roger Ruzek RC .07 .20
265 Darryl Clack .05 .15
266 Ed Too Tall Jones .15 .40
267 Jim Jeffcoat .05 .15
268 Everson Walls .05 .15
269 Bill Bates .07 .20
270 Michael Downs .05 .15
271 Giants TL .07 .20
(Mark Bavaro Drives Ahead)
272 Phil Simms .15 .40
273 Joe Morris .07 .20
274 Lee Rouson .05 .15
275 George Adams .05 .15
276 Lionel Manuel .05 .15
277 Mark Bavaro .07 .20
278 Raul Allegre .05 .15
279 Sean Landeta .05 .15
280 Erik Howard .05 .15
281 Leonard Marshall .07 .20
282 Carl Banks AP .07 .20
283 Pepper Johnson .07 .20
284 Harry Carson .07 .20
285 Lawrence Taylor .15 .40
286 Terry Kinard .05 .15
287 Rams TL .15 .40
(Jim Everett Races Downfield)
288 Jim Everett .15 .40
289 Charles White .07 .20
290 Ron Brown .07 .20
291 Henry Ellard .15 .40
292 Mike Lansford .05 .15
293 Dale Hatcher .05 .15
294 Doug Smith .05 .15
295 Jackie Slater .07 .20
296 Jim Collins .05 .15
297 Jerry Gray .05 .15
298 LeRoy Irvin .05 .15
299 Nolan Cromwell .07 .20
300 Kevin Greene RC .50 1.25
301 Jets TL .07 .20
(Ken O'Brien Reads Defense)
302 Ken O'Brien .07 .20
303 Freeman McNeil .07 .20
304 Johnny Hector .05 .15
305 Al Toon .07 .20
306 Jo Jo Townsell RC .07 .20
307 Mickey Shuler .05 .15
308 Pat Leahy .05 .15
309 Roger Vick .05 .15
310 Alex Gordon RC .05 .15
311 Troy Benson .05 .15
312 Bob Crable .05 .15
313 Harry Hamilton .05 .15
314 Packers TL .05 .15
(Phillip Epps Ready
for Contact)
315 Randy Wright .05 .15
316 Kenneth Davis .07 .20
317 Phillip Epps .05 .15
318 Walter Stanley .05 .15
319 Frankie Neal .05 .15
320 Don Bracken .05 .15
321 Brian Noble RC .07 .20
322 Johnny Holland SR RC .07 .20
323 Tim Harris .07 .20
324 Mark Murphy .05 .15
325 Raiders TL .20 .50
(Bo Jackson All Alone)
326 Marc Wilson .05 .15
327 Bo Jackson SR RC 2.00 5.00
328 Marcus Allen .15 .40
329 James Lofton .15 .40
330 Todd Christensen .07 .20
331 Chris Bahr .05 .15
332 Stan Talley .05 .15
333 Howie Long .15 .40
334 Sean Jones .15 .40
335 Matt Millen .07 .20
336 Stacey Toran .05 .15
337 Vann McElroy .05 .15
338 Greg Townsend .07 .20
339 Bengals TL .15 .40
(Boomer Esiason Calls Signals)
340 Boomer Esiason .15 .40
341 Larry Kinnebrew .05 .15
342 Stanford Jennings RC .05 .15
343 Eddie Brown .07 .20
344 Jim Breech .05 .15
345 Anthony Munoz AP .15 .40
346 Scott Fulhage RC .05 .15
347 Tim Krumrie RC .05 .15
348 Reggie Williams .07 .20
349 David Fulcher RC .05 .15
350 Buccaneers TL .05 .15
(James Wilder Free
and Clear)
351 Frank Garcia .05 .15
352 Vinny Testaverde RC 1.50 4.00
353 James Wilder .05 .15
354 Jeff Smith .05 .15
355 Gerald Carter .05 .15
356 Calvin Magee .05 .15
357 Donald Igwebuike .05 .15
358 Ron Holmes RC .05 .15
359 Chris Washington .05 .15
360 Ervin Randle .05 .15
361 Chiefs TL .05 .15
(Bill Kenney Ground Attack)
362 Bill Kenney .05 .15
363 Christian Okoye SR RC .15 .40
364 Paul Palmer .05 .15
365 Stephone Paige .07 .20
366 Carlos Carson .05 .15
367 Kelly Goodburn RC .05 .15
368 Bill Maas .05 .15
369 Mike Bell .05 .15
370 Dino Hackett RC .05 .15
371 Deron Cherry .05 .15
372 Lions TL .05 .15
(James Jones Stretches
For More)
373 Chuck Long .07 .20
374 Garry James .05 .15
375 James Jones .05 .15
376 Pete Mandley .05 .15
377 Gary Lee RC .05 .15
378 Eddie Murray .05 .15
379 Jim Arnold .05 .15
380 Dennis Gibson RC .05 .15
381 Mike Cofer .05 .15
382 James Griffin .05 .15
383 Falcons TL .05 .15
(Gerald Riggs Carries
Heavy Load)
384 Scott Campbell .05 .15
385 Gerald Riggs .07 .20
386 Floyd Dixon RC .05 .15
387 Rick Donnelly .05 .15
388 Bill Fralic .07 .20
389 Major Everett .05 .15
390 Mike Gann .05 .15
391 Tony Casillas RC .07 .20
392 Rick Bryan .05 .15
393 John Rade RC .05 .15
394 Checklist 1-132 .05 .15
395 Checklist 133-264 .05 .15
396 Checklist 265-396 .05 .15

1988 Topps Box Bottoms

This 16-card standard-size set was issued on the bottom of 1988 Topps wax pack boxes. These cards feature NFL players who had won major awards while in college and they are displayed two players per card. The back of the card features brief biographical blurbs about how the players won the awards while they were in school. The set includes cards of Cornelius Bennett, Bo Jackson, and Vinny Testaverde during their rookie years for cards.

COMPLETE SET (16) 4.00 10.00
A Vinny Testaverde .30 .75
Jason Buck
B Dean Steinkuhler .20 .50
Dave Rimington
C George Rogers .20 .50
Mark May
Washington Redskins
D Kenneth Sims .20 .50
Hugh Green
E Cornelius Bennett .25 .60
Tony Casillas
F Bo Jackson .30 .75
Mike Ruth
G Ross Browner .20 .50
Randy White
H Doug Flutie 1.25 3.00
Bruce Smith
I Herschel Walker .30 .75
Dave Rimington
J Jim Plunkett .30 .75
Randy White
K Charles White .20 .50
Jim Ritcher
L Brad Budde .20 .50
Bruce Clark
M Marcus Allen .60 1.50
Dave Rimington
N Mike Rozier .20 .50
Dean Steinkuhler
Houston Oilers
O Tony Dorsett .30 .75
Ross Browner
P Checklist .20 .50

1988 Topps 1000 Yard Club

COMPLETE SET (28) 2.00 5.00
1 Charles White .05 .15
2 Eric Dickerson .20 .50
3 J.T. Smith .05 .15
4 Jerry Rice 1.00 2.50
5 Gary Clark .10 .30
6 Carlos Carson .05 .15
7 Drew Hill .05 .15
8 Curt Warner UER .10 .30
(Reversed negative)
9 Al Toon .10 .30
10 Mike Rozier .05 .15
11 Ernest Givins .10 .30
12 Anthony Carter .10 .30
13 Rueben Mayes .05 .15
14 Steve Largent .20 .50
15 Herschel Walker .10 .30
16 James Lofton .20 .50
17 Gerald Riggs .05 .15
18 Mark Bavaro .05 .15
19 Roger Craig .10 .30
20 Webster Slaughter .05 .15
21 Henry Ellard .10 .30
22 Mike Quick .05 .15
23 Stump Mitchell .05 .15
24 Eric Martin .05 .15
25 Mark Clayton .10 .30
26 Chris Burkett .05 .15
27 Marcus Allen .30 .75
28 Andre Reed .20 .50

1989 Topps

This 396-card standard-size set was issued in 15-card wax packs as well as in factory set form. The 15-card wax packs also included an 1,000 yard club card. Card fronts have color stripes across the border one-quarter of the way down the card. The player's name, team name and position are toward the bottom of the photo. Horizontally designed backs have yearly statistics and highlights. The card are team order according to their finish in 1988. The Team Leader cards have an action scene on the front and a recap of the team's previous season on the back. Rookie Cards include Eric Allen, Steve Beuerlein, Brian Blades, Tim Brown, Mark Carrier (WR), Cris Carter, Michael Irvin, Keith Jackson, Anthony Miller, Chris Miller, Jay Novacek, Michael Dean Perry, Mark Rypien, Sterling Sharpe, Chris Spielman, John Taylor, Thurman Thomas and Rod Woodson.

COMPLETE SET (396) 7.50 20.00
COMP.FACT.SET (396) 12.00 30.00
1 Super Bowl XXIII .20 .50
(Joe Montana back
to pass)
2 Tim Brown RB .20 .50
Most Combined Net
Yards Gained:
Rookie Season
3 Eric Dickerson RB .05 .15
Most Consecutive
Seasons Start of
Career: 1000 or More
Yards Rushing
4 Steve Largent RB .08 .25
Most Yards Receiving:
Career
5 Dan Marino RB .30 .75
Most Seasons 4000 or
More Yards Passing
6 49ers Team .20 .50
Joe Montana On The Run
7 Jerry Rice .60 1.50
8 Roger Craig .08 .25
9 Ronnie Lott .08 .25
10 Michael Carter .02 .10
11 Charles Haley .08 .25
12 Joe Montana .75 2.00
13 John Taylor RC .20 .50
14 Michael Walter .02 .10
15 Mike Cofer RC .02 .10
16 Tom Rathman .05 .15
17 Daniel Stubbs RC .02 .10
18 Keena Turner .02 .10
19 Tim McKyer .02 .10
20 Larry Roberts .02 .10
21 Jeff Fuller .02 .10
22 Bubba Paris .02 .10
23 Bengals Team UER .02 .10
Boomer Esiason Measures
Up (Should be versus
Steelers in week three)
24 Eddie Brown .02 .10
25 Boomer Esiason .08 .25
26 Tim Krumrie .02 .10
27 Ickey Woods RC .15 .40
28 Anthony Munoz .08 .25
29 Tim McGee .02 .10
30 Max Montoya .02 .10
31 David Grant .02 .10
32 Rodney Holman RC .02 .10
(Cincinnati Bengals on
card front is subject to
various printing errors)
33 David Fulcher .02 .10
34 Jim Skow .02 .10
35 James Brooks .05 .15
36 Reggie Williams .02 .10
37 Eric Thomas RC .02 .10
38 Stanford Jennings .02 .10
39 Jim Breech .02 .10
40 Bills Team .08 .25
Jim Kelly Reads Defense
41 Shane Conlan .02 .10
42 Scott Norwood RC .02 .10
43 Cornelius Bennett .08 .25
44 Bruce Smith .08 .25
45 Thurman Thomas RC .50 1.25
46 Jim Kelly .20 .50
47 John Kidd .02 .10
48 Kent Hull RC .02 .10
49 Art Still .02 .10
50 Fred Smerlas .02 .10
51A Derrick Burroughs .02 .10
(White name plate)
51B Derrick Burroughs .02 .10
(Yellow name plate)
52 Andre Reed .08 .25
53 Robb Riddick .02 .10
54 Chris Burkett .02 .10
55 Ronnie Harmon .02 .10
56 Mark Kelso UER .02 .10
(team shown as Buffalo Bill)
57 Bears Team .02 .10
Thomas Sanders
* Changes Pace
58 Mike Singletary .08 .25
59 Jay Hilgenberg UER .02 .10
(letter g missing from Chicago)
60 Richard Dent .08 .25
61 Ron Rivera .02 .10
62 Jim McMahon .08 .25
63 Mike Tomczak .05 .15
64 Neal Anderson .08 .25
65 Dennis Gentry .02 .10
66 Dan Hampton .08 .25
67 David Tate .02 .10
68 Thomas Sanders RC .02 .10
69 Steve McMichael .05 .15
70 Dennis McKinnon .02 .10
71 Brad Muster RC .08 .25
72 Vestee Jackson RC .02 .10
73 Dave Duerson .02 .10
74 Vikings Team .02 .10
Millard Gets His Man
75 Joey Browner .05 .15
76 Carl Lee RC .02 .10
77 Gary Zimmerman .08 .25
78 Hassan Jones RC .02 .10
79 Anthony Carter .08 .25
80 Ray Berry .02 .10
81 Steve Jordan .02 .10
82 Issiac Holt .02 .10
83 Wade Wilson .05 .15
84 Chris Doleman .05 .15
85 Alfred Anderson .02 .10
86 Keith Millard .02 .10
87 Darrin Nelson .02 .10
88 D.J. Dozier .02 .10
89 Scott Studwell .02 .10
90 Oilers Team .02 .10
Tony Zendejas Big Boot
91 Bruce Matthews RC .30 .75
92 Curtis Duncan .02 .10
93 Warren Moon .08 .25
94 Johnny Meads RC .02 .10
95 Drew Hill .05 .15
96 Alonzo Highsmith .05 .15
97 Mike Munchak .08 .25
98 Mike Rozier .05 .15
99 Tony Zendejas .02 .10
100 Jeff Donaldson .02 .10
101 Ray Childress .05 .15
102 Sean Jones .02 .10
103 Ernest Givins .05 .15
104 William Fuller RC .08 .25
105 Allen Pinkett RC .02 .10
106 Eagles Team .02 .10
Randall Cunningham
Fakes Field
107 Keith Jackson RC .08 .25
108 Reggie White .08 .25
109 Clyde Simmons .05 .15
110 John Teltschik .02 .10
111 Wes Hopkins .05 .15
112 Keith Byars .05 .15
113 Jerome Brown .05 .15
114 Mike Quick .05 .15
115 Randall Cunningham .15 .40
116 Anthony Toney .02 .10
117 Ron Johnson .02 .10
118 Terry Hoage .02 .10
119 Seth Joyner .05 .15
120 Eric Allen RC .08 .25
121 Cris Carter RC .60 1.50
122 Rams Team .02 .10
Greg Bell Runs To Glory
123 Tom Newberry RC .02 .10
124 Pete Holohan .02 .10
125 Robert Delpino UER RC .02 .10
(Listed as Raider
on card back)
126 Carl Ekern .02 .10
127 Greg Bell .02 .10
128 Mike Lansford .02 .10
129 Jim Everett .08 .25
130 Mike Wilcher .02 .10
131 Jerry Gray .02 .10
132 Dale Hatcher .02 .10
133 Doug Smith .02 .10
134 Kevin Greene .08 .25
135 Jackie Slater .08 .25
136 Aaron Cox RC .02 .10
137 Henry Ellard .08 .25
138 Browns Team .02 .10
Bernie Kosar Quick
Release
139 Frank Minnifield .02 .10
140 Webster Slaughter .05 .15
141 Bernie Kosar .08 .25
142 Charles Buchanan .02 .10
143 Clay Matthews .05 .15
144 Reggie Langhorne RC .08 .25
145 Hanford Dixon .02 .10
146 Brian Brennan .02 .10
147 Earnest Byner .05 .15
148 Michael Dean Perry RC .05 .15
149 Kevin Mack .05 .15
150 Matt Bahr .02 .10
151 Ozzie Newsome .08 .25
152 Saints Team .02 .10
Craig Heyward Motors
Forward
153 Morten Andersen .05 .15
154 Pat Swilling .05 .15
155 Sam Mills .05 .15
156 Lonzell Hill .02 .10
157 Dalton Hilliard .02 .10
158 Craig Heyward RC .08 .25
159 Vaughan Johnson RC .05 .15
160 Rueben Mayes .02 .10
161 Gene Atkins RC .02 .10
162 Bobby Hebert .05 .15
163 Rickey Jackson .05 .15
164 Eric Martin .02 .10
165 Giants Team .02 .10
Joe Morris Up
The Middle
166 Lawrence Taylor .08 .25
167 Bart Oates .05 .15
168 Carl Banks .05 .15
169 Eric Moore RC .02 .10
170 Sheldon White RC .02 .10
171 Mark Collins RC .08 .25
172 Phil Simms .08 .25
173 Jim Burt .05 .15
174 Stephen Baker RC .08 .25
175 Mark Bavaro .05 .15
176 Pepper Johnson .05 .15
177 Lionel Manuel .05 .15
178 Joe Morris .05 .15
179 John Elliott RC .05 .15
180 Gary Reasons RC .02 .10
181 Seahawks Team .02 .10
Dave Krieg Winds Up
182 Brian Blades RC .08 .25
183 Steve Largent .08 .25
184 Rufus Porter RC .02 .10
185 Ruben Rodriguez .02 .10
186 Curt Warner .05 .15
187 Paul Moyer .02 .10
188 Dave Krieg .05 .15
189 Jacob Green .05 .15
190 John L. Williams .05 .15
191 Eugene Robinson RC .08 .25
192 Brian Bosworth .08 .25
193 Patriots Team .02 .10
Tony Eason Behind
Blocking
194 John Stephens RC .02 .10
195 Robert Perryman RC .02 .10
196 Andre Tippett .08 .25
197 Fred Marion .02 .10
198 Doug Flutie .40 1.00
199 Stanley Morgan .05 .15
200 Johnny Rembert RC .02 .10
201 Tony Eason .05 .15
202 Marvin Allen .02 .10
203 Raymond Clayborn .02 .10
204 Irving Fryar .08 .25
205 Colts Team .02 .10
Chris Chandler
All Alone
206 Eric Dickerson .08 .25
207 Chris Hinton .02 .10
208 Duane Bickett .02 .10
209 Chris Chandler RC .40 1.00
210 Jon Hand .02 .10
211 Ray Donaldson .02 .10
212 Dean Biasucci .02 .10
213 Bill Brooks .05 .15
214 Chris Goode RC .02 .10
215 Clarence Verdin RC .02 .10
216 Albert Bentley .02 .10
217 Passing Leaders .05 .15
Wade Wilson
Boomer Esiason
218 Receiving Leaders .05 .15
Henry Ellard
Al Toon
219 Rushing Leaders .05 .15
Herschel Walker
Eric Dickerson
220 Scoring Leaders .02 .10
Mike Cofer
Scott Norwood
221 Intercept Leaders .02 .10
Scott Case
Erik McMillan
222 Jets Team .02 .10
Ken O'Brien Surveys
Scene
223 Erik McMillan RC .02 .10
224 James Hasty RC .02 .10
225 Al Toon .05 .15
226 John Booty RC .02 .10
227 Johnny Hector .02 .10
228 Ken O'Brien .05 .15
229 Marty Lyons .02 .10
230 Mickey Shuler .02 .10
231 Robin Cole .02 .10
232 Freeman McNeil .05 .15
233 Marion Barber RC .08 .25
234 Jo Jo Townsell .02 .10
235 Wesley Walker .05 .15
236 Roger Vick .02 .10
237 Pat Leahy .02 .10
238 Broncos Team UER .20 .50
John Elway Ground Attack
(Score of week 15 says/42-21; should be 42-14)
239 Mike Horan .02 .10
240 Tony Dorsett .08 .25
241 John Elway .75 2.00
242 Mark Jackson .02 .10
243 Sammy Winder .02 .10
244 Rich Karlis .02 .10
245 Vance Johnson .02 .10
246 Steve Sewell RC .02 .10
247 Karl Mecklenburg UER .05 .15
(Drafted 2, should be 12)
248 Rulon Jones .02 .10
249 Simon Fletcher RC .02 .10
250 Redskins Team .05 .15
Doug Williams Sets Up
251 Chip Lohmiller RC .02 .10
252 Jamie Morris .05 .15
253 Mark Rypien RC UER .08 .25
(14 1988 completions;
should be 114)
254 Barry Wilburn .02 .10
255 Mark May RC .05 .15
256 Wilber Marshall .05 .15
257 Charles Mann .02 .10
258 Gary Clark .08 .25
259 Doug Williams .08 .25
260 Art Monk .08 .25
261 Kelvin Bryant .02 .10
262 Dexter Manley .05 .15
263 Ricky Sanders .05 .15
264 Raiders Team .08 .25
Marcus Allen Through
the Line
265 Tim Brown RC .60 1.50
266 Jay Schroeder .02 .10
267 Marcus Allen .08 .25
268 Mike Haynes .05 .15
269 Bo Jackson .10 .30
270 Steve Beuerlein RC .25 .60
271 Vann McElroy .02 .10
272 Willie Gault .05 .15
273 Howie Long .08 .25
274 Greg Townsend .02 .10
275 Mike Wise .02 .10
276 Cardinals Team .02 .10
Neil Lomax Looks Long
277 Luis Sharpe .02 .10
278 Scott Dill .02 .10
279 Vai Sikahema .02 .10
280 Ron Wolfley .02 .10
281 David Galloway .02 .10
282 Jay Novacek RC .20 .50
283 Neil Lomax .05 .15
284 Robert Awalt .02 .10
285 Cedric Mack .02 .10
286 Freddie Joe Nunn .02 .10
287 J.T. Smith .05 .15
288 Stump Mitchell .05 .15
289 Roy Green .05 .15
290 Dolphins Team .20 .50
Dan Marino High and Far
291 Jarvis Williams RC .02 .10
292 Troy Stradford .02 .10
293 Dan Marino .75 2.00
294 T.J. Turner .02 .10
295 John Offerdahl .02 .10
296 Ferrell Edmunds RC .02 .10
297 Scott Schwedes .02 .10
298 Lorenzo Hampton .02 .10
299 Jim C.Jensen RC .02 .10
300 Brian Sochia .02 .10
301 Reggie Roby .02 .10
302 Mark Clayton .05 .15
303 Chargers Team .02 .10
Tim Spencer Leads
the Way
304 Lee Williams .02 .10
305 Gary Plummer RC .05 .15
306 Gary Anderson RB .02 .10
307 Gill Byrd .02 .10
308 Jamie Holland RC .02 .10
309 Billy Ray Smith .05 .15
310 Lionel James .02 .10
311 Mark Vlasic RC .02 .10
312 Curtis Adams .02 .10
313 Anthony Miller RC .08 .25
314 Steelers Team .02 .10
Frank Pollard Set
for Action
315 Bubby Brister RC .08 .25
316 David Little .02 .10
317 Tunch Ilkin RC .02 .10
318 Louis Lipps .05 .15
319 Warren Williams RC .02 .10
320 Dwight Stone .02 .10
321 Merril Hoge RC .08 .25
322 Thomas Everett RC .02 .10
323 Rod Woodson RC .40 1.00
324 Gary Anderson K .02 .10
325 Buccaneers Team .02 .10
Ron Hall in Pursuit
326 Donnie Elder .02 .10
327 Vinny Testaverde .10 .30
328 Harry Hamilton .02 .10
329 James Wilder .02 .10
330 Lars Tate .02 .10
331 Mark Carrier RC .08 .25
332 Bruce Hill RC .02 .10
333 Paul Gruber RC .05 .15
334 Ricky Reynolds .02 .10
335 Eugene Marve .02 .10
336 Falcons Team .02 .10
Joel Williams Holds On
337 Aundray Bruce RC .02 .10
338 John Rade .02 .10
339 Scott Case RC .02 .10
340 Robert Moore .02 .10
341 Chris Miller RC .08 .25
342 Gerald Riggs .05 .15
343 Gene Lang .02 .10
344 Marcus Cotton .02 .10
345 Rick Donnelly .02 .10
346 John Settle RC .02 .10
347 Bill Fralic .05 .15
348 Chiefs Team .02 .10
Dino Hackett Zeros In
349 Steve DeBerg .05 .15
350 Mike Stensrud RC .02 .10
351 Dino Hackett .02 .10
352 Deron Cherry .02 .10
353 Christian Okoye .05 .15
354 Bill Maas .02 .10
355 Carlos Carson .05 .15
356 Albert Lewis .05 .15
357 Paul Palmer .02 .10
358 Nick Lowery .02 .10
359 Stephone Paige .05 .15
360 Lions Team .02 .10
Chuck Long Gets
the Snap
361 Chris Spielman RC .08 .25
362 Jim Arnold .02 .10
363 Devon Mitchell .02 .10
364 Mike Cofer .02 .10
365 Bennie Blades RC .02 .10
366 James Jones .02 .10
367 Garry James .02 .10
368 Pete Mandley .02 .10
369 Keith Ferguson .02 .10
370 Dennis Gibson .02 .10
371 Packers Team UER .02 .10
Johnny Holland Over
the Top (Week 16 has
vs. Vikings but
they played Bears)
372 Brent Fullwood RC .02 .10
373 Don Majkowski RC UER .08 .25
(3 TD's in 1987;
should be 5)
374 Tim Harris .02 .10
375 Keith Woodside RC .02 .10
376 Mark Murphy .02 .10
377 Dave Brown DB .02 .10
378 Perry Kemp RC .02 .10
379 Sterling Sharpe RC .30 .75
380 Chuck Cecil RC .05 .15
381 Walter Stanley .02 .10
382 Cowboys Team .02 .10
Steve Pelluer Lets
It Go
383 Michael Irvin RC .60 1.50
384 Bill Bates .05 .15
385 Herschel Walker .08 .25
386 Darryl Clack .02 .10
387 Danny Noonan .02 .10
388 Eugene Lockhart RC .02 .10
389 Ed Too Tall Jones .05 .15
390 Steve Pelluer .02 .10
391 Ray Alexander .02 .10
392 Nate Newton RC .08 .25
393 Garry Cobb .02 .10
394 Checklist 1-132 .02 .10
395 Checklist 133-264 .02 .10
396 Checklist 265-396 .02 .10

1989 Topps Box Bottoms

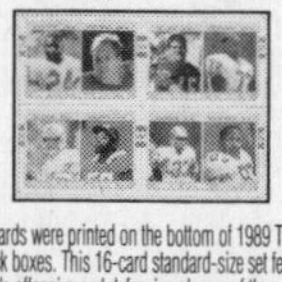

These cards were printed on the bottom of 1989 Topps wax pack boxes. This 16-card standard-size set features the NFL's offensive and defensive players of the week for each week in the 1989 season. Each card features two players on the front.

COMPLETE SET (16) 4.00 10.00
A Neal Anderson .20 .50
Terry Hoage
B Boomer Esiason .30 .75
Jacob Green
C Wesley Walker .20 .50
Gary Jeter
D Jim Everett .20 .50
Danny Noonan
E Neil Lomax .20 .50
Dexter Manley
F Kelvin Bryant .20 .50
Kevin Greene
G Roger Craig .30 .75
Tim Harris
H Dan Marino 1.25 3.00
Carl Banks
I Drew Hill .20 .50
Robin Cole
J Neil Lomax .30 .75
Lawrence Taylor
K Roy Green .20 .50
Tim Krumrie
L Bobby Hebert .20 .50
Aundray Bruce
M Ickey Woods .30 .75
Lawrence Taylor
N Louis Lipps .20 .50
Greg Townsend
O Curt Warner .20 .50
Tim Harris
P Dave Krieg .30 .75
Kevin Greene

1989 Topps 1000 Yard Club

COMPLETE SET (24) 1.50 4.00
1 Eric Dickerson .20 .50
2 Herschel Walker .10 .30
3 Roger Craig .10 .30
4 Henry Ellard .10 .30
5 Jerry Rice .75 2.00
6 Eddie Brown .05 .15
7 Anthony Carter .10 .30
8 Greg Bell .05 .15
9 John Stephens .05 .15
10 Ricky Sanders .05 .15
11 Drew Hill .05 .15
12 Mark Clayton .10 .30
13 Gary Anderson RB .05 .15
14 Neal Anderson .10 .30
15 Roy Green .05 .15
16 Eric Martin .05 .15
17 Joe Morris .05 .15
18 Al Toon .10 .30
19 Ickey Woods .05 .15
20 Bruce Hill .05 .15
21 Lionel Manuel .05 .15
22 Curt Warner .10 .30
23 John Settle .05 .15
24 Mike Rozier .05 .15

1989 Topps Traded

The 1989 Topps Traded set contains 132 standard-size cards featuring rookies and traded players in their new uniforms. The cards are nearly identical to the 1989 Topps regular issue football set, except this traded series was printed on white stock and was distributed only as a boxed set. The card are numbered with a "T" suffix. Rookie Cards include Troy Aikman, Marion Butts, Jim Harbaugh, Greg Lloyd, Dave Meggett, Eric Metcalf, Frank Reich, Andre Rison, Barry Sanders, Deion Sanders, Derrick Thomas, Steve Walsh and Lorenzo White.

COMP.FACT.SET (132) 6.00 15.00
1T Eric Ball RC * .05 .15
2T Tony Mandarich RC .05 .15
3T Shawn Collins RC .05 .15
4T Ray Bentley RC .02 .10
5T Tony Casillas .05 .15
6T Al Del Greco RC .05 .15
7T Dan Saleaumua RC .05 .15
8T Keith Bishop .02 .10
9T Rodney Peete RC .20 .50
10T Lorenzo White RC .08 .25
11T Steve Smith RC .02 .10
12T Pete Mandley .02 .10
13T Mervyn Fernandez RC .02 .10
14T Flipper Anderson RC .08 .25
15T Louis Oliver RC .05 .15
16T Rick Fenney .02 .10
17T Gary Jeter .02 .10
18T Greg Cox .02 .10
19T Bubba McDowell RC .02 .10
20T Ron Heller .02 .10
21T Tim McDonald RC .05 .15
22T Jerrol Williams RC .02 .10
23T Marion Butts RC .08 .25
24T Steve Young .30 .75
25T Mike Merriweather .05 .15
26T Richard Johnson .02 .10
27T Gerald Riggs .05 .15
28T Dave Waymer .02 .10
29T Issiac Holt .02 .10
30T Deion Sanders RC .60 1.50
31T Todd Blackledge .05 .15
32T Jeff Cross RC .05 .15
33T Steve Wisniewski RC .08 .25
34T Ron Brown .02 .10
35T Rod Bernstine RC .05 .15
36T Jeff Uhlenhake RC .02 .10
37T Donnell Woolford RC .08 .25
38T Bob Gagliano RC .02 .10
39T Ezra Johnson .02 .10
40T Ron Jaworski .08 .25
41T Lawyer Tillman RC .05 .15
42T Lorenzo Lynch RC .02 .10
43T Mike Alexander .02 .10
44T Tim Worley RC .05 .15
45T Guy Bingham .02 .10
46T Cleveland Gary RC .05 .15
47T Danny Peebles .02 .10
48T Clarence Weathers RC .08 .25
49T Jeff Lageman RC .08 .25
50T Eric Metcalf RC .08 .25
51T Myron Guyton RC .05 .15
52T Steve Atwater RC .08 .25
53T John Fourcade RC .05 .15
54T Randall McDaniel RC .40 1.00
55T Al Noga RC .02 .10
56T Sammie Smith RC .05 .15
57T Jesse Solomon .02 .10
58T Greg Kragen RC .02 .10
59T Don Beebe RC .08 .25
60T Hart Lee Dykes RC .02 .10
61T Trace Armstrong RC .05 .15
62T Steve Pelluer .02 .10
63T Barry Krauss .02 .10
64T Kevin Murphy RC .02 .10
65T Steve Tasker RC .08 .25
66T Jessie Small RC .05 .15
67T Dave Meggett RC .08 .25
68T Dean Hamel .02 .10
69T Jim Covert .05 .15
70T Troy Aikman RC 2.00 5.00
71T Raul Allegre .02 .10
72T Chris Jacke RC .02 .10
73T Leslie O'Neal .05 .15

74T Keith Taylor RC .02 .10
75T Steve Walsh RC .08 .25
76T Tracy Rocker .02 .10
77T Robert Massey RC .02 .10
78T Bryan Wagner .02 .10
79T Steve DeOssie .05 .15
80T Carnell Lake RC .08 .25
81T Frank Reich RC .08 .25
82T Tyrone Braxton RC .05 .15
83T Barry Sanders RC 2.50 6.00
84T Pete Stoyanovich RC .05 .15
85T Paul Palmer .02 .10
86T Billy Joe Tolliver RC .05 .15
87T Eric Hill RC .02 .10
88T Gerald McNeil .02 .10
89T Bill Hawkins RC .02 .10
90T Derrick Thomas RC .50 1.25
91T Jim Harbaugh RC .30 .75
92T Brian Williams OL RC .02 .10
93T Jack Trudeau .02 .10
94T Leonard Smith .02 .10
95T Gary Hogeboom .02 .10
96T A.J. Johnson RC .02 .10
97T Jim McMahon .05 .15
98T David Williams RC .02 .10
99T Rohn Stark .02 .10
100T Sean Landeta .05 .15
101T Tim Johnson RC .05 .15
102T Andre Rison RC .30 .75
103T Earnest Byner .05 .15
104T Don McPherson RC .02 .10
105T Zefross Moss RC .02 .10
106T Frank Stams RC .02 .10
107T Courtney Hall RC .02 .10
108T Marc Logan RC .02 .10
109T James Lofton .08 .25
110T Lewis Tillman RC .05 .15
111T Irv Pankey RC .02 .10
112T Ralf Mojsiejenko .02 .10
113T Bobby Humphrey RC .05 .15
114T Chris Burkett .02 .10
115T Greg Lloyd RC .08 .25
116T Matt Millen .05 .15
117T Carl Zander .02 .10
118T Wayne Martin RC .08 .25
119T Mike Saxon .02 .10
120T Herschel Walker .08 .25
121T Andy Heck RC .02 .10
122T Mark Robinson RC .02 .10
123T Keith Van Horne RC .02 .10
124T Ricky Hunley .02 .10
125T Timm Rosenbach RC .05 .15
126T Steve Grogan .08 .25
127T Stephen Braggs RC .02 .10
128T Terry Long .02 .10
129T Evan Cooper .02 .10
130T Robert Lyles .02 .10
131T Mike Webster .08 .25
132T Checklist 1-132 .02 .10

1989 Topps American/UK

This 33-card standard-size set was sold in the United Kingdom as a boxed set. The style of the cards is very similar to the 1989 Topps regular issue set. The backs are different as this set was printed on white card stock. The checklist for the set is on the back of the box. The set is populated with name players that, presumably, would be recognizable in England.

COMP.FACT SET (33) 8.00 20.00
1 Anthony Carter .25 .60
2 Jim Kelly .40 1.00
3 Bernie Kosar .25 .60
4 John Elway 2.00 5.00
5 Andre Tippett .15 .40
6 Henry Ellard .25 .60
7 Eddie Brown .15 .40
8 Gary Anderson RB .15 .40
9 Eric Martin .15 .40
10 Ickey Woods .15 .40
11 Mike Singletary .30 .75
12 Phil Simms .30 .75
13 Brian Bosworth .15 .40
14 Mark Clayton .25 .60
15 Eric Dickerson .30 .75
16 John Stephens .15 .40
17 Neal Anderson .25 .60
18 Al Toon .15 .40
19 Lionel Manuel .15 .40
20 Joe Montana 2.50 6.00
21 Reggie White .40 1.00
22 Randall Cunningham .40 1.00
23 Lawrence Taylor .30 .75
24 Jim Everett .25 .60
25 Neil Lomax .15 .40
26 Herschel Walker .25 .60
27 Roger Craig .25 .60
28 Greg Bell .15 .40
29 Ricky Sanders .15 .40
30 Joe Morris .15 .40
31 Curt Warner .15 .40
32 Boomer Esiason .30 .75
33 Dan Marino 2.00 5.00

1989 Topps Football Talk

LJN Toys distributed this set of cards to be used with their Sportstalk record player. Each player card features a reprint of a previously issued card on the fronts with a 1989 Topps football card style cardback along with a clear plastic audio record attached. Two program cover cards were included from historic NFL games. The eight cards were packaged in two seperate blister packs of four cards. Note that there were two card #1's produced and no #4.

COMPLETE SET (8) 60.00 120.00
1A 1958 Championship Program 5.00 10.00
1B Joe Greene (1971 Topps) 10.00 20.00
2 Bob Lilly (1966 Philadelphia Gum) 7.50 15.00
3 Super Bowl III Program 6.00 12.00
5 Franco Harris (1973 Topps) 12.50 25.00
6 Gale Sayers (1969 Topps) 12.50 25.00
7 Johnny Unitas (1961 Topps) 15.00 30.00
8 Billy Kilmer (1962 Topps) 5.00 10.00

1990 Topps

Returning to 528 cards for the first time since 1982, these standard size cards were available in factory sets, fifteen card wax packs and cello packs. Each pack included a 1,000 Yard Club card. The cardbacks can be found with variations: the NFL Properties disclaimer is either present or absent from the back of each card. The cards are arranged in team order and the teams themselves are ordered according to their finish in the 1989 standings. Subsets include Record Breakers (1-5) and Team Action (501-528) cards. League Leader cards are scattered throughout the set. A few leader cards (28, 193, 229, and 431) as well as all of the Team Action cards can be found with or without the hashmarks on the bottom of the card. Topps also produced a Tiffany or glossy edition of the set.

COMPLETE SET (528) 10.00 25.00
COMP.FACT.SET (528) 12.50 30.00
*DISCLAIMER BACK: .4X TO 1X
1 Joe Montana RB .20 .50
Most TD Passes: Super Bowl
2 Flipper Anderson RB .01 .05
Most Receiving Yards: Game
3 Troy Aikman RB .15 .40
Most Passing Yards in a Game: Rookie
4 Kevin Butler RB .01 .05
Most Consecutive Field Goals
5 Super Bowl XXIV/49ers 55 Broncos 10 .01 .05
(line of scrimmage)
6 Dexter Carter RC .01 .05
7 Matt Millen .02 .10
8 Jerry Rice .30 .75
9 Ronnie Lott .02 .10
10 John Taylor .02 .10
11 Guy McIntyre .01 .05
12 Roger Craig .02 .10
13 Joe Montana .50 1.25
14 Brent Jones RC .08 .25
15 Tom Rathman .01 .05
16 Harris Barton .01 .05
17 Charles Haley .02 .10
18 Pierce Holt RC .01 .05
19 Michael Carter .01 .05
20 Chet Brooks .01 .05
21 Eric Wright .01 .05
22 Mike Cofer .01 .05
23 Jim Fahnhorst .01 .05
24 Keena Turner .01 .05
25 Don Griffin .01 .05
26 Kevin Fagan RC .01 .05
27 Bubba Paris .01 .05
28A Rushing Leaders .20 .50
Barry Sanders
Christian Okoye
28B Rushing Leaders .20 .50
Barry Sanders
Christian Okoye
(missing hash marks on front)
29 Steve Atwater .01 .05
30 Tyrone Braxton .01 .05
31 Ron Holmes .01 .05
32 Bobby Humphrey .01 .05
33 Greg Kragen .01 .05
34 David Treadwell .01 .05
35 Karl Mecklenburg .01 .05
36 Dennis Smith .01 .05
37 John Elway .50 1.25
38 Vance Johnson .01 .05
39 Simon Fletcher UER .01 .05
(Front DL, back LB)
40 Jim Juriga .01 .05
41 Mark Jackson .01 .05
42 Melvin Bratton RC .01 .05
43 Wymon Henderson RC .01 .05
44 Ken Bell .01 .05
45 Sammy Winder .01 .05
46 Alphonso Carreker .01 .05
47 Orson Mobley RC .01 .05
48 Rodney Hampton RC .08 .25
49 Dave Meggett .02 .10
50 Myron Guyton .01 .05
51 Phil Simms .02 .10
52 Lawrence Taylor .08 .25
53 Carl Banks .01 .05
54 Pepper Johnson .01 .05
55 Leonard Marshall .01 .05
56 Mark Collins .01 .05
57 Erik Howard .01 .05
58 Eric Dorsey RC .01 .05
59 Ottis Anderson .02 .10
60 Mark Bavaro .01 .05
61 Odessa Turner RC .01 .05
62 Gary Reasons .01 .05
63 Maurice Carthon .01 .05
64 Lionel Manuel .01 .05
65 Sean Landeta .01 .05
66 Perry Williams .01 .05
67 Pat Terrell RC .01 .05
68 Flipper Anderson .01 .05
69 Jackie Slater .01 .05
70 Tom Newberry .01 .05
71 Jerry Gray .01 .05
72 Henry Ellard .02 .10
73 Doug Smith .01 .05
74 Kevin Greene .02 .10
75 Jim Everett .02 .10
76 Mike Lansford .01 .05
77 Greg Bell .01 .05
78 Pete Holohan .01 .05
79 Robert Delpino .01 .05
80 Mike Wilcher .01 .05
81 Mike Piel .01 .05
82 Mel Owens .01 .05
83 Michael Stewart RC .01 .05
84 Ben Smith RC .01 .05
85 Keith Jackson .02 .10
86 Reggie White .08 .25
87 Eric Allen .01 .05
88 Jerome Brown .01 .05
89 Robert Drummond .01 .05
90 Anthony Toney .01 .05
91 Keith Byars .01 .05
92 Cris Carter .20 .50
93 Randall Cunningham .08 .25
94 Ron Johnson .01 .05
95 Mike Quick .01 .05
96 Clyde Simmons .01 .05
97 Mike Pitts .01 .05
98 Izel Jenkins RC .01 .05
99 Seth Joyner .02 .10
100 Mike Schad .01 .05
101 Wes Hopkins .01 .05
102 Kirk Lowdermilk .01 .05
103 Rick Fenney .01 .05
104 Randall McDaniel .08 .25
105 Herschel Walker .02 .10
106 Al Noga .01 .05
107 Gary Zimmerman .02 .10
108 Chris Doleman .01 .05
109 Keith Millard .01 .05
110 Carl Lee .01 .05
111 Joey Browner .01 .05
112 Steve Jordan .01 .05
113 Reggie Rutland RC .01 .05
114 Wade Wilson .02 .10
115 Anthony Carter .02 .10
116 Rich Karlis .01 .05
117 Hassan Jones .01 .05
118 Henry Thomas .01 .05
119 Scott Studwell .01 .05
120 Ralf Mojsiejenko .01 .05
121 Earnest Byner .01 .05
122 Gerald Riggs .02 .10
123 Tracy Rocker .01 .05
124 A.J. Johnson .01 .05
125 Charles Mann .01 .05
126 Art Monk .02 .10
127 Ricky Sanders .01 .05
128 Gary Clark .08 .25
129 Jim Lachey .01 .05
130 Martin Mayhew RC .01 .05
131 Ravin Caldwell .01 .05
132 Don Warren .01 .05
133 Mark Rypien .02 .10
134 Ed Simmons RC .01 .05
135 Darryl Grant .01 .05
136 Darrell Green .02 .10
137 Chip Lohmiller .01 .05
138 Tony Bennett RC .08 .25
139 Tony Mandarich .01 .05
140 Sterling Sharpe .08 .25
141 Tim Harris .01 .05
142 Don Majkowski .01 .05
143 Rich Moran RC .01 .05
144 Jeff Query .01 .05
145 Brent Fullwood .01 .05
146 Chris Jacke .01 .05
147 Keith Woodside .01 .05
148 Perry Kemp .01 .05
149 Herman Fontenot .01 .05
150 Dave Brown DB .01 .05
151 Brian Noble .01 .05
152 Johnny Holland .01 .05
153 Mark Murphy .01 .05
154 Bob Nelson .01 .05
155 Darrell Thompson RC .01 .05
156 Lawyer Tillman .01 .05
157 Eric Metcalf .08 .25
158 Webster Slaughter .02 .10
159 Frank Minnifield .01 .05
160 Brian Brennan .01 .05
161 Thane Gash RC .01 .05
162 Robert Banks DE .01 .05
163 Bernie Kosar .02 .10
164 David Grayson .01 .05
165 Kevin Mack .01 .05
166 Mike Johnson .01 .05
167 Tim Manoa .01 .05
168 Ozzie Newsome .02 .10
169 Felix Wright .01 .05
170A Al Bubba Baker .02 .10
(orange Topps logo on front)
170B Al Bubba Baker .02 .10
(white Topps logo on front)
171 Reggie Langhorne .01 .05
172 Clay Matthews .02 .10
173 Andrew Stewart .01 .05
174 Barry Foster RC .08 .25
175 Tim Worley .01 .05
176 Tim Johnson .01 .05
177 Carnell Lake .01 .05
178 Greg Lloyd .08 .25
179 Rod Woodson .08 .25
180 Tunch Ilkin .01 .05
181 Dermontti Dawson .02 .10
182 Gary Anderson K .01 .05
183 Bubby Brister .01 .05
184 Louis Lipps .02 .10
185 Merril Hoge .01 .05
186 Mike Mularkey .01 .05
187 Derek Hill .01 .05
188 Rodney Carter .01 .05
189 Dwayne Woodruff .01 .05
190 Keith Willis .01 .05
191 Jerry Olsavsky .01 .05
192 Mark Stock .01 .05
193 Sacks Leaders .01 .05
Chris Doleman
Lee Williams
194 Leonard Smith .01 .05
195 Darryl Talley .01 .05
196 Mark Kelso .01 .05
197 Kent Hull .01 .05
198 Nate Odomes RC .02 .10
199 Pete Metzelaars .01 .05
200 Don Beebe .02 .10
201 Ray Bentley .01 .05
202 Steve Tasker .02 .10
203 Scott Norwood .01 .05
204 Andre Reed .08 .25
205 Bruce Smith .08 .25
206 Thurman Thomas .08 .25
207 Jim Kelly .08 .25
208 Cornelius Bennett .02 .10
209 Shane Conlan .01 .05
210 Larry Kinnebrew .01 .05
211 Jeff Alm RC .01 .05
212 Robert Lyles .01 .05
213 Bubba McDowell .01 .05
214 Mike Munchak .02 .10
215 Bruce Matthews .02 .10
216 Warren Moon .08 .25
217 Drew Hill .01 .05
218 Ray Childress .01 .05
219 Steve Brown .01 .05
220 Alonzo Highsmith .01 .05
221 Allen Pinkett .01 .05
222 Sean Jones .02 .10
223 Johnny Meads .01 .05
224 John Grimsley .01 .05
225 Haywood Jeffires RC .08 .25
226 Curtis Duncan .01 .05
227 Greg Montgomery RC .01 .05
228 Ernest Givins .02 .10
229A Passing Leaders .20 .50
Joe Montana
Boomer Esiason
229B Passing Leaders .20 .50
Joe Montana
Boomer Esiason
(missing hash marks on front)
230 Robert Massey .01 .05
231 John Fourcade .01 .05
232 Dalton Hilliard .01 .05
233 Vaughan Johnson .01 .05
234 Hoby Brenner .01 .05
235 Pat Swilling .02 .10
236 Kevin Haverdink .01 .05
237 Bobby Hebert .01 .05
238 Sam Mills .02 .10
239 Eric Martin .01 .05
240 Lonzell Hill .01 .05
241 Steve Trapilo .01 .05
242 Rickey Jackson .02 .10
243 Craig Heyward .02 .10
244 Rueben Mayes .01 .05
245 Morten Andersen .01 .05
246 Percy Snow RC .01 .05
247 Pete Mandley .01 .05
248 Derrick Thomas .08 .25
249 Dan Saleaumua .01 .05
250 Todd McNair RC .01 .05
251 Leonard Griffin RC .01 .05
252 Jonathan Hayes .01 .05
253 Christian Okoye .01 .05
254 Albert Lewis .01 .05
255 Nick Lowery .01 .05
256 Kevin Ross .01 .05
257 Steve DeBerg UER .01 .05
(Yardage Total 45,046 should be 25,046)
258 Stephone Paige .01 .05
259 James Saxon RC .01 .05
260 Herman Heard .01 .05
261 Deron Cherry .01 .05
262 Dino Hackett .01 .05
263 Neil Smith .08 .25
264 Steve Pelluer .01 .05
265 Eric Thomas .01 .05
266 Eric Ball .01 .05
267 Leon White .01 .05
268 Tim Krumrie .01 .05
269 Jason Buck .01 .05
270 Boomer Esiason .02 .10
271 Carl Zander .01 .05
272 Eddie Brown .01 .05
273 David Fulcher .01 .05
274 Tim McGee .01 .05
275 James Brooks .02 .10
276 Rickey Dixon RC .01 .05
277 Ickey Woods .01 .05
278 Anthony Munoz .02 .10
279 Rodney Holman .01 .05
280 Mike Alexander .01 .05
281 Mervyn Fernandez .01 .05
282 Steve Wisniewski .02 .10
283 Steve Smith .01 .05
284 Howie Long .08 .25
285 Bo Jackson .10 .30
286 Mike Dyal RC .01 .05
287 Thomas Benson RC .01 .05
288 Willie Gault .02 .10
289 Marcus Allen .08 .25
290 Greg Townsend .01 .05
291 Steve Beuerlein .02 .10
292 Scott Davis .01 .05
293 Eddie Anderson RC .01 .05
294 Terry McDaniel .01 .05
295 Tim Brown .08 .25
296 Bob Golic .01 .05
297 Jeff Jaeger RC .01 .05
298 Jeff George RC .20 .50
299 Chip Banks .01 .05
300 Andre Rison UER .08 .25
(Photo actually Clarence Weathers)
301 Rohn Stark .01 .05
302 Keith Taylor .01 .05
303 Jack Trudeau .01 .05
304 Chris Hinton .01 .05
305 Ray Donaldson .01 .05
306 Jeff Herrod RC .01 .05
307 Clarence Verdin .01 .05
308 Jon Hand .01 .05
309 Bill Brooks .01 .05
310 Albert Bentley .01 .05
311 Mike Prior .01 .05
312 Pat Beach .01 .05
313 Eugene Daniel .01 .05
314 Duane Bickett .01 .05
315 Dean Biasucci .01 .05
316 Richmond Webb RC .01 .05
317 Jeff Cross .01 .05
318 Louis Oliver .01 .05
319 Sammie Smith .01 .05
320 Pete Stoyanovich .01 .05
321 John Offerdahl .01 .05
322 Ferrell Edmunds .01 .05
323 Dan Marino .50 1.25
324 Andre Brown .01 .05
325 Reggie Roby .01 .05
326 Jarvis Williams .01 .05
327 Roy Foster .01 .05
328 Mark Clayton .02 .10
329 Brian Sochia .01 .05
330 Mark Duper .02 .10
331 T.J. Turner .01 .05
332 Jeff Uhlenhake .01 .05
333 Jim C.Jensen .01 .05
334 Cortez Kennedy RC .08 .25
335 Andy Heck .01 .05
336 Rufus Porter .01 .05
337 Brian Blades .02 .10
338 Dave Krieg .02 .10
339 John L. Williams .01 .05
340 David Wyman .01 .05
341 Paul Skansi RC .01 .05
342 Eugene Robinson .01 .05
343 Joe Nash .01 .05
344 Jacob Green .01 .05
345 Jeff Bryant .01 .05
346 Ruben Rodriguez .01 .05
347 Norm Johnson .01 .05
348 Darren Comeaux .01 .05
349 Andre Ware RC .02 .10
350 Richard Johnson .01 .05
351 Rodney Peete .02 .10
352 Barry Sanders .50 1.25
353 Chris Spielman .08 .25
354 Eddie Murray .01 .05
355 Jerry Ball .01 .05
356 Mel Gray .02 .10
357 Eric Williams RC .01 .05
358 Robert Clark RC .01 .05
359 Jason Phillips .01 .05
360 Terry Taylor RC .01 .05
361 Bennie Blades .01 .05
362 Michael Cofer .01 .05
363 Jim Arnold .01 .05
364 Marc Spindler RC .01 .05
365 Jim Covert .01 .05
366 Jim Harbaugh .08 .25
367 Neal Anderson .02 .10
368 Mike Singletary .02 .10
369 John Roper .01 .05
370 Steve McMichael .02 .10
371 Dennis Gentry .01 .05
372 Brad Muster .01 .05
373 Ron Morris .01 .05
374 James Thornton .01 .05
375 Kevin Butler .01 .05
376 Richard Dent .02 .10
377 Dan Hampton .02 .10
378 Jay Hilgenberg .01 .05
379 Donnell Woolford .01 .05
380 Trace Armstrong .01 .05
381 Junior Seau RC .50 1.25
382 Rod Bernstine .01 .05
383 Marion Butts .02 .10
384 Burt Grossman .01 .05
385 Darrin Nelson .01 .05
386 Leslie O'Neal .02 .10
387 Billy Joe Tolliver .01 .05
388 Courtney Hall .01 .05
389 Lee Williams .01 .05
390 Anthony Miller .08 .25
391 Gill Byrd .01 .05
392 Wayne Walker .01 .05
393 Billy Ray Smith .01 .05
394 Vencie Glenn .01 .05
395 Tim Spencer .01 .05
396 Gary Plummer .01 .05
397 Arthur Cox .01 .05
398 Jamie Holland .01 .05
399 Keith McCants RC .01 .05
400 Kevin Murphy .01 .05
401 Danny Peebles .01 .05
402 Mark Robinson .01 .05
403 Broderick Thomas .01 .05
404 Ron Hall .01 .05
405 Mark Carrier WR .08 .25
406 Paul Gruber .01 .05
407 Vinny Testaverde .02 .10
408 Bruce Hill .01 .05
409 Lars Tate .01 .05
410 Harry Hamilton .01 .05
411 Ricky Reynolds .01 .05
412 Donald Igwebuike .01 .05
413 Reuben Davis .01 .05
414 William Howard .01 .05
415 Winston Moss RC .01 .05
416 Chris Singleton RC .01 .05
417 Hart Lee Dykes .01 .05
418 Steve Grogan .02 .10
419 Bruce Armstrong .01 .05
420 Robert Perryman .01 .05
421 Andre Tippett .01 .05
422 Sammy Martin .01 .05
423 Stanley Morgan .01 .05
424 Cedric Jones .01 .05
425 Sean Farrell .01 .05
426 Marc Wilson .01 .05
427 John Stephens .01 .05
428 Eric Sievers RC .01 .05
429 Maurice Hurst RC .01 .05
430 Johnny Rembert .01 .05
431A Receiving Leaders .10 .30
Jerry Rice
Andre Reed
431B Receiving Leaders .10 .30
Jerry Rice
Andre Reed
(missing hash marks on front)
432 Eric Hill .01 .05
433 Gary Hogeboom .01 .05
434 Timm Rosenbach UER .01 .05
(Born 1967 in Everett, Wa., should be 1966 in Missoula, Montana)
435 Tim McDonald .01 .05
436 Rich Camarillo .01 .05
437 Luis Sharpe .01 .05
438 J.T. Smith .01 .05
439 Roy Green .02 .10
440 Ernie Jones RC .01 .05
441 Robert Awalt .01 .05
442 Vai Sikahema .01 .05
443 Joe Wolf .01 .05
444 Stump Mitchell .01 .05
445 David Galloway .01 .05
446 Ron Wolfley .01 .05
447 Freddie Joe Nunn .01 .05
448 Blair Thomas RC .02 .10
449 Jeff Lageman .01 .05
450 Tony Eason .01 .05
451 Erik McMillan .01 .05
452 Jim Sweeney .01 .05
453 Ken O'Brien .01 .05
454 Johnny Hector .01 .05
455 Jo Jo Townsell .01 .05
456 Roger Vick .01 .05
457 James Hasty .01 .05
458 Dennis Byrd RC .02 .10
459 Ron Stallworth .01 .05
460 Mickey Shuler .01 .05
461 Bobby Humphery .01 .05
462 Kyle Clifton .01 .05
463 Al Toon .02 .10
464 Freeman McNeil .01 .05
465 Pat Leahy .01 .05
466 Scott Case .01 .05
467 Shawn Collins .01 .05
468 Floyd Dixon .01 .05
469 Deion Sanders .20 .50
470 Tony Casillas .01 .05
471 Michael Haynes RC .08 .25
472 Chris Miller .08 .25
473 John Settle .01 .05
474 Aundray Bruce .01 .05
475 Gene Lang .01 .05
476 Tim Gordon RC .01 .05
477 Scott Fulhage .01 .05
478 Bill Fralic .01 .05
479 Jessie Tuggle RC .01 .05
480 Marcus Cotton .01 .05
481 Steve Walsh .02 .10
482 Troy Aikman .30 .75
483 Ray Horton .01 .05
484 Tony Tolbert RC .02 .10
485 Steve Folsom .01 .05
486 Ken Norton RC .08 .25
487 Kelvin Martin RC .01 .05
488 Jack Del Rio .02 .10
489 Daryl Johnston RC .40 1.00
490 Bill Bates .02 .10
491 Jim Jeffcoat .01 .05
492 Vince Albritton .01 .05
493 Eugene Lockhart .01 .05
494 Mike Saxon .01 .05
495 James Dixon .01 .05
496 Willie Broughton .01 .05
497 Checklist 1-132 .01 .05
498 Checklist 133-264 .01 .05
499 Checklist 265-396 .01 .05
500 Checklist 397-528 .01 .05
501A Bears Team .02 .10
(Jim) Harbaugh
Eludes the Pursuit
501B Bears Team Leaders .02 .10
(Jim) Harbaugh
Eludes the Pursuit/(missing hash marks on front)
502A Bengals Team .01 .05
Boomer (Esiason)
Studies the Defense
502B Bengals Team Leaders .01 .05
Boomer (Esiason)
Studies the Defense
(missing hash marks on front)
503A Bills Team .01 .05
(Shane) Conlan Calls
Defensive Scheme
503B Bills Team Leaders .01 .05
(Shane) Conlan Calls
Defensive Scheme/(missing hash marks on front)
504A Broncos Team .01 .05
(Melvin) Bratton
Breaks Away
504B Broncos Team Leaders .01 .05
(Melvin) Bratton Breaks Away/(missing hash marks on front)
505A Browns Team .01 .05
(Bernie) Kosar
Calls the Play
505B Browns Team Leaders .01 .05
(Bernie) Kosar Calls the Play/(missing hash marks on front)
506A Buccaneers Team .01 .05
(Winston) Moss Assists
in Squeeze Play
506B Buccaneers Team Leaders .01 .05
(Winston) Moss Assists
in Squeeze Play/(missing hash marks on front)
507A Cardinals Team .01 .05
(Michael) Zordich
Saves the Day
507B Cardinals Team Leaders .01 .05
(Michael) Zordich Saves the Day/(missing hash marks on front)
508A Chargers Team .01 .05
(Lee) Williams
Plugs the Hole
508B Chargers Team Leaders .01 .05
(Lee) Williams Plugs the Hole/(missing hash marks on front)
509A Chiefs Team .01 .05
(Deron Cherry
Applies The "D")
509B Chiefs Team Leaders .01 .05
(Deron Cherry Applies The "D")/(missing hash marks on front)
510A Colts Team .01 .05
(Jack) Trudeau
Begins a Reverse
510B Colts Team Leaders .01 .05
(Jack) Trudeau Begins a Reverse/(missing hash marks on front)
511A Cowboys Team .10 .30
(Troy) Aikman Directs
Ground Attack
511B Cowboys Team Leaders .10 .30
(Troy) Aikman Directs
Ground Attack/(missing hash marks on front)
512A Dolphins Team .01 .05
Double-Decker By
(Louis) Oliver
and (Jarvis) Williams
512B Dolphins Team Leaders .01 .05
Double-Decker By
(Louis) Oliver/(Jarvis) Williams/(missing hash marks on front)
513A Eagles Team .01 .05
(Anthony) Toney
Bangs into the Line
513B Eagles Team Leaders .01 .05
(Anthony) Toney
Bangs into the Line/(missing hash marks on front)
514A Falcons Team .01 .05
(Jessie) Tuggle
Falls on Fumble
514B Falcons Team Leaders .01 .05
(Jessie) Tuggle Falls on Fumble/(missing hash marks on front)
515A 49ers Team .10 .30
(Joe) Montana To /(Roger) Craig,
A Winning Duo
515B 49ers Team Leaders .10 .30
(Joe) Montana To /(Roger) Craig,
A Winning Duo/(missing hash marks on front)
516A Giants Team .01 .05
(Phil) Simms Likes
His O.J. (Anderson)
516B Giants Team Leaders .01 .05
(Phil) Simms Likes
His O.J. (Anderson)/(missing hash marks on front)
517A Jets Team .01 .05
A (James) Hasty Return
517B Jets Team Leaders .01 .05
A (James) Hasty Return
(missing hash marks on front)
518A Lions Team .01 .05
(Bob) Gagliano Orchestrates
The Offense
518B Lions Team Leaders .01 .05
(Bob) Gagliano Orchestrates
The Offense/(missing hash marks on front)
519A Oilers Team .02 .10
(Warren) Moon
Scrambles to Daylight
519B Oilers Team Leaders .02 .10
(Warren) Moon
Scrambles to Daylight/(missing hash marks on front)
520A Packers Team .01 .05
A Bit Of Packer "Majik"
Don Majkowski
520B Packers Team Leaders .01 .05
A Bit Of Packer "Majik"
(Don Majkowski)/(missing hash marks on front)
521A Patriots Team .01 .05
(John) Stephens
Steams Ahead
521B Patriots Team Leaders .01 .05
(John) Stephens
STeam Leaderss Ahead/(missing hash marks on front)
522A Raiders Team .02 .10
Bo (Jackson)
Knows Yardage
522B Raiders Team Leaders .02 .10
Bo (Jackson) Knows Yardage
(missing hash marks on front)
523A Rams Team .01 .05
(Jim) Everett
Rolls Right
523B Rams Team Leaders .01 .05
(Jim) Everett Rolls Right/(missing hash marks on front)
524A Redskins Team .01 .05
(Gerald) Riggs
Rumbles Downfield
524B Redskins Team Leaders .01 .05
(Gerald) Riggs Rumbles Downfield/(missing hash marks on front)
525A Saints Team .01 .05
(Sam) Mills
Takes A Stand
525B Saints Team Leaders .01 .05
(Sam) Mills Takes A Stand/(missing hash marks on front)
526A Seahawks Team .01 .05
(Grant) Feasel
Sets To Snap
526B Seahawks Team Leaders .01 .05
(Grant) Feasel Sets To Snap/(missing hash marks on front)
527A Steelers Team .01 .05
(Bubby) Brister
Has a Clear Lane
527B Steelers Team Leaders .01 .05
(Bubby) Brister Has a Clear Lane/(missing hash marks on front)
528A Vikings Team .01 .05
(Rick) Fenney
Spots Opening
528B Vikings Team Leaders .01 .05
(Rick) Fenney Spots Opening/(missing hash marks on front)

1990 Topps Tiffany

COMP.FACT.SET (528) 50.00 100.00
*VETERANS: 6X TO 15X BASIC CARDS
*ROOKIES: 3X TO 8X BASIC CARDS

1990 Topps Box Bottoms

These cards were printed on the bottom of the 1990 Topps Wax Boxes. This 16-card standard-size set features the NFL's offensive and defensive player of the week for each week of the 1989 season. Each card features two players on the front and the back explains why they were the player of the week and what they did to earn the title. The cards are lettered rather than numbered. The set is checklisted in order of weeks of the season and is arranged alphabetically.The cards in this set were released in two distinct varieties; the NFL Properties disclaimer is either present or absent from the back of each card.

COMPLETE SET (16) 3.00 8.00
*DISCLAIMER BACK: .4X TO 1X
A Jim Kelly .30 .75
David Grayson
B Henry Ellard .25 .60
Derrick Thomas
C Joe Montana .75 2.00
Vince Newsome
D Bubby Brister .15 .40
Tim Harris
E Christian Okoye .15 .40
Keith Millard
F Warren Moon .25 .60
Jerome Brown
G John Elway .75 2.00
Mike Merriweather
H Webster Slaughter .15 .40
Pat Swilling
I Rich Karlis .25 .60
Lawrence Taylor
J Dan Marino .75 2.00
Greg Kragen
K Boomer Esiason .15 .40
Brent Williams
L Flipper Anderson .15 .40
Pierce Holt
M Richard Johnson .15 .40
David Fulcher
N John Taylor .15 .40
Mike Prior
O Mark Rypien .15 .40
Brett Faryniarz
P Greg Bell .15 .40
Chris Doleman

1990 Topps 1000 Yard Club

COMPLETE SET (30) 2.00 5.00
*DISCLAIMER BACK: .4X TO 1X
ONE PER PACK
1 Jerry Rice .30 .75
2 Christian Okoye .01 .05
3 Barry Sanders .50 1.25
4 Sterling Sharpe .08 .25
5 Mark Carrier WR .08 .25
6 Henry Ellard .02 .10
7 Andre Reed .08 .25
8 Neal Anderson .02 .10
9 Dalton Hilliard .01 .05
10 Anthony Miller .08 .25
11 Thurman Thomas .08 .25
12 James Brooks .02 .10
13 Webster Slaughter .02 .10
14 Gary Clark .08 .25
15 Tim McGee .01 .05
16 Art Monk .02 .10
17 Bobby Humphrey .01 .05
18 Flipper Anderson .01 .05
19 Ricky Sanders .01 .05
20 Greg Bell .01 .05
21 Vance Johnson .01 .05
22 Richard Johnson UER .01 .05
(Topps logo in upper right corner)
23 Eric Martin .01 .05
24 John Taylor .02 .10
25 Mervyn Fernandez .01 .05
26 Anthony Carter .02 .10
27 Brian Blades .02 .10
28 Roger Craig .02 .10
29 Ottis Anderson .02 .10
30 Mark Clayton .02 .10

1990 Topps Traded

This 132-card standard-size set was released by Topps as an update to their regular issue set. The set features players who were traded after Topps printed their regular set and rookies who were not in the 1990 Topps football set. The set was issued in its own custom box and was distributed through the Topps hobby distribution system. The cards were printed on white card stock and are numbered on the back with a "T" suffix. Rookie Cards in the set inlcude Fred Barnett, Reggie Cobb, Harold Green, Stan Humphries, Johnny Johnson, Tony Martin, Terance Mathis, Rob Moore, Emmitt Smith and Calvin Williams.

COMP.FACT.SET (132)	6.00	15.00
1T Gerald McNeil	.01	.05
2T Andre Rison	.08	.25
3T Steve Walsh	.08	.25
4T Lorenzo White	.02	.10
5T Max Montoya	.01	.05
6T William Roberts RC	.01	.05
7T Alonzo Highsmith	.01	.05
8T Chris Hinton	.02	.10
9T Stanley Morgan	.02	.10
10T Mickey Shuler	.01	.05
11T Bobby Humphery	.01	.05
12T Gary Anderson RB	.01	.05
13T Mike Tomczak	.02	.10
14T Anthony Pleasant RC	.02	.10
15T Walter Stanley	.01	.05
16T Greg Bell	.01	.05
17T Tony Martin RC	.30	.75
18T Terry Kinard	.01	.05
19T Cris Carter	.20	.50
20T James Wilder	.01	.05
21T Jerry Kauric	.01	.05
22T Irving Fryar	.08	.25
23T Ken Harvey RC	.08	.25
24T James Williams DB RC	.01	.05
25T Ron Cox RC	.01	.05
26T Andre Ware	.08	.25
27T Emmitt Smith RC	4.00	10.00
28T Junior Seau	.30	.75
29T Mark Carrier RC	.08	.25
30T Rodney Hampton	.08	.25
31T Rob Moore RC	.20	.50
32T Bern Brostek RC	.01	.05
33T Dexter Carter	.02	.10
34T Blair Thomas	.02	.10
35T Harold Green RC	.08	.25
36T Darrell Thompson	.01	.05
37T Eric Green RC	.08	.25
38T Renaldo Turnbull RC	.08	.25
39T Leroy Hoard RC	.08	.25
40T Anthony Thompson RC	.02	.10
41T Jeff George	.08	.25
42T Alexander Wright RC	.01	.05
43T Richmond Webb	.01	.05
44T Cortez Kennedy	.08	.25
45T Ray Agnew RC	.01	.05
46T Percy Snow	.01	.05
47T Chris Singleton	.01	.05
48T James Francis RC	.02	.10
49T Tony Bennett	.02	.10
50T Reggie Cobb RC	.02	.10
51T Barry Foster	.08	.25
52T Ben Smith	.01	.05
53T Anthony Smith RC	.08	.25
54T Steve Christie RC	.01	.05
55T Johnny Bailey RC	.02	.10
56T Alan Grant RC	.01	.05
57T Eric Floyd RC	.01	.05
58T Robert Blackmon RC	.01	.05
59T Brent Williams	.01	.05
60T Raymond Clayborn	.01	.05
61T Dave Duerson	.01	.05
62T Derrick Fenner RC	.02	.10
63T Ken Willis	.01	.05
64T Brad Baxter RC	.02	.10
65T Tony Paige	.01	.05
66T Jay Schroeder	.01	.05
67T Jim Breech	.01	.05
68T Barry Word RC	.02	.10
69T Anthony Dilweg	.01	.05
70T Rich Gannon RC	.75	2.00
71T Stan Humphries RC	.08	.25
72T Jay Novacek	.08	.25
73T Tommy Kane RC	.01	.05
74T Everson Walls	.01	.05
75T Mike Rozier	.02	.10
76T Robb Thomas RC	.01	.05
77T Terance Mathis RC	.30	.75
78T LeRoy Irvin	.01	.05
79T Jeff Donaldson	.01	.05
80T Ethan Horton RC	.02	.10
81T J.B. Brown RC	.01	.05
82T Joe Kelly	.01	.05
83T John Carney RC	.01	.05
84T Dan Stryzinski RC	.01	.05
85T John Kidd	.01	.05
86T Al Smith	.02	.10
87T Travis McNeal	.01	.05
88T Reyna Thompson RC	.01	.05
89T Rick Donnelly	.01	.05
90T Marv Cook RC	.02	.10
91T Mike Farr RC	.01	.05
92T Daniel Stubbs	.01	.05
93T Jeff Campbell RC	.01	.05
94T Tim McKyer	.01	.05
95T Ian Beckles RC	.01	.05
96T Lemuel Stinson	.01	.05
97T Frank Cornish	.01	.05
98T Riki Ellison	.01	.05
99T Jamie Mueller RC	.01	.05
100T Brian Hansen	.01	.05
101T Warren Powers RC	.01	.05
102T Howard Cross RC	.01	.05
103T Tim Grunhard RC	.01	.05
104T Johnny Johnson RC	.08	.25
105T Calvin Williams RC	.08	.25
106T Keith McCants	.01	.05
107T Lamar Lathon RC	.02	.10
108T Steve Broussard RC	.02	.10
109T Glenn Parker RC	.01	.05
110T Alton Montgomery RC	.01	.05
111T Jim McMahon	.02	.10
112T Aaron Wallace RC	.01	.05
113T Keith Sims RC	.01	.05
114T Ervin Randle	.01	.05
115T Walter Wilson	.01	.05
116T Terry Wooden RC	.01	.05
117T Bernard Clark	.01	.05
118T Tony Stargell RC	.01	.05
119T Jimmie Jones RC	.01	.05
120T Andre Collins RC	.02	.10
121T Ricky Proehl RC	.08	.25
122T Darion Conner RC	.02	.10
123T Jeff Rutledge	.01	.05
124T Heath Sherman RC	.02	.10
125T Tommie Agee RC	.01	.05
126T Tory Epps RC	.01	.05
127T Tommy Hodson RC	.01	.05
128T Jessie Hester RC	.01	.05
129T Alfred Oglesby RC	.01	.05
130T Chris Chandler	.08	.25
131T Fred Barnett RC	.08	.25
132T Checklist 1-132	.01	.05

1991 Topps

This 660-card standard size set marked Topps' largest football card set to date. Factory sets were issued once again. The design of the card front was the same as the football and hockey sets of that year. A team-colored border outlines the photo with the player's name and position appearing in the bottom border. The team name is at the bottom right of the photo. The backs contain highlights and statistics. Subsets include Highlights (2-7), league leaders (8-12) and team cards (628-655). The cards are arranged by team in order of 1991 finish. Rookie Cards include Ricky Ervins, Alvin Harper, Russell Maryland, Herman Moore, Eric Turner and Harvey Williams.

COMPLETE SET (660)	10.00	20.00
COMP.FACT.SET (660)	15.00	30.00
1 Super Bowl XXV	.01	.05
2 Roger Craig HL	.02	.10
3 Derrick Thomas HL	.02	.10
4 Pete Stoyanovich HL	.01	.05
5 Ottis Anderson HL	.02	.10
6 Jerry Rice HL	.20	.50
7 Warren Moon HL	.02	.10
8 Leaders Passing Yards	.02	.10
Warren Moon		
Jim Everett		
9 B.Sanders	.15	.40
T.Thomas LL		
10 Leaders Receiving	.10	.30
Jerry Rice		
Haywood Jeffires		
11 Leaders Interceptions	.01	.05
Mark Carrier DB		
Richard Johnson		
12 Leaders Sacks	.02	.10
Derrick Thomas		
Charles Haley		
13 Jumbo Elliott	.01	.05
14 Leonard Marshall	.01	.05
15 William Roberts	.01	.05
16 Lawrence Taylor	.08	.25
17 Mark Ingram	.02	.10
18 Rodney Hampton	.08	.25
19 Carl Banks	.01	.05
20 Ottis Anderson	.02	.10
21 Mark Collins	.01	.05
22 Pepper Johnson	.01	.05
23 Dave Meggett	.02	.10
24 Reyna Thompson	.01	.05
25 Stephen Baker	.01	.05
26 Mike Fox	.01	.05
27 Maurice Carthon UER	.01	.05
(Herschel Walker mis-spelled as Herschell)		
28 Jeff Hostetler	.08	.25
29 Greg Jackson RC	.01	.05
30 Sean Landeta	.01	.05
31 Bart Oates	.01	.05
32 Phil Simms	.02	.10
33 Erik Howard	.01	.05
34 Myron Guyton	.01	.05
35 Mark Bavaro	.01	.05
36 Jarrod Bunch RC	.01	.05
37 Will Wolford	.01	.05
38 Ray Bentley	.01	.05
39 Nate Odomes	.01	.05
40 Scott Norwood	.01	.05
41 Darryl Talley	.01	.05
42 Carwell Gardner	.01	.05
43 James Lofton	.02	.10
44 Shane Conlan	.01	.05
45 Steve Tasker	.02	.10
46 James Williams	.01	.05
47 Kent Hull	.01	.05
48 Al Edwards	.01	.05
49 Frank Reich	.02	.10
50 Leon Seals	.01	.05
51 Keith McKeller	.01	.05
52 Thurman Thomas	.08	.25
53 Leonard Smith	.01	.05
54 Andre Reed	.02	.10
55 Kenneth Davis	.01	.05
56 Jeff Wright RC	.01	.05
57 Jamie Mueller	.01	.05
58 Jim Ritcher	.01	.05
59 Bruce Smith	.08	.25
60 Ted Washington RC	.01	.05
61 Guy McIntyre	.01	.05
62 Michael Carter	.01	.05
63 Pierce Holt	.01	.05
64 Darryl Pollard	.01	.05
65 Mike Sherrard	.01	.05
66 Dexter Carter	.01	.05
67 Bubba Paris	.01	.05
68 Harry Sydney	.01	.05
69 Tom Rathman	.01	.05
70 Jesse Sapolu	.01	.05
71 Mike Cofer	.01	.05
72 Keith DeLong	.01	.05
73 Joe Montana	.50	1.25
74 Bill Romanowski	.01	.05
75 John Taylor	.02	.10
76 Brent Jones	.08	.25
77 Harris Barton	.01	.05
78 Charles Haley	.02	.10
79 Eric Davis	.01	.05
80 Kevin Fagan	.01	.05
81 Jerry Rice	.30	.75
82 Dave Waymer	.01	.05
83 Todd Marinovich RC	.01	.05
84 Steve Smith	.01	.05
85 Tim Brown	.08	.25
86 Ethan Horton	.01	.05
87 Marcus Allen	.08	.25
88 Terry McDaniel	.01	.05
89 Thomas Benson	.01	.05
90 Roger Craig	.02	.10
91 Don Mosebar	.01	.05
92 Aaron Wallace	.01	.05
93 Eddie Anderson	.01	.05
94 Willie Gault	.02	.10
95 Howie Long	.08	.25
96 Jay Schroeder	.01	.05
97 Ronnie Lott	.02	.10
98 Bob Golic	.01	.05
99 Bo Jackson	.10	.30
100 Max Montoya	.01	.05
101 Scott Davis	.01	.05
102 Greg Townsend	.01	.05
103 Garry Lewis	.01	.05
104 Mervyn Fernandez	.01	.05
105 Steve Wisniewski UER	.01	.05
(Back has drafted, should be traded to)		
106 Jeff Jaeger	.01	.05
107 Nick Bell RC	.01	.05
108 Mark Dennis RC	.01	.05
109 Jarvis Williams	.01	.05
110 Mark Clayton	.02	.10
111 Harry Galbreath	.01	.05
112 Dan Marino	.50	1.25
113 Louis Oliver	.01	.05
114 Pete Stoyanovich	.01	.05
115 Ferrell Edmunds	.01	.05
116 Jeff Cross	.01	.05
117 Richmond Webb	.01	.05
118 Jim C. Jensen	.01	.05
119 Keith Sims	.01	.05
120 Mark Duper	.02	.10
121 Shawn Lee RC	.01	.05
122 Reggie Roby	.01	.05
123 Jeff Uhlenhake	.01	.05
124 Sammie Smith	.01	.05
125 John Offerdahl	.01	.05
126 Hugh Green	.01	.05
127 Tony Paige	.01	.05
128 David Griggs	.01	.05
129 J.B. Brown	.01	.05
130 Harvey Williams RC	.08	.25
131 John Alt	.01	.05
132 Albert Lewis	.01	.05
133 Robb Thomas	.01	.05
134 Neil Smith	.08	.25
135 Stephone Paige	.01	.05
136 Nick Lowery	.01	.05
137 Steve DeBerg	.01	.05
138 Rich Baldinger RC	.01	.05
139 Percy Snow	.01	.05
140 Kevin Porter	.01	.05
141 Chris Martin	.01	.05
142 Deron Cherry	.01	.05
143 Derrick Thomas	.08	.25
144 Tim Grunhard	.01	.05
145 Todd McNair	.01	.05
146 David Szott RC	.01	.05
147 Dan Saleaumua	.01	.05
148 Jonathan Hayes	.01	.05
149 Christian Okoye	.01	.05
150 Dino Hackett	.01	.05
151 Bryan Barker RC	.01	.05
152 Kevin Ross	.01	.05
153 Barry Word	.01	.05
154 Stan Thomas	.01	.05
155 Brad Muster	.01	.05
156 Donnell Woolford	.01	.05
157 Neal Anderson	.02	.10
158 Jim Covert	.01	.05
159 Jim Harbaugh	.08	.25
160 Shaun Gayle	.01	.05
161 William Perry	.02	.10
162 Ron Morris	.01	.05
163 Mark Bortz	.01	.05
164 James Thornton	.01	.05
165 Ron Rivera	.01	.05
166 Kevin Butler	.01	.05
167 Jay Hilgenberg	.01	.05
168 Peter Tom Willis	.01	.05
169 Johnny Bailey	.01	.05
170 Ron Cox	.01	.05
171 Keith Van Horne	.01	.05
172 Mark Carrier DB	.02	.10
173 Richard Dent	.02	.10
174 Wendell Davis	.01	.05
175 Trace Armstrong	.01	.05
176 Mike Singletary	.02	.10
177 Chris Zorich RC	.08	.25
178 Gerald Riggs	.01	.05
179 Jeff Bostic	.01	.05
180 Kurt Gouveia RC	.01	.05
181 Stan Humphries	.08	.25
182 Chip Lohmiller	.01	.05
183 Raleigh McKenzie RC	.01	.05
184 Alvin Walton	.01	.05
185 Earnest Byner	.01	.05
186 Markus Koch	.01	.05
187 Art Monk	.02	.10
188 Ed Simmons	.01	.05
189 Bobby Wilson RC	.01	.05
190 Charles Mann	.01	.05
191 Darrell Green	.01	.05
192 Mark Rypien	.02	.10
193 Ricky Sanders	.01	.05
194 Jim Lachey	.01	.05
195 Martin Mayhew	.01	.05
196 Gary Clark	.08	.25
197 Wilber Marshall	.01	.05
198 Darryl Grant	.01	.05
199 Don Warren	.01	.05
200 Ricky Ervins RC UER	.02	.10
(Front has Chiefs, back has Redskins)		
201 Eric Allen	.01	.05
202 Anthony Toney	.01	.05
203 Ben Smith UER	.01	.05
(Front CB; back S)		
204 David Alexander	.01	.05
205 Jerome Brown	.01	.05
206 Mike Golic	.01	.05
207 Roger Ruzek	.01	.05
208 Andre Waters	.01	.05
209 Fred Barnett	.08	.25
210 Randall Cunningham	.08	.25
211 Mike Schad	.01	.05
212 Reggie White	.08	.25
213 Mike Bellamy	.01	.05
214 Jeff Feagles RC	.01	.05
215 Wes Hopkins	.01	.05
216 Clyde Simmons	.01	.05
217 Keith Byars	.01	.05
218 Seth Joyner	.02	.10
219 Byron Evans	.01	.05
220 Keith Jackson	.02	.10
221 Calvin Williams	.02	.10
222 Mike Dumas RC	.01	.05
223 Ray Childress	.01	.05
224 Ernest Givins	.02	.10
225 Lamar Lathon	.01	.05
226 Greg Montgomery	.01	.05
227 Mike Munchak	.02	.10
228 Al Smith	.01	.05
229 Bubba McDowell	.01	.05
230 Haywood Jeffires	.02	.10
231 Drew Hill	.01	.05
232 William Fuller	.02	.10
233 Warren Moon	.08	.25
234 Doug Smith DT RC	.02	.10
235 Cris Dishman RC	.01	.05
236 Teddy Garcia RC	.01	.05
237 Richard Johnson RC	.01	.05
238 Bruce Matthews	.02	.10
239 Gerald McNeil	.01	.05
240 Johnny Meads	.01	.05
241 Curtis Duncan	.01	.05
242 Sean Jones	.02	.10
243 Lorenzo White	.01	.05
244 Rob Carpenter RC	.01	.05
245 Bruce Reimers	.01	.05
246 Ickey Woods	.01	.05
247 Lewis Billups	.01	.05
248 Boomer Esiason	.02	.10
249 Tim Krumrie	.01	.05
250 David Fulcher	.01	.05
251 Jim Breech	.01	.05
252 Mitchell Price RC	.01	.05
253 Carl Zander	.01	.05
254 Barney Bussey RC	.01	.05
255 Leon White	.01	.05
256 Eddie Brown	.01	.05
257 James Francis	.01	.05
258 Harold Green	.02	.10
259 Anthony Munoz	.02	.10
260 James Brooks	.02	.10
261 Kevin Walker RC UER	.01	.05
(Hometown should be West Milford Township)		
262 Bruce Kozerski	.01	.05
263 David Grant	.01	.05
264 Tim McGee	.01	.05
265 Rodney Holman	.01	.05
266 Dan McGwire RC	.01	.05
267 Andy Heck	.01	.05
268 Dave Krieg	.02	.10
269 David Wyman	.01	.05
270 Robert Blackmon	.01	.05
271 Grant Feasel	.01	.05
272 Patrick Hunter RC	.01	.05
273 Travis McNeal	.01	.05
274 John L. Williams	.01	.05
275 Tony Woods	.01	.05
276 Derrick Fenner	.01	.05
277 Jacob Green	.01	.05
278 Brian Blades	.02	.10
279 Eugene Robinson	.01	.05
280 Terry Wooden	.01	.05
281 Jeff Bryant	.01	.05
282 Norm Johnson	.01	.05
283 Joe Nash UER	.01	.05
Front DT; Back NT)		
284 Rick Donnelly	.01	.05
285 Chris Warren	.08	.25
286 Tommy Kane	.01	.05
287 Cortez Kennedy	.08	.25
288 Ernie Mills RC	.02	.10
289 Dermontti Dawson	.01	.05
290 Tunch Ilkin	.01	.05
291 Tim Worley	.01	.05
292 David Little	.01	.05
293 Gary Anderson K	.01	.05
294 Chris Calloway	.01	.05
295 Carnell Lake	.01	.05
296 Dan Stryzinski	.01	.05
297 Rod Woodson	.08	.25
298 John Jackson RC	.01	.05
299 Bubby Brister	.01	.05
300 Thomas Everett	.01	.05
301 Merril Hoge	.01	.05
302 Eric Green	.01	.05
303 Greg Lloyd	.08	.25
304 Gerald Williams	.01	.05
305 Bryan Hinkle	.01	.05
306 Keith Willis	.01	.05
307 Louis Lipps	.01	.05
308 Donald Evans	.01	.05
309 D.J. Johnson	.01	.05
310 Wesley Carroll RC	.01	.05
311 Eric Martin	.01	.05
312 Brett Maxie	.01	.05
313 Rickey Jackson	.01	.05
314 Robert Massey	.01	.05
315 Pat Swilling	.02	.10
316 Morten Andersen	.01	.05
317 Toi Cook RC	.01	.05
318 Sam Mills	.01	.05
319 Steve Walsh	.01	.05
320 Tommy Barnhardt RC	.01	.05
321 Vince Buck	.01	.05
322 Joel Hilgenberg	.01	.05
323 Rueben Mayes	.01	.05
324 Renaldo Turnbull	.01	.05
325 Brett Perriman	.08	.25
326 Vaughan Johnson	.01	.05
327 Gill Fenerty	.01	.05
328 Stan Brock	.01	.05
329 Dalton Hilliard	.01	.05
330 Hoby Brenner	.01	.05
331 Craig Heyward	.02	.10
332 Jon Hand	.01	.05
333 Duane Bickett	.01	.05
334 Jessie Hester	.01	.05
335 Rohn Stark	.01	.05
336 Zefross Moss	.01	.05
337 Bill Brooks	.01	.05
338 Clarence Verdin	.01	.05
339 Mike Prior	.01	.05
340 Chip Banks	.01	.05
341 Dean Biasucci	.01	.05
342 Ray Donaldson	.01	.05
343 Jeff Herrod	.01	.05
344 Donnell Thompson	.01	.05
345 Chris Goode	.01	.05
346 Eugene Daniel	.01	.05
347 Pat Beach	.01	.05
348 Keith Taylor	.01	.05
349 Jeff George	.08	.25
350 Tony Siragusa RC	.20	.50
351 Randy Dixon	.01	.05
352 Albert Bentley	.01	.05
353 Russell Maryland RC	.08	.25
354 Mike Saxon	.01	.05
355 Godfrey Myles RC UER	.01	.05
(Misspelled Miles on card front)		
356 Mark Stepnoski RC	.02	.10
357 James Washington RC	.01	.05
358 Jay Novacek	.08	.25
359 Kelvin Martin	.01	.05
360 Emmitt Smith UER	1.00	2.50
361 Jim Jeffcoat	.01	.05
362 Alexander Wright	.01	.05
363 James Dixon UER	.01	.05
(Photo is not Dixon on card front)		
364 Alonzo Highsmith	.01	.05
365 Daniel Stubbs	.01	.05
366 Jack Del Rio	.02	.10
367 Mark Tuinei RC	.01	.05
368 Michael Irvin	.08	.25
369 John Gesek RC	.01	.05
370 Ken Willis	.01	.05
371 Troy Aikman	.30	.75
372 Jimmie Jones	.01	.05
373 Nate Newton	.02	.10
374 Issiac Holt	.01	.05
375 Alvin Harper RC	.08	.25
376 Todd Kalis	.01	.05
377 Wade Wilson	.02	.10
378 Joey Browner	.01	.05
379 Chris Doleman	.01	.05
380 Hassan Jones	.01	.05
381 Henry Thomas	.01	.05
382 Darrell Fullington	.01	.05
383 Steve Jordan	.01	.05
384 Gary Zimmerman	.02	.10
385 Ray Berry	.01	.05
386 Cris Carter	.20	.50
387 Mike Merriweather	.01	.05
388 Carl Lee	.01	.05
389 Keith Millard	.01	.05
390 Reggie Rutland	.01	.05
391 Anthony Carter	.02	.10
392 Mark Dusbabek	.01	.05
393 Kirk Lowdermilk	.01	.05
394 Al Noga UER	.01	.05
(Card says DT should be DE)		
395 Herschel Walker	.02	.10
396 Randall McDaniel	.02	.10
397 Herman Moore RC	.08	.25
398 Eddie Murray	.01	.05
399 Lomas Brown	.01	.05
400 Marc Spindler	.01	.05
401 Bennie Blades	.01	.05
402 Kevin Glover	.01	.05
403 Aubrey Matthews RC	.01	.05
404 Michael Cofer	.01	.05
405 Robert Clark	.01	.05
406 Eric Andolsek	.01	.05
407 William White	.01	.05
408 Rodney Peete	.02	.10
409 Mel Gray	.02	.10
410 Jim Arnold	.01	.05
411 Jeff Campbell	.01	.05
412 Chris Spielman	.02	.10
413 Jerry Ball	.01	.05
414 Dan Owens	.01	.05
415 Barry Sanders	.50	1.25
416 Andre Ware	.02	.10
417 Stanley Richard RC	.01	.05
418 Gill Byrd	.01	.05
419 John Kidd	.01	.05
420 Sam Seale	.01	.05
421 Gary Plummer	.01	.05
422 Anthony Miller	.02	.10
423 Ronnie Harmon	.01	.05
424 Frank Cornish	.01	.05
425 Marion Butts	.02	.10
426 Leo Goeas	.01	.05
427 Junior Seau	.08	.25
428 Courtney Hall	.01	.05
429 Leslie O'Neal	.02	.10
430 Martin Bayless	.01	.05
431 John Carney	.01	.05
432 Lee Williams	.01	.05
433 Arthur Cox	.01	.05
434 Burt Grossman	.01	.05
435 Nate Lewis RC	.01	.05
436 Rod Bernstine	.01	.05
437 Henry Rolling RC	.01	.05
438 Billy Joe Tolliver	.01	.05
439 Vinnie Clark RC	.01	.05
440 Brian Noble	.01	.05
441 Charles Wilson	.01	.05
442 Don Majkowski	.01	.05
443 Tim Harris	.01	.05
444 Scott Stephen RC	.01	.05
445 Perry Kemp	.01	.05
446 Darrell Thompson	.01	.05
447 Chris Jacke	.01	.05
448 Mark Murphy	.01	.05
449 Ed West	.01	.05
450 LeRoy Butler	.02	.10
451 Keith Woodside	.01	.05
452 Tony Bennett	.02	.10
453 Mark Lee	.01	.05
454 James Campen RC	.01	.05
455 Robert Brown	.01	.05
456 Sterling Sharpe	.08	.25
457A Tony Mandarich ERR	1.25	2.50
Broncos listed as team		
457B Tony Mandarich COR	.01	.05
Packers listed as team		
458 Johnny Holland	.01	.05
459 Matt Brock RC	.01	.05
460A Esera Tuaolo RC ERR	.01	.05
(See also 462; no 1991 NFL Draft Pick logo)		
460B Esera Tuaolo RC COR	.01	.05
(See also 462; 1991 NFL Draft Pick logo on front)		
461 Freeman McNeil	.01	.05
462 Terance Mathis UER	.08	.25
(Card numbered in-correctly as 460)		
463 Rob Moore	.08	.25
464 Darrell Davis RC	.01	.05
465 Chris Burkett	.01	.05
466 Jeff Criswell	.01	.05
467 Tony Stargell	.01	.05
468 Ken O'Brien	.01	.05
469 Erik McMillan	.01	.05
470 Jeff Lageman UER	.01	.05
(Front DE; back LB)		
471 Pat Leahy	.01	.05
472 Dennis Byrd	.01	.05
473 Jim Sweeney	.01	.05
474 Brad Baxter	.01	.05
475 Joe Kelly	.01	.05
476 Al Toon	.02	.10
477 Joe Prokop	.01	.05
478 Mark Boyer	.01	.05
479 Kyle Clifton	.01	.05
480 James Hasty	.01	.05
481 Browning Nagle RC	.01	.05
482 Gary Anderson RB	.01	.05
483 Mark Carrier WR	.08	.25
484 Ricky Reynolds	.01	.05
485 Bruce Hill	.01	.05
486 Steve Christie	.01	.05
487 Paul Gruber	.01	.05
488 Jesse Anderson	.01	.05
489 Reggie Cobb	.01	.05
490 Harry Hamilton	.01	.05
491 Vinny Testaverde	.02	.10
492 Mark Royals RC	.01	.05
493 Keith McCants	.01	.05
494 Ron Hall	.01	.05
495 Ian Beckles	.01	.05
496 Mark Robinson	.01	.05
497 Reuben Davis	.01	.05
498 Wayne Haddix	.01	.05
499 Kevin Murphy	.01	.05
500 Eugene Marve	.01	.05
501 Broderick Thomas	.01	.05
502 Eric Swann RC UER	.08	.25
(Draft pick logo miss-ing from card front)		
503 Ernie Jones	.01	.05
504 Rich Camarillo	.01	.05
505 Tim McDonald	.01	.05
506 Freddie Joe Nunn	.01	.05
507 Tim Jorden RC	.01	.05
508 Johnny Johnson	.01	.05
509 Eric Hill	.01	.05
510 Derek Kennard	.01	.05
511 Ricky Proehl	.01	.05
512 Bill Lewis	.01	.05
513 Roy Green	.01	.05
514 Anthony Bell	.01	.05
515 Timm Rosenbach	.01	.05
516 Jim Wahler RC	.01	.05
517 Anthony Thompson	.01	.05
518 Ken Harvey	.02	.10
519 Luis Sharpe	.01	.05
520 Walter Reeves	.01	.05
521 Lonnie Young	.01	.05
522 Rod Saddler	.01	.05
523 Todd Lyght RC	.01	.05
524 Alvin Wright	.01	.05
525 Flipper Anderson	.01	.05
526 Jackie Slater	.01	.05
527 Damone Johnson RC	.01	.05
528 Cleveland Gary	.01	.05
529 Mike Piel	.01	.05
530 Buford McGee	.01	.05
531 Michael Stewart	.01	.05
532 Jim Everett	.02	.10
533 Mike Wilcher	.01	.05
534 Irv Pankey	.01	.05
535 Bern Brostek	.01	.05
536 Henry Ellard	.02	.10
537 Doug Smith	.01	.05
538 Larry Kelm	.01	.05
539 Pat Terrell	.01	.05
540 Tom Newberry	.01	.05
541 Jerry Gray	.01	.05
542 Kevin Greene	.02	.10
543 Duval Love RC	.01	.05
544 Frank Stams	.01	.05
545 Mike Croel RC	.01	.05
546 Mark Jackson	.01	.05
547 Greg Kragen	.01	.05
548 Karl Mecklenburg	.01	.05
549 Simon Fletcher	.01	.05
550 Bobby Humphrey	.01	.05
551 Ken Lanier	.01	.05
552 Vance Johnson	.01	.05
553 Ron Holmes	.01	.05
554 John Elway	.50	1.25
555 Melvin Bratton	.01	.05
556 Dennis Smith	.01	.05
557 Ricky Nattiel	.01	.05
558 Clarence Kay	.01	.05
559 Michael Brooks	.01	.05
560 Mike Horan	.01	.05
561 Warren Powers	.01	.05
562 Keith Kartz	.01	.05
563 Shannon Sharpe	.20	.50
564 Wymon Henderson	.01	.05
565 Steve Atwater	.01	.05
566 David Treadwell	.01	.05
567 Bruce Pickens RC	.01	.05
568 Jessie Tuggle	.01	.05
569 Chris Hinton	.01	.05
570 Keith Jones	.01	.05
571 Bill Fralic	.01	.05
572 Mike Rozier	.01	.05
573 Scott Fulhage	.01	.05
574 Floyd Dixon	.01	.05
575 Andre Rison	.02	.10
576 Darion Conner	.01	.05
577 Brian Jordan	.02	.10
578 Michael Haynes	.08	.25
579 Oliver Barnett	.01	.05
580 Shawn Collins	.01	.05
581 Tim Green	.01	.05
582 Deion Sanders	.15	.40
583 Mike Kenn	.01	.05
584 Mike Gann	.01	.05
585 Chris Miller	.02	.10
586 Tory Epps	.01	.05
587 Steve Broussard	.01	.05
588 Gary Wilkins	.01	.05
589 Eric Turner RC	.02	.10
590 Thane Gash	.01	.05
591 Clay Matthews	.02	.10
592 Mike Johnson	.01	.05
593 Raymond Clayborn	.01	.05
594 Leroy Hoard	.02	.10
595 Reggie Langhorne	.01	.05
596 Mike Baab	.01	.05
597 Anthony Pleasant	.01	.05
598 David Grayson	.01	.05
599 Rob Burnett RC	.02	.10
600 Frank Minnifield	.01	.05
601 Gregg Rakoczy	.01	.05
602 Eric Metcalf UER	.08	.25
(1989 stats given twice)		
603 Paul Farren	.01	.05
604 Brian Brennan	.01	.05
605 Tony Jones T RC	.01	.05
606 Stephen Braggs	.01	.05
607 Kevin Mack	.01	.05
608 Pat Harlow RC	.01	.05
609 Marv Cook	.01	.05
610 John Stephens	.01	.05
611 Ed Reynolds	.01	.05
612 Tim Goad	.01	.05
613 Chris Singleton	.01	.05
614 Bruce Armstrong	.01	.05
615 Tommy Hodson	.01	.05
616 Sammy Martin	.01	.05
617 Andre Tippett	.01	.05
618 Johnny Rembert	.01	.05
619 Maurice Hurst	.01	.05
620 Vincent Brown	.01	.05
621 Ray Agnew	.01	.05
622 Ronnie Lippett	.01	.05
623 Greg McMurtry	.01	.05
624 Brent Williams	.01	.05
625 Jason Staurovsky	.01	.05
626 Marvin Allen	.01	.05
627 Hart Lee Dykes	.01	.05
628 Atlanta Falcons	.01	.05
Team: (Keith) Jones		
Jumps for Yardage		
629 Buffalo Bills	.01	.05
Team: (Jeff) Wright		
Goes for a Block		
630 Chicago Bears	.02	.10
Team: (Jim) Harbaugh		
Makes Like a Halfback		
631 Cincinnati Bengals	.01	.05
Team: (Stanford) Jennings		
Cuts Through Hole		
632 Cleveland Browns	.01	.05
Team: (Eric) Metcalf		
Makes a Return		
633 Dallas Cowboys	.01	.05
Team: (Kelvin) Martin		
Makes a Move		
634 Denver Broncos	.01	.05
Team: (Shannon) Sharpe		
Into the Wedge		
635 Detroit Lions	.01	.05
Team: (Rodney) Peete		
Hunted by a Bear		
(Mike Singletary)		
636 Green Bay Packers	.01	.05
Team: (Don) Majkowski		
Orchestrates Some Magic		
637 Houston Oilers	.02	.10
Team: (Warren) Moon		
Monitors the Action		
638 Indianapolis Colts	.01	.05
Team: (Jeff) George		
Releases Just in Time		
639 Kansas City Chiefs	.01	.05
Team: (Christian) Okoye		
Powers Ahead		
640 Los Angeles Raiders	.02	.10
Team: (Marcus) Allen		
Crosses the Plane		
641 Los Angeles Rams	.01	.05
Team: (Jim) Everett		
Connects With Soft Touch		
642 Miami Dolphins	.01	.05
Team: (Pete) Stoyanovich		
Kicks It Through		
643 Minnesota Vikings	.02	.10
Team: (Rich) Gannon		
Loads Cannon		
644 New Eng. Patriots	.01	.05
Team: (John) Stephens		
Gets Stood Up		
645 New Orleans Saints	.01	.05
Team: (Gill) Fenerty		
Finds Opening		
646 New York Giants	.01	.05
Team: (Maurice) Carthon		
Inches Ahead		
647 New York Jets	.01	.05
Team: (Pat) Leahy		
Perfect on Extra Point		
648 Philadelphia Eagles	.01	.05
Team: (Randall) Cunningham		
Calls Own Play for TD		
649 Phoenix Cardinals	.01	.05
Team: (Bill) Lewis		
Provides the Protection		
650 Pittsburgh Steelers	.01	.05
Team: (Bubby) Brister		
Eyes Downfield Attack		
651 San Diego Chargers	.01	.05
Team: (John) Friesz		
Finds the Passing Lane		
652 San Francisco 49ers	.01	.05
Team: (Dexter) Carter		
Follows Rathman's Block		
653 Seattle Seahawks	.01	.05
Team: (Derrick) Fenner		
With Fancy Footwork		
654 Tampa Bay Buccaneers	.01	.05
Team: (Reggie) Cobb		
Hurdles His Way		
to First Down		
655 Washington Redskins	.01	.05
Team: (Earnest) Byner		
Cuts Back to		
Follow Block		
656 Checklist 1-132	.01	.05
657 Checklist 132-264	.01	.05
658 Checklist 265-396	.01	.05
659 Checklist 397-528	.01	.05
660 Checklist 529-660	.01	.05

1991 Topps 1000 Yard Club

COMPLETE SET (18)	2.00	5.00
ONE PER PACK		
1 Jerry Rice	.50	1.25
2 Barry Sanders	.75	2.00
3 Thurman Thomas	.15	.40
4 Henry Ellard	.05	.15
5 Marion Butts	.05	.15
6 Earnest Byner	.02	.10
7 Andre Rison	.05	.15
8 Bobby Humphrey	.02	.10
9 Gary Clark	.15	.40
10 Sterling Sharpe	.15	.40
11 Flipper Anderson	.02	.10
12 Neal Anderson	.05	.15
13 Haywood Jeffires	.05	.15
14 Stephone Paige	.02	.10
15 Drew Hill	.02	.10
16 Barry Word	.02	.10
17 Anthony Carter	.05	.15
18 James Brooks	.05	.15

1992 Topps

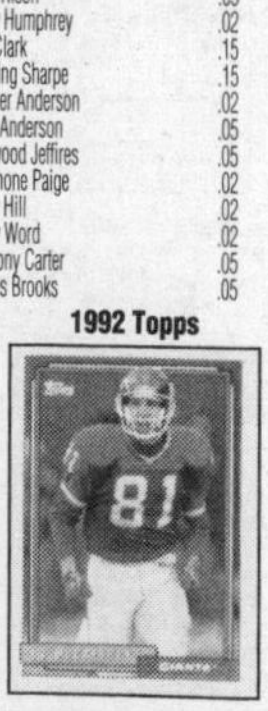

The 1992 Topps football set was issued in three series and totaled 759 standard-size cards. The first and second series consisted of 330 cards and a high series of 99 cards was released late in the season. A factory set was issued for the first 660 cards and it included 20 Topps

Gold cards. A separate high series factory set of 113 cards was issued. It included 10 Topps Gold cards and one four-card No. 1 Draft Picks set. .The key Rookie Cards in the set are Edgar Bennett, Steve Bono, Robert Brooks, Terrell Buckley, Quentin Coryatt, Steve Emtman, Amp Lee, Tommy Maddox, Carl Pickens and Tommy Vardell. Members of both NFL Properties and the NFL Players Association are included in the third series.

COMPLETE SET (759)	25.00	50.00
COMP.FACT.SET (680)	40.00	80.00
COMP.SERIES 1 (330)	10.00	20.00
COMP.SERIES 2 (330)	10.00	20.00
COMP.HIGH SER.(99)	5.00	10.00
COMP.FACT.HIGH SET (113)	5.00	12.00
1 Tim McGee	.01	.05
2 Rich Camarillo	.01	.05
3 Anthony Johnson	.02	.10
4 Larry Kelm	.01	.05
5 Irving Fryar	.02	.10
6 Joey Browner	.01	.05
7 Michael Walter	.01	.05
8 Cortez Kennedy	.02	.10
9 Reyna Thompson	.01	.05
10 John Friesz	.02	.10
11 Leroy Hoard	.02	.10
12 Steve McMichael	.02	.10
13 Marvin Washington	.01	.05
14 Clyde Simmons	.01	.05
15 Stephone Paige	.01	.05
16 Mike Utley	.02	.10
17 Tunch Ilkin	.01	.05
18 Lawrence Dawsey	.02	.10
19 Vance Johnson	.01	.05
20 Bryce Paup	.08	.25
21 Jeff Wright	.01	.05
22 Gill Fenerty	.01	.05
23 Lamar Lathon	.01	.05
24 Danny Copeland	.01	.05
25 Marcus Allen	.08	.25
26 Tim Green	.01	.05
27 Pete Stoyanovich	.01	.05
28 Alvin Harper	.02	.10
29 Roy Foster	.01	.05
30 Eugene Daniel	.01	.05
31 Luis Sharpe	.01	.05
32 Terry Wooden	.01	.05
33 Jim Breech	.01	.05
34 Randy Hilliard RC	.01	.05
35 Roman Phifer	.01	.05
36 Erik Howard	.01	.05
37 Chris Singleton	.01	.05
38 Matt Stover	.01	.05
39 Tim Irwin	.01	.05
40 Karl Mecklenburg	.01	.05
41 Joe Phillips	.01	.05
42 Bill Jones RC	.01	.05
43 Mark Carrier DB	.01	.05
44 George Jamison	.01	.05
45 Rob Taylor	.01	.05
46 Jeff Jaeger	.01	.05
47 Don Majkowski	.01	.05
48 Al Edwards	.01	.05
49 Curtis Duncan	.01	.05
50 Sam Mills	.01	.05
51 Terance Mathis	.02	.10
52 Brian Mitchell	.02	.10
53 Mike Pritchard	.02	.10
54 Calvin Williams	.02	.10
55 Hardy Nickerson	.02	.10
56 Nate Newton	.01	.05
57 Steve Wallace	.01	.05
58 John Offerdahl	.01	.05
59 Aeneas Williams	.02	.10
60 Lee Johnson	.01	.05
61 Ricardo McDonald RC	.01	.05
62 David Richards	.01	.05
63 Paul Gruber	.01	.05
64 Greg McMurtry	.01	.05
65 Jay Hilgenberg	.01	.05
66 Tim Grunhard	.01	.05
67 Dwayne White RC	.01	.05
68 Don Beebe	.01	.05
69 Simon Fletcher	.01	.05
70 Warren Moon	.08	.25
71 Chris Jacke	.01	.05
72 Steve Wisniewski UER (Traded to Raiders& not drafted by them)	.01	.05
73 Mike Cofer	.01	.05
74 Tim Johnson UER (No position listed on back)	.01	.05
75 T.J. Turner	.01	.05
76 Scott Case	.01	.05
77 Michael Jackson	.02	.10
78 Jon Hand	.01	.05
79 Stan Brock	.01	.05
80 Robert Blackmon	.01	.05
81 D.J. Johnson	.01	.05
82 Damone Johnson	.01	.05
83 Marc Spindler	.01	.05
84 Larry Brown DB	.01	.05
85 Ray Berry	.01	.05
86 Andre Waters	.01	.05
87 Carlos Huerta	.01	.05
88 Brad Muster	.01	.05
89 Chuck Cecil	.01	.05
90 Nick Lowery	.01	.05
91 Cornelius Bennett	.02	.10
92 Jessie Tuggle	.01	.05
93 Mark Schlereth RC	.01	.05
94 Vestee Jackson	.01	.05
95 Eric Bieniemy	.01	.05
96 Jeff Hostetler	.02	.10
97 Ken Lanier	.01	.05
98 Wayne Haddix	.01	.05
99 Lorenzo White	.01	.05
100 Mervyn Fernandez	.01	.05
101 Brent Williams	.01	.05
102 Ian Beckles	.01	.05
103 Harris Barton	.01	.05
104 Edgar Bennett RC	.08	.25
105 Mike Pitts	.01	.05
106 Fuad Reveiz	.01	.05
107 Vernon Turner	.01	.05
108 Tracy Hayworth RC	.01	.05
109 Checklist 1-110	.01	.05
110 Tom Waddle	.01	.05
111 Fred Stokes	.01	.05
112 Howard Ballard	.01	.05
113 David Szott	.01	.05
114 Tim McKyer	.01	.05
115 Kyle Clifton	.01	.05
116 Tony Bennett	.01	.05
117 Joel Hilgenberg	.01	.05
118 Dwayne Harper	.01	.05
119 Mike Baab	.01	.05
120 Mark Clayton	.02	.10
121 Eric Swann	.02	.10
122 Neil O'Donnell	.02	.10
123 Mike Munchak	.02	.10
124 Howie Long	.08	.25
125 John Elway UER (Card says 6-year vet, should be 9)	.50	1.25
126 Joe Prokop	.01	.05
127 Pepper Johnson	.01	.05
128 Richard Dent	.02	.10
129 Robert Porcher RC	.08	.25
130 Earnest Byner	.01	.05
131 Kent Hull	.01	.05
132 Mike Merriweather	.01	.05
133 Scott Fulhage	.01	.05
134 Kevin Porter	.01	.05
135 Tony Casillas	.01	.05
136 Dean Biasucci	.01	.05
137 Don Smith	.01	.05
138 Bruce Kozerski	.01	.05
139 Jeff Campbell	.01	.05
140 Kevin Greene	.02	.10
141 Gary Plummer	.01	.05
142 Vincent Brown	.01	.05
143 Ron Hall	.01	.05
144 Louie Aguiar RC	.01	.05
145 Mark Duper	.01	.05
146 Jesse Sapolu	.01	.05
147 Jeff Gossett	.01	.05
148 Brian Noble	.01	.05
149 Derek Russell	.01	.05
150 Carlton Bailey RC	.01	.05
151 Kelly Goodburn	.01	.05
152 Audray McMillian UER (Misspelled Audrey)	.01	.05
153 Neal Anderson	.01	.05
154 Bill Maas	.01	.05
155 Rickey Jackson	.01	.05
156 Chris Miller	.02	.10
157 Darren Comeaux	.01	.05
158 David Williams	.01	.05
159 Rich Gannon	.08	.25
160 Kevin Mack	.01	.05
161 Jim Arnold	.01	.05
162 Reggie White	.08	.25
163 Leonard Russell	.02	.10
164 Doug Smith	.01	.05
165 Tony Mandarich	.01	.05
166 Greg Lloyd	.02	.10
167 Jumbo Elliott	.01	.05
168 Jonathan Hayes	.01	.05
169 Jim Ritcher	.01	.05
170 Mike Kenn	.01	.05
171 James Washington	.01	.05
172 Tim Harris	.01	.05
173 James Thornton	.01	.05
174 John Brandes RC	.01	.05
175 Fred McAfee RC	.01	.05
176 Henry Rolling	.01	.05
177 Tony Paige	.01	.05
178 Jay Schroeder	.01	.05
179 Jeff Herrod	.01	.05
180 Emmitt Smith	.60	1.50
181 Wymon Henderson	.01	.05
182 Rob Moore	.02	.10
183 Robert Wilson	.01	.05
184 Michael Zordich RC	.01	.05
185 Jim Harbaugh	.08	.25
186 Vince Workman	.01	.05
187 Ernest Givins	.02	.10
188 Herschel Walker	.02	.10
189 Dan Fike	.01	.05
190 Seth Joyner	.01	.05
191 Steve Young	.25	.60
192 Dennis Gibson	.01	.05
193 Darryl Talley	.01	.05
194 Emile Harry	.01	.05
195 Bill Fralic	.01	.05
196 Michael Stewart	.01	.05
197 James Francis	.01	.05
198 Jerome Henderson	.01	.05
199 John L. Williams	.01	.05
200 Rod Woodson	.08	.25
201 Mike Farr	.01	.05
202 Greg Montgomery	.01	.05
203 Andre Collins	.01	.05
204 Scott Miller	.01	.05
205 Clay Matthews	.02	.10
206 Ethan Horton	.01	.05
207 Rich Miano	.01	.05
208 Chris Mims RC	.01	.05
209 Anthony Morgan	.01	.05
210 Rodney Hampton	.02	.10
211 Chris Hinton	.01	.05
212 Esera Tuaolo	.01	.05
213 Shane Conlan	.01	.05
214 John Carney	.01	.05
215 Kenny Walker	.01	.05
216 Scott Radecic	.01	.05
217 Chris Martin	.01	.05
218 Checklist 111-220 UER (152 Audray McMillian misspelled Audrey)	.01	.05
219 Wesley Carroll UER (Stats say 1st round pick, bio correctly has 2nd)	.01	.05
220 Bill Romanowski	.01	.05
221 Reggie Cobb	.01	.05
222 Alfred Anderson	.01	.05
223 Cleveland Gary	.01	.05
224 Eddie Blake RC	.01	.05
225 Chris Spielman	.02	.10
226 John Roper	.01	.05
227 George Thomas RC	.01	.05
228 Jeff Faulkner	.01	.05
229 Chip Lohmiller UER (RFK Stadium not identified on back)	.01	.05
230 Hugh Millen	.01	.05
231 Ray Horton	.01	.05
232 James Campen	.01	.05
233 Howard Cross	.01	.05
234 Keith McKeller	.01	.05
235 Dino Hackett	.01	.05
236 Jerome Brown	.01	.05
237 Andy Heck	.01	.05
238 Rodney Holman	.01	.05
239 Bruce Matthews	.01	.05
240 Jeff Lageman	.01	.05
241 Bobby Hebert	.01	.05
242 Gary Anderson K	.01	.05
243 Mark Bortz	.01	.05
244 Rich Moran	.01	.05
245 Jeff Uhlenhake	.01	.05
246 Ricky Sanders	.01	.05
247 Clarence Kay	.01	.05
248 Ed King	.01	.05
249 Eddie Anderson	.01	.05
250 Amp Lee RC	.01	.05
251 Norm Johnson	.01	.05
252 Michael Carter	.01	.05
253 Felix Wright	.01	.05
254 Leon Seals	.01	.05
255 Nate Lewis	.01	.05
256 Kevin Call	.01	.05
257 Darryl Henley	.01	.05
258 Jon Vaughn	.01	.05
259 Matt Bahr	.01	.05
260 Johnny Johnson	.01	.05
261 Ken Norton	.02	.10
262 Wendell Davis	.01	.05
263 Eugene Robinson	.01	.05
264 David Treadwell	.01	.05
265 Michael Haynes	.02	.10
266 Robb Thomas	.01	.05
267 Nate Odomes	.01	.05
268 Martin Mayhew	.01	.05
269 Perry Kemp	.01	.05
270 Jerry Ball	.01	.05
271 Tommy Vardell RC	.01	.05
272 Ernie Mills	.01	.05
273 Mo Lewis	.01	.05
274 Roger Ruzek	.01	.05
275 Steve Smith	.01	.05
276 Bo Orlando RC	.01	.05
277 Louis Oliver	.01	.05
278 Toi Cook	.01	.05
279 Eddie Brown	.01	.05
280 Keith McCants	.01	.05
281 Rob Burnett	.01	.05
282 Keith DeLong	.01	.05
283 Stan Thomas UER (9th line bio notes, the word of is in caps)	.01	.05
284 Robert Brown	.01	.05
285 John Alt	.01	.05
286 Randy Dixon	.01	.05
287 Siran Stacy RC	.01	.05
288 Ray Agnew	.01	.05
289 Darion Conner	.01	.05
290 Kirk Lowdermilk	.01	.05
291 Greg Jackson	.01	.05
292 Ken Harvey	.01	.05
293 Jacob Green	.01	.05
294 Mark Tuinei	.01	.05
295 Mark Rypien	.01	.05
296 Gerald Robinson RC	.01	.05
297 Broderick Thompson	.01	.05
298 Doug Widell	.01	.05
299 Carwell Gardner	.01	.05
300 Barry Sanders	.50	1.25
301 Eric Metcalf	.02	.10
302 Eric Thomas	.01	.05
303 Terrell Buckley RC	.01	.05
304 Byron Evans	.01	.05
305 Johnny Hector	.01	.05
306 Steve Broussard	.01	.05
307 Gene Atkins	.01	.05
308 Terry McDaniel	.01	.05
309 Charles McRae	.01	.05
310 Jim Lachey	.01	.05
311 Pat Harlow	.01	.05
312 Kevin Butler	.01	.05
313 Scott Stephen	.01	.05
314 Dermontti Dawson	.01	.05
315 Johnny Meads	.01	.05
316 Checklist 221-330	.01	.05
317 Aaron Craver	.01	.05
318 Michael Brooks	.01	.05
319 Guy McIntyre	.01	.05
320 Thurman Thomas	.08	.25
321 Courtney Hall	.01	.05
322 Dan Saleaumua	.01	.05
323 Vinson Smith RC	.01	.05
324 Steve Jordan	.01	.05
325 Walter Reeves	.01	.05
326 Erik Kramer	.02	.10
327 Duane Bickett	.01	.05
328 Tom Newberry	.01	.05
329 John Kasay	.01	.05
330 Dave Meggett	.02	.10
331 Kevin Ross	.01	.05
332 Keith Hamilton RC	.02	.10
333 Dwight Stone	.01	.05
334 Mel Gray	.02	.10
335 Harry Galbreath	.01	.05
336 William Perry	.02	.10
337 Brian Blades	.02	.10
338 Randall McDaniel	.02	.10
339 Pat Coleman RC	.02	.10
340 Michael Irvin	.08	.25
341 Checklist 331-440	.01	.05
342 Chris Mohr	.01	.05
343 Greg Davis	.01	.05
344 Dave Cadigan	.01	.05
345 Art Monk	.02	.10
346 Tim Goad	.01	.05
347 Vinnie Clark	.01	.05
348 David Fulcher	.01	.05
349 Craig Heyward	.02	.10
350 Ronnie Lott	.02	.10
351 Dexter Carter	.02	.10
352 Mark Jackson	.01	.05
353 Brian Jordan	.02	.10
354 Randy Donaldson	.01	.05
355 Jim Price	.01	.05
356 Rod Bernstine	.01	.05
357 Tony Mayberry RC	.01	.05
358 Richard Brown RC	.01	.05
359 David Alexander	.01	.05
360 Haywood Jeffires	.02	.10
361 Henry Thomas	.01	.05
362 Jeff Graham	.08	.25
363 Don Warren	.01	.05
364 Scott Davis	.01	.05
365 Harlon Barnett	.01	.05
366 Mark Collins	.01	.05
367 Rick Tuten	.01	.05
368 Lonnie Marts RC UER (Injured Reserved should be Reserve)	.01	.05
369 Dennis Smith	.01	.05
370 Steve Tasker	.02	.10
371 Robert Massey	.01	.05
372 Ricky Reynolds	.01	.05
373 Alvin Wright	.01	.05
374 Kelvin Martin	.01	.05
375 Vince Buck	.01	.05
376 John Kidd	.01	.05
377 William White	.01	.05
378 Bryan Cox	.02	.10
379 Jamie Dukes RC	.01	.05
380 Anthony Munoz	.02	.10
381 Mark Gunn RC	.01	.05
382 Keith Henderson	.01	.05
383 Charles Wilson	.01	.05
384 Shawn McCarthy RC	.01	.05
385 Ernie Jones	.01	.05
386 Nick Bell	.01	.05
387 Derrick Walker	.01	.05
388 Mark Stepnoski	.02	.10
389 Broderick Thomas	.01	.05
390 Reggie Roby	.01	.05
391 Bubba McDowell	.01	.05
392 Eric Martin	.01	.05
393 Toby Caston RC	.01	.05
394 Bern Brostek	.01	.05
395 Christian Okoye	.01	.05
396 Frank Minnifield	.01	.05
397 Mike Golic	.01	.05
398 Grant Feasel	.01	.05
399 Michael Ball	.01	.05
400 Mike Croel	.01	.05
401 Maury Buford	.01	.05
402 Jeff Bostic UER (Signed as free agent in 1980, not 1984)	.01	.05
403 Sean Landeta	.01	.05
404 Terry Allen	.08	.25
405 Donald Evans	.01	.05
406 Don Mosebar	.01	.05
407 D.J. Dozier	.01	.05
408 Bruce Pickens	.01	.05
409 Jim Dombrowski	.01	.05
410 Deron Cherry	.01	.05
411 Richard Johnson	.01	.05
412 Alexander Wright	.01	.05
413 Tom Rathman	.01	.05
414 Mark Dennis	.01	.05
415 Phil Hansen	.01	.05
416 Lonnie Young	.01	.05
417 Burt Grossman	.01	.05
418 Tony Covington	.01	.05
419 John Stephens	.01	.05
420 Jim Everett	.02	.10
421 Johnny Holland	.01	.05
422 Mike Barber RC	.01	.05
423 Carl Lee	.01	.05
424 Craig Patterson RC	.01	.05
425 Greg Townsend	.01	.05
426 Brett Perriman	.08	.25
427 Morten Andersen	.01	.05
428 John Gesek	.01	.05
429 Bryan Barker	.01	.05
430 John Taylor	.02	.10
431 Donnell Woolford	.01	.05
432 Ron Holmes	.01	.05
433 Lee Williams	.01	.05
434 Alfred Oglesby	.01	.05
435 Jarrod Bunch	.01	.05
436 Carlton Haselrig RC	.01	.05
437 Rufus Porter	.01	.05
438 Rohn Stark	.01	.05
439 Tony Jones	.01	.05
440 Andre Rison	.02	.10
441 Eric Hill	.01	.05
442 Jesse Solomon	.01	.05
443 Jackie Slater	.01	.05
444 Donnie Elder	.01	.05
445 Brett Maxie	.01	.05
446 Max Montoya	.01	.05
447 Will Wolford	.01	.05
448 Craig Taylor	.01	.05
449 Jimmie Jones	.01	.05
450 Anthony Carter	.02	.10
451 Brian Bollinger RC	.01	.05
452 Checklist 441-550	.01	.05
453 Brad Edwards	.01	.05
454 Gene Chilton RC	.01	.05
455 Eric Allen	.01	.05
456 William Roberts	.01	.05
457 Eric Green	.01	.05
458 Irv Eatman	.01	.05
459 Derrick Thomas	.08	.25
460 Tommy Kane	.01	.05
461 LeRoy Butler	.01	.05
462 Oliver Barnett	.01	.05
463 Anthony Smith	.01	.05
464 Cris Dishman	.01	.05
465 Pat Terrell	.01	.05
466 Greg Kragen	.01	.05
467 Rodney Peete	.02	.10
468 Willie Drewrey	.01	.05
469 Jim Wilks	.01	.05
470 Vince Newsome	.01	.05
471 Chris Gardocki	.01	.05
472 Chris Chandler	.08	.25
473 George Thornton	.01	.05
474 Albert Lewis	.01	.05
475 Kevin Glover	.01	.05
476 Joe Bowden RC	.01	.05
477 Harry Sydney	.01	.05
478 Bob Golic	.01	.05
479 Tony Zendejas	.01	.05
480 Brad Baxter	.01	.05
481 Steve Beuerlein	.02	.10
482 Mark Higgs	.01	.05
483 Drew Hill	.01	.05
484 Bryan Millard	.01	.05
485 Mark Kelso	.01	.05
486 David Grant	.01	.05
487 Gary Zimmerman	.01	.05
488 Leonard Marshall	.01	.05
489 Keith Jackson	.02	.10
490 Sterling Sharpe	.08	.25
491 Ferrell Edmunds	.01	.05
492 Wilber Marshall	.01	.05
493 Charles Haley	.02	.10
494 Riki Ellison	.01	.05
495 Bill Brooks	.01	.05
496 Bill Hawkins	.01	.05
497 Erik Williams	.01	.05
498 Leon Searcy RC	.01	.05
499 Mike Horan	.01	.05
500 Pat Swilling	.01	.05
501 Maurice Hurst	.01	.05
502 William Fuller	.01	.05
503 Tim Newton	.01	.05
504 Lorenzo Lynch	.01	.05
505 Tim Barnett	.01	.05
506 Tom Thayer	.01	.05
507 Chris Burkett	.01	.05
508 Ronnie Harmon	.01	.05
509 James Brooks	.02	.10
510 Bennie Blades	.01	.05
511 Roger Craig	.02	.10
512 Tony Woods	.02	.10
513 Greg Lewis	.01	.05
514 Eric Pegram	.02	.10
515 Elvis Patterson	.01	.05
516 Jeff Cross	.01	.05
517 Myron Guyton	.01	.05
518 Jay Novacek	.02	.10
519 Leo Barker RC	.01	.05
520 Keith Byars	.01	.05
521 Dalton Hilliard	.01	.05
522 Ted Washington	.01	.05
523 Dexter McNabb RC	.01	.05
524 Frank Reich	.02	.10
525 Henry Ellard	.02	.10
526 Barry Foster	.01	.05
527 Barry Word	.01	.05
528 Gary Anderson RB	.01	.05
529 Reggie Rutland	.01	.05
530 Stephen Baker	.01	.05
531 John Flannery	.01	.05
532 Steve Wright	.01	.05
533 Eric Sanders	.01	.05
534 Bob Whitfield RC	.01	.05
535 Gaston Green	.01	.05
536 Anthony Pleasant	.01	.05
537 Jeff Bryant	.01	.05
538 Jarvis Williams	.01	.05
539 Jim Morrissey	.01	.05
540 Andre Tippett	.01	.05
541 Gill Byrd	.01	.05
542 Raleigh McKenzie	.01	.05
543 Jim Sweeney	.01	.05
544 David Lutz	.01	.05
545 Wayne Martin	.01	.05
546 Karl Wilson	.01	.05
547 Pierce Holt	.01	.05
548 Doug Smith	.01	.05
549 Nolan Harrison RC	.01	.05
550 Freddie Joe Nunn	.01	.05
551 Eric Moore	.01	.05
552 Cris Carter	.20	.50
553 Kevin Gogan	.01	.05
554 Harold Green	.01	.05
555 Kenneth Davis	.01	.05
556 Travis McNeal	.01	.05
557 Jim C. Jensen	.01	.05
558 Willie Green	.01	.05
559 Scott Galbraith RC UER (Drafted in 1990, not 1989)	.01	.05
560 Louis Lipps	.01	.05
561 Matt Brock	.01	.05
562 Mike Prior	.01	.05
563 Checklist 551-660	.01	.05
564 Robert Delpino	.01	.05
565 Vinny Testaverde	.02	.10
566 Willie Gault	.02	.10
567 Quinn Early	.02	.10
568 Eric Moten	.01	.05
569 Lance Smith	.01	.05
570 Darrell Green	.01	.05
571 Moe Gardner	.01	.05
572 Steve Atwater	.01	.05
573 Ray Childress	.01	.05
574 Dave Krieg	.02	.10
575 Bruce Armstrong	.01	.05
576 Fred Barnett	.08	.25
577 Don Griffin	.01	.05
578 David Brandon RC	.01	.05
579 Robert Young	.01	.05
580 Keith Van Horne	.01	.05
581 Jeff Criswell	.01	.05
582 Lewis Tillman	.01	.05
583 Bubby Brister	.01	.05
584 Aaron Wallace	.01	.05
585 Chris Doleman	.01	.05
586 Marty Carter RC	.01	.05
587 Chris Warren	.08	.25
588 David Griggs	.01	.05
589 Darrell Thompson	.01	.05
590 Marion Butts	.01	.05
591 Scott Norwood	.01	.05
592 Lomas Brown	.01	.05
593 Daryl Johnston	.08	.25
594 Alonzo Mitz RC	.01	.05
595 Tommy Barnhardt	.01	.05
596 Tim Jorden	.01	.05
597 Neil Smith	.08	.25
598 Todd Marinovich	.01	.05
599 Sean Jones	.01	.05
600 Clarence Verdin	.01	.05
601 Trace Armstrong	.01	.05
602 Steve Bono RC	.08	.25
603 Mark Ingram	.01	.05
604 Flipper Anderson	.01	.05
605 James Jones	.01	.05
606 Al Noga	.01	.05
607 Rick Bryan	.01	.05
608 Eugene Lockhart	.01	.05
609 Charles Mann	.01	.05
610 James Hasty	.01	.05
611 Jeff Feagles	.01	.05
612 Tim Brown	.08	.25
613 David Little	.01	.05
614 Keith Sims	.01	.05
615 Kevin Murphy	.01	.05
616 Ray Crockett	.01	.05
617 Jim Jeffcoat	.01	.05
618 Patrick Hunter	.01	.05
619 Keith Kartz	.01	.05
620 Peter Tom Willis	.01	.05
621 Vaughan Johnson	.01	.05
622 Shawn Jefferson	.01	.05
623 Anthony Thompson	.01	.05
624 John Rienstra	.01	.05
625 Don Maggs	.01	.05
626 Todd Lyght	.01	.05
627 Brent Jones	.02	.10
628 Todd McNair	.01	.05
629 Winston Moss	.01	.05
630 Mark Carrier WR	.02	.10
631 Dan Owens	.01	.05
632 Sammie Smith UER (Old team front, correct new team back; acquired via trade, not draft)	.01	.05
633 James Lofton	.02	.10
634 Paul McJulien RC	.01	.05
635 Tony Tolbert	.01	.05
636 Carnell Lake	.01	.05
637 Gary Clark	.08	.25
638 Brian Washington	.01	.05
639 Jessie Hester	.01	.05
640 Doug Riesenberg	.01	.05
641 Joe Walter RC	.01	.05
642 John Rade	.01	.05
643 Wes Hopkins	.01	.05
644 Kelly Stouffer	.01	.05
645 Marv Cook	.01	.05
646 Ken Clarke	.01	.05
647 Bobby Humphrey UER (Old team front& correct new team back; acquired via trade& not draft)	.01	.05
648 Tim McDonald	.01	.05
649 Donald Frank RC	.01	.05
650 Richmond Webb	.01	.05
651 Lemuel Stinson	.01	.05
652 Merton Hanks	.02	.10
653 Frank Warren	.01	.05
654 Thomas Benson	.01	.05
655 Al Smith	.01	.05
656 Steve DeBerg	.01	.05
657 Jayice Pearson RC	.01	.05
658 Joe Morris	.01	.05
659 Fred Strickland	.01	.05
660 Kelvin Pritchett	.01	.05
661 Lewis Billups	.01	.05
662 Todd Collins RC	.01	.05
663 Corey Miller RC	.01	.05
664 Levon Kirkland RC	.01	.05
665 Jerry Rice	.30	.75
666 Mike Lodish RC	.01	.05
667 Chuck Smith RC	.01	.05
668 Lance Olberding RC	.01	.05
669 Kevin Smith RC	.01	.05
670 Dale Carter RC	.02	.10
671 Sean Gilbert RC	.02	.10
672 Ken O'Brien	.01	.05
673 Ricky Proehl	.01	.05
674 Junior Seau	.08	.25
675 Courtney Hawkins RC	.02	.10
676 Eddie Robinson RC	.01	.05
677 Tom Jeter RC	.01	.05
678 Jeff George	.08	.25
679 Cary Conklin	.01	.05
680 Rueben Mayes	.01	.05
681 Sean Lumpkin RC	.01	.05
682 Dan Marino	.50	1.25
683 Ed McDaniel RC	.01	.05
684 Greg Skrepenak RC	.01	.05
685 Tracy Scroggins RC	.01	.05
686 Tommy Maddox RC	.75	2.00
687 Mike Singletary	.02	.10
688 Patrick Rowe RC	.01	.05
689 Phillippi Sparks RC	.01	.05
690 Joel Steed RC	.01	.05
691 Kevin Fagan	.01	.05
692 Deion Sanders	.20	.50
693 Bruce Smith	.08	.25
694 David Klingler RC	.01	.05
695 Clayton Holmes RC	.01	.05
696 Brett Favre	2.50	6.00
697 Marc Boutte RC	.01	.05
698 Dwayne Sabb RC	.01	.05
699 Ed McCaffrey	.10	.30
700 Randall Cunningham	.08	.25
701 Quentin Coryatt RC	.01	.05
702 Bernie Kosar	.02	.10
703 Vaughn Dunbar RC	.01	.05
704 Browning Nagle	.01	.05
705 Mark Wheeler RC	.01	.05
706 Paul Siever RC	.01	.05
707 Anthony Miller	.02	.10
708 Corey Widmer RC	.01	.05
709 Eric Dickerson	.02	.10
710 Martin Bayless	.01	.05
711 Jason Hanson RC	.02	.10
712 Michael Dean Perry	.02	.10
713 Billy Joe Tolliver UER (Stats say 1991 Chargers, should be Falcons)	.01	.05
714 Chad Hennings RC	.02	.10
715 Bucky Richardson RC	.01	.05
716 Steve Israel RC	.01	.05
717 Robert Harris RC	.01	.05
718 Timm Rosenbach	.01	.05
719 Joe Montana	.50	1.25
720 Derek Brown TE RC	.01	.05
721 Robert Brooks RC	.30	.75
722 Boomer Esiason	.02	.10
723 Troy Auzenne RC	.01	.05
724 John Fina RC	.01	.05
725 Chris Crooms RC	.01	.05
726 Eugene Chung RC	.01	.05
727 Darren Woodson RC	.08	.25
728 Leslie O'Neal	.02	.10
729 Dan McGwire	.01	.05
730 Al Toon	.02	.10
731 Michael Brandon RC	.01	.05
732 Steve DeOssie	.01	.05
733 Jim Kelly	.08	.25
734 Webster Slaughter	.01	.05
735 Tony Smith RC	.01	.05
736 Shane Collins RC	.01	.05
737 Randal Hill	.01	.05
738 Chris Holder RC	.01	.05
739 Russell Maryland	.01	.05
740 Carl Pickens RC	.08	.25
741 Andre Reed	.02	.10
742 Steve Emtman RC	.01	.05
743 Carl Banks	.01	.05
744 Troy Aikman	.30	.75
745 Mark Royals	.01	.05
746 J.J. Birden	.01	.05
747 Michael Cofer	.01	.05
748 Darryl Ashmore RC	.01	.05
749 Dion Lambert RC	.01	.05
750 Phil Simms	.02	.10
751 Reggie E. White RC	.01	.05
752 Harvey Williams	.08	.25
753 Ty Detmer	.08	.25
754 Tony Brooks RC	.01	.05
755 Steve Christie	.01	.05
756 Lawrence Taylor	.08	.25
757 Merril Hoge	.01	.05
758 Robert Jones RC	.01	.05
759 Checklist 661-750	.01	.05

1992 Topps Gold

COMPLETE SET (759)	60.00	150.00
COMP.SERIES 1 (330)	20.00	50.00
COMP.SERIES 2 (330)	20.00	50.00
COMP.HI SERIES (99)	25.00	60.00
*VETERANS: 1.5X TO 4X BASIC CARDS		
*ROOKIES: 1.2X TO 3X BASIC CARDS		
ONE PER PACK/THREE PER RACK		
TWENTY PER LO FACTORY SET		
TEN PER HIGH FACTORY SET		
109 Freeman McNeil	.25	.60
218 David Daniels	.25	.60
316 Chris Hakel	.25	.60
341 Ottis Anderson	.25	.60
452 Shawn Moore	.25	.60
563 Mike Mooney	.25	.60
759 Curtis Whitley	.25	.60

1992 Topps No.1 Draft Picks

COMPLETE SET (4)	1.50	4.00
RANDOM INSERTS IN HIGH SERIES		
ONE SET PER HIGH SERIES FACTOR		
1 Jeff George	.60	1.50
2 Russell Maryland	.40	1.00
3 Steve Emtman	.40	1.00
4 Rocket Ismail	.40	1.00

1992 Topps 1000 Yard Club

COMPLETE SET (20)	6.00	15.00
*GOLDS: 1.5X TO 4X BASIC INSERTS		
GOLDS RANDOM INSERTS IN FACT.SETS		
1 Emmitt Smith	1.50	4.00
2 Barry Sanders	1.25	3.00
3 Michael Irvin	.25	.60
4 Thurman Thomas	.25	.60
5 Gary Clark	.25	.60
6 Haywood Jeffires	.08	.25
7 Michael Haynes	.08	.25
8 Drew Hill	.05	.15
9 Mark Duper	.05	.15
10 James Lofton	.08	.25
11 Rodney Hampton	.08	.25
12 Mark Clayton	.08	.25
13 Henry Ellard	.08	.25
14 Art Monk	.08	.25
15 Earnest Byner	.05	.15
16 Gaston Green	.05	.15
17 Christian Okoye	.05	.15
18 Irving Fryar	.08	.25
19 John Taylor	.08	.25
20 Brian Blades	.08	.25

1992 Topps Stadium of Stars

This 12-card standard-size set measures the standard size and features stars from different sports and entertainment. The cards have the same design as the regular 1992 Topps cards. The fronts feature color portraits with red and white inner borders and white outer borders. The star's name and the set name appear in two short color stripes respectively at the bottom. The backs carry a short biography and personal information. The cards are unnumbered and checklisted below in alphabetical order

COMPLETE SET (12)	5.00	12.00
3 Lou Holtz CO	.75	2.00

1993 Topps

The 1993 Topps football set consists of 660 standard-size cards that were issued in two series of 330. Each pack contained 14 cards plus one Topps Gold card. Factory sets of 673 cards contain 10 Topps Gold cards and three Topps Black Gold cards. Subsets featured are Record Breakers (1-2), Franchise Players (82-90), Team Leaders (171-184, 261-274), League Leaders (216-220) and Field Generals (291-300). Thirty Draft Pick cards are scattered throughout the set. Rookie Cards include Jerome Bettis, Drew Bledsoe, Reggie Brooks, Dave Brown, Curtis Conway, Garrison Hearst, Qadry Ismail, O.J. McDuffie, Natrone Means, Rick Mirer, Ronald Moore, Robert Smith and Dana Stubblefield.

COMPLETE SET (660)	15.00	40.00
COMP.FACT.SET (673)	90.00	150.00
COMP.SERIES 1 (330)	8.00	20.00
COMP.SERIES 2 (330)	8.00	20.00
1 Art Monk RB	.02	.10
2 Jerry Rice RB	.20	.50
3 Stanley Richard	.01	.05
4 Ron Hall	.01	.05
5 Daryl Johnston	.08	.25
6 Wendell Davis	.01	.05
7 Vaughn Dunbar	.01	.05
8 Mike Jones	.01	.05
9 Anthony Johnson	.02	.10
10 Chris Miller	.02	.10
11 Kyle Clifton	.01	.05
12 Curtis Conway RC	.15	.40
13 Lionel Washington	.01	.05
14 Reggie Johnson	.01	.05
15 David Little	.01	.05
16 Nick Lowery	.01	.05
17 Darryl Williams	.01	.05
18 Brent Jones	.02	.10
19 Bruce Matthews	.02	.10
20 Heath Sherman	.01	.05
21 John Kasay UER (Text on back states he did not attempt any FG's over 50 yds. but made 8)	.01	.05
22 Troy Drayton RC	.02	.10
23 Eric Metcalf	.02	.10
24 Andre Tippett	.02	.10
25 Rodney Hampton	.02	.10
26 Henry Jones	.01	.05
27 Jim Everett	.02	.10
28 Steve Jordan	.01	.05
29 LeRoy Butler	.01	.05
30 Troy Vincent	.01	.05
31 Nate Lewis	.01	.05
32 Rickey Jackson	.02	.10
33 Darion Conner	.01	.05
34 Tom Carter RC	.02	.10
35 Jeff George	.08	.25
36 Larry Centers RC	.08	.25
37 Reggie Cobb	.01	.05
38 Mike Saxon	.01	.05
39 Brad Baxter	.01	.05
40 Reggie White	.08	.25
41 Haywood Jeffires	.02	.10
42 Alfred Williams	.01	.05
43 Aaron Wallace	.01	.05
44 Tracy Simien	.01	.05
45 Pat Harlow	.01	.05
46 D.J. Johnson	.01	.05
47 Don Griffin	.01	.05
48 Flipper Anderson	.02	.10
49 Keith Kartz	.01	.05
50 Bernie Kosar	.02	.10
51 Kent Hull	.01	.05
52 Erik Howard	.01	.05
53 Pierce Holt	.01	.05
54 Dwayne Harper	.01	.05
55 Bennie Blades	.01	.05
56 Mark Duper	.01	.05
57 Brian Noble	.01	.05
58 Jeff Feagles	.01	.05
59 Michael Haynes	.02	.10
60 Junior Seau	.08	.25
61 Gary Anderson RB	.02	.10
62 Jon Hand	.01	.05
63 Lin Elliott RC	.01	.05
64 Dana Stubblefield RC	.08	.25
65 Vaughan Johnson	.01	.05
66 Mo Lewis	.01	.05
67 Aeneas Williams	.02	.10
68 David Fulcher	.01	.05
69 Chip Lohmiller	.01	.05
70 Greg Townsend	.02	.10
71 Simon Fletcher	.01	.05
72 Sean Salisbury	.02	.10
73 Christian Okoye	.02	.10
74 Jim Arnold	.01	.05
75 Bruce Smith	.08	.25
76 Fred Barnett	.02	.10
77 Bill Romanowski	.02	.10
78 Dermontti Dawson	.01	.05
79 Bern Brostek	.01	.05
80 Warren Moon	.08	.25
81 Bill Fralic	.01	.05
82 Lomas Brown FP	.01	.05
83 Duane Bickett FP	.01	.05
84 Neil Smith FP	.02	.10
85 Reggie White FP	.02	.10

86 Tim McDonald FP	.01	.05
87 Leslie O'Neal FP	.01	.05
88 Steve Young FP	.15	.40
89 Paul Gruber FP	.01	.05
90 Wilber Marshall FP	.01	.05
91 Trace Armstrong	.01	.05
92 Bobby Houston RC	.01	.05
93 George Thornton	.01	.05
94 Keith McCants	.01	.05
95 Ricky Sanders	.01	.05
96 Jackie Harris	.01	.05
97 Todd Marinovich	.01	.05
98 Henry Thomas	.01	.05
99 Jeff Wright	.01	.05
100 John Elway	.60	1.50
101 Garrison Hearst RC	.30	.75
102 Roy Foster	.01	.05
103 David Lang	.01	.05
104 Matt Stover	.01	.05
105 Lawrence Taylor	.08	.25
106 Pete Stoyanovich	.01	.05
107 Jessie Tuggle	.01	.05
108 William White	.01	.05
109 Andy Harmon RC	.02	.10
110 John L. Williams	.01	.05
111 Jon Vaughn	.01	.05
112 John Alt	.01	.05
113 Chris Jacke	.01	.05
114 Jim Breech	.01	.05
115 Eric Martin	.01	.05
116 Derrick Walker	.01	.05
117 Ricky Ervins	.01	.05
118 Roger Craig	.02	.10
119 Jeff Gossett	.01	.05
120 Emmitt Smith	.60	1.50
121 Bob Whitfield	.01	.05
122 Alonzo Spellman	.01	.05
123 David Klingler	.01	.05
124 Tommy Maddox	.08	.25
125 Robert Porcher	.01	.05
126 Edgar Bennett	.08	.25
127 Harvey Williams	.02	.10
128 Dave Brown RC	.08	.25
129 Johnny Mitchell	.01	.05
130 Drew Bledsoe RC	1.00	2.50
131 Zefross Moss	.01	.05
132 Nate Odomes	.01	.05
133 Rufus Porter	.01	.05
134 Jackie Slater	.02	.10
135 Steve Young	.30	.75
136 Chris Calloway	.02	.10
137 Steve Atwater	.02	.10
138 Mark Carrier DB	.01	.05
139 Marvin Washington	.01	.05
140 Barry Foster	.02	.10
141 Ricky Reynolds	.01	.05
142 Bubba McDowell	.01	.05
143 Dan Footman RC	.01	.05
144 Richmond Webb	.01	.05
145 Mike Pritchard	.02	.10
146 Chris Spielman	.02	.10
147 Dave Krieg	.02	.10
148 Nick Bell	.01	.05
149 Vincent Brown	.01	.05
150 Seth Joyner	.01	.05
151 Tommy Kane	.01	.05
152 Carlton Gray RC	.01	.05
153 Harry Newsome	.01	.05
154 Rohn Stark	.01	.05
155 Shannon Sharpe	.08	.25
156 Charles Haley	.02	.10
157 Cornelius Bennett	.02	.10
158 Doug Riesenberg	.01	.05
159 Amp Lee	.01	.05
160 Sterling Sharpe UER	.08	.25
(Card front pictures		
Edgar Bennett)		
161 Alonzo Mitz	.01	.05
162 Pat Terrell	.01	.05
163 Mark Schlereth	.01	.05
164 Gary Anderson K	.01	.05
165 Quinn Early	.02	.10
166 Jerome Bettis RC	2.50	5.00
167 Lawrence Dawsey	.01	.05
168 Derrick Thomas	.08	.25
169 Rodney Peete	.01	.05
170 Jim Kelly	.08	.25
171 Deion Sanders TL	.08	.25
172 Richard Dent TL	.01	.05
173 Emmitt Smith TL	.30	.75
174 Barry Sanders TL	.25	.60
175 Sterling Sharpe TL	.02	.10
176 Cleveland Gary TL	.01	.05
177 Terry Allen TL	.02	.10
178 Vaughan Johnson TL	.01	.05
179 Rodney Hampton TL	.01	.05
180 Randall Cunningham TL	.02	.10
181 Ricky Proehl TL	.01	.05
182 Jerry Rice TL	.20	.50
183 Reggie Cobb TL	.01	.05
184 Earnest Byner TL	.01	.05
185 Jeff Lageman	.01	.05
186 Carlos Jenkins	.01	.05
187 Cardinals Draft Picks	.15	.40
Ernest Dye RC		
Ronald Moore RC		
Garrison Hearst		
Ben Coleman RC		
188 Todd Lyght	.01	.05
189 Carl Simpson RC	.01	.05
190 Barry Sanders	.50	1.25
191 Jim Harbaugh	.08	.25
192 Roger Ruzek	.01	.05
193 Brent Williams	.01	.05
194 Chip Banks	.01	.05
195 Mike Croel	.01	.05
196 Marion Butts	.02	.10
197 James Washington	.01	.05
198 John Offerdahl	.01	.05
199 Tom Rathman	.02	.10
200 Joe Montana	.60	1.50
201 Pepper Johnson	.02	.10
202 Cris Dishman	.01	.05
203 Adrian White RC	.01	.05
204 Reggie Brooks RC	.02	.10
205 Cortez Kennedy	.02	.10
206 Robert Massey	.01	.05
207 Toi Cook	.01	.05
208 Harry Sydney	.01	.05
209 Lincoln Kennedy RC	.01	.05
210 Randall McDaniel	.05	.15
211 Eugene Daniel	.01	.05
212 Rob Burnett	.01	.05
213 Steve Broussard	.01	.05
214 Brian Washington	.01	.05
215 Leonard Renfro RC	.01	.05
216 Audray McMillian LL	.01	.05
Henry Jones		
217 Sterling Sharpe LL	.01	.05
Anthony Miller		
218 Clyde Simmons LL	.01	.05
Leslie O'Neal		
219 Emmitt Smith	.15	.40
B.Foster LL		
220 Steve Young LL	.08	.25
Warren Moon		
221 Mel Gray	.02	.10
222 Luis Sharpe	.01	.05
223 Eric Moten	.01	.05
224 Albert Lewis	.01	.05
225 Alvin Harper	.02	.10
226 Steve Wallace	.01	.05
227 Mark Higgs	.01	.05
228 Eugene Lockhart	.01	.05
229 Sean Jones	.01	.05
230 Buccaneers Draft Picks	.25	.60
Eric Curry		
Lamar Thomas RC		
Demetrious DuBose		
John Lynch RC		
231 Jimmy Williams	.01	.05
(Text states drafted in 1992;		
he was drafted in 1982)		
232 Demetrius DuBose RC	.01	.05
233 John Roper	.01	.05
234 Keith Hamilton	.01	.05
235 Donald Evans	.01	.05
236 Kenneth Davis	.02	.10
237 John Copeland RC	.02	.10
238 Leonard Russell	.02	.10
239 Ken Harvey	.01	.05
240 Dale Carter	.01	.05
241 Anthony Pleasant	.01	.05
242 Darrell Green	.02	.10
243 Natrone Means RC	.08	.25
244 Rob Moore	.02	.10
245 Chris Doleman	.01	.05
246 J.B. Brown	.01	.05
247 Ray Crockett	.01	.05
248 John Taylor	.02	.10
249 Russell Maryland	.01	.05
250 Brett Favre	.75	2.00
251 Carl Pickens	.02	.10
252 Andy Heck	.01	.05
253 Jerome Henderson	.01	.05
254 Deion Sanders	.20	.50
255 Steve Emtman	.01	.05
256 Calvin Williams	.02	.10
257 Sean Gilbert	.02	.10
258 Don Beebe	.01	.05
259 Robert Smith RC	.50	1.25
260 Robert Blackmon	.01	.05
261 Jim Kelly TL	.02	.10
262 Harold Green TL UER	.01	.05
(Harold Green is identified as		
Gaston Green)		
263 Clay Matthews TL	.01	.05
264 John Elway TL	.30	.75
265 Warren Moon TL	.02	.10
266 Jeff George TL	.02	.10
267 Derrick Thomas TL	.02	.10
268 Howie Long TL	.01	.05
269 Dan Marino TL	.30	.75
270 Jon Vaughn TL	.01	.05
271 Chris Burkett TL	.01	.05
272 Barry Foster TL	.01	.05
273 Marion Butts TL	.01	.05
274 Chris Warren TL	.01	.05
275 Michael Strahan RC	.75	2.00
Marcus Buckley RC		
(Giants Draft Picks)		
276 Tony Casillas	.01	.05
277 Jarrod Bunch	.01	.05
278 Eric Green	.01	.05
279 Stan Brock	.01	.05
280 Chester McGlockton	.02	.10
281 Ricky Watters	.08	.25
282 Dan Saleaumua	.01	.05
283 Rich Camarillo	.01	.05
284 Cris Carter	.08	.25
285 Rick Mirer RC	.08	.25
286 Matt Brock	.01	.05
287 Burt Grossman	.01	.05
288 Andre Collins	.01	.05
289 Mark Jackson	.01	.05
290 Dan Marino	.60	1.50
291 Cornelius Bennett FG	.01	.05
292 Steve Atwater FG	.01	.05
293 Bryan Cox FG	.01	.05
294 Sam Mills FG	.01	.05
295 Pepper Johnson FG	.01	.05
296 Seth Joyner FG	.01	.05
297 Chris Spielman FG	.01	.05
298 Junior Seau FG	.02	.10
299 Cortez Kennedy FG	.01	.05
300 Broderick Thomas FG	.01	.05
301 Todd McNair	.01	.05
302 Nate Newton	.02	.10
303 Michael Walter	.01	.05
304 Clyde Simmons	.01	.05
305 Ernie Mills	.01	.05
306 Steve Wisniewski	.01	.05
307 Coleman Rudolph RC	.01	.05
308 Thurman Thomas	.08	.25
309 Reggie Roby	.01	.05
310 Eric Swann	.02	.10
311 Mark Wheeler	.01	.05
312 Jeff Herrod	.01	.05
313 Leroy Hoard	.02	.10
314 Patrick Bates RC	.01	.05
315 Earnest Byner	.01	.05
316 Dave Meggett	.01	.05
317 George Teague RC	.02	.10
318 Ray Childress	.02	.10
319 Mike Kenn	.01	.05
320 Jason Hanson	.01	.05
321 Gary Clark	.02	.10
322 Chris Gardocki	.01	.05
323 Ken Norton	.02	.10
324 Eric Curry RC	.01	.05
325 Byron Evans	.01	.05
326 O.J. McDuffie RC	.08	.25
327 Dwight Stone	.01	.05
328 Tommy Barnhardt	.01	.05
329 Checklist 1-165	.01	.05
330 Checklist 166-329	.01	.05
331 Erik Williams	.01	.05
332 Phil Hansen	.01	.05
333 Martin Harrison RC	.01	.05
334 Mark Ingram	.01	.05
335 Mark Rypien	.02	.10
336 Anthony Miller	.02	.10
337 Antone Davis	.01	.05
338 Mike Munchak	.02	.10
339 Wayne Martin	.01	.05
340 Joe Montana	.60	1.50
341 Deon Figures RC	.01	.05
342 Ed McDaniel	.01	.05
343 Chris Burkett	.01	.05
344 Tony Smith	.01	.05
345 James Lofton	.02	.10
346 Courtney Hawkins	.01	.05
347 Dennis Smith	.01	.05
348 Anthony Morgan	.01	.05
349 Chris Goode	.01	.05
350 Phil Simms	.02	.10
351 Patrick Hunter	.01	.05
352 Brett Perriman	.08	.25
353 Corey Miller	.01	.05
354 Harry Galbreath	.01	.05
355 Mark Carrier WR	.02	.10
356 Troy Drayton	.02	.10
357 Greg Davis	.01	.05
358 Tim Krumrie	.01	.05
359 Tim McDonald	.01	.05
360 Webster Slaughter	.01	.05
361 Steve Christie	.01	.05
362 Courtney Hall	.01	.05
363 Charles Mann	.01	.05
364 Vestee Jackson	.01	.05
365 Robert Jones	.01	.05
366 Rich Miano	.01	.05
367 Morten Andersen	.02	.10
368 Jeff Graham	.02	.10
369 Martin Mayhew	.01	.05
370 Anthony Carter	.02	.10
371 Greg Kragen	.01	.05
372 Ron Cox	.01	.05
373 Perry Williams	.01	.05
374 Willie Gault	.02	.10
375 Chris Warren	.02	.10
376 Reyna Thompson	.01	.05
377 Bennie Thompson	.01	.05
378 Kevin Mack	.01	.05
379 Clarence Verdin	.01	.05
380 Marc Boutte	.01	.05
381 Marvin Jones RC	.01	.05
382 Greg Jackson	.01	.05
383 Steve Bono	.02	.10
384 Terrell Buckley	.01	.05
385 Garrison Hearst	.08	.25
386 Mike Brim	.01	.05
387 Jesse Sapolu	.01	.05
388 Carl Lee	.01	.05
389 Jeff Cross	.01	.05
390 Karl Mecklenburg	.02	.10
391 Chad Hennings	.01	.05
392 Oliver Barnett	.01	.05
393 Dalton Hilliard	.01	.05
394 Broderick Thompson	.01	.05
395 Rocket Ismail	.02	.10
396 John Kidd	.01	.05
397 Eddie Anderson	.01	.05
398 Lamar Lathon	.01	.05
399 Darren Perry	.01	.05
400 Drew Bledsoe	.50	1.25
401 Ferrell Edmunds	.01	.05
402 Lomas Brown	.01	.05
403 Drew Hill	.02	.10
404 David Whitmore	.01	.05
405 Mike Johnson	.01	.05
406 Paul Gruber	.01	.05
407 Kirk Lowdermilk	.01	.05
408 Curtis Conway	.08	.25
409 Bryce Paup	.02	.10
410 Boomer Esiason	.02	.10
411 Jay Schroeder	.01	.05
412 Anthony Newman	.01	.05
413 Ernie Jones	.01	.05
414 Carlton Bailey	.01	.05
415 Kenneth Gant	.01	.05
416 Todd Scott	.01	.05
417 Anthony Smith	.01	.05
418 Erik McMillan	.01	.05
419 Ronnie Harmon	.01	.05
420 Andre Reed	.02	.10
421 Wymon Henderson	.01	.05
422 Carnell Lake	.01	.05
423 Al Noga	.01	.05
424 Curtis Duncan	.01	.05
425 Mike Gann	.01	.05
426 Eugene Robinson	.02	.10
427 Scott Mersereau	.01	.05
428 Chris Singleton	.01	.05
429 Gerald Robinson	.01	.05
430 Pat Swilling	.02	.10
431 Ed McCaffrey	.08	.25
432 Neal Anderson	.02	.10
433 Joe Phillips	.01	.05
434 Jerry Ball	.01	.05
435 Tyronne Stowe	.01	.05
436 Dana Stubblefield	.08	.25
437 Eric Curry	.01	.05
438 Derrick Fenner	.01	.05
439 Mark Clayton	.02	.10
440 Quentin Coryatt	.02	.10
441 Willie Roaf RC	.02	.10
442 Ernest Dye	.01	.05
443 Jeff Jaeger	.01	.05
444 Stan Humphries	.02	.10
445 Johnny Johnson	.01	.05
446 Larry Brown DB	.01	.05
447 Kurt Gouveia	.01	.05
448 Qadry Ismail RC	.08	.25
449 Dan Footman	.01	.05
450 Tom Waddle	.01	.05
451 Kelvin Martin	.01	.05
452 Kanavis McGhee	.01	.05
453 Herman Moore	.08	.25
454 Jesse Solomon	.01	.05
455 Shane Conlan	.01	.05
456 Joel Steed	.01	.05
457 Charles Arbuckle	.01	.05
458 Shane Dronett	.01	.05
459 Steve Tasker	.02	.10
460 Herschel Walker	.02	.10
461 Willie Davis	.08	.25
462 Al Smith	.01	.05
463 O.J. McDuffie	.08	.25
464 Kevin Fagan	.01	.05
465 Hardy Nickerson	.02	.10
466 Leonard Marshall	.02	.10
467 John Baylor	.01	.05
468 Jay Novacek	.02	.10
469 Wayne Simmons RC	.01	.05
470 Tommy Vardell	.01	.05
471 Cleveland Gary	.01	.05
472 Mark Collins	.02	.10
473 Craig Heyward	.02	.10
474 John Copeland UER	.02	.10
(Bio states he was born 0-29-70		
instead of 9-29-70)		
475 Jeff Hostetler	.02	.10
476 Brian Mitchell	.02	.10
477 Natrone Means	.08	.25
478 Brad Muster	.01	.05
479 David Lutz	.01	.05
480 Andre Rison	.02	.10
481 Michael Zordich	.01	.05
482 Jim McMahon	.02	.10
483 Carlton Gray	.01	.05
484 Chris Mohr	.01	.05
485 Ernest Givins	.02	.10
486 Tony Tolbert	.01	.05
487 Vai Sikahema	.01	.05
488 Larry Webster	.01	.05
489 James Hasty	.01	.05
490 Reggie White	.08	.25
491 Reggie Rivers RC	.01	.05
492 Roman Phifer	.01	.05
493 Levon Kirkland	.01	.05
494 Demetrius DuBose	.01	.05
495 William Perry	.02	.10
496 Clay Matthews	.02	.10
497 Aaron Jones	.01	.05
498 Jack Trudeau	.01	.05
499 Michael Brooks	.01	.05
500 Jerry Rice	.40	1.00
501 Lonnie Marts	.01	.05
502 Tim McGee	.02	.10
503 Kelvin Pritchett	.01	.05
504 Bobby Hebert	.02	.10
505 Audray McMillian	.01	.05
506 Chuck Cecil	.01	.05
507 Leonard Renfro	.01	.05
508 Ethan Horton	.01	.05
509 Kevin Smith	.02	.10
510 Louis Oliver	.01	.05
511 John Stephens	.01	.05
512 Browning Nagle	.01	.05
513 Ricardo McDonald	.01	.05
514 Leslie O'Neal	.02	.10
515 Lorenzo White	.01	.05
516 Thomas Smith RC	.02	.10
517 Tony Woods	.01	.05
518 Darryl Henley	.01	.05
519 Robert Delpino	.01	.05
520 Rod Woodson	.08	.25
521 Phillippi Sparks	.01	.05
522 Jessie Hester	.01	.05
523 Shaun Gayle	.01	.05
524 Brad Edwards	.01	.05
525 Randall Cunningham	.08	.25
526 Marv Cook	.01	.05
527 Dennis Gibson	.01	.05
528 Erric Pegram	.02	.10
529 Terry McDaniel	.01	.05
530 Troy Aikman	.30	.75
531 Irving Fryar	.02	.10
532 Blair Thomas	.01	.05
533 Jim Wilks	.01	.05
534 Michael Jackson	.02	.10
535 Eric Davis	.01	.05
536 James Campen	.01	.05
537 Steve Beuerlein	.02	.10
538 Robert Smith	.20	.50
539 J.J. Birden	.01	.05
540 Broderick Thomas	.01	.05
541 Darryl Talley	.01	.05
542 Russell Freeman RC	.01	.05
543 David Alexander	.01	.05
544 Chris Mims	.01	.05
545 Coleman Rudolph	.01	.05
546 Steve McMichael	.02	.10
547 David Williams	.01	.05
548 Chris Hinton	.01	.05
549 Jim Jeffcoat	.01	.05
550 Howie Long	.08	.25
551 Roosevelt Potts RC	.01	.05
552 Bryan Cox	.01	.05
553 David Richards UER	.01	.05
(Photo on front is Stanley Richards)		
554 Reggie Brooks	.02	.10
555 Neil O'Donnell	.08	.25
556 Irv Smith RC	.01	.05
557 Henry Ellard	.02	.10
558 Steve DeBerg	.02	.10
559 Jim Sweeney	.01	.05
560 Harold Green	.01	.05
561 Darrell Thompson	.01	.05
562 Vinny Testaverde	.02	.10
563 Bubby Brister	.01	.05
564 Sean Landeta	.02	.10
565 Neil Smith	.08	.25
566 Craig Erickson	.02	.10
567 Jim Ritcher	.01	.05
568 Don Mosebar	.01	.05
569 John Gesek	.01	.05
570 Gary Plummer	.01	.05
571 Norm Johnson	.01	.05
572 Ron Heller	.01	.05
573 Carl Simpson	.01	.05
574 Greg Montgomery	.01	.05
575 Dana Hall	.01	.05
576 Vencie Glenn	.01	.05
577 Dean Biasucci	.01	.05
578 Rod Bernstine UER	.01	.05
(Name spelled Bernstein on front)		
579 Randal Hill	.01	.05
580 Sam Mills	.02	.10
581 Santana Dotson	.02	.10
582 Greg Lloyd	.02	.10
583 Eric Thomas	.01	.05
584 Henry Rolling	.01	.05
585 Tony Bennett	.01	.05
586 Sheldon White	.01	.05
587 Mark Kelso	.02	.10
588 Marc Spindler	.01	.05
589 Greg McMurtry	.01	.05
590 Art Monk	.02	.10
591 Marco Coleman	.01	.05
592 Tony Jones	.01	.05
593 Melvin Jenkins	.01	.05
594 Kevin Ross	.01	.05
595 William Fuller	.01	.05
596 James Joseph	.01	.05
597 Lamar McGriggs RC	.01	.05
598 Gill Byrd	.01	.05
599 Alexander Wright	.01	.05
600 Rick Mirer	.08	.25
601 Richard Dent	.02	.10
602 Thomas Everett	.01	.05
603 Jack Del Rio	.02	.10
604 Jerome Bettis	1.00	2.50
605 Ronnie Lott	.02	.10
606 Marty Carter	.01	.05
607 Arthur Marshall RC	.01	.05
608 Lee Johnson	.01	.05
609 Bruce Armstrong	.01	.05
610 Ricky Proehl	.02	.10
611 Will Wolford	.01	.05
612 Mike Prior	.01	.05
613 George Jamison	.01	.05
614 Gene Atkins	.01	.05
615 Merril Hoge	.02	.10
616 Desmond Howard UER	.02	.10
(Stats indicate 8 TD's receiving;		
he had 0)		
617 Jarvis Williams	.01	.05
618 Marcus Allen	.08	.25
619 Gary Brown	.01	.05
620 Bill Brooks	.01	.05
621 Eric Allen	.01	.05
622 Todd Kelly	.01	.05
623 Michael Dean Perry	.02	.10
624 David Braxton	.01	.05
625 Mike Sherrard	.01	.05
626 Jeff Bryant	.01	.05
627 Eric Bieniemy	.01	.05
628 Tim Brown	.08	.25
629 Troy Auzenne	.01	.05
630 Michael Irvin	.08	.25
631 Maurice Hurst	.01	.05
632 Duane Bickett	.01	.05
633 George Teague	.02	.10
634 Vince Workman	.01	.05
635 Renaldo Turnbull	.01	.05
636 Johnny Bailey	.01	.05
637 Dan Williams RC	.01	.05
638 James Thornton	.01	.05
639 Terry Allen	.08	.25
640 Kevin Greene	.02	.10
641 Tony Zendejas	.01	.05
642 Scott Kowalkowski RC	.01	.05
643 Jeff Query UER	.01	.05
(Text states he played for Packers		
in '92; he played for Bengals)		
644 Brian Blades	.02	.10
645 Keith Jackson	.02	.10
646 Monte Coleman	.01	.05
647 Guy McIntyre	.01	.05
648 Barry Word	.01	.05
649 Steve Everitt RC	.01	.05
650 Patrick Bates	.01	.05
651 Marcus Robertson RC	.01	.05
652 John Carney	.01	.05
653 Derek Brown TE	.01	.05
654 Carwell Gardner	.01	.05
655 Moe Gardner	.01	.05
656 Andre Ware	.02	.10
657 Keith Van Horne	.01	.05
658 Hugh Millen	.01	.05
659 Checklist 330-495	.01	.05
660 Checklist 496-660	.01	.05

1993 Topps Gold

*GOLD STARS: 1.5X TO 4X BASIC CARDS
*GOLD RCs: 1X TO 2.5X BASIC CARDS
ONE PER PACK

329 Terance Mathis	.40	1.00
330 John Wojciechowski	.20	.50
659 Pat Chaffey	.20	.50
660 Milton Mack	.20	.50

1993 Topps Black Gold

COMPLETE SET (44)	12.50	30.00
COMP.SERIES 1 SET (22)	5.00	12.00
COMP.SERIES 2 SET (22)	8.00	18.00
STATED ODDS 1:72H/R, 1:14JUM, 1:24RAK		
1 Kelvin Martin	.05	.15
2 Audray McMillian	.05	.15
3 Terry Allen	.30	.75
4 Vai Sikahema	.05	.15
5 Clyde Simmons	.05	.15
6 Lorenzo White	.05	.15
7 Michael Irvin	.30	.75
8 Troy Aikman	1.25	2.50
9 Mark Kelso	.05	.15
10 Cleveland Gary	.05	.15
11 Greg Montgomery	.05	.15
12 Jerry Rice	1.50	3.00
13 Rod Woodson	.30	.75
14 Leslie O'Neal	.10	.30
15 Harold Green	.05	.15
16 Randall Cunningham	.30	.75
17 Ricky Watters	.30	.75
18 Andre Rison	.10	.30
19 Eugene Robinson	.05	.15
20 Wayne Martin	.05	.15
21 Chris Warren	.10	.30
22 Anthony Miller	.10	.30
23 Steve Young	1.25	2.50
24 Tim Harris	.05	.15
25 Emmitt Smith	2.50	5.00
26 Sterling Sharpe	.30	.75
27 Henry Jones	.05	.15
28 Warren Moon	.30	.75
29 Barry Foster	.10	.30
30 Dale Carter	.05	.15
31 Mel Gray	.10	.30
32 Barry Sanders	2.00	4.00
33 Dan Marino	2.50	5.00
34 Fred Barnett	.10	.30
35 Deion Sanders	.75	1.50
36 Simon Fletcher	.05	.15
37 Donnell Woolford	.05	.15
38 Reggie Cobb	.05	.15
39 Brett Favre	3.00	6.00
40 Thurman Thomas	.30	.75
41 Rodney Hampton	.10	.30
42 Eric Martin	.05	.15
43 Pete Stoyanovich	.05	.15
44 Herschel Walker	.10	.30
A1 Winner A 1-11 EXCH Exp.	.40	1.00
B Winner B 12-22 EXCH Exp. UER	.40	1.00
(17 incorrectly Herschel Walker		
instead of Ricky Watters)		
C Winner C 23-33 EXCH Exp.	.40	1.00
D Winner D 34-44 EXCH Exp.	.40	1.00
AB Winner AB 1-22 EXCH Exp.	.60	1.50
CD Winner CD 23-44 EXCH Exp.	.60	1.50

1993 Topps FantaSports

This was the first interactive fantasy sports game that incorporated single player trading cards as a key playing element. The set included 200 cards with each produced with a black border and gold foil highlights. The card backs carried graphs of the players' three-year performances on all FantaSports criteria, comparisons with other players in that position, and scouting reports. The cards were issued in set form to contestants who paid the $159 entry fee. Included were the cards, entry into the league, stat book, worksheets, and instructions. The person who earned the best 18-game NFL fantasy score won four tickets to Super Bowl XXVIII. The game was test-marketed in four cities (Houston, Kansas City, Buffalo, and Washington D.C.) and the cards were not offered at retail in those cities. The cards are numbered on the back arranged by position, quarterbacks (1-30), running backs (31-89), wide receivers (90-137), tight ends (138-150), kickers (151-162), punters (163-172), and defensive players (173-200).

COMPLETE SET (200)	100.00	200.00
1 Chris Miller	.30	.75
2 Jim Kelly	.40	1.00
3 Jim Harbaugh	.30	.75
4 David Klingler	.30	.75
5 Bernie Kosar	.30	.75
6 Troy Aikman	6.00	15.00
7 John Elway	10.00	25.00
8 Tommy Maddox	.40	1.00
9 Rodney Peete	.30	.75
10 Andre Ware	.20	.50
11 Brett Favre	10.00	25.00
12 Warren Moon	.40	1.00
13 Jeff George	.40	1.00
14 Dave Krieg	.30	.75
15 Joe Montana	15.00	30.00
16 Todd Marinovich	.20	.50
17 Jim Everett	.30	.75
18 Dan Marino	10.00	25.00
19 Sean Salisbury	.20	.50
20 Drew Bledsoe	4.00	10.00
21 Dave Brown	.30	.75
22 Phil Simms	.30	.75
23 Boomer Esiason	.30	.75
24 Browning Nagle	.20	.50
25 Randall Cunningham	.40	1.00
26 Neil O'Donnell	.30	.75
27 Stan Humphries	.30	.75
28 Steve Young	4.80	12.00
29 Rick Mirer	.40	1.00
30 Mark Rypien	.30	.75
31 Kenneth Davis	.20	.50
32 Thurman Thomas	.80	2.00
33 Steve Broussard	.20	.50
34 Neal Anderson	.30	.75
35 Craig Heyward	.20	.50
36 Derrick Fenner	.20	.50
37 Harold Green	.20	.50
38 Leroy Hoard	.20	.50
39 Kevin Mack	.20	.50
40 Eric Metcalf	.30	.75
41 Tommy Vardell	.20	.50
42 Daryl Johnston	.30	.75
43 Emmitt Smith	10.00	25.00
44 Barry Sanders	8.00	20.00
45 Edgar Bennett	.40	1.00
46 Lorenzo White	.30	.75
47 Anthony Johnson	.30	.75
48 Todd McNair	.20	.50
49 Christian Okoye	.20	.50
50 Harvey Williams	.30	.75
51 Barry Word	.20	.50
52 Nick Bell	.20	.50
53 Eric Dickerson	.30	.75
54 Jerome Bettis	4.00	10.00
55 Cleveland Gary	.20	.50
56 Mark Higgs	.20	.50
57 Tony Paige	.20	.50
58 Terry Allen	.30	.75
59 Roger Craig	.30	.75
60 Robert Smith	.40	1.00
61 Leonard Russell	.30	.75
62 Jon Vaughn	.20	.50
63 Vaughn Dunbar	.20	.50
64 Dalton Hilliard	.20	.50
65 Jarrod Bunch	.20	.50
66 Rodney Hampton	.30	.75
67 Dave Meggett	.30	.75
68 Brad Baxter	.20	.50
69 Heath Sherman	.20	.50
70 Vai Sikahema	.20	.50
71 Johnny Bailey	.20	.50
72 Larry Centers	.30	.75
73 Garrison Hearst	2.40	6.00
74 Barry Foster	.30	.75
75 Eric Bieniemy	.20	.50
76 Marion Butts	.20	.50
77 Ronnie Harmon	.20	.50
78 Natrone Means	.30	.75
79 Amp Lee	.20	.50
80 Tom Rathman	.20	.50
81 Ricky Watters	.30	.75
82 Chris Warren	.30	.75
83 John L. Williams	.20	.50
84 Gary Anderson RB	.20	.50
85 Reggie Cobb	.20	.50
86 Vince Workman	.20	.50
87 Reggie Brooks	.30	.75
88 Earnest Byner	.20	.50
89 Ricky Ervins	.20	.50
90 Michael Haynes	.30	.75
91 Mike Pritchard	.30	.75
92 Andre Rison	.30	.75
93 Don Beebe	.20	.50
94 Andre Reed	.30	.75
95 Curtis Conway	.30	.75
96 Wendell Davis	.20	.50
97 Tom Waddle	.20	.50
98 Carl Pickens	.30	.75
99 Michael Jackson	.30	.75
100 Alvin Harper	.20	.50
101 Michael Irvin	1.20	3.00
102 Vance Johnson	.20	.50
103 Mel Gray	.20	.50
104 Sterling Sharpe	.30	.75
105 Curtis Duncan	.20	.50
106 Ernest Givins	.30	.75
107 Haywood Jeffires	.30	.75
108 Tim Brown	1.60	4.00
109 Willie Gault	.20	.50
110 Flipper Anderson	.20	.50
111 Henry Ellard	.30	.75
112 Mark Duper	.30	.75
113 O.J. McDuffie	.40	1.00
114 Anthony Carter	.30	.75
115 Cris Carter	2.40	6.00
116 Mike Farr	.20	.50
117 Quinn Early	.30	.75
118 Eric Martin	.20	.50
119 Chris Calloway	.20	.50
120 Mark Jackson	.20	.50
121 Rob Moore	.30	.75
122 Fred Barnett	.30	.75
123 Calvin Williams	.30	.75
124 Gary Clark	.30	.75
125 Randal Hill	.20	.50
126 Ricky Proehl	.20	.50
127 Jeff Graham	.30	.75
128 Ernie Mills	.30	.75
129 Dwight Stone	.20	.50
130 Nate Lewis	.20	.50
131 Jerry Rice	6.00	15.00
132 John Taylor	.30	.75
133 Tommy Kane	.20	.50
134 Kelvin Martin	.20	.50
135 Lawrence Dawsey	.30	.75
136 Courtney Hawkins	.30	.75
137 Art Monk	.30	.75
138 Pete Metzelaars	.20	.50
139 Jay Novacek	.30	.75
140 Reggie Johnson	.20	.50
141 Shannon Sharpe	.30	.75
142 Jackie Harris	.20	.50
143 Troy Drayton	.30	.75
144 Keith Jackson	.30	.75
145 Steve Jordan	.20	.50
146 Johnny Mitchell	.20	.50
147 Eric Green	.30	.75
148 Derrick Walker	.20	.50
149 Brent Jones	.30	.75
150 Ron Hall	.20	.50
151 Norm Johnson	.20	.50
152 Jim Breech	.20	.50
153 Matt Stover	.20	.50
154 Lin Elliott	.20	.50
155 Jason Hanson	.20	.50
156 Chris Jacke	.20	.50
157 Nick Lowery	.20	.50
158 Pete Stoyanovich	.20	.50
159 Roger Ruzek	.20	.50
160 Gary Anderson K	.20	.50
161 John Kasay	.20	.50
162 Chip Lohmiller	.20	.50
163 Chris Gardocki	.20	.50
164 Mike Saxon	.20	.50
165 Jim Arnold	.20	.50
166 Rohn Stark	.20	.50
167 Jeff Gossett	.20	.50
168 Reggie Roby	.20	.50
169 Harry Newsome	.20	.50
170 Tommy Barnhardt	.20	.50
171 Jeff Feagles	.20	.50
172 Rich Camarillo	.20	.50
173 Deion Sanders	4.00	10.00
Falcons Defense		
174 Cornelius Bennett	.30	.75
Bills Defense		
175 Mark Carrier DB	.30	.75
Bears Defense		
176 Darryl Williams	.20	.50
Bengals Defense		
177 Michael Dean Perry	.30	.75
Browns Defense		
178 Russell Maryland	.30	.75
Cowboys Defense		
179 Steve Atwater	.20	.50
Broncos Defense		
180 Bennie Blades	.20	.50
Lions Defense		
181 Reggie White	.40	1.00
Packers Defense		
182 Cris Dishman	.20	.50
Oilers Defense		
183 Steve Emtman	.20	.50
Colts Defense		
184 Derrick Thomas	.40	1.00
Chiefs Defense		
185 Howie Long	.40	1.00
Raiders Defense		
186 Sean Gilbert	.30	.75
Rams Defense		
187 John Offerdahl	.20	.50
Dolphins Defense		
188 Chris Doleman	.20	.50
Vikings Defense		
189 Andre Tippett	.20	.50
Patriots Defense		
190 Sam Mills	.20	.50
Saints Defense		
191 Lawrence Taylor	.30	.75
Giants Defense		
192 James Hasty	.20	.50
Jets Defense		
193 Clyde Simmons	.20	.50
Eagles Defense		
194 Eric Swann	.30	.75
Cardinals Defense		
195 Greg Lloyd	.20	.50
Steelers Defense		
196 Junior Seau	.40	1.00
Chargers Defense		
197 Kevin Fagan/49ers Defense	.20	.50
198 Cortez Kennedy	.30	.75
Seahawks Defense		
199 Broderick Thomas	.20	.50
Buccaneers Defense		
200 Darrell Green	.30	.75
Redskins Defense		

1993 Topps FantaSports Winners

Collectors who won weekly prizes in the Topps fantasy football league received one of these cards. The fantasy player whose team won a region for the year received a complete set. Reportedly, only 50-sets were produced. On a black card face with gray streaks radiating from the bottom, the front shows a color action player photo. The player's name is printed above the picture and "Fantastars '93" is printed vertically in the left border. The horizontal backs display week-by-week statistics, career highlights, and a second color action photo. The unnumbered cards are listed alphabetically below.

1 Boomer Esiason	35.00	60.00
2 Houston Oilers	25.00	40.00
3 Andre Rison	30.00	50.00
4 Jason Hanson	25.00	40.00
5 Troy Aikman	90.00	150.00
6 John Elway	125.00	200.00
7 Michael Irvin	35.00	60.00
8 Thurman Thomas	35.00	60.00
9 Emmitt Smith	150.00	250.00
10 Pittsburgh Steelers	30.00	50.00
11 Jerry Rice	90.00	150.00
12 Eric Green	25.00	40.00
13 Steve Young	75.00	125.00
14 Sterling Sharpe	30.00	50.00
14 Harold Alexander	25.00	40.00
15 Johnny Johnson	25.00	40.00
15 Shannon Sharpe	30.00	50.00
16 Jerome Bettis	35.00	60.00

1994 Topps

The 1994 Topps football set consists of 660 standard-size cards issued in two series of 330. Subsets include League Leaders (116-120), Tools of the Game (196-205/542-556), Career Active Leaders (272-275/470-476) and Measure of Greatness (316-319/611-615). Rookie Cards include Trent Dilfer, Bert Emanuel, Marshall Faulk, William Floyd, Greg Hill, Charles Johnson, Willie McGinest, Errict Rhett, Darnay Scott, Heath Shuler and Bryant Young. A nine-card promo sheet was produced to promote the set as was a three-card Special Effects promo sheet.

COMPLETE SET (660)	50.00	100.00
COMP.SERIES 1 (330)	20.00	50.00
COMP.SERIES 2 (330)	20.00	50.00
1 Emmitt Smith	.60	1.50
2 Russell Copeland	.01	.05
3 Jesse Sapolu	.01	.05
4 David Szott	.01	.05
5 Rodney Hampton	.02	.10
6 Bubba McDowell	.01	.05
7 Bryce Paup	.02	.10
8 Winston Moss	.01	.05
9 Brett Perriman	.02	.10
10 Rod Woodson	.02	.10
11 John Randle	.02	.10
12 David Wyman	.01	.05
13 Jeff Cross	.01	.05
14 Richard Cooper	.01	.05
15 Johnny Mitchell	.01	.05
16 David Alexander	.01	.05
17 Ronnie Harmon	.01	.05
18 Tyronne Stowe UER	.01	.05
Tyrone on both sides		
19 Chris Zorich	.01	.05
20 Rob Burnett	.01	.05
21 Harold Alexander	.01	.05
22 Rod Stephens	.01	.05
23 Mark Wheeler	.01	.05
24 Dwayne Sabb	.01	.05

1993 Topps Gold

25 Troy Drayton .01 .05
26 Kurt Gouveia .01 .05
27 Warren Moon .08 .25
28 Jeff Query .01 .05
29 Chuck Levy RC .01 .05
30 Bruce Smith .08 .25
31 Doug Riesenberg .01 .05
32 Willie Drewrey .01 .05
33 Nate Newton UER .01 .05
(Listed as Defensive End; should be guard)
34 James Jett .01 .05
35 George Teague .01 .05
36 Marc Spindler .01 .05
37 Jack Del Rio .01 .05
38 Dale Carter .01 .05
39 Steve Atwater .01 .05
40 Herschel Walker .02 .10
41 James Hasty .01 .05
42 Seth Joyner .01 .05
43 Keith Jackson .01 .05
44 Tommy Vardell .01 .05
45 Antonio Langham RC .02 .10
46 Derek Brown RBK .01 .05
47 John Wojciechowski .01 .05
48 Horace Copeland .01 .05
49 Luis Sharpe .01 .05
50 Pat Harlow .01 .05
51 David Palmer RC .08 .25
52 Tony Smith .01 .05
53 Tim Johnson .01 .05
54 Anthony Newman .01 .05
55 Terry Wooden .01 .05
56 Derrick Fenner .01 .05
57 Mike Fox .01 .05
58 Brad Hopkins .01 .05
59 Daryl Johnston UER .02 .10
(Johnson on front)
60 Steve Young .30 .75
61 Scottie Graham RC .02 .10
62 Nolan Harrison .01 .05
63 David Richards .01 .05
64 Chris Mohr .01 .05
65 Hardy Nickerson .02 .10
66 Heath Sherman .01 .05
67 Irving Fryar .02 .10
68 Ray Buchanan UER .01 .05
(Buchannan on front)
69 Jay Taylor .01 .05
70 Shannon Sharpe .02 .10
71 Vinny Testaverde .02 .10
72 Renaldo Turnbull .01 .05
73 Dwight Stone .01 .05
74 Willie McGinest RC .08 .25
75 Darrell Green .01 .05
76 Kyle Clifton .01 .05
77 Leo Goeas .01 .05
78 Ken Ruettgers .01 .05
79 Craig Heyward .02 .10
80 Andre Rison .02 .10
81 Chris Mims .01 .05
82 Gary Clark .02 .10
83 Ricardo McDonald .01 .05
84 Patrick Hunter .01 .05
85 Bruce Matthews .01 .05
86 Russell Maryland .01 .05
87 Gary Anderson K .01 .05
88 Brad Edwards .01 .05
89 Carlton Bailey .01 .05
90 Qadry Ismail .08 .25
91 Terry McDaniel .01 .05
92 Willie Green .01 .05
93 Cornelius Bennett .02 .10
94 Paul Gruber .01 .05
95 Pete Stoyanovich .01 .05
96 Merton Hanks .02 .10
97 Tre Johnson RC .01 .05
98 Jonathan Hayes .01 .05
99 Jason Elam .02 .10
100 Jerome Bettis .20 .50
101 Ronnie Lott .02 .10
102 Maurice Hurst .01 .05
103 Kirk Lowdermilk .01 .05
104 Tony Jones .01 .05
105 Steve Beuerlein .02 .10
106 Isaac Davis RC .01 .05
107 Vaughan Johnson .01 .05
108 Terrell Buckley .01 .05
109 Pierce Holt .01 .05
110 Alonzo Spellman .01 .05
111 Patrick Robinson .01 .05
112 Cortez Kennedy .02 .10
113 Kevin Williams .02 .10
114 Danny Copeland .01 .05
115 Chris Doleman .01 .05
116 Jerry Rice LL .20 .50
117 Neil Smith LL .02 .10
118 Emmitt Smith LL .30 .75
119 Eugene Robinson LL .01 .05
Nate Odomes
120 Steve Young LL .08 .25
121 Carnell Lake .01 .05
122 Ernest Givins UER .02 .10
(Givens on front)
123 Henry Jones .01 .05
124 Michael Brooks .01 .05
125 Jason Hanson .01 .05
126 Andy Harmon .01 .05
127 Errict Rhett RC .08 .25
128 Harris Barton .01 .05
129 Greg Robinson .01 .05
130 Derrick Thomas .08 .25
131 Keith Kartz .01 .05
132 Lincoln Kennedy .01 .05
133 Leslie O'Neal .01 .05
134 Tim Goad .01 .05
135 Rohn Stark .01 .05
136 O.J. McDuffie .08 .25
137 Donnell Woolford .01 .05
138 Jamir Miller RC .02 .10
139 Eric Thomas UER .01 .05
(Listed as tight end; he is a cornerback)
140 Willie Roaf .01 .05
141 Wayne Gandy RC .01 .05
142 Mike Brim .01 .05
143 Kelvin Martin .01 .05
144 Edgar Bennett .08 .25
145 Michael Dean Perry .02 .10
146 Shante Carver RC .01 .05
147 Jessie Armstead UER .01 .05
(Jesse on both sides)
148 Mo Elewonibi .01 .05
149 Dana Stubblefield .02 .10
150 Cody Carlson .01 .05
151 Vencie Glenn .01 .05
152 Levon Kirkland .01 .05
153 Derrick Moore .01 .05
154 John Fina .01 .05
155 Jeff Hostetler .02 .10
156 Courtney Hawkins .01 .05
157 Todd Collins .01 .05
158 Neil Smith .02 .10
159 Simon Fletcher .01 .05
160 Dan Marino .75 2.00
161 Sam Adams RC .02 .10
162 Marvin Washington .01 .05
163 John Copeland .01 .05
164 Eugene Robinson .01 .05
165 Mark Carrier DB .01 .05
166 Mike Kenn .01 .05
167 Tyrone Hughes .02 .10
168 Darren Carrington .01 .05
169 Shane Conlan .01 .05
170 Ricky Proehl .01 .05
171 Jeff Herrod .01 .05
172 Mark Carrier WR .02 .10
173 George Koonce .01 .05
174 Desmond Howard .02 .10
175 Dave Meggett .01 .05
176 Charles Haley .02 .10
177 Steve Wisniewski .01 .05
178 Dermontti Dawson .01 .05
179 Tim McDonald .01 .05
180 Broderick Thomas .01 .05
181 Bernard Dafney .01 .05
182 Bo Orlando .01 .05
183 Andre Reed .02 .10
184 Randall Cunningham .08 .25
185 Chris Spielman .02 .10
186 Keith Byars .01 .05
187 Ben Coates .02 .10
188 Tracy Simien .01 .05
189 Carl Pickens .02 .10
190 Reggie White .08 .25
191 Norm Johnson .01 .05
192 Brian Washington .01 .05
193 Stan Humphries .02 .10
194 Fred Stokes .01 .05
195 Dan Williams .01 .05
196 John Elway TOG .30 .75
197 Eric Allen TOG .01 .05
198 Hardy Nickerson TOG .02 .10
199 Jerome Bettis TOG .08 .25
200 Troy Aikman TOG .20 .50
201 Thurman Thomas TOG .08 .25
202 Cornelius Bennett TOG UER .02 .10
(card is numbered #450)
203 Michael Irvin TOG .02 .10
204 Jim Kelly TOG .02 .10
205 Junior Seau TOG .02 .10
206 Heath Shuler RC UER .08 .25
(Rifle spelled rife on back)
207 Howard Cross UER .01 .05
(Listed as linebacker; he plays tight end)
208 Pat Swilling .01 .05
209 Pete Metzelaars .01 .05
210 Tony McGee .01 .05
211 Neil O'Donnell .08 .25
212 Eugene Chung .01 .05
213 J.B. Brown .01 .05
214 Marcus Allen .08 .25
215 Harry Newsome .01 .05
216 Greg Hill RC .08 .25
217 Ryan Yarborough .01 .05
218 Marty Carter .01 .05
219 Bern Brostek .01 .05
220 Boomer Esiason .02 .10
221 Vince Buck .01 .05
222 Jim Jeffcoat .01 .05
223 Bob Dahl .01 .05
224 Marion Butts .01 .05
225 Ronald Moore .01 .05
226 Robert Blackmon .01 .05
227 Curtis Conway .08 .25
228 Jon Hand .01 .05
229 Shane Dronett .01 .05
230 Erik Williams UER .01 .05
(Misspelled Eric on front)
231 Dennis Brown .01 .05
232 Ray Childress .01 .05
233 Johnnie Morton RC .20 .50
234 Kent Hull .01 .05
235 John Elliott .01 .05
236 Ron Heller .01 .05
237 J.J. Birden .01 .05
238 Thomas Randolph RC .01 .05
239 Chip Lohmiller .01 .05
240 Tim Brown .08 .25
241 Steve Tovar .01 .05
242 Moe Gardner .01 .05
243 Vincent Brown .01 .05
244 Tony Zendejas .01 .05
245 Eric Allen .01 .05
246 Joe King RC .01 .05
247 Mo Lewis .01 .05
248 Rod Bernstine .01 .05
249 Tom Waddle .01 .05
250 Junior Seau .08 .25
251 Eric Metcalf .02 .10
252 Cris Carter .20 .50
253 Bill Hitchcock .01 .05
254 Zefross Moss .01 .05
255 Morten Andersen .01 .05
256 Keith Rucker RC .01 .05
257 Chris Jacke .01 .05
258 Richmond Webb .01 .05
259 Herman Moore .08 .25
260 Phil Simms .02 .10
261 Mark Tuinei .01 .05
262 Don Beebe .01 .05
263 Marc Logan .01 .05
264 Willie Davis .02 .10
265 David Klingler .01 .05
266 Martin Mayhew UER .01 .05
(Listed as wide receiver; he is a cornerback)
267 Mark Bavaro .01 .05
268 Greg Lloyd .02 .10
269 Al Del Greco .01 .05
270 Reggie Brooks .02 .10
271 Greg Townsend .01 .05
272 Rohn Stark CAL .01 .05
273 Marcus Allen CAL .02 .10
274 Ronnie Lott CAL .02 .10
275 Dan Marino CAL .30 .75
276 Sean Gilbert .01 .05
277 LeRoy Butler .01 .05
278 Troy Auzenne .01 .05
279 Eric Swann .02 .10
280 Quentin Coryatt .01 .05
281 Anthony Pleasant .01 .05
282 Brad Baxter .01 .05
283 Carl Lee .01 .05
284 Courtney Hall .01 .05
285 Quinn Early .01 .05
286 Eddie Robinson .01 .05
287 Marco Coleman .01 .05
288 Harold Green .01 .05
289 Santana Dotson .01 .05
290 Robert Porcher .01 .05
291 Joe Phillips .01 .05
292 Mark McMillian .01 .05
293 Eric Davis .01 .05
294 Mark Jackson .01 .05
295 Darryl Talley .01 .05
296 Curtis Duncan .01 .05
297 Bruce Armstrong .01 .05
298 Eric Hill .01 .05
299 Andre Collins .01 .05
300 Jay Novacek .02 .10
301 Roosevelt Potts .01 .05
302 Eric Martin .01 .05
303 Chris Warren .02 .10
304 Deral Boykin RC .01 .05
305 Jessie Tuggle .01 .05
306 Glyn Milburn .02 .10
307 Terry Obee .01 .05
308 Eric Turner .01 .05
309 Dewayne Washington RC .02 .10
310 Sterling Sharpe .02 .10
311 Jeff Gossett .01 .05
312 John Carney .01 .05
313 Aaron Glenn RC .08 .25
314 Nick Lowery .01 .05
315 Thurman Thomas .08 .25
316 Troy Aikman MG .20 .50
317 Thurman Thomas MG .02 .10
318 Michael Irvin MG .02 .10
319 Steve Beuerlein MG .02 .10
320 Jerry Rice .40 1.00
321 Alexander Wright .01 .05
322 Michael Bates .01 .05
323 Greg Davis .01 .05
324 Mark Bortz .01 .05
325 Kevin Greene .02 .10
326 Wayne Simmons .01 .05
327 Wayne Martin .01 .05
328 Michael Irvin UER .08 .25
(Stats on back have three career touchdowns; should be 34)
329 Checklist Card .01 .05
330 Checklist Card .01 .05
331 Doug Pelfrey .01 .05
332 Myron Guyton .01 .05
333 Howard Ballard .01 .05
334 Ricky Ervins .01 .05
335 Steve Emtman .01 .05
336 Eric Curry .01 .05
337 Bert Emanuel RC .08 .25
338 Darryl Ashmore .01 .05
339 Stevon Moore .01 .05
340 Garrison Hearst .08 .25
341 Vance Johnson .01 .05
342 Anthony Johnson .02 .10
343 Merril Hoge .01 .05
344 William Thomas .01 .05
345 Scott Mitchell .02 .10
346 Jim Everett .02 .10
347 Ray Crockett .01 .05
348 Bryan Cox .01 .05
349 Charles Johnson RC .08 .25
350 Randall McDaniel .01 .05
351 Micheal Barrow .01 .05
352 Darrell Thompson .01 .05
353 Kevin Gogan .01 .05
354 Brad Daluiso .01 .05
355 Mark Collins .01 .05
356 Bryant Young RC .15 .40
357 Steve Christie .01 .05
358 Derek Kennard .01 .05
359 Jon Vaughn .01 .05
360 Drew Bledsoe .30 .75
361 Randy Baldwin .01 .05
362 Kevin Ross .01 .05
363 Reuben Davis .01 .05
364 Chris Miller .01 .05
365 Tim McGee .01 .05
366 Tony Woods .01 .05
367 Dean Biasucci .01 .05
368 George Jamison .01 .05
369 Lorenzo Lynch .01 .05
370 Johnny Johnson .01 .05
371 Greg Kragen .01 .05
372 Vinson Smith .01 .05
373 Vince Workman .01 .05
374 Allen Aldridge .01 .05
375 Terry Kirby .08 .25
376 Mario Bates RC .08 .25
377 Dixon Edwards .01 .05
378 Leon Searcy .01 .05
379 Eric Guilford RC .01 .05
380 Gary Brown .01 .05
381 Phil Hansen .01 .05
382 Keith Hamilton .01 .05
383 John Alt .01 .05
384 John Taylor .02 .10
385 Reggie Cobb .01 .05
386 Rob Fredrickson RC .02 .10
387 Pepper Johnson .01 .05
388 Kevin Lee RC .01 .05
389 Stanley Richard .01 .05
390 Jackie Slater .01 .05
391 Derrick Brilz .01 .05
392 John Gesek .01 .05
393 Kelvin Pritchett .01 .05
394 Aeneas Williams .01 .05
395 Henry Ford .01 .05
396 Eric Mahlum .01 .05
397 Tom Rouen .01 .05
398 Vinnie Clark .01 .05
399 Jim Sweeney .01 .05
400 Troy Aikman UER .40 1.00
Threw for 56 TD's in 1993
401 Toi Cook .01 .05
402 Dan Saleaumua .01 .05
403 Andy Heck .01 .05
404 Deon Figures .01 .05
405 Henry Thomas .01 .05
406 Glenn Montgomery .01 .05
407 Trent Dilfer RC .40 1.00
408 Eddie Murray .01 .05
409 Gene Atkins .01 .05
410 Mike Sherrard .01 .05
411 Don Mosebar .01 .05
412 Thomas Smith .01 .05
413 Ken Norton Jr. .02 .10
414 Robert Brooks .08 .25
415 Jeff Lageman .01 .05
416 Tony Siragusa .01 .05
417 Brian Blades .02 .10
418 Matt Stover .01 .05
419 Jesse Solomon .01 .05
420 Reggie Roby .01 .05
421 Shawn Jefferson .01 .05
422 Marc Boutte .01 .05
423 William White .01 .05
424 Clyde Simmons .01 .05
425 Anthony Miller .02 .10
426 Brent Jones .02 .10
427 Tim Grunhard .01 .05
428 Alfred Williams .01 .05
429 Roy Barker RC .01 .05
430 Dante Jones .01 .05
431 Leroy Thompson .01 .05
432 Marcus Robertson .01 .05
433 Thomas Lewis RC .02 .10
434 Sean Jones .01 .05
435 Michael Haynes .02 .10
436 Albert Lewis .01 .05
437 Tim Bowens RC .02 .10
438 Marcus Patton .01 .05
439 Rich Miano .01 .05
440 Craig Erickson .01 .05
441 Larry Allen RC .08 .25
442 Fernando Smith .01 .05
443 D.J. Johnson .01 .05
444 Leonard Russell .01 .05
445 Marshall Faulk RC 2.00 5.00
446 Najee Mustafaa .01 .05
447 Brian Hansen .01 .05
448 Isaac Bruce RC 2.00 4.00
449 Kevin Scott .01 .05
450 Natrone Means .08 .25
451 Tracy Rogers RC .01 .05
452 Mike Croel .01 .05
453 Anthony Edwards .01 .05
454 Brenston Buckner RC .01 .05
455 Tom Carter .01 .05
456 Burt Grossman .01 .05
457 Jimmy Spencer RC .01 .05
458 Rocket Ismail .02 .10
459 Fred Strickland .01 .05
460 Jeff Burris RC .02 .10
461 Adrian Hardy .01 .05
462 Lamar McGriggs .01 .05
463 Webster Slaughter .01 .05
464 Demetrius DuBose .01 .05
465 Dave Brown .02 .10
466 Kenneth Gant .01 .05
467 Erik Kramer .02 .10
468 Mark Ingram .01 .05
469 Roman Phifer .01 .05
470 Steve Young .20 .50
471 Nick Lowery .01 .05
472 Irving Fryar .02 .10
473 Art Monk .02 .10
474 Mel Gray .01 .05
475 Reggie White .08 .25
476 Eric Ball .01 .05
477 Dwayne Harper .01 .05
478 Will Shields .01 .05
479 Roger Harper .01 .05
480 Rick Mirer .08 .25
481 Vincent Brisby .01 .05
482 John Jurkovic RC .02 .10
483 Michael Jackson .02 .10
484 Ed Cunningham .01 .05
485 Brad Ottis .01 .05
486 Sterling Palmer RC .01 .05
487 Tony Bennett .01 .05
488 Mike Pritchard .01 .05
489 Bucky Brooks RC .01 .05
490 Troy Vincent .01 .05
491 Eric Green .01 .05
492 Van Malone .01 .05
493 Marcus Spears RC .01 .05
494 Brian Williams OL .01 .05
495 Robert Smith .08 .25
496 Haywood Jeffires .02 .10
497 Darrin Smith .01 .05
498 Tommy Barnhardt .01 .05
499 Anthony Smith .01 .05
500 Ricky Watters .02 .10
501 Antono Davis .01 .05
502 David Braxton .01 .05
503 Donnell Bennett RC .08 .25
504 Donald Evans .01 .05
505 Lewis Tillman .01 .05
506 Lance Smith .01 .05
507 Aaron Taylor .01 .05
508 Ricky Sanders .01 .05
509 Dennis Smith .01 .05
510 Barry Foster .01 .05
511 Stan Brock .01 .05
512 Henry Rolling .01 .05
513 Walter Reeves .01 .05
514 John Booty .01 .05
515 Kenneth Davis .01 .05
516 Cris Dishman .01 .05
517 Bill Lewis .01 .05
518 Jeff Bryant .01 .05
519 Brian Mitchell .01 .05
520 Joe Montana .75 2.00
521 Keith Sims .01 .05
522 Harry Colon .01 .05
523 Leon Lett .01 .05
524 Carlos Jenkins .01 .05
525 Victor Bailey .01 .05
526 Harvey Williams .01 .05
527 Irv Smith .01 .05
528 Jason Sehorn RC .15 .40
529 John Thierry RC .01 .05
530 Brett Favre .75 2.00
531 Sean Dawkins RC .08 .25
532 Eric Pegram .01 .05
533 Jimmy Williams .01 .05
534 Michael Timpson .01 .05
535 Flipper Anderson .01 .05
536 John Parrella .01 .05
537 Freddie Joe Nunn .01 .05
538 Doug Dawson .01 .05
539 Michael Stewart .01 .05
540 John Elway .75 2.00
541 Ronnie Lott .02 .10
542 Barry Sanders TOG .30 .75
543 Andre Reed .02 .10
544 Deion Sanders .08 .25
545 Dan Marino .30 .75
546 Carlton Bailey .01 .05
547 Emmitt Smith .30 .75
548 Alvin Harper .01 .05
549 Eric Metcalf .02 .10
550 Jerry Rice .20 .50
551 Derrick Thomas .08 .25
552 Mark Collins .01 .05
553 Eric Turner .01 .05
554 Sterling Sharpe .02 .10
555 Steve Young .08 .25
556 Darnay Scott RC .20 .50
557 Joel Steed .01 .05
558 Dennis Gibson .01 .05
559 Charles Mincy .01 .05
560 Rickey Jackson .01 .05
561 Dave Cadigan .01 .05
562 Rick Tuten .01 .05
563 Mike Caldwell .01 .05
564 Todd Steussie RC .02 .10
565 Kevin Smith .01 .05
566 Arthur Marshall .01 .05
567 Aaron Wallace .01 .05
568 Calvin Williams .02 .10
569 Todd Kelly .01 .05
570 Barry Sanders .60 1.50
571 Shaun Gayle .01 .05
572 Will Wolford .01 .05
573 Ethan Horton .01 .05
574 Chris Slade .01 .05
575 Jeff Wright .01 .05
576 Toby Wright .01 .05
577 Lamar Thomas .01 .05
578 Chris Singleton .01 .05
579 Ed West .01 .05
580 Jeff George .08 .25
581 Kevin Mitchell .01 .05
582 Chad Brown .01 .05
583 Rich Camarillo .01 .05
584 Gary Zimmerman .01 .05
585 Randal Hill .01 .05
586 Keith Cash .01 .05
587 Sam Mills .01 .05
588 Shawn Lee .01 .05
589 Kent Graham .02 .10
590 Steve Everitt .01 .05
591 Rob Moore .02 .10
592 Kevin Mawae RC .08 .25
593 Jerry Ball .01 .05
594 Larry Brown DB .01 .05
595 Tim Krumrie .01 .05
596 Aubrey Beavers RC .01 .05
597 Chris Hinton .01 .05
598 Greg Montgomery .01 .05
599 Jimmie Jones .01 .05
600 Jim Kelly .08 .25
601 Joe Johnson RC .01 .05
602 Tim Irwin .01 .05
603 Steve Jackson .01 .05
604 James Williams RC .01 .05
605 Blair Thomas .01 .05
606 Danan Hughes .01 .05
607 Russell Freeman .01 .05
608 Andre Hastings .02 .10
609 Ken Harvey .01 .05
610 Jim Harbaugh .08 .25
611 Emmitt Smith MG .30 .75
612 Andre Rison MG .02 .10
613 Steve Young MG .08 .25
614 Anthony Miller MG .01 .05
615 Barry Sanders MG .30 .75
616 Bernie Kosar .02 .10
617 Chris Gardocki .01 .05
618 William Floyd RC .08 .25
619 Matt Brock .01 .05
620 Dan Wilkinson RC .02 .10
621 Tony Meola RC .02 .10
622 Tony Tolbert .01 .05
623 Mike Zandofsky .01 .05
624 William Fuller .01 .05
625 Steve Jordan .01 .05
626 Mike Johnson .01 .05
627 Ferrell Edmunds .01 .05
628 Gene Williams .01 .05
629 Willie Beamon .01 .05
630 Gerald Perry .01 .05
631 John Baylor .01 .05
632 Carwell Gardner .01 .05
633 Thomas Everett .01 .05
634 Lamar Lathon .01 .05
635 Michael Bankston .01 .05
636 Ray Crittenden RC .01 .05
637 Kimble Anders .02 .10
638 Robert Delpino .01 .05
639 Darren Perry .01 .05
640 Byron Evans .01 .05
641 Mark Higgs .01 .05
642 Lorenzo Neal .01 .05
643 Henry Ellard .02 .10
644 Trace Armstrong .01 .05
645 Greg McMurtry .01 .05
646 Steve McMichael .02 .10
647 Terance Mathis .02 .10
648 Eric Bieniemy .01 .05
649 Bobby Houston .01 .05
650 Alvin Harper .02 .10
651 James Folston RC .01 .05
652 Mel Gray .01 .05
653 Adrian Cooper .01 .05
654 Dexter Carter .01 .05
655 Don Griffin .01 .05
656 Corey Widmer .01 .05
657 Lee Johnson .01 .05
658 Nate Odomes .01 .05
659 Checklist Card .01 .05
660 Checklist Card .01 .05
P1 Promo Sheet 1.50 4.00
Stan Humphries
Darryl Talley
Rodney Hampton
Jerome Bettis
Chris Zorich
Harry Newsome
Tyrone Hughes
Rod Woodson
Chris Spielman
P2 Promo Sheet Spec. Eff. 1.50 4.00
Jerome Bettis
Chris Zorich
Harry Newsome

1994 Topps Special Effects

COMP.SERIES 1 (330)
*STARS: 3.5X TO 7X BASIC CARDS
*RCs: 2X TO 4X BASIC CARDS
STATED ODDS 1:2 H/R, 2:1 RACK PACK

1994 Topps All-Pros

COMPLETE SET (25) 20.00 50.00
STATED ODDS 1:36 SER.2
1 Michael Irvin 1.25 2.50
2 Erik Williams .20 .50
3 Steve Wisniewski .20 .50
4 Dermontti Dawson .20 .50
5 Nate Newton .20 .50
6 Harris Barton .20 .50
7 Shannon Sharpe .40 1.00
8 Jerry Rice 5.00 10.00
9 Troy Aikman 5.00 10.00
10 Barry Sanders 8.00 15.00
11 Jerome Bettis 2.50 5.00
12 Jason Hanson .20 .50
13 Eric Metcalf .40 1.00
14 Reggie White 1.25 2.50
15 Cortez Kennedy .40 1.00
16 Michael Dean Perry .40 1.00
17 Bruce Smith 1.25 2.50
18 Darryl Talley .20 .50
19 Hardy Nickerson .40 1.00
20 Derrick Thomas 1.25 2.50
21 Mark Collins .20 .50
22 Eric Allen .20 .50
23 Tim McDonald .20 .50
24 Marcus Robertson .20 .50
25 Greg Montgomery .20 .50

1994 Topps 1000/3000

COMPLETE SET (32) 25.00 60.00
STATED ODDS 1:36 SER.1
1 Jerry Rice 3.00 8.00
2 Chris Warren .30 .75
3 Leonard Russell .15 .40
4 Gary Brown .15 .40
5 Tim Brown .75 2.00
6 Erric Pegram .15 .40
7 Irving Fryar .30 .75
8 Anthony Miller .30 .75
9 Reggie Langhorne .15 .40
10 Thurman Thomas .75 2.00
11 Reggie Brooks .30 .75
12 Andre Rison .30 .75
13 Ronald Moore .15 .40
14 Michael Irvin .75 2.00
15 Barry Sanders 5.00 12.00
16 Cris Carter 1.50 4.00
17 Rodney Hampton .30 .75
18 Jerome Bettis 1.50 4.00
19 Sterling Sharpe .30 .75
20 Emmitt Smith 5.00 12.00
21 John Elway 6.00 15.00
22 Brett Favre 6.00 15.00
23 Jim Kelly .75 2.00
24 Warren Moon .75 2.00
25 Phil Simms .30 .75
26 Craig Erickson .15 .40
27 Neil O'Donnell .75 2.00
28 Steve Young 2.50 6.00
29 Steve Beuerlein .30 .75
30 Troy Aikman 3.00 8.00
31 Jeff Hostetler .30 .75
32 Boomer Esiason .30 .75

1995 Topps

This 468 card standard-size set was issued in two series, both in 13 count foil packs with a suggested retail price of $1.29. Similar to the '95 baseball issue, these cards feature color action photos with white borders on the front. Two subsets are included in this set: 1,000 Yard Club (1-29) and 3,000 Yard Club (30-41). Rookie Cards in this set include Ki-Jana Carter, Kerry Collins, Rashaan Salaam, J.J. Stokes and Michael Westbrook.

COMPLETE SET (468) 15.00 40.00
COMP.FACT.SET (478) 40.00 80.00
COMP.SERIES 1 (248) 8.00 20.00
COMP.SERIES 2 (220) 8.00 20.00
1 Barry Sanders TYC .30 .75
2 Chris Warren .07 .20
3 Jerry Rice .20 .50
4 Emmitt Smith .30 .75
5 Henry Ellard .07 .20
6 Natrone Means TYC .07 .20
7 Terance Mathis .07 .20
8 Tim Brown TYC .07 .20
9 Andre Reed .07 .20
10 Marshall Faulk .25 .60
11 Irving Fryar .07 .20
12 Cris Carter .10 .30
13 Michael Irvin .10 .30
14 Jake Reed .07 .20
15 Ben Coates .07 .20
16 Herman Moore .10 .30
17 Carl Pickens .07 .20
18 Fred Barnett .07 .20
19 Sterling Sharpe .07 .20
20 Anthony Miller .07 .20
21 Thurman Thomas .10 .30
22 Andre Rison .07 .20
23 Brian Blades .07 .20
24 Rodney Hampton .07 .20
25 Terry Allen .07 .20
26 Jerome Bettis .10 .30
27 Errict Rhett .07 .20
28 Rob Moore .07 .20
29 Shannon Sharpe .07 .20
30 Drew Bledsoe .10 .30
31 Dan Marino .40 1.00
32 Warren Moon .07 .20
33 Steve Young .15 .40
34 Brett Favre TYC .40 1.00
35 Jim Everett .02 .10
36 Jeff George .07 .20
37 John Elway .40 1.00
38 Jeff Hostetler .07 .20
39 Randall Cunningham .10 .30
40 Stan Humphries .07 .20
41 Jim Kelly .10 .30
42 Tommy Barnhardt .02 .10
43 Bob Whitfield .02 .10
44 William Thomas .02 .10
45 Glyn Milburn .02 .10
46 Steve Christie .02 .10
47 Kevin Mawae .02 .10
48 Vencie Glenn .02 .10
49 Eric Curry .02 .10
50 Jeff Hostetler .07 .20
51 Tyronne Stowe .02 .10
52 Steve Jackson .02 .10
53 Ben Coleman .02 .10
54 Brad Baxter .02 .10
55 Darryl Williams .02 .10
56 Troy Drayton .02 .10
57 George Teague .02 .10
58 Calvin Williams .07 .20
59 Jeff Cross .02 .10
60 Leroy Hoard .02 .10
61 John Carney .02 .10
62 Daryl Johnston .07 .20
63 Jim Jeffcoat .02 .10
64 Matt Stover .02 .10
65 LeRoy Butler .02 .10
66 Curtis Conway .10 .30
67 O.J. McDuffie .10 .30
68 Robert Massey .02 .10
69 Ed McDaniel .02 .10
70 William Floyd .07 .20
71 Willie Davis .07 .20
72 William Roberts .02 .10
73 Chester McGlockton .07 .20
74 D.J. Johnson .02 .10
75 Rondell Jones .02 .10
76 Morten Andersen .02 .10
77 Glenn Parker .02 .10
78 William Fuller .02 .10
79 Ray Buchanan .02 .10
80 Maurice Hurst .02 .10
81 Wayne Gandy .02 .10
82 Marcus Turner .02 .10
83 Greg Davis .02 .10
84 Terry Wooden .02 .10
85 Thomas Everett .02 .10
86 Steve Broussard .02 .10
87 Tom Carter .02 .10
88 Glenn Montgomery .02 .10
89 Larry Allen .07 .20
90 Donnell Woolford .02 .10
91 John Alt .02 .10
92 Phil Hansen .02 .10
93 Seth Joyner .02 .10
94 Michael Brooks .02 .10
95 Randall McDaniel .05 .15
96 Tydus Winans .02 .10
97 Rob Fredrickson .02 .10
98 Ray Crockett .02 .10
99 Courtney Hall .02 .10
100 Merton Hanks .02 .10
101 Aaron Glenn .02 .10
102 Roosevelt Potts .02 .10
103 Leon Lett .02 .10
104 Jessie Tuggle .02 .10
105 Martin Mayhew .02 .10
106 Willie Roaf .02 .10
107 Todd Lyght .02 .10
108 Ernest Givins .02 .10
109 Tony McGee .02 .10
110 Barry Sanders .60 1.50
111 Dermontti Dawson .07 .20
112 Rick Tuten .02 .10
113 Vincent Brisby .02 .10
114 Charlie Garner .10 .30
115 Irving Fryar .07 .20
116 Stevon Moore .02 .10
117 Matt Darby .02 .10
118 Howard Cross .02 .10
119 John Gesek .02 .10
120 Jack Del Rio .02 .10
121 Marcus Allen .10 .30
122 Torrance Small .02 .10
123 Chris Mims .02 .10
124 Don Mosebar .02 .10
125 Carl Pickens .07 .20
126 Tom Rouen .02 .10
127 Garrison Hearst .10 .30
128 Charles Johnson .07 .20
129 Derek Brown RBK .02 .10
130 Troy Aikman .40 1.00
131 Troy Vincent .02 .10
132 Ken Ruettgers .02 .10
133 Michael Jackson .07 .20
134 Dennis Gibson .02 .10
135 Brett Perriman .07 .20
136 Jeff Graham .02 .10
137 Chad Brown .07 .20
138 Ken Norton Jr. .07 .20
139 Chris Slade .02 .10
140 Dave Brown .07 .20
141 Bert Emanuel .10 .30
142 Renaldo Turnbull .02 .10
143 Jim Harbaugh .07 .20
144 Micheal Barrow .02 .10
145 Vincent Brown .02 .10
146 Bryant Young .07 .20
147 Boomer Esiason .07 .20
148 Sean Gilbert .07 .20
149 Greg Truitt .02 .10
150 Rod Woodson .07 .20
151 Robert Porcher .02 .10
152 Joe Phillips .02 .10
153 Gary Zimmerman .02 .10
154 Bruce Smith .10 .30
155 Randall Cunningham .10 .30
156 Fred Strickland .02 .10
157 Derrick Alexander WR .10 .30
158 James Williams .02 .10
159 Scott Dill .02 .10
160 Tim Bowens .02 .10
161 Floyd Turner .02 .10
162 Ronnie Harmon .02 .10
163 Wayne Martin .02 .10
164 John Randle .07 .20
165 Larry Centers .07 .20
166 Larry Brown DB .02 .10
167 Albert Lewis .02 .10
168 Michael Strahan .10 .30
169 Reggie Brooks .07 .20
170 Craig Heyward .07 .20
171 Pat Harlow .02 .10
172 Eugene Robinson .02 .10
173 Shane Conlan .02 .10
174 Bennie Blades .02 .10
175 Neil O'Donnell .07 .20
176 Steve Tovar .02 .10
177 Donald Evans .02 .10
178 Brent Jones .02 .10
179 Ray Childress .02 .10
180 Reggie White .10 .30
181 David Alexander .02 .10
182 Greg Hill .07 .20
183 Vinny Testaverde .07 .20
184 Jeff Burris .02 .10
185 Hardy Nickerson .02 .10
186 Terry Kirby .07 .20
187 Kirk Lowdermilk .02 .10
188 Eric Swann .07 .20
189 Chris Zorich .02 .10
190 Simon Fletcher .02 .10
191 Qadry Ismail .07 .20
192 Heath Shuler .07 .20
193 Michael Haynes .07 .20
194 Mike Sherrard .02 .10
195 Nolan Harrison .02 .10
196 Marcus Robertson .02 .10
197 Kevin Williams WR .07 .20
198 Moe Gardner .02 .10
199 Rick Mirer .07 .20
200 Junior Seau .10 .30
201 Byron Bam Morris .02 .10
202 Willie McGinest .07 .20
203 Chris Spielman .07 .20
204 Darnay Scott .07 .20
205 Jesse Sapolu .02 .10
206 Marvin Washington .02 .10
207 Anthony Newman .02 .10
208 Cortez Kennedy .07 .20
209 Quentin Coryatt .07 .20
210 Neil Smith .07 .20
211 Keith Sims .02 .10
212 Sean Jones .02 .10
213 Tony Jones .02 .10
214 Lewis Tillman .02 .10
215 Darren Woodson .07 .20
216 Jason Hanson .02 .10
217 John Taylor .02 .10
218 Shawn Lee .02 .10
219 Kevin Greene .07 .20
220 Jerry Rice .40 1.00
221 Ki-Jana Carter RC .10 .30
222 Tony Boselli RC .10 .30
223 Michael Westbrook RC .10 .30
224 Kerry Collins RC .75 2.00
225 Kevin Carter RC .10 .30
226 Kyle Brady RC .10 .30
227 J.J. Stokes RC .10 .30
228 Derr. Alexander DE RC .02 .10
229 Warren Sapp RC .60 1.50
230 Ruben Brown RC .10 .30
231 Hugh Douglas RC .10 .30
232 Luther Elliss RC .02 .10
233 Rashaan Salaam RC .07 .20
234 Tyrone Poole RC .10 .30
235 Korey Stringer RC .10 .30
236 Devin Bush RC .02 .10
237 Cory Raymer RC .02 .10
238 Zach Wiegert RC .02 .10
239 Ron Davis RC .02 .10
240 Todd Collins RC .50 1.25

241 Bobby Taylor RC .10 .30
242 Patrick Riley RC .02 .10
243 Scott Gragg .02 .10
244 Marvcus Patton .02 .10
245 Alvin Harper .02 .10
246 Ricky Watters .07 .20
247 Checklist 1 .02 .10
248 Checklist 2 .02 .10
249 Terance Mathis .07 .20
250 Mark Carrier DB .02 .10
251 Elijah Alexander .02 .10
252 George Koonce .02 .10
253 Tony Bennett .02 .10
254 Steve Wisniewski .02 .10
255 Bernie Parmalee .07 .20
256 Dwayne Sabb .02 .10
257 Lorenzo Neal .02 .10
258 Corey Miller .02 .10
259 Fred Barnett .07 .20
260 Greg Lloyd .07 .20
261 Robert Blackmon .02 .10
262 Ken Harvey .02 .10
263 Eric Hill .02 .10
264 Russell Copeland .02 .10
265 Jeff Blake RC .30 .75
266 Carl Banks .02 .10
267 Jay Novacek .07 .20
268 Mel Gray .02 .10
269 Kimble Anders .07 .20
270 Cris Carter .10 .30
271 Johnny Mitchell .02 .10
272 Shawn Jefferson .02 .10
273 Doug Brien .02 .10
274 Sean Landeta .02 .10
275 Scott Mitchell .07 .20
276 Charles Wilson .02 .10
277 Anthony Smith .02 .10
278 Anthony Miller .07 .20
279 Steve Walsh .02 .10
280 Drew Bledsoe .25 .60
281 Jamir Miller .02 .10
282 Robert Brooks UER .10 .30
Rushing and receiving totals are reversed
283 Sean Lumpkin .02 .10
284 Bryan Cox .02 .10
285 Byron Evans .02 .10
286 Chris Doleman .02 .10
287 Anthony Pleasant .02 .10
288 Stephen Grant RC .02 .10
289 Doug Riesenberg .02 .10
290 Natrone Means .07 .20
291 Henry Thomas .02 .10
292 Mike Pritchard .02 .10
293 Courtney Hawkins .02 .10
294 Bill Bates .07 .20
295 Jerome Bettis .10 .30
296 Russell Maryland .02 .10
297 Stanley Richard .02 .10
298 William White .02 .10
299 Dan Wilkinson .07 .20
300 Steve Young .30 .75
301 Gary Brown .02 .10
302 Jake Reed .07 .20
303 Carlton Gray .02 .10
304 Levon Kirkland .02 .10
305 Shannon Sharpe .07 .20
306 Luis Sharpe .02 .10
307 Marshall Faulk .50 1.25
308 Stan Humphries .07 .20
309 Chris Calloway .02 .10
310 Tim Brown .10 .30
311 Steve Everitt .02 .10
312 Raymont Harris .02 .10
313 Tim McDonald .02 .10
314 Trent Dilfer .10 .30
315 Jim Everett .02 .10
316 Ray Crittenden .02 .10
317 Jim Kelly .10 .30
318 Andre Reed .07 .20
319 Chris Miller .02 .10
320 Bobby Houston .02 .10
321 Charles Haley .07 .20
322 James Francis .02 .10
323 Bernard Williams .02 .10
324 Michael Bates .02 .10
325 Brian Mitchell .02 .10
326 Mike Johnson .02 .10
327 Eric Bieniemy .02 .10
328 Aubrey Beavers .02 .10
329 Dale Carter .07 .20
330 Emmitt Smith .60 1.50
331 Darren Perry .02 .10
332 Marquez Pope .02 .10
333 Clyde Simmons .02 .10
334 Corey Croom .02 .10
335 Thomas Randolph .02 .10
336 Harvey Williams .02 .10
337 Michael Timpson .02 .10
338 Eugene Daniel .02 .10
339 Shane Dronett .02 .10
340 Eric Turner .02 .10
341 Eric Metcalf .07 .20
342 Leslie O'Neal .07 .20
343 Mark Wheeler .02 .10
344 Mark Pike .02 .10
345 Brett Favre .75 2.00
346 Johnny Bailey .02 .10
347 Henry Ellard .07 .20
348 Chris Gardocki .02 .10
349 Henry Jones .02 .10
350 Dan Marino .75 2.00
351 Lake Dawson .07 .20
352 Mark McMillian .02 .10
353 Deion Sanders .25 .60
354 Antonio London .02 .10
355 Cris Dishman .02 .10
356 Ricardo McDonald .02 .10
357 Dexter Carter .02 .10
358 Kevin Smith .02 .10
359 Yancey Thigpen RC .07 .20
360 Chris Warren .07 .20
361 Quinn Early .07 .20
362 John Mangum .02 .10
363 Santana Dotson .02 .10
364 Rocket Ismail .07 .20
365 Aeneas Williams .02 .10
366 Dan Williams .02 .10
367 Sean Dawkins .07 .20
368 Pepper Johnson .02 .10
369 Roman Phifer .02 .10
370 Rodney Hampton .07 .20
371 Darrell Green .02 .10
372 Michael Zordich .02 .10
373 Andre Coleman .02 .10
374 Wayne Simmons .02 .10
375 Michael Irvin .10 .30
376 Clay Matthews .07 .20
377 Dewayne Washington .07 .20
378 Keith Byars .02 .10
379 Todd Collins LB .10 .30
380 Mark Collins .02 .10
381 Joel Steed .02 .10
382 Bart Oates .02 .10
383 Al Smith .02 .10
384 Rafael Robinson .02 .10
385 Mo Lewis .02 .10
386 Aubrey Matthews .02 .10
387 Corey Sawyer .02 .10
388 Bucky Brooks .02 .10
389 Erik Kramer .02 .10
390 Tyrone Hughes .07 .20
391 Terry McDaniel .02 .10
392 Craig Erickson .02 .10
393 Mike Flores .02 .10
394 Harry Swayne .02 .10
395 Irving Spikes .07 .20
396 Lorenzo Lynch .02 .10
397 Antonio Langham .02 .10
398 Edgar Bennett .07 .20
399 Thomas Lewis .07 .20
400 John Elway .75 2.00
401 Jeff George .07 .20
402 Errict Rhett .07 .20
403 Bill Romanowski .02 .10
404 Alexander Wright .02 .10
405 Warren Moon .07 .20
406 Eddie Robinson .02 .10
407 John Copeland .02 .10
408 Robert Jones .02 .10
409 Steve Bono .07 .20
410 Cornelius Bennett .07 .20
411 Ben Coates .07 .20
412 Dana Stubblefield .07 .20
413 Darryl Talley .02 .10
414 Brian Blades .07 .20
415 Herman Moore .10 .30
416 Nick Lowery .02 .10
417 Donnell Bennett .07 .20
418 Van Malone .02 .10
419 Pete Stoyanovich .02 .10
420 Joe Montana .75 2.00
421 Steve Young .20 .50
Super Bowl XXIX MVP
422 Steve Young .20 .50
Quarterback Rating Leaders
423 Steve Young .20 .50
Super Bowl Touchdown Record
424 Steve Young .20 .50
NFL League MVP
425 Steve Young .20 .50
Pro Bowl
426 Rod Stephens .02 .10
427 Ellis Johnson RC UER .02 .10
Card is numbered 436
428 Kordell Stewart RC .50 1.25
429 James O. Stewart RC .40 1.00
430 Steve McNair RC 1.00 2.50
431 Brian DeMarco .07 .20
432 Matt O'Dwyer .02 .10
433 Lorenzo Styles RC .02 .10
434 Anthony Cook RC .02 .10
435 Jesse James .02 .10
436 Darryl Pounds RC .02 .10
437 Derrick Graham RC .02 .10
438 Vernon Turner .02 .10
439 Carlton Bailey .02 .10
440 Darion Conner .02 .10
441 Randy Baldwin .02 .10
442 Tim McKyer .02 .10
443 Sam Mills .07 .20
444 Bob Christian .02 .10
445 Steve Lofton .02 .10
446 Lamar Lathon .02 .10
447 Tony Smith .02 .10
448 Don Beebe .02 .10
449 Barry Foster .07 .20
450 Frank Reich .02 .10
451 Pete Metzelaars .02 .10
452 Reggie Cobb .02 .10
453 Jeff Lageman .02 .10
454 Derek Brown TE .02 .10
455 Desmond Howard .07 .20
456 Vinnie Clark .02 .10
457 Keith Goganious .02 .10
458 Shawn Bouwens .02 .10
459 Rob Johnson RC .30 .75
460 Steve Beuerlein .07 .20
461 Mark Brunell .25 .60
462 Harry Colon .02 .10
463 Chris Hudson .02 .10
464 Darren Carrington .02 .10
465 Ernest Givins .02 .10
466 Kelvin Pritchett .02 .10
467 Checklist (249-358) .02 .10
468 Checklist (358-468) .02 .10

1995 Topps Factory Jaguars

COMP.FACT.SET (473) 20.00 50.00
*SINGLES: .4X TO 1X BASE CARD HI

1995 Topps Factory Panthers

COMP.FACT.SET (473) 20.00 50.00
*SINGLES: .4X TO 1X BASE CARD HI

1995 Topps 1000/3000 Boosters

COMPLETE SET (41) 30.00 80.00
STATED ODDS 1:36H,1:18J,1:72 SR SER.1
1 Barry Sanders 4.00 10.00
2 Chris Warren .50 1.25
3 Jerry Rice 2.50 6.00
4 Emmitt Smith 4.00 10.00
5 Henry Ellard .50 1.25
6 Natrone Means .50 1.25
7 Terance Mathis .50 1.25
8 Tim Brown .75 2.00
9 Andre Reed .50 1.25
10 Marshall Faulk 3.00 8.00
11 Irving Fryar .50 1.25
12 Cris Carter .75 2.00
13 Michael Irvin .75 2.00
14 Jake Reed .50 1.25
15 Ben Coates .50 1.25
16 Herman Moore .75 2.00
17 Carl Pickens .50 1.25
18 Fred Barnett .50 1.25
19 Sterling Sharpe .50 1.25
20 Anthony Miller .50 1.25
21 Thurman Thomas .75 2.00
22 Andre Rison .50 1.25
23 Brian Blades .50 1.25
24 Rodney Hampton .50 1.25
25 Terry Allen .50 1.25
26 Jerome Bettis .75 2.00
27 Errict Rhett .50 1.25
28 Rob Moore .50 1.25
29 Shannon Sharpe .50 1.25
30 Drew Bledsoe 1.50 4.00
31 Dan Marino 5.00 12.00
32 Warren Moon .50 1.25
33 Steve Young 2.00 5.00
34 Brett Favre 5.00 12.00
35 Jim Everett .25 .60
36 Jeff George .50 1.25
37 John Elway 5.00 12.00
38 Jeff Hostetler .50 1.25
39 Randall Cunningham .75 2.00
40 Stan Humphries .50 1.25
41 Jim Kelly .75 2.00

1995 Topps Air Raid

COMPLETE SET (10) 20.00 50.00
SER.2 STATED ODDS 1:20J,1:24R,1:48SP RET
1 Steve Young 5.00 10.00
Jerry Rice
2 Cris Carter 2.50 5.00
Warren Moon
3 Terance Mathis 1.50 3.00
Jeff George
4 Dave Brown 1.50 3.00
Michael Sherrard
5 Drew Bledsoe 2.50 6.00
Ben Coates
6 John Elway 6.00 15.00
Shannon Sharpe
7 Jeff Blake 2.50 5.00
Carl Pickens
8 Dan Marino 6.00 15.00
Irving Fryar
9 Fred Barnett 1.50 3.00
Randall Cunningham
10 Troy Aikman 5.00 10.00
Michael Irvin

1995 Topps All-Pros

COMPLETE SET (22) 20.00 50.00
SER.2 STATED ODDS 1:8 HOBBY
1 Jerry Rice 2.50 6.00
2 Lomas Brown .30 .75
3 Nate Newton .30 .75
4 Dermontti Dawson .30 .75
5 Keith Sims .30 .75
6 Richmond Webb .30 .75
7 Shannon Sharpe .75 2.00
8 Michael Irvin .75 2.00
9 Steve Young 2.00 5.00
10 Barry Sanders 4.00 10.00
11 Marshall Faulk 3.00 8.00
12 Bruce Smith .75 2.00
13 Dana Stubblefield .30 .75
14 John Randle .50 1.25
15 Reggie White .75 2.00
16 Greg Lloyd .30 .75
17 Junior Seau .75 2.00
18 Cornelius Bennett .50 1.25
19 Rod Woodson .50 1.25
20 Deion Sanders 2.00 5.00
21 Darren Woodson .50 1.25
22 Merton Hanks .30 .75

1995 Topps Expansion Team Boosters

COMPLETE SET (30) 25.00 60.00
SER.2 ODDS 1:36H/R,1:18J,1:72 SPEC.RET.
FIVE PER JAGUARS/PANTHERS FACT.SET
437 Derrick Graham .75 2.00
438 Vernon Turner .75 2.00
439 Carlton Bailey .75 2.00
440 Darion Conner .75 2.00
441 Randy Baldwin .75 2.00
442 Tim McKyer .75 2.00
443 Sam Mills .75 2.00
444 Bob Christian .75 2.00
445 Steve Lofton .75 2.00
446 Lamar Lathon .75 2.00
447 Tony Smith RB .75 2.00
448 Don Beebe 1.00 2.50
449 Barry Foster 1.00 2.50
450 Frank Reich 1.00 2.50
451 Pete Metzelaars .75 2.00
452 Reggie Cobb .75 2.00
453 Jeff Lageman .75 2.00
454 Derek Brown TE .75 2.00
455 Desmond Howard 1.00 2.50
456 Vinnie Clark .75 2.00
457 Keith Goganious .75 2.00
458 Shawn Bowens .75 2.00
459 Rob Johnson 1.50 4.00
460 Steve Beuerlein 1.00 2.50
461 Mark Brunell 6.00 15.00
462 Harry Colon .75 2.00
463 Chris Hudson .75 2.00
464 Darren Carrington .75 2.00
465 Ernest Givins .75 2.00
466 Kelvin Pritchett .75 2.00

1995 Topps Finest Boosters

COMPLETE SET (22) 40.00 80.00
STATED ODDS 1:36H/R,1:18J,1:72SR.SER.2
*REFRACTORS: 1.2X TO 3X BASIC INSERTS
STATED ODDS 1:36H,1:216J,1:432R SER.2
B166 Barry Sanders 4.00 10.00
B167 Bryant Young .50 1.25
B168 Boomer Esiason .50 1.25
B169 Terance Mathis .50 1.25
B170 Troy Aikman 2.50 6.00
B171 Junior Seau .75 2.00
B172 Rodney Hampton .50 1.25
B173 Jim Everett .25 .60
B174 Dan Marino 5.00 12.00
B175 Steve Young 2.00 5.00
B176 Cris Carter .75 2.00
B177 Eric Swann .50 1.25
B178 Rick Mirer .50 1.25
B179 Jerome Bettis .75 2.00
B180 Emmitt Smith 4.00 10.00
B181 Jim Kelly .75 2.00
B182 John Elway 5.00 12.00
B183 Dana Stubblefield .50 1.25
B184 Drew Bledsoe 1.50 4.00
B185 Jerry Rice 2.50 6.00
B186 Michael Irvin .75 2.00
B187 Bruce Smith .75 2.00

1995 Topps Florida Hot Bed

COMPLETE SET (15) 5.00 12.00
ONE PER SPECIAL RETAIL PACK
FH1 Deion Sanders 1.00 2.50
FH2 Brian Blades .30 .75
FH3 Errict Rhett .30 .75
FH4 Kevin Williams .30 .75
FH5 Cortez Kennedy .30 .75
FH6 Corey Sawyer .15 .40
FH7 Russell Maryland .15 .40
FH8 Emmitt Smith 2.50 6.00
FH9 Vinny Testaverde .30 .75
FH10 William Floyd .30 .75
FH11 Brett Perriman .30 .75
FH12 Nate Newton .15 .40
FH13 Jim Kelly .50 1.25
FH14 LeRoy Butler .15 .40
FH15 Michael Irvin .50 1.25

1995 Topps Hit List

COMPLETE SET (20) 2.50 6.00
STATED ODDS 1:4
1 Pepper Johnson .15 .40
2 Elijah Alexander .15 .40
3 Joe Cain .15 .40
4 Andre Collins .15 .40
5 Chris Spielman .30 .75
6 Bryan Cox .15 .40
7 Ed McDaniel .15 .40
8 Jack Del Rio .15 .40
9 Jeff Herrod .15 .40
10 Greg Lloyd .30 .75
11 Reggie White .50 1.25
12 Robert Jones .15 .40
13 Eric Turner .15 .40
14 Vincent Brown .15 .40
15 Kevin Greene .30 .75
16 Bruce Smith .50 1.25
17 Hardy Nickerson UER .15 .40
(incorrectly numbered 123)
18 Seth Joyner .15 .40
19 Darryl Talley .15 .40
20 Junior Seau .50 1.25

1995 Topps Mystery Finest

COMPLETE SET (27) 20.00 50.00
STATED ODDS 1:36H,1:12J,1:72SP RET SER.1
*REFRACTORS: .8X to 2X BASIC INSERTS
STATED ODDS 1:36H,1:216J,1:864R SER.1
1 Troy Aikman 2.00 5.00
2 Jerome Bettis .60 1.50
3 Drew Bledsoe 1.25 3.00
4 Tim Brown .60 1.50
5 Cris Carter .60 1.50
6 Henry Ellard .40 1.00
7 John Elway 4.00 10.00
8 Marshall Faulk 2.50 6.00
9 Brett Favre 4.00 10.00
10 Irving Fryar .40 1.00
11 Rodney Hampton .40 1.00
12 Stan Humphries .40 1.00
13 Michael Irvin .60 1.50
14 Jim Kelly .60 1.50
15 Dan Marino 4.00 10.00
16 Terance Mathis .40 1.00
17 Natrone Means .40 1.00
18 Warren Moon .40 1.00
19 Herman Moore .60 1.50
20 Andre Reed .40 1.00
21 Errict Rhett .40 1.00
22 Jerry Rice 2.00 5.00
23 Barry Sanders 3.00 8.00
24 Emmitt Smith 3.00 8.00
25 Chris Warren .40 1.00
26 Ricky Watters .40 1.00
27 Steve Young 1.50 4.00

1995 Topps Profiles

COMPLETE SET (15) 15.00 30.00
STATED ODDS 1:12H/R,1:6J,1:24SR SER.2
1 Emmitt Smith 5.00 10.00
2 Chris Spielman .60 1.25
3 Rod Woodson .60 1.25
4 Deion Sanders 2.00 4.00
5 Junior Seau 1.00 2.00
6 Byron Evans .25 .60
7 Jerome Bettis 1.00 2.00
8 Charles Haley .60 1.25
9 Jerry Rice 3.00 6.00
10 Barry Sanders 5.00 10.00
11 Hardy Nickerson .25 .60
12 Natrone Means .60 1.25
13 Darren Woodson .60 1.25
14 Reggie White 1.00 2.00
15 Troy Aikman 3.00 6.00

1995 Topps Sensational Sophomores

COMPLETE SET (10) 7.50 20.00
STATED ODDS 1:9JUM, 1:48 SP RET SER.1
1 Marshall Faulk 3.00 8.00
2 Heath Shuler 1.25 2.50
3 Tim Bowens .50 1.25
4 Bryant Young .50 1.25
5 Dan Wilkinson .50 1.25
6 Errict Rhett .50 1.25
7 Andre Coleman .50 1.25
8 Aaron Glenn .50 1.25
9 Trent Dilfer 1.25 2.50
10 Byron Bam Morris .50 1.25

1995 Topps Yesteryear

COMPLETE SET (15) 15.00 40.00
SER.1 STATED ODDS 1:72 HOBBY
1 Stan Humphries .60 1.50
2 Dan Marino 6.00 15.00
3 Irving Fryar .60 1.50
4 Warren Moon .60 1.50
5 Steve Young 2.50 6.00
6 Kevin Greene .60 1.50
7 Jeff Hostetler .60 1.50
8 Jack Del Rio .30 .75
9 Reggie White 1.00 2.50
10 Jerry Rice 3.00 8.00
11 Bruce Smith 1.00 2.50
12 Rod Woodson .60 1.50
13 Deion Sanders 2.00 5.00
14 Barry Sanders 5.00 12.00
15 Brett Favre 6.00 15.00

1995 Topps NPD Promo

This card was distributed to provide collectors with an early look at a possible upcoming new release. However, the set was never issued. The card is similar in design to the 1995 D3 baseball lenticular motion cards on the front and the back carries a blueprint design with no card number.

1 Glyn Milburn 2.00 5.00

1996 Topps

The 1996 Topps set was issued in one series totaling 440 standard-size cards. The 11-card hobby and retail foil packs carried a suggested retail price of $1.29 each. The packs were issued in 12-box foil cases which contained 36 packs in a box. Jumbo packs were also issued, these packs were in 8 box cases with 12 boxes per case and 39 cards per pack. The set contained the topical subsets: 1000 Yard Club (121-136/241-263) and 3000 Yard Club (371-386). Rookie Cards include Tim Biakabutuka, Eddie George, Marvin Harrison, Keyshawn Johnson, Leeland McLeroy, Eric Moulds and Lawrence Phillips. Topps produced a special promo card for the 1996 National Sports Collector's Convention. It featured Joe Namath and Steve Young printed in Finest technology with a Refractor version as well.

COMPLETE SET (440) 20.00 40.00
COMP.FACT.SET (448) 35.00 60.00
COMP.CEREAL FACT.SET (445) 20.00 40.00
1 Troy Aikman .40 1.00
2 Kevin Greene .07 .20
3 Robert Brooks .10 .30
4 Eugene Daniel .02 .10
5 Rodney Peete .02 .10
6 James Hasty .02 .10
7 Tim McDonald .02 .10
8 Darick Holmes .02 .10
9 Morten Andersen .02 .10
10 Junior Seau .10 .30
11 Brett Perriman .02 .10
12 Eric Green .02 .10
13 Jim Flanigan .02 .10
14 Cortez Kennedy .02 .10
15 Orlando Thomas .02 .10
16 Anthony Miller .07 .20
17 Sean Gilbert .02 .10
18 Rob Fredrickson .02 .10
19 Willie Green .02 .10
20 Jeff Blake .10 .30
21 Trent Dilfer .10 .30
22 Chris Chandler .07 .20
23 Renaldo Turnbull .02 .10
24 Dave Meggett .02 .10
25 Heath Shuler .07 .20
26 Michael Jackson .07 .20
27 Thomas Randolph .02 .10
28 Keith Goganious .02 .10
29 Seth Joyner .02 .10
30 Wayne Chrebet .25 .60
31 Craig Newsome .02 .10
32 William Fuller .02 .10
33 Merton Hanks .02 .10
34 Dale Carter .02 .10
35 Quentin Coryatt .02 .10
36 Robert Jones .02 .10
37 Eric Metcalf .02 .10
38 Byron Bam Morris .02 .10
39 Bill Brooks .02 .10
40 Barry Sanders .60 1.50
41 Michael Haynes .02 .10
42 Joey Galloway .10 .30
43 Robert Smith .07 .20
44 John Thierry .02 .10
45 Bryan Cox .02 .10
46 Anthony Parker .02 .10
47 Harvey Williams .02 .10
48 Terrell Davis .30 .75
49 Darnay Scott .07 .20
50 Kerry Collins .10 .30
51 Cris Dishman .02 .10
52 Dwayne Harper .02 .10
53 Warren Sapp .02 .10
54 Will Moore .02 .10
55 Earnest Byner .02 .10
56 Aaron Glenn .02 .10
57 Michael Westbrook .10 .30
58 Vencie Glenn .02 .10
59 Rob Moore .07 .20
60 Mark Brunell .25 .60
61 Craig Heyward .02 .10
62 Eric Allen .02 .10
63 Bill Romanowski .02 .10
64 Dana Stubblefield .07 .20
65 Steve Bono .02 .10
66 George Koonce .02 .10
67 Larry Brown .02 .10
68 Warren Moon .07 .20
69 Erric Pegram .02 .10
70 Jim Kelly .10 .30
71 Jason Belser .02 .10
72 Henry Thomas .02 .10
73 Mark Carrier DB .02 .10
74 Terry Wooden .02 .10
75 Terry McDaniel .02 .10
76 O.J. McDuffie .07 .20
77 Dan Wilkinson .02 .10
78 Blake Brockermeyer .02 .10
79 Micheal Barrow .02 .10
80 Dave Brown .02 .10
81 Todd Lyght .02 .10
82 Henry Ellard .02 .10
83 Jeff Lageman .02 .10
84 Anthony Pleasant .02 .10
85 Aeneas Williams .02 .10
86 Vincent Brisby .02 .10
87 Terrell Fletcher .02 .10
88 Brad Baxter .02 .10
89 Shannon Sharpe .07 .20
90 Errict Rhett .07 .20
91 Michael Zordich .02 .10
92 Dan Saleaumua .02 .10
93 Devin Bush .02 .10
94 Wayne Simmons .02 .10
95 Tyrone Hughes .02 .10
96 John Randle .07 .20
97 Tony Tolbert .02 .10
98 Yancey Thigpen .07 .20
99 J.J. Stokes .10 .30
100 Marshall Faulk .15 .40
101 Barry Minter RC .02 .10
102 Glenn Foley .07 .20
103 Chester McGlockton .02 .10
104 Carlton Gray .02 .10
105 Terry Kirby .07 .20
106 Darryll Lewis .02 .10
107 Thomas Smith .02 .10
108 Mike Fox .02 .10
109 Antonio Langham .02 .10
110 Drew Bledsoe .25 .60
111 Troy Drayton .02 .10
112 Marvcus Patton .02 .10
113 Tyrone Wheatley .07 .20
114 Desmond Howard .07 .20
115 Johnny Mitchell .02 .10
116 Dave Krieg .02 .10
117 Natrone Means .07 .20
118 Herman Moore .07 .20
119 Darren Woodson .07 .20
120 Ricky Watters .07 .20
121 Emmitt Smith TYC .30 .75
122 Barry Sanders TYC .30 .75
123 Curtis Martin TYC .10 .30
124 Chris Warren TYC .07 .20
125 Terry Allen TYC .07 .20
126 Ricky Watters TYC .07 .20
127 Errict Rhett TYC .07 .20
128 Rodney Hampton TYC .02 .10
129 Terrell Davis TYC .10 .30
130 Harvey Williams TYC .02 .10
131 Craig Heyward TYC .02 .10
132 Marshall Faulk TYC .10 .30
133 Rashaan Salaam TYC .02 .10
134 Garrison Hearst TYC .07 .20
135 Edgar Bennett TYC .07 .20
136 Thurman Thomas TYC .07 .20
137 Brian Washington .02 .10
138 Derek Loville .02 .10
139 Curtis Conway .10 .30
140 Isaac Bruce .10 .30
141 Ricardo McDonald .02 .10
142 Bruce Armstrong .02 .10
143 Will Wolford .02 .10
144 Thurman Thomas .10 .30
145 Mel Gray .02 .10
146 Napoleon Kaufman .10 .30
147 Terry Allen .07 .20
148 Chris Calloway .02 .10
149 Harry Colon .02 .10
150 Pepper Johnson .02 .10
151 Marco Coleman .02 .10
152 Shawn Jefferson .02 .10
153 Larry Centers .07 .20
154 Lamar Lathon .02 .10
155 Mark Chmura .07 .20
156 Dermontti Dawson .02 .10
157 Alvin Harper .02 .10
158 Randall McDaniel .05 .15
159 Allen Aldridge .02 .10
160 Chris Warren .07 .20
161 Jessie Tuggle .02 .10
162 Sean Lumpkin .02 .10
163 Bobby Houston .02 .10
164 Dexter Carter .02 .10
165 Erik Kramer .02 .10
166 Brock Marion .02 .10
167 Toby Wright .02 .10
168 John Copeland .02 .10
169 Sean Dawkins .02 .10
170 Tim Brown .10 .30
171 Darion Conner .02 .10
172 Aaron Hayden RC .02 .10
173 Charlie Garner .07 .20
174 Anthony Cook .02 .10
175 Derrick Thomas .10 .30
176 Willie McGinest .02 .10
177 Thomas Lewis .02 .10
178 Sherman Williams .02 .10
179 Cornelius Bennett .02 .10
180 Frank Sanders .10 .30
181 Leroy Hoard .02 .10
182 Bernie Parmalee .02 .10
183 Sterling Palmer .02 .10
184 Kelvin Pritchett .02 .10
185 Kordell Stewart .10 .30
186 Brent Jones .02 .10
187 Robert Blackmon .02 .10
188 Adrian Murrell .07 .20
189 Edgar Bennett .07 .20
190 Rashaan Salaam .07 .20
191 Ellis Johnson .02 .10
192 Andre Coleman .02 .10
193 Will Shields .02 .10
194 Derrick Brooks .10 .30
195 Carl Pickens .07 .20
196 Carlton Bailey .02 .10
197 Terance Mathis .07 .20
198 Carlos Jenkins .02 .10
199 Derrick Alexander DE .02 .10
200 Deion Sanders .25 .60
201 Glyn Milburn .02 .10
202 Chris Sanders .07 .20
203 Rocket Ismail .02 .10
204 Fred Barnett .02 .10
205 Quinn Early .02 .10
206 Henry Jones .02 .10
207 Herschel Walker .07 .20
208 James Washington .02 .10
209 Lee Woodall .02 .10
210 Neil Smith .07 .20
211 Tony Bennett .02 .10
212 Ernie Mills .02 .10
213 Clyde Simmons .02 .10
214 Chris Slade .02 .10
215 Tony Boselli .02 .10
216 Ryan McNeil .02 .10
217 Rob Burnett .02 .10
218 Stan Humphries .07 .20
219 Rick Mirer .07 .20
220 Troy Vincent .02 .10
221 Sean Jones .02 .10
222 Marty Carter .02 .10
223 Boomer Esiason .07 .20
224 Charles Haley .07 .20
225 Sam Mills .02 .10
226 Greg Biekert .02 .10
227 Bryant Young .07 .20
228 Ken Dilger .07 .20
229 Levon Kirkland .02 .10
230 Brian Mitchell .02 .10
231 Hardy Nickerson .02 .10
232 Elvis Grbac .07 .20
233 Kurt Schulz .02 .10
234 Chris Doleman .02 .10
235 Tamarick Vanover .07 .20
236 Jesse Campbell .02 .10
237 William Thomas .02 .10
238 Shane Conlan .02 .10
239 Jason Elam .07 .20
240 Steve McNair .30 .75
241 Jerry Rice TYC .20 .50
242 Isaac Bruce TYC .10 .30
243 Herman Moore TYC .07 .20
244 Michael Irvin TYC .07 .20
245 Robert Brooks TYC .10 .30
246 Brett Perriman TYC .02 .10
247 Cris Carter TYC .10 .30
248 Tim Brown TYC .07 .20
249 Yancey Thigpen TYC .07 .20
250 Jeff Graham TYC .02 .10
251 Carl Pickens TYC .07 .20
252 Tony Martin TYC .02 .10
253 Eric Metcalf TYC .02 .10
254 Jake Reed TYC .07 .20
255 Quinn Early TYC .02 .10
256 Anthony Miller TYC .07 .20
257 Joey Galloway TYC .10 .30
258 Bert Emanuel TYC .07 .20
259 Terance Mathis TYC .02 .10
260 Curtis Conway TYC .07 .20
261 Henry Ellard TYC .02 .10
262 Mark Carrier WR TYC .02 .10
263 Brian Blades TYC .02 .10
264 William Roaf .02 .10
265 Ed McDaniel .02 .10
266 Nate Newton .02 .10
267 Brett Maxie .02 .10
268 Anthony Smith .02 .10
269 Mickey Washington .02 .10
270 Jerry Rice .40 1.00
271 Shaun Gayle .02 .10
272 Gilbert Brown RC .10 .30
273 Mark Bruener .02 .10
274 Eugene Robinson .02 .10
275 Marvin Washington .02 .10
276 Keith Sims .02 .10
277 Ashley Ambrose .02 .10
278 Garrison Hearst .07 .20
279 Donnell Woolford .02 .10
280 Cris Carter .10 .30
281 Curtis Martin .30 .75
282 Scott Mitchell .07 .20
283 Stevon Moore .02 .10
284 Roman Phifer .02 .10
285 Ken Harvey .02 .10
286 Rodney Hampton .07 .20
287 Willie Davis .02 .10
288 Yonel Jourdain .02 .10
289 Brian DeMarco .02 .10
290 Reggie White .10 .30
291 Kevin Williams .02 .10
292 Gary Plummer .02 .10
293 Terrance Shaw .02 .10
294 Calvin Williams .02 .10
295 Eddie Robinson .02 .10
296 Tony McGee .02 .10
297 Clay Matthews .02 .10
298 Joe Cain .02 .10
299 Tim McKyer .02 .10
300 Greg Lloyd .07 .20
301 Steve Wisniewski .02 .10
302 Ray Buchanan .02 .10
303 Lake Dawson .02 .10
304 Kevin Carter .02 .10
305 Phillippi Sparks .02 .10
306 Emmitt Smith .60 1.50
307 Ruben Brown .02 .10
308 Tom Carter .02 .10
309 William Floyd .07 .20
310 Jim Everett .02 .10
311 Vincent Brown .02 .10
312 Dennis Gibson .02 .10
313 Lorenzo Lynch .02 .10
314 Corey Harris .02 .10
315 James O.Stewart .07 .20
316 Kyle Brady .02 .10
317 Irving Fryar .07 .20
318 Jake Reed .07 .20
319 Vinny Testaverde .07 .20
320 John Elway .75 2.00
321 Tracy Scroggins .02 .10
322 Chris Spielman .02 .10
323 Horace Copeland .02 .10
324 Chris Zorich .02 .10
325 Mike Mamula .02 .10
326 Henry Ford .02 .10
327 Steve Walsh .02 .10
328 Stanley Richard .07 .20
329 Mike Jones .02 .10
330 Jim Harbaugh .07 .20
331 Darren Perry .02 .10
332 Ken Norton .02 .10
333 Kimble Anders .07 .20
334 Harold Green .02 .10
335 Tyrone Poole .02 .10
336 Mark Fields .02 .10
337 Darren Bennett .02 .10
338 Mike Sherrard .02 .10
339 Terry Ray RC .02 .10
340 Bruce Smith .07 .20
341 Daryl Johnston .07 .20
342 Vinnie Clark .02 .10
343 Mike Caldwell .02 .10
344 Vinson Smith .02 .10
345 Mo Lewis .02 .10
346 Brian Blades .02 .10
347 Rod Stephens .02 .10
348 David Palmer .02 .10
349 Blaine Bishop .02 .10
350 Jeff George .07 .20
351 George Teague .02 .10
352 Jeff Hostetler .02 .10
353 Michael Strahan .07 .20
354 Eric Davis .02 .10
355 Jerome Bettis .10 .30
356 Irv Smith .02 .10
357 Jeff Herrod .02 .10
358 Jay Novacek .02 .10
359 Bryce Paup .02 .10
360 Neil O'Donnell .07 .20
361 Eric Swann .02 .10
362 Corey Sawyer .02 .10
363 Ty Law .10 .30
364 Bo Orlando .02 .10
365 Marcus Allen .10 .30
366 Mark McMillian .02 .10
367 Mark Carrier WR .02 .10
368 Jackie Harris .02 .10
369 Steve Atwater .02 .10
370 Steve Young .30 .75
371 Brett Favre TYC .40 1.00
372 Scott Mitchell TYC .02 .10
373 Warren Moon TYC .02 .10
374 Jeff George TYC .07 .20
375 Jim Everett TYC .02 .10
376 John Elway TYC .40 1.00
377 Erik Kramer TYC .02 .10
378 Jeff Blake TYC .07 .20
379 Dan Marino TYC .40 1.00
380 Dave Krieg TYC .02 .10
381 Drew Bledsoe TYC .10 .30
382 Stan Humphries TYC .02 .10
383 Troy Aikman TYC .20 .50
384 Steve Young TYC .10 .30
385 Jim Kelly TYC .10 .30
386 Steve Bono TYC .02 .10
387 David Sloan .02 .10
388 Jeff Graham .02 .10
389 Hugh Douglas .07 .20
390 Dan Marino .75 2.00
391 Winston Moss .02 .10
392 Darrell Green .02 .10
393 Mark Stepnoski .02 .10
394 Bert Emanuel .07 .20
395 Eric Zeier .02 .10
396 Willie Jackson .07 .20
397 Qadry Ismail .07 .20
398 Michael Brooks .02 .10
399 D'Marco Farr .02 .10
400 Brett Favre .75 2.00
401 Carnell Lake .02 .10
402 Pat Swilling .02 .10
403 Stephen Grant .02 .10
404 Steve Tasker .02 .10
405 Ben Coates .07 .20
406 Steve Tovar .02 .10
407 Tony Martin .07 .20
408 Greg Hill .07 .20
409 Eric Guliford .02 .10
410 Michael Irvin .10 .30
411 Eric Hill .02 .10
412 Mario Bates .07 .20
413 Brian Stablein RC .02 .10
414 Marcus Jones RC .02 .10
415 Reggie Brown LB RC .02 .10
416 Lawrence Phillips RC .10 .30
417 Alex Van Dyke RC .02 .10
418 Daryl Gardener RC .02 .10
419 Mike Alstott RC .40 1.00
420 Kevin Hardy RC .10 .30
421 Rickey Dudley RC .10 .30
422 Jerome Woods RC .02 .10

423 Eric Moulds RC	.50	1.25
424 Cedric Jones RC	.02	.10
425 Simeon Rice RC	.30	.75
426 Marvin Harrison RC	1.00	2.50
427 Tim Biakabutuka RC	.10	.30
428 Duane Clemons RC	.02	.10
429 Alex Molden RC	.02	.10
430 Keyshawn Johnson RC	.40	1.00
431 Willie Anderson RC	.02	.10
432 John Mobley RC	.02	.10
433 Leeland McElroy RC	.07	.20
434 Regan Upshaw RC	.02	.10
435 Eddie George RC	.50	1.25
436 Jonathan Ogden RC	.10	.30
437 Eddie Kennison RC	.10	.30
438 Jermaine Mayberry RC	.02	.10
439 Checklist 1 of 2	.02	.10
440 Checklist 2 of 2	.02	.10
P1 Joe Namath Promo Steve Young	7.50	15.00
P1R Joe Namath Promo Steve Young (Refractor version)	10.00	20.00

1996 Topps Broadway's Reviews

COMPLETE SET (10)	10.00	25.00
STATED ODDS 1:12H, 1:8R, 1:3J, 1:6 SP.RET		
BR1 Kerry Collins	.40	1.00
BR2 Drew Bledsoe	1.00	2.00
BR3 Jeff Blake	.40	1.00
BR4 Brett Favre	3.00	6.00
BR5 Scott Mitchell	.25	.60
BR6 Troy Aikman	1.50	3.00
BR7 Steve Young	1.25	2.50
BR8 Jim Harbaugh	.25	.60
BR9 John Elway	3.00	6.00
BR10 Dan Marino	3.00	6.00

1996 Topps 40th Anniversary Retros

COMPLETE SET (40)	25.00	60.00
STATED ODDS 1:6 HOB, 1:4 RET, 1:4 SP.RET		
1 Jim Harbaugh 1956	.30	.75
2 Greg Lloyd 1957	.30	.75
3 Barry Sanders 1958	3.00	6.00
4 Merton Hanks 1959	.15	.40
5 Herman Moore 1960	.30	.75
6 Tim Brown 1961	.60	1.25
7 Brett Favre 1962	4.00	8.00
8 Cris Carter 1963	.60	1.25
9 Curtis Martin 1964	1.50	3.00
10 Bryce Paup 1965	.15	.40
11 Steve Bono 1966	.15	.40
12 Blaine Bishop 1967	.15	.40
13 Emmitt Smith 1968	3.00	6.00
14 Carnell Lake 1969	.15	.40
15 Marshall Faulk 1970	.75	1.50
16 Mike Morris 1971	.15	.40
17 Shannon Sharpe 1972	.30	.75
18 Steve Young 1973	1.50	3.00
19 Jeff George 1974	.30	.75
20 Junior Seau 1975	.60	1.25
21 Chris Warren 1976	.30	.75
22 Heath Shuler 1977	.30	.75
23 Jeff Blake 1978	.60	1.25
24 Reggie White 1979	.60	1.25
25 Jeff Hostetler 1980	.15	.40
26 Errict Rhett 1981	.30	.75
27 Rodney Hampton 1982	.30	.75
28 Jerry Rice 1983	2.00	4.00
29 Jim Everett 1984	.15	.40
30 Isaac Bruce 1985	.60	1.25
31 Dan Marino 1986	4.00	8.00
32 Marcus Allen 1987	.60	1.25
33 Erik Kramer 1988	.15	.40
34 John Elway 1989	4.00	8.00
35 Ricky Watters 1990	.30	.75
36 Troy Aikman 1991	2.00	4.00
37 Drew Bledsoe 1992	1.25	2.50
38 Scott Mitchell 1993	.30	.75
39 Rashaan Salaam 1994	.30	.75
40 Kerry Collins 1995	.60	1.25

1996 Topps Hobby Masters

COMPLETE SET (20)	50.00	120.00
STATED ODDS 1:10 JUMBO		
HM1 Brett Favre	8.00	20.00
HM2 Emmitt Smith	6.00	15.00
HM3 Drew Bledsoe	2.50	6.00
HM4 Marshall Faulk	1.50	4.00
HM5 Steve Young	3.00	8.00
HM6 Barry Sanders	6.00	15.00
HM7 Troy Aikman	4.00	10.00
HM8 Jerry Rice	4.00	10.00
HM9 Michael Irvin	1.25	3.00
HM10 Dan Marino	8.00	20.00
HM11 Chris Warren	.75	2.00
HM12 Reggie White	1.25	3.00
HM13 Jeff Blake	1.25	3.00
HM14 Greg Lloyd	.75	2.00
HM15 Curtis Martin	3.00	8.00
HM16 Junior Seau	1.25	3.00
HM17 Kerry Collins	1.25	3.00
HM18 Deion Sanders	2.50	6.00
HM19 Joey Galloway	1.25	3.00
HM20 John Elway	8.00	20.00

1996 Topps Namath Reprints

COMPLETE SET (10)	20.00	50.00
COMMON NAMATH (1-10)	2.50	6.00
NAM.ODDS 1:18H,1:12R,1:5J,1:12 SP.RET		
1 Joe Namath 1965 (standard sized card)	4.00	8.00
NNO Joe Namath 1965 (large 1965 Topps size)	6.00	12.00
NNO Joe Namath Poster/4000	15.00	25.00

1996 Topps Turf Warriors

COMPLETE SET (22)	75.00	125.00
TW1 Bryce Paup	.50	1.25
TW2 Ben Coates	1.00	2.50
TW3 Jim Harbaugh	1.00	2.50
TW4 Brian Mitchell	.50	1.25
TW5 Brett Favre	10.00	25.00
TW6 Junior Seau	1.50	4.00
TW7 Michael Irvin	1.50	4.00
TW8 Steve Young	4.00	10.00
TW9 Terry McDaniel	.50	1.25
TW10 Curtis Martin	4.00	10.00
TW11 Greg Lloyd	1.00	2.50
TW12 Cris Carter	1.50	4.00
TW13 Emmitt Smith	8.00	20.00
TW14 Reggie White	1.50	4.00
TW15 Marshall Faulk	2.00	5.00
TW16 Jerry Rice	5.00	12.00
TW17 Shannon Sharpe	1.00	2.50
TW18 Dan Marino	10.00	25.00
TW19 Ken Norton	.50	1.25
TW20 Barry Sanders	8.00	20.00
TW21 Neil Smith	1.00	2.50
TW22 Troy Aikman	5.00	12.00

1997 Topps

This 1997 Topps set was issued in one series totaling 415 cards and distributed in 11-card packs with a suggested retail of $1.29. The first 385 cards feature the veteran players. The final 30-cards feature 1997 draft picks and were inserted 1:3 packs on average, making them short prints. The fronts feature color action player photos in a three-sided white border with a team color top and side margin. A special spot matte and gloss finish complement the design. The backs carry a small color player photo and career statistics. The set contains a 30-card subset of the 1997 NFL Draft Picks (#386-415) pictured in their new NFL team uniforms. Promo cards were released to promote the set and can only be differentiated by the green colored border on the cardback instead of gold.

COMPLETE SET (415)	25.00	50.00
COMP.FACT.SET (424)	50.00	80.00
1 Brett Favre	.75	2.00
2 Lawyer Milloy	.10	.30
3 Tim Biakabutuka	.10	.30
4 Clyde Simmons	.07	.20
5 Deion Sanders	.20	.50
6 Anthony Miller	.07	.20
7 Marquez Pope	.07	.20
8 Mike Tomczak	.07	.20
9 William Thomas	.07	.20
10 Marshall Faulk	.25	.60
11 John Randle	.10	.30
12 Jim Kelly	.20	.50
13 Steve Bono	.10	.30
14 Rod Stephens	.07	.20
15 Stan Humphries	.07	.20
16 Terrell Buckley	.07	.20
17 Ki-Jana Carter	.07	.20
18 Marcus Robertson	.07	.20
19 Corey Harris	.07	.20
20 Rashaan Salaam	.07	.20
21 Rickey Dudley	.10	.30
22 Jamir Miller	.07	.20
23 Martin Mayhew	.07	.20
24 Jason Sehorn	.10	.30
25 Isaac Bruce	.20	.50
26 Johnnie Morton	.10	.30
27 Antonio Langham	.07	.20
28 Cornelius Bennett	.07	.20
29 Joe Johnson	.07	.20
30 Keyshawn Johnson	.20	.50
31 Willie Green	.07	.20
32 Craig Newsome	.07	.20
33 Brock Marion	.07	.20
34 Corey Fuller	.07	.20
35 Ben Coates	.10	.30
36 Ty Detmer	.10	.30
37 Charles Johnson	.10	.30
38 Willie Jackson	.07	.20
39 Tyronne Drakeford	.07	.20
40 Gus Frerotte	.07	.20
41 Robert Blackmon	.07	.20
42 Andre Coleman	.07	.20
43 Mario Bates	.07	.20
44 Chris Calloway	.07	.20
45 Terry McDaniel	.07	.20
46 Anthony Davis	.07	.20
47 Stanley Pritchett	.07	.20
48 Ray Buchanan	.07	.20
49 Chris Chandler	.10	.30
50 Ashley Ambrose	.07	.20
51 Tyrone Braxton	.07	.20
52 Pepper Johnson	.07	.20
53 Frank Sanders	.10	.30
54 Clay Matthews	.07	.20
55 Bruce Smith	.10	.30
56 Jermaine Lewis	.20	.50
57 Mark Carrier WR UER (features the cardback for Mark Carrier DB)	.07	.20
58 Jeff Graham	.07	.20
59 Keith Lyle	.07	.20
60 Trent Dilfer	.20	.50
61 Trace Armstrong	.07	.20
62 Jeff Herrod	.07	.20
63 Tyrone Wheatley	.10	.30
64 Torrance Small	.07	.20
65 Chris Warren	.10	.30
66 Terry Kirby	.10	.30
67 Eric Pegram	.07	.20
68 Sean Gilbert	.07	.20
69 Greg Biekert	.07	.20
70 Ricky Watters	.10	.30
71 Chris Hudson	.07	.20
72 Tamarick Vanover	.10	.30
73 Orlando Thomas	.07	.20
74 Jimmy Spencer	.07	.20
75 John Mobley	.07	.20
76 Henry Thomas	.07	.20
77 Santana Dotson	.07	.20
78 Boomer Esiason	.10	.30
79 Bobby Hebert	.07	.20
80 Kerry Collins	.20	.50
81 Bobby Engram	.10	.30
82 Kevin Smith	.07	.20
83 Rick Mirer	.07	.20
84 Ted Johnson	.07	.20
85 Derrick Alexander WR	.10	.30
86 Hugh Douglas	.07	.20
87 Rodney Harrison RC	.40	1.00
88 Roman Phifer	.07	.20
89 Warren Moon	.20	.50
90 Thurman Thomas	.20	.50
91 Michael McCrary	.07	.20
92 Dana Stubblefield	.07	.20
93 Andre Hastings UER front reads Hasting	.07	.20
94 William Fuller	.07	.20
95 Jeff Hostetler	.07	.20
96 Danny Kanell	.07	.20
97 Mark Fields	.07	.20
98 Eddie Robinson	.07	.20
99 Daryl Gardener	.07	.20
100 Drew Bledsoe	.25	.60
101 Winslow Oliver	.07	.20
102 Raymont Harris	.07	.20
103 LeShon Johnson	.07	.20
104 Byron Bam Morris	.07	.20
105 Herman Moore	.10	.30
106 Keith Jackson	.07	.20
107 Chris Penn	.07	.20
108 Robert Griffith RC	.07	.20
109 Jeff Burris	.07	.20
110 Troy Aikman	.40	1.00
111 Allen Aldridge	.07	.20
112 Mel Gray	.07	.20
113 Aaron Bailey	.07	.20
114 Michael Strahan	.10	.30
115 Adrian Murrell	.10	.30
116 Chris Mims	.07	.20
117 Robert Jones	.07	.20
118 Derrick Brooks	.20	.50
119 Tom Carter	.07	.20
120 Carl Pickens	.10	.30
121 Tony Brackens	.07	.20
122 O.J. McDuffie	.10	.30
123 Napoleon Kaufman	.20	.50
124 Chris T. Jones	.07	.20
125 Kordell Stewart	.20	.50
126 Ray Zellars	.07	.20
127 Jessie Tuggle	.07	.20
128 Greg Kragen	.07	.20
129 Brett Perriman	.07	.20
130 Steve Young	.25	.60
131 Willie Clay	.07	.20
132 Kimble Anders	.10	.30
133 Eugene Daniel	.07	.20
134 Jevon Langford	.07	.20
135 Shannon Sharpe	.10	.30
136 Wayne Simmons	.07	.20
137 Leeland McElroy	.07	.20
138 Mike Caldwell	.07	.20
139 Eric Moulds	.20	.50
140 Eddie George	.20	.50
141 Jamal Anderson	.20	.50
142 Michael Timpson	.07	.20
143 Tony Tolbert	.07	.20
144 Robert Smith	.10	.30
145 Mike Alstott	.20	.50
146 Gary Jones	.07	.20
147 Terrance Shaw	.07	.20
148 Carlton Gray	.07	.20
149 Kevin Carter	.07	.20
150 Darrell Green	.10	.30
151 David Dunn	.07	.20
152 Ken Norton	.07	.20
153 Chad Brown	.07	.20
154 Pat Swilling	.07	.20
155 Irving Fryar	.10	.30
156 Michael Haynes	.07	.20
157 Shawn Jefferson	.07	.20
158 Stephen Grant	.07	.20
159 James O.Stewart	.10	.30
160 Derrick Thomas	.20	.50
161 Tim Bowens	.07	.20
162 Dixon Edwards	.07	.20
163 Micheal Barrow	.07	.20
164 Antonio Freeman	.20	.50
165 Terrell Davis	.25	.60
166 Henry Ellard	.10	.30
167 Daryl Johnston	.10	.30
168 Bryan Cox	.07	.20
169 Chad Cota	.07	.20
170 Vinny Testaverde	.10	.30
171 Andre Rison	.10	.30
172 Larry Centers	.10	.30
173 Craig Heyward	.07	.20
174 Glyn Milburn	.07	.20
175 Hardy Nickerson	.07	.20
176 Corey Miller	.07	.20
177 Bobby Houston	.07	.20
178 Marco Coleman	.07	.20
179 Winston Moss	.07	.20
180 Tony Banks	.10	.30
181 Jeff Lageman	.07	.20
182 Jason Belser	.07	.20
183 James Jett	.10	.30
184 Wayne Martin	.07	.20
185 Dave Meggett	.07	.20
186 Terrell Owens	.25	.60
187 Willie Williams	.07	.20
188 Eric Turner	.07	.20
189 Chuck Smith	.07	.20
190 Simeon Rice	.10	.30
191 Kevin Greene	.10	.30
192 Lance Johnstone	.07	.20
193 Marty Carter	.07	.20
194 Ricardo McDonald	.07	.20
195 Michael Irvin	.20	.50
196 George Koonce	.07	.20
197 Robert Porcher	.07	.20
198 Mark Collins	.07	.20
199 Louis Oliver	.07	.20
200 John Elway	.75	2.00
201 Jake Reed	.10	.30
202 Rodney Hampton	.10	.30
203 Aaron Glenn	.07	.20
204 Mike Mamula	.07	.20
205 Terry Allen	.20	.50
206 John Lynch	.10	.30
207 Todd Lyght	.07	.20
208 Dean Wells	.07	.20
209 Aaron Hayden	.07	.20
210 Blaine Bishop	.07	.20
211 Bert Emanuel	.10	.30
212 Mark Carrier DB UER (features the cardback for Mark Carrier WR)	.07	.20
213 Dale Carter	.07	.20
214 Jimmy Smith	.10	.30
215 Jim Harbaugh	.10	.30
216 Jeff George	.10	.30
217 Anthony Newman	.07	.20
218 Ty Law	.10	.30
219 Brent Jones	.07	.20
220 Emmitt Smith	.60	1.50
221 Bennie Blades	.07	.20
222 Alfred Williams	.07	.20
223 Eugene Robinson	.07	.20
224 Fred Barnett	.07	.20
225 Errict Rhett	.07	.20
226 Leslie O'Neal	.07	.20
227 Michael Sinclair	.07	.20
228 Marvcus Patton	.07	.20
229 Darrien Gordon	.07	.20
230 Jerome Bettis	.20	.50
231 Troy Vincent	.07	.20
232 Ray Mickens	.07	.20
233 Lonnie Johnson	.07	.20
234 Charles Way	.07	.20
235 Chris Sanders	.07	.20
236 Bracy Walker	.07	.20
237 Dave Krieg UER front has Bears logo	.07	.20
238 Kent Graham	.07	.20
239 Ray Lewis	.30	.75
240 Cris Carter	.20	.50
241 Elvis Grbac	.10	.30
242 Eric Davis	.07	.20
243 Harvey Williams	.07	.20
244 Eric Allen	.07	.20
245 Bryant Young	.07	.20
246 Terrell Fletcher	.07	.20
247 Darren Perry	.07	.20
248 Ken Harvey	.07	.20
249 Marvin Washington	.07	.20
250 Marcus Allen	.20	.50
251 Darrin Smith	.07	.20
252 James Francis	.07	.20
253 Michael Jackson	.10	.30
254 Ryan McNeil	.07	.20
255 Mark Chmura	.10	.30
256 Keenan McCardell	.10	.30
257 Tony Bennett	.07	.20
258 Irving Spikes	.07	.20
259 Jason Dunn	.07	.20
260 Joey Galloway	.10	.30
261 Eddie Kennison	.10	.30
262 Lonnie Marts	.07	.20
263 Thomas Lewis	.07	.20
264 Tedy Bruschi	.40	1.00
265 Steve Atwater	.07	.20
266 Dorsey Levens	.20	.50
267 Kurt Schulz	.07	.20
268 Rob Moore	.10	.30
269 Walt Harris	.07	.20
270 Steve McNair	.25	.60
271 Bill Romanowski	.07	.20
272 Sean Dawkins	.07	.20
273 Don Beebe	.07	.20
274 Fernando Smith	.07	.20
275 Willie McGinest	.07	.20
276 Levon Kirkland	.07	.20
277 Tony Martin	.10	.30
278 Warren Sapp	.10	.30
279 Lamar Smith	.20	.50
280 Mark Brunell	.25	.60
281 Jim Everett	.07	.20
282 Victor Green	.07	.20
283 Mike Jones	.07	.20
284 Charlie Garner	.10	.30
285 Karim Abdul-Jabbar	.10	.30
286 Michael Westbrook	.10	.30
287 Lawrence Phillips	.07	.20
288 Amani Toomer	.10	.30
289 Neil Smith	.10	.30
290 Barry Sanders	.60	1.50
291 Willie Davis	.07	.20
292 Bo Orlando	.07	.20
293 Alonzo Spellman	.07	.20
294 Eric Hill	.07	.20
295 Wesley Walls	.10	.30
296 Todd Collins	.07	.20
297 Stevon Moore	.07	.20
298 Eric Metcalf	.10	.30
299 Darren Woodson	.07	.20
300 Jerry Rice	.40	1.00
301 Scott Mitchell	.10	.30
302 Ray Crockett	.07	.20
303 Jim Schwantz RC UER back reads Schwartz	.07	.20
304 Steve Tovar	.07	.20
305 Terance Mathis	.10	.30
306 Earnest Byner	.07	.20
307 Chris Spielman	.07	.20
308 Curtis Conway	.10	.30
309 Cris Dishman	.07	.20
310 Marvin Harrison	.20	.50
311 Sam Mills	.07	.20
312 Brent Alexander RC	.07	.20
313 Shawn Wooden RC	.07	.20
314 Dewayne Washington	.07	.20
315 Terry Glenn	.20	.50
316 Winfred Tubbs	.07	.20
317 Dave Brown	.07	.20
318 Neil O'Donnell	.10	.30
319 Anthony Parker	.07	.20
320 Junior Seau	.20	.50
321 Brian Mitchell	.07	.20
322 Regan Upshaw	.07	.20
323 Darryl Williams	.07	.20
324 Chris Doleman	.07	.20
325 Rod Woodson	.10	.30
326 Derrick Witherspoon	.07	.20
327 Chester McGlockton	.07	.20
328 Mickey Washington	.07	.20
329 Greg Hill	.07	.20
330 Reggie White	.20	.50
331 John Copeland	.07	.20
332 Doug Evans	.07	.20
333 Lamar Lathon	.07	.20
334 Mark Maddox	.07	.20
335 Natrone Means	.10	.30
336 Corey Widmer	.07	.20
337 Terry Wooden	.07	.20
338 Merton Hanks	.07	.20
339 Cortez Kennedy	.07	.20
340 Tyrone Hughes	.07	.20
341 Tim Brown	.20	.50
342 John Jurkovic	.07	.20
343 Carnell Lake	.07	.20
344 Stanley Richard	.07	.20
345 Darryll Lewis	.07	.20
346 Dan Wilkinson	.07	.20
347 Broderick Thomas	.07	.20
348 Brian Williams	.07	.20
349 Eric Swann	.07	.20
350 Dan Marino	.75	2.00
351 Anthony Johnson	.07	.20
352 Joe Cain	.07	.20
353 Quinn Early	.07	.20
354 Seth Joyner	.07	.20
355 Garrison Hearst	.10	.30
356 Edgar Bennett	.10	.30
357 Brian Washington	.07	.20
358 Kevin Hardy	.07	.20
359 Quentin Coryatt	.07	.20
360 Tim McDonald	.07	.20
361 Brian Blades	.07	.20
362 Courtney Hawkins	.07	.20
363 Ray Farmer	.07	.20
364 Jessie Armstead	.07	.20
365 Curtis Martin	.25	.60
366 Zach Thomas	.20	.50
367 Frank Wycheck	.10	.30
368 Darnay Scott	.10	.30
369 Percy Ellsworth RC	.07	.20
370 Desmond Howard	.10	.30
371 Aeneas Williams	.07	.20
372 Bryce Paup	.07	.20
373 Michael Bates	.07	.20
374 Brad Johnson	.20	.50
375 Jeff Blake	.10	.30
376 Donnell Woolford UER front photo incorrect	.07	.20
377 Mo Lewis	.07	.20
378 Phillippi Sparks	.07	.20
379 Michael Bankston	.07	.20
380 LeRoy Butler	.07	.20
381 Tyrone Poole	.07	.20
382 Wayne Chrebet	.20	.50
383 Chris Slade	.07	.20
384 Checklist 1 (1-208)	.07	.20
385 Checklist 2 (209-415)	.07	.20
386 Will Blackwell SP RC	.10	.30
387 Tom Knight SP RC	.07	.20
388 Darnell Autry SP RC	.20	.50
389 Bryant Westbrook SP RC	.07	.20
390 David LaFleur RC SP	.10	.30
391 Antowain Smith SP RC	1.00	2.50
392 Kevin Lockett SP RC	.20	.50
393 Rae Carruth SP RC	.10	.30
394 Renaldo Wynn SP RC	.10	.30
395 Jim Druckenmiller SP RC	.20	.50
396 Kenny Holmes SP RC	.30	.75
397 Shawn Springs SP RC	.20	.50
398 Troy Davis SP RC	.20	.50
399 Dwayne Rudd SP RC	.30	.75
400 Orlando Pace SP RC	.30	.75
401 Byron Hanspard SP RC	.20	.50
402 Corey Dillon SP RC	1.50	4.00
403 Walter Jones SP RC	.30	.75
404 Reidel Anthony SP RC	.30	.75
405 Peter Boulware SP RC	.30	.75
406 Reinard Wilson SP RC	.20	.50
407 Pat Barnes SP RC	.30	.75
408 Yatil Green SP RC	.30	.75
409 Joey Kent SP RC	.30	.75
410 Ike Hilliard SP RC	.60	1.50
411 Jake Plummer SP RC	1.50	4.00
412 Darrell Russell SP RC	.10	.30
413 James Farrior SP RC	.30	.75
414 Tony Gonzalez SP RC	1.50	4.00
415 Warrick Dunn SP RC	1.25	3.00
P40 Gus Frerotte Promo green border on back	.08	.25
P170 V.Testaverde Promo green border on back	.08	.25
P240 Cris Carter Promo green border on back	.15	.40
P250 Marcus Allen Promo green border on back	.15	.40
P285 K.Abdul-Jabbar Promo green border on back	.08	.25
P356 Edgar Bennett Promo green border on back	.08	.25

1997 Topps Minted in Canton

COMPLETE SET (415)	250.00	500.00
*STARS: 5X TO 12X BASIC CARDS		
*RCs: 1.5X TO 3X BASIC CARDS		
STATED ODDS 1:6		

1997 Topps Autographs

CURRENT PLAYER ODDS 1:218H,1:60J		
SEAU ODDS 1:364 HOB, 1:100 JUM		
1 Karim Abdul-Jabbar	10.00	25.00
2 Terrell Davis	15.00	40.00
3 Eddie George	12.50	30.00
4 Jim Harbaugh	15.00	30.00
5 Desmond Howard	12.50	30.00
6 Herman Moore	7.50	20.00
7 Junior Seau	12.50	30.00
8 Chris Warren	7.50	20.00

1997 Topps Career Best

COMPLETE SET (5)	15.00	40.00
1 Dan Marino	10.00	25.00
2 Marcus Allen	2.50	6.00
3 Marcus Allen	2.50	6.00
4 Reggie White	2.50	6.00
5 Jerry Rice	5.00	12.00

1997 Topps Hall Bound

COMPLETE SET (15)	40.00	100.00
STATED ODDS 1:36 HOB, 1:8 JUM		
HB1 Jerry Rice	4.00	10.00
HB2 Rod Woodson	1.25	3.00
HB3 Marcus Allen	2.00	5.00
HB4 Reggie White	2.00	5.00
HB5 Emmitt Smith	6.00	15.00
HB6 Junior Seau	2.00	5.00
HB7 Troy Aikman	4.00	10.00
HB8 Bruce Smith	1.25	3.00
HB9 John Elway	8.00	20.00
HB10 Brett Favre	8.00	20.00
HB11 Thurman Thomas	2.00	5.00
HB12 Deion Sanders	2.00	5.00
HB13 Dan Marino	8.00	20.00
HB14 Steve Young	2.50	6.00
HB15 Barry Sanders	6.00	15.00

1997 Topps Hall of Fame Autographs

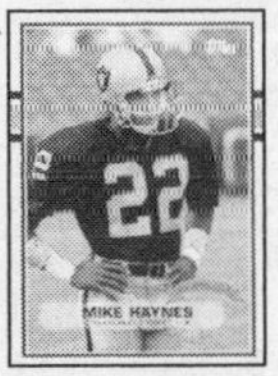

HAYNES/WEBSTER ODDS 1:436H,1:120J		
MARA ODDS 1:872 HOB,1:240 JUM		
SHULA ODDS 1:290HOB,1:80 JUM		
HF1 Mike Haynes	30.00	60.00
HF2 Don Shula	40.00	80.00
HF3 Wellington Mara	60.00	120.00
HF4 Mike Webster	150.00	300.00

1997 Topps High Octane

COMPLETE SET (15)	40.00	100.00
STATED ODDS 1:36 HOB, 1:8 JUM		
HO1 Brett Favre	8.00	20.00
HO2 Jerome Bettis	2.00	5.00
HO3 Jerry Rice	4.00	10.00
HO4 Junior Seau	2.00	5.00
HO5 Emmitt Smith	6.00	15.00
HO6 Herman Moore	1.25	3.00
HO7 Shannon Sharpe	1.25	3.00
HO8 Curtis Martin	2.50	6.00
HO9 Eddie George	2.00	5.00
HO10 Barry Sanders	6.00	15.00
HO11 John Elway	8.00	20.00
HO12 Steve Young	2.50	6.00
HO13 Drew Bledsoe	2.50	6.00
HO14 Troy Aikman	4.00	10.00
HO15 Dan Marino	8.00	20.00

1997 Topps Mystery Finest Bronze

COMPLETE SET (20)	25.00	60.00
*SINGLES: 2.5X TO 6X BASE CARD HI		
BRONZE STATED ODDS 1:36H, 1:8J		
*BRONZE REF: 1.2X TO 3X BASIC INSERTS		
BRONZE REF.ODDS 1:144H, 1:38J		
*GOLDS: 1.5X TO 4X BASIC INSERTS		
GOLD STATED ODDS 1:324 HOB, 1:88 JUM		
*GOLD REF: 5X TO 12 BASIC INSERTS		
GOLD REF.ODDS 1:1296 HOB, 1:354 JUM		
COMP.SILVER SET (20)	75.00	150.00
*SILVERS: .6X TO 1.5X BASIC INSERTS		
SILVER STATED ODDS 1:108 HOB, 1:28 JUM		
COMP.SILVER REF (20)	200.00	400.00
*SILVER REF: 2X TO 5X BASIC INSERTS		
SILVER REF.ODDS 1:432 HOB, 1:116 JUM		
M1 Barry Sanders	4.00	10.00
M2 Mark Brunell	1.50	4.00
M3 Terrell Davis	1.50	4.00
M4 Isaac Bruce	1.25	3.00
M5 Jerry Rice	2.50	6.00
M6 Drew Bledsoe	1.50	4.00
M7 Carl Pickens	.75	2.00
M8 Steve Young	1.50	4.00
M9 Cris Carter	1.25	3.00
M10 John Elway	5.00	12.00
M11 Junior Seau	1.25	3.00
M12 Herman Moore	.75	2.00
M13 Vinny Testaverde	.75	2.00
M14 Jerome Bettis	1.25	3.00
M15 Troy Aikman	2.50	6.00
M16 Reggie White	1.25	3.00
M17 Kerry Collins	1.25	3.00
M18 Curtis Martin	1.50	4.00
M19 Shannon Sharpe	.75	2.00
M20 Brett Favre	5.00	12.00

1997 Topps Season's Best

COMPLETE SET (25)	25.00	60.00
STATED ODDS: 1:16 HOB, 1:4 JUM		
1 Mark Brunell	1.50	4.00
2 Vinny Testaverde	.75	2.00
3 Drew Bledsoe	1.50	4.00
4 Brett Favre	5.00	12.00
5 Jeff Blake	.75	2.00
6 Barry Sanders	4.00	10.00
7 Terrell Davis	1.50	4.00
8 Jerome Bettis	1.25	3.00
9 Ricky Watters	.75	2.00
10 Eddie George	1.25	3.00
11 Brian Mitchell	.50	1.25
12 Tyrone Hughes	.50	1.25
13 Eric Metcalf	.75	2.00
14 Glyn Milburn	.50	1.25
15 Ricky Watters	.75	2.00
16 Kevin Greene	.75	2.00
17 Lamar Lathon	.50	1.25
18 Bruce Smith	.75	2.00
19 Michael Sinclair UER front reads Michael McCrary	.50	1.25
20 Derrick Thomas	1.25	3.00
21 Jerry Rice	2.50	6.00
22 Herman Moore	.75	2.00
23 Carl Pickens	.75	2.00
24 Cris Carter	1.25	3.00
25 Brett Perriman	.50	1.25

1997 Topps Underclassmen

COMPLETE SET (10)	15.00	40.00
STATED ODDS: 1:24 RET		
U1 Kerry Collins	2.50	6.00
U2 Karim Abdul-Jabbar	1.50	4.00
U3 Simeon Rice	1.50	4.00
U4 Keyshawn Johnson	2.50	6.00
U5 Eddie George	2.50	6.00
U6 Eddie Kennison	1.50	4.00
U7 Terry Glenn	2.50	6.00
U8 Kevin Hardy	1.00	2.50
U9 Steve McNair	3.00	8.00
U10 Kordell Stewart	2.50	6.00

1997 Topps Hall of Fame Class of 1997

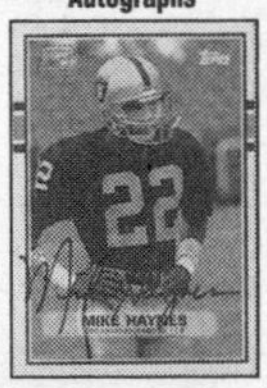

This five-card set was distributed at the 1997 induction ceremonies for the Pro Football Hall of Fame. Along with the set, two 1997 Topps promo cards were also distributed. Each card includes a photo of a 1997 inductee printed in the style of a Topps card from the past. A gold foil "Class of '97" logo is featured on the cardfronts and the Hall of Fame is pictured on the cardbacks. Versions of the cards were later included as signed inserts in Topps packs and unsigned inserts in Topps factory sets.

COMPLETE SET (5)	2.00	5.00
1 Mike Haynes	.40	1.00
2 Don Shula	.60	1.50
3 Wellington Mara	.40	1.00
4 Mike Webster	.40	1.00
NNO Header Card (Pro Football Hall of Fame)	.40	1.00

1998 Topps Promos

This set of six cards was released to preview the upcoming regular issue Topps football set for 1998. Each card closely resembles its base set counterpart and can be differentiated by the unique card number.

COMPLETE SET (6)	4.00	10.00
PP1 Mike Alstott	.30	.75
PP2 Eddie George	.50	1.25
PP3 Brett Favre	1.20	3.00
PP4 Terrell Davis	1.00	2.50
PP5 Dan Marino	1.20	3.00
PP6 Junior Seau	.20	.50

1998 Topps

The 1998 Topps series one was issued with a total of 360 standard size cards. The 11-card packs retail for $1.29 each. The fronts feature color game-action photography on 16 point stock. The backs carry complete career statistics and insightful text on the pictured player. The factory sets contained five assorted insert sets (not including the Giants Owner promo card).

COMPLETE SET (360)	30.00	60.00
COMP.FACT.SET (365)	50.00	80.00
1 Barry Sanders	.60	1.50
2 Derrick Rodgers	.07	.20
3 Chris Calloway	.07	.20
4 Bruce Armstrong	.07	.20
5 Horace Copeland	.07	.20
6 Chad Brown	.07	.20
7 Ken Harvey	.07	.20
8 Levon Kirkland	.07	.20
9 Glenn Foley	.10	.30
10 Corey Dillon	.20	.50
11 Sean Dawkins	.07	.20
12 Curtis Conway	.10	.30
13 Chris Chandler	.10	.30
14 Kerry Collins	.10	.30
15 Jonathan Ogden	.07	.20
16 Sam Shade	.07	.20
17 Vaughn Hebron	.07	.20
18 Quentin Coryatt	.07	.20
19 Jerris McPhail	.07	.20
20 Warrick Dunn	.20	.50
21 Wayne Martin	.07	.20
22 Chad Lewis	.10	.30
23 Danny Kanell	.10	.30
24 Shawn Springs	.07	.20
25 Emmitt Smith	.60	1.50
26 Todd Lyght	.07	.20
27 Donnie Edwards	.07	.20
28 Charlie Jones	.07	.20
29 Willie McGinest	.07	.20
30 Steve Young	.25	.60
31 Darrell Russell	.07	.20
32 Gary Anderson	.07	.20
33 Stanley Richard	.07	.20
34 Leslie O'Neal	.07	.20
35 Dermontti Dawson	.07	.20
36 Jeff Brady	.07	.20
37 Kimble Anders	.10	.30
38 Glyn Milburn	.07	.20
39 Greg Hill	.07	.20
40 Freddie Jones	.07	.20
41 Bobby Engram	.10	.30
42 Aeneas Williams	.07	.20
43 Antowain Smith	.20	.50
44 Reggie White	.20	.50
45 Rae Carruth	.07	.20
46 Leon Johnson	.07	.20
47 Bryant Young	.07	.20
48 Jamie Asher	.07	.20
49 Hardy Nickerson	.07	.20
50 Jerome Bettis	.20	.50
51 Michael Strahan	.10	.30
52 John Randle	.10	.30
53 Kevin Hardy	.07	.20
54 Eric Bjornson	.07	.20
55 Morten Andersen UER (misspelled Anderson)	.07	.20
56 Larry Centers	.07	.20
57 Bryce Paup	.07	.20
58 John Mobley	.07	.20
59 Michael Dates	.07	.20
60 Tim Brown	.20	.50
61 Doug Evans	.07	.20
62 Will Shields	.07	.20
63 Jeff Graham	.07	.20
64 Tony Martin	.07	.20
65 Steve Broussard	.07	.20
66 Blaine Bishop	.07	.20
67 Ernie Conwell	.07	.20
68 Heath Shuler	.07	.20
69 Eric Metcalf	.07	.20
70 Terry Glenn	.20	.50
71 James Hasty	.07	.20
72 Robert Porcher	.07	.20
73 Keenan McCardell	.10	.30
74 Tyrone Hughes	.07	.20
75 Troy Aikman	.40	1.00
76 Peter Boulware	.07	.20
77 Rob Johnson	.10	.30
78 Erik Kramer	.07	.20
79 Kevin Smith	.07	.20
80 Andre Rison	.10	.30
81 Jim Harbaugh	.10	.30
82 Chris Hudson	.07	.20
83 Ray Zellars	.07	.20
84 Jeff George	.10	.30
85 Willie Davis	.07	.20
86 Jason Gildon	.07	.20
87 Robert Brooks	.10	.30
88 Chad Cota	.07	.20
89 Simeon Rice	.10	.30
90 Mark Brunell	.20	.50
91 Jay Graham	.07	.20
92 Scott Greene	.07	.20
93 Jeff Blake	.10	.30
94 Jason Belser	.07	.20
95 Derrick Alexander DE	.07	.20
96 Ty Law	.10	.30
97 Charles Johnson	.07	.20
98 James Jett	.10	.30
99 Darrell Green	.10	.30
100 Brett Favre	.75	2.00
101 George Jones	.07	.20
102 Derrick Mason	.10	.30
103 Sam Adams	.07	.20
104 Lawrence Phillips	.07	.20
105 Randal Hill	.07	.20
106 John Mangum	.07	.20
107 Natrone Means	.10	.30
108 Bill Romanowski	.07	.20
109 Terance Mathis	.10	.30
110 Bruce Smith	.10	.30
111 Pete Mitchell	.07	.20
112 Duane Clemons	.07	.20
113 Willie Clay	.07	.20
114 Eric Allen	.07	.20
115 Troy Drayton	.07	.20
116 Derrick Thomas	.20	.50
117 Charles Way	.07	.20
118 Wayne Chrebet	.20	.50
119 Bobby Hoying	.10	.30
120 Michael Jackson	.07	.20
121 Gary Zimmerman	.07	.20
122 Yancey Thigpen	.07	.20
123 Dana Stubblefield	.07	.20
124 Keith Lyle	.07	.20
125 Marco Coleman	.07	.20
126 Karl Williams	.07	.20
127 Stephen Davis	.07	.20
128 Chris Sanders	.07	.20
129 Cris Dishman	.07	.20
130 Jake Plummer	.20	.50
131 Darryl Williams	.07	.20
132 Merton Hanks	.07	.20
133 Torrance Small	.07	.20
134 Aaron Glenn	.07	.20
135 Chester McGlockton	.07	.20
136 William Thomas	.07	.20
137 Kordell Stewart	.20	.50
138 Jason Taylor	.10	.30

139 Lake Dawson .07 .20
140 Carl Pickens .10 .30
141 Eugene Robinson .07 .20
142 Ed McCaffrey .10 .30
143 Lamar Lathon .07 .20
144 Ray Buchanan .07 .20
145 Thurman Thomas .20 .50
146 Andre Reed .10 .30
147 Wesley Walls .10 .30
148 Rob Moore .10 .30
149 Darren Woodson .07 .20
150 Eddie George .20 .50
151 Michael Irvin .20 .50
152 Johnnie Morton .10 .30
153 Ken Dilger .07 .20
154 Tony Boselli .07 .20
155 Randall McDaniel .07 .20
156 Mark Fields .07 .20
157 Phillippi Sparks .07 .20
158 Troy Davis .07 .20
159 Troy Vincent .07 .20
160 Cris Carter .20 .50
161 Amp Lee .07 .20
162 Will Blackwell .07 .20
163 Chad Scott .07 .20
164 Henry Ellard .10 .30
165 Robert Jones .07 .20
166 Garrison Hearst .20 .50
167 James McKnight .20 .50
168 Rodney Harrison .10 .30
169 Adrian Murrell .10 .30
170 Rod Smith WR .10 .30
171 Desmond Howard .10 .30
172 Ben Coates .10 .30
173 David Palmer .07 .20
174 Zach Thomas .20 .50
175 Dale Carter .07 .20
176 Mark Chmura .10 .30
177 Elvis Grbac .10 .30
178 Jason Hanson .07 .20
179 Walt Harris .07 .20
180 Ricky Watters .10 .30
181 Ray Lewis .20 .50
182 Lonnie Johnson .07 .20
183 Marvin Harrison .20 .50
184 Dorsey Levens .20 .50
185 Tony Gonzalez .20 .50
186 Andre Hastings .07 .20
187 Kevin Turner .07 .20
188 Mo Lewis .07 .20
189 Jason Sehorn .10 .30
190 Drew Bledsoe .30 .75
191 Michael Sinclair .07 .20
192 William Floyd .07 .20
193 Kenny Holmes .07 .20
194 Marvcus Patton .07 .20
195 Warren Sapp .10 .30
196 Junior Seau .20 .50
197 Ryan McNeil .07 .20
198 Tyrone Wheatley .10 .30
199 Robert Smith .20 .50
200 Terrell Davis .20 .50
201 Brett Perriman .07 .20
202 Tamarick Vanover .07 .20
203 Stephen Boyd .07 .20
204 Zack Crockett .07 .20
205 Sherman Williams .07 .20
206 Neil Smith .10 .30
207 Jermaine Lewis .10 .30
208 Kevin Williams .07 .20
209 Byron Hanspard .07 .20
210 Warren Moon .20 .50
211 Tony McGee .07 .20
212 Raymont Harris .07 .20
213 Eric Davis .07 .20
214 Darrien Gordon .07 .20
215 James Stewart .10 .30
216 Derrick Mayes .10 .30
217 Brad Johnson .20 .50
218 Karim Abdul-Jabbar UER .20 .50
(Jabbar missing from name)
219 Hugh Douglas .07 .20
220 Terry Allen .20 .50
221 Rhett Hall .07 .20
222 Terrell Fletcher .07 .20
223 Carnell Lake .07 .20
224 Darryll Lewis .07 .20
225 Chris Slade .07 .20
226 Michael Westbrook .10 .30
227 Willie Williams .07 .20
228 Tony Banks .10 .30
229 Keyshawn Johnson .20 .50
230 Mike Alstott .20 .50
231 Tiki Barber .20 .50
232 Jake Reed .10 .30
233 Eric Swann .07 .20
234 Eric Moulds .20 .50
235 Vinny Testaverde .10 .30
236 Jessie Tuggle .07 .20
237 Ryan Wetnight RC .07 .20
238 Tyrone Poole .07 .20
239 Bryant Westbrook .07 .20
240 Steve McNair .20 .50
241 Jimmy Smith .10 .30
242 Dewayne Washington .07 .20
243 Robert Harris .07 .20
244 Rod Woodson .10 .30
245 Reidel Anthony .10 .30
246 Jessie Armstead .07 .20
247 O.J. McDuffie .10 .30
248 Carlton Gray .07 .20
249 LeRoy Butler .07 .20
250 Jerry Rice .40 1.00
251 Frank Sanders .10 .30
252 Todd Collins .07 .20
253 Fred Lane .07 .20
254 David Dunn .07 .20
255 Micheal Barrow .07 .20
256 Luther Elliss .07 .20
257 Scott Mitchell .10 .30
258 Dave Meggett .07 .20
259 Rickey Dudley .07 .20
260 Isaac Bruce .20 .50
261 Henry Jones .10 .30
262 Leslie Shepherd .07 .20
263 Derrick Brooks .20 .50
264 Greg Lloyd .07 .20
265 Terrell Buckley .07 .20
266 Antonio Freeman .20 .50
267 Tony Brackens .07 .20
268 Mark McMillian .07 .20
269 Dexter Coakley .07 .20
270 Dan Marino .75 2.00
271 Bryan Cox .07 .20
272 Leeland McElroy .07 .20
273 Jeff Burris .07 .20
274 Eric Green .07 .20
275 Darnay Scott .10 .30
276 Greg Clark .07 .20
277 Mario Bates .10 .30
278 Eric Turner .07 .20
279 Neil O'Donnell .10 .30
280 Herman Moore .10 .30
281 Gary Brown .07 .20
282 Terrell Owens .20 .50
283 Frank Wycheck .07 .20
284 Trent Dilfer .20 .50
285 Curtis Martin .20 .50
286 Ricky Proehl .07 .20
287 Steve Atwater .07 .20
288 Aaron Bailey .07 .20
289 William Henderson .10 .30
290 Marcus Allen .20 .50
291 Tom Knight .07 .20
292 Quinn Early .07 .20
293 Michael McCrary .07 .20
294 Bert Emanuel .10 .30
295 Tom Carter .07 .20
296 Kevin Glover .07 .20
297 Marshall Faulk .25 .60
298 Harvey Williams .07 .20
299 Chris Warren .10 .30
300 John Elway .75 2.00
301 Eddie Kennison .10 .30
302 Gus Frerotte .07 .20
303 Regan Upshaw .07 .20
304 Kevin Gogan .07 .20
305 Napoleon Kaufman .20 .50
306 Charlie Garner .10 .30
307 Shawn Jefferson .07 .20
308 Tommy Vardell .07 .20
309 Mike Hollis .07 .20
310 Irving Fryar .10 .30
311 Shannon Sharpe .10 .30
312 Byron Bam Morris .07 .20
313 Jamal Anderson .20 .50
314 Chris Gedney .07 .20
315 Chris Spielman .07 .20
316 Derrick Alexander WR .10 .30
317 O.J. Santiago .07 .20
318 Anthony Miller .07 .20
319 Ki-Jana Carter .07 .20
320 Deion Sanders .20 .50
321 Joey Galloway .10 .30
322 J.J. Stokes .10 .30
323 Rodney Thomas .07 .20
324 John Lynch .10 .30
325 Mike Pritchard .07 .20
326 Terrance Shaw .07 .20
327 Ted Johnson .07 .20
328 Ashley Ambrose .07 .20
329 Checklist 1 .07 .20
330 Checklist 2 .07 .20
331 Jerome Pathon RC 1.00 2.50
332 Ryan Leaf RC 1.00 2.50
333 Duane Starks RC .50 1.25
334 Brian Simmons RC .75 2.00
335 Keith Brooking RC 1.00 2.50
336 Robert Edwards RC .75 2.00
337 Curtis Enis RC .50 1.25
338 John Avery RC .75 2.00
339 Fred Taylor RC 1.50 4.00
340 Germane Crowell RC .75 2.00
341 Hines Ward RC 4.00 10.00
342 Marcus Nash RC .50 1.25
343 Jacquez Green RC .75 2.00
344 Joe Jurevicius RC 1.00 2.50
345 Greg Ellis RC .50 1.25
346 Brian Griese RC 2.00 5.00
347 Tavian Banks RC .75 2.00
348 Robert Holcombe RC .75 2.00
349 Skip Hicks RC .75 2.00
350 Ahman Green RC 2.50 6.00
351 Takeo Spikes RC 1.00 2.50
352 Randy Moss RC 4.00 10.00
353 Andre Wadsworth RC .75 2.00
354 Jason Peter RC .50 1.25
355 Grant Wistrom RC .75 2.00
356 Charles Woodson RC 1.25 3.00
357 Kevin Dyson RC 1.00 2.50
358 Pat Johnson RC .75 2.00
359 Tim Dwight RC 1.00 2.50
360 Peyton Manning RC 8.00 20.00
P1 Robert Tisch 2.00 5.00
(Promo card of Giants' owner)

1998 Topps Autographs

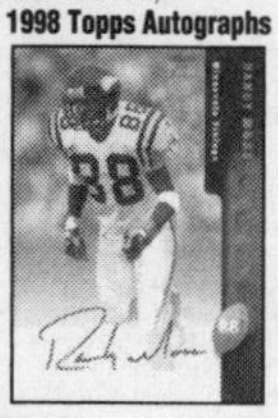

STATED ODDS 1:260 HOBBY
A1 Randy Moss 40.00 100.00
A2 Mike Alstott 10.00 25.00
A3 Jake Plummer 10.00 25.00
A4 Corey Dillon 8.00 20.00
A5 Kordell Stewart 10.00 25.00
A6 Eddie George 10.00 25.00
A7 Jason Sehorn 8.00 20.00
A8 Joey Galloway 8.00 20.00
A9 Ryan Leaf 6.00 15.00
A10B Peyton Manning Bronze 300.00 500.00
A10G Peyton Manning Gold 300.00 500.00
A11 Dwight Stephenson 20.00 50.00
A12 Anthony Munoz 25.00 50.00
A13 Mike Singletary 30.00 60.00
A14 Tommy McDonald 20.00 50.00
A15 Paul Krause 25.00 50.00

1998 Topps Generation 2000

COMPLETE SET (15) 25.00 50.00
STATED ODDS 1:18H/R, 1:12RET.JUM.
GE1 Warrick Dunn 1.50 4.00
GE2 Tony Gonzalez 1.50 4.00
GE3 Corey Dillon 1.50 4.00
GE4 Antowain Smith 1.50 4.00
GE5 Mike Alstott 1.50 4.00
GE6 Kordell Stewart 1.50 4.00
GE7 Peter Boulware .60 1.50
GE8 Jake Plummer 1.50 4.00
GE9 Tiki Barber 1.50 4.00
GE10 Terrell Davis 1.50 4.00
GE11 Steve McNair 1.50 4.00
GE12 Curtis Martin 1.50 4.00
GE13 Napoleon Kaufman 1.50 4.00
GE14 Terrell Owens 1.50 4.00
GE15 Eddie George 1.50 4.00

1998 Topps Gridiron Gods

COMPLETE SET (15) 40.00 80.00
STATED ODDS 1:36 HOBBY
G1 Barry Sanders 5.00 12.00
G2 Jerry Rice 3.00 8.00
G3 Herman Moore 1.00 2.50
G4 Drew Bledsoe 2.50 6.00
G5 Kordell Stewart 1.50 4.00
G6 Tim Brown 1.50 4.00
G7 Eddie George 1.50 4.00
G8 Dorsey Levens 1.50 4.00
G9 Warrick Dunn 1.50 4.00
G10 Brett Favre 6.00 15.00
G11 Terrell Davis 1.50 4.00
G12 Steve Young 2.00 5.00
G13 Jerome Bettis 1.50 4.00
G14 Mark Brunell 1.50 4.00
G15 John Elway 6.00 15.00

1998 Topps Hidden Gems

COMPLETE SET (15) 7.50 20.00
STATED ODDS 1:12RET,1:8RET.JUMBO
HG1 Andre Reed .40 1.00
HG2 Kevin Greene .40 1.00
HG3 Tony Martin .40 1.00
HG4 Shannon Sharpe .40 1.00
HG5 Terry Allen .60 1.50
HG6 Brett Favre 2.50 6.00
HG7 Ben Coates .40 1.00
HG8 Michael Sinclair .25 .60
HG9 Keenan McCardell .40 1.00
HG10 Brad Johnson .60 1.50
HG11 Mark Brunell .60 1.50
HG12 Dorsey Levens .60 1.50
HG13 Terrell Davis .60 1.50
HG14 Curtis Martin .60 1.50
HG15 Derrick Rodgers .25 .60

1998 Topps Measures of Greatness

COMPLETE SET (15) 40.00 80.00
STATED ODDS 1:36H/R, 1:24RET.JUM.
MG1 John Elway 6.00 15.00
MG2 Marcus Allen 1.50 4.00
MG3 Jerry Rice 3.00 8.00
MG4 Tim Brown 1.50 4.00
MG5 Warren Moon 1.50 4.00
MG6 Bruce Smith 1.00 2.50
MG7 Troy Aikman 3.00 8.00
MG8 Reggie White 1.50 4.00
MG9 Irving Fryar 1.00 2.50
MG10 Barry Sanders 5.00 12.00
MG11 Cris Carter 1.50 4.00
MG12 Emmitt Smith 5.00 12.00
MG13 Dan Marino 6.00 15.00
MG14 Rod Woodson 1.00 2.50
MG15 Brett Favre 6.00 15.00

1998 Topps Mystery Finest

COMPLETE SET (20) 75.00 150.00
STATED ODDS 1:36H/R, 1:24 RET.JUM.
*REFRACTORS: .8X TO 2X BASIC INSERTS
REFRACTOR STATED ODDS 1:144
M1 Steve Young 2.50 6.00
M2 Dan Marino 8.00 20.00
M3 Brett Favre 8.00 20.00
M4 Drew Bledsoe 3.00 8.00
M5 Mark Brunell 2.00 5.00
M6 Troy Aikman 4.00 10.00
M7 Kordell Stewart 2.00 5.00
M8 John Elway 8.00 20.00
M9 Barry Sanders 6.00 15.00
M10 Jerome Bettis 2.00 5.00
M11 Eddie George 2.00 5.00
M12 Emmitt Smith 6.00 15.00
M13 Curtis Martin 2.00 5.00
M14 Warrick Dunn 2.00 5.00
M15 Dorsey Levens 2.00 5.00
M16 Terrell Davis 2.00 5.00
M17 Herman Moore 1.25 3.00
M18 Jerry Rice 4.00 10.00
M19 Tim Brown 2.00 5.00
M20 Yancey Thigpen .75 2.00

1998 Topps Season's Best

COMPLETE SET (30) 30.00 60.00
STATED ODDS 1:12
1 Terrell Davis 1.00 2.50
2 Barry Sanders 3.00 8.00
3 Jerome Bettis 1.00 2.50
4 Dorsey Levens 1.00 2.50
5 Eddie George 1.00 2.50
6 Brett Favre 4.00 10.00
7 Mark Brunell 1.00 2.50
8 Jeff George .60 1.50
9 Steve Young 1.25 3.00
10 John Elway 4.00 10.00
11 Herman Moore .60 1.50
12 Rob Moore .60 1.50
13 Yancey Thigpen .40 1.00
14 Cris Carter 1.00 2.50
15 Tim Brown 1.00 2.50
16 Bruce Smith .60 1.50
17 Michael Sinclair .40 1.00
18 John Randle .60 1.50
19 Dana Stubblefield .40 1.00
20 Michael Strahan .60 1.50
21 Tamarick Vanover .40 1.00
22 Darrien Gordon .40 1.00
23 Michael Bates .40 1.00
24 David Meggett .40 1.00
25 Jermaine Lewis .60 1.50
26 Terrell Davis 1.00 2.50
27 Jerry Rice 2.00 5.00
28 Barry Sanders 3.00 8.00
29 John Randle .60 1.50
30 John Elway 4.00 10.00

1998 Topps Hall of Fame

This set was distributed at the Pro Football Hall of Fame in Canton, Ohio. Each card includes a photo of a 1998 inductee with a green colored border. The set is identical to the "Class of 98" version except for the lack of the gold foil logo on the cardfronts and the re-numbering.

COMPLETE SET (5) 4.00 10.00
11 Dwight Stephenson .75 2.00
12 Anthony Munoz 1.25 3.00
13 Mike Singletary 1.25 3.00
14 Tommy McDonald .75 2.00
15 Paul Krause .75 2.00

1998 Topps Hall of Fame Class of 1998

This set was distributed at the 1998 induction ceremonies for the Pro Football Hall of Fame. Along with the set, two 1998 Topps base cards were also distributed. Each card includes a photo of a 1998 inductee with a green colored border. A gold foil "Class of '98" logo is featured on the cardfronts and the Hall of Fame is pictured on the cardbacks.

COMPLETE SET (6) 4.00 10.00
HOF1 Dwight Stephenson 1.00 2.50
HOF2 Anthony Munoz 1.00 2.50
HOF3 Mike Singletary 1.25 3.00
HOF4 Tommy McDonald .75 2.00
HOF5 Paul Krause .75 2.00
NNO Cover Card .08 .25

1999 Topps Promos

This 6-card set was released at various Topps sponsored events and throuhg its dealer network to promote the 1999 football release. The cards look very similar to the base set except for the card numbering scheme.

COMPLETE SET (6) 2.00 5.00
PP1 Jamal Anderson .20 .50
PP2 Peyton Manning 1.60 4.00
PP3 Keenan McCardell .10 .30
PP4 Aeneas Williams .07 .20
PP5 Antowain Smith .20 .50
PP6 Andre Rison .10 .30

1999 Topps

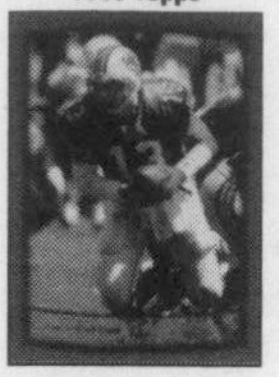

The 1999 Topps set was issued in one series for a total of 357 cards. The set features color action player photos printed on 16 pt. stock. The set contains the 10-card Season Highlights subset plus five cards showcasing five of the players selected in the Cleveland Browns Expansion Draft. Also included in the set were 27 cards of the 1999 NFL Draft Picks. The backs carry player information and career statistics.

COMPLETE SET (357) 20.00 50.00
COMP.SET w/o SP's (330) 10.00 20.00
1 Terrell Davis .25 .60
2 Adrian Murrell .20 .50
3 Ernie Mills .15 .40
4 Jimmy Hitchcock .15 .40
5 Charlie Garner .20 .50
6 Blaine Bishop .15 .40
7 Junior Seau .25 .60
8 Andre Rison .20 .50
9 Jake Reed .20 .50
10 Cris Carter .25 .60
11 Torrance Small .15 .40
12 Ronald McKinnon .15 .40
13 Tyrone Davis .15 .40
14 Warren Moon .25 .60
15 Joe Johnson .15 .40
16 Bert Emanuel .20 .50
17 Brad Culpepper .15 .40
18 Henry Jones .15 .40
19 Jonathan Ogden .15 .40
20 Terrell Owens .25 .60
21 Derrick Mason .20 .50
22 Jon Ritchie .15 .40
23 Eric Metcalf .15 .40
24 Kevin Carter .15 .40
25 Fred Taylor .20 .50
26 DeWayne Washington .15 .40
27 William Thomas .15 .40
28 Rocket Ismail .20 .50
29 Jason Taylor .20 .50
30 Doug Flutie .25 .60
31 Michael Sinclair .15 .40
32 Yancey Thigpen .15 .40
33 Darnay Scott .15 .40
34 Amani Toomer .20 .50
35 Edgar Bennett .20 .50
36 LeRoy Butler .20 .50
37 Jessie Tuggle .15 .40
38 Andrew Glover .15 .40
39 Tim McDonald .15 .40
40 Marshall Faulk .25 .60
41 Ray Mickens .15 .40
42 Kimble Anders .15 .40
43 Trent Green .20 .50
44 Dermontti Dawson .20 .50
45 Greg Ellis .15 .40
46 Hugh Douglas .20 .50
47 Amp Lee .15 .40
48 Lamar Thomas .15 .40
49 Curtis Conway .20 .50
50 Emmitt Smith .60 1.50
51 Elvis Grbac .15 .40
52 Tony Simmons .15 .40
53 Darrin Smith .15 .40
54 Donovin Darius .15 .40
55 Corey Chavous .15 .40
56 Phillippi Sparks .15 .40
57 Luther Elliss .15 .40
58 Tim Dwight .20 .50
59 Andre Hastings .15 .40
60 Dan Marino .75 2.00
61 Micheal Barrow .15 .40
62 Corey Fuller .15 .40
63 Bill Romanowski .20 .50
64 Derrick Rodgers .15 .40
65 Natrone Means .20 .50
66 Peter Boulware .15 .40
67 Brian Mitchell .20 .50
68 Cornelius Bennett .20 .50
69 Dedric Ward .15 .40
70 Drew Bledsoe .25 .60
71 Freddie Jones .15 .40
72 Derrick Thomas .25 .60
73 Willie Davis .15 .40
74 Larry Centers .20 .50
75 Mark Brunell .20 .50
76 Chuck Smith .15 .40
77 Desmond Howard .20 .50
78 Sedrick Shaw .15 .40
79 Tiki Barber .25 .60
80 Curtis Martin .25 .60
81 Barry Minter .15 .40
82 Skip Hicks .15 .40
83 O.J. Santiago .15 .40
84 Ed McCaffrey .20 .50
85 Terrell Buckley .20 .50
86 Charlie Jones .15 .40
87 Pete Mitchell .15 .40
88 La'Roi Glover RC .25 .60
89 Eric Davis .15 .40
90 John Elway .75 2.00
91 Kavika Pittman .15 .40
92 Fred Lane .15 .40
93 Warren Sapp .20 .50
94 Lorenzo Bromell RC .15 .40
95 Lawyer Milloy .20 .50
96 Aeneas Williams .15 .40
97 Michael McCrary .15 .40
98 Rickey Dudley .15 .40
99 Bryce Paup .15 .40
100 Jamal Anderson .20 .50
101 D'Marco Farr .15 .40
102 Johnnie Morton .20 .50
103 Jeff Graham .15 .40
104 Sam Cowart .15 .40
105 Bryant Young .20 .50
106 Jermaine Lewis .15 .40
107 Chad Bratzke .15 .40
108 Jeff Burris .15 .40
109 Roell Preston .15 .40
110 Vinny Testaverde .20 .50
111 Ruben Brown .15 .40
112 Darryll Lewis .15 .40
113 Billy Davis .15 .40
114 Bryant Westbrook .15 .40
115 Stephen Alexander .15 .40
116 Terrell Fletcher .15 .40
117 Terry Glenn .20 .50
118 Rod Smith .20 .50
119 Carl Pickens .20 .50
120 Tim Brown .25 .60
121 Mikhael Ricks .15 .40
122 Jason Gildon .20 .50
123 Charles Way .15 .40
124 Rob Moore .15 .40
125 Jerome Bettis .25 .60
126 Kerry Collins .20 .50
127 Bruce Smith .25 .60
128 James Hasty .15 .40
129 Ken Norton Jr. .15 .40
130 Charles Woodson .25 .60
131 Tony McGee .15 .40
132 Kevin Turner .15 .40
133 Jerome Pathon .15 .40
134 Garrison Hearst .20 .50
135 Craig Newsome .15 .40
136 Hardy Nickerson .15 .40
137 Ray Lewis .25 .60
138 Derrick Alexander .15 .40
139 Phil Hansen .15 .40
140 Joey Galloway .20 .50
141 Oronde Gadsden .15 .40
142 Herman Moore .20 .50
143 Bobby Taylor .20 .50
144 Mario Bates .15 .40
145 Kevin Dyson .15 .40
146 Aaron Glenn .15 .40
147 Ed McDaniel .15 .40
148 Terry Allen .20 .50
149 Ike Hilliard .20 .50
150 Steve Young .30 .75
151 Eugene Robinson .20 .50
152 John Mobley .15 .40
153 Kevin Hardy .15 .40
154 Lance Johnstone .15 .40
155 Willie McGinest .20 .50
156 Gary Anderson .15 .40
157 Dexter Coakley .15 .40
158 Mark Fields .15 .40
159 Steve McNair .25 .60
160 Corey Dillon .20 .50
161 Zach Thomas .25 .60
162 Kent Graham .15 .40
163 Tony Parrish .15 .40
164 Sam Gash .15 .40
165 Kyle Brady .15 .40
166 Donnell Bennett .15 .40
167 Tony Martin .20 .50
168 Michael Bates .15 .40
169 Bobby Engram .20 .50
170 Jimmy Smith .20 .50
171 Vonnie Holliday .15 .40
172 Simeon Rice .15 .40
173 Kevin Greene .20 .50
174 Mike Alstott .25 .60
175 Eddie George .20 .50
176 Michael Jackson .15 .40
177 Neil O'Donnell .20 .50
178 Sean Dawkins .15 .40
179 Courtney Hawkins .15 .40
180 Michael Irvin .25 .60
181 Thurman Thomas .25 .60
182 Cam Cleeland .15 .40
183 Ellis Johnson .15 .40
184 Will Blackwell .15 .40
185 Ty Law .20 .50
186 Merton Hanks .15 .40
187 Dan Wilkinson .20 .50
188 Andre Wadsworth .15 .40
189 Troy Vincent .15 .40
190 Frank Sanders .15 .40
191 Stephen Boyd .15 .40
192 Jason Elam .15 .40
193 Kordell Stewart .20 .50
194 Ted Johnson .20 .50
195 Glyn Milburn .15 .40
196 Gary Brown .15 .40
197 Travis Hall .15 .40
198 John Randle .20 .50
199 Jay Riemersma .15 .40
200 Barry Sanders .60 1.50
201 Chris Spielman .20 .50
202 Rod Woodson .25 .60
203 Darrell Russell .15 .40
204 Tony Boselli .20 .50
205 Darren Woodson .20 .50
206 Muhsin Muhammad .20 .50
207 Jim Harbaugh .20 .50
208 Isaac Bruce .25 .60
209 Mo Lewis .15 .40
210 Dorsey Levens .20 .50
211 Frank Wycheck .20 .50
212 Napoleon Kaufman .15 .40
213 Walt Harris .15 .40
214 Leon Lett .15 .40
215 Karim Abdul-Jabbar .20 .50
216 Carnell Lake .20 .50
217 Byron Bam Morris .15 .40
218 John Avery .15 .40
219 Chris Slade .15 .40
220 Robert Smith .20 .50
221 Mike Pritchard .15 .40
222 Ty Detmer .20 .50
223 Randall Cunningham .25 .60
224 Alonzo Mayes .15 .40
225 Jake Plummer .20 .50
226 Derrick Mayes .15 .40
227 Jeff Brady .15 .40
228 John Lynch .20 .50
229 Steve Atwater .20 .50
230 Warrick Dunn .20 .50
231 Shawn Jefferson .15 .40
232 Erik Kramer .20 .50
233 Ken Dilger .15 .40
234 Ryan Leaf .20 .50
235 Ray Buchanan .15 .40
236 Kevin Williams .15 .40
237 Ricky Watters .20 .50
238 Dwayne Rudd .15 .40
239 Duce Staley .20 .50
240 Charlie Batch .20 .50
241 Tim Biakabutuka .20 .50
242 Tony Gonzalez .25 .60
243 Bryan Still .15 .40
244 Donnie Edwards .15 .40
245 Troy Aikman .40 1.00
246 Tony Banks .20 .50
247 Curtis Enis .15 .40
248 Chris Chandler .20 .50
249 James Jett .15 .40
250 Brett Favre .75 2.00
251 Keith Poole .15 .40
252 Ricky Proehl .15 .40
253 Shannon Sharpe .25 .60
254 Robert Jones .15 .40
255 Chad Brown .15 .40
256 Ben Coates .20 .50
257 Jacquez Green .15 .40
258 Jessie Armstead .20 .50
259 Dale Carter .15 .40
260 Antowain Smith .15 .40
261 Mark Chmura .15 .40
262 Michael Westbrook .15 .40
263 Marvin Harrison .25 .60
264 Darrien Gordon .15 .40
265 Rodney Harrison .20 .50
266 Charles Johnson .15 .40
267 Roman Phifer .15 .40
268 Reidel Anthony .15 .40
269 Jerry Rice .50 1.25
270 Eric Moulds .20 .50
271 Robert Porcher .15 .40
272 Deion Sanders .25 .60
273 Germane Crowell .15 .40
274 Randy Moss .25 .60
275 Antonio Freeman .20 .50
276 Trent Dilfer .20 .50
277 Eric Turner .15 .40
278 Jeff George .15 .40
279 Levon Kirkland .15 .40
280 O.J. McDuffie .20 .50
281 Takeo Spikes .15 .40
282 Jim Flanigan .15 .40
283 Chris Warren .20 .50
284 J.J. Stokes .15 .40
285 Bryan Cox .20 .50
286 Sam Madison .15 .40
287 Priest Holmes .25 .60
288 Keenan McCardell .20 .50
289 Michael Strahan .20 .50
290 Robert Edwards .15 .40
291 Tommy Vardell .20 .50
292 Wayne Chrebet .20 .50
293 Chris Calloway .15 .40
294 Wesley Walls .20 .50
295 Derrick Brooks .25 .60
296 Trace Armstrong .15 .40
297 Brian Simmons .15 .40
298 Darrell Green .25 .60
299 Robert Brooks .20 .50
300 Peyton Manning .75 2.00
301 Dana Stubblefield .15 .40
302 Shawn Springs .15 .40
303 Leslie Shepherd .15 .40
304 Ken Harvey .15 .40
305 Jon Kitna .20 .50
306 Terance Mathis .15 .40
307 Andre Reed .25 .60
308 Jackie Harris .20 .50
309 Rich Gannon .20 .50
310 Keyshawn Johnson .20 .50
311 Victor Green .15 .40
312 Eric Allen .20 .50
313 Terry Fair .15 .40
314 Jason Elam SH .15 .40
315 Garrison Hearst SH .15 .40
316 Jake Plummer SH .15 .40
317 Randall Cunningham SH .20 .50
318 Randy Moss SH .20 .50
319 Jamal Anderson SH .15 .40
320 John Elway SH .60 1.50
321 Doug Flutie SH .20 .50
322 Emmitt Smith SH .50 1.25
323 Terrell Davis SH .20 .50
324 Jerris McPhail .15 .40
325 Damon Gibson .15 .40
326 Jim Pyne .15 .40
327 Antonio Langham .15 .40
328 Freddie Solomon .15 .40
329 Ricky Williams RC 1.50 4.00
330 Daunte Culpepper RC 1.00 2.50
331 Chris Claiborne RC .60 1.50
332 Amos Zereoue RC .75 2.00
333 Chris McAlister RC .75 2.00
334 Kevin Faulk RC 1.00 2.50
335 James Johnson RC .60 1.50
336 Mike Cloud RC .60 1.50
337 Jevon Kearse RC 1.00 2.50
338 Akili Smith RC .75 2.00
339 Edgerrin James RC 1.25 3.00
340 Cecil Collins RC .60 1.50
341 Donovan McNabb RC 3.00 8.00
342 Kevin Johnson RC .75 2.00
343 Torry Holt RC 1.50 4.00
344 Rob Konrad RC .60 1.50
345 Tim Couch RC 1.00 2.50
346 David Boston RC .75 2.00
347 Karsten Bailey RC .60 1.50
348 Troy Edwards RC .75 2.00
349 Sedrick Irvin RC .60 1.50
350 Shaun King RC .75 2.00
351 Peerless Price RC .75 2.00
352 Brock Huard RC .75 2.00
353 Cade McNown RC .75 2.00
354 Champ Bailey RC 2.00 5.00
355 D'Wayne Bates RC .60 1.50
356 Checklist Card .15 .40
357 Checklist Card .15 .40

1999 Topps Collection

COMP.FACT.SET (357) 20.00 50.00
*COLLECT.VETS: .3X TO 1X BASIC TOPPS
*COLLECT.ROOKIES: .3X TO .8X BASIC TOPPS

1999 Topps MVP Promotion

*1-328 VETS: 15X TO 40X BASIC CARDS
*314-324 SH: 20X TO 50X BASIC SH
*VET WINNER: 25X TO 60X BASIC CARDS
*329-355 ROOKIES: 4X TO 10X BASIC RC
*ROOKIE WINNER: 5X TO 12X BASIC RC
MVP STATED ODDS 1:253 H/R, 1:69 HTA
MVP STATED PRINT RUN 100 SETS

1999 Topps MVP Promotion Prizes

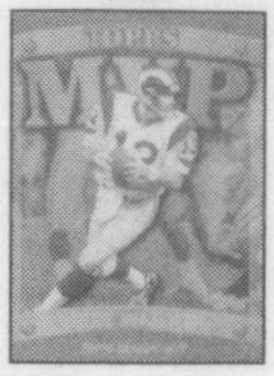

COMPLETE SET (22) 40.00 100.00
MVP1 Troy Aikman 4.00 10.00
MVP2 Drew Bledsoe 2.50 6.00
MVP3 Marvin Harrison 1.25 3.00
MVP4 Terry Glenn 1.25 3.00
MVP5 Isaac Bruce 1.25 3.00
MVP6 Marshall Faulk 2.00 5.00
MVP7 Tim Brown 1.25 3.00
MVP8 Edgerrin James 7.50 20.00
MVP9 Germane Crowell .60 1.50
MVP10 Jevon Kearse 2.00 5.00
MVP11 Jimmy Smith .60 1.50
MVP12 Jeff George .60 1.50
MVP13 Amani Toomer .60 1.50
MVP14 Corey Dillon 1.25 3.00
MVP15 Cade McNown 1.25 3.00
MVP16 Steve McNair 1.25 3.00
MVP17 Dorsey Levens 1.25 3.00
MVP18 Robert Smith 1.25 3.00
MVP19 Eddie George 1.25 3.00
MVP20 Ricky Proehl .60 1.50
MVP21 Kurt Warner 10.00 25.00
MVP22 Kurt Warner MVP 10.00 25.00

1999 Topps All Matrix

COMPLETE SET (30) 30.00 60.00
STATED ODDS 1:14 H/R, 1:9 JUM, 1:4 HTA
AM1 Fred Taylor 1.00 2.50
AM2 Ricky Watters .60 1.50
AM3 Curtis Martin 1.00 2.50
AM4 Eddie George 1.00 2.50
AM5 Marshall Faulk 1.25 3.00
AM6 Emmitt Smith 2.00 5.00
AM7 Barry Sanders 3.00 8.00
AM8 Garrison Hearst .60 1.50
AM9 Jamal Anderson 1.00 2.50
AM10 Terrell Davis 1.00 2.50
AM11 Chris Chandler .60 1.50
AM12 Steve McNair 1.00 2.50
AM13 Vinny Testaverde .60 1.50
AM14 Trent Green 1.00 2.50
AM15 Dan Marino 3.00 8.00
AM16 Drew Bledsoe 1.25 3.00
AM17 Randall Cunningham 1.00 2.50
AM18 Jake Plummer .60 1.50
AM19 Peyton Manning 3.00 8.00
AM20 Steve Young 1.25 3.00
AM21 Brett Favre 3.00 8.00
AM22 Tim Couch .75 2.00
AM23 Edgerrin James 2.50 6.00
AM24 David Boston .75 2.00
AM25 Akili Smith .60 1.50
AM26 Troy Edwards .60 1.50
AM27 Torry Holt 1.50 4.00
AM28 Donovan McNabb 3.00 8.00
AM29 Daunte Culpepper 2.50 6.00
AM30 Ricky Williams 1.25 3.00

1999 Topps Autographs

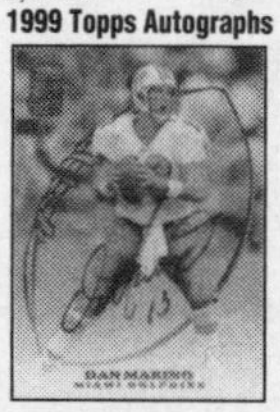

STATED ODDS 1:509 HOB, 1:140 HTA
R.WILL.AUTO ODDS 1:18,372H,1:5057HTA
A1 Randy Moss 30.00 60.00
A2 Wayne Chrebet 8.00 20.00
A3 Tim Couch 8.00 20.00
A4 Joey Galloway 10.00 25.00
A5 Ricky Williams 25.00 50.00
A6 Doug Flutie 12.00 30.00
A7 Terrell Owens 12.00 30.00
A8 Marshall Faulk 15.00 40.00
A9 Rod Smith 12.00 30.00
A10 Dan Marino 60.00 120.00

1999 Topps Hall of Fame Autographs

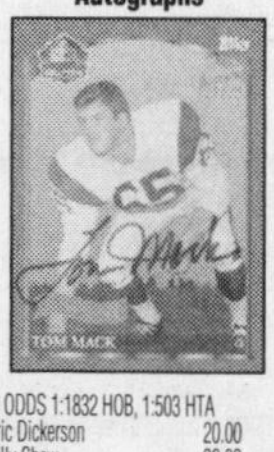

STATED ODDS 1:1832 HOB, 1:503 HTA
HOF1 Eric Dickerson 20.00 50.00
HOF2 Billy Shaw 20.00 50.00
HOF3 Lawrence Taylor 25.00 60.00
HOF4 Tom Mack 20.00 50.00
HOF5 Ozzie Newsome 20.00 50.00

1999 Topps Jumbos

COMPLETE SET (8) 10.00 20.00
ONE PER HOBBY BOX
1 Barry Sanders 2.00 5.00
2 Randy Moss 1.50 4.00
3 Terrell Davis .60 1.50
4 Dan Marino 2.00 5.00
5 Fred Taylor .60 1.50
6 John Elway 2.00 5.00
7 Brett Favre 2.00 5.00
8 Peyton Manning 2.00 5.00

1999 Topps Mystery Chrome

COMPLETE SET (20) 35.00 80.00
STATED ODDS 1:36 H/R, 1:24 JUM, 1:8 HTA
*REFRACTORS: 1X TO 2.5X BASIC INSERT
REFRACT.STATED ODDS 1:144H/R, 1:32 HTA
M1 Terrell Davis 1.50 4.00
M2 Steve Young 2.00 5.00
M3 Fred Taylor 1.50 4.00

M4 Chris Claiborne	.50	1.25
M5 Terrell Davis	1.50	4.00
M6 Randall Cunningham	1.50	4.00
M7 Charlie Batch	1.50	4.00
M8 Fred Taylor	1.50	4.00
M9 Vinny Testaverde	1.00	2.50
M10 Jamal Anderson	1.50	4.00
M11 Randy Moss	4.00	10.00
M12 Keyshawn Johnson	1.50	4.00
M13 Vinny Testaverde	1.00	2.50
M14 Chris Chandler	1.00	2.50
M15 Fred Taylor	1.50	4.00
M16 Ricky Williams	1.50	4.00
M17 Chris Chandler	1.00	2.50
M18 John Elway	5.00	12.00
M19 Randy Moss	4.00	10.00
M20 Troy Edwards	.75	2.00

1999 Topps Picture Perfect

COMPLETE SET (10)	10.00	25.00
STATED ODDS 1:14 H/R, 1:9 JUM, 1:4 HTA		
P1 Steve Young	.75	2.00
P2 Brett Favre	2.00	5.00
P3 Terrell Davis	.60	1.50
P4 Peyton Manning	2.00	5.00
P5 Jake Plummer	.40	1.00
P6 Fred Taylor	.60	1.50
P7 Barry Sanders	2.00	5.00
P8 Dan Marino	2.00	5.00
P9 John Elway	2.00	5.00
P10 Randy Moss	1.50	4.00

1999 Topps Record Numbers Silver

COMPLETE SET (10)	15.00	30.00
STATED ODDS 1:18 H/R, 1:8 JUM, 1:6 HTA		
RN1 Randy Moss	2.00	5.00
RN2 Terrell Davis	.75	2.00
RN3 Emmitt Smith	1.50	4.00
RN4 Barry Sanders	2.50	6.00
RN5 Dan Marino	2.50	6.00
RN6 Brett Favre	2.50	6.00
RN7 Doug Flutie	.75	2.00
RN8 Jerry Rice	1.50	4.00
RN9 Peyton Manning	2.50	6.00
RN10 Jason Elam	.30	.75

1999 Topps Record Numbers Gold

RN1 Randy Moss/17	100.00	250.00
RN2 Terrell Davis/56	20.00	50.00
RN3 Emmitt Smith/125	30.00	60.00
RN4 Barry Sanders/1000	20.00	40.00
RN5 Dan Marino/408	20.00	40.00
RN6 Brett Favre/30	75.00	200.00
RN7 Doug Flutie/3291	4.00	10.00
RN8 Jerry Rice/164	15.00	40.00
RN9 Peyton Manning/3739	7.50	20.00
RN10 Jason Elam/63	5.00	12.00

1999 Topps Season's Best

COMPLETE SET (30)	25.00	60.00
STATED ODDS 1:18 H/R, 1:12 JUM, 1:6 HTA		
SB1 Terrell Davis	1.00	2.50
SB2 Jamal Anderson	1.00	2.50
SB3 Garrison Hearst	.60	1.50
SB4 Barry Sanders	3.00	8.00
SB5 Emmitt Smith	2.00	5.00
SB6 Randall Cunningham	1.00	2.50
SB7 Brett Favre	3.00	8.00
SB8 Steve Young	1.25	3.00
SB9 Jake Plummer	.60	1.50
SB10 Peyton Manning	3.00	8.00
SB11 Antonio Freeman	1.00	2.50
SB12 Eric Moulds	1.00	2.50
SB13 Randy Moss	2.50	6.00
SB14 Rod Smith	.60	1.50
SB15 Jimmy Smith	.60	1.50
SB16 Michael Sinclair	.40	1.00
SB17 Kevin Greene	.40	1.00
SB18 Michael Strahan	.60	1.50
SB19 Michael McCrary	.40	1.00
SB20 Hugh Douglas	.40	1.00
SB21 Deion Sanders	1.00	2.50
SB22 Terry Fair	.40	1.00
SB23 Jacquez Green	.40	1.00
SB24 Corey Harris	.40	1.00
SB25 Tim Dwight	1.00	2.50
SB26 Dan Marino	3.00	8.00
SB27 Barry Sanders	3.00	8.00
SB28 Jerry Rice	2.00	5.00
SB29 Bruce Smith	.60	1.50
SB30 Darrien Gordon	.40	1.00

1999 Topps Hall of Fame

This set was distributed at various Topps sponsored events and through the Pro Football Hall of Fame. Each card includes a photo of a 1999 inductee printed in the style of the 1999 set except without the gold foil logo on the cardfront. The cards were not numbered and have been assigned numbers below alphabetically.

COMPLETE SET (5)	3.20	8.00
1 Eric Dickerson	.80	2.00
2 Tom Mack	.50	1.25
3 Ozzie Newsome	.80	2.00
4 Billy Shaw	.50	1.25
5 Lawrence Taylor	.80	2.00

1999 Topps Hall of Fame Class of 1999

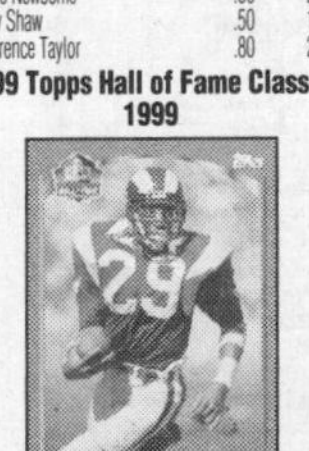

This set was distributed at various Topps sponsored events in 1999 including ceremonies for the Pro Football Hall of Fame. Each card includes a photo of a 1999 inductee printed in the style of the 1998 set except with a blue border instead of green. A gold foil "Class of '99" logo appears on the cardfronts.

COMPLETE SET (5)	3.00	8.00
HOF1 Eric Dickerson	.80	2.00
HOF2 Tom Mack	.60	1.50
HOF3 Lawrence Taylor	1.25	3.00
HOF4 Billy Shaw	.60	1.50
HOF5 Ozzie Newsome	.80	2.00

2000 Topps Promos

This 6-card set was released at various Topps sponsored events and through its dealer network to promote the 2000 football release. The cards look very similar to the base set except for the card numbering scheme.

COMPLETE SET (6)	2.00	5.00
PP1 Peyton Manning	1.00	2.50
PP2 Zach Thomas	.40	1.00
PP3 Eddie George	.30	.75
PP4 Rocket Ismail	.30	.75
PP5 Fred Taylor	.40	1.00
PP6 Shaun King	.25	.60

2000 Topps

Released as a 400-card set, 2000 Topps features 320 veteran cards, 10 Season Highlights, 10 Millennium Men, 20 NFL Europe Prospects, and 40 Draft Pick Cards seeded at one in five for Hobby and Retail and one in one for HTA packs. Hobby and Retail were packaged in 36-pack boxes with packs containing 10 cards and carried a suggested retail price of $1.29; and HTA was packaged in 12-pack boxes with packs containing 45 cards and carried a suggested retail price of $5.00.

COMPLETE SET (400)	25.00	60.00
COMP.SET w/o SP's (360)	8.00	20.00
361-400 ROOKIE ODDS 1:5H/R,1:1HTA		
SBMVP STATED ODDS 1:1287 HTA		
1 Kurt Warner	.40	1.00
2 Darrell Russell	.15	.40
3 Tai Streets	.15	.40
4 Bryant Young	.15	.40
5 Kent Graham	.15	.40
6 Shawn Jefferson	.15	.40
7 Wesley Walls	.15	.40
8 Jessie Armstead	.15	.40
9 Dedric Ward	.15	.40
10 Emmitt Smith	.60	1.50
11 James Stewart	.15	.40
12 Frank Sanders	.15	.40
13 Ray Buchanan	.15	.40
14 Olindo Mare	.15	.40
15 Andre Reed	.25	.60
16 Curtis Conway	.20	.50
17 Patrick Jeffers	.20	.50
18 Greg Hill	.15	.40
19 John Unitas	.60	1.50
20 Brett Favre	.75	2.00
21 Jerome Pathon	.15	.40
22 Jason Tucker	.15	.40
23 Charles Johnson	.15	.40
24 Brian Mitchell	.15	.40
25 Billy Miller	.15	.40
26 Jay Fiedler	.20	.50
27 Marcus Pollard	.15	.40
28 De'Mond Parker	.15	.40
29 Leslie Shepherd	.15	.40
30 Fred Taylor	.25	.60
31 Michael Pittman	.15	.40
32 Ricky Watters	.20	.50
33 Derrick Brooks	.25	.60
34 Junior Seau	.25	.60
35 Troy Vincent	.15	.40
36 Eric Allen	.15	.40
37 Pete Mitchell	.15	.40
38 Tony Simmons	.15	.40
39 Az-Zahir Hakim	.15	.40
40 Dan Marino	.75	2.00
41 Mac Cody	.15	.40
42 Scott Dreisbach	.15	.40
43 Al Wilson	.15	.40
44 Luther Broughton RC	.15	.40
45 Wane McGarity	.15	.40
46 Stephen Boyd	.15	.40
47 Michael Strahan	.20	.50
48 Chris Chandler	.20	.50
49 Tony Martin	.20	.50
50 Edgerrin James	.25	.60
51 John Randle	.20	.50
52 Warrick Dunn	.20	.50
53 Elvis Grbac	.15	.40
54 Champ Bailey	.20	.50
55 Kyle Brady	.15	.40
56 John Lynch	.20	.50
57 Kevin Carter	.15	.40
58 Mike Pritchard	.15	.40
59 Deon Mitchell RC	.20	.50
60 Randy Moss	.25	.60
61 Jermaine Fazande	.15	.40
62 Donovan McNabb	.25	.60
63 Richard Huntley	.15	.40
64 Rich Gannon	.20	.50
65 Aaron Glenn	.15	.40
66 Amani Toomer	.20	.50
67 Andre Hastings	.15	.40
68 Ricky Williams	.25	.60
69 Sam Madison	.15	.40
70 Drew Bledsoe	.25	.60
71 Eric Moulds	.20	.50
72 Justin Armour	.15	.40
73 Jamal Anderson	.20	.50
74 Mario Bates	.15	.40
75 Sam Gash	.15	.40
76 Macey Brooks	.15	.40
77 Tremain Mack	.15	.40
78 David LaFleur	.15	.40
79 Dexter Coakley	.15	.40
80 Cris Carter	.25	.60
81 Byron Chamberlain	.15	.40
82 David Sloan	.15	.40
83 Mike Devlin RC	.15	.40
84 Jimmy Smith	.20	.50
85 Derrick Alexander	.15	.40
86 Damon Huard	.20	.50
87 Jake Reed	.20	.50
88 Darrell Green	.20	.50
89 Derrick Mason	.20	.50
90 Curtis Martin	.25	.60
91 Donnie Abraham	.15	.40
92 D'Marco Farr	.15	.40
93 Ahman Green	.20	.50
94 Shane Matthews	.15	.40
95 Torrance Small	.15	.40
96 Duce Staley	.20	.50
97 Jon Ritchie	.15	.40
98 Victor Green	.15	.40
99 Kerry Collins	.20	.50
100 Peyton Manning	.60	1.50
101 Ben Coates	.15	.40
102 Thurman Thomas	.25	.60
103 Cornelius Bennett	.15	.40
104 Terance Mathis	.15	.40
105 Adrian Murrell	.15	.40
106 Donald Hayes	.15	.40
107 Terry Kirby	.15	.40
108 James Allen	.15	.40
109 Ty Law	.20	.50
110 Tim Brown	.25	.60
111 Chad Bratzke	.15	.40
112 Deion Sanders	.25	.60
113 James Johnson	.15	.40
114 Tony Richardson RC	.20	.50
115 Tony Brackens	.15	.40
116 Ken Dilger	.15	.40
117 Albert Connell	.15	.40
118 Neil O'Donnell	.15	.40
119 Selucio Sanford EP RC	.15	.40
120 Steve Young	.30	.75
121 Tony Horne	.15	.40
122 Charlie Rogers	.15	.40
123 J.J. Stokes	.20	.50
124 Kenny Bynum	.15	.40
125 Jeff Graham	.15	.40
126 Ike Hilliard	.20	.50
127 Ray Lucas	.15	.40
128 Terry Glenn	.20	.50
129 Rickey Dudley	.15	.40
130 Joey Galloway	.20	.50
131 Brian Dawkins	.25	.60
132 Rob Moore	.15	.40
133 Bob Christian	.15	.40
134 Anthony Wright RC	.25	.60
135 Antowain Smith	.20	.50
136 Kevin Johnson	.15	.40
137 Scott Covington	.15	.40
138 D'Wayne Bates	.15	.40
139 Sam Cowart	.15	.40
140 Isaac Bruce	.25	.60
141 Tony McGee	.15	.40
142 Dale Carter	.15	.40
143 Matt Hasselbeck	.25	.60
144 Torry Holt	.25	.60
145 Daunte Culpepper	.20	.50
146 Yatil Green	.15	.40
147 Chris Howard	.15	.40
148 Irving Fryar	.20	.50
149 Derrick Mayes	.15	.40
150 Warren Sapp	.20	.50
151 Ricky Proehl	.15	.40
152 Eric Kresser EP	.15	.40
153 Jeff Garcia	.20	.50
154 Freddie Jones	.15	.40
155 Mike Cloud	.15	.40
156 Wayne Chrebet	.20	.50
157 Joe Montgomery	.15	.40
158 Shannon Sharpe	.25	.60
159 Eddie Kennison	.15	.40
160 Eddie George	.20	.50
161 Jay Riemersma	.15	.40
162 Peter Boulware	.15	.40
163 Aeneas Williams	.15	.40
164 Jim Miller	.15	.40
165 Jamir Miller	.15	.40
166 Tim Biakabutuka	.20	.50
167 Kordell Stewart	.20	.50
168 Charlie Garner	.20	.50
169 Germane Crowell	.15	.40
170 Stephen Davis	.20	.50
171 Jeff George	.20	.50
172 Mark Brunell	.20	.50
173 Stephen Alexander	.15	.40
174 Mike Alstott	.25	.60
175 Terry Allen	.20	.50
176 Ed McCaffrey	.20	.50
177 Bobby Engram	.20	.50
178 Andre Cooper	.15	.40
179 Kevin Faulk	.20	.50
180 Errict Rhett	.20	.50
181 Jammi German	.15	.40
182 Oronde Gadsden	.20	.50
183 Jevon Kearse	.20	.50
184 Herman Moore	.20	.50
185 Terrence Wilkins	.15	.40
186 Rocket Ismail	.20	.50
187 Patrick Johnson	.15	.40
188 Simeon Rice	.20	.50
189 Mo Lewis	.15	.40
190 Qadry Ismail	.20	.50
191 Terry Jackson	.15	.40
192 Rashaan Shehee	.15	.40
193 Charles Woodson	.25	.60
194 Akili Smith	.15	.40
195 Yancey Thigpen	.15	.40
196 Michael Westbrook	.15	.40
197 Donnell Bennett	.15	.40
198 Sedrick Irvin	.15	.40
199 Keenan McCardell	.20	.50
200 Marshall Faulk	.25	.60
201 Jeff Blake	.20	.50
202 Rob Johnson	.20	.50
203 Vinny Testaverde	.20	.50
204 Andy Katzenmoyer	.15	.40
205 Michael Basnight	.15	.40
206 Lance Schulters	.15	.40
207 Shaun King	.15	.40
208 Bill Schroeder	.20	.50
209 Skip Hicks	.15	.40
210 Jake Plummer	.20	.50
211 Leroy Hoard	.15	.40
212 Reggie Barlow	.15	.40
213 E.G. Green	.15	.40
214 Fred Lane	.15	.40
215 Antonio Freeman	.20	.50
216 Grant Wistrom	.15	.40
217 Kevin Dyson	.20	.50
218 Mikhael Ricks	.15	.40
219 Rod Woodson	.25	.60
220 Tim Dwight	.20	.50
221 Darnay Scott	.20	.50
222 Curtis Enis	.15	.40
223 Sean Bennett	.15	.40
224 Napoleon Kaufman	.20	.50
225 Jonathan Linton	.15	.40
226 Jim Harbaugh	.20	.50
227 Hardy Nickerson	.15	.40
228 Todd Lyght	.15	.40
229 Dorsey Levens	.20	.50
230 Steve Beuerlein	.20	.50
231 Marty Booker	.20	.50
232 Andre Wadsworth	.15	.40
233 James Hasty	.15	.40
234 Shawn Bryson	.15	.40
235 Larry Centers	.15	.40
236 Charlie Batch	.20	.50
237 Steve McNair	.25	.60
238 Darrin Chiaverini	.15	.40
239 Jerome Bettis	.25	.60
240 Muhsin Muhammad	.20	.50
241 Terrell Fletcher	.15	.40
242 Jon Kitna	.20	.50
243 Frank Wycheck	.20	.50
244 Tony Gonzalez	.25	.60
245 Ron Rivers	.15	.40
246 Olandis Gary	.20	.50
247 Jermaine Lewis	.15	.40
248 Joe Jurevicius	.15	.40
249 Richie Anderson	.15	.40
250 Marcus Robinson	.20	.50
251 Shawn Springs	.15	.40
252 William Floyd	.15	.40
253 Bobby Shaw RC	.20	.50
254 Glyn Milburn	.15	.40
255 Brian Griese	.20	.50
256 Donnie Edwards	.15	.40
257 Joe Horn	.20	.50
258 Cameron Cleeland	.15	.40
259 Glenn Foley	.15	.40
260 Corey Dillon	.20	.50
261 Troy Brown	.20	.50
262 Stoney Case	.15	.40
263 Kevin Williams	.15	.40
264 London Fletcher RC	.25	.60
265 O.J. McDuffie	.20	.50
266 Jonathan Quinn	.15	.40
267 Trent Dilfer	.20	.50
268 Dameyune Craig	.15	.40
269 Terrell Owens	.25	.60
270 Tim Couch	.20	.50
271 Dameane Douglas	.15	.40
272 Moses Moreno	.15	.40
273 Bruce Smith	.25	.60
274 Peerless Price	.20	.50
275 Sam Garnes	.15	.40
276 Natrone Means	.20	.50
277 Na Brown	.15	.40
278 Dave Moore	.15	.40
279 Chris Sanders	.15	.40
280 Troy Aikman	.40	1.00
281 Cecil Collins	.15	.40
282 Matthew Hatchette	.15	.40
283 Bill Romanowski	.15	.40
284 Basil Mitchell	.15	.40
285 Tony Banks	.15	.40
286 Jake Delhomme RC	.60	1.50
287 Keyshawn Johnson	.20	.50
288 Dexter McCleon	.20	.50
289 Corey Bradford	.15	.40
290 Terrell Davis	.25	.60
291 Johnnie Morton	.20	.50
292 Kevin Lockett	.15	.40
293 Robert Smith	.20	.50
294 Jeff Lewis	.15	.40
295 Wali Rainer	.15	.40
296 Troy Edwards	.15	.40
297 Keith Poole	.15	.40
298 Priest Holmes	.25	.60
299 David Boston	.15	.40
300 Marvin Harrison	.25	.60
301 Levon Kirkland	.15	.40
302 Robert Holcombe	.15	.40
303 Autry Denson	.15	.40
304 Kevin Hardy	.15	.40
305 Rod Smith	.20	.50
306 Robert Porcher	.15	.40
307 Cade McNown	.15	.40
308 Craig Yeast	.15	.40
309 Doug Flutie	.25	.60
310 Jerry Rice	.50	1.25
311 Brad Johnson	.20	.50
312 Tiki Barber	.25	.60
313 Will Blackwell	.15	.40
314 Sean Dawkins	.15	.40
315 Jacquez Green	.15	.40
316 Zach Thomas	.25	.60
317 Gus Frerotte	.20	.50
318 Chris Warren	.15	.40
319 Carl Pickens	.20	.50
320 Tyrone Wheatley HL	.15	.40
321 Kurt Warner HL	.30	.75
322 Dan Marino HL	.60	1.50
323 Cris Carter HL	.20	.50
324 Brett Favre HL	.60	1.50
325 Marshall Faulk HL	.20	.50
326 Jevon Kearse HL	.15	.40
327 Edgerrin James HL	.20	.50
328 Emmitt Smith HL	.50	1.25
329 Andre Reed HL	.20	.50
330 Kevin Dyson	.15	.40
Frank Wycheck		
331 Olindo Mare MM	.15	.40
332 Marcus Coleman MM	.15	.40
333 James Johnson MM	.15	.40
334 Ray Lucas MM	.15	.40
335 Dedric Ward MM	.15	.40
336 Richie Cunningham MM	.15	.40
337 James Hasty MM	.15	.40
338 Sedrick Shaw MM	.15	.40
339 Kurt Warner MM	.30	.75
340 Marshall Faulk MM	.20	.50
341 Brian Shay EP	.15	.40
342 L.C. Stevens EP	.15	.40
343 Corey Thomas EP	.15	.40
344 Scott Milanovich EP	.15	.40
345 Pat Barnes EP	.20	.50
346 Danny Wuerffel EP	.25	.60
347 Kevin Daft EP	.15	.40
348 Ron Powlus EP RC	.25	.60
349 Tony Graziani EP	.20	.50
350 Norman Miller EP RC	.15	.40
351 Cory Sauter EP	.15	.40
352 Marcus Crandell EP RC	.15	.40
353 Sean Morey EP RC	.15	.40
354 Jeff Ogden EP	.15	.40
355 Ted White EP	.15	.40
356 Jim Kubiak EP RC	.15	.40
357 Aaron Stecker EP RC	.20	.50
358 Ronnie Powell EP	.15	.40
359 Matt Lytle EP RC	.15	.40
360 Kendrick Nord EP RC	.15	.40
361 Tim Rattay RC	.75	2.00
362 Rob Morris RC	.75	2.00
363 Chris Samuels RC	.75	2.00
364 Todd Husak RC	.60	1.50
365 Ahmed Plummer RC	.60	1.50
366 Frank Murphy RC	.60	1.50
367 Michael Wiley RC	.60	1.50
368 Giovanni Carmazzi RC	.60	1.50
369 Anthony Becht RC	.75	2.00
370 John Abraham RC	1.00	2.50
371 Shaun Alexander RC	1.25	3.00
372 Thomas Jones RC	1.25	3.00
373 Courtney Brown RC	.75	2.00
374 Curtis Keaton RC	.60	1.50
375 Jerry Porter RC	1.00	2.50
376 Corey Simon RC	.75	2.00
377 Dez White RC	.75	2.00
378 Jamal Lewis RC	1.00	2.50
379 Ron Dayne RC	1.00	2.50
380 R.Jay Soward RC	.60	1.50
381 Tee Martin RC	1.00	2.50
382 Shaun Ellis RC	1.00	2.50
383 Brian Urlacher RC	4.00	10.00
384 Reuben Droughns RC	1.00	2.50
385 Travis Taylor RC	.75	2.00
386 Plaxico Burress RC	1.00	2.50
387 Chad Pennington RC	1.50	4.00
388 Sylvester Morris RC	.60	1.50
389 Ron Dugans RC	.60	1.50
390 Joe Hamilton RC	.60	1.50
391 Chris Redman RC	.75	2.00
392 Trung Canidate RC	.75	2.00
393 J.R. Redmond RC	.60	1.50
394 Danny Farmer RC	.60	1.50
395 Todd Pinkston RC	.60	1.50
396 Dennis Northcutt RC	.75	2.00
397 Laveranues Coles RC	1.00	2.50
398 Bubba Franks RC	1.00	2.50
399 Travis Prentice RC	.75	2.00
400 Peter Warrick RC	1.00	2.50
SBMVP Kurt Warner FB AU	50.00	120.00

2000 Topps Collection

COMP.FACT.SET (400)	35.00	60.00
*VETS 1-360: .4X TO 1X BASIC TOPPS		
*ROOKIES 361-400: .2X TO .5X BASIC TOPPS		

2000 Topps MVP Promotion

*VET 1-360: 15X TO 40X BASIC CARDS
*VET WIN: 20X TO 50X BASIC CARDS
*ROOKIES 361-400: 3X TO 8X
STATED ODDS 1:234 HOB, 1:52 HTA

2000 Topps MVP Promotion Prizes

COMPLETE SET (17)	40.00	80.00
MVP1 Duce Staley	1.50	4.00
MVP2 Tony Banks	1.25	3.00
MVP3 Elvis Grbac	1.25	3.00
MVP4 Curtis Martin	2.00	5.00
MVP5 Randy Moss	2.00	5.00
MVP6 Tim Brown	2.00	5.00
MVP7 Edgerrin James	2.00	5.00
MVP8 Corey Dillon	1.50	4.00
MVP9 Marshall Faulk	2.00	5.00
MVP10 Antonio Freeman	1.50	4.00
MVP11 Daunte Culpepper	1.50	4.00
MVP12 Fred Taylor	2.00	5.00
MVP13 Jamal Lewis	2.00	5.00
MVP14 Warrick Dunn	1.50	4.00
MVP15 Donovan McNabb	2.00	5.00
MVP16 Terrell Owens	2.00	5.00
MVP17 Peyton Manning	5.00	12.00

2000 Topps Autographs

STATED ODDS 1:1015 H/R, 1:226HTA		
ANNOUNCED AUTO PRINT RUNS 250-700		
CP Chad Pennington	20.00	40.00
EJ Edgerrin James	20.00	40.00
JK Jon Kitna	8.00	20.00
JS Jimmy Smith	8.00	20.00
KC Kevin Carter	6.00	15.00
KW Kurt Warner	30.00	60.00
MF Marshall Faulk	12.00	30.00
MH Marvin Harrison	20.00	40.00
PM Peyton Manning	60.00	100.00
PW Peter Warrick SP	15.00	40.00
RD Ron Dayne	10.00	25.00
SA Shaun Alexander	20.00	40.00
SD Stephen Davis	8.00	20.00
SM Sylvester Morris	6.00	15.00
TJ Thomas Jones	20.00	40.00
ZT Zach Thomas	12.00	30.00

2000 Topps Chrome Previews

COMPLETE SET (20)	15.00	40.00
STATED ODDS 1:18 H/R, 1:5 HTA		
CP1 Kurt Warner	1.00	2.50
CP2 Shaun King	.40	1.00
CP3 Brad Johnson	.50	1.25
CP4 Daunte Culpepper	.50	1.25
CP5 Brett Favre	2.00	5.00
CP6 Eddie George	.50	1.25
CP7 Dan Marino	2.00	5.00
CP8 Randy Moss	.60	1.50
CP9 Troy Aikman	1.00	2.50
CP10 Peyton Manning	1.50	4.00
CP11 Fred Taylor	.60	1.50
CP12 Ricky Williams	.60	1.50
CP13 Jimmy Smith	.50	1.25
CP14 Jerry Rice	1.25	3.00
CP15 Marshall Faulk	.60	1.50
CP16 Marvin Harrison	.60	1.50
CP17 Stephen Davis	.50	1.25
CP18 Isaac Bruce	.60	1.50
CP19 Emmitt Smith	1.50	4.00
CP20 Edgerrin James	.60	1.50

2000 Topps Combos

COMPLETE SET (10)	6.00	15.00
STATED ODDS 1:12 H/R 1:4HTA		
TC1 Johnny Unitas	1.50	4.00
Peyton Manning		
TC2 Chris Carter	.60	1.50
Randy Moss		
TC3 Ricky Williams	.60	1.50
Edgerrin James		
TC4 Marvin Harrison	.60	1.50
Jimmy Smith		
TC5 Isaac Bruce	.60	1.50
Joey Galloway		
TC6 Donovan McNabb	.40	1.00
Tim Couch		
Shaun King		
Daunte Culpepper		
Akili Smith		
TC7 Stephen Davis	.60	1.50
Fred Taylor		
TC8 Marshall Faulk	.60	1.50
Eddie George		
TC9 Emmitt Smith	1.50	4.00
Troy Aikman		
TC10 Kurt Warner	2.00	5.00
Dan Marino		

2000 Topps Hall of Fame Autographs

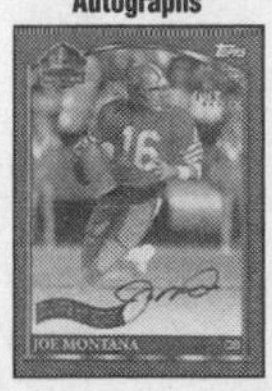

STATED ODDS 1:3551H/R, 1:790 HTA		
HOF1 Joe Montana	60.00	150.00
HOF2 Howie Long	50.00	120.00
HOF3 Ronnie Lott	50.00	100.00
HOF4 Dan Rooney	100.00	200.00
HOF5 Dave Wilcox	25.00	60.00

2000 Topps Hobby Masters

COMPLETE SET (10)	10.00	25.00
*CIRCULAR HOLO: .4X TO 1X BASIC INSERTS		
STATED ODDS 1:5 HTA		
HM1 Kurt Warner	1.25	3.00
HM2 Ricky Williams	.75	2.00
HM3 Eddie George	.60	1.50
HM4 Dan Marino	2.50	6.00
HM5 Edgerrin James	.75	2.00
HM6 Marshall Faulk	.75	2.00
HM7 Emmitt Smith	2.00	5.00
HM8 Jerry Rice	1.50	4.00
HM9 Brett Favre	2.50	6.00
HM10 Randy Moss	.75	2.00

2000 Topps Jumbos

COMPLETE SET (8)	6.00	15.00
ONE PER HOBBY BOX		
1 Peyton Manning	1.50	4.00
2 Marshall Faulk	.60	1.50
3 Dan Marino	2.00	5.00
4 Randy Moss	.60	1.50
5 Kurt Warner	1.00	2.50
6 Eddie George	.50	1.25
7 Brett Favre	2.00	5.00
8 Edgerrin James	.60	1.50

2000 Topps Own the Game

COMPLETE SET (30)	15.00	40.00
STATED ODDS 1:12 H/R, 1:4 HTA		
OTG1 Steve Beuerlein	.60	1.50
OTG2 Kurt Warner	1.25	3.00
OTG3 Peyton Manning	2.00	5.00
OTG4 Brett Favre	2.50	6.00
OTG5 Brad Johnson	.60	1.50
OTG6 Edgerrin James	.75	2.00
OTG7 Curtis Martin	.75	2.00
OTG8 Stephen Davis	.60	1.50
OTG9 Emmitt Smith	2.00	5.00
OTG10 Marshall Faulk	.75	2.00
OTG11 Eddie George	.60	1.50
OTG12 Duce Staley	.60	1.50
OTG13 Charlie Garner	.60	1.50
OTG14 Marvin Harrison	.75	2.00
OTG15 Jimmy Smith	.60	1.50
OTG16 Randy Moss	.75	2.00
OTG17 Marcus Robinson	.60	1.50
OTG18 Tim Brown	.75	2.00
OTG19 Germane Crowell	.50	1.25
OTG20 Muhsin Muhammad	.60	1.50
OTG21 Cris Carter	.75	2.00
OTG22 Michael Westbrook	.50	1.25
OTG23 Amani Toomer	.60	1.50
OTG24 Keyshawn Johnson	.60	1.50
OTG25 Isaac Bruce	.75	2.00
OTG26 Kurt Warner	1.25	3.00
OTG27 Stephen Davis	.60	1.50
OTG28 Edgerrin James	.75	2.00
OTG29 Cris Carter	.75	2.00
OTG30 Marvin Harrison	.75	2.00

2000 Topps Pro Bowl Jerseys

STATED ODDS 1:271 HOB, 1:60 HTA		
BMOG Bruce Matthews	8.00	20.00
CCWR Cris Carter	8.00	20.00
CDRB Corey Dillon	6.00	15.00
DRIL Darrell Russell	5.00	12.00
EGRB Eddie George	6.00	15.00
ESRB Emmitt Smith	20.00	50.00
JAOL Jessie Armstead	5.00	12.00
KCDE Kevin Carter	5.00	12.00
KHOL Kevin Hardy	5.00	12.00
KJWR Keyshawn Johnson	6.00	15.00
KWQB Kurt Warner	12.00	30.00
MAFB Mike Alstott	8.00	20.00
MBQB Mark Brunell	6.00	15.00
MHWR Marvin Harrison	8.00	20.00
MMWR Muhsin Muhammad	6.00	15.00
MSDE Michael Strahan	6.00	15.00
OMPK Olindo Mare	5.00	12.00
RGQB Rich Gannon	6.00	15.00
RWFS Rod Woodson	8.00	20.00
SBQB Steve Beuerlein	6.00	15.00
TBDE Tony Brackens	5.00	12.00
TGTE Tony Gonzalez	8.00	20.00
WSIL Warren Sapp	6.00	15.00
ZTIL Zach Thomas	8.00	20.00

2000 Topps Rookie Premier Autographs

STATED ODDS 1:5761 H, 1:1276 HTA		
STATED PRINT RUN 25 SER.#'d SETS		
AB Anthony Becht	30.00	80.00
BU Brian Urlacher	350.00	500.00
CB Courtney Brown	30.00	80.00
CK Curtis Keaton	25.00	60.00
CP Chad Pennington	150.00	300.00
CR Chris Redman	30.00	80.00
CS Corey Simon	30.00	80.00
DF Danny Farmer	25.00	60.00
DN Dennis Northcutt	30.00	80.00
DW Dez White	30.00	80.00
JH Joe Hamilton	25.00	60.00
JL Jamal Lewis	100.00	175.00
JP Jerry Porter	40.00	100.00
JR J.R. Redmond	25.00	60.00
LC Laveranues Coles	40.00	100.00
PB Plaxico Burress	60.00	120.00
PW Peter Warrick	40.00	100.00
RD Ron Dayne	40.00	100.00
SA Shaun Alexander	150.00	300.00
SM Sylvester Morris	25.00	60.00
TC Trung Canidate	30.00	80.00
TJ Thomas Jones	150.00	250.00
TM Tee Martin	40.00	100.00
TP Todd Pinkston	25.00	60.00
TT Travis Taylor	40.00	100.00
DFR Bubba Franks	40.00	100.00
RDR Reuben Droughns	40.00	100.00
RDU Ron Dugans	25.00	60.00
TPR Travis Prentice	30.00	80.00

2000 Topps Unitas Reprints

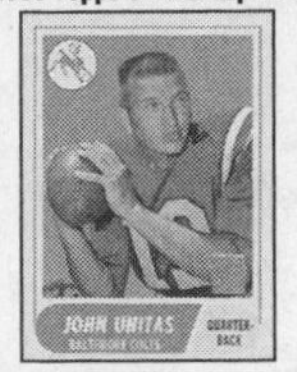

COMPLETE SET (18)	25.00	60.00
COMMON CARD (R1-R18)	1.50	4.00
STATED ODDS 1:19 HOB, 1:4 HTA		
*CHROME: .6X TO 1.5X BASIC INSERTS		
CHROME ODDS 1:72 H, 1:20 HTA		
R1 Johnny Unitas 1957	3.00	8.00

2000 Topps Unitas Reprints Autographs

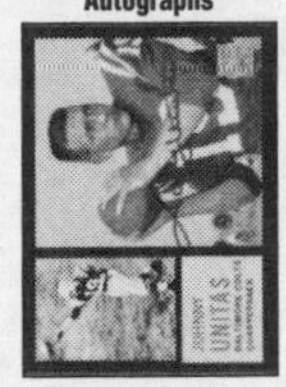

COMMON CARD (R1-R18)	175.00	350.00
AUTO ODDS 1:13,678 H, 1:3048 HTA		

2000 Topps Hall of Fame Class of 2000

This set was distributed by Topps at the 2000 Induction ceremonies for the Pro Football Hall of Fame. Each card includes a photo of a 2000 inductee printed with a border textured like a football. A gold foil "Class of 2000" logo also appears on the cardfronts. The cards are unnumbered and listed below alphabetically.

COMPLETE SET (5)	10.00	20.00
HOF1 Joe Montana	4.00	10.00
HOF2 Howie Long	1.50	4.00
HOF3 Ronnie Lott	1.50	4.00
HOF4 Dan Rooney	1.25	3.00
HOF5 Dave Wilcox	1.25	3.00

2001 Topps Promos

This set of 6-cards was released to promote the 2001 Topps base brand football release. Each card appears to be a parallel to the base set except for the card numbering on the backs.

COMPLETE SET (6)	2.00	5.00
P1 Emmitt Smith	1.00	2.50
P2 Warrick Dunn	.40	1.00
P3 Jeff Garcia	.30	.75
P4 Wayne Chrebet	.30	.75
P5 Jason Taylor	.40	1.00
P6 Tony Gonzalez	.40	1.00

2001 Topps

Released as a 385-card set, 2001 Topps features 310 veteran cards and 75 Draft Pick Cards Hobby and Retail were packaged in 36-pack boxes with packs containing 10 cards and carried a suggested retail price of $1.49; and HTA was packaged in 12-pack boxes with packs containing 45 cards and carried a suggested retail price of $5.00. This set included 3 no number checklists that were randomly inserted in packs.

COMPLETE SET (385)	45.00	75.00
1 Marshall Faulk	.25	.60
2 Lawyer Milloy	.20	.50
3 Rich Gannon	.20	.50
4 Rod Smith	.20	.50
5 David Boston	.15	.40
6 Jeremy McDaniel	.15	.40
7 Joey Galloway	.20	.50
8 Ron Dixon	.15	.40
9 Terrell Fletcher	.15	.40
10 Deion Sanders	.25	.60
11 Jevon Kearse	.20	.50
12 Charles Woodson	.25	.60
13 Brian Walker	.15	.40
14 Mike Peterson	.15	.40
15 Marcus Robinson	.20	.50
16 Duane Starks	.15	.40
17 KaRon Coleman	.15	.40
18 Randy Moss	.25	.60
19 Reggie Jones	.15	.40
20 Derrick Brooks	.25	.60
21 Eddie George	.25	.60
22 Wayne Chrebet	.20	.50
23 Kevin Hardy	.15	.40
24 Bill Schroeder	.20	.50
25 Doug Flutie	.25	.60
26 Tim Dwight	.20	.50
27 Eddie Kennison	.20	.50
28 Reggie Kelly	.15	.40
29 Ricky Watters	.20	.50
30 Stephen Alexander	.15	.40
31 Az-Zahir Hakim	.15	.40
32 Henri Crockett	.15	.40
33 Joe Horn	.20	.50
34 Danny Farmer	.15	.40

35 Shannon Sharpe .25 .60
36 Brad Hoover .20 .50
37 David Patten .15 .40
38 Kevin Faulk .20 .50
39 Freddie Jones .15 .40
40 Michael Westbrook .15 .40
41 Jacquez Green .15 .40
42 Torrance Small .15 .40
43 Terrence Wilkins .15 .40
44 Brett Favre .75 2.00
45 Tony Banks .15 .40
46 Johnnie Morton .20 .50
47 Jimmy Smith .20 .50
48 Jerry Rice .50 1.25
49 Jeff George .20 .50
50 Ray Lewis .25 .60
51 Joe Johnson .15 .40
52 Rocket Ismail .20 .50
53 Muhsin Muhammad .20 .50
54 Ken Dilger .15 .40
55 Ike Hilliard .20 .50
56 Joey Porter RC 1.25 3.00
57 Shaun Alexander .25 .60
58 Jeff Garcia .20 .50
59 Jay Fiedler .20 .50
60 Wane McGarity .15 .40
61 Steve Beuerlein .20 .50
62 Tywan Mitchell .15 .40
63 Travis Prentice .15 .40
64 Robert Griffith .15 .40
65 Napoleon Kaufman .15 .40
66 Randall Godfrey .15 .40
67 Junior Seau .25 .60
68 Willie Jackson .15 .40
69 Larry Foster .15 .40
70 Brandon Stokley .20 .50
71 Hugh Douglas .15 .40
72 James Thrash .20 .50
73 Vinny Testaverde .20 .50
74 Leslie Shepherd .15 .40
75 Terrell Davis .25 .60
76 Jake Plummer .20 .50
77 Corey Dillon .20 .50
78 Ron Dayne .20 .50
79 Brock Huard .15 .40
80 Todd Husak .15 .40
81 Richard Huntley .15 .40
82 Shaun Ellis .15 .40
83 Kyle Brady .15 .40
84 Corey Bradford .15 .40
85 Eric Moulds .20 .50
86 Brian Finneran .20 .50
87 Antonio Freeman .25 .60
88 Terry Glenn .20 .50
89 Tai Streets .15 .40
90 Chris Sanders .15 .40
91 Sylvester Morris .15 .40
92 Peter Warrick .20 .50
93 Chris Greisen .15 .40
94 Cade McNown .20 .50
95 Jerome Pathon .15 .40
96 John Randle .20 .50
97 Curtis Conway .20 .50
98 Keyshawn Johnson .20 .50
99 Trent Green .25 .60
100 Mike Anderson .20 .50
101 Jeff Blake .20 .50
102 Tee Martin .20 .50
103 Darrell Jackson .20 .50
104 Mark Brunell .20 .50
105 Charlie Batch .20 .50
106 Wesley Walls .15 .40
107 Edgerrin James .25 .60
108 Robert Wilson .15 .40
109 Donovan McNabb .25 .60
110 Champ Bailey .25 .60
111 Isaac Bruce .25 .60
112 Michael Strahan .25 .60
113 Donnie Edwards .15 .40
114 Randall Cunningham .25 .60
115 Germane Crowell .15 .40
116 Jermaine Lewis .15 .40
117 Dennis McKinley .15 .40
118 Ryan Leaf .15 .40
119 Samari Rolle .15 .40
120 Daunte Culpepper .20 .50
121 Tim Couch .15 .40
122 Greg Biekert .15 .40
123 Warrick Dunn .25 .60
124 Richie Anderson .15 .40
125 Trace Armstrong .15 .40
126 Bernardo Harris .15 .40
127 Kwame Cavil .15 .40
128 James Allen .15 .40
129 Anthony Becht .15 .40
130 Tiki Barber .25 .60
131 Brad Johnson .20 .50
132 Tyrone Wheatley .20 .50
133 Kurt Warner .40 1.00
134 Desmond Howard .20 .50
135 Thomas Jones .20 .50
136 Peyton Manning .60 1.50
137 Tony Richardson .15 .40
138 Chris Chandler .20 .50
139 Plaxico Burress .20 .50
140 J.R. Redmond .15 .40
141 Fred Taylor .25 .60
142 Akili Smith .15 .40
143 Sammy Morris .20 .50
144 Jessie Armstead .15 .40
145 Charlie Garner .20 .50
146 Steve McNair .25 .60
147 Charles Johnson .15 .40
148 Troy Aikman .40 1.00
149 Kevin Johnson .15 .40
150 Brian Urlacher .30 .75
151 Travis Taylor .15 .40
152 Aaron Shea .15 .40
153 Mike Cloud .15 .40
154 Donald Driver .25 .60
155 Chad Pennington .25 .60
156 Troy Edwards .15 .40
157 Reidel Anthony .15 .40
158 Michael Bishop .20 .50
159 Mo Lewis .15 .40
160 Damon Huard .20 .50
161 James McKnight .15 .40
162 Craig Yeast .15 .40
163 Michael Pittman .20 .50
164 Robert Smith .20 .50
165 Terrelle Smith .15 .40
166 Jeremiah Trotter .15 .40
167 Amani Toomer .20 .50
168 JaJuan Dawson .15 .40
169 Tim Biakabutuka .15 .40
170 Oronde Gadsden .15 .40
171 Ray Lucas .15 .40
172 Jermaine Fazande .15 .40
173 Todd Bouman .15 .40
174 Frank Wycheck .15 .40
175 Hines Ward .25 .60
176 Ahman Green .25 .60
177 Kaseem Sinceno .15 .40
178 Jamal Anderson .20 .50
179 Jay Riemersma .15 .40
180 Jarious Jackson .15 .40
181 Andre Rison .20 .50
182 Jerome Bettis .25 .60
183 Blaine Bishop .15 .40
184 Dorsey Levens .20 .50
185 James Stewart .15 .40
186 Chad Lewis .15 .40
187 Justin Watson .15 .40
188 Warren Sapp .20 .50
189 Rod Woodson .25 .60
190 Ricky Williams .25 .60
191 Marty Booker .20 .50
192 MarTay Jenkins .15 .40
193 Peerless Price .15 .40
194 Tony Gonzalez .25 .60
195 Jon Kitna .20 .50
196 Stephen Davis .20 .50
197 Curtis Martin .25 .60
198 Matt Hasselbeck .25 .60
199 Pat Johnson .15 .40
200 Emmitt Smith .60 1.50
201 Doug Johnson .15 .40
202 Autry Denson .15 .40
203 Troy Brown .20 .50
204 Jeff Graham .15 .40
205 Corey Simon .15 .40
206 Jamel White .15 .40
207 Jeff Lewis .15 .40
208 Frank Sanders .15 .40
209 Al Wilson .15 .40
210 Jason Sehorn .20 .50
211 Shaun King .15 .40
212 Torry Holt .20 .50
213 Kordell Stewart .20 .50
214 Keenan McCardell .20 .50
215 Dedric Ward .15 .40
216 Michael Wiley .15 .40
217 Rob Johnson .20 .50
218 Jamal Lewis .25 .60
219 Herman Moore .20 .50
220 Ron Dugans .15 .40
221 Jason Taylor .25 .60
222 Charles Lee .15 .40
223 J.J. Stokes .15 .40
224 Albert Connell .15 .40
225 Keith Poole .15 .40
226 Elvis Grbac .20 .50
227 Shawn Jefferson .15 .40
228 Jackie Harris .20 .50
229 Derrick Alexander .15 .40
230 Darnell Autry .15 .40
231 Bobby Shaw .15 .40
232 Aaron Brooks .20 .50
233 Cris Carter .25 .60
234 Desmond Clark .20 .50
235 Spergon Wynn .15 .40
236 Qadry Ismail .20 .50
237 Sam Cowart .15 .40
238 Zach Thomas .25 .60
239 Drew Bledsoe .25 .60
240 Ronney Jenkins .15 .40
241 Keith Mitchell RC .15 .40
242 Laveranues Coles .20 .50
243 Marcus Pollard .15 .40
244 Darren Sharper .20 .50
245 Donald Hayes .15 .40
246 Brian Griese .20 .50
247 Frank Moreau .15 .40
248 Bruce Smith .25 .60
249 Fred Beasley .15 .40
250 Mike Alstott .20 .50
251 Trent Dilfer .20 .50
252 Terance Mathis .15 .40
253 Shawn Bryson .15 .40
254 Dennis Northcutt .15 .40
255 Brandon Bennett .15 .40
256 Stacey Mack .15 .40
257 Tim Brown .25 .60
258 Duce Staley .20 .50
259 Sean Dawkins .15 .40
260 Ricky Proehl .15 .40
261 Chris Fuamatu-ma'afala .15 .40
262 La'Roi Glover .15 .40
263 Bubba Franks .20 .50
264 Kevin Lockett .15 .40
265 Lamar Smith .20 .50
266 Priest Holmes .25 .60
267 Macey Brooks .15 .40
268 Anthony Wright .15 .40
269 Ed McCaffrey .20 .50
270 Joe Jurevicius .15 .40
271 Terrell Owens .25 .60
272 Tony Simmons .15 .40
273 Itula Mili .15 .40
274 Chad Morton .15 .40
275 Marvin Harrison .25 .60
276 Jason Gildon .15 .40
277 Derrick Mason .20 .50
278 Greg Clark .15 .40
279 Casey Crawford .15 .40
280 Kerry Collins .20 .50
281 Terrell Owens SH .20 .50
282 Marshall Faulk SH .20 .50
283 Mike Anderson SH .15 .40
284 Cris Carter SH .20 .50
285 Corey Dillon SH .15 .40
286 Daunte Culpepper LL .15 .40
287 Peyton Manning LL .50 1.25
288 Torry Holt LL .15 .40
289 Marvin Harrison LL .20 .50
290 Edgerrin James LL .20 .50
291 Takeo Spikes .15 .40
292 John Lynch .20 .50
293 Sam Madison .15 .40
294 Stephen Boyd .15 .40
295 Tony Siragusa .20 .50
296 Robert Porcher .15 .40
297 Donnell Bennett .15 .40
298 Hardy Nickerson .15 .40
299 Jonathan Quinn .15 .40
300 Rob Morris .15 .40
301 E.G. Green .15 .40
302 David Sloan .15 .40
303 Jason Tucker .15 .40
304 Darrin Chiaverini .15 .40
305 Wali Rainer .15 .40
306 Jerry Azumah .15 .40
307 Jonathan Linton .15 .40
308 Dameyune Craig .15 .40
309 Courtney Brown .15 .40
310 Jammi German .15 .40
311 Michael Vick RC 5.00 12.00
312 Jamar Fletcher RC .30 .75
313 Will Allen RC .50 1.25
314 Jamal Reynolds RC .30 .75
315 Quincy Morgan RC .40 1.00
316 Eric Kelly RC .30 .75
317 Michael Stone RC .30 .75
318 Rod Gardner RC .40 1.00
319 Ken-Yon Rambo RC .30 .75
320 Eric Westmoreland RC .30 .75
321 Steve Smith RC 1.00 2.50
322 George Layne RC .30 .75
323 Justin McCareins RC .40 1.00
324 Adam Archuleta RC .40 1.00
325 Justin Smith RC .50 1.25
326 David Terrell RC .40 1.00
327 Correll Buckhalter RC .50 1.25
328 Drew Brees RC 7.50 15.00
329 Chris Barnes RC .30 .75
330 Santana Moss RC .60 1.50
331 Josh Heupel RC .50 1.25
332 Cedrick Wilson RC .40 1.00
333 Gerard Warren RC .40 1.00
334 Jamie Henderson RC .40 1.00
335 Onomo Ojo RC .30 .75
336 Marcus Stroud RC .40 1.00
337 Quincy Carter RC .40 1.00
338 Koren Robinson RC .40 1.00
339 Ryan Pickett RC .30 .75
340 Chad Johnson RC .75 2.00
341 Nate Clements RC .40 1.00
342 Jesse Palmer RC .40 1.00
343 Snoop Minnis RC .30 .75
344 Reggie Wayne RC 1.00 2.50
345 Kevin Kasper RC .30 .75
346 Will Peterson RC .40 1.00
347 Marques Tuiasosopo RC .40 1.00
348 Sage Rosenfels RC .50 1.25
349 Dan Alexander RC .40 1.00
350 LaDainian Tomlinson RC 6.00 12.00
351 Dan Morgan RC .40 1.00
352 Scotty Anderson RC .30 .75
353 Deuce McAllister RC .50 1.25
354 Todd Heap RC .50 1.25
355 Tony Dixon RC .30 .75
356 Chris Chambers RC .50 1.25
357 Eddie Berlin RC .30 .75
358 Anthony Thomas RC .50 1.25
359 James Jackson RC .30 .75
360 Richard Seymour RC .50 1.25
361 Andre Carter RC .40 1.00
362 Bobby Newcombe RC .40 1.00
363 Robert Ferguson RC .50 1.25
364 Jonathan Carter RC .30 .75
365 Damione Lewis RC .40 1.00
366 Darnerien McCants RC .40 1.00
367 Tim Hasselbeck RC .40 1.00
368 Derrick Gibson RC .30 .75
369 Rudi Johnson RC .50 1.25
370 Alge Crumpler RC .50 1.25
371 Derrick Blaylock RC .40 1.00
372 Moran Norris RC .30 .75
373 Travis Minor RC .40 1.00
374 LaMont Jordan RC .50 1.25
375 Kevan Barlow RC .40 1.00
376 Freddie Mitchell RC .30 .75
377 Shaun Rogers RC .50 1.25
378 Tay Cody RC .30 .75
379 Travis Henry RC .40 1.00
380 Chris Weinke RC .40 1.00
381 Willie Middlebrooks RC .40 1.00
382 Rashard Casey RC .30 .75
383 Mike McMahon RC .40 1.00
384 Michael Bennett RC .40 1.00
385 Jabari Holloway RC .30 .75
CL1 Checklist .02 .10
CL2 Checklist .02 .10
CL3 Checklist .02 .10
SBMVP Ray Lewis FB AU 150.00 300.00

2001 Topps Collection

COMP.FACT.SET (385) 50.00 80.00
*VETS: .4X TO 1X BASIC CARDS
*ROOKIES: .4X TO 1X BASIC CARDS

2001 Topps MVP Promotion

*VETS 1-310: 8X TO 20X BASIC CARDS
*VETS WIN: 10X TO 25X BASIC CARDS
*ROOKIES 311-385: 4X TO 10X
STATED ODDS 1:186H, 1:41HTA JUMBOS
311 Michael Vick 40.00 80.00
328 Drew Brees 40.00 80.00
350 LaDainian Tomlinson 30.00 80.00

2001 Topps MVP Promotion Prizes

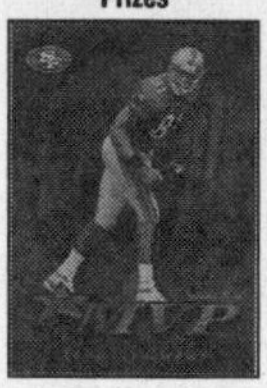

COMPLETE SET (17) 25.00 60.00
AVAILABLE ONLY VIA REDEMPTION
MVP1 Brian Griese 1.25 3.00
MVP2 Peyton Manning 4.00 10.00
MVP3 Kurt Warner 2.50 6.00
MVP4 Ricky Williams 1.50 4.00
MVP5 Terrell Owens 1.50 4.00
MVP6 David Patten 1.00 2.50
MVP7 Corey Dillon 1.25 3.00
MVP8 Ahman Green 1.50 4.00
MVP9 Shaun Alexander 1.50 4.00
MVP10 Randy Moss 1.50 4.00
MVP11 Jay Fiedler 1.25 3.00
MVP12 Steve McNair 1.50 4.00
MVP13 Todd Bouman 1.00 2.50
MVP14 Kordell Stewart 1.25 3.00
MVP15 Marshall Faulk 1.50 4.00
MVP16 Tim Couch 1.00 2.50
MVP17 Anthony Thomas 1.50 4.00

2001 Topps Autographs

GROUP 1 ODDS 1:21,614H, 1:4731HTA
GROUP 2 ODDS 1:12,763H, 1:2839HTA
GROUP 3 ODDS 1:4268H, 1:946HTA
GROUP 4 STATED ODDS 1:912H, 1:203HTA
GROUP 5 STATED ODDS 1:1418H, 1:315HTA
GROUP 6 STATED ODDS 1:1063H, 1:236HTA
OVERALL ODDS 1:322H, 1:72HTA JUMBOS
TABU Brian Urlacher 4 25.00 50.00
TACC Chris Chambers 4 8.00 20.00
TACJ Chad Johnson 6 12.00 30.00
TADB Drew Brees 3 75.00 135.00
TADC Daunte Culpepper 1 12.00 30.00
TADH Donald Hayes 4 5.00 12.00
TADJM Deuce McAllister 1 8.00 20.00
TADM Derrick Mason 4 6.00 15.00
TAEM Eric Moulds 4 6.00 15.00
TAES Emmitt Smith 2 100.00 200.00
TAJB Josh Booty 5 6.00 15.00
TAJH Joe Horn 4 6.00 15.00
TAJP Jesse Palmer 5 6.00 15.00
TAJS Jimmy Smith 4 6.00 15.00
TAJT James Thrash 6 6.00 15.00
TAKB Kevan Barlow 6 6.00 15.00
TAMV Michael Vick 1 60.00 120.00
TASM Santana Moss 3 10.00 25.00
TATM Travis Minor 5 6.00 15.00
TATW Terrence Wilkins 3 5.00 12.00

2001 Topps Combos

COMPLETE SET (19) 12.50 30.00
STATED ODDS 1:8H, 1:2HTA JUMBOS
TC1 Edgerrin James / Santana Moss .60 1.50
TC2 Torry Holt / Koren Robinson .60 1.50
TC3 Jamal Lewis / Travis Henry .75 2.00
TC4 Curtis Martin / Kevan Barlow .75 2.00
TC5 Cris Carter / Ken-Yon Rambo .75 2.00
TC6 Troy Aikman / Fred Mitchell 1.25 3.00
TC7 Brian Griese / David Terrell .60 1.50
TC8 Tyrone Wheatley / Anthony Thomas .75 2.00
TC9 Warrick Dunn / Travis Minor .75 2.00
TC10 Peter Warrick / Snoop Minnis .60 1.50
TC11 Warren Sapp / Dan Morgan .60 1.50
TC12 Tony Gonzalez / Andre Carter .75 2.00
TC13 Antonio Freeman / Michael Vick 2.00 5.00
TC14 Ron Dayne / Michael Bennett .60 1.50
TC15 Mike Alstott / Drew Brees 3.00 8.00
TC16 Ahman Green / Correll Buckhalter .75 2.00
TC17 Brad Johnson / Chris Weinke .60 1.50
TC18 Eric Moulds / Fred Smoot .75 2.00
TC19 Ray Lewis / Reggie Wayne 1.00 2.50

2001 Topps Hall of Fame Autographs

STATED ODDS 1:9242H, 1:2049HTA JUMBOS
TADJ Deacon Jones 60.00 120.00
TAJS Jackie Slater 60.00 120.00
TAJY Jack Youngblood 60.00 120.00
TAML Marv Levy 100.00 200.00
TARY Ron Yary 60.00 120.00
TAMM Mike Munchak 100.00 200.00

2001 Topps Hobby Masters

COMPLETE SET (10) 6.00 15.00
STATED ODDS 1:3 HTA JUMBOS
HM1 Jamal Lewis .75 2.00
HM2 Daunte Culpepper .60 1.50
HM3 Kurt Warner 1.25 3.00
HM4 Edgerrin James .75 2.00
HM5 Randy Moss .75 2.00
HM6 Eddie George .75 2.00
HM7 Mike Anderson .60 1.50
HM8 Peyton Manning 2.00 5.00
HM9 Marvin Harrison .75 2.00
HM10 Cris Carter .75 2.00

2001 Topps King of Kings Jerseys

STATED ODDS 1:580 H, 1:129HTA JUMBOS
KCD Corey Dillon 6.00 15.00
KDM Dan Marino 25.00 60.00
KES Emmitt Smith 20.00 50.00
KFT Fred Taylor 8.00 20.00
KJR Jerry Rice 15.00 40.00
KPM Peyton Manning 20.00 50.00
KRM Randy Moss 8.00 20.00
KTO Terrell Owens 8.00 20.00
KWP Walter Payton 25.00 60.00

2001 Topps King of Kings Jerseys Golden

STATED ODDS 1:1051 HTA JUMBOS
KGDT Corey Dillon / Fred Taylor 15.00 40.00
KGOR Terrell Owens / Jerry Rice 30.00 80.00
KGSP Emmitt Smith / Walter Payton 150.00 250.00

2001 Topps Own the Game

COMPLETE SET (30) 15.00 40.00
STATED ODDS 1:8H, 1:2HTA JUMBOS
AW1 Marvin Harrison .60 1.50
AW2 Muhsin Muhammad .50 1.25
AW3 Torry Holt .50 1.25
AW4 Rod Smith .50 1.25
AW5 Randy Moss .60 1.50
AW6 Cris Carter .60 1.50
AW7 Ed McCaffrey .50 1.25
AW8 Isaac Bruce .60 1.50
AW9 Terrell Owens .60 1.50
AW10 Tony Gonzalez .60 1.50
GW1 Edgerrin James .60 1.50
GW2 Robert Smith .50 1.25
GW3 Marshall Faulk .60 1.50
GW4 Mike Anderson .50 1.25
GW5 Eddie George .60 1.50
GW6 Corey Dillon .50 1.25
GW7 Fred Taylor .60 1.50
PS1 Brian Griese .50 1.25
PS2 Peyton Manning 1.50 4.00
PS3 Jeff Garcia .50 1.25
PS4 Daunte Culpepper .50 1.25
PS5 Brett Favre 2.00 5.00
PS6 Kurt Warner 1.00 2.50
PS7 Donovan McNabb .60 1.50
TI1 La'Roi Glover .40 1.00
TI2 Darren Sharper .50 1.25
TI3 Mike Peterson .40 1.00
TS1 Derrick Mason .50 1.25
TS2 Az-Zahir Hakim .40 1.00
TS3 Jermaine Lewis .40 1.00

2001 Topps Pro Bowl Jerseys

STATED ODDS 1:425H, 1:95HTA JUMBOS
TPCG Charlie Garner 8.00 20.00
TPCL Chad Lewis 6.00 15.00
TPDM Derrick Mason 8.00 20.00
TPEM Eric Moulds 8.00 20.00
TPJG Jeff Garcia 8.00 20.00
TPJL John Lynch 8.00 20.00
TPJS Junior Seau 10.00 25.00
TPJT Jason Taylor 10.00 25.00
TPMA Mike Alstott 8.00 20.00
TPRG Rich Gannon 8.00 20.00
TPRL Ray Lewis 12.00 30.00
TPTH Torry Holt 8.00 20.00

2001 Topps Pro Bowl Jerseys Autographs

STATED ODDS 1:9437H, 1:2114HTA JUMBOS
TPADC Daunte Culpepper 30.00 80.00
TPADM Derrick Mason 20.00 50.00
TPAEJ Edgerrin James 40.00 100.00

2001 Topps Rookie Premier Autographs

STATED ODDS 1:140HTA JUMBOS
RPAC Andre Carter 15.00 40.00
RPAT Anthony Thomas 20.00 50.00
RPCC Chris Chambers 15.00 40.00
RPCJ Chad Johnson SP 150.00 250.00
RPCW Chris Weinke 15.00 40.00
RPDB Drew Brees 300.00 500.00
RPDM Dan Morgan 15.00 40.00
RPDMC Deuce McAllister 20.00 50.00
RPDT David Terrell 15.00 40.00
RPDTM David Terrell / Santana Moss 60.00 150.00
RPDVB Michael Vick / Drew Brees 350.00 600.00
RPFM Freddie Mitchell 12.00 30.00
RPJH Josh Heupel 20.00 50.00
RPJJ James Jackson 12.00 30.00
RPJP Jesse Palmer 15.00 40.00
RPJS Justin Smith 20.00 50.00
RPKB Kevan Barlow 15.00 40.00
RPKR Koren Robinson 15.00 40.00
RPLD Leonard Davis 20.00 50.00
RPLT LaDainian Tomlinson 300.00 600.00
RPMB Michael Bennett 15.00 40.00
RPMMC Mike McMahon 15.00 40.00
RPMT Marques Tuiasosopo 15.00 40.00
RPMV Michael Vick 200.00 400.00
RPQC Quincy Carter 15.00 40.00
RPQM Quincy Morgan 15.00 40.00
RPRF Robert Ferguson 20.00 50.00
RPRG Rod Gardner 15.00 40.00
RPRJ Rudi Johnson 20.00 50.00
RPRS Richard Seymour 20.00 50.00
RPRW Reggie Wayne 40.00 100.00
RPSM Snoop Minnis 12.00 30.00
RPSM Santana Moss 25.00 60.00
RPSR Sage Rosenfels 20.00 50.00
RPTH Travis Henry 15.00 40.00
RPTM Travis Minor 15.00 40.00
RPGW Gerard Warren 15.00 40.00

2001 Topps Rookie Reprint Jerseys

STATED ODDS 1:11591:288 HOBBY JUMBO
TODM Dan Marino 40.00 100.00
TOES Emmitt Smith 30.00 80.00
TOJR Jerry Rice 30.00 80.00
TOWP Walter Payton 40.00 100.00

2001 Topps Super Bowl Bunting

ODDS 1:485 RET.JUMBO 1:968 RETAIL
SBB1 Kerry Collins 20.00 50.00
SBB2 Trent Dilfer 15.00 40.00
SBB3 Ike Hilliard 15.00 40.00
SBB4 Shannon Sharpe 15.00 40.00
SBB5 Ron Dayne 20.00 50.00
SBB6 Jason Sehorn 15.00 40.00

2001 Topps Super Bowl Ticket Stubs

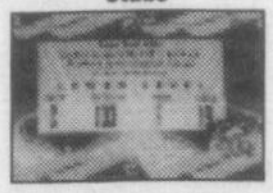

STATED ODDS 1:4702H, 1:1046HTA JUMBOS
LEWIS AU STATED ODDS 1:1380 HTA JUMBOS
1 Ron Dayne 50.00 100.00
2 Ron Dixon 25.00 60.00
3 Jamal Lewis 30.00 80.00
4 Jermaine Lewis 25.00 60.00
5 Ray Lewis 90.00 150.00
6 Brandon Stokley 30.00 80.00
7 Amani Toomer 25.00 60.00

2001 Topps Team Topps Legends Autographs

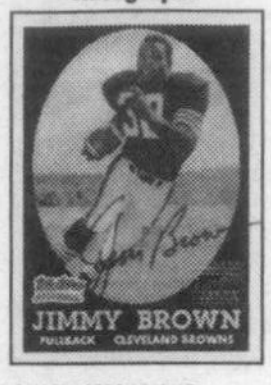

OVERALL GALLERY ODDS 1:310 H/R
OVERALL HERITAGE ODDS 1:282 H/R
OVERALL STADIUM ODDS 1:146 HOB/RET
OVERALL TOPPS ODDS 1:1597H/R,1:355HTA
TTF4 Tommy McDonald 68T 10.00 25.00
TTF6 Terry Metcalf 82T 5.00 12.00
TTF7 Art Donovan 59T 25.00 50.00
TTF9 Otis Sistrunk 79T 5.00 12.00
TTF10 Chuck Foreman 81T 5.00 12.00
TTF12 Don Maynard 73T 10.00 25.00
TTF13 Joe Namath 73T 60.00 120.00
TTF14 Charlie Joiner 87T 5.00 12.00
TTF16 Cliff Branch 85T 8.00 20.00
TTF19 Paul Hornung 57T 40.00 80.00
TTF20 Tom Dempsey 79T 5.00 12.00
TTF21 Billy Kilmer 78T 5.00 12.00
TTR1 Jim Brown 58T 125.00 200.00
TTR2 Dick Butkus 68T 40.00 80.00
TTR4 Tommy McDonald 57T 10.00 25.00
TTR5 John Hannah 74T 8.00 20.00
TTR6 Terry Metcalf 74T 5.00 12.00
TTR7 Art Donovan 56T 25.00 50.00
TTR9 Otis Sistrunk 74T 5.00 12.00
TTR10 Chuck Foreman 74T 5.00 12.00
TTR11 Sonny Jurgensen 58T 40.00 80.00
TTR12 Don Maynard 61T 10.00 25.00
TTR13 Joe Namath 65T 100.00 200.00
TTR14 Charlie Joiner 72T 8.00 20.00
TTR15 Mike Singletary 83T 15.00 40.00
TTR16 Cliff Branch 75T 8.00 20.00
TTR17 Johnny Unitas 57T 250.00 400.00
TTR18 Fred Biletnikoff 65T 20.00 40.00
TTR20 Tom Dempsey 70T 5.00 12.00
TTR21 Billy Kilmer 62T 5.00 12.00
TTR22 Barry Sanders 89TT 125.00 200.00
TTR23 Len Dawson 64T 20.00 40.00

2001 Topps Walter Payton Reprints

COMPLETE SET (12) 15.00 40.00
COMMON CARD (WP1-WP12) 1.50 4.00
STATED ODDS 1:12H, 1:3HTA JUMBO

2001 Topps Hall of Fame Class of 2001

This set was distributed by Topps at the 2001 Induction ceremonies for the Pro Football Hall of Fame. Each card includes a photo of a 2001 inductee printed in a very similar style to the 2001 Topps Hall of Fame Autographs inserts. A gold foil "Class of 2001" logo appears on the cardfronts. The cards are unnumbered and listed below alphabetically.

COMPLETE SET (7) 6.00 15.00
1 Nick Buoniconti 1.25 3.00
2 Marv Levy 1.25 3.00
3 Mike Munchak 1.00 2.50
4 Jackie Slater 1.00 2.50
5 Lynn Swann 2.00 5.00
6 Ron Yary 1.00 2.50
7 Jack Youngblood 1.25 3.00

2001 Topps Pro Bowl Promos

This set of 9-cards were issued on one unperforated sheet inside the 2001 Pro Bowl game program. The cards were printed on slick glossy thick stock and resemble the design of the 2000 Topps base set cards. The Pro Bowl logo appears on the cardfronts.

COMPLETE SET (9) 3.00 6.00
1 Peyton Manning .75 2.00
2 Donovan McNabb .30 .75
3 Marshall Faulk .30 .75
4 Randy Moss .30 .75
5 Edgerrin James .30 .75
6 Daunte Culpepper .25 .60
7 Jamal Lewis .30 .75
8 Jeff Garcia .25 .60
9 Warren Sapp .25 .60

2001 Topps Super Bowl XXXV Card Show

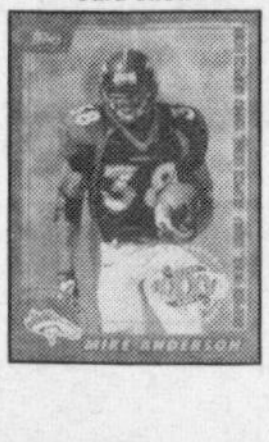

This 12-card set was issued one card at a time by completing the Treasure Hunt challenge at the Topps booth at the 2001 NFL Experience Super Bowl Card Show. Each card features a star player printed with an atomic refractor type design on the cardfront and a traditional cardback.

COMPLETE SET (12) 25.00 50.00
1 Peyton Manning 4.00 10.00
2 Donovan McNabb 1.50 4.00
3 Marshall Faulk 1.50 4.00
4 Jeff Garcia 1.25 3.00
5 Randy Moss 1.50 4.00
6 Fred Taylor 1.50 4.00
7 Robert Smith 1.25 3.00
8 Mike Anderson 1.25 3.00
9 Edgerrin James 1.50 4.00
10 Warren Sapp 1.25 3.00
11 Daunte Culpepper 1.25 3.00
12 Jamal Lewis 1.50 4.00

2002 Topps

This 385-card set was released in late June, 2002. This set contains 290 veteran cards, 20 Weekly Wrap-Up (291-310) and 75 rookies (311-385) . Boxes contained 36 packs of 10 cards with each pack having an $1.49 SRP. HTA packs were also produced for this product, each of those packs had an $5 SRP and came 12 packs per box and six boxes per case.

COMPLETE SET (385) 20.00 50.00
1 Kurt Warner .25 .60
2 Jeff Graham .15 .40
3 Todd Bouman .15 .40
4 Duce Staley .20 .50
5 Jon Kitna .20 .50
6 Shannon Sharpe .25 .60
7 Darrell Jackson .20 .50
8 Michael Pittman .20 .50
9 Tony Gonzalez .25 .60
10 Wayne Chrebet .20 .50
11 Jevon Kearse .20 .50
12 Bill Schroeder .15 .40
13 Jeremy McDaniel .15 .40
14 Todd Pinkston .15 .40
15 Maurice Smith .15 .40
16 Charlie Batch .15 .40
17 Olandis Gary .20 .50
18 Ron Dugans .15 .40
19 Brian Urlacher .25 .60
20 Amani Toomer .20 .50
21 Tim Couch .15 .40
22 Derrick Brooks .25 .60
23 Frank Sanders .15 .40
24 James Williams .15 .40
25 Lamar Smith .20 .50
26 Darrick Vaughn .15 .40
27 Cris Carter .25 .60
28 Roland Williams .15 .40
29 Bobby Shaw .15 .40
30 Jerome Pathon .15 .40
31 Rod Woodson .25 .60
32 Ronney Jenkins .15 .40
33 Chris Chandler .20 .50
34 Dez White .15 .40
35 Rod Smith .20 .50
36 Troy Brown .20 .50
37 JaJuan Dawson .15 .40
38 Reidel Anthony .15 .40
39 Mike Green .15 .40
40 Steve Smith .25 .60
41 Willie Jackson .15 .40
42 MarTay Jenkins .15 .40
43 Reggie Germany .15 .40
44 Desmond Howard .20 .50
45 Fred Taylor .20 .50
46 Scotty Anderson .15 .40
47 John Lynch .20 .50
48 Amos Zereoue .15 .40
49 Darnay Scott .20 .50
50 Anthony Thomas .20 .50
51 Jeff Garcia .20 .50
52 Charlie Garner .20 .50
53 Drew Bledsoe .25 .60
54 Donnie Edwards .15 .40
55 Corey Bradford .15 .40
56 Desmond Clark .20 .50
57 Courtney Brown .15 .40
58 Wesley Walls .20 .50
59 Chad Brown .15 .40
60 Shawn Jefferson .15 .40
61 Corey Dillon .20 .50
62 Johnnie Morton .20 .50
63 Marcus Pollard .15 .40
64 Jason Taylor .20 .50
65 Kevin Faulk .20 .50
66 Shane Matthews .15 .40
67 Hines Ward .25 .60
68 Garrison Hearst .20 .50
69 Trung Canidate .15 .40
70 Tony Banks .15 .40
71 Matt Hasselbeck .25 .60
72 Correll Buckhalter .20 .50
73 Ron Dayne .20 .50
74 Zach Thomas .25 .60
75 Emmitt Smith .60 1.50
76 Peter Warrick .20 .50
77 Rob Johnson .20 .50
78 Michael Strahan .25 .60
79 Ray Lewis .25 .60
80 Jamir Miller .15 .40
81 Brian Griese .20 .50
82 Stacey Mack .15 .40
83 Michael Bennett .20 .50
84 Ricky Williams .20 .50
85 Jamal Lewis .20 .50
86 Doug Flutie .25 .60
87 Jonathan Quinn .15 .40
88 Mike Alstott .20 .50
89 Samari Rolle .15 .40
90 LaMont Jordan .20 .50
91 Dominic Rhodes .20 .50
92 Quincy Carter .15 .40
93 Marcus Robinson .20 .50
94 Travis Henry .15 .40
95 Jason Brookins .15 .40
96 Nick Goings .15 .40
97 Brian Finneran .15 .40
98 Dorsey Levens .20 .50
99 Reggie Swinton .15 .40

100 Chris Chambers .20 .50
101 Kordell Stewart .20 .50
102 Tai Streets .15 .40
103 Chris Redman .15 .40
104 Jacquez Green .15 .40
105 Rod Gardner .15 .40
106 Kevin Kasper .15 .40
107 Anthony Henry .15 .40
108 Dan Morgan .15 .40
109 Ronald McKinnon .15 .40
110 Qadry Ismail .20 .50
111 Chad Johnson .25 .60
112 James Stewart .15 .40
113 Terrence Wilkins .15 .40
114 Joey Galloway .20 .50
115 Deuce McAllister .20 .50
116 Joe Jurevicius .15 .40
117 Tyrone Wheatley .20 .50
118 Jason Gildon .20 .50
119 LaDainian Tomlinson .30 .75
120 Grant Wistrom .15 .40
121 Eddie George .20 .50
122 Laveranues Coles .20 .50
123 Antowain Smith .20 .50
124 Larry Parker .15 .40
125 Bubba Franks .20 .50
126 Troy Hambrick .15 .40
127 Jamal Reynolds .15 .40
128 Doug Chapman .15 .40
129 Freddie Mitchell .15 .40
130 Tim Dwight .15 .40
131 Erron Kinney .15 .40
132 James Allen .15 .40
133 Eric Moulds .20 .50
134 Keenan McCardell .20 .50
135 David Sloan .15 .40
136 Dennis Northcutt .15 .40
137 Kevan Barlow .15 .40
138 Bobby Engram .20 .50
139 Champ Bailey .25 .60
140 Donald Hayes .15 .40
141 Brandon Bennett .15 .40
142 Deltha O'Neal .15 .40
143 James Jackson .15 .40
144 Shaun Rogers .15 .40
145 Joe Johnson .15 .40
146 Ricky Watters .20 .50
147 Warrick Dunn .20 .50
148 Steve McNair .25 .60
149 Marvin Harrison .25 .60
150 Kendrell Bell .15 .40
151 Jim Miller .15 .40
152 Terry Allen .20 .50
153 Jake Plummer .20 .50
154 James McKnight .15 .40
155 Curtis Martin .25 .60
156 Keyshawn Johnson .20 .50
157 Kevin Lockett .15 .40
158 Jeremiah Trotter .15 .40
159 Derrick Alexander .15 .40
160 Brandon Stokley .20 .50
161 J.J. Stokes .15 .40
162 Drew Bennett .20 .50
163 Drew Brees .40 1.00
164 Tim Brown .25 .00
165 Daunte Culpepper .20 .50
166 Rocket Ismail .20 .50
167 Alex Van Pelt .15 .40
168 Arnold Jackson .15 .40
169 Oronde Gadsden .15 .40
170 Isaac Bruce .25 .60
171 Warren Sapp .20 .50
172 Michael Westbrook .15 .40
173 John Abraham .20 .50
174 Jessie Armstead .15 .40
175 Brock Marion .15 .40
176 Brett Favre .60 1.50
177 Benjamin Gay .15 .40
178 Muhsin Muhammad .20 .50
179 Reggie Wayne .25 .60
180 Kailee Wong .15 .40
181 Rich Gannon .20 .50
182 Chris Fuamatu-Ma'afala .15 .40
183 Shaun Alexander .20 .50
184 Kevin Dyson .20 .50
185 Kwamie Lassiter .15 .40
186 Elvis Joseph .15 .40
187 Trent Dilfer .20 .50
188 Marty Booker .20 .50
189 Travis Taylor .15 .40
190 Michael Vick .40 1.00
191 Mike McMahon .15 .40
192 Jay Fiedler .20 .50
193 Zack Bronson .15 .40
194 Derrick Mason .20 .50
195 Anthony Becht .15 .40
196 Ahman Green .20 .50
197 Alge Crumpler .20 .50
198 Thomas Jones .25 .60
199 Tiki Barber .25 .60
200 Donovan McNabb .25 .60
201 Andre Carter .15 .40
202 Stephen Davis .20 .50
203 Troy Edwards .15 .40
204 Lawyer Milloy .15 .40
205 Peyton Manning .50 1.25
206 James Farrior .20 .50
207 Gerard Warren .15 .40
208 Peerless Price .15 .40
209 Avion Black .15 .40
210 Marcellus Wiley .15 .40
211 Torry Holt .25 .60
212 A.J. Feeley .15 .40
213 Travis Minor .15 .40
214 Darren Sharper .20 .50
215 Jerry Porter .15 .40
216 Randall Cunningham .25 .60
217 Chris Weinke .15 .40
218 Mike Anderson .20 .50
219 Snoop Minnis .15 .40
220 David Martin .15 .40
221 Vinny Sutherland .15 .40
222 Ki-Jana Carter .20 .50
223 Kevin Swayne .15 .40
224 Mark Brunell .20 .50
225 Quincy Morgan .15 .40
226 David Terrell .15 .40
227 Terance Mathis .15 .40
228 Frank Wycheck .15 .40
229 Az-Zahir Hakim .15 .40
230 Freddie Jones .15 .40
231 Jerry Rice .50 1.25
232 Ike Hilliard .20 .50
233 Terrell Davis .25 .60
234 Shawn Bryson .15 .40
235 David Boston .15 .40
236 Edgerrin James .20 .50
237 Trent Green .20 .50
238 Charlie Rogers .15 .40
239 Vinny Testaverde .20 .50
240 Koren Robinson .15 .40
241 Ronde Barber .20 .50
242 Dwayne Carswell .15 .40
243 Dedric Ward .15 .40
244 Richard Huntley .15 .40
245 Jamal Anderson .20 .50
246 Ryan Leaf .15 .40
247 Priest Holmes .25 .60
248 Tom Brady .60 1.50
249 Charles Woodson .25 .60
250 Jerome Bettis .25 .60
251 Tommy Polley .15 .40
252 Anthony Wright .15 .40
253 Chad Pennington .25 .60
254 David Patten .15 .40
255 Antonio Freeman .25 .60
256 Jamel White .15 .40
257 Jermaine Lewis .15 .40
258 Aaron Brooks .20 .50
259 Ron Dixon .15 .40
260 James Thrash .20 .50
261 Junior Seau .25 .60
262 Byron Chamberlain .15 .40
263 Ed McCaffrey .20 .50
264 Nate Clements .15 .40
265 Tony Martin .20 .50
266 Germane Crowell .15 .40
267 Terrell Owens .25 .60
268 Marshall Faulk .25 .60
269 Dat Nguyen .15 .40
270 Elvis Grbac .15 .40
271 Dante Hall .20 .50
272 Sylvester Morris .15 .40
273 Mike Brown .20 .50
274 Kevin Johnson .15 .40
275 Jimmy Smith .20 .50
276 Randy Moss .25 .60
277 Kerry Collins .20 .50
278 Santana Moss .20 .50
279 Plaxico Burress .20 .50
280 Brad Johnson .20 .50
281 Curtis Conway .20 .50
282 Eric Johnson .15 .40
283 Joe Horn .20 .50
284 Peter Boulware .15 .40
285 Larry Foster .15 .40
286 Nate Jacquet .15 .40
287 Terry Glenn .20 .50
288 Jarious Jackson .15 .40
289 Hugh Douglas .15 .40
290 Chad Lewis .15 .40
291 Ahman Green WW .15 .40
292 Peyton Manning WW .40 1.00
293 Kurt Warner WW .20 .50
294 Daunte Culpepper WW .15 .40
295 Tom Brady WW .50 1.25
296 Rod Gardner WW .12 .30
297 Corey Dillon WW .15 .40
298 Priest Holmes WW .20 .50
299 Shaun Alexander WW .15 .40
300 Randy Moss WW .20 .50
301 Eric Moulds WW .15 .40
302 Brett Favre WW .50 1.25
303 Todd Bouman WW .12 .30
304 Dominic Rhodes WW .15 .40
305 Marvin Harrison WW .20 .50
306 Torry Holt WW .20 .50
307 Derrick Mason WW .15 .40
308 Jerry Rice WW .40 1.00
309 Donovan McNabb WW .20 .50
310 Marshall Faulk WW .20 .50
311 David Carr RC .50 1.25
312 Quentin Jammer RC .50 1.25
313 Mike Williams RC .30 .75
314 Rocky Calmus RC .40 1.00
315 Travis Fisher RC .40 1.00
316 Dwight Freeney RC .60 1.50
317 Jeremy Shockey RC .75 2.00
318 Marquise Walker RC .30 .75
319 Eric Crouch RC .50 1.25
320 DeShaun Foster RC .50 1.25
321 Roy Williams RC .50 1.25
322 Andre Davis RC .40 1.00
323 Alex Brown RC .50 1.25
324 Michael Lewis RC .50 1.25
325 Terry Charles RC .30 .75
326 Clinton Portis RC .60 1.50
327 Dennis Johnson RC .30 .75
328 Lito Sheppard RC .50 1.25
329 Ryan Sims RC .50 1.25
330 Raonall Smith RC .30 .75
331 Albert Haynesworth RC .50 1.25
332 Eddie Freeman RC .30 .75
333 Levi Jones RC .30 .75
334 Josh McCown RC .50 1.25
335 Cliff Russell RC .30 .75
336 Maurice Morris RC .40 1.00
337 Antwaan Randle El RC .50 1.25
338 Ladell Betts RC .50 1.25
339 Daniel Graham RC .40 1.00
340 David Garrard RC .60 1.50
341 Antonio Bryant RC .50 1.25
342 Patrick Ramsey RC .50 1.25
343 Kelly Campbell RC .40 1.00
344 Will Overstreet RC .30 .75
345 Ryan Denney RC .30 .75
346 John Henderson RC .40 1.00
347 Freddie Milons RC .30 .75
348 Tim Carter RC .40 1.00
349 Kurt Kittner RC .30 .75
350 Joey Harrington RC .50 1.25
351 Ricky Williams RC .40 1.00
352 Bryant McKinnie RC .30 .75
353 Ed Reed RC 2.00 5.00
354 Josh Reed RC .40 1.00
355 Seth Burford RC .30 .75
356 Javon Walker RC .50 1.25
357 Jamar Martin RC .40 1.00
358 Leonard Henry RC .30 .75
359 Julius Peppers RC 1.00 2.50
360 Jabar Gaffney RC .50 1.25
361 Kalimba Edwards RC .40 1.00
362 Napoleon Harris RC .40 1.00
363 Ashley Lelie RC .40 1.00
364 Anthony Weaver RC .30 .75
365 Bryan Thomas RC .30 .75
366 Wendell Bryant RC .30 .75
367 Damien Anderson RC .30 .75
368 Travis Stephens RC .30 .75
369 Rohan Davey RC .50 1.25
370 Mike Pearson RC .30 .75
371 Marc Colombo RC .30 .75
372 Phillip Buchanon RC .50 1.25
373 T.J. Duckett RC .50 1.25
374 Ron Johnson RC .40 1.00
375 Larry Tripplett RC .30 .75
376 Randy Fasani RC .40 1.00
377 Keyuo Craver RC .30 .75
378 Marquand Manuel RC .30 .75
379 Jonathan Wells RC .50 1.25
380 Reche Caldwell RC .50 1.25
381 Luke Staley RC .30 .75
382 Donte Stallworth RC .50 1.25
383 Levar Fisher RC .30 .75
384 Lamar Gordon RC .40 1.00
385 William Green RC .40 1.00
SBMVP Tom Brady FB AU/150 350.00 600.00

2002 Topps Collection

COMP.FACT.SET (385) 40.00 75.00
*VETS: .4X TO 1X BASE TOPPS
*ROOKIES: .4X TO 1X BASE TOPPS

2002 Topps MVP Promotion

*1-310 VETS: 10X TO 25X BASIC CARDS
*311-385 ROOKIES: 4X TO 10X
STATED ODDS 1:112 HOB, 1:87 RET
40 Steve Smith WIN 10.00 25.00
51 Jeff Garcia WIN 10.00 25.00
53 Drew Bledsoe WIN 10.00 25.00
84 Ricky Williams WIN 10.00 25.00
94 Travis Henry WIN 10.00 25.00
149 Marvin Harrison WIN 10.00 25.00
176 Brett Favre WIN 25.00 50.00
183 Shaun Alexander WIN 10.00 25.00
190 Michael Vick WIN 10.00 25.00
200 Donovan McNabb WIN 10.00 25.00
247 Priest Holmes WIN 10.00 25.00
248 Tom Brady WIN 15.00 40.00
253 Chad Pennington WIN 10.00 25.00
267 Terrell Owens WIN 10.00 25.00
268 Marshall Faulk WIN 10.00 25.00
279 Plaxico Burress WIN 10.00 25.00
317 Jeremy Shockey WIN 10.00 25.00

2002 Topps MVP Promotion Prizes

COMPLETE SET (17) 20.00 50.00
MVP1 Priest Holmes 1.25 3.00
MVP2 Drew Bledsoe 1.25 3.00
MVP3 Tom Brady 3.00 8.00
MVP4 Shaun Alexander 1.00 2.50
MVP5 Brett Favre 3.00 8.00
MVP6 Travis Henry .75 2.00
MVP7 Marshall Faulk 1.25 3.00
MVP8 Terrell Owens 1.25 3.00
MVP9 Jeff Garcia 1.00 2.50
MVP10 Plaxico Burress 1.00 2.50
MVP11 Donovan McNabb 1.25 3.00
MVP12 Ricky Williams 1.00 2.50
MVP13 Michael Vick 2.00 5.00
MVP14 Steve Smith 1.25 3.00
MVP15 Marvin Harrison 1.25 3.00
MVP16 Kerry Collins 1.00 2.50
MVP17 Chad Pennington 1.25 3.00

2002 Topps Autographs

OVERALL ODDS 1:258 HOB, 1:80 HTA JUM
TAAT Anthony Thomas 6.00 15.00
TACC Chris Chambers 6.00 15.00
TADM Derrick Mason 6.00 15.00
TALT LaDainian Tomlinson 40.00 80.00
TARL Ray Lewis 25.00 50.00
TAWJ Willie Jackson 5.00 12.00

2002 Topps Hobby Masters

COMPLETE SET (10) 10.00 25.00
STATED ODDS 1:9 HOB, 1:3 HTA JUM
HM1 Kurt Warner .75 2.00
HM2 Tom Brady 2.00 5.00
HM3 Marshall Faulk .75 2.00
HM4 Marvin Harrison .75 2.00
HM5 Randy Moss .75 2.00
HM6 Jerome Bettis .75 2.00
HM7 Jerry Rice 1.50 4.00
HM8 Brett Favre 2.00 5.00
HM9 Donovan McNabb .75 2.00
HM10 Curtis Martin .75 2.00

2002 Topps King of Kings Super Bowl MVP Jerseys

STATED ODDS 1:4069 HOB, 1:3120 RET
KDA Terrell Davis 25.00 60.00
Marcus Allen
KME Joe Montana 50.00 120.00
John Elway
KMJ Joe Montana 50.00 120.00
Jerry Rice
KYR Steve Young 30.00 80.00
Jerry Rice

2002 Topps King of Kings Super Bowl MVP Autographs

STATED PRINT RUN 25 SER.#'d SETS
KDA Terrell Davis 100.00 175.00
Marcus Allen
KME Joe Montana 350.00 600.00
John Elway
KMJ Joe Montana 300.00 500.00
Jerry Rice
KYR Steve Young 250.00 400.00
Jerry Rice

2002 Topps Own The Game

COMPLETE SET (30) 30.00 80.00
STATED ODDS 1:12 HOB, 1:4 HTA JUM
OG1 Kurt Warner 1.25 3.00
OG2 Peyton Manning 2.50 6.00
OG3 Jeff Garcia 1.00 2.50
OG4 Brett Favre 3.00 8.00
OG5 Donovan McNabb 1.25 3.00
OG6 Rich Gannon 1.00 2.50
OG7 Tom Brady 3.00 8.00
OG8 Aaron Brooks 1.00 2.50
OG9 Priest Holmes 1.25 3.00
OG10 Curtis Martin 1.25 3.00
OG11 Stephen Davis 1.00 2.50
OG12 Ahman Green 1.00 2.50
OG13 Marshall Faulk 1.25 3.00
OG14 Shaun Alexander 1.00 2.50
OG15 Corey Dillon 1.00 2.50
OG16 Ricky Williams 1.00 2.50
OG17 David Boston .75 2.00
OG18 Marvin Harrison 1.25 3.00
OG19 Terrell Owens 1.25 3.00
OG20 Jimmy Smith 1.00 2.50
OG21 Torry Holt 1.25 3.00
OG22 Rod Smith 1.00 2.50
OG23 Keyshawn Johnson 1.00 2.50
OG24 Troy Brown 1.00 2.50
OG25 Michael Strahan 1.25 3.00
OG26 Ronald McKinnon .75 2.00
OG27 Ray Lewis 1.25 3.00
OG28 Zach Thomas 1.25 3.00
OG29 Ronde Barber 1.00 2.50
OG30 Anthony Henry .75 2.00

2002 Topps Pro Bowl Jerseys

STATED ODDS 1:399 HOB, 1:343 RET
APJE Jason Elam 6.00 15.00
APJL Jermaine Lewis 5.00 12.00
APLM Lawyer Milloy 5.00 12.00
APMF Marshall Faulk 8.00 20.00
APPH Priest Holmes 8.00 20.00
APRL Ray Lewis 8.00 20.00
APRW Rod Woodson 8.00 20.00
APSA Sam Adams 5.00 12.00
APSS Shannon Sharpe 8.00 20.00
APTB Tom Brady 15.00 40.00

2002 Topps Ring of Honor

COMPLETE SET (36) 30.00 80.00
STATED ODDS 1:9 HOB/RET, 1:3 HTA JUM
BS1 Bart Starr 2.50 6.00
BS2 Bart Starr 2.50 6.00
CH5 Chuck Howley .75 2.00
DH31 Desmond Howard 1.00 2.50
DW22 Doug Williams 1.00 2.50
ES28 Emmitt Smith 3.00 8.00
FB11 Fred Biletnikoff 1.25 3.00
FH9 Franco Harris 1.25 3.00
JE33 John Elway 2.50 6.00
JM16 Joe Montana 3.00 8.00
JM19 Joe Montana 3.00 8.00
JM24 Joe Montana 3.00 8.00
JN3 Joe Namath 2.00 5.00
JP15 Jim Plunkett 1.00 2.50
JR17 John Riggins 1.25 3.00
JR23 Jerry Rice 2.50 6.00
JS7 Jake Scott .75 2.00
KW34 Kurt Warner 1.25 3.00
LB30 Larry Brown .75 2.00
LC8 Larry Csonka 1.25 3.00
LD4 Len Dawson 1.25 3.00
MA18 Marcus Allen 1.25 3.00
MR26 Mark Rypien 1.00 2.50
OA25 Ottis Anderson .75 2.00
PS21 Phil Simms 1.00 2.50
RD20 Richard Dent 1.00 2.50
RL35 Ray Lewis 1.25 3.00
RS6 Roger Staubach 2.00 5.00
RW12 Randy White 1.00 2.50
SY29 Steve Young 1.50 4.00
TA27 Troy Aikman 2.00 5.00
TB13 Terry Bradshaw 2.00 5.00
TB14 Terry Bradshaw 2.00 5.00
TB36 Tom Brady 3.00 8.00
TD32 Terrell Davis 1.25 3.00

2002 Topps Ring of Honor Autographs

OVERALL HOB STATED ODDS 1:225
OVERALL RET STATED ODDS 1:1056
RHBS Bart Starr SB I 200.00 400.00
RHBS2 Bart Starr SB II 200.00 400.00
RHCH Chuck Howley 50.00 120.00
RHDH Desmond Howard SP 300.00 500.00
RHDW Doug Williams 100.00 200.00
RHES Emmitt Smith 300.00 450.00
RHFB Fred Biletnikoff 75.00 150.00
RHFH Franco Harris 100.00 200.00
RHJE John Elway 175.00 300.00
RHJM Joe Montana SB XVI 175.00 300.00
RHJM2 Joe Montana SB XIX 175.00 300.00
RHJM3 Joe Montana SB XXIV 175.00 300.00
RHJN Joe Namath 150.00 300.00
RHJP Jim Plunkett 100.00 200.00
RHJR Jerry Rice 200.00 350.00
RHJRI John Riggins 100.00 200.00
RHJS Jake Scott SP 500.00 750.00
RHKW Kurt Warner 100.00 200.00
RHLB Larry Brown 75.00 150.00
RHLC Larry Csonka 100.00 200.00
RHLD Len Dawson 100.00 200.00
RHMA Marcus Allen 100.00 200.00
RHMR Mark Rypien 100.00 200.00
RHOA Ottis Anderson 75.00 150.00
RHPS Phil Simms 100.00 200.00
RHRD Richard Dent 75.00 150.00
RHRL Ray Lewis 175.00 300.00
RHRS Roger Staubach 125.00 250.00
RHRW Randy White 50.00 120.00
RHSY Steve Young 125.00 225.00
RHTA Troy Aikman 150.00 250.00
RHTB Terry Bradshaw SB XIII 150.00 300.00
RHTBR Tom Brady SB XXXVI 300.00 600.00
RHTB2 Terry Bradshaw SB XIV 150.00 300.00
RHTD Terrell Davis 100.00 200.00

2002 Topps Rookie Premier Autographs

*HOLOGRAM MISSING: .2X TO .5X
RPAB Antonio Bryant 25.00 60.00
RPAD Andre Davis 20.00 50.00
RPAL Ashley Lelie 20.00 50.00
RPAR Antwaan Randle El 25.00 60.00
RPCP Clinton Portis 60.00 150.00
RPCR Cliff Russell 15.00 40.00
RPDC David Carr
RPDCH David Carr
Joey Harrington
RPDF DeShaun Foster 25.00 60.00
RPDG Daniel Graham 20.00 50.00
RPDGA David Garrard 30.00 80.00
RPDGD William Green 25.00 60.00
T.J. Duckett
RPDS Donte Stallworth 25.00 60.00
RPDSL Donte Stallworth 25.00 60.00
Ashley Lelie
RPEC Eric Crouch 25.00 60.00
RPJG Jabar Gaffney 25.00 60.00
RPJH Joey Harrington 25.00 60.00
RPJM Josh McCown 25.00 60.00
RPJP Julius Peppers 90.00 150.00
RPJR Josh Reed 20.00 50.00
RPJS Jeremy Shockey 75.00 150.00
RPJW Javon Walker 25.00 60.00
RPLB Ladell Betts 25.00 60.00
RPMM Maurice Morris 20.00 50.00
RPMW Marquise Walker 15.00 40.00
RPMWI Mike Williams 15.00 40.00
RPPR Patrick Ramsey 25.00 60.00
RPQJ Quentin Jammer 25.00 60.00
RPRC Reche Caldwell 25.00 60.00
RPRD Rohan Davey 25.00 60.00
RPRJ Ron Johnson 20.00 50.00
RPRW Roy Williams 25.00 60.00
RPTC Tim Carter 20.00 50.00
RPTJD T.J. Duckett 25.00 60.00
RPTS Travis Stephens 15.00 40.00
RPWG William Green 20.00 50.00

2002 Topps Super Bowl Goal Posts

COMPLETE SET (10) 150.00 300.00
STATED ODDS 1:410 HOB, 1:352 RET
VINATIERI AUTO ODDS 1:1621H
SBG1 Tom Brady 60.00 100.00
SBG2 Kurt Warner 12.00 30.00
SBG3 Antowain Smith 10.00 25.00
SBG4 Marshall Faulk 12.00 30.00
SBG5 Troy Brown 10.00 25.00
SBG6 Adam Vinatieri 40.00 80.00
SBG7 David Patten 8.00 20.00
SBG8 Torry Holt 12.00 30.00
SBG9 Ty Law 10.00 25.00
SBG10 Isaac Bruce 12.00 30.00
SBGAV Adam Vinatieri AUTO 125.00 250.00

2002 Topps Super Tix

STATED ODDS 1:929 HOB, 1:636 RET
SBT1 Tom Brady 40.00 80.00
SBT2 Kurt Warner 15.00 40.00
SBT3 Antowain Smith 12.00 30.00
SBT4 Marshall Faulk 15.00 40.00
SBT5 Troy Brown 12.00 30.00
SBT6 Az-Zahir Hakim 10.00 25.00
SBT7 David Patten 10.00 25.00
SBT8 Torry Holt 15.00 40.00
SBT9 Ty Law 12.00 30.00
SBT10 Isaac Bruce 15.00 40.00

2002 Topps Terry Bradshaw Reprints

COMPLETE SET (14) 15.00 40.00
COMMON CARD (1-14) 1.50 4.00
STATED ODDS 1:9 HOB/RET, 1:3 HTA JUM
AU STATED ODDS 1:8406 HOB, 1:7225 RET
1AU Terry Bradshaw '71 AUTO 60.00 120.00

2002 Topps Hall of Fame Class of 2002

This set was produced by Topps at issued at the 2002 Induction ceremonies for the Pro Football Hall of Fame. Each card includes a photo of a 2002 inductee printed with a gold colored border. A gold foil "Class of 2002" logo appears on the cardfronts as well. The cards are unnumbered and listed below alphabetically.

COMPLETE SET (5) 6.00 15.00
1 Dave Casper 1.25 3.00
2 Dan Hampton 1.25 3.00
3 Jim Kelly 2.00 5.00
4 John Stallworth 1.50 4.00
5 Hank Stram 1.25 3.00

2002 Topps Pro Bowl Card Show

This set was distributed to dealers who participated in the 2002 Pro Bowl Card Show in Hawaii. The cards are essentially identical to the Super Bowl Card Show set but include the 2002 Pro Bowl logo on the front. A Refractor parallel set was also produced with reportedly only 50-sets made.

COMPLETE SET (18) 10.00 20.00
*REFRACTOR: 1.5X TO 4X BASIC CARDS
1 Edgerrin James .40 1.00
2 Randy Moss .50 1.25
3 Peyton Manning 1.00 2.50
4 Ricky Williams .40 1.00
5 Aaron Brooks .40 1.00
6 Brian Griese .40 1.00
7 Ahman Green .40 1.00
8 Daunte Culpepper .40 1.00
9 Donovan McNabb .50 1.25
10 Anthony Thomas .40 1.00
11 Brett Favre 1.25 3.00
12 Marshall Faulk .50 1.25
13 Doug Flutie .50 1.25
14 Jeff Garcia .40 1.00
15 Kurt Warner .50 1.25
16 Chris Weinke .30 .75
17 LaDainian Tomlinson .60 1.50
18 Michael Vick .75 2.00

2002 Topps Pro Bowl Card Show Jumbos

Topps distributed these 6-cards at the 2002 Pro Bowl Card Show in Hawaii. Collectors could obtain one card at a time by completing various scavenger hunt type tasks as part of Topps' Treasure Hunt promotion. The cards are jumbo (roughly 3 1/4" by 4 1/5") sized versions of the basic Pro Bowl Card Show cards.

COMPLETE SET (6) 12.50 30.00
1 Anthony Thomas 1.50 4.00
2 Randy Moss 2.00 5.00
3 Marshall Faulk 2.00 5.00
4 LaDainian Tomlinson 2.50 6.00
5 Michael Vick 3.00 8.00
6 Donovan McNabb 2.00 5.00

2002 Topps Super Bowl XXXVI Card Show

This set was distributed directly to dealers who participated in the 2002 Super Bowl Card Show in New Orleans. Each card was printed on metallic foil card stock and included the Super Bowl XXXVI logo on the front. A reprint of the 1989 Topps Traded Troy Aikman card was distributed at the show via a wrapper redemption program. It is not considered part of the 18-card set. A Refractor parallel set was also produced with reportedly only 50-sets made.

COMPLETE SET (18) 10.00 20.00
*REFRACTORS: 2X TO 5X BASIC CARDS
1 Edgerrin James .40 1.00
2 Randy Moss .50 1.25
3 Peyton Manning 1.00 2.50
4 Ricky Williams .40 1.00
5 Aaron Brooks .40 1.00
6 Brian Griese .40 1.00
7 Ahman Green .40 1.00
8 Daunte Culpepper .40 1.00
9 Donovan McNabb .50 1.25
10 Anthony Thomas .40 1.00
11 Brett Favre 1.25 3.00
12 Marshall Faulk .50 1.25
13 Doug Flutie .50 1.25
14 Jeff Garcia .40 1.00
15 Kurt Warner .50 1.25
16 Chris Weinke .30 .75
17 LaDainian Tomlinson .60 1.50
18 Michael Vick .75 2.00

2003 Topps

Released in July of 2003, this set consists of 385 cards, including 310 veterans and 75 rookies. Boxes contained 36 packs of 10 cards. SRP was $2.99. Stated odds for the Dexter Jackson SBMVP37 card were 1:13590 hobby packs, and 1:3926 HTA packs.

COMPLETE SET (385) 25.00 60.00
SBMVP37 ODDS 1:13,590HOB, 1:3926HTA
1 Michael Vick .30 .75
2 Wesley Walls .20 .50
3 Josh Reed .15 .40
4 Josh McCown .20 .50
5 James Stewart .15 .40
6 Deltha O'Neal .15 .40
7 Quincy Morgan .15 .40
8 Tony Fisher .15 .40
9 Corey Bradford .15 .40
10 Byron Chamberlain .15 .40
11 James McKnight .15 .40
12 Fred Taylor .20 .50
13 David Patten .15 .40
14 Jerome Bettis .25 .60
15 Jerry Porter .15 .40
16 Anthony Becht .15 .40
17 Steve McNair .25 .60
18 Stephen Davis .20 .50
19 Terrence Wilkins .15 .40
20 Jamie Martin .15 .40
21 Tai Streets .15 .40
22 Frank Wycheck .15 .40
23 Sammy Knight .15 .40
24 Marcus Pollard .15 .40
25 Jamie Sharper .15 .40
26 T.J. Houshmandzadeh .25 .60
27 Javin Hunter .15 .40
28 Alge Crumpler .20 .50
29 Chris Weinke .20 .50
30 David Terrell .15 .40
31 Troy Hambrick .15 .40
32 Bubba Franks .20 .50
33 Todd Bouman .15 .40
34 Trent Green .20 .50
35 Mark Brunell .20 .50
36 James Thrash .15 .40
37 Donnie Edwards .15 .40
38 Mike Alstott .25 .60
39 Bobby Engram .15 .40
40 Deuce McAllister .20 .50
41 Santana Moss .20 .50
42 Kordell Stewart .20 .50
43 Jason Taylor .20 .50
44 Corey Dillon .20 .50
45 Damien Anderson .15 .40
46 Rodney Peete .15 .40
47 Jeff Blake .20 .50
48 Mike McMahon .15 .40
49 Ed McCaffrey .20 .50
50 Priest Holmes .25 .60
51 Moe Williams .15 .40
52 Brian Dawkins .20 .50
53 Tim Brown .25 .60
54 Curtis Martin .25 .60
55 Charles Stackhouse .15 .40
56 Derrius Thompson .15 .40
57 John Simon .15 .40
58 Joe Jurevicius .20 .50
59 Jonathan Wells .15 .40
60 William Green .15 .40
61 Ken-Yon Rambo .15 .40
62 Frank Sanders .15 .40
63 Chester Taylor .20 .50
64 Keith Brooking .20 .50
65 Bill Schroeder .15 .40
66 Travis Minor .15 .40
67 Eric Parker RC .30 .75
68 Phillip Buchanon .15 .40
69 Amos Zereoue .15 .40
70 Warren Sapp .20 .50
71 Ladell Betts .15 .40
72 Lamar Gordon .15 .40
73 Koren Robinson .20 .50
74 Ron Dayne .20 .50
75 Donovan McNabb .25 .60
76 Edgerrin James .25 .60
77 Stacey Mack .15 .40
78 Justin Smith .20 .50
79 Kelly Holcomb .15 .40
80 Thomas Jones .25 .60
81 Randy McMichael .15 .40
82 Daunte Culpepper .20 .50
83 Tommy Maddox .20 .50
84 Tyrone Wheatley .20 .50
85 Kevin Dyson .15 .40
86 Rod Gardner .15 .40
87 Wayne Chrebet .20 .50
88 Marc Boerigter .15 .40
89 Darnay Scott .20 .50
90 T.J. Duckett .20 .50
91 Marcel Shipp .15 .40
92 Ross Tucker .15 .40
93 Drew Bledsoe .25 .60
94 Scotty Anderson .15 .40
95 Rod Smith .20 .50
96 Jim Kleinsasser .15 .40
97 Peyton Manning .50 1.25
98 Junior Seau .25 .60
99 Darrell Jackson .20 .50
100 Brett Favre .60 1.50
101 Ashley Lelie .15 .40
102 Jajuan Dawson .15 .40
103 Kyle Brady .15 .40
104 Kevin Faulk .20 .50
105 Jeremy Shockey .25 .60
106 Hines Ward .25 .60
107 Jeff Garcia .20 .50
108 Shane Matthews .15 .40
109 Jevon Kearse .20 .50
110 Eddie Kennison .15 .40
111 Quincy Carter .15 .40
112 Brian Urlacher .25 .60
113 Charlie Rogers .15 .40
114 Robert Ferguson .15 .40
115 Christian Fauria .15 .40
116 Brian Westbrook .25 .60
117 Antwaan Randle El .20 .50
118 Eddie George .20 .50
119 Derrick Brooks .20 .50
120 Isaac Bruce .25 .60
121 Joe Horn .20 .50
122 Jermaine Lewis .15 .40
123 Jon Kitna .20 .50
124 David Boston .15 .40
125 Todd Heap .20 .50
126 Lamar Smith .20 .50
127 Marcus Robinson .20 .50
128 Germane Crowell .15 .40
129 Kevin Johnson .15 .40
130 Cris Carter .25 .60
131 Drew Brees .25 .60
132 Champ Bailey .25 .60
133 Brian Finneran .15 .40
134 Mike Anderson .20 .50
135 Derek Ross .15 .40
136 Javon Walker .20 .50
137 D'Wayne Bates .15 .40
138 Chad Lewis .20 .50
139 Charlie Garner .20 .50
140 Laveranues Coles .15 .40
141 Ron Dixon .15 .40
142 Rob Johnson .20 .50
143 Shaun Alexander .20 .50
144 Kevan Barlow .15 .40
145 Aaron Brooks .20 .50
146 Jay Foreman .15 .40
147 Mike Peterson .15 .40
148 Brandon Bennett .15 .40
149 Jake Plummer .20 .50
150 Emmitt Smith .60 1.50
151 Mikhael Ricks .15 .40
152 Terry Glenn .20 .50
153 Michael Bennett .20 .50
154 Deion Branch .20 .50
155 Justin McCareins .15 .40
156 Keyshawn Johnson .25 .60
157 Marc Bulger .25 .60
158 Matt Hasselbeck .20 .50
159 Garrison Hearst .20 .50
160 Jamel White .15 .40
161 Doug Johnson .15 .40
162 Larry Centers .20 .50
163 Dee Brown .15 .40

164 Dez White	.15	.40
165 Brian Griese	.20	.50
166 Johnnie Morton	.20	.50
167 Oronde Gadsden	.15	.40
168 Chad Morton	.15	.40
169 Rod Woodson	.25	.60
170 Ricky Proehl	.20	.50
171 Tim Dwight	.15	.40
172 Patrick Ramsey	.20	.50
173 Donald Driver	.25	.60
174 Joey Harrington	.15	.40
175 Ricky Williams	.20	.50
176 David Givens	.15	.40
177 Antonio Freeman	.20	.50
178 Dwight Freeney	.20	.50
179 Jabar Gaffney	.15	.40
180 Leon Johnson	.15	.40
181 Freddie Jones	.15	.40
182 Ron Johnson	.15	.40
183 Duce Staley	.20	.50
184 Charles Woodson	.25	.60
185 Trung Canidate	.15	.40
186 Jerome Pathon	.15	.40
187 Jimmy Smith	.20	.50
188 Reggie Wayne	.25	.60
189 Chad Johnson	.25	.60
190 Steve Beuerlein	.20	.50
191 Joey Galloway	.20	.50
192 Chris Walsh	.15	.40
193 Ty Law	.20	.50
194 Ike Hilliard	.15	.40
195 Curtis Conway	.15	.40
196 Kenny Watson	.15	.40
197 Brad Johnson	.20	.50
198 Shawn Jefferson	.15	.40
199 Jamal Lewis	.20	.50
200 Terrell Owens	.25	.60
201 Todd Pinkston	.15	.40
202 Maurice Morris	.15	.40
203 Dante Hall	.20	.50
204 Jeremiah Trotter UER	.20	.50
205 Keenan McCardell	.20	.50
206 Antonio Bryant	.15	.40
207 Trevor Gaylor	.15	.40
208 Eric Moulds	.20	.50
209 Jim Miller	.15	.40
210 Kabeer Gbaja-Biamila	.20	.50
211 James Mungro	.15	.40
212 Troy Brown	.20	.50
213 J.J. Stokes	.15	.40
214 Rich Gannon	.20	.50
215 Chad Pennington	.25	.60
216 Michael Strahan	.25	.60
217 David Garrard	.25	.60
218 Chris Chambers	.20	.50
219 Antowain Smith	.20	.50
220 Olandis Gary	.15	.40
221 Jason McAddley	.15	.40
222 Brandon Stokley	.20	.50
223 Derrick Alexander	.15	.40
224 Hugh Douglas	.15	.40
225 Danny Wuerffel	.20	.50
226 Derrick Mason	.20	.50
227 Michael Pittman	.15	.40
228 Torry Holt	.25	.60
229 Bobby Shaw	.15	.40
230 Tony Gonzalez	.25	.60
231 Ed Hartwell	.15	.40
232 Kris Mangum RC	.15	.40
233 Martay Jenkins	.15	.40
234 Marty Booker	.20	.50
235 London Fletcher	.15	.40
236 Shannon Sharpe	.25	.60
237 Zach Thomas	.25	.60
238 Plaxico Burress	.20	.50
239 Trent Dilfer	.20	.50
240 Kurt Warner	.25	.60
241 Vinny Testaverde	.20	.50
242 Al Wilson	.15	.40
243 Chris Redman	.15	.40
244 Warrick Dunn	.20	.50
245 Jay Fiedler	.15	.40
246 A.J. Feeley	.15	.40
247 LaMont Jordan	.20	.50
248 Kerry Collins	.20	.50
249 Michael Lewis	.15	.40
250 Jerry Rice	.50	1.25
251 Simeon Rice	.15	.40
252 Reche Caldwell	.15	.40
253 Randy Moss	.25	.60
254 Az-Zahir Hakim	.15	.40
255 Nate Wayne	.15	.40
256 James Allen	.15	.40
257 Qadry Ismail	.20	.50
258 Tom Brady	.60	1.50
259 Brian Kelly	.15	.40
260 Ray Lucas	.15	.40
261 Amani Toomer	.20	.50
262 Travis Henry	.15	.40
263 Chris Chandler	.20	.50
264 Peter Warrick	.20	.50
265 Ray Lewis	.25	.60
266 Sam Cowart	.15	.40
267 Donte Stallworth	.15	.40
268 David Carr	.20	.50
269 Andre Davis	.15	.40
270 Jake Delhomme	.25	.60
271 Travis Taylor	.15	.40
272 Steve Smith	.25	.60
273 Tiki Barber	.25	.60
274 Chad Hutchinson	.15	.40
275 Marshall Faulk	.25	.60
276 Chris Claiborne	.15	.40
277 Billy Miller	.15	.40
278 Peerless Price	.15	.40
279 Ed Reed	.25	.60
280 Ahman Green	.20	.50
281 Roy Williams	.20	.50
282 Dennis Northcutt	.15	.40
283 Julius Peppers	.25	.60
284 John Davis	.15	.40
285 LaDainian Tomlinson	.25	.60
286 Muhsin Muhammad	.20	.50
287 Tim Couch	.15	.40
288 Clinton Portis	.20	.50
289 Anthony Thomas	.20	.50
290 Marvin Harrison	.25	.60
291 Priest Holmes WW	.20	.50
292 Drew Bledsoe WW	.20	.50
293 Tom Brady WW	.50	1.25
294 Shaun Alexander WW	.15	.40
295 Brett Favre WW	.50	1.25
296 Travis Henry WW	.12	.30
297 Marshall Faulk WW	.20	.50
298 Terrell Owens WW	.20	.50
299 Jeff Garcia WW	.15	.40
300 Plaxico Burress WW	.15	.40
301 Donovan McNabb WW	.20	.50
302 Ricky Williams WW	.15	.40
303 Michael Vick WW	.25	.60
304 Steve Smith WW	.20	.50
305 Marvin Harrison WW	.20	.50
306 Chad Pennington WW	.20	.50
307 Jeremy Shockey WW	.20	.50
308 Tommy Maddox WW	.15	.40
309 Steve McNair WW	.20	.50
310 Rich Gannon WW	.15	.40
311 Carson Palmer RC	1.00	2.50
312 Keenan Howry RC	.30	.75
313 Michael Haynes RC	.30	.75
314 Terrell Suggs RC	.50	1.25
315 Rashean Mathis RC	.40	1.00
316 Chris Kelsay RC	.40	1.00
317 Brad Banks RC	.40	1.00
318 Jordan Gross RC	.30	.75
319 Lee Suggs RC	.40	1.00
320 Kliff Kingsbury RC	.40	1.00
321 William Joseph RC	.30	.75
322 Kelley Washington RC	.30	.75
323 Jerome McDougle RC	.30	.75
324 Osi Umenyiora RC	.60	1.50
325 Chris Simms RC	.50	1.25
326 Alonzo Jackson RC	.30	.75
327 L.J. Smith RC	.50	1.25
328 Mike Doss RC	.50	1.25
329 Bobby Wade RC	.40	1.00
330 Ken Hamlin RC	.50	1.25
331 Brandon Lloyd RC	.75	2.00
332 Justin Fargas RC	.50	1.25
333 DeWayne Robertson RC	.40	1.00
334 Bryant Johnson RC	.50	1.25
335 Boss Bailey RC	.40	1.00
336 Onterrio Smith RC	.30	.75
337 Doug Gabriel RC	.40	1.00
338 Jimmy Kennedy RC	.40	1.00
339 B.J. Askew RC	.40	1.00
340 Taylor Jacobs RC	.30	.75
341 Dallas Clark RC	.75	2.00
342 DeWayne White RC	.30	.75
343 Arnaz Battle RC	.50	1.25
344 Kareem Kelly RC	.30	.75
345 Terry Pierce RC	.30	.75
346 Billy McMullen RC	.30	.75
347 Talman Gardner RC	.30	.75
348 Anquan Boldin RC	.75	2.00
349 Travis Anglin RC	.30	.75
350 Byron Leftwich RC	.50	1.25
351 Marcus Trufant RC	.40	1.00
352 Sam Aiken RC	.40	1.00
353 LaBrandon Toefield RC	.40	1.00
354 J.R. Tolver RC	.40	1.00
355 Charles Rogers RC	.40	1.00
356 Chaun Thompson RC	.30	.75
357 Chris Brown RC	.30	.75
358 Justin Gage RC	.40	1.00
359 Kevin Williams RC	.50	1.25
360 Willis McGahee RC	.60	1.50
361 Victor Hobson RC	.30	.75
362 Brian St.Pierre RC	.40	1.00
363 Nate Burleson RC	.40	1.00
364 Calvin Pace RC	.40	1.00
365 Larry Johnson RC	.50	1.25
366 Andre Woolfolk RC	.40	1.00
367 Tyrone Calico RC	.40	1.00
368 Seneca Wallace RC	.50	1.25
369 Domanick Davis RC	.40	1.00
370 Rex Grossman RC	.50	1.25
371 Artose Pinner RC	.30	.75
372 Jason Witten RC	1.25	3.00
373 Bennie Joppru RC	.30	.75
374 Bethel Johnson RC	.30	.75
375 Kyle Boller RC	.50	1.25
376 Shaun McDonald RC	.40	1.00
377 Musa Smith RC	.30	.75
378 Ken Dorsey RC	.40	1.00
379 Johnathan Sullivan RC	.30	.75
380 Andre Johnson RC	1.25	3.00
381 Nick Barnett RC	.50	1.25
382 Teyo Johnson RC	.40	1.00
383 Terence Newman RC	.40	1.00
384 Kevin Curtis RC	.50	1.25
385 Dave Ragone RC	.30	.75
MVP Dex.Jackson FB AU/250	50.00	120.00
RH Dexter Jackson RH	.75	2.00
RHA Dexter Jackson RH AU	150.00	300.00

2003 Topps Black

*VETS 1-310: 6X TO 15X BASIC CARDS
*ROOKIES 311-385: 5X TO 12X
STATED PRINT RUN 150 SER.#'d SETS
BLACK/150 ODDS 1:21HOB, 1:8HTA

2003 Topps Collection

COMP.FACT SET (385)	30.00	50.00

*VETS 1-310: .4X TO 1X BASIC TOPPS
*ROOKIES 311-385: .4X TO 1X TOPPS

2003 Topps First Edition

*VETS 1-310: 1.5X TO 4X BASIC CARDS
*ROOKIES 311-385: 1.2X TO 3X
FOUND ONLY IN FIRST EDITION BOXES

2003 Topps Gold

*VETS 1-310: 2X TO 5X BASIC CARDS
*ROOKIES 311-385: 1.5X TO 4X
STATED PRINT RUN 499 SER.#'d SETS
GOLD/499 ODDS 1:17HOB, 1:5HTA

2003 Topps Autographs

GROUP A ODDS 1:11,293HOB, 1:3256HTA
GROUP B ODDS 1:8266HOB, 1:2383HTA
GROUP C ODDS 1:4334HOB, 1:1376HTA
GROUP D ODDS 1:1814HOB, 1:645HTA
GROUP E ODDS 1:684HOB, 1:191HTA
GROUP F ODDS 1:384HOB, 1:95HTA

TBL Byron Leftwich A	10.00	25.00
TCPA Carson Palmer A	30.00	80.00
TDD Donald Driver F	20.00	40.00
TDM Derrick Mason C	8.00	20.00
TDN Dennis Northcutt F	6.00	15.00
TJM James Mungro F	6.00	15.00
TJP Jerry Porter E	6.00	15.00
TJT Jason Taylor C	15.00	30.00
TLC Laveranues Coles E	6.00	15.00
TLJ Larry Johnson D	10.00	25.00
TMS Marcel Shipp F	6.00	15.00
TRL ReShard Lee E	10.00	25.00
TSS Steve Smith F	15.00	30.00
TTH Travis Henry D	6.00	15.00
TTM Tommy Maddox B	12.00	30.00

2003 Topps Fan Favorite Vintage Buy Backs

STATED ODDS 1:189HOB, 1:54HTA

1 Troy Aikman 89	3.00	8.00
2 Marcus Allen 87	2.00	5.00
3 Randall Cunningham 89	2.00	5.00
4 Eric Dickerson IR 84	2.00	5.00
5 Eric Dickerson 85	2.00	5.00
6 Eric Dickerson 89	2.00	5.00
7 Tony Dorsett 84	2.50	6.00
8 John Elway 89	5.00	12.00
9 Steve Largent 84	7.50	20.00
10 Steve Largent 86	6.00	15.00
11 Dan Marino 89	5.00	12.00
12 Joe Montana RB 88	10.00	20.00
13 Warren Moon 85	6.00	15.00
14 Warren Moon 89	2.00	5.00
15 Walter Payton RB 88	6.00	15.00
16 Deion Sanders 89	2.50	6.00
17 Lawrence Taylor 89	2.00	5.00
18 Reggie White 89	2.00	5.00
19 Steve Young 89	2.50	6.00

2003 Topps Game Breakers Relics

STATED ODDS 1:14,318HOB, 1:4306HTA

GB1 Brad Johnson	25.00	60.00
GB3 Keenan McCardell	25.00	60.00
GB5 Rich Gannon	25.00	60.00
GB6 Jerry Porter	20.00	50.00
GB7 Eric Johnson	25.00	60.00
GB8 Jerry Rice	50.00	120.00
GB9 Derrick Brooks	25.00	60.00

2003 Topps Hall of Fame Autographs

STATED ODDS 1:13,590 HOB, 1:3926 HTA

HOFEB Elvin Bethea	150.00	300.00
HOFHS Hank Stram	150.00	300.00
HOFJD Joe DeLamielleure	150.00	300.00
HOFJL James Lofton	150.00	300.00
HOFMA Marcus Allen	200.00	400:00

2003 Topps Hobby Masters

COMPLETE SET (10)	10.00	25.00
STATED ODDS 1:18HOB, 1:6HTA		
HM1 Michael Vick	1.25	3.00
HM2 Priest Holmes	1.00	2.50
HM3 Brett Favre	2.50	6.00
HM4 LaDainian Tomlinson	1.00	2.50
HM5 Terrell Owens	1.00	2.50
HM6 Marshall Faulk	1.00	2.50
HM7 Donovan McNabb	1.00	2.50
HM8 Peyton Manning	2.00	5.00
HM9 Deuce McAllister	.75	2.00
HM10 David Carr	.75	2.00

2003 Topps Own the Game

COMPLETE SET (30)	15.00	40.00
STATED ODDS 1:12 HOB, HTA		
OTG1 Brett Favre	2.50	6.00
OTG2 Rich Gannon	.75	2.00
OTG3 Drew Bledsoe	1.00	2.50
OTG4 Michael Vick	1.25	3.00
OTG5 Steve Mcnair	1.00	2.50
OTG6 Tom Brady	2.50	6.00
OTG7 Chad Pennington	1.00	2.50
OTG8 Peyton Manning	2.00	5.00
OTG9 Donovan McNabb	1.00	2.50
OTG10 Ricky Williams	.75	2.00
OTG11 LaDainian Tomlinson	1.00	2.50
OTG12 Priest Holmes	1.00	2.50
OTG13 Clinton Portis	.75	2.00
OTG14 Travis Henry	.60	1.50
OTG15 Deuce McAllister	.75	2.00
OTG16 Marshall Faulk	1.00	2.50
OTG17 Jamal Lewis	.75	2.00
OTG18 Marvin Harrison	1.00	2.50
OTG19 Randy Moss	1.00	2.50
OTG20 Amani Toomer	.75	2.00
OTG21 Hines Ward	1.00	2.50
OTG22 Plaxico Burress	.75	2.00
OTG23 Terrell Owens	1.00	2.50
OTG24 Eric Moulds	.75	2.00
OTG25 Jerry Rice	2.00	5.00
OTG26 Jason Taylor	.75	2.00
OTG27 Simeon Rice	.60	1.50
OTG28 Zach Thomas	1.00	2.50
OTG29 Brian Urlacher	1.00	2.50
OTG30 Rod Woodson	1.00	2.50

2003 Topps Pro Bowl Jerseys

STATED ODDS 1:200HOB, 1:28HTA

APBF Bubba Franks	5.00	12.00
APBU Brian Urlacher	6.00	15.00
APHW Hines Ward	6.00	15.00
APJG Jeff Garcia	5.00	12.00
APJH Joe Horn	5.00	12.00
APJP Joey Porter	6.00	15.00
APJR Jerry Rice	12.00	30.00
APLT LaDainian Tomlinson	6.00	15.00
APMA Mike Alstott	6.00	15.00
APMH Marvin Harrison	6.00	15.00
APML Michael Lewis	4.00	10.00
APMS Michael Strahan	6.00	15.00
APRG Rich Gannon	5.00	12.00
APRW Ricky Williams	5.00	12.00
APTH Todd Heap	5.00	12.00

2003 Topps Record Breakers

COMPLETE SET (29)	20.00	50.00
STATED ODDS 1:6		
RB1 Barry Sanders	2.00	5.00
RB2 Brett Favre	2.50	6.00
RB3 Brian Mitchell	.60	1.50
RB4 Bruce Matthews	.75	2.00
RB5 Clinton Portis	.75	2.00
RB6 Corey Dillon	.75	2.00
RB7 Dan Marino	2.50	6.00
RB8 Derrick Mason	.75	2.00
RB9 Emmitt Smith	2.50	6.00
RB10 Jason Elam	.75	2.00
RB11 Jason Taylor	.75	2.00
RB12 Jerry Rice	2.00	5.00
RB13 Jimmy Smith	.75	2.00
RB14 Terrell Owens	1.00	2.50
RB15 John Elway	2.50	6.00
RB16 LaDainian Tomlinson	1.00	2.50
RB17 Lawrence Taylor	1.00	2.50
RB18 Randy Moss	1.00	2.50
RB19 Marshall Faulk	1.00	2.50
RB20 Marvin Harrison	1.00	2.50
RB21 Michael Strahan	1.00	2.50
RB22 Peyton Manning	2.00	5.00
RB23 Priest Holmes	1.00	2.50
RB24 Rich Gannon	.75	2.00
RB25 Ricky Williams	.75	2.00
RB26 Rod Woodson	1.00	2.50
RB27 Jevon Kearse	.75	2.00
RB28 Tim Brown	1.00	2.50
RB29 Chris McAlister	.75	2.00

2003 Topps Record Breakers Autographs

GROUP A ODDS 1:13,590HOB, 1:3926HTA
GROUP B ODDS 1:4070HOB, 1:1112HTA
GROUP C ODDS 1:22,908HOB, 1:6357HTA
GROUP D ODDS 1:17,059HOB, 1:4603HTA

RBBF Brett Favre A	125.00	250.00
RBBS Barry Sanders A	125.00	250.00
RBCP Clinton Portis C	15.00	40.00
RBDM Dan Marino A	150.00	300.00
RBJE John Elway B	125.00	250.00
RBJS Jimmy Smith B	15.00	40.00
RBJT Jason Taylor B	15.00	40.00
RBLTO LaDainian Tomlinson A	75.00	150.00
RBMH Marvin Harrison B	20.00	50.00
RBMS Michael Strahan A	20.00	50.00
RBPH Priest Holmes D	20.00	50.00
RBSY Steve Young B	50.00	100.00

2003 Topps Record Breakers Autographs Duals

STATED ODDS 1:5492HOB, 1:552HTA

RBDEM John Elway / Dan Marino	300.00	550.00
RBDMS Derrick Mason / Jimmy Smith	15.00	40.00
RBDSS Barry Sanders / Emmitt Smith	400.00	600.00
RBDST Michael Strahan / Jason Taylor	25.00	50.00

2003 Topps Record Breakers Jerseys

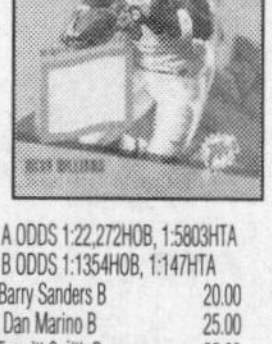

GROUP A ODDS 1:22,272HOB, 1:5803HTA
GROUP B ODDS 1:1354HOB, 1:147HTA

RBRBS Barry Sanders B	20.00	50.00
RBRDM Dan Marino B	25.00	60.00
RBRES Emmitt Smith B	25.00	60.00
RBRJE John Elway B	25.00	60.00
RBRJR Jerry Rice B	20.00	50.00
RBRKW Kurt Warner B	10.00	25.00
RBRLT LaDainian Tomlinson B	10.00	25.00
RBRMF Marshall Faulk B	10.00	25.00
RBRRW Ricky Williams B	8.00	20.00
RBRSY Steve Young B	12.00	30.00
RBRWP Walter Payton A	50.00	100.00

2003 Topps Record Breakers Jerseys Duals

GROUP A ODDS 1:14066HOB, 1:3814HTA
GROUP B ODDS 1:2344HOB, 1:602HTA

RDRDT Corey Dillon / LaDainian Tomlinson B	20.00	50.00
RDRFW Marshall Faulk / Ricky Williams	20.00	50.00
RDRME Dan Marino / John Elway	50.00	120.00
RDRPS Walter Payton / Emmitt Smith A	100.00	200.00
RDRSP Barry Sanders / Walter Payton A	100.00	200.00
RDRSR Emmitt Smith / Jerry Rice	40.00	100.00
RDRSS Barry Sanders / Emmitt Smith B	40.00	100.00
RDRYE Steve Young / John Elway	30.00	80.00

2003 Topps Rookie Premiere Autographs

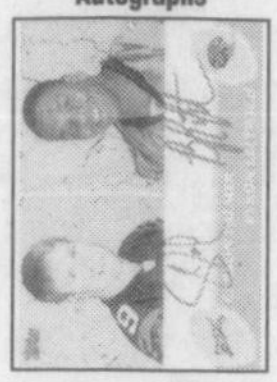

OVERALL STATED ODDS 1:196 TOPPS HTA
OVERALL DUAL ODDS 1:1963 TOPPS HTA
GROUP A ODDS 1:336,480 TOPPS CHROME
GROUP B ODDS 1:56,080 TOPPS CHROME
GROUP C ODDS 1:29,206 TOPPS CHROME
GROUP D ODDS 1:8628 TOPPS CHROME
GROUP E ODDS 1:1482 TOPPS CHROME
*HOLOGRAM MISSING: .2X TO .5X

RPAB Anquan Boldin E	50.00	120.00
RPAJ Andre Johnson C	125.00	200.00
RPAP Artose Pinner E	15.00	40.00
RPBJ Bethel Johnson E	15.00	40.00
RPBJ2 Bryant Johnson B		
RPBL Byron Leftwich A	25.00	60.00
RPBS Brian St.Pierre E	20.00	50.00
RPCB Chris Brown E	15.00	40.00
RPCP Carson Palmer A	100.00	200.00
RPDC Dallas Clark E	30.00	80.00
RPDMJ Willis McGahee / Larry Johnson	30.00	80.00
RPDPL Carson Palmer / Byron Leftwich	100.00	200.00
RPDR Dave Ragone E	15.00	40.00
RPDRJ Andre Johnson / Bryant Johnson	40.00	100.00
RPDR2 DeWayne Robertson C	20.00	50.00
RPJF Justin Fargas E	25.00	60.00
RPKB Kyle Boller E	25.00	60.00
RPKC Kevin Curtis E	25.00	60.00
RPKK Kliff Kingsbury E	20.00	50.00
RPKW Kelley Washington E	15.00	40.00
RPLJ Larry Johnson B	25.00	60.00
RPMS Musa Smith D	15.00	40.00
RPMT Marcus Trufant E	20.00	50.00
RPNB Nate Burleson E	20.00	50.00
RPOS Onterrio Smith E	15.00	40.00
RPRG Rex Grossman D	25.00	60.00
RPSW Seneca Wallace E	25.00	60.00
RPTC Tyrone Calico D	20.00	50.00
RPTJ Taylor Jacobs E	15.00	40.00
RPTJ2 Teyo Johnson E	20.00	50.00
RPTN Terence Newman E	20.00	50.00
RPTS Terrell Suggs D	30.00	80.00
RPWM Willis McGahee A	40.00	100.00

2003 Topps Split the Uprights

STATED ODDS 1:3383 HOB, 1:967 HTA

SU1 Martin Gramatica	15.00	40.00
SU2 Sebastian Janikowski	15.00	40.00

2003 Topps Super Tix

STATED ODDS 1:614 HOB, 1:89 HTA

ST1 Brad Johnson	10.00	25.00
ST2 Rich Gannon	10.00	25.00
ST3 Keyshawn Johnson	12.00	30.00
ST4 Jerry Rice	30.00	60.00
ST5 Michael Pittman	8.00	20.00
ST6 Charlie Garner	10.00	25.00
ST7 Derrick Brooks	10.00	25.00
ST8 Jerry Porter	8.00	20.00
ST9 Warren Sapp	10.00	25.00
ST10 Tim Brown	12.00	30.00

2003 Topps Hall of Fame Class of 2003

This set was distributed by Topps at the 2003 Induction ceremories for the Pro Football Hall of Fame. Each card includes a photo of a 2003 inductee printed in a very similar style to the 2003 Topps Hall of Fame Autographs inserts. A gold foil "Class of 2003" logo appears on the cardfronts. The cards are unnumbered and listed below alphabetically.

COMPLETE SET (5)	6.00	15.00
1 Marcus Allen	2.50	6.00
2 Elvin Bethea	1.00	2.50
3 Joe DeLamielleure	1.00	2.50
4 James Lofton	1.25	3.00
5 Hank Stram	1.25	3.00

2003 Topps Pro Bowl Card Show

This set was distributed directly to dealers who participated in the 2003 Pro Bowl Card Show in Hawaii. Each card was printed on metallic foil card stock and included the Pro Bowl logo on the front. A Gold foil parallel set was also produced of the set.

COMPLETE SET (18)	15.00	30.00
*GOLD CARDS: 1.2X TO 3X SILVER		
1 Brett Favre	2.00	5.00
2 Clinton Portis	.60	1.50
3 David Carr	.60	1.50
4 Deuce McAllister	.60	1.50
5 Donovan McNabb	.75	2.00
6 Donte Stallworth	.50	1.25
7 Edgerrin James	.75	2.00
8 Emmitt Smith	2.00	5.00
9 Joey Harrington	.50	1.25
10 LaDainian Tomlinson	.75	2.00
11 Marshall Faulk	.75	2.00
12 Peyton Manning	1.50	4.00
13 Priest Holmes	.75	2.00
14 Ricky Williams	.60	1.50
15 Tom Brady	2.00	5.00
16 Jeff Ulbrich	.50	1.25
17 Ashley Lelie	.50	1.25
18 Chris Fuamatu-Ma'afala	.60	1.50

2003 Topps Pro Bowl Card Show Jumbos

Topps distributed these 6-cards at the 2003 Pro Bowl Card Show in Hawaii. The cards are jumbo (roughly 3 1/4" by 4 1/5") sized versions of six of the basic Pro Bowl Card Show cards along with different card numbers.

COMPLETE SET (6)	15.00	30.00
1 Brett Favre	4.00	10.00
2 David Carr	1.25	3.00
3 LaDainian Tomlinson	1.50	4.00
4 Marshall Faulk	1.50	4.00
5 Priest Holmes	1.50	4.00
6 Tom Brady	4.00	10.00

2003 Topps Super Bowl XXXVII Card Show

This set was distributed directly to dealers who participated in the 2003 Super Bowl Card Show. Each card was printed on metallic foil card stock and included the Super Bowl XXXVII logo on the front. A Gold foil parallel set was also produced.

COMPLETE SET (18)	12.50	25.00
*GOLD CARDS: 1.5X TO 4X SILVERS		
1 Brett Favre	1.50	4.00
2 Clinton Portis	.50	1.25
3 David Carr	.50	1.25
4 Deuce McAllister	.50	1.25
5 Donovan McNabb	.60	1.50
6 Donte Stallworth	.40	1.00
7 Drew Bledsoe	.60	1.50
8 Drew Brees	.60	1.50
9 Edgerrin James	.60	1.50
10 Emmitt Smith	1.50	4.00
11 Joey Harrington	.40	1.00
12 LaDainian Tomlinson	.60	1.50
13 Marshall Faulk	.60	1.50
14 Michael Vick	.75	2.00
15 Peyton Manning	1.25	3.00
16 Priest Holmes	.60	1.50
17 Ricky Williams	.50	1.25
18 Tom Brady	1.50	4.00

2004 Topps

Topps initially released in mid-July 2004. The base set consists of 385-cards printed with silver foil highlights including 75-rookies. Hobby boxes contained 36-packs of 10-cards and carried an S.R.P. of $1.59 per pack. Two basic parallel sets and a variety of inserts can be found seeded in packs highlighted by the Premiere Prospects Autograph and Rookie Premiere Autograph inserts. Special First Edition packs included cards for one additional parallel set as did the gold foil Topps Collection factory sets.

COMPLETE SET (385)	30.00	60.00
RH38 STATED ODDS 1:36 H/HTA/R		
RH38A ODDS 1:13,494H, 1:3895HTA		
SBMVP ODDS 1:35,787H,1:10,710HTA,1:33,984R		
1 Peyton Manning	.50	1.25
2 Curtis Conway	.20	.50
3 Tim Brown	.25	.60
4 David Givens	.15	.40
5 Dorsey Levens	.20	.50
6 Jamal Robertson	.15	.40
7 Doug Flutie	.25	.60
8 Lamar Gordon	.15	.40
9 Leonard Little	.15	.40
10 Patrick Ramsey	.20	.50
11 Justin McCareins	.15	.40
12 Charles Lee	.15	.40
13 Matt Hasselbeck	.20	.50
14 Chris Chambers	.20	.50
15 Derrick Blaylock	.15	.40
16 Shannon Sharpe	.25	.60
17 Bubba Franks	.15	.40
18 London Fletcher	.15	.40
19 Eric Moulds	.20	.50
20 Anquan Boldin	.25	.60
21 Brian Urlacher	.25	.60
22 Stephen Davis	.20	.50
23 Mikhael Ricks	.15	.40
24 Jason Taylor	.20	.50
25 Michael Vick	.30	.75
26 Dante Hall	.20	.50
27 Marcus Pollard	.15	.40
28 Rick Mirer	.15	.40
29 David Tyree	.20	.50
30 Chad Pennington	.25	.60
31 Kevan Barlow	.15	.40
32 James Farrior	.20	.50
33 James Thrash	.15	.40
34 Darnerien McCants	.15	.40
35 L.J. Smith	.20	.50
36 Tommy Maddox	.20	.50
37 Tedy Bruschi	.25	.60
38 Moe Williams	.15	.40
39 Todd Bouman	.15	.40
40 Domanick Davis	.15	.40
41 Dwight Freeney	.20	.50
42 Kyle Brady	.20	.50
43 LaVar Arrington	.20	.50
44 Troy Hambrick	.15	.40
45 Jake Plummer	.20	.50
46 Freddie Jones	.15	.40
47 Chester Taylor	.20	.50
48 Willis McGahee	.25	.60
49 Bobby Wade	.20	.50
50 Steve McNair	.25	.60
51 Joe Jurevicius	.15	.40
52 Ladell Betts	.15	.40
53 LaMont Jordan	.20	.50
54 Kerry Collins	.20	.50
55 Hines Ward	.25	.60
56 Scott Fujita	.15	.40
57 Kevin Johnson	.15	.40
58 Troy Brown	.20	.50
59 Jerome Pathon	.15	.40
60 Andre Johnson	.25	.60
61 DeShaun Foster	.20	.50
62 Terrell Suggs	.20	.50
63 Marcel Shipp	.15	.40
64 Allen Rossum	.15	.40
65 Kyle Boller	.20	.50
66 Terence Newman	.20	.50
67 Javon Walker	.15	.40
68 Shawn Bryson	.15	.40
69 Travis Minor	.15	.40
70 Terrell Owens	.25	.60
71 Kassim Osgood	.15	.40
72 Bobby Engram	.20	.50
73 Drew Bennett	.20	.50
74 Rock Cartwright	.15	.40
75 Ahman Green	.20	.50
76 Steve Beuerlein	.20	.50
77 Takeo Spikes	.15	.40
78 Dez White	.20	.50
79 Tim Couch	.20	.50
80 Travis Henry	.15	.40
81 T.J. Duckett	.20	.50
82 LaBrandon Toefield	.15	.40
83 Randy McMichael	.15	.40
84 Jonathan Carter	.15	.40
85 Jerry Rice	.50	1.25
86 Maurice Morris	.20	.50
87 Kurt Warner	.25	.60
88 Josh Scobey	.15	.40
89 Travis Taylor	.15	.40
90 Fred Taylor	.20	.50
91 Zach Thomas	.25	.60
92 Kelly Campbell	.15	.40
93 Tim Carter	.15	.40
94 Marques Tuiasosopo	.15	.40
95 Laveranues Coles	.15	.40
96 Chris Brown	.15	.40
97 Thomas Jones	.25	.60
98 Dane Looker	.15	.40
99 Ross Tucker	.15	.40
100 Priest Holmes	.25	.60
101 Troy Walters	.15	.40
102 Jamie Sharper	.15	.40
103 Quincy Morgan	.15	.40
104 Aveion Cason	.15	.40
105 Joey Galloway	.20	.50
106 Bill Schroeder	.15	.40
107 Tony Fisher	.15	.40
108 Adewale Ogunleye	.20	.50
109 Justin Fargas	.20	.50
110 Daunte Culpepper	.20	.50
111 Donnie Edwards	.20	.50
112 Jed Weaver	.15	.40
113 Arlen Harris	.15	.40
114 Keenan McCardell	.15	.40
115 Chad Johnson	.25	.60
116 Marty Booker	.20	.50
117 Anthony Wright	.15	.40
118 Brian Finneran	.15	.40
119 Robert Ferguson	.15	.40
120 Ricky Williams	.20	.50
121 Shaun Ellis	.15	.40
122 Brian Westbrook	.25	.60
123 Sam Cowart	.15	.40
124 Tim Rattay	.15	.40
125 LaDainian Tomlinson	.25	.60
126 Simeon Rice	.15	.40
127 Jason Witten	.25	.60
128 Lee Suggs	.20	.50
129 Keith Brooking	.15	.40
130 Rex Grossman	.20	.50
131 Kelley Washington	.15	.40
132 Antonio Bryant	.20	.50
133 Dallas Clark	.25	.60
134 Stacey Mack	.15	.40
135 Charles Rogers	.15	.40
136 Donte' Stallworth	.15	.40
137 Deion Branch	.20	.50
138 Nate Burleson	.20	.50
139 Ike Hilliard	.20	.50
140 Randy Moss	.25	.60
141 Michael Strahan	.25	.60
142 John Abraham	.15	.40
143 Tim Dwight	.15	.40
144 Isaac Bruce	.20	.50
145 Brad Johnson	.20	.50
146 Trung Canidate	.15	.40
147 Warrick Dunn	.20	.50
148 Josh McCown	.20	.50
149 Muhsin Muhammad	.20	.50
150 Donovan McNabb	.25	.60
151 Tai Streets	.15	.40
152 Antonio Gates	.25	.60
153 Antwaan Randle El	.20	.50
154 Doug Jolley	.15	.40
155 Shaun Alexander	.20	.50
156 William Green	.15	.40
157 Carson Palmer	.25	.60
158 Quentin Griffin	.15	.40
159 Az-Zahir Hakim	.15	.40
160 Edgerrin James	.20	.50
161 Gus Frerotte	.20	.50
162 Brandon Lloyd	.20	.50
163 Brian Griese	.20	.50
164 Boo Williams	.15	.40
165 Santana Moss	.20	.50
166 Tyrone Wheatley	.20	.50
167 Eric Parker	.20	.50
168 Amos Zereoue	.15	.40
169 Itula Mili	.15	.40
170 Marshall Faulk	.25	.60
171 Tyrone Calico	.20	.50
172 Tim Hasselbeck	.15	.40
173 Anthony Becht	.15	.40
174 Larry Johnson	.20	.50
175 Marvin Harrison	.25	.60
176 Tony Gonzalez	.25	.60
177 Wayne Chrebet	.20	.50
178 Mike Barrow	.15	.40
179 Bethel Johnson	.15	.40
180 Deuce McAllister	.20	.50
181 Drew Brees	.25	.60
182 Teyo Johnson	.15	.40
183 Garrison Hearst	.20	.50
184 Todd Pinkston	.15	.40
185 Jeff Garcia	.20	.50
186 Darrell Jackson	.20	.50
187 Billy Volek	.15	.40
188 Ray Lewis	.25	.60
189 Ricky Proehl	.20	.50
190 Rudi Johnson	.20	.50
191 Emmitt Smith	.60	1.50
192 Cedrick Wilson	.15	.40
193 Julius Peppers	.20	.50
194 Peter Warrick	.20	.50
195 Trent Green	.20	.50
196 Derrius Thompson	.15	.40
197 Onterrio Smith	.15	.40
198 Jerome Bettis	.25	.60
199 Keyshawn Johnson	.20	.50
200 Jamal Lewis	.20	.50
201 Alge Crumpler	.20	.50
202 Justin Gage	.20	.50
203 Mike Rucker	.15	.40
204 Michael Bennett	.20	.50
205 Jimmy Smith	.20	.50
206 Ricky Williams TT	.15	.40
207 Corey Bradford	.15	.40

208 Jerry Porter .15 .40
209 Erron Kinney .15 .40
210 Marc Bulger .20 .50
211 Jeff Blake .20 .50
212 Terry Jones .15 .40
213 Kordell Stewart .20 .50
214 Andra Davis .15 .40
215 David Carr .15 .40
216 Nick Barnett .20 .50
217 Mark Brunell .20 .50
218 Daniel Graham .15 .40
219 Jim Kleinsasser .15 .40
220 Aaron Brooks .20 .50
221 Plaxico Burress .20 .50
222 Correll Buckhalter .20 .50
223 Jevon Kearse .20 .50
224 Michael Pittman .20 .50
225 Clinton Portis .25 .60
226 Corey Dillon .20 .50
227 Steve Smith .25 .60
228 David Thornton .15 .40
229 Eddie Kennison .20 .50
230 Amani Toomer .20 .50
231 Artose Pinner .15 .40
232 Kelly Holcomb .15 .40
233 Jay Fiedler .15 .40
234 Ernie Conwell .15 .40
235 Torry Holt .20 .50
236 Eddie George .20 .50
237 Jeremy Shockey .20 .50
238 Troy Edwards .15 .40
239 Antowain Smith .20 .50
240 Jon Kitna .20 .50
241 Bryant Johnson .15 .40
242 Todd Heap .20 .50
243 Doug Johnson .15 .40
244 Ashley Lelie .15 .40
245 Byron Leftwich .20 .50
246 Shawn Barber .15 .40
247 Duce Staley .20 .50
248 Rod Gardner .15 .40
249 Warren Sapp .20 .50
250 Brett Favre .60 1.50
251 Olandis Gary .15 .40
252 Reggie Wayne .25 .60
253 Billy Miller .15 .40
254 Johnnie Morton .20 .50
255 Joe Horn .20 .50
256 Curtis Martin .25 .60
257 Freddie Mitchell .15 .40
258 Charlie Garner .20 .50
259 Marcus Robinson .15 .40
260 Derrick Mason .20 .50
261 Bobby Shaw .15 .40
262 Desmond Clark .20 .50
263 James Jackson .15 .40
264 Josh Reed .15 .40
265 David Boston .15 .40
266 Drew Bledsoe .25 .60
267 Brock Forsey .15 .40
268 Dat Nguyen .15 .40
269 Mike Anderson .20 .50
270 Anthony Thomas .20 .50
271 Najeh Davenport .20 .50
272 Jabar Gaffney .15 .40
273 Tiki Barber .25 .60
274 Rich Gannon .20 .50
275 Tom Brady .50 1.25
276 Terry Glenn .20 .50
277 Dennis Northcutt .15 .40
278 A.J. Feeley .15 .40
279 Peerless Price .15 .40
280 Jake Delhomme .20 .50
281 Kevin Faulk .20 .50
282 Quincy Carter .15 .40
283 Andre' Davis .15 .40
284 Tony Hollings .15 .40
285 Joey Harrington .20 .50
286 Richie Anderson .15 .40
287 Donald Driver .25 .60
288 Koren Robinson .15 .40
289 Tony Banks .15 .40
290 Rod Smith .20 .50
291 Anquan Boldin WW .15 .40
292 Jamal Lewis WW .12 .30
293 Priest Holmes WW .15 .40
294 Peyton Manning WW .30 .75
295 Marvin Harrison WW .15 .40
296 Steve McNair WW .15 .40
297 Travis Henry WW .10 .25
298 Torry Holt WW .12 .30
299 Tom Brady WW .30 .75
300 Ahman Green WW .12 .30
301 Donovan McNabb WW .15 .40
302 Deuce McAllister WW .12 .30
303 Domanick Davis WW .10 .25
304 Clinton Portis WW .15 .40
305 Rudi Johnson WW .12 .30
306 Brett Favre WW .40 1.00
307 LaDainian Tomlinson WW .15 .40
308 Steve Smith WW .15 .40
309 Edgerrin James WW .12 .30
310 Ty Law WW .12 .30
311 Ben Roethlisberger RC 6.00 15.00
312 Ahmad Carroll RC .40 1.00
313 Johnnie Morant RC .40 1.00
314 Greg Jones RC .40 1.00
315 Michael Clayton RC .50 1.25
316 Josh Harris RC .40 1.00
317 Tatum Bell RC .50 1.25
318 Robert Gallery RC .60 1.50
319 B.J. Symons RC .40 1.00
320 Roy Williams RC .60 1.50
321 DeAngelo Hall RC .60 1.50
322 Jeff Smoker RC .50 1.25
323 Lee Evans RC .60 1.50
324 Michael Jenkins RC .60 1.50
325 Steven Jackson RC 1.00 2.50
326 Will Smith RC .50 1.25
327 Vince Wilfork RC .60 1.50
328 Ben Troupe RC .50 1.25
329 Chris Gamble RC .50 1.25
330 Kevin Jones RC .50 1.25
331 Jonathan Vilma RC .60 1.50
332 Dontarrious Thomas RC .50 1.25
333 Michael Boulware RC .60 1.50
334 Mewelde Moore RC .50 1.25
335 Drew Henson RC .40 1.00
336 D.J. Williams RC .60 1.50
337 Ernest Wilford RC .50 1.25
338 John Navarre RC .40 1.00
339 Jerricho Cotchery RC .50 1.25
340 Derrick Hamilton RC .40 1.00
341 Carlos Francis RC .40 1.00
342 Ben Watson RC .60 1.50
343 Reggie Williams RC .50 1.25
344 Devard Darling RC .40 1.00
345 Chris Perry RC .50 1.25
346 Derrick Strait RC .40 1.00
347 Sean Taylor RC 1.25 3.00
348 Michael Turner RC .75 2.00
349 Keary Colbert RC .40 1.00
350 Eli Manning RC 7.50 15.00
351 Julius Jones RC .50 1.25
352 Jason Babin RC .60 1.50
353 Cody Pickett RC .50 1.25
354 Kenechi Udeze RC .50 1.25
355 Rashaun Woods RC .40 1.00
356 Matt Schaub RC 1.25 3.00
357 Tommie Harris RC .60 1.50
358 Dwan Edwards RC .40 1.00
359 Shawn Andrews RC .50 1.25
360 Larry Fitzgerald RC 1.50 4.00
361 P.K. Sam RC .40 1.00
362 Teddy Lehman RC .40 1.00
363 Darius Watts RC .40 1.00
364 D.J. Hackett RC .50 1.25
365 Cedric Cobbs RC .40 1.00
366 Antwan Odom RC .50 1.25
367 Marquise Hill RC .40 1.00
368 Luke McCown RC .50 1.25
369 Triandos Luke RC .40 1.00
370 Kellen Winslow RC .60 1.50
371 Derek Abney RC .40 1.00
372 Chris Cooley RC .60 1.50
373 Dunta Robinson RC .40 1.00
374 Sean Jones RC .50 1.25
375 Philip Rivers RC 2.50 6.00
376 Craig Krenzel RC .50 1.25
377 Daryl Smith RC .40 1.00
378 Samie Parker RC .40 1.00
379 Ben Hartsock RC .40 1.00
380 J.P. Losman RC .50 1.25
381 Karlos Dansby RC .60 1.50
382 Ricardo Colclough RC .50 1.25
383 Bernard Berrian RC .60 1.50
384 Junior Siavii RC .40 1.00
385 Devery Henderson RC .60 1.50
TB38 Tom Brady RH 2.50 6.00
RHTBR2 Tom Brady RH AU 350.00 550.00
SBMVP Tom Brady FB AU/99 350.00 500.00
SAMV Michael Vick 40.00 80.00
Mr. Excitement AU

2004 Topps Black

*VETS: 5X TO 12X BASIC CARDS
*ROOKIES: 3X TO 8X BASIC CARDS
STATED ODDS 1:25 H/R, 1:6 HTA
STATED PRINT RUN 150 SER.#'d SETS

2004 Topps Collection

COMP.FACT SET (385) 40.00 70.00
*VETS: .4X TO 1X BASIC TOPPS
*ROOKIES: .4X TO 1X BASIC TOPPS

2004 Topps First Edition

COMPLETE SET (385) 75.00 150.00
*FIRST EDIT.VETS: 1.2X TO 3X BASIC CARDS
*FIRST EDITION RCs: .8X TO 2X BASIC CARDS

2004 Topps Gold

*VETERANS: 2X TO 5X BASIC CARDS
*ROOKIES: 1.5X TO 4X BASIC CARDS
STATED ODDS 1:18 H, 1:5 HTA, 1:15 R
STATED PRINT RUN 499 SER.#'d SETS

2004 Topps Autographs

GROUP A ODDS 1:8664H, 1:2472HTA, 1:7313R
GROUP B ODDS 1:6750H, 1:1890HTA, 1:5811R
GROUP C ODDS 1:3200H, 1:1212HTA, 1:5644R
GROUP D ODDS 1:3360H, 1:952HTA, 1:2913R
GROUP E ODDS 1:2230H, 1:636HTA, 1:1937R
GROUP F ODDS 1:983H, 1:280HTA, 1:859R
GROUP G ODDS 1:3724H, 1:1062HTA, 1:3234R
GROUP H ODDS 1:3346H, 1:952HTA, 1:2913R
GROUP I ODDS 1:1112H, 1:317HTA, 1:978R
TAG Ahman Green A 20.00 50.00
TBR Ben Roethlisberger B 75.00 150.00
TBS Brandon Stokley E 8.00 20.00
TCP Chad Pennington B 20.00 50.00
TCPE Chris Perry A 10.00 25.00
TCPI Cody Pickett H 8.00 20.00
TDD Domanick Davis E 6.00 15.00
TEM Eli Manning C 75.00 135.00
TGJ Greg Jones F 6.00 15.00
TKB Kevan Barlow D 6.00 15.00
TKJ Kevin Jones F 6.00 15.00
TLE Lee Evans G 10.00 25.00
TMC Michael Clayton I 8.00 20.00
TMS Matt Schaub I 25.00 50.00
TPM Peyton Manning A 60.00 120.00
TRW Roy Williams WR F 10.00 25.00
TRWI Reggie Williams F 8.00 20.00
TRWO Rashaun Woods C 6.00 15.00
TSJ Steven Jackson A 30.00 60.00

2004 Topps Game Breakers Relics

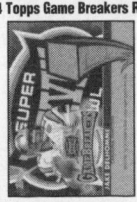

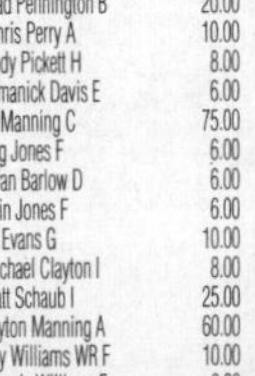

STATED ODDS 1:7035H, 1:1977HTA, 1:5997R
GB1 Deion Branch 20.00 50.00
GB2 Tom Brady 50.00 100.00
GB3 Steve Smith 25.00 60.00
GB4 Jake Delhomme 20.00 50.00
GB5 David Givens 15.00 40.00
GB6 Antowain Smith 20.00 50.00
GB7 DeShaun Foster 20.00 50.00
GB8 Muhsin Muhammad 20.00 50.00
GB9 Mike Vrabel 25.00 60.00
GB10 Ricky Proehl 20.00 50.00

2004 Topps Hall of Fame Autographs

STATED ODDS 1:17,513H, 1:4943HTA, 1:14,625R
HOFBB Bob Brown 100.00 200.00
HOFBS Barry Sanders 150.00 300.00
HOFCE Carl Eller 100.00 200.00
HOFJE John Elway 150.00 300.00

2004 Topps Hobby Masters

COMPLETE SET (10) 10.00 25.00
STATED ODDS 1:18 H/R, 1:6 HTA
HM1 Peyton Manning 1.50 4.00
HM2 Michael Vick 1.00 2.50
HM3 Steve McNair .75 2.00
HM4 Ricky Williams .60 1.50
HM5 Priest Holmes .75 2.00
HM6 Brett Favre 2.00 5.00
HM7 Clinton Portis .75 2.00
HM8 Donovan McNabb .75 2.00
HM9 Randy Moss .75 2.00
HM10 LaDainian Tomlinson .75 2.00

2004 Topps League Leaders Relics

STATED ODDS 1:538 H, 1:35 HTA
LLRJL Jamal Lewis 4.00 10.00
LLRMS Michael Strahan 5.00 12.00
LLRPM Peyton Manning 10.00 25.00
LLRRL Ray Lewis 5.00 12.00
LLRTH Torry Holt 4.00 10.00

2004 Topps Own the Game

COMPLETE SET (30) 20.00 50.00
STATED ODDS 1:12 H/HTA/R
OTG1 Brett Favre 2.50 6.00
OTG2 Donovan McNabb 1.00 2.50
OTG3 Trent Green .75 2.00
OTG4 Peyton Manning 2.00 6.00
OTG5 Matt Hasselbeck .75 2.00
OTG6 Jon Kitna .75 2.00
OTG7 Steve McNair 1.00 2.50
OTG8 Tom Brady 2.00 5.00
OTG9 Marc Bulger .75 2.00
OTG10 Jamal Lewis .75 2.00
OTG11 Deuce McAllister .75 2.00
OTG12 Ahman Green .75 2.00
OTG13 Stephen Davis .75 2.00
OTG14 Clinton Portis 1.00 2.50
OTG15 Priest Holmes 1.00 2.50
OTG16 LaDainian Tomlinson 1.00 2.50
OTG17 Fred Taylor .75 2.00
OTG18 Shaun Alexander .75 2.00
OTG19 Torry Holt .75 2.00
OTG20 Randy Moss 1.00 2.50
OTG21 Chad Johnson 1.00 2.50
OTG22 Anquan Boldin 1.00 2.50
OTG23 Laveranues Coles .60 1.50
OTG24 Derrick Mason .75 2.00
OTG25 Hines Ward 1.00 2.50
OTG26 Marvin Harrison 1.00 2.50
OTG27 Santana Moss .75 2.00
OTG28 Michael Strahan 1.00 2.50
OTG29 Ray Lewis 1.00 2.50
OTG30 Jamie Sharper .60 1.50

2004 Topps Premiere Prospects

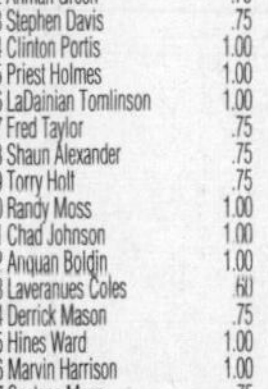

COMPLETE SET (20) 15.00 30.00
STATED ODDS 1:6 H/HTA/R
PP1 Ben Roethlisberger 6.00 15.00
PP2 Chris Perry .50 1.25
PP3 Darius Watts .40 1.00
PP4 Devery Henderson .60 1.50
PP5 Eli Manning 6.00 15.00
PP6 Greg Jones .40 1.00
PP7 J.P. Losman .50 1.25
PP8 Julius Jones .50 1.25
PP9 Kellen Winslow .60 1.50
PP10 Kevin Jones .50 1.25
PP11 Larry Fitzgerald 1.50 4.00
PP12 Lee Evans .60 1.50
PP13 Michael Clayton .50 1.25
PP14 Michael Jenkins .60 1.50
PP15 Philip Rivers 2.50 6.00
PP16 Rashaun Woods .40 1.00
PP17 Reggie Williams .50 1.25
PP18 Roy Williams WR .60 1.50
PP19 Steven Jackson 1.00 2.50
PP20 Tatum Bell .50 1.25

2004 Topps Premiere Prospects Autographs

SINGLE AU ODDS 1:3473H,1:996HTA,1:2913R
SINGLE PRINT RUN 100 SER.#'d SETS
DUAL AU ODDS 1:13,951H,1:4016HTA,1:11,622R
DUAL PRINT RUN 50 SER.#'d SETS
PPBR Ben Roethlisberger 150.00 250.00
PPCP Chris Perry 15.00 40.00
PPDFW Larry Fitzgerald 100.00 200.00
Roy Williams WR
PPDJJ Steven Jackson 75.00 150.00
Kevin Jones
PPDMR Eli Manning 250.00 450.00
Ben Roethlisberger
PPDPJ Chris Perry 20.00 50.00
Greg Jones
PPDWW Reggie Williams 20.00 50.00
Rashaun Woods
PPEM Eli Manning 150.00 250.00
PPGJ Greg Jones 12.00 30.00
PPKJ Kevin Jones 15.00 40.00
PPLE Lee Evans 20.00 50.00
PPRW Roy Williams WR 20.00 50.00
PPRWI Reggie Williams 15.00 40.00
PPRWO Rashaun Woods 12.00 30.00
PPSJ Steven Jackson 60.00 120.00

2004 Topps Pro Bowl Jerseys

STATED ODDS 1:204 H, 1:34 HTA, 1:190 R
PBAG Ahman Green 5.00 12.00
PBBU Brian Urlacher 8.00 20.00
PBCB Champ Bailey 5.00 12.00
PBCJ Chad Johnson 6.00 15.00
PBHW Hines Ward 10.00 25.00
PBKB Keith Brooking 4.00 10.00
PBLA LaVar Arrington 6.00 15.00
PBMH Marvin Harrison 6.00 15.00
PBMS Michael Strahan 6.00 15.00
PBPH Priest Holmes 6.00 15.00
PBPM Peyton Manning 12.00 30.00
PBSM Steve McNair 6.00 15.00
PBTG Trent Green 5.00 12.00
PBTGO Tony Gonzalez 6.00 15.00
PBTH Torry Holt 5.00 12.00

2004 Topps Ring of Honor Coaches' Cuts

STATED ODDS 1:102,888 H, 1:25,704 HTA
UNPRICED COACHES' CUTS #'d TO 1

2004 Topps Rookie Premiere Autographs

SINGLE AUTO ODDS 1:890 H, 1:225 HTA
DUAL AUTO ODDS 1.1977 HTA
AUTO 1/1 STATED ODDS 1:4016 HTA
*HOLOGRAM MISSING: .2X TO .5X
RPBB Bernard Berrian 25.00 60.00
RPBR Ben Roethlisberger 200.00 400.00
RPBT Ben Troupe 20.00 50.00
RPBW Ben Watson 20.00 50.00
RPCC Cedric Cobbs 15.00 40.00
RPCP Chris Perry 20.00 50.00
RPDD Devard Darling 15.00 40.00
RPDEH DeAngelo Hall 25.00 60.00
RPDFW Larry Fitzgerald 125.00 250.00
Roy Williams WR
RPDHA Derrick Hamilton 15.00 40.00
RPDHE Devery Henderson 25.00 60.00
RPDJJ Steven Jackson 40.00 100.00
Kevin Jones
RPDMR Eli Manning 200.00 400.00
Philip Rivers
RPDR Dunta Robinson 15.00 40.00
RPDW Darius Watts 15.00 40.00
RPEM Eli Manning 200.00 400.00
RPGJ Greg Jones 15.00 40.00
RPJJ Julius Jones 20.00 50.00
RPJPL J.P. Losman 20.00 50.00
RPKC Keary Colbert 15.00 40.00
RPKJ Kevin Jones 20.00 50.00
RPKW Kellen Winslow 25.00 60.00
RPLE Lee Evans 25.00 60.00
RPLF Larry Fitzgerald 75.00 200.00
RPLM Luke McCown 20.00 50.00
RPMC Michael Clayton 20.00 50.00
RPMJ Michael Jenkins 20.00 50.00
RPMM Mewelde Moore 20.00 50.00
RPMS Matt Schaub 30.00 80.00
RPPR Philip Rivers 100.00 200.00
RPRG Robert Gallery 25.00 60.00
RPRW Roy Williams WR 25.00 60.00
RPRWI Reggie Williams 20.00 50.00
RPRWO Rashaun Woods 15.00 40.00
RPSJ Steven Jackson 50.00 120.00
RPTB Tatum Bell 20.00 50.00

2004 Topps Super Tix

STATED ODDS 1:696 H, 1:199 HTA, 1:580 R
STATED ODDS 1:74,827H,1:21,420HTA,1:65,856R
ST1 Tom Brady 30.00 50.00
ST2 Jake Delhomme 10.00 25.00
ST3 Antowain Smith 10.00 25.00
ST4 Stephen Davis 10.00 25.00
ST5 Deion Branch 10.00 25.00
ST6 Steve Smith 12.00 30.00
ST7 Troy Brown 10.00 25.00
ST8 Muhsin Muhammad 10.00 25.00
ST9 Ty Law 10.00 25.00
ST10 Julius Peppers 10.00 25.00
STATB Tom Brady AU 500.00 800.00

2004 Topps Hall of Fame Class of 2004

This set was produced by Topps and distributed at the 2004 Induction ceremories for the Pro Football Hall of Fame. Each card includes a photo of a 2004 inductee printed in a very similar style to the 2004 Topps Hall of Fame Autographs inserts. A gold foil "Class of 2004" logo appears on the top of the cardfronts.

COMPLETE SET (4) 7.50 20.00
BB Bob Brown 1.25 3.00
BS Barry Sanders 3.00 8.00
CE Carl Eller 1.25 3.00
JE John Elway 3.00 8.00

2004 Topps Super Bowl XXXVIII Card Show

This set was distributed directly to dealers who participated in the 2004 Super Bowl Card Show in Houston. Each card was printed on metallic dufex card stock and included the Super Bowl XXXVIII logo on the front. A Gold foil parallel set was also produced.

COMPLETE SET (16) 15.00 25.00
*GOLDS: 1.2X TO 3X BASIC CARDS
1 David Carr .30 .75
2 Priest Holmes .50 1.25
3 Jamal Lewis .40 1.00
4 Steve McNair .50 1.25
5 Ricky Williams .40 1.00
6 Ahman Green .40 1.00
7 LaDainian Tomlinson .50 1.25
8 Clinton Portis .50 1.25
9 Peyton Manning 1.00 2.50
10 Michael Vick .60 1.50
11 Terrell Owens .50 1.25
12 Daunte Culpepper .40 1.00
13 Andre Johnson .75 2.00
14 Byron Leftwich .60 1.50
15 Anquan Boldin .75 2.00
16 Domanick Davis .50 1.25

2004 Topps Super Bowl XXXVIII Card Show Jumbos

This set was distributed by Topps one card at a time at the 2004 Super Bowl Card Show in Houston. Each card was printed on metallic dufex card stock and included the Super Bowl XXXVIII logo on the front. Each is essentially a jumbo (measuring roughly 3 1/4" by 5") version of five cards from the basic Super Bowl Card Show set.

COMPLETE SET (5) 20.00 35.00
1 Priest Holmes 2.50 6.00
2 Peyton Manning 3.00 8.00
3 Michael Vick 4.00 10.00
4 Byron Leftwich 4.00 10.00
5 Andre Johnson 2.50 6.00

2005 Topps Throwbacks Promos

These 7-cards were issued exclusively through Beckett Football magazines during the Fall 2005. Except for Alex Smith, the cards were designed like an older Topps card of a rookie player not featured in that year's set. These "cards that never were" have a card number on the back that reads "XX of 7" and cardback text written to reflect the player's rookie season.

COMPLETE SET (7) 12.50 25.00
1 Alex Smith QB 3.00 6.00
(1956 Topps Design)
2 Mike Williams WR 2.50 5.00
(2004 Topps design)
3 Priest Holmes 2.00 4.00
(1997 Topps design)
4 Brett Favre 3.00 6.00
(1991 Topps design)
5 Curtis Martin 2.00 4.00
(1995 Topps design)
6 Tom Brady 2.50 5.00
(2000 Topps design)
7 Cedric Benson 2.00 4.00
(1956 Topps design)

2005 Topps

COMP.COWBOYS SET (445) 30.00 60.00
COMP.EAGLES SET (445) 30.00 60.00
COMP.FACT.SET (445) 30.00 60.00
COMP.PACKERS SET (445) 30.00 60.00
COMP.RAIDERS SET (445) 30.00 60.00
COMP.SB XL SET (445) 50.00 80.00
COMPLETE SET (440) 30.00 50.00
RH39 STATED ODDS 1:275 HOB/HTA/RET
RH39A 1:62,233H, 1:15,547HTA, 1:51,346R
SBMVP 1:27,629H, 1:7774HTA, 1:43,632R
UNPRICED PLATINUM PRINT RUN 1 SET
1 Brian Westbrook .20 .50
2 Tim Rattay .15 .40
3 Domanick Davis .15 .40
4 Lee Suggs .15 .40
5 Keith Brooking .15 .40
6 Rex Grossman .20 .50
7 Chad Johnson .20 .50
8 Willis McGahee .25 .60
9 Eli Manning .40 1.00
10 Tom Brady .50 1.25
11 Ray Lewis .25 .60
12 Terence Newman .15 .40
13 Daunte Culpepper .20 .50
14 Marvin Harrison .25 .60
15 Greg Jones .15 .40
16 Anquan Boldin .20 .50
17 Julius Peppers .20 .50
18 Kevin Jones .15 .40
19 Javon Walker .15 .40
20 Michael Lewis .15 .40
21 Jamaar Taylor .15 .40
22 Hines Ward .25 .60
23 Drew Brees .25 .60
24 Marcus Trufant .15 .40
25 Derrick Brooks .20 .50
26 Sean Taylor .25 .60
27 Derrius Thompson .15 .40
28 Nick Barnett .20 .50
29 Dante Hall .15 .40
30 Mike Cloud .15 .40
31 Jake Plummer .20 .50
32 Donte Stallworth .15 .40
33 Shaun Ellis .15 .40
34 Jeremy Shockey .25 .60
35 Teyo Johnson .15 .40
36 Adam Archuleta .15 .40
37 Darius Watts .15 .40
38 Michael Pittman .15 .40
39 Drew Bennett .20 .50
40 Aaron Stecker .15 .40
41 Artose Pinner .15 .40
42 Dane Looker .15 .40
43 Jeff Garcia .20 .50
44 Travis Taylor .15 .40
45 Najeh Davenport .20 .50
46 Walter Jones .15 .40
47 Donnie Edwards .15 .40
48 Terrell Owens .25 .60
49 Matt Birk .15 .40
50 Chris Baker .15 .40
51 Brandon Lloyd .15 .40
52 Marshall Faulk .25 .60
53 Jonathan Vilma .20 .50
54 Dallas Clark .20 .50
55 David Carr .15 .40
56 Jerricho Cotchery .20 .50
57 Deuce McAllister .20 .50
58 Donald Driver .25 .60
59 Jeff Smoker .15 .40
60 Champ Bailey .20 .50
61 Jason Witten .25 .60
62 T.J. Houshmandzadeh .20 .50
63 Jay Fiedler .15 .40
64 Philip Rivers .25 .60
65 Jake Delhomme .20 .50
66 Terrence McGee RC .20 .50
67 Chester Taylor .20 .50
68 Tommy Maddox .20 .50
69 Bryant Johnson .15 .40
70 Justin Gage .15 .40
71 Troy Hambrick .15 .40
72 Kerry Collins .20 .50
73 Jeb Putzier .15 .40
74 Keary Colbert .15 .40
75 Jason Elam .15 .40
76 Jerramy Stevens .20 .50
77 Clinton Portis .20 .50
78 Sam Aiken .15 .40
79 Trent Green .20 .50
80 Dat Nguyen .15 .40
81 Ladell Betts .15 .40
82 Peter Warrick .15 .40
83 Dominic Rhodes .20 .50
84 Jason Taylor .20 .50
85 Antwaan Randle El .20 .50
86 Michael Jenkins .20 .50
87 Adam Vinatieri .25 .60
88 Mark Brunell .20 .50
89 Brian Finneran .15 .40
90 Ernie Conwell .15 .40
91 Chad Pennington .25 .60
92 Dan Morgan .15 .40
93 Kelly Holcomb .15 .40
94 Ronde Barber .20 .50
95 Torry Holt .20 .50
96 Bubba Franks .15 .40
97 Keyshawn Johnson .20 .50
98 J.P. Losman .15 .40
99 Ed Reed .20 .50
100 Chris McAlister .15 .40
101 Jamie Sharper .15 .40
102 Chad Lewis .15 .40
103 Chris Brown .15 .40
104 Marc Boerigter .15 .40
105 Zach Thomas .25 .60
106 Byron Leftwich .20 .50
107 Tatum Bell .15 .40
108 Tai Streets .15 .40
109 Tory James .15 .40
110 Cedrick Wilson .15 .40
111 Darrell Jackson .15 .40
112 Ben Roethlisberger .40 1.00
113 Quentin Jammer .15 .40
114 Maurice Morris .15 .40
115 Simeon Rice .15 .40
116 Tyrone Calico .15 .40
117 Patrick Ramsey .20 .50
118 Marcus Robinson .15 .40
119 Reggie Wayne .25 .60
120 Kevin Faulk .20 .50
121 Nate Burleson .15 .40
122 Aaron Brooks .15 .40
123 Willie Roaf .15 .40
124 Fred Taylor .20 .50
125 Dwight Freeney .20 .50
126 Olin Kreutz .20 .50
127 Dunta Robinson .15 .40
128 Warren Sapp .20 .50
129 Chris Perry .15 .40
130 Desmond Clark .15 .40
131 Takeo Spikes .15 .40
132 B.J. Sams .15 .40
133 Bertrand Berry .15 .40
134 Drew Henson .15 .40
135 Robert Ferguson .15 .40
136 Julius Jones .15 .40
137 Jeremiah Trotter .15 .40
138 Chris Simms .20 .50
139 Damerien McCants .15 .40
140 Robert Gallery .15 .40
141 Michael Strahan .25 .60
142 Reggie Williams .15 .40
143 Tony Gonzalez .20 .50
144 Priest Holmes .20 .50
145 Luke McCown .15 .40
146 Allen Rossum .15 .40
147 Eric Moulds .15 .40
148 Jonathan Wells .15 .40
149 Randy McMichael .15 .40
150 John Abraham .15 .40
151 Doug Gabriel .15 .40
152 Tiki Barber .25 .60
153 Marcel Shipp .15 .40
154 LaDainian Tomlinson .25 .60
155 Richard Seymour .15 .40
156 Mike Vanderjagt .15 .40
157 Roy Williams WR .20 .50
158 William Green .15 .40
159 DeAngelo Hall .20 .50
160 Josh McCown .20 .50
161 Terrell Suggs .20 .50
162 Brian Dawkins .20 .50
163 Lee Evans .20 .50
164 Nick Goings .15 .40
165 Carson Palmer .25 .60
166 Charles Woodson .25 .60
167 Keenan McCardell .20 .50
168 Kevan Barlow .15 .40
169 Matt Hasselbeck .20 .50
170 Steven Jackson .25 .60
171 Ben Troupe .15 .40
172 Jamal Lewis .20 .50
173 Sammy Morris .15 .40
174 Troy Polamalu .30 .75
175 Donovan McNabb .25 .60
176 Curtis Martin .25 .60
177 David Givens .15 .40
178 Kenechi Udeze .15 .40
179 A.J. Feeley .15 .40
180 Eddie Kennison .15 .40
181 LaBrandon Toefield .15 .40
182 Jabar Gaffney .15 .40
183 Bethel Johnson .15 .40
184 Eddie Drummond .15 .40
185 Rod Smith .20 .50
186 La'Roi Glover .15 .40
187 Onterrio Smith .15 .40
188 Antonio Bryant .15 .40
189 Lee Mays .15 .40
190 Michael Vick .25 .60
191 Samie Parker .15 .40
192 London Fletcher .15 .40
193 DeShaun Foster .20 .50
194 Rashaun Woods .15 .40
195 Marc Bulger .20 .50
196 Adrian Peterson .20 .50
197 Justin McCareins .15 .40
198 Corey Dillon .20 .50
199 James Farrior .15 .40
200 Antonio Gates .25 .60
201 Todd Pinkston .15 .40
202 Randy Hymes .15 .40
203 Peyton Manning .50 1.25
204 Ahman Green .20 .50
205 Charles Rogers .15 .40
206 John Lynch .20 .50
207 Larry Fitzgerald .25 .60
208 Jonathan Ogden .15 .40
209 Michael Bennett .20 .50
210 DeWayne Robertson .15 .40
211 Justin Fargas .20 .50
212 Duce Staley .20 .50
213 Koren Robinson .15 .40
214 Billy Volek .15 .40
215 Laveranues Coles .15 .40
216 Michael Clayton .15 .40
217 Amani Toomer .20 .50
218 Thomas Jones .25 .60
219 Todd Heap .20 .50
220 Ken Lucas .15 .40
221 Donovin Darius .15 .40
222 Ashley Lelie .15 .40
223 Warrick Dunn .20 .50
224 Doug Jolley .15 .40
225 Jimmy Smith .20 .50
226 Quentin Griffin .15 .40
227 Isaac Bruce .20 .50
228 Ronald Curry .15 .40
229 Corey Bradford .15 .40
230 LaVar Arrington .20 .50
231 William Henderson .20 .50
232 Brandon Stokley .15 .40
233 Alge Crumpler .20 .50
234 Joe Horn .20 .50
235 Bernard Berrian .20 .50
236 Michael Boulware .15 .40
237 Brett Favre .60 1.50
238 Dennis Northcutt .15 .40
239 Muhsin Muhammad .20 .50
240 Shawn Springs .15 .40
241 Kelly Campbell .15 .40
242 Johnnie Morton .20 .50
243 Derrick Blaylock .15 .40
244 Chris Chambers .20 .50
245 Joey Harrington .20 .50
246 Brian Urlacher .25 .60
247 T.J. Duckett .15 .40
248 Quincy Morgan .15 .40
249 Darren Sharper .20 .50
250 L.J. Smith .20 .50
251 Steve McNair .25 .60
252 Eric Parker .15 .40
253 Jerome Bettis .25 .60
254 LaMont Jordan .20 .50
255 Tedy Bruschi .25 .60
256 Ernest Wilford .15 .40
257 Reuben Droughns .15 .40
258 Lito Sheppard .20 .50
259 Steve Smith .25 .60
260 Shaun Alexander .20 .50
261 Kevin Curtis .20 .50
262 Drew Bledsoe .25 .60
263 Derrick Mason .20 .50
264 Jevon Kearse .20 .50
265 Jerry Porter .15 .40
266 Edgerrin James .20 .50
267 Santana Moss .20 .50
268 Kyle Boller .20 .50
269 Travis Henry .15 .40
270 Stephen Davis .20 .50
271 Gibril Wilson .15 .40
272 Plaxico Burress .20 .50
273 Deion Branch .15 .40
274 Larry Johnson .20 .50
275 Rudi Johnson .20 .50
276 Andre Johnson .25 .60
277 David Akers .15 .40
278 Randy Moss .25 .60
279 Roy Williams S .15 .40
280 Antoine Winfield .20 .50
281 Antonio Pierce .15 .40
282 Keith Bulluck .15 .40
283 Correll Buckhalter .20 .50
284 Troy Vincent .20 .50
285 D.J. Williams .15 .40
286 Matt Schaub .25 .60

287 Clarence Moore .15 .40
288 Billy Miller .15 .40
289 Terrence Holt .15 .40
290 Tony Hollings .15 .40
291 E.J. Henderson .15 .40
292 Fred Smoot .15 .40
293 Patrick Crayton .15 .40
294 Mike Alstott .20 .50
295 Mewelde Moore .15 .40
296 Shawn Bryson .15 .40
297 David Garrard .20 .50
298 Kurt Warner .25 .60
299 Nate Clements .20 .50
300 Kellen Winslow .20 .50
301 Eric Johnson .15 .40
302 Peerless Price .15 .40
303 Joey Galloway .20 .50
304 Sebastian Janikowski .15 .40
305 Jason McAddley .15 .40
306 Chris Gamble .15 .40
307 Brian Griese .20 .50
308 Greg Lewis .20 .50
309 Wes Welker .25 .60
310 Jesse Chatman .15 .40
311 Curtis Martin LL .20 .50
312 Daunte Culpepper LL .15 .40
313 Muhsin Muhammad LL .15 .40
314 Shaun Alexander LL .15 .40
315 Trent Green LL .15 .40
316 Joe Horn LL .15 .40
317 Corey Dillon LL .15 .40
318 Peyton Manning LL .40 1.00
319 Javon Walker LL .12 .30
320 Edgerrin James LL .15 .40
321 Jake Scott GM .15 .40
322 John Elway GM .50 1.25
323 Dwight Clark GM .20 .50
324 Lawrence Taylor GM .25 .60
325 Joe Namath GM .40 1.00
326 Richard Dent GM .20 .50
327 Peyton Manning GM .50 1.25
328 Don Maynard GM .20 .50
329 Joe Greene GM .25 .60
330 Roger Staubach GM .40 1.00
331 Daunte Culpepper AP .15 .40
332 Peyton Manning AP .40 1.00
333 Tiki Barber AP .20 .50
334 Antonio Gates AP .20 .50
335 Marvin Harrison AP .20 .50
336 Lito Sheppard AP .15 .40
337 LaDainian Tomlinson AP .20 .50
338 Muhsin Muhammad AP .15 .40
339 Allen Rossum AP .12 .30
340 Dwight Freeney AP .15 .40
341 Jerome Bettis AP .20 .50
342 Alge Crumpler AP .15 .40
343 Ed Reed AP .15 .40
344 Ronde Barber AP .15 .40
345 Takeo Spikes AP .12 .30
346 Rudi Johnson AP .15 .40
347 Adam Vinatieri AP .20 .50
348 Torry Holt AP .15 .40
349 Chad Johnson AP .15 .40
350 Brian Westbrook AP .15 .40
351 Michael Vick AP .20 .50
352 Tom Brady AP .40 1.00
353 Donovan McNabb AP .20 .50
354 Ahman Green AP .15 .40
355 Andre Johnson AP .20 .50
356 Drew Brees AP .20 .50
357 Hines Ward AP .20 .50
358 Deion Branch PH .12 .30
359 Philadelphia Eagles PH .20 .50
360 Tom Brady PH .40 1.00
361 Taylor Stubblefield RC .40 1.00
362 Dan Cody RC .50 1.25
363 Ryan Claridge RC .40 1.00
364 David Pollack RC .50 1.25
365 Craig Bragg RC .40 1.00
366 Alvin Pearman RC .40 1.00
367 Marcus Maxwell RC .40 1.00
368 Brock Berlin RC .50 1.25
369 Khalif Barnes RC .40 1.00
370 Eric King RC .40 1.00
371 Alex Smith TE RC .40 1.00
372 Dante Ridgeway RC .40 1.00
373 Shaun Cody RC .50 1.25
374 Donte Nicholson RC .40 1.00
375 DeMarcus Ware RC 1.25 3.00
376 Lionel Gates RC .40 1.00
377 Fabian Washington RC .50 1.25
378 Brandon Jacobs RC .75 2.00
379 Noah Herron RC .40 1.00
380 Derrick Johnson RC .50 1.25
381 J.R. Russell RC .40 1.00
382 Adrian McPherson RC .40 1.00
383 Marcus Spears RC .50 1.25
384 Justin Miller RC .50 1.25
385 Marion Barber RC .60 1.50
386 Anthony Davis RC .40 1.00
387 Chad Owens RC .50 1.25
388 Craphonso Thorpe RC .40 1.00
389 Travis Johnson RC .40 1.00
390 Erasmus James RC .50 1.25
391 Mike Patterson RC .40 1.00
392 Alphonso Hodge RC .40 1.00
393 Airese Currie RC .40 1.00
394 Justin Tuck RC .75 2.00
395 Dan Orlovsky RC .60 1.50
396 Thomas Davis RC .40 1.00
397 Derek Anderson RC .50 1.25
398 Matt Roth RC .50 1.25
399 Darryl Blackstock RC .40 1.00
400 Chris Henry RC .60 1.50
401 Rasheed Marshall RC .50 1.25
402 Anttaj Hawthorne RC .40 1.00
403 Bryant McFadden RC .50 1.25
404 Darren Sproles RC .60 1.50
405 Oshiomogho Atogwe RC .60 1.50
406 Fred Gibson RC .50 1.25
407 J.J. Arrington RC .50 1.25
408 Cedric Benson RC .60 1.50
409 Mark Bradley RC .40 1.00
410 Reggie Brown RC .40 1.00
411 Ronnie Brown RC .75 2.00
412 Jason Campbell RC .75 2.00
413 Maurice Clarett .40 1.00
414 Mark Clayton RC .50 1.25
415 Braylon Edwards RC .75 2.00
416 Ciatrick Fason RC .40 1.00
417 Charlie Frye RC .60 1.50
418 Frank Gore RC 1.00 2.50
419 David Greene RC .40 1.00
420 Vincent Jackson RC .75 2.00
421 Adam Jones RC .40 1.00
422 Matt Jones RC .50 1.25
423 Stefan LeFors RC .40 1.00
424 Heath Miller RC .75 2.00
425 Ryan Moats RC .40 1.00
426 Vernand Morency RC .40 1.00
427 Terrence Murphy RC .40 1.00
428 Kyle Orton RC .60 1.50
429 Roscoe Parrish RC .40 1.00
430 Courtney Roby RC .50 1.25
431 Aaron Rodgers RC 8.00 20.00
432 Carlos Rogers RC .60 1.50
433 Antrel Rolle RC .60 1.50
434 Eric Shelton RC .40 1.00
435 Alex Smith QB RC 1.00 2.50
436 Andrew Walter RC .50 1.25
437 Roddy White RC .75 2.00
438 Cadillac Williams RC .60 1.50
439 Mike Williams .60 1.50
440 Troy Williamson RC .50 1.25
RHDB Deion Branch RH 2.00 5.00
RHDBA Deion Branch RH AU 150.00 300.00
SBMVP Deion Branch FB AU/200 50.00 100.00

2005 Topps Black

*VETERANS: 2.5X TO 6X BASIC CARDS
*ROOKIES: 1X TO 2.5X BASIC CARDS
STATED ODDS 1:6 H/R, 1:2 HTA

2005 Topps First Edition

*VETERANS: 1.2X TO 3X BASIC CARDS
*ROOKIES: .8X TO 2X BASIC CARDS

2005 Topps Gold

*VETERANS: 12X TO 30X BASIC CARDS
*ROOKIES: 5X TO 12X BASIC CARDS
STATED ODDS 1:296H, 1:83HTA, 1:251R
STATED PRINT RUN 50 SER.#'d SETS
431 Aaron Rodgers 125.00 200.00

2005 Topps 50th Anniversary Rookies

*SINGLES: 5X TO 12X BASIC CARDS
STATED ODDS 1:1467H, 1:394HTA, 1:1238R
STATED PRINT RUN 50 SER.#'d SETS
431 Aaron Rodgers 125.00 200.00

2005 Topps 50th Anniversary Team Autographs

STATED ODDS 1:11,051 HOB, 1:2564 HTA
STATED PRINT RUN 50 SER.#'d SETS
TABF Brett Favre 200.00 400.00
TABS Barry Sanders 175.00 300.00
TACM Curtis Martin 125.00 250.00
TADM Dan Marino 200.00 400.00
TAEC Earl Campbell 75.00 150.00
TAED Eric Dickerson 75.00 150.00
TAES Emmitt Smith 200.00 400.00
TAGS Gale Sayers 125.00 250.00
TAJB Jim Brown 150.00 300.00
TAJE John Elway 175.00 350.00
TAJM Joe Montana 200.00 400.00
TAJN Joe Namath 125.00 250.00
TAJR Jerry Rice 150.00 300.00
TALM Lenny Moore 75.00 150.00
TALT Lawrence Taylor 75.00 150.00
TAMA Marcus Allen 125.00 250.00
TAMH Marvin Harrison 75.00 150.00
TAON Ozzie Newsome 75.00 150.00
TAPM Peyton Manning 150.00 300.00
TARL Ronnie Lott 100.00 200.00
TARS Roger Staubach 150.00 300.00
TASY Steve Young 75.00 150.00
TATB Terry Bradshaw 175.00 350.00
TATBR Tom Brady 200.00 400.00
TATD Tony Dorsett 100.00 200.00

2005 Topps Autographs

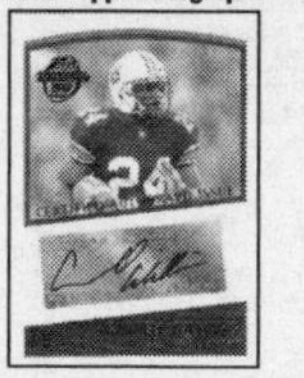

GROUP A 1:62,233H, 1:19,135HTA, 1:51,346R
GROUP B ODDS 1:9500H, 1:2795HTA, 1:9969R
GROUP C ODDS 1:3536H, 1:1050HTA, 1:3152R
GROUP D ODDS 1:3536H, 1:1050HTA, 1:3052R
GROUP E ODDS 1:1603H, 1:479HTA, 1:1400R
GROUP F ODDS 1:4041H, 1:1196HTA, 1:3491R
GROUP G ODDS 1:478H, 1:207HTA, 1:953R
GROUP H ODDS 1:1407H, 1:419HTA, 1:1238R
TAD Anthony Davis F 7.50 20.00
TAG Antonio Gates C 15.00 40.00
TAR Aaron Rodgers B 150.00 250.00
TAS Alex Smith QB C 50.00 100.00
TBE Braylon Edwards B 50.00 100.00
TCB Cedric Benson B 12.50 30.00
TCF Charlie Frye C 12.50 30.00
TCJ Chad Johnson C 12.50 30.00
TCW Cadillac Williams B 40.00 100.00
TDB Drew Bennett C 12.50 30.00
TDG David Greene D 12.50 30.00
TDJ Derrick Johnson G 12.50 30.00
TDM Darnerien McCants G 6.00 15.00
TDO Dan Orlovsky E 12.50 30.00
TDS Donte Stallworth C 12.50 30.00
TFG Fred Gibson G 6.00 15.00
TJF Justin Fargas E 12.50 30.00
TJS Junior Siavii E 7.50 20.00
TJW Jason White D 12.50 30.00
TKG Kevin Garrett G 6.00 15.00
TKK Kevin Kasper G 7.50 20.00
TKO Kyle Orton E 15.00 40.00
TLW LeVar Woods E 6.00 15.00
TMC Mark Clayton B 12.50 30.00
TMH Marquise Hill H 6.00 15.00
TMJ Marlin Jackson E 12.50 30.00
TMR Montae Reagor G 7.50 20.00
TMV Michael Vick A 75.00 150.00
TMW Mike Williams B 12.50 30.00
TNW Nate Wayne G 6.00 15.00
TPM Peyton Manning A 150.00 250.00
TRB Ronnie Brown D 30.00 80.00
TRJ Rudi Johnson C 7.50 20.00
TSM Santana Moss C 12.50 30.00
TTM Terrence Murphy G 12.50 30.00
TTS Trent Smith H 6.00 15.00
TTW Troy Williamson F 12.50 30.00
TCBR Chris Brown D 7.50 20.00
TJJA J.J. Arrington E 12.50 30.00

2005 Topps Golden Anniversary Glistening Gold

COMPLETE SET (15) 12.50 30.00
GOLDEN ANNIV.OVERALL ODDS 1:6 H/R
GG1 Priest Holmes 1.00 2.50
GG2 Michael Vick 1.25 3.00
GG3 Hines Ward 1.25 3.00
GG4 Terrell Owens 1.25 3.00
GG5 Randy Moss 1.25 3.00
GG6 Marvin Harrison 1.25 3.00
GG7 LaDainian Tomlinson 1.25 3.00
GG8 Donovan McNabb 1.25 3.00
GG9 Daunte Culpepper 1.00 2.50
GG10 Ahman Green 1.00 2.50
GG11 Shaun Alexander 1.00 2.50
GG12 Edgerrin James 1.00 2.50
GG13 Torry Holt 1.00 2.50
GG14 Clinton Portis 1.00 2.50
GG15 Jamal Lewis 1.00 2.50

2005 Topps Golden Anniversary Golden Greats

COMPLETE SET (10) 12.50 25.00
GOLDEN ANNIVERSARY OVERALL ODDS 1:6
GA1 Joe Montana 2.50 6.00
GA2 Joe Namath 1.50 4.00
GA3 Earl Campbell 1.00 2.50
GA4 Lawrence Taylor 1.00 2.50
GA5 John Elway 2.00 5.00
GA6 Barry Sanders 1.50 4.00
GA7 Jim Brown 1.25 3.00
GA8 Gale Sayers 1.25 3.00
GA9 Tony Dorsett .75 2.00
GA10 Ronnie Lott .75 2.00

2005 Topps Golden Anniversary Gold Nuggets

COMPLETE SET (10) 10.00 25.00
GOLDEN ANNIVERSARY OVERALL ODDS 1:6
GN1 Curtis Martin 1.25 3.00
GN2 Brett Favre 3.00 8.00
GN3 Jerome Bettis 1.25 3.00
GN4 Tom Brady 2.50 6.00
GN5 Ray Lewis 1.25 3.00
GN6 Marshall Faulk 1.25 3.00
GN7 Michael Strahan 1.25 3.00
GN8 Peyton Manning 2.50 6.00
GN9 Tony Gonzalez 1.00 2.50
GN10 Jonathan Ogden .75 2.00

2005 Topps Golden Anniversary Greats Autographs

GREATS/STARS 1:11,051H, 1:2795HTA, 1:8487R
UNPRICED RED INK AUTO PRINT RUN 5
GAGBS Barry Sanders 125.00 250.00
GAGEC Earl Campbell 50.00 100.00
GAGGS Gale Sayers 60.00 120.00
GAGJB Jim Brown 75.00 150.00
GAGJE John Elway 125.00 250.00
GAGJM Joe Montana 125.00 250.00
GAGJN Joe Namath 75.00 150.00
GAGLT Lawrence Taylor 50.00 100.00
GAGRL Ronnie Lott 50.00 100.00
GAGTD Tony Dorsett 50.00 100.00

2005 Topps Golden Anniversary Hidden Gold

COMPLETE SET (15) 15.00 30.00
GOLDEN ANNIVERSARY OVERALL ODDS 1:6
HG1 Nate Burleson .75 2.00
HG2 Julius Jones .75 2.00
HG3 Eli Manning 2.00 5.00
HG4 Kevin Jones .75 2.00
HG5 Lee Evans 1.00 2.50
HG6 Ben Roethlisberger 2.00 5.00
HG7 Willis McGahee 1.25 3.00
HG8 Dunta Robinson .75 2.00
HG9 Chris Brown .75 2.00
HG10 Roy Williams WR 1.00 2.50
HG11 Steven Jackson 1.25 3.00
HG12 Carson Palmer 1.25 3.00
HG13 Antonio Gates 1.25 3.00
HG14 Chris Gamble .75 2.00
HG15 LaMont Jordan 1.00 2.50

2005 Topps Golden Anniversary Prospects Autographs

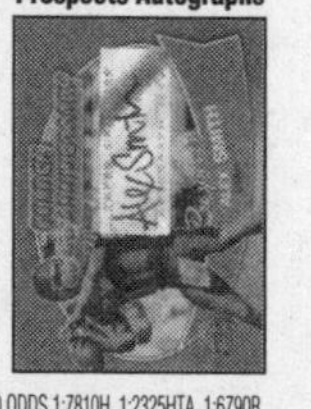

STATED ODDS 1:7810H, 1:2325HTA, 1:6790R
UNPRICED RED INK AUTO PRINT RUN 5
GAPAG Antonio Gates 30.00 60.00
GAPAR Aaron Rodgers 175.00 300.00
GAPAS Alex Smith QB 50.00 100.00
GAPBE Braylon Edwards 50.00 100.00
GAPCBE Cedric Benson 20.00 50.00
GAPMW Mike Williams 15.00 40.00
GAPRB Ronnie Brown 60.00 120.00
GAPTW Troy Williamson 15.00 40.00

2005 Topps Golden Anniversary Stars Autographs

GREATS/STARS 1:11,051H, 1:2795HTA, 1:8487R
UNPRICED RED INK AUTO PRINT RUN 5
GASBF Brett Favre 150.00 250.00
GASMH Marvin Harrison 30.00 80.00
GASMV Michael Vick 40.00 80.00
GASPM Peyton Manning 100.00 175.00
GASTB Tom Brady 150.00 250.00

2005 Topps Hall of Fame Autographs

ODDS 1:30,255H, 1:8464HTA, 1:43,632R
HOFDM Dan Marino 150.00 300.00
HOFSY Steve Young 100.00 200.00

2005 Topps Pro Bowl Jerseys

ODDS 1:539 H, 1:44 HTA, 1:1947 R
APAG Antonio Gates 6.00 15.00
APBB Bertrand Berry 5.00 12.00
APCB Champ Bailey 5.00 12.00
APDC Daunte Culpepper 6.00 15.00
APDM Dan Morgan 5.00 12.00
APER Ed Reed 6.00 15.00
APLT LaDainian Tomlinson 6.00 15.00
APMH Marvin Harrison 6.00 15.00
APPM Peyton Manning 10.00 25.00
APTB Tiki Barber 6.00 15.00

2005 Topps Rookie Premiere Autographs

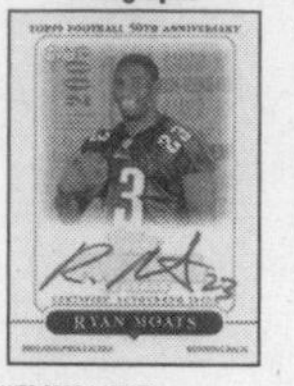

SINGLE AUTO ODDS 1:195 HTA
DUAL AUTO ODDS 1:16,584 HTA
QUAD AUTO ODDS 1:10,816 HTA
UNPRICED RED INK AUTO PRINT RUN 10
*HOLOGRAM MISSING: .2X TO .5X
RCBWA Maurice Clarett 60.00 150.00
Ronnie Brown
Cadillac Williams
J.J. Arrington
RCWBR Jason Campbell 75.00 150.00
Cadillac Williams
Ronnie Brown
Carlos Rogers
REJWC Braylon Edwards 50.00 100.00
Matt Jones
Troy Williamson
Mark Clayton
RPAJ Adam Jones 15.00 40.00
RPARO Antrel Rolle 25.00 60.00
RPAS Alex Smith QB 50.00 100.00
RPAW Andrew Walter 20.00 50.00
RPBE Braylon Edwards 50.00 120.00
RPCF Ciatrick Fason 15.00 40.00
RPCFR Charlie Frye
RPCR Courtney Roby 20.00 50.00
RPCRO Carlos Rogers 25.00 60.00
RPCW Cadillac Williams 25.00 60.00
RPDBW Ronnie Brown 75.00 150.00
Cadillac Williams
RPDEJ Braylon Edwards 60.00 120.00
Matt Jones
RPDEW Braylon Edwards 50.00 120.00
Troy Williamson
RPDJW Matt Jones 50.00 120.00
Roddy White
RPES Eric Shelton 15.00 40.00
RPFG Frank Gore 60.00 120.00
RPJC Jason Campbell 60.00 120.00
RPJJA J.J. Arrington 20.00 50.00
RPKO Kyle Orton 30.00 80.00
RPMB Mark Bradley 15.00 40.00
RPMC Maurice Clarett 15.00 40.00
RPMCL Mark Clayton 20.00 50.00
RPRB Ronnie Brown 50.00 120.00
RPRBR Reggie Brown 15.00 40.00
RPRM Ryan Moats 15.00 40.00
RPRP Roscoe Parrish 15.00 40.00
RPRW Roddy White 60.00 120.00
RPSL Stefan LeFors 15.00 40.00
RPTM Terrence Murphy 15.00 40.00
RPTW Troy Williamson 20.00 50.00
RPVJ Vincent Jackson 30.00 80.00
RPVM Vernand Morency 15.00 40.00
RSWCF Alex Smith QB 75.00 150.00
Andrew Walter
Jason Campbell
Charlie Frye
RWWEJ Troy Williamson 30.00 80.00
Roddy White
Braylon Edwards
Matt Jones

2005 Topps Rookie Throwback Jerseys

ODDS 1:361 H, 1:27 HTA, 1367 R
RTAJ Adam Jones 3.00 8.00
RTARO Antrel Rolle 4.00 10.00
RTAS Alex Smith QB 10.00 25.00
RTBE Braylon Edwards 5.00 12.00
RTCR Carlos Rogers 4.00 10.00
RTCW Cadillac Williams 4.00 10.00
RTJC Jason Campbell 5.00 12.00
RTJJA J.J. Arrington 3.00 8.00
RTMC Maurice Clarett 3.00 8.00
RTMCL Mark Clayton 4.00 10.00
RTMJ Matt Jones 4.00 10.00
RTRB Ronnie Brown 5.00 12.00
RTRW Roddy White 5.00 12.00
RTTM Terrence Murphy 2.50 6.00
RTTW Troy Williamson 3.00 8.00

2005 Topps Super Tix

STATED ODDS 1:588 H, 1:138 HTA, 1:489 R
ST1 Deion Branch 10.00 25.00
ST2 Donovan McNabb 12.50 30.00
ST3 Corey Dillon 10.00 25.00
ST4 Brian Westbrook 6.00 15.00
ST5 Rodney Harrison 6.00 15.00
ST6 Terrell Owens 10.00 25.00
ST7 Mike Vrabel 6.00 15.00
ST8 Jeremiah Trotter 6.00 15.00
ST9 Tom Brady 20.00 40.00
ST10 Brian Dawkins 6.00 15.00
STADB Deion Branch AU 75.00 135.00

2005 Topps Factory Set Rookie Bonus

COMP.COWBOYS SET (5) 4.00 10.00
COMP.EAGLES SET (5) 3.00 8.00
COMP.PACKERS SET (5) 3.00 8.00
COMP.RAIDERS SET (5) 3.00 8.00
COMP.MULTI TEAM (5) 6.00 12.00
FIVE PER TOPPS FACTORY SET
C1 Kevin Burnett .75 2.00
C2 Chris Canty 1.00 2.50
C3 Justin Beriault .60 1.50
C4 Rob Petitti .60 1.50
C5 Jay Ratliff 3.00 8.00
E1 Matt McCoy .75 2.00
E2 Sean Considine .60 1.50
E3 Calvin Armstrong .60 1.50
E4 Trent Cole 1.00 2.50
E5 David Bergeron .60 1.50
P1 Nick Collins 1.00 2.50
P2 Marviel Underwood .75 2.00
P3 Brady Poppinga 1.00 2.50
P4 Mike Montgomery 1.00 2.50
P5 Kurt Campbell .60 1.50
R1 Stanford Routt .75 2.00
R2 Kirk Morrison 1.00 2.50
R3 Ryan Riddle .60 1.50
R4 Pete McMahon .60 1.50
R5 Maurice Washington .60 1.50
T1 Jerome Mathis 1.00 2.50
T2 Mike Nugent .75 2.00
T3 Tab Perry .60 1.50
T4 Ryan Fitzpatrick 1.50 4.00
T5 Channing Crowder .75 2.00

2005 Topps Throwbacks

COMPLETE SET (49) 40.00 80.00
STATED ODDS 1:6 HOB/RET
TB1 LaDainian Tomlinson 1.25 3.00
TB2 Marvin Harrison 1.25 3.00
TB3 Shaun Alexander 1.00 2.50
TB4 Peyton Manning 2.50 6.00
TB5 Trent Green 1.00 2.50
TB6 Randy Moss 1.25 3.00
TB7 Brett Favre 3.00 8.00
TB8 Ben Roethlisberger 2.00 5.00
TB9 Donovan McNabb 1.25 3.00
TB10 Tom Brady 2.50 6.00
TB11 Dwight Freeney 1.00 2.50
TB12 Dante Hall .75 2.00
TB13 Edgerrin James 1.00 2.50
TB14 Daunte Culpepper 1.00 2.50
TB15 Ray Lewis 1.25 3.00
TB16 Joe Horn 1.00 2.50
TB17 Terrell Owens 1.25 3.00
TB18 Muhsin Muhammad 1.00 2.50
TB19 Curtis Martin 1.25 3.00
TB20 Michael Vick 1.25 3.00
TB21 Antonio Gates 1.25 3.00
TB22 Deuce McAllister 1.00 2.50
TB23 Javon Walker .75 2.00
TB24 Tony Gonzalez 1.00 2.50
TB25 Corey Dillon 1.00 2.50
TB26 Tiki Barber 1.25 3.00
TB27 Jamal Lewis 1.00 2.50
TB28 Reggie Wayne 1.25 3.00
TB29 Priest Holmes 1.00 2.50
TB30 Chris Brown .75 2.00
TB31 Marc Bulger 1.00 2.50
TB32 Hines Ward 1.25 3.00
TB33 Chad Johnson 1.00 2.50
TB34 Ahman Green 1.00 2.50
TB35 Willis McGahee 1.25 3.00
TB36 Rudi Johnson 1.00 2.50
TB37 Drew Brees 1.25 3.00
TB38 Isaac Bruce 1.00 2.50
TB39 Ed Reed 1.00 2.50
TB40 Domanick Davis .75 2.00
TB41 Jake Delhomme 1.00 2.50
TB42 Clinton Portis 1.00 2.50
TB43 Drew Bennett 1.00 2.50
TB44 Fred Taylor 1.00 2.50
TB45 Eric Moulds .75 2.00
TB46 Torry Holt 1.00 2.50
TB47 Brian Westbrook 1.00 2.50
TB48 Jake Plummer 1.00 2.50
TB49 Champ Bailey 1.00 2.50

2005 Topps Tribute

ONE PER HOBBY BOX
STATED PRINT RUN 1199 SER.#'d SETS
1 Daunte Culpepper 2.00 5.00
2 Marvin Harrison 2.50 6.00
3 Shaun Alexander 2.00 5.00
4 Peyton Manning 5.00 12.00
5 Corey Dillon 2.00 5.00
6 Terrell Owens 2.50 6.00
7 Antonio Gates 2.50 6.00
8 Ed Reed 2.00 5.00
9 Donovan McNabb 2.50 6.00
10 Tom Brady 5.00 12.00
11 Ray Lewis 2.50 6.00
12 LaDainian Tomlinson 2.50 6.00
13 Edgerrin James 2.00 5.00
14 Torry Holt 2.00 5.00
15 Michael Vick 2.50 6.00
16 Dwight Freeney 2.00 5.00
17 Ben Roethlisberger 4.00 10.00
18 Curtis Martin 2.50 6.00
19 Muhsin Muhammad 2.00 5.00
20 Joe Horn 2.00 5.00
21 Brett Favre 6.00 15.00
22 Deuce McAllister 2.00 5.00
23 Ahman Green 2.00 5.00
24 Randy Moss 2.50 6.00
25 Trent Green 2.00 5.00
26 Tiki Barber 2.50 6.00
27 Jamal Lewis 2.00 5.00
28 Reggie Wayne 2.50 6.00
29 Priest Holmes 2.00 5.00
30 Chris Brown 1.50 4.00
31 Marc Bulger 2.00 5.00
32 Hines Ward 2.50 6.00
33 Chad Johnson 2.00 5.00
34 Willis McGahee 2.50 6.00
35 Javon Walker 1.50 4.00
36 Rudi Johnson 2.00 5.00
37 Drew Brees 2.50 6.00
38 Isaac Bruce 2.00 5.00
39 Tony Gonzalez 2.00 5.00
40 Domanick Davis 1.50 4.00
41 Jake Delhomme 2.00 5.00
42 Clinton Portis 2.00 5.00
43 Drew Bennett 2.00 5.00
44 Fred Taylor 2.00 5.00
45 Eric Moulds 1.50 4.00
46 Dante Hall 1.50 4.00
47 Brian Westbrook 2.00 5.00
48 Plaxico Burress 2.00 5.00
49 Jake Plummer 2.00 5.00
50 Champ Bailey 2.00 5.00

2005 Topps Chronicles

TC6 New England Patriots Dynasty 4.00 10.00
TC42 Last Second Heroics 4.00 10.00
Matt Leinart
October 17, 2005

2005 Topps Hall of Fame Class of 2005

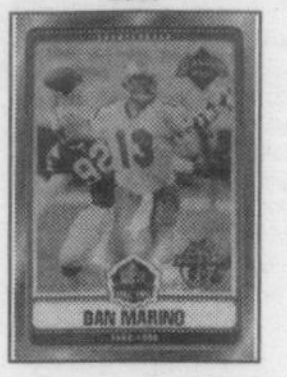

This set was produced by Topps and distributed at the 2005 Induction ceremories for the Pro Football Hall of Fame. Each card includes a photo of a 2005 inductee printed in a very similar style to the 2005 Topps Hall of Fame Autographs inserts. A gold foil "Class of 2005" logo appears on the top of the cardfronts and a Topps 50th Anniversary logo at the bottom.

COMPLETE SET (4) 7.50 20.00
BF Benny Friedman 1.25 3.00
DM Dan Marino 4.00 10.00
FP Fritz Pollard 1.25 3.00
SY Steve Young 2.00 5.00

2005 Topps Super Bowl XXXIX Card Show

This set was distributed directly to dealers who participated in the 2005 Super Bowl Card Show in Jacksonville. Each card was printed in the design of the basic issue 2004 Topps football release along with the Super Bowl XXXIX logo at the top of the cardfront. A Black bordered parallel set was also produced with each card serial numbered of 199.

COMPLETE SET (18) 20.00 40.00
*BLACK: 1.2X TO 3X BASE CARD HI
BLACK PRINT RUN 199 SER.#'d SETS
1 Donovan McNabb 1.00 2.50
2 LaDainian Tomlinson .60 1.50
3 Randy Moss .75 2.00
4 Brett Favre 1.50 4.00
5 Tom Brady 1.00 2.50
6 Eli Manning 2.50 6.00
7 Priest Holmes .60 1.50
8 Daunte Culpepper .60 1.50
9 Fred Taylor .60 1.50
10 Michael Vick 1.25 3.00
11 Terrell Owens .60 1.50
12 Peyton Manning 1.00 2.50
13 Michael Clayton .60 1.50
14 Byron Leftwich .60 1.50
15 Roy Williams WR 1.25 3.00
16 Brett Favre 1.50 4.00
17 Jimmy Smith .50 1.25
18 Ben Roethlisberger 3.00 8.00

2005 Topps Super Bowl XXXIX Card Show Promos

This set was issued at the Topps booth at the Super Bowl XXXIX Card Show in Jacksonville. A compete set was given to anyone making a purchase while supplies lasted. Each card was printed in the basic 2004 Topps football set design along with the Super Bowl logo at the top. The cardbacks featured a foil serial number out of 1000-sets produced.

COMPLETE SET (6) 7.50 20.00
1 Byron Leftwich .75 2.00
2 Tom Brady 1.25 3.00
3 Eli Manning 2.00 5.00
4 Fred Taylor .60 1.50
5 Ben Roethlisberger 2.50 6.00
6 Donovan McNabb 1.00 2.50

2005 Topps Turn Back the Clock

Cards from this set were issued during the 2005 NFL season directly to HTA hobby shop owners. Each card was produced in the design of the 1956 Topps football set to celebrate their 50th year as an NFL licensed trading card company. The first 5-cards in the set were issued in a pack with a retail price of just 5-cents to commemorate the first year pack price of 1956 Topps football. Each card thereafter was issued one-per week directly to hobby shops to be given to their customers who buy Topps products.

COMPLETE SET (22) 6.00 15.00
COMMON CARD .40 1.00
ISSUED ONE PER WEEK VIA HTA SHOPS
1 Joe Namath .50 1.25
2 Joe Montana .75 2.00
3 John Elway .60 1.50
4 Brett Favre 1.00 2.50
5 Peyton Manning .75 2.00
6 Tom Brady .75 2.00
7 Curtis Martin .40 1.00
8 Terrell Owens .40 1.00
9 Daunte Culpepper .30 .75
10 Randy Moss .40 1.00
11 Ben Roethlisberger .60 1.50
12 LaDainian Tomlinson .40 1.00
13 Donovan McNabb .40 1.00
14 Ronnie Brown .25 .60
15 Michael Vick .40 1.00
16 Alex Smith QB .30 .75
17 Eli Manning .60 1.50
18 Steven Jackson .40 1.00
19 Edgerrin James .30 .75
20 Braylon Edwards .25 .60
21 Julius Jones .25 .60
22 Cadillac Williams .20 .50

2006 Topps

This 385-card set was released in August, 2006. The set was released in a myriad of forms. The hobby form consisted of 12-card packs, with an $1.99 SRP, which came 36 packs to a box. Cards numbered 1-278 feature veterans, while cards numbered 279-286 are a league leader subset, cards numbered 287- 307 feature all pros, while cards numbered 308-310 are post-season highlight cards. The set concludes with a rookie card subset (Cards numbered 311-385). A special card of Hines Ward (#RH40) was inserted into packs at a stated rate of one in 36.

COMP.FACT.SET (390) 25.00 50.00
COMP.GIANTS SET (390) 25.00 50.00
COMP.PACKERS SET (390) 25.00 50.00
COMP.PATRIOTS SET (390) 25.00 50.00
COMP.STEELERS SET (390) 25.00 50.00
COMP.TARGET FACT.(391) 30.00 50.00
COMPLETE SET (385) 25.00 50.00
RH40 ODDS 1:36
RH40 AUTO ODDS 1:28,000 HOB
SB MVP AUTO ODDS 1:60,000 HOB
UNPRICED PLATINUM SER.#'d TO 1
UNPRICED PRINT PLATES SER.#'d TO 1
1 Jonathan Vilma .20 .50
2 Mewelde Moore .15 .40
3 Shaun McDonald .15 .40
4 Marcus Pollard .15 .40
5 Marcus Robinson .15 .40
6 David Garrard .20 .50
7 Chris Gamble .15 .40
8 Rex Grossman .20 .50
9 Lee Suggs .15 .40
10 Steve McNair .20 .50
11 Chester Taylor .20 .50
12 Randy Moss .25 .60
13 Jeremy Shockey .25 .60
14 Tedy Bruschi .25 .60
15 Walter Jones .15 .40
16 Troy Polamalu .30 .75
17 Ladell Betts .15 .40
18 DeMarcus Ware .20 .50
19 Erron Kinney .15 .40
20 Trent Cole .15 .40
21 Charlie Adams .15 .40
22 Brandon Jacobs .25 .60
23 Nathan Vasher .15 .40
24 Shawne Merriman .20 .50
25 Drew Carter .15 .40
26 Clinton Portis .25 .60
27 Alex Brown .15 .40
28 Osi Umenyiora .20 .50
29 Willie Parker .20 .50
30 Lofa Tatupu .20 .50
31 Odell Thurman .15 .40
32 Scottie Vines .15 .40
33 Sam Gado .20 .50
34 Todd DeVoe .15 .40
35 Keith Brooking .15 .40
36 Eddie Kennison .15 .40
37 Mike Williams .15 .40
38 Adam Jones .15 .40
39 Charlie Frye .20 .50
40 Reggie Wayne .20 .50
41 Donte Stallworth .15 .40
42 Vincent Jackson .20 .50
43 Alex Smith QB .25 .60
44 Greg Lewis .15 .40
45 Billy Volek .15 .40
46 Domonique Foxworth .15 .40
47 Terrell Owens .25 .60
48 Josh McCown .15 .40
49 Simeon Rice .15 .40
50 Curtis Martin .25 .60
51 Peyton Manning .40 1.00
52 Nick Barnett .20 .50
53 Marion Barber .25 .60
54 Chris McAlister .15 .40
55 Jerramy Stevens .20 .50
56 Jerome Bettis .25 .60
57 Chris Brown .15 .40
58 LeRon McCoy .15 .40
59 John Abraham .15 .40
60 LaMont Jordan .20 .50
61 Jason Taylor .20 .50
62 Michael Clayton .15 .40
63 Jake Plummer .20 .50
64 Travis Taylor .15 .40
65 Samie Parker .15 .40
66 Carlos Rogers .15 .40
67 Kevin Faulk .20 .50
68 Alvin Pearman .15 .40
69 Derrick Johnson .15 .40
70 Cedric Benson .20 .50
71 J.P. Losman .20 .50
72 Julius Peppers .20 .50
73 DeAngelo Hall .20 .50
74 Joey Galloway .20 .50
75 Marcus Trufant .15 .40
76 Frisman Jackson .15 .40
77 Jason Campbell .20 .50
78 Ron Dayne .20 .50
79 Ashley Lelie .15 .40
80 Drew Bennett .20 .50
81 Brandon Lloyd .15 .40
82 Trent Dilfer .20 .50
83 Marty Booker .15 .40

84 Aaron Rodgers	.50	1.25
85 Deltha O'Neal	.15	.40
86 Jon Kitna	.20	.50
87 Doug Gabriel	.15	.40
88 Keenan McCardell	.20	.50
89 Brian Griese	.20	.50
90 Michael Jenkins	.20	.50
91 Brian Westbrook	.20	.50
92 Terrence Holt	.15	.40
93 Justin Gage	.15	.40
94 Shayne Graham	.15	.40
95 D.J. Hackett	.15	.40
96 Kevan Barlow	.15	.40
97 Bob Sanders	.20	.50
98 Charles Rogers	.20	.50
99 Kevin Curtis	.20	.50
100 LaDainian Tomlinson	.25	.60
101 Plaxico Burress	.20	.50
102 Kyle Boller	.20	.50
103 Donald Driver	.25	.60
104 Jerome Mathis	.15	.40
105 Takeo Spikes	.15	.40
106 Tony Gonzalez	.20	.50
107 Keary Colbert	.15	.40
108 Derrick Burgess	.15	.40
109 T.J. Duckett	.15	.40
110 Chris Chambers	.20	.50
111 Cadillac Williams	.20	.50
112 Jerricho Cotchery	.20	.50
113 Ernest Wilford	.15	.40
114 Torry Holt	.20	.50
115 Corey Dillon	.20	.50
116 Chris Simms	.20	.50
117 Philip Rivers	.25	.60
118 LaVar Arrington	.20	.50
119 Andrew Walter	.15	.40
120 Joe Jurevicius	.15	.40
121 Kyle Vanden Bosch	.15	.40
122 London Fletcher	.15	.40
123 Deuce McAllister	.20	.50
124 Cedrick Wilson	.15	.40
125 Jason Witten	.25	.60
126 Troy Williamson	.15	.40
127 Dominic Rhodes	.20	.50
128 Koren Robinson	.15	.40
129 Eli Manning	.30	.75
130 Brian Finneran	.15	.40
131 Fabian Washington	.15	.40
132 Michael Boulware	.15	.40
133 Bernard Berrian	.20	.50
134 Stephen Davis	.20	.50
135 Reggie Brown	.15	.40
136 Chad Johnson	.20	.50
137 Ronnie Brown	.25	.60
138 Amani Toomer	.20	.50
139 Deion Branch	.20	.50
140 Darren Sproles	.25	.60
141 L.J. Smith	.15	.40
142 Arnaz Battle	.15	.40
143 Jerry Porter	.15	.40
144 Terry Glenn	.20	.50
145 Mike Vrabel	.20	.50
146 Chad Pennington	.20	.50
147 Allen Rossum	.15	.40
148 Greg Jones	.15	.40
149 Jake Delhomme	.20	.50
150 Tom Brady	.40	1.00
151 Neil Rackers	.15	.40
152 Charles Woodson	.25	.60
153 Carson Palmer	.25	.60
154 Kerry Collins	.20	.50
155 Brian Urlacher	.25	.60
156 Kevin Jones	.15	.40
157 Eric Parker	.15	.40
158 Daniel Graham	.15	.40
159 Dallas Clark	.20	.50
160 Matt Schaub	.20	.50
161 Drew Brees	.25	.60
162 Andre Johnson	.25	.60
163 Ray Lewis	.25	.60
164 Cato June	.20	.50
165 J.J. Arrington	.15	.40
166 Warren Sapp	.20	.50
167 T.J. Houshmandzadeh	.20	.50
168 Donnie Edwards	.15	.40
169 Thomas Jones	.20	.50
170 Mark Clayton	.20	.50
171 Kyle Orton	.25	.60
172 Najeh Davenport	.20	.50
173 Dan Morgan	.15	.40
174 David Pollack	.15	.40
175 D.J. Williams	.15	.40
176 Julius Jones	.15	.40
177 Roy Williams WR	.20	.50
178 Willis McGahee	.20	.50
179 Keyshawn Johnson	.20	.50
180 Dennis Northcutt	.15	.40
181 Courtney Roby	.15	.40
182 Jonathan Ogden	.15	.40
183 Kellen Winslow	.20	.50
184 Matt Jones	.15	.40
185 Robert Gallery	.15	.40
186 Mike Anderson	.20	.50
187 Frank Gore	.25	.60
188 Jimmy Smith	.20	.50
189 Antonio Pierce	.15	.40
190 Todd Heap	.20	.50
191 Champ Bailey	.20	.50
192 Roddy White	.20	.50
193 Rod Smith	.20	.50
194 Brian Dawkins	.20	.50
195 Larry Johnson	.20	.50
196 Ed Reed	.20	.50
197 Marc Bulger	.20	.50
198 Zach Thomas	.25	.60
199 Cedric Houston	.15	.40
200 Brett Favre	.50	1.25
201 Mark Brunell	.20	.50
202 Edgerrin James	.20	.50
203 Ronald Curry	.20	.50
204 Antonio Gates	.25	.60
205 Roscoe Parrish	.15	.40
206 Steve Smith	.25	.60
207 Reuben Droughns	.20	.50
208 Michael Vick	.25	.60
209 Chris Cooley	.20	.50
210 Chris Perry	.20	.50
211 Muhsin Muhammad	.20	.50
212 Trent Green	.20	.50
213 Matt Hasselbeck	.20	.50
214 Ben Roethlisberger	.30	.75
215 Tyrone Calico	.15	.40
216 Jamal Lewis	.20	.50
217 Antwaan Randle El	.20	.50
218 Byron Leftwich	.20	.50
219 Priest Holmes	.20	.50
220 Anquan Boldin	.20	.50
221 Drew Bledsoe	.25	.60
222 Randy McMichael	.15	.40
223 Tatum Bell	.15	.40
224 Daunte Culpepper	.20	.50
225 David Carr	.15	.40
226 Mark Bradley	.15	.40
227 Lee Evans	.20	.50
228 Domanick Davis	.15	.40
229 Robert Ferguson	.15	.40
230 Peter Warrick	.20	.50
231 Heath Miller	.20	.50
232 Derrick Brooks	.20	.50
233 Isaac Bruce	.20	.50
234 Aaron Brooks	.20	.50
235 Nate Burleson	.15	.40
236 Braylon Edwards	.20	.50
237 Ben Watson	.15	.40
238 Hines Ward	.25	.60
239 Shaun Alexander	.20	.50
240 Kurt Warner	.25	.60
241 Warrick Dunn	.20	.50
242 Rodney Harrison	.15	.40
243 Dante Hall	.20	.50
244 Tiki Barber	.25	.60
245 Santana Moss	.20	.50
246 Fred Taylor	.20	.50
247 Laveranues Coles	.15	.40
248 Darren Sharper	.20	.50
249 Brandon Stokley	.20	.50
250 Alge Crumpler	.20	.50
251 Derrick Mason	.20	.50
252 Antonio Bryant	.15	.40
253 Antrel Rolle	.15	.40
254 Eric Moulds	.15	.40
255 Bubba Franks	.15	.40
256 Joe Horn	.20	.50
257 Dunta Robinson	.15	.40
258 Larry Fitzgerald	.25	.60
259 Roy Williams S	.20	.50
260 Javon Walker	.20	.50
261 Alex Smith TE	.15	.40
262 Travis Henry	.15	.40
263 Luke McCown	.15	.40
264 James Farrior	.15	.40
265 Darrell Jackson	.20	.50
266 Marvin Harrison	.25	.60
267 Patrick Ramsey	.20	.50
268 Ernie Conwell	.15	.40
269 Ahman Green	.20	.50
270 Ryan Moats	.15	.40
271 Donovan McNabb	.25	.60
272 Steven Jackson	.25	.60
273 Ronde Barber	.20	.50
274 Michael Strahan	.20	.50
275 Dwight Freeney	.20	.50
276 DeShaun Foster	.20	.50
277 Terence Newman	.15	.40
278 Rudi Johnson	.20	.50
279 Shaun Alexander LL	.12	.30
280 Tom Brady LL	.25	.60
281 Steve Smith LL	.15	.40
282 Tiki Barber LL	.15	.40
283 Trent Green LL	.12	.30
284 Santana Moss LL	.12	.30
285 Larry Johnson LL	.12	.30
286 Brett Favre LL	.30	.75
287 Chad Johnson AP	.12	.30
288 Peyton Manning AP	.25	.60
289 Matt Hasselbeck AP	.12	.30
290 Edgerrin James AP	.12	.30
291 Shaun Alexander AP	.12	.30
292 Larry Johnson AP	.12	.30
293 Tiki Barber AP	.15	.40
294 Marvin Harrison AP	.15	.40
295 Santana Moss AP	.12	.30
296 Chad Johnson AP	.12	.30
297 Alge Crumpler AP	.12	.30
298 LaDainian Tomlinson AP	.15	.40
299 Derrick Brooks AP	.12	.30
300 Antonio Gates AP	.15	.40
301 Steve Smith AP	.15	.40
302 Shawne Merriman AP	.12	.30
303 Michael Vick AP	.15	.40
304 Tony Gonzalez AP	.12	.30
305 Jake Delhomme AP	.12	.30
306 Steve McNair AP	.12	.30
307 Larry Fitzgerald AP	.15	.40
308 Ben Roethlisberger HL	.20	.50
309 Seattle Seahawks HL	.25	.60
310 Pittsburgh Steelers HL	.25	.60
311 Tamba Hali RC	.60	1.50
312 Haloti Ngata RC	.60	1.50
313 Mike Hass RC	.50	1.25
314 Manny Lawson RC	.50	1.25
315 Reggie McNeal RC	.50	1.25
316 Kelly Jennings RC	.50	1.25
317 Jason Allen RC	.50	1.25
318 Joe Klopfenstein RC	.40	1.00
319 Willie Reid RC	.50	1.25
320 Brad Smith RC	.60	1.50
321 Bruce Gradkowski RC	.60	1.50
322 Ashton Youboty RC	.40	1.00
323 Abdul Hodge RC	.40	1.00
324 P.J. Daniels RC	.40	1.00
325 D'Qwell Jackson RC	.50	1.25
326 Johnathan Joseph RC	.50	1.25
327 Antonio Cromartie RC	.60	1.50
328 Elvis Dumervil RC	.60	1.50
329 Tye Hill RC	.40	1.00
330 Mathias Kiwanuka RC	.60	1.50
331 Leonard Pope RC	.60	1.50
332 DeMeco Ryans RC	.60	1.50
333 Brodrick Bunkley RC	.50	1.25
334 Devin Hester RC	1.00	2.50
335 Thomas Howard RC	.50	1.25
336 Cory Rodgers RC	.50	1.25
337 Ernie Sims RC	.50	1.25
338 Todd Watkins RC	.40	1.00
339 Rocky McIntosh RC	.50	1.25
340 Donte Whitner RC	.60	1.50
341 Anthony Schlegel RC	.50	1.25
342 Kamerion Wimbley RC	.60	1.50
343 Wali Lundy RC	.50	1.25
344 Bobby Carpenter RC	.40	1.00
345 Jimmy Williams RC ERR	.60	1.50
(College listed as Cavaliers)		
346 Michael Robinson RC	.50	1.25
347 Brandon Williams RC	.40	1.00
348 Skyler Green RC	.40	1.00
349 Jerious Norwood RC	.50	1.25
350 Travis Wilson RC	.40	1.00
351 Mario Williams RC	.60	1.50
352 Santonio Holmes RC	.75	2.00
353 Vince Young RC	.75	2.00
354 Matt Leinart RC	.60	1.50
355 D'Brickashaw Ferguson RC	.60	1.50
356 Michael Huff RC	.50	1.25
357 Chad Greenway RC	.60	1.50
358 Chad Jackson RC	.40	1.00
359A Reggie Bush RC	1.25	3.00
Topps logo in upper left		
359B Reggie Bush RC	1.25	3.00
(Topps logo in upper right,		
issued in factory sets)		
360 A.J. Hawk RC	.60	1.50
361 DeAngelo Williams RC	.75	2.00
362 Derek Hagan RC	.50	1.25
363 Vernon Davis RC	.75	2.00
364 Joseph Addai RC	.60	1.50
365 Jay Cutler RC	1.25	3.00
366 Jason Avant RC	.40	1.00
367 Brian Calhoun RC	.40	1.00
368 LenDale White RC	.50	1.25
369 Greg Jennings RC	1.00	2.50
370 Charlie Whitehurst RC	.60	1.50
371 Sinorice Moss RC	.60	1.50
372 Maurice Stovall RC	.40	1.00
373 Laurence Maroney RC	.50	1.25
374 Brodie Croyle RC	.60	1.50
375 Demetrius Williams RC	.50	1.25
376 Jerome Harrison RC	.60	1.50
377 Maurice Drew RC	1.00	2.50
378 Kellen Clemens RC	.50	1.25
379 Marcedes Lewis RC	.60	1.50
380 Leon Washington RC	.50	1.25
381 Anthony Fasano RC	.60	1.50
382 Jeremy Bloom RC	.50	1.25
383 Omar Jacobs RC	.40	1.00
384 Tarvaris Jackson RC	.60	1.50
385 Brandon Marshall RC	.60	1.50
RH40 Hines Ward	2.00	5.00
(Ring of Honor)		
RHAU Hines Ward AU	150.00	300.00
(Ring of Honor Autograph)		
SBMVP Hines Ward AU/100	150.00	300.00
(Super Bowl 40 MVP		
football swatch)		

2006 Topps Black

*VETS 1-310: 10X TO 25X BASIC CARDS
*ROOKIES 311-385: 4X TO 10X BASIC CARDS
BLACK/51 ODDS 1:134 HOB

2006 Topps Gold

*VETERANS: 4X TO 10X BASIC CARDS
*ROOKIES: 1.5X TO 4X BASIC CARDS
GOLD/2006 ODDS: 1:12 HOB, 1:8 RACK

2006 Topps Special Edition Rookies

*ROOKIES: 1.2X TO 3X BASIC CARDS
STATED ODDS 1:10 HOB/RACK

2006 Topps All-Pro Relics

GROUP A ODDS 1:1142
GROUP B ODDS 1:212

APAG Antonio Gates B	5.00	12.00
APBW Brian Waters B	3.00	8.00
APCC Chris Chambers B	4.00	10.00
APCJ Chad Johnson A	5.00	12.00
APDB Derrick Brooks B	4.00	10.00
APDF Dwight Freeney A	4.00	10.00
APDO Deltha O'Neal B	3.00	8.00
APEJ Edgerrin James B	5.00	12.00
APJD Jake Delhomme B	5.00	12.00
APJL John Lynch A	4.00	10.00
APJO Jonathan Ogden B	3.00	8.00
APJP Joey Porter B	5.00	12.00
APKB Keith Brooking B	3.00	8.00
APKV Kyle Vanden Bosch B	4.00	10.00
APLA Larry Allen B	3.00	8.00
APMH Matt Hasselbeck B	5.00	12.00
APMS Mack Strong B	3.00	8.00
APNV Nathan Vasher A	5.00	12.00
APPM Peyton Manning B	8.00	20.00
APSA Shaun Alexander B	6.00	15.00
APSH Steve Hutchinson B	3.00	8.00
APSS Steve Smith A	5.00	12.00
APTH Torry Holt B	4.00	10.00
APTL Ty Law B	3.00	8.00
APMST Michael Strahan B	3.00	8.00

2006 Topps Autographs

GROUP A ODDS 1:12,500 H, 1:8300 RACK
GROUP B ODDS 1:4470 H, 1:2980 RACK
GROUP C ODDS 1:3100 H, 1:2600 RACK
GROUP D ODDS 1:3300 H, 1:2400 RACK
GROUP E ODDS 1:2900 H, 1:2100 RACK
GROUP F ODDS 1:5800 H, 1:4200 RACK
GROUP G ODDS 1:292 H, 1:330 RACK

TAH A.J. Hawk C	25.00	60.00
TBC Brian Calhoun G	8.00	20.00
TBG Bruce Gradkowski G	8.00	20.00
TBJ Brandon Jacobs C	10.00	25.00
TCJ Chad Jackson G	10.00	25.00
TCT Chester Taylor E	8.00	20.00
TCW Charlie Whitehurst E	10.00	25.00
TDH Devin Hester G	15.00	40.00
TDW DeAngelo Williams B	20.00	50.00
TFG Frank Gore D	10.00	25.00
TFW Frank Walker G	6.00	15.00
TGL Greg Lewis E	6.00	15.00
TJA Joseph Addai C	12.00	30.00
TJB Jeremy Bloom D	8.00	20.00
TJC Jay Cutler B	40.00	80.00
TJH Jerome Harrison D	8.00	20.00
TJJ Julius Jones C	10.00	25.00
TKC Kellen Clemens G	10.00	25.00
TLM Laurence Maroney F	8.00	20.00
TLT LaDainian Tomlinson A	30.00	80.00
TLW LenDale White B	12.00	30.00
TMB Marc Bulger C	8.00	20.00
TMD Maurice Drew G	15.00	40.00
TML Matt Leinart B	15.00	40.00
TMT Michael Turner G	10.00	25.00
TOJ Omar Jacobs G	8.00	20.00
TPM Peyton Manning A	100.00	200.00
TRB Reggie Bush B	30.00	80.00
TSH Santonio Holmes B	12.00	30.00
TSM Sinorice Moss B	10.00	25.00
TSS Steve Smith A	40.00	80.00
TVD Vernon Davis C	12.00	30.00
TVY Vince Young A	30.00	80.00
TBCR Brodie Croyle G	10.00	25.00
TCHA Cortez Hankton G	6.00	15.00
TJAR J.J. Arrington G	6.00	15.00
TSME Shawne Merriman A	20.00	40.00

2006 Topps EA Sports Madden

COMPLETE SET (20)	12.00	30.00
STATED ODDS 1:18 HOB		
1 Shaun Alexander	1.25	3.00
2 Larry Johnson	1.25	3.00
3 LaDainian Tomlinson	1.50	4.00
4 Clinton Portis	1.50	4.00
5 Tiki Barber	1.50	4.00
6 Edgerrin James	1.25	3.00
7 Terrell Owens	1.50	4.00
8 Vince Young	1.00	2.50
9 Peyton Manning	2.50	6.00
10 Matt Leinart	.75	2.00
11 Jay Cutler	1.50	4.00
12 Tony Gonzalez	1.25	3.00
13 Tom Brady	2.50	6.00
14 Jeremy Shockey	1.50	4.00
15 Steve Smith	1.50	4.00
16 Chad Johnson	1.25	3.00
17 Torry Holt	1.25	3.00
18 Marvin Harrison	1.50	4.00
19 Randy Moss	1.50	4.00
20 Reggie Bush	1.50	4.00

2006 Topps EA Sports Street 3

COMPLETE SET (24)	8.00	20.00
INSERTS IN VIDEO GAME PACKAGES		
1 Chad Johnson	.50	1.25
2 Champ Bailey	.50	1.25
3 Tiki Barber	.60	1.50
4 Tom Brady	1.00	2.50
5 Tedy Bruschi	.60	1.50
6 Reggie Bush	.75	2.00
7 Brett Favre	1.25	3.00
8 Antonio Gates	.60	1.50
9 Edgerrin James	.50	1.25
10 Larry Johnson	.50	1.25
11 Matt Leinart	.40	1.00
12 Peyton Manning	1.00	2.50
13 Randy Moss	.60	1.50
14 Terrell Owens	.60	1.50
15 Julius Peppers	.50	1.25
16 Troy Polamalu	.75	2.00
17 Ben Roethlisberger	.75	2.00
18 Michael Strahan	.50	1.25
19 LaDainian Tomlinson	.60	1.50
20 Mario Williams	.40	1.00
21 Clinton Portis	.60	1.50
22 Byron Leftwich	.50	1.25
23 Brian Urlacher	.60	1.50
24 Shaun Alexander	.50	1.25

2006 Topps Factory Set Rookie Bonus

COMP.HOBBY SET (5)	4.00	10.00
COMP.RETAIL SET (5)	4.00	10.00
COMP.GIANTS SET (5)	4.00	10.00
COMP.PACKER SET (5)	4.00	10.00
COMP.PATRIOT SET (5)	4.00	10.00
COMP.STEELER SET (5)	4.00	10.00
COMP.SUPER BOWL (5)	6.00	15.00
G1 Gerris Wilkinson	.60	1.50
G2 Jai Lewis	.75	2.00
G3 Barry Cofield	1.00	2.50
G4 Charlie Prepah	.75	2.00
G5 Gerrick McPhearson	.60	1.50
H1 Marques Hagans	.60	1.50
H2 Devin Aromashodu	1.00	2.50
H3 Ingle Martin	.75	2.00
H4 Andre Hall	.75	2.00
H5 D.J. Shockley	.75	2.00
R1 Jonathan Orr	.75	2.00
R2 Cedric Humes	.60	1.50
R3 Dominique Byrd	.75	2.00
R4 Marcus Vick	.60	1.50
R5 Drew Olson	.60	1.50
S1 Cedric Humes	.60	1.50
S2 Anthony Smith	1.00	2.50
S3 Orien Harris	.75	2.00
S4 Charles Davis	.75	2.00
S5 Willie Colon	.60	1.50
PK1 Will Blackmon	.75	2.00
PK2 Ingle Martin	.75	2.00
PK3 Tony Moll	.60	1.50
PK4 Jason Spitz	1.00	2.50
PK5 Chris Francies	.75	2.00
PT1 David Thomas	.75	2.00
PT2 Garrett Mills	1.00	2.50
PT3 Freddie Roach	.75	2.00
PT4 Jeremy Mincey	.75	2.00
PT5 Willie Andrews	.75	2.00
SB1 Vince Young	.50	1.25
SB2 Matt Leinart	.40	1.00
SB3 Joseph Addai	.40	1.00
SB4 Jay Cutler	.75	2.00
SB5 Reggie Bush	.75	2.00
SB6 Laurence Maroney	.30	.75

2006 Topps Target Exclusive Factory Set Rookie Jerseys

1 Matt Leinart	8.00	20.00
2 Reggie Bush	10.00	25.00
3 Vince Young	8.00	20.00
5 Mario Williams	5.00	12.00

2006 Topps Game Breakers Super Bowl Pylons

STATED ODDS 1:37,500 HOB		
GBAR Antwaan Randle El	50.00	100.00
GBBR Ben Roethlisberger		
GBHW Hines Ward	60.00	100.00
GBJS Jerramy Stevens	20.00	40.00
GBMH Matt Hasselbeck	50.00	100.00
GBWP Willie Parker	60.00	100.00

2006 Topps Hall of Fame Autographs

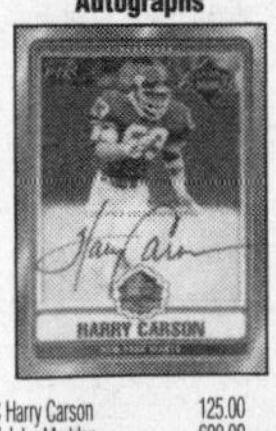

HOFHC Harry Carson	125.00	250.00
HOFJM John Madden	600.00	900.00
HOFTA Troy Aikman	250.00	500.00
HOFWM Warren Moon	250.00	400.00
HOFRWR Rayfield Wright	150.00	250.00

2006 Topps Hall of Fame Tribute

COMPLETE SET (9)	5.00	12.00
STATED ODDS 1:6 RACK		
UNPRICED CUT AUTOS SER.#'d 1-10		
BN Bronko Nagurski	.75	2.00
HC Harry Carson	.60	1.50
JM John Madden	.75	2.00
JT Jim Thorpe	1.00	2.50
RW Reggie White	.75	2.00
SB Sammy Baugh	.75	2.00
TA Troy Aikman	1.00	2.50
WM Warren Moon	.60	1.50
RWR Rayfield Wright	.60	1.50

2006 Topps Hall of Fame Tribute Cut Autographs

THORPE ODDS 1:1,612,656 HOBBY
BAUGH/NAGURSKI ODDS 1:150,000 HOBBY

2006 Topps Hobby Masters

COMPLETE SET (10)	6.00	15.00
STATED ODDS 1:18 HOB		
HM1 LaDainian Tomlinson	1.00	2.50
HM2 Peyton Manning	1.50	4.00
HM3 Tom Brady	1.50	4.00
HM4 Brett Favre	2.00	5.00
HM5 Cadillac Williams	.75	2.00
HM6 Ben Roethlisberger	1.25	3.00
HM7 Shaun Alexander	.75	2.00
HM8 Michael Vick	1.00	2.50
HM9 Tiki Barber	1.00	2.50
HM10 Larry Johnson	.75	2.00

2006 Topps NFL 8306

COMPLETE SET (10)	6.00	15.00
STATED ODDS 1:6 HOB/RACK		
NFL1 John Elway	2.00	5.00
NFL2 Jim Kelly	1.00	2.50
NFL3 Eric Dickerson	.60	1.50
NFL4 Dan Marino	2.50	6.00
NFL5 Reggie Bush	1.25	3.00
NFL6 Matt Leinart	.60	1.50
NFL7 Vince Young	.75	2.00
NFL8 Jay Cutler	1.25	3.00
NFL9 DeAngelo Williams	.75	2.00
NFL10 LenDale White	.60	1.50

2006 Topps NFL 8306 Autographs

AUTO/50 ODDS 1:18,800 H, 1:15,000 RACK		
DM Dan Marino	175.00	300.00
DW DeAngelo Williams	25.00	60.00
ED Eric Dickerson	100.00	175.00
JC Jay Cutler	50.00	100.00
JE John Elway	150.00	250.00
JK Jim Kelly	100.00	200.00
LW LenDale White	40.00	80.00
ML Matt Leinart	20.00	50.00
RB Reggie Bush	40.00	100.00
VY Vince Young	30.00	80.00

2006 Topps NFL 8306 Autographs Dual

DUAL AU/25 ODDS 1:85,000 H,1:60,000 RACK		
DB Eric Dickerson	100.00	200.00
Reggie Bush		
EL John Elway	100.00	200.00
Matt Leinart		
EY John Elway	100.00	200.00
Vince Young		
KC Jim Kelly	100.00	200.00
Jay Cutler		
ML Dan Marino	125.00	250.00
Matt Leinart		

2006 Topps NFL 8306 Relics

GROUP A ODDS 1:42,000 HOB		
GROUP B ODDS 1:2350 HOB		
8306RDM Dan Marino B	25.00	50.00
8306RDW DeAngelo Williams B	6.00	15.00
8306RED Eric Dickerson B	4.00	10.00
8306RJE John Elway A	15.00	40.00
8306RJK Jim Kelly B	8.00	20.00
8306RLW LenDale White B	6.00	15.00
8306RML Matt Leinart B	8.00	20.00
8306RRB Reggie Bush B	12.00	30.00
8306RVY Vince Young B	8.00	20.00

2006 Topps Own The Game

STATED ODDS 1:22 HOB, RACK		
OTG1 Tom Brady	2.50	6.00
OTG2 Trent Green	1.25	3.00
OTG3 Shaun Alexander	1.25	3.00
OTG4 Tiki Barber	1.50	4.00
OTG5 Steve Smith	1.50	4.00
OTG6 Santana Moss	1.25	3.00
OTG7 Derrick Burgess	1.00	2.50
OTG8 Osi Umenyiora	1.25	3.00
OTG9 Brett Favre	3.00	8.00
OTG10 Larry Johnson	1.25	3.00
OTG11 Chad Johnson	1.25	3.00
OTG12 Carson Palmer	1.50	4.00
OTG13 Clinton Portis	1.50	4.00
OTG14 Larry Fitzgerald	1.50	4.00
OTG15 Eli Manning	2.00	5.00
OTG16 Edgerrin James	1.25	3.00
OTG17 Anquan Boldin	1.25	3.00
OTG18 Ty Law	1.00	2.50
OTG19 Deltha O'Neal	1.00	2.50
OTG20 Drew Brees	1.50	4.00
OTG21 LaDainian Tomlinson	1.50	4.00
OTG22 Marvin Harrison	1.50	4.00
OTG23 Corey Dillon	1.25	3.00
OTG24 Matt Hasselbeck	1.25	3.00
OTG25 Chris Chambers	1.25	3.00
OTG26 Jonathan Vilma	1.25	3.00
OTG27 Jake Delhomme	1.25	3.00
OTG28 Rudi Johnson	1.25	3.00
OTG29 Zach Thomas	1.50	4.00
OTG30 Hines Ward	1.50	4.00

2006 Topps Red Hot Rookies

INSERTS IN TARGET RETAIL PACKS		
UNPRICED AU/10 ODDS 1:22,000 TARGET		
1 Reggie Bush	2.50	6.00
2 Tamba Hali	1.25	3.00
3 A.J. Hawk	1.25	3.00
4 Santonio Holmes	1.50	4.00
5 Matt Leinart	1.25	3.00
6 Brodie Croyle	1.25	3.00
7 Derek Hagan	1.00	2.50
8 Chad Jackson	.75	2.00
9 Vince Young	1.50	4.00
10 Sinorice Moss	1.25	3.00
11 DeAngelo Williams	1.50	4.00
12 Omar Jacobs	.75	2.00
13 Jay Cutler	2.50	6.00
14 Laurence Maroney	1.00	2.50
15 LenDale White	1.00	2.50
16 Brian Calhoun	.75	2.00

2006 Topps Red Hot Rookies Jerseys

JERSEY/199 ODDS 1:1260 TARGET		
AH A.J. Hawk	8.00	20.00
DW DeAngelo Williams	8.00	20.00
LW LenDale White	6.00	15.00
ML Matt Leinart	10.00	25.00
RB Reggie Bush	12.00	30.00
VY Vince Young	10.00	25.00

2006 Topps Red Hot Rookies Jerseys Dual

DUAL JSY/50 ODDS 1:12,000 TARGET RETAIL		
BL Reggie Bush	15.00	40.00
Matt Leinart		
WB DeAngelo Williams	15.00	40.00
Reggie Bush		
YL Vince Young	15.00	40.00
Matt Leinart		

2006 Topps Rookie Premiere Autographs

RED INK TOO SCARCE TO PRICE		
RPAH A.J. Hawk	20.00	50.00
RPBM Brandon Marshall	20.00	50.00
RPBW Brandon Williams	12.00	30.00
RPCJ Chad Jackson	12.00	30.00
RPCW Charlie Whitehurst	20.00	50.00
RPDH Derek Hagan	15.00	40.00
RPDW DeAngelo Williams	25.00	60.00
RPJK Joe Klopfenstein	12.00	30.00
RPJN Jerious Norwood	15.00	40.00
RPKC Kellen Clemens	15.00	40.00
RPLM Laurence Maroney	15.00	40.00
RPLW LenDale White	15.00	40.00
RPMD Maurice Drew	20.00	50.00
RPMH Michael Huff	15.00	40.00
RPML Matt Leinart	20.00	50.00
RPMR Michael Robinson	15.00	40.00
RPMS Maurice Stovall	12.00	30.00
RPMW Mario Williams	20.00	50.00
RPOJ Omar Jacobs	12.00	30.00
RPRB Reggie Bush	30.00	80.00
RPSH Santonio Holmes	25.00	60.00
RPSM Sinorice Moss	20.00	50.00
RPTJ Tarvaris Jackson	20.00	50.00
RPTW Travis Wilson	12.00	30.00
RPVD Vernon Davis	25.00	60.00
RPVY Vince Young	25.00	60.00
RPBCA Brian Calhoun	12.00	30.00
RPDEW Demetrius Williams	15.00	40.00
RPJAV Jason Avant	12.00	30.00
RPLWA Leon Washington	15.00	40.00
RPMLE Marcedes Lewis	20.00	50.00

2006 Topps Rookie Premiere Autographs Dual

RED INK TOO SCARCE TO PRICE		
LWML LenDale White	60.00	150.00
Matt Leinart		
LWVY LenDale White	60.00	150.00
Vince Young		
MLVY Matt Leinart	100.00	200.00
Vince Young		
MWRB Mario Williams	100.00	200.00
Reggie Bush		
RBLW Reggie Bush	100.00	200.00
LenDale White		
RBML Reggie Bush	100.00	200.00
Matt Leinart		

2006 Topps Rookie Premiere Autographs Quad

QUAD AUTOs TOO SCARCE TO PRICE
BMWW Reggie Bush
Laurence Maroney
DeAngelo Williams
LenDale White
BWLY Reggie Bush
LenDale White
Matt Leinart
Vince Young
HMJD Santonio Holmes
Sinorice Moss
Chad Jackson
Vernon Davis

2006 Topps Signature Series

SIG SERIES/50 ODDS 1:33,000 HOB		
TAAH A.J. Hawk	50.00	100.00
TABF Brett Favre	125.00	250.00
TACJ Chad Johnson	40.00	80.00
TACM Curtis Martin	60.00	120.00
TADM Dan Marino	125.00	250.00
TADMN Donovan McNabb	50.00	100.00
TAEM Eli Manning	60.00	120.00
TAES Emmitt Smith	125.00	250.00
TAGS Gale Sayers	50.00	100.00
TAJB Jim Brown	60.00	120.00
TAJC Jay Cutler	50.00	100.00
TAJM Joe Montana	100.00	200.00
TAJN Joe Namath	75.00	135.00
TALT LaDainian Tomlinson	50.00	100.00
TAML Matt Leinart	30.00	80.00
TAMV Michael Vick	60.00	120.00
TAPM Peyton Manning	100.00	200.00
TARB Reggie Bush	50.00	100.00
TASH Santonio Holmes	40.00	80.00
TASM Shawne Merriman	40.00	80.00
TASS Steve Smith	50.00	100.00
TASY Steve Young	60.00	120.00
TATA Troy Aikman	60.00	120.00
TATB Tom Brady	150.00	300.00
TAVY Vince Young	50.00	100.00

2006 Topps Super Tix

STATED ODDS 1:1750 HOB		
ST1 Ben Roethlisberger	25.00	60.00
ST2 Lofa Tatupu	8.00	20.00
ST3 Willie Parker	20.00	50.00
ST4 Darrell Jackson	8.00	20.00
ST5 Hines Ward	30.00	60.00
ST6 Matt Hasselbeck	10.00	25.00
ST7 Jerome Bettis	40.00	80.00
ST8 Shaun Alexander	10.00	25.00
ST9 Troy Polamalu	40.00	80.00
ST10 Joey Porter	20.00	50.00
STAHW Hines Ward AU	150.00	250.00

2006 Topps True Champions

INSERTS IN WAL-MART RETAIL PACKS		
1 Walter Payton	3.00	8.00
2 Reggie Bush	4.00	10.00
3 Brett Favre	3.00	8.00
4 Adam Vinatieri	1.00	2.50
5 Troy Aikman	1.50	4.00
6 Johnny Unitas	2.50	6.00
7 Matt Leinart	2.00	5.00
8 Tom Brady	2.00	5.00
9 John Elway	2.50	6.00
10 Ray Lewis	1.00	2.50
11 Joe Namath	1.50	4.00
12 Vince Young	3.00	8.00
13 Marshall Faulk	1.00	2.50
14 Terry Bradshaw	2.00	5.00
15 Joe Montana	3.00	8.00
16 Emmitt Smith	2.50	6.00
17 LenDale White	2.00	5.00
18 Torry Holt	1.00	2.50

2006 Topps True Champions Jerseys

JSY/199 INSERTS IN WAL-MART PACKS		
JN Joe Namath	20.00	40.00
JU Johnny Unitas	25.00	50.00
ML Matt Leinart		
RB Reggie Bush	15.00	40.00
VY Vince Young	12.00	30.00
WP Walter Payton	30.00	60.00

2006 Topps True Champions Jerseys Dual

DUALS/50 INSERTS IN WAL-MART PACKS		
NY Joe Namath	40.00	80.00
Vince Young		
PB Walter Payton	50.00	100.00
Reggie Bush		
UL Johnny Unitas	40.00	80.00
Matt Leinart		

2006 Topps Hall of Fame Class of 2006

This set was produced by Topps and distributed at the 2006 Induction ceremonies for the Pro Football Hall of Fame. Each card includes a photo of a 2006 inductee printed with a gold foil "Class of 2006" logo on the top of the cardfronts. This version of the cards is nearly identical to the basic 2006 Topps Hall of Fame Tribute inserts except for the difference in the prefix used for the card numbering on the backs. The induction ceremony version has a prefix that reads "HOF" versus "HOFT" for the pack insert.

COMPLETE SET (6)	5.00	10.00
HOFHC Harry Carson	.60	1.50
HOFJM John Madden	.75	2.00
HOFTA Troy Aikman	.60	2.50
HOFWM Warren Moon	.60	1.50
HOFRWR Rayfield Wright	.60	1.50
HOFRW Reggie White	.75	2.00

2006 Topps Super Bowl XL Card Show

This set was distributed directly to dealers who participated in the 2006 Super Bowl Card Show. Each card was printed in the design of the basic issue 2005 Topps football release along with the Super Bowl XL logo on the cardfront. The basic cards were printed with gold foil highlights and were serial numbered to 1000. A Platinum foil parallel set was also produced with each card serial numbered to 199.

COMPLETE SET (16)	15.00	30.00
GOLD PRINT RUN 1000 SER.#'d SETS		
*PLATINUM: .8X TO 2X BASIC GOLDS		
PLATINUM PRINT RUN 199 SER.#'d SETS		
1 Kevin Jones	.50	1.25
2 Cadillac Williams	.60	1.50
3 Peyton Manning	1.25	3.00
4 Mike Williams	.50	1.25
5 Ben Roethlisberger	1.00	2.50
6 Larry Johnson	.60	1.50
7 LaDainian Tomlinson	.75	2.00
8 Tom Brady	1.25	3.00
9 Eli Manning	1.00	2.50
10 Brett Favre	1.50	4.00
11 Shaun Alexander	.60	1.50
12 Michael Vick	.75	2.00
13 Ronnie Brown	.75	2.00
14 Edgerrin James	.60	1.50
15 Tiki Barber	.75	2.00
16 Carson Palmer	.75	2.00

2006 Topps Super Bowl XL Card Show Promos

These 6-cards were issued at the 2006 Super Bowl Card Show and produced by Topps. Cards were available at the Topps booth each day of event in exchange for football card wrappers from Topps products. Each card includes the Super Bowl XL logo on the front.

COMPLETE SET (6)	6.00	12.00
1 Mike Williams	.60	1.50
2 Peyton Manning	1.25	3.00
3 Shaun Alexander	.60	1.50
4 LaDainian Tomlinson	.75	2.00
5 Tom Brady	1.25	3.00
6 Ben Roethlisberger	2.50	6.00

2006 Topps Turn Back the Clock

COMPLETE SET (22)	6.00	15.00
ISSUED ONE PER WEEK VIA HTA SHOPS		
1 Sinorice Moss	.15	.40
2 Matt Leinart	.15	.40
3 DeAngelo Williams	.20	.50
4 Maurice Drew	.25	.60
5 Laurence Maroney	.12	.30
6 LenDale White	.25	.60
7 Mario Williams	.30	.75
8 Vernon Davis	.40	1.00
9 Reggie Bush	.60	1.50
10 Chad Jackson	.20	.50
11 Tarvaris Jackson	.30	.75
12 Michael Huff	.25	.60
13 Brian Calhoun	.20	.50
14 Santonio Holmes	.40	1.00
15 Jay Cutler	.60	1.50
16 Greg Jennings	.50	1.25
17 D'Brickashaw Ferguson	.30	.75
18 Joseph Addai	.30	.75
19 Derek Hagan	.25	.60
20 Kellen Clemens	.25	.60
21 Vince Young	.40	1.00
22 Marcedes Lewis	.30	.75

2007 Topps

This 440-card set was released in August, 2007. The set was issued into the hobby in nine-card packs, with a $1.99 SRP, which came 36 packs to a box. This set includes the following subsets: Rookies (286-395), League Leaders (396-404, 429), Pro Bowl (405-424), Award Winners (425-427), Post-Season Heroes (428, 430-440). A special card to commemorate Super Bowl MVP Peyton Manning was inserted into both hobby and retail packs at a stated rate of one in 36.

COMP.FACT.SET (445)	30.00	50.00
COMP.BEARS SET (445)	30.00	50.00
COMP.CHARGER SET (445)	30.00	50.00
COMP.COLTS SET (445)	30.00	50.00
COMP.JETS SET (445)	30.00	50.00
COMP.SUPER BOWL (446)	30.00	50.00
COMPLETE SET (440)	25.00	50.00
MANNING RH ODDS 1:36 HOB/RET		
MANNING RH AUTO ODDS 1:17,000		
MANNING SBMVP ODDS 1:500,000		
1 Matt Leinart	.20	.50
2 Kurt Warner	.20	.50
3 Matt Schaub	.20	.50
4 Michael Vick	.25	.60
5 Kyle Boller	.15	.40
6 Steve McNair	.20	.50
7 J.P. Losman	.15	.40
8 Jake Delhomme	.20	.50
9 Rex Grossman	.20	.50
10 Brian Griese	.20	.50
11 Carson Palmer	.20	.50
12 Charlie Frye	.20	.50
13 Drew Bledsoe	.25	.60
14 Tony Romo	.30	.75
15 Joey Harrington	.20	.50
16 Jay Cutler	.25	.60
17 Jon Kitna	.15	.40
18 Aaron Rodgers	.60	1.50
19 Brett Favre	.50	1.25
20 David Carr	.20	.50
21 Peyton Manning	.40	1.00
22 David Garrard	.20	.50
23 Byron Leftwich	.20	.50
24 Trent Green	.20	.50
25 Damon Huard	.20	.50
26 Daunte Culpepper	.20	.50
27 Tarvaris Jackson	.15	.40
28 Tom Brady	.40	1.00
29 Drew Brees	.25	.60
30 Eli Manning	.25	.60
31 Chad Pennington	.20	.50
32 Andrew Walter	.15	.40
33 Aaron Brooks	.15	.40
34 Donovan McNabb	.25	.60
35 Jeff Garcia	.20	.50
36 Ben Roethlisberger	.25	.60
37 Philip Rivers	.25	.60
38 Alex Smith QB	.25	.60
39 Matt Hasselbeck	.20	.50
40 Seneca Wallace	.15	.40
41 Marc Bulger	.20	.50
42 Chris Simms	.15	.40
43 Bruce Gradkowski	.15	.40
44 Vince Young	.20	.50
45 Jason Campbell	.20	.50
46 Jared Lorenzen	.15	.40
47 Mark Brunell	.20	.50
48 J.J. Arrington	.20	.50
49 Edgerrin James	.20	.50
50 Jerious Norwood	.20	.50
51 Warrick Dunn	.20	.50
52 Mike Anderson	.20	.50
53 Jamal Lewis	.20	.50
54 Willis McGahee	.20	.50
55 DeShaun Foster	.20	.50
56 DeAngelo Williams	.25	.60
57 Cedric Benson	.20	.50
58 Thomas Jones	.20	.50
59 Chris Perry	.15	.40
60 Rudi Johnson	.20	.50
61 Reuben Droughns	.20	.50
62 Jerome Harrison	.15	.40
63 Marion Barber	.25	.60
64 Julius Jones	.15	.40
65 Tatum Bell	.15	.40
66 Mike Bell	.20	.50
67 Kevin Jones	.15	.40
68 Brian Calhoun	.15	.40
69 Ahman Green	.20	.50
70 Vernand Morency	.20	.50
71 Ron Dayne	.20	.50
72 Wali Lundy	.15	.40
73 Dominic Rhodes	.20	.50
74 Joseph Addai	.20	.50
75 Fred Taylor	.20	.50
76 Maurice Jones-Drew	.25	.60
77 Larry Johnson	.15	.40
78 Sammy Morris	.15	.40
79 Ronnie Brown	.20	.50
80 Mewelde Moore	.15	.40
81 Chester Taylor	.15	.40
82 Kevin Faulk	.15	.40
83 Corey Dillon	.20	.50
84 Laurence Maroney	.20	.50
85 Deuce McAllister	.20	.50
86 Reggie Bush	.25	.60
87 Brandon Jacobs	.20	.50
88 Anthony Thomas	.15	.40
89 Cedric Houston	.15	.40
90 Leon Washington	.20	.50
91 Kevan Barlow	.20	.50
92 LaMont Jordan	.20	.50
93 Justin Fargas	.15	.40
94 Brian Westbrook	.20	.50
95 Correll Buckhalter	.20	.50
96 Willie Parker	.20	.50
97 Najeh Davenport	.15	.40
98 LaDainian Tomlinson	.25	.60
99 Darren Sproles	.20	.50
100 Frank Gore	.25	.60
101 Michael Robinson	.20	.50
102 Shaun Alexander	.20	.50
103 Maurice Morris	.15	.40
104 Steven Jackson	.25	.60
105 Stephen Davis	.20	.50
106 Cadillac Williams	.20	.50
107 Travis Henry	.20	.50
108 LenDale White	.20	.50
109 Ladell Betts	.15	.40
110 Clinton Portis	.20	.50
111 Michael Turner	.25	.60
112 T.J. Duckett	.15	.40
113 Anquan Boldin	.20	.50
114 Larry Fitzgerald	.25	.60
115 Bryant Johnson	.15	.40
116 Michael Jenkins	.20	.50
117 Ashley Lelie	.20	.50
118 Roddy White	.20	.50
119 Mark Clayton	.20	.50
120 Derrick Mason	.20	.50
121 Demetrius Williams	.15	.40
122 Peerless Price	.15	.40
123 Lee Evans	.20	.50
124 Drew Carter	.15	.40
125 Keyshawn Johnson	.20	.50
126 Steve Smith	.20	.50
127 Bernard Berrian	.15	.40
128 Mark Bradley	.15	.40
129 Muhsin Muhammad	.20	.50
130 Chad Johnson	.20	.50
131 T.J. Houshmandzadeh	.20	.50
132 Chris Henry	.15	.40
133 Joe Jurevicius	.15	.40
134 Braylon Edwards	.20	.50
135 Terrell Owens	.25	.60
136 Terry Glenn	.20	.50
137 Skyler Green	.15	.40
138 Rod Smith	.20	.50
139 Javon Walker	.20	.50
140 Brandon Marshall	.20	.50
141 Mike Furrey	.20	.50
142 Mike Williams	.15	.40
143 Roy Williams WR	.20	.50
144 Donald Driver	.25	.60
145 Greg Jennings	.25	.60
146 Andre Johnson	.20	.50
147 Eric Moulds	.20	.50
148 Reggie Wayne	.20	.50
149 Marvin Harrison	.25	.60
150 Ernest Wilford	.15	.40
151 Matt Jones	.20	.50
152 Reggie Williams	.20	.50
153 Eddie Kennison	.15	.40
154 Samie Parker	.15	.40
155 Marty Booker	.15	.40
156 Chris Chambers	.20	.50
157 Wes Welker	.25	.60
158 Travis Taylor	.15	.40
159 Troy Williamson	.15	.40
160 Reche Caldwell	.15	.40
161 Chad Jackson	.15	.40
162 Devery Henderson	.15	.40
163 Joe Horn	.20	.50
164 Marques Colston	.25	.60
165 Plaxico Burress	.20	.50
166 Amani Toomer	.20	.50
167 Sinorice Moss	.20	.50
168 Jerricho Cotchery	.20	.50
169 Laveranues Coles	.15	.40
170 Randy Moss	.25	.60
171 Ronald Curry	.20	.50
172 Donte Stallworth	.20	.50
173 Reggie Brown	.15	.40
174 Hines Ward	.25	.60
175 Nate Washington	.15	.40
176 Santonio Holmes	.20	.50
177 Keenan McCardell	.15	.40
178 Eric Parker	.15	.40
179 Arnaz Battle	.15	.40
180 Antonio Bryant	.15	.40
181 D.J. Hackett	.15	.40
182 Deion Branch	.20	.50
183 Darrell Jackson	.15	.40
184 Kevin Curtis	.15	.40
185 Torry Holt	.20	.50
186 Isaac Bruce	.20	.50
187 Michael Clayton	.15	.40
188 Joey Galloway	.20	.50
189 Drew Bennett	.15	.40
190 Bobby Wade	.15	.40
191 Antwaan Randle El	.15	.40
192 Santana Moss	.20	.50
193 Roscoe Parrish	.15	.40
194 Leonard Pope	.15	.40
195 Alge Crumpler	.20	.50
196 Todd Heap	.15	.40
197 Desmond Clark	.15	.40
198 Kellen Winslow	.20	.50
199 Jason Witten	.25	.60
200 Marcus Pollard	.15	.40
201 Bubba Franks	.15	.40
202 Dallas Clark	.15	.40
203 George Wrighster	.15	.40
204 Tony Gonzalez	.20	.50
205 Randy McMichael	.15	.40
206 Jermaine Wiggins	.15	.40
207 Ben Watson	.15	.40
208 Ernie Conwell	.15	.40
209 Jeremy Shockey	.20	.50
210 L.J. Smith	.15	.40
211 Heath Miller	.15	.40
212 Antonio Gates	.25	.60
213 Vernon Davis	.20	.50
214 Jerramy Stevens	.15	.40
215 Joe Klopfenstein	.15	.40
216 Alex Smith TE	.15	.40
217 Bo Scaife	.15	.40
218 Anthony Fasano	.15	.40
219 Chris Cooley	.20	.50
220 Robbie Gould	.15	.40
221 Adam Vinatieri	.20	.50
222 Devin Hester	.25	.60
223 Justin Miller	.15	.40
224 Sean Taylor	.25	.60
225 DeAngelo Hall	.20	.50
226 Chris McAlister	.15	.40
227 Nate Clements	.15	.40
228 Chris Gamble	.15	.40
229 Ricky Manning	.15	.40
230 Charles Tillman	.15	.40
231 Deltha O'Neal	.15	.40
232 Terence Newman	.15	.40
233 Champ Bailey	.20	.50
234 Charles Woodson	.25	.60
235 Dunta Robinson	.15	.40
236 Rashean Mathis	.15	.40
237 Antoine Winfield	.15	.40
238 Asante Samuel	.15	.40
239 Nnamdi Asomugha	.25	.60
240 Lito Sheppard	.15	.40
241 Walt Harris	.15	.40
242 Tye Hill	.15	.40
243 Ronde Barber	.20	.50
244 Quentin Jammer	.15	.40
245 Ed Reed	.20	.50
246 Roy Williams S	.20	.50
247 Troy Polamalu	.25	.60
248 Brian Dawkins	.20	.50
249 Terrell Suggs	.20	.50
250 Aaron Schobel	.15	.40
251 Julius Peppers	.20	.50
252 Alex Brown	.15	.40
253 Kamerion Wimbley	.15	.40
254 DeMarcus Ware	.20	.50
255 Elvis Dumervil	.15	.40
256 Mario Williams	.20	.50
257 Dwight Freeney	.20	.50
258 Tamba Hali	.15	.40
259 Jason Taylor	.20	.50
260 Michael Strahan	.20	.50
261 Aaron Kampman	.20	.50
262 Derrick Burgess	.15	.40
263 Leonard Little	.15	.40
264 Ty Warren	.15	.40
265 Warren Sapp	.20	.50
266 Luis Castillo	.15	.40
267 Keith Brooking	.15	.40
268 Ray Lewis	.25	.60
269 London Fletcher	.15	.40
270 Brian Urlacher	.25	.60
271 Ernie Sims	.15	.40
272 A.J. Hawk	.20	.50
273 DeMeco Ryans	.20	.50
274 Cato June	.15	.40
275 Derrick Johnson LB	.15	.40
276 Zach Thomas	.20	.50
277 Antonio Pierce	.15	.40
278 Jonathan Vilma	.20	.50
279 James Farrior	.15	.40
280 Shawne Merriman	.20	.50
281 Lofa Tatupu	.20	.50
282 Derrick Brooks	.20	.50
283 Jonathan Ogden	.15	.40
284 Steve Hutchinson	.20	.50
285 Walter Jones	.15	.40
286 JaMarcus Russell RC	.40	1.00
287 Brady Quinn RC	.60	1.50
288 Drew Stanton RC	.40	1.00
289 Troy Smith RC	.60	1.50
290 Kevin Kolb RC	1.00	2.50
291 Trent Edwards RC	.60	1.50
292 John Beck RC	.60	1.50
293 Jordan Palmer RC	.50	1.25
294 Chris Leak RC	.50	1.25
295 Isaiah Stanback RC	.40	1.00
296 Tyler Palko RC	.50	1.25
297 Jared Zabransky RC	.50	1.25
298 Jeff Rowe RC	.40	1.00
299 Zac Taylor RC	.50	1.25
300 Lester Ricard RC	.50	1.25
301 Adrian Peterson RC	2.50	6.00
302 Marshawn Lynch RC	.60	1.50
303 Brandon Jackson RC	.50	1.25
304 Michael Bush RC	.60	1.50
305 Kenny Irons RC	.40	1.00
306 Antonio Pittman RC	.40	1.00
307 Tony Hunt RC	.40	1.00
308 Darius Walker RC	.40	1.00
309 Dwayne Wright RC	.50	1.25
310 Lorenzo Booker RC	.50	1.25
311 Kenneth Darby RC	.50	1.25
312 Chris Henry RC	.50	1.25
313 Selvin Young RC	.50	1.25
314 Brian Leonard RC	.50	1.25
315 Ahmad Bradshaw RC	1.00	2.50
316 Gary Russell RC	.50	1.25
317 Kolby Smith RC	.50	1.25
318 Thomas Clayton RC	.50	1.25
319 Garrett Wolfe RC	.40	1.00
320 Calvin Johnson RC	2.00	5.00
321 Ted Ginn Jr. RC	.50	1.25
322 Dwayne Jarrett RC	.50	1.25
323 Dwayne Bowe RC	.75	2.00
324 Sidney Rice RC	.75	2.00
325 Robert Meachem RC	.60	1.50
326 Anthony Gonzalez RC	.60	1.50
327 Craig Buster Davis RC	.50	1.25
328 Aundrae Allison RC	.40	1.00
329 Chansi Stuckey RC	.60	1.50
330 David Clowney RC	.50	1.25
331 Steve Smith USC RC	.60	1.50
332 Courtney Taylor RC	.50	1.25
333 Paul Williams RC	.40	1.00
334 Johnnie Lee Higgins RC	.50	1.25
335 Rhema McKnight RC	.40	1.00
336 Jason Hill RC	.60	1.50
337 Dallas Baker RC	.40	1.00
338 Greg Olsen RC	.50	1.25
339 Yamon Figurs RC	.60	1.50
340 Scott Chandler RC	.60	1.50
341 Matt Spaeth RC	.60	1.50
342 Ben Patrick RC	.50	1.25
343 Clark Harris RC	.50	1.25
344 Martrez Milner RC	.40	1.00
345 Joe Newton RC	.40	1.00
346 Alan Branch RC	.50	1.25
347 Amobi Okoye RC	.60	1.50
348 DeMarcus Tank Tyler RC	.40	1.00
349 Justin Harrell RC	.50	1.25
350 Brandon Mebane RC	.50	1.25
351 Gaines Adams RC	.60	1.50
352 Jamaal Anderson RC	.50	1.25
353 Adam Carriker RC	.50	1.25
354 Jarvis Moss RC	.50	1.25
355 Charles Johnson RC	.40	1.00
356 Anthony Spencer RC	.60	1.50
357 Quentin Moses RC	.50	1.25
358 LaMarr Woodley RC	.60	1.50
359 Victor Abiamiri RC	.60	1.50
360 Ray McDonald RC	.50	1.25
361 Tim Crowder RC	.60	1.50
362 Patrick Willis RC	1.25	3.00
363 Brandon Siler RC	.40	1.00
364 David Harris RC	.50	1.25
365 Buster Davis RC	.50	1.25
366 Lawrence Timmons RC	.60	1.50
367 Paul Posluszny RC	.60	1.50
368 Jon Beason RC	.50	1.25
369 Rufus Alexander RC	.50	1.25
370 Earl Everett RC	.50	1.25
371 Stewart Bradley RC	.50	1.25
372 Prescott Burgess RC	.50	1.25
373 Leon Hall RC	.50	1.25
374 Darrelle Revis RC	1.00	2.50
375 Aaron Ross RC	.60	1.50
376 Daymeion Hughes RC	.50	1.25
377 Marcus McCauley RC	.50	1.25
378 Chris Houston RC	.50	1.25
379 Tanard Jackson RC	.40	1.00
380 Jonathan Wade RC	.50	1.25
381 Josh Wilson RC	.50	1.25
382 Eric Wright RC	.60	1.50
383 A.J. Davis RC	.40	1.00
384 David Irons RC	.40	1.00
385 LaRon Landry RC	.60	1.50
386 Reggie Nelson RC	.50	1.25
387 Michael Griffin RC	.60	1.50
388 Brandon Meriweather RC	.60	1.50
389 Eric Weddle RC	.60	1.50
390 Aaron Rouse RC	.50	1.25
391 Josh Gattis RC	.40	1.00
392 Joe Thomas RC	.60	1.50
393 Levi Brown RC	.60	1.50
394 Tony Ugoh RC	.50	1.25
395 Ryan Kalil RC	.50	1.25
396 Peyton Manning LL	.30	.75
397 Marc Bulger LL	.15	.40
398 LaDainian Tomlinson LL	.20	.50
399 Larry Johnson LL	.12	.30
400 Frank Gore LL	.20	.50
401 Chad Johnson LL	.15	.40
402 Marvin Harrison LL	.20	.50
403 Reggie Wayne LL	.15	.40
404 LaDainian Tomlinson LL	.20	.50
405 Peyton Manning PB	.30	.75
406 Marvin Harrison PB	.20	.50
407 LaDainian Tomlinson PB	.20	.50
408 Reggie Wayne PB	.15	.40
409 Antonio Gates PB	.20	.50
410 Jeff Saturday PB	.12	.30
411 Jason Taylor PB	.15	.40
412 Shawne Merriman PB	.15	.40
413 Champ Bailey PB	.15	.40
414 Troy Polamalu PB	.20	.50
415 Drew Brees PB	.20	.50
416 Frank Gore PB	.20	.50
417 Tony Gonzalez PB	.15	.40
418 Steve Smith PB	.15	.40
419 Walter Jones PB	.12	.30
420 Devin Hester PB	.20	.50
421 Julius Peppers PB	.15	.40
422 Tony Romo PB	.25	.60
423 Ronde Barber PB	.15	.40
424 Larry Johnson PB	.12	.30
425 LaDainian Tomlinson MVP	.20	.50
426 Vince Young OROY	.15	.40
427 DeMeco Ryans DROY	.15	.40
428 Peyton Manning	.30	.75
Reggie Wayne PSH		
429 Drew Brees LL	.20	.50
430 Asante Samuel PSH	.12	.30
431 New Orleans Saints PSH	.20	.50
432 Reggie Bush PSH	.20	.50
433 Peyton Manning PSH	.30	.75
434 Robbie Gould PSH	.12	.30
435 Thomas Jones	.15	.40
Cedric Benson PSH		
436 Joseph Addai PSH	.25	.60
437 Marlin Jackson PSH	.30	.75
438 Colts Defense PSH	.20	.50
439 Adam Vinatieri PSH	.15	.40
440 Devin Hester PSH	.20	.50
RH41 Peyton Manning RH	2.50	6.00
RH41A Peyton Manning RH AU	250.00	350.00
SBMVP Peyton Manning MVP FB/25	125.00	200.00
(Super Bowl football swatch)		

2007 Topps Copper

*VETS: 3X TO 8X BASIC CARDS
*ROOKIES: 1X TO 2.5X BASIC CARDS
COPPER/2007 ODDS 1:7 HOB, 1:9 RET

2007 Topps First Edition

*VETS: 5X TO 12X BASIC CARDS
*ROOKIES 286-395: 1.5X TO 4X
STATED ODDS 1:36 HOB

2007 Topps Gold

*VETS: 10X TO 25X BASIC CARDS
*ROOKIES 286-395: 4X TO 10X
GOLD/52 ODDS 1:76 HOB

2007 Topps Platinum

UNPRICED PLAT 1/1 ODDS 1:15,000 HOB

2007 Topps All Pro Relics

STATED ODDS 1:326 H, 1:410 R
UNPRICED IN THE NAME ODDS 1:32,800 HOB
*PATCH/99: 1.2X TO 3X BASIC INSERTS
PATCH/99 ODDS 1:3082 HOB

AG Antonio Gates	4.00	10.00
CB Champ Bailey	4.00	10.00
CP Carson Palmer	7.50	20.00
DB Drew Brees	7.50	20.00
DH Devin Hester	7.50	20.00
FG Frank Gore	5.00	12.00
JP Julius Peppers	4.00	10.00
JS Jeff Saturday	4.00	10.00
JT Jason Taylor	4.00	10.00
LJ Larry Johnson	6.00	15.00
LT LaDainian Tomlinson		
MH Marvin Harrison	6.00	15.00
PM Peyton Manning	12.50	30.00
RB Ronde Barber	4.00	10.00
RW Reggie Wayne	5.00	12.00
SM Shawne Merriman	5.00	12.00
SS Steve Smith	4.00	10.00
TG Tony Gonzalez	4.00	10.00
TP Troy Polamalu	10.00	25.00
TR Tony Romo	12.50	30.00
WJ Walter Jones	4.00	10.00

2007 Topps All Pro Team

COMPLETE SET (12)	10.00	25.00
ONE PER RACK PACK		
1 Drew Brees	1.25	3.00
2 Peyton Manning	2.00	5.00
3 Marc Bulger	1.00	2.50
4 LaDainian Tomlinson	1.25	3.00
5 Larry Johnson	.75	2.00
6 Frank Gore	1.25	3.00
7 Chad Johnson	1.00	2.50
8 Marvin Harrison	1.25	3.00
9 Roy Williams WR	1.00	2.50
10 Champ Bailey	1.00	2.50
11 Shawne Merriman	1.00	2.50
12 Zach Thomas	1.00	2.50

2007 Topps Brett Favre Collection

COMMON CARD (BF1-BF200)	1.25	3.00
STATED ODDS 1:6 HOB		

2007 Topps Brett Favre Collection Autographs

AUTO/18-39 ODDS 1:75,000 H,1:40,000 R		
BFA1 Brett Favre/18	100.00	200.00
BFA2 Brett Favre/19	100.00	200.00
BFA3 Brett Favre/33	100.00	200.00
BFA4 Brett Favre/38	100.00	200.00
BFA5 Brett Favre/39	100.00	200.00
BFA6 Brett Favre/35	100.00	200.00
BFA7 Brett Favre/18	100.00	200.00

2007 Topps Factory Set Rookie Bonus

COMP.HOBBY SET (5)	3.00	8.00
COMP.BEARS SET (5)	3.00	8.00
COMP.CHARGER SET (5)	3.00	8.00
COMP.COLTS SET (5)	3.00	8.00
COMP.JETS SET (5)	3.00	8.00
COMP.SUPER BOWL (6)	5.00	12.00
B1 Dan Bazuin	.60	1.50
B2 Michael Okwo	.60	1.50
B3 Kevin Payne	.50	1.25
B4 Corey Graham	.50	1.25
B5 Trumaine McBride	.60	1.50
C1 Roy Hall	.75	2.00
C2 Brannon Condren	.50	1.25
C3 Clint Session	.60	1.50
C4 Michael Coe	.50	1.25
C5 Keyunta Dawson	.60	1.50
J1 Jacob Bender	.50	1.25
J2 James Ihedigbo	.50	1.25
J3 Brett Ratliff	.75	2.00
J4 Kyle Steffes	.50	1.25
J5 Jesse Pellot	.50	1.25
CH1 Anthony Waters	.60	1.50
CH2 Legedu Naanee	.75	2.00
CH3 Brandon Siler	.50	1.25
CH4 Jarrett Hicks	.60	1.50
CH5 Sonny Shackelford	.50	1.25
SB1 JaMarcus Russell	.25	.60
SB2 Adrian Peterson	1.50	4.00
SB3 Brady Quinn	.40	1.00
SB4 Ted Ginn	.30	.75
SB5 Marshawn Lynch	.40	1.00
SB6 Calvin Johnson	1.25	3.00
111 James Jones	.75	2.00
112 Steve Breaston	.75	2.00
113 Jacoby Jones	.75	2.00
114 Ryne Robinson	.60	1.50
115 Chris Davis	.50	1.25

2007 Topps Game Breakers Super Bowl Pylons

PYLON/50 ODDS 1:15,000H, 1:30,000R		
GBADH Devin Hester	75.00	150.00
GBADR Dominic Rhodes	60.00	120.00
GBAKH Kelvin Hayden	50.00	100.00
GBAMM Muhsin Muhammad		
GBAPM Peyton Manning	75.00	150.00
GBARW Reggie Wayne	50.00	100.00

2007 Topps Generation Now

STATED ODDS 1:4 HOB		
UNPRICED AU ODDS 1:160,000 HOB		
AS1 Alex Smith QB	.75	2.00
AS2 Alex Smith QB	.75	2.00
AS3 Alex Smith QB	.75	2.00
AS4 Alex Smith QB	.75	2.00
BJ1 Brandon Jacobs	.60	1.50
BJ2 Brandon Jacobs	.75	2.00
BJ3 Brandon Jacobs	.60	1.50
BJ4 Brandon Jacobs	.60	1.50
BR1 Ben Roethlisberger	.75	2.00
BR2 Ben Roethlisberger	.75	2.00
BR3 Ben Roethlisberger	.75	2.00
BR4 Ben Roethlisberger	.75	2.00
CW1 Cadillac Williams	.60	1.50
CW2 Cadillac Williams	.60	1.50
CW3 Cadillac Williams	.60	1.50
CW4 Cadillac Williams	.60	1.50
DH1 Devin Hester	.75	2.00
DH2 Devin Hester	.75	2.00
DH3 Devin Hester	.75	2.00
DH4 Devin Hester	.75	2.00
DW1 DeAngelo Williams	.75	2.00
DW2 DeAngelo Williams	.75	2.00
DW3 DeAngelo Williams	.75	2.00
DW4 DeAngelo Williams	.75	2.00
EM1 Eli Manning	.75	2.00
EM2 Eli Manning	.75	2.00
EM3 Eli Manning	.75	2.00
EM4 Eli Manning	.75	2.00
FG1 Frank Gore	.75	2.00
FG2 Frank Gore	.75	2.00
FG3 Frank Gore	.75	2.00
FG4 Frank Gore	.75	2.00
GJ1 Greg Jennings	.75	2.00
GJ2 Greg Jennings	.75	2.00
GJ3 Greg Jennings	.75	2.00
GJ4 Greg Jennings	.75	2.00
JA1 Joseph Addai	.60	1.50
JA2 Joseph Addai	.60	1.50
JA3 Joseph Addai	.60	1.50
JA4 Joseph Addai	.60	1.50
JC1 Jay Cutler	.75	2.00
JC2 Jay Cutler	.75	2.00
JC3 Jay Cutler	.75	2.00
JC4 Jay Cutler	.75	2.00
JCO1 Jerricho Cotchery	.60	1.50
JCO2 Jerricho Cotchery	.60	1.50
JCO3 Jerricho Cotchery	.60	1.50
JCO4 Jerricho Cotchery	.60	1.50
JL1 J.P. Losman	.50	1.25
JL2 J.P. Losman	.50	1.25
JL3 J.P. Losman	.50	1.25
JL4 J.P. Losman	.50	1.25
KJ1 Kevin Jones	.50	1.25
KJ2 Kevin Jones	.50	1.25
KJ3 Kevin Jones	.50	1.25
KJ4 Kevin Jones	.50	1.25
LE1 Lee Evans	.60	1.50
LE2 Lee Evans	.60	1.50
LE3 Lee Evans	.60	1.50
LE4 Lee Evans	.60	1.50
LF1 Larry Fitzgerald	.75	2.00
LF2 Larry Fitzgerald	.75	2.00
LF3 Larry Fitzgerald	.75	2.00
LF4 Larry Fitzgerald	.75	2.00
LM1 Laurence Maroney	.60	1.50
LM2 Laurence Maroney	.60	1.50
LM3 Laurence Maroney	.60	1.50
LM4 Laurence Maroney	.60	1.50
MC1 Marques Colston	.75	2.00
MC2 Marques Colston	.75	2.00
MC3 Marques Colston	.75	2.00
MC4 Marques Colston	.75	2.00
MJ1 Maurice Jones-Drew	.75	2.00
MJ2 Maurice Jones-Drew	.75	2.00
MJ3 Maurice Jones-Drew	.75	2.00
MJ4 Maurice Jones-Drew	.75	2.00
ML1 Matt Leinart	.60	1.50
ML2 Matt Leinart	.60	1.50
ML3 Matt Leinart	.60	1.50
ML4 Matt Leinart	.60	1.50
PR1 Philip Rivers	.75	2.00
PR2 Philip Rivers	.75	2.00
PR3 Philip Rivers	.75	2.00
PR4 Philip Rivers	.75	2.00
RB1 Reggie Bush	.75	2.00
RB2 Reggie Bush	.75	2.00
RB3 Reggie Bush	.75	2.00
RB4 Reggie Bush	.75	2.00
RW1 Roy Williams WR	.60	1.50
RW2 Roy Williams WR	.60	1.50
RW3 Roy Williams WR	.60	1.50
RW4 Roy Williams WR	.60	1.50
SJ1 Steven Jackson	.75	2.00
SJ2 Steven Jackson	.75	2.00
SJ3 Steven Jackson	.75	2.00
SJ4 Steven Jackson	.75	2.00
VY1 Vince Young	.60	1.50
VY2 Vince Young	.60	1.50
VY3 Vince Young	.60	1.50
VY4 Vince Young	.60	1.50

2007 Topps Hall of Fame Class of 2007

COMPLETE SET (6)	4.00	10.00
STATED ODDS 1:12 HOB/RET		
HOFBM1 Bruce Matthews	1.00	2.50
(White jersey in photo; issued in Topps packs)		
HOFCS Charlie Sanders	1.00	2.50
HOFGH Gene Hickerson	1.00	2.50
HOFMI Michael Irvin	1.25	3.00
HOFRW Roger Wehrli	1.00	2.50
HOFTT Thurman Thomas	1.25	3.00
HOFBM2 Bruce Matthews	1.00	2.50
(Blue jersey in photo; issued at HOF induction)		

2007 Topps Hall of Fame Autographs

ODDS 1:50,700 HOB, 1:40,000 RET		
HOFABM Bruce Matthews	175.00	300.00
HOFACS Charlie Sanders	125.00	250.00
HOFAMI Michael Irvin	150.00	300.00
HOFATT Thurman Thomas	200.00	350.00

2007 Topps Hobby Masters

STATED ODDS 1:9 HOB		
HMCJ Chad Johnson	.75	2.00
HMCP Carson Palmer	.75	2.00
HMLJ Larry Johnson	.60	1.50
HMLT LaDainian Tomlinson	1.00	2.50
HMMV Michael Vick	1.00	2.50
HMPM Peyton Manning	1.50	4.00
HMSA Shaun Alexander	.75	2.00
HMSJ Steven Jackson	1.00	2.50
HMSS Steve Smith	.75	2.00
HMTB Tom Brady	1.50	4.00

2007 Topps League Leaders Relics

GROUP A ODDS 1:4300 H, 1:5700 R		
GROUP B ODDS 1:1172 H, 1:1525 R		
LLRAJ Andre Johnson B	4.00	10.00
LLRCB Champ Bailey B	5.00	12.00
LLRCJ Chad Johnson B	6.00	15.00
LLRCP Carson Palmer B	6.00	15.00
LLRDB Drew Brees B	5.00	12.00
LLRJK Jon Kitna B		
LLRLJ Larry Johnson A	12.00	30.00
LLRLJ2 Larry Johnson A	12.00	30.00
LLRLT LaDainian Tomlinson A	12.00	30.00
LLRLT2 LaDainian Tomlinson A	12.00	30.00
LLRMH Marvin Harrison B	5.00	12.00
LLRPM Peyton Manning A	15.00	40.00
LLRPM2 Peyton Manning A	15.00	40.00
LLRSM Shawne Merriman B	8.00	20.00
LLRTO Terrell Owens B	8.00	20.00

2007 Topps LT Touchdown Tribute

COMPLETE SET (31)	20.00	50.00
COMMON CARD	1.00	2.50
ODDS 1:4 TARGET RETAIL		

2007 Topps Own The Game

COMPLETE SET (30)	25.00	60.00
STATED ODDS 1:9 HOB/RET		
OTGAK Aaron Kampman	1.25	3.00
OTGAS Aaron Schobel	1.00	2.50
OTGASA Asante Samuel	1.00	2.50
OTGCB Champ Bailey	1.25	3.00
OTGCJ Chad Johnson	1.25	3.00
OTGCP Carson Palmer	1.25	3.00
OTGDB Drew Brees	1.50	4.00
OTGDB2 Drew Brees	1.50	4.00
OTGDH Devin Hester	1.50	4.00
OTGDR DeMeco Ryans	1.25	3.00
OTGFG Frank Gore	1.50	4.00
OTGJM Justin Miller	1.00	2.50
OTGLF London Fletcher	1.00	2.50
OTGLJ Larry Johnson	1.00	2.50
OTGLJ2 Larry Johnson	1.00	2.50
OTGLT LaDainian Tomlinson	1.50	4.00
OTGLT2 LaDainian Tomlinson	1.50	4.00
OTGMB Marc Bulger	1.25	3.00
OTGMBA Marion Barber	1.50	4.00
OTGMH Marvin Harrison	1.50	4.00
OTGMH2 Marvin Harrison	1.50	4.00
OTGPM Peyton Manning	2.50	6.00
OTGPM2 Peyton Manning	2.50	6.00
OTGRG Robbie Gould	1.00	2.50
OTGRM Rashean Mathis	1.00	2.50
OTGRW Roy Williams WR	1.25	3.00
OTGSM Shawne Merriman	1.25	3.00
OTGTH Torry Holt	1.25	3.00
OTGTO Terrell Owens	1.50	4.00
OTGZT Zach Thomas	1.25	3.00

2007 Topps Performance Highlights Autographs

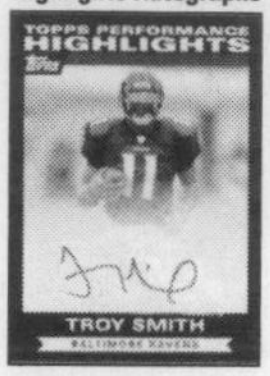

GROUP A ODDS 1:50,000H, 1:40,000R		
GROUP B ODDS 1:40,000H, 1:20,000R		
GROUP C/D ODDS 1:2500H, 1:5500R		
GROUP E ODDS 1:3381 H, 1:5500 R		
GROUP F ODDS 1:849 H, 1:2500 R		
THAAP Antonio Pittman F	4.00	10.00
THAAP Adrian Peterson A	100.00	200.00
THABJ Brandon Jackson E	5.00	12.00
THABL Brian Leonard F	5.00	12.00
THABQ Brady Quinn A		
THACJ Chad Johnson B	25.00	50.00
THACJ Calvin Johnson A	75.00	150.00
THADB Drew Brees A	50.00	100.00
THADB Dwayne Bowe C	8.00	20.00
THADJ Dwayne Jarrett C	5.00	12.00
THADS Drew Stanton C	4.00	10.00
THADT Drew Tate F	5.00	12.00
THAFG Frank Gore B	20.00	40.00
THAIS Isaiah Stanback F	4.00	10.00
THAJH Justise Hairston F	5.00	12.00
THAJP Jordan Palmer F	5.00	12.00
THAJR JaMarcus Russell A	20.00	50.00
THAJZ Jared Zabransky F	5.00	12.00
THAKI Kenny Irons C	4.00	10.00
THAKK Kevin Kolb D	10.00	25.00
THALG Luke Getsy F	6.00	15.00
THALJ Larry Johnson B	25.00	60.00
THALN Legedu Naanee F	6.00	15.00
THALT LaDainian Tomlinson A		
THAMB Michael Bush D	6.00	15.00
THAML Matt Leinart B		
THAML Marshawn Lynch B		
THARB Reggie Bush A	75.00	150.00
THARM Robert Meachem C	6.00	15.00
THARR Ryne Robinson F	5.00	12.00
THASJ Steven Jackson B	20.00	40.00
THASM Shawne Merriman B	30.00	60.00
THASR Sidney Rice C	12.50	25.00
THASS Steve Smith USC D	6.00	15.00
THASY Selvin Young F	8.00	20.00
THATB Tom Brady A	125.00	200.00
THATE Trent Edwards E	6.00	15.00
THATG Ted Ginn Jr. C	12.00	30.00
THATH Tony Hunt D	4.00	10.00
THATP Tyler Palko F	5.00	12.00
THATS Troy Smith C	6.00	15.00
THAVY Vince Young A		
THAWP Willie Parker B		

2007 Topps Performance Highlights Relics

GROUP A ODDS 1:8266 H, 1:12,000 R		
GROUP B ODDS 1:1400 H, 1:1800 R		
THRCJ Chad Johnson B	5.00	12.00
THRLJ Larry Johnson A	6.00	15.00
THRLT LaDainian Tomlinson A		
THRMH Marvin Harrison B	5.00	12.00
THRML Matt Leinart B	6.00	15.00
THRPM Peyton Manning A	10.00	25.00
THRRB Reggie Bush B	10.00	25.00
THRSJ Steven Jackson B	5.00	12.00
THRTB Tom Brady B	6.00	15.00
THRVY Vince Young B	7.50	20.00

2007 Topps Red Hot Rookies

RANDOM INSERTS IN WAL-MART PACKS		
1 JaMarcus Russell	.60	1.50
2 Calvin Johnson	3.00	8.00
3 Adrian Peterson	4.00	10.00
4 Ted Ginn	.75	2.00
5 Marshawn Lynch	1.00	2.50
6 Brady Quinn	1.00	2.50
7 Dwayne Bowe	1.25	3.00
8 Robert Meachem	1.00	2.50
9 Dwayne Jarrett	.75	2.00
10 Greg Olsen	.75	2.00
11 Anthony Gonzalez	1.00	2.50
12 Kevin Kolb	1.50	4.00
13 John Beck	1.00	2.50
14 Drew Stanton	.60	1.50
15 Sidney Rice	1.25	3.00

2007 Topps Red Hot Rookies Autographs

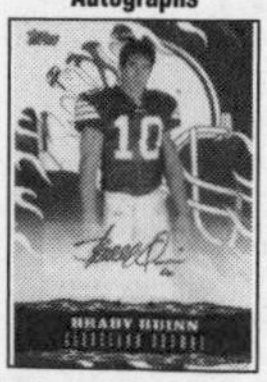

RANDOM INSERTS IN WAL-MART PACKS		
1 JaMarcus Russell	30.00	80.00
2 Ted Ginn Jr.	20.00	50.00
3 Marshawn Lynch	25.00	60.00
4 Brady Quinn	40.00	100.00
5 Dwayne Jarrett	12.00	30.00
6 Greg Olsen	20.00	40.00

2007 Topps Red Hot Rookies Jerseys

RANDOM INSERTS IN WAL-MART BLASTER

1 JaMarcus Russell	1.50	4.00
2 Calvin Johnson	8.00	20.00
3 Adrian Peterson	10.00	25.00
4 Ted Ginn	2.00	5.00
5 Marshawn Lynch	2.50	6.00
6 Brady Quinn	2.50	6.00
7 Dwayne Bowe	3.00	8.00
8 Robert Meachem	2.50	6.00
9 Dwayne Jarrett	2.00	5.00
10 Greg Olsen	2.00	5.00
11 Anthony Gonzalez	2.50	6.00
12 Kevin Kolb	4.00	10.00
13 John Beck	2.50	6.00
14 Drew Stanton	1.50	4.00
15 Sidney Rice	3.00	8.00

2007 Topps Rookie Fantasy Challenge

COMPLETE SET (20)	12.50	30.00
STATED ODDS 1:9 HOB		
1 JaMarcus Russell	.50	1.25
2 Adrian Peterson	3.00	8.00
3 Marshawn Lynch	.75	2.00
4 Brandon Jackson	.60	1.50
5 Calvin Johnson	2.50	6.00
6 Dwayne Bowe	1.00	2.50
7 Drew Stanton	.50	1.25
8 Chris Henry	.50	1.25
9 Robert Meachem	.75	2.00
10 Craig Buster Davis	.60	1.50
11 LaRon Landry	.75	2.00
12 Patrick Willis	1.50	4.00
13 Lawrence Timmons	.75	2.00
14 Anthony Gonzalez	.75	2.00
15 Kevin Kolb	1.25	3.00
16 Jason Hill	.75	2.00
17 Sidney Rice	1.00	2.50
18 Dwayne Jarrett	.60	1.50
19 Kenny Irons	.50	1.25
20 Lorenzo Booker	.60	1.50

2007 Topps Rookie Premiere Autographs

RANDOM INSERTS IN PACKS
RED INK TOO SCARCE TO PRICE

AG Anthony Gonzalez	15.00	40.00
AP Adrian Peterson	75.00	150.00
AP Antonio Pittman	10.00	26.00
BJ Brandon Jackson	12.00	30.00
BL Brian Leonard	12.00	30.00
BQ Brady Quinn	15.00	40.00
CH Chris Henry	10.00	25.00
CJ Calvin Johnson	50.00	120.00
DB Dwayne Bowe	20.00	50.00
DJ Dwayne Jarrett	12.00	30.00
DS Drew Stanton	10.00	25.00
GA Gaines Adams	15.00	40.00
GO Greg Olsen	12.00	30.00
GW Garrett Wolfe	10.00	25.00
JB John Beck	15.00	40.00
JH Jason Hill	15.00	40.00
JR JaMarcus Russell	10.00	25.00
JT Joe Thomas	15.00	40.00
KI Kenny Irons	10.00	25.00
KK Kevin Kolb	25.00	60.00
LB Lorenzo Booker	12.00	30.00
MB Michael Bush	15.00	40.00
ML Marshawn Lynch	15.00	40.00
PW Paul Williams	10.00	25.00
PW Patrick Willis	30.00	80.00
RM Robert Meachem	15.00	40.00
SR Sidney Rice	15.00	40.00
SS Steve Smith	15.00	40.00
TE Trent Edwards	15.00	40.00
TG Ted Ginn Jr.	12.00	30.00
TH Tony Hunt	10.00	25.00
TS Troy Smith	15.00	40.00
YF Yamon Figurs	10.00	25.00
JLH Johnnie Lee Higgins	12.00	30.00

2007 Topps Rookie Premiere Autographs Duals

RANDOM INSERTS IN PACKS
RED INK TOO SCARCE TO PRICE

JS Dwayne Jarrett	25.00	60.00
Steve Smith USC		
PJ Adrian Peterson	100.00	175.00
Calvin Johnson		
PL Adrian Peterson	40.00	100.00
Marshawn Lynch		
RJ JaMarcus Russell	30.00	80.00
Calvin Johnson		
RQ JaMarcus Russell	30.00	80.00
Brady Quinn		

2007 Topps Rookie Premiere Autographs Quads

RANDOM INSERTS IN PACKS
RED INK TOO SCARCE TO PRICE

JBGM Calvin Johnson	50.00	120.00
Dwayne Bowe		
Ted Ginn		
Robert Meachem		
JGLP Calvin Johnson	60.00	150.00
Ted Ginn Jr.		
Marshawn Lynch		
Adrian Peterson		
RQPJ JaMarcus Russell	60.00	150.00
Brady Quinn		
Adrian Peterson		
Calvin Johnson		
RQSB JaMarcus Russell	30.00	80.00
Brady Quinn		
Drew Stanton		
John Beck		
SGGP Troy Smith	50.00	120.00
Ted Ginn Jr.		
Anthony Gonzalez		
Antonio Pittman		

2007 Topps Running Back Royalty

COMPLETE SET (10)	6.00	15.00
STATED ODDS 1:12 HOB/RET		
TA LaDainian Tomlinson	1.00	2.50
Marcus Allen		
TB LaDainian Tomlinson	1.25	3.00
Jim Brown		
TC LaDainian Tomlinson	1.00	2.50
Earl Campbell		
TD LaDainian Tomlinson	1.00	2.50
Eric Dickerson		
TF LaDainian Tomlinson	1.00	2.50
Marshall Faulk		
TP LaDainian Tomlinson	2.00	5.00
Walter Payton		
TS LaDainian Tomlinson	1.50	4.00
Barry Sanders		
TDO LaDainian Tomlinson	1.00	2.50
Tony Dorsett		
TSA LaDainian Tomlinson	1.25	3.00
Gale Sayers		
TSM LaDainian Tomlinson	2.00	5.00
Emmitt Smith		

2007 Topps Running Back Royalty Autographs

AUTO/50 ODDS 1:20,000H, 1:17,000R		
BS Barry Sanders	100.00	175.00
EC Earl Campbell	40.00	80.00
ED Eric Dickerson	40.00	80.00
ES Emmitt Smith	125.00	200.00
GS Gale Sayers	50.00	100.00
JB Jim Brown	60.00	120.00
LT LaDainian Tomlinson	60.00	120.00
MA Marcus Allen	40.00	80.00
MF Marshall Faulk	40.00	80.00
TD Tony Dorsett	40.00	80.00

2007 Topps Running Back Royalty Autographs Dual

DUAL AU/25 ODDS 1:44,600H, 1:40,000R		
TA LaDainian Tomlinson	100.00	200.00
Marcus Allen		
TB LaDainian Tomlinson	125.00	250.00
Jim Brown		
TC LaDainian Tomlinson	100.00	200.00
Earl Campbell		
TD LaDainian Tomlinson	100.00	200.00
Eric Dickerson		
TDO LaDainian Tomlinson	100.00	200.00
Tony Dorsett		
TF LaDainian Tomlinson	100.00	200.00
Marshall Faulk		
TS LaDainian Tomlinson	150.00	300.00
Barry Sanders		
TSA LaDainian Tomlinson	100.00	200.00
Gale Sayers		
TSM LaDainian Tomlinson	200.00	400.00
Emmitt Smith		

2007 Topps Signature Series

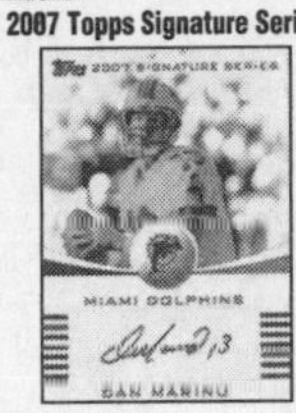

SIG SERIES/50 ODDS 1:85,000		
SSBF Brett Favre	150.00	300.00
SSBQ Brady Quinn	30.00	80.00
SSBS Barry Sanders	100.00	200.00
SSDB Drew Brees	50.00	100.00
SSDM Dan Marino	125.00	250.00
SSEC Earl Campbell	30.00	80.00
SSES Emmitt Smith	125.00	250.00
SSFG Frank Gore	25.00	50.00
SSGS Gale Sayers	50.00	100.00
SSJB Jim Brown	60.00	120.00
SSJM Joe Montana	125.00	250.00
SSJN Joe Namath	60.00	120.00
SSJR Jerry Rice	100.00	200.00
SSJRU JaMarcus Russell	25.00	60.00
SSLJ Larry Johnson	25.00	60.00
SSLT LaDainian Tomlinson	40.00	100.00
SSMA Marcus Allen	50.00	100.00
SSMF Marshall Faulk	30.00	80.00
SSML Matt Leinart	30.00	80.00
SSRB Reggie Bush	30.00	80.00
SSSA Shaun Alexander	25.00	50.00
SSSJ Steven Jackson	25.00	50.00
SSTB Tom Brady	175.00	300.00
SSTR Tony Romo	75.00	150.00
SSVY Vince Young	25.00	60.00

2007 Topps Stat Breakers Super Bowl Footballs

UNPRICED FB/10 ODDS 1:155,000 HOB

2007 Topps Target Exclusive Factory Set Rookie Jerseys

TWO PER TARGET FACTORY SET		
1 Brady Quinn	2.00	5.00
2 Calvin Johnson	6.00	15.00
3 Adrian Peterson	8.00	20.00
4 Dwayne Jarrett	1.50	4.00
5 JaMarcus Russell	1.25	3.00
6 Troy Smith	2.00	5.00

2007 Topps Retail Stars

This set of 12-cards was sold as a retail blister pack complete set through mass retail outlets. The cards are essentially the same as base 2007 Topps cards except that each has been re-numbered on the back.

COMPLETE SET (12)	4.00	8.00
1 Peyton Manning	.60	1.50
2 Brett Favre	.75	2.00
3 Reggie Bush	.40	1.00
4 Vince Young	.30	.75
5 Michael Vick	1.50	4.00
6 Ben Roethlisberger	.40	1.00
7 Tom Brady	.60	1.50
8 Brian Urlacher	.40	1.00
9 LaDainian Tomlinson	.40	1.00
10 Carson Palmer	.30	.75
11 Tony Romo	1.25	3.00
12 Donovan McNabb	.40	1.00

2007 Topps Super Bowl XLI Card Show

This set was distributed directly to dealers who participated in the 2007 Super Bowl Card Show in Miami. Each card was serial numbered to 1000, printed in the design of the basic issue 2006 Topps football release, and featured a Super Bowl XLI logo at the top of the cardfront. A Black bordered parallel set was also produced with each card serial numbered of 199.

COMPLETE SET (16)	15.00	30.00

2007 Topps Super Bowl XLI Card Show

*BLACK BORDER/199: .8X TO 2X		
1 Jason Taylor	.60	1.50
2 Larry Johnson	.50	1.25
3 Peyton Manning	1.25	3.00
4 Ronnie Brown	.60	1.50
5 LaDainian Tomlinson	.75	2.00
6 Tom Brady	1.25	3.00
7 Brian Urlacher	.75	2.00
8 Frank Gore	.75	2.00
9 Philip Rivers	.75	2.00
10 Brett Favre	1.50	4.00
11 Tiki Barber	.75	2.00
12 Marques Colston	.75	2.00
13 Dan Marino	1.50	4.00
14 Reggie Bush	.75	2.00
15 Vince Young	.60	1.50
16 Matt Leinart	.60	1.50

2007 Topps Turn Back The Clock

COMPLETE SET (22)	5.00	12.00
1 Brady Quinn	.15	.40
2 Ted Ginn Jr.	.25	.60
3 Greg Olsen	.25	.60
4 Vince Young	.25	.60
5 Joseph Addai	.25	.60
6 Robert Meachem	.30	.75
7 JaMarcus Russell	.10	.25
8 Calvin Johnson	.50	1.25
9 Adrian Peterson	.60	1.50
10 LaDainian Tomlinson	.30	.75
11 Frank Gore	.30	.75
12 Steven Jackson	.30	.75
13 Peyton Manning	.50	1.25
14 Reggie Bush	.30	.75
15 Marshawn Lynch	.15	.40
16 Joe Montana	.60	1.50
17 Joe Namath	.40	1.00
18 Dan Marino	.60	1.50
19 Jerry Rice	.50	1.25
20 Barry Sanders	.50	1.25
21 Roger Staubach	.50	1.25
22 Jim Brown	.40	1.00

2008 Topps

COMP.FACT.SET (445)	30.00	50.00
COMP.COWBOY SET (445)	30.00	50.00
COMP.GIANTS SET (445)	30.00	50.00
COMP.PACKER SET (445)	30.00	50.00
COMP.PATRIOT SET (445)	30.00	50.00
COMPLETE SET (440)	25.00	50.00
BASE CARD VARIATION ODDS 1:1722 H/R		
ELI RH ODDS 1:36		
ELI RH AUTO ODDS 1:40,000		
ELI SB FB/99 ODDS 1:12,175		
ELI SB FB AU ODDS 1:180,000		
UNPRICED PRINT PLATE 1/1 ODDS 1:910		
1 Drew Brees	.25	.60
2 Jon Kitna	.20	.50
3 Tom Brady	.40	1.00
4 Chad Pennington	.20	.50
5 Steve McNair	.20	.50
6 Josh McCown	.15	.40
7 Matt Hasselbeck	.20	.50
8 David Garrard	.20	.50
9 Jay Cutler	.25	.60
10 Matt Schaub	.20	.50
11 Daunte Culpepper	.20	.50
12 Kellen Clemens	.20	.50
13 John Beck	.15	.40
14 Trent Edwards	.15	.40
15 Brodie Croyle	.20	.50
16 Trent Dilfer	.20	.50
17 Chris Redman	.15	.40
18 Peyton Manning	.40	1.00
19 Carson Palmer	.25	.60
20 Ben Roethlisberger	.25	.60
21 Eli Manning	.25	.60
22 Tony Romo	.30	.75
23 Donovan McNabb	.25	.60
24 Joey Harrington	.15	.40
25 Jeff Garcia	.20	.50
26 Derek Anderson	.15	.40
27 Rex Grossman	.20	.50
28 Kyle Boller	.15	.40
29 Sage Rosenfels	.15	.40
30 JaMarcus Russell	.20	.50
31 Gus Frerotte	.15	.40
32 Luke McCown	.15	.40
33 Marc Bulger	.20	.50
34A Brett Favre	.60	1.50
34B Brett Favre Lombardi	150.00	300.00
(Vince Lombardi's face in background)		
34C Brett Favre Tractor	75.00	150.00
(Favre riding tractor; Packers helmet)		
34D Brett Favre Jets	5.00	12.00
(special factory set only)		
35 Philip Rivers	.25	.60
36 Vince Young	.20	.50
37 Kurt Warner	.25	.60
38 Cleo Lemon	.15	.40
39 Damon Huard	.15	.40
40 Jason Campbell	.20	.50
41 Brian Griese	.15	.40
42 Tarvaris Jackson	.20	.50
43 J.P. Losman	.15	.40
44 Troy Smith	.20	.50
45 Brady Quinn	.20	.50
46 Trent Green	.20	.50
47 Quinn Gray	.15	.40
48 Alex Smith QB	.25	.60
49 Todd Collins	.15	.40
50 Matt Moore	.20	.50
51 A.J. Feeley	.15	.40
52 Matt Leinart	.25	.60
53 Jake Delhomme	.20	.50
54 Steven Jackson	.25	.60
55 Willie Parker	.20	.50
56 Derrick Ward	.15	.40
57 Julius Jones	.15	.40
58 DeShaun Foster	.20	.50
59 Shaun Alexander	.20	.50
60 Reggie Bush	.25	.60
61 Clinton Portis	.20	.50
62 Ron Dayne	.15	.40
63 Maurice Jones-Drew	.20	.50
64 Warrick Dunn	.20	.50
65 Adrian Peterson	.40	1.00
66 Brian Leonard	.15	.40
67 Jerious Norwood	.20	.50
68 Thomas Jones	.20	.50
69 LaDainian Tomlinson	.25	.60
70 Cedric Benson	.20	.50
71 Marion Barber	.20	.50
72 Brian Westbrook	.20	.50
73 LenDale White	.20	.50
74 Ronnie Brown	.20	.50
75 Travis Henry	.15	.40
76 Kenny Watson	.15	.40
77 Fred Taylor	.20	.50
78 Ryan Grant	.25	.60
79 Marshawn Lynch	.20	.50
80 Selvin Young	.15	.40
81 Joseph Addai	.20	.50
82 Laurence Maroney	.20	.50
83 Brandon Jacobs	.20	.50
84 Willis McGahee	.20	.50
85 Frank Gore	.20	.50
86 Edgerrin James	.20	.50
87 Kevin Jones	.15	.40
88 DeAngelo Williams	.20	.50
89 Jamal Lewis	.20	.50
90 Chester Taylor	.15	.40
91 Earnest Graham	.15	.40
92 Justin Fargas	.15	.40
93 Kolby Smith	.15	.40
94 Maurice Morris	.15	.40
95 Larry Johnson	.20	.50
96 LaMont Jordan	.20	.50
97 Kenton Keith	.15	.40
98 Jesse Chatman	.15	.40
99 Adrian Peterson Bears	.40	1.00
100 Najeh Davenport	.15	.40
101 Rudi Johnson	.20	.50
102 Chris Brown	.15	.40
103 Aaron Stecker	.15	.40
104 Sammy Morris	.15	.40
105A Leon Washington	.20	.50
105B Brett Favre Tractor	30.00	80.00
(Favre riding tractor; Jets helmet/500,/ inserted in 2008 Bowman packs)		
106 T.J. Duckett	.15	.40
107 Ladell Betts	.15	.40
108 Michael Turner	.25	.60
109 Correll Buckhalter	.20	.50
110 Ahmad Bradshaw	.20	.50
111 Greg Jennings	.25	.60
112 Torry Holt	.20	.50
113 T.J. Houshmandzadeh	.20	.50
114 Jerricho Cotchery	.20	.50
115 Derrick Mason	.20	.50
116 Kevin Curtis	.15	.40
117 Kevin Walter	.20	.50
118 Joey Galloway	.20	.50
119 Anquan Boldin	.20	.60
120 Santonio Holmes	.20	.50
121 Lee Evans	.20	.50
122 Dwayne Bowe	.20	.50
123 Laurent Robinson	.15	.40
124 Wes Welker	.25	.60
125 Roy Williams WR	.20	.50
126 Randy Moss	.25	.60
127 Plaxico Burress	.20	.50
128 Terrell Owens	.25	.60
129 Andre Johnson	.20	.50
130 Roddy White	.20	.50
131 Brandon Marshall	.20	.50
132 Donald Driver	.20	.50
133 Hines Ward	.20	.50
134 Ike Hilliard	.15	.40
135 James Jones	.15	.40
136 Calvin Johnson	.25	.60
137 Marques Colston	.20	.50
138 Reggie Wayne	.20	.50
139 Chad Johnson	.20	.50
140 Amani Toomer	.20	.50
141 Bernard Berrian	.20	.50
142 Steve Smith	.20	.50
143 Larry Fitzgerald	.25	.60
144 Chris Chambers	.20	.50
145 Braylon Edwards	.20	.50
146 David Patten	.15	.40
147 Bobby Engram	.15	.40
148 Shaun McDonald	.15	.40
149 Anthony Gonzalez	.15	.40
150 Sidney Rice	.25	.60
151 Santana Moss	.15	.40
152 Reggie Brown	.15	.40
153 Justin Gage	.15	.40
154 Isaac Bruce	.20	.50
155 Antwaan Randle El	.15	.40
156 Roydell Williams	.15	.40
157 Ronald Curry	.20	.50
158 Jerry Porter	.15	.40
159 Patrick Crayton	.20	.50
160 Donte Stallworth	.15	.40
161 Nate Burleson	.15	.40
162 Mike Furrey	.20	.50
163 Deion Branch	.20	.50
164 Bobby Wade	.15	.40
165 Laveranues Coles	.15	.40
166 Brandon Stokley	.20	.50
167 Reggie Williams	.20	.50
168 Vincent Jackson	.15	.40
169 Joe Jurevicius	.15	.40
170 Dennis Northcutt	.15	.40
171 Arnaz Battle	.15	.40
172 Steve Smith USC	.20	.50
173 Ted Ginn Jr.	.20	.50
174 Antonio Gates	.25	.60
175 Chris Cooley	.20	.50
176 Owen Daniels	.15	.40
177 Kellen Winslow	.20	.50
178 Tony Gonzalez	.20	.50
179 Jason Witten	.25	.60
180 Greg Olsen	.20	.50
181 Jeremy Shockey	.20	.50
182 Dallas Clark	.20	.50
183 Donald Lee	.20	.50
184 Heath Miller	.15	.40
185 Tony Scheffler	.15	.40
186 Desmond Clark	.15	.40
187 Vernon Davis	.20	.50
188 Alge Crumpler	.20	.50
189 Zach Miller	.20	.50
190 Randy McMichael	.15	.40
191 Bo Scaife	.15	.40
192 Chris Baker	.15	.40
193 Jeff King	.15	.40
194 Marcedes Lewis	.15	.40
195 Ben Watson	.15	.40
196 Albert Haynesworth	.15	.40
197 Kevin Williams	.15	.40
198 Pat Williams	.15	.40
199 Tommie Harris	.15	.40
200 Darnell Dockett	.15	.40
201 Vince Wilfork	.15	.40
202 Jamal Williams	.15	.40
203 Casey Hampton	.15	.40
204 Amobi Okoye	.15	.40
205 Patrick Kerney	.15	.40
206 Gaines Adams	.15	.40
207 Osi Umenyiora	.20	.50
208 Mario Williams	.20	.50
209 Jared Allen	.25	.60
210 Trent Cole	.15	.40
211 Aaron Kampman	.20	.50
212 Kyle Vanden Bosch	.15	.40
213 Elvis Dumervil	.15	.40
214 Jason Taylor	.20	.50
215 Aaron Schobel	.15	.40
216 Andre Carter	.15	.40
217 John Abraham	.15	.40
218 Justin Tuck	.20	.50
219 Michael Strahan	.20	.50
220 Kabeer Gbaja-Biamila	.15	.40
221 Adewale Ogunleye	.15	.40
222 Julius Peppers	.20	.50
223 Tamba Hali	.15	.40
224 Luis Castillo	.15	.40
225 Jon Beason	.15	.40
226 D.J. Williams	.15	.40
227 Ernie Sims	.15	.40
228 DeMarcus Ware	.20	.50
229 Nick Barnett	.15	.40
230 Patrick Willis	.20	.50
231 Mike Vrabel	.15	.40
232 Shawne Merriman	.20	.50
233 Greg Ellis	.15	.40
234 Thomas Howard	.15	.40
235 Brian Urlacher	.25	.60
236 Keith Bulluck	.15	.40
237 London Fletcher	.15	.40
238 DeMeco Ryans	.20	.50
239 David Harris	.15	.40
240 Angelo Crowell	.15	.40
241 James Harrison RC	1.50	4.00
242 Julian Peterson	.15	.40
243 Lance Briggs	.15	.40
244 Lofa Tatupu	.20	.50
245 Ray Lewis	.25	.60
246 Shaun Phillips	.15	.40
247 Antonio Pierce	.15	.40
248 Antonio Cromartie	.15	.40
249 Marcus Trufant	.15	.40
250 Asante Samuel	.15	.40
251 Anthony Henry	.15	.40
252 Leigh Bodden	.15	.40
253 Antrel Rolle	.15	.40
254 Roderick Hood	.15	.40
255 DeAngelo Hall	.15	.40
256 Dre Bly	.15	.40
257 Leon Hall	.15	.40
258 Ronde Barber	.15	.40
259 Al Harris	.15	.40
260 Terence Newman	.15	.40
261 Champ Bailey	.20	.50
262 Aaron Ross	.15	.40
263 Bob Sanders	.20	.50
264 Reggie Nelson	.15	.40
265 Marvin Harrison	.25	.60
266 Ed Reed	.20	.50
267 O.J. Atogwe	.15	.40
268 Ken Hamlin	.15	.40
269 Kerry Rhodes	.15	.40
270 Clinton Hart	.15	.40
271 Atari Bigby	.15	.40
272 Sean Jones	.15	.40
273 Darren Sharper	.20	.50
274 Roy Williams S	.20	.50
275 Troy Polamalu	.25	.60
276 John Lynch	.20	.50
277 Antoine Bethea	.15	.40
278 LaRon Landry	.20	.50
279 Walter Jones	.15	.40
280 Jonathan Ogden	.15	.40
281 Joe Thomas	.20	.50
282 Nick Folk	.15	.40
283 Rob Bironas	.15	.40
284 Devin Hester	.25	.60
285 Josh Cribbs	.25	.60
286 Tom Brady LL	.30	.75
287 Drew Brees LL	.20	.50
288 Tony Romo LL	.25	.60
289 LaDainian Tomlinson LL	.20	.50
290 Adrian Peterson LL	.30	.75
291 Brian Westbrook LL	.20	.50
292 Reggie Wayne LL	.15	.40
293 Randy Moss LL	.20	.50
294 Chad Johnson LL	.15	.40
295 Randy Moss LL	.20	.50
296 Matt Hasselbeck PB	.15	.40
297 Tony Romo PB	.25	.60
298 Adrian Peterson PB	.30	.75
299 Marion Barber PB	.15	.40
300 Brian Westbrook PB	.15	.40
301 Larry Fitzgerald PB	.20	.50
302 Terrell Owens PB	.20	.50
303 Osi Umenyiora PB	.15	.40
304 Lofa Tatupu PB	.15	.40
305 Jason Witten PB	.20	.50
306 Torry Holt PB	.15	.40
307 Donald Driver PB	.15	.40
308 Peyton Manning PB	.30	.75
309 Ben Roethlisberger PB	.20	.50
310 Joseph Addai PB	.15	.40
311 Reggie Wayne PB	.15	.40
312 Braylon Edwards PB	.15	.40
313 Devin Hester PB	.20	.50
314 Champ Bailey PB	.15	.40
315 Ed Reed PB	.15	.40
316 Eli Manning PSH	.20	.50
317 David Tyree PSH	.15	.40
318 Plaxico Burress PSH	.15	.40
319 Lawrence Tynes PSH	.15	.40
320 Patriots Defense PSH	.20	.50
(Randy Moss		
Jabar Gaffney)		
321 R.W. McQuarters PSH	.15	.40
322 Ryan Grant PSH	.20	.50
323 Philip Rivers PSH	.20	.50
324 David Garrard PSH	.15	.40
325 Laurence Maroney PSH	.15	.40
326 Seattle Seahawks PSH	.15	.40
(Matt Hasselbeck)		
327 San Diego Chargers PSH	.15	.40
(Luis Castillo		
Jamal Williams)		
328 Tom Brady MVP	.30	.75
329 Adrian Peterson OROY	.30	.75
330 Patrick Willis DROY	.15	.40
331 Matt Ryan RC	2.50	6.00
331B Matt Ryan No Helm	60.00	100.00
(not wearing helmet in photo)		
332 Brian Brohm RC	.60	1.50
332B Brian Brohm No Helm	12.00	30.00
(not wearing helmet in photo)		
333 Andre Woodson RC	.60	1.50
334 Chad Henne RC	.60	1.50
335 Joe Flacco RC	2.00	5.00
336 John David Booty RC	.50	1.25
337 Colt Brennan RC	.60	1.50
338 Dennis Dixon RC	.60	1.50
339 Erik Ainge RC	.60	1.50
340 Josh Johnson RC	.60	1.50
341 Kevin O'Connell RC	.50	1.25
342 Matt Flynn RC	1.25	3.00
343 Sam Keller RC	.50	1.25
344 Harry Douglas RC	.50	1.25
345 Anthony Morelli RC	.50	1.25
346 Darren McFadden RC	1.50	4.00
346B Darren McFadden FB	25.00	50.00
(crushing football in photo)		
347 Rashard Mendenhall RC	1.25	3.00
347B Rashard Mendenhall FB	20.00	50.00
(pointing football outward)		
348 Jonathan Stewart RC	1.00	2.50
348B Jonathan Stewart No Helm	25.00	50.00
(not wearing helmet in photo)		
349 Felix Jones RC	1.00	2.50
350 Jamaal Charles RC	1.00	2.50
351 Chris Johnson RC	1.50	4.00
352 Ray Rice RC	1.25	3.00
353 Mike Hart RC	.60	1.50
354 Kevin Smith RC	.60	1.50
355 Steve Slaton RC	.60	1.50
356 Matt Forte RC	1.00	2.50
357 Tashard Choice RC	.50	1.25
358 Dominique Rodgers-Cromartie RC	.60	1.50
359 Cory Boyd RC	.40	1.00
360 Allen Patrick RC	.50	1.25
361 Thomas Brown RC	.50	1.25
362 Justin Forsett RC	.60	1.50
363 DeSean Jackson RC	1.25	3.00
364 Malcolm Kelly RC	.50	1.25
365 Limas Sweed RC UER 362	.60	1.50
(features back for card #362)		
366 Mario Manningham RC	.60	1.50
367 James Hardy RC	.50	1.25
368 Early Doucet RC	.50	1.25
369 Donnie Avery RC	.50	1.25
370 Dexter Jackson RC	.50	1.25
371 Devin Thomas RC	.50	1.25
372 Jordy Nelson RC	.75	2.00
373 Keenan Burton RC	.40	1.00
374 Chris Williams RC	.50	1.25
375 Earl Bennett RC	.60	1.50
376 Jerome Simpson RC	.60	1.50
377 Andre Caldwell RC	.50	1.25
378 Josh Morgan RC	.60	1.50
379 Fred Davis RC	.60	1.50
380 John Carlson RC	.60	1.50
381 Martellus Bennett RC	.50	1.25
382 Martin Rucker RC	.50	1.25
383 Jermichael Finley RC	.60	1.50
384 Dustin Keller RC	.60	1.50
385 Jacob Tamme RC	.60	1.50
386 Kellen Davis RC	.40	1.00
387 Jake Long RC	.60	1.50
388 Sam Baker RC	.40	1.00
389 Jeff Otah RC	.60	1.50
390 Owen Schmitt RC	.60	1.50
391 Chevis Jackson RC	.75	2.00
392 Jacob Hester RC	.60	1.50
393 Glenn Dorsey RC	.60	1.50
394 Sedrick Ellis RC	.60	1.50
395 Kentwan Balmer RC	.50	1.25
396 Pat Sims RC	.50	1.25
397 Marcus Harrison RC	.50	1.25
398 Dre Moore RC	.50	1.25
399 Red Bryant RC	.40	1.00
400 Trevor Laws RC	.60	1.50
401 Chris Long RC	.60	1.50
402 Vernon Gholston RC	.50	1.25
403 Derrick Harvey RC	.40	1.00
404 Calais Campbell RC	.50	1.25
405 Terrence Wheatley RC	.50	1.25
406 Phillip Merling RC	.50	1.25
407 Chris Ellis RC	.40	1.00
408 Lawrence Jackson RC	.50	1.25
409 Dan Connor RC	.60	1.50
410 Curtis Lofton RC	.50	1.25
411 Jerod Mayo RC	.60	1.50
412 Tavares Gooden RC	.50	1.25
413 Beau Bell RC	.50	1.25
414 Philip Wheeler RC	.50	1.25
415 Vince Hall RC	.40	1.00
416 Jonathan Goff RC	.40	1.00
417 Keith Rivers RC	.60	1.50
418 Ali Highsmith RC	.40	1.00
419 Xavier Adibi RC	.40	1.00
420 Erin Henderson RC	.60	1.50
421 Bruce Davis RC	.50	1.25
422 Jordon Dizon RC	.60	1.50
423 Shawn Crable RC	.40	1.00
424 Geno Hayes RC	.40	1.00
425 Mike Jenkins RC	.60	1.50
426 Aqib Talib RC	.60	1.50
427 Leodis McKelvin RC	.50	1.25
428 Terrell Thomas RC	.60	1.50
429 Reggie Smith RC	.50	1.25
430 Antoine Cason RC	.60	1.50
431 Patrick Lee RC	.50	1.25
432 Tracy Porter RC	.60	1.50
433 Kenny Phillips RC	.60	1.50
434 Simeon Castille RC	.50	1.25
435 Eddie Royal RC	.60	1.50
436 Thomas DeCoud RC	.40	1.00
437 Marcus Griffin RC	.40	1.00
438 Charles Godfrey RC	.60	1.50
439 Tyrell Johnson RC	.60	1.50
440 Jamar Adams RC	.50	1.25
RH42 Eli Manning RH	2.50	6.00
RHA42 Eli Manning RH AU	250.00	400.00
SBAEM Eli Manning FB AU/25	200.00	350.00
SBEM Eli Manning FB/99	50.00	100.00

2008 Topps Black

*VETS 1-330: 10X TO 25X BASIC CARDS		
*ROOKIES 331-440: 4X TO 10X BASIC CARDS		
BLACK/53 STATED ODDS 1:62		
241 James Harrison	25.00	60.00

2008 Topps Gold Border

*VETS 1-330: 3X TO 8X BASIC CARDS
*ROOKIES 331-440: 1.2X TO 3X BASIC CARDS
GOLD BORDER/2008 ODDS 1:7H, 1:8R

2008 Topps Gold Foil

*VETS 1-330: 1.5X TO 4X BASIC CARDS
*ROOKIES 331-440: .6X TO 1.5X BASIC CARDS

2008 Topps Platinum

UNPRICED PLATINUM 1/1 ODDS 1:12,000H

2008 Topps All-Stars

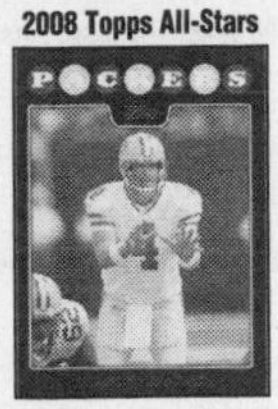

COMPLETE SET (12)	4.00	6.00
1 Peyton Manning	.50	1.25
2 Randy Moss	.30	.75
3 Devin Hester	.30	.75
4 Brett Favre	.75	2.00
5 Adrian Peterson	.50	1.25
6 Ben Roethlisberger	.30	.75
7 Tom Brady	.50	1.25
8 Derek Anderson	.20	.50
9 LaDainian Tomlinson	.30	.75
10 Darren McFadden	.75	2.00
11 Tony Romo	.40	1.00
12 Eli Manning	.30	.75

2008 Topps Brett Favre Collection

COMMON CARD	1.25	3.00
STATED ODDS 1:6 H/R		

2008 Topps Brett Favre Collection Autographs

COMMON CARD	100.00	200.00
FAVRE AU/13-32 ODDS 1:38,173		

2008 Topps Dynasties

STATED ODDS 1:4 H/R		
DYNAV Adam Vinatieri	1.00	2.50
DYNBB Bill Bates	.75	2.00
DYNBJ Brent Jones	.75	2.00
DYNCH Charles Haley	.75	2.00
DYNDB Deion Branch	.75	2.00
DYNDC Dwight Clark	.75	2.00
DYNDS Deion Sanders	1.00	2.50
DYNDSH Donnie Shell	.75	2.00
DYNDWH Dwight White	.75	2.00
DYNES Emmitt Smith	2.00	5.00
DYNES2 Emmitt Smith	2.00	5.00
DYNFH Franco Harris	1.00	2.50
DYNFH2 Franco Harris	1.00	2.50
DYNJG Joe Greene	1.00	2.50
DYNJM Joe Montana	2.00	5.00
DYNJM2 Joe Montana	2.00	5.00
DYNJM3 Joe Montana	2.00	5.00
DYNJN Jay Novacek	.75	2.00
DYNJR Jerry Rice	1.50	4.00
DYNJR2 Jerry Rice	1.50	4.00
DYNJT John Taylor	.75	2.00
DYNKT Keena Turner	.60	1.50
DYNLG L.C. Greenwood	.75	2.00
DYNLL Leon Lett	.60	1.50
DYNLM Lawyer Milloy	.60	1.50
DYNMB Mel Blount	.75	2.00
DYNRB Rocky Bleier	.75	2.00
DYNRC Randy Cross	.75	2.00
DYNRCR Roger Craig	.75	2.00
DYNRL Ronnie Lott	1.00	2.50
DYNTA Troy Aikman	1.25	3.00
DYNTA2 Troy Aikman	1.25	3.00
DYNTB Tom Brady	1.50	4.00
DYNTB2 Tom Brady	1.50	4.00
DYNTBR Terry Bradshaw	1.50	4.00
DYNTBR2 Terry Bradshaw	1.50	4.00
DYNTJ Ted Johnson	.60	1.50
DYNTL Ty Law	.60	1.50
DYNTR Tom Rathman	.75	2.00

2008 Topps Dynasties Autographs

GROUP A/25-100 ODDS 1:6482H, 1:20,734R		
GROUP B/200 ODDS 1:9200 H, 1:28,754 R		
GROUP C/500 ODDS 1:2350 H, 1:10,200 R		
DYNARL Ronnie Lott/50	30.00	60.00
DYNAAV Adam Vinatieri/100	40.00	80.00
DYNABB Bill Bates/500	8.00	20.00
DYNABJ Brent Jones/200	8.00	20.00
DYNACH Charles Haley/200	10.00	25.00
DYNADB Deion Branch/100	12.50	30.00
DYNADC Dwight Clark/100	15.00	40.00
DYNADS Deion Sanders/25	60.00	120.00
DYNADSH Donnie Shell/500	12.50	30.00
DYNADWH Dwight White/100	35.00	60.00
DYNAES Emmitt Smith/25	100.00	200.00
DYNAES2 Emmitt Smith/25	100.00	200.00
DYNAFH Franco Harris/25	50.00	100.00
DYNAFH2 Franco Harris/25	50.00	100.00
DYNAJG Joe Greene/50	20.00	50.00
DYNAJM Joe Montana/25	90.00	175.00
DYNAJM2 Joe Montana/25	90.00	175.00
DYNAJM3 Joe Montana/25	90.00	175.00
DYNAJN Jay Novacek/100	20.00	40.00
DYNAJR Jerry Rice/25	125.00	200.00
DYNAJR2 Jerry Rice/25	125.00	200.00
DYNAJT John Taylor/200	10.00	25.00
DYNAKT Keena Turner/500	6.00	15.00
DYNALG L.C. Greenwood/100	20.00	40.00
DYNALL Leon Lett/100	12.50	30.00
DYNALM Lawyer Milloy/500	6.00	15.00
DYNARB Rocky Bleier/200	20.00	40.00
DYNARC Randy Cross/100	10.00	25.00
DYNARCR Roger Craig/50	30.00	60.00
DYNATA Troy Aikman/25	60.00	120.00
DYNATA2 Troy Aikman/25	60.00	120.00
DYNATB Tom Brady/25	125.00	250.00
DYNATB2 Tom Brady/25	125.00	250.00
DYNATBR Terry Bradshaw/25	90.00	175.00
DYNATBR2 Terry Bradshaw/25	90.00	175.00
DYNATL Ty Law/200	10.00	25.00
DYNATR Tom Rathman/500	10.00	25.00

2008 Topps Dynasties Jerseys

DYNASTIES JSY/99 ODDS 1:2428		
JM Joe Montana	15.00	40.00
SY Steve Young	15.00	40.00
TA Troy Aikman	15.00	40.00
TB Terry Bradshaw	15.00	40.00
TBR Tom Brady	10.00	25.00

2008 Topps Dynasties Jerseys Autographs

JSY AUTO/25 ODDS 1:180,000
JM Joe Montana
SY Steve Young
TA Troy Aikman 75.00 150.00
TB Terry Bradshaw 100.00 200.00
TBR Tom Brady 175.00 300.00

2008 Topps Factory Set Rookie Bonus

COMP.HOBBY SET (5) 3.00 8.00
COMP.RETAIL SET (5) 3.00 8.00
COMP.COWBOY SET (5) 3.00 8.00
COMP.GIANTS SET (5) 3.00 8.00
COMP.PACKER SET (5) 3.00 8.00
COMP.PATRIOT SET (5) 3.00 8.00
H1 Marcus Smith .60 1.50
H2 Marcus Henry .60 1.50
H3 Ryan Torain .75 2.00
H4 Chauncey Washington .60 1.50
H5 Darius Reynaud .50 1.25
R1 Kyle Wright .60 1.50
R2 DJ Hall .60 1.50
R2 Adrian Arrington .60 1.50
R4 Lance Leggett .75 2.00
R5 Marcus Monk .60 1.50
DC1 Orlando Scandrick .75 2.00
DC2 Erik Walden .50 1.25
DC3 Danny Amendola 2.00 5.00
DC4 Mark Bradford .50 1.25
DC5 Keon Lattimore .60 1.50
GBP1 Jeremy Thompson .50 1.25
GBP2 Josh Sitton .60 1.50
GBP3 Breno Giacomini .50 1.25
GBP4 Brett Swain .60 1.50
GBP5 Kregg Lumpkin .75 2.00
NEP1 Jonathan Wilhite .60 1.50
NEP2 Matt Slater .75 2.00
NEP3 Bo Ruud .60 1.50
NEP4 Mark Dillard .50 1.25
NEP5 Casey Tyler .50 1.25
NYG1 Bryan Kehl .60 1.50
NYG2 Robert Henderson .50 1.25
NYG3 DJ Hall .60 1.50
NYG4 Taurean Rhetta .50 1.25
NYG5 Willie Copeland .50 1.25

2008 Topps Game Breakers Super Bowl Pylons

SB PYLON/50 ODDS 1:4040
GBDT David Tyree UER 20.00 40.00
(reads Game Worn Jersey on front))
GBEM Eli Manning UER 40.00 80.00
(reads Game Worn Jersey on front)
GBLM Laurence Maroney UER 12.50 30.00
(reads Game Worn Jersey on front)
GBPB Plaxico Burress UER 30.00 60.00
(reads Game Worn Jersey on front)
GBRM Randy Moss UER 30.00 60.00
(reads Game Worn Jersey on front)
GBTB Tom Brady UER 40.00 80.00
(reads Game Worn Jersey on front)

2008 Topps Hall of Fame Class of 2008

COMPLETE SET (6) 4.00 10.00
STATED ODDS 1:12 H/R
HOFAM-Art Monk 1.00 2.50
HOFAT Andre Tippett .75 2.00
HOFDG Darrell Green 1.00 2.50
HOFET Emmitt Thomas .75 2.00
HOFFD Fred Dean .75 2.00
HOFGZ Gary Zimmerman .75 2.00

2008 Topps Hall of Fame Autographs

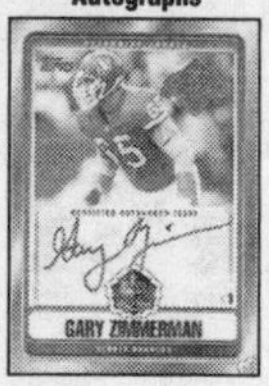

STATED ODDS 1:31,068
HOFAAM Art Monk 150.00 300.00
HOFAAT Andre Tippett 125.00 250.00
HOFADD Fred Dean 100.00 200.00
HOFADG Darrell Green 125.00 250.00
HOFAET Emmitt Thomas 125.00 250.00
HOFAGZ Gary Zimmerman 125.00 250.00

2008 Topps League Leaders Relics

GROUP A ODDS 1:298
GROUP B ODDS 1:248
LLRAC Antonio Cromartie B 3.00 8.00
LLRAP Adrian Peterson A 10.00 25.00
LLRDB Drew Brees A 3.00 8.00
LLRJA Jared Allen B 3.00 8.00
LLRLT LaDainian Tomlinson Yds A 3.00 8.00
LLRLT2 LaDainian Tomlinson TDs A 3.00 8.00
LLRPW Patrick Willis B 3.00 8.00
LLRRW Reggie Wayne A 3.00 8.00
LLRTB Tom Brady A 6.00 15.00
LLRTB2 Tom Brady A 6.00 15.00
LLRTR Tony Romo A 8.00 20.00
LLRWW Wes Welker B 4.00 10.00

2008 Topps Armed Forces Fans of the Game

COMPLETE SET (11) 3.00 8.00
STATED ODDS 1:6 H/R
AFFMH Col. Marc Hendler .40 1.00
AFFCA Srg. Christopher Ames .40 1.00
AFFMM SPC Mark Middlebrook .40 1.00
AFFRL Corp. Ryan Lenser .40 1.00
AFFJC Capt. John Cochrane Jr. .40 1.00
AFFJL Lance Corp. James Lenihan .40 1.00
AFFPL Srg. Phillip LaBonte .40 1.00
AFFTW Srg. Traci Williams .40 1.00
AFFSR Major Sean Ryan .40 1.00
AFFGB Sen. Airman Gabriel Bird .40 1.00
AFFWT Staff Srg. Wyat Tomlinson .40 1.00

2008 Topps Honor Roll

COMPLETE SET (9) 4.00 10.00
STATED ODDS 1:9 H/R
HRAD Art Donovan .60 1.50
HRCB Chuck Bednarik .75 2.00
HRGM Gino Marchetti .60 1.50
HRJM Johnny Blood McNally .60 1.50
HRLG Lou Groza .75 2.00
HRNB Norm Van Brocklin .75 2.00
HRRB Rocky Bleier .75 2.00
HRRS Roger Staubach 1.25 3.00
HRTF Tom Fears .60 1.50

2008 Topps Honor Roll Relic Patches

STATED ODDS 1:186
AD 101st Airborne Division 10.00 25.00
BA Blue Angels 10.00 25.00
CA 1st Cavalry 10.00 25.00
FF F-16 Fighting Falcon 10.00 25.00
IF Operation Iraqi Freedom Patch 10.00 25.00
MC Marines Eagle, Globe and Anchor 10.00 25.00
MR 7th Marine Regiment 10.00 25.00
MS Spade 10.00 25.00
NE 158th Fighter Wing/ Operation Noble Eagle 10.00
25.00
NI US Naval Intelligence 10.00 25.00
NS The Only Easy Day Was Yesterday 10.00 25.00
SO 82nd Airborne Division 10.00 25.00
TB Thunderbirds 10.00 25.00

2008 Topps Honor Roll Mini Medals

STATED ODDS 1:2715
HRRAD Art Donovan 20.00 50.00
HRRCB Chuck Bednarik 20.00 50.00
HRRGM Gino Marchetti 20.00 50.00
HRRJM Johnny Blood McNally 20.00 50.00
HRRLG Lou Groza 20.00 50.00
HRRNB Norm Van Brocklin 20.00 50.00
HRRRB Rocky Bleier 60.00 120.00
HRRRB2 Rocky Bleier 60.00 120.00
HRRRS Roger Staubach 75.00 150.00
HRRTF Tom Fears 20.00 50.00

2008 Topps Own The Game

COMPLETE SET (30) 10.00 25.00
STATED ODDS 1:9 H/R
OTGAC Antonio Cromartie .60 1.50
OTGAP Adrian Peterson 1.50 4.00
OTGAP2 Adrian Peterson 1.50 4.00
OTGBE Braylon Edwards .75 2.00
OTGBR Ben Roethlisberger 1.00 2.50
OTGBW Brian Westbrook .75 2.00
OTGCJ Chad Johnson .75 2.00
OTGDB Drew Brees 1.00 2.50
OTGDH Devin Hester 1.00 2.50
OTGDW D.J. Williams .60 1.50
OTGER Ed Reed .75 2.00
OTGJA Joseph Addai .75 2.00
OTGJAL Jared Allen 1.00 2.50
OTGJB Jon Beason .60 1.50
OTGLT LaDainian Tomlinson 1.00 2.50
OTGLT2 LaDainian Tomlinson 1.00 2.50
OTGLW Leon Washington .75 2.00
OTGMW Mario Williams .75 2.00
OTGOA O.J. Atogwe .60 1.50
OTGPK Patrick Kerney .60 1.50
OTGPW Patrick Willis .75 2.00
OTGRB Rob Bironas .60 1.50
OTGRM Randy Moss 1.00 2.50
OTGRM2 Randy Moss 1.00 2.50
OTGRW Reggie Wayne .75 2.00
OTGTB Tom Brady 1.50 4.00
OTGTB2 Tom Brady 1.50 4.00
OTGTO Terrell Owens 1.00 2.50
OTGTR Tony Romo 1.25 3.00
OTGTR2 Tony Romo 1.25 3.00

2008 Topps Performance Highlights Autographs

GROUP A ODDS 1:7500 H, 1:23,090 R
GROUP B ODDS 1:4200 H, 1:13,500 R
GROUP C ODDS 1:4600 H, 1:14,500 R
GROUP D ODDS 1:482 H, 1:1165 R
THAAA Adrian Arrington D 3.00 8.00
THAAC Andre Caldwell C 3.00 8.00
THAAM Anthony Morelli D 4.00 10.00
THAAP Allen Patrick D 3.00 8.00
THAAW Andre Woodson A 6.00 15.00
THABB Brian Brohm A 6.00 15.00
THABF Brett Favre A 150.00 250.00
THACH Chad Henne B 12.00 30.00
THADA Derek Anderson A 15.00 30.00
THADB Drew Brees A 30.00 60.00
THADF De'Cody Fagg D 3.00 8.00
THADJ DeSean Jackson B 10.00 25.00
THADM Darren McFadden A 15.00 40.00
THAFJ Felix Jones A 15.00 40.00
THAHD Harry Douglas C 3.00 8.00
THAJC Jamaal Charles B 8.00 20.00
THAJF Joe Flacco A 25.00 50.00
THAJS Jonathan Stewart A 10.00 25.00
THAKB Keenan Burton D 2.50 6.00
THAKW Kellen Winslow A 10.00 25.00
THALL Lance Leggett D 4.00 10.00
THALS Limas Sweed A 10.00 25.00
THAMB Marion Barber A 20.00 40.00
THAMF Matt Forte D 15.00 30.00
THAMG Marcus Griffin B 3.00 8.00
THAMK Malcolm Kelly B 4.00 10.00
THAML Marshawn Lynch A 20.00 40.00
THAMM Mario Manningham B 5.00 12.00
THAMMO Marcus Monk D 3.00 8.00
THAMR Matt Ryan A 25.00 60.00
THAPM Peyton Manning A 75.00 150.00
THAPW Patrick Willis A 10.00 25.00
THARM Rashard Mendenhall A 15.00 40.00
THARR Ray Rice B 10.00 25.00
THAWW Wes Welker B 20.00 40.00

2008 Topps Performance Highlights Relics

THRAG Antonio Gates A 4.00 10.00
THRBF Brett Favre A 10.00 25.00
THRBJ Brandon Jacobs B 3.00 8.00
THRDB Drew Brees A 4.00 10.00
THRDH Devin Hester B 4.00 10.00
THRML Marshawn Lynch B 3.00 8.00
THRPW Patrick Willis B 3.00 8.00
THRTH T.J. Houshmandzadeh B 3.00 8.00

2008 Topps Pro Bowl Jerseys

STATED ODDS 1:99
*PATCH/99: .6X TO 1.5X BASIC JSYs
PATCH/99 STATED ODDS 1:1214
UNPRICED IN THE NAME PRINT RUN 1
APRAP Adrian Peterson 8.00 20.00
APRBE Braylon Edwards 4.00 10.00
APRDH Devin Hester 5.00 12.00
APRJA Joseph Addai 4.00 10.00
APRLF Larry Fitzgerald 5.00 12.00
APRMB Marion Barber 4.00 10.00
APRPM Peyton Manning 8.00 20.00
APRRW Reggie Wayne 4.00 10.00
APRTO Terrell Owens 5.00 12.00
APRTR Tony Romo 6.00 15.00

2008 Topps Red Hot Rookies

RANDOM INSERTS IN WAL-MART PACKS
1 Matt Ryan 4.00 10.00
2 Joe Flacco 3.00 8.00
3 Brian Brohm 1.00 2.50
4 Chad Henne 1.00 2.50
5 Darren McFadden 2.50 6.00
6 Jonathan Stewart 1.50 4.00
7 Felix Jones 1.50 4.00
8 Rashard Mendenhall 2.00 5.00
9 Chris Johnson 2.50 6.00
10 Ray Rice 2.00 5.00
11 Donnie Avery .75 2.00
12 Devin Thomas .75 2.00
13 DeSean Jackson 2.00 5.00
14 Malcolm Kelly .75 2.00
15 Limas Sweed 1.00 2.50

2008 Topps Retail Game Jerseys

ONE PER SPECIAL RETAIL BOX
AC Antonio Cromartie 2.50 6.00
ACA Andre Caldwell 2.50 6.00
AF Alan Faneca 3.00 8.00
AG Andre Gurode 2.50 6.00
AGO Anthony Gonzalez 2.50 6.00
AJ Andre Johnson 3.00 8.00
AK Aaron Kampman 4.00 10.00
BA Brendon Ayanbadejo 2.50 6.00
BM Brian Moorman 2.50 6.00
BR Ben Roethlisberger 4.00 10.00
BW Brian Waters 2.50 6.00
CB Champ Bailey 3.00 8.00
CB2 Champ Bailey 3.00 8.00
CH Casey Hampton 2.50 6.00
CJ Chris Johnson 6.00 15.00
CP Chad Pennington 3.00 8.00
CS Chris Samuels 2.50 6.00
CS2 Chris Samuels 2.50 6.00
DBO Dwayne Bowe 3.00 8.00
DB Derrick Burgess 2.50 6.00
DJ Dwayne Jarrett 3.00 8.00
DK Dustin Keller 4.00 10.00
DM Derrick Mason 3.00 8.00
DT Devin Thomas 2.00 5.00
DW DeMarcus Ware 3.00 8.00
ED Early Doucet 2.00 5.00
FA Flozell Adams 2.50 6.00
GO Greg Olsen 3.00 8.00
HM Hank Milligan 2.50 6.00
JB John Beck 2.50 6.00
JC Josh Cribbs 5.00 12.00
JD Jake Delhomme 3.00 8.00
JDB John David Booty 2.00 5.00
JL J.P. Losman 2.50 6.00
JN Jordy Nelson 3.00 8.00
JT Joe Thomas 3.00 8.00
JW Jamal Williams 2.50 6.00
JW2 Jason Witten 4.00 10.00
KC Kellen Clemens 3.00 8.00
KD Kris Dielman 2.50 6.00
KK Kevin Kolb 3.00 8.00
KS Kevin Smith 2.50 6.00
KV Kyle Vanden Bosch 2.50 6.00
KW Kevin Williams 2.50 6.00
LA Larry Allen 2.50 6.00
LB LeCharles Bentley 2.50 6.00
LBO Lorenzo Booker 2.50 6.00
LD Leonard Davis 2.50 6.00
LJ LaMont Jordan 3.00 8.00
LN Lorenzo Neal 2.50 6.00
LS Limas Sweed 2.50 6.00
LT Lofa Tatupu 3.00 8.00
MB Matt Birk 2.50 6.00
MH Matt Hasselbeck 3.00 8.00
MK Malcolm Kelly 2.00 5.00
ML Marshawn Lynch 3.00 8.00
MMA Mario Manningham 2.50 6.00
MM2 Marcus McNeill 2.50 6.00
MS Marcus Stroud 2.50 6.00
MW Mike Wahle 2.50 6.00
OP Orlando Pace 2.50 6.00
OU Osi Umenyiora 3.00 8.00
PWIL Patrick Willis 3.00 8.00
PWI Paul Williams 2.50 6.00
PW Pat Williams 2.50 6.00
RJ Rudi Johnson 3.00 8.00
RR Ray Rice 5.00 12.00
RW1 Roy Williams S wht 3.00 8.00
RW2 Roy Williams S PB 3.00 8.00
SM Shawne Merriman 3.00 8.00
SM2 Shawne Merriman PB 3.00 8.00
SS Steve Smith USC 3.00 8.00
SS Steve Slaton 2.50 6.00
TE Trent Edwards 2.50 6.00
TGI Ted Ginn 3.00 8.00
TGL Tarik Glenn 2.50 6.00
TG Tony Gonzalez in hat 3.00 8.00
TGO Tony Gonzalez in helmet 3.00 8.00
TH Tony Hunt 3.00 8.00
TP Troy Polamalu 6.00 15.00
TR Tony Romo 5.00 12.00
TS Terrell Suggs 2.50 6.00
TSM Troy Smith 3.00 8.00
VD Vernon Davis 3.00 8.00
WA Willie Anderson 2.50 6.00
WJ Walter Jones 2.50 6.00
WJ2 Walter Jones PB 2.50 6.00

2008 Topps Retro Rookies

STATED ODDS 1:4 RETAIL
*COLOR/50: 1X TO 2.5X BASIC INSERTS
COLOR/50 ODDS 1:835 RETAIL
*SEPIA/199: .6X TO 1.5X BASIC INSERTS
SEPIA/199 ODDS 1:210 RETAIL
1 Matt Ryan 4.00 10.00
2 Joe Flacco 3.00 8.00
3 Brian Brohm 1.00 2.50
4 Chad Henne 1.00 2.50
5 Darren McFadden 2.50 6.00
6 Jonathan Stewart 1.50 4.00
7 Felix Jones 1.50 4.00
8 Rashard Mendenhall 2.00 5.00
9 Chris Johnson 2.50 6.00
10 Ray Rice 2.00 5.00
11 Donnie Avery .75 2.00
12 Devin Thomas .75 2.00
13 DeSean Jackson 2.00 5.00
14 Malcolm Kelly .75 2.00
15 Limas Sweed 1.00 2.50

2008 Topps Rookie Premiere Autographs

RED INK TOO SCARCE TO PRICE
RPAAW Andre Woodson 15.00 40.00
RPABB Brian Brohm 15.00 40.00
RPACH Chad Henne 15.00 40.00
RPACJ Chris Johnson 40.00 100.00
RPADA Donnie Avery 12.00 30.00
RPADD Dennis Dixon 15.00 40.00
RPADJ DeSean Jackson 30.00 80.00
RPADJA Dexter Jackson 12.00 30.00
RPADK Dustin Keller 15.00 40.00
RPADM Darren McFadden 25.00 60.00
RPADT Devin Thomas 12.00 30.00
RPAEB Earl Bennett 15.00 40.00
RPAED Early Doucet 12.00 30.00
RPAER Eddie Royal 15.00 40.00
RPAFJ Felix Jones 25.00 60.00
RPAHD Harry Douglas 12.00 30.00
RPAJB John David Booty 12.00 30.00
RPAJC Jamaal Charles 25.00 60.00
RPAJF Joe Flacco 30.00 80.00
RPAJH James Hardy 12.00 30.00
RPAJL Jake Long 15.00 40.00
RPAJN Jordy Nelson 20.00 50.00
RPAJS Jonathan Stewart 25.00 60.00
RPAJSI Jerome Simpson 15.00 40.00
RPAKO Kevin O'Connell 12.00 30.00
RPAKS Kevin Smith 15.00 40.00
RPALS Limas Sweed 15.00 40.00
RPAMF Matt Forte 25.00 60.00
RPAMK Malcolm Kelly 12.00 30.00
RPAMM Mario Manningham 15.00 40.00
RPAMR Matt Ryan 40.00 100.00
RPARM Rashard Mendenhall 30.00 80.00
RPARR Ray Rice 30.00 80.00
RPASS Steve Slaton 15.00 40.00

2008 Topps Rookie Premiere Autographs Dual

RED INK TOO SCARCE TO PRICE
FR Joe Flacco 60.00 120.00
Ray Rice
MJ Darren McFadden 40.00 100.00
Felix Jones
RB Matt Ryan 75.00 150.00
Brian Brohm
RM Matt Ryan 75.00 150.00
Darren McFadden
SM Jonathan Stewart 30.00 80.00
Rashard Mendenhall

2008 Topps Rookie Premiere Autographs Quads

RED INK TOO SCARCE TO PRICE
JMTK DeSean Jackson 60.00 150.00
Mario Manningham
Devin Thomas
Malcolm Kelly
JRCS Chris Johnson 75.00 150.00
Ray Rice
Jamaal Charles
Steve Slaton
MSJM Darren McFadden 75.00 150.00
Jonathan Stewart
Felix Jones
Rashard Mendenhall
RFBH Matt Ryan 100.00 200.00
Joe Flacco
Brian Brohm
Chad Henne
RFMS Matt Ryan 100.00 200.00
Joe Flacco
Darren McFadden
Jonathan Stewart

2008 Topps Rookie Premiere Jersey

GROUP A ODDS 1:247 BOW.HOB
GROUP B ODDS 1:520 BOW.HOB
GROUP C ODDS 1:371 BOW.HOB
GROUP D ODDS 1:325 BOW.HOB
*CHR.PATCH/25: .8X TO 2X BASIC JSY
CHROME PATCH/25 ODDS 1:2320 BOW.CHR
RPRBB Brian Brohm A 3.00 8.00
RPRCH Chad Henne C 3.00 8.00
RPRDA Donnie Avery C 2.50 6.00
RPRDM Darren McFadden A 8.00 20.00
RPRFJ Felix Jones B 8.00 20.00
RPRJF Joe Flacco C 6.00 15.00
RPRJH James Hardy C 2.50 6.00
RPRJS Jonathan Stewart A 6.00 15.00
RPRLS Limas Sweed A 3.00 8.00
RPRMK Malcolm Kelly A 2.50 6.00
RPRMR Matt Ryan A 10.00 25.00
RPRRM Rashard Mendenhall A 6.00 15.00
RPRRR Ray Rice B 6.00 15.00

2008 Topps Rookie Premiere Jersey Autographs

JSY AU/25 ODDS 1:2950 BOW, 1:5000 BOW.CHR
UNPRICED REFRAC/10 ODDS 1:2750 BOW.CHR
RPARBB Brian Brohm
RPARCH Chad Henne 25.00 50.00
RPARDA Donnie Avery
RPARDM Darren McFadden 50.00 100.00
RPARFJ Felix Jones
RPARJF Joe Flacco 50.00 120.00
RPARJH James Hardy
RPARJS Jonathan Stewart
RPARLS Limas Sweed
RPARMK Malcolm Kelly
RPARMR Matt Ryan 125.00 225.00
RPARRM Rashard Mendenhall 30.00 60.00
RPARRR Ray Rice 40.00 80.00

2008 Topps Signature Series

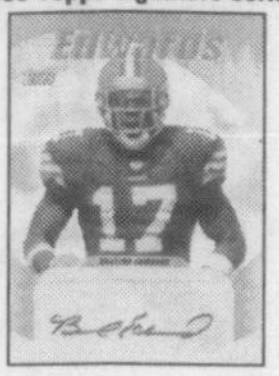

AUTO/50 ODDS 1:60,622 TOPPS
SSAP Adrian Peterson 100.00 200.00
SSBB Brian Brohm
SSBE Braylon Edwards 40.00 80.00
SSBS Bart Starr 100.00 175.00
SSDA Derek Anderson 30.00 60.00
SSDB Dwayne Bowe 30.00 60.00
SSDBR Drew Brees 40.00 80.00
SSDM Dan Marino 90.00 150.00
SSDMC Darren McFadden
SSEM Eli Manning 60.00 120.00
SSES Emmitt Smith 90.00 150.00
SSJB Jim Brown 60.00 120.00
SSJM Joe Montana 90.00 150.00
SSJR Jerry Rice 90.00 150.00
SSLT LaDainian Tomlinson 50.00 100.00
SSML Marshawn Lynch 40.00 80.00
SSMR Matt Ryan 100.00 175.00
SSPM Peyton Manning 90.00 150.00
SSRW Reggie Wayne 40.00 80.00
SSSJ Steven Jackson
SSTD Tony Dorsett 50.00 100.00
SSTT Thurman Thomas 40.00 80.00
SSTY Y.A. Tittle 40.00 80.00
SSVY Vince Young 40.00 80.00
SSWP Willie Parker 50.00 100.00

2008 Topps Stat Breakers Super Bowl Footballs

SB FB/40 ODDS 1:5400
SBAB Ahmad Bradshaw UER 20.00 40.00
(reads Game Worn Jersey on front)
SBEM Eli Manning UER 40.00 100.00
(reads Game Worn Jersey on front)
SBJT Justin Tuck UER 25.00 50.00
(reads Game Worn Jersey on front)
SBPB Plaxico Burress UER 25.00 50.00
(reads Game Worn Jersey on front)
SBTB Tom Brady UER 40.00 80.00
(reads Game Worn Jersey on front)
SBWW Wes Welker UER 30.00 60.00
(reads Game Worn Jersey on front)

2008 Topps Super Bowl XLII Card Show

COMPLETE SET (16) 12.50 25.00
MAROON BORDER PRINT RUN 1000
*BLACK BORDER/199: .8X TO 2X
1 Tom Brady 1.00 2.50
2 Brett Favre 1.50 4.00
3 Tony Romo .75 2.00
4 Peyton Manning 1.00 2.50
5 Vince Young .50 1.25
6 Willie Parker .50 1.25
7 Larry Fitzgerald .60 1.50
8 Willis McGahee .50 1.25
9 Frank Gore .50 1.25
10 Adrian Peterson 1.00 2.50
11 LaDainian Tomlinson .60 1.50
12 Randy Moss .60 1.50
13 Chad Johnson .50 1.25
14 Plaxico Burress .50 1.25
15 Calvin Johnson .60 1.50
16 Dwayne Bowe .50 1.25

2008 Topps Super Bowl XLII Card Show Promos

COMPLETE SET (6) 5.00 10.00
MAROON BORDER PRINT RUN 1000
*BLACK BORDER/199: .8X TO 2X
1 Tom Brady 1.00 2.50
2 Peyton Manning 1.00 2.50
3 Adrian Peterson 1.00 2.50
4 LaDainian Tomlinson .60 1.50
5 Tony Romo .75 2.00
6 Randy Moss .60 1.50

2008 Topps Tom Brady Tribute

COMPLETE SET (16) 10.00 25.00
COMMON CARD (TB1-TB16) .75 2.00
RANDOM INSERTS IN TARGET PACKS

2008 Topps Topps Chrome Gold Refractor Inserts

34 Brett Favre 6.00 15.00
298 Adrian Peterson 2.00 5.00
346 Darren McFadden 4.00 10.00

2008 Topps Turn Back the Clock

PACK P ODDS 1:9 HOB/RET
P ISSUED IN PACKS, S ISSUED AT SHOPS
1 Matt Ryan S 1.25 3.00
2 Rashard Mendenhall S .60 1.50
3 Eli Manning S .50 1.25
4 Tony Romo S .60 1.50
5 Eric Dickerson S .50 1.25
6 Felix Jones S .50 1.25
7 Malcolm Kelly P .40 1.00
8 Brian Westbrook S .40 1.00
9 Tom Brady P 1.25 3.00
10 Barry Sanders S 1.00 2.50
11 Dan Marino P 2.00 5.00
12 Brian Brohm S .30 .75
13 Darren McFadden P 1.25 3.00
14 Ben Roethlisberger S .50 1.25
15 Adrian Peterson P 1.25 3.00
16 Tony Dorsett S .60 1.50
17 Gale Sayers P 1.25 3.00
18 Jonathan Stewart S .50 1.25
19 Joe Flacco P 1.50 4.00
24 DeSean Jackson S .60 1.50
21 Randy Moss P .75 2.00
22 John Elway S 1.00 2.50
23 Terry Bradshaw P 1.50 4.00
20 LaDainian Tomlinson S .50 1.25
25 Ray Rice P 1.00 2.50
26 Peyton Manning S .75 2.00
27 Willie Parker P .60 1.50
28 Troy Aikman S .75 2.00
29 Vince Lombardi P 1.50 4.00
30 Limas Sweed S .30 .75
31 Drew Brees P .75 2.00
32 Jamal Lewis S .40 1.00
33 Brett Favre P 2.00 5.00
34 Emmitt Smith S 1.25 3.00
35 Carson Palmer P .75 2.00
36 Reggie Wayne S .40 1.00
37 Joe Namath P 1.25 3.00
38 Chad Johnson S .40 1.00
39 Larry Fitzgerald P .75 2.00
40 Terrell Owens P .75 2.00

2009 Topps

COMPLETE SET (440) 25.00 50.00
COMP.FACT.SET (445) 40.00 70.00
BASE SP ODDS 1:410 HOB
HOLMES RH ODDS 1:36
HOLMES RH AUTO ODDS 1:61,000
1 Hines Ward .20 .50
2 Ryan Torain .15 .40
3 Harry Douglas .15 .40
4 James Jones .15 .40
5 Willis McGahee .20 .50
6 Owen Daniels .15 .40
7 Peyton Hillis .25 .60
8 Hank Baskett .15 .40
9 Leonard Davis .15 .40
10 Peyton Manning .40 1.00
11 Shawne Merriman .20 .50
12 Laurence Maroney .20 .50
13 Chris Hope .15 .40
14 Joe Thomas .20 .50
15 Marshawn Lynch .20 .50
16 Kevin Williams .15 .40
17 London Fletcher .15 .40
18 Jason Campbell .15 .40
19 Antonio Bryant .15 .40
20 LaDainian Tomlinson .25 .60
21 Marc Bulger .20 .50
22 Vernon Davis .20 .50
23 Justin Tuck .20 .50
24 Deuce McAllister .20 .50
25 T.J. Houshmandzadeh .20 .50
26 Bernard Berrian .20 .50
27 Ryan Grant .20 .50
28 Tashard Choice .15 .40
29 Michael Jenkins .15 .40
30 Brian Dawkins .20 .50
31 Michael Turner .20 .50
32 Anquan Boldin .20 .50
33 Justin Gage .15 .40
34 Michael Bush .20 .50
35 Braylon Edwards .20 .50
36 Rashard Mendenhall .20 .50
37 Leon Washington .20 .50
38 Ricky Williams .20 .50
39 Rashean Mathis .15 .40
40 Ray Lewis .25 .60
41 Josh Cribbs .25 .60
42 James Hardy .20 .50
43 Joe Flacco .25 .60
44 Terrell Suggs .15 .40
45 Jay Cutler .25 .60
46 Glenn Holt .15 .40
47 D.J. Williams .15 .40
48 Andre Davis .15 .40
49 Dwayne Bowe .20 .50
50 DeAngelo Williams .25 .60
51 Wes Welker .25 .60
52 Willie Parker .15 .40
53 Dominique Rodgers-Cromartie .15 .40
54A Tony Romo .40 1.00
54B Tony Romo SP 30.00 60.00
playing golf)
55 Steve Slaton .20 .50
56 Jason Witten .25 .60
57 Terence Newman .15 .40
58 Jeff Garcia .20 .50
59 Barrett Ruud .15 .40
60 Andre Johnson .20 .50
61 Jordy Nelson .25 .60
62 Davone Bess .15 .40
63 Jacob Hester .15 .40
64 Jason Avant .15 .40
65 Joseph Addai .25 .60
66 Dennis Northcutt .15 .40
67 Maurice Morris .15 .40
68 Shaun Hill .15 .40
69 Dustin Keller .15 .40
70 Antonio Gates .20 .50
71 BenJarvus Green-Ellis RC 1.25 3.00
72 Brent Celek .20 .50
73 Ray Rice .25 .60
74 Vince Young .20 .50
75 Maurice Jones-Drew .20 .50
76 Devery Henderson .15 .40
77 Domenik Hixon .15 .40
78 Mike Walker .20 .50
79 Miles Austin .40 1.00
80 DeMarcus Ware .20 .50
81 Jordan Gross .15 .40
82 Chris Samuels .15 .40
83 Jay Ratliff .25 .60
84 Pat Williams .15 .40
85 Tony Gonzalez .20 .50
86 Andre Gurode .15 .40
87 Nick Mangold .15 .40
88 Bobby Engram .15 .40
89 Osi Umenyiora .20 .50
90 Brian Westbrook .20 .50
91 Jason Peters .15 .40
92 Shaun Rogers .15 .40
93 Kris Jenkins .15 .40
94 Kevin Mawae .15 .40
95 Ronnie Brown .20 .50
96 Joey Galloway .20 .50
97 Chris Snee .15 .40
98 Nick Collins .15 .40
99 Adrian Wilson .15 .40
100 Reggie Wayne .20 .50
101 Kellen Clemens .15 .40
102 LaRon Landry .15 .40
103 Walter Jones .15 .40
104 Josh Morgan .15 .40
105 Joey Porter .20 .50
106 Martellus Bennett .15 .40
107 Kirk Morrison .15 .40
108 Bradie James .15 .40
109 Le'Ron McClain .20 .50
110A Adrian Peterson .40 1.00
110B Adrian Peterson SP 25.00 50.00
(wearing a red shirt)
111 Trent Edwards .15 .40
112 Carson Palmer .25 .60
113 Jamal Lewis .20 .50
114 Champ Bailey .20 .50
115A Tom Brady .40 1.00
115B Tom Brady SP 50.00 100.00
(No helmet in photo)
116 Dominic Rhodes .15 .40
117 David Garrard .20 .50
118 Jamaal Charles .25 .60
119 Fred Taylor .20 .50
120 Matt Leinart .20 .50
121 Ted Ginn .20 .50
122 Sammy Morris .15 .40
123 Jerricho Cotchery .20 .50
124 JaMarcus Russell .15 .40
125 Thomas Jones .20 .50
126 Mewelde Moore .15 .40
127 Philip Rivers .25 .60
128 Antonio Cromartie .15 .40
129 Bo Scaife .15 .40
130 Jonathan Vilma .15 .40
131 Kurt Warner .25 .60
132 Steve Breaston .20 .50
133 Roddy White .20 .50
134 Jake Delhomme .20 .50
135 Darren McFadden .25 .60
136 Muhsin Muhammad .20 .50
137 Greg Olsen .15 .40
138 Felix Jones .25 .60
139 Ernie Sims .15 .40
140 Ed Reed .20 .50
141 Aaron Rodgers .50 1.25
142 Donald Lee .15 .40
143 Visanthe Shiancoe .20 .50
144 Drew Brees .25 .60
145A Ben Roethlisberger .25 .60
145B Ben Roethlisberger SP 30.00 60.00
(Holding Super Bowl Trophy)
146 Jason David .15 .40
147 Samari Rolle .15 .40
148 Brandon Jacobs .20 .50
149 DeSean Jackson .20 .50
150 Brady Quinn .20 .50
151 Isaac Bruce .20 .50
152 Matt Hasselbeck .20 .50
153 Lofa Tatupu .20 .50
154 Oshiomogho Atogwe .15 .40
155 Troy Polamalu .25 .60
156 Marvin Harrison .25 .60
157 Roscoe Parrish .15 .40
158 Paul Posluszny .20 .50
159 Eli Manning .25 .60
160 Randy Moss .25 .60
161 Earnest Graham .15 .40
162 Derrick Brooks .20 .50
163 Chris Cooley .20 .50
164 Antwaan Randle El .15 .40
165 Santonio Holmes .20 .50
166 Ronde Barber .15 .40
167 Donnie Avery .20 .50
168 Nate Clements .15 .40
169 Kevin Boss .20 .50
170 Jon Beason .15 .40
171 Jeremy Shockey .15 .40
172 Antoine Winfield .15 .40
173 Charles Woodson .25 .60
174 Terrell Owens .25 .60
175 Chris Johnson .25 .60
176 Charles Tillman .15 .40
177 Julius Peppers .20 .50
178 John Abraham .15 .40
179 Karlos Dansby .15 .40
180 Steve Smith USC .20 .50
181 Edgerrin James .20 .50
182 Cortland Finnegan .15 .40
183 Keith Bulluck .15 .40
184 Stephen Cooper RC .20 .50
185 LenDale White .20 .50
186 Vincent Jackson .20 .50
187 LaMarr Woodley .15 .40
188 Nnamdi Asomugha .20 .50
189 Calvin Pace .15 .40
190 Kellen Winslow Jr. .20 .50
191 Brandon Meriweather .15 .40
192 Matt Cassel .20 .50
193 Greg Camarillo .20 .50
194 Jarrad Page .15 .40
195 Tim Hightower .15 .40
196 Larry Johnson .20 .50
197 Matt Jones .20 .50
198 Bob Sanders .20 .50
199 Dwight Freeney .20 .50
200 Brandon Marshall .20 .50
201 Mario Williams .20 .50
202 Tony Scheffler .15 .40
203 D'Qwell Jackson .15 .40
204 Keith Rivers .15 .40
205 Larry Fitzgerald .25 .60
206 Chad Ochocinco .20 .50
207 Fred Jackson .25 .60
208 Bart Scott .15 .40
209 Todd Heap .15 .40
210 Clinton Portis .20 .50
211 Santana Moss .20 .50
212 Aqib Talib .15 .40
213 Warrick Dunn .20 .50
214 Torry Holt .20 .50
215 Matt Ryan .25 .60
216 Julius Jones .15 .40
217 Patrick Willis .20 .50
218 Correll Buckhalter .15 .40
219 Derrick Ward .15 .40
220 Steven Jackson .20 .50
221 Pierre Thomas .20 .50
222 Tarvaris Jackson .20 .50
223 Donald Driver .20 .50
224 Devin Hester .25 .60
225 Jonathan Stewart .20 .50
226 Steve Smith .20 .50
227 Jerious Norwood .20 .50
228 Albert Haynesworth .15 .40
229 Darren Sproles .20 .50
230 Frank Gore .20 .50
231 James Harrison .25 .60

232 Zach Miller	.15	.40
233 Darrelle Revis	.20	.50
234 Richard Seymour	.15	.40
235 Matt Forte	.25	.60
236 Ellis Hobbs	.15	.40
237 Anthony Fasano	.15	.40
238 Chad Pennington	.20	.50
239 Tyler Thigpen	.15	.40
240 Donovan McNabb	.25	.60
241 Robert Mathis	.15	.40
242 Kevin Walter	.20	.50
243 Matt Schaub	.20	.50
244 Brandon McDonald	.15	.40
245 Marion Barber	.20	.50
246 Cedric Benson	.20	.50
247 Lee Evans	.20	.50
248 Derrick Mason	.20	.50
249 Eddie Royal	.20	.50
250 Reggie Bush	.25	.60
251 Dallas Clark	.20	.50
252 Anthony Gonzalez	.15	.40
253 Derrick Johnson	.15	.40
254 Jerod Mayo	.20	.50
255 Kevin Smith	.20	.50
256 Laveranues Coles	.15	.40
257 Gibril Wilson	.15	.40
258 Justin Fargas	.15	.40
259 Lance Briggs	.20	.50
260 Greg Jennings	.25	.60
261 Kyle Orton	.20	.50
262 Michael Griffin	.15	.40
263 Kerry Collins	.20	.50
264 Chris Chambers	.20	.50
265 Jared Allen	.25	.60
266 Heath Miller	.20	.50
267 James Farrior	.15	.40
268 John Carlson	.20	.50
269 J.T. O'Sullivan	.15	.40
270 Calvin Johnson	.25	.60
271 Asante Samuel	.15	.40
272 Ahmad Bradshaw	.20	.50
273 Trent Cole	.15	.40
274 Lance Moore	.20	.50
275 Marques Colston	.20	.50
276 Chester Taylor	.15	.40
277 Aaron Kampman	.20	.50
278 Derrick Harvey	.15	.40
279 Brian Urlacher	.25	.60
280 Roy Williams WR	.20	.50
281 Drew Brees LL	.20	.50
282 Kurt Warner LL	.20	.50
283 Jay Cutler LL	.20	.50
284 Adrian Peterson LL	.30	.75
285 Michael Turner LL	.15	.40
286 DeAngelo Williams LL	.20	.50
287 Andre Johnson LL	.15	.40
288 Larry Fitzgerald LL	.20	.50
289 Steve Smith LL	.15	.40
290 Drew Brees PB	.20	.50
291 Adrian Peterson PB	.30	.75
292 Larry Fitzgerald PB	.20	.50
293 Anquan Boldin PB	.15	.40
294 Steve Smith PB	.15	.40
295 Jason Witten PB	.20	.50
296 DeMarcus Ware PB	.15	.40
297 Jon Beason PB	.12	.30
298 James Harrison PB	.20	.50
299 Michael Turner PB	.15	.40
300 Peyton Manning PB	.30	.75
301 Eli Manning PB	.20	.50
302 Thomas Jones PB	.15	.40
303 Andre Johnson PB	.15	.40
304 Brandon Marshall PB	.15	.40
305 Reggie Wayne PB	.15	.40
306 Tony Gonzalez PB	.15	.40
307 Ray Lewis PB	.20	.50
308 Darrelle Revis PB	.15	.40
309 Joey Porter PB	.15	.40
310 Donovan McNabb PH	.20	.50
311 Joe Flacco PH	.20	.50
312 Larry Fitzgerald PH	.20	.50
313 Darren Sproles PH	.15	.40
314 Ed Reed PH	.15	.40
315 Kurt Warner PH	.20	.50
316 Willie Parker PH	.12	.30
317 Asante Samuel PH	.12	.30
318 Troy Polamalu PH	.20	.50
319 Larry Fitzgerald PH	.20	.50
320 Santonio Holmes PH	.15	.40
321 Peyton Manning MVP	.30	.75
322 James Harrison D-POY	.20	.50
323 Matt Ryan O-ROY	.20	.50
324 Jerod Mayo D-ROY	.15	.40
325 J.Stewart	.20	.50
Williams CC		
326 E.Reed	.20	.50
R.Lewis CC		
327 L.White	.20	.50
C.Johnson CC		
328 T.Jones	.15	.40
Washington CC		
329 Roeth	.20	.50
W.Parker CC		
330 DeAngelo Williams LL	.20	.50
331 Aaron Brown RC	.60	1.50
332 B.J. Raji RC	.60	1.50
333 Aaron Maybin RC	.50	1.25
334 Alphonso Smith RC	.50	1.25
335 Hakeem Nicks RC	1.00	2.50
336 Andre Smith RC	.50	1.25
337 Andy Levitre RC	.50	1.25
338 Asher Allen RC	.50	1.25
339 Austin Collie RC	.60	1.50
340A Aaron Curry RC	.60	1.50
340B Aaron Curry SP	15.00	30.00
(Football in hand)		
341 Brandon Gibson RC	.60	1.50
342 Michael Oher RC	1.00	2.50
343 Brandon Tate RC	.60	1.50
344 Brandon Underwood RC	.60	1.50
345 Javon Ringer RC	.60	1.50
346 Brian Hartline RC	.60	1.50
347 Brian Orakpo RC	.60	1.50
348 Mike Wallace RC	1.25	3.00
349 Brooks Foster RC	.40	1.00
350 Brian Cushing RC	.60	1.50
351 Chase Coffman RC	.50	1.25
352 Darius Butler RC	.60	1.50
353 Clay Matthews RC	1.50	4.00
354 Clint Sintim RC	.60	1.50
355 Kenny Britt RC	.75	2.00
356 Patrick Turner RC	.50	1.25
357 Courtney Greene RC	.40	1.00
358 Curtis Painter RC	.60	1.50
359 D.J. Moore RC	.50	1.25
360 Chris Wells RC	1.00	2.50
361A Darrius Heyward-Bey RC	.60	1.50
(Leaping one-handed grab)		
361B Darrius Heyward-Bey SP	15.00	40.00
Catching pose, Football in hands)		
361C Darrius Heyward-Bey RET	.40	1.00
(Running to camera's left)		
362 Demetrius Byrd RC	.50	1.25
363 Deon Butler RC	.50	1.25
364 Derrick Williams RC	.50	1.25
365 Pat White RC	.60	1.50
366 Duke Robinson RC	.40	1.00
367 Eben Britton RC	.50	1.25
368 Eugene Monroe RC	.40	1.00
369 Everette Brown RC	.50	1.25
370A Donald Brown RC	.60	1.50
370B Donald Brown SP	15.00	40.00
(No helmet in photo)		
370C Donald Brown RET	.40	1.00
(Helmet on, Running to camera's left)		
371 Gartrell Johnson RC	.40	1.00
372 Glen Coffee RC	.50	1.25
373 Andre Brown RC	.40	1.00
374 James Casey RC	.50	1.25
375A Percy Harvin RC	1.00	2.50
375B Percy Harvin SP	25.00	50.00
(No helmet in photo)		
375C Percy Harvin RET	.60	1.50
(Cutting to his left)		
376 Roy Miller RC	.50	1.25
377 Jamon Meredith RC	.50	1.25
378 Jared Cook RC	.60	1.50
379 Jarett Dillard RC	.60	1.50
380A Jeremy Maclin RC	1.00	2.50
380B Jeremy Maclin SP	25.00	50.00
(Football in hand)		
381 Jason Williams RC	.60	1.50
382 Javarris Williams RC	.50	1.25
383 Cedric Peerman RC	.50	1.25
384 Jason Smith RC	.50	1.25
385 Fili Moala RC	.50	1.25
386 Rey Maualuga RC	.60	1.50
387 Travis Beckum RC	.50	1.25
388 Juaquin Iglesias RC	.50	1.25
389 Connor Barwin RC	.60	1.50
390A Knowshon Moreno RC	.60	1.50
390B Knowshon Moreno SP	20.00	40.00
(Cutting pose)		
391 Kenny McKinley RC	.60	1.50
392 Kevin Ellison RC	.50	1.25
393 Larry English RC	.60	1.50
394 Marko Mitchell RC	.50	1.25
395 Louis Delmas RC	.60	1.50
396 Shonn Greene RC	1.00	2.50
397 Malcolm Jenkins RC	.60	1.50
398 Manuel Johnson RC	.50	1.25
399 Marcus Freeman RC	.60	1.50
400 LeSean McCoy RC	1.25	3.00
401 Zack Follett RC	.40	1.00
402 Shawn Nelson RC	.50	1.25
403 Rashad Jennings RC	.60	1.50
404 Michael Hamlin RC	.50	1.25
405 Michael Johnson RC	.40	1.00
406 Brandon Pettigrew RC	.60	1.50
407 Mike Goodson RC	.60	1.50
408 Mike Mickens RC	.50	1.25
409 Mike Teel RC	.60	1.50
410 Mike Thomas RC	.60	1.50
411 Brian Robiskie RC	.60	1.50
412 Mohamed Massaquoi RC	.50	1.25
413 Nate Davis RC	.50	1.25
414 Patrick Chung RC	.60	1.50
415 Cornelius Ingram RC	.40	1.00
416 James Davis RC	.60	1.50
417 Peria Jerry RC	.50	1.25
418 Phil Loadholt RC	.50	1.25
419 Ramses Barden RC	.40	1.00
420A Michael Crabtree RC	1.25	3.00
420B Michael Crabtree SP	25.00	50.00
(No helmet in photo)		
421 Rashad Johnson RC	.50	1.25
422 Johnny Knox RC	1.00	2.50
423 Rhett Bomar RC	.50	1.25
424 Robert Ayers RC	.60	1.50
425 James Laurinaitis RC	.60	1.50
426 Sammie Stroughter RC	.60	1.50
427 Scott McKillop RC	.50	1.25
428 Sean Smith RC	.60	1.50
429 Sen'Derrick Marks RC	.40	1.00
430A Matthew Stafford RC	3.00	8.00
430B Matthew Stafford SP	30.00	60.00
(No helmet in photo)		
430C Matthew Stafford RET	2.00	5.00
(Helmet on, Football at chest)		
431 Louis Murphy RC	.60	1.50
432 Stephen McGee RC	.60	1.50
433 Tiquan Underwood RC	.50	1.25
434 Tom Brandstater RC	.60	1.50
435A Josh Freeman RC	1.25	3.00
435B Josh Freeman SP	20.00	40.00
No helmet in photo)		
436 Tyson Jackson RC	.50	1.25
437 Victor Harris RC	.60	1.50
438 Vontae Davis RC	.60	1.50
439 William Moore RC	.60	1.50
440A Mark Sanchez RC	2.00	5.00
no helmet in photo		
440B Mark Sanchez SP	25.00	50.00
(Helmet on, ball above shoulder)		
440C Mark Sanchez RET	1.25	3.00
(Helmet on, Football at chest)		
441 Barack Obama SP	30.00	80.00
RH43 Santonio Holmes RH	.60	1.50
RH43A Santonio Holmes RH AU	125.00	250.00

2009 Topps Black

*VETS 1-330: 10X TO 25X BASIC CARDS
*ROOKIES 331-440: 3X TO 8X BASIC CARDS
BLACK/54 ODDS 1:42 HOB

71 BenJarvus Green-Ellis	25.00	50.00
430 Matthew Stafford	50.00	100.00

2009 Topps Gold

*VETS 1-330: 3X TO 8X BASIC CARDS
*ROOKIES 331-440: 1X TO 2.5X BASIC CARDS
GOLD/2009 ODDS 1:3

2009 Topps Career Best Autographs

GROUP A ODDS 1:5700 HOB
GROUP B ODDS 1:1485 HOB
GROUP C ODDS 1:421 HOB

AB Ahmad Bradshaw A	5.00	12.00
AF Anthony Fasano C	4.00	10.00
AP Adrian Peterson A	75.00	150.00
BF Brett Favre A	150.00	250.00
BM Brandon Marshall A	5.00	12.00
CJ Chris Johnson C	6.00	15.00
CW Chris Wells A	20.00	40.00
DA Donnie Avery B	5.00	12.00
DB Donald Brown A	10.00	25.00
DB1 Drew Brees A	30.00	60.00
DH Devin Hester B	10.00	25.00
DJ DeSean Jackson B	5.00	12.00
DT Devin Thomas B	4.00	10.00
DW DeAngelo Williams A	15.00	40.00
EB Earl Bennett C	5.00	12.00
EM Eli Manning A	75.00	150.00
ER Eddie Royal B	5.00	12.00
HN Hakeem Nicks C	8.00	20.00
JA1 Joseph Addai A	6.00	15.00
JA2 Jason Avant B	6.00	15.00
JC Jay Cutler A	60.00	120.00
JF Joe Flacco A	25.00	50.00
JH Jacob Hester C	4.00	10.00
JH2 James Hardy B	5.00	12.00
JM Jeremy Maclin A	12.00	30.00
JM2 Josh Morgan B	4.00	10.00
JN Jordy Nelson C	6.00	15.00
JR Javon Ringer C	5.00	12.00
JS Jonathan Stewart A	15.00	40.00
JS2 Jerome Simpson B	4.00	10.00
KM Knowshon Moreno A	30.00	60.00
LM LeSean McCoy B	10.00	25.00
LT LaDainian Tomlinson A	40.00	80.00
MB Marion Barber A	12.00	30.00
MC Michael Crabtree A	75.00	150.00
MC1 Marques Colston A	10.00	25.00
MH Mike Hart C	5.00	12.00
MR Matt Ryan A	50.00	100.00
MS Mark Sanchez A	75.00	150.00
MS2 Matthew Stafford A	75.00	150.00
PC Patrick Crayton C	4.00	10.00
PH Percy Harvin C	15.00	40.00
PM Peyton Manning A	90.00	150.00
RR Ray Rice A	6.00	15.00
SG Shonn Greene C	10.00	25.00
SS Steve Slaton B	5.00	12.00
SS2 Steve Smith B	5.00	12.00
TC Tashard Choice C	3.00	8.00
TJ Tarvaris Jackson B	5.00	12.00

2009 Topps Career Best Dual Autographs

DUAL AUTO/25 ODDS 1:24,000 HOB

BM Tom Brady	250.00	400.00
Randy Moss		
BR Marion Barber	60.00	100.00
Tony Romo		
CM Michael Crabtree	75.00	150.00
Jeremy Maclin		
EM John Elway	175.00	300.00
Dan Marino		
HB Devin Hester	25.00	50.00
Earl Bennett		
JC Felix Jones	25.00	50.00
Tashard Choice		
JM Bo Jackson	90.00	150.00
Darren McFadden		
JW Chris Johnson	25.00	50.00
LenDale White		
MB Dan Marino	150.00	250.00
Drew Brees		
MM Peyton Manning	150.00	250.00
Eli Manning		
PT Adrian Peterson	125.00	250.00
LaDainian Tomlinson		
SS Matthew Stafford	175.00	300.00
Mark Sanchez		
SWH Steve Slaton	25.00	50.00
Pat White		
WJ Brian Westbrook	30.00	60.00
DeSean Jackson		
SW Jonathan Stewart	25.00	50.00
DeAngelo Williams		

2009 Topps Career Best Dual Jerseys

STATED ODDS 1:3000 HOB

BR1 Marion Barber	12.00	30.00
Tony Romo		
BR2 Drew Brees	10.00	25.00
Matt Ryan		
FB Larry Fitzgerald	8.00	20.00
Anquan Boldin		
HF Devin Hester	8.00	20.00
Matt Forte		
JA Steven Jackson		
Donnie Avery		
JS Andre Johnson	6.00	15.00
Steve Slaton		
JW Chris Johnson		
LenDale White		
MJ Donovan McNabb	8.00	20.00
DeSean Jackson		
MR Brandon Marshall		
Eddie Royal		
PT Adrian Peterson	12.00	30.00
LaDainian Tomlinson		
RH Ben Roethlisberger		
Santonio Holmes		
RJ Aaron Rodgers		
Greg Jennings		
RL Ed Reed	12.00	30.00
Ray Lewis		
WS DeAngelo Williams		
Jonathan Stewart		

2009 Topps Career Best Jerseys

GROUP A ODDS 1:137 HOB
GROUP B ODDS 1:97 HOB
*PLATINUM: .5X TO 1.2X BASIC JSY

AB1 Anquan Boldin A	3.00	8.00
AB2 Andre Brown B	2.00	5.00
AG Anthony Gonzalez A	2.50	6.00
BC Brian Cushing B	3.00	8.00
BG Brandon Gibson B	3.00	8.00
BM Brandon Marshall A	3.00	8.00
BP Brandon Pettigrew B	3.00	8.00
BR Brian Robiskie B	3.00	8.00
BU Brian Urlacher A	4.00	10.00
CJ Calvin Johnson A	4.00	10.00
CM Clay Matthews B	8.00	20.00
CP Cedric Peerman B	2.50	6.00
DA Donnie Avery A	3.00	8.00
DB Dwayne Bowe A	3.00	8.00
DK Dustin Keller A	2.50	6.00
DM Darren McFadden A	4.00	10.00
DW DeAngelo Williams A	4.00	10.00
ER Eddie Royal A	3.00	8.00
GJ Greg Jennings A	4.00	10.00
JC Jerricho Cotchery A	3.00	8.00
JD James Davis B	3.00	8.00
JF Joe Flacco A	4.00	10.00
JI Juaquin Iglesias B	4.00	10.00
LT LaDainian Tomlinson A	4.00	10.00
MF Matt Forte A	4.00	10.00
PW Pat White B	5.00	12.00
RB1 Ramses Barden B	2.00	5.00
RB2 Rhett Bomar B	2.50	6.00
RJ Rashad Jennings B	3.00	8.00
RL Ray Lewis A	5.00	12.00
RM Rey Maualuga B	4.00	10.00
RW Roddy White A	3.00	8.00
SJ Steven Jackson A	3.00	8.00
SM Shawne Merriman A	3.00	8.00
SS Steve Slaton A	3.00	8.00
WM William Moore B	3.00	8.00

2009 Topps Career Best Jerseys Autographs

JSY AUTO/50 ODDS 1:25,000 HOB

AP Adrian Peterson	100.00	200.00
CJ Chris Johnson		
DB Drew Brees	40.00	80.00
FG Frank Gore	15.00	40.00
LT LaDainian Tomlinson		
MR Matt Ryan	60.00	120.00
PM Peyton Manning	90.00	150.00
RW Reggie Wayne	15.00	40.00
SJ Steven Jackson	15.00	40.00
SS Steve Slaton		

2009 Topps Career Best Jumbo Jerseys

JUMBO SWATCH/20 ODDS 1:1425 HOB

AB Anquan Boldin	10.00	25.00
AB2 Andre Brown	10.00	25.00
AG Antonio Gates	12.00	30.00
AP Adrian Peterson	25.00	60.00
BC Brian Cushing	8.00	20.00
BG Brandon Gibson	8.00	20.00
BP Brandon Pettigrew	8.00	20.00
BR Brian Robiskie	8.00	20.00
CJ Chris Johnson	15.00	40.00
CJ2 Chad Ochocinco	12.00	30.00
CM Clay Matthews	20.00	50.00
CP Cedric Peerman	8.00	20.00
DA Donnie Avery	12.00	30.00
FG Frank Gore	12.00	30.00
JD James Davis	10.00	25.00
JI Juaquin Iglesias	6.00	15.00
LF Larry Fitzgerald	15.00	40.00
LT LaDainian Tomlinson	15.00	40.00
LW LenDale White	12.00	30.00
MB Marion Barber	12.00	30.00
MJD Maurice Jones-Drew	12.00	30.00
PM Peyton Manning	25.00	60.00
PW Pat White	8.00	20.00
RAB Reggie Bush	15.00	40.00
RB Rhett Bomar	6.00	15.00
RB1 Ramses Barden	5.00	12.00
RJ Rashad Jennings	10.00	25.00
RM Rey Maualuga	8.00	20.00
SJ Steven Jackson	12.00	30.00
SS Steve Slaton	12.00	30.00
TB Tom Brady	25.00	60.00
TG Ted Ginn	12.00	30.00
TH Todd Heap	10.00	25.00
WM William Moore	8.00	20.00

2009 Topps Cheerleaders

COMPLETE SET (15)	4.00	10.00
STATED ODDS 1:9 HOB		
C1 Tara	.40	1.00
C2 Amanda	.40	1.00
C3 Kelli	.40	1.00
C4 Emily C.	.40	1.00
C5 Kayla S.	.40	1.00
C6 Laurie	.40	1.00
C7 TaJonda	.40	1.00
C8 Amanda	.40	1.00
C9 Samantha	.40	1.00
C10 Amy	.40	1.00
C11 Fabiola	.40	1.00
C12 Johanna	.40	1.00
C13 Bibiana	.40	1.00
C14 Monica	.40	1.00
C15 Tiffany	.40	1.00

2009 Topps Chicle

COMPLETE SET (100)	50.00	80.00
STATED ODDS 1:6 HOB, 1:1 CEREAL		
1 Brian Westbrook	.75	2.00
2 Eli Manning	1.00	2.50
3 Thomas Jones	.75	2.00
4 Brandon Marshall	.75	2.00
5 Tony Gonzalez	.75	2.00
6 Jay Cutler	1.00	2.50
7 Darren McFadden	1.00	2.50
8 Steven Jackson	.75	2.00
9 Hines Ward	.75	2.00
10 Frank Gore	.75	2.00
11 Kurt Warner	1.00	2.50
12 Aaron Rodgers	2.00	5.00
13 Philip Rivers	1.00	2.50
14 Adrian Peterson	1.50	4.00
15 Clinton Portis	.75	2.00
16 Michael Turner	.75	2.00
17 DeAngelo Williams	1.00	2.50
18 Larry Fitzgerald	1.00	2.50
19 Steve Smith	.75	2.00
20 Andre Johnson	.75	2.00
21 Calvin Johnson	1.00	2.50
22 Roddy White	.75	2.00
23 Ed Reed	.75	2.00
24 Troy Polamalu	1.00	2.50
25 Willie Parker	.60	1.50
26 Steve Slaton	.75	2.00
27 Matt Forte	1.00	2.50
28 Chris Johnson	1.00	2.50
29 Ryan Grant	.75	2.00
30 Drew Brees	1.00	2.50
31 LaDainian Tomlinson	1.00	2.50
32 Brandon Jacobs	.75	2.00
33 Marshawn Lynch	.75	2.00
34 Kevin Smith	.75	2.00
35 Jamal Lewis	.75	2.00
36 Ronnie Brown	.75	2.00
37 Matthew Stafford	3.00	8.00
38 Donovan McNabb	1.00	2.50
39 DeSean Jackson	.75	2.00
40 Peyton Manning	1.50	4.00
41 Marion Barber	.75	2.00
42 Tony Romo	1.50	4.00
43 Jonathan Stewart	.75	2.00
44 Maurice Jones-Drew	.75	2.00
45 Warrick Dunn	.75	2.00
46 LenDale White	.75	2.00
47 Willis McGahee	.75	2.00
48 Joseph Addai	1.00	2.50
49 Reggie Bush	1.00	2.50
50 Tim Hightower	.60	1.50
51 Darren Sproles	.75	2.00
52 T.J. Houshmandzadeh	.75	2.00
53 Eddie Royal	.75	2.00
54 Anquan Boldin	.75	2.00
55 Dwayne Bowe	.75	2.00
56 Antonio Bryant	.60	1.50
57 Chris Cooley	.75	2.00
58 Reggie Wayne	.75	2.00
59 Jason Witten	1.00	2.50
60 Greg Jennings	1.00	2.50
61 Derrick Mason	.75	2.00
62 Santana Moss	.75	2.00
63 Randy Moss	1.00	2.50
64 Terrell Owens	1.00	2.50
65 Torry Holt	.75	2.00
66 Jerricho Cotchery	.75	2.00
67 Donald Driver	.75	2.00
68 Laveranues Coles	.60	1.50
69 Trent Edwards	.60	1.50
70 Antonio Gates	.75	2.00
71 Ted Ginn	.75	2.00
72 John Carlson	.75	2.00
73 Vincent Jackson	.75	2.00
74 Lee Evans	.75	2.00
75 Wes Welker	1.00	2.50
76 Ben Roethlisberger	1.00	2.50
77 LeSean McCoy	1.25	3.00
78 Braylon Edwards	.75	2.00
79 Kevin Walter	.75	2.00
80 Santonio Holmes	.75	2.00
81 Chris Wells	1.00	2.50
82 Donnie Avery	.75	2.00
83 Devin Hester	1.00	2.50
84 Anthony Gonzalez	.60	1.50
85 Matt Ryan	1.00	2.50
86 Joe Flacco	1.00	2.50
87 Michael Crabtree	1.25	3.00
88 Ray Lewis	1.00	2.50
89 Joey Porter	.75	2.00
90 Darrius Heyward-Bey	.60	1.50
91 DeMarcus Ware	.75	2.00
92 Hakeem Nicks	1.00	2.50
93 Jon Beason	.60	1.50
94 Knowshon Moreno	.60	1.50
95 Mark Sanchez	2.00	5.00
96 Aaron Curry	.60	1.50
97 Brian Orakpo	.60	1.50
98 Jeremy Maclin	1.00	2.50
99 Percy Harvin	1.00	2.50
100 Josh Freeman	1.25	3.00

2009 Topps Letter Patch Autographs

TOTAL PRINT RUNS 10-20 PER PLAYER
DHB Darrius Heyward-Bey/20*

2009 Topps Factory Set Rookie Bonus

COMPLETE SET (5)	6.00	15.00
1-5 INSERTS IN HOBBY FACTORY SETS		
1 Matthew Stafford HOB	2.00	5.00
2 Mark Sanchez HOB	1.25	3.00
3 Michael Crabtree HOB	.75	2.00
4 Knowshon Moreno HOB	.40	1.00
5 Chris Wells HOB	.60	1.50

2009 Topps Target Exclusive Factory Set Patches

TWO PER TARGET EXCLUSIVE FACTORY SET		
AP Adrian Peterson 07 Draft	2.50	6.00
KM Knowshon Moreno 09 Draft	.60	1.50
PM Peyton Manning 98 Draft	2.50	6.00
TB Tom Brady 00 Draft	2.50	6.00
MS1 Mark Sanchez 09 Draft	2.00	5.00
MS2 Matthew Stafford 09 Draft	3.00	8.00

2009 Topps Flashback

COMPLETE SET (15)	6.00	15.00
STATED ODDS 1:6 HOB		
FB1 Frank Tripucka	.50	1.25
FB2 Jack Kemp	.60	1.50
FB3 George Blanda	.60	1.50
FB4 Abner Haynes	.50	1.25
FB5 Billy Cannon	.50	1.25
FB6 Paul Lowe	.50	1.25
FB7 Don Maynard	.60	1.50
FB8 Bill Groman	.50	1.25
FB9 Jim Marshall	.50	1.25
FB10 Larry Grantham	.50	1.25
FB11 Tom Flores	.50	1.25
FB12 Babe Parilli	.50	1.25
FB13 Lionel Taylor	.50	1.25
FB14 Paul Maguire	.50	1.25
FB15 Wahoo McDaniel	.50	1.25

2009 Topps Letter Patch

GROUP A ODDS 1:3900 HOB
GROUP B ODDS 1:414 HOB
GROUP C ODDS 1:975 HOB

AC Andre Caldwell C	5.00	12.00
AP Adrian Peterson B	12.00	30.00
AT Aqib Talib B	5.00	12.00
BR Ben Roethlisberger B	8.00	20.00
CB Colt Brennan B	6.00	15.00
DD Dennis Dixon A	6.00	15.00
DM Dan Marino B	30.00	60.00
DT Devin Thomas B	5.00	12.00
FJ Felix Jones B	8.00	20.00
JE John Elway C	15.00	40.00
JF Joe Flacco B	8.00	20.00
JH Joe Montana C	20.00	50.00
JH Jacob Hester B	5.00	12.00
JN Jordy Nelson B	8.00	20.00
JS Jonathan Stewart A	6.00	15.00
LF Larry Fitzgerald B	10.00	25.00
MF Matt Forte A	10.00	25.00
MR Matt Ryan B	8.00	20.00
PM Peyton Manning B	15.00	40.00
SS Steve Slaton B	6.00	15.00
TB Tom Brady B	15.00	40.00
TD Tony Dorsett B	8.00	20.00
TR Tony Romo A	12.00	30.00
RM1 Rashard Mendenhall B	8.00	20.00
RM2 Randy Moss A	8.00	20.00

2009 Topps Postseason Patches

ONE PER RETAIL BLASTER BOX

PPR1 Terry Bradshaw SB XIV	12.00	30.00
PPR2 Terry Bradshaw SB XIII	12.00	30.00
PPR3 Terry Bradshaw SB X	12.00	30.00
PPR4 Terry Bradshaw SB IX	12.00	30.00
PPR5 Tony Dorsett SB XII	6.00	15.00
PPR6 Tony Dorsett SB XIII	6.00	15.00
PPR7 Tony Dorsett PB 1981	6.00	15.00
PPR8 Tony Dorsett PB 1983	6.00	15.00
PPR9 Joe Montana SB XXIV	15.00	40.00
PPR10 Joe Montana SB XXIII	15.00	40.00
PPR11 Joe Montana SB XIX	15.00	40.00
PPR12 Joe Montana SB XVI	15.00	40.00
PPR13 Eric Dickerson PB 1983	6.00	15.00
PPR14 Eric Dickerson PB 1984	6.00	15.00
PPR15 Eric Dickerson PB 1986	6.00	15.00
PPR16 Eric Dickerson PB 1988	6.00	15.00
PPR17 Earl Campbell PB 1980	8.00	20.00
PPR18 Earl Campbell PB 1981	8.00	20.00
PPR19 Earl Campbell PB 1983	8.00	20.00
PPR20 John Elway SB XXXIII	12.00	30.00
PPR21 John Elway SB XXXII	12.00	30.00
PPR22 John Elway SB XXIV	12.00	30.00
PPR23 John Elway SB XXI	12.00	30.00
PPR24 Dan Marino PB 1984	15.00	40.00
PPR25 Dan Marino PB 1985	15.00	40.00
PPR26 Dan Marino PB 1986	15.00	40.00
PPR27 Dan Marino SB XIX	15.00	40.00
PPR28 Peyton Manning SB XLI	12.00	30.00
PPR29 Peyton Manning PB 2005	12.00	30.00
PPR30 Peyton Manning PB 2007	12.00	30.00
PPR31 Tom Brady SB XXXVI	12.00	30.00
PPR32 Tom Brady SB XXXVIII	12.00	30.00
PPR33 Tom Brady SB XXXIX	12.00	30.00
PPR34 Eli Manning SB XLII	8.00	20.00
PPR35 Ray Lewis SB XXXV	8.00	20.00
PPR36 Ben Roethlisberger SB XL	8.00	20.00
PPR37 Ben Roethlisberger SB XLIII	8.00	20.00
PPR38 Larry Fitzgerald PB 2009	8.00	20.00
PPR39 Adrian Peterson PB 2008	12.00	30.00
PPR40 Randy Moss PB 2007	8.00	20.00
PPR41 LaDainian Tomlinson PB 2006	8.00	20.00
PPR42 LaDainian Tomlinson PB 2007	8.00	20.00
PPR43 Kurt Warner SB XXXV	8.00	20.00
PPR44 Hines Ward SB XL	6.00	15.00
PPR45 Drew Brees	8.00	20.00
PPR46 Chris Wells	4.00	10.00
PPR47 Percy Harvin	4.00	10.00
PPR48 Jeremy Maclin	4.00	10.00
PPR49 Matthew Stafford	12.00	30.00
PPR50 Mark Sanchez	8.00	20.00

2009 Topps Rookie Premiere Autographs

RED INK TOO SCARCE TO PRICE		
AB Andre Brown	5.00	12.00
AC Aaron Curry	8.00	20.00
BP Brandon Pettigrew	8.00	20.00
BR Brian Robiskie	8.00	20.00
CW Chris Wells	10.00	25.00
DB Deon Butler	6.00	15.00
DBR Donald Brown	8.00	20.00
DH Darrius Heyward-Bey	8.00	20.00
DW Derrick Williams	6.00	15.00
GC Glen Coffee	6.00	15.00
HN Hakeem Nicks	12.00	30.00
JF Josh Freeman	15.00	40.00
JI Juaquin Iglesias	6.00	15.00
JM Jeremy Maclin	12.00	30.00
JR Javon Ringer	8.00	20.00
JS Jason Smith	6.00	15.00
KB Kenny Britt	10.00	25.00
KM Knowshon Moreno	8.00	20.00
LM LeSean McCoy	15.00	40.00
MC Michael Crabtree	15.00	40.00
MM Mohamed Massaquoi	6.00	15.00
MS Mark Sanchez	25.00	60.00
MST Matthew Stafford	40.00	100.00
MT Mike Thomas	8.00	20.00
MW Mike Wallace	15.00	40.00
ND Nate Davis	6.00	15.00
PH Percy Harvin	12.00	30.00
PT Patrick Turner	6.00	15.00
PW Pat White	8.00	20.00
RB Ramses Barden	5.00	12.00
RMB Rhett Bomar	6.00	15.00
SG Shonn Greene	12.00	30.00
SM Stephen McGee	8.00	20.00
TJ Tyson Jackson	6.00	15.00

2009 Topps Rookie Premiere Autographs Dual

RED INK TOO SCARCE TO PRICE		
BM Donald Brown red	30.00	80.00
LeSean McCoy blue		
CH Michael Crabtree	50.00	120.00
Darrius Heyward-Bey		
MH Jeremy Maclin	75.00	150.00
Percy Harvin		
MW Knowshon Moreno	40.00	100.00
Chris Wells		
SS Matthew Stafford	100.00	200.00
Mark Sanchez		

2009 Topps Rookie Premiere Autographs Quads

RED INK TOO SCARCE TO PRICE		
BWGM Donald Brown	75.00	150.00
Chris Wells		
Shonn Greene		
LeSean McCoy		
CHMH Michael Crabtree	125.00	250.00
Darrius Heyward-Bey		
Jeremy Maclin		
Percy Harvin		
MWBM Knowshon Moreno	100.00	200.00
Chris Wells		
Donald Brown		
LeSean McCoy		
SSCM Matthew Stafford	150.00	300.00
Mark Sanchez		
Michael Crabtree		
Jeremy Maclin		
SSFW Mark Sanchez	150.00	300.00
Matthew Stafford		
Josh Freeman		
Pat White		

2009 Topps Target Exclusive Allen and Ginter

STATED ODDS 1:4 TARGET PACKS		
AG1 Earl Campbell	6.00	15.00
AG2 Matthew Stafford SP	20.00	40.00
AG3 Peyton Manning	8.00	20.00
AG4 Chris Johnson	5.00	12.00
AG5 John Elway DP	10.00	25.00
AG6 Mark Sanchez DP	8.00	20.00
AG7 Adrian Peterson	8.00	20.00
AG8 Matt Ryan DP	5.00	12.00
AG9 Ben Roethlisberger SP	12.00	30.00
AG10 Terry Bradshaw	6.00	15.00
AG11 Michael Crabtree SP	12.00	30.00
AG12 Bo Jackson	6.00	15.00
AG13 Gale Sayers	6.00	15.00
AG14 Chris Wells	3.00	8.00
AG15 Dan Marino	10.00	25.00

2009 Topps Topps Town Silver

COMPLETE SET (25)	4.00	10.00
ONE TOPPSTOWN PER PACK		
*GOLD: .8X TO 2X SILVER		
TTT1 Donovan McNabb	.30	.75
TTT2 Eli Manning	.30	.75
TTT3 Aaron Rodgers	.60	1.50
TTT4 Peyton Manning	.50	1.25
TTT5 Jay Cutler	.30	.75
TTT6 Joe Flacco	.30	.75
TTT7 Kurt Warner	.30	.75
TTT8 Philip Rivers	.30	.75
TTT9 Matt Ryan	.30	.75
TTT10 Tony Romo	.50	1.25
TTT11 Matt Hasselbeck	.25	.60
TTT12 Jason Campbell	.20	.50
TTT13 Trent Edwards	.20	.50
TTT14 Brady Quinn	.25	.60
TTT15 Matt Schaub	.25	.60
TTT16 Matt Cassel	.25	.60
TTT17 Tom Brady	.50	1.25
TTT18 Drew Brees	.30	.75
TTT19 Ben Roethlisberger	.30	.75
TTT20 Kerry Collins	.25	.60
TTT21 JaMarcus Russell	.20	.50
TTT22 Chad Pennington	.25	.60
TTT23 David Garrard	.25	.60
TTT24 Kyle Orton	.25	.60
TTT25 Carson Palmer	.30	.75

2009 Topps Wal-Mart Exclusive All Americans

STATED ODDS 1:4 WAL-MART PACKS		
AC Aaron Curry	1.00	2.50
AM Aaron Maybin	.75	2.00
BO Brian Orakpo	1.00	2.50
CW Chris Wells	1.50	4.00
DB Donald Brown	1.00	2.50
DW Derrick Williams	.75	2.00
JM Jeremy Maclin	1.50	4.00
JR Javon Ringer	1.00	2.50
JS Jason Smith	.75	2.00
KB Kenny Britt	1.25	3.00
KM Knowshon Moreno	1.00	2.50
MC Michael Crabtree	2.00	5.00
MS Matthew Stafford	5.00	12.00
PH Percy Harvin	1.50	4.00
RM Rey Maualuga	1.00	2.50

2009 Topps Wal-Mart Exclusive Factory Set Gold Refractors

W1 Peyton Manning	2.00	5.00
W2 Tom Brady	2.00	5.00

2010 Topps

COMPLETE SET (440)	25.00	50.00
COMP.FACT.SET (445)	30.00	60.00
COMP.SUPER BOWL (445)	50.00	80.00
ONE ROOKIE CARD PER PACK		
DREW BREES RH ODDS 1:36		
1 Peyton Manning	.40	1.00
2 Kareem Jackson RC	.50	1.25
3 Malcolm Kelly	.15	.40
4 Tim Hightower v	.15	.40
5 Derrick Ward	.15	.40
6 Marques Colston	.20	.50
7 Heath Miller	.20	.50
8 Mike Wallace	.20	.50
9 Carlos Dunlap RC	.50	1.25
10 Adrian Peterson	.40	1.00
11 DeMarcus Ware	.20	.50
12 Jairus Byrd	.20	.50
13 George Wilson	.15	.40
14 Kevin Smith	.20	.50
15 Arizona Cardinals Team	.20	.50
Tim Hightower		
Larry Fitzgerald		
16 Atlanta Falcons Team	.20	.50
Matt Ryan		
17 Jeremy Shockey	.20	.50
18 Jay Ratliff AP	.20	.50
19 Rennie Curran RC	.40	1.00
20 Randy Moss	.25	.60
21 Jermichael Finley	.20	.50
22 Matt Ryan	.25	.60
23 Jason Pierre-Paul RC	.75	2.00
24 Classic Matchups	.20	.50
Darrelle Revis vs. Randy Moss		
25 Ray Lewis AP	.25	.60
26 Will Smith	.15	.40
27 Bryan Bulaga RC	.50	1.25
28 Sergio Kindle RC	.50	1.25
29 Michael Turner	.15	.40
30 Tom Brady	.40	1.00
31 Dwayne Bowe	.20	.50
32 Amari Spievey RC	.50	1.25
33 Koa Misi RC	.50	1.25
34 Louis Murphy	.20	.50
35 Kansas City Chiefs Team	.15	.40
Matt Cassel		
Jamaal Charles		
36 Asante Samuel	.15	.40
37 DeMeco Ryans	.15	.40
38 Anthony Gonzalez	.15	.40
39 Mario Manningham	.20	.50
40 Chris Johnson	.25	.60
41 Charles Woodson AP	.25	.60
42 Roddy White	.20	.50
43 Nate Burleson	.15	.40
44A Mike Williams RC	.75	2.00
No helmet pose		
44B Mike Williams SP	10.00	25.00
Wearing a helmet		
45 Steve Smith	.20	.50
46 Major Wright RC	.50	1.25
47 Jacoby Jones	.15	.40
48 Nick Collins	.15	.40
49 Chad Greenway	.15	.40
50 Andre Johnson	.20	.50
51 Bob Sanders	.20	.50
52 Akwasi Owusu-Ansah RC	.50	1.25
53 Knowshon Moreno	.20	.50
54 Darrius Heyward-Bey	.20	.50

55 Jason Avant .15 .40
56 Tampa Bay Buccaneers Team .15 .40
Josh Johnson
Kellen Winslow Jr.
57 Ed Dickson RC .50 1.25
58 Taylor Price RC .50 1.25
59 Osi Umenyiora .15 .40
60 Brett Favre 1.00 2.50
61 Antonio Bryant .15 .40
62 Jason Witten .25 .60
63 Richard Seymour .15 .40
64 Jermaine Gresham RC .60 1.50
65 Nick Barnett .15 .40
66 Chicago Bears Team .20 .50
Matt Forte
Jay Cutler
67 Joey Porter .15 .40
68 Tyvon Branch .15 .40
69 Brandon Spikes RC .50 1.25
70 Maurice Jones-Drew .20 .50
71 Sheldon Brown .15 .40
72 Damian Williams RC .50 1.25
73 Philadelphia Eagles Team .20 .50
DeSean Jackson
74 Ernie Sims .15 .40
75 Javier Arenas RC .50 1.25
76 Donald Driver .20 .50
77 DeMarcus Ware AP .20 .50
78 Andre Johnson AP .20 .50
79 Indianapolis Colts Team .30 .75
Peyton Manning
Joseph Addai
80 Larry Fitzgerald .25 .60
81 Jared Odrick RC .50 1.25
82 Dustin Keller .20 .50
83 Deon Butler .15 .40
84 Willie Parker .15 .40
85 Brandon Ghee RC .40 1.00
86 Yeremiah Bell .15 .40
87 Chris Cooley .20 .50
88 Brian Cushing .15 .40
89 Leon Washington .20 .50
90 Steven Jackson .20 .50
91 Sean Canfield RC .40 1.00
92 Brandon Flowers .15 .40
93 Russell Okung RC .50 1.25
94 T.J. Houshmandzadeh .20 .50
95 Devin Hester .25 .60
96 Aaron Hernandez RC .75 2.00
97 New York Jets Team .20 .50
Mark Sanchez
Shonn Greene
98 Lee Evans .20 .50
99 Tony Gonzalez .20 .50
100 Drew Brees .25 .60
101A Arrelious Benn RC .50 1.25
Heisman pose
101B Arrelious Benn SP 5.00 12.00
Catching pass
102 Louis Delmas .15 .40
103 Adrian Peterson AP .40 1.00
104 Brandon Jacobs .20 .50
105 Buffalo Bills Team .20 .50
Fred Jackson
Lee Evans
106 Troy Polamalu .25 .60
107 Sean Lee RC .50 1.25
108 Brandon Meriweather .15 .40
109A Jordan Shipley RC .50 1.25
Wearing a helmet
109B Jordan Shipley SP 5.00 12.00
No Helmet
110 Wes Welker .25 .60
111 Michael Jenkins .15 .40
112 Marshawn Lynch .20 .50
113 Clay Matthews .25 .60
114 Mike Bell .15 .40
115 Hakeem Nicks .20 .50
116 New York Giants Team .20 .50
Eli Manning
Brandon Jacobs
117 Detroit Lions Team .20 .50
Matt Stafford
Kevin Smith
118 Curtis Lofton .15 .40
119 Jacksonville Jaguars Team .15 .40
Maurice Jones-Drew
120 Thomas Jones .20 .50
121 Darryl Sharpton RC .30 .75
122 Marcus Easley RC .40 1.00
123 Taylor Mays RC .50 1.25
124 Jon Beason .15 .40
125 Jonathan Vilma .15 .40
126 Felix Jones .20 .50
127 Maurkice Pouncey RC .50 1.25
128 Thomas DeCoud .15 .40
129 Dwight Freeney AP .20 .50
130 Dwight Freeney .20 .50
131 Donald Brown .20 .50
132A Montario Hardesty RC .50 1.25
Rushing forward
132B Montario Hardesty SP 6.00 15.00
Leaping pose
133 Chris Johnson AP .25 .60
134 Visanthe Shiancoe .20 .50
135 Brandon Gibson .15 .40
136 Darren Sharper .20 .50
137 New Orleans Saints Team .20 .50
Drew Brees
Marques Colston
138 Linval Joseph RC .40 1.00
139 John Conner RC .50 1.25
140 Matt Schaub .20 .50
141 Greg Jennings .20 .50
142 David Reed RC .40 1.00
143 Nate Kaeding AP .15 .40
144 Peyton Manning MVP .40 1.00
145 Brandon Pettigrew .15 .40
146 Washington Redskins Team .15 .40
Clinton Portis
Santana Moss
147A Joe McKnight RC .50 1.25
One handed catch
147B Joe McKnight SP 8.00 20.00
Leaping pose
148A Rob Gronkowski RC 1.25 3.00
Cutting to his right
148B Rob Gronkowski SP 12.00 30.00
Leaping catch
149 Levi Brown RC .40 1.00
150 Aaron Rodgers .50 1.25
151 Patrick Willis .20 .50
152 Calvin Johnson .25 .60
153 Kenny Britt .20 .50
154 Roscoe Parrish .15 .40
155 Karlos Dansby .15 .40
156 Sean Weatherspoon RC .50 1.25
157 Earl Thomas RC .50 1.25
158 Rashad Jennings .15 .40
159 Jermaine Cunningham RC .50 1.25
160 Ray Lewis .25 .60
161 Mike Thomas .20 .50
162 Aqib Talib .15 .40
163 Ahmad Bradshaw .20 .50
164 Donnie Avery .20 .50
165 Cortland Finnegan .15 .40
166 Elvis Dumervil .15 .40
167A C.J. Spiller RC .75 2.00
Rushing pose
167B C.J. Spiller SP 15.00 40.00
One handed catch
168 Tony Pike RC .50 1.25
169 Joe Haden RC .50 1.25
170 LaDainian Tomlinson .25 .60
171 Carolina Panthers Team .15 .40
Jonathan Stewart
Steve Smith
172 Brandon Graham RC .40 1.00
173 Anthony Davis RC .40 1.00
174 Devin Aromashodu .15 .40
175 Steve Slaton .15 .40
176 Chris Wells .20 .50
177 Brian Urlacher .25 .60
178 Willis McGahee .20 .50
179 Ted Ginn .20 .50
180 Reggie Wayne .20 .50
181 Adrian Wilson .15 .40
182 Johnathan Joseph .15 .40
183 Matthew Stafford .25 .60
184 Cincinnati Bengals Team .15 .40
Carson Palmer
Chad Ochocinco
185 David Harris .15 .40
186 Vince Young .15 .40
187 Torry Holt .20 .50
188 Minnesota Vikings Team .50 1.25
Brett Favre
Adrian Peterson
189 Kevin Kolb .20 .50
190 Brandon Marshall .20 .50
191 Braylon Edwards .20 .50
192 Carlton Mitchell RC .40 1.00
193 Nnamdi Asomugha .20 .50
194A Colt McCoy RC 1.00 2.50
Wearing helmet, empty stands
194B Colt McCoy SP 15.00 40.00
No helmet, jump pass pose
194C Colt McCoy FS .75 2.00
Wearing helmet, crowded stands
Factory set only
195 Walter McFadden RC .40 1.00
196 Brian Robiskie .15 .40
197 Myron Rolle RC .30 .75
198 Shonn Greene .20 .50
199 Jamaal Charles .20 .50
200 Tony Romo .30 .75
201 Denver Broncos Team .15 .40
Kyle Orton
Knowshon Moreno
202 Santana Moss .20 .50
203A Toby Gerhart RC .50 1.25
Running pose
203B Toby Gerhart SP 5.00 12.00
Leaping pose
204 James Harrison .25 .60
205 Stephen Cooper .15 .40
206 Brian Cushing ROY .15 .40
207 Zach Miller .20 .50
208 Ed Reed .20 .50
209 Chaz Schilens .15 .40
210 Chad Ochocinco .20 .50
211 Paul Posluszny .20 .50
212 Cadillac Williams .20 .50
213 Joe Webb RC .50 1.25
214 Vince Wilfork .15 .40
215 Terrence Cody RC .40 1.00
216 San Diego Chargers Team .20 .50
Philip Rivers
Antonio Gates
Vincent Jackson
217 Darren Sharper AP .20 .50
218 Davone Bess .15 .40
219 Laurence Maroney .20 .50
220 Dallas Clark .20 .50
221A Jimmy Clausen RC .50 1.25
Pointing his finger
221B Jimmy Clausen SP 10.00 25.00
Passing with ball in hands
221C Jimmy Clausen FS .40 1.00
Passing pose, no football
Factory set only
221D Jimmy Clausen FS .40 1.00
Dropping back with football
Factory set only
222 Michael Crabtree .25 .60
223 DeSean Jackson .20 .50
224 Jerome Harrison .15 .40
225 Trent Williams RC .50 1.25
226 Classic Matchups .25 .60
Eli Manning vs. Tony Romo
227 Mike Iupati RC .50 1.25
228 Jerry Hughes RC .50 1.25
229 Adrian Wilson AP .15 .40
230 Ray Rice .20 .50
231 Julius Jones .15 .40
232 Brent Celek .20 .50
233 Darnell Dockett .15 .40
234 Greg Olsen .15 .40
235 John Skelton RC .50 1.25
236 Darren Sproles .20 .50
237 Donte Stallworth .15 .40
238 Todd Heap .15 .40
239 Percy Harvin .25 .60
240 Ryan Grant .20 .50
241 Devery Henderson .15 .40
242 Riley Cooper RC .50 1.25
243 Jared Allen .25 .60
244 Mike Kafka RC .50 1.25
245 T.J. Ward RC .50 1.25
246 LeSean McCoy .20 .50
247 Miami Dolphins Team .15 .40
Ronnie Brown
248A Dexter McCluster RC .50 1.25
Wearing a helmet
248B Dexter McCluster SP 5.00 12.00
No helmet
249 David Garrard .20 .50
250 Philip Rivers .25 .60
251 Sidney Rice .20 .50
252 LaMarr Woodley .15 .40
253 Malcom Floyd .20 .50
254A Emmanuel Sanders RC .50 1.25
Running pose
254B Emmanuel Sanders SP 5.00 12.00
Leaping pose
255 Ronnie Brown .20 .50
256 Trent Cole .15 .40
257 Frank Gore .20 .50
258 Eric Decker RC .60 1.50
259 Chester Taylor .15 .40
260 Cedric Benson .20 .50
261 Justin Tuck .20 .50
262 Arian Foster .20 .50
263 Dan Williams RC .40 1.00
264 Mardy Gilyard RC .50 1.25
265 Jimmy Graham RC 1.00 2.50
266 Jay Cutler .25 .60
267 Baltimore Ravens Team .20 .50
Ray Lewis
268A Jahvid Best RC .75 2.00
Leaping pose, empty stands
268B Jahvid Best SP 8.00 20.00
Both arms raised, crowded stands
268C Jahvid Best FS .60 1.50
One arm raised, field in background
Factory set only
269 Austin Collie .20 .50
270 Steve Smith USC .20 .50
271 Jacoby Ford RC .50 1.25
272 Jerod Mayo .20 .50
273 Antwaan Randle El .15 .40
274 Josh Morgan .20 .50
275A Demaryius Thomas RC .60 1.50
Wearing a helmet
275B Demaryius Thomas SP 6.00 15.00
No helmet
276 Nate Washington .15 .40
277 Rashard Mendenhall .20 .50
278 Chris Cook RC .50 1.25
279 Josh Freeman .25 .60
280 Ben Roethlisberger .25 .60
281 Classic Matchups .50 1.25
Favre vs. Packers
282 Aaron Curry .20 .50
283 James Laurinaitis .20 .50
284 Shaun Phillips .15 .40
285 Kevin Thomas RC .40 1.00
286 Kellen Winslow .20 .50
287 Ryan Clady AP .15 .40
288 Pierre Garcon .20 .50
289 Darrelle Revis .20 .50
290 Jonathan Stewart .20 .50
291 Leon Hall .15 .40
292 Matt Cassel .20 .50
293 Earl Bennett .20 .50
294 Everson Griffen RC .50 1.25
295 Devin McCourty RC .50 1.25
296 Anquan Boldin .20 .50
297 Jonathan Crompton RC .40 1.00
298 Zac Robinson RC .40 1.00
299 Barrett Ruud .15 .40
300A Sam Bradford RC 3.00 8.00
Passing pose, stands in background
300B Sam Bradford SP 40.00 80.00
Taking snap
300C Sam Bradford FS 4.00 10.00
Rolling out pose
Factory set only
300D Sam Bradford FS 4.00 10.00
Passing pose, field in background
Factory set only
301 Chad Henne .20 .50
302 Clinton Portis .20 .50
303 Matt Leinart .20 .50
304 Dominique Rodgers-Cromartie .15 .40
305 Bradie James .15 .40
306 Julius Peppers .20 .50
307 Anthony Dixon RC .50 1.25
308 Lance Moore .20 .50
309 Pierre Thomas .20 .50
310 Joseph Addai .20 .50
311 Santonio Holmes .20 .50
312 Jerricho Cotchery .20 .50
313 Rashean Mathis .15 .40
314 Anthony McCoy RC .40 1.00
315A Armanti Edwards RC *.50 1.25
Catching a pass
315B Armanti Edwards SP 5.00 12.00
Leaping pose
316 Marion Barber .20 .50
317 Dallas Clark AP .20 .50
318 Jason Campbell .20 .50
319 Jahri Evans AP .15 .40
320 Hines Ward .20 .50
321 Houston Texans Team .15 .40
Matt Schaub
Andre Johnson
322 Ricky Williams .20 .50
323 Early Doucet .15 .40
324 Joe Thomas AP .15 .40
325 Julian Edelman .15 .40
326 Jerome Murphy RC .40 1.00
327 London Fletcher .15 .40
328 Dezmon Briscoe RC .40 1.00
329 Vernon Davis .20 .50
330 Joe Flacco .25 .60
331 Steve Breaston .15 .40
332 San Francisco 49ers Team .15 .40
Frank Gore
Alex Smith
333 Percy Harvin ROY .25 .60
334 James Davis .15 .40
335 LaRon Landry .15 .40
336 Alex Smith QB .20 .50
337 David Hawthorne .25 .60
338 Michael Bush .15 .40
339 Bernard Scott .15 .40
340 Vincent Jackson .15 .40
341 Peyton Manning AP .40 1.00
342 Matt Hasselbeck .15 .40
343 Josh Cribbs AP .25 .60
344 Nate Allen RC .50 1.25
345 D.J. Williams .15 .40
346 Super Bowl Champions .25 .60
Drew Brees
Jeremy Shockey
347 New England Patriots Team .30 .75
Tom Brady
Randy Moss
348 James Starks RC .75 2.00.
349 Charles Brown RC .40 1.00
350 Donovan McNabb .25 .60
351 Chad Jones RC .50 1.25
352 Kyle Orton .20 .50
353 St. Louis Rams Team .15 .40
Steven Jackson
354 Laurent Robinson .15 .40
355 Tennessee Titans Team .20 .50
Vince Young
Chris Johnson
356A Brandon LaFell RC .50 1.25
Running pose
356B Brandon LaFell SP 5.00 12.00
Catching a pose
357 Elvis Dumervil AP .15 .40
358 Darren McFadden .20 .50
359 John Carlson .15 .40
360A Ndamukong Suh RC 1.00 2.50
Wearing a helmet
360B Ndamukong Suh SP 10.00 25.00
No Helmet
361 Jeremy Maclin .20 .50
362 Derrick Morgan RC .40 1.00
363 Patrick Robinson RC .50 1.25
364A Jonathan Dwyer RC .50 1.25
Head and shoulders pose
364B Jonathan Dwyer SP 5.00 12.00
Running pose
365 Larry Johnson .20 .50
366 Justin Forsett .20 .50
367 Morgan Burnett RC UER .50 1.25
(team name missing on front)
368 Roy Williams WR .20 .50
369 Classic Matchups .20 .50
Steelers vs. Ravens
Troy Polamalu
Joe Flacco
370 Carson Palmer .20 .50
371 Ed Wang RC .50 1.25
372 Nick Mangold AP .15 .40
373 Kevin Boss .20 .50
374 Reggie Brown .15 .40
375 Matt Forte .20 .50
376 Robert Meachem .20 .50
377 Cleveland Browns Team .20 .50
Josh Cribbs
Mohamed Massaquoi
378 Green Bay Packers Team .40 1.00
Aaron Rodgers
Greg Jennings
379 Kirk Morrison .15 .40
380 Antonio Gates .20 .50
381 Torell Troup RC .40 1.00
382 Kevin Williams AP .15 .40
383 Jabar Gaffney .15 .40
384 Jake Long .15 .40
385 Seattle Seahawks Team .12 .30
Matt Hasselbeck
Julius Jones
386 Jerious Norwood .15 .40
387 Tyson Alualu RC .40 1.00
388 Daryl Washington RC .40 1.00
389 Ben Watson .15 .40
390 Reggie Bush .25 .60
391 Mike Sims-Walker .20 .50
392 Chris Chambers .20 .50
393 Haloti Ngata .15 .40
394 DeAngelo Williams .20 .50
395A Eric Berry RC .50 1.25
Ball in the air
395B Eric Berry SP 5.00 12.00
Ball in hand
396 Fred Jackson .25 .60
397 Pat Angerer RC .50 1.25
398A Golden Tate RC .50 1.25
Wearing a helmet
398B Golden Tate SP 5.00 12.00
No helmet
399 Kyle Wilson RC .50 1.25
400 Eli Manning .25 .60
401 Darrelle Revis AP .20 .50
402 Stephen Tulloch .15 .40
403A Ryan Mathews RC 1.00 2.50
Running pose twisting
403B Ryan Mathews SP 20.00 40.00
Leaping catch
403C Ryan Mathews FS .75 2.00
Running pose pointing
Factory set only
404 Jared Allen AP .25 .60
405 Patrick Willis AP .20 .50
406 Johnny Knox .20 .50
407 Tashard Choice .15 .40
408 Steve Hutchinson AP .20 .50
409 Anthony Becht .15 .40
410 Gerald McCoy RC .50 1.25
411 Wes Welker AP .25 .60
412 2010 Rookie Premiere CL .60 1.50
413 Leonard Weaver AP .15 .40
414 Eddie Royal .15 .40
415 Lamarr Houston RC .50 1.25
416A Ben Tate RC .60 1.50
Wearing a helmet
416B Ben Tate SP 6.00 15.00
No helmet
417 Shane Lechler AP .15 .40
418 Brian Dawkins .20 .50
419 Dallas Cowboys Team .25 .60
Tony Romo
Marion Barber
420 Mark Sanchez .25 .60
421 James Jones .15 .40
422 Kevin Walter .20 .50
423 Andre Roberts RC .50 1.25
424 Charles Scott RC .40 1.00
425A Dez Bryant RC 1.50 4.00
Leaping catch
425B Dez Bryant SP 20.00 40.00
Spiking ball over goalposts
425C Dez Bryant FS 1.25 3.00
Running pose
Factory set only
426 Glen Coffee .20 .50
427 Mohamed Massaquoi .20 .50
428 Rolando McClain RC .50 1.25
429 Dan LeFevour RC .50 1.25
430 Terrell Owens .25 .60
431 Phillip Dillard RC .30 .75
432 Rodger Saffold RC .30 .75
433 Devin Thomas .15 .40
434 Derrick Mason .20 .50
435 Miles Austin .25 .60
436 Oshiomogho Atogwe .15 .40
437 Pittsburgh Steelers Team .20 .50
Defensive line; James Harrison
438 Bernard Berrian .15 .40
439 Oakland Raiders Team .15 .40
Chaz Schilens
440A Tim Tebow RC 5.00 10.00
Leaping pose)
440B Tim Tebow SP 50.00 100.00
Pointing his finger
440C Tim Tebow FS 6.00 12.00
Passing with football
Factory set only
440D Tim Tebow FS 6.00 12.00
Passing without football
Factory set only
RH44DB Drew Brees RH .60 1.50

2010 Topps Black

*VETS/55: 10X TO 25X BASIC CARDS
*ROOKIES/55: 5X TO 12X BASIC CARDS
BLACK/55 STATED ODDS 1:70 HOB

2010 Topps Blue

*VETS/349: 5X TO 12X BASIC CARDS
*ROOKIE/349: 2X TO 5X BASIC CARDS
WAL-MART BLUE PRINT RUN 349

2010 Topps Gold

*VETS: 3X TO 8X BASIC CARDS
*ROOKIES: 1.2X TO 3X BASIC CARDS
GOLD/2010 ODDS 1:5 HOB, 1:10 RET
60 Brett Favre 5.00 12.00

2010 Topps 1952 Bowman

COMPLETE SET (50) 15.00 40.00
STATED ODDS 1:3 HOB/RET
*TAN BACK/52: 3X TO 8X BASIC INSERTS
TAN BACK/52 ODDS 1:2700 HOB/RET
52B1 Peyton Manning 1.00 2.50
52B2 Elvis Dumervil .40 1.00
52B3 Ronnie Brown .50 1.25
52B4 Golden Tate .40 1.00
52B5 Chris Wells .50 1.25
52B6 Aaron Rodgers 1.25 3.00
52B7 Matt Schaub .50 1.25
52B8 Frank Gore .50 1.25
52B9 Tim Tebow 3.00 8.00
52B10 Chris Johnson .60 1.50
52B11 Brandon Marshall .50 1.25
52B12 Philip Rivers .60 1.50
52B13 DeAngelo Williams .50 1.25
52B14 Ryan Grant .50 1.25
52B15 Dez Bryant 1.25 3.00
52B16 Knowshon Moreno .50 1.25
52B17 Jahvid Best .60 1.50
52B18 Randy Moss .60 1.50
52B19 Dexter McCluster .40 1.00
52B20 Adrian Peterson 1.00 2.50
52B21 Maurice Jones-Drew .50 1.25
52B22 Colt McCoy .75 2.00
52B23 C.J. Spiller .60 1.50
52B24 Sidney Rice .50 1.25
52B25 Greg Jennings .50 1.25
52B26 Joe McKnight .40 1.00
52B27 Ben Tate .50 1.25
52B28 Sam Bradford 1.50 4.00
52B29 Jimmy Clausen .40 1.00
52B30 Larry Fitzgerald .60 1.50
52B31 Steven Jackson .50 1.25
52B32 Jon Beason .40 1.00
52B33 DeSean Jackson .50 1.25
52B34 Toby Gerhart .40 1.00
52B35 Michael Turner .40 1.00
52B36 Ryan Mathews .75 2.00
52B37 Montario Hardesty .40 1.00
52B38 Ray Rice .50 1.25
52B39 Arrelious Benn .40 1.00
52B40 Andre Johnson .50 1.25
52B41 Eric Berry .40 1.00
52B42 Calvin Johnson .60 1.50
52B43 Tom Brady 1.00 2.50
52B44 Reggie Wayne .50 1.25
52B45 Miles Austin .60 1.50
52B46 Rashard Mendenhall .50 1.25
52B47 Darrelle Revis .50 1.25
52B48 Jamaal Charles .50 1.25
52B49 Demaryius Thomas .50 1.25
52B50 Drew Brees .60 1.50

2010 Topps Anniversary Reprints

COMPLETE SET (20) 8.00 20.00
STATED ODDS 1:9 HOB/RET
1 Drew Brees .75 2.00
2 Tom Brady 1.25 3.00
3 Eric Dickerson .75 2.00
4 Tony Dorsett 1.00 2.50
5 John Elway 1.50 4.00
6 Larry Fitzgerald .75 2.00
7 Frank Gore .60 1.50
8 Steven Jackson .60 1.50
9 Andre Johnson .60 1.50
10 Chris Johnson .75 2.00
11 Ray Lewis .75 2.00
12 Peyton Manning 1.25 3.00
13 Dan Marino 2.00 5.00
14 Joe Montana 2.00 5.00
15 Randy Moss .75 2.00
16 Adrian Peterson 1.25 3.00
17 Troy Polamalu .75 2.00
18 Aaron Rodgers 1.50 4.00
19 Gale Sayers 1.25 3.00
20 Reggie Wayne .60 1.50

2010 Topps Draft 75th Anniversary

COMPLETE SET (50) 15.00 40.00
STATED ODDS 1:6 HOB/RET
75DA1 Joe Montana 1.50 4.00
75DA2 Ray Lewis .75 2.00
75DA3 Tom Brady 1.25 3.00
75DA4 Sam Bradford 2.00 5.00
75DA5 Dexter McCluster .50 1.25
75DA6 Randy Moss .75 2.00
75DA7 Adrian Peterson 1.25 3.00
75DA8 C.J. Spiller .75 2.00
75DA9 Mark Sanchez .75 2.00
75DA10 Ben Tate .60 1.50
75DA11 LaDainian Tomlinson .75 2.00
75DA12 Tim Tebow 3.00 8.00
75DA13 Patrick Willis .60 1.50
75DA14 Demaryius Thomas .60 1.50
75DA15 Peyton Manning 1.25 3.00
75DA16 Brandon Marshall .60 1.50
75DA17 Cadillac Williams .60 1.50
75DA18 Gale Sayers 1.00 2.50
75DA19 Jimmy Clausen .50 1.25
75DA20 Dan Marino 1.50 4.00
75DA21 Rashard Mendenhall .60 1.50
75DA22 Brian Cushing .50 1.25
75DA23 Vince Young .50 1.25
75DA24 Matt Ryan .75 2.00
75DA25 Brett Favre 2.00 5.00
75DA26 Jamaal Charles .60 1.50
75DA27 Ray Rice .60 1.50
75DA28 Reggie Wayne .60 1.50
75DA29 John Elway 1.25 3.00
75DA30 Emmitt Smith 1.25 3.00
75DA31 Matt Leinart .60 1.50
75DA32 Frank Gore .60 1.50
75DA33 Eli Manning .75 2.00
75DA34 Golden Tate .50 1.25
75DA35 Eric Berry .50 1.25
75DA36 DeSean Jackson .60 1.50
75DA37 Jahvid Best .75 2.00
75DA38 Philip Rivers .75 2.00
75DA39 Dez Bryant 1.50 4.00
75DA40 Troy Aikman 1.00 2.50
75DA41 DeAngelo Williams .60 1.50
75DA42 Tony Dorsett .75 2.00
75DA43 Ryan Mathews 1.00 2.50
75DA44 Steven Jackson .60 1.50
75DA45 Eric Dickerson .60 1.50
75DA46 Shonn Greene .60 1.50
75DA47 Percy Harvin .75 2.00
75DA48 Colt McCoy 1.00 2.50
75DA49 Jim Brown 1.00 2.50
75DA50 Brian Westbrook .60 1.50

2010 Topps Gridiron Giveaway

COMPLETE SET (10) 12.00 30.00
STATED ODDS 1:6 HOB
GG1 Joe Montana 1.25 3.00
GG2 Drew Brees 1.25 3.00
GG3 Ray Lewis 1.25 3.00
GG4 Gale Sayers 1.25 3.00
GG5 John Elway 1.25 3.00
GG6 Peyton Manning 1.25 3.00
GG7 Tony Dorsett 1.25 3.00
GG8 Tom Brady 1.25 3.00
GG9 Eric Dickerson 1.25 3.00
GG10 Dan Marino 1.25 3.00

2010 Topps Gridiron Lineage

COMPLETE SET (20) 6.00 15.00
STATED ODDS 1:4 HOB/RET
GLAR Troy Aikman 1.00 2.50
Troy Romo
GLBP Jim Brown 1.00 2.50
Adrian Peterson
GLDA Eric Dickerson .50 1.25
Joseph Addai
GLDB Brian Dawkins .40 1.00
Eric Berry
GLDJ Eric Dickerson .50 1.25
Steven Jackson
GLDM Tony Dorsett .60 1.50
LeSean McCoy
GLET John Elway 2.50 6.00
Tim Tebow
GLJB Chris Johnson .60 1.50
Jahvid Best
GLMB Dan Marino 1.25 3.00
Drew Brees
GLMC Joe Montana 1.25 3.00
Jimmy Clausen
GLMT Brandon Marshall .50 1.25
Demaryius Thomas
GLNS Joe Namath .75 2.00
Mark Sanchez
GLPH Adrian Peterson 1.00 2.50
Percy Harvin
GLSF Gale Sayers .75 2.00
Matt Forte
GLST Emmitt Smith 1.00 2.50
LaDainian Tomlinson
GLTM LaDainian Tomlinson 1.00 2.50
Ryan Mathews
GLTS Thurman Thomas .60 1.50
C.J. Spiller
GLWM Patrick Willis .40 1.00
Rolando McClain
GLMBR Randy Moss 1.00 2.50
Dez Bryant
GLMOB Joe Montana 1.25 3.00
Tom Brady

2010 Topps Gridiron Lineage Autographs

DUAL AU/25 ODDS 1:17,000H, 1:48,000R
GLDAAR Troy Aikman 125.00 200.00
Troy Romo
GLDABP Jim Brown 125.00 200.00
Adrian Peterson
GLDADA Eric Dickerson 30.00 80.00
Joseph Addai
GLDADJ Eric Dickerson 50.00 100.00
Steven Jackson
GLDADM Tony Dorsett 30.00 60.00
LeSean McCoy
GLDAET John Elway 250.00 400.00
Tim Tebow
GLDAHM Percy Harvin 40.00 80.00
Dexter McCluster
GLDAMC Joe Montana 125.00 200.00
Jimmy Clausen
GLDAMT Brandon Marshall 30.00 80.00
Demaryius Thomas
GLDAPH Adrian Peterson 60.00 120.00
Percy Harvin
GLDASD Jonathan Stewart 30.00 60.00
Jonathan Dwyer
GLDASJ Emmitt Smith 125.00 200.00
Felix Jones
GLDAST Emmitt Smith 125.00 200.00
LaDainian Tomlinson
GLDATS Thurman Thomas 60.00 120.00
C.J. Spiller
GLDAWM Patrick Willis 30.00 60.00
Rolando McClain

2010 Topps Gridiron Lineage Relics

DUAL JSY/50 ODDS 1:20,000H, 1:22,000R
GLRDJ Eric Dickerson 8.00 20.00
Steven Jackson
GLRET John Elway 40.00 80.00
Tim Tebow
GLRFR Brett Favre 60.00 120.00
Aaron Rodgers
GLRMB LaDainian Tomlinson 20.00 40.00
Ryan Mathews
GLRMC Joe Montana 30.00 60.00
Jimmy Clausen
GLRNS Brian Dawkins 20.00 40.00
Eric Berry
GLRRC Steve Smith 8.00 20.00
Golden Tate
GLRSF Gale Sayers 12.00 30.00
Matt Forte
GLRSJ Chris Johnson 15.00 40.00
Jahvid Best
GLRMBR Randy Moss 15.00 40.00
Dez Bryant

2010 Topps Peak Performance

COMPLETE SET (50) 10.00 25.00
STATED ODDS 1:4 HOB/RET
PP1 Sam Bradford 1.50 4.00
PP2 Tim Tebow 2.50 6.00
PP3 C.J. Spiller .60 1.50
PP4 Ryan Mathews .75 2.00
PP5 Dez Bryant 1.25 3.00
PP6 Peyton Manning 1.00 2.50
PP7 Tom Brady 1.00 2.50
PP8 Brandon Marshall .50 1.25
PP9 Ray Rice .50 1.25
PP10 Reggie Wayne .50 1.25
PP11 Adrian Peterson 1.00 2.50
PP12 Steven Jackson .50 1.25
PP13 Eric Dickerson .50 1.25
PP14 Tony Dorsett .60 1.50
PP15 Frank Gore .50 1.25
PP16 Eli Manning .60 1.50
PP17 Kellen Winslow .50 1.25
PP18 Marques Colston .50 1.25
PP19 Joseph Addai .50 1.25
PP20 DeSean Jackson .50 1.25
PP21 Joe Flacco .60 1.50
PP22 Toby Gerhart .40 1.00
PP23 Arrelious Benn .40 1.00
PP24 Demaryius Thomas .50 1.25
PP25 Jamaal Charles .50 1.25
PP26 Jonathan Dwyer .40 1.00
PP27 Mike Williams .60 1.50
PP28 Dexter McCluster .40 1.00
PP29 Jerod Mayo .50 1.25
PP30 Jerome Harrison .40 1.00
PP31 Jonathan Stewart .50 1.25
PP32 Mike Sims-Walker .50 1.25
PP33 John Elway 1.00 2.50
PP34 Dan Marino 1.25 3.00
PP35 Brett Favre 1.50 4.00
PP36 Jahvid Best .60 1.50
PP37 Calvin Johnson .60 1.50
PP38 Darren McFadden .50 1.25
PP39 Rashard Mendenhall .50 1.25
PP40 Sidney Rice .50 1.25
PP41 DeMarcus Ware .50 1.25
PP42 Felix Jones .50 1.25
PP43 Michael Crabtree .60 1.50
PP44 Brian Dawkins .50 1.25
PP45 Dallas Clark .50 1.25
PP46 Golden Tate .40 1.00
PP47 Joe McKnight .40 1.00
PP48 Montario Hardesty .40 1.00
PP49 Jimmy Clausen .40 1.00
PP50 Colt McCoy .75 2.00

2010 Topps Peak Performance Autographs

GROUP A ODDS 1:1465 H, 1:4200 R
GROUP B ODDS 1:247 H, 1:735 R
PPAAB Arrelious Benn 4.00 10.00
PPAABR Ahmad Bradshaw 5.00 12.00
PPAAD Anthony Dixon 5.00 12.00
PPAAE Armanti Edwards 4.00 10.00
PPAAH Aaron Hernandez 6.00 15.00
PPAAR Andre Roberts 3.00 8.00
PPABF Brett Favre A 175.00 300.00
PPABM Brandon Marshall A 20.00 40.00
PPABT Ben Tate 5.00 12.00
PPACH Chad Henne 8.00 20.00
PPACM Carlton Mitchell 3.00 8.00
PPACS Charles Scott 3.00 8.00
PPACT Chester Taylor 4.00 10.00
PPADA Donnie Avery 4.00 10.00
PPADAM Darren McFadden 8.00 20.00
PPADBR Dezmon Briscoe 4.00 10.00
PPADD Dennis Dixon 8.00 20.00
PPADH David Harris 4.00 10.00
PPADJ DeSean Jackson 10.00 25.00
PPADM Dan Marino A 75.00 150.00
PPADMC Dexter McCluster 6.00 15.00
PPADR David Reed 4.00 10.00
PPADT Demaryius Thomas 6.00 15.00
PPAEM Eli Manning A 40.00 80.00
PPAES Emmanuel Sanders 5.00 12.00
PPAEW Ed Wang 6.00 15.00
PPAFD Fred Davis 3.00 8.00
PPAFG Frank Gore 8.00 20.00
PPAJA Joseph Addai 5.00 12.00
PPAJAF Jacoby Ford 6.00 15.00
PPAJC Jamaal Charles 8.00 20.00
PPAJD Jonathan Dwyer 5.00 12.00
PPAJDA James Davis 4.00 10.00
PPAJE John Elway A 75.00 150.00
PPAJF Joe Flacco 10.00 25.00
PPAJFO Justin Forsett 4.00 10.00
PPAJH Jerome Harrison 5.00 12.00
PPAJJ James Jones 4.00 10.00
PPAJM Joe McKnight 5.00 12.00
PPAJMA Jerod Mayo 4.00 10.00
PPAJN Jordy Nelson 4.00 10.00
PPAJS James Starks 8.00 20.00
PPAJSK John Skelton 5.00 12.00
PPAJST Jonathan Stewart A 6.00 15.00
PPAJW Joe Webb 4.00 10.00
PPAKW Kellen Winslow 4.00 10.00
PPAMC Marques Colston 5.00 12.00
PPAME Marcus Easley 4.00 10.00
PPAMG Mardy Gilyard 5.00 12.00
PPAMJ Michael Jenkins 4.00 10.00
PPAMM Mohamed Massaquoi 4.00 10.00
PPAMR Myron Rolle 5.00 12.00
PPAMSW Mike Sims-Walker 4.00 10.00
PPAMW Mike Williams 6.00 15.00
PPANB Nate Burleson 3.00 8.00
PPAPM Peyton Manning A 75.00 150.00
PPARC Riley Cooper 5.00 12.00
PPARW Reggie Wayne A 10.00 25.00
PPASB Sam Bradford 40.00 100.00
PPASS Steve Slaton 4.00 10.00
PPATC Tashard Choice 5.00 12.00
PPATG Toby Gerhart 8.00 20.00
PPATP Taylor Price 5.00 12.00
PPATT Tim Tebow 50.00 100.00

2010 Topps Peak Performance Relics

GROUP A ODDS 1:265 H, 1:1730 R
GROUP B ODDS 1:141 H, 1:908 R
GROUP B ODDS 1:91 H, 1:589
PPRAB Arrelious Benn 2.50 6.00
PPRAJH A.J. Hawk 3.00 8.00
PPRAR Aaron Rodgers 8.00 20.00
PPRBD Brian Dawkins 3.00 8.00
PPRBM Brandon Marshall 3.00 8.00
PPRBT Ben Tate 3.00 8.00
PPRCC Chris Cooley 4.00 10.00
PPRCJO Chris Johnson 4.00 10.00
PPRCM Colt McCoy 5.00 12.00
PPRDB Dez Bryant 5.00 12.00
PPRDC Dallas Clark 3.00 8.00
PPRDG David Garrard 3.00 8.00
PPRDH David Harris 2.50 6.00
PPRDM Dexter McCluster 3.00 8.00
PPRDMA Derrick Mason 3.00 8.00
PPRDMC Darren McFadden 3.00 8.00
PPRER Eddie Royal 2.50 6.00
PPRFJ Felix Jones 3.00 8.00
PPRGT Golden Tate 3.00 8.00
PPRJB Jahvid Best 4.00 10.00
PPRJC Jimmy Clausen 2.50 6.00
PPRJCU Jay Cutler 4.00 10.00
PPRJD Jonathan Dwyer 2.50 6.00
PPRJJ James Jones 2.50 6.00
PPRJM Joe McKnight 2.50 6.00
PPRKK Kevin Kolb 3.00 8.00
PPRKW Kellen Winslow 3.00 8.00
PPRLE Lee Evans 3.00 8.00
PPRLM Laurence Maroney 3.00 8.00
PPRME Marcus Easley 2.50 6.00
PPRMH Montario Hardesty 2.50 6.00
PPRML Matt Leinart 3.00 8.00
PPRMR Matt Ryan 4.00 10.00
PPRRL Ray Lewis 5.00 12.00
PPRRM Rashard Mendenhall 3.00 8.00
PPRRW Ricky Williams 3.00 8.00
PPRRWA Reggie Wayne 3.00 8.00
PPRSB Sam Bradford 6.00 15.00
PPRSBR Steve Breaston 2.50 6.00
PPRSR Sidney Rice 3.00 8.00
PPRSS Steve Slaton 2.50 6.00
PPRSSM Steve Smith 3.00 8.00
PPRTB Tom Brady 8.00 20.00
PPRTP Taylor Price 2.50 6.00
PPRTT Tim Tebow 10.00 25.00

2010 Topps Peak Performance Relics Autographs

JSY AU/50 ODDS 1:15,000 HOB
PPARAG Antonio Gates 25.00 50.00
PPARAP Adrian Peterson 75.00 150.00
PPARBM Brandon Marshall 25.00 50.00
PPARDB Dez Bryant 40.00 100.00
PPARED Eric Dickerson 40.00 80.00
PPARFJ Felix Jones 20.00 40.00
PPARPM Peyton Manning 90.00 150.00
PPARRM Ryan Mathews 30.00 80.00
PPARRR Ray Rice 30.00 60.00
PPARRW Reggie Wayne 20.00 40.00
PPARSB Sam Bradford 60.00 120.00
PPARSJ Steven Jackson 30.00 60.00
PPARTD Tony Dorsett 40.00 80.00
PPARTT Tim Tebow 75.00 150.00
PPARCJS C.J. Spiller 30.00 80.00

2010 Topps Peak Performance Relics Jumbo

JUMBO/20 ODDS 1:18,000 HOB		
PPJR1 Tim Tebow	25.00	60.00
PPJR2 Ryan Mathews	12.00	30.00
PPJR3 Dez Bryant	20.00	50.00
PPJR4 C.J. Spiller	10.00	25.00
PPJR5 Jimmy Clausen	6.00	15.00
PPJR6 Santana Moss	12.00	30.00
PPJR7 Jahvid Best	10.00	25.00
PPJR8 Jonathan Dwyer	6.00	15.00
PPJR9 Roddy White	12.00	30.00
PPJR10 Brandon Marshall	12.00	30.00
PPJR11 Ray Rice	12.00	30.00
PPJR12 Chris Johnson	15.00	40.00
PPJR13 Golden Tate	6.00	15.00
PPJR14 Steven Jackson	12.00	30.00
PPJR15 Maurice Jones-Drew	12.00	30.00
PPJR16 Reggie Bush	15.00	40.00
PPJR17 Colt McCoy	12.00	30.00
PPJR18 Calvin Johnson	15.00	40.00
PPJR19 Montario Hardesty	6.00	15.00
PPJR20 Jamaal Charles	12.00	30.00

2010 Topps Rookie Premiere Autographs

AUTO/90 ODDS 1:750 HOB		
RPAAB Arrelious Benn	15.00	40.00
RPAAE Armanti Edwards	15.00	40.00
RPAAR Andre Roberts	15.00	40.00
RPABL Brandon LaFell	15.00	40.00
RPABT Ben Tate	20.00	50.00
RPACM Colt McCoy	60.00	120.00
RPADB Dez Bryant	75.00	150.00
RPADM Dexter McCluster	30.00	80.00
RPADT Demaryius Thomas	20.00	50.00
RPADW Damian Williams	15.00	40.00
RPAEB Eric Berry	40.00	80.00
RPAED Eric Decker	20.00	50.00
RPAES Emmanuel Sanders	30.00	60.00
RPAGM Gerald McCoy	15.00	40.00
RPAGT Golden Tate	15.00	40.00
RPAJB Jahvid Best	25.00	60.00
RPAJC Jimmy Clausen	30.00	80.00
RPAJD Jonathan Dwyer	15.00	40.00
RPAJG Jermaine Gresham	20.00	50.00
RPAJM Joe McKnight	15.00	40.00
RPAJS Jordan Shipley	15.00	40.00
RPAME Marcus Easley	12.00	30.00
RPAMG Mardy Gilyard	15.00	40.00
RPAMH Montario Hardesty	15.00	40.00
RPAMK Mike Kafka	15.00	40.00
RPAMW Mike Williams	40.00	80.00
RPANS Ndamukong Suh	50.00	100.00
RPARG Rob Gronkowski	30.00	80.00
RPARM Rolando McClain	15.00	40.00
RPARM Ryan Mathews	40.00	100.00
RPASB Sam Bradford	125.00	250.00
RPATG Toby Gerhart	15.00	40.00
RPATP Taylor Price	15.00	40.00
RPATT Tim Tebow	125.00	250.00
RPACJS C.J. Spiller	50.00	120.00

2010 Topps Rookie Premiere Autographs Dual

DUAL AU/25 ODDS 1:18,000 HOB		
RPDABC Sam Bradford	150.00	250.00
Jimmy Clausen		
RPDABD Jahvid Best	40.00	100.00
Dexter McCluster		
RPDABT Dez Bryant	60.00	150.00
Demaryius Thomas		
RPDASM C.J Spiller	60.00	120.00
Ryan Mathews		
RPDATM Tim Tebow	150.00	250.00
Colt McCoy		

2010 Topps Rookie Redemption

COMPLETE SET (17)	8.00	20.00
ISSUED VIA MAIL REDEMPTION		
GR1 Jahvid Best	1.00	2.50
GR2 Demaryius Thomas	.75	2.00
GR3 C.J. Spiller	1.00	2.50
GR4 Sam Bradford	2.50	6.00
GR5 Max Hall	.60	1.50
GR6 Chris Ivory	.75	2.00
GR7 Jordan Shipley	.60	1.50
GR8 LeGarrette Blount	1.00	2.50
GR9 Colt McCoy	1.25	3.00
GR10 Rob Gronkowski	1.50	4.00
GR11 Mike Williams	1.00	2.50
GR12 Toby Gerhart	.60	1.50
GR13 Javarris James	.60	1.50
GR14 Arrelious Benn	.60	1.50
GR15 Tim Tebow	2.50	6.00
GR16 Ryan Mathews	1.25	3.00
GR17 Joe McKnight	.60	1.50

2010 Topps Rookie Red Zone Autographs

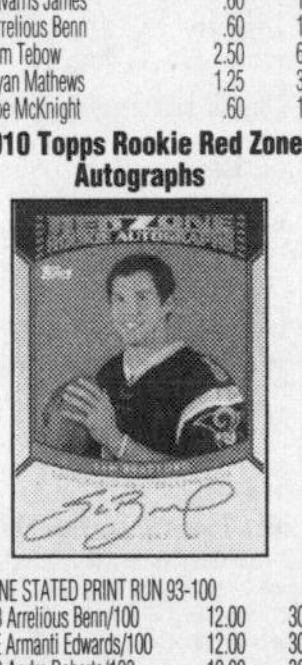

RED ZONE STATED PRINT RUN 93-100		
RZRAAB Arrelious Benn/100	12.00	30.00
RZRAAE Armanti Edwards/100	12.00	30.00
RZRAAR Andre Roberts/100	12.00	30.00
RZRABL Brandon LaFell/100	12.00	30.00
RZRABT Ben Tate/100	15.00	40.00
RZRACM Colt McCoy/100	25.00	60.00
RZRADB Dez Bryant/100	50.00	100.00
RZRADM Dexter McCluster/100	12.00	30.00
RZRADT Demaryius Thomas/100	15.00	40.00
RZRADW Damian Williams/100	12.00	30.00
RZRAEB Eric Berry/100	12.00	30.00
RZRAED Eric Decker/100	15.00	40.00
RZRAES Emmanuel Sanders/100	12.00	30.00
RZRAGM Gerald McCoy/99	12.00	30.00
RZRAGT Golden Tate/100	12.00	30.00
RZRAJB Jahvid Best/100	20.00	50.00
RZRAJC Jimmy Clausen/100	12.00	30.00
RZRAJD Jonathan Dwyer/93	12.00	30.00
RZRAJG Jermaine Gresham/100	15.00	40.00
RZRAJM Joe McKnight/100	12.00	30.00
RZRAJS Jordan Shipley/100	12.00	30.00
RZRAME Marcus Easley/100	10.00	25.00
RZRAMG Mardy Gilyard/98	12.00	30.00
RZRAMH Montario Hardesty/100	12.00	30.00
RZRAMK Mike Kafka/100	12.00	30.00
RZRAMW Mike Williams/100	25.00	60.00
RZRANS Ndamukong Suh/100	25.00	60.00
RZRARG Rob Gronkowski/100	30.00	80.00
RZRARM Ryan Mathews/100	25.00	60.00
RZRARM Rolando McClain/100	12.00	30.00
RZRASB Sam Bradford/100	75.00	150.00
RZRATG Toby Gerhart/100	12.00	30.00
RZRATP Taylor Price/100	12.00	30.00
RZRATT Tim Tebow/100	75.00	150.00
RZRACJS C.J. Spiller/100	20.00	50.00

2010 Topps Super Bowl Highlights

COMPLETE SET (5)	2.50	6.00
ONE SET PER TOPPS SB FACTORY		
SB1 Drew Brees	.60	1.50
SB2 Santonio Holmes	.50	1.25
SB3 David Tyree	.40	1.00
SB4 Tom Brady	1.00	2.50
SB5 Adam Vinatieri	.50	1.25

2010 Topps Target Exclusive Factory Set Patches

TWO PER TARGET EXCLUSIVE FACTORY SET		
TRGT1 Sam Bradford	6.00	15.00
TRGT2 Peyton Manning	4.00	10.00
TRGT3 Tim Tebow	7.50	20.00
TRGT4 Drew Brees	6.00	15.00
TRGT5 Jimmy Clausen	2.50	6.00
TRGT6 Tom Brady	4.00	10.00

2010 Topps Throwback Patch

ONE PER RETAIL BLASTER BOX		
LPC1 Santana Moss	4.00	10.00
LPC2 LeSean McCoy	4.00	10.00
LPC3 Ryan Grant	4.00	10.00
LPC4 Reggie Wayne	4.00	10.00
LPC5 Sam Bradford	10.00	25.00
LPC6 Randy Moss	5.00	12.00
LPC7 Darrelle Revis	4.00	10.00
LPC8 Brian Urlacher	5.00	12.00
LPC9 Mark Sanchez	5.00	12.00
LPC10 Steven Jackson	4.00	10.00
LPC11 Kenny Britt	4.00	10.00
LPC12 Mike Williams	5.00	12.00
LPC13 T.J. Houshmandzadeh	4.00	10.00
LPC14 Cedric Benson	4.00	10.00
LPC15 Montario Hardesty	4.00	10.00
LPC16 C.J. Spiller	8.00	20.00
LPC17 Chris Wells	4.00	10.00
LPC18 Brandon Jacobs	4.00	10.00
LPC19 Joe McKnight	4.00	10.00
LPC20 Knowshon Moreno	4.00	10.00
LPC21 Marques Colston	4.00	10.00
LPC22 Jahvid Best	6.00	15.00
LPC23 Peyton Manning	8.00	20.00
LPC24 Drew Brees	6.00	15.00
LPC25 Greg Jennings	4.00	10.00
LPC26 Pierre Thomas	4.00	10.00
LPC27 Colt McCoy	10.00	25.00
LPC28 Ryan Mathews	8.00	20.00
LPC29 Demaryius Thomas	3.00	8.00
LPC30 Larry Fitzgerald	5.00	12.00
LPC31 Matt Forte	4.00	10.00
LPC32 Jonathan Dwyer	5.00	12.00
LPC33 Matthew Stafford	5.00	12.00
LPC34 Vincent Jackson	3.00	8.00
LPC35 Rashard Mendenhall	5.00	12.00
LPC36 Tim Tebow	10.00	25.00
LPC37 Tom Brady	8.00	20.00
LPC38 Donovan McNabb	5.00	12.00
LPC39 Tony Romo	8.00	20.00
LPC40 Eli Manning	5.00	12.00
LPC41 Fred Jackson	5.00	12.00
LPC42 Aaron Rodgers	8.00	20.00
LPC43 Arrelious Benn	4.00	10.00
LPC44 Troy Polamalu	8.00	20.00
LPC45 Dez Bryant	8.00	20.00
LPC46 Golden Tate	5.00	12.00
LPC47 Chad Ochocinco	4.00	10.00
LPC48 Philip Rivers	6.00	15.00
LPC49 Chris Johnson	6.00	15.00
LPC50 DeSean Jackson	4.00	10.00

2011 Topps

COMP.FACT.HOBBY (485)	30.00	55.00
COMP.FACT.RETAIL (485)	30.00	55.00
COMP.FACT.SPCL RET (486)/(with Cam Newton patch)		
40.00	60.00	
COMP.SET w/o SP's (440)	25.00	50.00
ONE ROOKIE PER PACK		
RH EXCH EXPIRATION: 7/31/2014		
1A Aaron Rodgers	.40	1.00
1B Aaron Rodgers TB SP	30.00	60.00
(wearing throwback jersey)		
2 St. Louis Rams Team	.20	.50
Sam Bradford		
Steven Jackson		
3 Ben Watson	.15	.40
4 Reggie Bush	.20	.50
5 Lance Briggs	.20	.50
6A Kyle Rudolph RC	.50	1.25
(catching ball over head)		
6B Kyle Rudolph SP	5.00	12.00
(one-handed catch)		
7 Vincent Brown RC	.50	1.25
8 Blair White	.15	.40
9 Antonio Brown	.25	.60
10A Larry Fitzgerald	.20	.50
(white jersey)		
10B Larry Fitzgerald SP	8.00	20.00
(red jersey)		
11A Leonard Hankerson RC	.50	1.25
(no football in photo)		
11B Leonard Hankerson SP	10.00	25.00
(one-handed catch)		
12 Demaryius Thomas	.20	.50
13 Brian Cushing	.15	.40
14 Tyrod Taylor RC	.50	1.25
15 Brandon Harris RC	.30	.75
16 Colt McCoy	.20	.50
17 Denver Broncos Team	.40	1.00
Tim Tebow		
Brandon Lloyd		
18 Houston Texans Team	.15	.40
Matt Schaub		
Arian Foster		
19A Titus Young RC	.60	1.50
(football above head)		
19B Titus Young SP	6.00	15.00
(football at chest)		
20 Eli Manning	.25	.60
21 Jermaine Gresham	.20	.50
22 Austin Collie	.20	.50
23 Brandon Meriweather	.15	.40
24 Jake Long	.15	.40
25 Steve Smith	.20	.50
26 Robert Mathis	.15	.40
27 Phil Taylor RC	.40	1.00
28 New York Jets Team	.20	.50
Mark Sanchez		
Santonio Holmes		
Braylon Edwards		
29 Brooks Reed RC	.50	1.25
30 Maurice Jones-Drew	.20	.50
31 Knowshon Moreno	.20	.50
32 Brent Celek	.20	.50
33 Jonathan Stewart	.20	.50
34 David Harris	.15	.40
35 Tampa Bay Buccaneers Team	.20	.50
Josh Freeman		
LeGarrette Blount		
36 Devin Hester	.25	.60
37 Seyi Ajirotutu	.15	.40
38 Mike Tolbert	.20	.50
39 DeAngelo Williams	.20	.50
40 Greg Jennings	.20	.50
41 Akeem Ayers RC	.40	1.00
42 Philadelphia Eagles Team	.20	.50
Michael Vick		
LeSean McCoy		
43 Danny Watkins RC	.40	1.00
44 Davone Bess	.15	.40
45 Elvis Dumervil	.15	.40
46 Dion Lewis RC	.50	1.25
47 Derrick Johnson	.15	.40
48 Vonta Leach	.15	.40
49 DeMeco Ryans	.15	.40
50 Josh Freeman	.25	.60
51 Rob Housler RC	.40	1.00
52 Oakland Raiders Team	.15	.40
Jason Campbell		
Darren McFadden		
Marcell Reese		
53 Baltimore Ravens Team	.20	.50
Joe Flacco		
Anquan Boldin		
54 Sam Bradford ROY	.25	.60
55 Da'Rel Scott RC	.40	1.00
56 Mike Thomas	.20	.50
57 BenJarvus Green-Ellis	.20	.50
58 Prince Amukamara RC	.50	1.25
59 Cameron Wake	.15	.40
60A Chris Johnson	.20	.50
(blue jersey)		
60B Chris Johnson SP	8.00	20.00
(white jersey)		
61 Anthony Armstrong	.20	.50
62 Terrell Suggs	.15	.40
63 Vernon Davis	.20	.50
64 Dwayne Bowe	.20	.50
65 Billy Cundiff	.15	.40
66 Jay Ratliff	.20	.50
67 David Gettis	.15	.40
68 Beanie Wells	.20	.50
69 Tyron Smith RC	.60	1.50
70A Andy Dalton RC	1.25	3.00
(football in hand)		
70B Andy Dalton SP	12.00	30.00
(football in air)		
71 Alex Smith QB	.20	.50
72 Jacquizz Rodgers RC	.50	1.25
73 Aaron Williams RC	.40	1.00
74 T.J. Yates RC	.60	1.50
75 Percy Harvin	.20	.50
76 Donald Brown	.15	.40
77 Mike Goodson	.15	.40
78 Roy Williams WR	.20	.50
79 Keith Brooking	.15	.40
80 Calvin Johnson	.25	.60
81 Steve Smith USC	.20	.50
82 Anthony Allen RC	.30	.75
83 Kevin Boss	.20	.50
84 Green Bay Packers Team	.30	.75
Aaron Rodgers		
Jordy Nelson		
85A Troy Polamalu	.25	.60
(horizontal format)		
85B Troy Polamalu SP	10.00	25.00
(vertical format)		
86 Matthew Stafford	.25	.60
87 Asante Samuel	.15	.40
88 David Garrard	.20	.50
89 Chris Long	.15	.40
90 Ben Roethlisberger	.25	.60
91 Adrian Wilson	.15	.40
92 Dexter McCluster	.15	.40
93 Tramon Williams	.25	.60
94 Pierre Thomas	.20	.50
95 Jeremy Kerley RC	.50	1.25
96 Lofa Tatupu	.15	.40
97 Brandon LaFell	.15	.40
98 Zach Miller	.20	.50
99 Ryan Torain	.15	.40
100A Drew Brees	.25	.60
(white jersey)		
100B Drew Brees SP	10.00	25.00
(black jersey)		
101 Tandon Doss RC	.40	1.00
102 Chris Clemons	.15	.40
103 Karlos Dansby	.15	.40
104 Ndamukong Suh ROY	.25	.60
105 Brandon Pettigrew	.15	.40
106 Lee Evans	.20	.50
107 Marvin Austin RC	.40	1.00
108 Delone Carter RC	.40	1.00
109 Jermichael Finley	.20	.50
110 Sam Bradford	.25	.60
111 Michael Crabtree	.20	.50
112 Nathan Enderle RC	.50	1.25
113 James Starks	.20	.50
114 Darren Sproles	.20	.50
115 Malcom Floyd	.20	.50
116 Fred Jackson	.25	.60
117 Tennessee Titans Team	.15	.40
Chris Johnson		
118 Felix Jones	.20	.50
119 Atlanta Falcons Team	.15	.40
120 Frank Gore	.20	.50
121 Bernard Scott	.15	.40
122 Cincinnati Bengals Team	.15	.40
Chad Ochocinco		
Reggie Kelly		
123 Brian Dawkins	.20	.50
124 Nnamdi Asomugha	.20	.50
125 Buffalo Bills Team	.20	.50
Steve Johnson		
Fred Jackson		
Mansfield Wrotto		
126A DeMarco Murray RC	1.00	2.50
(football in both hands)		
126B DeMarco Murray SP	20.00	40.00
(football in left arm)		
127 Ryan Whalen RC	.40	1.00
128 T.J. Ward	.15	.40
129 Lawrence Timmons	.15	.40
130 Dez Bryant	.25	.60
131 Hines Ward	.20	.50
132 Julius Thomas RC	.40	1.00
133 Ryan Fitzpatrick	.20	.50
134 Ricky Stanzi RC	.60	1.50
135 Brian Hartline	.15	.40
136 Brandon Marshall	.20	.50
137 Seattle Seahawks Team	.15	.40
Matt Hasselbeck		
Marshawn Lynch		
138 James Harrison	.25	.60
139 James Jones	.15	.40
140 Jay Cutler	.20	.50
141 LaMarr Woodley	.15	.40
142 Brad Smith	.15	.40
143 Bilal Powell RC	.30	.75
144 Danny Amendola	.20	.50
145 Jason Campbell	.20	.50
146 Dontay Moch RC	.30	.75
147 Michael Bush	.15	.40
148 Nate Washington	.15	.40
149A Randall Cobb RC	.60	1.50
(leaping catch)		
149B Randall Cobb SP	10.00	25.00
(running catch)		
150 Mark Sanchez	.25	.60
151A A.J. Green RC	1.00	2.50
(running to the left)		
151B A.J. Green SP	10.00	25.00
(running forward)		
151C A.J. Green FS	.75	2.00
(overhead catch		
factory set only)		
152 Julius Peppers	.20	.50
153 Curtis Lofton	.15	.40
154 Vince Wilfork	.15	.40
155 Kendall Hunter RC	.50	1.25
156 New Orleans Saints Team	.20	.50
Drew Brees		
Lance Moore		
157 Rashad Jennings	.15	.40
158 Aaron Hernandez	.20	.50
159 Donovan McNabb	.25	.60
160A Blaine Gabbert RC	.75	2.00
(set to pass)		
160B Blaine Gabbert SP	15.00	30.00
(running pose)		
160C Blaine Gabbert FS	.60	1.50
(passing left, factory set only)		
161 Ronnie Brown	.20	.50
162 Mario Manningham	.20	.50
163 Dallas Cowboys Team	.15	.40
Miles Austin		
Roy Williams WR		
164 Ray Rice	.20	.50
165 Edmond Gates RC	.40	1.00
166 Vince Young	.15	.40
167 Champ Bailey	.20	.50
168 Ovie Mughelli	.15	.40
169 Mike Pouncey RC	.50	1.25
170 Jason Witten	.25	.60
171 Brian Urlacher	.25	.60
172 Derek Sherrod RC	.50	1.25
173 Jacoby Jones	.15	.40
174 Thomas Jones	.20	.50
175 Todd Heap	.15	.40
176 Osi Umenyiora	.15	.40
177 Ahmad Bradshaw	.20	.50
178 Aldon Smith RC	.75	2.00
179 Kevin Kolb	.20	.50
180 Peyton Hillis	.20	.50
181 Corey Liuget RC	.30	.75
182 Earl Thomas	.15	.40
183 Ray Lewis	.25	.60
184 Wes Welker	.25	.60
185 Stephen Tulloch	.15	.40
186 Jerricho Cotchery	.15	.40
187 2011 Rookie Premiere	.40	1.00
188 Kris Durham RC	.40	1.00
189 Jahvid Best	.20	.50
190 Miles Austin	.20	.50
191 Dwight Freeney	.20	.50
192 Emmanuel Sanders	.15	.40
193 Alex Green RC	.50	1.25
194 Deion Branch	.15	.40
195 Jahri Evans	.15	.40
196 Luke Stocker RC	.40	1.00
197 Steve Breaston	.15	.40
198 Jimmy Graham	.25	.60
199 Carolina Panthers Team	.15	.40
Jonathan Stewart		
Jeremy Shockey		
200A Cam Newton RC	3.00	8.00
(stands in background		
silver wall)		
200B Cam Newton SP	40.00	80.00
(field in background)		
200C Cam Newton FS	2.50	6.00
(stands in background		
blue wall, factory set only)		
201 Brandon Gibson	.15	.40
202 Paul Posluszny	.15	.40
203 A.J. Hawk	.20	.50
204 Tom Brady RB	.40	1.00
205 John Kuhn	.25	.60
206 Carson Palmer	.20	.50
207 Kenny Britt	.20	.50
208 Logan Mankins	.15	.40
209 Visanthe Shiancoe	.20	.50
210 Tim Tebow	.50	1.25
211 Chris Ivory	.20	.50
212 Nate Solder RC	.50	1.25
213 Gabe Carimi RC	.50	1.25
214 Curtis Brown RC	.50	1.25
215 Denarius Moore RC	.60	1.50
216 Pittsburgh Steelers Team	.20	.50
Ike Taylor		
Troy Polamalu		
217 Anquan Boldin RB	.20	.50
218 DeAngelo Hall	.15	.40
219 Nick Fairley RC	.60	1.50
220 Michael Turner	.20	.50
221 Jacob Tamme	.20	.50
222 Darren McFadden	.20	.50
223 Haloti Ngata	.15	.40
224 Brandon Jackson	.15	.40
225 B.J. Raji	.20	.50
226 Miami Dolphins Team	.15	.40
Davone Bess		
Chad Pennington		
Brandon Marshall		
227 Anquan Boldin	.20	.50
228 Ryan Kerrigan RC	.50	1.25
229 Quinton Carter RC	.30	.75
230 Rashard Mendenhall	.20	.50
231 Danny Woodhead	.25	.60
232 San Diego Chargers Team	.20	.50
Philip Rivers		
Antonio Gates		
233 Chris Snee	.15	.40
234 Devin McCourty	.15	.40
235A Jerrel Jernigan RC	.40	1.00
(catching pose)		
235B Jerrel Jernigan SP	6.00	15.00
(leaping pose)		
236 Mohamed Massaquoi	.20	.50
237 Trent Cole	.15	.40
238A Christian Ponder RC	1.25	3.00
(running pose)		
238B Christian Ponder SP	12.00	30.00
(passing pose)		
239 Brandon Tate	.15	.40
240 Tom Brady MVP	.40	1.00
241 Joe Flacco	.25	.60
242A Jon Baldwin RC	.50	1.25
(no football in photo)		
242B Jon Baldwin SP	8.00	20.00
(one-handed catch)		
243 Jerod Mayo	.15	.40
244 Arrelious Benn	.20	.50
245 Marcedes Lewis	.15	.40
246 Donald Driver	.20	.50
247 Packers SB Champs	.30	.75
Aaron Rodgers		
Clay Matthews		
248 Joseph Addai	.20	.50
249 Roy Helu RC	1.00	2.50
250A Andre Johnson	.20	.50
(white jersey)		
250B Andre Johnson SP	10.00	25.00
(red jersey)		
251 Justin Houston RC	.50	1.25
252 Takeo Spikes	.15	.40
253 Tony Moeaki	.15	.40
254 Chicago Bears Team	.15	.40
Julius Peppers		
Henry Melton		
255 Chad Henne	.20	.50
256 Marcell Dareus RC	.50	1.25
257 Eric Berry	.20	.50
258 Randy Moss	.20	.50
259 Lee Smith RC	.40	1.00
260A Roddy White	.20	.50
(red jersey)		
260B Roddy White SP	8.00	20.00
(white jersey)		
261 Charles Johnson	.15	.40
262 Justin Smith	.15	.40
263 Josh Cribbs	.20	.50
264 Shane Lechler	.15	.40
265 Brandon Lloyd	.20	.50
266 Dustin Keller	.20	.50
267 Patrick Peterson RC	.75	2.00
268 DeSean Jackson	.20	.50
269 John Abraham	.15	.40
270A Philip Rivers	.25	.60
(white jersey)		
270B Philip Rivers SP	10.00	25.00
(blue jersey)		
271 Robert Quinn RC	.50	1.25
272 Terrell Owens	.25	.60
273 LeGarrette Blount	.20	.50
274A Torrey Smith RC	.60	1.50
(no football in photo)		
274B Torrey Smith SP	8.00	20.00
(one-handed catch)		
275 James Carpenter RC	.50	1.25
276 Kris Dielman	.15	.40
277 Muhammad Wilkerson RC	.50	1.25
278 Ben Obomanu	.15	.40
279 Nick Collins	.15	.40
280A Antonio Gates	.20	.50
(horizontal format)		
280B Antonio Gates SP	8.00	20.00
(vertical format)		
281 Tim Hightower	.15	.40
282 Matt Schaub	.20	.50
283 Mario Williams	.15	.40
284 Antrel Rolle	.15	.40
285 Joe Thomas	.15	.40
286 Sam Bradford RB	.25	.60
287 Santana Moss	.20	.50
288 San Francisco 49ers Team	.15	.40
Alex Smith QB		
Vernon Davis		
289 Minnesota Vikings Team	.25	.60
Adrian Peterson		
Visanthe Shiancoe		
290 LaDainian Tomlinson	.25	.60
291 Greg Olsen	.15	.40
292 Niles Paul RC	.50	1.25
293 Tamba Hali	.15	.40
294 Jon Deason	.15	.40
295 Shaun Hill	.15	.40
296 LaRon Landry	.15	.40
297 Jordan Shipley	.20	.50
298 Ricky Williams	.20	.50
299 Cameron Heyward RC	.50	1.25
300A Peyton Manning	.40	1.00
(white jersey)		
300B Peyton Manning SP	20.00	40.00
(blue jersey)		
301 Derrick Mason	.15	.40
302 Joe Haden	.15	.40
303 Steve Johnson	.20	.50
304 Eddie Royal	.15	.40
305 Brent Grimes RC	.25	.60
306 Kevin Walter	.20	.50
307 Cortland Finnegan	.15	.40
308 Chris Cooley	.20	.50
309 Danario Alexander	.15	.40
310 Ndamukong Suh	.25	.60
311 Ras-I Dowling RC	.50	1.25
312 Jacoby Ford	.20	.50
313 Taiwan Jones RC	.50	1.25
314 Mike Williams USC	.20	.50
315 Sidney Rice	.20	.50
316 C.J. Spiller	.20	.50
317 Kansas City Chiefs Team	.15	.40
Matt Cassel and O-Line		
318 Matt Cassel	.20	.50
319 Chad Ochocinco	.20	.50
320 Santonio Holmes	.20	.50
321A Greg Little RC	.50	1.25
(Heisman style pose)		
321B Greg Little SP	6.00	15.00
(one-handed catch)		
322 Tony Gonzalez RB	.20	.50
323 Shaun Phillips	.15	.40
324 Lance Moore	.20	.50
325 Jordan Todman RC	.30	.75
326 Allen Bradford RC	.40	1.00
327 Cleveland Browns Team	.15	.40
Peyton Hillis		
Lawrence Vickers		
328 Jerome Simpson	.15	.40
329 Nick Mangold	.15	.40
330A Arian Foster	.20	.50
(white jersey)		
330B Arian Foster SP	8.00	20.00
(blue jersey)		
331 J.J. Watt RC	.60	1.50
332 Mike Sims-Walker	.20	.50
333 Johnny Knox	.20	.50
334 Patrick Willis	.20	.50
335 Carlos Dunlap	.15	.40
336 Marshawn Lynch	.20	.50
337 Anthony Castonzo RC	.30	.75
338 Kyle Orton	.20	.50
339 Cedric Benson	.20	.50
340 Hakeem Nicks	.20	.50
341 Braylon Edwards	.20	.50
342 Jimmy Smith RC	.50	1.25
343 London Fletcher	.15	.40
344 Jeremy Shockey	.20	.50
345 Jonathan Vilma	.15	.40
346 New England Patriots Team	.30	.75
Tom Brady		
Danny Woodhead		
347 Brandon Jacobs	.20	.50
348 Allen Bailey RC	.40	1.00
349 Cameron Jordan RC	.40	1.00
350A Julio Jones RC	1.00	2.50
(football at chest)		
350B Julio Jones SP	10.00	25.00
(ball over head, facing forward)		
350C Julio Jones SP	.75	2.00
(ball over head, facing left)		
351 Greg McElroy RC	.60	1.25
352 Pierre Garcon	.20	.50
353 Nate Burleson	.15	.40
354 Dallas Clark	.20	.50
355 Evan Royster RC	.50	1.25
356 Justin Tuck	.20	.50
357 Martez Wilson RC	.50	1.25
358 Robert Meachem	.20	.50
359 Andre Gurode	.15	.40
360 Tony Romo	.25	.60
361 James Laurinaitis	.15	.40
362 Adrian Clayborn RC	.50	1.25
363 Donte Whitner	.15	.40
364 Jason Snelling	.20	.50
365 Kealoha Pilares RC	.50	1.25
366A Daniel Thomas RC	.50	1.25
(football in right arm)		
366B Daniel Thomas SP	12.00	30.00
(football in left arm)		
367 Jabaal Sheard RC	.50	1.25
368 Indianapolis Colts Team	.30	.75
Peyton Manning		
Donald Brown		
369 Casey Matthews RC	.50	1.25
370 LeSean McCoy	.20	.50
371 Shonn Greene	.20	.50
372 Louis Murphy	.20	.50
373 Greg Salas RC	.50	1.25
374 Kellen Winslow	.20	.50
375 Arizona Cardinals Team	.15	.40
Larry Fitzgerald		
Max Komar		
Steve Breaston		
376 Jared Allen	.20	.50
377 Brian Orakpo	.20	.50
378 Virgil Green RC	.40	1.00
379 Matt Forte	.20	.50
380A Jamaal Charles	.20	.50
(red jersey)		
380B Jamaal Charles SP	6.00	15.00
(white jersey)		
381 Heath Miller	.20	.50
382A Jamie Harper RC	.50	1.25
(field in background)		
382B Jamie Harper SP	5.00	12.00
(stands in background)		
383 Mike Williams	.20	.50
384 Chad Greenway	.20	.50
385 Cecil Shorts RC	.40	1.00
386 Dwayne Harris RC	.50	1.25
387 Charles Woodson	.25	.60
388 Washington Redskins Team	.15	.40
Brian Orakpo		
London Fletcher		
389 Rob Gronkowski	.25	.60
390 Reggie Wayne	.20	.50
391 John Carlson	.15	.40
392 Clay Matthews	.25	.60
393 Jason Babin	.15	.40
394 Jeremy Maclin	.20	.50
395A Ryan Williams RC	.60	1.50
(cutting pose)		
395B Ryan Williams SP	6.00	15.00
(catching pose)		
396 Austin Pettis RC	.40	1.00
397 Da'Quan Bowers RC	.50	1.25
398 Joe Webb	.15	.40
399 Johnny White RC	.40	1.00
400A Tom Brady	.40	1.00
(red jersey)		
400B Tom Brady SP	15.00	40.00
(blue jersey)		
401 Jacksonville Jaguars Team	.15	.40
Maurice Jones-Drew		
David Garrard		
Zach Miller		
402A Shane Vereen RC	.50	1.25
(running pose)		
402B Shane Vereen SP	8.00	20.00
(leaping pose)		
403 Jordy Nelson	.20	.50
404 Bruce Carter RC	.50	1.25
405 Marques Colston	.20	.50
406 Jabar Gaffney	.15	.40
407 New York Giants Team	.15	.40
Justin Tuck		
Osi Umenyiora		
408 Ed Reed	.20	.50
409 D.J. Williams RC	.50	1.25
410A Adrian Peterson	.30	.75
(white pants)		
410B Adrian Peterson SP	12.00	30.00
(purple pants)		
411 Willis McGahee	.15	.40
412 Ronald Johnson RC	.40	1.00
413A Colin Kaepernick RC	.60	1.50
(passing the football)		
413B Colin Kaepernick SP	6.00	15.00
(holding the football)		
414 Steven Jackson	.20	.50
415 DeMarcus Ware	.20	.50
416 Darnell Dockett	.15	.40
417 Tony Gonzalez	.20	.50
418 Aldrick Robinson RC	.30	.75
419 Darrelle Revis	.20	.50
420 Matt Ryan	.25	.60
421 Lance Kendricks RC	.40	1.00
422 Ryan Mathews	.20	.50
423 Richard Seymour	.15	.40
424A Mikel Leshoure RC	.50	1.25
(running pose)		
424B Mikel Leshoure SP	5.00	12.00
(catching pose)		
425 Jordan Cameron RC	.40	1.00
426A Mark Ingram RC	1.00	2.50
(ball in left hand)		
426B Mark Ingram SP	10.00	25.00
(ball in right hand)		
426C Mark Ingram FS	.75	2.00
(ball in both hands		
factory set only)		
427A Von Miller RC	.60	1.50
(catching the ball)		
427B Von Miller SP	8.00	20.00
(no football in photo)		
428 Owen Daniels	.15	.40
429 Christian Ballard RC	.40	1.00
430A Jake Locker RC	1.25	3.00
(throwing pose)		
430B Jake Locker SP	12.00	30.00
(running pose)		
431 Vincent Jackson	.20	.50
432 Stevan Ridley RC	.50	1.25
433 Jimmy Clausen	.15	.40
434 Rahim Moore RC	.40	1.00
435 Matt Hasselbeck	.20	.50
436 Mike Wallace	.25	.60
437 Stephen Paea RC	.50	1.25
438A Ryan Mallett RC	1.00	2.50
(scrambling pose)		
438B Ryan Mallett SP	10.00	25.00
(passing pose)		
439 Detroit Lions Team	.20	.50
Ndamukong Suh		
Chris Houston		
440A Michael Vick	.25	.60
(white jersey)		
440B Michael Vick SP	15.00	30.00
(green jersey)		
RH45 Aaron Rodgers RH AU EXCH	250.00	450.00

2011 Topps Black

*VETS/55: 10X TO 25X BASIC CARDS		
*ROOKIES/55: 5X TO 12X BASIC RC		
STATED PRINT RUN 55 SER.#'d SETS		
200 Cam Newton	60.00	120.00

2011 Topps Gold

*VETS/2011: 3X TO 8X BASIC CARDS
*ROOKIES/2011: 1.5X TO 4X BASIC RC
GOLD/2011 ODDS 1:10

2011 Topps Red

*VETS/77: 6X TO 15X BASIC CARDS		
*ROOKIES/77: 3X TO 8X BASIC RC		
FIVE RED/77 PER HOBBY FACTORY SET		
200 Cam Newton	40.00	80.00

2011 Topps 1950 Bowman

COMPLETE SET (144)	50.00	100.00
STATED ODDS 1:3		
*SILVER/50: 3X TO 8X BASIC INSERTS		
1 Ndamukong Suh	.60	1.50
2 Calvin Johnson	.60	1.50
3 Ray Lewis	.60	1.50
4 Ray Rice	.50	1.25
5 Joe Flacco	.60	1.50
6 Colt McCoy	.50	1.25
7 Peyton Hillis	.50	1.25
8 Greg Little	.40	1.00
9 Clay Matthews	.60	1.50
10 Aaron Rodgers	1.00	2.50
11 A.J. Hawk	.50	1.25
12 Dallas Clark	.50	1.25
13 Peyton Manning	1.00	2.50
14 Reggie Wayne	.50	1.25
15 Sam Bradford	.60	1.50
16 Austin Pettis	.30	.75
17 Steven Jackson	.50	1.25
18 Ben Roethlisberger	.60	1.50
19 Mike Wallace	.60	1.50
20 Rashard Mendenhall	.50	1.25
21 Chris Wells	.50	1.25
22 Larry Fitzgerald	.50	1.25
23 DeSean Jackson	.50	1.25
24 LeSean McCoy	.50	1.25
25 Michael Vick	.60	1.50
26 Matt Forte	.50	1.25
27 Julius Peppers	.50	1.25
28 Greg Olsen	.40	1.00
29 Santana Moss	.50	1.25
30 Chris Cooley	.50	1.25
31 Leonard Hankerson	.40	1.00
32 Ahmad Bradshaw	.50	1.25
33 Eli Manning	.60	1.50
34 Frank Gore	.50	1.25
35 Michael Crabtree	.50	1.25
36 Vernon Davis	.50	1.25
37 Jahvid Best	.50	1.25
38 Brandon Pettigrew	.40	1.00
39 Matthew Stafford	.60	1.50
40 Matt Ryan	.60	1.50
41 Michael Turner	.50	1.25
42 Roddy White	.50	1.25
43 Benjamin Watson	.40	1.00
44 Mohamed Massaquoi	.50	1.25
45 Jason Avant	.40	1.00
46 Alex Green	.40	1.00
47 Charles Woodson	.60	1.50
48 Shonn Greene	.50	1.25
49 Dustin Keller	.50	1.25
50 Mark Sanchez	.60	1.50
51 Eric Berry	.50	1.25
52 Dwayne Bowe	.50	1.25
53 Jamaal Charles	.50	1.25
54 Troy Polamalu	.60	1.50
55 Emmanuel Sanders	.40	1.00
56 DeAngelo Williams	.50	1.25
57 Jonathan Stewart	.50	1.25
58 Jeremy Shockey	.50	1.25
59 Knowshon Moreno	.50	1.25
60 Tim Tebow	1.25	3.00
61 Jabar Gaffney	.40	1.00
62 C.J. Spiller	.50	1.25
63 Lee Evans	.50	1.25
64 Brandon Marshall	.50	1.25
65 Ronnie Brown	.50	1.25
66 Jake Long	.40	1.00
67 Hakeem Nicks	.50	1.25
68 Mario Manningham	.50	1.25
69 Steve Smith USC	.50	1.25
70 Darren McFadden	.50	1.25
71 Rolando McClain	.40	1.00
72 Jason Witten	.60	1.50
73 DeMarco Murray	.75	2.00
74 Felix Jones	.50	1.25
75 Dez Bryant	.60	1.50
76 Cecil Shorts	.30	.75
77 David Garrard	.50	1.25
78 Mike Thomas	.50	1.25
79 Maurice Jones-Drew	.50	1.25
80 Adrian Peterson	.75	2.00
81 Toby Gerhart	.50	1.25
82 Christian Ponder	.75	2.00
83 Andy Dalton	1.00	2.50
84 Jermaine Gresham	.50	1.25
85 Jon Baldwin	.40	1.00
86 Ricky Stanzi	.50	1.25
87 Devery Henderson	.40	1.00
88 Drew Brees	.60	1.50
89 Arian Foster	.50	1.25
90 Andre Johnson	.50	1.25
91 Mario Williams	.40	1.00
92 Patrick Peterson	.60	1.50
93 Ryan Williams	.50	1.25
94 Jordan Shipley	.50	1.25
95 A.J. Green	.75	2.00
96 Jamie Harper	.40	1.00
97 Chris Johnson	.50	1.25
98 Kenny Britt	.50	1.25
99 Jake Locker	1.00	2.50
100 Philip Rivers	.60	1.50
101 Antonio Gates	.50	1.25

102 Jordan Todman .25 .60
103 Joe McKnight .50 1.25
104 Bilal Powell .40 1.00
105 Santonio Holmes .50 1.25
106 Ryan Mathews .50 1.25
107 Vincent Brown .60 1.50
108 Stevan Ridley .40 1.00
109 Ryan Mallett .75 2.00
110 Tom Brady 1.00 2.50
111 Mikel Leshoure .40 1.00
112 Titus Young .50 1.25
113 Torrey Smith .50 1.25
114 Delone Carter .30 .75
115 Percy Harvin .50 1.25
116 Kyle Rudolph .40 1.00
117 Sidney Rice .50 1.25
118 Marshawn Lynch .50 1.25
119 Randall Cobb .50 1.25
120 Greg Jennings .50 1.25
121 Jerrel Jernigan .30 .75
122 Prince Amukamara .40 1.00
123 Colin Kaepernick .50 1.25
124 Kendall Hunter .40 1.00
125 Mike Williams .50 1.25
126 Josh Freeman .60 1.50
127 Julio Jones .75 2.00
128 Jacquizz Rodgers .40 1.00
129 Marcell Dareus .40 1.00
130 Blaine Gabbert .60 1.50
131 Marcedes Lewis .40 1.00
132 Shane Vereen .40 1.00
133 Rob Gronkowski .60 1.50
134 Daniel Thomas .40 1.00
135 Edmond Gates .30 .75
136 Kellen Winslow .50 1.25
137 Cadillac Williams .40 1.00
138 Von Miller .50 1.25
139 Reggie Bush .50 1.25
140 Mark Ingram .75 2.00
141 LaDainian Tomlinson .60 1.50
142 Braylon Edwards .50 1.25
143 Taiwan Jones .40 1.00
144 Cam Newton 2.00 5.00

2011 Topps End Zone Icons Patches

ONE PER SPECIAL BLASTER BOX
1 Tom Brady 8.00 20.00
2 Nick Collins 3.00 8.00
3 Braylon Edwards 4.00 10.00
4 Nate Burleson 3.00 8.00
5 Chris Johnson 4.00 10.00
6 Mike Thomas 4.00 10.00
7 Steve Johnson 4.00 10.00
8 Eli Manning 5.00 12.00
9 Mikel Leshoure 3.00 8.00
10 Larry Fitzgerald 4.00 10.00
11 LeSean McCoy 4.00 10.00
12 Rashard Mendenhall 4.00 10.00
13 Brandon Lloyd 4.00 10.00
14 Ricky Williams 4.00 10.00
15 Reggie Wayne 4.00 10.00
16 Peyton Hillis 4.00 10.00
17 Matt Cassel 4.00 10.00
18 Michael Crabtree 4.00 10.00
19 Darren McFadden 4.00 10.00
20 Drew Brees 5.00 12.00
21 Mark Ingram 6.00 15.00
22 Steve Smith 4.00 10.00
23 Rob Gronkowski 5.00 12.00
24 Felix Jones 4.00 10.00
25 Andre Johnson 4.00 10.00
26 Mike Williams 4.00 10.00
27 Greg Olsen 3.00 8.00
28 Jordy Nelson 4.00 10.00
29 Brandon Jacobs 4.00 10.00
30 Michael Vick 5.00 12.00
31 Jon Baldwin 3.00 8.00
32 Dominique Rodgers-Cromartie 3.00 8.00
33 Vernon Davis 4.00 10.00
34 Percy Harvin 4.00 10.00
35 LaDainian Tomlinson 5.00 12.00
36 Steven Jackson 4.00 10.00
37 Peyton Manning 8.00 20.00
38 Marcedes Lewis 3.00 8.00
39 Philip Rivers 5.00 12.00
40 A.J. Green 6.00 15.00
41 DeAngelo Hall 3.00 8.00
42 Jake Locker 8.00 20.00
43 Terrell Owens 5.00 12.00
44 LaMarr Woodley 3.00 8.00
45 Roddy White 4.00 10.00
46 Ryan Williams 4.00 10.00
47 Danny Woodhead 5.00 12.00
48 Mark Sanchez 5.00 12.00
49 Brent Celek 4.00 10.00
50 Aaron Rodgers 8.00 20.00
51 Antonio Gates 4.00 10.00
52 Matt Hasselbeck 4.00 10.00
53 Anquan Boldin 4.00 10.00
54 Randall Cobb 4.00 10.00
55 DeSean Jackson 4.00 10.00
56 Hakeem Nicks 4.00 10.00
57 Matt Forte 4.00 10.00
58 Zach Miller 4.00 10.00
59 Daniel Thomas 3.00 8.00
60 Blaine Gabbert 5.00 12.00
61 Kyle Rudolph 3.00 8.00
62 Greg Jennings 4.00 10.00
63 Mike Wallace 5.00 12.00
64 Mohamed Massaquoi 4.00 10.00
65 Maurice Jones-Drew 4.00 10.00
66 Miles Austin 4.00 10.00
67 Brandon Pettigrew 3.00 8.00
68 Pierre Garcon 4.00 10.00
69 Christian Ponder 6.00 15.00
70 Arian Foster 4.00 10.00
71 Lee Evans 4.00 10.00
72 Sam Bradford 5.00 12.00
73 Reggie Bush 4.00 10.00
74 Taylor Mays 3.00 8.00
75 Julio Jones 6.00 15.00
76 Cedric Benson 4.00 10.00
77 Santana Moss 4.00 10.00
78 Knowshon Moreno 4.00 10.00
79 Hines Ward 4.00 10.00
80 Tony Romo 5.00 12.00
81 Andy Dalton 8.00 20.00
82 Devin Hester 5.00 12.00
83 Malcom Floyd 4.00 10.00
85 Matt Ryan 5.00 12.00
86 Wes Welker 5.00 12.00
87 Tim Hightower 3.00 8.00
88 Kenny Britt 4.00 10.00
89 Ahmad Bradshaw 4.00 10.00
90 Adrian Peterson 6.00 15.00
91 Darrius Heyward-Bey 3.00 8.00
92 Ryan Mallett 6.00 15.00
93 Ray Rice 4.00 10.00
94 B.J. Raji 4.00 10.00
95 Jamaal Charles 4.00 10.00
96 Tim Tebow 10.00 25.00
97 Calvin Johnson 5.00 12.00
98 Marion Barber 4.00 10.00
99 Davone Bess 3.00 8.00
100 Cam Newton 12.00 30.00

2011 Topps Faces of the Franchise

STATED ODDS 1:4
BJ Sam Bradford .60 1.50
  Steven Jackson
BW Dez Bryant .60 1.50
  Jason Witten
FO Matt Forte .50 1.25
  Greg Olsen
FW Josh Freeman .60 1.50
  Mike Williams
JM DeSean Jackson .50 1.25
  LeSean McCoy
MA Darren McFadden .60 1.50
  Marcus Allen
MB Brandon Marshall .50 1.25
  Davone Bess
MW Peyton Manning 1.00 2.50
  Reggie Wayne
NS Joe Namath .75 2.00
  Mark Sanchez
NW Cam Newton 2.00 5.00
  DeAngelo Williams
PH Adrian Peterson .75 2.00
  Percy Harvin
RF Aaron Rodgers 1.25 3.00
  Brett Favre
RJ Aaron Rodgers 1.00 2.50
  Greg Jennings
RP Ben Roethlisberger .60 1.50
  Troy Polamalu
RW Matt Ryan .60 1.50
  Roddy White
SD C.J. Spiller .40 1.00
  Marcell Dareus
SF Ndamukong Suh .50 1.25
  Nick Fairley
UP Brian Urlacher .60 1.50
  Julius Peppers
WJ Roddy White .75 2.00
  Julio Jones
GJD Blaine Gabbert .60 1.50
  Maurice Jones-Drew

2011 Topps Faces of the Franchise Autographs

DUAL AUTO ODDS 1:20,840 RET
BJ Sam Bradford
  Steven Jackson
BW Dez Bryant 50.00 100.00
  Jason Witten
FO Matt Forte 25.00 50.00
  Greg Olsen
FW Josh Freeman 40.00 80.00
  Mike Williams
HG Percy Harvin 50.00 100.00
  Chad Greenway
JM DeSean Jackson 25.00 50.00
  LeSean McCoy
JN Greg Jennings
  Jordy Nelson
ML Brandon Marshall
  Jake Long
NS Joe Namath 75.00 150.00
  Mark Sanchez
NW Cam Newton 100.00 175.00
  DeAngelo Williams
RW Matt Ryan 40.00 80.00
  Roddy White
SD C.J. Spiller 30.00 60.00
  Marcell Dareus
SF Ndamukong Suh 40.00 80.00
  Nick Fairley
WJ Roddy White 50.00 100.00
  Julio Jones
GJD Blaine Gabbert 40.00 80.00
  Maurice Jones-Drew

2011 Topps Faces of the Franchise Relics

DUAL RELIC/50 ODDS 1:23,250 RET
FO Matt Forte 10.00 25.00
  Greg Olsen
MA Darren McFadden 12.00 30.00
  Marcus Allen
MW Peyton Manning 15.00 40.00
  Reggie Wayne
NW Cam Newton 15.00 40.00
  DeAngelo Williams
RF Aaron Rodgers 30.00 60.00
  Brett Favre
RP Ben Roethlisberger 12.00 30.00
  Troy Polamalu
RW Matt Ryan 8.00 20.00
  Roddy White
UP Brian Urlacher 8.00 20.00
  Julius Peppers
WJ Roddy White 10.00 25.00
  Julio Jones
GJD Blaine Gabbert 8.00 20.00
  Maurice Jones-Drew

2011 Topps Game Day

COMPLETE SET (50) 10.00 25.00
STATED ODDS 1:4
GDAG A.J. Green .50 1.25
GDAP Adrian Peterson .50 1.25
GDBF Brett Favre .75 2.00
GDBG Blaine Gabbert .40 1.00
GDBL Brandon Lloyd .30 .75
GDBR Ben Roethlisberger .40 1.00
GDCJ Calvin Johnson .40 1.00
GDCM Colt McCoy .30 .75
GDCN Cam Newton 1.25 3.00
GDCW Charles Woodson .40 1.00
GDDB Dwayne Bowe .30 .75
GDDBR Drew Brees .40 1.00
GDDM Dan Marino .75 2.00
GDEM Eli Manning .40 1.00
GDER Ed Reed .30 .75
GDFB Fred Biletnikoff .30 .75
GDFG Frank Gore .30 .75
GDGJ Greg Jennings .30 .75
GDHN Hakeem Nicks .30 .75
GDJA Jared Allen .30 .75
GDJB Jerome Bettis .40 1.00
GDJBE Jahvid Best .30 .75
GDJC Jamaal Charles .30 .75
GDJF Joe Flacco .40 1.00
GDJJ Julio Jones .50 1.25
GDJN Joe Namath .50 1.25
GDJW Jason Witten .40 1.00
GDLF Larry Fitzgerald .30 .75
GDMA Miles Austin .30 .75
GDMF Matt Forte .30 .75
GDMI Mark Ingram .50 1.25
GDMJD Maurice Jones-Drew .30 .75
GDMR Matt Ryan .40 1.00
GDMV Michael Vick .40 1.00
GDNA Nnamdi Asomugha .30 .75
GDNS Ndamukong Suh .40 1.00
GDPH Percy Harvin .30 .75
GDPM Peyton Manning .60 1.50
GDPW Patrick Willis .30 .75
GDRL Ray Lewis .40 1.00
GDRM Rashard Mendenhall .30 .75
GDRW Roddy White .30 .75
GDSB Sam Bradford .40 1.00
GDSG Shonn Greene .30 .75
GDSH Santonio Holmes .30 .75
GDSM Santana Moss .30 .75
GDTA Troy Aikman .50 1.25
GDTG Tony Gonzalez .30 .75
GDTP Troy Polamalu .40 1.00
GDTR Tony Romo .40 1.00

2011 Topps Game Day Autographs

GROUP A ODDS 1:10,340
GROUP B ODDS 1:2433
GROUP C ODDS 1:1061
GDAAG A.J. Green 15.00 30.00
GDAAH Aaron Hernandez 4.00 10.00
GDAAP Austin Pettis 3.00 8.00
GDABF Brett Favre 100.00 175.00
GDABP Bilal Powell 2.50 6.00
GDACG Chad Greenway 4.00 10.00
GDACK Colin Kaepernick 10.00 25.00
GDACM Colt McCoy 12.00 30.00
GDADB Drew Brees 50.00 100.00
GDAEB Eric Berry 5.00 12.00
GDAED Early Doucet 3.00 8.00
GDAER Ed Reed 15.00 30.00
GDAES Emmanuel Sanders 5.00 12.00
GDAFB Fred Biletnikoff 10.00 25.00
GDAFJ Fred Jackson 20.00 40.00
GDAGJ Greg Jennings 8.00 20.00
GDAHN Hakeem Nicks 6.00 15.00
GDAJB Jerome Bettis 30.00 60.00
GDAJC James Casey 3.00 8.00
GDAJJ James Jones 3.00 8.00
GDAJN Joe Namath 40.00 80.00
GDAJS James Starks 5.00 12.00
GDAJT Jordan Todman 2.50 6.00
GDAJW Joe Webb 5.00 12.00
GDAKH Kendall Hunter 4.00 10.00
GDAKR Kyle Rudolph 4.00 10.00
GDALH Leonard Hankerson 5.00 12.00
GDAMF Matt Forte 6.00 15.00
GDAMJ Malcolm Jenkins 4.00 10.00
GDANS Ndamukong Suh 15.00 30.00
GDARC Randall Cobb 5.00 12.00
GDARG Rob Gronkowski 15.00 30.00
GDARJ Rashad Jennings 3.00 8.00
GDARM Rashard Mendenhall 6.00 15.00
GDARW Roddy White 6.00 15.00
GDASB Sam Bradford 30.00 60.00
GDASG Shonn Greene 6.00 15.00
GDASH Santonio Holmes 8.00 20.00
GDATY Titus Young 5.00 12.00
GDAVJ Vincent Jackson 8.00 20.00
GDAVM Von Miller 8.00 20.00
GDABFL Brandon Flowers 3.00 8.00
GDAERO Eddie Royal 3.00 8.00
GDAJBE Jahvid Best 6.00 15.00
GDAJJO Julio Jones 15.00 30.00
GDAJNE Jordy Nelson 6.00 15.00
GDAJSM Jimmy Smith 4.00 10.00
GDAJWI Jason Witten 15.00 30.00
GDAKRI Keith Rivers 3.00 8.00
GDAMJE Michael Jenkins 3.00 8.00

2011 Topps Game Day Relics

GROUP A ODDS 1:444
GROUP B ODDS 1:1273
GDRAB Anquan Boldin 3.00 8.00
GDRAG A.J. Green 5.00 12.00
GDRAJH A.J. Hawk 3.00 8.00
GDRAS Asante Samuel 4.00 10.00
GDRBC Brent Celek 3.00 8.00
GDRBG Blaine Gabbert 4.00 10.00
GDRBJ Brandon Jacobs 3.00 8.00
GDRBL Brandon Lloyd 3.00 8.00
GDRBR Ben Roethlisberger 5.00 12.00
GDRCG Chad Greenway 4.00 10.00
GDRCJ Calvin Johnson 4.00 10.00
GDRCN Cam Newton 12.00 30.00
GDRCW Charles Woodson 6.00 15.00
GDRDB Dwayne Bowe 3.00 8.00
GDRDK Dustin Keller 3.00 8.00
GDRDM Dan Marino 10.00 25.00
GDRED Early Doucet 2.50 6.00
GDREM Eli Manning 4.00 10.00
GDRGO Greg Olsen 2.50 6.00
GDRJA Jared Allen 4.00 10.00
GDRJC Jamaal Charles 3.00 8.00
GDRJF Joe Flacco 4.00 10.00
GDRJJ Julio Jones 5.00 12.00
GDRJK Jake Locker 6.00 15.00
GDRKB Kenny Britt 3.00 8.00
GDRKR Kyle Rudolph 2.50 6.00
GDRLF Larry Fitzgerald 3.00 8.00
GDRMA Miles Austin 4.00 10.00
GDRMC Michael Crabtree 3.00 8.00
GDRMCA Matt Cassel 3.00 8.00
GDRMF Matt Forte 3.00 8.00
GDRMI Mark Ingram 5.00 12.00
GDRMJD Maurice Jones-Drew 3.00 8.00
GDRML Mikel Leshoure 2.50 6.00
GDRMV Michael Vick 4.00 10.00
GDRNA Nnamdi Asomugha 4.00 10.00
GDRPM Peyton Manning 6.00 15.00
GDRPW Patrick Willis 3.00 8.00
GDRRB Ronnie Brown 3.00 8.00
GDRRL Ray Lewis 4.00 10.00
GDRRW Ryan Williams 3.00 8.00
GDRSJ Steven Jackson 3.00 8.00
GDRSM Santana Moss 3.00 8.00
GDRSR Sidney Rice 3.00 8.00
GDRTA Troy Aikman 6.00 15.00
GDRTG Tony Gonzalez 3.00 8.00
GDRTP Troy Polamalu 6.00 15.00
GDRTR Tony Romo 4.00 10.00
GDRVJ Vincent Jackson 4.00 10.00
GDRVM Von Miller 4.00 10.00

2011 Topps Game Day Relics Jumbos

STATED PRINT RUN 20 SER.#'d SETS
GDJRAB Anquan Boldin 8.00 20.00
GDJRAP Adrian Peterson 12.00 30.00
GDJRBC Brent Celek 8.00 20.00
GDJRBJ Brandon Jacobs 8.00 20.00
GDJRBL Brandon Lloyd 8.00 20.00
GDJRCB Cedric Benson 10.00 25.00
GDJRDB Dwayne Bowe 8.00 20.00
GDJRJA John Abraham 8.00 20.00
GDJRJAL Jared Allen 12.00 30.00
GDJRJC Jamaal Charles 8.00 20.00
GDJRJF Joe Flacco 10.00 25.00
GDJRKB Kenny Britt 10.00 25.00
GDJRMA Miles Austin 12.00 30.00
GDJRMC Michael Crabtree 8.00 20.00
GDJRMCA Matt Cassel 8.00 20.00
GDJRMF Matt Forte 8.00 20.00
GDJRRB Ronnie Brown 8.00 20.00
GDJRRL Ray Lewis 10.00 25.00
GDJRTG Tony Gonzalez 8.00 20.00
GDJRWW Wes Welker 12.00 30.00

2011 Topps Game Day Relics Autographs

STATED PRINT RUN 50 SER.#'d SETS
GDARAP Adrian Peterson 50.00 100.00
GDARBF Brandon Flowers 12.00 30.00
GDARCB Champ Bailey 15.00 40.00
GDARCG Chad Greenway 25.00 50.00
GDARER Ed Reed 15.00 40.00
GDARFJ Fred Jackson 30.00 60.00
GDARGJ Greg Jennings 15.00 40.00
GDARGO Greg Olsen 12.00 30.00
GDARHN Hakeem Nicks 12.00 30.00
GDARJN Jordy Nelson 15.00 40.00
GDARKR Keith Rivers 6.00 15.00
GDARMR Matt Ryan 20.00 50.00
GDARPH Percy Harvin 15.00 40.00
GDARRW Roddy White 15.00 40.00
GDARVJ Vincent Jackson 15.00 40.00

2011 Topps Rookie Autographs

STATED ODDS 1:12,175
6 Kyle Rudolph 10.00 25.00
7 Vincent Brown 10.00 25.00
11 Leonard Hankerson 10.00 25.00
19 Titus Young 12.00 30.00
70 Andy Dalton 60.00 100.00
108 Delone Carter 15.00 30.00
126 DeMarco Murray 60.00 120.00
143 Bilal Powell 10.00 25.00
149 Randall Cobb 40.00 80.00
151 A.J. Green 75.00 125.00
155 Kendall Hunter 10.00 25.00
160 Blaine Gabbert 50.00 100.00
193 Alex Green 15.00 40.00
200 Cam Newton 175.00 300.00
235 Jerrel Jernigan 8.00 20.00
238 Christian Ponder
242 Jon Baldwin 12.00 30.00
256 Marcell Dareus 40.00 80.00
274 Torrey Smith 20.00 40.00
313 Taiwan Jones 10.00 25.00
321 Greg Little 10.00 25.00
325 Jordan Todman 12.00 30.00
350 Julio Jones 75.00 150.00
366 Daniel Thomas 25.00 50.00
382 Jamie Harper 12.00 30.00
395 Ryan Williams
396 Austin Pettis 12.00 30.00
402 Shane Vereen 10.00 25.00
413 Colin Kaepernick 50.00 100.00
424 Mikel Leshoure 10.00 25.00
426 Mark Ingram 90.00 150.00
427 Von Miller 25.00 50.00
430 Jake Locker 75.00 150.00
432 Stevan Ridley 15.00 40.00
438 Ryan Mallett 40.00 80.00

2011 Topps Rookie NFL Shield

ONE PER SPECIAL RETAIL FACTORY SET
LPR1 Cam Newton 10.00 25.00
LPR2 Jake Locker 5.00 12.00
LPR3 Julio Jones 4.00 10.00
LPR4 Mark Ingram 4.00 10.00

2011 Topps Rookie Patch

HRPAD Andy Dalton 10.00 25.00
HRPAG A.J. Green 8.00 20.00
HRPAGR Alex Green 4.00 10.00
HRPBG Blaine Gabbert 6.00 15.00
HRPBP Bilal Powell 2.50 6.00
HRPCK Colin Kaepernick 5.00 12.00
HRPCN Cam Newton 15.00 40.00
HRPCP Austin Pettis 3.00 8.00
HRPCP Christian Ponder 8.00 20.00
HRPDM Delone Carter 3.00 8.00
HRPDM DeMarco Murray 8.00 20.00
HRPGL Daniel Thomas 4.00 10.00
HRPGL Greg Little 4.00 10.00
HRPJH Jon Baldwin 4.00 10.00
HRPJH Jamie Harper 4.00 10.00
HRPJJE Jerrel Jernigan 3.00 8.00
HRPJL Jake Locker 10.00 25.00
HRPJL Julio Jones 8.00 20.00
HRPKH Kendall Hunter 4.00 10.00
HRPKH Jordan Todman 2.50 6.00
HRPKR Kyle Rudolph 4.00 10.00
HRPLH Leonard Hankerson 4.00 10.00
HRPMD Marcell Dareus 4.00 10.00
HRPMI Mark Ingram 8.00 20.00
HRPML Mikel Leshoure 4.00 10.00
HRPRC Randall Cobb 5.00 12.00
HRPRM Ryan Mallett 8.00 20.00
HRPRW Ryan Williams 5.00 12.00
HRPSR Stevan Ridley 4.00 10.00
HRPSV Shane Vereen 4.00 10.00
HRPTJ Taiwan Jones 4.00 10.00
HRPTS Torrey Smith 5.00 12.00
HRPTY Titus Young 6.00 15.00
HRPVB Vincent Brown 4.00 10.00
HRPVM Von Miller 5.00 12.00

2011 Topps Rookie Premiere Autographs

STATED PRINT RUN 90 SER.#'d SETS
RPAD Andy Dalton 60.00 120.00
RPAG Alex Green 15.00 40.00
RPAJG A.J. Green 60.00 120.00
RPAP Austin Pettis 12.00 30.00
RPBG Blaine Gabbert 25.00 60.00
RPBP Bilal Powell 10.00 25.00
RPCK Colin Kaepernick 20.00 50.00
RPCN Cam Newton 175.00 300.00
RPCP Christian Ponder 40.00 80.00
RPDC Delone Carter 12.00 30.00
RPDM DeMarco Murray 60.00 120.00
RPDT Daniel Thomas 30.00 60.00
RPEG Edmond Gates 12.00 30.00
RPGL Greg Little 15.00 40.00
RPJB Jon Baldwin 30.00 60.00
RPJH Jamie Harper 15.00 40.00
RPJJ Julio Jones 60.00 120.00
RPJJE Jerrel Jernigan 12.00 30.00
RPJL Jake Locker 75.00 150.00
RPJT Jordan Todman 10.00 25.00
RPKH Kendall Hunter 15.00 40.00
RPKR Kyle Rudolph 15.00 40.00
RPLH Leonard Hankerson 15.00 40.00
RPMD Marcell Dareus 15.00 40.00
RPMI Mark Ingram 60.00 120.00
RPML Mikel Leshoure 15.00 40.00
RPRC Randall Cobb 20.00 50.00
RPRM Ryan Mallett 30.00 80.00
RPRW Ryan Williams 20.00 50.00
RPSR Stevan Ridley 15.00 40.00
RPSV Shane Vereen 15.00 40.00
RPTJ Taiwan Jones 15.00 40.00
RPTS Torrey Smith 20.00 50.00
RPTY Titus Young 20.00 50.00
RPVB Vincent Brown 15.00 40.00
RPVM Von Miller 20.00 50.00

2011 Topps Rookie Premiere Autographs Dual

STATED PRINT RUN 25 SER.#'d SETS
DG Andy Dalton 60.00 120.00
  A.J. Green
GJ A.J. Green 60.00 120.00
  Julio Jones
GN Blaine Gabbert 125.00 250.00
  Cam Newton
IL Mark Ingram 50.00 100.00
  Mikel Leshoure
LY Mikel Leshoure 40.00 80.00
  Titus Young

2011 Topps Rookie Red Zone Autographs

STATED PRINT RUN 100 SER.#'d SETS
RZRAAD Andy Dalton 40.00 80.00
RZRAAG Alex Green 25.00 50.00
RZRAAJG A.J. Green 40.00 80.00
RZRAAP Austin Pettis 10.00 25.00
RZRABG Blaine Gabbert 20.00 50.00
RZRABP Bilal Powell 8.00 20.00
RZRACK Colin Kaepernick 15.00 40.00
RZRACN Cam Newton 125.00 200.00
RZRACP Christian Ponder 30.00 60.00
RZRADC Delone Carter 10.00 25.00
RZRADM DeMarco Murray 50.00 100.00
RZRADT Daniel Thomas 25.00 50.00
RZRAEG Edmond Gates 10.00 25.00
RZRAGL Greg Little 12.00 30.00
RZRAJB Jon Baldwin 25.00 50.00
RZRAJH Jamie Harper 12.00 30.00
RZRAJJ Julio Jones 40.00 80.00
RZRAJJE Jerrel Jernigan 10.00 25.00
RZRAJL Jake Locker 50.00 120.00
RZRAJT Jordan Todman 8.00 20.00
RZRAKH Kendall Hunter 12.00 30.00
RZRAKR Kyle Rudolph 12.00 30.00
RZRALH Leonard Hankerson 12.00 30.00
RZRAMD Marcell Dareus 12.00 30.00
RZRAMI Mark Ingram 40.00 100.00
RZRAML Mikel Leshoure 12.00 30.00
RZRARC Randall Cobb 25.00 60.00
RZRARM Ryan Mallett 25.00 60.00
RZRARW Ryan Williams 15.00 40.00
RZRASR Stevan Ridley 25.00 50.00
RZRASV Shane Vereen 12.00 30.00
RZRATJ Taiwan Jones 12.00 30.00
RZRATS Torrey Smith 15.00 40.00
RZRATY Titus Young 15.00 40.00
RZRAVB Vincent Brown 12.00 30.00
RZRAVM Von Miller 15.00 40.00

2011 Topps Rookie Refractors

ONE PER SPECIAL RETAIL BOX
TMB1 Cam Newton 4.00 10.00
TMB2 Blaine Gabbert 1.25 3.00

2011 Topps Super Bowl Legends

STATED ODDS 1:6
SBLI Bart Starr 1.00 2.50
SBLII Bart Starr 1.00 2.50
SBLIII Joe Namath .75 2.00
SBLIV Len Dawson .60 1.50
SBLV Chuck Howley .40 1.00
SBLVI Roger Staubach .75 2.00
SBLIX Franco Harris .60 1.50
SBLXI Fred Biletnikoff .50 1.25
SBLXIII Terry Bradshaw .75 2.00
SBLXIV Terry Bradshaw .75 2.00
SBLXL Hines Ward .60 1.50
SBLXV Jim Plunkett .50 1.25
SBLXVI Joe Montana 1.25 3.00
SBLXVIII Marcus Allen .60 1.50
SBLXIX Joe Montana 1.25 3.00
SBLXX Richard Dent .40 1.00
SBLXXI Phil Simms .50 1.25
SBLXXIII Jerry Rice 1.00 2.50
SBLXXIV Joe Montana 1.25 3.00
SBLXXV Ottis Anderson .40 1.00
SBLXXVII Troy Aikman .75 2.00
SBLXXVIII Emmitt Smith 1.00 2.50
SBLXXIX Steve Young .75 2.00
SBLXXX Larry Brown .40 1.00
SBLXXXIII John Elway 1.00 2.50
SBLXXXIV Kurt Warner .50 1.25
SBLXXXV Ray Lewis .60 1.50
SBLXXXVI Tom Brady 1.00 2.50
SBLXXXVIII Tom Brady 1.00 2.50
SBLXXXIX Deion Branch .40 1.00
SBLXLI Peyton Manning 1.00 2.50
SBLXLII Eli Manning .60 1.50
SBLXLIII Santonio Holmes .50 1.25
SBLXLIV Drew Brees .60 1.50
SBLXLV Aaron Rodgers 1.00 2.50

2011 Topps Super Bowl Legends Autographs

SB AUTO/25 ODDS 1:17,600
EXCH EXPIRATION: 7/31/2014
SBAI Bart Starr 125.00 200.00
SBAII Bart Starr 125.00 200.00
SBAIII Joe Namath 75.00 150.00
SBAIV Len Dawson 40.00 80.00
SBAV Chuck Howley EXCH 20.00 40.00
SBAVI Roger Staubach 75.00 150.00
SBAIX Franco Harris 40.00 80.00
SBAXI Fred Biletnikoff 40.00 80.00
SBAXIII Terry Bradshaw 100.00 175.00
SBAXIV Terry Bradshaw 100.00 175.00
SBAXV Jim Plunkett EXCH 30.00 60.00
SBAXVI Joe Montana 100.00 200.00
SBAXVIII Marcus Allen 40.00 80.00
SBAXIX Joe Montana 100.00 200.00
SBAXX Richard Dent 50.00 100.00
SBAXXI Phil Simms 25.00 50.00
SBAXXIII Jerry Rice 100.00 175.00
SBAXXIV Joe Montana 100.00 200.00
SBAXXV Ottis Anderson 20.00 40.00
SBAXXVII Troy Aikman 50.00 100.00
SBAXXVIII Emmitt Smith 100.00 175.00
SBAXXIX Steve Young 50.00 100.00
SBAXXX Larry Brown 30.00 60.00
SBAXXXIII John Elway 125.00 200.00
SBAXXXIV Kurt Warner EXCH 50.00 100.00
SBAXXXV Ray Lewis 40.00 80.00
SBAXXXIX Deion Branch 25.00 50.00
SBAXL Hines Ward 75.00 150.00
SBAXLI Peyton Manning 100.00 175.00
SBAXLIII Santonio Holmes 25.00 50.00
SBAXLIV Drew Brees 60.00 120.00
SBAXLV Aaron Rodgers 175.00 300.00

2011 Topps Super Bowl Legends Coins Pewter

PEWTER/75 STATED ODDS 1:3100
*BRONZE/50: .6X TO 1.5X PEWTER/75
*SILVER/25: .8X TO 2X PEWTER/75
SBLCI Bart Starr 12.00 30.00
SBLCII Bart Starr 12.00 30.00
SBLCIII Joe Namath 10.00 25.00
SBLCIV Len Dawson 10.00 25.00
SBLCVI Roger Staubach 10.00 25.00
SBLCIX Franco Harris 8.00 20.00
SBLCXI Fred Biletnikoff 6.00 15.00
SBLCXIII Terry Bradshaw 10.00 25.00
SBLCXIV Terry Bradshaw 10.00 25.00
SBLCXV Jim Plunkett 8.00 20.00
SBLCXVI Joe Montana 15.00 40.00
SBLCXVIII Marcus Allen 10.00 25.00
SBLCXIX Joe Montana 15.00 40.00
SBLCXXI Phil Simms 6.00 15.00
SBLCXXIV Joe Montana 15.00 40.00
SBLCXXVIII Emmitt Smith 12.00 30.00
SBLCXXVII Troy Aikman 10.00 25.00
SBLCXXIX Steve Young 10.00 25.00
SBLCXXXIII John Elway 15.00 40.00
SBLCXXXV Ray Lewis 8.00 20.00
SBLCXXXVI Tom Brady 12.00 30.00
SBLCXXXVIII Tom Brady 12.00 30.00
SBLCXXXIX Deion Branch 5.00 12.00
SBLCXL Hines Ward 6.00 15.00
SBLCXLI Peyton Manning 12.00 30.00
SBLCXLII Eli Manning 8.00 20.00
SBLCXLIII Santonio Holmes 8.00 20.00
SBLCXLIV Drew Brees 8.00 20.00
SBLCXLV Aaron Rodgers 12.00 30.00

2011 Topps Super Bowl Legends Giveaway

RANDOM INSERTS IN PACKS
SBLG1 Joe Namath 1.25 3.00
SBLG2 Terry Bradshaw 1.25 3.00
SBLG3 Joe Montana 1.25 3.00
SBLG4 Jerry Rice 1.25 3.00
SBLG5 Emmitt Smith 1.25 3.00
SBLG6 John Elway 1.25 3.00
SBLG7 Tom Brady 1.25 3.00
SBLG8 Peyton Manning 1.25 3.00
SBLG9 Drew Brees 1.25 3.00
SBLG110 Aaron Rodgers 1.25 3.00

2011 Topps Super Bowl Legends Giveaway Die Cut

ISSUED VIA MAIL REDEMPTION
*GOLD/99: .6X TO 1.5X BASIC CARD
1 Joe Namath 6.00 15.00
2 Terry Bradshaw 6.00 15.00
3 Joe Montana 10.00 25.00
4 Jerry Rice 8.00 20.00
5 Emmitt Smith 8.00 20.00
6 John Elway 8.00 20.00
7 Tom Brady 8.00 20.00
8 Peyton Manning 8.00 20.00
9 Drew Brees 5.00 12.00
10 Aaron Rodgers 12.00 30.00
11 Bart Starr 8.00 20.00
12 Bart Starr 8.00 20.00
13 Len Dawson 5.00 12.00
14 Chuck Howley 3.00 8.00
15 Roger Staubach 6.00 15.00
16 Franco Harris 5.00 12.00
17 Fred Biletnikoff 4.00 10.00
18 Terry Bradshaw 6.00 15.00
19 Jim Plunkett 4.00 10.00
20 Joe Montana 10.00 25.00
21 Marcus Allen 5.00 12.00
22 Richard Dent 3.00 8.00
23 Phil Simms 4.00 10.00
24 Joe Montana 10.00 25.00
25 Ottis Anderson 3.00 8.00
26 Troy Aikman 6.00 15.00
27 Steve Young 6.00 15.00
28 Larry Brown 3.00 8.00
29 Kurt Warner 4.00 10.00
30 Ray Lewis 5.00 12.00
31 Tom Brady 8.00 20.00
32 Deion Branch 3.00 8.00
33 Hines Ward 4.00 10.00
34 Eli Manning 5.00 12.00
35 Santonio Holmes 4.00 10.00
36 Greg Jennings 4.00 10.00
37 Clay Matthews 5.00 12.00
38 Jordy Nelson 4.00 10.00
39 Marques Colston 4.00 10.00
40 Terry Bradshaw 6.00 15.00
41 Hines Ward 4.00 10.00
42 Ben Roethlisberger 5.00 12.00
43 Steve Smith USC 5.00 12.00
44 Justin Tuck 4.00 10.00
45 Reggie Wayne 4.00 10.00
46 Joseph Addai 4.00 10.00
47 Jerome Bettis 5.00 12.00
48 Troy Polamalu 5.00 12.00
49 Tom Brady 8.00 20.00
50 Deion Branch 3.00 8.00
51 Terry Bradshaw 6.00 15.00
52 John Elway 8.00 20.00
53 Troy Aikman 6.00 15.00
54 Emmitt Smith 8.00 20.00
55 Jerry Rice 8.00 20.00
56 Troy Aikman 6.00 15.00
57 Emmitt Smith 8.00 20.00
58 Art Monk 4.00 10.00
59 Ronnie Lott 4.00 10.00
60 Jerry Rice 8.00 20.00
61 Ronnie Lott 4.00 10.00
62 Joe Montana 10.00 25.00
63 Art Monk 4.00 10.00
64 Ronnie Lott 4.00 10.00
65 Jim Plunkett 4.00 10.00
66 Howie Long 5.00 12.00
67 Ronnie Lott 4.00 10.00
68 Franco Harris 5.00 12.00
69 Franco Harris 5.00 12.00
70 Roger Staubach 6.00 15.00
71 Tony Dorsett 5.00 12.00
72 Ken Stabler 5.00 12.00
73 Franco Harris 5.00 12.00

2011 Topps Super Bowl Legends Jerseys

JERSEY/45 ODDS 1:8860
*GOLD/35: .4X TO 1X BASIC JSY/45
*HOLOFOIL/15: .6X TO 1.5X BASIC JSY/45
SBRIII Joe Namath 12.00 30.00
SBRVI Roger Staubach 12.00 30.00
SBRIX Franco Harris
SBRXI Fred Biletnikoff 10.00 25.00
SBRXIII Terry Bradshaw 12.00 30.00
SBRXIV Terry Bradshaw 12.00 30.00
SBRXV Jim Plunkett 8.00 20.00
SBRXVI Joe Montana 15.00 40.00
SBRXVIII Marcus Allen 10.00 25.00
SBRXIX Joe Montana 15.00 40.00
SBRXXI Phil Simms 8.00 20.00
SBRXXIII Jerry Rice 15.00 40.00
SBRXXIV Joe Montana 15.00 40.00
SBRXXVIII Emmitt Smith 15.00 40.00
SBRXXVII Troy Aikman 12.00 30.00
SBRXXIX Steve Young 12.00 30.00
SBRXXXIII John Elway 15.00 40.00
SBRXXXIV Kurt Warner 8.00 20.00
SBRXXXV Ray Lewis 10.00 25.00
SBRXXXVI Tom Brady 15.00 40.00
SBRXXXVIII Tom Brady 15.00 40.00
SBRXL Hines Ward 12.00 30.00
SBRXLI Peyton Manning 15.00 40.00
SBRXLII Eli Manning 10.00 25.00
SBRXLIII Santonio Holmes 10.00 25.00
SBRXLIV Drew Brees 10.00 25.00
SBRXLV Aaron Rodgers 15.00 40.00

2011 Topps Super Bowl Legends Logo Stamps

LOGO STAMP/100 ODDS 1:980
*PLAYER STAMP/100: .4X TO 1X LOGO/100
*RING/137: .4X TO 1X LOGO STAMP/100
*SB PATCH/50: .5X TO 1.2X LOGO STAMP/100
SBLSI Bart Starr 12.00 30.00
SBLSII Bart Starr 12.00 30.00
SBLSIII Joe Namath 10.00 25.00
SBLSIV Len Dawson 8.00 20.00
SBLSV Chuck Howley 5.00 12.00
SBLSVI Roger Staubach 10.00 25.00
SBLSIX Franco Harris 8.00 20.00
SBLSXI Fred Biletnikoff 8.00 20.00
SBLSXIII Terry Bradshaw 10.00 25.00
SBLSXIV Terry Bradshaw 10.00 25.00
SBLSXV Jim Plunkett 6.00 15.00
SBLSXVI Joe Montana 12.00 30.00
SBLSXVIII Marcus Allen 8.00 20.00
SBLSXIX Joe Montana 12.00 30.00
SBLSXX Richard Dent 8.00 20.00
SBLSXXI Phil Simms 6.00 15.00
SBLSXXIII Jerry Rice 12.00 30.00
SBLSXXIV Joe Montana 12.00 30.00
SBLSXXV Ottis Anderson 5.00 12.00
SBLSXXVII Troy Aikman 10.00 25.00
SBLSXXVIII Emmitt Smith 12.00 30.00
SBLSXXIX Steve Young 10.00 25.00
SBLSXXX Larry Brown 5.00 12.00
SBLSXXXIII John Elway 12.00 30.00
SBLSXXXIV Kurt Warner 6.00 15.00
SBLSXXXV Ray Lewis 10.00 25.00
SBLSXXXVI Tom Brady 12.00 30.00
SBLSXXXVIII Tom Brady 12.00 30.00
SBLSXXXIX Deion Branch 5.00 12.00
SBLSXL Hines Ward 8.00 20.00
SBLSXLI Peyton Manning 12.00 30.00
SBLSXLII Eli Manning 8.00 20.00
SBLSXLIII Santonio Holmes 8.00 20.00
SBLSXLIV Drew Brees 10.00 25.00
SBLSXLV Aaron Rodgers 20.00 50.00

2011 Topps Super Bowl Legends Venue Relics

VENUE RELIC/100 ODDS 1:14,500
SBVRII Bart Starr Seat 12.00 30.00
SBVRIII Joe Namath Seat 12.00 30.00
SBVRV Chuck Howley Seat 8.00 20.00
SBVRXIII Terry Bradshaw Seat 10.00 25.00
SBVRXV Jim Plunkett Turf 8.00 20.00
SBVRXX Richard Dent Turf 8.00 20.00
SBVRXXIV Joe Montana Turf 15.00 40.00
SBVRXXXVI Tom Brady Pylon 15.00 40.00
SBVRXXXIX Deion Branch Pylon 10.00 25.00
SBVRXLV Aaron Rodgers Pylon 15.00 40.00

2011 Topps Topps Town

STATED ODDS 1:6
TT1 Aaron Rodgers .50 1.25
TT2 Adrian Peterson .40 1.00
TT3 Andre Johnson .25 .60
TT4 Mark Ingram .50 1.25
TT5 Michael Vick .30 .75
TT6 Chris Johnson .25 .60
TT7 Tom Brady .50 1.25
TT8 Jake Locker .60 1.50
TT9 Roddy White .25 .60
TT10 Drew Brees .30 .75
TT11 Arian Foster .25 .60
TT12 Calvin Johnson .30 .75
TT13 Matt Schaub .25 .60
TT14 Peyton Manning .50 1.25
TT15 Maurice Jones-Drew .25 .60
TT16 Antonio Gates .25 .60
TT17 Torrey Smith .30 .75
TT18 Hakeem Nicks .25 .60
TT19 Philip Rivers .30 .75
TT20 A.J. Green .50 1.25
TT21 Ray Rice .25 .60
TT22 Greg Jennings .25 .60
TT23 Josh Freeman .30 .75
TT24 Christian Ponder .50 1.25
TT25 Jamaal Charles .25 .60
TT26 Mike Wallace .30 .75
TT27 Jerrel Jernigan .20 .50
TT28 Reggie Wayne .25 .60
TT29 Matt Ryan .30 .75
TT30 Blaine Gabbert .40 1.00
TT31 Rashard Mendenhall .25 .60
TT32 Ryan Mallett .50 1.25
TT33 Larry Fitzgerald .25 .60
TT34 Darren McFadden .25 .60
TT35 Mikel Leshoure .25 .60
TT36 Joe Flacco .30 .75
TT37 Kyle Rudolph .25 .60
TT38 LeSean McCoy .25 .60
TT39 Julio Jones .50 1.25
TT40 Dwayne Bowe .25 .60
TT41 Andy Dalton .60 1.50
TT42 DeSean Jackson .25 .60
TT43 Sam Bradford .30 .75
TT44 Michael Turner .25 .60
TT45 Ryan Williams .30 .75
TT46 Wes Welker .30 .75
TT47 Matt Forte .25 .60
TT48 Greg Little .25 .60
TT49 Jason Witten .30 .75
TT50 Cam Newton 1.25 3.00

2011 Topps Super Bowl XLV

This set was issued exclusively at the 2011 Super Bowl Card Show in Dallas via a wrapper redemption program. Each card features the Super Bowl logo at the top with Cowboys Stadium at the bottom.

COMPLETE SET (7) 20.00 40.00
SBWR1 Tom Brady 4.00 10.00
SBWR2 Drew Brees 2.50 6.00
SBWR3 Michael Vick 2.50 6.00
SBWR4 Miles Austin 2.00 5.00
SBWR5 Sam Bradford 2.50 6.00
SBWR6 Dez Bryant 2.50 6.00
SBWR7 Tony Romo 2.50 6.00

2012 Topps

COMPLETE SET (440) 25.00 50.00
VETERAN SP ODDS 1:335 HOB
ROOKIE SP ODDS 1:410 HOB
1A Aaron Rodgers .40 1.00
1B Aaron Rodgers SP 15.00 30.00
2 Jahvid Best .20 .50
3A Brandon Weeden RC .75 2.00
3B Brandon Weeden SP 10.00 25.00
4 Colt McCoy .20 .50
5 John Kuhn .20 .50
6 Robert Turbin RC .40 1.00
7 Rashard Mendenhall .20 .50
8 Eric Weddle .15 .40
9 C.J. Spiller .20 .50
10 Troy Polamalu .25 .60
11 Earl Thomas .15 .40
12 Owen Daniels .15 .40

13 Chicago Bears .15 .40
Jay Cutler
Matt Forte
14 T.Y. Hilton RC .40 1.00
15 Harrison Smith RC .40 1.00
16 Brian Cushing .15 .40
17 Brandon Lloyd .20 .50
18A Alshon Jeffery RC .60 1.50
18B Alshon Jeffery SP 8.00 20.00
19 T.J. Yates .20 .50
20 Andre Johnson .20 .50
21 Eric LeGrand RC .50 1.25
22 Melvin Ingram RC .50 1.25
23 Charles Johnson .15 .40
24 Jason Avant .15 .40
25 Ray Lewis .25 .60
26 Antonio Gates .20 .50
27 Adrian Wilson .15 .40
28 DeVier Posey RC .40 1.00
29 Titus Young .15 .40
30 Patrick Willis .20 .50
31 Sean Lee .15 .40
32 David DeCastro RC .50 1.25
33 Eric Decker .20 .50
34 Jeremy Maclin .20 .50
35 Justin Smith .15 .40
36 Ed Dickson .15 .40
37 T.J. Graham RC .40 1.00
38 Johnathan Joseph .15 .40
39 Reggie Wayne .20 .50
40 Dwayne Bowe .20 .50
41 Tamba Hali .15 .40
42 Vick Ballard RC .30 .75
43 New York Giants .20 .50
Eli Manning
44 Bruce Irvin RC .50 1.25
45 Dennis Pitta .15 .40
46 Malcom Floyd .15 .40
47 Mark Barron RC .60 1.50
48 Ryan Lindley RC .40 1.00
49 Eric Berry .20 .50
50A Tim Tebow .40 1.00
50B Tim Tebow SP 12.00 30.00
51 Gerell Robinson RC .40 1.00
52A Alex Smith .20 .50
52B Alex Smith SP 6.00 15.00
53 Jermichael Finley .20 .50
54 Kevin Kolb .20 .50
55 Roy Helu .20 .50
56 Buffalo Bills .12 .30
Brad Smith
57 Anquan Boldin .20 .50
58A Dwayne Allen RC .40 1.00
58B Dwayne Allen SP 5.00 12.00
59 Daniel Thomas .20 .50
60 Darren McFadden .20 .50
61 Brandon Gibson .15 .40
62 Steve Johnson .20 .50
63 Nick Toon RC .50 1.25
64 Andy Lee .15 .40
65 Marvin McNutt RC .40 1.00
66 Jerod Mayo .20 .50
67 Donald Brown .20 .50
68 Miami Dolphins .12 .30
Chris Long
Chad Henne
69 Dez Bryant .25 .60
70A Rob Gronkowski .20 .50
70B Rob Gronkowski SP 8.00 20.00
71 Nnamdi Asomugha .15 .40
72 Tampa Bay Buccaneers .15 .40
Josh Freeman
Kellen Winslow
73 Rookie Premiere .75 2.00
74 Doug Baldwin .20 .50
75 Carson Palmer .20 .50
76 Chandler Jones RC .40 1.00
77A Ryan Broyles RC .40 1.00
77B Ryan Broyles SP 6.00 15.00
78 Joe Flacco .20 .50
79 Fletcher Cox RC .40 1.00
80 Chris Johnson .20 .50
81 Kansas City Chiefs .15 .40
Matt Cassel
Branden Albert
82A DeMarco Murray .20 .50
82B DeMarco Murray SP 8.00 20.00
83 Kendall Reyes RC .30 .75
84 Pierre Garcon .20 .50
85 Joe Adams RC .40 1.00
86 Sebastian Janikowski .20 .50
87 Joe Haden .15 .40
88 Dexter McCluster .15 .40
89 Michael Brockers RC .40 1.00
90 Jason Pierre-Paul .20 .50
91A Michael Floyd RC .75 2.00
91B Michael Floyd SP 8.00 20.00
92 Chandler Harnish RC .40 1.00
93 Jason Peters .15 .40
94 Sidney Rice .20 .50
95 Rishard Matthews RC .40 1.00
96 Devery Henderson .15 .40
97 Jared Crick RC .40 1.00
98 Jon Baldwin .15 .40
99 Robert Meachem .20 .50
100A Drew Brees .25 .60
100B Drew Brees SP 10.00 25.00
101 San Diego Chargers .12 .30
Antoine Cason
Quentin Jammer
102 Jacksonville Jaguars .15 .40
Blaine Gabbert
Maurice Jones-Drew
103 Damian Williams .15 .40
104 Travis Benjamin RC .40 1.00
105 Knowshon Moreno .20 .50
106 Mark Ingram .20 .50
107 Matt Schaub .20 .50
108 Brent Celek .20 .50
109 Heath Miller .20 .50
110 Darrelle Revis .20 .50
111 Drew Brees POY .25 .60
112A A.J. Jenkins RC .50 1.25
112B A.J. Jenkins SP 6.00 15.00
113 Dallas Clark .20 .50
114 Jabaal Sheard .15 .40
115A Stephen Hill RC .40 1.00
115B Stephen Hill SP 5.00 12.00
116 Jake Ballard .15 .40
117 Early Doucet .15 .40
118 Denarius Moore .15 .40
119 Arrelious Benn .15 .40
120A Maurice Jones-Drew .20 .50
120B Maurice Jones-Drew SP 6.00 15.00
121 Marcedes Lewis .15 .40
122 Jared Cook .15 .40
123 Robert Mathis .15 .40
124 Sean Weatherspoon .15 .40
125 Mike Wallace .20 .50
126 Quinton Coples RC .40 1.00
127 DeSean Jackson .20 .50
128 Trent Cole .15 .40
129 Pat Angerer .15 .40
130A Hakeem Nicks .20 .50
130B Hakeem Nicks SP 6.00 15.00
131 Tavon Wilson RC .40 1.00
132A Coby Fleener RC .50 1.25
132B Coby Fleener SP 6.00 15.00
133 Fred Jackson .20 .50
134A Ryan Tannehill RC 1.00 2.50
134B Ryan Tannehill SP 15.00 40.00
135 Jay Cutler .20 .50
136 Josh Freeman .20 .50
137 Jermaine Gresham .20 .50
138 Matt Cassel .20 .50
139 Jerel Worthy RC .50 1.25
140A Andrew Luck RC 3.00 8.00
(passing sideways)
140B Andrew Luck SP 60.00 100.00
(passing forward, with rabbit foot)
140C Andrew Luck SP 35.00 60.00
(scrambling pose)
141 Cam Newton ROY .40 1.00
142 Darrius Heyward-Bey .15 .40
143 Steven Jackson .20 .50
144 John Abraham .15 .40
145 New Orleans Saints .20 .50
Drew Brees
146 Cyrus Gray RC .40 1.00
147 Detroit Lions .12 .30
Stephen Tulloch
148 Von Miller ROY .20 .50
149 Michael Egnew RC .30 .75
150A Larry Fitzgerald .20 .50
150B Larry Fitzgerald SP 6.00 15.00
151A Mohamed Sanu RC .40 1.00
151B Mohamed Sanu SP 5.00 12.00
152 Matt Ryan .20 .50
153 Santana Moss .20 .50
154 Stephon Gilmore RC .40 1.00
155 Paul Posluszny .20 .50
156 Whitney Mercilus RC .40 1.00
157 Kam Chancellor RC .25 .60
158 B.J. Raji .15 .40
159 Pittsburgh Steelers .20 .50
Ben Roethlisberger
Max Starks
160 Mark Sanchez .20 .50
161 Seattle Seahawks .15 .40
Mashawn Lynch
Sidney Rice
162 LaMarr Woodley .15 .40
163 Green Bay Packers .30 .75
Aaron Rodgers
James Starks
164A Vernon Davis .20 .50
164B Vernon Davis SP 5.00 12.00
165A Russell Wilson RC .60 1.50
165B Russell Wilson SP 8.00 20.00
166 Atlanta Falcons .15 .40
Matt Ryan
Roddy White
167 Christian Ponder .20 .50
168 Kyle Arrington .15 .40
169 Percy Harvin .20 .60
170 Ben Roethlisberger .25 .60
171 Vince Wilfork .15 .40
172 Carlos Rogers .15 .40
173 Michael Bush .15 .40
174 Nick Barnett .15 .40
175 Ed Reed .20 .60
176 John Skelton .15 .40
177 Aaron Rodgers MVP .40 1.00
178 Santonio Holmes .20 .50
179 Casey Hayward RC .40 1.00
180A Ray Rice .20 .50
180B Ray Rice SP 6.00 15.00
181 Chris Clemons .15 .40
182 Isaac Redman .20 .50
183 Ryan Grant .20 .50
184 Brandon Jacobs .20 .50
185A LaMichael James RC .75 2.00
185B LaMichael James SP 8.00 20.00
186A Nick Foles RC .60 1.50
186B Nick Foles SP 8.00 20.00
187 Torrey Smith .15 .40
188 Brooks Reed .15 .40
189 Haloti Ngata .15 .40
190 DeMarcus Ware .20 .50
191 Connor Barwin .15 .40
192 Jake Locker .20 .50
193 Kevin Zeitler RC .30 .75
194 Julio Jones .20 .50
195 Keshawn Martin RC .40 1.00
196 Curtis Lofton .15 .40
197 Ryan Fitzpatrick .20 .50
198 Joe Thomas .15 .40
199 Tommy Streeter RC .40 1.00
200 Adrian Peterson .25 .60
201 Peyton Hillis .15 .40
202 Marvin Jones RC .30 .75
203 Julius Peppers .20 .50
204A Doug Martin RC .60 1.50
204B Doug Martin SP 8.00 20.00
205 Greg Jennings .20 .50
206 George Iloka RC .30 .75
207 Plaxico Burress .20 .50
208 Alfonzo Dennard RC .40 1.00
209 Jahri Evans .15 .40
210A LeSean McCoy .20 .50
210B LeSean McCoy SP 6.00 15.00
211 Randall Cobb .20 .50
212 Courtney Upshaw RC .50 1.25
213 Asante Samuel .20 .50
214A Bernard Pierce RC .40 1.00
214B Bernard Pierce SP 5.00 12.00
215 Marques Colston .20 .50
216 Cincinnati Bengals .20 .50
Jermaine Gresham
Domata Peko
217 Stevan Ridley .15 .40
218 Tim Hightower .15 .40
219 Osi Umenyiora .15 .40
220A Wes Welker .25 .60
220B Wes Welker SP 8.00 20.00
221 Ben Tate .15 .40
222 Janoris Jenkins RC .40 1.00
223A Antonio Brown .20 .50
223B Antonio Brown SP 6.00 15.00
224 Jamaal Charles .20 .50
225 Matthew Stafford .25 .60
225B Matthew Stafford SP 8.00 20.00
226 Jonathan Martin RC .30 .75
227 Lance Briggs .15 .40
228 Brandon Boykin RC .40 1.00
229 Vinny Curry RC .40 1.00
230 Frank Gore .20 .50
231 Aldon Smith .20 .50
232 Steve Breaston .15 .40
233 Chris Long .15 .40
234 Davone Bess .15 .40
235 J.J. Watt .15 .40
236 Mychal Kendricks RC .40 1.00
237A Demaryius Thomas .20 .50
237B Demaryius Thomas SP 6.00 15.00
238 St. Louis Rams .12 .30
James Laurinaitus
Chris Long
Chris Chamberlain
239 Jake Bequette RC .40 1.00
240A Justin Blackmon RC .75 2.00
240B Justin Blackmon SP 10.00 25.00
241 James Anderson .15 .40
242 Lamar Miller RC .50 1.25
243 Peter Konz RC .25 .60
244 Andre Carter .15 .40
245 Devon Wylie RC .40 1.00
246 Blaine Gabbert .20 .50
247 Leonard Hankerson .15 .40
248 Bernard Scott .15 .40
249 James Jones .15 .40
250A Cam Newton .40 1.00
250B Cam Newton SP 12.00 30.00
251 Willis McGahee .15 .40
252 Jarius Wright RC .40 1.00
253 Akeem Ayers .15 .40
254 Baltimore Ravens .15 .40
Ray Rice
255 David Nelson .15 .40
256 Jordan White RC .30 .75
257 Lavonte David RC .50 1.25
258 Randy Moss .20 .50
259 Arizona Cardinals .12 .30
Todd Heap
Andre Roberts
260 Matt Forte .20 .50
261 Dustin Keller .15 .40
262 Kellen Winslow .20 .50
263 LeGarrette Blount .15 .40
264 Johnny Knox .20 .50
265A Reggie Bush .20 .50
265B Reggie Bush SP 6.00 15.00
266 Devon Still RC .40 1.00
267 Felix Jones .20 .50
268 Nate Burleson
269 Nick Mangold .15 .40
270 Philip Rivers .20 .50
271 Austin Collie .20 .50
272 DeAngelo Williams .20 .50
273 Nate Washington .15 .40
274 Maurkice Pouncey .20 .50
275 Andy Dalton .25 .60
276 Matt Moore .15 .40
277 Matt Flynn .20 .50
278 Juron Criner RC .30 .75
279A Brian Quick RC .50 1.25
279B Brian Quick SP 6.00 15.00
280A Jimmy Graham .20 .50
280B Jimmy Graham SP 8.00 20.00
281 Lance Moore .20 .50
282 Carolina Panthers .40 1.00
Cam Newton
Jonathan Stewart
283 Ronnie Hillman RC .50 1.25
284 Derrick Johnson .15 .40
285 Dontari Poe RC .40 1.00
286 Brandon Thompson RC .30 .75
287 Shea McClellin RC .50 1.25
288 Patrick Peterson .20 .50
289A David Wilson RC .75 2.00
289B David Wilson SP 8.00 20.00
290 Roddy White .20 .50
291 Toby Gerhart .15 .40
292 James Starks .20 .50
293 Brandon Pettigrew .15 .40
294 Fred Davis .15 .40
295 D'Qwell Jackson .15 .40
296 Geno Atkins .15 .40
297 Charles Tillman .15 .40
298 Ahmad Bradshaw .20 .50
299 James Harrison .25 .60
300A Eli Manning .25 .60
300B Eli Manning SP 8.00 20.00
301 Mike Williams .20 .50
302 Shane Lechler .15 .40
303 Devin Hester .25 .60
304 LaDainian Tomlinson .25 .60
305 Jason Babin .15 .40
306 Mario Williams .15 .40
307 Tarvaris Jackson .15 .40
308 Michael Turner .20 .50
309 Antwan Barnes .15 .40
310 Ndamukong Suh .25 .60
311 Oakland Raiders .15 .40
Carson Palmer
312 Greg Olsen .15 .40
313 Terrell Suggs POY .20 .50
314A Rueben Randle RC .40 1.00
314B Rueben Randle SP 6.00 15.00
315 Mike Tolbert .20 .50
316 Brandon Browner .15 .40
317 Jerome Simpson .15 .40
318 Dwight Bentley RC .25 .60
319 Matt Kalil RC .50 1.25
320A A.J. Green .20 .50
320B A.J. Green SP 8.00 20.00
321 Kenny Britt .20 .50
322 Dont'a Hightower RC .60 1.50
323 Aaron Hernandez .20 .50
324 Denver Broncos .12 .30
Matt Prater
Lonie Paxton
325 Von Miller .20 .50
326 Kirk Cousins RC .60 1.50
327 Jabar Gaffney .15 .40
328 Indianapolis Colts .15 .40
Dwight Freeney
Robert Mathis
329 Brian Urlacher .25 .60
330 Michael Vick .25 .60
331 Elvis Dumervil .15 .40
332 Nick Perry RC .40 1.00
333 Laurent Robinson .15 .40
334 BenJarvus Green-Ellis .20 .50
335 Michael Crabtree .20 .50
336 Kendall Hunter .20 .50
337 Dre Kirkpatrick RC .60 1.50
338 Anthony Fasano .15 .40
339 Billy Winn RC .40 1.00
340A Robert Griffin III RC 2.50 6.00
(passing pose)
340B Robert Griffin III SP 30.00 60.00
(scrambling pose)
341 Deion Branch .15 .40
342 Pierre Thomas .20 .50
343 San Francisco 49ers .20 .50
Vernon Davis and O-Line
344 James Laurinaitis .15 .40
345 Riley Reiff RC .40 1.00
346 Philadelphia Eagles .15 .40
LeSean McCoy
Riley Cooper
347 Matt Hasselbeck .20 .50
348 Clay Matthews .25 .60
349 Chris Ivory .20 .50
350 Peyton Manning .60 1.50
351 Jackie Battle .15 .40
352 Greg Little .15 .40
353 Dwight Freeney .20 .50
354 Chris Houston .15 .40
355 Morris Claiborne RC .75 2.00
356 Terrance Ganaway RC .30 .75
357 Chris Givens RC .30 .75
358 Kevin Smith .15 .40
359 Cliff Avril .15 .40
360A Arian Foster .20 .50
360B Arian Foster SP 6.00 15.00
361 London Fletcher .15 .40
362 Andre Branch RC .30 .75
363 Zach Brown RC .30 .75
364 Antonio Allen RC .30 .75
365A Brock Osweiler RC .50 1.25
365B Brock Osweiler SP 6.00 15.00
366 Markelle Martin RC .30 .75
367 Greg Childs RC .40 1.00
368 Orson Charles RC .40 1.00
369 Chris Rainey RC .40 1.00
370 Sam Bradford .25 .60
371 Vontae Davis .15 .40
372A Marshawn Lynch .20 .50
372B Marshawn Lynch SP 6.00 15.00
373 Justin Tuck .15 .40
374A Steve Smith .20 .50
374B Steve Smith SP 6.00 15.00
375 Tony Gonzalez .20 .50
376A Darren Sproles .20 .50
376B Darren Sproles SP 8.00 20.00
377 Kellen Moore RC .60 1.50
378A Kendall Wright RC .50 1.25
378B Kendall Wright SP 6.00 15.00
379 Jason Hill .15 .40
380A Trent Richardson RC 1.25 3.00
380B Trent Richardson SP 15.00 40.00
381 Champ Bailey .20 .50
382 David Akers .15 .40
383 Carlos Dunlap .15 .40
384 Brandon LaFell .15 .40
385 Miles Austin .20 .50
386 Jonathan Stewart .20 .50
387 Beanie Wells .20 .50
388 Minnesota Vikings .20 .50
Adrian Peterson
Kyle Rudolph
389 Mike Thomas .20 .50
390 Charles Woodson .25 .60
391 Washington Redskins .12 .30
London Fletcher
Brian Orakpo
392 Shonn Greene .20 .50
393 Tramon Williams .15 .40
394 Brian Orakpo .15 .40
395 Houston Texans .15 .40
Arian Foster
396 Adrian Clayborn .15 .40
397 Cedric Benson .20 .50
398 Ryan Mathews .20 .50
399A Isaiah Pead RC .40 1.00
399B Isaiah Pead SP 5.00 12.00
400A Calvin Johnson .25 .60
400B Calvin Johnson SP 8.00 20.00
401 Mike Adams RC .40 1.00
402 Josh Cribbs .15 .40
403 Dallas Cowboys .20 .50
Dez Bryant
Jason Witten
404 David Harris .15 .40
405 Richard Seymour .15 .40
406 Ryan Kerrigan .15 .40
407 Kelechi Osemele RC .40 1.00
408 Marcell Dareus .15 .40
409 New England Patriots .25 .60
Rob Gronkowski
Wes Welker
410 Tony Romo .25 .60
411 NaVorro Bowman .15 .40
412 Tennessee Titans .15 .40
Jake Locker
413 Aaron Corp RC .30 .75
414 Cam Johnson RC .40 1.00
415 Dashon Goldson .15 .40
416 Jordy Nelson .20 .50
417 Chad Greenway .20 .50
418 Cleveland Browns .15 .40
Colt McCoy
419 Derek Wolfe RC .30 .75
420A Jared Allen .20 .50
420B Jared Allen SP 6.00 15.00
421 Vincent Jackson .20 .50
422 NY Giants Champs .20 .50
Eli Manning
423 Scott Chandler .15 .40
424 Carl Nicks .15 .40
425 Terrell Suggs .20 .50
426 Mario Manningham .20 .50
427 Brandon Taylor RC .30 .75
428 Rex Grossman .20 .50
429 Dan Herron RC .40 1.00
430A Victor Cruz .25 .60
430B Victor Cruz SP 8.00 20.00
431 Andre Roberts .15 .40
432 Cordy Glenn RC .30 .75
433 Luke Kuechly RC .50 1.25
434 Jason Witten .25 .60
435 David Garrard .15 .40
436 Vonta Leach .15 .40
437 Cortland Finnegan .15 .40
438 Brandon Marshall .15 .40
439 New York Jets .15 .40
Santonio Holmes
440A Tom Brady .40 1.00
440B Tom Brady SP 12.00 30.00
RH46 Eli Manning RH .60 1.50

2012 Topps Black

*VETS/57: 10X TO 25X BASIC CARDS
*ROOKIES/57: 6X TO 15X BASIC RC
BLACK/57 ODDS 1:69 HOB
134 Ryan Tannehill 25.00 50.00
140 Andrew Luck 100.00 175.00
340 Robert Griffin III 50.00 100.00

2012 Topps Camo

*VETS/399: 5X TO 12X BASIC CARDS
*ROOKIES/399: 3X TO 8X BASIC RC
CAMO/399 ODDS 1:60 HOB
134 Ryan Tannehill 12.00 30.00
140 Andrew Luck 40.00 80.00
340 Robert Griffin III 30.00 60.00

2012 Topps Gold

*VETS/2012: 2.5X TO 6X BASIC CARDS
*ROOKIES/2012: 1.5X TO 4X BASIC RC
GOLD/2012 ODDS 1:12 HOB
134 Ryan Tannehill 6.00 15.00
140 Andrew Luck 15.00 40.00
340 Robert Griffin III 12.00 30.00

2012 Topps Pink

*VETS/399: 5X TO 12X BASIC CARDS
*ROOKIES/399: 3X TO 8X BASIC RC
PINK/399 STATED ODDS 1:60 HOB
134 Ryan Tannehill 12.00 30.00
140 Andrew Luck 40.00 80.00
340 Robert Griffin III 30.00 60.00

2012 Topps 1957 Green

EACH HAS TWO CARDS OF EQUAL VALUE
RANDOM INSERTS IN PACKS
*BLUE WAL-MART: .5X TO 1.2X GREEN
*RED TARGET: .5X TO 1.2X GREEN
1 Andrew Luck 6.00 15.00
2 Andrew Luck 6.00 15.00
3 Robert Griffin III 5.00 12.00
4 Robert Griffin III 5.00 12.00
5 Trent Richardson 3.00 8.00
6 Trent Richardson 3.00 8.00
7 Ryan Tannehill 2.50 6.00
8 Ryan Tannehill 2.50 6.00
9 Justin Blackmon 2.00 5.00
10 Justin Blackmon 2.00 5.00
11 Stephen Hill 1.00 2.50
12 Rueben Randle 1.00 2.50
13 Michael Floyd 2.00 5.00
14 Michael Floyd 2.00 5.00
15 Kendall Wright 1.25 3.00
16 Kendall Wright 1.25 3.00
17 Brandon Weeden 2.00 5.00
18 Brandon Weeden 2.00 5.00
19 Coby Fleener 1.25 3.00
20 Coby Fleener 1.25 3.00
21 David Wilson 2.00 5.00
22 David Wilson 2.00 5.00
23 Lamar Miller 1.25 3.00
24 Lamar Miller 1.25 3.00
25 Doug Martin 1.50 4.00
26 Doug Martin 1.50 4.00
27 Brock Osweiler 1.25 3.00
28 Brock Osweiler 1.25 3.00
29 Rueben Randle 1.00 2.50
30 Stephen Hill 1.00 2.50

2012 Topps 1965 Mini

COMPLETE SET (141) 75.00 150.00
STATED ODDS 1:3 HOB
1 Cam Newton 1.00 2.50
2 Brandon Jacobs .50 1.25
3 Jamaal Charles .50 1.25
4 Hakeem Nicks .50 1.25
5 Michael Turner .50 1.25
6 Tarvaris Jackson .40 1.00
7 Jeremy Maclin .50 1.25
8 Terrell Suggs .50 1.25
9 Nick Mangold .40 1.00
10 LeSean McCoy .50 1.25
11 Carson Palmer .50 1.25
12 Pat Angerer .40 1.00
13 Fred Jackson .50 1.25
14 Andy Dalton .60 1.50
15 Mark Ingram .50 1.25
16 Miles Austin .50 1.25
17 Joe Thomas .40 1.00
18 Kevin Kolb .50 1.25
19 Leonard Hankerson .40 1.00
20 Drew Brees .60 1.50
21 Ryan Fitzpatrick .50 1.25
22 Titus Young .40 1.00
23 Ed Reed .50 1.25
24 DeSean Jackson .50 1.25
25 Michael Vick .60 1.50
26 Pierre Thomas .50 1.25
27 Doug Baldwin .50 1.25
28 Jared Allen .50 1.25
29 Osi Umenyiora .40 1.00
30 Rob Gronkowski .50 1.25
31 Willis McGahee .40 1.00
32 Frank Gore .50 1.25
33 Matt Ryan .50 1.25
34 Cedric Benson .50 1.25
35 Jason Babin .40 1.00
36 Early Doucet .40 1.00
37 Devery Henderson .40 1.00
38 Kenny Britt .50 1.25
39 Ryan Grant .50 1.25
40 Adrian Peterson .60 1.50
41 Toby Gerhart .40 1.00
42 Brandon Marshall .40 1.00
43 Mike Wallace .50 1.25
44 Darrius Heyward-Bey .40 1.00
45 Sean Lee .40 1.00
46 Dallas Clark .50 1.25
47 Marcedes Lewis .40 1.00
48 Steve Johnson .50 1.25
49 Jake Locker .50 1.25
50 Tom Brady 1.00 2.50
51 Jason Witten .60 1.50
52 Tim Tebow 1.00 2.50
53 Darren Sproles .50 1.25
54 Elvis Dumervil .40 1.00
55 Sam Bradford .60 1.50
56 Jermichael Finley .50 1.25
57 Troy Polamalu .60 1.50
58 Devin Hester .60 1.50
59 Christian Ponder .50 1.25
60 Calvin Johnson .60 1.50
61 Greg Jennings .50 1.25
62 Mark Sanchez .50 1.25
63 Anquan Boldin .50 1.25
64 Donald Brown .50 1.25
65 Paul Posluszny .50 1.25
66 Marcell Dareus .40 1.00
67 Josh Freeman .50 1.25
68 Jon Baldwin .40 1.00
69 Patrick Peterson .50 1.25
70 Ray Rice .50 1.25
71 Marques Colston .50 1.25
72 Colt McCoy .50 1.25
73 Ryan Mathews .50 1.25
74 Nnamdi Asomugha .40 1.00
75 Arian Foster .50 1.25
76 Stevan Ridley .40 1.00
77 John Kuhn .50 1.25
78 David Akers .40 1.00
79 Chris Johnson .50 1.25
80 Larry Fitzgerald .50 1.25
81 Greg Little .40 1.00
82 Dustin Keller .40 1.00
83 Antonio Brown .50 1.25
84 Antonio Gates .50 1.25
85 Julio Jones .50 1.25
86 Malcom Floyd .40 1.00
87 Matt Schaub .50 1.25
88 Daniel Thomas .50 1.25
89 Marshawn Lynch .50 1.25
90 Ben Roethlisberger .60 1.50
91 DeMarcus Ware .50 1.25
92 Randall Cobb .50 1.25
93 Alex Smith .50 1.25
94 Jordy Nelson .50 1.25
95 Joe Flacco .50 1.25
96 Julius Peppers .50 1.25
97 Aaron Hernandez .50 1.25
98 Jason Pierre-Paul .50 1.25
99 Peyton Hillis .40 1.00
100 Eli Manning .60 1.50
101 Vernon Davis .50 1.25
102 Demaryius Thomas .50 1.25
103 Von Miller .50 1.25
104 Torrey Smith .40 1.00
105 Rashard Mendenhall .50 1.25
106 Ahmad Bradshaw .50 1.25
107 Heath Miller .50 1.25
108 Victor Cruz .60 1.50
109 Matthew Stafford .60 1.50
110 Maurice Jones-Drew .50 1.25
111 Matt Forte .50 1.25
112 Matt Moore .40 1.00
113 Blaine Gabbert .50 1.25
114 Darren McFadden .50 1.25
115 Kendall Hunter .50 1.25
116 Steven Jackson .50 1.25
117 Reggie Bush .50 1.25
118 Charles Tillman .40 1.00
119 B.J. Raji .40 1.00
120 Aaron Rodgers 1.00 2.50
121 Knowshon Moreno .50 1.25
122 Joe Namath 2.00 5.00
123 Santana Moss .50 1.25
124 Darrelle Revis .50 1.25
125 Andre Johnson .50 1.25
126 Beanie Wells .50 1.25
127 Eric Decker .50 1.25
128 DeMarco Murray .50 1.25
129 Percy Harvin .50 1.25
130 Jimmy Graham .50 1.25
131 Santonio Holmes .50 1.25
132 Robert Mathis .40 1.00
133 Mario Manningham .50 1.25
134 Dez Bryant .60 1.50
135 Patrick Willis .50 1.25
136 A.J. Green .50 1.25
137 Jermaine Gresham .50 1.25
138 Jay Cutler .50 1.25
139 Wes Welker .60 1.50
140 Philip Rivers .50 1.25
141 Peyton Manning 1.50 4.00

2012 Topps 1965 Mini Autographs

STATED ODDS 1:1650 HOB
142 Ryan Tannehill 125.00 200.00
143 Nick Foles 30.00 80.00
144 Michael Floyd 40.00 100.00
145 Kendall Wright
146 Brandon Weeden 60.00 120.00
147 Michael Egnew 15.00 40.00
148 David Wilson 50.00 100.00
149 Lamar Miller 30.00 60.00
150 Andrew Luck 300.00 500.00
151 Brock Osweiler
152 Russell Wilson 60.00 120.00
153 A.J. Jenkins 30.00 60.00
154 Chris Givens 15.00 40.00
154 Alshon Jeffery
155 Mohamed Sanu
156 Rueben Randle 30.00 60.00
157 Nick Toon
158 Isaiah Pead 30.00 60.00
159 Doug Martin
160 Robert Griffin III 300.00 450.00
161 LaMichael James 30.00 80.00
162 Brian Quick
163 Robert Turbin 15.00 40.00
164 DeVier Posey
165 Bernard Pierce EXCH 15.00 40.00
167 Coby Fleener 30.00 60.00
168 Jarius Wright 15.00 40.00
169 Dwayne Allen 25.00 50.00
170 Trent Richardson 75.00 125.00
171 Stephen Hill
172 Ryan Broyles 30.00 60.00
173 Joe Adams 15.00 40.00
174 Ronnie Hillman 20.00 50.00
175 Justin Blackmon 30.00 80.00
176 T.J. Graham 15.00 40.00

2012 Topps 1984 Autographs

AUTO/100 ODDS 1:1650 HOB
1 Andrew Luck 350.00 500.00
2 Kendall Wright 20.00 50.00
3 Michael Floyd 30.00 60.00
4 Nick Foles 40.00 80.00
5 Brandon Weeden 40.00 80.00
6 Lamar Miller 20.00 50.00
7 David Wilson 30.00 80.00
8 Dwayne Allen 15.00 40.00
9 Brock Osweiler 20.00 50.00
10 Robert Griffin III 300.00 500.00
11 Nick Toon 20.00 50.00
12 Rueben Randle 15.00 40.00
13 Mohamed Sanu 15.00 40.00
14 Russell Wilson 60.00 100.00
15 DeVier Posey 15.00 40.00
16 A.J. Jenkins 20.00 50.00
17 Isaiah Pead 15.00 40.00
19 Brian Quick 20.00 50.00
20 Trent Richardson 75.00 125.00
21 LaMichael James 30.00 80.00
22 Doug Martin 60.00 100.00
23 Bernard Pierce EXCH 15.00 40.00
24 Robert Turbin 15.00 40.00
25 Ryan Tannehill 50.00 100.00
26 Coby Fleener 30.00 60.00
27 Chris Givens 12.00 30.00
28 Stephen Hill 15.00 40.00
29 T.J. Graham 15.00 40.00
30 Justin Blackmon 30.00 80.00
31 Ryan Broyles 15.00 40.00
32 Joe Adams 15.00 40.00
33 Ronnie Hillman 30.00 60.00
34 Michael Egnew 12.00 30.00
35 Jarius Wright 15.00 40.00
36 Alshon Jeffery 25.00 60.00

2012 Topps Continuity Autographs

STATED PRINT RUN 100 SER.#'d SETS
AL Andrew Luck 150.00 250.00
RG Robert Griffin III 125.00 200.00

2012 Topps Field General Medals

STATED PRINT RUN 50 SER.#'d SETS
NFGAD Andy Dalton 15.00 40.00
NFGAR Aaron Rodgers 40.00 80.00
NFGBR Ben Roethlisberger 30.00 60.00
NFGCN Cam Newton 30.00 60.00
NFGCP Carson Palmer 15.00 40.00
NFGDB Drew Brees 30.00 60.00
NFGEM Eli Manning 30.00 60.00
NFGJC Jay Cutler 15.00 40.00
NFGJF Josh Freeman 12.00 30.00
NFGJFL Joe Flacco 15.00 40.00
NFGMR Matt Ryan 15.00 40.00
NFGMS Matthew Stafford 20.00 50.00
NFGMSA Mark Sanchez 15.00 40.00
NFGMSC Matt Schaub 15.00 40.00
NFGMV Michael Vick 20.00 50.00
NFGPM Peyton Manning 50.00 100.00
NFGPR Philip Rivers 12.00 30.00
NFGSB Sam Bradford 20.00 50.00
NFGTB Tom Brady 40.00 80.00
NFGTR Tony Romo 20.00 50.00

2012 Topps NFL Captains Patches

RANDOM INSERTS IN PACKS
*PINK/99: .8X TO 2X BASIC PATCH
NCPAJ Andre Johnson 5.00 12.00
NCPAJH A.J. Hawk 5.00 12.00
NCPAR Aaron Rodgers 10.00 25.00
NCPAW Adrian Wilson 4.00 10.00
NCPBD Brian Dawkins 5.00 12.00
NCPCB Champ Bailey 5.00 12.00
NCPCW Charles Woodson 6.00 15.00
NCPDB Drew Brees 8.00 20.00
NCPDH DeAngelo Hall 4.00 10.00
NCPDM Darren McFadden 5.00 12.00
NCPDR Darrelle Revis 5.00 12.00
NCPDW DeMarcus Ware 6.00 15.00
NCPEM Eli Manning 8.00 20.00
NCPFJ Fred Jackson 5.00 12.00
NCPJB Jon Beason 4.00 10.00
NCPJC Jay Cutler 5.00 12.00
NCPJF Josh Freeman 5.00 12.00
NCPJL Jake Long 4.00 10.00
NCPJP Julius Peppers 6.00 15.00
NCPJW Jason Witten 6.00 15.00
NCPLF Larry Fitzgerald 5.00 12.00
NCPMH Matt Hasselbeck 5.00 12.00
NCPMJD Maurice Jones-Drew 5.00 12.00
NCPML Marcedes Lewis 4.00 10.00
NCPMS Mark Sanchez 5.00 12.00
NCPMSC Matt Schaub 5.00 12.00
NCPMST Matthew Stafford 6.00 15.00
NCPPM Peyton Manning 12.00 30.00
NCPRF Ryan Fitzpatrick 5.00 12.00
NCPRS Richard Seymour 4.00 10.00
NCPSJ Steven Jackson 5.00 12.00
NCPSM Santana Moss 5.00 12.00
NCPSS Steve Smith 5.00 12.00
NCPTR Tony Romo 6.00 15.00
NCPWM Willis McGahee 4.00 10.00

2012 Topps NFL MVPs

MVP/50 ODDS 1:7000 HOB
LMVPAR Aaron Rodgers 15.00 40.00
LMVPBS Bart Starr 15.00 40.00
LMVPDM Dan Marino 30.00 60.00
LMVPJE John Elway 15.00 40.00
LMVPBF1 Brett Favre 25.00 60.00
LMVPBF2 Brett Favre 25.00 60.00
LMVPBF3 Brett Favre 25.00 60.00
LMVPJM1 Joe Montana 20.00 50.00
LMVPJM2 Joe Montana 20.00 50.00
LMVPKW1 Kurt Warner 10.00 25.00
LMVPKW2 Kurt Warner 10.00 25.00
LMVPPM1 Peyton Manning 25.00 60.00
LMVPPM2 Peyton Manning 25.00 60.00
LMVPPM3 Peyton Manning 25.00 60.00
LMVPPM4 Peyton Manning 25.00 60.00
LMVPSY1 Steve Young 12.00 30.00
LMVPSY2 Steve Young 12.00 30.00
LMVPTBR Terry Bradshaw 15.00 40.00
LMVPYAT Y.A. Tittle 10.00 25.00
LMVPTBR1 Tom Brady 15.00 40.00
LMVPTBR2 Tom Brady 15.00 40.00

2012 Topps Paramount Pairs

COMPLETE SET (22) 5.00 12.00
STATED ODDS 1:4 HOB
PABB Dez Bryant .40 1.00
Justin Blackmon
PABD Cedric Benson .30 .75
Andy Dalton
PABP Ahmad Bradshaw .25 .60
Jason Pierre-Paul
PABR Justin Blackmon .60 1.50
Trent Richardson
PACS Marques Colston .25 .60
Darren Sproles
PACT Marques Colston .25 .60
Pierre Thomas
PAEP John Elway .50 1.25
Jim Plunkett
PAFJ Ryan Fitzpatrick .25 .60
Steve Johnson
PAGM Frank Gore .25 .60
Lamar Miller
PAGW Robert Griffin III 1.00 2.50
Kendall Wright
PAHG Percy Harvin .25 .60
Jabar Gaffney
PAJW Vincent Jackson .25 .60
Mike Williams
PALE Andrew Luck 1.25 3.00
John Elway
PALF Ray Lewis .30 .75
Joe Flacco
PALG Andrew Luck 2.00 5.00
Robert Griffin III
PALP Andrew Luck 1.00 2.50
Jim Plunkett
PALW Brandon Lloyd .30 .75
Wes Welker
PAMM Willis McGahee .25 .60
Lamar Miller
PARJ Sidney Rice .30 .75
Alshon Jeffery
PATG Ryan Tannehill .50 1.25
Cyrus Gray
PABJA LeGarrette Blount .40 1.00
LaMichael James
PAWBL Brandon Weeden .40 1.00
Justin Blackmon

2012 Topps Paramount Pairs Autographs

AU PAIRS/25 ODDS 1:20,500 HOB
PAABB Dez Bryant 50.00 100.00
Justin Blackmon
PAABJ LeGarrette Blount
LaMichael James
PAABP Ahmad Bradshaw
Jason Pierre-Paul
PAABR Justin Blackmon 60.00 120.00
Trent Richardson
PAACS Marques Colston
Darren Sproles
PAAEP John Elway 60.00 120.00
Jim Plunkett
PAAGM Frank Gore
Lamar Miller
PAAGW Robert Griffin III
Kendall Wright
PAAHG Percy Harvin 12.00 30.00
Jabar Gaffney
PAAJW Vincent Jackson
Mike Williams
PAALE Andrew Luck 200.00 350.00
John Elway
PAALG Andrew Luck
Robert Griffin III
PAALP Andrew Luck 125.00 200.00
Jim Plunkett
PAAMM Willis McGahee
Lamar Miller
PAARJ Sidney Rice
Alshon Jeffery
PAATG Ryan Tannehill
Cyrus Gray
PAAWBL Brandon Weeden
Justin Blackmon

2012 Topps Paramount Pairs Relics

RELIC PAIRS/50 ODDS 1:11,900 HOB		
PARBD Cedric Benson Andy Dalton		
PARBR Justin Blackmon Trent Richardson	15.00	40.00
PARCT Marques Colston Pierre Thomas	6.00	15.00
PARFJ Ryan Fitzpatrick Steve Johnson	6.00	15.00
PARGW Robert Griffin III Kendall Wright	20.00	50.00
PARLF Ray Lewis Joe Flacco		
PARLG Andrew Luck Robert Griffin III	40.00	80.00
PARLW Brandon Lloyd Wes Welker	10.00	25.00
PARNC Hakeem Nicks Victor Cruz	15.00	40.00
PARTR Michael Turner Matt Ryan	6.00	15.00

2012 Topps Prolific Playmakers

COMPLETE SET (50)	8.00	20.00
STATED ODDS 1:4 HOB		
PPAB Anquan Boldin	.40	1.00
PPABR Ahmad Bradshaw	.40	1.00
PPAD Andy Dalton	.50	1.25
PPAF Arian Foster	.40	1.00
PPAJG A.J. Green	.40	1.00
PPAL Andrew Luck	2.00	5.00
PPANB Antonio Brown	.40	1.00
PPBL Brandon Lloyd	.40	1.00
PPBM Brandon Marshall	.30	.75
PPCB Cedric Benson	.40	1.00
PPCF Coby Fleener	.40	1.00
PPDB Dwayne Bowe	.40	1.00
PPDEB Dez Bryant	.50	1.25
PPDMO Denarius Moore	.30	.75
PPDS Darren Sproles	.40	1.00
PPFG Frank Gore	.40	1.00
PPJA Jared Allen	.40	1.00
PPJB Jahvid Best	.40	1.00
PPJBL Justin Blackmon	.60	1.50
PPJF Joe Flacco	.40	1.00
PPJG Jabar Gaffney	.30	.75
PPJGR Jimmy Graham	.40	1.00
PPJPP Jason Pierre-Paul	.40	1.00
PPKK Kevin Kolb	.40	1.00
PPLB LeGarrette Blount	.30	.75
PPLF Larry Fitzgerald	.40	1.00
PPLK Luke Kuechly	.40	1.00
PPLR Laurent Robinson	.30	.75
PPMA Miles Austin	.40	1.00
PPMC Marques Colston	.40	1.00
PPMF Matt Forte	.40	1.00
PPMI Mark Ingram	.40	1.00
PPMJD Maurice Jones-Drew	.40	1.00
PPMK Matt Kalil	.40	1.00
PPML Marshawn Lynch	.40	1.00
PPMWI Mike Williams	.40	1.00
PPPH Percy Harvin	.40	1.00
PPPHI Peyton Hillis.	.30	.75
PPPW Patrick Willis	.40	1.00
PPRF Ryan Fitzpatrick	.40	1.00
PPRG Robert Griffin III	1.50	4.00
PPRH Ronnie Hillman	.40	1.00
PPRL Ray Lewis	.50	1.25
PPSG Shonn Greene	.40	1.00
PPSJ Steven Jackson	.40	1.00
PPSR Sidney Rice	.40	1.00
PPTR Trent Richardson	1.00	2.50
PPVC Victor Cruz	.50	1.25
PPVJ Vincent Jackson	.40	1.00
PPWM Willis McGahee	.30	.75

2012 Topps Prolific Playmakers Autographs

STATED ODDS 1:550 HOB		
PPAAB Ahmad Bradshaw	5.00	12.00
PPAABR Antonio Brown	6.00	15.00
PPAAJG A.J. Green SP	12.50	25.00
PPAAL Andrew Luck SP	125.00	200.00
PPACF Coby Fleener	4.00	10.00
PPACM Colt McCoy	5.00	12.00
PPADB Dez Bryant	12.00	30.00
PPADM Denarius Moore	4.00	10.00
PPADS Darren Sproles	6.00	15.00
PPADST Devon Still	4.00	10.00
PPAFG Frank Gore SP	8.00	20.00
PPAGJ Greg Jennings	8.00	20.00
PPAJBL Justin Blackmon SP		
PPAJF Jermichael Finley	5.00	12.00
PPAJG Jimmy Graham	8.00	20.00
PPAJGA Jabar Gaffney	4.00	10.00
PPAJPP Jason Pierre-Paul	5.00	12.00
PPAJW Jerel Worthy	5.00	12.00
PPAKK Kevin Kolb SP	5.00	12.00
PPALB LeGarrette Blount	5.00	12.00
PPALK Luke Kuechly	5.00	12.00
PPALR Laurent Robinson	4.00	10.00
PPAMC Marques Colston SP	8.00	20.00
PPAMF Matt Forte SP	10.00	25.00
PPAMK Matt Kalil	4.00	10.00
PPAML Marshawn Lynch	5.00	12.00
PPAMWI Mike Williams	4.00	10.00
PPANT Nick Toon	4.00	10.00
PPAPG Pierre Garcon	5.00	12.00
PPAPH Percy Harvin	6.00	15.00
PPAPW Patrick Willis	8.00	20.00
PPARG Robert Griffin III SP	100.00	175.00
PPARH Ronnie Hillman	4.00	10.00
PPART Robert Turbin	4.00	10.00
PPASR Sidney Rice	4.00	10.00
PPATR Trent Richardson SP	25.00	50.00
PPAVJ Vincent Jackson	5.00	12.00
PPAWM Willis McGahee	4.00	10.00

2012 Topps Prolific Playmakers Relics

STATED ODDS 1:50 HOB		
PPRAB Anquan Boldin	3.00	8.00
PPRAD Andy Dalton	4.00	10.00
PPRAF Arian Foster	3.00	8.00
PPRBL Brandon Lloyd	3.00	8.00
PPRBM Brandon Marshall	2.50	6.00
PPRBT Ben Tate	2.50	6.00
PPRCB Cedric Benson	3.00	8.00
PPRCM Colt McCoy	3.00	8.00
PPRCP Carson Palmer	3.00	8.00
PPRDB Dwayne Bowe	3.00	8.00
PPRDBR Dez Bryant	4.00	10.00
PPRDM Darren McFadden	3.00	8.00
PPRHN Hakeem Nicks	3.00	8.00
PPRJA Jared Allen	3.00	8.00
PPRJB Jahvid Best	3.00	8.00
PPRJF Joe Flacco	3.00	8.00
PPRJFO Jacoby Ford	2.50	6.00
PPRLF Larry Fitzgerald	3.00	8.00
PPRMA Miles Austin	3.00	8.00
PPRMC Marques Colston	3.00	8.00
PPRMI Mark Ingram	3.00	8.00
PPRMJD Maurice Jones-Drew	3.00	8.00
PPRMR Matt Ryan	3.00	8.00
PPRMT Michael Turner	3.00	8.00
PPRMW Mike Wallace	3.00	8.00
PPRNS Ndamukong Suh	4.00	10.00
PPRPH Peyton Hillis	2.50	6.00
PPRRF Ryan Fitzpatrick	3.00	8.00
PPRRL Ray Lewis	4.00	10.00
PPRRM Ryan Mathews	3.00	8.00
PPRRW Roddy White	3.00	8.00
PPRSG Shonn Greene	3.00	8.00
PPRSJ Steven Jackson	3.00	8.00
PPRTT Tim Tebow	6.00	15.00
PPRVC Victor Cruz	5.00	12.00
PPRVJ Vincent Jackson	3.00	8.00

2012 Topps Prolific Playmakers Relics Autographs

RELIC AU/50 ODDS 1:2610 HOB		
PPARAB Ahmad Bradshaw	12.00	30.00
PPARAP Adrian Peterson	40.00	80.00
PPARDS Darren Sproles	15.00	40.00
PPARFJ Fred Jackson	12.00	30.00
PPARJM Jeremy Maclin	12.00	30.00
PPARMS Matt Schaub	12.00	30.00
PPARMV Michael Vick	25.00	50.00
PPARPB Plaxico Burress	10.00	25.00
PPARPH Percy Harvin	12.00	30.00
PPARRH Roy Helu	10.00	25.00
PPARSB Sam Bradford	30.00	60.00
PPARWM Willis McGahee	10.00	25.00
PPARMSA Mark Sanchez	15.00	40.00

2012 Topps Prolific Playmakers Relics Jumbo

JUMBO/20 ODDS 1:4244 HOB		
PPJRAD Andy Dalton	8.00	20.00
PPJRBL Brandon Lloyd	6.00	15.00
PPJRCB Cedric Benson	6.00	15.00
PPJRJA Jared Allen	8.00	20.00
PPJRJB Jahvid Best	6.00	15.00
PPJRJF Joe Flacco	6.00	15.00
PPJRMC Marques Colston	6.00	15.00
PPJRMW Mike Wallace	8.00	20.00
PPJRNS Ndamukong Suh	8.00	20.00
PPJRRF Ryan Fitzpatrick	6.00	15.00
PPJRRL Ray Lewis	8.00	20.00
PPJRRM Ryan Mathews	6.00	15.00
PPJRRW Roddy White	6.00	15.00
PPJRSG Shonn Greene	6.00	15.00
PPJRVJ Vincent Jackson	6.00	15.00

2012 Topps QB Immortals

COMPLETE SET (19)	5.00	12.00
STATED ODDS 1:6 HOB		
QIBG Bob Griese	.40	1.00
QIBS Bart Starr	.60	1.50
QIDF Dan Fouts	.40	1.00
QIDM Dan Marino	.75	2.00
QIJE John Elway	.60	1.50
QIJK Jim Kelly	.40	1.00
QIJM Joe Montana	.75	2.00
QIJN Joe Namath	.60	1.50
QIJP Jim Plunkett	.30	.75
QIKW Kurt Warner	.40	1.00
QILD Len Dawson	.40	1.00
QIPS Phil Simms	.30	.75
QIRS Roger Staubach	.50	1.25
QISJ Sonny Jurgensen	.30	.75
QISY Steve Young	.50	1.25
QITA Troy Aikman	.50	1.25
QITB Terry Bradshaw	.50	1.25
QIWM Warren Moon	.40	1.00
QIYAT Y.A. Tittle	.30	.75

2012 Topps QB Immortals Autographs

AUTO/25 ODDS 1:14,750 HOB		
*SILVER/15: .5X TO 1.2X BASIC AU/25		
QIABF Brett Favre	75.00	150.00
QIABG Bob Griese	25.00	50.00
QIABS Bart Starr	60.00	120.00
QIADF Dan Fouts		
QIADM Dan Marino	60.00	120.00
QIAJE John Elway	60.00	120.00
QIAJK Jim Kelly	30.00	60.00
QIAJM Joe Montana	60.00	120.00
QIAJN Joe Namath	50.00	100.00
QIAJP Jim Plunkett		
QIAKW Kurt Warner		
QIALD Len Dawson	30.00	60.00
QIAPS Phil Simms	30.00	60.00
QIARS Roger Staubach	40.00	80.00
QIASY Steve Young		
QIATA Troy Aikman		
QIATB Terry Bradshaw	60.00	120.00
QIAWM Warren Moon	25.00	50.00
QIAYAT Y.A. Tittle	25.00	50.00

2012 Topps QB Immortals Plaques

PLAQUE/50 ODDS 1:5050 HOB		
QIPBF Brett Favre	30.00	80.00
QIPBG Bob Griese	15.00	40.00
QIPBS Bart Starr	25.00	60.00
QIPDF Dan Fouts	20.00	50.00
QIPDM Dan Marino	30.00	80.00
QIPJE John Elway	25.00	60.00
QIPJK Jim Kelly	20.00	50.00
QIPJM Joe Montana	30.00	80.00
QIPJN Joe Namath	30.00	80.00
QIPJP Jim Plunkett	15.00	40.00
QIPKW Kurt Warner	20.00	50.00
QIPLD Len Dawson	15.00	40.00
QIPPS Phil Simms	15.00	40.00
QIPRS Roger Staubach	20.00	50.00
QIPTB Terry Bradshaw	20.00	50.00
QIPWM Warren Moon	15.00	40.00
QIPYAT Y.A. Tittle	12.00	30.00

2012 Topps QB Immortals Relics

RELIC/50 ODDS 1:7500 HOB		
*GOLD/15: .6X TO 1.5X BASIC JSY/50		
*SILVER/25: .5X TO 1.2X BASIC JSY/50		
QIRBF Brett Favre	12.00	30.00
QIRDM Dan Marino	12.00	30.00
QIRJE John Elway	10.00	25.00
QIRJM Joe Montana	12.00	30.00
QIRJN Joe Namath	20.00	50.00
QIRKW Kurt Warner	6.00	15.00
QIRSY Steve Young	8.00	20.00

2012 Topps Quarterback Milestones Medallions Touchdowns Bronze

TD BRONZE/75 ODDS 1:3400 HOB		
*GOLD/25: .6X TO 1.5X BRONZE/75		
*SILVER/50: .5X TO 1.2X BRONZE/75		
QMTBF Brett Favre	20.00	50.00
QMTBG Bob Griese	10.00	25.00
QMTDB Drew Brees	12.00	30.00
QMTDF Dan Fouts	10.00	25.00
QMTDM Dan Marino	20.00	50.00
QMTEM Eli Manning	10.00	25.00
QMTJE John Elway	15.00	40.00
QMTJK Jim Kelly	10.00	25.00
QMTJM Joe Montana	20.00	50.00
QMTKW Kurt Warner	10.00	25.00
QMTLD Len Dawson	10.00	25.00
QMTMH Matt Hasselbeck	8.00	20.00
QMTPM Peyton Manning	25.00	60.00
QMTPS Phil Simms	8.00	20.00
QMTSY Steve Young	12.00	30.00
QMTTB Terry Bradshaw	15.00	40.00
QMTWM Warren Moon	10.00	25.00
QMTDMC Donovan McNabb	8.00	20.00
QMTTBR Tom Brady	15.00	40.00
QMTYAT Y.A. Tittle	8.00	20.00

2012 Topps Quarterback Milestones Medallions Wins Bronze

BRONZE/75 ODDS 1:2800 HOB		
*GOLD/25: .6X TO 1.5X BRONZE/75		
*SILVER/50: .5X TO 1.2X BRONZE/75		
QMWBF Brett Favre	20.00	50.00
QMWBG Bob Griese	10.00	25.00
QMWBR Ben Roethlisberger	12.00	30.00
QMWBS Bart Starr	15.00	40.00
QMWDB Drew Brees	12.00	30.00
QMWDF Dan Fouts	10.00	25.00
QMWDM Dan Marino	20.00	50.00
QMWEM Eli Manning	10.00	25.00
QMWJE John Elway	15.00	40.00
QMWJK Jim Kelly	10.00	25.00
QMWJM Joe Montana	20.00	50.00
QMWJP Jim Plunkett	8.00	20.00
QMWLD Len Dawson	10.00	25.00
QMWMH Matt Hasselbeck	8.00	20.00
QMWPM Peyton Manning	25.00	60.00
QMWPS Phil Simms	8.00	20.00
QMWRS Roger Staubach	12.00	30.00
QMWSY Steve Young	12.00	30.00
QMWTA Troy Aikman	12.00	30.00
QMWTB Terry Bradshaw	15.00	40.00
QMWWM Warren Moon	10.00	25.00
QMWDMC Donovan McNabb	8.00	20.00
QMWTBR Tom Brady	15.00	40.00
QMWYAT Y.A. Tittle	8.00	20.00

2012 Topps Quarterback Milestones Medallions Yardage Bronze

YARDS BRONZE/75 ODDS 1:3450 HOB		
*GOLD/25: .6X TO 1.5X BRONZE/75		
*SILVER/50: .5X TO 1.2X BRONZE/75		
QMPBF Brett Favre	20.00	50.00
QMPDB Drew Brees	12.00	30.00
QMPDF Dan Fouts	10.00	25.00
QMPDM Dan Marino	20.00	50.00
QMPEM Eli Manning	10.00	25.00
QMPJE John Elway	15.00	40.00
QMPJK Jim Kelly	10.00	25.00
QMPJM Joe Montana	20.00	50.00
QMPKW Kurt Warner	10.00	25.00
QMPLD Len Dawson	10.00	25.00
QMPMH Matt Hasselbeck	8.00	20.00
QMPPM Peyton Manning	25.00	60.00
QMPPS Phil Simms	8.00	20.00
QMPSY Steve Young	12.00	30.00
QMPTA Troy Aikman	12.00	30.00
QMPTB Terry Bradshaw	15.00	40.00
QMPWM Warren Moon	10.00	25.00
QMPDMC Donovan McNabb	8.00	20.00
QMPTBR Tom Brady	15.00	40.00
QMPYAT Y.A. Tittle	8.00	20.00

2012 Topps Rookie Autographs

ROOKIE AU ODDS 1:1650 HOB		
3 Brandon Weeden SP		
6 Robert Turbin	5.00	12.00
14 T.Y. Hilton SP		
18 Alshon Jeffery SP	15.00	40.00
28 DeVier Posey SP		
37 T.J. Graham SP	10.00	25.00
58 Dwayne Allen	10.00	25.00
63 Nick Toon	6.00	15.00
77 Ryan Broyles SP		
85 Joe Adams SP	10.00	25.00
91 Michael Floyd SP	20.00	50.00
112 A.J. Jenkins SP	12.00	30.00
115 Stephen Hill SP	20.00	40.00
132 Coby Fleener	5.00	12.00
134 Ryan Tannehill SP		
140 Andrew Luck SP	300.00	450.00
146 Cyrus Gray SP	10.00	25.00
149 Michael Egnew SP		
151 Mohamed Sanu SP	12.00	30.00
165 Russell Wilson SP	20.00	50.00
185 LaMichael James SP	20.00	50.00
186 Nick Foles SP	15.00	40.00
204 Doug Martin SP		
214 Bernard Pierce SP EXCH	10.00	25.00
240 Justin Blackmon SP	15.00	40.00
242 Lamar Miller SP		
252 Jarius Wright SP		
279 Brian Quick SP		
283 Ronnie Hillman	4.00	10.00
289 David Wilson SP		
314 Rueben Randle SP	10.00	25.00
326 Kirk Cousins SP	15.00	40.00
340 Robert Griffin III SP	250.00	400.00
357 Chris Givens SP	8.00	20.00
365 Brock Osweiler SP	20.00	40.00
378 Kendall Wright SP	25.00	50.00
380 Trent Richardson SP		
399 Isaiah Pead SP	10.00	25.00

2012 Topps Rookie Patch

RPAJ Alshon Jeffery	5.00	12.00
RPAL Andrew Luck	20.00	50.00
RPBO Brock Osweiler	5.00	12.00
RPBP Bernard Pierce	4.00	10.00
RPBQ Brian Quick	5.00	12.00
RPBW Brandon Weeden	5.00	12.00
RPCF Coby Fleener	5.00	12.00
RPDM Doug Martin	5.00	12.00
RPDP DeVier Posey	4.00	10.00
RPDW David Wilson	5.00	12.00
RPIP Isaiah Pead	4.00	10.00
RPJA Joe Adams	4.00	10.00
RPJB Justin Blackmon	6.00	15.00
RPJW Jarius Wright	4.00	10.00
RPKW Kendall Wright	5.00	12.00
RPLJ LaMichael James	5.00	12.00
RPLM Lamar Miller	5.00	12.00
RPME Michael Egnew	4.00	10.00
RPMF Michael Floyd	5.00	12.00
RPMS Mohamed Sanu	4.00	10.00
RPNF Nick Foles	5.00	12.00
RPNT Nick Toon	5.00	12.00
RPRB Ryan Broyles	4.00	10.00
RPRG Robert Griffin III	15.00	40.00
RPRH Ronnie Hillman	5.00	12.00
RPRR Rueben Randle	4.00	10.00
RPRT Ryan Tannehill	8.00	20.00
RPRW Russell Wilson	5.00	12.00
RPSH Stephen Hill	4.00	10.00
RPTG T.J. Graham	4.00	10.00
RPTR Trent Richardson	6.00	15.00
RPAJJ A.J. Jenkins	5.00	12.00
RPCGI Chris Givens	3.00	8.00

2012 Topps Rookie Premiere Autographs

AUTO/90 ODDS 1:535 HOB		
RPAAJ Alshon Jeffery	25.00	60.00
RPAAJJ A.J. Jenkins	20.00	50.00
RPAAL Andrew Luck	250.00	400.00
RPABO Brock Osweiler	25.00	60.00
RPABP Bernard Pierce EXCH	15.00	40.00
RPABQ Brian Quick	15.00	40.00
RPABW Brandon Weeden	60.00	100.00
RPACF Coby Fleener	20.00	50.00
RPACGI Chris Givens	12.00	30.00
RPADA Dwayne Allen	12.00	30.00
RPADM Doug Martin	25.00	60.00
RPADP DeVier Posey	12.00	30.00
RPADW David Wilson	30.00	80.00
RPAIP Isaiah Pead	15.00	40.00
RPAJA Joe Adams	12.00	30.00
RPAJB Justin Blackmon	30.00	80.00
RPAJW Jarius Wright	15.00	40.00
RPAKW Kendall Wright	25.00	60.00
RPALJ LaMichael James	30.00	80.00
RPALM Lamar Miller	20.00	50.00
RPAME Michael Egnew	12.00	30.00
RPAMF Michael Floyd	40.00	80.00
RPAMS Mohamed Sanu	15.00	40.00
RPANF Nick Foles	20.00	50.00
RPANT Nick Toon	20.00	50.00
RPARB Ryan Broyles	15.00	40.00
RPARG Robert Griffin III	200.00	350.00
RPARH Ronnie Hillman	15.00	40.00
RPARR Rueben Randle	20.00	50.00
RPART Ryan Tannehill	60.00	100.00
RPARTU Robert Turbin	15.00	40.00
RPARW Russell Wilson	40.00	80.00
RPASH Stephen Hill	15.00	40.00
RPATG T.J. Graham	15.00	40.00
RPATR Trent Richardson	75.00	125.00

2012 Topps Rookie Premiere Autographs Dual

DUAL AU/25 ODDS 1:13,720 HOB		
RPDABR Justin Blackmon Trent Richardson		
RPDAGW Robert Griffin III Kendall Wright	100.00	175.00
RPDALG Andrew Luck Robert Griffin III		
RPDARH Rueben Randle Stephen Hill	20.00	40.00
RPDAWB Brandon Weeden Justin Blackmon		

2012 Topps Rookie Relic Jumbos

RJRAJ Alshon Jeffery	4.00	10.00
RJRAJJ A.J. Jenkins	4.00	10.00
RJRAL Andrew Luck	15.00	40.00
RJRBP Bernard Pierce	3.00	8.00
RJRBQ Brian Quick	4.00	10.00
RJRBW Brandon Weeden	4.00	10.00
RJRCF Coby Fleener	4.00	10.00
RJRCGI Chris Givens	2.50	6.00
RJRDA Dwayne Allen	3.00	8.00
RJRDM Doug Martin	5.00	12.00
RJRDP DeVier Posey	3.00	8.00
RJRDW David Wilson	4.00	10.00
RJRIP Isaiah Pead	3.00	8.00
RJRJA Joe Adams	3.00	8.00
RJRJB Justin Blackmon	5.00	12.00
RJRJW Jarius Wright	3.00	8.00
RJRKW Kendall Wright	4.00	10.00
RJRLJ LaMichael James	4.00	10.00
RJRLM Lamar Miller	4.00	10.00
RJRME Michael Egnew	2.50	6.00
RJRMF Michael Floyd	4.00	10.00
RJRMS Mohamed Sanu	3.00	8.00
RJRNF Nick Foles	4.00	10.00
RJRNT Nick Toon	4.00	10.00
RJRPBO Brock Osweiler	4.00	10.00
RJRRB Ryan Broyles	3.00	8.00
RJRRG Robert Griffin III	12.00	30.00
RJRRH Ronnie Hillman	4.00	10.00
RJRRR Rueben Randle	3.00	8.00
RJRRT Ryan Tannehill	8.00	20.00
RJRRTU Robert Turbin	3.00	8.00
RJRRW Russell Wilson	4.00	10.00
RJRSH Stephen Hill	3.00	8.00
RJRTG T.J. Graham	3.00	8.00
RJRTR Trent Richardson	8.00	20.00

2012 Topps Rookie Reprint

COMPLETE SET (21)	6.00	15.00
STATED ODDS 1:6 HOB		
63 John Elway 84	.60	1.50
65 Jim Plunkett 72	.30	.75
90 Sonny Jurgensen 58	.30	.75
119 Bart Starr 57	.60	1.50
122 Joe Namath 65	.60	1.50
123 Dan Marino 84	.75	2.00
156 Terry Bradshaw 71	.50	1.25
196 Bob Griese 68	.40	1.00
200 Roger Staubach 72	.50	1.25
216 Joe Montana 81	.75	2.00
225 Phil Simms 80	.30	.75
251 Warren Moon 85	.40	1.00
311 Michael Vick 01	.40	1.00
328 Drew Brees 01	.50	1.25
350 Eli Manning 04	.40	1.00
360 Peyton Manning 98	1.00	2.50
362 Jim Kelly 87	.40	1.00
367 Dan Fouts 75	.40	1.00
374 Steve Young 86	.50	1.25
430 Matthew Stafford 09	.40	1.00
431 Aaron Rodgers 05	.75	2.00

2012 Topps Rookie Reprint Autographs

AUTO/25 ODDS 1:16,600 HOB		
63 John Elway 84		
65 Jim Kelly 72		
119 Bart Starr 57		
122 Joe Namath 65		
123 Dan Fouts 75		
156 Terry Bradshaw 71		
196 Bob Griese 68		
200 Roger Staubach 72		
216 Joe Montana 81		
225 Phil Simms 80		
251 Warren Moon 85		
311 Michael Vick 01		
328 Drew Brees 01		
362 Jim Plunkett 72		
367 Dan Marino 84		
374 Steve Young 86		
430 Matthew Stafford 09		
431 Aaron Rodgers 05		

2012 Topps Rookie Reprint Relics

RELIC/25 ODDS 1:11,900 HOB		
63 John Elway 84		
122 Joe Namath 65		
216 Joe Montana 81		
311 Michael Vick 01		
350 Eli Manning 04		
367 Dan Marino 84		
374 Steve Young 86		

2012 Topps Super Bowl MVPs

MVP/46 ODDS 1:6750 HOB		
SBMVPAR Aaron Rodgers	40.00	80.00
SBMVPDB Drew Brees	25.00	50.00
SBMVPJE John Elway	15.00	40.00
SBMVPJN Joe Namath	15.00	40.00
SBMVPJP Jim Plunkett	8.00	20.00
SBMVPKW Kurt Warner	10.00	25.00
SBMVPLD Len Dawson	12.00	30.00
SBMVPPM Peyton Manning	25.00	60.00
SBMVPPS Phil Simms	8.00	20.00
SBMVPRS Roger Staubach	12.00	30.00
SBMVPSY Steve Young	12.00	30.00
SBMVPTA Troy Aikman	12.00	30.00
SBMVPBS1 Bart Starr	15.00	40.00
SBMVPBS2 Bart Starr	15.00	40.00
SBMVPEM1 Eli Manning	25.00	50.00
SBMVPEM2 Eli Manning	25.00	50.00
SBMVPJM1 Joe Montana	20.00	50.00
SBMVPJM2 Joe Montana	20.00	50.00
SBMVPJM3 Joe Montana	20.00	50.00
SBMVPTB1 Terry Bradshaw	15.00	40.00
SBMVPTB2 Terry Bradshaw	15.00	40.00
SBMVPTBR1 Tom Brady	30.00	60.00
SBMVPTBR2 Tom Brady	30.00	60.00

1998 Topps Action Flats Kickoff Edition

The 1998 Topps Action Flats set was issued in one series with a total of 8-statues/cards. The single-card/action figures retail for $2.99 each. The action figures are miniature plastic flat-sculpted silhouettes of NFL superstars. The accompanying 1998 Topps card features the player in the same pose as the action figure with a gold foil Action Flats logo and new card number.

COMPLETE SET (8)	7.50	15.00
K1 Troy Aikman	1.00	2.50
K2 Brett Favre	1.25	3.00
K3 John Elway	1.25	3.00
K4 Dan Marino	1.25	3.00
K5 Peyton Manning	2.50	6.00
K6 Ryan Leaf	.75	2.00
K7 Barry Sanders	1.25	3.00
K8 Jerry Rice	1.00	2.50

1999 Topps Action Flats

This set was issued in one series with a total of 12-statues and cards. The package with one card and an action figures originally retailed for $2.99. The action figures are miniature plastic flat-sculpted silhouettes of NFL superstars. The accompanying 1999 Topps card features the player in the same pose as the action figure with a gold foil Action Flats logo and new card number.

COMPLETE SET (12)	10.00	20.00
1 Jamal Anderson	.60	1.50
2 Jerome Bettis	.60	1.50
3 Mark Brunell	.80	2.00
4 Terrell Davis	1.20	3.00
5 Doug Flutie	.80	2.00
6 Eddie George	.80	2.00
7 Keyshawn Johnson	.60	1.50
8 Randy Moss	1.60	4.00
9 Jake Plummer	.60	1.50
10 Emmitt Smith	1.20	3.00
11 Fred Taylor	.75	2.00
12 Steve Young	.80	2.00

2003 Topps All American

Released in early June of 2003, this set contains 150 cards including 100 veterans and 50 rookies. The rookies were inserted at a rate of 1:4. Each pack contained 6 cards, including one Foil parallel. Boxes contained 20 packs. Each case held 8 boxes. Pack SRP was $4.00

COMPLETE SET (150)	50.00	100.00
COMP.SET w/o SP's (100)	10.00	25.00
ROOKIE STATED ODDS 1:4		
1 Marvin Harrison	.40	1.00
2 Tiki Barber	.40	1.00
3 Jamal Lewis	.30	.75
4 Tim Couch	.25	.60
5 Michael Bennett	.30	.75
6 Brad Johnson	.30	.75
7 Garrison Hearst	.30	.75
8 Plaxico Burress	.30	.75
9 Rod Gardner	.25	.60
10 Charlie Garner	.30	.75
11 Chad Pennington	.40	1.00
12 Brian Griese	.30	.75
13 Julius Peppers	.40	1.00
14 David Boston	.25	.60
15 Anthony Thomas	.30	.75
16 Ahman Green	.30	.75
17 Fred Taylor	.30	.75
18 Joe Horn	.30	.75
19 Joey Galloway	.30	.75
20 Eddie George	.30	.75
21 Jeff Garcia	.30	.75
22 Hines Ward	.40	1.00
23 Kurt Warner	.40	1.00
24 Marty Booker	.30	.75
25 Joey Harrington	.25	.60
26 Jay Fiedler	.25	.60
27 Troy Brown	.30	.75
28 David Carr	.30	.75
29 Eric Moulds	.30	.75
30 Michael Vick	.50	1.25
31 Keyshawn Johnson	.40	1.00
32 Torry Holt	.40	1.00
33 LaDainian Tomlinson	.40	1.00
34 Duce Staley	.30	.75
35 Curtis Martin	.40	1.00
36 Stephen Davis	.30	.75
37 Jim Miller	.25	.60
38 Travis Taylor	.25	.60
39 Jimmy Smith	.30	.75
40 Trent Green	.30	.75
41 Tom Brady	1.00	2.50
42 Randy Moss	.40	1.00
43 Clinton Portis	.30	.75
44 Emmitt Smith	1.00	2.50
45 Steve McNair	.40	1.00
46 Shaun Alexander	.30	.75
47 Jerome Bettis	.40	1.00
48 Rich Gannon	.30	.75
49 William Green	.25	.60
50 Priest Holmes	.40	1.00
51 James Stewart	.25	.60
52 Warrick Dunn	.30	.75
53 Jake Plummer	.30	.75
54 Antowain Smith	.30	.75
55 Peyton Manning	.75	2.00
56 Deuce McAllister	.30	.75
57 Jeremy Shockey	.40	1.00
58 Darrell Jackson	.30	.75
59 Derrick Mason	.30	.75
60 Terrell Owens	.40	1.00
61 Laveranues Coles	.25	.60
62 Amani Toomer	.30	.75
63 Tony Gonzalez	.40	1.00
64 Corey Bradford	.25	.60
65 Donald Driver	.40	1.00
66 Rod Smith	.30	.75
67 Chad Johnson	.40	1.00
68 Travis Henry	.25	.60
69 Mark Brunell	.30	.75
70 Edgerrin James	.40	1.00
71 Jerry Rice	.75	2.00
72 Aaron Brooks	.30	.75
73 Marshall Faulk	.40	1.00
74 Curtis Conway	.25	.60
75 Tommy Maddox	.30	.75
76 Isaac Bruce	.40	1.00
77 Matt Hasselbeck	.30	.75
78 Muhsin Muhammad	.30	.75
79 Drew Bledsoe	.40	1.00
80 Ricky Williams	.30	.75
81 Daunte Culpepper	.30	.75
82 Chad Hutchinson	.25	.60
83 Brian Urlacher	.40	1.00
84 Drew Brees	.40	1.00
85 Corey Dillon	.30	.75
86 Chris Chambers	.30	.75
87 Peerless Price	.25	.60
88 Kerry Collins	.30	.75
89 Donovan McNabb	.40	1.00
90 Brett Favre	1.00	2.50
91 Patrick Ramsey	.30	.75
92 T.J. Duckett	.30	.75
93 Derrick Brooks	.30	.75
94 Jon Kitna	.30	.75
95 Jerry Porter	.25	.60
96 Todd Pinkston	.25	.60
97 Tai Streets	.25	.60
98 Ray Lewis	.40	1.00
99 Michael Pittman	.25	.60
100 Brian Finneran	.25	.60
101 Carson Palmer RC	2.50	6.00
102 Terrell Suggs RC	1.25	3.00
103 Boss Bailey RC	1.00	2.50
104 Justin Gage RC	1.00	2.50
105 Bobby Wade RC	1.00	2.50
106 Larry Johnson RC	1.25	3.00
107 Ken Dorsey RC	1.00	2.50
108 Quentin Griffin RC	1.00	2.50
109 Musa Smith RC	.75	2.00
110 Chris Simms RC	1.25	3.00
111 Michael Haynes RC	.75	2.00
112 Charles Rogers RC	1.00	2.50
113 Kliff Kingsbury RC	1.00	2.50
114 Jerome McDougle RC	.75	2.00
115 ReShard Lee RC	1.25	3.00
116 Chris Brown RC	.75	2.00
117 Bryant Johnson RC	1.25	3.00
118 Teyo Johnson RC	1.00	2.50
119 Talman Gardner RC	.75	2.00
120 Brian St.Pierre RC	1.00	2.50
121 Onterrio Smith RC	.75	2.00
122 Marcus Trufant RC	1.00	2.50
123 Earnest Graham RC	1.25	3.00
124 Kareem Kelly RC	.75	2.00
125 Jason Witten RC	3.00	8.00
126 Brandon Lloyd RC	2.00	5.00
127 Anquan Boldin RC	2.00	5.00
128 Lee Suggs RC	1.00	2.50
129 Terry Pierce RC	.75	2.00
130 Dallas Clark RC	2.00	5.00
131 Kelley Washington RC	.75	2.00
132 Seneca Wallace RC	1.25	3.00
133 Domanick Davis RC	1.00	2.50
134 Terrence Edwards RC	.75	2.00
135 Dave Ragone RC	.75	2.00
136 Andre Johnson RC	3.00	8.00
137 Taylor Jacobs RC	.75	2.00
138 Kyle Boller RC	1.25	3.00
139 Willis McGahee RC	1.50	4.00
140 Byron Leftwich RC	1.25	3.00
141 Sam Aiken RC	1.00	2.50
142 Bennie Joppru RC	.75	2.00
143 Justin Fargas RC	1.25	3.00
144 Avon Cobourne RC	.75	2.00
145 Rex Grossman RC	1.25	3.00
146 LaBrandon Toefield RC	1.00	2.50
147 Tyrone Calico RC	1.00	2.50
148 Brad Banks RC	1.00	2.50
149 Terence Newman RC	1.00	2.50
150 Jimmy Kennedy RC	1.00	2.50

2003 Topps All American Foil

*VETS 1-100: 1X TO 2.5X BASIC CARDS
VETERAN ODDS: ONE PER PACK
*ROOKIES 101-150: .6X TO 1.5X
ROOKIE STATED ODDS 1:30

2003 Topps All American Foil Gold

*VETS 1-100: 5X TO 12X BASIC CARDS
*ROOKIES 101-150: 3X TO 8X
FOIL GOLD/55 ODDS 1:90
STATED PRINT RUN 55 SER.#'d SETS

2003 Topps All American Autographs

GROUP A STATED ODDS 1:856		
GROUP B STATED ODDS 1:2007		
GROUP C STATED ODDS 1:997		
GROUP D STATED ODDS 1:1198		
GROUP E STATED ODDS 1:598		
GROUP F STATED ODDS 1:460		
GROUP G STATED ODDS 1:332		
GROUP H STATED ODDS 1:315		
GROUP I STATED ODDS 1:28		
AAAC Avon Cobourne G	5.00	12.00
AAAJ Andre Johnson C	20.00	50.00
AABBE Brad Banks D	6.00	15.00
AABJ Bryant Johnson A	10.00	25.00
AABL Byron Leftwich C	8.00	20.00
AABM Billy McMullen I	5.00	12.00
AACB Chris Brown A	6.00	15.00
AACP Carson Palmer A	25.00	60.00
AACS Chris Simms A	15.00	40.00
AAEG Earnest Graham I	8.00	20.00
AAJF Justin Fargas I	8.00	20.00
AAJT Jason Thomas D	5.00	12.00
AAKB Kyle Boller B	8.00	20.00
AAKD Ken Dorsey A	8.00	20.00
AAKKE Kareem Kelly I	5.00	12.00
AAKW Kelley Washington E	5.00	12.00
AALJ Larry Johnson C	10.00	25.00
AALT LaBrandon Toefield I	6.00	15.00
AAOS Onterrio Smith I	5.00	12.00
AAQG Quentin Griffin H	6.00	15.00
AARG Rex Grossman A	12.00	30.00
AASW Seneca Wallace I	8.00	20.00
AATC Tyrone Calico I	6.00	15.00
AATG Talman Gardner I	5.00	12.00
AATJ Taylor Jacobs E	5.00	12.00
AAWM Willis McGahee F	10.00	25.00

2003 Topps All American Campus Connection Autographs

STATED ODDS 1:1208		
STATED PRINT RUN 100 SER.#'d SETS		
CCHS Priest Holmes Chris Simms	20.00	50.00
CCMD Ken Dorsey Santana Moss	15.00	40.00
CCPD Clinton Portis Ken Dorsey	20.00	50.00
CCZC Amos Zereoue Avon Cobourne	12.00	30.00

2003 Topps All American Conference Call Autographs

STATED ODDS 1:1208		
STATED PRINT RUN 100 SER.#'d SETS		
CCABP Carson Palmer Kyle Boller	40.00	80.00
CCACM Willis McGahee Avon Cobourne	20.00	50.00
CCAGB Chris Brown Quentin Griffin	15.00	40.00
CCASM Willis McGahee Lee Suggs	20.00	50.00

2003 Topps All American Fabric of America

GROUP A STATED ODDS 1:61		
GROUP B STATED ODDS 1:59		
GROUP C STATED ODDS 1:166		
GROUP D STATED ODDS 1:63		
GROUP E STATED ODDS 1:25		
GROUP F STATED ODDS 1:136		
FAAC Angelo Crowell A	3.00	8.00
FAAP Artose Pinner E	2.50	6.00
FAAW Andre Woolfolk E	3.00	8.00
FAAWA Aaron Walker A	3.00	8.00
FABJA Bradie James D	4.00	10.00
FABJO Bennie Joppru F	2.50	6.00
FABN Bruce Nelson A	2.50	6.00
FABW Brett Williams A	2.50	6.00
FACK Chris Kelsay C	3.00	8.00
FACP Carson Palmer E	7.50	20.00
FACS Chris Simms D	4.00	10.00
FADD Domanick Davis E	3.00	8.00
FADG Doug Gabriel E	3.00	8.00
FADR Dave Ragone B	2.50	6.00
FAEG Earnest Graham A	4.00	10.00
FAES Eric Steinbach B	2.50	6.00
FAJB Julian Battle E	3.00	8.00
FAJG DeJuan Groce F	4.00	10.00
FAJGR Justin Griffith E	3.00	8.00
FAJJ Jarret Johnson D	3.00	8.00
FAJM Jerome McDougle D	2.50	6.00
FAJS Jon Stinchcomb A	3.00	8.00
FAKG Kevin Garrett A	2.50	6.00
FAKK Kliff Kingsbury C	3.00	8.00
FAKW Kevin Williams B	4.00	10.00
FAMH Michael Haynes B	2.50	6.00
FAMT Marcus Trufant E	3.00	8.00
FAMW Matt Wilhelm D	3.00	8.00
FARM Rashean Mathis B	3.00	8.00
FASA Sam Aiken E	3.00	8.00
FATBC Tully Banta-Cain A	4.00	10.00
FATC Tyrone Calico E	3.00	8.00
FATG Talman Gardner A	2.50	6.00
FATJ Taylor Jacobs B	2.50	6.00
FATW Ty Warren E	3.00	8.00
FAVH Victor Hobson E	2.50	6.00
FAVM Vincent Manuwai A	2.50	6.00

2003 Topps All American Jersey Backs

STATED ODDS 1:2762		
STATED PRINT RUN 25 SER.#'d SETS		
JBBJ Bryant Johnson	20.00	50.00
JBCP Carson Palmer		

JBCS Chris Simms 20.00 50.00
JBDR Dave Ragone 12.00 30.00
JBJF Justin Fargas 20.00 50.00
JBKK Kliff Kingsbury 15.00 40.00
JBLJ Larry Johnson 20.00 50.00
JBTG Talman Gardner 12.00 30.00
JBTJ Taylor Jacobs 12.00 30.00

2005 Topps All American

This 91-card set was released in November, 2005. The set was issued through the hobby in six-card packs with an $5 SRP which came 24 packs to a box.

COMPLETE SET (91) 15.00 40.00
UNPRICED PRINT PLATE PRINT RUN 1 SET
ES5 STATED ODDS 1:1220 HOB/RET
ES5C STATED ODDS 1:27,245 HOB/RET
1 Dan Fouts .50 1.25
2 Kellen Winslow .40 1.00
3 Marty Lyons .50 1.25
4 Alan Page .40 1.00
5 Carl Eller .30 .75
6 Jake Scott .30 .75
7 William Perry .40 1.00
8 Joe Montana 1.25 3.00
9 Fred Biletnikoff .50 1.25
10 Dave Casper .40 1.00
11 Earl Campbell .50 1.25
12 Mark May .30 .75
13 Joe Greene .50 1.25
14 Ozzie Newsome .40 1.00
15 Joe Namath .75 2.00
16 Ted Hendricks .30 .75
17 Lawrence Taylor .50 1.25
18 Randy Gradishar .40 1.00
19 Reggie McKenzie .30 .75
20 Dave Foley .50 1.25
21 Mike Montler ERR .30 .75
(wrong player photo)
22 Merlin Olsen .40 1.00
23 John David Crow .30 .75
24 Paul Hornung .50 1.25
25 Jim Brown .60 1.50
26 Bob Lilly .40 1.00
27 Mel Renfro .30 .75
28 Dick Butkus .60 1.50
29 Roger Staubach .75 2.00
30 Gale Sayers .60 1.50
31 Bob Griese .50 1.25
32 Dick Anderson .30 .75
33 Jim Plunkett .40 1.00
34 Johnny Rodgers .50 1.25
35 Ed Marinaro .30 .75
36 Greg Pruitt .50 1.25
37 Johnny Musso .50 1.25
38 Johnny Majors .40 1.00
39 Bert Jones .30 .75
40 Steve Bartkowski .40 1.00
41 John Cappelletti .40 1.00
42 Archie Griffin .50 1.25
43 Randy White .40 1.00
44 Tommy Kramer .30 .75
45 Mike Singletary .50 1.25
46 Tony Dorsett .40 1.00
47 Tony Franklin .30 .75
48 John Jefferson .30 .75
49 Billy Sims .50 1.25
50 Charles White .40 1.00
51 Herschel Walker .40 1.00
52 Ronnie Lott .40 1.00
53 Anthony Carter .40 1.00
54 Jim McMahon .50 1.25
55 Marcus Allen .50 1.25
56 John Elway 1.00 2.50
57 Mike Rozier .50 1.25
58 Irving Fryar .50 1.25
59 Bo Jackson .60 1.50
60 Eric Dickerson .40 1.00
61 Kenny Easley .30 .75
62 Bruce Matthews .30 .75
63 Alex Karras .40 1.00
64 Bubba Smith .30 .75
65 Chuck Long .40 1.00
66 Lorenzo White .30 .75
67 Cris Carter .50 1.25
68 Brad Muster .30 .75
69 D.J. Dozier .40 1.00
70 Craig Heyward .30 .75
71 Chris Spielman .50 1.25
72 Chuck Cecil .30 .75
73 Hart Lee Dykes .30 .75
74 Tony Mandarich .30 .75
75 Barry Sanders .75 2.00
76 Troy Aikman .60 1.50
77 Andre Ware .30 .75
78 Desmond Howard .50 1.25
79 Gino Torretta .30 .75
80 Charlie Ward .30 .75
81 Danny Wuerffel .40 1.00
82 Tommie Frazier .50 1.25
83 Ty Detmer .30 .75
84 Wendell Davis .30 .75
85 Jay Novacek .40 1.00
86 Keith Byars .40 1.00
87 Steve Spurrier .50 1.25
88 Earl Morrall .40 1.00
89 Anthony Davis .30 .75
90 Brad Van Pelt .30 .75
91 Roland James .30 .75
ES5 Elvis Presley Shirt/500 50.00 100.00
ES5C Elvis Shirt Chr/25 125.00 200.00

2005 Topps All American Chrome

*SINGLES: 2X TO 5X BASIC CARDS
CHROME/555 STATED ODDS 1:12
UNPRICED XFRACTOR PRINT RUN 5 SETS

2005 Topps All American Chrome Refractor

*SINGLES: 5X TO 12X BASIC CARDS
CHROME REFRACTOR/55 ODDS 1:121

2005 Topps All American Chrome Xfractor

UNPRICED XFRACTOR/5 ODDS 1:1328

2005 Topps All American Gold Chrome

*SINGLES: 2X TO 5X BASIC CARDS
GOLD CHROME/555 STATED ODDS 1:12
UNPRICED GOLD XFRACT.PRINT RUN 5 SETS

2005 Topps All American Gold Chrome Refractor

*SINGLES: 5X TO 12X BASIC CARDS
GOLD CHROME REFRACT/55 ODDS 1:121

2005 Topps All American Gold Chrome Xfractor

UNPRICED XFRACTOR/5 ODDS 1:1328

2005 Topps All American Autographs

GROUP A/4 ODDS 1:58,000 HOB
GROUP B/19 ODDS 1:2000 H, 1:6024 R
GROUP C/44 ODDS 1:642 H, 1:3917 R
GROUP D/69 ODDS 1:5800 H, 1:9792 R
GROUP E/144 ODDS 1:1115 H, 1:305 R
GROUP F/194 ODDS 1:99 H, 1:280 R
GROUP G ODDS 1:2231 H, 1:1958 R
GROUP H ODDS 1:574 H, 1:593 R
GROUP I ODDS 1:71 H, 1:72 R
GROUP J ODDS 1:82 H, 1:122 R
GROUP K ODDS 1:57 H, 1:164 R
TOPPS ANNOUNCED PRINT RUNS BELOW
GROUPS A AND B TOO SCARCE TO PRICE
UNPRICED SUPERFRAC.PRINT RUN 1 SET
AJMA Johnny Majors J 12.50 30.00
AAC Anthony Carter/194* 15.00 40.00
AAD Anthony Davis J 10.00 25.00
AAG Archie Griffin/144* 30.00 60.00
AAK Alex Karras I 12.50 30.00
AAP Alan Page/194* 25.00 50.00
AAW Andre Ware/194* 15.00 30.00
ABG Bob Griese/144* 25.00 50.00
ABJ Bert Jones I 10.00 25.00
ABL Bob Lilly/144* 30.00 80.00
ABM Brad Muster J 6.00 15.00
ABMA Bruce Matthews/144* 30.00 60.00
ABOJ Bo Jackson/69* 75.00 135.00
ABS Bubba Smith/144* 25.00 50.00
ABSA Barry Sanders/4*
ABSI Billy Sims/144* 25.00 50.00
ABVP Brad Van Pelt I 7.50 20.00
ACC Cris Carter/144* 30.00 60.00
ACCE Chuck Cecil K 6.00 15.00
ACE Carl Eller/194* 25.00 50.00
ACH Craig Heyward J 15.00 30.00
ACL Chuck Long/194* 30.00 60.00
ACS Chris Spielman/194* 25.00 50.00
ACW Charles White I 15.00 30.00
ACWA Charlie Ward/144* 20.00 40.00
ADA Dick Anderson/144* 25.00 50.00
ADB Dick Butkus/144* 60.00 120.00
ADC Dave Casper H 10.00 25.00
ADD D.J. Dozier I 7.50 20.00
ADF Dan Fouts/44* 50.00 100.00
ADFO Dave Foley/194* 15.00 30.00
ADH Desmond Howard/144* 25.00 50.00
ADW Danny Wuerffel I 15.00 40.00
AEC Earl Campbell/44* 60.00 120.00
AED Eric Dickerson/44* 60.00 120.00
AEM Earl Morrall K 10.00 25.00
AEMA Ed Marinaro I 6.00 20.00
AFB Fred Biletnikoff/144* 40.00 80.00
AGP Greg Pruitt I 15.00 30.00
AGS Gale Sayers/19*
AGT Gino Torretta/194* 15.00 40.00
AHLD Hart Lee Dykes I 6.00 15.00
AHW Herschel Walker/144* 40.00 80.00
AIR Irving Fryar/144* 30.00 60.00
AJB Jim Brown/19*
AJC John Cappelletti K 10.00 25.00
AJDC John David Crow K 12.00 30.00
AJE John Elway/19*
AJG Joe Greene/144* 40.00 75.00
AJJ John Jefferson I 7.50 20.00
AJM Joe Montana/19*
AJMC Jim McMahon/144* 35.00 60.00
AJMU Johnny Musso J 10.00 25.00
AJN Joe Namath/19*
AJNO Jay Novacek/194* 15.00 40.00
AJP Jim Plunkett/194* 30.00 60.00
AJR Johnny Rodgers I 15.00 40.00
AJS Jake Scott/44* 50.00 100.00
AKB Keith Byars/194* 15.00 40.00
AKE Kenny Easley J 6.00 15.00
AKW Kellen Winslow/44* 30.00 80.00
ALT Lawrence Taylor/44* 60.00 120.00
ALW Lorenzo White/194* 15.00 30.00
AMA Marcus Allen/19*
AML Marty Lyons/194* 15.00 40.00
AMM Mark May/194* 15.00 30.00
AMMO Mike Montler ERR/194* 15.00 30.00
(wrong player photo)
AMO Merlin Olsen H 25.00 50.00
AMR Mel Renfro I 10.00 25.00
AMRO Mike Rozier/144* 30.00 60.00
AMS Mike Singletary/144* 25.00 50.00
AON Ozzie Newsome G 15.00 30.00
APH Paul Hornung/44* 50.00 100.00
ARG Randy Gradishar/194* 15.00 40.00
ARJ Roland James I 6.00 15.00
ARL Ronnie Lott/44* 60.00 120.00
ARM Reggie McKenzie/194* 15.00 30.00
ARS Roger Staubach/19*
ARW Randy White/144* 25.00 50.00
ASB Steve Bartkowski I 7.50 20.00
ASS Steve Spurrier/144* 40.00 80.00
ATA Troy Aikman/19*
ATD Tony Dorsett/19*
ATF Tony Franklin I 6.00 15.00
ATFR Tommie Frazier I 15.00 40.00
ATH Ted Hendricks/44* 40.00 80.00
ATK Tommy Kramer I 7.50 20.00
ATM Tony Mandarich/194* 15.00 30.00
ATYD Ty Detmer I 6.00 15.00
AWD Wendell Davis I 6.00 20.00
AWP William Perry H 12.50 30.00

2005 Topps All American Autographs Chrome Refractors

*CHROME REF/55: .6X TO 1.5X BASIC AUTOS
*CHROME REF/55: .5X TO 1.2X AUTO/144/194
*CHROME REF/55: .5X TO 1.2X AUTO/44
GROUP A/5 ODDS 1:12,429 H, 1:17,311 R
GROUP B/55 ODDS 1:63 H, 1:282 R
SERIAL #'d TO 5 TOO SCARCE TO PRICE

2005 Topps All American College Co-Signers

CO-SIGNER/25 ODDS 1:5612 H, 4896 R
AABJ Bo Jackson 150.00 250.00
Jim Brown
AABS Gale Sayers 125.00 250.00
Jim Brown
AAMA Joe Montana 200.00 350.00
Troy Aikman
AAME Joe Montana 200.00 400.00
John Elway
AASD Barry Sanders 150.00 250.00
Tony Dorsett

2006 Topps Allen and Ginter

This 350-card set was release in August, 2006. The set was issued in seven-card hobby packs with an $4 SRP. Those packs came 24 to a box and there were 12 boxes in a case. In addition, there were also six-card retail packs issued and those packs came 24 packs to a box and 20 boxes to a case. There were some subsets included in this set including Rookies (251-265); Retired Greats (266-290); Managers (291-300); Modern Personalities (301-314); Reprinted Allen and Ginters (316-319); Famous People of the Past (326-349).`

COMPLETE SET (350) 60.00 120.00
COMP.SET w/o SP's (300) 15.00 40.00
SP STATED ODDS 1:2 HOBBY, 1:2 RETAIL
SP CL: 5/15/25/35/45/50-59/65/85/105/115
SP CL: 125/135/145/150-159/165/175/185
SP CL: 205/215/235/245/251/255-256/265
SP CL: 285/295/305/315/325/335/345
FRAMED ORIGINALS ODDS 1:3227 H, 1:3227 R
314 Jim Thorpe .25 .60

2006 Topps Allen and Ginter Mini

*MINI 1-350: 1X TO 2.5X BASIC
*MINI 1-350: 1X TO 2.5X BASIC RC's
APPX.15 MINIS PER 24-CT SEALED BOX
*MINI SP 1-350: .6X TO 1.5X BASIC SP
*MINI SP 1-350: .6X TO 1.5X BASIC SP RC's
MINI SP ODDS 1:13 H, 1:13 R
COMMON CARD (351-375) 20.00 50.00
SEMISTARS 351-375 30.00 60.00
UNLISTED STARS 351-375 30.00 60.00
351-375 RANDOM WITHIN RIP CARDS
OVERALL PLATE ODDS 1:865 H, 1:865 R
PLATE PRINT RUN 1 SET PER COLOR
BLACK-CYAN-MAGENTA-YELLOW ISSUED
NO PLATE PRICING DUE TO SCARCITY

2006 Topps Allen and Ginter Mini A and G Back

*A & G BACK: 2X TO 5X BASIC
*A & G BACK: 1.5X TO 4X BASIC RC's
STATED ODDS 1:5 H, 1:5 R
*A & G BACK SP: 1X TO 2.5X BASIC SP
*A & G BACK SP: 1X TO 2.5X BASIC SP RC's
SP STATED ODDS 1:65 H, 1:65 R

2006 Topps Allen and Ginter Mini Black

*BLACK: 4X TO 10X BASIC
*BLACK: 2.5X TO 6X BASIC RC's
STATED ODDS 1:10 H, 1:10 R
*BLACK SP: 1.5X TO 4X BASIC SP
*BLACK SP: 1.5X TO 4X BASIC SP RC's
SP STATED ODDS 1:130 H, 1:130 R

2006 Topps Allen and Ginter Mini No Card Number

*NO NBR: 6X TO 15X BASIC
*NO NBR: 4X TO 10X BASIC RC's
*NO NBR: 2X TO 5X BASIC SP
*NO NBR: 2X TO 5X BASIC SP RC's
STATED ODDS 1:60 H, 1:168 R
STATED PRINT RUN 50 SETS
CARDS ARE NOT SERIAL-NUMBERED
PRINT RUN INFO PROVIDED BY TOPPS

2006 Topps Allen and Ginter National Promos

COMPLETE SET (8) 15.00 30.00
*MINIS: .6X TO 1.5X BASE CARDS
NCC1 Matt Leinart 1.50 4.00
NCC3 LenDale White 1.25 3.00
NCC5 Reggie Bush 2.50 6.00

2007 Topps Allen and Ginter National Mini Promos

NCC1 Brady Quinn 1.50 4.00
NCC2 Joe Thomas .60 1.50
NCC3 Ted Ginn Jr. .75 2.00

2007 Topps Allen and Ginter National Promos

NCC1 Brady Quinn 1.50 4.00
NCC2 Joe Thomas .60 1.50
NCC3 Ted Ginn Jr. .75 2.00

2008 Topps Allen and Ginter

COMP.SET w/o FUKU.(350) 30.00 60.00
COMP.SET w/o SPs (300) 15.00 40.00
COMMON CARD (1-300) .15 .40
COMMON RC (1-300) .40 1.00
COMMON SP (301-350) 1.25 3.00
SP STATED ODDS 1:2 HOBBY
FRAMED ORIG.ODDS 1:26,500 HOBBY
187 Les Miles .25 .60

2008 Topps Allen and Ginter Mini

*MINI 1-300: .75X TO 2X BASIC
*MINI 1-300 RC: .5X TO 1.2X BASIC RC's
APPX. ONE MINI PER PACK
*MINI SP 300-350: .75X TO 2X BASIC SP
MINI SP ODDS 1:13 HOBBY
351-390 RANDOM WITHIN RIP CARDS
OVERALL PLATE ODDS 1:961 HOBBY
PLATE PRINT RUN 1 SET PER COLOR
BLACK-CYAN-MAGENTA-YELLOW ISSUED
NO PLATE PRICING DUE TO SCARCITY

2008 Topps Allen and Ginter Mini A and G Back

*A & G BACK: 1X TO 2.5X BASIC
*A & G BACK RCs: .6X TO 1.5X BASIC RCs
STATED ODDS 1:5 HOBBY
*A & G BACK SP: 1X TO 2.5X BASIC SP
SP STATED ODDS 1:65 HOBBY

2008 Topps Allen and Ginter Mini Black

*BLACK: 1.5X TO 4X BASIC
*BLACK RCs: .75X TO 2X BASIC RCs
STATED ODDS 1:10 HOBBY
*BLACK SP: 1.2X TO 3X BASIC SP
SP STATED ODDS 1:130 HOBBY

2008 Topps Allen and Ginter Mini No Card Number

*NO NBR: 10X TO 25X BASIC
*NO NBR RCs: 4X TO 10X BASIC RCs
*NO NBR: 1.5X TO 4X BASIC SP
STATED ODDS 1:151 HOBBY
STATED PRINT RUN 50 SETS
CARDS ARE NOT SERIAL-NUMBERED
PRINT RUN INFO PROVIDED BY TOPPS

2008 Topps Allen and Ginter Autographs

GROUP A ODDS 1:277 HOBBY
GROUP B ODDS 1:256 HOBBY
GROUP C ODDS 1:135 HOBBY
GRP A PRINT RUNS B/W 90-240 COPIES PER
CARDS ARE NOT SERIAL-NUMBERED
PRINT RUNS PROVIDED BY TOPPS
EXCHANGE DEADLINE 7/31/2010
LM Les Miles A/190 * 30.00 60.00

2008 Topps Allen and Ginter Relics

GROUP A ODDS 1:280 HOBBY
GROUP B ODDS 1:71 HOBBY
GROUP C ODDS 1:20 HOBBY
RELIC AU ODDS 1:26,431 HOBBY
GROUP A B/W 100-250 COPIES PER
CARDS ARE NOT SERIAL NUMBERED
PRINT RUN INFO PROVIDED BY TOPPS
LM Les Miles A/250 * 10.00 25.00

2008 Topps Allen and Ginter National Convention

COMPLETE SET (7) 8.00 20.00
5 Johnny Unitas 2.50 6.00

2010 Topps Allen and Ginter

COMPLETE SET (350) 60.00 120.00
COMP.SET w/o SPs (300) 15.00 40.00
COMMON CARD (1-300) .15 .40
COMMON RC (1-300) .40 1.00
COMMON SP (301-350) 1.25 3.00
SP STATED ODDS 1:2 HOBBY
287 Drew Brees .40 1.00

2010 Topps Allen and Ginter Mini

*MINI 1-300: .75X TO 2X BASIC
*MINI 1-300 RC: .5X TO 1.2X BASIC RC's
APPX. ONE MINI PER PACK
*MINI SP 301-350: .5X TO 1.2X BASIC SP
MINI SP ODDS 1:13 HOBBY
COMMON CARD (351-400) 20.00 50.00
351-400 RANDOM WITHIN RIP CARDS
STRASBURG 401 ISSUED IN PACKS
OVERALL PLATE ODDS 1:799 HOBBY
PLATE PRINT RUN 1 SET PER COLOR
BLACK-CYAN-MAGENTA-YELLOW ISSUED
NO PLATE PRICING DUE TO SCARCITY

2010 Topps Allen and Ginter Mini A and G Back

*A & G BACK: 1X TO 2.5X BASIC
*A & G BACK RCs: .6X TO 1.5X BASIC RCs
STATED ODDS 1:5 HOBBY
*A & G BACK SP: .6X TO 1.5X BASIC SP
SP STATED ODDS 1:65 HOBBY

2010 Topps Allen and Ginter Mini Bazooka

STATED ODDS 1:280 HOBBY
STATED PRINT RUN 25 SER.#'D SETS
NO PRICING DUE TO SCARCITY

2010 Topps Allen and Ginter Mini Black

*BLACK: 2X TO 5X BASIC
*BLACK RCs: .75X TO 2X BASIC RCs
STATED ODDS 1:10 HOBBY
*BLACK SP: .75X TO 2X BASIC SP
SP STATED ODDS 1:130 HOBBY

2010 Topps Allen and Ginter Mini No Card Number

*NO NBR: 8X TO 20X BASIC
*NO NBR RCs: 3X TO 8X BASIC RCs
*NO NBR SP: 1.2X TO 3X BASIC SP
STATED ODDS 1:140 HOBBY

2010 Topps Allen and Ginter Mini Silk

STATED ODDS 1:365 HOBBY
STATED PRINT RUN 10 SER.#'D SET
NO PRICING DUE TO SCARCITY

2010 Topps Allen and Ginter Mini Wood

STATED ODDS 1:3542 HOBBY
STATED PRINT RUN 1 SER.#'D SET
NO PRICING DUE TO SCARCITY

2010 Topps Allen and Ginter Autographs

STATED ODDS 1:HOBBY
ASTERISK EQUALS PARTIAL EXCHANGE
DBR Drew Brees 60.00 120.00

2010 Topps Allen and Ginter Autographs Red Ink

RANDOM INSERTS IN RIP CARDS
STATED PRINT RUN 10 SER.#'D SETS
NO PRICING DUE TO SCARCITY

2010 Topps Allen and Ginter Relics

STATED ODDS 1:11 HOBBY
DBR Drew Brees 10.00 25.00

2011 Topps Allen and Ginter

COMPLETE SET (350) 50.00 100.00
COMP.SET w/o SP's (300) 12.50 30.00
COMMON CARD (1-300) .15 .40
COMMON RC (1-300) .40 1.00
COMMON SP (301-350) 1.25 3.00
SP ODDS 1:2 HOBBY
3 Lou Holtz .15 .40
238 Rudy Ruettiger .15 .40

2011 Topps Allen and Ginter Glossy

ISSUED VIA TOPPS ONLINE STORE
STATED PRINT RUN 999 SER.#'d SETS
3 Lou Holtz .75 2.00
238 Rudy Ruettiger .75 2.00

2011 Topps Allen and Ginter Mini

*MINI 1-300: .75X TO 2X BASIC
*MINI 1-300 RC: .5X TO 1.2X BASIC RC's
*MINI SP 301-350: .5X TO 1.2X BASIC SP
MINI SP ODDS 1:13 HOBBY
COMMON CARD (351-400) 15.00 40.00
351-400 RANDOM WITHIN RIP CARDS
STATED PLATE ODDS 1:751 HOBBY
PLATE PRINT RUN 1 SET PER COLOR
BLACK-CYAN-MAGENTA-YELLOW ISSUED
NO PLATE PRICING DUE TO SCARCITY

2011 Topps Allen and Ginter Mini A and G Back

*A & G BACK: 1X TO 2.5X BASIC
*A & G BACK RCs: .6X TO 1.5X BASIC RCs
A & G BACK ODDS 1:5 HOBBY
*A & G BACK SP: .6X TO 1.5X BASIC SP
A & G BACK SP ODDS 1:65 HOBBY

2011 Topps Allen and Ginter Mini Black

*BLACK: 2X TO 5X BASIC
*BLACK RCs: .75X TO 2X BASIC RCs
BLACK SP ODDS 1:130 HOBBY
BLACK ODDS 1:10 HOBBY
*BLACK SP: .75X TO 2X BASIC SP

2011 Topps Allen and Ginter Mini No Card Number

*NO NBR: 8X TO 20X BASIC
*NO NBR RCs: 3X TO 8X BASIC RCs
*NO NBR SP: 1.2X TO 3X BASIC SP
STATED ODDS 1:142 HOBBY

2011 Topps Allen and Ginter Autographs

STATED ODDS 1:68 HOBBY
DUAL AUTO ODDS 1:56,000 HOBBY
EXCHANGE DEADLINE 6/30/2014
LH Lou Holtz 30.00 60.00
RRU Rudy Ruettiger 30.00 60.00

2011 Topps Allen and Ginter Code Cards

*MINI 1-300: 1.5X TO 4X BASIC
*MINI 1-300 RC: .75X TO 2X BASIC RC's
OVERALL CODE ODDS 1:8 HOBBY

2011 Topps Allen and Ginter Relics

STATED ODDS 1:10 HOBBY
EXCHANGE DEADLINE 6/30/2014
LHO Lou Holtz 20.00 50.00
RRU Rudy Ruettiger 10.00 25.00

2012 Topps Allen and Ginter

COMPLETE SET (350) 40.00 80.00
COMP.SET w/o SP's (300) 15.00 40.00
SP ODDS 1:2 HOBBY
36 Kirk Herbstreit .15 .40
184 Ara Parseghian .15 .40
220 James Brown .15 .40

2012 Topps Allen and Ginter Mini

COMP.SET w/o EXT (350)
*MINI 1-300: .75X TO 2X BASIC
*MINI 1-300 RC: .5X TO 1.2X BASIC RC's
*MINI SP 301-350: .5X TO 1.2X BASIC SP
MINI SP ODDS 1:13 HOBBY
351-400 RANDOM WITHIN RIP CARDS
STATED PLATE ODDS 1:564 HOBBY

2012 Topps Allen and Ginter Mini A and G Back

*A & G BACK: 1X TO 2.5X BASIC
*A & G BACK RCs: .6X TO 1.5X BASIC RCs
A & G BACK ODDS 1:5 HOBBY
*A & G BACK SP: .6X TO 1.5X BASIC SP
A & G BACK SP ODDS 1:65 HOBBY

2012 Topps Allen and Ginter Mini Black

*BLACK: 1.5X TO 4X BASIC
*BLACK RCs: .6X TO 1.5X BASIC RCs
BLACK ODDS 1:10 HOBBY
*BLACK SP: 1X TO 2.5X BASIC SP
BLACK SP ODDS 1:130 HOBBY

2012 Topps Allen and Ginter Mini No Card Number

*NO NBR: 6X TO 15X BASIC
*NO NBR RCs: 2.5X TO 6X BASIC RCs
*NO NBR SP: 1.2X TO 3X BASIC SP
STATED ODDS 1:111 HOBBY

2012 Topps Allen and Ginter Autographs

STATED ODDS 1:51 HOBBY
EXCHANGE DEADLINE 06/30/2015
KH Kirk Herbstreit 15.00 40.00
APA Ara Parseghian 20.00 50.00
JBR James Brown 12.50 30.00

2012 Topps Allen and Ginter Relics

STATED ODDS 1:10 HOBBY
EXCHANGE DEADLINE 06/30/2015
KH Kirk Herbstreit 4.00 10.00
JBR James Brown 6.00 15.00

2009 Topps American Heritage

COMPLETE SET (150) 50.00 100.00
COMP.SET w/o SP's (125) 12.50 25.00
SP STATED ODDS 1:4
87 Joe Namath .40 1.00

2009 Topps American Heritage Chrome

COMPLETE SET (100) 25.00 50.00
STATED ODDS 1:2 H, 1:7 R
PRINT RUN 1776 SER. #'d SETS
*CHROME: .8X TO 2X BASE

2009 Topps American Heritage Chrome Refractors

COMPLETE SET (100)
STATED ODDS 1:53 H, 1:100 R
PRINT RUN 76 SER. #'d SETS
*REFRACTOR: 10X TO 25X BASE

2009 Topps American Heritage Relics

GROUP A ODDS 1:282 H, 1:1200 R
GROUP B ODDS 1:228 H, 1:925 R
GROUP C ODDS 1:33 H, 1:135 R
GROUP D ODDS 1:195 H, 1:825 R
NO PRICING ON PRINT RUN OF 10 OR LESS
JN Joe Namath 12.50 25.00
Shea Stadium Wall Padding

2009 Topps American Heritage Heroes Heroes of Sport

COMPLETE SET (25) 12.50 25.00
STATED ODDS 1:4
*GOLD/199: 3X TO 8X BASIC INSERTS
*PLATINUM/25: 5X TO 12X BASIC INSERTS
HS9 Tony Dorsett .40 1.00
HS13 Dan Marino .60 1.50
HS21 Jim Brown .60 1.50

2009 Topps American Heritage Heroes Heroes of Sport Autographs

STATED ODDS 1:6,000

2009 Topps American Heritage Heroes Heroes of Sport Cut Signatures

UNPRICED PRINT RUN 1
STATED ODDS 1:129,300

2009 Topps American Heritage Heroes Heroes of Sport Dual Relics

UNPRICED PRINT RUN 20
STATED ODDS 1:8,200

2009 Topps American Heritage Heroes Heroes of Sport 8-Piece Relics

UNPRICED PRINT RUN 1
STATED ODDS 1:191,448

2009 Topps American Heritage Heroes Heroes of Sport Relics

STATED ODDS 1:234
HSR6 Jim Brown Jsy 10.00 25.00
HSR13 Dan Marino Jsy 20.00 50.00
HSR15 Terry Bradshaw Jsy 10.00 25.00

1994 Topps Archives 1956

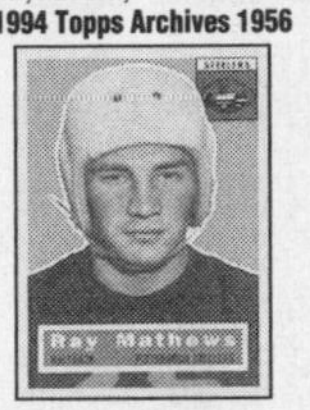

Topps reprinted all 274 standard-size cards in the original 1956 and 1957 sets. The 1956 reprint set contained 120 standard-siez cards, not including the unnumbered checklist card which was not reprinted. The suggested retail for a 12-card pack was 2.00. Factual and grammatical errors in the original cards were not changed in reprints. The fronts feature action player cutouts on bright color backgrounds. The backs were printed in red and black on gray card stock.

COMPLETE SET (120) 8.00 20.00
1 Johnny Carson .02 .10
2 Gordy Soltau .02 .10
3 Frank Varrichione .02 .10
4 Eddie Bell .02 .10
5 Alex Webster .07 .20
6 Norm Van Brocklin .80 2.00
7 Green Bay Packers .10 .30
Team Card
8 Lou Creekmur .07 .20
9 Lou Groza .60 1.50
10 Tom Bienemann .02 .10
11 George Blanda .50 1.25
12 Alan Ameche .15 .40
13 Vic Janowicz .15 .40
14 Dick Moegle .07 .20
15 Fran Rogel .02 .10
16 Harold Giancanelli .02 .10
17 Emlen Tunnell .25 .60
18 Paul(Tank) Younger .10 .30
19 Billy Howton .07 .20
20 Jack Christiansen .30 .75
21 Darrel Drewster .02 .10
22 Chicago Cardinals .10 .30
Team Card
23 Ed Brown .07 .20
24 Joe Campanella .02 .10
25 Leon Heath .02 .10
26 San Francisco 49ers .10 .30
Team Card
27 Dick Flanagan .02 .10
28 Chuck Bednarik .50 1.25
29 Kyle Rote .25 .60
30 Les Richter .07 .20
31 Howard Ferguson .02 .10
32 Dorne Dibble .02 .10
33 Kenny Konz .02 .10
34 Dave Mann .02 .10
35 Rick Casares .07 .20
36 Art Donovan .40 1.00
37 Chuck Drazenovich .02 .10
38 Joe Arenas .02 .10
39 Lynn Chandnois .02 .10
40 Philadelphia Eagles .10 .30
Team Card
41 Roosevelt Brown .25 .60
42 Tom Fears .30 .75
43 Gary Knafelc .02 .10
44 Joe Schmidt .40 1.00
45 Cleveland Browns .25 .60
Team Card UER
(Card back does not credit the Browns with being Champs in 1955)
46 Len Teeuws .02 .10
47 Bill George .25 .60
48 Baltimore Colts .10 .30
Team Card
49 Eddie LeBaron .15 .40
50 Hugh McElhenny .50 1.25
51 Ted Marchibroda .07 .20
52 Adrian Burk .02 .10
53 Frank Gifford 1.00 2.50
54 Charley Toogood .02 .10
55 Tobin Rote .07 .20
56 Bill Stits .02 .10
57 Don Colo .02 .10
58 Ollie Matson .50 1.25
59 Harlon Hill .02 .10
60 Lenny Moore .80 2.00
61 Washington Redskins .10 .30
Team Card
62 Billy Wilson .07 .20
63 Pittsburgh Steelers .10 .30
Team Card
64 Bob Pellegrini .02 .10
65 Ken MacAfee .07 .20
66 Willard Sherman .02 .10
67 Roger Zatkoff .02 .10
68 Dave Middleton .02 .10
69 Ray Renfro .07 .20
70 Don Stonesifer .02 .10
71 Stan Jones .25 .60
72 Jim Mutscheller .02 .10
73 Volney Peters .02 .10
74 Leo Nomellini .30 .75
75 Ray Mathews .02 .10
76 Dick Bielski .02 .10
77 Charley Conerly .50 1.25
78 Elroy Hirsch .50 1.25
79 Bill Forester .07 .20
80 Jim Doran .02 .10
81 Fred Morrison .02 .10
82 Jack Simmons .02 .10
83 Bill McColl .02 .10
84 Bert Rechichar .02 .10
85 Joe Scudero .02 .10
86 Y.A. Tittle 1.00 2.50
87 Ernie Stautner .40 1.00
88 Norm Willey .02 .10
89 Bob Schnelker .02 .10
90 Dan Towler .10 .30
91 John Martinkovic .02 .10
92 Detroit Lions .10 .30
Team Card
93 George Ratterman .02 .10
94 Chuck Ulrich .02 .10
95 Bobby Watkins .02 .10
96 Buddy Young .10 .30
97 Billy Wells .02 .10
98 Bob Toneff .02 .10
99 Bill McPeak .02 .10
100 Bobby Thomason .02 .10
101 Roosevelt Grier .25 .60
102 Ron Waller .02 .10
103 Bobby Dillon .02 .10
104 Leon Hart .10 .30
105 Mike McCormack .25 .60
106 John Olszewski .02 .10
107 Bill Wightkin .02 .10
108 George Shaw .07 .20
109 Dale Atkeson .02 .10
110 Joe Perry .50 1.25
111 Dale Dodrill .02 .10
112 Tom Scott .02 .10
113 New York Giants .12 .30
Team Card
114 Los Angeles Rams .10 .30
Team Card UER
(Back incorrect; Rams were not 1955 champs)
115 Al Carmichael .02 .10
116 Bobby Layne 1.00 2.50
117 Ed Modzelewski .07 .20
118 Lamar McHan .02 .10
119 Chicago Bears .10 .30
Team Card
120 Billy Vessels .20 .50

1994 Topps Archives 1956 Gold

COMPLETE SET (120) 20.00 50.00
*GOLD CARDS: .8X TO 2X BASIC CARDS

1994 Topps Archives 1957

Topps reprinted all 274 cards in the original 1956 and 1957 sets. The 1957 reprint set contained 154 standard-size cards, not including the unnumbered checklist card which was not reprinted. The suggested retail for a 12-card pack was 2.00. Factual and grammatical errors in the original cards were not changed in reprints. The fronts feature action player cutouts on bright color backgrounds. The backs were printed in red and black on gray card stock.

COMPLETE SET (154) 8.00 20.00
1 Eddie LeBaron .10 .30
2 Pete Retzlaff .07 .20
3 Mike McCormack .20 .50
4 Lou Baldacci .02 .10
5 Gino Marchetti .40 1.00
6 Leo Nomellini .30 .75
7 Bobby Watkins .02 .10
8 Dave Middleton .02 .10
9 Bobby Dillon .02 .10
10 Les Richter .07 .20
11 Roosevelt Brown .20 .50
12 Lavern Torgeson .02 .10
13 Dick Bielski .02 .10
14 Pat Summerall .40 1.00
15 Jack Butler .02 .10
16 John Henry Johnson .30 .75
17 Art Spinney .02 .10
18 Bob St. Clair .20 .50
19 Perry Jeter .02 .10
20 Lou Creekmur .10 .30
21 Dave Hanner .02 .10
22 Norm Van Brocklin .60 1.50
23 Don Chandler .02 .10
24 Al Dorow .02 .10
25 Tom Scott .02 .10
26 Ollie Matson .50 1.25
27 Fran Rogel .02 .10
28 Lou Groza .60 1.50
29 Billy Vessels .07 .20
30 Y.A. Tittle .80 2.00
31 George Blanda .60 1.50
32 Bobby Layne .80 2.00
33 Billy Howton .07 .20
34 Bill Wade .07 .20
35 Emlen Tunnell .30 .75
36 Leo Elter .02 .10
37 Clarence Peaks .07 .20
38 Don Stonesifer .02 .10
39 George Tarasovic .02 .10
40 Darrel Brewster .02 .10
41 Bert Rechichar .02 .10
42 Billy Wilson .07 .20
43 Ed Brown .07 .20
44 Gene Gedman .02 .10
45 Gary Knafelc .02 .10
46 Elroy Hirsch .50 1.25
47 Don Heinrich .02 .10
48 Gene Brito .02 .10
49 Chuck Bednarik .40 1.00
50 Dave Mann .02 .10
51 Bill McPeak .02 .10
52 Kenny Konz .02 .10
53 Alan Ameche .15 .40
54 Gordy Soltau .02 .10
55 Rick Casares .10 .30
56 Charlie Ane .02 .10
57 Al Carmichael .02 .10
58 Willard Sherman .02 .10
59 Kyle Rote .20 .50
60 Chuck Drazenovich .02 .10
61 Bobby Walston .02 .10
62 John Olszewski .02 .10
63 Ray Mathews .02 .10
64 Maurice Bassett .02 .10
65 Art Donovan .40 1.00
66 Joe Arenas .02 .10
67 Harlon Hill .02 .10
68 Yale Lary .25 .60
69 Bill Forester .07 .20
70 Bob Boyd .02 .10
71 Andy Robustelli .40 1.00
72 Sam Baker .07 .20
73 Bob Pellegrini .02 .10
74 Leo Sanford .02 .10
75 Sid Watson .02 .10
76 Ray Renfro .07 .20
77 Carl Taseff .02 .10
78 Clyde Conner .02 .10
79 J.C. Caroline .02 .10
80 Howard Cassady .10 .30
81 Tobin Rote .07 .20
82 Ron Waller .02 .10
83 Jim Patton .07 .20
84 Volney Peters .02 .10

85 Dick Lane .25 .60
86 Royce Womble .02 .10
87 Duane Putnam .02 .10
88 Frank Gifford .80 2.00
89 Steve Meilinger .02 .10
90 Buck Lansford .02 .10
91 Lindon Crow .02 .10
92 Ernie Stautner .30 .75
93 Preston Carpenter .07 .20
94 Raymond Berry .60 1.50
95 Hugh McElhenny .50 1.25
96 Stan Jones .20 .50
97 Dorne Dibble .02 .10
98 Joe Scudero .02 .10
99 Eddie Bell .02 .10
100 Joe Childress .02 .10
101 Elbert Nickel .02 .10
102 Walt Michaels .07 .20
103 Jim Mutscheller .02 .10
104 Earl Morrall .15 .40
105 Larry Strickland .02 .10
106 Jack Christiansen .30 .75
107 Fred Cone .02 .10
108 Bud McFadin .02 .10
109 Charley Conerly .50 1.25
110 Tom Runnels .02 .10
111 Ken Keller .02 .10
112 James Root .02 .10
113 Ted Marchibroda .10 .30
114 Don Paul .02 .10
115 George Shaw .07 .20
116 Dick Moegle .07 .20
117 Don Bingham .02 .10
118 Leon Hart .07 .20
119 Bart Starr 1.60 4.00
120 Paul Miller .02 .10
121 Alex Webster .07 .20
122 Ray Wietecha .02 .10
123 Johnny Carson .02 .10
124 Tommy McDonald .10 .30
125 Jerry Tubbs .02 .10
126 Jack Scarbath .02 .10
127 Ed Modzelewski .02 .10
128 Lenny Moore .50 1.25
129 Joe Perry .50 1.25
130 Bill Wightkin .02 .10
131 Jim Doran .02 .10
132 Howard Ferguson UER (Name misspelled Furgeson on front) .02 .10
133 Tom Wilson .02 .10
134 Dick James .02 .10
135 Jimmy Harris .02 .10
136 Chuck Ulrich .02 .10
137 Lynn Chandnois .02 .10
138 Johnny Unitas 1.60 4.00
139 Jim Ridlon .02 .10
140 Zeke Bratkowski .07 .20
141 Ray Krouse .02 .10
142 John Martinkovic .02 .10
143 Jim Cason .02 .10
144 Ken MacAfee .07 .20
145 Sid Youngelman .02 .10
146 Paul Larson .02 .10
147 Len Ford .40 1.00
148 Bob Toneff .02 .10
149 Ronnie Knox .02 .10
150 Jim David .02 .10
151 Paul Hornung 1.20 3.00
152 Paul(Tank) Younger .10 .30
153 Bill Svoboda .02 .10
154 Fred Morrison .10 .30

1994 Topps Archives 1957 Gold

COMPLETE SET (154) 20.00 50.00
*GOLD CARDS: .8X TO 2X BASIC CARDS

2001 Topps Archives Previews

COMPLETE SET (10) 6.00 15.00
1 Daunte Culpepper .50 1.25
2 Peyton Manning 1.25 3.00
3 Jerry Rice 1.00 2.50
4 Donovan McNabb .60 1.50
5 Emmitt Smith 1.00 2.50
6 Randy Moss 1.00 2.50
7 Eddie George .50 1.25
8 Cris Carter .50 1.25
9 Tim Brown .50 1.25
10 Edgerrin James .60 1.50

2001 Topps Archives

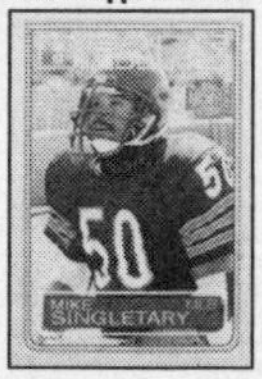

This 177 card set was issued in eight-card packs with a SRP of $4. The set was split up into three parts: Cards numbered one through 86 were issued in the players Rookie Card style, cards numbered 87 through 92 were issued in the style of the 1955 All-American set while cards numbered 93 through 179 were issued in the style of the players final card.

COMPLETE SET (178) 30.00 80.00
1 Warren Moon 85 .75 2.00
2 Alan Ameche 56 .50 1.25
3 Art Donovan 56 .50 1.25
4 Jackie Slater 84 .50 1.25
5 Bart Starr 57 1.50 4.00
6 Billy Howton 56 .50 1.25
7 Jack Youngblood 73 .50 1.25
8 Billy Kilmer 62 .60 1.50
9 Billy Sims 81 .60 1.50
10 Bo Jackson 88 1.00 2.50
11 Bob Griese 68 .75 2.00
12 Boomer Esiason 86 .60 1.50
13 Charley Conerly 56 .50 1.25
14 Charlie Joiner 72 .50 1.25
15 Christian Okoye 88 .50 1.25
16 Chuck Bednarik 56 .60 1.50
17 Cliff Branch 75 .60 1.50
18 Dan Fouts 75 .75 2.00
19 Dan Marino 84 2.00 5.00
20 Dave Casper 77 .50 1.25
21 Deacon Jones 63 .60 1.50
22 Dick Lane 57 .50 1.25
23 Don Maynard 61 .60 1.50
24 Doug Williams 79 .50 1.25
25 Barry Sanders 89 2.00 5.00
26 Bubba Smith 70 .50 1.25
27 Ed Too Tall Jones 76 .50 1.25
28 Chuck Foreman 74 .50 1.25
29 Elroy Hirsch 56 .60 1.50
30 Eric Dickerson 84 .60 1.50
31 Harold Carmichael 74 .50 1.25
32 Frank Gifford 56 .75 2.00
33 Fred Biletnikoff 65 .75 2.00
34 Gale Sayers 68 1.00 2.50
35 John Brodie 61 .50 1.25
36 Henry Ellard 85 .50 1.25
37 Jack Lambert 76 .75 2.00
38 Jim Brown 58 1.25 3.00
39 James Lofton 79 .50 1.25
40 Joe Montana 81 2.00 5.00
41 Joe Namath 65 1.25 3.00
42 Joe Theismann 75 .75 2.00
43 Tommy McDonald 57 .50 1.25
44 John Elway 84 2.00 5.00
45 John Riggins 72 .75 2.00
46 Johnny Unitas 57 1.50 4.00
47 Kellen Winslow 81 .60 1.50
48 Ken Anderson 73 .60 1.50
49 Ken Stabler 73 1.00 2.50
50 Drew Pearson 75 .60 1.50
51 Lawrence Taylor 82 .75 2.00
52 Len Dawson 64 .75 2.00
53 Lenny Moore 56 .60 1.50
54 Lester Hayes 80 .50 1.25
55 Troy Aikman 89 1.25 3.00
56 Mark Clayton 85 .50 1.25
57 John Taylor 89 .50 1.25
58 Norm Van Brocklin 56 .60 1.50
59 Gene Upshaw 72 .50 1.25
60 Otis Sistrunk 74 .50 1.25
61 Ottis Anderson 80 .50 1.25
62 Ozzie Newsome 79 .50 1.25
63 Paul Hornung 57 .75 2.00
64 Phil Simms 80 .60 1.50
65 Raymond Berry 57 .60 1.50
66 Roger Staubach 72 1.25 3.00
67 Ronnie Lott 82 .75 2.00
68 Roosevelt Brown 56 .50 1.25
69 Roosevelt Grier 56 .50 1.25
70 Sonny Jurgensen 58 .75 2.00
71 Marcus Allen 83 .75 2.00
72 Steve Grogan 76 .50 1.25
73 Roger Craig 84 .60 1.50
74 Ted Hendricks 72 .50 1.25
75 Jim Plunkett 72 .60 1.50
76 Terry Metcalf 74 .50 1.25
77 Tom Dempsey 70 .50 1.25
78 Tom Fears 56 .50 1.25
79 Tony Dorsett 78 .75 2.00
80 Walter Payton 76 2.00 5.00
81 Y.A. Tittle 56 .75 2.00
82 William Perry 86 .60 1.50
83 Steve Young 86 1.00 2.50
84 Rodney Hampton 90 .50 1.25
85 Jim Kelly 87 1.00 2.50
86 Gino Marchetti 57 .50 1.25
87 Sid Luckman 55 .60 1.50
88 Sammy Baugh 55 1.00 2.50
89 Red Grange 55 1.25 3.00
90 Otto Graham 55 .75 2.00
91 Knute Rockne 55 1.25 3.00
92 Jim Thorpe 55 1.25 3.00
93 Don Maynard 73 .40 1.00
94 Barry Sanders 99 1.25 3.00
95 Joe Theismann 86 .50 1.25
96 John Riggins 85 .50 1.25
97 William Perry 93 .40 1.00
98 Jim Brown 62 .75 2.00
99 Chuck Bednarik 61 .40 1.00
100 Warren Moon 99 .50 1.25
101 Frank Gifford 62 .50 1.25
102 Billy Sims 86 .40 1.00
103 Doug Williams 89 .30 .75
104 Lester Hayes 87 .30 .75
105 Jim Plunkett 87 .40 1.00
106 Dan Marino 00 1.25 3.00
107 Jack Youngblood 85 .30 .75
108 Tom Dempsey 79 .30 .75
109 Otis Sistrunk 79 .30 .75
110 Gale Sayers 72 .60 1.50
111 Billy Howton 62 .30 .75
112 Chuck Foreman 81 .30 .75
113 Jim Kelly 97 .60 1.50
114 Norm Van Brocklin 57 .40 1.00
115 Tommy McDonald 68 .30 .75
116 John Brodie 73 .30 .75
117 Art Donovan 59 .30 .75
118 Ted Hendricks 84 .30 .75
119 Henry Ellard 98 .30 .75
120 Bart Starr 71 1.00 2.50
121 Bo Jackson 91 .60 1.50
122 Tom Fears 56 .30 .75
123 Drew Pearson 84 .40 1.00
124 Ronnie Lott 94 .50 1.25
125 Terry Metcalf 82 .30 .75
126 Lenny Moore 63 .40 1.00
127 Raymond Berry 63 .40 1.00
128 John Elway 99 1.25 3.00
129 Steve Grogan 90 .30 .75
130 Roger Craig 93 .40 1.00
131 Bob Griese 81 .50 1.25
132 Johnny Unitas 74 1.00 2.50
133 Cliff Branch 85 .40 1.00
134 Billy Kilmer 78 .40 1.00
135 Boomer Esiason 97 .40 1.00
136 Fred Biletnikoff 79 .50 1.25
137 Marcus Allen 95 .50 1.25
138 Paul Hornung 62 .50 1.25
139 Kellen Winslow 88 .40 1.00
140 Joe Namath 73 .75 2.00
141 Jackie Slater 94 .30 .75
142 John Taylor 95 .30 .75
143 Phil Simms 94 .40 1.00
144 Ken Stabler 83 .60 1.50
145 Dave Casper 79 .30 .75
146 Dan Fouts 87 .50 1.25
147 Dick Lane 63 .30 .75
148 Alan Ameche 61 .30 .75
149 Sonny Jurgensen 72 .50 1.25
150 Harold Carmichael 84 .30 .75
151 Ed Too Tall Jones 89 .30 .75
152 Lawrence Taylor 93 .50 1.25
153 Ken Anderson 85 .40 1.00
154 Deacon Jones 74 .40 1.00
155 Ozzie Newsome 90 .30 .75
156 Steve Young 00 .60 1.50
157 Charlie Joiner 87 .30 .75
158 Tony Dorsett 89 .50 1.25
159 Christian Okoye 93 .30 .75
160 Charley Conerly 61 .30 .75
161 Elroy Hirsch 57 .40 1.00
162 Len Dawson 76 .50 1.25
163 Jack Lambert 85 .50 1.25
164 Mark Clayton 93 .30 .75
165 Y.A. Tittle 63 .50 1.25
166 Troy Aikman 01 .75 2.00
167 Roger Staubach 79 .75 2.00
168 Roosevelt Grier 63 .30 .75
169 Gino Marchetti 63 .30 .75
170 Walter Payton 87 1.25 3.00
171 Rodney Hampton 97 .30 .75
172 Eric Dickerson 92 .40 1.00
173 Ottis Anderson 91 .30 .75
174 James Lofton 93 .30 .75
175 Bubba Smith 76 .30 .75
176 Roosevelt Brown 61 .30 .75
177 Gene Upshaw 81 .30 .75
178 Joe Montana 95 1.25 3.00
NNO Checklist .07 .20

2001 Topps Archives Autoproofs

STATED PRINT RUN 100 SER.#'d SETS
NNO Lester Hayes EXCH
NNO Ken Anderson EXCH
NNO Ted Hendricks EXCH
NNO Ed Too Tall Jones
NNO Steve Grogan EXCH

2001 Topps Archives Relic Seats

COMPLETE SET (16) 75.00 200.00
GROUP A STATED ODDS 1:81
GROUP B STATED ODDS 1:32
GROUP C, D STATED ODDS 1:27
OVERALL STATED ODDS 1:9
ASBS Bubba Smith 5.00 12.00
ASBST Bart Starr 12.50 30.00
ASCB Chuck Bednarik 7.50 20.00
ASCO Christian Okoye 5.00 12.00
ASED Eric Dickerson 6.00 15.00
ASFG Frank Gifford 7.50 20.00
ASJB Jim Brown 10.00 25.00
ASJU Johnny Unitas 12.50 30.00
ASKA Ken Anderson 6.00 15.00
ASLD Len Dawson 7.50 20.00
ASLM Lenny Moore 6.00 15.00
ASMA Marcus Allen 7.50 20.00
ASPH Paul Hornung 7.50 20.00
ASRB Raymond Berry 6.00 15.00
ASSB Sammy Baugh 10.00 25.00
ASSJ Sonny Jurgensen 7.50 20.00

2001 Topps Archives Rookie Reprint Autographs

GROUP A STATED ODDS 1:10000
GROUP B STATED ODDS 1:1238
GROUP C STATED ODDS 1:2245
GROUP D STATED ODDS 1:4126
GROUP E STATED ODDS 1:1177
GROUP F STATED ODDS 1:330
GROUP G STATED ODDS 1:1653
GROUP H STATED ODDS 1:1102
GROUP I STATED ODDS 1:198
GROUP J STATED ODDS 1:35
GROUP K STATED ODDS 1:110
GROUP L STATED ODDS 1:309
OVERALL STATED ODDS 1:19
AABG Bob Griese C 50.00 100.00
AABK Billy Kilmer 10.00 25.00
AABS Barry Sanders C 125.00 250.00
AABSI Billy Sims J 12.00 30.00
AABSM Bubba Smith J 15.00 40.00
AACB Cliff Branch 12.00 30.00
AACBE Chuck Bednarik J 15.00 40.00
AACO Christian Okoye K 10.00 25.00
AADB Dick Butkus D 75.00 125.00
AADC Dave Casper J 12.00 30.00
AADF Dan Fouts F 30.00 50.00
AADJ Deacon Jones J 12.00 30.00
AADMA Don Maynard L 10.00 25.00
AADW Doug Williams I 12.00 30.00
AAED Eric Dickerson F 35.00 60.00
AAEJ Ed Too Tall Jones J 15.00 40.00
AAFG Frank Gifford E 25.00 50.00
AAGM Gino Marchetti I 15.00 40.00
AAGS Gale Sayers F 40.00 80.00
AAHE Henry Ellard I 10.00 25.00
AAJB Jim Brown B
AAJH John Hannah 10.00 25.00
AAJM Joe Montana B 400.00 600.00
AAJN Joe Namath A 150.00 300.00
AAJR John Riggins G 40.00 80.00
AAJU Johnny Unitas H 250.00 400.00
AAKA Ken Anderson J 12.00 30.00
AAKW Kellen Winslow F 15.00 40.00
AALD Len Dawson E 20.00 50.00
AALH Lester Hayes J 12.00 30.00
AALT Lawrence Taylor B 60.00 120.00
AAMA Marcus Allen B 40.00 100.00
AAMC Mark Clayton K 12.00 30.00
AAOA Ottis Anderson J 10.00 25.00
AAON Ozzie Newsome F 12.00 30.00
AARB Roosevelt Brown J 15.00 40.00
AARBE Raymond Berry I 12.00 30.00
AARG Roosevelt Grier J 12.00 30.00
AARH Rodney Hampton J 10.00 25.00
AARS Roger Staubach F 100.00 200.00
AASG Steve Grogan J 12.00 30.00
AATD Tom Dempsey 10.00 25.00
AATH Ted Hendricks K 10.00 25.00
AAWP William Perry J 12.00 30.00
AAYT Y.A. Tittle I 25.00 50.00

2001 Topps Archives Reserve

COMPLETE SET (94) 30.00 60.00
1 Warren Moon 85 1.25 3.00
2 Alan Ameche 56 .75 2.00
3 Art Donovan 56 .75 2.00
4 Jackie Slater 84 .75 2.00
5 Bart Starr 57 2.50 6.00
6 Billy Howton 56 .75 2.00
7 Jack Youngblood 73 .75 2.00
8 Billy Kilmer 62 1.00 2.50
9 Billy Sims 81 1.00 2.50
10 Bo Jackson 88 1.50 4.00
11 Bob Griese 68 1.25 3.00
12 Boomer Esiason 86 1.00 2.50
13 Charley Conerly 56 .75 2.00
14 Charlie Joiner 72 .75 2.00
15 Christian Okoye 88 .75 2.00
16 Chuck Bednarik 56 1.00 2.50
17 Cliff Branch 75 1.00 2.50
18 Dan Fouts 75 1.25 3.00
19 Dan Marino 84 3.00 8.00
20 Dave Casper 77 .75 2.00
21 Deacon Jones 63 1.00 2.50
22 Dick Lane 57 .75 2.00
23 Don Maynard 61 1.00 2.50
24 Doug Williams 79 .75 2.00
25 Barry Sanders 89 3.00 8.00
26 Bubba Smith 70 .75 2.00
27 Ed Too Tall Jones 76 .75 2.00
28 Chuck Foreman 74 .75 2.00
29 Elroy Hirsch 56 1.00 2.50
30 Eric Dickerson 84 1.00 2.50
31 Harold Carmichael 74 .75 2.00
32 Frank Gifford 56 1.25 3.00
33 Fred Biletnikoff 65 1.25 3.00
34 Gale Sayers 68 1.50 4.00
35 John Brodie 61 .75 2.00
36 Henry Ellard 85 .75 2.00
37 Jack Lambert 76 1.25 3.00
38 Jim Brown 58 2.00 5.00
39 James Lofton 79 .75 2.00
40 Joe Montana 81 3.00 8.00
41 Joe Namath 65 2.00 5.00
42 Joe Theismann 75 1.25 3.00
43 Tommy McDonald 57 .75 2.00
44 John Elway 84 3.00 8.00
45 John Riggins 72 1.25 3.00
46 Johnny Unitas 57 2.50 6.00
47 Kellen Winslow 81 1.00 2.50
48 Ken Anderson 73 1.00 2.50
49 Ken Stabler 73 1.50 4.00
50 Drew Pearson 75 1.00 2.50
51 Lawrence Taylor 82 1.25 3.00
52 Len Dawson 64 1.25 3.00
53 Lenny Moore 56 1.00 2.50
54 Lester Hayes 80 .75 2.00
55 Troy Aikman 89 2.00 5.00
56 Mark Clayton 85 .75 2.00
57 John Taylor 89 .75 2.00
58 Norm Van Brocklin 56 1.00 2.50
59 Gene Upshaw 72 .75 2.00
60 Otis Sistrunk 74 .75 2.00
61 Ottis Anderson 80 .75 2.00
62 Ozzie Newsome 79 .75 2.00
63 Paul Hornung 57 1.25 3.00
64 Phil Simms 80 1.00 2.50
65 Raymond Berry 57 1.00 2.50
66 Roger Staubach 72 2.00 5.00
67 Ronnie Lott 82 1.25 3.00
68 Roosevelt Brown 56 .75 2.00
69 Roosevelt Grier 56 .75 2.00
70 Sonny Jurgensen 58 1.25 3.00
71 Marcus Allen 83 1.25 3.00
72 Steve Grogan 76 .75 2.00
73 Roger Craig 84 1.00 2.50
74 Ted Hendricks 72 .75 2.00
75 Jim Plunkett 72 1.00 2.50
76 Terry Metcalf 74 .75 2.00
77 Tom Dempsey 70 .75 2.00
78 Tom Fears 56 .75 2.00
79 Tony Dorsett 78 1.25 3.00
80 Walter Payton 76 3.00 8.00
81 Y.A. Tittle 56 1.25 3.00
82 William Perry 86 1.00 2.50
83 Steve Young 86 1.50 4.00
84 Rodney Hampton 90 .75 2.00
85 Jim Kelly 87 1.50 4.00
86 Gino Marchetti 57 .75 2.00
87 Sid Luckman 55 1.00 2.50
88 Sammy Baugh 55 1.50 4.00
89 Red Grange 55 2.00 5.00
90 Otto Graham 55 1.25 3.00
91 Mike Singletary 83 1.25 3.00
92 Dick Butkus 68 1.50 4.00
93 John Hannah 74 .75 2.00
94 Derrick Thomas 89 1.25 3.00

2001 Topps Archives Reserve Jerseys

GROUP A STATED ODDS 1:8.5
GROUP B STATED ODDS 1:12
OVERALL STATED ODDS 1:3.3
ARRAT Al Toon 5.00 12.00
ARRBE Boomer Esiason 6.00 15.00
ARRBS Barry Sanders 12.50 30.00
ARRDM Dan Marino 20.00 50.00
ARRDT Derrick Thomas 25.00 50.00
ARRJE John Elway 15.00 40.00
ARRJK Jim Kelly 10.00 25.00
ARRJM Joe Montana 15.00 40.00
ARRLT Lawrence Taylor 8.00 20.00
ARRMA Marcus Allen 8.00 20.00
ARRPS Phil Simms 8.00 20.00
ARRSY Steve Young 10.00 25.00

2001 Topps Archives Reserve Mini Helmet Autographs

ONE PER BOX
1 Marcus Allen 30.00 60.00
2 Ottis Anderson 15.00 30.00
3 Jim Brown 75.00 125.00
4 Mark Clayton 15.00 30.00
5 Roger Craig 20.00 40.00
6 Eric Dickerson 20.00 40.00
8 Lester Hayes 15.00 30.00
9 Ed Too Tall Jones 20.00 40.00
10 Dan Marino 125.00 200.00
11 Don Maynard 15.00 30.00
12 Tommy McDonald 15.00 30.00
13 Terry Metcalf 15.00 30.00
14 Joe Montana 100.00 175.00
15 Joe Namath 90.00 150.00
16 Christian Okoye 15.00 30.00
17 Drew Pearson 15.00 30.00
18 Jim Plunkett 20.00 40.00
19 Mike Singletary 20.00 40.00
20 Lawrence Taylor 40.00 80.00
21 Doug Williams 20.00 40.00

2001 Topps Archives Reserve Rookie Reprint Autographs

ONE PER BOX
ARABK Billy Kilmer 12.50 25.00
ARABS Barry Sanders 75.00 150.00
ARACB Cliff Branch 12.50 25.00
ARACF Chuck Foreman 7.50 20.00
ARACJ Charlie Joiner 7.50 20.00
ARADB Dick Butkus 50.00 100.00
ARADC Dave Casper 12.50 25.00
ARADJ Deacon Jones 15.00 30.00
ARADM Don Maynard 12.50 25.00
ARADW Doug Williams 15.00 30.00
ARAED Eric Dickerson 30.00 60.00
ARAEJ Ed Too Tall Jones 20.00 40.00
ARAFG Frank Gifford 35.00 60.00
ARAHE Henry Ellard 7.50 20.00
ARAJH John Hannah 12.50 25.00
ARAJM Joe Montana 150.00 300.00
ARAJN Joe Namath 150.00 300.00
ARAJR John Riggins 30.00 60.00
ARAJU Johnny Unitas 250.00 400.00
ARALD Len Dawson 20.00 50.00
ARALH Lester Hayes 15.00 30.00
ARALT Lawrence Taylor 75.00 150.00
ARAMA Marcus Allen 50.00 100.00
ARAMC Mark Clayton 7.50 20.00
ARAON Ozzie Newsome 15.00 30.00
ARARB Raymond Berry 15.00 30.00
ARARH Rodney Hampton 7.50 20.00
ARATD Tom Dempsey 7.50 20.00
ARATH Ted Hendricks 7.50 20.00
ARATM Terry Metcalf 7.50 20.00
ARAWP William Perry 7.50 20.00

2010 Topps Attax

1 John Abraham .12 .30
2 Joseph Addai .15 .40
3 Jared Allen .20 .50
4 Nnamdi Asomugha .15 .40
5 Oshiomogho Atogwe .12 .30
6 Miles Austin .20 .50
7 Donnie Avery .15 .40
8 Jordan Babineaux .12 .30
9 Champ Bailey .15 .40
10 Nick Barnett .12 .30
11 Jon Beason .12 .30
12 Yeremiah Bell .12 .30
13 Arrelious Benn RC .60 1.50
14 Cedric Benson .15 .40
15 Eric Berry RC .60 1.50
16 Jahvid Best RC 1.00 2.50
17 Anquan Boldin .15 .40
18 Dwayne Bowe .15 .40
19 Sam Bradford RC 2.50 6.00
20 Stewart Bradley .12 .30
21 Tom Brady .30 .75
22 Tyvon Branch .12 .30
23 Drew Brees .20 .50
24 Lance Briggs .15 .40
25 Kenny Britt .15 .40
26 Keith Brooking .12 .30
27 Mike Brown .12 .30
28 Ronnie Brown .15 .40
29 Sheldon Brown .12 .30
30 Dez Bryant RC 2.00 5.00
31 Keith Bulluck .12 .30
32 Reggie Bush .20 .50
33 Darius Butler .12 .30
34 Jairus Byrd .15 .40
35 Calais Campbell .12 .30
36 Matt Cassel .15 .40
37 Brent Celek .15* .40
38 Jamaal Charles .15 .40
39 Dallas Clark .15 .40
40 Jimmy Clausen RC .60 1.50
41 Nate Clements .12 .30
42 Trent Cole .12 .30
43 Nick Collins .12 .30
44 Marques Colston .15 .40
45 Stephen Cooper .12 .30
46 Michael Crabtree .20 .50
47 Antonio Cromartie .12 .30
48 Aaron Curry .15 .40
49 Brian Cushing .12 .30
50 Jay Cutler .20 .50
51 Karlos Dansby .12 .30
52 Vernon Davis .15 .40
53 Vontae Davis .12 .30
54 Brian Dawkins .15 .40
55 Louis Delmas .12 .30
56 Darnell Dockett .12 .30
57 Donald Driver .15 .40
58 Elvis Dumervil .12 .30
59 Jonathan Dwyer RC .60 1.50
60 Braylon Edwards .15 .40
61 Shaun Ellis .12 .30
62 James Farrior .12 .30
63 Brett Favre 1.50 4.00
64 Cortland Finnegan .12 .30
65 Larry Fitzgerald .20 .50
66 Joe Flacco .20 .50
67 London Fletcher .12 .30
68 Brandon Flowers .12 .30
69 Matt Forte .15 .40
70 Josh Freeman .20 .50
71 Dwight Freeney .15 .40
72 Chris Gamble .12 .30
73 Pierre Garcon .15 .40
74 David Garrard .15 .40
75 Antonio Gates .15 .40
76 Tony Gonzalez .15 .40
77 Frank Gore .15 .40
78 Ryan Grant .15 .40
79 Shonn Greene .15* .40
80 Chad Greenway .12 .30
81 Cedric Griffin .12 .30
82 Leon Hall .12 .30
83 Casey Hampton .12 .30
84 David Harris .12 .30
85 James Harrison .20 .50
86 Percy Harvin .20 .50
87 Matt Hasselbeck .12 .30
88 A.J. Hawk .15 .40
89 David Hawthorne RC .60 1.50
90 Geno Hayes .12 .30
91 Chad Henne .15 .40
92 Devin Hester .20 .50
93 Santonio Holmes .15 .40
94 Chris Hope .12 .30
95 T.J. Houshmandzadeh .15 .40
96 DeSean Jackson .15 .40
97 Steven Jackson .15 .40
98 Vincent Jackson .12 .30
99 Brandon Jacobs .15 .40
100 Bradie James .12 .30
101 Malcolm Jenkins .12 .30
102 Mike Jenkins .12 .30
103 Greg Jennings .15 .40
104 Andre Johnson .15 .40
105 Calvin Johnson .20 .50
106 Chris Johnson .20 .50
107 Dhani Jones .12 .30
108 Felix Jones .15 .40
109 Maurice Jones-Drew .15 .40
110 Johnathan Joseph .12 .30
111 Kevin Kolb .15 .40
112 LaRon Landry .12 .30
113 James Laurinaitis .15 .40
114 Ray Lewis .20 .50
115 Curtis Lofton .12 .30
116 Chris Long .12 .30
117 Jeremy Maclin .15 .40
118 Eli Manning .20 .50
119 Peyton Manning .30 .75
120 Brandon Marshall .15 .40
121 Derrick Mason .15 .40
122 Mohamed Massaquoi .15 .40
123 Ryan Mathews RC 1.25 3.00
124 Robert Mathis .12 .30
125 Clay Matthews .20 .50
126 Rey Maualuga .12 .30
127 Jerod Mayo .15 .40
128 Dexter McCluster RC .60 1.50
129 Colt McCoy RC 1.25 3.00
130 LeSean McCoy .15 .40
131 Darren McFadden .15 .40
132 Donovan McNabb .20 .50
133 Rashard Mendenhall .15 .40
134 Brandon Meriweather .12 .30
135 Shawne Merriman .15 .40
136 Knowshon Moreno .15 .40
137 Kirk Morrison .12 .30
138 Randy Moss .20 .50
139 Santana Moss .15 .40
140 Terence Newman .12 .30
141 Hakeem Nicks .15 .40
142 Chad Ochocinco .15 .40
143 Brian Orakpo .12 .30
144 Kyle Orton .15 .40
145 Terrell Owens .20 .50
146 Carson Palmer .15 .40
147 Julius Peppers .15 .40
148 Adrian Peterson .30 .75
149 Julian Peterson .12 .30
150 Mike Peterson .12 .30
151 Kenny Phillips .12 .30
152 Shaun Phillips .12 .30
153 Troy Polamalu .20 .50
154 Joey Porter .12 .30
155 Clinton Portis .15 .40
156 Paul Posluszny .15 .40
157 Ed Reed .15 .40
158 Darrelle Revis .15 .40
159 Ray Rice .15 .40
160 Sidney Rice .15 .40
161 Philip Rivers .20 .50
162 Aaron Rodgers .40 1.00
163 Dominque Rodgers-Cromartie .12 .30
164 Ben Roethlisberger .20 .50
165 Antrel Rolle .12 .30
166 Tony Romo .25 .60
167 Barrett Ruud .12 .30
168 Matt Ryan .20 .50
169 DeMeco Ryans .12 .30
170 Asante Samuel .12 .30
171 Mark Sanchez .20 .50
172 Matt Schaub .15 .40
173 Aaron Schobel .12 .30
174 Bart Scott .12 .30
175 Clint Session .12 .30
176 Darren Sharper .15 .40
177 Ernie Sims .12 .30
178 Mike Sims-Walker .15 .40
179 Steve Slaton .12 .30
180 Alex Smith QB .15 .40
181 Sean Smith .12 .30
182 Steve Smith .15 .40
183 Steve Smith USC .15 .40
184 Will Smith .12 .30
185 C.J. Spiller RC 1.00 2.50
186 Matthew Stafford .20 .50
187 Terrell Suggs .12 .30
188 Ndamukong Suh RC 1.25 3.00
189 Aqib Talib .12 .30
190 Golden Tate RC .60 1.50
191 Tim Tebow RC 5.00 12.00
192 Demaryius Thomas RC .75 2.00
193 Charles Tillman .12 .30
194 Justin Tuck .15 .40
195 Stephen Tulloch .12 .30
196 Michael Turner .12 .30
197 Osi Umenyiora .12 .30
198 Brian Urlacher .20 .50
199 Jonathan Vilma .12 .30
200 Mike Wallace .15 .40
201 Hines Ward .15 .40
202 DeMarcus Ware .15 .40
203 Reggie Wayne .15 .40
204 Wes Welker .20 .50
205 Chris Wells .15 .40
206 Roddy White .15 .40
207 Vince Wilfork .12 .30
208 Cadillac Williams .15 .40
209 D.J. Williams .12 .30
210 DeAngelo Williams .15 .40
211 Demorrio Williams .12 .30
212 Kevin Williams .12 .30
213 Mario Williams .15 .40
214 Patrick Willis .15 .40
215 Adrian Wilson .12 .30
216 Kellen Winslow .15 .40
217 Jason Witten .20 .50
218 LaMarr Woodley .12 .30
219 Charles Woodson .20 .50
220 Vince Young .12 .30

2010 Topps Attax Code Cards

COMPLETE SET (50) 20.00 40.00
ONE FOIL OR CODE CARD PER BOOSTER
ONE CODE CARD PER 2010 TOPPS
1 Jared Allen .60 1.50
2 Nnamdi Asomugha .50 1.25
3 Oshiomogho Atogwe .40 1.00
4 Miles Austin .60 1.50
5 Jon Beason .40 1.00
6 Cedric Benson .50 1.25
7 Tom Brady 1.00 2.50
8 Drew Brees .60 1.50
9 Brian Dawkins .50 1.25
10 Brett Favre 3.00 8.00
11 Larry Fitzgerald .60 1.50
12 Dwight Freeney .50 1.25
13 Antonio Gates .50 1.25
14 Frank Gore .50 1.25
15 David Harris .40 1.00
16 James Harrison .60 1.50
17 DeSean Jackson .50 1.25
18 Steven Jackson .50 1.25
19 Andre Johnson .50 1.25
20 Calvin Johnson .60 1.50
21 Chris Johnson .60 1.50
22 Maurice Jones-Drew .50 1.25
23 James Laurinaitis .50 1.25
24 Ray Lewis .60 1.50
25 Peyton Manning 1.00 2.50
26 Brandon Marshall .50 1.25
27 Jerod Mayo .50 1.25
28 Rashard Mendenhall .50 1.25
29 Randy Moss .60 1.50
30 Julius Peppers .50 1.25
31 Adrian Peterson 1.00 2.50
32 Troy Polamalu .60 1.50
33 Ed Reed .50 1.25
34 Darrelle Revis .50 1.25
35 Ray Rice .50 1.25
36 Philip Rivers .60 1.50
37 Aaron Rodgers 1.25 3.00
38 DeMeco Ryans .40 1.00
39 Asante Samuel .40 1.00
40 Matt Schaub .50 1.25
41 Darren Sharper .50 1.25
42 Michael Turner .40 1.00
43 Osi Umenyiora .40 1.00
44 Brian Urlacher .60 1.50
45 Jonathan Vilma .40 1.00
46 DeMarcus Ware .50 1.25
47 Reggie Wayne .50 1.25
48 D.J. Williams .40 1.00
49 Patrick Willis .50 1.25
50 Adrian Wilson .40 1.00

2010 Topps Attax Legends Foil

COMPLETE SET (4) 10.00 25.00
ONE FOIL OR CODE CARD PER BOOSTER
1 John Elway 3.00 8.00
2 Ronnie Lott 2.00 5.00
3 Dan Marino 4.00 10.00
4 Emmitt Smith 3.00 8.00

2010 Topps Attax Red Zone

COMPLETE SET (70) 30.00 60.00
ONE FOIL OR CODE CARD PER BOOSTER
1 Joseph Addai .60 1.50
2 Oshiomogho Atogwe .50 1.25
3 Miles Austin .75 2.00
4 Champ Bailey .60 1.50
5 Cedric Benson .60 1.50
6 Eric Berry .60 1.50
7 Sam Bradford 2.50 6.00
8 Lance Briggs .60 1.50
9 Ronnie Brown .60 1.50
10 Dez Bryant 2.00 5.00
11 Jairus Byrd .60 1.50
12 Jamaal Charles .60 1.50
13 Dallas Clark .60 1.50
14 Trent Cole .50 1.25
15 Nick Collins .50 1.25
16 Marques Colston .60 1.50
17 Michael Crabtree .75 2.00
18 Aaron Curry .60 1.50
19 Brian Cushing .50 1.25
20 Karlos Dansby .50 1.25
21 Louis Delmas .50 1.25
22 Elvis Dumervil .50 1.25
23 Brett Favre 2.00 5.00
24 Joe Flacco .75 2.00
25 David Garrard .60 1.50
26 Antonio Gates .60 1.50
27 Ryan Grant .60 1.50
28 Shonn Greene .60 1.50
29 David Harris .50 1.25
30 Percy Harvin .75 2.00
31 A.J. Hawk .60 1.50
32 T.J. Houshmandzadeh .60 1.50
33 DeSean Jackson .60 1.50
34 Vincent Jackson .50 1.25
35 Brandon Jacobs .60 1.50
36 Greg Jennings .60 1.50
37 Calvin Johnson .75 2.00
38 James Laurinaitis .60 1.50
39 Robert Mathis .50 1.25
40 Clay Matthews .75 2.00
41 Rey Maualuga .50 1.25
42 Jerod Mayo .60 1.50
43 LeSean McCoy .60 1.50
44 Rashard Mendenhall .60 1.50
45 Brandon Meriweather .50 1.25
46 Knowshon Moreno .60 1.50
47 Terence Newman .50 1.25
48 Hakeem Nicks .60 1.50
49 Julius Peppers .60 1.50
50 Joey Porter .50 1.25
51 Ray Rice .60 1.50
52 Sidney Rice .60 1.50
53 Philip Rivers .75 2.00
54 Dominque Rodgers-Cromartie .50 1.25
55 Antrel Rolle .50 1.25
56 Tony Romo 1.00 2.50
57 Barrett Ruud .50 1.25
58 Matt Ryan .75 2.00
59 DeMeco Ryans .50 1.25
60 Steve Smith .60 1.50
61 C.J. Spiller 1.00 2.50
62 Ndamukong Suh 1.25 3.00
63 Aqib Talib .50 1.25
64 Michael Turner .50 1.25
65 Osi Umenyiora .50 1.25
66 Chris Wells .60 1.50
67 Roddy White .60 1.50
68 D.J. Williams .50 1.25
69 DeAngelo Williams .60 1.50
70 Mario Williams .60 1.50
71 Adrian Wilson .50 1.25
72 LaMarr Woodley .50 1.25
73 Charles Woodson .75 2.00

2010 Topps Attax Signed Stars Rookie Autographs

STATED ODDS 1:1393 B/J
1 Jahvid Best 40.00 80.00
2 Sam Bradford 75.00 135.00
3 Dez Bryant 60.00 120.00
4 Jimmy Clausen 25.00 60.00
5 Ryan Mathews 60.00 100.00
6 Colt McCoy 60.00 100.00
7 C.J. Spiller 25.00 60.00
8 Golden Tate 20.00 50.00
9 Tim Tebow 100.00 175.00

2010 Topps Attax Superstars

COMPLETE SET (30)* 20.00 40.00
ONE FOIL OR CODE CARD PER BOOSTER
1 Jared Allen 1.00 2.50
2 Nnamdi Asomugha .75 2.00
3 Jon Beason .60 1.50
4 Tom Brady 1.50 4.00
5 Drew Brees 1.00 2.50
6 Brian Dawkins .75 2.00
7 Larry Fitzgerald 1.00 2.50
8 Dwight Freeney .75 2.00
9 Frank Gore .75 2.00
10 James Harrison 1.00 2.50
11 Steven Jackson .75 2.00
12 Andre Johnson .75 2.00
13 Chris Johnson 1.00 2.50
14 Maurice Jones-Drew .75 2.00
15 Ray Lewis 1.00 2.50
16 Peyton Manning 1.50 4.00
17 Brandon Marshall .75 2.00
18 Randy Moss 1.00 2.50
19 Adrian Peterson 1.50 4.00
20 Ed Reed .75 2.00
21 Darrelle Revis .75 2.00
22 Aaron Rodgers 2.00 5.00
23 Asante Samuel .60 1.50
24 Matt Schaub .75 2.00
25 Darren Sharper .75 2.00
26 Brian Urlacher 1.00 2.50
27 Jonathan Vilma .60 1.50
28 DeMarcus Ware .75 2.00
29 Reggie Wayne .75 2.00
30 Patrick Willis .75 2.00

1996 Topps Chrome

The 1996 Topps Chrome set was issued in one series totalling 165 cards. The 4-card packs had a suggested retail of $3.00 each. These standard-sized cards are the same as the regular 1996 set except for numbering and the chrome foil treatment.

COMPLETE SET (165)	40.00	100.00
1 Troy Aikman	1.00	2.50
2 Kevin Greene	.20	.50
3 Robert Brooks	.40	1.00
4 Junior Seau	.40	1.00
5 Brett Perriman	.07	.20
6 Cortez Kennedy	.07	.20
7 Orlando Thomas	.07	.20
8 Anthony Miller	.20	.50
9 Jeff Blake	.40	1.00
10 Trent Dilfer	.40	1.00
11 Heath Shuler	.20	.50
12 Michael Jackson	.20	.50
13 Merton Hanks	.07	.20
14 Dale Carter	.07	.20
15 Eric Metcalf	.07	.20
16 Barry Sanders	1.50	4.00
17 Joey Galloway	.40	1.00
18 Bryan Cox	.07	.20
19 Harvey Williams	.07	.20
20 Terrell Davis	.60	1.50
21 Darnay Scott	.20	.50
22 Kerry Collins	.40	1.00
23 Warren Sapp	.07	.20
24 Michael Westbrook	.40	1.00
25 Mark Brunell	.60	1.50
26 Craig Heyward	.07	.20
27 Eric Allen	.07	.20
28 Dana Stubblefield	.20	.50
29 Steve Bono	.07	.20
30 Larry Brown	.07	.20
31 Warren Moon	.20	.50
32 Jim Kelly	.40	1.00
33 Terry McDaniel	.07	.20
34 Dan Wilkinson	.07	.20
35 Dave Brown	.07	.20
36 Todd Lyght	.07	.20
37 Aeneas Williams	.07	.20
38 Shannon Sharpe	.20	.50
39 Errict Rhett	.20	.50
40 Yancey Thigpen	.20	.50
41 J.J. Stokes	.40	1.00
42 Marshall Faulk	.50	1.25
43 Chester McGlockton	.07	.20
44 Darryll Lewis	.07	.20
45 Drew Bledsoe	.60	1.50
46 Tyrone Wheatley	.20	.50
47 Herman Moore	.20	.50
48 Darren Woodson	.20	.50
49 Ricky Watters	.20	.50
50 Emmitt Smith TYC	.60	1.50
51 Barry Sanders TYC	.60	1.50
52 Curtis Martin TYC	.40	1.00
53 Chris Warren TYC	.20	.50
54 Errict Rhett TYC	.20	.50
55 Rodney Hampton TYC	.07	.20
56 Terrell Davis TYC	.40	1.00
57 Marshall Faulk TYC	.40	1.00
58 Rashaan Salaam TYC	.20	.50
59 Curtis Conway	.40	1.00
60 Isaac Bruce	.40	1.00
61 Thurman Thomas	.40	1.00
62 Terry Allen	.20	.50
63 Lamar Lathon	.07	.20
64 Mark Chmura	.20	.50
65 Chris Warren	.20	.50
66 Jessie Tuggle	.07	.20
67 Erik Kramer	.07	.20
68 Tim Brown	.40	1.00
69 Derrick Thomas	.40	1.00
70 Willie McGinest	.07	.20
71 Frank Sanders	.20	.50
72 Bernie Parmalee	.07	.20
73 Kordell Stewart	.40	1.00
74 Brent Jones	.07	.20
75 Edgar Bennett	.20	.50
76 Rashaan Salaam	.20	.50
77 Carl Pickens	.20	.50
78 Terance Mathis	.07	.20
79 Deion Sanders	.50	1.25
80 Glyn Milburn	.07	.20
81 Lee Woodall	.07	.20
82 Neil Smith	.20	.50
83 Stan Humphries	.20	.50
84 Rick Mirer	.20	.50
85 Troy Vincent	.07	.20
86 Sam Mills	.07	.20
87 Brian Mitchell	.07	.20
88 Hardy Nickerson	.07	.20
89 Tamarick Vanover	.20	.50
90 Steve McNair	.60	1.50
91 Jerry Rice TYC	.40	1.00
92 Isaac Bruce TYC	.40	1.00
93 Herman Moore TYC	.20	.50
94 Cris Carter TYC	.40	1.00
95 Tim Brown TYC	.20	.50
96 Carl Pickens TYC	.20	.50
97 Joey Galloway TYC	.40	1.00
98 Jerry Rice	1.00	2.50
99 Cris Carter	.40	1.00
100 Curtis Martin	.60	1.50
101 Scott Mitchell	.20	.50
102 Ken Harvey	.07	.20
103 Rodney Hampton	.20	.50
104 Reggie White	.40	1.00
105 Eddie Robinson	.07	.20
106 Greg Lloyd	.20	.50
107 Phillippi Sparks	.07	.20
108 Emmitt Smith	1.50	4.00
109 Tom Carter	.07	.20
110 Jim Everett	.07	.20
111 James O.Stewart	.20	.50
112 Kyle Brady	.07	.20
113 Irving Fryar	.20	.50
114 Vinny Testaverde	.20	.50
115 John Elway	2.00	5.00
116 Chris Spielman	.07	.20
117 Mike Mamula	.07	.20
118 Jim Harbaugh	.20	.50
119 Ken Norton	.07	.20
120 Bruce Smith	.20	.50
121 Daryl Johnston	.20	.50
122 Blaine Bishop	.07	.20
123 Jeff George	.20	.50
124 Jeff Hostetler	.07	.20
125 Jerome Bettis	.40	1.00
126 Jay Novacek	.07	.20
127 Bryce Paup	.07	.20
128 Neil O'Donnell	.20	.50
129 Marcus Allen	.40	1.00
130 Steve Young	.60	1.50
131 Brett Favre TYC	.75	2.00
132 Scott Mitchell TYC	.07	.20
133 John Elway TYC	.75	2.00
134 Jeff Blake TYC	.20	.50
135 Dan Marino TYC	.75	2.00
136 Drew Bledsoe TYC	.40	1.00
137 Troy Aikman TYC	.40	1.00
138 Steve Young TYC	.40	1.00
139 Jim Kelly TYC	.40	1.00
140 Jeff Graham	.07	.20
141 Hugh Douglas	.20	.50
142 Dan Marino	2.00	5.00
143 Darrell Green	.07	.20
144 Eric Zeier	.07	.20
145 Brett Favre	2.00	5.00
146 Carnell Lake	.07	.20
147 Ben Coates	.20	.50
148 Tony Martin	.20	.50
149 Michael Irvin	.40	1.00
150 Lawrence Phillips RC	.40	1.00
151 Alex Van Dyke RC	.60	1.50
152 Kevin Hardy RC	.60	1.50
153 Rickey Dudley RC	2.00	5.00
154 Eric Moulds RC	4.00	10.00
155 Simeon Rice RC	1.50	4.00
156 Marvin Harrison RC	7.50	20.00
157 Tim Biakabutuka RC	1.50	4.00
158 Duane Clemons RC	.40	1.00
159 Keyshawn Johnson RC	5.00	12.00
160 John Mobley RC	.60	1.50
161 Leeland McElroy RC	.60	1.50
162 Eddie George RC	6.00	12.00
163 Jonathan Ogden RC	.75	2.00
164 Eddie Kennison RC	2.00	5.00
165 Checklist	.07	.20

1996 Topps Chrome Refractors

*REF.STARS: 2X TO 5X BASIC CARDS
*UNLISTED REF.RCs: .8X TO 2X
REF.STATED ODDS 1:12

156 Marvin Harrison	25.00	60.00

1996 Topps Chrome 40th Anniversary Retros

COMPLETE SET (40)	60.00	120.00

STATED ODDS 1:8
*REFRACTORS: .75X TO 2X BASIC INSERTS
REF.STATED ODDS 1:24

1 Jim Harbaugh 1956	.60	1.50
2 Greg Lloyd 1957	.60	1.50
3 Barry Sanders 1958	5.00	12.00
4 Merton Hanks 1959	.25	.60
5 Herman Moore 1960	.60	1.50
6 Tim Brown 1961	1.25	3.00
7 Brett Favre 1962	6.00	16.00
8 Cris Carter 1963	1.25	3.00
9 Curtis Martin 1964	2.00	5.00
10 Bryce Paup 1965	.25	.60
11 Steve Bono 1966	.25	.60
12 Blaine Bishop 1967	.25	.60
13 Emmitt Smith 1968	5.00	12.00
14 Carnell Lake 1969	.25	.60
15 Marshall Faulk 1970	1.50	4.00
16 Mike Morris 1971	.25	.60
17 Shannon Sharpe 1972	.60	1.50
18 Steve Young 1973	2.00	5.00
19 Jeff George 1974	.60	1.50
20 Junior Seau 1975	1.25	3.00
21 Chris Warren 1976	.60	1.50
22 Heath Shuler 1977	.60	1.50
23 Jeff Blake 1978	1.25	3.00
24 Reggie White 1979	1.25	3.00
25 Jeff Hostetler 1980	.25	.60
26 Errict Rhett 1981	.60	1.50
27 Rodney Hampton 1982	.60	1.50
28 Jerry Rice 1983	3.00	8.00
29 Jim Everett 1984	.25	.60
30 Isaac Bruce 1985	1.25	3.00
31 Dan Marino 1986	6.00	15.00
32 Marcus Allen 1987	1.25	3.00
33 Erik Kramer 1988	.25	.60
34 John Elway 1989	6.00	15.00
35 Ricky Watters 1990	.60	1.50
36 Troy Aikman 1991	3.00	8.00
37 Drew Bledsoe 1992	2.00	5.00
38 Scott Mitchell 1993	.60	1.50
39 Rashaan Salaam 1994	.60	1.50
40 Kerry Collins 1995	1.25	3.00

1996 Topps Chrome Tide Turners

COMPLETE SET (15)	20.00	50.00

STATED ODDS 1:12
*REFRACT: 1X TO 2.5X BASIC INSERTS
REF.STATED ODDS 1:48

TT1 Rashaan Salaam	.60	1.50
TT2 Warren Moon	.60	1.50
TT3 Marshall Faulk	1.50	4.00
TT4 Jeff Blake	1.25	3.00
TT5 Curtis Martin	2.00	5.00
TT6 Eric Metcalf	.25	.60
TT7 Errict Rhett	.60	1.50
TT8 Scott Mitchell	.60	1.50
TT9 Ricky Watters	.60	1.50
TT10 Jerry Rice	3.00	8.00
TT11 Emmitt Smith	5.00	12.00
TT12 Erik Kramer	.25	.60
TT13 Jim Harbaugh	.60	1.50
TT14 Barry Sanders	5.00	12.00
TT15 John Elway	6.00	15.00

1997 Topps Chrome

The 1997 Topps Chrome set was issued in one series totalling 165 cards and was distributed in four-card packs with a suggested retail price of $3. The fronts feature color action player photos printed with Chromium technology. The backs carry player information.

COMPLETE SET (165)	30.00	60.00
1 Brett Favre	2.50	6.00
2 Tim Biakabutuka	.40	1.00
3 Deion Sanders	.60	1.50
4 Marshall Faulk	.75	2.00
5 John Randle	.40	1.00
6 Stan Humphries	.40	1.00
7 Ki-Jana Carter	.25	.60
8 Rashaan Salaam	.25	.60
9 Rickey Dudley	.40	1.00
10 Isaac Bruce	.60	1.50
11 Keyshawn Johnson	.60	1.50
12 Ben Coates	.40	1.00
13 Ty Detmer	.40	1.00
14 Gus Frerotte	.25	.60
15 Mario Bates	.25	.60
16 Chris Calloway	.25	.60
17 Frank Sanders	.40	1.00
18 Bruce Smith	.40	1.00
19 Jeff Graham	.25	.60
20 Trent Dilfer	.60	1.50
21 Tyrone Wheatley	.40	1.00
22 Chris Warren	.40	1.00
23 Terry Kirby	.40	1.00
24 Tony Gonzalez RC	4.00	10.00
25 Ricky Watters	.40	1.00
26 Tamarick Vanover	.40	1.00
27 Kerry Collins	.60	1.50
28 Bobby Engram	.40	1.00
29 Derrick Alexander WR	.40	1.00
30 Hugh Douglas	.25	.60
31 Thurman Thomas	.60	1.50
32 Drew Bledsoe	.75	2.00
33 LeShon Johnson	.25	.60
34 Byron Bam Morris	.25	.60
35 Herman Moore	.40	1.00
36 Troy Aikman	1.25	3.00
37 Mel Gray	.25	.60
38 Adrian Murrell	.40	1.00
39 Carl Pickens	.40	1.00
40 Tony Brackens	.25	.60
41 O.J. McDuffie	.40	1.00
42 Napoleon Kaufman	.60	1.50
43 Chris T. Jones	.25	.60
44 Kordell Stewart	.60	1.50
45 Steve Young	.75	2.00
46 Shannon Sharpe	.40	1.00
47 Leeland McElroy	.25	.60
48 Eric Moulds	.60	1.50
49 Eddie George	.60	1.50
50 Jamal Anderson	.60	1.50
51 Robert Smith	.40	1.00
52 Mike Alstott	.60	1.50
53 Darrell Green	.40	1.00
54 Irving Fryar	.40	1.00
55 Derrick Thomas	.60	1.50
56 Antonio Freeman	.60	1.50
57 Terrell Davis	.75	2.00
58 Henry Ellard	.25	.60
59 Daryl Johnston	.40	1.00
60 Bryan Cox	.25	.60
61 Vinny Testaverde	.40	1.00
62 Andre Reed	.40	1.00
63 Larry Centers	.40	1.00
64 Hardy Nickerson	.25	.60
65 Tony Banks	.40	1.00
66 Dave Meggett	.25	.60
67 Simeon Rice	.40	1.00
68 Warrick Dunn RC	3.00	8.00
69 Michael Irvin	.60	1.50
70 John Elway	2.50	6.00
71 Jake Reed	.40	1.00
72 Rodney Hampton	.40	1.00
73 Aaron Glenn	.25	.60
74 Terry Allen	.60	1.50
75 Blaine Bishop	.25	.60
76 Bert Emanuel	.40	1.00
77 Mark Carrier WR	.25	.60
78 Jimmy Smith	.40	1.00
79 Jim Harbaugh	.40	1.00
80 Brent Jones	.40	1.00
81 Emmitt Smith	2.00	5.00
82 Fred Barnett	.25	.60
83 Errict Rhett	.25	.60
84 Michael Sinclair	.25	.60
85 Jerome Bettis	.60	1.50
86 Chris Sanders	.25	.60
87 Kent Graham	.25	.60
88 Cris Carter	.60	1.50
89 Harvey Williams	.25	.60
90 Eric Allen	.25	.60
91 Bryant Young	.25	.60
92 Marcus Allen	.60	1.50
93 Michael Jackson	.40	1.00
94 Mark Chmura	.40	1.00
95 Keenan McCardell	.40	1.00
96 Joey Galloway	.40	1.00
97 Eddie Kennison	.40	1.00
98 Steve Atwater	.25	.60
99 Dorsey Levens	.60	1.50
100 Rob Moore	.40	1.00
101 Steve McNair	.75	2.00
102 Sean Dawkins	.25	.60
103 Don Beebe	.25	.60
104 Willie McGinest	.25	.60
105 Tony Martin	.40	1.00
106 Mark Brunell	.75	2.00
107 Karim Abdul-Jabbar	.60	1.50
108 Michael Westbrook	.40	1.00
109 Lawrence Phillips	.25	.60
110 Barry Sanders	2.00	5.00
111 Willie Davis	.25	.60
112 Wesley Walls	.40	1.00
113 Todd Collins	.25	.60
114 Jerry Rice	1.25	3.00
115 Scott Mitchell	.40	1.00
116 Terance Mathis	.40	1.00
117 Chris Spielman	.25	.60
118 Curtis Conway	.40	1.00
119 Marvin Harrison	.60	1.50
120 Terry Glenn	.60	1.50
121 Dave Brown	.25	.60
122 Neil O'Donnell	.40	1.00
123 Junior Seau	.60	1.50
124 Reggie White	.60	1.50
125 Lamar Lathon	.25	.60
126 Natrone Means	.40	1.00
127 Tim Brown	.60	1.50
128 Eric Swann	.25	.60
129 Dan Marino	2.50	6.00
130 Anthony Johnson	.25	.60
131 Edgar Bennett	.40	1.00
132 Kevin Hardy	.25	.60
133 Brian Blades	.25	.60
134 Curtis Martin	.75	2.00
135 Zach Thomas	.60	1.50
136 Darnay Scott	.40	1.00
137 Desmond Howard	.40	1.00
138 Aeneas Williams	.25	.60
139 Bryce Paup	.25	.60
140 Brad Johnson	.60	1.50
141 Jeff Blake	.40	1.00
142 Wayne Chrebet	.60	1.50
143 Will Blackwell RC	.50	1.25
144 Tom Knight RC	.25	.60
145 Darnell Autry RC	.40	1.00
146 Bryant Westbrook RC	.25	.60
147 David LaFleur RC	.30	.75
148 Antowain Smith RC	2.50	6.00
149 Rae Carruth RC	.30	.75
150 Jim Druckenmiller RC	.40	1.00
151 Shawn Springs RC	.30	.75
152 Troy Davis RC	.50	1.25
153 Orlando Pace RC	.75	2.00
154 Byron Hanspard RC	.50	1.25
155 Corey Dillon RC	4.00	10.00
156 Reidel Anthony RC	.75	2.00
157 Peter Boulware RC	.75	2.00
158 Reinard Wilson RC	.50	1.25
159 Pat Barnes RC	.75	2.00
160 Joey Kent RC	.75	2.00
161 Ike Hilliard RC	1.25	3.00
162 Jake Plummer RC	3.00	8.00
163 Darrell Russell RC	.30	.75
164 Checklist Card	.25	.60
165 Checklist Card	.25	.60

1997 Topps Chrome Refractors

COMPLETE SET (165)	300.00	800.00

*STARS: 2X TO 5X BASIC CARDS
*RC'S: 1.2X TO 3X BASIC CARDS
STATED ODDS 1:12

24 Tony Gonzalez	20.00	50.00
68 Warrick Dunn	15.00	40.00
148 Antowain Smith	12.00	30.00
155 Corey Dillon	20.00	50.00
162 Jake Plummer	15.00	40.00

1997 Topps Chrome Career Best

COMPLETE SET (5)	30.00	60.00

*REFRACTORS: 1X TO 2X BASIC INSERTS

1 Dan Marino	12.50	30.00
2 Marcus Allen	3.00	8.00
3 Marcus Allen	3.00	8.00
4 Reggie White	3.00	8.00
5 Jerry Rice	6.00	15.00

1997 Topps Chrome Draft Year

COMPLETE SET (15)	75.00	150.00

STATED ODDS 1:48
*REFRACTORS: 1X TO 2X BASIC CARDS
REFRACTOR STATED ODDS 1:144

DR1 Dan Marino John Elway	12.50	30.00
DR2 Reggie White Steve Young	5.00	12.00
DR3 Bruce Smith Jerry Rice	6.00	15.00
DR4 Ronnie Harmon Pat Swilling	2.00	5.00
DR5 Jim Harbaugh Vinny Testaverde	2.00	5.00
DR6 Micheal Irvin Tim Brown	3.00	8.00
DR7 Troy Aikman Barry Sanders	10.00	25.00
DR8 Emmitt Smith Junior Seau	10.00	25.00
DR9 Brett Favre Ricky Watters	10.00	25.00
DR10 Carl Pickens Jeff Blake	3.00	8.00
DR11 Mark Brunell Drew Bledsoe	4.00	10.00
DR12 Marshall Faulk Isaac Bruce	4.00	10.00
DR13 Terrell Davis Curtis Martin	7.50	20.00
DR14 Eddie George Terry Glenn	3.00	8.00
DR15 Ike Hilliard Shawn Springs	3.00	8.00

1997 Topps Chrome Season's Best

COMPLETE SET (25)	50.00	100.00

STATED ODDS 1:12
*REFRACTORS: 1X TO 2X BASIC CARDS
REFRACTOR STATED ODDS 1:36

1 Mark Brunell	2.50	6.00
2 Vinny Testaverde	1.25	3.00
3 Drew Bledsoe	2.50	6.00
4 Brett Favre	8.00	20.00
5 Jeff Blake	1.25	3.00
6 Barry Sanders	6.00	15.00
7 Terrell Davis	2.50	6.00
8 Jerome Bettis	2.00	5.00
9 Ricky Watters	1.25	3.00
10 Eddie George	2.00	5.00
11 Brian Mitchell	.75	2.00
12 Tyrone Hughes	.75	2.00
13 Eric Metcalf	1.25	3.00
14 Glyn Milburn	.75	2.00
15 Ricky Watters	1.25	3.00
16 Kevin Greene	1.25	3.00
17 Lamar Lathon	.75	2.00
18 Bruce Smith	1.25	3.00
19 Michael Sinclair	.75	2.00
20 Derrick Thomas	2.00	5.00
21 Jerry Rice	4.00	10.00
22 Herman Moore	1.25	3.00
23 Carl Pickens	1.25	3.00
24 Cris Carter	2.00	5.00
25 Brett Perriman	.75	2.00

1997 Topps Chrome Underclassmen

COMPLETE SET (10)	12.00	30.00

STATED ODDS 1:16
*REFRACTORS: 1X TO 2X BASIC INSERTS
REFRACTOR STATED ODDS 1:48

U1 Kerry Collins	2.00	5.00
U2 Karim Abdul-Jabbar	2.00	5.00
U3 Simeon Rice	1.25	3.00
U4 Keyshawn Johnson	2.00	5.00
U5 Eddie George	2.00	5.00
U6 Eddie Kennison	1.25	3.00
U7 Terry Glenn	2.00	5.00
U8 Kevin Hardy	.75	2.00
U9 Steve McNair	2.50	6.00
U10 Kordell Stewart	2.00	5.00

1998 Topps Chrome

The 1998 Topps Chrome set was issued in one series totalling 165 cards. The four-card packs retail for $3.00 each. The cards feature action color player photos printed with chromium technology.

COMPLETE SET (165)	50.00	120.00
1 Barry Sanders	1.50	4.00
2 Duane Starks RC	.75	2.00
3 J.J. Stokes	.30	.75
4 Joey Galloway	.30	.75
5 Deion Sanders	.50	1.25
6 Anthony Miller	.20	.50
7 Jamal Anderson	.50	1.25
8 Shannon Sharpe	.30	.75
9 Irving Fryar	.30	.75
10 Curtis Martin	.50	1.25
11 Shawn Jefferson	.20	.50
12 Charlie Garner	.30	.75
13 Robert Edwards RC	1.25	3.00
14 Napoleon Kaufman	.50	1.25
15 Gus Frerotte	.20	.50
16 John Elway	2.00	5.00
17 Jerome Pathon RC	1.50	4.00
18 Marshall Faulk	.60	1.50
19 Michael McCrary	.20	.50
20 Marcus Allen	.50	1.25
21 Trent Dilfer	.50	1.25
22 Frank Wycheck	.20	.50
23 Terrell Owens	.50	1.25
24 Herman Moore	.30	.75
25 Neil O'Donnell	.30	.75
26 Darnay Scott	.30	.75
27 Keith Brooking RC	1.50	4.00
28 Eric Green	.20	.50
29 Dan Marino	2.00	5.00
30 Antonio Freeman	.50	1.25
31 Tony Martin	.30	.75
32 Isaac Bruce	.50	1.25
33 Rickey Dudley	.20	.50
34 Scott Mitchell	.30	.75
35 Randy Moss RC	8.00	20.00
36 Fred Lane	.20	.50
37 Frank Sanders	.30	.75
38 Jerry Rice	1.00	2.50
39 O.J. McDuffie	.30	.75
40 Jessie Armstead	.20	.50
41 Reidel Anthony	.30	.75
42 Steve McNair	.50	1.25
43 Jake Reed	.30	.75
44 Charles Woodson RC	2.50	6.00
45 Tiki Barber	.50	1.25
46 Mike Alstott	.50	1.25
47 Keyshawn Johnson	.50	1.25
48 Tony Banks	.30	.75
49 Michael Westbrook	.30	.75
50 Chris Slade	.20	.50
51 Terry Allen	.50	1.25
52 Karim Abdul-Jabbar	.50	1.25
53 Brad Johnson	.50	1.25
54 Tony McGee	.20	.50
55 Kevin Dyson RC	1.50	4.00
56 Warren Moon	.50	1.25
57 Byron Hanspard	.20	.50
58 Jermaine Lewis	.30	.75
59 Neil Smith	.30	.75
60 Tamarick Vanover	.20	.50
61 Terrell Davis	.50	1.25
62 Robert Smith	.50	1.25
63 Junior Seau	.50	1.25
64 Warren Sapp	.30	.75
65 Michael Sinclair	.20	.50
66 Ryan Leaf RC	1.50	4.00
67 Drew Bledsoe	.75	2.00
68 Jason Sehorn	.30	.75
69 Andre Hastings	.20	.50
70 Tony Gonzalez	.50	1.25
71 Dorsey Levens	.50	1.25
72 Ray Lewis	.50	1.25
73 Grant Wistrom RC	1.25	3.00
74 Elvis Grbac	.30	.75
75 Mark Chmura	.30	.75
76 Zach Thomas	.50	1.25
77 Ben Coates	.30	.75
78 Rod Smith WR	.30	.75
79 Andre Wadsworth RC	1.25	3.00
80 Garrison Hearst	.50	1.25
81 Will Blackwell	.20	.50
82 Cris Carter	.50	1.25
83 Mark Fields	.20	.50
84 Ken Dilger	.20	.50
85 Johnnie Morton	.30	.75
86 Michael Irvin	.50	1.25
87 Eddie George	.50	1.25
88 Rob Moore	.30	.75
89 Takeo Spikes RC	1.50	4.00
90 Wesley Walls	.30	.75
91 Andre Reed	.30	.75
92 Thurman Thomas	.50	1.25
93 Ed McCaffrey	.30	.75
94 Carl Pickens	.30	.75
95 Jason Taylor	.30	.75
96 Kordell Stewart	.50	1.25
97 Greg Ellis RC	.75	2.00
98 Aaron Glenn	.20	.50
99 Jake Plummer	.50	1.25
100 Checklist	.20	.50
101 Chris Sanders	.20	.50
102 Michael Jackson	.20	.50
103 Bobby Hoying	.30	.75
104 Wayne Chrebet	.50	1.25
105 Charles Way	.20	.50
106 Derrick Thomas	.50	1.25
107 Troy Drayton	.20	.50
108 Robert Holcombe RC	1.25	3.00
109 Pete Mitchell	.20	.50
110 Bruce Smith	.30	.75
111 Terance Mathis	.30	.75
112 Lawrence Phillips	.20	.50
113 Brett Favre	2.00	5.00
114 Darrell Green	.30	.75
115 Charles Johnson	.20	.50
116 Jeff Blake	.30	.75
117 Mark Brunell	.50	1.25
118 Simeon Rice	.30	.75
119 Robert Brooks	.30	.75
120 Jacquez Green RC	1.25	3.00
121 Willie Davis	.20	.50
122 Jeff George	.30	.75
123 Andre Rison	.30	.75
124 Erik Kramer	.20	.50
125 Peter Boulware	.20	.50
126 Marcus Nash RC	.75	2.00
127 Troy Aikman	1.00	2.50
128 Keenan McCardell	.30	.75
129 Bryant Westbrook	.20	.50
130 Terry Glenn	.50	1.25
131 Blaine Bishop	.20	.50
132 Tim Brown	.50	1.25
133 Brian Griese RC	2.50	6.00
134 John Mobley	.20	.50
135 Larry Centers	.20	.50
136 Eric Bjornson	.20	.50
137 Kevin Hardy	.20	.50
138 John Randle	.30	.75
139 Michael Strahan	.30	.75
140 Jerome Bettis	.50	1.25
141 Rae Carruth	.20	.50
142 Reggie White	.50	1.25
143 Antowain Smith	.50	1.25
144 Aeneas Williams	.20	.50
145 Bobby Engram	.30	.75
146 Germane Crowell RC	1.25	3.00
147 Freddie Jones	.20	.50
148 Kimble Anders	.30	.75
149 Steve Young	.60	1.50
150 Willie McGinest	.20	.50
151 Emmitt Smith	1.50	4.00
152 Fred Taylor RC	2.50	6.00
153 Danny Kanell	.30	.75
154 Warrick Dunn	.50	1.25
155 Kerry Collins	.30	.75
156 Chris Chandler	.30	.75
157 Curtis Conway	.30	.75
158 Curtis Enis RC	.75	2.00
159 Corey Dillon	.50	1.25
160 Glenn Foley	.30	.75
161 Marvin Harrison	.50	1.25
162 Chad Brown	.20	.50
163 Derrick Rodgers	.20	.50
164 Levon Kirkland	.20	.50
165 Peyton Manning RC	20.00	50.00

1998 Topps Chrome Refractors

*VETS: 4X TO 10X BASIC CARDS
*ROOKIE STARS: 1X TO 2.5X
STATED ODDS 1:12

165 Peyton Manning	100.00	200.00

1998 Topps Chrome Hidden Gems

COMPLETE SET (15)	15.00	30.00

STATED ODDS 1:12
*REFRACTORS: .6X TO 1.5X BASIC INSERTS
REFRACTOR ODDS 1:24

HG1 Andre Reed	.75	2.00
HG2 Kevin Greene	.75	2.00
HG3 Tony Martin	.75	2.00
HG4 Shannon Sharpe	.75	2.00
HG5 Terry Allen	1.25	3.00
HG6 Brett Favre	5.00	12.00
HG7 Ben Coates	.75	2.00
HG8 Michael Sinclair	.50	1.25
HG9 Keenan McCardell	.75	2.00
HG10 Brad Johnson	1.25	3.00
HG11 Mark Brunell	1.25	3.00
HG12 Dorsey Levens	1.25	3.00
HG13 Terrell Davis	1.25	3.00
HG14 Curtis Martin	1.25	3.00
HG15 Derrick Rodgers	.50	1.25

1998 Topps Chrome Measures of Greatness

COMPLETE SET (15)	30.00	60.00

STATED ODDS 1:12
*REFRACTORS: 1X TO 2.5X BASIC INSERTS
REFRACTOR ODDS 1:48

MG1 John Elway	5.00	12.00
MG2 Marcus Allen	1.25	3.00
MG3 Jerry Rice	2.50	6.00
MG4 Tim Brown	1.25	3.00
MG5 Warren Moon	1.25	3.00
MG6 Bruce Smith	.75	2.00
MG7 Troy Aikman	2.50	6.00
MG8 Reggie White	1.25	3.00
MG9 Irving Fryar	.75	2.00
MG10 Barry Sanders	4.00	10.00
MG11 Cris Carter	1.25	3.00
MG12 Emmitt Smith	4.00	10.00
MG13 Dan Marino	5.00	12.00
MG14 Rod Woodson	.75	2.00
MG15 Brett Favre	5.00	12.00

1998 Topps Chrome Season's Best

COMPLETE SET (30)	30.00	80.00

STATED ODDS 1:8
*REFRACTORS: .6X TO 1.5X BASIC INSERTS
REFRACTOR ODDS 1:24

1 Terrell Davis	1.25	3.00
2 Barry Sanders	4.00	10.00
3 Jerome Bettis	1.25	3.00
4 Dorsey Levens	1.25	3.00
5 Eddie George	1.25	3.00
6 Brett Favre	5.00	12.00
7 Mark Brunell	1.25	3.00
8 Jeff George	.75	2.00
9 Steve Young	1.50	4.00
10 John Elway	5.00	12.00
11 Herman Moore	.75	2.00
12 Rob Moore	.75	2.00
13 Yancey Thigpen	.75	2.00
14 Cris Carter	1.25	3.00
15 Tim Brown	1.25	3.00
16 Bruce Smith	.75	2.00
17 Michael Sinclair	.50	1.25
18 John Randle	.75	2.00
19 Dana Stubblefield	.50	1.25
20 Michael Strahan	.75	2.00
21 Tamarick Vanover	.50	1.25
22 Darrien Gordon	.50	1.25
23 Michael Bates	.50	1.25
24 David Meggett	.50	1.25
25 Jermaine Lewis	.75	2.00
26 Terrell Davis	1.25	3.00
27 Jerry Rice	2.50	6.00
28 Barry Sanders	4.00	10.00
29 John Randle	.75	2.00
30 John Elway	5.00	12.00

1999 Topps Chrome

The 1999 Topps Chrome set was released as a 165 card color action shot with an all chromium card front. Key rookies within the set include Tim Couch, Ricky Williams, and Cade McNown.

COMPLETE SET (165)	60.00	150.00
COMP.SET w/o SP's (135)	25.00	50.00
1 Randy Moss	.40	1.00
2 Keyshawn Johnson	.30	.75
3 Priest Holmes	.40	1.00
4 Warren Moon	.40	1.00
5 Joey Galloway	.30	.75
6 Zach Thomas	.40	1.00
7 Cam Cleeland	.25	.60
8 Jim Harbaugh	.30	.75
9 Napoleon Kaufman	.25	.60
10 Fred Taylor	.30	.75
11 Mark Brunell	.30	.75
12 Shannon Sharpe	.40	1.00
13 Jacquez Green	.25	.60
14 Adrian Murrell	.30	.75
15 Cris Carter	.40	1.00
16 Jerome Pathon	.25	.60
17 Drew Bledsoe	.40	1.00
18 Curtis Martin	.40	1.00
19 Johnnie Morton	.30	.75
20 Doug Flutie	.40	1.00
21 Carl Pickens	.30	.75
22 Jerome Bettis	.40	1.00
23 Derrick Alexander	.25	.60
24 Antowain Smith	.25	.60
25 Barry Sanders	1.00	2.50
26 Reidel Anthony	.25	.60
27 Wayne Chrebet	.30	.75
28 Terance Mathis	.25	.60
29 Shawn Springs	.25	.60
30 Emmitt Smith	1.00	2.50
31 Robert Smith	.30	.75
32 Charles Johnson	.25	.60
33 Mike Alstott	.40	1.00
34 Ike Hilliard	.30	.75
35 Ricky Watters	.30	.75
36 Charles Woodson	.40	1.00
37 Rod Smith	.30	.75
38 Pete Mitchell	.25	.60
39 Derrick Thomas	.40	1.00
40 Dan Marino	1.25	3.00
41 Darnay Scott	.25	.60
42 Jake Reed	.30	.75
43 Chris Chandler	.30	.75
44 Dorsey Levens	.30	.75
45 Kordell Stewart	.30	.75
46 Eddie George	.30	.75
47 Corey Dillon	.30	.75
48 Rich Gannon	.30	.75
49 Chris Spielman	.30	.75
50 Jerry Rice	.75	2.00
51 Trent Dilfer	.30	.75
52 Mark Chmura	.25	.60
53 Jimmy Smith	.30	.75
54 Isaac Bruce	.40	1.00
55 Karim Abdul-Jabbar	.30	.75
56 Sedrick Shaw	.25	.60
57 Jake Plummer	.30	.75
58 Tony Gonzalez	.40	1.00
59 Ben Coates	.30	.75
60 John Elway	1.25	3.00
61 Bruce Smith	.40	1.00
62 Tim Brown	.40	1.00
63 Tim Dwight	.30	.75
64 Yancey Thigpen	.25	.60
65 Terrell Owens	.40	1.00
66 Kyle Brady	.25	.60
67 Tony Martin	.30	.75
68 Michael Strahan	.30	.75
69 Deion Sanders	.40	1.00
70 Steve Young	.50	1.25
71 Dale Carter	.25	.60
72 Ty Law	.30	.75
73 Frank Wycheck	.30	.75
74 Marshall Faulk	.40	1.00
75 Vinny Testaverde	.30	.75
76 Chad Brown	.25	.60
77 Natrone Means	.30	.75
78 Bert Emanuel	.30	.75
79 Kerry Collins	.30	.75
80 Randall Cunningham	.40	1.00
81 Garrison Hearst	.30	.75
82 Curtis Enis	.25	.60
83 Steve Atwater	.30	.75
84 Kevin Greene	.30	.75
85 Steve McNair	.40	1.00
86 Andre Reed	.40	1.00
87 J.J. Stokes	.25	.60
88 Eric Moulds	.30	.75
89 Marvin Harrison	.40	1.00
90 Troy Aikman	.60	1.50
91 Herman Moore	.30	.75
92 Michael Irvin	.40	1.00
93 Frank Sanders	.25	.60
94 Duce Staley	.30	.75
95 James Jett	.25	.60
96 Ricky Proehl	.25	.60
97 Andre Rison	.30	.75
98 Leslie Shepherd	.25	.60
99 Trent Green	.30	.75
100 Terrell Davis	.40	1.00
101 Freddie Jones	.25	.60
102 Skip Hicks	.25	.60
103 Jeff Graham	.25	.60
104 Rob Moore	.25	.60
105 Torrance Small	.25	.60
106 Antonio Freeman	.30	.75
107 Robert Brooks	.30	.75
108 Jon Kitna	.30	.75
109 Curtis Conway	.30	.75
110 Brett Favre	1.25	3.00
111 Warrick Dunn	.30	.75
112 Elvis Grbac	.25	.60
113 Corey Fuller	.25	.60
114 Rickey Dudley	.25	.60
115 Jamal Anderson	.30	.75
116 Terry Glenn	.30	.75
117 Rocket Ismail	.30	.75
118 John Randle	.30	.75
119 Chris Calloway	.25	.60
120 Peyton Manning	1.25	3.00
121 Keenan McCardell	.30	.75
122 O.J. McDuffie	.30	.75
123 Ed McCaffrey	.30	.75
124 Charlie Batch	.30	.75
125 Jason Elam SH	.25	.60
126 Randy Moss SH	.30	.75
127 John Elway SH	1.00	2.50
128 Emmitt Smith SH	.75	2.00
129 Terrell Davis SH	.30	.75
130 Jerris McPhail	.25	.60
131 Damon Gibson	.25	.60
132 Jim Pyne	.25	.60
133 Antonio Langham	.25	.60
134 Freddie Solomon	.25	.60
135 Ricky Williams RC	3.00	8.00
136 Daunte Culpepper RC	2.00	5.00
137 Chris Claiborne RC	1.25	3.00
138 Amos Zereoue RC	1.50	4.00
139 Chris McAlister RC	1.50	4.00
140 Kevin Faulk RC	2.00	5.00
141 James Johnson RC	1.25	3.00
142 Mike Cloud RC	1.25	3.00
143 Jevon Kearse RC	2.00	5.00
144 Akili Smith RC	1.50	4.00
145 Edgerrin James RC	2.50	6.00
146 Cecil Collins RC	1.25	3.00
147 Donovan McNabb RC	8.00	20.00
148 Kevin Johnson RC	1.50	4.00
149 Torry Holt RC	3.00	8.00
150 Rob Konrad RC	1.25	3.00
151 Tim Couch RC	2.00	5.00
152 David Boston RC	1.50	4.00
153 Karsten Bailey RC	1.25	3.00
154 Troy Edwards RC	1.50	4.00
155 Sedrick Irvin RC	1.25	3.00
156 Shaun King RC	1.50	4.00
157 Peerless Price RC	1.50	4.00
158 Brock Huard RC	1.50	4.00
159 Cade McNown RC	1.50	4.00
160 Champ Bailey RC	4.00	10.00
161 D'Wayne Bates RC	1.25	3.00

162 Joe Germaine RC 1.50 4.00
163 Andy Katzenmoyer RC 1.50 4.00
164 Antoine Winfield RC 1.25 3.00
165 Checklist Card .25 .60

1999 Topps Chrome Refractors

*REF.VETS: 2.5X TO 6X BASIC CARDS
REFRACTOR VETERANS ODDS 1:12
REFRACTOR ROOKIES ODDS 1:32

1999 Topps Chrome All-Etch

COMPLETE SET (30) 100.00 200.00
STATED ODDS 1:24
*REF.STARS: 1.2X TO 3X BASIC INSERTS
*REF.ROOKIES: .8X TO 2X BASIC INSERTS
REFRACTOR STATED ODDS 1:120
AE1 Fred Taylor 2.00 5.00
AE2 Ricky Watters 1.25 3.00
AE3 Curtis Martin 2.00 5.00
AE4 Eddie George 2.00 5.00
AE5 Marshall Faulk 2.50 6.00
AE6 Emmitt Smith 4.00 10.00
AE7 Barry Sanders 6.00 15.00
AE8 Garrison Hearst 1.25 3.00
AE9 Jamal Anderson 2.00 5.00
AE10 Terrell Davis 2.00 5.00
AE11 Chris Chandler 1.25 3.00
AE12 Steve McNair 2.00 5.00
AE13 Vinny Testaverde 1.25 3.00
AE14 Trent Green 2.00 5.00
AE15 Dan Marino 6.00 15.00
AE16 Drew Bledsoe 2.50 6.00
AE17 Randall Cunningham 2.00 5.00
AE18 Jake Plummer 1.25 3.00
AE19 Peyton Manning 6.00 15.00
AE20 Steve Young 2.50 6.00
AE21 Brett Favre 6.00 15.00
AE22 Tim Couch .60 1.50
AE23 Edgerrin James 2.50 6.00
AE24 David Boston .60 1.50
AE25 Akili Smith .50 1.25
AE26 Troy Edwards .50 1.25
AE27 Torry Holt 2.00 5.00
AE28 Donovan McNabb 3.00 8.00
AE29 Daunte Culpepper 3.00 8.00
AE30 Ricky Williams 1.25 3.00

1999 Topps Chrome Hall of Fame

COMPLETE SET (30) 50.00 120.00
STATED ODDS 1:29
*REF.STARS: 2.5X TO 6X BASIC INSERTS
*REF.ROOKIES: 2X TO 5X BASIC INSERTS
REFRACTOR PRINT RUN 100 SERIAL #'d SETS
H1 Akili Smith .50 1.25
H2 Troy Edwards .50 1.25
H3 Donovan McNabb 3.00 8.00
H4 Cade McNown .50 1.25
H5 Ricky Williams 1.25 3.00
H6 David Boston .60 1.50
H7 Daunte Culpepper 3.00 8.00
H8 Edgerrin James 2.50 6.00
H9 Torry Holt 2.00 5.00
H10 Tim Couch .60 1.50
H11 Terrell Davis 2.00 5.00
H12 Fred Taylor 2.00 5.00
H13 Antonio Freeman 2.00 5.00
H14 Jamal Anderson 2.00 5.00
H15 Randy Moss 5.00 12.00
H16 Joey Galloway 1.25 3.00
H17 Eddie George 2.00 5.00
H18 Jake Plummer 1.25 3.00
H19 Curtis Martin 2.00 5.00
H20 Peyton Manning 6.00 15.00
H21 Barry Sanders 6.00 15.00
H22 Steve Young 2.50 6.00
H23 Cris Carter 2.00 5.00
H24 Emmitt Smith 4.00 10.00
H25 John Elway 6.00 15.00
H26 Drew Bledsoe 2.50 6.00
H27 Troy Aikman 4.00 10.00
H28 Brett Favre 6.00 15.00
H29 Jerry Rice 4.00 10.00
H30 Dan Marino 6.00 15.00

1999 Topps Chrome Record Numbers

COMPLETE SET (10) 40.00 80.00
STATED ODDS 1:72
REFRACTORS: 1.2X TO 3X BASIC INSERTS.
REFRACTOR STATED ODDS 1:360
RN1 Randy Moss 5.00 12.00
RN2 Terrell Davis 2.00 5.00
RN3 Emmitt Smith 4.00 10.00
RN4 Barry Sanders 6.00 15.00
RN5 Dan Marino 6.00 15.00
RN6 Brett Favre 6.00 15.00
RN7 Doug Flutie 2.00 5.00
RN8 Jerry Rice 4.00 10.00
RN9 Peyton Manning 6.00 15.00
RN10 Jason Elam .75 2.00

1999 Topps Chrome Season's Best

COMPLETE SET (30) 50.00 100.00
STATED ODDS: 1:24
*REFRACTORS: 1.2X TO 3X BASIC INSERTS
REFRACTOR STATED ODDS 1:120
SB1 Terrell Davis 1.50 4.00
SB2 Jamal Anderson 1.50 4.00
SB3 Garrison Hearst 1.00 2.50
SB4 Barry Sanders 5.00 12.00
SB5 Emmitt Smith 3.00 8.00
SB6 Randall Cunningham 1.50 4.00
SB7 Brett Favre 5.00 12.00
SB8 Steve Young 2.00 5.00
SB9 Jake Plummer 1.00 2.50
SB10 Peyton Manning 5.00 12.00
SB11 Antonio Freeman 1.50 4.00
SB12 Eric Moulds 1.50 4.00
SB13 Randy Moss 4.00 10.00
SB14 Rod Smith 1.00 2.50
SB15 Jimmy Smith 1.00 2.50
SB16 Michael Sinclair .60 1.50
SB17 Kevin Greene .60 1.50
SB18 Michael Strahan 1.00 2.50
SB19 Michael McCrary .60 1.50
SB20 Hugh Douglas .60 1.50
SB21 Deion Sanders 1.50 4.00
SB22 Terry Fair 1.00 2.50
SB23 Jacquez Green .60 1.50
SB24 Corey Harris .60 1.50
SB25 Tim Dwight 1.50 4.00
SB26 Dan Marino 5.00 12.00
SB27 Barry Sanders 5.00 12.00
SB28 Jerry Rice 3.00 8.00
SB29 Bruce Smith 1.00 2.50
SB30 Darrien Gordon .60 1.50

2000 Topps Chrome

Released as a 270-card set, the Topps Chrome card design parallels the regular Topps set with cards enhanced by foil card stock. Rookie cards are sequentially numbered to 1650. Chrome was packaged in 24-pack boxes with packs containing four cards and carried a suggested retail price of $3.00.

COMPLETE SET (270) 250.00 500.00
COMP.SET w/o SP's (180) 25.00 50.00
181-190/231-270 ROOKIE PRINT RUN 1650
1 Daunte Culpepper .40 1.00
2 Troy Edwards .30 .75
3 Terrell Owens .50 1.25
4 Ricky Proehl .30 .75
5 Shaun King .30 .75
6 Jeff George .40 1.00
7 Champ Bailey .40 1.00
8 Amani Toomer .40 1.00
9 Stephen Boyd .30 .75
10 Thurman Thomas .50 1.25
11 Patrick Jeffers .40 1.00
12 Jake Plummer .40 1.00
13 Peter Boulware .30 .75
14 Darrin Chiaverini .30 .75
15 Olandis Gary .40 1.00
16 Peyton Manning 1.25 3.00
17 Joe Horn .40 1.00
18 Wayne Chrebet .40 1.00
19 Freddie Jones .30 .75
20 Kurt Warner .75 2.00
21 Mike Alstott .50 1.25
22 Stephen Davis .40 1.00
23 Tim Brown .50 1.25
24 Damon Huard .40 1.00
25 Terry Glenn .40 1.00
26 Ricky Williams .50 1.25
27 Tim Dwight .40 1.00
28 Jay Riemersma .30 .75
29 Carl Pickens .40 1.00
30 Brett Favre 1.50 4.00
31 Oronde Gadsden .40 1.00
32 Steve McNair .50 1.25
33 Michael Pittman .30 .75
34 Emmitt Smith 1.25 3.00
35 Mark Brunell .40 1.00
36 Ed McCaffrey .40 1.00
37 Tyrone Wheatley .30 .75
38 Sean Dawkins .30 .75
39 Jevon Kearse .40 1.00
40 Tai Streets .30 .75
41 Keyshawn Johnson .40 1.00
42 Germane Crowell .30 .75
43 Yatil Green .30 .75
44 Anthony Wright RC .50 1.25
45 Jerry Rice 1.00 2.50
46 Az-Zahir Hakim .30 .75
47 Stephen Alexander .30 .75
48 Zach Thomas .50 1.25
49 Tony Simmons .30 .75
50 Jessie Armstead .30 .75
51 Kordell Stewart .40 1.00
52 Cade McNown .30 .75
53 Tony Gonzalez .50 1.25
54 John Randle .40 1.00
55 Donovan McNabb .50 1.25
56 Warrick Dunn .40 1.00
57 Dorsey Levens .40 1.00
58 Errict Rhett .40 1.00
59 Priest Holmes .50 1.25
60 Terrell Davis .50 1.25
61 Natrone Means .40 1.00
62 Brad Johnson .40 1.00
63 Rickey Dudley .30 .75
64 Billy Miller .30 .75
65 Randy Moss .50 1.25
66 Joe Montgomery .30 .75
67 Johnnie Morton .40 1.00
68 Peerless Price .40 1.00
69 Rocket Ismail .40 1.00
70 David Boston .30 .75
71 Fred Taylor .50 1.25
72 Jermaine Fazande .30 .75
73 Elvis Grbac .30 .75
74 Derrick Mayes .30 .75
75 Yancey Thigpen .30 .75
76 Ike Hilliard .40 1.00
77 Muhsin Muhammad .40 1.00
78 Shawn Jefferson .30 .75
79 Rod Smith .40 1.00
80 Darnay Scott .40 1.00
81 Cam Cleeland .30 .75
82 Steve Young .60 1.50
83 E.G. Green .30 .75
84 Robert Smith .40 1.00
85 Jermaine Lewis .30 .75
86 Tim Biakabutuka .40 1.00
87 Jerome Pathon .30 .75
88 Kent Graham .30 .75
89 Bruce Smith .50 1.25
90 Isaac Bruce .50 1.25
91 Curtis Enis .30 .75
92 D'Marco Farr .30 .75
93 Keith Poole .30 .75
94 Troy Aikman .75 2.00
95 Rich Gannon .40 1.00
96 Michael Westbrook .30 .75
97 Albert Connell .30 .75
98 James Johnson .30 .75
99 Jeff Blake .40 1.00
100 Joey Galloway .40 1.00
101 Rob Moore .30 .75
102 Chris Chandler .40 1.00
103 Fred Lane .30 .75
104 Eddie Kennison .30 .75
105 Kevin Hardy .30 .75
106 Napoleon Kaufman .40 1.00
107 Kevin Dyson .40 1.00
108 Keenan McCardell .40 1.00
109 Drew Bledsoe .50 1.25
110 Kevin Johnson .30 .75
111 Terance Mathis .30 .75
112 Gus Frerotte .40 1.00
113 Matthew Hatchette .30 .75
114 Herman Moore .40 1.00
115 Curtis Martin .50 1.25
116 Jacquez Green .30 .75
117 Jake Reed .40 1.00
118 Antonio Freeman .40 1.00
119 Jim Miller .30 .75
120 Frank Sanders .30 .75
121 Brian Griese .40 1.00
122 Troy Brown .40 1.00
123 Jeff Graham .30 .75
124 Marshall Faulk .50 1.25
125 Vinny Testaverde .40 1.00
126 Frank Wycheck .40 1.00
127 Kerry Collins .40 1.00
128 Jay Fiedler .40 1.00
129 Cris Carter .50 1.25
130 Jason Tucker .30 .75
131 Antowain Smith .40 1.00
132 Tony Banks .30 .75
133 Terrence Wilkins .30 .75
134 Tony Martin .40 1.00
135 Richard Huntley .30 .75
136 J.J. Stokes .40 1.00
137 Ricky Watters .40 1.00
138 Pete Mitchell .30 .75
139 Jimmy Smith .40 1.00
140 Doug Flutie .50 1.25
141 Corey Bradford .30 .75
142 Curtis Conway .40 1.00
143 Moses Moreno .30 .75
144 Torry Holt .50 1.25
145 Warren Sapp .40 1.00
146 Duce Staley .40 1.00
147 Mikhael Ricks .30 .75
148 Edgerrin James .50 1.25
149 Charlie Batch .40 1.00
150 Rob Johnson .40 1.00
151 Jamal Anderson .40 1.00
152 Tim Couch .40 1.00
153 O.J. McDuffie .40 1.00
154 Charles Woodson .50 1.25
155 Jake Delhomme RC 3.00 8.00
156 Eddie George .40 1.00
157 Jim Harbaugh .40 1.00
158 Jon Kitna .40 1.00
159 Derrick Alexander .30 .75
160 Marvin Harrison .50 1.25
161 James Stewart .30 .75
162 Qadry Ismail .40 1.00
163 Wesley Walls .30 .75
164 Steve Beuerlein .40 1.00
165 Marcus Robinson .40 1.00
166 Bill Schroeder .40 1.00
167 Charles Johnson .30 .75
168 Charlie Garner .40 1.00
169 Eric Moulds .40 1.00
170 Jerome Bettis .50 1.25
171 Tai Streets .30 .75
172 Akili Smith .30 .75
173 Jonathan Linton .30 .75
174 Corey Dillon .40 1.00
175 Junior Seau .50 1.25
176 Jonathan Quinn .30 .75
177 Bobby Engram .40 1.00
178 Shannon Sharpe .50 1.25
179 Michael Basnight .30 .75
180 Sedrick Irvin .30 .75
181 Sammy Morris RC 4.00 10.00
182 Ron Dixon RC 3.00 8.00
183 Trevor Gaylor RC 3.00 8.00
184 Chris Cole RC 4.00 10.00
185 Deltha O'Neal RC 4.00 10.00
186 Sebastian Janikowski RC 5.00 12.00
187 Kwame Cavil RC 3.00 8.00
188 Chad Morton RC 5.00 12.00
189 Terrelle Smith RC 3.00 8.00
190 Frank Moreau RC 3.00 8.00
191 Kurt Warner HL .60 1.50
192 Dan Marino HL 1.25 3.00
193 Cris Carter HL .40 1.00
194 Brett Favre HL 1.25 3.00
195 Marshall Faulk HL .40 1.00
196 Jevon Kearse HL .30 .75
197 Edgerrin James HL .40 1.00
198 Emmitt Smith HL 1.00 2.50
199 Andre Reed HL .40 1.00
200 Kevin Dyson HL .30 .75
Frank Wycheck HL
201 Olindo Mare MM .30 .75
202 Marcus Coleman MM .30 .75
203 James Johnson MM .30 .75
204 Ray Lucas MM .30 .75
205 Dedric Ward MM .30 .75
206 Richie Cunningham MM .30 .75
207 James Hasty MM .30 .75
208 Sedrick Shaw MM .30 .75
209 Kurt Warner MM .60 1.50
210 Marshall Faulk MM .40 1.00
211 Brian Shay EP .30 .75
212 L.C. Stevens EP .30 .75
213 Corey Thomas EP .30 .75
214 Scott Milanovich EP .30 .75
215 Pat Barnes EP .40 1.00
216 Danny Wuerffel EP .50 1.25
217 Kevin Daft EP .30 .75
218 Ron Powlus EP RC .50 1.25
219 Eric Kresser EP .30 .75
220 Norman Miller EP RC .30 .75
221 Cory Sauter EP .30 .75
222 Marcus Crandell EP RC .30 .75
223 Sean Morey EP RC .30 .75
224 Jeff Ogden EP .30 .75
225 Ted White EP .30 .75
226 Jim Kubiak EP RC .30 .75
227 Aaron Stecker EP RC .40 1.00
228 Ronnie Powell EP .30 .75
229 Matt Lytle EP RC .30 .75
230 Kendrick Nord EP RC .30 .75
231 Tim Rattay RC 4.00 10.00
232 Rob Morris RC 4.00 10.00
233 Chris Samuels RC 4.00 10.00
234 Todd Husak RC 3.00 8.00
235 Ahmed Plummer RC 3.00 8.00
236 Frank Murphy RC 3.00 8.00
237 Michael Wiley RC 3.00 8.00
238 Giovanni Carmazzi RC 3.00 8.00
239 Anthony Becht RC 4.00 10.00
240 John Abraham RC 5.00 12.00
241 Shaun Alexander RC 6.00 15.00
242 Thomas Jones RC 6.00 15.00
243 Courtney Brown RC 4.00 10.00
244 Curtis Keaton RC 3.00 8.00
245 Jerry Porter RC 5.00 12.00
246 Corey Simon RC 4.00 10.00
247 Dez White RC 4.00 10.00
248 Jamal Lewis RC 5.00 12.00
249 Ron Dayne RC 5.00 12.00
250 R.Jay Soward RC 3.00 8.00
251 Tee Martin RC 5.00 12.00
252 Shaun Ellis RC 5.00 12.00
253 Brian Urlacher RC 20.00 50.00
254 Reuben Droughns RC 5.00 12.00
255 Travis Taylor RC 4.00 10.00
256 Plaxico Burress RC 5.00 12.00
257 Chad Pennington RC 8.00 20.00
258 Sylvester Morris RC 3.00 8.00
259 Ron Dugans RC 3.00 8.00
260 Joe Hamilton RC 3.00 8.00
261 Chris Redman RC 4.00 10.00
262 Trung Canidate RC 4.00 10.00
263 J.R. Redmond RC 3.00 8.00
264 Danny Farmer RC 3.00 8.00
265 Todd Pinkston RC 3.00 8.00
266 Dennis Northcutt RC 4.00 10.00
267 Laveranues Coles RC 5.00 12.00
268 Bubba Franks RC 5.00 12.00
269 Travis Prentice RC 4.00 10.00
270 Peter Warrick RC 5.00 12.00

2000 Topps Chrome Refractors

*VETS: 2.5X TO 6X BASIC CARDS
VETERAN REFRACTOR ODDS 1:12
*ROOKIES: .6X TO 1.5X BASIC CARDS
ROOKIE STATED PRINT RUN 150

2000 Topps Chrome Combos

COMPLETE SET (10) 15.00 30.00
STATED ODDS 1:20
*REFRACTOR: 1.2X TO 3X BASIC INSERTS
REFRACTOR STATED ODDS 1:200
TC1 Johnny Unitas 2.50 6.00
Peyton Manning
TC2 Chris Carter 1.00 2.50
Randy Moss
TC3 Ricky Williams 1.00 2.50
Edgerrin James
TC4 Marvin Harrison 1.00 2.50
Jimmy Smith
TC5 Isaac Bruce 1.00 2.50
Joey Galloway
TC6 Donovan McNabb .60 1.50
Tim Couch
Shaun King
Daunte Culpepper
Akili Smith
TC7 Stephen Davis 1.00 2.50
Fred Taylor
TC8 Marshall Faulk 1.00 2.50
Eddie George
TC9 Emmitt Smith 2.50 6.00
Troy Aikman
TC10 Kurt Warner 3.00 8.00
Dan Marino

2000 Topps Chrome Own the Game

COMPLETE SET (30) 30.00 60.00
STATED ODDS 1:12
*REFRACTOR: 1.2X TO 3X BASIC INSERTS
REFRACTOR STATED ODDS 1:120
OTG1 Steve Beuerlein .75 2.00
OTG2 Kurt Warner 1.50 4.00
OTG3 Peyton Manning 2.50 6.00
OTG4 Brett Favre 3.00 8.00
OTG5 Brad Johnson .75 2.00
OTG6 Edgerrin James 1.00 2.50
OTG7 Curtis Martin 1.00 2.50
OTG8 Stephen Davis .75 2.00
OTG9 Emmitt Smith 2.50 6.00
OTG10 Marshall Faulk 1.00 2.50
OTG11 Eddie George .75 2.00
OTG12 Duce Staley .75 2.00
OTG13 Charlie Garner .75 2.00
OTG14 Marvin Harrison 1.00 2.50
OTG15 Jimmy Smith .75 2.00
OTG16 Randy Moss 1.00 2.50
OTG17 Marcus Robinson .75 2.00
OTG18 Tim Brown 1.00 2.50
OTG19 Germane Crowell .60 1.50
OTG20 Muhsin Muhammad .75 2.00
OTG21 Cris Carter 1.00 2.50
OTG22 Michael Westbrook .60 1.50
OTG23 Amani Toomer .75 2.00
OTG24 Keyshawn Johnson .75 2.00
OTG25 Isaac Bruce 1.00 2.50
OTG26 Kurt Warner 1.50 4.00
OTG27 Stephen Davis .75 2.00
OTG28 Edgerrin James 1.00 2.50
OTG29 Cris Carter 1.00 2.50
OTG30 Marvin Harrison 1.00 2.50

2000 Topps Chrome Preseason Picks

COMPLETE SET (31) 40.00 80.00
STATED ODDS 1:22 HOBBY
*REFRACTORS: 1.2X TO 3X BASIC INSERTS
REFRACTOR ODDS 1:220 HOB
P1 Jake Plummer .75 2.00
P2 Troy Aikman 1.50 4.00
P3 Kerry Collins .75 2.00
P4 Donovan McNabb 1.00 2.50
P5 Stephen Davis .75 2.00
P6 Cade McNown .75 2.00
Marcus Robinson
Curtis Enis
Bobby Engram
P7 Charlie Batch .75 2.00
P8 Brett Favre 3.00 8.00
P9 Randy Moss 1.00 2.50
P10 Shaun King .60 1.50
P11 Tim Couch .75 2.00
P12 Jamal Anderson .75 2.00
P13 Steve Beuerlein .75 2.00
P14 Ricky Williams 1.00 2.50
P15 Kurt Warner 1.50 4.00
P16 Jerry Rice 2.00 5.00
P17 Eric Moulds .75 2.00
P18 Peyton Manning 2.50 6.00
P19 Zach Thomas 1.00 2.50
P20 Drew Bledsoe 1.00 2.50
P21 Curtis Martin 1.00 2.50
P22 Tony Banks .60 1.50
P23 Akili Smith .60 1.50
P24 Jimmy Smith .75 2.00
P25 Jerome Bettis 1.00 2.50
P26 Eddie George .75 2.00
P27 Terrell Davis 1.00 2.50
P28 Tony Gonzalez 1.00 2.50
P29 Tim Brown 1.00 2.50
P30 Junior Seau 1.00 2.50
P31 Jon Kitna .75 2.00

2000 Topps Chrome Unitas Reprints Refractors

COMPLETE SET (18) 40.00 100.00
COMMON CARD (R1-R18) 2.50 6.00
STATED ODDS 1:14
R1 Johnny Unitas 1957 4.00 10.00

2001 Topps Chrome

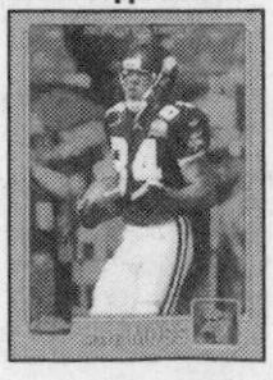

Topps released its Chrome set in August of 2001 as a 320-card set. The set was made up of 210 veterans and 110 short printed rookies. The rookies were serial numbered to 999 and were only available as refractors. The set looked identical to the base Topps set with the chromium technology.

COMP.SET w/o SP's (210) 20.00 50.00
ROOKIE/999 STATED ODDS 1:12
1 Randy Moss .50 1.25
2 Desmond Howard .40 1.00
3 Shawn Bryson .30 .75
4 Lamar Smith .40 1.00
5 Peter Warrick .40 1.00
6 Hines Ward .50 1.25
7 J.R. Redmond .30 .75
8 Reidel Anthony .30 .75
9 Rich Gannon .40 1.00
10 Ed McCaffrey .40 1.00
11 Jamel White .30 .75
12 Michael Pittman .40 1.00
13 Rob Johnson .40 1.00
14 Tim Couch .30 .75
15 Stephen Alexander .30 .75
16 Ricky Watters .40 1.00
17 Kerry Collins .40 1.00
18 Ricky Williams .50 1.25
19 Joey Galloway .40 1.00
20 Chris Chandler .40 1.00
21 Marty Booker .40 1.00
22 Mark Brunell .40 1.00
23 Antonio Freeman .50 1.25
24 Richie Anderson .30 .75
25 Amani Toomer .40 1.00
26 Trent Green .50 1.25
27 Terrell Fletcher .30 .75
28 Kevin Lockett .30 .75
29 Ron Dixon .30 .75
30 Charlie Batch .40 1.00
31 Oronde Gadsden .30 .75
32 Dorsey Levens .40 1.00
33 Jamal Lewis .50 1.25
34 Craig Yeast .30 .75
35 Muhsin Muhammad .40 1.00
36 Willie Jackson .30 .75
37 Isaac Bruce .50 1.25
38 Frank Wycheck .30 .75
39 Troy Brown .40 1.00
40 Anthony Wright .30 .75
41 Zach Thomas .50 1.25
42 Qadry Ismail .40 1.00
43 Jake Plummer .40 1.00
44 Keenan McCardell .40 1.00
45 Charles Johnson .30 .75
46 Brett Favre 1.50 4.00
47 Jacquez Green .30 .75
48 Matt Hasselbeck .50 1.25
49 Tiki Barber .50 1.25
50 Jeff Garcia .40 1.00
51 Shawn Jefferson .30 .75
52 Kevin Johnson .30 .75
53 Terrence Wilkins .30 .75
54 Mike Anderson .40 1.00
55 Tim Brown .50 1.25
56 Champ Bailey .50 1.25
57 Jimmy Smith .40 1.00
58 Trent Dilfer .40 1.00
59 James Allen .30 .75
60 David Boston .30 .75
61 Jeremiah Trotter .30 .75
62 Freddie Jones .30 .75
63 Deion Sanders .50 1.25
64 Darrell Jackson .40 1.00
65 David Patten .30 .75
66 Jeremy McDaniel .30 .75
67 Jay Fiedler .40 1.00
68 Chad Lewis .30 .75
69 Rocket Ismail .40 1.00
70 Cade McNown .40 1.00
71 Jevon Kearse .40 1.00
72 Jermaine Fazande .30 .75
73 Junior Seau .50 1.25
74 Rod Smith .40 1.00
75 Jermaine Lewis .30 .75
76 Dennis Northcutt .30 .75
77 Charlie Garner .40 1.00
78 Charles Woodson .50 1.25
79 Wayne Chrebet .40 1.00
80 Ahman Green .50 1.25
81 Donald Hayes .30 .75
82 Terance Mathis .30 .75
83 Warrick Dunn .50 1.25
84 Chris Sanders .30 .75
85 Albert Connell .30 .75
86 Robert Griffith .30 .75
87 Germane Crowell .30 .75
88 Tony Banks .30 .75
89 Travis Taylor .30 .75
90 Akili Smith .30 .75
91 Michael Westbrook .30 .75
92 Doug Flutie .50 1.25
93 Ike Hilliard .40 1.00
94 Terry Glenn .40 1.00
95 Leslie Shepherd .30 .75
96 Az-Zahir Hakim .30 .75
97 La'Roi Glover .30 .75
98 Peyton Manning 1.25 3.00
99 Jackie Harris .40 1.00
100 Edgerrin James .50 1.25
101 Peerless Price .30 .75
102 Jamal Anderson .40 1.00
103 Keyshawn Johnson .40 1.00
104 Derrick Mason .40 1.00
105 J.J. Stokes .30 .75
106 Kevin Faulk .40 1.00
107 Tony Richardson .30 .75
108 James Stewart .30 .75
109 Tim Biakabutuka .30 .75
110 Jon Kitna .40 1.00
111 Thomas Jones .40 1.00
112 Steve McNair .50 1.25
113 Sean Dawkins .30 .75
114 Jerome Bettis .50 1.25
115 Donovan McNabb .50 1.25
116 Bill Schroeder .40 1.00
117 Rod Woodson .50 1.25
118 James McKnight .30 .75
119 Daunte Culpepper .40 1.00
120 Todd Husak .30 .75
121 Shaun King .30 .75
122 Tyrone Wheatley .40 1.00
123 Curtis Martin .50 1.25
124 Terrell Davis .50 1.25
125 Steve Beuerlein .40 1.00
126 Brad Johnson .40 1.00
127 Joe Horn .40 1.00
128 Fred Taylor .50 1.25
129 Brian Urlacher .60 1.50
130 Ray Lewis .50 1.25
131 Marshall Faulk .50 1.25
132 Curtis Conway .40 1.00
133 Jason Sehorn .40 1.00
134 Jerome Pathon .30 .75
135 Derrick Alexander .30 .75
136 Jerry Rice 1.00 2.50
137 Jeff George .40 1.00
138 Johnnie Morton .40 1.00
139 Eric Moulds .40 1.00
140 Duce Staley .40 1.00
141 Vinny Testaverde .40 1.00
142 Eddie George .50 1.25
143 Shaun Alexander .50 1.25
144 Drew Bledsoe .50 1.25
145 Emmitt Smith 1.25 3.00
146 Marvin Harrison .50 1.25
147 Frank Sanders .30 .75
148 Aaron Shea .30 .75
149 Cris Carter .50 1.25
150 Tony Gonzalez .50 1.25
151 Marcus Robinson .40 1.00
152 Danny Farmer .30 .75
153 Warren Sapp .40 1.00
154 Kurt Warner .75 2.00
155 Jessie Armstead .30 .75
156 Lawyer Milloy .40 1.00
157 Brian Griese .40 1.00
158 Jason Taylor .50 1.25
159 Jeff Lewis .30 .75
160 Travis Prentice .30 .75
161 Tim Dwight .40 1.00
162 Kyle Brady .30 .75
163 Bubba Franks .40 1.00
164 James Thrash .40 1.00
165 Bobby Shaw .30 .75
166 Ron Dayne .40 1.00
167 Mike Alstott .40 1.00
168 Bruce Smith .50 1.25
169 Jeff Graham .30 .75
170 Jeff Blake .40 1.00
171 Laveranues Coles .40 1.00
172 Herman Moore .40 1.00
173 Shannon Sharpe .50 1.25
174 Corey Dillon .40 1.00
175 Ken Dilger .30 .75
176 Eddie Kennison .40 1.00
177 Andre Rison .40 1.00
178 Stephen Davis .40 1.00
179 Torry Holt .40 1.00
180 Samari Rolle .30 .75
181 Michael Strahan .50 1.25
182 Plaxico Burress .40 1.00
183 Darnell Autry .30 .75
184 Wesley Walls .30 .75
185 Elvis Grbac .40 1.00
186 Marcus Pollard .30 .75
187 Keith Poole .30 .75
188 Ryan Leaf .30 .75
189 Terrell Owens .50 1.25
190 Dedric Ward .30 .75
191 Donald Driver .50 1.25
192 Larry Foster .30 .75
193 Priest Holmes .50 1.25
194 Sammy Morris .40 1.00
195 Reggie Jones .30 .75
196 Kordell Stewart .40 1.00
197 Sylvester Morris .30 .75
198 Aaron Brooks .40 1.00
199 Tai Streets .30 .75
200 Chad Pennington .50 1.25
201 Terrell Owens SH .50 1.25
202 Marshall Faulk SH .50 1.25
203 Mike Anderson SH .40 1.00
204 Cris Carter SH .50 1.25
205 Corey Dillon SH .40 1.00
206 Daunte Culpepper SH .40 1.00
207 Peyton Manning SH 1.25 3.00
208 Torry Holt SH .40 1.00
209 Marvin Harrison SH .50 1.25
210 Edgerrin James SH .50 1.25
211 Sam Madison .30 .75
212 Jonathan Quinn .30 .75
213 Rob Morris .30 .75
214 E.G. Green .30 .75
215 David Sloan .30 .75
216 Jason Tucker .30 .75
217 Wali Rainer .30 .75
218 Jerry Azumah .30 .75
219 Dameyune Craig .30 .75
220 Jammi German .30 .75
221 LaDainian Tomlinson RC 40.00 100.00
222 Quincy Morgan RC 5.00 12.00
223 Steve Smith RC 12.00 30.00
224 Santana Moss RC 8.00 20.00
225 Koren Robinson RC 5.00 12.00
226 Kevin Kasper RC 4.00 10.00
227 Jamie Henderson RC 5.00 12.00
228 Adam Archuleta RC 5.00 12.00
229 Drew Brees RC 90.00 150.00
230 Michael Stone RC 4.00 10.00
231 Jamar Fletcher RC 4.00 10.00
232 Eric Westmoreland RC 4.00 10.00
233 Chris Barnes RC 4.00 10.00
234 Gerard Warren RC 5.00 12.00
235 Snoop Minnis RC 4.00 10.00
236 Chris Chambers RC 6.00 15.00
237 Damerien McCants RC 5.00 12.00
238 Kevan Barlow RC 5.00 12.00
239 Mike McMahon RC 5.00 12.00
240 Jabari Holloway RC 4.00 10.00
241 Travis Henry RC 5.00 12.00
242 Derrick Blaylock RC 5.00 12.00
243 Tim Hasselbeck RC 5.00 12.00
244 Andre Carter RC 5.00 12.00
245 Sage Rosenfels RC 6.00 15.00
246 Cedrick Wilson RC 5.00 12.00
247 Scotty Anderson RC 4.00 10.00
248 Ken-Yon Rambo RC 4.00 10.00
249 Marques Tuiasosopo RC 5.00 12.00
250 Reggie Wayne RC 12.00 30.00
251 Onomo Ojo RC 4.00 10.00
252 James Jackson RC 4.00 10.00
253 Moran Norris RC 4.00 10.00
254 Rashard Casey RC 4.00 10.00
255 Rudi Johnson RC 6.00 15.00
256 Willie Middlebrooks RC 5.00 12.00
257 Freddie Mitchell RC 4.00 10.00
258 Deuce McAllister RC 6.00 15.00
259 Chad Johnson RC 10.00 25.00
260 David Terrell RC 5.00 12.00
261 Jamal Reynolds RC 4.00 10.00
262 Michael Vick RC 50.00 120.00
263 Marcus Stroud RC 5.00 12.00
264 Dan Alexander RC 5.00 12.00
265 Jonathan Carter RC 4.00 10.00
266 Bobby Newcombe RC 5.00 12.00
267 Eddie Berlin RC 4.00 10.00
268 LaMont Jordan RC 6.00 15.00
269 Michael Bennett RC 5.00 12.00
270 Shaun Rogers RC 6.00 15.00
271 Travis Minor RC 5.00 12.00
272 Jesse Palmer RC 5.00 12.00
273 Derrick Gibson RC 4.00 10.00
274 Chris Weinke RC 5.00 12.00
275 Nate Clements RC 5.00 12.00
276 Eric Kelly RC 4.00 10.00
277 Justin Smith RC 6.00 15.00
278 Ryan Pickett RC 4.00 10.00
279 Anthony Thomas RC 6.00 15.00
280 Will Allen RC 6.00 15.00
281 Quincy Carter RC 5.00 12.00
282 Richard Seymour RC 6.00 15.00
283 Dan Morgan RC 5.00 12.00
284 Tay Cody RC 4.00 10.00
285 Alge Crumpler RC 6.00 15.00
286 Robert Ferguson RC 6.00 15.00
287 Will Peterson RC 5.00 12.00
288 Tony Dixon RC 4.00 10.00
289 Correll Buckhalter RC 6.00 15.00
290 Rod Gardner RC 5.00 12.00
291 Justin McCareins RC 5.00 12.00
292 Josh Heupel RC 6.00 15.00
293 Todd Heap RC 8.00 20.00
294 Damione Lewis RC 5.00 12.00
295 George Layne RC 4.00 10.00
296 Jamie Winborn RC 5.00 12.00
297 Billy Baber RC 4.00 10.00
298 T.J. Houshmandzadeh RC 8.00 20.00
299 Aaron Schobel RC 6.00 15.00
300 Gary Baxter RC 4.00 10.00
301 DeLawrence Grant RC 4.00 10.00
302 Morlon Greenwood RC 4.00 10.00
303 Shad Meier RC 4.00 10.00
304 Torrance Marshall RC 4.00 10.00
305 David Martin RC 4.00 10.00
306 Anthony Henry RC 6.00 15.00
307 Derrick Burgess RC 6.00 15.00
308 Andre Dyson RC 4.00 10.00
309 Ryan Helming RC 4.00 10.00
310 Fred Smoot RC 6.00 15.00
311 Arther Love RC 4.00 10.00
312 John Capel RC 4.00 10.00
313 Brandon Spoon RC 5.00 12.00
314 Karon Riley RC 4.00 10.00
315 Andre King RC 4.00 10.00
316 Quentin McCord RC 5.00 12.00
317 Zeke Moreno RC 5.00 12.00
318 Francis St. Paul RC 4.00 10.00
319 Richmond Flowers RC 4.00 10.00
320 Derek Combs RC 4.00 10.00

2001 Topps Chrome Refractors

*VETS: 2X TO 5X BASIC CARDS
*ROOKIES: 1X TO 2.5X
VETERAN/999 STATED ODDS 1:6
ROOKIE/100 STATED ODDS 1:125
ROOKIE PRINT RUN 100 SER.#'d SETS
221 LaDainian Tomlinson 50.00 120.00
229 Drew Brees 150.00 300.00
262 Michael Vick 75.00 200.00

2001 Topps Chrome Combos

COMPLETE SET (19) 15.00 40.00
STATED ODDS 1:12
TC1 Edgerrin James .75 2.00
Santana Moss
TC2 Tory Holt .75 2.00
Koren Robinson
TC3 Jamal Lewis 1.00 2.50
Travis Henry
TC4 Curtis Martin 1.00 2.50
Kevan Barlow
TC5 Cris Carter 1.00 2.50
Ken-Yon Rambo
TC6 Troy Aikman 1.50 4.00
Freddie Mitchell
TC7 Brian Griese .75 2.00
David Terrell
TC8 Tyrone Wheatley 1.00 2.50
Anthony Thomas
TC9 Warrick Dunn 1.00 2.50
Travis Minor
TC10 Peter Warrick .75 2.00
Snoop Minnis
TC11 Warren Sapp .75 2.00
Dan Morgan
TC12 Tony Gonzalez 1.00 2.50
Andre Carter
TC13 Antonio Freeman 2.50 6.00
Michael Vick
TC14 Ron Dayne .75 2.00
Michael Bennett
TC15 Mike Alstott 4.00 10.00
Drew Brees
TC16 Ahman Green 1.00 2.50
Correll Buckhalter
TC17 Brad Johnson .75 2.00
Chris Weinke
TC18 Eric Moulds 1.00 2.50
Fred Smoot
TC19 Ray Lewis 1.25 3.00
Reggie Wayne

2001 Topps Chrome King of Kings Jerseys

GROUP 1 ODDS 1:17766H
GROUP 2 ODDS 1:4890H
GROUP 3 ODDS 1:8094H
GROUP 4 ODDS 1:4834H
GROUP 5 ODDS 1:2194H
GROUP 6 ODDS 1:3215H
JSY/75-375 OVERALL ODDS 1:734H
KCD Corey Dillon/375 10.00 25.00
KDM Dan Marino/125 30.00 80.00
KES Emmitt Smith/150 30.00 80.00
KFT Fred Taylor/250 12.00 30.00
KJR Jerry Rice/125 25.00 60.00
KTO Terrell Owens/275 12.00 30.00
KWP Walter Payton/75 75.00 150.00

2001 Topps Chrome Own the Game

COMPLETE SET (10) 25.00 60.00
STATED ODDS 1:16
AW1 Marvin Harrison 1.00 2.50
AW2 Muhsin Muhammad .75 2.00
AW3 Torry Holt .75 2.00
AW4 Rod Smith .75 2.00
AW5 Randy Moss 1.00 2.50
AW6 Cris Carter 1.00 2.50
AW7 Ed McCaffrey .75 2.00
AW8 Isaac Bruce 1.00 2.50
AW9 Terrell Owens 1.00 2.50
AW10 Tony Gonzalez 1.00 2.50
GW1 Edgerrin James 1.00 2.50
GW2 Robert Smith .75 2.00
GW3 Marshall Faulk 1.00 2.50
GW4 Mike Anderson .75 2.00
GW5 Eddie George 1.00 2.50
GW6 Corey Dillon .75 2.00

GW7 Fred Taylor 1.00 2.50
PS1 Brian Griese .75 2.00
PS2 Peyton Manning 2.50 6.00
PS3 Jeff Garcia .75 2.00
PS4 Daunte Culpepper .75 2.00
PS5 Brett Favre 3.00 8.00
PS6 Kurt Warner 1.50 4.00
PS7 Donovan McNabb 1.00 2.50
TI1 La'Roi Glover .60 1.50
TI2 Darren Sharper .75 2.00
TI3 Mike Peterson .60 1.50
TS1 Derrick Mason .75 2.00
TS2 Az-Zahir Hakim .60 1.50
TS3 Jermaine Lewis .60 1.50

2001 Topps Chrome Pro Bowl Jerseys

GROUP 1 ODDS 1:4834H
GROUP 2 ODDS 1:1863H
GROUP 3 ODDS 1:1072H
GROUP 4 ODDS 1:602H
JSY/250-400 OVERALL ODDS 1:299H
TPCL Chad Lewis/400 8.00 20.00
TPDM Derrick Mason/400 10.00 25.00
TPEM Eric Moulds/375 10.00 25.00
TPJG Jeff Garcia/250 10.00 25.00
TPJL John Lynch/325 10.00 25.00
TPJS Junior Seau/375 12.00 30.00
TPJT Jason Taylor/400 12.00 30.00
TPMA Mike Alstott/400 10.00 25.00
TPRG Rich Gannon/325 10.00 25.00
TPRL Ray Lewis/375 15.00 40.00
TPTH Torry Holt/400 10.00 25.00

2001 Topps Chrome Rookie Reprint Jerseys

GROUP 1 ODDS 1:16766H
GROUP 2 ODDS 1:12354H
GROUP 3 ODDS 1:9780H
GROUP 4 ODDS 1:8094H
JSY/75-150 OVERALL ODDS 1:2729H
TODM Dan Marino/125 40.00 100.00
TOES Emmitt Smith/150 40.00 100.00
TOJR Jerry Rice/100 40.00 100.00
TOWP Walter Payton/75 40.00 100.00

2001 Topps Chrome Walter Payton Reprints Refractors

COMPLETE SET (12) 25.00 60.00
COMMON CARD (1-12) 3.00 8.00
STATED ODDS 1:20
JSY STATED ODDS 1:1204
JSY FEATURES 34 DIECUT SWATCH
WPR Walter Payton JSY 40.00 100.00

2002 Topps Chrome

Released in mid-August 2002, this 265-card set includes 165 veterans and 100 rookies. The rookies were inserted at a rate of 1:3. Boxes contained 24 packs of four cards. S.R.P. was $3.00 per pack.

COMPLETE SET (265) 150.00 300.00
COMP.SET w/o SP's (165) 20.00 50.00
166-265 ROOKIE ODDS 1:3 HOB/RET
1 Anthony Thomas .40 1.00
2 Jake Plummer .40 1.00
3 Maurice Smith .30 .75
4 Jamal Lewis .40 1.00
5 Ray Lewis .50 1.25
6 Alex Van Pelt .30 .75
7 Chris Weinke .30 .75
8 Corey Dillon .40 1.00
9 Quincy Morgan .30 .75
10 Rocket Ismail .40 1.00
11 Brian Griese .40 1.00
12 Johnnie Morton .40 1.00
13 Edgerrin James .40 1.00
14 Keenan McCardell .40 1.00
15 Travis Minor .30 .75
16 Sylvester Morris .30 .75
17 Randy Moss .50 1.25
18 Drew Bledsoe .50 1.25
19 Willie Jackson .30 .75
20 Michael Strahan .50 1.25
21 Santana Moss .40 1.00
22 Duce Staley .40 1.00
23 Kendrell Bell .30 .75
24 LaDainian Tomlinson .60 1.50
25 Terrell Owens .50 1.25
26 Shaun Alexander .40 1.00
27 Trung Canidate .30 .75
28 Mike Alstott .40 1.00
29 Kevin Dyson .40 1.00
30 Rod Gardner .30 .75
31 David Boston .30 .75
32 Michael Vick .75 2.00
33 Qadry Ismail .40 1.00
34 Peerless Price .30 .75
35 Rob Johnson .40 1.00
36 Marcus Robinson .40 1.00
37 Peter Warrick .40 1.00
38 Kevin Johnson .30 .75
39 Ed McCaffrey .40 1.00
40 Shaun Rogers .30 .75
41 Marvin Harrison .50 1.25
42 Priest Holmes .50 1.25
43 Oronde Gadsden .30 .75
44 Terry Glenn .40 1.00
45 Ike Hilliard .40 1.00
46 Charles Woodson .50 1.25
47 Freddie Mitchell .30 .75
48 Drew Brees .75 2.00
49 Jeff Garcia .40 1.00
50 Kurt Warner .50 1.25
51 Keyshawn Johnson .40 1.00
52 Jevon Kearse .40 1.00
53 Stephen Davis .40 1.00
54 Shannon Sharpe .50 1.25
55 Eric Moulds .40 1.00
56 Muhsin Muhammad .40 1.00
57 Brian Urlacher .50 1.25
58 Chad Johnson .50 1.25
59 Tim Couch .30 .75
60 Mike Anderson .40 1.00
61 James Stewart .30 .75
62 Corey Bradford .30 .75
63 Reggie Wayne .50 1.25
64 Mark Brunell .40 1.00
65 Trent Green .40 1.00
66 Zach Thomas .50 1.25
67 Michael Bennett .40 1.00
68 Troy Brown .40 1.00
69 Amani Toomer .40 1.00
70 Curtis Martin .50 1.25
71 Tim Brown .50 1.25
72 Correll Buckhalter .40 1.00
73 Kordell Stewart .40 1.00
74 Junior Seau .50 1.25
75 Kevan Barlow .30 .75
76 Matt Hasselbeck .50 1.25
77 Marshall Faulk .50 1.25
78 Warren Sapp .40 1.00
79 Frank Wycheck .30 .75
80 Michael Westbrook .30 .75
81 Travis Henry .30 .75
82 David Terrell .30 .75
83 Jon Kitna .40 1.00
84 James Jackson .30 .75
85 Joey Galloway .40 1.00
86 Rod Smith .40 1.00
87 Germane Crowell .30 .75
88 Bill Schroeder .30 .75
89 Dominic Rhodes .40 1.00
90 Fred Taylor .40 1.00
91 Snoop Minnis .30 .75
92 Chris Chambers .40 1.00
93 Daunte Culpepper .40 1.00
94 Deuce McAllister .40 1.00
95 Kerry Collins .40 1.00
96 John Abraham .40 1.00
97 Rich Gannon .40 1.00
98 Tiki Barber .50 1.25
99 Hines Ward .50 1.25
100 Tom Brady 1.25 3.00
101 Tim Dwight .30 .75
102 Garrison Hearst .40 1.00
103 Darrell Jackson .40 1.00
104 Isaac Bruce .50 1.25
105 Brad Johnson .40 1.00
106 Steve McNair .50 1.25
107 Champ Bailey .50 1.25
108 Emmitt Smith 1.25 3.00
109 Mike McMahon .30 .75
110 Terrell Davis .50 1.25
111 Antonio Freeman .50 1.25
112 Jimmy Smith .40 1.00
113 Tony Gonzalez .50 1.25
114 Jay Fiedler .40 1.00
115 Cris Carter .50 1.25
116 David Patten .30 .75
117 Joe Horn .40 1.00
118 Laveranues Coles .40 1.00
119 Charlie Garner .40 1.00
120 Donovan McNabb .50 1.25
121 Jerome Bettis .50 1.25
122 Curtis Conway .40 1.00
123 Az-Zahir Hakim .30 .75
124 Warrick Dunn .40 1.00
125 Eddie George .40 1.00
126 Quincy Carter .30 .75
127 Ahman Green .40 1.00
128 Peyton Manning 1.00 2.50
129 James McKnight .30 .75
130 Antowain Smith .40 1.00
131 Ricky Williams .40 1.00
132 Chad Pennington .50 1.25
133 Jerry Rice 1.00 2.50
134 Todd Pinkston .30 .75
135 Plaxico Burress .40 1.00
136 Doug Flutie .50 1.25
137 Koren Robinson .30 .75
138 Torry Holt .50 1.25
139 Aaron Brooks .40 1.00
140 Ron Dayne .40 1.00
141 Vinny Testaverde .40 1.00
142 Brett Favre 1.25 3.00
143 James Thrash .40 1.00
144 Wayne Chrebet .40 1.00
145 Derrick Mason .40 1.00
146 Ahman Green WW .30 .75
147 Peyton Manning WW .75 2.00
148 Kurt Warner WW .40 1.00
149 Daunte Culpepper WW .30 .75
150 Tom Brady WW 1.00 2.50
151 Rod Gardner WW .25 .60
152 Corey Dillon WW .30 .75
153 Priest Holmes WW .40 1.00
154 Shaun Alexander WW .30 .75
155 Randy Moss WW .40 1.00
156 Eric Moulds WW .30 .75
157 Brett Favre WW 1.00 2.50
158 Todd Bouman WW .25 .60
159 Dominic Rhodes WW .30 .75
160 Marvin Harrison WW .40 1.00
161 Torry Holt WW .40 1.00
162 Derrick Mason WW .30 .75
163 Jerry Rice WW .75 2.00
164 Donovan McNabb WW .40 1.00
165 Marshall Faulk WW .40 1.00
166 David Carr RC 3.00 8.00
167 Quentin Jammer RC 3.00 8.00
168 Mike Williams RC 2.00 5.00
169 Rocky Calmus RC 2.50 6.00
170 Travis Fisher RC 2.50 6.00
171 Dwight Freeney RC 4.00 10.00
172 Jeremy Shockey RC 5.00 12.00
173 Marquise Walker RC 2.00 5.00
174 Eric Crouch RC 3.00 8.00
175 DeShaun Foster RC 4.00 10.00
176 Roy Williams RC 3.00 8.00
177 Andre Davis RC 2.50 6.00
178 Alex Brown RC 3.00 8.00
179 Michael Lewis RC 3.00 8.00
180 Terry Charles RC 2.00 5.00
181 Clinton Portis RC 4.00 10.00
182 Dennis Johnson RC 2.00 5.00
183 Lito Sheppard RC 3.00 8.00
184 Ryan Sims RC 3.00 8.00
185 Raonall Smith RC 2.00 5.00
186 Albert Haynesworth RC 3.00 8.00
187 Eddie Freeman RC 2.00 5.00
188 Levi Jones RC 2.00 5.00
189 Josh McCown RC 3.00 8.00
190 Cliff Russell RC 2.00 5.00
191 Maurice Morris RC 2.50 6.00
192 Antwaan Randle El RC 3.00 8.00
193 Ladell Betts RC 3.00 8.00
194 Daniel Graham RC 2.50 6.00
195 David Garrard RC 4.00 10.00
196 Antonio Bryant RC 3.00 8.00
197 Patrick Ramsey RC 3.00 8.00
198 Kelly Campbell RC 2.50 6.00
199 Will Overstreet RC 2.00 5.00
200 Ryan Denney RC 2.00 5.00
201 John Henderson RC 2.50 6.00
202 Freddie Milons RC 2.00 5.00
203 Tim Carter RC 2.50 6.00
204 Kurt Kittner RC 2.00 5.00
205 Joey Harrington RC 3.00 8.00
206 Ricky Williams RC 2.50 6.00
207 Bryant McKinnie RC 2.00 5.00
208 Ed Reed RC 12.00 30.00
209 Josh Reed RC 2.50 6.00
210 Seth Burford RC 2.00 5.00
211 Javon Walker RC 3.00 8.00
212 Jamar Martin RC 2.50 6.00
213 Leonard Henry RC 2.00 5.00
214 Julius Peppers RC 6.00 15.00
215 Jabar Gaffney RC 3.00 8.00
216 Kalimba Edwards RC 2.50 6.00
217 Napoleon Harris RC 2.50 6.00
218 Ashley Lelie RC 2.50 6.00
219 Anthony Weaver RC 2.00 5.00
220 Bryan Thomas RC 2.00 5.00
221 Wendell Bryant RC 2.00 5.00
222 Damien Anderson RC 2.00 5.00
223 Travis Stephens RC 2.00 5.00
224 Rohan Davey RC 3.00 8.00
225 Mike Pearson RC 2.00 5.00
226 Marc Colombo RC 2.00 5.00
227 Phillip Buchanon RC 3.00 8.00
228 T.J. Duckett RC 3.00 8.00
229 Ron Johnson RC 2.50 6.00
230 Larry Tripplett RC 2.00 5.00
231 Randy Fasani RC 2.50 6.00
232 Keyuo Craver RC 2.00 5.00
233 Marquand Manuel RC 2.00 5.00
234 Jonathan Wells RC 3.00 8.00
235 Reche Caldwell RC 3.00 8.00
236 Luke Staley RC 2.00 5.00
237 Donte Stallworth RC 3.00 8.00
238 Levar Fisher RC 2.00 5.00
239 Lamar Gordon RC 2.50 6.00
240 William Green RC 2.50 6.00
241 Dusty Bonner RC 2.00 5.00
242 Craig Nall RC 2.50 6.00
243 Eric McCoo RC 2.00 5.00
244 David Thornton RC 2.00 5.00
245 Terry Jones RC 2.00 5.00
246 Lee Mays RC 2.00 5.00
247 Bryan Fletcher RC 2.00 5.00
248 Verron Haynes RC 2.00 5.00
249 Zak Kustok RC 2.00 5.00
250 Chad Hutchinson RC 2.00 5.00
251 Andra Davis RC 2.00 5.00
252 Wes Pate RC 2.00 5.00
253 Jon McGraw RC 2.00 5.00
254 Howard Green RC 2.00 5.00
255 Daryl Jones RC 2.00 5.00
256 David Priestley RC 2.00 5.00
257 Marques Anderson RC 2.50 6.00
258 Roosevelt Williams RC 2.00 5.00
259 Major Applewhite RC 3.00 8.00
260 Ronald Curry RC 2.50 6.00
261 Adrian Peterson RC 3.00 8.00
262 Tellis Redmon RC 2.00 5.00
263 Chester Taylor RC 3.00 8.00
264 Deion Branch RC 3.00 8.00
265 Tank Williams RC 2.50 6.00

2002 Topps Chrome Refractors

*VETS 1-165: 3X TO 8X BASIC CARDS
1-165 VET/599 ODDS 1:11 HOB/RET
1-165 STATED PRINT RUN 599 SER.#'d SETS
*ROOKIES 166-265: 1.2X TO 3X
166-265 ROOK/100 ODDS 1:109 HOB, 1:110 RET
166-265 STATED PRINT RUN 100 SER.#'d SETS

2002 Topps Chrome Gridiron Badges Jerseys

OVERALL ODDS 1:382 HOB, 1:384 RET
GBBF Brett Favre/200 15.00 40.00
GBCM Curtis Martin/200 6.00 15.00
GBDB David Boston/200 4.00 10.00
GBDC David Carr/50 8.00 20.00
GBDF Doug Flutie/100 6.00 15.00
GBDFO DeShaun Foster/100 6.00 15.00
GBDM Dan Marino/200 20.00 50.00
GBJG Jeff Garcia/100 5.00 12.00
GBJR Jerry Rice/150 12.00 30.00
GBKS Kordell Stewart/100 5.00 12.00
GBKW Kurt Warner/200 6.00 15.00
GBLT LaDainian Tomlinson/50 10.00 25.00
GBMF Marshall Faulk/50 8.00 20.00
GBMH Marvin Harrison/200 6.00 15.00
GBMS Michael Strahan/200 6.00 15.00
GBMW Marquise Walker/50 5.00 12.00
GBRL Ray Lewis/200 10.00 25.00
GBSY Steve Young/100 10.00 25.00
GBTB Tom Brady/200 15.00 40.00
GBTBR Tim Brown/100 6.00 15.00
GBTO Terrell Owens/100 6.00 15.00

2002 Topps Chrome King of Kings Super Bowl MVP Jerseys

OVERALL ODDS 1:3643 HOB, 1:3760 RET
ALL CARDS FEATURE REFRACTOR FRONTS
KDA Terrell Davis 25.00 60.00
Marcus Allen
KME Joe Montana 150.00 250.00
John Elway
KMR Joe Montana 175.00 350.00
Jerry Rice
KYR Steve Young 50.00 120.00
Jerry Rice

2002 Topps Chrome Own the Game

STATED ODDDS 1:8 HOB/RET
*REFRACT/100: 1X TO 2.5X BASIC INSERT
REFRACTOR/100 ODDS 1:364 H, 1:365 R
REFRACTOR PRINT RUN 100 SER.#'d SETS
OG1 Kurt Warner 1.25 3.00
OG2 Peyton Manning 2.50 6.00
OG3 Jeff Garcia 1.00 2.50
OG4 Brett Favre 3.00 8.00
OG5 Donovan McNabb 1.25 3.00
OG6 Rich Gannon 1.00 2.50
OG7 Tom Brady 3.00 8.00
OG8 Aaron Brooks 1.00 2.50
OG9 Priest Holmes 1.25 3.00
OG10 Curtis Martin 1.25 3.00
OG11 Stephen Davis 1.00 2.50
OG12 Ahman Green 1.00 2.50
OG13 Marshall Faulk 1.25 3.00
OG14 Shaun Alexander 1.00 2.50
OG15 Corey Dillon 1.00 2.50
OG16 Ricky Williams 1.00 2.50
OG17 David Boston .75 2.00
OG18 Marvin Harrison 1.25 3.00
OG19 Terrell Owens 1.25 3.00
OG20 Jimmy Smith 1.00 2.50
OG21 Torry Holt 1.25 3.00
OG22 Rod Smith 1.00 2.50
OG23 Keyshawn Johnson 1.00 2.50
OG24 Troy Brown 1.00 2.50
OG25 Michael Strahan 1.25 3.00
OG26 Ronald McKinnon .75 2.00
OG27 Ray Lewis 1.25 3.00
OG28 Zach Thomas 1.25 3.00
OG29 Ronde Barber 1.00 2.50
OG30 Anthony Henry .75 2.00

2002 Topps Chrome Pro Bowl Jerseys

STATED ODDS 1:109 HOB, 1:110 RET
PPAW Aeneas Williams 5.00 12.00
PPBD Brian Dawkins 6.00 15.00
PPDO Deltha O'Neal 4.00 10.00
PPJM Jamir Miller 4.00 10.00
PPLC Larry Centers 5.00 12.00
PPLG La'Roi Glover 4.00 10.00
PPRB Ruben Brown 4.00 10.00
PPRH Rodney Harrison 6.00 15.00
PPRP Robert Porcher 4.00 10.00
PPSK Sammy Knight 4.00 10.00

2002 Topps Chrome Ring of Honor

STATED ODDS 1:8 HOB/RET
*REF/100: 2X TO 5X BASIC INSERTS
REFRACTOR/100 STATED ODDS 1:312
REFRACTOR PRINT RUN 100 SER.#'d SETS
BS1 Bart Starr 2.50 6.00
BS2 Bart Starr 2.50 6.00
CH5 Chuck Howley .75 2.00
DH31 Desmond Howard 1.00 2.50
DJ37 Dexter Jackson 1.25 3.00
DW22 Doug Williams 1.00 2.50
ES28 Emmitt Smith 3.00 8.00
FB11 Fred Biletnikoff 1.25 3.00
FH9 Franco Harris 1.25 3.00
JE33 John Elway 2.50 6.00
JM16 Joe Montana 3.00 8.00
JM19 Joe Montana 3.00 8.00
JM24 Joe Montana 3.00 8.00
JN3 Joe Namath 2.00 5.00
JP15 Jim Plunkett 1.00 2.50
JR17 John Riggins 1.25 3.00
JR23 Jerry Rice 2.50 6.00
JS7 Jake Scott .75 2.00
KW34 Kurt Warner 1.25 3.00
LB30 Larry Brown .75 2.00
LC8 Larry Csonka 1.25 3.00
LD4 Len Dawson 1.25 3.00
MA18 Marcus Allen 1.25 3.00
MR26 Mark Rypien 1.00 2.50
OA25 Ottis Anderson .75 2.00
PS21 Phil Simms 1.00 2.50
RD20 Richard Dent 1.00 2.50
RL35 Ray Lewis 1.25 3.00
RS6 Roger Staubach 2.00 5.00
SY29 Steve Young 1.50 4.00
TA27 Troy Aikman 2.00 5.00
TB13 Terry Bradshaw 2.00 5.00
TB14 Terry Bradshaw 2.00 5.00
TB36 Tom Brady 3.00 8.00
TD32 Terrell Davis 1.25 3.00
WM12 Randy White 1.00 2.50

2002 Topps Chrome Super Bowl Goal Posts

STATED ODDS 1:437 HOB, 1:437 RET
ALL CARDS FEATURE REFRACTOR FRONTS
SBG1 Tom Brady 50.00 80.00
SBG2 Kurt Warner 15.00 40.00
SBG3 Antowain Smith 12.00 30.00
SBG4 Marshall Faulk 15.00 40.00
SBG5 Troy Brown 12.00 30.00
SBG6 Adam Vinatieri 35.00 60.00
SBG7 David Patten 10.00 25.00
SBG8 Torry Holt 15.00 40.00
SBG9 Ty Law 12.00 30.00
SBG10 Isaac Bruce 15.00 40.00

2002 Topps Chrome Terry Bradshaw Reprints

COMPLETE SET (14) 20.00 50.00
STATED ODDS 1:12 HOB/RET
*REFRACT/100: 1.2X TO 3X BASIC INSERT
REFRACTOR/100 ODDS 1:780 HOB, 1:783 RET
REFRACTOR PRINT RUN 100 SER.#'d SETS
*BLK.BORDER REFR/25: 3X TO 8X
BLACK BORD.REF/25.ODDS 1:3119 HOB, 1:3223 RET
BLK.BORDER PRINT RUN 25 SER.#'d SETS

2003 Topps Chrome

Released in September of 2003, this set consists of 275 cards including 165 veterans and 110 rookies. The rookies were inserted at a rate of 1:3. The URB1 card was inserted at a rate of 1:28040. Boxes contained 24 packs of 4 cards. Each box also contained one Xfractor parallel card, which was included in a silver foil pack, and was packaged in a hard plastic holder. Pack SRP was $3.

COMPLETE SET (275) 100.00 200.00
COMP.SET w/o SP's (165) 15.00 40.00
ROOKIE 166-275 ODDS 1:3
1 Michael Vick .60 1.50
2 Josh Reed .30 .75
3 James Stewart .30 .75
4 Quincy Morgan .30 .75
5 Corey Bradford .30 .75
6 Fred Taylor .40 1.00
7 David Patten .30 .75
8 Jerome Bettis .50 1.25
9 Jerry Porter .30 .75
10 Steve McNair .50 1.25
11 Stephen Davis .40 1.00
12 Frank Wycheck .30 .75
13 Marcus Pollard .30 .75
14 David Terrell .30 .75
15 Bubba Franks .40 1.00
16 Trent Green .40 1.00
17 Mark Brunell .40 1.00
18 James Thrash .30 .75
19 Mike Alstott .50 1.25
20 Deuce McAllister .40 1.00
21 Santana Moss .40 1.00
22 Jason Taylor .40 1.00
23 Corey Dillon .40 1.00
24 Jeff Blake .40 1.00
25 Ed McCaffrey .40 1.00
26 Priest Holmes .50 1.25
27 Tim Brown .50 1.25
28 Curtis Martin .50 1.25
29 Derrius Thompson .30 .75
30 Jonathan Wells .30 .75
31 William Green .30 .75
32 Bill Schroeder .30 .75
33 Amos Zereoue .30 .75
34 Warren Sapp .40 1.00
35 Koren Robinson .40 1.00
36 Donovan McNabb .50 1.25
37 Edgerrin James .50 1.25
38 Kelly Holcomb .30 .75
39 Daunte Culpepper .40 1.00
40 Tommy Maddox .40 1.00
41 Rod Gardner .30 .75
42 T.J. Duckett .40 1.00
43 Drew Bledsoe .50 1.25
44 Rod Smith .40 1.00
45 Peyton Manning 1.00 2.50
46 Darrell Jackson .40 1.00
47 Brett Favre 1.25 3.00
48 Ashley Lelie .30 .75
49 Jeremy Shockey .50 1.25
50 Hines Ward .50 1.25
51 Jeff Garcia .40 1.00
52 Eddie Kennison .30 .75
53 Brian Urlacher .50 1.25
54 Antwaan Randle El .40 1.00
55 Eddie George .40 1.00
56 Derrick Brooks .40 1.00
57 Isaac Bruce .50 1.25
58 Joe Horn .40 1.00
59 Jon Kitna .40 1.00
60 David Boston .30 .75
61 Todd Heap .40 1.00
62 Lamar Smith .40 1.00
63 Germane Crowell .30 .75
64 Kevin Johnson .30 .75
65 Drew Brees .50 1.25
66 Chad Lewis .40 1.00
67 Charlie Garner .40 1.00
68 Laveranues Coles .30 .75
69 Shaun Alexander .40 1.00
70 Kevan Barlow .30 .75
71 Aaron Brooks .40 1.00
72 Jake Plummer .40 1.00
73 Emmitt Smith 1.25 3.00
74 Terry Glenn .40 1.00
75 Michael Bennett .40 1.00
76 Deion Branch .40 1.00
77 Keyshawn Johnson .50 1.25
78 Marc Bulger .50 1.25
79 Matt Hasselbeck .40 1.00
80 Garrison Hearst .40 1.00
81 Brian Griese .40 1.00
82 Johnnie Morton .40 1.00
83 Patrick Ramsey .40 1.00
84 Donald Driver .50 1.25
85 Joey Harrington .30 .75
86 Ricky Williams .40 1.00
87 Jabar Gaffney .30 .75
88 Duce Staley .40 1.00
89 Jimmy Smith .40 1.00
90 Reggie Wayne .50 1.25
91 Chad Johnson .50 1.25
92 Steve Beuerlein .40 1.00
93 Joey Galloway .40 1.00
94 Curtis Conway .30 .75
95 Brad Johnson .40 1.00
96 Jamal Lewis .40 1.00
97 Terrell Owens .50 1.25
98 Todd Pinkston .30 .75
99 Keenan McCardell .40 1.00
100 Antonio Bryant .30 .75
101 Eric Moulds .40 1.00
102 Jim Miller .30 .75
103 Troy Brown .40 1.00
104 Rich Gannon .40 1.00
105 Chad Pennington .50 1.25
106 Michael Strahan .50 1.25
107 Chris Chambers .40 1.00
108 Antowain Smith .40 1.00
109 Derrick Mason .40 1.00
110 Michael Pittman .30 .75
111 Torry Holt .50 1.25
112 Tony Gonzalez .50 1.25
113 Marty Booker .40 1.00
114 Shannon Sharpe .50 1.25
115 Zach Thomas .50 1.25
116 Plaxico Burress .40 1.00
117 Kurt Warner .50 1.25
118 Warrick Dunn .40 1.00
119 Jay Fiedler .30 .75
120 LaMont Jordan .40 1.00
121 Kerry Collins .40 1.00
122 Jerry Rice 1.00 2.50
123 Randy Moss .50 1.25
124 Tom Brady 1.25 3.00
125 Amani Toomer .40 1.00
126 Travis Henry .30 .75
127 Chris Chandler .40 1.00
128 Ray Lewis .50 1.25
129 Donte Stallworth .30 .75
130 David Carr .40 1.00
131 Andre Davis .30 .75
132 Travis Taylor .30 .75
133 Steve Smith .50 1.25
134 Tiki Barber .50 1.25
135 Chad Hutchinson .30 .75
136 Marshall Faulk .50 1.25
137 Peerless Price .30 .75
138 Ahman Green .40 1.00
139 Julius Peppers .50 1.25
140 LaDainian Tomlinson .50 1.25
141 Muhsin Muhammad .40 1.00
142 Tim Couch .30 .75
143 Clinton Portis .40 1.00
144 Anthony Thomas .40 1.00
145 Marvin Harrison .50 1.25
146 Priest Holmes WW .40 1.00
147 Drew Bledsoe WW .40 1.00
148 Tom Brady WW 1.00 2.50
149 Shaun Alexander WW .30 .75
150 Brett Favre WW 1.00 2.50
151 Travis Henry WW .25 .60
152 Marshall Faulk WW .40 1.00
153 Terrell Owens WW .40 1.00
154 Jeff Garcia WW .30 .75
155 Plaxico Burress WW .30 .75
156 Donovan McNabb WW .40 1.00
157 Ricky Williams WW .30 .75
158 Michael Vick WW .50 1.25
159 Steve Smith WW .40 1.00
160 Marvin Harrison WW .40 1.00
161 Chad Pennington WW .40 1.00
162 Jeremy Shockey WW .40 1.00
163 Tommy Maddox WW .30 .75
164 Steve McNair WW .40 1.00
165 Rich Gannon WW .30 .75
166 Carson Palmer RC 4.00 10.00
167 J.R. Tolver RC 1.50 4.00
168 Michael Haynes RC 1.25 3.00
169 Terrell Suggs RC 2.00 5.00
170 Rashean Mathis RC 1.50 4.00
171 Chris Kelsay RC 1.50 4.00
172 Brad Banks RC 1.50 4.00
173 Jordan Gross RC 1.25 3.00
174 Lee Suggs RC 1.50 4.00
175 Kliff Kingsbury RC 1.50 4.00
176 William Joseph RC 1.25 3.00
177 Kelley Washington RC 1.25 3.00
178 Jerome McDougle RC 1.25 3.00
179 Keenan Howry RC 1.25 3.00
180 Chris Simms RC 2.00 5.00
181 Alonzo Jackson RC 1.25 3.00
182 L.J. Smith RC 2.00 5.00
183 Mike Doss RC 2.00 5.00
184 Bobby Wade RC 1.50 4.00
185 Ken Hamlin RC 2.00 5.00
186 Brandon Lloyd RC 3.00 8.00
187 Justin Fargas RC 2.00 5.00
188 DeWayne Robertson RC 1.50 4.00
189 Bryant Johnson RC 2.00 5.00
190 Boss Bailey RC 1.50 4.00
191 Onterrio Smith RC 1.25 3.00
192 Doug Gabriel RC 1.50 4.00
193 Jimmy Kennedy RC 1.50 4.00
194 B.J. Askew RC 1.50 4.00
195 Taylor Jacobs RC 1.25 3.00
196 Dallas Clark RC 3.00 8.00
197 DeWayne White RC 1.25 3.00
198 Arnaz Battle RC 2.00 5.00
199 Kareem Kelly RC 1.25 3.00
200 Talman Gardner RC 1.25 3.00
201 Billy McMullen RC 1.25 3.00
202 Travis Anglin RC 1.25 3.00
203 Anquan Boldin RC 3.00 8.00
204 Osi Umenyiora RC 2.50 6.00
205 Byron Leftwich RC 2.00 5.00
206 Marcus Trufant RC 1.50 4.00
207 Sam Aiken RC 1.50 4.00
208 LaBrandon Toefield RC 1.50 4.00
209 Terry Pierce RC 1.25 3.00
210 Charles Rogers RC 1.50 4.00
211 Chaun Thompson RC 1.25 3.00
212 Chris Brown RC 1.25 3.00
213 Justin Gage RC 1.50 4.00
214 Kevin Williams RC 2.00 5.00
215 Willis McGahee RC 2.50 6.00
216 Victor Hobson RC 1.25 3.00
217 Brian St.Pierre RC 1.50 4.00
218 Nate Burleson RC 1.50 4.00
219 Calvin Pace RC 1.50 4.00
220 Larry Johnson RC 3.00 8.00
221 Andre Woolfolk RC 1.50 4.00
222 Tyrone Calico RC 1.50 4.00
223 Seneca Wallace RC 2.00 5.00
224 Domanick Davis RC 1.50 4.00
225 Rex Grossman RC 2.00 5.00
226 Artose Pinner RC 1.25 3.00
227 Jason Witten RC 5.00 12.00
228 Bennie Joppru RC 1.25 3.00
229 Bethel Johnson RC 1.25 3.00
230 Kyle Boller RC 2.00 5.00
231 Shaun McDonald RC 1.50 4.00
232 Musa Smith RC 1.25 3.00
233 Ken Dorsey RC 1.50 4.00
234 Johnathan Sullivan RC 1.25 3.00
235 Andre Johnson RC 6.00 15.00
236 Nick Barnett RC 2.00 5.00
237 Teyo Johnson RC 1.50 4.00
238 Terence Newman RC 1.50 4.00
239 Kevin Curtis RC 2.00 5.00
240 Dave Ragone RC 1.25 3.00
241 Ty Warren RC 1.50 4.00
242 Walter Young RC 1.25 3.00
243 Kevin Walter RC 3.00 8.00
244 Carl Ford RC 1.25 3.00
245 Cecil Sapp RC 1.25 3.00
246 Sultan McCullough RC 1.25 3.00
247 Eugene Wilson RC 2.00 5.00
248 Ricky Manning RC 1.50 4.00
249 Andrew Williams RC 1.25 3.00
250 Juston Wood RC 1.25 3.00
251 Cory Redding RC 1.50 4.00
252 Charles Tillman RC 2.50 6.00
253 Terrence Edwards RC 1.25 3.00
254 Adrian Madise RC 1.25 3.00
255 David Kircus RC 2.00 5.00
256 Zuriel Smith RC 1.25 3.00
257 Earnest Graham RC 2.00 5.00
258 Ronald Bellamy RC 1.50 4.00
259 John Anderson RC 1.25 3.00
260 David Tyree RC 2.00 5.00
261 Malaefou MacKenzie RC 1.25 3.00
262 Ahmaad Galloway RC 1.50 4.00
263 Brooks Bollinger RC 1.50 4.00
264 Gibran Hamdan RC 1.25 3.00
265 Taco Wallace RC 1.25 3.00
266 LaTarence Dunbar RC 1.25 3.00
267 Justin Griffith RC 1.50 4.00
268 Bradie James RC 2.00 5.00
269 Danny Curley RC 1.25 3.00
270 Kenny Peterson RC 1.50 4.00
271 DeAndrew Rubin RC 1.25 3.00
272 Ryan Hoag RC 1.25 3.00
273 Rien Long RC 1.25 3.00
274 Troy Polamalu RC 25.00 50.00
275 Terrence Holt RC 1.50 4.00
URB1 Emmitt Smith JSY/25 200.00 350.00
Walter Payton JSY
Barry Sanders JSY

2003 Topps Chrome Black Refractors

*VETS 1-165: 2.5X TO 6X BASIC CARDS
1-165 VETERAN/599 ODDS 1:12
STATED PRINT RUN 599 SER.#'d SETS
*ROOKIES 166-275: 2X TO 5X
166-275 ROOKIE/100 ODDS 1:108
ROOKIES PRINT RUN 100 SER.#'d SETS
274 Troy Polamalu 150.00 250.00

2003 Topps Chrome Gold Xfractors

*VETS 1-165: 4X TO 10X BASIC CARDS
*ROOKIES 166-275: 1.5X TO 4X
GOLD XFRACT/101: ONE PER HOB BOX
STATED PRINT RUN 101 SER.#'d SETS
274 Troy Polamalu 150.00 250.00

2003 Topps Chrome Gridiron Badges Jerseys

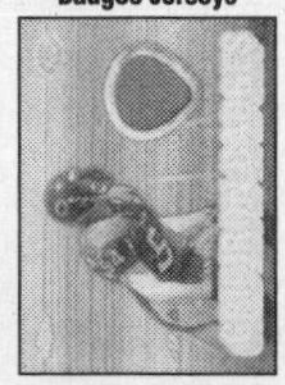

JERSEY/75 ODDS 1:674
GBBF Bubba Franks 6.00 15.00
GBBU Brian Urlacher 8.00 20.00
GBCB Champ Bailey 8.00 20.00
GBCD Corey Dillon 6.00 15.00
GBDB Drew Bledsoe 8.00 20.00
GBEM Eric Moulds 6.00 15.00
GBES Emmitt Smith 20.00 50.00
GBHW Hines Ward 8.00 20.00
GBJA John Abraham 6.00 15.00
GBJG Jeff Garcia 6.00 15.00
GBJH Joe Horn 6.00 15.00
GBJL John Lynch 6.00 15.00
GBJR Jerry Rice 15.00 40.00
GBJS Jeremy Shockey 8.00 20.00
GBJT Jason Taylor 6.00 15.00
GBMF Marshall Faulk 8.00 20.00
GBMH Marvin Harrison 8.00 20.00
GBMS Michael Strahan 8.00 20.00
GBPM Peyton Manning 15.00 40.00
GBRG Rich Gannon 6.00 15.00
GBRW Ricky Williams 6.00 15.00
GBRWO Rod Woodson 8.00 20.00
GBTD Todd Heap 6.00 15.00
GBTO Terrell Owens 8.00 20.00

2003 Topps Chrome Pro Bowl Jerseys

STATED ODDS 1:84
PBCB Champ Bailey 4.00 10.00
PBDB Drew Bledsoe 4.00 10.00
PBEM Eric Moulds 3.00 8.00
PBJL John Lynch 3.00 8.00
PBJP Julian Peterson 2.50 6.00
PBJS Jeremy Shockey 4.00 10.00
PBJT Jason Taylor 3.00 8.00
PBLG La'Roi Glover 2.50 6.00
PBMF Marshall Faulk 4.00 10.00
PBPM Peyton Manning 8.00 20.00
PBRW Rod Woodson 4.00 10.00
PBTL Ty Law 5.00 12.00

2003 Topps Chrome Record Breakers

COMPLETE SET (29) 20.00 50.00
STATED ODDS 1:8
*REFRACTOR/100: 1.5X TO 4X
REFRACTOR/100 ODDS 1:408
REFRACTOR PRINT RUN 100 SER.#'d SETS
RB1 Barry Sanders 2.50 6.00
RB2 Brett Favre 3.00 8.00
RB3 Brian Mitchell .75 2.00
RB4 Bruce Matthews 1.00 2.50
RB5 Clinton Portis 1.00 2.50
RB6 Corey Dillon 1.00 2.50
RB7 Dan Marino 3.00 8.00
RB8 Derrick Mason 1.00 2.50
RB9 Emmitt Smith 3.00 8.00
RB10 Jason Elam 1.00 2.50
RB11 Jason Taylor 1.00 2.50
RB12 Jerry Rice 2.50 6.00
RB13 Jimmy Smith 1.00 2.50
RB14 Terrell Owens 1.25 3.00
RB15 John Elway 3.00 8.00
RB16 LaDainian Tomlinson 1.25 3.00
RB17 Lawrence Taylor 1.25 3.00
RB18 Randy Moss 1.25 3.00
RB19 Marshall Faulk 1.25 3.00
RB20 Marvin Harrison 1.25 3.00
RB21 Michael Strahan 1.25 3.00
RB22 Peyton Manning 2.50 6.00
RB23 Priest Holmes 1.25 3.00
RB24 Rich Gannon 1.00 2.50
RB25 Ricky Williams 1.00 2.50
RB26 Rod Woodson 1.25 3.00
RB27 Jevon Kearse 1.00 2.50

RB28 Tim Brown 1.25 3.00
RB29 Chris McAlister 1.00 2.50

2003 Topps Chrome Record Breakers Jerseys

JERSEY/75 STATED ODDS 1:1467
STATED PRINT RUN 75 SER.#'d SETS
RBRBS Barry Sanders 15.00 40.00
RBRDM Dan Marino 30.00 80.00
RBRES Emmitt Smith 20.00 50.00
RBRJE John Elway 30.00 80.00
RBRJR Jerry Rice 15.00 40.00
RBRKW Kurt Warner 8.00 20.00
RBRLT LaDainian Tomlinson 8.00 20.00
RBRMF Marshall Faulk 8.00 20.00
RBRRW Ricky Williams 6.00 15.00
RBRSY Steve Young 15.00 40.00
RBRWP Walter Payton 50.00 120.00

2003 Topps Chrome Record Breakers Jerseys Duals

STATED ODDS 1:6425
STATED PRINT RUN 25 SER.#'d SETS
RDRDT Corey Dillon 20.00 50.00
LaDainian Tomlinson
RDRFW Marshall Faulk 20.00 50.00
Ricky Williams
RDRME Dan Marino 60.00 150.00
John Elway
RDRPS Walter Payton 100.00 200.00
Emmitt Smith
RDRSP Barry Sanders 100.00 200.00
Walter Payton
RDRSR Emmitt Smith 75.00 150.00
Jerry Rice
RDRSS Barry Sanders 50.00 120.00
Emmitt Smith
RDRYE Steve Young 50.00 120.00
John Elway

2004 Topps Chrome

Topps Chrome initially released in mid-September 2004. The base set consists of 275-cards including 110-rookies. Hobby boxes contained 24-packs of 8-cards and carried an S.R.P. of $3 per pack. Three very popular parallel sets and a variety of inserts can be found seeded in packs highlighted by the Premium Performers Autographed Jersey inserts.

COMPLETE SET (275) 100.00 200.00
COMP.SET w/o SP's (165) 12.50 30.00
ROOKIE STATED ODDS 1:2
1 Peyton Manning .75 2.00
2 Patrick Ramsey .30 .75
3 Justin McCareins .25 .60
4 Matt Hasselbeck .30 .75
5 Chris Chambers .30 .75
6 Bubba Franks .25 .60
7 Eric Moulds .30 .75
8 Anquan Boldin .40 1.00
9 Brian Urlacher .40 1.00
10 Stephen Davis .30 .75
11 Michael Vick .50 1.25
12 Dante Hall .30 .75
13 Chad Pennington .40 1.00
14 Kevan Barlow .25 .60
15 Tommy Maddox .30 .75
16 Domanick Davis .25 .60
17 Dwight Freeney .30 .75
18 LaVar Arrington .30 .75
19 Troy Hambrick .25 .60
20 Jake Plummer .30 .75
21 Willis McGahee .40 1.00
22 Steve McNair .40 1.00
23 Kerry Collins .30 .75
24 Hines Ward .40 1.00
25 Terrell Owens .40 1.00
26 Jerome Pathon .25 .60
27 Andre Johnson .40 1.00
28 DeShaun Foster .30 .75
29 Terrell Suggs .30 .75
30 Marcel Shipp .25 .60
31 Kyle Boller .30 .75
32 Javon Walker .25 .60
33 Ahman Green .30 .75
34 Travis Henry .25 .60
35 Randy McMichael .25 .60
36 Jerry Rice .75 2.00
37 Travis Taylor .25 .60
38 Fred Taylor .30 .75
39 Zach Thomas .40 1.00
40 Marques Tuiasosopo .25 .60
41 Laveranues Coles .25 .60
42 Thomas Jones .40 1.00
43 Jamie Sharper .25 .60
44 Quincy Morgan .25 .60
45 Troy Brown .30 .75
46 Joey Galloway .30 .75
47 Justin Fargas .30 .75
48 Daunte Culpepper .30 .75
49 Keenan McCardell .25 .60
50 Priest Holmes .40 1.00
51 Chad Johnson .40 1.00
52 Marty Booker .30 .75
53 Tim Rattay .25 .60
54 Brian Westbrook .40 1.00
55 Ricky Williams .30 .75
56 Lee Suggs .30 .75
57 Keith Brooking .25 .60
58 Rex Grossman .30 .75
59 Dallas Clark .40 1.00
60 Charles Rogers .25 .60
61 Donte' Stallworth .25 .60
62 Deion Branch .30 .75
63 Ike Hilliard .30 .75
64 Michael Strahan .40 1.00
65 Randy Moss .40 1.00
66 Isaac Bruce .30 .75
67 Brad Johnson .30 .75
68 Warrick Dunn .30 .75
69 Josh McCown .30 .75
70 Donovan McNabb .40 1.00
71 Shaun Alexander .30 .75
72 William Green .25 .60
73 Carson Palmer .40 1.00
74 Quentin Griffin .25 .60
75 LaDainian Tomlinson .40 1.00
76 Edgerrin James .30 .75
77 Santana Moss .30 .75
78 Marshall Faulk .40 1.00
79 Tyrone Calico .30 .75
80 Marvin Harrison .40 1.00
81 Tony Gonzalez .40 1.00
82 Deuce McAllister .30 .75
83 Drew Brees .40 1.00
84 Todd Pinkston .25 .60
85 Jeff Garcia .30 .75
86 Darrell Jackson .30 .75
87 Ray Lewis .40 1.00
88 Billy Volek .25 .60
89 Rudi Johnson .30 .75
90 Julius Peppers .30 .75
91 Peter Warrick .30 .75
92 Trent Green .30 .75
93 Onterrio Smith .25 .60
94 Jerome Bettis .40 1.00
95 Keyshawn Johnson .30 .75
96 Jamal Lewis .30 .75
97 Alge Crumpler .30 .75
98 Michael Bennett .30 .75
99 Jimmy Smith .30 .75
100 Brett Favre 1.00 2.50
101 Jerry Porter .25 .60
102 Marc Bulger .30 .75
103 David Carr .25 .60
104 Mark Brunell .30 .75
105 Aaron Brooks .30 .75
106 Plaxico Burress .30 .75
107 Correll Buckhalter .30 .75
108 Jevon Kearse .30 .75
109 Michael Pittman .30 .75
110 Clinton Portis .40 1.00
111 Corey Dillon .30 .75
112 Steve Smith .40 1.00
113 Eddie Kennison .30 .75
114 Amani Toomer .30 .75
115 Kelly Holcomb .25 .60
116 Torry Holt .30 .75
117 Eddie George .30 .75
118 Jeremy Shockey .30 .75
119 Jon Kitna .30 .75
120 Todd Heap .30 .75
121 Ashley Lelie .25 .60
122 Byron Leftwich .30 .75
123 Duce Staley .30 .75
124 Rod Gardner .25 .60
125 Tom Brady .75 2.00
126 Reggie Wayne .40 1.00
127 Joe Horn .30 .75
128 Curtis Martin .40 1.00
129 Charlie Garner .30 .75
130 Derrick Mason .30 .75
131 Marcus Robinson .25 .60
132 David Boston .25 .60
133 Drew Bledsoe .40 1.00
134 Anthony Thomas .30 .75
135 Tiki Barber .40 1.00
136 Terry Glenn .30 .75
137 A.J. Feeley .25 .60
138 Peerless Price .25 .60
139 Jake Delhomme .30 .75
140 Kevin Faulk .30 .75
141 Quincy Carter .25 .60
142 Joey Harrington .30 .75
143 Donald Driver .40 1.00
144 Koren Robinson .25 .60
145 Rod Smith .30 .75
146 Anquan Boldin WW .25 .60
147 Jamal Lewis WW .20 .50
148 Priest Holmes WW .25 .60
149 Peyton Manning WW .50 1.25
150 Marvin Harrison WW .25 .60
151 Steve McNair WW .25 .60
152 Travis Henry WW .15 .40
153 Torry Holt WW .20 .50
154 Tom Brady WW .50 1.25
155 Ahman Green WW .20 .50
156 Donovan McNabb WW .25 .60
157 Deuce McAllister WW .20 .50
158 Domanick Davis WW .15 .40
159 Clinton Portis WW .25 .60
160 Rudi Johnson WW .20 .50
161 Brett Favre WW .60 1.50
162 LaDainian Tomlinson WW .25 .60
163 Steve Smith WW .25 .60
164 Edgerrin James WW .20 .50
165 Ty Law WW .20 .50
166 Ben Roethlisberger RC 15.00 40.00
167 Ahmad Carroll RC 1.25 3.00
168 Johnnie Morant RC 1.25 3.00
169 Greg Jones RC 1.25 3.00
170 Michael Clayton RC 1.50 4.00
171 Josh Harris RC 1.25 3.00
172 Tatum Bell RC 1.50 4.00
173 Robert Gallery RC 2.00 5.00
174 B.J. Symons RC 1.25 3.00
175 Roy Williams RC 2.00 5.00
176 DeAngelo Hall RC 2.00 5.00
177 Jeff Smoker RC 1.50 4.00
178 Lee Evans RC 2.00 5.00
179 Michael Jenkins RC 2.00 5.00
180 Steven Jackson RC 3.00 8.00
181 Will Smith RC 1.50 4.00
182 Vince Wilfork RC 2.00 5.00
183 Ben Troupe RC 1.50 4.00
184 Chris Gamble RC 1.50 4.00
185 Kevin Jones RC 1.50 4.00
186 Jonathan Vilma RC 2.00 5.00
187 Dontarrious Thomas RC 1.50 4.00
188 Michael Boulware RC 2.00 5.00
189 Mewelde Moore RC 1.50 4.00
190 Drew Henson RC 1.25 3.00
191 D.J. Williams RC 2.00 5.00
192 Ernest Wilford RC 1.50 4.00
193 John Navarre RC 1.25 3.00
194 Jerricho Cotchery RC 1.50 4.00
195 Derrick Hamilton RC 1.25 3.00
196 Carlos Francis RC 1.25 3.00
197 Ben Watson RC 2.00 5.00
198 Reggie Williams RC 1.50 4.00
199 Devard Darling RC 1.25 3.00
200 Chris Perry RC 1.50 4.00
201 Derrick Strait RC 1.25 3.00
202 Sean Taylor RC 4.00 10.00
203 Michael Turner RC 2.50 6.00
204 Keary Colbert RC 1.25 3.00
205 Eli Manning RC 12.00 30.00
206 Julius Jones RC 1.50 4.00
207 Jason Babin RC 2.00 5.00
208 Cody Pickett RC 1.50 4.00
209 Kenechi Udeze RC 1.50 4.00
210 Rashaun Woods RC 1.25 3.00
211 Matt Schaub RC 4.00 10.00
212 Tommie Harris RC 2.00 5.00
213 Dwan Edwards RC 1.25 3.00
214 Shawn Andrews RC 1.50 4.00
215 Larry Fitzgerald RC 5.00 12.00
216 P.K. Sam RC 1.25 3.00
217 Teddy Lehman RC 1.25 3.00
218 Darius Watts RC 1.25 3.00
219 D.J. Hackett RC 1.50 4.00
220 Cedric Cobbs RC 1.25 3.00
221 Antwan Odom RC 1.50 4.00
222 Marquise Hill RC 1.25 3.00
223 Luke McCown RC 1.50 4.00
224 Triandos Luke RC 1.25 3.00
225 Kellen Winslow RC 2.00 5.00
226 Derek Abney RC 1.25 3.00
227 Chris Cooley RC 2.00 5.00
228 Dunta Robinson RC 1.25 3.00
229 Sean Jones RC 1.50 4.00
230 Philip Rivers RC 8.00 20.00
231 Craig Krenzel RC 1.50 4.00
232 Daryl Smith RC 1.25 3.00
233 Samie Parker RC 1.25 3.00
234 Ben Hartsock RC 1.25 3.00
235 J.P. Losman RC 1.50 4.00
236 Karlos Dansby RC 2.00 5.00
237 Ricardo Colclough RC 1.50 4.00
238 Bernard Berrian RC 2.00 5.00
239 Junior Siavii RC 1.25 3.00
240 Devery Henderson RC 2.00 5.00
241 Adimchinobe Echemandu RC 1.50 4.00
242 Patrick Crayton RC 2.00 5.00
243 Marcus Tubbs RC 1.25 3.00
244 Jamaar Taylor RC 1.25 3.00
245 Andy Hall RC 1.25 3.00
246 Darnell Dockett RC 1.25 3.00
247 Darrion Scott RC 1.50 4.00
248 Jim Sorgi RC 1.50 4.00
249 Jeff Dugan RC 1.25 3.00
250 Ryan Krause RC 1.25 3.00
251 Nate Lawrie RC 1.25 3.00
252 Casey Bramlet RC 1.25 3.00
253 Donnell Washington RC 1.50 4.00
254 Jonathan Smith RC 1.25 3.00
255 Tank Johnson RC 1.25 3.00
256 Keith Smith RC 1.25 3.00
257 Brandon Miree RC 1.25 3.00
258 Michael Gaines RC 1.25 3.00
259 Keiwan Ratliff RC 1.25 3.00
260 Stuart Schweigert RC 1.50 4.00
261 Derrick Ward RC 2.00 5.00
262 Matt Ware RC 2.00 5.00
263 Tim Anderson RC 1.50 4.00
264 Bradlee Van Pelt RC 1.50 4.00
265 Shawntae Spencer RC 1.25 3.00
266 Joey Thomas RC 1.25 3.00
267 Maurice Mann RC 1.25 3.00
268 Tim Euhus RC 1.25 3.00
269 Matt Mauck RC 1.25 3.00
270 Sloan Thomas RC 1.50 4.00
271 Jeris McIntyre RC 1.25 3.00
272 Randy Starks RC 1.25 3.00
273 Clarence Moore RC 1.25 3.00
274 Drew Carter RC 1.50 4.00
275 Sean Ryan RC 1.25 3.00
RH38 Tom Brady RH 2.00 5.00

2004 Topps Chrome Black Refractors

*VETS: 5X TO 12X BASIC CARDS
*ROOKIES: 2X TO 5X BASIC CARDS
BLACK REF/100 ODDS 1:45 HOB, 1:46 RET
STATED PRINT RUN 100 SER.#'d SETS
166 Ben Roethlisberger 125.00 250.00
205 Eli Manning 125.00 250.00

2004 Topps Chrome Gold Xfractors

*ROOKIES: 1.2X TO 3X BASIC CARDS
ONE PER HOBBY BOX
STATED PRINT RUN 279 SER.#'d SETS
166 Ben Roethlisberger 60.00 120.00
170AU Michael Clayton AU/250 15.00 40.00
172 Tatum Bell AU/250 10.00 25.00
186 Jonathan Vilma AU/250 12.50 30.00
203 Michael Turner AU/250 30.00 80.00
205 Eli Manning 75.00 150.00
216 P.K. Sam AU/250 12.50 30.00

2004 Topps Chrome Refractors

*VETS: 2.5X TO 6X BASIC CARDS
*ROOKIES: .8X TO 2X BASIC CARDS
STATED ODDS 1:6 HOB/RET
RH38 STATED ODDS 1:12,581H, 1:13,248R
166 Ben Roethlisberger 40.00 100.00
205 Eli Manning 50.00 100.00
RH38 Tom Brady RH/100 15.00 40.00

2004 Topps Chrome Gridiron Badges Jerseys

STATED ODDS 1:1707 HOB, 1:1816 RET
STATED PRINT RUN 50 SER.#'d SETS
GBAB Anquan Boldin 8.00 20.00
GBAG Ahman Green 6.00 15.00
GBBU Brian Urlacher 8.00 20.00
GBCJ Chad Johnson 8.00 20.00
GBHW Hines Ward 8.00 20.00
GBJL Jamal Lewis 6.00 15.00
GBLA LaVar Arrington 8.00 20.00
GBMH Marvin Harrison 8.00 20.00
GBPH Priest Holmes 8.00 20.00
GBPM Peyton Manning 15.00 40.00
GBRL Ray Lewis 8.00 20.00
GBSM Steve McNair 8.00 20.00
GBTH Torry Holt 6.00 15.00

2004 Topps Chrome Premiere Prospects

COMPLETE SET (20) 25.00 50.00
STATED ODDS 1:6 HOB/RET
*REFRACTOR/100: 2X TO 5X BASIC INSERTS
REFRACTOR STATED ODDS 1:627H, 1:629R
REFRACTOR PRINT RUN 100 SER.#'d SETS
PP1 Ben Roethlisberger 6.00 15.00
PP2 Chris Perry .75 2.00
PP3 Darius Watts .60 1.50
PP4 Devery Henderson 1.00 2.50
PP5 Eli Manning 6.00 15.00
PP6 Greg Jones .60 1.50
PP7 J.P. Losman .75 2.00
PP8 Julius Jones .75 2.00
PP9 Kellen Winslow 1.00 2.50
PP10 Kevin Jones .75 2.00
PP11 Larry Fitzgerald 2.50 6.00
PP12 Lee Evans 1.00 2.50
PP13 Michael Clayton .75 2.00
PP14 Michael Jenkins 1.00 2.50
PP15 Philip Rivers 4.00 10.00
PP16 Rashaun Woods .60 1.50
PP17 Reggie Williams .75 2.00
PP18 Roy Williams WR 1.00 2.50
PP19 Steven Jackson 1.50 4.00
PP20 Tatum Bell .75 2.00

2004 Topps Chrome Premium Performers Jersey Autographs

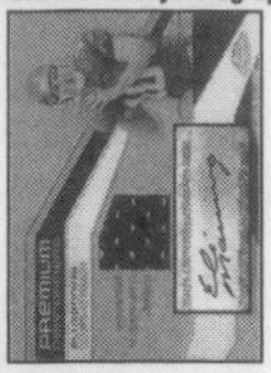

GROUP A/50 ODDS 1:25,611 H, 1:27,648 R
GROUP B/100 ODDS 1:3187 H, 1:3170 R
UNPRICED GOLD/10 1:27,581H, 1:32,496R
PPCP Chad Pennington/50 20.00 50.00
PPEM Eli Manning/100 175.00 300.00
PPMV Michael Vick/100 30.00 60.00
PPPM Peyton Manning/100 75.00 150.00
PPRW Roy Williams WR/100 20.00 50.00

2004 Topps Chrome Pro Bowl Jerseys

GROUP A STATED ODDS 1:1260H, 1:1273R
GROUP B STATED ODDS 1:965 H, 1:984 R
GROUP C STATED ODDS 1:89 H, 1:89 R
AB Anquan Boldin C 5.00 12.00
AO Adewale Ogunleye C 4.00 10.00
CB Champ Bailey B 5.00 12.00
DF Dwight Freeney C 4.00 10.00
DH Dante Hall C 4.00 10.00
JL Jamal Lewis C 4.00 10.00
KB Keith Brooking B 4.00 10.00
LL Leonard Little B 4.00 10.00
RL Ray Lewis C 5.00 12.00
SD Stephen Davis C 4.00 10.00
SE Shaun Ellis B 4.00 10.00
TH Todd Heap C 4.00 10.00
TL Ty Law A 4.00 10.00
ZT Zach Thomas C 5.00 12.00

2005 Topps Chrome

This 275-card set was released in September, 2005. The set was issued through the hobby in four-card packs with an $3 SRP which came 24 packs to a box. Cards numbered 1-145 featured veterans, while cards 146-155 are a league leader subset and cards numbered 156-165 is a golden moment subset. This set concludes with a rookie subset (166-275). The rookie cards were issued at a stated rate of one in two hobby or retail packs.

COMPLETE SET (275) 75.00 150.00
COMP.SET w/o RC's (165) 12.50 30.00
ROOKIE STATED ODDS 1:2 HOB/RET
RH STATED ODDS 1:288 HOB/RET
RH REFRACT.ODDS 1:17,884 H, 1:22,080 R
1 Deuce McAllister .30 .75
2 Sean Taylor .40 1.00
3 Koren Robinson .25 .60
4 Tiki Barber .40 1.00
5 LaDainian Tomlinson .40 1.00
6 Lee Evans .30 .75
7 Aaron Brooks .25 .60
8 LaMont Jordan .30 .75
9 Dante Hall .25 .60
10 Daunte Culpepper .30 .75
11 Thomas Jones .40 1.00
12 Warrick Dunn .30 .75
13 Willis McGahee .40 1.00
14 Ed Reed .30 .75
15 Derrick Mason .30 .75
16 Jason Witten .40 1.00
17 Chad Johnson .30 .75
18 Amani Toomer .30 .75
19 Joey Harrington .30 .75
20 Brian Urlacher .40 1.00
21 Brian Westbrook .30 .75
22 Matt Hasselbeck .30 .75
23 Michael Vick .40 1.00
24 Kevin Jones .25 .60
25 Julius Peppers .30 .75
26 Michael Clayton .25 .60
27 Javon Walker .25 .60
28 Santana Moss .30 .75
29 Travis Henry .25 .60
30 Stephen Davis .30 .75
31 Larry Johnson .30 .75
32 Terrell Owens .40 1.00
33 Ray Lewis .40 1.00
34 Jake Plummer .30 .75
35 Philip Rivers .40 1.00
36 Eli Manning .60 1.50
37 Tedy Bruschi .40 1.00
38 Adam Vinatieri .40 1.00
39 J.P. Losman .25 .60
40 Zach Thomas .40 1.00
41 Deion Branch .25 .60
42 Andre Johnson .40 1.00
43 Marshall Faulk .40 1.00
44 Bertrand Berry .25 .60
45 Terrell Suggs .30 .75
46 Tom Brady .75 2.00
47 Ashley Lelie .25 .60
48 Jonathan Wells .25 .60
49 Randy McMichael .25 .60
50 Charles Rogers .25 .60
51 Larry Fitzgerald .40 1.00
52 Hines Ward .40 1.00
53 Jason Taylor .30 .75
54 Ronde Barber .30 .75
55 T.J. Houshmandzadeh .30 .75
56 Keary Colbert .25 .60
57 DeAngelo Hall .30 .75
58 Chris Brown .25 .60
59 Chris Perry .25 .60
60 Steven Jackson .40 1.00
61 Kyle Boller .30 .75
62 Rudi Johnson .30 .75
63 Roy Williams S .25 .60
64 Onterrio Smith .25 .60
65 Roy Williams WR .30 .75
66 Jerry Porter .25 .60
67 Edgerrin James .30 .75
68 Randy Moss .40 1.00
69 Brian Griese .30 .75
70 Donovan McNabb .40 1.00
71 Joe Horn .30 .75
72 Muhsin Muhammad .30 .75
73 Johnnie Morton .30 .75
74 Chad Pennington .40 1.00
75 Torry Holt .30 .75
76 Marc Bulger .30 .75
77 Duce Staley .30 .75
78 Todd Heap .30 .75
79 Lee Suggs .25 .60
80 Patrick Ramsey .30 .75
81 Drew Bennett .30 .75
82 Michael Strahan .40 1.00
83 Priest Holmes .30 .75
84 DeShaun Foster .30 .75
85 Corey Dillon .30 .75
86 Antonio Gates .40 1.00
87 Trent Green .30 .75
88 Brandon Stokley .25 .60
89 Alge Crumpler .30 .75
90 Keyshawn Johnson .30 .75
91 Byron Leftwich .30 .75
92 Dunta Robinson .25 .60
93 Ben Roethlisberger .60 1.50
94 Rod Smith .30 .75
95 Robert Gallery .25 .60
96 Tony Gonzalez .30 .75
97 Steve McNair .40 1.00
98 Jeremy Shockey .40 1.00
99 Dominic Rhodes .30 .75
100 Michael Jenkins .30 .75
101 Jake Delhomme .30 .75
102 Jerome Bettis .40 1.00
103 Jevon Kearse .30 .75
104 Plaxico Burress .30 .75
105 Dwight Freeney .30 .75
106 Marcus Robinson .25 .60
107 Rex Grossman .30 .75
108 Drew Henson .25 .60
109 Julius Jones .25 .60
110 Jamal Lewis .30 .75
111 Justin McCareins .25 .60
112 Billy Volek .25 .60
113 Curtis Martin .40 1.00
114 Tatum Bell .25 .60
115 Domanick Davis .25 .60
116 Marvin Harrison .40 1.00
117 Anquan Boldin .30 .75
118 Jimmy Smith .30 .75
119 Drew Brees .40 1.00
120 Donte Stallworth .25 .60
121 Nate Burleson .25 .60
122 Fred Taylor .30 .75
123 Takeo Spikes .25 .60
124 Jonathan Ogden .25 .60
125 Michael Bennett .30 .75
126 Clinton Portis .30 .75
127 Ahman Green .30 .75
128 Drew Bledsoe .40 1.00
129 Darrell Jackson .25 .60
130 Jonathan Vilma .30 .75
131 David Carr .25 .60
132 Champ Bailey .30 .75
133 Derrick Blaylock .25 .60
134 T.J. Duckett .25 .60
135 Shaun Alexander .30 .75
136 Peyton Manning .75 2.00
137 Isaac Bruce .30 .75
138 LaVar Arrington .30 .75
139 Brett Favre 1.00 2.50
140 Allen Rossum .25 .60
141 Eric Moulds .25 .60
142 Carson Palmer .40 1.00
143 Laveranues Coles .25 .60
144 Chester Taylor .30 .75
145 Reggie Wayne .40 1.00
146 Curtis Martin LL .30 .75
147 Daunte Culpepper LL .25 .60
148 Muhsin Muhammad LL .25 .60
149 Shaun Alexander LL .25 *60
150 Trent Green LL .25 .60
151 Joe Horn LL .25 .60
152 Corey Dillon LL .25 .60
153 Peyton Manning LL .60 1.50
154 Javon Walker LL .20 .50
155 Edgerrin James LL .25 .60
156 Jake Scott GM .20 .50
157 John Elway GM .60 1.50
158 Dwight Clark GM .25 .60
159 Lawrence Taylor GM .30 .75
160 Joe Namath GM .50 1.25
161 Richard Dent GM .25 .60
162 Peyton Manning GM .60 1.50
163 Don Maynard GM .25 .60
164 Joe Greene GM .30 .75
165 Roger Staubach GM .50 1.25
166 J.J. Arrington RC 1.50 4.00
167 Cedric Benson RC 2.00 5.00
168 Mark Bradley RC 1.25 3.00
169 Reggie Brown RC 1.25 3.00
170 Ronnie Brown RC 2.50 6.00
171 Jason Campbell RC 2.50 6.00
172 Maurice Clarett 1.25 3.00
173 Mark Clayton RC 1.50 4.00
174 Braylon Edwards RC 2.50 6.00
175 Ciatrick Fason RC 1.25 3.00
176 Charlie Frye RC 2.00 5.00
177 Frank Gore RC 3.00 8.00
178 David Greene RC 1.25 3.00
179 Vincent Jackson RC 2.50 6.00
180 Adam Jones RC 1.25 3.00
181 Matt Jones RC 1.50 4.00
182 Stefan LeFors RC 1.25 3.00
183 Heath Miller RC 2.50 6.00
184 Ryan Moats RC 1.25 3.00
185 Vernand Morency RC 1.25 3.00
186 Terrence Murphy RC 1.25 3.00
187 Kyle Orton RC 2.00 5.00
188 Roscoe Parrish RC 1.25 3.00
189 Courtney Roby RC 1.50 4.00
190 Aaron Rodgers RC 50.00 100.00
191 Carlos Rogers RC 2.00 5.00
192 Antrel Rolle RC 2.00 5.00
193 Eric Shelton RC 1.25 3.00
194 Alex Smith QB RC 6.00 15.00
195 Andrew Walter RC 1.50 4.00
196 Roddy White RC 2.50 6.00
197 Cadillac Williams RC 2.00 5.00
198 Mike Williams 2.00 5.00
199 Troy Williamson RC 1.50 4.00
200 Taylor Stubblefield RC 1.25 3.00
201 Dan Cody RC 1.50 4.00
202 David Pollack RC 1.50 4.00
203 Craig Bragg RC 1.25 3.00
204 Alvin Pearman RC 1.25 3.00
205 Marcus Maxwell RC 1.25 3.00
206 Brock Berlin RC 1.50 4.00
207 Khalif Barnes RC 1.25 3.00
208 Eric King RC 1.25 3.00
209 Alex Smith TE RC 1.25 3.00
210 Dante Ridgeway RC 1.25 3.00
211 Shaun Cody RC 1.50 4.00
212 Donte Nicholson RC 1.25 3.00
213 DeMarcus Ware RC 4.00 10.00
214 Lionel Gates RC 1.25 3.00
215 Fabian Washington RC 1.50 4.00
216 Brandon Jacobs RC 2.50 6.00
217 Noah Herron RC 1.25 3.00
218 Derrick Johnson RC 1.50 4.00
219 J.R. Russell RC 1.25 3.00
220 Adrian McPherson RC 1.25 3.00
221 Marcus Spears RC 1.50 4.00
222 Justin Miller RC 1.50 4.00
223 Marion Barber RC 2.00 5.00
224 Anthony Davis RC 1.25 3.00
225 Chad Owens RC 1.50 4.00
226 Craphonso Thorpe RC 1.25 3.00
227 Travis Johnson RC 1.25 3.00
228 Erasmus James RC 1.50 4.00
229 Mike Patterson RC 1.25 3.00
230 Airese Currie RC 1.25 3.00
231 Justin Tuck RC 2.50 6.00
232 Dan Orlovsky RC 2.00 5.00
233 Thomas Davis RC 1.25 3.00
234 Derek Anderson RC 1.50 4.00
235 Matt Roth RC 1.50 4.00
236 Chris Henry RC 2.00 5.00
237 Rasheed Marshall RC 1.50 4.00
238 Bryant McFadden RC 1.50 4.00
239 Darren Sproles RC 2.00 5.00
240 Fred Gibson RC 1.50 4.00
241 Barrett Ruud RC 2.00 5.00
242 Kelvin Hayden RC 1.50 4.00
243 Ryan Fitzpatrick RC 3.00 8.00
244 Patrick Estes RC 1.25 3.00
245 Zach Tuiasosopo RC 1.25 3.00
246 Luis Castillo RC 1.50 4.00
247 Lance Mitchell RC 1.50 4.00
248 Ronald Bartell RC 1.50 4.00
249 Jerome Mathis RC 2.00 5.00
250 Marlin Jackson RC 1.25 3.00
251 James Kilian RC 1.25 3.00
252 Roydell Williams RC 1.50 4.00
253 Joel Dreessen RC 1.50 4.00
254 Paris Warren RC 1.50 4.00
255 Dustin Fox RC 1.50 4.00
256 Ellis Hobbs RC 2.00 5.00
257 Mike Nugent RC 1.50 4.00
258 Channing Crowder RC 1.50 4.00
259 Kerry Rhodes RC 1.50 4.00
260 Jerome Collins RC 1.50 4.00
261 Stanford Routt RC 1.50 4.00
262 Madison Hedgecock RC 2.00 5.00
263 Rian Wallace RC 1.50 4.00
264 Larry Brackins RC 1.25 3.00
265 Manuel White RC 1.50 4.00
266 Corey Webster RC 1.50 4.00
267 Eric Moore RC 1.25 3.00
268 Kirk Morrison RC 2.00 5.00
269 Atiyyah Ellison RC 1.25 3.00
270 Travis Daniels RC 1.50 4.00
271 Boomer Grigsby RC 2.00 5.00
272 Alex Barron RC 1.25 3.00
273 Tab Perry RC 1.25 3.00
274 Cedric Houston RC 2.00 5.00
275 Kevin Burnett RC 1.50 4.00
RH39 Deion Branch RH 2.00 5.00
RH39R Deion Branch RHR/100 6.00 15.00

2005 Topps Chrome Black Refractors

*VETS/100: 5X TO 12X BASIC CARDS
*ROOKIES/100: 2X TO 5X BASIC RC
STATED ODDS 1:66 HOB/RET
STATED PRINT RUN 100 SER.#'d SETS
190 Aaron Rodgers 300.00 500.00

2005 Topps Chrome 50th Anniversary Retro Rookie Refractors

*RETRO GOLD/50: 4X TO 10X BASIC RC
STATED ODDS 1:724 HOB, 1:727 RET
STATED PRINT RUN 50 SER.#'d SETS
190 Aaron Rodgers 350.00 600.00

2005 Topps Chrome Gold Xfractors

*GOLD XFRACT/399: 1.2X TO 3X BASIC RC
ONE PER HOBBY BOX
STATED PRINT RUN 399 SER.#'d SETS
174 Braylon Edwards AU 40.00 80.00
183 Heath Miller AU 20.00 50.00
185 Vernand Morency AU 12.50 30.00
190 Aaron Rodgers AU 600.00 800.00
198 Mike Williams AU 20.00 50.00

2005 Topps Chrome Refractors

*VETERANS: 2.5X TO 6X BASIC CARDS
*ROOKIES: .8X TO 2X BASIC CARDS
STATED ODDS 1:6 HOB/RET

2005 Topps Chrome Golden Anniversary Glistening Gold

COMPLETE SET (15) 15.00 30.00
GOLDEN ANNIV. OVERALL ODDS 1:6
*REFRACTORS: 1.5X TO 4X BASIC INSERTS
GOLDEN ANN. REFRACTOR ODDS 1:364
REFRACTOR PRINT RUN 100 SER.#'d SETS
GG1 Priest Holmes 1.00 2.50
GG2 Michael Vick 1.25 3.00
GG3 Hines Ward 1.25 3.00
GG4 Terrell Owens 1.25 3.00
GG5 Randy Moss 1.25 3.00
GG6 Marvin Harrison 1.25 3.00
GG7 LaDainian Tomlinson 1.25 3.00
GG8 Donovan McNabb 1.25 3.00
GG9 Daunte Culpepper 1.00 2.50
GG10 Ahman Green 1.00 2.50
GG11 Shaun Alexander 1.00 2.50
GG12 Edgerrin James 1.00 2.50
GG13 Torry Holt 1.00 2.50
GG14 Clinton Portis 1.00 2.50
GG15 Jamal Lewis 1.00 2.50

2005 Topps Chrome Golden Anniversary Gold Nuggets

COMPLETE SET (10) 10.00 25.00
GOLDEN ANNIV. OVERALL ODDS 1:6
*REFRACTORS: 1.5X TO 4X BASIC INSERTS
GOLDEN ANN. REFRACTOR ODDS 1:364
REFRACTOR PRINT RUN 100 SER.#'d SETS
GN1 Curtis Martin 1.25 3.00
GN2 Brett Favre 3.00 8.00
GN3 Jerome Bettis 1.25 3.00
GN4 Tom Brady 2.50 6.00
GN5 Ray Lewis 1.25 3.00
GN6 Marshall Faulk 1.25 3.00
GN7 Michael Strahan 1.25 3.00
GN8 Peyton Manning 2.50 6.00
GN9 Tony Gonzalez 1.00 2.50
GN10 Jonathan Ogden .75 2.00

2005 Topps Chrome Golden Anniversary Golden Greats

COMPLETE SET (10) 15.00 30.00
GOLDEN ANNIV. OVERALL ODDS 1:6
*REFRACTORS: 1.5X TO 4X BASIC INSERTS
GOLDEN ANN. REFRACTOR ODDS 1:364
REFRACTOR PRINT RUN 100 SER.#'d SETS
GA1 Joe Montana 4.00 10.00
GA2 Joe Namath 2.50 6.00
GA3 Earl Campbell 1.50 4.00
GA4 Lawrence Taylor 1.50 4.00
GA5 John Elway 3.00 8.00
GA6 Barry Sanders 2.50 6.00
GA7 Jim Brown 2.00 5.00
GA8 Gale Sayers 2.00 5.00
GA9 Tony Dorsett 1.25 3.00
GA10 Ronnie Lott 1.25 3.00

2005 Topps Chrome Golden Anniversary Hidden Gold

COMPLETE SET (15) 15.00 30.00
GOLDEN ANNIV. OVERALL ODDS 1:6
*REFRACTORS: 1.5X TO 4X BASIC INSERTS
GOLDEN ANN. REFRACTOR ODDS 1:364
REFRACTOR PRINT RUN 100 SER.#'d SETS
HG1 Nate Burleson .75 2.00
HG2 Julius Jones .75 2.00
HG3 Eli Manning 2.00 5.00
HG4 Kevin Jones .75 2.00
HG5 Lee Evans 1.00 2.50
HG6 Ben Roethlisberger 2.00 5.00
HG7 Willis McGahee 1.25 3.00
HG8 Dunta Robinson .75 2.00
HG9 Chris Brown .75 2.00
HG10 Roy Williams WR 1.00 2.50
HG11 Steven Jackson 1.25 3.00
HG12 Carson Palmer 1.25 3.00
HG13 Antonio Gates 1.25 3.00
HG14 Chris Gamble .75 2.00
HG15 LaMont Jordan 1.00 2.50

2005 Topps Chrome Gridiron Badges Jerseys

GROUP A/50 ODDS 1:7409 H, 1:8544 R
GROUP B/100 ODDS 1:1075 H, 1:1132 R
GBAG Antonio Gates/100 8.00 20.00
GBAGR Ahman Green/100 6.00 15.00
GBAV Adam Vinatieri/50 10.00 25.00
GBCB Champ Bailey/100 6.00 15.00
GBCJ Chad Johnson/100 6.00 15.00
GBDB Drew Brees/100 8.00 20.00
GBDC Daunte Culpepper/100 6.00 15.00
GBDF Dwight Freeney/100 6.00 15.00
GBDM Donovan McNabb/100 8.00 20.00
GBJP Julius Peppers/100 6.00 15.00
GBJW Javon Walker/100 5.00 12.00
GBJWI Jason Witten/100 8.00 20.00
GBLA Larry Allen/100 6.00 15.00
GBLT LaDainian Tomlinson/50 10.00 25.00
GBMC Mark Clayton/50 8.00 20.00
GBMM Muhsin Muhammad/100 6.00 15.00
GBMV Michael Vick/50 10.00 25.00
GBPM Peyton Manning/100 15.00 40.00
GBRW Roy Williams S/50 6.00 15.00
GBTB Tom Brady/100 15.00 40.00
GBTBA Tiki Barber/100 8.00 20.00
GBTG Tony Gonzalez/100 6.00 15.00

2005 Topps Chrome Premium Performers Jersey Autographs

STATED ODDS 1:7740 H, 1:8544 R
STATED PRINT RUN 40 SER.#'d SETS
UNPRICED GOLD REFRACT.SER.#'d TO 10
PPBF Brett Favre 175.00 300.00
PPBS Barry Sanders 125.00 250.00
PPES Emmitt Smith 200.00 350.00
PPJR Jerry Rice 125.00 250.00
PPPM Peyton Manning 150.00 300.00
PPTB Tom Brady 175.00 300.00

2005 Topps Chrome Pro Bowl Jerseys

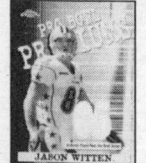

GROUP A ODDS 1:754 HOB/RET
GROUP B ODDS 1:258 HOB/RET
GROUP C ODDS 1:226 HOB/RET
GROUP D ODDS 1:335 HOB/RET
PBPAG Ahman Green B 5.00 12.00
PBPDM Donovan McNabb D 6.00 15.00
PBPJF James Farrior C 5.00 12.00
PBPJP Joey Porter B 6.00 15.00
PBPJT Jason Taylor A 3.00 8.00
PBPJW Jason Witten C 4.00 10.00
PBPJWA Javon Walker B 4.00 10.00
PBPKB Keith Brooking B 3.00 8.00
PBPKM Kevin Mawae C 3.00 8.00
PBPLA Larry Allen D 4.00 10.00
PBPMV Michael Vick C 7.50 20.00

PBPNC Nate Clements A	4.00	10.00
PBPRW Roy Williams S C	5.00	12.00
PBPSR Shaun Rogers D	3.00	8.00
PBPTR Tony Richardson B	4.00	10.00

2005 Topps Chrome Throwbacks

COMPLETE SET (49) 40.00 80.00
STATED ODDS 1:6 HOB/RET
*REFRACTORS: 1.5X TO 4X BASIC INSERTS
REFRACTOR ODDS 1:369 HOB, 1:371 RET
REFRACTOR PRINT RUN 100 SER.#'d SETS

TB1 LaDainian Tomlinson	1.25	3.00
TB2 Marvin Harrison	1.25	3.00
TB3 Shaun Alexander	1.00	2.50
TB4 Peyton Manning	2.50	6.00
TB5 Trent Green	1.00	2.50
TB6 Randy Moss	1.25	3.00
TB7 Brett Favre	3.00	8.00
TB8 Ben Roethlisberger	2.00	5.00
TB9 Donovan McNabb	1.25	3.00
TB10 Tom Brady	2.50	6.00
TB11 Dwight Freeney	1.00	2.50
TB12 Dante Hall	.75	2.00
TB13 Edgerrin James	1.00	2.50
TB14 Daunte Culpepper	1.00	2.50
TB15 Ray Lewis	1.25	3.00
TB16 Joe Horn	1.00	2.50
TB17 Terrell Owens	1.25	3.00
TB18 Muhsin Muhammad	1.00	2.50
TB19 Curtis Martin	1.25	3.00
TB20 Michael Vick	1.25	3.00
TB21 Antonio Gates	1.25	3.00
TB22 Deuce McAllister	1.00	2.50
TB23 Javon Walker	.75	2.00
TB24 Tony Gonzalez	1.00	2.50
TB25 Corey Dillon	1.00	2.50
TB26 Tiki Barber	1.25	3.00
TB27 Jamal Lewis	1.00	2.50
TB28 Reggie Wayne	1.25	3.00
TB29 Priest Holmes	1.00	2.50
TB30 Chris Brown	.75	2.00
TB31 Marc Bulger	1.00	2.50
TB32 Hines Ward	1.25	3.00
TB33 Chad Johnson	1.00	2.50
TB34 Ahman Green	1.00	2.50
TB35 Willis McGahee	1.25	3.00
TB36 Rudi Johnson	1.00	2.50
TB37 Drew Brees	1.25	3.00
TB38 Isaac Bruce	1.00	2.50
TB39 Ed Reed	1.00	2.50
TB40 Domanick Davis	.75	2.00
TB41 Jake Delhomme	1.00	2.50
TB42 Clinton Portis	1.00	2.50
TB43 Drew Bennett	1.00	2.50
TB44 Fred Taylor	1.00	2.50
TB45 Eric Moulds	.75	2.00
TB46 Torry Holt	1.00	2.50
TB47 Brian Westbrook	1.00	2.50
TB48 Jake Plummer	1.00	2.50
TB49 Champ Bailey	1.00	2.50

2006 Topps Chrome

This 270-card set was released in August, 2006. The set was issued into the hobby in four-cards packs which came 24 to a box. The first 165 cards in the set feature veterans while cards numbered 166-270 feature 2006 rookies. The rookies were inserted into packs at a stated rate of one in two. Similar to the basic topps set, a special card of Super Bowl XL hero Hines Ward (#RH40) was produced and that card was inserted at a stated rate of one in 36.

COMPLETE SET (270) 50.00 100.00
COMP.SET w/o RC's (165) 12.00 30.00
ROOKIE STATED ODDS 1:2
RH40 STATED ODDS 1:36

1 Jonathan Vilma	.30	.75
2 Chester Taylor	.30	.75
3 Troy Polamalu	.50	1.25
4 Nathan Vasher	.25	.60
5 Clinton Portis	.40	1.00
6 Willie Parker	.30	.75
7 Lofa Tatupu	.30	.75
8 Peyton Manning	.60	1.50
9 LaMont Jordan	.30	.75
10 Jason Taylor	.30	.75
11 Travis Taylor	.25	.60
12 Derrick Johnson	.25	.60
13 Jason Campbell	.30	.75
14 Aaron Rodgers	.75	2.00
15 Deltha O'Neal	.25	.60
16 LaDainian Tomlinson	.40	1.00
17 Keary Colbert	.25	.60
18 Chris Chambers	.30	.75
19 Chris Simms	.30	.75
20 Troy Williamson	.25	.60
21 Chad Johnson	.30	.75
22 Jake Delhomme	.30	.75
23 Willis McGahee	.30	.75
24 Roddy White	.30	.75
25 Rod Smith	.30	.75
26 Zach Thomas	.40	1.00
27 Antonio Gates	.40	1.00
28 Michael Vick	.40	1.00
29 Antwaan Randle El	.30	.75
30 Drew Bledsoe	.40	1.00
31 Randy McMichael	.25	.60
32 Heath Miller	.30	.75
33 Fred Taylor	.30	.75
34 Alge Crumpler	.30	.75
35 Roy Williams S	.30	.75
36 Ryan Moats	.25	.60
37 Dwight Freeney	.30	.75
38 Jeremy Shockey	.40	1.00
39 Shawne Merriman	.30	.75
40 Charlie Frye	.30	.75
41 Reggie Wayne	.30	.75
42 Alex Smith QB	.40	1.00
43 Jerome Bettis	.40	1.00
44 Chris Brown	.25	.60
45 Michael Clayton	.25	.60
46 Carlos Rogers	.25	.60
47 DeAngelo Hall	.30	.75
48 Drew Bennett	.30	.75
49 Brandon Lloyd	.25	.60
50 Corey Dillon	.30	.75
51 Eli Manning	.50	1.25
52 Jerry Porter	.25	.60
53 Carson Palmer	.40	1.00
54 Kevin Jones	.25	.60
55 Andre Johnson	.40	1.00
56 Ray Lewis	.40	1.00
57 Kyle Orton	.40	1.00
58 Julius Jones	.25	.60
59 Roy Williams WR	.30	.75
60 Jonathan Ogden	.25	.60
61 Antonio Pierce	.25	.60
62 Larry Johnson	.30	.75
63 Muhsin Muhammad	.30	.75
64 Trent Green	.30	.75
65 Tatum Bell	.25	.60
66 Lee Evans	.30	.75
67 Braylon Edwards	.30	.75
68 Hines Ward	.40	1.00
69 Warrick Dunn	.30	.75
70 Antonio Bryant	.25	.60
71 Mewelde Moore	.25	.60
72 Samkon Gado	.30	.75
73 Mike Williams	.25	.60
74 Marion Barber	.40	1.00
75 Samie Parker	.25	.60
76 Julius Peppers	.30	.75
77 Brian Westbrook	.30	.75
78 Kevan Barlow	.25	.60
79 Kyle Boller	.30	.75
80 Donnie Edwards	.25	.60
81 Courtney Roby	.25	.60
82 Marc Bulger	.30	.75
83 Steve Smith	.40	1.00
84 Ben Roethlisberger	.50	1.25
85 Byron Leftwich	.30	.75
86 Isaac Bruce	.30	.75
87 Kurt Warner	.40	1.00
88 Tiki Barber	.40	1.00
89 Derrick Mason	.30	.75
90 Joe Horn	.30	.75
91 Donovan McNabb	.40	1.00
92 DeShaun Foster	.30	.75
93 Rex Grossman	.30	.75
94 Randy Moss	.40	1.00
95 Tedy Bruschi	.40	1.00
96 Tony Gonzalez	.30	.75
97 Cadillac Williams	.30	.75
98 Torry Holt	.30	.75
99 Philip Rivers	.40	1.00
100 Deuce McAllister	.30	.75
101 Jason Witten	.40	1.00
102 Reggie Brown	.25	.60
103 Ronnie Brown	.40	1.00
104 Deion Branch	.30	.75
105 Terry Glenn	.30	.75
106 Tom Brady	.60	1.50
107 Dallas Clark	.30	.75
108 Mark Clayton	.30	.75
109 D.J. Williams	.25	.60
110 Matt Jones	.25	.60
111 Ed Reed	.30	.75
112 Reuben Droughns	.30	.75
113 Matt Hasselbeck	.30	.75
114 Anquan Boldin	.30	.75
115 David Carr	.25	.60
116 Domanick Davis	.25	.60
117 Nate Burleson	.25	.60
118 Shaun Alexander	.30	.75
119 Dante Hall	.30	.75
120 Santana Moss	.30	.75
121 Brandon Stokley	.30	.75
122 Larry Fitzgerald	.40	1.00
123 Marvin Harrison	.40	1.00
124 Steve McNair	.30	.75
125 Osi Umenyiora	.30	.75
126 Odell Thurman	.25	.60
127 Josh McCown	.25	.60
128 Curtis Martin	.40	1.00
129 Jake Plummer	.30	.75
130 Cedric Benson	.30	.75
131 J.P. Losman	.30	.75
132 Joey Galloway	.30	.75
133 Brian Griese	.30	.75
134 Plaxico Burress	.30	.75
135 Brian Urlacher	.40	1.00
136 T.J. Houshmandzadeh	.30	.75
137 Todd Heap	.30	.75
138 Champ Bailey	.30	.75
139 Mark Brunell	.30	.75
140 Chris Cooley	.30	.75
141 Priest Holmes	.30	.75
142 Aaron Brooks	.30	.75
143 Steven Jackson	.40	1.00
144 Michael Strahan	.30	.75
145 Rudi Johnson	.30	.75
146 Terrell Owens	.40	1.00
147 John Abraham	.25	.60
148 Jon Kitna	.30	.75
149 LaVar Arrington	.30	.75
150 Joe Jurevicius	.25	.60
151 Dominic Rhodes	.30	.75
152 Chad Pennington	.30	.75
153 Charles Woodson	.40	1.00
154 Kerry Collins	.30	.75
155 Drew Brees	.40	1.00
156 Keyshawn Johnson	.30	.75
157 Mike Anderson	.30	.75
158 Jimmy Smith	.30	.75
159 Brett Favre	.75	2.00
160 Edgerrin James	.30	.75
161 Jamal Lewis	.30	.75
162 Daunte Culpepper	.30	.75
163 Eric Moulds	.25	.60
164 Patrick Ramsey	.30	.75
165 Ahman Green	.30	.75
166 Kamerion Wimbley RC	2.00	5.00
167 Bobby Carpenter RC	1.25	3.00
168 Abdul Hodge RC	1.25	3.00
169 P.J. Daniels RC	1.25	3.00
170 D'Qwell Jackson RC	1.50	4.00
171 Johnathan Joseph RC	1.50	4.00
172 Antonio Cromartie RC	2.00	5.00
173 Elvis Dumervil RC	2.00	5.00
174 Tamba Hali RC	2.00	5.00
175 Derek Hagan RC	1.50	4.00
176 Haloti Ngata RC	2.00	5.00
177 Manny Lawson RC	1.50	4.00
178 Kelly Jennings RC	1.50	4.00
179 Jason Allen RC	1.50	4.00
180 Mathias Kiwanuka RC	2.00	5.00
181 Marques Hagans RC	1.25	3.00
182 Devin Aromashodu RC	2.00	5.00
183 Brandon Johnson RC	1.50	4.00
184 Ingle Martin RC	1.50	4.00
185 Claude Wroten RC	1.25	3.00
186 Tye Hill RC	1.25	3.00
187 Ashton Youboty RC	1.25	3.00
188 DeMeco Ryans RC	2.00	5.00
189 Brodrick Bunkley RC	1.50	4.00
190 Thomas Howard RC	1.50	4.00
191 Ernie Sims RC	1.50	4.00
192 Rocky McIntosh RC	1.50	4.00
193 Donte Whitner RC	2.00	5.00
194 Anthony Schlegel RC	1.50	4.00
195 Jimmy Williams RC	2.00	5.00
196 Brett Basanez RC	2.00	5.00
197 Ben Obomanu RC	2.00	5.00
198 Jonathan Orr RC	1.50	4.00
199 Andre Hall RC	1.50	4.00
200 James Anderson RC	1.25	3.00
201 Darnell Bing RC	1.50	4.00
202 Jovon Bouknight RC	1.50	4.00
203 Gabe Watson RC	1.25	3.00
204 Garrett Mills RC	2.00	5.00
205 Jeff Webb RC	1.50	4.00
206 Kevin McMahan RC	1.50	4.00
207 D.J. Shockley RC	1.50	4.00
208 A.J. Nicholson RC	1.25	3.00
209 Cedric Humes RC	1.25	3.00
210 Winston Justice RC	1.50	4.00
211 Lawrence Vickers RC	1.50	4.00
212 Daniel Bullocks RC	2.00	5.00
213 Tim Day RC	1.50	4.00
214 Ko Simpson RC	1.50	4.00
215 Dusty Dvoracek RC	2.00	5.00
216 Davin Joseph RC	1.50	4.00
217 Dominique Byrd RC	1.50	4.00
218 Marcus Vick RC	1.25	3.00
219 John McCargo RC	1.25	3.00
220 Danieal Manning RC	2.00	5.00
221 Reggie Bush RC	4.00	10.00
222 A.J. Hawk RC	2.00	5.00
223 Vince Young RC	2.50	6.00
224 Matt Leinart RC	2.00	5.00
225 Kellen Clemens RC	1.50	4.00
226 Sinorice Moss RC	2.00	5.00
227 Laurence Maroney RC	1.50	4.00
228 DeAngelo Williams RC	2.50	6.00
229 Jay Cutler RC	4.00	10.00
230 LenDale White RC	1.50	4.00
231 Leonard Pope RC	2.00	5.00
232 Chad Greenway RC	2.00	5.00
233 Chad Jackson RC	1.25	3.00
234 Vernon Davis RC	2.50	6.00
235 Todd Watkins RC	1.25	3.00
236 David Thomas RC	1.50	4.00
237 Marcedes Lewis RC	2.00	5.00
238 Leon Washington RC	1.50	4.00
239 Will Blackmon RC	1.50	4.00
240 Michael Huff RC	1.50	4.00
241 Jerious Norwood RC	1.50	4.00
242 Reggie McNeal RC	1.50	4.00
243 Wali Lundy RC	1.50	4.00
244 Santonio Holmes RC	2.50	6.00
245 Jerome Harrison RC	2.00	5.00
246 Bruce Gradkowski RC	2.00	5.00
247 Maurice Drew RC	3.00	8.00
248 Brandon Williams RC	1.25	3.00
249 Anthony Fasano RC	2.00	5.00
250 Omar Jacobs RC	1.25	3.00
251 Domenik Hixon RC	2.00	5.00
252 Devin Hester RC	4.00	10.00
253 Maurice Stovall RC	1.25	3.00
254 Tarvaris Jackson RC	2.00	5.00
255 Michael Robinson RC	1.50	4.00
256 Mario Williams RC	2.00	5.00
257 Jason Avant RC	1.25	3.00
258 Brian Calhoun RC	1.25	3.00
259 Skyler Green RC	1.25	3.00
260 Greg Jennings RC	4.00	10.00
261 Charlie Whitehurst RC	2.00	5.00
262 Mike Hass RC	1.50	4.00
263 Brandon Marshall RC	2.00	5.00
264 Drew Olson RC	1.25	3.00
265 Demetrius Williams RC	1.50	4.00
266 Travis Wilson RC	1.25	3.00
267 Joe Klopfenstein RC	1.25	3.00
268 Joseph Addai RC	2.00	5.00
269 Brad Smith RC	2.00	5.00
270 Willie Reid RC	1.50	4.00
RH40 Hines Ward RH	2.50	6.00

2006 Topps Chrome Black Refractors

*VETS 1-165: 4X TO 10X BASIC CARDS
*ROOKIES 166-270: 1.2X TO 3X BASIC CARDS
1-165 VET/199 ODDS 1:76H, 1:80R
166-270 ROOKIE/199 ODDS 1:227H, 1:242R
ALL ROOKIES HAVE SPECIAL EDITION LOGO

2006 Topps Chrome Blue

*VETS 1-165: 8X TO 20X BASIC CARDS
*ROOKIES 166-220: 2X TO 5X
1 220/50 ODDS 1:227 HOB, 1:240 RET

COMMON AUTO	10.00	25.00
AUTO SEMISTARS	12.00	30.00
AUTO UNL.STARS	15.00	40.00

221-270 ROOK.AU/50 ODDS 1:994H, 1:1100R

221 Reggie Bush AU	60.00	120.00
222 A.J. Hawk AU	40.00	100.00
223 Vince Young AU	40.00	100.00
224 Matt Leinart AU	30.00	60.00
228 DeAngelo Williams AU	50.00	100.00
229 Jay Cutler AU	75.00	150.00
234 Vernon Davis AU	30.00	60.00
244 Santonio Holmes AU	30.00	80.00
247 Maurice Drew AU	50.00	120.00
252 Devin Hester AU	50.00	100.00
256 Mario Williams AU	25.00	60.00
260 Greg Jennings AU	50.00	100.00

2006 Topps Chrome Red Refractors

*VETS 1-165: 4X TO 10X BASIC CARDS
*ROOKIES 166-270: 2.5X TO 6X
ONE PER HOBBY BOX
1-165 PRINT RUN 259 SER.#'d SETS
166-270 PRINT RUN 25 SER.#'d SETS

221 Reggie Bush	60.00	150.00
223 Vince Young	50.00	120.00
224 Matt Leinart	40.00	100.00
229 Jay Cutler	60.00	150.00

2006 Topps Chrome Refractors

*VETS 1-165: 2.5X TO 6X BASIC CARDS
*ROOKIES 166-270: .8X TO 2X BASIC CARDS
1-165 VET STATED ODDS 1:4 H, 1:6 R
166-270 ROOKIE ODDS 1:12 HOB/RET
ALL ROOKIES HAVE SPECIAL EDITION LOGO

RH40 Hines Ward RH/100	8.00	20.00

2006 Topps Chrome Special Edition Rookies

*SE ROOKIE: .5X TO 1.2X BASIC CARDS
STATED ODDS 1:6 HOB/RET

2006 Topps Chrome Rookie Autographs

GROUP A ODDS 1:850 H, 1:875 R
GROUP B ODDS 1:639 H, 1:450 R
GROUP C ODDS 1:400 H, 1:310 R
GROUP D ODDS 1:28 H, 1:72 R
UNPRICED PRINT.PLATES #'d TO 1

221 Reggie Bush A	30.00	80.00
222 A.J. Hawk A	25.00	50.00
223 Vince Young A	20.00	50.00
224 Matt Leinart A	15.00	40.00
225 Kellen Clemens D	5.00	12.00
226 Sinorice Moss A	12.00	30.00
227 Laurence Maroney B	5.00	12.00
228 DeAngelo Williams A	20.00	40.00
229 Jay Cutler A	30.00	80.00
230 LenDale White A	10.00	25.00
231 Leonard Pope D	6.00	15.00
232 Chad Greenway D	6.00	15.00
233 Chad Jackson C	4.00	10.00
234 Vernon Davis A	20.00	40.00
235 Todd Watkins D	4.00	10.00
236 David Thomas D	5.00	12.00
237 Marcedes Lewis D	6.00	15.00
238 Leon Washington D	8.00	20.00
239 Will Blackmon D	5.00	12.00
240 Michael Huff B	5.00	12.00
241 Jerious Norwood D	5.00	12.00
242 Reggie McNeal D	5.00	12.00
243 Wali Lundy D	5.00	12.00
244 Santonio Holmes A	15.00	40.00
245 Jerome Harrison D	6.00	15.00
246 Bruce Gradkowski D	6.00	15.00
247 Maurice Drew D	15.00	40.00
248 Brandon Williams D	4.00	10.00
249 Anthony Fasano D	6.00	15.00
250 Omar Jacobs B	4.00	10.00
251 Domenik Hixon D	6.00	15.00
252 Devin Hester D	20.00	50.00
253 Maurice Stovall D	4.00	10.00
254 Tarvaris Jackson D	6.00	15.00
255 Michael Robinson D	5.00	12.00
256 Mario Williams B	15.00	40.00
257 Jason Avant D	4.00	10.00
258 Brian Calhoun D	4.00	10.00
259 Skyler Green D	4.00	10.00
260 Greg Jennings D	15.00	30.00
261 Charlie Whitehurst C	6.00	15.00
262 Mike Hass C	5.00	12.00
263 Brandon Marshall D	15.00	30.00
264 Drew Olson D	4.00	10.00
265 Demetrius Williams C	5.00	12.00
266 Travis Wilson D	4.00	10.00
267 Joe Klopfenstein D	4.00	10.00
268 Joseph Addai B	10.00	25.00
269 Brad Smith C	6.00	15.00
270 Willie Reid D	5.00	12.00

2006 Topps Chrome Hall of Fame Tribute

COMPLETE SET (9) 6.00 15.00
STATED ODDS 1:12 HOB/RET
*REFRACTOR: 4X TO 10X BASIC INSERTS
REFRACTOR/100 ODDS 1:2600H, 1:3100R

BN Bronko Nagurski	1.25	3.00
HC Harry Carson	1.00	2.50
JM John Madden	1.25	3.00
JT Jim Thorpe	1.50	4.00
RW Reggie White	1.25	3.00
SB Sammy Baugh	1.25	3.00
TA Troy Aikman	1.50	4.00
WM Warren Moon	1.00	2.50
RWR Rayfield Wright	1.00	2.50

2006 Topps Chrome NFL 8306

STATED ODDS 1:12 HOB/RET
*VET REFRACT: 2.5X TO 6X BASIC INSERTS
*ROOKIE REF: 4X TO 10X BASIC INSERTS
REFRACTOR/100 ODDS 1:2500H, 1:2635R

NFL1 John Elway	2.50	6.00
NFL2 Jim Kelly	1.25	3.00
NFL3 Eric Dickerson	.75	2.00
NFL4 Dan Marino	3.00	8.00
NFL5 Reggie Bush	1.25	3.00
NFL6 Matt Leinart	.60	1.50
NFL7 Vince Young	.75	2.00
NFL8 Jay Cutler	1.25	3.00
NFL9 DeAngelo Williams	.75	2.00
NFL10 LenDale White	.75	2.00

2006 Topps Chrome Own The Game

COMPLETE SET (30) 10.00 25.00
STATED ODDS 1:6 HOB/RET
*REFRACTOR: 2X TO 5X BASIC INSERTS
REFRACTOR/100 ODDS 1:850H, 1:865R

OTG1 Tom Brady	1.50	4.00
OTG2 Trent Green	.75	2.00
OTG3 Shaun Alexander	.75	2.00
OTG4 Tiki Barber	1.00	2.50
OTG5 Steve Smith	1.00	2.50
OTG6 Santana Moss	.75	2.00
OTG7 Derrick Burgess	.60	1.50
OTG8 Osi Umenyiora	.75	2.00
OTG9 Brett Favre	2.00	5.00
OTG10 Larry Johnson	.75	2.00
OTG11 Chad Johnson	.75	2.00
OTG12 Carson Palmer	1.00	2.50
OTG13 Clinton Portis	1.00	2.50
OTG14 Larry Fitzgerald	1.00	2.50
OTG15 Eli Manning	1.25	3.00
OTG16 Edgerrin James	.75	2.00
OTG17 Anquan Boldin	.75	2.00
OTG18 Ty Law	.60	1.50
OTG19 Deltha O'Neal	.60	1.50
OTG20 Drew Brees	1.00	2.50
OTG21 LaDainian Tomlinson	1.00	2.50
OTG22 Marvin Harrison	1.00	2.50
OTG23 Corey Dillon	.75	2.00
OTG24 Matt Hasselbeck	.75	2.00
OTG25 Chris Chambers	.75	2.00
OTG26 Jonathan Vilma	.75	2.00
OTG27 Jake Delhomme	.75	2.00
OTG28 Rudi Johnson	.75	2.00
OTG29 Zach Thomas	1.00	2.50
OTG30 Hines Ward	1.00	2.50

2007 Topps Chrome

This 265-card set was released in August, 2007. The set was issued into the hobby in four-card packs, with a $2.99 SRP, which came 24 packs to a box. Cards numbered 1-165 feature veterans while cards numbered 166-265 feature 2007 NFL rookies. Those Rookie Cards were inserted into packs at a stated rate of one in two hobby or retail packs. In addition, just as in the regular Topps set, a special card to honor Super Bowl MVP Peyton Manning was created and that card was inserted into packs at a stated rate of one in 24.

COMPLETE SET (265) 60.00 150.00
COMP.SET w/o RC's (165) 12.50 30.00
ROOKIE STATED ODDS 1:2 H/R
MANNING RH ODDS 1:24
MANNING RH REF ODDS 1:12,565
MANN.RH WHITE REF ODDS 1:25,000

TC1 Matt Leinart	.30	.75
TC2 J.P. Losman	.25	.60
TC3 Carson Palmer	.30	.75
TC4 Jay Cutler	.40	1.00
TC5 Peyton Manning	.60	1.50
TC6 Tom Brady	.60	1.50
TC7 Chad Pennington	.30	.75
TC8 Philip Rivers	.40	1.00
TC9 Marc Bulger	.30	.75
TC10 Edgerrin James	.30	.75
TC11 Willis McGahee	.30	.75
TC12 Thomas Jones	.30	.75
TC13 Marion Barber	.30	.75
TC14 Fred Taylor	.30	.75
TC15 Chester Taylor	.25	.60
TC16 Reggie Bush	.40	1.00
TC17 Willie Parker	.30	.75
TC18 Shaun Alexander	.30	.75
TC19 LenDale White	.30	.75
TC20 Larry Fitzgerald	.40	1.00
TC21 Lee Evans	.30	.75
TC22 Muhsin Muhammad	.30	.75
TC23 Rod Smith	.30	.75
TC24 Andre Johnson	.30	.75
TC25 Matt Jones	.30	.75
TC26 Devery Henderson	.25	.60
TC27 Plaxico Burress	.30	.75
TC28 Randy Moss	.40	1.00
TC29 Santonio Holmes	.30	.75
TC30 Torry Holt	.30	.75
TC31 Antwaan Randle El	.25	.60
TC32 Todd Heap	.25	.60
TC33 Tony Gonzalez	.30	.75
TC34 Heath Miller	.25	.60
TC35 Alex Smith TE	.25	.60
TC36 Champ Bailey	.30	.75
TC37 Roy Williams S	.30	.75
TC38 Julius Peppers	.30	.75
TC39 Jason Taylor	.30	.75
TC40 Brian Urlacher	.40	1.00
TC41 Marc Bulger LL	.25	.60
TC42 Frank Gore LL	.30	.75
TC43 Reggie Wayne LL	.25	.60
TC44 Peyton Manning PB	.50	1.25
TC45 Reggie Wayne PB	.25	.60
TC46 Jason Taylor PB	.25	.60
TC47 Troy Polamalu PB	.30	.75
TC48 Tony Gonzalez PB	.25	.60
TC49 Devin Hester PB	.30	.75
TC50 LaDainian Tomlinson MVP	.30	.75
TC51 Peyton Manning / Reggie Wayne PSH	.50	1.25
TC52 New Orleans Saints PSH	.30	.75
TC53 Peyton Manning PSH	.50	1.25
TC54 Thomas Jones / Cedric Benson PSH	.25	.60
TC55 Colts Defense PSH	.25	.60
TC56 Steve McNair	.30	.75
TC57 Rex Grossman	.30	.75
TC58 Tony Romo	.50	1.25
TC59 David Carr	.30	.75
TC60 Tarvaris Jackson	.25	.60
TC61 Eli Manning	.40	1.00
TC62 Ben Roethlisberger	.40	1.00
TC63 Matt Hasselbeck	.30	.75
TC64 Jason Campbell	.30	.75
TC65 Warrick Dunn	.30	.75
TC66 Jamal Lewis	.30	.75
TC67 Cedric Benson	.30	.75
TC68 Reuben Droughns	.30	.75
TC69 Joseph Addai	.30	.75
TC70 Ronnie Brown	.30	.75
TC71 Deuce McAllister	.30	.75
TC72 Brian Westbrook	.30	.75
TC73 Frank Gore	.40	1.00
TC74 Cadillac Williams	.30	.75
TC75 Anquan Boldin	.30	.75
TC76 Mark Clayton	.30	.75
TC77 Bernard Berrian	.25	.60
TC78 Braylon Edwards	.30	.75
TC79 Donald Driver	.40	1.00
TC80 Marvin Harrison	.40	1.00
TC81 Troy Williamson	.25	.60
TC82 Marques Colston	.40	1.00
TC83 Laveranues Coles	.25	.60
TC84 Hines Ward	.40	1.00
TC85 Deion Branch	.30	.75
TC86 Alge Crumpler	.30	.75
TC87 Kellen Winslow	.30	.75
TC88 Dallas Clark	.25	.60
TC89 L.J. Smith	.25	.60
TC90 Vernon Davis	.30	.75
TC91 Sean Taylor	.40	1.00
TC92 Ronde Barber	.30	.75
TC93 Brian Dawkins	.30	.75
TC94 Dwight Freeney	.30	.75
TC95 Ray Lewis	.40	1.00
TC96 Peyton Manning LL	.50	1.25
TC97 Larry Johnson LL	.20	.50
TC98 Marvin Harrison LL	.30	.75
TC99 LaDainian Tomlinson PB	.30	.75
TC100 Jeff Saturday PB	.20	.50
TC101 Champ Bailey PB	.25	.60
TC102 Frank Gore PB	.30	.75
TC103 Walter Jones PB	.20	.50
TC104 Tony Romo PB	.40	1.00
TC105 Ronde Barber PB	.25	.60
TC106 Larry Johnson PB	.20	.50
TC107 Vince Young OROY	.25	.60
TC108 Asante Samuel PSH	.20	.50
TC109 Marlin Jackson PSH	.50	1.25
TC110 Devin Hester PSH	.30	.75
TC111 Michael Vick SP	40.00	80.00
TC112 Jake Delhomme	.30	.75
TC113 Charlie Frye	.30	.75
TC114 Brett Favre	.75	2.00
TC115 Trent Green	.30	.75
TC116 Drew Brees	.40	1.00
TC117 Donovan McNabb	.40	1.00
TC118 Alex Smith QB	.40	1.00
TC119 Vince Young	.30	.75
TC120 DeAngelo Williams	.40	1.00
TC121 Rudi Johnson	.30	.75
TC122 Julius Jones	.25	.60
TC123 Larry Johnson	.25	.60
TC124 Laurence Maroney	.30	.75
TC125 Brandon Jacobs	.30	.75
TC126 LaDainian Tomlinson	.40	1.00
TC127 Steven Jackson	.40	1.00
TC128 Clinton Portis	.30	.75
TC129 Michael Jenkins	.30	.75
TC130 Steve Smith	.30	.75
TC131 Chad Johnson	.30	.75
TC132 Roy Williams WR	.30	.75
TC133 Reggie Wayne	.30	.75
TC134 Reggie Williams	.30	.75
TC135 Chris Chambers	.30	.75
TC136 Sinorice Moss	.30	.75
TC137 Reggie Brown	.25	.60
TC138 Arnaz Battle	.25	.60
TC139 Michael Clayton	.25	.60
TC140 Santana Moss	.30	.75
TC141 Desmond Clark	.25	.60
TC142 Jeremy Shockey	.30	.75
TC143 Antonio Gates	.40	1.00
TC144 Chris Cooley	.30	.75
TC145 Devin Hester	.40	1.00
TC146 Asante Samuel	.25	.60
TC147 Troy Polamalu	.40	1.00
TC148 DeMarcus Ware	.30	.75
TC149 Michael Strahan	.30	.75
TC150 A.J. Hawk	.30	.75
TC151 LaDainian Tomlinson LL	.30	.75
TC152 Chad Johnson LL	.25	.60
TC153 LaDainian Tomlinson LL	.30	.75
TC154 Marvin Harrison PB	.30	.75
TC155 Antonio Gates PB	.30	.75
TC156 Shawne Merriman PB	.25	.60
TC157 Drew Brees PB	.30	.75
TC158 Steve Smith PB	.25	.60
TC159 Julius Peppers PB	.25	.60
TC160 DeMeco Ryans DROY	.25	.60
TC161 Drew Brees PSH	.30	.75
TC162 Reggie Bush PSH	.30	.75
TC163 Robbie Gould PSH	.20	.50
TC164 Joseph Addai PSH	.25	.60
TC165 Adam Vinatieri PSH	.25	.60
TC166 JaMarcus Russell RC	1.00	2.50
TC167 Brady Quinn RC	1.50	4.00
TC168 Drew Stanton RC	1.00	2.50
TC169 Troy Smith RC	1.50	4.00
TC170 Kevin Kolb RC	2.50	6.00
TC171 Trent Edwards RC	1.50	4.00
TC172 John Beck RC	1.50	4.00
TC173 Jordan Palmer RC	1.25	3.00
TC174 Chris Leak RC	1.25	3.00
TC175 Isaiah Stanback RC	1.00	2.50
TC176 Tyler Palko RC	1.25	3.00
TC177 Jared Zabransky RC	1.25	3.00
TC178 Jeff Rowe RC	1.00	2.50
TC179 Zac Taylor RC	1.25	3.00
TC180 Lester Ricard RC	1.25	3.00
TC181 Adrian Peterson RC	8.00	20.00
TC182 Marshawn Lynch RC	1.50	4.00
TC183 Brandon Jackson RC	1.25	3.00
TC184 Michael Bush RC	1.50	4.00
TC185 Kenny Irons RC	1.00	2.50
TC186 Antonio Pittman RC	1.00	2.50
TC187 Tony Hunt RC	1.00	2.50
TC188 Darius Walker RC	1.00	2.50
TC189 Dwayne Wright RC	1.25	3.00
TC190 Lorenzo Booker RC	1.25	3.00
TC191 Kenneth Darby RC	1.25	3.00
TC192 Chris Henry RB RC	1.00	2.50
TC193 Selvin Young RC	1.25	3.00
TC194 Brian Leonard RC	1.25	3.00
TC195 Ahmad Bradshaw RC	2.50	6.00
TC196 Gary Russell RC	1.25	3.00
TC197 Kolby Smith RC	1.25	3.00
TC198 Thomas Clayton RC	1.25	3.00
TC199 Garrett Wolfe RC	1.00	2.50
TC200 Calvin Johnson RC	5.00	12.00
TC201 Ted Ginn Jr. RC	1.25	3.00
TC202 Dwayne Jarrett RC	1.25	3.00
TC203 Dwayne Bowe RC	2.00	5.00
TC204 Sidney Rice RC	2.00	5.00
TC205 Robert Meachem RC	1.50	4.00
TC206 Anthony Gonzalez RC	1.50	4.00
TC207 Craig Buster Davis RC	1.25	3.00
TC208 Aundrae Allison RC	1.00	2.50
TC209 Chansi Stuckey RC	1.50	4.00
TC210 David Clowney RC	1.25	3.00
TC211 Steve Smith USC RC	1.50	4.00
TC212 Courtney Taylor RC	1.25	3.00
TC213 Paul Williams RC	1.00	2.50
TC214 Johnnie Lee Higgins RC	1.25	3.00
TC215 Rhema McKnight RC	1.00	2.50
TC216 Jason Hill RC	1.50	4.00
TC217 Dallas Baker RC	1.00	2.50
TC218 Greg Olsen RC	1.25	3.00
TC219 Yamon Figurs RC	1.00	2.50
TC220 Scott Chandler RC	1.50	4.00
TC221 Matt Spaeth RC	1.50	4.00
TC222 Ben Patrick RC	1.25	3.00
TC223 Clark Harris RC	1.25	3.00
TC224 Martrez Milner RC	1.00	2.50
TC225 Alan Branch RC	1.25	3.00
TC226 Amobi Okoye RC	1.50	4.00
TC227 DeMarcus Tank Tyler RC	1.00	2.50
TC228 Justin Harrell RC	1.25	3.00
TC229 Gaines Adams RC	1.50	4.00
TC230 Jamaal Anderson RC	1.25	3.00
TC231 Adam Carriker RC	1.25	3.00
TC232 Jarvis Moss RC	1.25	3.00
TC233 Charles Johnson RC	1.00	2.50
TC234 Anthony Spencer RC	1.50	4.00
TC235 Quentin Moses RC	1.25	3.00
TC236 LaMarr Woodley RC	1.50	4.00
TC237 Victor Abiamiri RC	1.50	4.00
TC238 Ray McDonald RC	1.25	3.00
TC239 Tim Crowder RC	1.50	4.00
TC240 Patrick Willis RC	3.00	8.00
TC241 David Harris RC	1.25	3.00
TC242 Buster Davis RC	1.25	3.00
TC243 Lawrence Timmons RC	1.50	4.00
TC244 Paul Posluszny RC	1.50	4.00
TC245 Jon Beason RC	1.25	3.00
TC246 Rufus Alexander RC	1.25	3.00
TC247 Prescott Burgess RC	1.25	3.00
TC248 Leon Hall RC	1.25	3.00
TC249 Darrelle Revis RC	2.50	6.00
TC250 Aaron Ross RC	1.50	4.00
TC251 Daymeion Hughes RC	1.25	3.00
TC252 Marcus McCauley RC	1.25	3.00
TC253 Chris Houston RC	1.25	3.00
TC254 Tanard Jackson RC	1.00	2.50
TC255 Jonathan Wade RC	1.25	3.00
TC256 Josh Wilson RC	1.25	3.00
TC257 Eric Wright RC	1.50	4.00
TC258 David Irons RC	1.00	2.50
TC259 Laron Landry RC	1.50	4.00
TC260 Reggie Nelson RC	1.25	3.00
TC261 Michael Griffin RC	1.50	4.00
TC262 Brandon Meriweather RC	1.50	4.00
TC263 Eric Weddle RC	1.50	4.00
TC264 Joe Thomas RC	1.50	4.00
TC265 Levi Brown RC	1.50	4.00
RH41 Peyton Manning RH	2.00	5.00

2007 Topps Chrome Blue Refractors

*VETS 1-165: 2.5X TO 6X BASIC CARDS
*ROOKIES 166-265: .8X TO 2X
STATED ODDS 1:6 RETAIL

TC111 Michael Vick SP	125.00	250.00
RH41 Peyton Manning RH/50	20.00	50.00

2007 Topps Chrome Red Refractors Uncirculated

*VETS 1-165: 5X TO 12X BASIC CARDS
*ROOKIES 166-265: 1.5X TO 4X
RED REF/139 ONE PER HOBBY BOX

TC181 Adrian Peterson	75.00	150.00
TC200 Calvin Johnson	40.00	100.00
RH41 Peyton Manning RH/10	60.00	120.00

2007 Topps Chrome Refractors

*VETS 1-165: 2X TO 5X BASIC CARDS
*ROOKIES 166-265: .6X TO 1.5X
STATED ODDS 1:3 HOB/RET

TC111 Michael Vick SP	100.00	200.00
RH41 Peyton Manning RH/199	15.00	40.00

2007 Topps Chrome White Refractors

*VETERANS 1-165: 3X TO 8X BASIC CARDS
*ROOKIES 166-265: 1X TO 2.5X
WHITE REF/869 ODDS 1:6 H, 1:24 R

RH41 Peyton Manning RH/100	20.00	50.00

2007 Topps Chrome Xfractors

*VETS 1-165: 3X TO 8X BASIC CARDS
*ROOKIES 166-265: 1X TO 2.5X
STATED ODDS 1:3 RETAIL

TC181 Adrian Peterson	25.00	60.00

2007 Topps Chrome Brett Favre Collection

COMMON CARD (1-200) 2.00 5.00
STATED ODDS 1:4 HOB, 1:6 RET
*BLUE REF/50: 2X TO 5X BASIC INSERTS
BLUE REFRACTOR/50 ODDS 1:149 RET
*REF/199: 1X TO 2.5X BASIC INSERTS
REFRACT/199 ODDS 1:63 H/R
*WHITE REF/100: 1.5X TO 4X BASIC INSERTS
WHITE REF/100 ODDS 1:125 H/R
*SUPERFRACT/1: 12X TO 30X BASIC INSERTS
*RED REF UNC/10: 6X TO 15X BASIC INSERTS
RED REFRACTORS UNCIRCULATED PRINT RUN 10 SER.#'d SETS

2007 Topps Chrome LaDainian Tomlinson

COMMON CARD 1.00 2.50
STATED ODDS 1:12 HOB/RET
*BLUE REFRACT: 1.2X TO 3X BASIC INSERTS
BLUE REFRACTOR ODDS 1:963 RET
*REF/199: 1.2X TO 3X BASIC INSERTS
REFRACTOR/199 ODDS 1:405 H/R
*WHITE REF/100: 1.5X TO 4X BASIC INSERTS
WHITE REF/100 ODDS 1:806 H/R
*RED REF UNC/10: 6X TO 15X BASIC INSERTS
RED REFRACTORS UNCIRCULATED PRINT RUN 10 SER.#'d SETS
UNPRICED SUPERFRACTORS #'d TO 1
UNPRICED AUTOGRAPHS #'d TO 1

2007 Topps Chrome Rookie Autographs

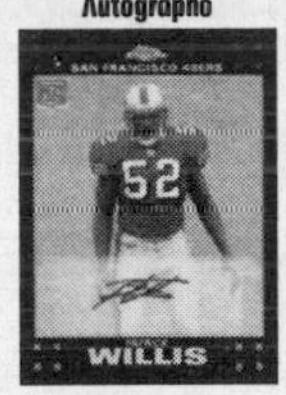

GROUP A ODDS 1:8816 H, 1:12,288 R
GROUP B ODDS 1:2380 H, 1:3072 R
GROUP C ODDS 1:240 H, 1:650 R
GROUP D ODDS 1:450 H, 1:1100 R
GROUP E ODDS 1:2017 H, 1:3500 R
GROUP F ODDS 1:153 H, 1:1500 R
GROUP G ODDS 1:43 H, 1:76 R
GROUP H ODDS 1:285 H, 1:338 R
GOLD SUPERFRACTORS UNCIRCULATED PRINT RUN 10 SER.#'d SETS
UNPRICED PRINTING PLATES #'d TO1
UNPRICED SUPERFRACTORS #'d TO1

TC166 JaMarcus Russell A	12.00	30.00
TC167 Brady Quinn B	15.00	40.00
TC168 Drew Stanton E	4.00	10.00
TC169 Troy Smith B	10.00	25.00
TC170 Kevin Kolb C	15.00	40.00
TC171 Trent Edwards F	6.00	15.00
TC172 John Beck D	6.00	15.00
TC174 Chris Leak D	5.00	12.00
TC175 Isaiah Stanback H	4.00	10.00
TC176 Tyler Palko G	5.00	12.00
TC181 Adrian Peterson A	150.00	300.00
TC182 Marshawn Lynch B	15.00	30.00
TC183 Brandon Jackson D	5.00	12.00
TC184 Michael Bush C	6.00	15.00
TC185 Kenny Irons A	12.00	30.00
TC186 Antonio Pittman C	4.00	10.00
TC187 Tony Hunt G	4.00	10.00
TC189 Dwayne Wright H	5.00	12.00
TC190 Lorenzo Booker D	5.00	12.00
TC192 Chris Henry G	4.00	10.00
TC193 Selvin Young G	5.00	12.00
TC196 Gary Russell G	5.00	12.00
TC198 Thomas Clayton G	5.00	12.00
TC199 Garrett Wolfe G	4.00	10.00
TC200 Calvin Johnson A	75.00	150.00
TC201 Ted Ginn Jr. B	8.00	20.00
TC202 Dwayne Jarrett C	5.00	12.00
TC203 Dwayne Bowe C	8.00	20.00
TC204 Sidney Rice C	8.00	20.00
TC205 Robert Meachem C	6.00	15.00
TC206 Anthony Gonzalez F	6.00	15.00
TC207 Craig Buster Davis C	5.00	12.00
TC208 Aundrae Allison G	4.00	10.00
TC209 Chansi Stuckey G	6.00	15.00
TC213 Paul Williams G	4.00	10.00
TC214 Johnnie Lee Higgins H	5.00	12.00
TC216 Jason Hill G	6.00	15.00
TC217 Dallas Baker G	4.00	10.00
TC218 Greg Olsen C	5.00	12.00
TC226 Amobi Okoye G	6.00	15.00
TC229 Gaines Adams G	6.00	15.00
TC230 Jamaal Anderson F	5.00	12.00
TC231 Adam Carriker F	5.00	12.00
TC240 Patrick Willis G	12.00	30.00
TC243 Lawrence Timmons G	6.00	15.00
TC244 Paul Posluszny H	6.00	15.00
TC248 Leon Hall G	5.00	12.00
TC250 Aaron Ross G	6.00	15.00
TC258 David Irons F	4.00	10.00
TC259 Laron Landry G	6.00	15.00

2007 Topps Chrome Rookie Autographs Refractors

*REFRACT/50: .6X TO 1.5X BASIC GROUP B
*REFRACT/50: .8X TO 2X BASIC GROUP C-G
*REFRACT/25: .5X TO 1.2X BASIC GROUP A
REFRACTORS PRINT RUN 25-50

TC181 Adrian Peterson/25 350.00 600.00
TC200 Calvin Johnson/25 175.00 300.00

2007 Topps Chrome Running Back Royalty

COMPLETE SET (10) 6.00 15.00
STATED ODDS 1:12 HOB/RET
*BLUE REFRACT: 1X TO 2.5X BASIC INSERTS
BLUE REFRACTOR ODDS 1:2987 RET
*REFRACT/199: 1X TO 2.5X BASIC INSERTS
REFRACTOR/199 ODDS 1:1256 H/R
*WHITE REF/100: 1.5X TO 4X BASIC INSERTS
WHITE REFRACT/100 ODDS 1:2500 H/R
*RED REF UNCIRC/10: 8X TO 20X BASIC INSERTS
RED REFRACT.UNCIRCULATED PRINT RUN 10
UNPRICED SUPERFRACTORS SER.#'d TO 1
TA LaDainian Tomlinson 1.00 2.50
Marcus Allen
TB LaDainian Tomlinson 1.25 3.00
Jim Brown
TC LaDainian Tomlinson 1.00 2.50
Earl Campbell
TD LaDainian Tomlinson 1.00 2.50
Eric Dickerson
TF LaDainian Tomlinson 1.00 2.50
Marshall Faulk
TP LaDainian Tomlinson 2.00 5.00
Walter Payton
TS LaDainian Tomlinson 1.50 4.00
Barry Sanders
TDO LaDainian Tomlinson 1.00 2.50
Tony Dorsett
TSA LaDainian Tomlinson 1.25 3.00
Gale Sayers
TSM LaDainian Tomlinson 2.00 5.00
Emmitt Smith

2008 Topps Chrome

This set was released on August 20, 2008. The base set consists of 275 cards. Cards 1-165 feature veterans, and cards 166-275 are rookies.

COMPLETE SET (275) 40.00 80.00
COMP.SET w/o RC's (165) 12.50 30.00
ONE ROOKIE PER PACK
UNPRICED PRINT.PLATE PRINT RUN 1
UNPRICED SUPERFRACTOR PRINT RUN 1
TC1 Drew Brees .40 1.00
TC2 Jon Kitna .30 .75
TC3 Tom Brady .60 1.50
TC4 Chad Pennington .30 .75
TC5 Matt Hasselbeck .30 .75
TC6 David Garrard .30 .75
TC7 Jay Cutler .40 1.00
TC8 Matt Schaub .30 .75
TC9 Trent Edwards .25 .60
TC10 Peyton Manning .60 1.50
TC11 Carson Palmer .40 1.00
TC12 Ben Roethlisberger .40 1.00
TC13 Eli Manning .40 1.00
TC14 Tony Romo .50 1.25
TC15 Donovan McNabb .40 1.00
TC16 Joey Harrington .25 .60
TC17 Jeff Garcia .30 .75
TC18 Derek Anderson .25 .60
TC19 Kyle Boller .25 .60
TC20 Sage Rosenfels .25 .60
TC21 Marc Bulger .30 .75
TC22 Brett Favre 1.00 2.50
TC23 Philip Rivers .40 1.00
TC24 Vince Young .30 .75
TC25 Kurt Warner .40 1.00
TC26 Cleo Lemon .25 .60
TC27 Damon Huard .25 .60
TC28 Jason Campbell .30 .75
TC29 Brian Griese .25 .60
TC30 Tarvaris Jackson .30 .75
TC31 Steven Jackson .40 1.00
TC32 Willie Parker .30 .75
TC33 DeShaun Foster .30 .75
TC34 Shaun Alexander .30 .75
TC35 Clinton Portis .30 .75
TC36 Ron Dayne .25 .60
TC37 Maurice Jones-Drew .30 .75
TC38 Warrick Dunn .30 .75
TC39 Adrian Peterson .60 1.50
TC40 Thomas Jones .30 .75
TC41 LaDainian Tomlinson .40 1.00
TC42 Marion Barber .30 .75
TC43 Brian Westbrook .30 .75
TC44 LenDale White .30 .75
TC45 Kenny Watson .25 .60
TC46 Fred Taylor .30 .75
TC47 Ryan Grant .40 1.00
TC48 Marshawn Lynch .30 .75
TC49 Selvin Young .25 .60
TC50 Joseph Addai .30 .75
TC51 Laurence Maroney .30 .75
TC52 Brandon Jacobs .30 .75
TC53 Willis McGahee .30 .75
TC54 Frank Gore .30 .75
TC55 Edgerrin James .30 .75
TC56 DeAngelo Williams .30 .75
TC57 Jamal Lewis .30 .75
TC58 Chester Taylor .25 .60
TC59 Earnest Graham .25 .60
TC60 Justin Fargas .25 .60
TC61 Greg Jennings .40 1.00
TC62 Torry Holt .30 .75
TC63 T.J. Houshmandzadeh .30 .75
TC64 Jerricho Cotchery .30 .75
TC65 Derrick Mason .30 .75
TC66 Kevin Curtis .25 .60
TC67 Joey Galloway .30 .75
TC68 Anquan Boldin .30 .75
TC69 Santonio Holmes .30 .75
TC70 Lee Evans .30 .75
TC71 Dwayne Bowe .30 .75
TC72 Wes Welker .40 1.00
TC73 Roy Williams WR .30 .75
TC74 Randy Moss .40 1.00
TC75 Plaxico Burress .30 .75
TC76 Terrell Owens .40 1.00
TC77 Andre Johnson .30 .75
TC78 Roddy White .30 .75
TC79 Brandon Marshall .30 .75
TC80 Donald Driver .30 .75
TC81 Marques Colston .30 .75
TC82 Reggie Wayne .30 .75
TC83 Chad Johnson .30 .75
TC84 Bernard Berrian .30 .75
TC85 Steve Smith .30 .75
TC86 Larry Fitzgerald .40 1.00
TC87 Braylon Edwards .30 .75
TC88 Bobby Engram .25 .60
TC89 Shaun McDonald .25 .60
TC90 Santana Moss .25 .60
TC91 Antonio Gates .40 1.00
TC92 Chris Cooley .30 .75
TC93 Owen Daniels .25 .60
TC94 Kellen Winslow .30 .75
TC95 Tony Gonzalez .30 .75
TC96 Jason Witten .40 1.00
TC97 Jeremy Shockey .30 .75
TC98 Dallas Clark .30 .75
TC99 Donald Lee .30 .75
TC100 Heath Miller .25 .60
TC101 Tony Scheffler .25 .60
TC102 Desmond Clark .25 .60
TC103 Vernon Davis .30 .75
TC104 Alge Crumpler .30 .75
TC105 Zach Miller .30 .75
TC106 Patrick Kerney .25 .60
TC107 Osi Umenyiora .30 .75
TC108 Mario Williams .30 .75
TC109 Jared Allen .40 1.00
TC110 Michael Strahan .30 .75
TC111 Ernie Sims .25 .60
TC112 DeMarcus Ware .30 .75
TC113 Patrick Willis .30 .75
TC114 Shawne Merriman .30 .75
TC115 Brian Urlacher .40 1.00
TC116 Ray Lewis .40 1.00
TC117 Antonio Cromartie .25 .60
TC118 Champ Bailey .30 .75
TC119 Bob Sanders .30 .75
TC120 Ed Reed .30 .75
TC121 Tom Brady LL .50 1.25
TC122 Drew Brees LL .30 .75
TC123 Tony Romo LL .40 1.00
TC124 LaDainian Tomlinson LL .30 .75
TC125 Adrian Peterson LL .50 1.25
TC126 Brian Westbrook LL .25 .60
TC127 Reggie Wayne LL .25 .60
TC128 Randy Moss LL .30 .75
TC129 Chad Johnson LL .25 .60
TC130 Randy Moss LL .30 .75
TC131 Matt Hasselbeck AP .25 .60
TC132 Tony Romo AP .40 1.00
TC133 Adrian Peterson AP .50 1.25
TC134 Marion Barber AP .25 .60
TC135 Brian Westbrook AP .25 .60
TC136 Larry Fitzgerald AP .30 .75
TC137 Terrell Owens AP .30 .75
TC138 Osi Umenyiora AP .25 .60
TC139 Lofa Tatupu AP .25 .60
TC140 Jason Witten AP .30 .75
TC141 Torry Holt AP .25 .60
TC142 Donald Driver AP .25 .60
TC143 Peyton Manning AP .50 1.25
TC144 Ben Roethlisberger AP .30 .75
TC145 Joseph Addai AP .25 .60
TC146 Reggie Wayne AP .25 .60
TC147 Braylon Edwards AP .25 .60
TC148 Devin Hester AP .30 .75
TC149 Champ Bailey AP .25 .60
TC150 Ed Reed AP .25 .60
TC151 Eli Manning PSH .30 .75
TC152 David Tyree PSH .25 .60
TC153 Plaxico Burress PSH .25 .60
TC154 Lawrence Tynes PSH .20 .50
TC155 Patriots Defense PSH .30 .75
(Randy Moss
Jabar Gaffney)
TC156 R.W. McQuarters PSH .20 .50
TC157 Ryan Grant PSH .30 .75
TC158 Philip Rivers PSH .30 .75
TC159 David Garrard PSH .25 .60
TC160 Laurence Maroney PSH .25 .60
TC161 Seattle Seahawks PSH .25 .60
(Matt Hasselbeck)
TC162 San Diego Chargers PSH .20 .50
(Luis Castillo
Jamal Williams)
TC163 Tom Brady MVP .50 1.25
TC164 Adrian Peterson OROY .50 1.25
TC165 Patrick Willis DROY .25 .60
TC166 Matt Ryan RC 5.00 12.00
TC167 Brian Brohm RC 1.25 3.00
TC168 Andre Woodson RC 1.25 3.00
TC169 Chad Henne RC 1.25 3.00
TC170 Joe Flacco RC 4.00 10.00
TC171 John David Booty RC 1.00 2.50
TC172 Colt Brennan RC 1.25 3.00
TC173 Dennis Dixon RC 1.25 3.00
TC174 Erik Ainge RC 1.25 3.00
TC175 Josh Johnson RC 1.25 3.00
TC176 Kevin O'Connell RC 1.00 2.50
TC177 Matt Flynn RC 2.50 6.00
TC178 Sam Keller RC 1.00 2.50
TC179 Harry Douglas RC 1.00 2.50
TC180 Anthony Morelli RC 1.00 2.50
TC181 Darren McFadden RC 3.00 8.00
TC182 Rashard Mendenhall RC 2.50 6.00
TC183 Jonathan Stewart RC 2.00 5.00
TC184 Felix Jones RC 2.00 5.00
TC185 Jamaal Charles RC 2.00 5.00
TC186 Chris Johnson RC 3.00 8.00
TC187 Ray Rice RC 2.50 6.00
TC188 Mike Hart RC 1.25 3.00
TC189 Kevin Smith RC 1.25 3.00
TC190 Steve Slaton RC 1.25 3.00
TC191 Matt Forte RC 2.00 5.00
TC192 Tashard Choice RC 1.00 2.50
TC193 Dominique Rodgers-Cromartie RC 1.25 3.00
TC194 Cory Boyd RC .75 2.00
TC195 Allen Patrick RC 1.00 2.50
TC196 Thomas Brown RC 1.00 2.50
TC197 Justin Forsett RC 1.25 3.00
TC198 DeSean Jackson RC 2.50 6.00
TC199 Malcolm Kelly RC 1.00 2.50
TC200 Limas Sweed RC 1.25 3.00
TC201 Mario Manningham RC 1.25 3.00
TC202 James Hardy RC 1.00 2.50
TC203 Early Doucet RC 1.00 2.50
TC204 Donnie Avery RC 1.00 2.50
TC205 Dexter Jackson RC 1.00 2.50
TC206 Devin Thomas RC 1.00 2.50
TC207 Jordy Nelson RC 1.50 4.00
TC208 Keenan Burton RC .75 2.00
TC209 Chris Williams RC 1.00 2.50
TC210 Earl Bennett RC 1.25 3.00
TC211 Jerome Simpson RC 1.25 3.00
TC212 Andre Caldwell RC 1.00 2.50
TC213 Josh Morgan RC 1.25 3.00
TC214 Fred Davis RC 1.25 3.00
TC215 John Carlson RC 1.25 3.00
TC216 Martellus Bennett RC 1.00 2.50
TC217 Martin Rucker RC 1.00 2.50
TC218 Jermichael Finley RC 1.25 3.00
TC219 Dustin Keller RC 1.25 3.00
TC220 Jacob Tamme RC 1.25 3.00
TC221 Kellen Davis RC .75 2.00
TC222 Jake Long RC 1.25 3.00
TC223 Sam Baker RC .75 2.00
TC224 Jeff Otah RC 1.00 2.50
TC225 Owen Schmitt RC 1.25 3.00
TC226 Chevis Jackson RC .75 2.00
TC227 Jacob Hester RC 1.25 3.00
TC228 Glenn Dorsey RC 1.25 3.00
TC229 Sedrick Ellis RC 1.25 3.00
TC230 Kentwan Balmer RC 1.00 2.50
TC231 Pat Sims RC 1.00 2.50
TC232 Marcus Harrison RC 1.00 2.50
TC233 Dre Moore RC 1.00 2.50
TC234 Red Bryant RC .75 2.00
TC235 Trevor Laws RC 1.25 3.00
TC236 Chris Long RC 1.25 3.00
TC237 Vernon Gholston RC 1.00 2.50
TC238 Derrick Harvey RC .75 2.00
TC239 Calais Campbell RC 1.00 2.50
TC240 Terrence Wheatley RC .75 2.00
TC241 Phillip Merling RC 1.00 2.50
TC242 Chris Ellis RC .75 2.00
TC243 Lawrence Jackson RC 1.00 2.50
TC244 Dan Connor RC 1.25 3.00
TC245 Curtis Lofton RC 1.00 2.50
TC246 Jerod Mayo RC 1.25 3.00
TC247 Tavares Gooden RC 1.00 2.50
TC248 Beau Bell RC 1.00 2.50
TC249 Philip Wheeler RC 1.00 2.50
TC250 Vince Hall RC .75 2.00
TC251 Jonathan Goff RC .75 2.00
TC252 Keith Rivers RC 1.25 3.00
TC253 Ali Highsmith RC .75 2.00
TC254 Xavier Adibi RC .75 2.00
TC255 Erin Henderson RC 1.25 3.00
TC256 Bruce Davis RC 1.00 2.50
TC257 Jordon Dizon RC 1.25 3.00
TC258 Shawn Crable RC .75 2.00
TC259 Geno Hayes RC .75 2.00
TC260 Mike Jenkins RC 1.25 3.00
TC261 Aqib Talib RC 1.25 3.00
TC262 Leodis McKelvin RC 1.00 2.50
TC263 Terrell Thomas RC 1.00 2.50
TC264 Reggie Smith RC 1.00 2.50
TC265 Antoine Cason RC 1.25 3.00
TC266 Patrick Lee RC 1.00 2.50
TC267 Tracy Porter RC 1.25 3.00
TC268 Kenny Phillips RC 1.25 3.00
TC269 Simeon Castille RC 1.00 2.50
TC270 Eddie Royal RC 1.25 3.00
TC271 Thomas DeCoud RC .75 2.00
TC272 Marcus Griffin RC .75 2.00
TC273 Charles Godfrey RC 1.25 3.00
TC274 Tyrell Johnson RC 1.25 3.00
TC275 Jamar Adams RC 1.00 2.50
RH42 Eli Manning RH 1.00 2.50

2008 Topps Chrome Blue Refractors

*BLUE REF VETS: 3X TO 8X BASIC CARDS
*BLUE REF ROOKIES: 1X TO 2.5X
RANDOM INSERTS IN RETAIL PACKS
RH Eli Manning RH/100 3.00 8.00

2008 Topps Chrome Copper Refractors

*VETS 1-165: 2.5X TO 6X BASIC CARDS
*ROOKIES 166-275: .8X TO 2X BASIC CARDS
COPPER REF/425 ODDS 1:22 HOB

2008 Topps Chrome Gold Refractors

*VETS 1-165: 4X TO 10X BASIC CARDS
*ROOKIES 166-275: 2X TO 5X BASIC CARDS
GOLD REF/199 ONE PER HOBBY BOX
TC166 Matt Ryan 30.00 80.00
TC177 Matt Flynn 25.00 60.00

2008 Topps Chrome Red Refractors

*VETS 1-165: 8X TO 20X BASIC CARDS
*ROOKIES 166-275: 3X TO 8X BASIC CARDS
RED REFRACTOR/25 ODDS 1:196 HOB
TC177 Matt Flynn 25.00 60.00

2008 Topps Chrome Refractors

*VETS 1-165: 1.5X TO 4X BASIC CARDS
*ROOKIES 166-275: .6X TO 1.5X BASIC CARDS
STATED ODDS 1:3
RH Eli Manning RH/199 6.00 15.00

2008 Topps Chrome Xfractors

*VETS: 1.5X TO 4X BASIC CARDS
*ROOKIES: .6X TO 1.5X BASIC CARDS
RANDOM INSERTS IN RETAIL PACKS

2008 Topps Chrome Brett Favre Collection

COMMON CARD (BF201-BF442) 1.25 3.00
STATED ODDS 1:4 HOB
*BLUE REFRACT/50: 3X TO 8X BASIC INSERTS
BLUE REF/50 INSERTED IN RETAIL PACKS
*REFRACT/199: 1X TO 2.5X BASIC INSERTS
REFRACTOR/199 ODDS 1:58 HOB
*RED REFRACT/10: 6X TO 15X BASIC INSERTS
RED REFRACTOR/10 ODDS 1:1158 HOB
UNPRICED SUPERFRACTOR PRINT RUN 1
*WHITE REFRACT/100: 2X TO 5X BASIC INSERTS
WHITE REFRACT/100 ODDS 1:114 HOB

2008 Topps Chrome Dynasties

COMPLETE SET (39) 15.00 40.00
STATED ODDS 1:6 HOB
*REFRACTOR/199: 1X TO 2.5X BASIC INSERTS
REFRACTOR/199 ODDS 1: HOB 1:304
*BLUE REF/50: 2X TO 5X BASIC INSERTS
BLUE REFRACTOR PRINT RUN 50
*RED REFRACT/10: 5X TO 12X BASIC INSERTS
RED REFRACTOR/10 ODDS 1:6089 HOB
UNPRICED SUPERFRACTOR/1 ODDS 1:29,400
*WHITE REFRACT/100: 1.5X TO 4X BASIC INSERTS
WHITE REFRACTOR/100 ODDS 1:608 HOB
DYNAV Adam Vinatieri 1.00 2.50
DYNBB Bill Bates .75 2.00
DYNBJ Brent Jones .75 2.00
DYNCH Charles Haley .75 2.00
DYNDB Deion Branch .75 2.00
DYNDC Dwight Clark .75 2.00
DYNDS Deion Sanders 1.00 2.50
DYNDSH Donnie Shell .75 2.00
DYNDWH Dwight White .75 2.00
DYNES Emmitt Smith 2.00 5.00
DYNES2 Emmitt Smith 2.00 5.00
DYNFH Franco Harris 1.00 2.50
DYNFH2 Franco Harris 1.00 2.50
DYNJG Joe Greene 1.00 2.50
DYNJM Joe Montana 2.00 5.00
DYNJM2 Joe Montana 2.00 5.00
DYNJM3 Joe Montana 2.00 5.00
DYNJN Jay Novacek .75 2.00
DYNJR Jerry Rice 1.50 4.00
DYNJR2 Jerry Rice 1.50 4.00
DYNJT John Taylor .75 2.00
DYNKT Keena Turner .60 1.50
DYNLG L.C. Greenwood .75 2.00
DYNLL Leon Lett .60 1.50
DYNLM Lawyer Milloy .60 1.50
DYNMB Mel Blount .75 2.00
DYNRB Rocky Bleier .75 2.00
DYNRC Randy Cross .75 2.00
DYNRCR Roger Craig .75 2.00
DYNRL Ronnie Lott 1.00 2.50
DYNTA Troy Aikman 1.25 3.00
DYNTA2 Troy Aikman 1.25 3.00
DYNTB Tom Brady 1.50 4.00
DYNTB2 Tom Brady 1.50 4.00
DYNTBR Terry Bradshaw 1.50 4.00
DYNTBR2 Terry Bradshaw 1.50 4.00
DYNTJ Ted Johnson .60 1.50
DYNTL Ty Law .60 1.50
DYNTR Tom Rathman .75 2.00

2008 Topps Chrome Hall of Fame

COMPLETE SET (6) 3.00 8.00
STATED ODDS 1:8
*REFRACTOR/199: 2X TO 5X BASIC INSERTS
REFRACTOR/199 ODDS 1:304 HOB
*WHITE REF/100: 3X TO 8X BASIC INSERTS
WHITE REFRACTOR/100 ODDS 1:608 HOB
*RED REFRACT/10: 8X TO 20X BASIC INSERTS
RED REFRACTOR/10 ODDS 1:6089 HOB
UNPRICED SUPERFRACT/1 ODDS 1:29,400
HOFAM Art Monk 1.25 3.00
HOFAT Andre Tippett .75 2.00
HOFDG Darrell Green 1.00 2.50
HOFET Emmitt Thomas .75 2.00
HOFFD Fred Dean .75 2.00
HOFGZ Gary Zimmerman .75 2.00

2008 Topps Chrome Honor Roll

COMPLETE SET (9) 4.00 10.00
STATED ODDS 1:6 HOB
HRAD Art Donovan .60 1.50
HRCB Chuck Bednarik .75 2.00
HRGM Gino Marchetti .60 1.50
HRJM Johnny Blood McNally .60 1.50
HRLG Lou Groza .75 2.00
HRNB Norm Van Brocklin .75 2.00
HRRB Rocky Bleier .75 2.00
HRRS Roger Staubach 1.25 3.00
HRTF Tom Fears .60 1.50

2008 Topps Chrome Honor Roll Relic Patches

STATED ODDS 1:4135 HOB
AD 101st Airborne Division 15.00 40.00
AD2 82nd Airborne Division 15.00 40.00
BA Blue Angels 15.00 40.00
CA 1st Cavalry 15.00 40.00
FF F-16 Fighting Falcon 15.00 40.00
IF Operation Iraqi Freedom Patch 15.00 40.00
MC Marine Corps Eagle 25.00 60.00
Globe and Anchor
MR 7th Marine Regiment 15.00 40.00
MS Semper Fidelis 15.00 40.00
NE 158th Fighter Wing 15.00 40.00
Operation Noble Eagle
NI United States Naval 15.00 40.00
Intelligence
NS The Only Easy 15.00 40.00
Day Was Yesterday
TB Thunderbirds 15.00 40.00

2008 Topps Chrome Rookie Autographs

GROUP A ODDS 1:862 HOB
GROUP B ODDS 1:143 HOB
GROUP C ODDS 1:458 HOB
GROUP D ODDS 1:191 HOB
GROUP E ODDS 1:42 HOB
UNPRICED GOLD REFRACTOR #'d TO 10
UNPRICED PRINT.PLATE PRINT RUN 1
TC166 Matt Ryan A 60.00 120.00
TC167 Brian Brohm A 10.00 25.00
TC168 Andre Woodson A 6.00 15.00
TC169 Chad Henne B 12.00 30.00
TC170 Joe Flacco A 40.00 100.00
TC171 John David Booty D 5.00 12.00
TC172 Colt Brennan A 12.00 30.00
TC173 Dennis Dixon B 10.00 25.00
TC174 Erik Ainge B 6.00 15.00
TC175 Josh Johnson E 6.00 15.00
TC176 Kevin O'Connell B 5.00 12.00
TC177 Matt Flynn E 25.00 60.00
TC179 Harry Douglas E 5.00 12.00
TC180 Anthony Morelli E 5.00 12.00
TC181 Darren McFadden A 40.00 80.00
TC182 Rashard Mendenhall A 20.00 50.00
TC183 Jonathan Stewart A 15.00 40.00
TC184 Felix Jones B 12.00 30.00
TC185 Jamaal Charles B 15.00 40.00
TC186 Chris Johnson E 20.00 50.00
TC187 Ray Rice B 25.00 60.00
TC188 Mike Hart B 6.00 15.00
TC189 Kevin Smith D 6.00 15.00
TC190 Steve Slaton B 6.00 15.00
TC191 Matt Forte E 15.00 40.00
TC192 Tashard Choice E 5.00 12.00
TC193 Dominique Rodgers-Cromartie D 6.00 15.00
TC195 Allen Patrick E 5.00 12.00
TC197 Justin Forsett E 6.00 15.00
TC198 DeSean Jackson B 25.00 50.00
TC199 Malcolm Kelly B 5.00 12.00
TC200 Limas Sweed B 6.00 15.00
TC201 Mario Manningham D 8.00 20.00
TC202 James Hardy B 5.00 12.00
TC203 Early Doucet B 5.00 12.00
TC204 Donnie Avery B 5.00 12.00
TC205 Dexter Jackson B 5.00 12.00
TC206 Devin Thomas B 5.00 12.00
TC207 Jordy Nelson B 15.00 30.00
TC208 Keenan Burton E 4.00 10.00
TC210 Earl Bennett E 6.00 15.00
TC211 Jerome Simpson B 6.00 15.00
TC212 Andre Caldwell E 5.00 12.00
TC214 Fred Davis E 6.00 15.00
TC219 Dustin Keller B 8.00 20.00
TC222 Jake Long B 6.00 15.00
TC225 Owen Schmitt E 6.00 15.00
TC227 Jacob Hester C 6.00 15.00
TC228 Glenn Dorsey B 6.00 15.00
TC236 Chris Long B 6.00 15.00
TC237 Vernon Gholston B 5.00 12.00
TC238 Derrick Harvey C 4.00 10.00
TC244 Dan Connor C 6.00 15.00
TC252 Keith Rivers C 6.00 15.00
TC253 Ali Highsmith E 4.00 10.00
TC260 Mike Jenkins E 6.00 15.00
TC261 Aqib Talib C 6.00 15.00
TC268 Kenny Phillips D 6.00 15.00
TC270 Eddie Royal D 6.00 15.00
TC272 Marcus Griffin E 4.00 10.00

2008 Topps Chrome Rookie Autographs Refractors

*REFRACTOR/50: .6X TO 1.5X BASIC AUTO
REFRACTOR/50 ODDS 1:584H
TC166 Matt Ryan 75.00 150.00
TC170 Joe Flacco 60.00 120.00
TC186 Chris Johnson 30.00 80.00
TC198 DeSean Jackson 50.00 100.00

2008 Topps Chrome Rookie Autographs Patch

PATCH AUTO/25 ODDS 1:1655 HOB
TC166 Matt Ryan 250.00 400.00
TC167 Brian Brohm 25.00 60.00
TC169 Chad Henne 50.00 120.00
TC170 Joe Flacco 125.00 250.00
TC171 John David Booty 20.00 50.00
TC176 Kevin O'Connell 20.00 50.00
TC179 Harry Douglas 20.00 50.00
TC181 Darren McFadden 125.00 200.00
TC182 Rashard Mendenhall 100.00 200.00
TC183 Jonathan Stewart 75.00 150.00
TC184 Felix Jones 75.00 150.00
TC185 Jamaal Charles 60.00 100.00
TC186 Chris Johnson 150.00 300.00
TC187 Ray Rice 100.00 200.00
TC189 Kevin Smith 25.00 60.00
TC190 Steve Slaton 25.00 60.00
TC191 Matt Forte 75.00 150.00
TC198 DeSean Jackson 100.00 200.00
TC199 Malcolm Kelly 20.00 50.00
TC200 Limas Sweed 25.00 60.00
TC201 Mario Manningham 40.00 80.00
TC202 James Hardy 20.00 50.00
TC203 Early Doucet 20.00 50.00
TC204 Donnie Avery 20.00 50.00
TC205 Dexter Jackson 20.00 50.00
TC206 Devin Thomas 15.00 40.00
TC207 Jordy Nelson 50.00 100.00
TC210 Earl Bennett 25.00 60.00
TC211 Jerome Simpson 25.00 60.00
TC212 Andre Caldwell 20.00 50.00
TC219 Dustin Keller 25.00 60.00
TC222 Jake Long 25.00 60.00
TC228 Glenn Dorsey 25.00 60.00
TC270 Eddie Royal 25.00 60.00

2008 Topps Chrome Tom Brady Tribute Autographs

UNPRICED BRADY AUTO PRINT RUN 1

2009 Topps Chrome

COMPLETE SET (220) 75.00 150.00
COMP.SET w/o RC's (110) 8.00 20.00
ROOKIE STATED ODDS 1:2
SP STATED ODDS 1:325 HOB
TC1 Santana Moss .25 .60
TC2 Vernon Davis .25 .60
TC3 Philip Rivers .30 .75
TC4 Santonio Holmes .25 .60
TC5 Jamarcus Russell .20 .50
TC6 Thomas Jones .25 .60
TC7 Randy Moss .30 .75
TC8 Tyler Thigpen .20 .50
TC9 Maurice Jones-Drew .25 .60
TC10 Calvin Johnson .30 .75
TC11 Champ Bailey .25 .60
TC12 Felix Jones .30 .75
TC13 Brady Quinn .25 .60
TC14 Carson Palmer .30 .75
TC15 Marshawn Lynch .25 .60
TC16 Ed Reed .25 .60
TC17 Tim Hightower .20 .50
TC18 Karlos Dansby .20 .50
TC19 Chris Cooley .25 .60
TC20 Donnie Avery .25 .60
TC21 John Carlson .25 .60
TC22 Hines Ward .25 .60
TC23 DeSean Jackson .25 .60
TC24 Justin Tuck .25 .60
TC25 Marques Colston .25 .60
TC26A Drew Brees .30 .75
(back to the camera)
TC26B Drew Brees SP 10.00 25.00
(facing camera)
TC27 Wes Welker .30 .75
TC28A Adrian Peterson .50 1.25
(white jersey)
TC28B Adrian Peterson SP 25.00 50.00
(purple jersey)
TC29 David Garrard .25 .60
TC30 Greg Jennings .30 .75
TC31 Kevin Smith .25 .60
TC32 Marion Barber .25 .60
TC33 Keith Rivers .20 .50
TC34 Devin Hester .30 .75
TC35 Trent Edwards .20 .50
TC36 Kurt Warner .30 .75
TC37 Clinton Portis .25 .60
TC38 LenDale White .25 .60
TC39 Chris Johnson .30 .75
TC40 Antonio Bryant .20 .50
TC41 Matt Hasselbeck .25 .60
TC42 Frank Gore .25 .60
TC43 Antonio Gates .25 .60
TC44 Troy Polamalu .30 .75
TC45 Brian Westbrook .25 .60
TC46 Steve Smith .25 .60
TC47 Darrelle Revis .25 .60
TC48 Kevin Boss .25 .60
TC49 Jeremy Shockey .20 .50
TC50 Tarvaris Jackson .25 .60
TC51 Ted Ginn Jr. .25 .60
TC52 Dwayne Bowe .25 .60
TC53 Bob Sanders .25 .60
TC54 Reggie Wayne .25 .60
TC55 DeMarcus Ware .25 .60
TC56A Tony Romo .50 1.25
(walking in tunnel)
TC56B Tony Romo SP 12.00 30.00
(passing the ball)
TC57 Matt Forte .30 .75
TC58 Jonathan Stewart .25 .60
TC59 Roddy White .25 .60
TC60 Anquan Boldin .25 .60
TC61 Kerry Collins .25 .60
TC62 Steven Jackson .25 .60
TC63 Darren Sproles .25 .60
TC64 Willie Parker .20 .50
TC65 Asante Samuel .20 .50
TC66 Donovan McNabb .30 .75
TC67 Jerricho Cotchery .25 .60
TC68 Brandon Jacobs .25 .60
TC69 Jerod Mayo .25 .60
TC70A Tom Brady .50 1.25
(passing)
TC70B Tom Brady SP 20.00 40.00
(dropping back)
TC71 Jared Allen .30 .75
TC72 Ronnie Brown .25 .60
TC73 Tony Gonzalez .25 .60
TC74A Andre Johnson .25 .60
(white jersey)
TC74B Andre Johnson SP 8.00 20.00
(blue jersey)
TC75A Aaron Rodgers .60 1.50
(passing)
TC75B Aaron Rodgers SP 20.00 40.00
(jogging)
TC76 Eddie Royal .25 .60
TC77 Terrell Owens .30 .75
TC78 Kellen Winslow Jr. .25 .60
TC79 Chad Ochocinco .25 .60
TC80 DeAngelo Williams .30 .75
TC81 Joe Flacco. .30 .75
TC82 Michael Turner .25 .60
TC83 Larry Fitzgerald .30 .75
TC84 Keith Bulluck .20 .50
TC85 Aqib Talib .20 .50
TC86 Patrick Willis .25 .60
TC87 LaDainian Tomlinson .30 .75
TC88 Ben Roethlisberger .30 .75
TC89 Darren McFadden .30 .75
TC90 Leon Washington .25 .60
TC91 Eli Manning .30 .75
TC92 Reggie Bush .30 .75
TC93 Chad Pennington .25 .60
TC94 Joey Porter .25 .60
TC95 Anthony Gonzalez .20 .50
TC96A Peyton Manning .50 1.25
(blue jersey)
TC96B Peyton Manning SP 20.00 40.00
(white jersey)
TC97 Matt Schaub .25 .60
TC98 Steve Slaton .25 .60
TC99 Aaron Kampman .25 .60
TC100 Ernie Sims .20 .50
TC101 Brandon Marshall .25 .60
TC102 Jay Cutler .30 .75
TC103 Jason Witten .30 .75
TC104 Braylon Edwards .25 .60
TC105 T.J. Houshmandzadeh .25 .60
TC106 Brian Urlacher .30 .75
TC107 Julius Peppers .25 .60
TC108 Willis McGahee .25 .60
TC109 Ray Lewis .30 .75
TC110 Matt Ryan .30 .75
TC111 Aaron Brown RC 1.25 3.00
TC112 B.J. Raji RC 1.25 3.00
TC113 Aaron Maybin RC 1.00 2.50
TC114 Alphonso Smith RC 1.00 2.50
TC115 Hakeem Nicks RC 2.00 5.00
TC116 Andre Smith RC 1.00 2.50
TC117 Andy Levitre RC 1.00 2.50
TC118 Asher Allen RC 1.00 2.50
TC119 Austin Collie RC 1.25 3.00
TC120 Aaron Curry RC 1.25 3.00
TC121 Brandon Gibson RC 1.25 3.00
TC122 Michael Oher RC 2.00 5.00
TC123 Brandon Tate RC 1.25 3.00
TC124 Brandon Underwood RC 1.25 3.00
TC125 Javon Ringer RC 1.25 3.00
TC126 Brian Hartline RC 1.25 3.00
TC127 Brian Orakpo RC 1.25 3.00
TC128 Mike Wallace RC 2.50 6.00
TC129 Brooks Foster RC .75 2.00
TC130 Brian Cushing RC 1.25 3.00
TC131 Chase Coffman RC 1.00 2.50
TC132 Darius Butler RC 1.25 3.00
TC133 Clay Matthews RC 4.00 10.00
TC134 Clint Sintim RC 1.25 3.00
TC135 Kenny Britt RC 1.50 4.00
TC136 Patrick Turner RC 1.00 2.50
TC137 Courtney Greene RC .75 2.00
TC138 Curtis Painter RC 1.25 3.00
TC139 D.J. Moore RC 1.00 2.50
TC140 Chris Wells RC 2.00 5.00
TC141 Darrius Heyward-Bey RC 1.25 3.00
TC142 Demetrius Byrd RC 1.00 2.50
TC143 Deon Butler RC 1.00 2.50
TC144 Derrick Williams RC 1.00 2.50
TC145A Pat White RC 1.25 3.00
(scrambling)
TC145B Pat White SP 15.00 30.00
(passing)
TC146 Duke Robinson RC .75 2.00
TC147 Eben Britton RC 1.00 2.50
TC148 Eugene Monroe RC .75 2.00
TC149 Everette Brown RC 1.00 2.50
TC150 Donald Brown RC 1.25 3.00
TC151 Gartrell Johnson RC .75 2.00
TC152 Glen Coffee RC 1.00 2.50
TC153 Andre Brown RC .75 2.00
TC154 James Casey RC 1.00 2.50
TC155 Percy Harvin RC 2.00 5.00
TC156 Roy Miller RC 1.00 2.50
TC157 Jamon Meredith RC 1.00 2.50
TC158 Jared Cook RC 1.25 3.00
TC159 Jarett Dillard RC 1.25 3.00
TC160 Jeremy Maclin RC 2.00 5.00
TC161 Jason Williams RC 1.25 3.00
TC162 Javarris Williams RC 1.00 2.50
TC163 Cedric Peerman RC 1.00 2.50
TC164 Jason Smith RC 1.00 2.50
TC165 Fili Moala RC 1.00 2.50
TC166 Rey Maualuga RC 1.25 3.00
TC167 Travis Beckum RC 1.00 2.50
TC168 Juaquin Iglesias RC 1.00 2.50
TC169 Connor Barwin RC 1.25 3.00
TC170 Knowshon Moreno RC 1.25 3.00
TC171 Kenny McKinley RC 1.25 3.00
TC172 Kevin Ellison RC 1.00 2.50
TC173 Larry English RC 1.25 3.00
TC174 Marko Mitchell RC 1.00 2.50
TC175 Louis Delmas RC 1.25 3.00
TC176 Shonn Greene RC 2.00 5.00
TC177 Malcolm Jenkins RC 1.25 3.00
TC178 Manuel Johnson RC 1.00 2.50
TC179 Marcus Freeman RC 1.25 3.00
TC180 LeSean McCoy RC 2.50 6.00
TC181 Zack Follett RC .75 2.00
TC182 Shawn Nelson RC 1.00 2.50
TC183 Rashad Jennings RC 1.25 3.00
TC184 Michael Hamlin RC 1.00 2.50
TC185 Michael Johnson RC .75 2.00
TC186 Brandon Pettigrew RC 1.25 3.00
TC187 Mike Goodson RC 1.25 3.00
TC188 Mike Mickens RC 1.00 2.50
TC189 Mike Teel RC 1.25 3.00
TC190 Mike Thomas RC 1.25 3.00
TC191 Brian Robiskie RC 1.25 3.00
TC192 Mohamed Massaquoi RC 1.00 2.50
TC193 Nate Davis RC 1.00 2.50
TC194 Patrick Chung RC 1.25 3.00
TC195 Cornelius Ingram RC .75 2.00
TC196 James Davis RC 1.25 3.00
TC197 Peria Jerry RC 1.00 2.50
TC198 Phil Loadholt RC 1.00 2.50
TC199 Ramses Barden RC .75 2.00
TC200A Michael Crabtree RC 2.50 6.00
(ball in hands above head)
TC200B Michael Crabtree SP 15.00 30.00
(ball in air)
TC201 Rashad Johnson RC 1.00 2.50
TC202 Johnny Knox RC 2.00 5.00
TC203 Rhett Bomar RC 1.00 2.50
TC204 Robert Ayers RC 1.25 3.00
TC205 James Laurinaitis RC 1.25 3.00
TC206 Sammie Stroughter RC 1.25 3.00
TC207 Scott McKillop RC 1.00 2.50
TC208 Sean Smith RC 1.25 3.00
TC209 Sen'Derrick Marks RC .75 2.00
TC210 Matthew Stafford RC 6.00 15.00
TC211 Louis Murphy RC 1.25 3.00
TC212 Stephen McGee RC 1.25 3.00
TC213 Tiquan Underwood RC 1.00 2.50
TC214 Tom Brandstater RC 1.25 3.00
TC215 Josh Freeman RC 2.50 6.00
TC216 Tyson Jackson RC 1.00 2.50
TC217 Victor Harris RC 1.25 3.00
TC218 Vontae Davis RC 1.25 3.00
TC219 William Moore RC 1.25 3.00
TC220A Mark Sanchez RC 6.00 15.00
(no helmet)
TC220B Mark Sanchez SP 30.00 60.00
(wearing helmet)
RHC43 Santonio Holmes RH .75 2.00

2009 Topps Chrome Copper Refractors

*VETS: 3X TO 8X BASIC CARDS
*ROOKIES: .8X TO 2X BASIC CARDS
COPPER REF/649 ODDS 1:12 HOB
TC210 Matthew Stafford 15.00 40.00
TC220 Mark Sanchez 12.00 30.00

2009 Topps Chrome Blue Refractors

*VETS: 5X TO 12X BASIC CARDS
*ROOKIES: 1.2X TO 3X BASIC CARDS
RANDOM INSERTS IN RETAIL PACKS
TC210 Matthew Stafford 30.00 60.00
TC220 Mark Sanchez 20.00 50.00
RH Santonio Holmes RH/100 5.00 12.00

2009 Topps Chrome Red Refractors

*VETS: 15X TO 40X BASIC CARDS
*ROOKIES: 3X TO 8X BASIC CARDS
RED REF/25 ODDS 1:138 HOB
TC210 Matthew Stafford 90.00 150.00
TC220 Mark Sanchez 60.00 120.00

2009 Topps Chrome Refractors

*VETS: 2.5X TO 6X BASIC CARDS
*ROOKIES: .6X TO 1.5X BASIC CARDS
REFRACTOR STATED ODDS 1:3 HOB
TC210 Matthew Stafford 12.00 30.00
TC220 Mark Sanchez 10.00 25.00
RH Santonio Holmes RH/199 4.00 10.00

2009 Topps Chrome Xfractors

*VETS: 2.5X TO 6X BASIC CARDS
*ROOKIES: .6X TO 1.5X BASIC CARDS
RANDOM INSERTS IN RETAIL PACKS
TC210 Matthew Stafford 15.00 30.00
TC220 Mark Sanchez 10.00 25.00

2009 Topps Chrome Cheerleaders

COMPLETE SET (15) 5.00 12.00
OVERALL STATED ODDS 1:8
*REFRACT/199: 4X TO 10X BASIC INSERTS
*BLUE REF/50: 6X TO 15X BASIC INSERTS
*WHITE REF/100: 5X TO 12X BASIC INSERTS
TCC1 Tara .50 1.25
TCC2 Amanda .50 1.25
TCC3 Kelli .50 1.25
TCC4 Emily C. .50 1.25
TCC5 Kayla S. .50 1.25
TCC6 Laurie .50 1.25
TCC7 TaJonda .50 1.25
TCC8 Amanda .50 1.25
TCC9 Samantha .50 1.25
TCC10 Amy .50 1.25
TCC11 Fabiola .50 1.25
TCC12 Johanna .50 1.25
TCC13 Bibiana .50 1.25
TCC14 Monica .50 1.25
TCC15 Tiffany .50 1.25

2009 Topps Chrome Chicle

COMPLETE SET (25) 8.00 20.00
OVERALL ODDS 1:4 HOB
*REFRACT/199: 1.5X TO 4X BASIC INSERTS
*BLUE REF/50: 2.5X TO 6X BASIC INSERTS
*WHITE REF/100: 2X TO 5X BASIC INSERTS
C1 Brian Westbrook .60 1.50
C5 Tony Gonzalez .60 1.50
C8 Steven Jackson .60 1.50
C14 Adrian Peterson 1.25 3.00
C21 Calvin Johnson .75 2.00
C24 Troy Polamalu .75 2.00
C30 Drew Brees .75 2.00
C31 LaDainian Tomlinson .75 2.00
C35 Jamal Lewis .60 1.50
C40 Peyton Manning 1.25 3.00
C42 Tony Romo 1.25 3.00
C46 LenDale White .60 1.50
C55 Dwayne Bowe .60 1.50
C59 Jason Witten .75 2.00
C66 Jerricho Cotchery .60 1.50
C71 Ted Ginn Jr. .50 1.25
C73 Vincent Jackson .60 1.50
C74 Lee Evans .60 1.50
C75 Wes Welker .75 2.00
C76 Ben Roethlisberger .75 2.00
C79 Kevin Walter .60 1.50
C83 Devin Hester .75 2.00
C89 Joey Porter .60 1.50
C90 Darrius Heyward-Bey .40 1.00
C93 Jon Beason .50 1.25

2009 Topps Chrome Rookie Autographs

GROUP A ODDS 1:7000 HOB
GROUP B ODDS 1:507 HOB
GROUP C ODDS 1:220 HOB
GROUP D ODDS 1:115 HOB
GROUP E ODDS 1:146 HOB
GROUP F ODDS 1:60 HOB
EXCH EXPIRATION: 8/31/2012
TC115 Hakeem Nicks D 12.50 25.00
TC120 Aaron Curry D 6.00 15.00
TC125 Javon Ringer F 6.00 15.00
TC127 Brian Orakpo E 6.00 15.00
TC130 Brian Cushing D 6.00 15.00
TC131 Chase Coffman E 5.00 12.00
TC135 Kenny Britt C 15.00 30.00
TC136 Patrick Turner F 5.00 12.00
TC140 Chris Wells C 20.00 50.00
TC141 Darrius Heyward-Bey B 12.00 30.00
TC142 Demetrius Byrd A 12.00 30.00
TC144 Derrick Williams C 5.00 12.00
TC145 Pat White C 10.00 25.00
TC150 Donald Brown C 6.00 15.00
TC151 Gartrell Johnson F 4.00 10.00
TC152 Glen Coffee F 5.00 12.00
TC153 Andre Brown F 4.00 10.00
TC154 James Casey E 5.00 12.00
TC155 Percy Harvin D 25.00 50.00
TC158 Jared Cook D 6.00 15.00
TC160 Jeremy Maclin C 15.00 40.00

TC163 Cedric Peerman E 5.00 12.00
TC166 Rey Maualuga E 6.00 15.00
TC168 Juaquin Iglesias F 5.00 12.00
TC170 Knowshon Moreno B 12.00 30.00
TC176 Shonn Greene F 10.00 25.00
TC177 Malcolm Jenkins D 6.00 15.00
TC181 LeSean McCoy D 25.00 50.00
TC183 Rashad Jennings F 6.00 15.00
TC185 Michael Johnson F 4.00 10.00
TC186 Brandon Pettigrew C 6.00 15.00
TC191 Brian Robiskie D 6.00 15.00
TC192 Mohamed Massaquoi F 5.00 12.00
TC193 Nate Davis F 5.00 12.00
TC195 Cornelius Ingram D 4.00 10.00
TC196 James Davis C 6.00 15.00
TC199 Ramses Barden D 4.00 10.00
TC200 Michael Crabtree B 25.00 60.00
TC202 Johnny Knox F 10.00 25.00
TC203 Rhett Bomar F 5.00 12.00
TC205 James Laurinaitis E 6.00 15.00
TC210 Matthew Stafford B 125.00 200.00
TC212 Stephen McGee E 6.00 15.00
TC213 Tiquan Underwood F 5.00 12.00
TC214 Tom Brandstater D 6.00 15.00
TC215 Josh Freeman B 40.00 80.00
TC220 Mark Sanchez B 50.00 100.00

2009 Topps Chrome Rookie Autographs Black Refractors

*BLACK REF/25: 1X TO 2.5X BASIC AU
BLACK REF/25 ODDS 1:788 HOB
TC210 Matthew Stafford 200.00 350.00
TC215 Josh Freeman 75.00 150.00
TC220 Mark Sanchez 125.00 250.00

2009 Topps Chrome Rookie Autographs Patch

PATCH AU/25 ODDS 1:1130 HOB
ARPAB Andre Brown 15.00 40.00
ARPAC Aaron Curry 25.00 60.00
ARPBP Brandon Pettigrew 25.00 60.00
ARPBR Brian Robiskie 25.00 60.00
ARPCW Chris Wells 40.00 100.00
ARPDB Donald Brown 25.00 60.00
ARPDH Darrius Heyward-Bey 25.00 60.00
ARPGC Glen Coffee 20.00 50.00
ARPHN Hakeem Nicks 40.00 100.00
ARPJF Josh Freeman 75.00 150.00
ARPJI Juaquin Iglesias 20.00 50.00
ARPJM Jeremy Maclin 40.00 100.00
ARPJR Javon Ringer 25.00 60.00
ARPKB Kenny Britt 30.00 80.00
ARPKM Knowshon Moreno 25.00 60.00
ARPLM LeSean McCoy 75.00 150.00
ARPMC Michael Crabtree 50.00 125.00
ARPMM Mohamed Massaquoi 20.00 50.00
ARPMS Mark Sanchez 125.00 250.00
ARPND Nate Davis 20.00 50.00
ARPPH Percy Harvin 60.00 120.00
ARPPT Patrick Turner 20.00 50.00
ARPPW Pat White 25.00 60.00
ARPRB Ramses Barden 15.00 40.00
ARPSG Shonn Greene 50.00 120.00
ARPSM Stephen McGee 25.00 60.00
ARPJMS Matthew Stafford 250.00 400.00
ARPRMD Rhett Bomar 20.00 50.00

2010 Topps Chrome

COMP.SET w/o SP's (220) 30.00 60.00
C1 Adrian Peterson .50 1.25
C2 Sidney Rice .25 .60
C3A Jahvid Best run RC 1.25 3.00
(running pose)
C3B Jahvid Best catch SP 10.00 25.00
(catching a pass)
C4 Terrell Owens .30 .75
C5 Brandon Marshall .25 .60
C6 Philip Rivers .30 .75
C7 Vernon Davis .25 .60
C8 Percy Harvin .30 .75
C9 Jamaal Charles .25 .60
C10 Donovan McNabb .30 .75
C11A Golden Tate helm RC .75 2.00
(wearing a helmet)
C11B Golden Tate no helm SP 6.00 15.00
(no helmet in photo)
C12 Myron Rolle RC .50 1.25
C13A Dexter McCluster helm RC .75 2.00
(wearing a helmet)
C13B Dexter McCluster no helm SP 6.00 15.00
(no helmet in photo)
C14 Morgan Burnett RC .75 2.00
C15 Jason Witten .30 .75
C16A Jonathan Dwyer rght RC .75 2.00
(holding ball in right arm)
C16B Jonathan Dwyer left SP 6.00 15.00
(holding ball in left arm)
C17 Dezmon Briscoe RC .60 1.50
C18 Brian Urlacher .30 .75
C19 DeAngelo Williams .25 .60
C20 Tony Romo .40 1.00
C21 Charles Scott RC .60 1.50
C22 Linval Joseph RC .60 1.50
C23 Ed Wang RC .75 2.00
C24 Tony Gonzalez .25 .60
C25 Darren McFadden .25 .60
C26 Matt Forte .25 .60
C27 Kenny Britt .25 .60
C28 Anthony Dixon RC .75 2.00
C29 Chad Jones RC .75 2.00
C30 Troy Polamalu .30 .75
C31 Taylor Mays RC .75 2.00
C32 Devin McCourty RC .75 2.00
C33 Matthew Stafford .30 .75
C34 London Fletcher .20 .50
C35 Darren Sproles .25 .60
C36 Dan LeFevour RC .75 2.00
C37 Michael Turner .20 .50
C38 Sean Lee RC .75 2.00
C39 Nnamdi Asomugha .25 .60
C40 Andre Johnson .25 .60
C41 Ryan Grant .25 .60
C42 Donald Driver .25 .60
C43 Eli Manning .30 .75
C44A Mike Williams RC 1.25 3.00
(no helmet in photo)
C44B Mike Williams SP 10.00 25.00
(wearing a helmet)
C45 Anquan Boldin .25 .60
C46A Ben Tate helm RC 1.00 2.50
((wearing a helmet)
C46B Ben Tate no helm SP 8.00 20.00
(no helmet in photo)
C47 Andre Roberts RC .75 2.00
C48 Kareem Jackson RC .75 2.00
C49 Zac Robinson RC .60 1.50
C50 Peyton Manning .50 1.25
C51A Brandon LaFell run RC .75 2.00
(running pose)
C51B Brandon LaFell catch SP 6.00 15.00
(catching a pass)
C52 Santana Moss .25 .60
C53 Russell Okung RC .75 2.00
C54 Julius Peppers .25 .60
C55 Hines Ward .25 .60
C56 Brandon Graham RC .60 1.50
C57 Steve Smith .25 .60
C58 Mike Iupati RC .75 2.00
C59 Joe Flacco .30 .75
C60A Dez Bryant RC 2.50 6.00
C60B Dez Bryant SP 30.00 60.00
C61 Rashard Mendenhall .25 .60
C62 James Harrison .30 .75
C63 Wes Welker .30 .75
C64 Jorod Mayo .25 .60
C65 Carlos Dunlap RC .75 2.00
C66 Taylor Price RC .75 2.00
C67 Jimmy Graham RC 1.50 4.00
C68 Walter McFadden RC .60 1.50
C69 Patrick Robinson RC .75 2.00
C70A Colt McCoy helm RC 1.50 4.00
(wearing a helmet)
C70B Colt McCoy no hlm SP 15.00 40.00
(no helmet in photo)
C71 Marion Barber .25 .60
C72 Tyson Alualu RC .60 1.50
C73 Chris Cook RC .75 2.00
C74 Joe Webb RC .75 2.00
C75 Brian Dawkins .25 .60
C76 Greg Jennings .25 .60
C77 Jonathan Stewart .25 .60
C78 Ronnie Brown .25 .60
C79 Willis McGahee .25 .60
C80 Tom Brady .50 1.25
C81 Clinton Portis .25 .60
C82 Jerry Hughes RC .75 2.00
C83 Knowshon Moreno .25 .60
C84 David Reed RC .60 1.50
C85 Brandon Spikes RC .75 2.00
C86 Joe Haden RC .75 2.00
C87 Aaron Hernandez RC 1.25 3.00
C88 Terrence Cody RC .60 1.50
C89 Felix Jones .25 .60
C90 Brett Favre .75 2.00
C91 Carson Palmer .25 .60
C92 Jay Cutler .30 .75
C93 Carlton Mitchell RC .60 1.50
C94 DeSean Jackson .25 .60
C95 LeSean McCoy .25 .60
C96 John Conner RC .75 2.00
C97 Charles Brown RC .60 1.50
C98 Eric Decker RC 1.00 2.50
C99 Brandon Ghee RC .60 1.50
C100A Tim Tebow RC 8.00 20.00
(leaping pose)
C100B Tim Tebow SP 60.00 100.00
(pointing his finger)
C101 Darren Sharper .25 .60
C102 Trent Williams RC .75 2.00
C103 Riley Cooper RC .75 2.00
C104 Brian Cushing .20 .50
C105 Miles Austin .30 .75
C106A Emmanuel Sanders RC .75 2.00
C106B Emmanuel Sanders SP 6.00 15.00
C107 Jermaine Gresham RC 1.00 2.50
C108 Vincent Jackson .20 .50
C109 Jermaine Cunningham RC .75 2.00
C110A Demaryius Thomas RC 1.00 2.50
C110B Demaryius Thomas SP 8.00 20.00
C111 Pierre Thomas .25 .60
C112A Rob Gronkowski RC 2.50 6.00
(running
cutting pose)
C112B Rob Gronkowski SP 10.00 25.00
(catching the ball)
C113 Major Wright RC .75 2.00
C114 Anthony Davis RC .60 1.50
C115 Darrelle Revis .25 .60
C116 Ray Lewis .30 .75
C117 Daryl Washington RC .60 1.50
C118 Kyle Wilson RC .75 2.00
C119 Koa Misi RC .75 2.00
C120A C.J. Spiller RC 1.25 3.00
C120B C.J. Spiller SP 10.00 25.00
C121 Pat Angerer RC .75 2.00
C122 Cadillac Williams .25 .60
C123 DeMarcus Ware UER 11 .25 .60
(Card numbered incorrectly #11)
C124 Aaron Rodgers .60 1.50
C125 Dan Williams RC .60 1.50
C126 Dallas Clark .25 .60
C127 Santonio Holmes .25 .60
C128 Michael Crabtree .30 .75
C129 Bryan Bulaga RC .75 2.00
C130A Jimmy Clausen point RC .75 2.00
(pointing his finger)
C130B Jimmy Clausen pass SP 6.00 15.00
(passing the football)
C131 Chad Ochocinco .25 .60
C132 Ben Roethlisberger .30 .75
C133 Steve Smith USC .25 .60
C134 Everson Griffen RC .75 2.00
C135 Earl Thomas RC .75 2.00
C136A Armanti Edwards RC .75 2.00
C136B Armanti Edwards SP 6.00 15.00
C137 Kevin Kolb .25 .60
C138 Akwasi Owusu-Ansah RC .75 2.00
C139 Mike Kafka RC .75 2.00
C140A Ryan Mathews run RC 1.50 4.00
(running pose)
C140B Ryan Mathews catch SP 12.00 30.00
(catching a pass)
C141 T.J. Houshmandzadeh .25 .60
C142 Chris Cooley .25 .60
C143 Randy Moss .30 .75
C144 Rodger Saffold RC .50 1.25
C145 Maurice Jones-Drew .25 .60
C146 Jonathan Vilma .20 .50
C147 Matt Schaub .25 .60
C148 Jacoby Ford RC .75 2.00
C149 T.J. Ward RC .75 2.00
C150A Sam Bradford run RC 4.00 10.00
(running pose)
C150B Sam Bradford snap SP 40.00 80.00
(taking a snap pose)
C151 Joey Porter .20 .50
C152 Ray Rice .25 .60
C153 James Starks RC 1.25 3.00
C154 Joseph Addai .25 .60
C155 Matt Hasselbeck .20 .50
C156 Antonio Gates .25 .60
C157 Mardy Gilyard RC .75 2.00
C158 Jerome Murphy RC .60 1.50
C159A Joe McKnight catch RC .75 2.00
(catching a pass)
C159B Joe McKnight jump SP 6.00 15.00
(jumping pose)
C160A Ndamukong Suh RC 2.00 5.00
C160B Ndamukong Suh SP 20.00 40.00
C161 Marcus Easley RC .60 1.50
C162 Marques Colston .25 .60
C163 Torell Troup RC .60 1.50
C164 Amari Spievey RC .75 2.00
C165 Sergio Kindle RC .75 2.00
C166 Jonathan Crompton RC .60 1.50
C167 James Laurinaitis .25 .60
C168A Montario Hardesty run RC .75 2.00
(running pose)
C168B Montario Hardesty jump SP 6.00 15.00
(jumping stiff arm pose)
C169 Frank Gore .25 .60
C170 Gerald McCoy RC .75 2.00
C171 Sean Weatherspoon RC .75 2.00
C172 Damian Williams RC .75 2.00
C173 Reggie Bush .30 .75
C174 Kellen Winslow .25 .60
C175 Tony Pike RC .75 2.00
C176 Reggie Wayne .25 .60
C177 Dwayne Bowe .25 .60
C178 Brandon Jacobs .25 .60
C179 Levi Brown RC .60 1.50
C180 Larry Fitzgerald .30 .75
C181 Cedric Benson .25 .60
C182 Patrick Willis .25 .60
C183 Maurkice Pouncey RC .75 2.00
C184 Sean Canfield RC .60 1.50
C185 Ed Dickson RC .75 2.00
C186A Arrelious Benn RC .75 2.00
C186B Arrelious Benn SP 6.00 15.00
C187 Matt Ryan .30 .75
C188 Jared Odrick RC .75 2.00
C189 Phillip Dillard RC .50 1.25
C190 Steven Jackson .25 .60
C191 Jeremy Maclin .25 .60
C192 Ed Reed .25 .60
C193 Calvin Johnson .30 .75
C194 Chris Wells .25 .60
C195A Eric Berry catch RC .75 2.00
(catching; ball not in hands)
C195B Eric Berry leap SP 6.00 15.00
(leaping one hand grab)
C196 Shonn Greene .25 .60
C197 Rennie Curran RC .60 1.50
C198 Javier Arenas RC .75 2.00
C199 Kevin Thomas UER RC .60 1.50
(No C prefix on card number)
C200 Chris Johnson .30 .75
C201 Jason Pierre-Paul RC 1.25 3.00
C202 Jared Allen .30 .75
C203 Steve Slaton .20 .50
C204 Lamarr Houston RC .75 2.00
C205 Anthony McCoy RC .60 1.50
C206 Mark Sanchez .30 .75
C207 Derrick Morgan RC .60 1.50
C208A Jordan Shipley helm RC .75 2.00
(wearing a helmet)
C208B Jordan Shipley no helm SP 6.00 15.00
(no photo in photo)
C209 Dwight Freeney .25 .60
C210 LaDainian Tomlinson .30 .75
C211 Matt Cassel .25 .60
C212 Rolando McClain RC .75 2.00
C213 Nate Allen RC .75 2.00
C214 Thomas Jones .25 .60
C215 Darryl Sharpton RC .50 1.25
C216A Toby Gerhart cut RC .75 2.00
(running
cutting pose)
C216B Toby Gerhart leap SP 6.00 15.00
(running
leaping pose)
C217 Jon Beason .20 .50
C218 John Skelton RC .75 2.00
C219 D.J. Williams .20 .50
C220 Drew Brees .30 .75

2010 Topps Chrome Blue Refractors

*VETS: 6X TO 15X BASIC CARDS
*ROOKIES: 2.5X TO 6X BASIC CARDS
BLUE/199 STATED ODDS 1:52
C100 Tim Tebow 50.00 100.00
C150 Sam Bradford 25.00 60.00

2010 Topps Chrome Gold Refractors

*VETS: 10X TO 25X BASIC CARDS
*ROOKIES: 4X TO 10X BASIC CARDS
GOLD/50 STATED ODDS 1:208
C100 Tim Tebow 125.00 200.00
C150 Sam Bradford 75.00 150.00

2010 Topps Chrome Orange Refractors

*VETS: 3X TO 8X BASIC CARDS
*ROOKIES: 1.2X TO 3X BASIC CARDS
RANDOM INSERTS IN RETAIL PACKS

2010 Topps Chrome Purple Refractors

*VETS: 4X TO 10X BASIC CARDS
*ROOKIES: 1.5X TO 4X BASIC CARDS
RETAIL INSERT PRINT RUN 555
C100 Tim Tebow 40.00 80.00
C150 Sam Bradford 12.00 30.00

2010 Topps Chrome Red Refractors

*VETS: 12X TO 30X BASIC CARDS
*ROOKIES: 5X TO 12X BASIC CARDS
RED REFRACTOR/25 ODDS 1:204
C100 Tim Tebow 150.00 300.00
C150 Sam Bradford 100.00 200.00

2010 Topps Chrome Refractors

*VETS: 2X TO 5X BASIC CARDS
*ROOKIES: .8X TO 2X BASIC CARDS
STATED ODDS 1:3 HOB/RET

2010 Topps Chrome Xfractors

*VETS: 3X TO 8X BASIC CARDS
*ROOKIES: 1.2X TO 3X BASIC CARDS
STATED ODDS 1:3 RETAIL

2010 Topps Chrome Anniversary Reprints

*REFRACT/99: 1X TO 2.5X BASIC INSERTS
1 Jim Brown 1.50 4.00
2 Eric Dickerson 1.00 2.50
3 Tony Dorsett 1.25 3.00
4 John Elway 2.00 5.00
5 Frank Gore .75 2.00
6 Steven Jackson .75 2.00
7 Chad Johnson .75 2.00
8 Felix Jones .75 2.00
9 Ray Lewis 1.00 2.50
10 Eli Manning 1.00 2.50
11 Peyton Manning 1.50 4.00
12 Dan Marino 2.50 6.00
13 Brandon Marshall .75 2.00
14 LeSean McCoy .75 2.00
15 Joe Montana 2.50 6.00
16 Adrian Peterson 1.50 4.00
17 Mark Sanchez 1.00 2.50
18 Gale Sayers 1.50 4.00
19 LaDainian Tomlinson 1.00 2.50
20 Reggie Wayne .75 2.00

2010 Topps Chrome Gridiron Lineage

*REFRACT/99: 1.2X TO 3X BASIC INSERTS
CGLAR Troy Aikman 1.25 3.00
Tony Romo
CGLBL Dwayne Bowe .75 2.00
Brandon LaFell
CGLDA Eric Dickerson .60 1.50
Joseph Addai
CGLDJ Eric Dickerson .60 1.50
Steven Jackson
CGLDM Tony Dorsett .75 2.00
LeSean McCoy
CGLET John Elway 3.00 8.00
Tim Tebow
CGLGG Antonio Gates 1.00 2.50
Jermaine Gresham
CGLGS Anthony Gonzalez .50 1.25
Jordan Shipley
CGLHM Percy Harvin .50 1.25
Dexter McCluster
CGLMC Joe Montana 1.50 4.00
Jimmy Clausen
CGLMT Brandon Marshall .60 1.50
Demaryius Thomas
CGLNS Joe Namath 1.00 2.50
Mark Sanchez
CGLPB Adrian Peterson .75 2.00
Jahvid Best
CGLPH Adrian Peterson 1.25 3.00
Percy Harvin
CGLSD Jonathan Stewart .50 1.25
Jonathan Dwyer
CGLSJ Emmitt Smith 1.25 3.00
Felix Jones
CGLST Emmitt Smith 1.25 3.00
LaDainian Tomlinson
CGLTM LaDainian Tomlinson 1.25 3.00
Ryan Mathews
CGLTS Thurman Thomas .75 2.00
C.J. Spiller
CGLWM Patrick Willis .50 1.25
Rolando McClain

2010 Topps Chrome Retail Exclusive Rookie Refractors

INSERTS IN SPECIAL RETAIL BOXES
TMB1 Sam Bradford 3.00 8.00
TMB2 Jimmy Clausen .75 2.00

2010 Topps Chrome Rookie Autographs

GROUP A ODDS 1:200 HOB
GROUP B ODDS 1:31 HOB
C3 Jahvid Best A 20.00 40.00
C13 Dexter McCluster B 5.00 12.00
C16 Jonathan Dwyer B 5.00 12.00
C17 Dezmon Briscoe B 4.00 10.00
C23 Ed Wang B 5.00 12.00
C36 Dan LeFevour B 5.00 12.00
C46 Ben Tate B 6.00 15.00
C47 Andre Roberts B 5.00 12.00
C49 Zac Robinson B 4.00 10.00
C51 Brandon LaFell B 5.00 12.00
C60 Dez Bryant A 40.00 80.00
C66 Taylor Price B 5.00 12.00
C70 Colt McCoy A 15.00 40.00
C74 Joe Webb B 5.00 12.00
C84 David Reed B 4.00 10.00
C87 Aaron Hernandez B 8.00 20.00
C98 Eric Decker B 8.00 20.00
C100 Tim Tebow A 100.00 175.00
C103 Riley Cooper B 5.00 12.00
C106 Emmanuel Sanders A 8.00 20.00
C110 Demaryius Thomas A 20.00 40.00
C112 Rob Gronkowski B 20.00 50.00
C120 C.J. Spiller A 12.00 30.00
C130 Jimmy Clausen A 8.00 20.00
C135 Earl Thomas B 5.00 12.00
C136 Armanti Edwards B 5.00 12.00
C139 Mike Kafka B 5.00 12.00
C140 Ryan Mathews A 25.00 50.00
C148 Jacoby Ford B 5.00 12.00
C150 Sam Bradford A 75.00 150.00
C159 Joe McKnight A 8.00 20.00
C160 Ndamukong Suh A 25.00 50.00
C161 Marcus Easley B 4.00 10.00
C168 Montario Hardesty B 5.00 12.00
C170 Gerald McCoy B 5.00 12.00
C172 Damian Williams B 5.00 12.00
C175 Tony Pike B 5.00 12.00
C186 Arrelious Benn B 5.00 12.00
C208 Jordan Shipley B 5.00 12.00
C218 John Skelton B 6.00 15.00

2010 Topps Chrome Rookie Autographs Black Refractors

*BLACK REF/25: 1X TO 2.5X BASIC GRP A
*BLACK REF/25: 1.5X TO 4X BASIC GRP B
BLACK REFRCTOR PRINT RUN 25
C60 Dez Bryant 175.00 300.00
C70 Colt McCoy 125.00 250.00
C100 Tim Tebow 350.00 600.00
C112 Rob Gronkowski 125.00 200.00
C140 Ryan Mathews 60.00 150.00
C150 Sam Bradford 350.00 600.00
C160 Ndamukong Suh 75.00 150.00

2010 Topps Chrome Rookie Autographs Refractors

*REFRACT/50: .6X TO 1.5X BASIC GRP A
*REFRACT/50: 1X TO 2.5X BASIC GRP B
REFRACTOR AU PRINT RUN 50
C60 Dez Bryant 100.00 175.00
C70 Colt McCoy 75.00 150.00
C100 Tim Tebow 175.00 300.00
C112 Rob Gronkowski 60.00 120.00
C140 Ryan Mathews 40.00 100.00
C150 Sam Bradford 150.00 300.00

2010 Topps Chrome Rookie Autographs Dual

STATED PRINT RUN 25 SER.#'d SETS
CDRA1 Colt McCoy 50.00 100.00
Montario Hardesty
CDRA2 Tim Tebow 125.00 200.00
Aaron Hernandez
CDRA3 Sam Bradford 100.00 200.00
Jimmy Clausen
CDRA4 C.J. Spiller 100.00 175.00
Ryan Mathews
CDRA5 Dez Bryant 50.00 100.00
Demaryius Thomas

2010 Topps Chrome Rookie Autographs Patch

PATCH AU/25 ODDS 1:1561 HOB
C3 Jahvid Best 50.00 120.00
C11 Golden Tate 20.00 50.00
C13 Dexter McCluster 20.00 50.00
C16 Jonathan Dwyer 20.00 50.00
C46 Ben Tate 25.00 60.00
C47 Andre Roberts 20.00 50.00
C51 Brandon LaFell 20.00 50.00
C60 Dez Bryant 125.00 250.00
C70 Colt McCoy 75.00 150.00
C86 Joe Haden 20.00 50.00
C98 Eric Decker 30.00 80.00
C100 Tim Tebow 250.00 500.00
C106 Emmanuel Sanders 20.00 50.00
C107 Jermaine Gresham 25.00 60.00
C110 Demaryius Thomas 75.00 125.00
C112 Rob Gronkowski 75.00 150.00
C120 C.J. Spiller 50.00 120.00
C130 Jimmy Clausen 20.00 50.00
C136 Armanti Edwards 20.00 50.00
C140 Ryan Mathews 60.00 150.00
C150 Sam Bradford 250.00 500.00
C159 Joe McKnight 20.00 50.00
C160 Ndamukong Suh 100.00 200.00
C168 Montario Hardesty 20.00 50.00
C170 Gerald McCoy 20.00 50.00
C172 Damian Williams 20.00 50.00
C186 Arrelious Benn 20.00 50.00
C195 Eric Berry 20.00 50.00
C208 Jordan Shipley 20.00 50.00
C212 Rolando McClain 20.00 50.00
C216 Toby Gerhart 20.00 50.00

2011 Topps Chrome

COMP.SET w/o SP's (220) 30.00 80.00
ROOKIE SP ODDS 1:330 HOB
1A Cam Newton RC 6.00 12.00
(football over right shoulder)
1B Cam Newton SP 40.00 80.00
(football at chest)
2 Ray Lewis .30 .75
3 Rob Housler RC .60 1.50
4 Matthew Stafford .30 .75
5 Gabe Carimi RC .75 2.00
6 Prince Amukamara RC .75 2.00
7 Beanie Wells .25 .60
8 Calvin Johnson .30 .75
9 Ryan Kerrigan RC .75 2.00
10 Arian Foster .25 .60
11 Ryan Torain .20 .50
12 Eli Manning .30 .75
13 Lance Kendricks RC .60 1.50
14 Adrian Clayborn RC .75 2.00
15 Darrelle Revis .25 .60
16 Percy Harvin .25 .60
17 Santana Moss .25 .60
18 Marshawn Lynch .25 .60
19 Lee Smith RC .60 1.50
20 Tom Brady .50 1.25
21 Matt Schaub .25 .60
22 Edmond Gates RC .60 1.50
23 Steve Smith .25 .60
24 Nathan Enderle RC .75 2.00
25A Colin Kaepernick RC 1.00 2.50
(passing the football)
25B Colin Kaepernick SP 8.00 20.00
(set to throw)
26 Tyrod Taylor RC .75 2.00
27 Patrick Willis .25 .60
28 Peyton Hillis .25 .60
29 Antonio Gates .25 .60
30 Chris Johnson .25 .60
31 Virgil Green RC .60 1.50
32 Da'Rel Scott RC .60 1.50
33 Denarius Moore RC 1.00 2.50
34 Sam Bradford .30 .75
35 Johnny White RC .60 1.50
36 Jason Witten .30 .75
37 Aldon Smith RC 1.25 3.00
38 Tyron Smith RC 1.00 2.50
39 Cameron Jordan RC .60 1.50
40 Maurice Jones-Drew .25 .60
41 Derrick Mason .20 .50
42 Vincent Brown RC .75 2.00
43 Felix Jones .25 .60
44 Rahim Moore RC .60 1.50
45 Kenny Britt .25 .60
46 Curtis Brown RC .75 2.00
47 Luke Stocker RC .60 1.50
48 Derek Sherrod RC .75 2.00
49 Brandon Pettigrew .20 .50
50A Mark Ingram RC 1.50 4.00
(football in both hands)
50B Mark Ingram SP 12.00 30.00
(football in right arm)
51A Andy Dalton RC 2.00 5.00
(football in right hand)
51B Andy Dalton SP 25.00 50.00
(football in air)
52 James Harrison .30 .75
53 Ricky Stanzi RC 1.00 2.50
54 Joseph Addai .25 .60
55A Blaine Gabbert RC 1.25 3.00
(set to throw)
55B Blaine Gabbert SP 10.00 25.00
(running the football)
56 Jeremy Kerley RC .75 2.00
57 Chad Ochocinco .25 .60
58 Jordan Cameron RC .60 1.50
59 Brandon Marshall .25 .60
60 Andre Johnson .25 .60
61 Taiwan Jones RC .75 2.00
62 Kendall Hunter RC .75 2.00
63 Jimmy Smith RC .75 2.00
64 LeSean McCoy .25 .60
65 D.J. Williams RC .75 2.00
66 Mike Pouncey RC .75 2.00
67 Greg Jennings .25 .60
68 Owen Daniels .20 .50
69 Darren McFadden .25 .60
70 Michael Vick .30 .75
71A Ryan Williams RC 1.00 2.50
(running the football)
71B Ryan Williams SP 8.00 20.00
(one handed catch)
72 Da'Quan Bowers RC .75 2.00
73 Jamaal Charles .25 .60
74A Mikel Leshoure RC .75 2.00
(running the football)
74B Mikel Leshoure SP 6.00 15.00
(catching the football)
75 Ronnie Brown .25 .60
76 Jimmy Graham .30 .75
77 Jermichael Finley .25 .60
78 DeSean Jackson .25 .60
79 Brian Urlacher .30 .75
80 Larry Fitzgerald .25 .60
81 Hakeem Nicks .25 .60
82 Evan Royster RC .75 2.00
83 Matt Forte .25 .60
84 Sidney Rice .25 .60
85 Hines Ward .25 .60
86 Greg McElroy RC .75 2.00
87 Tony Gonzalez .25 .60
88A Greg Little RC .75 2.00
(running the football)
88B Greg Little SP 6.00 15.00
(one handed catch)
89 Kris Durham RC .60 1.50
90 Philip Rivers .30 .75
91 Dez Bryant .30 .75
92 Julius Thomas RC .60 1.50
93A Randall Cobb RC 1.00 2.50
(overhead catch)
93B Randall Cobb SP 8.00 20.00
(football at chest)
94 Niles Paul RC .75 2.00
95 Joe Flacco .30 .75
96 C.J. Spiller .25 .60
97A Torrey Smith RC 1.00 2.50
(looking up for football)
97B Torrey Smith SP 8.00 20.00
(one handed catch)
98 Wes Welker .30 .75
99 Dwayne Bowe .25 .60
100 Aaron Rodgers .50 1.25
101 Randy Moss .25 .60
102 Brooks Reed RC .75 2.00
103 Ryan Mathews .25 .60
104 J.J. Watt RC 1.00 2.50
105 Dallas Clark .25 .60
106 Delone Carter RC .60 1.50
107 Matt Cassel .25 .60
108 Knowshon Moreno .25 .60
109 Ras-I Dowling RC .75 2.00
110 Peyton Manning .50 1.25
111A Leonard Hankerson RC .75 2.00
(reaching up for football)
111B Leonard Hankerson SP 6.00 15.00
(one handed catch)
112 Corey Liuget RC .50 1.25
113 Dontay Moch RC .50 1.25
114 Reggie Wayne .25 .60
115 Justin Houston RC .75 2.00
116 Greg Salas RC .75 2.00
117 Cameron Heyward RC .75 2.00
118 Anthony Allen RC .50 1.25
119 Anquan Boldin .25 .60
120 Ben Roethlisberger .30 .75
121 Santonio Holmes .25 .60
122A Ryan Mallett RC 1.50 4.00
scrambling pose)
122B Ryan Mallett SP 12.00 30.00
(passing pose)
123A Jon Baldwin RC .75 2.00
(hands at chest)
123B Jon Baldwin SP 6.00 15.00
(one handed catch)
124 Marcell Dareus RC .75 2.00
125 Jabaal Sheard RC .75 2.00
126 Phil Taylor RC .60 1.50
127 Danny Watkins RC .60 1.50
128 Bilal Powell RC .50 1.25
129 Martez Wilson RC .75 2.00
130 Drew Brees .30 .75
131A Julio Jones RC 1.50 4.00
(hands at chest)
131B Julio Jones SP 12.00 30.00
(hands above head)
132 Rob Gronkowski .30 .75
133 Mike Wallace .30 .75
134 Kellen Winslow .25 .60
135 Jordan Todman RC .50 1.25
136A Daniel Thomas RC .75 2.00
(football in right arm)
136B Daniel Thomas SP 6.00 15.00
(football in left arm)
137A Titus Young RC 1.00 2.50
(football above head)
137B Titus Young SP 8.00 20.00
(football at chest)
138 Braylon Edwards .25 .60
139 Malcom Floyd .25 .60
140 Matt Ryan .30 .75
141 Jay Cutler .25 .60
142 Jeremy Maclin .25 .60
143 LaDainian Tomlinson .30 .75
144 Allen Bailey RC .60 1.50
145 Dwayne Harris RC .75 2.00
146 Mike Williams .25 .60
147 Steve Johnson .25 .60
148 Tim Tebow .60 1.50
149 Alex Green RC .75 2.00
150A A.J. Green RC 1.50 4.00
(running to the left)
150B A.J. Green SP 12.00 30.00
(running forward)
151 Quinton Carter RC .50 1.25
152 Cedric Benson .25 .60
153 Julius Peppers .25 .60
154 Marques Colston .25 .60
155 Clay Matthews .30 .75
156 Aaron Williams RC .60 1.50
157 Vincent Jackson .25 .60
158 Ed Reed .25 .60
159 T.J. Yates RC 1.00 2.50
160 Tony Romo .30 .75
161 DeAngelo Williams .25 .60
162 Brandon Lloyd .25 .60
163 Jacquizz Rodgers RC .75 2.00
164 James Carpenter RC .75 2.00
165A Christian Ponder RC 1.50 4.00
(football in right hand)
165B Christian Ponder SP 12.00 30.00
(football in both hands)
166 Akeem Ayers RC .60 1.50
167 Christian Ballard RC .60 1.50
168 Dion Lewis RC .75 2.00
169 Ryan Whalen RC .60 1.50
170 Mark Sanchez .30 .75
171 Marvin Austin RC .60 1.50
172 Deion Branch .20 .50
173A DeMarco Murray RC 1.50 4.00
(football in both hands)
173B DeMarco Murray SP 20.00 40.00
(football in left arm)
174 Tandon Doss RC .60 1.50
175 Bruce Carter RC .75 2.00
176 Chris Cooley .25 .60
177 Josh Freeman .30 .75
178 Robert Quinn RC .75 2.00
179 DeMarcus Ware .25 .60
180 Troy Polamalu .30 .75
181A Jamie Harper RC .75 2.00
(left hand visible)
181B Jamie Harper SP 5.00 12.00
(left hand cropped out)
182 Brandon Harris RC .50 1.25
183 Jonathan Stewart .25 .60
184A Shane Vereen RC .75 2.00
(running the football)
184B Shane Vereen SP 6.00 15.00
(leaping catch)
185A Jake Locker RC 2.00 5.00
(passing the football)
185B Jake Locker SP 15.00 40.00
(running the football)
186 Brandon Jacobs .25 .60
187 Shonn Greene .25 .60
188 Jordan Shipley .25 .60
189 Casey Matthews RC .75 2.00
190 Michael Turner .25 .60
191A Jerrel Jernigan RC .60 1.50
(catching football pose)
191B Jerrel Jernigan SP 5.00 12.00
(leaping pose)
192 Muhammad Wilkerson RC .75 2.00
193 Stevan Ridley RC .75 2.00
194 Kealoha Pilares RC .75 2.00
195 Miles Austin .25 .60
196 Cecil Shorts RC .60 1.50
197 Jahvid Best .25 .60
198 Donovan McNabb .30 .75
199 Vernon Davis .25 .60
200 Steven Jackson .25 .60
201 Frank Gore .25 .60
202 Pierre Garcon .25 .60
203A Kyle Rudolph RC .75 2.00
(overhead catch)
203B Kyle Rudolph SP 6.00 15.00
(one handed catch)
204 Ronald Johnson RC .60 1.50
205 Aldrick Robinson RC .50 1.25
206 Roy Helu RC 1.50 4.00
207 Ahmad Bradshaw .25 .60
208 Austin Pettis RC .60 1.50
209 Roddy White .25 .60
210 Ray Rice .25 .60
211 Patrick Peterson RC 1.25 3.00
212A Von Miller RC 1.00 2.50
(making an interception)
212B Von Miller SP 8.00 20.00
(set to cover a receiver)
213 Anthony Castonzo RC .50 1.25
214 Carson Palmer .25 .60
215 Nate Solder RC .75 2.00
216 Stephen Paea RC .75 2.00
217 Nick Fairley RC 1.00 2.50
218 Rashard Mendenhall .25 .60
219 Allen Bradford RC .60 1.50
220 Adrian Peterson .40 1.00

2011 Topps Chrome Black Refractors

*VETS/299: 5X TO 12X BASIC CARDS
*ROOKIES/299: 2X TO 5X BASIC CARDS
BLACK REF/299 ODDS 1:30 HOB
1 Cam Newton 30.00 80.00

2011 Topps Chrome Blue Refractors

*VETS/199: 6X TO 15X BASIC CARDS
*ROOKIES/199: 2.5X TO 6X BASIC CARDS
BLUE REF/199 ODDS 1:47
1 Cam Newton 40.00 100.00

2011 Topps Chrome Crystal Atomic Refractors

*VETS/139: 8X TO 20X BASIC CARDS
*ROOKIES/139: 3X TO 8X BASIC CARDS
CRYSTAL ATOMIC/139 ODDS 1:24 HOB
1 Cam Newton 50.00 100.00

2011 Topps Chrome Gold Refractors

*VETS/50: 10X TO 25X BASIC CARDS
*ROOKIES/50: 4X TO 10X BASIC CARDS
GOLD REF/50 ODDS 1:188 HOB
1 Cam Newton 100.00 175.00
51 Andy Dalton 50.00 100.00
165 Christian Ponder 40.00 80.00
173 DeMarco Murray 50.00 100.00
185 Jake Locker 40.00 80.00

2011 Topps Chrome Orange Refractors

*VETS: 3X TO 8X BASIC CARDS
*ROOKIES: 1.2X TO 3X BASIC CARDS
THREE ORANGE REF PER RETAIL JUMBO
1 Cam Newton 15.00 40.00

2011 Topps Chrome Purple Refractors

*VETS/499: 4X TO 10X BASIC CARDS
*ROOKIES/499: 1.5X TO 4X BASIC CARDS
PURPLE/499 INSERTED IN RETAIL BLASTER
1 Cam Newton 30.00 60.00

2011 Topps Chrome Red Refractors

*VETS/25: 12X TO 30X BASIC CARDS
*ROOKIES/25: 6X TO 15X BASIC CARDS
RED REF/25 ODDS 1:375 HOB
1 Cam Newton 150.00 250.00
51 Andy Dalton 75.00 150.00
150 A.J. Green 40.00 80.00
165 Christian Ponder 75.00 150.00
173 DeMarco Murray 75.00 150.00
185 Jake Locker 75.00 150.00

2011 Topps Chrome Refractors

*VETS: 2.5X TO 6X BASIC CARDS
*ROOKIES: 1X TO 2.5X BASIC CARDS
STATED ODDS 1:3 HOB
1 Cam Newton 12.00 30.00

2011 Topps Chrome Sepia Refractors

*VETS/99: 6X TO 15X BASIC CARDS
*ROOKIES/99: 2.5X TO 6X BASIC CARDS
SEPIA REF/99 ODDS 1:33 HOB
1 Cam Newton 75.00 150.00
165 Christian Ponder 12.00 30.00

2011 Topps Chrome Xfractors

*VETS: 3X TO 8X BASIC CARDS
*ROOKIES: 1.2X TO 3X BASIC CARDS
RANDOM INSERTS IN RETAIL BLASTER
1 Cam Newton 20.00 50.00

2011 Topps Chrome Finest Freshman

COMPLETE SET (36) 12.00 30.00
STATED ODDS 1:6 HOB
*ATOMIC REF/50: 3X TO 8X BASIC INSERTS
*GOLD REF/75: 2.5X TO 6X BASIC INSERTS
*REFRACT/99: 2X TO 5X BASIC INSERTS
FFAD Andy Dalton 1.50 4.00
FFAG Alex Green .60 1.50
FFAJG A.J. Green 1.25 3.00
FFAP Austin Pettis .50 1.25
FFBG Blaine Gabbert 1.00 2.50
FFBP Bilal Powell .40 1.00
FFCK Colin Kaepernick .75 2.00
FFCM Cam Newton 3.00 8.00
FFCP Christian Ponder 1.25 3.00

FFDC Delone Carter .50 1.25
FFDM DeMarco Murray 1.25 3.00
FFDT Daniel Thomas .60 1.50
FFEG Edmond Gates .50 1.25
FFGL Greg Little .60 1.50
FFJB Jon Baldwin .60 1.50
FFJH Jamie Harper .60 1.50
FFJJ Julio Jones 1.25 3.00
FFJE Jerrel Jernigan .50 1.25
FFJL Jake Locker 1.50 4.00
FFJT Jordan Todman .40 1.00
FFKH Kendall Hunter .60 1.50
FFKR Kyle Rudolph .60 1.50
FFLH Leonard Hankerson .60 1.50
FFMD Marcell Dareus .60 1.50
FFMI Mark Ingram 1.25 3.00
FFML Mikel Leshoure .60 1.50
FFRC Randall Cobb .75 2.00
FFRM Ryan Mallett. 1.25 3.00
FFRW Ryan Williams .75 2.00
FFSR Stevan Ridley .60 1.50
FFSV Shane Vereen .60 1.50
FFTJ Taiwan Jones .60 1.50
FFTS Torrey Smith .75 2.00
FFTY Titus Young .75 2.00
FFVB Vincent Brown .60 1.50
FFVM Von Miller .75 2.00

2011 Topps Chrome Rookie Autographs

GROUP A ODDS 1:502 HOB
GROUP B ODDS 1:153 HOB
GROUP C ODDS 1:50 HOB
EXCH EXPIRATION: 10/31/2014
1 Cam Newton A 175.00 300.00
9 Ryan Kerrigan C 5.00 12.00
13 Lance Kendricks 4.00 10.00
22 Edmond Gates C 4.00 10.00
25 Colin Kaepernick A 15.00 40.00
37 Aldon Smith C 8.00 20.00
42 Vincent Brown C 5.00 12.00
50 Mark Ingram A 40.00 80.00
51 Andy Dalton A 50.00 100.00
55 Blaine Gabbert A 30.00 60.00
61 Taiwan Jones C 5.00 12.00
62 Kendall Hunter C 6.00 15.00
65 D.J. Williams B 5.00 12.00
71 Ryan Williams A 8.00 20.00
74 Mikel Leshoure B 6.00 15.00
86 Greg McElroy C 5.00 12.00
88 Greg Little B 6.00 15.00
93 Randall Cobb B 8.00 20.00
97 Torrey Smith B 8.00 20.00
106 Delone Carter C 4.00 10.00
111 Leonard Hankerson B 5.00 12.00
116 Greg Salas C 5.00 12.00
122 Ryan Mallett A 20.00 40.00
123 Jon Baldwin B 8.00 20.00
124 Marcell Dareus B 5.00 12.00
128 Bilal Powell C 3.00 8.00
135 Jordan Todman C 3.00 8.00
136 Daniel Thomas C 6.00 15.00
137 Titus Young B 8.00 20.00
145 Dwayne Harris B 5.00 12.00
149 Alex Green C 5.00 12.00
150 A.J. Green A 30.00 60.00
165 Christian Ponder A 50.00 100.00
166 Akeem Ayers C 4.00 10.00
168 Dion Lewis C 4.00 10.00
173 DeMarco Murray C 40.00 80.00
181 Jamie Harper C 5.00 12.00
184 Shane Vereen C 5.00 12.00
185 Jake Locker A 50.00 100.00
191 Jerrel Jernigan C 4.00 10.00
193 Stevan Ridley C 5.00 12.00
203 Kyle Rudolph C 5.00 12.00
204 Ronald Johnson C 4.00 10.00
208 Austin Pettis C 4.00 10.00
212 Von Miller B 10.00 25.00

2011 Topps Chrome Rookie Autographs Black Refractors

*BLK REF/25: 1.2X TO 3X BASE AU GRP A
*BLK REF/25: 1.5X TO 4X BASE AU GRP B-C
BLACK REF/25 ODDS 1:836 HOB
1 Cam Newton 600.00 900.00
50 Mark Ingram 150.00 250.00
51 Andy Dalton 200.00 350.00
165 Christian Ponder 125.00 250.00
173 DeMarco Murray 250.00 400.00
185 Jake Locker 175.00 350.00

2011 Topps Chrome Rookie Autographs Crystal Atomic Refractors

*ATOM.REF/50: .8X TO 2X BASE AU GRP A
*ATOM.REF/50: 1X TO 2.5X BASE AU GRP B-C
ATOMIC REF/50 ODDS 1:341 HOB
1 Cam Newton 500.00 800.00
50 Mark Ingram 60.00 150.00
51 Andy Dalton 125.00 200.00
165 Christian Ponder 150.00 250.00
173 DeMarco Murray 150.00 250.00
185 Jake Locker 100.00 200.00

2011 Topps Chrome Rookie Autographs Refractors

*REF/99: .6X TO 1.5X BASE AU GRP A
*REF/99: .8X TO 2X BASE AU GRP B-C
REFRACTOR/99 ODDS 1:462 HOB
1 Cam Newton 300.00 500.00
50 Mark Ingram 75.00 150.00
51 Andy Dalton 100.00 175.00
165 Christian Ponder 75.00 150.00
173 DeMarco Murray 100.00 200.00
185 Jake Locker 100.00 175.00

2011 Topps Chrome Rookie Autographs Refractors Variations

*UNNUMBERED REF: .4X TO 1X REF AU/99
UNNUMBERED REF ODDS 1:572 HOB
1 Cam Newton 300.00 450.00
131 Julio Jones 90.00 150.00

2011 Topps Chrome Rookie Autographs Dual

DUAL AUTO/25 ODDS 1:16,500 HOB
CDRA1 Cam Newton 150.00 250.00
Jake Locker
CDRA2 A.J. Green 60.00 120.00
Julio Jones
CDRA3 Mark Ingram 75.00 150.00
Julio Jones
CDRA4 Blaine Gabbert 75.00 150.00
Christian Ponder
CDRA5 A.J. Green 40.00 80.00
Jon Baldwin

2011 Topps Chrome Rookie Autographs Patch

PATCH AU/25 ODDS 1:795 HOB
AD Andy Dalton 150.00 250.00
AG Alex Green 20.00 50.00
AJG A.J. Green 100.00 175.00
AP Austin Pettis 15.00 40.00
BG Blaine Gabbert 60.00 150.00
BP Bilal Powell 12.00 30.00
CK Colin Kaepernick 40.00 100.00
CN Cam Newton 300.00 500.00
CP Christian Ponder 125.00 250.00
DC Delone Carter 15.00 40.00
DM DeMarco Murray 175.00 300.00
DT Daniel Thomas 20.00 50.00
EG Edmond Gates 15.00 40.00
GL Greg Little 20.00 50.00
JB Jon Baldwin 30.00 80.00
JH Jamie Harper 20.00 50.00
JH Leonard Hankerson 20.00 50.00
JJ Julio Jones 90.00 150.00
JJE Jerrel Jernigan 15.00 40.00
JL Jake Locker 125.00 250.00
JT Jordan Todman 12.00 30.00
KH Kendall Hunter 25.00 60.00
KR Kyle Rudolph
MD Marcell Dareus 20.00 50.00
MI Mark Ingram 100.00 200.00
ML Mikel Leshoure 20.00 50.00
RC Randall Cobb EXCH
RM Ryan Mallett 50.00 100.00
RW Ryan Williams 25.00 60.00
SR Stevan Ridley 20.00 50.00
SV Shane Vereen 20.00 50.00
TJ Taiwan Jones 20.00 50.00
TS Torrey Smith 25.00 60.00
TY Titus Young 25.00 60.00
VB Vincent Brown 20.00 50.00
VM Von Miller 25.00 60.00

2011 Topps Chrome Rookie Recognition

COMPLETE SET (36) 20.00 50.00
STATED ODDS 1:12 HOB
RRAD Andy Dalton 2.00 5.00
RRAG Alex Green .75 2.00
RRAJG A.J. Green 1.50 4.00
RRAP Austin Pettis .75 2.00
RRBG Blaine Gabbert 1.25 3.00
RRBP Bilal Powell .50 1.25
RRCK Colin Kaepernick 1.00 2.50
RRCM Cam Newton 4.00 10.00
RRCP Christian Ponder 1.50 4.00
RRDC Delone Carter .60 1.50
RRDM DeMarco Murray 1.50 4.00
RRDT Daniel Thomas .75 2.00
RREG Edmond Gates .60 1.50
RRGL Greg Little .75 2.00
RRJB Jon Baldwin .75 2.00
RRJH Jamie Harper 1.00 2.50
RRJJ Julio Jones 1.50 4.00
RRJE Jerrel Jernigan .60 1.50
RRJL Jake Locker 2.00 5.00
RRJT Jordan Todman .50 1.25
RRKH Kendall Hunter .75 2.00
RRKR Kyle Rudolph .75 2.00
RRLH Leonard Hankerson .75 2.00
RRMD Marcell Dareus .75 2.00
RRMI Mark Ingram 1.50 4.00
RRML Mikel Leshoure .75 2.00
RRRC Randall Cobb 1.00 2.50
RRRM Ryan Mallett 1.50 4.00
RRRW Ryan Williams 1.00 2.50
RRSR Stevan Ridley .75 2.00
RRSV Shane Vereen .75 2.00
RRTJ Taiwan Jones .75 2.00
RRTS Torrey Smith 1.00 2.50
RRTY Titus Young 1.00 2.50
RRVB Vincent Brown .75 2.00
RRVM Von Miller 1.00 2.50

2011 Topps Chrome Rookie Recognition Autographs

STATED ODDS 1:818 HOB
RRAAD Andy Dalton EXCH 60.00 120.00
RRAAG Alex Green
RRAAJG A.J. Green 40.00 80.00
RRAAP Austin Pettis 6.00 15.00
RRABG Blaine Gabbert 30.00 80.00
RRABP Bilal Powell 5.00 12.00
RRACK Colin Kaepernick 15.00 40.00
RRACM Cam Newton 250.00 400.00
RRACP Christian Ponder 60.00 120.00
RRADC Delone Carter 6.00 15.00
RRADM DeMarco Murray 60.00 120.00
RRADT Daniel Thomas 25.00 50.00
RRAEG Edmond Gates 6.00 15.00
RRAGL Greg Little 10.00 25.00
RRAJB Jon Baldwin 20.00 40.00
RRAJH Jamie Harper 8.00 20.00
RRAJJ Julio Jones
RRAJJE Jerrel Jernigan 6.00 15.00
RRAJL Jake Locker 40.00 80.00
RRAJT Jordan Todman 5.00 12.00
RRAKH Kendall Hunter 10.00 25.00
RRAKR Kyle Rudolph 8.00 20.00
RRALH Leonard Hankerson 8.00 20.00
RRAMI Mark Ingram 60.00 100.00
RRAML Mikel Leshoure 8.00 20.00
RRARC Randall Cobb 10.00 25.00
RRARM Ryan Mallett 25.00 50.00
RRARW Ryan Williams 12.00 30.00
RRASR Stevan Ridley 8.00 20.00
RRASV Shane Vereen 8.00 20.00
RRATJ Taiwan Jones 10.00 25.00
RRATS Torrey Smith 12.00 30.00
RRATY Titus Young 12.00 30.00
RRAVB Vincent Brown 8.00 20.00
RRAVM Von Miller 12.00 30.00

2011 Topps Chrome Superlative Rookies

STATED ODDS 1:24 HOB
*BLUE REF/50: 1.5X TO 4X BASIC INSERTS
SRAD Andy Dalton 3.00 8.00
SRAG Alex Green 1.25 3.00
SRAJG A.J. Green 2.50 6.00
SRAP Austin Pettis 1.00 2.50
SRBG Blaine Gabbert 2.00 5.00
SRBP Bilal Powell .75 2.00
SRCK Colin Kaepernick 1.50 4.00
SRCM Cam Newton 6.00 15.00
SRCP Christian Ponder 2.50 6.00
SRDC Delone Carter 1.00 2.50
SRDM DeMarco Murray 2.50 6.00
SRDT Daniel Thomas 1.25 3.00
SREG Edmond Gates 1.00 2.50
SRGL Greg Little 1.25 3.00
SRJB Jon Baldwin 1.25 3.00
SRJH Jamie Harper 1.25 3.00
SRJJ Julio Jones 2.50 6.00
SRJE Jerrel Jernigan 1.00 2.50
SRJL Jake Locker 3.00 8.00
SRJT Jordan Todman .75 2.00
SRKH Kendall Hunter 1.25 3.00
SRKR Kyle Rudolph 1.25 3.00
SRLH Leonard Hankerson 1.25 3.00
SRMD Marcell Dareus 1.25 3.00
SRMI Mark Ingram 2.50 6.00
SRML Mikel Leshoure 1.25 3.00
SRRC Randall Cobb 1.50 4.00
SRRM Ryan Mallett 2.50 6.00
SRRW Ryan Williams 1.50 4.00
SRSR Stevan Ridley 1.25 3.00
SRSV Shane Vereen 1.25 3.00
SRTJ Taiwan Jones 1.25 3.00
SRTS Torrey Smith 1.50 4.00
SRTY Titus Young 1.50 4.00
SRVB Vincent Brown 1.25 3.00
SRVM Von Miller 1.50 4.00

2011 Topps Chrome Superlative Rookies Red Refractors

*RED REF/25: 2.6X TO 6X BASIC INSERTS
RED REF/25 ODDS 1:2360 HOB
SRCM Cam Newton 100.00 175.00

2007 Topps Co-Signers

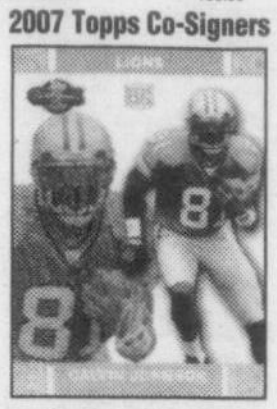

This 100-card set was released in November, 2007. The set was issued into the hobby in six-card packs, with a $10 SRP, which came 12 packs to a box. The set contains veteran players (1-35); retired greats (36-50) and 2007 NFL rookies (51-100). The Rookie Cards were issued to a stated print run of 2249 serial numbered cards and were inserted into packs at a stated rate of one in three.

COMP.SET w/o RC's (50) 8.00 20.00
ROOKIE/2249 ODDS 1:3
UNPRICED PRINT PLATE/1 ODDS 1:838
1 Peyton Manning .75 2.00
2 Brett Favre 1.00 2.50
3 Carson Palmer .40 1.00
4 Tom Brady .75 2.00
5 Eli Manning .50 1.25
6 Philip Rivers .50 1.25
7 Matt Leinart .40 1.00
8 Vince Young .40 1.00
9 Jay Cutler .50 1.25
10 Ben Roethlisberger .50 1.25
11 Drew Brees .50 1.25
12 LaDainian Tomlinson .50 1.25
13 Larry Johnson .30 .75
14 Frank Gore .50 1.25
15 Steven Jackson .50 1.25
16 Willie Parker .40 1.00
17 Rudi Johnson .40 1.00
18 Thomas Jones .40 1.00
19 Edgerrin James .40 1.00
20 Julius Jones .30 .75
21 Joseph Addai .40 1.00
22 Maurice Jones-Drew .50 1.25
23 Shaun Alexander .40 1.00
24 Laurence Maroney .40 1.00
25 Cedric Benson .40 1.00
26 Reggie Bush .50 1.25
27 Chad Johnson .40 1.00
28 Marvin Harrison .50 1.25
29 Steve Smith .40 1.00
30 Randy Moss .50 1.25
31 Terrell Owens .50 1.25
32 Andre Johnson .40 1.00
33 Greg Jennings .50 1.25
34 Marques Colston .50 1.25
35 Jerricho Cotchery .40 1.00
36 Troy Aikman .75 2.00
37 Terry Bradshaw 1.00 2.50
38 John Elway 1.00 2.50
39 Roger Staubach 1.00 2.50
40 Dan Marino 1.25 3.00
41 Joe Namath .75 2.00
42 Joe Montana 1.25 3.00
43 Paul Hornung .60 1.50
44 Emmitt Smith 1.25 3.00
45 Jim Brown .75 2.00
46 Barry Sanders 1.00 2.50
47 Marcus Allen .60 1.50
48 Tony Dorsett .60 1.50
49 Fred Biletnikoff .60 1.50
50 Jerry Rice 1.00 2.50
51 JaMarcus Russell RC .75 2.00
52 John Beck RC 1.25 3.00
53 Trent Edwards RC 1.25 3.00
54 Chris Leak RC 1.00 2.50
55 Brady Quinn RC 1.25 3.00
56 Jeff Rowe RC .75 2.00
57 Troy Smith RC 1.25 3.00
58 Kevin Kolb RC 2.00 5.00
59 Drew Stanton RC .75 2.00
60 Jordan Palmer RC 1.00 2.50
61 Luke Getsy RC 1.25 3.00
62 Brian Leonard RC 1.00 2.50
63 Lorenzo Booker RC 1.00 2.50
64 Michael Bush RC 1.25 3.00
65 Chris Henry RC .75 2.00
66 Tony Hunt RC .75 2.00
67 Kenny Irons RC .75 2.00
68 Brandon Jackson RC 1.00 2.50
69 Marshawn Lynch RC 1.25 3.00
70 Adrian Peterson RC 5.00 12.00
71 Garrett Wolfe RC .75 2.00
72 Antonio Pittman RC .75 2.00
73 Kolby Smith RC 1.00 2.50
74 Greg Olsen RC 1.00 2.50
75 Zach Miller RC 1.25 3.00
76 Dwayne Bowe RC 1.50 4.00
77 Steve Breaston RC 1.25 3.00
78 David Clowney RC 1.00 2.50
79 Craig Buster Davis RC 1.00 2.50
80 Chris Davis RC .75 2.00
81 Yamon Figurs RC .75 2.00
82 Ted Ginn RC 1.00 2.50
83 Anthony Gonzalez RC 1.25 3.00
84 Jason Hill RC 1.25 3.00
85 Dwayne Jarrett RC 1.00 2.50
86 Calvin Johnson RC 4.00 10.00
87 Robert Meachem RC 1.25 3.00
88 Sidney Rice RC 1.50 4.00
89 Steve Smith RC 1.25 3.00
90 Mike Walker RC 1.25 3.00
91 Roy Hall RC 1.25 3.00
92 Dallas Baker RC .75 2.00
93 Johnnie Lee Higgins RC 1.00 2.50
94 Ryne Robinson RC 1.00 2.50
95 Chansi Stuckey RC 1.25 3.00
96 Gaines Adams RC 1.25 3.00
97 Adam Carriker RC 1.00 2.50
98 Paul Posluszny RC 1.25 3.00
99 Patrick Willis RC 2.50 6.00
100 LaRon Landry RC 1.25 3.00

2007 Topps Co-Signers Changing Faces Gold Red

GOLD RED PRINT RUN 399 SER.#'d SETS
*GOLD BLUE/349: .4X TO 1X GOLD RED/399
GOLD BLUE/349 ODDS 1:5
*GOLD GREEN/249: .5X TO 1.2X GOLD RED/399
GOLD GREEN/249 ODDS 1:7
*HOLOGOLD BLUE/25: 2X TO 5X GOLD RED/399
HOLOGOLD BLUE/25 ODDS 1:68
UNPRICED HOLOGOLD GREEN/1 ODDS 1:676
*HOLOGOLD RED/50: 1X TO 2.5X GOLD RED/399
HOLOGOLD RED/50 ODDS 1:34
*HOLOSLVR BLUE/99: .8X TO 2X GOLD RED/399
HOLOSILVER BLUE/99 ODDS 1:17
*HLSLVR GREEN/75: .8X TO 2X GOLD RED/399
HOLOSILVER GREEN/75 1:23
*HLSLVR RED/150: .6X TO 1.5X GOLD RED/399
HOLOSILVER RED/150 ODDS 1:12
1A Peyton Manning 2.00 5.00
Marvin Harrison
1B Peyton Manning 2.00 5.00
Anthony Gonzalez
2A Brett Favre 2.50 6.00
Paul Hornung
2B Brett Favre 1.00 2.50
Brandon Jackson
3A Carson Palmer 1.00 2.50
Chad Johnson
3B Carson Palmer 1.00 2.50
Jeff Rowe
4A Tom Brady 2.50 6.00
Randy Moss
4B Tom Brady 2.00 5.00
Steve Breaston
5A Eli Manning 1.50 4.00
Peyton Manning
5B Eli Manning 1.25 3.00
Steve Smith USC
6A Philip Rivers 1.25 3.00
LaDainian Tomlinson
6B Philip Rivers 1.25 3.00
Craig Buster Davis
7A Matt Leinart 1.00 2.50
Edgerrin James
7B Matt Leinart 1.25 3.00
Steve Breaston
8A Vince Young 2.50 6.00
John Elway
8B Vince Young 1.00 2.50
Chris Henry
9A Jay Cutler 3.00 8.00
John Elway
9B Jay Cutler 1.25 3.00
Chris Leak
10A Ben Roethlisberger 2.00 5.00
Terry Bradshaw
10B Ben Roethlisberger 1.25 3.00
Dallas Baker
11A Drew Brees 1.25 3.00
Reggie Bush
11B Drew Brees 1.25 3.00
Robert Meachem
12A LaDainian Tomlinson 1.50 4.00
Barry Sanders
12B LaDainian Tomlinson 1.25 3.00
Craig Buster Davis
13A Larry Johnson 1.25 3.00
Marcus Allen
13B Larry Johnson .75 2.00
Kolby Smith
14A Frank Gore 1.25 3.00
Joe Montana
14B Frank Gore 1.25 3.00
Jason Hill
15A Steven Jackson 1.25 3.00
Shaun Alexander
15B Steven Jackson 1.25 3.00
Brian Leonard
16A Willie Parker 1.25 3.00
Ben Roethlisberger
16B Willie Parker 1.00 2.50
Dallas Baker
17A Rudi Johnson 1.00 2.50
Carson Palmer
17B Rudi Johnson 1.00 2.50
Kenny Irons
18A Thomas Jones 1.00 2.50
Jerricho Cotchery
18B Thomas Jones 1.25 3.00
Chansi Stuckey
19A Edgerrin James 1.00 2.50
Matt Leinart
19B Edgerrin James 1.25 3.00
Steve Breaston
20A Julius Jones 2.00 5.00
Emmitt Smith
20B Julius Jones .75 2.00
Brady Quinn
21A Joseph Addai 2.00 5.00
Peyton Manning
21B Joseph Addai 1.25 3.00
Roy Hall
22A Maurice Jones-Drew 1.25 3.00
Laurence Maroney
22B Maurice Jones-Drew 1.25 3.00
Mike Walker
23A Shaun Alexander 1.00 2.50
Larry Johnson
23B Shaun Alexander 1.00 2.50
Kenny Irons
24A Laurence Maroney 1.50 4.00
Tom Brady
24B Laurence Maroney 1.00 2.50
Tony Hunt
25A Cedric Benson .75 2.00
Vince Young
25B Cedric Benson 1.00 2.50
Garrett Wolfe
26A Reggie Bush 1.25 3.00
Drew Brees
26B Reggie Bush .75 2.00
Antonio Pittman
27A Chad Johnson 1.00 2.50
Rudi Johnson
27B Chad Johnson 1.00 2.50
Jeff Rowe
28A Marvin Harrison 1.25 3.00
Joseph Addai
28B Marvin Harrison 1.25 3.00
Anthony Gonzalez
29A Steve Smith 1.50 4.00
Jerry Rice
29B Steve Smith 1.00 2.50
Dwayne Jarrett
30A Randy Moss 1.25 3.00
Laurence Maroney
30B Randy Moss 2.50 6.00
Calvin Johnson
31A Terrell Owens 1.25 3.00
Troy Aikman
31B Terrell Owens .75 2.00
Ted Ginn Jr.
32A Andre Johnson 1.25 3.00
Fred Biletnikoff
32B Andre Johnson 1.00 2.50
Greg Olsen
33A Greg Jennings 2.00 5.00
Brett Favre
33B Greg Jennings 1.00 2.50
David Clowney
34A Marques Colston 1.00 2.50
Reggie Bush
34B Marques Colston 1.25 3.00
Robert Meachem
35A Jerricho Cotchery 1.00 2.50
Thomas Jones
35B Jerricho Cotchery 1.25 3.00
Chansi Stuckey
36A Troy Aikman 2.50 6.00
Emmitt Smith
36B Troy Aikman 1.00 2.50
Brady Quinn
37A Terry Bradshaw 2.00 5.00
Willie Parker
37B Terry Bradshaw 2.00 5.00
Dallas Baker
38A John Elway 2.50 6.00
Jay Cutler
38B John Elway 1.50 4.00
Trent Edwards
39A Roger Staubach 2.50 6.00
Troy Aikman
39B Roger Staubach 1.25 3.00
JaMarcus Russell
40A Dan Marino 3.00 8.00
John Elway
40B Dan Marino 2.50 6.00
John Beck
41A Joe Namath 1.50 4.00
Jerricho Cotchery
41B Joe Namath 1.25 3.00
Chansi Stuckey
42A Joe Montana 4.00 10.00
Jerry Rice
42B Joe Montana 3.00 8.00
Luke Getsy
43A Paul Hornung 1.25 3.00
Greg Jennings
43B Paul Hornung 1.00 2.50
Brandon Jackson
44A Emmitt Smith 2.50 6.00
Tony Dorsett
44B Emmitt Smith 2.50 6.00
Chris Leak
45A Jim Brown 1.50 4.00
LaDainian Tomlinson
45B Jim Brown 1.25 3.00
Brady Quinn
46A Barry Sanders 2.50 6.00
Emmitt Smith
46B Barry Sanders 2.50 6.00
Calvin Johnson
47A Marcus Allen 1.25 3.00
Fred Biletnikoff
47B Marcus Allen 1.00 2.50
Michael Bush
48A Tony Dorsett 2.00 5.00
Roger Staubach
48B Tony Dorsett 3.00 8.00
Adrian Peterson
49A Fred Biletnikoff 1.25 3.00
Marcus Allen
49B Fred Biletnikoff 1.25 3.00
Johnnie Lee Higgins
50A Jerry Rice 1.25 3.00
Frank Gore
50B Jerry Rice 2.00 5.00
Jason Hill
51A JaMarcus Russell 1.00 2.50
Michael Bush
51B JaMarcus Russell .75 2.00
Joseph Addai
52A John Beck 1.00 2.50
Lorenzo Booker
52B John Beck 1.00 2.50
Jay Cutler
53A Trent Edwards 1.00 2.50
Marshawn Lynch
53B Trent Edwards 1.00 2.50
Matt Leinart
54A Chris Leak .75 2.00
Garrett Wolfe
54B Chris Leak .75 2.00
Cedric Benson
55A Brady Quinn 1.00 2.50
JaMarcus Russell
55B Brady Quinn 1.50 4.00
Peyton Manning
56A Jeff Rowe .60 1.50
Kenny Irons
56B Jeff Rowe .75 2.00
Chad Johnson
57A Troy Smith 1.00 2.50
Yamon Figurs
57B Troy Smith 1.00 2.50
Vince Young
58A Kevin Kolb 1.50 4.00
Tony Hunt
58B Kevin Kolb 1.50 4.00
Ben Roethlisberger
59A Drew Stanton 2.50 6.00
Calvin Johnson
59B Drew Stanton 1.00 2.50
Drew Brees
60A Jordan Palmer 1.00 2.50
LaRon Landry
60B Jordan Palmer .75 2.00
Carson Palmer
61A Luke Getsy 1.00 2.50
Jason Hill
61B Luke Getsy 1.00 2.50
Frank Gore
62A Brian Leonard .75 2.00
Adam Carriker
62B Brian Leonard 1.00 2.50
Steven Jackson
63A Lorenzo Booker .60 1.50
Ted Ginn Jr.
63B Lorenzo Booker .75 2.00
Laurence Maroney
64A Michael Bush 1.00 2.50
Zach Miller
64B Michael Bush 1.00 2.50
Maurice Jones-Drew
65A Chris Henry .60 1.50
Chris Davis
65B Chris Henry .60 1.50
Vince Young
66A Tony Hunt 1.50 4.00
Kevin Kolb
66B Tony Hunt .60 1.50
Larry Johnson
67A Kenny Irons .60 1.50
Jeff Rowe
67B Kenny Irons .75 2.00
Carson Palmer
68A Brandon Jackson .75 2.00
David Clowney
68B Brandon Jackson .75 2.00
Greg Jennings
69A Marshawn Lynch 1.00 2.50
Paul Posluszny
69B Marshawn Lynch 1.00 2.50
Joseph Addai
70A Adrian Peterson 4.00 10.00
Sidney Rice
70B Adrian Peterson 4.00 10.00
LaDainian Tomlinson
71A Garrett Wolfe .75 2.00
Greg Olsen
71B Garrett Wolfe .75 2.00
Cedric Benson
72A Antonio Pittman 1.00 2.50
Robert Meachem
72B Antonio Pittman .60 1.50
Drew Brees
73A Kolby Smith 1.00 2.50
Dwayne Bowe
73B Kolby Smith .75 2.00
Larry Johnson
74A Greg Olsen .75 2.00
Chris Leak
74B Greg Olsen .75 2.00
Cedric Benson
75A Zach Miller 1.00 2.50
Johnnie Lee Higgins
75B Zach Miller 1.00 2.50
Randy Moss
76A Dwayne Bowe 1.25 3.00
Kolby Smith
76B Dwayne Bowe 1.25 3.00
Larry Johnson
77A Steve Breaston 1.00 2.50
Craig Buster Davis
77B Steve Breaston 1.00 2.50
Edgerrin James
78A David Clowney .75 2.00
Brandon Jackson
78B David Clowney .75 2.00
Brett Favre
79A Craig Buster Davis 1.00 2.50
Dwayne Bowe
79B Craig Buster Davis 1.00 2.50
LaDainian Tomlinson
80A Chris Davis .60 1.50
Chris Henry
80B Chris Davis .60 1.50
Vince Young
81A Yamon Figurs 1.00 2.50
Troy Smith
81B Yamon Figurs .75 2.00
Steve Smith
82A Ted Ginn Jr. .75 2.00
John Beck
82B Ted Ginn Jr. 1.00 2.50
Randy Moss
83A Anthony Gonzalez 1.00 2.50
Roy Hall
83B Anthony Gonzalez 1.00 2.50
Marvin Harrison
84A Jason Hill 1.50 4.00
Patrick Willis
84B Jason Hill 1.00 2.50
Frank Gore
85A Dwayne Jarrett .75 2.00
Ryne Robinson
85B Dwayne Jarrett .75 2.00
Steve Smith
86A Calvin Johnson 3.00 8.00
Drew Stanton
86B Calvin Johnson 3.00 8.00
Terrell Owens
87A Robert Meachem 1.00 2.50
Antonio Pittman
87B Robert Meachem .75 2.00
Reggie Bush
88A Sidney Rice 3.00 8.00
Adrian Peterson
88B Sidney Rice 1.25 3.00
Andre Johnson
89A Steve Smith USC 1.00 2.50
Dwayne Jarrett
89B Steve Smith USC 1.00 2.50
Eli Manning
90A Mike Walker 1.00 2.50
Dallas Baker
90B Mike Walker 1.00 2.50
Maurice Jones-Drew
91A Roy Hall .75 2.00
Anthony Gonzalez
91B Roy Hall 1.00 2.50
Marvin Harrison
92A Dallas Baker 1.00 2.50
Steve Breaston
92B Dallas Baker .75 2.00
Willie Parker
93A Johnnie Lee Higgins .60 1.50
JaMarcus Russell
93B Johnnie Lee Higgins 1.00 2.50
Greg Jennings
94A Ryne Robinson .75 2.00
Dwayne Jarrett
94B Ryne Robinson .75 2.00
Steve Smith
95A Chansi Stuckey 1.00 2.50
Steve Smith USC
95B Chansi Stuckey 1.00 2.50
Jerricho Cotchery
96A Gaines Adams 1.00 2.50
Chansi Stuckey
96B Gaines Adams 1.00 2.50
Andre Johnson
97A Adam Carriker .75 2.00
Brian Leonard
97B Adam Carriker 1.00 2.50
Steven Jackson
98A Paul Posluszny .75 2.00
Trent Edwards
98B Paul Posluszny 1.00 2.50
Larry Johnson
99A Patrick Willis 2.00 5.00
Luke Getsy
99B Patrick Willis 1.00 2.50
Frank Gore
100A LaRon Landry 1.00 2.50
Jordan Palmer
100B LaRon Landry 1.00 2.50
Joseph Addai

2007 Topps Co-Signers Co-Signer Autographs

GROUP A/20 ODDS 1:886
GROUP B/25 ODDS 1:13,842
GROUP C/50 ODDS 1:1378
GROUP D/75 ODDS 1:4548
GROUP E/100 ODDS 1:1702
GROUP F/200 ODDS 1:846
GROUP G/250 ODDS 1:677
GROUP H ODDS 1:675
GROUP I ODDS 1:562
GROUP J ODDS 1:449
GROUP K ODDS 1:374
GROUP L ODDS 1:364
GROUP M ODDS 1:112
GROUP N ODDS 1:269
GROUP O ODDS 1:112
GROUP P ODDS 1:56
GROUP Q ODDS 1:45
TOPPS ANNOUNCED SOME PRINT RUNS
UNPRICED HOLOGOLD/1 ODDS 1:6774
UNPRICED HOLOSILVER/10 ODDS 1:674
UNPRICED PRINT PLATE/1 ODDS 1:1684
AB Mike Alstott E/100 25.00 50.00
Derrick Brooks
AS Troy Aikman A/20 100.00 200.00
Roger Staubach
BB Deion Branch D/75 10.00 25.00
Michael Bush
BC Drew Brees C/50 50.00 100.00
Marques Colston
BH Terry Bradshaw A/20 100.00 200.00
Franco Harris
BHA Alan Branch M 6.00 15.00
Leon Hall
BJ Brandon Jackson M 6.00 15.00
Chris Henry
BM Tom Brady A/20 250.00 500.00
Joe Montana
BP Tim Brown A/20 40.00 80.00
Jim Plunkett
BS Reggie Bush A/20 100.00 200.00
Barry Sanders UER
Text reverses the years
that Bush and Sanders
won the Heisman
CB Ronald Curry H 8.00 20.00
Michael Bush
CC Jerricho Cotchery F/200 8.00 20.00
Marques Colston
CJ David Clowney O 6.00 15.00
Brandon Jackson
DL Craig Buster Davis Q 8.00 20.00
LaRon Landry
DS Eric Dickerson A/20 100.00 200.00
Barry Sanders
FJ Yamon Figurs Q 8.00 20.00
Jacoby Jones
FS Brett Favre A/20 250.00 400.00
Bart Starr
GC Frank Gore F/200 10.00 25.00
Thomas Clayton
GG Joey Galloway G/250 8.00 20.00
Ted Ginn
GJ Frank Gore A/20 12.00 30.00
Larry Johnson
GT Tarik Glenn L 8.00 20.00
Joe Thomas
HH DeAngelo Hall C/50 8.00 20.00
Leon Hall
HI DeAngelo Hall C/50 8.00 20.00
David Irons
HP Tony Hunt O 8.00 20.00
Paul Posluszny
HW Steve Hutchinson K 6.00 15.00
Walter Jones
JA Steven Jackson A/20 12.00 30.00
Shaun Alexander
JH Greg Jennings C/50 10.00 25.00
Santonio Holmes
JJ Julius Jones C/50 8.00 20.00
Thomas Jones
JJO Jacoby Jones P 8.00 20.00
James Jones
JP Ron Jaworski E/100 40.00 80.00
Vince Papale
KH Brad Kassell N 6.00 15.00
David Harris
KT Jim Kelly A/20 75.00 150.00
Thurman Thomas
MC Robert Meachem G/250 10.00 25.00
Marques Colston
MH Peyton Manning A/20 100.00 200.00
Marvin Harrison
MN Dan Marino A/20 125.00 250.00
Joe Namath
MR Joe Montana A/20 175.00 300.00
Jerry Rice
NE Joe Namath A/20 100.00 200.00
John Elway
PH Antonio Pittman P 5.00 12.00
Tony Hunt
RS Tony Romo J 20.00 50.00
Isaiah Stanback
SB Gale Sayers A/20 100.00 200.00
Barry Sanders
SC Chansi Stuckey I 8.00 20.00
Jerricho Cotchery
SD Emmitt Smith A/20 150.00 300.00
Tony Dorsett
SDA Bart Starr A/20 75.00 150.00
Len Dawson
SJ Steve Smith USC B/25 12.00 30.00
Dwayne Jarrett
TB LaDainian Tomlinson A/20 50.00 120.00
Reggie Bush
TL Drew Tate Q 6.00 15.00
Brian Leonard
WH LaMarr Woodley P 8.00 20.00
David Harris
WP Kyle Williams M 8.00 20.00
Paul Posluszny
YM Steve Young A/20 125.00 250.00
Joe Montana
YT Vince Young A/20 25.00 60.00
LaDainian Tomlinson

2007 Topps Co-Signers Co-Signer Autographs Gold

*GOLD/25: .75X TO 1.5X BASE AU GROUP E-Q
*GOLD/25: .6X TO 1.2X BASE AU GROUP C-D
*GOLD/25: .5X TO 1X BASE AU GROUP A-B
GOLD/25 ODDS 1:281
BM Tom Brady 250.00 400.00
Joe Montana
BS Reggie Bush 125.00 250.00
Barry Sanders
FS Brett Favre 250.00 400.00
Bart Starr
MH Peyton Manning 150.00 250.00
Marvin Harrison
MN Dan Marino 150.00 250.00
Joe Namath
MR Joe Montana 175.00 300.00
Jerry Rice
SD Emmitt Smith 150.00 300.00
Tony Dorsett
YM Steve Young 125.00 250.00
Joe Montana

2007 Topps Co-Signers Rookie Autographs

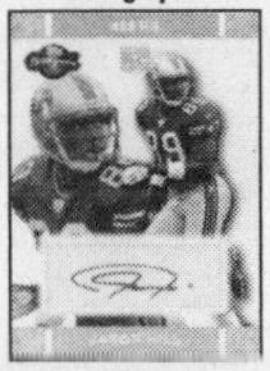

GROUP A/25 ODDS 1:4682
GROUP B/50 ODDS 1:6921
GROUP C/100 ODDS 1:3425
GROUP D/150 ODDS 1:188
GROUP E/250 ODDS 1:169
GROUP F ODDS 1:84
GROUP G ODDS 1:374
GROUP H ODDS 1:48
GROUP I ODDS 1:32
TOPPS ANNOUNCED SOME PRINT RUNS
UNPRICED PRINT PLATE/1 ODDS 1:3387

AC Adam Carriker D	5.00	12.00
AG Anthony Gonzalez D	6.00	15.00
AP Adrian Peterson A	100.00	200.00
API Antonio Pittman F	3.00	8.00
BJ Brandon Jackson E	5.00	12.00
BL Brian Leonard E	5.00	12.00
BQ Brady Quinn B	25.00	60.00
CD Craig Buster Davis H	4.00	10.00
CDA Chris Davis F	3.00	8.00
CH Chris Henry F	3.00	8.00
CJ Calvin Johnson A	60.00	100.00
CL Chris Leak F	4.00	10.00
CS Chansi Stuckey H	5.00	12.00
DB Dwayne Bowe D	15.00	40.00
DBA Dallas Baker I	3.00	8.00
DC David Clowney H	4.00	10.00
DJ Dwayne Jarrett D	5.00	12.00
DS Drew Stanton D	4.00	10.00
GO Greg Olsen D	5.00	12.00
GS Gaines Adams F	5.00	12.00
GW Garrett Wolfe F	3.00	8.00
JB John Beck F	5.00	12.00
JH Jason Hill H	5.00	12.00
JHI Johnnie Lee Higgins I	4.00	10.00
JP Jordan Palmer I	4.00	10.00
JR JaMarcus Russell A	25.00	60.00
JRO Jeff Rowe H	3.00	8.00
KK Kevin Kolb D	10.00	25.00
KS Kolby Smith H	4.00	10.00
LB Lorenzo Booker E	5.00	12.00
LL LaRon Landry E	6.00	15.00
MB Michael Bush D	6.00	15.00
ML Marshawn Lynch C	15.00	40.00
MW Mike Walker I	5.00	12.00
PP Paul Posluszny F	5.00	12.00
PW Patrick Willis E	12.00	30.00
RH Roy Hall H	5.00	12.00
RM Robert Meachem D	6.00	15.00
RR Ryne Robinson I	4.00	10.00
SB Steve Breaston I	5.00	12.00
SR Sidney Rice D	8.00	20.00
SS Steve Smith E	6.00	15.00
TE Trent Edwards E	6.00	15.00
TG Ted Ginn D	5.00	12.00
TH Tony Hunt E	4.00	10.00
TS Troy Smith D	6.00	15.00
YF Yamon Figurs I	3.00	8.00
ZM Zach Miller G	5.00	12.00

2007 Topps Co-Signers Rookie Autographs Gold

*GOLD/25: .8X TO 2X BASE AU GROUP F-I
*GOLD/25: .6X TO 1.5X BASE AU GROUP D-E
GOLD GROUP A/10 ODDS 1:12,735
GOLD GROUP B/25 ODDS 1:312
UNPRICED HOLOGOLD/1 ODDS 1:6921
UNPRICED HOLOSILVER GRP A ODDS 1:22,741
UNPRICED HOLOSILVER GRP B/10 ODDS 1:749

AP Adrian Peterson/10	200.00	350.00
BQ Brady Quinn/25	40.00	100.00
CJ Calvin Johnson/10	75.00	150.00
JR JaMarcus Russell/10	40.00	100.00
ML Marshawn Lynch/25	25.00	60.00

2007 Topps Co-Signers Rookie Co-Signer Autographs

GROUP A/10 ODDS 1:12,735
GROUP B/25 ODDS 1:936
GROUP C/50 ODDS 1:982
UNPRICED GOLD/10 ODDS 1:1349
UNPRICED HOLOGOLD/1 ODDS 1:13,842
UNPRICED HOLOSILVER/5 ODDS 1:2698
UNPRICED PRINT PLATES/1 ODDS 1:3387
SER.#'d UNDER 10 NOT PRICED

AA Gaines Adams/25	12.00	30.00
Jamaal Anderson		
BB Lorenzo Booker/25	12.00	30.00
John Beck		
BD Dwayne Bowe/50	10.00	25.00
Craig Buster Davis		
BM Dwayne Bowe/25	12.00	30.00
Robert Meachem		
BS Michael Bush/25	12.00	30.00
Kolby Smith		
DW Chris Davis/25	8.00	20.00
Paul Williams		
GJ Ted Ginn/50	6.00	15.00
Dwayne Jarrett		
HH Leon Hall/25	10.00	25.00
David Harris		
HW Chris Henry/25	8.00	20.00
Paul Williams		
JT Brandon Jackson/25	10.00	25.00
Zac Taylor		
KH Kevin Kolb/25	20.00	50.00
Tony Hunt		
LO Chris Leak/50	6.00	15.00
Greg Olsen		
MW Rhema McKnight/25	8.00	20.00
Darius Walker		
OM Greg Olsen/25	12.00	30.00
Zach Miller		
PH Antonio Pittman/25	8.00	20.00
Tony Hunt		
QT Brady Quinn/25	12.00	30.00
Joe Thomas		
RR Ryne Robinson/25	12.00	30.00
Laurent Robinson		
SE Drew Stanton/50	8.00	20.00
Trent Edwards		
SG Troy Smith/50	8.00	20.00
Ted Ginn		
TW Lawrence Timmons/50	15.00	40.00
Patrick Willis		
WB LaMarr Woodley/25	15.00	40.00
Alan Branch		
WL Dwayne Wright/50	8.00	20.00
Marshawn Lynch		

2007 Topps Co-Signers Tri-Signer Autographs

GROUP A/15 ODDS 1:8163
GROUP B/20 ODDS 1:2211
GROUP C/150 ODDS 1:2258
GROUP D/175 ODDS 1:1941
GROUP E/200 ODDS 1:846
UNPRICED GOLD/10 ODDS 1:2242
UNPRICED HOLOGOLD/1 ODDS 1:22,741
UNPRICED HOLOSILVER/5 ODDS 1:4484
UNPRICED PRINT PLATES/1 ODDS 1:5685

AWL Gaines Adams/150	15.00	40.00
Patrick Willis		
LaRon Landry		
BIL Lorenzo Booker/20	30.00	60.00
Kenny Irons		
Brian Leonard		
BMB Terry Bradshaw/20	400.00	600.00
Joe Montana		
Tom Brady		
BMD Dwayne Bowe/175	15.00	40.00
Robert Meachem		
Craig Buster Davis		
BSS Jim Brown/20	400.00	600.00
Barry Sanders		
Emmitt Smith		
DDA Tony Dorsett/20		
Eric Dickerson		
Marcus Allen		
DFJ Eric Dickerson/20	50.00	120.00
Marshall Faulk		
Steven Jackson		
HJH Chris Henry/200	15.00	40.00
Brandon Jackson		
Tony Hunt		
JGJ Calvin Johnson/15	50.00	100.00
Ted Ginn Jr.		
Dwayne Jarrett		
JTA Larry Johnson/20	40.00	100.00
LaDainian Tomlinson		
Shaun Alexander		
LPB Marshawn Lynch/15	200.00	400.00
Adrian Peterson		
Michael Bush		
MEN Dan Marino/20	250.00	400.00
John Elway		
Joe Namath		
PTP Paul Posluszny/200	15.00	40.00
Lawrence Timmons		
Patrick Willis		
RQS JaMarcus Russell/15		
Brady Quinn		
Drew Stanton		
SDP Bart Starr/20	125.00	250.00
Len Dawson		
Jim Plunkett		

2001 Topps Debut

This 175-card base set features 100 veterans and 75 short-printed rookies. Cards 101-110 are rookie autographs and serial numbered to 499, 111-150 are rookie game-worn jersey cards and serial numbered to 999, and 151-175 are rookies and serial numbered to 1499. No rookies had more than one version of their cards.

COMP.SET w/o SP's (100)	7.50	20.00
1 Marshall Faulk	.30	.75
2 Ricky Watters	.25	.60
3 Bill Schroeder	.25	.60
4 Muhsin Muhammad	.25	.60
5 Peter Warrick	.25	.60
6 Marvin Harrison	.30	.75
7 Stephen Davis	.25	.60
8 Cris Carter	.30	.75
9 Charlie Batch	.25	.60
10 David Boston	.20	.50
11 Ike Hilliard	.25	.60
12 Steve McNair	.30	.75
13 Kordell Stewart	.25	.60
14 Travis Prentice	.20	.50
15 Sammy Morris	.25	.60
16 Vinny Testaverde	.25	.60
17 Tyrone Wheatley	.25	.60
18 Jeff Garcia	.25	.60
19 Brett Favre	1.00	2.50
20 Jake Plummer	.25	.60
21 Cade McNown	.25	.60
22 Rob Johnson	.25	.60
23 Tim Couch	.20	.50
24 Jerome Bettis	.30	.75
25 Ricky Williams	.30	.75
26 Darrell Jackson	.25	.60
27 Troy Brown	.25	.60
28 Jamal Lewis	.30	.75
29 Isaac Bruce	.30	.75
30 Lamar Smith	.25	.60
31 Qadry Ismail	.25	.60
32 Elvis Grbac	.25	.60
33 Shaun Alexander	.30	.75
34 Peyton Manning	.75	2.00
35 Curtis Martin	.30	.75
36 Jamal Anderson	.25	.60
37 Mark Brunell	.25	.60
38 Emmitt Smith	.75	2.00
39 Chad Lewis	.20	.50
40 Randy Moss	.30	.75
41 Kurt Warner	.50	1.25
42 Terrence Wilkins	.20	.50
43 Corey Dillon	.25	.60
44 Brian Griese	.25	.60
45 Jon Kitna	.25	.60
46 Eric Moulds	.25	.60
47 Steve Beuerlein	.25	.60
48 James Allen	.20	.50
49 Amani Toomer	.25	.60
50 Daunte Culpepper	.25	.60
51 Michael Pittman	.25	.60
52 Warrick Dunn	.30	.75
53 Terrell Owens	.30	.75
54 Donald Hayes	.20	.50
55 Keenan McCardell	.25	.60
56 Tony Gonzalez	.30	.75
57 Freddie Jones	.20	.50
58 Charlie Garner	.25	.60
59 Shawn Jefferson	.20	.50
60 Brian Urlacher	.40	1.00
61 Donovan McNabb	.30	.75
62 Az-Zahir Hakim	.20	.50
63 James Thrash	.25	.60
64 Hines Ward	.30	.75
65 Shawn Bryson	.20	.50
66 Wayne Chrebet	.25	.60
67 Kevin Johnson	.20	.50
68 Eddie George	.30	.75
69 Derrick Alexander	.20	.50
70 Tim Brown	.30	.75
71 Jay Fiedler	.25	.60
72 Aaron Brooks	.25	.60
73 Torry Holt	.25	.60
74 Edgerrin James	.30	.75
75 Shannon Sharpe	.30	.75
76 Oronde Gadsden	.20	.50
77 Rod Smith	.25	.60
78 Rich Gannon	.25	.60
79 Fred Taylor	.30	.75
80 Derrick Mason	.25	.60
81 Joe Horn	.25	.60
82 Robert Smith	.25	.60
83 James Stewart	.20	.50
84 Jeff George	.25	.60
85 Troy Aikman	.50	1.25
86 Charles Johnson	.20	.50
87 Ahman Green	.30	.75
88 Shaun King	.20	.50
89 Ray Lewis	.30	.75
90 Trent Dilfer	.25	.60
91 Drew Bledsoe	.30	.75
92 Jimmy Smith	.25	.60
93 Ed McCaffrey	.25	.60
94 Kerry Collins	.25	.60
95 Terry Glenn	.25	.60
96 Ron Dayne	.25	.60
97 Keyshawn Johnson	.25	.60
98 Antonio Freeman	.30	.75
99 Tiki Barber	.30	.75
100 Mike Anderson	.25	.60
101 Drew Brees AU RC	90.00	150.00
102 Chris Weinke AU RC	6.00	15.00
103 LaDainian Tomlinson AU RC	40.00	100.00
104 Michael Bennett AU RC	6.00	15.00
105 Anthony Thomas AU RC	8.00	20.00
106 LaMont Jordan AU RC	8.00	20.00
107 David Terrell AU RC	6.00	15.00
108 Michael Vick AU RC	60.00	120.00
109 Deuce McAllister AU RC	8.00	20.00
110 James Jackson AU RC	5.00	12.00
111 Mike McMahon JSY RC	5.00	12.00
112 Cedrick Wilson JSY RC	5.00	12.00
113 Ken Lucas JSY RC	5.00	12.00
114 Fred Smoot JSY RC	6.00	15.00
115 Alge Crumpler JSY RC	6.00	15.00
116 Sage Rosenfels JSY RC	6.00	15.00
117 Rashard Casey JSY RC	4.00	10.00
118 David Allen JSY RC	4.00	10.00
119 Bobby Newcombe JSY RC	5.00	12.00
120 Jesse Palmer JSY RC	5.00	12.00
121 Tommy Polley JSY RC	4.00	10.00
122 Kevan Barlow JSY RC	5.00	12.00
123 Scotty Anderson JSY RC	4.00	10.00
124 Travis Minor JSY RC	5.00	12.00
125 Snoop Minnis JSY RC	4.00	10.00
126 Moran Norris JSY RC	4.00	10.00
127 Alex Lincoln JSY RC	4.00	10.00
128 Chad Johnson JSY RC	10.00	25.00
129 Boo Williams JSY RC	4.00	10.00
130 Brian Natkin JSY RC	4.00	10.00
131 Orlando Huff JSY RC	4.00	10.00
132 Derrick Gibson JSY RC	4.00	10.00
133 Tony Driver JSY RC	5.00	12.00
134 Torrance Marshall JSY RC	4.00	10.00
135 Alex Bannister JSY RC	4.00	10.00
136 Morlon Greenwood JSY RC	4.00	10.00
137 Ennis Davis JSY RC	4.00	10.00
138 Mike Cerimele JSY RC	4.00	10.00
139 David Rivers JSY RC	4.00	10.00
140 Dustin McClintock JSY RC	5.00	12.00
141 Tay Cody JSY RC	4.00	10.00
142 Arther Love JSY RC	4.00	10.00
143 Sly Johnson JSY RC	4.00	10.00
144 Dan Alexander JSY RC	5.00	12.00
145 Will Allen JSY RC	6.00	15.00
146 Andre Dyson JSY RC	4.00	10.00
147 Margin Hooks JSY RC	4.00	10.00
148 Adam Archuleta JSY RC	5.00	12.00
149 Sedrick Hodge JSY RC	4.00	10.00
150 Kendrell Bell JSY RC	6.00	15.00
151 Reggie Wayne RC	4.00	10.00
152 Rod Gardner RC	1.50	4.00
153 Chris Chambers RC	2.00	5.00
154 Jamal Reynolds RC	1.25	3.00
155 Ben Hamilton RC	1.25	3.00
156 Dan Morgan RC	1.50	4.00
157 Quincy Morgan RC	1.50	4.00
158 Travis Henry RC	1.50	4.00
159 Ken-Yon Rambo RC	1.25	3.00
160 Josh Heupel RC	2.00	5.00
161 Marcus Stroud RC	1.50	4.00
162 Marques Tuiasosopo RC	1.50	4.00
163 Reggie Germany RC	1.25	3.00
164 Robert Ferguson RC	2.00	5.00
165 Jabari Holloway RC	1.25	3.00
166 Ben Leard RC	1.25	3.00
167 Bhawoh Jue RC	1.50	4.00
168 Freddie Mitchell RC	1.25	3.00
169 Vinny Sutherland RC	1.25	3.00
170 Jeff Backus RC	1.25	3.00
171 Correll Buckhalter RC	2.00	5.00
172 Mario Fatafehi RC	1.25	3.00
173 Rudi Johnson RC	2.00	5.00
174 Koren Robinson RC	1.50	4.00
175 Santana Moss RC	2.50	6.00

2002 Topps Debut

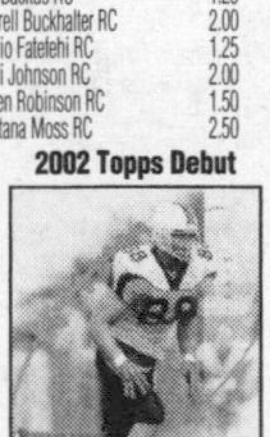

This 200-card set contains 150 veterans and 50 rookies. Cards 151-155 are rookie autographs, cards 156-160 are rookie jersey cards, and both groups of cards are serial #'d to 1499. Rookies 161-200 were inserted at a rate of 1:3. Boxes contained 24 packs of 5 cards. SRP was $2.99

COMP.SET w/o SP's (150)	10.00	25.00
1 Kurt Warner	.30	.75
2 James Thrash	.25	.60
3 Aaron Brooks	.25	.60
4 Mark Brunell	.25	.60
5 Mike Anderson	.25	.60
6 Benjamin Gay	.20	.50
7 Marvin Harrison	.30	.75
8 Randy Moss	.30	.75
9 Ron Dayne	.25	.60
10 Tim Brown	.30	.75
11 Vinny Testaverde	.25	.60
12 Mike Alstott	.25	.60
13 Tony Banks	.20	.50
14 Plaxico Burress	.25	.60
15 Chris Chambers	.25	.60
16 Brett Favre	.75	2.00
17 Quincy Carter	.20	.50
18 Brian Urlacher	.30	.75
19 Byron Chamberlain	.20	.50
20 Tony Gonzalez	.30	.75
21 Troy Brown	.25	.60
22 Drew Brees	.50	1.25
23 Koren Robinson	.20	.50
24 Donald Hayes	.20	.50
25 Michael Vick	.50	1.25
26 Travis Taylor	.20	.50
27 Peerless Price	.20	.50
28 Chad Johnson	.30	.75
29 Tim Couch	.20	.50
30 Edgerrin James	.25	.60
31 Willie Jackson	.20	.50
32 Hines Ward	.30	.75
33 Terrell Owens	.30	.75
34 Eddie George	.25	.60
35 Michael Westbrook	.20	.50
36 Kerry Collins	.25	.60
37 Terrell Davis	.30	.75
38 Marcus Robinson	.25	.60
39 Charlie Batch	.20	.50
40 Jake Plummer	.25	.60
41 Qadry Ismail	.25	.60
42 Snoop Minnis	.20	.50
43 Jimmy Smith	.25	.60
44 Charlie Garner	.25	.60
45 Jeff Graham	.20	.50
46 Torry Holt	.30	.75
47 Kevin Dyson	.25	.60
48 Maurice Smith	.20	.50
49 Muhsin Muhammad	.25	.60
50 Curtis Martin	.30	.75
51 Todd Pinkston	.20	.50
52 Matt Hasselbeck	.30	.75
53 Corey Dillon	.25	.60
54 Michael Pittman	.25	.60
55 Antonio Freeman	.30	.75
56 Oronde Gadsden	.20	.50
57 Tiki Barber	.30	.75
58 Isaac Bruce	.30	.75
59 Rod Gardner	.20	.50
60 Derrick Mason	.25	.60
61 Joe Horn	.25	.60
62 Antowain Smith	.25	.60
63 Johnnie Morton	.25	.60
64 Kevin Johnson	.20	.50
65 Nick Goings	.20	.50
66 Jason Brookins	.20	.50
67 Travis Henry	.20	.50
68 Brian Griese	.25	.60
69 Priest Holmes	.30	.75
70 Daunte Culpepper	.25	.60
71 Amani Toomer	.25	.60
72 Rich Gannon	.25	.60
73 Correll Buckhalter	.25	.60
74 Kevan Barlow	.20	.50
75 Stephen Davis	.25	.60
76 Keenan McCardell	.25	.60
77 Jon Kitna	.25	.60
78 Eric Moulds	.25	.60
79 Dez White	.20	.50
80 Rocket Ismail	.25	.60
81 Dominic Rhodes	.25	.60
82 Lamar Smith	.25	.60
83 David Patten	.20	.50
84 Duce Staley	.25	.60
85 Curtis Conway	.25	.60
86 Kordell Stewart	.25	.60
87 Brad Johnson	.25	.60
88 Wayne Chrebet	.25	.60
89 Michael Bennett	.25	.60
90 Quincy Morgan	.20	.50
91 Steve Smith	.30	.75
92 David Boston	.20	.50
93 Shannon Sharpe	.30	.75
94 Mike McMahon	.20	.50
95 Stacey Mack	.20	.50
96 Santana Moss	.25	.60
97 Jeff Garcia	.25	.60
98 Keyshawn Johnson	.25	.60
99 Rod Smith	.25	.60
100 Jerome Bettis	.30	.75
101 LaDainian Tomlinson	.40	1.00
102 Warrick Dunn	.25	.60
103 Ray Lewis	.30	.75
104 Chris Chandler	.25	.60
105 Jim Miller	.20	.50
106 Ahman Green	.25	.60
107 Jay Fiedler	.25	.60
108 Tom Brady	.75	2.00
109 Michael Strahan	.30	.75
110 James Jackson	.20	.50
111 Rob Johnson	.25	.60
112 Elvis Grbac	.20	.50
113 Troy Hambrick	.20	.50
114 Corey Bradford	.20	.50
115 Trent Green	.25	.60
116 Cris Carter	.30	.75
117 Chris Fuamatu-Ma'afala	.20	.50
118 Chris Weinke	.20	.50
119 MarTay Jenkins	.20	.50
120 Laveranues Coles	.25	.60
121 Donovan McNabb	.30	.75
122 Jerry Rice	.60	1.50
123 Garrison Hearst	.25	.60
124 Steve McNair	.30	.75
125 Trung Canidate	.20	.50
126 Doug Flutie	.30	.75
127 Ricky Williams	.25	.60
128 Peyton Manning	.60	1.50
129 Kevin Kasper	.20	.50
130 Emmitt Smith	.75	2.00
131 Peter Warrick	.25	.60
132 Anthony Thomas	.25	.60
133 Ike Hilliard	.25	.60
134 Kendrell Bell	.20	.50
135 Shaun Alexander	.25	.60
136 Wesley Walls	.25	.60
137 Gerard Warren	.20	.50
138 James Stewart	.20	.50
139 Drew Bledsoe	.30	.75
140 Fred Taylor	.25	.60
141 Marshall Faulk	.30	.75
142 Marcus Pollard	.20	.50
143 Bill Schroeder	.20	.50
144 Marty Booker	.25	.60
145 Amos Zereoue	.20	.50
146 Darrell Jackson	.25	.60
147 Brian Finneran	.20	.50
148 Alex Van Pelt	.20	.50
149 Andre Carter	.20	.50
150 Joey Galloway	.25	.60
151 Joey Harrington AU RC	6.00	15.00
152 Andre Davis AU RC	5.00	12.00
153 Eric Crouch AU RC	6.00	15.00
154 Kelly Campbell AU RC	5.00	12.00
155 Ron Johnson AU RC	5.00	12.00
156 David Carr JSY RC	5.00	12.00
157 Kurt Kittner JSY RC	3.00	8.00
158 Javon Walker JSY RC	5.00	12.00
159 DeShaun Foster JSY RC	5.00	12.00
160 Lamar Gordon JSY RC	4.00	10.00
161 Antwaan Randle El RC	1.25	3.00
162 Clinton Portis RC	1.50	4.00
163 Luke Staley RC	.75	2.00
164 Daniel Graham RC	1.00	2.50
165 Ashley Lelie RC	1.00	2.50
166 Ladell Betts RC	1.25	3.00
167 Rocky Calmus RC	1.00	2.50
168 Ryan Sims RC	1.25	3.00
169 Jeremy Shockey RC	2.00	5.00
170 Damien Anderson RC	.75	2.00
171 Bryant McKinnie RC	.75	2.00
172 Kahlil Hill RC	.75	2.00
173 John Henderson RC	1.00	2.50
174 Donte Stallworth RC	1.25	3.00
175 Kalimba Edwards RC	1.00	2.50
176 Freddie Milons RC	.75	2.00
177 Antonio Bryant RC	1.25	3.00
178 Cliff Russell RC	.75	2.00
179 T.J. Duckett RC	1.25	3.00
180 Roy Williams RC	1.25	3.00
181 Patrick Ramsey RC	1.25	3.00
182 Josh Reed RC	1.00	2.50
183 Wendell Bryant RC	.75	2.00
184 Jabar Gaffney RC	1.25	3.00
185 Napoleon Harris RC	1.00	2.50
186 Adrian Peterson RC	1.25	3.00
187 David Garrard RC	1.50	4.00
188 Levar Fisher RC	.75	2.00
189 Quentin Jammer RC	1.25	3.00
190 Anthony Weaver RC	.75	2.00
191 Dwight Freeney RC	1.50	4.00
192 Reche Caldwell RC	1.25	3.00
193 Larry Tripplett RC	.75	2.00
194 Rohan Davey RC	1.25	3.00
195 Marquise Walker RC	.75	2.00
196 William Green RC	1.00	2.50
197 Tracey Wistrom RC	1.00	2.50
198 Alan Harper RC	.75	2.00
199 Lito Sheppard RC	1.25	3.00
200 Albert Haynesworth RC	1.25	3.00

2002 Topps Debut Red

*VETS 1/150: 3X TO 8X BASIC CARDS
*151-155 ROOKIE AU: 1X TO 2.5X
151-155 ROOKIE AU ODDS 1:642
*156-160 ROOKIE JSY: 1X TO 2.5X
156-160 ROOKIE JSY ODDS 1:645
*161-200 ROOKIES: 1.2X TO 3X
161-200 ROOKIE ODDS 1:17
STATED PRINT RUN 199 SER.#'d SETS

2002 Topps Debut All-Star Materials

STATED ODDS 1:14
*GOLD: 1.2X TO 3X BASIC INSERTS
GOLD STATED ODDS 1:525
GOLD STATED PRINT RUN 25 SER.#'d SETS

AMAA Akin Ayodele	3.00	8.00
AMAD Andra Davis	2.50	6.00
AMAP Adrian Peterson	4.00	10.00
AMAR Antwaan Randle El	4.00	10.00
AMAW Anthony Weaver	2.50	6.00
AMBF Bryan Fletcher	2.50	6.00
AMBT Bryan Thomas	2.50	6.00
AMBW Brian Westbrook	6.00	15.00
AMCH Chris Hope	4.00	10.00
AMCR Cliff Russell	2.50	6.00
AMDG David Garrard	5.00	12.00
AMDGR Daniel Graham	3.00	8.00
AMFM Freddie Milons	2.50	6.00
AMJMC Jason McAddley	3.00	8.00
AMKC Kenyon Coleman	2.50	6.00
AMMW Marquise Walker	2.50	6.00
AMNH Napoleon Harris	3.00	8.00
AMPR Patrick Ramsey	4.00	10.00
AMRC Rocky Calmus	3.00	8.00
AMRD Rohan Davey	4.00	10.00
AMRJ Ron Johnson	3.00	8.00
AMRS Ryan Sims	4.00	10.00
AMTW Tracey Wistrom	3.00	8.00

2002 Topps Debut Collegiate Classics

COMPLETE SET (19)	15.00	40.00
STATED ODDS 1:12		
1 Randy Moss	1.00	2.50
2 Antonio Bryant	1.00	2.50
3 David Carr	1.00	2.50
4 William Green	.75	2.00
5 Eric Crouch	1.00	2.50
6 Jabar Gaffney	1.00	2.50
7 Andre Davis	.75	2.00
8 Joey Harrington	1.00	2.50
9 T.J. Duckett	1.00	2.50
10 Josh Reed	.75	2.00
11 DeShaun Foster	1.00	2.50
12 Kurt Kittner	.60	1.50
13 Marquise Walker	.60	1.50
14 Clinton Portis	1.25	3.00
15 Woody Dantzler	.75	2.00
16 David Boston	.60	1.50
17 Donovan McNabb	1.00	2.50
18 Peyton Manning	2.00	5.00
19 Keyshawn Johnson	.75	2.00

2002 Topps Debut Dynamite Debuts

COMPLETE SET (20)	12.00	30.00
STATED ODDS 1:8		
DD1 Anthony Thomas	.75	2.00
DD2 Kendrell Bell	.60	1.50
DD3 LaDainian Tomlinson	1.25	3.00
DD4 Chris Chambers	.75	2.00
DD5 Travis Henry	.60	1.50
DD6 Chris Weinke	.60	1.50
DD7 Koren Robinson	.60	1.50
DD8 James Jackson	.60	1.50
DD9 Dominic Rhodes	.75	2.00
DD10 Michael Bennett	.75	2.00
DD11 Correll Buckhalter	.75	2.00
DD12 Rod Gardner	.60	1.50
DD13 Kevan Barlow	.60	1.50
DD14 Michael Vick	1.50	4.00
DD15 Mike Anderson	.75	2.00
DD16 Brian Urlacher	1.00	2.50
DD17 Jamal Lewis	.75	2.00
DD18 Ron Dayne	.75	2.00
DD19 Darrell Jackson	.75	2.00
DD20 Sylvester Morris	.60	1.50

2002 Topps Debut Heads of Class Jerseys

STATED ODDS 1:281
*GOLD/25: 1X TO 2.5X BASIC DUAL
GOLD/25 STATED ODDS 1:2297
GOLD STATED PRINT RUN 25 SER.#'d SETS

HCDO Stephen Davis	8.00	20.00
Terrell Owens		
HCFD Antonio Freeman	8.00	20.00
Terrell Davis		
HCJT Keyshawn Johnson	8.00	20.00
Zach Thomas		
HCSD Warren Sapp	8.00	20.00
Terrell Davis		
HCTB LaDainian Tomlinson	12.00	30.00
Drew Brees		

2003 Topps Draft Picks and Prospects

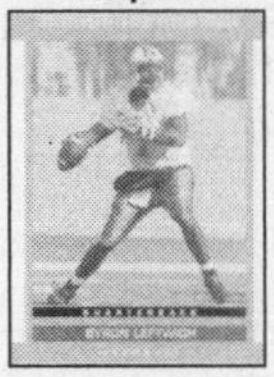

This 165-card set was released in May, 2003. This set was issued in five card packs with a $3 SRP. The packs came 24 to a box and 10 boxes to a case. Cards numbered 1-110 featured veterans while cards 111-165 featured rookies.

COMPLETE SET (165)	25.00	50.00
1 Priest Holmes	.30	.75
2 Tommy Maddox	.25	.60
3 Donald Driver	.30	.75
4 Drew Bledsoe	.30	.75
5 Tiki Barber	.30	.75
6 Terrell Owens	.30	.75
7 Rich Gannon	.25	.60
8 Isaac Bruce	.30	.75
9 Stephen Davis	.25	.60
10 Peyton Manning	.60	1.50
11 Tony Gonzalez	.30	.75
12 Marty Booker	.25	.60
13 Warrick Dunn	.25	.60
14 Jimmy Smith	.25	.60
15 Troy Brown	.25	.60
16 Jerry Rice	.60	1.50
17 Curtis Conway	.20	.50
18 Kurt Warner	.30	.75
19 Steve McNair	.30	.75
20 Edgerrin James	.30	.75
21 Aaron Brooks	.25	.60
22 Joey Galloway	.25	.60
23 Peerless Price	.20	.50
24 Torry Holt	.30	.75
25 Derrick Mason	.25	.60
26 Curtis Martin	.30	.75
27 Daunte Culpepper	.25	.60
28 Ahman Green	.25	.60
29 Tim Couch	.20	.50
30 Ricky Williams	.25	.60
31 Darrell Jackson	.25	.60
32 Keyshawn Johnson	.30	.75
33 Jeff Garcia	.25	.60
34 Charlie Garner	.25	.60
35 Randy Moss	.30	.75
36 Rod Smith	.25	.60
37 Jamal Lewis	.25	.60
38 Corey Dillon	.25	.60
39 Marvin Harrison	.30	.75
40 Joe Horn	.25	.60
41 Laveranues Coles	.20	.50
42 Hines Ward	.30	.75
43 Brad Johnson	.25	.60
44 Eddie George	.25	.60
45 Donovan McNabb	.30	.75
46 Marshall Faulk	.30	.75
47 Amani Toomer	.25	.60
48 Trent Green	.25	.60
49 Emmitt Smith	.75	2.00
50 Brett Favre	.75	2.00
51 Brian Griese	.25	.60
52 Eric Moulds	.25	.60
53 Plaxico Burress	.25	.60
54 Fred Taylor	.25	.60
55 Tom Brady	.75	2.00
56 Michael Vick	.40	1.00
57 Andre Davis	.20	.50
58 Chris Chambers	.25	.60
59 Javon Walker	.25	.60
60 Marc Bulger	.30	.75
61 LaDainian Tomlinson	.30	.75
62 Chad Pennington	.30	.75
63 Marc Boerigter	.20	.50
64 Rod Gardner	.20	.50
65 DeShaun Foster	.25	.60
66 Chris Redman	.20	.50
67 Chad Hutchinson	.20	.50
68 Deion Branch	.25	.60
69 Jeremy Shockey	.30	.75
70 Shaun Alexander	.25	.60
71 Derrius Thompson	.20	.50
72 A.J. Feeley	.20	.50
73 Reggie Wayne	.30	.75
74 William Green	.20	.50
75 Julius Peppers	.30	.75
76 Travis Henry	.20	.50
77 Marcel Shipp	.20	.50
78 Michael Bennett	.25	.60
79 Maurice Morris	.20	.50
80 Josh Reed	.20	.50
81 David Terrell	.20	.50
82 Drew Brees	.30	.75
83 Jonathan Wells	.20	.50
84 Anthony Thomas	.25	.60
85 Quincy Morgan	.20	.50
86 Jerry Porter	.20	.50
87 Ron Johnson	.20	.50
88 Najeh Davenport	.25	.60
89 Lamar Gordon	.20	.50
90 Joey Harrington	.20	.50
91 Donte Stallworth	.20	.50
92 Kenny Watson	.20	.50
93 LaMont Jordan	.25	.60
94 Antonio Bryant	.20	.50
95 Steve Smith	.30	.75
96 T.J. Duckett	.25	.60
97 Patrick Ramsey	.25	.60
98 Santana Moss	.25	.60
99 Chad Johnson	.30	.75
100 Clinton Portis	.25	.60
101 Reche Caldwell	.20	.50
102 Kevan Barlow	.20	.50
103 Deuce McAllister	.25	.60
104 Koren Robinson	.25	.60
105 Todd Heap	.25	.60
106 Jabar Gaffney	.20	.50
107 Randy McMichael	.20	.50
108 Dwight Freeney	.25	.60
109 Antwaan Randle El	.25	.60
110 David Carr	.25	.60
111 Carson Palmer RC	1.25	3.00
112 Dahrran Diedrick RC	.40	1.00
113 Kyle Boller RC	.60	1.50
114 Terrell Suggs RC	.60	1.50
115 Rien Long RC	.40	1.00
116 Justin Gage RC	.50	1.25
117 William Joseph RC	.40	1.00
118 Chris Simms RC	.60	1.50
119 Avon Cobourne RC	.40	1.00
120 Victor Hobson RC	.40	1.00
121 Jason Gesser RC	.50	1.25
122 Ronald Bellamy RC	.50	1.25
123 Terence Newman RC	.50	1.25
124 Terrence Edwards RC	.40	1.00
125 Sultan McCullough RC	.40	1.00
126 Kareem Kelly RC	.40	1.00
127 Jason Witten RC	1.50	4.00
128 Mike Doss RC	.60	1.50
129 Seneca Wallace RC	.60	1.50
130 Chris Brown RC	.40	1.00
131 Larry Johnson RC	.60	1.50
132 Taylor Jacobs RC	.40	1.00
133 Jerome McDougle RC	.40	1.00
134 Kelley Washington RC	.40	1.00
135 Brad Banks RC	.50	1.25
136 DeWayne White RC	.40	1.00
137 LaBrandon Toefield RC	.50	1.25
138 Brian St.Pierre RC	.50	1.25
139 Kindal Moorehead RC	.50	1.25
140 Willis McGahee RC	.75	2.00
141 Jimmy Kennedy RC	.50	1.25
142 Talman Gardner RC	.40	1.00
143 Chris Kelsay RC	.50	1.25
144 Cory Redding RC	.50	1.25
145 Dave Ragone RC	.40	1.00
146 Earnest Graham RC	.60	1.50
147 Andre Johnson RC	1.50	4.00
148 Boss Bailey RC	.50	1.25
149 Sam Aiken RC	.50	1.25
150 Byron Leftwich RC	.60	1.50
151 Teyo Johnson RC	.50	1.25
152 Quentin Griffin RC	.50	1.25
153 Justin Fargas RC	.60	1.50
154 Bradie James RC	.60	1.50
155 Andre Woolfolk RC	.50	1.25
156 Marcus Trufant RC	.50	1.25
157 Ken Dorsey RC	.50	1.25
158 Onterrio Smith RC	.40	1.00
159 Bryant Johnson RC	.60	1.50
160 Charles Rogers RC	.50	1.25
161 Kliff Kingsbury RC	.50	1.25
162 Michael Haynes RC	.40	1.00
163 Bennie Joppru RC	.40	1.00
164 Brandon Lloyd RC	1.00	2.50
165 Jarret Johnson RC	.50	1.25

2003 Topps Draft Picks and Prospects Chrome

*VETS 1-110: .8X TO 2X BASIC CARDS
*ROOKIES 111-165: 1.2X TO 3X
ONE CHROME PER PACK

2003 Topps Draft Picks and Prospects Chrome Gold Refractors

*VETS 1-110: 2X TO 5X BASIC CARDS
*ROOKIES 111-165: 3X TO 8X
STATED ODDS 1:4

2003 Topps Draft Picks and Prospects Class Marks Autographs

GROUP A STATED ODDS 1:7647
GROUP B STATED ODDS 1:826
GROUP C STATED ODDS 1:4904
GROUP D STATED ODDS 1:1825
GROUP E STATED ODDS 1:839
GROUP F STATED ODDS 1:559
GROUP G STATED ODDS 1:93
OVERALL AUTOGRAPH ODDS 1:44
*SILVER/100: .8X TO 2X BASIC AU/D-G
*SILVER/100: .6X TO 1.5X BASIC AU/A-C

CMAC Avon Cobourne G	4.00	10.00
CMAJ Andre Johnson B	20.00	50.00
CMBJ Bryant Johnson C	8.00	20.00
CMBL Byron Leftwich A	15.00	40.00
CMCB Chris Brown B	5.00	12.00
CMCP Carson Palmer A	40.00	80.00
CMJT Jason Thomas B	5.00	12.00
CMKB Kyle Boller B	8.00	20.00
CMKD Ken Dorsey B	6.00	15.00
CMKKE Kareem Kelly G	4.00	10.00
CMKW Kelley Washington D	4.00	10.00
CMLJ Larry Johnson B	8.00	20.00
CMLS Lee Suggs B	6.00	15.00
CMLT LaBrandon Toefield G	5.00	12.00
CMMB Marquel Blackwell B	5.00	12.00
CMOS Onterrio Smith E	4.00	10.00
CMQB Quentin Griffin G	5.00	12.00
CMSW Seneca Wallace G	6.00	15.00
CMTG Talman Gardner G	4.00	10.00
CMTJ Taylor Jacobs D	4.00	10.00
CMWM Willis McGahee F	8.00	20.00

2003 Topps Draft Picks and Prospects Classmate Cuts

STATED PRINT RUN 75 SER.#'d SETS
STATED ODDS 1:1951
*FOIL/25: .6X TO 1.5X BASIC DUAL/75
FOIL STATED ODDS 1:5854
FOIL PRINT RUN 25 SER.#'d SETS

CCDCW Kevin Curtis Kelley Washington	10.00	25.00
CCDDG Ken Dorsey Jason Gesser	8.00	20.00
CCDFJ Justin Fargas Larry Johnson	10.00	25.00
CCDJL Bryant Johnson Brandon Lloyd	15.00	40.00
CCDRB Dave Ragone Kyle Boller	10.00	25.00

2003 Topps Draft Picks and Prospects Collegiate Cuts

GROUP A STATED ODDS 1:811
GROUP B STATED ODDS 1:135
GROUP C STATED ODDS 1:487
GROUP D STATED ODDS 1:90
GROUP E STATED ODDS 1:192
GROUP F STATED ODDS 1:98
GROUP G STATED ODDS 1:90
GROUP H STATED ODDS 1:292
*FOIL: .6X TO 1.5X BASIC JSY
FOIL STATED ODDS 1:96
*PATCH/75: 1X TO 2.5X BASIC JSY
PATCH/75 STATED ODDS 1:427
PATCH PRINT RUN 75 SER.#'d SETS
*FOIL PATCH/25: 1.2X TO 3X BASIC JSY
FOIL PATCH PRINT RUN 25

CCAJ Andre Johnson B	10.00	25.00
CCBJ Bryant Johnson C	4.00	10.00
CCBLL Brandon Lloyd B	6.00	15.00
CCDC Dallas Clark B	6.00	15.00
CCDR Dave Ragone F	2.50	6.00
CCJF Justin Fargas D	4.00	10.00
CCJG Justin Gage D	3.00	8.00
CCJGE Jason Gesser E	3.00	8.00
CCJJ Jarret Johnson D	3.00	8.00
CCJW Jason Witten G	10.00	25.00
CCKB Kyle Boller H	4.00	10.00
CCKC Kevin Curtis F	4.00	10.00
CCKD Ken Dorsey B	3.00	8.00
CCKK Kliff Kingsbury A	3.00	8.00
CCKM Kindal Moorehead G	3.00	8.00
CCKW Kelley Washington D	2.50	6.00
CCLJ Larry Johnson F	6.00	15.00
CCRL ReShard Lee D	4.00	10.00
CCSW Seneca Wallace G	4.00	10.00
CCTC Tyrone Calico F	3.00	8.00
CCTE Terrence Edwards G	2.50	6.00
CCTS Terrell Suggs E	4.00	10.00
CCWM Willis McGahee B	5.00	12.00

2003 Topps Draft Picks and Prospects Pen Pals Autographs

STATED ODDS 1:1979
STATED PRINT RUN 75 SER.#'d SETS
*FOIL/25: .5X TO 1.2X BASIC DUAL/75
FOIL PRINT RUN 25 SER.#'d SETS
FOIL STATED ODDS 1:6180

PPDS Ken Dorsey Chris Simms	15.00	40.00
PPJM Larry Johnson Willis McGahee	20.00	50.00
PPLP Byron Leftwich Carson Palmer	30.00	80.00
PPSS Lee Suggs Onterrio Smith	10.00	25.00

2004 Topps Draft Picks and Prospects

Topps Draft Picks and Prospects released in May of 2004 making it Topps' first football card release of the year. The base set consists of 165-cards including 110-veterans and prospects and 55-rookies. Note that Mike Williams made an apearance in this product although he was declared ineligible for the NFL Draft. Hobby boxes contained 24-packs of 5-cards with an SRP of $3 per pack. Two parallel sets and a variety of game-used inserts can be found seeded in packs highlighted by the Class Marks (rookie) Autographs and the triple signed Mannings Legacy card

COMPLETE SET (165)	40.00	80.00
1 Steve McNair	.40	1.00
2 Stephen Davis	.30	.75
3 Chris Chambers	.30	.75
4 Curtis Martin	.40	1.00
5 Shaun Alexander	.30	.75
6 Jon Kitna	.30	.75
7 Jimmy Smith	.30	.75
8 Travis Henry	.25	.60
9 Torry Holt	.30	.75
10 Jamal Lewis	.30	.75
11 Clinton Portis	.40	1.00
12 Aaron Brooks	.30	.75
13 Plaxico Burress	.30	.75
14 Trent Green	.30	.75
15 Chad Johnson	.40	1.00
16 Jake Delhomme	.30	.75
17 David Boston	.25	.60
18 Joe Horn	.30	.75
19 Ahman Green	.30	.75
20 Fred Taylor	.30	.75
21 Terrell Owens	.40	1.00
22 Brad Johnson	.30	.75
23 Laveranues Coles	.25	.60
24 Ricky Williams	.30	.75
25 Peyton Manning	.75	2.00
26 Hines Ward	.40	1.00
27 Matt Hasselbeck	.30	.75
28 Marshall Faulk	.40	1.00
29 Tony Gonzalez	.40	1.00
30 Marvin Harrison	.40	1.00
31 Eric Moulds	.30	.75
32 Chad Pennington	.40	1.00
33 Jerry Porter	.25	.60
34 Jeff Garcia	.30	.75
35 Derrick Mason	.30	.75
36 Anthony Thomas	.30	.75
37 Drew Bledsoe	.40	1.00
38 Jake Plummer	.30	.75
39 Tiki Barber	.40	1.00
40 Brett Favre	1.00	2.50
41 Joey Harrington	.30	.75
42 Daunte Culpepper	.30	.75
43 LaVar Arrington	.30	.75
44 Santana Moss	.30	.75
45 David Carr	.25	.60
46 Randy Moss	.40	1.00
47 LaDainian Tomlinson	.40	1.00
48 Deuce McAllister	.30	.75
49 Amani Toomer	.30	.75
50 Donovan McNabb	.40	1.00
51 Priest Holmes	.40	1.00
52 Corey Dillon	.30	.75
53 Tom Brady	.75	2.00
54 Edgerrin James	.30	.75
55 Michael Vick	.50	1.25
56 Anquan Boldin	.40	1.00
57 Robert Ferguson	.25	.60
58 Onterrio Smith	.25	.60
59 Marques Tuiasosopo	.25	.60
60 Rudi Johnson	.30	.75
61 Alge Crumpler	.30	.75
62 Antonio Bryant	.30	.75
63 LaMont Jordan	.30	.75
64 Lamar Gordon	.25	.60
65 Tim Rattay	.25	.60
66 Antwaan Randle El	.30	.75
67 Ladell Betts	.25	.60
68 LaBrandon Toefield	.25	.60
69 Ashley Lelie	.25	.60
70 Marc Bulger	.30	.75
71 Reggie Wayne	.40	1.00
72 William Green	.25	.60
73 Josh Reed	.25	.60
74 T.J. Duckett	.30	.75
75 Andre Johnson	.40	1.00
76 Deion Branch	.30	.75
77 Tyrone Calico	.30	.75
78 Jeremy Shockey	.30	.75
79 Najeh Davenport	.30	.75
80 Byron Leftwich	.30	.75
81 Correll Buckhalter	.30	.75
82 Justin McCareins	.25	.60
83 Carson Palmer	.40	1.00
84 Bryant Johnson	.25	.60
85 Patrick Ramsey	.30	.75
86 Justin Fargas	.30	.75
87 Dallas Clark	.40	1.00
88 Kelly Campbell	.25	.60
89 DeShaun Foster	.30	.75
90 Charles Rogers	.25	.60
91 Donte' Stallworth	.25	.60
92 Dante Hall	.30	.75
93 Randy McMichael	.25	.60
94 Marcel Shipp	.25	.60
95 Kyle Boller	.30	.75
96 Steve Smith	.40	1.00
97 Brian Westbrook	.40	1.00
98 Kevan Barlow	.25	.60
99 Darnerien McCants	.25	.60
100 Domanick Davis	.25	.60
101 Andre' Davis	.25	.60
102 Nate Burleson	.30	.75
103 Larry Johnson	.30	.75
104 Drew Brees	.40	1.00
105 Koren Robinson	.25	.60
106 Quincy Carter	.25	.60
107 Javon Walker	.25	.60
108 Willis McGahee	.40	1.00
109 Chris Simms	.30	.75
110 Rex Grossman	.30	.75
111 Steven Jackson RC	1.25	3.00
112 Greg Jones RC	.50	1.25
113 Brandon Everage RC	.50	1.25
114 DeAngelo Hall RC	.75	2.00
115 Tatum Bell RC	.60	1.50
116 B.J. Symons RC	.50	1.25
117 Michael Clayton RC	.60	1.50
118 Jared Lorenzen RC	.60	1.50
119 Josh Harris RC	.50	1.25
120 Roy Williams RC	.75	2.00
121 Mewelde Moore RC	.60	1.50
122 Jeff Smoker RC	.60	1.50
123 Lee Evans RC	.75	2.00
124 Michael Jenkins RC	.75	2.00
125 Drew Henson RC	.50	1.25
126 Ben Watson RC	.75	2.00
127 Jerricho Cotchery RC	.60	1.50
128 Ben Troupe RC	.60	1.50
129 Chris Gamble RC	.60	1.50
130 Kevin Jones RC	.60	1.50
131 Cody Pickett RC	.60	1.50
132 J.P. Losman RC	.60	1.50
133 Michael Boulware RC	.75	2.00
134 Julius Jones RC	.60	1.50
135 Keary Colbert RC	.50	1.25
136 Vince Wilfork RC	.75	2.00
137 Ernest Wilford RC	.60	1.50
138 John Navarre RC	.50	1.25
139 D.J. Williams RC	.75	2.00
140 Larry Fitzgerald RC	2.00	5.00
141 Quincy Wilson RC	.60	1.50
142 James Newson RC	.75	2.00
143 Reggie Williams RC	.60	1.50
144 Devard Darling RC	.50	1.25
145 Chris Perry RC	.60	1.50
146 Derrick Strait RC	.50	1.25
147 Teddy Lehman RC	.50	1.25
148 Michael Turner RC	1.00	2.50
149 Will Smith RC	.60	1.50
150 Eli Manning RC	8.00	20.00
151 Cedric Cobbs RC	.50	1.25
152 Ell Roberson UER RC (name misspelled Eli)	.75	2.00
153 Matt Schaub RC	1.50	4.00
154 Derrick Knight RC	.50	1.25
155 Rashaun Woods RC	.50	1.25
156 Jonathan Vilma RC	.75	2.00
157 Tommie Harris RC	.75	2.00
158 Dwan Edwards RC	.50	1.25
159 Will Poole RC	.75	2.00
160 Mike Williams RC	.60	1.50
161 Philip Rivers RC	3.00	8.00
162 Sean Taylor RC	1.50	4.00
163 Darius Watts RC	.50	1.25
164 Casey Clausen RC	.60	1.50
165 Ben Roethlisberger RC	8.00	20.00

2004 Topps Draft Picks and Prospects Chrome

COMPLETE SET (165)	75.00	150.00

*VETS: .8X TO 2X BASIC CARDS
*ROOKIES: .6X TO 1.5X BASIC CARDS
STATED ODDS 1:1

2004 Topps Draft Picks and Prospects Gold Chrome

*VETS: 3X TO 8X BASIC CARDS
*ROOKIES: 2.5X TO 6X BASIC CARDS
STATED ODDS 1:12 H/R

2004 Topps Draft Picks and Prospects Big Dog Relics

GROUP A STATED ODDS 1:207H, 1:204R
GROUP B STATED ODDS 1:275H, 1:272R
GROUP C STATED ODDS 1:158H, 1:155R
GROUP D STATED ODDS 1:259H, 1:239R
GROUP E STATED ODDS 1:242H, 1:236R
GROUP F STATED ODDS 1:68H, 1:49R
GROUP G STATED ODDS 1:161H,1:156R
GROUP H STATED ODDS 1:99H, 1:97R
*SILVER: .6X TO 1.5X BASIC INSERTS
SILVER STATED ODDS 1:245H, 1:175R
SILVER PRINT RUN 100 SER.#'d SETS
UNPRICED SLVR PATCH ODDS 1:574H, 1:541R

BDAS Antonio Smith F	4.00	10.00
BDBE Brandon Everage G	3.00	8.00
BDBH Bryan Hickman F	3.00	8.00
BDBM Bobby McCray F	3.00	8.00
BDBW Ben Watson E	5.00	12.00
BDCC Cedric Cobbs C	3.00	8.00
BDCCO Chris Cooley H	5.00	12.00
BDCP Cody Pickett A	4.00	10.00
BDCW Courtney Watson F	3.00	8.00
BDDC Darrell Campbell G	3.00	8.00
BDDE Dwan Edwards H	3.00	8.00
BDDH Devery Henderson H	5.00	12.00
BDDM DeMarco McNeil F	3.00	8.00
BDDS Derrick Strait E	3.00	8.00
BDDSM Daryl Smith F	3.00	8.00
BDDT Dontarrious Thomas F	4.00	10.00
BDDW Demorrio Williams F	5.00	12.00
BDEW Ernest Wilford A	4.00	10.00
BDGJ Greg Jones A	3.00	8.00
BDJC Jerricho Cotchery D	4.00	10.00
BDJH Josh Harris B	3.00	8.00
BDJJ Julius Jones B	4.00	10.00
BDJM Johnnie Morant F	3.00	8.00
BDJN John Navarre D	3.00	8.00
BDJNE James Newson E	5.00	12.00
BDJPL J.P. Losman C	4.00	10.00
BDKC Keary Colbert C	3.00	8.00
BDKF Keyaron Fox F	4.00	10.00
BDKW Kris Wilson F	4.00	10.00
BDMB Michael Boulware G	5.00	12.00
BDMBR Maurice Brown F	3.00	8.00
BDMJ Michael Jenkins A	5.00	12.00
BDMM Mewelde Moore C	4.00	10.00
BDMS Matt Schaub C	10.00	25.00
BDMT Michael Turner B	6.00	15.00
BDNK Niko Koutouvides H	3.00	8.00
BDPR Philip Rivers A	12.00	30.00
BDRL Rodney Leisle H	3.00	8.00
BDTB Tatum Bell D	4.00	10.00
BDTL Teddy Lehman G	3.00	8.00
BDTLU Triandos Luke H	3.00	8.00

2004 Topps Draft Picks and Prospects Class Marks Autographs

GROUP A STATED ODDS 1:5702H, 1:5561R
GROUP B STATED ODDS 1:1026H, 1:1029R
GROUP C STATED ODDS 1:457H/R
GROUP D STATED ODDS 1:165H, 1:325R
GROUP E STATED ODDS 1:97H, 1:273R
GROUP F STATED ODDS 1:421H/R

CMBR Ben Roethlisberger B	60.00	120.00
CMCC Cedric Cobbs E	6.00	15.00
CMCP Chris Perry C	8.00	20.00
CMCPI Cody Pickett C	8.00	20.00
CMEM Eli Manning A	75.00	135.00
CMEW Ernest Wilford D	8.00	20.00
CMGJ Greg Jones B	6.00	15.00
CMJC Jerricho Cotchery D	8.00	20.00
CMKJ Kevin Jones E	8.00	20.00
CMLE Lee Evans D	10.00	25.00
CMLF Larry Fitzgerald A	50.00	80.00
CMMC Michael Clayton E	8.00	20.00
CMMJ Michael Jenkins D	10.00	25.00
CMMS Matt Schaub C	20.00	50.00
CMPR Philip Rivers B	40.00	80.00
CMRW Roy Williams WR C	10.00	25.00
CMRWI Reggie Williams E	8.00	20.00
CMRWO Rashaun Woods B	6.00	15.00
CMSJ Steven Jackson A	20.00	50.00
CMTB Tatum Bell F	8.00	20.00

2004 Topps Draft Picks and Prospects Class Marks Autographs Silver

SILVER/50 ODDS 1:847 H, 1:824 R
SILVER PRINT RUN 50 SER.#'d SETS

CMBR Ben Roethlisberger	75.00	150.00
CMCC Cedric Cobbs	8.00	20.00
CMCP Chris Perry	10.00	25.00
CMCPI Cody Pickett	10.00	25.00
CMEM Eli Manning	90.00	150.00
CMEW Ernest Wilford	10.00	25.00
CMGJ Greg Jones	8.00	20.00
CMJC Jerricho Cotchery	10.00	25.00
CMKJ Kevin Jones	10.00	25.00
CMLE Lee Evans	12.00	30.00
CMLF Larry Fitzgerald	60.00	100.00
CMMC Michael Clayton	10.00	25.00
CMMJ Michael Jenkins	12.00	30.00
CMMS Matt Schaub	25.00	60.00
CMPR Philip Rivers	40.00	100.00
CMRW Roy Williams WR	12.00	30.00
CMRWO Rashaun Woods	8.00	20.00
CMSJ Steven Jackson	20.00	50.00
CMTB Tatum Bell	10.00	25.00

2004 Topps Draft Picks and Prospects Old School Dual Relics

STATED ODDS 1:846H, 1:820R

OSBJ Anquan Boldin Greg Jones	8.00	20.00
OSDP Corey Dillon Cody Pickett	8.00	20.00
OSDW Andre Davis Ernest Wilford	6.00	15.00
OSGJ Eddie George Michael Jenkins	8.00	20.00
OSHR Torry Holt Philip Rivers	30.00	50.00

2004 Topps Draft Picks and Prospects Quarterback Legacy Autographs

SINGLE AUTO ODDS 1:2753H, 1:2780R
TRIPLE SILVER ODDS 1:16,630H, 1:46,320R
TRIPLE GOLD 1/1 STATED ODDS 1:399,120

QBS Archie Manning Peyton Manning Eli Manning Silver/50	300.00	500.00
QBAM Archie Manning/100	25.00	40.00
QBEM Eli Manning/100	100.00	175.00
QBPM Peyton Manning/100	50.00	100.00

2005 Topps Draft Picks and Prospects

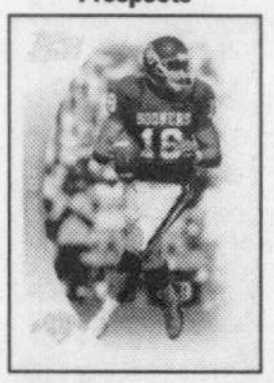

Topps Draft Picks and Prospects initially released in late-May 2005 as Topps?ÇÖ first football product of the year. The base set consists of 170-cards including 55-rookies issued one per pack and five autographed draft picks cards. Hobby boxes contained 14-packs of 5-cards and carried an S.R.P. of $2.99 per pack. Four parallel sets and a variety of inserts can be found seeded in packs highlighted by the Class Marks Autographs and Double Feature Dual Autographs inserts.

COMP.SET w/o AU's (165)	15.00	40.00
COMP.SET w/o RC's (110)	10.00	25.00
ONE ROOKIE PER PACK		
DRAFT PICK AUTO ODDS 1:1179		
UNPRICED GOLD SUPERFRACTORS #'d TO 1		
UNPRICED PRINTING PLATES #'d TO 1		
1 Marvin Harrison	.40	1.00
2 Rudi Johnson	.30	.75
3 Matt Hasselbeck	.30	.75
4 Plaxico Burress	.30	.75
5 Chad Pennington	.40	1.00
6 Jamal Lewis	.30	.75
7 Terrell Owens	.40	1.00
8 LaDainian Tomlinson	.40	1.00
9 Tiki Barber	.40	1.00
10 Dante Hall	.25	.60
11 Peyton Manning	.75	2.00
12 Marshall Faulk	.40	1.00
13 Donovan McNabb	.40	1.00
14 Randy Moss	.40	1.00
15 Muhsin Muhammad	.30	.75
16 Deuce McAllister	.30	.75
17 Fred Taylor	.30	.75
18 Jake Plummer	.30	.75
19 Javon Walker	.25	.60
20 Tony Gonzalez	.30	.75
21 Michael Vick	.40	1.00
22 Brett Favre	1.00	2.50
23 Joe Horn	.30	.75
24 Jeremy Shockey	.40	1.00
25 Laveranues Coles	.25	.60
26 Trent Green	.30	.75
27 Alge Crumpler	.30	.75
28 Curtis Martin	.40	1.00
29 Torry Holt	.30	.75
30 Daunte Culpepper	.30	.75
31 Aaron Brooks	.25	.60
32 Priest Holmes	.30	.75
33 Eric Moulds	.25	.60
34 Jerome Bettis	.40	1.00
35 David Carr	.25	.60
36 Chad Johnson	.30	.75
37 Ahman Green	.30	.75
38 Clinton Portis	.30	.75
39 Drew Brees	.40	1.00
40 Darrell Jackson	.25	.60
41 Corey Dillon	.30	.75
42 Reggie Wayne	.40	1.00
43 Shaun Alexander	.30	.75
44 Hines Ward	.40	1.00
45 Tom Brady	.75	2.00
46 Isaac Bruce	.30	.75
47 Byron Leftwich	.30	.75
48 Chris Chambers	.30	.75
49 Marc Bulger	.30	.75
50 Edgerrin James	.30	.75
51 Jake Delhomme	.30	.75
52 Koren Robinson	.25	.60
53 Brian Westbrook	.30	.75
54 Reuben Droughns	.25	.60
55 Joey Harrington	.30	.75
56 Eli Manning	.60	1.50
57 Julius Jones	.25	.60
58 Nick Goings	.25	.60
59 T.J. Houshmandzadeh	.30	.75
60 Ben Roethlisberger	.60	1.50
61 Charles Rogers	.25	.60
62 Billy Volek	.25	.60
63 Drew Henson	.25	.60
64 Andre Johnson	.40	1.00
65 Carson Palmer	.40	1.00
66 Anquan Boldin	.30	.75
67 Lee Suggs	.25	.60
68 Jerry Porter	.25	.60
69 J.P. Losman	.25	.60
70 Nate Burleson	.25	.60
71 Lee Evans	.30	.75
72 Tatum Bell	.25	.60
73 Chester Taylor	.30	.75
74 Philip Rivers	.40	1.00
75 Rex Grossman	.30	.75
76 Willis McGahee	.40	1.00
77 Antonio Gates	.40	1.00
78 Steven Jackson	.40	1.00
79 Roy Williams WR	.30	.75
80 Chris Simms	.30	.75
81 Najeh Davenport	.30	.75
82 Kevin Jones	.25	.60
83 Jason Witten	.40	1.00
84 Brandon Lloyd	.25	.60
85 Larry Johnson	.30	.75
86 Ronald Curry	.25	.60
87 Chris Brown	.25	.60
88 Kyle Boller	.30	.75
89 Chris Perry	.25	.60
90 Keary Colbert	.25	.60
91 Sean Taylor	.40	1.00
92 Greg Jones	.25	.60
93 Larry Fitzgerald	.40	1.00
94 Michael Clayton	.25	.60
95 Mewelde Moore	.25	.60
96 Drew Bennett	.30	.75
97 Reggie Williams	.25	.60
98 Quentin Griffin	.25	.60
99 Josh McCown	.30	.75
100 Santana Moss	.30	.75
101 Kellen Winslow	.30	.75
102 Michael Jenkins	.30	.75
103 Dunta Robinson	.25	.60
104 Luke McCown	.25	.60
105 Brandon Stokley	.25	.60
106 Derrick Blaylock	.25	.60
107 Ernest Wilford	.25	.60
108 Domanick Davis	.25	.60
109 Jonathan Vilma	.30	.75
110 Dwight Freeney	.30	.75
111 Alex Smith QB AU RC	30.00	60.00
112 Derrick Johnson AU RC	15.00	40.00
113 Charlie Frye AU RC	20.00	50.00
114 Ronnie Brown AU RC	30.00	60.00
115 Mike Williams AU	15.00	40.00
116 Erasmus James RC	.60	1.50
117 Alex Smith TE RC	.50	1.25
118 Dan Orlovsky RC	.75	2.00
119 Eric Shelton RC	.50	1.25
120 Reggie Brown RC	.50	1.25
121 Carlos Rogers RC	.75	2.00
122 Dan Cody RC	.60	1.50
123 J.J. Arrington RC	.60	1.50
124 Travis Johnson RC	.50	1.25
125 Antrel Rolle RC	.75	2.00
126 Andrew Walter RC	.60	1.50
127 Craphonso Thorpe RC	.50	1.25
128 Bryan Randall RC	.60	1.50
129 Anttaj Hawthorne RC	.50	1.25
130 David Pollack RC	.60	1.50
131 Heath Miller RC	1.00	2.50
132 Charles Frederick RC	.50	1.25
133 Anthony Davis RC	.50	1.25
134 Chris Rix RC	.60	1.50
135 T.A. McLendon RC	.50	1.25
136 David Greene RC	.50	1.25
137 Timmy Chang RC	.60	1.50
138 Marcus Spears RC	.60	1.50
139 Airese Currie RC	.50	1.25
140 Chris Henry RC	.75	2.00
141 Josh Davis RC	.50	1.25
142 Jason Campbell RC	1.00	2.50
143 Barrett Ruud RC	.75	2.00
144 Courtney Roby RC	.60	1.50
145 Mike Patterson RC	.50	1.25
146 Jason White RC	.75	2.00
147 Fred Gibson RC	.60	1.50
148 Marion Barber RC	.75	2.00
149 Braylon Edwards RC	1.00	2.50
150 Cadillac Williams RC	.75	2.00
151 Kyle Orton RC	.75	2.00
152 Aaron Rodgers RC	6.00	15.00
153 Alvin Pearman RC	.50	1.25
154 Stefan LeFors RC	.50	1.25
155 Marlin Jackson RC	.50	1.25
156 Taylor Stubblefield RC	.50	1.25
157 Ciatrick Fason RC	.50	1.25
158 Kay-Jay Harris RC	.50	1.25
159 Frank Gore RC	1.25	3.00
160 Vernand Morency RC	.60	1.50
161 Adam Jones RC	.60	1.50
162 Troy Williamson RC	.60	1.50
163 Roddy White RC	1.00	2.50
164 Thomas Davis RC	.50	1.25
165 Mark Clayton RC	.75	2.00
166 Craig Bragg RC	.50	1.25
167 Noah Herron RC	.50	1.25
168 Darren Sproles RC	.75	2.00
169 Terrence Murphy RC	.50	1.25
170 Walter Reyes RC	.50	1.25

2005 Topps Draft Picks and Prospects Chrome Black Refractors

*VETERANS: 8X TO 20X BASIC CARDS
*ROOKIES: 5X TO 12X BASIC CARDS
STATED ODDS 1:284 HOB, 1:285 RET
STATED PRINT RUN 25 SER.#'d SETS

152 Aaron Rodgers	150.00	250.00

2005 Topps Draft Picks and Prospects Chrome

COMPLETE SET (165)	60.00	120.00

*VETERANS: 1X TO 2.5X BASIC CARDS
*ROOKIES: .8X TO 2X BASIC CARDS
ONE PER PACK

2005 Topps Draft Picks and Prospects Chrome Gold Refractors

*VETERANS: 5X TO 12X BASIC CARDS
*ROOKIES: 3X TO 8X BASIC CARDS
STATED ODDS 1:35 HOB, 1:36 RET
STATED PRINT RUN 199 SER.#'d SETS

2005 Topps Draft Picks and Prospects Class Marks Autographs

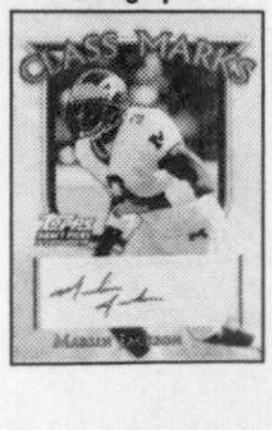

GROUP A ODDS 1:555 HOB, 1:556 RET
GROUP B ODDS 1:227 HOB/RET
GROUP C ODDS 1:778 HOB, 1:768 RET
GROUP D ODDS 1:173 HOB/RET
GROUP E ODDS 1:240 HOB, 1:219 RET
GROUP F ODDS 1:68 HOB, 1:80 RET
GOLD STATED ODDS 1:5241 HOB/RET
UNPRICED GOLD PRINT RUN 10 SETS
UNPRICED PRINT PLATE PRINT RUN 1 SET
RAINBOW STATED ODDS 1:22,990 HOB
UNPRICED RAINBOW PRINT RUN 1 SET

CMAD Anthony Davis B	5.00	12.00
CMAR Aaron Rodgers A	150.00	250.00
CMAW Andrew Walter A	6.00	15.00
CMBE Braylon Edwards A	25.00	60.00
CMCB Cedric Benson A	12.00	30.00
CMCF Charles Frederick F	5.00	12.00
CMCH Chris Henry D	8.00	20.00
CMCHO Cedric Houston F	8.00	20.00
CMCR Chris Rix D	6.00	15.00
CMCT Craphonso Thorpe B	5.00	12.00
CMCW Cadillac Williams A	15.00	40.00
CMDC Dan Cody A	6.00	15.00
CMDG David Greene B	5.00	12.00
CMES Eric Shelton E	5.00	12.00
CMFG Fred Gibson F	6.00	15.00
CMJA J.J. Arrington E	6.00	15.00
CMJC Jason Campbell A	12.00	30.00
CMJW Jason White A	8.00	20.00
CMKO Kyle Orton B	15.00	40.00
CMMB Marion Barber F	8.00	20.00
CMMC Mark Clayton A	8.00	20.00
CMMJ Marlin Jackson D	5.00	12.00
CMRBR Reggie Brown B	5.00	12.00
CMTAM T.A. McLendon C	5.00	12.00
CMWR Walter Reyes F	5.00	12.00

2005 Topps Draft Picks and Prospects Class Marks Autographs Silver

SILVER/50 ODDS 1:940 HOB, 1:942 RET
SILVER PRINT RUN 50 SER.#'d SETS

CMAD Anthony Davis	8.00	20.00
CMAR Aaron Rodgers	200.00	350.00
CMAW Andrew Walter	10.00	25.00
CMBE Braylon Edwards	30.00	80.00
CMCB Cedric Benson	20.00	50.00
CMCF Charles Frederick	8.00	20.00
CMCH Chris Henry	12.00	30.00
CMCHO Cedric Houston	12.00	30.00
CMCR Chris Rix	10.00	25.00
CMCT Craphonso Thorpe	8.00	20.00
CMCW Cadillac Williams	20.00	50.00
CMDC Dan Cody	10.00	25.00
CMDG David Greene	8.00	20.00
CMES Eric Shelton	8.00	20.00
CMFG Fred Gibson	10.00	25.00
CMJA J.J. Arrington	10.00	25.00
CMJC Jason Campbell	20.00	50.00
CMJW Jason White	12.00	30.00
CMKO Kyle Orton	20.00	50.00
CMMB Marion Barber	12.00	30.00
CMMC Mark Clayton	10.00	25.00
CMMJ Marlin Jackson	8.00	20.00
CMRBR Reggie Brown	8.00	20.00
CMTAM T.A. McLendon	8.00	20.00
CMWR Walter Reyes	8.00	20.00

2005 Topps Draft Picks and Prospects Double Feature Dual Autographs

STATED ODDS 1:5108 HOB, 1:4702 RET

BW Cedric Benson Cadillac Williams	30.00	80.00
EC Braylon Edwards Mark Clayton	25.00	60.00
EW Braylon Edwards Mike Williams	40.00	100.00
SR Alex Smith QB Aaron Rodgers	150.00	250.00
WB Cadillac Williams Ronnie Brown	50.00	120.00

2005 Topps Draft Picks and Prospects Senior Standout Jersey

GROUP A ODDS 1:1304 HOB, 1:1309
GROUP B ODDS 1:275 HOB/RET
GROUP C ODDS 1:188 HOB/RET
GROUP D ODDS 1:171 HOB/RET
GROUP E ODDS 1:869 HOB, 1:874
GROUP F ODDS 1:270 HOB/RET
GROUP G ODDS 1:535 HOB/RET
GROUP H ODDS 1:245 HOB/RET
GROUP I ODDS 1:470 HOB/RET
GROUP J ODDS 1:107 HOB, 1:103 RET
GROUP K ODDS 1:250 HOB, 1:185 RET
GROUP L ODDS 1:385 HOB, 1:379 RET
GROUP M ODDS 1:356 HOB/RET
UNPRICED GOLD PRINT RUN 10 SETS
UNPRICED PRINT PLATE PRINT RUN 1 SET
*SILVER: .6X TO 1.5X GROUP A-B JSYs
*SILVER: .8X TO 2X GROUP C-M JSYs
SILVER ODDS 1:207 HOB, 1:181 RET
SILVER PRINT RUN 50 SER.#'d SETS

SSAR Antrel Rolle SB A	5.00	12.00
SSAR2 Antrel Rolle Mia G	4.00	10.00
SSAS Alex Smith TE F	2.50	6.00
SSBJ Brandon Jones C	3.00	8.00
SSBR Barrett Ruud L	4.00	10.00
SSCF Charlie Frye C	4.00	10.00
SSCH Cedric Houston C	4.00	10.00
SSCR Carlos Rogers SB D	4.00	10.00
SSCR2 Carlos Rogers Aub J	4.00	10.00
SSCT Craphonso Thorpe C	2.50	6.00
SSCW Cadillac Williams Aub J	4.00	10.00
SSCW2 Cadillac Williams SB D	4.00	10.00
SSDG David Greene D	2.50	6.00
SSDS Darren Sproles E	4.00	10.00
SSFG Fred Gibson D	3.00	8.00
SSFGO Frank Gore M	6.00	15.00
SSJA J.J. Arrington D	3.00	8.00
SSJC Jason Campbell B	6.00	15.00
SSKO Kyle Orton K	4.00	10.00
SSMC Mark Clayton H	4.00	10.00
SSMJ Marlin Jackson H	2.50	6.00
SSMS Marcus Spears LSU K	3.00	8.00
SSMS2 Marcus Spears SB B	4.00	10.00
SSRB Reggie Brown C	2.50	6.00
SSRBR Ronnie Brown I	10.00	25.00
SSSC Shaun Cody F	3.00	8.00
SSSCU Sonny Cumbie I	2.50	6.00
SSTS Taylor Stubblefield J	2.50	6.00
SSVJ Vincent Jackson J	5.00	12.00
SSMSC Morgan Scalley J	2.50	6.00

2005 Topps Draft Picks and Prospects Senior Standout Jersey Autographs

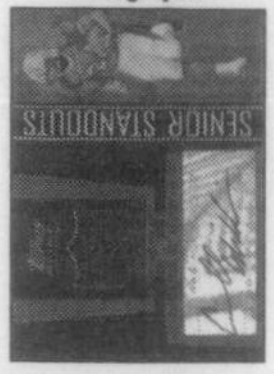

SILVER STATED ODDS 1:2398 HOB/RET
SILVER PRINT RUN 50 SER.#'d SETS
GOLD STATED ODDS 1:13,457 HOB/RET
UNPRICED GOLD PRINT RUN 10 SETS
RAINBOW STATED ODDS 1:61,307 HOB
RAINBOW PRINT RUN 1 SER.#'d SETS

SSAAR Antrel Rolle	20.00	50.00
SSACF Charlie Frye	20.00	50.00
SSACW Cadillac Williams	20.00	50.00
SSADG David Greene	15.00	40.00
SSAJA J.J. Arrington	15.00	40.00
SSAJC Jason Campbell	40.00	80.00
SSAKO Kyle Orton	25.00	50.00
SSAMC Mark Clayton	15.00	40.00
SSARB Reggie Brown	20.00	50.00
SSARBR Ronnie Brown	40.00	100.00

2006 Topps Draft Picks and Prospects

This 175-card set was released in May, 2006. The set was issued into the hobby in five-card packs, with an $3 SRP, which came 24 packs to a box. The first 109 cards in this set are veterans while the rest of the set features 2006 NFL rookies. The overall odds of finding a rookie was stated to be one per pack. The final 10 cards (#166-175(in the set were all signed by the rookie. Those signed rookie cards were issued to a stated print run of 199 serial numbered copies and those cards were inserted into packs at a stated rate of one in 1282.

COMP.SET w/o SP's (165)	12.50	30.00
COMP.SET w/o RC's (110)	6.00	15.00
ONE ROOKIE CARD PER PACK		
166-175 ROOKIE AU/199 ODDS 1:1282		
UNPRICED PRINT PLATES SER.#'d TO 1		
1 Plaxico Burress	.30	.75
2 Ahman Green	.30	.75
3 Domanick Davis	.25	.60
4 Andre Johnson	.40	1.00
5 Donovan McNabb	.40	1.00
6 Marvin Harrison	.40	1.00
7 Michael Vick	.40	1.00
8 Priest Holmes	.30	.75
9 Torry Holt	.30	.75
10 Marc Bulger	.30	.75
11 Ben Roethlisberger	.50	1.25
12 Larry Fitzgerald	.40	1.00
13 Peyton Manning	.60	1.50
14 Chris Perry	.30	.75
15 Antonio Gates	.40	1.00
16 Eli Manning	.50	1.25
17 Brett Favre	.75	2.00
18 Reggie Brown	.25	.60
19 Curtis Martin	.40	1.00
20 Charlie Frye	.30	.75
21 Tom Brady	.60	1.50
22 Cadillac Williams	.30	.75
23 Trent Green	.30	.75
24 Matt Jones	.25	.60
25 Anquan Boldin	.30	.75
26 Larry Johnson	.30	.75
27 Rudi Johnson	.30	.75
28 Marion Barber	.40	1.00
29 Jake Delhomme	.30	.75
30 Philip Rivers	.40	1.00
31 Fred Taylor	.30	.75
32 Frank Gore	.40	1.00
33 Shaun Alexander	.30	.75
34 Chris Simms	.30	.75
35 LaDainian Tomlinson	.40	1.00
36 Troy Williamson	.25	.60
37 Clinton Portis	.40	1.00
38 Kyle Orton	.40	1.00
39 Tony Gonzalez	.30	.75
40 Mark Clayton	.30	.75
41 Steve Smith	.40	1.00
42 Heath Miller	.30	.75
43 Warrick Dunn	.30	.75
44 Alex Smith TE	.25	.60
45 Chris Brown	.25	.60
46 Billy Volek	.25	.60
47 Tiki Barber	.40	1.00
48 Julius Jones	.25	.60
49 Drew Bledsoe	.40	1.00
50 Charles Rogers	.30	.75
51 Jake Plummer	.30	.75
52 Greg Jones	.25	.60
53 Chad Johnson	.30	.75
54 Braylon Edwards	.30	.75
55 Carson Palmer	.40	1.00
56 Scottie Vines	.25	.60
57 Keary Colbert	.25	.60
58 Alex Smith QB	.40	1.00
59 Roy Williams WR	.30	.75
60 Roddy White	.30	.75
61 Willis McGahee	.30	.75
62 Michael Clayton	.25	.60
63 Edgerrin James	.30	.75
64 Aaron Rodgers	.75	2.00
65 Byron Leftwich	.30	.75
66 Tatum Bell	.25	.60
67 Daunte Culpepper	.30	.75
68 Chris Henry	.25	.60
69 Corey Dillon	.30	.75
70 Ronnie Brown	.40	1.00
71 Kevin Jones	.25	.60
72 J.P. Losman	.30	.75
73 Steven Jackson	.40	1.00
74 Mike Williams	.25	.60
75 Jeremy Shockey	.40	1.00
76 DeMarcus Ware	.30	.75
77 LaMont Jordan	.30	.75

78 Cedric Benson .30 .75
79 Ricky Williams .25 .60
80 Brandon Jones .25 .60
81 Brian Westbrook .30 .75
82 Willie Parker .30 .75
83 Hines Ward .40 1.00
84 Ernest Wilford .25 .60
85 Matt Hasselbeck .30 .75
86 Jason Campbell .30 .75
87 Joey Galloway .30 .75
88 Odell Thurman .25 .60
89 Santana Moss .30 .75
90 Courtney Roby .25 .60
91 Deuce McAllister .30 .75
92 Derrick Johnson .25 .60
93 Drew Brees .40 1.00
94 Michael Jenkins .30 .75
95 Jerome Bettis .40 1.00
96 Osi Umenyiora .30 .75
97 Reggie Wayne .30 .75
98 Ryan Moats .25 .60
99 Randy Moss .40 1.00
100 Samie Parker .25 .60
101 Mark Bradley .25 .60
102 Samkon Gado .30 .75
103 Matt Schaub .30 .75
104 Shaun McDonald .25 .60
105 D.J. Hackett .25 .60
106 Mewelde Moore .25 .60
107 Chester Taylor .30 .75
108 Greg Lewis .25 .60
109 Chris Cooley .30 .75
110 Todd DeVoe RC .25 .60
111 Joel Klopfenstein RC .60 1.50
112 Devin Hester RC 1.50 4.00
113 Brad Smith RC 1.00 2.50
114 Jason Avant RC .60 1.50
115 Michael Robinson RC .75 2.00
116 Kellen Clemens RC .75 2.00
117 Anthony Fasano RC 1.00 2.50
118 Leon Washington RC .75 2.00
119 Laurence Maroney RC .75 2.00
120 Martin Nance RC .75 2.00
121 Demetrius Williams RC .75 2.00
122 A.J. Nicholson RC .60 1.50
123 Jimmy Williams RC 1.00 2.50
124 Michael Huff RC .75 2.00
125 Chad Jackson RC .60 1.50
126 Mike Hass RC .75 2.00
127 Brodie Croyle RC 1.00 2.50
128 Jerome Harrison RC 1.00 2.50
129 Hank Baskett RC 1.00 2.50
130 Santonio Holmes RC 1.25 3.00
131 Chad Greenway RC 1.00 2.50
132 Mario Williams RC 1.00 2.50
133 Charlie Whitehurst RC 1.00 2.50
134 Darrell Hackney RC .75 2.00
135 DeMeco Ryans RC 1.00 2.50
136 Mathias Kiwanuka RC 1.00 2.50
137 Omar Jacobs RC .60 1.50
138 Bruce Gradkowski RC 1.00 2.50
139 Drew Olson RC .60 1.50
140 Maurice Stovall RC .60 1.50
141 Greg Jennings RC 1.50 4.00
142 D'Brickashaw Ferguson RC 1.00 2.50
143 Manny Lawson RC .75 2.00
144 Tamba Hali RC 1.00 2.50
145 Vernon Davis RC 1.25 3.00
146 Greg Lee RC .60 1.50
147 Dominique Byrd RC .75 2.00
148 Leonard Pope RC 1.00 2.50
149 Bobby Carpenter RC .60 1.50
150 Haloti Ngata RC 1.00 2.50
151 Marcedes Lewis RC 1.00 2.50
152 Ernie Sims RC .75 2.00
153 Ashton Youboty RC .60 1.50
154 D.J. Shockley RC .75 2.00
155 Paul Pinegar RC .60 1.50
156 Maurice Drew RC 1.50 4.00
157 Jeremy Bloom RC .75 2.00
158 Cory Rodgers RC .75 2.00
159 Abdul Hodge RC .60 1.50
160 Tye Hill RC .60 1.50
161 D'Qwell Jackson RC .75 2.00
162 Jonathan Orr RC .75 2.00
163 Antonio Cromartie RC 1.00 2.50
164 Todd Watkins RC .60 1.50
165 Gerald Riggs RC .75 2.00
166 Matt Leinart AU RC 15.00 40.00
167 Reggie Bush AU RC 30.00 80.00
168 DeAngelo Williams AU RC 20.00 50.00
169 A.J. Hawk AU RC 20.00 50.00
170 Vince Young AU RC 20.00 50.00
171 Derek Hagan AU RC 12.00 30.00
172 Joseph Addai AU RC 15.00 40.00
173 Jay Cutler AU RC 40.00 100.00
174 Sinorice Moss AU RC 15.00 40.00
175 LenDale White AU RC 12.00 30.00
RBML Reggie Bush AU/25 100.00 200.00
Matt Leinart AU

2006 Topps Draft Picks and Prospects Chrome Black

COMPLETE SET (165) 60.00 120.00
*VETS 1-110: 1X TO 2.5X BASIC CARDS
*ROOKIES 111-165: .6X TO 1.5X
OVERALL CHROME PARALLEL ODDS 1:1

2006 Topps Draft Picks and Prospects Chrome Black Refractors

*VETS 1-110: 1.5X TO 4X BASIC CARDS
*ROOKIES 111-165: 1X TO 2.5X BASIC CARDS
STATED ODDS 1:4

2006 Topps Draft Picks and Prospects Chrome Bronze

*VETS 1-110: 3X TO 8X BASIC CARDS
*ROOKIES 111-165: 2X TO 5X BASIC CARDS
BRONZE/449 STATED ODDS 1:31

2006 Topps Draft Picks and Prospects Chrome Bronze Refractors

*VETS 1-110: 4X TO 10X BASIC CARDS
*ROOKIES 111-165: 2.5X TO 6X BASIC CARDS
BRONZE REF/299 STATED ODDS 1:52

2006 Topps Draft Picks and Prospects Chrome Gold

*VETS 1-110: 8X TO 20X BASIC CARDS
*ROOKIES 111-165: 6X TO 15X BASIC CARDS
GOLD/25 STATED ODDS 1:617

2006 Topps Draft Picks and Prospects Chrome Gold Refractors

UNPRICED GOLD REF PRINT RUN 1 SET

2006 Topps Draft Picks and Prospects Chrome Silver

*VETS 1-110: 5X TO 12X BASIC CARDS
*ROOKIES 111-165: 4X TO 10X BASIC CARDS
SILVER/199 STATED ODDS 1:78

2006 Topps Draft Picks and Prospects Chrome Silver Refractors

*VETS 1-110: 6X TO 15X BASIC CARDS
*ROOKIES 111-165: 5X TO 12X BASIC CARDS
SILVER REF/99 STATED ODDS 1:156

2006 Topps Draft Picks and Prospects Class Marks Autographs

GROUP A ODDS 1:4275
GROUP B ODDS 1:1664
GROUP C ODDS 1:385
GROUP D ODDS 1:1275
GROUP E ODDS 1:278
GROUP F ODDS 1:93
UNPRICED GOLD/10 ODDS 1:9000
UNPRICED HOLOFOIL/1 ODDS 1:60,206
UNPRICED PRINT PLATES SER.#'d TO 1
*SILVER/50: .8X TO 2X AU GRP B-F
*SILVER/50: .6X TO 1.5X AU GRP A
SILVER/50 STATED ODDS 1:1185
CMBB Brett Basanez F 6.00 15.00
CMBC Brian Calhoun B 4.00 10.00
CMBG Bruce Gradkowski D 6.00 15.00
CMCG Chad Greenway F 6.00 15.00
CMCJ Chad Jackson C 4.00 10.00
CMCR Cory Rodgers F 5.00 12.00
CMCW Charlie Whitehurst C 6.00 15.00
CMDH Derek Hagan B 5.00 12.00
CMDM DonTrell Moore F 5.00 12.00
CMDO Drew Olson E 4.00 10.00
CMDS D.J. Shockley E 5.00 12.00
CMDW DeAngelo Williams A 15.00 40.00
CMDW Demetrius Williams C 5.00 12.00
CMGJ Greg Jennings F 15.00 30.00
CMGL Greg Lee F 4.00 10.00
CMGR Gerald Riggs F 5.00 12.00
CMJA Jason Avant D 4.00 10.00
CMJB Jeremy Bloom C 5.00 12.00
CMJC Jay Cutler A 30.00 60.00
CMJH Jerome Harrison E 6.00 15.00
CMLM Laurence Maroney B 5.00 12.00
CMLW Leon Washington 5.00 12.00
CMMD Maurice Drew C 15.00 40.00
CMML Matt Leinart A 12.00 30.00
CMMN Martin Nance E 5.00 12.00
CMMR Michael Robinson E 5.00 12.00
CMMS Maurice Stovall F 4.00 10.00
CMOJ Omar Jacobs C 4.00 10.00
CMPP Paul Pinegar C 4.00 10.00
CMRB Reggie Bush A 25.00 50.00
CMRM Reggie McNeal F 5.00 12.00
CMSH Santonio Holmes B 12.00 30.00
CMSM Sinorice Moss B 6.00 15.00
CMTW Todd Watkins E 4.00 10.00
CMTW Travis Wilson F 4.00 10.00
CMVD Vernon Davis C 8.00 20.00
CMVY Vince Young A 12.00 30.00
CMAMH Mike Hass C 5.00 12.00
CMBCR Brodie Croyle C 6.00 15.00
CMDHA Darrell Hackney C 5.00 12.00
CMDHE Devin Hester C 15.00 40.00
CMJAD Joseph Addai B 6.00 15.00
CMLEW LenDale White A 8.00 20.00

2006 Topps Draft Picks and Prospects First and Ten Autographs

FIRST AND TEN AUTO/50 ODDS 1:4900
UNPRICED DUAL AUTO/10 ODDS 1:32,000
UNPRICED DUAL GLD AU ODDS 1:1,400,000
BJ Bo Jackson 40.00 80.00
EC Earl Campbell 25.00 50.00
EM Eli Manning 50.00 100.00
JE John Elway 75.00 150.00
JP Jim Plunkett 25.00 50.00
MV Michael Vick 30.00 60.00
PH Paul Hornung 40.00 80.00
PM Peyton Manning 60.00 120.00
RB Reggie Bush 40.00 80.00
TA Troy Aikman 50.00 100.00
TB Terry Bradshaw 50.00 100.00

2006 Topps Draft Picks and Prospects Senior Standout Jersey

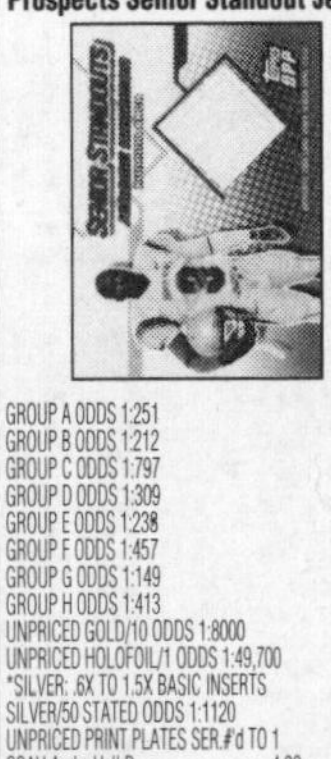

GROUP A ODDS 1:251
GROUP B ODDS 1:212
GROUP C ODDS 1:797
GROUP D ODDS 1:309
GROUP E ODDS 1:238
GROUP F ODDS 1:457
GROUP G ODDS 1:149
GROUP H ODDS 1:413
UNPRICED GOLD/10 ODDS 1:8000
UNPRICED HOLOFOIL/1 ODDS 1:49,700
*SILVER: .6X TO 1.5X BASIC INSERTS
SILVER/50 STATED ODDS 1:1120
UNPRICED PRINT PLATES SER.#'d TO 1
SSAH Andre Hall D 4.00 10.00
SSAM Anthony Mix E 4.00 10.00
SSAP Anwar Phillips A 5.00 12.00
SSBB Broderick Bunkley G 5.00 12.00
SSBC Brodie Croyle D 6.00 15.00
SSCG Chad Greenway G 5.00 12.00
SSDA Devin Aromashodu E 4.00 10.00
SSDB Dominique Byrd E 5.00 12.00
SSDD Dusty Dvoracek G 4.00 10.00
SSDF D'Brickashaw Ferguson H 5.00 12.00
SSDJ D'Qwell Jackson B 4.00 10.00
SSDM DeMario Minter B 4.00 10.00
SSDR DeMeco Ryans D 6.00 15.00
SSDS D.J. Shockley E 5.00 12.00
SSDW DeAngelo Williams B 10.00 25.00
SSED Elvis Dumervil F 3.00 8.00
SSEW Eric Winston H 3.00 8.00
SSGM Garrett Mills C 3.00 8.00
SSHB Hank Baskett D 5.00 12.00
SSJA Joseph Addai A 8.00 20.00
SSJC Jay Cutler E 12.00 30.00
SSJH Jerome Harrison E 5.00 12.00
SSJK Joe Klopfenstein G 4.00 10.00
SSJM Jesse Mahelona H 4.00 10.00
SSJN Jerious Norwood A 8.00 20.00
SSLW Lawrence Vickers E 4.00 10.00
SSMB Mike Bell E 5.00 12.00
SSMK Mathias Kiwanuka G 6.00 15.00
SSML Manny Lawson G 5.00 12.00
SSMN Martin Nance A 4.00 10.00
SSMR Michael Robinson E 5.00 12.00
SSMS Maurice Stovall E 5.00 12.00
SSOH Orien Harris F 3.00 8.00
SSSG Skyler Green A 5.00 12.00
SSSH Spencer Havner F 4.00 10.00
SSSM Sinorice Moss A 5.00 12.00
SSTH Tye Hill B 5.00 12.00
SSTJ T.J. Williams G 5.00 12.00
SSTW Terrence Whitehead E 4.00 10.00
SSWB Will Blackmon B 4.00 10.00
SSAHO Abdul Hodge C 5.00 12.00
SSDEW Demetrius Williams B 5.00 12.00
SSDH1 Darrell Hackney E 4.00 10.00
SSDH2 Derek Hagan A 4.00 10.00
SSJAV Jason Avant B 5.00 12.00
SSMLE Marcedes Lewis G 5.00 12.00
SSTHA Tamba Hali G 5.00 12.00
SSTHO Thomas Howard D 5.00 12.00
SSTRW Travis Wilson B 5.00 12.00

2006 Topps Draft Picks and Prospects Senior Standout Jersey Autographs Silver

SILVER/50 STATED ODDS 1:5150
UNPRICED HOLOFOIL/1 ODDS 1:1,400,000
UNPRICED GOLD/10 ODDS 1:37,000
SSADF D'Brickashaw Ferguson 15.00 40.00
SSADS D.J. Shockley 12.50 30.00
SSADW DeAngelo Williams 25.00 60.00
SSAJA Joseph Addai 30.00 80.00
SSAJC Jay Cutler 60.00 120.00
SSAMN Martin Nance 15.00 30.00
SSAMR Michael Robinson 15.00 40.00
SSAMS Maurice Stovall 15.00 40.00
SSASM Sinorice Moss 15.00 40.00
SSADHA Derek Hagan 15.00 40.00

2006 Topps Draft Picks and Prospects Upperclassmen Jersey

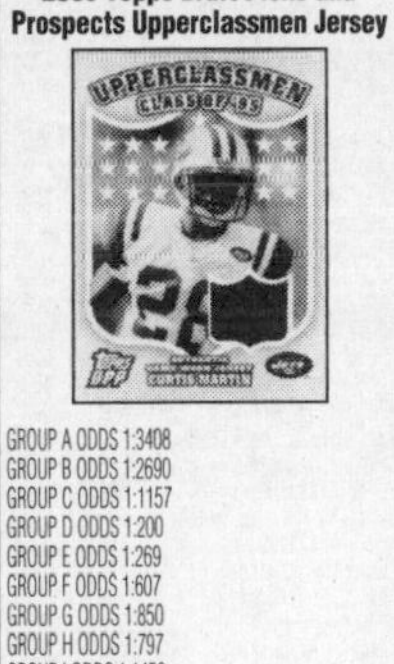

GROUP A ODDS 1:3408
GROUP B ODDS 1:2690
GROUP C ODDS 1:1157
GROUP D ODDS 1:200
GROUP E ODDS 1:269
GROUP F ODDS 1:607
GROUP G ODDS 1:850
GROUP H ODDS 1:797
GROUP I ODDS 1:1459
GROUP J ODDS 1:1380
GROUP K ODDS 1:207
GROUP L ODDS 1:378
GROUP M ODDS 1:114
*SILVER: .6X TO 1.5X BASIC INSERTS
SILVER/50 STATED ODDS 1:1175
UNPRICED PRINT PLATES SER.#'d TO 1
UCAJ Andre Johnson M 3.00 8.00
UCAL Ashley Lelie D 2.50 6.00
UCAM Amani Toomer E 3.00 8.00
UCBL Byron Leftwich L 4.00 10.00
UCBR Ben Roethlisberger K 10.00 25.00
UCBU Brian Urlacher H 4.00 10.00
UCCB Cedric Benson E 4.00 10.00
UCCC Chris Chambers D 3.00 8.00
UCCD Corey Dillon K 3.00 8.00
UCCJ Chad Johnson D 4.00 10.00
UCCM Curtis Martin D 4.00 10.00
UCCP Clinton Portis E 4.00 10.00
UCCS Chris Simms G 3.00 8.00
UCCW Cadillac Williams D 4.00 10.00
UCDB Drew Brees D 4.00 10.00
UCDD Domanick Davis 3.00 8.00
UCDF DeShaun Foster I 3.00 8.00
UCDH DeAngelo Hall C 3.00 8.00
UCDM Deuce McAllister K 3.00 8.00
UCEM Eric Moulds K 3.00 8.00
UCHW Hines Ward K 4.00 10.00
UCIB Isaac Bruce M 3.00 8.00
UCJB Jerome Bettis M 6.00 15.00
UCJS Jeremy Shockey D 4.00 10.00
UCJT Jason Taylor F 2.50 6.00
UCLA LaVar Arrington F 4.00 10.00
UCLT LaDainian Tomlinson D 4.00 10.00
UCMH Marvin Harrison M 4.00 10.00
UCPH Priest Holmes M 3.00 8.00
UCRM Randy Moss C 4.00 10.00
UCSA Shaun Alexander A 5.00 12.00
UCSD Stephen Davis J 3.00 8.00
UCSJ Steven Jackson E 4.00 10.00
UCSM Santana Moss E 3.00 8.00
UCTB Tatum Bell M 3.00 8.00
UCTG Tony Gonzalez F 3.00 8.00
UCTH Torry Holt L 3.00 8.00
UCTS Terrell Suggs G 2.50 6.00
UCWD Warrick Dunn K 3.00 8.00
UCWM Willis McGahee B 3.00 8.00
UCZT Zach Thomas D 4.00 10.00
UCARE Antwaan Randle El D 5.00 12.00
UCCBA Champ Bailey D 3.00 8.00
UCDBR Drew Brees L 4.00 10.00
UCTBA Tiki Barber E 4.00 10.00
UCTBE Tom Brady M 6.00 15.00
UCTGR Trent Green H 3.00 8.00
UCTHE Todd Heap E 2.50 6.00

2007 Topps Draft Picks and Prospects

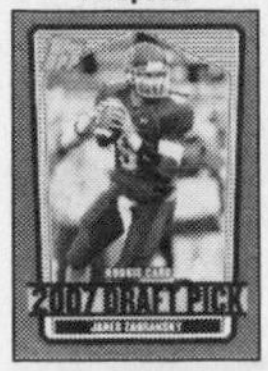

This 155-card set was released in May, 2007. The set was issued into the hobby in five-card packs, with a $3 SRP, which came 24 packs to a box. Cards numbered 1-100 feature veterans while cards numbered 101-155 feature 2007 NFL rookies.

COMPLETE SET (155) 20.00 50.00
1 Donovan McNabb .40 1.00
2 Larry Johnson .25 .60
3 Willis McGahee .30 .75
4 Tom Brady .60 1.50
5 Anquan Boldin .30 .75
6 Steve Smith .30 .75
7 Philip Rivers .40 1.00
8 LaDainian Tomlinson .40 1.00
9 Reuben Droughns .30 .75
10 Julius Jones .25 .60
11 Drew Brees .40 1.00
12 Chad Johnson .30 .75
13 Ronnie Brown .30 .75
14 Brett Favre .75 2.00
15 J.P. Losman .25 .60
16 Clinton Portis .30 .75
17 Edgerrin James .30 .75
18 Andre Johnson .30 .75
19 Fred Taylor .30 .75
20 Marc Bulger .30 .75
21 Peyton Manning .60 1.50
22 Reggie Wayne .30 .75
23 Hines Ward .40 1.00
24 Michael Vick .40 1.00
25 Santana Moss .30 .75
26 Torry Holt .30 .75
27 Jake Delhomme .30 .75
28 Brian Westbrook .30 .75
29 Tony Gonzalez .30 .75
30 Larry Fitzgerald .40 1.00
31 Matt Hasselbeck .30 .75
32 Kevin Jones .25 .60
33 Willie Parker .30 .75
34 Jeremy Shockey .30 .75
35 Marvin Harrison .40 1.00
36 Warrick Dunn .30 .75
37 Ahman Green .30 .75
38 Ben Roethlisberger .40 1.00
39 Randy Moss .40 1.00
40 Rudi Johnson .30 .75
41 Carson Palmer .30 .75
42 Trent Green .30 .75
43 Plaxico Burress .30 .75
44 Steven Jackson .40 1.00
45 Deuce McAllister .30 .75
46 Antonio Gates .40 1.00
47 Cadillac Williams .30 .75
48 Eli Manning .40 1.00
49 Rex Grossman .30 .75
50 Shaun Alexander .30 .75
51 DeAngelo Williams .40 1.00
52 Joseph Addai .30 .75
53 Vince Young .30 .75
54 Matt Leinart .30 .75
55 Sinorice Moss .30 .75
56 Matt Jones .30 .75
57 Tony Romo .50 1.25
58 Jay Cutler .40 1.00
59 Marques Colston .40 1.00
60 Vernon Davis .30 .75
61 Cedric Benson .30 .75
62 Mario Williams .30 .75
63 Hank Baskett .30 .75
64 Alex Smith QB .40 1.00
65 Jason Campbell .30 .75
66 Mike Furrey .30 .75
67 Greg Jennings .40 1.00
68 Laurence Maroney .30 .75
69 Charlie Frye .30 .75
70 Michael Robinson .30 .75
71 Michael Huff .30 .75
72 A.J. Hawk .30 .75
73 Marion Barber .40 1.00
74 Santonio Holmes .30 .75
75 Kellen Winslow .30 .75
76 Reggie Bush .40 1.00
77 Charlie Whitehurst .25 .60
78 Brad Smith .25 .60
79 Leon Washington .30 .75
80 Wali Lundy .25 .60
81 Owen Daniels .25 .60
82 Devin Hester .40 1.00
83 Chad Jackson .25 .60
84 Braylon Edwards .30 .75
85 Bruce Gradkowski .25 .60
86 Tarvaris Jackson .25 .60
87 Derek Hagan .25 .60
88 Mike Bell .30 .75
89 Frank Gore .40 1.00
90 LenDale White .30 .75
91 Chris Henry .25 .60
92 Kellen Clemens .30 .75
93 Nate Washington .25 .60
94 Jerious Norwood .30 .75
95 Maurice Jones-Drew .40 1.00
96 Mark Clayton .30 .75
97 Jason Avant .25 .60
98 Mathias Kiwanuka .25 .60
99 Brandon Jacobs .30 .75
100 Chris Cooley .30 .75
101 Brady Quinn RC 1.00 2.50
102 Michael Bush RC 1.00 2.50
103 Leon Hall RC .75 2.00
104 Jason Hill RC 1.00 2.50
105 Patrick Willis RC 2.00 5.00
106 Brian Leonard RC .75 2.00
107 Gaines Adams RC 1.00 2.50
108 Kenneth Darby RC .75 2.00
109 Marcus McCauley RC .75 2.00
110 Paul Posluszny RC 1.00 2.50
111 Drew Stanton RC .60 1.50
112 Troy Smith RC 1.00 2.50
113 Garrett Wolfe RC .60 1.50
114 Chris Leak RC .75 2.00
115 Joe Thomas RC 1.00 2.50
116 Paul Williams RC .60 1.50
117 LaRon Landry RC 1.00 2.50
118 Aundrae Allison RC .60 1.50
119 Kenny Irons RC .60 1.50
120 Kevin Kolb RC 1.50 4.00
121 Tyler Palko RC .75 2.00
122 Steve Smith USC RC 1.00 2.50
123 Steve Breaston RC 1.00 2.50
124 Tyrone Moss RC .60 1.50
125 LaMarr Woodley RC 1.00 2.50
126 Brandon Meriweather RC 1.00 2.50
127 Rhema McKnight RC .60 1.50
128 Daymeion Hughes RC .75 2.00
129 Jared Zabransky RC .75 2.00
130 Chansi Stuckey RC 1.00 2.50
131 Amobi Okoye RC 1.00 2.50
132 Calvin Johnson RC 3.00 8.00
133 Marshawn Lynch RC 1.00 2.50
134 Ted Ginn Jr. RC .75 2.00
135 Adrian Peterson RC 4.00 10.00
136 Dwayne Jarrett RC .75 2.00
137 Greg Olsen RC .75 2.00
138 Adam Carriker RC .75 2.00
139 Darius Walker RC .60 1.50
140 Robert Meachem RC 1.00 2.50
141 Jordan Palmer RC .75 2.00
142 JaMarcus Russell RC .60 1.50
143 DeShawn Wynn RC .75 2.00
144 Zach Miller RC 1.00 2.50
145 Lorenzo Booker RC .75 2.00
146 Selvin Young RC .75 2.00
147 Courtney Lewis RC .75 2.00
148 Tony Hunt RC .60 1.50
149 Dwayne Bowe RC 1.25 3.00
150 Aaron Ross RC 1.00 2.50
151 Antonio Pittman RC .60 1.50
152 Anthony Gonzalez RC 1.00 2.50
153 John Beck RC 1.00 2.50
154 Sidney Rice RC 1.25 3.00
155 Lawrence Timmons RC 1.00 2.50

2007 Topps Draft Picks and Prospects Chrome Black

*VETS 1-100: 1X TO 2.5X BASIC CARDS
*ROOKIES 101-155: .5X TO 1.2X
OVERALL CHROME ODDS ONE PER PACK

2007 Topps Draft Picks and Prospects Chrome Bronze

*VETS 1-100: 1.2X TO 3X BASIC CARDS
*ROOKIES 101-155: .6X TO 1.5X
STATED ODDS 1:6

2007 Topps Draft Picks and Prospects Chrome Gold

*VETS 1-100: 4X TO 10X BASIC CARDS
*ROOKIES 101-155: 2X TO 5X BASIC CARDS
GOLD/99 ODDS 1:145

2007 Topps Draft Picks and Prospects Chrome Silver

*VETS 1-100: 2.5X TO 6X BASIC CARDS
*ROOKIES 101-155: 1.2X TO 3X BASIC CARDS
SILVER/299 ODDS 1:48

2007 Topps Draft Picks and Prospects Chrome Black Refractors

*VETS 1-100: 2X TO 5X BASIC CARDS
*ROOKIES 101-155: 1X TO 2.5X BASIC CARDS
STATED ODDS 1:12

2007 Topps Draft Picks and Prospects Chrome Bronze Refractors

*VETS 1-100: 2.5X TO 6X BASIC CARDS
*ROOKIES 101-155: 1.2X TO 3X BASIC CARDS
BRONZE REFRACTOR/250 ODDS 1:58

2007 Topps Draft Picks and Prospects Chrome Gold Refractors

*VETS 1-100: 8X TO 20X BASIC CARDS
*ROOKIES 101-155: 4X TO 10X BASIC CARDS
GOLD REFRACTOR/25 ODDS 1:577

2007 Topps Draft Picks and Prospects Chrome Silver Refractors

*VETS 1-100: 4X TO 10X BASIC CARDS
*ROOKIES 101-155: 2X TO 5X BASIC CARDS
SILVER REFRACTOR/125 ODDS 1:115

2007 Topps Draft Picks and Prospects All-Star Alumni Autographs

SINGLE AUTO/50 ODDS 1:4900
AP Adrian Peterson 100.00 200.00
BQ Brady Quinn 25.00 60.00
CJ Calvin Johnson 75.00 150.00
DJ Dwayne Jarrett 15.00 40.00
JM Joe Montana 125.00 200.00
ML Matt Leinart 20.00 50.00
RB Reggie Bush 25.00 60.00
TB Tim Brown 25.00 60.00
TG Ted Ginn Jr. 20.00 50.00
VY Vince Young 25.00 60.00

2007 Topps Draft Picks and Prospects All-Star Alumni Autographs Dual

DUAL AUTO/25 ODDS 1:19,000
BJ Reggie Bush 100.00 200.00
Dwayne Jarrett
BM Tim Brown 125.00 250.00
Joe Montana
LB Matt Leinart 100.00 200.00
Reggie Bush
QM Brady Quinn 150.00 300.00
Joe Montana
SG Troy Smith 50.00 120.00
Ted Ginn Jr.
SP Billy Sims 250.00 400.00
Adrian Peterson

2007 Topps Draft Picks and Prospects Class Marks Autographs

GROUP A ODDS 1:3470
GROUP B ODDS 1:1440
GROUP C ODDS 1:1985
GROUP D ODDS 1:520
GROUP E ODDS 1:164
GROUP F ODDS 1:155
UNPRICED HOLOFOIL/10 ODDS 1:5690
AA Aundrae Allison E 4.00 10.00
AO Amobi Okoye B 8.00 20.00
AP1 Adrian Peterson A 75.00 150.00
AP2 Antonio Pittman B 5.00 12.00
BL Brian Leonard E 5.00 12.00
BQ Brady Quinn A 30.00 80.00
CLE Chris Leak D 5.00 12.00
CS Chansi Stuckey E 6.00 15.00
DB Dwayne Bowe B 10.00 25.00
DC David Clowney D 5.00 12.00
DJ Dwayne Jarrett A 8.00 20.00
DS Drew Stanton B 5.00 12.00
DW Darius Walker E 4.00 10.00
GA Gaines Adams E 6.00 15.00
GO Greg Olsen B 6.00 15.00
GW Garrett Wolfe F 4.00 10.00
JH Jason Hill F 6.00 15.00
JP Jordan Palmer C 5.00 12.00
JR JaMarcus Russell A 6.00 15.00
JZ Jared Zabransky C 5.00 12.00
KD Kenneth Darby E 5.00 12.00
KI Kenny Irons B 5.00 12.00
KK Kevin Kolb B 12.00 30.00
LH Leon Hall B 6.00 15.00
LL Laron Landry D 6.00 15.00
LT Lawrence Timmons D 6.00 15.00
LW LaMarr Woodley C 6.00 15.00
MB Michael Bush B 8.00 20.00
ML Marshawn Lynch A 10.00 25.00
PP Paul Posluszny D 6.00 15.00
PW Paul Williams F 4.00 10.00
RM Rhema McKnight F 4.00 10.00
RME Robert Meachem B 8.00 20.00
SB Steve Breaston F 6.00 15.00
SR Sidney Rice B 10.00 25.00
SS Steve Smith USC E 6.00 15.00
TG Ted Ginn Jr. A 8.00 20.00
TH Tony Hunt E 4.00 10.00
TP Tyler Palko F 5.00 12.00
TS Troy Smith A 12.00 30.00

2007 Topps Draft Picks and Prospects Class Marks Autographs Gold

*GOLD/25: .75X TO 1.5X BASE AU GRP A
*GOLD/25: .8X TO 2X BASE AU GRP B
*GOLD/25: 1X TO 2.5X BASE AU GRP C-F
GOLD/25 ODDS 1:2300
AP1 Adrian Peterson 125.00 250.00
BQ Brady Quinn 40.00 100.00

2007 Topps Draft Picks and Prospects Class Marks Autographs Silver

*SILVER/75: .4X TO 1X BASE AU GRP A
*SILVER/75: .5X TO 1.2X BASE AU GRP B
*SILVER/75: .6X TO 1.5X BASE AU GRP C-F
SILVER/75 ODDS 1:810
AP1 Adrian Peterson 75.00 150.00

2007 Topps Draft Picks and Prospects Class of 2006 Unsigned

*CHR.BLACK: .5X TO 1.2X BASIC INSERTS
*CHR.BLACK REF: .8X TO 2X BASIC INSERTS
*CHR.BRONZE: .6X TO 1.5X BASIC INSERTS
*CHR.BRONZE REF/250: 1.2X TO 3X
*CHR.GOLD/99: 2X TO 5X BASIC INSERTS
*CHR.GOLD REF/25: 4X TO 10X BASIC INSERTS
*CHR.SILVER/299: 1X TO 2.5X BASIC INSERTS
*CHR.SILVER REF/125: 1.5X TO 4X
166 Matt Leinart 1.25 3.00
167 Reggie Bush 1.50 4.00
170 Vince Young 1.25 3.00
172 Joseph Addai 1.25 3.00
173 Jay Cutler 1.50 4.00

2007 Topps Draft Picks and Prospects Rookie Autographs

AUTO/100 STATED ODDS 1:610
101 Brady Quinn 30.00 80.00
102 Michael Bush 12.00 30.00
103 Leon Hall 10.00 25.00
104 Jason Hill 12.00 30.00
106 Brian Leonard 10.00 25.00
107 Gaines Adams 12.00 30.00
108 Kenneth Darby 10.00 25.00
110 Paul Posluszny 12.00 30.00
111 Drew Stanton 8.00 20.00
112 Troy Smith 12.00 30.00
116 Paul Williams 8.00 20.00
118 Aundrae Allison 8.00 20.00
119 Kenny Irons 8.00 20.00
120 Kevin Kolb 20.00 50.00
122 Steve Smith USC 12.00 30.00
123 Steve Breaston 12.00 30.00
127 Rhema McKnight 8.00 20.00
130 Chansi Stuckey 12.00 30.00
132 Calvin Johnson 75.00 150.00
133 Marshawn Lynch 12.00 30.00
134 Ted Ginn Jr. 10.00 25.00
135 Adrian Peterson 100.00 200.00
136 Dwayne Jarrett 10.00 25.00
142 JaMarcus Russell 8.00 20.00
147 Courtney Lewis 10.00 25.00

2007 Topps Draft Picks and Prospects Senior Standout Jersey

STATED ODDS 1:23
*GOLD/25: 1X TO 2.5X BASIC JSYs
UNPRICED HOLOFOIL SER.#'d TO 10
*PRIME/99: .6X TO 1.5X BASIC JSYs
*SILVER/75: .6X TO 1.5X BASIC JSYs
AA Aundrae Allison 3.00 8.00
AC Adam Carriker 4.00 10.00
AO Amobi Okoye 5.00 12.00
AR Aaron Ross 5.00 12.00
AS Anthony Spencer 5.00 12.00
BD Buster Davis 4.00 10.00
BL Brian Leonard 4.00 10.00
BM Brandon Myles 4.00 10.00
BME Brandon Meriweather 5.00 12.00
BP Ben Patrick 4.00 10.00
CD Chris Davis 3.00 8.00
CL Chris Leak 5.00 12.00
CS Chansi Stuckey 5.00 12.00
CT Courtney Taylor 4.00 10.00
DB Dallas Baker 3.00 8.00
DBO Dwayne Bowe 6.00 15.00
DC David Clowney 4.00 10.00
DH David Harris 4.00 10.00
DI David Irons 3.00 8.00
DS Drew Stanton 3.00 8.00
DT DeMarcus Tank Tyler 3.00 8.00
EE Earl Everett 4.00 10.00
EW Eric Weddle 5.00 12.00
HB H.B. Blades 3.00 8.00
JG Josh Gattis 3.00 8.00
JH Johnnie Lee Higgins 4.00 10.00
JHL Jason Hill 5.00 12.00
JN Joe Newton 3.00 8.00
JP Jordan Palmer 4.00 10.00
JW Josh Wilson 4.00 10.00
JWI Jonathan Wade 3.00 8.00
KD Kenneth Darby 4.00 10.00
KI Kenny Irons 3.00 8.00
KK Kevin Kolb 8.00 20.00
KS Kolby Smith 4.00 10.00
LB Levi Brown 5.00 12.00
LB Lorenzo Booker 4.00 10.00
LH Leon Hall 4.00 10.00
LM Le'Ron McClain 5.00 12.00
MG Michael Griffin 5.00 12.00
MM Martrez Milner 3.00 8.00
MM Marcus McCauley 4.00 10.00
PB Prescott Burgess 4.00 10.00
PP Paul Posluszny 5.00 12.00
PW Patrick Willis 10.00 25.00
PWI Paul Williams 3.00 8.00
QM Quentin Moses 4.00 10.00
QP Quinn Pitcock 4.00 10.00
RK Ryan Kalil 4.00 10.00
RM Rhema McKnight 3.00 8.00
RMC Ray McDonald 4.00 10.00
SC Scott Chandler 5.00 12.00
TC Tim Crowder 5.00 12.00
TCL Thomas Clayton 4.00 10.00
TH Tony Hunt 3.00 8.00
TJ Tanard Jackson 3.00 8.00
TP Tyler Palko 4.00 10.00
TT Tony Taylor 4.00 10.00
VA Victor Abiamiri 5.00 12.00

2007 Topps Draft Picks and Prospects Senior Standout Jersey Combos

STATED PRINT RUN 199 SER.#'d SETS
*PRIME/49: 1X TO 2.5X BASIC JSYs
*SILVER/35: .8X TO 2X BASIC JSYs
UNPRICED GOLD SERIAL #'d TO 10
UNPRICED HOLOFOIL SERIAL #'d TO 5
AH Aundrae Allison 5.00 12.00
Jason Hill
BB Dallas Baker 6.00 15.00
Dwayne Bowe
BD Lorenzo Booker 4.00 10.00
Chris Davis
CC Adam Carriker 5.00 12.00
Tim Crowder
DM Kenneth Darby 5.00 12.00
Le'Ron McClain
GW Josh Gattis 4.00 10.00
Josh Wilson
HB Leon Hall 4.00 10.00
Prescott Burgess
IT Kenny Irons 4.00 10.00
Courtney Taylor
IW Kenny Irons 4.00 10.00
Jonathan Wade
LC Brian Leonard 4.00 10.00
Thomas Clayton
MCM Rhema McKnight 4.00 10.00
Brandon Myles
ME Ray McDonald 4.00 10.00
Earl Everett
MM Martrez Milner 4.00 10.00
Quentin Moses
NC Joe Newton 5.00 12.00
Scott Chandler
PB Tyler Palko 4.00 10.00
H.B. Blades
PH Jordan Palmer 4.00 10.00
Johnnie Lee Higgins
PHU Paul Posluszny 5.00 12.00
Tony Hunt
RG Aaron Ross 5.00 12.00
Michael Griffin
SC Chansi Stuckey 5.00 12.00
David Clowney
SK Drew Stanton 8.00 20.00
Kevin Kolb
SO Kolby Smith 5.00 12.00
Amobi Okoye
TB DeMarcus Tank Tyer 5.00 12.00
Levi Brown
WM Paul Williams 3.00 8.00
Marcus McCuley
WME Patrick Willis 10.00 25.00
Brandon Meriweather

2007 Topps Draft Picks and Prospects Senior Standout Jersey Autographs Silver

SILVER/75 STATED ODDS 1:912
*GOLD/25: .5X TO 1.2X SILVER AUTO/75
UNPRICED HOLOFOIL/10 ODDS 1:9200
AA Aundrae Allison 10.00 25.00
AO Amobi Okoye 15.00 40.00
BL Brian Leonard 12.00 30.00
CL Chris Leak 12.00 30.00
CS Chansi Stuckey 15.00 40.00
CT Courtney Taylor 12.00 30.00
DB Dallas Baker 10.00 25.00
DC David Clowney 12.00 30.00
DS Drew Stanton 10.00 25.00
JH Johnnie Lee Higgins 12.00 30.00
JH Jason Hill 15.00 40.00
JP Jordan Palmer 12.00 30.00
KD Kenneth Darby 12.00 30.00
KI Kenny Irons 10.00 25.00
KK Kevin Kolb 25.00 60.00
KS Kolby Smith 12.00 30.00
LB Lorenzo Booker 12.00 30.00
LH Leon Hall 12.00 30.00
PP Paul Posluszny 15.00 40.00
PW Paul Williams 10.00 25.00
RM Rhema McKnight 10.00 25.00
TC Thomas Clayton 12.00 30.00
TH Tony Hunt 10.00 25.00
TP Tyler Palko 12.00 30.00

2007 Topps Draft Picks And Prospects Upperclassmen Jersey

GROUP A ODDS 1:220
GROUP B ODDS 1:330
GROUP C ODDS 1:288
*SILVER/50: .6X TO 1.5X BASIC JSYs
AJ Andre Johnson A 4.00 10.00
BW Brian Westbrook A 4.00 10.00
CJ Chad Johnson C 4.00 10.00
CT Chester Taylor A 3.00 8.00
CW Cadillac Williams A 4.00 10.00
DB Drew Brees A 5.00 12.00
DW DeAngelo Williams B 5.00 12.00
FG Frank Gore A 5.00 12.00
JS Jeremy Shockey B 4.00 10.00
LJ Larry Johnson C 3.00 8.00
LM Laurence Maroney A 4.00 10.00

MV Michael Vick B	5.00	12.00
RJ Rudi Johnson B	4.00	10.00
SJ Steven Jackson C	5.00	12.00
TB Tom Brady C	8.00	20.00

2007 Topps Exclusive Rookies

COMP.FACTORY SET (31)	15.00	25.00
COMPLETE SET (30)	6.00	12.00
1 JaMarcus Russell	.30	.75
2 Calvin Johnson	1.50	4.00
3 Adrian Peterson	2.00	5.00
4 Ted Ginn	.40	1.00
5 Marshawn Lynch	.50	1.25
6 Brady Quinn	.50	1.25
7 Dwayne Bowe	.60	1.50
8 Robert Meachem	.50	1.25
9 Greg Olsen	.40	1.00
10 Brandon Jackson	.40	1.00
11 Anthony Gonzalez	.50	1.25
12 Kevin Kolb	.75	2.00
13 John Beck	.50	1.25
14 Drew Stanton	.30	.75
15 Sidney Rice	.60	1.50
16 Dwayne Jarrett	.40	1.00
17 Chris Henry	.30	.75
18 Steve Smith	.50	1.25
19 Brian Leonard	.40	1.00
20 Lorenzo Booker	.40	1.00
21 Jason Hill	.50	1.25
22 Paul Williams	.30	.75
23 Tony Hunt	.30	.75
24 Trent Edwards	.50	1.25
25 Johnnie Lee Higgins	.40	1.00
26 Joe Thomas	.50	1.25
27 Gaines Adams	.50	1.25
28 Patrick Willis	1.00	2.50
29 Troy Smith	.50	1.25
30 Michael Bush	.50	1.25

2007 Topps Exclusive Rookies Autographs

RANDOM INSERT IN FACTORY SETS
TOO SCARCE TO PRICE

2007 Topps Exclusive Rookies Jerseys

ONE PER FACTORY SET

1 JaMarcus Russell	1.25	3.00
2 Calvin Johnson	6.00	15.00
3 Adrian Peterson	8.00	20.00
4 Ted Ginn	1.50	4.00
5 Marshawn Lynch	2.00	5.00
6 Brady Quinn	2.00	5.00
7 Dwayne Bowe	2.50	6.00
8 Robert Meachem	2.00	5.00
9 Greg Olsen	1.50	4.00
10 Brandon Jackson	1.50	4.00
11 Anthony Gonzalez	2.00	5.00
12 Kevin Kolb	3.00	8.00
13 John Beck	2.00	5.00
14 Drew Stanton	1.25	3.00
15 Sidney Rice	2.50	6.00
16 Dwayne Jarrett	1.50	4.00
17 Chris Henry	1.25	3.00
18 Steve Smith	2.00	5.00
19 Brian Leonard	1.50	4.00
20 Lorenzo Booker	1.50	4.00
21 Jason Hill	2.00	5.00
22 Paul Williams	1.25	3.00
23 Tony Hunt	1.25	3.00
24 Trent Edwards	2.00	5.00
25 Johnnie Lee Higgins	2.00	5.00
26 Joe Thomas	2.00	5.00
27 Gaines Adams	2.00	5.00
28 Patrick Willis	4.00	10.00
29 Troy Smith	2.00	5.00
30 Michael Bush	2.00	5.00

2004 Topps Fan Favorites

Topps Fan Favorites was initially released in early March 2005 making it Topps?ÇÖ final football product of the 2004 NFL season. The base set consists entirely of retired players grouped thematically in famous offensive and defensive units of the past. Hobby boxes contained 24-packs of 6-cards and carried an S.R.P. of $5 per pack. Two parallel sets can be found seeded in packs as well as one of the more popular Autograph insert sets of the season.

COMPLETE SET (85)	20.00	50.00
1 Alan Page	.50	1.25
2 Abdul Salaam	.40	1.00
3 Bob Baumhower	.40	1.00
4 Bob Brudzinski	.40	1.00
5 Billy Johnson	.40	1.00
6 Cliff Branch	.50	1.25
7 Carl Banks	.40	1.00
8 Charles Bowser	.40	1.00
9 Clint Didier	.40	1.00
10 Carl Eller	.40	1.00
11 Charlie Joiner	.40	1.00
12 Dick Anderson	.40	1.00
13 Doug Betters	.40	1.00
14 Dave Casper	.50	1.25
15 Dwight Clark	.50	1.25
16 Dan Fouts	.60	1.50
17 Dave Foley	.40	1.00
18 Donnie Green	.40	1.00
19 Deacon Jones	.50	1.25
20 Don Maynard	.50	1.25
21 Dan Pastorini	.40	1.00
22 Drew Pearson	.50	1.25
23 Dwight White	.40	1.00
24 Emerson Boozer	.40	1.00
25 Earl Campbell	.60	1.50
26 Ernie Holmes	.50	1.25
27 Fred Biletnikoff	.60	1.50
28 Glenn Blackwood	.40	1.00
29 Gary Larsen	.40	1.00
30 Greg Lloyd	.50	1.25
31 George Martin	.40	1.00
32 Gene Upshaw	.40	1.00
33 Harry Carson	.40	1.00
34 Harold Jackson	.40	1.00
35 Hugh McElhenny	.40	1.00
36 Jeff Bostic	.40	1.00
37 Jim Burt	.40	1.00
38 Joe Greene	.60	1.50
39 John Hannah	.40	1.00
40 John Henry Johnson	.40	1.00
41 Joe Jacoby	.40	1.00
42 Jim Kiick	.40	1.00
43 Joe Klecko	.40	1.00
44 Joe Delamielleure	.40	1.00
45 Joe Montana	1.50	4.00
46 Jim Marshall	.40	1.00
47 Joe Namath	1.00	2.50
48 Jake Scott	.40	1.00
49 John Taylor	.40	1.00
50 Kim Bokamper	.40	1.00
51 Kevin Greene	.50	1.25
52 Karl Mecklenburg	.40	1.00
53 Ken Stabler	.75	2.00
54 Kellen Winslow	.60	1.50
55 Lyle Blackwood	.40	1.00
56 Larry Csonka	.60	1.50
57 L.C. Greenwood	.50	1.25
58 Lamar Lundy	.40	1.00
59 Leonard Marshall	.40	1.00
60 Lawrence Taylor	.60	1.50
61 Mark Clayton	.40	1.00
62 Mark Duper	.40	1.00
63 Manny Fernandez	.40	1.00
64 Mark Gastineau	.40	1.00
65 Marty Lyons	.40	1.00
66 Mark May	.40	1.00
67 Mike Montler	.40	1.00
68 Merlin Olsen	.50	1.25
69 Matt Snell	.40	1.00
70 Ozzie Newsome	.50	1.25
71 Otis Sistrunk	.40	1.00
72 Phil Villapiano UER (name spelled Villipiano)	.40	1.00
73 Roger Craig	.60	1.50
74 Richard Dent	.40	1.00
75 Randy Gradishar	.40	1.00
76 Russ Grimm	.40	1.00
77 Reggie McKenzie	.40	1.00
78 Roosevelt Grier	.40	1.00
79 Roger Staubach	1.00	2.50
80 Steve Grogan	.40	1.00
81 Stanley Morgan	.40	1.00
82 Tony Dorsett	.60	1.50
83 Ted Hendricks	.40	1.00
84 Tony Hill	.40	1.00
85 Y.A. Tittle	.60	1.50

2004 Topps Fan Favorites Chrome

*CHROME/499: 3X TO 8X BASIC CARDS
STATED ODDS 1:14 H/R
STATED PRINT RUN 499 SER.#'d SETS

2004 Topps Fan Favorites Chrome Refractors

*CHR.REF/99: 5X TO 12X BASIC CARDS
STATED ODDS 1:74 HOB, 1:123 RET
STATED PRINT RUN 99 SER.#'d SETS

2004 Topps Fan Favorites Autographs

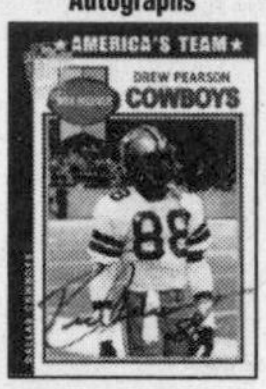

GROUP A ODDS 1:5362 H, 1:6144 R
GROUP B ODDS 1:2289 H, 1:2458 R
GROUP C ODDS 1:1014 H, 1:1024 R
GROUP D ODDS 1:3754 H, 1:4096 R
GROUP E ODDS 1:3412 H, 1:3520 R
GROUP F ODDS 1:140 H, 1:141 R
GROUP G ODDS 1:2208 H, 1:2261 R
GROUP H ODDS 1:22 H, 1:193 R
GROUP I ODDS 1:168 H/R
GROUP J ODDS 1:1188 H, 1:1229 R
GROUP K ODDS 1:1031 H, 1:1039 R
GROUP L ODDS 1:500 H, 1:503 R
GROUP M ODDS 1:67 H, 1:66 R
ANNOUNCED PRINT RUNS BELOW
UNPRICED NOTATIONS PRINT RUN 10 SETS

AP Alan Page K	12.00	30.00
AS Abdul Salaam M	8.00	20.00
BB Bob Baumhower H	15.00	40.00
BBR Bob Brudzinski H	15.00	40.00
BJ Billy Johnson M	8.00	20.00
CB Cliff Branch H	10.00	25.00
CBA Carl Banks F	12.00	30.00
CBO Charles Bowser H	8.00	20.00
CBR Charlie Brown H	8.00	20.00
CD Clint Didier F	8.00	20.00
CE Carl Eller L	12.00	30.00
CJ Charlie Joiner M	8.00	20.00
DA Dick Anderson F	8.00	20.00
DB Doug Betters H	8.00	20.00
DC Dave Casper/90* C	30.00	60.00
DCL Dwight Clark F	10.00	25.00
DF Dan Fouts/190* E	20.00	50.00
DFO Dave Foley F	8.00	20.00
DG Donnie Green H	8.00	20.00
DH Dan Hampton I	8.00	20.00
DJ Deacon Jones/90* C	40.00	80.00
DM Don Maynard/170* D	15.00	40.00
DP Dan Pastorini H	8.00	20.00
DPE Drew Pearson M	12.00	30.00
DW Dwight White H	40.00	80.00
EB Emerson Boozer H	15.00	40.00
EC Earl Campbell/90* C	50.00	100.00
EH Ernie Holmes H	50.00	100.00
FB Fred Biletnikoff/70* B	40.00	100.00
GB Glenn Blackwood H	8.00	20.00
GF Gary Fencik M	8.00	20.00
GL Gary Larsen M	8.00	20.00
GLL Greg Lloyd F	25.00	50.00
GM George Martin H	8.00	20.00
GU Gene Upshaw F	30.00	50.00
HC Harry Carson F	15.00	40.00
HJ Harold Jackson M	8.00	20.00
HM Hugh McElhenny H	8.00	20.00
JB Jeff Bostic H	8.00	20.00
JBU Jim Burt H	12.00	30.00
JG Joe Greene/70* B	75.00	150.00
JH John Hannah I	8.00	20.00
JHJ John Henry Johnson H	15.00	40.00
JJ Joe Jacoby H	8.00	20.00
JKI Jim Kiick G	15.00	40.00
JKL Joe Klecko L	12.00	30.00
JL Joe Delamielleure H	8.00	20.00
JM Joe Montana/90* C	100.00	200.00
JMA Jim Marshall M	12.00	30.00
JN Joe Namath/40* A	100.00	200.00
JS Jake Scott/90* C	75.00	150.00
JT John Taylor F	10.00	25.00
KB Kim Bokamper H	8.00	20.00
KG Kevin Greene F	25.00	60.00
KM Karl Mecklenburg H	8.00	20.00
KS Ken Stabler F	25.00	50.00
KW Kellen Winslow F	12.00	30.00
LB Lyle Blackwood H	8.00	20.00
LC Larry Csonka/90* C	40.00	80.00
LCG L.C. Greenwood H	20.00	50.00
LL Lamar Lundy I	15.00	40.00
LM Leonard Marshall H	8.00	20.00
LT Lawrence Taylor/90* C	40.00	80.00
MC Mark Clayton I	10.00	25.00
MD Mark Duper I	12.00	30.00
MF Manny Fernandez F	15.00	40.00
MG Mark Gastineau H	15.00	40.00
MJ Mark Jackson M	8.00	20.00
ML Marty Lyons M	8.00	20.00
MM Mark May F	20.00	40.00
MMO Mike Montler F	12.00	30.00
MO Merlin Olsen I	15.00	40.00
MS Matt Snell H	8.00	20.00
ON Ozzie Newsome/90* C	25.00	60.00
OS Otis Sistrunk H	8.00	20.00
PV Phil Villapiano H	8.00	20.00
RC Roger Craig F	12.00	30.00
RD Richard Dent I	8.00	20.00
RG Randy Gradishar F	8.00	20.00
RGR Russ Grimm I	20.00	40.00
RM Reggie McKenzie F	8.00	20.00
RN Ricky Nattiel M	8.00	20.00
ROG Roosevelt Grier H	12.00	30.00
RS Roger Staubach/40* A	90.00	150.00
SG Steve Grogan J	8.00	20.00
SM Stanley Morgan M	8.00	20.00
TD Tony Dorsett/40* A	75.00	150.00
TH Ted Hendricks F	10.00	25.00
THI Tony Hill H	8.00	20.00
VJ Vance Johnson M	8.00	20.00
WP William Perry M	8.00	20.00
YAT Y.A. Tittle/70* B	60.00	100.00

2004 Topps Fan Favorites Buy Back Autographs

STATED ODDS 1:4692 H, 1:4200 R
NOT PRICED DUE TO SCARCITY
FB Fred Biletnikoff 71T
JG Joe Greene 81T
DM1 Don Maynard 64T
DM3 Don Maynard 67T
DM2 Don Maynard 66T
DM4 Don Maynard 68T
HM1 Hugh McElhenny 58T
HM2 Hugh McElhenny 60T
HM3 Hugh McElhenny 62T
KS1 Ken Stabler 75T
KS2 Ken Stabler HL 75T
KS3 Ken Stabler 76T
YT1 Y.A.Tittle 59T
YT2 Y.A.Tittle 60T

2004 Topps Fan Favorites Co-Signers

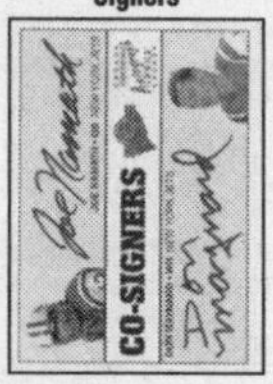

STATED ODDS 1:2288 H, 1:2148 R
ANNOUNCED PRINT RUN 50 SETS

CODC Mark Duper / Mark Clayton	50.00	100.00
COFW Dan Fouts / Kellen Winslow	60.00	120.00
COKG Joe Klecko / Mark Gastineau	50.00	100.00
CONM Joe Namath / Don Maynard	125.00	200.00
COPE Alan Page / Carl Eller	50.00	100.00
COSD Roger Staubach / Tony Dorsett	125.00	200.00

2004 Topps Fan Favorites Jumbos

COMPLETE SET (10)	40.00	80.00
ONE PER BOX		
1 Charlie Joiner / Dan Fouts / Kellen Winslow	3.00	8.00
2 Drew Pearson / Roger Staubach / Tony Dorsett / Tony Hill	6.00	15.00
3 Deacon Jones / Lamar Lundy / Merlin Olsen / Roosevelt Grier	2.50	6.00
4 Mark Clayton / Mark Duper	2.00	5.00
5 Hugh McElhenny / John Henry Johnson / Y.A. Tittle	3.00	8.00
6 Abdul Salaam / Joe Klecko / Mark Gastineau / Marty Lyons	2.00	5.00
7 Alan Page / Carl Eller / Gary Larsen / Jim Marshall	2.50	6.00
8 Cliff Branch / Dave Casper / Fred Biletnikoff / Ken Stabler	5.00	12.00
9 Don Maynard / Emerson Boozer / Joe Namath / Matt Snell	6.00	15.00
10 Dwight White / Ernie Holmes / Joe Greene / L.C. Greenwood	3.00	8.00

2010 Topps Five Star

1-150 VET/LEGEND PRINT RUN 79
151-180 ROOKIE JSY AU PRINT RUN 50-90

1 Peyton Manning	15.00	40.00
2 Franco Harris	6.00	15.00
3 Rashard Mendenhall	4.00	10.00
4 Roger Staubach	6.00	15.00
5 BenJarvus Green-Ellis	8.00	20.00
6 Michael Turner	3.00	8.00
7 Joe Flacco	5.00	12.00
8 Dallas Clark	4.00	10.00
9 Tony Dorsett	5.00	12.00
10 Adrian Peterson	8.00	20.00
11 LeSean McCoy	4.00	10.00
12 Eli Manning	5.00	12.00
13 Patrick Willis	4.00	10.00
14 Calvin Johnson	5.00	12.00
15 Brandon Pettigrew	3.00	8.00
16 Chris Cooley	4.00	10.00
17 Percy Harvin	5.00	12.00
18 Jerome Bettis	10.00	25.00
19 Peyton Hillis	10.00	25.00
20 Brandon Marshall	4.00	10.00
21 Matt Forte	4.00	10.00
22 Jon Beason	3.00	8.00
23 Cris Carter	8.00	20.00
24 DeAngelo Hall	3.00	8.00
25 Dwayne Bowe	4.00	10.00
26 Matthew Stafford	5.00	12.00
27 Fred Jackson	5.00	12.00
28 Danny Woodhead RC	30.00	80.00
29 Jermichael Finley	4.00	10.00
30 Chris Johnson	5.00	12.00
31 Randy Moss	5.00	12.00
32 Thomas Jones	4.00	10.00
33 Dwight Freeney	4.00	10.00
34 Ed Reed	4.00	10.00
35 Steve Smith USC	4.00	10.00
36 Jay Cutler	5.00	12.00
37 Jerod Mayo	4.00	10.00
38 Frank Gore	4.00	10.00
39 Ronnie Brown	4.00	10.00
40 Jim Brown	5.00	12.00
41 Ray Lewis	5.00	12.00
42 Felix Jones	4.00	10.00
43 Tim Hightower	3.00	8.00
44 Braylon Edwards	4.00	10.00
45 Terrell Owens	5.00	12.00
46 Hines Ward	5.00	12.00
47 Darrelle Revis	4.00	10.00
48 Chad Henne	4.00	10.00
49 Joseph Addai	4.00	10.00
50 Drew Brees	6.00	15.00
51 Jared Allen	5.00	12.00
52 Jason Witten	5.00	12.00
53 Andre Johnson	4.00	10.00
54 Mike Tolbert	5.00	12.00
55 Santana Moss	4.00	10.00
56 Ricky Williams	4.00	10.00
57 Miles Austin	5.00	12.00
58 Jeremy Maclin	4.00	10.00
59 Tony Romo	6.00	15.00
60 Dan Marino	15.00	40.00
61 Beanie Wells	4.00	10.00
62 Jabar Gaffney	3.00	8.00
63 Carson Palmer	4.00	10.00
64 Clay Matthews	6.00	15.00
65 Dustin Keller	4.00	10.00
66 Michael Vick	6.00	15.00
67 Matt Cassel	4.00	10.00
68 Ray Rice	4.00	10.00
69 Greg Jennings	4.00	10.00
70 Larry Fitzgerald	5.00	12.00
71 Wes Welker	5.00	12.00
72 Hakeem Nicks	4.00	10.00
73 Johnny Knox	4.00	10.00
74 Knowshon Moreno	4.00	10.00
75 Eric Dickerson	4.00	10.00
76 Julius Peppers	4.00	10.00
77 Davone Bess	3.00	8.00
78 Kellen Winslow	4.00	10.00
79 Kyle Orton	4.00	10.00
80 Joe Namath	6.00	15.00
81 DeMeco Ryans	3.00	8.00
82 Pierre Garcon	4.00	10.00
83 Junior Seau	4.00	10.00
84 Donovan McNabb	5.00	12.00
85 Howie Long	5.00	12.00
86 Lance Moore	4.00	10.00
87 Louis Murphy	4.00	10.00
88 Matt Ryan	5.00	12.00
89 Josh Freeman	5.00	12.00
90 Tom Brady	20.00	50.00
91 Sidney Rice	5.00	12.00
92 Malcom Floyd	4.00	10.00
93 Antonio Gates	4.00	10.00
94 Marion Barber	4.00	10.00
95 Lee Evans	4.00	10.00
96 Kenny Britt	4.00	10.00
97 Philip Rivers	5.00	12.00
98 Troy Polamalu	8.00	20.00
99 Reggie Wayne	4.00	10.00
100 Aaron Rodgers	25.00	50.00
101 Brian Urlacher	5.00	12.00
102 Ahmad Bradshaw	4.00	10.00
103 Steve Young	8.00	20.00
104 Troy Aikman	6.00	15.00
105 DeSean Jackson	4.00	10.00
106 Pierre Thomas	4.00	10.00
107 Jamaal Charles	4.00	10.00
108 Anquan Boldin	4.00	10.00
109 Thurman Thomas	5.00	12.00
110 LaDainian Tomlinson	5.00	12.00
111 Clinton Portis	4.00	10.00
112 Mario Manningham	4.00	10.00
113 Brett Favre	20.00	50.00
114 Kevin Kolb	4.00	10.00
115 Zach Miller	4.00	10.00
116 Mario Williams	4.00	10.00
117 Matt Schaub	4.00	10.00
118 Marques Colston	4.00	10.00
119 Vince Young	3.00	8.00
120 Joe Montana	15.00	40.00
121 Michael Crabtree	5.00	12.00
122 Mark Sanchez	5.00	12.00
123 Austin Collie	4.00	10.00
124 Mike Wallace	4.00	10.00
125 Osi Umenyiora	3.00	8.00
126 Paul Posluszny	5.00	12.00
127 Art Monk	8.00	20.00
128 Brandon Lloyd	4.00	10.00
129 Eddie Royal	3.00	8.00
130 Arian Foster	4.00	10.00
131 Steven Jackson	4.00	10.00
132 Vernon Davis	4.00	10.00
133 Roddy White	4.00	10.00
134 Chad Ochocinco	4.00	10.00
135 DeAngelo Williams	4.00	10.00
136 Steve Breaston	3.00	8.00
137 Shonn Greene	4.00	10.00
138 Darren McFadden	4.00	10.00
139 Ryan Torain	3.00	8.00
140 Maurice Jones-Drew	4.00	10.00
141 Steve Johnson	4.00	10.00
142 Ronnie Lott	5.00	12.00
143 Steve Smith	4.00	10.00
144 Emmitt Smith	12.00	30.00
145 Tony Gonzalez	4.00	10.00
146 DeMarcus Ware	4.00	10.00
147 Cedric Benson	4.00	10.00
148 Gale Sayers	6.00	15.00
149 Santonio Holmes	4.00	10.00
150 John Elway	12.00	30.00
151 Emmanuel Sanders JSY AU/90 RC	12.00	30.00
152 Andre Roberts JSY AU/90 RC	10.00	25.00
153 Taylor Price JSY AU/90 RC	12.00	30.00
154 Mardy Gilyard JSY AU/90 RC	12.00	30.00
155 Damian Williams JSY AU/90 RC	12.00	30.00
156 Armanti Edwards JSY AU/90 RC	10.00	25.00
157 Jonathan Dwyer JSY AU/90 RC	12.00	30.00
158 Brandon LaFell JSY AU/90 RC	12.00	30.00
159 Jordan Shipley JSY AU/90 RC	12.00	30.00
160 Colt McCoy JSY AU/50 RC	50.00	100.00
161 Rob Gronkowski JSY AU/90 RC	40.00	80.00
162 Arrelious Benn JSY AU/75 RC	12.00	30.00
163 Toby Gerhart JSY AU/75 RC	12.00	30.00
164 Montario Hardesty JSY AU/90 RC	12.00	30.00
166 Ben Tate JSY AU/75 RC	20.00	40.00
167 Golden Tate JSY AU/90 RC	12.00	30.00
168 Jermaine Gresham JSY AU/90 RC	12.00	30.00
169 Gerald McCoy JSY AU/75 RC	12.00	30.00
170 Sam Bradford JSY AU/50 RC	150.00	300.00
171 Ndamukong Suh JSY AU/50 RC	60.00	120.00
172 Jahvid Best JSY AU/50 RC	25.00	50.00
173 Demaryius Thomas JSY AU/50 RC	25.00	50.00
174 Ryan Mathews JSY AU/50 RC	60.00	120.00
175 C.J. Spiller JSY AU/50 RC	20.00	50.00
176 Mike Kafka JSY AU/60 RC	12.00	30.00
177 Eric Decker JSY AU/90 RC	15.00	40.00
178 Marcus Easley JSY AU/75 RC	8.00	20.00
179 Eric Berry JSY AU/75 RC	12.00	30.00
180 Tim Tebow JSY AU/50 RC	175.00	300.00
189 Jimmy Clausen JSY AU/90 RC	12.00	30.00
RHA Drew Brees RH AU/50	125.00	200.00

2010 Topps Five Star Jumbo Jerseys

JUMBO JERSEY PRINT RUN 40-65
*PATCH/20: .5X TO 1.2X JMBO JSY VET
*PATCH/20: .4X TO 1X JMBO JSY LGND
*PATCH/20: .5X TO 1.2X JMBO JSY ROOK

JJRAB Arrelious Benn/40	5.00	12.00
JJRAE Armanti Edwards/40	5.00	12.00
JJRAG Antonio Gates/40	6.00	15.00
JJRAP Adrian Peterson/40	15.00	40.00
JJRBL Brandon LaFell/40	5.00	12.00
JJRBT Ben Tate/40	6.00	15.00
JJRCJ Calvin Johnson/40	8.00	20.00
JJRCJO Chris Johnson/40	8.00	20.00
JJRCJS C.J. Spiller/40	8.00	20.00
JJRCM Colt McCoy/40	10.00	25.00
JJRDB Dez Bryant/40	15.00	40.00
JJRDJ DeSean Jackson/65	6.00	15.00
JJRDM Dan Marino/40	30.00	80.00
JJRDMC Dexter McCluster/40	5.00	12.00
JJRDR Darrelle Revis/40	6.00	15.00
JJRDT Demaryius Thomas/40	6.00	15.00
JJREB Eric Berry/40	5.00	12.00
JJRES Emmanuel Sanders/40	5.00	12.00
JJRFH Franco Harris/40	15.00	40.00
JJRGM Gerald McCoy/40	5.00	12.00
JJRGT Golden Tate/40	5.00	12.00
JJRJB Jahvid Best/40	10.00	25.00
JJRJC Jimmy Clausen/40	5.00	12.00
JJRJD Jonathan Dwyer/40	5.00	12.00
JJRJG Jermaine Gresham/40	6.00	15.00
JJRJM Joe Montana/40	30.00	80.00
JJRJMC Joe McKnight/40	5.00	12.00
JJRJS Jordan Shipley/40	5.00	12.00
JJRLF Larry Fitzgerald/40	8.00	20.00
JJRLT LaDainian Tomlinson/40	8.00	20.00
JJRMG Mardy Gilyard/40	5.00	12.00
JJRMH Montario Hardesty/40	5.00	12.00
JJRMJD Maurice Jones-Drew/40	6.00	15.00
JJRMS Mark Sanchez/40	8.00	20.00
JJRMW Mike Williams/40	8.00	20.00
JJRNS Ndamukong Suh/40	10.00	25.00
JJRPR Philip Rivers/40	10.00	25.00
JJRRG Rob Gronkowski/40	12.00	30.00
JJRRL Ray Lewis/40	10.00	25.00
JJRRM Randy Moss/40	8.00	20.00
JJRRMA Ryan Mathews/40	10.00	25.00
JJRRMC Rolando McClain/40	5.00	12.00
JJRRR Ray Rice/65	6.00	15.00
JJRRS Roger Staubach/40	20.00	50.00
JJRSB Sam Bradford/40	25.00	50.00
JJRSJ Steven Jackson/40	6.00	15.00
JJRSY Steve Young/40	20.00	40.00
JJRTG Toby Gerhart/40	5.00	12.00
JJRTP Taylor Price/40	5.00	12.00
JJRTT Tim Tebow/40	25.00	50.00

2010 Topps Five Star Rookie Autographed Patch Gold

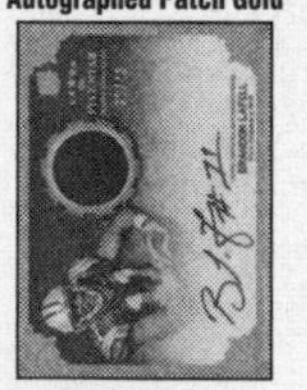

*AU GLD/40: .4X TO 1X BASIC JSY AU
STATED PRINT RUN 40 SER.#'d SETS

160 Colt McCoy JSY AU	75.00	150.00
170 Sam Bradford JSY AU	200.00	400.00
180 Tim Tebow JSY AU	175.00	300.00

2010 Topps Five Star Rookie Autographed Patch Platinum

*AU PLAT/20: .5X TO 1.2X JSY AU RC
STATED PRINT RUN 20 SER.#'d SETS

170 Sam Bradford JSY AU	250.00	500.00
180 Tim Tebow JSY AU	300.00	500.00

2010 Topps Five Star Rookie Autographed Triple Patch Silver

TRIPLE SILVER AU PRINT RUN 20-25
*QUAD SLV AU/20-25: .4X TO 1X TRP/20-25

3RAB Arrelious Benn/25	25.00	60.00
3RAE Armanti Edwards/25	15.00	40.00
3RAR Andre Roberts/25	15.00	40.00
3RBL Brandon LaFell/25	15.00	40.00
3RBT Ben Tate/25	20.00	50.00
3RCJS C.J. Spiller/20	50.00	120.00
3RCM Colt McCoy/20	75.00	150.00
3RDT Demaryius Thomas/25	20.00	50.00
3RDW Damian Williams/25	15.00	40.00
3REB Eric Berry/25	40.00	80.00
3RED Eric Decker/25	20.00	50.00
3RES Emmanuel Sanders/25	20.00	50.00
3RGM Gerald McCoy/25	25.00	60.00
3RGT Golden Tate/25	15.00	40.00
3RJB Jahvid Best/25	25.00	60.00
3RJC Jimmy Clausen/25	15.00	40.00
3RJD Jonathan Dwyer/25	15.00	40.00
3RJG Jermaine Gresham/25	20.00	50.00
3RJS Jordan Shipley/25	15.00	40.00
3RME Marcus Easley/25	12.00	30.00
3RMG Mardy Gilyard/25	15.00	40.00
3RMH Montario Hardesty/25	20.00	50.00
3RMK Mike Kafka/25	20.00	50.00
3RNS Ndamukong Suh/20	75.00	150.00
3RRG Rob Gronkowski/25	75.00	125.00
3RRM Ryan Mathews/20	50.00	120.00
3RSB Sam Bradford/20	250.00	500.00
3RTG Toby Gerhart/25	15.00	40.00
3RTP Taylor Price/25	15.00	40.00
3RTT Tim Tebow/20	300.00	500.00

2010 Topps Five Star Rookie Autographs Gold

ROOKIE GOLD AUTO PRINT RUN 50-100

AAB Arrelious Benn/100	10.00	25.00
AAE Armanti Edwards/100	8.00	20.00
ABL Brandon LaFell/100	10.00	25.00
ABT Ben Tate/100	12.00	30.00
ACI Chris Ivory/100	12.00	30.00
ACJS C.J. Spiller/100	15.00	40.00
ACM Colt McCoy/100	25.00	60.00
ADT Demaryius Thomas/75	12.00	30.00
ADW Damian Williams/100	10.00	25.00
AEB Eric Berry/75	20.00	50.00
AED Eric Decker/100	12.00	30.00
AES Emmanuel Sanders/100	10.00	25.00
AET Earl Thomas/100	10.00	25.00
AGM Gerald McCoy/75	10.00	25.00
AGT Golden Tate/100	10.00	25.00
AJB Jahvid Best/75	15.00	40.00
AJC Jimmy Clausen/100	10.00	25.00
AJD Jonathan Dwyer/100	10.00	25.00
AJG Jermaine Gresham/75	12.00	30.00
AJPP Jason Pierre-Paul/50	35.00	60.00
AJS Jordan Shipley/100	10.00	25.00
AMG Mardy Gilyard/100	8.00	20.00
AMH Montario Hardesty/100	12.00	30.00
ANS Ndamukong Suh/75	50.00	120.00
ARG Rob Gronkowski/100	30.00	60.00
ARM Ryan Mathews/100	30.00	80.00
ASB Sam Bradford/100	100.00	200.00
ASW Sean Weatherspoon/75	10.00	25.00
ATG Toby Gerhart/100	10.00	25.00
ATT Tim Tebow/100	125.00	200.00

2010 Topps Five Star Rookie Quotable Autographs

ROOKIE QUOTE AU PRINT RUN 15
EXCH EXPIRATION: 2/28/2014

AAB Arrelious Benn	25.00	60.00
AAE Armanti Edwards	25.00	60.00
ABL Brandon LaFell	25.00	60.00
ABT Ben Tate	30.00	80.00
ACI Chris Ivory	30.00	80.00
ACJS C.J. Spiller	50.00	120.00
ACM Colt McCoy	125.00	250.00
ADT Demaryius Thomas	75.00	125.00
ADW Damian Williams	25.00	60.00
AEB Eric Berry	25.00	60.00
AED Eric Decker	30.00	80.00
AES Emmanuel Sanders	25.00	60.00
AET Earl Thomas	25.00	60.00
AGM Gerald McCoy	25.00	60.00
AGT Golden Tate	25.00	60.00
AJB Jahvid Best	50.00	120.00
AJC Jimmy Clausen	25.00	60.00
AJD Jonathan Dwyer	25.00	60.00
AJG Jermaine Gresham	30.00	80.00
AJPP Jason Pierre-Paul	40.00	100.00
AJS Jordan Shipley	25.00	60.00
AMG Mardy Gilyard	25.00	60.00
AMH Montario Hardesty	25.00	60.00
ANS Ndamukong Suh	100.00	200.00
ARG Rob Gronkowski	75.00	150.00
ARM Ryan Mathews	50.00	125.00
ASB Sam Bradford EXCH	250.00	500.00
ASW Sean Weatherspoon	25.00	60.00
ATG Toby Gerhart	40.00	100.00
ATT Tim Tebow	350.00	600.00

2010 Topps Five Star Veteran Autographed Patch Gold

GOLD PATCH AU PRINT RUN 30
*PLATINUM/15: .5X TO 1.2X GOLD AU/30
*SILVER/50-60: .3X TO .8X GOLD AU/30
*SILVER/35: .4X TO 1X GOLD AU/30

SPAM Art Monk	40.00	80.00
SPBM Brandon Marshall	15.00	40.00
SPCP Clinton Portis	12.00	30.00
SPDB Drew Brees	60.00	120.00
SPDR Darrelle Revis	20.00	50.00
SPER Ed Reed	50.00	100.00
SPFG Frank Gore	15.00	40.00
SPFJ Felix Jones	15.00	40.00
SPHL Howie Long	40.00	80.00
SPJB Jerome Bettis	75.00	150.00
SPJS Junior Seau	30.00	60.00
SPJW Jason Witten	30.00	60.00
SPLM LeSean McCoy	20.00	50.00
SPMF Matt Forte	15.00	40.00
SPRL Ronnie Lott	50.00	100.00
SPRM Rashard Mendenhall	15.00	40.00
SPRR Ray Rice	15.00	40.00
SPTO Terrell Owens	20.00	50.00
SPVJ Vincent Jackson	12.00	30.00

2010 Topps Five Star Veteran Autographed Triple Patch Silver

SILVER PATCH AU PRINT RUN 20
EXCH EXPIRATION: 2/28/2014

SBAM Art Monk	60.00	120.00
SBAP Adrian Peterson	100.00	200.00
SBBF Brett Favre	175.00	300.00
SBCO Chad Ochocinco	25.00	60.00
SBCP Clinton Portis	25.00	60.00
SBDB Drew Brees	75.00	150.00
SBDR Darrelle Revis	40.00	100.00
SBEM Eli Manning	90.00	150.00
SBES Emmitt Smith	150.00	250.00
SBFG Frank Gore	30.00	80.00
SBGJ Greg Jennings	30.00	80.00
SBHL Howie Long	30.00	80.00
SBJB Jerome Bettis	100.00	200.00
SBJE John Elway	150.00	250.00
SBJN Joe Namath	100.00	175.00
SBJS Junior Seau	40.00	100.00
SBKM Knowshon Moreno	30.00	80.00
SBLT LaDainian Tomlinson	40.00	100.00
SBMR Matt Ryan	40.00	100.00
SBMS Mark Sanchez	60.00	120.00
SBPM Peyton Manning	150.00	250.00
SBRL Ronnie Lott	60.00	120.00
SBRM Rashard Mendenhall	30.00	80.00
SBRR Ray Rice	30.00	80.00
SBRW Roddy White	30.00	80.00
SBSY Steve Young	100.00	175.00
SBTO Terrell Owens	40.00	100.00
SBTR Tony Romo	50.00	125.00
SBVJ Vincent Jackson	25.00	60.00
SBMST Matthew Stafford	60.00	120.00

2010 Topps Five Star Veteran Autographs Gold

GOLD AU STATED PRINT RUN 35
*PLATINUM/20: .5X TO 1.2X GOLD AU/35
*SILVER/50: .3X TO .8X GOLD AU/35
*SILVER/40: .4X TO 1X GOLD AU/35
EXCH EXPIRATION: 2/28/2014

SAM Art Monk	30.00	60.00
SBM Brandon Marshall	12.00	30.00
SBW Beanie Wells	12.00	30.00
SCP Clinton Portis	10.00	25.00
SDB Drew Brees	50.00	100.00
SDR Darrelle Revis	20.00	50.00
SER Ed Reed	25.00	60.00
SHL Howie Long	30.00	60.00
SJB Jim Brown	50.00	100.00
SJS Junior Seau	25.00	50.00
SJW Jason Witten	15.00	40.00
SLM LeSean McCoy	12.00	30.00
SMF Matt Forte	12.00	30.00
SMS Mark Sanchez	40.00	80.00
SMST Matthew Stafford	30.00	60.00
SRM Rashard Mendenhall	15.00	40.00
SRR Ray Rice	12.00	30.00
SRW Roddy White	15.00	40.00
SSH Santonio Holmes	12.00	30.00
SSY Steve Young	50.00	100.00
SVJ Vincent Jackson	10.00	25.00

2010 Topps Five Star Veteran Quotable Autographs

EXCH EXPIRATION: 2/28/2014

2011 Topps Five Star

1-150 STATED PRINT RUN 129
ROOKIE JSY AU PRINT RUN 65-199
EXCH EXPIRATION: 2/28/2015

1 Bart Starr	8.00	20.00
2 Jermaine Gresham	4.00	10.00
3 Ben Roethlisberger	5.00	12.00
4 Jim Plunkett	4.00	10.00
5 Dez Bryant	5.00	12.00
6 Greg Jennings	5.00	12.00
7 Charles Woodson	6.00	15.00
8 Antonio Gates	4.00	10.00
9 Richard Dent	3.00	8.00
10 Larry Fitzgerald	4.00	10.00
11 Rob Gronkowski	5.00	12.00
12 James Starks	4.00	10.00
13 Jermichael Finley	4.00	10.00
14 Tim Hightower	3.00	8.00
15 Anquan Boldin	4.00	10.00
16 BenJarvus Green-Ellis	4.00	10.00
17 Ndamukong Suh	5.00	12.00
18 Deion Branch	3.00	8.00
19 Sam Bradford	5.00	12.00
20 Arian Foster	4.00	10.00
21 Kenny Britt	4.00	10.00
22 Ray Lewis	5.00	12.00
23 Darren McFadden	4.00	10.00
24 Owen Daniels	3.00	8.00
25 Patrick Willis	4.00	10.00
26 Joe Flacco	5.00	12.00
27 Brandon Lloyd	4.00	10.00
28 Frank Gore	4.00	10.00
29 Jeremy Maclin	4.00	10.00
30 Andre Johnson	4.00	10.00
31 Brandon Marshall	4.00	10.00
32 LeGarrette Blount	4.00	10.00
33 Hines Ward	4.00	10.00
34 Eli Manning	6.00	15.00
35 Nate Burleson	3.00	8.00
36 Tony Romo	6.00	15.00
37 Mike Thomas	4.00	10.00
38 Vernon Davis	4.00	10.00
39 Santana Moss	4.00	10.00
40 Michael Vick	5.00	12.00
41 Mike Wallace	5.00	12.00
42 Ryan Torain	3.00	8.00
43 Ed Reed	4.00	10.00
44 Robert Meachem	4.00	10.00
45 Devery Henderson	3.00	8.00
46 Colt McCoy	4.00	10.00
47 Dallas Clark	4.00	10.00
48 Rashard Mendenhall	4.00	10.00
49 Jason Pierre-Paul	5.00	12.00
50 Terry Bradshaw	6.00	15.00
51 Joseph Addai	4.00	10.00
52 Plaxico Burress	4.00	10.00
53 Tony Gonzalez	4.00	10.00
54 Troy Polamalu	6.00	15.00
55 Clay Matthews	6.00	15.00
56 Pierre Thomas	4.00	10.00
57 Santonio Holmes	4.00	10.00
58 Fred Davis	4.00	10.00
59 Steven Jackson	4.00	10.00
60 Adrian Peterson	6.00	15.00
61 Cedric Benson	4.00	10.00
62 Brandon Jacobs	4.00	10.00
63 Matt Schaub	4.00	10.00
64 Maurice Jones-Drew	4.00	10.00
65 Darrius Heyward-Bey	3.00	8.00
66 Greg Olsen	3.00	8.00
67 Jamaal Charles	4.00	10.00
68 Kurt Warner	4.00	10.00
69 Ryan Grant	4.00	10.00
70 Joe Namath	6.00	15.00
71 Hakeem Nicks	4.00	10.00
72 LaDainian Tomlinson	5.00	12.00
73 Matthew Stafford	5.00	12.00
74 Chris Johnson	4.00	10.00
75 Reggie Bush	4.00	10.00
76 Darrelle Revis	4.00	10.00
77 Jordy Nelson	5.00	12.00
78 Devin Hester	5.00	12.00
79 Matt Cassel	4.00	10.00
80 Jerry Rice	8.00	20.00
81 Mark Sanchez	5.00	12.00
82 Jimmy Graham	5.00	12.00
83 Jared Allen	5.00	12.00
84 Steve Johnson	4.00	10.00
85 Eric Decker	4.00	10.00
86 Phil Simms	4.00	10.00
87 Michael Crabtree	4.00	10.00
88 Fred Jackson	5.00	12.00
89 Beanie Wells	4.00	10.00
90 Dan Marino	10.00	25.00
91 Malcom Floyd	4.00	10.00
92 Kevin Kolb	4.00	10.00
93 Mike Tolbert	4.00	10.00
94 Tarvaris Jackson	3.00	8.00
95 Davone Bess	3.00	8.00
96 Percy Harvin	4.00	10.00
97 Jason Witten	5.00	12.00
98 Carson Palmer	4.00	10.00
99 Marques Colston	4.00	10.00
100 Joe Montana	10.00	25.00
101 Matt Hasselbeck	4.00	10.00
102 Felix Jones	4.00	10.00
103 Aaron Hernandez	4.00	10.00
104 Ryan Fitzpatrick	4.00	10.00
105 Chuck Howley	3.00	8.00
106 Steve Breaston	3.00	8.00
107 Mario Manningham	4.00	10.00

108 Michael Turner 4.00 10.00
109 Dustin Keller 4.00 10.00
110 Peyton Hillis 4.00 10.00
111 Tom Brady 15.00 30.00
112 Ahmad Bradshaw 4.00 10.00
113 Mike Williams 4.00 10.00
114 Jahvid Best 4.00 10.00
115 Victor Cruz 6.00 15.00
116 Dwayne Bowe 4.00 10.00
117 Jay Cutler 4.00 10.00
118 Shonn Greene 4.00 10.00
119 Brandon Pettigrew 3.00 8.00
120 Roddy White 4.00 10.00
121 Wes Welker 5.00 12.00
122 Calvin Johnson 5.00 12.00
123 Vincent Jackson 4.00 10.00
124 Josh Freeman 5.00 12.00
125 Matt Forte 4.00 10.00
126 DeMarcus Ware 4.00 10.00
127 Jonathan Stewart 4.00 10.00
128 Matt Ryan 5.00 12.00
129 Nate Washington 3.00 8.00
130 Peyton Manning 12.50 25.00
131 Miles Austin 4.00 10.00
132 LeSean McCoy 4.00 10.00
133 Alex Smith QB 4.00 10.00
134 Marshawn Lynch 4.00 10.00
135 DeSean Jackson 4.00 10.00
136 DeAngelo Williams 4.00 10.00
137 Reggie Wayne 4.00 10.00
138 Ray Rice 4.00 10.00
139 Kellen Winslow Jr. 4.00 10.00
140 Drew Brees 6.00 15.00
141 Tim Tebow 10.00 25.00
142 Knowshon Moreno 4.00 10.00
143 Sidney Rice 4.00 10.00
144 Philip Rivers 5.00 12.00
145 Ryan Mathews 4.00 10.00
146 Willis McGahee 3.00 8.00
147 Steve Smith WR 4.00 10.00
148 Pierre Garcon 4.00 10.00
149 Darren Sproles 4.00 10.00
150 Aaron Rodgers 15.00 30.00
151 Daniel Thomas JSY AU/120 RC 12.00 30.00
152 Jonathan Baldwin JSY AU/75 RC 12.00 30.00
153 Christian Ponder JSY AU/65 RC 60.00 120.00
154 Alex Green JSY AU/175 RC 12.00 30.00
155 Blaine Gabbert JSY AU/65 RC 30.00 80.00
156 Jordan Todman JSY AU/199 RC 8.00 20.00
157 Kendall Hunter JSY AU/199 RC 15.00 40.00
158 Bilal Powell JSY AU/175 RC 8.00 20.00
159 Greg Little JSY AU/65 RC 12.00 30.00
160 Mark Ingram JSY AU/65 RC 40.00 100.00
161 Andy Dalton JSY AU/75 RC 75.00 150.00
162 Delone Carter JSY AU/175 RC 10.00 25.00
163 Austin Pettis JSY AU/199 RC 8.00 20.00
164 Jake Locker JSY AU/75 RC 75.00 150.00
165 Kyle Rudolph JSY AU/120 RC 12.00 30.00
166 Jerrel Jernigan JSY AU/120 RC 10.00 25.00
167 Ryan Mallett JSY AU/65 RC 50.00 100.00
168 Vincent Brown JSY AU/199 RC 12.00 30.00
169 Jamie Harper JSY AU/199 RC 12.00 30.00
170 Cam Newton JSY AU/199 RC 250.00 500.00
171 Von Miller JSY AU/65 RC 25.00 60.00
172 DeMarco Murray JSY AU/130 RC 50.00 100.00
173 Ryan Williams JSY AU/75 RC 15.00 40.00
174 Stevan Ridley JSY AU/99 RC 12.00 30.00
175 Torrey Smith JSY AU/75 RC 25.00 60.00
176 Mikel Leshoure JSY AU/75 RC 20.00 50.00
177 Titus Young JSY AU/75 RC 20.00 50.00
178 Randall Cobb JSY AU/99 RC 15.00 40.00
179 Marcell Dareus JSY AU/75 RC 15.00 40.00
180 A.J. Green JSY AU/65 RC 50.00 100.00
181 Colin Kaepernick JSY AU/65 RC 30.00 60.00
182 Leonard Hankerson JSY AU/99 RC 12.00 30.00
183 Shane Vereen JSY AU/130 RC 12.00 30.00

2011 Topps Five Star Dual Patches

STATED PRINT RUN 15 SER.#'d SETS
FSDPBC Dwayne Bowe 15.00 40.00
Jamaal Charles
FSDPBS Jonathan Baldwin 10.00 25.00
Torrey Smith
FSDPCG Randall Cobb 15.00 40.00
Alex Green
FSDPDP Andy Dalton 20.00 50.00
Christian Ponder
FSDPGD A.J. Green 20.00 50.00
Andy Dalton
FSDPGJ A.J. Green 15.00 40.00
Julio Jones
FSDPGL Blaine Gabbert 15.00 40.00
Jake Locker
FSDPGN Blaine Gabbert 30.00 80.00
Cam Newton
FSDPGP Blaine Gabbert 15.00 40.00
Christian Ponder
FSDPID Mark Ingram 15.00 40.00
Marcell Dareus
FSDPIJ Mark Ingram 15.00 40.00
Julio Jones
FSDPIL Mark Ingram 15.00 40.00
Mikel Leshoure
FSDPJD Julio Jones 12.00 30.00
Marcell Dareus
FSDPKH Colin Kaepernick 10.00 25.00
Kendall Hunter
FSDPLD Jake Locker 20.00 50.00
Andy Dalton
FSDPLG Greg Little 12.00 30.00
A.J. Green
FSDPLH Jake Locker 20.00 50.00
Jamie Harper
FSDPLM Jake Locker 20.00 50.00
Ryan Mallett
FSDPMD Von Miller 12.00 30.00
Marcell Dareus
FSDPMR Ryan Mallett 15.00 40.00
Stevan Ridley
FSDPMV Ryan Mallett 15.00 40.00
Shane Vereen
FSDPNI Cam Newton 30.00 80.00
Mark Ingram
FSDPNJ Cam Newton 30.00 80.00
Julio Jones
FSDPRJ Matt Ryan 20.00 50.00
Julio Jones
FSDPRP Kyle Rudolph 15.00 40.00
Christian Ponder
FSDPVR Shane Vereen 8.00 20.00
Stevan Ridley
FSDPWL Ryan Williams 12.00 30.00
Mikel Leshoure
FSDPYP Titus Young 12.00 30.00
Austin Pettis

2011 Topps Five Star Dual Rookie Autographed Patch

STATED PRINT RUN 15 SER.#'d SETS
EXCH EXPIRATION: 2/28/2015
FSFDAPBS Jonathan Baldwin 40.00 80.00
Torrey Smith
FSFDAPCAJ Cam Newton 250.00 500.00
A.J. Green
FSFDAPCG Randall Cobb 40.00 80.00
Alex Green
FSFDAPCY Randall Cobb 30.00 60.00
Titus Young
FSFDAPDG Andy Dalton EXCH 150.00 250.00
A.J. Green
FSFDAPDM Marcell Dareus 50.00 100.00
Von Miller
FSFDAPGL Blaine Gabbert 100.00 200.00
Jake Locker
FSFDAPHC Jamie Harper 20.00 50.00
Delone Carter
FSFDAPHJ Leonard Hankerson 20.00 50.00
Jerrel Jernigan
FSFDAPHS Leonard Hankerson 25.00 60.00
Torrey Smith
FSFDAPIL Mark Ingram 50.00 100.00
Mikel Leshoure
FSFDAPKH Colin Kaepernick 60.00 120.00
Kendall Hunter
FSFDAPLH Greg Little 20.00 50.00
Leonard Hankerson
FSFDAPLHA Jake Locker 60.00 120.00
Jamie Harper
FSFDAPLS Greg Little 25.00 60.00
Torrey Smith
FSFDAPLY Mikel Leshoure
Titus Young
FSFDAPMH DeMarco Murray 75.00 150.00
Kendall Hunter
FSFDAPMR Ryan Mallett 60.00 120.00
Stevan Ridley
FSFDAPMT DeMarco Murray 50.00 100.00
Daniel Thomas
FSFDAPMV Ryan Mallett 60.00 120.00
Shane Vereen
FSFDAPNG Cam Newton 200.00 400.00
Blaine Gabbert
FSFDAPNI Cam Newton 200.00 400.00
Mark Ingram
FSFDAPPR Christian Ponder 60.00 120.00
Kyle Rudolph
FSFDAPSG Torrey Smith 60.00 120.00
A.J. Green
FSFDAPTB Jordan Todman 20.00 50.00
Vincent Brown
FSFDAPTG Daniel Thomas 20.00 50.00
Edmond Gates
FSFDAPTP Daniel Thomas 20.00 50.00
Bilal Powell
FSFDAPVR Shane Vereen 20.00 50.00
Stevan Ridley
FSFDAPWH Ryan Williams 40.00 80.00
Kendall Hunter
FSFDAPYP Titus Young EXCH 25.00 60.00
Austin Pettis

2011 Topps Five Star Dual Rookie Autographs

STATED PRINT RUN 20 SER.#'d SETS
EXCH EXPIRATION: 2/28/2015
FSFDABB Jonathan Baldwin 15.00 40.00
Vincent Brown
FSFDABJ Jonathan Baldwin 15.00 40.00
Taiwan Jones
FSFDABS Jonathan Baldwin 20.00 50.00
Torrey Smith
FSFDACG Randall Cobb 30.00 60.00
Alex Green
FSFDACT Delone Carter 12.00 30.00
Jordan Todman
FSFDACY Randall Cobb 30.00 60.00
Titus Young
FSFDADG Andy Dalton 125.00 200.00
A.J. Green
FSFDADM Marcell Dareus 30.00 60.00
Von Miller
FSFDAGL Blaine Gabbert 60.00 120.00
Jake Locker
FSFDAGS A.J. Green 50.00 100.00
Torrey Smith
FSFDAHC Jamie Harper 15.00 40.00
Delone Carter
FSFDAHJ Leonard Hankerson 15.00 40.00
Jerrel Jernigan
FSFDAHS Leonard Hankerson 20.00 50.00
Torrey Smith
FSFDAID Mark Ingram 30.00 80.00
Marcell Dareus
FSFDAIR Mark Ingram 30.00 80.00
Stevan Ridley
FSFDAJP Jerrel Jernigan 12.00 30.00
Bilal Powell
FSFDAKG Colin Kaepernick 25.00 60.00
Alex Green
FSFDAKH Colin Kaepernick 40.00 80.00
Kendall Hunter
FSFDAKW Colin Kaepernick 25.00 60.00
Ryan Williams
FSFDALG Mikel Leshoure 20.00 50.00
Alex Green
FSFDALH Greg Little 20.00 50.00
Leonard Hankerson
FSFDALS Greg Little 25.00 60.00
Torrey Smith
FSFDALY Mikel Leshoure 25.00 60.00
Titus Young
FSFDAMH DeMarco Murray 50.00 100.00
Kendall Hunter
FSFDAMR Ryan Mallett 30.00 80.00
Stevan Ridley
FSFDAMT DeMarco Murray 50.00 100.00
Daniel Thomas
FSFDAMV Ryan Mallett 30.00 80.00
Shane Vereen
FSFDANG Cam Newton 150.00 300.00
Blaine Gabbert
FSFDANI Cam Newton 150.00 300.00
Mark Ingram
FSFDAPG Bilal Powell 12.00 30.00
Edmond Gates
FSFDAPR Christian Ponder 50.00 100.00
Kyle Rudolph
FSFDASG Torrey Smith 50.00 100.00
A.J. Green
FSFDATB Jordan Todman 15.00 40.00
Vincent Brown
FSFDATG Daniel Thomas 15.00 40.00
Edmond Gates
FSFDATJ Jordan Todman 15.00 40.00
Taiwan Jones
FSFDATP Daniel Thomas 15.00 40.00
Bilal Powell
FSFDAVP Shane Vereen 12.00 30.00
Bilal Powell
FSFDAVR Shane Vereen 15.00 40.00
Stevan Ridley
FSFDAWH Ryan Williams 20.00 50.00
Kendall Hunter
FSFDAWL Ryan Williams 20.00 50.00
Mikel Leshoure
FSFDAYP Titus Young 15.00 40.00
Austin Pettis
FSFDACAJ Cam Newton 150.00 300.00
A.J. Green
FSFDAGLI A.J. Green 30.00 80.00
Greg Little
FSFDALHA Jake Locker 50.00 100.00
Jamie Harper
FSFDAPRI Bilal Powell 12.00 30.00
Stevan Ridley

2011 Topps Five Star Patches

STATED PRINT RUN 40 SER.#'d SETS
*JUMBO JSY/88: .3X TO .8X PATCH/40
FSPAD Andy Dalton 12.00 30.00
FSPAF Arian Foster 12.00 30.00
FSPAGA Antonio Gates 6.00 15.00
FSPAJG A.J. Green 10.00 25.00
FSPAP Adrian Peterson 12.00 30.00
FSPAR Aaron Rodgers 25.00 50.00
FSPBG Blaine Gabbert 8.00 20.00
FSPBP Bilal Powell 3.00 8.00
FSPCB Cedric Benson 8.00 20.00
FSPCK Colin Kaepernick 6.00 15.00
FSPCN Cam Newton 30.00 60.00
FSPCP Christian Ponder 10.00 25.00
FSPDB Dwayne Bowe 6.00 15.00
FSPDC Delone Carter 4.00 10.00
FSPDH Devin Hester 10.00 25.00
FSPDMU DeMarco Murray 10.00 25.00
FSPDT Daniel Thomas 5.00 12.00
FSPDW DeAngelo Williams 8.00 20.00
FSPGL Greg Little 5.00 12.00
FSPHN Hakeem Nicks 8.00 20.00
FSPHW Hines Ward 10.00 25.00
FSPJB Jonathan Baldwin 5.00 12.00
FSPJC Jamaal Charles 8.00 20.00
FSPJE John Elway 15.00 40.00
FSPJJ Julio Jones 8.00 20.00
FSPJJE Jerrel Jernigan 4.00 10.00
FSPJL Jake Locker 12.00 30.00
FSPKH Kendall Hunter 6.00 15.00
FSPKR Kyle Rudolph 5.00 12.00
FSPLF Larry Fitzgerald 8.00 20.00
FSPLH Leonard Hankerson 5.00 12.00
FSPMD Marcell Dareus 5.00 12.00
FSPMI Mark Ingram 10.00 25.00
FSPML Mikel Leshoure 6.00 15.00
FSPMR Matt Ryan 10.00 25.00
FSPMS Mark Sanchez 8.00 20.00
FSPMV Michael Vick 8.00 20.00
FSPRC Randall Cobb 8.00 20.00
FSPRL Ray Lewis 12.00 30.00
FSPRM Ryan Mallett 10.00 25.00
FSPRW Ryan Williams 6.00 15.00
FSPSR Stevan Ridley 5.00 12.00
FSPSV Shane Vereen 5.00 12.00
FSPTR Tony Romo 10.00 25.00
FSPTS Torrey Smith 6.00 15.00
FSPTY Titus Young 6.00 15.00
FSPVM Von Miller 8.00 20.00

2011 Topps Five Star Rookie Autographed Patch Gold

*GOLD AU/55: .5X TO 1.2X BASIC JSY AU
STATED PRINT RUN 55 SER.#'d SETS
170 Cam Newton 300.00 600.00

2011 Topps Five Star Rookie Autographed Patch Rainbow

*RAINBOW AU/25: .6X TO 1.5X BASIC JSY AU
STATED PRINT RUN 25 SER.#'d SETS
167 Ryan Mallett 100.00 175.00
170 Cam Newton 400.00 800.00
172 DeMarco Murray 100.00 200.00

2011 Topps Five Star Rookie Autographed Quad Jersey

QUAD JSY AU PRINT RUN 35-95
*QUAD GOLD/15: .5X TO 1.2X QUAD AU
*TRIPLE AU/30-50: .4X TO 1X QUAD AU
*TRIPLE GLD/15: .5X TO 1.2X QUAD AU
EXCH EXPIRATION: 2/28/2015
FSFA4AD Andy Dalton/35 60.00 120.00
FSFA4AJG A.J. Green/35 50.00 100.00
FSFA4BG Blaine Gabbert/35 40.00 80.00
FSFA4BP Bilal Powell/35 10.00 25.00
FSFA4CK Colin Kaepernick/35 30.00 60.00
FSFA4CN Cam Newton/50 200.00 350.00
FSFA4CP Christian Ponder/35 50.00 100.00
FSFA4DC Delone Carter/35 12.00 30.00
FSFA4DM DeMarco Murray/35 50.00 100.00
FSFA4DT Daniel Thomas/35 15.00 40.00
FSFA4GL Greg Little/35 15.00 40.00
FSFA4JB Jonathan Baldwin/35 15.00 40.00
FSFA4JJE Jerrel Jernigan/35 12.00 30.00
FSFA4JL Jake Locker/35 50.00 120.00
FSFA4JT Jordan Todman/35 10.00 25.00
FSFA4KR Kyle Rudolph/35 20.00 50.00
FSFA4LH Leonard Hankerson/35 15.00 40.00
FSFA4MD Marcell Dareus/35 15.00 40.00
FSFA4MI Mark Ingram/35 50.00 100.00
FSFA4ML Mikel Leshoure/35 25.00 60.00
FSFA4RC Randall Cobb/50 20.00 50.00
FSFA4RM Ryan Mallett/35 40.00 80.00
FSFA4RW Ryan Williams/35 20.00 50.00
FSFA4SR Stevan Ridley/35 15.00 40.00
FSFA4SV Shane Vereen/35 15.00 40.00
FSFA4TJ Taiwan Jones/95 15.00 40.00
FSFA4TS Torrey Smith/50 25.00 60.00
FSFA4TY Titus Young/35 20.00 50.00
FSFA4VM Von Miller/35 40.00 80.00

2011 Topps Five Star Rookie Autographs

STATED PRINT RUN 55-199
EXCH EXPIRATION: 2/28/2015
FSFAAD Andy Dalton/55 50.00 100.00
FSFAAGR Alex Green/190 8.00 20.00
FSFAAJG A.J. Green/165 40.00 80.00
FSFAAP Austin Pettis/199 5.00 12.00
FSFABG Blaine Gabbert/110 20.00 50.00
FSFABP Bilal Powell/199 5.00 12.00
FSFACK Colin Kaepernick/90 20.00 50.00
FSFACN Cam Newton/110 125.00 250.00
FSFACP Christian Ponder/90 40.00 80.00
FSFADC Delone Carter/199 6.00 15.00
FSFADM DeMarco Murray/199 30.00 60.00
FSFADT Daniel Thomas/199 8.00 20.00
FSFAGL Greg Little/175 8.00 20.00
FSFAJB Jonathan Baldwin/165 8.00 20.00
FSFAJH Jamie Harper/199 6.00 15.00
FSFAJJE Jerrel Jernigan/175 6.00 15.00
FSFAJL Jake Locker/110 40.00 80.00
FSFAJT Jordan Todman/175 5.00 12.00
FSFAKH Kendall Hunter/190 10.00 25.00
FSFAKR Kyle Rudolph/199 10.00 25.00
FSFALH Leonard Hankerson/165 8.00 20.00
FSFAMD Marcell Dareus/155 8.00 20.00
FSFAMI Mark Ingram/55 25.00 60.00
FSFAML Mikel Leshoure/145 10.00 25.00
FSFARC Randall Cobb/160 15.00 40.00
FSFARH Roy Helu/110 20.00 50.00
FSFARM Ryan Mallett/90 20.00 50.00
FSFARW Ryan Williams/155 10.00 25.00
FSFASR Stevan Ridley/199 8.00 20.00
FSFASV Shane Vereen/199 8.00 20.00
FSFATJ Taiwan Jones/199 8.00 20.00
FSFATP Terrelle Pryor/110 30.00 60.00
FSFATS Torrey Smith/160 12.00 30.00
FSFATY Titus Young/145 10.00 25.00
FSFAVB Vincent Brown/199 8.00 20.00
FSFAVM Von Miller/165 20.00 40.00

2011 Topps Five Star Rookie Quotable Autographs

STATED PRINT RUN 25 SER.#'d SETS
FSFQAAD Andy Dalton 250.00 400.00
FSFQAAJG A.J. Green 150.00 300.00
FSFQABG Blaine Gabbert 60.00 120.00
FSFQABP Bilal Powell 20.00 50.00
FSFQACK Colin Kaepernick 60.00 120.00
FSFQACN Cam Newton 400.00 600.00
FSFQACP Christian Ponder 150.00 250.00
FSFQADC Delone Carter 25.00 60.00
FSFQADM DeMarco Murray 150.00 300.00
FSFQADT Daniel Thomas 30.00 80.00
FSFQAGL Greg Little 30.00 80.00
FSFQAJB Jonathan Baldwin 30.00 80.00
FSFQAJJE Jerrel Jernigan 25.00 60.00
FSFQAJL Jake Locker 200.00 350.00
FSFQAKH Kendall Hunter 30.00 80.00
FSFQAKR Kyle Rudolph 30.00 80.00
FSFQALH Leonard Hankerson 30.00 80.00
FSFQAMD Marcell Dareus 30.00 80.00
FSFQAMI Mark Ingram 150.00 250.00
FSFQARC Randall Cobb 60.00 120.00
FSFQARM Ryan Mallett 75.00 150.00
FSFQARW Ryan Williams 50.00 100.00
FSFQASR Stevan Ridley 30.00 80.00
FSFQASV Shane Vereen 30.00 80.00
FSFQATJ Taiwan Jones 30.00 80.00
FSFQATS Torrey Smith 50.00 100.00
FSFQATY Titus Young 40.00 100.00
FSFQAVM Von Miller 75.00 150.00

2011 Topps Five Star Super Bowl MVP Autograph

SBMVPAR Aaron Rodgers 250.00 500.00

2011 Topps Five Star Super Bowl MVP Relics

STATED PRINT RUN 16-20
SBMVPAR Aaron Rodgers FB/20 200.00 400.00
SBMVPRAR Aaron Rodgers Pylon/16 300.00 500.00

2011 Topps Five Star Veteran Autographed Patch

PATCH AUTO PRINT RUN 50-99
*GOLD/40: .5X TO 1.2X PATCH AU/50-99
*RAINBOW/25: .6X TO 1.5X PATCH AU/50-99
EXCH EXPIRATION: 2/28/2015
FSSPAG Antonio Gates/90 15.00 40.00
FSSPAR Aaron Rodgers/70 175.00 300.00
FSSPCB Champ Bailey/50 30.00 60.00
FSSPDB Dwayne Bowe/99 12.00 30.00
FSSPDM Darren McFadden/99 20.00 50.00
FSSPDR Darrelle Revis/99 15.00 40.00
FSSPHW Hines Ward/99 50.00 100.00
FSSPJC Jamaal Charles/70 15.00 40.00
FSSPJR Jerry Rice/50 125.00 200.00
FSSPKN Knowshon Moreno/99 15.00 40.00
FSSPKW Kurt Warner/50 40.00 80.00
FSSPLM LeSean McCoy 20.00 50.00
FSSPMA Miles Austin EXCH 20.00 50.00
FSSPMJ Maurice Jones-Drew/99 20.00 50.00
FSSPMS Mark Sanchez EXCH 20.00 50.00
FSSPMT Michael Turner/50 15.00 40.00
FSSPMV Michael Vick/50 30.00 80.00
FSSPPW Patrick Willis/70 25.00 60.00
FSSPRL Ray Lewis/50 50.00 100.00
FSSPTB Terry Bradshaw/50 75.00 150.00

2011 Topps Five Star Veteran Autographed Triple Jersey

STATED PRINT RUN 25-35
*GOLD/10: .5X TO 1.2X TRIP JSY AU/25-35
FSSBAG Antonio Gates/35 20.00 50.00
FSSBAR Aaron Rodgers/35 200.00 350.00
FSSBCB Champ Bailey/35 30.00 60.00
FSSBDB Dwayne Bowe/35 15.00 40.00
FSSBDM Dan Marino/25 150.00 250.00
FSSBDMC Darren McFadden/35 25.00 60.00
FSSBDR Darrelle Revis/35 20.00 50.00
FSSBHW Hines Ward/35 60.00 120.00
FSSBJC Jamaal Charles/35 20.00 50.00
FSSBJM Joe Montana/25 150.00 250.00
FSSBJN Joe Namath/25 125.00 200.00
FSSBJR Jerry Rice/25 125.00 200.00
FSSBKM Knowshon Moreno/35 20.00 50.00
FSSBKW Kurt Warner/35 50.00 100.00
FSSBLM LeSean McCoy EXCH 25.00 60.00
FSSBMA Miles Austin EXCH 25.00 60.00
FSSBMS Mark Sanchez EXCH 25.00 60.00
FSSBMT Michael Turner/35 20.00 50.00
FSSBMV Michael Vick/35 50.00 100.00
FSSBPM Peyton Manning/25 125.00 200.00
FSSBPW Patrick Willis/35 40.00 80.00
FSSBRL Ray Lewis/35 60.00 120.00
FSSBSG Shonn Greene/35 20.00 50.00
FSSBSM Santana Moss/35 20.00 50.00
FSSBTR Tony Romo/25 50.00 100.00
FSSBVD Vernon Davis/35 25.00 60.00

2011 Topps Five Star Veteran Autographs

STATED PRINT RUN 35-190
*GOLD/25: .6X TO 1.5X BASIC AU/150-190
*GOLD/25: .5X TO 1.2X BASIC AU/35-70
*RAINBOW/15: .6X TO 1.5X BASIC AU/150-190
*RAINBOW/15: .5X TO 1.X BASIC AU/35-70
EXCH EXPIRATION: 2/28/2015
FSSAF Arian Foster/190 25.00 50.00
FSSBS Bart Starr/50 75.00 150.00
FSSCB Champ Bailey/70 20.00 40.00
FSSCH Chuck Howley/50 12.00 30.00
FSSDM Dan Marino/40 100.00 200.00
FSSJC Jamaal Charles/60 12.00 30.00
FSSJM Joe Montana/40 100.00 200.00
FSSJMA Jeremy Maclin/190 8.00 20.00
FSSJN Joe Namath/40 75.00 150.00
FSSJR Jerry Rice/35 100.00 200.00
FSSKW Kurt Warner/150 30.00 60.00
FSSKWI Kellen Winslow Jr./150 6.00 15.00
FSSLM LeSean McCoy EXCH 30.00 60.00
FSSMC Marques Colston/150 10.00 25.00
FSSMJ Maurice Jones-Drew/50 12.00 30.00
FSSMT Michael Turner/35 12.00 30.00
FSSMW Mike Wallace/190 15.00 40.00
FSSPH Peyton Hillis/150 10.00 25.00
FSSPM Peyton Manning/40 75.00 150.00
FSSPS Phil Simms/60 25.00 50.00
FSSPW Patrick Willis/60 15.00 40.00
FSSRD Richard Dent/150 15.00 30.00
FSSSG Shonn Greene/150 8.00 20.00
FSSSM Santana Moss/150 8.00 20.00
FSSTB Terry Bradshaw/60 75.00 150.00
FSSVD Vernon Davis/190 12.00 30.00

1997 Topps Gallery

The 1997 Topps Gallery set was issued in one series totalling 135 cards and was distributed in six-card packs with a suggested retail price of $3. The fonts feature color photos of young stars, future stars, and veterans with bright colored frame-like borders and printed on 24 pt. card stock. Randomly inserted into packs was a "John Elway Feel the Power Instant Win" card. Every card was a winner, but the prize was unknown until the card was redeemed. Prizes included: a Pro Bowl/Super Bowl trip, trips to the Super Bowl, John Elway autographs, free packs of trading cards.

COMPLETE SET (135) 12.50 30.00
1 Orlando Pace RC .25 .60
2 Darrell Russell RC .10 .30
3 Shawn Springs RC .20 .50
4 Peter Boulware RC .25 .60
5 Bryant Westbrook RC .10 .30
6 Walter Jones RC .25 .60
7 Ike Hilliard RC .75 2.00
8 James Farrior RC .25 .60
9 Tom Knight RC .10 .30
10 Warrick Dunn RC 2.00 5.00
11 Tony Gonzalez RC 2.50 6.00
12 Reinard Wilson RC .20 .50
13 Yatil Green RC .20 .50
14 Reidel Anthony RC .25 .60
15 Kenny Holmes RC .25 .60
16 Dwayne Rudd RC .25 .60
17 Renaldo Wynn RC .10 .30
18 David LaFleur RC .40 1.00
19 Antowain Smith RC 1.50 4.00
20 Jim Druckenmiller RC .20 .50
21 Rae Carruth RC .10 .30
22 Byron Hanspard RC .20 .50
23 Jake Plummer RC 2.50 6.00
24 Corey Dillon RC 2.50 6.00
25 Darnell Autry RC .20 .50
26 Kevin Lockett RC .20 .50
27 Troy Davis RC .20 .50
28 Mike Alstott .25 .60
29 Napoleon Kaufman .25 .60
30 Terrell Davis .30 .75
31 Byron Bam Morris .10 .30
32 Dana Stubblefield .10 .30
33 Ki-Jana Carter .10 .30
34 Hugh Douglas .10 .30
35 Natrone Means .20 .50
36 Marshall Faulk .30 .75
37 Tyrone Wheatley .20 .50
38 Tony Banks .20 .50
39 Marvin Harrison .25 .60
40 Eddie George .25 .60
41 Eddie Kennison .20 .50
42 Ray Mickens .10 .30
43 Mike Mamula .10 .30
44 Tamarick Vanover .20 .50
45 Rashaan Salaam .10 .30
46 Trent Dilfer .25 .60
47 John Mobley .10 .30
48 Gus Frerotte .10 .30
49 Isaac Bruce .25 .60
50 Mark Brunell .30 .75
51 Jamal Anderson .25 .60
52 Keyshawn Johnson .25 .60
53 Curtis Conway .20 .50
54 Zach Thomas .25 .60
55 Simeon Rice .20 .50
56 Lawrence Phillips .10 .30
57 Ty Detmer .20 .50
58 Bobby Engram .20 .50
59 Joey Galloway .20 .50
60 Curtis Martin .30 .75
61 Kevin Hardy .10 .30
62 Eric Moulds .25 .60
63 Michael Westbrook .20 .50
64 Robert Smith .20 .50
65 Karim Abdul-Jabbar .25 .60
66 Errict Rhett .10 .30
67 Ray Lewis .40 1.00
68 Terry Glenn .25 .60
69 Leeland McElroy .10 .30
70 Kerry Collins .25 .60
71 Steve McNair .30 .75
72 Kordell Stewart .25 .60
73 Terry Allen .25 .60
74 Michael Irvin .25 .60
75 John Elway 1.00 2.50
76 Lamar Lathon .10 .30
77 Rob Moore .20 .50
78 Irving Fryar .20 .50
79 Jim Everett .10 .30
80 Steve Young .30 .75
81 Bryan Cox .10 .30
82 Dale Carter .10 .30
83 Chris Warren .20 .50
84 Shannon Sharpe .20 .50
85 Reggie White .25 .60
86 Deion Sanders .25 .60
87 Hardy Nickerson .10 .30
88 Edgar Bennett .20 .50
89 Kent Graham .10 .30
90 Dan Marino 1.00 2.50
91 Kevin Greene .20 .50
92 Derrick Thomas .25 .60
93 Carl Pickens .20 .50
94 Neil O'Donnell .20 .50
95 Drew Bledsoe .30 .75
96 Michael Haynes .10 .30
97 Tony Martin .20 .50
98 Scott Mitchell .20 .50
99 Rodney Hampton .20 .50
100 Brett Favre 1.00 2.50
101 Darrell Green .20 .50
102 Rod Woodson .20 .50
103 Chris Spielman .10 .30
104 Jake Reed .20 .50
105 Jerry Rice .50 1.25
106 Jeff Hostetler .10 .30
107 Anthony Johnson .10 .30
108 Keenan McCardell .20 .50
109 Ben Coates .20 .50
110 Emmitt Smith .75 2.00
111 LeRoy Butler .10 .30
112 Steve Atwater .10 .30
113 Ricky Watters .20 .50
114 Jim Harbaugh .20 .50
115 Marcus Allen .25 .60
116 Levon Kirkland .10 .30
117 Jessie Tuggle .10 .30
118 Ken Norton .10 .30
119 Thurman Thomas .25 .60
120 Junior Seau .25 .60
121 Tim Brown .25 .60
122 Michael Jackson .20 .50
123 Eric Metcalf .20 .50
124 Herman Moore .20 .50
125 Bruce Smith .20 .50
126 Cris Carter .25 .60
127 Dave Brown .10 .30
128 Jeff Blake .20 .50
129 Robert Blackmon .10 .30
130 Barry Sanders .75 2.00
131 Blaine Bishop .10 .30
132 Jerome Bettis .25 .60
133 Stan Humphries .20 .50
134 Vinny Testaverde .20 .50
135 Troy Aikman .50 1.25
P54 Zach Thomas Promo .40 1.00
(on back HT
WT in yellow
box instead of team name)

1997 Topps Gallery Player's Private Issue

COMPLETE SET (135) 1,000.00 2,000.00
*STARS: 8X TO 20X BASIC CARDS
*RCs: 2.5X TO 6X BASIC CARDS
STATED ODDS 1:12
STATED PRINT RUN 250 #'d SETS

1997 Topps Gallery Critics Choice

COMPLETE SET (20) 60.00 120.00
STATED ODDS 1:24
CC1 Barry Sanders 6.00 15.00
CC2 Jeff Blake 1.50 4.00
CC3 Vinny Testaverde 1.50 4.00
CC4 Ricky Watters 1.50 4.00
CC5 John Elway 8.00 20.00
CC6 Drew Bledsoe 2.50 6.00
CC7 Kordell Stewart 2.00 5.00
CC8 Mark Brunell 2.50 6.00
CC9 Troy Aikman 4.00 10.00
CC10 Brett Favre 8.00 20.00
CC11 Kevin Hardy 1.00 2.50
CC12 Shannon Sharpe 1.50 4.00
CC13 Emmitt Smith 6.00 15.00
CC14 Rob Moore 1.50 4.00
CC15 Eddie George 2.00 5.00
CC16 Herman Moore 1.50 4.00
CC17 Terry Glenn 2.00 5.00
CC18 Jim Harbaugh 1.50 4.00
CC19 Terrell Davis 2.50 6.00
CC20 Junior Seau 2.00 5.00

1997 Topps Gallery Gallery of Heroes

COMPLETE SET (15) 100.00 200.00
STATED ODDS 1:36
GH1 Desmond Howard 3.00 8.00
GH2 Marcus Allen 2.00 5.00
GH3 Kerry Collins 2.00 5.00
GH4 Troy Aikman 7.50 20.00
GH5 Jerry Rice 7.50 20.00
GH6 Drew Bledsoe 6.00 15.00
GH7 John Elway 15.00 40.00
GH8 Mark Brunell 6.00 15.00
GH9 Junior Seau 2.00 5.00
GH10 Brett Favre 15.00 40.00
GH11 Dan Marino 15.00 40.00
GH12 Barry Sanders 12.50 30.00
GH13 Reggie White 2.00 5.00
GH14 Emmitt Smith 12.50 30.00
GH15 Steve Young 6.00 15.00

1997 Topps Gallery Peter Max Serigraphs

COMPLETE SET (10) 50.00 100.00
STATED ODDS 1:24
PM1 Brett Favre 8.00 20.00
PM2 Jerry Rice 4.00 10.00
PM3 Emmitt Smith 6.00 15.00
PM4 John Elway 8.00 20.00
PM5 Barry Sanders 6.00 15.00
PM6 Reggie White 2.00 5.00
PM7 Steve Young 2.50 6.00
PM8 Troy Aikman 4.00 10.00
PM9 Drew Bledsoe 2.50 6.00
PM10 Dan Marino 8.00 20.00

1997 Topps Gallery Peter Max Serigraphs Max Signatures

RANDOM INSERTS IN PACKS
PM1 Brett Favre 175.00 350.00
PM2 Jerry Rice 175.00 350.00
PM3 Emmitt Smith 175.00 350.00
PM4 John Elway 175.00 350.00
PM5 Barry Sanders 175.00 350.00
PM6 Reggie White 175.00 350.00
PM7 Steve Young 175.00 350.00
PM8 Troy Aikman 175.00 350.00
PM9 Drew Bledsoe 175.00 350.00
PM10 Dan Marino 175.00 350.00

1997 Topps Gallery Photo Gallery

COMPLETE SET (15) 75.00 150.00
STATED ODDS 1:24
PG1 Eddie George 2.00 5.00
PG2 Drew Bledsoe 2.50 6.00
PG3 Brett Favre 8.00 20.00
PG4 Emmitt Smith 6.00 15.00
PG5 Dan Marino 8.00 20.00
PG6 Terrell Davis 2.50 6.00
PG7 Kevin Greene 1.50 4.00
PG8 Troy Aikman 4.00 10.00
PG9 Curtis Martin 2.50 6.00
PG10 Barry Sanders 6.00 15.00
PG11 Junior Seau 2.00 5.00
PG12 Deion Sanders 2.00 5.00
PG13 Steve Young 2.50 6.00
PG14 Reggie White 2.00 5.00
PG15 Jerry Rice 4.00 10.00

2000 Topps Gallery

Released as a 175-card set, 2000 Topps Gallery is comprised of 125 base veteran cards, 25 Apprentices which feature rookies from the 2000 draft, 13 Artisans which feature young stars, and 12 Masters which picture top NFL veterans. Either one subset or Rookie Card was included in each pack. Gallery was packaged in 24-pack boxes where packs contained six cards and carried a suggested retail price of $3.00.

COMPLETE SET (175) 20.00 50.00
COMP.SET w/o SP's (125) 7.50 20.00
UNPRICED PRESS PLATE PRINT RUN 1
1 Marshall Faulk .30 .75
2 Kordell Stewart .25 .60
3 Priest Holmes .30 .75
4 James Johnson .20 .50
5 Charlie Garner .25 .60
6 Jeff Blake .25 .60
7 Joey Galloway .25 .60
8 Terrell Davis .30 .75
9 Jerome Bettis .30 .75
10 Bobby Engram .25 .60
11 Muhsin Muhammad .25 .60
12 Marcus Robinson .25 .60
13 Kerry Collins .25 .60
14 Jake Plummer .25 .60
15 J.J. Stokes .25 .60
16 Tim Couch .25 .60
17 Napoleon Kaufman .25 .60
18 Az-Zahir Hakim .20 .50
19 Jimmy Smith .25 .60
20 Eddie George .25 .60
21 Jacquez Green .20 .50
22 Champ Bailey .25 .60
23 Wesley Walls .20 .50
24 Eric Moulds .25 .60
25 Corey Dillon .25 .60
26 Freddie Jones .20 .50
27 Jevon Kearse .25 .60
28 Ray Lucas .20 .50
29 Germane Crowell .20 .50
30 Randy Moss .30 .75
31 Patrick Jeffers .25 .60
32 Zach Thomas .30 .75
33 Shannon Sharpe .30 .75
34 Derrick Mayes .20 .50
35 Antonio Freeman .25 .60
36 Terance Mathis .20 .50
37 Herman Moore .25 .60
38 Tony Banks .20 .50
39 Jerry Rice .60 1.50
40 Troy Aikman .50 1.25
41 Rickey Dudley .20 .50
42 Troy Edwards .20 .50
43 Curtis Martin .30 .75
44 Eddie Kennison .20 .50
45 Mark Brunell .25 .60
46 Shaun King .20 .50
47 Duce Staley .25 .60
48 Darnay Scott .25 .60
49 Sean Dawkins .20 .50
50 Edgerrin James .30 .75
51 Olandis Gary .25 .60
52 Peerless Price .25 .60
53 Akili Smith .20 .50
54 Charlie Batch .25 .60
55 Tim Biakabutuka .25 .60
56 Rob Moore .20 .50
57 Keenan McCardell .25 .60
58 Dan Marino 1.00 2.50
59 Tony Gonzalez .30 .75
60 Stephen Davis .25 .60
61 Ricky Watters .25 .60
62 Frank Wycheck .25 .60
63 Kevin Johnson .20 .50
64 Isaac Bruce .30 .75
65 Andre Reed .30 .75
66 Jamal Anderson .25 .60
67 Dorsey Levens .25 .60
68 Rocket Ismail .25 .60
69 Albert Connell .20 .50
70 Brett Favre 1.00 2.50
71 Wayne Chrebet .25 .60
72 Jon Kitna .25 .60
73 Brian Griese .25 .60
74 Rob Johnson .25 .60
75 Qadry Ismail .25 .60
76 Derrick Alexander .20 .50
77 Tim Dwight .25 .60
78 Ike Hilliard .25 .60
79 Frank Sanders .20 .50
80 Fred Taylor .30 .75
81 Robert Smith .25 .60
82 Vinny Testaverde .25 .60
83 Steve Young .40 1.00
84 Tyrone Wheatley .20 .50
85 Mikhael Ricks .20 .50
86 Tony Martin .25 .60
87 Carl Pickens .25 .60
88 Warrick Dunn .25 .60
89 Emmitt Smith .75 2.00
90 Keyshawn Johnson .25 .60
91 James Stewart .20 .50
92 Doug Flutie .30 .75
93 Torry Holt .30 .75
94 Jeff Graham .20 .50
95 Steve McNair .30 .75
96 Erriet Rhett .25 .60
97 Terrell Owens .30 .75
98 Terry Glenn .25 .60
99 Steve Beuerlein .25 .60
100 Kurt Warner .50 1.25
101 Jeff George .25 .60
102 Deion Sanders .30 .75
103 Johnnie Morton .25 .60
104 Antowain Smith .25 .60
105 O.J. McDuffie .25 .60
106 Rod Smith .25 .60
107 Jim Harbaugh .25 .60
108 Marvin Harrison .30 .75
109 Curtis Enis .20 .50
110 Drew Bledsoe .30 .75
111 Mike Alstott .30 .75
112 Amani Toomer .25 .60
113 Elvis Grbac .20 .50
114 Tim Brown .30 .75
115 Cris Carter .30 .75
116 Donovan McNabb .30 .75
117 Chris Chandler .25 .60
118 Kevin Dyson .25 .60
119 Rich Gannon .25 .60
120 Ricky Williams .30 .75
121 Brad Johnson .25 .60
122 Cade McNown .20 .50
123 Ed McCaffrey .25 .60
124 Michael Westbrook .20 .50
125 Peyton Manning .75 2.00
126 Brett Favre MAS 1.25 3.00
127 Emmitt Smith MAS 1.00 2.50
128 Tim Brown MAS .40 1.00
129 Troy Aikman MAS .60 1.50
130 Jimmy Smith MAS .30 .75
131 Dan Marino MAS 1.25 3.00
132 Cris Carter MAS .40 1.00
133 Jerry Rice MAS .75 2.00
134 Steve Young MAS .50 1.25
135 Marshall Faulk MAS .40 1.00
136 Eddie George MAS .30 .75
137 Drew Bledsoe MAS .40 1.00
138 Randy Moss ART .40 1.00

139 Germane Crowell ART	.25	.60
140 Akili Smith ART	.25	.60
141 Tim Couch ART	.30	.75
142 Marcus Robinson ART	.30	.75
143 Daunte Culpepper ART	.30	.75
144 Jevon Kearse ART	.30	.75
145 Edgerrin James ART	.40	1.00
146 Tony Gonzalez ART	.40	1.00
147 Cade McNown ART	.25	.60
148 Fred Taylor ART	.40	1.00
149 Donovan McNabb ART	.40	1.00
150 Ricky Williams ART	.40	1.00
151 Jamal Lewis RC	.60	1.50
152 Tee Martin RC	.60	1.50
153 Plaxico Burress RC	.60	1.50
154 Chad Pennington RC	1.00	2.50
155 Curtis Keaton RC	.40	1.00
156 Thomas Jones RC	.75	2.00
157 Courtney Brown RC	.50	1.25
158 Ron Dayne RC	.60	1.50
159 Shaun Alexander RC	.75	2.00
160 Travis Taylor RC	.50	1.25
161 Sylvester Morris RC	.40	1.00
162 Giovanni Carmazzi RC	.40	1.00
163 Laveranues Coles RC	.60	1.50
164 Chris Redman RC	.50	1.25
165 Bubba Franks RC	.60	1.50
166 R.Jay Soward RC	.40	1.00
167 Reuben Droughns RC	.60	1.50
168 Todd Pinkston RC	.40	1.00
169 Trung Canidate RC	.50	1.25
170 Danny Farmer RC	.40	1.00
171 Ron Dugans RC	.40	1.00
172 Dennis Northcutt RC	.50	1.25
173 J.R. Redmond RC	.40	1.00
174 Travis Prentice RC	.50	1.25
175 Peter Warrick RC	.60	1.50

2000 Topps Gallery Player's Private Issue

*VETS 1-125: 2.5X TO 6X BASIC CARDS
*SUBSET 126-150: 2X TO 5X
*ROOKIES 151-175: 1.5X TO 4X
PRIVATE ISSUE/250 ODDS 1:16H
STATED PRINT RUN 250 SER.#'d SETS

2000 Topps Gallery Autographs

GROUP A STATED ODDS 1:236H
GROUP B STATED ODDS 1:2849H
OVERALL STATED ODDS 1:218H

JK Jon Kitna	6.00	15.00
JL Jamal Lewis	12.50	30.00
MF Marshall Faulk	25.00	50.00
SM Sylvester Morris	5.00	12.00
TJ Thomas Jones	10.00	25.00
ZT Zach Thomas	8.00	20.00

2000 Topps Gallery Exhibitions

COMPLETE SET (15)	15.00	40.00
STATED ODDS 1:32H		
GE1 Marshall Faulk	1.25	3.00
GE2 Muhsin Muhammad	1.00	2.50
GE3 Marvin Harrison	1.25	3.00
GE4 Stephen Davis	1.00	2.50
GE5 Eddie George	1.00	2.50
GE6 Antonio Freeman	1.00	2.50
GE7 Isaac Bruce	1.25	3.00
GE8 Jevon Kearse	1.00	2.50
GE9 Curtis Martin	1.25	3.00
GE10 Troy Aikman	2.00	5.00
GE11 Jimmy Smith	1.00	2.50
GE12 Edgerrin James	1.25	3.00
GE13 Randy Moss	1.25	3.00
GE14 Steve Beuerlein	1.00	2.50
GE15 Kurt Warner	2.00	5.00

2000 Topps Gallery Gallery of Heroes

COMPLETE SET (10)	15.00	40.00
STATED ODDS 1:24H		
GH1 Emmitt Smith	3.00	8.00
GH2 Troy Aikman	2.00	5.00
GH3 Brett Favre	4.00	10.00
GH4 Edgerrin James	1.25	3.00
GH5 Peyton Manning	3.00	8.00
GH6 Randy Moss	1.25	3.00
GH7 Marshall Faulk	1.25	3.00
GH8 Jerry Rice	2.50	6.00
GH9 Kurt Warner	2.00	5.00
GH10 Eddie George	1.00	2.50

2000 Topps Gallery Heritage

COMPLETE SET (10)	15.00	40.00
STATED ODDS 1:12H		
*PROOF: .6X TO 1.5X BASIC INSERT		
PROOFS STATED ODDS 1:48H		
*ART.SIGN/175: 2.5X TO 6X BASIC INSERT		
H1 Marshall Faulk	1.00	2.50
H2 Troy Aikman	1.50	4.00
H3 Randy Moss	1.00	2.50
H4 Brett Favre	3.00	8.00
H5 Jerry Rice	2.00	5.00
H6 Dan Marino	3.00	8.00
H7 Peyton Manning	2.50	6.00
H8 Emmitt Smith	2.50	6.00
H9 Edgerrin James	1.25	3.00
H10 Kurt Warner	1.50	4.00

2000 Topps Gallery Proof Positive

COMPLETE SET (10)	15.00	40.00
STATED ODDS 1:48H		
P1 Dan Marino Kurt Warner	4.00	10.00
P2 Eddie George Ricky Williams	1.25	3.00
P3 Jerry Rice Keyshawn Johnson	2.50	6.00
P4 Bruce Smith Jevon Kearse	1.25	3.00
P5 Marshall Faulk Edgerrin James	1.25	3.00
P6 Marvin Harrison Marcus Robinson	1.25	3.00
P7 Emmitt Smith Stephen Davis	3.00	8.00
P8 Isaac Bruce Randy Moss	1.25	3.00
P9 Steve Young Mark Brunell	1.50	4.00
P10 Drew Bledsoe Peyton Manning	3.00	8.00

2001 Topps Gallery

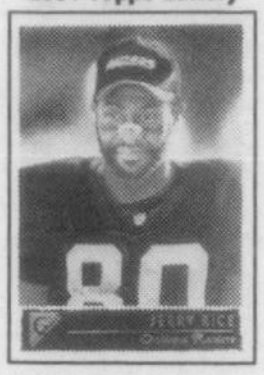

Topps Gallery was released in mid-August of 2001. The set design was a hand painted theme. This 145-card set included 140 base cards along with five short printed cards. There were 40 rookies and 100 veterans in the base set and the five short printed legends cards which were highlighted with a copper-foil along the nameplate. Please note the Joe Namath legends card was available in both a hobby and retail version.

COMPLETE SET (145)	30.00	80.00
COMP.SET w/o SP's (100)	10.00	25.00
1 Donovan McNabb	.30	.75
2 Jamal Anderson	.25	.60
3 Steve McNair	.30	.75
4 Peyton Manning	.75	2.00
5 Curtis Martin	.30	.75
6 Joey Galloway	.25	.60
7 Daunte Culpepper	.25	.60
8 Corey Dillon	.25	.60
9 Brad Johnson	.25	.60
10 Doug Flutie	.30	.75
11 Jerome Bettis	.30	.75
12 Elvis Grbac	.25	.60
13 Aaron Brooks	.25	.60
14 Ray Lewis	.30	.75
15 Tim Dwight	.25	.60
16 Robert Smith	.25	.60
17 Jake Plummer	.25	.60
18 Jay Fiedler	.25	.60
19 Fred Taylor	.30	.75
20 Jerry Rice	.60	1.50
21 Shaun King	.20	.50
22 Cade McNown	.25	.60
23 Drew Bledsoe	.30	.75
24 Ricky Watters	.25	.60
25 Muhsin Muhammad	.25	.60
26 Shawn Jefferson	.20	.50
27 Tiki Barber	.30	.75
28 Derrick Alexander	.20	.50
29 Stephen Davis	.25	.60
30 James Stewart	.20	.50
31 Terrell Owens	.30	.75
32 Ed McCaffrey	.25	.60
33 Jeff Graham	.20	.50
34 Jamal Lewis	.30	.75
35 Edgerrin James	.30	.75
36 Tim Couch	.20	.50
37 Marshall Faulk	.30	.75
38 Ike Hilliard	.25	.60
39 Ahman Green	.30	.75
40 Tim Biakabutuka	.20	.50
41 Akili Smith	.20	.50
42 David Boston	.20	.50
43 Eddie George	.30	.75
44 Hines Ward	.30	.75
45 Chad Lewis	.20	.50
46 Brian Urlacher	.40	1.00
47 Eric Moulds	.25	.60
48 Ricky Williams	.30	.75
49 Warrick Dunn	.30	.75
50 Kerry Collins	.25	.60
51 Isaac Bruce	.30	.75
52 Jimmy Smith	.25	.60
53 Emmitt Smith	.75	2.00
54 Cris Carter	.30	.75
55 Jeff Garcia	.25	.60
56 Mike Anderson	.25	.60
57 Lamar Smith	.25	.60
58 Brett Favre	1.00	2.50
59 Steve Beuerlein	.25	.60
60 Terry Glenn	.25	.60
61 Tyrone Wheatley	.25	.60
62 Charlie Batch	.25	.60
63 Chris Chandler	.25	.60
64 Sylvester Morris	.20	.50
65 Joe Horn	.25	.60
66 Kevin Johnson	.20	.50
67 Rob Johnson	.25	.60
68 Jeff George	.25	.60
69 Keyshawn Johnson	.25	.60
70 Wayne Chrebet	.25	.60
71 Randy Moss	.30	.75
72 Marvin Harrison	.30	.75
73 Peter Warrick	.25	.60
74 Darrell Jackson	.25	.60
75 Derrick Mason	.25	.60
76 Oronde Gadsden	.20	.50
77 Charles Johnson	.20	.50
78 James Allen	.20	.50
79 Torry Holt	.25	.60
80 Troy Brown	.25	.60
81 Amani Toomer	.25	.60
82 Junior Seau	.30	.75
83 Troy Aikman	.50	1.25
84 Mark Brunell	.25	.60
85 Brian Griese	.25	.60
86 Charlie Garner	.25	.60
87 Rich Gannon	.25	.60
88 Jeff Blake	.25	.60
89 Donald Hayes	.20	.50
90 Germane Crowell	.20	.50
91 Tony Gonzalez	.30	.75
92 Jon Kitna	.25	.60
93 Vinny Testaverde	.25	.60
94 Kordell Stewart	.25	.60
95 Keenan McCardell	.25	.60
96 Kurt Warner	.50	1.25
97 Bill Schroeder	.25	.60
98 Rod Smith	.25	.60
99 Tim Brown	.30	.75
100 Trent Dilfer	.25	.60
101 Michael Vick RC	2.50	6.00
102 Koren Robinson RC	.50	1.25
103 LaDainian Tomlinson RC	2.00	5.00
104 Todd Heap RC	.60	1.50
105 Correll Buckhalter RC	.60	1.50
106 Freddie Mitchell RC	.40	1.00
107 Josh Booty RC	.50	1.25
108 Chris Chambers RC	.60	1.50
109 Chris Weinke RC	.50	1.25
110 Steve Smith RC	1.25	3.00
111 Travis Minor RC	.50	1.25
112 Ken-Yon Rambo RC	.40	1.00
113 Marques Tuiasosopo RC	.50	1.25
114 Bobby Newcombe RC	.50	1.25
115 Drew Brees RC	4.00	10.00
116 LaMont Jordan RC	.60	1.50
117 Dan Morgan RC	.50	1.25
118 Reggie Wayne RC	1.25	3.00
119 Dan Alexander RC	.50	1.25
120 Alge Crumpler RC	.60	1.50
121 Robert Ferguson RC	.60	1.50
122 Rod Gardner RC	.50	1.25
123 Mike McMahon RC	.50	1.25
124 Kevan Barlow RC	.50	1.25
125 Snoop Minnis RC	.40	1.00
126 Sage Rosenfels RC	.60	1.50
127 Jesse Palmer RC	.50	1.25
128 Michael Bennett RC	.50	1.25
129 Rudi Johnson RC	.60	1.50
130 Deuce McAllister RC	.60	1.50
131 Santana Moss RC	.75	2.00
132 Josh Heupel RC	.60	1.50
133 Quincy Morgan RC	.50	1.25
134 Quincy Carter RC	.50	1.25
135 Anthony Thomas RC	.60	1.50
136 James Jackson RC	.40	1.00
137 Kevin Kasper RC	.40	1.00
138 Alex Bannister RC	.40	1.00
139 David Terrell RC	.50	1.25
140 Chad Johnson RC	1.00	2.50
141 Walter Payton	1.50	4.00
142 Bart Starr	1.25	3.00
143 Sonny Jurgensen	.60	1.50
144 Jim Brown	1.00	2.50
145A Joe Namath HTA (pictured in a Jets jersey)	4.00	10.00
145B Joe Namath RETAIL (pictured in a fur coat)	6.00	15.00
NNO Joe Namath Bucks	1.50	4.00

2001 Topps Gallery Autographs

GROUP A ODDS 1:669HTA
GROUP B ODDS 1:502HTA
GROUP C ODDS 1:668HTA
GROUP D ODDS 1:250HTA
GROUP E ODDS 1:334HTA
OVERALL ODDS 1:84

AB Aaron Brooks E	6.00	15.00
DC Daunte Culpepper A	15.00	40.00
EG Eddie George A	15.00	40.00
JG Jeff Garcia B	8.00	20.00
JL Jamal Lewis B	8.00	20.00
MA Mike Anderson C	6.00	15.00
TB Tim Brown A	20.00	40.00
TD Tim Dwight D	6.00	15.00
WC Wayne Chrebet D	6.00	15.00

2001 Topps Gallery Heritage

COMPLETE SET (9)	7.50	20.00
STATED ODDS 1:12		
GH1 Johnny Unitas	1.50	4.00
GH2 Bart Starr	1.50	4.00
GH3 Y.A. Tittle	1.00	2.50
GH4 Chuck Bednarik	.60	1.50
GH5 Randy Moss	1.25	3.00
GH6 Jerry Rice	1.25	3.00
GH7 Peyton Manning	1.50	4.00
GH8 Brett Favre	2.00	5.00
GH9 Marshall Faulk	.75	2.00

2001 Topps Gallery Heritage Relics

STATED ODDS 1:211		
GRBF Brett Favre	15.00	40.00
GRBS Bart Starr Seat	10.00	25.00
GRFG Frank Gifford Seat	7.50	20.00
GRJR Jerry Rice	12.50	30.00
GRRM Randy Moss	15.00	30.00

2001 Topps Gallery Heritage Relics Autographs

STATED ODDS 1:4166		
GRABF Brett Favre	125.00	250.00
GRABS Bart Starr (stadium seat swatch)	150.00	250.00
GRAFG Frank Gifford (stadium seat swatch)	40.00	80.00
GRAJR Jerry Rice		
GRARM Randy Moss		

2001 Topps Gallery Originals Relics

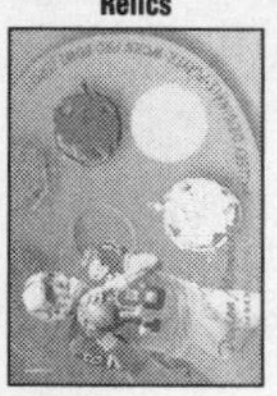

GROUP A ODDS 1:685HTA
GROUP B ODDS 1:668HTA
GROUP C ODDS 1:557HTA
GROUP D ODDS 1:501HTA
GROUP E ODDS 1:76HTA
OVERALL ODDS 1:50

GOCC Cris Carter	8.00	20.00
GOCD Corey Dillon	6.00	15.00
GOCJ Chad Johnson	8.00	20.00
GODA Dan Alexander	6.00	15.00
GOKB Kevan Barlow	6.00	15.00
GOKW Kurt Warner	12.00	30.00
GOPM Peyton Manning	20.00	50.00
GORC Rashard Casey	5.00	12.00
GORG Rod Gardner	6.00	15.00
GOWS Warren Sapp	6.00	15.00

2001 Topps Gallery Star Gallery

COMPLETE SET (10)	5.00	12.00
STATED ODDS 1:8		
SG1 Daunte Culpepper	.40	1.00
SG2 Jamal Lewis	.50	1.25
SG3 Peyton Manning	1.25	3.00
SG4 Edgerrin James	.50	1.25
SG5 Randy Moss	.50	1.25
SG6 Marshall Faulk	.50	1.25
SG7 Mike Anderson	.40	1.00
SG8 Eddie George	.50	1.25
SG9 Donovan McNabb	.50	1.25
SG10 Cris Carter	.50	1.25

2002 Topps Gallery

Released in September, 2002, this set contains 150 veterans and 50 rookies. The Hobby S.R.P. is $3.00/per pack. Each pack contains 5 cards. There were 24 packs per box, eight boxes per case.

COMPLETE SET (200)	25.00	60.00
COMP.SET w/o SP's (150)	15.00	40.00
UNPRICED PRESS PLATE/1 ODDS 1:617		
1 Marshall Faulk	.40	1.00
2 Mark Brunell	.30	.75
3 Jeff Garcia	.30	.75
4 David Terrell	.25	.60
5 Curtis Martin	.40	1.00
6 Terrell Davis	.40	1.00
7 Jake Plummer	.30	.75
8 Eric Moulds	.30	.75
9 Peyton Manning	.75	2.00
10 Hines Ward	.40	1.00
11 Koren Robinson	.25	.60
12 Eddie George	.30	.75
13 Shane Matthews	.25	.60
14 Trent Green	.30	.75
15 Marcus Robinson	.30	.75
16 Michael Vick	.60	1.50
17 Muhsin Muhammad	.30	.75
18 Rocket Ismail	.30	.75
19 Quincy Morgan	.25	.60
20 Mike McMahon	.25	.60
21 Randy Moss	.40	1.00
22 Willie Jackson	.25	.60
23 Freddie Mitchell	.25	.60
24 LaDainian Tomlinson	.50	1.25
25 Warrick Dunn	.30	.75
26 Zach Thomas	.40	1.00
27 Bill Schroeder	.25	.60
28 Jon Kitna	.30	.75
29 Rob Johnson	.30	.75
30 Drew Bledsoe	.40	1.00
31 Ron Dayne	.30	.75
32 Tim Brown	.40	1.00
33 Michael Westbrook	.25	.60
34 Terrell Owens	.40	1.00
35 Santana Moss	.30	.75
36 Edgerrin James	.30	.75
37 Ray Lewis	.40	1.00
38 Chris Weinke	.25	.60
39 Brian Griese	.30	.75
40 Trent Dilfer	.30	.75
41 Jay Fiedler	.30	.75
42 Joe Horn	.30	.75
43 Chad Johnson	.40	1.00
44 Plaxico Burress	.30	.75
45 Trung Canidate	.25	.60
46 Steve McNair	.40	1.00
47 Curtis Conway	.30	.75
48 James Stewart	.25	.60
49 James Jackson	.25	.60
50 Tom Brady	1.00	2.50
51 Emmitt Smith	1.00	2.50
52 Michael Pittman	.30	.75
53 Tony Gonzalez	.40	1.00
54 Daunte Culpepper	.30	.75
55 Michael Strahan	.40	1.00
56 Keyshawn Johnson	.30	.75
57 Marvin Harrison	.40	1.00
58 Brian Urlacher	.40	1.00
59 Jeff Blake	.30	.75
60 Chris Redman	.25	.60
61 James McKnight	.25	.60
62 Jerome Bettis	.40	1.00
63 Shaun Alexander	.30	.75
64 Rod Gardner	.25	.60
65 Jimmy Smith	.30	.75
66 Thomas Jones	.40	1.00
67 Peter Warrick	.30	.75
68 Mike Anderson	.30	.75
69 Ahman Green	.30	.75
70 Amani Toomer	.30	.75
71 Rich Gannon	.30	.75
72 Vinny Testaverde	.30	.75
73 Isaac Bruce	.40	1.00
74 Derrick Mason	.30	.75
75 John Abraham	.30	.75
76 Shannon Sharpe	.40	1.00
77 Quincy Carter	.25	.60
78 Todd Pinkston	.25	.60
79 Drew Brees	.60	1.50
80 Brad Johnson	.30	.75
81 Garrison Hearst	.30	.75
82 Anthony Thomas	.30	.75
83 Brett Favre	1.00	2.50
84 Troy Brown	.30	.75
85 Charlie Garner	.30	.75
86 Kendrell Bell	.25	.60
87 Darrell Jackson	.30	.75
88 Ricky Williams	.30	.75
89 Duce Staley	.30	.75
90 Stephen Davis	.30	.75
91 Dominic Rhodes	.30	.75
92 Travis Henry	.25	.60
93 David Boston	.25	.60
94 Deuce McAllister	.30	.75
95 Ike Hilliard	.30	.75
96 Doug Flutie	.40	1.00
97 Torry Holt	.40	1.00
98 Keenan McCardell	.30	.75
99 Rod Smith	.30	.75
100 Donovan McNabb	.40	1.00
101 Corey Bradford	.25	.60
102 Germane Crowell	.25	.60
103 Michael Bennett	.30	.75
104 Wayne Chrebet	.30	.75
105 Mike Alstott	.30	.75
106 Kevin Dyson	.30	.75
107 Tim Couch	.25	.60
108 Donald Hayes	.25	.60
109 Maurice Smith	.25	.60
110 Snoop Minnis	.25	.60
111 Antowain Smith	.30	.75
112 Kordell Stewart	.30	.75
113 Kurt Warner	.40	1.00
114 Jerry Rice	.75	2.00
115 Aaron Brooks	.30	.75
116 Tiki Barber	.40	1.00
117 Marty Booker	.30	.75
118 Qadry Ismail	.30	.75
119 Peerless Price	.25	.60
120 Marcus Pollard	.25	.60
121 James Allen	.25	.60
122 Junior Seau	.40	1.00
123 Fred Taylor	.30	.75
124 Corey Dillon	.30	.75
125 Lamar Smith	.30	.75
126 Laveranues Coles	.30	.75
127 James Thrash	.30	.75
128 Kevan Barlow	.25	.60
129 Matt Hasselbeck	.40	1.00
130 David Patten	.25	.60
131 Antonio Freeman	.40	1.00
132 Johnnie Morton	.30	.75
133 Priest Holmes	.40	1.00
134 Cris Carter	.40	1.00
135 Kevin Johnson	.25	.60
136 Jim Miller	.25	.60
137 Kerry Collins	.30	.75
138 Joey Galloway	.30	.75
139 Correll Buckhalter	.30	.75
140 Chris Chambers	.30	.75
141 Travis Taylor	.25	.60
142 Ed McCaffrey	.30	.75
143 J.J. Stokes	.25	.60
144 Reggie Wayne	.40	1.00
145 Az-Zahir Hakim	.25	.60
146 Tim Dwight	.25	.60
147 Jevon Kearse	.30	.75
148 Jamal Lewis	.30	.75
149 Warren Sapp	.30	.75
150 Jermaine Lewis	.25	.60
151 William Green RC	.50	1.25
152 Roy Williams RC	.60	1.50
153 Kurt Kittner RC	.40	1.00
154 Daniel Graham RC	.50	1.25
155 Andre Davis RC	.50	1.25
156 Donte Stallworth RC	.60	1.50
157 Josh Reed RC	.50	1.25
158 Rohan Davey RC	.60	1.50
159 Wendell Bryant RC	.40	1.00
160 Lito Sheppard RC	.60	1.50
161 Najeh Davenport RC	.60	1.50
162 Freddie Milons RC	.40	1.00
163 Patrick Ramsey RC	.60	1.50
164 Luke Staley RC	.40	1.00
165 Maurice Morris RC	.50	1.25
166 Dwight Freeney RC	.75	2.00
167 Jeremy Shockey RC	1.00	2.50
168 Jabar Gaffney RC	.60	1.50
169 DeShaun Foster RC	.60	1.50
170 Chad Hutchinson RC	.40	1.00
171 Tim Carter RC	.50	1.25
172 Napoleon Harris RC	.50	1.25
173 Kahlil Hill RC	.40	1.00
174 Josh McCown RC	.60	1.50
175 Ron Johnson RC	.50	1.25
176 Marquise Walker RC	.40	1.00
177 Joey Harrington RC	.60	1.50
178 Travis Stephens RC	.40	1.00
179 Julius Peppers RC	1.25	3.00
180 Ryan Sims RC	.60	1.50
181 Albert Haynesworth RC	.60	1.50
182 Phillip Buchanon RC	.60	1.50
183 Jonathan Wells RC	.60	1.50
184 Chester Taylor RC	.60	1.50
185 Antonio Bryant RC	.60	1.50
186 Adrian Peterson RC	.60	1.50
187 Clinton Portis RC	.75	2.00
188 Lamar Gordon RC	.50	1.25
189 Reche Caldwell RC	.60	1.50
190 Ashley Lelie RC	.50	1.25
191 T.J. Duckett RC	.60	1.50
192 Eric Crouch RC	.60	1.50
193 David Garrard RC	.75	2.00
194 Quentin Jammer RC	.60	1.50
195 Ladell Betts RC	.60	1.50
196 Antwaan Randle El RC	.60	1.50
197 Cliff Russell RC	.40	1.00
198 Javon Walker RC	.60	1.50
199 John Henderson RC	.50	1.25
200 David Carr RC	.60	1.50

2002 Topps Gallery Rookie Variations

*VARIATIONS: 1X TO 2.5X BASIC CARDS
STATED ODDS 1:12 HOB/RET

2002 Topps Gallery Autographs

GROUP A STATED ODDS 1:3281H, 1:3283R
GROUP B STATED ODDS 1:155 HOB/RET
*ART.PROOF/100: .6X TO 1.5X BASIC AU
ART.PROOF/100 ODDS 1:550 H, 1:551 R
AP PRINT RUN 100 SER.#'d SETS

GAB Aaron Brooks B	8.00	20.00
GAT Anthony Thomas B	8.00	20.00
GCC Chris Chambers B	8.00	20.00
GDS Duce Staley B	8.00	20.00
GHW Hines Ward B	30.00	60.00
GJA John Abraham B	8.00	20.00
GKB Kendrell Bell B	6.00	15.00
GMB Marty Booker B	8.00	20.00
GTB Tom Brady A	150.00	250.00

2002 Topps Gallery Heritage

STATED ODDS 1:12		
NAMATH AU STATED ODDS 1:18701		
GHBF Brett Favre	2.50	6.00
GHCD Corey Dillon	.75	2.00
GHDC Daunte Culpepper	.75	2.00
GHDM Dan Marino	3.00	8.00
GHDMC Donovan McNabb	1.00	2.50
GHEJ Edgerrin James	.75	2.00
GHES Emmitt Smith	2.50	6.00
GHJL Jamal Lewis	.75	2.00
GHJM Joe Montana	3.00	8.00
GHJN Joe Namath	2.00	5.00
GHJR Jerry Rice	2.00	5.00
GHKW Kurt Warner	1.00	2.50
GHMJ Marshall Faulk	1.00	2.50
GHMV Michael Vick	1.50	4.00
GHPM Peyton Manning	2.00	5.00
GHRM Randy Moss	1.00	2.50
GHTB Terry Bradshaw	2.00	5.00
GHTBR Tom Brady	2.50	6.00
GHAJN Joe Namath AU/25*	60.00	120.00

2002 Topps Gallery Heritage Relics

STATED ODDS 1:198 HOB/RET		
GHRBF Brett Favre	20.00	50.00
GHRCD Corey Dillon	6.00	15.00
GHRDM Dan Marino	25.00	60.00
GHREJ Edgerrin James	6.00	15.00
GHRES Emmitt Smith	20.00	50.00
GHRJM Joe Montana	25.00	60.00
GHRJN Joe Namath	15.00	40.00
GHRJR Jerry Rice	15.00	40.00
GHRKW Kurt Warner	8.00	20.00
GHRMF Marshall Faulk	8.00	20.00

2002 Topps Gallery Originals Relics

GROUP A ODDS 1:66 HOB/RET
GROUP B ODDS 1:82 HOB, 1:83 RET

GOAL Ashley Lelie B	5.00	12.00
GOBU Brian Urlacher A	6.00	15.00
GOCC Cris Carter A	6.00	15.00
GOCCH Chris Chambers A	5.00	12.00
GODB Drew Brees A	10.00	25.00
GODC David Carr B	6.00	15.00
GOEG Eddie George A	5.00	12.00
GOFT Fred Taylor A		
GOJG Jeff Garcia A	5.00	12.00
GOJS Jimmy Smith A	5.00	12.00
GOKJ Keyshawn Johnson A	5.00	12.00
GOLT LaDainian Tomlinson A	8.00	20.00
GORD Rohan Davey B	6.00	15.00
GORJ Ron Johnson B	5.00	12.00
GOSD Stephen Davis A	5.00	12.00
GOSM Steve McNair A	6.00	15.00
GOTB Tim Brown A	6.00	15.00
GOTO Terrell Owens A	6.00	15.00
GOTS Travis Stephens B	4.00	10.00
GOWS Warren Sapp A	5.00	12.00

1996 Topps Gilt Edge

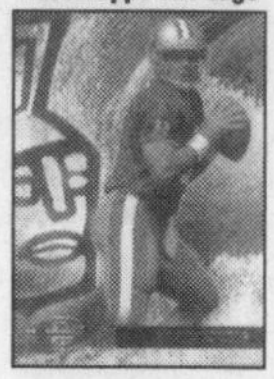

The 1996 Topps Gilt Edge set was issued in one series. This 90-card standard-size set was released in April 1996 and features the 84 members of the 1996 Pro Bowl roster, plus five players who had Pro Bowl-caliber seasons and one checklist card. Each card features Topps' new "gilt-edge" technology, placing gold foil edging around every card. The cards were issued in nine-card packs with a suggested retail price of $3.50 which included seven regular cards, a platinum card as well as a definitive edge card. Each case consisted of six boxes with 20 packs in each box. There are no Rookie Cards in this set.

COMPLETE SET (90)	6.00	15.00
1 Brett Favre	1.00	2.50
2 Kevin Glover	.02	.10
3 Nate Newton	.02	.10
4 Randall McDaniel	.05	.15
5 William Roaf	.02	.10
6 Lomas Brown	.02	.10
7 Jay Novacek	.02	.10
8 Emmitt Smith	.75	2.00
9 Barry Sanders	.75	2.00
10 Jerry Rice	.50	1.25
11 Herman Moore	.08	.25
12 Larry Centers	.08	.25
13 Chester McGlockton	.02	.10
14 Dan Saleaumua	.02	.10
15 Bruce Smith	.08	.25
16 Neil Smith	.08	.25
17 Junior Seau	.20	.50
18 Bryce Paup	.02	.10
19 Greg Lloyd	.08	.25
20 Terry McDaniel	.02	.10
21 Dale Carter	.02	.10
22 Carnell Lake	.02	.10
23 Steve Atwater	.02	.10
24 Elbert Shelley	.02	.10
25 Brian Mitchell	.02	.10
26 Jeff Feagles	.02	.10
27 Morten Andersen	.02	.10
28 Dan Marino	1.00	2.50
29 Dermontti Dawson	.02	.10
30 Steve Wisniewski	.02	.10
31 Bruce Matthews	.02	.10
32 Bruce Armstrong	.02	.10
33 Richmond Webb	.02	.10
34 Ben Coates	.08	.25
35 Marshall Faulk	.25	.60
36 Chris Warren	.08	.25
37 Carl Pickens	.08	.25
38 Tim Brown	.20	.50
39 Kimble Anders	.08	.25
40 John Randle	.08	.25
41 Eric Swann	.02	.10
42 Reggie White	.20	.50
43 Charles Haley	.08	.25
44 Ken Norton	.02	.10
45 Lee Woodall	.02	.10
46 Ken Harvey	.02	.10
47 Aeneas Williams	.02	.10
48 Eric Davis	.02	.10
49 Darren Woodson	.08	.25
50 Merton Hanks	.02	.10
51 Steve Tasker	.02	.10
52 Glyn Milburn	.02	.10
53 Jason Elam	.08	.25
54 Darren Bennett	.02	.10
55 Steve Young	.40	1.00
56 Bart Oates	.02	.10
57 Larry Allen	.02	.10
58 Mark Tuinei	.02	.10
59 Mark Chmura	.08	.25
60 Michael Irvin	.20	.50
61 Ricky Watters	.08	.25
62 Cortez Kennedy	.02	.10
63 Leslie O'Neal	.02	.10
64 Bryan Cox	.02	.10
65 Derrick Thomas	.20	.50
66 Darryll Lewis	.02	.10
67 Blaine Bishop	.02	.10
68 Dana Stubblefield	.08	.25
69 William Fuller	.02	.10
70 Jessie Tuggle	.02	.10
71 William Thomas	.02	.10
72 Eric Allen	.02	.10
73 Tim McDonald	.02	.10
74 Jim Harbaugh	.08	.25
75 Mark Stepnoski	.02	.10
76 Keith Sims	.02	.10
77 Gary Zimmerman	.02	.10
78 Shannon Sharpe	.08	.25
79 Anthony Miller	.08	.25
80 Curtis Martin	.40	1.00
81 Troy Aikman	.50	1.25
82 Cris Carter	.20	.50
83 Jeff Blake	.20	.50
84 Yancey Thigpen	.08	.25
85 Isaac Bruce	.20	.50
86 Sam Mills	.02	.10
87 Terrell Davis	.40	1.00
88 Larry Brown	.02	.10
89 Joey Galloway	.20	.50
90 Checklist	.02	.10

1996 Topps Gilt Edge Platinum

COMPLETE SET (90)	20.00	50.00
*PLATINUM: 1X TO 2.5X BASIC CARDS		
ONE PLATINUM PER PACK		

1996 Topps Gilt Edge Definitive Edge

COMPLETE SET (15)	10.00	25.00
STATED ODDS 1:4		
1 Bruce Smith	.30	.75
2 Brett Favre	3.00	8.00
3 Marcus Allen	.60	1.50
4 Junior Seau	.60	1.50
5 Deion Sanders	.60	1.50
6 Jerry Rice	1.50	4.00
7 Steve Young	1.25	3.00
8 Drew Bledsoe	1.25	3.00
9 Michael Irvin	.60	1.50
10 Reggie White	.60	1.50
11 Dan Marino	3.00	8.00
12 John Alt	.10	.30
13 Barry Sanders	2.50	6.00
14 Orlando Thomas	.10	.30
15 Kordell Stewart	.60	1.50

1998 Topps Gold Label Class 1

The 1998 Topps Gold Label set was printed on a prismatic 35 pt. Spectra-reflective rainbow stock and are gold foiled-stamped with the player's name and the Gold Label logo. In the foreground of each card is found a photo of a league standout with the background featuring quarterbacks passing and defensive players tackling. The backs carry career statistics and an insightful player commentary. Two parallel background variations for this set were also produced with the quarterbacks running (Class 2) and handing off the ball (Class 3) and defensive players running (Class 2) and pictured set before the snap (Class 3).

COMP.GOLD CLASS 1 (100)	30.00	60.00
1 John Elway	2.00	5.00
2 Rob Moore	.30	.75
3 Jamal Anderson	.50	1.25
4 Pat Johnson RC	1.00	2.50
5 Troy Aikman	1.00	2.50
6 Antowain Smith	.50	1.25
7 Wesley Walls	.30	.75
8 Curtis Enis RC	.60	1.50
9 Jimmy Smith	.30	.75
10 Terrell Davis	.50	1.25
11 Marshall Faulk	.60	1.50
12 Germane Crowell RC	1.00	2.50
13 Marcus Nash RC	.60	1.50
14 Deion Sanders	.50	1.25
15 Dorsey Levens	.50	1.25
16 Corey Dillon	.50	1.25
17 Fred Taylor RC	2.00	5.00
18 Derrick Thomas	.50	1.25
19 Kevin Dyson RC	1.25	3.00
20 Peyton Manning RC	10.00	25.00
21 Warren Sapp	.30	.75
22 Robert Holcombe RC	1.00	2.50
23 Joey Galloway	.30	.75
24 Garrison Hearst	.50	1.25
25 Brett Favre	2.00	5.00
26 Aeneas Williams	.20	.50
27 Danny Kanell	.30	.75
28 Robert Smith	.50	1.25
29 Brad Johnson	.50	1.25
30 Dan Marino	2.00	5.00
31 Elvis Grbac	.30	.75
32 Terry Allen	.50	1.25
33 Frank Sanders	.30	.75
34 Peter Boulware	.20	.50
35 Tim Brown	.50	1.25
36 Keyshawn Johnson	.50	1.25
37 Rae Carruth	.20	.50
38 Michael Irvin	.50	1.25
39 Brian Griese RC	2.00	6.00
40 Kordell Stewart	.50	1.25
41 Johnnie Morton	.30	.75
42 Robert Brooks	.30	.75
43 Keenan McCardell	.30	.75
44 Ben Coates	.30	.75
45 Jerry Rice	1.00	2.50
46 Tony Simmons RC	1.00	2.50
47 Irving Fryar	.30	.75
48 Jerome Pathon RC	1.25	3.00
49 Steve McNair	.50	1.25
50 Warrick Dunn	.50	1.25
51 Skip Hicks RC	1.00	2.50
52 Andre Wadsworth RC	1.00	2.50
53 Chris Chandler	.30	.75
54 Curtis Conway	.30	.75
55 Eddie George	.50	1.25
56 Jeff Blake	.30	.75
57 Greg Ellis RC	.60	1.50
58 Scott Mitchell	.30	.75
59 Antonio Freeman	.50	1.25
60 Drew Bledsoe	.75	2.00
61 Mark Brunell	.50	1.25
62 Andre Rison	.30	.75
63 Cris Carter	.50	1.25
64 Jake Reed	.30	.75
65 Napoleon Kaufman	.50	1.25
66 Terry Glenn	.50	1.25
67 Jason Sehorn	.30	.75
68 Rickey Dudley	.20	.50
69 Junior Seau	.50	1.25
70 Jerome Bettis	.50	1.25
71 Curtis Martin	.50	1.25
72 Warren Moon	.50	1.25
73 Isaac Bruce	.50	1.25
74 Mike Alstott	.50	1.25
75 Steve Young	.60	1.50
76 Jacquez Green RC	1.00	2.50
77 Gus Frerotte	.20	.50
78 Michael Jackson	.20	.50
79 Carl Pickens	.50	1.25
80 Bruce Smith	.30	.75
81 Shannon Sharpe	.30	.75
82 Herman Moore	.30	.75

83 Reggie White	.50	1.25
84 Marvin Harrison	.50	1.25
85 Jake Plummer	.50	1.25
86 Karim Abdul-Jabbar	.50	1.25
87 John Randle	.30	.75
88 Robert Edwards RC	1.00	2.50
89 Jeff George	.30	.75
90 Emmitt Smith	1.50	4.00
91 Terrell Owens	.50	1.25
92 Trent Dilfer	.50	1.25
93 Darrell Green	.30	.75
94 Andre Reed	.30	.75
95 Ryan Leaf RC	1.25	3.00
96 Rod Smith WR	.30	.75
97 O.J. McDuffie	.30	.75
98 John Avery RC	1.00	2.50
99 Charles Way	.20	.50
100 Barry Sanders	1.50	4.00

1998 Topps Gold Label Class 1 Black

COMPLETE SET (100)	200.00	400.00
*STARS: 2X TO 5X GOLD CLASS 1		
*ROOKIES: 1X TO 2X GOLD CLASS 1		
STATED ODDS 1:8		

1998 Topps Gold Label Class 1 Red

*STARS: 15X TO 40X GOLD CLASS 1
*ROOKIES: 4X TO 10X GOLD CLASS 1
RED/100 STATED ODDS 1:94

1998 Topps Gold Label Class 2

COMP.CLASS 2 GOLD (100)	75.00	150.00
*STARS: .8X TO 2X GOLD CLASS 1		
*ROOKIES: .6X TO 1.2X GOLD CLASS 1		
GOLD CLASS 2 STATED ODDS 1:2		

1998 Topps Gold Label Class 2 Black

COMPLETE SET (100)	300.00	600.00
*STARS: 4X TO 10X GOLD CLASS 1		
*ROOKIES: 1.2X TO 3X GOLD CLASS 1		
STATED ODDS 1:16		

1998 Topps Gold Label Class 2 Red

*STARS: 15X TO 40X GOLD CLASS 1
*ROOKIES: 5X TO 12X GOLD CLASS 1
STATED ODDS 1:187
STATED PRINT RUN 50 SER.#'d SETS

1998 Topps Gold Label Class 3

COMP.CLASS 3 GOLD (100)	125.00	250.00
*STARS: 1.5X TO 3X GOLD CLASS 1		
*ROOKIES: .75X TO 1.5X GOLD CLASS 1		
GOLD CLASS 3 STATED ODDS 1:4		

1998 Topps Gold Label Class 3 Black

*STARS: 6X TO 15X GOLD CLASS 1
*ROOKIES: 2X TO 5X GOLD CLASS 1
STATED ODDS 1:32

1998 Topps Gold Label Class 3 Red

*STARS: 50X TO 120X GOLD CLASS 1		
*ROOKIES: 10X TO 25X GOLD CLASS 1		
STATED ODDS 1:375		
STATED PRINT RUN 25 SER.#'d SETS		
20 Peyton Manning	300.00	600.00

1999 Topps Gold Label Class 1

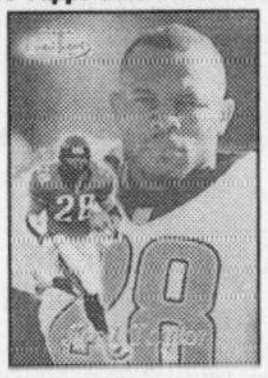

This 100 card standard-size set was issued in five card packs. A large number of parallels were issued and randomly inserted. Key Rookie Cards included Donovan McNabb, Edgerrin James, and Ricky Williams.

COMPLETE SET (100)	25.00	60.00
1 Terrell Davis	.40	1.00
2 Jake Plummer	.30	.75
3 Mike Cloud RC	.30	.75
4 D'Wayne Bates RC	.30	.75
5 Jamal Anderson	.30	.75
6 Cecil Collins RC	.30	.75
7 Keyshawn Johnson	.30	.75
8 Jerome Bettis	.40	1.00
9 Ricky Watters	.30	.75
10 Brett Favre	1.25	3.00
11 Joe Germaine RC	.40	1.00
12 Eddie George	.30	.75
13 Jevon Kearse RC	.50	1.25
14 Skip Hicks	.25	.60
15 James Johnson RC	.30	.75
16 Terry Glenn	.30	.75
17 Troy Edwards RC	.40	1.00
18 Karsten Bailey RC	.30	.75
19 Trent Dilfer	.30	.75
20 Barry Sanders	1.00	2.50
21 Vinny Testaverde	.30	.75
22 Ed McCaffrey	.30	.75
23 Shannon Sharpe	.40	1.00
24 Robert Smith	.30	.75
25 Emmitt Smith	1.00	2.50
26 Rob Moore	.25	.60
27 J.J. Stokes	.25	.60
28 Champ Bailey RC	1.00	2.50
29 Napoleon Kaufman	.25	.60
30 Fred Taylor	.30	.75
31 Corey Dillon	.30	.75
32 Sedrick Irvin RC	.30	.75
33 Chris McAlister RC	.40	1.00
34 Warrick Dunn	.30	.75
35 Isaac Bruce	.40	1.00
36 Peerless Price RC	.40	1.00
37 Dorsey Levens	.30	.75
38 Wayne Chrebet	.30	.75
39 Randall Cunningham	.40	1.00
40 Dan Marino	1.25	3.00
41 Chris Chandler	.30	.75
42 Mark Brunell	.30	.75
43 Kevin Johnson RC	.40	1.00
44 Natrone Means	.30	.75
45 Jerome Pathon	.25	.60
46 Daunte Culpepper RC	.50	1.25
47 Akili Smith RC	.40	1.00
48 Keenan McCardell	.30	.75
49 Steve McNair	.40	1.00
50 Randy Moss	.40	1.00
51 Terance Mathis	.25	.60
52 Eric Moulds	.30	.75
53 Rocket Ismail	.30	.75
54 Cade McNown RC	.40	1.00
55 Kordell Stewart	.30	.75
56 Rob Konrad RC	.30	.75
57 Andre Rison	.30	.75
58 Curtis Conway	.30	.75
59 Chris Claiborne RC	.30	.75
60 Jerry Rice	.75	2.00
61 Peyton Manning	1.25	3.00
62 Jimmy Smith	.30	.75
63 Doug Flutie	.40	1.00
64 Frank Sanders	.25	.60
65 Antowain Smith	.25	.60
66 Curtis Enis	.25	.60
67 Charlie Batch	.30	.75
68 Marvin Harrison	.40	1.00
69 Garrison Hearst	.30	.75
70 Ricky Williams RC	.75	2.00
71 Torry Holt RC	.75	2.00
72 Mike Alstott	.40	1.00
73 Drew Bledsoe	.40	1.00
74 O.J. McDuffie	.30	.75
75 Donovan McNabb RC	2.50	6.00
76 Curtis Martin	.40	1.00
77 Priest Holmes	.40	1.00
78 Antonio Freeman	.30	.75
79 Herman Moore	.30	.75
80 Tim Couch RC	.50	1.25
81 Troy Aikman	.60	1.50
82 David Boston RC	.40	1.00
83 Tim Brown	.40	1.00
84 Kevin Faulk RC	.50	1.25
85 Cris Carter	.40	1.00
86 Marshall Faulk	.40	1.00
87 Shaun King RC	.40	1.00
88 Terrell Owens	.40	1.00
89 Carl Pickens	.30	.75
90 Steve Young	.50	1.25
91 Rod Smith	.30	.75
92 Michael Irvin	.40	1.00
93 Ike Hilliard	.30	.75
94 Jon Kitna	.30	.75
95 Brock Huard RC	.40	1.00
96 Joey Galloway	.30	.75
97 Amos Zereoue RC	.40	1.00
98 Duce Staley	.30	.75
99 John Elway	1.25	3.00
100 Edgerrin James RC	.60	1.50

1999 Topps Gold Label Class 1 One to One

OVERALL ONE TO ONE STATED ODDS 1:839
NOT PRICED DUE TO SCARCITY

1999 Topps Gold Label Class 1 Black

COMPLETE SET (100)	100.00	200.00
*BLACK 1 VETS: 1.2X TO 3X CLASS 1		
*BLACK 1 ROOKIES: 1X TO 2.5X CLS 1		
BLACK CLASS 1 ODDS 1:8		

1999 Topps Gold Label Class 1 Red

COMPLETE SET (100)	500.00	1,000.00
*RED 1 VETS: 6X TO 15X CLASS 1		
*RED 1 ROOKIES: 5X TO 12X CLS 1		
CLASS 1 RED/100 ODDS 1:79		

1999 Topps Gold Label Class 2

COMPLETE SET (100)	75.00	150.00
*CLASS 2 VETS: .6X TO 1.5X CLASS 1		
*CLASS 2 ROOKIES: .5X TO 1.2X CLS 1		
CLASS 2 STATED ODDS 1:2		

1999 Topps Gold Label Class 2 One to One

OVERALL ONE TO ONE STATED ODDS 1:839
NOT PRICED DUE TO SCARCITY

1999 Topps Gold Label Class 2 Black

*BLACK 2 VETS: 2X TO 5X CLASS 1
*BLACK 2 ROOKIES: 1.5X TO 4X CLS 1
BLACK CLASS 2 ODDS 1:16

1999 Topps Gold Label Class 2 Red

*RED 2 VETS: 8X TO 20X CLASS 1
*RED 2 ROOKIES: 3X TO 15X CLS 1
CLASS 2 RED/50 ODDS 1:157
STATED PRINT RUN 50 SER.#'d SETS

1999 Topps Gold Label Class 3

COMPLETE SET (100)	125.00	250.00
*CLASS 3 VETS: 1X TO 2.5X CLASS 1		
*CLASS 3 ROOKIES: .8X TO 2X CLS 1		
CLASS 3 STATED ODDS 1:4		

1999 Topps Gold Label Class 3 One to One

OVERALL ONE TO ONE STATED ODDS 1:839
NOT PRICED DUE TO SCARCITY

1999 Topps Gold Label Class 3 Black

*BLACK 3 VETS: 2.5X TO 6X CLASS 1
*BLACK 3 ROOKIES: 2X TO 5X CLS 1
BLACK CLASS 3 ODDS 1:32

1999 Topps Gold Label Class 3 Red

*RED 3 VETS: 12X TO 30X CLASS 1
*RED 3 ROOKIES: 10X TO 25X CLS 1
STATED PRINT RUN 25 SER.#'d SETS
CLASS 3 RED/25 ODDS 1:314

1999 Topps Gold Label Race to Gold

COMP.GOLD SET (15)	20.00	50.00
GOLD LABEL STATED ODDS 1:12		
*BLACK LABEL: .8X TO 2X GOLD LABEL		
BLACK LABEL STATED ODDS 1:48		
*R1-R5 RED LABELS: 15X TO 35X GOLDS		
R1-R5 RED LABEL PRINT RUN 13 SER.#'d SETS		
R1-R5 RED LABEL STATED ODDS 1:11,867		
*R6-R10 RED LABELS: 7X TO 20X GOLDS		
R6-R10 RED LAB.PRINT RUN 34 SER.#'d SETS		
R6-R10 RED LABEL STATED ODDS 1:4638		
*R11-R15 RED LABELS: 3X TO 8X GOLDS		
R11-R15 RED LAB.PRINT RUN 80 SER.#'d SETS		
R11-R15 RED LABEL STATED ODDS 1:1968		
R1 Brett Favre	5.00	12.00
R2 Peyton Manning	5.00	12.00
R3 Drew Bledsoe	2.00	5.00
R4 Randall Cunningham	1.50	4.00
R5 Jake Plummer	1.00	2.50
R6 Emmitt Smith	3.00	8.00
R7 Terrell Davis	1.50	4.00
R8 Barry Sanders	5.00	12.00
R9 Eddie George	1.50	4.00
R10 Curtis Martin	1.50	4.00
R11 Antonio Freeman	1.50	4.00
R12 Eric Moulds	1.50	4.00
R13 Joey Galloway	1.00	2.50
R14 Rod Smith	1.00	2.50
R15 Randy Moss	4.00	10.00

2000 Topps Gold Label Class 1

Released in late October, Gold Label Features a 100-card set divided up into 80 veteran cards and 20 rookie cards. Base card stock is thick foilboard with two photos of each player; one close up, and a smaller action shot in the corner. Each card has a divider through the middle running from the top left corner to the bottom right corner stating which class each card is in. Gold Label was packaged in 24-pack boxes with packs containing five cards and carried a suggested retail price of $5.00.

COMPLETE SET (100)	15.00	40.00
1 Eric Moulds	.25	.60
2 Muhsin Muhammad	.25	.60
3 Patrick Jeffers	.25	.60
4 Joey Galloway	.25	.60
5 Edgerrin James	.30	.75
6 Germane Crowell	.20	.50
7 Ed McCaffrey	.25	.60
8 Dorsey Levens	.25	.60
9 Marcus Robinson	.25	.60
10 Tony Gonzalez	.30	.75
11 Robert Smith		
12 Rich Gannon	.25	.60
13 Jerry Rice	.60	1.50
14 Mike Alstott	.30	.75
15 Brad Johnson	.25	.60
16 Emmitt Smith	.75	2.00
17 Marvin Harrison	.30	.75
18 Duce Staley	.25	.60
19 Terry Glenn	.25	.60
20 Terrell Owens	.30	.75
21 Antonio Freeman	.25	.60
22 Curtis Enis	.20	.50
23 Michael Westbrook	.20	.50
24 Cris Carter	.30	.75
25 Tim Brown	.30	.75
26 Terrell Davis	.30	.75
27 Fred Taylor	.30	.75
28 Amani Toomer	.25	.60
29 Donovan McNabb	.30	.75
30 Charlie Garner	.25	.60
31 Kurt Warner	.50	1.25
32 Antowain Smith	.25	.60
33 Torry Holt	.30	.75
34 Jake Plummer	.25	.60
35 Steve Beuerlein	.25	.60
36 Rocket Ismail	.25	.60
37 Brett Favre	1.00	2.50
38 Mark Brunell	.25	.60
39 Qadry Ismail	.25	.60
40 Carl Pickens	.25	.60
41 James Stewart	.20	.50
42 Drew Bledsoe	.30	.75
43 Keenan McCardell	.25	.60
44 Jerome Bettis	.30	.75
45 Jon Kitna	.25	.60
46 Warrick Dunn	.25	.60
47 Jevon Kearse	.25	.60
48 Jamal Anderson	.25	.60
49 Shaun King	.20	.50
50 Ricky Williams	.30	.75
51 Elvis Grbac	.20	.50
52 Corey Dillon	.25	.60
53 Brian Griese	.25	.60
54 Steve Young	.40	1.00
55 Tyrone Wheatley	.20	.50
56 Daunte Culpepper	.25	.60
57 Troy Aikman	.50	1.25
58 Peyton Manning	.75	2.00
59 Stephen Davis	.25	.60
60 Keyshawn Johnson	.25	.60
61 Doug Flutie	.30	.75
62 Yancey Thigpen	.20	.50
63 Jeff Blake	.25	.60
64 Tony Banks	.20	.50
65 Tim Couch	.25	.60
66 Charlie Batch	.25	.60
67 Rob Johnson	.25	.60
68 Cade McNown	.20	.50
69 Steve McNair	.30	.75
70 Eddie George	.25	.60
71 Isaac Bruce	.30	.75
72 Ricky Watters	.25	.60
73 Kordell Stewart	.25	.60
74 Wayne Chrebet	.25	.60
75 Curtis Martin	.30	.75
76 Jimmy Smith	.25	.60
77 Randy Moss	.30	.75
78 Akili Smith	.20	.50
79 Marshall Faulk	.30	.75
80 Kerry Collins	.25	.60
81 Ron Dayne RC	.40	1.00
82 Chad Pennington RC	.60	1.50
83 Sylvester Morris RC	.25	.60
84 Thomas Jones RC	.50	1.25
85 Shaun Alexander RC	.50	1.25
86 Chris Redman RC	.30	.75
87 Courtney Brown RC	.30	.75
88 Jerry Porter RC	.40	1.00
89 Ron Dugans RC	.25	.60
90 Jamal Lewis RC	.40	1.00
91 Travis Prentice RC	.30	.75
92 Travis Taylor RC	.30	.75
93 R.Jay Soward RC	.25	.60
94 Peter Warrick RC	.40	1.00
95 Trung Canidate RC	.30	.75
96 Tee Martin RC	.40	1.00
97 Bubba Franks RC	.40	1.00
98 Plaxico Burress RC	.40	1.00
99 J.R. Redmond RC	.25	.60
100 Dennis Northcutt RC	.30	.75

2000 Topps Gold Label Class 2

COMPLETE SET (100)	15.00	40.00
*CLASS 2: SAME VALUE AS CLASS 1		

2000 Topps Gold Label Class 3

COMPLETE SET (100)	15.00	40.00
*CLASS 3: SAME VALUE AS CLASS 1		

2000 Topps Gold Label Premium Parallel

COMPLETE SET (100)	125.00	250.00
*1-80 PREMIUM VETS: 2.5X TO 6X CLASS 1		
*81-100 PREMIUM ROOKIES: 2X TO 5X		
PREMIUM PRINT RUN 1000 SER.#'d SETS		

2000 Topps Gold Label After Burners

COMPLETE SET (14)	20.00	40.00
STATED ODDS 1:23		
UNPRICED 1/1 ISSUED		
A1 Brett Favre	5.00	12.00
A2 Corey Dillon	1.25	3.00
A3 Drew Bledsoe	1.50	4.00
A4 Cris Carter	1.50	4.00
A5 Jimmy Smith	1.25	3.00
A6 Edgerrin James	1.50	4.00
A7 Fred Taylor	1.50	4.00
A8 Tim Brown	1.50	4.00
A9 Marshall Faulk	1.50	4.00
A10 Steve Beuerlein	1.25	3.00
A11 Antonio Freeman	1.25	3.00
A12 Peyton Manning	4.00	10.00
A13 Mike Alstott	1.50	4.00
A14 Mark Brunell	1.25	3.00

2000 Topps Gold Label Bullion

COMPLETE SET (10)	25.00	50.00
STATED ODDS 1:32		
UNPRICED 1/1 ISSUED		
B1 Daunte Culpepper	1.25	3.00
Randy Moss		
Cris Carter		
B2 Edgerrin James	3.00	8.00
Peyton Manning		
Marvin Harrison		
B3 Brad Johnson	1.00	2.50
Stephen Davis		
Michael Westbrook		
B4 Fred Taylor	1.25	3.00
Mark Brunell		
Jimmy Smith		
B5 Emmitt Smith	3.00	8.00
Troy Aikman		
Joey Galloway		
B6 Akili Smith	1.25	3.00
Corey Dillon		
Peter Warrick		
B7 Marshall Faulk	2.00	5.00
Kurt Warner		
Isaac Bruce		
B8 Steve McNair	1.25	3.00
Eddie George		
Jevon Kearse		
B9 Warren Sapp	1.00	2.50
Shaun King		
Keyshawn Johnson		
B10 Dorsey Levens	4.00	10.00
Brett Favre		
Antonio Freeman		

2000 Topps Gold Label Graceful Giants

COMPLETE SET (20)	25.00	50.00
STATED ODDS 1:16		
UNPRICED 1/1 ISSUED		
G1 Eddie George	1.00	2.50
G2 Randy Moss	1.25	3.00
G3 Keyshawn Johnson	1.00	2.50
G4 Warrick Dunn	1.00	2.50
G5 Jevon Kearse	1.00	2.50
G6 Sylvester Morris	.75	2.00
G7 Ron Dayne	1.25	3.00
G8 Wayne Chrebet	1.00	2.50
G9 Steve McNair	1.25	3.00
G10 Courtney Brown	1.00	2.50
G11 Jacquez Green	.75	2.00
G12 Daunte Culpepper	1.00	2.50
G13 Tony Gonzalez	1.25	3.00
G14 Mike Alstott	1.25	3.00
G15 Plaxico Burress	1.25	3.00
G16 Drew Bledsoe	1.25	3.00
G17 Travis Prentice	1.00	2.50
G18 Jerome Bettis	1.25	3.00
G19 Ricky Williams	1.25	3.00
G20 Jamal Lewis	1.25	3.00

2000 Topps Gold Label Holiday Match-Ups Fall

COMPLETE SET (14)	20.00	40.00
STATED ODDS 1:6		
UNPRICED 1/1 ISSUED		
T1 Randy Moss	1.50	4.00
Troy Aikman		
T2 Drew Bledsoe	1.00	2.50
Germane Crowell		
T3 Chris Chandler	1.00	2.50
Tim Brown		
T4 Rob Johnson	1.00	2.50
Mike Alstott		
T5 Cade McNown	.75	2.00
Wayne Chrebet		
T6 Courtney Brown	1.00	2.50
Jamal Lewis		
T7 Terrell Davis	1.00	2.50
Jon Kitna		
T8 Tony Gonzalez	1.00	2.50
Junior Seau		
T9 Zach Thomas	2.50	6.00
Peyton Manning		
T10 Ricky Williams	1.00	2.50
Marshall Faulk		
T11 Duce Staley	.75	2.00
Brad Johnson		
T12 Jerome Bettis	1.00	2.50
Corey Dillon		
T13 Steve McNair	1.00	2.50
Mark Brunell		
T14 Ron Dayne	1.00	2.50
Thomas Jones		

2000 Topps Gold Label Holiday Match-Ups Winter

COMPLETE SET (14)	15.00	30.00
STATED ODDS 1:6		
UNPRICED 1/1 ISSUED		
C1 Jimmy Smith	.75	2.00
Kerry Collins		
C2 Charlie Garner	.75	2.00
Ed McCaffrey		
C3 Antowain Smith	1.25	3.00
Shaun Alexander		
C4 Jake Plummer	.75	2.00
Michael Westbrook		
C5 Steve Beuerlein	.75	2.00
Rich Gannon		
C6 Curtis Enis	.75	2.00
Charlie Batch		
C7 Akili Smith	1.00	2.50
Donovan McNabb		
C8 Sylvester Morris	.60	1.50
J.Anderson		
C9 O.J. McDuffie	.75	2.00
Terry Glenn		
C10 Cris Carter	1.00	2.50
Edgerrin James		
C11 Curtis Martin	1.00	2.50
Travis Taylor		
C12 Plaxico Burress	1.00	2.50
Jeff Graham		
C13 Kurt Warner	1.50	4.00
Jeff Blake		
C14 Shaun King	3.00	8.00
Brett Favre		

2000 Topps Gold Label Rookie Autographs

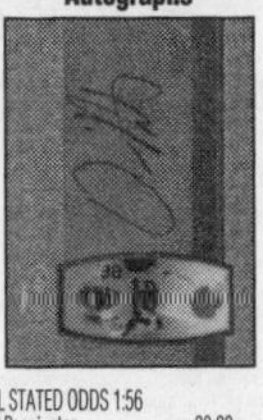

OVERALL STATED ODDS 1:56		
CP Chad Pennington	20.00	50.00
CR Chris Redman	6.00	15.00
DF Bubba Franks	8.00	20.00
DN Dennis Northcutt	6.00	15.00
JL Jamal Lewis	8.00	20.00
JP Jerry Porter	8.00	20.00
JR J.R. Redmond	5.00	12.00
PB Plaxico Burress	8.00	20.00
PW Peter Warrick	8.00	20.00
RD Ron Dayne	8.00	20.00
RS R.Jay Soward	5.00	12.00
SA Shaun Alexander	10.00	25.00
SM Sylvester Morris	5.00	12.00
TC Trung Canidate	6.00	15.00
TJ Thomas Jones	10.00	25.00
TM Tee Martin	8.00	20.00
TP Travis Prentice	6.00	15.00
TT Travis Taylor	6.00	15.00
RDU Ron Dugans	5.00	12.00

2012 Topps Gypsy Queen Mini National Convention

4 Andrew Luck	6.00	15.00
5 Robert Griffin III	6.00	15.00
6 Ryan Tannehill	2.50	6.00
7 Trent Richardson	4.00	10.00
8 Michael Floyd	1.50	4.00
9 Justin Blackmon	1.50	4.00

2001 Topps Heritage

In the summer of 2001 Topps released its Heritage set. The 146-card set featured the look of the 1956 Topps set and it included 110 veterans and 36 short printed rookies. The rookies were numbered to 1956. The cards were distributed in 8-card packs in boxes containing 24 packs. The cases contained 8 boxes. The packs carried a $3.00 SRP.

COMPLETE SET (146)	125.00	250.00
COMP.SET w/o SP's (110)	10.00	25.00
1 Ray Lewis	.40	1.00
2 Peter Warrick	.30	.75
3 James Stewart	.25	.60
4 Junior Seau	.40	1.00
5 Jeff George	.30	.75
6 Amani Toomer	.30	.75
7 Elvis Grbac	.30	.75
8 David Boston	.25	.60
9 Jimmy Smith	.30	.75
10 Warrick Dunn	.40	1.00
11 Hines Ward	.40	1.00
12 Joe Horn	.30	.75
13 Stephen Davis	.30	.75
14 Tyrone Wheatley	.30	.75
15 Brian Urlacher	.50	1.25
16 Fred Taylor	.40	1.00
17 Jerry Rice	.75	2.00
18 Keyshawn Johnson	.30	.75
19 Jay Fiedler	.30	.75
20 Jamal Anderson	.30	.75
21 Emmitt Smith	1.00	2.50
22 Tiki Barber	.40	1.00
23 Daunte Culpepper	.30	.75
24 Torry Holt	.30	.75
25 Peyton Manning	1.00	2.50
26 Eddie George	.40	1.00
27 Jamal Lewis	.40	1.00
28 Ricky Williams	.40	1.00
29 Ahman Green	.40	1.00
30 Ed McCaffrey	.30	.75
31 Curtis Martin	.40	1.00
32 Isaac Bruce	.40	1.00
33 Doug Flutie	.40	1.00
34 Steve McNair	.40	1.00
35 Donovan McNabb	.40	1.00
36 Keenan McCardell	.30	.75
37 Charlie Batch	.30	.75
38 Cade McNown	.30	.75
39 Terrell Owens	.40	1.00
40 Brad Johnson	.30	.75
41 Robert Smith	.30	.75
42 Muhsin Muhammad	.30	.75
43 Kurt Warner	.60	1.50
44 Lamar Smith	.30	.75
45 Brian Griese	.30	.75
46 Trent Dilfer	.30	.75
47 Jeff Garcia	.30	.75
48 Derrick Mason	.30	.75
49 Drew Bledsoe	.40	1.00
50 Marshall Faulk	.40	1.00
51 Corey Dillon	.30	.75
52 Tony Gonzalez	.40	1.00
53 Chad Lewis	.25	.60
54 Shaun Alexander	.40	1.00
55 Edgerrin James	.40	1.00
56 Eric Moulds	.30	.75
57 Aaron Brooks	.30	.75
58 Zach Thomas	.40	1.00
59 Jerome Bettis	.40	1.00
60 Shannon Sharpe	.40	1.00
61 Kerry Collins	.30	.75
62 Ricky Watters	.30	.75
63 Tim Couch	.25	.60
64 Marvin Harrison	.40	1.00
65 Tim Brown	.40	1.00
66 Mark Brunell	.30	.75
67 Wayne Chrebet	.30	.75
68 Terry Glenn	.30	.75
69 Mike Anderson	.30	.75
70 Randy Moss	.40	1.00
71 Freddie Jones	.25	.60
72 Ike Hilliard	.30	.75
73 Derrick Alexander	.25	.60
74 Travis Prentice	.25	.60
75 Brett Favre	1.25	3.00
76 Rod Smith	.30	.75
77 Troy Aikman	.60	1.50
78 Cris Carter	.40	1.00
79 Rich Gannon	.30	.75
80 Charlie Garner	.30	.75
81 Michael Pittman	.30	.75
82 Jeff Graham	.25	.60
83 Albert Connell	.25	.60
84 Bill Schroeder	.30	.75
85 Jeff Blake	.30	.75
86 Jon Kitna	.30	.75
87 Qadry Ismail	.30	.75
88 Joey Galloway	.30	.75
89 Charles Johnson	.25	.60
90 Troy Brown	.30	.75
91 Johnnie Morton	.30	.75
92 Chris Chandler	.30	.75
93 Donald Hayes	.25	.60
94 Shaun King	.25	.60
95 Vinny Testaverde	.30	.75
96 James Allen	.25	.60
97 Jake Plummer	.30	.75
98 Antonio Freeman	.40	1.00
99 Sean Dawkins	.25	.60
100 Ron Dayne	.30	.75
101 Rob Johnson	.30	.75
102 Kordell Stewart	.30	.75
103 Akili Smith	.25	.60
104 Shawn Jefferson	.25	.60
105 Germane Crowell	.25	.60
106 Kevin Johnson	.25	.60
107 Steve Beuerlein	.30	.75
108 Marcus Robinson	.30	.75
109 Peerless Price	.25	.60
110 Jerome Pathon	.25	.60
111 Sage Rosenfels RC	2.50	6.00
112 Quincy Morgan RC	2.00	5.00
113 Chad Johnson RC	4.00	10.00
114 Josh Heupel RC	2.50	6.00
115 Anthony Thomas RC	2.50	6.00
116 Drew Brees RC	15.00	40.00
117 Kevan Barlow RC	2.00	5.00
118 Chris Chambers RC	2.50	6.00
119 Mike McMahon RC	2.00	5.00
120 Todd Heap RC	2.50	6.00
121 Leonard Davis RC	2.50	6.00
122 Richard Seymour RC	2.50	6.00
123 Robert Ferguson RC	2.50	6.00
124 Andre Carter RC	2.00	5.00
125 Jesse Palmer RC	2.00	5.00
126 Travis Minor RC	2.00	5.00
127 Rudi Johnson RC	2.50	6.00
128 Rod Gardner RC	2.00	5.00
129 Snoop Minnis RC	1.50	4.00
130 Koren Robinson RC	2.00	5.00
131 Chris Weinke RC	2.00	5.00
132 James Jackson RC	1.50	4.00
133 Michael Vick RC	10.00	25.00
134 Marques Tuiasosopo RC	2.00	5.00
135 Michael Bennett RC	2.00	5.00
136 LaDainian Tomlinson RC	8.00	20.00
137 Freddie Mitchell RC	1.50	4.00
138 Deuce McAllister RC	2.50	6.00
139 Quincy Carter RC	2.00	5.00
140 Santana Moss RC	3.00	8.00
141 David Terrell RC	2.00	5.00
142 Reggie Wayne RC	5.00	12.00
143 Justin Smith RC	2.50	6.00
144 Gerard Warren RC	2.00	5.00
145 Travis Henry RC	2.00	5.00
146 Dan Morgan RC	2.00	5.00
NNO Checklist CL	.20	.50

2001 Topps Heritage Retrofractor

*VETS 1-110: 4X TO 10X BASIC CARDS
*ROOKIES 111-146: .6X TO 1.5X
STATED PRINT RUN 556 SER.#'d SETS

2001 Topps Heritage 1956 All-Stars

COMPLETE SET (3)	2.50	6.00
STATED ODDS 1:12		
HACB Chuck Bednarik	.75	2.00
HALM Lenny Moore	.75	2.00
HAYT Y.A. Tittle	1.25	3.00

2001 Topps Heritage Classic Renditions

COMPLETE SET (10)	6.00	15.00
STATED ODDS 1:8		
CR1 Donovan McNabb	.60	1.50
CR2 Brett Favre	2.00	5.00
CR3 Edgerrin James	.60	1.50
CR4 Peyton Manning	1.50	4.00
CR5 Marvin Harrison	.60	1.50
CR6 Kurt Warner	1.00	2.50
CR7 Marshall Faulk	.60	1.50
CR8 Brian Urlacher	.75	2.00
CR9 Jeff Garcia	.50	1.25
CR10 Terrell Owens	.60	1.50
CRABF Brett Favre AU	125.00	250.00
CRABU Brian Urlacher AU/25	60.00	120.00
CRAEJ Edgerrin James AU	100.00	200.00

2001 Topps Heritage Gridiron Collection Jersey

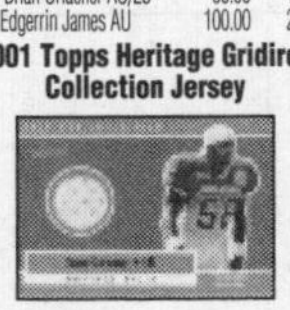

STATED ODDS 1:287		
GC1 Daunte Culpepper	6.00	15.00
GC2 Eddie George	8.00	20.00
GC3 Edgerrin James	8.00	20.00
GC4 Tony Gonzalez	8.00	20.00
GC5 Marvin Harrison	8.00	20.00
GC6 Jimmy Smith	6.00	15.00
GC7 Sam Cowart	5.00	12.00
GC9 Rod Woodson	10.00	25.00
GC10 Mo Lewis	5.00	12.00
GC11 Charles Woodson	8.00	20.00
GC12 Derrick Brooks	8.00	20.00

2001 Topps Heritage New Age Performers

COMPLETE SET (15)	12.50	30.00
STATED ODDS 1:8		
NA1 Marshall Faulk	1.00	2.50
NA2 Jerry Rice	2.00	5.00
NA3 Marvin Harrison	1.00	2.50
NA4 Peyton Manning	2.50	6.00
NA5 Torry Holt	.75	2.00
NA6 Isaac Bruce	1.00	2.50
NA7 Eddie George	1.00	2.50
NA8 Daunte Culpepper	.75	2.00
NA9 Edgerrin James	1.00	2.50
NA10 Randy Moss	1.00	2.50
NA11 Jeff Garcia	.75	2.00
NA12 Mike Anderson	.75	2.00
NA13 Terrell Owens	1.00	2.50
NA14 Rod Smith	.75	2.00
NA15 Cris Carter	1.00	2.50

2001 Topps Heritage Real One Autographs

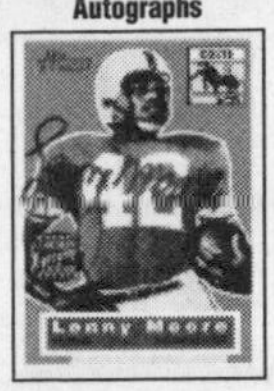

STATED ODDS 1:377		
*RED INK/56: 1X TO 2.5X BASIC AUTO		
RED INK SER.#'d PRINT RUN 56 SETS		
THROAB Aaron Brooks	8.00	20.00
THROBU Brian Urlacher	30.00	50.00
THROCB Chuck Bednarik	10.00	25.00
THRODC Daunte Culpepper	8.00	20.00
THROEH Elroy Hirsch	60.00	120.00
THROEJ Edgerrin James	10.00	25.00
THROEM Eric Moulds	8.00	20.00
THROJL Jamal Lewis	10.00	25.00
THROJS Jimmy Smith	8.00	20.00
THROLM Lenny Moore	25.00	50.00
THROMA Mike Anderson	8.00	20.00
THROMH Marvin Harrison	10.00	25.00
THROOM Ollie Matson	30.00	50.00
THRORB Roosevelt Brown	25.00	50.00
THRORG Roosevelt Grier	12.00	30.00
THRORW Ricky Williams	10.00	25.00
THROSD Stephen Davis	8.00	20.00
THROTO Terrell Owens	10.00	25.00
THROWC Wayne Chrebet	8.00	20.00
THROYT Y.A. Tittle	25.00	50.00
THROJSC Joe Schmidt	20.00	40.00

2001 Topps Heritage Souvenir Seating

STATED ODDS 1:263		
SS1 Charley Conerly SP	30.00	60.00
SS2 Frank Gifford SP	30.00	60.00
SS3 Bart Starr	12.50	30.00
SS4 Paul Hornung SP	30.00	60.00
SS5 Johnny Unitas	12.50	30.00
SS6 Raymond Berry	6.00	15.00
SS7 Lenny Moore	6.00	15.00
SS8 Jim Brown	10.00	25.00
SS10 Chuck Bednarik	6.00	15.00

2001 Topps Heritage Then and Now

COMPLETE SET (3)	3.00	8.00
STATED ODDS 1:8		
TNBL Chuck Bednarik	1.00	2.50
Ray Lewis		
TNMJ Lenny Moore	1.25	3.00
Edgerrin James		
TNTG Y.A. Tittle	1.25	3.00
Jeff Garcia		

2002 Topps Heritage

This 194-card set contains 154 veterans and 40 rookies. The rookies were inserted at a rate of 1:2. In addition, there were also several veteran SP's whose odds are not known. Boxes contained 24 packs of 8 cards. SRP was $3.00.

COMPLETE SET (194)	75.00	150.00
COMP.SET w/o SP's (154)	20.00	50.00
ROOKIE STATED ODDS 1:2		
1 Jerome Bettis	.50	1.25
2 Jeff Blake SP	.60	1.50
3 Rod Smith	.40	1.00
4 Eric Moulds	.40	1.00
5 Michael Vick	.75	2.00
6 Randy Moss	.50	1.25
7 Todd Pinkston	.30	.75
8 Trung Canidate SP	.50	1.25
9 Steve McNair	.50	1.25
10 J.J. Stokes SP	.50	1.25
11 Ricky Williams	.40	1.00
12 Germane Crowell SP	.50	1.25
13 Muhsin Muhammad SP	.60	1.50
14 Michael Pittman SP	.60	1.50
15 James Jackson SP	.50	1.25
16 Dominic Rhodes	.40	1.00
17 Jay Fiedler	.40	1.00
18 Marcus Robinson	.40	1.00
19 Qadry Ismail SP	.60	1.50
20 Michael Strahan	.50	1.25
21 Koren Robinson	.30	.75
22 James Allen SP	.50	1.25
23 Chad Pennington	.50	1.25
24 Fred Taylor	.40	1.00
25 Corey Dillon	.40	1.00
26 Thomas Jones SP	.75	2.00
27 Anthony Thomas	.40	1.00
28 Priest Holmes	.50	1.25
29 Troy Brown	.40	1.00
30 Jerry Rice	1.00	2.50
31 Correll Buckhalter	.40	1.00
32 Drew Brees	.75	2.00
33 Isaac Bruce	.50	1.25
34 Warrick Dunn SP	.60	1.50
35 Chris Chambers	.40	1.00
36 Antonio Freeman	.50	1.25
37 Joey Galloway SP	.60	1.50
38 Rob Johnson SP	.60	1.50
39 Reggie Wayne	.50	1.25
40 Santana Moss	.40	1.00
41 Plaxico Burress	.40	1.00
42 Frank Wycheck SP	.50	1.25
43 Johnnie Morton	.40	1.00
44 Chris Weinke	.30	.75
45 Rocket Ismail SP	.60	1.50
46 Daunte Culpepper	.40	1.00
47 Deuce McAllister SP	.60	1.50
48 Terrell Owens	.50	1.25

49 Michael Westbrook	.30	.75
50 Tom Brady	1.25	3.00
51 Mike Anderson	.40	1.00
52 Jake Plummer	.40	1.00
53 Travis Taylor SP	.50	1.25
54 Marcus Pollard SP	.50	1.25
55 Zach Thomas	.50	1.25
56 Duce Staley	.40	1.00
57 Trent Dilfer	.40	1.00
58 Keyshawn Johnson	.40	1.00
59 Amani Toomer SP	.60	1.50
60 David Terrell	.30	.75
61 Robert Ferguson SP	.60	1.50
62 Jeff Garcia	.40	1.00
63 Eddie George	.40	1.00
64 Marshall Faulk	.50	1.25
65 Travis Henry	.30	.75
66 Tim Couch	.30	.75
67 Mike McMahon	.30	.75
68 John Abraham SP	.60	1.50
69 James Thrash	.40	1.00
70 Shaun Alexander	.40	1.00
71 Ike Hilliard SP	.60	1.50
72 Brian Griese	.40	1.00
73 Ray Lewis	.50	1.25
74 Jon Kitna	.40	1.00
75 Az-Zahir Hakim SP	.50	1.25
76 Oronde Gadsden SP	.50	1.25
77 Joe Horn	.40	1.00
78 Tim Brown	.50	1.25
79 Kendrell Bell	.30	.75
80 LaDainian Tomlinson	.60	1.50
81 Brad Johnson	.40	1.00
82 Tony Gonzalez	.50	1.25
83 Bill Schroeder	.30	.75
84 Quincy Carter	.30	.75
85 Donald Hayes SP	.50	1.25
86 Peyton Manning	1.00	2.50
87 Drew Bledsoe	.50	1.25
88 Darrell Jackson	.40	1.00
89 Rod Gardner	.30	.75
90 Derrick Mason	.40	1.00
91 Byron Chamberlain SP	.50	1.25
92 James McKnight SP	.50	1.25
93 Kevin Johnson	.30	.75
94 Terry Glenn	.40	1.00
95 Marty Booker SP	.60	1.50
96 Terrell Davis	.50	1.25
97 Vinny Testaverde	.40	1.00
98 Hines Ward	.50	1.25
99 Chad Lewis SP	.50	1.25
100 Kurt Warner	.50	1.25
101 Michael Bennett	.40	1.00
102 Edgerrin James	.40	1.00
103 Corey Bradford SP	.50	1.25
104 Chad Johnson SP	.75	2.00
105 Alex Van Pelt	.30	.75
106 Antowain Smith	.40	1.00
107 Rich Gannon	.40	1.00
108 Kevan Barlow SP	.50	1.25
109 Mike Alstott SP	.60	1.50
110 Kerry Collins SP	.60	1.50
111 Jimmy Smith	.40	1.00
112 Jermaine Lewis SP	.50	1.25
113 Quincy Morgan SP	.50	1.25
114 Maurice Smith SP	.50	1.25
115 Willie Jackson	.30	.75
116 Doug Flutie	.50	1.25
117 Matt Hasselbeck	.50	1.25
118 Amos Zereoue SP	.50	1.25
119 Lamar Smith	.40	1.00
120 Snoop Minnis	.30	.75
121 Troy Hambrick SP	.50	1.25
122 Shannon Sharpe SP	.75	2.00
123 Laveranues Coles	.40	1.00
124 Freddie Mitchell	.30	.75
125 Kevin Dyson SP	.60	1.50
126 Torry Holt	.50	1.25
127 James Stewart SP	.50	1.25
128 Brian Urlacher	.50	1.25
129 David Boston	.30	.75
130 Ron Dayne	.40	1.00
131 Garrison Hearst	.40	1.00
132 Stephen Davis	.40	1.00
133 Donovan McNabb	.50	1.25
134 David Patten	.30	.75
135 Travis Minor SP	.50	1.25
136 Peerless Price SP	.50	1.25
137 Chris Redman SP	.50	1.25
138 Ahman Green	.40	1.00
139 Mark Brunell	.40	1.00
140 Charlie Garner	.40	1.00
141 Curtis Conway	.40	1.00
142 Wayne Chrebet	.40	1.00
143 Kordell Stewart	.40	1.00
144 Peter Warrick	.40	1.00
145 Emmitt Smith	1.25	3.00
146 Jim Miller SP	.50	1.25
147 Trent Green	.40	1.00
148 Cris Carter	.50	1.25
149 Aaron Brooks	.40	1.00
150 Curtis Martin	.50	1.25
151 Tiki Barber SP	.75	2.00
152 Marvin Harrison	.50	1.25
153 Tyrone Wheatley SP	.60	1.50
154 Brett Favre	1.25	3.00
155 David Carr RC	1.00	2.50
156 Quentin Jammer RC	1.00	2.50
157 Julius Peppers RC	2.00	5.00
158 Mike Williams RC	.60	1.50
159 Antwaan Randle El RC	1.00	2.50
160 Joey Harrington RC	1.00	2.50
161 Ashley Lelie RC	.75	2.00
162 Marquise Walker RC	.60	1.50
163 Rohan Davey RC	1.00	2.50
164 Patrick Ramsey RC	1.00	2.50
165 T.J. Duckett RC	1.00	2.50
166 DeShaun Foster RC	1.00	2.50
167 Donte Stallworth RC	1.00	2.50
168 William Green RC	.75	2.00
169 Ron Johnson RC	.75	2.00
170 Maurice Morris RC	.75	2.00
171 Travis Stephens RC	.60	1.50
172 Eric Crouch RC	1.00	2.50
173 David Garrard RC	1.25	3.00
174 Daniel Graham RC	.75	2.00
175 Roy Williams RC	1.00	2.50
176 Jeremy Shockey RC	1.50	4.00
177 Josh McCown RC	1.00	2.50
178 Josh Reed RC	.75	2.00
179 Andre Davis RC	.75	2.00
180 Antonio Bryant RC	1.00	2.50
181 Clinton Portis RC	1.25	3.00
182 Javon Walker RC	1.00	2.50
183 Jabar Gaffney RC	1.00	2.50
184 Ladell Betts RC	1.00	2.50
185 Tim Carter RC	.75	2.00
186 Reche Caldwell RC	1.00	2.50
187 Cliff Russell RC	.60	1.50
188 Brian Westbrook SP RC	2.50	6.00
189 Freddie Milons RC	.60	1.50
190 Phillip Buchanon RC	1.00	2.50
191 Lamar Gordon RC	.75	2.00
192 Luke Staley RC	.60	1.50
193 Albert Haynesworth RC	1.00	2.50
194 Kurt Kittner RC	.60	1.50

2002 Topps Heritage Retrofractors

*VETS: 3X TO 8X BASIC CARDS
*VETS: 2X TO 5X BASIC SP
RETRO/557 ODDS 1:13 HOB, 1:14 RET
STATED PRINT RUN 557 SER.#'d SETS

2002 Topps Heritage Black Backs

STATED ODDS 1:2

1 Jerome Bettis	.75	2.00
6 Randy Moss	.75	2.00
27 Anthony Thomas	.60	1.50
28 Priest Holmes	.75	2.00
48 Terrell Owens	.75	2.00
50 Tom Brady	2.00	5.00
62 Jeff Garcia	.60	1.50
64 Marshall Faulk	.75	2.00
70 Shaun Alexander	.60	1.50
86 Peyton Manning	1.50	4.00
100 Kurt Warner	.75	2.00
102 Edgerrin James	.60	1.50
129 David Boston	.50	1.25
133 Donovan McNabb	.75	2.00
138 Ahman Green	.60	1.50
150 Curtis Martin	.75	2.00
152 Marvin Harrison	.75	2.00
154 Brett Favre	2.00	5.00
155 David Carr	1.25	3.00
160 Joey Harrington	1.25	3.00
161 Ashley Lelie	1.00	2.50
163 Rohan Davey	1.25	3.00
164 Patrick Ramsey	1.25	3.00
166 DeShaun Foster	1.25	3.00
175 Roy Williams	1.25	3.00
179 Andre Davis	1.00	2.50
180 Antonio Bryant	1.25	3.00
184 Ladell Betts	1.25	3.00

2002 Topps Heritage 1957 Reprints

COMPLETE SET (10)	8.00	20.00
STATED ODDS 1:6 HOB, 1:12 RET		
RAD Art Donovan	.75	2.00
RBS Bart Starr	2.00	5.00
RCB Chuck Bednarik	1.00	2.50
RGB George Blanda	1.00	2.50
RGM Gino Marchetti	.75	2.00
RPH Paul Hornung	1.00	2.50
RPS Pat Summerall	1.00	2.50
RRB Raymond Berry	.75	2.00
RTM Tommy McDonald	.75	2.00
RYT Y.A. Tittle	.75	2.00

2002 Topps Heritage Classic Renditions

COMPLETE SET (10)	8.00	20.00
STATED ODDS 1:6 HOB, 1:12 RET		
CRAT Anthony Thomas	.75	2.00
CRDB David Boston	.60	1.50
CREJ Edgerrin James	.75	2.00
CRKB Kendrell Bell	.60	1.50
CRKS Kordell Stewart	.75	2.00
CRKW Kurt Warner	1.00	2.50
CRMF Marshall Faulk	1.00	2.50
CRMS Michael Strahan	1.00	2.50
CRPM Peyton Manning	2.00	5.00
CRTH Torry Holt	1.00	2.50

2002 Topps Heritage Classic Renditions Autographs

STATED ODDS 1:10990 HOB, 1:11904 RET
STATED PRINT RUN 25 SER.#'d SETS

CRAAT Anthony Thomas	15.00	40.00
CRAKB Kendrell Bell	12.00	30.00
CRAKW Kurt Warner	75.00	150.00

2002 Topps Heritage Gridiron Collection Jerseys

JERSEY/999 ODDS 1:64 HOB/RET
STATED PRINT RUN 999 SER.#'d SETS
*FOIL/25: 1X TO 2.5X BASIC JSY/999
FOIL/25 ODDS 1:2572 H, 1:2580 R
FOIL PRINT RUN 25 SER.#'d SETS

GCBF Bubba Franks	3.00	8.00
GCCM Curtis Martin	4.00	10.00
GCEG Eddie George	3.00	8.00
GCES Emmitt Smith	10.00	25.00
GCJA John Abraham	3.00	8.00
GCJK Jevon Kearse	3.00	8.00
GCJN Joe Namath	12.00	30.00
GCJT Jeremiah Trotter	2.50	6.00
GCKJ Keyshawn Johnson	3.00	8.00
GCOK Olin Kreutz	5.00	12.00
GCRB Ronde Barber	3.00	8.00
GCTC Tim Couch	2.50	6.00
GCTO Terrell Owens	4.00	10.00

2002 Topps Heritage Hall of Fame Autographs

STATED ODDS 1:8337 HOB, 1:8928 RET

HOFDC Dave Casper	60.00	120.00
HOFDH Dan Hampton	125.00	200.00
HOFJK Jim Kelly	125.00	250.00
HOFJS John Stallworth	90.00	150.00

2002 Topps Heritage New Age Performers

COMPLETE SET (15)	15.00	40.00
STATED ODDS 1:8 HOB, 1:15 RET		
NAP1 Donovan McNabb	1.25	3.00
NAP2 Kurt Warner	1.25	3.00
NAP3 Brett Favre	3.00	8.00
NAP4 Peyton Manning	2.50	6.00
NAP5 Stephen Davis	1.00	2.50
NAP6 Terrell Owens	1.25	3.00
NAP7 Anthony Thomas	1.00	2.50
NAP8 Jeff Garcia	1.00	2.50
NAP9 Marshall Faulk	1.25	3.00
NAP10 Edgerrin James	1.00	2.50
NAP11 David Boston	.75	2.00
NAP12 Tim Couch	.75	2.00
NAP13 Chris Chambers	1.00	2.50
NAP14 Marvin Harrison	1.25	3.00
NAP15 Curtis Martin	1.25	3.00

2002 Topps Heritage Real One Autographs

STATED ODDS 1:199 HOB/RET

HRAD Art Donovan	12.00	30.00
HRAT Anthony Thomas	10.00	25.00
HRBS Bart Starr	125.00	200.00
HRCB Chuck Bednarik	15.00	40.00
HRDB David Boston	8.00	20.00
HRDR Dominic Rhodes	10.00	25.00
HRGB George Blanda	30.00	60.00
HRGH Garrison Hearst	10.00	25.00
HRGM Gino Marchetti	20.00	40.00
HRHW Hines Ward	30.00	60.00
HRJA John Abraham	10.00	25.00
HRKB Kendrell Bell	8.00	20.00
HRMB Marty Booker	10.00	25.00
HRPH Paul Hornung	30.00	60.00
HRPHO Priest Holmes	12.00	30.00
HRPS Pat Summerall	30.00	60.00
HRRB Raymond Berry	15.00	40.00
HRTB Tom Brady	175.00	300.00
HRTM Tommy McDonald	12.00	30.00
HRYT Y.A. Tittle	25.00	50.00
HRZT Zach Thomas	12.00	30.00

2002 Topps Heritage Real One Autographs Red Ink

*RED INK/57: .6X TO 1.5X BASIC AU
RED INK/57 ODDS 1:699 H. 1:700 R

HRBS Bart Starr	125.00	250.00
HRTB Tom Brady	200.00	350.00

2005 Topps Heritage

This 400-card set was released in November, 2005. The set was issued in the hobby through eight-card packs with an $3 SRP which came 24 packs to a box. This set included 35 variations, most of which featured rookies in the style of the 1958 Topps football set. If the variations did not involve the 58 design; they were instead pictures of the players in throwback jerseys. There were also a grouping of short prints from cards 301-365 outside of the variations.

COMPLETE SET (400)	75.00	150.00
COMP.SET w/o SPs (300)	15.00	40.00
58T SP PRINTED WITH 1958 TOPPS DESIGN		
TBJ SP PRINTED W/THROWBACK JER.PHOTO		
1 Curtis Martin	.40	1.00
2 Javon Walker	.25	.60
3 Derrick Mason	.30	.75
4 Julius Jones	.25	.60
5 Marc Bulger	.30	.75
6 Reggie Wayne	.40	1.00
7 Isaac Bruce	.30	.75
8 Ray Lewis	.40	1.00
9 Drew Bledsoe	.40	1.00
10 Michael Vick	.40	1.00
11 Charles Rogers	.25	.60
12 Lee Evans	.30	.75
13 Jake Plummer	.30	.75
14 Edgerrin James	.30	.75
15 Hines Ward	.40	1.00
16 Peyton Manning	.75	2.00
17 Andre Johnson	.40	1.00
18 Trent Green	.30	.75
19 Brian Westbrook	.30	.75
20 Kevin Jones	.25	.60
21 Deuce McAllister	.30	.75
22 Marvin Harrison	.40	1.00
23 Dwight Freeney	.30	.75
24 Ahman Green	.30	.75
25 Plaxico Burress	.30	.75
26 Daunte Culpepper	.30	.75
27 Corey Dillon	.30	.75
28 Joe Horn	.30	.75
29 Torry Holt	.30	.75
30 Randy Moss	.40	1.00
31 Drew Brees	.40	1.00
32 Jonathan Vilma	.30	.75
33 Jerome Bettis	.40	1.00
34 Byron Leftwich	.30	.75
35 Marshall Faulk	.40	1.00
36 Brett Favre	1.00	2.50
37 Steve McNair	.40	1.00
38 Rudi Johnson	.30	.75
39 Tiki Barber	.40	1.00
40 Muhsin Muhammad	.30	.75
41 Tony Gonzalez	.30	.75
42 Chad Pennington	.40	1.00
43 Shaun Alexander	.30	.75
44 Jamal Lewis	.30	.75
45 Antonio Gates	.40	1.00
46 LaDainian Tomlinson	.40	1.00
47 Matt Hasselbeck	.30	.75
48 Jake Delhomme	.30	.75
49 Chad Johnson	.30	.75
50 Willis McGahee	.40	1.00
51 Jason Witten	.40	1.00
52 J.P. Losman	.25	.60
53 Donovan McNabb	.40	1.00
54A Eric Shelton RC	.60	1.50
54B Eric Shelton 58T SP	.75	2.00
55A Alex Smith QB RC	1.50	4.00
55B Alex Smith QB TBJ SP	2.00	5.00
56A Kyle Orton RC	1.00	2.50
56B Kyle Orton 58T SP	1.25	3.00
57A Andrew Walter RC	.75	2.00
57B Andrew Walter TBJ SP	1.00	2.50
58A Ryan Moats RC	.60	1.50
58B Ryan Moats 58T SP	.75	2.00
59A Ciatrick Fason RC	.60	1.50
59B Ciatrick Fason 58T SP	.75	2.00
60A Vincent Jackson RC	1.25	3.00
60B Vincent Jackson 58T SP	1.50	4.00
61A Heath Miller RC	1.25	3.00
61B Heath Miller 58T SP	1.50	4.00
62A Carlos Rogers RC	1.00	2.50
62B Carlos Rogers TBJ SP	1.25	3.00
63A Terrence Murphy RC	.60	1.50
63B Terrence Murphy 58T SP	.75	2.00
64A Mike Williams	1.00	2.50
64B Mike Williams 58T SP	1.25	3.00
65A Vernand Morency RC	.60	1.50
65B Vernand Morency 58T SP	.75	2.00
66A Maurice Clarett	.60	1.50
66B Maurice Clarett 58T SP	.75	2.00
67A Roscoe Parrish RC	.60	1.50
67B Roscoe Parrish 58T SP	.75	2.00
68A Courtney Roby RC	.75	2.00
68B Courtney Roby 58T SP	1.00	2.50
69 Tom Brady	.75	2.00
70A David Greene RC	.60	1.50
70B David Greene 58T SP	.75	2.00
71A Antrel Rolle RC	1.00	2.50
71B Antrel Rolle 58T SP	1.25	3.00
72A Mark Bradley RC	.60	1.50
72B Mark Bradley 58T SP	.75	2.00
73A Frank Gore RC	1.50	4.00
73B Frank Gore 58T SP	2.00	5.00
74A Cedric Benson RC	1.00	2.50
74B Cedric Benson 58T SP	1.25	3.00
75A Derrick Johnson 62T RC	.75	2.00
75B Derrick Johnson 58T SP	1.00	2.50
76A Reggie Brown RC	.60	1.50
76B Reggie Brown 58T SP	.75	2.00
77A Ronnie Brown RC	1.25	3.00
77B Ronnie Brown TBJ SP	1.50	4.00
78A Jason Campbell RC	1.25	3.00
78B Jason Campbell TBJ SP	1.50	4.00
79A Charlie Frye RC	1.00	2.50
79B Charlie Frye 58T SP	1.25	3.00
80 Jamie Sharper	.25	.60
81 Tony Romo	6.00	15.00
82 Rod Smith	.30	.75
83 Chester Taylor	.30	.75
84 Marcus Robinson	.25	.60
85 Terence Newman	.25	.60
86 Aaron Brooks	.25	.60
87 Kerry Collins	.30	.75
88 Brandon Lloyd	.25	.60
89 Michael Pittman	.25	.60
90 Sean Taylor	.40	1.00
91 Michael Lewis	.25	.60
92 Jeremy Shockey	.40	1.00
93 Zach Thomas	.40	1.00
94 David Carr	.25	.60
95 Champ Bailey	.30	.75
96 Julius Peppers	.30	.75
97 Brandon Stokley	.25	.60
98 Deion Branch	.25	.60
99 Charles Woodson	.40	1.00
100 Darrell Jackson	.25	.60
101 Ronde Barber	.30	.75
102 Patrick Ramsey	.30	.75
103 Warrick Dunn	.30	.75
104 Takeo Spikes	.25	.60
105 Thomas Jones	.40	1.00
106 T.J. Houshmandzadeh	.30	.75
107 Najeh Davenport	.30	.75
108 Nate Burleson	.25	.60
109 Kelly Campbell	.25	.60
110 LaVar Arrington	.30	.75
111 Joey Harrington	.30	.75
112 DeAngelo Hall	.30	.75
113 Derrick Blaylock	.25	.60
114 Michael Clayton	.25	.60
115 Adam Archuleta	.25	.60
116 Jason Taylor	.30	.75
117 Donald Driver	.40	1.00
118 Dan Morgan	.25	.60
119 Michael Jenkins	.30	.75
120 Drew Henson	.25	.60
121 Jay Fiedler	.25	.60
122 Ladell Betts	.25	.60
123 Jonathan Ogden	.25	.60
124 Domanick Davis	.25	.60
125 Sebastian Janikowski	.25	.60
126 Cedrick Wilson	.25	.60
127 Marcus Trufant	.25	.60
128 Santana Moss	.30	.75
129 Tatum Bell	.25	.60
130 Jonathan Wells	.25	.60
131 Laveranues Coles	.25	.60
132 Josh McCown	.30	.75
133 Antonio Bryant	.25	.60
134 John Lynch	.30	.75
135 Roy Williams WR	.30	.75
136 Adam Vinatieri	.40	1.00
137 Dominic Rhodes	.30	.75
138 Tyrone Calico	.25	.60
139 Keenan McCardell	.30	.75
140 Antonio Pierce	.25	.60
141 Chris Chambers	.30	.75
142 Bubba Franks	.25	.60
143 Mike Vanderjagt	.25	.60
144 Ernest Wilford	.25	.60
145 Bertrand Berry	.25	.60
146 David Garrard	.30	.75
147 DeShaun Foster	.30	.75
148 Rashaun Woods	.25	.60
149 Wes Welker	.40	1.00
150 Allen Rossum	.25	.60
151 Mike Anderson	.25	.60
152 Keyshawn Johnson	.30	.75
153 Alge Crumpler	.30	.75
154 Dunta Robinson	.25	.60
155 Kyle Boller	.30	.75
156 William Green	.25	.60
157 Peter Warrick	.25	.60
158 Doug Gabriel	.25	.60
159 Ashley Lelie	.25	.60
160 Ronald Curry	.25	.60
161 Keary Colbert	.25	.60
162 Shawn Bryson	.25	.60
163 Tim Rattay	.25	.60
164 Jabar Gaffney	.25	.60
165 Doug Jolley	.25	.60
166 Keith Brooking	.25	.60
167 Brian Urlacher	.40	1.00
168 Chris Gamble	.25	.60
169 Kurt Warner	.40	1.00
170 Duce Staley	.30	.75
171 Steve Smith	.40	1.00
172 Anquan Boldin	.30	.75
173 Fred Taylor	.30	.75
174 Donnie Edwards	.25	.60
175 Clarence Moore	.25	.60
176 Corey Bradford	.25	.60
177 Dante Hall	.25	.60
178 Warren Sapp	.30	.75
179 Todd Heap	.30	.75
180 Mewelde Moore	.25	.60
181 John Abraham	.25	.60
182 Rex Grossman	.30	.75
183 Stephen Davis	.30	.75
184 Greg Jones	.25	.60
185 Jeremiah Trotter	.25	.60
186 Carson Palmer	.40	1.00
187 Simeon Rice	.25	.60
188 A.J. Feeley	.25	.60
189 Matt Schaub	.40	1.00
190 Jamaar Taylor	.25	.60
191 Joey Galloway	.30	.75
192 Quentin Griffin	.25	.60
193 Amani Toomer	.30	.75
194 Michael Strahan	.40	1.00
195 Travis Henry	.25	.60
196 Billy Volek	.25	.60
197 Robert Ferguson	.25	.60
198 Reggie Williams	.25	.60
199 Jeff Garcia	.30	.75
200 Mark Brunell	.30	.75
201 Derrick Brooks	.30	.75
202 Tommy Maddox	.30	.75
203 William Henderson	.30	.75
204 Bryant Johnson	.25	.60
205 Philip Rivers	.40	1.00
206 James Farrior	.25	.60
207 Terrence McGee	.30	.75
208 Bernard Berrian	.30	.75
209 Gus Frerotte	.25	.60
210 Mike Alstott	.30	.75
211 Luke McCown	.25	.60
212 Michael Bennett	.30	.75
213 Kenechi Udeze	.25	.60
214 Chris Perry	.25	.60
215 Robert Gallery	.25	.60
216 Lito Sheppard	.30	.75
217 Brian Finneran	.25	.60
218 Brian Griese	.30	.75
219 Kevin Curtis	.30	.75
220 LaMont Jordan	.30	.75
221 Jerry Porter	.25	.60
222 Reuben Droughns	.25	.60
223 Dallas Clark	.30	.75
224 Kevan Barlow	.25	.60
225 Ken Lucas	.25	.60
226 Lee Suggs	.25	.60
227 Marcus Pollard	.25	.60
228 David Givens	.25	.60
229 T.J. Duckett	.25	.60
230 Chris Simms	.30	.75
231 Maurice Morris	.25	.60
232 Chris McAllister	.25	.60
233 Justin Fargas	.30	.75
234 Jimmy Smith	.30	.75
235 Aaron Stecker	.25	.60
236 Donte Stallworth	.25	.60
237 Darren Sproles RC	1.00	2.50
238 Justin McCareins	.25	.60
239 Adrian McPherson RC	.60	1.50
240 Brian Dawkins	.30	.75
241 Travis Taylor	.25	.60
242 Fabian Washington RC	.75	2.00
243 Jerramy Stevens	.30	.75
244 Anthony Davis RC	.60	1.50
245 Alex Smith TE RC	.60	1.50
246 Ricky Williams	.30	.75
247 Marion Barber RC	1.00	2.50
248 Marcus Spears RC	.75	2.00
249 Mike Nugent RC	.75	2.00
250 Dat Nguyen	.25	.60
251 Derek Anderson RC	.75	2.00
252 Terrence Holt	.25	.60
253 Dane Looker	.25	.60
254 Randy McMichael	.25	.60
255 Craig Bragg RC	.60	1.50
256 James Kilian RC	.60	1.50
257 Airese Currie RC	.60	1.50
258 Noah Herron RC	.60	1.50
259 Dan Cody RC	.75	2.00
260 Willie Parker	.30	.75
261 Travis Johnson RC	.60	1.50
262 Dan Orlovsky RC	1.00	2.50
263 Chris Baker	.25	.60
264 Luis Castillo RC	.75	2.00
265 Travis Daniels RC	.75	2.00
266 Justin Miller RC	.75	2.00
267 J.R. Russell RC	.60	1.50
268 Lance Mitchell RC	.75	2.00
269 T.A. McLendon RC	.60	1.50
270 Jerricho Cotchery	.30	.75
271 Chad Owens RC	.75	2.00
272 Tab Perry RC	.60	1.50
273 Corey Webster RC	.75	2.00
274 Fred Gibson RC	.75	2.00
275 Brandon Jones RC	.75	2.00
276 DeWayne Robertson	.25	.60
277 Brock Berlin RC	.75	2.00
278 Nehemiah Broughton RC	.75	2.00
279 Shaun Cody RC	.75	2.00
280 Anthony Wright	.25	.60
281 Damien Nash RC	.75	2.00
282 Ryan Fitzpatrick RC	1.50	4.00
283 Paris Warren RC	.75	2.00
284 Justin Tuck RC	1.25	3.00
285 Cedric Houston RC	1.00	2.50
286 Odell Thurman RC	1.00	2.50
287 Kirk Morrison RC	1.00	2.50
288 Josh Davis RC	.60	1.50
289 Craphonso Thorpe RC	.60	1.50
290 Sam Aiken	.25	.60
291 Stanley Wilson RC	.75	2.00
292 Jonathan Babineaux RC	.75	2.00
293 Darryl Blackstock RC	.60	1.50
294 Roydell Williams RC	.75	2.00
295 Channing Crowder RC	.75	2.00
296 Deandra Cobb RC	.60	1.50
297 Larry Brackins RC	.60	1.50
298 Bryant McFadden RC	.75	2.00
299 Kevin Burnett RC	.75	2.00
300 Barrett Ruud RC	1.00	2.50
301 Terrell Owens SP	1.50	4.00
302 Ben Roethlisberger SP	2.50	6.00
303 Eric Moulds SP	1.00	2.50
304 Eli Manning SP	2.50	6.00
305 Ed Reed SP	1.25	3.00
306 Larry Fitzgerald SP	1.50	4.00
307 Clinton Portis SP	1.25	3.00
308 Priest Holmes SP	1.25	3.00
309 Drew Bennett SP	1.25	3.00
310 Steven Jackson SP	1.50	4.00
311 Roy Williams S SP	1.00	2.50
312 Marcel Shipp SP	1.00	2.50
313 Peerless Price SP	1.00	2.50
314 Troy Vincent SP	1.25	3.00
315 Justin Gage SP	1.00	2.50
316 Nick Goings SP	1.00	2.50
317 Dennis Northcutt SP	1.00	2.50
318 Quincy Morgan SP	1.00	2.50
319 Darius Watts SP	1.00	2.50
320 Jason Elam SP	1.00	2.50
321 Nick Barnett SP	1.25	3.00
322 Tony Hollings SP	1.00	2.50
323 Samie Parker SP	1.00	2.50
324 Kelly Campbell SP	1.00	2.50
325 Kelly Holcomb SP	1.00	2.50
326 Darren Sharper SP	1.25	3.00
327 Tedy Bruschi SP	1.50	4.00
328 Ernie Conwell SP	1.00	2.50
329 Shaun Ellis SP	1.00	2.50
330 Teyo Johnson SP	1.00	2.50
331 Chris Brown SP	1.00	2.50
332 Quentin Jammer SP	1.00	2.50
333 Fred Smoot SP	1.00	2.50
334 Eric Parker SP	1.00	2.50
335 Steve Heiden SP	1.00	2.50
336 Troy Polamalu SP	2.00	5.00
337 Todd Pinkston SP	1.00	2.50
338 L.J. Smith SP	1.25	3.00
339 London Fletcher SP	1.00	2.50
340 Devery Henderson SP	1.00	2.50
341A Troy Williamson SP RC	1.00	2.50
341B Troy Williamson TBJ SP	1.25	3.00
342A J.J. Arrington SP RC	1.00	2.50
342B J.J. Arrington 58T SP	1.25	3.00
343A Cadillac Williams SP SP	1.25	3.00
343B Cadillac Williams TBJ SP	1.50	4.00
344A Aaron Rodgers SP RC	12.50	25.00
344B Aaron Rodgers 58T SP	12.00	30.00
345A Matt Jones SP RC	1.00	2.50
345B Matt Jones 58T SP	1.25	3.00
346A Roddy White SP RC	1.50	4.00
346B Roddy White 58T SP	2.00	5.00
347A Braylon Edwards SP RC	1.50	4.00
347B Braylon Edwards TBJ SP	2.00	5.00
348A Adam Jones SP RC	1.00	2.50
348B Adam Jones TBJ SP	1.00	2.50
349A Mark Clayton SP RC	1.00	2.50
349B Mark Clayton TBJ SP	1.25	3.00
350A Stefan LeFors SP RC	.75	2.00
350B Stefan LeFors 58T SP	1.00	2.50
351 Alvin Pearman SP RC	.75	2.00
352 Erasmus James SP RC	1.00	2.50
353 David Pollack SP RC	1.00	2.50
354 Brandon Jacobs SP RC	1.50	4.00
355 Chris Henry SP RC	1.25	3.00
356 Thomas Davis SP RC	.75	2.00
357 Rasheed Marshall SP RC	1.00	2.50
358 Matt Roth SP RC	1.00	2.50
359 DeMarcus Ware SP RC	2.50	6.00
360 Matt Cassel SP RC	2.50	6.00
361 Stanford Routt SP RC	1.00	2.50
362 Marlin Jackson SP RC	.75	2.00
363 Derrick Johnson 59T SP ERR (card is misnumbered #75)	1.00	2.50
364 Jerome Mathis SP RC	1.25	3.00
365 Lionel Gates SP RC	.75	2.00

2005 Topps Heritage Felt Back Flashback

FELT BACK/199 ODDS 1:367 HOB		
1 Michael Vick	10.00	25.00
2 Peyton Manning	10.00	25.00
3 Terrell Owens	6.00	15.00
4 Marvin Harrison	6.00	15.00
5 Shaun Alexander	7.50	20.00
6 Randy Moss	6.00	15.00
7 Tom Brady	15.00	40.00
8 LaDainian Tomlinson	6.00	15.00
9 Brett Favre	15.00	40.00
10 Donovan McNabb	7.50	20.00
11 Alex Smith QB	20.00	50.00
12 Ronnie Brown	20.00	50.00
13 Braylon Edwards	15.00	40.00
14 Cadillac Williams	12.00	30.00
15 Troy Williamson	8.00	20.00

2005 Topps Heritage Flashback Relics

GROUP A GOAL POST ODDS 1:151 HOB
GROUP B SEAT ODDS 1:837 HOB
GROUP C SEAT ODDS 1:725 HOB

FAV Adam Vinatieri A	12.50	30.00
FBF Brett Favre A	12.50	30.00
FJB Jim Brown C	7.50	20.00
FJE John Elway A	10.00	25.00
FJP Jim Plunkett A	6.00	15.00
FJR Jerry Rice A	7.50	20.00
FRS Roger Staubach A	7.50	20.00
FTB Tom Brady A	15.00	40.00
FTBR Terry Bradshaw B	10.00	25.00
FWP William Perry A	6.00	15.00

2005 Topps Heritage Foil

*VETERANS: 1.5X TO 4X BASIC VETS 1-300
*VETERANS: .3X TO .8X BASIC VET 301-340
*ROOKIES: .4X TO 1X BASIC ROOKIES 1-300
*ROOKIES: .3X TO .8X BASIC ROOK.341-365
FOIL SP ROOKIES TOO SCARCE TO PRICE
OVERALL FOIL STATED ODDS 1:4
58T SP PRINTED WITH 1958 TOPPS DESIGN
TBJ SP PRINTED W/THROWBACK JER.PHOTO

THC27A Aaron Rodgers	15.00	40.00

2005 Topps Heritage Foil Rainbow

*VETERANS: 8X TO 20X BASIC VETS 1-300
*VETERANS: 1.5X TO 4X BASIC VETS 301-340
*ROOKIES: 2.5X TO 6X BASIC ROOKIES 1-300
*ROOKIES: 2X TO 5X BASIC ROOKIES 341-365
FOIL RAINBOW/50 STATED ODDS 1:217

THC27 Aaron Rodgers	125.00	200.00

2005 Topps Heritage Gridiron Collection Relics

GROUP A ODDS 1:48, 911 HOB
GROUP B ODDS 1:124 HOB
GROUP C ODDS 1:121 HOB

GCRAS Alex Smith QB B	7.50	20.00
GCRBE Braylon Edwards B	6.00	15.00
GCRBS Barry Sanders C	10.00	25.00
GCRCW Cadillac Williams B	5.00	12.00
GCRJC Jason Campbell B	5.00	12.00
GCRJE John Elway C	10.00	25.00
GCRJM Joe Montana C	12.50	30.00
GCRJN Joe Namath A		
GCRMA Marcus Allen C	5.00	12.00
GCRMC Mark Clayton B	5.00	12.00
GCRMJ Matt Jones B	4.00	10.00
GCRRB Ronnie Brown B	7.50	20.00
GCRRL Ronnie Lott C	4.00	10.00
GCRSY Steve Young C	6.00	15.00
GCRTW Troy Williamson B	5.00	12.00

2005 Topps Heritage New Age Performers

COMPLETE SET (15)	20.00	40.00
STATED ODDS 1:15		
NAP1 Peyton Manning	1.50	4.00
NAP2 LaDainian Tomlinson	1.00	2.50
NAP3 Ben Roethlisberger	2.50	6.00
NAP4 Daunte Culpepper	1.00	2.50
NAP5 Randy Moss	1.00	2.50
NAP6 Shaun Alexander	1.25	3.00
NAP7 Marvin Harrison	1.00	2.50
NAP8 Brett Favre	2.50	6.00
NAP9 Tom Brady	2.50	6.00
NAP10 Michael Vick	1.50	4.00
NAP11 Terrell Owens	1.00	2.50
NAP12 Alex Smith QB	2.50	6.00
NAP13 Ronnie Brown	2.50	6.00
NAP14 Braylon Edwards	2.00	5.00
NAP15 Cadillac Williams	1.50	4.00

2005 Topps Heritage Real One Autographs

GROUP A ODDS 1:48,911 H
GROUP B ODDS 1:5675 H
GROUP C ODDS 1:3708 H
GROUP D ODDS 1:2451 H
GROUP E ODDS 1:1097 H
GROUP F ODDS 1:925 H
GROUP G ODDS 1:910 H
GROUP H ODDS 1:2185 H
GROUP I ODDS 1:202 H
GROUP J ODDS 1:1088 H
GROUP K ODDS 1:362 H
GROUP L ODDS 1:272 H

ROAAJ Adam Jones K	5.00	12.00
ROAAR Aaron Rodgers F	200.00	350.00
ROAAS Alex Smith QB D	25.00	50.00
ROAAW Andrew Walter G	8.00	20.00
ROAASM Alex Smith TE L	6.00	15.00
ROABA B.J. Askew I	5.00	12.00
ROABE Braylon Edwards G	15.00	40.00
ROABF Brett Favre A	150.00	300.00
ROABJ Brandon Jones L	5.00	12.00
ROACB Craig Bragg I	5.00	12.00
ROACF Ciatrick Fason F	8.00	20.00
ROACO Chad Owens J	5.00	12.00
ROACR Courtney Roby I	5.00	12.00
ROACW Cadillac Williams B	15.00	40.00
ROADJ Derrick Johnson I	8.00	20.00
ROADJ Deacon Jones F	15.00	30.00
ROAEC Earl Campbell D	25.00	50.00
ROAFG Frank Gore E	20.00	50.00
ROAHM Heath Miller F	10.00	25.00
ROAJA Joe Andruzzi I	5.00	12.00
ROAJB Jim Brown C	60.00	120.00
ROAJE John Elway B	100.00	200.00
ROAJM Joe Montana C	100.00	200.00
ROAJN Joe Namath C	60.00	120.00
ROAJMA Jerome Mathis K	5.00	12.00
ROAJMU James Mungro I	6.00	15.00
ROALM Lenny Moore E	15.00	30.00
ROALT Lawrence Taylor E	30.00	60.00
ROAMC Mark Clayton E	8.00	20.00
ROAMJ Matt Jones G	8.00	20.00
ROARB Ronnie Brown H	25.00	50.00
ROARC Ronald Curry I	6.00	15.00
ROARG Randall Gay I	6.00	15.00
ROARL Ronnie Lott B	40.00	80.00
ROARP Roscoe Parrish I	8.00	20.00
ROARW Roddy White D	12.50	25.00
ROATB Tatum Bell B	8.00	20.00
ROATW Troy Williamson E	8.00	20.00

2005 Topps Heritage Team Pennants

ONE PER BOX		
1 Arizona Cardinals	2.00	5.00
2 Chicago Bears	2.50	6.00
3 Cleveland Browns	2.00	5.00
4 Detroit Lions	2.00	5.00
5 Green Bay Packers	3.00	8.00
6 Indianapolis Colts	2.00	5.00
7 New York Giants	2.50	6.00
8 Philadelphia Eagles	2.00	5.00
9 Pittsburgh Steelers	3.00	8.00
10 San Francisco 49ers	2.50	6.00
11 St. Louis Rams	2.00	5.00
12 Washington Redskins	2.50	6.00

2005 Topps Heritage Then and Now

COMPLETE SET (10)	12.50	30.00
STATED ODDS 1:15		
TN1 Brian Westbrook / Lenny Moore	1.25	3.00
TN2 Joe Montana / Tom Brady	4.00	10.00
TN3 Gale Sayers / LaDainian Tomlinson	2.00	5.00
TN4 Ben Roethlisberger / Joe Namath	3.00	8.00
TN5 Earl Campbell / Edgerrin James	1.25	3.00
TN6 Jamal Lewis / Jim Brown	2.00	5.00
TN7 Brian Dawkins / Ronnie Lott	1.25	3.00
TN8 Lawrence Taylor / Ray Lewis	1.25	3.00
TN9 Ozzie Newsome / Tony Gonzalez	1.25	3.00
TN10 Deacon Jones / Dwight Freeney	1.25	3.00

2006 Topps Heritage

This 407-card set was released in November, 2006. The set was issued into the hobby in eight-card packs, with a $3 SRP, which came 24 packs to a box. Some cards numbered between 1-133 and all cards numbered 311-407 were issued in shorter quantity then the other players in this set.

COMPLETE SET (497)	75.00	150.00
COMP.SET w/o SP's (207)	15.00	40.00
SPs: 1-90/95/100/101/107/109/111/121		
SPs: 123/125/127/129/131/133/311-407		
1 LaVar Arrington SP	.50	1.25
2 Justin McCareins SP	.40	1.00

2002 Topps Heritage Retrofractors

3 Simeon Rice SP .40 1.00
4 Dennis Northcutt SP .40 1.00
5 Jason Campbell SP .50 1.25
6 Ricardo Colclough SP .40 1.00
7 Marion Barber SP .60 1.50
8 Samie Parker SP .40 1.00
9 Nick Barnett SP .50 1.25
10 David Garrard SP .50 1.25
11 Roy Williams S SP .50 1.25
12 Adrian Peterson SP .50 1.25
13 Marcus Robinson SP .40 1.00
14 Andrew Walter SP .40 1.00
15 Cedric Houston SP .40 1.00
16 John Abraham SP .40 1.00
17 Alex Smith TE SP .40 1.00
18 Travis Henry SP .40 1.00
19 Craig Krenzel SP .30 .75
20 Brian Dawkins SP .50 1.25
21 Bryant Young SP .40 1.00
22 Al Wilson SP .40 1.00
23 Nick Goings SP .40 1.00
24 Shaun Ellis SP .40 1.00
25 Marty Booker SP .40 1.00
26 Daniel Graham SP .40 1.00
27 Jim Sorgi SP .40 1.00
28 Sebastian Janikowski SP .40 1.00
29 Allen Rossum SP .40 1.00
30 Jim Kleinsasser SP .40 1.00
31 Lee Evans SP .50 1.25
32 Alex Brown SP .40 1.00
33 Steve Hutchinson SP .50 1.25
34 Sam Madison SP .40 1.00
35 Aaron Rodgers SP 1.25 3.00
36 Justin Griffith SP .30 .75
37 Terrence McGee SP .40 1.00
38 Odell Thurman SP .40 1.00
39 Marcus Trufant SP .40 1.00
40 Courtney Roby SP .40 1.00
41 Isaac Bruce SP .50 1.25
42 Ben Watson SP .40 1.00
43 Brandon Stokley SP .50 1.25
44 Koren Robinson SP .40 1.00
45 Mark Clayton SP .50 1.25
46 Darren Sproles SP .60 1.50
47 Matt Leinart SP RC 1.25 3.00
48 Terrell Owens SP .60 1.50
49 Antonio Pierce SP .40 1.00
50 Mark Brunell SP .50 1.25
51 T.J. Houshmandzadeh SP .50 1.25
52 Chris Gamble SP .40 1.00
53 Jason Witten SP .60 1.50
54 Michael Huff SP RC 1.00 2.50
55 Joey Porter SP .40 1.00
56 Eli Manning SP .75 2.00
57 Ladell Betts SP .40 1.00
58 Kevin Curtis SP .50 1.25
59 Reggie Williams SP .50 1.25
60 Alge Crumpler SP .50 1.25
61 Joseph Addai SP RC 1.25 3.00
62 Todd Heap SP .50 1.25
63 Trent Green SP .50 1.25
64 Muhsin Muhammad SP .50 1.25
65 Drew Bledsoe SP .60 1.50
66 LenDale White SP RC 1.00 2.50
67 Kris Mangum SP .30 .75
68 Troy Vincent SP .40 1.00
69 DeMarcus Ware SP .50 1.25
70 Brian Westbrook SP .50 1.25
71 Brandon Lloyd SP .40 1.00
72 Corey Dillon SP .50 1.25
73 Ernie Conwell SP .40 1.00
74 Laveranues Coles SP .40 1.00
75 Santana Moss SP .50 1.25
76 Alvis Whitted SP .30 .75
77 Demorrio Williams SP .75 2.00
78 Matt Hasselbeck SP .50 1.25
79 Billy Volek SP .40 1.00
80 Sean Taylor SP .60 1.50
81 Plaxico Burress SP .50 1.25
82 Frank Gore SP .60 1.50
83 Chris McAlister SP .40 1.00
84 Donnie Edwards SP .40 1.00
85 Ed Reed SP .50 1.25
86 Tarvaris Jackson SP RC 1.25 3.00
87 T.J. Duckett SP .40 1.00
88 Rex Grossman SP .50 1.25
89 Ronnie Brown SP .60 1.50
90 James Farrior SP .40 1.00
91 Mike Alstott .25 .60
92 Eddie Kennison .25 .60
93 Charlie Frye .30 .75
94 Deion Branch .30 .75
95 Brandon Jacobs SP .75 2.00
96 Larry Fitzgerald .40 1.00
97 Domanick Davis .25 .60
98 Terrence Holt .25 .60
99 Dan Morgan .25 .60
100 Shaun Alexander SP .60 1.50
101 Shawne Merriman SP .60 1.50
102 Roddy White .30 .75
103 Ashley Lelie .25 .60
104 Jevon Kearse .30 .75
105 Andre Johnson .40 1.00
106 Matt Mauck .25 .60
107 Dwight Freeney SP .60 1.50
108 Robert Gallery .25 .60
109 Chad Jackson SP RC 1.00 2.50
110 Marques Tuiasosopo .25 .60
111 LaMont Jordan SP .60 1.50
112 Taylor Jacobs .25 .60
113 Byron Leftwich .30 .75
114 Fabian Washington .25 .60
115 Michael Jenkins .30 .75
116 Steven Jackson .40 1.00
117 Ronald Curry .30 .75
118 J.P. Losman .30 .75
119 Patrick Crayton .25 .60
120 Javon Walker .30 .75
121 Daunte Culpepper SP .60 1.50
122 Marc Bulger .30 .75
123 Kevin Jones SP .50 1.25
124 Tom Brady .60 1.50
125 Jay Cutler SP RC 3.00 8.00
126 Tony Gonzalez .30 .75
127 Warrick Dunn SP .60 1.50
128 Michael Strahan .30 .75
129 Demetrius Williams SP RC 1.25 3.00
130 Charles Woodson .40 1.00
131 Tiki Barber SP .75 2.00
132 Hines Ward .40 1.00
133 Brian Calhoun SP RC 1.00 2.50
134 Torry Holt .30 .75
135 Priest Holmes .30 .75
136 Philip Rivers .40 1.00
137 Joey Harrington .25 .60
138 Donte Stallworth .25 .60
139 Ken Lucas .25 .60
140 Chad Morton .25 .60
141 Osi Umenyiora .30 .75
142 Jamal Lewis .30 .75
143 Derek Hagan RC .75 2.00
144 Deshaun Foster .30 .75
145 Michael Lewis .25 .60
146 Anquan Boldin .30 .75
147 Derrick Brooks .30 .75
148 Michael Turner .40 1.00
149 Zach Thomas .40 1.00
150 Carson Palmer .40 1.00
151 Ryan Moats .25 .60
152 William Henderson .25 .60
153 Marcus Spears .25 .60
154 Travis Minor .25 .60
155 Scottie Vines .25 .60
156 Maurice Stovall RC .60 1.50
157 Dante Hall .30 .75
158 Chris Simms .30 .75
159 Zack Crockett .25 .60
160 Thomas Jones .30 .75
161 Marcus Pollard .25 .60
162 Troy Polamalu .50 1.25
163 LeRon McCoy .25 .60
164 Najeh Davenport .30 .75
165 Keenan McCardell .30 .75
166 Chris Brown .25 .60
167 Derrick Johnson .25 .60
168 Chad Pennington .30 .75
169 Adam Jones .25 .60
170 Terry Glenn .30 .75
171 Antonio Bryant .25 .60
172 Jerramy Stevens .30 .75
173 Antrel Rolle .25 .60
174 Randy McMichael .25 .60
175 Orlando Pace .25 .60
176 Chris Perry .30 .75
177 Drew Bennett .30 .75
178 Cedric Benson .30 .75
179 Ernest Wilford .25 .60
180 Dunta Robinson .25 .60
181 Reggie Wayne .30 .75
182 Lito Sheppard .30 .75
183 Maurice Drew RC 1.50 4.00
184 Todd Bouman .25 .60
185 Marlin Jackson .25 .60
186 D.J. Williams .25 .60
187 DeAngelo Hall .30 .75
188 Bubba Franks .25 .60
189 Greg Jones .25 .60
190 Dominic Rhodes .30 .75
191 Dallas Clark .30 .75
192 Dre Bly .25 .60
193 Charlie Whitehurst .40 1.00
194 Will Demps RC .40 1.00
195 Champ Bailey .30 .75
196 Sinorice Moss RC 1.00 2.50
197 Jonathan Ogden .25 .60
198 Mike Peterson .25 .60
199 D.D. Lewis RC .60 1.50
200 Vincent Jackson .30 .75
201 Stefan Lefors .25 .60
202 Willie Parker .30 .75
203 Antwaan Randle El .30 .75
204 Keary Colbert .25 .60
205 Tyrone Calico .25 .60
206 Mike Williams .25 .60
207 David Carr .25 .60
208 Braylon Edwards .30 .75
209 Michael Clayton .25 .60
210 Jerome Mathis .25 .60
211 Fred Taylor .30 .75
212 Jake Delhomme .30 .75
213 Roy Williams WR .30 .75
214 Curtis Martin .40 1.00
215 Terrell Suggs .30 .75
216 Troy Williamson .25 .60
217 Marshall Faulk .30 .75
218 D'Brickashaw Ferguson RC 1.00 2.50
219 Kelly Holcomb .25 .60
220 Matt Jones .25 .60
221 Michael Vick .40 1.00
222 Deuce McAllister .30 .75
223 Eric Moulds .25 .60
224 Ike Taylor .25 .60
225 D.J. Hackett .25 .60
226 Keyshawn Johnson .30 .75
227 Josh McCown .25 .60
228 Joe Horn .30 .75
229 Jonathan Vilma .30 .75
230 Warren Sapp .30 .75
231 Reggie Brown .25 .60
232 Clinton Portis .40 1.00
233 Derrick Burgess .25 .60
234 Bob Sanders .30 .75
235 Lofa Tatupu .30 .75
236 Justin Fargas .30 .75
237 Kellen Clemens RC .75 2.00
238 Richard Seymour .25 .60
239 Jeff Garcia .30 .75
240 Shaun Cody .25 .60
241 Brad Johnson .30 .75
242 Edgerrin James .30 .75
243 Terence Newman .25 .60
244 Bernard Berrian .30 .75
245 Mike Anderson .30 .75
246 Ahman Green .30 .75
247 Erron Kinney .25 .60
248 David Pollack .25 .60
249 Kevin Faulk .30 .75
250 Laurence Maroney RC .75 2.00
251 Chad Johnson .30 .75
252 Antonio Gates .40 1.00
253 Drew Brees .40 1.00
254 Jake Plummer .30 .75
255 Mario Williams RC 1.00 2.50
256 Chester Taylor .30 .75
257 Shawn Bryson .25 .60
258 J.J. Arrington .25 .60
259 Robert Ferguson .25 .60
260 Reuben Droughns .30 .75
261 Tab Perry .25 .60
262 Troy Brown .25 .60
263 Luis Castillo .25 .60
264 Quincy Morgan .25 .60
265 Damon Huard .25 .60
266 Walter Jones .25 .60
267 Kyle Vanden Bosch .25 .60
268 Doug Gabriel .25 .60
269 Deltha O'Neal .25 .60
270 Randy Moss .40 1.00
271 Omar Jacobs RC .60 1.50
272 Kevan Barlow .25 .60
273 John Lynch .25 .60
274 Chris Cooley .30 .75
275 Zach Hilton .25 .60
276 Peter Warrick .30 .75
277 London Fletcher .25 .60
278 Nate Burleson .25 .60
279 Larry Foote .25 .60
280 Justin Miller .25 .60
281 Darius Watts .25 .60
282 Aaron Brooks .30 .75
283 Joey Galloway .30 .75
284 Darrell Jackson .30 .75
285 Alex Smith QB .40 1.00
286 Vonnie Holliday .25 .60
287 Nathan Vasher .25 .60
288 Tatum Bell .25 .60
289 Olin Kreutz .25 .60
290 Duce Staley .25 .60
291 Courtney Anderson .25 .60
292 Tory James .25 .60
293 Mike Vanderjagt .25 .60
294 Mark Bradley .25 .60
295 Kurt Warner .40 1.00
296 Ray Lewis .40 1.00
297 Kassim Osgood .25 .60
298 Trent Dilfer .30 .75
299 Justin Gage .25 .60
300 DeAngelo Williams RC 1.25 3.00
301 Luke McCown .25 .60
302 Charles Rogers .30 .75
303 Marcedes Lewis RC 1.00 2.50
304 Samari Rolle .25 .60
305 Greg Lewis .25 .60
306 Peter Boulware .30 .75
307 Donald Driver .40 1.00
308 Travis Taylor .25 .60
309 Quentin Jammer .25 .60
310 Carlos Rogers .25 .60
311 Peyton Manning SP 3.00 8.00
312 Reggie Bush SP RC 2.50 6.00
313 Vernon Davis SP RC 1.50 4.00
314 Brett Favre SP 4.00 10.00
315 Cadillac Williams SP 1.50 4.00
316 Donovan McNabb SP 2.00 5.00
317 Jason Avant SP RC .75 2.00
318 Ben Roethlisberger SP 2.50 6.00
319 Steve Smith SP 2.00 5.00
320 Vince Young SP RC 1.50 4.00
321 Willis McGahee SP 1.50 4.00
322 Jeremy Shockey SP 2.00 5.00
323 Rudi Johnson SP 1.50 4.00
324 Brian Urlacher SP 2.00 5.00
325 Rod Smith SP 1.50 4.00
326 Santonio Holmes SP RC 1.50 4.00
327 Larry Johnson SP 1.50 4.00
328 Julius Jones SP 1.25 3.00
329 Marvin Harrison SP 2.00 5.00
330 Chris Chambers SP 1.50 4.00
331 Takeo Spikes SP 1.25 3.00
332 Brian Griese SP 1.50 4.00
333 Steve McNair SP 1.50 4.00
334 Willie McGinest SP 1.25 3.00
335 Tedy Bruschi SP 2.00 5.00
336 Roydell Williams SP 1.25 3.00
337 Patrick Ramsey SP 1.50 4.00
338 Kyle Boller SP 1.50 4.00
339 Bethel Johnson SP 1.25 3.00
340 Jerry Porter SP 1.25 3.00
341 Shawntae Spencer SP 1.25 3.00
342 Drew Carter SP 1.25 3.00
343 Jason Elam SP 1.25 3.00
344 Michael Pittman SP 1.25 3.00
345 Edell Shepherd SP RC .75 2.00
346 Maurice Hicks SP 1.25 3.00
347 Ron Dayne SP 1.50 4.00
348 Josh Reed SP 1.25 3.00
349 Lorenzo Neal SP 1.25 3.00
350 LaDainian Tomlinson SP 2.00 5.00
351 David Tyree SP 1.50 4.00
352 Keith Brooking SP 1.25 3.00
353 Devery Henderson SP 1.25 3.00
354 Daylon McCutcheon SP 1.25 3.00
355 Derrick Mason SP 1.50 4.00
356 Fred Smoot SP 1.25 3.00
357 Ronde Barber SP 1.50 4.00
358 Dan Kreider SP 1.25 3.00
359 Shayne Graham SP 1.25 3.00
360 Vernand Morency SP 1.25 3.00
361 Shawn Springs SP 1.25 3.00
362 Amani Toomer SP 1.50 4.00
363 Eric Parker SP 1.25 3.00
364 Jason Taylor SP 1.50 4.00
365 Keith Bulluck SP 1.25 3.00
366 Sam Gado SP 1.50 4.00
367 Cedrick Wilson SP 1.25 3.00
368 Mewelde Moore SP 1.25 3.00
369 Travis Daniels SP 1.25 3.00
370 Arnaz Battle SP 1.25 3.00
371 Kyle Orton SP 2.00 5.00
372 Dane Looker SP 1.25 3.00
373 Kellen Winslow SP 1.50 4.00
374 Julius Peppers SP 1.50 4.00
375 Jeremiah Trotter SP 1.25 3.00
376 L.J. Smith SP 1.25 3.00
377 Gibril Wilson SP 1.25 3.00
378 Adam Archuleta SP 1.25 3.00
379 Darren Sharper SP 1.50 4.00
380 Joe Jurevicius SP 1.25 3.00
381 Patrick Pass SP 1.25 3.00
382 A.J. Feeley SP 1.25 3.00
383 Leroy Hill SP 1.25 3.00
384 Corey Webster SP 1.25 3.00
385 Heath Miller SP 1.50 4.00
386 Cato June SP 1.50 4.00
387 Brad Hoover SP 1.25 3.00
388 Michael Boulware SP 1.25 3.00
389 Matt Schaub SP 1.50 4.00
390 Kirk Morrison SP 1.25 3.00
391 Kevin Carter SP 1.25 3.00
392 David Givens SP 1.50 4.00
393 Alvin Pearman SP 1.25 3.00
394 Brian Finneran SP 1.25 3.00
395 Ike Hilliard SP 1.25 3.00
396 Angelo Crowell SP 1.25 3.00
397 Charlie Adams SP 1.25 3.00
398 Neil Rackers SP 1.25 3.00
399 Brandon Jones SP 1.25 3.00
400 B.J. Sams SP 1.25 3.00
401 Kyle Johnson SP 1.25 3.00
402 Adam Vinatieri SP 1.50 4.00
403 Bryant Johnson SP 1.25 3.00
404 Bryan Fletcher SP 1.25 3.00
405 Channing Crowder SP 1.25 3.00
406 Jerricho Cotchery SP 1.50 4.00
407 A.J. Hawk SP RC 1.25 3.00

2006 Topps Heritage Black Backs

*BLACK BACKS: .4X TO 1X RED BACKS

2006 Topps Heritage Chrome

CHROME/1952 ODDS 1:6 HOB
*REF.VETS: .6X TO 1.5X BASIC CHROME
*REF.ROOKIES: .6X TO 1.5X BASIC CHROME
REFRACT/552 ODDS 1:27 HOB
*BLACK REF.VETS: 1.2X TO 3X
*BLACK REF.ROOKIE: 1.5X TO 4X
BLK REFRACT/52 ODDS 1:294 HOB
THC1 Jeremy Shockey 2.00 5.00
THC2 Maurice Stovall 1.25 3.00
THC3 Donte Stallworth 1.25 3.00
THC4 Zach Thomas 2.00 5.00
THC5 Daunte Culpepper 1.50 4.00
THC6 Carson Palmer 2.00 5.00
THC7 Vernon Davis 2.50 6.00
THC8 A.J. Hawk 2.00 5.00
THC9 Plaxico Burress 1.50 4.00
THC10 Jamal Lewis 1.50 4.00
THC11 Shaun Alexander 1.50 4.00
THC12 LaMont Jordan 1.50 4.00
THC13 Marc Bulger 1.50 4.00
THC14 Chris Simms 1.50 4.00
THC15 Muhsin Muhammad 1.50 4.00
THC16 Ahman Green 1.50 4.00
THC17 Drew Bledsoe 2.00 5.00
THC18 David Carr 1.25 3.00
THC19 LenDale White 1.50 4.00
THC20 Joey Galloway 1.50 4.00
THC21 Michael Vick 2.00 5.00
THC22 Ray Lewis 2.00 5.00
THC23 Deuce McAllister 1.50 4.00
THC24 Marcedes Lewis 2.00 5.00
THC25 Eric Moulds 1.25 3.00
THC26 Julius Jones 1.25 3.00
THC27 Rudi Johnson 1.50 4.00
THC28 Chester Taylor 1.50 4.00
THC29 Todd Heap 1.50 4.00
THC30 Dante Hall 1.50 4.00
THC31 Trent Green 1.50 4.00
THC32 Rod Smith 1.50 4.00
THC33 Javon Walker 1.50 4.00
THC34 Omar Jacobs 1.25 3.00
THC35 Kevin Jones 1.25 3.00
THC36 Derek Hagan 1.50 4.00
THC37 Jason Avant 1.25 3.00
THC38 Deshaun Foster 1.50 4.00
THC39 Chris Brown 1.25 3.00
THC40 Takeo Spikes 1.25 3.00
THC41 Alge Crumpler 1.50 4.00
THC42 Tarvaris Jackson 2.00 5.00
THC43 Joseph Addai 2.00 5.00
THC44 Ben Roethlisberger 2.50 6.00
THC45 Chad Johnson 1.50 4.00
THC46 Ronnie Brown 2.00 5.00
THC47 Brian Urlacher 2.00 5.00
THC48 Laurence Maroney 1.50 4.00
THC49 Maurice Drew 3.00 8.00
THC50 Shawne Merriman 1.50 4.00
THC51 Vince Young 2.50 6.00
THC52 Corey Dillon 1.50 4.00
THC53 Steve Smith 2.00 5.00
THC54 Matt Hasselbeck 1.50 4.00
THC55 Willis McGahee 1.50 4.00
THC56 D'Brickashaw Ferguson 2.00 5.00
THC57 Chad Jackson 1.25 3.00
THC58 Clinton Portis 2.00 5.00
THC59 Santana Moss 1.50 4.00
THC60 Larry Johnson 1.50 4.00
THC61 Cadillac Williams 1.50 4.00
THC62 Tom Brady 3.00 8.00
THC63 Peyton Manning 3.00 8.00
THC64 Jay Cutler 4.00 10.00
THC65 Reggie Bush 4.00 10.00
THC66 Eli Manning 2.50 6.00
THC67 Brett Favre 4.00 10.00
THC68 Tony Gonzalez 1.50 4.00
THC69 Matt Leinart 2.00 5.00
THC70 Warrick Dunn 1.50 4.00
THC71 Terrell Owens 2.00 5.00
THC72 Anquan Boldin 1.50 4.00
THC73 LaDainian Tomlinson 2.00 5.00
THC74 Michael Strahan 1.50 4.00
THC75 Donovan McNabb 2.00 5.00
THC76 Demetrius Williams 1.50 4.00
THC77 Michael Huff 1.50 4.00
THC78 Charles Woodson 2.00 5.00
THC79 Byron Leftwich 1.50 4.00
THC80 Tiki Barber 2.00 5.00
THC81 Curtis Martin 2.00 5.00
THC82 Hines Ward 2.00 5.00
THC83 DeAngelo Williams 2.50 6.00
THC84 Brian Calhoun 1.25 3.00
THC85 Randy Moss 2.00 5.00
THC86 Torry Holt 1.50 4.00
THC87 Steven Jackson 2.00 5.00
THC88 Priest Holmes 1.50 4.00
THC89 Larry Fitzgerald 2.00 5.00
THC90 Philip Rivers 2.00 5.00
THC91 Domanick Davis 1.25 3.00
THC92 Santonio Holmes 2.50 6.00
THC93 Charlie Whitehurst 2.00 5.00
THC94 Antonio Gates 2.00 5.00
THC95 Fred Taylor 1.50 4.00
THC96 Drew Brees 2.00 5.00
THC97 Jake Delhomme 1.50 4.00
THC98 Jake Plummer 1.50 4.00
THC99 Roy Williams WR 1.50 4.00
THC100 Mario Williams 2.00 5.00
THC101 Drew Bennett 1.50 4.00
THC102 Sinorice Moss 2.00 5.00
THC103 Reggie Wayne 1.50 4.00
THC104 Willie Parker 1.50 4.00
THC105 Marvin Harrison 2.00 5.00
THC106 Joe Horn 1.50 4.00
THC107 Jonathan Vilma 1.50 4.00
THC108 Chris Chambers 1.50 4.00
THC109 Kellen Clemens 1.50 4.00
THC110 Edgerrin James 1.50 4.00

2006 Topps Heritage Flashbacks

COMPLETE SET (6) 5.00 12.00
STATED ODDS 1:5 HOB
FL1 Frank Gifford 1.25 3.00
FL2 Chuck Bednarik 1.00 2.50
FL3 Y.A. Tittle 1.25 3.00
FL4 Art Donovan 1.00 2.50
FL5 Hugh McElhenny 1.00 2.50
FL6 Lou Creekmur .60 1.50

2006 Topps Heritage Flashbacks Autographs

AUTO/25 ODDS 1:17,600 HOB
FAAD Art Donovan
FACB Chuck Bednarik 25.00 60.00
FAYT Y.A. Tittle 30.00 80.00

2006 Topps Heritage Flashbacks Relics

GIFFORD ODDS 1:17,150 HOB
BEDNARIK ODDS 1:1680 HOB
FRCB Chuck Bednarik 5.00 12.00
FRFG Frank Gifford 20.00 50.00

2006 Topps Heritage Gridiron Collection Jersey

STATED ODDS 1:45 HOB
GCAH A.J. Hawk 6.00 15.00
GCBC Brian Calhoun 3.00 8.00
GCCW Charlie Whitehurst 3.00 8.00
GCDH Derek Hagan 3.00 8.00
GCJA Jason Avant 3.00 8.00
GCJK Joe Klopfenstein 3.00 8.00
GCLW LenDale White 5.00 12.00
GCMH Michael Huff 3.00 8.00
GCMS Maurice Stovall 4.00 10.00
GCMW Mario Williams 4.00 10.00
GCRB Reggie Bush 10.00 25.00
GCSH Santonio Holmes 4.00 10.00
GCSM Sinorice Moss 3.00 8.00
GCTJ Tarvaris Jackson 3.00 8.00
GCTW Travis Wilson 3.00 8.00
GCVY Vince Young 8.00 20.00

2006 Topps Heritage Gridiron Collection Jersey Autographs

AUTO/25 ODDS 1:5850 HOB
GCRAAH A.J. Hawk 40.00 80.00
GCRABC Brian Calhoun 20.00 40.00
GCRADH Derek Hagan 15.00 40.00
GCRAJK Joe Klopfenstein
GCRALW LenDale White 40.00 80.00
GCRAMS Maurice Stovall
GCRAMW Mario Williams 25.00 50.00
GCRARB Reggie Bush 75.00 200.00
GCRASH Santonio Holmes
GCRASM Sinorice Moss 15.00 40.00
GCRATJ Tarvaris Jackson 30.00 80.00
GCRAVY Vince Young 50.00 120.00

2006 Topps Heritage Gridiron Collection Jersey Duals

DUAL/52 ODDS 1:5500 HOB
BL Reggie Bush 20.00 50.00
Matt Leinart
BW Reggie Bush 25.00 60.00
LenDale White
HM Sinorice Moss 12.00 30.00
Santonio Holmes
HS Santonio Holmes 20.00 40.00
Maurice Stovall
HW A.J. Hawk 25.00 50.00
Mario Williams
YL Vince Young 20.00 50.00
Matt Leinart

2006 Topps Heritage In the Cards Autographs

GROUP A ODDS 1:70,000 HOB
GROUP B ODDS 1:5725 HOB
GROUP C ODDS 1:17,500 HOB
GROUP D ODDS 1:1208 HOB
GROUP E ODDS 1:1600 HOB
GROUP F ODDS 1:420 HOB
GROUP G ODDS 1:1680 HOB
UNPRICED SPECIAL EDITION #'d TO 6
HCAAH A.J. Hawk G 12.00 30.00
HCABF Brett Favre B 125.00 200.00
HCACJ Chad Jackson G 6.00 15.00
HCADA DeAngelo Williams D 12.00 30.00
HCADF D'Brickashaw Ferguson E 10.00 25.00
HCADM Dan Marino B 100.00 200.00
HCAES Emmitt Smith A 150.00 250.00
HCAJA Joseph Addai G 10.00 25.00
HCAJC Jay Cutler E 20.00 50.00
HCAJE John Elway B 75.00 150.00
HCAJK Joe Klopfenstein F 6.00 15.00
HCAJN Jerious Norwood G 8.00 20.00
HCAJN Joe Namath C 60.00 100.00
HCALP Leonard Pope E 10.00 25.00
HCALT LaDainian Tomlinson B 25.00 60.00
HCALW Leon Washington G 8.00 20.00
HCAMK Mathias Kiwanuka G 10.00 25.00
HCAML Matt Leinart D 10.00 25.00
HCAMW Mario Williams G 10.00 25.00
HCAPM Peyton Manning D 60.00 100.00
HCARB Reggie Bush D 20.00 50.00
HCASH Santonio Holmes D 12.00 30.00
HCATB Terry Bradshaw B 60.00 100.00
HCAVD Vernon Davis G 12.00 30.00
HCAVY Vince Young D 12.00 30.00
HCACJO Chad Johnson B 12.00 30.00
HCALWH LenDale White D 8.00 20.00

2006 Topps Heritage New Age Performers

COMPLETE SET (15) 8.00 20.00
STATED ODDS 1:8 HOB
NAP1 Brett Favre 2.50 6.00
NAP2 Steve Smith 1.25 3.00
NAP3 Tiki Barber 1.25 3.00
NAP4 Chad Johnson 1.00 2.50
NAP5 Tom Brady 2.00 5.00
NAP6 Carson Palmer 1.25 3.00
NAP7 LaDainian Tomlinson 1.25 3.00
NAP8 Larry Johnson 1.00 2.50
NAP9 Matt Hasselbeck 1.00 2.50
NAP10 Shaun Alexander 1.00 2.50
NAP11 Peyton Manning 2.00 5.00
NAP12 Ben Roethlisberger 1.50 4.00
NAP13 Reggie Bush 1.00 2.50
NAP14 Matt Leinart .50 1.25
NAP15 Vince Young .60 1.50

2006 Topps Heritage Real One Autographs

AUTO/200 ODDS 1:1055 HOB
*SPECIAL EDIT/52: .6X TO 1.5X BASIC INSERTS
SPEC.EDIT.AU/52 ODDS 1:4120 HOB
ROAAD Art Donovan 25.00 50.00
ROACB Chuck Bednarik 25.00 50.00
ROACT Charley Trippi 25.00 50.00
ROAGM Gino Marchetti 25.00 50.00
ROAHM Hugh McElhenny 25.00 50.00
ROAYA Y.A. Tittle UER 30.00 60.00
(birth year incorrect on back)

2006 Topps Heritage Then and Now

COMPLETE SET (5) 5.00 12.00
STATED ODDS 1:0 HOB
TN1 Reggie Bush 3.00 8.00
Frank Gifford
TN2 Brian Urlacher 1.50 4.00
Chuck Bednarik
TN3 Drew Brees 2.00 5.00
Y.A. Tittle
TN4 Michael Vick 2.00 5.00
Charley Trippi
TN5 Warren Sapp 1.25 3.00
Art Donovan

1956 Topps Hocus Focus

The 1956 Topps Hocus Focus set is very similar in size and design to the 1948 Topps Magic Photos set. It contains at least 96 small (approximately 7/8" by 1 5/8") individual cards featuring a variety of sports and non-sport subjects. They were printed with both a series card number (by subject matter) on the back as well as a card number reflecting the entire set. The fronts were developed, much like a photograph, from a blank appearance by using moisture and sunlight. Due to varying degrees of photographic sensitivity, the clarity of these cards ranges from fully developed to poorly developed. A premium album holding 126-cards was also issued leading to the theory that there are actually 126 different cards. A few High Series (#97-126) cards have been discovered and cataloged below although a full 126-card checklist is yet unknown. The cards do reference the set name "Hocus Focus" on the backs unlike the 1948 Magic Photos. Finally, a slightly smaller version (roughly 7/8" by 1 7/16") of some of the cards has also been found, but a full checklist is not known.

10 Southern Cal Football 12.50 25.00

2011 Topps Inception

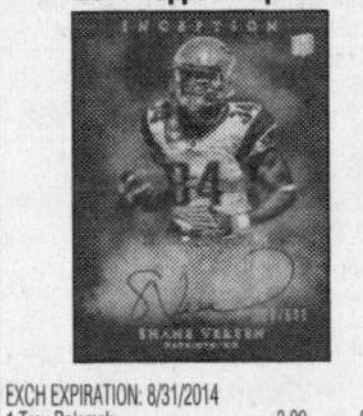

EXCH EXPIRATION: 8/31/2014
1 Troy Polamalu 3.00 8.00
2 Darren McFadden 2.00 5.00
3 Hakeem Nicks 2.00 5.00
4 Ryan Mathews 2.00 5.00
5 Mark Sanchez 2.50 6.00
6 Mike Williams 2.00 5.00
7 James Harrison 2.50 6.00
8 Dwight Freeney 2.00 5.00
9 Mike Wallace 2.50 6.00
10 Peyton Manning 4.00 10.00
11 Charles Woodson 2.50 6.00
12 Marshawn Lynch 2.00 5.00
13 Marcedes Lewis 1.50 4.00
14 Sidney Rice 2.00 5.00
15 Jonathan Stewart 2.00 5.00
16 Jerod Mayo 1.50 4.00
17 Dwayne Bowe 2.00 5.00
18 Matt Cassel 2.00 5.00
19 Peyton Hillis 2.00 5.00
20 Tom Brady 4.00 10.00
21 Santonio Holmes 2.00 5.00
22 Reggie Wayne 2.00 5.00
23 Josh Freeman 2.50 6.00
24 Knowshon Moreno 2.00 5.00
25 Ed Reed 2.00 5.00
26 Ronnie Brown 2.00 5.00
27 Sam Bradford 2.50 6.00
28 Jay Cutler 2.00 5.00
29 Eli Manning 2.50 6.00
30 Adrian Peterson 3.00 8.00
31 Beanie Wells 2.00 5.00
32 Arian Foster 2.00 5.00
33 Brian Urlacher 2.50 6.00
34 Greg Jennings 2.00 5.00
35 Pierre Garcon 2.00 5.00
36 Colt McCoy 2.00 5.00
37 Fred Jackson 2.50 6.00
38 Tony Gonzalez 2.00 5.00
39 Chris Ivory 2.00 5.00
40 Michael Vick 2.50 6.00
41 Ray Rice 2.00 5.00
42 Miles Austin 2.00 5.00
43 Hines Ward 2.00 5.00
44 Matthew Stafford 2.50 6.00
45 Ahmad Bradshaw 2.00 5.00
46 Rob Gronkowski 2.50 6.00
47 Marques Colston 2.00 5.00
48 Andre Johnson 2.00 5.00
48 Matt Schaub 2.00 5.00
49 Calvin Johnson 2.50 6.00
50 Roddy White 2.00 5.00
51 Antonio Gates 2.00 5.00
52 Larry Fitzgerald 2.00 5.00
53 LeSean McCoy 2.00 5.00
54 Ndamukong Suh 2.50 6.00
55 LeGarrette Blount 2.00 5.00
56 Philip Rivers 2.50 6.00
57 Steve Johnson 2.00 5.00
58 Santana Moss 2.00 5.00
59 Jason Witten 2.50 6.00
60 Maurice Jones-Drew 2.00 5.00
61 Matt Forte 2.00 5.00
62 Wes Welker 2.50 6.00
63 Tim Tebow 5.00 12.00
64 Jermichael Finley 2.00 5.00
65 Jordan Shipley 2.00 5.00
66 Matt Ryan 2.50 6.00
67 BenJarvus Green-Ellis 2.00 5.00
68 Matt Hasselbeck 2.00 5.00
69 Tony Romo 2.50 6.00
70 Ray Lewis 2.50 6.00
71 Vernon Davis 2.00 5.00
72 Dez Bryant 2.50 6.00
73 Chris Cooley 2.00 5.00
74 Shonn Greene 2.00 5.00
75 Brandon Lloyd 2.00 5.00
76 Jared Allen 2.00 5.00
77 Joe Flacco 2.50 6.00
78 Clay Matthews 2.50 6.00
79 Rashard Mendenhall 2.00 5.00
81 Darrelle Revis 2.00 5.00
82 Chris Johnson 2.00 5.00
83 Ben Roethlisberger 2.50 6.00
84 Malcom Floyd 2.00 5.00
85 Michael Turner 2.00 5.00
86 DeSean Jackson 2.00 5.00
87 James Starks 2.00 5.00
88 Zach Miller 2.00 5.00
89 Kenny Britt 2.00 5.00
90 Drew Brees 2.50 6.00
91 Danny Woodhead 2.50 6.00
92 Steven Jackson 2.00 5.00
93 Frank Gore 2.00 5.00
94 Percy Harvin 2.00 5.00
95 Braylon Edwards 2.00 5.00
96 Jamaal Charles 2.00 5.00
97 Julius Peppers 2.00 5.00
98 Brandon Marshall 2.00 5.00
99 Patrick Willis 2.00 5.00
100 Aaron Rodgers 5.00 12.00
101 Leonard Hankerson AU/199 RC 6.00 15.00
102 Ryan Mallett AU/199 RC 30.00 60.00
103 Ryan Williams AU RC EXCH 12.00 30.00
104 Mikel Leshoure AU RC EXCH 6.00 15.00
106 Jon Baldwin AU/500 RC 5.00 12.00
107 Torrey Smith AU/200 RC 8.00 20.00
108 Delone Carter AU/900 RC 4.00 10.00
109 Kyle Rudolph AU/900 RC 5.00 12.00
112 Randall Cobb AU/200 RC 15.00 30.00
113 Von Miller AU/199 RC 10.00 25.00
114 Daniel Thomas AU/200 RC 15.00 30.00
115 Jerrel Jernigan AU/500 RC 4.00 10.00
116 Shane Vereen AU/500 RC 5.00 12.00
117 DeMarco Murray AU/800 RC 25.00 50.00
118 Greg Little AU/800 RC 6.00 15.00
121 Titus Young AU/500 RC 10.00 25.00
122 Stevan Ridley AU/600 RC 5.00 12.00
123 Jordan Todman AU/900 RC 3.00 8.00
124 Alex Green AU/900 RC 5.00 12.00
126 Colin Kaepernick AU/500 RC 12.00 30.00
127 Austin Pettis AU/900 RC 4.00 10.00
128 Kendall Hunter AU/600 RC 5.00 12.00
129 Vincent Brown AU/900 RC 5.00 12.00
131 Taiwan Jones AU/900 RC 5.00 12.00
132 Bilal Powell AU/900 RC 3.00 8.00
133 Marcell Dareus AU/500 RC 5.00 12.00
134 Jamie Harper AU/600 RC 5.00 12.00
137 Edmond Gates AU/600 RC 4.00 10.00

2011 Topps Inception Blue

COMPLETE SET (125)
*1-100 VETS/209: .5X TO 1.2X BASIC CARDS
VETERAN STATED PRINT RUN 209
*ROOK.AU/150: .5X TO 1.2X AU RC/500-900
*ROOK.AU/150: .4X TO 1X AU RC/199-200
101-136 ROOKIE AU PRINT RUN 150
EXCH EXPIRATION: 8/31/2014

2011 Topps Inception Gray

*1-100 VETS/106: .6X TO 1.5X BASIC CARDS
VETERAN STATED PRINT RUN 106
*ROOK.AU/99: .6X TO 1.5X AU RC/500-900
*ROOK.AU/99: .5X TO 1.2X AU RC/199-200
101-136 ROOKIE AU PRINT RUN 99
EXCH EXPIRATION: 8/31/2014

2011 Topps Inception Green

*1-100 VETS/75: .8X TO 2X BASIC CARDS
1-100 VETERAN PRINT RUN 75
*ROOK.AU/50: .8X TO 2X AU RC/500 900
*ROOK.AU/50: .6X TO 1.5X AU RC/199-200
101-150 ROOKIE AU PRINT RUN 50
EXCH EXPIRATION: 8/31/2014
105 Julio Jones AU 50.00 100.00
111 Andy Dalton AU 50.00 100.00
135 Cam Newton AU 100.00 200.00

2011 Topps Inception Red

*1-100 VETS/25: 1.2X TO 3X BASIC CARDS
*ROOK.AU/25: 1X TO 2.5X AU RC/500-900
*ROOK.AU/25: .8X TO 2X AU RC/199-200
STATED PRINT RUN 25 SER.#'d SETS
EXCH EXPIRATION: 8/31/2014
105 Julio Jones AU 75.00 150.00
110 Mark Ingram AU EXCH 100.00 200.00
111 Andy Dalton AU 75.00 150.00
119 Christian Ponder AU 75.00 150.00
120 Jake Locker AU 100.00 200.00
125 Blaine Gabbert AU 75.00 150.00
130 A.J. Green AU 75.00 150.00
135 Cam Newton AU 200.00 350.00

2011 Topps Inception Dual Autographs

STATED PRINT RUN 25 SER.#'d SETS
EXCH EXPIRATION: 8/31/2014
DABS Jon Baldwin EXCH 25.00 60.00
Torrey Smith
DACJ Randall Cobb 25.00 60.00
Jerrel Jernigan
DADG Andy Dalton 100.00 200.00
A.J. Green
DADP Andy Dalton 75.00 150.00
Christian Ponder
DAGJ A.J. Green 100.00 200.00
Julio Jones
DAGL Blaine Gabbert 100.00 200.00
Jake Locker
DAGN Blaine Gabbert 150.00 250.00
Cam Newton
DAIJ Mark Ingram 100.00 200.00
Julio Jones
DAIL Mark IngramH 50.00 100.00
Mikel Leshoure
DALM Jake Locker 100.00 200.00
Ryan Mallett
DAMV Ryan Mallett 60.00 120.00
Shane Vereen
DANI Cam Newton EXCH 125.00 250.00
Mark Ingram
DAPR Christian Ponder 60.00 120.00
Kyle Rudolph
DAVR Shane Vereen 25.00 60.00
Stevan Ridley
DAWL Ryan Williams EXCH 25.00 60.00
Mikel Leshoure

2011 Topps Inception Rookie Autographs Silver Ink

*SILVER INK/25: .4X TO 1X RED AU/25
STATED PRINT RUN 25 SER.#'d SETS
SSAD Andy Dalton 125.00 200.00
SSAG A.J. Green EXCH 90.00 150.00
SSBG Blaine Gabbert 100.00 200.00
SSCK Colin Kaepernick 40.00 100.00
SSCN Cam Newton 250.00 400.00
SSCP Christian Ponder 125.00 200.00
SSDM DeMarco Murray 100.00 200.00
SSJJ Julio Jones 100.00 175.00
SSJL Jake Locker 100.00 200.00
SSMI Mark Ingram EXCH 100.00 200.00
SSRC Randall Cobb 40.00 80.00
SSRM Ryan Mallett 75.00 150.00

2011 Topps Inception Rookie Dual Jumbo Relics

STATED PRINT RUN 15 SER.#'d SETS
DJRBB Jon Baldwin 8.00 20.00
Vincent Brown
DJRBS Jon Baldwin 12.00 30.00
Torrey Smith
DJRCG Randall Cobb 10.00 25.00
Alex Green
DJRCJ Randall Cobb 10.00 25.00
Jerrel Jernigan
DJRDB Andy Dalton 20.00 50.00
Vincent Brown
DJRDK Andy Dalton 20.00 50.00
Colin Kaepernick
DJRDP Andy Dalton 20.00 50.00
Christian Ponder
DJRGD A.J. Green 20.00 50.00
Andy Dalton
DJRGJ A.J. Green 15.00 40.00
Julio Jones
DJRGL Blaine Gabbert 20.00 50.00
Jake Locker
DJRGN Blaine Gabbert 25.00 60.00
Cam Newton
DJRGT Edmond Gates 8.00 20.00
Daniel Thomas
DJRID Mark Ingram 15.00 40.00
Marcell Dareus
DJRIJ Mark Ingram 15.00 40.00
Julio Jones
DJRIL Mark Ingram 15.00 40.00
Mikel Leshoure
DJRJD Julio Jones 15.00 40.00
Marcell Dareus
DJRJH Jerrel Jernigan 8.00 20.00
Leonard Hankerson
DJRJP Jerrel Jernigan 6.00 15.00
Bilal Powell
DJRKG Colin Kaepernick 10.00 25.00
Alex Green
DJRKH Colin Kaepernick 10.00 25.00
Kendall Hunter
DJRKP Colin Kaepernick 10.00 25.00
Austin Pettis
DJRKW Colin Kaepernick 10.00 25.00
Ryan Williams
DJRLG Greg Little 15.00 40.00
A.J. Green

DJRLH Jake Locker	15.00	40.00
Jamie Harper		
DJRLJ Jake Locker	15.00	40.00
Taiwan Jones		
DJRLM Jake Locker	20.00	50.00
Ryan Mallett		
DJRLY Mikel Leshoure	10.00	25.00
Titus Young		
DJRMD Von Miller	10.00	25.00
Marcell Dareus		
DJRMH DeMarco Murray	15.00	40.00
Kendall Hunter		
DJRMJ Von Miller	10.00	25.00
Taiwan Jones		
DJRMR Ryan Mallett	20.00	50.00
Stevan Ridley		
DJRMV Ryan Mallett	20.00	50.00
Shane Vereen		
DJRND Cam Newton	25.00	60.00
Andy Dalton		
DJRNI Cam Newton	25.00	60.00
Mark Ingram		
DJRNJ Cam Newton	25.00	60.00
Julio Jones		
DJRNM Cam Newton	25.00	60.00
Ryan Mallett		
DJRPH Christian Ponder	15.00	40.00
Leonard Hankerson		
DJRPT Bilal Powell	8.00	20.00
Daniel Thomas		
DJRRG Kyle Rudolph	8.00	20.00
Alex Green		
DJRRP Kyle Rudolph	15.00	40.00
Christian Ponder		
DJRSL Torrey Smith	12.00	30.00
Greg Little		
DJRTB Jordan Todman	8.00	20.00
Vincent Brown		
DJRTC Daniel Thomas	8.00	20.00
Delone Carter		
DJRTJ Jordan Todman	8.00	20.00
Taiwan Jones		
DJRTM Daniel Thomas	10.00	25.00
Von Miller		
DJRTP Jordan Todman	5.00	12.00
Bilal Powell		
DJRVR Shane Vereen	8.00	20.00
Stevan Ridley		
DJRWH Ryan Williams	10.00	25.00
Jamie Harper		
DJRWL Ryan Williams	10.00	25.00
Mikel Leshoure		
DJRYP Titus Young	10.00	25.00
Austin Pettis		

2011 Topps Inception Rookie Jumbo Patch Autographs Red

RED JSY AU STATED PRINT RUN 25
*BASE AU/399-599: .2X TO .5X RED JSY AU/25
*BASE AU/150: .25X TO .5X RED JSY AU/25
*GRAY/75: .25X TO .6X RED JSY AU/25
*GREEN/50: .3X TO .8X RED JSY AU/25

AJPAD Andy Dalton	100.00	200.00
AJPAG A.J. Green	100.00	175.00
AJPAGR Alex Green	15.00	40.00
AJPAP Austin Pettis	12.00	30.00
AJPBG Blaine Gabbert	100.00	200.00
AJPBP Bilal Powell	10.00	25.00
AJPCK Colin Kaepernick	50.00	100.00
AJPCN Cam Newton	250.00	400.00
AJPCP Christian Ponder	100.00	200.00
AJPDB Da'Quan Bowers	15.00	40.00
AJPDC Delone Carter	12.00	30.00
AJPDM DeMarco Murray	75.00	200.00
AJPDT Daniel Thomas	30.00	80.00
AJPEG Edmond Gates	12.00	30.00
AJPGL Greg Little	20.00	50.00
AJPJB Jon Baldwin	15.00	40.00
AJPJH Jamie Harper	15.00	40.00
AJPJJ Julio Jones	100.00	200.00
AJPJJE Jerrel Jernigan	12.00	30.00
AJPJL Jake Locker	100.00	200.00
AJPJT Jordan Todman	10.00	25.00
AJPKH Kendall Hunter	15.00	40.00
AJPKR Kyle Rudolph	15.00	40.00
AJPLH Leonard Hankerson	15.00	40.00
AJPMD Marcell Dareus	15.00	40.00
AJPMI Mark Ingram	100.00	200.00
AJPML Mikel Leshoure	15.00	40.00
AJPRC Randall Cobb	30.00	80.00
AJPRM Ryan Mallett	100.00	175.00
AJPRW Ryan Williams	30.00	80.00
AJPSR Stevan Ridley	15.00	40.00
AJPSV Shane Vereen	15.00	40.00
AJPTJ Taiwan Jones	15.00	40.00
AJPTS Torrey Smith	20.00	50.00
AJPTY Titus Young	20.00	50.00
AJPVB Vincent Brown	15.00	40.00
AJPVM Von Miller	25.00	60.00

2011 Topps Inception Rookie Quad Patches

STATED PRINT RUN 15 SER.#'d SETS

GJBY A.J. Green	40.00	80.00
Julio Jones		
Jon Baldwin		
Titus Young		
GJCH A.J. Green	30.00	80.00
Julio Jones		
Randall Cobb		
Leonard Hankerson		
GLMD Blaine Gabbert	40.00	80.00
Jake Locker		
Ryan Mallett		
Andy Dalton		
ILWT Mark Ingram	40.00	80.00
Mikel Leshoure		
Ryan Williams		
Jordan Todman		
JCHS Julio Jones	40.00	80.00
Randall Cobb		
Leonard Hankerson		
Torrey Smith		
LWTV Mikel Leshoure	20.00	50.00
Ryan Williams		
Jordan Todman		
Shane Vereen		
NDGM Cam Newton	50.00	100.00
Marcell Dareus		
Blaine Gabbert		
Von Miller		
NGLM Cam Newton	50.00	100.00
Blaine Gabbert		
Jake Locker		
Ryan Mallett		
NLGP Cam Newton	60.00	120.00
Jake Locker		
Blaine Gabbert		
Christian Ponder		
TVRP Daniel Thomas	30.00	60.00
Shane Vereen		
Stevan Ridley		
Bilal Powell		

2011 Topps Inception Rookie Relics Jumbo Swatch

STATED PRINT RUN 158 SER.#'d SETS
*JUMBO PATCH/15: 1X TO 2.5X JUM.JSY/158
*JUMBO GRAY/75: .5X TO 1.2X JUM.JSY/158
*JUMBO GREEN/25: .6X TO 1.5X JUM.JSY/158
*JUMBO RED/10: .8X TO 2X JUMBO JSY/158
*PATCH/158: .5X TO 1.2X JUMBO JSY/158
*PATCH GRAY/75: .6X TO 1.5X JUM.JSY/158
*PATCH GREEN/25: .8X TO 2X JUM.JSY/158
*PATCH RED/10: 1X TO 2.5X JUMBO JSY/158

JRAD Andy Dalton	8.00	20.00
JRAG A.J. Green	6.00	15.00
JRAGR Alex Green	3.00	8.00
JRAP Austin Pettis	2.50	6.00
JRBG Blaine Gabbert	5.00	12.00
JRBP Bilal Powell	2.00	5.00
JRCK Colin Kaepernick	4.00	10.00
JRCN Cam Newton	15.00	40.00
JRCP Christian Ponder	8.00	20.00
JRDC Delone Carter	2.50	6.00
JRDM DeMarco Murray	6.00	15.00
JRDT Daniel Thomas	3.00	8.00
JREG Edmond Gates	2.50	6.00
JRGL Greg Little	3.00	8.00
JRJB Jon Baldwin	3.00	8.00
JRJH Jamie Harper	3.00	8.00
JRJJ Julio Jones	6.00	15.00
JRJJE Jerrel Jernigan	2.50	6.00
JRJL Jake Locker	8.00	20.00
JRJT Jordan Todman	2.00	5.00
JRKH Kendall Hunter	3.00	8.00
JRKR Kyle Rudolph	3.00	8.00
JRLH Leonard Hankerson	3.00	8.00
JRMD Marcell Dareus	3.00	8.00
JRMI Mark Ingram	6.00	15.00
JRML Mikel Leshoure	3.00	8.00
JRRC Randall Cobb	4.00	10.00
JRRM Ryan Mallett	6.00	15.00
JRRW Ryan Williams	4.00	10.00
JRSR Stevan Ridley	3.00	8.00
JRSV Shane Vereen	3.00	8.00
JRTJ Taiwan Jones	3.00	8.00
JRTS Torrey Smith	4.00	10.00
JRTY Titus Young	4.00	10.00
JRVB Vincent Brown	3.00	8.00
JRVM Von Miller	4.00	10.00

2012 Topps Inception

*ROOKIE AU: .25X TO .6X BLUE AU/150
TWO AUTOS PER BOX OVERALL
EXCH EXPIRATION: 6/30/2015

1 Cam Newton	2.50	6.00
2 Joe Flacco	1.25	3.00
3 Darren Sproles	1.25	3.00
4 Miles Austin	1.25	3.00
5 Josh Freeman	1.25	3.00
6 Steve Smith	1.25	3.00
7 Steven Jackson	1.25	3.00
8 Shonn Greene	1.25	3.00
9 Wes Welker	1.50	4.00
10 Calvin Johnson	1.50	4.00
11 Mike Wallace	1.25	3.00
12 Marques Colston	1.25	3.00
13 DeMarco Murray	1.25	3.00
14 Patrick Willis	1.25	3.00
15 C.J. Spiller	1.25	3.00
16 Ray Lewis	1.50	4.00
17 Jimmy Graham	1.25	3.00
18 Von Miller	1.25	3.00
19 Jason Witten	1.50	4.00
20 Aaron Rodgers	2.50	6.00
21 Chris Johnson	1.25	3.00
22 Michael Turner	1.25	3.00
23 LaDainian Tomlinson	1.50	4.00
24 Titus Young	1.00	2.50
25 Philip Rivers	1.25	3.00
26 Greg Jennings	1.25	3.00
27 Christian Ponder	1.25	3.00
28 Ryan Mathews	1.25	3.00
29 Matt Flynn	1.25	3.00
30 Adrian Peterson	1.50	4.00
31 Stevan Ridley	1.00	2.50
32 Reggie Bush	1.25	3.00
33 LeGarrette Blount	1.00	2.50
34 Tony Romo	1.50	4.00
35 Mark Sanchez	1.25	3.00
36 Antonio Gates	1.25	3.00
37 Jordy Nelson	1.25	3.00
38 Willis McGahee	1.00	2.50
39 Jake Locker	1.25	3.00
40 Tom Brady	2.50	6.00
41 Ben Roethlisberger	1.50	4.00
42 Darren McFadden	1.25	3.00
43 Matt Schaub	1.25	3.00
44 Beanie Wells	1.25	3.00
45 Steve Johnson	1.25	3.00
46 Julius Peppers	1.25	3.00
47 Vernon Davis	1.25	3.00
48 Roy Helu	1.25	3.00
49 Sidney Rice	1.25	3.00
50 Drew Brees	1.50	4.00
51 Fred Davis	1.00	2.50
52 Carson Palmer	1.25	3.00
53 Michael Bush	1.00	2.50
54 Jamaal Charles	1.25	3.00
55 Jared Allen	1.25	3.00
56 Marshawn Lynch	1.25	3.00
57 Andre Johnson	1.25	3.00
58 Jermichael Finley	1.25	3.00
59 LeSean McCoy	1.25	3.00
60 Eli Manning	1.50	4.00
61 Rob Gronkowski	1.25	3.00
62 Maurice Jones-Drew	1.25	3.00
63 Matthew Stafford	1.50	4.00
64 Ray Rice	1.25	3.00
65 Matt Ryan	1.25	3.00
66 Dez Bryant	1.50	4.00
67 Larry Fitzgerald	1.25	3.00
68 Ahmad Bradshaw	1.25	3.00
69 Jay Cutler	1.25	3.00
70 Michael Vick	1.50	4.00
71 Frank Gore	1.25	3.00
72 DeAngelo Williams	1.25	3.00
73 Vincent Jackson	1.25	3.00
74 Ryan Fitzpatrick	1.25	3.00
75 Matt Forte	1.25	3.00
76 Julio Jones	1.25	3.00
77 Fred Jackson	1.25	3.00
78 Alex Smith	1.25	3.00
79 Sam Bradford	1.50	4.00
80 Arian Foster	1.25	3.00
81 Hakeem Nicks	1.25	3.00
82 Tony Gonzalez	1.25	3.00
83 Andy Dalton	1.50	4.00
84 A.J. Green	1.25	3.00
85 Percy Harvin	1.25	3.00
86 Ben Tate	1.00	2.50
87 Tim Tebow	2.50	6.00
88 Aaron Hernandez	1.25	3.00
89 Mario Manningham	1.25	3.00
90 Troy Polamalu	1.50	4.00
91 Roddy White	1.25	3.00
92 BenJarvus Green-Ellis	1.25	3.00
93 Victor Cruz	1.50	4.00
94 Brandon Marshall	1.00	2.50
95 Ndamukong Suh	1.50	4.00
96 Jeremy Maclin	1.25	3.00
97 Kevin Kolb	1.25	3.00
98 Dwayne Bowe	1.25	3.00
99 Antonio Brown	1.25	3.00
100 Peyton Manning	4.00	10.00
102 Nick Foles AU RC	6.00	15.00
106 Ryan Broyles AU RC	5.00	12.00
108 Lamar Miller AU RC	5.00	12.00
113 Alshon Jeffery AU RC EXCH	8.00	20.00
114 Mohamed Sanu AU RC	4.00	10.00
115 Rueben Randle AU RC	5.00	12.00
116 Nick Toon AU RC	5.00	12.00
117 Doug Martin AU RC	6.00	15.00
118 LaMichael James AU RC	10.00	25.00
119 Bernard Pierce AU RC EXCH	4.00	10.00
121 Brian Quick AU RC	5.00	12.00
122 Jarius Wright AU RC	3.00	8.00
123 DeVier Posey AU RC	3.00	8.00
124 Dwayne Allen AU RC	3.00	8.00
125 Coby Fleener AU RC	5.00	12.00
126 Isaiah Pead AU RC	4.00	10.00
127 Robert Turbin AU RC	4.00	10.00
131 T.J. Graham AU RC	3.00	8.00
132 Joe Adams AU RC	4.00	10.00
133 Ronnie Hillman AU RC	4.00	10.00
134 Michael Egnew AU RC	3.00	8.00
141 Chris Givens AU RC EXCH	3.00	8.00

2012 Topps Inception Blue

*1-100 VETS/252: .6X TO 1.5X BASIC CARDS
1-100 VETERAN PRINT RUN 252
101-141 ROOKIE AU PRINT RUN 150

101 Ryan Tannehill AU	30.00	60.00
102 Nick Foles AU	10.00	25.00
103 Michael Floyd AU	12.00	30.00
104 Kendall Wright AU	8.00	20.00
105 Brandon Weeden AU	20.00	40.00
106 Ryan Broyles AU	6.00	15.00
107 David Wilson AU	12.00	30.00
108 Lamar Miller AU	8.00	20.00
109 A.J. Jenkins AU	8.00	20.00
110 Andrew Luck AU	150.00	250.00
111 Brock Osweiler AU	8.00	20.00
112 Russell Wilson AU	10.00	25.00
113 Alshon Jeffery AU	15.00	30.00
114 Mohamed Sanu AU	6.00	15.00
115 Rueben Randle AU	8.00	20.00
116 Nick Toon AU	8.00	20.00
117 Doug Martin AU	10.00	25.00
118 LaMichael James AU	15.00	40.00
119 Bernard Pierce AU EXCH	6.00	15.00
120 Robert Griffin III AU	125.00	200.00
121 Brian Quick AU	8.00	20.00
122 Jarius Wright AU	5.00	12.00
123 DeVier Posey AU	5.00	12.00
124 Dwayne Allen AU	5.00	12.00
125 Coby Fleener AU	8.00	20.00
126 Isaiah Pead AU	6.00	15.00
127 Robert Turbin AU	6.00	15.00
129 Stephen Hill AU	6.00	15.00
130 Trent Richardson AU	40.00	80.00
131 T.J. Graham AU	5.00	12.00
132 Joe Adams AU	6.00	15.00
133 Ronnie Hillman AU	6.00	15.00
134 Michael Egnew AU	5.00	12.00
135 Justin Blackmon AU	20.00	40.00
141 Chris Givens AU	5.00	12.00

2012 Topps Inception Gold

*1-100 VETS/252: .8X TO 2X BASIC CARDS
1-100 VETERAN PRINT RUN 252
*ROOKIE AU/99: .4X TO 1X BLUE AU/150
101-141 ROOKIE AU PRINT RUN 99

2012 Topps Inception Green

*1-100 VETS/75: 1X TO 2.5X BASIC CARDS
1-100 VETERAN PRINT RUN 75
*ROOKIE AU/50: .5X TO 1.2X BLUE AU/150
101-141 ROOKIE AU PRINT RUN 50

110 Andrew Luck AU	175.00	300.00
120 Robert Griffin III AU	150.00	250.00

2012 Topps Inception Red

*1-100 VETS/50: 1.5X TO 4X BASIC CARDS
1-100 VETERAN PRINT RUN 50
*ROOKIE AU/25: .8X TO 2X BLUE AU/150
101-141 ROOKIE AU PRINT RUN 25

110 Andrew Luck AU	250.00	400.00
120 Robert Griffin III AU	200.00	350.00

2012 Topps Inception Rookie Autographs Silver Ink

*SILVER INK/25: .8X TO 2X BLUE AU/150
STATED PRINT RUN 25 SER.#'d SETS
EXCH EXPIRATION: 6/30/2015

SSAL Andrew Luck	250.00	400.00
SSRG Robert Griffin III	200.00	350.00

2012 Topps Inception Dual Autographs

STATED PRINT RUN 25 SER.#'d SETS
EXCH EXPIRATION: 6/30/2015

DABF Justin Blackmon		
Michael Floyd		
DABR Justin Blackmon	90.00	150.00
Trent Richardson		
DAGW Robert Griffin III	125.00	200.00
Kendall Wright		
DAJP LaMichael James	25.00	60.00
Isaiah Pead		
DAJS Alshon Jeffery	25.00	60.00
Mohamed Sanu		
DALG Andrew Luck	400.00	550.00
Robert Griffin III		
DAOF Brock Osweiler		
Nick Foles		
DATH Nick Toon	25.00	60.00
Stephen Hill		
DATW Ryan Tannehill	50.00	100.00
Brandon Weeden		
DAWB Brandon Weeden EXCH	75.00	125.00
Justin Blackmon		
DAWM David Wilson	25.00	60.00
Lamar Miller		

2012 Topps Inception Rookie Dual Jumbo Relics

STATED PRINT RUN 15 SER.#'d SETS

DJRBF Justin Blackmon	12.00	30.00
Michael Floyd		
DJRBJ Ryan Broyles	10.00	25.00
Alshon Jeffery		
DJRBR Justin Blackmon	20.00	50.00
Trent Richardson		
DJRFA Coby Fleener	8.00	20.00
Dwayne Allen		
DJRFW Michael Floyd	12.00	30.00
Kendall Wright		
DJRGT Robert Griffin III	30.00	60.00
Ryan Tannehill		
DJRGW Robert Griffin III	25.00	60.00
Kendall Wright		
DJRHG Stephen Hill	6.00	15.00
T.J. Graham		
DJRJJ A.J. Jenkins	12.00	30.00
LaMichael James		
DJRJP LaMichael James	12.00	30.00
Isaiah Pead		
DJRJS Alshon Jeffery	10.00	25.00
Mohamed Sanu		
DJRLA Andrew Luck	30.00	60.00
Dwayne Allen		
DJRLF Andrew Luck	30.00	60.00
Coby Fleener		
DJRLG Andrew Luck	40.00	80.00
Robert Griffin III		
DJRME Lamar Miller	8.00	20.00
Michael Egnew		
DJRMW Doug Martin	12.00	30.00
David Wilson		
DJROF Brock Osweiler	10.00	25.00
Nick Foles		
DJROH Brock Osweiler	8.00	20.00
Ronnie Hillman		
DJRQP Brian Quick	8.00	20.00
Isaiah Pead		
DJRRH Rueben Randle	6.00	15.00
Stephen Hill		
DJRRM Trent Richardson	20.00	50.00
Doug Martin		
DJRRW Trent Richardson	20.00	50.00
David Wilson		
DJRTE Ryan Tannehill	15.00	40.00
Michael Egnew		
DJRTH Nick Toon	8.00	20.00
Stephen Hill		
DJRTM Ryan Tannehill	15.00	40.00
Lamar Miller		
DJRTS Ryan Tannehill	15.00	40.00
Brock Osweiler		
DJRTW Nick Toon	10.00	25.00
Russell Wilson		
DJRWA Jarius Wright	6.00	15.00
Joe Adams		
DJRWB Brandon Weeden	12.00	30.00
Justin Blackmon		
DJRWJ Kendall Wright	10.00	25.00
Alshon Jeffery		
DJRWM David Wilson	12.00	30.00
Lamar Miller		
DJRWT Russell Wilson	10.00	25.00
Robert Turbin		
DJRRWE Trent Richardson	20.00	50.00
Brandon Weeden		
DJRRWI Rueben Randle	12.00	30.00
David Wilson		
DJRTWE Ryan Tannehill	15.00	40.00
Brandon Weeden		
DJRWBR Jarius Wright	6.00	15.00
Ryan Broyles		
DJRWJE Kendall Wright	8.00	20.00
A.J. Jenkins		

2012 Topps Inception Rookie Jumbo Patch Autographs

TWO AUTOS PER BOX OVERALL
*GOLD AU/75: .5X TO 1.2X PATCH AU

AJPAJ Alshon Jeffery	15.00	40.00
AJPBO Brock Osweiler	12.00	30.00
AJPBP Bernard Pierce EXCH	8.00	20.00
AJPBQ Brian Quick	10.00	25.00
AJPCF Coby Fleener	8.00	20.00
AJPDA Dwayne Allen	6.00	15.00
AJPDM Doug Martin	12.00	30.00
AJPDP DeVier Posey	6.00	15.00
AJPIP Isaiah Pead	8.00	20.00
AJPJA Joe Adams	8.00	20.00
AJPJW Jarius Wright	6.00	15.00
AJPLJ LaMichael James	20.00	50.00
AJPLM Lamar Miller	12.00	30.00
AJPME Michael Egnew	6.00	15.00
AJPMS Mohamed Sanu	8.00	20.00
AJPNF Nick Foles	12.00	30.00
AJPNT Nick Toon	10.00	25.00
AJPRB Ryan Broyles	8.00	20.00
AJPRH Ronnie Hillman	8.00	20.00
AJPRR Rueben Randle	10.00	25.00
AJPRW Russell Wilson	12.00	30.00
AJPSH Stephen Hill	8.00	20.00
AJPTG T.J. Graham	6.00	15.00
AJPAJJ A.J. Jenkins	10.00	25.00
AJPCGI Chris Givens	6.00	15.00
AJPRTU Robert Turbin	8.00	20.00
AJPTYH T.Y. Hilton EXCH	8.00	20.00

2012 Topps Inception Rookie Jumbo Patch Autographs Green

*GREEN AU/50: .6X TO 1.5X PATCH AU
STATED PRINT RUN 50 SER.#'d SETS

AJPKW Kendall Wright	15.00	40.00
AJPMF Michael Floyd	25.00	60.00

2012 Topps Inception Rookie Jumbo Patch Autographs Red

*RED AU/25: .8X TO 2X PATCH AU
RED PATCH AU PRINT RUN 25

AJPAL Andrew Luck	300.00	500.00
AJPBW Brandon Weeden		
AJPDW David Wilson	50.00	100.00
AJPJB Justin Blackmon	60.00	120.00
AJPKW Kendall Wright	25.00	50.00
AJPMF Michael Floyd	40.00	80.00
AJPRG Robert Griffin III	250.00	400.00
AJPRT Ryan Tannehill	60.00	120.00
AJPTR Trent Richardson	100.00	175.00

2012 Topps Inception Rookie Patch Autographs Gold Ink

*GOLD INK/25: .4X TO 1X RED PATCH AU/25
STATED PRINT RUN 25 SER.#'d SETS

GAPAL Andrew Luck	300.00	500.00
GAPRG Robert Griffin III	250.00	400.00
GAPTR Trent Richardson	100.00	175.00

2012 Topps Inception Rookie Quad Patches

STATED PRINT RUN 15 SER.#'d SETS

QPBFRW Justin Blackmon	20.00	50.00
Michael Floyd		
Trent Richardson		
David Wilson		
QPBFWJ Justin Blackmon	15.00	40.00
Michael Floyd		
Kendall Wright		
A.J. Jenkins		
QPGWWB Robert Griffin III	50.00	100.00
Kendall Wright		
Brandon Weeden		
Justin Blackmon		
QPLGBR Andrew Luck	75.00	150.00
Robert Griffin III		
Justin Blackmon		
Trent Richardson		
QPLGTW Andrew Luck	75.00	150.00
Robert Griffin III		
Ryan Tannehill		
Brandon Weeden		
QPRMWP Trent Richardson		
Doug Martin		
David Wilson		
Isaiah Pead		
QPWRMM Kendall Wright	12.00	30.00
Rueben Randle		
Lamar Miller		
Doug Martin		

2012 Topps Inception Rookie Relics Patch

STATED PRINT RUN 210 SER.#'d SETS
*PATCH BLUE/75: .4X TO 1X PATCH/210
*PATCH GOLD/50: .4X TO 1X PATCH/210
*PATCH GREEN/25: .5X TO 1.2X PATCH/210
*PATCH RED/10: .8X TO 2X PATCH/210
*JUMBO/165-169: .3X TO .8X PTCH/210
*JUMBO BLUE/75: .4X TO 1X PATCH/210
*JUMBO GOLD/50: .4X TO 1X PATCH/210
*JUM.PTCH GRN/25: .8X TO 2X PATCH/210
*JUM.PTCH RED/10: 1X TO 2.5X PATCH/210

RPAJ Alshon Jeffery	6.00	15.00
RPAL Andrew Luck	25.00	60.00
RPBO Brock Osweiler	5.00	12.00
RPBP Bernard Pierce	4.00	10.00
RPBQ Brian Quick	5.00	12.00
RPBW Brandon Weeden	8.00	20.00
RPCF Coby Fleener	5.00	12.00
RPDA Dwayne Allen	4.00	10.00
RPDM Doug Martin	6.00	15.00
RPDP DeVier Posey	4.00	10.00
RPDW David Wilson	8.00	20.00
RPIP Isaiah Pead	4.00	10.00
RPJA Joe Adams	4.00	10.00
RPJB Justin Blackmon	8.00	20.00
RPJW Jarius Wright	4.00	10.00
RPKW Kendall Wright	5.00	12.00
RPLJ LaMichael James	8.00	20.00
RPLM Lamar Miller	5.00	12.00
RPME Michael Egnew	3.00	8.00
RPMF Michael Floyd	6.00	15.00
RPMS Mohamed Sanu	4.00	10.00
RPNF Nick Foles	6.00	15.00
RPNT Nick Toon	5.00	12.00
RPRB Ryan Broyles	4.00	10.00
RPRG Robert Griffin III	20.00	50.00
RPRH Ronnie Hillman	5.00	12.00
RPRR Rueben Randle	4.00	10.00
RPRT Ryan Tannehill	10.00	25.00
RPRW Russell Wilson	6.00	15.00
RPSH Stephen Hill	4.00	10.00
RPTG T.J. Graham	4.00	10.00
RPTR Trent Richardson	12.00	30.00
RPAJJ A.J. Jenkins	5.00	12.00
RPCGI Chris Givens	3.00	8.00
RPRTU Robert Turbin	4.00	10.00

2008 Topps Kickoff

This set was released on September 3, 2008. The base set consists of 220 cards. Cards 1-165 feature veterans, and cards 166-220 are rookies.

COMPLETE SET (220)	20.00	40.00
UNPRICED PRINT PLATE 1/1 ODDS 1:340		
1 Drew Brees	.20	.50
2 Peyton Manning	.30	.75
3 Eli Manning	.20	.50
4 Steven Jackson	.20	.50
5 Brian Westbrook	.15	.40
6 Fred Taylor	.15	.40
7 Terrell Owens	.20	.50
8 Reggie Wayne	.15	.40
9 Steve Smith	.15	.40
10 Chad Pennington	.15	.40
11 Jay Cutler	.20	.50
12 Joey Harrington	.12	.30
13 Kyle Boller	.12	.30
14 Brett Favre	.50	1.25
15 Kurt Warner	.20	.50
16 Jason Campbell	.15	.40
17 Shaun Alexander	.15	.40
18 Maurice Jones-Drew	.15	.40
19 Thomas Jones	.15	.40
20 Selvin Young	.12	.30
21 Brandon Jacobs	.15	.40
22 Edgerrin James	.15	.40
23 Chester Taylor	.12	.30
24 Greg Jennings	.20	.50
25 Jerricho Cotchery	.15	.40
26 Joey Galloway	.15	.40
27 Lee Evans	.15	.40
28 Roy Williams WR	.15	.40
29 Brandon Marshall	.15	.40
30 Bobby Engram	.12	.30
31 Antonio Gates	.20	.50
32 Kellen Winslow	.15	.40
33 Jeremy Shockey	.15	.40
34 Heath Miller	.12	.30
35 Vernon Davis	.15	.40
36 Patrick Kerney	.12	.30
37 Jared Allen	.20	.50
38 DeMarcus Ware	.15	.40
39 Brian Urlacher	.20	.50
40 Champ Bailey	.15	.40
41 Kellen Clemens	.15	.40
42 JaMarcus Russell	.15	.40
43 Matt Leinart	.20	.50
44 Julius Jones	.12	.30
45 Jerious Norwood	.15	.40
46 James Jones	.12	.30
47 Chris Chambers	.15	.40
48 Sidney Rice	.20	.50
49 Donte Stallworth	.12	.30
50 Isaac Bruce	.15	.40
51 Albert Haynesworth	.12	.30
52 Julius Peppers	.15	.40
53 Jon Beason	.12	.30
54 Asante Samuel	.12	.30
55 Roy Williams S	.15	.40
56 Carson Palmer	.20	.50
57 Tony Romo	.25	.60
58 Willie Parker	.15	.40
59 Clinton Portis	.15	.40
60 LaDainian Tomlinson	.20	.50
61 Joseph Addai	.15	.40
62 Willis McGahee	.15	.40
63 Anquan Boldin	.15	.40
64 Randy Moss	.20	.50
65 Andre Johnson	.15	.40
66 Chad Johnson	.15	.40
67 Larry Fitzgerald	.20	.50
68 Jon Kitna	.15	.40
69 Matt Hasselbeck	.15	.40
70 Matt Schaub	.15	.40
71 Jeff Garcia	.15	.40
72 Sage Rosenfels	.12	.30
73 Philip Rivers	.20	.50
74 Cleo Lemon	.12	.30
75 Brian Griese	.12	.30
76 Warrick Dunn	.15	.40
77 LenDale White	.15	.40
78 Ryan Grant	.20	.50
79 DeAngelo Williams	.15	.40
80 Earnest Graham	.12	.30
81 Torry Holt	.15	.40
82 Derrick Mason	.15	.40
83 Dwayne Bowe	.15	.40
84 Donald Driver	.15	.40
85 Shaun McDonald	.12	.30
86 Chris Cooley	.15	.40
87 Tony Gonzalez	.15	.40
88 Dallas Clark	.15	.40
89 Tony Scheffler	.12	.30
90 Alge Crumpler	.15	.40
91 Osi Umenyiora	.15	.40
92 Michael Strahan	.15	.40
93 Patrick Willis	.15	.40
94 Ray Lewis	.20	.50
95 Bob Sanders	.15	.40
96 Troy Smith	.15	.40
97 Jake Delhomme	.15	.40
98 John Beck	.12	.30
99 Reggie Bush	.20	.50
100 Larry Johnson	.15	.40
101 Rudi Johnson	.15	.40
102 Ahmad Bradshaw	.15	.40
103 Hines Ward	.15	.40
104 Calvin Johnson	.20	.50
105 Jerry Porter	.12	.30
106 Reggie Williams	.15	.40
107 Ted Ginn Jr.	.15	.40
108 Terence Newman	.12	.30
109 Troy Polamalu	.20	.50
110 Devin Hester	.20	.50
111 Tom Brady	.30	.75
112 Ben Roethlisberger	.20	.50
113 Vince Young	.15	.40
114 Adrian Peterson	.30	.75
115 Marion Barber	.15	.40
116 Marshawn Lynch	.15	.40
117 Frank Gore	.15	.40
118 Plaxico Burress	.15	.40
119 Braylon Edwards	.15	.40
120 David Garrard	.15	.40
121 Trent Edwards	.12	.30
122 Donovan McNabb	.20	.50
123 Derek Anderson	.12	.30
124 Marc Bulger	.15	.40
125 Damon Huard	.12	.30
126 Tarvaris Jackson	.15	.40
127 DeShaun Foster	.15	.40
128 Ron Dayne	.12	.30
129 Kenny Watson	.12	.30
130 Laurence Maroney	.15	.40
131 Jamal Lewis	.15	.40
132 Justin Fargas	.12	.30
133 T.J. Houshmandzadeh	.15	.40
134 Kevin Curtis	.12	.30
135 Santonio Holmes	.15	.40
136 Wes Welker	.20	.50
137 Roddy White	.15	.40
138 Marques Colston	.15	.40
139 Bernard Berrian	.15	.40
140 Santana Moss	.12	.30
141 Owen Daniels	.12	.30
142 Jason Witten	.20	.50
143 Donald Lee	.15	.40
144 Desmond Clark	.12	.30
145 Zach Miller	.15	.40
146 Mario Williams	.15	.40
147 Ernie Sims	.12	.30
148 Shawne Merriman	.15	.40
149 Antonio Cromartie	.12	.30
150 Ed Reed	.15	.40
151 Brodie Croyle	.15	.40
152 Rex Grossman	.15	.40
153 Alex Smith QB	.20	.50
154 Ronnie Brown	.15	.40
155 Michael Turner	.20	.50
156 Anthony Gonzalez	.12	.30
157 Laveranues Coles	.12	.30
158 Vincent Jackson	.12	.30
159 Greg Olsen	.15	.40
160 Jason Taylor	.15	.40
161 Lofa Tatupu	.15	.40
162 Marcus Trufant	.12	.30
163 DeAngelo Hall	.12	.30
164 Ronde Barber	.12	.30
165 John Lynch	.15	.40
166 Matt Ryan RC	1.50	4.00
167 Brian Brohm RC	.40	1.00
168 Andre Woodson RC	.40	1.00
169 Chad Henne RC	.40	1.00
170 Joe Flacco RC	1.25	3.00
171 John David Booty RC	.30	.75
172 Colt Brennan RC	.40	1.00
173 Dennis Dixon RC	.40	1.00
174 Erik Ainge RC	.40	1.00
175 Josh Johnson RC	.40	1.00
176 Kevin O'Connell RC	.30	.75
177 Anthony Morelli RC	.30	.75
178 Darren McFadden RC	1.00	2.50
179 Rashard Mendenhall RC	.75	2.00
180 Jonathan Stewart RC	.60	1.50
181 Felix Jones RC	.60	1.50
182 Jamaal Charles RC	.60	1.50
183 Chris Johnson RC	1.00	2.50
184 Ray Rice RC	.75	2.00
185 Mike Hart RC	.40	1.00
186 Kevin Smith RC	.40	1.00
187 Steve Slaton RC	.40	1.00
188 Matt Forte RC	.60	1.50
189 Tashard Choice RC	.30	.75
190 Justin Forsett RC	.40	1.00
191 Harry Douglas RC	.30	.75
192 DeSean Jackson RC	.75	2.00
193 Malcolm Kelly RC	.30	.75
194 Limas Sweed RC	.40	1.00
195 Mario Manningham RC	.40	1.00
196 James Hardy RC	.30	.75
197 Early Doucet RC	.30	.75
198 Donnie Avery RC	.30	.75
199 Dexter Jackson RC	.30	.75
200 Devin Thomas RC	.30	.75
201 Jordy Nelson RC	.50	1.25
202 Eddie Royal RC	.40	1.00
203 Earl Bennett RC	.40	1.00
204 Jerome Simpson RC	.40	1.00
205 Andre Caldwell RC	.30	.75
206 Keenan Burton RC	.25	.60
207 Dustin Keller RC	.40	1.00
208 Fred Davis RC	.40	1.00
209 John Carlson RC	.40	1.00
210 Jake Long RC	.40	1.00
211 Dominique Rodgers-Cromartie RC	.40	1.00
212 Glenn Dorsey RC	.40	1.00
213 Sedrick Ellis RC	.40	1.00
214 Chris Long RC	.40	1.00
215 Vernon Gholston RC	.30	.75
216 Derrick Harvey RC	.25	.60
217 Jerod Mayo RC	.40	1.00
218 Keith Rivers RC	.40	1.00
219 Leodis McKelvin RC	.30	.75
220 Aqib Talib RC	.40	1.00
CL1 Checklist 1	.02	.10
CL2 Checklist 2	.02	.10

2008 Topps Kickoff Silver Holofoil

*VETS 1-165: 3X TO 8X BASIC CARDS
*ROOKIES 166-220: .8X TO 2X BASIC CARDS
STATED PRINT RUN 1349 SER.#'d SETS

2008 Topps Kickoff Autographs

GROUP A ODDS 1:25,762 H, 1:15,237 J
GROUP B ODDS 1:1491 H, 1:997 J
GROUP C ODDS 1:900 H, 1:600 J
GROUP D ODDS 1:1975 H, 1:1350 J
GROUP A AU TOO SCARCE TO PRICE

KAAA Anthony Alridge C	3.00	8.00
KAAG Anthony Gonzalez B	5.00	12.00
KAAM Anthony Madison D	10.00	25.00
KAAV Adam Vinatieri B	8.00	20.00
KADH David Harris B	5.00	12.00
KADM Darren McFadden A	40.00	100.00
KAMK Mathias Kiwanuka B	5.00	12.00
KAMR Matt Ryan A	75.00	150.00
KAPS Paul Smith C	4.00	10.00
KART Ryan Torain C	4.00	10.00

2008 Topps Kickoff Puzzle

STATED ODDS 1:3

1 Peyton Manning	1.50	4.00
2 Tom Brady	1.50	4.00
3 Eli Manning	1.00	2.50
4 Tony Romo	1.25	3.00
5 Ben Roethlisberger	1.00	2.50
6 Drew Brees	1.00	2.50
7 LaDainian Tomlinson	1.00	2.50
8 Adrian Peterson	1.50	4.00
9 Willie Parker	.75	2.00
10 Frank Gore	.75	2.00
11 Willis McGahee	.75	2.00
12 Steven Jackson	1.00	2.50
13 Chad Johnson	.75	2.00
14 Reggie Wayne	.75	2.00
15 Terrell Owens	1.00	2.50
16 Randy Moss	1.00	2.50
17 Braylon Edwards	.75	2.00
18 Steve Smith	.75	2.00
19 Antonio Gates	1.00	2.50
20 Tony Gonzalez	.75	2.00
21 Matt Ryan	2.50	6.00
22 Brian Brohm	.60	1.50
23 Darren McFadden	1.50	4.00
24 Rashard Mendenhall	1.25	3.00
25 Jonathan Stewart	1.00	2.50
26 Chad Henne	.60	1.50
27 Felix Jones	1.00	2.50
28 Ray Rice	1.25	3.00

2008 Topps Kickoff Stars of the Game

STATED ODDS 1:6 HOB, 1:2 JUM

SGAG Antonio Gates	1.25	3.00
SGAP Adrian Peterson	2.00	5.00
SGBB Brian Brohm	.75	2.00
SGBE Braylon Edwards	1.00	2.50
SGBR Ben Roethlisberger	1.25	3.00
SGCJ Chad Johnson	1.00	2.50
SGDB Drew Brees	1.25	3.00
SGDM Darren McFadden	2.00	5.00
SGEM Eli Manning	1.25	3.00
SGFG Frank Gore	1.00	2.50
SGJS Jonathan Stewart	1.25	3.00
SGLT LaDainian Tomlinson	1.25	3.00
SGMR Matt Ryan	3.00	8.00
SGPM Peyton Manning	2.00	5.00
SGRM Randy Moss	1.25	3.00
SGRM Rashard Mendenhall	1.50	4.00
SGRW Reggie Wayne	1.00	2.50
SGSJ Steven Jackson	1.25	3.00
SGSS Steve Smith	1.00	2.50
SGTB Tom Brady	2.00	5.00
SGTG Tony Gonzalez	1.00	2.50
SGTO Terrell Owens	1.25	3.00
SGTR Tony Romo	1.50	4.00
SGWM Willis McGahee	1.00	2.50
SGWP Willie Parker	1.00	2.50

2008 Topps Kickoff Tattoos

STATED ODDS 1:36 HOB, 1:9 JUM

TT1 Buffalo Bills	.30	.75
TT2 Miami Dolphins	.40	1.00
TT3 New England Patriots	.40	1.00
TT4 New York Jets	.40	1.00
TT5 Baltimore Ravens	.30	.75
TT6 Cincinnati Bengals	.30	.75
TT7 Cleveland Browns	.30	.75
TT8 Pittsburgh Steelers	.50	1.25
TT9 Houston Texans	.30	.75
TT10 Indianapolis Colts	.40	1.00
TT11 Jacksonville Jaguars	.30	.75
TT12 Tennessee Titans	.30	.75
TT13 Denver Broncos	.40	1.00
TT14 Kansas City Chiefs	.30	.75
TT15 Oakland Raiders	.50	1.25
TT16 San Diego Chargers	.30	.75
TT17 Dallas Cowboys	.50	1.25
TT18 New York Giants	.40	1.00
TT19 Philadelphia Eagles	.30	.75
TT20 Washington Redskins	.40	1.00
TT21 Chicago Bears	.40	1.00
TT22 Detroit Lions	.30	.75
TT23 Green Bay Packers	.50	1.25
TT24 Minnesota Vikings	.30	.75
TT25 Atlanta Falcons	.30	.75
TT26 Carolina Panthers	.30	.75
TT27 New Orleans Saints	.30	.75
TT28 Tampa Bay Buccaneers	.30	.75
TT29 Arizona Cardinals	.30	.75
TT30 San Francisco 49ers	.40	1.00
TT31 Seattle Seahawks	.30	.75
TT32 St. Louis Rams	.30	.75

2009 Topps Kickoff

COMPLETE SET (165)	15.00	40.00
TWO ROOKIES PER PACK		
1 Larry Fitzgerald	.20	.50
2 Anquan Boldin	.15	.40
3 Roddy White	.15	.40
4 Terrell Owens	.20	.50
5 Steve Smith	.15	.40
6 Chad Ochocinco	.15	.40
7 Laveranues Coles	.12	.30
8 Braylon Edwards	.15	.40
9 Brandon Marshall	.15	.40
10 Eddie Royal	.15	.40
11 Calvin Johnson	.20	.50
12 Greg Jennings	.20	.50
13 Andre Johnson	.15	.40
14 Anthony Gonzalez	.12	.30

15 Reggie Wayne .15 .40
16 Dwayne Bowe .15 .40
17 Randy Moss .20 .50
18 Marques Colston .15 .40
19 Steve Smith .15 .40
20 Jerricho Cotchery .15 .40
21 DeSean Jackson .15 .40
22 Hines Ward .15 .40
23 Santonio Holmes .15 .40
24 Chris Chambers .15 .40
25 T.J. Houshmandzadeh .15 .40
26 Donnie Avery .15 .40
27 Antonio Bryant .12 .30
28 Santana Moss .15 .40
29 Jason Witten .20 .50
30 Dallas Clark .15 .40
31 Tony Gonzalez .15 .40
32 Jeremy Shockey .12 .30
33 Heath Miller .15 .40
34 Antonio Gates .15 .40
35 Vernon Davis .15 .40
36 John Carlson .15 .40
37 Kellen Winslow Jr. .15 .40
38 Chris Cooley .15 .40
39 Ed Reed .15 .40
40 Troy Polamalu .20 .50
41 Michael Turner .15 .40
42 Willis McGahee .15 .40
43 Marshawn Lynch .15 .40
44 DeAngelo Williams .20 .50
45 Jonathan Stewart .15 .40
46 Matt Forte .20 .50
47 Jamal Lewis .15 .40
48 Marion Barber .15 .40
49 Kevin Smith .15 .40
50 Steve Slaton .15 .40
51 Joseph Addai .20 .50
52 Maurice Jones-Drew .15 .40
53 Larry Johnson .15 .40
54 Jamaal Charles .20 .50
55 Ronnie Brown .15 .40
56 Adrian Peterson .30 .75
57 Chester Taylor .12 .30
58 Wes Welker .20 .50
59 Reggie Bush .20 .50
60 Brandon Jacobs .15 .40
61 Leon Washington .15 .40
62 Thomas Jones .15 .40
63 Darren McFadden .20 .50
64 Justin Fargas .12 .30
65 Brian Westbrook .15 .40
66 Willie Parker .12 .30
67 LaDainian Tomlinson .20 .50
68 Darren Sproles .15 .40
69 Frank Gore .15 .40
70 Steven Jackson .15 .40
71 Warrick Dunn .15 .40
72 Earnest Graham .12 .30
73 Chris Johnson .20 .50
74 LenDale White .15 .40
75 Clinton Portis .15 .40
76 Kurt Warner .20 .50
77 Matt Ryan .20 .50
78 Joe Flacco .20 .50
79 Trent Edwards .12 .30
80 Kyle Orton .15 .40
81 Carson Palmer .20 .50
82 Brady Quinn .15 .40
83 Tony Romo .30 .75
84 Jay Cutler .20 .50
85 Aaron Rodgers .40 1.00
86 Matt Schaub .15 .40
87 Peyton Manning .30 .75
88 David Garrard .15 .40
89 Matt Cassel .15 .40
90 Chad Pennington .15 .40
91 Tarvaris Jackson .15 .40
92 Tom Brady .30 .75
93 Drew Brees .20 .50
94 Eli Manning .20 .50
95 JaMarcus Russell .12 .30
96 Donovan McNabb .20 .50
97 Ben Roethlisberger .20 .50
98 Philip Rivers .20 .50
99 Matt Hasselbeck .15 .40
100 Marc Bulger .15 .40
101 Jason Campbell .12 .30
102 Ray Lewis .20 .50
103 Brian Urlacher .20 .50
104 Ernie Sims .12 .30
105 Joey Porter .15 .40
106 Jerod Mayo .15 .40
107 James Harrison .20 .50
108 Patrick Willis .15 .40
109 Julius Peppers .15 .40
110 DeMarcus Ware .15 .40
111 Brian Orakpo RC .40 1.00
112 Pat White RC .40 1.00
113 Malcolm Jenkins RC .40 1.00
114 Nate Davis RC .30 .75
115 Rhett Bomar RC .30 .75
116 Matthew Stafford RC 2.00 5.00
117 Stephen McGee RC .40 1.00
118 Aaron Maybin RC .30 .75
119 Josh Freeman RC .75 2.00
120 Mark Sanchez RC 1.25 3.00
121 B.J. Raji RC .40 1.00
122 Javon Ringer RC .40 1.00
123 Chris Wells RC .60 1.50
124 Donald Brown RC .40 1.00
125 Gartrell Johnson RC .25 .60
126 Glen Coffee RC .30 .75
127 Andre Brown RC .40 1.00
128 Aaron Curry RC .40 1.00
129 Cedric Peerman RC .30 .75
130 Knowshon Moreno RC .40 1.00
131 Shonn Greene RC .60 1.50
132 LeSean McCoy RC .75 2.00
133 Rashad Jennings RC .40 1.00
134 Brian Cushing RC .40 1.00
135 James Davis RC .40 1.00
136 Hakeem Nicks RC .60 1.50
137 Austin Collie RC .40 1.00
138 Eugene Monroe RC .25 .60
139 Brandon Tate RC .40 1.00
140 Clay Matthews RC 1.00 2.50
141 Chase Coffman RC .30 .75
142 Brooks Foster RC .25 .60
143 Kenny Britt RC .50 1.25
144 Patrick Turner RC .30 .75
145 Darrius Heyward-Bey RC .40 1.00
146 Rey Maualuga RC .40 1.00
147 Deon Butler RC .30 .75
148 Derrick Williams RC .30 .75
149 Percy Harvin RC .60 1.50
150 Jarett Dillard RC .40 1.00
151 Jeremy Maclin RC .60 1.50
152 Juaquin Iglesias RC .30 .75
153 Jared Cook RC .40 1.00
154 James Laurinaitis RC .40 1.00
155 Brandon Pettigrew RC .40 1.00
156 Andre Smith RC .30 .75
157 Brian Robiskie RC .40 1.00
158 Mohamed Massaquoi RC .30 .75
159 Ramses Barden RC .25 .60
160 Michael Crabtree RC .75 2.00
161 Michael Oher RC .60 1.50
162 Patrick Chung RC .40 1.00
163 Louis Murphy RC .40 1.00
164 William Moore RC .40 1.00
165 Victor Harris RC .40 1.00

2009 Topps Kickoff Silver Holofoil

*VETS 1-110: 3X TO 8X BASIC CARDS
*ROOKIES 111-165: .8X TO 2X
STATED PRINT RUN 2009 SER.#'d SETS

2009 Topps Kickoff Komics

STATED ODDS 1:4
1 Matt Ryan 1.00 2.50
2 Joe Flacco 1.00 2.50
3 Steve Slaton .75 2.00
4 Matt Forte 1.00 2.50
5 Chris Johnson 1.00 2.50
6 Jerod Mayo .75 2.00
7 Eddie Royal .75 2.00
8 Jake Long .60 1.50
9 Ryan Clady .60 1.50
10 Adrian Peterson 1.50 4.00
11 Drew Brees 1.00 2.50
12 Kurt Warner 1.00 2.50
13 Larry Fitzgerald 1.00 2.50
14 Michael Turner .75 2.00
15 James Harrison 1.00 2.50
16 Ben Roethlisberger 1.00 2.50
17 Philip Rivers 1.00 2.50
18 Santonio Holmes .75 2.00
19 Matt Cassel .75 2.00
20 Antonio Gates .75 2.00
21 Peyton Manning 1.50 4.00
22 Terrell Owens 1.00 2.50
23 Ed Reed .75 2.00
24 LaDainian Tomlinson 1.00 2.50
25 DeMarcus Ware .75 2.00
26 DeAngelo Williams 1.00 2.50
27 Brett Favre 2.50 6.00
28 Matthew Stafford 3.00 8.00
29 Michael Crabtree 1.25 3.00
30 Jeremy Maclin 1.00 2.50

2009 Topps Kickoff Stars of the Game

STATED ODDS 1:4
1 Peyton Manning 2.00 5.00
2 Larry Fitzgerald 1.25 3.00
3 Steve Slaton 1.00 2.50
4 Chris Johnson 1.25 3.00
5 Adrian Peterson 2.00 5.00
6 Aaron Rodgers 2.50 6.00
7 Jay Cutler 1.25 3.00
8 Steve Smith 1.00 2.50
9 Maurice Jones-Drew 1.00 2.50
10 Andre Johnson 1.00 2.50
11 Philip Rivers 1.25 3.00
12 Michael Turner 1.00 2.50
13 Calvin Johnson 1.25 3.00
14 Tony Romo 2.00 5.00
15 Reggie Wayne 1.00 2.50
16 Matt Forte 1.25 3.00
17 DeAngelo Williams 1.25 3.00
18 Frank Gore 1.00 2.50
19 Matt Ryan 1.25 3.00
20 Brian Westbrook 1.00 2.50
21 Kurt Warner 1.25 3.00
22 Clinton Portis 1.00 2.50
23 Brandon Jacobs 1.00 2.50
24 Steven Jackson 1.00 2.50
25 Drew Brees 1.25 3.00

1996 Topps Laser

The 1996 Topps Laser set was issued in one series totalling 128 cards. The 4-card packs carried a suggested retail of $5.00 each. The cards are all etch foil stamped, die-cut and UV coated.

COMPLETE SET (128) 15.00 40.00
1 Marshall Faulk .40 1.00
2 Alonzo Spellman .07 .20
3 Frank Sanders .15 .40
4 Anthony Pleasant .07 .20
5 Scott Mitchell .15 .40
6 Robert Brooks .30 .75
7 Robert Jones .07 .20
8 Phillippi Sparks .07 .20
9 Rodney Peete .07 .20
10 Kordell Stewart .30 .75
11 Ken Norton .07 .20
12 Brian Mitchell .07 .20
13 Ben Coates .15 .40
14 Quinn Early .07 .20
15 Emmitt Smith 1.25 3.00
16 Steve Bono .07 .20
17 Anthony Miller .15 .40
18 Mel Gray .07 .20
19 Neil O'Donnell .15 .40
20 Tim Brown .30 .75
21 Terrell Fletcher .07 .20
22 John Randle .15 .40
23 Fred Barnett .07 .20
24 Craig Heyward .07 .20
25 Ki-Jana Carter .15 .40
26 Eric Allen .07 .20
27 Warren Sapp .07 .20
28 Terry Wooden .07 .20
29 Darion Conner .07 .20
30 Mark Brunell .50 1.25
31 Vinny Testaverde .15 .40
32 Chris Calloway .07 .20
33 Steve Walsh .07 .20
34 Ken Dilger .15 .40
35 Bryan Cox .07 .20
36 Rob Moore .15 .40
37 Henry Thomas .07 .20
38 Henry Ellard .07 .20
39 Mark Chmura .15 .40
40 Jerry Rice .75 2.00
41 Michael Irvin .30 .75
42 Willie McGinest .07 .20
43 Steve McNair .60 1.50
44 Tamarick Vanover .15 .40
45 Cris Carter .30 .75
46 Levon Kirkland .07 .20
47 Terry McDaniel .07 .20
48 Jessie Tuggle .07 .20
49 O.J. McDuffie .15 .40
50 Bruce Smith .15 .40
51 Tyrone Hughes .07 .20
52 Tony Martin .15 .40
53 Hardy Nickerson .07 .20
54 Garrison Hearst .15 .40
55 Sam Mills .07 .20
56 Mark Carrier DB .07 .20
57 Quentin Coryatt .07 .20
58 Neil Smith .15 .40
59 Michael Westbrook .30 .75
60 Greg Lloyd .15 .40
61 Jeff Hostetler .07 .20
62 Wayne Chrebet .40 1.00
63 Herschel Walker .15 .40
64 Pepper Johnson .07 .20
65 John Elway 1.50 4.00
66 Reggie White .30 .75
67 James O.Stewart .15 .40
68 Bernie Parmalee .07 .20
69 Robert Smith .15 .40
70 Drew Bledsoe .50 1.25
71 Marvcus Patton .07 .20
72 Stan Humphries .15 .40
73 Darnay Scott .15 .40
74 Jim Kelly .30 .75
75 Terance Mathis .07 .20
76 Erik Kramer .07 .20
77 Marcus Allen .30 .75
78 Ernie Mills .07 .20
79 Harvey Williams .07 .20
80 Brett Favre 1.50 4.00
81 Seth Joyner .07 .20
82 Tyrone Poole .07 .20
83 Troy Aikman .75 2.00
84 Warren Moon .15 .40
85 Isaac Bruce .30 .75
86 Errict Rhett .15 .40
87 Rick Mirer .15 .40
88 Anthony Smith .07 .20
89 Bert Emanuel .15 .40
90 Junior Seau .30 .75
91 Terry Allen .15 .40
92 Brent Jones .07 .20
93 Adrian Murrell .15 .40
94 Dave Brown .07 .20
95 Bryce Paup .07 .20
96 Jim Everett .07 .20
97 Brian Washington .07 .20
98 Jim Harbaugh .15 .40
99 Shannon Sharpe .15 .40
100 Dan Marino 1.50 4.00
101 Curtis Martin .60 1.50
102 Ricky Watters .15 .40
103 Yancey Thigpen .15 .40
104 Trent Dilfer .30 .75
105 Joey Galloway .30 .75
106 Edgar Bennett .15 .40
107 Willie Jackson .15 .40
108 Mark Collins .07 .20
109 Rashaan Salaam .15 .40
110 Eric Metcalf .07 .20
111 Terrell Davis .60 1.50
112 Darryll Lewis .07 .20
113 Ken Harvey .07 .20
114 Rob Fredrickson .07 .20
115 Rodney Hampton .15 .40
116 Chris Slade .07 .20
117 Jeff George .15 .40
118 Lamar Lathon .07 .20
119 Curtis Conway .30 .75
120 Barry Sanders 1.25 3.00
121 Eric Zeier .07 .20
122 Jeff Blake .30 .75
123 Derrick Thomas .30 .75
124 Tyrone Wheatley .15 .40
125 Steve Young .60 1.50
126 Napoleon Kaufman .30 .75
127 Dave Meggett .07 .20
128 Kerry Collins .30 .75
P77 Marcus Allen Prototype .30 .75
(die cut team name is
much larger than base card)

1996 Topps Laser Bright Spots

COMPLETE SET (16) 25.00 60.00
STATED ODDS 1:24
1 Curtis Martin 3.00 8.00
2 Tom Carter .40 1.00
3 Dave Brown .40 1.00
4 Wayne Chrebet 2.00 5.00
5 Rashaan Salaam .75 2.00
6 Mark Brunell 2.50 6.00
7 Elvis Grbac .75 2.00
8 Errict Rhett .75 2.00
9 Isaac Bruce 1.50 4.00
10 Kerry Collins 1.50 4.00
11 Mario Bates .40 1.00
12 Joey Galloway 1.50 4.00
13 Napoleon Kaufman 1.50 4.00
14 Tamarick Vanover .75 2.00
15 Marshall Faulk 2.00 5.00
16 Terrell Davis 3.00 8.00

1996 Topps Laser Draft Picks

COMPLETE SET (16) 15.00 40.00
STATED ODDS 1:12
1 Keyshawn Johnson 2.50 6.00
2 Lawrence Phillips 1.25 3.00
3 Bobby Hoying 1.50 4.00
4 Marco Battaglia .75 2.00
5 Kevin Hardy .75 2.00
6 Jerome Woods .75 2.00
7 Ray Mickens .75 2.00
8 John Mobley .75 2.00
9 Marvin Harrison 5.00 12.00
10 Walt Harris .75 2.00
11 Duane Clemons .75 2.00
12 Regan Upshaw .75 2.00
13 Brian Dawkins 3.00 8.00
14 Bobby Engram 1.25 3.00
15 Eddie Kennison 1.50 4.00
16 Jeff Lewis 1.25 3.00

1996 Topps Laser Stadium Stars

COMPLETE SET (16) 75.00 200.00
STATED ODDS 1:48
1 Barry Sanders 12.50 30.00
2 Jim Harbaugh 1.50 4.00
3 Tim Brown 3.00 8.00
4 Jim Everett .75 2.00
5 Brett Favre 15.00 40.00
6 Junior Seau 3.00 8.00
7 Greg Lloyd 1.50 4.00
8 Cris Carter 3.00 8.00
9 Emmitt Smith 12.50 30.00
10 Dan Marino 15.00 40.00
11 Jeff Blake 3.00 8.00
12 Darrell Green 1.50 4.00
13 John Elway 15.00 40.00
14 Marcus Allen 3.00 8.00
15 Steve Young 6.00 15.00
16 Drew Bledsoe 5.00 12.00

2011 Topps Legends

COMPLETE SET (165) 20.00 40.00
1 Joe Namath .30 .75
2 Junior Seau .25 .60
3 Vincent Brown RC .50 1.25
4 Ray Rice .20 .50
5 Matt Ryan .25 .60
6 Roddy White .20 .50
7 Miles Austin .20 .50
8 Delone Carter RC .40 1.00
9 Howie Long .25 .60
10 Roger Staubach .30 .75
11 Brian Urlacher .25 .60
12 Darrelle Revis .20 .50
13 Santana Moss .20 .50
14 Mikel Leshoure RC .50 1.25
15 Jon Baldwin RC .50 1.25
16 Niles Paul RC .50 1.25
17 Felix Jones .20 .50
18 Matt Schaub .20 .50
19 Kurt Warner .20 .50
20 Marcus Allen .25 .60
21 Shane Vereen RC .50 1.25
22 Cecil Shorts RC .40 1.00
23 Phil Simms .20 .50
24 Antonio Gates .20 .50
25 Jerrel Jernigan RC .40 1.00
26 Champ Bailey .20 .50
27 Mark Sanchez .25 .60
28 Blaine Gabbert RC .75 2.00
29 Jeremy Kerley RC .50 1.25
30 John Elway .40 1.00
31 Stevan Ridley RC .50 1.25
32 Ndamukong Suh .25 .60
33 Drew Brees .25 .60
34 Ronald Johnson RC .40 1.00
35 Virgil Green RC .50 1.25
36 Hakeem Nicks .20 .50
37 Richard Dent .15 .40
38 Torrey Smith RC .60 1.50
39 Tony Romo .25 .60
40 Franco Harris .25 .60
41 Christian Ponder RC 1.00 2.50
42 Andy Dalton RC 1.25 3.00
43 Matt Cassel .20 .50
44 Dwayne Bowe .20 .50
45 Mark Ingram RC 1.00 2.50
46 Bilal Powell RC .30 .75
47 Jamaal Charles .20 .50
48 Greg Little RC .50 1.25
49 Luke Stocker RC .40 1.00
50 Joe Montana .50 1.25
51 Len Dawson .25 .60
52 Andre Johnson .20 .50
53 Reggie Wayne .20 .50
54 Charles Woodson .25 .60
55 Eli Manning .25 .60
56 Marcell Dareus RC .50 1.25
57 Maurice Jones-Drew .20 .50
58 Wes Welker .25 .60
59 Sam Bradford .25 .60
60 Terry Bradshaw .30 .75
61 Leonard Hankerson RC .50 1.25
62 Anquan Boldin .20 .50
63 Ryan Mallett RC 1.00 2.50
64 Ryan Williams RC .60 1.50
65 Troy Polamalu .25 .60
66 Kendall Hunter RC .50 1.25
67 Julio Jones RC 1.00 2.50
68 LeGarrette Blount .20 .50
69 Julius Peppers .20 .50
70 Eric Dickerson .20 .50
71 Ahmad Bradshaw .20 .50
72 Ronnie Lott .20 .50
73 Da'Quan Bowers RC .50 1.25
74 Edmond Gates RC .40 1.00
75 Cam Newton RC 3.00 8.00
76 Fred Jackson .25 .60
77 Aldon Smith RC .75 2.00
78 LaDainian Tomlinson .25 .60
79 Tandon Doss RC .40 1.00
80 Jim Brown .30 .75
81 Jamie Harper RC .50 1.25
82 A.J. Green RC 1.00 2.50
83 Michael Vick .25 .60
84 Chad Ochocinco .20 .50
85 Hines Ward .20 .50
86 Randall Cobb RC .60 1.50
87 Tim Tebow .50 1.25
88 Chris Johnson .20 .50
89 Ed Reed .20 .50
90 Troy Aikman .30 .75
91 Nick Fairley RC .60 1.50
92 Prince Amukamara RC .50 1.25
93 Patrick Peterson RC .75 2.00
94 DeSean Jackson .20 .50
95 DeMarco Murray RC 1.00 2.50
96 Michael Turner .20 .50
97 Titus Young RC .60 1.50
98 Daniel Thomas RC .50 1.25
99 Kellen Winslow .20 .50
100 Dan Marino .50 1.25
101 Steve Young .30 .75
102 Matt Forte .20 .50
103 LeSean McCoy .20 .50
104 Dion Lewis RC .50 1.25
105 Mike Williams .20 .50
106 Thomas Jones .20 .50
107 Jacquizz Rodgers RC .50 1.25
108 Aaron Rodgers .40 1.00
109 Mike Wallace .25 .60
110 Emmitt Smith .40 1.00
111 Arian Foster .20 .50
112 Josh Freeman .25 .60
113 Dwight Freeney .20 .50
114 Joe Flacco .25 .60
115 Tom Brady .40 1.00
116 Vernon Davis .20 .50
117 Kyle Rudolph RC .50 1.25
118 Art Monk .20 .50
119 J.J. Watt RC .60 1.50
120 Bart Starr .40 1.00
121 Peyton Hillis .20 .50
122 Tony Gonzalez .20 .50
123 Jermichael Finley .20 .50
124 Marques Colston .20 .50
125 Jonathan Stewart .20 .50
126 Jim Plunkett .20 .50
127 Ray Lewis .25 .60
128 Steve Smith .20 .50
129 Austin Pettis RC .40 1.00
130 Earl Campbell .25 .60
131 Calvin Johnson .25 .60
132 Steven Jackson .20 .50
133 Ben Roethlisberger .25 .60
134 Marshawn Lynch .20 .50
135 Ricky Stanzi RC .60 1.50
136 Darren McFadden .20 .50
137 Jordan Todman RC .30 .75
138 Philip Rivers .25 .60
139 Adrian Peterson .30 .75
140 Tony Dorsett .25 .60
141 Jerome Bettis .25 .60
142 Larry Fitzgerald .20 .50
143 Steve Johnson .20 .50
144 Alex Green RC .50 1.25
145 Tim Brown .25 .60
146 Frank Gore .20 .50
147 Percy Harvin .20 .50
148 Matt Hasselbeck .20 .50
149 Peyton Manning .40 1.00
150 Jerry Rice .40 1.00
151 Brandon Lloyd .20 .50
152 Von Miller RC .60 1.50
153 Santonio Holmes .20 .50
154 Brandon Marshall .20 .50
155 David Garrard .20 .50
156 Rashard Mendenhall .20 .50
157 Taiwan Jones RC .50 1.25
158 Jimmy Smith RC .50 1.25
159 Rob Housler RC .40 1.00
160 Gale Sayers .25 .60
161 Jake Locker RC 1.25 3.00
162 Colin Kaepernick RC .60 1.50
163 Patrick Willis .20 .50
164 Greg Salas RC .50 1.25
165 Y.A. Tittle .25 .60

2011 Topps Legends Blue

*BLUE: .8X TO 2X BASIC CARDS
ONE PER PACK

2011 Topps Legends Bronze

*BRONZE/299: 2.5X TO 6X BASIC CARDS
BRONZE/299 ODDS 1:16 H, 1:22 R

2011 Topps Legends Gold

*GOLD/99: 4X TO 10X BASIC CARDS
GOLD/99 ODDS 1:49H, 1:65R

2011 Topps Legends Green

*GREEN/150: 3X TO 8X BASIC CARDS
GREEN/150 ODDS 1:32H, 1:44R

2011 Topps Legends Orange

*ORANGE/50: 6X TO 15X BASIC CARDS
ORANGE/50 ODDS 1:97H, 1;127R

2011 Topps Legends Purple

*PURPLE/10: 12X TO 30X BASIC CARDS
PURPLE PRINT RUN 10 SER.#'d SETS

2011 Topps Legends Red

*RED/75: 5X TO 12X BASIC CARDS
RED/75 ODDS 1:65H, 1:86R

2011 Topps Legends Aspiring Legacies

STATED ODDS 1:5 HOB/RET
ALAD Andy Dalton 1.25 3.00
ALAJG A.J. Green 1.00 2.50
ALAG Alex Green .50 1.25
ALAP Austin Pettis .40 1.00
ALBG Blaine Gabbert .75 2.00
ALBP Bilal Powell .30 .75
ALCK Colin Kaepernick .60 1.50
ALCN Cam Newton 2.50 6.00
ALCP Christian Ponder 1.00 2.50
ALDC Delone Carter .40 1.00
ALDM DeMarco Murray 1.00 2.50
ALDT Daniel Thomas .50 1.25
ALEG Edmond Gates .40 1.00
ALGL Greg Little .50 1.25
ALJB Jon Baldwin .50 1.25
ALJH Jamie Harper .50 1.25
ALJJE Jerrel Jernigan .40 1.00
ALJJ Julio Jones 1.00 2.50
ALJL Jake Locker 1.25 3.00
ALJT Jordan Todman .30 .75
ALKH Kendall Hunter .50 1.25
ALKR Kyle Rudolph .50 1.25
ALLH Leonard Hankerson .50 1.25
ALMD Marcell Dareus .50 1.25
ALMI Mark Ingram 1.00 2.50
ALML Mikel Leshoure .50 1.25
ALRC Randall Cobb .60 1.50
ALRM Ryan Mallett 1.00 2.50
ALRW Ryan Williams .60 1.50
ALSR Stevan Ridley .50 1.25
ALSV Shane Vereen .50 1.25
ALTJ Taiwan Jones .50 1.25
ALTS Torrey Smith .60 1.50
ALTY Titus Young .60 1.50
ALVB Vincent Brown .50 1.25
ALVM Von Miller .60 1.50

2011 Topps Legends Aspiring Legacies Jerseys

STATED ODDS 1:110 RET
*GOLD/50: .6X TO 1.5X BASIC JSY
*GREEN/150: .5X TO 1.2X BASIC JSY
*JUMBO/99: .6X TO 1.5X BASIC JSY
*RED/99: .5X TO 1.2X BASIC JSY
ALRAD Andy Dalton 5.00 12.00
ALRAG Alex Green 2.00 5.00
ALRAJG A.J. Green 4.00 10.00
ALRAP Austin Pettis 1.50 4.00
ALRBG Blaine Gabbert 3.00 8.00
ALRBP Bilal Powell 2.00 5.00
ALRCK Colin Kaepernick 2.50 6.00
ALRCN Cam Newton 10.00 25.00
ALRCP Christian Ponder 4.00 10.00
ALRDC Delone Carter 1.50 4.00
ALRDM DeMarco Murray 4.00 10.00
ALRDT Daniel Thomas 2.00 5.00
ALREG Edmond Gates 1.50 4.00
ALRGL Greg Little 2.50 6.00
ALRJB Jon Baldwin 2.00 5.00
ALRJH Jamie Harper 2.00 5.00
ALRJJ Julio Jones 4.00 10.00
ALRJJE Jerrel Jernigan 1.50 4.00
ALRJL Jake Locker 5.00 12.00
ALRJT Jordan Todman 1.25 3.00
ALRKH Kendall Hunter 2.00 5.00
ALRKR Kyle Rudolph 2.00 5.00
ALRLH Leonard Hankerson 2.00 5.00
ALRMD Marcell Dareus 2.00 5.00
ALRMI Mark Ingram 4.00 10.00
ALRML Mikel Leshoure 2.00 5.00
ALRRC Randall Cobb 2.50 6.00
ALRRM Ryan Mallett 4.00 10.00
ALRRW Ryan Williams 3.00 8.00
ALRSR Stevan Ridley 2.00 5.00
ALRSV Shane Vereen 2.00 5.00
ALRTJ Taiwan Jones 2.00 5.00
ALRTS Torrey Smith 2.50 6.00
ALRTY Titus Young 2.50 6.00
ALRVB Vincent Brown 2.00 5.00
ALRVM Von Miller 2.50 6.00

2011 Topps Legends Autographed Relics

JSY AU/25 ODDS 1:1065H, 1:3200R
EXCH EXPIRATION: 9/30/2014
AM Art Monk 50.00 100.00
EC Earl Campbell 25.00 50.00
ED Eric Dickerson 30.00 60.00
FH Franco Harris 30.00 60.00
GS Gale Sayers 30.00 60.00
HL Howie Long 30.00 60.00
JS Junior Seau 40.00 80.00
KS Ken Stabler 40.00 80.00
KW Kurt Warner 30.00 60.00
RL Ronnie Lott 40.00 80.00
SY Steve Young 40.00 80.00
TB Tim Brown 30.00 60.00
TBR Terry Bradshaw 50.00 100.00
TD Tony Dorsett 25.00 50.00
TT Thurman Thomas 20.00 40.00

2011 Topps Legends Autographs

STATED ODDS 1:1605 HOB, 1:4750 RET
EXCH EXPIRATION: 9/30/2014
LAAM Art Monk 40.00 80.00
LACH Chuck Howley
LAEC Earl Campbell 20.00 40.00
LAED Eric Dickerson 40.00 80.00
LAFB Fred Biletnikoff
LAFH Franco Harris 30.00 60.00
LAGS Gale Sayers 25.00 50.00
LAHL Howie Long 20.00 40.00
LAJB Jerome Bettis 40.00 80.00
LAJP Jim Plunkett
LAJS Junior Seau
LAKS Ken Stabler
LAKW Kurt Warner EXCH 25.00 50.00
LALB Larry Brown
LALD Len Dawson 25.00 50.00
LAMA Marcus Allen
LAOA Ottis Anderson EXCH 25.00 50.00
LAPS Phil Simms 15.00 30.00
LARD Richard Dent
LARL Ronnie Lott 15.00 30.00
LASY Steve Young 30.00 60.00
LATB Tim Brown 25.00 50.00
LATD Tony Dorsett
LATT Thurman Thomas
LAYT Y.A. Tittle 15.00 30.00

2011 Topps Legends Canton Hopefuls Autographs

STATED ODDS 1:2000H, 1:6000R
EXCH EXPIRATION: 9/30/2014
CHAAG Antonio Gates
CHAAJ Andre Johnson 15.00 30.00
CHAAP Adrian Peterson 40.00 80.00
CHACB Champ Bailey
CHADM Darren McFadden
CHAHN Hakeem Nicks
CHAHW Hines Ward 30.00 60.00
CHAJC Jamaal Charles
CHAKW Kellen Winslow 15.00 30.00
CHAMJ Maurice Jones-Drew
CHAMT Michael Turner 16.00 30.00
CHAPM Peyton Manning 60.00 120.00
CHAPW Patrick Willis 20.00 40.00
CHARL Ray Lewis
CHARW Reggie Wayne 15.00 30.00
CHASH Santonio Holmes
CHASJ Steven Jackson 15.00 30.00
CHASM Santana Moss
CHATJ Thomas Jones
CHATR Tony Romo 30.00 60.00

2011 Topps Legends Canton Hopefuls Autographed Relics

JSY AU/25 ODDS 1:1602H, 1:4750R
EXCH EXPIRATION: 9/30/2014
AG Antonio Gates 20.00 40.00
AJ Andre Johnson 20.00 40.00
DM Darren McFadden
HW Hines Ward 50.00 100.00
JC Jamaal Charles
MT Michael Turner 12.00 30.00
PM Peyton Manning 75.00 150.00
PW Patrick Willis 15.00 40.00
RL Ray Lewis 60.00 120.00
RW Reggie Wayne 20.00 40.00
TJ Thomas Jones

2011 Topps Legends Combo

STATED ODDS 1:10 HOB/RET
LCAC Joseph Addai .75 2.00
Delone Carter
LCAM Marcus Allen 1.50 4.00
Darren McFadden
LCBM Tom Brady 1.50 4.00
Ryan Mallet
LCCG Randall Cobb .75 2.00
Alex Green
LCCJ Earl Campbell 1.00 2.50
Chris Johnson
LCGD A.J. Green 1.50 4.00
Andy Dalton
LCGG David Garrard 1.00 2.50
Blaine Gabbert
LCGJ A.J. Green 1.25 3.00
Julio Jones
LCGN Blaine Gabbert 2.50 6.00
Cam Newton
LCGT Edmond Gates .60 1.50
Daniel Thomas
LCID Mark Ingram 1.25 3.00
Marcell Dareus
LCIJ Mark Ingram 1.25 3.00
Julio Jones
LCJP Jerrel Jernigan .50 1.25
Bilal Powell
LCJY Calvin Johnson .75 2.00
Titus Young
LCKH Colin Kaepernick 1.00 2.50
Kendall Hunter
LCLH Jake Locker 1.50 4.00
Jamie Harper
LCLY Mikel Leshoure .75 2.00
Titus Young
LCMR Joe Montana 2.50 6.00
Jerry Rice
LCPP Adrian Peterson 1.50 5.00
Christian Ponder
LCRF Aaron Rodgers 2.50 6.00
Brett Favre
LCRP Kyle Rudolph 1.25 3.00
Christian Ponder
LCTB Jordan Todman .60 1.50
Vincent Brown
LCVR Shane Vereen .60 1.50
Stevan Ridley
LCWB Kurt Warner 1.00 2.50
Sam Bradford
LCYP Titus Young .75 2.00
Austin Pettis

2011 Topps Legends Combo Relics

STATED PRINT RUN 25 SER.#'d SETS
AC Joseph Addai 5.00 12.00
Delone Carter
AM Marcus Allen 8.00 20.00
Darren McFadden
BM Tom Brady 15.00 40.00
Ryan Mallet
CG Randall Cobb 5.00 12.00
Alex Green
CJ Earl Campbell 10.00 25.00
Chris Johnson
GD A.J. Green 10.00 25.00
Andy Dalton
GG David Garrard 6.00 15.00
Blaine Gabbert
GJ A.J. Green 12.00 30.00
Julio Jones
GN Blaine Gabbert 15.00 40.00
Cam Newton
GT Edmond Gates 4.00 10.00
Daniel Thomas
ID Mark Ingram 8.00 20.00
Marcell Dareus
IJ Mark Ingram 8.00 20.00
Julio Jones
JP Jerrel Jernigan 3.00 8.00
Bilal Powell
JY Calvin Johnson 6.00 15.00
Titus Young
KH Colin Kaepernick 5.00 12.00
Kendall Hunter
LH Jake Locker 10.00 25.00
Jamie Harper
LY Mikel Leshoure 5.00 12.00
Titus Young
MR Joe Montana 25.00 60.00
Jerry Rice
PP Adrian Peterson 12.00 30.00
Christian Ponder
RF Aaron Rodgers 40.00 80.00
Brett Favre
RP Kyle Rudolph 8.00 20.00
Christian Ponder
TB Jordan Todman 6.00 15.00
Vincent Brown
VR Shane Vereen 4.00 10.00
Stevan Ridley
WB Kurt Warner 30.00 60.00
Sam Bradford
YP Titus Young 5.00 12.00
Austin Pettis

2011 Topps Legends Dual Autographs

DUAL AU/25 ODDS 1:1885H, 1:3400R
EXCH EXPRATION: 9/30/2014
AM Marcus Allen 50.00 100.00
Darren McFadden
BT Vincent Brown 12.00 30.00
Jordan Todman
CG Randall Cobb 20.00 50.00
Alex Green
CH Earl Campbell
Jamie Harper
JC Taiwan Jones
Delone Carter
JH Taiwan Jones 15.00 40.00
Kendall Hunter
MM Art Monk 40.00 80.00
Santana Moss
PR Bilal Powell 15.00 40.00
Stevan Ridley
TG Daniel Thomas 15.00 40.00
Edmond Gates
WB Kurt Warner 60.00 120.00
Sam Bradford
YK Steve Young 50.00 100.00
Colin Kaepernick

2011 Topps Legends Future Legends Autographs

STATED ODDS 1:1275H, 1:4000R
EXCH EXPIRATION: 9/30/2014
FLAAD Andy Dalton 25.00 50.00
FLAAJG A.J. Green 25.00 50.00
FLAAG Alex Green EXCH 8.00 20.00
FLAAP Austin Pettis
FLABG Blaine Gabbert 20.00 50.00
FLABP Bilal Powell
FLACK Colin Kaepernick
FLACN Cam Newton 75.00 150.00
FLACP Christian Ponder 20.00 40.00
FLADC Delone Carter
FLADM DeMarco Murray 25.00 50.00
FLADT Daniel Thomas
FLAEG Edmond Gates
FLAGL Greg Little 8.00 20.00
FLAJB Jon Baldwin
FLAJH Jamie Harper 8.00 20.00
FLAJJ Julio Jones
FLAJJE Jerrel Jernigan
FLAJL Jake Locker 30.00 60.00
FLAJT Jordan Todman
FLAKH Kendall Hunter
FLAKR Kyle Rudolph 8.00 20.00
FLALH Leonard Hankerson
FLAMD Marcell Dareus
FLAMI Mark Ingram
FLAML Mikel Leshoure
FLARC Randall Cobb 10.00 25.00
FLARM Ryan Mallett 30.00 60.00
FLARW Ryan Williams
FLASR Stevan Ridley
FLASV Shane Vereen 8.00 20.00
FLATJ Taiwan Jones
FLATS Torrey Smith 10.00 25.00
FLATY Titus Young
FLAVB Vincent Brown 8.00 20.00
FLAVM Von Miller 10.00 25.00

2011 Topps Legends Future Legends Autographed Relics

JSY AU/25 ODDS 1:600H, 1:3650R
EXCH EXPIRATION: 9/30/2014
AG Alex Green 12.00 30.00
AJG A.J. Green 40.00 80.00
AP Austin Pettis 10.00 25.00
BG Blaine Gabbert 40.00 80.00
BP Bilal Powell
CN Cam Newton 100.00 200.00
DC Delone Carter
DM DeMarco Murray 30.00 60.00
DT Daniel Thomas 12.00 30.00
EG Edmond Gates
GL Greg Little 12.00 30.00
JH Jamie Harper
JJ Julio Jones 50.00 100.00
JJE Jerrel Jernigan
JL Jake Locker 60.00 120.00
JT Jordan Todman
KH Kendall Hunter 12.00 30.00
KR Kyle Rudolph EXCH 12.00 30.00

LH Leonard Hankerson
MD Marcell Dareus
ML Mikel Leshoure
RC Randall Cobb 15.00 40.00
SR Stevan Ridley
SV Shane Vereen 12.00 30.00
TJ Taiwan Jones
TS Torrey Smith 15.00 40.00
TY Titus Young
VB Vincent Brown
VM Von Miller 15.00 40.00

2011 Topps Legends Gridiron Legacies

STATED ODDS 1:4 HOB/RET
GLAM Art Monk .50 1.25
GLBF Brett Favre 1.25 3.00
GLCC Chris Cooley .50 1.25
GLCJ Chris Johnson .50 1.25
GLDB Drew Brees .60 1.50
GLDM Dan Marino 1.25 3.00
GLES Emmitt Smith 1.00 2.50
GLJE John Elway 1.00 2.50
GLJM Joe Montana 1.25 3.00
GLJN Joe Namath .75 2.00
GLJR Jerry Rice 1.00 2.50
GLKS Ken Stabler .60 1.50
GLLF Larry Fitzgerald .50 1.25
GLLT LaDainian Tomlinson .60 1.50
GLMA Marcus Allen .60 1.50
GLMF Matt Forte .50 1.25
GLMR Matt Ryan .60 1.50
GLMV Michael Vick .60 1.50
GLRS Roger Staubach .75 2.00
GLTA Troy Aikman .75 2.00
GLTB Terry Bradshaw .75 2.00
GLTBR Tim Brown .60 1.50
GLTG Tony Gonzalez .50 1.25
GLTOB Tom Brady 1.00 2.50
GLWW Wes Welker .60 1.50

2011 Topps Legends Gridiron Legacies Relics

STATED PRINT RUN 150 SER.#'d SETS
*OVERSIZE/15: 1X TO 2.5X BASIC JSY/150
GLRAM Art Monk 6.00 15.00
GLRBF Brett Favre 10.00 25.00
GLRCC Chris Cooley 4.00 10.00
GLRDB Drew Brees 4.00 10.00
GLRDM Dan Marino 10.00 25.00
GLRES Emmitt Smith 8.00 20.00
GLRJE John Elway 8.00 20.00
GLRJM Joe Montana 10.00 25.00
GLRKS Ken Stabler 6.00 15.00
GLRLF Larry Fitzgerald 3.00 8.00
GLRLT LaDainian Tomlinson 4.00 10.00
GLRMA Marcus Allen 5.00 12.00
GLRMF Matt Forte 3.00 8.00
GLRMR Matt Ryan 4.00 10.00
GLRMV Michael Vick 4.00 10.00
GLRRS Roger Staubach 6.00 15.00
GLRTA Troy Aikman 6.00 15.00
GLRTB Tim Brown 5.00 12.00
GLRTG Tony Gonzalez 3.00 8.00
GLRWW Wes Welker 4.00 10.00

2011 Topps Legends Reprint Autographs

RANDOM INSERTS IN HOBBY PACKS
EXCH EXPIRATION: 9/30/2014
36 Art Donovan 12.00 30.00
60 Lenny Moore 12.00 30.00
81 Fred Morrison 12.00 30.00
86 Y.A. Tittle 30.00 60.00
105 Mike McCormack 12.00 30.00

2011 Topps Legends Rookie Autographs

*BASE AUTO: .3X TO .8X BRONZE/99
GROUP A ODDS 1:253 H, 1:1307 R
GROUP B ODDS 1:79 H, 1:363 R
GROUP C ODDS 1:44 H, 1:238 R
RACN Cam Newton A 90.00 150.00

2011 Topps Legends Rookie Autographs Bronze

STATED PRINT RUN 99 SER.#'d SETS
RAAC Anthony Castonzo 3.00 8.00
RAAS Aldon Smith 10.00 25.00
RADB Da'Quan Bowers 5.00 12.00
RADE Darren Evans 4.00 10.00
RADH Dwayne Harris 5.00 12.00
RADL Derrick Locke 4.00 10.00
RADLE Dion Lewis 5.00 12.00
RADS Da'Rel Scott 4.00 10.00
RADT Daniel Thomas 8.00 20.00
RADW D.J. Williams 5.00 12.00
RAGL Greg Little 5.00 12.00
RAGS Greg Salas 5.00 12.00
RAJB Jon Baldwin 5.00 12.00
RAJH Jamie Harper 6.00 15.00
RAJHO Justin Houston 5.00 12.00
RAJJE Jerrel Jernigan 4.00 10.00
RAJK Jeremy Kerley 6.00 15.00
RAJR Jacquizz Rodgers 5.00 12.00
RAJW J.J. Watt 8.00 20.00
RALH Leonard Hankerson 5.00 12.00
RALS Luke Stocker 4.00 10.00
RAMH Mark Herzlich 4.00 10.00
RAMM Mike McNeill 6.00 15.00
RAMP Mike Pouncey 5.00 12.00
RANF Nick Fairley 6.00 15.00
RARH Robert Housler 4.00 10.00
RARJ Ronald Johnson 4.00 10.00
RARMO Rahim Moore 4.00 10.00
RARS Ricky Stanzi 6.00 15.00
RARW Ryan Williams 8.00 20.00
RASR Stevan Ridley 5.00 12.00
RASV Shane Vereen 5.00 12.00
RATS Torrey Smith 6.00 15.00
RATT Terrence Toliver 4.00 10.00
RATTA Tyrod Taylor 5.00 12.00
RAVG Virgil Green 4.00 10.00
RAVM Von Miller 8.00 20.00

2011 Topps Legends Rookie Autographs Red

*RED/50: .5X TO 1.2X BRONZE/99
RED PRINT RUN 50 SER.#'d SETS
RAAD Andy Dalton 40.00 80.00
RAAG Alex Green 10.00 25.00
RAAJG A.J. Green 40.00 80.00
RABG Blaine Gabbert 40.00 80.00
RACK Colin Kaepernick 10.00 25.00
RACP Christian Ponder 30.00 60.00
RAJJ Julio Jones 40.00 80.00
RAMI Mark Ingram 40.00 80.00
RARC Randall Cobb 20.00 40.00
RARM Ryan Mallett 25.00 50.00
RATS Torrey Smith 10.00 25.00

2011 Topps Legends Stamp of Approval Relics

STATED ODDS 1:580 H, 1:650 R
AP Austin Pettis 4.00 10.00
CH Chad Henne 6.00 15.00
CN Cam Newton 25.00 50.00
DB Dwayne Bowe 6.00 15.00
DC Delone Carter 4.00 10.00
EC Earl Campbell 15.00 30.00
EG Edmond Gates 4.00 10.00
JA Joseph Addai 6.00 15.00
JF Joe Flacco 8.00 20.00
JH Jamie Harper 5.00 12.00
JK Johnny Knox 6.00 15.00
JM Jeremy Maclin 6.00 15.00
JN Jordy Nelson 6.00 15.00
JT Jordan Todman 3.00 8.00
KH Kendall Hunter 5.00 12.00
LL LaRon Landry 5.00 12.00
MC Matt Cassel 6.00 15.00
TB Tim Brown 8.00 20.00
TJ Taiwan Jones 5.00 12.00
VB Vincent Brown 5.00 12.00

2011 Topps Legends Triple Autographs

STATED PRINT RUN 15 SER.#'d SETS
TAHBM Franco Harris 100.00 175.00
Jerome Bettis
Rashard Mendenhall
TAHMM Leonard Hankerson 60.00 120.00
Art Monk
Santana Moss
TAJAM Taiwan Jones 60.00 120.00
Marcus Allen
Darren McFadden
TALYF Mikel Leshoure 40.00 80.00
Titus Young
Nick Fairley
TAMVR Ryan Mallett 50.00 100.00
Shane Vereen
Stevan Ridley

2008 Topps Letterman

This set was released on November 28, 2008. The base set consists of 100 cards. Cards 1-50 feature veterans serial numbered of 949, and cards 51-100 are rookies serial numbered of 419.

VETERAN PRINT RUN 949 SER.#'d SETS
ROOKIE PRINT RUN 419 SER.#'d SETS
1 Drew Brees 1.00 2.50
2 Tom Brady 1.50 4.00
3 Peyton Manning 1.50 4.00
4 Carson Palmer 1.00 2.50
5 Ben Roethlisberger 1.00 2.50
6 Eli Manning 1.00 2.50
7 Tony Romo 1.25 3.00
8 Vince Young .75 2.00
9 Matt Hasselbeck .75 2.00
10 Derek Anderson .60 1.50
11 Jay Cutler 1.00 2.50
12 Philip Rivers 1.00 2.50
13 Steven Jackson 1.00 2.50
14 Willie Parker .75 2.00
15 Clinton Portis .75 2.00
16 Adrian Peterson 1.50 4.00
17 LaDainian Tomlinson 1.00 2.50
18 Marion Barber .75 2.00
19 Brian Westbrook .75 2.00
20 Fred Taylor .75 2.00
21 Marshawn Lynch .75 2.00
22 Joseph Addai .75 2.00
23 Willis McGahee .75 2.00
24 Frank Gore .75 2.00
25 Larry Johnson .75 2.00
26 Brandon Jacobs .75 2.00
27 Ryan Grant 1.00 2.50
28 Chester Taylor .60 1.50
29 Laurence Maroney .75 2.00
30 Thomas Jones .75 2.00
31 Chad Johnson .75 2.00
32 Reggie Wayne .75 2.00
33 Anquan Boldin .75 2.00
34 Randy Moss 1.00 2.50
35 Plaxico Burress .75 2.00
36 Terrell Owens 1.00 2.50
37 Andre Johnson .75 2.00
38 Larry Fitzgerald 1.00 2.50
39 Braylon Edwards .75 2.00
40 Steve Smith .75 2.00
41 T.J. Houshmandzadeh .75 2.00
42 Torry Holt .75 2.00
43 Brandon Marshall .75 2.00
44 Wes Welker 1.00 2.50
45 Dwayne Bowe .75 2.00
46 Terry Bradshaw 2.00 5.00
47 Brett Favre 6.00 15.00
48 John Elway 2.00 5.00
49 Lawrence Taylor 1.25 3.00
50 Joe Namath 1.50 4.00
51 Matt Ryan RC 6.00 15.00
52 Brian Brohm RC 1.50 4.00
53 Chad Henne RC 1.50 4.00
54 Joe Flacco RC 5.00 12.00
55 Andre Woodson RC 1.50 4.00
56 John David Booty RC 1.25 3.00
57 Josh Johnson RC 1.50 4.00
58 Colt Brennan RC 1.50 4.00
59 Dennis Dixon RC 1.50 4.00
60 Erik Ainge RC 1.50 4.00
61 Kevin O'Connell RC 1.25 3.00
62 Darren McFadden RC 4.00 10.00
63 Rashard Mendenhall RC 3.00 8.00
64 Jonathan Stewart RC 2.50 6.00
65 Felix Jones RC 2.50 6.00
66 Jamaal Charles RC 2.50 6.00
67 Ray Rice RC 3.00 8.00
68 Chris Johnson RC 4.00 10.00
69 Mike Hart RC 1.50 4.00
70 Matt Forte RC 2.50 6.00
71 Kevin Smith RC 1.50 4.00
72 Steve Slaton RC 1.50 4.00
73 Malcolm Kelly RC 1.25 3.00
74 Limas Sweed RC 1.50 4.00
75 DeSean Jackson RC 3.00 8.00
76 James Hardy RC 1.25 3.00
77 Mario Manningham RC 1.50 4.00
78 Devin Thomas RC 1.25 3.00
79 Early Doucet RC 1.25 3.00
80 Andre Caldwell RC 1.25 3.00
81 Jordy Nelson RC 2.00 5.00
82 Eddie Royal RC 1.50 4.00
83 Earl Bennett RC 1.50 4.00
84 Donnie Avery RC 1.25 3.00
85 Dexter Jackson RC 1.25 3.00
86 Jerome Simpson RC 1.50 4.00
87 Harry Douglas RC 1.25 3.00
88 Keenan Burton RC 1.00 2.50
89 Marcus Smith RC 1.25 3.00
90 Dustin Keller RC 1.50 4.00
91 John Carlson RC 1.50 4.00
92 Jake Long RC 1.50 4.00
93 Chris Long RC 1.50 4.00
94 Vernon Gholston RC 1.25 3.00
95 Glenn Dorsey RC 1.50 4.00
96 Sedrick Ellis RC 1.50 4.00
97 Keith Rivers RC 1.50 4.00
98 Leodis McKelvin RC 1.25 3.00
99 Dominique Rodgers-Cromartie RC 1.50 4.00
100 Aqib Talib RC 1.50 4.00

2008 Topps Letterman Refractors

*VETS 1-45: 1.5X TO 4X BASIC CARDS
*LEGENDS 46-50: 1.2X TO 3X BASIC CARDS
*ROOKIES 51-100: .8X TO 2X BASIC CARDS
STATED PRINT RUN 99 SER.#'d SETS
47 Brett Favre 10.00 25.00

2008 Topps Letterman Superfractors

UNPRICED SUPERFRACTOR PRINT RUN 1

2008 Topps Letterman Xfractors

*VETS 1-45: 3X TO 8X BASIC CARDS
*LEGENDS 46-50: 2X TO 5X BASIC CARDS
*ROOKIES 51-100: 1.2X TO 3X BASIC CARDS
STATED PRINT RUN 25 SER.#'d SETS
47 Brett Favre 15.00 40.00

2008 Topps Letterman 14K Gold Letterman

SER.#'d TO 1, TOTAL PRINT RUNS 4-9

2008 Topps Letterman Authentic Letterman Patches

SER.#'d TO 1, TOTAL PRINT RUNS 4-10
UNPRICED AU/1 PRINT RUNS 4-10
UNPRICED JERSEY TAG PRINT RUN 1
UNPRICED JSY TAG AU PRINT RUN 1

2008 Topps Letterman Authentic Relics Quad Autographs

BASE AUTO PRINT RUN 25-75
*REFRACTOR/15: .5X TO 1.2X BASE AU/75
REFRACTOR PRINT RUN 5-15
UNPRICED XFRACTOR AU PRINT RUN 3-5
UNPRICED SPRFRCTR AU PRINT RUN 1
AQRAC Andre Caldwell/75 8.00 20.00
AQRAG Anthony Gonzalez/25 10.00 25.00
AQRBE Braylon Edwards/25 12.00 30.00
AQRBM Brandon Marshall/25 12.00 30.00
AQRDA Donnie Avery/75 8.00 20.00
AQRDB Dwayne Bowe/25 12.00 30.00
AQRDH David Harris/75 8.00 20.00
AQREB Earl Bennett/75 10.00 25.00
AQRER Eddie Royal/75 10.00 25.00
AQRGD Glenn Dorsey/75 EXCH 10.00 25.00
AQRHD Harry Douglas/75 8.00 20.00
AQRJB John David Booty/75 8.00 20.00
AQRJC Jamaal Charles/75 15.00 40.00
AQRJL Jake Long/75 10.00 25.00
AQRJS Jerome Simpson/75 10.00 25.00
AQRMB Marion Barber/25 12.00 30.00
AQRMC Marques Colston/25 12.00 30.00
AQRMF Matt Forte/75 15.00 40.00
AQRML Marshawn Lynch/25 12.00 30.00
AQRRR Ray Rice/75 20.00 40.00
AQRSJ Steven Jackson/25 15.00 40.00
AQRSS Steve Slaton/75 10.00 25.00
AQRWW Wes Welker/25 30.00 60.00

2008 Topps Letterman Authentic Relics Quad Patch

UNPRICED QUAD PRINT RUN 10
UNPRICED REFRACTOR PRINT RUN 5
UNPRICED XFRACTOR PRINT RUN 3
UNPRICED SUPERFRACT PRINT RUN 1

2008 Topps Letterman Booklet Autographs

BASE AUTO PRINT RUN 15-46
UNPRICED REFRCTR PRINT RUN 10
UNPRICED XFRACTOR PRINT RUN 3
UNPRICED SUPERFRCTR PRINT RUN 1
ALBBE Braylon Edwards/46 25.00 60.00
ALBCB Colt Brennan/46 30.00 80.00
ALBCH Chad Henne/46 60.00 100.00
ALBDB Dwayne Bowe/46 25.00 60.00
ALBDD Dennis Dixon/46 30.00 60.00
ALBES Emmitt Smith/15 200.00 350.00
ALBFB Brett Favre/15 200.00 400.00
ALBFJ Felix Jones/46 30.00 80.00
ALBJA Joseph Addai/46 25.00 60.00
ALBJE John Elway/15 250.00 400.00
ALBJF Joe Flacco/46 125.00 250.00
ALBJH James Hardy/46 15.00 40.00
ALBJL Jake Long/46 20.00 50.00
ALBJM Joe Montana/15 200.00 400.00
ALBJN Joe Namath/15 125.00 200.00
ALBLS Limas Sweed/46 20.00 50.00
ALBLT Lawrence Taylor/15 60.00 120.00
ALBMB Marion Barber/46 50.00 100.00
ALBMF Matt Forte/46 90.00 150.00
ALBMR Matt Ryan/15 200.00 400.00
ALBPM Peyton Manning/15 150.00 250.00
ALBRR Ray Rice/15 50.00 100.00
ALBSJ Steven Jackson/46 30.00 80.00
ALBTBR Tom Brady/15 175.00 300.00

2008 Topps Letterman Dual Patch Autographs RC Logo

UNPRICED BASE AU PRINT RUN 5-10
UNPRICED REFRCTR PRINT RUN 3
UNPRICED XFRACTOR PRINT RUN 3
UNPRICED SUPERFRCTR PRINT RUN 1

2008 Topps Letterman Patches

SER.#'d TO 9, TOTAL PRINT RUNS 36-126
*REFRACT/6: .5X TO 1.2X BASIC INSERT/9
REF.#'d TO 6, TOTAL PRINT RUNS 24-84
*XFRACT/3: .6X TO 1.5X BASIC INSERT/9
XFR.#'d TO 3, TOTAL PRINT RUNS 12-42
UNPRICED SUPR 1/1 TTL PRINT RUNS 4-14
LPAB Anquan Boldin/54* 8.00 20.00
LPAC Andre Caldwell/72* 5.00 12.00
LPAT Aqib Talib/45* 6.00 15.00
LPAW Andre Woodson/63* 6.00 15.00
LPBB Brian Brohm/45* 6.00 15.00
LPBR Ben Roethlisberger/126* 10.00 25.00
LPBS Barry Sanders/63* 20.00 50.00
LPBW Brian Westbrook/81* 8.00 20.00
LPCB Colt Brennan/63* 6.00 15.00
LPCL Chris Long/36* 6.00 15.00
LPCP Carson Palmer/54* 10.00 25.00
LPCW Chauncey Washington/90* 5.00 12.00
LPDA Donnie Avery/45* 5.00 12.00
LPDJ DeSean Jackson/63* 12.00 30.00
LPDM Dan Marino/54* 40.00 100.00
LPDT Devin Thomas/54* 5.00 12.00
LPES Emmitt Smith/45* 25.00 60.00
LPFG Frank Gore/36* 8.00 20.00
LPFJ Felix Jones/45* 10.00 25.00
LPFT Fred Taylor/54* 8.00 20.00
LPJC Jay Cutler/54* 10.00 25.00
LPJE John Elway/45* 30.00 80.00
LPJF Joe Flacco/54* 20.00 50.00
LPJH James Hardy/45* 5.00 12.00
LPJH Jacob Hester/54* 6.00 15.00
LPJJ Josh Johnson/63* 6.00 15.00
LPJM Joe Montana/63* 25.00 60.00
LPJN Jordy Nelson/54* 8.00 20.00
LPJN Joe Namath/54* 15.00 40.00
LPJR Jerry Rice/36* 30.00 80.00
LPJS Jonathan Stewart/63* 10.00 25.00
LPKW Kyle Wright/54* 5.00 12.00
LPLF Larry Fitzgerald/90* 10.00 25.00
LPLH Lavelle Hawkins/63* 4.00 10.00
LPLP Adrian Peterson/90* 15.00 40.00
LPLT Lawrence Taylor/54* 12.00 30.00
LPMF Matt Forte/45* 10.00 25.00
LPMH Marcus Henry/45* 5.00 12.00
LPMH Mike Hart/36* 6.00 15.00
LPMK Malcolm Kelly/45* 5.00 12.00
LPMR Matt Ryan/36* 25.00 60.00
LPRM Rashard Mendenhall/90* 12.00 30.00
LPRM Randy Moss/36* 10.00 25.00
LPSS Steve Slaton/54* 6.00 15.00
LPTA Troy Aikman/54* 15.00 40.00
LPTD Tony Dorsett/63* 15.00 40.00
LPTR Tony Romo/36* 12.00 30.00

2008 Topps Letterman Patches Autograph

SER.#'d TO 5-35; TOTAL PRINT RUNS 25-350
*REFRACTOR: .5X TO 1.2X BASIC AUTO
REF SER.#'d 4-9; TOTAL PRINT RUNS 16-190
*XFRACTOR: .6X TO 1.5X BASIC AUTO
XFR SER.#'d 3-15; TOTAL PRINT RUNS 12-150
SPRFRCT SER.#'d TO 1; TTL PRINT RUN 4-10
APAA Anthony Alridge/245* 8.00 20.00
APAC Andre Caldwell/280* 8.00 20.00
APAP Adrian Peterson/40* 75.00 150.00
APAT Aqib Talib/175* 10.00 25.00
APAW Andre Woodson/140* 10.00 25.00
APBB Brian Brohm/25* 10.00 25.00
APBS Barry Sanders/35* 75.00 150.00
APCB Colt Brennan/35* 15.00 40.00
APCW Chauncey Washington/350* 8.00 20.00
APDA Derek Anderson/40* 8.00 20.00
APDD Dennis Dixon/100* 12.00 30.00
APDM Darren McFadden/40* 50.00 100.00
APDM Dan Marino/30* 125.00 250.00
APDR Darius Reynaud/245* 6.00 15.00
APDT Devin Thomas/120* 8.00 20.00
APES Emmitt Smith/25* 125.00 250.00
APFJ Felix Jones/100* 25.00 60.00
APJA Joseph Addai/25* 15.00 40.00
APJE John Elway/25* 125.00 250.00
APJF Joe Flacco/120* 50.00 100.00
APJH Jacob Hester/120* 10.00 25.00
APJJ Josh Johnson/245* 10.00 25.00
APJM Joe Montana/35* 125.00 250.00
APJN Jordy Nelson/120* 25.00 50.00
APJR Jerry Rice/20* 100.00 200.00
APJS Jonathan Stewart/35* 30.00 60.00
APLH Lavelle Hawkins/245* 6.00 15.00
APLT Lawrence Taylor/30* 30.00 60.00
APMH Mike Hart/80* 10.00 25.00
APMH Marcus Henry/175* 8.00 20.00
APMR Matt Ryan/20* 100.00 200.00
APPA Allen Patrick/245* 8.00 20.00
APRM Rashard Mendenhall/200* 20.00 50.00
APSS Steve Slaton/120* 10.00 25.00

2008 Topps Letterman Patches Autograph Jersey Number

JERSEY # AU PRINT RUN 7-75
*REFRACTOR/25: .5X TO 1.2X BASIC AU/75
REFRACTORS PRINT RUN 5-25 SER.#'d SETS
UNPRICED XFRACTOR PRINT RUN 3-10
SUPERFRACTOR PRINT RUN 1
SERIAL #'d UNDER 25 NOT PRICED
ANPAA Jake Long/75 10.00 25.00
ANPAB Ahmad Bradshaw/75 15.00 40.00
ANPAW Andre Woodson/75 10.00 25.00
ANPCH Chad Henne/75 10.00 25.00
ANPCJ Chris Johnson/75 25.00 60.00
ANPDD Dennis Dixon/75 12.00 30.00
ANPDK Dustin Keller/75 10.00 25.00
ANPDM Ray Rice/75 20.00 50.00
ANPDS Dantrell Savage/75 8.00 20.00
ANPFJ Felix Jones/75 15.00 40.00
ANPHD Harry Douglas/75 8.00 20.00
ANPJH Jacob Hester/75 10.00 25.00
ANPJJ Josh Johnson/75 10.00 25.00
ANPJM Jerod Mayo/75 10.00 25.00
ANPKB Chris Long/75 10.00 25.00
ANPLL Kevin O'Connell/75 8.00 20.00
ANPMS Keith Rivers/75 10.00 25.00
ANPRM Rashard Mendenhall/75 20.00 50.00
ANPRT Ryan Torain/75 10.00 25.00
ANPXO Xavier Omon/75 10.00 25.00

2008 Topps Letterman Patches Autograph RC Logo

RC LOGO AU PRINT RUN 19-79
UNPRICED REFRACT PRINT RUN 5-10
UNPRICED XFRACTOR PRINT RUN 3
UNPRICED SUPERFRACT PRINT RUN 1
RAPAA Adrian Arrington/79 8.00 20.00
RAPAC Andre Caldwell/79 8.00 20.00
RAPAP Allen Patrick/79 8.00 20.00
RAPBB Brian Brohm/19 12.00 30.00
RAPCH Chad Henne/19 20.00 50.00
RAPCJ Chris Johnson/79 30.00 60.00
RAPDA Donnie Avery/79 8.00 20.00
RAPDJ DeSean Jackson/79 20.00 50.00
RAPDM Jake Long/79 10.00 25.00
RAPDM Darren McFadden/19 50.00 100.00
RAPDR Darius Reynaud/79 6.00 15.00
RAPED Early Doucet/79 8.00 20.00
RAPFJ Felix Jones/19 40.00 80.00
RAPJB John David Booty/79 8.00 20.00
RAPJC Jamaal Charles/79 15.00 40.00
RAPJF Joe Flacco/19 60.00 120.00
RAPJH James Hardy/79 8.00 20.00
RAPJS Jonathan Stewart/19 30.00 60.00
RAPKO Kevin O'Connell/79 8.00 20.00
RAPKS Kevin Smith/79 10.00 25.00
RAPLH Lavelle Hawkins/79 6.00 15.00
RAPLS Limas Sweed/19 12.00 30.00
RAPMH Mike Hart/79 10.00 25.00
RAPMK Malcolm Kelly/79 8.00 20.00
RAPMR Matt Ryan/19 125.00 250.00
RAPOS Owen Schmitt/79 10.00 25.00
RAPPS Paul Smith/79 10.00 25.00
RAPRM Rashard Mendenhall/19 25.00 60.00
RAPRR Ray Rice/19 15.00 40.00
RAPSE Sedrick Ellis/79 10.00 25.00
RAPSS Steve Slaton/79 10.00 25.00

2008 Topps Letterman Patches Autograph Team Logo

TEAM LOGO AU PRINT RUN 7-75
*REFRACTOR/25: .5X TO 1.2X BASIC AU/75
REFRACTORS PRINT RUN 5-25
UNPRICED XFRACTOR PRINT RUN 3-10
UNPRICED SUPERFRACT PRINT RUN 1
SERIAL #'d UNDER 25 NOT PRICED
ATPBB Brian Brohm/75 10.00 25.00
ATPCJ Chris Johnson/75 30.00 60.00
ATPDA Donnie Avery/75 8.00 20.00
ATPDH David Harris/75 8.00 20.00
ATPDJ Dexter Jackson/75 8.00 20.00
ATPDJ DeSean Jackson/75 20.00 50.00
ATPDT Devin Thomas/75 8.00 20.00
ATPER Eddie Royal/75 10.00 25.00
ATPFJ Felix Jones/75 15.00 40.00
ATPGD Glenn Dorsey/75 10.00 25.00
ATPJH James Hardy/75 8.00 20.00
ATPJL Jake Long/75 10.00 25.00
ATPJN Jordy Nelson/75 25.00 50.00
ATPJS Jerome Simpson/75 10.00 25.00
ATPKS Kevin Smith/75 10.00 25.00
ATPMF Matt Forte/75 30.00 60.00
ATPRM Rashard Mendenhall/75 20.00 50.00
ATPRR Ray Rice/75 20.00 40.00
ATPSS Steve Slaton/75 10.00 25.00

2008 Topps Letterman Patches Jersey Number

STATED PRINT RUN 25 SER.#'d SETS
UNPRICED REFRACTOR PRINT RUN 5
UNPRICED XFRACTOR PRINT RUN 3
UNPRICED SUPERFRACTOR PRINT RUN 1
JNPAB Ahmad Bradshaw 8.00 20.00
JNPAP Adrian Peterson 12.00 30.00
JNPBB Brian Brohm 5.00 12.00
JNPBR Ben Roethlisberger 8.00 20.00
JNPBS Barry Sanders 12.00 30.00
JNPCB Colt Brennan 5.00 12.00
JNPCH Chad Henne 5.00 12.00
JNPCL Chris Long 5.00 12.00
JNPDA Derek Anderson 5.00 12.00
JNPDB Drew Brees 8.00 20.00
JNPDJ DeSean Jackson 10.00 25.00
JNPDK Dustin Keller 5.00 12.00
JNPDM Dan Marino 20.00 50.00
JNPDMC Darren McFadden 12.00 30.00
JNPEM Eli Manning 8.00 20.00
JNPES Emmitt Smith 20.00 50.00
JNPFJ Felix Jones 8.00 20.00
JNPHD Harry Douglas 4.00 10.00
JNPJA Joseph Addai 6.00 15.00
JNPJC Jamaal Charles 8.00 20.00
JNPJE John Elway 15.00 40.00
JNPJF Joe Flacco 15.00 40.00
JNPJH James Hardy 4.00 10.00
JNPJHE Jacob Hester 5.00 12.00
JNPJJ Josh Johnson 5.00 12.00
JNPJM Joe Montana 20.00 50.00
JNPJMA Jerod Mayo 5.00 12.00
JNPJS Jonathan Stewart 8.00 20.00
JNPKO Kevin O'Connell 4.00 10.00
JNPLF Larry Fitzgerald 8.00 20.00
JNPLT LaDainian Tomlinson 8.00 20.00
JNPMD Maurice Jones-Drew 6.00 15.00
JNPMF Matt Forte 8.00 20.00
JNPMH Matt Hasselbeck 6.00 15.00
JNPMR Matt Ryan 20.00 50.00
JNPPM Peyton Manning 12.00 30.00
JNPPR Philip Rivers 8.00 20.00
JNPRM Randy Moss 8.00 20.00
JNPRME Rashard Mendenhall 10.00 25.00
JNPRR Ray Rice 10.00 25.00
JNPRW Reggie Wayne 6.00 15.00
JNPSS Steve Slaton 5.00 12.00
JNPSY Selvin Young 5.00 12.00
JNPTB Tom Brady 12.00 30.00
JNPTO Terrell Owens 8.00 20.00

2008 Topps Letterman Patches Team Logos

STATED PRINT RUN 25 SER.#'d SETS
UNPRICED REFRACTOR PRINT RUN 5
UNPRICED XFRACTOR PRINT RUN 3
UNPRICED SUPERFRACTOR PRINT RUN 1
TLPAP Adrian Peterson 12.00 30.00
TLPBB Brian Brohm 5.00 12.00
TLPBE Braylon Edwards 6.00 15.00
TLPBJ Brandon Jacobs 6.00 15.00
TLPBS Barry Sanders 15.00 40.00
TLPBU Brian Urlacher 8.00 20.00
TLPCJ Chris Johnson 12.00 30.00
TLPCPO Clinton Portis 6.00 15.00
TLPDA Donnie Avery 4.00 10.00
TLPDJ Dexter Jackson 4.00 10.00
TLPDJA DeSean Jackson 10.00 25.00
TLPDM Darren McFadden 12.00 30.00
TLPDT Devin Thomas 4.00 10.00
TLPED Early Doucet 4.00 10.00
TLPER Eddie Royal 5.00 12.00
TLPFG Frank Gore 6.00 15.00
TLPFJ Felix Jones 8.00 20.00
TLPGD Glenn Dorsey 5.00 12.00
TLPJE John Elway 15.00 40.00
TLPJF Joe Flacco 15.00 40.00
TLPJH James Hardy 4.00 10.00
TLPJL Jake Long 5.00 12.00
TLPJN Joe Namath 12.00 30.00
TLPJNE Jordy Nelson 6.00 15.00
TLPJR JaMarcus Russell 6.00 15.00
TLPJS Jonathan Stewart 8.00 20.00
TLPJSI Jerome Simpson 5.00 12.00
TLPLT LaDainian Tomlinson 8.00 20.00
TLPMF Matt Forte 8.00 20.00
TLPMH Matt Hasselbeck 6.00 15.00
TLPML Marshawn Lynch 6.00 15.00
TLPMR Matt Ryan 20.00 50.00
TLPPM Peyton Manning 12.00 30.00
TLPRB Reggie Bush 8.00 20.00
TLPRG Ryan Grant 8.00 20.00
TLPRM Rashard Mendenhall 10.00 25.00
TLPRR Ray Rice 10.00 25.00
TLPSJ Steven Jackson 8.00 20.00
TLPSS Steve Smith 6.00 15.00
TLPSSL Steve Slaton 5.00 12.00
TLPTB Tom Brady 12.00 30.00
TLPTR Tony Romo 10.00 25.00
TLPVY Vince Young 6.00 15.00
TLPWM Willis McGahee 6.00 15.00
TLPWP Willie Parker 6.00 15.00

1948 Topps Magic Photos

The 1948 Topps Magic Photos set contains 252 small (approximately 7/8" by 1 7/16") individual cards featuring sport and non-sport subjects. They were issued in 19 lettered series with cards numbered within each series. The fronts were developed, much like a photograph, from a "blank" appearance by using moisture and sunlight. Due to varying degrees of photographic sensitivity, the clarity of these cards ranges from fully developed to poorly developed. This set contains Topps' first baseball cards. A premium album holding 126-cards was also issued. The set is sometimes confused with Topps' 1956 Hocus-Focus set, although the cards in this set are slightly smaller than those in the Hocus-Focus set. The checklist below is presented by series. Poorly developed cards are considered in lesser condition and hence have lesser value. The catalog designation for this set is R714-27. Each type of card subject has a letter prefix as follows: Boxing Champions (A), All-American Basketball (B), All-American Football (C), Wrestling Champions (D), Track and Field Champions (E), Stars of Stage and Screen (F), American Dogs (G), General Sports (H), Movie Stars (J), Baseball Hall of Fame (K), Aviation Pioneers (L), Famous Landmarks (M), American Inventors (N), American Military Leaders (O), American Explorers (P), Basketball Thrills (Q), Football Thrills (R), Figures of the Wild West (S), and General Sports (T).

COMPLETE SET (252) 3,000.00 5,000.00
C1 Barney Poole 12.50 25.00
C2 Pete Elliott 7.50 15.00
C3 Doak Walker 25.00 50.00
C4 Bill Swiacki 10.00 20.00
C5 Bill Fischer 7.50 15.00
C6 Johnny Lujack 25.00 50.00
C7 Chuck Bednarik 25.00 50.00
C8 Joe Steffy 7.50 15.00
C9 George Connor 15.00 30.00
C10 Steve Suhey 10.00 20.00
C11 Bob Chappuis 10.00 20.00
C12 Bill Swiacki 7.50 15.00
Columbia 23
Navy 14
C13 Army-Notre Dame 12.50 25.00
R1 Wally Triplett 5.00 10.00
R2 Gil Stevenson 5.00 10.00
R3 Northwestern 5.00 10.00
R4 Yale vs. Columbia 5.00 10.00
R5 Cornell 5.00 10.00
NNO Sid Luckman Ad Poster 175.00 300.00

2009 Topps Magic

COMPLETE SET (250) 60.00 120.00
COMP.SET w/o SP's (200) 15.00 40.00
SP STATED ODDS 1:3
1 Domenik Hixon .20 .50
2 Brodie Croyle SP 1.50 4.00
3 LaDainian Tomlinson .30 .75
4 Glen Coffee RC .50 1.25
5 Cullen Harper RC .60 1.50
6 DeMeco Ryans SP 2.00 5.00
7 Roddy White .25 .60
8 Dexter Jackson .20 .50
9 Derek Hagan .20 .50
10 Zach Miller .20 .50
11 Ryan Torain .20 .50
12 Andrew Walter .20 .50
13 Tarvaris Jackson .25 .60
14 Felix Jones .30 .75
15 Darren McFadden .30 .75
16 Jason Campbell .20 .50
17 Peyton Manning .75 2.00
18 Kenny Irons SP 1.50 4.00
19 Bo Jackson .60 1.50
20 Gartrell Johnson RC .40 1.00
21 Ben Obomanu SP 2.00 5.00
22 Jerod Mayo .25 .60
23 Courtney Taylor .20 .50
24 Cadillac Williams .25 .60
25 Nate Davis RC .50 1.25
26 Robert Meachem SP 2.00 5.00
27 Isaiah Stanback SP 1.50 4.00
28 Earl Campbell .50 1.25
29 Mathias Kiwanuka .20 .50
30 Rashad Jennings RC .60 1.50
31 Matt Ryan .30 .75
32 Jamaal Charles .30 .75
33 Marcus Griffin .20 .50
34 John Beck SP 1.50 4.00
35 Justin Forsett SP 1.50 4.00
36 Lavelle Hawkins SP 1.50 4.00
37 DeSean Jackson .25 .60
38 Marshawn Lynch .25 .60
39 Brandon Marshall .25 .60
40 Chase Coffman RC .50 1.25
41 Kevin Smith .25 .60
42 Aaron Ross .20 .50
43 Gaines Adams .20 .50
44 Tye Hill SP 1.50 4.00
45 Winston Justice .20 .50
46 Chris Simms SP 1.50 4.00
47 Chris Brown SP 1.50 4.00
48 Limas Sweed .25 .60
49 David Anderson .20 .50
50 Donald Brown RC .60 1.50
51 Joe Flacco .30 .75
52 Dave Thomas SP 1.50 4.00
53 Dallas Baker .20 .50
54 Andre Caldwell .20 .50
55 Derrick Harvey SP 1.50 4.00
56 David Clowney .20 .50
57 Percy Harvin RC 1.00 2.50
58 Fred Taylor SP 2.00 5.00
59 DeShawn Wynn .20 .50
60 Lorenzo Booker SP 1.50 4.00
61 Roy Williams WR .25 .60
62 Chris Davis .20 .50
63 Sebastian Janikowski SP 1.50 4.00
64 Greg Jones .20 .50
65 James Laurinaitis RC .60 1.50
66 Ernie Sims SP 1.50 4.00
67 Lawrence Timmons .20 .50
68 Leon Washington .25 .60
69 Kamerion Wimbley .20 .50
70 Bernard Berrian .25 .60
71 Selvin Young .20 .50
72 Vince Young .25 .60
73 Paul Williams .20 .50
74 Reggie Brown .20 .50
75 Sean Jones SP 1.50 4.00
76 Knowshon Moreno RC .60 1.50
77 Matthew Stafford RC 3.00 8.00
78 Mohamed Massaquoi RC .50 1.25
79 Leonard Pope SP 1.50 4.00
80 D.J. Shockley .20 .50
81 Tashard Choice .20 .50
82 P.J. Daniels SP 1.50 4.00
83 Colt Brennan .25 .60
84 John Parker Wilson RC .60 1.50
85 Donnie Avery .25 .60
86 Kevin Kolb SP 1.50 4.00
87 Graham Harrell RC .60 1.50
88 Rashard Mendenhall .25 .60
89 Laurent Robinson .20 .50
90 James Hardy .25 .60
91 Antwaan Randle El .20 .50
92 Scott Chandler .20 .50
93 Chad Greenway .20 .50
94 Ramses Barden RC .40 1.00
95 Shonn Greene RC 1.00 2.50
96 Aqib Talib .20 .50
97 Michael Crabtree RC 1.25 3.00
98 Yamon Figurs SP 1.50 4.00
99 Josh Freeman RC 1.25 3.00
100 Jordy Nelson .30 .75
101 Zach Thomas .25 .60
102 Antonio Gates .25 .60
103 Keenan Burton .20 .50
104 Matt Forte .30 .75
105 Terry Bradshaw SP 3.00 8.00
106 Ryan Moats .20 .50
107 John David Booty .25 .60
108 Brian Brohm .20 .50
109 Michael Bush .25 .60
110 Amobi Okoye .20 .50
111 Kolby Smith SP 1.50 4.00
112 Joseph Addai .30 .75
113 Dwayne Bowe .25 .60
114 Michael Clayton .20 .50
115 Craig Buster Davis .20 .50
116 Early Doucet .25 .60
117 Reggie Bush .30 .75
118 Matt Flynn .30 .75
119 Fred Davis .25 .60
120 Kory Sheets RC .50 1.25
121 Jacob Hester .20 .50
122 LaRon Landry .20 .50
123 Justin Fargas .20 .50
124 Dwayne Jarrett .20 .50
125 Ahmad Bradshaw SP 2.00 5.00
126 Randy Moss .30 .75
127 Chad Pennington .25 .60
128 Darrius Heyward-Bey RC .60 1.50
129 Matt Leinart .25 .60
130 Shawne Merriman SP 2.00 5.00
131 DeAngelo Williams SP 2.50 6.00
132 Frank Gore .25 .60
133 Devin Hester .30 .75
134 Ray Lewis .30 .75
135 Willis McGahee .25 .60
136 Greg Olsen SP 1.50 4.00
137 Roscoe Parrish .20 .50
138 Antrel Rolle SP 1.50 4.00
139 Reggie Wayne .25 .60
140 Kellen Winslow .25 .60
141 Adrian Arrington .20 .50
142 B.J. Askew .20 .50
143 Jason Avant .20 .50
144 Mark Sanchez RC 2.00 5.00
145 Tom Brady .75 2.00
146 Steve Breaston .25 .60
147 Braylon Edwards .25 .60
148 Leon Hall .20 .50
149 Steve Smith USC .25 .60
150 Mike Hart .25 .60
151 Chad Henne .25 .60
152 Drew Henson .20 .50
153 Steve Hutchinson .25 .60
154 Marlin Jackson SP 1.50 4.00
155 Ty Law .20 .50
156 Mario Manningham .25 .60
157 LaMarr Woodley .20 .50
158 Javon Ringer RC .60 1.50
159 LenDale White .25 .60
160 Drew Stanton .20 .50
161 Devin Thomas .20 .50
162 Laurence Maroney .25 .60
163 Alex Smith QB .25 .60
164 Eli Manning .40 1.00
165 Deuce McAllister SP 2.00 5.00
166 Patrick Willis .25 .60
167 Jerious Norwood .25 .60
168 Jordan Palmer .20 .50
169 Chase Daniel RC .60 1.50
170 Jeremy Maclin RC 1.00 2.50
171 Jay Cutler .30 .75
172 Brad Smith SP 1.50 4.00
173 Thomas Jones .25 .60
174 Brandon Jackson SP 2.00 5.00
175 Nate Burleson .20 .50
176 Alvin Pearman SP 1.50 4.00
177 Marcus Smith .20 .50
178 Matt Schaub SP 2.00 5.00
179 DeAngelo Hall .25 .60
180 Ronald Curry SP 1.50 4.00
181 Hakeem Nicks RC 1.00 2.50
182 Kevin Jones .20 .50
183 Willie Parker .20 .50
184 Andre Brown RC .40 1.00
185 DaJuan Morgan SP 1.50 4.00
186 Philip Rivers .30 .75
187 Mario Williams .25 .60
188 Vincent Jackson .25 .60
189 Garrett Wolfe .20 .50
190 Xavier Omon .20 .50
191 John Carlson .25 .60
192 Anthony Fasano .20 .50
193 Julius Jones SP 1.50 4.00
194 Brady Quinn .25 .60
195 Maurice Stovall SP 1.50 4.00
196 Bobby Carpenter .20 .50
197 Chris Wells RC 1.00 2.50
198 Joey Galloway .25 .60
199 Vernon Gholston SP 1.50 4.00
200 Ted Ginn .25 .60
201 Anthony Gonzalez .20 .50
202 Eddie Royal .25 .60
203 Michael Jenkins .20 .50
204 Jason Hill .20 .50
205 Troy Smith .25 .60
206 Marc Bulger SP 2.00 5.00
207 Mark Bradley SP 1.50 4.00
208 Owen Schmitt SP 1.50 4.00
209 Juaquin Iglesias RC .50 1.25
210 Malcolm Kelly .20 .50
211 Allen Patrick SP 1.50 4.00
212 Adrian Peterson .75 2.00
213 Tatum Bell .20 .50
214 Brandon Pettigrew RC .60 1.50
215 Kelleh Clemens .20 .50
216 Dennis Dixon .25 .60
217 Jonathan Stewart .25 .60
218 Demetrius Williams .20 .50
219 Derek Anderson .20 .50
220 Steven Jackson .25 .60
221 Chad Johnson .25 .60
222 Reggie Williams SP 1.50 4.00
223 Dan Connor .20 .50
224 Derrick Williams SP RC 1.50 4.00
225 Larry Johnson .25 .60
226 Pat White RC .60 1.50
227 Paul Posluszny .25 .60
228 Tony Dorsett .50 1.25
229 LeSean McCoy RC 1.25 3.00
230 Dan Marino 1.25 3.00
231 Drew Brees .30 .75
232 Dustin Keller .20 .50
233 Kyle Orton SP 2.00 5.00
234 Steve Slaton .25 .60

235 Kenny Britt RC	.75	2.00
236 Brian Leonard SP	1.50	4.00
237 Ray Rice	.30	.75
238 Kevin O'Connell	.20	.50
239 Lee Evans SP	2.00	5.00
240 James Jones	.20	.50
241 Eric Dickerson	.40	1.00
242 Jared Cook RC	.60	1.50
243 P.J. Hill RC	.50	1.25
244 Andre Hall	.20	.50
245 Rhett Bomar RC	.50	1.25
246 Trent Edwards	.20	.50
247 John Elway	1.00	2.50
248 Jim Brown	.60	1.50
249 Dwight Freeney	.25	.60
250 Joe Thomas	.25	.60
TMJR Jackie Robinson	8.00	20.00

2009 Topps Magic Mini

*VETS: 1.2X TO 3X BASIC CARDS
*VET SPs: .5X TO 1.2X BASIC CARDS
*RETIRED: 1.2X TO 3X BASIC CARDS
*RETIRED SPs: .5X TO 1.2X BASIC CARDS
*ROOKIES: .6X TO 1.5X BASIC CARDS
*ROOKIE SPs: .5X TO 1.2X BASIC CARDS
ONE MINI PER PACK OVERALL
MINI SP ODDS 1:12

2009 Topps Magic Mini Black

*VETS: 2.5X TO 6X BASIC CARDS
*VET SPs: .6X TO 1.5X BASIC CARDS
*RETIRED: 2.5X TO 6X BASIC CARDS
*RETIRED SPs: .6X TO 1.5X BASIC CARDS
*ROOKIES: 1X TO 2.5X BASIC CARDS
*ROOKIE SPs: .6X TO 1.5X BASIC CARDS
BLACK MINI ODDS 1:8
BLACK MINI SP ODDS 1:24

2009 Topps Magic 1948 Magic

STATED ODDS 1:6

M1 Vince Young	1.00	2.50
M2 McCollum vs. Board of Educ.	.75	2.00
M3 Adrian Peterson	2.00	5.00
M4 Percy Harvin	1.00	2.50
M5 Terry Bradshaw	1.50	4.00
M6 Marshall Plan	.75	2.00
M7 Tony Dorsett	1.25	3.00
M8 Knowshon Moreno	.60	1.50
M9 Bo Jackson	1.50	4.00
M10 World Heath Organization	.75	2.00
M11 Michael Crabtree	1.25	3.00
M12 Berlin Blockage	.75	2.00
M13 Earl Campbell	1.25	3.00
M14 LeSean McCoy	1.25	3.00
M15 John Elway	2.00	5.00
M16 Israel Dec. Of Independ.	.75	2.00
M17 Jim Brown	1.50	4.00
M18 Harry Truman	.75	2.00
Dewey defeats Truman		
M19 Dan Marino	2.50	6.00
M20 Jeremy Maclin	1.00	2.50
M21 Chris Johnson	1.25	3.00
M22 Harry Truman	.75	2.00
Executive Order 9981		
M23 Steve Slaton	1.00	2.50
M24 Arthur Miller Author	.75	2.00
Death of a Salesman		
M25 Reggie Bush	1.25	3.00
M26 Matthew Stafford	3.00	8.00
M27 Mark Sanchez	2.00	5.00
M28 LP Record	.75	2.00
M29 Eric Dickerson	1.00	2.50
M30 Maria Telkes	.75	2.00

2009 Topps Magic 1948 Magic Autographs

STATED ODDS 1:1480

AP Adrian Peterson	100.00	175.00
BJ Bo Jackson	60.00	120.00
DM Dan Marino	100.00	200.00
EC Earl Campbell	40.00	80.00
ED Eric Dickerson	50.00	100.00
JB Jim Brown	50.00	100.00
JE John Elway	75.00	150.00
MC Michael Crabtree	60.00	120.00
TB Terry Bradshaw	50.00	100.00
TD Tony Dorsett	30.00	60.00

2009 Topps Magic All Americans

STATED ODDS 1:8

AA1 John Elway	2.50	6.00
AA2 Knowshon Moreno	.75	2.00
AA3 Bo Jackson	2.00	5.00
AA4 LaDainian Tomlinson	1.50	4.00
AA5 Kevin Smith	1.25	3.00
AA6 Earl Campbell	1.50	4.00
AA7 Jeremy Maclin	1.25	3.00
AA8 DeAngelo Williams	1.50	4.00
AA9 Shonn Greene	1.25	3.00
AA10 Matt Ryan	1.50	4.00
AA11 Dan Marino	3.00	8.00
AA12 Peyton Manning	3.00	8.00
AA13 Donald Brown	.75	2.00
AA14 Eric Dickerson	1.25	3.00
AA15 Vince Young	1.25	3.00
AA16 Gale Sayers	2.00	5.00
AA17 Michael Crabtree	1.50	4.00
AA18 Jim Brown	2.00	5.00
AA19 Larry Fitzgerald	1.50	4.00
AA20 Adrian Peterson	2.50	6.00
AA21 Terry Bradshaw	2.00	5.00
AA22 Javon Ringer	1.50	4.00
AA23 Tony Dorsett	1.50	4.00
AA24 Darren McFadden	1.50	4.00
AA25 Reggie Bush	1.50	4.00

2009 Topps Magic Alumni

STATED ODDS 1:12

AB Joseph Addai	1.50	4.00
Dwayne Bowe		
BE Tom Brady	2.50	6.00
Braylon Edwards		
CH Michael Crabtree	1.25	3.00
Graham Harrell		
CV Earl Campbell	1.50	4.00
Vince Young		
DS Dennis Dixon	1.25	3.00
Jonathan Stewart		
GM Frank Gore	1.25	3.00
Willis McGahee		
JJ Chad Johnson	1.25	3.00
Steven Jackson		
JL DeSean Jackson	1.25	3.00
Marshawn Lynch		
MC Jeremy Maclin	1.00	2.50
Chase Coffman		
MD Dan Marino	3.00	8.00
Tony Dorsett		
PM Chad Pennington	1.50	4.00
Randy Moss		
SM Matthew Stafford	3.00	8.00
Knowshon Moreno		
SW Steve Slaton	2.00	5.00
Pat White		
WW Reggie Wayne	1.25	3.00
Kellen Winslow		

2009 Topps Magic Alumni Autographs Dual

DUAL AUTO/25 ODDS 1:1025

AB Joseph Addai	20.00	50.00
Dwayne Bowe		
BE Tom Brady	150.00	250.00
Braylon Edwards		
CH Michael Crabtree	50.00	100.00
Graham Harrell		
CV Earl Campbell	75.00	150.00
Vince Young		
DS Dennis Dixon	30.00	60.00
Jonathan Stewart		
GM Frank Gore	30.00	60.00
Willis McGahee		
JJ Steven Jackson	30.00	60.00
Chad Johnson		
JL DeSean Jackson	20.00	50.00
Marshawn Lynch		
MC Jeremy Maclin	30.00	60.00
Chase Coffman		
MD Dan Marino	150.00	250.00
Tony Dorsett		
PM Chad Pennington	75.00	150.00
Randy Moss		
SM Matthew Stafford	75.00	150.00
Knowshon Moreno		
SW Steve Slaton	50.00	100.00
Pat White		
WW Reggie Wayne	30.00	60.00
Kellen Winslow		

2009 Topps Magic Alumni Autographs Triple

TRIPLE AUTO/25 ODDS 1:1480

BBO Michael Bush		
Brian Brohm		
Amobi Okoye		
BSW Reggie Bush	100.00	200.00
Mark Sanchez		
LenDale White		
CDM Chase Coffman	40.00	80.00
Chase Daniel		
Jeremy Maclin		
DMM Tony Dorsett	175.00	300.00
Dan Marino		
LeSean McCoy		
GSG Ted Ginn Jr.	50.00	100.00
Troy Smith		
Anthony Gonzalez		
JWL Malcolm Jenkins	60.00	120.00
Chris Wells		
James Laurinaitis		
LBE Ty Law	175.00	300.00
Tom Brady		
Braylon Edwards		
MMW Deuce McAllister	100.00	200.00
Eli Manning		
Patrick Willis		
MSM Knowshon Moreno	100.00	200.00
Matthew Stafford		
Mohamed Massaquoi		
WLW Reggie Wayne	75.00	150.00
Ray Lewis		
Kellen Winslow		

2009 Topps Magic Autographs

GROUP 1A/25* ODDS 1:438
GROUP 1B/50* ODDS 1:650
GROUP 1C/250* ODDS 1:76
GROUP 1D ODDS 1:389
GROUP 1E ODDS 1:179
GROUP 1F ODDS 1:148
GROUP 2A/20* ODDS 1:35,000
GROUP 2B/25* ODDS 1:870
GROUP 2C/100* ODDS 1:91
GROUP 2D/150* ODDS 1:43
GROUP 2E ODDS 1:185
GROUP 2F ODDS 1:168
GROUP 2G ODDS 1:158
GROUP 2H ODDS 1:31

1 Domenik Hixon/100*	8.00	20.00
2 Brodie Croyle/150*	8.00	20.00
3 LaDainian Tomlinson/25*	125.00	250.00
4 Glen Coffee/150*	8.00	20.00
5 Cullen Harper/150*	10.00	25.00
6 DeMeco Ryans/150*	10.00	25.00
7 Roddy White/100*	10.00	25.00
8 Dexter Jackson 2H	4.00	10.00
9 Derek Hagan/150*	8.00	20.00
10 Zach Miller/25*	75.00	150.00
11 Ryan Torain 2E	4.00	10.00
12 Andrew Walter/100*	8.00	20.00
13 Tarvaris Jackson 2H	5.00	12.00
14 Felix Jones/250*	12.00	30.00
15 Darren McFadden/25*	60.00	120.00
16 Jason Campbell/25*	50.00	100.00
17 Peyton Manning/25*	175.00	300.00
18 Kenny Irons/20*	125.00	250.00
19 Bo Jackson/25*	125.00	200.00
20 Gartrell Johnson/150*	6.00	15.00
21 Ben Obomanu/100*	10.00	25.00
22 Jerod Mayo/150*	10.00	25.00
23 Courtney Taylor 2H	4.00	10.00
24 Cadillac Williams/25*	50.00	100.00
25 Nate Davis/250*	6.00	15.00
26 Robert Meachem/25*	75.00	150.00
27 Isaiah Stanback/100*	8.00	20.00
28 Earl Campbell/25*	75.00	150.00
29 Mathias Kiwanuka 2F	4.00	10.00
30 Rashad Jennings/150*	10.00	25.00
31 Matt Ryan/25*	125.00	250.00
32 Jamaal Charles/150*	12.00	30.00
33 Marcus Griffin 2H	4.00	10.00
34 John Beck/150*	8.00	20.00
35 Justin Forsett 2F	4.00	10.00
36 Lavelle Hawkins/150*	8.00	20.00
37 DeSean Jackson 1E	6.00	15.00
38 Marshawn Lynch/50*	25.00	50.00
39 Brandon Marshall/150*	10.00	25.00
40 Chase Coffman/150*	8.00	20.00
41 Kevin Smith 1G	6.00	15.00
42 Aaron Ross/150*	8.00	20.00
43 Gaines Adams/100*	8.00	20.00
44 Tye Hill/100*	8.00	20.00
45 Winston Justice/100*	8.00	20.00
46 Chris Simms/100*	8.00	20.00
47 Chris Brown/150*	8.00	20.00
48 Limas Sweed/100*	10.00	25.00
49 David Anderson/100*	8.00	20.00
50 Donald Brown/250*	15.00	40.00
51 Joe Flacco 1D	15.00	40.00
52 Dave Thomas/100*	8.00	20.00
53 Dallas Baker/100*	8.00	20.00
54 Andre Caldwell 2H	4.00	10.00
55 Derrick Harvey/150*	8.00	20.00
56 David Clowney 2E	4.00	10.00
57 Percy Harvin/250*	30.00	50.00
58 Fred Taylor/25*	50.00	100.00
59 DeShawn Wynn 2E	4.00	10.00
60 Lorenzo Booker/150*	8.00	20.00
61 Roy Williams WR 1E	6.00	15.00
62 Chris Davis 2F	4.00	10.00
63 Sebastian Janikowski/100*	12.00	30.00
64 Greg Jones/100*	8.00	20.00
65 James Laurinaitis/150*	10.00	25.00
66 Ernie Sims/150*	8.00	20.00
67 Lawrence Timmons/150*	8.00	20.00
68 Leon Washington 2G	5.00	12.00
69 Kamerion Wimbley/150*	8.00	20.00
70 Bernard Berrian/100*	10.00	25.00
71 Selvin Young/25*	90.00	150.00
72 Vince Young/25*	125.00	200.00
73 Paul Williams/150*	8.00	20.00
74 Reggie Brown/150*	8.00	20.00
75 Sean Jones/100*	8.00	20.00
76 Knowshon Moreno/50*	60.00	100.00
77 Matthew Stafford/50*	75.00	150.00
78 Mohamed Massaquoi/150*	8.00	20.00
79 Leonard Pope 2H	4.00	10.00
80 D.J. Shockley/100*	8.00	20.00
81 Tashard Choice/150*	8.00	20.00
82 P.J. Daniels 2H	4.00	10.00
83 Colt Brennan/100*	20.00	40.00
84 John Parker Wilson 2H	6.00	15.00
85 Donnie Avery/150*	10.00	25.00
86 Kevin Kolb/100*	10.00	25.00
87 Graham Harrell/150*	15.00	40.00
88 Rashard Mendenhall/250*	8.00	20.00
89 Laurent Robinson/150*	8.00	20.00
90 James Hardy/150*	10.00	25.00
91 Antwaan Randle El/100*	8.00	20.00
92 Scott Chandler 2H	4.00	10.00
93 Chad Greenway/100*	8.00	20.00
94 Ramses Barden/150*	6.00	15.00
95 Shonn Greene/150*	20.00	50.00
96 Aqib Talib 2G	4.00	10.00
97 Michael Crabtree/25*	60.00	120.00
98 Yamon Figurs 2E	4.00	10.00
99 Josh Freeman/50*	30.00	60.00
100 Jordy Nelson/150*	12.00	30.00
101 Zach Thomas/25*	60.00	120.00
102 Antonio Gates/50*	20.00	40.00
103 Keenan Burton 2G	4.00	10.00
104 Matt Forte 1G	10.00	25.00
105 Terry Bradshaw/25*	125.00	250.00
106 Ryan Moats/100*	8.00	20.00
107 John David Booty/100*	10.00	25.00
108 Brian Brohm/100*	8.00	20.00
109 Michael Bush/150*	10.00	25.00
110 Amobi Okoye/150*	8.00	20.00
111 Kolby Smith/50*	25.00	50.00
112 Joseph Addai/250*	10.00	25.00
113 Dwayne Bowe/250*	8.00	20.00
114 Michael Clayton/25*	40.00	80.00
115 Craig Buster Davis 2H	4.00	10.00
116 Early Doucet/150*	10.00	25.00
117 Reggie Bush/25*	125.00	200.00
118 Matt Flynn/150*	15.00	40.00
119 Fred Davis 2F	5.00	12.00
120 Kory Sheets/150*	8.00	20.00
121 Jacob Hester/150*	8.00	20.00
122 LaRon Landry/150*	8.00	20.00
123 Justin Fargas/100*	8.00	20.00
124 Dwayne Jarrett/100*	8.00	20.00
125 Ahmad Bradshaw/100*	12.00	30.00
126 Randy Moss/25*	125.00	200.00
127 Chad Pennington/25*	50.00	100.00
128 Darrius Heyward-Bey/50*	20.00	50.00
129 Matt Leinart/250*	20.00	40.00
130 Shawne Merriman/25*	50.00	100.00
131 DeAngelo Williams/50*	25.00	60.00
132 Frank Gore/250*	8.00	20.00
133 Devin Hester/150*	25.00	40.00
134 Ray Lewis/25*	125.00	200.00
135 Willis McGahee/25*	50.00	100.00
136 Greg Olsen/150*	8.00	20.00
137 Roscoe Parrish/100*	8.00	20.00
138 Antrel Rolle/100*	8.00	20.00
139 Reggie Wayne/25*	50.00	100.00
140 Kellen Winslow/25*	50.00	100.00
141 Adrian Arrington 2H	4.00	10.00
142 B.J. Askew/100*	8.00	20.00
143 Jason Avant/150*	8.00	20.00
144 Mark Sanchez/25*	150.00	250.00
145 Tom Brady/25*	150.00	250.00
146 Steve Breaston 2G	5.00	12.00
147 Braylon Edwards/25*	75.00	150.00
148 Leon Hall/100*	8.00	20.00
149 Steve Smith/100*	12.00	30.00
150 Mike Hart/150*	12.00	30.00
151 Chad Henne/150*	10.00	25.00
152 Drew Henson/100*	10.00	25.00
153 Steve Hutchinson/25*	125.00	250.00
154 Marlin Jackson/150*	8.00	20.00
155 Ty Law/100*	15.00	40.00
156 Mario Manningham/150*	10.00	25.00
157 LaMarr Woodley/150*	8.00	20.00
158 Javon Ringer/150*	15.00	30.00
159 LenDale White/100*	12.00	30.00
160 Drew Stanton/100*	8.00	20.00
161 Devin Thomas/150*	8.00	20.00
162 Laurence Maroney/25*	50.00	100.00
163 Alex Smith QB/150*	10.00	25.00
164 Eli Manning/25*	90.00	150.00
165 Deuce McAllister/25*	50.00	100.00
166 Patrick Willis 1D	8.00	20.00
167 Jerious Norwood/25*	50.00	100.00
168 Jordan Palmer/100*	8.00	20.00
169 Chase Daniel/150*	10.00	25.00
170 Jeremy Maclin/250*	12.00	30.00
171 Jay Cutler/50*	50.00	80.00
172 Brad Smith/100*	8.00	20.00
173 Thomas Jones/25*	60.00	120.00
174 Brandon Jackson/150*	10.00	25.00
175 Nate Burleson/150*	8.00	20.00
176 Alvin Pearman/100*	8.00	20.00
177 Marcus Smith 2E	4.00	10.00
178 Matt Schaub/100*	75.00	125.00
179 DeAngelo Hall/25*	40.00	80.00
180 Ronald Curry/100*	8.00	20.00
181 Hakeem Nicks/250*	12.00	30.00
182 Kevin Jones/25*	40.00	80.00
183 Willie Parker/25*	50.00	100.00
184 Andre Brown/150*	6.00	15.00
185 DaJuan Morgan 2G	4.00	10.00
186 Philip Rivers/50*	50.00	80.00
187 Mario Williams/100*	10.00	25.00
188 Vincent Jackson/25*	50.00	100.00
189 Garrett Wolfe/150*	8.00	20.00
190 Xavier Omon 2H	4.00	10.00
191 John Carlson 2H	5.00	12.00
192 Anthony Fasano/150*	8.00	20.00
193 Julius Jones/100*	12.00	30.00
194 Brady Quinn/25*	60.00	120.00
195 Maurice Stovall/100*	8.00	20.00
196 Bobby Carpenter/150*	8.00	20.00
197 Chris Wells/250*	20.00	40.00
198 Joey Galloway/100*	10.00	25.00
199 Vernon Gholston/150*	8.00	20.00
200 Ted Ginn/50*	25.00	50.00
201 Anthony Gonzalez/150*	8.00	20.00
202 Eddie Royal 1F	6.00	15.00
203 Michael Jenkins/150*	8.00	20.00
204 Jason Hill 2E	4.00	10.00
205 Troy Smith/100*	20.00	40.00
206 Marc Bulger/100*	10.00	25.00
207 Mark Bradley/100*	8.00	20.00
208 Owen Schmitt 2H	4.00	10.00
209 Juaquin Iglesias/150*	8.00	20.00
210 Malcolm Kelly/150*	8.00	20.00
211 Allen Patrick 2H	4.00	10.00
212 Adrian Peterson/25*	175.00	300.00
213 Tatum Bell/100*	8.00	20.00
214 Brandon Pettigrew/250*	8.00	20.00
215 Kellen Clemens/100*	8.00	20.00
216 Dennis Dixon/100*	15.00	30.00
217 Jonathan Stewart/250*	8.00	20.00
218 Demetrius Williams/150*	8.00	20.00
219 Derek Anderson/50*	20.00	40.00
220 Steven Jackson/25*	60.00	120.00
221 Chad Johnson/25*	75.00	150.00
222 Reggie Williams 2F	4.00	10.00
223 Dan Connor/150*	8.00	20.00
224 Derrick Williams/150*	8.00	20.00
225 Larry Johnson/25*	50.00	100.00
226 Pat White/250*	8.00	20.00
227 Paul Posluszny 2H	6.00	15.00
228 Tony Dorsett/25*	75.00	150.00
229 LeSean McCoy/250*	15.00	40.00
230 Dan Marino/25*	150.00	250.00
231 Drew Brees/25*	175.00	300.00
232 Dustin Keller/150*	8.00	20.00
233 Kyle Orton/100*	20.00	40.00
234 Steve Slaton 1F	10.00	25.00
235 Kenny Britt/250*	10.00	25.00
236 Brian Leonard/150*	8.00	20.00
237 Ray Rice/250*	12.00	30.00
238 Kevin O'Connell/150*	8.00	20.00
239 Lee Evans/100*	10.00	25.00
240 James Jones 2H	4.00	10.00
241 Eric Dickerson/25*	75.00	150.00
242 Jared Cook/150*	10.00	25.00
243 P.J. Hill/150*	8.00	20.00
244 Andre Hall/150*	8.00	20.00
245 Rhett Bomar/150*	8.00	20.00
246 Trent Edwards/150*	12.00	30.00
247 John Elway/25*	125.00	200.00
248 Jim Brown/25*	75.00	150.00
249 Dwight Freeney/100*	20.00	40.00
250 Joe Thomas/25*	60.00	120.00

2009 Topps Magic Thrills

STATED ODDS 1:10

MT1 2007 Fiesta Bowl	.75	2.00
MT2 2006 Rose Bowl	1.00	2.50
Vince Young		
MT3 2003 Fiesta Bowl	.75	2.00
MT4 2005 Rose Bowl	1.00	2.50
Vince Young		
MT5 2006 Sugar Bowl	1.00	2.50
Steve Slaton		
MT6 2000 Orange Bowl	2.00	5.00
Tom Brady		
MT7 2006 Orange Bowl	.75	2.00
Michael Robinson		
MT8 2004 Sugar Bowl	.75	2.00
Marcus Spears		
MT9 2005 Sugar Bowl	.75	2.00
Jason Campbell		
MT10 1980 Holiday Bowl	1.00	2.50
Eric Dickerson		
MT11 2008 Meineke Bowl	.60	1.50
Pat White		
MT12 2009 Rose Bowl	2.00	5.00
Mark Sanchez		
MT13 2008 Alamo Bowl	1.00	2.50
Jeremy Maclin		
MT14 2007 Hawaii Bowl	1.25	3.00
Chris Johnson		
MT15 2006 Insight Bowl	.75	2.00
MT16 2009 National Championship	1.00	2.50
Percy Harvin		
MT17 2008 Orange Bowl	.75	2.00
MT18 2008 Papajohns.com Bowl	.75	2.00
Kenny Britt		
MT19 2008 Capital One Bowl	1.25	3.00
Mike Hart		
MT20 2009 Fiesta Bowl	.75	2.00
Quan Cosby		

2010 Topps Magic

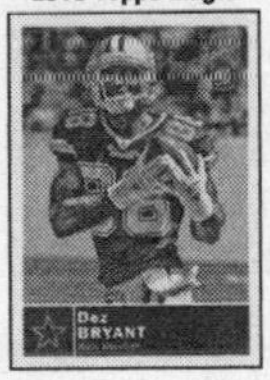

COMPLETE SET (248)	60.00	120.00
COMP.SET w/o SP's (200)	15.00	30.00
SP STATED ODDS 1:3 HOB		
1 Jared Allen SP	2.50	6.00
2 Earl Thomas RC	.60	1.50
3 Ricky Williams	.20	.50
4 Fred Jackson	.25	.60
5 Charles Scott SP RC	1.50	4.00
6 Matt Ryan	.25	.60
7 Chad Ochocinco	.20	.50
8 LeSean McCoy	.20	.50
9 Brent Celek	.20	.50
10 Myron Rolle RC	.40	1.00
11 Emmitt Smith	.60	1.50
12 Joe Namath SP	3.00	8.00
13 Knowshon Moreno	.20	.50
14 Hines Ward	.20	.50
15 Dwayne Bowe	.20	.50
16 Ndamukong Suh SP RC	3.00	8.00
17 Eric Berry RC	.60	1.50
18 Paul Hornung	.40	1.00
19 John Elway	.60	1.50
20 Marcus Easley RC	.50	1.25
21 Frank Gore SP	2.00	5.00
22 John Abraham	.15	.40
23 Chester Taylor	.15	.40
24 James Starks SP RC	3.00	8.00
25 Tim Tebow RC	3.00	8.00
26 Rob Gronkowski RC	1.50	4.00
27 Jerry Hughes SP RC	2.00	5.00
28 Kevin Smith	.20	.50
29 Todd Heap	.15	.40
30 Dezmon Briscoe SP RC	1.50	4.00
31 Braylon Edwards	.20	.50
32 Dan Marino	.75	2.00
33 Michael Bush	.15	.40
34 Brian Westbrook	.20	.50
35 Alex Smith QB SP	2.00	5.00
36 Kellen Clemens	.15	.40
37 James Hardy	.15	.40
38 Chad Henne	.20	.50
39 Bobby Carpenter SP	1.50	4.00
40 Ramses Barden	.15	.40
41 Marques Colston	.20	.50
42 Darren McFadden SP	2.00	5.00
43 Brooks Foster	.15	.40
44 Drew Brees	.25	.60
45 Jordan Shipley SP RC	2.00	5.00
46 James Casey	.15	.40
47 DeMarcus Ware	.20	.50
48 Reggie Wayne	.20	.50
49 Andre Johnson SP	2.00	5.00
50 Tony Romo	.30	.75
51 Jermaine Gresham RC	.75	2.00
52 Mike Williams RC	1.00	2.50
53 Thomas Jones SP	2.00	5.00
54 Tony Gonzalez SP	2.00	5.00
55 David Anderson SP	1.50	4.00
56 Aaron Hernandez SP RC	3.00	8.00
57 Ed Wang RC	.60	1.50
58 David Harris SP	1.50	4.00
59 Juaquin Iglesias SP	1.50	4.00
60 Bob Sanders SP	2.00	5.00
61 Brian Orakpo	.15	.40
62 Jahvid Best RC	1.00	2.50
63 Ed Reed	.20	.50
64 Gale Sayers SP	2.50	6.00
65 Sean Lee SP RC	2.00	5.00
66 Brandon LaFell RC	.60	1.50
67 Gerald McCoy RC	.60	1.50
68 Roddy White SP	2.00	5.00
69 Joey Galloway SP	2.00	5.00
70 Jonathan Crompton SP RC	1.50	4.00
71 Peyton Manning	.40	1.00
72 Deion Branch	.15	.40
73 Keith Rivers	.15	.40
74 William Moore	.15	.40
75 Jimmy Clausen RC	.60	1.50
76 Aaron Curry SP	2.00	5.00
77 Jared Odrick RC	.60	1.50
78 Sidney Rice SP	2.00	5.00
79 Santana Moss	.20	.50
80 Jimmy Graham SP RC	4.00	10.00
81 Rolando McClain RC	.60	1.50
82 Quan Cosby SP	1.50	4.00
83 Justin Gage	.15	.40
84 Andre Roberts SP RC	2.00	5.00
85 Rey Maualuga SP	1.50	4.00
86 LaDainian Tomlinson SP	2.50	6.00
87 Bernard Berrian	.15	.40
88 Chris Ogbonnaya	.15	.40
89 Dustin Keller SP	2.00	5.00
90 Mardy Gilyard RC	.60	1.50
91 Jacoby Ford RC	.60	1.50
92 Kevin Kolb	.20	.50
93 Antonio Gates	.20	.50
94 Joe McKnight RC	.60	1.50
95 Eli Manning	.25	.60
96 Ryan Mathews RC	1.25	3.00
97 Armanti Edwards RC	.60	1.50
98 Arrelious Benn RC	.60	1.50
99 Cadillac Williams	.20	.50
100 Mark Sanchez	.25	.60
101 Joe Flacco	.25	.60
102 Philip Rivers	.25	.60
103 Tom Brady SP	3.00	8.00
104 Brandon Jacobs	.20	.50
105 Clinton Portis SP	2.00	5.00
106 Jason Witten	.25	.60
107 Willie Parker	.15	.40
108 Champ Bailey	.20	.50
109 Shonn Greene	.20	.50
110 Damian Williams RC	.60	1.50
111 Greg Jennings	.20	.50
112 Troy Polamalu	.25	.60
113 Jordy Nelson	.25	.60
114 Emmanuel Sanders RC	.60	1.50
115 Felix Jones	.20	.50
116 Carson Palmer	.20	.50
117 Derrick Morgan RC	.50	1.25
118 D.J. Williams	.15	.40
119 Steve Young SP	3.00	8.00
120 Percy Harvin SP	2.50	6.00
121 Dan LeFevour RC	.60	1.50
122 Richard Seymour	.15	.40
123 Mike Sims-Walker	.20	.50
124 Dexter McCluster RC	.60	1.50
125 Donovan McNabb	.25	.60
126 Patrick Willis	.20	.50
127 Brian Cushing	.15	.40
128 Marion Barber	.20	.50
129 Ben Tate RC	.75	2.00
130 Ahmad Bradshaw SP	2.00	5.00
131 Brian Urlacher SP	2.50	6.00
132 Steven Jackson	.20	.50
133 Chris Wells	.20	.50
134 James Jones	.15	.40
135 Robert Meachem	.20	.50
136 Brandon Gibson SP	1.50	4.00
137 Vernon Davis SP	2.00	5.00
138 Taylor Price SP RC	2.00	5.00
139 Montario Hardesty RC	.60	1.50
140 David Reed SP RC	1.50	4.00
141 Eddie Royal	.15	.40
142 Anthony Gonzalez	.15	.40
143 Riley Cooper RC	.60	1.50
144 Jacoby Jones	.15	.40
145 Marc Bulger SP	1.50	4.00
146 Sean Canfield RC	.50	1.25
147 Matt Cassel	.20	.50
148 Colt McCoy SP RC	3.00	8.00
149 Justin Forsett	.20	.50
150 Ronnie Lott	.40	1.00
151 Mathias Kiwanuka	.15	.40
152 Joe Webb SP RC	2.00	5.00
153 Jerome Harrison	.15	.40
154 Tony Dorsett	.40	1.00
155 Brandon Marshall SP	2.00	5.00
156 Elvis Dumervil	.15	.40
157 Y.A. Tittle	.40	1.00
158 Greg Olsen	.15	.40
159 Josh Freeman	.25	.60
160 Darren Sproles	.20	.50
161 Chris Johnson	.25	.60
162 Hakeem Nicks	.20	.50
163 Matt Leinart	.20	.50
164 Bryan Bulaga RC	.60	1.50
165 Marcus Allen	.40	1.00
166 Johnny Knox	.20	.50
167 Jarett Dillard	.15	.40
168 Amobi Okoye	.15	.40
169 Dwight Freeney	.20	.50
170 Brett Favre	1.00	2.50
171 Ray Rice	.20	.50
172 Malcolm Kelly	.15	.40
173 Vincent Jackson	.15	.40
174 Adrian Peterson	.40	1.00
175 Kellen Winslow Jr.	.20	.50
176 Darrius Heyward-Bey	.20	.50
177 John Carlson	.15	.40
178 Carlton Mitchell RC	.50	1.25
179 Marshawn Lynch	.20	.50
180 Santonio Holmes	.20	.50
181 Matt Forte	.20	.50
182 Fred Davis	.20	.50
183 Trent Edwards	.15	.40
184 Brian Brohm	.15	.40
185 Jonathan Dwyer RC	.60	1.50
186 Dez Bryant RC	2.00	5.00
187 Joseph Addai	.20	.50
188 Nate Burleson	.15	.40
189 Troy Aikman	.50	1.25
190 Maurice Jones-Drew	.20	.50
191 Zac Robinson RC	.50	1.25
192 DeAngelo Williams	.20	.50
193 Roger Staubach	.50	1.25
194 Wes Welker SP	2.50	6.00
195 Steve Smith	.20	.50
196 Vince Young	.15	.40
197 Tony Pike RC	.60	1.50
198 C.J. Spiller RC	1.00	2.50
199 Demaryius Thomas RC	.75	2.00
200 Rashard Mendenhall	.20	.50
201 Ray Lewis	.25	.60
202 Anthony Dixon RC	.60	1.50
203 Nnamdi Asomugha	.20	.50
204 Chad Greenway	.15	.40
205 Jim Brown	.50	1.25
206 Mike Kafka RC	.60	1.50
207 Michael Jenkins	.15	.40
208 Eric Decker RC	.75	2.00
209 Steve Slaton	.15	.40
210 Toby Gerhart RC	.60	1.50
211 Rashad Jennings	.15	.40
212 Malcolm Jenkins	.15	.40
213 Franco Harris	.40	1.00
214 Matthew Stafford	.25	.60
215 Paul Posluszny	.20	.50
216 Jerod Mayo	.20	.50
217 Fred Biletnikoff	.40	1.00
218 Aaron Rodgers	.50	1.25
219 Jake Long	.15	.40
220 Jamaal Charles	.20	.50
221 Willis McGahee	.20	.50
222 Tashard Choice	.15	.40
223 Larry Fitzgerald	.25	.60
224 Ben Roethlisberger	.25	.60
225 LaRon Landry	.15	.40
226 Early Doucet	.15	.40
227 Sammy Morris	.15	.40
228 Randy Moss	.25	.60
229 Chris Cooley	.20	.50
230 Cedric Benson	.20	.50
231 Mario Williams	.20	.50
232 Calvin Johnson	.25	.60
233 Cedric Peerman	.15	.40
234 Kyle Orton	.20	.50
235 Darrelle Revis	.20	.50
236 Golden Tate RC	.60	1.50
237 Reggie Bush	.25	.60
238 Jeremy Maclin	.20	.50
239 Derek Anderson	.15	.40
240 Devin Thomas	.15	.40
241 Sam Bradford RC	3.00	8.00
242 T.J. Houshmandzadeh	.20	.50
243 DeSean Jackson	.20	.50
244 Mohamed Massaquoi	.20	.50
245 Dennis Dixon	.20	.50
246 John Skelton RC	.60	1.50
247 Jonathan Stewart	.20	.50
248 James Davis	.15	.40

2010 Topps Magic Mini

*VETS: 1.2X TO 3X BASIC CARDS
*VET SP: .5X TO 1.2X BASIC SP
*ROOKIES: .5X TO 1.2X BASIC CARDS
*ROOKIE SP: .5X TO 1.2X BASIC SP RC
OVERALL MINI ODDS 1:1 HOB
MINI SP STATED ODDS 1:12 HOB

2010 Topps Magic Mini Black

*VETS: 2.5X TO 6X BASIC CARDS
*VET SP: .6X TO 1.5X BASIC SP
*ROOKIES: 1X TO 2.5X BASIC CARDS
*ROOKIE SP: .5X TO 1.5X BASIC RC SP
MINI BLACK STATED ODDS 1:8 HOB
MINI BLACK SP ODDS 1:24 HOB

2010 Topps Magic Mini Pigskin 50

*VETS/50: 4X TO 10X BASIC CARDS
*VETS/50: .6X TO 1.5X BASIC SP
*ROOKIE/50: 1.5X TO 4X BASIC RC
*ROOKIE/50: .6X TO 1.5X BASIC RC SP
MINI PIGSKIN/50 ODDS 1:37 HOB

2010 Topps Magic Autographs

TIER 1 GROUP A/15* ODDS 1:882 HOB
TIER 1 GROUP B/50* ODDS 1:333 HOB
TIER 1 GROUP C/100* ODDS 1:201 HOB
TIER 1 GROUP D ODDS 1:100 HOB
TIER 1 GROUP E ODDS 1:73 HOB
TIER 2 GROUP A/15* ODDS 1:1525 HOB
TIER 2 GROUP B/50* ODDS 1:615 HOB
TIER 2 GROUP C/100* ODDS 1:423 HOB
TIER 2 GROUP D ODDS 1:70 HOB
TIER 2 GROUP E ODDS 1:201 HOB
TIER 2 GROUP F ODDS 1:84 HOB
TIER 2 GROUP G ODDS 1:21 HOB
EXCH EXPIRATION: 12/31/2013

2 Earl Thomas 1C/100*	8.00	20.00
5 Charles Scott 2A/15*	30.00	60.00
6 Matt Ryan 1A/15*	75.00	135.00
7 Chad Ochocinco 1B/50*	30.00	60.00
8 LeSean McCoy 1C/100*	20.00	40.00
10 Myron Rolle 2D	6.00	15.00
11 Emmitt Smith 1A/15*	125.00	200.00
12 Joe Namath 1A/15*	100.00	175.00
15 Dwayne Bowe 1B/50*	20.00	40.00
16 Ndamukong Suh 1D	20.00	40.00
17 Eric Berry 1E	12.00	30.00
18 Paul Hornung 1C/100*	25.00	50.00
19 John Elway 1A/15*	100.00	200.00
20 Marcus Easley 2D	5.00	12.00
21 Frank Gore 1B/50*	12.00	30.00
23 Chester Taylor 2C/100*	8.00	20.00
24 James Starks 2D	15.00	30.00
25 Tim Tebow 1A/15*	200.00	350.00
26 Rob Gronkowski 2C/100*	20.00	40.00
27 Jerry Hughes 2D	6.00	15.00
30 Dezmon Briscoe 2A/15*	30.00	60.00
31 Braylon Edwards 1C/100*	10.00	25.00
32 Dan Marino 1A/15*	175.00	300.00
34 Brian Westbrook 1B/50*	10.00	25.00
36 Kellen Clemens 2F	6.00	15.00
37 James Hardy 2G	4.00	10.00
38 Chad Henne 2D	10.00	25.00
39 Bobby Carpenter 2G	4.00	10.00
40 Ramses Barden 2E	5.00	12.00
42 Darren McFadden 1A/15*	75.00	150.00
43 Brooks Foster 2G	5.00	12.00
44 Drew Brees 1D	40.00	80.00
45 Jordan Shipley 1E	6.00	15.00
46 James Casey 2A/15*	40.00	80.00
48 Reggie Wayne 1C/100*	20.00	40.00
50 Tony Romo 1A/15*	60.00	120.00
55 David Anderson 2F	5.00	12.00
56 Aaron Hernandez 2D	10.00	25.00
57 Ed Wang 2A/15*	50.00	100.00
58 David Harris 2F	4.00	10.00
59 Juaquin Iglesias 2G	5.00	12.00
62 Jahvid Best 1E	15.00	40.00
63 Ed Reed 1C/100*	30.00	60.00
64 Gale Sayers 1B/50*	50.00	100.00
65 Sean Lee 2C/100*	6.00	15.00
66 Brandon LaFell 2B/50*	10.00	25.00
67 Gerald McCoy 2B/50*	10.00	25.00
68 Roddy White 1D	10.00	25.00
69 Joey Galloway 2F	8.00	20.00
70 Jonathan Crompton 2F	5.00	12.00
71 Peyton Manning 1A/15*	100.00	200.00
72 Deion Branch 2E	8.00	20.00
73 Keith Rivers 2G	4.00	10.00
74 William Moore 2F	5.00	12.00
75 Jimmy Clausen 1A/15*	40.00	80.00
76 Aaron Curry 2E	8.00	20.00
77 Jared Odrick 2D	8.00	20.00
78 Sidney Rice 1B/50*	20.00	40.00
80 Jimmy Graham 2C/100*	15.00	40.00
82 Quan Cosby 2G	5.00	12.00
84 Andre Roberts 2D	5.00	12.00
85 Rey Maualuga 2B/50*	10.00	25.00
86 LaDainian Tomlinson 1B/50*	40.00	80.00
87 Bernard Berrian 2E	6.00	15.00
88 Chris Ogbonnaya 2A/15*	40.00	80.00
89 Dustin Keller 2A/15*	40.00	80.00
90 Mardy Gilyard 2D	6.00	15.00
91 Jacoby Ford 2D	10.00	25.00
92 Kevin Kolb 2A/15*	40.00	80.00
93 Antonio Gates 1B/50*	30.00	60.00
95 Eli Manning 1A/15*	75.00	150.00
96 Ryan Mathews 1D	15.00	40.00
97 Armanti Edwards 2D	6.00	15.00
98 Arrelious Benn 1E	6.00	15.00
101 Joe Flacco 1D	15.00	30.00
107 Willie Parker 2A/15*	75.00	150.00
109 Shonn Greene 1C/100*	15.00	40.00
110 Damian Williams 2B/50*	20.00	40.00
111 Greg Jennings 1C/100*	15.00	30.00
113 Jordy Nelson 2G	6.00	15.00
114 Emmanuel Sanders 2D	8.00	20.00
115 Felix Jones 1B/50*	12.00	30.00
117 Derrick Morgan 2B/50*	10.00	25.00
119 Steve Young 1B/50*	40.00	80.00
121 Dan LeFevour 2A/15*	40.00	80.00
123 Mike Sims-Walker 2C	6.00	15.00
124 Dexter McCluster 2B/50*	12.00	30.00
126 Patrick Willis 1B/50*	12.00	30.00
127 Brian Cushing 1E	5.00	12.00
129 Ben Tate 2A/15*	60.00	120.00
130 Ahmad Bradshaw 1B/50*	12.00	30.00
133 Chris Wells 1C/100*	10.00	25.00
134 James Jones 2G	5.00	12.00
136 Brandon Gibson 2A/15*	40.00	80.00
138 Taylor Price 2C/100*	6.00	15.00
139 Montario Hardesty 2A/15*	40.00	80.00
140 David Reed 2C/100*	6.00	15.00
142 Anthony Gonzalez 2B/50*	12.00	30.00
143 Riley Cooper 2D	6.00	15.00
144 Jacoby Jones 2E	6.00	15.00
145 Marc Bulger 2D	6.00	15.00
146 Sean Canfield 2D	5.00	12.00
148 Colt McCoy 1C/100*	40.00	80.00
149 Justin Forsett 2B/50*	8.00	20.00
150 Ronnie Lott 1D	25.00	50.00
151 Mathias Kiwanuka 2F	5.00	12.00
152 Joe Webb 2D	6.00	15.00
153 Jerome Harrison 2E	6.00	15.00
154 Tony Dorsett 1B/50*	40.00	80.00
155 Brandon Marshall 1A/15*	50.00	100.00
157 Y.A. Tittle 1B/50*	30.00	60.00
159 Josh Freeman 2A/15*	75.00	150.00
162 Hakeem Nicks 1D	8.00	20.00
163 Matt Leinart 2A/15*		
164 Bryan Bulaga 2B/50*	12.00	30.00
165 Marcus Allen 1B/50*	40.00	80.00
167 Jarett Dillard 2D	5.00	12.00
168 Amobi Okoye 2G	4.00	10.00
170 Brett Favre 1A/15*	200.00	400.00
171 Ray Rice 1A/15*	50.00	100.00
172 Malcolm Kelly 2G	4.00	10.00
174 Adrian Peterson 1A/15*	100.00	200.00
175 Kellen Winslow Jr. 1E	8.00	20.00
177 John Carlson 2B/50*	25.00	50.00
178 Carlton Mitchell 2D	5.00	12.00
179 Marshawn Lynch 2F	8.00	20.00
182 Fred Davis 2G	6.00	15.00
183 Trent Edwards 2A/15*		
184 Brian Brohm 2G	6.00	15.00
185 Jonathan Dwyer 2D	6.00	15.00
188 Nate Burleson 2A/15*	30.00	60.00
189 Troy Aikman 1A/15*	75.00	150.00
191 Zac Robinson 2D	5.00	12.00
192 DeAngelo Williams 1A/15*	40.00	80.00
193 Roger Staubach 1A/15*	60.00	120.00
196 Vince Young 1A/15*	50.00	100.00
197 Tony Pike 2B/50*	12.00	30.00
198 C.J. Spiller 1E	12.00	30.00
199 Demaryius Thomas 1E	8.00	20.00
201 Ray Lewis 1C/100*	50.00	80.00
202 Anthony Dixon 2D	8.00	20.00
205 Jim Brown 1A/15*	100.00	175.00
206 Mike Kafka 2A/15*	40.00	80.00
207 Michael Jenkins 2C	6.00	15.00
208 Eric Decker 2D	8.00	20.00
209 Steve Slaton 2B/50*	8.00	20.00
210 Toby Gerhart 2C/100*	20.00	40.00
211 Rashad Jennings 2G	5.00	12.00
212 Malcolm Jenkins 2G	5.00	12.00
213 Franco Harris 1C/100*	30.00	60.00
214 Matthew Stafford 1B/50*	30.00	60.00
215 Paul Posluszny 2B/50*	10.00	25.00
216 Jerod Mayo 1E	6.00	15.00
217 Fred Biletnikoff 1D	20.00	40.00
219 Jake Long 2F	6.00	15.00
220 Jamaal Charles 1D	12.00	30.00
221 Willis McGahee 1D	8.00	20.00
222 Tashard Choice 2B/50*	10.00	25.00
225 LaRon Landry 2F	6.00	15.00
226 Early Doucet 2G	5.00	12.00
227 Sammy Morris 2G	6.00	15.00
231 Mario Williams 1D	5.00	12.00
233 Cedric Peerman 2G	4.00	10.00
236 Golden Tate 1E	6.00	15.00
237 Reggie Bush 1A/15*	50.00	100.00
238 Jeremy Maclin 1C/100*	12.00	30.00
239 Derek Anderson 2G	6.00	15.00
240 Devin Thomas 2G	4.00	10.00
241 Sam Bradford 1B/50*	100.00	200.00
243 DeSean Jackson 1C/100*	12.00	30.00
244 Mohamed Massaquoi 2D	5.00	12.00
245 Dennis Dixon 2G	5.00	12.00
246 John Skelton 2A/15*	40.00	80.00
247 Jonathan Stewart 1D	8.00	20.00
248 James Davis 2D	5.00	12.00

2010 Topps Magic Autographs Dual

DUAL AU/25 ODDS 1:775 HOB
EXCH EXPIRATION: 12/31/2013
DAAJ Troy Aikman 75.00 150.00
Maurice Jones-Drew
DABA Fred Biletnikoff 40.00 80.00
Marcus Allen
DABB Drew Brees 60.00 120.00
Reggie Bush
DABH Jim Brown 50.00 100.00
Montario Hardesty
DAJD Felix Jones 50.00 100.00
Tony Dorsett
DALW Ronnie Lott 75.00 150.00
Patrick Willis
DAMAN Peyton Manning 100.00 200.00
Eli Manning
DAMH Rashard Mendenhall 60.00 120.00
Franco Harris
DAMM Dan Marino 100.00 175.00
Brandon Marshall
DANS Joe Namath 100.00 175.00
Mark Sanchez
DARS Tony Romo 75.00 150.00
Roger Staubach
DASH Gale Sayers 50.00 100.00
Paul Hornung
DASP Emmitt Smith 125.00 250.00
Adrian Peterson
DATE Tim Tebow 200.00 350.00
John Elway
DATG LaDainian Tomlinson 60.00 120.00
Shonn Greene

2010 Topps Magic Autographs Triple

TRIPLE AU/25 ODDS 1:1150 HOB
EXCH EXPIRATION: 12/31/2013
TABME Sam Bradford 200.00 350.00
Peyton Manning
John Elway
TABMS Drew Brees 125.00 250.00
Eli Manning
Roger Staubach
TADBA Tony Dorsett 60.00 120.00
Reggie Bush
Marcus Allen
TAFPR Brett Favre 150.00 250.00
Adrian Peterson
Sidney Rice
TALGW Ray Lewis 60.00 120.00
Frank Gore
Reggie Wayne
TASSF Matthew Stafford 60.00 120.00
Mark Sanchez
Joe Flacco
TASTH Emmitt Smith 150.00 250.00
Tim Tebow
Percy Harvin
TASTS C.J. Spiller 75.00 150.00
LaDainian Tomlinson
Gale Sayers
TATEB Golden Tate 40.00 80.00
Braylon Edwards
Fred Biletnikoff
TATYA Y.A. Tittle 100.00 200.00
Steve Young
Troy Aikman

2010 Topps Magic Historical Stamp of Approval

HISTORICAL STAMP/25 ODDS 1:358 HOB
HSAE Amelia Earhart 30.00 80.00
HSAES Albert Einstein 30.00 80.00
HSAGB Alexander Graham Bell 25.00 60.00
HSAH Alexander Hamilton 25.00 60.00
HSAJ Andrew Jackson 25.00 60.00
HSAL Abraham Lincoln 40.00 80.00
HSBC Buffalo Bill Cody 20.00 50.00
HSBF Benjamin Franklin 50.00 100.00
HSCP Casimir Pulaski 20.00 50.00
HSDMC Douglas MacArthur 25.00 60.00
HSEAP Edgar Allen Poe 25.00 60.00
HSEB Elizabeth Blackwell 20.00 50.00
HSER Eleanor Roosevelt 20.00 50.00
HSFAB Frederic Bartholdi 20.00 50.00
HSFD Frederick Douglas 20.00 50.00
HSFDR Franklin D. Roosevelt 25.00 60.00
HSFSF F. Scott Fitzgerald 20.00 50.00
HSFSK Francis Scott Key 25.00 60.00
HSGC Grover Cleveland 25.00 60.00
HSGE Geronimo 25.00 60.00
HSGP General Patton 25.00 60.00
HSGW George Washington 30.00 80.00
HSGWC George Washington Carver 25.00 60.00
HSHDT Henry David Thoreau 20.00 50.00
HSHK Helen Keller 20.00 50.00
HSJA Johnny Appleseed 20.00 50.00
HSJB James Buchanan 25.00 60.00
HSJFK John F. Kennedy 60.00 120.00
HSJH John Hanson 25.00 60.00
HSJJA John James Audubon 25.00 60.00
HSJM John Muir 20.00 50.00
HSJMO James Monroe 20.00 50.00
HSJPJ John Paul Jones 20.00 50.00
HSJQA John Quincy Adams 30.00 80.00
HSLC Lewis and Clark 20.00 50.00
HSLE Leif Erikson 20.00 50.00
HSMEW Mary Edwards Walker 20.00 50.00
HSMLK Martin Luther King 25.00 60.00
HSMMB Mary McLeod Bethune 20.00 50.00
HSNC Nicolaus Copernicus 20.00 50.00
HSNH Nathan Hale 20.00 50.00
HSOWW Orville and Wilbur Wright 20.00 50.00
HSPB Pearl Buck 20.00 50.00
HSPDL Ponce de Leon 20.00 50.00
HSRG Robert Goddard 20.00 50.00
HSRK Robert Kennedy 50.00 100.00
HSSB Simon Bolivar 20.00 50.00
HSSH Sam Houston 25.00 60.00
HSTE Thomas Edison 25.00 60.00
HSTJ Thomas Jefferson 25.00 60.00

2010 Topps Magic History's Best

COMPLETE SET (10) 8.00 20.00
STATED ODDS 1:12 HOBBY
HB1 Emmitt Smith 1.50 4.00
HB2 Tom Brady 1.50 4.00
HB3 Ray Lewis 1.00 2.50
HB4 Brett Favre 2.50 6.00
HB5 Dan Marino 2.00 5.00
HB6 Peyton Manning 1.50 4.00
HB7 John Elway 1.50 4.00
HB8 Steve Young 1.25 3.00
HB9 Paul Hornung 1.00 2.50
HB10 LaDainian Tomlinson 1.00 2.50

2010 Topps Magic Magical Moments

COMPLETE SET (20) 8.00 20.00
STATED ODDS 1:4 HOBBY
MM1 Andre Johnson .60 1.50
MM2 Terrell Owens .75 2.00
MM3 Wes Welker .75 2.00
MM4 Brett Favre 2.00 5.00
MM5 Tony Romo 1.00 2.50
MM6 Brandon Marshall .60 1.50
MM7 Adrian Wilson .50 1.25
MM8 Jamaal Charles .60 1.50
MM9 LaDainian Tomlinson .75 2.00
MM10 Peyton Manning 1.25 3.00
MM11 Matt Schaub .60 1.50
MM12 Tom Brady 1.25 3.00
MM13 Fred Jackson .75 2.00
MM14 Knowshon Moreno .60 1.50
MM15 Elvis Dumervil .50 1.25
MM16 Drew Brees .75 2.00
MM17 Patrick Willis .60 1.50
MM18 Shonn Greene .60 1.50
MM19 Randy Moss .75 2.00
MM20 Chris Johnson .75 2.00

2010 Topps Magic Relics

RELIC/25 ODDS 1:153 HOBBY
1 Jared Allen 6.00 15.00
3 Ricky Williams 5.00 12.00
4 Fred Jackson 8.00 20.00
9 Brent Celek 5.00 12.00
13 Knowshon Moreno 5.00 12.00
14 Hines Ward 6.00 12.00
22 John Abraham 4.00 10.00
28 Kevin Smith 5.00 12.00
29 Todd Heap 4.00 10.00
33 Michael Bush 4.00 10.00
35 Alex Smith QB 5.00 12.00
41 Marques Colston 5.00 12.00
47 DeMarcus Ware 6.00 15.00
49 Andre Johnson 5.00 12.00
51 Jermaine Gresham 5.00 12.00
52 Mike Williams 6.00 15.00
53 Thomas Jones 5.00 12.00
54 Tony Gonzalez 5.00 12.00
60 Bob Sanders 6.00 15.00
61 Brian Orakpo 4.00 10.00
79 Santana Moss 5.00 12.00
81 Rolando McClain 4.00 10.00
83 Justin Gage 4.00 10.00
94 Joe McKnight 4.00 10.00
99 Cadillac Williams 5.00 12.00
100 Mark Sanchez 6.00 15.00
102 Philip Rivers 6.00 15.00
103 Tom Brady 12.00 30.00
104 Brandon Jacobs 5.00 12.00
105 Clinton Portis 5.00 12.00
106 Jason Witten 6.00 15.00
108 Champ Bailey 6.00 12.00
112 Troy Polamalu 8.00 20.00
116 Carson Palmer 5.00 12.00
118 D.J. Williams 4.00 10.00
120 Percy Harvin 6.00 15.00
122 Richard Seymour 4.00 10.00
125 Donovan McNabb 6.00 15.00
128 Marion Barber 5.00 12.00
131 Brian Urlacher 6.00 15.00
132 Steven Jackson 5.00 12.00
135 Robert Meachem 5.00 12.00
137 Vernon Davis 5.00 12.00
141 Eddie Royal 4.00 10.00
147 Matt Cassel 5.00 12.00
156 Elvis Dumervil 5.00 12.00
158 Greg Olsen 4.00 10.00
160 Darren Sproles 5.00 12.00
161 Chris Johnson 6.00 15.00
166 Johnny Knox 5.00 12.00
169 Dwight Freeney 5.00 12.00
173 Vincent Jackson 4.00 10.00
176 Darrius Heyward-Bey 5.00 12.00
180 Santonio Holmes 5.00 12.00
181 Matt Forte 5.00 12.00
186 Dez Bryant 10.00 25.00
187 Joseph Addai 5.00 12.00
190 Maurice Jones-Drew 5.00 12.00
194 Wes Welker 12.50 25.00
195 Steve Smith 5.00 12.00
200 Rashard Mendenhall 5.00 12.00
203 Nnamdi Asomugha 5.00 12.00
204 Chad Greenway 15.00 30.00
218 Aaron Rodgers 25.00 50.00
223 Larry Fitzgerald 6.00 15.00
224 Ben Roethlisberger
228 Randy Moss 6.00 15.00
229 Chris Cooley 6.00 12.00
230 Cedric Benson 5.00 12.00
232 Calvin Johnson 6.00 15.00
234 Kyle Orton 5.00 12.00
235 Darrelle Revis 5.00 12.00
242 T.J. Houshmandzadeh 5.00 12.00

2010 Topps Magic Rookie Stars

COMPLETE SET (20) 12.00 30.00
STATED ODDS 1:6 HOBBY
RS1 Arrelious Benn .75 2.00
RS2 Toby Gerhart .75 2.00
RS3 Tim Tebow 3.00 8.00
RS4 C.J. Spiller 1.25 3.00
RS5 Joe McKnight .75 2.00
RS6 Jermaine Gresham 1.00 2.50
RS7 Jahvid Best 1.25 3.00
RS8 Golden Tate .75 2.00
RS9 Ndamukong Suh 1.50 4.00
RS10 Montario Hardesty .75 2.00
RS11 Ryan Mathews 1.50 4.00
RS12 Demaryius Thomas 1.00 2.50
RS13 Rolando McClain .75 2.00
RS14 Colt McCoy 1.50 4.00
RS15 Jimmy Clausen .75 2.00
RS16 Sam Bradford 3.00 8.00
RS17 Rob Gronkowski 2.00 5.00
RS18 Dez Bryant 2.50 6.00
RS19 Dexter McCluster .75 2.00
RS20 Eric Berry .75 2.00

2011 Topps Magic Rookies

1A A.J. Green blue 2.00 5.00
1B A.J. Green orng SP 8.00 20.00
2 Aldon Smith 1.50 4.00
3 Niles Paul 1.00 2.50
4 Jon Baldwin 1.00 2.50
5 Justin Houston 1.00 2.50
6 Akeem Ayers .75 2.00
7 Brandon Browner .60 1.50
8 Dion Lewis 1.00 2.50
9 DeMarco Murray 2.00 5.00
10A Mark Ingram purple 2.00 5.00
10B Mark Ingram red SP 8.00 20.00
11 Ryan Kerrigan 1.00 2.50
12 Lance Kendricks .75 2.00
13 Marcell Dareus 1.00 2.50
14 Stephen Paea 1.00 2.50
15 Mike Pouncey 1.00 2.50
16 Terrence Toliver .75 2.00
17 Terrelle Pryor 1.25 3.00
18 Muhammad Wilkerson 1.00 2.50
19 Brooks Reed 1.00 2.50
20A Jake Locker purple 2.50 6.00
20B Jake Locker blue SP 10.00 25.00
21 Vincent Brown 1.00 2.50
22 Jacquizz Rodgers 1.00 2.50
23 Ras-I Dowling 1.00 2.50
24 Rahim Moore .75 2.00
25 Patrick Peterson 1.50 4.00
26 Jeremy Kerley 1.00 2.50
27 Terrell McClain .75 2.00
28 Dane Sanzenbacher 1.00 2.50
29 Cecil Shorts .75 2.00
30A Daniel Thomas purple 1.00 2.50
30B Daniel Thomas grn SP 4.00 10.00
31 Cameron Jordan .75 2.00
32 Casey Matthews 1.00 2.50
33 Virgil Green .75 2.00
34 Owen Marecic 1.00 2.50
35 Austin Pettis .75 2.00
36 Darvin Adams .75 2.00
37 Prince Amukamara 1.00 2.50
38 Corey Liuget .60 1.50
39 Luke Stocker .75 2.00
40 Ryan Mallett 2.00 5.00
41 Cameron Heyward 1.00 2.50
42 Robert Quinn 1.00 2.50
43 Aaron Williams .75 2.00
44 Roy Helu 2.00 5.00
45 Rob Housler .75 2.00
46A Von Miller blue 1.25 3.00
46B Von Miller orng SP 5.00 12.00
47 Jamie Harper 1.00 2.50
48 Mark Herzlich .75 2.00
49 Edmond Gates .75 2.00
50A Julio Jones purple 2.00 5.00
50B Julio Jones red SP 8.00 20.00
51 Alex Green 1.00 2.50
52 Jordan Todman .60 1.50
53 J.J. Watt 1.25 3.00
54 Jimmy Smith 1.00 2.50
55 Leonard Hankerson 1.00 2.50
56 Greg Salas 1.00 2.50
57 Nick Fairley 1.25 3.00
58 Ryan Williams 1.25 3.00
59 Tandon Doss .75 2.00
60 Randall Cobb 1.25 3.00
61 Bilal Powell .60 1.50
62 Denarius Moore 1.25 3.00
63 Kyle Rudolph 1.00 2.50
64 Dwayne Harris 1.00 2.50
65 Jabaal Sheard 1.00 2.50
66 Kendall Hunter 1.00 2.50
67 Ronald Johnson .75 2.00
68 Greg Jones .75 2.00
69 K.J. Wright 1.00 2.50
70A Christian Ponder purple 2.00 5.00
70B Christian Ponder red SP 8.00 20.00
71 Greg McElroy 1.00 2.50
72 Tyrod Taylor 1.00 2.50
73 Da'Quan Bowers 1.00 2.50
74 Colin Kaepernick 1.25 3.00
75 John Clay 1.00 2.50
76 Adrian Clayborn 1.00 2.50
77 Mike McNeill 1.00 2.50
78 Kris Durham .75 2.00
79 Titus Young 1.25 3.00
80A Blaine Gabbert purple 1.50 4.00
80B Blaine Gabbert blue SP 6.00 15.00
81 Dontay Moch .60 1.50
82 D.J. Williams 1.00 2.50
83 Delone Carter .75 2.00
84 Taiwan Jones 1.00 2.50
85 Stevan Ridley 1.00 2.50
86 Darren Evans .75 2.00
87 Jerrel Jernigan .75 2.00
88 Sione Fua .75 2.00
89 Derrick Locke .75 2.00
90A Andy Dalton purple 2.50 6.00
90B Andy Dalton orng SP 10.00 25.00
91 Greg Little 1.00 2.50
92 Phil Taylor .75 2.00
93 Da'Rel Scott .75 2.00
94 Shane Vereen 1.00 2.50
95 Ricky Stanzi 1.25 3.00
96 Brian Rolle 1.00 2.50
97 Doug Baldwin 3.00 8.00
98 Mikel Leshoure 1.00 2.50
99 Torrey Smith 1.25 3.00
100A Cam Newton purple 5.00 12.00
100B Cam Newton blue SP 20.00 50.00

2011 Topps Magic Rookies Autographs

ONE AUTOGRAPH PER BOX
1 A.J. Green SP 50.00 100.00
2 Aldon Smith 15.00 30.00
3 Niles Paul 6.00 15.00
4 Jon Baldwin 6.00 15.00
5 Justin Houston 5.00 12.00
6 Akeem Ayers 4.00 10.00
8 Dion Lewis 6.00 15.00
10 Mark Ingram SP 60.00 100.00
11 Ryan Kerrigan 8.00 20.00
12 Lance Kendricks 4.00 10.00
13 Marcell Dareus 6.00 15.00
14 Stephen Paea 6.00 15.00
15 Mike Pouncey 5.00 12.00
16 Terrence Toliver 4.00 10.00
20 Jake Locker SP 60.00 120.00
21 Vincent Brown 5.00 12.00
22 Jacquizz Rodgers 6.00 15.00
24 Rahim Moore 4.00 10.00
26 Jeremy Kerley 5.00 12.00
29 Cecil Shorts 4.00 10.00
30 Daniel Thomas 8.00 20.00
31 Cameron Jordan 4.00 10.00
33 Virgil Green 4.00 10.00
35 Austin Pettis 4.00 10.00
36 Darvin Adams 4.00 10.00
37 Prince Amukamara 6.00 15.00
39 Luke Stocker 4.00 10.00
40 Ryan Mallett SP 25.00 50.00
43 Aaron Williams 4.00 10.00
45 Rob Housler 4.00 10.00
46 Von Miller SP 20.00 40.00
47 Jamie Harper 6.00 15.00
48 Mark Herzlich 4.00 10.00
49 Edmond Gates 4.00 10.00
51 Alex Green
52 Jordan Todman 4.00 10.00
53 J.J. Watt SP 8.00 20.00
55 Leonard Hankerson 5.00 12.00
56 Greg Salas 5.00 12.00
57 Nick Fairley 6.00 15.00
58 Ryan Williams 8.00 20.00
59 Tandon Doss 4.00 10.00
60 Randall Cobb SP 20.00 40.00
61 Bilal Powell 4.00 10.00
64 Dwayne Harris 5.00 12.00
66 Kendall Hunter 6.00 15.00
67 Ronald Johnson 4.00 10.00
70 Christian Ponder SP 60.00 100.00
71 Greg McElroy 6.00 15.00
72 Tyrod Taylor 5.00 12.00
73 Da'Quan Bowers 8.00 20.00
74 Colin Kaepernick
75 John Clay 15.00 30.00
76 Adrian Clayborn 5.00 12.00
77 Mike McNeill 5.00 12.00
79 Titus Young 15.00 30.00
80 Blaine Gabbert SP 20.00 40.00
82 D.J. Williams 5.00 12.00
83 Delone Carter 4.00 10.00
84 Taiwan Jones 8.00 20.00
86 Darren Evans 4.00 10.00
87 Jerrel Jernigan 4.00 10.00
89 Derrick Locke 4.00 10.00
93 Da'Rel Scott 4.00 10.00
94 Shane Vereen 5.00 12.00
95 Ricky Stanzi 15.00 30.00
98 Mikel Leshoure 5.00 12.00
100 Cam Newton SP 250.00 350.00

2011 Topps Magic Rookies Cut Autographs Black

1 A.J. Green 100.00 175.00
9 DeMarco Murray 125.00 200.00
10 Mark Ingram 90.00 150.00
50 Julio Jones 75.00 125.00
79 Titus Young 50.00 100.00
83 Delone Carter 50.00 100.00
91 Greg Little 30.00 60.00
100 Cam Newton 300.00 450.00

2008 Topps Mayo

This set was released on January 28, 2009. The base set consists of 330 cards. Rookies and short prints are scattered throughout the set. This product was released with 8 cards per pack and 24 packs per hobby box.

COMPLETE SET (330) 60.00 120.00
COMP.SET w/o SP's (275) 20.00 40.00
UNPRICED PRINT PLATE PRINT RUN 1
1 Drew Brees .30 .75
2 Kyle Orton SP 1.25 3.00
3 LenDale White SP 1.25 3.00
4 Shaun McDonald .20 .50
5 Bobby Wade .20 .50
6 Javon Walker .25 .60
7 Owen Daniels .20 .50
8 Justin Tuck SP 1.25 3.00
9 Amobi Okoye .20 .50
10 Rich Eisen .20 .50
11 Fred Taylor SP 1.25 3.00
12 Ryan Torain SP RC 1.25 3.00
13 Steve Slaton RC 1.00 2.50
14 Jake Long SP RC 1.25 3.00
15 Peyton Manning .50 1.25
16 Jon Kitna .25 .60
17 Ryan Grant .30 .75
18 Brandon Stokley .25 .60
19 Troy Williamson SP 1.00 2.50
20 Reggie Brown .20 .50
21 Zach Miller .25 .60
22 Aaron Kampman SP 1.25 3.00
23 Albert Haynesworth .20 .50
24 Matt Cassel .30 .75
25 Selvin Young SP 1.00 2.50
26 Will Franklin SP RC 1.00 2.50
27 Matt Forte RC 1.50 4.00
28 Glenn Dorsey RC 1.00 2.50
29 Marc Bulger .25 .60
30 Jeff Garcia .25 .60
31 DeAngelo Williams .25 .60
32 Roydell Williams .20 .50
33 Sidney Rice .30 .75
34 James Jones SP 1.00 2.50
35 L.J. Smith .20 .50
36 Aaron Schobel .20 .50
37 Tommie Harris .20 .50
38 Tyler Thigpen .25 .60
39 LaDainian Tomlinson SP 1.50 4.00
40 Marcus Smith SP RC 1.00 2.50
41 Tashard Choice RC .75 2.00
42 Chris Long RC 1.00 2.50
43 Matt Moore SP 1.25 3.00
44 Chris Redman .20 .50
45 Laurence Maroney .25 .60
46 Larry Fitzgerald .30 .75
47 Donte Stallworth .20 .50
48 Marty Booker .20 .50
49 Greg Olsen .25 .60
50 Terrell Suggs .20 .50
51 Kevin Williams .20 .50
52 Derrick Ward .20 .50
53 Steven Jackson SP 1.50 4.00
54 Adrian Arrington SP RC 1.00 2.50
55 Tim Hightower RC 1.00 2.50
56 Chauncey Washington RC .75 2.00
57 Joe Thomas .25 .60
58 Matt Leinart SP 1.50 4.00
59 Jamal Lewis .25 .60
60 Braylon Edwards .25 .60
61 Steve Smith USC .25 .60
62 Mark Bradley .20 .50
63 Leonard Pope .20 .50
64 Dwight Freeney .25 .60
65 Adam Carriker .20 .50
66 Devery Henderson .20 .50
67 Willis McGahee SP 1.25 3.00
68 Fred Davis SP RC 1.25 3.00
69 Harry Douglas RC .75 2.00
70 Anthony Alridge SP RC 1.00 2.50
71 Rex Grossman .25 .60
72 Kellen Clemens .25 .60
73 Justin Fargas .20 .50
74 Steve Smith .25 .60
75 Hines Ward .25 .60
76 Muhsin Muhammad .25 .60
77 Randy McMichael .20 .50
78 Tamba Hali .20 .50
79 Archie Manning .30 .75
80 Orville Wright .20 .50
81 Michael Turner SP 1.50 4.00
82 Paul Smith RC 1.00 2.50
83 DeSean Jackson RC 2.00 5.00
84 Josh McCown .20 .50
85 John Beck .20 .50
86 LaMont Jordan SP 1.25 3.00
87 Greg Jennings .30 .75
88 Deion Branch .25 .60
89 David Patten .20 .50
90 Bob Sanders .25 .60
91 Luis Castillo .20 .50
92 Troy Aikman .40 1.00
93 Le'Ron McClain .30 .75
94 Todd Heap SP 1.00 2.50
95 Kyle Wright RC .75 2.00
96 Malcolm Kelly RC .75 2.00
97 Vince Young .25 .60
98 Troy Smith .25 .60
99 Reggie Bush .30 .75
100 Jerricho Cotchery .25 .60
101 Jerry Porter .20 .50
102 Ike Hilliard .20 .50
103 Ed Reed .25 .60
104 John Abraham .20 .50
105 Sterling Sharpe .25 .60
106 Brodie Croyle .25 .60
107 Jeremy Shockey SP 1.25 3.00
108 Andre Woodson RC 1.00 2.50
109 Limas Sweed RC 1.00 2.50
110 Jay Cutler .30 .75
111 Adrian Peterson .50 1.25
112 Larry Johnson .25 .60
113 Joey Galloway .25 .60
114 Reggie Williams .25 .60
115 Justin McCareins .20 .50
116 Roy Williams S .25 .60
117 Julius Peppers .25 .60
118 Terry Bradshaw .50 1.25
119 James Harrison RC 5.00 12.00
120 Heath Miller SP 1.00 2.50
121 Chad Henne RC 1.00 2.50
122 Mario Manningham RC 1.00 2.50
123 J.P. Losman .20 .50
124 Willie Parker .25 .60
125 Rudi Johnson .25 .60
126 Lee Evans .25 .60
127 Marvin Harrison .30 .75
128 Isaac Bruce .25 .60
129 Kerry Rhodes .20 .50
130 Brian Urlacher SP 1.50 4.00
131 John Elway .50 1.25
132 LaMarr Woodley .25 .60
133 Calvin Johnson SP 1.50 4.00
134 Joe Flacco RC 3.00 8.00
135 James Hardy SP RC 1.00 2.50
136 Jason Campbell .25 .60
137 DeShaun Foster .25 .60
138 Ahmad Bradshaw .25 .60
139 Roy Williams WR .25 .60
140 Amani Toomer .25 .60
141 Bryant Johnson .20 .50
142 Troy Polamalu .30 .75
143 DeMarcus Ware .25 .60
144 Dan Marino .60 1.50
145 Grover Cleveland .20 .50
146 Plaxico Burress SP 1.25 3.00
147 Colt Brennan RC 1.00 2.50
148 Early Doucet RC .75 2.00
149 Matt Hasselbeck .25 .60
150 Jerious Norwood .25 .60
151 Leon Washington .25 .60
152 Arnaz Battle .20 .50
153 Ted Ginn Jr. .25 .60
154 Drew Bennett .20 .50
155 Brian Dawkins .25 .60
156 Patrick Willis .25 .60
157 Sonny Jurgensen .25 .60
158 Susan B. Anthony .20 .50
159 Terrell Owens SP 1.50 4.00
160 Dennis Dixon RC 1.00 2.50
161 Donnie Avery RC .75 2.00
162 Matt Schaub .25 .60
163 Kerry Collins .25 .60
164 Ronnie Brown .25 .60
165 Bobby Engram .20 .50
166 Laveranues Coles .20 .50
167 Antonio Gates .30 .75
168 LaRon Landry .25 .60
169 Ray Lewis .30 .75
170 Joe Namath .40 1.00
171 William Cody .20 .50
172 Andre Johnson SP 1.25 3.00
173 Erik Ainge RC 1.00 2.50
174 Dexter Jackson RC .75 2.00
175 Philip Rivers .30 .75
176 Marion Barber .25 .60
177 Chris Perry .20 .50
178 Torry Holt .25 .60
179 Anthony Gonzalez .20 .50
180 Kellen Winslow .25 .60
181 Adrian Wilson .20 .50
182 Shawne Merriman .25 .60
183 Lawrence Taylor .30 .75
184 William Rockefeller .20 .50
185 Brandon Marshall SP 1.25 3.00
186 Josh Johnson RC 1.00 2.50
187 Devin Thomas RC .75 2.00
188 Chad Pennington .25 .60
189 Brian Westbrook .25 .60
190 Ahman Green .25 .60
191 Derrick Mason .25 .60
192 Ernest Wilford .20 .50
193 Tony Scheffler .20 .50
194 Champ Bailey .25 .60
195 DeMeco Ryans .25 .60
196 Gale Sayers .40 1.00
197 Gus Frerotte .20 .50
198 Dwayne Bowe SP 1.25 3.00
199 Kevin O'Connell RC .75 2.00
200 Jordy Nelson RC 1.25 3.00
201 Trent Edwards .20 .50
202 Kolby Smith .20 .50
203 Brian Leonard .20 .50
204 Mike Furrey .25 .60
205 Jabar Gaffney .20 .50
206 Donald Lee .25 .60
207 Antonio Cromartie .20 .50
208 Joey Porter .20 .50
209 Norman Rockwell .20 .50
210 Tom Brady SP 2.50 6.00
211 Nate Burleson SP 1.00 2.50
212 Funkmaster Flex SP 1.00 2.50
213 Keenan Burton RC .60 1.50
214 Donovan McNabb .30 .75
215 Marshawn Lynch .25 .60
216 Earnest Graham .20 .50
217 Donald Driver .25 .60
218 Mark Clayton .25 .60
219 Vernon Davis .25 .60
220 Asante Samuel .20 .50
221 Mike Vrabel .20 .50
222 King Edward VIII .20 .50
223 Warren Haynes SP 1.00 2.50
224 Antwaan Randle El SP 1.00 2.50
225 Darren McFadden RC 2.50 6.00
226 Earl Bennett RC 1.00 2.50
227 Derek Anderson .20 .50
228 Joseph Addai .25 .60
229 Julius Jones .20 .50
230 T.J. Houshmandzadeh .25 .60
231 Kevin Walter .25 .60
232 Chris Cooley .25 .60
233 Leon Hall .20 .50
234 D.J. Williams .20 .50
235 Guglielmo Marconi .20 .50
236 David Garrard SP 1.25 3.00
237 Vincent Jackson SP 1.00 2.50
238 Jonathan Stewart RC 1.50 4.00
239 Jerome Simpson RC 1.00 2.50
240 Kyle Boller .20 .50
241 Warrick Dunn .25 .60
242 Ricky Williams .25 .60
243 Kevin Curtis .20 .50
244 Justin Gage .20 .50
245 Tony Gonzalez .25 .60
246 DeAngelo Hall .20 .50
247 Antonio Pierce .20 .50
248 Claude Monet .20 .50
249 Carson Palmer SP 1.50 4.00
250 Laurent Robinson SP 1.00 2.50
251 Felix Jones RC 1.50 4.00
252 Andre Caldwell RC .75 2.00
253 JaMarcus Russell .25 .60
254 Frank Gore .25 .60
255 Dominic Rhodes .20 .50
256 Santonio Holmes .25 .60
257 J.T. O'Sullivan .20 .50
258 Dallas Clark .25 .60
259 Terence Newman .20 .50
260 Ernie Sims .20 .50
261 Paul Gauguin .20 .50
262 Ben Roethlisberger SP 1.50 4.00
263 Chris Chambers SP 1.25 3.00
264 John David Booty RC .75 2.00
265 Eddie Royal RC 1.00 2.50
266 Brady Quinn .25 .60
267 Maurice Jones-Drew .25 .60
268 Deuce McAllister .25 .60
269 Wes Welker .30 .75
270 Darrell Jackson .20 .50
271 Jason Witten .30 .75
272 Nate Clements .20 .50
273 A.J. Hawk .25 .60
274 Dr. John Harvey Kellogg .20 .50
275 Eli Manning SP 1.50 4.00
276 Matt Ryan SP RC 5.00 12.00
277 Jamaal Charles RC 1.50 4.00
278 Lavelle Hawkins RC .60 1.50
279 Jake Delhomme .25 .60
280 Thomas Jones .25 .60
281 Chad Johnson .25 .60
282 Roddy White .25 .60
283 Devard Darling .20 .50
284 Alge Crumpler .25 .60
285 Jared Allen .30 .75
286 Jonathan Vilma .25 .60
287 Milton Hershey .20 .50
288 Tony Romo SP 2.00 5.00
289 Brian Brohm SP RC 1.25 3.00
290 Chris Johnson RC 2.50 6.00
291 Vernon Gholston RC .75 2.00
292 Alex Smith QB .30 .75
293 Brandon Jacobs .25 .60
294 Reggie Wayne .25 .60
295 Marques Colston .25 .60
296 Ronald Curry .25 .60
297 Ben Watson .20 .50
298 Mario Williams .25 .60
299 Derrick Brooks .25 .60
300 Thomas Edison .20 .50
301 Brett Favre SP 4.00 10.00
302 Anthony Morelli SP RC 1.00 2.50
303 Ray Rice RC 2.00 5.00
304 Dustin Keller RC 1.00 2.50
305 Aaron Rodgers .60 1.50
306 Edgerrin James .25 .60
307 Anquan Boldin .25 .60
308 Bernard Berrian .25 .60
309 Dennis Northcutt .20 .50
310 Marcedes Lewis .20 .50
311 Jason Taylor .25 .60
312 Lofa Tatupu .25 .60
313 Arthur Conan Doyle .20 .50
314 Kurt Warner SP 1.50 4.00
315 Rashard Mendenhall SP RC 2.50 6.00
316 Mike Hart SP RC 1.25 3.00
317 Owen Schmitt RC 1.00 2.50
318 Tarvaris Jackson .25 .60
319 Chester Taylor .20 .50
320 Randy Moss .30 .75
321 Santana Moss .20 .50
322 Patrick Crayton .25 .60
323 Chris Baker .20 .50
324 Osi Umenyiora .25 .60
325 Shaun Rogers .20 .50
326 Rudyard Kipling .20 .50
327 Clinton Portis SP 1.25 3.00
328 Xavier Omon SP RC 1.25 3.00
329 Kevin Smith RC 1.00 2.50
330 Jacob Hester RC 1.00 2.50

2008 Topps Mayo Mini 1894 Sepia Backs

UNPRICED SEPIA BACK PRINT RUN 5
STATED ODDS 1:250 HOB

2008 Topps Mayo Mini Harvard Red Backs

*VETS: 8X TO 20X BASIC CARDS
*VET SPs: 1.5X TO 4X BASIC CARDS
*ROOKIES: 1.5X TO 4X BASIC CARDS
*ROOKIE SPs: 2X TO 5X BASIC CARDS
HARVARD RED BACK/25 ODDS 1:50 HOB
119 James Harrison 10.00 25.00

2008 Topps Mayo Mini Black Backs

*VETS: 1.5X TO 4X BASIC CARDS
*VET SPs: .5X TO 1.2X BASIC CARDS
*ROOKIES: .4X TO 1X BASIC CARDS
*ROOKIE SPs: .4X TO 1X BASIC CARDS
OVERALL MINI ODDS 1:1 HOBBY
SP MINI STATED ODDS 1:12 HOBBY
119 James Harrison 4.00 10.00

2008 Topps Mayo Mini Princeton Orange Backs

*VETS: 4X TO 10X BASIC CARDS
*VET SPs: .8X TO 2X BASIC CARDS
*ROOKIES: .8X TO 2X BASIC CARDS
*ROOKIE SPs: .6X TO 1.5X BASIC CARDS
PRINCETON ORANGE BACK ODDS 1:24 HOB
119 James Harrison 8.00 20.00

2008 Topps Mayo Mini Yale Blue Backs

*VETS: 3X TO 8X BASIC CARDS
*VET SPs: .6X TO 1.5X BASIC CARDS
*ROOKIES: .6X TO 1.5X BASIC CARDS
*ROOKIE SPs: .5X TO 1.2X BASIC CARDS
YALE BLUE BACK ODDS 1:13 HOB
119 James Harrison 6.00 15.00

2008 Topps Mayo Americana Autographs

GROUP A/190* ODDS 1:1000 HOB
GROUP B ODDS 1:1600 HOB
UNPRICED RED INK/10 ODDS 1:12,500 HOB
AAFF Funkmaster Flex/190* 15.00 40.00
AARE Rich Eisen/190* 15.00 40.00
AAWH Warren Haynes B 15.00 40.00

2008 Topps Mayo Americana Relics

GROUP A/50* ODDS 1:400 HOB
GROUP B ODDS 1:600 HOB
ARAF Al Franken A 12.00 30.00
(subway token)
ARCP Colin Powell A 12.00 30.00
(subway token)
ARCV Cornelius Vanderbilt A 12.00 30.00
(subway token)
ARER Eleanor Roosevelt A 12.00 30.00
(subway token)
ARFF Funkmaster Flex B 4.00 10.00
(suit swatch)
ARFL Fiorello LaGuardia A 12.00 30.00
(subway token)
ARGG George Gershwin A 12.00 30.00
(subway token)
ARHF Hamilton Fish A 12.00 30.00
(subway token)
ARHM Herman Melville A 12.00 30.00
(subway token)
ARHS Henry Stimson A 12.00 30.00
(subway token)
ARJJ John Jay A 12.00 30.00
(subway token)
ARJS Jonas Salk A 12.00 30.00
(subway token)
ARNR Norman Rockwell A 12.00 30.00
(subway token)
ARRE Rich Eisen A 8.00 20.00
(tie swatch)
ARRG Rudy Giuliani A 12.00 30.00
(subway token)
ARRL Robert Livingston A 12.00 30.00
(subway token)
ARTR Theodore Roosevelt A 12.00 30.00
(subway token)
ARWH Warren Haynes B 12.00 30.00
(guitar strap)

2008 Topps Mayo Autographs

GROUP A/40* ODDS 1:1950 HOB
GROUP B/65* ODDS 1:3000 HOB
GROUP C/90* ODDS 1:4300 HOB
GROUP D/140* ODDS 1:920 HOB
GROUP E/190* ODDS 1:1000 HOB
GROUP F ODDS 1:193 HOB
GROUP G ODDS 1:1350 HOB
GROUP H ODDS 1:188 HOB
GROUP I ODDS 1:250 HOB
UNPRICED RED INK/10 ODDS 1:1420 HOB
EXCH EXPIRATION: 12/31/2011
AAH Ali Highsmith F 5.00 12.00
AAM Archie Manning/40* 20.00 40.00
AAW Andre Woodson F 6.00 15.00
ABF Brandon Flowers H 6.00 15.00
ACB Colt Brennan/65* 15.00 40.00
ACJ Chad Johnson/190* 10.00 25.00
ADA Donnie Avery H 5.00 12.00
ADBR Drew Brees/90* 30.00 60.00
ADJ DeSean Jackson H 12.00 30.00
ADMC Darren McFadden/65* 30.00 60.00
AEM Eli Manning/40* 50.00 100.00
AER Eddie Royal F 6.00 15.00
AFD Fred Davis/190* 6.00 15.00
AJC John Carlson I 6.00 15.00
AJE John Elway/40* 75.00 150.00
AJJ James Jones F 6.00 15.00
AJMO Josh Morgan I 6.00 15.00
AMC Marques Colston F 10.00 25.00
AMF Matt Forte H 15.00 40.00
AMK Malcolm Kelly F 5.00 12.00
AMR Matt Ryan/140* 50.00 100.00
APM Peyton Manning/40* 60.00 120.00
ASJ Sonny Jurgensen/140*
ASS Sterling Sharpe/140* 12.00 30.00
ATD Tony Dorsett/40* 30.00 60.00
AWF Will Franklin F 5.00 12.00
AWW Wes Welker G 25.00 50.00

2008 Topps Mayo Century Series Relics

GROUP A/50* ODDS 1:1200 HOB
GROUP B/100* ODDS 1:650 HOB
CSRAO Annie Oakley Stamp/100* 15.00 50.00
CSRFD Frederick Douglass Stamp/100* 15.00 40.00
CSRFS Ben Franklin Stamp/50* 20.00 50.00
CSRGC Grover Cleveland Hankerchief/50* 20.00 50.00
CSRGS Ulysses S. Grant Stamp/50* 20.00 50.00
CSRLD Statue of Liberty Dime/50* 35.00 60.00
CSRSA Susan B. Anthony Stamp/100* 15.00 40.00
CSRTE Thomas Edison Stamp/100* 15.00 40.00
CSRUSM U.S.S. Maine Deck/100* 40.00 80.00
CSRWC William Cody Stamp/100* 15.00 40.00
CSRWS Daniel Webster Stamp/50* 20.00 50.00

2008 Topps Mayo Cut Signatures

UNPRICED CUT SIG/1 ODDS 1:35,328 HOB

2008 Topps Mayo Famous Ships

COMPLETE SET (19) 15.00 40.00
STATED ODDS 1:12 HOB
S1 Victoria 1.25 3.00
S2 Nina 1.25 3.00
S3 Pinta 1.25 3.00
S4 Santa Maria 1.25 3.00
S5 RMS Titanic 2.00 5.00
S6 Cutty Sark 1.25 3.00
S7 Queen Mary 2 1.25 3.00
S8 USS Arizona 1.25 3.00
S9 USS Monitor 1.25 3.00
S10 HMS Victory 1.25 3.00
S11 Appomattox 1.25 3.00
S12 Andrea Gail 1.25 3.00
S13 Andrea Doria 1.25 3.00
S14 RMS Carpathia 1.25 3.00
S15 RV Calypso 1.25 3.00
S16 Nimrod 1.25 3.00
S17 HMS Beagle 1.25 3.00
S18 HMS Bounty 1.25 3.00
S19 Golden Hind 1.25 3.00

2008 Topps Mayo Horses

STATED ODDS 1:48 HOB
H1 Appaloosa Horse 2.50 6.00
H2 Shetland Pony 2.50 6.00
H3 Tennessee Walking Horse 2.50 6.00
H4 Mustang 2.50 6.00
H5 Belgian Draft Horse 2.50 6.00
H6 American Miniature Horse 2.50 6.00
H7 Clydesdale 2.50 6.00
H8 Missouri Fox Trotter 2.50 6.00
H9 Morgan Horse 2.50 6.00
H10 American Paint Horse 2.50 6.00
H11 Chincoteague Pony 2.50 6.00
H12 Arabian Horse 2.50 6.00

H13 Canadian Horse	2.50	6.00
H14 Zebra	2.50	6.00
H15 Unicorn	2.50	6.00

2008 Topps Mayo Relics

GROUP A ODDS 1:38 HOB
GROUP B ODDS 1:32 HOB

RAB Anquan Boldin A	3.00	8.00
RAG Antonio Gates A	4.00	10.00
RAP Adrian Peterson A	6.00	15.00
RBB Brian Brohm B	3.00	8.00
RCH Chad Henne B	3.00	8.00
RCJ Chad Johnson A	3.00	8.00
RCJO Chris Johnson B	6.00	15.00
RCP Carson Palmer A	4.00	10.00
RCPO Clinton Portis A	3.00	8.00
RDA Donnie Avery B	2.50	6.00
RDG David Garrard A	3.00	8.00
RDM Darren McFadden B	6.00	15.00
RDW DeAngelo Williams A	3.00	8.00
REM Eli Manning A	5.00	12.00
RFG Frank Gore A	3.00	8.00
RFJ Felix Jones B	6.00	15.00
RGD Glenn Dorsey B	3.00	8.00
RJB John David Booty B	2.50	6.00
RJF Joe Flacco B	6.00	15.00
RJG Jeff Garcia A	3.00	8.00
RJH James Hardy B	2.50	6.00
RJL Jake Long B	3.00	8.00
RJS Jonathan Stewart B	6.00	15.00
RLF Larry Fitzgerald A	6.00	15.00
RLT LaDainian Tomlinson A	6.00	15.00
RLW LenDale White A	3.00	8.00
RMB Marion Barber A	5.00	12.00
RMF Matt Forte B	6.00	15.00
RMH Matt Hasselbeck A	3.00	8.00
RMK Malcolm Kelly B	2.50	6.00
RML Marshawn Lynch A	3.00	8.00
RMR Matt Ryan B	10.00	25.00
RPM Peyton Manning A	8.00	20.00
RRG Ryan Grant A	4.00	10.00
RRM Randy Moss A	4.00	10.00
RRME Rashard Mendenhall B	5.00	12.00
RRR Ray Rice B	6.00	15.00
RRW Reggie Wayne A	4.00	10.00
RSS Steve Slaton B	3.00	8.00
RTG Tony Gonzalez A	4.00	10.00
RTJ Thomas Jones A	3.00	8.00
RWW Wes Welker A	4.00	10.00

2008 Topps Mayo Super Bowl Match-ups

COMPLETE SET (33)	6.00	15.00
OVERALL ODDS 1:1 HOBBY		
SB32A Denver Broncos	.30	.75
SB32B Super Bowl XXXII	.30	.75
SB32C Green Bay Packers	.30	.75
SB33A Denver Broncos	.30	.75
SB33B Super Bowl XXXIII	.30	.75
SB33C Atlanta Falcons	.30	.75
SB34A St. Louis Rams	.30	.75
SB34B Super Bowl XXXIV	.30	.75
SB34C Tennessee Titans	.30	.75
SB35A Baltimore Ravens	.30	.75
SB35B Super Bowl XXXV	.30	.75
SB35C New York Giants	.30	.75
SB36A New England Patriots	.30	.75
SB36B Super Bowl XXXVI	.30	.75
SB36C St. Louis Rams	.30	.75
SB37A Tampa Bay Buccaneers	.30	.75
SB37B Super Bowl XXXVII	.30	.75
SB37C Oakland Raiders	.30	.75
SB38A New England Patriots	.30	.75
SB38B Super Bowl XXXVIII	.30	.75
SB38C Carolina Panthers	.30	.75
SB39A New England Patriots	.30	.75
SB39B Super Bowl XXXIX	.30	.75
SB39C Philadelphia Eagles	.30	.75
SB40A Pittsburgh Steelers	.30	.75
SB40B Super Bowl XL	.30	.75
SB40C Seattle Seahawks	.30	.75
SB41A Indianapolis Colts	.30	.75
SB41B Super Bowl XLI	.30	.75
SB41C Chicago Bears	.30	.75
SB42A New York Giants	.30	.75
SB42B Super Bowl XLII	.30	.75
SB42C New England Patriots	.30	.75

2009 Topps Mayo

COMPLETE SET (330)	75.00	135.00
COMP.SET w/o SP's (275)	20.00	40.00
276-330 SP ODDS 1:2 HOB		
1 Benjamin Harrison Pres.	.20	.50
2 Aaron Curry RC	.60	1.50
3 Aaron Kampman	.25	.60
4 Aaron Maybin RC	.50	1.25
5 Aaron Rodgers	.60	1.50
6 Adrian Peterson	.50	1.25
7 Adrian Wilson	.20	.50
8 Ahmad Bradshaw	.25	.60
9 Al Harris	.20	.50
10 Albert Haynesworth	.20	.50
11 Alex Smith QB	.25	.60
12 Andre Brown RC	.40	1.00
13 Andre Caldwell	.20	.50
14 Andre Johnson	.25	.60
15 Anquan Boldin	.25	.60
16 Anthony Gonzalez	.20	.50
17 Antoine Winfield	.20	.50
18 Antonio Gates	.25	.60
19 Antonio Pierce	.20	.50
20 Antwaan Randle El	.20	.50
21 Asante Samuel	.20	.50
22 Austin Collie RC	.60	1.50
23 B.J. Raji RC	.60	1.50
24 Barry Sanders	.60	1.50
25 Ben Roethlisberger	.30	.75
26 Bernard Berrian	.25	.60
27 Bo Scaife	.20	.50
28 Bobby Engram	.20	.50
29 Bobby Wade	.20	.50
30 Bradie James	.20	.50
31 Brady Quinn	.25	.60
32 Brandon Marshall	.25	.60
33 Brandon Pettigrew RC	.60	1.50
34 Brandon Tate RC	.60	1.50
35 Brian Cushing RC	.60	1.50
36 Brian Dawkins	.25	.60
37 Brian Hartline RC	.60	1.50
38 Brian Orakpo RC	.60	1.50
39 Brian Robiskie RC	.60	1.50
40 Brian Urlacher	.30	.75
41 Brian Westbrook	.25	.60
42 Brooks Foster RC	.40	1.00
43 Buffalo Bill	.20	.50
44 Carson Palmer	.30	.75
45 Cedric Benson	.25	.60
46 Chad Ochocinco	.25	.60
47 Champ Bailey	.25	.60
48 Charles Woodson	.30	.75
49 Chester Taylor	.20	.50
50 Chris Chambers	.25	.60
51 Chris Cooley	.25	.60
52 Chris Johnson	.30	.75
53 Chris Wells RC	1.00	2.50
54 Clay Matthews RC	1.50	4.00
55 Clinton Portis	.25	.60
56 Grover Cleveland Pres.	.20	.50
57 D'Qwell Jackson	.20	.50
58 Dallas Clark	.25	.60
59 Dan Marino	.75	2.00
60 Darrelle Revis	.25	.60
61 Darren McFadden	.30	.75
62 Darrius Heyward-Bey RC	.60	1.50
63 Daunte Culpepper	.25	.60
64 DeAngelo Hall	.25	.60
65 DeAngelo Williams	.30	.75
66 Deion Branch	.25	.60
67 DeMarcus Ware	.25	.60
68 Derek Anderson	.20	.50
69 Derrick Mason	.25	.60
70 Derrick Ward	.20	.50
71 Derrick Williams RC	.50	1.25
72 DeSean Jackson	.25	.60
73 Devery Henderson	.20	.50
74 Devin Hester	.30	.75
75 Domenik Hixon	.20	.50
76 Donald Brown RC	.60	1.50
77 Donald Driver	.25	.60
78 Donnie Avery	.25	.60
79 Donovan McNabb	.30	.75
80 Drew Brees	.30	.75
81 Dustin Keller	.20	.50
82 Dwayne Bowe	.25	.60
83 Dwight Freeney	.25	.60
84 Orville Wright inventor	.20	.50
85 Ed Reed	.25	.60
86 Eddie Royal	.25	.60
87 Eli Manning	.30	.75
88 Ernie Sims	.20	.50
89 Evander Hood RC	.75	2.00
90 Annie Oakley	.20	.50
91 Felix Jones	.30	.75
92 Frank Gore	.25	.60
93 Fred Jackson	.30	.75
94 Fred Taylor	.25	.60
95 Nikola Tesla engineer	.20	.50
96 Gaines Adams	.20	.50
97 Glen Coffee RC	.50	1.25
98 Greg Camarillo	.25	.60
99 Greg Jennings	.30	.75
100 Greg Olsen	.20	.50
101 William McKinley Pres.	.20	.50
102 Heath Miller	.25	.60
103 Hines Ward	.25	.60
104 George Westinghouse entrepren.	.20	.50
105 Isaac Bruce	.25	.60
106 Theodore Roosevelt Pres.	.20	.50
107 Jake Delhomme	.25	.60
108 Jamaal Charles	.30	.75
109 Jamal Lewis	.25	.60
110 JaMarcus Russell	.20	.50
111 James Farrior	.20	.50
112 James Harrison	.30	.75
113 Jared Allen	.30	.75
114 Jared Cook RC	.60	1.50
115 Jason Witten	.30	.75
116 Jay Cutler	.30	.75
117 Jeremy Maclin RC	1.00	2.50
118 Jeremy Shockey	.20	.50
119 Jerious Norwood	.25	.60
120 Jerod Mayo	.25	.60
121 Jerricho Cotchery	.25	.60
122 Jerry Rice	.60	1.50
123 Jim Brown	.50	1.25
124 Joe Flacco	.30	.75
125 Joe Montana	.75	2.00
126 Joey Galloway	.25	.60
127 Joey Porter	.25	.60
128 John Abraham	.20	.50
129 John Carlson	.25	.60
130 John Elway	.60	1.50
131 Johnny Knox RC	1.00	2.50
132 Jon Beason	.20	.50
133 Jonathan Stewart	.25	.60
134 Jonathan Vilma	.20	.50
135 Joseph Addai	.30	.75
136 Josh Freeman RC	1.25	3.00
137 Josh Reed	.20	.50
138 Juaquin Iglesias RC	.50	1.25
139 Julian Peterson	.20	.50
140 Julius Peppers	.25	.60
141 Justin Fargas	.20	.50
142 Justin Gage	.20	.50
143 Justin Tuck	.25	.60
144 Clara Barton nurse	.20	.50
145 Kellen Winslow Jr.	.25	.60
146 Kenny Britt RC	.75	2.00
147 Kenny McKinley RC	.60	1.50
148 Kerry Collins	.25	.60
149 Kevin Faulk	.20	.50
150 Kevin Smith	.25	.60
151 Kevin Walter	.25	.60
152 Kevin Williams	.20	.50
153 Knowshon Moreno RC	.60	1.50
154 Kris Jenkins	.20	.50
155 Kurt Warner	.30	.75
156 Kyle Orton	.25	.60
157 LaDainian Tomlinson	.30	.75
158 LaMarr Woodley	.20	.50
159 Lance Briggs	.25	.60
160 Lance Moore	.25	.60
161 Larry English RC	.60	1.50
162 Larry Fitzgerald	.30	.75
163 Larry Johnson	.25	.60
164 Laurence Maroney	.25	.60
165 Laveranues Coles	.20	.50
166 Le'Ron McClain	.25	.60
167 Lee Evans	.25	.60
168 LenDale White	.25	.60
169 Leon Washington	.25	.60
170 LeSean McCoy RC	1.25	3.00
171 London Fletcher	.20	.50
172 Thomas Edison inventor	.20	.50
173 Malcolm Jenkins RC	.60	1.50
174 Marc Bulger	.25	.60
175 Mario Williams	.25	.60
176 Marion Barber	.25	.60
177 Mark Clayton	.20	.50
178 Mark Sanchez RC	2.00	5.00
179 Marques Colston	.25	.60
180 Marshawn Lynch	.25	.60
181 Mathias Kiwanuka	.20	.50
182 Matt Cassel	.25	.60
183 Matt Forte	.30	.75
184 Matt Hasselbeck	.25	.60
185 Matt Ryan	.30	.75
186 Matt Schaub	.25	.60
187 Matthew Stafford RC	3.00	8.00
188 Maurice Jones-Drew	.25	.60
189 Mewelde Moore	.20	.50
190 Michael Bush	.25	.60
191 Michael Crabtree RC	1.25	3.00
192 Michael Jenkins	.20	.50
193 Michael Turner	.25	.60
194 Mike Goodson RC	.60	1.50
195 Mike Thomas RC	.60	1.50
196 Mike Wallace RC	1.25	3.00
197 Mohamed Massaquoi RC	.50	1.25
198 Muhsin Muhammad	.25	.60
199 Andrew Mellon banker	.20	.50
200 Nate Davis RC	.50	1.25
201 Nate Washington	.20	.50
202 Nnamdi Asomugha	.25	.60
203 Fred Grandy Congress	.20	.50
204 Owen Daniels	.20	.50
205 Barack Obama	.30	.75
206 Pat White RC	.60	1.50
207 Patrick Turner RC	.50	1.25
208 Patrick Willis	.25	.60
209 Percy Harvin RC	1.00	2.50
210 Peria Jerry RC	.50	1.25
211 Peyton Manning	.50	1.25
212 Philip Rivers	.30	.75
213 Pierre Thomas	.25	.60
214 Jay Ratliff	.30	.75
215 Robert Jarvik inventor	.20	.50
216 Ramses Barden RC	.40	1.00
217 Randy Moss	.30	.75
218 Rashard Mendenhall	.25	.60
219 Ray Lewis	.30	.75
220 Ray Rice	.30	.75
221 Reggie Bush	.30	.75
222 Reggie Wayne	.25	.60
223 Rhett Bomar RC	.50	1.25
224 Richard Seymour	.20	.50
225 Ricky Williams	.25	.60
226 Robert Ayers RC	.60	1.50
227 Roddy White	.25	.60
228 Ronde Barber	.20	.50
229 Ronnie Brown	.25	.60
230 Roscoe Parrish	.20	.50
231 Roy Williams WR	.25	.60
232 Ryan Grant	.25	.60
233 Pawnee Bill	.20	.50
234 Sage Rosenfels	.20	.50
235 Santana Moss	.25	.60
236 Shaun Hill	.20	.50
237 Shaun Rogers	.20	.50
238 Shonn Greene RC	1.00	2.50
239 Stephen McGee RC	.60	1.50
240 Steve Slaton	.25	.60
241 Steve Smith	.25	.60
242 Steve Smith USC	.25	.60
243 Steven Jackson	.25	.60
244 Richmond Hobson Admiral	.20	.50
245 T.J. Houshmandzadeh	.25	.60
246 Tarvaris Jackson	.25	.60
247 Tashard Choice	.20	.50
248 Ted Ginn Jr.	.25	.60
249 Terence Newman	.20	.50
250 Terrell Owens	.30	.75
251 Terrell Suggs	.20	.50
252 Terry Bradshaw	.50	1.25
253 Thomas Jones	.25	.60
254 Tim Hightower	.20	.50
255 Tom Brady	.50	1.25
256 Tony Dorsett	.40	1.00
257 Tony Gonzalez	.25	.60
258 Tony Romo	.50	1.25
259 Torry Holt	.25	.60
260 Edgerrin James	.25	.60
261 Travis Beckum RC	.50	1.25
262 Troy Aikman	.50	1.25
263 Troy Polamalu	.30	.75
264 Tyson Jackson RC	.50	1.25
265 Paddy Doyle athlete	.20	.50
266 John D. Rockefeller tycoon	.20	.50
267 Vince Young	.25	.60
268 Vincent Jackson	.25	.60
269 Vontae Davis RC	.60	1.50
270 Kevin Young track	.20	.50
271 Wes Welker	.30	.75
272 Willie Parker	.20	.50
273 Willis McGahee	.25	.60
274 Booker T. Washington	.20	.50
275 Zach Miller	.20	.50
276 Anthony Fasano	1.00	2.50
277 Antonio Bryant	1.00	2.50
278 Mike Powell track	1.00	2.50
279 Barrett Ruud	1.00	2.50
280 Brandon Jacobs	1.25	3.00
281 Braylon Edwards	1.25	3.00
282 Calvin Johnson	1.50	4.00
283 Chad Pennington	1.25	3.00
284 Chase Coffman RC	1.00	2.50
285 Chris Hope	1.00	2.50
286 Cortland Finnegan	1.00	2.50
287 Brett Favre	6.00	15.00
288 Darren Howard	1.00	2.50
289 Darren Sproles	1.25	3.00
290 David Garrard	1.25	3.00
291 Deon Butler RC	1.00	2.50
292 Dominic Rhodes	1.00	2.50
293 Earnest Graham	1.00	2.50
294 Gartrell Johnson RC	.75	2.00
295 Gibril Wilson	1.00	2.50
296 Hakeem Nicks RC	2.00	5.00
297 J.T. O'Sullivan	1.00	2.50
298 James Casey RC	1.00	2.50
299 Jarett Dillard RC	1.25	3.00
300 Jason Campbell	1.00	2.50
301 Jason Smith RC	1.00	2.50
302 Michael Vick	2.00	5.00
303 Jeff Garcia	1.25	3.00
304 Joe Namath	2.00	5.00
305 Jon Kitna	1.00	2.50
306 Josh Cribbs	1.50	4.00
307 Julius Jones	1.00	2.50
308 Kenny Phillips	1.00	2.50
309 Kirk Morrison	1.00	2.50
310 Maurice Greene track	1.00	2.50
311 Louis Murphy RC	1.25	3.00
312 Manuel Johnson RC	1.00	2.50
313 Matt Leinart	1.25	3.00
314 Maurice Morris	1.00	2.50
315 Michael Griffin	1.00	2.50
316 Nick Collins	1.00	2.50
317 Pat Williams	1.00	2.50
318 Robert Mathis	1.00	2.50
319 Ryan Fitzpatrick	1.50	4.00
320 Sammy Morris	1.00	2.50
321 Santonio Holmes	1.25	3.00
322 Seneca Wallace	1.00	2.50
323 Ted Kennedy	1.25	3.00
324 Shawn Nelson RC	1.00	2.50
325 Steve Breaston	1.25	3.00
326 Tony Scheffler	1.00	2.50
327 Trent Cole	1.00	2.50
328 Trent Edwards	1.00	2.50
329 Tyler Thigpen	1.00	2.50
330 Jackie Joyner-Kersee track	1.00	2.50

2009 Topps Mayo Mini

*VETS 1-275: 1.5X TO 4X BASIC CARDS
*ROOKIES 1-275: .5X TO 1.2X BASIC CARDS
*VETS 276-330: .5X TO 1.2X BASIC CARDS
*ROOKIES 276-330: .4X TO 1X BASIC CARDS
276-330 STATED ODDS 1:12 HOB
331-360 SP INSERTED INSIDE RIP CARDS

287 Brett Favre	6.00	15.00
331 Adrian Peterson SP	12.00	30.00
332 Andre Johnson SP	6.00	15.00
333 Ben Roethlisberger SP	8.00	20.00
334 Brandon Marshall SP	6.00	15.00
335 Brian Westbrook SP	6.00	15.00
336 Calvin Johnson SP	8.00	20.00
337 Chris Wells SP	8.00	20.00
338 Clinton Portis SP	6.00	15.00
339 Donovan McNabb SP	8.00	20.00
340 Drew Brees SP	8.00	20.00
341 Eli Manning SP	8.00	20.00
342 Jay Cutler SP	8.00	20.00
343 Jeremy Maclin SP	8.00	20.00
344 Josh Freeman SP	10.00	25.00
345 Knowshon Moreno SP	5.00	12.00
346 LaDainian Tomlinson SP	8.00	20.00
347 Larry Fitzgerald SP	8.00	20.00
348 Mark Sanchez SP	15.00	40.00
349 Matt Ryan SP	8.00	20.00
350 Matthew Stafford SP	25.00	60.00
351 Michael Crabtree SP	10.00	25.00
352 Michael Turner SP	6.00	15.00
353 Peyton Manning SP	12.00	30.00
354 Philip Rivers SP	8.00	20.00
355 Reggie Wayne SP	6.00	15.00
356 Steve Smith SP	6.00	15.00
357 Steven Jackson SP	6.00	15.00
358 Terrell Owens SP	8.00	20.00
359 Tom Brady SP	12.00	30.00
360 Tony Romo SP	12.00	30.00

2009 Topps Mayo Mini Blue Back

*VETS 1-275: 4X TO 10X BASIC CARDS
*ROOKIES 1-275: 1X TO 2.5X BASIC CARDS
*VETS 276-330: .8X TO 2X BASIC CARDS
*ROOKIES 276-330: .6X TO 1.5X BASIC CARDS
BLUE BACK ODDS 1:24 HOB

287 Brett Favre	10.00	25.00

2009 Topps Mayo Mini Gold

*VETS 1-275: 4X TO 10X BASIC CARDS
*ROOKIES 1-275: 1X TO 2.5X BASIC CARDS
*VETS 276-330: .8X TO 2X BASIC CARDS
*ROOKIES 276-330: .6X TO 1.5X BASIC CARDS
GOLD STATED ODDS 1:21 HOB

287 Brett Favre	10.00	25.00

2009 Topps Mayo Mini Red Back

*VETS 1-275: 10 TO 25X BASIC CARDS
*ROOKIES 1-275: 2X TO 5X BASIC CARDS
*VETS 276-330: 2X TO 5X BASIC CARDS
*ROOKIES 276-330: 1X TO 2.5X BASIC CARDS
RED BACK/25 ODDS 1:82 HOB

287 Brett Favre	30.00	60.00

2009 Topps Mayo Silver

*VETS 1-275: 1.5X TO 4X BASIC CARDS
*ROOKIES 1-275: .5X TO 1.2X BASIC CARDS
*VETS 276-330: .5X TO 1.2X BASIC CARDS
*ROOKIES 276-330: .4X TO 1X BASIC CARDS
ONE SILVER PER PACK

287 Brett Favre	6.00	15.00

2009 Topps Mayo Americana Relics

GROUP A ODDS 1:33,000 HOB
GROUP B ODDS 1:1540 HOB
GROUP D ODDS 1:2100 HOB

MRAO Annie Oakley Brick B	25.00	50.00
MRBB Buffalo Bill Nickel A	30.00	60.00
MRBW Booker T. Washington Brick B	25.00	50.00
MRCE Columbian Exposition Handkerchief B	30.00	60.00
MRGC Grover Cleveland Floor B	30.00	60.00
MRHR Adm. H.G. Rickover Wood B	30.00	60.00
MRNT Nikola Tesla Brick B	25.00	50.00
MRRR Soldier Table B	30.00	60.00
MRTE Thomas Edison Brick B	25.00	50.00
MRTK Ted Kennedy Floor B	40.00	80.00
MRTR Theodore Roosevelt Floor B	40.00	80.00
MRWD William R. Day Tree A	30.00	60.00
MRWH Benjamin Harrsion Floor B	30.00	60.00
MRWM William McKinley Floor B	30.00	60.00
MRWN Wendell Neville Pants B	30.00	60.00
MRBB2 Buffalo Bill Brick B	25.00	50.00
MRRR2 Soldier Blanket B (from Spanish-American War)	30.00	60.00
MRRR3 Soldier Knapsack B	50.00	100.00
MRTK2 Ted Kennedy Banner D	30.00	60.00

2009 Topps Mayo Autographs

GROUP A ODDS 1:529 HOB
GROUP B ODDS 1:1330 HOB
GROUP C ODDS 1:160 HOB
GROUP D ODDS 1:90 HOB
GROUP E ODDS 1:96 HOB
GROUP F ODDS 1:86 HOB
UNPRICED RED INK INSERTED IN RIP CARDS

MAAC Austin Collie F	5.00	12.00
MAAP Adrian Peterson A	125.00	200.00
MABP Brandon Pettigrew E	4.00	10.00
MABR Brian Robiskie D	6.00	15.00
MACJ Chris Johnson A	40.00	80.00
MACL Chris Long A	8.00	20.00
MACWE Chris Wells C	12.00	30.00
MADA Donnie Avery C	6.00	15.00
MADB Donald Brown A	20.00	40.00
MADBR Drew Brees A	75.00	135.00
MADH Darrius Heyward-Bey A	12.00	30.00
MADJ DeSean Jackson C	8.00	20.00
MADW1 DeAngelo Williams A	15.00	40.00
MADW2 Derrick Williams E	3.00	8.00
MAGC Glen Coffee E	3.00	8.00
MAGJ1 Greg Jennings C	10.00	25.00
MAGJ2 Gartrell Johnson F	2.50	6.00
MAHN Hakeem Nicks D	10.00	25.00
MAJCU Jay Cutler A	40.00	80.00
MAJF1 Joe Flacco B	25.00	50.00
MAJF2 Josh Freeman A	20.00	40.00
MAJJK Jackie Joyner-Kersee Track C	8.00	20.00
MAJL James Laurinaitis E	6.00	15.00
MAJLO Jake Long F	5.00	12.00
MAJM Jeremy Maclin B	12.00	30.00
MAJS Jonathan Stewart A	12.00	30.00
MAKB Kenny Britt D	5.00	12.00
MAKM Knowshon Moreno A	30.00	60.00
MAKY Kevin Young Track C	5.00	12.00
MALF Larry Fitzgerald A	25.00	50.00
MALM LeSean McCoy D	12.00	30.00
MAMC Michael Crabtree A	30.00	80.00
MAMG Maurice Greene Track C	6.00	15.00
MAMM Mohamed Massaquoi	6.00	15.00
MAMP Mike Powell Track C	6.00	15.00
MAMR Matt Ryan A	30.00	60.00
MAMS Matthew Stafford A	60.00	120.00
MAMSA Mark Sanchez A	60.00	120.00
MAMT Michael Turner A	12.00	30.00
MAMW Mario Williams A	8.00	20.00
MAPD Paddy Doyle Rec.Holder C	5.00	12.00
MAPH Percy Harvin D	15.00	40.00
MAPM Peyton Manning A	125.00	200.00
MAPR Philip Rivers A	25.00	50.00
MAPW1 Pat White D	12.00	30.00
MAPW2 Patrick Willis A	12.00	30.00
MARB Randy Barnes Track C		
MARB2 Russell Byars Rec.Holder C	4.00	10.00
MARJ Robert Jarvik Inventor C	10.00	25.00
MARM Rey Maualuga F	4.00	10.00
MARW Roddy White B	8.00	20.00
MASGR Shonn Greene D	10.00	25.00

2009 Topps Mayo Cabinet Cards

ONE CABINET CARD PER HOBBY BOX

MCC1 Drew Brees	3.00	8.00
MCC2 Philip Rivers	3.00	8.00
MCC3 Peyton Manning	5.00	12.00
MCC4 Tom Brady	5.00	12.00
MCC5 Tony Romo	5.00	12.00
MCC6 Eli Manning	3.00	8.00
MCC7 Ben Roethlisberger	3.00	8.00
MCC8 Matt Ryan	3.00	8.00
MCC9 Adrian Peterson	5.00	12.00
MCC10 Clinton Portis	2.50	6.00
MCC11 LaDainian Tomlinson	3.00	8.00
MCC12 Steven Jackson	2.50	6.00
MCC13 Andre Johnson	2.50	6.00
MCC14 Larry Fitzgerald	3.00	8.00
MCC15 Knowshon Moreno	1.00	2.50
MCC16 Steve Smith	2.50	6.00
MCC17 Calvin Johnson	3.00	8.00
MCC18 Reggie Wayne	2.50	6.00
MCC19 Matthew Stafford	5.00	12.00
MCC20 Mark Sanchez	3.00	8.00

2009 Topps Mayo Cabinet Relics

STATED ODDS 1:73 HOBBY BOXES

MCR1 Drew Brees	20.00	40.00
MCR2 Aaron Rodgers	20.00	40.00
MCR3 Philip Rivers	12.00	30.00
MCR4 Peyton Manning	20.00	50.00
MCR5 Donovan McNabb	12.00	30.00
MCR6 Tony Romo	20.00	50.00
MCR7 Matt Ryan	12.00	30.00
MCR8 Ben Roethlisberger	12.00	30.00
MCR9 Adrian Peterson	20.00	50.00
MCR10 DeAngelo Williams	12.00	30.00
MCR11 Clinton Portis		
MCR12 Thomas Jones		
MCR13 Andre Johnson	10.00	25.00
MCR14 Larry Fitzgerald		
MCR15 Steve Smith	10.00	25.00
MCR16 Calvin Johnson		
MCR17 Matthew Stafford		
MCR18 Mark Sanchez	15.00	40.00
MCR19 Knowshon Moreno		
MCR20 Chris Wells	8.00	20.00

2009 Topps Mayo Celebrated Citizens

COMPLETE SET (15)	8.00	20.00
STATED ODDS 1:12		
CC1 Samuel Adams	1.25	3.00
CC2 William Penn	1.25	3.00
CC3 Barack Obama	2.00	5.00
CC4 Andrew Hallidie	1.25	3.00
CC5 Henry Ford	1.25	3.00
CC6 Andrew Carnegie	1.25	3.00
CC7 Franklin D. Roosevelt	1.25	3.00
CC8 Stephen F. Austin	1.25	3.00
CC9 Janet Reno	1.25	3.00
CC10 John D. Rockefeller tycoon	1.25	3.00
CC11 Edgar Allan Poe	1.25	3.00
CC12 Henry Hudson	1.25	3.00
CC13 George Washington	1.25	3.00
CC14 David Crockett	1.25	3.00
CC15 William Tecumseh Sherman	1.25	3.00

2009 Topps Mayo Namesakes

COMPLETE SET (13)	15.00	40.00
STATED ODDS 1:48 HOB		
NFL1 Bills	1.50	4.00
NFL2 Dolphins	1.50	4.00
NFL3 Eagles	1.50	4.00
NFL4 Falcons	1.50	4.00
NFL5 Colts	1.50	4.00
NFL6 Jaguars	1.50	4.00
NFL7 Lions	1.50	4.00
NFL8 Ravens	1.50	4.00
NFL9 Seahawks	1.50	4.00
NFL10 Bengals	1.50	4.00
NFL11 Jets	1.50	4.00
NFL12 Patriots	1.50	4.00
NFL13 Titans	1.50	4.00

2009 Topps Mayo Relics

GROUP A ODDS 1:239 HOB
GROUP B ODDS 1:85 HOB
GROUP C ODDS 1:38 HOB

MRAB Andre Brown C	2.50	6.00
MRABO Anquan Boldin A	4.00	10.00
MRAC Aaron Curry C	2.50	6.00
MRAG Antonio Gates A	4.00	10.00
MRAR Aaron Rodgers B	8.00	20.00
MRBM Brandon Marshall B	4.00	10.00
MRBP Brandon Pettigrew C	2.50	6.00
MRBR Brian Robiskie C	2.50	6.00
MRBRO Ben Roethlisberger B	5.00	12.00
MRBW Brian Westbrook B	4.00	10.00
MRCJ Calvin Johnson A	5.00	12.00
MRCW Chris Wells C	5.00	12.00
MRDA Donnie Avery B	4.00	10.00
MRDB Dwayne Bowe B	4.00	10.00
MRDB2 Donald Brown C	4.00	10.00
MRDBU Deon Butler C	2.00	5.00
MRDH Darrius Heyward-Bey C	2.50	6.00
MRDM Donovan McNabb B	5.00	12.00
MRDW DeAngelo Williams A	5.00	12.00
MRDW2 Derrick Williams C	2.00	5.00
MRER Eddie Royal B	4.00	10.00
MRGC Glen Coffee C	2.00	5.00
MRHN Hakeem Nicks C	4.00	10.00
MRJF Josh Freeman C	5.00	12.00
MRJI Juaquin Iglesias C	2.00	5.00
MRJM Jeremy Maclin C	4.00	10.00
MRJR Javon Ringer C	2.50	6.00
MRJS Jason Smith C	2.50	6.00
MRKB Kenny Britt C	3.00	8.00
MRKM Knowshon Moreno C	5.00	12.00
MRLF Larry Fitzgerald A	5.00	12.00
MRLM LeSean McCoy C	4.00	10.00
MRMC Marques Colston B	4.00	10.00
MRMC2 Michael Crabtree C	5.00	12.00
MRMF Matt Forte B	5.00	12.00
MRMJ Maurice Jones-Drew B	4.00	10.00
MRMM Mohamed Massaquoi C	2.00	5.00
MRMS Mark Sanchez C	8.00	20.00
MRMS2 Matthew Stafford C	6.00	15.00
MRMT Mike Thomas C	2.50	6.00
MRMW Mike Wallace C	5.00	12.00
MRND Nate Davis C	2.00	5.00
MRPH Percy Harvin C	6.00	15.00
MRPR Philip Rivers A	5.00	12.00
MRPT Patrick Turner C	2.50	6.00
MRPW Pat White C	2.50	6.00
MRRB Ramses Barden C	1.50	4.00
MRRB2 Ronnie Brown B	4.00	10.00
MRRBO Rhett Bomar C	2.50	6.00
MRRG Ryan Grant B	4.00	10.00
MRRRI Ray Rice B	5.00	12.00
MRSG Shonn Greene C	4.00	10.00
MRSJ Steven Jackson A	4.00	10.00
MRSM Stephen McGee C	2.50	6.00
MRSM2 Santana Moss B	4.00	10.00
MRSS1 Steve Smith B	4.00	10.00
MRSS2 Steve Smith USC B	4.00	10.00
MRTJ Tyson Jackson C	2.00	5.00
MRTJO Thomas Jones A	4.00	10.00

2009 Topps Mayo Rip Cards Ripped

PRICED WITH CLEANLY RIPPED BACKS

RC1 Drew Brees	3.00	8.00
RC2 Jay Cutler	3.00	8.00
RC3 Philip Rivers	3.00	8.00
RC4 Peyton Manning	5.00	12.00
RC5 Tom Brady	5.00	12.00
RC6 Donovan McNabb	3.00	8.00
RC7 Tony Romo	5.00	12.00
RC8 Eli Manning	3.00	8.00
RC9 Ben Roethlisberger	3.00	8.00
RC10 Matt Ryan	3.00	8.00
RC11 Adrian Peterson	5.00	12.00
RC12 Clinton Portis	2.50	6.00
RC13 LaDainian Tomlinson	3.00	8.00
RC14 Steven Jackson	2.50	6.00
RC15 Brian Westbrook	2.50	6.00
RC16 Michael Turner	2.50	6.00
RC17 Andre Johnson	2.50	6.00
RC18 Larry Fitzgerald	3.00	8.00
RC19 Steve Smith	2.50	6.00
RC20 Calvin Johnson	3.00	8.00
RC21 Brandon Marshall	2.50	6.00
RC22 Reggie Wayne	2.50	6.00
RC23 Terrell Owens	3.00	8.00
RC24 Matthew Stafford	5.00	12.00
RC25 Mark Sanchez	3.00	8.00
RC26 Josh Freeman	2.00	5.00
RC27 Knowshon Moreno	1.00	2.50
RC28 Chris Wells	1.50	4.00
RC29 Michael Crabtree	2.00	5.00
RC30 Jeremy Maclin	1.50	4.00

2009 Topps Mayo Rip Cards Unripped

STATED ODDS 1:192 HOB

RC1 Drew Brees	25.00	60.00
RC2 Jay Cutler	25.00	60.00
RC3 Philip Rivers	25.00	60.00
RC4 Peyton Manning	40.00	80.00
RC5 Tom Brady	40.00	80.00
RC6 Donovan McNabb	25.00	60.00
RC7 Tony Romo	40.00	80.00
RC8 Eli Manning	25.00	60.00
RC9 Ben Roethlisberger	40.00	80.00
RC10 Matt Ryan	25.00	60.00
RC11 Adrian Peterson	40.00	80.00
RC12 Clinton Portis	20.00	50.00
RC13 LaDainian Tomlinson	25.00	60.00
RC14 Steven Jackson	20.00	50.00
RC15 Brian Westbrook	20.00	50.00
RC16 Michael Turner	20.00	50.00
RC17 Andre Johnson	20.00	50.00
RC18 Larry Fitzgerald	25.00	60.00
RC19 Steve Smith	20.00	50.00
RC20 Calvin Johnson	25.00	60.00
RC21 Brandon Marshall	20.00	50.00
RC22 Reggie Wayne	20.00	50.00
RC23 Terrell Owens	25.00	60.00
RC24 Matthew Stafford	25.00	60.00
RC25 Mark Sanchez	40.00	80.00
RC26 Josh Freeman	20.00	50.00
RC27 Knowshon Moreno	10.00	25.00
RC28 Chris Wells	15.00	40.00
RC29 Michael Crabtree	20.00	50.00
RC30 Jeremy Maclin	15.00	40.00

2009 Topps Mayo Stamp Relics

STATED ODDS 1:985

S1 1492 Landing of Columbus	15.00	40.00
S2 1901 East Express	15.00	40.00
S3 1898 Farming in the West	15.00	40.00
S4 Documentary Series of 1898	15.00	40.00
S5 1492 Columbus in Sight of Land	15.00	40.00

2009 Topps Mayo United States Governors

STATED ODDS 1:12 HOB

USG1 Bob Riley	1.00	2.50
USG2 Sean Parnell	1.00	2.50
USG3 Jan Brewer	1.00	2.50
USG4 Michael Dale Beebe	1.00	2.50
USG5 Arnold Schwarzenegger	1.00	2.50
USG6 Bill Ritter Jr.	1.00	2.50
USG7 M. Jodi Rell	1.00	2.50
USG8 Jack Markell	1.00	2.50
USG9 Charles Joseph Crist Jr.	1.00	2.50
USG10 Sonny Perdue	1.00	2.50
USG11 Linda Lingle	1.00	2.50
USG12 Butch Otter	1.00	2.50
USG13 Pat Quinn	1.00	2.50
USG14 Mitch Daniels	1.00	2.50
USG15 Chet Culver	1.00	2.50
USG16 Mark Parkinson	1.00	2.50
USG17 Steven L. Beshear	1.00	2.50
USG18 Bobby Jindal	1.00	2.50
USG19 John Elias Baldacci	1.00	2.50
USG20 Martin Joseph O'Malley	1.00	2.50
USG21 Deval Laurdine Patrick	1.00	2.50
USG22 Jennifer M. Granholm	1.00	2.50
USG23 Timothy Pawlenty	1.00	2.50
USG24 Haley Barbour	1.00	2.50
USG25 Jay Nixon	1.00	2.50
USG26 Brian Schweitzer	1.00	2.50
USG27 Dave Heineman	1.00	2.50
USG28 Jim Gibbons	1.00	2.50
USG29 John Lynch	1.00	2.50
USG30 Jon Stevens Corzine	1.00	2.50
USG31 Bill Richardson	1.00	2.50
USG32 David A. Paterson	1.00	2.50
USG33 Beverly Perdue	1.00	2.50
USG34 John Hoeven	1.00	2.50
USG35 Ted Strickland	1.00	2.50
USG36 Brad Henry	1.00	2.50
USG37 Ted Kulongoski	1.00	2.50
USG38 Edward G. Rendell	1.00	2.50
USG39 Donald L. Carcieri	1.00	2.50
USG40 Mark Sanford, Jr.	1.00	2.50
USG41 M. Michael Rounds	1.00	2.50
USG42 Phil Bredesen	1.00	2.50
USG43 Rick Perry	1.00	2.50
USG44 Gary Herbert	1.00	2.50
USG45 James H. Douglas	1.00	2.50
USG46 Tim Kaine	1.00	2.50
USG47 Christine Gregoire	1.00	2.50
USG48 Joe Manchin III	1.00	2.50
USG49 Jim Doyle	1.00	2.50
USG50 Dave Freudenthal	1.00	2.50

2009 Topps Mayo World's Fair Attractions

COMPLETE SET (14)	8.00	20.00
STATED ODDS 1:12 HOB		
WF1 Ferris Wheel	.75	2.00
WF2 1893 Chicago World's Fair	.75	2.00
WF3 Court of Honor and the Grand Basin	.75	2.00
WF4 Buffalo Bill	.75	2.00
WF5 The White City	.75	2.00
WF6 Thomas Edison inventor	.75	2.00
WF7 Idaho Building	.75	2.00
WF8 John Bull Locomotive	.75	2.00
WF9 Nikola Tesla engineer	.75	2.00
WF10 Viking	.75	2.00
WF11 Eadweard Muybridge	.75	2.00
WF12 Hamburger	.75	2.00
WF13 Scott Joplin	.75	2.00
WF14 Frederick Law Olmstead	.75	2.00

2009 Topps National Chicle

COMP.SET w/o SP's (173)	40.00	80.00
SP STATED ODDS 1:6		
BASE CARDS #59, 99, 191 NOT ISSUED		
1 Maurice Jones-Drew	.25	.60
2 Nnamdi Asomugha	.25	.60
3 Asante Samuel	.20	.50
4 Vontae Davis RC	.75	2.00
5 Brandon Jacobs	.25	.60
6 Malcolm Jenkins RC	.75	2.00
7 Mario Williams	.25	.60
8 Julius Peppers	.25	.60
9 Aaron Maybin RC	.60	1.50
10 Matt Forte	.30	.75
11 Tyson Jackson RC	.60	1.50
12 Justin Tuck	.25	.60
13 Jared Allen	.30	.75
14 Brian Orakpo RC	.75	2.00
15 Reggie Bush	.30	.75
16 DeMarcus Ware	.25	.60
17 Kris Jenkins	.20	.50
18 B.J. Raji RC	.75	2.00
19 Lance Briggs	.25	.60
20 Drew Brees	.30	.75
21 Jon Beason	.20	.50
22 Johnny Knox SP RC	4.00	10.00
23 Aaron Curry RC	.75	2.00
24 James Harrison SP	3.00	8.00
25 Anquan Boldin	.25	.60
26 Clay Matthews SP RC	6.00	15.00
27 Brian Cushing RC	.75	2.00
28 Joey Porter	.25	.60
29 Patrick Willis	.25	.60
30 Adrian Peterson	.50	1.25
31 Jason Smith RC	.60	1.50
32 Nate Davis RC	.60	1.50
33 Josh Freeman SP RC	4.00	10.00
34 Matt Cassel	.25	.60
35 Ronnie Brown	.25	.60
36 Dan Marino	1.00	2.50
37 Matthew Stafford RC	4.00	10.00
38 Matt Hasselbeck	.25	.60
39 Brady Quinn	.25	.60
40 LaDainian Tomlinson	.30	.75
41 John Elway SP	5.00	12.00
42 JaMarcus Russell	.20	.50
43 Joe Namath	.60	1.50
44 Terry Bradshaw	.60	1.50
45 Ryan Grant	.25	.60
46 Joe Montana	1.00	2.50
47 Dan Marino SP	6.00	15.00
48 Troy Aikman	.60	1.50
49 Stephen McGee RC	.75	2.00
50 Steven Jackson	.25	.60
51 Trent Edwards	.20	.50
52 Mark Sanchez RC	2.50	6.00
53 David Garrard	.25	.60
54 Chad Pennington SP	2.50	6.00
55 Kurt Warner	.30	.75
56 Vince Young	.25	.60
57 Jason Campbell	.20	.50
58 Shonn Greene RC	1.25	3.00
60 DeAngelo Williams	.30	.75
61 Tim Hightower	.20	.50
62 Michael Turner	.20	.50
63 Larry Johnson	.25	.60
64 Jamal Lewis	.25	.60
65 Donovan McNabb	.30	.75
66 Cedric Peerman SP	2.50	6.00
67 Willis McGahee	.25	.60
68 Mike Goodson	.30	.75
69 Donald Brown SP RC	2.50	6.00
70 Patrick Turner RC	.60	1.50
71 LenDale White	.25	.60
72 Jerious Norwood SP	2.50	6.00
73 Barry Sanders SP	5.00	12.00
74 Felix Jones SP	3.00	8.00
75 Jay Cutler	.30	.75
76 Rashard Mendenhall	.25	.60
77 Ray Rice	.30	.75
78 Darren Sproles	.25	.60
79 Jim Brown	.60	1.50
80 Larry Fitzgerald	.30	.75
81 Tony Dorsett	.50	1.25
82 Fred Taylor	.25	.60
83 Andre Brown RC	.50	1.25
84 Chris Wells RC	1.25	3.00
85 Matt Schaub	.25	.60
86 Marshawn Lynch	.25	.60
87 Jamaal Charles	.30	.75
88 Chester Taylor	.20	.50
89 Pierre Thomas	.25	.60
90 Andre Johnson	.25	.60
91 LeSean McCoy RC	1.50	4.00
92 Willie Parker	.20	.50
93 Julius Jones	.20	.50
94 Troy Polamalu	.30	.75
95 Eli Manning	.30	.75
96 Ed Reed SP	3.00	8.00
97 Brian Dawkins	.25	.60
98 Tony Gonzalez	.25	.60
100 Michael Vick	.40	1.00
101 Antonio Gates	.25	.60
102 Greg Olsen	.20	.50
103 Tony Scheffler	.20	.50
104 Chris Cooley	.20	.50
105 Ben Roethlisberger	.30	.75
106 Dustin Keller SP	2.00	5.00
107 Shawn Nelson RC	.60	1.50

108 Travis Beckum RC	.60	1.50
109 Dallas Clark	.25	.60
110 Chris Johnson	.30	.75
111 John Carlson	.25	.60
112 Chase Coffman RC	.60	1.50
113 James Casey RC	.60	1.50
114 Kellen Winslow Jr.	.25	.60
115 Joe Flacco	.30	.75
116 Jared Cook SP RC	2.50	6.00
117 Michael Jenkins	.20	.50
118 Mike Thomas RC	.75	2.00
119 Ted Ginn	.25	.60
120 Reggie Wayne	.25	.60
121 Percy Harvin RC	1.25	3.00
122 Hakeem Nicks RC	1.25	3.00
123 Mike Wallace RC	1.50	4.00
124 T.J. Houshmandzadeh	.25	.60
125 Marques Colston	.25	.60
126 Deion Branch	.25	.60
127 Derrick Mason	.25	.60
128 Brian Westbrook	.25	.60
129 Roscoe Parrish	.20	.50
130 Philip Rivers	.30	.75
131 Brian Robiskie RC	.75	2.00
132 Ramses Barden RC	.50	1.25
133 Darrius Heyward-Bey RC	.75	2.00
134 Jeremy Maclin SP RC	3.00	8.00
135 Kevin Smith	.25	.60
136 Devery Henderson SP	2.00	5.00
137 Steve Smith USC	.25	.60
138 Donnie Avery	.25	.60
139 Santonio Holmes	.25	.60
140 Matt Ryan	.30	.75
141 Clinton Portis	.25	.60
142 Manuel Johnson RC	.60	1.50
143 Austin Collie RC	.75	2.00
144 Jarett Dillard RC	.75	2.00
145 Terrell Owens	.30	.75
146 Braylon Edwards	.25	.60
147 Chris Chambers	.25	.60
148 Brian Hartline RC	.75	2.00
149 Louis Murphy RC	.75	2.00
150 Frank Gore	.25	.60
151 Michael Crabtree RC	1.50	4.00
152 Jerry Rice	.75	2.00
153 Torry Holt SP	2.50	6.00
154 Justin Gage	.20	.50
155 Dwayne Bowe	.25	.60
156 Juaquin Iglesias RC	.60	1.50
157 Mohamed Massaquoi RC	.60	1.50
158 Kevin Walter	.25	.60
159 Isaac Bruce	.25	.60
160 Tony Romo	.50	1.25
161 Donald Driver	.25	.60
162 Mark Clayton	.20	.50
163 Laveranues Coles	.20	.50
164 Roy Williams WR	.25	.60
165 Wes Welker	.30	.75
166 Bobby Engram	.20	.50
167 Joey Galloway	.25	.60
168 Brooks Foster SP RC	1.50	4.00
169 Brandon Tate RC	.75	2.00
170 Calvin Johnson	.30	.75
171 Jerricho Cotchery	.25	.60
172 DeSean Jackson	.25	.60
173 Hines Ward	.25	.60
174 Deon Butler RC	.60	1.50
175 Roddy White	.25	.60
176 Santana Moss	.25	.60
177 Lee Evans SP	2.50	6.00
178 Andre Caldwell	.20	.50
179 Brandon Marshall	.25	.60
180 Aaron Rodgers	.60	1.50
181 Derrick Williams SP RC	2.00	5.00
182 Devin Hester	.30	.75
183 Anthony Gonzalez	.20	.50
184 Bernard Berrian SP	2.50	6.00
185 Vincent Jackson	.25	.60
186 Antonio Bryant	.20	.50
187 Kenny Britt RC	1.00	2.50
188 Thomas Jones	.25	.60
189 Eddie Royal	.25	.60
190 Peyton Manning SP	5.00	12.00
192 Knowshon Moreno RC	.75	2.00
193 Marion Barber	.25	.60
194 Chad Ochocinco SP	2.50	6.00
195 Jason Witten	.30	.75
196 Greg Jennings	.30	.75
197 Joseph Addai	.30	.75
198 Steve Smith	.25	.60
199 Tom Brady	.50	1.25
200 Randy Moss	.30	.75

2009 Topps National Chicle Mini

*VETS: 1.2X TO 3X BASIC CARDS
*RETIRED: 1X TO 2.5X BASIC CARDS
*VETS: .1X TO .3X BASIC SP
*RETIRED: .1X TO .3X BASIC SP
*ROOKIES: .5X TO 1.2X BASIC RC
*ROOKIES: .15X TO .4X BASIC SP RC
ONE MINI PER HOBBY PACK

2009 Topps National Chicle Mini Bazooka Back

*VETS: 2.5X TO 6X BASIC CARDS
*RETIRED: 2X TO 5X BASIC CARDS
*VETS: .25X TO .6X BASIC SP
*RETIRED: .3X TO .8X BASIC SP
*ROOKIES: .8X TO 2X BASIC RC
*ROOKIES: .25X TO .6X BASIC SP RC
STATED ODDS 1:12

2009 Topps National Chicle Mini Chicle Back

*VETS: 2X TO 5X BASIC CARDS
*VETS: .2X TO .5X BASIC SP
*RETIRED: 1.4X TO 4X BASIC CARDS
*RETIRED: .25X TO .6X BASIC SP
*ROOKIES: .6X TO 1.5X BASIC RC
*ROOKIES: .2X TO .5X BASIC SP RC
STATED ODDS 1:6

2009 Topps National Chicle Mini Topps Back

*VETS: 8X TO 20X BASIC CARDS
*VETS: .8X TO 2X BASIC SP
*RETIRED: 6X TO 15X BASIC CARDS
*RETIRED: 1X TO 2.5X BASIC SP
*ROOKIES: 2.5X TO 6X BASIC RC
*ROOKIES: .8X TO 2X BASIC SP RC
TOPPS/UMBRELLA BACK/25 ODDS 1:92 HOB

2009 Topps National Chicle Autographs

GROUP A ODDS 1:437 HOB
GROUP B ODDS 1:142 HOB
GROUP C ODDS 1:60 HOB
GROUP D ODDS 1:56 HOB
GROUP E ODDS 1:25 HOB

MCAMG Mike Goodson D	5.00	12.00
NCAAB Andre Brown E	3.00	8.00
NCAAC Aaron Curry C	5.00	12.00
NCAACB Drew Brees A	40.00	80.00
NCAACO Austin Collie E	8.00	20.00
NCAAP Adrian Peterson A	100.00	200.00
NCABB Bernard Berrian B	8.00	20.00
NCABF Brett Favre A	200.00	300.00
NCABH Brian Hartline D	5.00	12.00
NCABM Brandon Marshall B	8.00	20.00
NCABO Brian Orakpo D	5.00	12.00
NCABS Barry Sanders A	125.00	200.00
NCABT Brandon Tate C	6.00	15.00
NCACC Chase Coffman E	4.00	10.00
NCACW Chris Wells B	12.00	30.00
NCADBR Donald Brown A	12.00	30.00
NCADHB Darrius Heyward-Bey A		
NCADJ DeSean Jackson B	10.00	25.00
NCADM Darren McFadden A		
NCADMA Dan Marino A	125.00	200.00
NCADW Derrick Williams B	4.00	10.00
NCAGJ Greg Jennings B	10.00	25.00
NCAHN Hakeem Nicks C	8.00	20.00
NCAJA Joseph Addai A	10.00	25.00
NCAJB Jim Brown A	60.00	100.00
NCAJC1 Jamaal Charles C	8.00	20.00
NCAJC2 Jared Cook E	5.00	12.00
NCAJC3 Jay Cutler A	60.00	100.00
NCAJD Jarett Dillard E	4.00	10.00
NCAJE John Elway A	100.00	175.00
NCAJF Joe Flacco B	20.00	40.00
NCAJF Josh Freeman A	15.00	40.00
NCAJI Juaquin Iglesias D	4.00	10.00
NCAJM1 Jeremy Maclin A	25.00	50.00
NCAJM2 Joe Montana A	125.00	200.00
NCAJN Joe Namath A	75.00	150.00
NCAJR Jerry Rice A	125.00	200.00
NCAJS Jason Smith C	4.00	10.00
NCAKM Knowshon Moreno A	30.00	60.00
NCALJ Larry Johnson A	10.00	25.00
NCALM LeSean McCoy B	15.00	40.00
NCAMC Michael Crabtree A	40.00	80.00
NCAMJ Michael Jenkins E	4.00	10.00
NCAMS Matthew Stafford A	60.00	120.00
NCAMSA Mark Sanchez A	50.00	100.00
NCAMW Mike Wallace A	25.00	50.00
NCAND Nate Davis D	4.00	10.00
NCAPH Percy Harvin C	20.00	50.00
NCAPT Patrick Turner E	4.00	10.00
NCAPW Pat White B	5.00	12.00
NCARB Ramses Barden E	3.00	8.00
NCARR Ray Rice C	15.00	30.00
NCARW Reggie Wayne A	15.00	30.00
NCASG Shonn Greene C	15.00	30.00
NCASM Stephen McGee B	6.00	15.00
NCATA Troy Aikman A	60.00	120.00
NCATB1 Travis Beckum D	4.00	10.00
NCATB2 Terry Bradshaw A	60.00	100.00
NCATD Tony Dorsett A	25.00	50.00
NCATJ Tyson Jackson C	4.00	10.00
NCAWW Wes Welker C	20.00	40.00

2009 Topps National Chicle Cabinet

ONE CABINET PER HOBBY BOX
*ARTIST SIGN/50: 2X TO 5X BASIC CABINET

NCCC1 Peyton Manning	5.00	12.00
NCCC2 Andre Johnson	2.50	6.00
NCCC3 Clinton Portis	2.50	6.00
NCCC4 Jim Brown	4.00	10.00
NCCC5 Barry Sanders	5.00	12.00
NCCC6 Joe Namath	4.00	10.00
NCCC7 Tony Dorsett	3.00	8.00
NCCC8 Chris Wells	2.50	6.00
NCCC9 Donald Brown	1.50	4.00
NCCC10 Knowshon Moreno	1.50	4.00
NCCC11 Chris Johnson	3.00	8.00
NCCC12 Santonio Holmes	2.50	6.00
NCCC13 DeSean Jackson	2.50	6.00
NCCC14 Chad Ochocinco	2.50	6.00
NCCC15 Felix Jones	3.00	8.00
NCCC16 Matthew Stafford	8.00	20.00
NCCC17 Greg Jennings	3.00	8.00
NCCC18 Eli Manning	3.00	8.00
NCCC19 Terry Bradshaw	4.00	10.00
NCCC20 Aaron Rodgers	6.00	15.00
NCCC21 Michael Turner	2.50	6.00
NCCC22 Brian Westbrook	2.50	6.00
NCCC23 Joe Flacco	3.00	8.00
NCCC24 Tom Brady	5.00	12.00
NCCC25 Jay Cutler	3.00	8.00

2009 Topps National Chicle Dual Autographs

DUAL AUTO/20-25 ODDS 1:1690 HOB

CB Matt Cassel Dwayne Bowe	25.00	50.00
FP Brett Favre Adrian Peterson	250.00	400.00
MM Jeremy Maclin LeSean McCoy	30.00	80.00
MS Matthew Stafford Michael Crabtree	60.00	120.00
MW Peyton Manning Reggie Wayne	90.00	150.00
MWE Knowshon Moreno Chris Wells	25.00	60.00
PH Adrian Peterson Percy Harvin	125.00	250.00
SC Mark Sanchez Matt Cassel	40.00	100.00
SM Matthew Stafford Knowshon Moreno	50.00	100.00
SS Matthew Stafford Mark Sanchez	75.00	150.00

2009 Topps National Chicle Dual Relics

DUAL RELIC/25 ODDS 1:1150 HOB

BC Drew Brees Marques Colston	15.00	30.00
BW Ronnie Brown Pat White		
FB Larry Fitzgerald Anquan Boldin	10.00	25.00
ME Dan Marino John Elway	40.00	80.00
MN Eli Manning Hakeem Nicks	10.00	25.00
MP Santana Moss Clinton Portis	8.00	20.00
MW Peyton Manning Reggie Wayne	20.00	40.00
PH Adrian Peterson Percy Harvin	20.00	40.00
RB Tony Romo Marion Barber	15.00	40.00
RG Philip Rivers Antonio Gates	10.00	25.00
RJ Aaron Rodgers Greg Jennings	15.00	40.00
SG Mark Sanchez Shonn Greene	15.00	40.00
SJ Matthew Stafford Calvin Johnson	12.00	30.00
SW Steve Smith DeAngelo Williams	8.00	20.00
WM Brian Westbrook LeSean McCoy	8.00	20.00

2009 Topps National Chicle Era Icons

COMPLETE SET (14)	5.00	12.00
STATED ODDS 1:3 HOB		
EI1 Amelia Earhart	.50	1.25
EI2 Pennsylvania Railroad	.50	1.25
EI3 Caroline Mikkelson	.50	1.25
EI4 Sir Watson-Watt	.50	1.25
EI5 Boulder Dam	.50	1.25
EI6 Omaha (race horse)	.50	1.25
EI7 Franklin D. Roosevelt	.50	1.25
EI8 Fort Knox	.50	1.25
EI9 Danno O'Mahoney	.50	1.25
EI10 Helen Jacobs	.50	1.25
EI11 Roller Derby	.50	1.25
EI12 Sir Malcolm Campbell	.50	1.25
EI13 Porgy and Bess	.50	1.25
EI14 China Clipper	.50	1.25

2009 Topps National Chicle Era Icons Relics

ICON RELIC ODDS 1:139 HOB

AE Amelia Earhart Stamp	10.00	25.00
BD Boulder Dam Stamp	8.00	20.00
CL Charles Lindbergh Stamp	8.00	20.00
YS Yankee Stadium Stamp (Babe Ruth stamp)	12.00	30.00
FDR Franklin D. Roosevelt Stamp	8.00	20.00
FDR2 Franklin D. Roosevelt A Shirt	20.00	40.00

2009 Topps National Chicle Greatest Thrills

COMPLETE SET (10)	10.00	25.00
STATED ODDS 1:12 HOB		
GT1 Santonio Holmes	1.25	3.00
GT2 David Tyree	.75	2.00
GT3 Eli Manning	1.25	3.00
GT4 Kurt Warner	1.25	3.00
GT5 Terry Bradshaw	2.00	5.00
GT6 James Harrison	1.50	4.00
GT7 Tom Brady	2.00	5.00
GT8 John Elway	2.00	5.00
GT9 Willie Parker	1.00	2.50
GT10 Adam Vinatieri	1.00	2.50

2009 Topps National Chicle Greats of the Gridiron

STATED ODDS 1:24 HOB

GG1 Troy Aikman	2.50	6.00
GG2 Jerry Rice	3.00	8.00
GG3 Joe Montana	4.00	10.00
GG4 Joe Namath	2.50	6.00
GG5 Barry Sanders	3.00	8.00
GG6 Terry Bradshaw	2.50	6.00
GG7 John Elway	3.00	8.00
GG8 Brett Favre	5.00	12.00
GG9 Jim Brown	2.50	6.00
GG10 Tony Dorsett	2.00	5.00

2009 Topps National Chicle Relics

GROUP A ODDS 1:1285 HOB
GROUP B ODDS 1:25 HOB

NCRAB Andre Brown B	2.00	5.00
NCRAC Aaron Curry B	2.00	5.00
NCRAR Aaron Rodgers B	8.00	20.00
NCRBM Brandon Marshall B	3.00	8.00
NCRBP Brandon Pettigrew B	2.00	5.00
NCRBR Brian Robiskie B	2.00	5.00
NCRBS Barry Sanders A	12.00	30.00
NCRCW Chris Wells B	3.00	8.00
NCRDA Donnie Avery B	3.00	8.00
NCRDB1 Drew Brees B	4.00	10.00
NCRDB2 Deon Butler B	1.50	4.00
NCRDBR Donald Brown B	2.00	5.00
NCRDC Dallas Clark B	3.00	8.00
NCRDEW DeAngelo Williams B	4.00	10.00
NCRDHB Darrius Heyward-Bey B	2.00	5.00
NCRDM1 Dan Marino A	15.00	40.00
NCRDM2 Donovan McNabb B	4.00	10.00
NCRDMC Darren McFadden B	4.00	10.00
NCRDW Derrick Williams B	1.50	4.00
NCRFJ Felix Jones B	4.00	10.00
NCRHN Hakeem Nicks B	3.00	8.00
NCRJE John Elway A	12.00	30.00
NCRJF Josh Freeman B	4.00	10.00
NCRJI Juaquin Iglesias B	2.50	6.00
NCRJM Jeremy Maclin B	3.00	8.00
NCRJMO Joe Montana A	15.00	40.00
NCRJR Jerry Rice B	6.00	15.00
NCRJS Jason Smith B	2.00	5.00
NCRKB Kenny Britt B	2.50	6.00
NCRKM Knowshon Moreno B	2.00	5.00
NCRLE Lee Evans B	3.00	8.00
NCRLM LeSean McCoy B	4.00	10.00
NCRMC Michael Crabtree B	4.00	10.00
NCRMF Matt Forte B	4.00	10.00
NCRMJD Maurice Jones-Drew B	3.00	8.00
NCRMM Mohamed Massaquoi B	1.50	4.00
NCRMS Matthew Stafford B	10.00	25.00
NCRMSA Mark Sanchez B	6.00	15.00
NCRMT Mike Thomas B	2.00	5.00
NCRMW Mike Wallace B	4.00	10.00
NCRND Nate Davis B	1.50	4.00
NCRPH Percy Harvin B	3.00	8.00
NCRPT Patrick Turner B	2.00	5.00
NCRPW Pat White B	2.00	5.00
NCRRB Ramses Barden B	1.25	3.00
NCRRM Randy Moss B	5.00	12.00
NCRRR Ray Rice B	4.00	10.00
NCRSG Shonn Greene B	3.00	8.00
NCRSM Stephen McGee B	2.50	6.00
NCRSMO Santana Moss B	3.00	8.00
NCRTA Troy Aikman A	10.00	25.00
NCRTB Tom Brady B	6.00	15.00
NCRTBR Terry Bradshaw A	10.00	25.00
NCRTJ Tyson Jackson B	1.50	4.00

2009 Topps National Chicle Stars of the Gridiron

COMPLETE SET (10)	8.00	20.00
STATED ODDS 1:6 HOB		
SG1 Tom Brady	1.50	4.00
SG2 Andre Johnson	.75	2.00
SG3 Adrian Peterson	1.50	4.00
SG4 LaDainian Tomlinson	1.00	2.50
SG5 Brian Westbrook	.75	2.00
SG6 Randy Moss	1.00	2.50
SG7 Clinton Portis	.75	2.00
SG8 Steven Jackson	.75	2.00
SG9 Larry Fitzgerald	1.00	2.50
SG10 Peyton Manning	1.50	4.00

2009 Topps National Chicle Youngsters of the Gridiron

COMPLETE SET (20)	20.00	50.00
STATED ODDS 1:4 HOB		
YG1 Mark Sanchez	2.50	6.00
YG2 Chris Johnson	1.00	2.50
YG3 Pat White	.75	2.00
YG4 Steve Slaton	.75	2.00
YG5 Matthew Stafford	4.00	10.00
YG6 Eddie Royal	.75	2.00
YG7 LeSean McCoy	1.50	4.00
YG8 Hakeem Nicks	1.25	3.00
YG9 Kevin Smith	.75	2.00
YG10 Knowshon Moreno	.75	2.00
YG11 Matt Forte	1.00	2.50
YG12 Jeremy Maclin	1.25	3.00
YG13 Darren McFadden	1.00	2.50
YG14 Percy Harvin	1.25	3.00
YG15 Donald Brown	.75	2.00
YG16 Matt Ryan	1.00	2.50
YG17 Jonathan Stewart	.75	2.00
YG18 Chris Wells	1.25	3.00
YG19 Joe Flacco	1.00	2.50
YG20 Michael Crabtree	1.50	4.00

2006 Topps Paradigm

This 98-card set was released in April, 2007. The first 40 cards in this set feature a mix of active and retired greats while cards numbered 41-98 feature 2006 NFL rookies. Cards numbered 1-40 were issued to a stated print run of 169 serial numbered sets. The rookies are broken down into the following subsets; Cards with jersey swatches (41-59) issued to a stated print run of 249 serial numbered sets which were inserted at a stated rate of one in two; carrds with autographs (60-76) issued to a stated print run of 199 serial numbered sets which were inserted at a stated rate of one in three; and cards with both player-worn jersey swatches and autographs were issued to a stated print run of 99 serial numbered set which were inserted at a stated rate of one in eight. Cards numbered 61, 63, 66, 78 and 98 were never produced for this set.

1-40 PRINT RUN 169 SER.#'d SETS
JSY RC/249 STATED ODDS 1:2
JSY RC PRINT RUN 249 SER.#'d SETS
AU/199 RC STATED ODDS 1:3
AU/149 RC STATED ODDS 1:4
AUTO RC PRINT RUN 149-199
JSY AU/99 RC STATED ODDS 1:8
JSY AU RC PRINT RUN 99 SER.#'d SETS

1 Joe Namath	6.00	15.00
2 Dan Marino	10.00	25.00
3 Joe Montana	10.00	25.00
4 Terry Bradshaw	8.00	20.00
5 John Elway	8.00	20.00
6 Bart Starr	8.00	20.00
7 Barry Sanders	8.00	20.00
8 Emmitt Smith	10.00	25.00
9 Eric Dickerson	4.00	10.00
10 Earl Campbell	5.00	12.00
11 Jim Brown	6.00	15.00
12 Gale Sayers	6.00	15.00
13 Tony Dorsett	5.00	12.00
14 Jerry Rice	8.00	20.00
15 Brett Favre	10.00	25.00
16 Peyton Manning	8.00	20.00
17 Tom Brady	8.00	20.00
18 Michael Vick	5.00	12.00
19 Carson Palmer	5.00	12.00
20 Shaun Alexander	4.00	10.00
21 LaDainian Tomlinson	5.00	12.00
22 Larry Johnson	4.00	10.00
23 Frank Gore	5.00	12.00
24 Steve Smith	5.00	12.00
25 Chad Johnson	4.00	10.00
26 Johnny Unitas	8.00	20.00
27 Steve McNair	4.00	10.00
28 Donovan McNabb	5.00	12.00
29 Ben Roethlisberger	6.00	15.00
30 Tiki Barber	5.00	12.00
31 Corey Dillon	4.00	10.00
32 Edgerrin James	4.00	10.00
33 Clinton Portis	5.00	12.00
34 Tony Gonzalez	4.00	10.00
35 Jeremy Shockey	5.00	12.00
36 Marvin Harrison	5.00	12.00
37 Terrell Owens	5.00	12.00
38 Randy Moss	5.00	12.00
39 Torry Holt	4.00	10.00
40 Hines Ward	5.00	12.00
41 Kamerion Wimbley JSY RC	6.00	15.00
42 DeMeco Ryans JSY RC	6.00	15.00
43 Mathias Kiwanuka JSY RC	6.00	15.00
44 Ingle Martin JSY RC	5.00	12.00
45 Jerome Harrison JSY RC	6.00	15.00
46 Derek Hagan JSY RC	5.00	12.00
47 Joe Klopfenstein JSY RC	4.00	10.00
48 Willie Reid JSY RC	5.00	12.00
49 Devin Hester JSY RC	10.00	25.00
50 Tarvaris Jackson JSY RC	6.00	15.00
51 D.J. Shockley JSY RC	5.00	12.00
52 Brian Calhoun JSY RC	4.00	10.00
53 Anthony Fasano JSY RC	6.00	15.00
54 Hank Baskett JSY RC	6.00	15.00
55 Maurice Stovall JSY RC	4.00	10.00
56 Brad Smith JSY RC	6.00	15.00
57 Brandon Williams JSY RC	4.00	10.00
58 Travis Wilson JSY RC	4.00	10.00
59 Jason Avant JSY RC	4.00	10.00
60 Tye Hill AU/199 RC	5.00	12.00
62 Adam Jennings AU/199 RC	6.00	15.00
64 Cedric Humes AU/199 RC	5.00	12.00
65 P.J. Daniels AU/199 RC	5.00	12.00
67 David Thomas AU/199 RC	6.00	15.00
68 Dominique Byrd AU/199 RC	6.00	15.00
69 Quinton Ganther AU/199 RC	5.00	12.00
70 Ashton Youboty AU/199 RC	5.00	12.00
71 Bobby Carpenter AU/199 RC	5.00	12.00
72 Kellen Clemens AU/199 RC	6.00	15.00
73 Charlie Whitehurst AU/199 RC	8.00	20.00
74 Reggie McNeal AU/199 RC	6.00	15.00
75 Demetrius Williams AU/199 RC	6.00	15.00
76 Skyler Green AU/199 RC	5.00	12.00
77 Michael Huff AU/149 RC	8.00	20.00
79 Brodie Croyle AU/149 RC	10.00	25.00
80 Bruce Gradkowski AU/149 RC	10.00	25.00
81 Wali Lundy AU/149 RC	8.00	20.00
82 Jerious Norwood AU/149 RC	8.00	20.00
83 Mike Bell AU/99 RC	10.00	25.00
84 Marcedes Lewis AU/149 RC	10.00	25.00
85 Leonard Pope AU/149 RC	10.00	25.00
86 Chad Jackson AU/149 RC	6.00	15.00
87 Leon Washington AU/149 RC	8.00	20.00
88 Michael Robinson AU/149 RC	8.00	20.00
89 Mario Williams AU/149 RC	15.00	30.00
90 Joseph Addai AU/149 RC	10.00	25.00
91 Marques Colston AU/149 RC	20.00	50.00
92 Sinorice Moss AU/149 RC	10.00	25.00
93 Greg Jennings AU/149 RC	15.00	40.00
94 Matt Leinart JSY AU/99 RC	12.00	30.00
95 Vince Young JSY AU/99 RC	25.00	60.00
96 Sinorice Moss JSY AU/99	25.00	60.00
97 Reggie Bush JSY AU/99 RC	30.00	80.00
99 DeAngelo Williams JSY AU/99 RC	25.00	60.00
100 LenDale White JSY AU/99 RC	10.00	25.00
101 Santonio Holmes JSY AU/99 RC	15.00	40.00
102 Vernon Davis JSY AU/99 RC	15.00	40.00
103 A.J. Hawk JSY AU/99 RC	12.00	30.00

2006 Topps Paradigm Gold

*VETS 1-40: .8X TO 2X BASIC CARDS
VETS/25 STATED ODDS 1:8
VETERANS PRINT RUN 25 SER.#'d SETS
*JSY ROOK/25 #41-59: .5X TO 1.2X
ROOKIE JSY/25 ODDS 1:17
*AUTO ROOK/50: .5X TO 1.2X BASE AU/199
AUTO ROOKIE/50 ODDS 1:10-1:12
ROOKIE AUTO PRINT RUN 50

2006 Topps Paradigm Autographed NFL Logos

UNPRICED VETERAN 1/1 ODDS 1:825
UNPRICED ROOKIE 1/1 ODDS 1:298

2006 Topps Paradigm Autographed NFL Logos Dual

UNPRICED VETERAN 1/1 ODDS 1:1856
UNPRICED ROOKIE 1/1 ODDS 1:745

2006 Topps Paradigm Autographs

AUTO/149 STATED ODDS 1:11
STATED PRINT RUN 149 SER.#'d SETS
*GOLD/50: .6X TO 1.2X BASIC AUTO/149
GOLD/50 STATED ODDS 1:31
GOLD PRINT RUN 50 SER.#'d SETS

TPABS Barry Sanders	60.00	120.00
TPAJB Jim Brown	50.00	100.00
TPAJM Joe Montana	75.00	150.00
TPAJN Joe Namath	50.00	100.00

2006 Topps Paradigm Career Highs Triple Jersey Autographs

PASSING/RUSHING YARDS ODDS 1:5
RECEIVING YARDS ODDS 1:6
TOUCHDOWNS STATED ODDS 1:9
STATED PRINT RUN 99 UNLESS NOTED
*GOLD/25: .6X TO 1.2X BASIC INSERTS
GOLD PASSING YARDS/25 ODDS 1:19
GOLD RUSHING YARDS/25 ODDS 1:20
GOLD RECEIVING YARDS/25 ODDS 1:23

PBF Brett Favre	100.00	200.00
PBG Bruce Gradkowski	15.00	40.00
PDM Dan Marino/56	150.00	250.00
PEM Eli Manning	50.00	100.00
PJC Jay Cutler	40.00	100.00
PJE John Elway	75.00	150.00
PJK Jim Kelly	30.00	60.00
PJM Joe Montana	75.00	150.00
PJN Joe Namath	60.00	120.00
PML Matt Leinart	15.00	40.00
PMV Michael Vick	40.00	80.00
PPM Peyton Manning	75.00	150.00
PTA Troy Aikman	60.00	120.00
PTB Terry Bradshaw	75.00	150.00
PTBR Tom Brady	100.00	200.00
PTR Tony Romo	40.00	100.00
PVY Vince Young	30.00	80.00
RBG Paul Hornung	30.00	60.00
RBS Barry Sanders	75.00	150.00
RDW DeAngelo Williams	15.00	40.00
REC Earl Campbell	30.00	60.00
RED Eric Dickerson	30.00	60.00
RES Emmitt Smith	100.00	200.00
RFG Frank Gore	20.00	50.00
RJN Jerious Norwood	20.00	50.00
RLJ Larry Johnson	20.00	50.00
RLT LaDainian Tomlinson/62	30.00	80.00
RMF Marshall Faulk	30.00	60.00
RRB Reggie Bush	40.00	100.00
RSA Shaun Alexander	15.00	40.00
REAG Antonio Gates	15.00	30.00
RECJ Chad Johnson	20.00	40.00
REFB Fred Biletnikoff	30.00	60.00
REGJ Greg Jennings	30.00	60.00
REHB Hank Baskett	15.00	40.00
REJR Jerry Rice	75.00	150.00
RELJ Larry Johnson	20.00	50.00
RELT LaDainian Tomlinson/61	40.00	100.00
REMC Marques Colston	25.00	60.00
REMH Marvin Harrison	30.00	60.00
RERB Reggie Bush	40.00	100.00
RESS Steve Smith/93	30.00	60.00
RETIB Tim Brown	30.00	60.00
RMJD Maurice Drew	40.00	80.00
TDBS Barry Sanders	75.00	150.00
TDDM Dan Marino		
TDES Emmitt Smith/23	125.00	250.00
TDJR Jerry Rice	75.00	150.00
TDLJ Larry Johnson	20.00	50.00
TDMF Marshall Faulk	30.00	60.00
TDPM Peyton Manning	75.00	150.00
TDSA Shaun Alexander	15.00	40.00
TDTB Terry Bradshaw	75.00	150.00

2006 Topps Paradigm Dual Autograph Dual Patches

UNPRICED DUAL/10 ODDS 1:168
STATED PRINT RUN 10 SER.#'d SETS

2006 Topps Paradigm Dual Jersey Numbers Autographs

DUAL JSY AUTO/25 STATED ODDS 1:21
STATED PRINT RUN 25 SER.#'d SETS

JNABF Brett Favre	125.00	250.00
JNABS Barry Sanders	100.00	200.00
JNADM Dan Marino		
JNAES Emmitt Smith		
JNAJE John Elway	100.00	200.00
JNAJM Joe Montana	100.00	200.00
JNAJN Joe Namath	75.00	150.00
JNALM Laurence Maroney		
JNAML Matt Leinart	30.00	80.00
JNAPM Peyton Manning	100.00	200.00
JNARB Reggie Bush	75.00	150.00
JNASA Shaun Alexander	40.00	80.00
JNATB Terry Bradshaw	100.00	200.00
JNATBR Tom Brady	150.00	250.00
JNAVY Vince Young	75.00	150.00

2006 Topps Paradigm Dual Jerseys

SILVER/99 STATED ODDS 1:4
SILVER PRINT RUN 99 SER.#'d SETS
*GOLD/25: .5X TO 1.2X BASIC DUAL JSY/99
GOLD/25 STATED ODDS 1:16
GOLD PRINT RUN 25 SER.#'d SETS

TPBSA Barry Sanders	15.00	40.00
TPCJ Chad Johnson	5.00	12.00
TPCP Carson Palmer	6.00	15.00
TPDM Dan Marino	25.00	60.00
TPES Emmitt Smith	20.00	50.00
TPFG Frank Gore	6.00	15.00
TPJE John Elway	15.00	40.00
TPJM Joe Montana	20.00	50.00
TPJN Joe Namath	12.00	30.00
TPJR Jerry Rice	15.00	40.00
TPJS Jeremy Shockey	6.00	15.00
TPJU Johnny Unitas	20.00	50.00
TPLJ Larry Johnson	5.00	12.00
TPLT LaDainian Tomlinson	6.00	15.00
TPMH Marvin Harrison	6.00	15.00
TPMV Michael Vick	6.00	15.00
TPPM Peyton Manning	10.00	25.00
TPSM Steve McNair	5.00	12.00
TPSS Steve Smith	6.00	15.00
TPTBR Tom Brady	10.00	25.00

2006 Topps Paradigm Namesake Relics Autographs

UNPRICED SILVER STATED ODDS 1:47
SILVER STATED PRINT RUN 2-4
UNPRICED GOLD 1/1 ODDS 1:115
GOLD STATED PRINT RUN 1

2006 Topps Paradigm Patch Frame Autographs

UNPRICED FRAMED AUTO/5 ODDS 1:190
STATED PRINT RUN 5 SER.#'d SETS

2006 Topps Paradigm Rookie Dual Jersey Autographs

SILVER/149 STATED ODDS 1:9
SILVER/249/250 STATED ODDS 1:6
SILVER/299 STATED ODDS 1:3
*GOLD/50: .6X TO 1.2X BASIC INSERTS
GOLD/50 STATED ODDS 1:16-1:28
GOLD PRINT RUN 50 SER.#'d SETS

AF Anthony Fasano/299	8.00	20.00
BG Bruce Gradkowski/249	8.00	20.00
BS Brad Smith/299	8.00	20.00
BW Brandon Williams/299	5.00	12.00
CJ Chad Jackson/249	5.00	12.00
CW Charlie Whitehurst/299	8.00	20.00
DH Devin Hester/299	15.00	40.00
DW Demetrius Williams/299	6.00	15.00
GJ Greg Jennings/149	25.00	50.00
HB Hank Baskett/250	8.00	20.00
JA Jason Avant/299	5.00	12.00
JN Jerious Norwood/249	6.00	15.00
MB Mike Bell/249	8.00	20.00
MC Marques Colston/149	25.00	60.00
ML Marcedes Lewis/249	8.00	20.00
MS Maurice Stovall/299	5.00	12.00
MW Mario Williams/149	8.00	20.00
SM Sinorice Moss/149	8.00	20.00
TJ Tarvaris Jackson/299	10.00	25.00
WL Wali Lundy/249	6.00	15.00
AD Joseph Addai/149	8.00	20.00
CA Brian Calhoun/299	5.00	12.00
MJD Maurice Drew/149	30.00	80.00

2007 Topps Performance

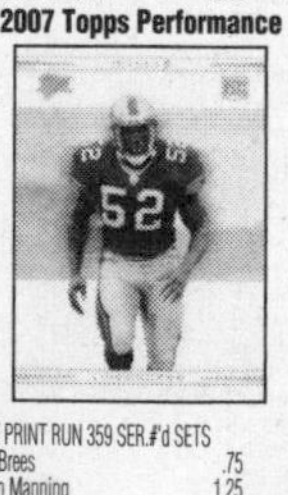

ROOKIE PRINT RUN 359 SER.#'d SETS

1 Drew Brees	.75	2.00
2 Peyton Manning	1.25	3.00
3 Marc Bulger	.60	1.50
4 Jon Kitna	.50	1.25
5 Carson Palmer	.60	1.50
6 Brett Favre	1.50	4.00
7 Tom Brady	1.25	3.00
8 Ben Roethlisberger	.75	2.00
9 Philip Rivers	.75	2.00
10 Chad Pennington	.60	1.50
11 Eli Manning	.75	2.00
12 Vince Young	.60	1.50
13 Steve McNair	.60	1.50
14 Tony Romo	1.00	2.50
15 Kurt Warner	.60	1.50
16 Kyle Boller	.50	1.25
17 Donovan McNabb	.75	2.00
18 J.P. Losman	.50	1.25
19 Matt Hasselbeck	.60	1.50
20 Joey Harrington	.60	1.50
21 Damon Huard	.60	1.50
22 David Garrard	.60	1.50
23 Trent Green	.60	1.50
24 Jeff Garcia	.60	1.50
25 Jason Campbell	.60	1.50
26 Jay Cutler	.75	2.00
27 Derek Anderson	.50	1.25
28 Brian Griese	.60	1.50
29 Matt Schaub	.60	1.50
30 Daunte Culpepper	.60	1.50
31 Joseph Addai	.60	1.50
32 Maurice Jones-Drew	.75	2.00
33 Steven Jackson	.75	2.00
34 Brandon Jacobs	.60	1.50
35 Willie Parker	.60	1.50
36 LaDainian Tomlinson	.75	2.00
37 Thomas Jones	.60	1.50
38 Derrick Ward	.60	1.50
39 Cedric Benson	.60	1.50
40 Willis McGahee	.60	1.50
41 Chester Taylor	.50	1.25
42 Marion Barber	.75	2.00
43 Frank Gore	.75	2.00
44 DeShaun Foster	.60	1.50
45 Brian Westbrook	.60	1.50
46 Edgerrin James	.60	1.50
47 Shaun Alexander	.60	1.50
48 Warrick Dunn	.60	1.50
49 LenDale White	.60	1.50
50 Justin Fargas	.50	1.25
51 Larry Johnson	.50	1.25
52 Ronnie Brown	.60	1.50
53 Fred Taylor	.60	1.50
54 Clinton Portis	.60	1.50
55 Travis Henry	.60	1.50
56 Jamal Lewis	.60	1.50
57 LaMont Jordan	.60	1.50
58 Earnest Graham	.60	1.50
59 Kenny Watson	.60	1.50
60 Reggie Bush	.75	2.00
61 Reggie Wayne	.60	1.50
62 Torry Holt	.60	1.50
63 Roy Williams WR	.60	1.50
64 Chad Johnson	.60	1.50
65 T.J. Houshmandzadeh	.60	1.50
66 Randy Moss	.75	2.00
67 Antwaan Randle El	.50	1.25
68 Jerricho Cotchery	.60	1.50
69 Plaxico Burress	.60	1.50
70 Bernard Berrian	.50	1.25
71 Derrick Mason	.60	1.50
72 Terrell Owens	.75	2.00
73 Steve Smith	.60	1.50
74 Kevin Curtis	.50	1.25
75 Shaun McDonald	.50	1.25
76 Larry Fitzgerald	.75	2.00
77 Santonio Holmes	.60	1.50
78 Roddy White	.60	1.50
79 Chris Chambers	.60	1.50
80 Joey Galloway	.60	1.50
81 Brandon Marshall	.60	1.50
82 Braylon Edwards	.60	1.50
83 Wes Welker	.75	2.00
84 Donald Driver	.75	2.00
85 Lee Evans	.60	1.50
86 Greg Jennings	.75	2.00
87 Kevin Walter	.60	1.50
88 Ike Hilliard	.50	1.25
89 Bobby Engram	.50	1.25
90 Marques Colston	.75	2.00
91 Antonio Gates	.75	2.00
92 Kellen Winslow	.60	1.50
93 Jason Witten	.75	2.00
94 Dallas Clark	.50	1.25
95 Tony Gonzalez	.60	1.50
96 Jason Taylor	.60	1.50
97 Ray Lewis	.75	2.00
98 Shawne Merriman	.60	1.50
99 Brian Urlacher	.75	2.00
100 Champ Bailey	.60	1.50
101 Trent Edwards RC	2.00	5.00
102 Kevin Kolb RC	3.00	8.00
103 JaMarcus Russell RC	1.25	3.00
104 Brady Quinn RC	2.00	5.00
105 John Beck RC	2.00	5.00
106 Drew Stanton RC	1.25	3.00
107 Troy Smith RC	2.00	5.00
108 Chris Leak RC	1.50	4.00
109 Adrian Peterson RC	8.00	20.00
110 Marshawn Lynch RC	2.00	5.00
111 Brandon Jackson RC	1.50	4.00
112 DeShawn Wynn RC	1.50	4.00
113 Tony Hunt RC	1.25	3.00
114 Dwayne Bowe RC	2.50	6.00
115 James Jones RC	2.00	5.00
116 Calvin Johnson RC	6.00	15.00
117 Sidney Rice RC	2.50	6.00
118 Laurent Robinson RC	2.00	5.00
119 Jacoby Jones RC	2.00	5.00
120 Greg Olsen RC	1.50	4.00
121 Steve Smith USC RC	2.00	5.00
122 Chris Davis RC	1.25	3.00
123 Ted Ginn Jr. RC	1.50	4.00
124 Dwayne Jarrett RC	1.50	4.00
125 Robert Meachem RC	2.00	5.00
126 Chris Henry RB RC	1.25	3.00
127 David Harris RC	1.50	4.00
128 Michael Bush RC	2.00	5.00
129 Yamon Figurs RC	1.25	3.00
130 Gaines Adams RC	2.00	5.00
131 Amobi Okoye RC	2.00	5.00
132 Patrick Willis RC	4.00	10.00
133 Paul Posluszny RC	2.00	5.00
134 LaMarr Woodley RC	2.00	5.00
135 LaRon Landry RC	2.00	5.00
136 Selvin Young RC	1.50	4.00
137 Brian Leonard RC	1.50	4.00
138 Scott Chandler RC	2.00	5.00
139 Anthony Gonzalez RC	2.00	5.00
140 Courtney Taylor RC	1.50	4.00
141 Mike Walker RC	2.00	5.00
142 Thomas Clayton RC	1.50	4.00
143 Ryne Robinson RC	1.50	4.00
144 Johnnie Lee Higgins RC	1.50	4.00
145 Lorenzo Booker RC	1.50	4.00
146 Craig Buster Davis RC	1.50	4.00
147 Antonio Pittman RC	1.25	3.00
148 Kolby Smith RC	1.50	4.00
149 Joe Thomas RC	2.00	5.00
150 Garrett Wolfe RC	1.25	3.00

2007 Topps Performance Bronze

*VETS/99: 1.5X TO 4X BASIC CARDS
*ROOKIES/199: .5X TO 1.2X BASIC CARDS
BRONZE STATED ODDS 1:2
1-100 BRONZE PRINT RUN 99 SER.#'d SETS
101-150 BRONZE PRINT RUN 199 SER.#'d SETS

2007 Topps Performance Gold

1-100 VETERAN/10 ODDS 1:20
101-150 ROOKIE/10 ODDS 1:39
UNPRICED GOLD PRINT RUN 10

2007 Topps Performance Silver

*VETS/50: 2.5X TO 6X BASIC CARDS
*ROOKIES/50: 1X TO 2.5X BASIC CARDS
1-100 VETERAN/50 ODDS 1:4
101-150 ROOKIE/50 ODDS 1:8
SILVER PRINT RUN 50 SER.#'d SETS

2007 Topps Performance Breakout Autographs

GROUP A ODDS 1:60
GROUP B ODDS 1:28
GROUP C ODDS 1:20
GROUP D ODDS 1:70
GROUP E ODDS 1:65
GROUP F ODDS 1:25
GROUP G ODDS 1:30
GROUP H ODDS 1:9
*BRONZE/50: .4X TO 1X BASE GROUP A-B
*BRONZE/50: .5X TO 1.2X BASE GROUP C-H
BRONZE/50 ODDS 1:16
*SILVER/25: .5X TO 1.2X BASE GROUP A-B
*SILVER/25: .6X TO 1.5X BASE GROUP C-H
SILVER/25 ODDS 1:33
UNPRICED GOLD/5 ODDS 1:155

BAAO Amobi Okoye C	4.00	10.00
BABJ Brandon Jackson E	3.00	8.00
BACW Cadillac Williams A	8.00	20.00
BADH David Harris B	4.00	10.00
BADS Drew Stanton B	3.00	8.00
BADW DeShawn Wynn H	3.00	8.00
BADWI DeAngelo Williams A	10.00	25.00
BAGJ Greg Jennings D	8.00	20.00
BAGO Greg Olsen C	3.00	8.00
BAJB John Beck C	4.00	10.00
BAJJO James Jones H	4.00	10.00
BAKK Kevin Kolb B	8.00	20.00
BALR Laurent Robinson F	4.00	10.00
BAMD Maurice Jones-Drew G	8.00	20.00
BAML Marshawn Lynch B	5.00	12.00
BAPW Patrick Willis C	10.00	25.00
BARW Roy Williams WR A	8.00	20.00
BASH Santonio Holmes A	8.00	20.00
BASJ Steven Jackson A	10.00	25.00
BASS Steve Smith USC F	4.00	10.00
BATE Trent Edwards C	4.00	10.00
BATG Ted Ginn Jr. B	8.00	20.00
BATH Tony Hunt B	3.00	8.00
BATR Tony Romo A	30.00	80.00
BAYF Yamon Figurs B	3.00	8.00

2007 Topps Performance Breakout Relics

BREAKOUT RELIC/50 ODDS 1:16
*BRONZE/25: .6X TO 1.5X BASIC JSY/50
BRONZE RELIC/25 ODDS 1:33
UNPRICED SILVER/10 ODDS 1:86
UNPRICED GOLD/5 ODDS 1:154

BADH David Harris	2.50	6.00
BRAO Amobi Okoye	3.00	8.00
BRBJ Brandon Jackson	2.50	6.00
BRCW Cadillac Williams	4.00	10.00
BRDS Drew Stanton	2.00	5.00
BRDW DeShawn Wynn	2.50	6.00
BRDWI DeAngelo Williams	5.00	12.00
BRGJ Greg Jennings	5.00	12.00
BRGO Greg Olsen	2.50	6.00
BRJB John Beck	3.00	8.00
BRJJO James Jones	3.00	8.00
BRKK Kevin Kolb	5.00	12.00
BRLR Laurent Robinson	3.00	8.00
BRMD Maurice Jones-Drew	5.00	12.00
BRML Marshawn Lynch	3.00	8.00
BRPW Patrick Willis	6.00	15.00
BRRW Roy Williams WR	4.00	10.00
BRSH Santonio Holmes	4.00	10.00
BRSJ Steven Jackson	5.00	12.00
BRSS Steve Smith USC	3.00	8.00
BRTE Trent Edwards	3.00	8.00
BRTG Ted Ginn Jr.	2.50	6.00
BRTH Tony Hunt	2.00	5.00
BRTR Tony Romo	15.00	40.00
BRYF Yamon Figurs	2.00	5.00

2007 Topps Performance Hall of Fame Autographed Relics

HOF RELIC AU/20 ODDS 1:102
UNPRICED DUAL RELIC AU/10 ODDS 1:194
UNPRICED QUAD RELIC AU/10 ODDS 1:387

HFARDM Dan Marino	175.00	300.00
HFARED Eric Dickerson	25.00	60.00
HFARFH Franco Harris	40.00	80.00
HFARJE John Elway	125.00	250.00
HFARJK Jim Kelly	60.00	120.00
HFARJM Joe Montana	150.00	250.00
HFARMA Marcus Allen	25.00	60.00
HFARSY Steve Young	75.00	150.00
HFARTA Troy Aikman	75.00	150.00
HFARTD Tony Dorsett	40.00	80.00

2007 Topps Performance Hall of Fame Autographed Relics Dual

UNPRICED DUAL RELIC AU/10 ODDS 1:194

2007 Topps Performance Hall of Fame Autographed Relics Quad

UNPRICED QUAD RELIC AU/10 ODDS 1:387

2007 Topps Performance Hall of Fame Autographs

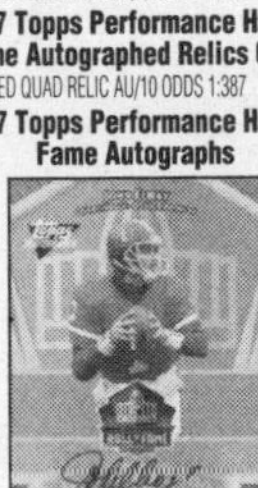

HOF AUTO/20 ODDS 1:68
UNPRICED AUTO CUT/1 ODDS 1:1935

HFABS Barry Sanders	60.00	120.00
HFADM Dan Marino	100.00	200.00
HFAED Eric Dickerson	40.00	80.00
HFAFH Franco Harris	40.00	80.00
HFAGS Gale Sayers	50.00	100.00
HFAJB Jim Brown	60.00	120.00
HFAJE John Elway	75.00	150.00
HFAJM Joe Montana	75.00	150.00
HFAJN Joe Namath	60.00	120.00
HFAMA Marcus Allen	40.00	80.00
HFAPH Paul Hornung	30.00	60.00
HFARS Roger Staubach	60.00	120.00
HFATA Troy Aikman	60.00	120.00
HFATB Terry Bradshaw	60.00	120.00
HFATD Tony Dorsett	40.00	80.00

2007 Topps Performance Hall of Fame Autographs Dual

UNPRICED DUAL AU/10 ODDS 1:215

2007 Topps Performance Hall of Fame Cuts

UNPRICED AUTO CUT/1 ODDS 1:1935

2007 Topps Performance Rookie Autographed NFL Logos

UNPRICED NFL LOGO/1 ODDS 1:968

2007 Topps Performance Rookie Autographed NFL Logos Dual

UNPRICED NFL LOGO DUAL/1 ODDS 1:1935

2007 Topps Performance Rookie Autographed Relics

GROUP A ODDS 1:450
GROUP B ODDS 1:7
GROUP C ODDS 1:14
GROUP D/E ODDS 1:6
GROUP F ODDS 1:13
GROUP G ODDS 1:5
*BRONZE/50: .5X TO 1.2X AU JSY GRP B-H
*BRONZE/25: .6X TO 1.5X AU JSY GRP B
UNPRICED BRONZE GRP A/15 ODDS 1:691
BRONZE GROUP B/50 ODDS 1:101
BRONZE GROUP C/50 ODDS 1:17
*SILVER/25: .6X TO 1.5X AU JSY GRP B-H
UNPRICED SLVR GRP A/15 ODDS 1:1076
UNPRICED SLVR GRP B/15 ODDS 1:173
SILVER GRP C/25 ODDS 1:34
UNPRICED GOLD/5 ODDS 1:114
UNPRICED PRINT PLATE/1 ODDS 1:138
UNPRICED NFL LOGO/1 ODDS 1:968
UNPRICED NFL LOGO DUAL/1 ODDS 1:1935

101 Trent Edwards D	6.00	15.00
102 Kevin Kolb B	10.00	25.00
103 JaMarcus Russell A	8.00	20.00
104 Brady Quinn B	10.00	25.00
105 John Beck D	6.00	15.00
106 Drew Stanton B	4.00	10.00
107 Troy Smith B	6.00	15.00
108 Chris Leak C	5.00	12.00
109 Adrian Peterson A	125.00	250.00
110 Marshawn Lynch B	6.00	15.00
111 Brandon Jackson B	5.00	12.00
112 DeShawn Wynn F	5.00	12.00
113 Tony Hunt B	4.00	10.00
114 Dwayne Bowe B	8.00	20.00
115 James Jones G	6.00	15.00
117 Sidney Rice B	8.00	20.00
118 Laurent Robinson D	6.00	15.00
119 Jacoby Jones B	6.00	15.00
120 Greg Olsen B	5.00	12.00
121 Steve Smith USC C	6.00	15.00
122 Chris Davis E	4.00	10.00
123 Ted Ginn Jr. B	5.00	12.00
124 Dwayne Jarrett B	5.00	12.00
125 Robert Meachem B	6.00	15.00
126 Chris Henry F	4.00	10.00
127 David Harris G	5.00	12.00
128 Michael Bush B	6.00	15.00
129 Yamon Figurs E	4.00	10.00
130 Gaines Adams B	6.00	15.00
131 Amobi Okoye D	6.00	15.00
132 Patrick Willis C	12.00	30.00
133 Paul Posluszny C	6.00	15.00
134 LaMarr Woodley D	8.00	20.00
135 LaRon Landry B	6.00	15.00

2007 Topps Performance Rookie Autographs

GROUP A ODDS 1:370
GROUP B ODDS 1:40
GROUP C ODDS 1:10
GROUP D ODDS 1:12
GROUP E ODDS 1:5
GROUP F/G ODDS 1:3
GROUP H ODDS 1:6
A.PETERSON OVERALL ODDS 1:78

101 Trent Edwards D	5.00	12.00
102 Kevin Kolb C	8.00	20.00
103 JaMarcus Russell A	20.00	50.00
104 Brady Quinn C	20.00	50.00
105 John Beck E	5.00	12.00
106 Drew Stanton D	3.00	8.00
107 Troy Smith B	6.00	15.00
108 Chris Leak C	4.00	10.00
109A Adrian Peterson/169	60.00	120.00
109B Adrian Peterson ROY/169	60.00	120.00
110 Marshawn Lynch C	12.00	30.00
111 Brandon Jackson C	4.00	10.00
112 DeShawn Wynn E	4.00	10.00
113 Tony Hunt B	4.00	10.00
114 Dwayne Bowe C	6.00	15.00
115 James Jones H	5.00	12.00
116 Calvin Johnson A	50.00	100.00
117 Sidney Rice B	8.00	20.00
118 Laurent Robinson F	5.00	12.00
119 Jacoby Jones E	5.00	12.00
120 Greg Olsen C	4.00	10.00
121 Steve Smith USC G	5.00	12.00
122 Chris Davis F	3.00	8.00
123 Ted Ginn Jr. B	5.00	12.00
124 Dwayne Jarrett C	4.00	10.00
125 Robert Meachem B	6.00	15.00
126 Chris Henry F	3.00	8.00
127 David Harris F	4.00	10.00
128 Michael Bush D	5.00	12.00
129 Yamon Figurs F	3.00	8.00
130 Gaines Adams D	5.00	12.00
131 Amobi Okoye E	5.00	12.00
132 Patrick Willis E	10.00	25.00
133 Paul Posluszny G	5.00	12.00
134 LaMarr Woodley E	6.00	15.00
135 LaRon Landry G	5.00	12.00

2007 Topps Performance Rookie Autographs Bronze

*BRONZE/50: .5X TO 1.2X BASIC AUTO
*BRONZE/25: .5X TO 1.2X BASE GRP A-B
*BRONZE/25: .6X TO 1.5X BASE GRP C-H
GROUP A/15 ODDS 1:692
GROUP B/25 ODDS 1:100
GROUP C/50 ODDS 1:17
A.PETERSON BRONZE OVERALL ODDS 1:197
BRONZE PRINT RUN 15-99

104 Brady Quinn/50	25.00	60.00
109A Adrian Peterson/99	60.00	120.00
109B Adrian Peterson ROY/99	60.00	120.00
110 Marshawn Lynch/50	10.00	25.00

2007 Topps Performance Rookie Autographs Gold

UNPRICED GOLD/5 ODDS 1:114
A.PETERSON GOLD OVERALL ODDS 1:807
GOLD STATED PRINT RUN 5-25

109A Adrian Peterson/25	125.00	250.00
109B Adrian Peterson ROY/25	125.00	250.00

2007 Topps Performance Rookie Autographs Red

A.PETERSON OVERALL RED ODDS 1:109

109A Adrian Peterson/135	60.00	120.00
109B Adrian Peterson ROY/135	60.00	120.00

2007 Topps Performance Rookie Autographs Silver

*SILVER/25: .6X TO 1.5X BASE GRP C-H
GROUP A/10 ODDS 1:1076
GROUP B/15 ODDS 1:173
GROUP C/25 ODDS 1:34
A.PETERSON SILVER OVERALL ODDS 1:262
SILVER PRINT RUN 10-75

104 Brady Quinn/25	30.00	80.00
109A Adrian Peterson/75	60.00	120.00
109B Adrian Peterson ROY/75	60.00	120.00
110 Marshawn Lynch/25	12.00	30.00

2007 Topps Performance Rookie Relics

ROOKIE RELIC/30 ODDS 1:20
*BRONZE/25: .4X TO 1X BASIC JSY/30
BRONZE/25 ODDS 1:23
UNPRICED SILVER/10 ODDS 1:62
UNPRICED GOLD/5 ODDS 1:110

101 Trent Edwards	3.00	8.00
102 Kevin Kolb	5.00	12.00
103 JaMarcus Russell	2.00	5.00
104 Brady Quinn	3.00	8.00
105 John Beck	3.00	8.00
106 Drew Stanton	2.00	5.00
107 Troy Smith	3.00	8.00
108 Chris Leak	2.50	6.00
109 Adrian Peterson	12.00	30.00
110 Marshawn Lynch	3.00	8.00
111 Brandon Jackson	2.50	6.00
112 DeShawn Wynn	2.50	6.00
113 Tony Hunt	2.00	5.00
114 Dwayne Bowe	4.00	10.00
115 James Jones	3.00	8.00
116 Calvin Johnson	10.00	25.00
117 Sidney Rice	4.00	10.00
118 Laurent Robinson	3.00	8.00
119 Jacoby Jones	3.00	8.00
120 Greg Olsen	2.50	6.00
121 Steve Smith USC	3.00	8.00
122 Chris Davis	2.00	5.00
123 Ted Ginn Jr.	2.50	6.00
124 Dwayne Jarrett	2.50	6.00
125 Robert Meachem	3.00	8.00
126 Chris Henry RB	2.00	5.00
127 David Harris	2.50	6.00
128 Michael Bush	3.00	8.00
129 Yamon Figurs	2.00	5.00
130 Gaines Adams	3.00	8.00
131 Amobi Okoye	3.00	8.00
132 Patrick Willis	6.00	15.00
133 Paul Posluszny	3.00	8.00
134 LaMarr Woodley	3.00	8.00
135 LaRon Landry	3.00	8.00

2007 Topps Performance Skill Sets Quarterbacks Triple Relics

SKILL SET QB/60 ODDS 1:22
*BRONZE/50: .4X TO 1X BASE JSY/60
BRONZE/50 ODDS 1:27
*SILVER/25: .5X TO 1.2X BASE JSY/60
SILVER/25 ODDS 1:54
UNPRICED RED/5 ODDS 1:258
UNPRICED GOLD/1 ODDS 1:1290

SSQBF Brett Favre	15.00	40.00
SSQBQ Brady Quinn	4.00	10.00
SSQBR Ben Roethlisberger	8.00	20.00
SSQDS Drew Stanton	2.50	6.00
SSQEM Eli Manning	8.00	20.00
SSQJB John Beck	4.00	10.00
SSQJE John Elway	15.00	40.00
SSQJR JaMarcus Russell	2.50	6.00
SSQKK Kevin Kolb	6.00	15.00
SSQML Matt Leinart	6.00	15.00
SSQTA Troy Aikman	12.00	30.00
SSQTE Trent Edwards	4.00	10.00
SSQTP Tom Brady	12.00	30.00
SSQTR Tony Romo	10.00	25.00
SSQTS Troy Smith	4.00	10.00

2007 Topps Performance Skill Sets Receivers Triple Relics

SKILL SET REC/60 ODDS 1:22
*BRONZE/50: .4X TO 1X BASE JSY/60
BRONZE/50 ODDS 1:27
*SILVER/25: .5X TO 1.2X BASE JSY/60
SILVER/25 ODDS 1:54
UNPRICED RED/5 ODDS 1:258
UNPRICED GOLD/1 ODDS 1:1290

SSWAG Anthony Gonzalez	4.00	10.00
SSWCJ Calvin Johnson	12.00	30.00
SSWDB Dwayne Bowe	5.00	12.00
SSWDJ Dwayne Jarrett	3.00	8.00
SSWJH Jason Hill	4.00	10.00
SSWJR Jerry Rice	15.00	40.00
SSWLF Larry Fitzgerald	8.00	20.00
SSWPW Paul Williams	2.50	6.00
SSWRM Robert Meachem	4.00	10.00
SSWRM Randy Moss	8.00	20.00
SSWSR Sidney Rice	5.00	12.00
SSWSS Steve Smith USC	4.00	10.00
SSWTB Tim Brown	10.00	25.00
SSWTG Ted Ginn Jr.	3.00	8.00
SSWYF Yamon Figurs	2.50	6.00

2007 Topps Performance Skill Sets Running Backs Triple Relics

SKILL SET RB/60 ODDS 1:22
*BRONZE/50: .4X TO 1X BASE JSY/60
BRONZE/50 ODDS 1:27
*SILVER/25: .5X TO 1.2X BASE JSY/60
SILVER/25 ODDS 1:54
UNPRICED RED/5 ODDS 1:258
UNPRICED GOLD/1 ODDS 1:1290

SSRAP Adrian Peterson	15.00	40.00
SSRBJ Brandon Jackson	3.00	8.00
SSRBL Brian Leonard	3.00	8.00
SSRDW DeAngelo Williams	8.00	20.00
SSRES Emmitt Smith	20.00	50.00
SSRGW Garrett Wolfe	2.50	6.00
SSRJA Joseph Addai	6.00	15.00
SSRKI Kenny Irons	2.50	6.00
SSRLB Lorenzo Booker	3.00	8.00
SSRLM Laurence Maroney	6.00	15.00
SSRMB Michael Bush	4.00	10.00
SSRML Marshawn Lynch	4.00	10.00
SSRPH Paul Hornung	10.00	25.00
SSRSA Shaun Alexander	6.00	15.00
SSRAPI Antonio Pittman	2.50	6.00

2007 Topps Performance Triple Relic Signatures

UNPRICED TRIPLE RELIC/5 ODDS 1:387

2007 Topps Performance Triple Signatures

UNPRICED TRIPLE AU/5 ODDS 1:387
UNPRICED TRIP.RELIC AU/5 ODDS 1:387

2009 Topps Platinum

COMPLETE SET (165)	25.00	50.00
TWO ROOKIES PER HOBBY PACK		
1 Drew Brees	.25	.60
2 Kurt Warner	.25	.60
3 Jay Cutler	.25	.60
4 Aaron Rodgers	.50	1.25
5 Philip Rivers	.25	.60
6 Peyton Manning	.40	1.00
7 Donovan McNabb	.25	.60
8 Matt Cassel	.20	.50
9 David Garrard	.20	.50
10 Brett Favre	4.00	10.00
11 Tony Romo	.40	1.00
12 Matt Ryan	.25	.60
13 Ben Roethlisberger	.25	.60
14 Eli Manning	.25	.60
15 Matt Schaub	.20	.50
16 Joe Flacco	.25	.60
17 Carson Palmer	.25	.60
18 Tom Brady	.40	1.00
19 Adrian Peterson	.40	1.00
20 Michael Turner	.20	.50
21 DeAngelo Williams	.25	.60
22 Clinton Portis	.20	.50
23 Thomas Jones	.20	.50
24 Steve Slaton	.20	.50
25 Matt Forte	.25	.60
26 Chris Johnson	.25	.60
27 Ryan Grant	.20	.50
28 LaDainian Tomlinson	.25	.60
29 Brandon Jacobs	.20	.50
30 Steven Jackson	.20	.50
31 Marshawn Lynch	.20	.50
32 Frank Gore	.20	.50
33 Kevin Smith	.20	.50
34 Brian Westbrook	.20	.50
35 Ronnie Brown	.20	.50
36 Marion Barber	.20	.50
37 Jonathan Stewart	.20	.50
38 Maurice Jones-Drew	.20	.50
39 Willie Parker	.15	.40
40 Darren McFadden	.25	.60
41 Reggie Bush	.25	.60
42 Joseph Addai	.25	.60
43 LenDale White	.20	.50
44 Felix Jones	.25	.60
45 Ray Rice	.25	.60
46 Fred Jackson	.25	.60
47 Leon Washington	.20	.50
48 Andre Johnson	.20	.50
49 Larry Fitzgerald	.25	.60
50 Steve Smith	.20	.50
51 Roddy White	.20	.50
52 Calvin Johnson	.25	.60
53 Greg Jennings	.25	.60
54 Brandon Marshall	.20	.50
55 Antonio Bryant	.15	.40
56 Wes Welker	.25	.60
57 Reggie Wayne	.20	.50
58 Marques Colston	.20	.50
59 Terrell Owens	.25	.60
60 Santana Moss	.20	.50
61 Hines Ward	.20	.50
62 Anquan Boldin	.20	.50
63 Dwayne Bowe	.20	.50
64 Roy Williams WR	.20	.50
65 Donald Driver	.20	.50
66 Randy Moss	.25	.60
67 Eddie Royal	.20	.50
68 DeSean Jackson	.20	.50
69 T.J. Houshmandzadeh	.20	.50
70 Jerricho Cotchery	.20	.50
71 Santonio Holmes	.20	.50
72 Chad Ochocinco	.20	.50
73 Vincent Jackson	.20	.50
74 Lee Evans	.20	.50
75 Devin Hester	.25	.60
76 Anthony Gonzalez	.15	.40
77 Tony Gonzalez	.20	.50
78 Jason Witten	.25	.60
79 Dallas Clark	.20	.50
80 Antonio Gates	.20	.50
81 Chris Cooley	.20	.50
82 Zach Miller	.20	.50
83 Greg Olsen	.15	.40
84 John Carlson	.20	.50
85 Willis McGahee	.20	.50
86 Fred Taylor	.20	.50
87 John Abraham	.15	.40
88 Jared Allen	.25	.60
89 Julius Peppers	.20	.50
90 Mario Williams	.20	.50
91 Dwight Freeney	.20	.50
92 DeMarcus Ware	.20	.50
93 Joey Porter	.20	.50
94 James Harrison	.25	.60
95 LaMarr Woodley	.15	.40
96 Patrick Willis	.20	.50
97 Brian Urlacher	.25	.60
98 Terrell Suggs	.15	.40
99 Jerod Mayo	.20	.50
100 Ray Lewis	.25	.60
101 Charles Woodson	.25	.60
102 Darrelle Revis	.20	.50
103 Antoine Winfield	.15	.40
104 Asante Samuel	.15	.40
105 Chris Johnson CB	.25	.60
106 Nnamdi Asomugha	.20	.50
107 Champ Bailey	.20	.50
108 Ed Reed	.20	.50
109 Troy Polamalu	.25	.60
110 Adrian Wilson	.15	.40
111 Andre Brown RC	.60	1.50
112 Aaron Curry RC	1.00	2.50
113 Brandon Pettigrew RC	1.00	2.50
114 Brian Robiskie RC	1.00	2.50
115 Chris Wells RC	1.50	4.00
116 Deon Butler RC	.75	2.00
117 Donald Brown RC	1.00	2.50
118 Darrius Heyward-Bey RC	1.00	2.50
119 Derrick Williams RC	.75	2.00
120 Glen Coffee RC	.75	2.00
121 Hakeem Nicks RC	1.50	4.00
122 Josh Freeman RC	2.00	5.00
123 Juaquin Iglesias RC	.75	2.00
124 Jeremy Maclin RC	1.50	4.00
125 Matthew Stafford RC	5.00	12.00
126 Javon Ringer RC	1.00	2.50
127 Jason Smith RC	.75	2.00
128 Kenny Britt RC	1.25	3.00
129 Knowshon Moreno RC	1.00	2.50
130 LeSean McCoy RC	2.00	5.00
131 Michael Crabtree RC	2.00	5.00
132 Mohamed Massaquoi RC	.75	2.00
133 Mark Sanchez RC	3.00	8.00
134 Mike Thomas RC	1.00	2.50
135 Mike Wallace RC	2.00	5.00
136 Nate Davis RC	.75	2.00
137 Percy Harvin RC	1.50	4.00
138 Patrick Turner RC	.75	2.00
139 Pat White RC	1.00	2.50
140 Ramses Barden RC	.60	1.50
141 Rhett Bomar RC	.75	2.00
142 Shonn Greene RC	1.50	4.00
143 Stephen McGee RC	1.00	2.50
144 Tyson Jackson RC	.75	2.00
145 Chase Coffman RC	.75	2.00
146 Tom Brandstater RC	1.00	2.50
147 Brian Orakpo RC	1.00	2.50
148 Malcolm Jenkins RC	1.00	2.50
149 Brian Cushing RC	1.00	2.50
150 Brian Hartline RC	1.00	2.50
151 Mike Goodson RC	1.00	2.50
152 Shawn Nelson RC	.75	2.00
153 Austin Collie RC	1.00	2.50
154 Louis Murphy RC	1.00	2.50
155 Johnny Knox RC	1.50	4.00
156 Rashad Jennings RC	1.00	2.50
157 Jarett Dillard RC	1.00	2.50
158 Quan Cosby RC	.75	2.00
159 Julian Edelman RC	1.00	2.50
160 James Laurinaitis RC	1.00	2.50
161 Gartrell Johnson RC	.60	1.50
162 Brandon Gibson RC	1.00	2.50
163 James Davis RC	1.00	2.50
164 Rey Maualuga RC	1.00	2.50
165 Sammie Stroughter RC	1.00	2.50

2009 Topps Platinum Rookie Blue Refractors

*ROOKIES: 1.2X TO 3X BASIC CARDS
BLUE REFRACTOR/99 ODDS 1:76 HOB

2009 Topps Platinum Rookie Platinum Refractors 1549

*ROOKIES: .6X TO 1.5X BASIC CARDS
PLATINUM REF/1549 ODDS 1:5 HOB

2009 Topps Platinum Rookie Platinum Refractors 99

*ROOKIES: 1.2X TO 3X BASIC CARDS
PLATINUM REF/99 ODDS 1:40 HOB

2009 Topps Platinum Rookie Red Refractors

*ROOKIES: 3X TO 8X BASIC CARDS
RED REFRACTOR/25 ODDS 1:300 HOB

125 Matthew Stafford	60.00	120.00
133 Mark Sanchez	30.00	80.00

2009 Topps Platinum Rookie Refractors

*ROOKIES: .8X TO 2X BASIC CARDS
REFRACTOR/999 ODDS 1:8 HOB

2009 Topps Platinum Rookie White Refractors

*ROOKIES: 1X TO 2.5X BASIC CARDS
WHITE REFRACT/499 ODDS 1:15 HOB

2009 Topps Platinum Autographed Patches

STATED PRINT RUN 8-550

ARPAB Andre Brown/200	6.00	15.00
ARPAC Aaron Curry/450	6.00	15.00
ARPAP Adrian Peterson/90	90.00	150.00
ARPBM Brandon Marshall/150	10.00	25.00
ARPBP Brandon Pettigrew/150	8.00	20.00
ARPBR Brian Robiskie/300	6.00	15.00
ARPBW Chris Wells/450	20.00	50.00
ARPDB Deon Butler/150	5.00	12.00
ARPDBO Dwayne Bowe/150	8.00	20.00
ARPDBR Donald Brown/150	6.00	15.00
ARPDHB Darrius Heyward-Bey/110	6.00	15.00
ARPDM Dan Marino/110	75.00	135.00
ARPDW Derrick Williams/150	5.00	12.00
ARPGC Glen Coffee/150	5.00	12.00
ARPHN Hakeem Nicks/200	10.00	25.00
ARPJA Joseph Addai/110	12.00	30.00
ARPJF Josh Freeman/150	30.00	60.00
ARPJI Juaquin Iglesias/350	5.00	12.00
ARPJM Jeremy Maclin/150	10.00	25.00
ARPJR Javon Ringer/150	6.00	15.00
ARPJS Jason Smith/550	5.00	12.00
ARPKB Kenny Britt/200	8.00	20.00
ARPKM Knowshon Moreno/25	30.00	80.00
ARPLE Lee Evans/150	8.00	20.00
ARPLM LeSean McCoy/350	20.00	50.00
ARPMC Michael Crabtree/40	40.00	100.00
ARPMS Matt Stafford/8		
ARPMSA Mark Sanchez/110	60.00	120.00
ARPMT Mike Thomas/150	6.00	15.00
ARPMW Mike Wallace/150	25.00	50.00
ARPPH Percy Harvin/300	25.00	60.00
ARPPT Patrick Turner/450	6.00	15.00
ARPPW Pat White/110	6.00	15.00
ARPRM Rashard Mendenhall/350	12.00	30.00
ARPRR Ray Rice/350	20.00	50.00
ARPSG Shonn Greene/150	20.00	50.00
ARPSS Steve Smith/350	10.00	25.00
ARPSSL Steve Slaton/150	8.00	20.00
ARPTJ Tyson Jackson/550	5.00	12.00

2009 Topps Platinum Autographed Patches Black Refractors

BLACK REF/25 ODDS 1:240 HOB
*RED REF/10: .5X TO 1.2X BLK REF/25

ARPAB Andre Brown	6.00	15.00
ARPAC Aaron Curry	10.00	25.00
ARPAP Adrian Peterson		
ARPBM Brandon Marshall	12.00	30.00
ARPBP Brandon Pettigrew	10.00	25.00
ARPBR Brian Robiskie	10.00	25.00
ARPBW Chris Wells	15.00	40.00
ARPDB Deon Butler	8.00	20.00
ARPDBO Dwayne Bowe	12.00	30.00
ARPDBR Donald Brown	10.00	25.00
ARPDHB Darrius Heyward-Bey	10.00	25.00
ARPDM Dan Marino	100.00	200.00
ARPDW Derrick Williams	8.00	20.00
ARPGC Glen Coffee	8.00	20.00
ARPHN Hakeem Nicks	15.00	40.00
ARPJA Joseph Addai	15.00	40.00
ARPJF Josh Freeman	60.00	120.00
ARPJI Juaquin Iglesias	8.00	20.00
ARPJM Jeremy Maclin	15.00	40.00
ARPJR Javon Ringer	10.00	25.00
ARPJS Jason Smith	8.00	20.00
ARPKB Kenny Britt	12.00	30.00
ARPKM Knowshon Moreno	30.00	80.00
ARPLE Lee Evans	12.00	30.00
ARPLM LeSean McCoy	30.00	60.00
ARPMC Michael Crabtree	60.00	150.00
ARPMSA Mark Sanchez	100.00	200.00
ARPMT Mike Thomas	10.00	25.00
ARPMW Mike Wallace	40.00	80.00
ARPPH Percy Harvin	50.00	120.00
ARPPT Patrick Turner	8.00	20.00
ARPPW Pat White	10.00	25.00
ARPRM Rashard Mendenhall	12.00	30.00
ARPRR Ray Rice	30.00	80.00
ARPSG Shonn Greene	30.00	80.00
ARPSS Steve Smith	12.00	30.00
ARPSSL Steve Slaton	12.00	30.00
ARPTJ Tyson Jackson	8.00	20.00

2009 Topps Platinum Rookie Autographs

AUTO PRINT RUN 90-1550

111 Andre Brown/850	3.00	8.00
112 Aaron Curry/350	6.00	15.00
113 Brandon Pettigrew/100	6.00	15.00
114 Brian Robiskie/150	6.00	15.00
115 Chris Wells/50	15.00	40.00
116 Deon Butler/100	5.00	12.00
117 Donald Brown/90	8.00	20.00
118 Darrius Heyward-Bey/150	6.00	15.00
119 Derrick Williams/350	5.00	12.00
120 Glen Coffee/550	4.00	10.00
121 Hakeem Nicks/450	10.00	25.00
122 Josh Freeman/150	12.00	30.00
123 Juaquin Iglesias/550	4.00	10.00
124 Jeremy Maclin/150	10.00	25.00
126 Javon Ringer/1500	5.00	12.00
127 Jason Smith/650	4.00	10.00
128 Kenny Britt/150	8.00	20.00
130 LeSean McCoy/350	12.00	30.00
131 Michael Crabtree/50	30.00	80.00
133 Mark Sanchez/50	60.00	120.00
134 Mike Thomas/100	6.00	15.00
135 Mike Wallace/100	15.00	40.00
136 Nate Davis/650	4.00	10.00
137 Percy Harvin/850	15.00	40.00
138 Patrick Turner/450	5.00	12.00
139 Pat White/100	6.00	15.00
140 Ramses Barden/850	3.00	8.00
141 Rhett Bomar/850	4.00	10.00
142 Shonn Greene/550	8.00	20.00
143 Stephen McGee/450	6.00	15.00
144 Tyson Jackson/100	5.00	12.00
146 Tom Brandstater/450	6.00	15.00
148 Malcolm Jenkins/850	5.00	12.00
149 Brian Cushing/1550	5.00	12.00
152 Shawn Nelson/550	4.00	10.00
153 Austin Collie/450	8.00	20.00
155 Johnny Knox/1550	8.00	20.00
156 Rashad Jennings/1050	5.00	12.00
157 Jarett Dillard/1050	5.00	12.00
158 Quan Cosby/850	4.00	10.00
160 James Laurinaitis/850	5.00	12.00
162 Brandon Gibson/1050	5.00	12.00
163 James Davis/1050	5.00	12.00
164 Rey Maualuga/850	5.00	12.00

2009 Topps Platinum Rookie Autographs Black Refractors

BLACK REF AU/25 ODDS 1:270 HOB
*RED REF/10: .5X TO 1.2X BLACK REF/25
RED REFRACT/10 ODDS 1:535 HOB

111 Andre Brown	6.00	15.00
112 Aaron Curry	10.00	25.00
113 Brandon Pettigrew	10.00	25.00
114 Brian Robiskie	10.00	25.00
115 Chris Wells	15.00	40.00
116 Deon Butler	8.00	20.00
117 Donald Brown	10.00	25.00
118 Darrius Heyward-Bey	10.00	25.00
119 Derrick Williams	8.00	20.00
120 Glen Coffee	8.00	20.00
121 Hakeem Nicks	15.00	40.00
122 Josh Freeman	30.00	60.00
123 Juaquin Iglesias	8.00	20.00
124 Jeremy Maclin	15.00	40.00
126 Javon Ringer	10.00	25.00
127 Jason Smith	8.00	20.00
128 Kenny Britt	12.00	30.00
130 LeSean McCoy	20.00	50.00
131 Michael Crabtree	50.00	120.00
133 Mark Sanchez	125.00	200.00
134 Mike Thomas	10.00	25.00
135 Mike Wallace	30.00	60.00
136 Nate Davis	8.00	20.00
137 Percy Harvin	50.00	120.00
138 Patrick Turner	8.00	20.00
139 Pat White	10.00	25.00
140 Ramses Barden	6.00	15.00
141 Rhett Bomar	8.00	20.00
142 Shonn Greene	15.00	40.00
143 Stephen McGee	10.00	25.00
144 Tyson Jackson	8.00	20.00
146 Tom Brandstater	10.00	25.00
148 Malcolm Jenkins	10.00	25.00
149 Brian Cushing	10.00	25.00
152 Shawn Nelson	8.00	20.00
153 Austin Collie	12.00	30.00
155 Johnny Knox	15.00	40.00
156 Rashad Jennings	10.00	25.00
157 Jarett Dillard	10.00	25.00
158 Quan Cosby	8.00	20.00
160 James Laurinaitis	10.00	25.00
162 Brandon Gibson	10.00	25.00
163 James Davis	10.00	25.00
164 Rey Maualuga	10.00	25.00

2010 Topps Platinum

COMPLETE SET (165)	20.00	50.00
OVERALL TWO ROOKIES PER HOBBY PACK		
1 Peyton Manning	.40	1.00
2 Pierre Thomas	.20	.50
3 Vernon Davis	.20	.50
4 Chris Wells	.20	.50
5 Eddie Royal	.15	.40
6 Derrick Morgan RC	.60	1.50
7 Jordan Shipley RC	.75	2.00
8 James Starks RC	1.25	3.00
9 Matthew Stafford	.25	.60
10 Larry Fitzgerald	.25	.60
11 Tony Pike RC	.75	2.00
12 Santonio Holmes	.20	.50
13 Vince Young	.15	.40
14 Rashard Mendenhall	.20	.50
15 C.J. Spiller RC	1.25	3.00
16 Montario Hardesty RC	.75	2.00
17 Reggie Wayne	.20	.50
18 Matt Ryan	.25	.60
19 Tom Brady	.40	1.00
20 Tony Romo	.30	.75
21 Sean Canfield RC	.60	1.50
22 Mike Sims-Walker	.20	.50
23 Mike Williams RC	1.25	3.00
24 Philip Rivers	.25	.60
25 Marion Barber	.20	.50
26 Kellen Winslow	.20	.50
27 Greg Jennings	.20	.50
28 Toby Gerhart RC	.75	2.00
29 Anthony Dixon RC	.75	2.00
30 Knowshon Moreno	.20	.50
31 Jamaal Charles	.20	.50
32 Ricky Williams	.20	.50
33 Vincent Jackson	.15	.40
34 Andre Roberts RC	.75	2.00
35 Zac Robinson RC	.60	1.50
36 Ryan Mathews RC	1.50	4.00
37 T.J. Houshmandzadeh	.20	.50
38 Carson Palmer	.20	.50
39 D.J. Williams	.15	.40
40 Andre Johnson	.20	.50
41 Armanti Edwards RC	.75	2.00
42 Kevin Kolb	.20	.50
43 Darrelle Revis	.20	.50
44 LeSean McCoy	.20	.50
45 Josh Freeman	.25	.60
46 Antonio Bryant	.15	.40
47 Brian Cushing	.15	.40
48 LaDainian Tomlinson	.25	.60
49 Steve Smith	.20	.50
50 Brandon Marshall	.20	.50
51 Dan LeFevour RC	.75	2.00
52 Steve Slaton	.15	.40
53 Ray Lewis	.25	.60
54 Charles Scott RC	.60	1.50
55 Felix Jones	.20	.50
56 Terrell Owens	.25	.60
57 Jonathan Stewart	.20	.50
58 Tony Gonzalez	.20	.50
59 Earl Thomas RC	.75	2.00
60 Michael Turner	.15	.40
61 Carlton Mitchell RC	.60	1.50
62 Jerome Harrison	.15	.40
63 Matt Cassel	.20	.50
64 Arrelious Benn RC	.75	2.00
65 Dezmon Briscoe RC	.60	1.50
66 Clinton Portis	.20	.50
67 Jon Beason	.15	.40
68 Troy Polamalu	.25	.60
69 Aaron Hernandez RC	1.25	3.00
70 Drew Brees	.25	.60
71 Chad Ochocinco	.20	.50
72 Jonathan Dwyer RC	.75	2.00
73 Jermaine Gresham RC	1.00	2.50
74 Hakeem Nicks	.20	.50
75 Emmanuel Sanders RC	.75	2.00
76 DeMarcus Ware	.20	.50
77 Fred Jackson	.25	.60
78 Golden Tate RC	.75	2.00
79 Tim Tebow RC	3.00	8.00
80 Dallas Clark	.20	.50
81 Brandon Jacobs	.20	.50
82 Donald Driver	.20	.50
83 Brandon LaFell RC	.75	2.00
84 James Harrison	.25	.60
85 Kenny Britt	.20	.50
86 Miles Austin	.25	.60
87 Dexter McCluster RC	.75	2.00
88 Matt Schaub	.20	.50
89 Steven Jackson	.20	.50
90 Maurice Jones-Drew	.20	.50
91 Eric Berry RC	.75	2.00
92 Ed Reed	.20	.50
93 Jimmy Clausen RC	.75	2.00
94 Chris Johnson	.25	.60
95 David Reed RC	.60	1.50
96 Lee Evans	.20	.50
97 Santana Moss	.20	.50
98 Rolando McClain RC	.75	2.00
99 Jonathan Vilma	.15	.40
100 Aaron Rodgers	.50	1.25
101 Demaryius Thomas RC	1.00	2.50
102 Joe Webb RC	.75	2.00
103 Jimmy Graham RC	1.50	4.00
104 Joseph Addai	.20	.50
105 Mohamed Massaquoi	.20	.50
106 Marques Colston	.20	.50
107 Ndamukong Suh RC	1.50	4.00
108 Jason Campbell	.20	.50
109 Damian Williams RC	.75	2.00
110 DeAngelo Williams	.20	.50
111 Steve Smith USC	.20	.50
112 Taylor Price RC	.75	2.00
113 Mike Wallace	.20	.50
114 Jason Witten	.25	.60
115 Roddy White	.20	.50
116 Riley Cooper RC	.75	2.00
117 Shonn Greene	.20	.50
118 DeSean Jackson	.20	.50
119 Patrick Willis	.20	.50
120 Sam Bradford RC	3.00	8.00
121 Eli Manning	.25	.60
122 Rob Gronkowski RC	2.00	5.00
123 Hines Ward	.20	.50
124 Jay Cutler	.25	.60
125 Marcus Easley RC	.60	1.50
126 Jonathan Crompton RC	.60	1.50
127 Jeremy Maclin	.20	.50
128 Gerald McCoy RC	.75	2.00
129 Ryan Grant	.20	.50
130 Brett Favre	1.00	2.50
131 Mark Sanchez	.25	.60
132 Mike Kafka RC	.75	2.00
133 Colt McCoy RC	1.50	4.00
134 Anquan Boldin	.20	.50
135 Mardy Gilyard RC	.75	2.00
136 Reggie Bush	.25	.60
137 Antonio Gates	.20	.50
138 John Skelton RC	.75	2.00
139 Darren McFadden	.20	.50
140 Percy Harvin	.25	.60
141 Thomas Jones	.20	.50
142 Jacoby Ford RC	.75	2.00
143 Michael Crabtree	.25	.60
144 Joe McKnight RC	.75	2.00
145 Braylon Edwards	.20	.50
146 Ben Tate RC	1.00	2.50
147 Anthony McCoy RC	.60	1.50
148 Cedric Benson	.20	.50

149 Wes Welker .25 .60
150 Randy Moss .25 .60
151 Eric Decker RC 1.00 2.50
152 Dez Bryant RC 2.50 6.00
153 Matt Forte .20 .50
154 Willis McGahee .20 .50
155 Sidney Rice .20 .50
156 Dwayne Bowe .20 .50
157 Jahvid Best RC 1.25 3.00
158 Cadillac Williams .20 .50
159 Donovan McNabb .25 .60
160 Calvin Johnson .25 .60
161 Ronnie Brown .20 .50
162 Frank Gore .20 .50
163 Ray Rice .20 .50
164 Joe Flacco .25 .60
165 Adrian Peterson .40 1.00

2010 Topps Platinum Rookie Blue Refractors

*ROOKIES: 1.5X TO 4X BASIC CARDS
BLUE REF/99 ODDS 1:175 HOB

2010 Topps Platinum Rookie Platinum Black Refractors

*ROOKIES: 3X TO 8X BASIC CARDS
BLACK REFRACTOR/25 ODDS 1:765 HOB

2010 Topps Platinum Rookie Platinum Refractors

*ROOKIES: .6X TO 1.5X BASIC CARDS
PLATINUM REFRACTOR ODDS 1:6 HOB

2010 Topps Platinum Rookie Red Refractors

*ROOKIES: 3X TO 8X BASIC CARDS
RED REFRACTOR/25 ODDS 1:740 HOB

2010 Topps Platinum Rookie Refractors

*ROOKIES: .8X TO 2X BASIC CARDS
REFRACTOR/999 ODDS 1:116

2010 Topps Platinum Rookie White Refractors

*ROOKIES: 1X TO 2.5X BASIC CARDS
WHITE REFRACTOR/499 ODDS 1:34 HOB

2010 Topps Platinum Autographed Patch Duals

DUAL AU PATCH/25 ODDS 1:3340 HOB
BT Jahvid Best 75.00 150.00
Ben Tate
ET John Elway 250.00 400.00
Tim Tebow
HM Montario Hardesty 20.00 50.00
Joe McKnight
JR Felix Jones 30.00 80.00
Ray Rice
MC Dexter McCluster 40.00 80.00
Jamaal Charles
PG Adrian Peterson 125.00 200.00
Toby Gerhart
SM C.J. Spiller 125.00 200.00
Ryan Mathews
TB Demaryius Thomas 60.00 120.00
Dez Bryant
WM Patrick Willis 40.00 80.00
Rolando McClain
BMC Eric Berry 50.00 100.00
Dexter McCluster

2010 Topps Platinum Autographed Patches

VETERAN PRINT RUN 120-300
ROOKIE PRINT RUN 200-800
EXCH EXPIRATION: 8/31/2013
*BLACK REF/99: .5X TO 1.2X VET/120-300
*BLACK REF/99: .8X TO 2X ROOKIE/500-800
*BLACK REF/99: .5X TO 1.2X ROOKIE/200-300
AB Arrelious Benn/800 8.00 20.00
AE Armanti Edwards/800 8.00 20.00
AG Anthony Gonzalez/140 8.00 20.00
AR Andre Roberts/800 8.00 20.00
BJ Brandon Jacobs/160 10.00 25.00
BL Brandon LaFell/500 8.00 20.00
BT Ben Tate/800 10.00 25.00
CH Chad Henne/120 10.00 25.00
CJS C.J. Spiller/200 20.00 50.00
CM Colt McCoy/200 20.00 50.00
CW Cadillac Williams/160 10.00 25.00
DB Dez Bryant/300 50.00 100.00
DBO Dwayne Bowe/160 10.00 25.00
DJ DeSean Jackson/180 12.00 30.00
DM Dexter McCluster/800 12.00 30.00
DM Darren McFadden/130 10.00 25.00
DT Demaryius Thomas/200 30.00 60.00
DW Damian Williams/500 8.00 20.00
EB Eric Berry/500 15.00 40.00
ED Eric Decker/800 10.00 25.00
ES Emmanuel Sanders/500 8.00 20.00
GM Gerald McCoy/500 8.00 20.00
GT Golden Tate/500 8.00 20.00
JA Joseph Addai/160 10.00 25.00
JB Jahvid Best/200 20.00 50.00
JC Jimmy Clausen/200 12.00 30.00
JD Jonathan Dwyer/500 8.00 20.00
JFR Josh Freeman/140 12.00 30.00
JG Jermaine Gresham/800 10.00 25.00
JM Joe McKnight EXCH 8.00 20.00
JMA Jerod Mayo/120 10.00 25.00
JS Jordan Shipley/500 8.00 20.00
KK Kevin Kolb/200 10.00 25.00
MC Marques Colston/200 10.00 25.00
ME Marcus Easley/800 6.00 15.00
MG Mardy Gilyard/800 8.00 20.00
MH Montario Hardesty/500 8.00 20.00
MK Mike Kafka/800 8.00 20.00
ML Marshawn Lynch/140 10.00 25.00
MW Mike Williams/800 15.00 40.00
MWI Mario Williams/120 10.00 25.00
NS Ndamukong Suh/500 25.00 60.00
PW Patrick Willis/300 12.00 30.00
RG Rob Gronkowski/800 20.00 50.00
RM Rolando McClain/500 8.00 20.00
RMA Ryan Mathews/200 30.00 80.00
SB Sam Bradford/200 75.00 150.00
TG Toby Gerhart/500 15.00 40.00
TP Taylor Price/800 8.00 20.00
TT Tim Tebow/300 75.00 150.00

2010 Topps Platinum Rookie Autographs

STATED PRINT RUN 400-1225
EXCH EXPIRATION: 8/31/2013
*BLACK REF/99: .8X TO 2X AUTO/900-1225
*BLACK REF/99: .6X TO 1.5X AUTO/400
*BLUE REF/599: .5X TO 1.2X AUTO/900-1225
6 Derrick Morgan/1099 4.00 10.00
7 Jordan Shipley/999 5.00 12.00
8 James Starks/1099 12.00 30.00
11 Tony Pike/1225 5.00 12.00
16 Montario Hardesty/999 5.00 12.00
21 Sean Canfield/1099 4.00 10.00
23 Mike Williams/900 10.00 25.00
28 Toby Gerhart/999 5.00 12.00
29 Anthony Dixon/900 5.00 12.00
34 Andre Roberts/900 5.00 12.00
35 Zac Robinson/1099 4.00 10.00
36 Ryan Mathews/400 20.00 50.00
41 Armanti Edwards/900 5.00 12.00
51 Dan LeFevour/1225 5.00 12.00
54 Charles Scott/1099 4.00 10.00
59 Earl Thomas/1099 5.00 12.00
61 Carlton Mitchell/1099 4.00 10.00
64 Arrelious Benn/400 6.00 15.00
65 Dezmon Briscoe/1099 4.00 10.00
69 Aaron Hernandez/1099 8.00 20.00
72 Jonathan Dwyer/400 6.00 15.00
73 Jermaine Gresham/999 6.00 15.00
75 Emmanuel Sanders/900 5.00 12.00
78 Golden Tate/400 6.00 15.00
83 Brandon LaFell/900 5.00 12.00
87 Dexter McCluster/400 10.00 25.00
91 Eric Berry/400 15.00 40.00
95 David Reed/900 4.00 10.00
98 Rolando McClain/900 5.00 12.00
101 Demaryius Thomas/400 8.00 20.00
102 Joe Webb/1099 5.00 12.00
103 Jimmy Graham/999 15.00 30.00
107 Ndamukong Suh/400 25.00 50.00
109 Damian Williams/1099 5.00 12.00
112 Taylor Price/900 5.00 12.00
116 Riley Cooper/1099 5.00 12.00
122 Rob Gronkowski/999 15.00 40.00
125 Marcus Easley/900 4.00 10.00
126 Jonathan Crompton/999 4.00 10.00
128 Gerald McCoy/400 6.00 15.00
132 Mike Kafka/999 5.00 12.00
135 Mardy Gilyard/999 5.00 12.00
138 John Skelton/999 5.00 12.00
142 Jacoby Ford/1099 5.00 12.00
144 Joe McKnight/999 5.00 12.00
146 Ben Tate/400 8.00 20.00
147 Anthony McCoy/1099 4.00 10.00
151 Eric Decker/900 6.00 15.00
152 Dez Bryant/400 40.00 80.00
157 Jahvid Best/400 15.00 40.00

2010 Topps Platinum Rookie Autographs Dual

STATED PRINT RUN 25 SER.#'d SETS
EXCH EXPIRATION: 8/31/2013
BB Sam Bradford 75.00 150.00
Dez Bryant
BC Sam Bradford 60.00 120.00
Jimmy Clausen
BM Jahvid Best 25.00 60.00
Dexter McCluster
CT Jimmy Clausen 30.00 80.00
Golden Tate
GM Toby Gerhart EXCH 25.00 50.00
Joe McKnight
MS Ryan Mathews 50.00 120.00
C.J. Spiller
TC Tim Tebow 100.00 175.00
Jimmy Clausen
TH Ben Tate 20.00 40.00
Montario Hardesty
BMC Sam Bradford 60.00 120.00
Colt McCoy
BW Arrelious Benn 40.00 80.00
Mike Williams

2011 Topps Platinum

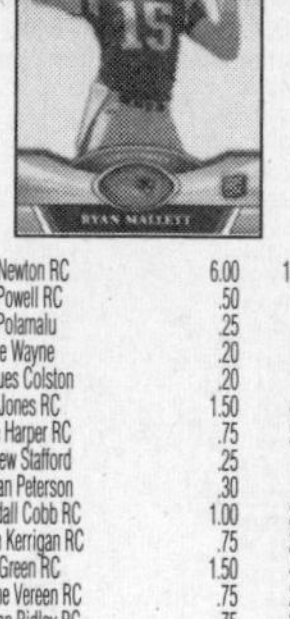

1 Cam Newton RC 6.00 15.00
2 Bilal Powell RC .50 1.25
3 Troy Polamalu .25 .60
4 Reggie Wayne .20 .50
6 Marques Colston .20 .50
7 Julio Jones RC 1.50 4.00
8 Jamie Harper RC .75 2.00
9 Matthew Stafford .25 .60
10 Adrian Peterson .30 .75
11 Randall Cobb RC 1.00 2.50
12 Ryan Kerrigan RC .75 2.00
13 A.J. Green RC 1.50 4.00
14 Shane Vereen RC .75 2.00
15 Stevan Ridley RC .75 2.00
16 Jeremy Kerley RC .75 2.00
17 Miles Austin .20 .50
18 Matt Schaub .20 .50
19 Jon Baldwin RC .75 2.00
20 Ray Rice .20 .50
21 Alex Green RC .75 2.00
22 Michael Turner .20 .50
23 Mike Williams .20 .50
24 Beanie Wells .20 .50
25 Ryan Mathews .20 .50
26 Kellen Winslow .20 .50
27 Von Miller RC 1.00 2.50
28 Tandon Doss RC .60 1.50
29 Roddy White .20 .50
30 Chris Johnson .20 .50
31 Percy Harvin .20 .50
32 DeAngelo Williams .20 .50
33 Dallas Clark .20 .50
35 Jonathan Stewart .20 .50
36 Knowshon Moreno .20 .50
38 Nick Fairley RC 1.00 2.50
39 Lance Kendricks RC .60 1.50
40 Andre Johnson .20 .50
41 Ray Lewis .25 .60
42 Jahvid Best .20 .50
44 Daniel Thomas RC .75 2.00
45 Brandon Marshall .20 .50
46 Dez Bryant .25 .60
47 Sidney Rice .20 .50
48 Shonn Greene .20 .50
49 LaDainian Tomlinson .25 .60
50 Blaine Gabbert RC 1.25 3.00
51 Jimmy Smith RC .75 2.00
53 Steven Jackson .20 .50
54 Cedric Benson .20 .50
55 Brian Urlacher .25 .60
56 Tony Romo .25 .60
58 D.J. Williams RC .75 2.00
59 Colin Kaepernick RC 1.00 2.50
60 Arian Foster .20 .50
61 Chris Cooley .20 .50
62 Edmond Gates RC .60 1.50
63 Santana Moss .20 .50
64 Marcell Dareus RC .75 2.00
65 Frank Gore .20 .50
66 Aldon Smith RC 1.25 3.00
67 Champ Bailey .20 .50
68 Jay Cutler .20 .50
69 Santonio Holmes .20 .50
70 Tom Brady .40 1.00
71 Greg Jennings .20 .50
72 Pierre Thomas .20 .50
73 Prince Amukamara RC .75 2.00
74 Ben Roethlisberger .25 .60
75 Matt Ryan .25 .60
76 Antonio Gates .20 .50
77 Thomas Jones .20 .50
78 Jordan Todman RC .50 1.25
79 Felix Jones .20 .50
80 Michael Vick .25 .60
81 Philip Rivers .25 .60
82 Darren McFadden .20 .50
83 Sam Bradford .25 .60
84 Josh Freeman .25 .60
85 Brandon Pettigrew .15 .40
86 J.J. Watt RC 1.00 2.50
88 Joseph Addai .20 .50
89 Joe Flacco .25 .60
90 Larry Fitzgerald .20 .50
91 Delone Carter RC .60 1.50
92 Calvin Johnson .25 .60
93 Jeremy Maclin .20 .50
94 Mikel Leshoure RC .75 2.00
95 Kenny Britt .20 .50
96 Austin Pettis RC .60 1.50
97 Kyle Rudolph RC .75 2.00
98 Mike Wallace .25 .60
99 Cameron Jordan RC .60 1.50
100 Peyton Manning .40 1.00
101 Vincent Brown RC .75 2.00
102 Braylon Edwards .20 .50
103 Jermichael Finley .20 .50
104 Hakeem Nicks .20 .50
105 Jerrel Jernigan RC .60 1.50
106 Ryan Williams RC 1.00 2.50
107 Da'Quan Bowers RC .75 2.00
108 Vincent Jackson .20 .50
109 Christian Ponder RC 1.50 4.00
110 Jamaal Charles .20 .50
111 Taiwan Jones RC .75 2.00
112 Marshawn Lynch .20 .50
113 LeSean McCoy .20 .50
114 DeMarco Murray RC 1.50 4.00
115 Cecil Shorts RC .60 1.50
116 Titus Young RC 1.00 2.50
117 Patrick Willis .20 .50
118 Brandon Lloyd .20 .50
119 Torrey Smith RC 1.00 2.50
120 Mark Ingram RC 1.50 4.00
121 Dwayne Bowe .20 .50
123 Matt Forte .20 .50
125 Jake Locker RC 2.00 5.00
126 Zach Miller .20 .50
127 Rashard Mendenhall .20 .50
129 Eli Manning .25 .60
130 Drew Brees .25 .60
131 Fred Jackson .25 .60
132 Andy Dalton RC 2.00 5.00
133 Jason Witten .25 .60
134 Ricky Stanzi RC 1.00 2.50
135 Steve Johnson .20 .50
136 Ryan Mallett RC 1.50 4.00
137 Leonard Hankerson RC .75 2.00
138 Ahmad Bradshaw .20 .50
139 Kendall Hunter RC .75 2.00
140 Maurice Jones-Drew .20 .50
142 Wes Welker .25 .60
143 Michael Crabtree .20 .50
144 DeSean Jackson .20 .50
145 Peyton Hillis .20 .50
146 Matt Cassel .20 .50
147 Vernon Davis .20 .50
148 Greg Little RC .75 2.00
150 Aaron Rodgers .40 1.00

2011 Topps Platinum Blue Refractors

*BLUE REF/299: 1.2X TO 3X BASIC INSERTS
BLUE REF/299 ODDS 1:49 HOB

2011 Topps Platinum Gold

*VETS: 1X TO 2.5X BASIC CARDS
ONE VETERAN PER HOBBY PACK
*ROOKIES: 3X TO 8X BASIC CARDS
ROOKIE/50 ODDS 1:293 HOB
1 Cam Newton/50 60.00 120.00

2011 Topps Platinum Green

*VETS: 2X TO 5X BASIC CARDS
VETERAN STATED ODDS 1:10 HOB
*ROOKIES: 1X TO 2.5X BASIC CARDS
ROOKIE/499 ODDS 1:29 HOB

2011 Topps Platinum Red

*VETS: 3X TO 8X BASIC CARDS
VETERAN STATED ODDS 1:20 HOB
*ROOKIES/25: 4X TO 10X BASIC CARDS
ROOKIE/25 ODDS 1:586 HOB
1 Cam Newton/25 150.00 250.00

2011 Topps Platinum Purple Refractors

*PURPLE REF/99: 2X TO 5X BASIC INSERTS
PURPLE REF/99 ODDS 1:48 HOB
1 Cam Newton 40.00 100.00

2011 Topps Platinum Xfractors

*ROOKIES: .8X TO 2X BASIC INSERTS
STATED ODDS 1:4 HOB

2011 Topps Platinum Die Cuts

STATED ODDS 1:20 HOB
PDCAD Andy Dalton 4.00 10.00
PDCAF Arian Foster 2.00 5.00
PDCAG A.J. Green 3.00 8.00
PDCAJ Andre Johnson 2.00 5.00
PDCAP Adrian Peterson 3.00 8.00
PDCAR Aaron Rodgers 4.00 10.00
PDCBG Blaine Gabbert 2.50 6.00
PDCCJ Chris Johnson 2.00 5.00
PDCCJO Calvin Johnson 2.50 6.00
PDCCN Cam Newton 12.00 30.00
PDCJB Jon Baldwin 1.50 4.00
PDCJJ Julio Jones 3.00 8.00
PDCJL Jake Locker 4.00 10.00
PDCKR Kyle Rudolph 1.50 4.00
PDCLF Larry Fitzgerald 2.00 5.00
PDCMD Marcell Dareus 1.50 4.00
PDCML Mikel Leshoure 1.50 4.00
PDCMV Michael Vick 2.50 6.00
PDCPA Prince Amukamara 1.50 4.00
PDCPP Patrick Peterson 2.50 6.00
PDCRM Ryan Mallett 3.00 8.00
PDCRW Ryan Williams 2.00 5.00
PDCTB Tom Brady 4.00 10.00
PDCTP Troy Polamalu 2.50 6.00
PDCTS Torrey Smith 2.00 5.00

2011 Topps Platinum Patch Autographs

STATED PRINT RUN 30 SER.#'d SETS
*GOLD REF/10: .5X TO 1.2X PATCH AU/30
*PURPLE REF/25: .4X TO 1X PATCH AU/30
EXCH EXPIRATION: 8/31/2014
AVPAG Antonio Gates 15.00 40.00
AVPCB Champ Bailey 25.00 50.00
AVPDM Darren McFadden 25.00 50.00
AVPDR Darrelle Revis 15.00 40.00
AVPGJ Greg Jennings 25.00 50.00
AVPJM Jerod Mayo EXCH 12.00 30.00
AVPJMA Jeremy Maclin 15.00 40.00
AVPJW Jason Witten 25.00 50.00
AVPLM LeSean McCoy 15.00 40.00
AVPMJD Maurice Jones-Drew 15.00 40.00
AVPPM Peyton Manning
AVPPW Patrick Willis EXCH 15.00 40.00
AVPRL Ray Lewis 50.00 100.00
AVPSJ Steven Jackson
AVPSR Sidney Rice 15.00 40.00

2011 Topps Platinum Rookie Autographs

STATED PRINT RUN 250-2175
*GREEN REF/150: .6X TO 1.5X AU/1450-2175
*GREEN REF/150: .5X TO 1.2X AU/808-1050
*GREEN REF/150: .4X TO 1X AU/250
EXCH EXPIRATION: 8/31/2014
2 Bilal Powell/250 4.00 10.00
5 Darvin Adams/1725 3.00 8.00
8 Jamie Harper/250 6.00 15.00
12 Ryan Kerrigan/1450 5.00 12.00
15 Stevan Ridley/250 6.00 15.00
16 Jeremy Kerley/2175 4.00 10.00
21 Alex Green/250 6.00 15.00
28 Tandon Doss/1725 3.00 8.00
34 Derrick Locke/1000 4.00 10.00
37 Justin Houston/1450 4.00 10.00
39 Lance Kendricks/808 4.00 10.00
43 Niles Paul/1450 4.00 10.00
44 Daniel Thomas/250 6.00 15.00
51 Jimmy Smith/1450 4.00 10.00
52 Da'Rel Scott/1050 4.00 10.00
57 Virgil Green/1000 4.00 10.00
58 D.J. Williams/1000 5.00 12.00
62 Edmond Gates/1000 4.00 10.00
66 Aldon Smith/808 8.00 20.00
73 Prince Amukamara/2175 4.00 10.00
78 Jordan Todman/250 4.00 10.00
86 J.J. Watt/1550 5.00 12.00
87 Rob Housler/1050 4.00 10.00
91 Delone Carter/250 5.00 12.00
96 Austin Pettis/1000 4.00 10.00
97 Kyle Rudolph/250 6.00 15.00
99 Cameron Jordan/1550 3.00 8.00
101 Vincent Brown/1000 5.00 12.00
105 Jerrel Jernigan/250 5.00 12.00
107 Da'Quan Bowers/250 6.00 15.00
111 Taiwan Jones/2175 4.00 10.00
114 DeMarco Murray/250 40.00 80.00
115 Cecil Shorts/1000 4.00 10.00
122 John Clay/1550 4.00 10.00
124 Rahim Moore/1000 4.00 10.00
128 Dwayne Harris EXCH 4.00 10.00
139 Kendall Hunter/1000 5.00 12.00
141 Terrence Toliver/1000 4.00 10.00
149 Darren Evans/1000 4.00 10.00

2011 Topps Platinum Rookie Autographs Blue Refractors

*BLUE REF/99: .8X TO 2X AU/1450-2175
*BLUE REF/99: .6X TO 1.5X AU/808-1050
*BLUE REF/99: .5X TO 1.2X AU/250
11 Randall Cobb 25.00 50.00
134 Ricky Stanzi
137 Leonard Hankerson 8.00 20.00
148 Greg Little 8.00 20.00

2011 Topps Platinum Rookie Autographs Dual

STATED PRINT RUN 25 SER.#'d SETS
AP Prince Amukamara 25.00 50.00
Niles Paul
BL Jon Baldwin
Dion Lewis
CG Randall Cobb 60.00 120.00
Alex Green
DM Marcell Dareus 25.00 50.00
Von Miller
DP Andy Dalton 75.00 150.00
Christian Ponder
FB Nick Fairley 12.00 30.00
Da'Quan Bowers
GT Edmond Gates
Daniel Thomas
HT Kendall Hunter EXCH 10.00 25.00
Jordan Todman
JD Julio Jones 40.00 80.00
Marcell Dareus
JG Jerrel Jernigan 15.00 40.00
Edmond Gates
KG Colin Kaepernick 30.00 80.00
Virgil Green
LW Mikel Leshoure 20.00 50.00
Ryan Williams
MA Von Miller 20.00 50.00
Prince Amukamara
MK Ryan Mallett 40.00 80.00
Colin Kaepernick
MT DeMarco Murray 40.00 80.00
Daniel Thomas
NF Cam Newton 125.00 200.00
Nick Fairley
SH Torrey Smith 20.00 50.00
Leonard Hankerson
SS Torrey Smith 15.00 40.00
Da'Rel Scott
VR Shane Vereen 15.00 40.00
Jacquizz Rodgers
YP Titus Young
Austin Pettis

2011 Topps Platinum Rookie Jumbo Patch

STATED PRINT RUN 36 SER.#'d SETS
PRPAD Andy Dalton 15.00 40.00
PRPAG Alex Green 6.00 15.00
PRPAJG A.J. Green 15.00 40.00
PRPAP Austin Pettis 5.00 12.00
PRPBG Blaine Gabbert 10.00 25.00
PRPBP Bilal Powell 4.00 10.00
PRPCK Colin Kaepernick 8.00 20.00
PRPCN Cam Newton 40.00 80.00
PRPCP Christian Ponder 12.00 30.00
PRPDC Delone Carter 5.00 12.00
PRPDM DeMarco Murray 12.00 30.00
PRPDT Daniel Thomas 6.00 15.00
PRPEG Edmond Gates 5.00 12.00
PRPGL Greg Little 6.00 15.00
PRPJB Jon Baldwin 6.00 15.00
PRPJH Jamie Harper 6.00 15.00
PRPJJ Julio Jones 15.00 40.00
PRPJJE Jerrel Jernigan 5.00 12.00
PRPJL Jake Locker 15.00 40.00
PRPJT Jordan Todman 4.00 10.00
PRPKH Kendall Hunter 6.00 15.00
PRPKR Kyle Rudolph 6.00 15.00
PRPLH Leonard Hankerson 6.00 15.00
PRPMD Marcell Dareus 6.00 15.00
PRPMI Mark Ingram 12.00 30.00
PRPML Mikel Leshoure 6.00 15.00
PRPRC Randall Cobb 8.00 20.00
PRPRM Ryan Mallett 12.00 30.00
PRPRW Ryan Williams 8.00 20.00
PRPSR Stevan Ridley 6.00 15.00
PRPSV Shane Vereen 6.00 15.00
PRPTJ Taiwan Jones 6.00 15.00
PRPTS Torrey Smith 8.00 20.00
PRPTY Titus Young 8.00 20.00
PRPVB Vincent Brown 6.00 15.00
PRPVM Von Miller 8.00 20.00

2011 Topps Platinum Rookie Patch Autographs

STATED PRINT RUN 150-475
2 Bilal Powell/356 4.00 10.00
8 Jamie Harper/475 6.00 15.00
11 Randall Cobb/150 25.00 50.00
15 Stevan Ridley/199 8.00 20.00
16 Shane Vereen/199 8.00 20.00
21 Alex Green/475 6.00 15.00
27 Von Miller/150 10.00 25.00
28 Tandon Doss/356 5.00 12.00
37 Greg Salas/356 6.00 15.00
43 Niles Paul/356 6.00 15.00
44 Daniel Thomas/199 8.00 20.00
51 Dion Lewis/356 6.00 15.00
62 Edmond Gates/475 5.00 12.00
64 Marcell Dareus/150 8.00 20.00
73 Prince Amukamara/475 6.00 15.00
78 Jordan Todman/475 4.00 10.00
86 Torrey Smith/150 10.00 25.00
91 Delone Carter/475 5.00 12.00
94 Mikel Leshoure/150 8.00 20.00
96 Austin Pettis/475 5.00 12.00
97 Kyle Rudolph/150 8.00 20.00
101 Vincent Brown/475 6.00 15.00
105 Jerrel Jernigan/199 6.00 15.00
111 Taiwan Jones/475 8.00 20.00
114 DeMarco Murray/199 50.00 100.00
115 Cecil Shorts/356 5.00 12.00
116 Titus Young/150 10.00 25.00
137 Leonard Hankerson/150 8.00 20.00
139 Kendall Hunter/475 6.00 15.00
148 Greg Little/150 8.00 20.00

2011 Topps Platinum Rookie Patch Autographs Blue Refractors

*BLUE AU/75: .6X TO 1.5X BASIC AU/356-475
*BLUE AU/75: .5X TO 1.2X BASIC AU/150-199
1 Cam Newton 175.00 300.00
106 Ryan Williams 30.00 60.00

2011 Topps Platinum Rookie Patch Autographs Green Refractors

*GREEN AU/125: .5X TO 1.2X BASIC AU/356-475
*GREEN AU/125: .4X TO 1X BASIC AU/150-199
1 Cam Newton 150.00 300.00

2011 Topps Platinum Rookie Patch Autographs Purple Refractors

*PURPLE AU/25: 1.2X TO 3X BASIC AU/356-475
*PURPLE AU/25: 1X TO 2.5X BASIC AU/150-199
1 Cam Newton 300.00 450.00
11 Randall Cobb 60.00 120.00
50 Blaine Gabbert 100.00 175.00
59 Colin Kaepernick 40.00 100.00
106 Ryan Williams 40.00 80.00
120 Mark Ingram 125.00 200.00
132 Andy Dalton 100.00 175.00
136 Ryan Mallett 90.00 150.00

2011 Topps Platinum Rookie Patch Autographs Dual

STATED PRINT RUN 25 SER.#'d SETS
AP Prince Amukamara 25.00 60.00
Niles Paul
BL Jon Baldwin 20.00 50.00
Dion Lewis
CG Randall Cobb 75.00 135.00
Alex Green
DM Marcell Dareus 25.00 60.00
Von Miller
DP Andy Dalton 100.00 200.00
Christian Ponder
FB Nick Fairley 15.00 40.00
Da'Quan Bowers
GJ A.J. Green 125.00 200.00
Julio Jones
GT Edmond Gates 25.00 60.00
Daniel Thomas
HT Kendall Hunter
Jordan Todman
JD Julio Jones 50.00 100.00
Marcell Dareus
JH Jerrel Jernigan 15.00 40.00
Leonard Hankerson
KH Colin Kaepernick 40.00 80.00
Kendall Hunter
LW Mikel Leshoure 25.00 60.00
Ryan Williams
MK Ryan Mallett 50.00 100.00
Colin Kaepernick
MT DeMarco Murray 40.00 100.00
Daniel Thomas
NF Cam Newton 175.00 300.00
Nick Fairley
PT Bilal Powell 20.00 50.00
Daniel Thomas
VR Shane Vereen 20.00 50.00
Jacquizz Rodgers
YL Titus Young EXCH 25.00 60.00
Mikel Leshoure
YP Titus Young EXCH 25.00 60.00
Austin Pettis

2011 Topps Precision

ONE AUTO PER PACK OVERALL
EXCH EXPIRATION: 1/31/2015
1 Adrian Peterson 2.00 5.00
2 Sidney Rice 1.25 3.00
3 Sam Bradford 1.50 4.00
4 Patrick Willis 1.25 3.00
5 Roger Staubach 2.00 5.00
6 Jim Brown 2.00 5.00
7 Maurice Jones-Drew 1.25 3.00
8 Frank Gore 1.25 3.00
9 Marques Colston 1.25 3.00
10 Larry Fitzgerald 1.25 3.00
11 DeAngelo Williams 1.25 3.00
12 Greg Jennings 1.25 3.00
13 Tony Dorsett 1.50 4.00
14 DeMarcus Ware 1.25 3.00
15 DeSean Jackson 1.25 3.00
16 Mike Wallace 1.50 4.00
17 Calvin Johnson 1.50 4.00
18 Reggie Bush 1.25 3.00
19 Dwayne Bowe 1.25 3.00
20 Roddy White 1.25 3.00
21 Peyton Hillis 1.25 3.00
22 Shonn Greene 1.25 3.00
23 Earl Campbell 1.50 4.00
24 Jason Witten 1.50 4.00
25 Knowshon Moreno 1.25 3.00
26 Rashard Mendenhall 1.25 3.00
27 Vincent Jackson 1.25 3.00
28 Ben Roethlisberger 1.50 4.00
29 Phil Simms 1.25 3.00
30 Chris Johnson 1.25 3.00
31 Brandon Lloyd 1.25 3.00
32 Charles Woodson 1.50 4.00
33 Ndamukong Suh 1.50 4.00
34 Tony Romo 1.50 4.00
35 Philip Rivers 1.50 4.00
36 Vernon Davis 1.25 3.00
37 Miles Austin 1.25 3.00
38 Dez Bryant 1.50 4.00
39 Jimmy Graham 1.50 4.00
40 Andre Johnson 1.25 3.00
41 Chad Ochocinco 1.25 3.00
42 Percy Harvin 1.25 3.00
43 Terry Bradshaw 2.00 5.00
44 Brandon Marshall 1.25 3.00
45 Joe Flacco 1.50 4.00
46 Peyton Manning 2.50 6.00
47 Mike Williams 1.25 3.00
48 Cedric Benson 1.25 3.00
49 Josh Freeman 1.50 4.00
50 Aaron Rodgers 3.00 8.00
51 Mario Manningham 1.25 3.00
52 Pierre Thomas 1.25 3.00
53 Kenny Britt 1.25 3.00
54 Santonio Holmes 1.25 3.00
55 Clay Matthews 1.50 4.00
56 Felix Jones 1.25 3.00
57 LeSean McCoy 1.25 3.00
58 Thurman Thomas 1.50 4.00
59 Ray Lewis 1.50 4.00
60 Jamaal Charles 1.25 3.00
61 Joe Namath 2.00 5.00
62 Dallas Clark 1.25 3.00
63 Ahmad Bradshaw 1.25 3.00
64 Ryan Mathews 1.25 3.00
65 Eli Manning 1.50 4.00
66 Matt Schaub 1.25 3.00
67 Darren McFadden 1.25 3.00
68 Ray Rice 1.25 3.00
69 Gale Sayers 1.50 4.00
70 Arian Foster 1.25 3.00
71 Matt Forte 1.25 3.00
72 Steve Smith 1.25 3.00
73 Hakeem Nicks 1.25 3.00
74 Franco Harris 1.50 4.00
75 Steven Jackson 1.25 3.00
76 Matthew Stafford 1.50 4.00
77 Steve Johnson 1.25 3.00
78 Antonio Gates 1.25 3.00
79 Anquan Boldin 1.25 3.00
80 Tom Brady 2.50 6.00
81 Len Dawson 1.50 4.00
82 Marshawn Lynch 1.25 3.00
83 Austin Collie 1.25 3.00
84 Kurt Warner 1.25 3.00
85 Beanie Wells 1.25 3.00
86 Owen Daniels 1.00 2.50
87 Michael Turner 1.25 3.00
88 Eric Dickerson 1.25 3.00
89 LeGarrette Blount 1.25 3.00
90 Drew Brees 1.50 4.00
91 Tim Hightower 1.00 2.50
92 Marcus Allen 1.50 4.00
93 Santana Moss 1.25 3.00
94 Jermichael Finley 1.25 3.00
95 Reggie Wayne 1.25 3.00
96 Jahvid Best 1.25 3.00
97 Joseph Addai 1.25 3.00
98 Matt Ryan 1.50 4.00
99 Jeremy Maclin 1.25 3.00
100 Michael Vick 1.50 4.00
105 Colin Kaepernick AU RC 10.00 25.00
106 Ryan Mallett AU RC 15.00 40.00
107 Jonathan Baldwin AU RC 8.00 20.00
108 Ryan Williams AU RC 10.00 25.00
109 Mikel Leshoure AU RC 8.00 20.00
111 Marcell Dareus AU RC 8.00 20.00
112 Von Miller AU RC 10.00 25.00
113 Randall Cobb AU RC 10.00 25.00
114 Leonard Hankerson AU RC 6.00 15.00
115 Greg Little AU RC 6.00 15.00
116 Torrey Smith AU RC 8.00 20.00
117 Alex Green AU RC 8.00 20.00
118 Jerrel Jernigan AU RC 5.00 12.00
119 DeMarco Murray AU RC 25.00 50.00
121 Shane Vereen AU RC 6.00 15.00
122 Stevan Ridley AU RC 6.00 15.00
123 Delone Carter AU RC 5.00 12.00
124 Jamie Harper AU RC 5.00 12.00
125 Taiwan Jones AU RC 5.00 12.00
126 Bilal Powell AU RC 4.00 10.00
127 Jordan Todman AU RC 4.00 10.00
128 Edmond Gates AU RC 4.00 10.00
129 Kendall Hunter AU RC 8.00 20.00
131 Vincent Brown AU RC 5.00 12.00
132 Roy Helu AU RC 10.00 25.00
133 Terrelle Pryor AU RC EXCH 15.00 40.00
134 Titus Young AU RC 8.00 20.00
135 Kyle Rudolph AU RC 6.00 15.00
136 Austin Pettis AU RC 4.00 10.00
137 Daniel Thomas AU RC 5.00 12.00

2011 Topps Precision Autographs Gold

*GOLD VETS/50: .5X TO 1.2X RED AU/99
GOLD VETERANS PRINT RUN 50
UNPRICED GOLD LEGEND PRINT RUN 10
PCVADB Drew Brees/50 40.00 80.00

2011 Topps Precision Autographs Green

*GREEN VETS/25: .6X TO 1.5X RED AU/99
GREEN PRINT RUN 25 SER.#'d SETS
PCVADB Drew Brees 40.00 100.00

2011 Topps Precision Autographs Red

VETERAN STATED PRINT RUN 99
LEGEND STATED PRINT RUN 25
*BASE VETS: .3X TO .8X RED AU/99
*BASE LEGENDS: .3X TO .8X RED AU/99
PCRAAM Art Monk/25 20.00 50.00
PCRAEC Earl Campbell/25 20.00 50.00
PCRAED Eric Dickerson/25 20.00 50.00
PCRAFB Fred Biletnikoff/25 20.00 50.00
PCRAFH Franco Harris/25 20.00 50.00
PCRAGS Gale Sayers/25 25.00 60.00
PCRAJB Jerome Bettis/25 75.00 150.00
PCRAJBR Jim Brown/25 40.00 80.00
PCRAJN Joe Namath/25 50.00 100.00
PCRAKS Ken Stabler/25 20.00 50.00
PCRAKW Kurt Warner/25
PCRALD Len Dawson/25 15.00 40.00
PCRAMA Marcus Allen/25 20.00 50.00
PCRAPS Phil Simms/25 15.00 40.00
PCRARL Ronnie Lott/25 20.00 50.00
PCRARS Roger Staubach/25 50.00 100.00
PCRATB Terry Bradshaw/25 50.00 100.00
PCRATBR Tim Brown/25 20.00 50.00
PCRATD Tony Dorsett/25 30.00 60.00
PCRATT Thurman Thomas/25 15.00 40.00
PCRAYT Y.A. Tittle/25 15.00 40.00
PCVAAB Ahmad Bradshaw/99 6.00 15.00
PCVAABE Arrelious Benn/99 5.00 12.00
PCVAAR Antrel Rolle/99 4.00 10.00
PCVAAW Adrian Wilson/99 4.00 10.00
PCVABL Brandon Lloyd/99 5.00 12.00
PCVACS C.J. Spiller/99 5.00 12.00
PCVADBE Davone Bess/99 4.00 10.00
PCVADH DeAngelo Hall/99 4.00 10.00
PCVADM Derrick Mason/99 4.00 10.00
PCVAEB Eric Berry/99 6.00 15.00
PCVAGO Greg Olsen/99 5.00 12.00
PCVAJF Jacoby Ford/99 5.00 12.00
PCVAJG Jermaine Gresham/99 5.00 12.00
PCVAJGR Jimmy Graham/99 12.00 30.00
PCVAJM Jerod Mayo/99 5.00 12.00
PCVAJP Jason Pierre-Paul/99 10.00 25.00
PCVALB LeGarrette Blount/99 5.00 12.00
PCVAML Marshawn Lynch/99 8.00 20.00
PCVAMW Mike Wallace/99 10.00 25.00
PCVANW Nate Washington/99 5.00 12.00
PCVARM Robert Mathis/99 6.00 15.00
PCVARW Roddy White/99 6.00 15.00
PCVASB Steve Breaston/99 4.00 10.00
PCVASJ Steve Johnson/99 6.00 15.00
PCVATH Todd Heap/99 4.00 10.00
PCVATJ Thomas Jones/99 6.00 15.00
PCVATP Taylor Price/99 4.00 10.00
PCVATW T.J. Ward/99 6.00 15.00
PCVAVD Vernon Davis/99 8.00 20.00

2011 Topps Precision Autographs Dual

STATED PRINT RUN 25 SER.#'d SETS
PCDABS Jonathan Baldwin 15.00 40.00
Torrey Smith
PCDACG Randall Cobb 15.00 40.00
Alex Green
PCDADG Andy Dalton 75.00 150.00
A.J. Green
PCDADM Marcell Dareus EXCH 20.00 50.00
Von Miller
PCDAFJ Jacoby Ford 12.00 30.00
Taiwan Jones
PCDAGJ A.J. Green 60.00 120.00
Julio Jones
PCDAGL Blaine Gabbert 40.00 100.00
Jake Locker
PCDAIL Mark Ingram
Mikel Leshoure
PCDAKH Colin Kaepernick 25.00 50.00
Kendall Hunter
PCDAKW Kevin Kolb 15.00 40.00
Ryan Williams
PCDALH Greg Little 12.00 30.00
Leonard Hankerson
PCDALY Mikel Leshoure 15.00 40.00
Titus Young
PCDAMR Ryan Mallett 20.00 50.00
Stevan Ridley
PCDAMT Brandon Marshall 15.00 40.00
Daniel Thomas
PCDAMV Ryan Mallett
Shane Vereen
PCDANG Cam Newton 125.00 200.00
A.J. Green
PCDANI Cam Newton 125.00 200.00
Mark Ingram
PCDANJ Cam Newton 125.00 200.00
Julio Jones
PCDAPR Christian Ponder 25.00 60.00
Kyle Rudolph
PCDASY Matt Stafford 40.00 80.00
Titus Young
PCDATB Jordan Todman 12.00 30.00
Vincent Brown
PCDATG Daniel Thomas 12.00 30.00
Edmond Gates
PCDAVR Shane Vereen 12.00 30.00
Stevan Ridley
PCDALHA Jake Locker 40.00 100.00
Jamie Harper
PCDANGA Cam Newton 100.00 200.00
Blaine Gabbert

2011 Topps Precision Autographs Triple

STATED PRINT RUN 15 SER.#'d SETS
BCI Drew Brees 150.00 250.00
Marques Colston
Mark Ingram
CJC Matt Cassel 15.00 40.00
Thomas Jones
Jamaal Charles
FMB Nick Fairley 25.00 50.00
Von Miller
Da'Quan Bowers
GSL A.J. Green 50.00 100.00
Torrey Smith
Greg Little
JCG Greg Jennings
Randall Cobb
Alex Green
KWW Kevin Kolb 30.00 60.00
Beanie Wells
Ryan Williams
LYF Mikel Leshoure 25.00 50.00
Titus Young
Nick Fairley
MHL Colt McCoy 25.00 50.00
Peyton Hillis
Greg Little
MVR Ryan Mallett 30.00 80.00
Shane Vereen
Stevan Ridley
RBM Tony Romo 125.00 200.00
Dez Bryant
DeMarco Murray
RML Stevan Ridley 30.00 80.00
DeMarco Murray
Dion Lewis
RPC Stevan Ridley 15.00 40.00
Bilal Powell
Delone Carter
RWJ Matt Ryan 60.00 120.00
Roddy White
Julio Jones
TMR Daniel Thomas
DeMarco Murray
Stevan Ridley
YHL Titus Young 15.00 40.00
Leonard Hankerson
Greg Little

2011 Topps Precision Rookie Autographs Gold Ink

*GOLD INK/50: .6X TO 1.5X BASIC AU
GOLD INK STATED PRINT RUN 50
EXCH EXPIRATION: 1/31/2015
101 Jake Locker 50.00 120.00
102 Blaine Gabbert 25.00 60.00
104 Andy Dalton 40.00 100.00
120 A.J. Green 40.00 100.00
138 Cam Newton 150.00 300.00

2011 Topps Precision Rookie Autographs Red Ink

*RED INK/75: .5X TO 1.2X BASIC AU
RED INK STATED PRINT RUN 75

103 Christian Ponder	30.00	60.00
104 Andy Dalton	30.00	80.00
110 Mark Ingram	30.00	60.00

2011 Topps Precision Rookie Autographs White Ink

*WHITE INK/25: .8X TO 2X BASIC AU
WHITE INK STATED PRINT RUN 25

101 Jake Locker	75.00	150.00
102 Blaine Gabbert	30.00	80.00
103 Christian Ponder	40.00	100.00
110 Mark Ingram	40.00	100.00

2011 Topps Precision Rookie Jumbo Relic Autographs Green

GREEN PRINT RUN 25 SER.#'d SETS
*BASE JSY AU: .25X TO .6X GREEN JSY AU/25
*GOLD/30: .3X TO .8X GREEN JSY AU/25
*RED/50: .3X TO .8X GREEN JSY AU/25
EXCH EXPIRATION: 1/31/2015

RAJRAD Andy Dalton	60.00	120.00
RAJRAG A.J. Green	50.00	100.00
RAJRAGR Alex Green	12.00	30.00
RAJRAP Austin Pettis	10.00	25.00
RAJRBG Blaine Gabbert	20.00	50.00
RAJRBP Bilal Powell	8.00	20.00
RAJRCK Colin Kaepernick	15.00	40.00
RAJRCN Cam Newton	250.00	400.00
RAJRCP Christian Ponder	40.00	80.00
RAJRDC Delone Carter	10.00	25.00
RAJRDM DeMarco Murray EXCH	40.00	100.00
RAJRDT Daniel Thomas	12.00	30.00
RAJREG Edmond Gates	10.00	25.00
RAJRGL Greg Little	12.00	30.00
RAJRJB Jonathan Baldwin	12.00	30.00
RAJRJH Jamie Harper	10.00	25.00
RAJRJJE Jerrel Jernigan	10.00	25.00
RAJRJL Jake Locker	50.00	120.00
RAJRJT Jordan Todman	8.00	20.00
RAJRKH Kendall Hunter	15.00	40.00
RAJRKR Kyle Rudolph	12.00	30.00
RAJRLH Leonard Hankerson	12.00	30.00
RAJRMD Marcell Dareus	12.00	30.00
RAJRMI Mark Ingram	50.00	100.00
RAJRML Mikel Leshoure	12.00	30.00
RAJRRC Randall Cobb	15.00	40.00
RAJRRM Ryan Mallett	40.00	80.00
RAJRRW Ryan Williams	15.00	40.00
RAJRSR Stevan Ridley	12.00	30.00
RAJRSV Shane Vereen	12.00	30.00
RAJRTJ Taiwan Jones	12.00	30.00
RAJRTS Torrey Smith	15.00	40.00
RAJRTY Titus Young	15.00	40.00
RAJRVB Vincent Brown	12.00	30.00
RAJRVM Von Miller EXCH	25.00	60.00

2011 Topps Precision Veteran Patch Relic Autographs

STATED PRINT RUN 15 SER.#'d SETS

VAPAB Ahmad Bradshaw	12.00	30.00
VAPAG Antonio Gates	12.00	30.00
VAPBL Brandon Lloyd	12.00	30.00
VAPDM Darren McFadden	15.00	40.00
VAPHW Hines Ward	50.00	100.00
VAPJC Jamaal Charles	12:00	30.00
VAPLM LeSean McCoy	15.00	40.00
VAPMS Mark Sanchez		
VAPSJ Steve Johnson		
VAPVD Vernon Davis		

2010 Topps Prime

COMPLETE SET (150)	40.00	80.00
COMP.SET w/o RC's (100)	15.00	30.00

ROOKIE/999 STATED ODDS 1:4 HOB
HOBBY CARDS PRINTED ON THICK STOCK

1 Tim Tebow RC	4.00	10.00
2 Trent Williams RC	1.00	2.50
3 Miles Austin	.30	.75
4 Matt Forte	.25	.60
5 Armanti Edwards RC	1.00	2.50
6 Mike Wallace	.25	.60
7 Donovan McNabb	.30	.75
8 Jay Cutler	.30	.75
9 Derrick Morgan RC	.75	2.00
10 Jimmy Clausen RC	1.00	2.50
11 Knowshon Moreno	.25	.60
12 Arrelious Benn RC	1.00	2.50
13 James Laurinaitis	.25	.60
14 Kellen Winslow	.25	.60
15 Reggie Bush	.30	.75
16 Jacoby Ford RC	1.00	2.50
17 Carlton Mitchell RC	.75	2.00
18 Beanie Wells	.25	.60
19 Troy Polamalu	.30	.75
20 Colt McCoy RC	2.00	5.00
21 Kevin Kolb	.25	.60
22 Eric Berry RC	1.00	2.50
23 Joe Webb RC	1.00	2.50
24 Jared Allen	.30	.75
25 Ed Wang RC	1.00	2.50
26 Randy Moss	.30	.75
27 Santana Moss	.25	.60
28 Rolando McClain RC	1.00	2.50
29 Felix Jones	.25	.60
30 Ryan Mathews RC	2.00	5.00
31 Darrelle Revis	.25	.60
32 Damian Williams RC	1.00	2.50
33 Shonn Greene	.25	.60
34 Marion Barber	.25	.60
35 LeSean McCoy	.25	.60
36 Matt Ryan	.30	.75
37 Brent Celek	.25	.60
38 Rashard Mendenhall	.25	.60
39 Clinton Portis	.25	.60
40 C.J. Spiller RC	1.50	4.00
41 Joe Flacco	.30	.75
42 Rob Gronkowski RC	2.50	6.00
43 Ronnie Brown	.25	.60
44 Ryan Grant	.25	.60
45 Fred Jackson	.30	.75
46 Andre Roberts RC	1.00	2.50
47 Josh Freeman	.30	.75
48 Mike Kafka RC	1.00	2.50
49 Gerald McCoy RC	1.00	2.50
50 Dez Bryant RC	3.00	8.00
51 Vincent Jackson	.20	.50
52 DeAngelo Williams	.25	.60
53 Dexter McCluster RC	1.00	2.50
54 Jonathan Dwyer RC	1.00	2.50
55 Earl Thomas RC	1.00	2.50
56 Sean Lee RC	1.00	2.50
57 Montario Hardesty RC	1.00	2.50
58 Cedric Benson	.25	.60
59 Chad Ochocinco	.25	.60
60 Demaryius Thomas RC	1.25	3.00
61 Jerry Hughes RC	1.00	2.50
62 Mario Williams	.25	.60
63 Dwight Freeney	.25	.60
64 Brandon LaFell RC	1.00	2.50
65 Emmanuel Sanders RC	1.00	2.50
66 Riley Cooper RC	1.00	2.50
67 Jamaal Charles	.25	.60
68 David Reed RC	.75	2.00
69 Mardy Gilyard RC	1.00	2.50
70 Jahvid Best RC	1.50	4.00
71 Devin Hester	.30	.75
72 Jared Odrick RC	1.00	2.50
73 Nnamdi Asomugha	.25	.60
74 Michael Turner	.20	.50
75 Eric Decker RC	1.25	3.00
76 Ray Rice	.25	.60
77 Robert Meachem	.25	.60
78 Steve Smith	.25	.60
79 Cadillac Williams	.25	.60
80 Ndamukong Suh RC	2.00	5.00
81 John Skelton RC	1.00	2.50
82 Sean Canfield RC	.75	2.00
83 Jonathan Stewart	.25	.60
84 DeMeco Ryans	.20	.50
85 Brian Dawkins	.25	.60
86 Brandon Marshall	.25	.60
87 Santonio Holmes	.25	.60
88 Brett Favre	.75	2.00
89 Jason Witten	.30	.75
90 Ben Tate RC	1.25	3.00
91 Dallas Clark	.25	.60
92 Jordan Shipley RC	1.00	2.50
93 Steven Jackson	.25	.60
94 Marcus Easley RC	.75	2.00
95 Joe McKnight RC	1.00	2.50
96 Mike Williams RC	1.50	4.00
97 Sidney Rice	.25	.60
98 Jermaine Gresham RC	1.25	3.00
99 Greg Jennings	.25	.60
100 Sam Bradford RC	4.00	10.00
101 Pierre Thomas	.25	.60
102 Roddy White	.25	.60
103 Reggie Wayne	.25	.60
104 Brandon Jacobs	.25	.60
105 Patrick Willis	.25	.60
106 Hakeem Nicks	.25	.60
107 Pierre Garcon	.25	.60
108 Frank Gore	.25	.60
109 Carson Palmer	.25	.60
110 Peyton Manning	.50	1.25
111 Antonio Gates	.25	.60
112 Bryan Bulaga RC	1.00	2.50
113 Mark Sanchez	.30	.75
114 Dwayne Bowe	.25	.60
115 DeMarcus Ware	.25	.60
116 Steve Smith USC	.25	.60
117 LaDainian Tomlinson	.30	.75
118 Chad Henne	.25	.60
119 Calvin Johnson	.30	.75
120 Adrian Peterson	.50	1.25
121 Tony Gonzalez	.25	.60
122 Michael Crabtree	.30	.75
123 Jon Beason	.20	.50
124 Vernon Davis	.25	.60
125 Philip Rivers	.30	.75
126 DeSean Jackson	.25	.60
127 Aaron Rodgers	.60	1.50
128 Larry Fitzgerald	.30	.75
129 Percy Harvin	.30	.75
130 Tom Brady	.50	1.25
131 Taylor Price RC	1.00	2.50
132 Hines Ward	.25	.60
133 Eli Manning	.30	.75
134 Wes Welker	.30	.75
135 Kenny Britt	.25	.60
136 Andre Johnson	.25	.60
137 Tony Romo	.40	1.00
138 Jeremy Maclin	.25	.60
139 Toby Gerhart RC	1.00	2.50
140 Chris Johnson	.30	.75
141 Matthew Stafford	.30	.75
142 Mike Sims-Walker	.25	.60
143 Golden Tate RC	1.00	2.50
144 Joseph Addai	.25	.60
145 Matt Schaub	.25	.60
146 Marques Colston	.25	.60
147 Thomas Jones	.25	.60
148 Maurice Jones-Drew	.25	.60
149 Anquan Boldin	.25	.60
150 Drew Brees	.30	.75

2010 Topps Prime Black

*ROOKIES: 1.5X TO 4X BASIC CARDS
BLACK/25 ODDS 1:133 HOBBY

2010 Topps Prime Blue

*VETS/50: 4X TO 10X BASIC CARDS
VETS/50 STATED ODDS 1:34 HOB
*ROOKIES/199: .8X TO 2X BASIC CARDS
ROOKIE/199 STATED ODDS 1:17 HOB

2010 Topps Prime Gold

*VETS/199: 2.5X TO 6X BASIC CARDS
VET/199 STATED ODDS 1:9 HOB
*ROOKIES/699: .5X TO 1.2X BASIC CARDS
ROOKIE/699 STATED ODDS 1:5 HOB

2010 Topps Prime Red

*ROOKIES: 1X TO 2.5X BASIC CARDS
RED/75 STATED ODDS 1:45 HOB

2010 Topps Prime Retail

*RETAIL VETS: .3X TO .8X HOBBY
*RETAIL ROOKIES: .2X TO .5X HOBBY
RETAIL CARDS PRINTED ON THIN STOCK

2010 Topps Prime Retail Bronze

*VETS: 1.5X TO 4X BASIC HOBBY
*ROOKIES: .4X TO 1X BASIC HOBBY
RETAIL BRONZE PRINT RUN 1379

2010 Topps Prime 2nd Quarter

*GOLD/25: .6X TO 1.5X BASIC INSERTS

2Q1 Tim Tebow	5.00	12.00
Sam Bradford		
2Q2 Peyton Manning	2.50	6.00
Joseph Addai		
2Q3 Joe McKnight	1.00	2.50
Anthony McCoy		
2Q4 Rolando McClain	1.00	2.50
Jacoby Ford		
2Q5 Tony Romo	3.00	8.00
Dez Bryant		
2Q6 Jimmy Clausen	1.00	2.50
Golden Tate		
2Q7 Eric Berry	1.00	2.50
Montario Hardesty		
2Q8 Jahvid Best	2.00	5.00
Ndamukong Suh		
2Q9 Dexter McCluster	1.00	2.50
Eric Berry		
2Q10 Bob Sanders	1.00	2.50
Eric Berry		
2Q11 Mike Kafka	1.00	2.50
Riley Cooper		
2Q12 Jonathan Dwyer	1.00	2.50
Emmanuel Sanders		
2Q13 Sam Bradford	4.00	10.00
Mardy Gilyard		
2Q14 Arrelious Benn	1.50	4.00
Mike Williams		
2Q15 Rob Gronkowski	2.50	6.00
Taylor Price		
2Q16 Ndamukong Suh	2.00	5.00
Gerald McCoy		
2Q17 Dez Bryant	3.00	8.00
Demaryius Thomas		
2Q18 Dexter McCluster	1.00	2.50
Arrelious Benn		
2Q19 C.J. Spiller	1.50	4.00
Marcus Easley		
2Q20 C.J. Spiller	2.00	5.00
Ryan Mathews		
2Q21 Rolando McClain	1.00	2.50
Richard Seymour		
2Q22 Colt McCoy	2.00	5.00
Montario Hardesty		
2Q23 Tim Tebow	4.00	10.00
Demaryius Thomas		
2Q24 Tim Tebow	4.00	10.00
Eric Decker		
2Q25 Demaryius Thomas	1.25	3.00
Eric Decker		
2Q26 Jermaine Gresham	1.25	3.00
Jordan Shipley		
2Q27 Brandon LaFell	1.00	2.50
Armanti Edwards		
2Q28 Jermaine Gresham	2.50	6.00
Rob Gronkowski		
2Q29 Alex Smith QB	1.25	3.00
Patrick Willis		
2Q30 Jimmy Clausen	1.00	2.50
Brandon LaFell		

2010 Topps Prime 2nd Quarter Relics

DUAL JSY/275-355 ODDS 1:20 HOB
*GOLD/25: .6X TO 1.5X BASIC JSY/275

BG Sam Bradford/355	6.00	15.00
Mardy Gilyard		
BH Eric Berry/355	2.50	6.00
Montario Hardesty		
BS Jahvid Best/355	5.00	12.00
Ndamukong Suh		
BT Dez Bryant/355	5.00	12.00
Demaryius Thomas		
BW Arrelious Benn/355	4.00	10.00
Mike Williams		
CL Jimmy Clausen/355	2.50	6.00
Brandon LaFell		
CT Jimmy Clausen/355	2.50	6.00
Golden Tate		
DS Jonathan Dwyer/355	2.50	6.00
Emmanuel Sanders		
GG Jermaine Gresham/355	6.00	15.00
Rob Gronkowski		
GP Rob Gronkowski/355	6.00	15.00
Taylor Price		
GS Jermaine Gresham/355	3.00	8.00
Jordan Shipley		
KC Mike Kafka/275	2.50	6.00
Riley Cooper		
LE Brandon LaFell/355	2.50	6.00
Armanti Edwards		
MA Peyton Manning/275	6.00	15.00
Joseph Addai		
MB Dexter McCluster/355	2.50	6.00
Eric Berry		
MCB Dexter McCluster/355	2.50	6.00
Arrelious Benn		
MF Rolando McClain/275	4.00	10.00
Jacoby Ford		
MH Colt McCoy/355	5.00	12.00
Montario Hardesty		
MM Joe McKnight/275	2.50	6.00
Anthony McCoy		
MS Rolando McClain/275	2.50	6.00
Richard Seymour		
RB Tony Romo/275	8.00	20.00
Dez Bryant		
SB Bob Sanders/275	2.50	6.00
Eric Berry		
SE C.J. Spiller/355	4.00	10.00
Marcus Easley		
SM Ndamukong Suh/355	5.00	12.00
Gerald McCoy		
SM C.J. Spiller/355	5.00	12.00
Ryan Mathews		
SW Alex Smith QB/275	3.00	8.00
Patrick Willis		
TB Tim Tebow/355	8.00	20.00
Sam Bradford		
TD Tim Tebow/355	6.00	15.00
Eric Decker		
THD Demaryius Thomas/355	3.00	8.00
Eric Decker		
TT Tim Tebow/355	6.00	15.00
Demaryius Thomas		

2010 Topps Prime 3rd Quarter

*GOLD/25: .6X TO 1.5X BASIC INSERTS

3Q1 Tim Tebow	4.00	10.00
Demaryius Thomas		
Eric Decker		
3Q2 Tim Tebow	4.00	10.00
Riley Cooper		
Aaron Hernandez		
3Q3 Sam Bradford	4.00	10.00
Gerald McCoy		
Jermaine Gresham		
3Q4 Adrian Peterson	2.50	6.00
Chris Johnson		
Maurice Jones-Drew		
3Q5 Jimmy Clausen	1.00	2.50
Armanti Edwards		
Brandon LaFell		
3Q6 Colt McCoy	2.00	5.00
Montario Hardesty		
Carlton Mitchell		
3Q7 Arrelious Benn	1.50	4.00
Gerald McCoy		
Mike Williams		
3Q8 Colt McCoy	2.00	5.00
Jordan Shipley		
Earl Thomas		
3Q9 Vince Young	1.50	4.00
Justin Gage		
Damian Williams		
3Q10 Jahvid Best	1.50	4.00
Toby Gerhart		
Joe McKnight		
3Q11 Demaryius Thomas	1.25	3.00
Jonathan Dwyer		
Derrick Morgan		
3Q12 Sam Bradford	5.00	12.00
Tim Tebow		
Jimmy Clausen		
3Q13 C.J. Spiller	2.00	5.00
Ryan Mathews		
Jahvid Best		
3Q14 Toby Gerhart	2.00	5.00
Ben Tate		
Montario Hardesty		
3Q15 Dez Bryant	3.00	8.00
Demaryius Thomas		
Arrelious Benn		
3Q16 Golden Tate	1.00	2.50
Damian Williams		
Brandon LaFell		
3Q17 Cedric Benson	1.25	3.00
Jermaine Gresham		
Jordan Shipley		
3Q18 Mardy Gilyard	1.50	4.00
Mike Williams		
Taylor Price		
3Q19 Ndamukong Suh	2.00	5.00
Gerald McCoy		
Eric Berry		
3Q20 Jahvid Best	1.50	4.00
Toby Gerhart		
Damian Williams		
3Q21 C.J. Spiller	1.50	4.00
Joe McKnight		
Taylor Price		
3Q22 Jermaine Gresham	1.25	3.00
Jonathan Dwyer		
Montario Hardesty		
3Q23 Demaryius Thomas	2.00	5.00
Ryan Mathews		
Rolando McClain		
3Q24 Sam Bradford	4.00	10.00
Demaryius Thomas		
C.J. Spiller		
3Q25 Tim Tebow	4.00	10.00
Dez Bryant		
Ryan Mathews		
3Q26 Jimmy Clausen	1.50	4.00
Dexter McCluster		
Jahvid Best		
3Q27 Colt McCoy	2.00	5.00
Arrelious Benn		
Toby Gerhart		
3Q28 Braylon Edwards	1.50	4.00
LaDainian Tomlinson		
Joe McKnight		
3Q29 Tom Brady	4.00	10.00
Rob Gronkowski		
Taylor Price		
3Q30 Golden Tate	1.00	2.50
Earl Thomas		
Anthony McCoy		

2010 Topps Prime 3rd Quarter Relics

TRIPLE JSY/199-275 ODDS 1:27 HOB
*GOLD/25: .6X TO 1.5X BASIC TRIPLE

BGM Jahvid Best/275	6.00	15.00
Toby Gerhart		
Joe McKnight		
BGP Tom Brady/199	12.00	30.00
Rob Gronkowski		
Taylor Price		
BGS Cedric Benson/199	4.00	10.00
Jermaine Gresham		
Jordan Shipley		
BGW Jahvid Best/275	6.00	15.00
Toby Gerhart		
Damian Williams		
BMG Sam Bradford/275	8.00	20.00
Gerald McCoy		
Jermaine Gresham		
BMW Arrelious Benn/275	5.00	12.00
Gerald McCoy		
Mike Williams		
BTB Dez Bryant/275	6.00	15.00
Demaryius Thomas		
Arrelious Benn		
BTC Sam Bradford/275	8.00	20.00
Tim Tebow		
Jimmy Clausen		
BTS Sam Bradford/275	8.00	20.00
Demaryius Thomas		
C.J. Spiller		
CEL Jimmy Clausen/199	5.00	12.00
Armanti Edwards		
Brandon LaFell		
CMB Jimmy Clausen/275	5.00	12.00
Dexter McCluster		
Jahvid Best		
ETM Braylon Edwards/199	5.00	12.00
LaDainian Tomlinson		
Joe McKnight		
GDH Jermaine Gresham/275	4.00	10.00
Jonathan Dwyer		
Montario Hardesty		
GTH Toby Gerhart/275	4.00	10.00
Ben Tate		
Montario Hardesty		
GWP Mardy Gilyard/275	5.00	12.00
Mike Williams		
Taylor Price		
MBG Colt McCoy/275	6.00	15.00
Arrelious Benn		
Toby Gerhart		
MHM Colt McCoy/199	6.00	15.00
Montario Hardesty		
Carlton Mitchell		
MST Colt McCoy/199	6.00	15.00
Jordan Shipley		
Earl Thomas		
PJJ Adrian Peterson/199	8.00	20.00
Chris Johnson		
Maurice Jones-Drew		
SMB C.J. Spiller/275	6.00	15.00
Ryan Mathews		
Jahvid Best		
SMCB Ndamukong Suh/275	6.00	15.00
Gerald McCoy		
Eric Berry		
SMP C.J. Spiller/275	5.00	12.00
Joe McKnight		
Taylor Price		
TBM Tim Tebow/275	8.00	20.00
Dez Bryant		
Ryan Mathews		
TCH Tim Tebow/199	8.00	20.00
Riley Cooper		
Aaron Hernandez		
TDM Demaryius Thomas/199	4.00	10.00
Jonathan Dwyer		
Derrick Morgan		
TMM Demaryius Thomas/275	6.00	15.00
Ryan Mathews		
Rolando McClain		
TTD Tim Tebow/275	8.00	20.00
Demaryius Thomas		
Eric Decker		
TTM Golden Tate/199	3.00	8.00
Earl Thomas		
Anthony McCoy		
TWL Golden Tate/275	3.00	8.00
Damian Williams		
Brandon LaFell		
YGW Vince Young/199	5.00	12.00
Justin Gage		
Damian Williams		

2010 Topps Prime 4th Quarter

*GOLD/25: .6X TO 1.5X BASIC INSERTS

4Q1 C.J. Spiller	2.00	5.00
Jahvid Best		
Ryan Mathews		
Ben Tate		
4Q2 Toby Gerhart	2.00	5.00
Joe McKnight		
Montario Hardesty		
Anthony Dixon		
4Q3 Tim Tebow	4.00	10.00
Jimmy Clausen		
Sam Bradford		
Colt McCoy		
4Q4 Dez Bryant	3.00	8.00
Dexter McCluster		
Demaryius Thomas		
Arrelious Benn		
4Q5 Golden Tate	1.00	2.50
Brandon LaFell		
Damian Williams		
Emmanuel Sanders		
4Q6 Carson Palmer	2.50	6.00
Jordan Shipley		
Tom Brady		
Taylor Price		
4Q7 Mardy Gilyard	1.50	4.00
Marcus Easley		
Mike Williams		
Jacoby Ford		
4Q8 Jermaine Gresham	2.50	6.00
Aaron Hernandez		
Rob Gronkowski		
Jimmy Graham		
4Q9 Ndamukong Suh	2.00	5.00
Eric Berry		
Gerald McCoy		
Earl Thomas		
4Q10 Braylon Edwards	1.50	4.00
LaDainian Tomlinson		
Jonathan Dwyer		
Emmanuel Sanders		
4Q11 C.J. Spiller	2.00	5.00
Jonathan Dwyer		
Demaryius Thomas		
Jimmy Graham		
4Q12 Sam Bradford	4.00	10.00
Dez Bryant		
Colt McCoy		
Jordan Shipley		
4Q13 Adrian Peterson	2.50	6.00
Toby Gerhart		
Steve Slaton		
Ben Tate		
4Q14 Jimmy Clausen	2.00	5.00
Golden Tate		
Colt McCoy		
Jordan Shipley		
4Q15 Jahvid Best	2.50	6.00
Rob Gronkowski		
Toby Gerhart		
Damian Williams		
4Q16 Dexter McCluster	1.00	2.50
Anthony Dixon		
Eric Berry		
Rolando McClain		
4Q17 Dexter McCluster	1.25	3.00
Brandon LaFell		
Montario Hardesty		
Ben Tate		
4Q18 C.J. Spiller	1.50	4.00
Ricky Williams		
Joe McKnight		
Taylor Price		
4Q19 Ndamukong Suh	2.00	5.00
Jahvid Best		
Gerald McCoy		
Arrelious Benn		
4Q20 Brandon LaFell	1.25	3.00
Armanti Edwards		
Jermaine Gresham		
Jordan Shipley		
4Q21 Marion Barber	1.25	3.00
Felix Jones		
Santana Moss		
Clinton Portis		
4Q22 Dexter McCluster	2.00	5.00
Demaryius Thomas		
Ryan Mathews		
Rolando McClain		
4Q23 Tim Tebow	4.00	10.00
C.J. Spiller		
Dez Bryant		
Jermaine Gresham		
4Q24 Sam Bradford	4.00	10.00
C.J. Spiller		
Ndamukong Suh		
Gerald McCoy		
4Q25 Sam Bradford	4.00	10.00
C.J. Spiller		
Tim Tebow		
Ryan Mathews		
4Q26 Sam Bradford	4.00	10.00
Dez Bryant		
Tim Tebow		
Demaryius Thomas		
4Q27 Dez Bryant	3.00	8.00
C.J. Spiller		
Demaryius Thomas		
Ryan Mathews		
4Q28 Peyton Manning	4.00	10.00
Tom Brady		
Tony Romo		
Sam Bradford		
4Q29 Sam Bradford	4.00	10.00
Mardy Gilyard		
Tim Tebow		
Eric Decker		
4Q30 Jahvid Best	1.50	4.00
Toby Gerhart		
Montario Hardesty		
Jonathan Dwyer		

2010 Topps Prime 4th Quarter Relics

QUAD JSY/124-175 ODDS 1:43 HOB
*GOLD/25: .6X TO 1.5X BASIC QUAD

BBMS Sam Bradford/175	10.00	25.00
Dez Bryant		
Colt McCoy		
Jordan Shipley		
BBTT Sam Bradford/175	12.00	30.00
Dez Bryant		
Tim Tebow		
Demaryius Thomas		
BGGW Jahvid Best/175	8.00	20.00
Rob Gronkowski		
Toby Gerhart		
Damian Williams		
BGHD Jahvid Best/175	6.00	15.00
Toby Gerhart		
Montario Hardesty		
Jonathan Dwyer		
BGTD Sam Bradford/175	12.00	30.00
Mardy Gilyard		
Tim Tebow		
Eric Decker		
BJMP Marion Barber/124	5.00	12.00
Felix Jones		
Santana Moss		
Clinton Portis		
BMTB Dez Bryant/175	8.00	20.00
Dexter McCluster		
Demaryius Thomas		
Arrelious Benn		
BSSM Sam Bradford/175	10.00	25.00
C.J. Spiller		
Ndamukong Suh		
Gerald McCoy		
BSTM Sam Bradford/175	12.00	30.00
C.J. Spiller		
Tim Tebow		
Ryan Mathews		
CTMS Jimmy Clausen/175	8.00	20.00
Golden Tate		
Colt McCoy		
Jordan Shipley		
DSTM Dez Bryant/175	8.00	20.00
C.J. Spiller		
Demaryius Thomas		
Ryan Mathews		
ETDS Braylon Edwards/124	5.00	12.00
LaDainian Tomlinson		
Jonathan Dwyer		
Emmanuel Sanders		
GEWF Mardy Gilyard/124	6.00	15.00
Marcus Easley		
Mike Williams		
Jacoby Ford		
GHGG Jermaine Gresham/124	10.00	25.00
Aaron Hernandez		
Rob Gronkowski		
Jimmy Graham		
GMHD Toby Gerhart/175	5.00	12.00
Joe McKnight		
Montario Hardesty		
Anthony Dixon		
LEGS Brandon LaFell/175	5.00	12.00
Armanti Edwards		
Jermaine Gresham		
Jordan Shipley		
MBRB Peyton Manning/124	15.00	40.00
Tom Brady		
Tony Romo		
Sam Bradford		
MDBM Dexter McCluster/124	6.00	15.00
Anthony Dixon		
Eric Berry		
Rolando McClain		
MLHT Dexter McCluster/175	6.00	15.00
Brandon LaFell		
Montario Hardesty		
Ben Tate		
MTMM Dexter McCluster/175	6.00	15.00
Demaryius Thomas		
Ryan Mathews		
Rolando McClain		
PGST Adrian Peterson/124	6.00	15.00
Toby Gerhart		
Steve Slaton		
Ben Tate		
PSBP Carson Palmer/124	6.00	15.00
Jordan Shipley		
Tom Brady		
Taylor Price		
SBMB Ndamukong Suh/175	10.00	25.00
Jahvid Best		
Gerald McCoy		
Arrelious Benn		
SBMT C.J. Spiller/175	8.00	20.00
Jahvid Best		
Ryan Mathews		
Ben Tate		
SBMTH Ndamukong Suh/124	8.00	20.00
Eric Berry		
Gerald McCoy		
Earl Thomas		
SDTG C.J. Spiller/124	8.00	20.00
Jonathan Dwyer		
Demaryius Thomas		
Jimmy Graham		
SWMP C.J. Spiller/124	6.00	15.00
Ricky Williams		
Joe McKnight		
Taylor Price		
TCBM Tim Tebow/175	12.00	30.00
Jimmy Clausen		
Sam Bradford		
Colt McCoy		
TLWS Golden Tate/175	4.00	10.00
Brandon LaFell		
Damian Williams		
Emmanuel Sanders		
TSBG Tim Tebow/175	10.00	25.00
C.J. Spiller		
Dez Bryant		
Jermaine Gresham		

2010 Topps Prime Autographed Relics Level 1

*LEVEL 1/20: .8X TO 2X LEVEL 4
*LEVEL 1/10: 1X TO 2.5X LEVEL 4
LEVEL 1 PRINT RUN 10-20

PL1CM Colt McCoy/20	100.00	200.00
PL1DB Dez Bryant/10		
PL1SB Sam Bradford/20	150.00	300.00
PL1TT Tim Tebow/20	175.00	300.00

2010 Topps Prime Autographed Relics Level 4

STATED PRINT RUN 30 SER.#'d SETS
*LEVEL 3/25: .6X TO 1.5X LEVEL 4
*LEVEL 2/15: .8X TO 2X LEVEL 4
EXCH EXPIRATION: 11/30/2013

PL4AB Arrelious Benn	10.00	25.00
PL4AE Armanti Edwards	10.00	25.00
PL4AR Andre Roberts	10.00	25.00
PL4BL Brandon LaFell	10.00	25.00
PL4BT Ben Tate	12.00	30.00
PL4CM Colt McCoy	50.00	100.00
PL4CS C.J. Spiller	15.00	40.00
PL4DB Dez Bryant	50.00	120.00
PL4DM Dexter McCluster	10.00	25.00
PL4DT Demaryius Thomas	12.00	30.00
PL4DW Damian Williams	10.00	25.00
PL4EB Eric Berry	10.00	25.00
PL4ED Eric Decker	12.00	30.00
PL4ES Emmanuel Sanders	10.00	25.00
PL4GT Golden Tate	10.00	25.00
PL4JB Jahvid Best	15.00	40.00
PL4JC Jimmy Clausen	15.00	40.00
PL4JD Jonathan Dwyer	10.00	25.00
PL4JG Jermaine Gresham	12.00	30.00
PL4JS Jordan Shipley	10.00	25.00
PL4ME Marcus Easley	8.00	20.00
PL4MG Mardy Gilyard	10.00	25.00
PL4MH Montario Hardesty	10.00	25.00
PL4MK Mike Kafka	10.00	25.00
PL4MW Mike Williams	20.00	50.00
PL4NS Ndamukong Suh	30.00	60.00
PL4RG Rob Gronkowski.	25.00	60.00
PL4RM Ryan Mathews	30.00	60.00
PL4SB Sam Bradford	100.00	200.00
PL4TG Toby Gerhart	10.00	25.00
PL4TP Taylor Price	10.00	25.00
PL4TT Tim Tebow	100.00	200.00

2010 Topps Prime Autographed Relics Level 5

STATED PRINT RUN 75-499
EXCH EXPIRATION: 11/30/2013

PL5AB Arrelious Benn/499	5.00	12.00
PL5AD Anthony Dixon/299	8.00	20.00
PL5AE Armanti Edwards/499	5.00	12.00
PL5AG Antonio Gates/150	12.00	30.00
PL5AH Aaron Hernandez/299	12.00	30.00
PL5AM Anthony McCoy/299	6.00	15.00
PL5AP Adrian Peterson/75	60.00	120.00
PL5AR Andre Roberts/499	5.00	12.00
PL5BL Brandon LaFell/499	5.00	12.00
PL5BT Ben Tate/499	6.00	15.00
PL5CH Chad Henne/75	12.00	30.00
PL5CM Colt McCoy/150	40.00	80.00
PL5CS C.J. Spiller/399	10.00	25.00
PL5CT Chester Taylor/150	10.00	25.00
PL5DL Dan LeFevour/299	8.00	20.00
PL5DM Darren McFadden/150	15.00	40.00
PL5DMC Dexter McCluster/499	5.00	12.00
PL5DMO Derrick Morgan/299	6.00	15.00
PL5DT Demaryius Thomas/399	8.00	20.00
PL5DW Damian Williams/499	5.00	12.00
PL5ED Eric Decker/499	6.00	15.00
PL5ES Emmanuel Sanders/499	5.00	12.00
PL5FJ Felix Jones/150	15.00	40.00
PL5GRA Jimmy Graham/299	25.00	50.00
PL5GT Golden Tate/499	5.00	12.00
PL5JB Jahvid Best/399	10.00	25.00
PL5JC Jimmy Clausen/150	15.00	40.00
PL5JD Jonathan Dwyer/499	5.00	12.00
PL5JF Jacoby Ford/299	10.00	25.00
PL5JG Jermaine Gresham/499	6.00	15.00
PL5JS Jordan Shipley/499	5.00	12.00
PL5KK Kevin Kolb/150	10.00	25.00
PL5KM Knowshon Moreno/150	12.00	30.00
PL5MC Marques Colston/150	10.00	25.00
PL5ME Marcus Easley/399	5.00	12.00
PL5MG Mardy Gilyard/499	5.00	12.00
PL5MH Montario Hardesty/499	5.00	12.00
PL5MJD Maurice Jones-Drew/150	12.00	30.00
PL5MK Mike Kafka/499	5.00	12.00
PL5NS Ndamukong Suh/299	20.00	50.00
PL5PM Peyton Manning/150	60.00	120.00
PL5RC Riley Cooper/299	8.00	20.00
PL5RG Rob Gronkowski/499	15.00	40.00
PL5RM Ryan Mathews/399	12.00	30.00
PL5SB Sam Bradford/150	60.00	150.00
PL5SR Sidney Rice/150	12.00	30.00
PL5SS Steve Slaton/75	10.00	25.00
PL5TG Toby Gerhart/499	5.00	12.00
PL5TP Taylor Price/150	10.00	25.00
PL5TR Tony Romo/150	30.00	60.00

2010 Topps Prime Rookie

*GOLD/25: .8X TO 2X BASIC INSERTS

PR1 Sam Bradford	3.00	8.00
PR2 Ndamukong Suh	1.50	4.00
PR3 Eric Berry	.75	2.00
PR4 C.J. Spiller	1.25	3.00
PR5 Ryan Mathews	1.50	4.00
PR6 Jermaine Gresham	1.00	2.50
PR7 Demaryius Thomas	1.00	2.50
PR8 Dez Bryant	2.50	6.00
PR9 Tim Tebow	3.00	8.00
PR10 Jahvid Best	1.25	3.00
PR11 Dexter McCluster	.75	2.00
PR12 Arrelious Benn	.75	2.00
PR13 Rob Gronkowski	2.00	5.00
PR14 Jimmy Clausen	.75	2.00
PR15 Toby Gerhart	.75	2.00
PR16 Ben Tate	1.00	2.50
PR17 Montario Hardesty	.75	2.00
PR18 Golden Tate	.75	2.00
PR19 Damian Williams	.75	2.00
PR20 Brandon LaFell	.75	2.00
PR21 Jordan Shipley	.75	2.00
PR22 Colt McCoy	1.50	4.00
PR23 Eric Decker	1.00	2.50
PR24 Joe McKnight	.75	2.00
PR25 Jonathan Dwyer	.75	2.00
PR26 Emmanuel Sanders	.75	2.00
PR27 Mike Williams	1.25	3.00
PR28 Mardy Gilyard	.75	2.00
PR29 Taylor Price	.75	2.00
PR30 Rolando McClain	.75	2.00
PR31 Gerald McCoy	.75	2.00
PR32 Marcus Easley	.60	1.50
PR33 Andre Roberts	.75	2.00
PR34 Mike Kafka	.75	2.00
PR35 Armanti Edwards	.75	2.00

2010 Topps Prime Rookie Autographs

STATED PRINT RUN 149-599
EXCH EXPIRATION: 11/30/2013

PARAB Arrelious Benn/399	5.00	12.00
PARADX Anthony Dixon/599	4.00	10.00
PARAE Armanti Edwards/599	4.00	10.00
PARAM Anthony McCoy/599	3.00	8.00
PARAR Andre Roberts/149	6.00	15.00
PARBB Bryan Bulaga/599	4.00	10.00
PARBL Brandon LaFell/149	6.00	15.00
PARBT Ben Tate/299	6.00	15.00
PARCM Carlton Mitchell/599	3.00	8.00
PARCMC Colt McCoy/149	30.00	60.00
PARCS C.J. Spiller/299	12.00	30.00
PARCSC Charles Scott/149	5.00	12.00
PARDL Dan LeFevour/399	5.00	12.00
PARDMC Dexter McCluster/399	5.00	12.00
PARDR David Reed/149	5.00	12.00
PARDT Demaryius Thomas/149	8.00	20.00
PARDW Damian Williams/299	5.00	12.00
PARED Eric Decker/299	6.00	15.00
PARES Emmanuel Sanders/599	4.00	10.00
PARET Earl Thomas/399	5.00	12.00
PARGRA Jimmy Graham/149	20.00	40.00
PARGT Golden Tate/399	5.00	12.00
PARJB Jahvid Best/299	8.00	20.00
PARJC Jimmy Clausen/149	6.00	15.00
PARJCR Jonathan Crompton/599	3.00	8.00
PARJD Jonathan Dwyer/299	5.00	12.00
PARJF Jacoby Ford/599	6.00	15.00
PARJG Jermaine Gresham/399	6.00	15.00

PARJH Jerry Hughes/599 4.00 10.00
PARJO Jared Odrick/599 6.00 15.00
PARJS John Skelton/599 6.00 15.00
PARJSH Jordan Shipley/599 4.00 10.00
PARJST James Starks/599 12.00 30.00
PARJW Joe Webb/149 6.00 15.00
PARME Marcus Easley/599 3.00 8.00
PARMG Mardy Gilyard/599 4.00 10.00
PARMH Montario Hardesty/149 6.00 15.00
PARMK Mike Kafka/149 6.00 15.00
PARNS Ndamukong Suh/149 20.00 40.00
PARRC Riley Cooper/599 4.00 10.00
PARRG Rob Gronkowski/299 15.00 40.00
PARRM Ryan Mathews/299 10.00 25.00
PARSB Sam Bradford/149 50.00 120.00
PARSC Sean Canfield/599 3.00 8.00
PARSL Sean Lee/149 8.00 20.00
PARTG Toby Gerhart/149 6.00 15.00
PARTP Tony Pike/149 6.00 15.00
PARTPR Taylor Price/599 4.00 10.00
PARTT Tim Tebow/149 60.00 120.00
PARTW Trent Williams/599 4.00 10.00

2010 Topps Prime Rookie Autographs Gold

*GOLD/25: 1X TO 2.5X BASIC AU/599
*GOLD/25: .8X TO 2X BASIC AU/299-399
*GOLD/25: .6X TO 1.5X BASIC AU/149
GOLD/25 STATED ODDS 1:196 HOB
PARCMC Colt McCoy 50.00 100.00
PARSB Sam Bradford 100.00 200.00
PARTT Tim Tebow 125.00 200.00

2010 Topps Prime Rookie Relics

ROOKIE RELIC/420 ODDS 1:14 HOB
*GOLD/25: .6X TO 1.5X BASIC JSY/420
PRRAB Arrelious Benn 2.00 5.00
PRRAE Armanti Edwards 2.00 5.00
PRRAR Andre Roberts 2.00 5.00
PRRBL Brandon LaFell 2.00 5.00
PRRBT Ben Tate 2.50 6.00
PRRCM Colt McCoy 4.00 10.00
PRRCS C.J. Spiller 3.00 8.00
PRRDB Dez Bryant 5.00 12.00
PRRDM Dexter McCluster 2.00 5.00
PRRDT Demaryius Thomas 2.50 6.00
PRRDW Damian Williams 2.00 5.00
PRREB Eric Berry 2.00 5.00
PRRED Eric Decker 2.50 6.00
PRRES Emmanuel Sanders 2.00 5.00
PRRGM Gerald McCoy 2.00 5.00
PRRGT Golden Tate 2.00 5.00
PRRJB Jahvid Best 4.00 10.00
PRRJC Jimmy Clausen 2.00 5.00
PRRJD Jonathan Dwyer 2.00 5.00
PRRJG Jermaine Gresham 2.50 6.00
PRRJM Joe McKnight 2.00 5.00
PRRJS Jordan Shipley 2.00 5.00
PRRME Marcus Easley 1.50 4.00
PRRMG Mardy Gilyard 2.00 5.00
PRRMH Montario Hardesty 2.00 5.00
PRRMK Mike Kafka 2.00 5.00
PRRMW Mike Williams 3.00 8.00
PRRNS Ndamukong Suh 4.00 10.00
PRRRG Rob Gronkowski 5.00 12.00
PRRRM Ryan Mathews 4.00 10.00
PRRRM Rolando McClain 2.00 5.00
PRRSB Sam Bradford 8.00 20.00
PRRTG Toby Gerhart 2.00 5.00
PRRTP Taylor Price 2.00 5.00
PRRTT Tim Tebow 8.00 20.00

2011 Topps Prime

COMPLETE SET (150) 30.00 80.00
COMP.SET w/o RC's (100) 12.00 30.00
ROOKIE/930 STATED ODDS 1:4 HOB
1 Aaron Rodgers .50 1.25
2 Jamie Harper RC 1.00 2.50
3 Bilal Powell RC .60 1.50
4 Brandon Lloyd .25 .60
5 Sam Bradford .30 .75
6 Antonio Gates .25 .60
7 Mark Ingram RC 2.00 5.00
8 Shonn Greene .25 .60
9 DeMarco Murray RC 2.00 5.00
10 Andre Johnson .25 .60
11 Rashard Mendenhall .25 .60
12 Rob Housler RC .75 2.00
13 Jonathan Stewart .25 .60
14 Delone Carter RC .75 2.00
15 Prince Amukamara RC 1.00 2.50
16 Michael Turner .25 .60
17 LaDainian Tomlinson .30 .75
18 Dwayne Harris RC 1.00 2.50
19 Philip Rivers .30 .75
20 Adrian Peterson .40 1.00
21 Nick Fairley RC 1.25 3.00
22 Percy Harvin .25 .60
23 Titus Young RC 1.25 3.00
24 D.J. Williams RC 1.00 2.50
25 Lee Evans .25 .60
26 Jeremy Maclin .25 .60
27 Jordan Todman RC .60 1.50
28 Calvin Johnson .30 .75
29 Jacquizz Rodgers RC 1.00 2.50
30 Arian Foster .25 .60
31 A.J. Green RC 2.00 5.00
32 Josh Freeman .30 .75
33 Ryan Mathews .25 .60
34 Austin Pettis RC .75 2.00
35 Jared Allen .25 .60
36 Anquan Boldin .25 .60
37 Kyle Rudolph RC 1.00 2.50
38 LeGarrette Blount .25 .60
39 Cedric Benson .25 .60
40 Chris Johnson .25 .60
41 Steven Jackson .25 .60
42 Troy Polamalu .30 .75
43 Mike Williams .25 .60
44 Ryan Mallett RC 2.00 5.00
45 Torrey Smith RC 1.25 3.00
46 Tony Gonzalez .25 .60
47 Colin Kaepernick RC 1.25 3.00
48 Brandon Jacobs .25 .60
49 Eli Manning .30 .75
50 Cam Newton RC 6.00 15.00
51 Rahim Moore RC .75 2.00
52 Julio Jones RC 2.00 5.00
53 Da'Rel Scott RC .75 2.00
54 Greg Salas RC 1.00 2.50
55 Randall Cobb RC 1.25 3.00
56 Marcell Dareus RC 1.00 2.50
57 Alex Green RC 1.00 2.50
58 Matt Forte .25 .60
59 Mike Williams .25 .60
60 Clay Matthews .30 .75
61 Christian Ponder RC 2.00 5.00
62 Greg Jennings .25 .60
63 Shane Vereen RC 1.00 2.50
64 Ray Rice .25 .60
65 Marshawn Lynch .25 .60
66 Peyton Hillis .25 .60
67 Ben Roethlisberger .30 .75
68 Jon Baldwin RC 1.00 2.50
69 Joe Flacco .30 .75
70 Drew Brees .30 .75
71 Jamaal Charles .25 .60
72 Pierre Garcon .25 .60
73 Stephen Tulloch .20 .50
74 Dion Lewis RC 1.00 2.50
75 Michael Crabtree .25 .60
76 Hakeem Nicks .25 .60
77 Beanie Wells .25 .60
78 Von Miller RC 1.25 3.00
79 Miles Austin .25 .60
80 Larry Fitzgerald .25 .60
81 Jahvid Best .25 .60
82 Jake Locker RC 2.50 6.00
83 Blaine Gabbert RC 1.50 4.00
84 Chad Ochocinco .25 .60
85 DeSean Jackson .25 .60
86 Dwayne Bowe .25 .60
87 Ricky Stanzi RC 1.25 3.00
88 James Starks .25 .60
89 Jimmy Graham .30 .75
90 Mark Sanchez .30 .75
91 Leonard Hankerson RC 1.00 2.50
92 Knowshon Moreno .25 .60
93 Taiwan Jones RC 1.00 2.50
94 Ed Reed .25 .60
95 Dez Bryant .30 .75
96 Kendall Hunter RC 1.00 2.50
97 Vincent Jackson .25 .60
98 Kenny Britt .25 .60
99 Jerod Mayo .20 .50
100 Peyton Manning .50 1.25
101 Darren McFadden .25 .60
102 C.J. Spiller .25 .60
103 Santana Moss .25 .60
104 Ray Lewis .30 .75
105 Matt Schaub .25 .60
106 Marcedes Lewis .20 .50
107 Marques Colston .25 .60
108 Ryan Williams RC 1.25 3.00
109 Steve Johnson .25 .60
110 Matt Ryan .30 .75
111 Roddy White .25 .60
112 Austin Collie .25 .60
113 Andy Dalton RC 2.50 6.00
114 Stevan Ridley RC 1.00 2.50
115 Jason Witten .30 .75
116 Matt Cassel .25 .60
117 Daniel Thomas RC 1.00 2.50
118 Luke Stocker RC .75 2.00
119 Virgil Green RC .75 2.00
120 Maurice Jones-Drew .25 .60
121 Santonio Holmes .25 .60
122 Brandon Marshall .25 .60
123 Felix Jones .25 .60
124 LeSean McCoy .25 .60
125 Mike Wallace .30 .75
126 Patrick Willis .25 .60
127 Jeremy Kerley RC 1.00 2.50
128 Reggie Wayne .25 .60
129 DeMarcus Ware .25 .60
130 Michael Vick .30 .75
131 Dallas Clark .25 .60
132 Brian Urlacher .30 .75
133 Sidney Rice .25 .60
134 Steve Smith .25 .60
135 Wes Welker .30 .75
136 Frank Gore .25 .60
137 Jerrel Jernigan RC .75 2.00
138 Davone Bess .20 .50
139 Malcom Floyd .25 .60
140 Tony Romo .30 .75
141 Braylon Edwards .25 .60
142 Ahmad Bradshaw .25 .60
143 Vincent Brown RC 1.00 2.50
144 Vernon Davis .25 .60
145 Edmond Gates RC .75 2.00
146 Mikel Leshoure RC 1.00 2.50
147 Jay Cutler .25 .60
148 Greg Little RC 1.00 2.50
149 Hines Ward .25 .60
150 Tom Brady .50 1.25

2011 Topps Prime Aqua

*AQUA VETS: .8X TO 2X BASIC CARDS
RANDOM INSERTS IN HOBBY PACKS

2011 Topps Prime Blue

*BLUE/599: .5X TO 1.2X BASIC ROOKIES
BLUE/599 STATED ODDS 1:6

2011 Topps Prime Gold

*GOLD/699: .5X TO 1.2X BASIC ROOKIES
GOLD/699 STATED ODDS 1:5

2011 Topps Prime Green

*GREEN/99: 1X TO 2.5X BASIC ROOKIES
GREEN/99 STATED ODDS 1:33

2011 Topps Prime Powder Blue

*BLUE VETS/75: 3X TO 8X BASIC CARDS
POWDER BLUE/75 ODDS 1:22

2011 Topps Prime Purple

*PURPLE/399: .6X TO 1.5X BASIC ROOKIES
PURPLE/399 STATED ODDS 1:9

2011 Topps Prime Rainbow

*RAINBOW/25: 1.5X TO 4X BASIC ROOKIES
RAINBOW/25 STATED ODDS 1:130
50 Cam Newton 40.00 80.00

2011 Topps Prime Red

*RED/499: .5X TO 1.2X BASIC ROOKIES
RED/499 STATED ODDS 1:7

2011 Topps Prime Retail

*VETS: .3X TO .8X BASIC CARDS
*ROOKIES: .2X TO .5X BASIC CARDS

2011 Topps Prime Retail Bronze

*VETS: 1.2X TO 3X BASIC HOBBY
*ROOKIES: .4X TO 1X BASIC HOBBY
RANDOM INSERTS IN RETAIL PACKS

2011 Topps Prime Autographed Relics Level 3

*LEV.THREE/25: 1X TO 2.5X LEV.SIX/515
*LEV.THREE/25: .8X TO 2X LEV.SIX/199
*LEV.THREE/25: .5X TO 1.2X LEV.SIX/50
LEVEL THREE PRINT RUN 25

2011 Topps Prime Autographed Relics Level 4

LEVEL FOUR STATED PRINT RUN 15
*LEVEL TWO/15: .5X TO 1.2X LEV.FOUR/15
*LEVEL THREE/25: .4X TO 1X LEV.FOUR/15
PIVAD Andy Dalton 125.00 200.00
PIVAG Alex Green 15.00 40.00
PIVAJG A.J. Green 75.00 150.00
PIVAP Austin Pettis 12.00 30.00
PIVBG Blaine Gabbert 100.00 200.00
PIVBP Bilal Powell 10.00 25.00
PIVCK Colin Kaepernick 40.00 80.00
PIVCN Cam Newton 250.00 400.00
PIVCP Christian Ponder 125.00 200.00
PIVDC Delone Carter 12.00 30.00
PIVDM DeMarco Murray 125.00 200.00
PIVDT Daniel Thomas 30.00 60.00
PIVEG Edmond Gates 12.00 30.00
PIVGL Greg Little 15.00 40.00
PIVJB Jon Baldwin 20.00 50.00
PIVJH Jamie Harper 15.00 40.00
PIVJJ Julio Jones 100.00 200.00
PIVJJE Jerrel Jernigan 12.00 30.00
PIVJL Jake Locker 125.00 200.00
PIVJT Jordan Todman EXCH 10.00 25.00
PIVKH Kendall Hunter 20.00 50.00
PIVKR Kyle Rudolph 15.00 40.00
PIVLH Leonard Hankerson 15.00 40.00
PIVMD Marcell Dareus 15.00 40.00
PIVMI Mark Ingram 100.00 200.00
PIVML Mikel Leshoure 15.00 40.00
PIVRC Randall Cobb 20.00 50.00
PIVRM Ryan Mallett 100.00 175.00
PIVRW Ryan Williams 25.00 60.00
PIVSR Stevan Ridley 15.00 40.00
PIVSV Shane Vereen 20.00 50.00
PIVTJ Taiwan Jones 25.00 60.00
PIVTS Torrey Smith 20.00 50.00
PIVTY Titus Young 20.00 50.00
PIVVB Vincent Brown 15.00 40.00
PIVVM Von Miller 25.00 60.00

2011 Topps Prime Autographed Relics Level 6

STATED PRINT RUN 50-515
EXCH EXPIRATION: 9/30/2014
PVIAD Andy Dalton/515 25.00 60.00
PVIAG Alex Green/515 6.00 15.00
PVIAGA Antonio Gates/50 12.00 30.00
PVIAJ Andre Johnson/50 30.00 60.00
PVIAJG A.J. Green/199 25.00 50.00
PVIAP Austin Pettis/50 10.00 25.00
PVIAR Antrel Rolle/100 8.00 20.00
PVIBG Blaine Gabbert/199 30.00 60.00
PVIBP Bilal Powell/199 5.00 12.00
PVICB Champ Bailey/100 12.00 30.00
PVICK Colin Kaepernick/199 12.00 30.00
PVICN Cam Newton/199 100.00 200.00
PVICP Christian Ponder/515 25.00 50.00
PVIDC Delone Carter/199 6.00 15.00
PVIDM DeMarco Murray/199 40.00 80.00
PVIDMC Darren McFadden/100 25.00 50.00
PVIDR Darrelle Revis/50 25.00 50.00
PVIDT Daniel Thomas/515 10.00 25.00
PVIEG Edmond Gates/515 5.00 12.00
PVIGJ Greg Jennings/100 12.00 30.00
PVIGL Greg Little/515 6.00 15.00
PVIHW Hines Ward/50 30.00 60.00
PVIJB Jon Baldwin/515 8.00 20.00
PVIJH Jamie Harper/515 6.00 15.00
PVIJJ Julio Jones/515 20.00 50.00
PVIJJE Jerrel Jernigan/515 5.00 12.00
PVIJL Jake Locker/199 40.00 80.00
PVIJT Jordan Todman EXCH 5.00 12.00
PVIJW Jason Witten/100 20.00 40.00
PVIKH Kendall Hunter/515 8.00 20.00
PVIKM Knowshon Moreno/50 12.00 30.00
PVIKR Kyle Rudolph/515 8.00 20.00
PVILH Leonard Hankerson/515 6.00 15.00
PVIMD Marcell Dareus/199 8.00 20.00
PVIMI Mark Ingram/199 40.00 80.00
PVIMJ Maurice Jones-Drew/50 12.00 30.00
PVIML Mikel Leshoure EXCH 8.00 20.00
PVIRC Randall Cobb/515 8.00 20.00
PVIRL Ray Lewis/100 30.00 60.00
PVIRM Ryan Mallett/515 15.00 40.00
PVIRW Ryan Williams/515 10.00 25.00
PVISG Shonn Greene/100 10.00 25.00
PVISR Sidney Rice/100 10.00 25.00
PVISRI Stevan Ridley/515 6.00 15.00
PVISV Shane Vereen/515 8.00 20.00
PVITJ Taiwan Jones/199 10.00 25.00
PVITS Torrey Smith/515 8.00 20.00
PVITY Titus Young 10.00 25.00
PVIVB Vincent Brown/515 6.00 15.00
PVIVM Von Miller/515 10.00 25.00

2011 Topps Prime Autographed Relics Level 6 Gold

*GOLD/25: .8X TO 2X LEVEL SIX/515
*GOLD/25: .6X TO 1.5X LEVEL SIX/199
*GOLD/25: .5X TO 1.2X LEVEL SIX/100
*GOLD/25: .4X TO 1X LEVEL SIX/50 VETS
*GOLD/25: .4X TO 1X LEVEL SIX/50 ROOK
GOLD STATED PRINT RUN 25
PVICN Cam Newton 150.00 250.00

2011 Topps Prime Dual

COMPLETE SET (20) 10.00 25.00
RANDOM INSERTS IN PACKS
*GOLD/50: .8X TO 2X BASIC INSERTS
*SILVER HOLO/25: 1X TO 2.5X BASIC INSERTS
AR Joseph Addai / Stevan Ridley .75 2.00
BP Michael Bush / Bilal Powell .50 1.25
CG Randall Cobb / Alex Green 2.00 5.00
GD A.J. Green / Andy Dalton 2.00 5.00
GJ A.J. Green / Julio Jones 1.50 4.00
ID Mark Ingram / Marcell Dareus 1.50 4.00
JD Julio Jones / Marcell Dareus 1.50 4.00
JP Jerrel Jernigan / Bilal Powell .60 1.50
KH Colin Kaepernick / Kendall Hunter 1.00 2.50
LH Jake Locker / Jamie Harper 2.00 5.00
LY Mikel Leshoure / Titus Young 1.00 2.50
MB LeSean McCoy / Jon Baldwin .75 2.00
MH Santana Moss / Leonard Hankerson .75 2.00
MV Ryan Mallett / Shane Vereen 1.50 4.00
NL Hakeem Nicks / Greg Little .75 2.00
PM Adrian Peterson / DeMarco Murray 1.50 4.00
RP Kyle Rudolph / Christian Ponder 1.50 4.00
TB Jordan Todman / Vincent Brown .75 2.00
VR Shane Vereen / Stevan Ridley .75 2.00
YP Titus Young / Austin Pettis 1.00 2.50

2011 Topps Prime Dual Relics

STATED PRINT RUN 398 SER.#'d SETS
*GOLD/50: .6X TO 1.5X BASIC DUAL JSY
*SLVR HOLO/25: .8X TO 2X BASIC DUAL JSY
AR Joseph Addai / Stevan Ridley 2.50 6.00
BP Michael Bush / Bilal Powell 2.50 6.00
CG Randall Cobb / Alex Green 3.00 8.00
GD A.J. Green / Andy Dalton 6.00 15.00
GJ A.J. Green / Julio Jones 6.00 15.00
ID Mark Ingram / Marcell Dareus 5.00 12.00
JD Julio Jones / Marcell Dareus 5.00 12.00
JP Jerrel Jernigan / Bilal Powell 2.00 5.00
KH Colin Kaepernick / Kendall Hunter 4.00 10.00
LH Jake Locker / Jamie Harper 5.00 12.00
LY Mikel Leshoure / Titus Young 3.00 8.00
MB LeSean McCoy / Jon Baldwin 2.50 6.00
MH Santana Moss / Leonard Hankerson 2.50 6.00
MV Ryan Mallett / Shane Vereen 5.00 12.00
NL Hakeem Nicks / Greg Little 2.50 6.00
PM Adrian Peterson / DeMarco Murray 5.00 12.00
RP Kyle Rudolph / Christian Ponder 5.00 12.00
TB Jordan Todman / Vincent Brown 2.50 6.00
VR Shane Vereen / Stevan Ridley 2.50 6.00
YP Titus Young / Austin Pettis 3.00 8.00

2011 Topps Prime Quad

RANDOM INSERTS IN PACKS
*GOLD/50: .8X TO 2X BASIC INSERTS
*SILVER HOLO/25: 1X TO 2.5X BASIC INSERTS
BWMV Tom Brady / Wes Welker / Ryan Mallett / Shane Vereen 2.50 6.00
GJCH A.J. Green / Julio Jones / Randall Cobb / Leonard Hankerson 2.00 5.00
GLMD Blaine Gabbert / Jake Locker / Ryan Mallett / Andy Dalton 2.50 6.00
ILWT Mark Ingram / Mikel Leshoure / Ryan Williams / Jordan Todman 2.00 5.00
JCHS Julio Jones / Randall Cobb / Leonard Hankerson / Torrey Smith 2.00 5.00
LWTV Mikel Leshoure / Ryan Williams / Jordan Todman / Shane Vereen 1.25 3.00
NGGJ Cam Newton / Blaine Gabbert / A.J. Green / Julio Jones 5.00 12.00
NLGP Cam Newton / Jake Locker / Blaine Gabbert / Christian Ponder 5.00 12.00
PDKM Christian Ponder / Andy Dalton / Colin Kaepernick / Ryan Mallett 2.50 6.00
PHPR Adrian Peterson / Percy Harvin / Christian Ponder / Kyle Rudolph 2.00 5.00

2011 Topps Prime Quad Relics

STATED PRINT RUN 350 SER.#'d SETS
*GOLD/50: .5X TO 1.2X BASIC QUAD
*SLVR HOLO/25: .6X TO 1.5X BASIC QUAD
BWMV Tom Brady / Wes Welker / Ryan Mallett / Shane Vereen 12.00 30.00
GJCH A.J. Green / Julio Jones / Randall Cobb / Leonard Hankerson 6.00 15.00
GLMD Blaine Gabbert / Jake Locker / Ryan Mallett / Andy Dalton 8.00 20.00
ILWT Mark Ingram / Mikel Leshoure / Ryan Williams / Jordan Todman 6.00 15.00
JCHS Julio Jones / Randall Cobb / Leonard Hankerson / Torrey Smith 8.00 20.00
LWTV Mikel Leshoure / Ryan Williams / Jordan Todman / Shane Vereen 5.00 12.00
NGGJ Cam Newton / Blaine Gabbert / A.J. Green / Julio Jones 12.00 30.00
NLGP Cam Newton / Jake Locker / Blaine Gabbert / Christian Ponder 12.00 30.00
PDKM Christian Ponder / Andy Dalton / Colin Kaepernick / Ryan Mallett 10.00 25.00
PHPR Adrian Peterson / Percy Harvin / Christian Ponder / Kyle Rudolph 10.00 25.00

2011 Topps Prime Rookie

COMPLETE SET (35) 15.00 40.00
RANDOM INSERTS IN PACKS
*GOLD/50: .8X TO 2X BASIC INSERTS
*SILVER HOLO/25: 1X TO 2.5X BASIC INSERTS
PRAD Andy Dalton 2.00 5.00
PRAG Alex Green .75 2.00
PRAJG A.J. Green 1.50 4.00
PRAP Austin Pettis .60 1.50
PRBG Blaine Gabbert 1.25 3.00
PRBP Bilal Powell .50 1.25
PRCK Colin Kaepernick 1.00 2.50
PRCN Cam Newton 5.00 12.00
PRCP Christian Ponder 1.50 4.00
PRDC Delone Carter .60 1.50
PRDM DeMarco Murray 1.50 4.00
PRDT Daniel Thomas .75 2.00
PRGL Greg Little .75 2.00
PRJB Jon Baldwin .75 2.00
PRJH Jamie Harper .75 2.00
PRJJ Julio Jones 1.50 4.00
PRJJE Jerrel Jernigan .60 1.50
PRJL Jake Locker 2.00 5.00
PRJT Jordan Todman .50 1.25
PRKH Kendall Hunter .75 2.00
PRKR Kyle Rudolph .75 2.00
PRLH Leonard Hankerson .75 2.00
PRMD Marcell Dareus .75 2.00
PRMI Mark Ingram 1.50 4.00
PRML Mikel Leshoure .75 2.00
PRRC Randall Cobb 1.00 2.50
PRRM Ryan Mallett 1.50 4.00
PRRW Ryan Williams 1.00 2.50
PRSR Stevan Ridley .75 2.00
PRSV Shane Vereen .75 2.00
PRTJ Taiwan Jones .75 2.00
PRTS Torrey Smith 1.00 2.50
PRTY Titus Young 1.00 2.50
PRVB Vincent Brown .75 2.00
PRVM Von Miller 1.00 2.50

2011 Topps Prime Rookie Autographs

STATED PRINT RUN 99-450
EXCH EXPIRATION: 9/30/2014
2 Jamie Harper/250 6.00 15.00
3 Bilal Powell/99 5.00 12.00
7 Mark Ingram/99 25.00 60.00
9 DeMarco Murray/200 25.00 50.00
12 Rob Housler/450 4.00 10.00
14 Delone Carter/99 6.00 15.00
15 Prince Amukamara/450 5.00 12.00
18 Dwayne Harris/450 5.00 12.00
21 Nick Fairley/400 6.00 15.00
23 Titus Young 8.00 20.00
24 D.J. Williams/450 5.00 12.00
27 Jordan Todman
29 Jacquizz Rodgers/450 5.00 12.00
31 A.J. Green/99 25.00 50.00
37 Kyle Rudolph/250 6.00 15.00
44 Ryan Mallett/99 15.00 40.00
45 Torrey Smith/270 8.00 20.00
47 Colin Kaepernick/99 10.00 25.00
50 Cam Newton/200 90.00 150.00
51 Rahim Moore/450 4.00 10.00
52 Julio Jones/99 30.00 60.00
53 Da'Rel Scott/450 4.00 10.00
54 Greg Salas/450 5.00 12.00
55 Randall Cobb/270 8.00 20.00
56 Marcell Dareus
57 Alex Green/400 5.00 12.00
61 Christian Ponder/99 25.00 50.00
63 Shane Vereen/250 6.00 15.00
68 Jon Baldwin/99 8.00 20.00
74 Dion Lewis/450 5.00 12.00
78 Von Miller/99 10.00 25.00
82 Jake Locker/99 30.00 60.00
83 Blaine Gabbert/99 20.00 50.00
87 Ricky Stanzi/400 6.00 15.00
91 Leonard Hankerson/270 6.00 15.00
93 Taiwan Jones/99 8.00 20.00
96 Kendall Hunter/250 6.00 15.00
108 Ryan Williams/99 10.00 25.00
113 Andy Dalton/99 30.00 60.00
114 Stevan Ridley/250 6.00 15.00
117 Daniel Thomas/250 6.00 15.00
118 Luke Stocker/450 4.00 10.00
119 Virgil Green/450 4.00 10.00
127 Jeremy Kerley/450 5.00 12.00
137 Jerrel Jernigan/250 5.00 12.00
143 Vincent Brown
145 Edmond Gates/250 5.00 12.00
146 Mikel Leshoure EXCH 6.00 15.00
148 Greg Little/270 6.00 15.00
151 Aldon Smith/400 8.00 20.00
152 J.J. Watt/450 6.00 15.00
153 Adrian Clayborn EXCH 6.00 15.00
154 Ryan Kerrigan/450 5.00 12.00
155 Aaron Williams/450 4.00 10.00

2011 Topps Prime Rookie Autographs Gold

*GOLD/50: .8X TO 2X BASIC AU/400-450
*GOLD/50: .6X TO 1.5X BASIC AU/200-270
*GOLD/50: .5X TO 1.2X BASIC AU/99
STATED PRINT RUN 50 SER.#'d SETS
50 Cam Newton 125.00 200.00

2011 Topps Prime Rookie Autographs Silver Holofoil

*SLV HOLO/25: 1X TO 2.5X BASIC AU/400-450
*SLV HOLO/25: .8X TO 2X BASIC AU/200-270
*SLV HOLO/25: .6X TO 1.5X BASIC AU/99
STATED PRINT RUN 25 SER.#'d SETS
50 Cam Newton 150.00 250.00

2011 Topps Prime Rookie Jumbo Relics

SILVER PRINT RUN 318 SER.#'d SETS
*GOLD/50: .6X TO 1.5X BASIC JSY/318
*SLVR HOLO/25: .8X TO 2X BASIC JSY/318
PRJAD Andy Dalton 6.00 15.00
PRJAG Alex Green 2.50 6.00
PRJAP Austin Pettis 2.00 5.00
PRJBG Blaine Gabbert 4.00 10.00
PRJBP Bilal Powell 1.50 4.00
PRJCK Colin Kaepernick 3.00 8.00
PRJCN Cam Newton 15.00 40.00
PRJCP Christian Ponder 5.00 12.00
PRJDC Delone Carter 2.00 5.00
PRJDM DeMarco Murray 6.00 15.00
PRJDT Daniel Thomas 2.50 6.00
PRJEG Edmond Gates 2.00 5.00
PRJGL Greg Little 2.50 6.00
PRJJB Jon Baldwin 2.50 6.00
PRJJH Jamie Harper 2.50 6.00
PRJJJ Julio Jones 6.00 15.00
PRJJJE Jerrel Jernigan 2.00 5.00
PRJJL Jake Locker 6.00 15.00
PRJJT Jordan Todman 1.50 4.00
PRJKH Kendall Hunter 2.50 6.00
PRJKR Kyle Rudolph 2.50 6.00
PRJLH Leonard Hankerson 2.50 6.00
PRJMD Marcell Dareus 2.50 6.00
PRJMI Mark Ingram 5.00 12.00
PRJML Mikel Leshoure 2.50 6.00
PRJRC Randall Cobb 5.00 12.00
PRJRM Ryan Mallett 5.00 12.00
PRJRW Ryan Williams 3.00 8.00
PRJSR Stevan Ridley 2.50 6.00
PRJSV Shane Vereen 2.50 6.00
PRJTJ Taiwan Jones 2.50 6.00
PRJTS Torrey Smith 3.00 8.00
PRJTY Titus Young 3.00 8.00
PRJVB Vincent Brown 2.50 6.00
PRJVM Von Miller 3.00 8.00
PRJAJG A.J. Green 5.00 12.00

2011 Topps Prime Triple

RANDOM INSERTS IN PACKS
*GOLD/50: .8X TO 2X BASIC INSERTS
*SILVER HOLO/25: 1X TO 2.5X BASIC INSERTS
CJH Delone Carter / Taiwan Jones / Jamie Harper .75 2.00
GJB A.J. Green / Julio Jones / Jon Baldwin 1.50 4.00
HCJ Kendall Hunter / Delone Carter / Taiwan Jones .75 2.00
IWV Mark Ingram / Ryan Williams / Shane Vereen 1.50 4.00
JBP Jerrel Jernigan / Vincent Brown / Austin Pettis .75 2.00
JDI Julio Jones / Marcell Dareus / Mark Ingram 1.50 4.00
JLY Calvin Johnson / Mikel Leshoure / Titus Young 1.00 2.50
LTM Mikel Leshoure / Daniel Thomas / DeMarco Murray 1.50 4.00
MRB Peyton Manning / Aaron Rodgers / Tom Brady 2.50 6.00
MVR Ryan Mallett / Shane Vereen / Stevan Ridley 1.50 4.00
NLG Cam Newton / Jake Locker / Blaine Gabbert 4.00 10.00
NMD Cam Newton / Von Miller / Marcell Dareus 4.00 10.00
PDK Christian Ponder / Andy Dalton / Colin Kaepernick 2.00 5.00
RBT Philip Rivers / Vincent Brown / Jordan Todman .75 2.00
YSL Titus Young / Torrey Smith / Greg Little 1.00 2.50

2011 Topps Prime Triple Relics

STATED PRINT RUN 388
*GOLD/50: .6X TO 1.5X BASIC TRIPLE
*SLVR HOLO/25: .8X TO 2X BASIC TRIPLE
CJH Delone Carter / Taiwan Jones / Jamie Harper 3.00 8.00
GJB A.J. Green / Julio Jones / Jon Baldwin 6.00 15.00
HCJ Kendall Hunter / Delone Carter / Taiwan Jones 3.00 8.00
IWV Mark Ingram / Ryan Williams / Shane Vereen 5.00 12.00
JBP Jerrel Jernigan / Vincent Brown / Austin Pettis 3.00 8.00
JDI Julio Jones / Marcell Dareus / Mark Ingram 8.00 20.00
JLY Calvin Johnson / Mikel Leshoure / Titus Young 5.00 12.00
LTM Mikel Leshoure / Daniel Thomas / DeMarco Murray 5.00 12.00
MRB Peyton Manning / Aaron Rodgers / Tom Brady 12.00 30.00
MVR Ryan Mallett / Shane Vereen / Stevan Ridley 5.00 12.00
NLG Cam Newton / Jake Locker / Blaine Gabbert 10.00 25.00
NMD Cam Newton / Von Miller / Marcell Dareus 10.00 25.00
PDK Christian Ponder / Andy Dalton / Colin Kaepernick 6.00 15.00
RBT Philip Rivers / Vincent Brown / Jordan Todman 4.00 10.00
YSL Titus Young / Torrey Smith / Greg Little 4.00 10.00

2011 Topps Prime Veteran

COMPLETE SET (20) 8.00 20.00
RANDOM INSERTS IN PACKS
*GOLD/50: 1X TO 2.5X BASIC INSERTS
*SILVER HOLO/25: 1.2X TO 3X BASIC INSERTS
PVAP Adrian Peterson 1.25 3.00
PVBU Brian Urlacher 1.00 2.50
PVCJ Calvin Johnson 1.00 2.50
PVER Eddie Royal .60 1.50
PVHN Hakeem Nicks .75 2.00
PVJA Joseph Addai .75 2.00
PVJW Jason Witten 1.00 2.50
PVKM Knowshon Moreno .75 2.00
PVLF Larry Fitzgerald .75 2.00
PVLM LeSean McCoy .75 2.00
PVMB Michael Bush .60 1.50
PVPH Percy Harvin .75 2.00
PVPR Philip Rivers 1.00 2.50
PVRL Ray Lewis 1.00 2.50
PVSM Santana Moss .75 2.00
PVTB Tom Brady 1.50 4.00
PVTG Tony Gonzalez .75 2.00
PVTP Troy Polamalu 1.00 2.50
PVTR Tony Romo 1.00 2.50
PVWW Wes Welker 1.00 2.50

2011 Topps Prime Veteran Relics

STATED PRINT RUN 99 SER.#'d SETS
*GOLD/50: .5X TO 1.2X BASIC JSY
*SILVER HOLO/25: .8X TO 2X BASIC JSY
PVRAP Adrian Peterson 6.00 15.00
PVRBU Brian Urlacher 5.00 12.00
PVRCJ Calvin Johnson 5.00 12.00
PVRER Eddie Royal 3.00 8.00
PVRHN Hakeem Nicks 4.00 10.00
PVRJA Joseph Addai 4.00 10.00
PVRJW Jason Witten 5.00 12.00
PVRKM Knowshon Moreno 4.00 10.00
PVRLF Larry Fitzgerald 4.00 10.00
PVRLM LeSean McCoy 4.00 10.00
PVRMB Michael Bush 3.00 8.00
PVRPH Percy Harvin 4.00 10.00
PVRPR Philip Rivers 5.00 12.00
PVRRL Ray Lewis 5.00 12.00
PVRSM Santana Moss 4.00 10.00
PVRTB Tom Brady 8.00 20.00
PVRTG Tony Gonzalez 4.00 10.00
PVRTP Troy Polamalu 6.00 15.00
PVRTR Tony Romo 5.00 12.00
PVRWW Wes Welker 5.00 12.00

2002 Topps Pristine

Released in December 2002, this set features 50 veterans and 120 rookies. The rookie portion of the set, cards 51-170 were broken into three tiers: common (C), uncommon (U), and rare (R). The uncommon cards were serial #'d to 999, and the rares were serial #d to 499. Boxes contained 5 triple packs, containing a total of 8 cards. The first pack contained an uncirculated refractor, the second pack contained a memorabilia card, and the third pack contained veteran and rookie cards.

COMP.SET w/o SP's (50) 20.00 50.00
1 Peyton Manning 2.00 5.00
2 Darrell Jackson .75 2.00
3 Donovan McNabb 1.00 2.50
4 Rod Smith .75 2.00
5 Daunte Culpepper .75 2.00
6 Drew Brees 1.50 4.00
7 Stephen Davis .75 2.00
8 Kurt Warner 1.00 2.50
9 Eric Moulds .75 2.00
10 Jake Plummer .75 2.00
11 Chris Weinke .60 1.50
12 Brian Griese .75 2.00
13 Corey Bradford .60 1.50
14 Trent Green .75 2.00
15 Tom Brady 2.50 6.00
16 Jeff Garcia .75 2.00
17 Tiki Barber 1.00 2.50
18 Eddie George .75 2.00
19 Jamal Lewis .75 2.00
20 Troy Brown .75 2.00
21 Priest Holmes 1.00 2.50
22 Jimmy Smith .75 2.00
23 Tim Brown 1.00 2.50
24 Plaxico Burress .75 2.00
25 Aaron Brooks .75 2.00
26 Marshall Faulk 1.00 2.50
27 Steve McNair 1.00 2.50
28 Curtis Martin 1.00 2.50
29 Corey Dillon .75 2.00
30 Tim Couch .60 1.50
31 Michael Vick 1.50 4.00
32 David Boston .60 1.50
33 Kordell Stewart .75 2.00
34 Jerome Bettis 1.00 2.50
35 Keyshawn Johnson .75 2.00
36 Torry Holt 1.00 2.50
37 Shaun Alexander .75 2.00
38 Brett Favre 2.50 6.00
39 Marvin Harrison 1.00 2.50
40 Randy Moss 1.00 2.50
41 Jerry Rice 2.00 5.00
42 LaDainian Tomlinson 1.25 3.00
43 Terrell Owens 1.00 2.50
44 Edgerrin James .75 2.00
45 Anthony Thomas .75 2.00
46 Drew Bledsoe 1.00 2.50
47 Ahman Green .75 2.00
48 Ricky Williams .75 2.00
49 Tony Gonzalez 1.00 2.50
50 Emmitt Smith 2.50 6.00
51 Joey Harrington C RC 1.00 2.50
52 Joey Harrington U 1.25 3.00
53 Joey Harrington R 1.50 4.00
54 Josh McCown C RC 1.00 2.50
55 Josh McCown U 1.25 3.00
56 Josh McCown R 1.50 4.00
57 Antwaan Randle El C RC 1.00 2.50
58 Antwaan Randle El U 1.25 3.00
59 Antwaan Randle El R 1.50 4.00
60 Reche Caldwell C RC 1.00 2.50
61 Reche Caldwell U 1.25 3.00
62 Reche Caldwell R 1.50 4.00
63 Jason McAddley C RC .75 2.00
64 Jason McAddley U 1.00 2.50
65 Jason McAddley R 1.25 3.00
66 Ashley Lelie C RC .75 2.00
67 Ashley Lelie U 1.00 2.50
68 Ashley Lelie R 1.25 3.00
69 Travis Stephens C RC .60 1.50
70 Travis Stephens U .75 2.00
71 Travis Stephens R 1.00 2.50
72 Chad Hutchinson C RC .60 1.50
73 Chad Hutchinson U .75 2.00
74 Chad Hutchinson R 1.00 2.50
75 Quentin Jammer C RC 1.00 2.50
76 Quentin Jammer U 1.25 3.00
77 Quentin Jammer R 1.50 4.00
78 Tim Carter C RC .75 2.00
79 Tim Carter U 1.00 2.50
80 Tim Carter R 1.25 3.00
81 Antonio Bryant C RC 1.00 2.50
82 Antonio Bryant U 1.25 3.00
83 Antonio Bryant R 1.50 4.00
84 Cliff Russell C RC .60 1.50
85 Cliff Russell U .75 2.00
86 Cliff Russell R 1.00 2.50
87 Rohan Davey C RC 1.00 2.50
88 Rohan Davey U 1.25 3.00
89 Rohan Davey R 1.50 4.00
90 Javon Walker C RC 1.00 2.50
91 Javon Walker U 1.25 3.00
92 Javon Walker R 1.50 4.00
93 T.J. Duckett C RC 1.00 2.50
94 T.J. Duckett U 1.25 3.00
95 T.J. Duckett R 1.50 4.00
96 Donte Stallworth C RC 1.00 2.50
97 Donte Stallworth U 1.25 3.00
98 Donte Stallworth R 1.50 4.00
99 Andre Davis C RC .75 2.00
100 Andre Davis U 1.00 2.50
101 Andre Davis R 1.25 3.00
102 Mike Williams C RC .60 1.50
103 Mike Williams U .75 2.00
104 Mike Williams R 1.00 2.50
105 Freddie Milons C RC .60 1.50
106 Freddie Milons U .75 2.00
107 Freddie Milons R 1.00 2.50

108 John Henderson C RC	.75	2.00
109 John Henderson U	1.00	2.50
110 John Henderson R	1.25	3.00
111 DeShaun Foster C RC	1.00	2.50
112 DeShaun Foster U	1.25	3.00
113 DeShaun Foster R	1.50	4.00
114 Josh Reed C RC	.75	2.00
115 Josh Reed U	1.00	2.50
116 Josh Reed R	1.25	3.00
117 Jabar Gaffney C RC	1.00	2.50
118 Jabar Gaffney U	1.25	3.00
119 Jabar Gaffney R	1.50	4.00
120 Clinton Portis C RC	1.25	3.00
121 Clinton Portis U	1.50	4.00
122 Clinton Portis R	2.00	5.00
123 Jeremy Shockey C RC	1.50	4.00
124 Jeremy Shockey U	2.50	6.00
125 Jeremy Shockey R	2.50	6.00
126 Dwight Freeney C RC	1.25	3.00
127 Dwight Freeney U	1.50	4.00
128 Dwight Freeney R	2.00	5.00
129 Brian Westbrook C RC	1.50	4.00
130 Brian Westbrook U	2.00	5.00
131 Brian Westbrook R	2.50	6.00
132 Randy Fasani C RC	.75	2.00
133 Randy Fasani U	1.00	2.50
134 Randy Fasani R	1.25	3.00
135 Julius Peppers C RC	2.00	5.00
136 Julius Peppers U	2.50	6.00
137 Julius Peppers R	3.00	8.00
138 Patrick Ramsey C RC	1.00	2.50
139 Patrick Ramsey U	1.25	3.00
140 Patrick Ramsey R	1.50	4.00
141 William Green C RC	.75	2.00
142 William Green U	1.00	2.50
143 William Green R	1.25	3.00
144 Daniel Graham C RC	.75	2.00
145 Daniel Graham U	1.00	2.50
146 Daniel Graham R	1.25	3.00
147 Ron Johnson C RC	.75	2.00
148 Ron Johnson U	1.00	2.50
149 Ron Johnson R	1.25	3.00
150 Maurice Morris C RC	.75	2.00
151 Maurice Morris U	1.00	2.50
152 Maurice Morris R	1.25	3.00
153 Eric Crouch C RC	1.00	2.50
154 Eric Crouch U	1.25	3.00
155 Eric Crouch R	1.50	4.00
156 Roy Williams C RC	1.00	2.50
157 Roy Williams U	1.25	3.00
158 Roy Williams R	1.50	4.00
159 Ladell Betts C RC	1.00	2.50
160 Ladell Betts U	1.25	3.00
161 Ladell Betts R	1.50	4.00
162 David Garrard C RC	1.25	3.00
163 David Garrard U	1.50	4.00
164 David Garrard R	2.00	5.00
165 Marquise Walker C RC	.60	1.50
166 Marquise Walker U	.75	2.00
167 Marquise Walker R	1.00	2.50
168 David Carr C RC	1.00	2.50
169 David Carr U	1.25	3.00
170 David Carr R	1.50	4.00
ESA1 Emmitt Smith AU	175.00	300.00
ESJ1 Emmitt Smith JSY	15.00	40.00

2002 Topps Pristine Gold Refractors

*1-50 VETS: 3X TO 8X BASIC CARDS
*ROOKIE C 51-170: 2.5X TO 6X
*ROOKIE U 51-170: 2X TO 5X
*ROOKIE R 51-170: 1.5X TO 4X
ONE PER HOBBY BOX
STATED PRINT RUN 79 SER.#'d SETS

2002 Topps Pristine Refractors

*1-50 VET/349: 2X TO 5X BASIC CARDS
1-50 VET/349 ODDS 1:5
1-50 VET PRINT RUN 349
*51-170 ROOKIE C/999: 1X TO 2.5X
51-170 ROOKIE C PRINT RUN 999
*51-170 ROOKIE U/499: 1X TO 2.5X
51-170 ROOKIE U/499 ODDS 1:5
51-170 ROOKIE U PRINT RUN 499
*51-170 ROOKIE R/199: 1.2X TO 3X
51-170 ROOKIE R/199 ODDS 1:11
51-170 ROOKIE R PRINT RUN 199

2002 Topps Pristine All-Rookie Team Jerseys

GROUP A STATED ODDS 1:30
GROUP B STATED ODDS 1:50
GROUP C STATED ODDS 1:46

TRRAL Ashley Lelie A	3.00	8.00
TRRCP Clinton Portis A	5.00	12.00
TRRJG Jabar Gaffney A	4.00	10.00
TRRJP Julius Peppers B	8.00	20.00
TRRMW Mike Williams C	2.50	6.00

2002 Topps Pristine Autographs

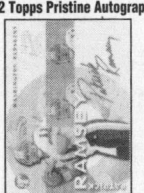

GROUP A STATED ODDS 1:637
GROUP B STATED ODDS 1:36
GROUP C STATED ODDS 1:160
GROUP D STATED ODDS 1:26
GROUP E STATED ODDS 1:154
GROUP F STATED ODDS 1:41
GROUP G STATED ODDS 1:64

PAD Andre Davis B	6.00	15.00
PAL Ashley Lelie D	6.00	15.00
PBF Brett Favre C	125.00	200.00
PBM Bryant McKinnie F	5.00	12.00
PCR Cliff Russell G	5.00	12.00
PDC David Carr B	8.00	20.00
PDF DeShaun Foster B	8.00	20.00
PDG David Garrard D	15.00	40.00
PJH Joey Harrington A	12.00	30.00
PJM Josh McCown D	8.00	20.00
PJR Josh Reed D	6.00	15.00
PJW Javon Walker B	8.00	20.00
PKC Kelly Campbell B	6.00	15.00
PKK Kurt Kittner B	5.00	12.00
PPR Patrick Ramsey B	8.00	20.00
PRD Rohan Davey F	8.00	20.00
PRJ Ron Johnson B	6.00	15.00
PTS Travis Stephens D	5.00	12.00
PWG William Green C	6.00	15.00
PDRC Reche Caldwell D	8.00	20.00
PTJD T.J. Duckett B	12.00	30.00

2002 Topps Pristine Driving Force Jerseys

GROUP A STATED ODDS 1:126
GROUP B STATED ODDS 1:110
GROUP C STATED ODDS 1:31
GROUP D STATED ODDS 1:18
GROUP E STATED ODDS 1:25
GROUP F STATED ODDS 1:33

DFAB Aaron Brooks D	3.00	8.00
DFAT Anthony Thomas D	3.00	8.00
DFBF Brett Favre B	10.00	25.00
DFCM Curtis Martin C	4.00	10.00
DFDF Doug Flutie E	4.00	10.00
DFKW Kurt Warner E	4.00	10.00
DFLT LaDainian Tomlinson D	5.00	12.00
DFMB Mark Brunell F	3.00	8.00
DFMF Marshall Faulk C	4.00	10.00
DFSD Stephen Davis A	3.00	8.00

2002 Topps Pristine Nickel Package Jerseys

GROUP A STATED ODDS 1:238
GROUP B STATED ODDS 1:185
GROUP C STATED ODDS 1:60
GROUP D STATED ODDS 1:49
GROUP E STATED ODDS 1:35

NPJK Jevon Kearse B	3.00	8.00
NPJP Julius Peppers D	8.00	20.00
NPJS Justin Smith C	2.50	6.00
NPRW Roy Williams E	4.00	10.00
NPTV Troy Vincent A	3.00	8.00

2002 Topps Pristine Patches

PATCH/100 STATED ODDS 1:49
STATED PRINT RUN 100 SER.#'d SETS

PPAB Aaron Brooks	5.00	12.00
PPAT Anthony Thomas	5.00	12.00
PPBF Brett Favre	15.00	40.00
PPBG Brian Griese	5.00	12.00
PPCM Curtis Martin	6.00	15.00
PPDF Doug Flutie	6.00	15.00
PPDG Darrell Green	6.00	15.00
PPDS Duce Staley	5.00	12.00
PPEG Eddie George	5.00	12.00
PPES Emmitt Smith	15.00	40.00
PPJG Jeff Garcia	5.00	12.00
PPJR Jerry Rice	12.00	30.00
PPKJ Keyshawn Johnson	5.00	12.00
PPKW Kurt Warner	6.00	15.00
PPMB Mark Brunell	5.00	12.00
PPMF Marshall Faulk	6.00	15.00
PPTO Terrell Owens	6.00	15.00

2002 Topps Pristine Portions Jerseys

GROUP A STATED ODDS 1:74
GROUP B STATED ODDS 1:63
GROUP C STATED ODDS 1:29
GROUP D STATED ODDS 1:55
GROUP E STATED ODDS 1:46
GROUP F STATED ODDS 1:46
GROUP G STATED ODDS 1:40

PPBRG Brian Griese D	3.00	8.00
PPRDB Drew Brees G	6.00	15.00
PPRDG Darrell Green F	4.00	10.00
PPREG Eddie George C	3.00	8.00
PPRES Emmitt Smith A	15.00	40.00
PPRJG Jeff Garcia E	3.00	8.00
PPRJR Jerry Rice F	8.00	20.00
PPRKJ Keyshawn Johnson D	3.00	8.00
PPRTO Terrell Owens D	4.00	10.00

2002 Topps Pristine Rookie Premiere Jerseys

GROUP A STATED ODDS 1:97
GROUP B STATED ODDS 1:72
GROUP C STATED ODDS 1:63
GROUP D STATED ODDS 1:55
GROUP E STATED ODDS 1:49
GROUP F STATED ODDS 1:15
GROUP G STATED ODDS 1:21
GROUP H STATED ODDS 1:20
GROUP I STATED ODDS 1:18
GROUP J STATED ODDS 1:18
GROUP K STATED ODDS 1:31

RPRAB Antonio Bryant I	4.00	10.00
RPRAD Andre Davis H	3.00	8.00
RPRCP Clinton Portis F	5.00	12.00
RPRDC Reche Caldwell E	4.00	10.00
RPRDF DeShaun Foster L	4.00	10.00
RPRDG David Garrard G	5.00	12.00
RPRDS Donte Stallworth I	4.00	10.00
RPREC Eric Crouch G	4.00	10.00
RPRGR Daniel Graham D	3.00	8.00
RPRJG Jabar Gaffney I	4.00	10.00
RPRJH Joey Harrington F	4.00	10.00
RPRJM Josh McCown H	4.00	10.00
RPRJR Josh Reed K	3.00	8.00
RPRJS Jeremy Shockey K	6.00	15.00
RPRJW Javon Walker J	4.00	10.00
RPRMW Marquise Walker A	2.50	6.00
RPRPR Patrick Ramsey B	4.00	10.00
RPRTC Tim Carter F	3.00	8.00
RPRTD T.J. Duckett C	4.00	10.00
RPRWG William Green J	3.00	8.00

2003 Topps Pristine

Released in November of 2003, this set features 50 veterans and 99 rookies. The rookie portion of this set, cards 51-149, is broken into three tiers: common, uncommon, and rare. Uncommon rookies were inserted at a rate of 1:2, and are serial numbered to 1499. Rare rookies were inserted at a rate of 1:5, and are serial numbered to 499. Boxes contained 5 triple packs, and each pack contained a total of 8 cards. The first pack contained an uncirculated refractor, the second pack contained a memorabilia card, and the third pack contained veteran and rookie cards. The pack SRP was $30.

COMP.SET w/o SP's (50)	15.00	40.00

U ROOKIE/1499 ODDS 1:2
R ROOKIE/499 ODDS 1:5

1 Brett Favre	2.00	5.00
2 Rich Gannon	.60	1.50
3 Randy Moss	.75	2.00
4 Travis Henry	.50	1.25
5 Troy Brown	.60	1.50
6 Darrell Jackson	.60	1.50
7 Steve McNair	.75	2.00
8 Plaxico Burress	.60	1.50
9 Jerry Rice	1.50	4.00
10 Donovan McNabb	.75	2.00
11 Marty Booker	.60	1.50
12 Joey Galloway	.60	1.50
13 Peerless Price	.50	1.25
14 Emmitt Smith	2.00	5.00
15 David Carr	.60	1.50
16 Priest Holmes	.75	2.00
17 LaDainian Tomlinson	.75	2.00
18 Hines Ward	.75	2.00
19 Tiki Barber	.75	2.00
20 Fred Taylor	.60	1.50
21 Marvin Harrison	.75	2.00
22 Marshall Faulk	.75	2.00
23 Terrell Owens	.75	2.00
24 Patrick Ramsey	.60	1.50
25 Michael Vick	1.00	2.50
26 Tom Brady	2.00	5.00
27 Shaun Alexander	.60	1.50
28 Derrick Mason	.60	1.50
29 Keyshawn Johnson	.75	2.00
30 Ricky Williams	.60	1.50
31 Ahman Green	.60	1.50
32 Joey Harrington	.50	1.25
33 Corey Dillon	.60	1.50
34 Jamal Lewis	.60	1.50
35 Drew Bledsoe	.75	2.00
36 Tommy Maddox	.60	1.50
37 Kurt Warner	.75	2.00
38 Deuce McAllister	.60	1.50
39 Curtis Martin	.75	2.00
40 Chad Pennington	.75	2.00
41 Trent Green	.60	1.50
42 Edgerrin James	.75	2.00
43 Clinton Portis	.60	1.50
44 Eric Moulds	.60	1.50
45 Peyton Manning	1.50	4.00
46 Jeff Garcia	.60	1.50
47 Daunte Culpepper	.60	1.50
48 Tim Couch	.50	1.25
49 Drew Brees	.75	2.00
50 Aaron Brooks	.60	1.50
51 Anquan Boldin C RC	2.00	5.00
52 Anquan Boldin U	2.50	6.00
53 Anquan Boldin R	4.00	10.00
54 Andre Johnson C RC	3.00	8.00
55 Andre Johnson U	4.00	10.00
56 Andre Johnson R	6.00	15.00
57 Artose Pinner C RC	.75	2.00
58 Artose Pinner U	1.00	2.50
59 Artose Pinner R	1.50	4.00
60 Bryant Johnson C RC	1.25	3.00
61 Bryant Johnson U	1.50	4.00
62 Bryant Johnson R	2.50	6.00
63 Bethel Johnson C RC	.75	2.00
64 Bethel Johnson U	1.00	2.50
65 Bethel Johnson R	1.50	4.00
66 Byron Leftwich C RC	1.25	3.00
67 Byron Leftwich U	1.50	4.00
68 Byron Leftwich R	2.50	6.00
69 Brian St.Pierre C RC	1.00	2.50
70 Brian St.Pierre U	1.25	3.00
71 Brian St.Pierre R	2.00	5.00
72 Chris Brown C RC	.75	2.00
73 Chris Brown U	1.00	2.50
74 Chris Brown R	1.50	4.00
75 Carson Palmer C RC	2.50	6.00
76 Carson Palmer U	3.00	8.00
77 Carson Palmer R	5.00	12.00
78 Charles Rogers C RC	1.00	2.50
79 Charles Rogers U	1.25	3.00
80 Charles Rogers R	2.00	5.00
81 Chris Simms C RC	1.25	3.00
82 Chris Simms U	1.50	4.00
83 Chris Simms R	2.50	6.00
84 Dallas Clark C RC	2.00	5.00
85 Dallas Clark U	2.50	6.00
86 Dallas Clark R	4.00	10.00
87 Dave Ragone C RC	.75	2.00
88 Dave Ragone U	1.00	2.50
89 Dave Ragone R	1.50	4.00
90 DeWayne Robertson C RC	1.00	2.50
91 DeWayne Robertson U	1.25	3.00
92 DeWayne Robertson R	2.00	5.00
93 Justin Fargas C RC	1.25	3.00
94 Justin Fargas U	1.50	4.00
95 Justin Fargas R	2.50	6.00
96 Kyle Boller C RC	1.25	3.00
97 Kyle Boller U	1.50	4.00
98 Kyle Boller R	2.50	6.00
99 Kevin Curtis C RC	1.25	3.00
100 Kevin Curtis U	1.50	4.00
101 Kevin Curtis R	2.50	6.00
102 Ken Dorsey C RC	1.00	2.50
103 Ken Dorsey U	1.25	3.00
104 Ken Dorsey R	2.00	5.00
105 Kelley Washington C RC	.75	2.00
106 Kelley Washington U	1.00	2.50
107 Kelley Washington R	1.50	4.00
108 Kliff Kingsbury C RC	1.00	2.50
109 Kliff Kingsbury U	1.25	3.00
110 Kliff Kingsbury R	2.00	5.00
111 Larry Johnson C RC	1.25	3.00
112 Larry Johnson U	1.50	4.00
113 Larry Johnson R	2.50	6.00
114 Musa Smith C RC	.75	2.00
115 Musa Smith U	1.00	2.50
116 Musa Smith R	1.50	4.00
117 Marcus Trufant C RC	1.00	2.50
118 Marcus Trufant U	1.25	3.00
119 Marcus Trufant R	2.00	5.00
120 Nate Burleson C RC	1.00	2.50
121 Nate Burleson U	1.25	3.00
122 Nate Burleson R	2.00	5.00
123 Onterrio Smith C RC	.75	2.00
124 Onterrio Smith U	1.00	2.50
125 Onterrio Smith R	1.50	4.00
126 Rex Grossman C RC	1.25	3.00
127 Rex Grossman U	1.50	4.00
128 Rex Grossman R	2.50	6.00
129 Seneca Wallace C RC	1.25	3.00
130 Seneca Wallace U	1.50	4.00
131 Seneca Wallace R	2.50	6.00
132 Tyrone Calico C RC	1.00	2.50
133 Tyrone Calico U	1.25	3.00
134 Tyrone Calico R	2.00	5.00
135 Taylor Jacobs C RC	.75	2.00
136 Taylor Jacobs U	1.00	2.50
137 Taylor Jacobs R	1.50	4.00
138 Teyo Johnson C RC	1.00	2.50
139 Teyo Johnson U	1.25	3.00
140 Toyo Johnson R	2.00	5.00
141 Terence Newman C RC	1.00	2.50
142 Terence Newman U	1.25	3.00
143 Terence Newman R	2.00	5.00
144 Terrell Suggs C RC	1.25	3.00
145 Terrell Suggs U	1.50	4.00
146 Terrell Suggs R	2.50	6.00
147 Willis McGahee C RC	1.50	4.00
148 Willis McGahee U	2.00	5.00
149 Willis McGahee R	3.00	8.00

2003 Topps Pristine Gold Refractors

*VETS 1-50: 2X TO 5X BASIC CARDS
1-50 VETERAN PRINT RUN 150
*C ROOKIES 51-149: 1.5X TO 4X
C ROOKIES PRINT RUN 75
*U ROOKIES 51-149: 1.5X TO 4X
U ROOKIES PRINT RUN 50
*R ROOKIES 51-149: 1.5X TO 4X
R ROOKIES PRINT RUN 25
ONE PER HOBBY BOX

2003 Topps Pristine Refractors

*VETS 1-50: 2.5X TO 6X BASIC CARDS
1-50 VETERAN/99 ODDS 1:15
1-50 PRINT RUN 99 SER.#'d SETS
*C ROOKIES 51-149: .8X TO 2X
C ROOKIE/1499 ODDS 1:2
C ROOKIE PRINT RUN 1499 SER.#'d SETS
*U ROOKIES 51-149: .8X TO 2X
U ROOKIE/499 ODDS 1:25
U ROOKIE PRINT RUN 499 SER.#'d SETS
*R ROOKIES 51-149: 1X TO 2.5X
R ROOKIE/99 ODDS 1:23
R ROOKIE PRINT RUN 99 SER.#'d SETS

2003 Topps Pristine All-Rookie Team Jerseys

GROUP A STATED ODDS 1:88
GROUP B STATED ODDS 1:74
GROUP C STATED ODDS 1:14
*REFRACTOR/25: 1.5X TO 4X BASIC JSY
REFRACTOR/25 STATED ODDS 1:345

ARTAJ Andre Johnson C	10.00	25.00
ARTBJ Bryant Johnson A	4.00	10.00
ARTBL Byron Leftwich C	4.00	10.00
ARTCP Carson Palmer C	10.00	25.00
ARTCR Charles Rogers C	3.00	8.00
ARTKB Kyle Boller C	4.00	10.00
ARTLJ Larry Johnson A	4.00	10.00
ARTRG Rex Grossman A	8.00	20.00
ARTWM Willis McGahee B	8.00	20.00

2003 Topps Pristine All-Star Endorsements Jersey Autographs

GROUP A STATED ODDS 1:138
GROUP B STATED ODDS 1:34
GROUP C STATED ODDS 1:44

ASEDM Deuce McAllister A	10.00	25.00
ASELK Lincoln Kennedy B	8.00	20.00
ASEMB Marty Booker B	10.00	25.00
ASEOK Olin Kreutz C	12.00	30.00
ASETG Tony Gonzalez A	12.00	30.00
ASEWR Willie Roaf C	25.00	50.00

2003 Topps Pristine Autographs

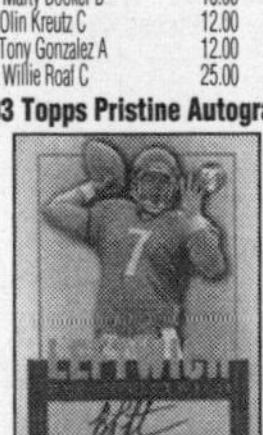

GROUP A STATED ODDS 1:3350
GROUP B STATED ODDS 1:455
GROUP C STATED ODDS 1:20
GROUP D STATED ODDS 1:110
GROUP E STATED ODDS 1:48
GROUP F STATED ODDS 1:31

PEBJ Bryant Johnson C	8.00	20.00
PEBL Byron Leftwich C	8.00	20.00
PEBS Barry Sanders B	50.00	100.00
PECB Chris Brown C	5.00	12.00
PECS Chris Simms F	12.00	30.00
PEDM Dan Marino A	125.00	250.00
PEJF Justin Fargas E	8.00	20.00
PEJR Jerry Rice B	75.00	150.00
PEKB Kyle Boller E	8.00	20.00
PEKW Kelly Washington C	5.00	12.00
PELJ Larry Johnson C	8.00	20.00
PERG Rex Grossman C	15.00	40.00
PETC Tyrone Calico D	6.00	15.00
PETJ Taylor Jacobs C	5.00	12.00
PETJO Teyo Johnson F	6.00	15.00
PETS Terrell Suggs F	10.00	25.00

2003 Topps Pristine Autographs Gold

*GOLD/25: .8X TO 2X BASIC AUTO
GOLD PRINT RUN 25 SERIAL #'d SETS

PEBS Barry Sanders	100.00	200.00
PEDM Dan Marino	125.00	250.00
PEJR Jerry Rice	100.00	200.00

2003 Topps Pristine Gems Relics

GROUP A STATED ODDS 1:248
GROUP B STATED ODDS 1:121
GROUP C STATED ODDS 1:57
GROUP D STATED ODDS 1:51

PGABU Brian Urlacher C	5.00	12.00
PGACP Clinton Portis C	4.00	10.00
PGADM Deuce McAllister D	4.00	10.00
PGADS Duce Staley C	4.00	10.00
PGAJK Jevon Kearse D	4.00	10.00
PGAJS Jeremy Shockey B	5.00	12.00
PGAJT Jason Taylor D	4.00	10.00
PGARW Ricky Williams C	4.00	10.00
PGAT Amani Toomer B	4.00	10.00
PGATH Anthony Thomas B	4.00	10.00
PGATO Terrell Owens C	5.00	12.00
PGAZT Zach Thomas C	5.00	12.00
PGCP Chad Pennington A	6.00	15.00
PGDC David Carr A	5.00	12.00
PGJH Joey Harrington A	4.00	10.00

2003 Topps Pristine Igniters Relics

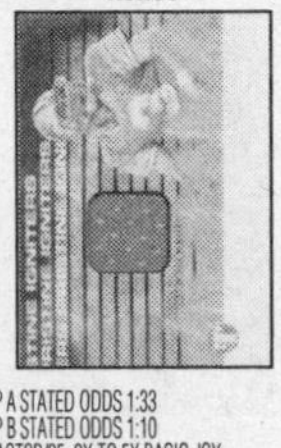

GROUP A STATED ODDS 1:33
GROUP B STATED ODDS 1:10
*REFRACTOR/25: 2X TO 5X BASIC JSY
REFRACTOR/25 ODDS 1:634

PICP Chad Pennington A	5.00	12.00
PIJH Joey Harrington B	3.00	8.00
PIJS Jeremy Shockey B	5.00	12.00
PIJT Jason Taylor B	4.00	10.00
PITO Terrell Owens A	5.00	12.00

2003 Topps Pristine Minis

STATED ODDS ONE PER BOX
RICE AU STATED ODDS 1:648

PM1 Michael Vick	1.25	3.00
PM2 Brett Favre	2.50	6.00
PM3 Marvin Harrison	1.00	2.50
PM4 Chad Pennington	1.00	2.50
PM5 Priest Holmes	1.00	2.50
PM6 LaDainian Tomlinson	1.00	2.50
PM7 Drew Bledsoe	1.00	2.50
PM8 Ricky Williams	.75	2.00
PM9 Randy Moss	1.00	2.50
PM10 Donovan McNabb	1.00	2.50
PM11 Peyton Manning	2.00	5.00
PM12 Deuce McAllister	.75	2.00
PM13 Steve McNair	1.00	2.50
PM14 Clinton Portis	.75	2.00
PM15 Jerry Rice	2.00	5.00
PM16 Terrell Owens	1.00	2.50
PM17 Marshall Faulk	1.00	2.50
PM18 Rich Gannon	.75	2.00
PM19 Tom Brady	2.50	6.00
PM20 Jamal Lewis	.75	2.00
PM21 Carson Palmer	2.00	5.00
PM22 Andre Johnson	2.50	6.00
PM23 Willis McGahee	1.25	3.00
PM24 Bryant Johnson	1.00	2.50
PM25 Byron Leftwich	1.00	2.50
PM26 Justin Fargas	1.00	2.50
PM27 Anquan Boldin	1.50	4.00
PM28 Rex Grossman	1.00	2.50
PM29 Larry Johnson	1.00	2.50
PM30 Taylor Jacobs	.60	1.50
PM31 Kyle Boller	1.00	2.50
PM32 Tyrone Calico	.75	2.00
PM33 Bethel Johnson	.60	1.50
PM34 Charles Rogers	.75	2.00
PM35 Teyo Johnson	.75	2.00
PM36 Musa Smith	.60	1.50
PM37 Kelley Washington	.60	1.50
PM38 Chris Brown	.60	1.50
PM39 Dallas Clark	1.50	4.00
PM40 Chris Simms	1.00	2.50
NNO Jerry Rice AUTO	60.00	120.00

2003 Topps Pristine Performance

GROUP A STATED ODDS 1:37
GROUP B STATED ODDS 1:33
GROUP C STATED ODDS 1:4
*REFRACTOR/25: 2X TO 5X BASIC JSY
REFRACTOR/25 ODDS 1:311

PPAT Amani Toomer C	3.00	8.00
PPATH Anthony Thomas C	3.00	8.00
PPBU Brian Urlacher C	4.00	10.00
PPCP Clinton Portis C	3.00	8.00
PPDC David Carr A	3.00	8.00
PPDM Deuce McAllister C	3.00	8.00
PPDS Duce Staley C	3.00	8.00
PPJK Jevon Kearse C	3.00	8.00
PPRW Ricky Williams C	3.00	8.00
PPZT Zach Thomas B	4.00	10.00

2003 Topps Pristine Rookie Premiere Jerseys

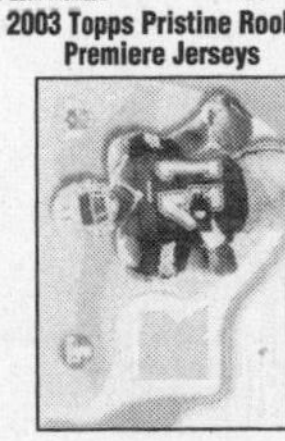

GROUP A STATED ODDS 1:137
GROUP B STATED ODDS 1:46
GROUP C STATED ODDS 1:74
GROUP D STATED ODDS 1:27
GROUP E STATED ODDS 1:7
GROUP F STATED ODDS 1:36
GROUP G STATED ODDS 1:6
*REFRACTOR/25: 1.5X TO 4X BASIC JSY
REFRACTOR/25 STATED ODDS 1:179
REFRACTOR PRINT RUN 25 #'d SETS

RPRAJ Andre Johnson E	10.00	25.00
RPRAP Artose Pinner G	2.50	6.00
RPRBJ Bethel Johnson G	2.50	6.00
RPRBL Byron Leftwich E	4.00	10.00
RPRCR Charles Rogers E	3.00	8.00
RPRDC Dallas Clark A	6.00	15.00
RPRDR DeWayne Robertson E	3.00	8.00
RPRKB Kyle Boller G	4.00	10.00
RPRKC Kevin Curtis E	4.00	10.00
RPRKD Ken Dorsey E	3.00	8.00
RPRKK Kliff Kingsbury G	3.00	8.00
RPRKW Kelly Washington D	2.50	6.00
RPRLJ Larry Johnson D	4.00	10.00
RPRMS Musa Smith G	2.50	6.00
RPRMT Marcus Trufant C	3.00	8.00
RPRNB Nate Burleson G	3.00	8.00
RPRSW Seneca Wallace R	4.00	10.00
RPRTC Tyrone Calico B	3.00	8.00
RPRTN Terence Newman E	3.00	8.00
RPRTS Terrell Suggs F	4.00	10.00

2004 Topps Pristine

Topps Pristine was initially released in mid-November 2004. The base set consists of 149-cards including 33-rookies produced with three levels of base set cards (common - C, Rare - R, and Uncommon - U). Hobby boxes contained 5-packs of 8-cards and carried an S.R.P. of $30 per pack. Two parallel sets and a variety of inserts can be found seeded in packs highlighted by the Personal Endorsement Autograph inserts.

COMP.SET w/o SP's (50)	15.00	40.00

R/499 STATED ODDS 1:4
R STATED PRINT RUN 499 SER.#'d SETS
UNPRICED PRESS PLATES #'d OF 1

1 Michael Vick	1.00	2.50
2 Tony Gonzalez	.75	2.00
3 Terrell Owens	.75	2.00
4 Brett Favre	2.00	5.00
5 Jamal Lewis	.60	1.50
6 Tim Rattay	.50	1.25
7 Ricky Williams	.60	1.50
8 Edgerrin James	.60	1.50
9 Torry Holt	.60	1.50
10 Randy Moss	.75	2.00
11 Derrick Mason	.60	1.50
12 Joe Horn	.60	1.50
13 Marvin Harrison	.75	2.00
14 Carson Palmer	.75	2.00
15 Anquan Boldin	.75	2.00
16 Quincy Carter	.50	1.25
17 Byron Leftwich	.60	1.50
18 Eric Moulds	.60	1.50
19 Marc Bulger	.60	1.50
20 Ahman Green	.60	1.50
21 Jeff Garcia	.60	1.50
22 Laveranues Coles	.50	1.25
23 Hines Ward	.75	2.00
24 Santana Moss	.60	1.50
25 LaDainian Tomlinson	.75	2.00
26 Domanick Davis	.50	1.25
27 Stephen Davis	.60	1.50
28 Tiki Barber	.75	2.00
29 Chris Chambers	.60	1.50
30 Priest Holmes	.75	2.00
31 Chad Pennington	.75	2.00
32 Shaun Alexander	.60	1.50
33 Brad Johnson	.60	1.50
34 Marshall Faulk	.75	2.00
35 Peyton Manning	1.50	4.00
36 Jake Plummer	.60	1.50
37 Clinton Portis	.75	2.00
38 Matt Hasselbeck	.60	1.50
39 Amani Toomer	.60	1.50
40 Steve McNair	.75	2.00
41 Daunte Culpepper	.60	1.50
42 Fred Taylor	.60	1.50
43 Joey Harrington	.60	1.50
44 Jake Delhomme	.60	1.50
45 Deuce McAllister	.60	1.50
46 Chad Johnson	.75	2.00
47 Travis Henry	.50	1.25
48 Corey Dillon	.60	1.50
49 Tom Brady	1.50	4.00
50 Donovan McNabb	.75	2.00
51 Ben Roethlisberger C RC	8.00	20.00
52 Ben Roethlisberger U	10.00	25.00
53 Ben Roethlisberger R	12.00	30.00
54 Ben Troupe C RC	1.00	2.50
55 Ben Troupe U	1.25	3.00
56 Ben Troupe R	1.50	4.00
57 Ben Watson C RC	1.25	3.00
58 Ben Watson U	1.50	4.00
59 Ben Watson R	2.00	5.00
60 Bernard Berrian C RC	1.25	3.00
61 Bernard Berrian U	1.50	4.00
62 Bernard Berrian R	2.00	5.00
63 Cedric Cobbs C RC	.75	2.00
64 Cedric Cobbs U	1.00	2.50
65 Cedric Cobbs R	1.25	3.00
66 Chris Perry C RC	1.00	2.50
67 Chris Perry U	1.25	3.00
68 Chris Perry R	1.50	4.00
69 Darius Watts C RC	.75	2.00
70 Darius Watts U	1.00	2.50
71 Darius Watts R	1.25	3.00
72 DeAngelo Hall C RC	1.25	3.00
73 DeAngelo Hall U	1.50	4.00
74 DeAngelo Hall R	2.00	5.00
75 Derrick Hamilton C RC	.75	2.00
76 Derrick Hamilton U	1.00	2.50
77 Derrick Hamilton R	1.25	3.00
78 Devard Darling C RC	.75	2.00
79 Devard Darling U	1.00	2.50
80 Devard Darling R	1.25	3.00
81 Devery Henderson C RC	1.25	3.00
82 Devery Henderson U	1.50	4.00
83 Devery Henderson R	2.00	5.00
84 Dunta Robinson C RC	.75	2.00
85 Dunta Robinson U	1.00	2.50
86 Dunta Robinson R	1.25	3.00
87 Eli Manning C RC	8.00	20.00
88 Eli Manning U	10.00	25.00
89 Eli Manning R	12.00	30.00
90 Greg Jones C RC	.75	2.00
91 Greg Jones U	1.00	2.50
92 Greg Jones R	1.25	3.00
93 J.P. Losman C RC	1.00	2.50
94 J.P. Losman U	1.25	3.00
95 J.P. Losman R	1.50	4.00
96 Julius Jones C RC	1.00	2.50
97 Julius Jones U	1.25	3.00
98 Julius Jones R	1.50	4.00
99 Keary Colbert C RC	.75	2.00
100 Keary Colbert U	1.00	2.50
101 Keary Colbert R	1.25	3.00
102 Kellen Winslow C RC	1.25	3.00
103 Kellen Winslow U	1.50	4.00
104 Kellen Winslow R	2.00	5.00
105 Kevin Jones C RC	1.00	2.50
106 Kevin Jones U	1.00	2.50
107 Kevin Jones R	1.50	4.00
108 Larry Fitzgerald C RC	3.00	8.00
109 Larry Fitzgerald U	4.00	10.00
110 Larry Fitzgerald R	5.00	12.00
111 Lee Evans C RC	1.25	3.00
112 Lee Evans U	1.50	4.00
113 Lee Evans R	2.00	5.00
114 Luke McCown C RC	1.00	2.50
115 Luke McCown U	1.25	3.00
116 Luke McCown R	1.50	4.00
117 Matt Schaub C RC	2.50	6.00
118 Matt Schaub U	3.00	8.00
119 Matt Schaub R	4.00	10.00
120 Mewelde Moore C RC	1.00	2.50
121 Mewelde Moore U	1.25	3.00
122 Mewelde Moore R	1.50	4.00
123 Michael Clayton C RC	1.00	2.50
124 Michael Clayton U	1.25	3.00
125 Michael Clayton R	1.50	4.00
126 Michael Jenkins C RC	1.25	3.00
127 Michael Jenkins U	1.50	4.00
128 Michael Jenkins R	2.00	5.00
129 Philip Rivers C RC	5.00	12.00
130 Philip Rivers U	6.00	15.00
131 Philip Rivers R	8.00	20.00
132 Rashaun Woods C RC	.75	2.00
133 Rashaun Woods U	1.00	2.50
134 Rashaun Woods R	1.25	3.00
135 Reggie Williams C RC	1.00	2.50
136 Reggie Williams U	1.25	3.00
137 Reggie Williams R	1.50	4.00
138 Robert Gallery C RC	1.25	3.00
139 Robert Gallery U	1.50	4.00
140 Robert Gallery R	2.00	5.00
141 Roy Williams C RC	1.25	3.00
142 Roy Williams U	1.50	4.00
143 Roy Williams R	2.00	5.00
144 Steven Jackson C RC	2.00	5.00
145 Steven Jackson U	2.50	6.00
146 Steven Jackson R	3.00	8.00
147 Tatum Bell C RC	1.00	2.50
148 Tatum Bell U	1.25	3.00
149 Tatum Bell R	1.50	4.00

2004 Topps Pristine Gold Refractors

*VETS 1-50: 1.5X TO 4X BASIC CARDS
*C ROOKIES 51-149: 2X TO 5X BASE CARD
1-50/C ROOKIES/99: ONE PER HOBBY BOX
*U ROOKIES 51-149: 3X TO 8X BASE CARD
U ROOKIES PRINT RUN 25 SER.#'d SETS
UNPRICED R ROOKIES PRINT RUN 10

2004 Topps Pristine Refractors

*VETSS 1-50: 1.5X TO 4X BASIC CARDS
1-50 VETERAN/99 ODDS 1:13
*C ROOKIES 51-149: .8X TO 2X BASE CARD
51-149 C ROOKIE PRINT RUN 1099
*U ROOKIES 51-149: .8X TO 2X BASE CARD
51-149 U ROOKIES/499 ODDS 1:4
*R ROOKIES 51-149: 1.2X TO 3X BASE CARD
51-149 R ROOKIE/99 ODDS 1:19
ONE REFRACTOR PER HOBBY PACK

2004 Topps Pristine All-Pro Endorsement Jersey Autographs

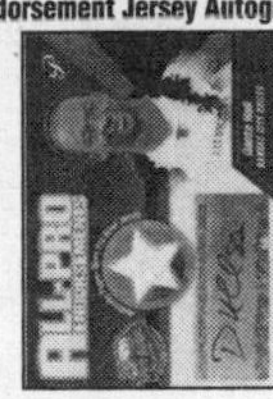

GROUP A STATED ODDS 1:308
GROUP 8 STATED ODDS 1:202
GROUP C STATED ODDS 1:175
GROUP D STATED ODDS 1:86

APEAC Alge Crumpler D	10.00	25.00
APEDF Dwight Freeney B	15.00	40.00
APEDH Dante Hall C	10.00	25.00
APEPM Peyton Manning A	75.00	135.00
APESE Shaun Ellis A	10.00	25.00

2004 Topps Pristine Clutch Performers Jersey

GROUP A STATED ODDS 1:20
GROUP B STATED ODDS 1:19
GROUP C STATED ODDS 1:31
*REFRACTOR/25: 1.5X TO 4X BASIC JSY
REFRACTOR/25 STATED ODDS 1:510

CPAB Aaron Brooks A	3.00	8.00
CPDB Deion Branch B	3.00	8.00
CPDH Dante Hall A	3.00	8.00
CPJH Joey Harrington C	3.00	8.00
CPTL Ty Law B	3.00	8.00

2004 Topps Pristine Fantasy Favorites Jersey

GROUP A STATED ODDS 1:121
GROUP B STATED ODDS 1:77
GROUP C STATED ODDS 1:67
GROUP D STATED ODDS 1:48
GROUP E STATED ODDS 1:42

GROUP F STATED ODDS 1:37
GROUP G STATED ODDS 1:18
GROUP H STATED ODDS 1:33
GROUP I STATED ODDS 1:28
*REFRACTOR/25: 2X TO 5X BASIC JSY
REFRACTOR/25 STATED ODDS 1:254
FFCM Curtis Martin C 3.00 8.00
FFDM Donovan McNabb I 3.00 8.00
FFJW Javon Walker D 2.00 5.00
FFMF Marshall Faulk H 3.00 8.00
FFMV Michael Vick A 6.00 15.00
FFPB Plaxico Burress B 2.50 6.00
FFPM Peyton Manning G 6.00 15.00
FFRJ Rudi Johnson G 2.50 6.00
FFRM Randy Moss F 3.00 8.00
FFSM Santana Moss E 2.50 6.00

2004 Topps Pristine Minis

STATED ODDS 1:6
VICK AUTO STATED ODDS 1:472
PM1 Michael Vick 2.50 6.00
PM2 Randy Moss 2.00 5.00
PM3 Marshall Faulk 2.00 5.00
PM4 Deuce McAllister 1.50 4.00
PM5 Peyton Manning 4.00 10.00
PM6 Donovan McNabb 2.00 5.00
PM7 Jamal Lewis 1.50 4.00
PM8 Tom Brady 4.00 10.00
PM9 Torry Holt 1.50 4.00
PM10 Priest Holmes 2.00 5.00
PM11 Clinton Portis 2.00 5.00
PM12 Terrell Owens 2.00 5.00
PM13 Anquan Boldin 2.00 5.00
PM14 Ahman Green 1.50 4.00
PM15 Brett Favre 5.00 12.00
PM16 Chris Perry 1.50 4.00
PM17 Greg Jones 1.25 3.00
PM18 Derrick Hamilton 1.25 3.00
PM19 Keary Colbert 1.25 3.00
PM20 Reggie Williams 1.50 4.00
PM21 Philip Rivers 6.00 15.00
PM22 Steven Jackson 2.50 6.00
PM23 Luke McCown 1.50 4.00
PM24 Kevin Jones 1.25 3.00
PM25 Darius Watts 1.25 3.00
PM26 Eli Manning 10.00 25.00
PM27 Michael Jenkins 2.00 5.00
PM28 Lee Evans 2.00 5.00
PM29 Julius Jones 1.25 3.00
PM30 Matt Schaub 3.00 8.00
PM31 Roy Williams WR 1.50 4.00
PM32 Tatum Bell 1.50 4.00
PM33 Rashaun Woods 1.25 3.00
PM34 Michael Clayton 1.50 4.00
PM35 Devery Henderson 2.00 5.00
PM36 Larry Fitzgerald 4.00 10.00
PM37 J.P. Losman 1.50 4.00
PM38 Kellen Winslow 2.00 5.00
PM39 Ben Roethlisberger 10.00 25.00
PMAMV Michael Vick AU 30.00 60.00

2004 Topps Pristine Minis Jersey

JERSEY STATED ODDS 1:312
PMRBR Ben Roethlisberger 100.00 200.00
PMRDM Donovan McNabb 25.00 60.00
PMREM Eli Manning 75.00 150.00
PMRMF Marshall Faulk 20.00 50.00
PMRMV Michael Vick 60.00 120.00
PMRPM Peyton Manning 75.00 150.00
PMRRM Randy Moss 50.00 100.00
PMRRW Roy Williams WR 20.00 50.00
PMRSJ Steven Jackson 40.00 80.00

2004 Topps Pristine Personal Endorsement Autographs

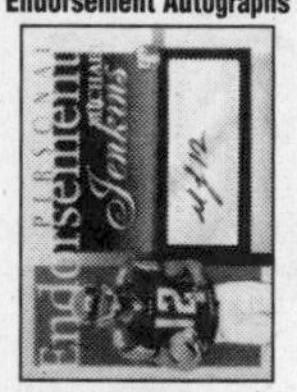

GROUP A STATED ODDS 1:829
GROUP B STATED ODDS 1:734
GROUP C STATED ODDS 1:480
GROUP D STATED ODDS 1:412
GROUP E STATED ODDS 1:97
GROUP F STATED ODDS 1:167
GROUP G STATED ODDS 1:24
GROUP H STATED ODDS 1:8
PEBB Bernard Berrian F 8.00 20.00
PECPE Chris Perry D 6.00 15.00
PEDF Dwight Freeney G 8.00 20.00
PEDHA Derrick Hamilton H 5.00 12.00
PEDHE Devery Henderson H 8.00 20.00
PEDRH Drew Henson E 5.00 12.00
PEEM Eli Manning E 60.00 120.00
PEGJ Greg Jones G 5.00 12.00
PEJC Jerricho Cotchery H 6.00 15.00
PEJPL J.P. Losman G 6.00 15.00
PEJV Jonathan Vilma G 8.00 20.00
PEKJ Kevin Jones G 6.00 15.00
PEMJ Michael Jenkins H 8.00 20.00
PEMV Michael Vick C 25.00 50.00
PEPKS P.K. Sam H 5.00 12.00
PEPM Peyton Manning B 75.00 150.00
PEPR Philip Rivers E 25.00 50.00
PERW Roy Williams WR A 8.00 20.00
PESE Shaun Ellis H 5.00 12.00
PETB Tatum Bell H 6.00 15.00

2004 Topps Pristine Personal Endorsement Autographs Gold

*GOLD/25: 1X TO 2.5X BASIC AUTO
GOLD/25 STATED ODDS 1:127 HOB
PEEM Eli Manning 150.00 300.00
PEPM Peyton Manning 175.00 300.00

2004 Topps Pristine Pristine Gems Jersey

GROUP A STATED ODDS 1:624
GROUP B STATED ODDS 1:87
GROUP C STATED ODDS 1:102
PGAB Aaron Brooks C 3.00 8.00
PGDM Donovan McNabb C 4.00 10.00
PGJPL J.P. Losman B 3.00 8.00
PGKJ Kevin Jones B 3.00 8.00
PGLF Larry Fitzgerald B 8.00 20.00
PGMF Marshall Faulk C 4.00 10.00
PGMV Michael Vick A 5.00 12.00
PGPM Peyton Manning B 8.00 20.00
PGRJ Rudi Johnson B 3.00 8.00
PGRM Randy Moss B 4.00 10.00
PGRW Roy Williams WR B 3.00 8.00
PGSM Santana Moss A 3.00 8.00

2004 Topps Pristine Real Deal Jersey

GROUP A STATED ODDS 1:1263
GROUP B STATED ODDS 1:154
*REFRACTOR/25: 1.5X TO 4X BASIC DUAL
REFRACTOR/25 ODDS 1:510
RDEL Eli Manning 12.00 30.00
J.P. Losman
RDFW Larry Fitzgerald 6.00 15.00
Roy Williams WR
RDMR Eli Manning 15.00 40.00
Ben Roethlisberger
RDPJ Chris Perry 5.00 12.00
Kevin Jones
RDRC Philip Rivers 10.00 20.00
Michael Clayton

2004 Topps Pristine Rookie Revolution Jersey

GROUP A STATED ODDS 1:123
GROUP B STATED ODDS 1:30
GROUP C STATED ODDS 1:16
GROUP D STATED ODDS 1:23
GROUP E STATED ODDS 1:41
GROUP F STATED ODDS 1:19
GROUP G STATED ODDS 1:18
GROUP H STATED ODDS 1:6
GROUP I STATED ODDS 1:30
GROUP J STATED ODDS 1:10
*REFRACTOR/25: 1.5X TO 4X BASIC JSY
REFRACTOR/25 ODDS 1:111
RRBB Bernard Berrian E 3.00 8.00
RRBR Ben Roethlisberger A 15.00 40.00
RRBW Ben Watson G 3.00 8.00
RRCC Cedric Cobbs E 2.00 5.00
RRCP Chris Perry H 2.50 6.00
RRDD Devard Darling G 2.00 5.00
RRDHA Derrick Hamilton D 2.00 5.00
RRDHE Devery Henderson G 3.00 8.00
RRDR Dunta Robinson E 2.00 5.00
RRDW Darius Watts F 2.00 5.00
RREM Eli Manning B 20.00 40.00
RRGJ Greg Jones F 2.00 5.00
RRJJ Julius Jones I 2.50 6.00
RRJPL J.P. Losman G 2.50 6.00
RRKC Keary Colbert I 2.00 5.00
RRKJ Kevin Jones D 2.50 6.00
RRLF Larry Fitzgerald G 6.00 15.00
RRMC Michael Clayton C 2.50 6.00
RRMM Mewelde Moore I 2.50 6.00
RRMS Matt Schaub B 6.00 15.00
RRRG Robert Gallery C 3.00 8.00
RRRW Roy Williams WR C 3.00 8.00
RRRWO Rashaun Woods G 2.00 5.00

2005 Topps Pristine

This 172-card set was released in November, 2005. The set was issued in the hobby in seven-card packs with an $30 SRP Which came five packs to a box, Cards number 1-100 were the heaviest printed cards with cards numbered 101-166 had either a game-worn jersey relic (101-145) ; an autograph (146-167) or both a game-worn jersey relic and an autograph (168-172),

COMP.SET w/o SP's (100) 25.00 60.00
OVERALL JSY U STATED ODDS 1:6
JSY U PRINT RUN 900 UNLESS NOTED
AU R/100 STATED ODDS 1:37
JSY AU S/25 STATED ODDS 1:675
UNPRICED PRINT.PLATES PRINT RUN 1 SET
1 Tiki Barber C 1.00 2.50
2 LaDainian Tomlinson C 1.00 2.50
3 Drew Bennett C .75 2.00
4 Jake Delhomme C .75 2.00
5 Deuce McAllister C .75 2.00
6 Jerome Bettis C 1.00 2.50
7 Javon Walker C .60 1.50
8 Marshall Faulk C 1.00 2.50
9 Trent Green C .75 2.00
10 Travis Henry C .60 1.50
11 Eli Manning C 1.50 4.00
12 Donovan McNabb C 1.00 2.50
13 Priest Holmes C .75 2.00
14 Brandon Stokley C .60 1.50
15 Curtis Martin C 1.00 2.50
16 Muhsin Muhammad C .75 2.00
17 Corey Dillon C .75 2.00
18 Fred Taylor C .75 2.00
19 Michael Vick C 1.00 2.50
20 Michael Jenkins C .75 2.00
21 Chris Brown C .60 1.50
22 Willis McGahee C 1.00 2.50
23 Drew Bledsoe C 1.00 2.50
24 Michael Clayton C .60 1.50
25 Kerry Collins C .75 2.00
26 Jason Witten C 1.00 2.50
27 Clinton Portis C .75 2.00
28 Marc Bulger C .75 2.00
29 Julius Jones C .60 1.50
30 Chad Pennington C 1.00 2.50
31 Kevin Jones C .60 1.50
32 Domanick Davis C .60 1.50
33 Reggie Wayne C 1.00 2.50
34 Jimmy Smith C .75 2.00
35 Byron Leftwich C .75 2.00
36 Randy Moss C 1.00 2.50
37 Isaac Bruce C .75 2.00
38 LaMont Jordan C .75 2.00
39 Edgerrin James C .75 2.00
40 Aaron Brooks C .60 1.50
41 Steven Jackson C 1.00 2.50
42 Cedric Benson C RC 1.50 4.00
43 Brian Westbrook C .75 2.00
44 Andrew Walter C RC 1.25 3.00
45 Andre Johnson C 1.00 2.50
46 David Greene C RC 1.00 2.50
47 David Carr C .60 1.50
48 Marion Barber C RC 1.50 4.00
49 Warrick Dunn C .75 2.00
50 Terrence Murphy C RC 1.00 2.50
51 Dante Hall C .60 1.50
52 Willie Parker C .75 2.00
53 Laveranues Coles C .60 1.50
54 DeMarcus Ware C RC 3.00 8.00
55 Santana Moss C .75 2.00
56 Alvin Pearman C RC 1.00 2.50
57 Keary Colbert C .60 1.50
58 Carlos Rogers C RC 1.50 4.00
59 Jeremy Shockey C 1.00 2.50
60 Craig Bragg C RC 1.00 2.50
61 Daunte Culpepper C .75 2.00
62 Charlie Frye C RC 1.50 4.00
63 DeShaun Foster C .75 2.00
64 Chad Owens C RC 1.25 3.00
65 Dunta Robinson C .60 1.50
66 Mike Nugent C RC 1.25 3.00
67 Jonathan Vilma C .75 2.00
68 Erasmus James C RC 1.25 3.00
69 Randy McMichael C .60 1.50
70 Stefan LeFors C RC 1.00 2.50
71 Ben Roethlisberger C 1.50 4.00
72 Tab Perry C RC 1.00 2.50
73 Joey Harrington C .75 2.00
74 Adrian McPherson C RC 1.00 2.50
75 Roy Williams WR C .75 2.00
76 Vincent Jackson C RC 2.00 5.00
77 Lee Suggs C .60 1.50
78 Ryan Moats C RC 1.00 2.50
79 Plaxico Burress C .75 2.00
80 Chris Henry C RC 1.50 4.00
81 Larry Fitzgerald C 1.00 2.50
82 Travis Johnson C RC 1.00 2.50
83 Terrell Owens C 1.00 2.50
84 Fabian Washington C RC 1.25 3.00
85 Stephen Davis C .75 2.00
86 Odell Thurman C RC 1.50 4.00
87 Tatum Bell C .60 1.50
88 Roddy White C RC 2.00 5.00
89 J.P. Losman C .60 1.50
90 J.J. Arrington C RC 1.25 3.00
91 Thomas Jones C 1.00 2.50
92 Eric Shelton C RC 1.00 2.50
93 Charles Rogers C .60 1.50
94 Matt Jones C RC 1.25 3.00
95 Chris Chambers C .75 2.00
96 Jerome Mathis C RC 1.50 4.00
97 Darrell Jackson C .60 1.50
98 Justin Miller C RC 1.25 3.00
99 Donte Stallworth C .60 1.50
100 Brandon Jacobs C RC 2.00 5.00
101 Alex Smith QB JSY U RC 5.00 12.00
102 Mark Clayton JSY U RC 2.50 6.00
103 Antrel Rolle JSY U RC 3.00 8.00
104 Kyle Orton JSY/500 U RC 3.00 8.00
105 Roscoe Parrish JSY U RC 2.00 5.00
106 Vernand Morency JSY U RC 2.00 5.00
107 Maurice Clarett JSY U 2.00 5.00
108 Mark Bradley JSY U RC 2.00 5.00
109 Reg.Brown JSY/500 U RC 2.00 5.00
110 Ronnie Brown JSY U RC 4.00 10.00
111 B.Edwards JSY/500 U RC 4.00 10.00
112 T.Williamson JSY/500 U RC 2.50 6.00
113 Cadillac Williams JSY U RC 3.00 8.00
114 Ricky Williams JSY/500 U 3.00 8.00
115 Jake Plummer JSY/500 U 3.00 8.00
116 Brian Urlacher JSY U 4.00 10.00
117 Joe Horn JSY/500 U 3.00 8.00
118 Anquan Boldin JSY/500 U 3.00 8.00
119 Carson Palmer JSY U 4.00 10.00
120 Rudi Johnson JSY/500 U 3.00 8.00
121 Matt Hasselbeck JSY/500 U 3.00 8.00
123 Steve McNair JSY/500 U 4.00 10.00
124 Shaun Alexander JSY U 3.00 8.00
125 Julius Peppers JSY/500 U 3.00 8.00
126 Dwight Freeney JSY/500 U 3.00 8.00
127 Patrick Kerney JSY U 3.00 8.00
128 Drew Brees JSY U 4.00 10.00
129 Tony Gonzalez JSY/500 U 3.00 8.00
130 Alge Crumpler JSY/500 U 3.00 8.00
131 Chad Johnson JSY/500 U 3.00 8.00
132 M.Muhammad JSY/500 U 3.00 8.00
133 Zach Thomas JSY/500 U 4.00 10.00
134 Marvin Harrison JSY U 4.00 10.00
135 LaVar Arrington JSY U 3.00 8.00
136 Eric Moulds JSY U 2.50 6.00
137 Michael Strahan JSY U 4.00 10.00
138 Jamal Lewis JSY/500 U 3.00 8.00
139 Ray Lewis JSY U 4.00 10.00
140 Hines Ward JSY/500 U 4.00 10.00
141 Peyton Manning JSY/500 U 8.00 20.00
142 Tom Brady JSY/500 U 8.00 20.00
143 Ahman Green JSY/500 U 3.00 8.00
144 Trent Green JSY/500 U 3.00 8.00
145 Brett Favre JSY/500 U 10.00 25.00
146 Aaron Rodgers AU R RC 250.00 400.00
147 Adam Jones AU R RC 5.00 12.00
148 Alex Smith QB AU R 30.00 60.00
149 Antrel Rolle AU R 8.00 20.00
150 Braylon Edwards AU R 10.00 25.00
151 Ciatrick Fason AU R RC 5.00 12.00
152 Courtney Roby AU R RC 6.00 15.00
153 Craphonso Thorpe AU R RC 5.00 12.00
154 Dan Cody AU R RC 6.00 15.00
155 Dan Orlovsky AU R RC 8.00 20.00
156 Darren Sproles AU R RC 20.00 40.00
157 David Pollack AU R RC 6.00 15.00
158 Derrick Johnson AU R RC 6.00 15.00
159 Frank Gore AU R RC 12.00 30.00
160 Heath Miller AU R RC 10.00 25.00
161 Jason Campbell AU R RC 10.00 25.00
162 Kyle Orton AU R 20.00 40.00
163 Mike Williams AU R 10.00 25.00
164 Ronnie Brown AU R 10.00 25.00
165 Troy Williamson AU R 6.00 15.00
166 Vernand Morency AU R 5.00 12.00
167 Deion Branch AU R 5.00 12.00
168 Brett Favre JSY AU S 175.00 300.00
169 Joe Montana JSY AU S 175.00 300.00
170 Barry Sanders JSY AU S 125.00 250.00
171 Tom Brady JSY AU S 175.00 300.00
172 Dan Marino JSY AU S 175.00 300.00

2005 Topps Pristine Die Cuts

*VETERANS 1-100: 1.2X TO 3X BASIC CARDS
*ROOKIES 1-100: .8X TO 2X BASIC CARDS
1-100 C/115 STATED ODDS 1:2
*VET.JSYs 114-145: .6X TO 1.5X BASIC CARDS
*ROOKIE JSY 101-113: .6X TO 1.5X
101-145 U JSY/45 STATED ODDS 1:18
*ROOKIE AUs 146-167: .6X TO 1.5X
146-167 R AU/20 STATED ODDS 1:193
UNPRICED S JSY AU/5 ODDS 1:3837
146 Aaron Rodgers AU R 400.00 600.00

2005 Topps Pristine In The Name Letter Patches

STATED ODDS 1:1145
UNPRICED PER LETTER PRINT RUN 1

2005 Topps Pristine Personal Endorsements Autographs

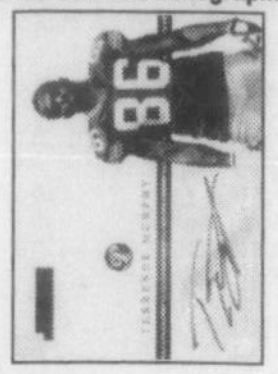

C/1500 STATED ODDS 1:3
U/250 STATED ODDS 1:36
R/50 STATED ODDS 1:276
S/25 STATED ODDS 1:1705
UNPRICED UNCIRC.PRINT RUN 3 SETS
UNPRICED DUAL/5 STATED ODDS 1:1023
AJ Adam Jones/250 U 6.00 15.00
AR Antrel Rolle/250 U 6.00 15.00
AW Andrew Walter/250 U 6.00 15.00
CB Craig Bragg/1500 C 4.00 10.00
CC Channing Crowder/1500 C 5.00 12.00
CH Chris Henry/250 U 6.00 15.00
CL Chase Lyman/1500 C 4.00 10.00
CW Cadillac Williams/250 U 30.00 80.00
DA Derek Anderson/1500 C 5.00 12.00
DB Deion Branch/50 R 20.00 40.00
DC Deandra Cobb/1500 C 4.00 10.00
DJ Derrick Johnson/1500 C 5.00 12.00
DN Damien Nash/1500 C 5.00 12.00
DR Dante Ridgeway/1500 C 4.00 10.00
EC Earl Campbell/50 R 25.00 50.00
HM Heath Miller/250 U 10.00 25.00
JC Jason Campbell/250 U 15.00 30.00
JM Joe Montana/25 S 125.00 250.00
JN Joe Namath/25 S 125.00 200.00
JR J.R. Russell/1500 C 4.00 10.00
KH Kay-Jay Harris/1500 C 4.00 10.00
LT Lawrence Taylor/50 R 40.00 80.00
MB Marion Barber/1500 C 6.00 15.00
MC Matt Cassel/1500 C 12.00 30.00
MC Mark Clayton/250 U 8.00 20.00
MH Marvin Harrison/50 R 30.00 60.00
MW Mike Williams/50 R 10.00 25.00
NB Nate Burleson/250 U 6.00 15.00
NH Noah Herron/1500 C 4.00 10.00
RF Ryan Fitzpatrick/1500 C 15.00 30.00
RM Rasheed Marshall/1500 C 5.00 12.00
RP Roscoe Parrish/1500 C 4.00 10.00
RW Roydell Williams/1500 C 5.00 12.00
SL Stefan LeFors/1500 C 4.00 10.00
TM Terrence Murphy/1500 C 4.00 10.00
DJO Deacon Jones/50 R 15.00 40.00

2005 Topps Pristine Personal Pieces Common

GROUP A ODDS 1:14
GROUP B ODDS 1:16
GROUP C/750 ODDS 1:3
UNPRICED UNCIRC/3 ODDS 1:533
AC Alge Crumpler/750 4.00 10.00
AG Antonio Gates/500 4.00 10.00
AR Antrel Rolle/1000 4.00 10.00
AS Alex Smith QB/1000 8.00 20.00
BE Braylon Edwards/500 5.00 12.00
BL Byron Leftwich/1000 4.00 10.00
BU Brian Urlacher/1000 4.00 10.00
CJ Chad Johnson/500 5.00 12.00
CP Carson Palmer/1000 5.00 12.00
CW Cadillac Williams/1000 4.00 10.00
DB Drew Brees/750 4.00 10.00
DF Dwight Freeney/1000 4.00 10.00
DM Deuce McAllister/500 4.00 10.00
EM Eric Moulds/1000 3.00 8.00
FT Fred Taylor/1000 3.00 8.00
JH Joe Horn/750 4.00 10.00
JL J.P. Losman/1000 4.00 10.00
JP Jake Plummer/750 4.00 10.00
JT Jason Taylor/1000 3.00 8.00
JV Jonathan Vilma/1000 4.00 10.00
KO Kyle Orton/1000 4.00 10.00
LA LaVar Arrington/1000 4.00 10.00
LE Lee Evans/1000 3.00 8.00
LT LaDainian Tomlinson/500 5.00 12.00
MB Mark Bradley/1000 3.00 8.00
MC Mark Clayton/1000 3.00 8.00
MH Matt Hasselbeck/500 5.00 12.00
MM Muhsin Muhammad/750 3.00 8.00
MS Michael Strahan/1000 3.00 8.00
PK Patrick Kerney/1000 3.00 8.00
RB Ronnie Brown/1000 6.00 15.00
RJ Rudi Johnson/500 4.00 10.00
RP Roscoe Parrish/1000 4.00 10.00
RW Ricky Williams/500 4.00 10.00
SA Shaun Alexander/1000 5.00 12.00
SM Steve McNair/500 4.00 10.00
TG Tony Gonzalez/750 4.00 10.00
TS Takeo Spikes/1000 3.00 8.00
TW Troy Williamson/1000 3.00 8.00
VM Vernand Morency/1000 3.00 8.00
WM Willis McGahee/1000 3.00 8.00
ZT Zach Thomas/500 5.00 12.00
DMA Derrick Mason/1000 3.00 8.00
JPE Julius Peppers/1000 4.00 10.00
MBU Marc Bulger/1000 3.00 8.00
MCL Maurice Clarett/750 3.00 8.00
MHA Marvin Harrison/1000 4.00 10.00
RBR Reggie Brown/1000 3.00 8.00
TGR Trent Green/500 4.00 10.00

2005 Topps Pristine Personal Pieces Rare

RARE/75 STATED ODDS 1:120
UNPRICED UNCIRC/3 ODDS 1:1163
PPRAS Alex Smith QB 15.00 40.00
PPRBE Braylon Edwards 10.00 25.00
PPRCW Cadillac Williams 10.00 25.00
PPRLT LaDainian Tomlinson 10.00 25.00
PPRMHA Marvin Harrison 8.00 20.00
PPRPM Peyton Manning 10.00 25.00
PPRRB Ronnie Brown 12.50 30.00
PPRSA Shaun Alexander 10.00 25.00
PPRTW Troy Williamson 6.00 15.00

2005 Topps Pristine Personal Pieces Scarce

UNPRICED SCARCE/10 ODDS 1:2257
UNPRICED UNCIRC/3 ODDS 1:6396

2005 Topps Pristine Personal Pieces Uncommon

UNCOMMON/200 STATED ODDS 1:18
UNPRICED UNCIRC/3 ODDS 1:1163
PPUAG Antonio Gates 5.00 12.00
PPUAR Antrel Rolle 5.00 12.00
PPUAS Alex Smith QB 10.00 25.00
PPUCJ Chad Johnson 6.00 15.00
PPUCP Carson Palmer 8.00 20.00
PPUCW Cadillac Williams 6.00 15.00
PPUDB Drew Brees 5.00 12.00
PPUDM Deuce McAllister 5.00 12.00
PPULT LaDainian Tomlinson 6.00 15.00
PPUMC Mark Clayton 4.00 10.00
PPUMCL Maurice Clarett 4.00 10.00
PPUMHA Marvin Harrison 5.00 12.00
PPUPM Peyton Manning 7.50 20.00
PPURB Ronnie Brown 8.00 20.00
PPURJ Rudi Johnson 5.00 12.00
PPURW Ricky Williams 5.00 12.00
PPURBR Reggie Brown 4.00 10.00
PPUSA Shaun Alexander 8.00 20.00
PPUSM Steve McNair 5.00 12.00
PPUTG Tony Gonzalez 5.00 12.00
PPUTW Troy Williamson 4.00 10.00
PPUTGR Trent Green 5.00 12.00
PPUZT Zach Thomas 6.00 15.00

2005 Topps Pristine Pro Bowl Leather

PRO BOWL LEATHER/50 ODDS 1:164
PBLDC Daunte Culpepper 7.50 20.00
PBLDM Donovan McNabb 10.00 25.00
PBLJB Jerome Bettis 10.00 25.00
PBLLT LaDainian Tomlinson 8.00 20.00
PBLMH Marvin Harrison 7.50 20.00
PBLMV Michael Vick
PBLPM Peyton Manning 12.50 30.00
PBLTB Tom Brady 15.00 40.00
PBLTG Tony Gonzalez
PBLTBA Tiki Barber 7.50 20.00

2005 Topps Pristine Pro Bowl Paydirt

PRO BOWL PAYDIRT/25 ODDS 1:419
PBPAG Antonio Gates 10.00 25.00
PBPBW Brian Westbrook 10.00 25.00
PBPHW Hines Ward 10.00 25.00
PBPLT LaDainian Tomlinson
PBPMH Marvin Harrison 10.00 25.00
PBPMV Michael Vick 12.50 30.00
PBPPM Peyton Manning 15.00 40.00
PBPTH Torry Holt 10.00 25.00

2005 Topps Pristine Selective Swatch

UNPRICED SELECT.SWATCH/1 ODDS 1:4263

2005 Topps Pristine Uncirculated

*VETERANS 1-100: 1.2X TO 3X BASIC CARDS
*ROOKIES 1-100: .8X TO 2X BASIC CARDS
1-100 C PRINT RUN 750 SER.#'d SETS
*VET.JSYs 114-145: .6X TO 1.5X BASIC CARDS
*ROOKIE JSY 101-113: .6X TO 1.5X
101-145 U JSY PRINT RUN 100 SER.#'d SETS
*ROOKIE AU 146-167: .6X TO 1.5X BASIC AUTO
146-167 R AU PRINT RUN 20 SER.#'d SETS
UNPRICED S JSY AU PRINT RUN 5 SETS
ONE UNCIRCULATED CARD PER BOX
146 Aaron Rodgers AU R 500.00 800.00

2005 Topps Pristine 50th Anniversary Patches

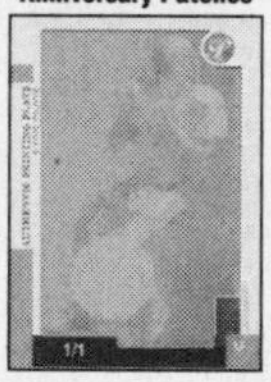

50TH ANNIV.PATCH/150 ODDS 1:27
PRAJ Adam Jones 3.00 8.00
PRARO Antrel Rolle 3.00 8.00
PRAS Alex Smith QB 10.00 25.00
PRAW Andrew Walter 3.00 8.00
PRBE Braylon Edwards 6.00 15.00
PRCF Charlie Frye 3.00 8.00
PRCR Carlos Rogers 3.00 8.00
PRCW Cadillac Williams 6.00 15.00
PRJC Jason Campbell 5.00 12.00
PRJJA J.J. Arrington 3.00 8.00
PRKO Kyle Orton 4.00 10.00
PRMB Mark Bradley 3.00 8.00
PRMC Maurice Clarett 3.00 8.00
PRMCL Mark Clayton 3.00 8.00
PRMJ Matt Jones 4.00 10.00
PRRB Ronnie Brown 10.00 25.00
PRRBR Reggie Brown 3.00 8.00
PRRW Roddy White 4.00 10.00
PRTM Terrence Murphy 3.00 8.00
PRTW Troy Williamson 3.00 8.00

2001 Topps Reserve

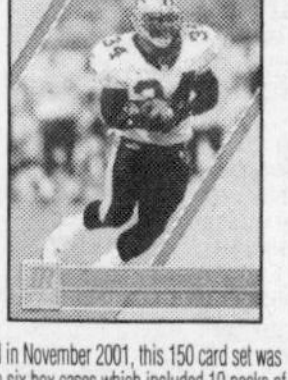

Realesed in November 2001, this 150 card set was issued in six box cases which included 10 packs of cards per box. A dealer ordering this product also received one autographed mini-helmet on top of each box as a premium for ordering the product. The base cards 1-100 feature veterans, while the rookie cards were short printed (serial numbered of 999) and inserted at a 1:5 ratio for hobby packs and 1:9 for retail.

COMP.SET w/o SP's (100) 30.00 60.00
ROOKIE/999 ODDS 1:5 HOB, 1:9 RET
1 Jeff Garcia .40 1.00
2 Joe Horn .40 1.00
3 Jeff George .40 1.00
4 Ed McCaffrey .40 1.00
5 Keenan McCardell .40 1.00
6 Jerome Bettis .50 1.25
7 Jake Plummer .40 1.00
8 Doug Flutie .50 1.25
9 Wayne Chrebet .40 1.00
10 Brett Favre 1.50 4.00
11 Emmitt Smith 1.25 3.00
12 Derrick Mason .40 1.00
13 Lamar Smith .40 1.00
14 Brian Urlacher .60 1.50
15 Kurt Warner .75 2.00
16 Jerry Rice 1.00 2.50
17 Tony Gonzalez .50 1.25
18 Jeff Blake .40 1.00
19 Warrick Dunn .50 1.25
20 Vinny Testaverde .40 1.00
21 Peyton Manning 1.25 3.00
22 Drew Bledsoe .50 1.25
23 Tim Dwight .40 1.00
24 Brad Johnson .40 1.00
25 Peter Warrick .40 1.00
26 Steve McNair .50 1.25
27 James Thrash .40 1.00
28 Kordell Stewart .40 1.00
29 Randy Moss .50 1.25
30 Brian Griese .40 1.00
31 Curtis Martin .50 1.25
32 Ike Hilliard .40 1.00
33 Torry Holt .40 1.00
34 James Allen .30 .75
35 Jay Fiedler .40 1.00
36 Junior Seau .50 1.25
37 Troy Brown .40 1.00
38 Ricky Williams .50 1.25
39 Charlie Garner .40 1.00
40 Eddie George .50 1.25
41 Stephen Davis .40 1.00
42 Tim Couch .30 .75
43 Jimmy Smith .40 1.00
44 Trent Green .50 1.25
45 Rod Smith .40 1.00
46 Isaac Bruce .50 1.25
47 Oronde Gadsden .30 .75
48 Keyshawn Johnson .40 1.00
49 Jeff Graham .30 .75
50 Mark Brunell .40 1.00
51 Cade McNown .40 1.00
52 Terry Glenn .40 1.00
53 Derrick Alexander .30 .75
54 Ron Dayne .40 1.00
55 Shaun Alexander .50 1.25
56 Chris Chandler .40 1.00
57 Rob Johnson .40 1.00
58 Germane Crowell .30 .75
59 Cris Carter .50 1.25
60 Ahman Green .50 1.25
61 Marshall Faulk .50 1.25
62 Darrell Jackson .40 1.00
63 Duce Staley .40 1.00
64 Kevin Johnson .30 .75
65 Muhsin Muhammad .40 1.00
66 Elvis Grbac .40 1.00
67 Fred Taylor .50 1.25
68 Marcus Robinson .40 1.00
69 Edgerrin James .50 1.25
70 Kerry Collins .40 1.00
71 Daunte Culpepper .40 1.00
72 Matt Hasselbeck .50 1.25
73 Akili Smith .30 .75
74 Aaron Brooks .40 1.00
75 Tim Biakabutuka .30 .75
76 Ray Lewis .50 1.25
77 David Boston .30 .75
78 Donovan Mcnabb .50 1.25
79 Marvin Harrison .50 1.25
80 Rich Gannon .40 1.00
81 Tony Richardson .30 .75
82 Peerless Price .30 .75
83 Jamal Anderson .40 1.00
84 Mike Anderson .40 1.00
85 Terrell Owens .50 1.25
86 Antonio Freeman .50 1.25
87 Charlie Batch .40 1.00
88 Jamal Lewis .50 1.25
89 Jon Kitna .40 1.00
90 Joey Galloway .40 1.00
91 Tyrone Wheatley .40 1.00
92 Jeff Lewis .30 .75
93 Eric Moulds .40 1.00
94 Shawn Jefferson .30 .75
95 Tiki Barber .50 1.25
96 Tim Brown .50 1.25
97 Corey Dillon .40 1.00
98 Tony Banks .30 .75
99 James Stewart .30 .75
100 Amani Toomer .40 1.00
101 Freddie Mitchell RC 1.25 3.00
102 James Jackson RC 1.25 3.00
103 Michael Bennett RC 1.50 4.00
104 LaDainian Tomlinson RC 6.00 15.00
105 Gerard Warren RC 1.50 4.00
106 Dan Morgan RC 1.50 4.00
107 Alge Crumpler RC 2.00 5.00
108 Mike McMahon RC 1.50 4.00
109 Justin Smith RC 2.00 5.00
110 Chris Weinke RC 1.50 4.00
111 Rudi Johnson RC 2.00 5.00
112 Rod Gardner RC 1.50 4.00
113 Koren Robinson RC 1.50 4.00
114 Andre Carter RC 1.50 4.00
115 Kevan Barlow RC 1.50 4.00
116 Jesse Palmer RC 1.50 4.00
117 Anthony Thomas RC 2.00 5.00
118 Michael Vick RC 8.00 20.00
119 Sage Rosenfels RC 2.00 5.00
120 Chad Johnson RC 3.00 8.00
121 Robert Ferguson RC 2.00 5.00
122 Quincy Carter RC 1.50 4.00
123 Travis Minor RC 1.50 4.00
124 Travis Henry RC 1.50 4.00
125 Reggie Wayne RC 4.00 10.00
126 David Terrell RC 1.50 4.00
127 Josh Heupel RC 2.00 5.00
128 Deuce McAllister RC 2.00 5.00
129 Todd Heap RC 2.00 5.00
130 Drew Brees RC 12.00 30.00
131 Snoop Minnis RC 1.25 3.00
132 Marques Tuiasosopo RC 1.50 4.00
133 Santana Moss RC 2.50 6.00
134 Quincy Morgan RC 1.50 4.00
135 Chris Chambers RC 2.00 5.00
136 Richard Seymour RC 2.00 5.00
137 LaMont Jordan RC 2.00 5.00
138 Eddie Berlin RC 1.25 3.00
139 Correll Buckhalter RC 2.00 5.00
140 Justin McCareins RC 1.50 4.00
141 Vinny Sutherland RC 1.25 3.00
142 Chris Taylor RC 1.25 3.00
143 Scotty Anderson RC 1.25 3.00
144 Nate Clements RC 1.50 4.00
145 Darnerien McCants RC 1.50 4.00
146 Dan Alexander RC 1.50 4.00
147 A.J. Feeley RC 1.50 4.00
148 Chris Barnes RC 1.25 3.00
149 Dee Brown RC 1.25 3.00
150 Milton Wynn RC 1.25 3.00
NNO Checklist Card .02 .10

2001 Topps Reserve Autographs

OVERALL STATED ODDS 1:9 HOB, 1:37 RET
TRAB Aaron Brooks 5.00 12.00
TRCC Chris Chambers 12.50 25.00
TRCJ Chad Johnson 15.00 40.00
TRCW Chris Weinke 5.00 12.00
TRDB Drew Brees 90.00 150.00
TRDC Daunte Culpepper 5.00 12.00
TRDM Derrick Mason 5.00 12.00
TRDMO Dan Morgan 5.00 12.00
TRDT David Terrell 5.00 12.00
TREM Eric Moulds 5.00 12.00
TRJB Josh Booty 5.00 12.00
TRJH Joe Horn 5.00 12.00
TRJJ James Jackson 4.00 10.00
TRJL Jamal Lewis 6.00 15.00
TRJP Jesse Palmer 5.00 12.00
TRJS Jimmy Smith 5.00 12.00
TRJT James Thrash 5.00 12.00
TRKB Kevan Barlow 5.00 12.00
TRKR Koren Robinson 5.00 12.00
TRLS Lamar Smith 5.00 12.00
TRLT LaDainian Tomlinson 60.00 120.00
TRMA Mike Anderson 5.00 12.00
TRMB Michael Bennett 5.00 12.00
TRMV Michael Vick 75.00 150.00
TRQM Quincy Morgan 5.00 12.00
TRRG Rod Gardner 5.00 12.00
TRRWA Reggie Wayne 25.00 50.00
TRSM Santana Moss 10.00 25.00
TRSMO Sammy Morris 5.00 12.00
TRTH Travis Henry 5.00 12.00
TRWJ Willie Jackson 4.00 10.00

2001 Topps Reserve Jerseys

REGULAR JERSEY ODDS 1:39H, 1:107R
PRO BOWL JERSEY ODDS 1:33H, 1:97R
TRRBB Blaine Bishop PB 4.00 10.00
TRRDB Derrick Brooks PB 6.00 15.00
TRRFW Frank Wycheck PB 4.00 10.00
TRRMA Mike Alstott 5.00 12.00
TRRMB Mark Brunell 5.00 12.00
TRRML Mo Lewis PB 4.00 10.00
TRRSM Sam Madison PB 4.00 10.00
TRRSR Samari Rolle PB 4.00 10.00
TRRSS Shannon Sharpe 6.00 15.00
TRRTH Torry Holt 5.00 12.00

2001 Topps Reserve Mini Helmet Autographs

ONE PER HOBBY BOX
RETAIL REDEMPTION CARD ODDS 1:108
1 Dan Alexander 10.00 25.00
2 Kevan Barlow 10.00 25.00
4 Drew Brees 40.00 80.00
5 Rod Gardner 10.00 25.00
6 Travis Henry 10.00 25.00
7 Josh Heupel 12.00 30.00
8 James Jackson 8.00 20.00
9 Peyton Manning 40.00 80.00
10 Justin McCareins 10.00 25.00
11 Travis Minor 10.00 25.00
12 Dan Morgan 10.00 25.00
13 Santana Moss 20.00 50.00
14 Bobby Newcombe 10.00 25.00
15 Jesse Palmer 10.00 25.00
16 Ken-Yon Rambo 8.00 20.00
17 Koren Robinson 10.00 25.00
18 Vinny Sutherland 8.00 20.00
19 Michael Vick 50.00 125.00
20 Chris Weinke 10.00 25.00

2001 Topps Reserve Rookie Premier Jerseys

COMPLETE SET (8) 30.00 60.00
STATED ODDS 1:23 HOB, 1:66 RET
TRRDM Dan Morgan 4.00 10.00
TRRJJ James Jackson 3.00 8.00
TRRMM Snoop Minnis 3.00 8.00
TRRMT Marques Tuiasosopo 4.00 10.00
TRRQM Quincy Morgan 4.00 10.00
TRRRJ Rudi Johnson 5.00 12.00
TRRTM Travis Minor 4.00 10.00

2002 Topps Reserve

This 150 card set consists of 100 veterans and 50 rookies. The rookies were randomly inserted packs, and were serial #'d to 999. Boxes contained 10 packs of 5 cards and one mini-helmet. The box SRP was $75.

COMP.SET w/o SP's (100) 15.00 40.00
ROOKIE PRINT RUN 999 SER.#'d SETS
1 Michael Vick .75 2.00
2 Chris Chambers .40 1.00
3 Laveranues Coles .40 1.00
4 Koren Robinson .30 .75
5 Rod Gardner .30 .75
6 James Thrash .40 1.00
7 Michael Bennett .40 1.00
8 Rocket Ismail .40 1.00
9 Peter Warrick .40 1.00
10 Drew Bledsoe .50 1.25
11 Marcus Robinson .40 1.00
12 Tiki Barber .50 1.25
13 LaDainian Tomlinson .60 1.50
14 Eddie George .40 1.00
15 Mike McMahon .30 .75
16 Joe Horn .40 1.00
17 Tom Brady 1.25 3.00
18 Edgerrin James .40 1.00
19 Mike Anderson .40 1.00
20 Lamar Smith .40 1.00
21 Chris Redman .30 .75
22 David Boston .30 .75

23 Ike Hilliard .40 1.00
24 Jeff Garcia .40 1.00
25 Michael Pittman .40 1.00
26 Torry Holt .50 1.25
27 Priest Holmes .50 1.25
28 Germane Crowell .30 .75
29 David Terrell .30 .75
30 Tim Couch .30 .75
31 Terry Glenn .40 1.00
32 Qadry Ismail .40 1.00
33 Aaron Brooks .40 1.00
34 Donovan McNabb .50 1.25
35 Jerome Bettis .50 1.25
36 Stephen Davis .40 1.00
37 Trent Green .40 1.00
38 Chris Weinke .30 .75
39 Derrick Alexander .30 .75
40 Ahman Green .40 1.00
41 Antowain Smith .40 1.00
42 Garrison Hearst .40 1.00
43 Keyshawn Johnson .40 1.00
44 Plaxico Burress .40 1.00
45 Marvin Harrison .50 1.25
46 Ray Lewis .50 1.25
47 Jake Plummer .40 1.00
48 Daunte Culpepper .40 1.00
49 Troy Brown .40 1.00
50 Emmitt Smith 1.25 3.00
51 Jerry Rice 1.00 2.50
52 Duce Staley .40 1.00
53 Kurt Warner .50 1.25
54 Derrick Mason .40 1.00
55 Brad Johnson .40 1.00
56 Fred Taylor .40 1.00
57 Jimmy Smith .40 1.00
58 Sylvester Morris .30 .75
59 Quincy Morgan .30 .75
60 Jamal Lewis .40 1.00
61 Warrick Dunn .40 1.00
62 Rod Smith .40 1.00
63 Deuce McAllister .40 1.00
64 Hines Ward .50 1.25
65 Steve McNair .50 1.25
66 Ricky Williams .40 1.00
67 Anthony Thomas .40 1.00
68 Eric Moulds .40 1.00
69 Travis Taylor .30 .75
70 Tim Brown .50 1.25
71 Kordell Stewart .40 1.00
72 Shaun Alexander .40 1.00
73 Peyton Manning 1.00 2.50
74 Marty Booker .40 1.00
75 Brett Favre 1.25 3.00
76 Santana Moss .40 1.00
77 James Allen .30 .75
78 Tony Gonzalez .50 1.25
79 Mark Brunell .40 1.00
80 Randy Moss .50 1.25
81 Jay Fiedler .40 1.00
82 Muhsin Muhammad .40 1.00
83 Travis Henry .30 .75
84 Amani Toomer .40 1.00
85 Freddie Mitchell .30 .75
86 Terrell Owens .50 1.25
87 Drew Brees .75 2.00
88 Darrell Jackson .40 1.00
89 Curtis Martin .50 1.25
90 Snoop Minnis .30 .75
91 Quincy Carter .30 .75
92 Corey Dillon .40 1.00
93 Rich Gannon .40 1.00
94 Vinny Testaverde .40 1.00
95 Jim Miller .30 .75
96 Kevin Johnson .30 .75
97 Brian Griese .40 1.00
98 Kerry Collins .40 1.00
99 Brian Urlacher .50 1.25
100 Marshall Faulk .50 1.25
101 David Carr RC 2.00 5.00
102 Donte Stallworth RC 2.00 5.00
103 Marquise Walker RC 1.25 3.00
104 Eric Crouch RC 2.00 5.00
105 Jake Schifino RC 1.25 3.00
106 Rohan Davey RC 2.00 5.00
107 David Garrard RC 2.50 6.00
108 Julius Peppers RC 4.00 10.00
109 DeShaun Foster RC 2.00 5.00
110 Roy Williams RC 2.00 5.00
111 Javon Walker RC 2.00 5.00
112 Matt Schobel RC 2.00 5.00
113 Clinton Portis RC 2.50 6.00
114 Albert Haynesworth RC 2.00 5.00
115 Jeremy Shockey RC 3.00 8.00
116 Antwaan Randle El RC 2.00 5.00
117 Maurice Morris RC 1.50 4.00
118 Andre Davis RC 1.50 4.00
119 Chad Hutchinson RC 1.25 3.00
120 Lito Sheppard RC 2.00 5.00
121 Daniel Graham RC 1.50 4.00
122 Jabar Gaffney RC 2.00 5.00
123 Josh McCown RC 2.00 5.00
124 Randy Fasani RC 1.50 4.00
125 Patrick Ramsey RC 2.00 5.00
126 Tim Carter RC 1.50 4.00
127 Ladell Betts RC 2.00 5.00
128 Jonathan Wells RC 2.00 5.00
129 Jason McAddley RC 1.50 4.00
130 Kurt Kittner RC 1.25 3.00
131 Josh Reed RC 1.50 4.00
132 T.J. Duckett RC 2.00 5.00
133 John Henderson RC 1.50 4.00
134 Travis Stephens RC 1.25 3.00
135 William Green RC 1.50 4.00
136 Freddie Milons RC 1.25 3.00
137 Ashley Lelie RC 1.50 4.00
138 Brian Westbrook RC 3.00 8.00
139 Antonio Bryant RC 2.00 5.00
140 Cliff Russell RC 1.25 3.00
141 Reche Caldwell RC 2.00 5.00
142 Aaron Lockett RC 1.25 3.00
143 Mike Williams RC 1.25 3.00
144 Ron Johnson RC 1.50 4.00
145 Herb Haygood RC 1.25 3.00
146 Dwight Freeney RC 2.50 6.00
147 Josh Scobey RC 1.50 4.00
148 Luke Staley RC 1.25 3.00
149 Jerramy Stevens RC 2.00 5.00
150 Joey Harrington RC 2.00 5.00
NNO Joe Namath AUTO

2002 Topps Reserve Autographs

GROUP A STATED ODDS 1:134
GROUP B STATED ODDS 1:67
GROUP C STATED ODDS 1:14
GROUP D STATED ODDS 1:17
GROUP E STATED ODDS 1:13
GROUP F STATED ODDS 1:6
GROUP G STATED ODDS 1:17
GROUP H STATED ODDS 1:14
GROUP I STATED ODDS 1:12
GROUP J STATED ODDS 1:8
RAAT Anthony Thomas F 5.00 12.00
RABF Brett Favre B 125.00 200.00
RABS Bill Schroeder H 4.00 10.00
RABU Brian Urlacher C 20.00 40.00
RACC Chris Chambers G 5.00 12.00
RADM Derrick Mason J 5.00 12.00
RADT David Terrell C 4.00 10.00
RAJG Jeff Garcia C 6.00 12.00
RAJR Jerry Rice A 75.00 125.00
RALJ LaMont Jordan E 6.00 12.00
RALS Lamar Smith D 5.00 12.00
RALT LaDainian Tomlinson I 30.00 60.00
RAMR Marcus Robinson D
RARD Richard Dent E 10.00 25.00
RASM Sammy Morris F 5.00 12.00
RATS Tai Streets F 4.00 10.00
RAWJ Willie Jackson F 4.00 10.00

2002 Topps Reserve Jerseys

GROUP A STATED ODDS 1:64
GROUP B STATED ODDS 1:52
GROUP C STATED ODDS 1:16
GROUP D STATED ODDS 1:46
GROUP E STATED ODDS 1:35
GROUP F STATED ODDS 1:26
RRCD Corey Dillon C 3.00 8.00
RRCG Charlie Garner B 3.00 8.00
RRDB Drew Brees C 6.00 15.00
RRDC Daunte Culpepper D 3.00 8.00
RRDM Dan Marino F DP 12.00 30.00
RRDS Duce Staley E DP 3.00 8.00
RREG Eddie George A 3.00 8.00
RREJ Edgerrin James D 3.00 8.00
RREM Eric Moulds A 3.00 8.00
RRFT Fred Taylor C 3.00 8.00
RRJN Joe Namath C 15.00 40.00
RRJS Jimmy Smith C 3.00 8.00
RRKJ Keyshawn Johnson C 3.00 8.00
RRMA Mike Alstott F 3.00 8.00
RRMB Mark Brunell A 3.00 8.00
RRPM Peyton Manning C 8.00 20.00
RRRG Rich Gannon B 3.00 8.00
RRSC Sam Cowart B 2.50 6.00
RRSM Steve McNair C 4.00 10.00
RRTG Tony Gonzalez D 4.00 10.00
RRTM Travis Minor C 2.50 6.00
RRTO Terrell Owens C 4.00 10.00

2002 Topps Reserve Mini Helmet Autographs

STATED ODDS ONE PER BOX
SERIAL #'d/25 OR LESS NOT PRICED
3 Mike Anderson/250 20.00 40.00
5 Kevan Barlow/80 30.00 60.00
8 Deion Branch/500 20.00 40.00
9 Drew Brees/65 40.00 80.00
12 Antonio Bryant/800 20.00 40.00
13 Tim Carter/1000 12.50 25.00
14 Dave Casper/500 15.00 30.00
15 Mark Clayton/570 20.00 40.00
16 Laveranues Coles/229 15.00 30.00
18 Roger Craig/66 25.00 50.00
20 Andre Davis/900 15.00 30.00
21 Eric Dickerson/41 50.00 100.00
22 Rod Gardner/70 25.00 50.00
24 Roosevelt Grier/480 15.00 30.00
26 Rodney Hampton/480 15.00 30.00
27 Lester Hayes/35 20.00 50.00
29 Travis Henry/160 25.00 50.00
31 Darrell Jackson/214 15.00 30.00
36 Deacon Jones/551 20.00 40.00
42 Don Maynard/55 25.00 50.00
43 Justin McCareins/55 15.00 30.00
44 Tommy McDonald/543 12.50 25.00
47 Travis Minor/144 15.00 30.00
48 Joe Montana/30 150.00 260.00
49 Dan Morgan/55 20.00 40.00
50 Santana Moss/48 30.00 60.00
52 Christian Okoye/189 15.00 30.00
53 Jesse Palmer/154 12.50 25.00
54 Drew Pearson/451 15.00 30.00
59 Gale Sayers/260 35.00 60.00
63 Otis Sistrunk/500 12.50 25.00
64 Steve Smith/500 20.00 40.00
69 Chris Weinke/178 15.00 30.00

2011 Topps Rising Rookies

COMPLETE SET (200) 15.00 40.00
FIVE ROOKIES PER PACK ON AVERAGE
UNPRICED PRINT PLATE PRINT RUN 1
1 Aaron Rodgers .40 1.00
2 Calvin Johnson .25 .60
3 Philip Rivers .25 .60
4 Frank Gore .20 .50
5 Patrick Willis .20 .50
6 Colt McCoy .20 .50
7 Maurice Jones-Drew .20 .50
8 Miles Austin .20 .50
9 Andre Johnson .20 .50
10 Chris Johnson .20 .50
11 Jason Witten .25 .60
12 DeAngelo Williams .20 .50
13 Ray Rice .20 .50
14 Steven Jackson .20 .50
15 Jay Cutler .20 .50
16 Tony Romo .25 .60
17 Vernon Davis .20 .50
18 Anquan Boldin .20 .50
19 Brandon Lloyd .20 .50
20 Peyton Manning .40 1.00
21 LeGarrette Blount .20 .50
22 Steve Smith USC .20 .50
23 Brian Urlacher .25 .60
24 David Garrard .20 .50
25 Arian Foster .20 .50
26 Knowshon Moreno .20 .50
27 Mark Sanchez .25 .60
28 Tim Tebow .50 1.25
29 LaDainian Tomlinson .25 .60
30 Adrian Peterson .30 .75
31 Reggie Wayne .20 .50
32 Matt Cassel .20 .50
33 Percy Harvin .20 .50
34 DeMarcus Ware .20 .50
35 Jared Allen .20 .50
36 Brandon Marshall .20 .50
37 Darrelle Revis .20 .50
38 Joe Flacco .25 .60
39 Mike Williams .20 .50
40 Tom Brady .40 1.00
41 Dallas Clark .20 .50
42 Darren McFadden .20 .50
43 Jeremy Maclin .20 .50
44 Dez Bryant .25 .60
45 Hakeem Nicks .20 .50
46 Peyton Hillis .20 .50
47 Ray Lewis .25 .60
48 Justin Tuck .20 .50
49 Marques Colston .20 .50
50 Michael Vick .25 .60
51 Ben Roethlisberger .25 .60
52 Rob Gronkowski .25 .60
53 Matt Forte .20 .50
54 Braylon Edwards .20 .50
55 BenJarvus Green-Ellis .20 .50
56 Matt Schaub .20 .50
57 Wes Welker .25 .60
58 Charles Woodson .25 .60
59 Matthew Stafford .25 .60
60 Matt Ryan .25 .60
61 Austin Collie .20 .50
62 Danny Woodhead .25 .60
63 Eli Manning .25 .60
64 Greg Jennings .20 .50
65 Ed Reed .20 .50
66 Ryan Mathews .20 .50
67 Hines Ward .20 .50
68 Jonathan Stewart .20 .50
69 Jermichael Finley .20 .50
70 Roddy White .20 .50
71 Jerod Mayo .15 .40
72 Marshawn Lynch .20 .50
73 Santana Moss .20 .50
74 DeSean Jackson .20 .50
75 Kenny Britt .20 .50
76 Clay Matthews .25 .60
77 Sam Bradford .25 .60
78 Santonio Holmes .20 .50
79 Michael Turner .20 .50
80 Larry Fitzgerald .20 .50
81 Antonio Gates .20 .50
82 Jamaal Charles .20 .50
83 Ryan Torain .15 .40
84 Ndamukong Suh .25 .60
85 Ahmad Bradshaw .20 .50
86 Malcom Floyd .20 .50
87 Julius Peppers .20 .50
88 Rashard Mendenhall .20 .50
89 Marcedes Lewis .15 .40
90 Drew Brees .25 .60
91 LeSean McCoy .20 .50
92 Dwight Freeney .20 .50
93 Tony Gonzalez .20 .50
94 James Harrison .25 .60
95 Dwayne Bowe .20 .50
96 Mike Wallace .25 .60
97 Steve Johnson .20 .50
98 Josh Freeman .25 .60
99 Deion Branch .15 .40
100 Troy Polamalu .25 .60
101 Patrick Peterson RC .75 2.00
102 Aldon Smith RC .75 2.00
103 Daniel Thomas RC .50 1.25
104 Ryan Mallett RC 1.00 2.50
105 Greg Little RC .50 1.25
106 Mike Pouncey RC .60 1.50
107 Greg Salas RC .50 1.25
108 Delone Carter RC .40 1.00
109 Julio Jones RC 1.00 2.50
110 Da'Quan Bowers RC .60 1.50
111 Torrey Smith RC .60 1.50
112 Kyle Rudolph RC .50 1.25
113 Kendall Hunter RC .50 1.25
114 Prince Amukamara RC .50 1.25
115 Jon Baldwin RC .50 1.25
116 Aldrick Robinson RC .30 .75
117 T.J. Yates RC .60 1.50
118 Stephen Paea RC .50 1.25
119 Aaron Williams RC .40 1.00
120 Jake Locker RC 1.25 3.00
121 Robert Quinn RC .50 1.25
122 Adrian Clayborn RC .50 1.25
123 Marcell Dareus RC .50 1.25
124 Akeem Ayers RC .40 1.00
125 Christian Ponder RC 1.25 3.00
126 Andy Dalton RC 1.25 3.00
127 Ricky Stanzi RC .60 1.50
128 Colin Kaepernick RC .60 1.50
129 Randall Cobb RC .60 1.50
130 Cam Newton RC 2.50 6.00
131 Shane Vereen RC .50 1.25
132 DeMarco Murray RC 1.00 2.50
133 Stevan Ridley RC .50 1.25
134 Christian Ballard RC .40 1.00
135 Dion Lewis RC .50 1.25
136 Luke Stocker RC .40 1.00
137 Lance Kendricks RC .40 1.00
138 D.J. Williams RC .50 1.25
139 Jerrel Jernigan RC .40 1.00
140 Mark Ingram RC 1.00 2.50
141 Tandon Doss RC .40 1.00
142 Titus Young RC .60 1.50
143 Austin Pettis RC .40 1.00
144 Ryan Kerrigan RC .50 1.25
145 Cameron Jordan RC .40 1.00
146 J.J. Watt RC .60 1.50
147 Dontay Moch RC .30 .75
148 Marvin Austin RC .40 1.00
149 Vincent Brown RC .60 1.50
150 A.J. Green RC 1.00 2.50
151 Brandon Harris RC .30 .75
152 Curtis Brown RC .50 1.25
153 Brooks Reed RC .50 1.25
154 Jabaal Sheard RC .50 1.25
155 Leonard Hankerson RC .50 1.25
156 Dwayne Harris RC .50 1.25
157 Roy Helu RC 1.00 2.50
158 Cameron Heyward RC .50 1.25
159 Justin Houston RC .50 1.25
160 Blaine Gabbert RC .75 2.00
161 Ronald Johnson RC .40 1.00
162 Taiwan Jones RC .50 1.25
163 Bruce Carter RC .50 1.25
164 Greg McElroy RC .50 1.25
165 Colin McCarthy RC .40 1.00
166 Rahim Moore RC .40 1.00
167 Niles Paul RC .50 1.25
168 Bilal Powell RC .30 .75
169 Jacquizz Rodgers RC .50 1.25
170 Mikel Leshoure RC .50 1.25
171 Cecil Shorts RC .40 1.00
172 Tyrod Taylor RC .50 1.25
173 Jordan Todman RC .30 .75
174 Brandon Burton RC .40 1.00
175 Martez Wilson RC .50 1.25
176 Anthony Allen RC .30 .75
177 Allen Bailey RC .40 1.00
178 Quan Sturdivant RC .50 1.25
179 Jordan Cameron RC .40 1.00
180 Ryan Williams RC .60 1.50
181 Nathan Enderle RC .50 1.25
182 Ras-I Dowling RC .50 1.25
183 Edmond Gates RC .40 1.00
184 Jamie Harper RC .50 1.25
185 Robert Housler RC .40 1.00
186 Jeremy Kerley RC .50 1.25
187 Denarius Moore RC .60 1.50
188 Anthony Castonzo RC .30 .75
189 Casey Matthews RC .50 1.25
190 Nick Fairley RC .60 1.50
191 Evan Royster RC .50 1.25
192 Quinton Carter RC .30 .75
193 Jimmy Smith RC .50 1.25
194 Virgil Green RC .40 1.00
195 Ryan Whalen RC .40 1.00
196 Da'Rel Scott RC .40 1.00
197 Alex Green RC .50 1.25
198 Phil Taylor RC .40 1.00
199 Muhammad Wilkerson RC .50 1.25
200 Von Miller RC .60 1.50

2011 Topps Rising Rookies Black

UNPRICED BLACK/1 ODDS 1:2856 HOB

2011 Topps Rising Rookies Blue

*BLUE/1339: .8X TO 2X BASIC CARDS
BLUE/1399 STATED ODDS 1:6 HOB

2011 Topps Rising Rookies Gold

*GOLD: .5X TO 1.2X BASIC CARDS
GOLD STATED ODDS 1:1 HOB

2011 Topps Rising Rookies Green

*GREEN/25: 4X TO 10X BASIC CARDS
GREEN/25 STATED ODDS 1:322 HOB

2011 Topps Rising Rookies Orange

*ORANGE: 1.2X TO 3X BASIC CARDS
ORANGE STATED PRINT RUN 1:65 HOB

2011 Topps Rising Rookies Red

*RED/99: 2X TO 5X BASIC CARDS
RED/99 STATED ODDS 1:81 HOB

2011 Topps Rising Rookies Combine Competition

RANDOM INSERTS IN PACKS
CCBL Jon Baldwin .60 1.50
Greg Little
CCCJ Randall Cobb .75 2.00
Jerrel Jernigan
CCGJ A.J. Green 1.25 3.00
Julio Jones
CCHY Leonard Hankerson .75 2.00
Titus Young
CCIL Mark Ingram 1.25 3.00
Mikel Leshoure
CCLP Jake Locker 1.50 4.00
Christian Ponder
CCMW Von Miller .75 2.00
Martez Wilson
CCNG Cam Newton 3.00 8.00
Blaine Gabbert
CCPA Patrick Peterson 1.00 2.50
Prince Amukamara
CCSG Torrey Smith .75 2.00
Edmond Gates
CCVC Shane Vereen .60 1.50
Delone Carter
CCWG D.J. Williams .60 1.50
Virgil Green
CCWT Ryan Williams .75 2.00
Jordan Todman

2011 Topps Rising Rookies Draft Selection

RANDOM INSERTS IN PACKS
DSAB Ahmad Bradshaw .75 2.00
DSAR Aaron Rodgers 1.50 4.00
DSBJ Brandon Jacobs .75 2.00
DSBL Brandon Lloyd .75 2.00
DSBR Ben Roethlisberger 1.00 2.50
DSBU Brian Urlacher 1.00 2.50
DSCB Champ Bailey .75 2.00
DSCC Chris Cooley .75 2.00
DSCJ Calvin Johnson 1.00 2.50
DSDF D'Brickashaw Ferguson .60 1.50
DSDG David Garrard .75 2.00
DSDH Devery Henderson .60 1.50
DSDK Dustin Keller .75 2.00
DSDM Derrick Mason .60 1.50
DSER Ed Reed .75 2.00
DSFJ Felix Jones .75 2.00
DSGO Greg Olsen .60 1.50
DSJA Jared Allen .75 2.00
DSJC Jerricho Cotchery .60 1.50
DSJK Johnny Knox .75 2.00
DSJL James Laurinaitis .60 1.50
DSJP Julius Peppers .75 2.00
DSKB Kenny Britt .75 2.00
DSKO Kyle Orton .75 2.00
DSLM LaMarr Woodley .60 1.50
DSLT Lawrence Timmons .60 1.50
DSMB Michael Bush .60 1.50
DSMC Michael Crabtree .75 2.00
DSMH Matt Hasselbeck .75 2.00
DSMT Michael Turner .75 2.00
DSMW Mario Williams .60 1.50
DSNA Nnamdi Asomugha .75 2.00
DSPH Percy Harvin .75 2.00
DSPM Peyton Manning 1.50 4.00
DSPP Paul Posluszny .60 1.50
DSPR Philip Rivers 1.00 2.50
DSPW Patrick Willis .75 2.00
DSRM Robert Meachem .75 2.00
DSRS Richard Seymour .60 1.50
DSSB Steve Breaston .60 1.50
DSTG Tony Gonzalez .75 2.00
DSTH Todd Heap .60 1.50
DSABO Anquan Boldin .75 2.00
DSAJH A.J. Hawk .75 2.00
DSCBE Cedric Benson .75 2.00
DSCHJ Chris Johnson .75 2.00
DSDHT Devin Hester 1.00 2.50
DSDMC Darren McFadden .75 2.00
DSJAV Jason Avant .60 1.50
DSJCU Jay Cutler .75 2.00

2011 Topps Rising Rookies Draft Selection Jerseys

RANDOM INSERTS IN PACKS
DSSAB Ahmad Bradshaw 3.00 8.00
DSSAR Aaron Rodgers 8.00 20.00
DSSBJ Brandon Jacobs 3.00 8.00
DSSBL Brandon Lloyd 3.00 8.00
DSSBR Ben Roethlisberger 4.00 10.00
DSSBU Brian Urlacher 4.00 10.00
DSSCB Champ Bailey 3.00 8.00
DSSCC Chris Cooley 3.00 8.00
DSSCJ Calvin Johnson 4.00 10.00
DSSDF D'Brickashaw Ferguson 2.50 6.00
DSSDG David Garrard 3.00 8.00
DSSDH Devery Henderson 2.50 6.00
DSSDK Dustin Keller 3.00 8.00
DSSDM Derrick Mason 2.50 6.00
DSSER Ed Reed 3.00 8.00
DSSFJ Felix Jones 3.00 8.00
DSSGO Greg Olsen 2.50 6.00
DSSJA Jared Allen 3.00 8.00
DSSJC Jerricho Cotchery 2.50 6.00
DSSJK Johnny Knox 3.00 8.00
DSSJL James Laurinaitis 2.50 6.00
DSSJP Julius Peppers 3.00 8.00
DSSKB Kenny Britt 3.00 8.00
DSSKO Kyle Orton 3.00 8.00
DSSLM LaMarr Woodley 4.00 10.00
DSSLT Lawrence Timmons 4.00 10.00
DSSMB Michael Bush 2.50 6.00
DSSMC Michael Crabtree 3.00 8.00
DSSMH Matt Hasselbeck 3.00 8.00
DSSMT Michael Turner 3.00 8.00
DSSMW Mario Williams 2.50 6.00
DSSNA Nnamdi Asomugha 3.00 8.00
DSSPH Percy Harvin 3.00 8.00
DSSPM Peyton Manning 10.00 25.00
DSSPP Paul Posluszny 2.50 6.00
DSSPR Philip Rivers 4.00 10.00
DSSPW Patrick Willis 3.00 8.00
DSSRM Robert Meachem 3.00 8.00
DSSRS Richard Seymour 2.50 6.00
DSSSB Steve Breaston 2.50 6.00
DSSTG Tony Gonzalez 3.00 8.00
DSSTH Todd Heap 2.50 6.00
DSSABO Anquan Boldin 3.00 8.00
DSSAJH A.J. Hawk 3.00 8.00
DSSCBE Cedric Benson 3.00 8.00
DSSCHJ Chris Johnson 3.00 8.00
DSSDHT Devin Hester 4.00 10.00
DSSDMC Darren McFadden 3.00 8.00
DSSJAV Jason Avant 2.50 6.00
DSSJCU Jay Cutler 3.00 8.00

2011 Topps Rising Rookies Dual Autographs

STATED PRINT RUN 25 SER.#'d SETS
UNPRICED GOLD AU PRINT RUN 5
EXCH EXPIRATION: 5/31/2014
DAAS Prince Amukamara 30.00 60.00
Ndamukong Suh
DABF Da'Quan Bowers 15.00 40.00
Nick Fairley
DABS Jon Baldwin 20.00 50.00
Torrey Smith
DAGB Blaine Gabbert 50.00 100.00
Sam Bradford
DAGJ A.J. Green EXCH 60.00 120.00
Julio Jones
DAGN Blaine Gabbert 100.00 200.00
Cam Newton
DAIL Mark Ingram EXCH 30.00 60.00
Mikel Leshoure
DAIM Mark Ingram
Ryan Mathews
DALM Mikel Leshoure EXCH 20.00 50.00
Rashard Mendenhall
DAMP DeMarco Murray 100.00 175.00
Adrian Peterson
DANF Cam Newton 100.00 200.00
Nick Fairley
DANT Cam Newton 175.00 300.00
Tim Tebow
DARG Kyle Rudolph EXCH 15.00 40.00
Jermaine Gresham
DASH Torrey Smith 20.00 50.00
Leonard Hankerson
DAGBR A.J. Green 40.00 80.00
Dez Bryant

2011 Topps Rising Rookies Freshman Impressions Autograph Jerseys

STATED PRINT RUN 25 SER.#'d SETS
UNPRICED JUMBO AU PRINT RUN 5
UNPRICED JUMBO PATCH AU PRINT RUN 1
UNPRICED PATCH AU PRINT RUN 10
FIARAD Arrelious Benn 8.00 20.00
FIARAE Armanti Edwards 6.00 15.00
FIARAH Aaron Hernandez 10.00 25.00
FIARAR Andre Roberts 6.00 15.00
FIARBL Brandon LaFell 6.00 15.00
FIARBT Ben Tate 10.00 25.00
FIARCJS C.J. Spiller 8.00 20.00
FIARCM Colt McCoy 15.00 40.00
FIARDB Dez Bryant 25.00 50.00
FIARDM Dexter McCluster 10.00 25.00
FIARDT Demaryius Thomas
FIARDW Damian Williams
FIAREB Eric Berry 10.00 25.00
FIARED Eric Decker 10.00 25.00
FIARES Emmanuel Sanders 6.00 15.00
FIARET Earl Thomas 6.00 15.00
FIARGM Gerald McCoy 6.00 15.00
FIARGT Golden Tate 6.00 15.00
FIARJB Jahvid Best 8.00 20.00
FIARJC Jimmy Clausen 10.00 25.00
FIARJG Jermaine Gresham
FIARJGR Jimmy Graham 25.00 50.00
FIARJM Joe McKnight 10.00 25.00
FIARJS Jordan Shipley
FIARME Marcus Easley
FIARMH Montario Hardesty 8.00 20.00
FIARMK Mike Kafka 6.00 15.00
FIARMW Mike Williams 12.00 30.00
FIARNS Ndamukong Suh 25.00 50.00
FIARRG Rob Gronkowski 25.00 50.00
FIARRM Ryan Mathews 15.00 40.00
FIARSB Sam Bradford 50.00 100.00
FIARTG Toby Gerhart 10.00 25.00
FIARTP Taylor Price 6.00 15.00
FIARTT Tim Tebow 75.00 135.00

2011 Topps Rising Rookies Freshman Impressions Autographs

RANDOM INSERTS IN PACKS
FIAAB Arrelious Benn 5.00 12.00
FIAAE Armanti Edwards 4.00 10.00
FIAAH Aaron Hernandez 6.00 15.00
FIAAR Andre Roberts 4.00 10.00
FIABL Brandon LaFell 4.00 10.00
FIABT Ben Tate 5.00 12.00
FIACJS C.J. Spiller 5.00 12.00
FIACM Colt McCoy 15.00 40.00
FIADB Dez Bryant 20.00 40.00
FIADM Dexter McCluster 6.00 15.00
FIADT Demaryius Thomas 5.00 12.00
FIADW Damian Williams 4.00 10.00
FIAEB Eric Berry 6.00 15.00
FIAED Eric Decker 5.00 12.00
FIAES Emmanuel Sanders 5.00 12.00
FIAGM Gerald McCoy 4.00 10.00
FIAGT Golden Tate 4.00 10.00
FIAJB Jahvid Best 5.00 12.00
FIAJC Jimmy Clausen 8.00 20.00
FIAJF Jacoby Ford 5.00 12.00
FIAJG Jermaine Gresham 5.00 12.00
FIAJGR Jimmy Graham 20.00 40.00
FIAJM Joe McKnight 6.00 15.00
FIAJS Jordan Shipley 6.00 15.00
FIAME Marcus Easley 4.00 10.00
FIAMH Montario Hardesty 5.00 12.00
FIAMK Mike Kafka 5.00 12.00
FIAMW Mike Williams 8.00 20.00
FIANS Ndamukong Suh 12.00 30.00
FIARG Rob Gronkowski 15.00 30.00
FIARM Ryan Mathews
FIASB Sam Bradford 30.00 60.00
FIATG Toby Gerhart 5.00 12.00
FIATP Taylor Price 4.00 10.00
FIATT Tim Tebow 40.00 80.00

2011 Topps Rising Rookies Freshman Impressions Jerseys

RANDOM INSERTS IN PACKS
*JUMBO/10: .8X TO 2X BASIC JSY
UNPRICED JUMBO PATCH PRINT RUN 1
FIRAB Arrelious Benn 4.00 10.00
FIRAE Armanti Edwards 3.00 8.00
FIRAR Andre Roberts 3.00 8.00
FIRBL Brandon LaFell 3.00 8.00
FIRBT Ben Tate 4.00 10.00
FIRCJS C.J. Spiller 4.00 10.00
FIRCM Colt McCoy 4.00 10.00
FIRDB Dez Bryant 5.00 12.00
FIRDM Dexter McCluster 3.00 8.00
FIRDT Demaryius Thomas 4.00 10.00
FIRDW Damian Williams 3.00 8.00
FIREB Eric Berry 4.00 10.00
FIRED Eric Decker 4.00 10.00
FIRES Emmanuel Sanders 3.00 8.00
FIRET Earl Thomas 3.00 8.00
FIRGM Gerald McCoy 3.00 8.00
FIRGT Golden Tate 3.00 8.00
FIRJB Jahvid Best 4.00 10.00
FIRJC Jimmy Clausen 3.00 8.00
FIRJG Jermaine Gresham 4.00 10.00
FIRJGR Jimmy Graham 5.00 12.00
FIRJM Joe McKnight 4.00 10.00
FIRJS Jordan Shipley 4.00 10.00
FIRME Marcus Easley 3.00 8.00
FIRMG Mardy Gilyard 3.00 8.00
FIRMH Montario Hardesty 4.00 10.00
FIRMK Mike Kafka 3.00 8.00
FIRMW Mike Williams 4.00 10.00
FIRNS Ndamukong Suh 5.00 12.00
FIRRG Rob Gronkowski 5.00 12.00
FIRRM Ryan Mathews 4.00 10.00
FIRSB Sam Bradford 5.00 12.00
FIRTG Toby Gerhart 4.00 10.00
FIRTP Taylor Price 3.00 8.00
FIRTT Tim Tebow 8.00 20.00

2011 Topps Rising Rookies Freshman Impressions Jerseys Patch

*PATCH/25: .8X TO 2X BASIC JSY
STATED PRINT RUN 25 SER.#'d SETS
FIRSB Sam Bradford 25.00 60.00
FIRTT Tim Tebow 25.00 60.00

2011 Topps Rising Rookies NFL Draft

RANDOM INSERTS IN PACKS
DRAD Andy Dalton 1.50 4.00
DRAJG A.J. Green 1.25 3.00
DRAP Austin Pettis .50 1.25
DRBG Blaine Gabbert 1.00 2.50
DRCK Colin Kaepernick .75 2.00
DRCN Cam Newton 3.00 8.00
DRCP Christian Ponder 1.25 3.00
DRCS Cecil Shorts .50 1.25
DRDB Da'Quan Bowers .60 1.50
DRDL Dion Lewis .60 1.50
DRDM DeMarco Murray 1.25 3.00
DRDT Daniel Thomas .60 1.50
DRGL Greg Little .60 1.50
DRGS Greg Salas .60 1.50
DRJB Jon Baldwin .60 1.50
DRJJ Julio Jones 1.25 3.00
DRJJE Jerrel Jernigan .50 1.25
DRJL Jake Locker 1.50 4.00
DRJR Jacquizz Rodgers .60 1.50
DRJT Jordan Todman .40 1.00
DRKH Kendall Hunter .60 1.50
DRKR Kyle Rudolph .60 1.50
DRLH Leonard Hankerson .60 1.50
DRLK Lance Kendricks .50 1.25
DRLS Luke Stocker .50 1.25
DRMI Mark Ingram 1.25 3.00
DRML Mikel Leshoure .60 1.50
DRNF Nick Fairley .75 2.00
DRNP Niles Paul .60 1.50
DRPA Prince Amukamara .60 1.50
DRPP Patrick Peterson 1.00 2.50
DRRC Randall Cobb .75 2.00
DRRM Ryan Mallett 1.25 3.00
DRRW Ryan Williams .75 2.00
DRSR Stevan Ridley .60 1.50
DRSV Shane Vereen .60 1.50
DRTD Tandon Doss .50 1.25
DRTS Torrey Smith .75 2.00
DRTY Titus Young .75 2.00
DRVM Von Miller .75 2.00

2011 Topps Rising Rookies NFL Draft Autographs

STATED PRINT RUN 10-260
*NFL SHIELD AU: .4X TO 1X DRAFT AU
UNPRICED RED INK PRINT RUN 5
EXCH EXPIRATION: 5/31/2014
DRAAD Andy Dalton/50 25.00 50.00
DRAAJG A.J. Green/25 30.00 60.00
DRAAP Austin Pettis/260 6.00 15.00
DRABG Blaine Gabbert EXCH 20.00 50.00
DRACK Colin Kaepernick/100 12.00 30.00
DRACN Cam Newton/10
DRACP Christian Ponder/50 25.00 50.00
DRACS Cecil Shorts/260 4.00 10.00
DRADB Da'Quan Bowers
DRADC Delone Carter EXCH 5.00 12.00
DRADL Dion Lewis/260 5.00 12.00
DRADM DeMarco Murray/100 25.00 50.00
DRADT Daniel Thomas/260 8.00 20.00
DRAGL Greg Little/100 6.00 15.00
DRAGS Greg Salas/260 5.00 12.00
DRAJB Jon Baldwin/50 8.00 20.00
DRAJJ Julio Jones/25 25.00 50.00
DRAJJE Jerrel Jernigan/100 5.00 12.00
DRAJL Jake Locker/25 50.00 100.00
DRAJR Jacquizz Rodgers/260 5.00 12.00
DRAJT Jordan Todman/260 3.00 8.00
DRAKH Kendall Hunter/260 5.00 12.00
DRAKR Kyle Rudolph/100 6.00 15.00
DRALH Leonard Hankerson/100 8.00 20.00
DRALK Lance Kendricks/260 4.00 10.00
DRALS Luke Stocker/100 5.00 12.00
DRAMI Mark Ingram/10
DRAML Mikel Leshoure EXCH 10.00 25.00
DRANF Nick Fairley
DRANP Niles Paul/260 5.00 12.00
DRAPA Prince Amukamara/100 6.00 15.00
DRARC Randall Cobb/100 8.00 20.00
DRARM Ryan Mallett/25 40.00 80.00
DRARW Ryan Williams/50 20.00 40.00
DRASR Stevan Ridley/260 5.00 12.00
DRASV Shane Vereen/260 5.00 12.00
DRATD Tandon Doss/260 4.00 10.00
DRATS Torrey Smith/50 10.00 25.00
DRATY Titus Young/100 8.00 20.00
DRAVM Von Miller/50 12.00 30.00

2011 Topps Rising Rookies NFL Draft Patch Autographs

STATED PRINT RUN 10-170
*NFL SHLD PATCH: .4X TO 1X DRFT PCH AU
UNPRICED RED INK PRINT RUN 5
EXCH EXPIRATION: 5/31/2014
RAPAD Andy Dalton/40 40.00 80.00
RAPAJG A.J. Green/25 25.00 60.00
RAPAP Austin Pettis/170 8.00 20.00
RAPBG Blaine Gabbert/10
RAPCK Colin Kaepernick/65 25.00 60.00
RAPCN Cam Newton/10
RAPCP Christian Ponder/25 40.00 80.00
RAPCS Cecil Shorts/170 5.00 12.00
RAPDB Da'Quan Bowers/40 10.00 25.00
RAPDC Delone Carter EXCH 6.00 15.00
RAPDL Dion Lewis/170 6.00 15.00
RAPDM DeMarco Murray 40.00 80.00
RAPDT Daniel Thomas/115 10.00 25.00
RAPGL Greg Little/65 10.00 25.00
RAPGS Greg Salas/170 6.00 15.00
RAPJB Jon Baldwin/40 10.00 25.00
RAPJJ Julio Jones/25 25.00 60.00
RAPJJE Jerrel Jernigan/65 8.00 20.00
RAPJL Jake Locker/25 60.00 120.00
RAPJR Jacquizz Rodgers/170 6.00 15.00
RAPJT Jordan Todman/115 5.00 12.00
RAPKH Kendall Hunter/170 6.00 15.00
RAPKR Kyle Rudolph/65 10.00 25.00
RAPLH Leonard Hankerson 10.00 25.00
RAPLK Lance Kendricks/170 5.00 12.00
RAPLS Luke Stocker/115 6.00 15.00
RAPMI Mark Ingram
RAPML Mikel Leshoure EXCH 12.00 30.00
RAPNF Nick Fairley/40 12.00 30.00
RAPNP Niles Paul/170 6.00 15.00
RAPPA Prince Amukamara/40 10.00 25.00
RAPRC Randall Cobb/40 15.00 30.00
RAPRM Ryan Mallett/25 40.00 80.00
RAPRW Ryan Williams
RAPSR Stevan Ridley/170 6.00 15.00
RAPSV Shane Vereen/115 8.00 20.00
RAPTD Tandon Doss/115 6.00 15.00
RAPTS Torrey Smith/40 12.00 30.00
RAPTY Titus Young/40 12.00 30.00
RAPVM Von Miller/40 15.00 40.00

2011 Topps Rising Rookies Playmaker

RANDOM INSERTS IN PACKS
PAG Antonio Gates .75 2.00
PAP Adrian Peterson 1.25 3.00
PBE Braylon Edwards .75 2.00
PCG Chad Greenway .75 2.00
PCP Clinton Portis .75 2.00
PDB Dwayne Bowe .75 2.00
PDBR Drew Brees 1.00 2.50
PDH David Harris .60 1.50
PDJ DeSean Jackson .75 2.00
PDR Darrelle Revis .75 2.00
PER Eddie Royal .60 1.50
PFJ Fred Jackson 1.00 2.50
PGJ Greg Jennings .75 2.00
PHN Hakeem Nicks .75 2.00
PJA Joseph Addai .75 2.00
PJC Jamaal Charles .75 2.00
PJF Joe Flacco 1.00 2.50
PJN Jordy Nelson .75 2.00
PJW Jason Witten 1.00 2.50
PLL LaRon Landry .60 1.50
PLM LeSean McCoy .75 2.00
PMF Matt Forte .75 2.00
PMJD Maurice Jones-Drew .75 2.00
PMS Matthew Stafford 1.00 2.50
PRL Ray Lewis 1.00 2.50
PRM Rashard Mendenhall .75 2.00
PRW Reggie Wayne .75 2.00
PRWH Roddy White .75 2.00
PSH Santonio Holmes .75 2.00
PSJ Steven Jackson .75 2.00

2011 Topps Rising Rookies Playmaker Autograph Jerseys

STATED PRINT RUN 25 SER.#'d SETS
UNPRICED JUMBO PRINT RUN 5
UNPRICED JUMBO PATCH PRINT RUN 1
UNPRICED PATCH PRINT RUN 10
PARAG Antonio Gates 10.00 25.00
PARAP Adrian Peterson 60.00 120.00
PARBE Braylon Edwards 10.00 25.00
PARCG Chad Greenway 20.00 40.00
PARCP Clinton Portis 10.00 25.00
PARDB Dwayne Bowe 10.00 25.00
PARDBR Drew Brees 30.00 60.00
PARDH David Harris
PARDJ DeSean Jackson 12.00 30.00
PARDR Darrelle Revis 12.00 30.00
PARER Eddie Royal 8.00 20.00
PARFJ Fred Jackson 40.00 80.00
PARGJ Greg Jennings 12.00 30.00
PARHN Hakeem Nicks 10.00 25.00
PARJA Joseph Addai 10.00 25.00
PARJC Jamaal Charles 12.00 30.00
PARJF Joe Flacco 15.00 40.00
PARJN Jordy Nelson 10.00 25.00
PARJW Jason Witten
PARLL LaRon Landry
PARLM LeSean McCoy 12.00 30.00
PARMF Matt Forte 10.00 25.00
PARMJD Maurice Jones-Drew 10.00 25.00
PARMS Matthew Stafford 40.00 80.00
PARRL Ray Lewis 50.00 100.00
PARRM Rashard Mendenhall 10.00 25.00
PARRW Reggie Wayne 12.00 30.00
PARRWH Roddy White 12.00 30.00
PARSH Santonio Holmes 10.00 25.00
PARSJ Steven Jackson 10.00 25.00

2011 Topps Rising Rookies Playmaker Autographs

STATED PRINT RUN 20 SER.#'d SETS
PAAG Antonio Gates 10.00 25.00
PAAP Adrian Peterson 50.00 100.00
PABE Braylon Edwards 8.00 20.00
PACG Chad Greenway 15.00 30.00
PACP Clinton Portis 8.00 20.00
PADB Dwayne Bowe 8.00 20.00
PADBR Drew Brees 30.00 60.00
PADH David Harris 6.00 15.00
PADJ DeSean Jackson 10.00 25.00
PADR Darrelle Revis 8.00 20.00
PAER Eddie Royal
PAFJ Fred Jackson 40.00 80.00
PAGJ Greg Jennings 10.00 25.00

PAHN Hakeem Nicks 10.00 25.00
PAJA Joseph Addai 8.00 20.00
PAJC Jamaal Charles
PAJF Joe Flacco 15.00 30.00
PAJN Jordy Nelson 10.00 25.00
PAJW Jason Witten 15.00 30.00
PALL LaRon Landry 6.00 15.00
PALM LeSean McCoy 10.00 25.00
PAMF Matt Forte 8.00 20.00
PAMJD Maurice Jones-Drew 8.00 20.00
PAMS Matthew Stafford 25.00 50.00
PARL Ray Lewis 30.00 60.00
PARM Rashard Mendenhall 8.00 20.00
PARW Reggie Wayne 8.00 20.00
PARWH Roddy White 8.00 20.00
PASH Santonio Holmes 8.00 20.00
PASJ Steven Jackson 8.00 20.00

2011 Topps Rising Rookies Playmaker Jerseys

RANDOM INSERTS IN PACKS
*PATCH/25: .8X TO 2X BASIC JSY
*JUMBO/10: 1X TO 2.5X BASIC JSY
UNPRICED JUMBO PATCH PRINT RUN 1
PSAG Antonio Gates 3.00 8.00
PSAP Adrian Peterson 5.00 12.00
PSBE Braylon Edwards 3.00 8.00
PSCG Chad Greenway 3.00 8.00
PSCP Clinton Portis 3.00 8.00
PSDB Dwayne Bowe 3.00 8.00
PSDBR Drew Brees 4.00 10.00
PSDH David Harris 2.50 6.00
PSDJ DeSean Jackson 3.00 8.00
PSDR Darrelle Revis 3.00 8.00
PSER Eddie Royal 2.50 6.00
PSFJ Fred Jackson 5.00 12.00
PSGJ Greg Jennings 3.00 8.00
PSHN Hakeem Nicks 3.00 8.00
PSJA Joseph Addai 3.00 8.00
PSJC Jamaal Charles 3.00 8.00
PSJF Joe Flacco 4.00 10.00
PSJN Jordy Nelson 3.00 8.00
PSJW Jason Witten 4.00 10.00
PSLL LaRon Landry 2.50 6.00
PSLM LeSean McCoy 3.00 8.00
PSMF Matt Forte 3.00 8.00
PSMJD Maurice Jones-Drew 3.00 8.00
PSMS Matthew Stafford 4.00 10.00
PSRL Ray Lewis 4.00 10.00
PSRM Rashard Mendenhall 3.00 8.00
PSRW Reggie Wayne 3.00 8.00
PSRWH Roddy White 3.00 8.00
PSSH Santonio Holmes 3.00 8.00
PSSJ Steven Jackson 3.00 8.00

2011 Topps Rising Rookies Rookie Autographs

RANDOM INSERTS IN PACKS
*RED INK/15: .6X TO 1.5X BASIC AU
EXCH EXPIRATION: 5/31/2014
102 Aldon Smith 8.00 20.00
103 Daniel Thomas 10.00 25.00
104 Ryan Mallett 20.00 50.00
105 Greg Little 5.00 12.00
106 Mike Pouncey 10.00 25.00
107 Greg Salas 5.00 12.00
108 Delone Carter 4.00 10.00
109 Julio Jones EXCH 20.00 50.00
110 Da'Quan Bowers 5.00 12.00
111 Torrey Smith 8.00 20.00
112 Kyle Rudolph EXCH 5.00 12.00
113 Kendall Hunter 5.00 12.00
114 Prince Amukamara 5.00 12.00
115 Jon Baldwin 5.00 12.00
118 Stephen Paea 5.00 12.00
119 Aaron Williams 4.00 10.00
120 Jake Locker 40.00 80.00
123 Marcell Dareus 5.00 12.00
125 Christian Ponder EXCH 20.00 40.00
126 Andy Dalton 20.00 50.00
127 Ricky Stanzi 20.00 40.00
128 Colin Kaepernick 25.00 50.00
129 Randall Cobb
130 Cam Newton 60.00 120.00
131 Shane Vereen 5.00 12.00
132 DeMarco Murray 25.00 50.00
133 Stevan Ridley 5.00 12.00
135 Dion Lewis 5.00 12.00
136 Luke Stocker 4.00 10.00
137 Lance Kendricks 4.00 10.00
139 Jerrel Jernigan 4.00 10.00
140 Mark Ingram 25.00 60.00
141 Tandon Doss 4.00 10.00
142 Titus Young 6.00 15.00
143 Austin Pettis 6.00 15.00
146 J.J. Watt 6.00 15.00
149 Vincent Brown 5.00 12.00
150 A.J. Green 25.00 50.00
155 Leonard Hankerson 5.00 12.00
159 Justin Houston 5.00 12.00
160 Blaine Gabbert
161 Ronald Johnson 4.00 10.00
162 Taiwan Jones 5.00 12.00
166 Rahim Moore 4.00 10.00
167 Niles Paul 5.00 12.00
168 Bilal Powell 3.00 8.00
169 Jacquizz Rodgers 5.00 12.00
170 Mikel Leshoure 5.00 12.00
171 Cecil Shorts 4.00 10.00
172 Tyrod Taylor 5.00 12.00
173 Jordan Todman 3.00 8.00
180 Ryan Williams 25.00 50.00
183 Edmond Gates 4.00 10.00
184 Jamie Harper 5.00 12.00
186 Jeremy Kerley 5.00 12.00
188 Anthony Castonzo 3.00 8.00
190 Nick Fairley 6.00 15.00
193 Jimmy Smith 6.00 15.00
194 Virgil Green 6.00 15.00
196 Da'Rel Scott 6.00 15.00
197 Alex Green 5.00 12.00
200 Von Miller 6.00 15.00

2011 Topps Rising Rookies Rookie Team Patches

STATED PRINT RUN 1074 SER.#'d SETS
RTPAS Aldon Smith 5.00 12.00
RTPBG Blaine Gabbert 5.00 12.00
RTPCH Cameron Heyward 3.00 8.00
RTPCL Corey Liuget 2.00 5.00
RTPCN Cam Newton 20.00 50.00
RTPCP Christian Ponder 6.00 15.00
RTPDB Da'Quan Bowers 3.00 8.00
RTPDW Dan Watkins 3.00 8.00
RTPGC Gabe Carimi 3.00 8.00
RTPJB Jon Baldwin 3.00 8.00
RTPJJ Julio Jones 6.00 15.00
RTPJL Jake Locker 8.00 20.00
RTPJS Jimmy Smith 3.00 8.00
RTPMD Marcell Dareus 3.00 8.00
RTPMI Mark Ingram 6.00 15.00
RTPMP Mike Pouncey 3.00 8.00
RTPMW Muhammad Wilkerson 3.00 8.00
RTPNF Nick Fairley 4.00 10.00
RTPNS Nate Solder 3.00 8.00
RTPPA Prince Amukamara 3.00 8.00
RTPPP Patrick Peterson 6.00 15.00
RTPPT Phil Taylor 3.00 8.00
RTPRC Randall Cobb 4.00 10.00
RTPRK Ryan Kerrigan 3.00 8.00
RTPRM Ryan Mallett 6.00 15.00
RTPRQ Robert Quinn 3.00 8.00
RTPVM Von Miller 4.00 10.00
RTPACA Anthony Castonzo 2.00 5.00
RTPAJG A.J. Green 6.00 15.00
RTPJJW J.J. Watt 4.00 10.00
RTPTSM Tyron Smith 4.00 10.00

2011 Topps Rising Rookies Triple Autographs

STATED PRINT RUN 25 SER.#'d SETS
UNPRICED GOLD PRINT RUN 5
EXCH EXPIRATION: 5/31/2014
TABDF Da'Quan Bowers
Marcell Dareus
Nick Fairley
TABMS Da'Quan Bowers
Von Miller
Aldon Smith
TAGJS A.J. Green 60.00 120.00
Julio Jones
Torrey Smith
TAHCB Leonard Hankerson 25.00 50.00
Randall Cobb
Jon Baldwin
TAIJD Mark Ingram EXCH 60.00 120.00
Julio Jones
Marcell Dareus
TAILW Mark Ingram EXCH 50.00 100.00
Mikel Leshoure
Ryan Williams
TAMSI Knowshon Moreno 40.00 80.00
C.J. Spiller
Mark Ingram
TANGL Cam Newton 175.00 300.00
Blaine Gabbert
Jake Locker
TASBG Matthew Stafford 75.00 150.00
Sam Bradford
Blaine Gabbert
TASHL Torrey Smith 30.00 60.00
Leonard Hankerson
Greg Little

2008 Topps Rookie Progression

This set was released on May 21, 2008. The base set consists of 220 cards, which have some rookie cards scattered among the veterans and legends. Each pack contained at least one rookie card.

COMPLETE SET (220) 30.00 60.00
1 Drew Brees .40 1.00
2 Jon Kitna .30 .75
3 Tom Brady .60 1.50
4 Chad Pennington .30 .75
5 Steve McNair .30 .75
6 Josh McCown .25 .60
7 Matt Hasselbeck .30 .75
8 David Garrard .30 .75
9 Jay Cutler .40 1.00
10 Matt Schaub .30 .75
11 Daunte Culpepper .30 .75
12 Kellen Clemens .30 .75
13 John Beck .25 .60
14 Trent Edwards .25 .60
15 Steven Jackson .40 1.00
16 Willie Parker .30 .75
17 Derrick Ward .25 .60
18 Julius Jones .25 .60
19 DeShaun Foster .30 .75
20 Shaun Alexander .30 .75
21 Reggie Bush .40 1.00
22 Clinton Portis .30 .75
23 Ron Dayne .25 .60
24 Maurice Jones-Drew .30 .75
25 Warrick Dunn .30 .75
26 Adrian Peterson .60 1.50
27 Brian Leonard .25 .60
28 Greg Jennings .40 1.00
29 Torry Holt .30 .75
30 T.J. Houshmandzadeh .30 .75
31 Jerricho Cotchery .30 .75
32 Derrick Mason .30 .75
33 Kevin Curtis .25 .60
34 Kevin Walter .30 .75
35 Joey Galloway .30 .75
36 Anquan Boldin .30 .75
37 Santonio Holmes .30 .75
38 Lee Evans .30 .75
39 Dwayne Bowe .30 .75
40 Laurent Robinson .25 .60
41 Antonio Gates .40 1.00
42 Chris Cooley .30 .75
43 Owen Daniels .25 .60
44 Patrick Kerney .25 .60
45 Gaines Adams .25 .60
46 Jon Beason .25 .60
47 Antonio Cromartie .25 .60
48 Bob Sanders .30 .75
49 Reggie Nelson .25 .60
50 John Elway .75 2.00
51 Allen Patrick RC .60 1.50
52 Steve Young .60 1.50
53 Bruce Davis RC .60 1.50
54 Cliff Avril RC .60 1.50
55 Chevis Jackson RC .50 1.25
56 Peyton Manning .60 1.50
57 Carson Palmer .40 1.00
58 Ben Roethlisberger .40 1.00
59 Eli Manning .40 1.00
60 Tony Romo .50 1.25
61 Donovan McNabb .40 1.00
62 Joey Harrington .25 .60
63 Jeff Garcia .30 .75
64 Derek Anderson .25 .60
65 Rex Grossman .30 .75
66 Kyle Boller .25 .60
67 Sage Rosenfels .25 .60
68 JaMarcus Russell .30 .75
69 Jerious Norwood .30 .75
70 Thomas Jones .30 .75
71 LaDainian Tomlinson .40 1.00
72 Cedric Benson .30 .75
73 Marion Barber .30 .75
74 Brian Westbrook .30 .75
75 LenDale White .30 .75
76 Ronnie Brown .30 .75
77 Travis Henry .25 .60
78 Kenny Watson .25 .60
79 Fred Taylor .30 .75
80 Ryan Grant .40 1.00
81 Marshawn Lynch .30 .75
82 Selvin Young .25 .60
83 Wes Welker .40 1.00
84 Roy Williams WR .30 .75
85 Randy Moss .40 1.00
86 Plaxico Burress .30 .75
87 Terrell Owens .40 1.00
88 Andre Johnson .30 .75
89 Roddy White .30 .75
90 Brandon Marshall .30 .75
91 Donald Driver .30 .75
92 Hines Ward .30 .75
93 Ike Hilliard .25 .60
94 James Jones .25 .60
95 Calvin Johnson .40 1.00
96 Kellen Winslow .30 .75
97 Tony Gonzalez .30 .75
98 Osi Umenyiora .30 .75
99 Mario Williams .30 .75
100 D.J. Williams .25 .60
101 Ernie Sims .25 .60
102 Marcus Trufant .25 .60
103 Sean Taylor .40 1.00
104 Troy Aikman .60 1.50
105 Dan Marino 1.00 2.50
106 Dantrell Savage RC .60 1.50
107 DJ Hall RC .60 1.50
108 Eddie Royal RC .75 2.00
109 Harry Douglas RC .60 1.50
110 Marcus Griffin RC .50 1.25
111 Marc Bulger .30 .75
112 Peyton Hillis RC 2.00 5.00
113 Philip Rivers .40 1.00
114 Vince Young .30 .75
115 Kurt Warner .40 1.00
116 Cleo Lemon .25 .60
117 Damon Huard .25 .60
118 Jason Campbell .30 .75
119 Brian Griese .25 .60
120 Tarvaris Jackson .30 .75
121 J.P. Losman .25 .60
122 Troy Smith .30 .75
123 Brady Quinn .30 .75
124 Joseph Addai .30 .75
125 Laurence Maroney .30 .75
126 Brandon Jacobs .30 .75
127 Willis McGahee .30 .75
128 Frank Gore .30 .75
129 Edgerrin James .30 .75
130 Kevin Jones .25 .60
131 DeAngelo Williams .30 .75
132 Jamal Lewis .30 .75
133 Chester Taylor .25 .60
134 Earnest Graham .25 .60
135 Justin Fargas .25 .60
136 Kolby Smith .25 .60
137 Marques Colston .30 .75
138 Reggie Wayne .30 .75
139 Chad Johnson .30 .75
140 Amani Toomer .30 .75
141 Bernard Berrian .30 .75
142 Steve Smith .30 .75
143 Larry Fitzgerald .40 1.00
144 Chris Chambers .30 .75
145 Braylon Edwards .30 .75
146 David Patten .25 .60
147 Bobby Engram .25 .60
148 Shaun McDonald .25 .60
149 Anthony Gonzalez .25 .60
150 Sidney Rice .40 1.00
151 Jason Witten .40 1.00
152 Greg Olsen .30 .75
153 Jared Allen .40 1.00
154 DeMarcus Ware .30 .75
155 Nick Barnett .25 .60
156 Patrick Willis .30 .75
157 Ed Reed .30 .75
158 Asante Samuel .25 .60
159 Rafael Little RC .60 1.50
160 Joe Montana 1.00 2.50
161 Lawrence Jackson RC .60 1.50
162 Chauncey Washington RC .60 1.50
163 Keenan Burton RC .50 1.25
164 John Carlson RC .75 2.00
165 Dorien Bryant RC .60 1.50
166 Adarius Bowman RC .60 1.50
167 Ali Highsmith RC .50 1.25
168 Andre Woodson RC .75 2.00
169 Darren McFadden RC 2.00 5.00
170 Brian Brohm RC .75 2.00
171 Brandon Flowers RC .75 2.00
172 Matt Ryan RC 3.00 8.00
173 Calais Campbell RC .60 1.50
174 Quentin Groves RC .60 1.50
175 Curtis Lofton RC .60 1.50
176 Justin Forsett RC .75 2.00
177 Lavelle Hawkins RC .50 1.25
178 DeSean Jackson RC 1.50 4.00
179 Dan Connor RC .75 2.00
180 Dennis Dixon RC .75 2.00
181 Derrick Harvey RC .50 1.25
182 Erik Ainge RC .75 2.00
183 Earl Bennett RC .75 2.00
184 Early Doucet RC .60 1.50
185 Erin Henderson RC .75 2.00
186 Felix Jones RC 1.25 3.00
187 James Hardy RC .60 1.50
188 Jonathan Stewart RC 1.25 3.00
189 Kenny Phillips RC .75 2.00
190 Keith Rivers RC .75 2.00
191 Kevin Smith RC .75 2.00
192 Mike Jenkins RC .75 2.00
193 Malcolm Kelly RC .60 1.50
194 Mike Hart RC .75 2.00
195 Chad Henne RC .75 2.00
196 Jake Long RC .75 2.00
197 Mario Manningham RC .75 2.00
198 Rashard Mendenhall RC 1.50 4.00
199 Reggie Smith RC .60 1.50
200 Ray Rice RC 1.50 4.00
201 Steve Slaton RC .75 2.00
202 Tracy Porter RC .75 2.00
203 Jerod Mayo RC .75 2.00
204 John David Booty RC .60 1.50
205 Fred Davis RC .75 2.00
206 Sedrick Ellis RC .75 2.00
207 Chris Johnson RC 2.00 5.00
208 Andre Caldwell RC .60 1.50
209 Tashard Choice RC .60 1.50
210 Glenn Dorsey RC .75 2.00
211 Vernon Gholston RC .60 1.50
212 Chris Long RC .75 2.00
213 Xavier Adibi RC .50 1.25
214 Donnie Avery RC .60 1.50
215 Colt Brennan RC .75 2.00
216 Kentwan Balmer RC .60 1.50
217 Jamaal Charles RC 1.25 3.00
218 Limas Sweed RC .75 2.00
219 Matt Forte RC 1.25 3.00
220 Owen Schmitt RC .75 2.00

2008 Topps Rookie Progression Bronze

*VETS: 1.5X TO 4X BASIC CARDS
*ROOKIES: .6X TO 1.5X BASIC CARDS
BRONZE/389 STATED ODDS 1:8S

2008 Topps Rookie Progression Gold

*VETS: 2.5X TO 6X BASIC CARDS
*ROOKIES: 1X TO 2.5X BASIC CARDS
GOLD/199 STATED ODDS 1:15

2008 Topps Rookie Progression Platinum

*VETS: 3X TO 8X BASIC CARDS
*ROOKIES: 1.2X TO 3X BASIC CARDS
PLATINUM/99 STATED ODDS 1:29

2008 Topps Rookie Progression Silver

*VETS: 2X TO 5X BASIC CARDS
*ROOKIES: .8X TO 2X BASIC CARDS
SILVER/299 STATED ODDS 1:10

2008 Topps Rookie Progression Game Worn Jerseys

GROUP A ODDS 1:2300
GROUP B ODDS 1:3117
GROUP C ODDS 1:1400
GROUP D ODDS 1:4950
GROUP E ODDS 1:263
GROUP F ODDS 1:623
GROUP G ODDS 1:207
GROUP H ODDS 1:339
AB Adarius Bowman A 4.00 10.00
AC Andre Caldwell A 4.00 10.00
AH Ali Highsmith A 3.00 8.00
AP Adrian Peterson E 6.00 15.00
AW Andre Woodson A 5.00 12.00
BD Bruce Davis H 2.50 6.00
BU Brian Urlacher E 4.00 10.00
BW Brian Westbrook E 3.00 8.00
CB Colt Brennan B 4.00 10.00
CH Chad Henne B 8.00 20.00
CW Chauncey Washington D 2.50 6.00
DA Donnie Avery A 4.00 10.00
DB Dorien Bryant B 3.00 8.00
DBO Dwayne Bowe E 3.00 8.00
DC Dan Connor A 5.00 12.00
DD Donald Driver E 3.00 8.00
DH DJ Hall C 2.50 6.00
DJ Dexter Jackson G 2.50 6.00
DM Donovan McNabb E 4.00 10.00
DR Dominique Rodgers-Cromartie C 3.00 8.00
DS Dantrell Savage C 2.50 6.00
DST Donte Stallworth E 2.50 6.00
EA Erik Ainge B 6.00 15.00
ER Eddie Royal A 5.00 12.00
FT Fred Taylor E 3.00 8.00
HD Harry Douglas A 4.00 10.00
JA Joseph Addai E 3.00 8.00
JB John David Booty B 3.00 8.00
JF Justin Forsett A 5.00 12.00
JF Joe Flacco C 6.00 15.00
JG Joey Galloway E 3.00 8.00
JH Jacob Hester A 5.00 12.00
JN Jordy Nelson G 4.00 10.00
KR Keith Rivers A 5.00 12.00
LH Lavelle Hawkins A 3.00 8.00
LJ Lawrence Jackson G 3.00 8.00
LM Leodis McKelvin F 2.50 6.00
LT LaDainian Tomlinson E 4.00 10.00
MF Matt Forte A 8.00 20.00
MG Marcus Griffin C 2.00 5.00
ML Marshawn Lynch E 3.00 8.00
MS Marcus Smith H 2.50 6.00
PH Peyton Hillis G 8.00 20.00
RL Rafael Little E 2.50 6.00
SE Sedrick Ellis F 3.00 8.00
SM Shawne Merriman E 3.00 8.00
TC Tashard Choice A 4.00 10.00
TO Terrell Owens E 4.00 10.00
VY Vince Young E 3.00 8.00
YB Yvenson Bernard C 3.00 8.00

2008 Topps Rookie Progression Game Worn Jerseys Bronze

BRONZE/189 GRP A ODDS 1:284
BRONZE/249 GRP B ODDS 1:84
*GOLD/99: .5X TO 1.2X BRONZE JSYs
GOLD/99 ODDS 1:154
*PLATINUM/29: .8X TO 2X BRONZE JSYs
PLATINUM/29 ODDS 1:650
*SILVER/179: .4X TO 1X BRONZE JSYs
SILVER/179 ODDS 1:84
AB Adarius Bowman/189 2.50 6.00
AC Andre Caldwell/189 2.50 6.00
AH Ali Highsmith/249 2.50 6.00
AP Adrian Peterson/249 6.00 15.00
AW Andre Woodson/189 4.00 10.00
BD Bruce Davis/249 2.50 6.00
BU Brian Urlacher/249 4.00 10.00
BW Brian Westbrook/249 3.00 8.00
CB Colt Brennan/189 3.00 8.00
CH Chad Henne/189 6.00 15.00
CW Chauncey Washington/249 2.50 6.00
DA Donnie Avery/189 2.50 6.00
DB Dorien Bryant/189 2.50 6.00
DBO Dwayne Bowe/249 3.00 8.00
DC Dan Connor/189 3.00 8.00
DD Donald Driver/249 3.00 8.00
DH DJ Hall/249 2.50 6.00
DJ Dexter Jackson/249 2.50 6.00
DM Donovan McNabb/249 4.00 10.00
DR Dominique Rodgers-Cromartie/249 3.00 8.00
DS Dantrell Savage/249 2.50 6.00
DST Donte Stallworth/249 2.50 6.00
EA Erik Ainge/189 5.00 12.00
ER Eddie Royal/189 3.00 8.00
FT Fred Taylor/249 3.00 8.00
HD Harry Douglas/189 2.50 6.00
JA Joseph Addai/249 3.00 8.00
JB John David Booty/189 2.50 6.00
JF Joe Flacco/249 6.00 15.00
JFO Justin Forsett/189 3.00 8.00
JG Joey Galloway/249 3.00 8.00
JH Jacob Hester/189 3.00 8.00
JN Jordy Nelson/249 4.00 10.00
KR Keith Rivers/189 3.00 8.00
LH Lavelle Hawkins/189 2.00 5.00
LJ Lawrence Jackson/249 3.00 8.00
LM Leodis McKelvin/249 2.50 6.00
LT LaDainian Tomlinson/249 4.00 10.00
MF Matt Forte/189 5.00 12.00
MG Marcus Griffin/249 2.00 5.00
ML Marshawn Lynch/249 3.00 8.00
MS Marcus Smith/249 2.50 6.00
PH Peyton Hillis/249 8.00 20.00
RL Rafael Little/249 2.50 6.00
SE Sedrick Ellis/249 3.00 8.00
SM Shawne Merriman/249 3.00 8.00
TC Tashard Choice/189 2.50 6.00
TO Terrell Owens/249 4.00 10.00
VY Vince Young/249 3.00 8.00
YB Yvenson Bernard/249 3.00 8.00

2008 Topps Rookie Progression Game Worn Jerseys Dual

GROUP A ODDS 1:4650
GROUP B ODDS 1:861
*BRONZE/99: .3X TO .8X BASIC DUAL
BRONZE/99 ODDS 1:306
*SILVER/50: .4X TO 1X BASIC DUAL
SILVER/50 ODDS 1:620
*GOLD/25: .5X TO 1.2X BASIC DUAL
GOLD/25 ODDS 1:1300
UNPRICED PLATINUM/10 ODDS 1:2950
PDRAB Donnie Avery A 4.00 10.00
Dorien Bryant
PDRAF Erik Ainge A 15.00 40.00
Joe Flacco
PDRAH Joseph Addai B 5.00 12.00
Jacob Hester
PDRBH John David Booty B 4.00 10.00
Chad Henne
PDRCF Tashard Choice A 5.00 12.00
Justin Forsett
PDRCH Andre Caldwell B 4.00 10.00
DJ Hall
PDRCR Dan Connor A 5.00 12.00
Keith Rivers
PDRDG Thomas DeCoud B 3.00 8.00
Marcus Griffin
PDREJ Sedrick Ellis B 5.00 12.00
Lawrence Jackson
PDRHB Lavelle Hawkins A 4.00 10.00
Adarius Bowman
PDRJH Chevis Jackson B 3.00 8.00
Ali Highsmith
PDRLF Marshawn Lynch B 5.00 12.00
Justin Forsett
PDRMR Leodis McKelvin B 5.00 12.00
Dominique Rodgers-Cromartie
PDRMW Donovan McNabb B 5.00 12.00
Brian Westbrook
PDRPT Adrian Peterson B 15.00 40.00
LaDainian Tomlinson
PDRPW Tracy Porter B 5.00 12.00
D.J. Wolfe
PDRRD Eddie Royal B 5.00 12.00
Harry Douglas
PDRSB Dantrell Savage B 5.00 12.00
Yvenson Bernard
PDRTC Fred Taylor B 4.00 10.00
Andre Caldwell
PDRTT Terrell Thomas B 4.00 10.00
DeJuan Tribble
PDRUC Brian Urlacher B 5.00 12.00
Dan Connor
PDRUM Brian Urlacher B 5.00 12.00
Shawne Merriman
PDRWB Andre Woodson A 5.00 12.00
Colt Brennan
PDRWF Chauncey Washington A 8.00 20.00
Matt Forte
PDRYP Vince Young B 15.00 40.00
Adrian Peterson

2008 Topps Rookie Progression Game Worn Jerseys Triple

BASE TRIPLE ODDS 1:1035
*BRONZE/99: .3X TO .8X BASIC TRIPLE
BRONZE/99 ODDS 1:512
*SILVER/50: .4X TO 1X BASIC TRIPLE
SILVER/50 ODDS 1:1035
*GOLD/25: .5X TO 1.2X BASIC TRIPLE
GOLD/25 ODDS 1:2150
UNPRICED PLATINUM/10 ODDS 1:5050
BAF Colt Brennan 15.00 40.00
Erik Ainge
Joe Flacco
BAH Dorien Bryant 4.00 10.00
Donnie Avery
DJ Hall
BHW John David Booty 4.00 10.00
Chad Henne
Andre Woodson
CFF Tashard Choice 8.00 20.00
Justin Forsett
Matt Forte
CRH Dan Connor 5.00 12.00
Keith Rivers
Ali Highsmith
DWM Bruce Davis 4.00 10.00
Phillip Wheeler
Ben Moffitt
HCB Lavelle Hawkins 4.00 10.00
Andre Caldwell
Adarius Bowman
HHJ Jacob Hester 5.00 12.00
Ali Highsmith
Chevis Jackson
JER Lawrence Jackson 5.00 12.00
Sedrick Ellis
Keith Rivers
JTT Chevis Jackson 4.00 10.00
DeJuan Tribble
Terrell Thomas
LRA Trevor Laws 5.00 12.00
Darrell Robertson
Cliff Avril
NRD Jordy Nelson 6.00 15.00
Eddie Royal
Harry Douglas
OBD Terrell Owens 8.00 20.00
Dwayne Bowe
Donald Driver
RMP Dominique Rodgers-Cromartie 5.00 12.00
Leodis McKelvin
Tracy Porter
WHH Chauncey Washington 12.00 30.00
Jacob Hester
Peyton Hillis

2008 Topps Rookie Progression Game Worn Jerseys Quad

BASE QUAD ODDS 1:3225
*BRONZE/50: .3X TO .8X BASIC QUAD
BRONZE/50 ODDS 1:1558
*SILVER/25: .4X TO 1X BASIC QUAD
SILVER/25 ODDS 1:3250
UNPRICED GOLD/10 ODDS 1:7550
UNPRICED PLATINUM/1 ODDS 1:90,000
1 Tashard Choice 20.00 50.00
Matt Forte
Adrian Peterson
Marshawn Lynch
2 Chad Henne 6.00 15.00
Andre Woodson
Vince Young
Donovan McNabb
3 Justin Forsett 6.00 15.00
Lavelle Hawkins
Dantrell Savage
Adarius Bowman
4 Joe Flacco 5.00 12.00
Erik Ainge
Colt Brennan
John David Booty
5 Joey Galloway 5.00 12.00
Donte Stallworth
Marcus Smith
Dexter Jackson
6 Andre Caldwell 5.00 12.00
Donnie Avery
Dorien Bryant
DJ Hall
7 Shawne Merriman 6.00 15.00
Brian Urlacher
Dan Connor
Keith Rivers
8 Fred Taylor 6.00 15.00
Brian Westbrook
Joseph Addai
LaDainian Tomlinson
9 Marcus Griffin 5.00 12.00
Simeon Castille
Thomas DeCoud
D.J. Wolfe
10 John David Booty 5.00 12.00
Chauncey Washington
Andre Woodson
Rafael Little

2008 Topps Rookie Progression Legends

*BRONZE/389: .5X TO 1.2X BASIC INSERTS
L/R/V BRONZE/389 ODDS 1:16
*SILVER/299: .6X TO 1.5X BASIC INSERTS
L/R/V SILVER/299 ODDS 1:21
*GOLD/199: .8X TO 2X BASIC INSERTS
L/R/V GOLD/199 ODDS 1:32
*PLATINUM/50: 1X TO 2.5X BASIC INSERTS
L/R/V PLATINUM/50 ODDS 1:125
PLAG Antonio Gates 1.00 2.50
PLBE Braylon Edwards .75 2.00
PLBR Ben Roethlisberger 1.00 2.50
PLBW Brian Westrbook .75 2.00
PLCP Carson Palmer 1.00 2.50
PLDB Drew Brees 1.00 2.50
PLDM Dan Marino 2.50 6.00
PLFT Fred Taylor .75 2.00
PLJE John Elway 2.00 5.00
PLJL Jamal Lewis .75 2.00
PLJM Joe Montana 2.50 6.00
PLLF Larry Fitzgerald 1.00 2.50
PLLT LaDainian Tomlinson 1.00 2.50
PLPM Peyton Manning 1.50 4.00
PLRM Randy Moss 1.00 2.50
PLSJ Steven Jackson 1.00 2.50
PLSY Steve Young 1.50 4.00
PLTA Troy Aikman 1.50 4.00
PLTB Tom Brady 1.50 4.00
PLTO Terrell Owens 1.00 2.50

2008 Topps Rookie Progression Legends Game Worn Jerseys Bronze

BRONZE/99 ODDS 1:1525
*SILVER/79: .4X TO 1X BRONZE JSY
SILVER/79 ODDS 1:1942
*GOLD/50: .5X TO 1.2X BRONZE JSY
GOLD/50 ODDS 1:3117
UNPRICED L/V/R PLAT.AU/20 ODDS 1:554
PLDM Dan Marino 12.00 30.00
PLJE John Elway 10.00 25.00
PLJM Joe Montana 12.00 30.00
PLSY Steve Young 6.00 15.00
PLTA Troy Aikman 8.00 20.00

2008 Topps Rookie Progression Rookie Autographs Blue

BLUE GROUP A/79 ODDS 1:290
BLUE GROUP B/299 ODDS 1:1505
BLUE GROUP C/499 ODDS 1:895
BLUE GROUP D/999 ODDS 1:149
*RED VERSION: SAME PRICE
166 Adarius Bowman/999 3.00 8.00
168 Andre Woodson/79 6.00 15.00
169 Darren McFadden/79 25.00 50.00
170 Brian Brohm/79 6.00 15.00
172 Matt Ryan/79 40.00 100.00
178 DeSean Jackson/79 12.00 30.00
180 Dennis Dixon/79 8.00 20.00
184 Early Doucet/79 5.00 12.00
186 Felix Jones/79 25.00 50.00
188 Jonathan Stewart/79 10.00 25.00
189 Kenny Phillips/499 4.00 10.00
193 Malcolm Kelly/79 5.00 12.00
194 Mike Hart/79 6.00 15.00
195 Chad Henne/79 20.00 40.00
196 Jake Long/299 5.00 12.00
197 Mario Manningham/79 8.00 20.00
198 Rashard Mendenhall/79 25.00 50.00
200 Ray Rice/79 12.00 30.00
201 Steve Slaton/79 6.00 15.00
204 John David Booty/79 5.00 12.00
205 Fred Davis/999 4.00 10.00
207 Chris Johnson/999 25.00 50.00
215 Colt Brennan/79 12.00 30.00
218 Limas Sweed/79 6.00 15.00

2008 Topps Rookie Progression Rookie Autographs Blue Bronze

BRONZE/35 ODDS 1:271
*SILVER/20: .6X TO 1.5X BRONZE AU/35
SILVER/20 ODDS 1:497
UNPRICED GOLD/10 ODDS 1:892
UNPRICED PLATINUM/1 ODDS 1:9000
RED VERSION SAME PRICE
166 Adarius Bowman 6.00 15.00
168 Andre Woodson 8.00 20.00
169 Darren McFadden 20.00 50.00
170 Brian Brohm 8.00 20.00
172 Matt Ryan 40.00 100.00
178 DeSean Jackson 15.00 40.00
180 Dennis Dixon 8.00 20.00
184 Early Doucet 6.00 15.00
186 Felix Jones 12.00 30.00
188 Jonathan Stewart 12.00 30.00
189 Kenny Phillips 8.00 20.00
193 Malcolm Kelly 6.00 15.00
194 Mike Hart 8.00 20.00
195 Chad Henne 8.00 20.00
196 Jake Long 8.00 20.00
197 Mario Manningham 8.00 20.00
198 Rashard Mendenhall 15.00 40.00
200 Ray Rice 15.00 40.00
201 Steve Slaton 8.00 20.00
204 John David Booty 6.00 15.00
205 Fred Davis 8.00 20.00
207 Chris Johnson 30.00 60.00
210 Glenn Dorsey
215 Colt Brennan 8.00 20.00
218 Limas Sweed 8.00 20.00

2008 Topps Rookie Progression Rookies

*BRONZE/389: .5X TO 1.2X BASIC INSERTS
L/R/V BRONZE/389 ODDS 1:16
*SILVER/299: .6X TO 1.5X BASIC INSERTS
L/R/V SILVER/299 ODDS 1:21
*GOLD/199: .8X TO 2X BASIC INSERTS
L/R/V GOLD/199 ODDS 1:32
*PLATINUM/50: 1X TO 2.5X BASIC INSERTS
L/R/V PLATINUM/50 ODDS 1:125
PRAB Adarius Bowman .60 1.50
PRAC Andre Caldwell .60 1.50
PRAH Ali Highsmith .50 1.25
PRAW Andre Woodson .75 2.00
PRBB Brian Brohm .75 2.00
PRBM Ben Moffitt .50 1.25
PRCB Colt Brennan .75 2.00
PRCG Charles Godfrey .75 2.00
PRCH Chad Henne .75 2.00
PRCJ Chris Johnson 2.00 5.00
PRCW Chauncey Washington .60 1.50
PRDA Donnie Avery .60 1.50
PRDB Dorien Bryant .60 1.50
PRDC Dan Connor .75 2.00
PRDH DJ Hall .60 1.50
PRDR Darrell Robertson .50 1.25
PRDRC Dominique Rodgers-Cromartie .75 2.00
PRDS Dantrell Savage .60 1.50
PREA Erik Ainge .75 2.00
PRED Early Doucet .60 1.50
PRER Eddie Royal .75 2.00
PRFD Fred Davis .75 2.00
PRHD Harry Douglas .60 1.50
PRJB John David Booty .60 1.50
PRJF Joe Flacco 2.50 6.00
PRJFO Justin Forsett .75 2.00
PRJH Jacob Hester .75 2.00
PRJN Jordy Nelson 1.00 2.50
PRKB Keenan Burton .50 1.25
PRKD Kellen Davis .50 1.25
PRKR Keith Rivers .75 2.00
PRLH Lavelle Hawkins .50 1.25
PRLJ Lawrence Jackson .60 1.50
PRLM Leodis McKelvin .60 1.50
PRLS Limas Sweed .75 2.00
PRMF Matt Forte 1.25 3.00
PRMG Marcus Griffin .50 1.25
PRMJ Mike Jenkins .75 2.00
PRMR Matt Ryan 3.00 8.00
PRMRU Martin Rucker .60 1.50
PRMS Marcus Smith .60 1.50
PRPH Peyton Hillis 1.50 4.00
PRQG Quentin Groves .60 1.50
PRRL Rafael Little .60 1.50
PRSE Sedrick Ellis .75 2.00
PRTC Tashard Choice .60 1.50
PRTD Thomas DeCoud .50 1.25
PRTP Tracy Porter .75 2.00
PRTZ Tom Zbikowski .75 2.00
PRYB Yvenson Bernard .75 2.00

2008 Topps Rookie Progression Rookies Game Worn Jerseys Bronze

BRONZE PRINT RUN 299 SER.#'d SETS
*SILVER/199: .5X TO 1.2X BRONZE JSY
SILVER PRINT RUN 199 SER.#'d SETS
*GOLD/99: .6X TO 1.5X BRONZE JSY
GOLD PRINT RUN 99 SER.#'d SETS
UNPRICED L/V/R PLAT.AU/20 ODDS 1:554
PRAB Adarius Bowman 2.50 6.00
PRAC Andre Caldwell 2.50 6.00
PRAH Ali Highsmith 2.00 5.00
PRAW Andre Woodson 3.00 8.00
PRCB Colt Brennan 3.00 8.00
PRCH Chad Henne 6.00 15.00
PRCJ Chris Johnson 8.00 20.00
PRCW Chauncey Washington 2.50 6.00
PRDA Donnie Avery 2.50 6.00
PRDB Dorien Bryant 2.50 6.00
PRDC Dan Connor 3.00 8.00
PRDH DJ Hall 2.50 6.00
PRDS Dantrell Savage 2.50 6.00
PREA Erik Ainge 3.00 8.00
PRED Early Doucet 2.50 6.00
PRER Eddie Royal 3.00 8.00
PRFD Fred Davis 3.00 8.00
PRHD Harry Douglas 2.50 6.00
PRJB John David Booty 2.50 6.00
PRJF Joe Flacco 6.00 15.00
PRJFO Justin Forsett 3.00 8.00
PRJH Jacob Hester 3.00 8.00
PRKB Keenan Burton 2.00 5.00
PRKR Keith Rivers 3.00 8.00
PRLH Lavelle Hawkins 2.00 5.00
PRLS Limas Sweed 3.00 8.00
PRMF Matt Forte 5.00 12.00
PRRL Rafael Little 2.50 6.00
PRTC Tashard Choice 2.50 6.00
PRYB Yvenson Bernard 3.00 8.00

2008 Topps Rookie Progression Signatures

GROUP A ODDS 1:1664
GROUP B ODDS 1:381
GROUP C ODDS 1:602
GROUP D ODDS 1:179
GROUP E ODDS 1:150
GROUP F ODDS 1:449
GROUP G ODDS 1:299
GROUP H ODDS 1:112
GROUP I ODDS 1:45
GROUP J ODDS 1:149
AB Adarius Bowman I 3.00 8.00
AW Andre Woodson B 5.00 12.00
BB Brian Brohm A 8.00 20.00
BJ Brandon Jacobs A 6.00 15.00
BW Brian Westbrook A 12.00 30.00
CB Colt Brennan A 15.00 40.00
CH Chad Henne A
CJ Chris Johnson J 15.00 40.00
CL Chris Long D 4.00 10.00
DA Derek Anderson A 8.00 20.00

DC Dan Connor E	4.00	10.00
DD Dennis Dixon B	8.00	20.00
DF De'Cody Fagg H	3.00	8.00
DH DJ Hall I	3.00	8.00
DJ DeSean Jackson B	10.00	25.00
DM Darren McFadden A	25.00	60.00
EA Erik Ainge E	4.00	10.00
EB Earl Bennett I	4.00	10.00
ED Early Doucett C	3.00	8.00
ES Ernie Sims E	3.00	8.00
FD Fred Davis H	4.00	10.00
FJ Felix Jones A	25.00	60.00
GD Glenn Dorsey D EXCH		
GJ Greg Jennings B	8.00	20.00
JB John David Booty B	4.00	10.00
JF Joe Flacco B	30.00	60.00
JH James Hardy D	3.00	8.00
JL Jake Long F	4.00	10.00
JS Jonathan Stewart A	25.00	50.00
KR Keith Rivers D	4.00	10.00
KS Kevin Smith G	4.00	10.00
LS Limas Sweed B	5.00	12.00
LT LaDainian Tomlinson A	25.00	50.00
MB Marion Barber A	15.00	40.00
MH Mike Hart B	5.00	12.00
MK Malcolm Kelly C	3.00	8.00
ML Marshawn Lynch A	10.00	25.00
MM Mario Manningham D	6.00	15.00
MR Matt Ryan A	50.00	100.00
PM Peyton Manning A		
PW Patrick Willis B	6.00	15.00
RG Ryan Grant B EXCH		
RM Rashard Mendenhall A	25.00	60.00
RR Ray Rice E	8.00	20.00
RW Roddy White B	4.00	10.00
SS Steve Slaton B	6.00	15.00
TC Tashard Choice I	3.00	8.00
WW Wes Welker C	15.00	30.00

2008 Topps Rookie Progression Signatures Bronze

BRONZE/35 ODDS 1:282
*SILVER/20: .6X TO 1.5X BRONZE AU/35
SILVER/20 ODDS 1:519
UNPRICED GOLD/10 ODDS 1:932
UNPRICED PLAT/1 ODDS 1:9502

AB Adarius Bowman	6.00	15.00
AW Andre Woodson	10.00	25.00
BB Brian Brohm	10.00	25.00
BJ Brandon Jacobs	10.00	25.00
BW Brian Westbrook	12.00	30.00
CB Colt Brennan	15.00	40.00
CH Chad Henne	8.00	20.00
CJ Chris Johnson	40.00	80.00
CL Chris Long	8.00	20.00
DA Derek Anderson	8.00	20.00
DC Dan Connor	8.00	20.00
DD Dennis Dixon	12.00	30.00
DF De'Cody Fagg	6.00	15.00
DH DJ Hall	6.00	15.00
DJ DeSean Jackson	15.00	40.00
DM Darren McFadden	25.00	60.00
EA Erik Ainge	8.00	20.00
EB Earl Bennett	8.00	20.00
ED Early Doucett	6.00	15.00
ES Ernie Sims	8.00	20.00
FD Fred Davis	8.00	20.00
FJ Felix Jones	25.00	60.00
GD Glenn Dorsey EXCH		
GJ Greg Jennings	12.00	30.00
JB John David Booty	6.00	15.00
JF Joe Flacco	40.00	80.00
JH James Hardy	6.00	15.00
JL Jake Long	8.00	20.00
JS Jonathan Stewart	12.00	30.00
KR Keith Rivers	8.00	20.00
KS Kevin Smith	8.00	20.00
LS Limas Sweed	8.00	20.00
LT LaDainian Tomlinson	30.00	60.00
MB Marion Barber	30.00	50.00
MH Mike Hart	8.00	20.00
MK Malcolm Kelly	6.00	15.00
ML Marshawn Lynch	15.00	40.00
MM Mario Manningham	12.00	30.00
MR Matt Ryan	50.00	100.00
PM Peyton Manning	60.00	100.00
PW Patrick Willis	10.00	25.00
RG Ryan Grant EXCH		
RM Rashard Mendenhall	25.00	60.00
RR Ray Rice	12.00	30.00
RW Roddy White	10.00	25.00
SS Steve Slaton	8.00	20.00
TC Tashard Choice	6.00	15.00
WW Wes Welker	25.00	50.00

2008 Topps Rookie Progression Signatures Dual

DUAL AUTO/20 ODDS 1:1663

GJ Ryan Grant Greg Jennings	50.00	100.00
HJ Lavelle Hawkins DeSean Jackson	25.00	50.00
HM Mike Hart Mario Manningham	25.00	50.00
JB Brandon Jacobs Marion Barber	25.00	60.00
LF Marshawn Lynch Justin Forsett	25.00	50.00
MA Peyton Manning Erik Ainge	75.00	150.00
MJ Darren McFadden Felix Jones	60.00	150.00
RB Matt Ryan Brian Brohm	100.00	200.00
RS Ray Rice Steve Slaton	40.00	80.00
SB Dontrell Savage Adarius Bowman	20.00	40.00
SK Limas Sweed Malcolm Kelly	20.00	50.00
SM Jonathan Stewart Rashard Mendenhall	30.00	80.00
TM LaDainian Tomlinson Darren McFadden	60.00	120.00
WB Andre Woodson Colt Brennan	20.00	50.00
WJ Brian Westbrook Chris Johnson	60.00	100.00

2008 Topps Rookie Progression Signatures Triple

UNPRICED TRIPLE AU/10 ODDS 1:5030

2008 Topps Rookie Progression Veterans

*BRONZE/389: .5X TO 1.2X BASIC INSERTS
L/R/V BRONZE/389 ODDS 1:16
*SILVER/299: .6X TO 1.5X BASIC INSERTS
L/R/V SILVER/299 ODDS 1:21
*GOLD/199: .8X TO 2X BASIC INSERTS
L/R/V GOLD/199 ODDS 1:32
*PLATINUM/50: 1X TO 2.5X BASIC INSERTS
L/R/V PLATINUM/50 ODDS 1:125

PVAG Antonio Gates	1.00	2.50
PVAP Adrian Peterson	1.50	4.00
PVBE Braylon Edwards	.75	2.00
PVBJ Brandon Jacobs	.75	2.00
PVBM Brandon Marshall	.75	2.00
PVBR Ben Roethlisberger	1.00	2.50
PVBW Brian Westrbook	.75	2.00
PVCP Carson Palmer	1.00	2.50
PVCPO Clinton Portis	.75	2.00
PVDA Derek Anderson	.60	1.50
PVDB Drew Brees	1.00	2.50
PVDH Devin Hester	1.00	2.50
PVFT Fred Taylor	.75	2.00
PVJA Joseph Addai	.75	2.00
PVJL Jamal Lewis	.75	2.00
PVKW Kellen Winslow	.75	2.00
PVLF Larry Fitzgerald	1.00	2.50
PVLT LaDainian Tomlinson	1.00	2.50
PVPM Peyton Manning	1.50	4.00
PVRM Randy Moss	1.00	2.50
PVRW Reggie Wayne	.75	2.00
PVSH Santonio Holmes	.75	2.00
PVSJ Steven Jackson	1.00	2.50
PVTB Tom Brady	1.50	4.00
PVTH T.J. Houshmandzadeh	.75	2.00
PVTO Terrell Owens	1.00	2.50
PVTR Tony Romo	1.25	3.00
PVVY Vince Young	.75	2.00
PVWP Willie Parker	.75	2.00

2008 Topps Rookie Progression Veterans Game Worn Jerseys Bronze

BRONZE PRINT RUN 299 SER.#'d SETS
*SILVER/199: .5X TO 1.2X BRONZE JSYs
SILVER PRINT RUN 199 SER.#'d SETS
*GOLD/99: .6X TO 1.5X BRONZE JSYs
GOLD PRINT RUN 99 SER.#'d SETS
UNPRICED L/V/R PLAT.AU/20 ODDS 1:554

PVAG Antonio Gates	4.00	10.00
PVBE Braylon Edwards	3.00	8.00
PVBJ Brandon Jacobs	3.00	8.00
PVBM Brandon Marshall	3.00	8.00
PVDA Derek Anderson	2.50	6.00
PVDB Drew Brees	4.00	10.00
PVDH Devin Hester	5.00	12.00
PVJA Joseph Addai	3.00	8.00
PVKW Kellen Winslow	3.00	8.00
PVLT LaDainian Tomlinson	4.00	10.00
PVPM Peyton Manning	6.00	15.00
PVRM Randy Moss	4.00	10.00
PVRW Reggie Wayne	3.00	8.00
PVSH Santonio Holmes	3.00	8.00
PVSJ Steven Jackson	4.00	10.00
PVTH T.J. Houshmandzadeh	3.00	8.00
PVTR Tony Romo	5.00	12.00
PVVY Vince Young	3.00	8.00
PVWP Willie Parker	3.00	8.00

2008 Topps Rookie Progression Veterans Game Worn Jerseys Platinum Autographs

VETERAN PLAT.AU/20 ODDS 1:554

PVAG Antonio Gates	20.00	50.00
PVBE Braylon Edwards	15.00	40.00
PVBJ Brandon Jacobs	15.00	40.00
PVBM Brandon Marshall	15.00	40.00
PVDA Derek Anderson	12.00	30.00
PVDB Drew Brees	40.00	80.00
PVDH Devin Hester	20.00	50.00
PVJA Joseph Addai	15.00	40.00
PVKW Kellen Winslow	15.00	40.00
PVLT LaDainian Tomlinson	30.00	60.00
PVPM Peyton Manning	75.00	150.00
PVRM Randy Moss	40.00	80.00
PVRW Reggie Wayne	15.00	40.00
PVSH Santonio Holmes	15.00	40.00
PVSJ Steven Jackson	20.00	50.00
PVTH T.J. Houshmandzadeh	15.00	40.00
PVTR Tony Romo	50.00	100.00
PVVY Vince Young	15.00	40.00
PVWP Willie Parker	15.00	40.00

1998 Topps Season Opener

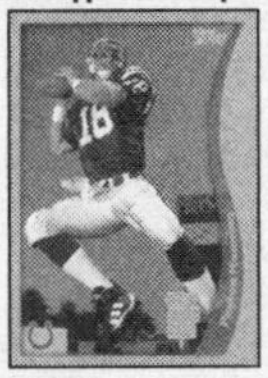

COMPLETE SET (165)	30.00	80.00
*STARS: .4X TO 1X BASE TOPPS		
SEASON OPENER RETAIL ONLY PRODUCT		
1 Peyton Manning RC	8.00	20.00
2 Jerome Pathon RC	1.00	2.50
3 Duane Starks RC	.50	1.25
4 Brian Simmons RC	.75	2.00
5 Keith Brooking RC	1.00	2.50
6 Robert Edwards RC	.75	2.00
7 Curtis Enis RC	.50	1.25
8 John Avery RC	.75	2.00
9 Fred Taylor RC	1.50	4.00
10 Germane Crowell RC	.75	2.00
11 Hines Ward RC	4.00	10.00
12 Marcus Nash RC	.50	1.25
13 Jacquez Green RC	.75	2.00
14 Joe Jurevicius RC	1.00	2.50
15 Greg Ellis RC	.50	1.25
16 Brian Griese RC	1.50	4.00
17 Tavian Banks RC	.75	2.00
18 Robert Holcombe RC	.75	2.00
19 Skip Hicks RC	.75	2.00
20 Ahman Green RC	2.00	5.00
21 Takeo Spikes RC	1.00	2.50
22 Randy Moss RC	5.00	12.00
23 Andre Wadsworth RC	.75	2.00
24 Jason Peter RC	.50	1.25
25 Grant Wistrom RC	.75	2.00
26 Charles Woodson RC	1.25	3.00
27 Kevin Dyson RC	1.00	2.50
28 Pat Johnson RC	.75	2.00
29 Tim Dwight RC	1.00	2.50
30 Ryan Leaf RC	1.00	2.50

1999 Topps Season Opener

Released as a retail product, this 165-card set incorporates the 1999 Topps card-stock but is enhanced with a foil "Season Opener" stamp.

COMPLETE SET (165)	20.00	40.00
1 Jerry Rice	.40	1.00
2 Emmitt Smith	.50	1.25
3 Curtis Martin	.20	.50
4 Ed McCaffrey	.15	.40
5 Oronde Gadsden	.12	.30
6 Byron Bam Morris	.12	.30
7 Michael Irvin	.20	.50
8 Shannon Sharpe	.20	.50
9 Levon Kirkland	.12	.30
10 Fred Taylor	.15	.40
11 Andre Reed	.20	.50
12 Chad Brown	.12	.30
13 Skip Hicks	.12	.30
14 Tim Dwight	.15	.40
15 Michael Sinclair	.12	.30
16 Carl Pickens	.15	.40
17 Derrick Alexander WR	.12	.30
18 Kevin Greene	.15	.40
19 Duce Staley	.15	.40
20 Dan Marino	.60	1.50
21 Frank Sanders	.12	.30
22 Ricky Proehl	.12	.30
23 Frank Wycheck	.15	.40
24 Andre Rison	.15	.40
25 Natrone Means	.15	.40
26 Steve McNair	.20	.50
27 Vonnie Holliday	.12	.30
28 Charles Woodson	.20	.50
29 Rob Moore	.12	.30
30 John Elway	.60	1.50
31 Derrick Thomas	.20	.50
32 Jake Plummer	.15	.40
33 Mike Alstott	.20	.50
34 Keenan McCardell	.15	.40
35 Mark Chmura	.12	.30
36 Keyshawn Johnson	.15	.40
37 Priest Holmes	.20	.50
38 Antonio Freeman	.15	.40
39 Ty Law	.15	.40
40 Jamal Anderson	.15	.40
41 Courtney Hawkins	.12	.30
42 James Jett	.12	.30
43 Aaron Glenn	.12	.30
44 Jimmy Smith	.15	.40
45 Michael McCrary	.12	.30
46 Junior Seau	.20	.50
47 Bill Romanowski	.15	.40
48 Mark Brunell	.15	.40
49 Yancey Thigpen	.12	.30
50 Steve Young	.25	.60
51 Cris Carter	.20	.50
52 Vinny Testaverde	.15	.40
53 Zach Thomas	.20	.50
54 Kordell Stewart	.15	.40
55 Tim Biakabutuka	.15	.40
56 J.J. Stokes	.12	.30
57 Jon Kitna	.15	.40
58 Jacquez Green	.12	.30
59 Marvin Harrison	.20	.50
60 Barry Sanders	.50	1.25
61 Darrell Green	.20	.50
62 Terance Mathis	.12	.30
63 Ricky Watters	.15	.40
64 Chris Chandler	.15	.40
65 Cameron Cleeland	.12	.30
66 Rod Smith	.15	.40
67 Freddie Jones	.12	.30
68 Adrian Murrell	.15	.40
69 Terrell Owens	.20	.50
70 Troy Aikman	.30	.75
71 John Mobley	.12	.30
72 Corey Dillon	.15	.40
73 Rickey Dudley	.12	.30
74 Randall Cunningham	.20	.50
75 Muhsin Muhammad	.15	.40
76 Stephen Boyd	.12	.30
77 Tony Gonzalez	.20	.50
78 Deion Sanders	.20	.50
79 Ben Coates	.15	.40
80 Brett Favre	.60	1.50
81 Shawn Springs	.12	.30
82 Dorsey Levens	.15	.40
83 Ray Buchanan	.12	.30
84 Charlie Batch	.15	.40
85 John Randle	.15	.40
86 Eddie George	.15	.40
87 Ray Lewis	.20	.50
88 Johnnie Morton	.15	.40
89 Kevin Hardy	.12	.30
90 O.J. McDuffie	.15	.40
91 Herman Moore	.15	.40
92 Tim Brown	.20	.50
93 Bert Emanuel	.15	.40
94 Elvis Grbac	.12	.30
95 Peter Boulware	.12	.30
96 Curtis Conway	.15	.40
97 Doug Flutie	.20	.50
98 Jake Reed	.15	.40
99 Ike Hilliard	.15	.40
100 Randy Moss	.20	.50
101 Warren Sapp	.15	.40
102 Bruce Smith	.20	.50
103 Joey Galloway	.15	.40
104 Napoleon Kaufman	.12	.30
105 Warrick Dunn	.15	.40
106 Wayne Chrebet	.15	.40
107 Robert Brooks	.15	.40
108 Antowain Smith	.12	.30
109 Trent Dilfer	.15	.40
110 Peyton Manning	.60	1.50
111 Isaac Bruce	.20	.50
112 John Lynch	.15	.40
113 Terry Glenn	.15	.40
114 Garrison Hearst	.15	.40
115 Jerome Bettis	.20	.50
116 Damay Scott	.12	.30
117 Lamar Thomas	.12	.30
118 Chris Spielman	.15	.40
119 Robert Smith	.15	.40
120 Drew Bledsoe	.20	.50
121 Reidel Anthony	.12	.30
122 Wesley Walls	.15	.40
123 Eric Moulds	.15	.40
124 Terrell Davis	.20	.50
125 Dale Carter	.12	.30
126 Charles Johnson	.12	.30
127 Steve Atwater	.15	.40
128 Jim Harbaugh	.15	.40
129 Tony Martin	.15	.40
130 Kerry Collins	.15	.40
131 Trent Green	.15	.40
132 Marshall Faulk	.20	.50
133 Rocket Ismail	.15	.40
134 Warren Moon	.20	.50
135 Jerris McPhail	.12	.30
136 Damon Gibson	.12	.30
137 Jim Pyne	.12	.30
138 Antonio Langham	.12	.30
139 Freddie Solomon	.12	.30
140 Randy Moss SH	.20	.50
141 John Elway SH	.60	1.50
142 Doug Flutie SH	.20	.50
143 Emmitt Smith SH	.50	1.25
144 Terrell Davis SH	.20	.50
145 Troy Edwards RC	.50	1.25
146 Torry Holt RC	1.00	2.50
147 Tim Couch RC	.60	1.50
148 Sedrick Irvin RC	.40	1.00
149 Ricky Williams RC	1.00	2.50
150 Peerless Price RC	.50	1.25
151 Mike Cloud RC	.40	1.00
152 Kevin Faulk RC	.60	1.50
153 Kevin Johnson RC	.50	1.25
154 James Johnson RC	.40	1.00
155 Edgerrin James RC	.75	2.00
156 D'Wayne Bates RC	.40	1.00
157 Donovan McNabb RC	2.50	6.00
158 David Boston RC	.50	1.25
159 Daunte Culpepper RC	.60	1.50
160 Champ Bailey RC	1.25	3.00
161 Cecil Collins RC	.40	1.00
162 Cade McNown RC	.50	1.25
163 Brock Huard RC	.50	1.25
164 Akili Smith RC	.50	1.25
165 Checklist Card	.10	.30

1999 Topps Season Opener Autographs

STATED ODDS 1:7126

A1 Tim Couch	30.00	80.00
A2 Peyton Manning	60.00	150.00

1999 Topps Season Opener Football Fever

COMPLETE SET (55)	10.00	20.00
ONE PER PACK		
F1A Brett Favre 9/26 W	.75	2.00
F1B Brett Favre 10/17	.40	1.00
F1C Brett Favre 11/07	.40	1.00
F1D Brett Favre 11/29	.40	1.00
F2A Jake Plummer 9/27	.07	.20
F2B Jake Plummer 10/03	.07	.20
F2C Jake Plummer 10/31	.07	.20
F2D Jake Plummer 12/05	.07	.20
F3A Drew Bledsoe 9/19	.15	.40
F3B Drew Bledsoe 10/03 W	.30	.75
F3C Drew Bledsoe 10/24	.15	.40
F3D Drew Bledsoe 12/05	.15	.40
F4A Peyton Manning 9/12	.30	.75
F4B Peyton Manning 10/17	.30	.75
F4C Peyton Manning 10/24	.30	.75
F4D Peyton Manning 12/12	.30	.75
F5A Tim Couch 10/10	.08	.25
F5B Tim Couch 11/21	.08	.25
F5C Tim Couch 11/28	.08	.25
F5D Tim Couch 12/05	.08	.25
F6A Terrell Davis 9/13	.10	.30
F6B Terrell Davis 10/03	.10	.30
F6C Terrell Davis 10/31	.10	.30
F6D Terrell Davis 12/19	.10	.30
F7A Jamal Anderson 9/12	.10	.30
F7B Jamal Anderson 10/17	.10	.30
F7C Jamal Anderson 10/25	.10	.30
F7D Jamal Anderson 12/05	.10	.30
F8A Curtis Martin 9/12	.10	.30
F8B Curtis Martin 10/17 W	.25	.60
F8C Curtis Martin 10/24 W	.25	.80
F8D Curtis Martin 11/21	.10	.30
F9A Fred Taylor 9/26	.08	.25
F9B Fred Taylor 10/17	.08	.25
F9C Fred Taylor 10/31 W	.20	.50
F9D Fred Taylor 12/12	.08	.25
F10A Ricky Williams 10/3	.20	.50
F10B Ricky Williams 10/10	.20	.50
F10C Ricky Williams 10/31 W	.40	1.00
F10D Ricky Williams 12/12	.20	.50
F11A Antonio Freeman 9/26	.10	.30
F11B Antonio Freeman 11/29	.10	.30
F11C Antonio Freeman 12/12	.10	.30
F12A Jerry Rice 9/19	.25	.60
F12B Jerry Rice 10/24	.25	.60
F12C Jerry Rice 11/29	.25	.60
F13A Jimmy Smith 10/17	.07	.20
F13B Jimmy Smith 10/31	.07	.20
F13C Jimmy Smith 12/13	.07	.20
F14A Randy Moss 10/24	.30	.75
F14B Randy Moss 11/08	.30	.75
F14C Randy Moss 12/20 W	.60	1.50
F15A Torry Holt 10/03	.20	.50
F15B Torry Holt 10/24	.20	.50
F15C Torry Holt 12/05	.20	.50

2000 Topps Season Opener

Released as a retail product, Topps Season Opener utilizes the same card stock as the regular Topps Set but replaced the blue border with a burgandy one and each card has a silver foil Season Opener stamp. Topps Season Opener was packaged in 24-pack boxes with each pack containing seven cards plus one Football Fever card.

COMPLETE SET (220)	15.00	40.00
1 Tyrone Wheatley	.10	.25
2 Carl Pickens	.12	.30
3 Zach Thomas	.15	.40
4 Jacquez Green	.10	.25
5 Sean Dawkins	.10	.25
6 Brad Johnson	.12	.30
7 Jerry Rice	.30	.75
8 Doug Flutie	.15	.40
9 Cade McNown	.10	.25
10 Rod Smith	.12	.30
11 Kevin Hardy	.10	.25
12 Marvin Harrison	.15	.40
13 David Boston	.10	.25
14 Priest Holmes	.15	.40
15 Keith Poole	.10	.25
16 Troy Edwards	.10	.25
17 Robert Smith	.12	.30
18 Kevin Lockett	.10	.25
19 Johnnie Morton	.12	.30
20 Terrell Davis	.15	.40
21 Corey Bradford	.10	.25
22 Keyshawn Johnson	.12	.30
23 Tony Banks	.10	.25
24 Matthew Hatchette	.10	.25
25 Troy Aikman	.25	.60
26 Natrone Means	.12	.30
27 Peerless Price	.12	.30
28 Bruce Smith	.15	.40
29 Tim Couch	.12	.30
30 Terrell Owens	.15	.40
31 O.J. McDuffie	.12	.30
32 Troy Brown	.12	.30
33 Corey Dillon	.12	.30
34 Cam Cleeland	.10	.25
35 Brian Griese	.12	.30
36 Shawn Springs	.10	.25
37 Marcus Robinson	.12	.30
38 Jermaine Lewis	.10	.25
39 Olandis Gary	.12	.30
40 Tony Gonzalez	.15	.40
41 Frank Wycheck	.12	.30
42 Jon Kitna	.12	.30
43 Muhsin Muhammad	.12	.30
44 Jerome Bettis	.15	.40
45 Darrin Chiaverini	.10	.25
46 Steve McNair	.15	.40
47 Charlie Batch	.12	.30
48 Steve Beuerlein	.12	.30
49 Dorsey Levens	.12	.30
50 Jim Harbaugh	.12	.30
51 Jonathan Linton	.10	.25
52 Napoleon Kaufman	.12	.30
53 Curtis Enis	.10	.25
54 Darnay Scott	.12	.30
55 Tim Dwight	.12	.30
56 Mikhael Ricks	.10	.25
57 Kevin Dyson	.12	.30
58 Antonio Freeman	.12	.30
59 E.G. Green	.10	.25
60 Jake Plummer	.12	.30
61 Bill Schroeder	.12	.30
62 Shaun King	.10	.25
63 Michael Basnight	.10	.25
64 Vinny Testaverde	.12	.30
65 Rob Johnson	.12	.30
66 Jeff Blake	.12	.30
67 Marshall Faulk	.15	.40
68 Keenan McCardell	.12	.30
69 Michael Westbrook	.10	.25
70 Yancey Thigpen	.10	.25
71 Akili Smith	.10	.25
72 Charles Woodson	.15	.40
73 Qadry Ismail	.12	.30
74 Pat Johnson	.10	.25
75 Rocket Ismail	.12	.30
76 Terrence Wilkins	.10	.25
77 Herman Moore	.12	.30
78 Jevon Kearse	.12	.30
79 Oronde Gadsden	.12	.30
80 Errict Rhett	.12	.30
81 Ed McCaffrey	.12	.30
82 Mike Alstott	.15	.40
83 Stephen Alexander	.10	.25
84 Mark Brunell	.12	.30
85 Jeff George	.12	.30
86 Stephen Davis	.12	.30
87 Germane Crowell	.10	.25
88 Charlie Garner	.12	.30
89 Kordell Stewart	.12	.30
90 Tim Biakabutuka	.12	.30
91 Jim Miller	.10	.25
92 Eddie George	.12	.30
93 Joe Montgomery	.10	.25
94 Wayne Chrebet	.12	.30
95 Freddie Jones	.10	.25
96 Ricky Proehl	.10	.25
97 Warren Sapp	.12	.30
98 Derrick Mayes	.10	.25
99 Daunte Culpepper	.12	.30
100 Torry Holt	.15	.40
101 Isaac Bruce	.15	.40
102 Kevin Johnson	.10	.25
103 Antowain Smith	.12	.30
104 Rob Moore	.10	.25
105 Joey Galloway	.12	.30
106 Rickey Dudley	.10	.25
107 Terry Glenn	.12	.30
108 Ike Hilliard	.12	.30
109 Jeff Graham	.10	.25
110 J.J. Stokes	.12	.30
111 Steve Young	.20	.50
112 Albert Connell	.10	.25
113 Tony Brackens	.10	.25
114 James Johnson	.10	.25
115 Tim Brown	.15	.40
116 Terance Mathis	.10	.25
117 Peyton Manning	.40	1.00
118 Kerry Collins	.12	.30
119 Duce Staley	.12	.30
120 Torrance Small	.10	.25
121 Curtis Martin	.15	.40
122 Damon Huard	.12	.30
123 Derrick Alexander	.10	.25
124 Jimmy Smith	.12	.30
125 Cris Carter	.15	.40
126 Jamal Anderson	.12	.30
127 Eric Moulds	.12	.30
128 Drew Bledsoe	.15	.40
129 Ricky Williams	.15	.40
130 Andre Hastings	.10	.25
131 Amani Toomer	.12	.30
132 Rich Gannon	.12	.30
133 Richard Huntley	.10	.25
134 Donovan McNabb	.15	.40
135 Jermaine Fazande	.10	.25
136 Randy Moss	.15	.40
137 Champ Bailey	.12	.30
138 Elvis Grbac	.10	.25
139 Warrick Dunn	.12	.30
140 John Randle	.12	.30
141 Edgerrin James	.15	.40
142 Tony Martin	.12	.30
143 Chris Chandler	.12	.30
144 Stephen Boyd	.10	.25
145 Az-Zahir Hakim	.10	.25
146 Tony Simmons	.10	.25
147 Pete Mitchell	.10	.25
148 Junior Seau	.15	.40
149 Ricky Watters	.12	.30
150 Michael Pittman	.10	.25
151 Fred Taylor	.15	.40
152 Charles Johnson	.10	.25
153 Jason Tucker	.10	.25
154 Brett Favre	.50	1.25
155 Patrick Jeffers	.12	.30
156 Curtis Conway	.12	.30
157 Frank Sanders	.10	.25
158 James Stewart	.10	.25
159 Emmitt Smith	.40	1.00
160 Jessie Armstead	.10	.25
161 Wesley Walls	.10	.25
162 Kent Graham	.10	.25
163 Kurt Warner	.25	.60
164 Shawn Jefferson	.10	.25
165 Jammi German	.10	.25
166 Jay Riemersma	.10	.25
167 Fred Lane	.10	.25
168 Jamir Miller	.10	.25
169 David LaFleur	.10	.25
170 David Sloan	.10	.25
171 Jerome Pathon	.10	.25
172 Sam Madison	.10	.25
173 Tiki Barber	.15	.40
174 Yatil Green	.10	.25
175 Checklist	.08	.25
176 Kurt Warner HL	.20	.50
177 Brett Favre HL	.40	1.00
178 Marshall Faulk HL	.12	.30
179 Jevon Kearse HL	.10	.25
180 Edgerrin James CL	.12	.30
181 Troy Aikman CS	.20	.50
182 Terrell Davis CS	.12	.30
183 Steve Beuerlein CS	.10	.25
184 Tim Brown CS	.12	.30
185 Randy Moss CS	.12	.30
186 Drew Bledsoe CS	.12	.30
187 Curtis Martin CS	.12	.30
188 Shannon Sharpe CS	.12	.30
189 Brett Favre CS	.40	1.00
190 Brad Johnson CS	.10	.25
191 Tony Gonzalez CS	.12	.30
192 Jon Kitna CS	.10	.25
193 Peyton Manning CS	.30	.75
194 Mark Brunell CS	.10	.25
195 Cade McNown CS	.08	.25
196 Jim Harbaugh CS	.10	.25
197 Shaun King CS	.08	.25
198 Kurt Warner CS	.20	.50
199 Eddie George CS	.10	.25
200 Ricky Williams CS	.12	.30
201 Curtis Keaton RC	.25	.60
202 Tee Martin RC	.40	1.00
203 Thomas Jones RC	.50	1.25
204 Giovanni Carmazzi RC	.25	.60
205 Courtney Brown RC	.30	.75
206 Shaun Alexander RC	.50	1.25
207 Travis Taylor RC	.30	.75
208 Dennis Northcutt RC	.30	.75
209 Trung Canidate RC	.30	.75
210 Jamal Lewis RC	.40	1.00
211 R.Jay Soward RC	.25	.60
212 Sylvester Morris RC	.25	.60
213 Ron Dugans RC	.25	.60
214 Chris Redman RC	.30	.75
215 Plaxico Burress RC	.40	1.00
216 Peter Warrick RC	.40	1.00
217 Travis Prentice RC	.30	.75
218 Ron Dayne RC	.40	1.00
219 J.R. Redmond RC	.25	.60
220 Chad Pennington RC	.60	1.50

2000 Topps Season Opener Autographs

AUTO/100-300 OVERALL ODDS 1:2296

A1 Kurt Warner/100	30.00	60.00
A2 Marvin Harrison/300	15.00	30.00
A3 Stephen Davis/300	10.00	25.00
A4 Joe Montana/200	60.00	120.00

2000 Topps Season Opener Football Fever

COMPLETE SET (55)	6.00	15.00
F1A Brett Favre	.50	1.25
F1B Brett Favre	.50	1.25
F1C Brett Favre	.50	1.25
F1D Brett Favre	.50	1.25
F2A Kurt Warner	.25	.60
F2B Kurt Warner	.25	.60
F2C Kurt Warner	.25	.60
F2D Kurt Warner	.25	.60
F3A Brad Johnson	.12	.30
F3B Brad Johnson	.12	.30
F3C Brad Johnson	.12	.30
F3D Brad Johnson	.12	.30
F4A Peyton Manning	.40	1.00
F4B Peyton Manning	.40	1.00
F4C Peyton Manning	.40	1.00
F4D Peyton Manning	.40	1.00
F5A Drew Bledsoe	.15	.40
F5B Drew Bledsoe	.15	.40
F5C Drew Bledsoe	.15	.40
F5D Drew Bledsoe	.15	.40
F6A Terrell Davis	.15	.40
F6B Terrell Davis	.15	.40
F6C Terrell Davis	.15	.40
F6D Terrell Davis	.15	.40
F7A Edgerrin James	.15	.40
F7B Edgerrin James	.15	.40
F7C Edgerrin James	.15	.40
F7D Edgerrin James	.15	.40
F8A Stephen Davis	.12	.30
F8B Stephen Davis	.12	.30
F8C Stephen Davis	.12	.30
F8D Stephen Davis	.12	.30
F9A Fred Taylor	.15	.40
F9B Fred Taylor	.15	.40
F9C Fred Taylor	.15	.40
F9D Fred Taylor	.15	.40
F10A Jamal Lewis	.10	.25
F10B Jamal Lewis	.10	.25
F10C Jamal Lewis	.10	.25
F10D Jamal Lewis	.10	.25
F11A Marvin Harrison	.15	.40
F11B Marvin Harrison	.15	.40
F11C Marvin Harrison	.15	.40
F11D Marvin Harrison	.15	.40
F12A Isaac Bruce	.15	.40
F12B Isaac Bruce	.15	.40
F12C Isaac Bruce	.15	.40
F12D Isaac Bruce	.15	.40
F13A Jimmy Smith	.12	.30
F13B Jimmy Smith	.12	.30
F13C Jimmy Smith	.12	.30
F13D Jimmy Smith	.12	.30
F14A Randy Moss	.15	.40
F14B Randy Moss	.15	.40
F14C Randy Moss	.15	.40
F14D Randy Moss	.15	.40
F15A Peter Warrick	.15	.40
F15B Peter Warrick	.15	.40
F15C Peter Warrick	.15	.40
F15D Peter Warrick	.15	.40

2004 Topps Signature

Topps Signature was initially released in late-December 2004. The base set consists of 96-cards including 20-rookies serial numbered to 499 and 21-signed rookie cards serial numbered between 299 and 1499. Hobby boxes contained 4-packs of 5-cards and carried an S.R.P. of $50 per pack with one autographed card per pack. Two parallel sets and a variety of autographed inserts can be found seeded in packs highlighted by the Canton Cuts 1/1 autographs.

COMP.SET w/o SP's (55)	15.00	40.00
56-75 ROOKIE/499 STATED ODDS 1:3		
ROOKIE AU/299 GROUP A ODDS 1:15		
ROOKIE AU/999 GROUP B ODDS 1:11		
ROOKIE AU/1099 GROUP C ODDS 1:4		
ROOKIE AU/1499 GROUP D ODDS 1:3		
1 Tom Brady	2.00	5.00
2 Chad Johnson	1.00	2.50
3 Amani Toomer	.75	2.00
4 Shaun Alexander	.75	2.00
5 Terrell Owens	1.00	2.50
6 Jake Delhomme	.75	2.00
7 Eric Moulds	.75	2.00
8 Fred Taylor	.75	2.00
9 Mark Brunell	.75	2.00
10 Priest Holmes	1.00	2.50
11 Marvin Harrison	1.00	2.50
12 Jeff Garcia	.75	2.00
13 Brad Johnson	.75	2.00
14 Laveranues Coles	.60	1.50
15 LaDainian Tomlinson	1.00	2.50
16 Anquan Boldin	1.00	2.50
17 Curtis Martin	1.00	2.50
18 Joe Horn	.75	2.00
19 Domanick Davis	.60	1.50
20 Jamal Lewis	.75	2.00
21 Steve Smith	1.00	2.50
22 Aaron Brooks	.75	2.00
23 Hines Ward	1.00	2.50
24 Marc Bulger	.75	2.00
25 Randy Moss	1.00	2.50
26 Jerry Rice	2.00	5.00
27 Tiki Barber	1.00	2.50
28 Jake Plummer	.75	2.00
29 Travis Henry	.60	1.50
30 Michael Vick	1.25	3.00
31 Matt Hasselbeck	.75	2.00
32 Santana Moss	.75	2.00
33 Corey Dillon	.75	2.00
34 Byron Leftwich	.75	2.00
35 Clinton Portis	1.00	2.50
36 Derrick Mason	.75	2.00
37 Tim Rattay	.60	1.50
38 Chris Chambers	.75	2.00
39 Joey Harrington	.75	2.00
40 Deuce McAllister	.75	2.00
41 Tony Gonzalez	1.00	2.50
42 Kurt Warner	1.00	2.50
43 Carson Palmer	1.00	2.50
44 Marshall Faulk	1.00	2.50
45 Peyton Manning	2.00	5.00
46 Ahman Green	.75	2.00
47 Torry Holt	.75	2.00
48 Chad Pennington	1.00	2.50
49 Trent Green	.75	2.00
50 Brett Favre	2.50	6.00
51 Stephen Davis	.75	2.00
52 Steve McNair	1.00	2.50
53 Daunte Culpepper	.75	2.00
54 Edgerrin James	.75	2.00
55 Donovan McNabb	1.00	2.50
56 Sean Taylor RC	5.00	12.00
57 Darius Watts RC	1.50	4.00
58 Ben Troupe RC	2.00	5.00
59 Josh Harris RC	1.50	4.00
60 Jeff Smoker RC	2.00	5.00
61 Mewelde Moore RC	2.00	5.00
62 Reggie Williams RC	2.00	5.00
63 Ben Watson RC	2.50	6.00
64 Rashaun Woods RC	1.50	4.00
65 Kellen Winslow RC	2.50	6.00
66 Robert Gallery RC	2.50	6.00
67 Steven Jackson RC	4.00	10.00
68 Craig Krenzel RC	2.00	5.00
69 DeAngelo Hall RC	2.50	6.00
70 Devard Darling RC	1.50	4.00
71 Julius Jones RC	2.00	5.00
72 Derrick Hamilton RC	1.50	4.00
73 Devery Henderson RC	2.50	6.00
74 Dunta Robinson RC	1.50	4.00
75 Larry Fitzgerald RC	6.00	15.00
76 Chris Perry AU/999 RC	6.00	15.00
77 J.P. Losman AU/1099 RC	6.00	15.00
78 Lee Evans AU/1099 RC	8.00	20.00
79 Cedric Cobbs AU/1499 RC	5.00	12.00
80 Philip Rivers AU/299 RC	50.00	100.00
81 Greg Jones AU/1499 RC	5.00	12.00
82 Michael Clayton AU/1099 RC	6.00	15.00
83 Jonathan Vilma AU/1499 RC	8.00	20.00
84 Jerricho Cotchery AU/1499 RC	6.00	15.00
85 Roy Williams AU/299 RC	15.00	40.00
86 Keary Colbert AU/1499 RC	5.00	12.00
87 Luke McCown AU/1499 RC	6.00	15.00
88 Bernard Berrian AU/1499 RC	8.00	20.00
89 Michael Jenkins AU/1499 RC	8.00	20.00
90 Eli Manning AU/299 RC	125.00	250.00
91 Matt Schaub AU/1499 RC	20.00	40.00
92 Tatum Bell AU/1099 RC	6.00	15.00
93 Ben Roethlisberger AU/299 RC	100.00	175.00
94 Kevin Jones AU/1099 RC	6.00	15.00
95 Cody Pickett AU/999 RC	6.00	15.00
96 Drew Henson AU/299 RC	10.00	25.00

2004 Topps Signature Blue

*BLUE VETS 1-55: 2.5X TO 6X BASE CARDS
*BLUE ROOKIES 56-75: .6X TO 1.5X
1-75 PRINT RUN 50; ODDS 1:6
*ROOKIE AU: 1X TO 2.5X BASE AU
ROOKIE AU/50 ODDS 1:39
ROOKIE JSY AU/50 ODDS 1:43

77 J.P. Losman JSY AU	15.00	40.00
78 Lee Evans JSY AU	20.00	50.00
80 Philip Rivers JSY AU	75.00	150.00
82 Michael Clayton JSY AU	15.00	40.00
85 Roy Williams WR JSY AU	25.00	60.00
90 Eli Manning JSY AU	250.00	400.00
91 Matt Schaub AU	60.00	120.00
92 Tatum Bell JSY AU	15.00	40.00
93 Ben Roethlisberger JSY AU	175.00	350.00

94 Kevin Jones JSY AU 15.00 40.00
96 Drew Henson JSY AU 20.00 50.00

2004 Topps Signature Gold

1-75 GOLD STATED ODDS 1:286
ROOKIE AU STATED ODDS 1:1847
ROOKIE JSY AU STATED ODDS 1:2032
UNPRICED GOLD PRINT RUN 1 SET

2004 Topps Signature Autographs Green

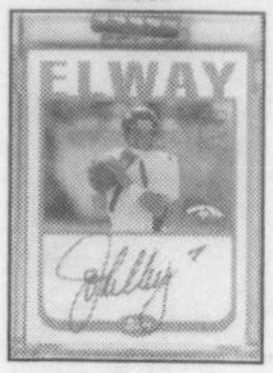

GROUP A STATED ODDS 1:72
GROUP B STATED ODDS 1:12
*BLUE/50: .5X TO 1.2X GRP A AU
*BLUE/50: .6X TO 1.5X GRP B AU
BLUE/50 STATED ODDS 1:62
UNPRICED GOLD/1 ODDS 1:2903
ACB Chris Brown A 8.00 20.00
ADD Domanick Davis B 6.00 15.00
AJE John Elway A 100.00 200.00
AJM Justin McCareins B 6.00 15.00
AKB Kevan Barlow B 6.00 15.00
AMV Michael Vick A 30.00 60.00
ASS Steve Smith B 10.00 25.00

2004 Topps Signature Buy Back Autographs

STATED ODDS 1:813
JE1 John Elway 87T 75.00 150.00
JE2 John Elway 88T 75.00 150.00

1997 Topps Stars

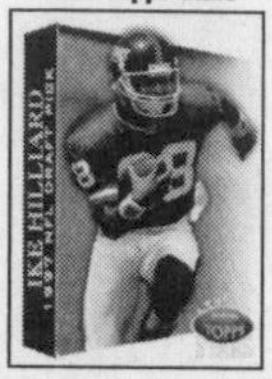

The 1997 Topps Stars hobby only set was issued in one series of 125-cards and was distributed in seven-card packs with a suggested retail price of $3. The set features color photos of 100 current NFL stars and 25 1997 NFL draft picks printed on heavy 20 point card stock with diffraction and matte gold foil stamping. The backs carry player and statistical information.

COMPLETE SET (125) 10.00 25.00
1 Brett Favre 1.00 2.50
2 Michael Jackson .15 .40
3 Simeon Rice .15 .40
4 Thurman Thomas .25 .60
5 Karim Abdul-Jabbar .25 .60
6 Marvin Harrison .25 .60
7 John Elway 1.00 2.50
8 Carl Pickens .15 .40
9 Rod Woodson .15 .40
10 Kerry Collins .25 .60
11 Cortez Kennedy .08 .25
12 William Fuller .08 .25
13 Michael Irvin .25 .60
14 Tyrone Braxton .08 .25
15 Steve Young .30 .75
16 Keith Lyle .08 .25
17 Blaine Bishop .08 .25
18 Jeff Hostetler .08 .25
19 Levon Kirkland .08 .25
20 Barry Sanders .75 2.00
21 Deion Sanders .25 .60
22 Jamal Anderson .25 .60
23 Eric Davis .08 .25
24 Hardy Nickerson .08 .25
25 LeRoy Butler .08 .25
26 Mark Brunell .30 .75
27 Aeneas Williams .08 .25
28 Curtis Martin .30 .75
29 Wayne Chrebet .25 .60
30 Jerry Rice .50 1.25
31 Jake Reed .15 .40
32 Wayne Martin .08 .25
33 Derrick Alexander WR .15 .40
34 Isaac Bruce .25 .60
35 Terrell Davis .30 .75
36 Jerome Bettis .25 .60
37 Keenan McCardell .15 .40
38 Derrick Thomas .25 .60
39 Jason Sehorn .15 .40
40 Keyshawn Johnson .25 .60
41 Jeff Blake .15 .40
42 Terry Allen .25 .60
43 Ben Coates .15 .40
44 William Thomas .08 .25
45 Bryce Paup .08 .25
46 Bryant Young .08 .25
47 Eric Swann .08 .25
48 Tim Brown .25 .60
49 Tony Martin .15 .40
50 Eddie George .25 .60
51 Sam Mills .08 .25
52 Terry McDaniel .08 .25
53 Darren Woodson .08 .25
54 Ashley Ambrose .08 .25
55 Drew Bledsoe .30 .75
56 Larry Centers .15 .40
57 Ty Detmer .15 .40
58 Merton Hanks .08 .25
59 Charles Johnson .15 .40
60 Dan Marino 1.00 2.50
61 Joey Galloway .15 .40
62 Junior Seau .25 .60
63 Brett Perriman .08 .25
64 Wesley Walls .15 .40
65 Chad Brown .08 .25
66 Henry Ellard .08 .25
67 Keith Jackson .08 .25
68 John Randle .15 .40
69 Chester McGlockton .08 .25
70 Emmitt Smith .75 2.00
71 Vinny Testaverde .15 .40
72 Steve Atwater .08 .25
73 Irving Fryar .15 .40
74 Gus Frerotte .08 .25
75 Terry Glenn .25 .60
76 Anthony Johnson .08 .25
77 Jimmy Smith .15 .40
78 Terrell Buckley .08 .25
79 Kimble Anders .15 .40
80 Cris Carter .25 .60
81 Dave Meggett .08 .25
82 Shannon Sharpe .15 .40
83 Adrian Murrell .15 .40
84 Herman Moore .15 .40
85 Bruce Smith .15 .40
86 Lamar Lathon .08 .25
87 Ken Harvey .08 .25
88 Curtis Conway .15 .40
89 Alfred Williams .08 .25
90 Troy Aikman .50 1.25
91 Carnell Lake .08 .25
92 Michael Sinclair .08 .25
93 Ricky Watters .15 .40
94 Kevin Greene .15 .40
95 Reggie White .25 .60
96 Tyrone Hughes .08 .25
97 Dale Carter .08 .25
98 Rob Moore .15 .40
99 Tony Tolbert .08 .25
100 Willie McGinest .08 .25
101 Orlando Pace RC .40 1.00
102 Yatil Green RC .20 .50
103 Antowain Smith RC 1.50 4.00
104 David LaFleur RC .08 .25
105 Jake Plummer RC 2.50 6.00
106 Will Blackwell RC .20 .50
107 Dwayne Rudd RC .40 1.00
108 Corey Dillon RC 2.50 6.00
109 Pat Barnes RC .40 1.00
110 Peter Boulware RC .40 1.00
111 Tony Gonzalez RC 2.50 6.00
112 Renaldo Wynn RC .08 .25
113 Darrell Russell RC .08 .25
114 Bryant Westbrook RC .08 .25
115 James Farrior RC .40 1.00
116 Joey Kent RC .20 .50
117 Rae Carruth RC .08 .25
118 Jim Druckenmiller RC .20 .50
119 Byron Hanspard RC .15 .40
120 Ike Hilliard RC .75 2.00
121 Kevin Lockett RC .20 .50
122 Tom Knight RC .08 .25
123 Shawn Springs RC .20 .50
124 Troy Davis RC .20 .50
125 Darnell Autry RC .20 .50
NNO Checklist Card .08 .25
PP36 Jerome Bettis Promo .60 1.50

1997 Topps Stars Foil

COMPLETE SET (125) 400.00 800.00
*STARS: 10X TO 25X BASIC CARDS
*RCs: 3X TO 8X BASIC CARDS
STATED ODDS 1:18

1997 Topps Stars Future Pro Bowlers

COMPLETE SET (15) 15.00 40.00
STATED ODDS 1:12 HOBBY
FPB1 Ike Hilliard 1.50 4.00
FPB2 Tom Knight .75 2.00
FPB3 David LaFleur .75 2.00
FPB4 Byron Hanspard 1.25 3.00
FPB5 Kevin Lockett 1.25 3.00
FPB6 Rae Carruth .75 2.00
FPB7 Jim Druckenmiller 1.25 3.00
FPB8 Darnell Autry 1.25 3.00
FPB9 Joey Kent 1.50 4.00
FPB10 Peter Boulware 1.25 3.00
FPB11 Orlando Pace 1.50 4.00
FPB12 Troy Davis 1.25 3.00
FPB13 Antowain Smith 4.00 8.00
FPB14 Bryant Westbrook .75 2.00
FPB15 Yatil Green 1.25 3.00

1997 Topps Stars Rookie Reprints

COMPLETE SET (10) 30.00 60.00
STATED ODDS 1:64
AUTOGRAPH STATED ODDS 1:128
1 George Blanda 2.50 6.00
2 Dick Butkus 4.00 10.00
3 Len Dawson UER 2.50 6.00
(Card numbered 4 of 10)
4 Jack Ham 2.00 5.00
5 Sam Huff 2.00 5.00
6 Deacon Jones 2.50 6.00
7 Ray Nitschke 2.50 6.00
8 Gale Sayers 4.00 10.00
(1968 Topps card)
9 Randy White 2.00 5.00
10 Kellen Winslow 2.00 5.00

1997 Topps Stars Rookie Reprints Autographs

STATED ODDS 1:128 HOBBY
1 George Blanda 40.00 80.00
2 Dick Butkus 50.00 80.00
3 Len Dawson 15.00 40.00
4 Jack Ham 30.00 60.00
5 Sam Huff 30.00 60.00
6 Deacon Jones 15.00 40.00
7 Ray Nitschke 125.00 200.00
8 Gale Sayers 40.00 80.00
9 Randy White 25.00 50.00
10 Kellen Winslow 20.00 40.00

1997 Topps Stars Pro Bowl Memories

COMPLETE SET (10) 25.00 60.00
STATED ODDS 1:24
PBM1 Barry Sanders 6.00 15.00
PBM2 Jeff Blake 1.25 3.00
PBM3 Ken Harvey .75 2.00
PBM4 Brett Favre 8.00 20.00
PBM5 Jerry Rice 4.00 10.00
PBM6 John Elway 8.00 20.00
PBM7 Marshall Faulk 2.00 5.00
PBM8 Steve Young 2.50 6.00
PBM9 Mark Brunell 2.50 6.00
PBM10 Troy Aikman 4.00 10.00

1997 Topps Stars Pro Bowl Stars

COMPLETE SET (30) 40.00 100.00
STATED ODDS 1:24
PB1 Brett Favre 10.00 25.00
PB2 Mark Brunell 3.00 8.00
PB3 Kerry Collins 2.50 6.00
PB4 Drew Bledsoe 3.00 8.00
PB5 Barry Sanders 8.00 20.00
PB6 Terrell Davis 3.00 8.00
PB7 Terry Allen 2.50 6.00
PB8 Jerome Bettis 2.50 6.00
PB9 Ricky Watters 1.50 4.00
PB10 Curtis Martin 3.00 8.00
PB11 Emmitt Smith 8.00 20.00
PB12 Kimble Anders 1.50 4.00
PB13 Jerry Rice 5.00 12.00
PB14 Carl Pickens 1.50 4.00
PB15 Herman Moore 1.50 4.00
PB16 Tony Martin 1.50 4.00
PB17 Isaac Bruce 2.50 6.00
PB18 Tim Brown 2.50 6.00
PB19 Wesley Walls 1.50 4.00
PB20 Shannon Sharpe 1.50 4.00
PB21 Dana Stubblefield 1.00 2.50
PB22 Reggie White 2.50 6.00
PB23 Bruce Smith 1.50 4.00
PB24 Bryant Young 1.00 2.50
PB25 Junior Seau 2.50 6.00
PB26 Kevin Greene 1.50 4.00
PB27 Derrick Thomas 2.50 6.00
PB28 Chad Brown 1.00 2.50
PB29 Deion Sanders 2.50 6.00
PB30 Rod Woodson 1.50 4.00

1998 Topps Stars Promos

COMPLETE SET (6) 2.50 6.00
PP1 Terrell Davis .40 1.00
PP2 Herman Moore .30 .75
PP3 Brett Favre 1.25 3.00
PP4 Eddie George .30 .75
PP5 Jerome Bettis .40 1.00
PP6 Barry Sanders .75 2.00

1998 Topps Stars

The 1998 Topps Stars set was issued in one series totalling 150 standard size cards. The six-card packs retail for $3.00 each. The 20 pt. stock cards are borderless with a matte gold-foil stamping and UV coating. The set is sequentially numbered within one of five groups: Red Star (1 of 8799), Bronze Star (1 of 8799), Silver Star (1 of 3999), Gold Star (1 of 1999) and Gold Star Rainbow (1 of 99). Red Star and Bronze Star are considered regular cards. The player selection and categories are also based upon the five-star system which includes: Arm Strength, Accuracy, Mobility, Consistency and Leadership. A complete checklist card of the 1998 Topps Stars set was seeded in packs at the rate of 1:5.

COMP.RED SET (150) 30.00 80.00
1 John Elway 2.00 5.00
2 Duane Starks RC .40 1.00
3 Bruce Smith .30 .75
4 Jeff Blake .30 .75
5 Carl Pickens .30 .75
6 Shannon Sharpe .30 .75
7 Jerome Pathon RC 1.00 2.50
8 Jimmy Smith .30 .75
9 Elvis Grbac .30 .75
10 Mark Brunell .50 1.25
11 Karim Abdul-Jabbar .50 1.25
12 Terry Glenn .50 1.25
13 Larry Centers .20 .50
14 Jeff George .30 .75
15 Terry Allen .50 1.25
16 Charles Johnson .20 .50
17 Chris Spielman .20 .50
18 Ahman Green RC 2.50 6.00
19 Kevin Dyson RC 1.00 2.50
20 Dan Marino 2.00 5.00
21 Andre Wadsworth RC .60 1.50
22 Chris Chandler .30 .75
23 Kerry Collins .30 .75
24 Erik Kramer .20 .50
25 Warrick Dunn .50 1.25
26 Michael Irvin .50 1.25
27 Herman Moore .30 .75
28 Dorsey Levens .50 1.25
29 Cris Carter .50 1.25
30 Drew Bledsoe .75 2.00
31 Kevin Greene .30 .75
32 Charles Way .20 .50
33 Bobby Hoying .30 .75
34 Tony Banks .30 .75
35 Steve Young .60 1.50
36 Trent Dilfer .50 1.25
37 Warren Sapp .30 .75
38 Skip Hicks RC .60 1.50
39 Michael Jackson .20 .50
40 Curtis Martin .50 1.25
41 Thurman Thomas .50 1.25
42 Corey Dillon .50 1.25
43 Brian Griese RC 2.00 5.00
44 Marshall Faulk .60 1.50
45 Isaac Bruce .50 1.25
46 Fred Taylor RC 1.50 4.00
47 Andre Rison .30 .75
48 O.J. McDuffie .30 .75
49 John Avery RC .60 1.50
50 Terrell Davis .50 1.25
51 Robert Edwards RC .60 1.50
52 Keyshawn Johnson .50 1.25
53 Rickey Dudley .20 .50
54 Hines Ward RC 5.00 10.00
55 Irving Fryar .30 .75
56 Freddie Jones .20 .50
57 Michael Sinclair .20 .50
58 Darnay Scott .30 .75
59 Tim Dwight RC 1.00 2.50
60 Tim Brown .50 1.25
61 Ray Lewis .50 1.25
62 Curtis Enis RC .40 1.00
63 Emmitt Smith 1.50 4.00
64 Scott Mitchell .30 .75
65 Antonio Freeman .50 1.25
66 Randy Moss RC 4.00 10.00
67 Peyton Manning RC 8.00 20.00
68 Danny Kanell .30 .75
69 Charlie Garner .30 .75
70 Mike Alstott .50 1.25
71 Grant Wistrom RC .60 1.50
72 Jacquez Green RC .60 1.50
73 Gus Frerotte .20 .50
74 Peter Boulware .20 .50
75 Jerry Rice 1.00 2.50
76 Antowain Smith .50 1.25
77 Brian Simmons RC .60 1.50
78 Rod Smith .30 .75
79 Marvin Harrison .50 1.25
80 Ryan Leaf RC 1.00 2.50
81 Keenan McCardell .30 .75
82 Derrick Thomas .50 1.25
83 Zach Thomas .50 1.25
84 Ben Coates .30 .75
85 Rob Moore .30 .75
86 Wayne Chrebet .50 1.25
87 Napoleon Kaufman .50 1.25
88 Levon Kirkland .20 .50
89 Junior Seau .50 1.25
90 Eddie George .50 1.25
91 Warren Moon .50 1.25
92 Anthony Simmons RC .60 1.50
93 Steve McNair .50 1.25
94 Frank Sanders .30 .75
95 Joey Galloway .30 .75
96 Jamal Anderson .50 1.25
97 Rae Carruth .20 .50
98 Curtis Conway .30 .75
99 Greg Ellis RC .40 1.00
100 Kordell Stewart .50 1.25
101 Germane Crowell RC .60 1.50
102 Mark Chmura .30 .75
103 Robert Smith .50 1.25
104 Andre Hastings .20 .50
105 Reggie White .50 1.25
106 Jessie Armstead .20 .50
107 Kevin Hardy .20 .50
108 Robert Holcombe RC .60 1.50
109 Garrison Hearst .50 1.25
110 Jerome Bettis .50 1.25
111 Reidel Anthony .30 .75
112 Michael Westbrook .30 .75
113 Pat Johnson RC .60 1.50
114 Andre Reed .30 .75
115 Charles Woodson RC 1.50 4.00
116 Takeo Spikes RC 1.00 2.50
117 Marcus Nash RC .40 1.00
118 Tavian Banks RC .30 .75
119 Tony Gonzalez .50 1.25
120 Jake Plummer .50 1.25
121 Tony Simmons RC .60 1.50
122 Aaron Glenn .20 .50
123 Ricky Watters .30 .75
124 Kimble Anders .30 .75
125 Barry Sanders 1.50 4.00
126 Terance Mathis .30 .75
127 Wesley Walls .30 .75
128 Bobby Engram .30 .75
129 Johnnie Morton .30 .75
130 Brett Favre 2.00 5.00
131 Brad Johnson .50 1.25
132 John Randle .30 .75
133 Chris Sanders .20 .50
134 Joe Jurevicius RC 1.00 2.50
135 Deion Sanders .50 1.25
136 Terrell Owens .50 1.25
137 Darrell Green .30 .75
138 Jermaine Lewis .30 .75
139 James Stewart .30 .75
140 Troy Aikman 1.00 2.50
141 Hardy Nickerson .20 .50
142 Blaine Bishop .20 .50
143 Keith Brooking RC 1.00 2.50
144 Jason Peter RC .40 1.00
145 Jake Reed .30 .75
146 Jason Sehorn .30 .75
147 Robert Brooks .30 .75
148 J.J. Stokes .30 .75
149 Michael Strahan .30 .75
150 Glenn Foley .30 .75
NNO Checklist Card .20 .50

1998 Topps Stars Bronze

COMPLETE SET (150) 30.00 80.00
*BRONZE CARDS: SAME PRICE AS RED
STATED PRINT RUN 8799 SER.#'d SETS

1998 Topps Stars Gold

COMP.GOLD SET (150) 125.00 250.00
*GOLD VETS: 1.2X TO 3X BASIC CARDS
*GOLD ROOKIES: .8X TO 2X BASIC CARDS
GOLD/1999 ODDS 1:2

1998 Topps Stars Gold Rainbow

*GOLD RBW.VETS: 8X TO 20X BASIC CARDS
*GOLD RBW.ROOKIES: 2.5X TO 6X
GOLD RAINBOW/99 ODDS 1:41

1998 Topps Stars Silver

COMP.SILVER SET (150) 50.00 120.00
*SILVER/3999: .6X TO 1.5X BASIC CARDS
SILVER PRINT RUN 3999 SER.#'d SETS

1998 Topps Stars Galaxy

BRONZE/100 STATED ODDS 1:611
*SILVER/75: .5X TO 1.2X BRONZE/100
SILVER/75 STATED ODDS 1:814
*GOLD/50: .6X TO 1.5X BRONZE/100
GOLD/50 STATED ODDS 1:1222
UNPRICED GOLD RBW/5 ODDS 1:12,215
G1 Brett Favre 30.00 80.00
G2 Barry Sanders 25.00 60.00
G3 Jerry Rice 15.00 40.00
G4 Herman Moore 5.00 12.00
G5 Tim Brown 8.00 20.00
G6 Steve Young 10.00 25.00
G7 Cris Carter 8.00 20.00
G8 John Elway 30.00 80.00
G9 Mark Brunell 6.00 15.00
G10 Terrell Davis 8.00 20.00

1998 Topps Stars Luminaries

BRONZE/100 STATED ODDS 1:407
*SILVER/75: .4X TO 1X BRONZE/100
SILVER/75 STATED ODDS 1:543
*GOLD/50: .5X TO 1.2X BRONZE/100
GOLD/50 STATED ODDS 1:814
UNPRICED GOLD RBW/5 ODDS 1:8144
L1 Brett Favre 40.00 100.00
L2 Steve Young 12.50 30.00
L3 John Elway 40.00 100.00
L4 Barry Sanders 30.00 80.00
L5 Terrell Davis 10.00 25.00
L6 Eddie George 10.00 25.00
L7 Herman Moore 2.50 6.00
L8 Tim Brown 10.00 25.00
L9 Jerry Rice 20.00 50.00
L10 Junior Seau 10.00 25.00
L11 Bruce Smith 10.00 25.00
L12 John Randle 6.00 15.00
L13 Peyton Manning 75.00 150.00
L14 Ryan Leaf 6.00 15.00
L15 Curtis Enis 2.50 6.00

1998 Topps Stars Rookie Reprints

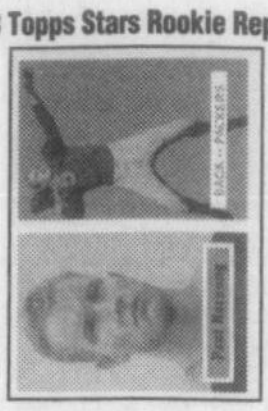

COMPLETE SET (8) 12.50 25.00
STATED ODDS 1:24
1 Walter Payton 6.00 15.00
2 Don Maynard 1.50 4.00
3 Charlie Joiner 1.25 3.00
4 Fred Biletnikoff 1.50 4.00
5 Paul Hornung 1.50 4.00
6 Gale Sayers 2.50 6.00
7 John Hannah .75 2.00
8 Paul Warfield 1.50 4.00

1998 Topps Stars Rookie Reprints Autographs

STATED ODDS 1:153
1 Walter Payton 300.00 600.00
2 Don Maynard 15.00 30.00
3 Charlie Joiner 15.00 30.00
4 Fred Biletnikoff 30.00 60.00
5 Paul Hornung 35.00 60.00
6 Gale Sayers 35.00 60.00
7 John Hannah 15.00 30.00
8 Paul Warfield 20.00 40.00

1998 Topps Stars Supernovas

BRONZE/100 STATED ODDS 1:611
*SILVER/75: .5X TO 1.2X BRONZE/100
SILVER/75 STATED ODDS 1:814
*GOLD/50: .6X TO 1.5X BRONZE/100
GOLD/50 STATED ODDS 1:1222
UNPRICED GOLD RBW/5 ODDS 1:12,215
S1 Ryan Leaf 4.00 10.00
S2 Curtis Enis 2.50 6.00
S3 Kevin Dyson 4.00 10.00
S4 Randy Moss 30.00 80.00
S5 Peyton Manning 75.00 150.00
S6 Duane Starks 2.50 6.00
S7 Grant Wistrom 2.50 6.00
S8 Charles Woodson 10.00 25.00
S9 Fred Taylor 8.00 20.00
S10 Andre Wadsworth 4.00 10.00

1999 Topps Stars Promos

Sent out for promotional purposes, this 6-card set previewed the base card product for the 1999 Topps Stars release.

COMPLETE SET (6) 2.50 6.00
PP1 Chris Chandler .40 1.00
PP2 Charlie Batch .40 1.00
PP3 Jake Plummer .50 1.25
PP4 Terrell Davis .75 2.00
PP5 Keyshawn Johnson .50 1.25
PP6 Warrick Dunn .50 1.25

1999 Topps Stars

Released as a 140-card set, the 1999 Topps Stars set was printed on thick 24 point card stock with foil stamping and a flood-gloss finish. Four different versions, destinguished by the number of foil stars on the card front, of the base set were released ranging from one star to four stars, and parallels for each set level were released also. Topps stars was packaged in 24-pack boxes containing 6-card packs and carried a suggested retail price of $3.00.

COMPLETE SET (140) 20.00 50.00
1 Champ Bailey RC .75 2.00
2 Akili Smith RC .30 .75
3 Randy Moss .30 .75
4 Cade McNown RC .30 .75
5 Torry Holt RC .60 1.50
6 Troy Edwards RC .30 .75
7 David Boston RC .30 .75
8 Edgerrin James RC .50 1.25
9 Daunte Culpepper RC .40 1.00
10 Tim Couch RC .40 1.00
11 Ricky Williams RC .60 1.50
12 Fred Taylor .25 .60
13 Barry Sanders .75 2.00
14 Emmitt Smith .75 2.00
15 Jerry Rice .60 1.50
16 Jake Plummer .25 .60
17 Terrell Owens .30 .75
18 Eric Moulds .25 .60
19 Dan Marino 1.00 2.50
20 Steve McNair .30 .75
21 Donovan McNabb RC 2.00 5.00
22 Curtis Martin .30 .75
23 Peyton Manning 1.00 2.50
24 Garrison Hearst .25 .60
25 Eddie George .25 .60
26 Antonio Freeman .25 .60
27 Doug Flutie .30 .75
28 Kevin Faulk RC .40 1.00
29 Brett Favre 1.00 2.50
30 Randall Cunningham .30 .75
31 Mark Brunell .25 .60
32 Keyshawn Johnson .25 .60
33 Terrell Davis .30 .75
34 Drew Bledsoe .30 .75
35 Jerome Bettis .30 .75
36 Charlie Batch .25 .60
37 Steve Young .40 1.00
38 Jamal Anderson .25 .60
39 Troy Aikman .50 1.25
40 John Elway 1.00 2.50
41 Amos Zereoue RC .30 .75
42 J.J. Stokes .20 .50
43 Antowain Smith .20 .50
44 Jimmy Smith .25 .60
45 Shaun King RC .30 .75
46 Jevon Kearse RC .40 1.00
47 Sedrick Irvin RC .25 .60
48 Rod Smith .25 .60
49 Kevin Johnson RC .30 .75
50 Joey Galloway .25 .60
51 Mike Cloud RC .25 .60
52 D'Wayne Bates RC .25 .60
53 Peerless Price RC .30 .75
54 Herman Moore .25 .60
55 Rob Konrad RC .25 .60
56 James Johnson RC .25 .60
57 Cecil Collins RC .25 .60
58 Wayne Chrebet .25 .60
59 Cris Carter .30 .75
60 Tim Brown .30 .75
61 Frank Wycheck .25 .60
62 Charles Woodson .30 .75
63 Antoine Winfield RC .25 .60
64 Ryan Leaf .25 .60
65 Ricky Watters .25 .60
66 Yancey Thigpen .20 .50
67 Michael Westbrook .20 .50
68 Vinny Testaverde .25 .60
69 Kordell Stewart .25 .60
70 Duce Staley .25 .60
71 Shannon Sharpe .30 .75
72 Junior Seau .30 .75
73 Bruce Smith .30 .75
74 Frank Sanders .20 .50
75 Lawrence Phillips .25 .60
76 Robert Smith .25 .60
77 Andre Reed .30 .75
78 Darnay Scott .20 .50
79 Adrian Murrell .25 .60
80 Ricky Proehl .20 .50
81 Zach Thomas .30 .75
82 Deion Sanders .30 .75
83 Andre Rison .25 .60
84 Jake Reed .25 .60
85 Carl Pickens .25 .60
86 John Randle .25 .60
87 Jerome Pathon .20 .50
88 Brock Huard RC .30 .75
89 Elvis Grbac .20 .50
90 Curtis Enis .20 .50
91 Rickey Dudley .20 .50
92 Amani Toomer .25 .60
93 Robert Brooks .25 .60
94 Derrick Alexander .20 .50
95 Reidel Anthony .20 .50
96 Mark Chmura .20 .50
97 Trent Dilfer .25 .60
98 Ebenezer Ekuban RC .25 .60
99 Tony Banks .25 .60
100 Terry Glenn .25 .60
101 Andre Hastings .20 .50
102 Ike Hilliard .25 .60
103 Michael Irvin .30 .75
104 Napoleon Kaufman .20 .50
105 Dorsey Levens .25 .60
106 Ed McCaffrey .25 .60
107 Natrone Means .25 .60
108 Skip Hicks .20 .50
109 James Jett .20 .50
110 Priest Holmes .30 .75
111 Tim Dwight .25 .60
112 Curtis Conway .25 .60
113 Jeff Blake .25 .60
114 Karim Abdul-Jabbar .25 .60
115 Karsten Bailey RC .25 .60
116 Chris Chandler .25 .60
117 Germane Crowell .20 .50
118 Warrick Dunn .25 .60
119 Bert Emanuel .25 .60
120 Jermaine Fazande RC .25 .60
121 Joe Germaine RC .30 .75
122 Tony Gonzalez .30 .75
123 Jacquez Green .20 .50
124 Marvin Harrison .30 .75
125 Corey Dillon .25 .60
126 Ben Coates .25 .60
127 Chris Claiborne RC .25 .60
128 Isaac Bruce .30 .75
129 Mike Alstott .30 .75
130 Andy Katzenmoyer RC .30 .75
131 Jon Kitna .25 .60
132 Keenan McCardell .25 .60
133 Johnnie Morton .25 .60
134 O.J. McDuffie .25 .60
135 Chris McAlister .25 .60
136 Terance Mathis .20 .50
137 Thurman Thomas .30 .75
138 Jermaine Lewis .20 .50
139 Rob Moore .20 .50
140 Brad Johnson .25 .60

1999 Topps Stars Parallel

COMPLETE SET (140) 250.00 500.00
*STARS: 3X TO 8X BASE CARDS
*RCs: 1.2X TO 3X
STATED ODDS 1:15
CARDS SERIAL NUMBERED TO 299

1999 Topps Stars Two Star

COMPLETE SET (60) 15.00 40.00
*TWO STARS: SAME PRICE AS 1 STAR
ONE OR TWO CARDS PER PACK

1999 Topps Stars Two Star Parallel

COMPLETE SET (60) 250.00 500.00
*STARS: 4X TO 10X HI COL.
*ROOKIES: 1.5X TO 4X
STATED ODDS 1:42
CARDS SERIAL NUMBERED TO 249

1999 Topps Stars Three Star

COMPLETE SET (40) 12.50 30.00
*THREE STARS: SAME PRICE AS 1 STAR
ONE PER PACK

1999 Topps Stars Three Star Parallel

COMPLETE SET (40) 250.00 500.00
*STARS: 5X TO 12X BASIC CARDS
*ROOKIES: 2X TO 5X
STATED ODDS 1:79
CARDS SERIAL NUMBERED TO 199

1999 Topps Stars Four Star

COMPLETE SET (10) 10.00 25.00
*FOUR STARS: SAME PRICE AS 1 STAR
STATED ODDS 1:4

1999 Topps Stars Four Star Parallel

COMPLETE SET (10) 75.00 150.00
*STARS: 5X TO 12X
*ROOKIES: 2.5X TO 6X
STATED ODDS 1:634
CARDS SERIAL NUMBERED TO 99

1999 Topps Stars Autographs

BLUE BACKGROUND STATED ODDS 1:419
GOLD BACKGROUND STATED ODDS 1:2528
RED BACKGROUND STATED ODDS 1:629
A1 Tim Couch B 10.00 25.00
A2 Torry Holt B 12.00 30.00
A3 David Boston B 8.00 30.00
A4 Fred Taylor R 12.00 30.00
A5 Marshall Faulk R 20.00 50.00
A6 Randy Moss G 30.00 80.00

1999 Topps Stars New Dawn

COMPLETE SET (20) 50.00 100.00
STATED ODDS 1:31
STATED PRINT RUN 1000 SER.#'d SETS
N1 Tim Couch 1.25 3.00
N2 Kevin Faulk 1.25 3.00
N3 Troy Edwards 1.00 2.50
N4 Champ Bailey 1.50 4.00
N5 Peerless Price 1.25 3.00
N6 Kevin Johnson 1.25 3.00
N7 Edgerrin James 5.00 12.00
N8 Daunte Culpepper 5.00 12.00
N9 Torry Holt 3.00 8.00
N10 Donovan McNabb 6.00 15.00
N11 Shaun King 1.00 2.50
N12 Mike Cloud 1.00 2.50
N13 Cade McNown 1.00 2.50
N14 David Boston 1.25 3.00
N15 James Johnson 1.00 2.50
N16 Karsten Bailey 1.00 2.50
N17 Sedrick Irvin .60 1.50
N18 Akili Smith 1.00 2.50
N19 D'Wayne Bates 1.00 2.50
N20 Ricky Williams 2.50 6.00

1999 Topps Stars Rookie Relics

COMPLETE SET (3) 40.00 100.00
STATED ODDS 1:209
RR1 Kurt Warner 15.00 40.00
RR2 Torry Holt 12.50 30.00
RR3 Donovan McNabb 15.00 40.00

1999 Topps Stars Rookie Reprints

COMPLETE SET (2) 4.00 10.00
STATED ODDS 1:16
1 Roger Staubach 2.00 5.00
2 Terry Bradshaw 2.00 5.00

1999 Topps Stars Rookie Reprints Autographs

STATED ODDS 1:629
RA1 Roger Staubach 60.00 120.00
RA2 Terry Bradshaw 75.00 150.00

1999 Topps Stars Stars of the Game

COMPLETE SET (10) 40.00 80.00
STATED ODDS 1:31
STATED PRINT RUN 1999 SER.#'d SETS
S1 Jamal Anderson 1.50 4.00
S2 Dan Marino 5.00 12.00
S3 Barry Sanders 5.00 12.00
S4 Brett Favre 5.00 12.00
S5 Emmitt Smith 3.00 8.00
S6 Fred Taylor 1.50 4.00
S7 Kurt Warner 7.50 20.00
S8 Randy Moss 4.00 10.00
S9 Peyton Manning 6.00 15.00
S10 Terrell Davis 1.50 4.00

1999 Topps Stars Zone of Their Own

COMPLETE SET (10) 20.00 50.00
STATED ODDS 1:31
STATED PRINT RUN 1999 SER.#'d SETS
Z1 Randy Moss 4.00 10.00
Z2 Eddie George 1.50 4.00
Z3 Tim Brown 1.50 4.00
Z4 Curtis Martin 1.50 4.00
Z5 Brett Favre 5.00 12.00
Z6 Barry Sanders 5.00 12.00
Z7 Warrick Dunn 1.50 4.00
Z8 Terrell Davis 1.50 4.00
Z9 Ricky Williams 2.00 5.00
Z10 Doug Flutie 1.50 4.00

2000 Topps Stars Promos

Sent out for promotional purposes, this 6-card set previewed the base card product for the 2000 Topps Stars release.

COMPLETE SET (6) 2.50 6.00
PP1 Keyshawn Johnson .50 1.25
PP2 Dorsey Levens .50 1.25
PP3 Rich Gannon .50 1.25
PP4 Michael Westbrook .40 1.00
PP5 Mike Alstott .60 1.50
PP6 Edgerrin James .60 1.50

2000 Topps Stars

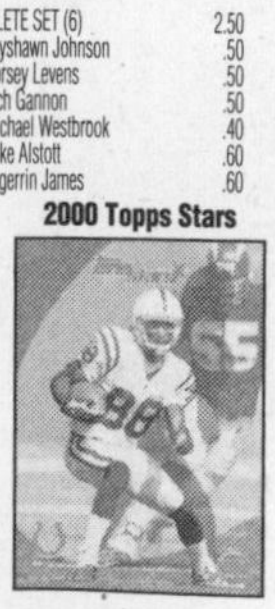

Issued as a 175-card base set, Topps Stars is comprised of 120 regular issue player cards, five Retired Stars, 20 Heroes of Hawaii, five Hawaiian Future, and 25 Rookie cards. Base cards are borderless and feature player action shots and silver foil highlights. Topps Stars was packaged in 24-pack boxes with packs containing six cards and carried a suggested retail price of $3.00.

COMPLETE SET (175)	15.00	40.00
1 Keyshawn Johnson	.25	.60
2 Marcus Robinson	.25	.60
3 Antonio Freeman	.25	.60
4 Jake Plummer	.25	.60
5 Zach Thomas	.30	.75
6 Kordell Stewart	.25	.60
7 Mike Alstott	.30	.75
8 Fred Taylor	.30	.75
9 J.J. Stokes	.25	.60
10 Emmitt Smith	.75	2.00
11 Derrick Mayes	.20	.50
12 Stephen Davis	.25	.60
13 Jamal Anderson	.25	.60
14 Antowain Smith	.25	.60
15 Steve Beuerlein	.25	.60
16 Olandis Gary	.25	.60
17 Rickey Dudley	.20	.50
18 Sean Dawkins	.20	.50
19 Mark Brunell	.25	.60
20 Brett Favre	1.00	2.50
21 Jim Harbaugh	.25	.60
22 Darnay Scott	.25	.60
23 Herman Moore	.25	.60
24 Drew Bledsoe	.30	.75
25 Priest Holmes	.30	.75
26 Albert Connell	.20	.50
27 Ike Hilliard	.25	.60
28 Charlie Garner	.25	.60
29 Jimmy Smith	.25	.60
30 Randy Moss	.30	.75
31 Peerless Price	.25	.60
32 Terrell Davis	.30	.75
33 Troy Edwards	.20	.50
34 Kevin Dyson	.25	.60
35 O.J. McDuffie	.25	.60
36 Troy Aikman	.50	1.25
37 Frank Sanders	.20	.50
38 Bobby Engram	.25	.60
39 Tyrone Wheatley	.20	.50
40 Ricky Williams	.30	.75
41 Warrick Dunn	.25	.60
42 Elvis Grbac	.20	.50
43 Dorsey Levens	.25	.60
44 Curtis Conway	.25	.60
45 Johnnie Morton	.25	.60
46 Ed McCaffrey	.25	.60
47 Kevin Johnson	.20	.50
48 Muhsin Muhammad	.25	.60
49 Terance Mathis	.20	.50
50 Eddie George	.25	.60
51 Daunte Culpepper	.25	.60
52 Jeff Graham	.20	.50
53 Jon Kitna	.25	.60
54 Marvin Harrison	.30	.75
55 Steve McNair	.30	.75
56 Jeff Blake	.25	.60
57 Carl Pickens	.25	.60
58 Germane Crowell	.20	.50
59 Rob Moore	.20	.50
60 Marshall Faulk	.30	.75
61 Jerome Bettis	.30	.75
62 Michael Westbrook	.20	.50
63 Keenan McCardell	.25	.60
64 Shannon Sharpe	.30	.75
65 Rod Smith	.25	.60
66 Curtis Enis	.20	.50
67 Vinny Testaverde	.25	.60
68 Freddie Jones	.20	.50
69 Jevon Kearse	.25	.60
70 Jerry Rice	.60	1.50
71 Champ Bailey	.25	.60
72 Peyton Manning	.75	2.00
73 Rich Gannon	.25	.60
74 Cris Carter	.30	.75
75 Doug Flutie	.30	.75
76 Corey Dillon	.25	.60
77 Tony Gonzalez	.30	.75
78 Shaun King	.20	.50
79 Terrell Owens	.30	.75
80 Dan Marino	1.00	2.50
81 Curtis Martin	.30	.75
82 Patrick Jeffers	.25	.60
83 Brian Griese	.25	.60
84 Akili Smith	.20	.50
85 Charlie Batch	.25	.60
86 Tim Dwight	.25	.60
87 Robert Smith	.25	.60
88 Duce Staley	.25	.60
89 Jacquez Green	.20	.50
90 Steve Young	.40	1.00
91 Tony Martin	.25	.60
92 Az-Zahir Hakim	.20	.50
93 Tim Brown	.30	.75
94 Donovan McNabb	.30	.75
95 Chris Chandler	.25	.60
96 Tim Couch	.25	.60
97 Tim Biakabutuka	.25	.60
98 Terry Glenn	.25	.60
99 Wayne Chrebet	.25	.60
100 Kurt Warner	.50	1.25
101 Qadry Ismail	.25	.60
102 Torry Holt	.30	.75
103 Ray Lucas	.20	.50
104 James Johnson	.20	.50
105 Errict Rhett	.25	.60
106 James Stewart	.20	.50
107 Tony Banks	.20	.50
108 Amani Toomer	.25	.60
109 Isaac Bruce	.30	.75
110 Brad Johnson	.25	.60
111 Kerry Collins	.25	.60
112 Eric Moulds	.25	.60
113 Rocket Ismail	.25	.60
114 Keith Poole	.20	.50
115 Rob Johnson	.25	.60
116 Deion Sanders	.30	.75
117 Ricky Watters	.25	.60
118 Cade McNown	.20	.50
119 Joey Galloway	.25	.60
120 Edgerrin James	.30	.75
121 Franco Harris	.30	.75
122 Steve Largent	.30	.75
123 Joe Montana	1.00	2.50
124 Deacon Jones	.25	.60
125 Ronnie Lott	.30	.75
126 Mark Brunell HH	.20	.50
127 Rich Gannon HH	.20	.50
128 Tony Gonzalez HH	.25	.60
129 Randy Moss HH	.25	.60
130 Kurt Warner HH	.40	1.00
131 Marvin Harrison HH	.25	.60
132 Jimmy Smith HH	.20	.50
133 Edgerrin James HH	.25	.60
134 Corey Dillon HH	.20	.50
135 Peyton Manning HH	.60	1.50
136 Brad Johnson HH	.20	.50
137 Steve Beuerlein HH	.20	.50
138 Emmitt Smith HH	.60	1.50
139 Marshall Faulk HH	.25	.60
140 Mike Alstott HH	.25	.60
141 Deacon Jones HH	.20	.50
142 Joe Montana HH	.75	2.00
143 Franco Harris HH	.25	.60
144 Steve Largent HH	.25	.60
145 Ronnie Lott HH	.25	.60
146 Chad Pennington HF	.40	1.00
147 Peter Warrick HF	.25	.60
148 Plaxico Burress HF	.25	.60
149 Thomas Jones HF	.30	.75
150 Jamal Lewis HF	.25	.60
151 Travis Taylor RC	.25	.60
152 Shaun Alexander RC	.40	1.00
153 Dez White RC	.25	.60
154 Thomas Jones RC	.40	1.00
155 Curtis Keaton RC	.20	.50
156 Courtney Brown RC	.25	.60
157 Danny Farmer RC	.20	.50
158 Trung Canidate RC	.25	.60
159 R.Jay Soward RC	.20	.50
160 Jamal Lewis RC	.30	.75
161 Todd Pinkston RC	.20	.50
162 Reuben Droughns RC	.30	.75
163 Ron Dugans RC	.20	.50
164 Ron Dayne RC	.30	.75
165 Laveranues Coles RC	.30	.75
166 Sylvester Morris RC	.20	.50
167 Peter Warrick RC	.30	.75
168 Dennis Northcutt RC	.25	.60
169 Tee Martin RC	.30	.75
170 Brian Urlacher RC	1.25	3.00
171 Chris Redman RC	.25	.60
172 Chad Pennington RC	.50	1.25
173 J.R. Redmond RC	.20	.50
174 Travis Prentice RC	.25	.60
175 Plaxico Burress RC	.30	.75

2000 Topps Stars Green

*VETS 1-125: 3X TO 8X BASIC CARDS
1-125 VETERAN PRINT RUN 299
*VETS 126-150: 10X TO 25X
*ROOKIES 126-150: 10X TO 25X
*ROOKIES 151-175: 8X TO 20X
126-175 STATED PRINT RUN 99

2000 Topps Stars Pro Bowl Jerseys

STATED ODDS 1:85		
KMC Kevin Mawae	6.00	15.00
MBP Mitch Berger	8.00	20.00
TTP Tom Tupa	6.00	15.00
AZTI Zach Thomas	10.00	25.00
BDFS Brian Dawkins	10.00	25.00
BJQB Brad Johnson	8.00	20.00
BMOG Bruce Matthews	8.00	20.00
CDOLD Chad Drown	6.00	15.00
CCWR Cris Carter	10.00	25.00
CDRB Corey Dillon	8.00	20.00
CKILB Curtez Kennedy	6.00	15.00
CLFS Carnell Lake	6.00	15.00
CWCB Charles Woodson	10.00	25.00
DBOLB Derrick Brooks	10.00	25.00
DCOLB Dexter Coakley	6.00	15.00
DRILM Darrell Russell	6.00	15.00
DSST Detron Smith	6.00	15.00
DSTE David Sloan	6.00	15.00
EGRB Eddie George	8.00	20.00
EJRB Edgerrin James	10.00	25.00
ESRB Emmitt Smith	25.00	60.00
FWTE Frank Wycheck	8.00	20.00
GMKR Glyn Milburn	6.00	15.00
HNILB Hardy Nickerson	6.00	15.00
IBWR Isaac Bruce	10.00	25.00
JKDE Jevon Kearse	8.00	20.00
JSWR Jimmy Smith	8.00	20.00
KCDE Kevin Carter	6.00	15.00
KHOLB Kevin Hardy	6.00	15.00
KJWR Keyshawn Johnson	8.00	20.00
KWQB Kurt Warner	15.00	40.00
LEILM Luther Elliss	6.00	15.00
LMSS Lawyer Milloy	6.00	15.00
LSFS Lance Schulters	6.00	15.00
LSOT Leon Searcy	6.00	15.00
MAFB Mike Alstott	10.00	25.00
MBQB Mark Brunell	8.00	20.00
MFRB Marshall Faulk	10.00	25.00
MHWR Marvin Harrison	10.00	25.00
MMDE Michael McCrary	6.00	15.00
MMWR Muhsin Muhammad	8.00	20.00
MSDE Michael Strahan	8.00	20.00
OMPK Olindo Mare	6.00	15.00
OPOT Orlando Pace	8.00	20.00
PBOL Peter Boulware	6.00	15.00
RGQB Rich Gannon	8.00	20.00
RMOG Randall McDaniel	8.00	20.00
RMWR Randy Moss	10.00	25.00
RPDE Robert Porcher	6.00	15.00
RWFS Rod Woodson	10.00	25.00
SBIL Stephen Boyd	6.00	15.00
SBQB Steve Beuerlein	8.00	20.00
SDRB Stephen Davis	8.00	20.00
SGFB Sam Gash	6.00	15.00
SLOT Leon Searcy	6.00	15.00
SMCB Sam Madison	6.00	15.00
TBDE Tony Brackens	6.00	15.00
TGTE Tony Gonzalez	10.00	25.00
TJOG Tre Johnson	6.00	15.00
TLCB Todd Lyght	6.00	15.00
TMKR Tremain Mack	6.00	15.00
TPILM Trevor Pryce	6.00	15.00
WROT William Roaf	6.00	15.00
WSIL Warren Sapp	8.00	20.00
WWTE Wesley Walls	6.00	15.00

2000 Topps Stars Autographs

STATED ODDS 1:411		
CC Cris Carter	15.00	40.00
CR Chris Redman	12.00	30.00
DG Darrell Green	30.00	60.00
DJ Deacon Jones	15.00	40.00
EJ Edgerrin James	15.00	40.00
JM Joe Montana	50.00	120.00
KC Kevin Carter	10.00	25.00
KW Kurt Warner	20.00	50.00
RD Ron Dayne	15.00	40.00
RL Ronnie Lott	20.00	50.00
SL Steve Largent	20.00	50.00

2000 Topps Stars Pro Bowl Powerhouse

COMPLETE SET (15)	7.50	20.00
STATED ODDS 1:12		
PB1 Kurt Warner	1.00	2.50
PB2 Warren Sapp	.50	1.25
PB3 Marvin Harrison	.60	1.50
PB4 Kevin Carter	.40	1.00
PB5 Jimmy Smith	.50	1.25
PB6 Stephen Davis	.50	1.25
PB7 Edgerrin James	.60	1.50
PB8 Tony Gonzalez	.60	1.50
PB9 Sam Madison	.40	1.00
PB10 Mike Alstott	.60	1.50
PB11 Marshall Faulk	.60	1.50
PB12 Jevon Kearse	.50	1.25
PB13 Kevin Hardy	.40	1.00
PB14 Peyton Manning	1.50	4.00
PB15 Randy Moss	.60	1.50

2000 Topps Stars Progression

COMPLETE SET (5)	4.00	10.00
STATED ODDS 1:15		
P1 Joe Montana Brett Favre Chad Pennington	1.00	2.50
P2 Deacon Jones Jevon Kearse Courtney Brown	.50	1.25
P3 Ronnie Lott John Lynch Deon Grant	.40	1.00
P4 Steve Largent Randy Moss Peter Warrick	.60	1.50
P5 Franco Harris Edgerrin James Thomas Jones	.75	2.00

2000 Topps Stars Walk of Fame

COMPLETE SET (15)	7.50	20.00
STATED ODDS 1:8		
W1 Randy Moss	.50	1.25
W2 Kurt Warner	.75	2.00
W3 Jimmy Smith	.40	1.00
W4 Cris Carter	.50	1.25
W5 Brett Favre	1.50	4.00
W6 Ricky Williams	.50	1.25
W7 Marvin Harrison	.50	1.25
W8 Fred Taylor	.50	1.25
W9 Eddie George	.40	1.00
W10 Edgerrin James	.50	1.25
W11 Jevon Kearse	.40	1.00
W12 Emmitt Smith	1.25	3.00
W13 Marshall Faulk	.50	1.25
W14 Terrell Davis	.50	1.25
W15 Peyton Manning	1.25	3.00

1981 Topps Red Border Stickers

This set of 28 red-bordered stickers was distributed as a separate issue (inside a football capsule) unlike the "Coming Soon" subsets, which were inserted in with the regular football card wax packs. The stickers were actually sold in vending machines for 25 cents a sticker. They are the same size as the regular Topps stickers (1 15/16" by 2 9/16") and tougher to find than the other "Coming Soon" sticker subsets distributed in later years. The numbering in this set is completely different from the sticker numbering in the 1981 Topps 262-sticker set. There was one sticker issued for each team.

COMPLETE SET (28)	20.00	40.00
1 Steve Bartkowski	.50	1.25
2 Bert Jones	.50	1.25
3 Joe Cribbs	.50	1.25
4 Walter Payton	7.50	15.00
5 Ross Browner	.40	1.00
6 Brian Sipe	.50	1.25
7 Tony Dorsett	2.50	5.00
8 Randy Gradishar	.50	1.25
9 Billy Sims	.60	1.50
10 James Lofton	.60	1.50
11 Mike Barber	.40	1.00
12 Art Still	.40	1.00
13 Jack Youngblood	.50	1.25
14 David Woodley	.40	1.00
15 Ahmad Rashad	.60	1.50
16 Russ Francis	.40	1.00
17 Archie Manning	.60	1.50
18 Dave Jennings	.40	1.00
19 Richard Todd	.40	1.00
20 Lester Hayes	.50	1.25
21 Ron Jaworski	.50	1.25
22 Franco Harris	1.25	3.00
23 Ottis Anderson	.60	1.50
24 John Jefferson	.50	1.25
25 Freddie Solomon	.40	1.00
26 Steve Largent	1.25	3.00
27 Lee Roy Selmon	.60	1.50
28 Art Monk	1.50	4.00

1981 Topps Stickers

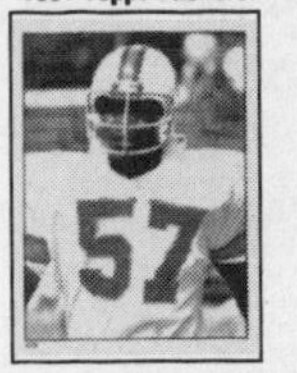

Like the 1981 baseball stickers, the 1981 Topps football stickers were also printed in Italy, each sticker measuring 1 15/16" by 2 9/16". The 262-card (sticker) set contains 22 All-Pro foil cards (numbers 121-142). The foil cards are somewhat more difficult to obtain, and a premium price is placed upon them. The card numbers begin with players from the AFC East teams and continue through the AFC Central and West divisions with teams within each division listed alphabetically. Card number 151 begins the NFC East teams, and a similar progression through the NFC divisions completes the remaining cards of the set. The backs contain a 1981 copyright date. On the inside back cover of the sticker album the company offered (via direct mail-order) any ten different stickers (but no more than two foil) of your choice for 1.00; this is one reason why the values of the most popular players in these sticker sets are somewhat depressed compared to traditional card set prices. The front cover of the sticker album features a Buffalo Bills player. The following players are shown in their Rookie Card year or earlier: Dwight Clark, Jacob Green (two years early), Dan Hampton, Art Monk, Anthony Munoz (one year early), and Kellen Winslow.

COMPLETE SET (262)	10.00	25.00
1 Brian Sipe LL	.02	.10
2 Dan Fouts LL	.10	.30
3 John Jefferson LL	.02	.10
4 Bruce Harper LL	.02	.10
5 J.T. Smith LL	.02	.10
6 Luke Prestridge LL	.02	.10
7 Lester Hayes LL	.02	.10
8 Gary Johnson LL	.02	.10
9 Bert Jones	.07	.20
10 Fred Cook	.02	.10
11 Roger Carr	.02	.10
12 Greg Landry	.02	.10
13 Raymond Butler	.02	.10
14 Bruce Laird	.02	.10
15 Ed Simonini	.02	.10
16 Curtis Dickey	.02	.10
17 Joe Cribbs	.02	.10
18 Joe Ferguson	.02	.10
19 Ben Williams	.02	.10
20 Jerry Butler	.02	.10
21 Roland Hooks	.02	.10
22 Fred Smerlas	.02	.10
23 Frank Lewis	.02	.10
24 Mark Brammer	.02	.10
25 David Woodley	.02	.10
26 Nat Moore	.02	.10
27 Uwe Von Schamann	.02	.10
28 Vern Den Herder	.02	.10
29 Tony Nathan	.02	.10
30 Duriel Harris	.02	.10
31 Don McNeal	.02	.10
32 Delvin Williams	.02	.10
33 Stanley Morgan	.02	.10
34 John Hannah	.07	.20
35 Horace Ivory	.02	.10
36 Steve Nelson	.02	.10
37 Steve Grogan	.07	.20
38 Vagas Ferguson	.02	.10
39 John Smith	.02	.10
40 Mike Haynes	.02	.10
41 Mark Gastineau	.02	.10
42 Wesley Walker	.02	.10
43 Joe Klecko	.02	.10
44 Chris Ward	.02	.10
45 Johnny Lam Jones	.02	.10
46 Marvin Powell	.02	.10
47 Richard Todd	.02	.10
48 Greg Buttle	.02	.10
49 Eddie Edwards	.02	.10
50 Dan Ross	.02	.10
51 Ken Anderson	.10	.30
52 Ross Browner	.02	.10
53 Don Bass	.02	.10
54 Jim LeClair	.02	.10
55 Pete Johnson	.02	.10
56 Anthony Munoz	.40	1.00
57 Brian Sipe	.02	.10
58 Mike Pruitt	.02	.10
59 Greg Pruitt	.02	.10
60 Thom Darden	.02	.10
61 Ozzie Newsome	.10	.30
62 Dave Logan	.02	.10
63 Lyle Alzado	.07	.20
64 Reggie Rucker	.02	.10
65 Robert Brazile	.02	.10
66 Mike Barber	.02	.10
67 Carl Roaches	.02	.10
68 Ken Stabler	.40	1.00
69 Gregg Bingham	.02	.10
70 Mike Renfro	.02	.10
71 Leon Gray	.02	.10
72 Rob Carpenter	.02	.10
73 Franco Harris	.15	.40
74 Jack Lambert	.10	.30
75 Jim Smith	.02	.10
76 Mike Webster	.07	.20
77 Sidney Thornton	.02	.10
78 Joe Greene	.10	.30
79 John Stallworth	.07	.20
80 Tyrone McGriff	.02	.10
81 Randy Gradishar	.02	.10
82 Haven Moses	.02	.10
83 Riley Odoms	.02	.10
84 Matt Robinson	.02	.10
85 Craig Morton	.02	.10
86 Rulon Jones	.02	.10
87 Rick Upchurch	.02	.10
88 Jim Jensen	.02	.10
89 Art Still	.02	.10
90 J.T. Smith	.02	.10
91 Steve Fuller	.02	.10
92 Gary Barbaro	.02	.10
93 Ted McKnight	.02	.10
94 Bob Grupp	.02	.10
95 Henry Marshall	.02	.10
96 Mike Williams	.02	.10
97 Jim Plunkett	.07	.20
98 Lester Hayes	.02	.10
99 Cliff Branch	.07	.20
100 John Matuszak	.02	.10
101 Matt Millen	.02	.10
102 Kenny King	.02	.10
103 Ray Guy	.02	.10
104 Ted Hendricks	.07	.20
105 John Jefferson	.07	.20
106 Fred Dean	.07	.20
107 Dan Fouts	.15	.40
108 Charlie Joiner	.10	.30
109 Kellen Winslow	.60	1.50
110 Gary Johnson	.02	.10
111 Mike Thomas	.02	.10
112 Louie Kelcher	.02	.10
113 Jim Zorn	.02	.10
114 Terry Beeson	.02	.10
115 Jacob Green	.07	.20
116 Steve Largent	.30	.75
117 Dan Doornink	.02	.10
118 Manu Tuiasosopo	.02	.10
119 John Sawyer	.02	.10
120 Jim Jodat	.02	.10
121 Walter Payton FOIL	1.50	4.00
122 Brian Sipe FOIL	.10	.30
123 Joe Cribbs FOIL	.10	.30
124 James Lofton FOIL	.20	.50
125 John Jefferson FOIL	.10	.30
126 Leon Gray FOIL	.07	.20
127 Joe DeLamielleure FOIL	.10	.30
128 Mike Webster FOIL	.10	.30
129 John Hannah FOIL	.10	.30
130 Mike Kenn FOIL	.07	.20
131 Kellen Winslow FOIL	.60	1.50
132 Lee Roy Selmon FOIL	.20	.50
133 Randy White FOIL	.20	.50
134 Gary Johnson FOIL	.07	.20
135 Art Still FOIL	.07	.20
136 Robert Brazile FOIL	.07	.20
137 Nolan Cromwell FOIL	.07	.20
138 Ted Hendricks FOIL	.10	.30
139 Lester Hayes FOIL	.10	.30
140 Randy Gradishar FOIL	.10	.30
141 Lemar Parrish FOIL	.07	.20
142 Donnie Shell FOIL	.10	.30
143 Ron Jaworski LL	.02	.10
144 Archie Manning LL	.02	.10
145 Walter Payton LL	.40	1.00
146 Billy Sims LL	.07	.20
147 James Lofton LL	.07	.20
148 Dave Jennings LL	.02	.10
149 Nolan Cromwell LL	.02	.10
150 Al(Bubba) Baker LL	.02	.10
151 Tony Dorsett	.50	1.25
152 Harvey Martin	.02	.10
153 Danny White	.07	.20
154 Pat Donovan	.02	.10
155 Drew Pearson	.07	.20
156 Robert Newhouse	.02	.10
157 Randy White	.10	.30
158 Butch Johnson	.02	.10
159 Dave Jennings	.02	.10
160 Brad Van Pelt	.02	.10
161 Phil Simms	.20	.50
162 Mike Friede	.02	.10
163 Billy Taylor	.02	.10
164 Gary Jeter	.02	.10
165 George Martin	.02	.10
166 Earnest Gray	.02	.10
167 Ron Jaworski	.07	.20
168 Bill Bergey	.02	.10
169 Wilbert Montgomery	.02	.10
170 Charlie Smith	.02	.10
171 Jerry Robinson	.02	.10
172 Herman Edwards	.02	.10
173 Harold Carmichael	.07	.20
174 Claude Humphrey	.02	.10
175 Ottis Anderson	.08	.25
176 Jim Hart	.02	.10
177 Pat Tilley	.02	.10
178 Rush Brown	.02	.10
179 Tom Brahaney	.02	.10
180 Dan Dierdorf	.08	.25
181 Wayne Morris	.02	.10
182 Doug Marsh	.02	.10
183 Art Monk	.60	1.50
184 Clarence Harmon	.02	.10
185 Lemar Parrish	.02	.10
186 Joe Theismann	.15	.40
187 Joe Lavender	.02	.10
188 Wilbur Jackson	.02	.10
189 Dave Butz	.02	.10
190 Coy Bacon	.02	.10
191 Walter Payton	1.25	3.00
192 Alan Page	.07	.20
193 Vince Evans	.07	.20
194 Roland Harper	.02	.10
195 Dan Hampton	.25	.60
196 Gary Fencik	.02	.10
197 Mike Hartenstine	.02	.10
198 Robin Earl	.02	.10
199 Billy Sims	.08	.25
200 Leonard Thompson	.02	.10
201 Jeff Komlo	.02	.10
202 Al(Bubba) Baker	.02	.10
203 Eddie Murray	.02	.10
204 Dexter Bussey	.02	.10
205 Tom Ginn	.02	.10
206 Freddie Scott	.02	.10
207 James Lofton	.15	.40
208 Mike Butler	.02	.10
209 Lynn Dickey	.02	.10
210 Gerry Ellis	.02	.10
211 Eddie Lee Ivery	.02	.10
212 Ezra Johnson	.02	.10
213 Paul Coffman	.02	.10
214 Aundra Thompson	.02	.10
215 Ahmad Rashad	.07	.20
216 Tommy Kramer	.02	.10
217 Matt Blair	.02	.10
218 Sammie White	.02	.10
219 Ted Brown	.02	.10
220 Joe Senser	.02	.10
221 Rickey Young	.02	.10
222 Randy Holloway	.02	.10
223 Lee Roy Selmon	.10	.30
224 Doug Williams	.02	.10
225 Ricky Bell	.02	.10
226 David Lewis	.02	.10
227 Gordon Jones	.02	.10
228 Dewey Selmon	.02	.10
229 Jimmie Giles	.02	.10
230 Mike Washington	.02	.10
231 William Andrews	.02	.10
232 Jeff Van Note	.02	.10
233 Steve Bartkowski	.02	.10
234 Junior Miller	.02	.10
235 Lynn Cain	.02	.10
236 Joel Williams	.02	.10
237 Alfred Jenkins	.02	.10
238 Kenny Johnson	.02	.10
239 Jack Youngblood	.07	.20
240 Elvis Peacock	.02	.10
241 Cullen Bryant	.02	.10
242 Dennis Harrah	.02	.10
243 Billy Waddy	.02	.10
244 Nolan Cromwell	.02	.10
245 Doug France	.02	.10
246 Johnnie Johnson	.02	.10
247 Archie Manning	.07	.20
248 Tony Galbreath	.02	.10
249 Wes Chandler	.02	.10
250 Stan Brock	.02	.10
251 Ike Harris	.02	.10
252 Russell Erxleben	.02	.10
253 Jimmy Rogers	.02	.10
254 Tom Myers	.02	.10
255 Dwight Clark	.30	.75
256 Earl Cooper	.02	.10
257 Steve DeBerg	.07	.20
258 Randy Cross	.02	.10
259 Freddie Solomon	.02	.10
260 Jim Miller P	.02	.10
261 Charle Young	.02	.10
262 Bobby Leopold	.02	.10
NNO Sticker Album	.75	2.00

1982 Topps Coming Soon Stickers

This 16-sticker set advertises "Coming Soon" on the sticker backs. All stickers in this small set were gold bordered foil stickers; these "Coming Soon" stickers were inserted in the regular issue 1982 Topps football card wax packs. They are the same size as the regular Topps stickers with the same sticker numbers as well; hence the set is skip-numbered.

COMPLETE SET (16)	2.00	5.00
5 MVP Super Bowl XVI (Joe Montana)	.75	2.00
6 NFC Championship	.07	.20
9 Super Bowl XVI (Joe Montana handing off)	.60	1.50
71 Tommy Kramer	.07	.20
73 George Rogers	.10	.30
75 Tom Skladany	.07	.20
139 Nolan Cromwell AP	.07	.20
143 Jack Lambert AP	.20	.50
144 Lawrence Taylor AP	.40	1.00
150 Billy Sims AP	.15	.40
154 Ken Anderson AP	.20	.50
159 John Hannah AP	.15	.40
160 Anthony Munoz AP	.40	1.00
220 Ken Anderson	.20	.50
221 Dan Fouts	.20	.50
222 Frank Lewis	.07	.20

1982 Topps Stickers

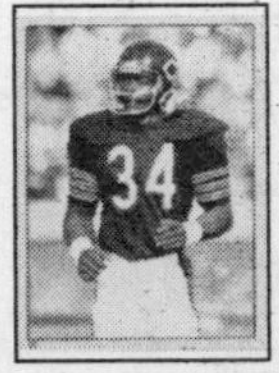

The 1982 Topps football sticker set contains 288 stickers and is similar in format to the 1981 sticker set. The stickers measure 1 15/16" by 2 9/16". This year's stickers have yellow borders compared to the white borders of the previous year. Stickers numbered 1-10, 70-77, 139-160, and 220-227 are foils. Stickers numbered 1 and 2 combine to portray the San Francisco 49ers, Super Bowl XVI Champions. Sticker numbers 3 and 4 combine to form the Super Bowl XVI theme art trophy. Stickers are numbered essentially in team order, with the teams themselves ordered alphabetically by team name within conference. Those stickers that are asterisked in the checklist below are those that were also included in the "Coming Soon" sticker set inserted in early 1982 football wax packs. The backs contain a 1982 copyright date. On the inside back cover of the sticker album the company offered (via direct mail-order) any ten different stickers (but no more than two foil) of your choice for 1.00; this is one reason why the values of the most popular players in these sticker sets are somewhat depressed compared to traditional card set prices. The front cover of the sticker album features Joe Montana. The following players are shown in their Rookie Card year: James Brooks, Cris Collinsworth, Ronnie Lott, Anthony Munoz, Lawrence Taylor, and Everson Walls.

COMPLETE SET (288)	10.00	25.00
1 Super Bowl XVI Champs, San Francisco/49ers Team (L) FOIL	.40	1.00
2 Super Bowl XVI Champs, San Francisco/49ers Team (R) FOIL	.30	.75
3 Super Bowl XVI Theme Art trophy (top) FOIL	.07	.20
4 Super Bowl XVI Theme Art trophy (bottom) FOIL	.07	.20
5 MVP Joe Montana Super Bowl XVI * FOIL	2.00	5.00
6 1981 NFC Champions/49'ers * FOIL	.02	.10
7 1981 AFC Champions (Ken Anderson handing off) FOIL	.07	.20
8 Super Bowl XVI (Ken Anderson dropping back) FOIL	.08	.25
9 Super Bowl XVI (Joe Montana handing off) * FOIL	1.50	4.00
10 Super Bowl XVI (line blocking) FOIL	.20	.50
11 Steve Bartkowski	.02	.10
12 William Andrews	.02	.10
13 Lynn Cain	.02	.10
14 Wallace Francis	.02	.10
15 Alfred Jackson	.02	.10
16 Alfred Jenkins	.02	.10
17 Mike Kenn	.02	.10
18 Junior Miller	.02	.10
19 Vince Evans	.02	.10
20 Walter Payton	1.25	3.00
21 Dave Williams	.02	.10
22 Brian Baschnagel	.02	.10
23 Rickey Watts	.02	.10
24 Ken Margerum	.02	.10
25 Revie Sorey	.02	.10
26 Gary Fencik	.02	.10
27 Matt Suhey	.02	.10
28 Danny White	.07	.20
29 Tony Dorsett	.15	.40
30 Drew Pearson	.07	.20
31 Rafael Septien	.02	.10
32 Pat Donovan	.02	.10
33 Herb Scott	.02	.10
34 Ed Too Tall Jones	.07	.20
35 Randy White	.08	.25
36 Tony Hill	.02	.10
37 Eric Hipple	.02	.10
38 Billy Sims	.07	.20
39 Dexter Bussey	.02	.10
40 Freddie Scott	.02	.10
41 David Hill	.02	.10
42 Eddie Murray	.02	.10
43 Tom Skladany	.02	.10
44 Doug English	.02	.10
45 Al(Bubba) Baker	.02	.10
46 Lynn Dickey	.02	.10
47 Gerry Ellis	.02	.10
48 Harlan Huckleby	.02	.10
49 James Lofton	.15	.40
50 John Jefferson	.02	.10
51 Paul Coffman	.02	.10
52 Jan Stenerud	.02	.10
53 Rich Wingo	.02	.10
54 Wendell Tyler	.02	.10
55 Preston Dennard	.02	.10
56 Billy Waddy	.02	.10
57 Frank Corral	.02	.10
58 Jack Youngblood	.02	.10
59 Pat Thomas	.02	.10
60 Rod Perry	.02	.10
61 Nolan Cromwell	.02	.10
62 Tommy Kramer	.02	.10
63 Rickey Young	.02	.10
64 Ted Brown	.02	.10
65 Ahmad Rashad	.08	.25
66 Sammie White	.02	.10
67 Joe Senser	.02	.10
68 Ron Yary	.02	.10
69 Matt Blair	.02	.10
70 Joe Montana FOIL NFC Passing Leader	2.50	6.00
71 Tommy Kramer * FOIL NFC Passing Yardage Leader	.05	.15
72 Alfred Jenkins FOIL NFC Receiving Yardage Leader	.05	.15
73 George Rogers * FOIL NFC Rushing Yardage Leader	.05	.15
74 Wendell Tyler FOIL NFC Rushing Touchdowns Leader	.05	.15
75 Tom Skladany * FOIL NFC Punting Leader	.05	.15
76 Everson Walls FOIL NFC Interceptions Leader	.08	.25
77 Curtis Greer FOIL NFC Sacks Leader	.05	.15
78 Archie Manning	.07	.20
79 Dave Waymer	.02	.10
80 George Rogers	.07	.20
81 Jack Holmes	.02	.10
82 Toussaint Tyler	.02	.10
83 Wayne Wilson	.02	.10
84 Russell Erxleben	.02	.10
85 Elois Grooms	.02	.10
86 Phil Simms	.07	.20
87 Scott Brunner	.02	.10
88 Rob Carpenter	.02	.10
89 Johnny Perkins	.02	.10
90 Dave Jennings	.02	.10
91 Harry Carson	.02	.10
92 Lawrence Taylor	.60	1.50
93 Beasley Reece	.02	.10
94 Mark Haynes	.02	.10
95 Ron Jaworski	.02	.10
96 Wilbert Montgomery	.02	.10
97 Hubie Oliver	.02	.10
98 Harold Carmichael	.02	.10
99 Jerry Robinson	.02	.10
100 Stan Walters	.02	.10
101 Charlie Johnson	.02	.10
102 Roynell Young	.02	.10
103 Tony Franklin	.02	.10
104 Neil Lomax	.07	.20
105 Jim Hart	.02	.10
106 Ottis Anderson	.07	.20
107 Stump Mitchell	.02	.10
108 Pat Tilley	.02	.10
109 Rush Brown	.02	.10
110 E.J. Junior	.02	.10
111 Ken Greene	.02	.10
112 Mel Gray	.02	.10
113 Joe Montana	2.00	5.00
114 Ricky Patton	.02	.10
115 Earl Cooper	.02	.10
116 Dwight Clark	.08	.25
117 Freddie Solomon	.02	.10
118 Randy Cross	.02	.10
119 Fred Dean	.07	.20
120 Ronnie Lott	.40	1.00
121 Dwight Hicks	.02	.10
122 Doug Williams	.02	.10
123 Jerry Eckwood	.02	.10
124 James Owens	.02	.10
125 Kevin House	.02	.10
126 Jimmie Giles	.02	.10
127 Charley Hannah	.02	.10
128 Lee Roy Selmon	.08	.25
129 Hugh Green	.02	.10
130 Joe Theismann	.10	.30
131 Joe Washington	.02	.10
132 John Riggins	.08	.25
133 Art Monk	.20	.50
134 Ricky Thompson	.02	.10
135 Don Warren	.02	.10
136 Perry Brooks	.02	.10
137 Mike Nelms	.02	.10
138 Mark Moseley	.02	.10
139 Nolan Cromwell * AP FOIL	.05	.15
140 Dwight Hicks AP FOIL	.05	.15
141 Ronnie Lott AP FOIL	.60	1.50
142 Harry Carson AP FOIL	.08	.25
143 Jack Lambert * AP FOIL	.15	.40
144 Lawrence Taylor * AP FOIL	.75	2.00
145 Mel Blount AP FOIL	.10	.30
146 Joe Klecko AP FOIL	.05	.15
147 Randy White AP FOIL	.15	.40
148 Doug English AP FOIL	.05	.15
149 Fred Dean AP FOIL	.07	.20
150 Billy Sims * AP FOIL	.10	.30
151 Tony Dorsett AP FOIL	.50	1.25
152 James Lofton AP FOIL	.25	.60
153 Alfred Jenkins AP FOIL	.08	.25
154 Ken Anderson * AP FOIL	.15	.40
155 Kellen Winslow AP FOIL	.25	.60

156 Marvin Powell AP FOIL	.05	.15
157 Randy Cross AP FOIL	.05	.15
158 Mike Webster AP FOIL	.08	.25
159 John Hannah * AP FOIL	.10	.30
160 Anthony Munoz * AP FOIL	.40	1.00
161 Curtis Dickey	.02	.10
162 Randy McMillan	.02	.10
163 Roger Carr	.02	.10
164 Raymond Butler	.02	.10
165 Reese McCall	.02	.10
166 Ed Simonini	.02	.10
167 Herb Orvis	.02	.10
168 Nesby Glasgow	.02	.10
169 Joe Ferguson	.02	.10
170 Joe Cribbs	.02	.10
171 Jerry Butler	.02	.10
172 Frank Lewis	.02	.10
173 Mark Brammer	.02	.10
174 Fred Smerlas	.02	.10
175 Jim Haslett	.02	.10
176 Charles Romes	.02	.10
177 Bill Simpson	.02	.10
178 Ken Anderson	.08	.25
179 Charles Alexander	.02	.10
180 Pete Johnson	.02	.10
181 Isaac Curtis	.02	.10
182 Cris Collinsworth	.20	.50
183 Pat McInally	.02	.10
184 Anthony Munoz	.20	.50
185 Louis Breeden	.02	.10
186 Jim Breech	.02	.10
187 Brian Sipe	.02	.10
188 Charles White	.02	.10
189 Mike Pruitt	.02	.10
190 Reggie Rucker	.02	.10
191 Dave Logan	.02	.10
192 Ozzie Newsome	.08	.25
193 Dick Ambrose	.02	.10
194 Joe DeLamielleure	.02	.10
195 Ricky Feacher	.02	.10
196 Craig Morton	.02	.10
197 Dave Preston	.02	.10
198 Rick Parros	.02	.10
199 Rick Upchurch	.02	.10
200 Steve Watson	.02	.10
201 Riley Odoms	.02	.10
202 Randy Gradishar	.02	.10
203 Steve Foley	.02	.10
204 Ken Stabler	.15	.40
205 Gifford Nielsen	.02	.10
206 Tim Wilson	.02	.10
207 Ken Burrough	.02	.10
208 Mike Renfro	.02	.10
209 Greg Stemrick	.02	.10
210 Robert Brazile	.02	.10
211 Gregg Bingham	.02	.10
212 Steve Fuller	.02	.10
213 Bill Kenney	.02	.10
214 Joe Delaney	.02	.10
215 Henry Marshall	.02	.10
216 Nick Lowery	.02	.10
217 Art Still	.02	.10
218 Gary Green	.02	.10
219 Gary Barbaro	.02	.10
220 Ken Anderson * FOIL AFC Passing Leader	.15	.40
221 Dan Fouts * FOIL AFC Passing Yardage Leader	.20	.50
222 Frank Lewis * FOIL AFC Receiving Yardage Leader	.05	.15
222 Steve Watson FOIL AFC Receiving Yardage Leader	.05	.15
223 James Brooks FOIL AFC Kickoff Return Yardage Leader	.25	.60
224 Chuck Muncie FOIL AFC Rushing Touchdowns Leader	.05	.15
225 Pat McInally FOIL AFC Punting Leader	.05	.15
226 John Harris FOIL AFC Interceptions Leader	.05	.15
227 Joe Klecko FOIL AFC Sacks Leader	.05	.15
228 David Woodley	.02	.10
229 Tony Nathan	.02	.10
230 Andra Franklin	.02	.10
231 Nat Moore	.02	.10
232 Duriel Harris	.02	.10
233 Uwe Von Schamann	.02	.10
234 Bob Baumhower	.02	.10
235 Glenn Blackwood	.02	.10
236 Tommy Vigorito	.02	.10
237 Steve Grogan	.02	.10
238 Matt Cavanaugh	.02	.10
239 Tony Collins	.02	.10
240 Vagas Ferguson	.02	.10
241 John Smith	.02	.10
242 Stanley Morgan	.02	.10
243 John Hannah	.02	.10
244 Steve Nelson	.02	.10
245 Don Hasselbeck	.02	.10
246 Richard Todd	.02	.10
247 Bruce Harper	.02	.10
248 Wesley Walker	.02	.10
249 Jerome Barkum	.02	.10
250 Marvin Powell	.02	.10
251 Mark Gastineau	.02	.10
252 Joe Klecko	.02	.10
253 Darrol Ray	.02	.10
254 Marty Lyons	.02	.10
255 Marc Wilson	.02	.10
256 Kenny King	.02	.10
257 Mark Van Eeghen	.02	.10
258 Cliff Branch	.02	.10
259 Bob Chandler	.02	.10
260 Ray Guy	.02	.10
261 Ted Hendricks	.07	.20
262 Lester Hayes	.02	.10
263 Terry Bradshaw	.40	1.00
264 Franco Harris	.15	.40
265 John Stallworth	.07	.20
266 Jim Smith	.02	.10
267 Mike Webster	.02	.10
268 Jack Lambert	.08	.25
269 Mel Blount	.07	.20
270 Donnie Shell	.02	.10
271 Bennie Cunningham	.02	.10
272 Dan Fouts	.10	.30
273 Chuck Muncie	.02	.10
274 James Brooks	.10	.30
275 Charlie Joiner	.07	.20
276 Wes Chandler	.02	.10
277 Kellen Winslow	.15	.40
278 Doug Wilkerson	.02	.10
279 Gary Johnson	.02	.10
280 Rolf Benirschke	.02	.10
281 Jim Zorn	.02	.10
282 Theotis Brown	.02	.10
283 Dan Doornink	.02	.10
284 Steve Largent	.40	1.00
285 Sam McCullum	.02	.10
286 Efren Herrera	.02	.10
287 Manu Tuiasosopo	.02	.10
288 John Harris	.02	.10
288 Sticker Album (Joe Montana)	1.25	3.00

1983 Topps Stickers

The 1983 Topps football sticker set (330) is similar to the previous years in that it contains stickers, foil stickers, and an accompanying album to house one's sticker collection. The foil stickers are noted in the checklist below by "FOIL"; foils are numbers 1-4, 73-80, 143-152, and 264-271. On the inside back cover of the sticker album the company offered (via direct mail-order) any ten different stickers (but no more than two foil) of your choice for 1.00; this is one reason why the values of the most popular players in these sticker sets are somewhat depressed compared to traditional card set prices. The following players are shown in their Rookie Card year: Marcus Allen, Jim McMahon, and Mike Singletary.

COMPLETE SET (330)	10.00	25.00
1 Franco Harris (Left half) FOIL	.30	.75
2 Franco Harris (Right half) FOIL	.15	.40
3 Walter Payton FOIL	1.50	4.00
4 Walter Payton FOIL	1.50	4.00
5 John Riggins	.10	.30
6 Tony Dorsett	.20	.50
7 Mark Van Eeghen	.02	.10
8 Chuck Muncie	.02	.10
9 Wilbert Montgomery	.02	.10
10 Greg Pruitt	.02	.10
11 Sam Cunningham	.02	.10
12 Ottis Anderson	.07	.20
13 Mike Pruitt	.02	.10
14 Dexter Bussey	.02	.10
15 Mike Pagel	.02	.10
16 Curtis Dickey	.02	.10
17 Randy McMillan	.02	.10
18 Raymond Butler	.02	.10
19 Nesby Glasgow	.02	.10
20 Zachary Dixon	.02	.10
21 Matt Bouza	.02	.10
22 Johnie Cooks	.02	.10
23 Curtis Brown	.02	.10
24 Joe Cribbs	.02	.10
25 Roosevelt Leaks	.02	.10
26 Jerry Butler	.02	.10
27 Frank Lewis	.02	.10
28 Fred Smerlas	.02	.10
29 Ben Williams	.02	.10
30 Joe Ferguson	.02	.10
31 Isaac Curtis	.02	.10
32 Cris Collinsworth	.07	.20
33 Anthony Munoz	.07	.20
34 Max Montoya	.02	.10
35 Ross Browner	.02	.10
36 Reggie Williams	.02	.10
37 Ken Riley	.02	.10
38 Pete Johnson	.02	.10
39 Ken Anderson	.08	.25
40 Charles White	.02	.10
41 Dave Logan	.02	.10
42 Doug Dieken	.02	.10
43 Ozzie Newsome	.07	.20
44 Tom Cousineau	.02	.10
45 Bob Golic	.02	.10
46 Brian Sipe	.02	.10
47 Paul McDonald	.02	.10
48 Mike Pruitt	.02	.10
49 Luke Prestridge	.02	.10
50 Randy Gradishar	.02	.10
51 Rulon Jones	.02	.10
52 Rick Parros	.02	.10
53 Steve DeBerg	.02	.10
54 Tom Jackson	.02	.10
55 Rick Upchurch	.02	.10
56 Steve Watson	.02	.10
57 Robert Brazile	.02	.10
58 Willie Tullis	.02	.10
59 Archie Manning	.07	.20
60 Gifford Nielsen	.02	.10
61 Harold Bailey	.02	.10
62 Carl Roaches	.02	.10
63 Gregg Bingham	.02	.10
64 Daryl Hunt	.02	.10
65 Gary Green	.02	.10
66 Gary Barbaro	.02	.10
67 Bill Kenney	.02	.10
68 Joe Delaney	.02	.10
69 Henry Marshall	.02	.10
70 Nick Lowery	.02	.10
71 Jeff Gossett	.02	.10
72 Art Still	.02	.10
73 Ken Anderson FOIL AFC Passing Leader	.08	.25
74 Dan Fouts FOIL AFC Passing Yardage Leader	.15	.40
75 Wes Chandler FOIL AFC Receiving Yardage Leader	.08	.25
76 James Brooks FOIL AFC Kickoff Return Yardage Leader	.08	.25
77 Rick Upchurch FOIL AFC Punt Return Yardage Leader	.02	.10
78 Luke Prestridge FOIL AFC Punting Leader	.02	.10
79 Jesse Baker FOIL AFC Sacks Leader	.02	.10
80 Freeman McNeil FOIL AFC Rushing Yardage Leader	.08	.25
81 Ray Guy	.02	.10
82 Jim Plunkett	.07	.20
83 Lester Hayes	.02	.10
84 Kenny King	.02	.10
85 Cliff Branch	.07	.20
86 Todd Christensen	.02	.10
87 Lyle Alzado	.07	.20
88 Ted Hendricks	.07	.20
89 Rod Martin	.02	.10
90 David Woodley	.02	.10
91 Ed Newman	.02	.10
92 Earnie Rhone	.02	.10
93 Don McNeal	.02	.10
94 Glenn Blackwood	.02	.10
95 Andra Franklin	.02	.10
96 Nat Moore	.02	.10
97 Lyle Blackwood	.02	.10
98 A.J. Duhe	.02	.10
99 Tony Collins	.02	.10
100 Stanley Morgan	.02	.10
101 Pete Brock	.02	.10
102 Steve Nelson	.02	.10
103 Steve Grogan	.02	.10
104 Mark Van Eeghen	.02	.10
105 Don Hasselbeck	.02	.10
106 John Hannah	.07	.20
107 Mike Haynes	.02	.10
108 Wesley Walker	.02	.10
109 Marvin Powell	.02	.10
110 Joe Klecko	.02	.10
111 Bobby Jackson	.02	.10
112 Richard Todd	.02	.10
113 Lance Mehl	.02	.10
114 Johnny Lam Jones	.02	.10
115 Mark Gastineau	.02	.10
116 Freeman McNeil	.02	.10
117 Franco Harris	.15	.40
118 Mike Webster	.07	.20
119 Mel Blount	.07	.20
120 Donnie Shell	.02	.10
121 Terry Bradshaw	.40	1.00
122 John Stallworth	.07	.20
123 Jack Lambert	.08	.25
124 Dwayne Woodruff	.02	.10
125 Bennie Cunningham	.02	.10
126 Charlie Joiner	.07	.20
127 Kellen Winslow	.10	.30
128 Rolf Benirschke	.02	.10
129 Louie Kelcher	.02	.10
130 Chuck Muncie	.02	.10
131 Wes Chandler	.02	.10
132 Gary Johnson	.02	.10
133 James Brooks	.07	.20
134 Dan Fouts	.15	.40
135 Jacob Green	.02	.10
136 Michael Jackson	.02	.10
137 Jim Zorn	.02	.10
138 Sherman Smith	.02	.10
139 Keith Simpson	.02	.10
140 Steve Largent	.40	1.00
141 John Harris	.02	.10
142 Jeff West	.02	.10
143 Ken Anderson (top) FOIL	.08	.25
144 Ken Anderson (bottom) FOIL	.08	.25
145 Tony Dorsett (top) FOIL	.30	.75
146 Tony Dorsett (bottom) FOIL	.30	.75
147 Dan Fouts (top) FOIL	.15	.40
148 Dan Fouts (bottom) FOIL	.15	.40
149 Joe Montana (top) FOIL	2.00	5.00
150 Joe Montana (bottom) FOIL	2.00	5.00
151 Mark Moseley (top) FOIL	.02	.10
152 Mark Moseley (bottom) FOIL	.02	.10
153 Richard Todd	.02	.10
154 Butch Johnson	.02	.10
155 Gary Hogeboom UER (Bill on back)	.02	.10
156 A.J. Duhe	.02	.10
157 Kurt Sohn	.02	.10
158 Drew Pearson	.07	.20
159 John Riggins	.08	.25
160 Pat Donovan	.02	.10
161 John Hannah	.07	.20
162 Jeff Van Note	.02	.10
163 Randy Cross	.02	.10
164 Marvin Powell	.02	.10
165 Kellen Winslow	.08	.25
166 Dwight Clark	.07	.20
167 Wes Chandler	.02	.10
168 Tony Dorsett	.15	.40
169 Freeman McNeil	.02	.10
170 Ken Anderson	.07	.20
171 Mark Moseley	.02	.10
172 Mark Gastineau	.02	.10
173 Gary Johnson	.02	.10
174 Randy White	.08	.25
175 Ed Too Tall Jones	.07	.20
176 Hugh Green	.02	.10
177 Harry Carson	.02	.10
178 Lawrence Taylor	.15	.40
179 Lester Hayes	.02	.10
180 Mark Haynes	.02	.10
181 Dave Jennings	.02	.10
182 Nolan Cromwell	.02	.10
183 Tony Peters	.02	.10
184 Jimmy Cefalo	.02	.10
185 A.J. Duhe	.02	.10
186 John Riggins	.08	.25
187 Charlie Brown	.02	.10
188 Mike Nelms	.02	.10
189 Mark Murphy	.02	.10
190 Fulton Walker	.02	.10
191 Marcus Allen	1.25	3.00
192 Chip Banks	.02	.10
193 Charlie Brown	.02	.10
194 Bob Crable	.02	.10
195 Vernon Dean	.02	.10
196 Jim McMahon	.40	1.00
197 Tootie Robbins	.02	.10
198 Luis Sharpe	.02	.10
199 Rohn Stark	.02	.10
200 Lester Williams	.02	.10
201 Leo Wisniewski	.02	.10
202 Butch Woolfolk	.02	.10
203 Mike Kenn	.02	.10
204 R.C. Thielemann	.02	.10
205 Buddy Curry	.02	.10
206 Steve Bartkowski	.02	.10
207 Alfred Jackson	.02	.10
208 Don Smith	.02	.10
209 Alfred Jenkins	.02	.10
210 Fulton Kuykendall	.02	.10
211 William Andrews	.02	.10
212 Gary Fencik	.02	.10
213 Walter Payton	1.25	3.00
214 Mike Singletary	.40	1.00
215 Otis Wilson	.02	.10
216 Matt Suhey	.02	.10
217 Dan Hampton	.08	.25
218 Emery Moorehead	.02	.10
219 Mike Hartenstine	.02	.10
220 Danny White	.07	.20
221 Drew Pearson	.07	.20
222 Rafael Septien	.02	.10
223 Ed Too Tall Jones	.07	.20
224 Everson Walls	.02	.10
225 Randy White	.08	.25
226 Harvey Martin	.02	.10
227 Tony Hill	.02	.10
228 Tony Dorsett	.15	.40
229 Billy Sims	.07	.20
230 Leonard Thompson	.02	.10
231 Eddie Murray	.02	.10
232 Doug English	.02	.10
233 Ken Fantetti	.02	.10
234 Tom Skladany	.02	.10
235 Freddie Scott	.02	.10
236 Eric Hipple	.02	.10
237 David Hill	.02	.10
238 John Jefferson	.02	.10
239 Paul Coffman	.02	.10
240 Ezra Johnson	.02	.10
241 Mike Douglass	.02	.10
242 Mark Lee	.02	.10
243 John Anderson	.02	.10
244 Jan Stenerud	.07	.20
245 Lynn Dickey	.02	.10
246 James Lofton	.10	.30
247 Vince Ferragamo	.02	.10
248 Preston Dennard	.02	.10
249 Jack Youngblood	.07	.20
250 Mike Guman	.02	.10
251 LeRoy Irvin	.02	.10
252 Mike Lansford	.02	.10
253 Kent Hill	.02	.10
254 Nolan Cromwell	.02	.10
255 Doug Martin	.02	.10
256 Greg Coleman	.02	.10
257 Ted Brown	.02	.10
258 Mark Mullaney	.02	.10
259 Joe Senser	.02	.10
260 Randy Holloway	.02	.10
261 Matt Blair	.02	.10
262 Sammie White	.02	.10
263 Tommy Kramer	.02	.10
264 Joe Theismann FOIL NFC Passing Leader	.15	.40
265 Joe Montana FOIL NFC Passing Yardage Leader	2.50	6.00
266 Dwight Clark FOIL NFC Receiving Yardage Leader	.08	.25
267 Mike Nelms FOIL NFC Kickoff Return Yardage Leader	.02	.10
268 Carl Birdsong FOIL NFC Punting Leader	.02	.10
269 Everson Walls FOIL NFC Interceptions Leader	.02	.10
270 Doug Martin FOIL NFC Sacks Leader	.02	.10
271 Tony Dorsett FOIL NFC Rushing Yardage Leader	.50	1.25
272 Russell Erxleben	.02	.10
273 Stan Brock	.02	.10
274 Jeff Groth	.02	.10
275 Bruce Clark	.02	.10
276 Ken Stabler	.15	.40
277 George Rogers	.02	.10
278 Derland Moore	.02	.10
279 Wayne Wilson	.02	.10
280 Lawrence Taylor	.15	.40
281 Harry Carson	.02	.10
282 Brian Kelley	.02	.10
283 Brad Van Pelt	.02	.10
284 Earnest Gray	.02	.10
285 Dave Jennings	.02	.10
286 Rob Carpenter	.02	.10
287 Scott Brunner	.02	.10
288 Ron Jaworski	.02	.10
289 Jerry Robinson	.02	.10
290 Frank LeMaster	.02	.10
291 Wilbert Montgomery	.02	.10
292 Tony Franklin	.02	.10
293 Harold Carmichael	.07	.20
294 John Spagnola	.02	.10
295 Herman Edwards	.02	.10
296 Ottis Anderson	.02	.10
297 Carl Birdsong	.02	.10
298 Doug Marsh	.02	.10
299 Neil Lomax	.02	.10
300 Rush Brown	.02	.10
301 Pat Tilley	.02	.10
302 Wayne Morris	.02	.10
303 Dan Dierdorf	.07	.20
304 Roy Green	.07	.20
305 Joe Montana	1.50	4.00
306 Randy Cross	.02	.10
307 Freddie Solomon	.02	.10
308 Jack Reynolds	.02	.10
309 Ronnie Lott	.15	.40
310 Renaldo Nehemiah	.02	.10
311 Russ Francis	.02	.10
312 Dwight Clark	.07	.20
313 Doug Williams	.02	.10
314 Bill Capece	.02	.10
315 Mike Washington	.02	.10
316 Hugh Green	.02	.10
317 Kevin House	.02	.10
318 Lee Roy Selmon	.08	.25
319 Neal Colzie	.02	.10
320 Jimmie Giles	.02	.10
321 Cedric Brown	.02	.10
322 Tony Peters	.02	.10
323 Neal Olkewicz	.02	.10
324 Dexter Manley	.02	.10
325 Joe Theismann	.10	.30
326 Rich Milot	.02	.10
327 Mark Moseley	.02	.10
328 Art Monk	.15	.40
329 Mike Nelms	.02	.10
330 John Riggins	.08	.25
NNO Sticker Album	.75	2.00

1983 Topps Sticker Boxes

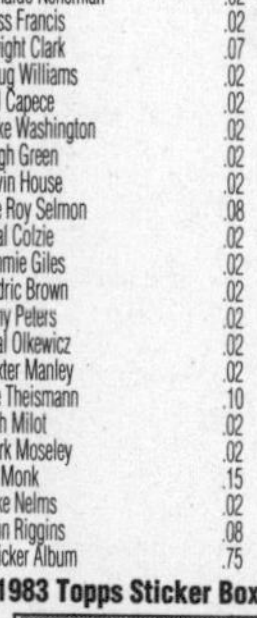

The 1983 Topps Sticker Box set contains 12 boxes each containing two large cards (24 cards total) on the side of the box itself and 35 stickers inside. Cards, when cut, measure approximately 2 1/2" by 3 1/2". These blank-backed cards are unnumbered but each box is numbered on a white box tab. The player on top is offense and the lower player is defense. Number 10 was not issued. Prices below reflect the value of the uncut boxes not including the stickers inside the box.

COMPLETE SET (12)	50.00	100.00
1 Pat Donovan and Mark Gastineau	4.00	8.00
2 Wes Chandler and Nolan Cromwell	4.00	8.00
3 Marvin Powell and Ed Too Tall Jones	5.00	10.00
4 Ken Anderson and Tony Peters	5.00	10.00
5 Freeman McNeil and Lawrence Taylor	7.50	15.00
6 Mark Moseley and Dave Jennings	4.00	8.00
7 Dwight Clark and Mike Haynes	5.00	10.00
8 Jeff Van Note and Harry Carson	4.00	8.00
9 Tony Dorsett and Hugh Green	10.00	20.00
11 Randy Cross and Gary Johnson	4.00	8.00
12 Kellen Winslow and Lester Hayes	5.00	10.00
13 John Hannah and Randy White	7.50	15.00

1984 Topps Stickers

The 1984 Topps Football sticker set is similar to the previous years in that it contains stickers, foil stickers, and an accompanying album to house one's collection. Many of these stickers were printed two players per card. In the checklist below the dual player stickers are listed according to the player with the lowest sticker number. The foil stickers are noted by "FOIL" in the checklist below. On the inside back cover of the sticker album the company offered (via direct mail-order) any 10 different stickers of your choice for 1.00; this is one reason why the values of the most popular players in these sticker sets are somewhat depressed compared to traditional card set prices. The sticker album features Charlie Joiner on the front cover and Dan Fouts on the back cover. The following players are shown in their Rookie Card year: Deron Cherry, Roger Craig, Eric Dickerson, Mark Duper, John Elway, Chris Hinton, Howie Long, Dan Marino, and Jackie Slater.

COMPLETE SET (186)	15.00	35.00
1 Super Bowl XVIII FOIL Plunkett Allen UL	.10	.30
2 Super Bowl XVIII FOIL Plunkett Allen UR	.07	.20
3 Super Bowl XVIII FOIL Plunkett Allen LL	.07	.20
4 Super Bowl XVIII FOIL Plunkett Allen LR	.07	.20
5 Marcus Allen FOIL (Super Bowl MVP)	.50	1.25
6 Walter Payton	1.25	3.00
7 Mike Richardson/157 Pete Johnson	.02	.10
8 Jim McMahon/158 Reggie Williams	.02	.10
9 Mike Hartenstine/159 Isaac Curtis	.02	.10
10 Mike Singletary	.07	.20
11 Willie Gault	.02	.10
12 Terry Schmidt/162 Charles Alexander	.02	.10
13 Emery Moorehead/163 Ray Horton	.02	.10
14 Leslie Frazier/164 Steve Kreider	.02	.10
15 Jack Thompson/165 Ben Williams	.02	.10
16 Booker Reese/166 Frank Lewis	.02	.10
17 James Wilder/167 Roosevelt Leaks	.02	.10
18 Lee Roy Selmon	.07	.20
19 Hugh Green	.02	.10
20 Gerald Carter/170 Joe Danelo	.02	.10
21 Steve Wilson/171 Chris Keating	.02	.10
22 Michael Morton/172 Jerry Butler	.02	.10
23 Kevin House	.02	.10
24 Ottis Anderson	.02	.10
25 Lionel Washington/175 Barney Chavous	.02	.10
26 Pat Tilley/176 Zach Thomas WR	.02	.10
27 Curtis Greer/177 Luke Prestridge	.02	.10
28 Roy Green	.02	.10
29 Carl Birdsong	.02	.10
30 Neil Lomax/180 Steve Foley	.02	.10
31 Lee Nelson/181 Sammy Winder	.02	.10
32 Stump Mitchell/182 Rick Upchurch	.02	.10
33 Tony Hill/183 Bobby Jones	.02	.10
34 Everson Walls/184 Matt Bahr	.02	.10
35 Danny White/185 Doug Dieken	.02	.10
36 Tony Dorsett	.20	.50
37 Ed Too Tall Jones	.07	.20
38 Rafael Septien/188 Tom Cousineau	.02	.10
39 Doug Cosbie/189 Paul McDonald	.02	.10
40 Drew Pearson/190 Clay Matthews	.07	.20
41 Randy White	.07	.20
42 Ron Jaworski	.02	.10
43 Anthony Griggs/193 Chuck Muncie	.02	.10
44 Hubie Oliver/194 Linden King	.02	.10
45 Wilbert Montgomery/195 Charlie Joiner	.07	.20
46 Dennis Harrison	.02	.10
47 Mike Quick	.02	.10
48 Jerry Robinson/198 James Brooks	.02	.10
49 Michael Williams/199 Mike Green LB	.02	.10
50 Herman Edwards/200 Rolf Benirschke	.02	.10
51 Steve Bartkowski/201 Henry Marshall	.02	.10
52 Mick Luckhurst/202 Nick Lowery	.02	.10
53 Mike Pitts/203 Jerry Blanton	.02	.10
54 William Andrews	.02	.10
55 R.C. Thielemann	.02	.10
56 Buddy Curry/206 Billy Jackson	.02	.10
57 Billy Johnson/207 Art Still	.02	.10
58 Ralph Giacomarro/208 Theotis Brown	.02	.10
59 Mike Kenn	.02	.10
60 Joe Montana	1.50	4.00
61 Fred Dean/211 Nesby Glasgow	.05	.15
62 Dwight Clark/212 Mike Pagel	.02	.10
63 Wendell Tyler/213 Ray Donaldson	.02	.10
64 Dwight Hicks	.02	.10
65 Ronnie Lott	.10	.30
66 Roger Craig/216 Rohn Stark	.10	.30
67 Fred Solomon/217 Randy McMillan	.02	.10
68 Ray Wersching/218 Vernon Maxwell	.02	.10
69 Brad Van Pelt/219 A.J. Duhe	.02	.10
70 Butch Woolfolk/220 Andra Franklin	.02	.10
71 Terry Kinard/221 Ed Newman	.02	.10
72 Lawrence Taylor	.15	.40
73 Ali Haji-Sheikh	.02	.10
74 Mark Haynes/224 Bob Baumhower	.02	.10
75 Rob Carpenter/225 Reggie Roby	.02	.10
76 Earnest Gray/226 Dwight Stephenson	.02	.10
77 Harry Carson	.02	.10
78 Billy Sims	.07	.20
79 Eddie Murray/229 Freeman McNeil	.02	.10
80 William Gay/230 Bruce Harper	.02	.10
81 Leonard Thompson/231 Wesley Walker	.02	.10
82 Doug English	.02	.10
83 Eric Hipple	.02	.10
84 Ken Fantetti/234 Johnny Lam Jones	.02	.10
85 Bruce McNorton/235 Lance Mehl	.02	.10
86 James Jones/236 Pat Ryan	.02	.10
87 Lynn Dickey/237 Florian Kempf	.02	.10
88 Ezra Johnson/238 Carl Roaches	.02	.10
89 Jan Stenerud/239 Gregg Bingham	.02	.10
90 James Lofton	.07	.20
91 Larry McCarren	.02	.10
92 John Jefferson/242 Doug France	.02	.10
93 Mike Douglass/243 Chris Dressel	.02	.10
94 Gerry Ellis/244 Willie Tullis	.02	.10
95 Paul Coffman	.02	.10
96 Eric Dickerson	.30	.75
97 Jackie Slater/247 Brian Holloway	.07	.20
98 Carl Ekern/248 Stanley Morgan	.02	.10
99 Vince Ferragamo/249 Rick Sanford	.02	.10
100 Kent Hill	.02	.10
101 Nolan Cromwell	.02	.10
102 Jack Youngblood/252 Andre Tippett	.07	.20
103 John Misko/253 Steve Grogan	.02	.10
104 Mike Barber/254 Clayton Weishuhn.	.02	.10
105 Jeff Bostic/255 Jim Plunkett	.07	.20
106 Mark Murphy/256 Rod Martin	.02	.10
107 Joe Jacoby/257 Lester Hayes	.02	.10
108 John Riggins	.07	.20
109 Joe Theismann	.07	.20
110 Russ Grimm/260 Ted Hendricks	.07	.20
111 Neal Olkewicz/261 Greg Pruitt	.02	.10
112 Charlie Brown WR/262 Howie Long	.25	.60
113 Dave Butz	.02	.10
114 George Rogers	.02	.10
115 Jim Kovach/265 Jacob Green	.02	.10
116 Dave Wilson/266 Bruce Scholtz	.02	.10
117 Johnnie Poe/267 Steve Largent	.20	.50
118 Russell Erxleben	.02	.10
119 Rickey Jackson	.30	.75
120 Jeff Groth/270 Dave Brown DB	.02	.10
121 Richard Todd/271 Zachary Dixon	.02	.10
122 Wayne Wilson/272 Norm Johnson	.02	.10
123 Steve Dils/273 Terry Bradshaw	.15	.40
124 Benny Ricardo/274 Keith Willis	.02	.10
125 John Turner/275 Gary Anderson K	.02	.10
126 Ted Brown	.02	.10
127 Greg Coleman	.02	.10
128 Darrin Nelson/278 Calvin Sweeney	.02	.10
129 Scott Studwell/279 Rick Woods	.02	.10
130 Tommy Kramer/280 Bennie Cunningham	.02	.10
131 Doug Martin	.02	.10
132 Nolan Cromwell/144 Dan Marino All-Pro FOIL	2.50	6.00
133 Carl Birdsong/145 Ali Haji-Sheikh All-Pro FOIL	.02	.10
134 Deron Cherry/146 Eric Dickerson All-Pro FOIL	.07	.20
135 Ronnie Lott/147 Curt Warner All-Pro FOIL	.10	.30
136 Lester Hayes/148 James Lofton All-Pro FOIL	.07	.20
137 Lawrence Taylor/149 Todd Christensen All-Pro FOIL	.15	.40
138 Jack Lambert/150 Cris Collinsworth All-Pro FOIL	.07	.20
139 Chip Banks/151 Mike Kenn All-Pro FOIL	.02	.10
140 Lee Roy Selmon/152 Russ Grimm All-Pro FOIL	.07	.20
141 Fred Smerlas/153 Jeff Bostic All-Pro FOIL	.02	.10
142 Doug English/154 John Hannah All-Pro FOIL	.07	.20
143 Doug Betters/155 Anthony Munoz All-Pro FOIL	.07	.20
156 Ken Anderson	.07	.20
160 Anthony Munoz	.07	.20
161 Cris Collinsworth	.02	.10
168 Joe Ferguson	.02	.10
169 Fred Smerlas	.02	.10
173 Eugene Marve	.02	.10
174 Louis Wright	.02	.10
178 Steve Watson	.02	.10
179 John Elway	2.50	6.00
186 Mike Pruitt	.02	.10
187 Chip Banks	.02	.10
191 Ozzie Newsome	.07	.20
192 Dan Fouts	.10	.30
196 Wes Chandler	.02	.10
197 Kellen Winslow	.07	.20
204 Bill Kenney	.02	.10
205 Carlos Carson	.02	.10
209 Deron Cherry	.07	.20
210 Curtis Dickey	.02	.10
214 Raul Allegre	.02	.10
215 Chris Hinton	.02	.10
222 Dan Marino	2.50	6.00
223 Doug Betters	.02	.10
227 Mark Duper	.15	.40
228 Mark Gastineau	.02	.10
232 Marvin Powell	.02	.10
233 Joe Klecko	.02	.10
240 Tim Smith	.02	.10
241 Jesse Baker	.02	.10
245 Robert Brazile	.02	.10
246 Tony Collins	.02	.10
250 John Hannah	.07	.20
251 Rich Camarillo	.02	.10
258 Marcus Allen	.30	.75
259 Todd Christensen	.02	.10
263 Vann McElroy	.02	.10
264 Curt Warner	.07	.20
268 Kenny Easley	.02	.10
269 Dave Krieg	.07	.20
276 Franco Harris	.07	.20
277 Mike Webster	.02	.10
281 Jack Lambert	.07	.20
282 Curt Warner/283 Todd Christensen FOIL	.07	.20
NNO Sticker Album (Charlie Joiner and Dan Fouts)	.75	2.00

1985 Topps Coming Soon Stickers

This set of 30 white-bordered stickers are usually referred to as the "Coming Soon" stickers as they were inserted in the regular issue 1985 Topps football card wax packs and prominently mention "Coming Soon" on the sticker backs. They are the same size as the regular Topps stickers (approximately 2 1/8" by 3") and were not very difficult to find. Unlike many of the sticker cards in the regular set, this subset only contains one player per sticker. This is a skip-numbered set due to the fact that these stickers have the same numbers as the regular sticker issue.

COMPLETE SET (30)	3.00	8.00
6 Ken Anderson	.07	.20
15 Greg Bell	.02	.10
24 John Elway	1.00	2.50
33 Ozzie Newsome	.07	.20
42 Charlie Joiner	.07	.20
51 Bill Kenney	.05	.15
60 Randy McMillan	.02	.10
69 Dan Marino	1.00	2.50
77 Mark Clayton	.07	.20
78 Mark Gastineau	.05	.15
87 Warren Moon	.40	1.00
96 Tony Eason	.02	.10
105 Marcus Allen	.25	.60
114 Steve Largent	.20	.50
123 John Stallworth	.05	.15
156 Walter Payton	.50	1.25
165 James Wilder	.02	.10
174 Neil Lomax	.05	.15
183 Tony Dorsett	.15	.40
192 Mike Quick	.02	.10
201 William Andrews	.05	.15
210 Joe Montana	1.00	2.50
214 Dwight Clark	.07	.20
219 Lawrence Taylor	.10	.30
228 Billy Sims	.05	.15
237 James Lofton	.10	.30
246 Eric Dickerson	.10	.30
255 John Riggins	.08	.25
268 George Rogers	.05	.15
281 Tommy Kramer	.05	.15

1985 Topps Stickers

The 1985 Topps Football sticker set is similar to the previous years in that it contains stickers and an accompanying album to house one's sticker collection. However, there are no foil stickers in this set. Some of the stickers are half the size of others; those paired stickers sharing a card with another player are indicated parenthetically by the other player's sticker number in the checklist below. On the inside back cover of the sticker album the company offered (via direct mail-order) any ten different stickers of your choice for 1.00; this is one reason why the values of the most popular players in these sticker sets are somewhat depressed compared to traditional card set prices. The front cover of the sticker album features Dan Marino, Joe Montana, Walter Payton, Eric Dickerson, Art Monk, and Charlie Joiner; the back cover shows a team photo of the San Francisco 49ers. The stickers are checklisted below according to special subsets and teams. The following players are shown in their Rookie Card year or earlier: Mark Clayton, Richard Dent, Henry Ellard, Boomer Esiason (one year early), Craig James, Louis Lipps, Warren Moon, Ken O'Brien, and Darryl Talley.

COMPLETE SET (173)	20.00	40.00
1 Super Bowl XIX Joe Montana LH	1.50	4.00
2 Super Bowl XIX Joe Montana RH	.75	2.00
3 Super Bowl XIX Roger Craig LH	.02	.10
4 Super Bowl XIX Roger Craig RH	.02	.10
5 Super Bowl XIX Wendell Tyler	.02	.10
6 Ken Anderson	.07	.20
7 M.L. Harris/157 Dan Hampton	.07	.20
8 Eddie Edwards/158 Wille Gault	.02	.10
9 Louis Breeden/159 Matt Suhey	.02	.10
10 Larry Kinnebrew	.02	.10
11 Isaac Curtis/161 Mike Singletary	.02	.10
12 James Brooks/162 Gary Fencik	.02	.10
13 Jim Breech/163 Jim McMahon	.07	.20
14 Boomer Esiason/164 Bob Thomas	.20	.50
15 Greg Bell	.02	.10
16 Fred Smerlas/166 Steve DeBerg	.02	.10
17 Joe Ferguson/167 Mark Cotney	.02	.10
18 Ken Johnson DE/168 Adger Armstrong	.02	.10
19 Darryl Talley/169 Gerald Carter	.07	.20
20 Preston Dennard/170 David Logan	.02	.10
21 Charles Romes/171 Hugh Green	.02	.10
22 Jim Haslett/172 Lee Roy Selmon	.07	.20
23 Byron Franklin	.02	.10
24 John Elway	2.00	5.00
25 Rulon Jones/175 Otis Armstrong	.02	.10
26 Butch Johnson/176 Al Bubba Baker	.02	.10
27 Rich Karlis/177 E.J. Junior	.02	.10
28 Sammy Winder	.02	.10
29 Tom Jackson/179 Pat Tilley	.02	.10
30 Mike Harden/180 Stump Mitchell	.02	.10
31 Steve Watson/181 Lionel Washington	.02	.10
32 Steve Foley/182 Curtis Greer	.02	.10
33 Ozzie Newsome	.07	.20
34 Al Gross/184 Gary Hogeboom	.02	.10
35 Paul McDonald/185 Jim Jeffcoat	.02	.10
36 Matt Bahr/186 Danny White	.02	.10
37 Charles White/187 Michael Downs	.02	.10
38 Don Rogers/188 Doug Cosbie	.02	.10
39 Mike Pruitt/189 Tony Hill	.02	.10
40 Reggie Camp/190 Rafael Septien	.02	.10
41 Boyce Green	.02	.10
42 Charlie Joiner	.02	.10
43 Dan Fouts/193 Ray Ellis	.07	.20
44 Keith Ferguson/194 John Spagnola	.02	.10
45 Pete Holohan/195 Dennis Harrison	.02	.10
46 Earnest Jackson	.02	.10
47 Wes Chandler/197 Greg Brown	.02	.10
48 Gill Byrd/198 Ron Jaworski	.07	.20
49 Kellen Winslow/199 Paul McFadden	.07	.20
50 Billy Ray Smith/200 Wes Hopkins	.02	.10
51 Bill Kenney	.02	.10
52 Herman Heard/202 Mike Pitts	.02	.10
53 Art Still/203 Steve Bartkowski	.02	.10
54 Nick Lowery/204 Gerald Riggs	.02	.10
55 Deron Cherry/205 Alfred Jackson	.02	.10
56 Henry Marshall/206 Don Smith DE	.02	.10
57 Mike Bell/207 Mike Kenn	.02	.10
58 Todd Blackledge/208 Kenny Johnson	.02	.10
59 Carlos Carson	.02	.10
60 Randy McMillan	.02	.10
61 Donnell Thompson/211 Wendell Tyler	.02	.10
62 Raymond Butler/212 Keena Turner	.02	.10
63 Ray Donaldson/213 Ray Wersching	.02	.10
64 Art Schlichter	.02	.10

65 Rohn Stark/215 Dwaine Board .02 .10
66 Johnie Cooks/216 Roger Craig .07 .20
67 Mike Pagel/217 Ronnie Lott .07 .20
68 Eugene Daniel/218 Freddie Solomon .02 .10
69 Dan Marino 2.00 5.00
70 Pete Johnson/220 Zeke Moyatt .02 .10
71 Tony Nathan/221 Harry Carson .02 .10
72 Glenn Blackwood/222 Rob Carpenter RB .02 .10
73 Woody Bennett/223 Bobby Johnson WR .02 .10
74 Dwight Stephenson/224 Joe Morris .02 .10
75 Mark Duper/225 Mark Haynes .02 .10
76 Doug Betters/226 Lionel Manuel .02 .10
77 Mark Clayton .10 .30
78 Mark Gastineau .02 .10
79 Johnny Lam Jones/229 Leonard Thompson .02 .10
80 Mickey Shuler/230 James Jones FB .02 .10
81 Tony Paige/231 Eddie Murray .07 .20
82 Freeman McNeil .02 .10
83 Russell Carter/233 Gary Danielson .02 .10
84 Wesley Walker/234 Curtis Green .02 .10
85 Bruce Harper/235 Bobby Watkins .02 .10
86 Ken O'Brien/236 Doug English .07 .20
87 Warren Moon .30 .75
88 Jesse Baker/238 Eddie Lee Ivery .02 .10
89 Carl Roaches/239 Mike Douglass .02 .10
90 Carter Hartwig/240 Gerry Ellis .02 .10
91 Larry Moriarty/241 Tim Lewis .02 .10
92 Robert Brazile/242 Paul Coffman .02 .10
93 Oliver Luck/243 Tom Flynn .02 .10
94 Willie Tullis/244 Ezra Johnson .02 .10
95 Tim Smith .02 .10
96 Tony Eason .02 .10
97 Stanley Morgan/247 Jack Youngblood .02 .10
98 Mosi Tatupu/248 Doug Smith C .02 .10
99 Raymond Clayborn/249 Jeff Kemp .02 .10
100 Andre Tippett .02 .10
101 Craig James/251 Mike Lansford .07 .20
102 Derrick Ramsey/252 Henry Ellard .02 .10
103 Tony Collins/253 LeRoy Irvin .02 .10
104 Tony Franklin/254 Ron Brown .02 .10
105 Marcus Allen .20 .50
106 Chris Bahr/256 Dexter Manley .02 .10
107 Marc Wilson/257 Darrell Green .02 .10
108 Howie Long/258 Joe Theismann .07 .20
109 Bill Pickel/259 Mark Malone .02 .10
110 Mike Haynes/260 Clint Didier .02 .10
111 Malcolm Barnwell/261 Vernon Dean .02 .10
112 Rod Martin/262 Calvin Muhammad .02 .10
113 Todd Christensen .02 .10
114 Steve Largent .20 .50
115 Curt Warner/265 Hoby Brenner .02 .10
116 Kenny Easley/266 Dave Wilson .02 .10
117 Jacob Green/267 Hokie Gajan .02 .10
118 Daryl Turner .02 .10
119 Norm Johnson/269 Rickey Jackson .05 .15
120 Dave Krieg/270 Brian Hansen .07 .20
121 Eric Lane/271 Dave Waymer .02 .10
122 Jeff Bryant/272 Richard Todd .02 .10
123 John Stallworth .02 .10
124 Donnie Shell/274 Ted Brown .02 .10
125 Gary Anderson/275 Leo Lewis .02 .10
126 Mark Malone/276 Scott Studstill .02 .10
127 Sam Washington/277 Alfred Anderson .02 .10
128 Frank Pollard/278 Rufus Bess .02 .10
129 Mike Merriweather/279 Darrin Nelson .02 .10
130 Walter Abercrombie/280 Greg Coleman .02 .10
131 Louis Lipps .02 .10
132 Mark Clayton/144 Todd Bell .07 .20
133 Randy Cross/145 Richard Dent .02 .10
134 Eric Dickerson/146 Kenny Easley .10 .30
135 John Hannah/147 Mark Gastineau .02 .10
136 Mike Kenn/148 Dan Hampton .07 .20
137 Dan Marino/149 Mark Haynes 1.50 4.00
138 Art Monk/150 Mike Haynes .07 .20
139 Anthony Munoz/151 E.J. Junior .02 .10
140 Ozzie Newsome/152 Rod Martin .02 .10
141 Walter Payton/153 Steve Nelson 1.25 3.00
142 Jan Stenerud/154 Reggie Roby .02 .10
143 Dwight Stephenson/155 Lawrence Taylor .07 .20
156 Walter Payton 1.50 4.00
160 Richard Dent .20 .50
165 James Wilder .02 .10
173 Kevin House .02 .10
174 Neil Lomax .02 .10
178 Roy Green .02 .10
183 Tony Dorsett .20 .50
191 Randy White .07 .20
192 Mike Quick .02 .10
196 Wilbert Montgomery .02 .10
201 William Andrews .02 .10
209 Stacey Bailey .02 .10
210 Joe Montana 2.00 5.00
214 Dwight Clark .02 .10
219 Lawrence Taylor .10 .30
227 Phil Simms .07 .20
228 Billy Sims .02 .10
232 William Gay .02 .10
237 James Lofton .07 .20
245 Lynn Dickey .02 .10
246 Eric Dickerson .10 .30
250 Kent Hill .02 .10
255 John Riggins .07 .20
263 Art Monk .07 .20
264 Bruce Clark .02 .10
268 George Rogers .02 .10
273 Jan Stenerud .02 .10
281 Tommy Kramer .02 .10
282 Joe Montana/283 Dan Marino 2.50 6.00
284 Brian Hansen/285 Jim Arnold .02 .10
NNO Sticker Album .75 2.00

1986 Topps Stickers

The 1986 Topps Football sticker set is similar to the previous years in that it contains stickers, foil stickers, and an accompanying album to house one's sticker collection. The stickers measure approximately 2 1/8" by 3". The sticker design shows an inverted L-shaped border in an accent color. The stickers are numbered on the front and on the back. The sticker backs are printed in brown ink on white stock. Sticker pairs are identified below by parenthetically listing the other member of the pair. On the inside back cover of the sticker album the company offered (via direct mail-order) any ten different stickers of your choice for 1.00; this is one reason why the values of the most popular players in these sticker sets are somewhat depressed compared to traditional card set prices. The front cover of the sticker album features Walter Payton and several other Chicago Bears players; the back cover shows a team photo of the Chicago Bears. The stickers are checklisted below according to special subsets and teams. The following players are shown in their Rookie Card year: Anthony Carter, Gary Clark, Bernie Kosar, Andre Reed, Bruce Smith, Al Toon, Reggie White, and Steve Young.

COMPLETE SET (173) 12.50 25.00
1 Walter Payton LH .50 1.25
2 Walter Payton RH .40 1.00
3 Richard Dent LH .02 .10
4 Richard Dent RH .02 .10
5 Richard Dent FOIL .07 .20
Super Bowl MVP
6 Walter Payton 1.25 3.00
7 William Perry .02 .10
8 Jim McMahon/158 Cris Collinsworth .02 .10
9 Richard Dent/159 Eddie Edwards .02 .10
10 Jim Covert/160 James Griffin .02 .10
11 Dan Hampton/161 Jim Breech .02 .10
12 Mike Singletary/162 Eddie Brown WR .02 .10
13 Jay Hilgenberg/163 Ross Browner .02 .10
14 Otis Wilson/164 James Brooks .02 .10
15 Jimmie Giles .02 .10
16 Kevin House/166 Jerry Butler .02 .10
17 Jeremiah Castille/167 Don Wilson .02 .10
18 James Wilder .02 .10
19 Donald Igwebuike/169 Jim Haslett .02 .10
20 David Logan/170 Bruce Mathison .02 .10
21 Jeff Davis/171 Bruce Smith .30 .75
22 Frank Garcia/172 Joe Cribbs .02 .10
23 Steve Young/173 Charles Romes .75 2.00
24 Stump Mitchell .02 .10
25 E.J. Junior .02 .10
26 J.T. Smith/176 John Elway 1.00 2.50
27 Pat Tilley/177 Sammy Winder .02 .10
28 Neil Lomax/178 Louis Wright .02 .10
29 Leonard Smith/179 Steve Watson .02 .10
30 Ottis Anderson/180 Dennis Smith .02 .10
31 Curtis Greer/181 Mike Harden .02 .10
32 Roy Green/182 Vance Johnson .02 .10
33 Tony Dorsett .15 .40
34 Tony Hill/184 Chip Banks .02 .10
35 Doug Cosbie/185 Bob Golic .02 .10
36 Everson Walls .02 .10
37 Randy White/187 Ozzie Newsome .07 .20
38 Rafael Septien/188 Bernie Kosar .10 .30
39 Mike Renfro/189 Don Rogers .02 .10
40 Danny White/190 Al Gross .02 .10
41 Ed Too Tall Jones/191 Clarence Weathers .02 .10
42 Earnest Jackson .02 .10
43 Mike Quick .02 .10
44 Wes Hopkins/194 Wes Chandler .02 .10
45 Reggie White/195 Kellen Winslow .40 1.00
46 Greg Brown/196 Gary Anderson RB .02 .10
47 Paul McFadden/197 Charlie Joiner .02 .10
48 John Spagnola/198 Ralf Mojsiejenko .02 .10
49 Ron Jaworski/199 Bob Thomas .02 .10
50 Herman Hunter/200 Tim Spencer .02 .10
51 Gerald Riggs .02 .10
52 Mike Pitts/202 Bill Maas .02 .10
53 Buddy Curry/203 Herman Heard .02 .10
54 Billy Johnson .02 .10
55 Rick Donnelly/205 Nick Lowery .02 .10
56 Rick Bryan/206 Bill Kenney .02 .10
57 Bobby Butler/207 Albert Lewis .02 .10
58 Mick Luckhurst/208 Art Still .02 .10
59 Mike Kenn/209 Stephone Paige .02 .10
60 Roger Craig .07 .20
61 Joe Montana 1.50 4.00
62 Michael Carter/212 Albert Bentley .02 .10
63 Eric Wright/213 Eugene Daniel .02 .10
64 Dwight Clark/214 Pat Beach .02 .10
65 Ronnie Lott/215 Cliff Odom .02 .10
66 Carlton Williamson/216 Duane Bickett .02 .10
67 Wendell Tyler/217 George Wonsley .02 .10
68 Dwaine Board/218 Randy McMillan .02 .10
69 Joe Morris .02 .10
70 Leonard Marshall/220 Dwight Stephenson .02 .10
71 Lionel Manue/221 Roy Foster .02 .10
72 Harry Carson .02 .10
73 Phil Simms/223 Mark Duper .02 .10
74 Sean Landeta/224 Fuad Reveiz .02 .10
75 Lawrence Taylor/225 Reggie Roby .07 .20
76 Elvis Patterson/226 Tony Nathan .02 .10
77 George Adams/227 Ron Davenport .02 .10
78 James Jones .02 .10
79 Leonard Thompson .02 .10
80 William Graham/230 Mark Gastineau .02 .10
81 Mark Nichols/231 Ken O'Brien .02 .10
82 William Gay/232 Lance Mehl .02 .10
83 Jimmy Williams/233 Al Toon .02 .10
84 Billy Sims/234 Mickey Shuler .02 .10
85 Bobby Watkins/235 Pat Leahy .02 .10
86 Eddie Murray/236 Wesley Walker .02 .10
87 James Lofton .07 .20
88 Jessie Clark/238 Warren Moon .10 .30
89 Tim Lewis/239 Mike Rozier .02 .10
90 Eddie Lee Ivery .02 .10
91 Phillip Epps/241Tim Smith .02 .10
92 Ezra Johnson/242 Butch Woolfolk .02 .10
93 Mike Douglass/243 Willie Drewrey .02 .10
94 Paul Coffman/244 Keith Bostic .02 .10
95 Randy Scott/245 Jesse Baker .02 .10
96 Eric Dickerson .07 .20
97 Dale Hatcher .02 .10
98 Ron Brown/248 Tony Eason .02 .10
99 LeRoy Irvin/249 Andre Tippett .02 .10
100 Kent Hill/250 Tony Collins .02 .10
101 Dennis Harrah/251 Brian Holloway .02 .10
102 Jackie Slater/252 Irving Fryar .02 .10
103 Mike Wilcher/253 Raymond Clayborn .02 .10
104 Doug Smith/254 Steve Nelson .02 .10
105 Art Monk .07 .20
106 Joe Jacoby/256 Mike Haynes .02 .10
107 Russ Grimm/257 Todd Christensen .02 .10
108 George Rogers .02 .10
109 Dexter Manley/259 Lester Hayes .02 .10
110 Jay Schroeder/260 Rod Martin .02 .10
111 Gary Clark/261 Dokie Williams .15 .40
112 Curtis Jordan/262 Chris Bahr .02 .10
113 Charles Mann/263 Bill Pickel .02 .10
114 Morten Andersen .02 .10
115 Rickey Jackson .02 .10
116 Glen Redd/266 Fredd Young .02 .10
117 Bobby Hebert/267 Dave Krieg .07 .20
118 Hoby Brenner/268 Daryl Turner .02 .10
119 Brian Hansen/269 John Harris .02 .10
120 Dave Waymer/270 Randy Edwards .02 .10
121 Bruce Clark/271 Kenny Easley .02 .10
122 Wayne Wilson/272 Jacob Green .02 .10
123 Joey Browner .07 .20
124 Darrin Nelson/274 Mike Webster .02 .10
125 Keith Millard/275 Walter Abercrombie .02 .10
126 Anthony Carter .10 .30
127 Buster Rhymes/277 Frank Pollard .02 .10
128 Steve Jordan/278 Mike Merriweather .07 .20
129 Greg Coleman/279 Mark Malone .02 .10
130 Ted Brown/280 Donnie Shell .02 .10
131 John Turner/281 John Stallworth .07 .20
132 Harry Carson/144 Marcus Allen .15 .40
AP FOIL
133 Deron Cherry/145 Gary Anderson K .02 .10
AP FOIL
134 Richard Dent/146 Doug Cosbie .07 .20
AP FOIL
135 Mike Haynes/147 Jim Covert .07 .20
AP FOIL
136 Wes Hopkins/148 John Hannah .07 .20
AP FOIL
137 Joe Klecko/149 Jay Hilgenberg .02 .10
AP FOIL
138 Leonard Marshall/150 Kent Hill .02 .10
AP FOIL
139 Karl Mecklenburg/151 Brian Holloway .02 .10
AP FOIL
140 Rohn Stark/152 Steve Largent .20 .50
AP FOIL
141 Lawrence Taylor/153 Dan Marino 1.00 2.50
AP FOIL
142 Andre Tippett/154 Art Monk .07 .20
AP FOIL
143 Everson Walls/155 Walter Payton .75 2.00
156 Anthony Munoz .07 .20
157 Boomer Esiason .10 .30
165 Greg Bell .02 .10
168 Andre Reed .30 .75
174 Karl Mecklenburg .02 .10
175 Rulon Jones .02 .10
183 Kevin Mack .02 .10
186 Earnest Byner .07 .20
192 Lionel James .02 .10
193 Dan Fouts .10 .30
201 Deron Cherry .02 .10
204 Carlos Carson .02 .10
210 Rohn Stark .02 .10
211 Chris Hinton .02 .10
219 Dan Marino 1.50 4.00
222 Mark Clayton .07 .20
228 Freeman McNeil .02 .10
229 Joe Klecko .02 .10
237 Drew Hill .02 .10
240 Mike Munchak .02 .10
246 Craig James .07 .20
247 John Hannah .07 .20
255 Marcus Allen .15 .40
258 Howie Long .07 .20
264 Curt Warner .02 .10
265 Steve Largent .20 .50
273 Gary Anderson K .02 .10
276 Louis Lipps .02 .10
282 Marcus Allen/284 Kevin Butler .20 .50
FOIL
283 Ken O'Brien/285 Roger Craig .07 .20
FOIL
NNO Sticker Album .75 2.00

1987 Topps Stickers

The 1987 Topps Football sticker set is similar to the previous years in that it contains stickers, foil stickers, and an accompanying album to house one's sticker collection. The stickers are approximately 2 1/8" by 3" and are in full-color with a white border with little footballs in each corner. The stickers are numbered on the front in the lower left hand border. Several feature two players per sticker card; they are designated in the checklist below along with the card number of the paired player. The sticker backs are printed in red on white stock. On the inside back cover of the sticker album the company offered (via direct mail-order) any ten different stickers of your choice for 1.00; this is one reason why the values of the most popular players in these sticker sets are somewhat depressed compared to traditional card set prices. The front cover of the sticker album shows New York Giants art. The following players are shown in their Rookie Card year: Keith Byars, Randall Cunningham, Kenneth Davis, Jim Everett, Doug Flutie, Ernest Givins, Jim Kelly, Leslie O'Neal and Herschel Walker.

COMPLETE SET (173) 10.00 20.00
1 Phil Simms .07 .20
Super Bowl MVP
2 Super Bowl XXI .02 .10
Phil Simms UL
3 Super Bowl XXI .02 .10
Phil Simms UR
4 Super Bowl XXI .02 .10
Phil Simms LL
5 Super Bowl XXI .02 .10
Phil Simms LR
6 Mike Singletary .07 .20
7 Jim Covert/156 Boomer Esiason .07 .20
8 Willie Gault/157 Anthony Munoz .07 .20
9 Jim McMahon/158 Tim McGee .07 .20
10 Doug Flutie/159 Max Montoya .40 1.00
11 Richard Dent/160 Jim Breach .02 .10
12 Kevin Butler/161 Tim Krumrie .02 .10
13 Wilber Marshall/162 Eddie Brown WR .02 .10
14 Walter Payton .75 2.00
15 Calvin Magee .02 .10
16 David Logan/165 Charles Romes .02 .10
17 Jeff Davis/166 Robb Riddick .02 .10
18 Gerald Carter/167 Eugene Marve .02 .10
19 James Wilder .02 .10
20 Chris Washington/168 Chris Burkett .02 .10
21 Phil Freeman/169 Bruce Smith .08 .25
22 Frank Garcia/170 Greg Bell .02 .10
23 Donald Igwebuike/171 Pete Metzelaars .02 .10
24 Al(Bubba) Baker/175 Mike Harden .02 .10
25 Vai Sikahema/176 Gerald Willhite .02 .10
26 Leonard Smith/177 Rulon Jones .02 .10
27 Ron Wolfley/178 Rick Hunley .02 .10
28 J.T. Smith .02 .10
29 Roy Green/179 Mark Jackson .02 .10
30 Cedric Mack/180 Rich Karlis .02 .10
31 Neil Lomax/181 Sammy Winder .02 .10
32 Stump Mitchell .02 .10
33 Herschel Walker .15 .40
34 Danny White/184 Kevin Mack .02 .10
35 Michael Downs/185 Bob Golic .02 .10
36 Randy White/186 Ozzie Newsome .07 .20
37 Eugene Lockhart/188 Gerald McNeil .02 .10
38 Mike Sherrard/189 Hanford Dixon .07 .20
39 Jim Jeffcoat/190 Cody Risien .02 .10
40 Tony Hill/191 Chris Rockins .02 .10
41 Tony Dorsett .10 .30
42 Keith Byars/192 Gill Byrd .02 .10
43 Andre Waters/193 Kellen Winslow .07 .20
44 Kenny Jackson/194 Billy Ray Smith .02 .10
45 John Teltschik/195 Wes Chandler .02 .10
46 Roynell Young/196 Leslie O'Neal .07 .20
47 Randall Cunningham/197 Ralf Mojsiejenko .20 .50
48 Mike Reichenbach/198 Lee Williams .02 .10
49 Reggie White .20 .50
50 Mike Quick .02 .10
51 Bill Fralic/201 Stephone Paige .02 .10
52 Sylvester Stamps/202 Irv Eatman .02 .10
53 Bret Clark/203 Bill Kenney .02 .10
54 William Andrews/204 Dino Hackett .02 .10
55 Buddy Curry/205 Carlos Carson .02 .10
56 David Archer/206 Art Still .02 .10
57 Rick Bryan/207 Lloyd Burruss .02 .10
58 Gerald Riggs .02 .10
59 Charlie Brown .02 .10
60 Joe Montana 1.00 2.50
61 Jerry Rice .75 2.00
62 Carlton Williamson/212 Cliff Odom .02 .10
63 Roger Craig/213 Randy McMillan .07 .20
64 Ronnie Lott/214 Chris Hinton .07 .20
65 Dwight Clark/215 Matt Bouza .02 .10
66 Jeff Stover/216 Ray Donaldson .02 .10
67 Charles Haley/217 Bill Brooks .07 .20
68 Ray Wersching/218 Jack Trudeau .02 .10
69 Lawrence Taylor .10 .30
70 Joe Morris .02 .10
71 Carl Banks/221 Dwight Stephenson .02 .10
72 Mark Bavaro/222 Mark Clayton .02 .10
73 Harry Carson/223 Roy Foster .02 .10
74 Phil Simms/224 John Offerdahl .07 .20
75 Jim Burt/225 Lorenzo Hampton .02 .10
76 Brad Benson/226 Reggie Roby .02 .10
77 Leonard Marshall/227 Tony Nathan .02 .10
78 Jeff Chadwick .02 .10
79 Devon Mitchell/228 Johnny Hector .02 .10
80 Chuck Long/229 Wesley Walker .02 .10
81 Demetrious Johnson/230 Mark Gastineau .02 .10
82 Herman Hunter/231 Ken O'Brien .02 .10
83 Keith Ferguson/232 Dave Jennings .02 .10
84 Garry James/233 Mickey Shuler .02 .10
85 Leonard Thompson/234 Joe Klecko .02 .10
86 James Jones .02 .10
87 Kenneth Davis .07 .20
88 Brian Noble/237 Warren Moon .07 .20
89 Al Del Greco/238 Dean Steinkuhler .02 .10
90 Mark Lee/239 Mike Rozier .02 .10
91 Randy Wright .02 .10
92 Tim Harris/240 Ray Childress .07 .20
93 Phillip Epps/241 Tony Zendejas .02 .10
94 Walter Stanley/242 John Grimsley .02 .10
95 Eddie Lee Ivery/243 Jesse Baker .02 .10
96 Doug Smith/247 Steve Grogan .07 .20
97 Jerry Gray/248 Garin Veris .02 .10
98 Dennis Harrah/249 Stanley Morgan .02 .10
99 Jim Everett/250 Fred Marion .07 .20
100 Jackie Slater/251 Raymond Clayborn .02 .10
101 Vince Newsome/252 Mosi Tatupu .02 .10
102 LeRoy Irvin/253 Tony Eason .02 .10
103 Henry Ellard .02 .10
104 Eric Dickerson .10 .30
105 George Rogers/256 Howie Long .07 .20
106 Darrell Green/257 Marcus Allen .07 .20
107 Art Monk/258 Vann McElroy .07 .20
108 Neal Olkewicz/260 Mike Haynes .07 .20
109 Russ Grimm/261 Sean Jones .02 .10
110 Dexter Manley/262 Jim Plunkett .07 .20
111 Kelvin Bryant/263 Chris Bahr .02 .10
112 Jay Schroeder .02 .10
113 Gary Clark .07 .20
114 Rickey Jackson .02 .10
115 Eric Martin/264 Dave Krieg .02 .10
116 Dave Waymer/265 Jacob Green .02 .10
117 Morten Andersen/266 Norm Johnson .02 .10
118 Bruce Clark/267 Fredd Young .02 .10
119 Hoby Brenner/269 Dave Brown DB .02 .10
120 Brian Hansen/270 Kenny Easley .02 .10
121 Dave Wilson/271 Bobby Joe Edmonds .02 .10
122 Rueben Mayes .02 .10
123 Tommy Kramer .02 .10
124 Joey Browner/274 Mark Malone .02 .10
125 Anthony Carter/275 Bryan Hinkle .07 .20
126 Keith Millard/276 Earnest Jackson .02 .10
127 Steve Jordan .02 .10
128 Chuck Nelson/277 Keith Willis .02 .10
129 Isslac Holt/278 Walter Abercrombie .02 .10
130 Darrin Nelson/279 Donnie Shell .02 .10
131 Gary Zimmerman/280 John Stallworth .20 .50
132 Mark Bavaro/146 Darrell Green .02 .10
All-Pro FOIL
133 Jim Covert/147 Ronnie Lott .10 .30
All-Pro FOIL
134 Eric Dickerson/148 Bill Maas .07 .20
All-Pro FOIL
135 Bill Fralic/149 Dexter Manley .02 .10
All-Pro FOIL
136 Tony Franklin/150 Karl Mecklenburg .02 .10
All-Pro FOIL
137 Dennis Harrah/151 Mike Singletary .10 .30
All-Pro FOIL
138 Dan Marino/152 Rohn Stark .75 2.00
All-Pro FOIL
139 Joe Morris/153 Lawrence Taylor .10 .30
All-Pro FOIL
140 Jerry Rice/154 Andre Tippett .60 1.50
All-Pro FOIL
141 Cody Risien/155 Reggie White .15 .40
All-Pro FOIL
142 Dwight Stephenson/282 Eric Dickerson .07 .20
All-Pro FOIL
143 Al Toon/283 Dan Marino .75 2.00
All-Pro FOIL
144 Deron Cherry/284 Tony Franklin .02 .10
All-Pro FOIL
145 Hanford Dixon/285 Todd Christensen .02 .10
All-Pro FOIL
163 James Brooks .02 .10
164 Cris Collinsworth .02 .10
172 Jim Kelly .40 1.00
173 Andre Reed .15 .40
174 John Elway .75 2.00
182 Karl Mecklenburg .02 .10
183 Bernie Kosar .07 .20
187 Brian Brennan .02 .10
199 Gary Anderson RB .02 .10
200 Dan Fouts .10 .30
208 Deron Cherry .02 .10
209 Bill Maas .02 .10
210 Gary Hogeboom .02 .10
211 Rohn Stark .02 .10
219 Mark Duper .02 .10
220 Dan Marino .75 2.00
235 Freeman McNeil .02 .10
236 Al Toon .02 .10
244 Ernest Givins .07 .20
245 Drew Hill .02 .10
246 Tony Franklin .02 .10
254 Andre Tippett .02 .10
255 Todd Christensen .02 .10
259 Dokie Williams .02 .10
268 Steve Largent .20 .50
272 Curt Warner .02 .10
273 Mike Merriweather .02 .10
281 Louis Lipps .02 .10
NNO Sticker Album .75 2.00

1988 Topps Stickers

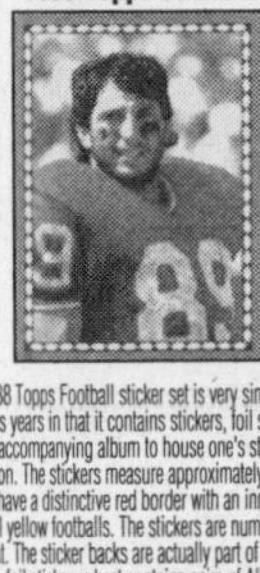

The 1988 Topps Football sticker set is very similar to the previous years in that it contains stickers, foil stickers, and an accompanying album to house one's sticker collection. The stickers measure approximately 2 1/8" by 3" and have a distinctive red border with an inner frame of small yellow footballs. The stickers are numbered on the front. The foil sticker subset contains pairs of All-Pros (AP) and are so indicated in the checklist below. Stickers 2-5 are actually a large four-part action photo of Super Bowl XXII action with Doug Williams handing off to Timmy Smith. On the inside back cover of the sticker album the company offered (via direct mail-order) any ten different stickers of your choice for 1.00; this is one reason why the values of the most popular players in these sticker sets are somewhat depressed compared to traditional card set prices. The front cover of the sticker album features an action photo of the Washington Redskins; the back cover depicts Doug Williams artwork. The following players are shown in their Rookie Card year: Neal Anderson, Cornelius Bennett, Brian Bosworth, Ronnie Harmon, Bo Jackson, Clyde Simmons, Webster Slaughter, Pat Swilling, Vinny Testaverde, and Wade Wilson.

COMPLETE SET (173) 4.00 10.00
1 Super Bowl XXII MVP .02 .10
Doug Williams
2 Super Bowl XXII .02 .10
Redskins vs. Broncos
Doug Williams UL
3 Super Bowl XXII .02 .10
Redskins vs. Broncos
Doug Williams UR
4 Super Bowl XXII .02 .10
Redskins vs. Broncos
Doug Williams LL
5 Super Bowl XXII .02 .10
Redskins vs. Broncos
Doug Williams LR
6 Neal Anderson/234 Alex Gordon .02 .10
7 Willie Gault/224 Paul Lankford .02 .10
8 Dennis Gentry/219 Dwight Stephenson .02 .10
9 Dave Duerson/197 Lee Williams .02 .10
10 Steve McMichael/266 Norm Johnson .02 .10
11 Dennis McKinnon/230 Freeman McNeil .02 .10
12 Mike Singletary/209 Paul Palmer .02 .10
13 Jim McMahon .02 .10
14 Richard Dent .02 .10
15 Vinny Testaverde/167 Ronnie Harmon .20 .50
16 Gerald Carter/187 Brian Brennan .02 .10
17 Jeff Smith/185 Earnest Byner .02 .10
18 Chris Washington/212 Bill Brooks .02 .10
19 Bobby Futrell/231 Johnny Hector .02 .10
20 Calvin Magee/182 Mike Harden .02 .10
21 Ron Holmes/169 Chris Burkett .02 .10
22 Ervin Randle .02 .10
23 James Wilder .02 .10
24 Neil Lomax .02 .10
25 Robert Awalt/161 Tim Krumrie .02 .10
26 Leonard Smith/177 Karl Mecklenburg .02 .10
27 Stump Mitchell/178 Mark Haynes .02 .10
28 Vai Sikahema/280 Harry Newsome .02 .10
29 Freddie Joe Nunn/222 John Bosa .02 .10
30 Earl Ferrell/223 Jackie Shipp .02 .10
31 Roy Green/157 Stanford Jennings .02 .10
32 J.T. Smith .02 .10
33 Michael Downs .02 .10
34 Herschel Walker .07 .20
35 Roger Ruzek/269 Dave Krieg .02 .10
36 Ed Too Tall Jones/245 Sean Jones .02 .10
37 Everson Walls/252 Ronnie Lippett .02 .10
38 Bill Bates/213 Dean Biasucci .02 .10
39 Doug Cosbie/179 Rulon Jones .02 .10
40 Eugene Lockhart/186 Webster Slaughter .02 .10
41 Danny White/205 Dino Hackett .02 .10
42 Randall Cunningham .20 .50
43 Reggie White .20 .50
44 Anthony Toney/256 James Lofton .07 .20
45 Mike Quick/248 Stephen Starring .02 .10
46 John Spagnola/235 Harry Hamilton .02 .10
47 Clyde Simmons/275 Dwight Stone .02 .10
48 Andre Waters/261 Greg Townsend .02 .10
49 Keith Byars/265 Jacob Green .02 .10
50 Jerome Brown/240 Warren Moon .07 .20
51 John Rade .02 .10
52 Rick Donnelly .02 .10
53 Scott Campbell/160 Boomer Esiason .02 .10
54 Floyd Dixon/246 Stanley Morgan .02 .10
55 Gerald Riggs/236 Mickey Shuler .02 .10
56 Bill Fralic/267 Brian Bosworth .02 .10
57 Mike Gann/165 Andre Reed .02 .10
58 Tony Casillas/168 Shane Conlan .02 .10
59 Rick Bryan/257 Vance Mueller .02 .10
60 Jerry Rice .50 1.25
61 Ronnie Lott .07 .20
62 Ray Wersching/220 John Offerdahl .02 .10
63 Charles Haley/281 Dwayne Woodruff .02 .10
64 Joe Montana/190 Clay Matthews .75 2.00
65 Joe Cribbs/221 Troy Stradford .02 .10
66 Mike Wilson/203 Christian Okoye .02 .10
67 Roger Craig/251 Rich Camarillo .02 .10
68 Michael Walter/162 Anthony Munoz .02 .10
69 Mark Bavaro .02 .10
70 Carl Banks .02 .10
71 George Adams/274 Frank Pollard .02 .10
72 Phil Simms/216 Mike Prior .02 .10
73 Lawrence Taylor/181 Vance Johnson .07 .20
74 Joe Morris/198 Curtis Adams .02 .10
75 Lionel Manuel/204 Deron Cherry .02 .10
76 Sean Landeta/210 Jack Trudeau .02 .10
77 Harry Carson/159 Scott Fulhage .02 .10
78 Chuck Long/166 Cornelius Bennett .10 .30
79 James Jones/259 Todd Christensen .02 .10
80 Garry James/158 Eddie Brown WR .02 .10
81 Gary Lee/176 Sammy Winder .02 .10
82 Jim Arnold/260 Vann McElroy .02 .10
83 Dennis Gibson/232 Pat Leahy .02 .10
84 Mike Cofer/242 Alonzo Highsmith .02 .10
85 Pete Mandley .02 .10
86 James Griffin .02 .10
87 Randy Wright/206 Mike Bell .02 .10
88 Phillip Epps/191 Kevin Mack .02 .10
89 Brian Noble/249 Steve Grogan .02 .10
90 Johnny Holland/258 Jerry Robinson .02 .10
91 Dave Brown/156 Larry Kinnebrew .02 .10
92 Brent Fullwood/207 Stephone Paige .02 .10
93 Kenneth Davis/194 Gary Anderson RB .02 .10
94 Tim Harris .02 .10
95 Walter Stanley .02 .10
96 Charles White .02 .10
97 Jackie Slater .02 .10
98 Jim Everett/271 Steve Largent .10 .30
99 Mike Lansford/200 Ralf Mojsiejenko .02 .10
100 Henry Ellard/199 Vencie Glenn .02 .10
101 Dale Hatcher/170 Mark Kelso .02 .10
102 Jim Collins/268 Bobby Joe Edmonds .02 .10
103 Jerry Gray/214 Cliff Odom .02 .10
104 LeRoy Irvin/276 Mike Merriweather .02 .10
105 Darrell Green .02 .10
106 Doug Williams .02 .10
107 Gary Clark/247 Garin Veris .02 .10
108 Charles Mann/171 Robb Riddick .02 .10
109 Art Monk/270 Kenny Easley .07 .20
110 Barry Wilburn/196 Elvis Patterson .02 .10
111 Alvin Walton/188 Carl Hairston .02 .10
112 Dexter Manley/233 Ken O'Brien .02 .10
113 Kelvin Bryant/180 Ricky Nattiel .02 .10
114 Morten Andersen .02 .10
115 Rueben Mayes/244 Keith Bostic .02 .10
116 Brian Hansen/279 Gary Anderson K .02 .10
117 Dalton Hilliard/241 Drew Hill .02 .10
118 Rickey Jackson/195 Chip Banks .02 .10
119 Eric Martin/189 Mike Johnson LB .02 .10
120 Mel Gray/278 Delton Hall .02 .10
121 Bobby Hebert/215 Barry Krauss .02 .10
122 Pat Swilling .07 .20
123 Anthony Carter .02 .10
124 Wade Wilson/225 Mark Duper .02 .10
125 Darrin Nelson/250 Irving Fryar .02 .10
126 D.J. Dozier/239 Ernest Givins .02 .10
127 Chris Doleman .07 .20
128 Henry Thomas/255 Howie Long .02 .10
129 Jesse Solomon/211 Albert Bentley .02 .10
130 Neal Guggemos/243 Mike Munchak .02 .10
131 Joey Browner/208 Bill Kenney .02 .10
132 Carl Banks/152 Jackie Slater .02 .10
AP FOIL
133 Joey Browner/145 Mark Bavaro .02 .10
AP FOIL
134 Hanford Dixon/147 John Elway .60 1.50
AP FOIL
135 Rick Donnelly/149 Mike Munchak .02 .10
AP FOIL
136 Kenny Easley/155 Charles White .02 .10
AP FOIL
137 Darrell Green/151 Jerry Rice .40 1.00
AP FOIL
138 Bill Maas/148 Bill Fralic .02 .10
AP FOIL
139 Mike Singletary/153 J.T. Smith .10 .30
140 Bruce Smith/154 Dwight Stephenson .10 .30
AP FOIL
141 Andre Tippett/146 Eric Dickerson .07 .20
AP FOIL
142 Reggie White/150 Anthony Munoz .15 .40
AP FOIL
143 Fredd Young/144 Morten Andersen .02 .10
AP FOIL
163 Jim Breech .02 .10
164 Reggie Williams .02 .10
172 Bruce Smith .07 .20
173 Jim Kelly .20 .50
174 Jim Ryan .02 .10
175 John Elway .75 2.00
183 Frank Minnifield .02 .10
184 Bernie Kosar .02 .10
192 Kellen Winslow .02 .10
193 Billy Ray Smith .02 .10
201 Carlos Carson .02 .10
202 Bill Maas .02 .10
217 Eric Dickerson .07 .20
218 Duane Bickett .02 .10
226 Dan Marino .75 2.00
227 Mark Clayton .02 .10
228 Bob Crable .02 .10
229 Al Toon .02 .10
237 Mike Rozier .02 .10
238 Al Smith .02 .10
253 Andre Tippett .02 .10
254 Fred Marion .02 .10
262 Bo Jackson .30 .75
263 Marcus Allen .15 .40
264 Curt Warner .02 .10
272 Fredd Young .02 .10
273 David Little .02 .10
277 Earnest Jackson .02 .10
282 J.T. Smith/283 Charles White .02 .10
284 Reggie White/285 Morten Andersen .07 .20
NNO Sticker Album .75 2.00

1988 Topps Sticker Backs

These cards are actually the backs of the Topps stickers. These cards are numbered in fine print in the statistical section of the card. The 67 cards in the set are generally a selection of popular players with all of them being quarterbacks, running backs, or receivers. The cards measure approximately 2 1/8" by 3". The cards are checklisted below alphabetically according to teams.

COMPLETE SET (67) 2.00 5.00
1 Doug Williams .02 .10
2 Gary Clark .02 .10
3 John Elway .50 1.25
4 Sammy Winder .02 .10
5 Vance Johnson .02 .10
6 Joe Montana .50 1.25
7 Roger Craig .02 .10
8 Jerry Rice .30 .75
9 Rueben Mayes .02 .10
10 Eric Martin .02 .10
11 Neal Anderson .02 .10
12 Willie Gault .02 .10
13 Bernie Kosar .02 .10
14 Kevin Mack .02 .10
15 Webster Slaughter .07 .20
16 Warren Moon .10 .30
17 Mike Rozier .02 .10
18 Drew Hill .02 .10
19 Eric Dickerson .07 .20
20 Bill Brooks .02 .10
21 Curt Warner .02 .10
22 Steve Largent .10 .30
23 Darrin Nelson .02 .10
24 Anthony Carter .02 .10
25 Earnest Jackson .02 .10
26 Weegie Thompson .02 .10
27 Stephen Starring .02 .10
28 Stanley Morgan .02 .10
29 Dan Marino .50 1.25
30 Troy Stradford .02 .10
31 Mark Clayton .02 .10
32 Curtis Adams .02 .10
33 Kellen Winslow .07 .20
34 Jim Kelly .15 .40
35 Ronnie Harmon .02 .10
36 Chris Burkett .02 .10
37 Randall Cunningham .10 .30
38 Anthony Toney .02 .10
39 Mike Quick .02 .10
40 Neil Lomax .02 .10
41 Stump Mitchell .02 .10
42 J.T. Smith .02 .10
43 Herschel Walker .07 .20
44 Herschel Walker .07 .20
45 Joe Morris .02 .10
46 Mark Bavaro .02 .10
47 Charles White .02 .10
48 Henry Ellard .07 .20
49 Ken O'Brien .02 .10
50 Freeman McNeil .02 .10
51 Al Toon .02 .10
52 Kenneth Davis .02 .10
53 Walter Stanley .02 .10
54 Marcus Allen .10 .30
55 James Lofton .07 .20
56 Boomer Esiason .07 .20
57 Larry Kinnebrew .02 .10
58 Eddie Brown .02 .10
59 James Wilder .02 .10
60 Gerald Carter .02 .10
61 Christian Okoye .02 .10
62 Carlos Carson .02 .10
63 James Jones .02 .10
64 Pete Mandley .02 .10
65 Gerald Riggs .02 .10
66 Floyd Dixon .02 .10
67 Checklist Card .02 .10

2010 Topps Supreme

STATED PRINT RUN 209 SER.#'d SETS
1 Drew Brees 2.00 5.00
2 Armanti Edwards RC 2.00 5.00
3 Jahvid Best RC 3.00 8.00
4 Colt McCoy RC 4.00 10.00
5 C.J. Spiller RC 3.00 8.00
6 Ben Tate RC 2.50 6.00
7 Hakeem Nicks 1.50 4.00
8 LeSean McCoy 1.50 4.00
9 Troy Polamalu 2.50 6.00
10 Larry Fitzgerald 2.00 5.00
11 Emmitt Smith 3.00 8.00
12 Aaron Rodgers 4.00 10.00
13 Antonio Gates 1.50 4.00
14 Toby Gerhart RC 2.00 5.00
15 Roddy White 1.50 4.00
16 Mark Sanchez 2.00 5.00
17 Kenny Britt 1.50 4.00
18 Kareem Jackson RC 2.00 5.00
19 Major Wright RC 2.00 5.00
20 Ray Lewis 2.00 5.00
21 Jared Allen 2.00 5.00
22 LaDainian Tomlinson 2.00 5.00
23 Matt Schaub 1.50 4.00
24 Donovan McNabb 2.00 5.00
25 Dez Bryant RC 6.00 15.00
26 Tyson Alualu RC 1.50 4.00
27 Darren McFadden 1.50 4.00
28 Jermaine Gresham RC 2.50 6.00
29 Joe Namath 2.50 6.00
30 Peyton Manning 3.00 8.00
31 Damian Williams RC 2.00 5.00
32 Jordan Shipley RC 2.00 5.00
33 Dexter McCluster RC 2.00 5.00
34 Dwight Freeney 1.50 4.00
35 Michael Turner 1.25 3.00
36 Marques Colston 1.50 4.00
37 Golden Tate RC 2.00 5.00
38 Jimmy Clausen RC 2.00 5.00
39 Mardy Gilyard RC 2.00 5.00
40 Eric Dickerson 1.50 4.00
41 Ray Rice 1.50 4.00
42 Art Monk 1.50 4.00
43 Rolando McClain RC 2.00 5.00
44 Emmanuel Sanders RC 2.00 5.00
45 Tony Romo 2.50 6.00
46 Rob Gronkowski RC 5.00 12.00
47 Joe Flacco 2.00 5.00
48 Gerald McCoy RC 2.00 5.00
49 Marcus Allen 2.00 5.00
50 Dan Marino 4.00 10.00
51 Wes Welker 2.00 5.00
52 Sean Weatherspoon RC 2.00 5.00
53 Shonn Greene 1.50 4.00
54 Andre Roberts RC 2.00 5.00
55 Philip Rivers 2.00 5.00
56 Tim Brown 2.00 5.00
57 Anquan Boldin 1.50 4.00
58 Ryan Torain 1.50 4.00
59 Franco Harris 2.00 5.00
60 Vernon Davis 1.50 4.00
61 Brett Favre 5.00 12.00
62 Josh Freeman 2.00 5.00
63 Rashard Mendenhall 1.50 4.00
64 Ryan Mathews RC 4.00 10.00
65 Taylor Price RC 2.00 5.00
66 Patrick Willis 1.50 4.00
67 Brandon Marshall 1.50 4.00
68 Arian Foster 1.50 4.00
69 Brandon LaFell RC 2.00 5.00
70 Demaryius Thomas RC 2.50 6.00
71 Tom Brady 3.00 8.00
72 Mike Kafka RC 2.00 5.00
73 DeAngelo Williams 1.50 4.00
74 Jonathan Dwyer RC 2.00 5.00
75 Tim Tebow RC 15.00 30.00
76 Jamaal Charles 1.50 4.00
77 Jason Pierre-Paul RC 3.00 8.00
78 Eric Decker RC 2.50 6.00
79 Eli Manning 2.00 5.00
80 Cris Carter 2.00 5.00
81 Joe Montana 4.00 10.00
82 Andre Johnson 1.50 4.00
83 Darrelle Revis 1.50 4.00
84 Marcus Easley RC 1.50 4.00
85 Joe McKnight RC 2.00 5.00
86 Mario Williams 1.50 4.00
87 Mike Williams RC 3.00 8.00

88 Eric Berry RC 2.00 5.00
89 Montario Hardesty RC 2.00 5.00
90 Sam Bradford RC 12.00 30.00
91 Randy Moss 2.50 6.00
92 Reggie Wayne 1.50 4.00
93 Maurice Jones-Drew 1.50 4.00
94 Arrelious Benn RC 2.00 5.00
95 Ndamukong Suh RC 4.00 10.00
96 Howie Long 2.00 5.00
97 Justin Tuck 1.50 4.00
98 Adrian Peterson 3.00 8.00
99 Jay Cutler 2.00 5.00
100 Chris Johnson 2.00 5.00

2010 Topps Supreme Black
*VETS/25: 1.2X TO 3X BASIC CARDS
*ROOKIES/25: .8X TO 2X BASIC CARDS
STATED PRINT RUN 25 SER.#'d SETS

2010 Topps Supreme Blue
*VETS/62: .8X TO 2X BASIC CARDS
*ROOKIES/62: .5X TO 1.2X BASIC CARDS
BLUE STATED PRINT RUN 62

2010 Topps Supreme Autographed Dual Relics
STATED PRINT RUN 10-50
*TRIPLE AU/50: .4X TO 1X DUAL JSY AU/50
TRIPLE JSY AU PRINT RUN 10-50
SADRBF Brett Favre/15 150.00 250.00
SADRCM Colt McCoy/50 40.00 60.00
SADRCS C.J. Spiller/25 20.00 50.00
SADRDB Drew Brees/15 40.00 80.00
SADRDR Darrelle Revis/15 25.00 50.00
SADRDT Demaryius Thomas/25 15.00 40.00
SADRED Eric Dickerson/15 25.00 50.00
SADREM Eli Manning/50 50.00 100.00
SADRJB Jahvid Best/25 25.00 60.00
SADRJC Jimmy Clausen/50 10.00 25.00
SADRJF Joe Flacco/15 30.00 60.00
SADRJM Joe Montana/25 100.00 175.00
SADRJN Joe Namath/25 60.00 120.00
SADRNS Ndamukong Suh/25 40.00 80.00
SADRPM Peyton Manning/50 60.00 120.00
SADRRM Ryan Mathews/25 25.00 60.00
SADRSB Sam Bradford/50 75.00 150.00
SADRSH Santonio Holmes/15 15.00 40.00
SADRTR Tony Romo/15 40.00 80.00
SADRTT Tim Tebow/50 100.00 175.00

2010 Topps Supreme Autographs
STATED PRINT RUN 10-75
EXCH EXPIRATION: 1/31/2014
SAAG Antonio Gates/25 12.00 30.00
SABM Brandon Marshall/25 12.00 30.00
SADJ DeSean Jackson/25 15.00 40.00
SAEM Eli Manning/55 30.00 60.00
SAFG Frank Gore/25 12.00 30.00
SAJE John Elway/55 60.00 120.00
SAJM Joe Montana/55 60.00 120.00
SAJN Joe Namath/55 40.00 80.00
SAMS Matthew Stafford/25 30.00 60.00
SAPM Peyton Manning/55 50.00 100.00
SARL Ray Lewis/25 40.00 80.00
SATR Tony Romo/55 30.00 60.00
SARCM Colt McCoy/50 30.00 60.00
SARCS C.J. Spiller/50 12.00 30.00
SARDM Dexter McCluster/15 12.00 30.00
SARDT Demaryius Thomas/50 10.00 25.00
SAREB Eric Berry/15 30.00 60.00
SARGM Gerald McCoy/15 12.00 30.00
SARJB Jahvid Best/50 12.00 30.00
SARJC Jimmy Clausen/50 8.00 20.00
SARJG Jermaine Gresham/15 15.00 40.00
SARJS Jordan Shipley/15 12.00 30.00
SARNS Ndamukong Suh/50 30.00 60.00
SARRM Ryan Mathews/50 15.00 40.00
SARSB Sam Bradford/50 75.00 150.00
SARTT Tim Tebow/75 90.00 150.00

2010 Topps Supreme Dual Autographs
STATED PRINT RUN 10-50
MM Peyton Manning/50 100.00 200.00
Eli Manning
TM LaDainian Tomlinson/50 50.00 100.00
Ryan Mathews

2010 Topps Supreme Rookie Quad Relics
STATED PRINT RUN 15 SER.#'d SETS
EACH HAS 2 CARDS OF EQUAL VALUE
*TRIPLE/15: .4X TO 1X QUAD/15
SRQRAB Arrelious Benn 8.00 20.00
SRQRBL Brandon LaFell 8.00 20.00
SRQRCM Colt McCoy 15.00 40.00
SRQRCS C.J. Spiller 10.00 25.00
SRQRDB Dez Bryant 20.00 50.00
SRQRDM Dexter McCluster 8.00 20.00
SRQRDT Demaryius Thomas 10.00 25.00
SRQREB Eric Berry 8.00 20.00
SRQRGM Gerald McCoy 8.00 20.00
SRQRGT Golden Tate 8.00 20.00
SRQRJD Jonathan Dwyer 8.00 20.00
SRQRJG Jermaine Gresham 8.00 20.00
SRQRJM Joe McKnight 8.00 20.00
SRQRJS Jordan Shipley 8.00 20.00
SRQRMK Mike Kafka 8.00 20.00
SRQRMW Mike Williams 12.00 30.00
SRQRNS Ndamukong Suh 15.00 40.00
SRQRRG Rob Gronkowski 20.00 50.00
SRQRRM Ryan Mathews 12.00 30.00
SRQRABE Arrelious Benn 8.00 20.00
SRQRBLA Brandon LaFell 8.00 20.00
SRQRCMC Colt McCoy 15.00 40.00
SRQRCSP C.J. Spiller 10.00 25.00
SRQRDBR Dez Bryant 20.00 50.00
SRQRDMC Dexter McCluster 8.00 20.00
SRQRDTH Demaryius Thomas 10.00 25.00
SRQREBE Eric Berry 8.00 20.00
SRQRGMC Gerald McCoy 8.00 20.00
SRQRGTA Golden Tate 8.00 20.00
SRQRJDW Jonathan Dwyer 8.00 20.00
SRQRJGR Jermaine Gresham 8.00 20.00
SRQRJMC Joe McKnight 8.00 20.00
SRQRJSH Jordan Shipley 8.00 20.00
SRQRMKA Mike Kafka 8.00 20.00
SRQRMWI Mike Williams 12.00 30.00
SRQRNSU Ndamukong Suh 15.00 40.00
SRQRRGR Rob Gronkowski 20.00 50.00
SRQRRMA Ryan Mathews 12.00 30.00
SRQRRMC Rolando McClain 8.00 20.00
SRQRRMCL Rolando McClain 8.00 20.00

2010 Topps Supreme Rookie Relic Quad Combos
STATED PRINT RUN 15 SER.#'d SETS
BBMS Sam Bradford 15.00 40.00
Dez Bryant
Colt McCoy
Jordan Shipley
BGGW Jahvid Best 10.00 25.00
Toby Gerhart
Rob Gronkowski
Damian Williams
BGTT Sam Bradford 15.00 40.00
Mardy Gilyard
Tim Tebow
Demaryius Thomas
BGWL Jahvid Best 10.00 25.00
Toby Gerhart
Mike Williams
Brandon LaFell
BMBR Sam Bradford 15.00 40.00
Gerald McCoy
Dez Bryant
Zac Robinson
BRBK Sam Bradford 15.00 40.00
Andre Roberts
Dez Bryant
Mike Kafka
BSMM Dez Bryant 12.00 30.00
C.J. Spiller
Dexter McCluster
Ryan Mathews
BSTM Sam Bradford 15.00 40.00
C.J. Spiller
Tim Tebow
Ryan Mathews
BSWM Jahvid Best 10.00 25.00
Ndamukong Suh
Mike Williams
Gerald McCoy
BTMT Dez Bryant 12.00 30.00
Demaryius Thomas
Dexter McCluster
Golden Tate
BTSG Sam Bradford 15.00 40.00
Demaryius Thomas
C.J. Spiller
Jermaine Gresham
BWLS Arrelious Benn 6.00 15.00
Damian Williams
Brandon LaFell
Emmanuel Sanders
CMBG Jimmy Clausen 8.00 20.00
Dexter McCluster
Jahvid Best
Jimmy Graham
CMMT Jimmy Clausen 10.00 25.00
Colt McCoy
Dexter McCluster
Golden Tate
CTMS Jimmy Clausen 10.00 25.00
Golden Tate
Colt McCoy
Jordan Shipley
GEWS Mardy Gilyard 6.00 15.00
Marcus Easley
Mike Williams
Jordan Shipley
GPGS Rob Gronkowski 6.00 15.00
Taylor Price
Jermaine Gresham
Jordan Shipley
GSDS Jermaine Gresham 6.00 15.00
Jordan Shipley
Jonathan Dwyer
Emmanuel Sanders
GSLE Jermaine Gresham 6.00 15.00
Jordan Shipley
Brandon LaFell
Armanti Edwards
GTHM Toby Gerhart 8.00 20.00
Ben Tate
Montario Hardesty
Joe McKnight
HSTW Montario Hardesty 8.00 20.00
Emmanuel Sanders
Ben Tate
Damian Williams
KCDS Mike Kafka 6.00 15.00
Riley Cooper
Jonathan Dwyer
Emmanuel Sanders
MBFM Dexter McCluster 8.00 20.00
Eric Berry
Jacoby Ford
Rolando McClain
MHDS Colt McCoy 10.00 25.00
Montario Hardesty
Jonathan Dwyer
Emmanuel Sanders
MHGS Colt McCoy 10.00 25.00
Montario Hardesty
Jermaine Gresham
Jordan Shipley
MTMM Dexter McCluster 12.00 30.00
Demaryius Thomas
Ryan Mathews
Rolando McClain
MTMT Colt McCoy 10.00 25.00
Golden Tate
Gerald McCoy
Ben Tate
SEGP C.J. Spiller 8.00 20.00
Marcus Easley
Rob Gronkowski
Taylor Price
SEMH C.J. Spiller 10.00 25.00
Marcus Easley
Colt McCoy
Montario Hardesty
SMBT C.J. Spiller 10.00 25.00
Ryan Mathews
Jahvid Best
Ben Tate
STDG C.J. Spiller 8.00 20.00
Demaryius Thomas
Jonathan Dwyer
Jimmy Graham
TBBM Tim Tebow 20.00 50.00
Dez Bryant
Sam Bradford
Dexter McCluster
TBCM Tim Tebow 15.00 40.00
Sam Bradford
Jimmy Clausen
Colt McCoy
TBMG Demaryius Thomas 8.00 20.00
Eric Berry
Joe McKnight
Rob Gronkowski
TBSM Demaryius Thomas 12.00 30.00
Dez Bryant
C.J. Spiller
Ryan Mathews
TBTB Tim Tebow 20.00 50.00
Sam Bradford
Demaryius Thomas
Dez Bryant
TDBG Tim Tebow 15.00 40.00
Eric Decker
Sam Bradford
Mardy Gilyard
TDFS Demaryius Thomas 8.00 20.00
Jonathan Dwyer
Jacoby Ford
C.J. Spiller
TDMB Demaryius Thomas 8.00 20.00
Eric Decker
Dexter McCluster
Eric Berry
TDWB Demaryius Thomas 8.00 20.00
Eric Decker
Mike Williams
Arrelious Benn
THCT Tim Tebow 15.00 40.00
Aaron Hernandez
Jimmy Clausen
Golden Tate
THDG Ben Tate 8.00 20.00
Montario Hardesty
Jonathan Dwyer
Toby Gerhart
TMLT Tim Tebow 15.00 40.00
Dexter McCluster
Brandon LaFell
Ben Tate
TTCL Tim Tebow 15.00 40.00
Demaryius Thomas
Jimmy Clausen
Brandon LaFell
TWTW Golden Tate 8.00 20.00
Mike Williams
Ben Tate
Damian Williams
WBGP Mike Williams 6.00 15.00
Arrelious Benn
Rob Gronkowski
Taylor Price
WBLE Mike Williams 6.00 15.00
Arrelious Benn
Brandon LaFell
Armanti Edwards
WGEM Mike Williams 6.00 15.00
Mardy Gilyard
Marcus Easley
Carlton Mitchell
SMBTH Ndamukong Suh 8.00 20.00
Gerald McCoy
Eric Berry
Earl Thomas
TBMGR Tim Tebow 15.00 40.00
Dez Bryant
Ryan Mathews
Rob Gronkowski

2011 Topps Supreme
STATED PRINT RUN 429 SER.#'d SETS
1 Joe Namath 2.50 6.00
2 Vincent Brown RC 2.00 5.00
3 Jon Baldwin RC 2.00 5.00
4 Mark Sanchez 2.00 5.00
5 Sam Bradford 2.00 5.00
6 Mikel Leshoure RC 2.00 5.00
7 LeSean McCoy 1.50 4.00
8 Matt Ryan 2.00 5.00
9 Mark Ingram RC 4.00 10.00
10 Terry Bradshaw 2.50 6.00
11 Howie Long 2.00 5.00
12 Knowshon Moreno 1.50 4.00
13 Taiwan Jones RC 2.00 5.00
14 Peyton Hillis 1.50 4.00
15 Dwayne Bowe 1.50 4.00
16 Franco Harris 2.00 5.00
17 Leonard Hankerson RC 2.00 5.00
18 Marcell Dareus RC 2.00 5.00
19 Eric Berry 1.50 4.00
20 Emmitt Smith 3.00 8.00
21 Mike Wallace 2.00 5.00
22 Arian Foster 1.50 4.00
23 Philip Rivers 2.00 5.00
24 Shane Vereen RC 2.00 5.00
25 Andy Dalton RC 5.00 12.00
26 Bart Starr 3.00 8.00
27 Dez Bryant 2.00 5.00
28 DeSean Jackson 1.50 4.00
29 Ronnie Lott 1.50 4.00
30 Tom Brady 3.00 8.00
31 Phil Simms 1.50 4.00
32 Charles Woodson 2.00 5.00
33 A.J. Green RC 4.00 10.00
34 Matt Schaub 1.50 4.00
35 Randall Cobb RC 2.50 6.00
36 Marques Colston 1.50 4.00
37 Andre Johnson 1.50 4.00
38 Bilal Powell RC 1.25 3.00
39 Jeremy Maclin 1.50 4.00
40 Adrian Peterson 2.50 6.00
41 Reggie Wayne 1.50 4.00
42 DeMarco Murray RC 5.00 12.00
43 Kendall Hunter RC 2.00 5.00
44 Maurice Jones-Drew 1.50 4.00
45 Jamie Harper RC 2.00 5.00
46 Daniel Thomas RC 2.00 5.00
47 Patrick Willis 1.50 4.00
48 Kyle Rudolph RC 2.00 5.00
49 Drew Brees 2.00 5.00
50 Dan Marino 4.00 10.00
51 Frank Gore 1.50 4.00
52 Greg Little RC 2.00 5.00
53 Larry Fitzgerald 1.50 4.00
54 Alex Green RC 2.00 5.00
55 Ben Roethlisberger 2.00 5.00
56 Von Miller RC 2.50 6.00
57 Jordan Todman RC 1.25 3.00
58 Edmond Gates RC 1.50 4.00
59 Jared Allen 1.50 4.00
60 Peyton Manning 3.00 8.00
61 Austin Pettis RC 1.50 4.00
62 Tony Dorsett 2.00 5.00
63 Torrey Smith RC 2.50 6.00
64 Ray Rice 1.50 4.00
65 Ryan Mallett RC 4.00 10.00
66 Titus Young RC 2.50 6.00
67 Tony Romo 2.00 5.00
68 Delone Carter RC 1.50 4.00
69 Miles Austin 1.50 4.00
70 Aaron Rodgers 3.00 8.00
71 Julio Jones RC 4.00 10.00
72 Ahmad Bradshaw 1.50 4.00
73 Colin Kaepernick RC 2.50 6.00
74 Jerrel Jernigan RC 2.00 5.00
75 Ray Lewis 2.00 5.00
76 Roddy White 1.50 4.00
77 Hakeem Nicks 1.50 4.00
78 Darren McFadden 1.50 4.00
79 Kevin Kolb 1.50 4.00
80 Jerry Rice 3.00 8.00
81 Rashard Mendenhall 1.50 4.00
82 Jake Locker RC 5.00 12.00
83 Chris Johnson 1.50 4.00
84 Christian Ponder RC 4.00 10.00
85 DeAngelo Williams 1.50 4.00
86 Roger Staubach 2.50 6.00
87 Ryan Williams RC 2.50 6.00
88 Ndamukong Suh 2.00 5.00
89 Eli Manning 2.00 5.00
90 Michael Vick 2.00 5.00
91 Jamaal Charles 1.50 4.00
92 Cam Newton RC 15.00 30.00
93 Steven Jackson 1.50 4.00
94 Stevan Ridley RC 2.00 5.00
95 Blaine Gabbert RC 3.00 8.00
96 Greg Jennings 1.50 4.00
97 Michael Turner 1.50 4.00
98 Calvin Johnson 2.00 5.00
99 Mike Williams 1.50 4.00
100 Joe Montana 4.00 10.00

2011 Topps Supreme Green
*VETS/15: 1.5X TO 4X BASIC CARDS
*RETIRED/15: 1.5X TO 4X BASIC CARDS
*ROOKIES/15: 1.2X TO 3X BASIC CARDS
STATED PRINT RUN 15 SER.#'d SETS

2011 Topps Supreme Purple
*VETS/75: .8X TO 2X BASIC CARDS
*RETIRED/75: .8X TO 2X BASIC CARDS
*ROOKIES/75: .6X TO 1.5X BASIC CARDS
STATED PRINT RUN 75 SER.#'d SETS

2011 Topps Supreme Red
*VETS/99: .8X TO 2X BASIC CARDS
*RETIRED/99: .8X TO 2X BASIC CARDS
*ROOKIES/99: .6X TO 1.5X BASIC CARDS
STATED PRINT RUN 99 SER.#'d SETS

2011 Topps Supreme Sepia
*VETS/30: 1X TO 2.5X BASIC CARDS
*RETIRED/30: 1X TO 2.5X BASIC CARDS
*ROOKIES/30: .8X TO 2X BASIC CARDS
STATED PRINT RUN 30 SER.#'d SETS

2011 Topps Supreme Autographed Dual Relics
*DUAL VETS/15: .5X TO 1.2X AU RELIC/50
*DUAL ROOKIE/15: .6X TO 1.5X AU RELIC/50
STATED PRINT RUN 15 SER.#'d SETS
UNPRICED DUAL JUMBO AU PRINT RUN 15
UNPRICED DUAL PATCH AU PRINT RUN 10
SADRCN Cam Newton 200.00 300.00
SADRDM DeMarco Murray 50.00 100.00
SADRJJ Julio Jones 50.00 100.00

2011 Topps Supreme Autographed Relics
STATED PRINT RUN 50 SER.#'d SETS
UNPRICED JUMBO AU PRINT RUN 10
UNPRICED QUAD AU PRINT RUN 10
UNPRICED SIX AU PRINT RUN 8
EXCH EXPIRATION: 12/31/2014
SARAD Andy Dalton 40.00 80.00
SARAJG A.J. Green 40.00 80.00
SARAP Austin Pettis 10.00 25.00
SARBG Blaine Gabbert 20.00 50.00
SARCK Colin Kaepernick 15.00 40.00
SARCN Cam Newton 125.00 200.00
SARCP Christian Ponder 25.00 60.00
SARDB Drew Brees 40.00 80.00
SARDM DeMarco Murray EXCH 40.00 80.00
SARDT Daniel Thomas 12.00 30.00
SARGL Greg Little 12.00 30.00
SARJB Jon Baldwin 12.00 30.00
SARJJE Jerrel Jernigan 10.00 25.00
SARJL Jake Locker 30.00 60.00
SARJM Joe Montana 75.00 150.00
SARJR Jerry Rice 90.00 150.00
SARKH Kendall Hunter 20.00 50.00
SARKR Kyle Rudolph 12.00 30.00
SARLH Leonard Hankerson 12.00 30.00
SARMD Marcell Dareus 12.00 30.00
SARMF Matt Forte 12.00 30.00
SARMI Mark Ingram 30.00 60.00
SARML Mikel Leshoure 12.00 30.00
SARMR Matt Ryan 25.00 50.00
SARMT Michael Turner 12.00 30.00
SARMV Michael Vick 40.00 80.00
SARRC Randall Cobb 20.00 50.00
SARRL Ray Lewis 40.00 80.00
SARRM Ryan Mallett 25.00 60.00
SARRW Ryan Williams 15.00 40.00
SARSJ Steve Johnson 12.00 30.00
SARSR Stevan Ridley 12.00 30.00
SARSV Shane Vereen 12.00 30.00
SARTR Tony Romo 30.00 80.00
SARTS Torrey Smith 15.00 40.00
SARTY Titus Young 15.00 40.00
SARVM Von Miller 15.00 40.00

2011 Topps Supreme Autographed Relics Red
*RED VETS/20: .5X TO 1.2X AU RELIC/50
*RED ROOKIES/20: .6X TO 1.5X AU RELIC/50
AUTO RED PRINT RUN 20 SER.#'d SETS
EXCH EXPIRATION: 12/31/2014
SARCN Cam Newton 175.00 300.00
SARDM DeMarco Murray EXCH 50.00 100.00

2011 Topps Supreme Autographs
BLUE STATED PRINT RUN 27
UNPRICED GREEN PRINT RUN 10
*RED/20: .4X TO 1X BLUE AU/27
EXCH EXPIRATION: 12/31/2014
SAAF Arian Foster 15.00 40.00
SAAJ Andre Johnson 15.00 40.00
SAAP Adrian Peterson 50.00 100.00
SABS Bart Starr 60.00 120.00
SADB Drew Brees 40.00 80.00
SADJ DeSean Jackson 12.00 30.00
SADM Dan Marino 75.00 150.00
SAGJ Greg Jennings 15.00 40.00
SAHL Howie Long 20.00 50.00
SAJM Joe Montana 75.00 150.00
SAJMA Jeremy Maclin 12.00 30.00
SAJN Joe Namath 50.00 100.00
SAJR Jerry Rice 90.00 150.00
SAMA Miles Austin EXCH 12.00 30.00
SAMC Marques Colston 15.00 40.00
SAMV Michael Vick 40.00 80.00
SAMW Mike Wallace 20.00 50.00
SAPH Peyton Hillis 12.00 30.00
SAPM Peyton Manning 60.00 120.00
SAPS Phil Simms 15.00 40.00
SARR Ray Rice 15.00 40.00
SARW Roddy White 12.00 30.00
SASB Sam Bradford 30.00 60.00
SATB Terry Bradshaw 50.00 100.00
SATR Tony Romo 30.00 60.00
SATT Tim Tebow 60.00 120.00

2011 Topps Supreme Dual Autographs
STATED PRINT RUN 25 SER.#'d SETS
UNPRICED JSY AU PRINT RUN 5
UNPRICED PATCH AU PRINT RUN 1
SDABB Dwayne Bowe 15.00 40.00
Jon Baldwin
SDABS Jon Baldwin 20.00 50.00
Torrey Smith
SDACG Randall Cobb 20.00 50.00
Alex Green
SDACJ Matt Cassel 15.00 40.00
Thomas Jones
SDADB Andy Dalton 50.00 100.00
Vincent Brown
SDADK Andy Dalton 50.00 100.00
Colin Kaepernick
SDADP Andy Dalton 75.00 150.00
Christian Ponder
SDADS Tony Dorsett 125.00 200.00
Emmitt Smith
SDAGD A.J. Green 75.00 150.00
Andy Dalton
SDAGL Blaine Gabbert 40.00 100.00
Jake Locker
SDAGN Blaine Gabbert 100.00 200.00
Cam Newton
SDAID Mark Ingram 30.00 80.00
Marcell Dareus
SDAIL Mark Ingram 30.00 80.00
Mikel Leshoure
SDAJB Vincent Jackson 15.00 40.00
Vincent Brown
SDAJH Jerrel Jernigan 15.00 40.00
Leonard Hankerson
SDAJP Jerrel Jernigan 12.00 30.00
Bilal Powell
SDAKG Colin Kaepernick 20.00 50.00
Alex Green
SDAKH Colin Kaepernick 20.00 50.00
Kendall Hunter
SDALG Greg Little 40.00 80.00
A.J. Green
SDALH Jake Locker 40.00 100.00
Jamie Harper
SDALM Jake Locker 50.00 100.00
Ryan Mallett
SDALY Mikel Leshoure 20.00 50.00
Titus Young
SDAMH Santana Moss 15.00 40.00
Leonard Hankerson
SDAMR Joe Montana 200.00 300.00
Jerry Rice
SDAMV Ryan Mallett 30.00 60.00
Shane Vereen
SDANM Cam Newton 100.00 200.00
Ryan Mallett
SDANS Joe Namath 90.00 150.00
Mark Sanchez
SDAPH Christian Ponder 30.00 80.00
Leonard Hankerson
SDAPJ Adrian Peterson 60.00 120.00
Maurice Jones-Drew
SDARG Kyle Rudolph 15.00 40.00
Alex Green
SDARP Kyle Rudolph 30.00 80.00
Christian Ponder
SDASL Torrey Smith 20.00 50.00
Greg Little
SDATB Jordan Todman 15.00 40.00
Vincent Brown
SDATC Daniel Thomas
Delone Carter
SDATJ Jordan Todman 15.00 40.00
Taiwan Jones
SDATM Daniel Thomas
Von Miller
SDATP Jordan Todman 10.00 25.00
Bilal Powell
SDAVR Shane Vereen 15.00 40.00
Stevan Ridley
SDAWH Ryan Williams 15.00 40.00
Jamie Harper
SDAWL Ryan Williams 15.00 40.00
Mikel Leshoure
SDAYP Titus Young 20.00 50.00
Austin Pettis
SDACJE Randall Cobb 15.00 40.00
Jerrel Jernigan
SDAMHU DeMarco Murray
Kendall Hunter
SDAMRI Ryan Mallett 30.00 60.00
Stevan Ridley
SDAMRO Peyton Manning EXCH 250.00 400.00
Aaron Rodgers

2011 Topps Supreme Eight Piece Relics
STATED PRINT RUN 20 SER.#'d SETS
UNPRICED PLATINUM PRINT RUN 1
1 Adrian Peterson 30.00 60.00
Chris Johnson
Jamaal Charles
Michael Turner
Mark Ingram
Daniel Thomas
Ryan Williams
DeMarco Murray
2 Michael Vick 40.00 80.00
Tom Brady
Mark Sanchez
Tony Romo
Cam Newton
Jake Locker
Blaine Gabbert
Christian Ponder
3 Julio Jones 25.00 50.00
Torrey Smith
Leonard Hankerson
Austin Pettis
Mark Ingram
Daniel Thomas
Jordan Todman
Kendall Hunter
4 Christian Ponder 30.00 60.00
Blaine Gabbert
Andy Dalton
Jake Locker
Julio Jones
Torrey Smith
Leonard Hankerson
Austin Pettis
5 Blaine Gabbert 25.00 50.00
Jake Locker
Ryan Mallett
Colin Kaepernick
Jon Baldwin
Torrey Smith
Randall Cobb
Greg Little
6 Blaine Gabbert
Cam Newton
Ryan Mallett
Colin Kaepernick
A.J. Green
Julio Jones
Titus Young
Edmond Gates
7 Jake Locker 30.00 60.00
Ryan Mallett
Andy Dalton
Colin Kaepernick
Torrey Smith
Greg Little
Titus Young
Leonard Hankerson
8 Blaine Gabbert 40.00 80.00
Jake Locker
Cam Newton
Andy Dalton
A.J. Green
Torrey Smith
Randall Cobb
Vincent Brown
9 Jake Locker
Cam Newton
Andy Dalton
Colin Kaepernick
Mark Ingram
Daniel Thomas
Jordan Todman
Kendall Hunter
10 Blaine Gabbert 40.00 80.00
Jake Locker
Cam Newton
Ryan Mallett
DeMarco Murray
Jordan Todman
Kendall Hunter
Stevan Ridley
11 Blaine Gabbert 40.00 80.00
Jake Locker
Cam Newton
Colin Kaepernick
Mark Ingram
Daniel Thomas
Shane Vereen
Kendall Hunter
12 Jon Baldwin 25.00 50.00
Torrey Smith
Randall Cobb
Greg Little
DeMarco Murray
Jordan Todman
Kendall Hunter
Stevan Ridley
13 Cam Newton 40.00 80.00
Andy Dalton
Christian Ponder
Colin Kaepernick
Ryan Williams
Daniel Thomas
Shane Vereen
Stevan Ridley

2011 Topps Supreme Rookie Autographs
STATED PRINT RUN 55-175
EXCH EXPIRATION: 12/31/2014
SRAAD Andy Dalton/55 25.00 50.00
SRAAG Alex Green/55 10.00 25.00
SRAAJG A.J. Green/90 20.00 40.00
SRAAP Austin Pettis/55 8.00 20.00
SRABG Blaine Gabbert/90 12.00 30.00
SRABP Bilal Powell/55 6.00 15.00
SRACK Colin Kaepernick/90 10.00 25.00
SRACN Cam Newton/175 90.00 150.00
SRACP Christian Ponder/90 20.00 40.00
SRADC Delone Carter 8.00 20.00
SRADM DeMarco Murray/55 30.00 60.00
SRADT Daniel Thomas/55 10.00 25.00
SRAEG Edmond Gates/55 8.00 20.00
SRAGL Greg Little/55 10.00 25.00
SRAJB Jon Baldwin/90 8.00 20.00
SRAJH Jamie Harper/55 10.00 25.00
SRAJJE Jerrel Jernigan/55 8.00 20.00
SRAJL Jake Locker/175 30.00 60.00
SRAJT Jordan Todman/55 6.00 15.00
SRAKH Kendall Hunter/55 12.00 30.00
SRALH Leonard Hankerson/55 8.00 20.00
SRALK Lance Kendricks/55 8.00 20.00
SRAMD Marcell Dareus/90 8.00 20.00
SRAMI Mark Ingram/175 20.00 40.00
SRAML Mikel Leshoure/90 8.00 20.00
SRARC Randall Cobb/55 15.00 30.00
SRARH Roy Helu/90 15.00 40.00
SRARM Ryan Mallett/90 15.00 40.00
SRARW Ryan Williams/90 10.00 25.00
SRASR Stevan Ridley/55 10.00 25.00
SRASV Shane Vereen/55 10.00 25.00
SRATJ Taiwan Jones/55 10.00 25.00
SRATP Terrelle Pryor/90 15.00 40.00
SRATS Torrey Smith/55 12.00 30.00
SRATY Titus Young/90 10.00 25.00
SRAVB Vincent Brown/55 8.00 20.00
SRAVM Von Miller 12.00 30.00

2011 Topps Supreme Rookie Autographs Green
*GREEN/15: .8X TO 2X BASIC AU/90-175
*GREEN/15: .6X TO 1.5X BASIC AU/55
GREEN PRINT RUN 15 SER.#'d SETS
SRACN Cam Newton 200.00 350.00

2011 Topps Supreme Rookie Autographs Purple
*PURPLE/25: .6X TO 1.5X BASIC AU/90-175
*PURPLE/25: .5X TO 1.2X BASIC AU/55
PURPLE STATED PRINT RUN 25
SRAAD Andy Dalton 50.00 100.00
SRACN Cam Newton 175.00 300.00

2011 Topps Supreme Rookie Autographs Red
*RED/50: .5X TO 1.2X BASIC AU/90-175
*RED/50: .4X TO 1X BASIC AU/55
RED PRINT RUN 50 SER.#'d SETS
SRACN Cam Newton 100.00 175.00

2011 Topps Supreme Rookie Quad Relics
STATED PRINT RUN 25-30
MOST HAVE TWO CARDS OF EQUAL VALUE
SRQRAD1 Andy Dalton/25 12.00 30.00
SRQRAD2 Andy Dalton/30 12.00 30.00
SRQRAJG1 A.J. Green/30 10.00 25.00
SRQRAJG2 A.J. Green
SRQRBG1 Blaine Gabbert/25 8.00 20.00
SRQRBG2 Blaine Gabbert/30 8.00 20.00
SRQRCK1 Colin Kaepernick/25 6.00 15.00
SRQRCK2 Colin Kaepernick/30 6.00 15.00
SRQRCN1 Cam Newton/30 25.00 60.00
SRQRCN2 Cam Newton/30 25.00 60.00
SRQRCP1 Christian Ponder/25 10.00 25.00
SRQRCP2 Christian Ponder/30 10.00 25.00
SRQRGL1 Greg Little/25 5.00 12.00
SRQRGL2 Greg Little/30 5.00 12.00
SRQRJB1 Jon Baldwin/25 8.00 20.00
SRQRJB2 Jon Baldwin/25 8.00 20.00
SRQRJJ1 Julio Jones/30 10.00 25.00
SRQRJJ2 Julio Jones/25 10.00 25.00
SRQRJL1 Jake Locker/25 12.00 30.00
SRQRJL2 Jake Locker 12.00 30.00
SRQRLH1 Leonard Hankerson/25 5.00 12.00
SRQRLH2 Leonard Hankerson
SRQRMD1 Marcell Dareus/30 5.00 12.00
SRQRMD2 Marcell Dareus
SRQRMI1 Mark Ingram/30 10.00 25.00
SRQRMI2 Mark Ingram/25 10.00 25.00
SRQRML1 Mikel Leshoure/30 5.00 12.00
SRQRML2 Mikel Leshoure/25 5.00 12.00
SRQRRC1 Randall Cobb/30 6.00 15.00
SRQRRC2 Randall Cobb/25 6.00 15.00
SRQRRM1 Ryan Mallett/30 10.00 25.00
SRQRRM2 Ryan Mallett/25 10.00 25.00
SRQRRW1 Ryan Williams/30 6.00 15.00
SRQRRW2 Ryan Williams/25 6.00 15.00
SRQRTS1 Torrey Smith/30 6.00 15.00
SRQRTS2 Torrey Smith/25 6.00 15.00
SRQRTY1 Titus Young/30 6.00 15.00
SRQRTY2 Titus Young/25 6.00 15.00
SRQRVM1 Von Miller/30 6.00 15.00
SRQRVM2 Von Miller/25 6.00 15.00

2011 Topps Supreme Rookie Relic Die Cuts
STATED PRINT RUN 55 SER.#'d SETS
SRDCAD Andy Dalton 10.00 25.00
SRDCAG Alex Green 4.00 10.00
SRDCAP Austin Pettis 3.00 8.00
SRDCBG Blaine Gabbert 6.00 15.00
SRDCBP Bilal Powell 2.50 6.00
SRDCCK Colin Kaepernick 5.00 12.00
SRDCCN Cam Newton 20.00 50.00
SRDCCP Christian Ponder 8.00 20.00
SRDCDC Delone Carter 3.00 8.00
SRDCDM DeMarco Murray 8.00 20.00
SRDCDT Daniel Thomas 4.00 10.00
SRDCGL Greg Little 4.00 10.00
SRDCJB Jon Baldwin 4.00 10.00
SRDCJH Jamie Harper 4.00 10.00
SRDCJJ Julio Jones 8.00 20.00
SRDCJL Jake Locker 10.00 25.00
SRDCJT Jordan Todman 2.50 6.00
SRDCKH Kendall Hunter 4.00 10.00
SRDCKR Kyle Rudolph 4.00 10.00
SRDCLH Leonard Hankerson 4.00 10.00
SRDCMD Marcell Dareus 4.00 10.00
SRDCMI Mark Ingram 8.00 20.00
SRDCML Mikel Leshoure 4.00 10.00
SRDCRC Randall Cobb 5.00 12.00
SRDCRM Ryan Mallett 8.00 20.00
SRDCRW Ryan Williams 5.00 12.00
SRDCSR Stevan Ridley 4.00 10.00
SRDCSV Shane Vereen 4.00 10.00
SRDCTS Torrey Smith 5.00 12.00
SRDCTY Titus Young 5.00 12.00
SRDCVB Vincent Brown 4.00 10.00
SRDCVM Von Miller 5.00 12.00
SRDCAJG A.J. Green 8.00 20.00
SRDCJJE Jerrel Jernigan 3.00 8.00

2011 Topps Supreme Rookie Relic Quad Combos
STATED PRINT RUN 25 SER.#'d SETS
BCGR Jon Baldwin 5.00 12.00
Randall Cobb
Alex Green
Stevan Ridley
BSCL Jon Baldwin 5.00 12.00
Torrey Smith
Randall Cobb
Greg Little
CLBG Randall Cobb 5.00 12.00
Greg Little
Vincent Brown
Edmond Gates
CYPB Randall Cobb 5.00 12.00
Titus Young
Austin Pettis
Vincent Brown
GBJY A.J. Green 8.00 20.00
Jon Baldwin
Jerrel Jernigan
Titus Young
GDPK Blaine Gabbert 10.00 25.00
Andy Dalton
Christian Ponder
Colin Kaepernick
GJIT A.J. Green 10.00 25.00
Julio Jones
Mark Ingram
Daniel Thomas
GJLP A.J. Green 8.00 20.00
Jerrel Jernigan
Greg Little
Austin Pettis
GJYG A.J. Green 10.00 25.00
Julio Jones
Titus Young
Edmond Gates
GLDK Blaine Gabbert 10.00 25.00
Jake Locker
Andy Dalton
Colin Kaepernick
GLMK Blaine Gabbert 10.00 25.00
Jake Locker
Ryan Mallett
Colin Kaepernick
GLMP Blaine Gabbert 10.00 25.00
Jake Locker
Ryan Mallett
Christian Ponder
GLND Blaine Gabbert 20.00 50.00
Jake Locker
Cam Newton
Andy Dalton
GLNK Blaine Gabbert 20.00 50.00
Jake Locker
Cam Newton
Colin Kaepernick
GLNM Blaine Gabbert 20.00 50.00
Jake Locker
Cam Newton
Ryan Mallett
GLNP Blaine Gabbert 20.00 50.00
Jake Locker
Cam Newton
Christian Ponder
GLPK Blaine Gabbert 10.00 25.00
Jake Locker
Christian Ponder
Colin Kaepernick
GNMD Blaine Gabbert 20.00 50.00
Cam Newton
Ryan Mallett
Andy Dalton
GNMK Blaine Gabbert 20.00 50.00
Cam Newton
Ryan Mallett
Colin Kaepernick
GSCB A.J. Green 8.00 20.00
Torrey Smith
Randall Cobb
Jon Baldwin
ITRG Mark Ingram 8.00 20.00
Jordan Todman
Stevan Ridley
Alex Green
ITTH Mark Ingram 8.00 20.00
Daniel Thomas
Jordan Todman
Kendall Hunter
ITVH Mark Ingram 8.00 20.00
Daniel Thomas
Shane Vereen
Kendall Hunter
JBLY Julio Jones 8.00 20.00
Jon Baldwin
Greg Little
Titus Young
JCJH Julio Jones 8.00 20.00

Randall Cobb
Jerrel Jernigan
Leonard Hankerson
JSHP Julio Jones 8.00 20.00
Torrey Smith
Leonard Hankerson
Austin Pettis
JSLH Julio Jones 8.00 20.00
Torrey Smith
Greg Little
Leonard Hankerson
LMDK Jake Locker 10.00 25.00
Ryan Mallett
Andy Dalton
Colin Kaepernick
LMDP Jake Locker 10.00 25.00
Ryan Mallett
Andy Dalton
Christian Ponder
LNDK Jake Locker 20.00 50.00
Cam Newton
Andy Dalton
Colin Kaepernick
LNMP Jake Locker 20.00 50.00
Cam Newton
Ryan Mallett
Christian Ponder
LSVH Greg Little 5.00 12.00
Torrey Smith
Shane Vereen
Jamie Harper
MDPK Ryan Mallett 10.00 25.00
Andy Dalton
Christian Ponder
Colin Kaepernick
MHCP DeMarco Murray 8.00 20.00
Kendall Hunter
Delone Carter
Bilal Powell
MTHR DeMarco Murray 8.00 20.00
Jordan Todman
Kendall Hunter
Stevan Ridley
NDPK Cam Newton 20.00 50.00
Andy Dalton
Christian Ponder
Colin Kaepernick
PGDL Christian Ponder 10.00 25.00
Blaine Gabbert
Andy Dalton
Jake Locker
SLYH Torrey Smith 5.00 12.00
Greg Little
Titus Young
Leonard Hankerson
SYBG Torrey Smith 5.00 12.00
Titus Young
Vincent Brown
Edmond Gates
TMHG Daniel Thomas 8.00 20.00
DeMarco Murray
Kendall Hunter
Alex Green
WMHR Ryan Williams 8.00 20.00
DeMarco Murray
Jamie Harper
Stevan Ridley
WTVC Ryan Williams 5.00 12.00
Daniel Thomas
Shane Vereen
Delone Carter
WTVR Ryan Williams 5.00 12.00
Daniel Thomas
Shane Vereen
Stevan Ridley

2011 Topps Supreme Six Piece Relics

STATED PRINT RUN 25 SER.#'d SETS
1 Daniel Thomas 20.00 50.00
DeMarco Murray
Jordan Todman
Bilal Powell
Stevan Ridley
Alex Green
2 Dwayne Dowe
Chris Johnson
Calvin Johnson
Jon Baldwin
Jamie Harper
Titus Young
3 A.J. Green 15.00 40.00
Torrey Smith
Greg Little
Titus Young
Leonard Hankerson
Austin Pettis
4 Darren McFadden 25.00 50.00
Adrian Peterson
Dwayne Bowe
Ryan Mallett
DeMarco Murray
Stevan Ridley
5 A.J. Green 12.00 30.00
Randall Cobb
Jerrel Jernigan
Greg Little
Titus Young
Austin Pettis
6 Blaine Gabbert 25.00 60.00
Jake Locker
Cam Newton
Andy Dalton
Christian Ponder
Colin Kaepernick
7 Blaine Gabbert 25.00 60.00
Jake Locker
Cam Newton
Ryan Mallett
Christian Ponder
Colin Kaepernick
8 Cam Newton 25.00 60.00
Blaine Gabbert
Jake Locker
A.J. Green
Julio Jones
Mark Ingram
9 Jake Locker 25.00 60.00
Cam Newton
Ryan Mallett
Andy Dalton
Christian Ponder
Colin Kaepernick
10 Blaine Gabbert 25.00 60.00
Jake Locker
Cam Newton
Ryan Mallett
Andy Dalton
Christian Ponder
11 Blaine Gabbert
Jake Locker
Ryan Mallett
Andy Dalton
Christian Ponder
Colin Kaepernick
12 Mark Ingram 15.00 40.00
Daniel Thomas
Jordan Todman
Jamie Harper
Kendall Hunter
Bilal Powell
13 Daniel Thomas 12.00 30.00
Jordan Todman
Kendall Hunter
Bilal Powell
Stevan Ridley
Alex Green

2011 Topps Supreme Veteran Quad Relics

STATED PRINT RUN 20 SER.#'d SETS
EACH HAS TWO CARDS OF EQUAL VALUE
SVQRAG1 Antonio Gates 6.00 15.00
SVQRAG2 Antonio Gates 6.00 15.00
SVQRCJ1 Chris Johnson 6.00 15.00
SVQRCJ2 Chris Johnson 6.00 15.00
SVQRDB1 Dwayne Bowe 6.00 15.00
SVQRDB2 Dwayne Bowe 6.00 15.00
SVQRDM1 Darren McFadden 6.00 15.00
SVQRDM2 Darren McFadden 6.00 15.00
SVQRDR1 Darrelle Revis 6.00 15.00
SVQRDR2 Darrelle Revis 6.00 15.00
SVQRJC1 Jamaal Charles 6.00 15.00
SVQRJC2 Jamaal Charles 6.00 15.00
SVQRMS1 Mark Sanchez 8.00 20.00
SVQRMS2 Mark Sanchez 8.00 20.00
SVQRMV1 Michael Vick 8.00 20.00
SVQRMV2 Michael Vick 8.00 20.00
SVQRTB1 Tom Brady 15.00 40.00
SVQRTB2 Tom Brady 15.00 40.00
SVQRTR1 Tony Romo 8.00 20.00
SVQRTR2 Tony Romo 8.00 20.00

2003 Topps Total

Released in August of 2003, this 550-card set includes 440 veterans and 110 rookies. Boxes contained 36 packs of 10 cards. Pack SRP was $1.

COMPLETE SET (550) 40.00 80.00
1 Rich Gannon .20 .50
2 Travis Henry .15 .40
3 Brian Finneran .15 .40
4 Ed Hartwell .15 .40
5 Az-Zahir Hakim .15 .40
6 Rodney Peete .15 .40
7 David Terrell .15 .40
8 Matt Schobel .20 .50
9 Andre Davis .15 .40
10 Dexter Coakley .20 .50
11 Rod Smith .20 .50
12 Damerien McCants .15 .40
13 Robert Ferguson .15 .40
14 Kailee Wong .15 .40
15 James Mungro .15 .40
16 Fred Taylor .20 .50
17 Tony Gonzalez .25 .60
18 Randall Godfrey .15 .40
19 Robert Thomas .15 .40
20 Rohan Davey .15 .40
21 Terrell Owens .25 .60
22 Ron Dayne .20 .50
23 Charlie Batch .15 .40
24 Brian Westbrook .25 .60
25 Plaxico Burress .20 .50
26 Reche Caldwell .15 .40
27 Frod Boosloy .15 .40
28 Anthony Simmons .15 .40
29 Rod Woodson .25 .60
30 Derrick Brooks .20 .50
31 Shaun Ellis .15 .40
32 Ladell Betts .15 .40
33 Russell Davis .15 .40
34 Warrick Dunn .20 .50
35 Jeremy Shockey .25 .60
36 Alex Van Pelt .15 .40
37 Todd Bouman .15 .40
38 Kelly Campbell .15 .40
39 Justin Smith .20 .50
40 Jamel White .15 .40
41 La'Roi Glover .15 .40
42 Ian Gold .15 .40
43 Robert Porcher .15 .40
44 Jermaine Lewis .15 .40
45 Marvin Harrison .25 .60
46 Darren Sharper .20 .50
47 Jamie Sharper .15 .40
48 Tony Richardson .15 .40
49 Moe Williams .15 .40
50 Ricky Williams .20 .50
51 Ty Law .20 .50
52 Donte Stallworth .15 .40
53 Shannon Sharpe .25 .60
54 Santana Moss .20 .50
55 Charlie Garner .20 .50
56 Brian Dawkins .20 .50
57 Dan Campbell .15 .40
58 William Green .15 .40
59 Ron Dugans .15 .40
60 Darrell Jackson .20 .50
61 Marc Bulger .25 .60
62 Joe Jurevicius .20 .50
63 Erron Kinney .15 .40
64 Champ Bailey .25 .60
65 Peerless Price .15 .40
66 Gary Baxter .15 .40
67 Chris Redman .15 .40
68 London Fletcher .15 .40
69 Dee Brown .15 .40
70 Anthony Thomas .20 .50
71 Jake Delhomme .25 .60
72 Dorsey Levens .20 .50
73 Roy Williams .20 .50
74 Ashley Lelie .15 .40
75 Joey Harrington .15 .40
76 William Henderson .20 .50
77 Corey Bradford .15 .40
78 Reggie Wayne .25 .60
79 Kyle Brady .15 .40
80 Trent Green .20 .50
81 Bill Romanowski .20 .50
82 Chike Okeafor RC .30 .75
83 David Patten .15 .40
84 Terrelle Smith .15 .40
85 Kerry Collins .20 .50
86 Derrick Mason .20 .50
87 Trung Canidate .15 .40
88 A.J. Feeley .15 .40
89 Jason Gildon .20 .50
90 Doug Flutie .25 .60
91 Tai Streets .15 .40
92 Keith Newman .15 .40
93 Adam Archuleta .15 .40
94 Simeon Rice .15 .40
95 Eddie George .20 .50
96 Frank Sanders .15 .40
97 Freddie Jones .15 .40
98 Charles Johnson .15 .40
99 Keith Traylor .20 .50
100 Drew Bledsoe .25 .60
101 Muhsin Muhammad .20 .50
102 Marques Anderson .15 .40
103 Donald Hayes .15 .40
104 Quincy Morgan .15 .40
105 Chad Hutchinson .15 .40
106 Mike Anderson .20 .50
107 Randy McMichael .15 .40
108 Vonnie Holliday .15 .40
109 Marcus Coleman .15 .40
110 Edgerrin James .25 .60
111 Michael Lewis .15 .40
112 Wayne Chrebet .20 .50
113 Antwaan Randle El .20 .50
114 Byron Chamberlain .15 .40
115 Jeff Garcia .20 .50
116 Kim Herring .15 .40
117 Kenny Holmes .15 .40
118 John Lynch .20 .50
119 Doug Jolley .15 .40
120 Duce Staley .20 .50
121 Kordell Stewart .20 .50
122 Stephen Alexander .15 .40
123 Andre Carter .15 .40
124 Bobby Engram .15 .40
125 Marshall Faulk .25 .60
126 Peter Simon RC .15 .40
127 Alge Crumpler .20 .50
128 Kenny Watson .15 .40
129 Duane Starks .15 .40
130 Jeff Blake .20 .50
131 Todd Heap .20 .50
132 Bobby Shaw .15 .40
133 Ricky Proehl .20 .50
134 John Abraham .20 .50
135 T.J. Houshmandzadeh .25 .60
136 Brian Urlacher .25 .60
137 Darren Woodson .20 .50
138 Steve Beuerlein .20 .50
139 Cory Schlesinger .15 .40
140 Ahman Green .20 .50
141 Jabar Gaffney .15 .40
142 Eddie Drummond .15 .40
143 Stacey Mack .15 .40
144 Johnnie Morton .20 .50
145 Chris Chambers .20 .50
146 Jim Kleinsasser .15 .40
147 Tebucky Jones .15 .40
148 Marcus Pollard .15 .40
149 Tony Brackens .15 .40
150 Chad Pennington .25 .60
151 Kevin Faulk .20 .50
152 Michael Lewis .15 .40
153 Mark Bruener .15 .40
154 Tim Dwight .15 .40
155 Jerry Rice .50 1.25
156 Trent Dilfer .20 .50
157 Jon Ritchie .15 .40
158 Michael Pittman .15 .40
159 Lamar Gordon .15 .40
160 Rod Gardner .15 .40
161 Ken Dilger .20 .50
162 Doug Johnson .15 .40
163 Peter Boulware .20 .50
164 Jevon Kearse .20 .50
165 Julius Peppers .25 .60
166 Chris Chandler .20 .50
167 Lorenzo Neal .20 .50
168 Kevin Johnson .15 .40
169 Kevin Hardy .15 .40
170 KaRon Coleman .15 .40
171 James Stewart .15 .40
172 Tony Fisher .15 .40
173 Billy Miller .15 .40
174 Phillip Crosby .15 .40
175 Priest Holmes .25 .60
176 Elvis Joseph .15 .40
177 Bryan Gilmore .15 .40
178 D'Wayne Bates .15 .40
179 Quincy Carter .15 .40
180 Joe Horn .20 .50
181 Anthony Henry .15 .40
182 Anthony Becht .15 .40
183 Mike Peterson .15 .40
184 James Thrash .15 .40
185 Jerome Bettis .25 .60
186 Marcellus Wiley .15 .40
187 Tim Rattay .15 .40
188 Maurice Morris .15 .40
189 Jason Taylor .20 .50
190 Keyshawn Johnson .25 .60
191 John Simon .15 .40
192 Fred Smoot .15 .40
193 Wendell Bryant .15 .40
194 Brandon Stokley .20 .50
195 Kurt Warner .25 .60
196 Steve Smith .25 .60
197 Dez White .15 .40
198 Jim Miller .15 .40
199 Robert Griffith .15 .40
200 Michael Vick .30 .75
201 Antonio Bryant .15 .40
202 Laveranues Coles .15 .40
203 Kalimba Edwards .15 .40
204 Bubba Franks .20 .50
205 David Carr .20 .50
206 Dwight Freeney .20 .50
207 Eric Johnson .20 .50
208 Reggie Tongue .15 .40
209 Cam Cleeland .15 .40
210 Michael Bennett .20 .50
211 Antowain Smith .20 .50
212 Warren Sapp .20 .50
213 Ike Hilliard .15 .40
214 Olandis Gary .15 .40
215 Tim Brown .25 .60
216 Kevin Dyson .15 .40
217 Eddie Kennison .15 .40
218 Junior Seau .25 .60
219 Donnie Edwards .15 .40
220 Shaun Alexander .20 .50
221 Terrence Wilkins .15 .40
222 Garrison Hearst .20 .50
223 Keith Bulluck .15 .40
224 Zeron Flemister .15 .40
225 Jake Plummer .20 .50
226 Chad Johnson .25 .60
227 Travis Taylor .15 .40
228 Josh Reed .15 .40
229 James Farrior .20 .50
230 Marty Booker .20 .50
231 Todd Pinkston .15 .40
232 Dennis Northcutt .15 .40
233 Troy Hambrick .15 .40
234 Roland Williams .15 .40
235 Bill Schroeder .15 .40
236 Javon Walker .20 .50
237 Kevin Swayne .15 .40
238 Dominic Rhodes .20 .50
239 David Garrard .25 .60
240 Mike Maslowski RC .15 .40
241 Travis Minor .15 .40
242 Terry Glenn .20 .50
243 Deion Branch .20 .50
244 Adrian Peterson .15 .40
245 Tiki Barber .25 .60
246 Ray Lewis .25 .60
247 Marques Tuiasosopo .15 .40
248 Chad Lewis .20 .50
249 Takeo Spikes .15 .40
250 LaDainian Tomlinson .25 .60
251 Stephen Davis .20 .50
252 Koren Robinson .20 .50
253 Daylon McCutcheon .15 .40
254 Rob Johnson .20 .50
255 Donovan McNabb .25 .60
256 Derrius Thompson .15 .40
257 Marcel Shipp .15 .40
258 Keith Brooking .20 .50
259 Chris McAlister .20 .50
260 Eric Moulds .20 .50
261 Amos Zereoue .15 .40
262 Drew Brees .25 .60
263 Jon Kitna .20 .50
264 Brad Johnson .20 .50
265 Emmitt Smith .60 1.50
266 Trevor Pryce .20 .50
267 Mike McMahon .15 .40
268 Patrick Ramsey .20 .50
269 Jonathan Wells .15 .40
270 Mark Brunell .20 .50
271 Marc Boerigter .15 .40
272 Rob Konrad .15 .40
273 Derrick Alexander .15 .40
274 Joey Galloway .20 .50
275 Peyton Manning .50 1.25
276 Najeh Davenport .20 .50
277 Jesse Palmer .15 .40
278 LaMont Jordan .20 .50
279 Ernie Conwell .15 .40
280 Hines Ward .25 .60
281 Freddie Mitchell .20 .50
282 Curtis Conway .15 .40
283 Cedrick Wilson .15 .40
284 Troy Brown .20 .50
285 Torry Holt .25 .60
286 Mike Alstott .25 .60
287 Frank Wycheck .15 .40
288 Jeremiah Trotter .20 .50
289 Tyrone Wheatley .20 .50
290 David Boston .15 .40
291 Jay Fiedler .15 .40
292 Troy Walters .15 .40
293 Warrick Holdman .15 .40
294 Peter Warrick .20 .50
295 Tim Couch .15 .40
296 Aaron Glenn .15 .40
297 Deuce McAllister .20 .50
298 Michael Strahan .25 .60
299 Tom Brady .60 1.50
300 Brett Favre .60 1.50
301 Isaac Bruce .25 .60
302 Jimmy Smith .20 .50
303 Dante Hall .20 .50
304 James McKnight .15 .40
305 Daunte Culpepper .20 .50
306 Lawyer Milloy .20 .50
307 Jerome Pathon .15 .40
308 Steve McNair .25 .60
309 Vinny Testaverde .20 .50
310 Tommy Maddox .20 .50
311 Amani Toomer .20 .50
312 Aaron Brooks .20 .50
313 Gus Frerotte .20 .50
314 Kevan Barlow .15 .40
315 Matt Hasselbeck .20 .50
316 Clinton Portis .20 .50
317 Keenan McCardell .20 .50
318 Zach Thomas .25 .60
319 Curtis Martin .25 .60
320 Jamal Lewis .20 .50
321 T.J. Duckett .20 .50
322 Jerry Porter .15 .40
323 Randy Moss .25 .60
324 Rosevelt Colvin .20 .50
325 Corey Dillon .20 .50
326 Kelly Holcomb .15 .40
327 Josh McCown .20 .50
328 Ed McCaffrey .20 .50
329 Mikhael Ricks .15 .40
330 Donald Driver .25 .60
331 James Darling .15 .40
Ray Thompson
Ronald McKinnon
332 Cory Hall .15 .40
Keion Carpenter
Ray Buchanon
333 Adalius Thomas .15 .40
Anthony Weaver
Kelly Gregg RC
334 Antoine Winfield .20 .50
Coy Wire
Nate Clements
335 Dan Morgan .20 .50
Mark Fields
Will Witherspoon
336 Alex Brown .15 .40
Bryan Robinson RC
Phillip Daniels
337 Carl Powell RC .15 .40
John Thornton
Tony Williams RC
338 Ben Taylor RC .15 .40
Earl Little
Kevin Bentley
339 Ebenezer Ekuban .25 .60
Greg Ellis
Michael Myers
340 Daryl Gardener .30 .75
Lional Dalton RC
Bertrand Berry RC
341 Barrett Green .15 .40
Donte Curry RC
Earl Holmes
342 Cletidus Hunt RC .20 .50
Kabeer Gbaja-Biamila
Rod Walker RC
343 Gary Walker .15 .40
Jerry Deloach RC
Seth Payne
344 Chad Bratzke .15 .40
Marcus Washington
Rob Morris
345 John Henderson .20 .50
Marco Coleman
Marcus Stroud
346 Eric Hicks .15 .40
John Browning RC
Ryan Sims
347 Adewale Ogunleye RC .75 2.00
Larry Chester RC
Tim Bowens
348 Fred Robbins .15 .40
Kenny Mixon
Lance Johnstone
349 Roman Phifer .25 .60
Ted Johnson
Tedy Bruschi
350 Charles Grant .20 .50
Martin Chase RC
Darren Howard
351 Brandon Short .25 .60
Dhani Jones RC
Mike Barrow
352 Marvin Jones .15 .40
Mo Lewis
Sam Cowart
353 Eric Barton .15 .40
John Parrella
Napoleon Harris
354 Brandon Whiting .20 .50
Corey Simon
Darwin Walker
355 Aaron Smith .40 1.00
Casey Hampton
Kimo von Oelhoffen
356 Jamal Williams RC .15 .40
Jason Fisk
Raylee Johnson
357 Derek Smith .15 .40
Jeff Ulbrich
Julian Peterson
358 Antonio Cochran RC .20 .50
Chad Eaton
John Randle
359 Damione Lewis .15 .40
Grant Wistrom
Leonard Little
360 Dwayne Rudd .15 .40
Greg Spires
Shelton Quarles RC
361 Albert Haynesworth .25 .60
Kevin Carter
Robaire Smith
362 Bruce Smith .20 .50
Jessie Armstead
Regan Upshaw
363 Adrian Wilson .25 .60
Dexter Jackson RC
364 Fred Wakefield .15 .40
Kyle Vanden Bosch
365 Kevin Kasper .15 .40
Jason McAddley
366 Brady Smith .20 .50
Patrick Kerney
367 Martay Jenkins .15 .40
Trevor Gaylor
368 Chris Draft .15 .40
Matt Stewart
369 Javin Hunter .15 .40
Ron Johnson
370 Corey Fuller .25 .60
Ed Reed
371 Aaron Schobel .20 .50
Jeff Posey RC
372 Pat Williams .20 .50
Sam Adams
373 Deon Grant .15 .40
Mike Minter
374 Brentson Buckner .15 .40
Kris Jenkins
375 Reggie Howard RC .15 .40
Terry Cousin RC
376 Mike Brown .20 .50
Mike Green
377 Jerry Azumah .15 .40
R.W. McQuarters
378 Brian Simmons .15 .40
Steve Foley
379 Artrell Hawkins .15 .40
Jeff Burris
380 JoJuan Armour RC .15 .40
Marquand Manuel
381 Gerard Warren .15 .40
Orpheus Roye
382 Courtney Brown .15 .40
Kenard Lang
383 Derek Ross .15 .40
Mario Edwards
384 Al Singleton RC .20 .50
Dat Nguyen
385 Al Wilson .15 .40
John Mobley
386 Deltha O'Neal .15 .40
Kenoy Kennedy
387 Luther Elliss .15 .40
Shaun Rogers
388 Chris Cash .15 .40
Dre Bly
389 Brian Walker .15 .40
Corey Harris
390 Hannibal Navies RC .15 .40
Na'Il Diggs
391 Al Harris .20 .50
Mike McKenzie
392 Charlie Clemons .15 .40
Jay Foreman
393 Eric Brown .15 .40
Matt Stevens
394 Brad Scioli .15 .40
Larry Tripplett
395 David Macklin .15 .40
Walt Harris
396 Akin Ayodele .15 .40
Hugh Douglas
397 Fernando Bryant .15 .40
Jason Craft RC
398 Donovin Darius .15 .40
Marlon McCree
399 Scott Fujita .15 .40
Shawn Barber
400 Eric Warfield RC .20 .50
William Bartee
401 Greg Wesley .15 .40
Jerome Woods
402 Patrick Surtain .20 .50
Sam Madison
403 Brock Marion .15 .40
Sammy Knight
404 Greg Biekert .15 .40
Henri Crockett
405 Chris Claiborne .20 .50
Chris Hovan
406 Corey Chavous .15 .40
Ken Irvin
407 Christian Fauria .15 .40
Daniel Graham
408 Otis Smith .20 .50
Rodney Harrison
409 Anthony Pleasant .20 .50
Richard Seymour
410 Darrin Smith .15 .40
Sedrick Hodge
411 Ashley Ambrose .15 .40
Dale Carter
412 Mel Mitchell .15 .40
Derrick Rodgers
413 Will Allen .20 .50
William Peterson
414 Cornelius Griffin .15 .40
Keith Hamilton
415 Omar Stoutmire .15 .40
Shaun Williams
416 Aaron Beasley .20 .50
Donnie Abraham
417 Jon McGraw .15 .40
Sam Garnes
418 Charles Woodson .25 .60
Phillip Buchanon
419 Tony Bryant .15 .40
Trace Armstrong
420 Bobby Taylor .20 .50
Troy Vincent
421 Carlos Emmons .15 .40
Nate Wayne
422 Brent Alexander .15 .40
Chris Hope
423 Joey Porter .25 .60
Kendrell Bell
424 Chad Scott .15 .40
Dewayne Washington
425 Ben Leber .15 .40
Ryan McNeil
426 Quentin Jammer .15 .40
Tay Cody
427 Ahmed Plummer .15 .40
Jason Webster
428 Tony Parrish .15 .40
Zack Bronson
429 Itula Mili .20 .50
Jerramy Stevens
430 Ken Lucas .15 .40
Shawn Springs
431 Chad Brown .15 .40
Orlando Huff
432 Jamie Duncan .15 .40
Tommy Polley
433 Aeneas Williams .20 .50
Travis Fisher
434 Brian Kelly .20 .50
Ronde Barber
435 Aaron Stecker .15 .40
Karl Williams
436 Drew Bennett .20 .50
Justin McCareins
437 Lance Schulters .15 .40
Tank Williams
438 Andre Dyson .20 .50
Samari Rolle
439 Ifeanyi Ohalete .15 .40
Matt Bowen
440 Brandon Noble .20 .50
Dan Wilkinson
441 Charles Rogers RC .40 1.00
442 Jimmy Kennedy RC .40 1.00
443 Kelley Washington RC .30 .75
444 Trent Smith RC .40 1.00
445 Rashean Mathis RC .40 1.00
446 Brian St.Pierre RC .40 1.00
447 Bethel Johnson RC .30 .75
448 Alonzo Jackson RC .30 .75
449 Arnaz Battle RC .50 1.25
450 Carson Palmer RC 1.00 2.50
451 Michael Haynes RC .30 .75
452 LaBrandon Toefield RC .40 1.00
453 Earnest Graham RC .50 1.25
454 Walter Young RC .30 .75
455 Terry Pierce RC .30 .75
456 Talman Gardner RC .30 .75
457 J.T. Wall RC .30 .75
458 DeWayne Robertson RC .40 1.00
459 Bradie James RC .50 1.25
460 Andre Johnson RC 1.25 3.00
461 Bobby Wade RC .40 1.00
462 Chris Davis RC .40 1.00
463 Kliff Kingsbury RC .40 1.00
464 Osi Umenyiora RC .60 1.50
465 Domanick Davis RC .40 1.00
466 Sam Aiken RC .40 1.00
467 Ty Warren RC .40 1.00
468 Terence Newman RC .50 1.25
469 Zuriel Smith RC .30 .75
470 Willis McGahee RC .60 1.50
471 David Kircus RC .50 1.25
472 Billy McMullen RC .30 .75
473 Antwoine Sanders RC .30 .75
474 Adrian Madise RC .30 .75
475 Byron Leftwich RC .50 1.25
476 Justin Gage RC .40 1.00
477 Jason Witten RC 1.25 3.00
478 Lee Suggs RC .40 1.00
479 Kareem Kelly RC .30 .75
480 Rex Grossman RC .50 1.25
481 Nate Burleson RC .40 1.00
482 Chris Brown RC .30 .75
483 Julian Battle RC .40 1.00
484 Carl Ford RC .30 .75
485 Angelo Crowell RC .40 1.00
486 Bennie Joppru RC .30 .75
487 Aaron Walker RC .40 1.00
488 Brandon Green RC .30 .75
489 L.J. Smith RC .50 1.25
490 Ken Dorsey RC .40 1.00
491 Eugene Wilson RC .50 1.25
492 Chaun Thompson RC .30 .75
493 Kevin Curtis RC .50 1.25
494 Marcus Trufant RC .40 1.00
495 Andrew Williams RC .30 .75
496 Visanthe Shiancoe RC .50 1.25
497 Terrence Edwards RC .30 .75
498 Rien Long RC .30 .75
499 Nick Barnett RC .50 1.25
500 Larry Johnson RC .50 1.25
501 Ken Hamlin RC .50 1.25
502 Johnathan Sullivan RC .30 .75
503 Jeremi Johnson RC .30 .75
504 William Joseph RC .30 .75
505 Boss Bailey RC .40 1.00
506 Anquan Boldin RC .75 2.00
507 Dave Ragone RC .30 .75
508 DeJuan Groce RC .50 1.25
509 Rashad Moore RC .30 .75
510 Mike Doss RC .50 1.25
511 Kenny Peterson RC .40 1.00
512 Justin Griffith RC .40 1.00
513 Jordan Gross RC .30 .75
514 Terrence Holt RC .40 1.00
515 Seneca Wallace RC .50 1.25
516 Ovie Mughelli RC .40 1.00
517 Jerome McDougle RC .30 .75
518 Kevin Williams RC .50 1.25
519 Musa Smith RC .30 .75
520 Teyo Johnson RC .40 1.00
521 Victor Hobson RC .30 .75
522 Cory Redding RC .40 1.00
523 Cecil Sapp RC .30 .75
524 Brandon Lloyd RC .75 2.00
525 Chris Simms RC .50 1.25
526 Artose Pinner RC .30 .75
527 DeWayne White RC .30 .75
528 Doug Gabriel RC .40 1.00
529 Calvin Pace RC .40 1.00
530 Onterrio Smith RC .30 .75
531 Terrell Suggs RC .50 1.25
532 Ronald Bellamy RC .40 1.00
533 Jimmy Wilkerson RC .40 1.00
534 Travis Anglin RC .30 .75
535 Tyrone Calico RC .40 1.00
536 Keenan Howry RC .30 .75
537 Gibran Hamdan RC .30 .75
538 Bryant Johnson RC .50 1.25
539 Brad Banks RC .40 1.00
540 Justin Fargas RC .50 1.25
541 B.J. Askew RC .40 1.00
542 J.R. Tolver RC .40 1.00
543 Tully Banta-Cain RC .50 1.25
544 Shaun McDonald RC .40 1.00
545 Taylor Jacobs RC .30 .75
546 Ricky Manning RC .40 1.00
547 Dallas Clark RC .75 2.00
548 Juston Wood RC .30 .75
549 Andre Woolfolk RC .40 1.00
550 Kyle Boller RC .50 1.25
CL1 Checklist Card 1 .02 .10
CL2 Checklist Card 2 .02 .10
CL3 Checklist Card 3 .02 .10
CL4 Checklist Card 4 .02 .10

2003 Topps Total Silver

*VETS 1-440: 1X TO 2.5X BASIC CARDS
*ROOKIES 441-550: .8X TO 2X
ONE SILVER PER PACK

2003 Topps Total Award Winners

COMPLETE SET (20) 7.50 20.00
STATED ODDS 1:6
AW1 Rich Gannon .50 1.25
AW2 Derrick Brooks .50 1.25
AW3 Clinton Portis .50 1.25
AW4 Julius Peppers .60 1.50
AW5 Priest Holmes .60 1.50
AW6 Kerry Collins .50 1.25
AW7 Tom Brady 1.50 4.00
AW8 Brett Favre 1.50 4.00
AW9 Chad Pennington .60 1.50
AW10 Ricky Williams .50 1.25
AW11 Deuce Mcallister .50 1.25
AW12 Shaun Alexander .50 1.25
AW13 Marvin Harrison .60 1.50
AW14 Randy Moss .60 1.50
AW15 Terrell Owens .60 1.50
AW16 Hines Ward .60 1.50
AW17 Jason Taylor .50 1.25
AW18 Brian Urlacher .60 1.50
AW19 Rod Woodson .60 1.50
AW20 Brian Kelly .40 1.00

2003 Topps Total Signatures

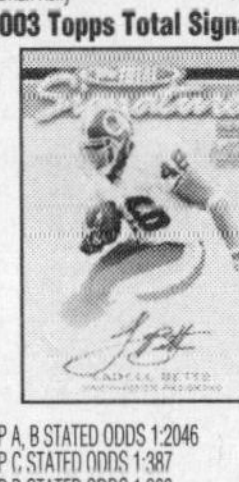

GROUP A, B STATED ODDS 1:2046
GROUP C STATED ODDS 1:387
GROUP D STATED ODDS 1:268
OVERALL STATED ODDS 1:185
TSCJ Chad Johnson C 10.00 25.00
TSDN Dennis Northcutt B 6.00 15.00
TSJJ Joe Jurevicius A 8.00 20.00
TSJT Jason Taylor A 20.00 40.00
TSLB Ladell Betts D 6.00 15.00
TSMB Marc Boerigter D 6.00 15.00
TSTB Todd Bouman D 6.00 15.00

2003 Topps Total Team Checklists

COMPLETE SET (32) 10.00 25.00
TC1 Emmitt Smith 1.00 2.50
TC2 Michael Vick .50 1.25
TC3 Ray Lewis .40 1.00
TC4 Drew Bledsoe .40 1.00
TC5 Stephen Davis .30 .75
TC6 Brian Urlacher .40 1.00
TC7 Corey Dillon .30 .75
TC8 Tim Couch .25 .60
TC9 Keyshawn Johnson .40 1.00
TC10 Clinton Portis .30 .75
TC11 Joey Harrington .25 .60
TC12 Brett Favre 1.00 2.50
TC13 David Carr .30 .75
TC14 Peyton Manning .75 2.00
TC15 Jimmy Smith .30 .75
TC16 Priest Holmes .40 1.00
TC17 Ricky Williams .30 .75
TC18 Randy Moss .40 1.00
TC19 Tom Brady 1.00 2.50
TC20 Deuce Mcallister .30 .75
TC21 Jeremy Shockey .40 1.00
TC22 Chad Pennington .40 1.00
TC23 Rich Gannon .30 .75
TC24 Donovan Mcnabb .40 1.00
TC25 Hines Ward .40 1.00
TC26 LaDainian Tomlinson .40 1.00
TC27 Terrell Owens .40 1.00
TC28 Shaun Alexander .30 .75
TC29 Marshall Faulk .40 1.00
TC30 Warren Sapp .30 .75
TC31 Steve Mcnair .40 1.00
TC32 Patrick Ramsey .30 .75

2003 Topps Total Total Production

COMPLETE SET (10) 5.00 12.00
STATED ODDDS 1:12
TP1 Tom Brady 1.50 4.00
TP2 Peyton Manning 1.25 3.00
TP3 Brett Favre 1.50 4.00
TP4 Priest Holmes .60 1.50
TP5 Shaun Alexander .50 1.25
TP6 Ricky Williams .50 1.25
TP7 Clinton Portis .50 1.25
TP8 Terrell Owens .60 1.50
TP9 Hines Ward .60 1.50
TP10 Marvin Harrison .60 1.50

2003 Topps Total Total Topps

COMPLETE SET (20) 10.00 25.00
STATED ODDS 1:6

TT1 Rich Gannon	.50	1.25
TT2 Peyton Manning	1.25	3.00
TT3 Brett Favre	1.50	4.00
TT4 Steve McNair	.60	1.50
TT5 Chad Pennington	.60	1.50
TT6 Michael Vick	.75	2.00
TT7 Ricky Williams	.40	1.00
TT8 Priest Holmes	.60	1.50
TT9 LaDainian Tomlinson	.60	1.50
TT10 Clinton Portis	.50	1.25
TT11 Travis Henry	.40	1.00
TT12 Deuce McAllister	.50	1.25
TT13 Marvin Harrison	.60	1.50
TT14 Jerry Rice	1.25	3.00
TT15 Randy Moss	.60	1.50
TT16 Hines Ward	.60	1.50
TT17 Terrell Owens	.60	1.50
TT18 Derrick Brooks	.50	1.25
TT19 Brian Urlacher	.60	1.50
TT20 Jason Taylor	.50	1.25

2004 Topps Total

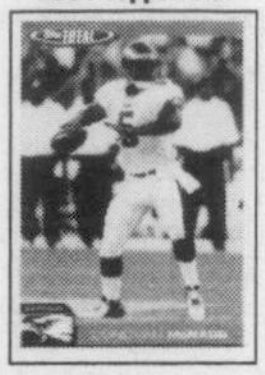

Topps Total was initially released in mid-August 2004. The base set consists of 440-cards including 110-rookies making it the largest base set of the year. Hobby boxes contained 36-packs of 10-cards and carried an S.R.P. of $1 per pack. Two parallel sets and a variety of inserts can be found seeded in packs.

COMPLETE SET (440)	40.00	80.00
1 Donovan McNabb	.30	.75
2 Zach Thomas	.30	.75
3 Randy Moss	.30	.75
4 Kerry Collins	.25	.60
5 Hines Ward	.30	.75
6 Tyrone Calico	.25	.60
7 Patrick Ramsey	.25	.60
8 Jeff Garcia	.25	.60
9 Aveion Cason	.20	.50
10 Stephen Davis	.25	.60
11 Marcel Shipp	.20	.50
12 T.J. Duckett	.25	.60
13 Chris McAlister	.20	.50
14 Peter Warrick	.25	.60
15 Ahman Green	.25	.60
16 Deion Branch	.25	.60
17 David Boston	.20	.50
18 Wayne Chrebet	.25	.60
19 Michael Strahan	.30	.75
20 Arnaz Battle	.25	.60
21 Darrell Jackson	.25	.60
22 Chris Chandler	.25	.60
23 Charlie Garner	.25	.60
24 James Thrash	.20	.50
25 LaDainian Tomlinson	.30	.75
26 Jerry Porter	.20	.50
27 Jerome Pathon	.20	.50
28 Jerome Bettis	.30	.75
29 Eddie George	.25	.60
30 Jamal Lewis	.25	.60
31 Ricky Proehl	.25	.60
32 Josh Reed	.20	.50
33 David Terrell	.20	.50
34 Antonio Bryant	.25	.60
35 Domanick Davis	.20	.50
36 Artose Pinner	.20	.50
37 Jed Weaver	.20	.50
38 Johnnie Morton	.25	.60
39 Troy Edwards	.20	.50
40 Marvin Harrison	.30	.75
41 Chris Hovan	.20	.50
42 Boo Williams	.20	.50
43 Ike Hilliard	.25	.60
44 Sam Cowart	.20	.50
45 Shaun Alexander	.25	.60
46 Freddie Mitchell	.20	.50
47 Garrison Hearst	.25	.60
48 Joe Jurevicius	.20	.50
49 Freddie Jones	.20	.50
50 Michael Vick	.40	1.00
51 Mike Rucker	.20	.50
52 Carson Palmer	.30	.75
53 Az-Zahir Hakim	.20	.50
54 Billy Miller	.20	.50
55 Chad Pennington	.30	.75
56 Charles Woodson	.30	.75
57 Andre Carter	.20	.50
58 Maurice Morris	.25	.60
59 Leonard Little	.20	.50
60 Travis Henry	.20	.50
61 Thomas Jones	.30	.75
62 Dennis Northcutt	.20	.50
63 Quentin Griffin	.20	.50
64 Joey Harrington	.25	.60
65 Edgerrin James	.25	.60
66 Cortez Hankton	.20	.50
67 Jason Taylor	.25	.60
68 Eddie Kennison	.25	.60
69 Ty Law	.25	.60
70 Aaron Brooks	.25	.60
71 Antonio Gates	.30	.75
72 Antwaan Randle El	.25	.60
73 Kevan Barlow	.20	.50
74 Chris Brown	.20	.50
75 Clinton Portis	.30	.75
76 Rod Gardner	.20	.50
77 Isaac Bruce	.25	.60
78 Mike Alstott	.25	.60
79 Brian Westbrook	.30	.75
80 Amani Toomer	.25	.60
81 Justin Fargas	.25	.60
82 Michael Bennett	.25	.60
83 Dante Hall	.25	.60
84 Marcus Pollard	.20	.50
85 Fred Taylor	.25	.60
86 Tai Streets	.20	.50
87 Robert Ferguson	.20	.50
88 Roy Williams S	.25	.60
89 Lee Suggs	.25	.60
90 Chad Johnson	.30	.75
91 DeShaun Foster	.25	.60
92 Alge Crumpler	.25	.60
93 Travis Taylor	.20	.50
94 London Fletcher	.20	.50
95 Priest Holmes	.30	.75
96 A.J. Feeley	.20	.50
97 Kevin Faulk	.25	.60
98 Shaun Ellis	.20	.50
99 Tim Dwight	.20	.50
100 Peyton Manning	.60	1.50
101 Dane Looker	.20	.50
102 Mark Brunell	.25	.60
103 Bryant Johnson	.20	.50
104 Kelley Washington	.20	.50
105 Rex Grossman	.25	.60
106 William Green	.20	.50
107 Keyshawn Johnson	.25	.60
108 Trevor Pryce	.20	.50
109 Donald Driver	.30	.75
110 David Carr	.20	.50
111 Marcus Robinson	.20	.50
112 Justin McCareins	.20	.50
113 Tim Brown	.30	.75
114 James Farrior	.25	.60
115 Deuce McAllister	.25	.60
116 Simeon Rice	.20	.50
117 Koren Robinson	.20	.50
118 Kassim Osgood	.20	.50
119 Tim Rattay	.20	.50
120 Laveranues Coles	.20	.50
121 Brian Finneran	.20	.50
122 Todd Heap	.25	.60
123 Bobby Shaw	.20	.50
124 Anthony Thomas	.25	.60
125 Brett Favre	.75	2.00
126 Dwight Freeney	.25	.60
127 Randy McMichael	.20	.50
128 David Givens	.20	.50
129 Rich Gannon	.25	.60
130 Tiki Barber	.30	.75
131 Terrell Owens	.30	.75
132 Drew Bennett	.25	.60
133 Shawn Bryson	.20	.50
134 Jabar Gaffney	.20	.50
135 Jake Delhomme	.25	.60
136 Warrick Dunn	.25	.60
137 Brandon Lloyd	.25	.60
138 Brad Johnson	.25	.60
139 Jon Kitna	.25	.60
140 Marshall Faulk	.30	.75
141 Javon Walker	.20	.50
142 Nate Burleson	.25	.60
143 Jimmy Smith	.25	.60
144 Adewale Ogunleye	.25	.60
145 Trent Green	.25	.60
146 Richard Seymour	.20	.50
147 Donte' Stallworth	.20	.50
148 Curtis Martin	.30	.75
149 Todd Pinkston	.20	.50
150 Steve McNair	.30	.75
151 Josh McCown	.25	.60
152 Ray Lewis	.30	.75
153 Muhsin Muhammad	.25	.60
154 Quincy Morgan	.20	.50
155 Jake Plummer	.25	.60
156 Jason Witten	.30	.75
157 Dallas Clark	.30	.75
158 Onterrio Smith	.20	.50
159 Jeremy Shockey	.25	.60
160 Ricky Williams	.25	.60
161 Jevon Kearse	.25	.60
162 Plaxico Burress	.25	.60
163 Drew Brees	.30	.75
164 Bobby Engram	.25	.60
165 Torry Holt	.25	.60
166 Ladell Betts	.20	.50
167 Kelly Holcomb	.20	.50
168 Vinny Testaverde	.25	.60
169 Marty Booker	.25	.60
170 Rudi Johnson	.25	.60
171 Andra Davis	.20	.50
172 Kurt Warner	.30	.75
173 Troy Brown	.25	.60
174 Jerry Rice	.60	1.50
175 Daunte Culpepper	.25	.60
176 Darren Sharper	.25	.60
177 Charles Rogers	.20	.50
178 Ashley Lelie	.20	.50
179 Correll Buckhalter	.25	.60
180 Anquan Boldin	.30	.75
181 Terrell Suggs	.25	.60
182 Reggie Wayne	.30	.75
183 Duce Staley	.25	.60
184 Donnie Edwards	.25	.60
185 Joe Horn	.25	.60
186 LaVar Arrington	.25	.60
187 Keenan McCardell	.20	.50
188 Cedrick Wilson	.20	.50
189 Bubba Franks	.20	.50
190 Santana Moss	.25	.60
191 Peerless Price	.20	.50
192 Kyle Boller	.25	.60
193 Julius Peppers	.25	.60
194 Drew Bledsoe	.30	.75
195 Marc Bulger	.25	.60
196 Brian Urlacher	.30	.75
197 Andre' Davis	.20	.50
198 Terry Glenn	.25	.60
199 Champ Bailey	.25	.60
200 Tom Brady	.60	1.50
201 Chris Chambers	.25	.60
202 Tommy Maddox	.25	.60
203 Derrick Brooks	.25	.60
204 Corey Dillon	.25	.60
205 Matt Hasselbeck	.25	.60
206 Keith Brooking	.20	.50
207 Steve Smith	.30	.75
208 Tony Gonzalez	.30	.75
209 Joey Galloway	.25	.60
210 Derrick Mason	.25	.60
211 Quincy Carter	.20	.50
212 Rod Smith	.25	.60
213 Andre Johnson	.30	.75
214 Rod Woodson	.25	.60
215 Byron Leftwich	.25	.60
216 Kevin Dyson	.20	.50
217 Keith Bulluck	.20	.50
218 Eric Moulds	.25	.60
219 Jamie Sharper	.20	.50
220 Takeo Spikes	.20	.50
221 Calvin Pace	.20	.50
Fred Wakefield		
222 Brady Smith	.25	.60
Patrick Kerney		
223 Ed Reed	.25	.60
Gary Baxter		
224 Aaron Schobel	.20	.50
Jeff Posey		
225 Kris Jenkins	.25	.60
Brentson Buckner		
226 Justin Smith	.20	.50
Duane Clemons		
227 Michael Haynes	.20	.50
Bryan Robinson		
228 Courtney Brown	.25	.60
Gerard Warren		
229 Terence Newman	.25	.60
Darren Woodson		
230 Raylee Johnson	.20	.50
Mario Fatafehi		
231 Robert Porcher	.30	.75
James Hall RC		
232 Kabeer Gbaja-Biamila	.25	.60
Cletidus Hunt		
233 Aaron Glenn	.25	.60
Marcus Coleman		
234 Nick Harper RC	.25	.60
Joseph Jefferson		
235 Hugh Douglas	.20	.50
Tony Brackens		
236 Vonnie Holliday	.20	.50
Eric Hicks		
237 Sammy Knight	.20	.50
Arturo Freeman		
238 Steve Martin	.20	.50
Nick Rogers		
239 Rosevelt Colvin	.25	.60
Willie McGinest		
240 Omar Stoutmire	.20	.50
Shaun Williams		
241 Eric Barton	.20	.50
Victor Hobson		
242 Warren Sapp	.25	.60
Ted Washington		
243 Corey Simon	.25	.60
Darwin Walker		
244 Troy Polamalu	1.00	2.50
Mike Logan		
245 Jamal Williams	.20	.50
Adrian Dingle RC		
246 Bryant Young	.25	.60
Brandon Whiting		
247 Ken Hamlin	.20	.50
Damien Robinson RC		
248 Damione Lewis	.20	.50
Ryan Pickett		
249 Anthony McFarland	.20	.50
Greg Spires		
250 Albert Haynesworth	.20	.50
Rien Long		
251 Ifeanyi Ohalete	.20	.50
Matt Bowen		
252 Bertrand Berry	.25	.60
Kenny King		
253 Ellis Johnson	.20	.50
Ed Jasper		
254 Charles Tillman	.25	.60
Jerry Azumah		
255 Marcellus Wiley	.25	.60
La'Roi Glover		
256 Shaun Rogers	.25	.60
Dan Wilkinson		
257 Gary Walker	.20	.50
Robaire Smith		
258 Mike Doss	.25	.60
Idrees Bashir		
259 Marcus Stroud	.20	.50
John Henderson		
260 Ryan Sims	.25	.60
John Browning		
261 Junior Seau	.30	.75
Morlon Greenwood		
262 Kevin Williams	.20	.50
Kenny Mixon		
263 Ty Warren	.20	.50
Keith Traylor		
264 Will Allen	.20	.50
William Peterson		
265 David Barrett	.20	.50
Reggie Tongue		
266 Phillip Buchanon	.25	.60
Derrick Gibson		
267 Lito Sheppard	.20	.50
Sheldon Brown		
268 Bobby Taylor	.25	.60
Marcus Trufant		
269 Marcus Washington	.20	.50
Micheal Barrow		
270 Chris Draft	.20	.50
Matt Stewart		
271 Mike Brown	.25	.60
Mike Green		
272 Eric Brown	.20	.50
Marlon McCree		
273 Patrick Surtain	.20	.50
Sam Madison		
274 Brian Dawkins	.25	.60
Michael Lewis		
275 Shawn Springs	.20	.50
Fred Smoot		
276 Ronald McKinnon	.20	.50
Levar Fisher		
Ray Thompson		
277 Jason Webster	.30	.75
Tod McBride RC		
Bryan Scott RC		
278 Peter Boulware	.25	.60
Ed Hartwell		
Adalius Thomas		
279 Troy Vincent	.25	.60
Lawyer Milloy		
Nate Clements		
280 Will Witherspoon	.25	.60
Dan Morgan		
Mark Fields		
281 Brian Simmons	.25	.60
Kevin Hardy		
Nate Webster		
282 Joe Odom RC	1.00	2.50
Alex Brown		
Lance Briggs		
283 Warrick Holdman	.20	.50
Chaun Thompson		
Kenard Lang		
284 Dat Nguyen	.20	.50
Dexter Coakley		
Al Singleton		
285 Al Wilson	.20	.50
Donnie Spragan RC		
Darius Holland		
286 Earl Holmes	.20	.50
James Davis RC		
Boss Bailey		
287 Nick Barnett	.25	.60
Na'il Diggs		
Hannibal Navies		
288 Jay Foreman	.20	.50
Antwan Peek		
Kailee Wong		
289 Raheem Brock RC	.25	.60
Montae Reagor		
Larry Tripplett		
290 Akin Ayodele	.20	.50
Greg Favors		
Mike Peterson		
291 Shawn Barber	.20	.50
Mike Maslowski		
Scott Fujita		
292 Chris Claiborne	.25	.60
E.J. Henderson		
Mike Nattiel		
293 Tedy Bruschi	.30	.75
Roman Phifer		
Mike Vrabel		
294 Charles Grant	.20	.50
Darren Howard		
Johnathan Sullivan		
295 Fred Robbins	.30	.75
William Joseph		
Osi Umenyiora		
296 John Abraham	.50	1.25
DeWayne Robertson		
Jason Ferguson RC		
297 Napoleon Harris	.25	.60
Dwayne Rudd		
Tyler Brayton		
298 Mark Simoneau	.20	.50
Nate Wayne		
Dhani Jones		
299 Joey Porter	.40	1.00
Kendrell Bell		
Clark Haggans RC		
300 Quentin Jammer	.20	.50
Sammy Davis		
Drayton Florence		
301 Julian Peterson	.25	.60
Jeff Ulbrich		
Derek Smith		
302 Anthony Simmons	.20	.50
Orlando Huff		
Chad Brown		
303 Pisa Tinoisamoa	.20	.50
Tommy Polley		
Robert Thomas		
304 Shelton Quarles	.20	.50
Ellis Wyms		
Ryan Nece		
305 Kevin Carter	.25	.60
Carlos Hall		
Peter Sirmon		
306 Cornelius Griffin	.20	.50
Phillip Daniels		
Renaldo Wynn		
307 Dexter Jackson	.20	.50
Adrian Wilson		
David Macklin		
308 Kelly Gregg	.20	.50
Marques Douglas		
Anthony Weaver		
309 Pat Williams	.25	.60
Ryan Denney		
Sam Adams		
310 Artrell Hawkins	.20	.50
Mike Minter		
Ricky Manning		
311 Tory James	.20	.50
Kim Herring		
Rogers Beckett		
312 Robert Griffith	.20	.50
Earl Little		
Anthony Henry		
313 John Lynch	.25	.60
Nick Ferguson RC		
Kelly Herndon RC		
314 Dre Bly	.20	.50
Brock Marion		
Fernando Bryant		
315 Al Harris	.25	.60
Mark Roman		
Mike McKenzie		
316 David Thornton	.30	.75
Rob Morris		
Gary Brackett RC		
317 Rashean Mathis	.20	.50
Donovin Darius		
Juran Bolden RC		
318 Eric Warfield	.20	.50
Greg Wesley		
Jerome Woods		
319 Antoine Winfield	.25	.60
Brian Russell RC		
Corey Chavous		
320 Rodney Harrison	.25	.60
Eugene Wilson		
Tyrone Poole		
321 Derrick Rodgers	.20	.50
Orlando Ruff		
Sedrick Hodge		
322 Barrett Green	.20	.50
Nick Greisen		
Carlos Emmons		
323 Kimo Von Oelhoffen	.20	.50
Aaron Smith		
Casey Hampton		
324 Randall Godfrey	.20	.50
Steve Foley		
Ben Leber		
325 Ahmed Plummer	.20	.50
Tony Parrish		
Mike Rumph		
326 Chike Okeafor	.25	.60
Grant Wistrom		
Rashad Moore		
327 Adam Archuleta	.20	.50
Aeneas Williams		
Jerametrius Butler		
328 Ronde Barber	.25	.60
Dwight Smith		
Jermaine Phillips		
329 Andre Dyson	.20	.50
Lance Schulters		
Tank Williams		
330 Fred Thomas	.20	.50
Jay Bellamy		
Tebucky Jones		
331 Philip Rivers RC	2.50	6.00
332 Dwan Edwards RC	.40	1.00
333 Ben Watson RC	.60	1.50
334 Karlos Dansby RC	.60	1.50
335 Cedric Cobbs RC	.40	1.00
336 Chris Perry RC	.50	1.25
337 Darius Watts RC	.40	1.00
338 Ricardo Colclough RC	.50	1.25
339 Derrick Hamilton RC	.40	1.00
340 Devard Darling RC	.40	1.00
341 Daryl Smith RC	.40	1.00
342 Luke McCown RC	.50	1.25
343 Dunta Robinson RC	.40	1.00
344 Keith Smith RC	.40	1.00
345 Ben Hartsock RC	.40	1.00
346 J.P. Losman RC	.50	1.25
347 Chris Cooley RC	.60	1.50
348 Keary Colbert RC	.40	1.00
349 Tommie Harris RC	.60	1.50
350 Eli Manning RC	4.00	10.00
351 Kevin Jones RC	.50	1.25
352 Lee Evans RC	.60	1.50
353 D.J. Williams RC	.60	1.50
354 Ben Troupe RC	.50	1.25
355 Mewelde Moore RC	.50	1.25
356 Michael Clayton RC	.50	1.25
357 Michael Jenkins RC	.60	1.50
358 Adimchinobe Echemandu RC	.50	1.25
359 Rashaun Woods RC	.40	1.00
360 Bernard Berrian RC	.60	1.50
361 Carlos Francis RC	.40	1.00
362 Roy Williams RC	.60	1.50
363 Sean Taylor RC	1.25	3.00
364 Steven Jackson RC	1.00	2.50
365 Tatum Bell RC	.50	1.25
366 Jonathan Vilma RC	.60	1.50
367 Derrick Strait RC	.40	1.00
368 Andy Hall RC	.40	1.00
369 Jason Babin RC	.60	1.50
370 Will Smith RC	.50	1.25
371 Kenechi Udeze RC	.50	1.25
372 Vince Wilfork RC	.60	1.50
373 Ahmad Carroll RC	.40	1.00
374 Marquise Hill RC	.40	1.00
375 Ben Roethlisberger RC	4.00	10.00
376 Chris Gamble RC	.50	1.25
377 Junior Siavii RC	.40	1.00
378 Teddy Lehman RC	.40	1.00
379 Antwan Odom RC	.50	1.25
380 DeAngelo Hall RC	.60	1.50
381 Nathan Vasher RC	.60	1.50
382 B.J. Symons RC	.40	1.00
383 Reggie Williams RC	.50	1.25
384 Michael Boulware RC	.60	1.50
385 Matt Schaub RC	1.25	3.00
386 Sean Jones RC	.50	1.25
387 Courtney Watson RC	.40	1.00
388 Nathaniel Adibi RC	.40	1.00
389 Devery Henderson RC	.60	1.50
390 Greg Jones RC	.40	1.00
391 Joey Thomas RC	.40	1.00
392 Drew Carter RC	.50	1.25
393 Julius Jones RC	.50	1.25
394 Keyaron Fox RC	.50	1.25
395 Darrion Scott RC	.50	1.25
396 Rich Gardner RC	.50	1.25
397 Jeff Smoker RC	.50	1.25
398 Will Poole RC	.60	1.50
399 Samie Parker RC	.40	1.00
400 Larry Fitzgerald RC	1.50	4.00
401 Jerricho Cotchery RC	.50	1.25
402 Ernest Wilford RC	.50	1.25
403 Johnnie Morant RC	.40	1.00
404 Craig Krenzel RC	.50	1.25
405 Michael Turner RC	.75	2.00
406 D.J. Hackett RC	.50	1.25
407 P.K. Sam RC	.40	1.00
408 Triandos Luke RC	.40	1.00
409 Josh Harris RC	.40	1.00
410 Drew Henson RC	.40	1.00
411 John Navarre RC	.40	1.00
412 Cody Pickett RC	.50	1.25
413 Clarence Moore RC	.40	1.00
414 Michael Gaines RC	.40	1.00
415 Derek Abney RC	.40	1.00
416 Dontarrious Thomas RC	.50	1.25
417 Reggie Torbor RC	.40	1.00
418 Ryan Krause RC	.40	1.00
419 Travis LaBoy RC	.50	1.25
420 Kellen Winslow RC	.60	1.50
421 Keiwan Ratliff RC	.40	1.00
422 Gilbert Gardner RC	.40	1.00
423 Jamaar Taylor RC	.40	1.00
424 Matt Ware RC	.60	1.50
425 Stuart Schweigert RC	.50	1.25
426 Marcus Tubbs RC	.40	1.00
427 Brandon Chillar RC	.50	1.25
428 Shawntae Spencer RC	.40	1.00
429 Marquis Cooper RC	.40	1.00
430 Derrick Ward RC	.60	1.50
431 Tim Euhus RC	.40	1.00
432 Patrick Crayton RC	.60	1.50
433 Caleb Miller RC	.40	1.00
434 Donnell Washington RC	.50	1.25
435 Thomas Tapeh RC	.50	1.25
436 Randy Starks RC	.40	1.00
437 Sloan Thomas RC	.50	1.25
438 Maurice Mann RC	.40	1.00
439 Jim Sorgi RC	.50	1.25
440 Nate Lawrie RC	.40	1.00

2004 Topps Total First Edition

COMPLETE SET (440)	60.00	150.00
*FRST EDIT.VETS: 1X TO 2.5X BASIC CARDS		
*FE ROOKIES: .8X TO 2X BASIC CARDS		

2004 Topps Total Silver

COMPLETE SET (440)	100.00	200.00
*SILVER VETS: 1.2X TO 3X BASIC CARDS		
*SLVR ROOK: 1X TO 2.5X BASIC CARDS		
ONE PER PACK		

2004 Topps Total Award Winners

COMPLETE SET (20)	10.00	25.00
STATED ODDS 1:9 HOB/RET		
AW1 Jamal Lewis	.75	2.00
AW2 Ahman Green	.75	2.00
AW3 Priest Holmes	1.00	2.50
AW4 Torry Holt	.75	2.00
AW5 Randy Moss	1.00	2.50
AW6 Chris Chambers	.75	2.00
AW7 LaDainian Tomlinson	1.00	2.50
AW8 Peyton Manning	2.00	5.00
AW9 Marc Bulger	.75	2.00
AW10 Brett Favre	2.50	6.00
AW11 Steve McNair	1.00	2.50
AW12 Daunte Culpepper	.75	2.00
AW13 Michael Strahan	1.00	2.50
AW14 Adewale Ogunleye	.75	2.00
AW15 Jamie Sharper	.60	1.50
AW16 Micheal Barrow	.60	1.50
AW17 Mike Vanderjagt	.60	1.50
AW18 Anquan Boldin	1.00	2.50
AW19 Terrell Suggs	.75	2.00
AW20 Tom Brady	2.00	5.00

2004 Topps Total Signatures

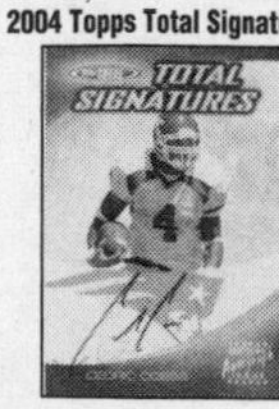

GROUP A ODDS 1:33,480 H, 1:17,383 R		
GROUP B ODDS 1:11,160 H, 1:6773 R		
GROUP C ODDS 1:427 HOB, 1:3369 RET		
GROUP D ODDS 1:4058 HOB, 1:2173 RET		
GROUP E ODDS 1:2829 HOB, 1:1644 RET		
OVERALL AUTO ODDS 1:327 HOB, 1:605 RET		
TSBS Brandon Stokley D	10.00	25.00
TSCC Cedric Cobbs C	8.00	20.00
TSCP Chad Pennington A	15.00	40.00
TSDD Domanick Davis B	8.00	20.00
TSKC Keary Colbert C	8.00	20.00
TSMCL Michael Clayton E	10.00	25.00
TSNB Nate Burleson C	10.00	25.00

2004 Topps Total Team Checklists

COMPLETE SET (32)	15.00	40.00
TTC1 Anquan Boldin	.50	1.25
TTC2 Michael Vick	.60	1.50
TTC3 Jamal Lewis	.40	1.00
TTC4 Travis Henry	.30	.75
TTC5 Jake Delhomme	.40	1.00
TTC6 Brian Urlacher	.50	1.25
TTC7 Chad Johnson	.50	1.25
TTC8 Jeff Garcia	.40	1.00
TTC9 Keyshawn Johnson	.40	1.00
TTC10 Jake Plummer	.40	1.00
TTC11 Joey Harrington	.40	1.00
TTC12 Brett Favre	1.25	3.00
TTC13 Domanick Davis	.30	.75
TTC14 Peyton Manning	1.00	2.50
TTC15 Byron Leftwich	.40	1.00
TTC16 Priest Holmes	.50	1.25
TTC17 Ricky Williams	.40	1.00
TTC18 Randy Moss	.50	1.25
TTC19 Tom Brady	1.00	2.50
TTC20 Deuce McAllister	.40	1.00
TTC21 Amani Toomer	.40	1.00
TTC22 Chad Pennington	.50	1.25
TTC23 Jerry Rice	1.00	2.50
TTC24 Donovan McNabb	.50	1.25
TTC25 Hines Ward	.50	1.25
TTC26 LaDainian Tomlinson	.50	1.25
TTC27 Kevan Barlow	.30	.75
TTC28 Matt Hasselbeck	.40	1.00
TTC29 Torry Holt	.40	1.00
TTC30 Keenan McCardell	.30	.75
TTC31 Steve McNair	.50	1.25
TTC32 Clinton Portis	.50	1.25

2004 Topps Total Total Production

COMPLETE SET (10)	6.00	15.00
STATED ODDS 1:18 HOB/RET		
TP1 Brett Favre	2.50	6.00
TP2 Peyton Manning	2.00	5.00
TP3 Priest Holmes	1.00	2.50
TP4 Jon Kitna	.75	2.00
TP5 Matt Hasselbeck	.75	2.00
TP6 Daunte Culpepper	.75	2.00
TP7 Ahman Green	.75	2.00
TP8 LaDainian Tomlinson	1.00	2.50
TP9 Randy Moss	1.00	2.50
TP10 Shaun Alexander	.75	2.00

2004 Topps Total Total Topps

COMPLETE SET (20)	10.00	25.00
STATED ODDS 1:9 HOB/RET		
TT1 Peyton Manning	2.00	5.00
TT2 Steve McNair	1.00	2.50
TT3 Torry Holt	.75	2.00
TT4 Brett Favre	2.50	6.00
TT5 Jamal Lewis	.75	2.00
TT6 Deuce McAllister	.75	2.00
TT7 Randy Moss	1.00	2.50
TT8 Marvin Harrison	1.00	2.50
TT9 Ahman Green	.75	2.00
TT10 Tom Brady	2.00	5.00
TT11 Shaun Alexander	.75	2.00
TT12 LaDainian Tomlinson	1.00	2.50
TT13 Daunte Culpepper	.75	2.00
TT14 Hines Ward	1.00	2.50
TT15 Anquan Boldin	1.00	2.50
TT16 Priest Holmes	1.00	2.50
TT17 Derrick Mason	.75	2.00
TT18 Donovan McNabb	1.00	2.50
TT19 Clinton Portis	1.00	2.50
TT20 Terrell Owens	1.00	2.50

2005 Topps Total

This 550-card set was released in August, 2005. The hobby version of this product was issued in 10-card packs with an 99 cent SPR which came 36 packs to a box. An 110-card rookie subset (441-550) is included in this set. An interesting aspect of this set is the inclusion of many multi-player cards, which expands the number of players in this set by a sigificant amoun t.

COMPLETE SET (550)	30.00	80.00
COMP.PACKERS TIN (20)	10.00	20.00
COMP.STEELERS TIN (20)	10.00	20.00
1 Michael Vick	.30	.75
2 Olin Kreutz	.25	.60
Qasim Mitchell RC		
3 Reggie Williams	.25	.60
David Garrard		
Troy Edwards		
4 Terence Newman	.20	.50
5 Doug Jolley	.20	.50
Chris Baker		
6 Danny Clark	.20	.50
Sam Williams RC		
Bobby Hamilton		
7 Terrell Owens	.30	.75
8 Ifeanyi Ohalete	.20	.50
Adrian Wilson		
9 Gary Walker	.20	.50
Seth Payne		
Robaire Smith		
10 Quentin Jammer	.20	.50
11 Keith Smith	.20	.50
Dre Bly		
12 Chester Taylor	.25	.60
Jonathan Ogden		
B.J. Sams		
13 Torry Holt	.25	.60
14 William Henderson	.25	.60
Najeh Davenport		
15 Junior Siavii	.30	.75
Eric Hicks		
Jared Allen		
16 Keith Bulluck	.20	.50
17 Ken Irvin	.20	.50
Corey Chavous		
18 Frisman Jackson	.20	.50
Antonio Bryant		
Andre Davis		
19 Michael Pittman	.20	.50
20 Mike Vanderjagt	.20	.50
Hunter Smith RC		
21 Jamie Winborn	.20	.50
Jeff Ulbrich		
Derek Smith		
22 Reggie Wayne	.30	.75
23 Shane Lechler	.20	.50
Sebastian Janikowski		
24 Kevin Mathis RC	.20	.50
Jason Webster		
Bryan Scott		
25 Daunte Culpepper	.25	.60
26 Will Peterson	.20	.50
Will Allen		
27 Tyson Walter	.25	.60
Flozell Adams		
Larry Allen		
28 Mark Tauscher	.20	.50
Mike Flanagan		
Chad Clifton RC		
29 Jerome Bettis	.30	.75
30 Mike Brown	.20	.50
R.W. McQuarters		
31 Andre Johnson	.30	.75
32 Labrandon Toefield	.20	.50
Greg Jones		
Chris Fuamatu-Ma'Afala		
33 Greg Lewis	.25	.60
Billy McMullen		
34 Kyle Boller	.25	.60
35 Isaiah Kacyvenski	.20	.50
Tracy White RC		
Solomon Bates		
36 Chris Brown	.20	.50
37 Jermaine Phillips	.20	.50
Brian Kelly		
38 Jeff Saturday RC	.30	.75
Ryan Diem RC		
Tarik Glenn		
39 Clinton Portis	.25	.60
40 Mike Scifres	.20	.50
Nate Kaeding		
41 Kevin Williams	.20	.50
Kenechi Udeze		
Lance Johnstone		
42 Tony Parrish	.20	.50
43 Derick Armstrong	.20	.50
Jabar Gaffney		
44 Fernando Bryant	.20	.50
Chris Cash		
Terrence Holt		
45 Kerry Collins	.25	.60
46 Mack Strong	.20	.50
Maurice Morris		
47 DeWayne Robertson	.20	.50
John Abraham		
Shaun Ellis		
48 Darrell Jackson	.20	.50
49 Peerless Price	.20	.50
Allen Rossum		
50 Anthony Henry	.20	.50
Nate Jones RC		
Lance Frazier RC		
51 Steven Jackson	.30	.75
52 Ryan Sims	.20	.50
John Browning		
53 Fred Robbins	.30	.75
Osi Umenyiora		
William Joseph		
54 Billy Volek	.20	.50
55 Akin Ayodele	.20	.50
Daryl Smith		
56 Ian Scott RC	.20	.50
Joe Odom		
Tank Johnson		
57 Onterrio Smith	.20	.50
58 Matt Stover	.20	.50
Dave Zastudil RC		
59 Cletidus Hunt	.30	.75
Kabeer Gbaja-Biamila		
Aaron Kampman RC		
60 Dante Hall	.20	.50
61 Julian Peterson	.20	.50
Bryant Young		
62 Nick Hardwick RC	.20	.50
Shane Olivea RC		
Roman Oben		
63 Chad Pennington	.30	.75
64 Dallas Clark	.25	.60
Aaron Moorehead		
65 Bobby Taylor	.20	.50
Kris Richard RC		
66 Kenyatta Walker	.20	.50
John Wade RC		
67 Jeremy Shockey	.30	.75
68 Daylon McCutcheon	.20	.50
69 Dexter Coakley	.20	.50
Chris Claiborne		
Pisa Tinoisamoa		
70 Roy Williams WR	.25	.60
71 Lance Schulters	.20	.50
Tank Williams		
72 Sheldon Brown	.30	.75
Roderick Hood RC		
Dexter Wynn		
73 Sean Taylor	.30	.75
74 Leonard Little	.20	.50
Brandon Chillar		
75 Rocky Boiman	.20	.50
Randy Starks		
Jared Clauss RC		
76 Lee Suggs	.20	.50
77 Patrick Crayton	.20	.50
Terry Glenn		
78 Karlos Dansby	.20	.50
James Darling		
Gerald Hayes		
79 Nick Barnett	.25	.60
80 Rod Coleman	.20	.50
Antwan Lake RC		
81 Bernard Berrian	.25	.60
Justin Gage		
Desmond Clark		
82 Dominic Rhodes	.25	.60
83 Clarence Moore	.20	.50
Randy Hymes		
84 Hank Fraley RC	.20	.50
Jon Runyan		
Tra Thomas		
85 Philip Rivers	.30	.75
86 Al Harris	.20	.50
Ahmad Carroll		
87 Bob Sanders	.50	1.25
Mike Doss		
Joseph Jefferson		
88 Jacques Cesaire RC	.20	.50
Jamal Williams		
Adrian Dingle		
89 Eric Moulds	.20	.50
90 Peppi Zellner RC	.20	.50
Russell Davis		
91 Kailee Wong	.20	.50
Jason Babin		
Antwan Peek		
92 Tony Richardson	.20	.50
93 Greg Wesley	.20	.50
Jerome Woods		
94 Jason Fabini	.20	.50
Jonathan Goodwin RC		
Kevin Mawae		
95 Tatum Bell	.20	.50
96 Kevin Lewis RC	.20	.50
Carlos Emmons		
97 Joey Galloway	.25	.60
Will Heller		
98 Tom Brady	.60	1.50
99 Rod Babers	.20	.50
Bracy Walker		
100 Ray Mickens	.20	.50

Jon McGraw
Terrell Buckley
101 Zach Thomas .30 .75
102 Cornell Brown RC .20 .50
Anthony Weaver
103 Aeneas Williams .20 .50
Jerametrius Butler
Kevin Garrett
104 Troy Polamalu .40 1.00
105 Warren Sapp .25 .60
Ted Washington
106 Teyo Johnson .20 .50
Zack Crockett
Johnnie Morant
107 Chris McAlister .20 .50
108 Chad Stanley RC .20 .50
Kris Brown
109 Drew Henson .20 .50
110 James Hall .20 .50
111 Scott Player .20 .50
Neil Rackers
112 Darius Watts .20 .50
Ashley Lelie
113 Jason David .20 .50
Nick Harper
114 Ronald Curry .20 .50
Doug Gabriel
115 Ricardo Colclough .25 .60
Willie Williams
116 Charles Tillman .20 .50
Jerry Azumah
117 Ma'Ake Kemoeatu RC .30 .75
Adalius Thomas
118 Mark Roman .20 .50
Joey Thomas
119 Devery Henderson .20 .50
Michael Lewis
120 Mike Furrey .30 .75
Brandon Manumaleuna
121 Reno Mahe .25 .60
Correll Buckhalter
122 Erron Kinney .20 .50
Troy Fleming
123 Warrick Dunn .25 .60
T.J. Duckett
124 Tim Euhus .20 .50
Mark Campbell
125 Pete Hunter .20 .50
Aaron Glenn
126 Reggie Tongue .20 .50
David Barrett
127 Sammy Morris .20 .50
Lamar Gordon
128 Ryan Clark RC .60 1.50
Shawn Springs
129 Josh Miller .30 .75
Adam Vinatieri
130 Eric Warfield .20 .50
William Bartee
131 Mewelde Moore .25 .60
Michael Bennett
132 Nick Goings .20 .50
Brad Hoover
133 Quentin Harris .20 .50
David Macklin
134 Eddie Drummond .20 .50
Reggie Swinton
135 Justin Fargas .25 .60
Alvis Whitted
136 Nate Clements .25 .60
Terrence McGee RC
137 Tony Hollings .20 .50
Jonathan Wells
138 Deke Cooper RC .20 .50
Kiwaukee Thomas RC
139 Phil Dawson .20 .50
Derrick Frost RC
140 Josh McCown .25 .60
John Navarre
141 Greg Ellis .20 .50
Kenyon Coleman
142 Gibril Wilson .20 .50
Brent Alexander
143 Andre Woolfolk .20 .50
Lamont Thompson
144 Ernie Conwell .20 .50
Boo Williams
145 David Akers .20 .50
Dirk Johnson RC
146 Hunter Hillenmeyer RC .50 1.25
Lance Briggs
147 Robert Mathis RC .50 1.25
Gary Brackett
148 Jerry Rice .60 1.50
Roc Alexander
149 Erik Coleman .20 .50
Derrick Strait
150 Justin Hartwig RC .20 .50
Ben Troupe
151 Sammy Davis .20 .50
Drayton Florence
152 Phillip Buchanon .20 .50
Marcus Coleman
153 Steve Heiden .20 .50
Aaron Shea
154 Takeo Spikes .20 .50
London Fletcher
155 Travis Laboy .20 .50
Antwan Odom
156 Amani Toomer .25 .60
Mike Cloud
157 Lawrence Tynes RC .25 .60
Chris Horn
158 Na'll Diggs .20 .50
Paris Lenon RC
159 Rien Long .20 .50
Albert Haynesworth
160 B.J. Askew .20 .50
Jerald Sowell
161 John Carney .20 .50
Mitch Berger
162 Kelly Campbell .20 .50
Jermaine Wiggins
163 Jerramy Stevens .25 .60
164 Willis McGahee .30 .75
165 Ed Rood .25 .60
166 Muhsin Muhammad .25 .60
167 Donovin Darius .20 .50
168 E.J. Henderson .20 .50
169 Tony Banks .20 .50
170 Fred Taylor .25 .60
171 Jeremiah Trotter .20 .50
172 Adam Archuleta .20 .50
173 Marcus Trufant .20 .50
174 Steve McNair .30 .75
175 Ben Roethlisberger .50 1.25
176 Derrick Blaylock .20 .50
177 Michael Strahan .30 .75
178 Robert Gallery .20 .50
179 Drew Brees .30 .75
180 David Kircus .20 .50
181 Robert Ferguson .20 .50
182 Jim Sorgi .20 .50
183 Alge Crumpler .25 .60
184 DeShaun Foster .25 .60
185 Reuben Droughns .20 .50
186 Charles Grant .20 .50
187 Jason Taylor .25 .60
188 James Thrash .25 .60
189 LaDainian Tomlinson .30 .75
190 Tim Rattay .20 .50
191 Jeff Garcia .25 .60
192 Jerricho Cotchery .25 .60
193 Chris Simms .25 .60
194 Jevon Kearse .25 .60
195 Kyle Brady .20 .50
196 Trent Green .25 .60
197 Antoine Winfield .25 .60
198 Deion Branch .20 .50
199 Rudi Johnson .25 .60
200 Lee Evans .25 .60
201 Stephen Davis .25 .60
202 Darnell Dockett .20 .50
203 Kurt Warner .30 .75
204 Quincy Morgan .20 .50
205 Daimon Shelton .20 .50
206 Champ Bailey .25 .60
207 Jamal Lewis .25 .60
208 Brett Favre .75 2.00
209 Charles Woodson .30 .75
210 Koren Robinson .20 .50
211 Chris Chambers .25 .60
212 Dave Ragone .20 .50
213 Travis Minor .20 .50
214 Simeon Rice .20 .50
215 Tommy Maddox .25 .60
216 Aaron Stecker .20 .50
217 Dwight Freeney .25 .60
218 Thomas Jones .30 .75
219 Patrick Ramsey .25 .60
220 Travis Taylor .20 .50
221 Chris Weinke .20 .50
222 Marc Bulger .25 .60
223 James Farrior .20 .50
224 Billy Miller .20 .50
225 Mike Peterson .20 .50
226 Eddie Kennison .20 .50
227 Aaron Brooks .20 .50
228 Plaxico Burress .25 .60
229 Jerry Porter .20 .50
230 Joey Harrington .25 .60
231 Bubba Franks .20 .50
232 Michael Jenkins .25 .60
233 Larry Fitzgerald .30 .75
234 Troy Vincent .25 .60
235 Chad Johnson .25 .60
236 Roy Williams S .20 .50
237 Corey Dillon .25 .60
238 Donovan McNabb .30 .75
239 Marcus Robinson .20 .50
240 Derrick Brooks .25 .60
241 David Bowens RC .20 .50
242 Renaldo Wynn .20 .50
243 Kevan Barlow .20 .50
244 Antonio Gates .30 .75
245 Duce Staley .25 .60
246 Ernest Wilford .20 .50
247 Kevin Jones .20 .50
248 Julius Peppers .25 .60
249 Terrell Suggs .25 .60
250 Bertrand Berry .20 .50
251 Brian Simmons .20 .50
252 Jake Plummer .25 .60
253 Brian Urlacher .30 .75
254 Justin McCareins .20 .50
255 L.J. Smith .25 .60
256 Matt Hasselbeck .25 .60
257 Rashaun Woods .20 .50
258 Rodney Harrison .25 .60
259 Brandon Stokley .20 .50
260 Tony Gonzalez .25 .60
261 J.P. Losman .20 .50
262 DeAngelo Hall .25 .60
263 Jake Delhomme .25 .60
264 Shaun Rogers .20 .50
265 Donald Driver .30 .75
266 Will Smith .20 .50
267 Brian Westbrook .25 .60
268 A.J. Feeley .20 .50
269 Marshall Faulk .30 .75
270 Marques Tuiasosopo .20 .50
271 Curtis Martin .30 .75
272 Jason Witten .30 .75
273 Kellen Winslow .25 .60
274 Corey Bradford .20 .50
275 Samari Rolle .20 .50
276 Anquan Boldin .25 .60
277 Adrian Peterson .25 .60
278 Javon Walker .20 .50
279 Fred Smoot .20 .50
280 Mike Alstott .25 .60
281 Randy McMichael .20 .50
282 Jay Fiedler .20 .50
283 Jamie Sharper .20 .50
284 Eli Manning .50 1.25
285 Todd Pinkston .20 .50
286 La'Roi Glover .20 .50
287 Chris Perry .20 .50
288 David Carr .20 .50
289 Bryant Johnson .20 .50
290 Ray Lewis .30 .75
291 Tommie Harris .20 .50
292 Joe Horn .25 .60
293 Rod Smith .25 .60
294 Michael Clayton .20 .50
295 Tyrone Calico .20 .50
296 Santana Moss .25 .60
297 Hines Ward .30 .75
298 Jonathan Vilma .25 .60
299 Randy Moss .30 .75
300 Donte Stallworth .20 .50
301 Isaac Bruce .25 .60
302 Brian Griese .25 .60
303 Dennis Northcutt .20 .50
304 Michael Green .20 .50
305 Marvin Harrison .30 .75
306 Jimmy Smith .25 .60
307 Patrick Kerney .25 .60
308 Todd Heap .25 .60
309 Dan Morgan .20 .50
310 Charles Rogers .20 .50
311 Dunta Robinson .20 .50
312 Deuce McAllister .25 .60
313 Ronde Barber .25 .60
314 Brandon Lloyd .20 .50
315 Tiki Barber .30 .75
316 LaMont Jordan .25 .60
317 Lito Sheppard .25 .60
318 Laveranues Coles .20 .50
319 Drew Bennett .25 .60
320 Julius Jones .20 .50
321 Ahman Green .25 .60
322 Domanick Davis .20 .50
323 Byron Leftwich .25 .60
324 Nate Burleson .20 .50
325 David Givens .20 .50
326 Trent Dilfer .25 .60
327 T.J. Houshmandzadeh .25 .60
328 Keith Brooking .20 .50
329 Derrick Mason .25 .60
330 Ken Lucas .20 .50
331 Rex Grossman .25 .60
332 Edgerrin James .25 .60
333 Priest Holmes .25 .60
334 Donnie Edwards .20 .50
335 Pierson Prioleau RC .20 .50
336 Shaun Alexander .25 .60
337 D.J. Williams .20 .50
338 Peyton Manning .60 1.50
339 Carson Palmer .30 .75
340 Keyshawn Johnson .25 .60
341 Tory James .20 .50
342 Drew Bledsoe .30 .75
343 Chris Gamble .20 .60
344 Michael Lewis .25 .60
Brian Dawkins
345 Kynan Forney .20 .50
Todd McClure RC
Todd Weiner RC
346 Rod Smart .20 .50
Jon Kasay
Jason Kyle
347 Jason Ferguson .20 .50
Jacques Reeves
Dat Nguyen
348 Chris Crocker .20 .50
Michael Lehan RC
Michael Jameson
349 David Tyree .20 .50
Jamaar Taylor
Tim Carter
350 Hollis Thomas .20 .50
Dhani Jones
Mark Simoneau
351 Robert Royal .20 .50
Darnerien McCants
Taylor Jacobs
352 Wes Welker .30 .75
Derrius Thompson
Bryan Gilmore
353 Damione Lewis .20 .50
Ryan Pickett
Tyoka Jackson
354 Fakhir Brown .20 .50
Fred Thomas
Jay Bellamy
355 Nnamdi Asomugha .30 .75
Marques Anderson
Stuart Schweigert
356 Marcus Stroud .20 .50
John Henderson
Greg Favors
357 Will Shields .20 .50
Willie Roaf
Brian Waters RC
358 Ben Hamilton .20 .50
Tom Nalen
Matt Lepsis
359 Justin Smith .20 .50
Robert Geathers
Duane Clemons
360 Coy Wire .25 .60
Rashad Baker
Lawyer Milloy
361 Obafemi Ayanbadejo .20 .50
Josh Scobey
Troy Hambrick
362 Steve Smith .30 .75
Ricky Proehl
Keary Colbert
363 Napoleon Harris .20 .50
Dontarrious Thomas
Willie Offord
364 Lorenzo Neal .30 .75
Michael Turner
Andrew Pinnock
365 Alan Faneca .50 1.25
Marvel Smith RC
Jeff Hartings
366 Eddie Moore .25 .60
Derrick Pope
Brendon Ayanbadejo RC
367 Ahmed Plummer .20 .50
Joselio Hanson RC
Shawntae Spencer
368 Ladell Betts .25 .60
Mark Brunell
Chad Morton
369 Orlando Pace .20 .50
Adam Timmerman
Andy McCollum
370 Bryan Thomas .20 .50
Eric Barton
Victor Hobson
371 Shawn Barber .20 .50
Keyaron Fox
Kawika Mitchell
372 Kalimba Edwards .20 .50
Dan Wilkinson
Cory Redding
373 Corey Jackson RC .20 .50
Kenard Lang
Alvin McKinley
374 Justin Bannan .20 .50
Ron Edwards
Sam Adams
375 Matt Schaub .30 .75
Dez White
Brian Finneran
376 Brandon Short .20 .50
Al Wallace RC
Kris Jenkins
377 Mike Leach .20 .50
Dwayne Carswell
Jeb Putzier
378 Mike Vrabel .30 .75
Ted Johnson
Tedy Bruschi
379 Terrence Kiel .20 .50
Jerry Wilson RC
Jamar Fletcher
380 John Engelberger .20 .50
Tony Brown RC
Anthony Adams
381 Shelton Quarles .20 .50
Jeff Gooch
DeWayne White
382 Sam Madison .20 .50
Will Poole
Reggie Howard
383 Mike Schneck RC .20 .50
Chris Gardocki
Jeff Reed
384 Jeff Mitchell RC .20 .50
Jordan Gross
Doug Brzezinski RC
385 Nick Greisen .20 .50
Barrett Green
Antonio Pierce
386 Corey Simon .20 .50
Darwin Walker
Jerome McDougle
387 Daniel Graham .25 .60
Christian Fauria
Ben Watson
388 Ellis Johnson .20 .50
Raylee Johnson
Marco Coleman
389 Cato June .25 .60
David Thornton
Von Hutchins
390 Trey Teague .20 .50
Ross Tucker
Mike Williams T
391 Michael Haynes .20 .50
Alex Brown
Adewale Ogunleye
392 Artio Ulmor RC .20 .50
Brady Smith
Demorrio Williams
393 Kevin Faulk .25 .60
Patrick Pass
Bethel Johnson
394 Robbie Tobeck RC .25 .60
Walter Jones
Steve Hutchinson
395 Vonnie Holliday .20 .50
Yeremiah Bell RC
Kevin Carter
396 Larry Foote .20 .50
Joey Porter
Alonzo Jackson
397 Dane Looker .25 .60
Kevin Curtis
Shaun McDonald
398 Lemar Marshall RC .25 .60
Cornelius Griffin
Demetric Evans
399 Dan Klecko .20 .50
Larry Izzo
Rosevelt Colvin
400 Montrae Holland .20 .50
LeCharles Bentley
Wayne Gandy
401 Luke Petitgout .20 .50
Kareem McKenzie RC
Jason Whittle RC
402 Jashon Sykes RC .20 .50
Mario Fatafehi
Al Wilson
403 Brad Meester RC .20 .50
Maurice Williams
Vince Manuwai RC
404 Matt Schobel .20 .50
Kelley Washington
Peter Warrick
405 Mike Minter .20 .50
Ricky Manning
Colin Branch
406 Josh Reed .20 .50
Jonathan Smith
Sam Aiken
407 Matt Birk .20 .50
Chris Liwienski
Bryant McKinnie
408 Randall Godfrey .20 .50
Steve Foley
Ben Leber
409 Anthony McFarland .20 .50
Ellis Wyms
Greg Spires
410 Ed Perry .20 .50
Donald Lee
Marty Booker
411 Kimo Von Oelhoffen .25 .60
Chris Hoke RC
Aaron Smith
412 Brandon Mitchell .20 .50
Grant Wistrom
Rashad Moore
413 Jarvis Green .25 .60
Vince Wilfork
Ty Warren
414 Willie Middlebrooks .25 .60
John Lynch
Nick Ferguson
415 Montae Reagor .20 .50
Raheem Brock
Josh Williams
416 Jason Dunn .25 .60
Samie Parker
Larry Johnson
417 Landon Johnson .20 .50
Marcus Wilkins RC
Caleb Miller
418 Brentson Buckner .20 .50
Kindal Moorehead
Mike Rucker
419 Ryan Denney .20 .50
Chris Kelsay
Aaron Schobel
420 Al Singleton .20 .50
Bradie James
Keith O'Neil RC
421 Chaun Thompson .20 .50
Brant Boyer
Andra Davis
422 Deon Grant .20 .50
David Richardson RC
Rashean Mathis
423 Cory Schlesinger .20 .50
Shawn Bryson
Artose Pinner
424 Spencer Johnson RC .20 .50
Rod Davis
Rushen Jones
425 Roman Phifer .25 .60
Tully Banta-Cain
Willie McGinest
426 Keenan McCardell .25 .60
Kassim Osgood
Eric Parker
427 Cedric Woodard .20 .50
Rocky Bernard
Antonio Cochran
428 Arnaz Battle .20 .50
Aaron Walker
Eric Johnson
429 Joe Salave'a RC .25 .60
Marcus Washington
LaVar Arrington
430 Lee Mays .25 .60
Cedrick Wilson
Antwaan Randle El
431 Duane Starks .20 .50
Eugene Wilson
Randall Gay
432 Quentin Griffin .20 .50
Mike Anderson
Cecil Sapp
433 John Thornton .20 .50
Langston Moore RC
Carl Powell
434 Michael Gaines .20 .50
Karl Hankton
Mike Seidman
435 Mario Haggan RC .20 .50
Jeff Posey
Angelo Crowell
436 Deltha O'Neal .20 .50
Madieu Williams
Keiwan Ratliff
437 Matt Light .20 .50
Dan Koppen RC
Steve Neal RC
438 Courtney Watson .20 .50
Derrick Rodgers
James Allen
439 Michael Boulware .20 .50
Ken Hamlin
Terreal Bierria RC
440 Tyrone Rogers RC .20 .50
Mason Unck RC
Orpheus Roye
441 Frank Gore RC 1.00 2.50
442 Mike Patterson RC .40 1.00
443 DeMarcus Ware RC 1.25 3.00
444 Chris Henry RC .60 1.50
445 Thomas Davis RC .40 1.00
446 Justin Miller RC .50 1.25
447 Shaun Cody RC .50 1.25
448 Alex Barron RC .40 1.00
449 Brock Berlin RC .50 1.25
450 Travis Johnson RC .40 1.00
451 Jerome Mathis RC .60 1.50
452 Lance Mitchell RC .50 1.25
453 Marlin Jackson RC .40 1.00
454 Charlie Frye RC .60 1.50
455 Luis Castillo RC .50 1.25
456 Fred Gibson RC .50 1.25
457 Dustin Fox RC .50 1.25
458 Ryan Fitzpatrick RC 1.00 2.50
459 Dan Orlovsky RC .60 1.50
460 Justin Tuck RC .75 2.00
461 Corey Webster RC .50 1.25
462 Travis Daniels RC .50 1.25
463 J.J. Arrington RC .50 1.25
464 David Greene RC .40 1.00
465 Alvin Pearman RC .40 1.00
466 Manuel White RC .50 1.25
467 Paris Warren RC .50 1.25
468 Patrick Estes RC .40 1.00
469 Cedric Houston RC .60 1.50
470 David Pollack RC .50 1.25
471 Craig Bragg RC .40 1.00
472 Vincent Jackson RC .75 2.00
473 Adam Jones RC .50 1.25
474 Matt Jones RC .60 1.50
475 Stefan LeFors RC .40 1.00
476 Heath Miller RC .75 2.00
477 Ryan Moats RC .50 1.25
478 Vernand Morency RC .50 1.25
479 Terrence Murphy RC .40 1.00
480 Kyle Orton RC .60 1.50
481 Roscoe Parrish RC .40 1.00
482 Courtney Roby RC .50 1.25
483 Aaron Rodgers RC 6.00 12.00
484 Carlos Rogers RC .60 1.50
485 Antrel Rolle RC .60 1.50
486 Eric Shelton RC .40 1.00
487 Alex Smith QB RC 1.00 2.50
488 Andrew Walter RC .50 1.25
489 Roddy White RC .75 2.00
490 Cadillac Williams RC .60 1.50
491 Mike Williams .60 1.50
492 Troy Williamson RC .50 1.25
493 Kirk Morrison RC .60 1.50
494 Tab Perry RC .40 1.00
495 Chad Owens RC .50 1.25
496 Lofa Tatupu RC .60 1.50
497 Craphonso Thorpe RC .40 1.00
498 Ryan Riddle RC .40 1.00
499 Marcus Maxwell RC .40 1.00
500 Barrett Ruud RC .60 1.50
501 Stanley Wilson RC .50 1.25
502 Mike Nugent RC .50 1.25
503 Eric King RC .40 1.00
504 Darryl Blackstock RC .40 1.00
505 Attiyah Ellison RC .40 1.00
506 Donte Nicholson RC .40 1.00
507 Airese Currie RC .40 1.00
508 Larry Brackins RC .40 1.00
509 Joel Dreessen RC .50 1.25
510 Cedric Benson RC .60 1.50
511 Mark Bradley RC .40 1.00
512 Reggie Brown RC .40 1.00
513 Ronnie Brown RC .75 2.00
514 Jason Campbell RC .75 2.00
515 Maurice Clarett .50 1.25
516 Mark Clayton RC .60 1.50
517 Braylon Edwards RC .75 2.00
518 Ciatrick Fason RC .40 1.00
519 Dan Cody RC .50 1.25
520 Taylor Stubblefield RC .40 1.00
521 J.R. Russell RC .40 1.00
522 Rian Wallace RC .50 1.25
523 Anthony Davis RC .40 1.00
524 Derek Anderson RC .50 1.25
525 Boomer Grigsby RC .60 1.50
526 Rasheed Marshall RC .50 1.25
527 Adrian McPherson RC .40 1.00
528 Noah Herron RC .40 1.00
529 Bryant McFadden RC .50 1.25
530 Lionel Gates RC .40 1.00
531 Matt Roth RC .50 1.25
532 Derrick Johnson RC .50 1.25
533 Stanford Routt RC .50 1.25
534 Brandon Jacobs RC .75 2.00
535 Kevin Burnett RC .50 1.25
536 Ryan Claridge RC .40 1.00
537 James Kilian RC .40 1.00
538 Oshiomogho Atogwe RC .60 1.50
539 Fabian Washington RC .50 1.25
540 Marion Barber RC .60 1.50
541 Anttaj Hawthorne RC .40 1.00
542 Zach Tuiasosopo RC .40 1.00
543 Ellis Hobbs RC .60 1.50
544 Alex Smith TE RC .40 1.00
545 Erasmus James RC .50 1.25
546 Channing Crowder RC .50 1.25
547 Kelvin Hayden RC .50 1.25
548 Darren Sproles RC .60 1.50
549 Marcus Spears RC .50 1.25
550 Dante Ridgeway RC .40 1.00
CL1 Checklist 1 .02 .10
CL2 Checklist 2 .02 .10
CL3 Checklist 3 .02 .10
CL4 Checklist 4 .02 .10
BR1 Ben Roethlisberger Jumbo 3.00 6.00
(Steelers Tin insert)
VL1 Vince Lombardi Jumbo 3.00 6.00
(Packers Tin insert)

2005 Topps Total First Edition

COMPLETE SET (55) 125.00 250.00
*STARS: 1X TO 2.5X BASIC CARDS
*ROOKIES: .8X TO 2X BASIC CARDS

2005 Topps Total Silver

COMPLETE SET (550) 60.00 150.00
*STARS: 1.2X TO 3X BASIC CARDS
*ROOKIES: .8X TO 2X BASIC CARDS
ONE SILVER PER PACK

2005 Topps Total Award Winners

COMPLETE SET (20) 12.50 25.00
STATED ODDS 1:12 HOB/RET
AW1 Curtis Martin 1.00 2.50
AW2 Shaun Alexander .75 2.00
AW3 Daunte Culpepper .75 2.00
AW4 Trent Green .75 2.00
AW5 Muhsin Muhammad .75 2.00
AW6 Chad Johnson .75 2.00
AW7 LaDainian Tomlinson 1.00 2.50
AW8 Marvin Harrison 1.00 2.50
AW9 Dwight Freeney .75 2.00
AW10 Adam Vinatieri 1.00 2.50
AW11 Dante Hall .60 1.50
AW12 Joe Horn .75 2.00
AW13 Tony Gonzalez .75 2.00
AW14 Donovan McNabb 1.00 2.50
AW15 Corey Dillon .75 2.00
AW16 Peyton Manning 2.00 5.00
AW17 Ed Reed .75 2.00
AW18 Ben Roethlisberger 1.50 4.00
AW19 Jonathan Vilma .75 2.00
AW20 Deion Branch .60 1.50

2005 Topps Total Rookie Jerseys

STATED ODDS 1:8 SPECIAL RETAIL
1 Alex Smith QB 7.50 20.00
2 Mark Clayton 3.00 8.00
3 Antrel Rolle 3.00 8.00
4 Kyle Orton 3.00 8.00
5 Roscoe Parrish 3.00 8.00
6 Vernand Morency 3.00 8.00
7 Maurice Clarett 3.00 8.00
8 Mark Bradley 3.00 8.00
9 Reggie Brown 3.00 8.00

2005 Topps Total Signatures

GROUP A ODDS 1:18,092 H, 1:3860 R
GROUP B ODDS 1:234 H, 1:1924 R
GROUP C ODDS 1:1528 H, 1:1522 R
TSAG Antonio Gates A 10.00 25.00
TSDB Drew Bennett A 20.00 40.00
TSJS Junior Siavii C 5.00 12.00
TSLW LeVar Woods B 5.00 12.00
TSMH Marquise Hill B 5.00 12.00
TSTS Trent Smith B 5.00 12.00

2005 Topps Total Team Checklists

COMPLETE SET (32) 12.50 30.00
TC1 Larry Fitzgerald .50 1.25
TC2 Michael Vick .50 1.25
TC3 Jamal Lewis .40 1.00
TC4 Willis McGahee .50 1.25
TC5 Jake Delhomme .40 1.00
TC6 Muhsin Muhammad .40 1.00
TC7 Rudi Johnson .40 1.00
TC8 Reuben Droughns .30 .75
TC9 Drew Bledsoe .50 1.25
TC10 Jake Plummer .40 1.00
TC11 Kevin Jones .30 .75
TC12 Brett Favre 1.25 3.00
TC13 Domanick Davis .30 .75
TC14 Peyton Manning 1.00 2.50
TC15 Byron Leftwich .40 1.00
TC16 Trent Green .40 1.00
TC17 Chris Chambers .40 1.00
TC18 Daunte Culpepper .40 1.00
TC19 Tom Brady 1.00 2.50
TC20 Joe Horn .40 1.00
TC21 Tiki Barber .50 1.25
TC22 Curtis Martin .50 1.25
TC23 Randy Moss .50 1.25
TC24 Donovan McNabb .50 1.25
TC25 Ben Roethlisberger .75 2.00
TC26 LaDainian Tomlinson .50 1.25
TC27 Brandon Lloyd .30 .75
TC28 Shaun Alexander .40 1.00
TC29 Torry Holt .40 1.00
TC30 Michael Clayton .30 .75
TC31 Drew Bennett .40 1.00
TC32 Clinton Portis .40 1.00

2005 Topps Total Total Production

COMPLETE SET (10) 10.00 20.00
STATED ODDS 1:18 HOB/RET
TP1 Peyton Manning 2.00 5.00
TP2 Daunte Culpepper .75 2.00
TP3 LaDainian Tomlinson 1.00 2.50
TP4 Muhsin Muhammad .75 2.00
TP5 Shaun Alexander .75 2.00
TP6 Marvin Harrison 1.00 2.50
TP7 Priest Holmes .75 2.00
TP8 Donovan McNabb 1.00 2.50
TP9 Terrell Owens 1.00 2.50
TP10 Brett Favre 2.50 6.00

2005 Topps Total Total Topps

COMPLETE SET (20) 15.00 30.00
STATED ODDS 1:6 HOB/RET
TT1 Tom Brady 2.00 5.00
TT2 LaDainian Tomlinson 1.00 2.50
TT3 Terrell Owens 1.00 2.50
TT4 Priest Holmes .75 2.00
TT5 Daunte Culpepper .75 2.00
TT6 Curtis Martin 1.00 2.50
TT7 Joe Horn .75 2.00
TT8 Trent Green .75 2.00
TT9 Edgerrin James .75 2.00
TT10 Randy Moss 1.00 2.50
TT11 Michael Vick 1.00 2.50
TT12 Tony Gonzalez .75 2.00
TT13 Marvin Harrison 1.00 2.50
TT14 Corey Dillon .75 2.00
TT15 Rudi Johnson .75 2.00
TT16 Peyton Manning 2.00 5.00
TT17 Muhsin Muhammad .75 2.00
TT18 Shaun Alexander .75 2.00
TT19 Brett Favre 2.50 6.00
TT20 Donovan McNabb 1.00 2.50

2006 Topps Total

This 550-card set was released in August, 2006. The set was issued into the hobby in 30-card packs with an $3 SRP which came 24 packs to a box. The first 440 cards in this set feature a mix of single and multi-player veteran cards, while cards numbered 441-550 feature 2006 rookies.

COMPLETE SET (550) 25.00 60.00
1 Corey Webster .20 .50
Sam Madison
2 Randy Moss .30 .75
3 Jeff Garcia .25 .60
Josh Parry
Koy Detmer
4 Matt Jones .20 .50
5 C.C. Brown .20 .50
Glenn Earl
6 Willie Anderson .20 .50
Eric Steinbach
Rich Braham
7 DeAngelo Hall .25 .60
8 J.P. Losman .25 .60
9 Kevin Jones .20 .50
10 Ken Dorsey .30 .75
Frank Gore
11 Donte Nicholson .20 .50
Kalvin Pearson RC
Will Allen
12 Brandon Lloyd .20 .50
13 Jeremiah Trotter .20 .50
14 Ron Stone .20 .50
Jake Grove
Barry Sims
15 Drew Brees .30 .75
16 Jason Taylor .25 .60
17 Tony Gonzalez .25 .60
18 Brandon Stokley .25 .60
19 Jake Plummer .25 .60
20 Braylon Edwards .25 .60
21 Bernard Berrian .25 .60
Brad Maynard
Robbie Gould RC
22 B.J. Sams .20 .50
Matt Stover
23 James Darling .20 .50
Orlando Huff
Karlos Dansby
24 Julius Peppers .25 .60
25 Jason Ferguson .20 .50
Marcus Spears
Greg Ellis
26 Donald Lee .20 .50
David Martin
27 Brad Johnson .25 .60
Bethel Johnson
28 Bethel Johnson .20 .50
29 Shaun Ellis .20 .50
Dewayne Robertson
Bryan Thomas
30 Willie Parker .25 .60
31 Edell Shepherd .20 .50
Ike Hilliard
32 Ben Troupe .20 .50
Bo Scaife
Matt Mauck
33 Marc Bulger .25 .60
34 Marcus Trufant .20 .50
Michael Boulware
35 Nick Hardwick .20 .50
Roman Oben
Shane Olivea
36 Ray Lewis .30 .75
37 Stefan Lefors .20 .50
Chris Weinke
38 Kevin Kaesviharn .20 .50
David Pollack
Ifeanyi Ohalete
39 Greg Jones .20 .50
Alvin Pearman
40 Jared Allen .30 .75
Eric Hicks
Ryan Sims
41 Tiki Barber .30 .75
42 Nnamdi Asomugha .30 .75
Fabian Washington
43 Keith Lewis .20 .50
Mike Adams
Ben Emanuel
44 Rodney Harrison .20 .50
45 Hunter Smith .25 .60
Adam Vinatieri
46 Dan Orlovsky .25 .60
Jon Kitna
Shawn Bryson
47 Bubba Franks .20 .50
48 Al Wilson .20 .50
Ian Gold
49 Andra Davis .20 .50
Chaun Thompson
Willie McGinest
50 Nathan Vasher .20 .50
51 Jabari Greer .20 .50
Troy Vincent
52 Allen Rossum .20 .50
Todd Peterson
Michael Koenen RC
53 DeMarcus Ware .25 .60
54 Lorenzo Diamond RC .20 .50
Marty Booker
55 Bryant McKinnie .25 .60
Matt Birk
Steve Hutchinson
56 Trent Cole .25 .60
Jevon Kearse
Mike Patterson
57 Marcus Tubbs .20 .50
Grant Wistrom
Bryce Fisher
58 Curtis Martin .30 .75
59 David Macklin .20 .50
Antrel Rolle
60 Norman Lejeune .20 .50

Reggie Howard
Yeremiah Bell
61 Reggie Brown .20 .50
62 Mike McKenzie .20 .50
Fred Thomas
63 Bryan Fletcher .20 .50
Ben Hartsock
Jim Sorgi
64 Larry Fitzgerald .30 .75
65 Eric Moulds .20 .50
Vernand Morency
66 Maurice Wiliams .20 .50
Khalif Barnes
Chris Naeole
67 Trent Green .25 .60
68 Darren Sproles .30 .75
Michael Turner
69 Brandon Chillar .25 .60
Laroi Glover
Pisa Tinoisamoa
70 Chris Gamble .20 .50
71 Adam Jones .20 .50
Michael Waddell
72 Lemar Marshall .20 .50
Marcus Washington
Phillip Daniels
73 Hines Ward .30 .75
74 Sammy Knight .20 .50
Patrick Surtain
75 Steve McKinney .20 .50
Todd Wade
Zach Wiegert
76 Rod Smith .25 .60
77 Drew Henson 2.00 5.00
Tony Romo
78 Aubrayo Franklin RC .20 .50
Kelly Gregg
Trevor Pryce
79 David Garrard .25 .60
80 Daryl Smith .20 .50
Mike Peterson
81 David Bowens .20 .50
Keith Traylor
Matt Roth
82 Simeon Rice .20 .50
83 Marques Douglas .20 .50
Bryant Young
84 David Thornton .20 .50
Rob Reynolds RC
Peter Sirmon
85 T.J. Houshmandzadeh .25 .60
86 Ladell Betts .25 .60
Jason Campbell
87 Marvel Smith .25 .60
Jeff Hartings
Alan Faneca
88 Antonio Pierce .20 .50
89 Chris Kluwe .20 .50
Ryan Longwell
90 Robert Thomas .20 .50
Roy Manning
Brady Poppinga
91 Willis McGahee .25 .60
92 Keith Smith .20 .50
Terrence Holt
93 Eugene Wilson .25 .60
Asante Samuel
Ellis Hobbs
94 Orlando Pace .20 .50
Adam Timmerman
Alex Barron
95 Fred Taylor .25 .60
96 Mike Doss .25 .60
Bob Sanders
97 Leon Joe .25 .60
Lance Briggs
Brendon Ayanbadejo
98 Daunte Culpepper .25 .60
99 Chris Perry .25 .60
Tab Perry
100 Alvis Whitted .20 .50
Sebastian Janikowski
Shane Lechler
101 Julius Jones .20 .50
102 Chad Lavalais .20 .50
Rod Coleman
103 Mike Rucker .20 .50
Vinny Ciurciu RC
Al Wallace
104 Rex Grossman .25 .60
105 Dunta Robinson .20 .50
106 Colby Bockwoldt .20 .50
Jason Craft
Steve Gleason
107 Chad Pennington .25 .60
108 Heath Miller .25 .60
109 D.J. Hackett .20 .50
Nate Burleson
110 Drew Bennett .25 .60
111 Jamal Williams .20 .50
Randall Godfrey
Luis Castillo
112 Doug Gabriel .20 .50
113 Amani Toomer .30 .75
Brandon Jacobs
114 Travis Taylor .20 .50
115 Terrell Suggs .25 .60
116 Todd Heap .25 .60
117 Ike Reese .20 .50
Demorrio Williams
Michael Boley
118 Odell Thurman .20 .50
119 Darius Watts .25 .60
Javon Walker
120 Josh Scobee .20 .50
Chris Hanson RC
LaBrandon Toefield
121 Donovan McNabb .30 .75
122 Alex Smith TE .20 .50
Anthony Becht
123 Adam Archuleta .20 .50
124 J.J. Arrington .20 .50
125 Landon Johnson .20 .50
Brian Simmons
Caleb Miller
126 Joe Andruzzi .20 .50
LeCharles Bentley
Ryan Tucker
127 Aaron Rodgers .60 1.50
128 Mark Brown .20 .50
Barry Gardner
Victor Hobson
129 Antonio Bryant .20 .50
130 Isaac Bruce .25 .60
131 Shelton Quarles .20 .50
Ryan Nece
Barrett Ruud
132 Darrent Williams .20 .50
Jason Elam
Todd Sauerbrun
133 Brad Hoover .20 .50
Nick Goings
134 B.J. Ward .20 .50
Dale Carter
Samari Rolle
135 Dante Hall .25 .60
136 Tom Brady .50 1.25
137 Ryan Moats .20 .50
Correll Buckhalter
138 Arnaz Battle .20 .50
139 Rocky Bernard .20 .50
Leroy Hill
D.D. Lewis RC
140 Aaron Kampman .25 .60
Kabeer Gbaja-Biamila
Cullen Jenkins
141 Ryan Fowler RC .20 .50
Bradie James
Kevin Burnett
142 Warrick Dunn .25 .60
143 Eli Manning .40 1.00
144 Danny Clark .20 .50
Tyler Brayton
Kirk Morrison
145 Zach Thomas .30 .75
146 Charlie Anderson .20 .50
Jason Babin
Morlon Greenwood
147 Ron Dayne .25 .60
148 Dave Zastudil .20 .50
Phil Dawson
149 Pat Williams .20 .50
C.J. Mosley
Spencer Johnson
150 Donte Stallworth .20 .50
151 Shawne Merriman .25 .60
152 Lamont Thompson .20 .50
Craig Hentrich
Rob Bironas
153 Clinton Portis .30 .75
154 Ronald Curry .25 .60
Johnnie Morant
155 Dwight Freeney .25 .60
156 Brian Russell .20 .50
Daylon McCutcheon
157 Mike Brown .25 .60
Mike Green
Charles Tillman
158 Takeo Spikes .20 .50
159 Kurt Warner .30 .75
160 Jonathan Vilma .25 .60
161 James Farrior .20 .50
162 Drayton Florence .20 .50
Quentin Jammer
163 Kevan Barlow .20 .50
164 Clark Haggans .20 .50
Casey Hampton
Aaron Smith
165 Walter Jones .20 .50
166 Jermane Mayberry .20 .50
Kendyl Jacox RC
Montrae Holland
167 Byron Leftwich .25 .60
168 Mike Williams WR .20 .50
169 Jason Witten .30 .75
170 Dennis Northcutt .20 .50
171 Rashad Baker .20 .50
Nate Clements
Coy Wire
172 Ronnie Cruz .20 .50
173 E.J. Henderson .20 .50
Erasmus James
174 LaMont Jordan .25 .60
175 Tyrone Calico .20 .50
176 Tom Nalen .20 .50
George Foster
Ben Hamilton
177 Sam Gado .25 .60
178 Randy McMichael .20 .50
179 Sheldon Brown .25 .60
Lito Sheppard
Matt Ware
180 Leonard Little .20 .50
Anthony Hargrove
181 Cadillac Williams .25 .60
182 Jay Feely .25 .60
Chad Morton
David Tyree
183 Dallas Clark .25 .60
184 Demarcus Faggins .20 .50
Lewis Sanders
Marcus Coleman
185 Vonnie Holliday .20 .50
Kevin Carter
186 Derek Smith .20 .50
Jeff Ulbrich
Jamie Winborn
187 Scott Player .20 .50
Neil Rackers
188 Steve Smith .30 .75
189 Matt Cassel .30 .75
Daniel Graham
Ben Watson
190 Joey Porter .20 .50
Larry Foote
191 Jamal Lewis .25 .60
192 Michael Jenkins .25 .60
193 Michael Strahan .25 .60
194 Kyle Vanden Bosch .20 .50
195 Will Shields .20 .50
Willie Roaf
Brian Waters
196 Terry Glenn .25 .60
197 Robert Griffith .20 .50
Eric Green
Adrian Wilson
198 Philip Rivers .30 .75
199 Justin Tuck .25 .60
William Joseph
Fred Robbins
200 LaDainian Tomlinson .30 .75
201 Jason David .20 .50
Nick Harper
202 James Hall .20 .50
Boss Bailey
Shaun Rogers
203 Donald Driver .30 .75
204 Reuben Droughns .25 .60
205 Mike Wahle .20 .50
Jordan Gross
Travelle Wharton
206 Jonathan Ogden .20 .50
207 Josh Bullocks .20 .50
Dwight Smith
208 Mike Nugent .20 .50
Justin Miller
Ben Graham RC
209 Matt Hasselbeck .25 .60
210 Derrick Brooks .25 .60
211 Domonique Foxworth .20 .50
John Lynch
Nick Ferguson
212 Matt Stewart .20 .50
Mason Unck
Jason Fisk
213 Mike Williams T .20 .50
Bennie Anderson RC
Chris Villarrial
214 Jeff Saturday .20 .50
Tarik Glenn
Ryan Diem
215 Larry Johnson .25 .60
216 Marcus Robinson .20 .50
217 Aaron Brooks .25 .60
218 L.J. Smith .20 .50
Mike Bartrum
Stephen Spach
219 Steven Jackson .30 .75
220 Roy Williams WR .25 .60
221 Lousaka Polite .20 .50
Patrick Crayton
222 Carson Palmer .30 .75
223 Ruben Brown .20 .50
Olin Kreutz
John Tait
224 Charles Woodson .30 .75
225 Jarrett Payton .20 .50
Travis Henry
226 Kerry Rhodes .20 .50
Erik Coleman
227 Ronnie Brown .30 .75
228 David Carr .20 .50
229 Terence Newman .20 .50
230 Boomer Grigsby .20 .50
Kendrell Bell
Kawika Mitchell
231 Mike Vrabel .25 .60
Rosevelt Colvin
232 Eric Heitmann .20 .50
Justin Smiley
Kwame Harris
233 Joey Galloway .25 .60
234 Keith Bulluck .20 .50
235 John Hall .20 .50
Derrick Frost
Antonio Brown
236 Darnell Dockett .20 .50
Antonio Smith
Chike Okeafor
237 Mike Anderson .25 .60
238 Kellen Winslow .25 .60
239 Tatum Bell .20 .50
240 Artose Pinner .20 .50
Cory Schlesinger
241 Mark Roman .25 .60
Marviel Underwood
Nick Collins
242 Reggie Wayne .25 .60
243 Reggie Williams .25 .60
244 Derrick Pope .20 .50
Donnie Spragan
Channing Crowder
245 Courtney Watson .20 .50
246 Greg Lewis .20 .50
Billy McMullen
247 Troy Polamalu .40 1.00
248 Jeff Smoker .25 .60
Marshall Faulk
Dane Looker
249 Keyshawn Johnson .25 .60
250 Jonathan Babineaux .20 .50
Chauncey Davis
251 Marcel Shipp .20 .50
252 Brian Urlacher .30 .75
253 Albert Hayhesworth .20 .50
Travis LaBoy
Randy Starks
254 Derrick Burgess .20 .50
255 Napoleon Harris .20 .50
Dontarrious Thomas
Ben Leber
256 John Henderson .20 .50
Marcus Stroud
Reggie Hayward
257 Travis Minor .20 .50
258 Marco Rivera .20 .50
Rob Petitti
Al Johnson
259 D.J. Williams .20 .50
260 Terrell Owens .30 .75
261 Cedrick Wilson .20 .50
Dan Kreider
262 Antonio Gates .30 .75
263 Ronde Barber .25 .60
264 Bryant Johnson .20 .50
265 Brett Favre .60 1.50
266 Chad Stanley .20 .50
Kris Brown
267 Kareem McKenzie .40 1.00
Luke Petitgout
Shaun O'Hara RC
268 Chris Cooley .25 .60
269 Steve McNair .25 .60
270 Justin Smith .20 .50
John Thornton
Robert Geathers
271 Todd McClure .15 .40
Kynan Forney
Matt Lehr RC
272 Benny Sapp RC .15 .40
Dexter McCleon
Eric Warfield
273 Jeremy Shockey .30 .75
274 Chad Johnson .25 .60
275 Keydrick Vincent RC .20 .50
Mike Flynn RC
Edwin Mulitalo
276 Deuce McAllister .25 .60
277 Warren Sapp .25 .60
Tommy Kelly
Bobby Hamilton
278 Brandon Manumaleuna .30 .75
Ryan Fitzpatrick
279 Greg Spires .20 .50
Dewayne White
Ellis Wyms
280 Josh McCown .20 .50
281 Derrick Johnson LB .20 .50
282 Tony Bryant .20 .50
Charles Grant
283 Cedric Houston .20 .50
Derrick Blaylock
284 David Givens .25 .60
285 Rian Lindell .20 .50
Terrence McGee
Brian Moorman
286 Charlie Frye .25 .60
287 Ahman Green .25 .60
288 Darren Sharper .25 .60
289 Justin McCareins .20 .50
290 Lofa Tatupu .25 .60
291 Raheem Brock .20 .50
Montae Reagor
Josh Thomas
292 Muhsin Muhammad .25 .60
293 Derrick Mason .25 .60
294 Donnie Jones .30 .75
Olindo Mare
Wes Welker
295 Aaron Stecker .20 .50
Devery Henderson
Ernie Conwell
296 Kevin Mawae .20 .50
Michael Roos
Benji Olson
297 Mark Bradley .25 .60
Adrian Peterson
298 John Abraham .20 .50
299 Derrick Dockery .20 .50
Casey Rabach
Chris Samuels
300 Peyton Manning .50 1.25
301 Alge Crumpler .25 .60
302 Rashean Mathis .20 .50
David Richardson
Deon Grant
303 Tedy Bruschi .30 .75
304 Chris Snee .40 1.00
David Diehl RC
Grey Ruegamer RC
305 Jerramy Stevens .25 .60
Peter Warrick
306 Trent Dilfer .25 .60
307 Marion Barber .25 .60
308 Robert Ferguson .20 .50
309 Chester Taylor .25 .60
310 Jerry Porter .20 .50
311 Dan Buenning .20 .50
Kenyatta Walker
John Wade
312 DeShaun Foster .25 .60
313 Roscoe Parrish .20 .50
Kelly Holcomb
314 Chris Brown .20 .50
315 Damien Woody .20 .50
Jeff Backus
Dominic Raiola
316 Andre Johnson .30 .75
317 Shayne Graham .20 .50
Kyle Larson
318 Kris Mangum .20 .50
Michael Gaines
Eric Shelton
319 Ben Roethlisberger .40 1.00
320 Todd Devoe .20 .50
Charlie Adams
321 Jake Delhomme .25 .60
322 Chris Chambers .25 .60
323 Chris Simms .25 .60
324 Ed Reed .25 .60
325 Charles Rogers .25 .60
326 Eddie Kennison .20 .50
327 Richard Seymour .25 .60
Ty Warren
Vince Wilfork
328 Lorenzo Neal .20 .50
329 Taylor Jacobs .20 .50
330 Kevin Mathis .20 .50
Lawyer Milloy
331 Aaron Glenn .20 .50
Anthony Henry
Jacques Reeves
332 Brian Dawkins .25 .60
Michael Lewis
333 Edgerrin James .25 .60
334 Lee Evans .25 .60
335 Pat Williams .20 .50
336 LaVar Arrington .25 .60
Reggie Torbor
Eric Moore
337 Roy Williams S .25 .60
338 Joe Horn .25 .60
339 Keenan McCardell .25 .60
340 Andy Lee RC .20 .50
Joe Nedney
Maurice Hicks
341 Mark Brunell .25 .60
342 Jimmy Smith .25 .60
343 Deltha O'Neal .20 .50
344 Chris McAlister .20 .50
345 Troy Williamson .20 .50
Jim Kleinsasser
346 Noah Herron .20 .50
Andrae Thurman
347 Alex Brown .20 .50
Adewale Ogunleye
348 Michael Vick .30 .75
349 Laveranues Coles .20 .50
350 Alex Smith QB .30 .75
351 Billy Volek .20 .50
352 Cato June .25 .60
353 Joe Jurevicius .20 .50
Frisman Jackson
354 Keary Colbert .20 .50
355 Justin Griffith .25 .60
Matt Schaub
Roddy White
356 Robaire Smith .20 .50
Seth Payne
Gary Walker
357 Samie Parker .20 .50
358 Plaxico Burress .25 .60
359 Ronald Bartell .20 .50
Oshiomogho Atogwe
360 Courtney Roby .20 .50
Roydell Williams
361 Shawn Springs .20 .50
Walt Harris
Pierson Prioleau
362 Angelo Crowell .20 .50
London Fletcher
363 Nick Barnett .25 .60
364 Antoine Winfield .20 .50
365 Will Smith .20 .50
366 Jerricho Cotchery .25 .60
B.J. Askew
367 Brian Westbrook .25 .60
368 Jerome Mathis .20 .50
369 Clarence Moore .20 .50
Devard Darling
370 Eric Parker .20 .50
371 Dre Bly .20 .50
Stanley Wilson
Kenoy Kennedy
372 Champ Bailey .25 .60
373 Cedric Benson .25 .60
374 Chris Gray RC .20 .50
Robbie Tobeck
Sean Locklear
375 Lawrence Tynes .20 .50
Dustin Colquitt
376 Dan Morgan .20 .50
377 Jeff Posey .20 .50
Aaron Schobel
Chris Kelsay
378 Ebenezer Ekuban .20 .50
Courtney Brown
Michael Myers
379 Jeff Reed .20 .50
Ricardo Colclough
Chris Gardocki
380 Marcus Pollard .20 .50
Scottie Vines
381 R.W. McQuarters .20 .50
James Butler
Curtis Deloatch
382 Fred Smoot .20 .50
383 Andrew Walter .20 .50
Courtney Anderson
Zack Crockett
384 Dominic Rhodes .25 .60
385 Tyson Thompson .25 .60
Mike Vanderjagt
386 Johnathan Sullivan .20 .50
Terrence Melton
Tony Bryant
387 Mike Scifres .20 .50
Nate Kaeding
388 Erron Kinney .20 .50
389 Adam Bergen .20 .50
Eric Edwards
Leron McCoy
390 Brian Jones .20 .50
Kyle Brady
391 Alvin McKinley .20 .50
Brodney Pool
Gary Baxter
392 Marlin Jackson .20 .50
Matt Giordano
Kelvin Hayden
393 Keith Brooking .20 .50
394 Josh Reed .20 .50
395 Thomas Jones .25 .60
396 Derrick Johnson CB .20 .50
Shawntae Spencer
397 Andre Woolfolk .20 .50
Jared Clauss
Rich Gardner
398 Kyle Boller .25 .60
399 Patrick Pass .25 .60
Kevin Faulk
400 Stanford Routt .20 .50
Stuart Schweigert
Ryan Riddle
401 Donnie Edwards .20 .50
402 Michael Clayton .20 .50
403 John Kasay .20 .50
Jason Kyle
Jamal Robertson
404 Ahmad Carroll .25 .60
Al Harris
405 Priest Holmes .25 .60
406 Jabar Gaffney .20 .50
407 Mewelde Moore .20 .50
408 Torry Holt .25 .60
409 Mark Clayton .25 .60
410 Shaun Alexander .25 .60
411 Travares Tillman .20 .50
Travis Daniels
412 Deion Branch .25 .60
413 Hank Fraley .20 .50
Shawn Andrews
Trey Darilek RC
414 Anquan Boldin .25 .60
415 Tory James .20 .50
Keiwan Ratliff
416 Ernest Wilford .20 .50
417 Brandon Moore .20 .50
Adrian Jones
Pete Kendall
418 Brian Griese .25 .60
419 Brian Kelly .20 .50
Jermaine Phillips
420 Patrick Ramsey .25 .60
421 Corey Dillon .25 .60
422 Santana Moss .25 .60
423 Adalius Thomas .25 .60
Dwan Edwards
Peter Boulware
424 Ashley Lelie .20 .50
425 Gibril Wilson .30 .75
Will Demps
426 Darrell Jackson .25 .60
427 Kevin Williams .20 .50
Kenechi Udeze
Darrion Scott
428 Ken Lucas .20 .50
Mike Minter
429 Lee Suggs .20 .50
430 Nick Kaczur .20 .50
Gene Mruczkowski
Brandon Gorin
431 Robert Gallery .20 .50
432 Kassim Osgood .25 .60
A.J. Feeley
Vincent Jackson
433 Domanick Davis .20 .50
434 Osi Umenyiora .25 .60
435 Drew Bledsoe .30 .75
436 Justin Gage .20 .50
Eddie Berlin
437 Rudi Johnson .25 .60
438 Justin Fargas .25 .60
Marques Tuiasosopo
439 Antwaan Randle El .25 .60
440 Marvin Harrison .30 .75
441 Brandon Marshall RC .60 1.50
442 Wali Lundy RC .50 1.25
443 Bruce Gradkowski RC .60 1.50
444 Leonard Pope RC .60 1.50
445 Omar Jacobs RC .40 1.00
446 Travis Wilson RC .40 1.00
447 Derek Hagan RC .50 1.25
448 Devin Hester RC 1.00 2.50
449 Willie Reid RC .50 1.25
450 A.J. Hawk RC .60 1.50
451 DeAngelo Williams RC .75 2.00
452 Ashton Youboty RC .40 1.00
453 Abdul Hodge RC .40 1.00
454 Leon Washington RC .50 1.25
455 D'Qwell Jackson RC .50 1.25
456 Johnathan Joseph RC .50 1.25
457 Antonio Cromartie RC .60 1.50
458 Michael Robinson RC .50 1.25
459 Tye Hill RC .40 1.00
460 Mathias Kiwanuka RC .60 1.50
461 Vince Young RC .75 2.00
462 DeMeco Ryans RC .60 1.50
463 Brodrick Bunkley RC .50 1.25
464 Jay Cutler RC 1.25 3.00
465 Brad Smith RC .60 1.50
466 Elvis Dumervil RC .60 1.50
467 Cory Rodgers RC .50 1.25
468 Davin Joseph RC .50 1.25
469 Rocky McIntosh RC .50 1.25
470 Jason Avant RC .40 1.00
471 Anthony Schlegel RC .50 1.25
472 Kamerion Wimbley RC .60 1.50
473 Joseph Addai RC .60 1.50
474 Ernie Sims RC .50 1.25
475 Jimmy Williams RC .60 1.50
476 LenDale White RC .50 1.25
477 Brandon Williams RC .40 1.00
478 Ko Simpson RC .50 1.25
479 Jerious Norwood RC .50 1.25
480 P.J. Daniels RC .40 1.00
481 Mario Williams RC .60 1.50
482 Santonio Holmes RC .75 2.00
483 Joe Klopfenstein RC .40 1.00
484 Matt Leinart RC .60 1.50
485 Danieal Manning RC .60 1.50
486 Andre Hall RC .50 1.25
487 Chad Greenway RC .60 1.50
488 Chad Jackson RC .40 1.00
489 Skyler Green RC .40 1.00
490 Donte Whitner RC .60 1.50
491 Bobby Carpenter RC .40 1.00
492 Jovon Bouknight RC .50 1.25
493 Vernon Davis RC .75 2.00
494 Kevin McMahan RC .50 1.25
495 D.J. Shockley RC .50 1.25
496 A.J. Nicholson RC .40 1.00
497 Brian Calhoun RC .40 1.00
498 Tim Day RC .50 1.25
499 Devin Aromashodu RC .60 1.50
500 Charlie Whitehurst RC .60 1.50
501 Sinorice Moss RC .60 1.50
502 Maurice Stovall RC .40 1.00
503 Laurence Maroney RC .50 1.25
504 James Anderson RC .40 1.00
505 Darnell Bing RC .50 1.25
506 Jerome Harrison RC .60 1.50
507 Daniel Bullocks RC .60 1.50
508 Will Blackmon RC .50 1.25
509 Marcedes Lewis RC .60 1.50
510 Lawrence Vickers RC .50 1.25
511 Marques Hagans RC .40 1.00
512 Jeremy Bloom RC .50 1.25
513 Dominique Byrd RC .50 1.25
514 Tarvaris Jackson RC .60 1.50
515 Dusty Dvoracek RC .60 1.50
516 Brodie Croyle RC .60 1.50
517 Demetrius Williams RC .50 1.25
518 Jason Allen RC .50 1.25
519 Mike Hass RC .50 1.25
520 Nick Mangold RC .50 1.25
521 Brett Basanez RC .60 1.50
522 Ben Obomanu RC .60 1.50
523 Tamba Hali RC .60 1.50
524 Gabe Watson RC .40 1.00
525 Kelly Jennings RC .50 1.25
526 Reggie Bush RC 1.25 3.00
527 Bernard Pollard RC .50 1.25
528 Reggie McNeal RC .50 1.25
529 Jonathan Orr RC .50 1.25
530 Haloti Ngata RC .60 1.50
531 David Thomas RC .50 1.25
532 Ingle Martin RC .50 1.25
533 Anthony Fasano RC .60 1.50
534 Winston Justice RC .50 1.25
535 Manny Lawson RC .50 1.25
536 Kellen Clemens RC .50 1.25
537 Adam Jennings RC .50 1.25
538 Thomas Howard RC .50 1.25
539 Cedric Humes RC .40 1.00
540 Garrett Mills RC .60 1.50
541 Jeff Webb RC .50 1.25
542 Michael Huff RC .50 1.25
543 Gerris Wilkinson RC UER .40 1.00
(photo on back Barry Cofield)
544 Maurice Drew RC 1.00 2.50
545 John McCargo RC .40 1.00
546 Todd Watkins RC .40 1.00
547 Marcus Vick RC .40 1.00
548 Greg Jennings RC 1.00 2.50
549 P.J. Pope RC .60 1.50
550 D'Brickashaw Ferguson RC .60 1.50

2006 Topps Total Black

*VETS 1-440: 3X TO 8X BASIC CARDS
*ROOKIES 441-550: 1.5X TO 4X BASIC CARDS
BLACK/50 STATED ODDS 1:11

2006 Topps Total Blue

*VETS 1-440: .8X TO 2X BASIC CARDS
*ROOKIES 441-550: .5X TO 1.2X
STATED ODDS 1.5:1

2006 Topps Total Gold

*VETS 1-440: 2.5X TO 6X BASIC CARDS
*ROOKIES 441-550: 1.2X TO 3X BASIC CARDS
STATED ODDS 1:10 HOB, 1:12 RET

2006 Topps Total Red

*VETERANS 1-440: 1X TO 2.5X BASIC CARDS
*ROOKIES 441-550: .6X TO 1.5X
STATED ODDS 1:1 HOB, 1:4 RET

2006 Topps Total Silver

*VETERANS 1-440: 1.5X TO 4X BASIC CARDS
*ROOKIES 441-550: .8X TO 2X BASIC CARDS
STATED ODDS 1:4 HOB, 1:6 RET

2006 Topps Total Award Winners

COMPLETE SET (20) 10.00 25.00
STATED ODDS 1:8 HOB/RET
AW1 Carson Palmer .75 2.00
AW2 Tom Brady 1.25 3.00
AW3 Brett Favre 1.50 4.00
AW4 Larry Johnson .60 1.50
AW5 Ben Roethlisberger 1.00 2.50
AW6 Chad Johnson .60 1.50
AW7 Derrick Burgess .50 1.25
AW8 Cadillac Williams .60 1.50
AW9 Shaun Alexander .60 1.50
AW10 Tedy Bruschi .75 2.00
AW11 Marvin Harrison .75 2.00
AW12 Brian Urlacher .75 2.00
AW13 Steve Smith .75 2.00
AW14 Matt Hasselbeck .60 1.50
AW15 Jonathan Vilma .60 1.50
AW16 Shawne Merriman .60 1.50
AW17 Peyton Manning 1.25 3.00
AW18 Larry Fitzgerald .75 2.00
AW19 Shaun Alexander .60 1.50
AW20 Hines Ward .75 2.00

2006 Topps Total Rookie Jerseys

ODDS 1:8 TARGET RETAIL PACKS
32TE A.J. Hawk 3.00 8.00
33TE Brandon Marshall 3.00 8.00
34TE Brandon Williams 2.00 5.00
35TE Brian Calhoun 2.00 5.00
36TE Chad Jackson 2.00 5.00
37TE Charlie Whitehurst 3.00 8.00
38TE DeAngelo Williams 4.00 10.00
39TE Demetrius Williams 2.50 6.00
40TE Derek Hagan 2.50 6.00
41TE Jason Avant 2.00 5.00
42TE Jerious Norwood 2.50 6.00
43TE Joe Klopfenstein 2.00 5.00
44TE Kellen Clemens 2.50 6.00
45TE Laurence Maroney 2.50 6.00
46TE LenDale White 2.50 6.00
47TE Leon Washington 2.50 6.00
48TE Marcedes Lewis 3.00 8.00
49TE Mario Williams 3.00 8.00
50TE Matt Leinart 3.00 8.00
51TE Maurice Drew 5.00 12.00
52TE Maurice Stovall 2.00 5.00
53TE Michael Huff 2.50 6.00
54TE Michael Robinson 2.50 6.00
55TE Omar Jacobs 2.00 5.00
56TE Reggie Bush 6.00 15.00
57TE Santonio Holmes 4.00 10.00
58TE Sinorice Moss 3.00 8.00
59TE Tarvaris Jackson 3.00 8.00
60TE Travis Wilson 2.00 5.00
61TE Vernon Davis 4.00 10.00
62TE Vince Young 4.00 10.00

2006 Topps Total Signatures

GROUP A ODDS 1:5100 H, 1:7400 R
GROUP B ODDS 1:1310 H, 1:2550
GROUP C ODDS 1:385 H, 1:1000 R
TSBS Brad Smith 10.00 25.00
TSCT Chester Taylor 15.00 40.00
TSDH Devin Hester 25.00 50.00
TSJA Jason Avant 8.00 20.00
TSMD Maurice Drew 20.00 40.00
TSMH Michael Huff 10.00 25.00
TSSM Shawne Merriman 12.00 30.00
TSSS Steve Smith 30.00 60.00
TSTP Troy Polamalu

2006 Topps Total Sports Illustrated For Kids

COMPLETE SET (25) 8.00 20.00
STATED ODDS 1:1
1 Shaun Alexander .40 1.00
2 Larry Johnson .40 1.00
3 LaDainian Tomlinson .50 1.25
4 Clinton Portis .50 1.25
5 Tiki Barber .50 1.25
6 Edgerrin James .40 1.00
7 Rudi Johnson .40 1.00
8 Cadillac Williams .40 1.00
9 Peyton Manning .75 2.00
10 Ronnie Brown .50 1.25
11 Steven Jackson .50 1.25
12 Tony Gonzalez .40 1.00
13 LaMont Jordan .40 1.00
14 Terrell Owens .50 1.25
15 Steve Smith .50 1.25
16 Chad Johnson .40 1.00
17 Torry Holt .40 1.00
18 Marvin Harrison .50 1.25
19 Larry Fitzgerald .50 1.25
20 Randy Moss .50 1.25
21 Antonio Gates .50 1.25
22 Reggie Bush 1.00 2.50
23 Tom Brady .75 2.00
24 Jeremy Shockey .50 1.25
25 Donovan McNabb .50 1.25

2006 Topps Total Team Checklists

STATED ODDS 1:4
1 Edgerrin James .25 .60
2 Michael Vick .30 .75
3 Steve McNair .25 .60
4 Willis McGahee .25 .60
5 Steve Smith .30 .75
6 Brian Urlacher .30 .75
7 Carson Palmer .30 .75
8 Charlie Frye .25 .60
9 Terrell Owens .30 .75
10 Jake Plummer .25 .60
11 Roy Williams WR .25 .60
12 Brett Favre .60 1.50
13 Mario Williams .40 1.00
14 Peyton Manning .50 1.25
15 Byron Leftwich .25 .60
16 Larry Johnson .25 .60
17 Daunte Culpepper .25 .60
18 Chester Taylor .25 .60
19 Tom Brady .50 1.25
20 Reggie Bush .75 2.00
21 Tiki Barber .30 .75
22 Curtis Martin .30 .75
23 Randy Moss .30 .75
24 Donovan McNabb .30 .75
25 Ben Roethlisberger .40 1.00
26 LaDainian Tomlinson .30 .75
27 Vernon Davis .50 1.25
28 Shaun Alexander .25 .60
29 Marc Bulger .25 .60
30 Cadillac Williams .25 .60
31 Vince Young .50 1.25
32 Clinton Portis .30 .75

2006 Topps Total Total Production

COMPLETE SET (10) 6.00 15.00
STATED ODDS 1:16 HOB/RET
TP1 Shaun Alexander .60 1.50
TP2 Larry Johnson .60 1.50
TP3 Carson Palmer .75 2.00
TP4 Peyton Manning 1.25 3.00
TP5 Tom Brady 1.25 3.00
TP6 Drew Brees .75 2.00
TP7 LaDainian Tomlinson .75 2.00
TP8 Chris Chambers .60 1.50
TP9 Marvin Harrison .75 2.00
TP10 Steve Smith .75 2.00

2006 Topps Total Total Topps

COMPLETE SET (20) 10.00 25.00
STATED ODDS 1:8 HOB/RET
TT1 Peyton Manning 1.25 3.00
TT2 Ben Roethlisberger 1.00 2.50
TT3 Steve Smith .75 2.00
TT4 Carson Palmer .75 2.00
TT5 Larry Johnson .60 1.50
TT6 Tiki Barber .60 1.50
TT7 Chad Johnson .60 1.50
TT8 LaDainian Tomlinson .75 2.00
TT9 Michael Vick .75 2.00
TT10 Edgerrin James .60 1.50
TT11 Cadillac Williams .60 1.50
TT12 Tom Brady 1.25 3.00
TT13 Antonio Gates .75 2.00
TT14 Hines Ward .75 2.00
TT15 Trent Green .60 1.50
TT16 Rudi Johnson .60 1.50
TT17 Donovan Mcnabb .75 2.00
TT18 Shaun Alexander .60 1.50
TT19 Marvin Harrison .75 2.00
TT20 Brett Favre 1.50 4.00

2007 Topps Total

This 550-card set was released in August, 2007. The set was issued into the hobby in 10-card packs, with a 99 cent SRP, which came 36 packs to a box. Cards numbered 1-440 feature veteran players in a mix of single and multi-player cards while cards numbered 441-550 feature 2007 NFL rookies.

COMPLETE SET (550)	35.00	60.00
UNPRICED PRINT PLATES SER.#'d TO 1		
1 Cadillac Williams	.25	.60
2 Marcel Shipp	.20	.50
Troy Walters		
3 Kerry Collins	.20	.50
Brandon Jones		
4 J.J. Arrington	.25	.60
5 Albert Haynesworth	.20	.50
6 DeAngelo Hall	.25	.60
7 Kyle Vanden Bosch	.20	.50
Travis LaBoy		
Andre Woolfolk		
8 Kyle Boller	.20	.50
Justin Green		
Demetrius Williams		
9 Anquan Boldin	.25	.60
10 Anthony Thomas	.20	.50
11 Orlando Huff	.20	.50
Leonard Pope		
Darnell Dockett		
12 Mike Rucker	.20	.50
Kris Jenkins		
13 Musa Smith	.25	.60
Mike Anderson		
14 DeShaun Foster	.25	.60
15 Mark Clayton	.25	.60
16 Mike Minter		
Ken Lucas		
Richard Marshall		
17 Ed Reed	.25	.60
18 Devin Hester	.30	.75
19 Brian Moorman	.20	.50
Craig Nall		
Rian Lindell		
20 Jamal Lewis	.25	.60
21 Chris Gamble	.20	.50
22 Kenny Wright	.20	.50
Leigh Bodden		
Tim Carter		
23 Tommie Harris	.20	.50
Tank Johnson		
24 Ryan Tucker	.20	.50
Kevin Shaffer RC		
Hank Fraley		
25 Brad Maynard	.20	.50
Robbie Gould		
Adrian Peterson Bears		
26 Terence Newman	.20	.50
Anthony Henry		
27 T.J. Houshmandzadeh	.25	.60
28 Travis Henry	.25	.60
29 Julius Jones	.20	.50
30 Kyle Johnson	.20	.50
Nick Ferguson		
Dre Bly		
31 Leonard Davis	.20	.50
Marco Rivera		
Andre Gurode		
32 Aaron Kampman	.25	.60
Kabeer Gbaja-Biamila		
33 Demetrin Veal RC	.20	.50
Gerard Warren		
34 Brett Favre	.60	1.50
35 Mike Bell	.25	.60
36 Ron Dayne	.25	.60
37 Jon Kitna	.20	.50
38 Kris Brown	.20	.50
Dexter Wynn		
Samkon Gado		
39 Daniel Bullocks	.20	.50
Fernando Bryant		
Kenoy Kennedy		
40 Peyton Manning	.50	1.25
41 Matt Schaub	.25	.60
42 Matt Jones	.25	.60
43 Jim Sorgi	.20	.50
Ben Utecht		
44 Dennis Northcutt	.20	.50
Josh Scobee		
Alvin Pearman		
45 Dallas Clark	.20	.50
46 Kris Wilson	.20	.50
Michael Bennett		
47 Jeff Saturday	.20	.50
Tarik Glenn		
Ryan Diem		
48 Daunte Culpepper	.25	.60
49 Damon Huard	.25	.60
50 Bryant McKinnie	.25	.60
Matt Birk		
Steve Hutchinson		
51 Ty Law	.25	.60
52 Rosevelt Colvin	.25	.60
Mike Vrabel		
53 Brian Waters	.20	.50
Casey Wiegmann RC		
Will Shields		
54 Chad Jackson	.20	.50
55 Bobby Wade	.20	.50
Tony Richardson		
56 Tedy Bruschi	.30	.75
57 Antoine Winfield	.20	.50
58 Jammal Brown	.20	.50
Jeff Faine		
Jon Stinchcomb		
59 Matt Light	.20	.50
Logan Mankins		
Dan Koppen		
60 Michael Strahan	.25	.60
61 Marques Colston	.30	.75
62 Johnnie Morant	.25	.60
Ronald Curry		
63 Will Demps	.20	.50
Gibril Wilson		
64 Warren Sapp	.25	.60
65 William Joseph	.20	.50
Fred Robbins		
Barry Cofield		
66 Chris Carr	.20	.50
Sebastian Janikowski		
Shane Lechler		
67 Cedric Houston	.20	.50
68 Nate Washington	.20	.50
69 Jonathan Vilma	.25	.60
70 Willie Parker	.25	.60
71 Sheldon Brown	.20	.50
Lito Sheppard		
72 Najeh Davenport	.20	.50
Charlie Batch		
Dan Kreider		
73 Jevon Kearse	.25	.60
74 Luis Castillo	.20	.50
Jamal Williams		
75 Darren Howard	.20	.50
Jerome McDougle		
Trent Cole		
76 Vernon Davis	.25	.60
77 Antonio Gates	.30	.75
78 Chris Gray	.20	.50
Chris Spencer		
Walter Jones		
79 Terrence Kiel	.20	.50
Drayton Florence		
Marlon McCree		
80 Victor Adeyanju	.20	.50
La'Roi Glover		
81 Ashley Lelie	.25	.60
82 Torry Holt	.25	.60
83 Maurice Morris	.20	.50
Mack Strong		
84 Jermaine Phillips	.20	.50
Will Allen		
Shelton Quarles		
85 Shaun Alexander	.25	.60
86 Vince Young	.25	.60
87 Orlando Pace	.20	.50
Alex Barron		
Andy McCollum		
88 Brandon Lloyd	.25	.60
89 Joey Galloway	.25	.60
90 Neil Rackers	.20	.50
Scott Player		
91 Peter Sirmon	.20	.50
David Thornton		
92 Bryant Johnson	.20	.50
93 Bo Scaife	.20	.50
Cortland Finnegan		
Reynaldo Hill		
94 John Abraham	.20	.50
95 Jason Campbell	.25	.60
96 Kelly Gregg	.25	.60
Bart Scott		
Haloti Ngata		
97 Adrian Wilson	.20	.50
98 Drew Carter	.20	.50
Keary Colbert		
99 Michael Jenkins	.25	.60
D.J. Shockley		
Roddy White		
100 Jake Delhomme	.25	.60
101 Terrell Suggs	.25	.60
Trevor Pryce		
102 Thomas Davis	.20	.50
James Anderson RC		
Dan Morgan		
103 Todd Heap	.20	.50
104 Bernard Berrian	.20	.50
105 Peerless Price	.20	.50
106 Chris Henry	.20	.50
107 Daimon Shelton	.20	.50
Robert Royal		
Ryan Neufeld		
108 Kellen Winslow	.25	.60
109 Rex Grossman	.25	.60
110 Kamerion Wimbley	.20	.50
D'Qwell Jackson		
Andra Davis		
111 Levi Jones	.20	.50
Willie Anderson		
112 Bradie James	.20	.50
Akin Ayodele		
113 Deltha O'Neal	.20	.50
114 Javon Walker	.25	.60
115 Jeremi Johnson	.20	.50
Doug Johnson		
Reggie Kelly		
116 Quincy Morgan	.20	.50
Jason Elam		
Paul Ernster		
117 Roy Williams S	.25	.60
118 Donald Driver	.30	.75
119 Miles Austin	.50	1.25
Mat McBriar		
Sam Hurd		
120 Dunta Robinson	.20	.50
Dexter McCleon		
121 Devale Ellis RC	.20	.50
Shaun McDonald		
122 Wali Lundy	.20	.50
123 Tatum Bell	.20	.50
124 Owen Daniels	.20	.50
Mark Bruener		
Jeb Putzier		
125 Marquand Manuel	.20	.50
Nick Collins		
Al Harris		
126 Morlon Greenwood	.20	.50
Shawn Barber		
Shantee Orr		
127 Ahman Green	.25	.60
128 Marvin Harrison	.30	.75
129 Josh Thomas	.20	.50
Corey Simon		
Raheem Brock		
130 Chris Naeole	.20	.50
Brad Meester		
Maurice Williams		
131 Marcus Stroud	.20	.50
John Henderson		
132 Kendrell Bell	.20	.50
Derrick Johnson		
133 Byron Leftwich	.25	.60
134 Trent Green	.25	.60
135 Samie Parker	.20	.50
136 Mewelde Moore	.20	.50
137 Chris Chambers	.25	.60
138 Chris Kluwe	.20	.50
Artrose Pinner		
Ryan Longwell		
139 Travis Daniels	.20	.50
Michael Lehan		
Keith Adams		
140 Richard Seymour	.20	.50
141 Jim Kleinsasser	.20	.50
Brooks Bollinger		
142 Fred Thomas	.20	.50
Mike McKenzie		
143 Darren Sharper	.25	.60
144 Will Smith	.20	.50
145 Ellis Hobbs	.20	.50
Asante Samuel		
Chad Scott		
146 Brian Simmons	.20	.50
Scott Shanle RC		
Scott Fujita		
147 Devery Henderson	.20	.50
148 Jeremy Shockey	.25	.60
149 Antonio Pierce	.20	.50
Reggie Torbor		
150 Zack Crockett	.20	.50
Justin Fargas		
151 Jerricho Cotchery	.25	.60
152 Dominic Rhodes	.25	.60
153 D'Brickashaw Ferguson	.20	.50
Nick Mangold		
Pete Kendall		
154 Nnamdi Asomugha	.30	.75
Fabian Washington		
Stuart Schweigart		
155 Andrew Walter	.20	.50
156 Cedrick Wilson	.20	.50
157 Dirk Johnson	.20	.50
David Akers		
Reno Mahe		
158 Troy Polamalu	.30	.75
159 Casey Hampton	.20	.50
Aaron Smith		
160 Alan Faneca	.20	.50
Max Starks		
Marvel Smith		
161 Shawne Merriman	.25	.60
162 Shaun Phillips	.20	.50
Randall Godfrey		
163 Jonas Jennings	.20	.50
Larry Allen		
Kwame Harris		
164 Nate Clements	.20	.50
165 Marcus Pollard	.20	.50
Seneca Wallace		
166 Marcus Trufant	.20	.50
Jordan Babineaux		
Kelly Jennings		
167 Nate Burleson	.20	.50
168 Isaac Bruce	.25	.60
169 Deion Branch	.25	.60
170 Alex Smith TE	.20	.50
Anthony Becht		
171 Brandon Chillar	.20	.50
Pisa Tinoisamoa		
Will Witherspoon		
172 Mark Jones	.20	.50
Matt Bryant		
Josh Bidwell		
173 Michael Clayton	.20	.50
174 LenDale White	.25	.60
175 Lamont Thompson	.20	.50
Chris Hope		
176 Chris Cooley	.25	.60
177 Santana Moss	.25	.60
178 Chike Okeafor	.20	.50
Bertrand Berry		
179 Chris Samuels	.20	.50
Jon Jansen		
Randy Thomas		
180 Matt Leinart	.25	.60
181 Michael Vick	.30	.75
182 Antrel Rolle	.20	.50
Roderick Hood		
Terrence Holt		
183 Michael Koenen	.20	.50
Morten Andersen		
Allen Rossum		
184 Joe Horn	.25	.60
185 Chris McAlister	.20	.50
Samari Rolle		
186 Steve McNair	.25	.60
187 Roscoe Parrish	.20	.50
188 Sam Koch	.20	.50
Jonathan Ogden		
Matt Stover		
189 J.P. Losman	.20	.50
190 John Kasay	.20	.50
Jason Baker RC		
191 Kiwaukee Thomas	.20	.50
Ko Simpson		
Donte Whitner		
192 Steve Smith WR	.25	.60
193 Cedric Benson	.25	.60
194 Rashied Davis	.20	.50
195 Bryan Robinson	.20	.50
Justin Smith		
196 Mark Bradley	.25	.60
Brian Griese		
Desmond Clark		
197 Dexter Jackson	.20	.50
Keiwan Ratliff		
Johnathan Joseph		
198 Carson Palmer	.25	.60
199 Joe Jurevicius	.20	.50
200 Willie McGinest	.20	.50
201 Terry Glenn	.25	.60
202 Joshua Cribbs	.30	.75
Phil Dawson		
Dave Zastudil		
203 DeMarcus Ware	.25	.60
Greg Ellis		
Marcus Spears		
204 Bobby Carpenter	.20	.50
Aaron Glenn		
205 Cory Redding	.20	.50
Shaun Rogers		
206 Champ Bailey	.25	.60
207 T.J. Duckett	.20	.50
208 Damien Woody	.20	.50
Dominic Raiola		
Jeff Backus		
209 Kevin Jones	.20	.50
210 Greg Jennings	.30	.75
211 Cullen Jenkins	.20	.50
Corey Williams		
Ryan Pickett		
212 Anthony Weaver	.20	.50
Jason Babin		
213 Andre Johnson	.25	.60
214 Kevin Walter	.25	.60
Jameel Cook		
Derrick Lewis		
215 Hunter Smith	.25	.60
Terrence Wilkins		
Adam Vinatieri		
216 Bob Sanders	.25	.60
217 Greg Jones	.25	.60
David Garrard		
218 Reggie Wayne	.25	.60
219 Fred Taylor	.25	.60
220 Eddie Kennison	.20	.50
221 Marty Booker	.20	.50
222 Jeff Webb	.20	.50
Rod Gardner		
Dustin Colquitt		
223 Ronnie Brown	.25	.60
224 Channing Crowder	.20	.50
Joey Porter		
225 Jason Allen	.20	.50
Renaldo Hill		
Yeremiah Bell		
226 Tarvaris Jackson	.20	.50
227 Kevin Williams	.20	.50
Pat Williams		
228 Kenechi Udeze	.20	.50
Darrion Scott		
Dwight Smith		
229 Tom Brady	.50	1.25
230 Roman Harper	.20	.50
Josh Bullocks		
231 James Sanders	.20	.50
Rodney Harrison		
Stephen Gostkowski		
232 Terrance Copper	.25	.60
233 Brandon Jacobs	.25	.60
234 Drew Brees	.30	.75
235 Bryan Thomas	.20	.50
Shaun Ellis		
236 Amani Toomer	.25	.60
237 Justin Miller	.20	.50
238 Jared Lorenzen	.25	.60
David Tyree		
Sinorice Moss		
239 Brad Smith	.20	.50
Chris Baker		
240 Derrick Burgess	.20	.50
Tyler Brayton		
241 Jerry Porter	.25	.60
242 Michael Huff	.25	.60
243 Jeremiah Trotter	.20	.50
244 Kirk Morrison	.20	.50
Sam Williams		
Thomas Howard		
245 Shawn Andrews	.20	.50
William Thomas		
Jon Runyan		
246 Santonio Holmes	.25	.60
247 Jerame Tuman	.20	.50
Heath Miller		
248 Eric Parker	.20	.50
249 Quentin Jammer	.20	.50
250 Marcus McNeill	.20	.50
Nick Hardwick		
Mike Goff RC		
251 Mark Roman	.20	.50
Jeff Ulbrich		
Shawntae Spencer		
252 Walt Harris	.20	.50
Michael Lewis		
253 LeRoy Hill	.25	.60
Lofa Tatupu		
254 Bryant Young	.20	.50
255 Darrell Jackson	.20	.50
256 Deon Grant	.20	.50
Brian Russell		
Michael Boulware		
257 Drew Bennett	.20	.50
258 Steven Jackson	.30	.75
259 Dane Looker	.20	.50
Gus Frerotte		
Corey Chavous		
260 Ike Hilliard	.20	.50
Michael Pittman		
261 Simeon Rice	.20	.50
262 Roydell Williams	.20	.50
263 Mark Brunell	.25	.60
James Thrash		
264 Ben Troupe	.20	.50
Kevin Mawae		
Erron Kinney		
265 Clinton Portis	.25	.60
266 Larry Fitzgerald	.30	.75
267 Carlos Rogers	.20	.50
Fred Smoot		
Shawn Springs		
268 Gerald Hayes	.20	.50
Calvin Pace		
Karlos Dansby		
269 Warrick Dunn	.25	.60
270 Keith Brooking	.20	.50
Brian Finneran		
271 Kynan Forney	.20	.50
Wayne Gandy		
Todd McClure		
272 Jerious Norwood	.25	.60
273 Josh Reed	.20	.50
Shaud Williams		
274 Willis McGahee	.25	.60
275 Terrence McGee	.20	.50
276 Ronnie Prude	.20	.50
Jarret Johnson		
Dawan Landry		
277 Lee Evans	.25	.60
278 Keyshawn Johnson	.25	.60
279 Jordan Gross	.20	.50
Mike Wahle		
Will Montgomery		
280 Alex Brown	.20	.50
Adewale Ogunleye		
281 Muhsin Muhammad	.25	.60
282 Olin Kreutz	.20	.50
John Tait		
Fred Miller		
283 Glenn Holt RC	.25	.60
Kyle Larson		
Shayne Graham		
284 Chris Perry	.20	.50
285 Derek Anderson	.20	.50
Ken Dorsey		
286 Chad Johnson	.25	.60
287 Charlie Frye	.25	.60
288 Orpheus Roye	.20	.50
Ted Washington		
Robaire Smith		
289 Jason Witten	.30	.75
290 Tony Romo	.40	1.00
291 D.J. Williams	.20	.50
Ian Gold		
Al Wilson		
292 Ebenezer Ekuban	.20	.50
Kenard Lang		
293 Paris Lenon	.20	.50
Boss Bailey		
294 Rod Smith	.25	.60
295 Mike Furrey	.25	.60
296 Nick Harris	.20	.50
Jason Hansen		
Eddie Drummond		
297 Robert Ferguson	.20	.50
298 Charles Woodson	.30	.75
299 Chad Clifton	.20	.50
Mark Tauscher		
Rob Davis		
300 Travis Johnson	.20	.50
C.C. Brown		
Glenn Earl		
301 Mario Williams	.25	.60
302 Anthony McFarland	.20	.50
Robert Mathis		
303 George Wrighster	.20	.50
Marcedes Lewis		
304 Joseph Addai	.25	.60
305 Maurice Jones-Drew	.30	.75
306 Ernest Wilford	.20	.50
307 Donovin Darius	.20	.50
Nick Griesen		
Mike Peterson		
308 Larry Johnson	.20	.50
309 Derek Hagan	.20	.50
310 Ron Edwards	.20	.50
James Reed		
Jimmy Wilkerson		
311 Zach Thomas	.25	.60
312 Vonnie Holliday	.20	.50
Keith Traylor		
313 Jason Rader	.20	.50
L.J. Shelton		
Cleo Lemon		
314 Chester Taylor	.20	.50
315 Jabar Gaffney	.20	.50
Reche Caldwell		
316 E.J. Henderson	.20	.50
Dontarrious Thomas		
Ben Leber		
317 Donte Stallworth	.25	.60
318 Jamie Martin	.20	.50
Mike Karney		
319 Hollis Thomas	.20	.50
Brian Young		
Charles Grant		
320 Reuben Droughns	.25	.60
321 Eli Manning	.30	.75
322 Corey Webster	.20	.50
R.W. McQuarters		
Sam Madison		
323 Erik Coleman	.20	.50
Kerry Rhodes		
324 Chad Pennington	.25	.60
325 DeWayne Robertson	.20	.50
Kimo Van Oelhoffen		
Andre Dyson		
326 Courtney Anderson	.20	.50
Robert Gallery		
Randal Williams		
327 Randy Moss	.30	.75
328 Brodrick Bunkley	.20	.50
Mike Patterson		
329 Correll Buckhalter	.25	.60
330 Donovan McNabb	.30	.75
331 Chris Gardocki	.20	.50
Jeff Reed		
332 Vincent Jackson	.25	.60
333 Ben Roethlisberger	.30	.75
334 Philip Rivers	.30	.75
335 Larry Foote	.20	.50
Clark Haggans		
James Farrior		
336 Billy Volek	.20	.50
Brandon Manumaleuna		
Nate Kaeding		
337 Alex Smith QB	.30	.75
338 Marques Douglas	.20	.50
Manny Lawson		
339 Maurice Hicks	.20	.50
Joe Nedney		
Andy Lee		
340 D.J. Hackett	.20	.50
341 Julian Peterson	.20	.50
342 Patrick Kerney	.20	.50
Bryce Fisher		
Rocky Bernard		
343 Randy McMichael	.20	.50
Joe Klopfenstein		
344 Leonard Little	.20	.50
345 Jeff Garcia	.25	.60
346 Cato June	.25	.60
Derrick Brooks		
347 Mike Alstott	.25	.60
348 Keith Bulluck	.20	.50
349 Kevin Carter	.20	.50
Greg Spires		
Chris Hovan		
350 Courtney Roby	.20	.50
Craig Hentrich		
Rob Bironas		
351 London Fletcher	.20	.50
Marcus Washington		
352 Edgerrin James	.25	.60
353 Antwaan Randle El	.20	.50
354 Kurt Warner	.25	.60
Gabe Watson		
Sean Morey		
355 Renaldo Wynn	.20	.50
Phillip Daniels		
Andre Carter		
356 Roy Williams WR	.25	.60
357 Alge Crumpler	.25	.60
358 Brian Dawkins	.25	.60
359 Chris Crocker	.20	.50
Lawyer Milloy		
Jimmy Williams		
360 Reggie Bush	.30	.75
361 Chris Kelsay	.20	.50
Angelo Crowell		
362 Sean Taylor	.30	.75
363 Aaron Schobel	.20	.50
364 Rock Cartwright	.20	.50
Ladell Betts		
Mike Sellers		
365 DeAngelo Williams	.30	.75
366 Grady Jackson	.20	.50
Rod Coleman		
367 David Carr	.25	.60
Brad Hoover		
Michael Gaines		
368 Derrick Mason	.25	.60
369 Brian Urlacher	.30	.75
370 Ray Lewis	.30	.75
371 Robert Geathers	.20	.50
Madieu Williams		
Landon Johnson		
372 Langston Walker	.20	.50
Jason Peters		
Derrick Dockery		
373 Jason Wright	.20	.50
Jerome Harrison		
374 Julius Peppers	.25	.60
375 Braylon Edwards	.25	.60
376 Lance Briggs	.25	.60
Mark Anderson		
377 Jay Cutler	.30	.75
378 Nathan Vasher	.20	.50
Charles Tillman		
Ricky Manning Jr		
379 Brandon Marshall	.25	.60
Daniel Graham		
Patrick Ramsey		
380 Rudi Johnson	.25	.60
381 Ernie Sims	.20	.50
382 Marion Barber	.30	.75
383 Bubba Franks	.75	2.00
Aaron Rodgers		
384 Terrell Owens	.30	.75
385 Vernand Morency	.25	.60
386 Brad Johnson	.25	.60
Anthony Fasano		
Patrick Crayton		
387 Nick Barnett	.20	.50
Will Blackmon		
Abdul Hodge		
388 John Engelberger	.20	.50
Elvis Dumervil		
389 DeMeco Ryans	.25	.60
390 John Lynch	.25	.60
391 Rashean Mathis	.20	.50
392 Shawn Bryson	.20	.50
Brian Calhoun		
Dan Campbell		
393 Brian Williams	.20	.50
Paul Spicer		
Reggie Hayward		
394 A.J. Hawk	.25	.60
395 Tamba Hali	.30	.75
Jared Allen		
396 Gary Brackett	.20	.50
Rob Morris		
397 Jason Taylor	.25	.60
398 Dwight Freeney	.25	.60
399 Donnie Spragan	.20	.50
Matt Roth		
Travares Tillman		
400 Marlin Jackson	.20	.50
Matt Giordano		
Antoine Bethea		
401 Ty Warren	.20	.50
Vince Wilfork		
402 Reggie Williams	.25	.60
403 Wes Welker	.30	.75
404 Tony Gonzalez	.25	.60
405 Laurence Maroney	.25	.60
406 Patrick Surtain	.20	.50
Greg Wesley		
Sammy Knight		
407 Steve Weatherford RC	.20	.50
Michael Lewis		
John Carney		
408 Will Allen	.20	.50
Andre Goodman		
409 Plaxico Burress	.25	.60
410 Troy Williamson	.20	.50
411 Victor Hobson	.20	.50
Eric Barton		
412 Ben Watson	.30	.75
Matt Cassell		
Kevin Faulk		
413 Justin McCareins	.20	.50
Mike Nugent		
Ben Graham		
414 Deuce McAllister	.25	.60
415 LaMont Jordan	.25	.60
416 Osi Umenyiora	.25	.60
Mathias Kiwanuka		
417 Reggie Brown	.20	.50
418 Shaun O'Hara	.20	.50
Kareem McKenzie		
Chris Snee		
419 Hines Ward	.30	.75
420 Leon Washington	.25	.60
421 Ike Taylor	.20	.50
Deshea Townsend		
Bryant McFadden		
422 Laveranues Coles	.20	.50
423 Lorenzo Neal	.30	.75
Michael Turner		
424 Dhani Jones	.20	.50
Takeo Spikes		
425 Frank Gore	.30	.75
426 Brian Westbrook	.25	.60
427 Michael Robinson	.25	.60
Moran Norris		
Trent Dilfer		
428 Kevin Curtis	.25	.60
Hank Baskett		
Greg Lewis		
429 Fakhir Brown	.20	.50
Tye Hill		
430 LaDainian Tomlinson	.30	.75
431 Marc Bulger	.25	.60
432 Matt Wilhelm	.20	.50
Igor Olshansky		
Antonio Cromartie		
433 Chris Simms	.20	.50
434 Derek Smith LB	.20	.50
Tully Banta-Cain		
435 Ronde Barber	.25	.60
Brian Kelly		
Phillip Buchanon		
436 Arnaz Battle	.20	.50
437 David Givens	.20	.50
438 Matt Hasselbeck	.25	.60
439 Cornelius Griffin	.20	.50
Roger McIntosh		
440 Dominique Byrd	.20	.50
Jeff Wilkins		
Aaron Walker		
441 JaMarcus Russell RC	.40	1.00
442 Brady Quinn RC	.60	1.50
443 Drew Stanton RC	.40	1.00
444 Troy Smith RC	.60	1.50
445 Kevin Kolb RC	1.00	2.50
446 Trent Edwards RC	.60	1.50
447 John Beck RC	.60	1.50
448 Jordan Palmer RC	.50	1.25
449 Chris Leak RC	.50	1.25
450 Isiah Stanback RC	.40	1.00
451 Tyler Palko RC	.50	1.25
452 Jared Zabransky RC	.50	1.25
453 Jeff Rowe RC	.40	1.00
454 Zac Taylor RC	.50	1.25
455 Lester Ricard RC	.50	1.25
456 Adrian Peterson RC	2.50	6.00
457 Marshawn Lynch RC	.60	1.50
458 Brandon Jackson RC	.50	1.25
459 Michael Bush RC	.60	1.50
460 Kenny Irons RC	.40	1.00
461 Antonio Pittman RC	.40	1.00
462 Tony Hunt RC	.40	1.00
463 Darius Walker RC	.40	1.00
464 Dwayne Wright RC	.50	1.25
465 Lorenzo Booker RC	.50	1.25
466 Kenneth Darby RC	.50	1.25
467 Chris Henry RC	.40	1.00
468 Selvin Young RC	.50	1.25
469 Brian Leonard RC	.50	1.25
470 Ahmad Bradshaw RC	1.00	2.50
471 Gary Russell RC	.50	1.25
472 Kolby Smith RC	.50	1.25
473 Thomas Clayton RC	.50	1.25
474 Garrett Wolfe RC	.40	1.00
475 Calvin Johnson RC	2.00	5.00
476 Ted Ginn Jr. RC	.50	1.25
477 Dwayne Jarrett RC	.50	1.25
478 Dwayne Bowe RC	.75	2.00
479 Sidney Rice RC	.75	2.00
480 Robert Meachem RC	.60	1.50
481 Anthony Gonzalez RC	.60	1.50
482 Craig Buster Davis RC	.50	1.25
483 Aundrae Allison RC	.40	1.00
484 Chansi Stuckey RC	.60	1.50
485 David Clowney RC	.50	1.25
486 Steve Smith RC	.60	1.50
487 Courtney Taylor RC	.50	1.25
488 Paul Williams RC	.40	1.00
489 Johnnie Lee Higgins RC	.50	1.25
490 Rhema McKnight RC	.40	1.00
491 Jason Hill RC	.60	1.50
492 Dallas Baker RC	.40	1.00
493 Greg Olsen RC	.50	1.25
494 Yamon Figurs RC	.40	1.00
495 Scott Chandler RC	.60	1.50
496 Matt Spaeth RC	.60	1.50
497 Ben Patrick RC	.50	1.25
498 Clark Harris RC	.50	1.25
499 Martrez Milner RC	.40	1.00
500 Joe Newton RC	.40	1.00
501 Alan Branch RC	.50	1.25
502 Amobi Okoye RC	.60	1.50
503 DeMarcus Tank Tyler RC	.40	1.00
504 Justin Harrell RC	.50	1.25
505 Brandon Mebane RC	.50	1.25
506 Gaines Adams RC	.60	1.50
507 Jamaal Anderson RC	.50	1.25
508 Adam Carriker RC	.50	1.25
509 Jarvis Moss RC	.50	1.25
510 Charles Johnson RC	.40	1.00
511 Anthony Spencer RC	.60	1.50
512 Quentin Moses RC	.50	1.25
513 LaMarr Woodley RC	.60	1.50
514 Victor Abiamiri RC	.60	1.50
515 Ray McDonald RC	.50	1.25
516 Tim Crowder RC	.60	1.50
517 Patrick Willis RC	1.25	3.00
518 Brandon Siler RC	.40	1.00
519 David Harris RC	.50	1.25
520 Buster Davis RC	.50	1.25
521 Lawrence Timmons RC	.60	1.50
522 Paul Posluszny RC	.60	1.50
523 Jon Beason RC	.50	1.25
524 Rufus Alexander RC	.50	1.25
525 Earl Everett RC	.50	1.25
526 Stewart Bradley RC	.50	1.25
527 Prescott Burgess RC	.50	1.25
528 Leon Hall RC	.50	1.25
529 Darrelle Revis RC	1.00	2.50
530 Aaron Ross RC	.60	1.50
531 Daymeion Hughes RC	.50	1.25
532 Marcus McCauley RC	.50	1.25
533 Chris Houston RC	.50	1.25
534 Tanard Jackson RC	.40	1.00
535 Jonathan Wade RC	.50	1.25
536 Josh Wilson RC	.50	1.25
537 Eric Wright RC	.60	1.50
538 A.J. Davis RC	.40	1.00
539 David Irons RC	.40	1.00
540 LaRon Landry RC	.60	1.50
541 Reggie Nelson RC	.50	1.25
542 Michael Griffin RC	.60	1.50
543 Brandon Meriweather RC	.60	1.50
544 Eric Weddle RC	.60	1.50
545 Aaron Rouse RC	.50	1.25
546 Josh Gattis RC	.40	1.00
547 Joe Thomas RC	.60	1.50
548 Levi Brown RC	.60	1.50
549 Tony Ugoh RC	.50	1.25
550 Ryan Kalil RC	.50	1.25

2007 Topps Total 1st Edition Copper

*1ST EDIT.VETS: 1.2X TO 3X BASIC CARDS
*1ST EDIT.ROOKIE: .5X TO 1.5X BASIC CARDS
1ST EDITION ODDS 1:2

2007 Topps Total Black

*BLACK VETS: 4X TO 10X BASIC CARDS
*BLACK ROOKIES: 2X TO 5X BASIC CARDS
BLACK/50 STATED ODDS 1:18

2007 Topps Total Blue

*BLUE VETS: 1.2X TO 3X BASIC CARDS
*BLUE ROOKIES: .6X TO 1.5X BASIC CARDS
BLUE STATED ODDS 1:2

2007 Topps Total Gold

*GOLD VETS: 3X TO 8X BASIC CARDS
*GOLD ROOKIES: 1.5X TO 4X BASIC CARDS
GOLD STATED ODDS 1:12

2007 Topps Total Red

*RED VETS: 1.5X TO 4X BASIC CARDS
*RED ROOKIES: .8X TO 2X BASIC CARDS
STATED ODDS 1:4

2007 Topps Total Silver

*SILVER VETS: 2X TO 5X BASIC CARDS
*SILVER ROOKIES: 1X TO 2.5X BASIC CARDS
STATED ODDS 1:6

2007 Topps Total Award Winners

STATED ODDS 1:8		
AW1 Indianapolis Colts	1.25	3.00
AW2 New Orleans Saints	.75	2.00
AW3 San Diego Chargers	.75	2.00
AW4 San Diego Chargers	.75	2.00
AW5 Cincinnati Bengals	.60	1.50
AW6 Dallas Cowboys	.75	2.00
AW7 San Diego Chargers	.60	1.50
AW8 Tennessee Titans	.60	1.50
AW9 Houston Texans	.60	1.50
AW10 New York Jets	.60	1.50
AW11 Miami Dolphins	.60	1.50
AW12 San Diego Chargers	.75	2.00
AW13 Denver Broncos	.60	1.50
AW14 Miami Dolphins	.60	1.50
AW15 Indianapolis Colts	1.25	3.00
AW16 Detroit Lions	.50	1.25
AW17 Indianapolis Colts	1.25	3.00
AW18 Houston Texans	.60	1.50
AW19 Philadelphia Eagles	.60	1.50
AW20 Minnesota Vikings	.50	1.25

2007 Topps Total Signatures

GROUP A ODDS 1:10,750		
GROUP B ODDS 1:2175		
GROUP C ODDS 1:400		
UNPRICED PRINT PLATES SER.#'d TO 1		
DW Darius Walker C	6.00	15.00
FG Frank Gore A	40.00	80.00
GJ Greg Jennings B	8.00	20.00
JC Jerricho Cotchery A	10.00	25.00
JH Jason Hill B	8.00	20.00
KJ Kevin Jones B	6.00	15.00
MC Marques Colston A		
MJ Maurice Jones-Drew A	10.00	25.00
SJ Steven Jackson A		
SS Steve Smith USC B	10.00	25.00
SY Selvin Young C	10.00	25.00
TJ Thomas Jones A		
TP Tyler Palko C	6.00	15.00
DWI DeAngelo Williams A		

2007 Topps Total Team Checklists

TC1 Matt Leinart	.40	1.00
TC2 Michael Vick	.50	1.25
TC3 Ray Lewis	.50	1.25
TC4 Lee Evans	.40	1.00
TC5 Steve Smith WR	.40	1.00
TC6 Brian Urlacher	.50	1.25
TC7 Chad Johnson	.40	1.00
TC8 Braylon Edwards	.40	1.00
TC9 Tony Romo	.60	1.50
TC10 Jay Cutler	.50	1.25
TC11 Roy Williams WR	.40	1.00
TC12 Brett Favre	1.00	2.50
TC13 Andre Johnson	.40	1.00
TC14 Peyton Manning	.75	2.00
TC15 Fred Taylor	.40	1.00
TC16 Larry Johnson	.30	.75
TC17 Ronnie Brown	.40	1.00
TC18 Chester Taylor	.30	.75
TC19 Tom Brady	.75	2.00
TC20 Reggie Bush	.50	1.25
TC21 Eli Manning	.50	1.25
TC22 Chad Pennington	.40	1.00
TC23 JaMarcus Russell	.30	.75
TC24 Donovan McNabb	.50	1.25
TC25 Willie Parker	.40	1.00
TC26 LaDainian Tomlinson	.50	1.25
TC27 Frank Gore	.50	1.25
TC28 Shaun Alexander	.40	1.00
TC29 Torry Holt	.40	1.00
TC30 Cadillac Williams	.40	1.00
TC31 Vince Young	.40	1.00
TC32 Clinton Portis	.40	1.00

2007 Topps Total Total Production

STATED ODDS 1:16
TP1 LaDainian Tomlinson .75 2.00
TP2 Peyton Manning 1.25 3.00
TP3 Carson Palmer .60 1.50
TP4 Drew Brees .75 2.00
TP5 Marc Bulger .60 1.50
TP6 Tom Brady 1.25 3.00
TP7 Eli Manning .75 2.00
TP8 Rex Grossman .60 1.50
TP9 Philip Rivers .75 2.00
TP10 Jon Kitna .50 1.25

2007 Topps Total Total Topps

STATED ODDS 1:8
TT1 Peyton Manning 1.25 3.00
TT2 Tom Brady 1.25 3.00
TT3 Carson Palmer .60 1.50
TT4 LaDainian Tomlinson .75 2.00
TT5 Shaun Alexander .60 1.50
TT6 Larry Johnson .50 1.25
TT7 Chad Johnson .60 1.50
TT8 Marvin Harrison .75 2.00
TT9 Steve Smith .60 1.50
TT10 Drew Brees .75 2.00
TT11 Donovan McNabb .75 2.00
TT12 Steven Jackson .75 2.00
TT13 Frank Gore .75 2.00
TT14 Torry Holt .60 1.50
TT15 Terrell Owens .75 2.00
TT16 Brett Favre 1.50 4.00
TT17 Willie Parker .60 1.50
TT18 Philip Rivers .75 2.00
TT19 Rudi Johnson .60 1.50
TT20 Roy Williams WR .60 1.50

2010 Topps Tribute

1 Drew Brees 1.50 4.00
2 Ray Lewis 1.50 4.00
3 Devin McCourty RC 1.25 3.00
4 Tony Romo 2.00 5.00
5 Percy Harvin 1.50 4.00
6 Joe Namath 2.00 5.00
7 Ahmad Bradshaw 1.25 3.00
8 John Conner RC 1.25 3.00
9 Sean Weatherspoon RC 1.25 3.00
10 Chris Johnson 1.50 4.00
11 Arian Foster 1.25 3.00
12 Kyle Wilson RC 1.25 3.00
13 Arrelious Benn RC 1.25 3.00
14 Anquan Boldin 1.25 3.00
15 LaDainian Tomlinson 1.50 4.00
16 Kareem Jackson RC 1.25 3.00
17 LeGarrette Blount RC 2.00 5.00
18 Rashard Mendenhall 1.25 3.00
19 Chris Ivory RC 1.50 4.00
20 Sam Bradford RC 8.00 20.00
21 Anthony Dixon RC 1.25 3.00
22 Dan Marino 3.00 8.00
23 Rob Gronkowski RC 3.00 8.00
24 Mark Sanchez 1.50 4.00
25 Eric Dickerson 1.25 3.00
26 Chad Ochocinco 1.25 3.00
27 Eli Manning 1.50 4.00
28 Jason Pierre-Paul RC 2.00 5.00
29 Miles Austin 1.50 4.00
30 Frank Gore 1.25 3.00
31 Jimmy Clausen RC 1.25 3.00
32 Patrick Robinson RC 1.25 3.00
33 DeSean Jackson 1.25 3.00
34 Derrick Morgan RC 1.00 2.50
35 Troy Polamalu 1.50 4.00
36 Franco Harris 1.50 4.00
37 Jerry Hughes RC 1.25 3.00
38 Aaron Hernandez RC 2.00 5.00
39 Emmitt Smith 2.50 6.00
40 Adrian Peterson 2.50 6.00
41 Tyson Alualu RC 1.00 2.50
42 Michael Turner 1.00 2.50
43 T.J. Ward RC 1.25 3.00
44 Jordan Shipley RC 1.25 3.00
45 Michael Vick 2.00 5.00
46 Jahvid Best RC 2.00 5.00
47 Larry Fitzgerald 1.50 4.00
48 Austin Collie 1.25 3.00
49 Darrelle Revis 1.25 3.00
50 Tim Tebow RC 10.00 20.00
51 Reggie Wayne 1.25 3.00
52 Donovan McNabb 1.50 4.00
53 Joe Haden RC 1.25 3.00
54 Gale Sayers 2.00 5.00
55 Rolando McClain RC 1.25 3.00
56 Patrick Willis 1.25 3.00
57 John Elway 2.50 6.00
58 Jermaine Gresham RC 1.50 4.00
59 Eric Berry RC 1.25 3.00
60 Peyton Manning 2.50 6.00
61 Brandon Marshall 1.25 3.00
62 Ndamukong Suh RC 2.50 6.00
63 Joe Montana 3.00 8.00
64 Colt McCoy RC 2.50 6.00
65 LeSean McCoy 1.25 3.00
66 Kyle Orton 1.25 3.00
67 Steve Young 2.00 5.00
68 Hakeem Nicks 1.25 3.00
69 Steven Jackson 1.25 3.00
70 Maurice Jones-Drew 1.25 3.00
71 Troy Aikman 2.00 5.00
72 Tony Dorsett 1.50 4.00
73 Mike Williams RC 2.00 5.00
74 Ryan Mathews RC 2.50 6.00
75 Wes Welker 1.50 4.00
76 Thurman Thomas 1.50 4.00
77 Nate Allen RC 1.25 3.00
78 Max Hall RC 1.25 3.00
79 Dallas Clark 1.25 3.00
80 Dez Bryant RC 4.00 10.00
81 Brett Favre 4.00 10.00
82 Roger Staubach 2.00 5.00
83 Toby Gerhart RC 1.25 3.00
84 Ray Rice 1.25 3.00
85 Calvin Johnson 1.50 4.00
86 Demaryius Thomas RC 1.50 4.00
87 Joe Flacco 1.50 4.00
88 C.J. Spiller RC 2.00 5.00
89 Philip Rivers 1.50 4.00
90 Tom Brady 2.50 6.00
91 Golden Tate RC 1.25 3.00
92 Dexter McCluster RC 1.25 3.00
93 Matt Ryan 1.50 4.00
94 Earl Campbell 1.50 4.00
95 Gerald McCoy RC 1.25 3.00
96 Matt Schaub 1.25 3.00
97 Earl Thomas RC 1.25 3.00
98 Andre Johnson 1.25 3.00
99 Terrell Owens 1.50 4.00
100 Aaron Rodgers 2.00 5.00

2010 Topps Tribute Black

*VETS: .8X TO 2X BASIC CARDS
*ROOKIES: .8X TO 2X BASIC CARDS
BLACK PRINT RUN 75 SER.#'d SETS

2010 Topps Tribute Blue

*VETS: .8X TO 2X BASIC CARDS
*ROOKIES: .8X TO 2X BASIC CARDS
BLUE PRINT RUN 89 SER.#'d SETS

2010 Topps Tribute Gold

*VETS: 2X TO 5X BASIC CARDS
*ROOKIES: 2.5X TO 6X BASIC CARDS
GOLD PRINT RUN 20 SER.#'d SETS
20 Sam Bradford 60.00 100.00
50 Tim Tebow 60.00 120.00

2010 Topps Tribute Green

*VETS: 1X TO 2.5X BASIC CARDS
*ROOKIES: 1X TO 2.5X BASIC CARDS
GREEN PRINT RUN 50 SER.#'d SETS

2010 Topps Tribute Autographed Dual Relics

DUAL JSY AUTO PRINT RUN 20-99
*BLACK/30: .5X TO 1.2X BASIC INSERT/55-99
*BLACK/30: .4X TO 1X BASIC INSERT/20
*BLUE/50: .4X TO 1X BASIC INSERT/55-99
EXCH EXPIRATION: 1/31/2014
ADRAB Arrelious Benn/55 8.00 20.00
ADRABE Arrelious Benn/55 8.00 20.00
ADRAD Anthony Dixon/99 8.00 20.00
ADRAH Aaron Hernandez/99 12.00 30.00
ADRBL Brandon LaFell/60 8.00 20.00
ADRBLA Brandon LaFell/99 8.00 20.00
ADRBT Ben Tate/55 10.00 25.00
ADRBTA Ben Tate/55 10.00 25.00
ADRCM Colt McCoy/20 50.00 100.00
ADRCMI Carlton Mitchell/99 6.00 15.00
ADRCP Clinton Portis/20 15.00 40.00
ADRCS C.J. Spiller/20 15.00 40.00
ADRCSP C.J. Spiller/20 15.00 40.00
ADRDB Drew Brees/20 40.00 80.00
ADRDM Dexter McCluster/60 8.00 20.00
ADRDMC Dexter McCluster/55 8.00 20.00
ADRDT Demaryius Thomas/20 25.00 50.00
ADRDTH Demaryius Thomas/20 25.00 50.00
ADRDW Damian Williams/55 8.00 20.00
ADRDWI Damian Williams/55 8.00 20.00
ADREB Eric Berry/55 8.00 20.00
ADREM Eli Manning/20 50.00 100.00
ADRFH Franco Harris/20 30.00 60.00
ADRGTA Golden Tate/55 8.00 20.00
ADRJB Jahvid Best/20 15.00 40.00
ADRJBE Jahvid Best/20 15.00 40.00
ADRJC Jimmy Clausen/20 10.00 25.00
ADRJD Jonathan Dwyer/99 8.00 20.00
ADRJDW Jonathan Dwyer/99 8.00 20.00
ADRJF Joe Flacco/55 20.00 40.00
ADRJG Jermaine Gresham/55 6.00 15.00
ADRJGR Jermaine Gresham/55 6.00 15.00
ADRJK Johnny Knox/60 10.00 25.00
ADRJN Joe Namath/20 50.00 100.00
ADRJS Jordan Shipley/99 8.00 20.00
ADRJSH Jordan Shipley/99 8.00 20.00
ADRJST James Starks/99 12.00 30.00
ADRKS Ken Stabler/20 30.00 60.00
ADRLT LaDainian Tomlinson/20 20.00 50.00
ADRMF Matt Forte/20 12.00 30.00
ADRMG Mardy Gilyard EXCH 8.00 20.00
ADRMH Montario Hardesty/55 8.00 20.00
ADRMHA Montario Hardesty/55 8.00 20.00
ADRMK Mike Kafka/55 6.00 15.00
ADRMKA Mike Kafka/55 6.00 15.00
ADRNS Ndamukong Suh/20 40.00 80.00
ADRNSU Ndamukong Suh/20 40.00 80.00
ADRPM Peyton Manning/20 100.00 200.00
ADRRC Riley Cooper/99 8.00 20.00
ADRRG Rob Gronkowski/99 30.00 60.00
ADRRM Ryan Mathews/20 20.00 50.00
ADRRMA Ryan Mathews/20 20.00 50.00
ADRSB Sam Bradford/20 100.00 200.00
ADRSC Sean Canfield/60 6.00 15.00
ADRSY Steve Young/20 50.00 100.00
ADRTG Toby Gerhart/55 8.00 20.00
ADRTGE Toby Gerhart/55 8.00 20.00
ADRTP Taylor Price/99 8.00 20.00
ADRTPR Taylor Price/99 8.00 20.00
ADRTT Tim Tebow/20 125.00 200.00
ADRTTH Thurman Thomas/20 20.00 50.00

2010 Topps Tribute Autographed Dual Relics Gold

*GOLD/15: .5X TO 1.2X BASIC INSERT/55-99
*GOLD/15: .4X TO 1X BASIC INSERT/20
GOLD PRINT RUN 15 SER.#'d SETS
ADRBF Brett Favre 125.00 250.00
ADRER Ed Reed 40.00 80.00
ADRES Emmitt Smith 125.00 200.00
ADRKK Kevin Kolb 20.00 40.00
ADRRL Ray Lewis 40.00 80.00

2010 Topps Tribute Autographed Quad Relics

*QUAD JSY AU: .4X TO 1X DUAL JSY AU
QUAD JSY AUTO PRINT RUN 20-99
*BLACK/30: .5X TO 1.2X BASIC INSERT/55-99
*BLUE/50: .4X TO 1X BASIC INSERT/55-99
*GOLD/15: .5X TO 1.2X BASIC INSERT/55-99
*GOLD/15: .4X TO 1X BASIC INSERT/20
EXCH EXPIRATION: 1/31/2014
AQRDR Darrelle Revis/20 20.00 40.00
AQRGMC Gerald McCoy/55 8.00 20.00

2010 Topps Tribute Autographed Triple Relics

*TRIPLE JSY AU: .4X TO 1X DUAL JSY AU
TIPLE JSY AUTO PRINT RUN 20-99
*BLACK/30: .5X TO 1.2X BASIC TRIPLE/55-99
*BLACK/30: .4X TO 1X BASIC TRIPLE/20
*BLUE/50: .4X TO 1X BASIC TRIPLE/55-99
*GOLD/15: .5X TO 1.2X BASIC TRIPLE/55-99
*GOLD/15: .4X TO 1X BASIC TRIPLE/20
EXCH EXPIRATION: 1/31/2014
ATRDR Darrelle Revis/20 20.00 40.00
ATRDRE David Reed/99 6.00 15.00
ATREC Earl Campbell/20 30.00 60.00
ATRED Eric Decker/99 10.00 25.00
ATREDK Eric Decker/99 10.00 25.00
ATRJSK John Skelton/99 8.00 20.00

2010 Topps Tribute Dual Autographs

STATED PRINT RUN 20 SER.#'d SETS
DABS Jahvid Best 25.00 60.00
  C.J. Spiller
DABT Sam Bradford 200.00 350.00
  Tim Tebow
DADB Eric Dickerson 100.00 200.00
  Sam Bradford
DAET John Elway 200.00 350.00
  Tim Tebow
DAGD Frank Gore 25.00 60.00
  Anthony Dixon
DAHG Aaron Hernandez 50.00 100.00
  Rob Gronkowski
DAMM Peyton Manning 100.00 200.00
  Eli Manning
DAMS Dexter McCluster 30.00 80.00
  C.J. Spiller
DATM Demaryius Thomas 15.00 40.00
  Dexter McCluster

2010 Topps Tribute Dual Player Relics

STATED PRINT RUN 15 SER.#'d SETS
DCRBM Tom Brady
  Randy Moss
DCRBR Drew Brees 20.00 50.00
  Aaron Rodgers
DCRBT Dez Bryant 12.00 30.00
  Demaryius Thomas
DCRET John Elway 40.00 80.00
  Tim Tebow
DCRFP Brett Favre 30.00 60.00
  Adrian Peterson
DCRGD Frank Gore
  Anthony Dixon
DCRBSP Jahvid Best
  C.J. Spiller

2010 Topps Tribute Relic Dual Swatch

STATED PRINT RUN 45 SER.#'d SETS
*BLACK/15: .5X TO 1.2X BASIC DUAL JSY/45
*BLUE/30: .4X TO 1X BASIC DUAL JSY/45
*QUAD JSY/45: .4X TO 1X BASIC DUAL JSY/45
*QUAD BLACK/15: .5X TO 1.2X DUAL JSY/45
*QUAD BLUE/30: .4X TO 1X DUAL JSY/45
DRAB Arrelious Benn 4.00 10.00
DRAR Aaron Rodgers 12.00 30.00
DRBC Brent Celek 6.00 15.00
DRBL Brandon LaFell 4.00 10.00
DRBR Ben Roethlisberger 8.00 20.00
DRBT Ben Tate 5.00 12.00
DRCC Chris Cooley 6.00 15.00
DRCM Colt McCoy 8.00 20.00
DRCS C.J. Spiller 6.00 15.00
DRCSP C.J. Spiller 6.00 15.00
DRDB Dez Bryant 12.00 30.00
DRDBR Dez Bryant 12.00 30.00
DRDM Dexter McCluster 4.00 10.00
DRDMC Dexter McCluster 4.00 10.00
DRDT Demaryius Thomas 5.00 12.00
DRDTH Demaryius Thomas 5.00 12.00
DRDW Damian Williams 4.00 10.00
DREB Eric Berry 4.00 10.00
DREM Eli Manning 8.00 20.00
DRGT Golden Tate 4.00 10.00
DRJB Jahvid Best 8.00 20.00
DRJBE Jahvid Best 8.00 20.00
DRJC Jimmy Clausen 4.00 10.00
DRJCL Jimmy Clausen 4.00 10.00
DRJD Jonathan Dwyer 4.00 10.00
DRJG Jermaine Gresham 5.00 12.00
DRJGR Jermaine Gresham 5.00 12.00
DRJS Jordan Shipley 4.00 10.00
DRMC Matt Cassel 6.00 15.00
DRMH Montario Hardesty 4.00 10.00
DRMJD Maurice Jones-Drew 6.00 15.00
DRRG Rob Gronkowski 10.00 25.00
DRRM Ryan Mathews 8.00 20.00
DRRMA Ryan Mathews 8.00 20.00
DRRMO Randy Moss 8.00 20.00
DRSB Sam Bradford 15.00 40.00
DRSBR Sam Bradford 15.00 40.00
DRSM Santana Moss 6.00 15.00
DRTG Toby Gerhart 4.00 10.00
DRTT Tim Tebow 15.00 40.00
DRTTE Tim Tebow 15.00 40.00

2010 Topps Tribute Relic Triple Swatch

*TRIPLE JSY/45: .4X TO 1X DUAL JSY/45
STATED PRINT RUN 45 SER.#'d SETS
*BLACK/15: .5X TO 1.2X BASIC DUAL JSY/45
*BLUE/30: .4X TO 1X BASIC DUAL JSY/45
TRKK Kevin Kolb 6.00 15.00

2006 Topps Triple Threads

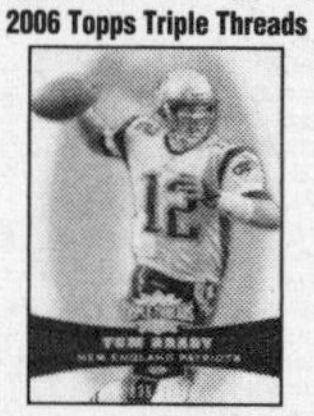

This 149-card set was released in January, 2007. This set was issued into the hobby in six-card packs, with an $100 SRP, which came 2 packs to a box. Cards numbered 1-100 feature veterans while cards numbered 102-150 are 2006 with both player-worn jersey swatches and signatures. The veteran cards were issued to a stated print run of 1199 serial numbered sets while cards numbered 102-150 were issued to a stated print run of 99 serial numbered sets. Interesting, card number 101, which was intended to be Vince Young, was never released.

COMP.SET w/o RC's (100) 75.00 150.00
1-100 PRINT RUN 1199 SER.#'d SETS
JSY AU/99 ROOKIE ODDS 1:8
JSY AU ROOKIE PRINT RUN 99 SER.#'d SETS
UNPRICED PRINT PLATE PRINT RUN 1
1 Shaun Alexander 1.25 3.00
2 Carson Palmer 1.50 4.00
3 Randy Moss 1.50 4.00
4 Dan Marino 4.00 10.00
5 Terrell Owens 1.50 4.00
6 Trent Green 1.25 3.00
7 Brian Westbrook 1.25 3.00
8 Terry Bradshaw 3.00 8.00
9 Steven Jackson 1.50 4.00
10 Emmitt Smith 4.00 10.00
11 Ben Roethlisberger 2.00 5.00
12 Daunte Culpepper 1.25 3.00
13 Edgerrin James 1.25 3.00
14 Santana Moss 1.25 3.00
15 Larry Johnson 1.25 3.00
16 Johnny Unitas 3.00 8.00
17 Eric Moulds 1.00 2.50
18 LaDainian Tomlinson 1.50 4.00
19 Donovan McNabb 1.50 4.00
20 Fred Taylor 1.25 3.00
21 Hines Ward 1.50 4.00
22 Eli Manning 2.00 5.00
23 Tatum Bell 1.00 2.50
24 Donald Driver 1.50 4.00
25 Drew Bledsoe 1.50 4.00
26 Clinton Portis 1.50 4.00
27 Tony Gonzalez 1.25 3.00
28 Plaxico Burress 1.25 3.00
29 Shawne Merriman 1.25 3.00
30 Cadillac Williams 1.25 3.00
31 Larry Fitzgerald 1.50 4.00
32 Jake Plummer 1.25 3.00
33 Willis McGahee 1.25 3.00
34 Joe Namath 2.50 6.00
35 Ahman Green 1.25 3.00
36 Marvin Harrison 1.50 4.00
37 Ronnie Brown 1.50 4.00
38 Joe Montana 4.00 10.00
39 Deuce McAllister 1.25 3.00
40 Philip Rivers 1.50 4.00
41 Marion Barber 1.25 3.00
42 Chris Chambers 1.25 3.00
43 Jason Witten 1.50 4.00
44 Brett Favre 3.00 8.00
45 Anquan Boldin 1.25 3.00
46 Tiki Barber 1.50 4.00
47 Byron Leftwich 1.25 3.00
48 Steve Smith 1.50 4.00
49 Willie Parker 1.25 3.00
50 Darrell Jackson 1.25 3.00
51 David Carr 1.00 2.50
52 Chris Brown 1.00 2.50
53 Aaron Brooks 1.25 3.00
54 Donte Stallworth 1.00 2.50
55 Michael Vick 1.50 4.00
56 Curtis Martin 1.50 4.00
57 T.J. Houshmandzadeh 1.25 3.00
58 Steve McNair 1.25 3.00
59 Reggie Wayne 1.25 3.00
60 DeShaun Foster 1.25 3.00
61 Chad Johnson 1.25 3.00
62 Domanick Davis 1.00 2.50
63 Braylon Edwards 1.25 3.00
64 Drew Brees 1.50 4.00
65 Kevin Jones 1.00 2.50
66 Alge Crumpler 1.25 3.00
67 Lee Evans 1.25 3.00
68 Matt Hasselbeck 1.25 3.00
69 Jamal Lewis 1.25 3.00
70 Aaron Rodgers 3.00 8.00
71 Joey Galloway 1.25 3.00
72 LaMont Jordan 1.25 3.00
73 Mark Brunell 1.25 3.00
74 Torry Holt 1.25 3.00
75 Chester Taylor 1.25 3.00
76 Jake Delhomme 1.25 3.00
77 Doak Walker 2.00 5.00
78 Corey Dillon 1.25 3.00
79 Antonio Gates 1.50 4.00
80 Marc Bulger 1.25 3.00
81 Walter Payton 4.00 10.00
82 Mark Clayton 1.25 3.00
83 Brian Urlacher 1.50 4.00
84 Julius Jones 1.00 2.50
85 Tom Brady 2.50 6.00
86 Joe Horn 1.25 3.00
87 John Elway 3.00 8.00
88 Reggie Brown 1.00 2.50
89 Warrick Dunn 1.25 3.00
90 Charlie Frye 1.25 3.00
91 Isaac Bruce 1.25 3.00
92 Jim Thorpe 2.50 6.00
93 Drew Bennett 1.25 3.00
94 Brad Johnson 1.25 3.00
95 Chad Pennington 1.25 3.00
96 Andre Johnson 1.50 4.00
97 Todd Heap 1.25 3.00
98 Rudi Johnson 1.25 3.00
99 Jeremy Shockey 1.50 4.00
100 Peyton Manning 2.50 6.00
102 A.J. Hawk JSY AU RC 15.00 40.00
103 Reggie Bush JSY AU RC 40.00 100.00
104 Matt Leinart JSY AU RC 15.00 40.00
105 Mario Williams JSY AU RC 15.00 40.00
106 Santonio Holmes JSY AU RC 20.00 50.00
107 DeAngelo Williams JSY AU RC 20.00 50.00
108 Jay Cutler JSY AU RC 40.00 100.00
109 Jerious Norwood JSY AU RC 12.00 30.00
110 Chad Jackson JSY AU RC 10.00 25.00
111 Tarvaris Jackson JSY AU RC 15.00 40.00
112 Brian Calhoun JSY AU RC 10.00 25.00
113 Laurence Maroney JSY AU RC 12.00 30.00
114 Maurice Stovall JSY AU RC 10.00 25.00
115 Travis Wilson JSY AU RC 10.00 25.00
116 Omar Jacobs JSY AU RC 10.00 25.00
117 Michael Huff JSY AU RC 12.00 30.00
118 Brandon Williams JSY AU RC 10.00 25.00
119 Kellen Clemens JSY AU RC 12.00 30.00
120 Jason Avant JSY AU RC 10.00 25.00
121 Michael Robinson JSY AU RC 12.00 30.00
122 Marcedes Lewis JSY AU RC 15.00 40.00
123 Brandon Marshall JSY AU RC 15.00 40.00
124 Vernon Davis JSY AU RC 20.00 50.00
125 Demetrius Williams JSY AU RC 12.00 30.00
126 Charlie Whitehurst JSY AU RC 15.00 40.00
127 Sinorice Moss JSY AU RC 15.00 40.00
128 Maurice Drew JSY AU RC 25.00 60.00
129 Derek Hagan JSY AU RC 12.00 30.00
130 Leon Washington JSY AU RC 12.00 30.00
131 Joseph Addai JSY AU RC 15.00 40.00
132 Joe Klopfenstein JSY AU RC 10.00 25.00
133 LenDale White JSY AU RC 12.00 30.00
134 Anthony Fasano JSY AU RC 15.00 40.00
135 Mike Bell JSY AU RC 15.00 40.00
136 Will Blackmon JSY AU RC 12.00 30.00
137 Bruce Gradkowski JSY AU RC 15.00 40.00
138 Marques Hagans JSY AU RC 10.00 25.00
139 Jerome Harrison JSY AU RC 15.00 40.00
140 Devin Hester JSY AU RC 25.00 60.00
141 Greg Jennings JSY AU RC 25.00 60.00
142 Mathias Kiwanuka JSY AU RC 15.00 40.00
143 Ingle Martin JSY AU RC 12.00 30.00
144 Willie Reid JSY AU RC 12.00 30.00
145 Cory Rodgers JSY AU RC 15.00 40.00
146 Brad Smith JSY AU RC 15.00 40.00
147 Hank Baskett JSY AU RC 15.00 40.00
148 Kamerion Wimbley JSY AU RC 15.00 40.00
149 DeMeco Ryans JSY AU RC 15.00 40.00
150 David Anderson JSY AU RC 12.00 30.00

2006 Topps Triple Threads Emerald

*VETS 1-100: .6X TO 1.5X BASIC CARDS
*RETIRED: .6X TO 1.5X BASIC CARDS
1-100 #'d OF 199 STATED ODDS 1:2
1-100 PRINT RUN 199 SER.#'d SETS
*ROOKIE JSY AU: .5X TO 1.2X BASIC CARDS
ROOKIE JSY AU/50 ODDS 1:16
ROOKIE PRINT RUN 50 SER.#'d SETS
101 Vince Young JSY AU 40.00 100.00

2006 Topps Triple Threads Gold

*VETS 1-100: .8X TO 2X BASIC CARDS
*RETIRED: .8X TO 2X BASIC CARDS
1-100 #'d OF 99 STATED ODDS 1:2
VETERANS PRINT RUN 99 SER.#'d SETS
*ROOKIE JSY AU: .8X TO 2X BASIC CARDS
ROOKIE JSY AU/25 STATED ODDS 1:32
ROOKIES PRINT RUN 25 SER.#'d SETS
101 Vince Young JSY AU 60.00 150.00

2006 Topps Triple Threads Platinum

VETERANS STATED ODDS 1:399
ROOKIES STATED ODDS 1:798
UNPRICED PLATINUM PRINT RUN 1

2006 Topps Triple Threads Sapphire

*VETS 1-100: 2X TO 5X BASIC CARDS
*RETIRED: 2X TO 5X BASIC CARDS
1-100 #'d OF 25 STATED ODDS 1:16
VETERANS PRINT RUN 25 SER.#'d SETS
UNPRICED ROOKIE JSY AU/10 ODDS 1:79
ROOKIES PRINT RUN 10 SER.#'d SETS

2006 Topps Triple Threads Sepia

*VETS 1-100: .5X TO 1.2X BASIC CARDS
*RETIRED 1-100: .5X TO 1.2X BASIC CARDS
1-100 PRINT RUN 499 SER.#'d SETS
*ROOKIE JSY AU: .5X TO 1.2X BASIC CARDS
ROOKIE JSY AU/75 ODDS 1:11
ROOKIES PRINT RUN 75 SER.#'d SETS
101 Vince Young JSY AU 30.00 100.00

2006 Topps Triple Threads Autographed Relic Combos Red

RED/36 STATED ODDS 1:94
RED PRINT RUN 36 SER.#'d SETS
*SEPIA/27: .5X TO 1.2X RED/36
SEPIA/27 STATED ODDS 1:127
SEPIA PRINT RUN 27 SER.#'d SETS
*EMERALD/18: .5X TO 1.2X RED/36
EMERALD/18 STATED ODDS 1:182
EMERALD PRINT RUN 18 SER.#'d SETS
UNPRICED GOLD/9 ODDS 1:368
GOLD PRINT RUN 9 SER.#'d SETS
UNPRICED SAPPHIRE/3 ODDS 1:1136
SAPPHIRE PRINT RUN 3 SER.#'d SETS
UNPRICED PLATINUM 1/1 ODDS 1:3126
UNPRICED PRINT.PLATE 1/1 ODDS 1:1137
1 Matt Leinart 40.00 100.00
  Reggie Bush
  LenDale White
2 Joe Klopfenstein 30.00 80.00
  Marcedes Lewis
  Vernon Davis
3 Sinorice Moss 25.00 60.00
  Santonio Holmes
  Derek Hagan
4 Brian Calhoun 30.00 80.00
  Laurence Maroney
  Joseph Addai
5 Mario Williams 50.00 120.00
  Reggie Bush
  Vince Young
6 Peyton Manning 125.00 250.00
  Marvin Harrison
  Joseph Addai
7 Joe Namath 125.00 250.00
  Peyton Manning
  Eli Manning
8 Brett Favre 300.00 500.00
  John Elway
  Dan Marino
9 LaDainian Tomlinson 50.00 120.00
  Philip Rivers
  Shawne Merriman
10 Omar Jacobs 25.00 60.00
  Tarvaris Jackson
  Kellen Clemens
11 Vernon Davis 30.00 80.00
  Charlie Whitehurst
  Leon Washington
12 Vince Young 40.00 100.00
  Michael Huff
  Chris Simms

2006 Topps Triple Threads Autographed Relic Red

RED/18 STATED ODDS 1:15
RED PRINT RUN 18 SER.#'d SETS
*GOLD/9: .6X TO 1.2X RED/18
GOLD/9 STATED ODDS 1:28
GOLD PRINT RUN 9 SER.#'d SETS
UNPRICED SAPPHIRE/3 ODDS 1:83
SAPPHIRE PRINT RUN 3 SER.#'d SETS
UNPRICED PLATINUM/1 ODDS 1:248
UNPRICED PRINT PLATE/1 ODDS 1:62
EACH PLAYER HAS 3 CARDS PRICED EQUALLY
1 Peyton Manning 125.00 225.00
4 LaDainian Tomlinson 25.00 60.00
7 Michael Vick 40.00 80.00
10 Emmitt Smith 125.00 250.00
13 Matt Leinart 20.00 50.00
16 Reggie Bush 40.00 100.00
19 Vince Young 30.00 80.00
22 Chad Johnson 20.00 40.00
25 A.J. Hawk 40.00 80.00
28 Eli Manning 60.00 120.00
31 Steve Smith 20.00 40.00
34 LenDale White 20.00 40.00
37 Santonio Holmes 30.00 60.00
40 Mario Williams 20.00 40.00
43 Vernon Davis 20.00 50.00
46 Sinorice Moss 15.00 30.00
49 Joe Namath 75.00 150.00
52 Chad Jackson 15.00 30.00
55 DeAngelo Williams 25.00 60.00
58 Laurence Maroney 15.00 40.00
61 Brett Favre 125.00 250.00
64 Joe Montana 100.00 200.00
67 Dan Marino 125.00 250.00
70 John Elway 100.00 200.00
73 Jim Kelly 50.00 100.00
76 Eric Dickerson 50.00 100.00
79 Shawne Merriman 20.00 40.00
82 Rudi Johnson 20.00 40.00
85 Marc Bulger 20.00 40.00
88 Chris Brown 12.50 25.00
91 Tatum Bell 15.00 30.00
94 Brian Calhoun 15.00 30.00
97 Maurice Drew 30.00 80.00
100 Derek Hagan 15.00 30.00
103 Michael Huff 15.00 30.00
106 Tarvaris Jackson 15.00 30.00
109 Joseph Addai 20.00 40.00
112 Jay Cutler 50.00 120.00
115 Maurice Stovall 20.00 40.00
118 Demetrius Williams 15.00 30.00
121 Kellen Clemens 20.00 40.00
124 Omar Jacobs 15.00 30.00
127 Brandon Marshall 15.00 40.00
130 Michael Robinson 15.00 30.00
133 Brandon Williams 20.00 40.00
136 Jerious Norwood 20.00 40.00
139 Travis Wilson 20.00 40.00
142 Jason Avant 15.00 30.00
145 Marcedes Lewis 15.00 30.00
148 Mike Bell 15.00 30.00
151 Joe Klopfenstein 12.50 25.00
154 Charlie Whitehurst 20.00 40.00
157 Larry Johnson 20.00 40.00
160 Philip Rivers 40.00 80.00

2006 Topps Triple Threads Relic Combos Red

RED/36 STATED ODDS 1:15
*SEPIA/27: .4X TO 1X RED/36
SEPIA/27 STATED ODDS 1:19
*EMERALD/18: .5X TO 1.2X RED/36
EMERALD/18 STATED ODDS 1:28
UNPRICED GOLD/9 ODDS 1:55
UNPRICED SAPPHIRE/3 ODDS 1:165
SAPPHIRE PRINT RUN 3 SER.#'d SETS
UNPRICED PLATINUM 1/1 ODDS 1:494
1 Marcus Allen 30.00 80.00
  Barry Sanders
  Emmitt Smith
2 Johnny Unitas 40.00 100.00
  John Elway
  Joe Namath
3 Emmitt Smith 30.00 80.00
  Shaun Alexander
  Barry Sanders
4 Shaun Alexander 12.00 30.00
  Priest Holmes
  Marshall Faulk
5 Eric Dickerson 20.00 50.00
  Jamal Lewis
  Barry Sanders
6 Michael Strahan 10.00 25.00
  Dwight Freeney
  Jason Taylor
7 Ed Reed 10.00 25.00
  Deltha O'Neal
  Ty Law
8 Brett Favre 40.00 100.00
  John Elway
  Dan Marino
9 Edgerrin James 12.00 30.00
  Randy Moss
  Clinton Portis
10 Joe Montana 40.00 100.00
  Dan Marino
  Lawrence Taylor
11 Kurt Warner 20.00 50.00
  Peyton Manning
  Steve McNair
12 Jonathan Vilma 15.00 40.00
  Brian Urlacher
  Zach Thomas
13 Jamal Lewis 25.00 60.00
  Corey Dillon
  Walter Payton
14 Marcus Allen 30.00 80.00
  Barry Sanders
  Walter Payton
15 Emmitt Smith 30.00 80.00
  Jerry Rice
  Marcus Allen
16 Matt Leinart 25.00 60.00
  Reggie Bush
  LenDale White
17 Eli Manning 15.00 40.00
  Tiki Barber
  Michael Strahan
18 Joe Montana 25.00 60.00
  Maurice Stovall
  Julius Jones
19 Reggie Bush 25.00 60.00
  DeAngelo Williams
  Laurence Maroney
20 Ben Roethlisberger 40.00 80.00
  Hines Ward
  Santonio Holmes
21 Carson Palmer 15.00 40.00
  Marcus Allen
  Mike Williams
22 Matt Leinart 25.00 60.00
  Jay Cutler
  Vince Young
23 Tom Brady 15.00 40.00
  Chad Jackson
  Laurence Maroney
24 Joe Klopfenstein 12.00 30.00
  Marcedes Lewis
  Vernon Davis
25 Donovan McNabb 12.00 30.00
  Reggie Brown
  Jason Avant
26 Curtis Martin 25.00 60.00
  Dan Marino
  Larry Fitzgerald
27 Brett Favre 40.00 100.00
  Joe Montana
  Dan Marino
28 Anquan Boldin 20.00 50.00
  Ben Roethlisberger
  Cadillac Williams
29 Walter Payton 30.00 80.00
  Marshall Faulk
  Marcus Allen
30 LaDainian Tomlinson 20.00 50.00
  Philip Rivers
  Antonio Gates
31 Donovan McNabb 12.00 30.00
  Dwight Freeney
  Marvin Harrison
32 Drew Bledsoe 15.00 40.00
  Jason Witten
  Julius Jones
33 Edgerrin James 12.00 30.00
  Jeremy Shockey
  Clinton Portis
34 Vince Young 12.00 30.00
  Cedric Benson
  Chris Simms
35 Omar Jacobs 10.00 25.00
  Tarvaris Jackson
  Kellen Clemens
36 Emmitt Smith 25.00 60.00
  Chad Jackson
  Fred Taylor
37 Larry Johnson 12.00 30.00
  Tony Gonzalez
  Trent Green
38 Ben Roethlisberger 20.00 50.00
  Randy Moss
  Chad Pennington
39 Carson Palmer 12.00 30.00
  Chad Johnson
  Rudi Johnson
40 Peyton Manning 20.00 50.00
  Shaun Alexander
  Steve Smith
41 Maurice Drew 12.00 30.00
  Marcedes Lewis
  Matt Jones
42 Sinorice Moss 12.00 30.00
  Santonio Holmes
  Derek Hagan
43 Tom Brady 20.00 50.00
  Larry Johnson
  Chad Johnson
44 Brett Favre 25.00 60.00
  Shaun Alexander
  Steve Smith
45 Sinorice Moss 12.00 30.00
  Santana Moss
  Frank Gore
46 Brian Calhoun 12.00 30.00
  Laurence Maroney
  Joseph Addai
47 Terrell Suggs 12.00 30.00
  Julius Peppers
  Jonathan Vilma
48 Torry Holt 10.00 25.00
  Steven Jackson
  Marc Bulger
49 Reggie Bush 25.00 60.00
  Joe Horn
  Donte Stallworth
50 Michael Strahan 12.00 30.00
  Lawrence Taylor
  Osi Umenyiora
51 Mario Williams 30.00 80.00
  Reggie Bush
  Vince Young
52 Lawrence Taylor 15.00 40.00
  Julius Peppers
  Warrick Dunn
53 Brett Favre 30.00 80.00
  Ahman Green
  AJ Hawk
54 Jake Delhomme 12.00 30.00
  DeShaun Foster
  Steve Smith
55 Vernon Davis 12.00 30.00
  Charlie Whitehurst
  Leon Washington
56 Todd Heap 10.00 25.00
  Ray Lewis
  Jamal Lewis
57 Chad Pennington 12.00 30.00
  Curtis Martin
  Kellen Clemens
58 Warrick Dunn 12.00 30.00
  Leon Washington
  Anquan Boldin
59 Larry Fitzgerald 10.00 25.00
  Antrel Rolle
  Anquan Boldin
60 Kurt Warner 12.00 30.00
  Tom Brady
  Hines Ward
61 Shaun Alexander 25.00 60.00
  Priest Holmes
  Emmitt Smith
62 Peyton Manning 20.00 50.00
  Marvin Harrison
  Dwight Freeney
63 J.P. Losman 10.00 25.00
  Lee Evans
  Willis McGahee
64 Cadillac Williams 12.00 30.00
  Chris Simms
  Maurice Stovall
65 Jake Plummer 15.00 40.00
  Jay Cutler
  Tatum Bell
66 Larry Johnson 12.00 30.00
  Michael Robinson
  LaVar Arrington
67 Michael Vick 12.00 30.00
  Alge Crumpler
  Roddy White
68 Travis Wilson 10.00 25.00
  Brandon Marshall
  Demetrius Williams
69 Joe Namath 30.00 80.00
  Peyton Manning
  Eli Manning
70 Joseph Addai 12.00 30.00
  Domanick Davis
  Michael Clayton
71 Dan Marino 40.00 100.00
  Jerry Rice
  Emmitt Smith
72 Mario Williams 10.00 25.00
  Andre Johnson
  David Carr
73 Kevin Jones 12.00 30.00
  Mike Williams
  Roy Williams
74 Tarvaris Jackson 10.00 25.00
  Troy Williamson
  Mewelde Moore
75 Braylon Edwards 12.00 30.00
  Charlie Frye
  Travis Wilson
76 Shaun Alexander 12.00 30.00
  Matt Hasselbeck
  Marcus Trufant
77 Vince Young 12.00 30.00
  Adam Jones
  LenDale White
78 Randy Moss 12.00 30.00
  Michael Huff
  Andrew Walter
79 Ronnie Brown 10.00 25.00
  Derek Hagan
  Chris Chambers
80 Jonathan Vilma 20.00 50.00
  Ray Lewis
  Ed Reed

2006 Topps Triple Threads Relic Red

RED/36 STATED ODDS 1:9
RED PRINT RUN 36 SER.#'d SETS
*SEPIA/27: .4X TO 1X RED/36
SEPIA/27 STATED ODDS 1:12
SEPIA PRINT RUN 27 SER.#'d SETS
*EMERALD/18: .5X TO 1.2X RED/36
EMERALD/18 ODDS 1:17
EMERALD PRINT RUN 18 SER.#'d SETS
*GOLD/9: .6X TO 1.5X RED/36
GOLD/9 STATED ODDS 1:33
GOLD PRINT RUN 9 SER.#'d SETS
UNPRICED SAPPHIRE/3 ODDS 1:98
SAPPHIRE PRINT RUN 3 SER.#'d SETS
UNPRICED PLATINUM 1/1 ODDS 1:293
EACH PLAYER HAS 3 CARDS PRICED EQUALLY
TTR1 Peyton Manning 15.00 40.00
TTR4 LaDainian Tomlinson 10.00 25.00
TTR7 Michael Vick 10.00 25.00
TTR10 Emmitt Smith 30.00 80.00
TTR13 Matt Leinart 8.00 20.00
TTR16 Randy Moss 10.00 25.00
TTR19 Cadillac Williams 8.00 20.00
TTR22 Tom Brady 15.00 40.00
TTR25 Lawrence Taylor 15.00 40.00
TTR28 Reggie Bush 15.00 40.00
TTR31 Carson Palmer 10.00 25.00
TTR34 Hines Ward 10.00 25.00
TTR37 Ronnie Brown 10.00 25.00
TTR40 Vince Young 10.00 25.00

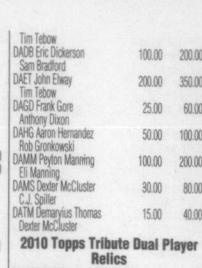

TTR43 Chad Johnson 8.00 20.00
TTR46 A.J. Hawk 8.00 20.00
TTR49 Johnny Unitas 25.00 60.00
TTR52 Eli Manning 12.00 30.00
TTR55 Steve Smith 10.00 25.00
TTR58 Shaun Alexander 8.00 20.00
TTR61 LenDale White 6.00 15.00
TTR64 Donovan McNabb 10.00 25.00
TTR67 Santonio Holmes 10.00 25.00
TTR70 Mario Williams 8.00 20.00
TTR73 Vernon Davis 10.00 25.00
TTR76 Jeremy Shockey 10.00 25.00
TTR79 Marvin Harrison 10.00 25.00
TTR82 Ben Roethlisberger 12.00 30.00
TTR85 Tiki Barber 10.00 25.00
TTR88 Sinorice Moss 8.00 20.00
TTR91 Joe Namath 20.00 50.00
TTR94 Jerry Rice 25.00 60.00
TTR97 Curtis Martin 10.00 25.00
TTR100 Chad Jackson 5.00 12.00
TTR103 Clinton Portis 10.00 25.00
TTR106 DeAngelo Williams 10.00 25.00
TTR109 Barry Sanders 25.00 60.00
TTR112 Edgerrin James 8.00 20.00
TTR115 Laurence Maroney 6.00 15.00
TTR118 Brett Favre 20.00 50.00
TTR121 Walter Payton 30.00 80.00
TTR124 Joe Montana 30.00 80.00
TTR127 Larry Johnson 8.00 20.00
TTR130 Dan Marino 30.00 80.00
TTR133 John Elway 25.00 60.00

2007 Topps Triple Threads

This 149-card set was released in January, 2008. The set was issued into the hobby in six-card packs with an $100 SRP which came two packs to a box. Cards numbered 1-80 feature veterans and cards numbered 81-100 feature retired greats. All cards numbered 1-100 were issued to a stated print run of 1449 serial numbered sets. Cards numbered 101-149 are 2007 NFL rookies with both player-worn swatches and a signature. All cards numbered 101-149 were issued to a stated print run of 99 serial numbered sets.

1-100 PRINT RUN 1449 SER.#'d SETS
JSY AU ROOKIE PRINT RUN 99
1 Peyton Manning 2.50 6.00
2 Carson Palmer 1.25 3.00
3 Tom Brady 2.50 6.00
4 Drew Brees 1.50 4.00
5 Marc Bulger 1.25 3.00
6 Donovan McNabb 1.50 4.00
7 Eli Manning 1.50 4.00
8 Jay Cutler 1.50 4.00
9 Vince Young 1.25 3.00
10 Brett Favre 3.00 8.00
11 Matt Hasselbeck 1.25 3.00
12 Tony Romo 2.00 5.00
13 Philip Rivers 1.50 4.00
14 Matt Leinart 1.25 3.00
15 Ben Roethlisberger 1.50 4.00
16 Chad Pennington 1.25 3.00
17 Alex Smith QB 1.50 4.00
18 Matt Schaub 1.25 3.00
19 Steve McNair 1.25 3.00
20 Rex Grossman 1.25 3.00
21 Jason Campbell 1.25 3.00
22 Trent Green 1.25 3.00
23 J.P. Losman 1.00 2.50
24 Byron Leftwich 1.25 3.00
25 Jake Delhomme 1.25 3.00
26 LaDainian Tomlinson 1.50 4.00
27 Steven Jackson 1.50 4.00
28 Shaun Alexander 1.25 3.00
29 Larry Johnson 1.00 2.50
30 Brian Westbrook 1.25 3.00
31 Joseph Addai 1.25 3.00
32 Reggie Bush 1.50 4.00
33 Frank Gore 1.50 4.00
34 Willie Parker 1.25 3.00
35 Laurence Maroney 1.25 3.00
36 Maurice Jones-Drew 1.50 4.00
37 Travis Henry 1.25 3.00
38 Clinton Portis 1.25 3.00
39 Ronnie Brown 1.25 3.00
40 Thomas Jones 1.25 3.00
41 Willis McGahee 1.25 3.00
42 Edgerrin James 1.25 3.00
43 Brandon Jacobs 1.25 3.00
44 Ahman Green 1.25 3.00
45 Cedric Benson 1.25 3.00
46 Cadillac Williams 1.25 3.00
47 Warrick Dunn 1.25 3.00
48 Jamal Lewis 1.25 3.00
49 Julius Jones 1.00 2.50
50 DeAngelo Williams 1.50 4.00
51 Fred Taylor 1.25 3.00
52 Chester Taylor 1.00 2.50
53 DeShaun Foster 1.25 3.00
54 Chad Johnson 1.25 3.00
55 Marvin Harrison 1.50 4.00
56 Torry Holt 1.25 3.00
57 Terrell Owens 1.50 4.00
58 Reggie Wayne 1.25 3.00
59 Steve Smith 1.25 3.00
60 Roy Williams WR 1.25 3.00
61 Randy Moss 1.50 4.00
62 Andre Johnson 1.25 3.00
63 Larry Fitzgerald 1.50 4.00
64 Anquan Boldin 1.25 3.00
65 Javon Walker 1.25 3.00
66 Laveranues Coles 1.00 2.50
67 Hines Ward 1.50 4.00
68 Lee Evans 1.25 3.00
69 Marques Colston 1.50 4.00
70 Braylon Edwards 1.25 3.00
71 Santana Moss 1.25 3.00
72 Jerricho Cotchery 1.25 3.00
73 Greg Jennings 1.50 4.00
74 Antonio Gates 1.50 4.00
75 Tony Gonzalez 1.25 3.00
76 Jeremy Shockey 1.25 3.00
77 Alge Crumpler 1.25 3.00
78 Champ Bailey 1.25 3.00
79 Shawne Merriman 1.25 3.00
80 Jason Taylor 1.25 3.00
81 Troy Aikman 2.00 5.00
82 Terry Bradshaw 2.50 6.00
83 Jim Brown 2.00 5.00
84 Earl Campbell 1.50 4.00
85 Len Dawson 1.50 4.00
86 Eric Dickerson 1.25 3.00
87 Tony Dorsett 1.50 4.00
88 John Elway 2.50 6.00
89 Marshall Faulk 1.25 3.00
90 Franco Harris 1.50 4.00
91 Dan Marino 3.00 8.00
92 Joe Montana 3.00 8.00
93 Joe Namath 2.00 5.00
94 Walter Payton 3.00 8.00
95 Jerry Rice 2.50 6.00
96 Barry Sanders 2.50 6.00
97 Gale Sayers 2.00 5.00
98 Bart Starr 2.50 6.00
99 Roger Staubach 2.50 6.00
100 Steve Young 2.00 5.00
101 Gaines Adams JSY AU RC 10.00 25.00
102 David Harris JSY AU RC 8.00 20.00
103 Paul Posluszny JSY AU RC 10.00 25.00
104 Lawrence Timmons JSY AU RC 10.00 25.00
105 Patrick Willis JSY AU RC 20.00 50.00
106 John Beck JSY AU RC 10.00 25.00
107 Trent Edwards JSY AU RC 10.00 25.00
108 Kevin Kolb JSY AU RC 15.00 40.00
109 Chris Leak JSY AU RC 8.00 20.00
110 Jordan Palmer JSY AU RC 8.00 20.00
111 Brady Quinn JSY AU RC 10.00 25.00
112 JaMarcus Russell JSY AU RC 6.00 15.00
113 Troy Smith JSY AU RC 10.00 25.00
114 Isaiah Stanback JSY AU RC 6.00 15.00
115 Drew Stanton JSY AU RC 6.00 15.00
116 Lorenzo Booker JSY AU RC 8.00 20.00
117 Michael Bush JSY AU RC 10.00 25.00
118 Chris Henry RB JSY AU RC 6.00 15.00
119 Tony Hunt JSY AU RC 6.00 15.00
120 Brandon Jackson JSY AU RC 8.00 20.00
121 Brian Leonard JSY AU RC 8.00 20.00
122 Marshawn Lynch JSY AU RC 15.00 30.00
123 Adrian Peterson JSY AU RC 125.00 250.00
124 Antonio Pittman JSY AU RC 6.00 15.00
125 Garrett Wolfe JSY AU RC 6.00 15.00
126 LaRon Landry JSY AU RC 10.00 25.00
127 Greg Olsen JSY AU RC 8.00 20.00
128 Aundrae Allison JSY AU RC 6.00 15.00
129 Dwayne Bowe JSY AU RC 12.00 30.00
130 Steve Breaston JSY AU RC 10.00 25.00
131 Craig Buster Davis JSY AU RC 8.00 20.00
132 Chris Davis JSY AU RC 6.00 15.00
133 Yamon Figurs JSY AU RC 6.00 15.00
134 Joel Filani JSY AU RC 8.00 20.00
135 Ted Ginn JSY AU RC 8.00 20.00
136 Anthony Gonzalez JSY AU RC 10.00 25.00
137 Roy Hall JSY AU RC 10.00 25.00
138 Jason Hill JSY AU RC 10.00 25.00
139 Dwayne Jarrett JSY AU RC 8.00 20.00
140 Calvin Johnson JSY AU RC 75.00 150.00
141 Jacoby Jones JSY AU RC 10.00 25.00
142 Johnnie Lee Higgins JSY AU RC 8.00 20.00
143 Robert Meachem JSY AU RC 10.00 25.00
144 Sidney Rice JSY AU RC 12.00 30.00
145 Ryne Robinson JSY AU RC 8.00 20.00
146 Steve Smith JSY AU RC 10.00 25.00
147 Chansi Stuckey JSY AU RC 10.00 25.00
148 Paul Williams JSY AU RC 6.00 15.00
149 Joe Thomas JSY AU RC 10.00 25.00

2007 Topps Triple Threads Emerald

*VETS/199 1-100: .6X TO 1.5X BASIC CARDS
*RETIRED/199 1-100: .6X TO 1.5X BASIC CARDS
*ROOKIES/69 101-150: .4X TO 1X
EMERALD 1-100 PRINT RUN 199
EMERALD 101-150 PRINT RUN 69
123 Adrian Peterson JSY AU 125.00 250.00

2007 Topps Triple Threads Gold

*VETS/99 1-100: .8X TO 2X BASIC CARDS
*RETIRED/99 1-100: .8X TO 2X BASIC CARDS
*ROOKIES/25 101-150: .5X TO 1.2X
GOLD 1-100 PRINT RUN 99
GOLD 101-150 PRINT RUN 25
123 Adrian Peterson JSY AU 150.00 300.00
140 Calvin Johnson JSY AU 125.00 200.00

2007 Topps Triple Threads Platinum

UNPRICED PLATINUM PRINT RUN 1

2007 Topps Triple Threads Rookie Autographed Relic Prime

*ROOKIES/25: .6X TO 1.5X BASIC CARDS
STATED PRINT RUN 25 SER.#'d SETS
UNPRICED PRIME BLACK PRINT RUN 1
UNPRICED PRINT PLATE PRINT RUN 1
123 Adrian Peterson JSY AU 250.00 500.00
140 Calvin Johnson JSY AU 75.00 150.00

2007 Topps Triple Threads Rookie Autographed Relic Prime Red

*ROOKIES/10: 1X TO 2.5X BASIC CARDS
PRIME RED PRINT RUN 10
123 Adrian Peterson JSY AU 400.00 750.00

2007 Topps Triple Threads Sapphire

*VETS/25 1-100: 2X TO 5X BASIC CARDS
*RETIRED/25 1-100: 2X TO 5X BASIC CARDS
*ROOKIES/10 101-150: .75X TO 1.5X
SAPPHIRE 1-100 PRINT RUN 25
SAPPHIRE 101-150 PRINT RUN 10
123 Adrian Peterson JSY AU 250.00 500.00
140 Calvin Johnson JSY AU 175.00 300.00

2007 Topps Triple Threads Sepia

*VETS/639 1-80: .5X TO 1.2X BASIC CARDS
*RETIRED/639 81-100: .5X TO 1.2X BASE CARD
*ROOKIES/89 101-150: .4X TO 1X
SEPIA 1-100 PRINT RUN 639
SEPIA 101-149 PRINT RUN 89

2007 Topps Triple Threads Autographed Relic Red

RED PRINT RUN 18 SER.#'d SETS
*GOLD/9: .5X TO 1.2X RED/18
GOLD STATED PRINT RUN 9
UNPRICED SAPPHIRE PRINT RUN 3
UNPRICED PLATINUM PRINT RUN 1
UNPRICED PRINT PLATES PRINT RUN 1
EACH PLAYER HAS 3 CARDS PRICED EQUALLY
1 John Beck 12.00 30.00
4 Lorenzo Booker 10.00 25.00
7 Dwayne Bowe 15.00 40.00
10 Michael Bush 12.00 30.00
13 Trent Edwards 12.00 30.00
16 JaMarcus Russell 8.00 20.00
19 Ted Ginn Jr. 10.00 25.00
22 Anthony Gonzalez 12.00 30.00
25 Chris Henry RB 8.00 20.00
28 Jason Hill 12.00 30.00
31 Tony Hunt 8.00 20.00
34 Brandon Jackson 10.00 25.00
37 Dwayne Jarrett 10.00 25.00
40 Kevin Kolb 20.00 50.00
43 Brian Leonard 10.00 25.00
46 Marshawn Lynch 12.00 30.00
49 Robert Meachem 12.00 30.00
52 Greg Olsen 10.00 25.00
55 Antonio Pittman 8.00 20.00
58 Brady Quinn 15.00 40.00
61 Steve Smith USC 12.00 30.00
64 Drew Stanton 8.00 20.00
67 Calvin Johnson 60.00 120.00
70 Adrian Peterson 150.00 300.00
73 Paul Williams 8.00 20.00
76 Terry Bradshaw 75.00 150.00
79 Jim Brown 50.00 120.00
82 Eric Dickerson 50.00 100.00
85 Tony Dorsett 40.00 100.00
88 Dan Marino 125.00 250.00
91 Joe Montana 100.00 200.00
94 Jerry Rice 100.00 175.00
97 Barry Sanders 100.00 175.00
100 Paul Hornung 30.00 80.00
103 Joe Namath 60.00 120.00
106 Shaun Alexander 20.00 50.00
109 Tom Brady 175.00 300.00
112 Drew Brees 40.00 80.00
115 Reggie Bush 25.00 60.00
118 Marques Colston 25.00 60.00
121 Brett Favre 150.00 250.00
124 Maurice Jones-Drew 25.00 60.00
127 Joey Galloway 20.00 50.00
130 Antonio Gates 25.00 60.00
133 Tony Gonzalez 20.00 50.00
136 Frank Gore 25.00 60.00
139 Marvin Harrison 25.00 60.00
142 Steven Jackson 25.00 60.00
145 Chad Johnson 20.00 50.00
148 Larry Johnson 15.00 40.00
151 Julius Jones 15.00 40.00
154 Matt Leinart 20.00 50.00
157 Peyton Manning 100.00 175.00
160 Eli Manning 50.00 100.00
163 Shawne Merriman 20.00 50.00
166 Willie Parker 20.00 50.00
169 Tony Romo 30.00 80.00
172 Reggie Wayne 20.00 50.00
175 LaDainian Tomlinson 50.00 100.00
178 Vince Young 20.00 50.00

2007 Topps Triple Threads Autographed Relic Combos Red

RED PRINT RUN 36 SER.#'d SETS
*SEPIA/27: .6X TO 1.2X RED/36
SEPIA PRINT RUN 27 SER.#'d SETS
*EMERALD/18: .75X TO 1.5X RED/36
EMERALD PRINT RUN 18 SER.#'d SETS
UNPRICED GOLD PRINT RUN 9
UNPRICED SAPPHIRE PRINT RUN 3
UNPRICED PLATINUM PRINT RUN 1
UNPRICED PRINT PLATES PRINT RUN 1
1 Marcus Allen 40.00 100.00
Matt Leinart
Reggie Bush
2 Ted Ginn Jr. 40.00 80.00
Troy Smith
Anthony Gonzalez
3 Peyton Manning 200.00 400.00
Tom Brady
John Elway
4 Steve Young 250.00 400.00
Joe Montana
Jerry Rice
5 Peyton Manning 250.00 400.00
Steve Young
Joe Montana
6 Julius Peppers 50.00 100.00
Tony Gonzalez
Antonio Gates
7 Eli Manning 50.00 120.00
Brady Quinn
Vince Young
8 Kevin Kolb 40.00 80.00
Drew Stanton
John Beck
9 Dwayne Bowe 20.00 50.00
Robert Meachem
Dwayne Jarrett
10 Michael Bush 20.00 50.00
Chris Henry RB
Brandon Jackson
11 John Beck 15.00 40.00
Lorenzo Booker
Ted Ginn Jr.
12 Paul Hornung 100.00 175.00
Terry Bradshaw
Joe Namath
13 Barry Sanders 175.00 300.00
Jim Brown
Tony Dorsett

2007 Topps Triple Threads Dual Crest Rookie Autographed Relic Combos

UNPRICED DUAL AUTO PRINT RUN 1

2007 Topps Triple Threads HOF Autographed Relic Red

RED PRINT RUN 18 SER.#'d SETS
*GOLD/9: .5X TO 1.2X RED/18
GOLD STATED PRINT RUN 9
UNPRICED SAPPHIRE PRINT RUN 3
UNPRICED PLATINUM PRINT RUN 1
UNPRICED PRINT PLATES PRINT RUN 1
TTH1 Marcus Allen 40.00 80.00
TTH2 Jim Brown 60.00 120.00
TTH3 Tony Dorsett 50.00 100.00
TTH4 Joe Namath 60.00 120.00
TTH5 Barry Sanders 100.00 175.00
TTH6 Terry Bradshaw 75.00 150.00
TTH7 Eric Dickerson 50.00 100.00
TTH8 Paul Hornung 30.00 80.00
TTH9 Joe Montana 125.00 200.00
TTH10 Dan Marino 150.00 250.00

2007 Topps Triple Threads Relic Red

RED PRINT RUN 36 SER.#'d SETS
*SEPIA/27: .4X TO 1X RED/36
SEPIA PRINT RUN 27 SER.#'d SETS
*EMERALD/18: .5X TO 1.2X RED/36
EMERALD PRINT RUN 18 SER.#'d SETS
*GOLD/9: .6X TO 1.5X RED/36
GOLD STATED PRINT RUN 9
UNPRICED SAPPHIRE PRINT RUN 3
UNPRICED PLATINUM PRINT RUN 1
*PRIME RED/18: .6X TO 1.5X RED/36
PRIME RED PRINT RUN 18
*PRIME GOLD/9: .8X TO 2X RED/36
PRIME GOLD PRINT RUN 9
UNPRICED PRIME PLAT.PRINT RUN 1
UNPRICED PRIME SAPPHIRE PRINT RUN 3
PLAYERS HAVE THREE CARDS OF EQUAL VALUE
TTR1 JaMarcus Russell 2.50 6.00
TTR4 Brady Quinn 4.00 10.00
TTR7 Adrian Peterson 15.00 40.00
TTR10 Marshawn Lynch 4.00 10.00
TTR13 Calvin Johnson 12.00 30.00
TTR16 Ted Ginn Jr. 3.00 8.00
TTR19 Dwayne Bowe 5.00 12.00
TTR22 Robert Meachem 4.00 10.00
TTR25 Drew Stanton 2.50 6.00
TTR28 Dwayne Jarrett 3.00 8.00
TTR31 John Elway 25.00 60.00
TTR34 Dan Marino 30.00 80.00
TTR37 Joe Montana 25.00 60.00
TTR40 Joe Namath 20.00 50.00
TTR43 Jim Brown 20.00 50.00
TTR46 Barry Sanders 25.00 60.00
TTR49 Eric Dickerson 12.00 30.00
TTR52 Tony Dorsett 15.00 40.00
TTR55 Terry Bradshaw 20.00 50.00
TTR58 Roger Staubach 20.00 50.00
TTR61 Peyton Manning 20.00 50.00
TTR64 Drew Brees 10.00 25.00
TTR67 Carson Palmer 8.00 20.00
TTR70 Brett Favre 20.00 50.00
TTR73 Vince Young 8.00 20.00
TTR76 Tom Brady 15.00 40.00
TTR79 Philip Rivers 10.00 25.00
TTR82 Matt Leinart 8.00 20.00
TTR85 LaDainian Tomlinson 10.00 25.00
TTR88 Larry Johnson 6.00 15.00
TTR91 Steven Jackson 10.00 25.00
TTR94 Frank Gore 10.00 25.00
TTR97 Reggie Bush 10.00 25.00
TTR100 Willie Parker 8.00 20.00
TTR103 Rudi Johnson 8.00 20.00
TTR106 Shaun Alexander 8.00 20.00
TTR109 Laurence Maroney 8.00 20.00
TTR112 Chad Johnson 8.00 20.00
TTR115 Marvin Harrison 10.00 25.00
TTR118 Roy Williams WR 8.00 20.00
TTR121 Reggie Wayne 8.00 20.00
TTR124 Torry Holt 8.00 20.00
TTR127 Terrell Owens 10.00 25.00
TTR130 Andre Johnson 8.00 20.00
TTR133 Steve Smith 8.00 20.00

2007 Topps Triple Threads Relic Combos Red

RED PRINT RUN 36 SER.#'d SETS
*SEPIA/27: .5X TO 1.2X RED/36
SEPIA PRINT RUN 27 SER.#'d SETS
*EMERALD/18: .6X TO 1.5X RED/36
EMERALD PRINT RUN 18 SER.#'d SETS
UNPRICED GOLD PRINT RUN 9
UNPRICED SAPPHIRE PRINT RUN 3
UNPRICED PLATINUM PRINT RUN 1
1 Drew Brees 12.00 30.00
Marques Colston
Reggie Bush
2 Tom Brady 20.00 50.00
Laurence Maroney
Randy Moss
3 Peyton Manning 20.00 50.00
Marvin Harrison
Reggie Wayne
4 Philip Rivers 12.00 30.00
LaDainian Tomlinson
Antonio Gates
5 Chad Johnson 10.00 25.00
Rudi Johnson
Carson Palmer
6 Tony Romo 20.00 50.00
Terrell Owens
Julius Jones
7 Marc Bulger 12.00 30.00
Torry Holt
Steven Jackson
8 Eli Manning 15.00 40.00
Plaxico Burress
Jeremy Shockey
9 Ben Roethlisberger 12.00 30.00
Willie Parker
Hines Ward
10 Jay Cutler 12.00 30.00
Travis Henry
Javon Walker
11 Dan Marino 50.00 100.00
Brett Favre
John Elway
12 Drew Brees 20.00 50.00
Peyton Manning
Marc Bulger
13 Emmitt Smith 50.00 100.00
Walter Payton
Barry Sanders
14 LaDainian Tomlinson 12.00 30.00
Larry Johnson
Frank Gore
15 Chad Johnson 12.00 30.00
Marvin Harrison
Roy Williams WR
16 Emmitt Smith 40.00 80.00
Marcus Allen
Walter Payton
17 Eli Manning 15.00 40.00
Deuce McAllister
Patrick Willis
18 Anquan Boldin 10.00 25.00
Laveranues Coles
Javon Walker
19 Leon Hall 12.00 30.00
Ty Law
Charles Woodson
20 JaMarcus Russell 10.00 25.00
Dwayne Bowe
Craig Buster Davis
21 Brady Quinn 8.00 20.00
Darius Walker
Rhema McKnight
22 John Elway 50.00 100.00
Dan Marino
Tom Brady
23 Steven Jackson 12.00 30.00
Chad Johnson
T.J. Houshmandzadeh
24 Matt Leinart 12.00 30.00
Reggie Bush
Carson Palmer
25 Greg Olsen 10.00 25.00
Kellen Winslow
Jeremy Shockey
26 Frank Gore 12.00 30.00
Willis McGahee
Edgerrin James
27 Cadillac Williams 10.00 25.00
Ronnie Brown
Kenny Irons
28 Philip Rivers 12.00 30.00
Torry Holt
Jerricho Cotchery
29 Shawne Merriman 10.00 25.00
Vernon Davis
LaMont Jordan
30 Robert Meachem 12.00 30.00
Peerless Price
Donte Stallworth
31 Ted Ginn Jr. 6.00 15.00
Joey Galloway
Terry Glenn
32 Ted Ginn Jr. 8.00 20.00
Troy Smith
Anthony Gonzalez
33 Dwight Freeney 12.00 30.00
Donovan McNabb
Marvin Harrison
34 Alge Crumpler 10.00 25.00
Willie Parker
Julius Peppers
35 Julius Peppers 12.00 30.00
Tony Gonzalez
Antonio Gates
36 Adrian Peterson 25.00 60.00
Roy Williams S
Mark Clayton
37 Santana Moss 10.00 25.00
Andre Johnson
Reggie Wayne
38 Barry Sanders 20.00 50.00
Marcus Allen
Reggie Bush
39 Marques Colston 12.00 30.00
T.J. Houshmandzadeh
Donald Driver
40 JaMarcus Russell 20.00 50.00
Calvin Johnson
Joe Thomas
41 Vince Young 12.00 30.00
Matt Leinart
Jay Cutler
42 Reggie Bush 12.00 30.00
Laurence Maroney
Joseph Addai
43 Calvin Johnson 15.00 40.00
Ted Ginn Jr.
Dwayne Bowe
44 Drew Stanton 12.00 30.00
John Beck
Kevin Kolb
45 Eli Manning 12.00 30.00
Philip Rivers
Ben Roethlisberger
46 Chad Pennington 12.00 30.00
Byron Leftwich
Randy Moss
47 Ben Roethlisberger 12.00 30.00
Cadillac Williams
Vince Young
48 Clinton Portis 10.00 25.00
Edgerrin James
Jonathan Vilma
49 Jamal Lewis 10.00 25.00
Thomas Jones
Shaun Alexander
50 Thomas Jones 10.00 25.00
Jamal Lewis
Willis McGahee
51 Peyton Manning 50.00 100.00
Tom Brady
John Elway
52 Steve Young 50.00 100.00
Joe Montana
Jerry Rice
53 Matt Leinart 12.00 30.00
Reggie Bush
Dwayne Jarrett
54 Troy Aikman 40.00 80.00
John Elway
Dan Marino
55 Matt Jones 10.00 25.00
Antwaan Randle El
Brad Smith
56 Arnaz Battle 12.00 30.00
Anquan Boldin
Hines Ward
57 Peyton Manning 40.00 00.00
Joe Montana
Steve Young
58 Ben Roethlisberger 12.00 30.00
J.P. Losman
Matt Leinart
59 Carson Palmer 20.00 50.00
Drew Brees
Tony Romo
60 LaDainian Tomlinson 12.00 30.00
Frank Gore
Julius Jones
61 Edgerrin James 10.00 25.00
Cedric Benson
Rudi Johnson
62 Willie Parker 12.00 30.00
Steven Jackson
Laurence Maroney
63 Fred Taylor 25.00 60.00
Adrian Peterson
Warrick Dunn
64 Jim Brown 20.00 50.00
Marcus Allen
Franco Harris
65 Chris Chambers 10.00 25.00
Javon Walker
Joey Galloway
66 Braylon Edwards 12.00 30.00
Plaxico Burress
Philip Rivers
67 Calvin Johnson 15.00 40.00
Torry Holt
Terrell Owens
68 Roy Williams WR 12.00 30.00
Larry Fitzgerald
Alex Smith QB
69 Antonio Gates 12.00 30.00
Greg Jennings
Chad Johnson
70 Willis McGahee 12.00 30.00
Ronnie Brown
Devin Hester
71 Marcus Allen 12.00 30.00
Terrell Davis
Reggie Bush
72 Larry Johnson 10.00 25.00
Chad Johnson
Andre Johnson
73 Terry Bradshaw 40.00 80.00
Franco Harris
Hines Ward
74 Matt Leinart 12.00 30.00
Anquan Boldin
Larry Fitzgerald
75 LaDainian Tomlinson 20.00 50.00
Barry Sanders
Curtis Martin
76 Eli Manning 15.00 40.00
Tony Romo
Donovan McNabb
77 Ben Roethlisberger 20.00 50.00
Carson Palmer
Brady Quinn
78 Philip Rivers 15.00 40.00
JaMarcus Russell
Jay Cutler
79 Peyton Manning 20.00 50.00
Carson Palmer
JaMarcus Russell
80 Andre Johnson 12.00 30.00
Larry Fitzgerald
Braylon Edwards
81 Joe Namath 40.00 80.00
Terry Bradshaw
Tom Brady
82 Paul Hornung 20.00 50.00
Joe Montana
Brady Quinn
83 Barry Sanders 25.00 60.00
Tony Dorsett
Jim Brown
84 Jim Brown 30.00 60.00
Joe Namath
Terry Bradshaw
85 John Elway 50.00 100.00
Dan Marino
Joe Montana

2007 Topps Triple Threads Relic Double Combos Red

RED STATED PRINT RUN 36
*SEPIA/27: .4X TO 1X RED/36
SEPIA STATED PRINT RUN 27
*EMERALD/18: .5X TO 1.2X RED/36
EMERALD STATED PRINT RUN 18
UNPRICED GOLD PRINT RUN 9
UNPRICED SAPPHIRE PRINT RUN 3
UNPRICED PLATINUM PRINT RUN 1
1 Peyton Manning 6X Jsy 30.00 80.00
2 Eric Dickerson 30.00 80.00
Jim Brown
Barry Sanders
Tony Dorsett
Marcus Allen
Paul Hornung
3 Tom Brady 60.00 120.00
Terry Bradshaw
Joe Namath
Jim Kelly
Roger Staubach
Ken Stabler
4 Peyton Manning 60.00 120.00
Tom Brady
John Elway
Steve Young
Troy Aikman
Joe Montana
5 JaMarcus Russell 50.00 100.00
Carson Palmer
Eli Manning
Peyton Manning
Troy Aikman
John Elway
6 Terry Bradshaw 75.00 150.00
Joe Namath
Joe Montana
Dan Marino
Johnny Unitas
John Elway
7 Carson Palmer 30.00 80.00
Matt Leinart
Steven Jackson
Reggie Bush
Chad Johnson
Tony Gonzalez
8 Tom Brady 40.00 100.00
Drew Brees
Larry Johnson
Laurence Maroney
Plaxico Burress
Lee Evans
9 Rudi Johnson 20.00 50.00
Shaun Alexander
Joseph Addai
Deuce McAlister
Chris Henry
Fred Taylor
10 Jim Brown 6X Jsy 20.00 50.00
11 Tom Brady 40.00 100.00
Carson Palmer
Philip Rivers
Peyton Manning
Vince Young
Ben Roethlisberger
12 Eli Manning 40.00 100.00
Donovan McNabb
Brett Favre
Matt Leinart
Drew Brees
Marc Bulger
13 JaMarcus Russell 25.00 60.00
Brady Quinn
Drew Stanton
John Beck
Kevin Kolb
Troy Smith
14 Johnny Unitas 6X Jsy 30.00 80.00
15 Terry Bradshaw 6X Jsy 25.00 60.00
16 Calvin Johnson 20.00 40.00
Ted Ginn
Robert Meachem
Dwayne Bowe
Dwayne Jarrett
Steve Smith USC
17 Brady Quinn 15.00 40.00
Alex Smith QB
Matt Leinart
Vince Young
Jay Cutler
JaMarcus Russell
18 Troy Aikman 75.00 150.00
Emmitt Smith
Tony Dorsett
Roger Staubach
Tony Romo
Terrell Owens
19 Terry Bradshaw 75.00 150.00
Franco Harris
Ben Roethlisberger
Willie Parker
Hines Ward
Santonio Holmes
20 Joe Montana 50.00 100.00
Steve Young
Jerry Rice
Frank Gore
Alex Smith QB
Patrick Willis

2008 Topps Triple Threads

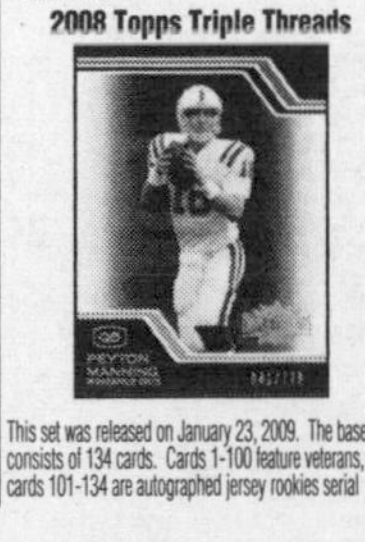

This set was released on January 23, 2009. The base set consists of 134 cards. Cards 1-100 feature veterans, and cards 101-134 are autographed jersey rookies serial numbered of 89. This product was released with 6 cards per pack and 2 packs per hobby box.

1-100 PRINT RUN 779 SER.#'d SETS
101-134 JSY AU RC/89 ODDS 1:10
1 Drew Brees 1.50 4.00
2 Tom Brady 2.50 6.00
3 Peyton Manning 2.50 6.00
4 Carson Palmer 1.50 4.00
5 Ben Roethlisberger 1.50 4.00
6 Eli Manning 1.50 4.00
7 Tony Romo 2.00 5.00
8 Vince Young 1.25 3.00
9 Jon Kitna 1.25 3.00
10 Matt Hasselbeck 1.25 3.00
11 Derek Anderson 1.00 2.50
12 Jay Cutler 1.50 4.00
13 Donovan McNabb 1.50 4.00
14 Philip Rivers 1.50 4.00
15 Jason Campbell 1.25 3.00
16 David Garrard 1.25 3.00
17 Jeff Garcia 1.25 3.00
18 Marc Bulger 1.25 3.00
19 Matt Schaub 1.25 3.00
20 Tarvaris Jackson 1.25 3.00
21 Matt Leinart 1.50 4.00
22 Trent Edwards 1.00 2.50
23 JaMarcus Russell 1.25 3.00
24 Brodie Croyle 1.25 3.00
25 Aaron Rodgers 3.00 8.00
26 Steven Jackson 1.50 4.00
27 Willie Parker 1.25 3.00
28 Clinton Portis 1.25 3.00
29 Adrian Peterson 2.50 6.00
30 LaDainian Tomlinson 1.50 4.00
31 Marion Barber 1.25 3.00
32 Brian Westbrook 1.25 3.00
33 Fred Taylor 1.25 3.00
34 Marshawn Lynch 1.25 3.00
35 Joseph Addai 1.25 3.00
36 Willis McGahee 1.25 3.00
37 Frank Gore 1.25 3.00
38 Jamal Lewis 1.25 3.00
39 Edgerrin James 1.25 3.00
40 Thomas Jones 1.25 3.00
41 LenDale White 1.25 3.00
42 Justin Fargas 1.00 2.50
43 Brandon Jacobs 1.25 3.00
44 Ryan Grant 1.50 4.00
45 Larry Johnson 1.25 3.00
46 Laurence Maroney 1.25 3.00
47 Maurice Jones-Drew 1.25 3.00
48 Ronnie Brown 1.25 3.00
49 Reggie Bush 1.50 4.00
50 DeAngelo Williams 1.25 3.00
51 Chad Johnson 1.25 3.00
52 Reggie Wayne 1.25 3.00
53 Anquan Boldin 1.25 3.00
54 Randy Moss 1.50 4.00
55 Plaxico Burress 1.25 3.00
56 Terrell Owens 1.50 4.00
57 Andre Johnson 1.25 3.00
58 Larry Fitzgerald 1.50 4.00
59 Braylon Edwards 1.25 3.00
60 Steve Smith 1.25 3.00
61 Brandon Marshall 1.25 3.00
62 Roddy White 1.25 3.00
63 Marques Colston 1.25 3.00
64 Torry Holt 1.25 3.00
65 Wes Welker 1.50 4.00
66 Bobby Engram 1.00 2.50
67 T.J. Houshmandzadeh 1.25 3.00
68 Jerricho Cotchery 1.25 3.00
69 Kevin Curtis 1.00 2.50
70 Derrick Mason 1.25 3.00
71 Donald Driver 1.25 3.00
72 Joey Galloway 1.25 3.00
73 Dwayne Bowe 1.25 3.00
74 Chris Chambers 1.25 3.00
75 Santonio Holmes 1.25 3.00
76 Tony Gonzalez 1.25 3.00
77 Jason Witten 1.50 4.00
78 Kellen Winslow 1.25 3.00
79 Antonio Gates 1.50 4.00
80 Chris Cooley 1.25 3.00
01 Vernon Davis 1.25 3.00
82 Dallas Clark 1.25 3.00
83 Jason Taylor 1.25 3.00
84 Shawne Merriman 1.25 3.00
85 Champ Bailey 1.25 3.00
86 Patrick Willis 1.25 3.00
87 Ray Lewis 1.50 4.00
88 DeMarcus Ware 1.25 3.00
89 Bob Sanders 1.25 3.00
90 Devin Hester 1.50 4.00
91 Brett Favre 4.00 10.00
92 John Elway 2.50 6.00
93 Joe Montana 3.00 8.00
94 Barry Sanders 2.50 6.00
95 Walter Payton 3.00 8.00
96 Joe Namath 2.00 5.00
97 Paul Hornung 1.50 4.00
98 Troy Aikman 2.00 5.00
99 Lawrence Taylor 1.50 4.00
100 Emmitt Smith 3.00 8.00
101 Matt Ryan JSY AU RC 50.00 120.00
102 Darren McFadden JSY AU RC 25.00 50.00
103 Jonathan Stewart JSY AU RC 12.00 30.00
104 Joe Flacco JSY AU RC 40.00 100.00
105 Felix Jones JSY AU RC 20.00 50.00
106 Rashard Mendenhall JSY AU RC 15.00 40.00
107 Brian Brohm JSY AU RC 8.00 20.00
108 Chris Johnson JSY AU RC 40.00 100.00
109 Donnie Avery JSY AU RC 6.00 15.00
110 Devin Thomas JSY AU RC 6.00 15.00
111 Chad Henne JSY AU RC 30.00 60.00
112 Ray Rice JSY AU RC 20.00 50.00
113 DeSean Jackson JSY AU RC 15.00 40.00
114 Malcolm Kelly JSY AU RC 6.00 15.00
115 Limas Sweed JSY AU RC 8.00 20.00
116 Kevin Smith JSY AU RC 8.00 20.00
117 Jamaal Charles JSY AU RC 12.00 30.00
118 Steve Slaton JSY AU RC 8.00 20.00
119 Jordy Nelson JSY AU RC 20.00 40.00
120 James Hardy JSY AU RC 6.00 15.00
121 Jake Long JSY AU RC 8.00 20.00
122 Glenn Dorsey JSY AU RC 8.00 20.00
123 Eddie Royal JSY AU RC 8.00 20.00
124 Matt Forte JSY AU RC 15.00 40.00
125 Jerome Simpson JSY AU RC 8.00 20.00
126 Dexter Jackson JSY AU RC 6.00 15.00
127 Earl Bennett JSY AU RC 8.00 20.00
128 Early Doucet JSY AU RC 6.00 15.00
129 Harry Douglas JSY AU RC 6.00 15.00
130 Kevin O'Connell JSY AU RC 6.00 15.00
131 Mario Manningham JSY AU RC 15.00 30.00
132 Andre Caldwell JSY AU RC 6.00 15.00
133 Dustin Keller JSY AU RC 8.00 20.00
134 John David Booty JSY AU RC 6.00 15.00

2008 Topps Triple Threads Emerald

*VETS 1-100: .6X TO 1.5X BASIC CARDS
1-100 VETERAN/149 ODDS 1:2

*ROOKIES 101-134: .5X TO 1.2X BASIC CARDS
1-100 ROOKIE JSY AU/50 ODDS 1:16

2008 Topps Triple Threads Gold

*VETS 1-100: .8X TO 2X BASIC CARDS
1-100 VETERAN/99 ODDS 1:3
*ROOKIES 101-134: .8X TO 2X BASIC CARDS
101-134 ROOKIE JSY AU/25 ODDS 1:32
101 Matt Ryan JSY AU 125.00 250.00
104 Joe Flacco JSY AU 100.00 200.00
108 Chris Johnson JSY AU 125.00 200.00

2008 Topps Triple Threads Platinum

UNPRICED PLATINUM VET.ODDS 1:262
UNPRICED PLAT JSY AU ODDS 1:752

2008 Topps Triple Threads Rookie Autographed Relic Prime

*PRIME.25: .8X TO 2X BASE JSY AU/89
PRIME SILVER/25 ODDS 1:32
UNPRICED PRIME BLACK/1 ODDS 1:752
UNPRICED PRINT PLATE PRINT RUN 1
101 Matt Ryan 100.00 200.00
104 Joe Flacco 75.00 150.00
108 Chris Johnson 75.00 150.00

2008 Topps Triple Threads Rookie Autographed Relic Prime Red

*RED/10: 1X TO 2.5X BASIC JSY AU/89
RED JSY AU PRINT RUN 10
101 Matt Ryan 300.00 500.00
104 Joe Flacco 125.00 250.00
105 Felix Jones 100.00 175.00
108 Chris Johnson 250.00 400.00
111 Chad Henne 125.00 200.00
112 Ray Rice 100.00 175.00

2008 Topps Triple Threads Sapphire

*VETS 1-100: 1.2X TO 3X BASIC CARDS
1-100 VETERAN/25 ODDS 1:11
*ROOKIES 101-134: .8X TO 2X BASIC CARDS
101-134 ROOKIE JSY AU/10 ODDS 1:76
101 Matt Ryan JSY AU 150.00 300.00
104 Joe Flacco JSY AU 125.00 250.00
108 Chris Johnson JSY AU 125.00 250.00

2008 Topps Triple Threads Sepia

*VETS 1-100: .5X TO 1.2X BASIC CARDS
1-100 VETERAN/249 ODDS 1:2
*ROOKIES 101-134: .4X TO 1X BASIC CARDS
101-134 ROOKIE JSY AU/75 ODDS 1:11

2008 Topps Triple Threads Autographed Relic Triple Red

RED STATED PRINT RUN 6-36
*SEPIA/15: .5X TO 1.2X RED/36
SEPIA STATED PRINT RUN 5-15
UNPRICED EMERALD PRINT RUN 4
UNPRICED GOLD PRINT RUN 3
UNPRICED SAPPHIRE PRINT RUN 2
UNPRICED PLATINUM PRINT RUN 1
UNPRICED PRINT PLATE PRINT RUN 1
4 Felix Jones/36 60.00 120.00
Chris Johnson
Ray Rice
5 Matt Forte/36 50.00 100.00
Kevin Smith
Steve Slaton
6 Eddie Royal/36 40.00 80.00
DeSean Jackson
James Hardy
11 Joe Flacco/36 60.00 120.00
Dexter Jackson
Jerome Simpson
12 Matt Forte/36 60.00 120.00
Chris Johnson
Kevin Smith

2008 Topps Triple Threads Relic Red

RED/17 STATED ODDS 1:12
*SEPIA/12: .4X TO 1X RED/17
SEPIA/12 STATED ODDS 1:16
*EMERALD/9: .4X TO 1X RED/17
EMERALD/9 STATED ODDS 1:22
*GOLD/6: .5X TO 1.2X RED/17
GOLD/6 STATED ODDS 1:32
UNPRICED SAPPHIRE/3 ODDS 1:64
UNPRICED PLATINUM/1 ODDS 1:194
UNPRICED PRIME RED/9 ODDS 1:64
UNPRICED PRIME GOLD/6 ODDS 1:96
UNPRICED PRIME SAPPHIRE/3 ODDS 1:194
UNPRICED PRIME PLATINUM/1 ODDS 1:564
PLAYERS HAVE THREE CARDS OF EQUAL VALUE
TTR1 Matt Ryan 40.00 80.00
TTR4 Darren McFadden 20.00 50.00
TTR7 Jonathan Stewart 12.00 30.00
TTR10 Joe Flacco 25.00 60.00
TTR13 Felix Jones 12.00 30.00
TTR16 Rashard Mendenhall 15.00 40.00
TTR19 Brian Brohm 8.00 20.00
TTR22 Chad Henne 8.00 20.00
TTR25 Devin Thomas 6.00 15.00
TTR28 Limas Sweed 8.00 20.00
TTR31 Brett Favre 30.00 80.00
TTR34 John Elway 25.00 60.00
TTR37 Joe Montana 30.00 80.00
TTR40 Barry Sanders 25.00 60.00
TTR43 Walter Payton 30.00 80.00
TTR46 Joe Namath 20.00 50.00
TTR49 Matt Leinart 12.00 30.00
TTR52 Troy Aikman 20.00 50.00
TTR55 Lawrence Taylor 15.00 40.00
TTR58 Emmitt Smith 30.00 80.00
TTR61 Eli Manning 12.00 30.00
TTR64 Peyton Manning 20.00 50.00
TTR67 Ben Roethlisberger 25.00 60.00
TTR70 Tom Brady 20.00 50.00
TTR73 Tony Romo 15.00 40.00
TTR76 Drew Brees 12.00 30.00
TTR79 Philip Rivers 12.00 30.00
TTR82 Jay Cutler 12.00 30.00
TTR85 Vince Young 10.00 25.00
TTR88 LaDainian Tomlinson 12.00 30.00
TTR91 Adrian Peterson 30.00 80.00
TTR94 Marshawn Lynch 10.00 25.00
TTR97 Steven Jackson 12.00 30.00
TTR100 Willie Parker 10.00 25.00
TTR103 Willis McGahee 10.00 25.00
TTR106 Frank Gore 10.00 25.00
TTR109 Joseph Addai 10.00 25.00
TTR112 Terrell Owens 12.00 30.00
TTR115 Randy Moss 12.00 30.00
TTR118 Chad Johnson 10.00 25.00
TTR121 Reggie Wayne 10.00 25.00
TTR124 Andre Johnson 10.00 25.00
TTR127 Larry Fitzgerald 12.00 30.00
TTR130 Braylon Edwards 10.00 25.00
TTR133 Plaxico Burress 10.00 25.00

2008 Topps Triple Threads Relic Combos Red

RED/22 STATED ODDS 1:16
*SEPIA/15: .5X TO 1.2X RED/22
SEPIA/15 STATED ODDS 1:22
UNPRICED EMERALD/9 ODDS 1:36
UNPRICED GOLD/6 ODDS 1:54
UNPRICED SAPPHIRE/3 ODDS 1:107
UNPRICED PLATINUM/1 ODDS 1:322
TTRC1 Tom Brady 20.00 50.00
Randy Moss
Laurence Maroney
TTRC2 Tony Romo 12.00 30.00
Marion Barber
Terrell Owens
TTRC3 Eli Manning 12.00 30.00
Brandon Jacobs
Plaxico Burress
TTRC4 Drew Brees 10.00 25.00
Reggie Bush
Marques Colston
TTRC5 Matt Leinart 10.00 25.00
Larry Fitzgerald
Anquan Boldin
TTRC6 Marc Bulger 10.00 25.00
Steven Jackson
Torry Holt
TTRC7 Ben Roethlisberger 20.00 50.00
Willie Parker
Hines Ward
TTRC8 Carson Palmer 10.00 25.00
Chad Johnson
T.J. Houshmandzadeh
TTRC9 Derek Anderson 8.00 20.00
Braylon Edwards
Kellen Winslow
TTRC10 Peyton Manning 15.00 40.00
Joseph Addai
Reggie Wayne
TTRC11 Philip Rivers 10.00 25.00
LaDainian Tomlinson
Antonio Gates
TTRC12 Brett Favre 40.00 80.00
Dan Marino
John Elway
TTRC13 Tom Brady 15.00 40.00
Drew Brees
Tony Romo
TTRC14 Emmitt Smith 40.00 80.00
Walter Payton
Barry Sanders
TTRC15 LaDainian Tomlinson 15.00 40.00
Adrian Peterson
Brian Westbrook
TTRC16 Jerry Rice 20.00 50.00
Tim Brown
Isaac Bruce
TTRC17 Reggie Wayne 10.00 25.00
Randy Moss
Chad Johnson
TTRC18 Tom Brady 15.00 40.00
Tony Romo
Ben Roethlisberger
TTRC19 Emmitt Smith 25.00 60.00
Marcus Allen
LaDainian Tomlinson
TTRC20 LaDainian Tomlinson 15.00 40.00
Adrian Peterson
Joseph Addai
TTRC21 Randy Moss 10.00 25.00
Braylon Edwards
Terrell Owens
TTRC22 Chad Henne 5.00 12.00
Mario Manningham
Jake Long
TTRC23 JaMarcus Russell 8.00 20.00
Joseph Addai
Dwayne Bowe
TTRC24 Jake Long 15.00 40.00
Chris Long
Matt Ryan
TTRC25 Kevin Smith 5.00 12.00
Brandon Marshall
Asante Samuel
TTRC26 Matt Ryan 15.00 40.00
Chad Henne
Brian Brohm
TTRC27 Joe Flacco 12.00 30.00
Kevin O'Connell
John David Booty
TTRC28 Darren McFadden 12.00 30.00
Jonathan Stewart
Rashard Mendenhall
TTRC29 Felix Jones 12.00 30.00
Chris Johnson
Ray Rice
TTRC30 Matt Forte 8.00 20.00
Kevin Smith
Steve Slaton
TTRC31 Malcolm Kelly 6.00 15.00
Devin Thomas
Limas Sweed
TTRC32 DeSean Jackson 10.00 25.00
Mario Manningham
Early Doucet
TTRC33 James Hardy 6.00 15.00
Donnie Avery
Jordy Nelson
TTRC34 Carson Palmer 8.00 20.00
Matt Leinart
John David Booty
TTRC35 Terrell Owens 10.00 25.00
Randy Moss
Marvin Harrison
TTRC36 Aaron Rodgers 10.00 25.00
Marshawn Lynch
DeSean Jackson
TTRC37 Tony Romo 15.00 40.00
Brian Westbrook
Terrell Owens
TTRC38 Braylon Edwards 10.00 25.00
Amani Toomer
Mario Manningham
TTRC39 Ben Roethlisberger 15.00 40.00
Vince Young
Adrian Peterson
TTRC40 Brian Urlacher 10.00 25.00
Shawne Merriman
Patrick Willis
TTRC41 Plaxico Burress 8.00 20.00
Derrick Mason
Devin Thomas
TTRC42 Santana Moss 8.00 20.00
Devin Thomas
Malcolm Kelly
TTRC43 Vince Young 10.00 25.00
Roy Williams WR
Limas Sweed
TTRC44 LaDainian Tomlinson 10.00 25.00
Fred Taylor
Warrick Dunn
TTRC45 Ryan Grant 10.00 25.00
Julius Jones
Darius Walker
TTRC46 Mario Williams 6.00 15.00
Gaines Adams
Chris Long
TTRC47 Reggie Bush 25.00 60.00
Adrian Peterson
Darren McFadden
TTRC48 Adrian Peterson 15.00 40.00
Malcolm Kelly
Roy Williams S
TTRC49 Dwayne Bowe 8.00 20.00
Buster Davis
Early Doucet
TTRC50 Tom Brady 15.00 40.00
Chad Henne
Brian Griese
TTRC51 Derek Anderson 10.00 25.00
Steven Jackson
Chad Johnson
TTRC52 Plaxico Burress 10.00 25.00
Amani Toomer
Mario Manningham
TTRC53 Adrian Peterson 40.00 80.00
Jamal Lewis
Walter Payton
TTRC54 Hines Ward 10.00 25.00
Santonio Holmes
Limas Sweed
TTRC55 Tom Brady 15.00 40.00
LaDainian Tomlinson
Peyton Manning
TTRC56 Ben Roethlisberger 15.00 40.00
Jason Taylor
Antonio Gates
TTRC57 Matt Ryan 15.00 40.00
Malcolm Kelly
Jamaal Charles
TTRC58 Adrian Peterson 15.00 40.00
Jonathan Stewart
Felix Jones
TTRC59 Willis McGahee 8.00 20.00
Ronnie Brown
Marshawn Lynch
TTRC60 Ben Roethlisberger 10.00 25.00
Matt Leinart
Chad Henne
TTRC61 LenDale White 10.00 25.00
Justin Fargas
Ryan Grant
TTRC62 Terrell Owens 10.00 25.00
Randy Moss
Torry Holt
TTRC63 Dan Marino 40.00 80.00
Tony Dorsett
Larry Fitzgerald
TTRC64 Larry Fitzgerald 10.00 25.00
Roy Williams WR
Devin Thomas
TTRC65 Adrian Peterson 15.00 40.00
Terrell Owens
LaDainian Tomlinson
TTRC66 Jerry Rice 20.00 50.00
Terrell Owens
Randy Moss
TTRC67 Tony Romo 12.00 30.00
Willie Parker
Antonio Gates
TTRC68 Reggie Bush 10.00 25.00
LenDale White
Justin Fargas
TTRC69 Derek Anderson 10.00 25.00
Ryan Grant
Wes Welker
TTRC70 Darren McFadden 12.00 30.00
Willis McGahee
Deuce McAllister
TTRC71 Brian Brohm 10.00 25.00
Ray Rice
Steve Slaton
TTRC72 Joe Flacco 12.00 30.00
Dexter Jackson
Jerome Simpson
TTRC73 Reggie Bush 12.00 30.00
LaDainian Tomlinson
Darren McFadden
TTRC74 Adrian Peterson 15.00 40.00
Patrick Willis
Joe Thomas
TTRC75 Matt Forte 12.00 30.00
Chris Johnson
Kevin Smith
TTRC76 Steven Jackson 8.00 20.00
Marshawn Lynch
Jonathan Stewart
TTRC77 Clinton Portis 8.00 20.00
Willis McGahee
Edgerrin James
TTRC78 Plaxico Burress 8.00 20.00
Reggie Wayne
Hines Ward
TTRC79 Adrian Peterson 15.00 40.00
Marshawn Lynch
Dwayne Bowe
TTRC80 Tom Brady 40.00 80.00
John Elway
Joe Montana

2009 Topps Triple Threads

1-100 VETERAN PRINT RUN 799
101-134 ROOKIE JSY AU PRINT RUN 35-70
1 Drew Brees 1.50 4.00
2 Kurt Warner 1.50 4.00
3 Jay Cutler 1.50 4.00
4 Aaron Rodgers 3.00 8.00
5 Philip Rivers 1.50 4.00
6 Peyton Manning 2.50 6.00
7 Donovan McNabb 1.50 4.00
8 Matt Cassel 1.25 3.00
9 Chad Pennington 1.25 3.00
10 David Garrard 1.25 3.00
11 Brett Favre 6.00 15.00
12 Tony Romo 2.50 6.00
13 Matt Ryan 1.50 4.00
14 Ben Roethlisberger 1.50 4.00
15 Jake Delhomme 1.25 3.00
16 Jason Campbell 1.00 2.50
17 Eli Manning 1.50 4.00
18 Matt Schaub 1.25 3.00
19 Kyle Orton 1.25 3.00
20 Joe Flacco 1.50 4.00
21 Marc Bulger 1.25 3.00
22 JaMarcus Russell 1.00 2.50
23 Trent Edwards 1.00 2.50
24 Kerry Collins 1.25 3.00
25 Matt Hasselbeck 1.25 3.00
26 Brady Quinn 1.25 3.00
27 Carson Palmer 1.50 4.00
28 Tom Brady 2.50 6.00
29 Adrian Peterson 2.50 6.00
30 Michael Turner 1.25 3.00
31 DeAngelo Williams 1.50 4.00
32 Clinton Portis 1.25 3.00
33 Thomas Jones 1.25 3.00
34 Steve Slaton 1.25 3.00
35 Matt Forte 1.50 4.00
36 Chris Johnson 1.50 4.00
37 Ryan Grant 1.25 3.00
38 LaDainian Tomlinson 1.50 4.00
39 Brandon Jacobs 1.25 3.00
40 Steven Jackson 1.25 3.00
41 Marshawn Lynch 1.25 3.00
42 Frank Gore 1.25 3.00
43 Derrick Ward 1.00 2.50
44 Jamal Lewis 1.25 3.00
45 Kevin Smith 1.25 3.00
46 Brian Westbrook 1.25 3.00
47 Ronnie Brown 1.25 3.00
48 Marion Barber 1.25 3.00
49 Larry Johnson 1.25 3.00
50 Cedric Benson 1.25 3.00
51 Jonathan Stewart 1.25 3.00
52 Maurice Jones-Drew 1.25 3.00
53 Willie Parker 1.00 2.50
54 Darren McFadden 1.50 4.00
55 Reggie Bush 1.50 4.00
56 Joseph Addai 1.50 4.00
57 Andre Johnson 1.25 3.00
58 Larry Fitzgerald 1.50 4.00
59 Steve Smith 1.25 3.00
60 Roddy White 1.25 3.00
61 Calvin Johnson 1.50 4.00
62 Greg Jennings 1.50 4.00
63 Brandon Marshall 1.25 3.00
64 Antonio Bryant 1.00 2.50
65 Wes Welker 1.50 4.00
66 Reggie Wayne 1.25 3.00
67 Marques Colston 1.25 3.00
68 Terrell Owens 1.50 4.00
69 Santana Moss 1.25 3.00
70 Hines Ward 1.25 3.00
71 Anquan Boldin 1.25 3.00
72 Dwayne Bowe 1.25 3.00
73 Roy Williams WR 1.25 3.00
74 Donald Driver 1.25 3.00
75 Randy Moss 1.50 4.00
76 Eddie Royal 1.25 3.00
77 Bernard Berrian 1.25 3.00
78 DeSean Jackson 1.25 3.00
79 T.J. Houshmandzadeh 1.25 3.00
80 Braylon Edwards 1.25 3.00
81 Jerricho Cotchery 1.25 3.00
82 Santonio Holmes 1.25 3.00
83 Torry Holt 1.25 3.00
84 Chad Ochocinco 1.25 3.00
85 Tony Gonzalez 1.25 3.00
86 Jason Witten 1.50 4.00
87 Dallas Clark 1.25 3.00
88 DeMarcus Ware 1.25 3.00
89 Ed Reed 1.25 3.00
90 Patrick Willis 1.25 3.00
91 Terry Bradshaw 2.00 5.00
92 Earl Campbell 1.50 4.00
93 Bo Jackson 2.00 5.00
94 Joe Montana 3.00 8.00
95 Dan Marino 3.00 8.00
96 Jim Brown 2.00 5.00
97 Tony Dorsett 1.50 4.00
98 Joe Namath 2.00 5.00
99 Jerry Rice 2.50 6.00
100 John Elway 2.50 6.00
101 Andre Brown JSY AU/70 RC 6.00 15.00
102 Aaron Curry JSY AU/70 RC 10.00 25.00
103 Brandon Pettigrew JSY AU/70 RC 10.00 25.00
104 Brian Robiskie JSY AU/70 RC 10.00 25.00
105 Chris Wells JSY AU/35 RC 20.00 50.00
106 Deon Butler JSY AU/70 RC 8.00 20.00
107 Donald Brown JSY AU/35 RC 12.00 30.00
108 Darrius Heyward-Bey JSY AU/35 RC 12.00 30.00
109 Derrick Williams JSY AU/70 RC 8.00 20.00
110 Glen Coffee JSY AU/70 RC 8.00 20.00
111 Hakeem Nicks JSY AU/70 RC 15.00 40.00
112 Josh Freeman JSY AU/35 RC 25.00 60.00
113 Juaquin Iglesias JSY AU/70 RC 8.00 20.00
114 Jeremy Maclin JSY AU/35 RC 20.00 50.00
115 Matthew Stafford JSY AU/35 RC 60.00 120.00
116 Javon Ringer JSY AU/70 RC 10.00 25.00
117 Jason Smith JSY AU/70 RC 8.00 20.00
118 Kenny Britt JSY AU/70 RC 12.00 30.00
119 Knowshon Moreno JSY AU/35 RC 12.00 30.00
120 LeSean McCoy JSY AU/70 RC 20.00 50.00
121 Michael Crabtree JSY AU/35 RC 25.00 60.00
122 Mohamed Massaquoi JSY AU/70 RC 8.00 20.00
123 Mark Sanchez JSY AU/35 RC 40.00 100.00
124 Mike Thomas JSY AU/70 RC 10.00 25.00
125 Mike Wallace JSY AU/70 RC 20.00 50.00
126 Nate Davis JSY AU/70 RC 8.00 20.00
127 Percy Harvin JSY AU/70 RC 15.00 40.00
128 Patrick Turner JSY AU/70 RC 8.00 20.00
129 Pat White JSY AU/70 RC 10.00 25.00
130 Ramses Barden JSY AU/70 RC 6.00 15.00
131 Rhett Bomar JSY AU/70 RC 8.00 20.00
132 Shonn Greene JSY AU/70 RC 15.00 40.00
133 Stephen McGee JSY AU/70 RC 10.00 25.00
134 Tyson Jackson JSY AU/70 RC 8.00 20.00

2009 Topps Triple Threads Emerald

*VETS 1-100: .6X TO 1.5X BASIC CARDS
1-100 VETERAN PRINT RUN 149
*ROOKIE: .6X TO 1.5X BASIC JSY AU/70
*ROOKIE: .5X TO 1.2X BASIC JSY AU/35
101-134 ROOKIE JSY AU PRINT RUN 50

2009 Topps Triple Threads Gold

*VETS 1-100: .8X TO 2X BASIC CARDS
1-100 VETERAN PRINT RUN 99
*ROOKIE: .6X TO 1.5X BASIC JSY AU/70
*ROOKIE: .5X TO 1.2X BASIC JSY AU/35
101-134 ROOKIE JSY AU PRINT RUN 15

2009 Topps Triple Threads Sapphire

*VETS 1-100: 1.5X TO 4X BASIC CARDS
1-100 VETERAN PRINT RUN 25
*ROOKIE: .8X TO 2X BASIC JSY AU/70
*ROOKIE: .6X TO 1.5X BASIC JSY AU/35
101-134 ROOKIE JSY AU PRINT RUN 10

2009 Topps Triple Threads Sepia

*VETS 1-100: .5X TO 1.2X BASIC CARDS
1-100 VETERAN PRINT RUN 249
*ROOKIE: .5X TO 1.2X BASIC JSY AU/70
*ROOKIE: .4X TO 1X BASIC JSY AU/35
101-134 ROOKIE JSY AU PRINT RUN 30

2009 Topps Triple Threads Rookie Autographed Relic Prime Sepia

*ROOKIE/30: .6X TO 1.5X BASIC JSY AU/70
*ROOKIE/20: .6X TO 1.5X BASIC JSY AU/35
PRIME SEPIA PRINT RUN 20-30

2009 Topps Triple Threads Rookie Autographed Relic Prime Sapphire

*ROOKIE/15: .8X TO 2X BASIC JSY AU/70
*ROOKIE/15: .6X TO 1.5X BASIC JSY AU/35
PRIME SAPPHIRE PRINT RUN 15

2009 Topps Triple Threads Autographed Relic Combos Red

RED STATED PRINT RUN 25
*SEPIA/12: .5X TO 1.2X RED/36
*SEPIA/12: .4X TO 1X RED/15
1 Gale Sayers/15 100.00 200.00
Jim Brown
Barry Sanders
2 Matthew Stafford/15 100.00 200.00
Mark Sanchez
Josh Freeman
3 Knowshon Moreno/36 25.00 60.00
Chris Wells
Donald Brown
4 Michael Crabtree/15 50.00 100.00
Darius Heyward-Bey
Jeremy Maclin
5 Troy Aikman/15 100.00 200.00
Peyton Manning
Matthew Stafford
6 Tom Brady/15 250.00 400.00
Joe Montana
Terry Bradshaw
7 LaDainian Tomlinson/15 100.00 200.00
Adrian Peterson
Reggie Bush
8 Dan Marino/15 150.00 250.00
Tony Dorsett
LeSean McCoy
9 Drew Brees/36 60.00 120.00
Matt Hasselbeck
Tony Romo
10 Chris Wells/36 40.00 80.00
Donald Brown
LeSean McCoy
11 Percy Harvin/36 50.00 100.00
Hakeem Nicks
Kenny Britt
12 Darius Heyward-Bey/36 20.00 50.00
Aaron Curry
Hakeem Nicks

2009 Topps Triple Threads Autographed Relics Red

RED STATED PRINT RUN 15-25
*GOLD/10: .6X TO 1.5X RED/25
*GOLD/10: .5X TO 1.2X RED/15
EACH HAS THREE CARDS OF EQUAL VALUE
TTRA1 Drew Brees/15 60.00 120.00
TTRA4 Matt Ryan/15 40.00 80.00
TTRA7 Eli Manning/15 40.00 80.00
TTRA10 Frank Gore/25 12.00 30.00
TTRA13 Matthew Stafford/15 60.00 150.00
TTRA16 Joe Flacco/25 25.00 50.00
TTRA19 Mark Sanchez/15 40.00 100.00
TTRA22 Brady Quinn/15 15.00 40.00
TTRA28 Pat White/25 10.00 25.00
TTRA31 Eric Dickerson/15 30.00 60.00
TTRA34 Peyton Manning/15 100.00 175.00
TTRA37 Josh Freeman/15 25.00 60.00
TTRA40 Bo Jackson/15 50.00 100.00
TTRA49 Knowshon Moreno/15 12.00 30.00
TTRA52 Darren McFadden/15 25.00 50.00
TTRA61 Chris Wells/25 15.00 40.00
TTRA67 Donald Brown/25 10.00 25.00
TTRA70 LeSean McCoy/25 25.00 60.00
TTRA73 Percy Harvin/25 15.00 40.00
TTRA76 Jeremy Maclin/25 15.00 40.00
TTRA79 Darrius Heyward-Bey/25 10.00 25.00
TTRA82 Shonn Greene/25 15.00 40.00
TTRA85 Hakeem Nicks/25 20.00 50.00
TTRA88 Kenny Britt/25 12.00 30.00
TTRA91 Michael Crabtree/15 25.00 60.00
TTRA94 Dan Marino/15 100.00 200.00
TTRA106 Terry Bradshaw/15 50.00 100.00

2009 Topps Triple Threads Relic Red

RED STATED PRINT RUN 25
*EMERALD/9: .5X TO 1.2X RED/25
*PURPLE/20: .4X TO 1X RED/25
*SEPIA/18: .4X TO 1X RED/25
*PRIME/15: .6X TO 1.5X RED/25
EACH HAS THREE CARDS OF EQUAL VALUE
TTR1 Matthew Stafford 10.00 25.00
TTR2 Matthew Stafford 10.00 25.00
TTR3 Matthew Stafford 10.00 25.00
TTR4 Mark Sanchez 12.00 30.00
TTR5 Mark Sanchez 12.00 30.00
TTR6 Mark Sanchez 12.00 30.00
TTR7 Josh Freeman 8.00 20.00
TTR8 Josh Freeman 8.00 20.00
TTR9 Josh Freeman 8.00 20.00
TTR10 Knowshon Moreno 4.00 10.00
TTR11 Knowshon Moreno 4.00 10.00
TTR12 Knowshon Moreno 4.00 10.00
TTR13 Donald Brown 4.00 10.00
TTR14 Donald Brown 4.00 10.00
TTR15 Donald Brown 4.00 10.00
TTR16 Chris Wells 8.00 20.00
TTR17 Chris Wells 8.00 20.00
TTR18 Chris Wells 8.00 20.00
TTR19 Darrius Heyward-Bey 4.00 10.00
TTR20 Darrius Heyward-Bey 4.00 10.00
TTR21 Darrius Heyward-Bey 4.00 10.00
TTR22 Michael Crabtree 8.00 20.00
TTR23 Michael Crabtree 8.00 20.00
TTR24 Michael Crabtree 8.00 20.00
TTR25 Jeremy Maclin 6.00 15.00
TTR26 Jeremy Maclin 8.00 20.00
TTR27 Jeremy Maclin 6.00 15.00
TTR28 Percy Harvin 6.00 15.00
TTR29 Percy Harvin 6.00 15.00
TTR30 Percy Harvin 6.00 15.00
TTR31 Drew Brees 10.00 25.00
TTR32 Drew Brees 10.00 25.00
TTR33 Drew Brees 10.00 25.00
TTR34 Peyton Manning 15.00 40.00
TTR35 Peyton Manning 15.00 40.00
TTR36 Peyton Manning 15.00 40.00
TTR37 Tom Brady 20.00 50.00
TTR38 Tom Brady 20.00 50.00
TTR39 Tom Brady 20.00 50.00
TTR40 Philip Rivers 10.00 25.00
TTR41 Philip Rivers 10.00 25.00
TTR42 Philip Rivers 10.00 25.00
TTR43 Ben Roethlisberger 10.00 25.00
TTR44 Ben Roethlisberger 10.00 25.00
TTR45 Ben Roethlisberger 10.00 25.00
TTR46 Adrian Peterson 15.00 40.00
TTR47 Adrian Peterson 15.00 40.00
TTR48 Adrian Peterson 15.00 40.00
TTR49 LaDainian Tomlinson 10.00 25.00
TTR50 LaDainian Tomlinson 10.00 25.00
TTR51 LaDainian Tomlinson 10.00 25.00
TTR52 Clinton Portis 8.00 20.00
TTR53 Clinton Portis 8.00 20.00
TTR54 Clinton Portis 8.00 20.00
TTR55 Matt Forte 10.00 25.00
TTR56 Matt Forte 10.00 25.00
TTR57 Matt Forte 10.00 25.00
TTR58 Frank Gore 8.00 20.00
TTR59 Frank Gore 8.00 20.00
TTR60 Frank Gore 8.00 20.00
TTR61 Andre Johnson 8.00 20.00
TTR62 Andre Johnson 8.00 20.00
TTR63 Andre Johnson 8.00 20.00
TTR64 Larry Fitzgerald 10.00 25.00
TTR65 Larry Fitzgerald 10.00 25.00
TTR66 Larry Fitzgerald 10.00 25.00
TTR67 Steve Smith 8.00 20.00
TTR68 Steve Smith 8.00 20.00
TTR69 Steve Smith 8.00 20.00
TTR70 DeAngelo Williams 10.00 25.00
TTR71 DeAngelo Williams 10.00 25.00
TTR72 DeAngelo Williams 10.00 25.00
TTR73 Randy Moss 10.00 25.00
TTR74 Randy Moss 10.00 25.00
TTR75 Randy Moss 10.00 25.00
TTR76 Terry Bradshaw 12.00 30.00
TTR77 Terry Bradshaw 12.00 30.00
TTR78 Terry Bradshaw 12.00 30.00
TTR79 Earl Campbell 10.00 25.00
TTR80 Earl Campbell 10.00 25.00
TTR81 Earl Campbell 10.00 25.00
TTR82 Bo Jackson 12.00 30.00
TTR83 Bo Jackson 12.00 30.00
TTR84 Bo Jackson 12.00 30.00
TTR85 Dan Marino 25.00 60.00
TTR86 Dan Marino 25.00 60.00
TTR87 Dan Marino 25.00 60.00
TTR88 John Elway 20.00 50.00
TTR89 John Elway 20.00 50.00
TTR90 John Elway 20.00 50.00

2009 Topps Triple Threads Relic Combos Red

RED STATED PRINT RUN 25
*SEPIA/15: .5X TO 1.2X RED/25
1 Peyton Manning 15.00 40.00
Joseph Addai
Reggie Wayne
2 Tony Romo 15.00 40.00
Marion Barber
Roy Williams
3 Larry Fitzgerald 10.00 25.00
Anquan Boldin
Steve Breaston
4 Dwayne Bowe 8.00 20.00
Glenn Dorsey
Tyson Jackson
5 Tom Brady 15.00 40.00
Randy Moss
Wes Welker
6 Terry Bradshaw 15.00 40.00
Hines Ward
Santonio Holmes
7 Drew Brees 10.00 25.00
Reggie Bush
Marques Colston
8 Troy Aikman 25.00 60.00
Peyton Manning
Matthew Stafford
9 Jim Brown 15.00 40.00
Eric Dickerson
Tony Dorsett
10 Pat White 5.00 12.00
Ronnie Brown
Ted Ginn Jr.
11 Joe Montana 25.00 60.00
Jerry Rice
Terrell Owens
12 Mark Sanchez 12.00 30.00
Thomas Jones
Jerricho Cotchery
13 Jake Delhomme 10.00 25.00
DeAngelo Williams
Steve Smith
14 Knowshon Moreno 10.00 25.00
Donald Brown
Kenny Britt
15 Maurice Jones-Drew 10.00 25.00
Ray Rice
Brian Westbrook
16 John Elway 20.00 50.00
Ben Roethlisberger
Roger Staubach
17 Eric Dickerson 10.00 25.00
Marshall Faulk
Steven Jackson
18 Brett Favre 30.00 80.00
Dan Marino
Peyton Manning
19 Ben Roethlisberger 10.00 25.00
Matt Ryan
Joe Flacco
20 Chris Johnson 10.00 25.00
Matt Forte
Steve Slaton
21 Frank Gore 10.00 25.00
Steven Jackson
LaDainian Tomlinson
22 Aaron Rodgers 20.00 50.00
Ryan Grant
Greg Jennings
23 Andre Johnson 10.00 25.00
Larry Fitzgerald
Steve Smith
24 Matthew Stafford 12.00 30.00
Barry Sanders
Calvin Johnson
25 DeAngelo Williams 10.00 25.00
Brandon Jacobs
LenDale White
26 Matthew Stafford 12.00 30.00
Mark Sanchez
Josh Freeman
27 Pat White 5.00 12.00
Stephen McGee
Nate Davis
28 Knowshon Moreno 10.00 25.00
Donald Brown
Chris Wells
29 LeSean McCoy 10.00 25.00
Shonn Greene
Glen Coffee
30 Darrius Heyward-Bey 10.00 25.00
Michael Crabtree
Jeremy Maclin
31 Percy Harvin 12.00 30.00
Hakeem Nicks
Kenny Britt
32 Matthew Stafford 12.00 30.00
Brandon Pettigrew
Derrick Williams
33 Nate Davis 10.00 25.00
Glen Coffee
Michael Crabtree
34 Hakeem Nicks 8.00 20.00
Ramses Barden
Andre Brown
35 Matthew Stafford 12.00 30.00
Knowshon Moreno
Mohamed Massaquoi
36 Carson Palmer 12.00 30.00
Matt Leinart
Mark Sanchez
37 Santana Moss 5.00 12.00
Chris Johnson
Darrius Heyward-Bey
38 Chad Ochocinco 10.00 25.00
Greg Jennings
Antonio Gates
39 Tim Brown 12.00 30.00
Marcus Allen
Howie Long
40 Donovan McNabb 8.00 20.00
LeSean McCoy
Jeremy Maclin
41 JaMarcus Russell 5.00 12.00
Darren McFadden
Darrius Heyward-Bey
42 Ray Lewis 10.00 25.00
Shawne Merriman
Aaron Curry
43 Joe Namath 15.00 40.00
Eli Manning
Mark Sanchez
44 Walter Payton 25.00 60.00
Jim Brown
Emmitt Smith
45 Adrian Peterson 15.00 40.00
Clinton Portis
Eric Dickerson
46 Willie Parker 8.00 20.00
Julius Peppers
Hakeem Nicks
47 Willis McGahee 10.00 25.00
Ray Lewis
Ed Reed
48 Eli Manning 10.00 25.00
Philip Rivers
Ben Roethlisberger
49 Aaron Rodgers 20.00 50.00
Marshawn Lynch
DeSean Jackson
50 Donnie Avery 10.00 25.00
Devin Hester
Eddie Royal
51 Jonathan Stewart 10.00 25.00
Rashard Mendenhall
Felix Jones
52 LaDainian Tomlinson 10.00 25.00
Lawrence Taylor
Lawrence Timmons
53 Johnny Unitas 30.00 80.00
Joe Namath
Brett Favre
54 Brian Urlacher 10.00 25.00
Patrick Willis
Ray Lewis
55 Jerry Rice 20.00 50.00
Reggie White
Lawrence Taylor
56 Brian Urlacher 8.00 20.00
A.J. Hawk
Aaron Curry
57 Larry Johnson 8.00 20.00
Derrick Williams
Deon Butler
58 DeMarcus Ware 8.00 20.00
Julius Peppers
Mario Williams
59 Jerry Rice 20.00 50.00
Hines Ward
Santonio Holmes
60 Dan Marino 25.00 60.00
LeSean McCoy
Larry Fitzgerald

2009 Topps Triple Threads Relic Double Combos Red

STATED PRINT RUN 20
*SEPIA/15: .4X TO 1X RED/20
1 Tom Brady 100.00 200.00
Peyton Manning
Brett Favre
Dan Marino
John Elway
Joe Montana
2 Matthew Stafford 30.00 80.00
Mark Sanchez
Josh Freeman
Pat White
Stephen McGee
Nate Davis
3 Knowshon Moreno 20.00 50.00
Donald Brown
Chris Wells
LeSean McCoy
Shonn Greene
Glen Coffee
4 Darrius Heyward-Bey 25.00 60.00
Michael Crabtree
Jeremy Maclin
Percy Harvin
Hakeem Nicks
Kenny Britt
5 Mohamed Massaquoi 15.00 40.00
Brian Robiskie
Ramses Barden
Mike Wallace
Patrick Turner
Derrick Williams
6 Andre Brown 15.00 40.00
Javon Ringer
Deon Butler
Juaquin Iglesias
Mike Thomas
Brandon Pettigrew
7 Aaron Rodgers 25.00 60.00
Matt Schaub
Maurice Jones-Drew
DeAngelo Williams
Greg Jennings
Dwayne Bowe
8 Philip Rivers 40.00 100.00
Peyton Manning
Tom Brady
Ben Roethlisberger
Carson Palmer
Mark Sanchez
9 Drew Brees 30.00 80.00
Tony Romo
Matt Ryan
Eli Manning
Aaron Rodgers
Matthew Stafford
10 LaDainian Tomlinson 25.00 60.00
Thomas Jones
Steve Slaton
Chris Johnson
Marshawn Lynch
Maurice Jones-Drew
11 Adrian Peterson 30.00 80.00

DeAngelo Williams
Clinton Portis
Matt Forte
Ryan Grant
Brandon Jacobs
12 Emmitt Smith
LaDainian Tomlinson
Marcus Allen
Walter Payton
Jim Brown
Marshall Faulk

2009 Topps Triple Threads Relic XXIV Red

RED PRINT RUN 15
*SEPIA/9: .4X TO 1X RED/15
TFR1 Matthew Stafford 40.00 100.00
TFR2 Mark Sanchez 60.00 120.00
TFR3 Jerry Rice 75.00 150.00
TFR4 Earl Campbell 40.00 80.00
TFR5 Bo Jackson 50.00 100.00
TFR6 Dan Marino 100.00 175.00
TFR7 Knowshon Moreno 30.00 80.00
TFR8 Chris Wells 25.00 60.00
TFR9 Michael Crabtree 30.00 80.00
TFR10 Jeremy Maclin 20.00 50.00
TFR11 Tom Brady 75.00 150.00
TFR13 Peyton Manning 75.00 150.00
TFR14 Andre Johnson 30.00 60.00
TFR15 Aaron Rodgers 40.00 80.00

2010 Topps Triple Threads

101A-135B ROOKIE JSY AU PRINT RUN 99
A FEATURE RC DIE CUT/B TEAM DIE CUT
A/B JSY AU ROOKIES OF EQUAL VALE
EXCH EXPIRATION: 10/31/2013
1 Peyton Manning 1.50 4.00
2 Ray Rice .75 2.00
3 Marques Colston .75 2.00
4 LeSean McCoy .75 2.00
5 Aaron Rodgers 2.00 5.00
6 Anquan Boldin .75 2.00
7 Antonio Gates .75 2.00
8 Steve Smith USC .75 2.00
9 Jonathan Stewart .75 2.00
10 Drew Brees 1.00 2.50
11 Hakeem Nicks .75 2.00
12 Steven Jackson .75 2.00
13 Pierre Garcon .75 2.00
14 Matt Ryan 1.00 2.50
15 Pierre Thomas .75 2.00
16 Shonn Greene .75 2.00
17 Matt Schaub .75 2.00
18 Cedric Benson .75 2.00
19 Mark Sanchez 1.00 2.50
20 Adrian Peterson 1.50 4.00
21 Kyle Orton .75 2.00
22 Jerome Harrison .60 1.50
23 Kevin Kolb .75 2.00
24 Randy Moss 1.00 2.50
25 Vince Young .60 1.50
26 Miles Austin 1.00 2.50
27 Chad Henne .75 2.00
28 Chris Johnson 1.00 2.50
29 Carson Palmer .75 2.00
30 Chad Ochocinco .75 2.00
31 DeAngelo Williams .75 2.00
32 Thomas Jones .75 2.00
33 Donald Driver .75 2.00
34 Matt Forte .75 2.00
35 Philip Rivers 1.00 2.50
36 Ryan Grant .75 2.00
37 Joe Flacco 1.00 2.50
38 Brandon Jacobs .75 2.00
39 LaDainian Tomlinson 1.00 2.50
40 Brett Favre 4.00 8.00
41 Frank Gore .75 2.00
42 Dwayne Bowe .75 2.00
43 Beanie Wells .75 2.00
44 Ben Roethlisberger 1.00 2.50
45 Felix Jones .75 2.00
46 Percy Harvin 1.00 2.50
47 Knowshon Moreno .75 2.00
48 Sidney Rice .75 2.00
49 Ronnie Brown .75 2.00
50 Eli Manning 1.00 2.50
51 Joseph Addai .75 2.00
52 Tony Romo 1.25 3.00
53 Larry Fitzgerald 1.00 2.50
54 Jared Allen 1.00 2.50
55 Rashard Mendenhall .75 2.00
56 Reggie Wayne .75 2.00
57 Darren McFadden .75 2.00
58 Lee Evans .75 2.00
59 Reggie Bush 1.00 2.50
60 Troy Polamalu 1.00 2.50
61 Andre Johnson .75 2.00
62 Dallas Clark .75 2.00
63 Greg Jennings .75 2.00
64 Donovan McNabb 1.00 2.50
65 Steve Smith .75 2.00
66 Fred Jackson 1.00 2.50
67 Calvin Johnson 1.00 2.50
68 Patrick Willis .75 2.00
69 Brandon Marshall .75 2.00
70 Tom Brady 1.50 4.00
71 Vincent Jackson .60 1.50
72 Clinton Portis .75 2.00
73 Wes Welker 1.00 2.50
74 Jamaal Charles .75 2.00
75 Jay Cutler 1.00 2.50
76 Mike Sims-Walker .75 2.00
77 Hines Ward .75 2.00
78 David Garrard .75 2.00
79 Eddie Royal .60 1.50
80 Maurice Jones-Drew .75 2.00
81 DeSean Jackson .75 2.00
82 Matthew Stafford 1.00 2.50
83 Michael Turner .60 1.50
84 Santonio Holmes .75 2.00
85 Roddy White .75 2.00
86 Tony Gonzalez .75 2.00
87 DeMarcus Ware .75 2.00
88 Jason Witten 1.00 2.50
89 Santana Moss .75 2.00
90 Darrelle Revis .75 2.00
91 Troy Aikman 1.50 4.00
92 Marcus Allen 1.25 3.00
93 Ronnie Lott 1.25 3.00
94 Dan Marino 2.50 6.00
95 Emmitt Smith 2.00 5.00
96 Thurman Thomas 1.25 3.00
97 Eric Dickerson 1.00 2.50
98 Gale Sayers 1.50 4.00
99 Jim Brown 1.50 4.00
100 John Elway 2.00 5.00
101A Sam Bradford JSY AU RC 75.00 150.00
101B Sam Bradford JSY AU RC 75.00 150.00
102A Ndamukong Suh JSY AU RC 40.00 80.00
102B Ndamukong Suh JSY AU RC 40.00 80.00
103B Charles Scott JSY AU RC 8.00 20.00
104A C.J. Spiller JSY AU RC 15.00 40.00
104B C.J. Spiller JSY AU RC 15.00 40.00
105A Ryan Mathews JSY AU RC 20.00 50.00
105B Ryan Mathews JSY AU RC 20.00 60.00
106A Anthony McCoy JSY AU RC 8.00 20.00
106B Anthony McCoy JSY AU RC 8.00 20.00
107A Demaryius Thomas JSY AU RC 12.00 30.00
107B Demaryius Thomas JSY AU RC 12.00 30.00
108B Dez Bryant JSY AU RC 50.00 100.00
109A Tim Tebow JSY AU RC 75.00 150.00
110A Jahvid Best JSY AU RC 15.00 40.00
110B Jahvid Best JSY AU RC 15.00 40.00
111A Dexter McCluster JSY AU RC 10.00 25.00
111B Dexter McCluster JSY AU RC 10.00 25.00
112A Arrelious Benn JSY AU RC 10.00 25.00
112B Arrelious Benn JSY AU RC 10.00 25.00
113A Rob Gronkowski JSY AU RC 25.00 50.00
113B Rob Gronkowski JSY AU RC 25.00 50.00
114A Jimmy Clausen JSY AU RC 10.00 25.00
114B Jimmy Clausen JSY AU RC 10.00 25.00
115A Toby Gerhart JSY AU RC 10.00 25.00
115B Toby Gerhart JSY AU RC 10.00 25.00
116A Ben Tate JSY AU RC 12.00 30.00
116B Ben Tate JSY AU RC 12.00 30.00
117A Montario Hardesty JSY AU RC 10.00 25.00
117B Montario Hardesty JSY AU RC 10.00 25.00
118A Golden Tate JSY AU RC 10.00 25.00
118B Golden Tate JSY AU RC 10.00 25.00
119A Damian Williams JSY AU RC 10.00 25.00
119B Damian Williams JSY AU RC 10.00 25.00
120A Brandon LaFell JSY AU RC 8.00 20.00
120B Brandon LaFell JSY AU RC 8.00 20.00
121A Jordan Shipley JSY AU RC 10.00 25.00
121B Jordan Shipley JSY AU RC 10.00 25.00
122A Colt McCoy JSY AU RC 25.00 60.00
122B Colt McCoy JSY AU RC 25.00 60.00
123A Eric Decker JSY AU RC 12.00 30.00
123B Eric Decker JSY AU RC 12.00 30.00
124A Derrick Morgan JSY AU RC 8.00 20.00
124B Derrick Morgan JSY AU RC 8.00 20.00
125A Jonathan Dwyer JSY AU RC 10.00 25.00
125B Jonathan Dwyer JSY AU RC 10.00 25.00
126A Emmanuel Sanders JSY AU RC 10.00 25.00
126B Emmanuel Sanders JSY AU RC 10.00 25.00
127A Mike Williams JSY AU RC 15.00 40.00
127B Mike Williams JSY AU RC 15.00 40.00
128A Mardy Gilyard JSY AU RC 10.00 25.00
128B Mardy Gilyard JSY AU RC 10.00 25.00
129A Gerald McCoy JSY AU RC 10.00 25.00
129B Gerald McCoy JSY AU RC 10.00 25.00
130A Marcus Easley JSY AU RC 8.00 20.00
130B Marcus Easley JSY AU RC 8.00 20.00
131A Andre Roberts JSY AU RC 6.00 15.00
131B Andre Roberts JSY AU RC 6.00 15.00
132A Mike Kafka JSY AU RC 8.00 20.00
132B Mike Kafka JSY AU RC 8.00 20.00
133A Armanti Edwards JSY AU RC 8.00 20.00
133B Armanti Edwards JSY AU RC 8.00 20.00
134A Earl Thomas JSY AU RC 10.00 25.00
135A Sean Canfield JSY AU RC 8.00 20.00

2010 Topps Triple Threads Emerald

*VETS 1-90: .6X TO 1.5X BASIC CARDS
*RETIRED 91-100: .6X TO 1.5X BASIC CARDS
1-100 STATED PRINT RUN 299
*ROOKIE JSY AU: .5X TO 1.2X BASIC CARDS
101-135 ROOKIE JSY AU PRINT RUN 50
101A Sam Bradford JSY AU 75.00 150.00
101B Sam Bradford JSY AU 75.00 150.00
109A Tim Tebow JSY AU 100.00 200.00

2010 Topps Triple Threads Gold

*VETS 1-90: 1X TO 2.5X BASIC CARDS
*RETIRED 91-100: 1X TO 2.5X BASIC CARDS
1-100 STATED PRINT RUN 99
*ROOKIE JSY AU: .6X TO 1.5X BASIC CARDS
101-135 ROOKIE JSY AU PRINT RUN 25
101A Sam Bradford JSY AU 100.00 250.00
101B Sam Bradford JSY AU 100.00 250.00
108B Dez Bryant JSY AU 60.00 120.00
109A Tim Tebow JSY AU 125.00 250.00
109B Tim Tebow JSY AU 150.00 250.00

2010 Topps Triple Threads Ruby

*VETS 1-90: 2X TO 5X BASIC CARDS
*RETIRED 91-100: 2X TO 5X BASIC CARDS
1-100 STATED PRINT RUN 25
101-135 UNPRICED JSY AU PRINT RUN 10

2010 Topps Triple Threads Autographed Relic Combos

STATED PRINT RUN 27 SER.#'d SETS
*EMERALD/18: .5X TO 1.2X BASIC INSERTS
EXCH EXPIRATION: 10/13/2012
1 Joe Montana 100.00 200.00
Steve Young
Ronnie Lott
2 Sam Bradford 75.00 150.00
Colt McCoy
Jimmy Clausen
3 C.J. Spiller 40.00 80.00
Ryan Mathews
Jahvid Best
4 Demaryius Thomas 25.00 50.00
Dexter McCluster
Arrelious Benn
5 Ray Lewis 40.00 80.00
Patrick Willis
Jerod Mayo
6 Sam Bradford 75.00 150.00
Colt McCoy
Jordan Shipley
7 Peyton Manning 75.00 150.00
Joseph Addai
Reggie Wayne
8 Maurice Jones-Drew 40.00 80.00
Ryan Mathews
Jahvid Best
9 Ben Tate 25.00 50.00
Montario Hardesty
Dexter McCluster
10 Jimmy Clausen 30.00 60.00
DeAngelo Williams
Brandon LaFell
11 Gerald McCoy 40.00 80.00
Arrelious Benn
Mike Williams
12 Josh Freeman 30.00 60.00
Mike Williams
Arrelious Benn
13 Arrelious Benn 25.00 50.00
Eric Decker
Mike Kafka
14 C.J. Spiller 25.00 50.00
Demaryius Thomas
Jonathan Dwyer
15 Damian Williams 30.00 60.00
Toby Gerhart
Jahvid Best
16 Andre Roberts 20.00 40.00
Golden Tate
Mardy Gilyard
17 Frank Gore 25.00 50.00
Maurice Jones-Drew
Steven Jackson
18 Ryan Mathews 40.00 80.00
Demaryius Thomas
Dexter McCluster
19 Drew Brees 50.00 100.00
Reggie Bush
Marques Colston
20 Mike Williams EXCH 20.00 50.00
Marcus Easley
Mardy Gilyard
21 Sam Bradford 60.00 120.00
Demaryius Thomas
C.J. Spiller

2010 Topps Triple Threads Autographed Relics

STATED PRINT RUN 18 SER.#'d SETS
*GOLD/9: .5X TO 1.2X BASIC AU/18
EXCH EXPIRATION: 10/31/2013
EACH HAS 2-3 CARDS OF EQUAL VALUE
TTRA1 Peyton Manning 100.00 200.00
TTRA2 Peyton Manning 100.00 200.00
TTRA3 Peyton Manning 100.00 200.00
TTRA4 Mark Sanchez 40.00 80.00
TTRA5 Mark Sanchez 40.00 80.00
TTRA6 Mark Sanchez 40.00 80.00
TTRA7 Sam Bradford 125.00 250.00
TTRA8 Sam Bradford 125.00 250.00
TTRA9 Sam Bradford 125.00 250.00
TTRA10 John Elway 75.00 150.00
TTRA11 John Elway 75.00 150.00
TTRA12 John Elway 75.00 150.00
TTRA13 Knowshon Moreno 20.00 40.00
TTRA14 Knowshon Moreno 20.00 40.00
TTRA15 Knowshon Moreno 20.00 40.00
TTRA16 Sidney Rice 20.00 40.00
TTRA17 Sidney Rice 20.00 40.00
TTRA18 Sidney Rice 20.00 40.00
TTRA19 Adrian Peterson 100.00 200.00
TTRA20 Adrian Peterson 100.00 200.00
TTRA21 Adrian Peterson 100.00 200.00
TTRA22 Earl Campbell 30.00 60.00
TTRA23 Earl Campbell 30.00 60.00
TTRA24 Earl Campbell 30.00 60.00
TTRA25 Matt Ryan 30.00 60.00
TTRA26 Matt Ryan 30.00 60.00
TTRA27 Matt Ryan 30.00 60.00
TTRA28 Marques Colston 20.00 40.00
TTRA29 Marques Colston 20.00 40.00
TTRA30 Franco Harris 30.00 60.00
TTRA31 Dan Marino 100.00 200.00
TTRA32 Dan Marino 100.00 200.00
TTRA33 Dan Marino 100.00 200.00
TTRA34 Eli Manning 50.00 100.00
TTRA35 Eli Manning 50.00 100.00
TTRA36 Eli Manning 50.00 100.00
TTRA37 Jimmy Clausen 20.00 60.00
TTRA38 Jimmy Clausen 20.00 50.00
TTRA39 Jimmy Clausen 20.00 50.00
TTRA40 Ryan Mathews 25.00 60.00
TTRA41 Ryan Mathews 25.00 60.00
TTRA42 Ryan Mathews 25.00 60.00
TTRA43 Ben Tate 15.00 40.00
TTRA44 Ben Tate 15.00 40.00
TTRA45 Ben Tate 15.00 40.00
TTRA46 C.J. Spiller 30.00 60.00
TTRA47 C.J. Spiller 30.00 60.00
TTRA48 C.J. Spiller 30.00 60.00
TTRA49 Kevin Kolb 12.00 30.00
TTRA50 Kevin Kolb 12.00 30.00
TTRA51 Kevin Kolb 12.00 30.00
TTRA52 Emmitt Smith 100.00 200.00
TTRA53 Emmitt Smith 100.00 200.00
TTRA54 Emmitt Smith 100.00 200.00
TTRA55 Joe Flacco 30.00 60.00
TTRA56 Joe Flacco 30.00 60.00
TTRA57 Joe Flacco 30.00 60.00
TTRA58 Marcus Allen 25.00 50.00
TTRA59 Marcus Allen 25.00 50.00
TTRA60 Marcus Allen 25.00 50.00
TTRA61 Montario Hardesty 12.00 30.00
TTRA62 Montario Hardesty 12.00 30.00
TTRA63 Montario Hardesty 12.00 30.00
TTRA64 Jahvid Best 20.00 50.00
TTRA65 Jahvid Best 20.00 50.00
TTRA66 Jahvid Best 20.00 50.00
TTRA67 Jonathan Dwyer 15.00 40.00
TTRA68 Jonathan Dwyer 15.00 40.00
TTRA69 Jonathan Dwyer 15.00 40.00
TTRA70 Dexter McCluster 15.00 40.00
TTRA71 Dexter McCluster 15.00 40.00
TTRA72 Dexter McCluster 15.00 40.00
TTRA73 LaDainian Tomlinson 30.00 60.00
TTRA74 LaDainian Tomlinson 30.00 60.00
TTRA75 LaDainian Tomlinson 30.00 60.00
TTRA76 Percy Harvin 20.00 40.00
TTRA77 Percy Harvin 20.00 40.00
TTRA78 Percy Harvin 20.00 40.00
TTRA79 Demaryius Thomas 12.00 30.00
TTRA80 Demaryius Thomas 12.00 30.00
TTRA81 Demaryius Thomas 12.00 30.00
TTRA82 Rashard Mendenhall 25.00 50.00
TTRA83 Rashard Mendenhall 25.00 50.00
TTRA84 Rashard Mendenhall 25.00 50.00
TTRA85 Frank Gore 20.00 40.00
TTRA86 Frank Gore 20.00 40.00
TTRA87 Frank Gore 20.00 40.00
TTRA88 Tim Tebow 150.00 250.00
TTRA89 Thurman Thomas 30.00 60.00
TTRA90 Matthew Stafford 30.00 80.00
TTRA91 Brett Favre 175.00 300.00
TTRA92 Brett Favre 175.00 300.00
TTRA93 Brett Favre 175.00 300.00
TTRA94 Eric Dickerson 25.00 50.00
TTRA95 Eric Dickerson 25.00 50.00
TTRA96 Eric Dickerson 25.00 50.00
TTRA97 Drew Brees 50.00 100.00
TTRA98 Drew Brees 50.00 100.00
TTRA99 Drew Brees 50.00 100.00
TTRA100 Colt McCoy 30.00 80.00
TTRA101 Colt McCoy 30.00 80.00
TTRA102 Colt McCoy 30.00 80.00
TTRA103 DeAngelo Williams 20.00 40.00
TTRA104 DeAngelo Williams 20.00 40.00
TTRA105 DeAngelo Williams 20.00 40.00
TTRA106 Matthew Stafford 30.00 80.00
TTRA107 Matthew Stafford 30.00 80.00

2010 Topps Triple Threads Relic

STATED PRINT RUN 36 SER.#'d SETS
*EMERALD/18: .5X TO 1.2X BASIC JSY/36
*GOLD/9: .6X TO 1.5X BASIC JSY/36
*SEPIA/27: .4X TO 1X BASIC JSY/36
EACH HAS THREE CARDS OF EQUAL VALUE
TTR1 Tony Romo 10.00 25.00
TTR2 Tony Romo 10.00 25.00
TTR3 Tony Romo 10.00 25.00
TTR4 Sam Bradford 20.00 50.00
TTR5 Sam Bradford 20.00 50.00
TTR6 Sam Bradford 20.00 50.00
TTR7 Jimmy Clausen 5.00 12.00
TTR8 Jimmy Clausen 5.00 12.00
TTR9 Jimmy Clausen 5.00 12.00
TTR10 Tim Tebow 20.00 50.00
TTR11 Tim Tebow 20.00 50.00
TTR12 Tim Tebow 20.00 50.00
TTR13 C.J. Spiller 8.00 20.00
TTR14 C.J. Spiller 8.00 20.00
TTR15 C.J. Spiller 8.00 20.00
TTR16 Ryan Mathews 10.00 25.00
TTR17 Ryan Mathews 10.00 25.00
TTR18 Ryan Mathews 10.00 25.00
TTR19 Jahvid Best 8.00 20.00
TTR20 Jahvid Best 8.00 20.00
TTR21 Jahvid Best 8.00 20.00
TTR22 Demaryius Thomas 6.00 15.00
TTR23 Demaryius Thomas 6.00 15.00
TTR24 Demaryius Thomas 6.00 15.00
TTR25 Dez Bryant 15.00 40.00
TTR26 Dez Bryant 15.00 40.00
TTR27 Dez Bryant 15.00 40.00
TTR28 Golden Tate 5.00 12.00
TTR29 Golden Tate 5.00 12.00
TTR30 Golden Tate 5.00 12.00
TTR31 Dexter McCluster 8.00 20.00
TTR32 Dexter McCluster 8.00 20.00
TTR33 Dexter McCluster 8.00 20.00
TTR34 Ben Tate 6.00 15.00
TTR35 Ben Tate 6.00 15.00
TTR36 Ben Tate 6.00 15.00
TTR37 Colt McCoy 10.00 25.00
TTR38 Colt McCoy 10.00 25.00
TTR39 Colt McCoy 10.00 25.00
TTR40 Jonathan Dwyer 5.00 12.00
TTR41 Jonathan Dwyer 5.00 12.00
TTR42 Jonathan Dwyer 5.00 12.00
TTR43 Toby Gerhart 5.00 12.00
TTR44 Toby Gerhart 5.00 12.00
TTR45 Toby Gerhart 5.00 12.00
TTR46 Montario Hardesty 5.00 12.00
TTR47 Montario Hardesty 5.00 12.00
TTR48 Montario Hardesty 5.00 12.00
TTR49 Joe McKnight 5.00 12.00
TTR50 Joe McKnight 5.00 12.00
TTR51 Joe McKnight 5.00 12.00
TTR52 Mike Williams 8.00 20.00
TTR53 Mike Williams 8.00 20.00
TTR54 Mike Williams 8.00 20.00
TTR55 Eric Decker 6.00 15.00
TTR56 Eric Decker 6.00 15.00
TTR57 Eric Decker 6.00 15.00
TTR58 Arrelious Benn 5.00 12.00
TTR59 Arrelious Benn 5.00 12.00
TTR60 Arrelious Benn 5.00 12.00
TTR61 Steven Jackson 6.00 15.00
TTR62 Steven Jackson 6.00 15.00
TTR63 Steven Jackson 6.00 15.00
TTR64 Brandon Jacobs 8.00 20.00
TTR65 Brandon Jacobs 8.00 20.00
TTR66 Brandon Jacobs 8.00 20.00
TTR67 Tom Brady 15.00 40.00
TTR68 Tom Brady 15.00 40.00
TTR69 Tom Brady 15.00 40.00
TTR70 Peyton Manning 15.00 40.00
TTR71 Peyton Manning 15.00 40.00
TTR72 Peyton Manning 15.00 40.00
TTR73 Maurice Jones-Drew 6.00 15.00
TTR74 Maurice Jones-Drew 6.00 15.00
TTR75 Maurice Jones-Drew 6.00 15.00
TTR76 Larry Fitzgerald 8.00 20.00
TTR77 Larry Fitzgerald 8.00 20.00
TTR78 Larry Fitzgerald 8.00 20.00
TTR79 Eric Dickerson 10.00 25.00
TTR80 Eric Dickerson 10.00 25.00
TTR81 Eric Dickerson 10.00 25.00
TTR82 Tony Dorsett 12.00 30.00
TTR83 Tony Dorsett 12.00 30.00
TTR84 Tony Dorsett 12.00 30.00
TTR85 Marcus Allen 12.00 30.00
TTR86 Marcus Allen 12.00 30.00
TTR87 Marcus Allen 12.00 30.00
TTR88 Dan Marino 25.00 60.00
TTR89 Dan Marino 25.00 60.00
TTR90 Dan Marino 25.00 60.00
TTR91 Dwayne Bowe 6.00 15.00
TTR92 Dwayne Bowe 6.00 15.00
TTR93 Dwayne Bowe 6.00 15.00
TTR94 Andre Johnson 6.00 15.00
TTR95 Andre Johnson 6.00 15.00
TTR96 Andre Johnson 6.00 15.00
TTR97 Chris Johnson 8.00 20.00
TTR98 Chris Johnson 8.00 20.00
TTR99 Chris Johnson 8.00 20.00
TTR100 Mike Kafka 5.00 12.00
TTR101 Mike Kafka 5.00 12.00
TTR102 Mike Kafka 5.00 12.00
TTR103 Ray Lewis 10.00 25.00
TTR104 Ray Lewis 10.00 25.00
TTR105 Ray Lewis 10.00 25.00
TTR106 Jeremy Maclin 6.00 15.00
TTR107 Jeremy Maclin 6.00 15.00
TTR108 Jeremy Maclin 6.00 15.00
TTR109 Knowshon Moreno 6.00 15.00
TTR110 Knowshon Moreno 6.00 15.00
TTR111 Knowshon Moreno 6.00 15.00
TTR112 Rashard Mendenhall 6.00 15.00
TTR113 Rashard Mendenhall 6.00 15.00
TTR114 Rashard Mendenhall 6.00 15.00
TTR115 Joe Montana 25.00 60.00
TTR116 Joe Montana 25.00 60.00
TTR117 Joe Montana 25.00 60.00
TTR118 Santana Moss 6.00 15.00
TTR119 Santana Moss 6.00 15.00
TTR120 Santana Moss 6.00 15.00
TTR121 Willis McGahee 6.00 15.00
TTR122 Willis McGahee 6.00 15.00
TTR123 Willis McGahee 6.00 15.00
TTR124 Adrian Peterson 15.00 40.00
TTR125 Adrian Peterson 15.00 40.00
TTR126 Adrian Peterson 15.00 40.00
TTR127 Troy Polamalu 10.00 25.00
TTR128 Troy Polamalu 10.00 25.00
TTR129 Troy Polamalu 10.00 25.00
TTR130 Ed Reed 10.00 25.00
TTR131 Ed Reed 10.00 25.00
TTR132 Ed Reed 10.00 25.00
TTR133 Philip Rivers 8.00 20.00
TTR134 Philip Rivers 8.00 20.00
TTR135 Philip Rivers 8.00 20.00
TTR136 Steve Smith 6.00 15.00
TTR137 Steve Smith 6.00 15.00
TTR138 Steve Smith 6.00 15.00
TTR139 Roddy White 6.00 15.00
TTR140 Roddy White 6.00 15.00
TTR141 Roddy White 6.00 15.00
TTR142 Thurman Thomas 12.00 30.00
TTR143 Thurman Thomas 12.00 30.00
TTR144 Thurman Thomas 12.00 30.00
TTR145 Matthew Stafford 8.00 20.00
TTR146 Matthew Stafford 8.00 20.00
TTR147 Matthew Stafford 8.00 20.00
TTR148 Earl Campbell 12.00 30.00
TTR149 Earl Campbell 12.00 30.00
TTR150 Earl Campbell 12.00 30.00
TTR151 Troy Aikman 15.00 40.00
TTR152 Troy Aikman 15.00 40.00
TTR153 Troy Aikman 15.00 40.00
TTR154 Roger Staubach 15.00 40.00
TTR155 Roger Staubach 15.00 40.00
TTR156 Roger Staubach 15.00 40.00
TTR157 Eric Berry 5.00 12.00
TTR158 Eric Berry 5.00 12.00
TTR159 Eric Berry 5.00 12.00

2010 Topps Triple Threads Relic Combos

STATED PRINT RUN 36 SER.#'d SETS
*EMERALD/18: .5X TO 1.2X BASIC JSY/36
*SEPIA/27: .4X TO 1X BASIC JSY/36
TTRC1 Andre Johnson 8.00 20.00
Larry Fitzgerald
Randy Moss
TTRC2 Chris Johnson 12.00 30.00
Adrian Peterson
Maurice Jones-Drew
TTRC3 Mark Sanchez 8.00 20.00
Matthew Stafford
Joe Flacco
TTRC4 Peyton Manning 15.00 40.00
Reggie Wayne
Eric Dickerson
TTRC5 Tony Romo 10.00 25.00
Felix Jones
Jason Witten
TTRC6 Eli Manning 10.00 25.00
Tony Romo
Kevin Kolb
TTRC7 Frank Gore 6.00 15.00
Maurice Jones-Drew
Steven Jackson
TTRC8 Eddie Royal 6.00 15.00
Demaryius Thomas
Eric Decker
TTRC9 Matthew Stafford 20.00 50.00
Sam Bradford
Jimmy Clausen
TTRC10 Roger Staubach 20.00 50.00
Tony Dorsett
Emmitt Smith
TTRC11 Matt Ryan 8.00 20.00
Roddy White
Tony Gonzalez
TTRC12 Elvis Dumervil 10.00 25.00
Jared Allen
Ndamukong Suh
TTRC13 Joe Montana 30.00 80.00
Dan Marino
John Elway
TTRC14 Joe Montana 15.00 40.00
Tom Brady
Jimmy Clausen
TTRC15 Ronnie Lott 12.00 30.00
Troy Polamalu
Ed Reed
TTRC16 Carson Palmer 6.00 16.00
Jordan Shipley
Jermaine Gresham
TTRC17 Matt Leinart 8.00 20.00
Larry Fitzgerald
Andre Roberts
TTRC18 Mark Sanchez 8.00 20.00
LaDainian Tomlinson
Joe McKnight
TTRC19 Matt Cassel 5.00 12.00
Dwayne Bowe
Dexter McCluster
TTRC20 DeMarcus Ware 6.00 15.00
Dwight Freeney
Mario Williams
TTRC21 Chad Henne 6.00 15.00
Brandon Marshall
Ricky Williams
TTRC22 Matthew Stafford 8.00 20.00
Calvin Johnson
Jahvid Best
TTRC23 Tom Brady 12.00 30.00
Wes Welker
Laurence Maroney
TTRC24 Santana Moss 6.00 15.00
Clinton Portis
Devin Thomas
TTRC25 Ben Roethlisberger 8.00 20.00
Rashard Mendenhall
Jonathan Dwyer
TTRC26 Matt Forte 8.00 20.00
Devin Hester
Earl Bennett
TTRC27 Patrick Willis 5.00 12.00
Rolando McClain
Jerod Mayo
TTRC28 Vince Young 8.00 20.00
Chris Johnson
Damian Williams
TTRC29 Ben Roethlisberger 8.00 20.00
Hines Ward
Emmanuel Sanders
TTRC30 Tim Tebow 20.00 50.00
{Demaryius Thomas
Eric Decker
TTRC31 Ryan Mathews 10.00 25.00
Jahvid Best
Toby Gerhart
TTRC32 Gerald McCoy 8.00 20.00
Arrelious Benn
Mike Williams
TTRC33 Rob Gronkowski 12.00 30.00
Taylor Price
Aaron Hernandez
TTRC34 Tim Tebow 20.00 50.00
Aaron Hernandez
Anthony Dixon
TTRC35 Nnamdi Asomugha 8.00 20.00
Darrelle Revis
Champ Bailey
TTRC36 Carson Palmer 10.00 25.00
Joe Flacco
Colt McCoy
TTRC37 Philip Rivers 20.00 50.00
Tim Tebow
Matt Cassel
TTRC38 Dexter McCluster 5.00 12.00
Montario Hardesty
Brandon LaFell
TTRC39 Jimmy Clausen 10.00 25.00
Brandon LaFell
Armanti Edwards
TTRC40 C.J. Spiller 10.00 25.00
Ryan Mathews
Jahvid Best
TTRC41 Andre Johnson 10.00 25.00
Steve Slaton
Ben Tate
TTRC42 Andre Roberts 5.00 12.00
Armanti Edwards
Taylor Price
TTRC43 Devin Hester 10.00 25.00
Greg Olsen
Matt Forte
TTRC44 Marques Colston 6.00 15.00
Roddy White
Steve Smith
TTRC45 C.J. Spiller 8.00 20.00
Demaryius Thomas
Jonathan Dwyer
TTRC46 Sam Bradford 20.00 50.00
Colt McCoy
Dez Bryant
TTRC47 Arrelious Benn 6.00 15.00
Eric Decker
Mike Kafka
TTRC48 Mike Williams 8.00 20.00
Marcus Easley
Mardy Gilyard
TTRC49 Damian Williams 8.00 20.00
Joe McKnight
Jahvid Best
TTRC50 Sam Bradford 20.00 50.00
Jimmy Clausen
Colt McCoy
TTRC51 Damian Williams 5.00 12.00
Brandon LaFell
Emmanuel Sanders
TTRC52 Jahvid Best 8.00 20.00
Toby Gerhart
*Damian Williams
TTRC53 Ben Tate 6.00 15.00
Montario Hardesty
Anthony Dixon
TTRC54 Sam Bradford 20.00 50.00
Gerald McCoy
Jermaine Gresham
TTRC55 Ben Tate 6.00 15.00
Montario Hardesty
Dexter McCluster
TTRC56 Jermaine Gresham 15.00 40.00
Demaryius Thomas
Dez Bryant
TTRC57 Sam Bradford 20.00 50.00
Tim Tebow
Jimmy Clausen
TTRC58 Ndamukong Suh 10.00 25.00
Gerald McCoy
Eric Berry
TTRC59 Toby Gerhart 6.00 15.00
Ben Tate
Montario Hardesty
TTRC60 Dez Bryant 15.00 40.00
Demaryius Thomas
Dexter McCluster

2010 Topps Triple Threads Relic Double Combos

STATED PRINT RUN 36 SER.#'d SETS
*EMERALD/18: .5X TO 1.2X BASIC JSY/36
*SEPIA/27: .4X TO 1X BASIC JSY/36
1 Adrian Peterson 40.00 80.00
Larry Fitzgerald
Peyton Manning
O.J. Spiller
Dez Bryant
Sam Bradford
2 Roger Staubach 50.00 100.00
Troy Aikman
Tony Romo
Tony Dorsett
Emmitt Smith
Felix Jones
3 Dan Marino 60.00 120.00
Joe Montana
John Elway
Joe Namath
Steve Young
Troy Aikman
4 C.J. Spiller 25.00 60.00
Ryan Mathews
Jahvid Best
Toby Gerhart
Ben Tate
Montario Hardesty
5 Sam Bradford 40.00 100.00
Tim Tebow
Jimmy Clausen
C.J. Spiller
Ryan Mathews
Jahvid Best
6 Tim Tebow 40.00 80.00
Dexter McCluster
Montario Hardesty
Ben Tate
Brandon LaFell
Anthony Dixon
7 Sam Bradford 40.00 80.00
Dez Bryant
Gerald McCoy
Colt McCoy
Jordan Shipley
Ndamukong Suh
8 Mike Williams 25.00 60.00
Mardy Gilyard
Marcus Easley
Demaryius Thomas
Jimmy Graham
Jacoby Ford
9 C.J. Spiller 25.00 60.00
Demaryius Thomas
Jonathan Dwyer
Ben Tate
Brandon LaFell
Montario Hardesty
10 Peyton Manning 60.00 120.00
Tom Brady
Philip Rivers
Brett Favre
Eli Manning
Matt Ryan
11 Roger Staubach 40.00 80.00
Tony Dorsett
12 Brett Favre 50.00 100.00
Aaron Rodgers
13 Ray Lewis 25.00 50.00
Ed Reed
14 Marcus Allen 20.00 40.00
Reggie Bush
15 Dan Marino 50.00 100.00
Larry Fitzgerald

2010 Topps Triple Threads Relic XXIV

STATED PRINT RUN 18 SER.#'d SETS
*GOLD/9: .6X TO 1.5X BASIC JSY/18
TFR1 Brett Favre 50.00 120.00
TFR2 Sam Bradford 25.00 60.00
TFR3 Peyton Manning 15.00 40.00
TFR4 DeMarcus Ware 8.00 20.00
TFR5 Dan Marino 25.00 60.00
TFR6 C.J. Spiller 10.00 25.00
TFR7 Chris Johnson 10.00 25.00
TFR8 Hines Ward 8.00 20.00
TFR9 Demaryius Thomas 10.00 25.00
TFR10 Marcus Allen 12.00 30.00
TFR11 Dez Bryant 20.00 50.00
TFR12 LaDainian Tomlinson 15.00 40.00
TFR13 Jimmy Clausen 6.00 15.00
TFR14 Clinton Portis 8.00 20.00
TFR15 Thurman Thomas 12.00 30.00
TFR16 Ryan Mathews 12.00 30.00
TFR17 Tim Tebow 25.00 60.00
TFR18 Steve Young 15.00 40.00

2010 Topps Triple Threads Rookie and Rising Star Autographed Relic Dual

STATED PRINT RUN 50 SER.#'d SETS
*GOLD/25: .5 X TO 1.2X BASIC AU/50
1 Sam Bradford 100.00 200.00
Dez Bryant
2 Percy Harvin
Dexter McCluster
3 C.J. Spiller 30.00 60.00
Jonathan Dwyer
4 Ryan Mathews 30.00 80.00
Jahvid Best
5 Troy Aikman 100.00 200.00
Sam Bradford
6 Mark Sanchez 40.00 100.00
Jimmy Clausen

2010 Topps Triple Threads Sepia

*VETS 1-90: .5X TO 1.2X BASIC CARDS
*RETIRED 91-100: .5X TO 1.2X BASIC CARDS
1-100 STATED PRINT RUN 499
*ROOKIE JSY AU: .4X TO 1X BASIC CARDS
101-135 ROOKIE JSY AU PRINT RUN 70

2011 Topps Triple Threads

1-100 VETERAN PRINT RUN 999
101-136 ROOKIE JSY AU PRINT RUN 99
EXCH EXPIRATION: 11/30/2014
1 Tom Brady 2.00 5.00
2 LeGarrette Blount 1.00 2.50
3 Jamaal Charles 1.00 2.50
4 Brian Urlacher 1.25 3.00
5 Matt Schaub 1.00 2.50
6 Ed Reed 1.00 2.50
7 Marshawn Lynch 1.00 2.50
8 Jay Cutler 1.00 2.50
9 Jahvid Best 1.00 2.50
10 Drew Brees 1.25 3.00
11 Frank Gore 1.00 2.50
12 Mike Williams 1.00 2.50
13 Hakeem Nicks 1.00 2.50
14 Steven Jackson 1.00 2.50
15 Rob Gronkowski 1.25 3.00
16 Roddy White 1.00 2.50
17 Mark Sanchez 1.25 3.00
18 Maurice Jones-Drew 1.00 2.50
19 LeSean McCoy 1.00 2.50
20 LaDainian Tomlinson 1.25 3.00
21 Michael Turner 1.00 2.50
22 Nnamdi Asomugha 1.00 2.50
23 Chad Ochocinco 1.00 2.50
24 Sam Bradford 1.25 3.00
25 Calvin Johnson 1.25 3.00
26 Tim Tebow 2.50 6.00
27 Fred Jackson 1.25 3.00
28 Jerome Bettis 1.25 3.00
29 Dwayne Bowe 1.00 2.50
30 Adrian Peterson 1.50 4.00
31 Brandon Lloyd 1.00 2.50
32 Junior Seau 1.25 3.00
33 Sidney Rice 1.00 2.50
34 Gale Sayers 1.25 3.00
35 Matt Hasselbeck 1.00 2.50
36 Ryan Mathews 1.00 2.50
37 Josh Freeman 1.25 3.00
38 Greg Jennings 1.00 2.50
39 Jonathan Stewart 1.00 2.50
40 Larry Fitzgerald 1.00 2.50
41 Brandon Marshall 1.00 2.50
42 Clay Matthews 1.25 3.00
43 Matt Forte 1.00 2.50
44 Jerod Mayo .75 2.00
45 Dan Marino 2.50 6.00
46 David Garrard 1.00 2.50
47 Wes Welker 1.25 3.00
48 Jerry Rice 2.00 5.00
49 Chris Johnson 1.00 2.50
50 Aaron Rodgers 2.00 5.00
51 Dez Bryant 1.25 3.00
52 DeSean Jackson 1.00 2.50
53 Anquan Boldin 1.00 2.50
54 John Elway 2.00 5.00
55 Brett Favre 2.50 6.00
56 Arian Foster 1.00 2.50
57 Jeremy Maclin 1.00 2.50
58 Percy Harvin 1.00 2.50
59 Tony Romo 1.25 3.00
60 Tony Gonzalez 1.00 2.50
61 Joe Flacco 1.25 3.00
62 Terry Bradshaw 1.50 4.00
63 Antonio Gates 1.00 2.50
64 Matt Ryan 1.25 3.00
65 Steve Johnson 1.00 2.50
66 Santana Moss 1.00 2.50
67 Jordy Nelson 1.00 2.50
68 Andre Johnson 1.00 2.50
69 Knowshon Moreno 1.00 2.50
70 Philip Rivers 1.25 3.00
71 Steve Smith 1.00 2.50
72 Vernon Davis 1.00 2.50
73 DeMarcus Ware 1.00 2.50
74 Austin Collie 1.00 2.50
75 Matthew Stafford 1.25 3.00
76 Marcedes Lewis .75 2.00
77 Joe Montana 2.50 6.00
78 Marques Colston 1.00 2.50
79 Reggie Wayne 1.00 2.50
80 Troy Polamalu 1.25 3.00
81 Peyton Hillis 1.00 2.50
82 Mike Wallace 1.25 3.00
83 Shonn Greene 1.00 2.50
84 Darren McFadden 1.00 2.50
85 Eli Manning 1.25 3.00
86 Pierre Thomas 1.00 2.50
87 Matt Cassel 1.00 2.50
88 Rashard Mendenhall 1.00 2.50
89 Miles Austin 1.00 2.50
90 Michael Vick 1.25 3.00
91 BenJarvus Green-Ellis 1.00 2.50
92 Ahmad Bradshaw 1.00 2.50
93 Ndamukong Suh 1.25 3.00
94 Santonio Holmes 1.00 2.50
95 Justin Tuck 1.00 2.50
96 Ben Roethlisberger 1.25 3.00
97 Joseph Addai 1.00 2.50
98 Ray Rice 1.00 2.50
99 Joe Namath 1.50 4.00
100 Peyton Manning 2.00 5.00
103A Vincent Brown JSY AU RC 8.00 20.00

103B Vincent Brown SD JSY AU RC 8.00 20.00
103C Vincent Brown MFL JSY AU RC 8.00 20.00
104A Daniel Thomas JSY AU RC 12.00 30.00
104B Daniel Thomas NFL JSY AU RC 12.00 30.00
104C Daniel Thomas MIA JSY AU RC 12.00 30.00
105A Kyle Rudolph JSY AU RC 8.00 20.00
105B Kyle Rudolph NFL JSY AU RC 8.00 20.00
105C Kyle Rudolph MIN JSY AU RC 8.00 20.00
106A Bilal Powell JSY AU RC 5.00 12.00
106B Bilal Powell NFL JSY AU RC 5.00 12.00
106C Bilal Powell NYJ JSY AU RC 5.00 12.00
107A Jordan Todman JSY AU RC 5.00 12.00
107B Jordan Todman NFL JSY AU RC 5.00 12.00
107C Jordan Todman SD JSY AU RC 5.00 12.00
109A Shane Vereen JSY AU RC 8.00 20.00
109B Shane Vereen NFL JSY AU RC 8.00 20.00
109C Shane Vereen NE JSY AU RC 8.00 20.00
110 Cam Newton JSY AU RC 175.00 300.00
112A Kendall Hunter JSY AU RC 12.00 30.00
112B Kendall Hunter NFL JSY AU RC 12.00 30.00
112C Kendall Hunter SF JSY AU RC 12.00 30.00
115A Jerrel Jernigan JSY AU RC 6.00 15.00
115B Jerrel Jernigan NFL JSY AU RC 6.00 15.00
115C Jerrel Jernigan NYG JSY AU RC 6.00 15.00
119A Alex Green JSY AU RC 8.00 20.00
119B Alex Green NFL JSY AU RC 8.00 20.00
119C Alex Green GB JSY AU RC 8.00 20.00
125A Edmond Gates JSY AU RC 6.00 15.00
125B Edmond Gates NFL JSY AU RC 6.00 15.00
125C Edmond Gates MIA JSY AU RC 6.00 15.00
126A Austin Pettis JSY AU RC 6.00 15.00
126B Austin Pettis NFL JSY AU RC 6.00 15.00
126C Austin Pettis STL JSY AU RC 6.00 15.00
127A Jamie Harper JSY AU RC 8.00 20.00
127B Jamie Harper NFL JSY AU RC 8.00 20.00
127C Jamie Harper TEN JSY AU RC 8.00 20.00
129A Stevan Ridley JSY AU RC 10.00 25.00
129B Stevan Ridley NFL JSY AU RC 10.00 25.00
129C Stevan Ridley NE JSY AU RC 10.00 25.00
132A Delone Carter JSY AU RC 6.00 15.00
132B Delone Carter NFL JSY AU RC 6.00 15.00
132C Delone Carter IND JSY AU RC 6.00 15.00
134A DeMarco Murray JSY AU RC 40.00 80.00
134B DeMarco Murray NFL JSY AU RC 40.00 80.00
134C DeMarco Murray DAL JSY AU RC 40.00 80.00
135A Taiwan Jones JSY AU RC 8.00 20.00
135B Taiwan Jones NFL JSY AU RC 8.00 20.00
135C Taiwan Jones OAK JSY AU RC 8.00 20.00

2011 Topps Triple Threads Emerald

*VETS/250: .6X TO 1.5X BASIC CARDS
1-100 VETERAN PRINT RUN 250
*ROOKIE JSY AU/50: .5X TO 1.2X BASIC AU
101-136 ROOKIE JSY AU PRINT RUN 50
101A Torrey Smith JSY AU 15.00 40.00
113A Leonard Hankerson JSY AU 10.00 25.00
116A Greg Little JSY AU 10.00 25.00
121A Randall Cobb JSY AU 12.00 30.00

2011 Topps Triple Threads Gold

*VETS/99: 1X TO 2.5X BASIC CARDS
1-100 VETERAN PRINT RUN 9
*ROOKIE JSY AU/25: .8X TO 2X BASIC AU
101-136 ROOKIE JSY AU PRINT RUN 25

2011 Topps Triple Threads Ruby

*VETS/25: 2X TO 5X BASIC CARDS
1-100 VETERAN PRINT RUN 25
UNPRICED ROOKIE JSY AU PRINT RUN 10

2011 Topps Triple Threads Sepia

*VETS/300: .5X TO 1.2X BASIC CARDS
1-100 VETERAN PRINT RUN 300
*ROOKIE AU/70: .4X TO 1X BASIC JSY AU
101-136 ROOKIE JSY AU PRINT RUN 70

2011 Topps Triple Threads Autographed Relic Combos

STATED PRINT RUN 27 SER.#'d SETS
*EMERALD/18: .5X TO 1.2X COMBO AU/27
RC1 Michael Vick 40.00 80.00
DeSean Jackson
Jeremy Maclin
RC3 Knowshon Moreno 60.00 120.00
Tim Tebow
Von Miller
RC4 Randall Cobb 30.00 60.00
Mikel Leshoure
Kyle Rudolph
RC5 Cam Newton 125.00 250.00
Von Miller
Marcell Dareus
RC6 Cam Newton 150.00 250.00
Jake Locker
Blaine Gabbert
RC8 Mark Ingram 40.00 100.00
Ryan Williams
Shane Vereen
RC9 Christian Ponder 60.00 120.00
Andy Dalton
Colin Kaepernick
RC10 Ryan Mallett 30.00 80.00
Shane Vereen
Stevan Ridley
RC11 Jerrel Jernigan 15.00 40.00
Vincent Brown
Austin Pettis
RC13 Titus Young 20.00 50.00
Torrey Smith
Greg Little
RC14 Mikel Leshoure 30.00 80.00
Daniel Thomas
DeMarco Murray
RC15 Colin Kaepernick 20.00 50.00
Titus Young
Austin Pettis
RC16 Leonard Hankerson 30.00 80.00
Jerrel Jernigan
DeMarco Murray
RC17 Drew Brees 90.00 150.00
Marques Colston
Mark Ingram
RC19 Kendall Hunter 20.00 50.00
Delone Carter
Taiwan Jones
RC21 A.J. Green 30.00 80.00
Torrey Smith
Greg Little

2011 Topps Triple Threads Autographed Relic Duals

STATED PRINT RUN 18 SER.#'d SETS
EXCH EXPIRATION: 11/30/2014
TTARP1 Michael Vick 60.00 120.00
DeSean Jackson
TTARP2 Adrian Peterson 125.00 200.00
DeMarco Murray
TTARP3 John Elway 250.00 400.00
Tim Tebow
TTARP4 Drew Brees 175.00 300.00
Peyton Manning
TTARP5 Brett Favre 400.00 600.00
Aaron Rodgers
TTARP6 Roger Staubach 75.00 150.00
Tony Romo

2011 Topps Triple Threads Autographed Relics

STATED PRINT RUN 18 SER.#'d SETS
*SEPIA/9: .5X TO 1.2X BASIC AU/18
TTAR1 Vincent Brown 12.00 30.00
TTAR2 Vincent Brown 12.00 30.00
TTAR3 Knowshon Moreno 15.00 40.00
TTAR4 Knowshon Moreno 15.00 40.00
TTAR5 Jerrel Jernigan 10.00 25.00
TTAR6 Jerrel Jernigan 10.00 25.00
TTAR10 Phil Simms 15.00 40.00
TTAR11 A.J. Green 50.00 100.00
TTAR12 A.J. Green 50.00 100.00
TTAR13 Hines Ward 50.00 100.00
TTAR14 Hines Ward 50.00 100.00
TTAR15 Drew Brees 75.00 150.00
TTAR16 Drew Brees 75.00 150.00
TTAR17 Daniel Thomas 12.00 30.00
TTAR18 Daniel Thomas 12.00 30.00
TTAR19 Santana Moss 15.00 40.00
TTAR20 Santana Moss 15.00 40.00
TTAR21 Darrelle Revis
TTAR22 Darrelle Revis
TTAR23 Matt Cassel 15.00 40.00
TTAR24 Matt Cassel 15.00 40.00
TTAR25 Christian Ponder 50.00 100.00
TTAR26 Christian Ponder 50.00 100.00
TTAR27 Kendall Hunter 12.00 30.00
TTAR28 Kendall Hunter 12.00 30.00
TTAR29 Earl Campbell 40.00 80.00
TTAR30 Earl Campbell 40.00 80.00
TTAR31 Julio Jones 40.00 80.00
TTAR32 Julio Jones 40.00 80.00
TTAR33 Andy Dalton 50.00 100.00
TTAR34 Andy Dalton 50.00 100.00
TTAR35 Jamaal Charles 15.00 40.00
TTAR36 Jamaal Charles 15.00 40.00
TTAR37 Colin Kaepernick 15.00 40.00
TTAR38 Colin Kaepernick 15.00 40.00
TTAR39 Ryan Mallett 25.00 60.00
TTAR40 Ryan Mallett 25.00 60.00
TTAR41 Zach Miller 15.00 40.00
TTAR42 Zach Miller 15.00 40.00
TTAR43 Joe Flacco 30.00 60.00
TTAR44 Joe Flacco 30.00 60.00
TTAR45 Jon Baldwin 12.00 30.00
TTAR46 Jon Baldwin 12.00 30.00
TTAR47 Ryan Williams 15.00 40.00
TTAR48 Ryan Williams 15.00 40.00
TTAR49 DeSean Jackson 15.00 40.00
TTAR50 DeSean Jackson 15.00 40.00
TTAR51 Mikel Leshoure 12.00 30.00
TTAR52 Mikel Leshoure 12.00 30.00
TTAR53 Alex Green 12.00 30.00
TTAR54 Alex Green 12.00 30.00
TTAR55 DeMarco Murray 60.00 120.00
TTAR56 DeMarco Murray 60.00 120.00
TTAR57 Greg Little 12.00 30.00
TTAR58 Greg Little 12.00 30.00
TTAR59 Kyle Rudolph 12.00 30.00
TTAR60 Kyle Rudolph 12.00 30.00
TTAR61 Leonard Hankerson 12.00 30.00
TTAR62 Leonard Hankerson 12.00 30.00
TTAR63 Marcell Dareus 12.00 30.00
TTAR64 Marcell Dareus 12.00 30.00
TTAR65 Randall Cobb 30.00 60.00
TTAR66 Randall Cobb 30.00 60.00
TTAR67 Titus Young 15.00 40.00
TTAR68 Titus Young 15.00 40.00
TTAR69 Torrey Smith 15.00 40.00
TTAR70 Torrey Smith 15.00 40.00
TTAR71 Von Miller 25.00 50.00
TTAR72 Von Miller 25.00 50.00

2011 Topps Triple Threads Autographed Unity Relics

STATED PRINT RUN 90 SER.#'d SETS
*EMERALD/50: .5X TO 1.2X BASIC AU/90
*GOLD/25: .6X TO 1.5X BASIC AU/90
*SEPIA/75: .4X TO 1X BASIC AU/90
TTUAR1 Steve Breaston 5.00 12.00
TTUAR2 Steve Breaston 5.00 12.00
TTUAR3 Steve Breaston 5.00 12.00
TTUAR4 Ryan Williams 8.00 20.00
TTUAR5 Ryan Williams 8.00 20.00
TTUAR6 Ryan Williams 8.00 20.00
TTUAR7 Chris Cooley 8.00 20.00
TTUAR8 DeAngelo Hall 6.00 15.00
TTUAR9 Leonard Hankerson 6.00 15.00
TTUAR10 Jon Baldwin 6.00 15.00
TTUAR11 Jon Baldwin 6.00 15.00
TTUAR12 Jon Baldwin 6.00 15.00
TTUAR13 Titus Young 8.00 20.00
TTUAR14 Brandon Pettigrew 6.00 15.00
TTUAR15 Mikel Leshoure 6.00 15.00
TTUAR16 Jamie Harper 6.00 15.00
TTUAR17 Earl Campbell 20.00 40.00
TTUAR18 Jake Locker 30.00 60.00
TTUAR19 Dwayne Bowe 8.00 20.00
TTUAR20 Matt Cassel 8.00 20.00
TTUAR21 Jon Baldwin 6.00 15.00
TTUAR22 Kyle Rudolph 6.00 15.00
TTUAR23 Kyle Rudolph 6.00 15.00
TTUAR24 Kyle Rudolph 6.00 15.00
TTUAR25 Marques Colston 8.00 20.00
TTUAR26 Marques Colston 8.00 20.00
TTUAR27 Marques Colston 8.00 20.00
TTUAR28 Shonn Greene 8.00 20.00
TTUAR29 Dustin Keller 5.00 12.00
TTUAR30 Bilal Powell 4.00 10.00
TTUAR31 Bilal Powell 4.00 10.00
TTUAR32 Shonn Greene 8.00 20.00
TTUAR33 Dustin Keller 5.00 12.00
TTUAR34 Dustin Keller 5.00 12.00
TTUAR35 Bilal Powell 4.00 10.00
TTUAR36 Shonn Greene 8.00 20.00
TTUAR37 Tony Dorsett 20.00 40.00
TTUAR38 Tony Dorsett 20.00 40.00
TTUAR39 Tony Dorsett 20.00 40.00
TTUAR40 Jordan Todman 4.00 10.00
TTUAR41 Antonio Gates 8.00 20.00
TTUAR42 Vincent Brown 6.00 15.00
TTUAR43 Vernon Davis 8.00 20.00
TTUAR44 Patrick Willis 12.00 30.00
TTUAR45 Colin Kaepernick 8.00 20.00
TTUAR46 Colin Kaepernick 8.00 20.00
TTUAR47 Vernon Davis 8.00 20.00
TTUAR48 Patrick Willis 12.00 30.00
TTUAR49 Patrick Willis 12.00 30.00
TTUAR50 Colin Kaepernick 8.00 20.00
TTUAR51 Vernon Davis 8.00 20.00
TTUAR52 DeAngelo Hall 6.00 15.00
TTUAR53 Leonard Hankerson 6.00 15.00
TTUAR54 Chris Cooley 8.00 20.00
TTUAR55 Stevan Ridley 6.00 15.00
TTUAR56 Ryan Mallett 15.00 40.00
TTUAR57 Shane Vereen 6.00 15.00
TTUAR58 Shane Vereen 6.00 15.00
TTUAR59 Stevan Ridley 6.00 15.00
TTUAR60 Ryan Mallett 15.00 40.00
TTUAR61 Ryan Mallett 15.00 40.00
TTUAR62 Shane Vereen 6.00 15.00
TTUAR63 Stevan Ridley 6.00 15.00
TTUAR64 A.J. Green 25.00 50.00
TTUAR65 A.J. Green 25.00 50.00
TTUAR66 A.J. Green 25.00 50.00

2011 Topps Triple Threads Relic

STATED PRINT RUN 36 SER.#'d SETS
*EMERALD/18: .5X TO 1.2X BASIC JSY/36
*GOLD/9: .6X TO 1.5X BASIC JSY/36
*SEPIA/27: .4X TO 1X BASIC JSY/36
MOST HAVE THREE CARDS OF EQUAL VALUE
TTR1 Cam Newton 25.00 60.00
TTR2 Cam Newton 25.00 60.00
TTR3 Cam Newton 25.00 60.00
TTR4 Jake Locker 15.00 40.00
TTR5 Jake Locker 15.00 40.00
TTR6 Jake Locker 15.00 40.00
TTR7 Mark Ingram 12.00 30.00
TTR8 Mark Ingram 12.00 30.00
TTR9 Mark Ingram 12.00 30.00
TTR10 Blaine Gabbert 10.00 25.00
TTR11 Blaine Gabbert 10.00 25.00
TTR12 Blaine Gabbert 10.00 25.00
TTR13 A.J. Green 12.00 30.00
TTR14 A.J. Green 12.00 30.00
TTR15 A.J. Green 12.00 30.00
TTR16 Christian Ponder 12.00 30.00
TTR17 Christian Ponder 12.00 30.00
TTR18 Christian Ponder 12.00 30.00
TTR19 Julio Jones 12.00 30.00
TTR20 Julio Jones 12.00 30.00
TTR21 Julio Jones 12.00 30.00
TTR22 Andy Dalton 15.00 40.00
TTR23 Andy Dalton 15.00 40.00
TTR24 Andy Dalton 15.00 40.00
TTR25 Colin Kaepernick 8.00 20.00
TTR26 Colin Kaepernick 8.00 20.00
TTR27 Colin Kaepernick 8.00 20.00
TTR28 Ryan Mallett 10.00 25.00
TTR29 Ryan Mallett 10.00 25.00
TTR30 Ryan Mallett 10.00 25.00
TTR31 Jon Baldwin 6.00 15.00
TTR32 Jon Baldwin 6.00 15.00
TTR33 Jon Baldwin 6.00 15.00
TTR34 Ryan Williams 8.00 20.00
TTR35 Ryan Williams 8.00 20.00
TTR36 Ryan Williams 8.00 20.00
TTR37 Mikel Leshoure 6.00 15.00
TTR38 Mikel Leshoure 6.00 15.00
TTR39 Mikel Leshoure 6.00 15.00
TTR40 Titus Young 8.00 20.00
TTR41 Titus Young 8.00 20.00
TTR42 Titus Young 8.00 20.00
TTR43 Marcell Dareus 6.00 15.00
TTR44 Marcell Dareus 6.00 15.00
TTR45 Marcell Dareus 6.00 15.00
TTR46 DeMarco Murray 12.00 30.00
TTR47 DeMarco Murray 12.00 30.00
TTR48 DeMarco Murray 12.00 30.00
TTR49 Greg Little 6.00 15.00
TTR50 Greg Little 6.00 15.00
TTR51 Greg Little 6.00 15.00
TTR52 Leonard Hankerson 6.00 15.00
TTR53 Leonard Hankerson 6.00 15.00
TTR54 Leonard Hankerson 6.00 15.00
TTR55 Randall Cobb 8.00 20.00
TTR56 Randall Cobb 8.00 20.00
TTR57 Randall Cobb 8.00 20.00
TTR58 Torrey Smith 8.00 20.00
TTR59 Torrey Smith 8.00 20.00
TTR60 Torrey Smith 8.00 20.00
TTR61 Kyle Rudolph 6.00 15.00
TTR62 Kyle Rudolph 6.00 15.00
TTR63 Kyle Rudolph 6.00 15.00
TTR64 Daniel Thomas 6.00 15.00
TTR65 Daniel Thomas 6.00 15.00
TTR66 Daniel Thomas 6.00 15.00
TTR67 Nnamdi Asomugha 6.00 15.00
TTR68 Nnamdi Asomugha 6.00 15.00
TTR69 Nnamdi Asomugha 6.00 15.00
TTR70 Marion Barber 6.00 15.00
TTR71 Marion Barber 6.00 15.00
TTR72 Marion Barber 6.00 15.00
TTR73 Tom Brady 12.00 30.00
TTR74 Tom Brady 12.00 30.00
TTR75 Tom Brady 12.00 30.00
TTR76 Jay Cutler 6.00 15.00
TTR77 Jay Cutler 6.00 15.00
TTR78 Jay Cutler 6.00 15.00
TTR79 Larry Fitzgerald 6.00 15.00
TTR80 Larry Fitzgerald 6.00 15.00
TTR81 Larry Fitzgerald 6.00 15.00
TTR82 Matt Forte 6.00 15.00
TTR83 Matt Forte 6.00 15.00
TTR84 Matt Forte 6.00 15.00
TTR85 Alex Green 6.00 15.00
TTR86 Alex Green 6.00 15.00
TTR87 Alex Green 6.00 15.00
TTR88 Tony Gonzalez 6.00 15.00
TTR89 Tony Gonzalez 6.00 15.00
TTR90 Tony Gonzalez 6.00 15.00
TTR91 Frank Gore 6.00 15.00
TTR92 Frank Gore 6.00 15.00
TTR93 Frank Gore 6.00 15.00
TTR94 LaDainian Tomlinson 8.00 20.00
TTR95 LaDainian Tomlinson 8.00 20.00
TTR96 Terry Bradshaw 15.00 40.00
TTR97 Devin Hester 8.00 20.00
TTR98 Devin Hester 8.00 20.00
TTR99 Devin Hester 8.00 20.00
TTR100 Brian Urlacher 8.00 20.00
TTR101 Brian Urlacher 8.00 20.00
TTR102 Brian Urlacher 8.00 20.00
TTR103 Chris Johnson 6.00 15.00
TTR104 Chris Johnson 6.00 15.00
TTR105 Chris Johnson 6.00 15.00
TTR106 Felix Jones 6.00 15.00
TTR107 Felix Jones 6.00 15.00
TTR108 Felix Jones 6.00 15.00
TTR109 Jim Plunkett 10.00 25.00
TTR110 Jim Plunkett 10.00 25.00
TTR111 Jim Plunkett 10.00 25.00
TTR112 Troy Polamalu 10.00 25.00
TTR113 Troy Polamalu 10.00 25.00
TTR114 Troy Polamalu 10.00 25.00
TTR115 Ed Reed 8.00 20.00
TTR116 Ed Reed 8.00 20.00
TTR117 Ed Reed 8.00 20.00

2011 Topps Triple Threads Relic Combos

STATED PRINT RUN 36 SER.#'d SETS
*EMERALD/18: .5X TO 1.2X COMBO/36
*SEPIA/27: .4X TO 1X COMBO/36
TTRC1 Joe Namath 40.00 80.00
Joe Montana
John Elway
TTRC2 Matt Ryan 10.00 25.00
Matthew Stafford
Mark Sanchez
TTRC3 Jordy Nelson 6.00 15.00
Eddie Royal
DeSean Jackson
TTRC4 DeMarco Murray 10.00 25.00
Kendall Hunter
Daniel Thomas
TTRC5 Taiwan Jones 8.00 20.00
Darren McFadden
Michael Bush
TTRC6 Paul Posluszny 6.00 15.00
Patrick Willis
David Harris
TTRC7 Mario Williams 6.00 15.00
Reggie Bush
Vince Young
TTRC8 DeAngelo Williams 6.00 15.00
Maurice Jones-Drew
Joseph Addai
TTRC9 Darren McFadden 6.00 15.00
Chris Johnson
Jamaal Charles
TTRC10 Patrick Willis 12.00 30.00
Ray Lewis
Brian Urlacher
TTRC11 Andre Caldwell 6.00 15.00
Percy Harvin
Louis Murphy
TTRC12 Torrey Smith 6.00 15.00
Greg Little
Leonard Hankerson
TTRC13 Cam Newton 25.00 60.00
A.J. Green
Julio Jones
TTRC14 John Elway 15.00 40.00
Tim Tebow
Kyle Orton
TTRC15 Tom Brady 30.00 60.00
Peyton Manning
Dan Marino
TTRC16 Jerry Rice 15.00 40.00
Emmitt Smith
LaDainian Tomlinson
TTRC17 Emmitt Smith 15.00 40.00
LaDainian Tomlinson
Marcus Allen
TTRC18 Steve Young 12.00 30.00
Philip Rivers
Tony Romo
TTRC19 Peyton Manning 20.00 50.00
Tom Brady
Steve Young
TTRC20 Brett Favre 30.00 80.00
Dan Marino
John Elway
TTRC21 Ben Roethlisberger 10.00 25.00
Matt Ryan
Joe Flacco
TTRC22 Jerry Rice 15.00 40.00
Thurman Thomas
Emmitt Smith
TTRC23 Emmitt Smith 15.00 40.00
Franco Harris
Thurman Thomas
TTRC24 Joe Montana 30.00 80.00
Brett Favre
Dan Marino
TTRC25 Cam Newton 25.00 60.00
Von Miller
Marcell Dareus
TTRC26 Cam Newton 25.00 60.00
Jake Locker
Blaine Gabbert
TTRC27 A.J. Green 10.00 25.00
Julio Jones
Jon Baldwin
TTRC28 Mark Ingram 10.00 25.00
Ryan Williams
Shane Vereen
TTRC29 Kendall Hunter 5.00 12.00
Delone Carter
Taiwan Jones
TTRC30 Christian Ponder 12.00 30.00
Andy Dalton
Colin Kaepernick
TTRC31 Ryan Mallett 10.00 25.00
Shane Vereen
Stevan Ridley
TTRC32 Jerrel Jernigan 5.00 12.00
Vincent Brown
Austin Pettis
TTRC33 Julio Jones 10.00 25.00
Marcell Dareus
Mark Ingram
TTRC34 Titus Young 6.00 15.00
Torrey Smith
Greg Little
TTRC35 Mikel Leshoure 10.00 25.00
Daniel Thomas
DeMarco Murray
TTRC36 Delone Carter 6.00 15.00
Taiwan Jones
Jamie Harper
TTRC37 Colin Kaepernick 6.00 15.00
Titus Young
Austin Pettis
TTRC38 Bilal Powell 5.00 12.00
Shane Vereen
Daniel Thomas
TTRC39 A.J. Green 10.00 25.00
Torrey Smith
Greg Little
TTRC40 Leonard Hankerson 10.00 25.00
Jerrel Jernigan
DeMarco Murray

2011 Topps Triple Threads Relic Double Combos

STATED PRINT RUN 36 SER.#'d SETS
*EMERALD/18: .5X TO 1.2X DOUBLE COMBO/36
*SEPIA/27: .4X TO 1X DOUBLE COMBO/36
TTRDC1 Michael Vick 15.00 40.00
TTRDC2 Dan Marino 25.00 60.00
TTRDC3 Brett Favre 30.00 80.00
TTRDC4 Brian Urlacher 15.00 40.00
TTRDC5 Louis Murphy 12.00 30.00
TTRDC6 Wes Welker 15.00 40.00
TTRDC7 Devin Hester 15.00 40.00
TTRDC8 Jay Cutler 12.00 30.00
TTRDC9 Tim Tebow 30.00 80.00
TTRDC10 Tony Romo 15.00 40.00
TTRDC11 Maurice Jones-Drew 12.00 30.00
TTRDC12 Calvin Johnson 15.00 40.00
Titus Young
TTRDC13 Chris Johnson 12.00 30.00
Jamie Harper
TTRDC14 Darren Sproles 12.00 30.00
Daniel Thomas
TTRDC15 Jason Campbell 12.00 30.00

2011 Topps Triple Threads Rookies and Rising Stars Autographed Relics

STATED PRINT RUN 50 SER.#'d SETS
*SEPIA/25: .5X TO 1.2X DUAL AU/50
1 Roddy White 40.00 80.00
Julio Jones
2 DeSean Jackson 15.00 40.00
Shane Vereen
3 Jeremy Maclin 40.00 80.00
Blaine Gabbert
4 LeSean McCoy 15.00 40.00
Jon Baldwin
5 Brandon Pettigrew 15.00 40.00
Kyle Rudolph
6 Shonn Greene 15.00 40.00
Bilal Powell

2011 Topps Triple Threads Super Bowl Legends Relics

STATED PRINT RUN 18 SER.#'d SETS
TTSBL1 Jerry Rice 20.00 50.00
TTSBL2 Joe Namath 15.00 40.00
TTSBL3 Roger Staubach 15.00 40.00
TTSBL4 Tom Brady 15.00 40.00
TTSBL5 Aaron Rodgers 50.00 100.00
TTSBL6 Kurt Warner 15.00 40.00
TTSBL7 Drew Brees 12.00 30.00
TTSBL8 Joe Montana 25.00 60.00
TTSBL9 Marcus Allen 12.00 30.00
TTSBL10 Peyton Manning 15.00 40.00
TTSBL11 Phil Simms 10.00 25.00
TTSBL12 Troy Aikman 15.00 40.00
TTSBL13 Emmitt Smith 20.00 50.00
TTSBL14 Steve Young 15.00 40.00
TTSBL15 John Elway 20.00 50.00

2011 Topps Triple Threads Unity Relics

STATED PRINT RUN 36 SER.#'d SETS
*EMERALD/18: .5X TO 1.2X BASIC JSY/36
*GOLD/9: .6X TO 1.5X BASIC JSY/36
*SEPIA/27: .4X TO 1X BASIC JSY/36
MOST HAVE THREE CARDS OF EQUAL VALUE
TTUSR1 Dan Marino 15.00 40.00
TTUSR2 Dan Marino 15.00 40.00
TTUSR3 Dan Marino 15.00 40.00
TTUSR4 Cam Newton 15.00 40.00
TTUSR5 Cam Newton 15.00 40.00
TTUSR6 Cam Newton 15.00 40.00
TTUSR7 Phil Simms 5.00 12.00
TTUSR8 Phil Simms 5.00 12.00
TTUSR9 Phil Simms 5.00 12.00
TTUSR10 Brett Favre 12.00 30.00
TTUSR11 Brett Favre 12.00 30.00
TTUSR12 Brett Favre 12.00 30.00
TTUSR13 Mark Sanchez 5.00 12.00
TTUSR14 Mark Sanchez 5.00 12.00
TTUSR15 Mark Sanchez 5.00 12.00
TTUSR16 Jason Witten 5.00 12.00
TTUSR17 Jason Witten 5.00 12.00
TTUSR18 Jason Witten 5.00 12.00
TTUSR19 Jason Avant 3.00 8.00
TTUSR20 Jason Avant 3.00 8.00
TTUSR21 Jason Avant 3.00 8.00
TTUSR22 Jordy Nelson 5.00 12.00
TTUSR23 Jordy Nelson 5.00 12.00
TTUSR24 Jordy Nelson 5.00 12.00
TTUSR25 Tom Brady 8.00 20.00
TTUSR26 Tom Brady 8.00 20.00
TTUSR27 Tom Brady 8.00 20.00
TTUSR28 Austin Pettis 3.00 8.00
TTUSR29 Austin Pettis 3.00 8.00
TTUSR30 Austin Pettis 3.00 8.00
TTUSR31 Steven Jackson 4.00 10.00
TTUSR32 Steven Jackson 4.00 10.00
TTUSR33 Steven Jackson 4.00 10.00
TTUSR34 Taiwan Jones 4.00 10.00
TTUSR35 Taiwan Jones 4.00 10.00
TTUSR36 Taiwan Jones 4.00 10.00
TTUSR37 Bilal Powell 2.50 6.00
TTUSR38 Bilal Powell 2.50 6.00
TTUSR39 Bilal Powell 2.50 6.00
TTUSR40 Delone Carter 3.00 8.00
TTUSR41 Delone Carter 3.00 8.00
TTUSR42 Delone Carter 3.00 8.00
TTUSR43 Jordan Todman 2.50 6.00
TTUSR44 Jordan Todman 2.50 6.00
TTUSR45 Jordan Todman 2.50 6.00
TTUSR46 Jason Campbell 4.00 10.00
TTUSR47 Ken Stabler 6.00 15.00
TTUSR48 Jim Plunkett 6.00 15.00
TTUSR49 Jim Plunkett 6.00 15.00
TTUSR50 Jason Campbell 4.00 10.00
TTUSR51 Ken Stabler 6.00 15.00
TTUSR52 Ken Stabler 6.00 15.00
TTUSR53 Jim Plunkett 6.00 15.00
TTUSR54 Jason Campbell 4.00 10.00
TTUSR55 Fred Biletnikoff 6.00 15.00
TTUSR56 Louis Murphy 4.00 10.00
TTUSR57 Darrius Heyward-Bey 3.00 8.00
TTUSR58 Darrius Heyward-Bey 3.00 8.00
TTUSR59 Fred Biletnikoff 6.00 15.00
TTUSR60 Louis Murphy 4.00 10.00
TTUSR61 Louis Murphy 4.00 10.00
TTUSR62 Darrius Heyward-Bey 3.00 8.00
TTUSR63 Fred Biletnikoff 6.00 15.00
TTUSR64 Champ Bailey 4.00 10.00
TTUSR65 Eddie Royal 3.00 8.00
TTUSR66 Von Miller 5.00 12.00
TTUSR67 Von Miller 5.00 12.00
TTUSR68 Champ Bailey 4.00 10.00
TTUSR69 Eddie Royal 3.00 8.00
TTUSR70 Eddie Royal 3.00 8.00
TTUSR71 Von Miller 5.00 12.00
TTUSR72 Champ Bailey 4.00 10.00
TTUSR73 Richard Seymour 3.00 8.00
TTUSR74 Howie Long 8.00 20.00
TTUSR75 Rolando McClain 3.00 8.00
TTUSR76 Rolando McClain 3.00 8.00
TTUSR77 Richard Seymour 3.00 8.00
TTUSR78 Howie Long 8.00 20.00
TTUSR79 Howie Long 8.00 20.00
TTUSR80 Rolando McClain 3.00 8.00
TTUSR81 Richard Seymour 3.00 8.00
TTUSR82 Andre Caldwell 3.00 8.00
TTUSR83 Andy Dalton 10.00 25.00
TTUSR84 A.J. Green 8.00 20.00
TTUSR85 A.J. Green 8.00 20.00
TTUSR86 Andre Caldwell 3.00 8.00
TTUSR87 Andy Dalton 10.00 25.00
TTUSR88 Andy Dalton 10.00 25.00
TTUSR89 A.J. Green 8.00 20.00
TTUSR90 Andre Caldwell 3.00 8.00
TTUSR91 DeMarco Murray 8.00 20.00
TTUSR92 DeMarco Murray 8.00 20.00
TTUSR93 DeMarco Murray 8.00 20.00
TTUSR94 Ryan Williams 5.00 12.00
TTUSR95 Ryan Williams 5.00 12.00
TTUSR96 Ryan Williams 5.00 12.00
TTUSR97 Jon Baldwin 4.00 10.00
TTUSR98 Jon Baldwin 4.00 10.00
TTUSR99 Jon Baldwin 4.00 10.00
TTUSR100 Marcell Dareus 4.00 10.00
TTUSR101 Marcell Dareus 4.00 10.00
TTUSR102 Marcell Dareus 4.00 10.00
TTUSR103 Jerrel Jernigan 3.00 8.00
TTUSR104 Jerrel Jernigan 3.00 8.00
TTUSR105 Jerrel Jernigan 3.00 8.00
TTUSR106 Mario Williams 3.00 8.00
TTUSR107 Mario Williams 3.00 8.00
TTUSR108 Mario Williams 3.00 8.00
TTUSR109 Art Monk 10.00 25.00
TTUSR110 Santana Moss 4.00 10.00
TTUSR111 Leonard Hankerson 4.00 10.00
TTUSR112 Leonard Hankerson 4.00 10.00
TTUSR113 Art Monk 10.00 25.00
TTUSR114 Santana Moss 4.00 10.00
TTUSR115 Santana Moss 4.00 10.00
TTUSR116 Leonard Hankerson 4.00 10.00
TTUSR117 Art Monk 10.00 25.00
TTUSR118 Torrey Smith 5.00 12.00
TTUSR119 Torrey Smith 5.00 12.00
TTUSR120 Torrey Smith 5.00 12.00
TTUSR121 Titus Young 5.00 12.00
TTUSR122 Titus Young 5.00 12.00
TTUSR123 Titus Young 5.00 12.00
TTUSR124 Greg Little 4.00 10.00
TTUSR125 Greg Little 4.00 10.00
TTUSR126 Greg Little 4.00 10.00
TTUSR127 Edmond Gates 3.00 8.00
TTUSR128 Edmond Gates 3.00 8.00
TTUSR129 Edmond Gates 3.00 8.00
TTUSR130 Daniel Thomas 4.00 10.00
TTUSR131 Daniel Thomas 4.00 10.00
TTUSR132 Daniel Thomas 4.00 10.00
TTUSR133 Dustin Keller 4.00 10.00
TTUSR134 Dustin Keller 4.00 10.00
TTUSR135 Dustin Keller 4.00 10.00
TTUSR136 Stevan Ridley 4.00 10.00
TTUSR137 Ryan Mallett 8.00 20.00
TTUSR138 Shane Vereen 4.00 10.00
TTUSR139 Shane Vereen 4.00 10.00
TTUSR140 Stevan Ridley 4.00 10.00
TTUSR141 Ryan Mallett 8.00 20.00
TTUSR142 Ryan Mallett 8.00 20.00
TTUSR143 Shane Vereen 4.00 10.00
TTUSR144 Stevan Ridley 4.00 10.00
TTUSR145 Joe Montana 15.00 40.00
TTUSR146 Colin Kaepernick 5.00 12.00
TTUSR147 Kendall Hunter 4.00 10.00
TTUSR148 Kendall Hunter 4.00 10.00
TTUSR149 Joe Montana 15.00 40.00
TTUSR150 Colin Kaepernick 5.00 12.00
TTUSR151 Colin Kaepernick 5.00 12.00
TTUSR152 Kendall Hunter 4.00 10.00
TTUSR153 Joe Montana 15.00 40.00
TTUSR154 Jared Allen 5.00 12.00
TTUSR155 Christian Ponder 8.00 20.00
TTUSR156 Kyle Rudolph 4.00 10.00
TTUSR157 Kyle Rudolph 4.00 10.00
TTUSR158 Jared Allen 5.00 12.00
TTUSR159 Christian Ponder 8.00 20.00
TTUSR160 Christian Ponder 8.00 20.00
TTUSR161 Kyle Rudolph 4.00 10.00
TTUSR162 Jared Allen 5.00 12.00
TTUSR163 Devery Henderson 3.00 8.00
TTUSR164 Robert Meachem 4.00 10.00
TTUSR165 Mark Ingram 8.00 20.00
TTUSR166 Mark Ingram 8.00 20.00
TTUSR167 Devery Henderson 3.00 8.00
TTUSR168 Robert Meachem 4.00 10.00
TTUSR169 Robert Meachem 4.00 10.00
TTUSR170 Mark Ingram 8.00 20.00
TTUSR171 Devery Henderson 3.00 8.00
TTUSR172 Blaine Gabbert 6.00 15.00
TTUSR173 Blaine Gabbert 6.00 15.00
TTUSR174 Blaine Gabbert 6.00 15.00
TTUSR175 Randall Cobb 5.00 12.00
TTUSR176 Alex Green 4.00 10.00
TTUSR177 A.J. Hawk 4.00 10.00

2005 Topps Turkey Red

This 299-card set was released in January, 2006. The set was issued in the hobby in eight-card packs with an $4 SRP which came 24 packs to a box. Cards numbered 181-230 form a rookie subset.

COMPLETE SET (299) 125.00 250.00
COMP.SET w/o SP's (249) 25.00 60.00
SP STATED ODDS 1:4
1A Eli Manning .60 1.50
1B Eli Manning Ad Back 3.00 8.00
2 Clinton Portis .30 .75
3 Charles Woodson .40 1.00
4A Ray Lewis .40 1.00
4B Ray Lewis Ad Back 2.00 5.00
5 Michael Clayton .25 .60
6 Eric Moulds .25 .60
7 Derrick Blaylock .25 .60
8 Carson Palmer .40 1.00
9 Zach Thomas .40 1.00
10 Dallas Clark .30 .75
11 DeAngelo Hall .30 .75
12 Terrell Owens .40 1.00
13 Brian Griese .30 .75
14 Dunta Robinson .25 .60
15 Kevan Barlow .25 .60
16 Jake Plummer .30 .75
17 James Farrior .25 .60
18A Peyton Manning .75 2.00
18B Peyton Manning Ad Back 4.00 10.00
19 Michael Bennett .30 .75
20 Brian Urlacher .40 1.00
21 Dante Hall .25 .60
22 Deion Branch .25 .60
23 Billy Volek .25 .60
24 Donald Driver .40 1.00
25 LaDainian Tomlinson CL .30 .75
26 Donte Stallworth CL .20 .50
27 Joey Galloway .30 .75
28 Joey Harrington .30 .75
29 T.J. Houshmandzadeh .30 .75
30 LaDainian Tomlinson .40 1.00
31 Darius Watts .25 .60
32 Chris Gamble .25 .60
33 Javon Walker .25 .60
34 Kevin Curtis .30 .75
35 Steven Jackson .40 1.00
36 J.P. Losman .25 .60
37A Champ Bailey .30 .75
37B Champ Bailey Ad Back 1.50 4.00
38 Tiki Barber .40 1.00
39 LaVar Arrington .30 .75
40 Byron Leftwich .30 .75
41 Edgerrin James .30 .75
42 DeShaun Foster .30 .75
43 Darrell Jackson .25 .60
44 Julius Peppers .30 .75
45 David Carr .25 .60
46 Drew Bennett .30 .75
47 Antonio Gates .40 1.00
48A Deuce McAllister .30 .75
48B Deuce McAllister Ad Back 1.50 4.00
49 Patrick Ramsey .30 .75
50 Antonio Bryant .25 .60
51 Quentin Jammer .25 .60
52 Chris Brown .25 .60
53 Eddie Kennison .25 .60
54 Steve McNair .40 1.00
55 Corey Bradford .25 .60
56 Chris Perry .25 .60
57 Curtis Martin .40 1.00
58 Mewelde Moore .25 .60
59 Travis Taylor .25 .60
60 Chad Pennington .40 1.00
61 Chad Johnson .30 .75
62 Kyle Boller .30 .75
63 Tyrone Calico .25 .60
64 Michael Pittman .25 .60
65 Kerry Collins .30 .75
66 Keary Colbert .25 .60
67 LaMont Jordan CL .25 .60
LaMont Slips A Tackle
68 Robert Gallery .25 .60
69 Derrick Mason .30 .75
70 Brian Dawkins .30 .75
71 Chris Simms .30 .75
72 Marc Bulger .30 .75
73 Stephen Davis .30 .75
74 Kurt Warner .40 1.00
75 Todd Heap .30 .75
76 Domanick Davis CL .20 .50
Davis Hits the Hole
77 Shaun Alexander .30 .75
78 Jerry Porter .25 .60
79 Chester Taylor .30 .75
80A Michael Vick .40 1.00
80B Michael Vick Ad Back 2.00 5.00
81 Justin McCareins .25 .60
82 Fred Taylor .30 .75
83 Laveranues Coles .25 .60
84 Steve Smith .40 1.00
85 Sean Taylor .40 1.00
86 Marvin Harrison .40 1.00
87 Ashley Lelie .25 .60
88 Willis McGahee .40 1.00
89 Terence Newman .25 .60
90 Joe Horn .30 .75
91 Lee Suggs .25 .60
92 Keyshawn Johnson .30 .75
93 Desmond Clark .25 .60
94 T.J. Duckett .25 .60
95 Reggie Wayne .40 1.00
96 Donte Stallworth .25 .60
97 Clarence Moore .25 .60
98 Jason Witten .40 1.00
99 Jake Delhomme .30 .75
100 Julius Jones .25 .60
101 Ben Troupe .25 .60
102 Hines Ward .40 1.00
103 Domanick Davis .25 .60
104 B.J. Sams .25 .60
105 Marcus Robinson .25 .60
106 Devery Henderson .25 .60
107 Matt Hasselbeck .30 .75
108 Antonio Pierce .25 .60
109 Santana Moss .30 .75
110 Adam Vinatieri .40 1.00
111 Michael Strahan .40 1.00
112 Greg Jones .25 .60
113 Drew Brees .40 1.00
114 Marcus Robinson .25 .60
115 Michael Jenkins .30 .75
116 Randy McMichael .25 .60
117 Jonathan Vilma .30 .75
118 Greg Lewis .30 .75
119 Ernest Wilford .25 .60
120 Warrick Dunn .30 .75
121 Shaun Alexander CL .25 .60
122 Donnie Edwards .25 .60
123 Antwaan Randle El .30 .75
124 Rod Smith .30 .75
125 Ed Reed .30 .75
126 Muhsin Muhammad .30 .75
127 L.J. Smith .30 .75
128 Chris Chambers .30 .75
129 Matt Schaub .40 1.00
130 Andre Johnson .40 1.00
131 Thomas Jones .40 1.00
132 Robert Ferguson .25 .60
133 Jeremy Shockey .40 1.00
134 William Green .25 .60
135A Ben Roethlisberger .60 1.50
135B Ben Roethlisberger Ad Back 3.00 8.00
136A Donovan McNabb .40 1.00
136B Donovan McNabb Ad Back 2.00 5.00
137 Duce Staley .30 .75
138 Larry Fitzgerald .40 1.00
139 Charles Rogers .25 .60
140 Mark Brunell .30 .75
141 Kevin Jones .25 .60
142 LaMont Jordan .30 .75
143 Aaron Brooks .25 .60
144 Brian Westbrook .30 .75
145 Larry Johnson .30 .75
146 Tommy Maddox .30 .75
147 Corey Dillon .30 .75
148 William Henderson .30 .75
149 Tony Hollings .25 .60
150 Lee Evans .30 .75
151 Kelly Holcomb .25 .60
152 Reuben Droughns .25 .60
153 Keenan McCardell .30 .75
154 Ricky Williams .30 .75
155 Rashaun Woods .25 .60
156 D.J. Williams .25 .60
157 Tom Brady .75 2.00
158 Eric Parker .25 .60
159 Mike Anderson .25 .60
160 Roy Williams WR .30 .75
161 Mike Vanderjagt .25 .60
162 Ronald Curry .25 .60
163 Priest Holmes .30 .75
164 Bernard Berrian .30 .75
165 Brian Finneran .25 .60
166 Tony Gonzalez .30 .75
167 Chris McAlister .25 .60
168 Gus Frerotte .25 .60
169 Bryant Johnson .25 .60
170 Jay Fiedler .25 .60
171 Bubba Franks .25 .60
172 Tony Romo 5.00 10.00
173 Jamal Lewis .30 .75
174 Torry Holt .30 .75
175 Ladell Betts .25 .60
176 Bertrand Berry .25 .60
177 Josh McCown .30 .75
178 Jonathan Wells .25 .60
179 Plaxico Burress .30 .75
180 Rudi Johnson .30 .75
181 Cedric Benson RC .75 2.00
182 Carlos Rogers RC .75 2.00
183 Terrence Murphy RC .50 1.25
184 Frank Gore RC 1.25 3.00
185 Vincent Jackson RC 1.00 2.50
186 Ciatrick Fason RC .50 1.25
187 Alex Smith QB RC 1.25 3.00

188 Mike Williams .75 2.00
189 Kyle Orton RC .75 2.00
190A Ronnie Brown RC 1.00 2.50
190B Ronnie Brown 4.00 10.00
191 Charlie Frye RC .75 2.00
192 Mark Bradley RC .50 1.25
193 Antrel Rolle RC .75 2.00
194 Roscoe Parrish RC .50 1.25
195 Ryan Moats RC .60 1.50
196 Andrew Walter RC .60 1.50
197 Troy Williamson RC .60 1.50
198 Cadillac Williams RC .75 2.00
199 Adam Jones RC .60 1.50
200 Braylon Edwards RC 1.00 2.50
201 Vernand Morency RC .60 1.50
202 Ryan Fitzpatrick RC 1.25 3.00
203 Heath Miller RC 1.00 2.50
204 Eric Shelton RC .50 1.25
205 Jason Campbell RC .75 2.00
206 David Pollack RC .60 1.50
207 Stefan LeFors RC .50 1.25
208 DeMarcus Ware RC 1.50 4.00
209 J.J. Arrington RC .60 1.50
210 Marion Barber RC .75 2.00
211 Samkon Gado RC .75 2.00
212 Roddy White RC 1.00 2.50
213 Brandon Jacobs RC 1.00 2.50
214 Mark Clayton RC .75 2.00
215 Alex Smith TE RC .50 1.25
216 Darren Sproles RC .75 2.00
217 Fabian Washington RC .60 1.50
218 Brandon Jones RC .60 1.50
219 Derrick Johnson RC .60 1.50
220 Dan Orlovsky RC .75 2.00
221 Aaron Rodgers RC 10.00 20.00
222 Cedric Houston RC .75 2.00
223 Reggie Brown RC .50 1.25
224 Scottie Vines RC .75 2.00
225 Willie Parker .30 .75
226 Matt Jones RC .75 2.00
227 Odell Thurman RC .75 2.00
228 Alvin Pearman RC .50 1.25
229 Chris Henry RC .75 2.00
230 Courtney Roby RC .60 1.50
231 Isaac Bruce .30 .75
232 Warrick Dunn CL .25 .60
233 Willis McGahee CL .30 .75
234 Marcus Pollard .25 .60
235 Jason Taylor .30 .75
236 Joe Namath 2.50 6.00
237 Joe Montana 4.00 10.00
238 Barry Sanders 2.50 6.00
239 Jim Brown 2.00 5.00
240 Terry Bradshaw 2.50 6.00
241 Ahman Green .30 .75
242 Tiki Barber CL .30 .75
243 Julius Jones CL .20 .50
244 Daunte Culpepper .30 .75
245 Edgerrin James CL .25 .60
246 Trent Green 2.50 6.00
247 Dwight Freeney 2.50 6.00
248A Brett Favre 5.00 12.00
248B Brett Favre Ad Back 6.00 15.00
249 Marshall Faulk 3.00 8.00
250 Jerome Bettis 3.00 8.00
251 Nate Burleson 2.00 5.00
252 Brandon Lloyd 2.00 5.00
253 Randy Moss 3.00 8.00
254 Drew Bledsoe 3.00 8.00
255 Brandon Stokley 2.00 5.00
256 Takeo Spikes 2.00 5.00
257 Philip Rivers 3.00 8.00
258 Lito Sheppard 2.50 6.00
259 Jimmy Smith 2.50 6.00
260 Tatum Bell 2.00 5.00
261 Allen Rossum 2.00 5.00
262 Amani Toomer 2.50 6.00
263 Jabar Gaffney 2.00 5.00
264 Jonathan Ogden 2.00 5.00
265 John Abraham 2.00 5.00
266 Aaron Stecker 2.00 5.00
267 Jason Elam 2.00 5.00
268 Najeh Davenport 2.50 6.00
269 Alge Crumpler 2.50 6.00
270 Roy Williams S 2.00 5.00
271 Trent Dilfer 2.50 6.00
272 Anquan Boldin 2.50 6.00
273 Artose Pinner 2.00 5.00
274 David Garrard 2.50 6.00
275 Terry Glenn 2.00 5.00
276 Adam Archuleta 2.00 5.00
277 Jeremiah Trotter 2.00 5.00
278 Travis Henry 2.00 5.00
279 Rex Grossman 2.50 6.00
280 Maurice Morris 2.00 5.00
281 Mike Alstott 2.50 6.00
282 Justin Gage 2.00 5.00
283 Dennis Northcutt 2.00 5.00
284 David Givens 2.00 5.00
285 Dominic Rhodes 2.50 6.00
286 Gerald Ford 2.00 5.00
287 Ronald Reagan 2.00 5.00
288 John F. Kennedy 2.00 5.00
289 Ulysses S. Grant 2.00 5.00
CL1 Jumbo Checklist 1 .40 1.00
CL2 Jumbo Checklist 2 .40 1.00

2005 Topps Turkey Red Black

*VETERANS 1-245: 4X TO 10X BASIC CARDS
*VETS 1-245: .8X TO 2X BASIC AD BACKS
*ROOKIES: 1.2X TO 3X BASIC CARDS
*RETIRED 236-240: 1X TO 2.5X BASIC CARDS
*VETERANS 246-285: .5X TO 1.2X
*PRESIDENTS 286-289: .6X TO 1.5X
BLACK STATED ODDS 1:20 HOB/RET
190B Ronnie Brown Ad Back 6.00 15.00
248A Brett Favre
248B Brett Favre Ad Back 10.00 25.00

2005 Topps Turkey Red Gold

*VETERANS 1-245: 8X TO 20X BASIC CARDS
*VETS 1-245: 1.5X TO 4X BASIC AD BACKS
*ROOKIES: 2.5X TO 6X BASIC CARDS
*RETIRED 236-240: 2X TO 5X BASIC CARDS
*VETERANS 246-285: 1X TO 2.5X
*PRESIDENTS 286-289: 1.2X TO 3X
GOLD/50 ODDS 1:41 HOB, 1:42 RET
190B Ronnie Brown Ad Back 20.00 50.00
248A Brett Favre 20.00 50.00
248B Brett Favre Ad Back 20.00 50.00

2005 Topps Turkey Red Red

*VETERANS 1-245: 1.2X TO 3X BASIC CARDS
*VETS 1-245: .3X TO .8X BASIC AD BACKS
*ROOKIES: .6X TO 1.5X BASIC CARDS
*RETIRED 236-240: .4X TO 1X BASIC CARDS
*VETERANS 246-285: .15X TO .4X
*PRESIDENTS 286-289: .4X TO 1X
OVERALL PARALLEL ODDS 1:1
190B Ronnie Brown Ad Back 2.50 6.00
248A Brett Favre 2.50 6.00
248B Brett Favre Ad Back 3.00 8.00

2005 Topps Turkey Red White

VETERANS 1-245: 1.5X TO 4X BASIC CARDS
*VETS 1-245: .4X TO 1X BASIC AD BACKS
*ROOKIES: .8X TO 2X BASIC CARDS
*RETIRED 236-240: .5X TO 1.2X BASIC CARDS
*VETERANS 246-285: .2X TO .5X
*PRESIDENTS 286-289: .5X TO 1.2X
STATED ODDS 1:4 HOB/RET

2005 Topps Turkey Red Autographs Gray

GROUP A ODDS 1:1514 H, 1:8042 R
GROUP B ODDS 1:1020 H, 1:4530 R
GROUP C ODDS 1:237 H, 1:1292 R
GROUP D ODDS 1:342 H, 1:2096 R
GROUP E ODDS 1:458 H, 1:2432 R
GROUP F ODDS 1:79 H, 1:1565 R
TRAAR Aaron Rodgers B 175.00 300.00
TRABB Bernard Berrian C 6.00 15.00
TRABE Braylon Edwards C 20.00 40.00
TRACB Craig Bragg C 6.00 15.00
TRACP Chad Pennington A 20.00 40.00
TRADJ Deacon Jones C 10.00 25.00
TRADS Darren Sproles D 12.00 30.00
TRADBO David Bowens F 4.00 10.00
TRAEC Earl Campbell A 20.00 50.00
TRAEH Ed Hartwell F 4.00 10.00
TRAEW Ernest Wilford E 4.00 10.00
TRAJB Jim Brown A 60.00 100.00
TRAJC Jason Campbell C 15.00 40.00
TRAJN Joe Namath A 60.00 100.00
TRAKO Kyle Orton 10.00 25.00
TRAMC Mark Clayton A 20.00 40.00
TRAMJ Matt Jones B 12.00 30.00
TRAMS Mark Simoneau F 5.00 12.00
TRAPM Peyton Manning A 75.00 135.00
TRARB Ronnie Brown A 60.00 100.00
TRARC Ronald Curry 6.00 15.00
TRARM Ryan Moats B 10.00 25.00
TRASL Stefan LeFors C 6.00 15.00
TRASM Santana Moss C 10.00 25.00
TRATB Terry Bradshaw A 60.00 100.00
TRATBR Tom Brady A 100.00 200.00

2005 Topps Turkey Red Autographs Red

RED/199 GROUP A ODDS 1:144 H, 1:765 R
RED/50 GROUP B ODDS 1: 353 H, 1:2165 R
*BLACK/50: .6X TO 1.5X REDS
BLACK/10 NOT PRICED DUE TO SCARCITY
BLACK GROUP A ODDS 1:566H, 1:3417R
BLACK GROUP B ODDS 1:2236H, 1:8089R
*GOLD/25: .8X TO 2X REDS
GOLD/5 NOT PRICED DUE TO SCARCITY
GOLD/25 GROUP A ODDS 1:1278H, 1:5430R
GOLD/5 GROUP B ODDS 1:7029H, 1:12,010R
*WHITE/25: .5X TO 1.2X REDS
*WHITE/99: .5X TO 1.2X REDS
WHITE/99 GROUP A ODDS 1:266H, 1:2120R
WHITE/25 GROUP B ODDS 1: 775H, 1:3570R
WOOD 1/1 ODDS 1:24,600H,1:24,628 R
TRAAR Aaron Rodgers/50 B 300.00 450.00
TRABB Bernard Berrian/199 A 6.00 15.00
TRABE Braylon Edwards/50 B 20.00 50.00
TRACB Craig Bragg/199 A 6.00 15.00
TRACP Chad Pennington/50 B 12.50 30.00
TRADJ Deacon Jones/50 B 12.50 30.00
TRADS Darren Sproles/199 12.00 30.00
TRADBO David Bowens/199 A 5.00 12.00
TRAEC Earl Campbell/50 B 30.00 50.00
TRAEH Ed Hartwell/199 A 5.00 12.00
TRAFW Ernest Wilford/199 A 6.00 15.00
TRAJB Jim Brown/50 B 60.00 100.00
TRAJC Jason Campbell/50 B 25.00 50.00
TRAJN Joe Namath/50 B 60.00 100.00
TRAKO Kyle Orton/50 B 12.50 30.00
TRAMC Mark Clayton/199 A 10.00 25.00
TRAMJ Matt Jones/50 B 15.00 40.00
TRAMS Mark Simoneau/199 A 5.00 12.00
TRAPM Peyton Manning/50 B 75.00 150.00
TRARB Ronnie Brown/50 B 40.00 80.00
TRARC Ronald Curry/199 A 5.00 12.00
TRARM Ryan Moats/199 A 8.00 20.00
TRASL Stefan LeFors/50 B 10.00 25.00
TRASM Santana Moss/50 B 12.50 30.00
TRATB Terry Bradshaw/50 B 60.00 100.00
TRATBR Tom Brady/50 B 150.00 250.00

2005 Topps Turkey Red B-18 Blankets Yellow

STATED ODDS 1:2 BOXES
*WHITE BACKGROUND: .4X TO 1X YELLOW
BF Brett Favre 10.00 25.00
CW Cadillac Williams 4.00 10.00
LT LaDainian Tomlinson 4.00 10.00
MV Michael Vick 6.00 15.00
PM Peyton Manning 8.00 20.00
RB Ronnie Brown 5.00 12.00
RM Randy Moss 4.00 10.00
TB Tom Brady 8.00 20.00

2005 Topps Turkey Red Cabinet

STATED ODDS 1:BOX
TRAL Abraham Lincoln 6.00 15.00
TRBC Bill Clinton 12.50 30.00
TRBF Brett Favre 15.00 40.00
TRBR Ben Roethlisberger 15.00 40.00
TRCP Carson Palmer 8.00 20.00
TRCW Cadillac Williams 8.00 20.00
TREM Eli Manning 10.00 25.00
TRJA John Adams 6.00 15.00
TRJJ Jack Johnson 6.00 15.00
TRLT LaDainian Tomlinson 8.00 20.00
TRMV Michael Vick 10.00 25.00
TRPM Peyton Manning 10.00 25.00
TRRB Ronnie Brown 12.00 30.00
TRRM Randy Moss 6.00 15.00
TRSA Shaun Alexander 8.00 20.00
TRTB Tom Brady 10.00 25.00

2005 Topps Turkey Red Cabinet Autographed Relics

OVERALL CABINET ODDS 1:2 BOXES
TRARBR Ben Roethlisberger/50 125.00 250.00
TRARCW Cadillac Williams/75 30.00 80.00
TRARDM Dan Marino/25 200.00 350.00
TRARJA J.J. Arrington/175 15.00 40.00
TRARJE John Elway/25 175.00 300.00
TRARJM Joe Montana/25 175.00 300.00
TRARKO Kyle Orton/100 25.00 50.00
TRARLT Lawrence Taylor/50 60.00 120.00
TRARMB Mark Bradley/175 15.00 40.00
TRARMC Mark Clayton/100 15.00 40.00
TRARMJ Matt Jones/100 25.00 60.00
TRARPM Peyton Manning/25 175.00 300.00
TRARRB Ronnie Brown/50 60.00 120.00
TRARTB Tom Brady/25 200.00 350.00
TRARTW Troy Williamson/75 20.00 50.00

2005 Topps Turkey Red Cut Signatures

UNPRICED CUT AU/1 ODDS 1:21,866 HOB

2005 Topps Turkey Red Relics Gray

STATED ODDS 1:67 HOB, 1:75 RET
*BLACK/99: .8X TO 2X BASIC CARDS
BLACK/99 ODDS 1:220 HOB, 1:278 RET
*GOLD/25: 1.2X TO 3X BASIC CARDS
GOLD/25 ODDS 1:1009 H, 1:1059 R
*RED/299: .5X TO 1.2X BASIC CARDS
RED/299 ODDS 1:84 HOB/RET
*WHITE/199: .6X TO 1.5X BASIC CARDS
WHITE/199 ODDS 1:86 HOB, 1:265 RET
UNPRICED WOOD/1 ODDS 1:25,689H,1:26,270R
TRRAJ Andre Johnson 4.00 10.00
TRRBR Ben Roethlisberger 12.50 30.00
TRRCB Chris Brown 4.00 10.00
TRRCC Chris Chambers 4.00 10.00
TRRCD Corey Dillon 4.00 10.00
TRRCJ Chad Johnson 5.00 12.00
TRRDB Drew Brees 5.00 12.00
TRRDC Daunte Culpepper 5.00 12.00
TRRDD Domanick Davis 4.00 10.00
TRRDM Deuce McAllister 4.00 10.00
TRRDCA David Carr 4.00 10.00
TRRHW Hines Ward 6.00 15.00
TRRIB Isaac Bruce 4.00 10.00
TRRJA John Abraham 4.00 10.00
TRRJL J.P. Losman 4.00 10.00
TRRJS Jeremy Shockey 5.00 12.00
TRRPH Priest Holmes 5.00 12.00
TRRRW Roy Williams S 5.00 12.00
TRRSA Shaun Alexander 6.00 15.00
TRRSD Stephon Davis 4.00 10.00
TRRTB Tom Brady 8.00 20.00
TRRTG Tony Gonzalez 4.00 10.00
TRRTH Torry Holt 5.00 12.00
TRRTS Terrell Suggs 4.00 10.00
TRRWD Warrick Dunn 4.00 10.00

2006 Topps Turkey Red

This 328-card set was released in November, 2006. The set was issued into the hobby eight-card packs, with a $4 SRP, which came 24 packs to a box. Cards numbered 1-180 and 231-315 are veterans while cards numbered 181-230 feature 2006 rookies. Some of the cards in this set were produced to shorter quantities than the other cards in the set are those cards are notated in our checklist with an SP.

COMPLETE SET (328) 100.00 200.00
COMP.SET w/o SP's (274) 20.00 50.00
UNPRICED PRINT PLATES #'d TO 1
UNPRICED SUEDE PRINT RUN 1
1 LaVar Arrington .25 .60
2 Heath Miller .25 .60
3 Antwaan Randle El .25 .60
4 Derrick Mason .25 .60
5 Deshaun Foster .25 .60
6 Andre Johnson .30 .75
7 Jonathan Vilma .25 .60
8 Trent Dilfer .25 .60
9 Tatum Bell .20 .50
10 Bubba Franks .20 .50
11 T.J. Houshmandzadeh .25 .60
12 Adam Vinatieri .25 .60
13 Quentin Jammer .20 .50
14 Jim Kleinsasser .20 .50
15 Priest Holmes .25 .60
16 Courtney Roby .20 .50
17 Chris Simms .25 .60
18 Terry Glenn .25 .60
19 Jonathan Ogden .20 .50
20 Andrew Walter .20 .50
21 Lito Sheppard .25 .60
22 Kevan Barlow .20 .50
23 Santana Moss .25 .60
24 Kelly Holcomb .20 .50
25 Thomas Jones .25 .60
26 Dennis Northcutt .20 .50
27 Najeh Davenport .25 .60
28 Edgerrin James .25 .60
29 Kevin Curtis .25 .60
30 Brian Griese .25 .60
31 Jason Taylor .25 .60
32 T.J. Duckett .20 .50
33 Antonio Bryant .20 .50
34 Donald Driver .30 .75
35 Brian Westbrook .25 .60
36 Lofa Tatupu .25 .60
37 Ben Troupe .20 .50
38 Chris Cooley .25 .60
39 Josh McCown .20 .50
40 Chris Perry .25 .60
41 Joe Horn .25 .60
42 Kyle Boller .25 .60
43 Keyshawn Johnson .25 .60
44 Frank Gore .30 .75
45 Terence Newman .20 .50
46 Devery Henderson .20 .50
47 Michael Strahan .25 .60
48 Ladell Betts .20 .50
49 Patrick Ramsey .25 .60
50 Anquan Boldin .25 .60
51 Nathan Vasher .20 .50
52 Dominic Rhodes .25 .60
53 Travis Minor .20 .50
54 Torry Holt .25 .60
55 Sam Gado .25 .60
56 Fred Taylor .25 .60
57 Braylon Edwards .25 .60
58 Tyrone Calico .20 .50
59 Derrick Burgess .20 .50
60 Chester Taylor .25 .60
61 Julius Peppers .25 .60
62 L.J. Smith .20 .50
63 Keenan McCardell .25 .60
64 Lee Evans .25 .60
65 Champ Bailey .25 .60
66 Alex Smith QB .30 .75
67 Tedy Bruschi .30 .75
68 Roddy White .25 .60
69 Marty Booker .20 .50
70 Fred Smoot .20 .50
71 A.J. Feeley .20 .50
72 Kellen Winslow .25 .60
73 Curtis Martin .30 .75
74 Ronald Curry .25 .60
75 Sam Madison .20 .50
76 Keary Colbert .20 .50
77 Marcus Pollard .20 .50
78 James Farrior .20 .50
79 Travis Henry .20 .50
80 Samari Rolle .20 .50
81 Rodney Harrison .20 .50
82 Matt Schaub .25 .60
83 Philip Rivers .30 .75
84 DeMarcus Ware .25 .60
85 Reggie Wayne .25 .60
86 Derrick Johnson .20 .50
87 Travis Taylor .20 .50
88 Antonio Pierce .20 .50
89 Jamal Lewis .25 .60
90 Aaron Brooks .25 .60
91 Michael Pittman .20 .50
92 Jerricho Cotchery .25 .60
93 Shayne Graham .20 .50
94 Dante Hall .25 .60
95 Warrick Dunn .25 .60
96 Mewelde Moore .20 .50
97 Brandon Lloyd .20 .50
98 Chris Gamble .20 .50
99 Odell Thurman .20 .50
100 Osi Umenyiora .25 .60
101 Jerry Porter .20 .50
102 Brandon Stokley .25 .60
103 Clinton Portis .30 .75
104 Quentin Jammer .20 .50
105 Reuben Droughns .25 .60
106 Jason Campbell .25 .60
107 LaBrandon Toefield .20 .50
108 Nate Burleson .20 .50
109 Antrel Rolle .20 .50
110A Steve McNair .25 .60
(purple sky)
110B Steve McNair .25 .60
(yellow sky)
111A Chad Johnson .25 .60
(press box in background)
111B Chad Johnson .25 .60
(only stands in background)
112 Steven Jackson .30 .75
113 Ron Dayne .25 .60
114 Deion Branch .25 .60
115 Ed Reed .25 .60
116 Ty Law .20 .50
117 Drew Bledsoe .30 .75
118 Chris McAlister .20 .50
119 Plaxico Burress .25 .60
120 Aaron Rodgers .60 1.50
121 Tony Gonzalez .25 .60
122 David Givens .25 .60
123 Michael Vick .30 .75
124 Antonio Gates .30 .75
125 Darrell Jackson .25 .60
126 Adam Jones .20 .50
127 (LaDainian) Tomlinson Dashes Down The Gridiron .25 .60
(checklist back)
128 Chad Pennington .25 .60
129 Kevin Faulk .25 .60
130 Isaac Bruce .25 .60
131 (Tom) Brady Throws Downfield .40 1.00
(checklist back)
132 Deuce McAllister .25 .60
133 Laveranues Coles .20 .50
134 Donnie Edwards .20 .50
135 (Brian) Urlacher Tracks/'Em Down .25 .60
(checklist back)
136 Dallas Clark .25 .60
137 Drew Bennett .25 .60
138 Domanick Davis .20 .50
139 Cadillac (Williams) Drives Through The Opposition .20 .50
(checklist back)
140 David Garrard .25 .60
141 (Shaun) Alexander Runs For The End Zone .20 .50
(checklist back)
142 Troy Williamson .20 .50
143 (Steve) Smith Breaks Away From The DB .25 .60
(checklist back)
144 Jake Plummer .25 .60
145 (Carson) Palmer Runs Out Of The Pocket .25 .60
(checklist back)
146 DeAngelo Hall .25 .60
147 (Michael) Vick Decides To Run .25 .60
(checklist back)
148 Kyle Vanden Bosch .20 .50
149 (Larry) Johnson Slips The Defenders .20 .50
(checklist back)
150 LaDainian Tomlinson .30 .75
151 Dunta Robinson .20 .50
152 Muhsin Muhammad .25 .60
153 (Steven) Jackson Dives For The End Zone .25 .60
(checklist back)
154 David Pollack .20 .50
155 Mark Brunell .25 .60
156 Donovan McNabb .30 .75
157 Jeremy Shockey .30 .75
158 Corey Dillon .25 .60
159 Mark Clayton .25 .60
160 Vincent Jackson .25 .60
161 Kurt Warner .30 .75
162 Marcus Robinson .20 .50
163 Takeo Spikes .20 .50
164 Charles Rogers .25 .60
165 J.P. Losman .25 .60
166 Matt Jones .20 .50
167 Rod Smith .25 .60
168 Steve Smith .30 .75
169 Michael Vick .30 .75
170 Mike Vanderjagt .20 .50
171 Amani Toomer .25 .60
172 Deltha O'Neal .20 .50
173 Michael Jenkins .25 .60
174 David Carr .20 .50
175 Chris Brown .20 .50
176 Kevin Jones .20 .50
177 Roy Williams S .25 .60
178 Marvin Harrison .30 .75
179 Drew Brees .30 .75
180 John Abraham .20 .50
181 Joseph Addai RC SP 2.00 5.00
182 Sinorice Moss RC SP 2.00 5.00
183A Vince Young RC 1.00 2.50
(purple sky)
183B Vince Young SP 2.50 6.00
(orange sky)
184 Vernon Davis RC SP 2.50 6.00
185 Brandon Williams RC SP 1.25 3.00
186 Derek Hagan RC SP 1.50 4.00
187 Brian Calhoun RC SP 1.25 3.00
188 Mario Williams RC SP 2.00 5.00
189 DeAngelo Williams RC SP 2.50 6.00
190 Jay Cutler RC SP 4.00 10.00
191 A.J. Hawk RC SP 2.00 5.00
192 Reggie Bush RC 1.50 4.00
193 Laurence Maroney RC SP 1.50 4.00
194 D'Brickashaw Ferguson RC SP 2.00 5.00
195 Jason Avant RC SP 1.25 3.00
196 Brodie Croyle RC SP 2.00 5.00
197 Michael Huff RC SP 1.50 4.00
198 LenDale White RC SP 1.50 4.00
199 Marcedes Lewis RC SP 2.00 5.00
200 Travis Wilson RC SP 1.25 3.00
201 Haloti Ngata RC SP 2.00 5.00
202 Greg Jennings RC SP 3.00 8.00
203 Leon Washington RC SP 1.50 4.00
204 Tamba Hali RC SP 2.00 5.00
205 Santonio Holmes RC SP 2.50 6.00
206 Jerome Harrison RC SP 2.00 5.00
207 Tarvaris Jackson RC SP 2.00 5.00
208 Mathias Kiwanuka RC SP 2.00 5.00
209 Omar Jacobs RC SP 1.25 3.00
210 Alan Zemaitis RC SP 2.00 5.00
211 Demetrius Williams RC SP 1.50 4.00
212 Bobby Carpenter RC SP 1.25 3.00
213 Tye Hill RC SP 1.25 3.00
214 Chad Jackson RC SP 1.25 3.00
215 Joe Klopfenstein RC SP 1.25 3.00
216 Kamerion Wimbley RC SP 2.00 5.00
217 Michael Robinson RC SP 1.50 4.00
218 David Thomas RC SP 1.50 4.00
219 Charlie Whitehurst RC SP 2.00 5.00
220 Jerious Norwood RC SP 1.50 4.00
221 Bruce Gradkowski RC SP 2.00 5.00
222 Kellen Clemens RC SP 1.50 4.00
223 Thomas Howard RC SP 1.50 4.00
224 Anthony Fasano RC SP 2.00 5.00
225 Maurice Drew RC SP 3.00 8.00
226 Antonio Cromartie RC SP 2.00 5.00
227 Mike Bell RC SP 2.00 5.00
228 D'Qwell Jackson RC SP 2.00 5.00
229A Matt Leinart RC .75 2.00
(trees in background)
229B Matt Leinart SP 2.00 5.00
(stands in background, blue sky)
230 Maurice Stovall RC SP 1.25 3.00
231A Carson Palmer .30 .75
(white jersey)
231A Carson Palmer .30 .75
(black jersey)
232 Courtney Anderson .20 .50
233 D.J. Williams .20 .50
234 Chris Chambers .25 .60
235 Zach Thomas .30 .75
236 Reggie Brown .20 .50
237 Cadillac Williams .25 .60
238 Randy McMichael .20 .50
239 Brian Urlacher .30 .75
240 Cedric Houston .20 .50
241 Marc Bulger .25 .60
242 Mike Anderson .25 .60
243 Allen Rossum .20 .50
244 William Henderson .20 .50
245 Eddie Kennison .20 .50
246 Adam Archuleta .20 .50
247 Ryan Moats .20 .50
248 D.J. Hackett .20 .50
249 Marion Barber .30 .75
250 Mike Alstott .20 .50
251 Shawne Merriman .25 .60
252 Byron Leftwich .25 .60
253 Dan Morgan .20 .50
254 Ronnie Brown .30 .75
255 Mark Bradley .20 .50
256 Mike Williams .20 .50
257 Ronde Barber .25 .60
258 Bernard Berrian .25 .60
259 Gibril Wilson .20 .50
260 Scottie Vines .20 .50
261 Rex Grossman .25 .60
262 Daniel Graham .20 .50
263 Ernest Wilford .20 .50
264 Javon Walker .25 .60
265 Corey Webster .20 .50
266 Jon Kitna .25 .60
267 Arnaz Battle .20 .50
268 Robert Ferguson SP 1.50 4.00
269 Cedric Benson .25 .60
270 Michael Clayton .20 .50
271 Brandon Jacobs .30 .75
272 Jason Witten SP 2.50 6.00
273A Randy Moss .30 .75
(blue sky)
273B Randy Moss .30 .75
(purple sky)
274 Daunte Culpepper SP 2.00 5.00
275 Ronnie Brown .30 .75
276 Dwight Freeney .25 .60
277 LaMont Jordan .25 .60
278 Jeremiah Trotter .20 .50
279A Hines Ward .30 .75
(purple orange sky)
279B Hines Ward .30 .75
(blue yellow sky)
280A Tom Brady .50 1.25
(press box in background)
280B Tom Brady .50 1.25
(only stands in background)
281 Charles Woodson .30 .75
282A Shaun Alexander .25 .60
(green jersey)
282B Shaun Alexander .25 .60
(white jersey)
283 Eric Moulds .20 .50
284A Ben Roethlisberger .40 1.00
(blue sky)
284B Ben Roethlisberger .40 1.00
(purple sky)
285 Matt Hasselbeck .25 .60
286 Willis McGahee .25 .60
287 Carlos Rogers .20 .50
288 Brett Favre .60 1.50
289 Larry Fitzgerald .30 .75
290 Billy Volek .20 .50
291 Julius Jones .20 .50
292 Trent Green .25 .60
293 Ashley Lelie .20 .50
294 Eli Manning .40 1.00
295 Alge Crumpler .25 .60
296 Rudi Johnson .25 .60
297 Troy Polamalu .40 1.00
298 Roy Williams WR .25 .60
299 Willie Parker .25 .60
300 Jake Delhomme .25 .60
301 Champ Bailey .25 .60
302 Ahman Green .25 .60
303 Robert Gallery .20 .50
304 Todd Heap .25 .60
305 Joey Harrington .20 .50
306 Terrell Owens .30 .75
307 Joey Galloway .25 .60
308A Larry Johnson .25 .60
(purple sky)
308A Larry Johnson .25 .60
(orange sky)
309 Brian Dawkins .25 .60
310 Ray Lewis .30 .75
311A Tiki Barber .30 .75
(orange sky)
311B Tiki Barber SP 2.50 6.00
(blue sky)
312 Donte Stallworth .20 .50
313 Eric Parker .20 .50
314 Charlie Frye .25 .60
315A Peyton Manning .50 1.25
(blue yellow sky)
315B Peyton Manning SP 15.00 40.00
(orange sky)

2006 Topps Turkey Red Black

*VETERANS: 3X TO 8X BASIC CARDS
*VETERAN SPs: .5X TO 1.2X BASIC CARDS
*ROOKIES: 1X TO 2.5X BASIC CARDS
*ROOKIE SPs: .4X TO 1X BASIC CARDS
BLACK STATED ODDS 1:24

2006 Topps Turkey Red Gold

*VETERANS: 6X TO 15X BASIC CARDS
*VETERAN SPs: 1X TO 2.5X BASIC CARDS
*ROOKIES: 2.5X TO 6X BASIC CARDS
*ROOKIE SPs: 1X TO 2.5X BASIC CARDS
GOLD/50 STATED ODDS 1:78

2006 Topps Turkey Red Red

*VETERANS: 1.2X TO 3X BASIC CARDS
*VETERAN SPs: .2X TO .5X BASIC CARDS
*ROOKIES: .5X TO 1.2X BASIC CARDS
*ROOKIE SPs: .2X TO .5X BASIC CARDS
OVERALL PARALLEL ODDS 1:1

2006 Topps Turkey Red Suede

UNPRICED SUEDE PRINT RUN 1

2006 Topps Turkey Red White

*VETERANS: 1.5X TO 4X BASIC CARDS
*VETERAN SPs: .25X TO .6X BASIC CARDS
*ROOKIES: .6X TO 1.5X BASIC CARDS
*ROOKIE SPs: .25X TO .6X BASIC CARDS
STATED ODDS 1:4

2006 Topps Turkey Red Cabinet

UNPRICED SUEDE PRINT RUN 1
AH A.J. Hawk 2.00 5.00
BF Brett Favre 8.00 20.00
BR Ben Roethlisberger 5.00 12.00
CJ Chad Johnson 3.00 8.00
CJA Chad Jackson 1.25 3.00
CP Carson Palmer 4.00 10.00
CW Cadillac Williams 3.00 8.00
DC Daunte Culpepper 3.00 8.00
DW DeAngelo Williams 2.50 6.00
EJ Edgerrin James 3.00 8.00
HW Hines Ward 4.00 10.00
JA Joseph Addai 2.00 5.00
JC Jay Cutler 4.00 10.00
LJ Larry Johnson 3.00 8.00
LM Laurence Maroney 1.50 4.00
LT LaDainian Tomlinson 4.00 10.00
LW LenDale White 1.50 4.00
MH Marvin Harrison 4.00 10.00
ML Matt Leinart 2.00 5.00
MW Mario Williams 2.00 5.00
PM Peyton Manning 6.00 15.00
RB Ronnie Brown 4.00 10.00
RBU Reggie Bush 4.00 10.00
RM Randy Moss 4.00 10.00
SA Shaun Alexander 3.00 8.00
SH Santonio Holmes 2.50 6.00
SM Sinorice Moss 2.00 5.00
TB Tiki Barber 4.00 10.00
TBR Tom Brady 6.00 15.00
TO Terrell Owens 4.00 10.00
VD Vernon Davis 2.50 6.00
VY Vince Young 2.50 6.00

2006 Topps Turkey Red Cabinet Autographed Relics

STATED PRINT RUN 75-500
UNPRICED SUEDE PRINT RUN 1
CJ Chad Jackson/500 10.00 25.00
CW Charlie Whitehurst/500 10.00 25.00
ES Emmitt Smith/75 125.00 250.00
JM Joe Montana/75 100.00 200.00
LM Laurence Maroney/300 12.00 30.00
LT LaDainian Tomlinson/75 90.00 150.00
MD Maurice Drew/500 20.00 50.00
ML Matt Leinart/150 25.00 60.00
PM Peyton Manning/75 125.00 200.00
RB Reggie Bush/75 50.00 120.00
SH Santonio Holmes/150 25.00 50.00
TB Tatum Bell/225 15.00 30.00
VD Vernon Davis/225 12.00 30.00
VY Vince Young/150 40.00 100.00

2006 Topps Turkey Red Cabinet Autographed Relics Duals

STATED PRINT RUN 25 SER.#'d SETS
UNPRICED SUEDE PRINT RUN 1
BS Reggie Bush 200.00 350.00
Emmitt Smith
ML Peyton Manning 150.00 300.00
Matt Leinart
MM Joe Montana 300.00 450.00
Peyton Manning
TB LaDainian Tomlinson 100.00 200.00
Reggie Bush
YL Vince Young 40.00 100.00
Matt Leinart

2006 Topps Turkey Red Autographs Red

GROUP B/199 ODDS 1:308
GROUP A/50 ODDS 1:720
*WHITE/25-99: .5X TO 1.2X RED/50-199
*BLACK/50: .6X TO 1.5X RED/199
*GOLD/25: .8X TO 2X RED/199
*GRAY GRP E-G: .4X TO 1X RED/199
*GRAY GRP B-C: .5X TO 1.2X RED/199
*GRAY GRP B-C: .4X TO 1X RED/50
*GRAY GRP A: .5X TO 1.2X RED/50
AH A.J. Hawk/50 15.00 40.00
BF Brett Favre/50 90.00 150.00
BM Brandon Marshall/199 8.00 20.00
BW Brandon Williams/199 5.00 12.00
CG Chad Greenway/199 8.00 20.00
CJ Chad Jackson/199 5.00 12.00
DW DeAngelo Williams/50 15.00 40.00
DWI Demetrius Williams/199 6.00 15.00
ES Emmitt Smith/50 75.00 150.00
JA Joseph Addai/50 12.00 30.00
JC Jay Cutler/50 40.00 80.00
JE John Elway/50 75.00 150.00
JM Joe Montana/50 90.00 150.00
LM Laurence Maroney/199 6.00 15.00
LW LenDale White/199 6.00 15.00
MD Maurice Drew/50 20.00 50.00
MK Mathias Kiwanuka/50 12.00 30.00
ML Matt Leinart/50 12.00 30.00
MLE Marcedes Lewis/199 8.00 20.00
MW Mario Williams/199 8.00 20.00
PM Peyton Manning/50 60.00 120.00
RB Reggie Bush/50 30.00 80.00
SH Santonio Holmes/199 10.00 25.00
SM Sinorice Moss/199 8.00 20.00
TW Travis Wilson/199 5.00 12.00
VY Vince Young/50 15.00 40.00
WR Willie Reid/199 6.00 15.00

2006 Topps Turkey Red Relics Gray

*BLACK/99: .8X TO 2X GRAY RELIC
BLACK/99 STATED ODDS 1:524
*GOLD/25: 1.2X TO 3X GRAY RELIC
GOLD/25 STATED ODDS 1:2144
*RED/399: .5X TO 1.2X GRAY RELIC
RED/399 STATED ODDS 1:83
UNPRICED SUEDE PRINT RUN 1
*WHITE/199: .6X TO 1.5X GRAY RELIC
WHITE/199 STATED ODDS 1:260
AB Anquan Boldin G 3.00 8.00
AH A.J. Hawk G 5.00 12.00
BU Brian Urlacher F 4.00 10.00
CC Chris Chambers F 3.00 8.00
DD Domanick Davis C 2.50 6.00
EM Eric Moulds F 2.50 6.00
FG Frank Gore E 3.00 8.00
JV Jonathan Vilma F 3.00 8.00
LA LaVar Arrington G 3.00 8.00
MB Marc Bulger F 3.00 8.00
MC Michael Clayton G 3.00 8.00
MF Marshall Faulk B 3.00 8.00
MH Marvin Harrison F 4.00 10.00
MJ Matt Jones F 2.50 6.00
ML Matt Leinart G 4.00 10.00
RB Reggie Bush C 8.00 20.00
RL Ray Lewis F 4.00 10.00
SD Stephen Davis D 2.50 6.00
SH Santonio Holmes A 4.00 10.00
SJ Steven Jackson G 3.00 8.00
TB Tatum Bell G 3.00 8.00
TBR Tom Brady C 5.00 12.00
TG Trent Green F 3.00 8.00
VD Vernon Davis F 5.00 12.00
VY Vince Young E 6.00 15.00

2006 Topps Turkey Red B-18 Blankets White

*YELLOW: .4X TO 1X WHITE
BR Ben Roethlisberger 4.00 10.00
CP Carson Palmer 3.00 8.00
LT LaDainian Tomlinson 3.00 8.00
ML Matt Leinart 1.25 3.00
PM Peyton Manning 5.00 12.00
RB Reggie Bush 2.50 6.00
SA Shaun Alexander 2.50 6.00
TB Tom Brady 5.00 12.00
TB Tiki Barber 3.00 8.00
VY Vince Young 1.50 4.00

2007 Topps TX Exclusive

This 225-card set was released in August, 2007. The set was issued into the hobby in five-card packs, with a $20 SRP, which came 12 packs to a box. Cards numbered 1-100 feature veterans, while cards 101-200 feature 2007 NFL Rookie Cards issued to stated print runs between 399 and 1049 cards and the set concludes with cards 201-225 which feature retired greats and were issued to a stated print run of 1099 serial numbered cards and were inserted into packs at a stated rate of one in six.

COMP.SET w/o SP's (100) 10.00 25.00
101-200 ROOKIE PRINT RUN 399-1049
201-225 RETIRED/1099 ODDS 1:6
1 Peyton Manning .75 2.00
2 Carson Palmer .40 1.00
3 Tom Brady .75 2.00
4 Drew Brees .50 1.25
5 Rex Grossman .40 1.00
6 Donovan McNabb .50 1.25
7 Eli Manning .50 1.25
8 Philip Rivers .50 1.25
9 Brett Favre 1.00 2.50
10 Marc Bulger .40 1.00
11 Michael Vick .50 1.25
12 Tony Romo .60 1.50
13 Matt Hasselbeck .40 1.00
14 Jake Delhomme .40 1.00
15 Ben Roethlisberger .50 1.25
16 Alex Smith QB .50 1.25
17 Chad Pennington .40 1.00
18 Steve McNair .40 1.00
19 Trent Green .40 1.00
20 David Carr .40 1.00
21 Vince Young .40 1.00
22 Jay Cutler .50 1.25
23 Matt Leinart .40 1.00
24 Jason Campbell .40 1.00
25 Bruce Gradkowski .30 .75
26 Larry Johnson .30 .75
27 Frank Gore .50 1.25
28 LaDainian Tomlinson .50 1.25
29 Cedric Benson .40 1.00
30 Chester Taylor .30 .75
31 Thomas Jones .40 1.00
32 Steven Jackson .50 1.25
33 Willie Parker .40 1.00
34 Rudi Johnson .40 1.00
35 Fred Taylor .40 1.00
36 Warrick Dunn .40 1.00
37 Julius Jones .30 .75
38 Brian Westbrook .40 1.00
39 Ronnie Brown .40 1.00
40 Travis Henry .40 1.00
41 Jamal Lewis .40 1.00
42 Cadillac Williams .40 1.00
43 Edgerrin James .40 1.00
44 Ahman Green .40 1.00
45 Deuce McAllister .40 1.00
46 Deshaun Foster .40 1.00
47 Tatum Bell .30 .75
48 Willis McGahee .40 1.00
49 Kevin Jones .30 .75
50 Corey Dillon .40 1.00
51 Clinton Portis .40 1.00
52 Shaun Alexander .40 1.00
53 Laurence Maroney .40 1.00
54 Maurice Jones-Drew .50 1.25
55 Jerious Norwood .40 1.00
56 Mike Bell .40 1.00
57 Leon Washington .40 1.00

58 Chad Johnson .40 1.00
59 Roy Williams WR .40 1.00
60 Andre Johnson .40 1.00
61 Reggie Wayne .40 1.00
62 Steve Smith .40 1.00
63 Donald Driver .50 1.25
64 Anquan Boldin .40 1.00
65 Lee Evans .40 1.00
66 Eric Moulds .40 1.00
67 Javon Walker .40 1.00
68 Terrell Owens .50 1.25
69 Laveranues Coles .30 .75
70 Marvin Harrison .50 1.25
71 Darrell Jackson .30 .75
72 Torry Holt .40 1.00
73 Hines Ward .50 1.25
74 Joey Galloway .40 1.00
75 T.J. Houshmandzadeh .40 1.00
76 Plaxico Burress .40 1.00
77 Jerricho Cotchery .40 1.00
78 Joe Horn .40 1.00
79 Mike Furrey .40 1.00
80 Braylon Edwards .40 1.00
81 Mark Bradley .30 .75
82 Larry Fitzgerald .50 1.25
83 Terry Glenn .40 1.00
84 Michael Clayton .30 .75
85 Muhsin Muhammad .40 1.00
86 Randy Moss .50 1.25
87 Chris Chambers .40 1.00
88 Santana Moss .40 1.00
89 Keyshawn Johnson .40 1.00
90 Santonio Holmes .40 1.00
91 Marques Colston .50 1.25
92 Greg Jennings .50 1.25
93 Vernon Davis .40 1.00
94 Chris Cooley .40 1.00
95 Alge Crumpler .40 1.00
96 Tony Gonzalez .40 1.00
97 Ben Watson .30 .75
98 Todd Heap .30 .75
99 Antonio Gates .50 1.25
100 Jeremy Shockey .40 1.00
101 Brady Quinn/399 RC 2.50 6.00
102 Joe Thomas/1049 RC 1.50 4.00
103 Calvin Johnson/399 RC 8.00 20.00
104 Adrian Peterson/399 RC 10.00 25.00
105 JaMarcus Russell/399 RC 1.50 4.00
106 Marshawn Lynch/399 RC 2.50 6.00
107 Alan Branch/1049 RC 1.25 3.00
108 Levi Brown/799 RC 1.50 4.00
109 Gaines Adams/599 RC 2.00 5.00
110 Trent Edwards/1049 RC 1.50 4.00
111 Dwayne Jarrett/1049 RC 1.25 3.00
112 Leon Hall/1049 RC 1.25 3.00
113 Kenneth Darby/599 RC 1.50 4.00
114 John Beck/599 RC 2.00 5.00
115 Marcus McCauley/1049 RC 1.25 3.00
116 Ted Ginn Jr./399 RC 2.00 5.00
117 Kenny Irons/1049 RC 1.00 2.50
118 LaRon Landry/599 RC 2.00 5.00
119 Reggie Nelson/1049 RC 1.25 3.00
120 Quentin Moses/1049 RC 1.25 3.00
121 Ray McDonald/1049 RC 1.25 3.00
122 Drew Stanton/599 RC 1.25 3.00
123 Garrett Wolfe/1049 RC 1.00 2.50
124 Greg Olsen/799 RC 1.25 3.00
125 Troy Smith/599 RC 2.00 5.00
126 Chris Henry/1049 RC 1.00 2.50
127 Patrick Willis/1049 RC 3.00 8.00
128 Chris Leak/799 RC 1.25 3.00
129 Paul Posluszny/799 RC 1.50 4.00
130 Steve Breaston/599 RC 2.00 5.00
131 Brandon Meriweather/799 RC 1.50 4.00
132 Thomas Clayton/1049 RC 1.25 3.00
133 Rhema McKnight/1049 RC 1.00 2.50
134 Anthony Spencer/1049 RC 1.50 4.00
135 Amobi Okoye/799 RC 1.50 4.00
136 Daymeion Hughes/1049 RC 1.25 3.00
137 Michael Bush/1049 RC 1.50 4.00
138 H.B. Blades/1049 RC 1.00 2.50
139 Michael Griffin/799 RC 1.50 4.00
140 Justin Harrell/1049 RC 1.25 3.00
141 Victor Abiamiri/1049 RC 1.50 4.00
142 Aundrae Allison/799 RC 1.00 2.50
143 Jared Zabransky/799 RC 1.25 3.00
144 Martrez Milner/799 RC 1.00 2.50
145 Adam Carriker/799 RC 1.25 3.00
146 Paul Williams/599 RC 1.25 3.00
147 Tanard Jackson/1049 RC 1.00 2.50
148 Marcus Thomas/1049 RC 1.25 3.00
149 Selvin Young/1049 RC 1.25 3.00
150 Jamaal Anderson/799 RC 1.25 3.00
151 David Harris/1049 RC 1.25 3.00
152 Vincent Marshall/1049 RC 1.25 3.00
153 Buster Davis/1049 RC 1.25 3.00
154 Jon Beason/799 RC 1.25 3.00
155 Tim Crowder/1049 RC 1.50 4.00
156 Brian Leonard/1049 RC 1.25 3.00
157 LaMarr Woodley/1049 RC 1.50 4.00
158 DeMarcus Tank Tyler/1049 RC 1.00 2.50
159 John Wendling/1049 RC 1.25 3.00
160 Aaron Ross/1049 RC 1.50 4.00
161 Earl Everett/1049 RC 1.25 3.00
162 Tony Hunt/599 RC 1.25 3.00
163 Craig Buster Davis/1049 RC 1.25 3.00
164 Rufus Alexander/1049 RC 1.25 3.00
165 Aaron Rouse/799 RC 1.25 3.00
166 Lorenzo Booker/599 RC 1.50 4.00
167 Kevin Kolb/1049 RC 2.50 6.00
168 David Irons/799 RC 1.00 2.50
169 Sidney Rice/599 RC 2.50 6.00
170 Johnnie Lee Higgins/799 RC 1.25 3.00
171 Tyler Palko/1049 RC 1.25 3.00
172 Robert Meachem/1049 RC 1.50 4.00
173 Prescott Burgess/1049 RC 1.25 3.00
174 Jordan Palmer/799 RC 1.25 3.00
175 Darius Walker/799 RC 1.00 2.50
176 Drew Tate/799 RC 1.25 3.00
177 Chris Davis/1049 RC 1.00 2.50
178 Michael Johnson/1049 RC 1.25 3.00
179 Matt Spaeth/1049 RC 1.50 4.00
180 Yamon Figurs/1049 RC 1.00 2.50
181 Joel Filani/1049 RC 1.25 3.00
182 Jason Hill/599 RC 2.00 5.00
183 Anthony Gonzalez/1049 RC 1.50 4.00
184 Chansi Stuckey/1049 RC 1.50 4.00
185 Antonio Pittman/799 RC 1.00 2.50
186 Dallas Baker/1049 RC 1.00 2.50
187 Sabby Piscitelli/1049 RC 1.50 4.00
188 Brandon Jackson/1049 RC 1.25 3.00
189 Darrelle Revis/1049 RC 2.50 6.00
190 David Clowney/1049 RC 1.25 3.00
191 Courtney Taylor/1049 RC 1.25 3.00
192 Eric Weddle/1049 RC 1.50 4.00
193 Lawrence Timmons/799 RC 1.50 4.00
194 Scott Chandler/1049 RC 1.50 4.00
195 Dwayne Bowe/399 RC 3.00 8.00
196 Kolby Smith/1049 RC 1.25 3.00
197 Jarvis Moss/1049 RC 1.25 3.00
198 Isaiah Stanback/1049 RC 1.00 2.50
199 Steve Smith USC/599 RC 2.00 5.00
200 Joe Newton/1049 RC 1.00 2.50
201 Troy Aikman 2.50 6.00
202 Terry Bradshaw 3.00 8.00
203 John Elway 3.00 8.00
204 Roger Staubach 3.00 8.00
205 Steve Young 2.50 6.00
206 Jim Plunkett 1.50 4.00
207 Dan Marino 4.00 10.00
208 Jim Kelly 2.50 6.00
209 Joe Namath 2.50 6.00
210 Joe Montana 4.00 10.00
211 Earl Campbell 2.00 5.00
212 Paul Hornung 2.00 5.00
213 Eric Dickerson 1.50 4.00
214 Emmitt Smith 4.00 10.00
215 Jim Brown 2.50 6.00
216 Marshall Faulk 1.50 4.00
217 Barry Sanders 3.00 8.00
218 Thurman Thomas 1.50 4.00
219 Marcus Allen 2.00 5.00
220 Tony Dorsett 2.00 5.00
221 Fred Biletnikoff 2.00 5.00
222 Tim Brown 2.00 5.00
223 Jerry Rice 3.00 8.00
224 Lawrence Taylor 2.00 5.00
225 Rod Woodson 1.25 3.00

2007 Topps TX Exclusive Bronze

*VETS 1-100: 2.5X TO 6X BASIC CARDS
*ROOKIES: .6X TO 1.5X BASIC RC/1049
*ROOKIES: .6X TO 1.5X BASIC RC/799
*ROOKIES: .5X TO 1.2X BASIC RC/599
*ROOKIES: .4X TO 1X BASIC RC/399
*RETIRED 201-225: .4X TO 1X BASIC CARDS
BRONZE/149 STATED ODDS 1:5 HOB

2007 Topps TX Exclusive Gold

*VETS 1-100: 10X TO 25X BASIC CARDS
*ROOKIES: 3X TO 8X BASIC RC/1049
*ROOKIES: 3X TO 8X BASIC RC/799
*ROOKIES: 2.5X TO 6X BASIC RC/599
*ROOKIES: 2X TO 5X BASIC RC/399
*RETIRED 201-225: 2.5X TO 6X
GOLD/10 STATED ODDS 1:74 HOB

2007 Topps TX Exclusive Silver

*VETS 1-100: 4X TO 10X BASIC CARDS
*ROOKIES: 1.2X TO 3X BASIC RC/1049
*ROOKIES: 1.2X TO 3X BASIC RC/799
*ROOKIES: 1X TO 2.5X BASIC RC/599
*ROOKIES: .8X TO 2X BASIC RC/399
*RETIRED 201-225: 1X TO 2.5X
SILVER/49 STATED ODDS 1:15 HOB

2007 Topps TX Exclusive Franchise Winning Ticket

WIN.TICKET/299 ODDS 1:9
*BRONZE/99: .5X TO 1.2X BASIC INSERTS
BRONZE PRINT RUN 99 SER.#'d SETS
*SILVER/49: .6X TO 1.5X BASIC INSERTS
SILVER/49 ODDS 1:113
*GOLD/25: 1X TO 2.5X BASIC INSERTS
GOLD/25 ODDS 1:221
AG Antonio Gates 2.00 5.00
AJ Andre Johnson 1.50 4.00
CJ Chad Johnson 1.50 4.00
CP Carson Palmer 1.50 4.00
DB Drew Brees 2.00 5.00
FG Frank Gore 2.00 5.00
GJ Greg Jennings 2.00 5.00
JA Joseph Addai 1.50 4.00
JC Jay Cutler 2.00 5.00
JS Jeremy Shockey 1.50 4.00
JW Javon Walker 1.50 4.00
LF Larry Fitzgerald 2.00 5.00
LJ Larry Johnson 1.25 3.00
LM Laurence Maroney 1.50 4.00
LT LaDainian Tomlinson 2.00 5.00
MC Marques Colston 2.00 5.00
MH Marvin Harrison 2.00 5.00
MJD Maurice Jones-Drew 2.00 5.00
ML Matt Leinart 1.50 4.00
PM Peyton Manning 3.00 8.00
PR Philip Rivers 2.00 5.00
RB Reggie Bush 2.00 5.00
RW Roy Williams WR 1.50 4.00
SA Shaun Alexander 1.50 4.00
SS Steve Smith 1.50 4.00
TG Tony Gonzalez 1.50 4.00
TM Tom Brady 3.00 8.00
TR Tony Romo 2.50 6.00
VY Vince Young 1.50 4.00
WM Willis McGahee 1.50 4.00

2007 Topps TX Exclusive Franchise Winning Ticket Dual

DUAL/149 STATED ODDS 1:74
*BRONZE/49: .5X TO 1.2X BASIC INSERTS
BRONZE PRINT RUN 49 SER.#'d SETS
*SILVER/25: .6X TO 1.5X BASIC INSERTS
SILVER/25 STATED ODDS 1:442
*GOLD/10: 1.5X TO 4X BASIC INSERTS
GOLD/10 STATED ODDS 1:1100
BM Tom Brady 5.00 12.00
Laurence Maroney
CB Reggie Bush 3.00 8.00
Drew Brees
CW Jay Cutler 3.00 8.00
Javon Walker
DS Jake Delhomme 2.50 6.00
Steve Smith
GS Frank Gore 3.00 8.00
Alex Smith QB
HA Matt Hasselbeck 2.50 6.00
Shaun Alexander
JG Larry Johnson 2.50 6.00
Tony Gonzalez
LF Matt Leinart 3.00 8.00
Larry Fitzgerald
MH Peyton Manning 5.00 12.00
Marvin Harrison
MS Eli Manning 3.00 8.00
Jeremy Shockey
PJ Carson Palmer 2.50 6.00
Chad Johnson
RJ Tony Romo 4.00 10.00
Julius Jones
TR LaDainian Tomlinson 3.00 8.00
Philip Rivers
VD Michael Vick 3.00 8.00
Warrick Dunn
YW Vince Young 2.50 6.00
LenDale White

2007 Topps TX Exclusive Franchise Winning Ticket Jersey

BASE JSY/199 ODDS 1:28
*PATCH/15: 1.2X TO 3X BASIC JSY/199
PATCH/15 ODDS 1:395
AG Antonio Gates 4.00 10.00
AJ Andre Johnson 3.00 8.00
CJ Chad Johnson 3.00 8.00
CP Carson Palmer 3.00 8.00
DB Drew Brees 4.00 10.00
FG Frank Gore 4.00 10.00
GJ Greg Jennings 4.00 10.00
JA Joseph Addai 3.00 8.00
JC Jay Cutler 4.00 10.00
JS Jeremy Shockey 3.00 8.00
JW Javon Walker 3.00 8.00
LF Larry Fitzgerald 4.00 10.00
LJ Larry Johnson 2.50 6.00
LM Laurence Maroney 3.00 8.00
LT LaDainian Tomlinson 4.00 10.00
MC Marques Colston 4.00 10.00
MH Marvin Harrison 4.00 10.00
MJD Maurice Jones-Drew 4.00 10.00
ML Matt Leinart 3.00 8.00
PM Peyton Manning 6.00 15.00
PR Philip Rivers 4.00 10.00
RB Reggie Bush 4.00 10.00
RW Roy Williams WR 3.00 8.00
SA Shaun Alexander 3.00 8.00
SS Steve Smith 3.00 8.00
TB Tom Brady 6.00 15.00
TG Tony Gonzalez 3.00 8.00
TR Tony Romo 5.00 12.00
VY Vince Young 3.00 8.00
WM Willis McGahee 3.00 8.00

2007 Topps TX Exclusive Franchise Winning Ticket Jersey Autographs

STATED PRINT RUN 10 SER.#'d SETS
UNPRICED PATCH AU PRINT RUN 5
AG Antonio Gates 15.00 40.00
CJ Chad Johnson 20.00 50.00
DB Drew Brees 60.00 120.00
FG Frank Gore 25.00 60.00
GJ Greg Jennings 20.00 50.00
JA Joseph Addai 25.00 60.00
LJ Larry Johnson 25.00 60.00
LM Laurence Maroney 25.00 60.00
LT LaDainian Tomlinson 60.00 120.00
MC Marques Colston 25.00 60.00
MH Marvin Harrison 40.00 80.00
MJD Maurice Jones-Drew 20.00 50.00
ML Matt Leinart 30.00 80.00
PM Peyton Manning 125.00 250.00
RW Roy Williams WR 20.00 50.00
SA Shaun Alexander 25.00 60.00
SS Steve Smith 20.00 50.00
TB Tom Brady 150.00 300.00
TG Tony Gonzalez 15.00 40.00
TR Tony Romo 125.00 250.00
VY Vince Young 40.00 100.00
WM Willis McGahee 15.00 40.00

2007 Topps TX Exclusive Franchise Winning Ticket Dual Jersey

DUAL JSY/49 ODDS 1:230
PATCH/5 ODDS 1:2209
BB Reggie Bush 12.50 30.00
Drew Brees
BM Tom Brady 12.50 30.00
Laurence Maroney
CW Jay Cutler 10.00 25.00
Javon Walker
DS Jake Delhomme 6.00 15.00
Steve Smith
GS Frank Gore 8.00 20.00
Alex Smith QB
HA Matt Hasselbeck 6.00 15.00
Shaun Alexander
JG Larry Johnson 6.00 15.00
Tony Gonzalez
LF Matt Leinart 10.00 25.00
Larry Fitzgerald
MH Peyton Manning 12.00 30.00
Marvin Harrison
MS Eli Manning 8.00 20.00
Jeremy Shockey
PJ Carson Palmer 8.00 20.00
Chad Johnson
RJ Tony Romo 20.00 50.00
Julius Jones
TR LaDainian Tomlinson 10.00 25.00
Philip Rivers
VD Michael Vick 6.00 15.00
Warrick Dunn
YW Vince Young 10.00 25.00
LenDale White

2007 Topps TX Exclusive Post Season Ticket

BASE/499 STATED ODDS 1:20
*BRONZE/99: .6X TO 1.5X BASIC INSERTS
BRONZE/99 ODDS 1:99
*SILVER/49: .8X TO 2X BASIC INSERTS
SILVER/49 ODDS 1:199
*GOLD/10: 2X TO 5X BASIC INSERTS
GOLD/10 ODDS 1:972
BF Brett Favre 3.00 8.00
BU Brian Urlacher 1.50 4.00
DJ Darrell Jackson 1.00 2.50
FT Fred Taylor 1.25 3.00
JD Jake Delhomme 1.25 3.00
LT LaDainian Tomlinson 1.50 4.00
MH Marvin Harrison 1.50 4.00
MHA Matt Hasselbeck 1.25 3.00
PM Peyton Manning 2.50 6.00
RS Rod Smith 1.25 3.00
SA Shaun Alexander 1.25 3.00
SM Steve McNair 1.25 3.00
SS Steve Smith 1.25 3.00
TB Tom Brady 2.50 6.00
TBR Troy Brown 1.25 3.00
TG Tony Gonzalez 1.25 3.00
TH Torry Holt 1.25 3.00

2007 Topps TX Exclusive Post Season Ticket Jersey

JSY/199 ODDS 1:50
*PATCH/25: 1X TO 2.5X BASIC JSY/199
PATCH/25 ODDS 1:406
BF Brett Favre 8.00 20.00
BU Brian Urlacher 4.00 10.00
DJ Darrell Jackson 2.50 6.00
FT Fred Taylor 3.00 8.00
JD Jake Delhomme 3.00 8.00
LT LaDainian Tomlinson 4.00 10.00
MH Matt Hasselbeck 3.00 8.00
MH Marvin Harrison 4.00 10.00
PM Peyton Manning 6.00 15.00
RS Rod Smith 3.00 8.00
SA Shaun Alexander 3.00 8.00
SM Steve McNair 3.00 8.00
SS Steve Smith 3.00 8.00
TB Troy Brown 3.00 8.00
TB Tom Brady 6.00 15.00
TG Tony Gonzalez 3.00 8.00
TH Torry Holt 3.00 8.00

2007 Topps TX Exclusive Post Season Ticket Jersey Autographs

STATED PRINT RUN 15 SER.#'d SETS
UNPRICED PATCH PRINT RUN 5
BF Brett Favre 175.00 300.00
FT Fred Taylor 20.00 40.00
JD Jake Delhomme 30.00 60.00
LT LaDainian Tomlinson 40.00 100.00
MH Marvin Harrison 40.00 80.00
MH Matt Hasselbeck 30.00 60.00
PM Peyton Manning 125.00 250.00
SS Steve Smith 20.00 40.00
TB Tom Brady 150.00 300.00
TG Tony Gonzalez 20.00 40.00

2007 Topps TX Exclusive Pro Bowl Ticket Stub Autographs

PRO BOWL AUTO/25 ODDS 1:691
UNPRICED GOLD SER.#'d TO 1
AG Antonio Gates 30.00 60.00
BDR Drew Brees 50.00 100.00
CJ Chad Johnson 40.00 80.00
LJ Larry Johnson 50.00 100.00
LT LaDainian Tomlinson 75.00 150.00
MH Marvin Harrison 50.00 100.00
PM Peyton Manning 150.00 300.00
SM Shawne Merriman 50.00 100.00
SS Steve Smith 30.00 60.00
TG Tony Gonzalez 30.00 60.00

2007 Topps TX Exclusive Rookie Autographs

GROUP A ODDS 1:1691
GROUP B ODDS 1:837
GROUP C ODDS 1:222
GROUP D ODDS 1:70
GROUP E ODDS 1:166
GROUP F ODDS 1:42
GROUP G ODDS 1:18
GROUP H ODDS 1:17
AA Aundrae Allison G 3.00 8.00
AG Anthony Gonzalez E 5.00 12.00
AO Amobi Okoye G 5.00 12.00
AP Adrian Peterson A 150.00 300.00
API Antonio Pittman G 3.00 8.00
BQ Brady Quinn B 30.00 80.00
CJ Calvin Johnson A 100.00 200.00
CL Chris Leak G 4.00 10.00
DB Dwayne Bowe D 10.00 25.00
DJ Dwayne Jarrett C 4.00 10.00
DS Drew Stanton D 3.00 8.00
DW Darius Walker H 3.00 8.00
GO Greg Olsen D 4.00 10.00
GW Garrett Wolfe F 3.00 8.00
IS Isaiah Stanback H 3.00 8.00
JH Jason Hill F 5.00 12.00
JR JaMarcus Russell B 15.00 40.00
LG Luke Getsy H 5.00 12.00
LH Leon Hall F 4.00 10.00
LL LaRon Landry G 5.00 12.00
MB Michael Bush D 5.00 12.00
ML Marshawn Lynch C 12.00 30.00
RM Robert Meachem G 5.00 12.00
SR Sidney Rice D 6.00 15.00
SS Steve Smith USC H 5.00 12.00
SY Selvin Young F 4.00 10.00
TG Ted Ginn Jr. C 10.00 25.00
TH Tony Hunt E 3.00 8.00
TP Tyler Palko H 4.00 10.00
TS Troy Smith D 5.00 12.00

2007 Topps TX Exclusive Season Ticket

BASE/399 STATED ODDS 1:22
*BRONZE/99: .6X TO 1.5X BASIC INSERTS
BRONZE/99 ODDS 1:88
*SILVER/49: .8X TO 2X BASIC INSERTS
SILVER/49 ODDS 1:199
*GOLD/10: 2X TO 5X BASIC INSERTS
GOLD/10 ODDS 1:972
BD Brian Dawkins 1.25 3.00
BF Brett Favre 3.00 8.00
BU Brian Urlacher 1.50 4.00
CJ Chad Johnson 1.25 3.00
CP Chad Pennington 1.25 3.00
DB Derrick Brooks 1.25 3.00
DD Donald Driver 1.50 4.00
DM Deuce McAllister 1.25 3.00
FT Fred Taylor 1.25 3.00
JH Joe Horn 1.25 3.00
LT LaDainian Tomlinson 1.50 4.00
MH Marvin Harrison 1.50 4.00
MHA Matt Hasselbeck 1.25 3.00
PM Peyton Manning 2.50 6.00
RL Ray Lewis 1.50 4.00
SA Shaun Alexander 1.25 3.00
TG Tony Gonzalez 1.25 3.00
TH Torry Holt 1.25 3.00
ZT Zach Thomas 1.25 3.00

2007 Topps TX Exclusive Season Ticket Jersey

JSY/199 ODDS 1:44
*PATCH/25: 1X TO 2.5X BASIC JSY/199
PATCH/25 ODDS 1:363
BD Brian Dawkins 3.00 8.00
BF Brett Favre 8.00 20.00
BU Brian Urlacher 4.00 10.00
CJ Chad Johnson 3.00 8.00
CP Chad Pennington 3.00 8.00
DB Derrick Brooks 3.00 8.00
DD Donald Driver 4.00 10.00
DM Deuce McAllister 3.00 8.00
FT Fred Taylor 3.00 8.00
JH Joe Horn 3.00 8.00
LT LaDainian Tomlinson 4.00 10.00
MH Matt Hasselbeck 3.00 8.00
MH Marvin Harrison 4.00 10.00
PM Peyton Manning 6.00 15.00
RL Ray Lewis 4.00 10.00
SA Shaun Alexander 3.00 8.00
TG Tony Gonzalez 3.00 8.00
TH Torry Holt 3.00 8.00
ZT Zach Thomas 3.00 8.00

2007 Topps TX Exclusive Season Ticket Jersey Autographs

STATED PRINT RUN 10 SER.#'d SETS
UNPRICED PATCH PRINT RUN 5
CJ Chad Johnson 25.00 50.00
CP Chad Pennington 25.00 50.00
DB Derrick Brooks 25.00 50.00
DM Deuce McAllister 25.00 50.00
FT Fred Taylor 30.00 60.00
JH Joe Horn 15.00 40.00
LT LaDainian Tomlinson 75.00 150.00
MH Matt Hasselbeck 30.00 60.00
PM Peyton Manning 150.00 300.00
RL Ray Lewis 60.00 120.00
SA Shaun Alexander 30.00 60.00
TG Tony Gonzalez 15.00 40.00
ZT Zach Thomas 40.00 80.00

2007 Topps TX Exclusive Super Bowl Ticket Stub

STATED ODDS 1:6
ARE Antwaan Randle El 6.00 15.00
AV Adam Vinatieri 6.00 15.00
BR Ben Roethlisberger 10.00 25.00
BU Brian Urlacher 8.00 20.00
DF Dwight Freeney 5.00 12.00
DH Devin Hester 6.00 15.00
DJ Darrell Jackson 5.00 12.00
HM Heath Miller 5.00 12.00
JA Joseph Addai 8.00 20.00
LT Lofa Tatupu 5.00 12.00
MH Matt Hasselbeck 5.00 12.00
MH Marvin Harrison 6.00 15.00
MM Muhsin Muhammad 5.00 12.00
PM Peyton Manning 12.50 30.00
RW Reggie Wayne 5.00 12.00
SA Shaun Alexander 5.00 12.00
TJ Thomas Jones 5.00 12.00
TP Troy Polamalu 8.00 20.00
WP Willie Parker 6.00 15.00

2007 Topps TX Exclusive Super Bowl Ticket Stub Autographs

GROUP A ODDS 1:483
GROUP B ODDS 1:167
GROUP C ODDS 1:371
GROUP D ODDS 1:222
GROUP E ODDS 1:42
GROUP F ODDS 1:93
GROUP G ODDS 1:34
GROUP H ODDS 1:28
GROUP I ODDS 1:21
ARE Antwaan Randle El E 10.00 25.00
AS Asante Samuel D 20.00 50.00
BD Brian Dawkins E 15.00 40.00
CW Cedrick Wilson I 8.00 20.00
DB Derrick Brooks B 40.00 80.00
DB Deion Branch B 12.00 30.00
DJ2 Dexter Jackson B 12.00 30.00
DJ3 Dhani Jones E 6.00 15.00
DM Dan Morgan G 5.00 12.00
GW Grant Wistrom H 6.00 15.00
HM Heath Miller I 12.00 30.00
JA Joseph Addai C 25.00 60.00
JD Jake Delhomme B 12.00 30.00
JF James Farrior I 10.00 25.00
JJ Joe Jurevicius B 12.00 30.00
JR Jerry Rice A 125.00 200.00
JS Jerramy Stevens H 5.00 12.00
JT Jeremiah Trotter E 8.00 20.00
KF Kevin Faulk G 8.00 20.00
KJ Kris Jenkins F 8.00 20.00
LJS L.J. Smith G 6.00 15.00
LT Lofa Tatupu G 8.00 20.00
MA Mike Alstott B 40.00 80.00
MB Michael Boulware H 5.00 12.00
MH1 Marvin Harrison A 30.00 80.00
MH2 Matt Hasselbeck B 15.00 40.00
MM1 Muhsin Muhammad XXXVIII C 8.00 20.00
MM2 Muhsin Muhammad XLI D 8.00 20.00
MS Mack Strong H 6.00 15.00
PM Peyton Manning A 200.00 400.00
RC Rosevelt Colvin G 8.00 20.00
RH Rodney Harrison E 15.00 40.00
RW Reggie Wayne C 30.00 60.00
SA Shaun Alexander A 30.00 60.00
SJ Sebastian Janikowski B 20.00 40.00
SS Steve Smith B 30.00 60.00
TB Tim Brown A 40.00 80.00
TBR Tom Brady A 250.00 500.00
TJ Thomas Jones E 12.00 30.00
TL Ty Law E 8.00 20.00
VW Vince Wilfork E 8.00 20.00
WJ Walter Jones I 6.00 15.00
WP Willie Parker D 30.00 60.00

2007 Topps TX Exclusive Ticket 2 Stardom

BASE/499 STATED ODDS 1:16
*BRONZE/99: .6X TO 1.5X BASIC INSERTS
BRONZE/99 ODDS 1:76
*SILVER/49: .8X TO 2X BASIC INSERTS
SILVER/49 ODDS 1:154
*GOLD/10: 2X TO 5X BASIC INSERTS
GOLD/10 ODDS 1:751
AS Alex Smith QB 1.50 4.00
BJ Brandon Jacobs 1.25 3.00
BR Ben Roethlisberger 1.50 4.00
CW Cadillac Williams 1.25 3.00
DH DeAngelo Hall 1.25 3.00
DW DeAngelo Williams 1.50 4.00
FG Frank Gore 1.50 4.00
GJ Greg Jennings 1.50 4.00
JA Joseph Addai 1.25 3.00
JCO Jerricho Cotchery 1.25 3.00
JCU Jay Cutler 1.50 4.00
KJ Kevin Jones 1.00 2.50
LF Larry Fitzgerald 1.50 4.00
LM Laurence Maroney 1.25 3.00
MC Marques Colston 1.50 4.00
ML Matt Leinart 1.25 3.00
PR Philip Rivers 1.50 4.00
RB Reggie Bush 1.50 4.00
RW Roy Williams WR 1.25 3.00
SJ Steven Jackson 1.50 4.00
SM Shawne Merriman 1.25 3.00
VY Vince Young 1.25 3.00

2007 Topps TX Exclusive Ticket 2 Stardom Jersey

STATED PRINT RUN 199 SER.#'d SETS
*PATCH/49: .8X TO 2X BASIC JSY/199
PATCH PRINT RUN 49 SER.#'d SETS
AS Alex Smith QB 4.00 10.00
BJ Brandon Jacobs 3.00 8.00
BR Ben Roethlisberger 4.00 10.00
CW Cadillac Williams 3.00 8.00
DH DeAngelo Hall 3.00 8.00
DW DeAngelo Williams 4.00 10.00
FG Frank Gore 4.00 10.00
GJ Greg Jennings 4.00 10.00
JA Joseph Addai 3.00 8.00
JC Jay Cutler 4.00 10.00
JC Jerricho Cotchery 3.00 8.00
KJ Kevin Jones 2.50 6.00
LF Larry Fitzgerald 4.00 10.00
LM Laurence Maroney 3.00 8.00
MC Marques Colston 4.00 10.00
ML Matt Leinart 3.00 8.00
PR Philip Rivers 4.00 10.00
RB Reggie Bush 4.00 10.00
RW Roy Williams WR 3.00 8.00
SJ Steven Jackson 4.00 10.00
SM Shawne Merriman 3.00 8.00
VY Vince Young 3.00 8.00

2007 Topps TX Exclusive Ticket 2 Stardom Jersey Autographs

STATED PRINT RUN 25 SER.#'d SETS
UNPRICED PATCH PRINT RUN 5
AS Alex Smith QB 25.00 50.00
CW Cadillac Williams 25.00 50.00
DH DeAngelo Hall 12.50 30.00
DW DeAngelo Williams 20.00 40.00
FG Frank Gore 25.00 50.00
GJ Greg Jennings 20.00 40.00
JA Joseph Addai 30.00 60.00
JC Jerricho Cotchery 12.50 30.00
KJ Kevin Jones 12.50 30.00
LM Laurence Maroney 25.00 50.00
MC Marques Colston 25.00 50.00
ML Matt Leinart 40.00 80.00
RB Reggie Bush 50.00 120.00
RW Roy Williams WR 20.00 40.00
SJ Steven Jackson 25.00 50.00
SM Shawne Merriman 25.00 50.00
VY Vince Young 50.00 100.00

2007 Topps TX Exclusive Ticket to Hawaii

BASE/499 STATED ODDS 1:14
*BRONZE/99: .6X TO 1.5X BASIC INSERTS
BRONZE/99 ODDS 1:70
*SILVER/49: .8X TO 2X BASIC INSERTS
SILVER/49 ODDS 1:141
*GOLD/10: 2X TO 5X BASIC INSERTS
GOLD/10 ODDS 1:698
AC Alge Crumpler 1.25 3.00
AJ Andre Johnson 1.25 3.00
CJ Chad Johnson 1.25 3.00
CP Carson Palmer 1.25 3.00
DB Drew Brees 1.50 4.00
DD Donald Driver 1.50 4.00
DH Devin Hester 1.50 4.00
DHA DeAngelo Hall 1.25 3.00
ER Ed Reed 1.25 3.00
FG Frank Gore 1.50 4.00
JP Julius Peppers 1.25 3.00
JPE Julian Peterson 1.00 2.50
JT Jason Taylor 1.25 3.00
LJ Larry Johnson 1.00 2.50
LT LaDainian Tomlinson 1.50 4.00
PM Peyton Manning 2.50 6.00
RW Reggie Wayne 1.25 3.00
SH Steve Hutchinson 1.25 3.00
SJ Steven Jackson 1.50 4.00
SM Shawne Merriman 1.25 3.00
SS Steve Smith 1.25 3.00
TG Tarik Glenn 1.00 2.50
TR Tony Romo 2.00 5.00
VY Vince Young 1.25 3.00

2007 Topps TX Exclusive Ticket to Hawaii Jersey

STATED PRINT RUN 249 SER.#'d SETS
*PATCH/49: .8X TO 2X BASIC JSY/199
PATCH PRINT RUN 49 SER.#'d SETS
AC Alge Crumpler 3.00 8.00
AJ Andre Johnson 3.00 8.00
CJ Chad Johnson 3.00 8.00
CP Carson Palmer 3.00 8.00
DB Drew Brees 4.00 10.00
DD Donald Driver 4.00 10.00
DH Devin Hester 6.00 15.00
DHA DeAngelo Hall 3.00 8.00
ER Ed Reed 3.00 8.00
FG Frank Gore 4.00 10.00
JP Julius Peppers 3.00 8.00
JPE Julian Peterson 4.00 10.00
JT Jason Taylor 3.00 8.00
LJ Larry Johnson 2.50 6.00
LT LaDainian Tomlinson 4.00 10.00
PM Peyton Manning 6.00 15.00
RW Reggie Wayne 3.00 8.00
SH Steve Hutchinson 3.00 8.00
SJ Steven Jackson 4.00 10.00
SM Shawne Merriman 3.00 8.00
SS Steve Smith 3.00 8.00
TG Tarik Glenn 3.00 8.00
TR Tony Romo 12.50 30.00
VY Vince Young 3.00 8.00

2007 Topps TX Exclusive Ticket to Hawaii Jersey Autographs

STATED PRINT RUN 25 SER.#'d SETS
UNPRICED PATCH PRINT RUN 5
CJ Chad Johnson 20.00 40.00
DB Drew Brees 40.00 80.00
DHA DeAngelo Hall 20.00 40.00
FG Frank Gore 25.00 50.00
JP Julius Peppers
LJ Larry Johnson 30.00 60.00
LT LaDainian Tomlinson 60.00 120.00
PM Peyton Manning 150.00 250.00
RW Reggie Wayne 30.00 60.00
SH Steve Hutchinson 20.00 40.00
SJ Steven Jackson 25.00 50.00
SM Shawne Merriman 25.00 50.00
SS Steve Smith
TG Tarik Glenn 20.00 40.00
TR Tony Romo 100.00 175.00
VY Vince Young 50.00 120.00

2009 Topps Unique

COMPLETE SET (200) 50.00 100.00
COMP.SET w/o SP's (150) 15.00 30.00
SHORT PRINT/1829 ODDS 1:2
1 Drew Brees/1829 1.25 3.00
2 Julius Jones .20 .50
3 Ray Lewis .30 .75
4 Devin Hester .30 .75
5 Jamal Lewis .25 .60
6 Darren Sharper .25 .60
7 Brian Urlacher .30 .75
8 Darren Sproles .25 .60
9 Greg Olsen .20 .50
10 Ted Ginn .25 .60
11 Tony Gonzalez/1829 1.00 2.50
12 Fred Jackson .30 .75
13 Owen Daniels .20 .50
14 Patrick Willis .25 .60
15 DeMarcus Ware .25 .60
16 Earl Bennett/1829 1.00 2.50
17 Chris Cooley .25 .60
18 Nate Burleson .20 .50
19 Laurent Robinson .20 .50
20 Matt Forte .30 .75
21 Willis McGahee/1829 1.00 2.50
22 Muhsin Muhammad .25 .60
23 Antonio Cromartie/1829 .75 2.00
24 Patrick Crayton .20 .50
25 Steve Breaston .25 .60
26 Steve Smith USC .25 .60
27 Chris Chambers .25 .60
28 Zach Miller .25 .60
29 Fred Taylor .25 .60
30 Adrian Peterson .50 1.25
31 Kellen Winslow/1829 1.00 2.50
32 Vernon Davis .25 .60
33 Visanthe Shiancoe .25 .60
34 Jerious Norwood .25 .60
35 Dustin Keller/1829 .75 2.00
36 Donnie Avery/1829 1.00 2.50
37 Michael Vick .40 1.00
38 Josh Morgan .20 .50
39 Rashard Mendenhall/1829 1.00 2.50
40 Steven Jackson/1829 1.00 2.50
41 Ahmad Bradshaw .25 .60
42 Michael Bush .25 .60
43 Jeremy Shockey/1829 .75 2.00
44 Jairus Byrd RC .75 2.00
45 Darrelle Revis .25 .60
46 Dallas Clark/1829 1.00 2.50
47 Chester Taylor/1829 .75 2.00
48 Chaz Schilens .20 .50
49 Ricky Williams .25 .60
50 Tom Brady .50 1.25
51 Mark Clayton/1829 .75 2.00
52 John Carlson/1829 1.00 2.50
53 Asante Samuel .20 .50
54 Peyton Manning .50 1.25
55 Aaron Rodgers .60 1.50
56 Philip Rivers/1829 1.25 3.00
57 Kurt Warner .30 .75
58 Donovan McNabb .30 .75
59 Matt Ryan .30 .75
60 DeAngelo Williams .30 .75
61 Tony Romo .50 1.25
62 Carson Palmer .30 .75
63 Matt Schaub .25 .60
64 Matt Hasselbeck/1829 1.00 2.50
65 Brett Favre 1.25 3.00
66 David Garrard .25 .60
67 Chad Pennington .25 .60
68 Ben Roethlisberger/1829 1.25 3.00
69 Kyle Orton .25 .60
70 Michael Turner .25 .60
71 Joe Flacco .30 .75
72 Trent Edwards/1829 .75 2.00
73 Eli Manning .30 .75
74 Matt Cassel .25 .60
75 Jake Delhomme .25 .60
76 Kerry Collins/1829 1.00 2.50
77 JaMarcus Russell .20 .50
78 Brady Quinn .25 .60
79 Marc Bulger .25 .60
80 Larry Fitzgerald .30 .75
81 Domenik Hixon .20 .50
82 Isaac Bruce .25 .60
83 LaDainian Tomlinson .30 .75
84 Tim Hightower .20 .50
85 Jay Cutler/1829 1.25 3.00
86 Jason Campbell .20 .50
87 Maurice Jones-Drew/1829 1.00 2.50
88 Roddy White .25 .60
89 Brandon Jacobs/1829 1.00 2.50
90 Andre Johnson/1829 1.00 2.50
91 T.J. Houshmandzadeh/1829 1.00 2.50
92 Santonio Holmes .25 .60
93 Cedric Benson/1829 1.00 2.50
94 Calvin Johnson .30 .75
95 Steve Slaton .25 .60
96 Greg Jennings/1829 1.25 3.00
97 Marion Barber .25 .60
98 Steve Smith .25 .60
99 Clinton Portis .25 .60
100 Brian Westbrook .25 .60
101 Reggie Bush .30 .75
102 Anquan Boldin .25 .60
103 Pierre Thomas .25 .60
104 Ronnie Brown/1829 1.00 2.50
105 Ryan Grant .25 .60
106 Marques Colston .25 .60
107 Kevin Smith .25 .60
108 Wes Welker/1829 1.25 3.00
109 Dwayne Bowe .25 .60
110 Chris Johnson .30 .75
111 Vincent Jackson .25 .60
112 Thomas Jones/1829 1.00 2.50
113 Jason Witten .30 .75
114 Eddie Royal .25 .60
115 Ed Reed .25 .60
116 Chad Ochocinco/1829 1.00 2.50
117 Joseph Addai .30 .75
118 Terrell Owens .30 .75
119 Anthony Gonzalez .20 .50
120 Randy Moss .30 .75
121 DeSean Jackson .25 .60
122 Braylon Edwards .25 .60
123 LenDale White .25 .60
124 Darren McFadden/1829 1.25 3.00
125 Derrick Mason .25 .60
126 Laveranues Coles .20 .50
127 Antonio Gates .25 .60
128 Felix Jones/1829 1.25 3.00
129 Antonio Bryant .20 .50
130 Reggie Wayne/1829 1.00 2.50
131 Donald Driver .25 .60
132 Hines Ward/1829 1.00 2.50
133 Leon Washington .25 .60
134 Brandon Marshall .25 .60
135 Troy Polamalu .30 .75
136 Roy Williams WR/1829 1.00 2.50
137 Jerricho Cotchery .25 .60
138 Ray Rice .30 .75
139 Kevin Walter .25 .60
140 Frank Gore .25 .60
141 Lee Evans .25 .60
142 Bernard Berrian .25 .60
143 Derrick Ward/1829 .75 2.00
144 Marshawn Lynch/1829 1.00 2.50
145 Jonathan Stewart .25 .60
146 Larry Johnson .25 .60
147 Willie Parker .20 .50
148 Santana Moss .25 .60
149 Torry Holt .25 .60
150 Matthew Stafford RC 4.00 10.00
151 Aaron Curry RC .75 2.00
152 Rashad Jennings RC .75 2.00
153 Brian Robiskie/1829 RC 1.00 2.50
154 Deon Butler RC .60 1.50
155 Chris Wells RC 1.25 3.00
156 Aaron Maybin/1829 RC .75 2.00
157 Darrius Heyward-Bey/1829 RC 1.00 2.50
158 Derrick Williams RC .60 1.50
159 Glen Coffee RC .60 1.50
160 Hakeem Nicks RC 1.25 3.00
161 Josh Freeman/1829 RC 2.00 5.00
162 Juaquin Iglesias RC .60 1.50
163 Mike Goodson RC .75 2.00
164 Andre Brown RC .50 1.25
165 Percy Harvin RC 1.25 3.00
166 Jason Smith RC .60 1.50
167 Kenny Britt RC 1.00 2.50
168 Rhett Bomar RC .60 1.50
169 Nate Davis RC .60 1.50
170 Knowshon Moreno RC .75 2.00
171 Mohamed Massaquoi RC .60 1.50
172 Bernard Scott RC .75 2.00
173 Mike Thomas/1829 RC 1.00 2.50
174 Mike Wallace RC 1.50 4.00
175 LeSean McCoy/1829 RC 2.00 5.00
176 Javon Ringer/1829 RC 1.00 2.50
177 Patrick Turner/1829 RC .75 2.00
178 Pat White RC .75 2.00
179 Ramses Barden RC .50 1.25
180 Michael Crabtree RC 1.50 4.00
181 Shonn Greene/1829 RC 1.50 4.00
182 Stephen McGee RC .75 2.00
183 Tyson Jackson RC .60 1.50
184 B.J. Raji RC .75 2.00
185 Donald Brown RC .75 2.00
186 Brian Orakpo RC .75 2.00
187 Malcolm Jenkins RC .75 2.00
188 Brian Cushing RC .75 2.00
189 Brian Hartline/1829 RC 1.00 2.50
190 Jeremy Maclin RC 1.25 3.00
191 Louis Murphy RC .75 2.00
192 Austin Collie RC .75 2.00
193 Gartrell Johnson/1829 RC .60 1.50
194 Jared Cook RC .75 2.00
195 Brandon Pettigrew RC .75 2.00
196 Shawn Nelson RC .60 1.50
197 Sammie Stroughter/1829 RC 1.00 2.50

198 Chase Coffman RC .60 1.50
199 James Davis RC .75 2.00
200 Mark Sanchez RC 2.50 6.00

2009 Topps Unique Bronze
*VETS: 2.5X TO 6X BASIC CARDS
*VETS: .6X TO 1.5X BASIC SP
*ROOKIES: .8X TO 2X BASIC CARDS
*ROOKIES: .6X TO 1.5X BASIC SP RC
BRONZE/99 ODDS 1:10

2009 Topps Unique Gold
*VETS: 4X TO 10X BASIC CARDS
*VETS: 1X TO 2.5X BASIC SP
*ROOKIES: 1.2X TO 3X BASIC CARDS
*ROOKIES: 1X TO 2.5X BASIC SP RC
GOLD/25 ODDS 1:37

2009 Topps Unique Red
*VETS: 2X TO 5X BASIC CARDS
*VETS: .5X TO 1.2X BASIC SP
*ROOKIES: .5X TO 1.2X BASIC CARDS
*ROOKIES: .4X TO 1X BASIC SP RC
RED/799 ODDS 1:2

2009 Topps Unique Alone At The Top
COMPLETE SET (10) 8.00 20.00
STATED ODDS 1:12
*BRONZE/99: 1X TO 2.5X BASIC INSERTS
*GOLD/25: 1.2X TO 3X BASIC INSERTS
AT1 Adrian Peterson 1.50 4.00
AT2 Drew Brees 1.00 2.50
AT3 Andre Johnson .75 2.00
AT4 DeAngelo Williams 1.00 2.50
AT5 Philip Rivers 1.00 2.50
AT6 Larry Fitzgerald 1.00 2.50
AT7 D'Qwell Jackson .60 1.50
AT8 DeMarcus Ware .75 2.00
AT9 Ed Reed .75 2.00
AT10 Drew Brees 1.00 2.50

2009 Topps Unique Dynamic Dual Autographs
DUAL AUTO/25 ODDS 1:729
BB Tom Brady 150.00 300.00
Drew Brees
BM Dwayne Bowe 20.00 40.00
Brandon Marshall
BN Kenny Britt
Hakeem Nicks
CH Michael Crabtree 30.00 60.00
Darrius Heyward-Bey
MW Randy Moss 40.00 80.00
Reggie Wayne
OE Chad Ochocinco 20.00 40.00
Braylon Edwards
PH Adrian Peterson 75.00 150.00
Percy Harvin
PT Adrian Peterson 75.00 150.00
LaDainian Tomlinson
RW Matt Ryan 40.00 80.00
Roddy White
WM Chris Wells 25.00 60.00
Knowshon Moreno

2009 Topps Unique Dynamic Dual Jerseys
DUAL JERSEY/79 ODDS 1:93
JA Joseph Addai 4.00 10.00
Donald Brown
BB Drew Brees 6.00 15.00
Reggie Bush
BM Tom Brady 10.00 25.00
Randy Moss
NB Ramses Barden 6.00 15.00
Hakeem Nicks
BF Larry Fitzgerald 5.00 12.00
Anquan Boldin
GG Frank Gore 3.00 8.00
Glen Coffee
HF Devin Hester 5.00 12.00
Matt Forte
BJ Felix Jones 6.00 15.00
Marion Barber
JS Andre Johnson 4.00 10.00
Steve Slaton
MJ Eli Manning 6.00 15.00
Brandon Jacobs
MM LeSean McCoy 6.00 15.00
Jeremy Maclin
MS Santana Moss 4.00 10.00
Clinton Portis
MW Donovan McNabb 5.00 12.00
Brian Westbrook
PH Adrian Peterson 6.00 15.00
Percy Harvin
RB Javon Ringer 5.00 12.00
Kenny Britt
RG Philip Rivers 5.00 12.00
Antonio Gates
RJ Aaron Rodgers 8.00 20.00
Greg Jennings
RMA Brian Robiskie 4.00 10.00
Mohamad Massaquoi
SK Mark Sanchez 10.00 25.00
Dustin Keller
SP Matthew Stafford 8.00 20.00
Brandon Pettigrew
WS DeAngelo Williams 5.00 12.00
Steve Smith
MR Brandon Marshall 4.00 10.00
Eddie Royal
RM Knowshon Moreno 6.00 15.00
Eddie Royal
RW Tony Romo 8.00 20.00
Jason Witten
RWH Matt Ryan 5.00 12.00
Roddy White

2009 Topps Unique Game Breakers Autographs
STATED PRINT RUN 25-1000
BB Bernard Berrian/150 6.00 15.00
BF Brett Favre/25 175.00 300.00
BQ Brady Quinn/25 15.00 40.00
DB Drew Brees/50 40.00 80.00
EM Eli Manning/50 40.00 80.00
FG Frank Gore/100 6.00 15.00
GC Glen Coffee/250 4.00 10.00
HN Hakeem Nicks/100 8.00 20.00
JA Joseph Addai/100 8.00 20.00
JC Jamaal Charles/500 8.00 20.00
JD James Davis/1000 4.00 10.00
JF1 Joe Flacco/200 10.00 25.00
JF2 Josh Freeman/100 10.00 25.00
JK Johnny Knox/750 6.00 15.00
JM Jeremy Maclin/100 10.00 25.00
JS Jonathan Stewart/100 8.00 20.00
LE Lee Evans/100 5.00 12.00
LM LeSean McCoy/400 10.00 25.00
MC Matt Cassel/100 8.00 20.00
MR Matt Ryan/50 25.00 50.00
PH Percy Harvin/200 20.00 50.00
PM Peyton Manning/25 75.00 150.00
PW Pat White/400 5.00 12.00
RJ Rashad Jennings/500 4.00 10.00
RR Ray Rice/400 10.00 25.00
SS Steve Smith USC/500 5.00 12.00
TE Trent Edwards/250 5.00 12.00
WW Wes Welker/50 20.00 40.00

2009 Topps Unique Game Breakers Jersey
GAME BREAKER JERSEY/199 ODDS 1:37
AJ Andre Johnson 3.00 8.00
AP Adrian Peterson 6.00 15.00
BJ Brandon Jacobs 3.00 8.00
BM Brandon Marshall 3.00 8.00
BR Ben Roethlisberger 4.00 10.00
BW Brian Westbrook 3.00 8.00
CP Clinton Portis 3.00 8.00
DW DeAngelo Williams 4.00 10.00
EM Eli Manning 4.00 10.00
FG Frank Gore 3.00 8.00
GJ Greg Jennings 4.00 10.00
JA Joseph Addai 4.00 10.00
JS Jonathan Stewart 3.00 8.00
LF Larry Fitzgerald 4.00 10.00
MB Marion Barber 3.00 8.00
MF Matt Forte 4.00 10.00
MJD Maurice Jones-Drew 3.00 8.00
PM Peyton Manning 6.00 15.00
PR Philip Rivers 4.00 10.00
RB Reggie Bush 4.00 10.00
RM Randy Moss 4.00 10.00
RW Reggie Wayne 3.00 8.00
SH Santonio Holmes 3.00 8.00
SS Steve Slaton 3.00 8.00
TR Tony Romo 6.00 15.00

2009 Topps Unique Game Breakers Jersey Autographs
GAME BREAKER JSY AU/25 ODDS 1:729
BJ Brandon Jacobs 10.00 25.00
BW Brian Westbrook
DW DeAngelo Williams 12.00 30.00
FG Frank Gore
JC Jay Cutler 12.00 30.00
JF Joe Flacco 20.00 40.00
JS Jonathan Stewart 10.00 25.00
MB Marion Barber
MR Matt Ryan 25.00 50.00
MS Mark Sanchez
SS Steve Slaton 10.00 25.00

2009 Topps Unique Jumbo Relic Patch
JUMBO PATCH/10-20 ODDS 1:289
SERIAL #'d UNDER 20 NOT PRICED
AJ Andre Johnson/20 12.00 30.00
AV Adam Vinatieri/20 20.00 50.00
BF Brett Favre/20 50.00 120.00
BR B.J. Raji/20 15.00 40.00
BU Brian Urlacher/20 20.00 50.00
DW Derrick Williams/20 12.00 30.00
EH Evander Hood/20 20.00 50.00
JPW John Parker Wilson/20 15.00 40.00
JS1 Jeremy Shockey/20 12.00 30.00
KC Kevin Curtis/20 12.00 30.00
KS Kevin Smith/20 15.00 40.00
MO Michael Oher/20 25.00 60.00
MT Mike Thomas/20 15.00 40.00
MTH Mike Thomas/20 15.00 40.00
PT Patrick Turner/20 12.00 30.00
QC Quan Cosby/20 15.00 40.00
SN Shawn Nelson/20 15.00 40.00
SS2 Steve Smith/20 15.00 40.00
TG Tony Gonzalez/20 15.00 40.00
TH1 Todd Heap/20 12.00 30.00
TH2 Torry Holt/20 15.00 40.00
TP Troy Polamalu/20 20.00 50.00

2009 Topps Unique Prime Time Patches
STATED PRINT RUN 25-99
PTP1 Joseph Addai/50 6.00 15.00
PTP2 Donnie Avery/50 5.00 12.00
PTP3 Donnie Avery/40 5.00 12.00
PTP4 Marion Barber/99 5.00 12.00
PTP5 Anquan Boldin/50 5.00 12.00
PTP6 Anquan Boldin/40 5.00 12.00
PTP7 Dwayne Bowe/50 5.00 12.00
PTP8 Dwayne Bowe/40 5.00 12.00
PTP9 Terry Bradshaw/50 8.00 20.00
PTP10 Tom Brady/99 10.00 25.00
PTP11 Tom Brady/40 10.00 25.00
PTP12 Drew Brees/75 6.00 15.00
PTP13 Kenny Britt/50 4.00 10.00
PTP14 Kenny Britt/40 4.00 10.00
PTP16 Ronnie Brown/50 5.00 12.00
PTP17 Ronnie Brown/40 5.00 12.00
PTP18 Reggie Bush/50 6.00 15.00
PTP19 Reggie Bush/40 6.00 15.00
PTP20 Brian Westbrook/50 5.00 12.00
PTP21 Brian Westbrook/40 5.00 12.00
PTP22 Dallas Clark/50 5.00 12.00
PTP23 Dallas Clark/40 5.00 12.00
PTP25 Laveranues Coles/75 4.00 10.00
PTP26 Marques Colston/50 5.00 12.00
PTP27 Chris Cooley/75 5.00 12.00
PTP28 Jerricho Cotchery/50 5.00 12.00
PTP29 Jerricho Cotchery/40 5.00 12.00
PTP33 Brian Dawkins/50 6.00 15.00
PTP34 Brian Dawkins/40 6.00 15.00
PTP35 Donald Driver/75 5.00 12.00
PTP36 Braylon Edwards/50 5.00 12.00
PTP37 Trent Edwards/50 4.00 10.00
PTP38 Trent Edwards/40 4.00 10.00
PTP39 John Elway/50 10.00 25.00
PTP40 Lee Evans/50 5.00 12.00
PTP41 Lee Evans/40 5.00 12.00
PTP42 Brett Favre/25 25.00 60.00
PTP43 Larry Fitzgerald/50 6.00 15.00
PTP44 Joe Flacco/50 6.00 15.00
PTP46 Antonio Gates/50 5.00 12.00
PTP47 Antonio Gates/40 5.00 12.00
PTP48 Ted Ginn/50 5.00 12.00
PTP49 Ted Ginn/40 5.00 12.00
PTP50 Anthony Gonzalez/50 4.00 10.00
PTP51 Anthony Gonzalez/50 4.00 10.00
PTP52 Tony Gonzalez/50 5.00 12.00
PTP53 Tony Gonzalez/40 5.00 12.00
PTP54 Frank Gore/99 5.00 12.00
PTP55 Frank Gore/40 5.00 12.00
PTP56 Marvin Harrison/50 6.00 15.00
PTP57 Marvin Harrison/40 6.00 15.00
PTP59 Matt Hasselbeck/50 5.00 12.00
PTP60 Matt Hasselbeck/40 5.00 12.00
PTP61 Devin Hester/75 6.00 15.00
PTP62 Santonio Holmes/50 5.00 12.00
PTP63 T.J. Houshmandzadeh/50 5.00 12.00
PTP64 T.J. Houshmandzadeh/40 5.00 12.00
PTP65 DeSean Jackson/50 5.00 12.00
PTP66 Steven Jackson/99 5.00 12.00
PTP67 Steven Jackson/40 5.00 12.00
PTP68 Vincent Jackson/75 5.00 12.00
PTP69 Edgerrin James/50 5.00 12.00
PTP70 Edgerrin James/40 5.00 12.00
PTP71 Greg Jennings/75 6.00 15.00
PTP72 Andre Johnson/50 5.00 12.00
PTP73 Andre Johnson/40 5.00 12.00
PTP74 Calvin Johnson/50 6.00 15.00
PTP75 Calvin Johnson/40 6.00 15.00
PTP76 Chad Ochocinco/50 5.00 12.00
PTP77 Chad Ochocinco/40 5.00 12.00
PTP78 Felix Jones/50 6.00 15.00
PTP79 Felix Jones/40 6.00 15.00
PTP80 Maurice Jones-Drew/50 5.00 12.00
PTP81 Maurice Jones-Drew/40 5.00 12.00
PTP82 Jamal Lewis/50 5.00 12.00
PTP83 Ray Lewis/50 6.00 15.00
PTP84 Ray Lewis/40 6.00 15.00
PTP85 Marshawn Lynch/50 5.00 12.00
PTP86 Marshawn Lynch/40 5.00 12.00
PTP89 Peyton Manning/50 10.00 25.00
PTP90 Dan Marino/50 15.00 40.00
PTP91 DeAngelo Williams/50 6.00 15.00
PTP92 DeAngelo Williams/40 6.00 15.00
PTP94 Darren McFadden/75 6.00 15.00
PTP95 Willis McGahee/50 5.00 12.00
PTP96 Willis McGahee/40 5.00 12.00
PTP97 Donovan McNabb/50 6.00 15.00
PTP98 Donovan McNabb/40 6.00 15.00
PTP99 Rashard Mendenhall/50 5.00 12.00
PTP100 Rashard Mendenhall/40 5.00 12.00
PTP101 Joe Montana/25 25.00 60.00
PTP103 Randy Moss/50 6.00 15.00
PTP104 Randy Moss/40 6.00 15.00
PTP105 Santana Moss/75 5.00 12.00
PTP106 Hakeem Nicks/50 6.00 15.00
PTP107 Greg Olsen/75 4.00 10.00
PTP108 Terrell Owens/50 6.00 15.00
PTP109 Terrell Owens/40 6.00 15.00
PTP110 Terrell Owens/50 6.00 15.00
PTP111 Terrell Owens/40 6.00 15.00
PTP112 Carson Palmer/50 6.00 15.00
PTP113 Carson Palmer/40 6.00 15.00
PTP114 Willie Parker/50 4.00 10.00
PTP115 Willie Parker/40 4.00 10.00
PTP116 Adrian Peterson/50 10.00 25.00
PTP117 Adrian Peterson/40 10.00 25.00
PTP118 Clinton Portis/50 5.00 12.00
PTP119 Clinton Portis/40 5.00 12.00
PTP120 Brady Quinn/50 5.00 12.00
PTP121 Brady Quinn/40 5.00 12.00
PTP122 Ed Reed/50 5.00 12.00
PTP123 Ed Reed/40 5.00 12.00
PTP125 Ray Rice/50 6.00 15.00
PTP126 Ray Rice/50 6.00 15.00
PTP127 Aaron Rodgers/75 10.00 25.00
PTP128 Ben Roethlisberger/50 6.00 15.00
PTP129 Eddie Royal/50 5.00 12.00
PTP130 Eddie Royal/40 5.00 12.00
PTP131 JaMarcus Russell/50 4.00 10.00
PTP132 JaMarcus Russell/40 4.00 10.00
PTP133 Matt Ryan/50 6.00 15.00
PTP135 Jeremy Shockey/50 4.00 10.00
PTP136 Jeremy Shockey/40 4.00 10.00
PTP137 Steve Slaton/50 5.00 12.00
PTP139 Steve Smith/50 5.00 12.00
PTP140 Steve Smith/40 5.00 12.00
PTP141 Matthew Stafford/50 30.00 80.00
PTP142 Jonathan Stewart/50 5.00 12.00
PTP143 Fred Taylor/50 5.00 12.00
PTP144 Fred Taylor/40 5.00 12.00
PTP145 LaDainian Tomlinson/50 6.00 15.00
PTP146 LaDainian Tomlinson/40 6.00 15.00
PTP147 Brian Urlacher/50 6.00 15.00
PTP148 Brian Urlacher/40 6.00 15.00
PTP149 Michael Vick/50 8.00 20.00
PTP150 Michael Vick/40 8.00 20.00
PTP151 Hines Ward/50 5.00 12.00
PTP152 Hines Ward/40 5.00 12.00
PTP153 Kurt Warner/75 6.00 15.00
PTP154 Reggie Wayne/50 5.00 12.00

2009 Topps Unique Triple Threat Jersey
TRIPLE JERSEY/25 ODDS 1:260
BBB Rhett Bomar 6.00 15.00
Andre Brown
Ramses Barden
BBC Drew Brees 8.00 20.00
Reggie Bush
Marques Colston
BMW Tom Brady 12.00 30.00
Randy Moss
Wes Welker
CHM Michael Crabtree 15.00 40.00
Percy Harvin
Jeremy Maclin
CPM Jason Campbell 6.00 15.00
Clinton Portis
Santana Moss
DCC Nate Davis 10.00 25.00
Glen Coffee
Michael Crabtree
ELE Trent Edwards 6.00 15.00
Marshawn Lynch
Lee Evans
FRM Joe Flacco 8.00 20.00
Ray Rice
Willis McGahee
GJT David Garrard 8.00 20.00
Maurice Jones-Drew
Mike Thomas
JMM DeSean Jackson 8.00 20.00
Jeremy Maclin
LeSean McCoy
JWR Chris Johnson 8.00 20.00
LenDale White
Javon Ringer
MBW Knowshon Moreno 10.00 25.00
Donald Brown
Chris Wells
MJN Eli Manning 8.00 20.00
Brandon Jacobs
Hakeem Nicks
MRM Knowshon Moreno 10.00 25.00
Eddie Royal
Brandon Marshall
MWB Peyton Manning 8.00 20.00
Reggie Wayne
Donald Brown
MWJ Donovan McNabb 8.00 20.00
Brian Westbrook
DeSean Jackson
QEM Brady Quinn 6.00 15.00
Braylon Edwards
Mohamed Massaquoi
RBJ Tony Romo 12.00 30.00
Marion Barber
Felix Jones
RGJ Aaron Rodgers 12.00 30.00
Ryan Grant
Greg Jennings
RMH JaMarcus Russell 5.00 12.00
Darren McFadden
Darrius Heyward-Bey
RMW Ben Roethlisberger 10.00 25.00
Rashard Mendenhall
Mike Wallace
RTG Philip Rivers 8.00 20.00
LaDainian Tomlinson
Antonio Gates
SGK Mark Sanchez 10.00 25.00
Shonn Greene
Dustin Keller
SPW Matthew Stafford 10.00 25.00
Brandon Pettigrew
Derrick Williams
SSF Matthew Stafford 15.00 40.00
Mark Sanchez
Josh Freeman
BGW Pat White 5.00 12.00
Ronnie Brown
Ted Ginn
WFB Kurt Warner 8.00 20.00
Larry Fitzgerald
Anquan Boldin
WSS DeAngelo Williams 8.00 20.00
Steve Smith
Jonathan Stewart

2009 Topps Unique Unique Unis
COMPLETE SET (20) 12.00 30.00
STATED ODDS 1:6
*BRONZE/99: 1X TO 2.5X BASIC INSERTS
*GOLD/25: 1.2X TO 3X BASIC INSERTS
UU1 Donovan McNabb 1.00 2.50
UU2 Brett Favre 4.00 10.00
UU3 Frank Gore .75 2.00
UU4 Tom Brady 1.50 4.00
UU5 Brian Westbrook .75 2.00
UU6 Tony Romo 1.50 4.00
UU7 Josh Freeman 2.00 5.00
UU8 LaDainian Tomlinson 1.00 2.50
UU9 Mark Sanchez 2.00 5.00
UU10 Terrell Owens 1.00 2.50
UU11 Philip Rivers 1.00 2.50
UU12 Ronnie Brown .75 2.00
UU13 Chris Johnson 1.00 2.50
UU14 Matt Forte 1.00 2.50
UU15 Adrian Peterson 1.50 4.00
UU16 Kyle Orton .75 2.00
UU17 Zach Miller .75 2.00
UU18 Steven Jackson .75 2.00
UU19 Dwayne Bowe .75 2.00
UU20 Ben Roethlisberger 1.00 2.50

2009 Topps Unique Unparalled Performances
STATED ODDS 1:6
*BRONZE/99: 1X TO 2.5X BASIC INSERTS
*GOLD/25: 1.2X TO 3X BASIC INSERTS
UP1 Drew Brees 1.00 2.50
UP2 Andre Johnson .75 2.00
UP3 Michael Turner .75 2.00
UP4 Matt Forte 1.00 2.50
UP5 Tom Brady 1.50 4.00
UP6 Steven Jackson .75 2.00
UP7 Philip Rivers 1.00 2.50
UP8 Terrell Owens 1.00 2.50
UP9 Steve Smith .75 2.00
UP10 Adrian Peterson 1.50 4.00
UP11 Larry Fitzgerald 1.00 2.50
UP12 Frank Gore .75 2.00
UP13 Reggie Wayne .75 2.00
UP14 Brian Westbrook .75 2.00
UP15 Peyton Manning 1.50 4.00
UP16 DeAngelo Williams 1.00 2.50
UP17 Randy Moss 1.00 2.50
UP18 Maurice Jones-Drew .75 2.00
UP19 Clinton Portis .75 2.00
UP20 LaDainian Tomlinson 1.00 2.50

2010 Topps Unrivaled

COMP.SET w/o RC's (100) 8.00 20.00
151-200 ROOKIE/999 ODDS 1:8 HOB
1 Steven Jackson .25 .60
2 Joseph Addai .25 .60
3 Matthew Stafford .30 .75
4 Randy Moss .30 .75
5 Brandon Marshall .25 .60
6 Ray Lewis .30 .75
7 Nnamdi Asomugha .25 .60
8 Vincent Jackson .20 .50
9 Beanie Wells .25 .60
10 Ryan Grant .25 .60
11 Pierre Garcon .25 .60
12 Jonathan Vilma .20 .50
13 Shonn Greene .25 .60
14 Tony Romo .40 1.00
15 Jon Beason .20 .50
16 Marques Colston .25 .60
17 Vince Young .20 .50
18 Vernon Davis .25 .60
19 Mike Wallace .25 .60
20 Patrick Willis .25 .60
21 Eli Manning .30 .75
22 DeAngelo Williams .25 .60
23 Mike Sims-Walker .25 .60
24 Troy Polamalu .30 .75
25 Jamaal Charles .25 .60
26 Knowshon Moreno .25 .60
27 LeSean McCoy .25 .60
28 Cedric Benson .25 .60
29 Dallas Clark .25 .60
30 Pierre Thomas .25 .60
31 DeSean Jackson .25 .60
32 Jonathan Stewart .25 .60
33 Lee Evans .25 .60
34 Darren McFadden .25 .60
35 Jay Cutler .30 .75
36 Philip Rivers .30 .75
37 Roddy White .25 .60
38 Calvin Johnson .30 .75
39 Ronnie Brown .25 .60
40 Chris Cooley .25 .60
41 Percy Harvin .30 .75
42 Carson Palmer .25 .60
43 Drew Brees .30 .75
44 Clinton Portis .25 .60
45 Reggie Wayne .25 .60
46 Hines Ward .25 .60
47 Mark Sanchez .30 .75
48 Brian Urlacher .30 .75
49 Jerome Harrison .20 .50
50 Kevin Kolb .25 .60
51 Tony Gonzalez .25 .60
52 Steve Smith .25 .60
53 T.J. Houshmandzadeh .25 .60
54 Justin Forsett .25 .60
55 Jeremy Maclin .25 .60
56 Ricky Williams .25 .60
57 Chad Henne .25 .60
58 Steve Smith .25 .60
59 Steve Slaton .20 .50
60 Brent Celek .25 .60
61 Asante Samuel .20 .50
62 Hakeem Nicks .25 .60
63 Matt Schaub .25 .60
64 Miles Austin .30 .75
65 Michael Crabtree .30 .75
66 Maurice Jones-Drew .25 .60
67 Rashard Mendenhall .25 .60
68 Joe Flacco .30 .75
69 Sidney Rice .25 .60
70 Donovan McNabb .30 .75
71 Aaron Rodgers .60 1.50
72 Fred Jackson .30 .75
73 Felix Jones .25 .60
74 Brett Favre .75 2.00
75 Chris Johnson .30 .75
76 Matt Ryan .30 .75
77 Adrian Peterson .50 1.25
78 Andre Johnson .25 .60
79 Antonio Gates .25 .60
80 Tom Brady .50 1.25
81 Frank Gore .25 .60
82 Kellen Winslow .25 .60
83 Matt Forte .25 .60
84 Anquan Boldin .25 .60
85 Chad Ochocinco .25 .60
86 Greg Jennings .25 .60
87 Reggie Bush .30 .75
88 Jared Allen .30 .75
89 Santana Moss .25 .60
90 Braylon Edwards .25 .60
91 Brandon Jacobs .25 .60
92 Darrelle Revis .25 .60
93 Dwayne Bowe .25 .60
94 Peyton Manning .50 1.25
95 Thomas Jones .25 .60
96 James Laurinaitis .25 .60
97 Michael Turner .20 .50
98 Ray Rice .25 .60
99 Donald Brown .25 .60
100 Larry Fitzgerald .30 .75
101 Anthony McCoy RC 1.25 3.00
102 Anthony Dixon RC 1.50 4.00
103 Ryan Mathews RC 3.00 8.00
104 Mike Kafka RC 1.50 4.00
105 Brandon Ghee RC 1.25 3.00
106 Ndamukong Suh RC 3.00 8.00
107 C.J. Spiller RC 2.50 6.00
108 Montario Hardesty RC 1.50 4.00
109 Dan Williams RC 1.25 3.00
110 Eric Decker RC 2.00 5.00
111 Brandon LaFell RC 1.50 4.00
112 Rob Gronkowski RC 4.00 10.00
113 Aaron Hernandez RC 2.50 6.00
114 Jacoby Ford RC 1.50 4.00
115 Mike Williams RC 2.50 6.00
116 Demaryius Thomas RC 2.00 5.00
117 Tony Pike RC 1.50 4.00
118 Jimmy Clausen RC 1.50 4.00
119 John Skelton RC 1.50 4.00
120 Jonathan Crompton RC 1.25 3.00
121 Andre Roberts RC 1.50 4.00
122 Bryan Bulaga RC 1.50 4.00
123 Jimmy Graham RC 3.00 8.00
124 Jahvid Best RC 2.50 6.00
125 Taylor Price RC 1.50 4.00
126 Colt McCoy RC 3.00 8.00
127 Armanti Edwards RC 1.50 4.00
128 Carlton Mitchell RC 1.25 3.00
129 Dez Bryant RC 5.00 12.00
130 Damian Williams RC 1.50 4.00
131 Jonathan Dwyer RC 1.50 4.00
132 Jordan Shipley RC 1.50 4.00
133 Arrelious Benn RC 1.50 4.00
134 Charles Scott RC 1.25 3.00
135 Toby Gerhart RC 1.50 4.00
136 Tim Tebow RC 6.00 15.00
137 Ben Tate RC 2.00 5.00
138 Dexter McCluster RC 1.50 4.00
139 Sean Lee RC 1.50 4.00
140 Dan LeFevour RC 1.50 4.00
141 Jerry Hughes RC 1.50 4.00
142 Gerald McCoy RC 1.50 4.00
143 Sam Bradford RC 6.00 15.00
144 Riley Cooper RC 1.50 4.00
145 James Starks RC 2.50 6.00
146 Emmanuel Sanders RC 1.50 4.00
147 Marcus Easley RC 1.25 3.00
148 Mardy Gilyard RC 1.50 4.00
149 Trent Williams RC 1.50 4.00
150 Golden Tate RC 1.50 4.00

2010 Topps Unrivaled Black
*VETS 1-100: 4X TO 10X BASIC CARDS
*ROOKIES 101-150: .6X TO 1.5X BASIC CARDS
BLACK/99 STATED ODDS 1:37 HOB

2010 Topps Unrivaled Gold 499
*VETS: 2X TO 5X BASIC CARDS
*ROOKIES: .4X TO 1X BASIC CARDS
GOLD/499 STATED ODDS 1:8 HOB

2010 Topps Unrivaled Gold 759
*VETS: 1.5X TO 4X BASIC CARDS
VETS GOLD/759 ODDS 1:6 HOB

2010 Topps Unrivaled Red
*VETS 1-100: 8X TO 20X BASIC CARDS
*ROOKIES 101-150: 1.5X TO 4X BASIC CARDS
RED/25 STATED ODDS 1:140 HOB

2010 Topps Unrivaled Silver
*VETS: 2.5X TO 6X BASIC CARDS
*ROOKIES: .5X TO 1.2X BASIC CARDS
SILVER PRINT RUN 299 SER.#'d SETS

2010 Topps Unrivaled Autographed Patch
GROUP A ODDS 1:1052 HOB
GROUP B ODDS 1:334 HOB
GROUP C ODDS 1:153 HOB
GROUP D ODDS 1:183 HOB
GROUP E ODDS 1:65 HOB
EXCH EXPIRATION: 10/31/2013
UAPAB Arrelious Benn/349 10.00 25.00
UAPAD Anthony Dixon/249 8.00 20.00
UAPAE Armanti Edwards/349 8.00 20.00
UAPAH Aaron Hernandez/149 12.00 30.00
UAPAP Adrian Peterson/149 60.00 120.00
UAPAR Andre Roberts/349 8.00 20.00
UAPBB Bernard Berrian/149 6.00 15.00
UAPBE Braylon Edwards/149 10.00 25.00
UAPBL Brandon LaFell/349 8.00 20.00
UAPBT Ben Tate/249 10.00 25.00
UAPCMC Colt McCoy/50 25.00 60.00
UAPCO Chad Ochocinco/100 10.00 25.00
UAPCS C.J. Spiller/100 20.00 40.00
UAPCSC Charles Scott/249 6.00 15.00
UAPCT Chester Taylor/149 6.00 15.00
UAPDB Dez Bryant/30 75.00 150.00
UAPDBO Dwayne Bowe/149 10.00 25.00
UAPDMC Dexter McCluster/349 8.00 20.00
UAPDT Demaryius Thomas/100 25.00 50.00
UAPDW DeAngelo Williams/100 10.00 25.00
UAPDWI Damian Williams/349 8.00 20.00
UAPED Eric Decker/349 10.00 25.00
UAPES Emmanuel Sanders/349 8.00 20.00
UAPFG Frank Gore/50 12.00 30.00
UAPFJ Felix Jones/50 12.00 30.00
UAPGM Gerald McCoy/149 8.00 20.00
UAPGT Golden Tate/349 8.00 20.00
UAPJB Jahvid Best/100 20.00 50.00
UAPJC Jimmy Clausen/50 12.00 30.00
UAPJD Jonathan Dwyer/249 8.00 20.00
UAPJF Jacoby Ford/349 10.00 25.00
UAPJG1 Jermaine Gresham/249 8.00 20.00
(brown background)
UAPJG2 Jermaine Gresham/221 8.00 20.00
(silver background)
UAPJGR Jimmy Graham/349 25.00 50.00
UAPJM Jeremy Maclin/149 8.00 20.00
UAPJN Jordy Nelson/149 10.00 25.00
UAPJS James Starks/249 25.00 50.00
UAPJSH Jordan Shipley/349 8.00 20.00
UAPKM Knowshon Moreno/100 10.00 25.00
UAPLL LaRon Landry/149 6.00 15.00
UAPLT LaDainian Tomlinson/50 30.00 60.00
UAPMC Matt Cassel/149 12.00 30.00
UAPME Marcus Easley/349 6.00 15.00
UAPMG Mardy Gilyard/349 8.00 20.00
UAPMH Montario Hardesty/249 8.00 20.00
UAPMK Mike Kafka/349 6.00 15.00
UAPMR Matt Ryan/149 25.00 60.00
UAPMW Mike Williams/249 15.00 40.00
(silver background)
UAPNS Ndamukong Suh/100 30.00 60.00
UAPPH Percy Harvin/100 20.00 40.00
(silver background)
UAPPP Paul Posluszny/149 8.00 20.00
UAPRG Rob Gronkowski/149 30.00 80.00
UAPRM Ryan Mathews/100 30.00 80.00
UAPRMA Rey Maualuga/149 6.00 15.00
UAPSB Sam Bradford/50 75.00 150.00
UAPSJ Steven Jackson/100 12.00 30.00
UAPSR Sidney Rice/100 15.00 40.00
UAPTG Toby Gerhart/349 8.00 20.00
UAPTT Tim Tebow/30 100.00 200.00
UAPWM Willis McGahee/149 8.00 20.00

2010 Topps Unrivaled Autographed Patch Black
*VETS: .6X TO 1.5X BASIC AU/149
*VETS: .5X TO 1.2X BASIC AU/100
*VETS: .4X TO 1X BASIC AU/50
*ROOKIES: .6X TO 1.5X BASIC AU/149-349
*ROOKIES: .5X TO 1.2X BASIC AU/100
*ROOKIES: .4X TO 1X BASIC AU/30-50
AU PATCH BLACK/50 ODDS 1:157 HOB
UAPAP Adrian Peterson 60.00 120.00
UAPCMC Colt McCoy 25.00 60.00
UAPSB Sam Bradford 75.00 150.00

2010 Topps Unrivaled Greats
GREATS/499 ODDS 1:39 HOB
UGDM Dan Marino 3.00 8.00
UGED Eric Dickerson 1.25 3.00
UGES Emmitt Smith 2.50 6.00
UGET Earl Campbell 1.50 4.00
UGGS Gale Sayers 2.00 5.00
UGJE John Elway 2.50 6.00
UGJM Joe Montana 3.00 8.00
UGJN Joe Namath 2.00 5.00
UGMA Marcus Allen 1.50 4.00
UGRL Ronnie Lott 1.50 4.00
UGRS Roger Staubach 2.00 5.00
UGSY Steve Young 2.00 5.00
UGTA Troy Aikman 2.00 5.00
UGTD Tony Dorsett 1.50 4.00
UGTT Thurman Thomas 1.50 4.00

2010 Topps Unrivaled Greats Jerseys
GREATS JSY/199 ODDS 1:422 HOB
UGRDM Dan Marino 12.00 30.00
UGREC Earl Campbell 6.00 15.00
UGRED Eric Dickerson 5.00 12.00
UGRES Emmitt Smith 10.00 25.00
UGRGS Gale Sayers 8.00 20.00
UGRJE John Elway 10.00 25.00
UGRJM Joe Montana 12.00 30.00
UGRJN Joe Namath 8.00 20.00
UGRMA Marcus Allen 6.00 15.00
UGRRL Ronnie Lott 6.00 15.00
UGRRS Roger Staubach 8.00 20.00
UGRSY Steve Young 8.00 20.00
UGRTA Troy Aikman 8.00 20.00
UGRTD Tony Dorsett 6.00 15.00
UGRTT Thurman Thomas 5.00 12.00

2010 Topps Unrivaled Rookie Autographs
GROUP A ODDS 1:10,175 HOB
GROUP B ODDS 1:321 HOB
GROUP C ODDS 1:36 HOB
GROUP D ODDS 1:53 HOB
GROUP E ODDS 1:58 HOB
EXCH EXPIRATION: 10/31/2013
101 Anthony McCoy/780 3.00 8.00
102 Anthony Dixon/680 4.00 10.00
103 Ryan Mathews/125 15.00 40.00
104 Mike Kafka/480 4.00 10.00
105 Brandon Ghee/780 3.00 8.00
106 Ndamukong Suh/125 25.00 50.00
107 C.J. Spiller/125 15.00 40.00
108 Montario Hardesty/480 4.00 10.00
109 Dan Williams/780 3.00 8.00
110 Eric Decker/480 5.00 12.00
111 Brandon LaFell/680 4.00 10.00
112 Rob Gronkowski/480 15.00 40.00
113 Aaron Hernandez/480 6.00 15.00
114 Jacoby Ford/680 4.00 10.00
115 Mike Williams/480 8.00 20.00
116 Demaryius Thomas/125 6.00 15.00
117 Tony Pike/480 4.00 10.00
118 Jimmy Clausen/125 8.00 20.00
119 John Skelton/480 4.00 10.00
120 Jonathan Crompton/480 3.00 8.00
121 Andre Roberts/680 4.00 10.00
122 Bryan Bulaga/780 4.00 10.00
123 Jimmy Graham/480 15.00 30.00
124 Jahvid Best/125 8.00 20.00
125 Taylor Price/680 4.00 10.00
126 Colt McCoy/125 15.00 40.00
127 Armanti Edwards/480 4.00 10.00
128 Carlton Mitchell/780 3.00 8.00
129 Dez Bryant EXCH 30.00 60.00
130 Damian Williams/680 4.00 10.00
131 Jonathan Dwyer/480 4.00 10.00
132 Jordan Shipley/480 4.00 10.00
133 Arrelious Benn/480 4.00 10.00
134 Charles Scott/780 3.00 8.00
135 Toby Gerhart/480 4.00 10.00
136 Tim Tebow/20 125.00 200.00
137 Ben Tate/480 5.00 12.00
138 Dexter McCluster/680 4.00 10.00
139 Sean Lee/480 4.00 10.00
140 Dan LeFevour/480 4.00 10.00
141 Jerry Hughes/480 4.00 10.00
142 Gerald McCoy/125 5.00 12.00
143 Sam Bradford/125 50.00 120.00
144 Riley Cooper/480 4.00 10.00
145 James Starks/780 12.00 30.00
146 Emmanuel Sanders/680 6.00 15.00
147 Marcus Easley/680 3.00 8.00
148 Mardy Gilyard/680 4.00 10.00
149 Trent Williams/780 4.00 10.00
150 Golden Tate/480 4.00 10.00

2010 Topps Unrivaled Rookie Autographs Black
*BLACK AU: .5X TO 1.2X BASIC AU/480-780
*BLACK AU: .4X TO 1X BASIC AU/125
BLACK AU/99 ODDS 1:78 HOB
126 Colt McCoy 15.00 40.00
129 Dez Bryant EXCH 30.00 60.00
136 Tim Tebow
143 Sam Bradford 60.00 120.00

2010 Topps Unrivaled Rookie Autographs Dual
DUAL AUTO/25 ODDS 1:1040 HOB
BM1 Sam Bradford 60.00 120.00
Colt McCoy
BM2 Jahvid Best 20.00 50.00
Dexter McCluster
BW Arrelious Benn 20.00 50.00
Mike Williams
CL Jimmy Clausen
Brandon LaFell
CT Jimmy Clausen 20.00 50.00
Golden Tate
DB Dexter McCluster 25.00 60.00
C.J. Spiller
DG Jonathan Dwyer 15.00 40.00
Toby Gerhart
MB Ryan Mathews 30.00 80.00
Jahvid Best
MG Ryan Mathews 30.00 80.00
Toby Gerhart
MH Colt McCoy 25.00 60.00
Montario Hardesty
SC Sam Bradford 60.00 120.00
Jimmy Clausen
SM C.J. Spiller
Ryan Mathews
TH Ben Tate 15.00 40.00
Montario Hardesty
BBR Sam Bradford 60.00 120.00
C.J. Spiller
SMC Ndamukong Suh 25.00 60.00
Gerald McCoy

2010 Topps Unrivaled Rookies
ROOKIE/199 ODDS 1:105 HOB
URAB Arrelious Benn 2.00 5.00
URCM Colt McCoy 4.00 10.00
URCS C.J. Spiller 3.00 8.00
URDB Dez Bryant 6.00 15.00
URDT Demaryius Thomas 2.50 6.00
URDW Damian Williams 2.00 5.00
UREB Eric Berry 2.00 5.00
URGM Gerald McCoy 2.00 5.00
URGT Golden Tate 2.00 5.00
URJB Jahvid Best 3.00 8.00
URJC Jimmy Clausen 2.00 5.00
URJD Jonathan Dwyer 2.00 5.00
URJG Jermaine Gresham 2.50 6.00
URJM Joe McKnight 2.00 5.00
URJS Jordan Shipley 2.00 5.00
URMG Mardy Gilyard 2.00 5.00
URMH Montario Hardesty 2.00 5.00
URMW Mike Williams 3.00 8.00
URNS Ndamukong Suh 4.00 10.00
URRG Rob Gronkowski 5.00 12.00
URRM Rolando McClain 2.00 5.00
URSB Sam Bradford 8.00 20.00
URTT Tim Tebow 8.00 20.00
URDMC Dexter McCluster 2.00 5.00
URRMA Ryan Mathews 4.00 10.00

2010 Topps Unrivaled Rookies Jerseys
ROOKIE JSY/99 ODDS 1:507 HOB
URRAB Arrelious Benn 4.00 10.00
URRCM Colt McCoy 8.00 20.00
URRCS C.J. Spiller 6.00 15.00
URRDB Dez Bryant 12.00 30.00
URRDT Demaryius Thomas 5.00 12.00
URRDW Damian Williams 4.00 10.00
URREB Eric Berry 4.00 10.00
URRGM Gerald McCoy 4.00 10.00
URRGT Golden Tate 4.00 10.00
URRJB Jahvid Best 6.00 15.00
URRJC Jimmy Clausen 4.00 10.00
URRJD Jonathan Dwyer 4.00 10.00
URRJG Jermaine Gresham 5.00 12.00
URRJM Joe McKnight 4.00 10.00
URRJS Jordan Shipley 4.00 10.00
URRMG Mardy Gilyard 4.00 10.00
URRMH Montario Hardesty 4.00 10.00
URRMW Mike Williams 6.00 15.00
URRNS Ndamukong Suh 8.00 20.00
URRRG Rob Gronkowski 10.00 25.00
URRRM Rolando McClain 4.00 10.00
URRSB Sam Bradford 15.00 40.00
URRTT Tim Tebow 15.00 40.00
URRDMC Dexter McCluster 4.00 10.00
URRRMA Ryan Mathews 8.00 20.00

2010 Topps Unrivaled Trio
TRIO/299 ODDS 1:174 HOB
ABM Marcus Allen 2.50 6.00
Reggie Bush
Joe McKnight
DPB Eric Dickerson 2.50 6.00
Clinton Portis
Jahvid Best
DTM Tony Dorsett 3.00 8.00
LaDainian Tomlinson
Ryan Mathews
EBT John Elway 5.00 12.00
Tom Brady
Tim Tebow
HFG Paul Hornung 2.50 6.00
Matt Forte
Toby Gerhart
MMB Joe Montana 5.00 12.00
Peyton Manning
Sam Bradford
MRC Dan Marino 4.00 10.00
Tony Romo
Jimmy Clausen
SGM Gale Sayers 3.00 8.00
Frank Gore
Ryan Mathews
SPS Emmitt Smith 4.00 10.00
Adrian Peterson
C.J. Spiller
SRB Roger Staubach 4.00 10.00
Matt Ryan
Sam Bradford

2010 Topps Unrivaled Trio Jerseys
TRIO JSY STATED ODDS 1:1300 HOB
ABM Marcus Allen 6.00 15.00
Reggie Bush
Joe McKnight
DPB Eric Dickerson 5.00 12.00
Clinton Portis
Jahvid Best
DTM Tony Dorsett
LaDainian Tomlinson
Ryan Mathews
EBT John Elway 25.00 50.00
Tom Brady
Tim Tebow
HFG Paul Hornung 6.00 15.00
Matt Forte
Toby Gerhart
MMB Joe Montana 25.00 50.00
Peyton Manning
Sam Bradford
MRC Dan Marino 20.00 40.00
Tony Romo
Jimmy Clausen
SGM Gale Sayers 12.00 30.00
Frank Gore
Ryan Mathews
SPS Emmitt Smith 10.00 25.00
Adrian Peterson
C.J. Spiller
SRB Roger Staubach 20.00 40.00
Matt Ryan
Sam Bradford

2010 Topps Unrivaled Veterans
VETERANS/999 ODDS 1:21 HOB
UVAG Antonio Gates 1.25 3.00
UVAP Adrian Peterson 2.50 6.00
UVBD Brian Dawkins 1.25 3.00
UVBE Braylon Edwards 1.25 3.00
UVCP Carson Palmer 1.25 3.00
UVCP Clinton Portis 1.25 3.00
UVDH Devin Hester 1.50 4.00
UVDM DeMarcus Ware 1.25 3.00
UVED Elvis Dumervil 1.00 2.50
UVFJ Fred Jackson 1.50 4.00
UVHW Hines Ward 1.25 3.00
UVJA Jared Allen 1.50 4.00
UVLT LaDainian Tomlinson 1.50 4.00
UVMF Matt Forte 1.25 3.00
UVMR Matt Ryan 1.50 4.00
UVNA Nnamdi Asomugha 1.25 3.00
UVRM Robert Meachem 1.25 3.00
UVSH Santonio Holmes 1.25 3.00
UVSR Sidney Rice 1.25 3.00
UVTH T.J. Houshmandzadeh 1.25 3.00
UVTJ Thomas Jones 1.25 3.00
UVVJ Vincent Jackson 1.00 2.50
UVVY Vince Young 1.00 2.50
UVWW Wes Welker 1.50 4.00
UVC.J. Calvin Johnson 1.50 4.00

2010 Topps Unrivaled Veterans Jerseys
VETERANS JSY/199 ODDS 1:140 HOB
UVRAG Antonio Gates 3.00 8.00
UVRAP Adrian Peterson 6.00 15.00
UVRBD Brian Dawkins 3.00 8.00
UVRBE Braylon Edwards 3.00 8.00
UVRCP Carson Palmer 3.00 8.00
UVRCP Clinton Portis 3.00 8.00
UVRDH Devin Hester 4.00 10.00
UVRDW DeMarcus Ware 3.00 8.00
UVRED Elvis Dumervil 2.50 6.00
UVRFJ Fred Jackson 5.00 12.00
UVRHW Hines Ward 3.00 8.00
UVRJA Jared Allen 4.00 10.00
UVRLT LaDainian Tomlinson 5.00 12.00
UVRMF Matt Forte 3.00 8.00
UVRMR Matt Ryan 4.00 10.00
UVRNA Nnamdi Asomugha 3.00 8.00
UVRRM Robert Meachem 3.00 8.00
UVRSH Santonio Holmes 3.00 8.00
UVRSR Sidney Rice 3.00 8.00
UVRTJ Thomas Jones 3.00 8.00
UVRVJ Vincent Jackson 2.50 6.00
UVRVY Vince Young 2.50 6.00
UVRWW Wes Welker 4.00 10.00
UVRTJH T.J. Houshmandzadeh 3.00 8.00
UVRC.J. Calvin Johnson 4.00 10.00

2009 Topps Update
COMP.SET w/o VAR (330) 20.00 50.00
COMMON CARD (1-330) .12 .30
COMMON SP VAR (1-330) 5.00 12.00
SP VAR ODDS 1:32 HOBBY
COMMON RC (1-330) .30 .75
PRINTING PLATE ODDS 1:615 HOBBY
PLATE PRINT RUN 1 SET PER COLOR
BLACK-CYAN-MAGENTA-YELLOW ISSUED
NO PLATE PRICING DUE TO SCARCITY
UH320 Mark Schlereth .12 .30
Daniel Schlereth

2009 Topps Update Black
STATED ODDS 1:44 HOBBY
STATED PRINT RUN 58 SER.#'d SETS
UH320 Mark Schlereth 5.00 12.00
Daniel Schlereth

2009 Topps Update Gold Border
*GOLD VET: 2.5X TO 6X BASIC
*GOLD RC: 1X TO 2.5X BASIC RC
STATED ODDS 1:3 HOBBY
STATED PRINT RUN 2009 SER.#'d SETS

2009 Topps Update Platinum
STATED ODDS 1:6250 HOBBY
STATED PRINT RUN 1 SER.#'d SET
NO PRICING DUE TO SCARCITY

2001 Topps XFL Promos
Distributed to hobby dealers and at various wrestling events, these cards were produced to promote the release of the 2001 Topps XFL footbal card product.

COMPLETE SET (8) 2.00 4.00
P1 Scott Milanovich .30 .75
P2 James Bostic .20 .50
P3 Rashaan Salaam .40 1.00
P4 Jeff Brohm .30 .75
P5 Chuck Clements .20 .50
P6 Pat Barnes .30 .75
P7 Charles Puleri .20 .50
P8 John Avery .40 1.00

2001 Topps XFL

Topps issued the first set featuring players from the XFL in April 2001. This would prove to be the only year the XFL existed. The cards were released in 8-card packs. The set was broken down into: 79-player cards, 4-team vs. team (LB) cards, 16-Girls on Fire cheerleader cards and 1-checklist. Many players in the set had previous NFL cards.

COMPLETE SET (100) 12.50 25.00
1 Mike Pawlawski .50 1.25
2 Todd Doxzon .10 .30
3 James Bostic .30 .75
4 Jim Druckenmiller .20 .50
5 Mario Bailey .10 .30
6 Mike Cawley .20 .50
7 Dino Philyaw .10 .30
8 Aaron Bailey .20 .50
9 Juan Johnson .20 .50
10 Kaipo McGuire .10 .30
11 Toya Jones .10 .30
12 Todd Floyd .10 .30
13 Jamie Baisley .10 .30
14 Brian Shay .20 .50
15 Eric England .10 .30
16 Curtis Alexander .10 .30
17 Tim Lester .30 .75
18 Dialleo Burks .10 .30
19 Charles Puleri .30 .75
20 Zechariah Lord .10 .30
21 Chrys Chukwuma .10 .30
22 Rickey Brady .20 .50
23 Rashaan Salaam .60 1.50
24 Jermaine Copeland .20 .50
25 Butler By'not'e .10 .30
26 Tommy Maddox 1.25 3.00
27 Mike Furrey 1.25 3.00
28 Ed Smith .10 .30
29 Pat Barnes .40 1.00
30 James Hundon .20 .50
31 John Avery .40 1.00
32 James Willis .10 .30
33 Larry Ryans .10 .30
34 Vaughn Dunbar .10 .30
35 John Williams .10 .30
36 Casey Weldon .40 1.00
37 Roell Preston .20 .50
38 Jeff Brohm .40 1.00
39 Rashaan Shehee .20 .50
40 Kevin Swayne .20 .50
41 Ben Snell .10 .30
42 James Williams UER .10 .30
College listed as NC)
43 Corte McGuffey .20 .50
44 Charles Jordan .20 .50
45 Frank Leatherwood .10 .30
46 Dwayne Sabb .10 .30
47 Shannon Culver .10 .30
48 Brent Moss .20 .50
49 Zola Davis .10 .30
50 Ryan Clement .30 .75
51 Tyji Armstrong .10 .30
52 Paul Failla .10 .30
53 Michael Blair .20 .50
54 Corey Ivy .30 .75
55 Daryl Hobbs .20 .50
56 Paul Lacoste .10 .30
57 Damon Gourdine .10 .30
58 Wendell Davis .10 .30
59 Joe Cummings .10 .30
60 Stephen Fisher .10 .30
61 Stepfret Williams .30 .75
62 Brandon Sanders .10 .30
63 Michael Black .20 .50
64 Scott Milanovich .40 1.00
65 Brian Roche .10 .30
66 Darnell McDonald .20 .50
67 Marcus Hinton .10 .30
68 Quincy Jackson .10 .30
69 Roosevelt Potts .20 .50
70 Rod Smart .75 2.00
71 Keith Elias .10 .30
72 Latario Rachal .10 .30
73 Mike Sutton .10 .30
74 Kirby DarDar .20 .50
75 Derrick Clark .20 .50
76 Antonio Edwards .10 .30
77 Marcus Crandell .20 .50
78 Jerry Crafts .10 .30
79 Brian Roberson .20 .50
80 Las Vegas vs New York LB .10 .30
81 Orlando vs Chicago LB .10 .30
82 San Francisco vs Los Angeles LB .10 .30
83 Memphis vs Birmingham LB .10 .30
84 Kat GF .10 .30
85 Rose GF .10 .30
86 Dana GF .10 .30
87 Lisa Michelle GF .10 .30
88 Kiushin GF .10 .30
89 Youn GF .10 .30
90 Sunni GF .10 .30
91 Cicely GF .10 .30
92 Tanisha GF .10 .30
93 Krissy GF .10 .30
94 TK GF .10 .30
95 Jensi GF .10 .30
96 Jenny GF .10 .30
97 Karla GF .10 .30
98 Jenny GF .10 .30
99 Susanne GF .10 .30
100 Checklist .10 .30

2001 Topps XFL Endzone Autographs
1 Tommy Maddox 30.00 50.00
2 Tim Lester 6.00 15.00
3 Rickey Brady 6.00 15.00
4 Wally Richardson 7.50 20.00
5 Michael Black 6.00 15.00
6 Jermaine Copeland 7.50 20.00
7 LeShon Johnson 6.00 15.00
8 Chrys Chukwuma 6.00 15.00
9 Mike Archie 6.00 15.00
10 Rashaan Shehee 6.00 15.00
11 Roell Preston 6.00 15.00
12 Mike Furrey 20.00 40.00
13 Keith Elias 5.00 12.00
14 Ken Oxendine 6.00 15.00
15 Paul Failla 5.00 12.00
16 Dino Philyaw 5.00 12.00
17 Todd Doxzon 5.00 12.00
18 Chris Brantley 5.00 12.00

2001 Topps XFL Gridiron Gear
1F John Avery FB 20.00 40.00
1J John Avery JSY 10.00 25.00
2F Rashaan Salaam FB 12.50 25.00
2J Rashaan Salaam JSY 6.00 15.00
3F Jeff Brohm FB 12.50 25.00
3J Jeff Brohm JSY 6.00 15.00
4F James Bostic FB 12.50 25.00
4J James Bostic JSY 6.00 15.00
5F Pat Barnes FB 12.50 25.00
5J Pat Barnes JSY 6.00 15.00
6F Scott Milanovich FB 12.50 25.00
6J Scott Milanovich JSY 6.00 15.00
7F Charles Puleri FB 12.50 25.00
7J Charles Puleri JSY 6.00 15.00
8F Chuck Clements FB 12.50 25.00
8J Chuck Clements JSY 6.00 15.00

2001 Topps XFL Loaded Cannon
COMPLETE SET (8) 10.00 25.00
1 Tommy Maddox 3.00 8.00
2 Casey Weldon 2.50 6.00
3 Marcus Crandell 2.00 5.00
4 Jeff Brohm 2.50 6.00
5 Ryan Clement 2.00 5.00
6 Mike Pawlawski 2.00 5.00
7 Charles Puleri 2.00 5.00
8 Tim Lester 2.00 5.00

2001 Topps XFL Logo Stickers
COMPLETE SET (10) 1.50 4.00
1 Los Angeles Xtreme .20 .50
2 Birmingham Thunderbolts .20 .50
3 Memphis Maniax .20 .50
4 Orlando Rage .20 .50
5 Las Vegas Outlaws .20 .50
6 San Francisco Demons .20 .50
7 New York Hitmen .20 .50
8 Chicago Enforcers .20 .50
9 XFL Logo .20 .50
10 XFL Football .20 .50

2004 Toronto Sun Superstar Quarterbacks Stickers

This set of stickers was sponsored by the Toronto Sun and Mac's Stores and released in Canada. The stickers were issued on numbered blankbacked sheets of seven or eight stickers per sheet. When seperated, each sticker measures roughly 1 1/2" by 2 /18" and each includes its own sticker number on the front. An album was issued to house the set with one page devoted to each of the 12-quarterbacks in the set. Each player has six-different stickers featuring different photos. We've cataloged them below as full sheets instead of cut out stickers.

COMPLETE SET (10) 10.00 20.00
1 Sheet 1 1.25 3.00
2 Sheet 2 .75 2.00
3 Sheet 3 1.00 2.50
4 Sheet 4 .75 2.00
5 Sheet 5 1.25 3.00
6 Sheet 6 1.00 2.50
7 Sheet 7 1.25 3.00
8 Sheet 8 .75 2.00
9 Sheet 9 1.25 3.00
10 Sheet 10 1.25 3.00
NNO Album 2.00 5.00

2011 Totally Certified
COMP.SET w/o RC's (100) 10.00 25.00
151-200 ROOKIE AU PRINT RUN 299
201-236 ROOKIE JSY AU PRINT RUN 99-499
EXCH EXPIRATION: 9/14/2013
1 Fred Jackson .50 1.25
2 Ryan Fitzpatrick .40 1.00
3 Steve Johnson .40 1.00
4 BenJarvus Green-Ellis .40 1.00
5 Tom Brady .75 2.00
6 Wes Welker .50 1.25
7 Mark Sanchez .50 1.25
8 Santonio Holmes .40 1.00
9 Shonn Greene .40 1.00
10 Brandon Marshall .40 1.00
11 Brian Hartline .30 .75
12 Reggie Bush .40 1.00
13 Ben Roethlisberger .50 1.25
14 Mike Wallace .50 1.25
15 Rashard Mendenhall .40 1.00
16 Troy Polamalu .50 1.25
17 Cedric Benson .40 1.00
18 Jermaine Gresham .40 1.00
19 Jerome Simpson .30 .75
20 Anquan Boldin .40 1.00
21 Joe Flacco .50 1.25
22 Ray Lewis .50 1.25
23 Ray Rice .40 1.00
24 Colt McCoy .40 1.00
25 Josh Cribbs .40 1.00
26 Peyton Hillis .40 1.00
27 Andre Johnson .40 1.00
28 Arian Foster .40 1.00
29 Matt Schaub .40 1.00
30 Chris Johnson .40 1.00
31 Kenny Britt .40 1.00
32 Matt Hasselbeck .40 1.00
33 Maurice Jones-Drew .40 1.00
34 Mike Thomas .40 1.00
35 Paul Posluszny .30 .75
36 Dallas Clark .40 1.00
37 Joseph Addai .40 1.00
38 Peyton Manning .75 2.00
39 Reggie Wayne .40 1.00
40 Dwayne Bowe .40 1.00
41 Jamaal Charles .40 1.00
42 Matt Cassel .40 1.00
43 Philip Rivers .50 1.25
44 Ryan Mathews .40 1.00
45 Vincent Jackson .40 1.00
46 Carson Palmer .40 1.00
47 Darren McFadden .40 1.00
48 Darrius Heyward-Bey .30 .75
49 Eric Decker .40 1.00
50 Tim Tebow 1.00 2.50
51 Willis McGahee .30 .75
52 Ahmad Bradshaw .40 1.00
53 Eli Manning .50 1.25
54 Hakeem Nicks .40 1.00
55 DeSean Jackson .40 1.00
56 LeSean McCoy .40 1.00
57 Michael Vick .50 1.25
58 DeMarcus Ware .40 1.00
59 Dez Bryant .50 1.25
60 Tony Romo .50 1.25
61 Fred Davis .40 1.00
62 London Fletcher .30 .75
63 Ryan Torain .30 .75
64 Aaron Rodgers .75 2.00
65 Greg Jennings .40 1.00
66 James Starks .40 1.00
67 Calvin Johnson .50 1.25
68 Jahvid Best .40 1.00
69 Matthew Stafford .50 1.25
70 Brian Urlacher .50 1.25
71 Jay Cutler .40 1.00
72 Matt Forte .40 1.00
73 Adrian Peterson .60 1.50
74 Jared Allen .40 1.00
75 Percy Harvin .40 1.00
76 Drew Brees .50 1.25
77 Jimmy Graham .50 1.25
78 Marques Colston .40 1.00
79 Josh Freeman .50 1.25
80 LeGarrette Blount .40 1.00
81 Mike Williams .40 1.00
82 Matt Ryan .50 1.25
83 Michael Turner .40 1.00
84 Roddy White .40 1.00
85 DeAngelo Williams .40 1.00
86 Greg Olsen .30 .75
87 Jonathan Stewart .40 1.00
88 Steve Smith WR .40 1.00
89 Alex Smith QB .40 1.00
90 Frank Gore .40 1.00
91 Vernon Davis .40 1.00
92 Leon Washington .30 .75
93 Marshawn Lynch .40 1.00
94 Sidney Rice .40 1.00
95 Brandon Lloyd .40 1.00
96 Sam Bradford .50 1.25
97 Steven Jackson .40 1.00
98 Beanie Wells .40 1.00
99 Kevin Kolb .40 1.00
100 Larry Fitzgerald .40 1.00
151 Aaron Williams AU/299 RC EXCH 4.00 10.00
152 Adrian Clayborn AU/299 RC EXCH 5.00 12.00
153 Akeem Ayers AU/299 RC EXCH 4.00 10.00
154 Aldon Smith AU/299 RC EXCH 12.00 30.00
155 Allen Bradford AU/299 RC 4.00 10.00
156 Brandon Harris AU/299 RC 3.00 8.00
157 Cameron Heyward AU/299 RC 5.00 12.00
158 Cameron Jordan AU/299 RC 4.00 10.00
159 Cecil Shorts AU/299 RC 4.00 10.00
160 Corey Liuget AU/299 RC 3.00 8.00
161 D.J. Williams AU/299 RC EXCH 5.00 12.00
162 Da'Quan Bowers AU/299 RC EXCH 5.00 12.00
163 Da'Rel Scott AU/299 RC 4.00 10.00
164 Denarius Moore AU/299 RC EXCH 8.00 20.00
165 Dion Lewis AU/299 RC 5.00 12.00
166 Greg Jones AU/299 RC 4.00 10.00
167 Greg Salas AU/299 RC 5.00 12.00
168 J.J. Watt AU/299 RC 6.00 15.00
169 Jacquizz Rodgers AU/299 RC 5.00 12.00
170 Jeremy Kerley AU/299 RC 5.00 12.00
171 Jimmy Smith AU/299 RC EXCH 5.00 12.00
172 Johnny White AU/299 RC 4.00 10.00
173 Julius Thomas AU/299 RC 4.00 10.00
174 Justin Houston AU/299 RC 5.00 12.00
175 Kris Durham AU/299 RC 4.00 10.00
176 Lance Kendricks AU/299 RC 4.00 10.00
177 Luke Stocker AU/299 RC 4.00 10.00
178 Nathan Enderle AU/299 RC EXCH 5.00 12.00
179 Niles Paul AU/299 RC 5.00 12.00
180 Phil Taylor AU/299 RC 4.00 10.00
181 Prince Amukamara AU/299 RC 5.00 12.00
182 Rahim Moore AU/299 RC 4.00 10.00
183 Ricky Stanzi AU/299 RC 6.00 15.00
184 Roy Helu AU/299 RC EXCH 10.00 25.00
185 Ryan Kerrigan AU/299 RC 5.00 12.00
186 T.J. Yates AU/299 RC 6.00 15.00
187 Tandon Doss AU/299 RC 4.00 10.00
188 Terrelle Pryor AU/299 RC 10.00 25.00
189 Tyrod Taylor AU/299 RC 5.00 12.00
190 Joe Lefeged AU/299 RC 4.00 10.00
191 Jacquian Williams AU/299 RC EXCH 5.00 12.00
192 K.J. Wright AU/299 RC 5.00 12.00
193 Mason Foster AU/299 RC 5.00 12.00
194 Casey Matthews AU/299 RC 5.00 12.00
195 Anthony Allen AU/299 RC 3.00 8.00
196 Armond Smith AU/299 RC 4.00 10.00
197 Dane Sanzenbacher AU/299 RC 5.00 12.00
198 Doug Baldwin AU/299 RC 8.00 20.00
199 LaQuan Williams AU/299 RC 4.00 10.00
200 Mark Herzlich AU/299 RC 4.00 10.00
201 A.J. Green JSY AU/299 RC 20.00 40.00
202 Alex Green JSY AU/499 RC 6.00 15.00
203 Andy Dalton JSY AU/399 RC 30.00 60.00
204 Austin Pettis JSY AU/499 RC EXCH 5.00 12.00
205 Bilal Powell JSY AU/99 RC EXCH 8.00 20.00
206 Blaine Gabbert JSY AU/299 RC 12.00 30.00
207 Cam Newton JSY AU/299 RC 100.00 200.00
208 Christian Ponder JSY AU/299 RC 25.00 50.00
209 Clyde Gates JSY AU/499 RC 5.00 12.00
210 Colin Kaepernick JSY AU/399 RC 8.00 20.00
211 Daniel Thomas JSY AU/499 RC EXCH 6.00 15.00
212 Delone Carter JSY AU/499 RC 5.00 12.00
213 DeMarco Murray JSY AU/99 RC 40.00 80.00
214 Greg Little JSY AU/499 RC EXCH 6.00 15.00
215 Jake Locker JSY AU/299 RC 30.00 60.00
216 Jamie Harper JSY AU/499 RC EXCH 6.00 15.00
217 Jerrel Jernigan JSY AU/499 RC EXCH 5.00 12.00
218 Jonathan Baldwin JSY AU/499 RC 6.00 15.00
219 Jordan Todman JSY AU/499 RC 4.00 10.00
220 Julio Jones JSY AU/399 RC EXCH 15.00 40.00
221 Kendall Hunter JSY AU/499 RC 8.00 20.00
222 Kyle Rudolph JSY AU/499 RC 6.00 15.00
223 Leonard Hankerson JSY AU/499 RC 6.00 15.00
224 Marcell Dareus JSY AU/499 RC EXCH 6.00 15.00
225 Mark Ingram JSY AU/299 RC 20.00 50.00
226 Mikel Leshoure JSY AU/399 RC EXCH 6.00 15.00
227 Randall Cobb JSY AU/99 RC 12.00 30.00
228 Ryan Mallett JSY AU/299 RC 15.00 40.00
229 Ryan Williams JSY AU/399 RC EXCH 8.00 20.00
230 Shane Vereen JSY AU/499 RC EXCH 6.00 15.00
231 Stevan Ridley JSY AU/499 RC 8.00 20.00
232 Taiwan Jones JSY AU/499 RC 6.00 15.00
233 Titus Young JSY AU/499 RC 8.00 20.00
234 Torrey Smith JSY AU/499 RC 10.00 25.00
235 Vincent Brown JSY AU/499 RC 6.00 15.00
236 Von Miller JSY AU/499 RC 10.00 25.00

2011 Totally Certified Blue
*1-100 VETS/50: 3X TO 8X BASIC CARDS
STATED PRINT RUN 50 SER.#'d SETS

2011 Totally Certified Blue Materials
STATED PRINT RUN 12-249
1 Fred Jackson/25 6.00 15.00
2 Ryan Fitzpatrick/249 3.00 8.00
3 Steve Johnson/199 3.00 8.00
4 BenJarvus Green-Ellis/99 5.00 12.00
5 Tom Brady/249 6.00 15.00
6 Wes Welker/99 5.00 12.00
7 Mark Sanchez/249 4.00 10.00
9 Shonn Greene/249 3.00 8.00
10 Brandon Marshall/249 3.00 8.00
11 Brian Hartline/249 2.50 6.00
14 Mike Wallace/249 4.00 10.00
17 Cedric Benson/249 3.00 8.00
18 Jermaine Gresham/249 3.00 8.00
20 Anquan Boldin/249 3.00 8.00
21 Joe Flacco/249 4.00 10.00
22 Ray Lewis/249 4.00 10.00
23 Ray Rice/249 3.00 8.00
24 Colt McCoy/249 3.00 8.00
25 Josh Cribbs/249 3.00 8.00
26 Peyton Hillis/99 4.00 10.00
27 Andre Johnson/99 4.00 10.00
28 Arian Foster/49 5.00 12.00
29 Matt Schaub/249 3.00 8.00
30 Chris Johnson/199 3.00 8.00
31 Kenny Britt/249 3.00 8.00
32 Matt Hasselbeck/249 3.00 8.00
33 Maurice Jones-Drew/249 3.00 8.00
34 Mike Thomas/249 3.00 8.00
36 Dallas Clark/249 3.00 8.00
37 Joseph Addai/249 3.00 8.00
38 Peyton Manning/49 8.00 20.00
39 Reggie Wayne/99 4.00 10.00
40 Dwayne Bowe/249 3.00 8.00
41 Jamaal Charles/249 3.00 8.00
42 Matt Cassel/249 3.00 8.00
43 Philip Rivers/249 4.00 10.00
44 Ryan Mathews/199 3.00 8.00
45 Vincent Jackson/249 3.00 8.00
47 Darren McFadden/249 3.00 8.00
50 Tim Tebow/249 8.00 20.00
52 Ahmad Bradshaw/249 3.00 8.00
53 Eli Manning/249 4.00 10.00
54 Hakeem Nicks/249 3.00 8.00
55 DeSean Jackson/12 6.00 15.00
56 LeSean McCoy/80 4.00 10.00
57 Michael Vick/99 5.00 12.00
58 DeMarcus Ware/249 4.00 10.00
59 Dez Bryant/99 5.00 12.00
60 Tony Romo/249 4.00 10.00
62 London Fletcher/249 2.50 6.00
63 Ryan Torain/249 2.50 6.00
64 Aaron Rodgers/99 10.00 25.00
67 Calvin Johnson/99 5.00 12.00
68 Jahvid Best/199 3.00 8.00
69 Matthew Stafford/99 5.00 12.00
70 Brian Urlacher/249 4.00 10.00
71 Jay Cutler/249 3.00 8.00
72 Matt Forte/249 3.00 8.00
73 Adrian Peterson/49 6.00 15.00
74 Jared Allen/249 4.00 10.00
75 Percy Harvin/199 3.00 8.00
76 Drew Brees/249 4.00 10.00
78 Marques Colston/249 3.00 8.00
82 Matt Ryan/249 4.00 10.00
83 Michael Turner/249 3.00 8.00
84 Roddy White/99 4.00 10.00
85 DeAngelo Williams/199 3.00 8.00
90 Frank Gore/249 3.00 8.00
91 Vernon Davis/199 3.00 8.00
96 Sam Bradford/249 4.00 10.00
97 Steven Jackson/249 3.00 8.00
98 Beanie Wells/99 4.00 10.00
100 Larry Fitzgerald/249 3.00 8.00

2011 Totally Certified Gold
*1-100 VETS/25: 5X TO 12X BASIC CARDS
*151-200 ROOK.AU25: .8X TO 2X AU RC/299
*RK.JSY AU/20-25: 1.2X TO 3X JSY AU/399-499
*ROOK.JSY AU/20-25: 1X TO 2.5X JSY AU/299
*ROOK.JSY AU/20-25: .8X TO 2X JSY AU/99
GOLD STATED PRINT RUN 12-25
201 A.J. Green JSY AU/25 60.00 120.00
203 Andy Dalton JSY AU/25 100.00 200.00
207 Cam Newton JSY AU/25 250.00 450.00
208 Christian Ponder JSY AU/25 90.00 150.00
215 Jake Locker JSY AU/25 100.00 175.00
220 Julio Jones JSY AU/12 EXCH
225 Mark Ingram JSY AU/25 75.00 135.00

2011 Totally Certified Gold Materials Prime
GOLD STATED PRINT RUN 1-49
2 Ryan Fitzpatrick/49 6.00 15.00
4 BenJarvus Green-Ellis/49 8.00 20.00
6 Wes Welker/49 8.00 20.00
7 Mark Sanchez/49 8.00 20.00
8 Santonio Holmes/49 6.00 15.00
9 Shonn Greene/49 6.00 15.00
10 Brandon Marshall/49 6.00 15.00
11 Brian Hartline/49 5.00 12.00
17 Cedric Benson/49 6.00 15.00
20 Anquan Boldin/49 6.00 15.00
21 Joe Flacco/49 8.00 20.00
22 Ray Lewis/49 8.00 20.00
23 Ray Rice/49 6.00 15.00
25 Josh Cribbs/49 6.00 15.00
30 Chris Johnson/49 6.00 15.00
32 Matt Hasselbeck/49 6.00 15.00
33 Maurice Jones-Drew/49 6.00 15.00
34 Mike Thomas/49 6.00 15.00
37 Joseph Addai/25 8.00 20.00
40 Dwayne Bowe/49 6.00 15.00
41 Jamaal Charles/49 6.00 15.00
42 Matt Cassel/49 6.00 15.00
43 Philip Rivers/49 8.00 20.00
44 Ryan Mathews/49 6.00 15.00
45 Vincent Jackson/49 6.00 15.00
47 Darren McFadden/49 6.00 15.00
50 Tim Tebow/49 15.00 40.00
52 Ahmad Bradshaw/49 6.00 15.00
53 Eli Manning/49 8.00 20.00
54 Hakeem Nicks/49 6.00 15.00
55 DeSean Jackson/49 6.00 15.00
58 DeMarcus Ware/49 8.00 20.00
59 Dez Bryant/49 8.00 20.00
60 Tony Romo/49 8.00 20.00
62 London Fletcher/49 5.00 12.00
63 Ryan Torain/25 6.00 15.00
67 Calvin Johnson/49 8.00 20.00
70 Brian Urlacher/49 8.00 20.00
71 Jay Cutler/25 8.00 20.00
72 Matt Forte/49 6.00 15.00
76 Drew Brees/49 8.00 20.00
78 Marques Colston/49 6.00 15.00
83 Michael Turner/49 6.00 15.00
84 Roddy White/49 6.00 15.00
90 Frank Gore/49 6.00 15.00
97 Steven Jackson/49 6.00 15.00
100 Larry Fitzgerald/49 6.00 15.00

2011 Totally Certified Gold Signatures
STATED PRINT RUN 8-15
1 Aaron Rodgers/15 150.00 250.00
4 Charles Woodson/15 150.00 250.00
5 Drew Brees/15 50.00 100.00
6 Larry Fitzgerald/15 30.00 60.00
7 Mark Sanchez/15 25.00 50.00
8 Matthew Stafford/15 30.00 60.00
10 Peyton Manning/15 75.00 150.00
11 Ray Rice/15 EXCH 30.00 60.00
12 Tim Tebow/15 60.00 120.00
14 Troy Polamalu/15 60.00 120.00
15 Antonio Gates/15 10.00 25.00
16 Matt Forte/15 10.00 25.00
17 Ben Roethlisberger/15
18 Brandon Lloyd/15 10.00 25.00
19 Clay Matthews/15 30.00 60.00
20 Roddy White/15 10.00 25.00
21 Dwayne Bowe/15 EXCH 8.00 20.00
22 Greg Jennings/15 20.00 40.00
23 Hakeem Nicks/15 10.00 25.00
24 LeSean McCoy/15 12.00 30.00
25 Jahvid Best/15 10.00 25.00
26 Jerod Mayo/15 8.00 20.00
27 Marques Colston/15 10.00 25.00
28 Matt Schaub/15 10.00 25.00
29 Mike Tolbert/15 10.00 25.00
30 Mike Wallace/15 12.00 30.00
31 Nnamdi Asomugha/15 12.00 30.00
32 Peyton Hillis/15 10.00 25.00
33 Pierre Thomas/15 12.00 30.00
34 Ryan Mathews/15 EXCH 10.00 25.00
35 Shonn Greene/15 10.00 25.00
36 Vernon Davis/15 12.00 30.00
37 Tony Romo/15 40.00 80.00
38 Brian Hartline/15 8.00 20.00
39 C.J. Spiller/15 10.00 25.00
40 Chad Greenway/15 12.00 30.00
41 Chris Cooley/15 10.00 25.00
43 DeAngelo Williams/15 10.00 25.00
44 DeSean Jackson/15 10.00 25.00
45 Donald Driver/15 20.00 40.00
46 Eli Manning/15 60.00 120.00
47 Fred Davis/15 8.00 20.00
48 Greg Olsen/15 8.00 20.00
49 Jared Allen/15 20.00 40.00
50 Joe Flacco/15
101 Archie Manning AU/15 20.00 50.00
102 Ace Parker AU/15 15.00 40.00
103 Doug Williams AU/15 15.00 40.00
104 Floyd Little AU/15 12.00 30.00
105 Frank Gifford AU/15 15.00 40.00
106 Fred Williamson AU/15 12.00 30.00
107 Gary Collins AU/15 12.00 30.00
108 Henry Ellard AU/15 12.00 30.00
109 Jim Taylor AU/15 15.00 40.00
110 John Taylor AU/15 15.00 40.00
111 Lydell Mitchell AU/15 12.00 30.00
112 Mel Renfro AU/15 12.00 30.00
113 Ottis Anderson AU/15 12.00 30.00
114 Rosey Grier AU/15 15.00 40.00
115 Russ Grimm AU/15 12.00 30.00
116 Willie Davis AU/15 12.00 30.00
117 Alan Page AU/15 15.00 40.00
119 Bart Starr AU/15 90.00 150.00
120 Bob Lilly AU/15 15.00 40.00
121 Bobby Bell AU/15 12.00 30.00
122 Charley Taylor AU/15 12.00 30.00
123 Charlie Joiner AU/15 15.00 40.00
124 Chuck Bednarik AU/15 12.00 30.00
125 Dave Casper AU/15 12.00 30.00
126 Deion Sanders AU/15 40.00 80.00
127 Earl Campbell AU/15 20.00 50.00
128 Forrest Gregg AU/15 12.00 30.00
130 Hugh McElhenny AU/15 15.00 40.00
131 Jack Lambert AU/15 40.00 80.00
132 Jack Youngblood AU/15 12.00 30.00
133 James Lofton AU/15 12.00 30.00
134 Jan Stenerud AU/15 15.00 40.00
135 Jim Otto AU/15 12.00 30.00
136 Joe Greene AU/15 40.00 80.00
138 Barry Sanders AU/15 60.00 120.00
140 Cris Carter AU/15 20.00 50.00
141 Dan Marino AU/15 125.00 200.00
145 Jim Kelly AU/15 20.00 50.00
146 Joe Montana AU/15 90.00 150.00
147 Joe Namath AU/15 60.00 120.00
148 John Elway AU/15 60.00 120.00

2011 Totally Certified Freshman Fabric Signatures Red
*RED/200-300: .5X TO 1.2X JSY AU/399-499
*RED/175-300: .4X TO 1X JSY AU/299
RED STATED PRINT RUN 175-300
207 Cam Newton JSY AU/175 100.00 200.00

2011 Totally Certified Future Materials
STATED PRINT RUN 499 SER.#'d SETS
*PRIME/17-49: .8X TO 2X BASIC JSY/499
1 Randall Cobb 3.00 8.00
2 Blaine Gabbert 4.00 10.00
3 Ryan Mallett 5.00 12.00
4 Julio Jones 5.00 12.00
5 A.J. Green 5.00 12.00
6 Colin Kaepernick 3.00 8.00
7 Austin Pettis 2.00 5.00
8 Marcell Dareus 2.50 6.00
9 Titus Young 3.00 8.00
10 Von Miller 3.00 8.00
11 Mark Ingram 5.00 12.00
12 Christian Ponder 5.00 12.00
13 DeMarco Murray 5.00 12.00
14 Jake Locker 5.00 12.00
15 Mikel Leshoure 2.50 6.00
16 Jonathan Baldwin 2.50 6.00
17 Ryan Williams 3.00 8.00
18 Delone Carter 2.00 5.00
19 Alex Green 3.00 8.00
20 Kyle Rudolph 2.50 6.00
21 Stevan Ridley 2.50 6.00
22 Vincent Brown 2.50 6.00
23 Clyde Gates 2.00 5.00
24 Daniel Thomas 2.50 6.00
25 Andy Dalton 6.00 15.00
26 Kendall Hunter 2.50 6.00
27 Jamie Harper 2.50 6.00
28 Greg Little 2.50 6.00
29 Leonard Hankerson 2.50 6.00
30 Shane Vereen 2.50 6.00
31 Jerrel Jernigan 2.00 5.00
32 Bilal Powell 1.50 4.00
33 Cam Newton 12.00 30.00
34 Jordan Todman 1.50 4.00
35 Torrey Smith 3.00 8.00
36 Taiwan Jones 2.50 6.00

2011 Totally Certified Heritage Collection Jerseys
STATED PRINT RUN 50-249
*PRIME/30-49: .6X TO 1.5X BASIC JSY/199-249
*PRIME/15-25: .8X TO 2X BASIC JSY/199-249
*PRIME/49: .6X TO 1.5X BASIC JSY/100
*PRIME/45: .5X TO 1.2X BASIC JSY/50
1 Alan Page/249 4.00 10.00
2 Y.A. Tittle/249 5.00 12.00
3 Bo Jackson/249 8.00 20.00
4 Bob Hayes/199 5.00 12.00
5 Boomer Esiason/249 4.00 10.00
6 Buck Buchanan/249 3.00 8.00
7 Chuck Howley/249 5.00 12.00
8 Cris Carter/249 5.00 12.00
9 Curtis Martin/249 5.00 12.00
10 Dan Marino/249 10.00 25.00
11 Deion Sanders/249 6.00 15.00
12 Doak Walker/249 6.00 15.00
13 Don Maynard/249 4.00 10.00
14 Don Meredith/249 8.00 20.00
15 Doug Flutie/249 4.00 10.00
16 Ed Too Tall Jones/249 3.00 8.00
17 Eddie George/249 4.00 10.00
18 Eric Dickerson/249 4.00 10.00
19 Ernie Davis/50 15.00 40.00
20 Fran Tarkenton/249 5.00 12.00
21 Franco Harris/249 5.00 12.00
22 Gale Sayers/249 5.00 12.00
23 George Blanda/249 4.00 10.00
24 Irving Fryar/249 3.00 8.00
25 Jay Novacek/249 4.00 10.00
26 Jerome Bettis/249 8.00 20.00
27 Jerry Rice/249 8.00 20.00
28 Jerry Rice/249 8.00 20.00
29 Jim Brown/249 6.00 15.00
30 Jim McMahon/249 4.00 10.00
31 Jim Otto/249 4.00 10.00
32 Jim Parker/249 3.00 8.00
33 Jim Plunkett/249 4.00 10.00
34 Jim Thorpe/100 50.00 100.00
35 Joe Greene/249 5.00 12.00
36 Joe Montana/200 10.00 25.00
37 Joe Montana/249 10.00 25.00
38 Joe Namath/240 6.00 15.00
39 Joe Perry/100 5.00 12.00
40 John Fuqua/249 6.00 15.00
41 John Hadl/249 3.00 8.00
42 Keith Jackson/249 3.00 8.00
43 Ken Stabler/249 5.00 12.00
44 Keyshawn Johnson/249 4.00 10.00
45 Larry Csonka/249 4.00 10.00
46 Len Dawson/249 5.00 12.00
47 Marshall Faulk/249 4.00 10.00
48 Mike Ditka/249 6.00 15.00
49 Mike Singletary/249 5.00 12.00
50 Warren Sapp/215 4.00 10.00
51 Paul Warfield/249 4.00 10.00
52 Phil Simms/249 4.00 10.00
53 Randall Cunningham/249 5.00 12.00
54 Richard Dent/249 3.00 8.00
55 Rickey Jackson/199 3.00 8.00
56 Rod Woodson/249 4.00 10.00
57 Roger Staubach/249 6.00 15.00
58 Ronnie Lott/249 4.00 10.00
59 Shannon Sharpe/249 5.00 12.00
60 Steve Young/249 6.00 15.00
61 Tony Dorsett/249 5.00 12.00
62 Troy Aikman/249 6.00 15.00
63 Walter Payton/249 15.00 30.00
64 Warren Moon/249 4.00 10.00

2011 Totally Certified HRX Video Cards
STATED PRINT RUN 40 SER.#'d SETS
UNPRICED AUTO PRINT RUN 10
EXCH EXPIRATION: 9/14/2013
1 Andy Dalton 100.00 175.00
2 Cam Newton 125.00 250.00
3 Mark Ingram 75.00 150.00
4 Tim Tebow 150.00 300.00

2011 Totally Certified Pepsi Elite Rookie of the Week
1 Randall Cobb 1.00 2.50
2 Denarius Moore 1.00 2.50
3 Stefen Wisniewski .75 2.00
4 Cam Newton 4.00 10.00
5 Aldon Smith 1.25 3.00
6 Aldon Smith 1.25 3.00
7 DeMarco Murray 1.50 4.00
8 Marcell Dareus .75 2.00
9 Andy Dalton 2.00 5.00
10 Denarius Moore 1.00 2.50
11 Torrey Smith 1.00 2.50
12 Andy Dalton 2.00 5.00
13 Colin McCarthy .60 1.50
14 T.J. Yates 1.00 2.50
15 Cam Newton 4.00 10.00
16 Cam Newton 4.00 10.00
17 Sterling Moore 1.50 4.00
18 Cam Newton 4.00 10.00

2011 Totally Certified Piece of the Game
STATED PRINT RUN 7-199
*PRIME/38-49: .8X TO 2X BASIC JSY/125-199
*PRIME/15-25: 1X TO 2.5X BASIC JSY/125-199
1 Matt Ryan/199 4.00 10.00
2 Roddy White/7
3 Anquan Boldin/199 3.00 8.00
4 Joe Flacco/199 4.00 10.00
5 Ray Lewis/199 4.00 10.00
6 Ray Rice/199 3.00 8.00
7 C.J. Spiller/199 3.00 8.00
8 Ryan Fitzpatrick/199 3.00 8.00
9 Brian Urlacher/199 4.00 10.00
10 Devin Hester/199 4.00 10.00
11 Johnny Knox/199 3.00 8.00
12 Felix Jones/199 3.00 8.00
13 Eddie Royal/199 2.50 6.00
14 Knowshon Moreno/199 3.00 8.00
15 Tim Tebow/199 8.00 20.00
16 Matthew Stafford/148 4.00 10.00
17 Clay Matthews/199 5.00 12.00
18 Matt Schaub/199 3.00 8.00
19 Dwight Freeney/125 3.00 8.00
20 Pierre Garcon/145 3.00 8.00
21 Reggie Wayne/177 3.00 8.00
22 Maurice Jones-Drew/172 3.00 8.00
23 Dexter McCluster/190 2.50 6.00
24 Matt Cassel/149 3.00 8.00
25 Tamba Hali/149 2.50 6.00
26 Anthony Fasano/149 2.50 6.00
27 Brian Hartline/149 2.50 6.00
28 Chad Greenway/149 3.00 8.00
29 Devery Henderson/149 2.50 6.00
30 Marques Colston/149 3.00 8.00
31 Pierre Thomas/149 3.00 8.00
32 Ahmad Bradshaw/149 3.00 8.00
33 Brandon Jacobs/149 3.00 8.00
34 Eli Manning/149 4.00 10.00
35 Hakeem Nicks/149 3.00 8.00
36 Darrelle Revis/149 3.00 8.00
37 LaDainian Tomlinson/149 4.00 10.00
38 Mark Sanchez/149 4.00 10.00
39 Darren McFadden/149 3.00 8.00
40 Jacoby Ford/149 3.00 8.00
41 Antonio Gates/149 3.00 8.00
42 Malcom Floyd/149 3.00 8.00
43 Vincent Jackson/149 3.00 8.00
44 Frank Gore/149 3.00 8.00
45 Patrick Willis/149 3.00 8.00
46 Steven Jackson/149 3.00 8.00
47 Earnest Graham/149 2.50 6.00
48 Kellen Winslow Jr./195 3.00 8.00
49 Chris Johnson/149 3.00 8.00
50 Cortland Finnegan/149 2.50 6.00
51 Marc Mariani/149 3.00 8.00
52 Brian Orakpo/149 4.00 10.00
53 Chris Cooley/149 3.00 8.00
54 Santana Moss/149 3.00 8.00

55 Beanie Wells/149 3.00 8.00
56 Larry Fitzgerald/149 3.00 8.00
57 Tony Gonzalez/149 3.00 8.00
58 Jay Cutler/149 3.00 8.00
59 Julius Peppers/149 3.00 8.00
60 Cedric Benson/149 3.00 8.00
61 Jordan Shipley/149 3.00 8.00
62 Josh Cribbs/149 3.00 8.00
63 Miles Austin/149 3.00 8.00
64 Owen Daniels/149 2.50 6.00
65 Dallas Clark/149 3.00 8.00
66 Joseph Addai/149 3.00 8.00
67 Mike Thomas/149 3.00 8.00
68 Tom Brady/149 6.00 15.00
69 Sebastian Janikowski/149 6.00 15.00
70 Brent Celek/149 3.00 8.00
71 Sam Bradford/149 4.00 10.00
72 Kenny Britt/149 3.00 8.00
73 Michael Turner/149 3.00 8.00
74 Ed Reed/149 3.00 8.00
75 Haloti Ngata/149 2.50 6.00

2011 Totally Certified Stitches In Time

STATED PRINT RUN 35-200
*PRIME/25: .6X TO 1.5X QUAD/115-200
*PRIME/25: .5X TO 1.2X QUAD/35
1 Emmitt Smith/35 30.00 60.00
Walter Payton
Barry Sanders
Curtis Martin
2 Jerome Bettis/200 10.00 25.00
LaDainian Tomlinson
Eric Dickerson
Tony Dorsett
3 Brett Favre/100 40.00 80.00
Dan Marino
Peyton Manning
John Elway
4 Jerry Rice/199 12.00 30.00
Terrell Owens
Randy Moss
Cris Carter
5 Clyde Bulldog Turner/70 20.00 40.00
Dick Butkus
Mike Singletary
Brian Urlacher
6 Roger Craig/125 8.00 20.00
Frank Gore
Brent Jones
Vernon Davis
7 Don Meredith/150 30.00 60.00
Roger Staubach
Troy Aikman
Tony Romo
8 Jim Kelly/75 15.00 40.00
Thurman Thomas
Andre Reed
Bruce Smith
9 John Elway/150 15.00 40.00
Terrell Davis
Ed McCaffrey
Shannon Sharpe
10 Bart Starr/150 15.00 40.00
Forrest Gregg
Henry Jordan
Paul Hornung
11 Jim Plunkett/150 12.00 30.00
Ken Stabler
Willie Brown
Ted Hendricks
12 Reggie White/115 10.00 25.00
Bruce Smith
Michael Strahan
DeMarcus Ware
13 Rod Woodson/150 12.00 30.00
Deion Sanders
Ed Reed
Nnamdi Asomugha
14 Eli Manning/85 20.00 40.00
Ben Roethlisberger
Drew Brees
Aaron Rodgers
15 Terry Bradshaw/145 20.00 40.00
John Stallworth
Joe Greene
Franco Harris
16 Adrian Peterson/150 12.00 30.00
Chuck Foreman
Cris Carter
Percy Harvin
17 Maurice Jones-Drew/150 10.00 25.00
Ray Rice
Michael Turner
Frank Gore
18 Calvin Johnson/150 10.00 25.00
Wes Welker
Andre Johnson
Larry Fitzgerald
19 Tony Gonzalez/150 6.00 15.00
Jason Witten
Antonio Gates
Vernon Davis
20 Hines Ward/150 8.00 20.00
Matthew Stafford
Knowshon Moreno
A.J. Green
21 Ray Lewis/150 10.00 25.00
Ed Reed
Frank Gore
Devin Hester
22 Tom Brady/150 8.00 20.00
Chad Henne
David Harris
Mario Manningham
23 Eli Manning/35 12.00 30.00
Dexter McCluster
Patrick Willis
BenJarvus Green-Ellis
24 Colt McCoy/150 6.00 15.00
Jordan Shipley
Cedric Benson
Jamaal Charles
25 Matt Cassel/150 8.00 20.00
Ronnie Lott
Clay Matthews
Mark Sanchez

2011 Totally Certified Team Panini Material Autographs

STATED PRINT RUN 25-30
1 Anquan Boldin/30 10.00 25.00
2 Arian Foster/25 25.00 50.00
3 BenJarvus Green-Ellis/30 25.00 50.00
4 Colt McCoy/25 12.00 30.00
5 Darren McFadden/30 12.00 30.00
6 Dez Bryant/30 15.00 40.00
7 Jamaal Charles/25 15.00 40.00
8 Jay Cutler/25 12.00 30.00
10 LaDainian Tomlinson/30 40.00 80.00
11 Percy Harvin/30 12.00 30.00
12 Philip Rivers/25 25.00 50.00
13 Sam Bradford/25 25.00 50.00
14 Santonio Holmes/30 10.00 25.00

2000 Totino's Pizza

These cards were actually part of a contest in which one had to accumulate more than one player to qualify for various prizes. The Eddie George card was good for the Grand Prize of which only 5 were made. The cards were printed on the inside of Totino's Pizza boxes are were to be cut off of the box by the collector. Each card features a small black and white photo with a brief write-up on the player. There are two versions of each card: white stock cards measure roughly 3 1/2" by 3 1/2" when cut from the product package and the brown stock cards measure roughly 3 1/2" by 4 1/4" when cut. The contest expired 2/29/2000.

COMPLETE SET (4) 1.20 3.00
1 Mike Alstott .40 1.00
2 Eddie George WIN
3 Marshall Faulk .50 1.25
4 John Randle .40 1.00
5 Charles Woodson .20 .50

1977 Touchdown Club

This 50-card set was initially targeted toward football autograph collectors as the set featured only living (at the time) ex-football players many of whom were or are now in the Pro Football Hall of Fame in Canton, Ohio. The set was originally sold for $5.95 along with a printed address list for the players in the set. The cards are black and white (typically showing the player in his prime) and are numbered on the back. The cards measure approximately 2 1/4" by 3 1/4". Card backs list career honors the player received.

COMPLETE SET (50) 60.00 120.00
1 Red Grange 4.00 8.00
2 George Halas 4.00 8.00
3 Benny Friedman UER 1.00 2.50
Card Pictures Cliff Montgomery
4 Cliff Battles 1.25 3.00
5 Mike Michalske 1.25 3.00
6 George McAfee 1.50 3.00
7 Beattie Feathers 1.25 3.00
8 Ernie Caddel 1.00 2.50
9 George Musso 1.25 3.00
10 Sid Luckman 2.50 5.00
11 Cecil Isbell 1.25 3.00
12 Bronko Nagurski 4.00 8.00
13 Hunk Anderson 1.00 2.50
14 Dick Farman 1.00 2.50
15 Aldo Forte 1.00 2.50
16 Ki Aldrich 1.00 2.50
17 Jim Lee Howell 1.00 2.50
18 Ray Flaherty 1.25 3.00
19 Hampton Pool 1.00 2.50
20 Alex Wojciechowicz 1.25 3.00
21 Bill Osmanski 1.00 2.50
22 Hank Soar 1.00 2.50
23 Dutch Clark 1.50 3.00
24 Joe Muha 1.00 2.50
25 Don Hutson 2.00 4.00
26 Jim Poole 1.00 2.50
27 Charley Malone 1.00 2.50
28 Charley Trippi 1.50 3.00
29 Andy Farkas 1.00 2.50
30 Clarke Hinkle 1.25 3.00
31 Gary Famiglietti 1.00 2.50
32 Bulldog Turner 1.50 3.00
33 Sammy Baugh 4.00 8.00
34 Pat Harder 1.00 2.50
35 Tuffy Leemans 1.00 2.50
36 Ken Strong 1.50 3.00
37 Barney Poole 1.00 2.50
38 Frank(Bruiser) Kinard 1.25 3.00
39 Buford Ray 1.00 2.50
40 Clarence(Ace) Parker 1.25 3.00
41 Buddy Parker 1.00 2.50
42 Mel Hein 1.25 3.00
43 Ed Danowski 1.00 2.50
44 Bill Dudley 1.50 3.00
45 Paul Stenn 1.00 2.50
46 George Connor 1.25 3.00
47 George Sauer Sr. 1.00 2.50
48 Armand Niccolai 1.00 2.50
49 Tony Canadeo 1.25 3.00
50 Bill Willis 1.50 4.00

1989 Touchdown UK

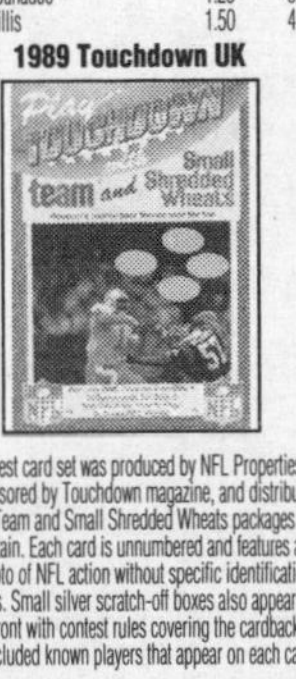

This contest card set was produced by NFL Properties UK, sponsored by Touchdown magazine, and distributed through Team and Small Shredded Wheats packages in Great Britain. Each card is unnumbered and features a color photo of NFL action without specific identification of players. Small silver scratch-off boxes also appear on the cardfront with contest rules covering the cardback. We've included known players that appear on each card below.

COMPLETE SET (30) 300.00 500.00
1 Duel for the Ball 7.50 15.00
Rams vs. Chargers
2 Safety Blitz Pressures QB 7.50 15.00
Todd Blackledge vs. Oilers
3 Powerful Kick-off 7.50 15.00
Scott Norwood
4 Kick-off Starts the Game 7.50 15.00
Gary Anderson K
5 Receiver and Defender in Combat 7.50 15.00
Dennis Gentry,
Joey Browner
6 Field Goal Attempt Sails 10.00 20.00
Packers vs. 49ers
7 Atlanta's QB Finds Receiver 10.00 20.00
Chris Miller
8 Loose Ball on the Gridiron 10.00 20.00
Afred Anderson
Bill Bates
9 End Zone Ballet for a TD 7.50 15.00
Jonathan Hayes vs. Bears
10 Bengals' QB Throws a Pass 12.50 25.00
Boomer Esiason
11 Breaking up a Reception 7.50 15.00
Gill Byrd
Ron Heller TE
12 Catching a Long Bomb 7.50 15.00
for TD, Mark Clayton
Dwayne Woodruff
13 Cincinnati's QB Let's 12.50 25.00
One Fly, Boomer Esiason
14 Catching a Pass 7.50 15.00
Behind Defense
Eddie Brown WR vs Steelers
15 Fighting for a Fumble 7.50 15.00
Delton Hall
16 Houston's QB Throws 15.00 30.00
Over Top, Warren Moon,
Reggie Williams
17 Juggling the Ball 10.00 20.00
Gary Anderson RB vs. Cowboys
18 Reaching High for 7.50 15.00
Completion, Chris Burkett
19 Saints' QB Fires a Bomb 10.00 20.00
Bobby Hebert
20 Splitting Defense 7.50 15.00
for Reception
James Pruitt
Ray Horton
21 Ball Pops Loose 10.00 20.00
Dino Hackett
Neal Anderson
22 Bears Attempt Field Goal 10.00 20.00
Kevin Butler
Steve McMichael
23 Ball Flies Loose After Punt 7.50 15.00
Bill Renner vs. Giants
24 Giants QB Unloads 15.00 30.00
Before Sack
Phil Simms
Jumbo Elliott
Jesse Penn
25 Raiders QB Has Ball 10.00 20.00
Stripped, Marc Wilson
Leslie O'Neal
26 Steelers Defense 7.50 15.00
Causes Fumble
John Swain
27 Threading the Needle 7.50 15.00
Mark Malone
Markus Koch
Craig Wolfley
28 Long Pass From 40.00 80.00
Broncos QB, John Elway
29 Punt From the End Zone 7.50 15.00
30 Bears Pass 10.00 20.00
Defense Crashes In

2005 Tri-Cities Fever NIFL

COMPLETE SET (26) 7.50 15.00
1 Jeremy Bohannon .30 .75
2 Antar Brame .30 .75
3 Ron Childs .30 .75
4 Jason Cobb .30 .75
5 Jarvis Dunn .30 .75
6 Zach Fife .30 .75
7 Thomas Ford .30 .75
8 Nick Hannah .30 .75
9 Michael Hodges Jr. .30 .75
10 Josh Jelinek .30 .75
11 Josh Jelmberg .30 .75
12 Rhodri Kirwan .30 .75
13 Nick Lano .30 .75
14 Karl Kuhau-Ieftee .30 .75
15 Scott Lunde .30 .75
16 Ray Marshall .30 .75
17 Brian Meier .30 .75
18 Paris Moore .30 .75
19 Mike Rigell .30 .75
20 Michael Che Romero .30 .75
21 Brandon Schillinger .30 .75
22 Lucien Scott .30 .75
23 Tyler Thomas .30 .75
24 Mac Tuiaea .30 .75
25 Cheerleaders Card .30 .75
26 Cover Card .30 .75

2010 TRISTAR Obak

COMMON CARD (1-109) .20 .50
COMMON VAR (1-109) .40 1.00
COMMON SP (110-120) 1.50 4.00
THREE SPs PER BOX
73 Andy Farkas .20 .50
101 Howard Cassady .20 .50
104 Kyle Rote Sr. .20 .50
105 Charlie Ward .20 .50

2010 TRISTAR Obak Black

*BLACK: 2.5X TO 6X BASIC
*BLACK VAR: 1.2X TO 3X BASIC VAR
*BLACK SP: .5X TO 1.2X BASIC SP
OVERALL PARALLEL ODDS 1:10
STATED PRINT RUN 50 SER.#'d SETS

2010 TRISTAR Obak Green

OVERALL PARALLEL ODDS 1:10
VARIATIONS RANDOMLY INSERTED
STATED PRINT RUN 25 SER.#'d SETS
NO PRICING DUE TO SCARCITY

2010 TRISTAR Obak Mini T212

STATED ODDS ONE PER PACK
35 Charlie Ward .30 .75

2010 TRISTAR Obak Mini T212 Black

*BLACK: 1X TO 2.5X BASIC
*BLACK VAR: .6X TO 1.5X BASIC VAR
STATED ODDS 1:20
STATED PRINT RUN 50 SER.#'d SETS

2010 TRISTAR Obak Mini T212 Green

OVERALL MINI PARALLEL ODDS 1:20
VARIATIONS RANDOMLY INSERTED
STATED PRINT RUN 25 SER.#'d SETS
NO PRICING DUE TO SCARCITY

2010 TRISTAR Obak Mini T212 Purple

OVERALL MINI PARALLEL ODDS 1:20
VARIATIONS RANDOMLY INSERTED
STATED PRINT RUN 1 SER.#'d SET
NO PRICING DUE TO SCARCITY

2010 TRISTAR Obak Mini T212 Red

OVERALL MINI PARALLEL ODDS 1:20
VARIATIONS RANDOMLY INSERTED
STATED PRINT RUN 5 SER.#'d SETS
NO PRICING DUE TO SCARCITY

2010 TRISTAR Obak Purple

OVERALL PARALLEL ODDS 1:10
VARIATIONS RANDOMLY INSERTED
STATED PRINT RUN 1 SER.#'d SET
NO PRICING DUE TO SCARCITY

2010 TRISTAR Obak Red

OVERALL PARALLEL ODDS 1:10
VARIATIONS RANDOMLY INSERTED
STATED PRINT RUN 5 SER.#'d SETS
NO PRICING DUE TO SCARCITY

2010 TRISTAR Obak Autographs

OVERALL AUTO ODDS 1:5
STATED PRINT RUN 125 SER.#'d SETS
A81 Charlie Ward 4.00 10.00

2010 TRISTAR Obak Autographs Black

*BLACK: .5X TO 1.2X BROWN
OVERALL AUTO ODDS 1:5
STATED PRINT RUN 50 SER.#'d SETS
A58 Toby Gerhart 8.00 20.00

2010 TRISTAR Obak Autographs Brown

*BROWN: .5X TO 1.2X BASIC
OVERALL AUTO ODDS 1:5
STATED PRINT RUN 75 SER.#'d SETS
A54 Howard Cassady 8.00 20.00

2010 TRISTAR Obak Autographs Green

OVERALL AUTO ODDS 1:5
VARIATIONS RANDOMLY INSERTED
STATED PRINT RUN 25 SER.#'d SETS
NO PRICING DUE TO SCARCITY

2010 TRISTAR Obak Autographs Purple

OVERALL AUTO ODDS 1:5
VARIATIONS RANDOMLY INSERTED
STATED PRINT RUN 1 SER.#'d SET
NO PRICING DUE TO SCARCITY

2010 TRISTAR Obak Autographs Red

OVERALL AUTO ODDS 1:5
VARIATIONS RANDOMLY INSERTED
STATED PRINT RUN 5 SER.#'d SETS
NO PRICING DUE TO SCARCITY

2010 TRISTAR Obak National Convention VIP

COMPLETE SET (12)
N6 Andy Farkas 1.50 4.00

2011 TRISTAR Obak National Convention VIP

NP4 Roger Staubach
NP5 Terry Bradshaw
NP6 Gale Sayers
NP9 Stan Musial 2.50 6.00
Bob Kalsu

2011 TRISTAR Pursuit Obak Preview

TWO OBAK CARDS PER BOX
ANNC'D PRINT RUN OF 311 SETS
P6A Billy Johnson .60 1.50
P6B Billy Johnson .60 1.50
Square Around Number
P7 William Heffelfinger .60 1.50

2011 TRISTAR Obak

COMP.SET w/o SP's (110)
1 Sammy Baugh .30 .75
2 Dutch Clark .20 .50
3 Red Grange .40 1.00
4 Mel Hein .20 .50
5 Fats Henry .20 .50
6 Cal Hubbard .20 .50
7 Don Hutson .25 .60
8 Curly Lambeau .30 .75
9 Tim Mara .20 .50
10 George Preston Marshall .20 .50
11 Johnny Blood McNally .20 .50
12 Bronko Nagurski .30 .75
13 Ernie Nevers .25 .60
14 Bart Starr .50 1.25
15 Johnny Unitas .50 1.25
16 Paul Hornung .30 .75
17 Terry Bradshaw .40 1.00
18 Earl Campbell .30 .75
19 Morten Andersen .20 .50
20 Roger Staubach .40 1.00
21 Gale Sayers .30 .75
22 Gino Cappelletti .20 .50
23 Jim Otto .20 .50
24 Jim Parker .20 .50
25 Norm Van Brocklin .25 .60
26 Vince Lombardi .50 1.25
27 John Heisman .20 .50
28 Paul Bear Bryant .30 .75
29 Doak Walker .30 .75
30 Douglas MacArthur .20 .50
31 Joe Carr .20 .50
32 Bert Bell .20 .50
33 Robert Maxwell .20 .50
34 John Outland .20 .50
35 Henry Rutgers .20 .50
36 King Camp Gillette .20 .50
37 Darrell Royal .20 .50
38 Angelo Bertelli .20 .50
39 Bo Jackson .50 1.25
40 John Cappelletti .20 .50
41 John David Crow .20 .50
42 Howard Cassady .20 .50
43 Billy Sims .25 .60
44 Johnny Lattner .30 .75
45 Steve Owens .20 .50
46 Frank Sinkwich .20 .50
47 Mike Rozier .30 .75
48 Larry Kelley .20 .50
49 Andre Ware .25 .60
50 Charlie Ward .20 .50
51 Tom Dempsey .20 .50
52 Benny Friedman .20 .50
53 Paul Robeson .20 .50
54 Corbett Davis .20 .50
55 Sam Francis .20 .50
56 Tommy Nobis .20 .50
57 Lem Barney .20 .50
58 Dennis Byrd .20 .50
59 Bobby Douglass .20 .50
60 Kurt Warner .25 .60
61 Quentin Coryatt .20 .50
62 Poe Brothers .20 .50
Samuel Poe
Edgar Allan Poe
Johnny Poe
Neilson Poe
Arthur Poe
Gresham Poe
63 Ray Childress .20 .50
64 Lydell Mitchell .20 .50
65 Chuck Hughes .20 .50
66 Johanna Spyri .20 .50
67 Caspar Whitney .20 .50
68 John Moses Brunswick .20 .50
69 Bob Lilly .25 .60
70 Elroy Hirsch .25 .60
71 Dante Hall .20 .50
72 Christian Okoye .20 .50
73 Ickey Woods .20 .50
74 Harry Beecher .20 .50
75 Roger Craig .25 .60
76 Beattie Feathers .20 .50
77 Joe Foss .20 .50
78 Ray Guy .20 .50
79 Graham McNamee .20 .50
80 Joe Perry .25 .60
81 Emlen Tunnell .20 .50
82 Emory Bellard .20 .50
83 Walter Camp .20 .50
84 Eddie Cochems .20 .50
85 William Webb Ellis .20 .50
86 Ray Flaherty .20 .50
87 Charles Follis .20 .50
88 Ralph Hay .20 .50
89 Pudge Heffelfinger .20 .50
90 Fritz Pollard .20 .50
91 Cadet Joseph Reeves .20 .50
92 John Tate Riddell .20 .50
93 Bradbury Robinson .20 .50
94 Amos?âAlonzo Stagg .20 .50
95 A.E. Staley .20 .50
96 George Taliaferro .20 .50
97 Fielding Yost .20 .50
98 Lyndon B. Johnson .20 .50
99 Dwight Eisenhower .20 .50
100 Gerald Ford .25 .60
101 John Kennedy .30 .75
102 Richard Nixon .20 .50
103 Ronald Reagan .30 .75
104 Rocky Bleier .25 .60
105 Maurice Footsie Britt .20 .50
106 Jack Chevigney .20 .50
107 Bob Kalsu .20 .50
108 Yale Lary .20 .50
109 Eddie LeBaron .20 .50
110 Jack Lummus .20 .50
111 Charlie Ward SP 1.25 3.00
112 Rocky Bleier SP 1.50 4.00
113 Maurice Footsie Britt SP 1.25 3.00
114 Al Blozis SP 1.25 3.00
115 Jack Chevigney SP 1.25 3.00
116 Bob Kalsu SP 1.25 3.00
117 Eddie LeBaron SP 1.25 3.00
118 Jack Lummus SP 1.25 3.00
119 Johnny Poe SP 1.25 3.00
120 Fritz Pollard SP 1.25 3.00

2011 TRISTAR Obak Gold

*111-120 GOLD/50: .6X TO 1.5X BASIC SP

2011 TRISTAR Obak Green

*1-110 GREEN/25: 3X TO 8X BASIC CARDS
*111-120 GREEN/25: .8X TO 2X BASIC CARDS

2011 TRISTAR Obak Orange

*1-110 ORANGE/10: 5X TO 12X BASIC CARDS
*111-120 ORANGE/10: 1.2X TO 3X BASIC SP

2011 TRISTAR Obak Orange 75

*111-120 ORANGE/75: .5X TO 1.2X BASIC SP

2011 TRISTAR Obak Autographs

*BASE AU/100: .3X TO .8X BROWN/50
STATED PRINT RUN 100 SER.#'d SETS
A1 Morten Andersen 5.00 12.00
A5 Dennis Byrd 5.00 12.00
A7 Gino Cappelletti 5.00 12.00
A8 John Cappelletti 5.00 12.00
A12 Eric Crouch 6.00 15.00
A14 Tom Dempsey 5.00 12.00
A15 Bobby Douglass 5.00 12.00
A17 Ray Guy 6.00 15.00
A18 Dante Hall 5.00 12.00
A19 Paul Hornung 8.00 20.00
A22 Johnny Lattner 6.00 15.00
A23 Eddie LeBaron 6.00 15.00
A26 Lydell Mitchell 5.00 12.00
A29 Christian Okoye 5.00 12.00
A30 Jim Otto 5.00 12.00
A34 Mike Rozier 5.00 12.00
A36 Billy Sims 6.00 15.00
A39 Charlie Ward 6.00 15.00

2011 TRISTAR Obak Autographs Brown

STATED PRINT RUN 50 SER.#'d SETS
A1 Morten Andersen 6.00 15.00
A2 Lem Barney 6.00 15.00
A3 Rocky Bleier 10.00 25.00
A5 Dennis Byrd 6.00 15.00
A7 Gino Cappelletti 6.00 15.00
A8 John Cappelletti 6.00 15.00
A9 Ray Childress 6.00 15.00
A10 Quentin Coryatt 6.00 15.00
A11 Roger Craig 8.00 20.00
A12 Eric Crouch 8.00 20.00
A14 Tom Dempsey 6.00 15.00
A15 Bobby Douglass 6.00 15.00
A16 Toby Gerhart 8.00 20.00
A17 Ray Guy 8.00 20.00
A18 Dante Hall 6.00 15.00
A19 Paul Hornung 10.00 25.00
A21 Yale Lary 6.00 15.00
A22 Johnny Lattner 8.00 20.00
A23 Eddie LeBaron 8.00 20.00
A25 Bob Lilly 8.00 20.00
A26 Lydell Mitchell 6.00 15.00
A27 Ozzie Newsome 8.00 20.00
A28 Tommy Nobis 6.00 15.00
A29 Christian Okoye 6.00 15.00
A30 Jim Otto 6.00 15.00
A31 Steve Owens 6.00 15.00
A32 Mel Renfro 6.00 15.00
A34 Mike Rozier 6.00 15.00
A36 Billy Sims 8.00 20.00
A38 George Taliaferro 6.00 15.00
A39 Charlie Ward 6.00 15.00
A40 Andre Ware 8.00 20.00
A41 Ickey Woods 6.00 15.00

2011 TRISTAR Obak Autographs Green

*GREEN AU/25: .5X TO 1.2X BROWN/50
STATED PRINT RUN 25 SER.#'d SETS
A13 John David Crow 8.00 20.00
A35 Gale Sayers 15.00 40.00

2011 TRISTAR Obak Autographs Orange

*ORANGE AU/75: .3X TO .8X BROWN/50
STATED PRINT RUN 75 SER.#'d SETS

2011 TRISTAR Obak Cut Signatures Blue

BLUE PRINT RUN 50 SER.#'d SETS
*BRONZE/75: .4X TO 1X BLUE/50
24 Bob Gain 6.00 15.00
34 Brad Johnson 6.00 15.00
37 Lee Roy Jordan 6.00 15.00
59 Philip Rivers 12.00 30.00
62 Junior Seau 25.00 50.00
64 Don Shula 15.00 30.00
69 Jim Stillwagon 6.00 15.00
72 Pat Summerall 10.00 25.00
75 Vinny Testaverde 8.00 20.00
79 Charley Trippi 6.00 15.00
84 Charles White 6.00 15.00

2011 TRISTAR Obak Cut Signatures Green

GREEN AUTO PRINT RUN 25
4 Terry Baker 12.00 30.00
6 Sammy Baugh 40.00 80.00
7 Joe Bellino 8.00 20.00
13 David Carr 8.00 20.00
18 Richard Dent 12.00 30.00
37 Lee Roy Jordan 8.00 20.00
50 Craig Morton 8.00 20.00
51 Jay Novacek 10.00 25.00
59 Philip Rivers 15.00 40.00
55 William Perry 10.00 25.00
60 George Rogers 8.00 20.00
62 Junior Seau 30.00 60.00
63 Jerry Sherk 8.00 20.00
64 Don Shula 15.00 40.00
69 Jim Stillwagon 8.00 20.00
72 Pat Summerall 10.00 25.00
78 Y.A. Tittle 12.00 30.00
79 Charley Trippi 8.00 20.00
84 Charles White 8.00 20.00
89 Danny Wuerffel 8.00 20.00

1983 Tudor Figurines

Produced by Tudor Games, these figurines were produced for each NFL team's quarterback. Although the statues are not specifically identified, they were designed to represent that team's 1983 quarterback. The pieces were rather crudely done with each appearing to be exact in design save for the team uniform. They are listed below by the product code number on the package (also in team alphabetical order) and are priced as opened statues. Complete sealed packages are valued at double the prices below.

COMPLETE SET (28) 220.00 550.00
2001 Jim McMahon 8.00 20.00
2002 Ken Anderson 8.00 20.00
2003 Joe Ferguson 6.00 15.00
2004 John Elway 40.00 100.00
2005 Brian Sipe 6.00 15.00
2006 Doug Williams 6.00 15.00
2007 Jim Hart 6.00 15.00
2008 Dan Fouts 10.00 25.00
2009 Steve Fuller 6.00 15.00
2010 Bert Jones 8.00 20.00
2011 Danny White 8.00 20.00
2012 David Woodley 6.00 15.00
2013 Ron Jaworski 6.00 15.00
2014 Steve Bartkowski 8.00 20.00
2015 Joe Montana 50.00 125.00
2016 Phil Simms 8.00 20.00
2017 Richard Todd 6.00 15.00
2018 Eric Hipple 6.00 15.00
2019 Archie Manning 20.00 40.00
2020 Lynn Dickey 6.00 15.00
2021 Steve Grogan 8.00 20.00
2022 Jim Plunkett 8.00 20.00
2023 Vince Ferragamo 6.00 15.00
2024 Joe Theismann 20.00 40.00
2025 Ken Stabler 12.00 30.00
2026 Jim Zorn 6.00 15.00
2027 Terry Bradshaw 25.00 50.00
2028 Tommy Kramer 6.00 15.00

2011 TRISTAR Obak T212 Mini

ONE MINI PER PACK
*BROWN/75: 1.5X TO 4X BASIC INSERTS
*GREEN/25: 2.5X TO 6X BASIC INSERTS
1 Sammy Baugh .50 1.25
2 Bronko Nagurski .50 1.25
3 Earl Campbell .50 1.25
4 Terry Bradshaw .60 1.50
5 Bart Starr .75 2.00
6 Johnny Unitas .75 2.00
7 Bob Lilly .40 1.00
8 Vince Lombardi .75 2.00
9 John Heisman .30 .75
10 Bo Jackson .60 1.50
11 John Cappelletti .30 .75
12 Benny Friedman .30 .75
13 Gale Sayers .50 1.25
14 Walter Camp .30 .75
15 Kurt Warner .40 1.00
16 Poe Brothers .30 .75
Samuel Poe
Edgar Allan Poe
Johnny Poe
Neilson Poe
Arthur Poe
Gresham Poe
17 Harry Beecher .30 .75
18 Paul Bear Bryant .50 1.25
19 Charles Follis .30 .75
20 Pudge Heffelfinger .30 .75
21 Fritz Pollard .30 .75
22 Gerald Ford .40 1.00
23 John Kennedy .50 1.25
24 Rocky Bleier .40 1.00

2011 TRISTAR Obak T4 Cabinets

ONE T4 CABINET PER HOBBY BOX
*BROWN/50: .5X TO 1.2X BASIC INSERTS
*GREEN/25: .6X TO 1.5X BASIC INSERTS
T4F1 Gerald Ford 1.50 4.00
Fielding Yost
T4F2 Charles Follis 1.50 4.00
Emlen Tunnell
T4F3 Rocky Bleier 2.00 5.00
Terry Bradshaw
T4F4 Eddie LeBaron 1.50 4.00
Amos Alonzo Stagg
T4F5 Paul Hornung 4.00 10.00
Bart Starr
T4F6 Darrell Royal 2.50 6.00
Earl Campbell
T4F7 John Cappelletti 1.50 4.00
John Heisman
T4F8 Toby Gerhart 2.00 5.00
Walter Camp
T4F9 Roger Staubach 3.00 8.00
Terry Bradshaw
T4F10 Charlie Ward 1.50 4.00
Robert Maxwell
T4F11 Paul Hornung 2.50 6.00
Bert Bell
T4F12 Gale Sayers 3.00 8.00
Red Grange
T4F13 Yale Lary 1.50 4.00
John David Crow
T4F14 Johnny Lattner 1.50 4.00
Jack Chevigney
T4F15 Bob Lilly 2.50 6.00
Sammy Baugh

1989 TV-4 NFL Quarterbacks

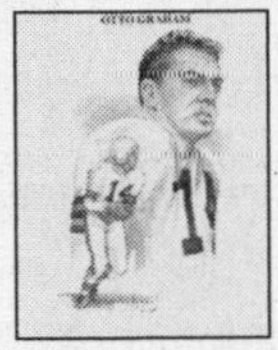

The 1989 TV-4 NFL Quarterbacks set features 20 cards measuring approximately 2 7/16" by 3 1/8". The fronts are borderless and show attractive color action and portrait drawings of each quarterback. The drawings were performed by artist J.C. Ford. The vertically oriented backs list career highlights. The TV-4 refers to a London (England) television station, which distributed the cards. The cards were distributed in England and were intended to promote the National Football League, which had begun playing pre-season games there.

COMPLETE SET (20) 20.00 40.00
1 Dutch Clark .50 1.25
2 Sammy Baugh .60 1.50
3 Bob Waterfield .50 1.25
4 Sid Luckman .60 1.50
5 Otto Graham .60 1.50
6 Bobby Layne .60 1.50
7 Norm Van Brocklin .50 1.25
8 George Blanda .50 1.25
9 Y.A. Tittle .50 1.25
10 Johnny Unitas 1.50 4.00
11 Bart Starr 1.50 4.00
12 Sonny Jurgensen .50 1.25
13 Joe Namath 1.50 4.00
14 Fran Tarkenton .60 1.50
15 Roger Staubach 1.25 3.00
16 Terry Bradshaw 1.25 3.00
17 Dan Fouts .50 1.25
18 Joe Montana 4.00 10.00
19 John Elway 3.00 8.00
20 Dan Marino 3.00 8.00

1997 UD3

The 1997 Upper Deck UD3 set was issued in one series totalling 90 cards. The set contains the topical subsets: Prime Choice Rookie (1-30), Eye of a Champion (31-60), and Pigskin Heroes (61-90). Each of the three subsets were printed using different insert quality printing technologies. Prime Choice Rookies display color action player photos using Light F/X technology. Eye of a Champion utilizes CEL Chrome technology. Pigskin Heroes features color player action photos and player images using Electric embossed technology and printed on a pigskin-look background.

COMPLETE SET (90) 20.00 50.00
1 Orlando Pace RC .50 1.25
2 Walter Jones RC .50 1.25
3 Tony Gonzalez RC 1.50 4.00
4 David LaFleur RC .20 .50
5 Jim Druckenmiller RC .30 .75
6 Jake Plummer RC 1.50 4.00
7 Pat Barnes RC .30 .75
8 Ike Hilliard RC .60 1.50
9 Reidel Anthony RC .50 1.25
10 Rae Carruth RC .20 .50
11 Yatil Green RC .30 .75
12 Joey Kent RC .50 1.25
13 Will Blackwell RC .30 .75
14 Kevin Lockett RC .30 .75
15 Warrick Dunn RC 1.25 3.00
16 Antowain Smith RC 1.25 3.00
17 Troy Davis RC .30 .75
18 Byron Hanspard RC .30 .75
19 Corey Dillon RC 1.50 4.00
20 Darnell Autry RC .30 .75
21 Peter Boulware RC .50 1.25
22 Darrell Russell RC .20 .50
23 Kenny Holmes RC .50 1.25
24 Reinard Wilson RC .30 .75
25 Renaldo Wynn RC .20 .50
26 Dwayne Rudd RC .50 1.25
27 James Farrior RC .50 1.25
28 Shawn Springs RC .30 .75
29 Bryant Westbrook RC .20 .50
30 Tom Knight RC .20 .50
31 Barry Sanders EC 1.50 4.00
32 Brett Favre EC 2.00 5.00
33 Brian Mitchell EC .20 .50
34 Curtis Martin EC .60 1.50
35 Dan Marino EC 2.00 5.00
36 Deion Sanders EC .50 1.25
37 Drew Bledsoe EC .60 1.50
38 Eddie George EC .50 1.25
39 Edgar Bennett EC .20 .50
40 Emmitt Smith EC 1.50 4.00
41 Isaac Bruce EC .50 1.25
42 Jerome Bettis EC .50 1.25
43 Jerry Rice EC 1.00 2.50
44 John Elway EC 2.00 5.00
45 Junior Seau EC .50 1.25
46 Karim Abdul-Jabbar EC .50 1.25
47 Kerry Collins EC .50 1.25
48 Marshall Faulk EC .60 1.50
49 Marvin Harrison EC .50 1.25
50 Michael Irvin EC .50 1.25
51 Natrone Means EC .30 .75
52 Reggie White EC .50 1.25
53 Ricky Watters EC .30 .75
54 Stan Humphries EC .30 .75
55 Steve Young EC .60 1.50
56 Terry Glenn EC .50 1.25
57 Thurman Thomas EC .50 1.25
58 Tony Martin EC .30 .75
59 Troy Aikman EC 1.00 2.50
60 Vinny Testaverde EC .30 .75

61 Anthony Johnson PH .20 .50
62 Bobby Engram EC .30 .75
63 Carl Pickens PH .30 .75
64 Cris Carter PH .30 .75
65 Derrick Witherspoon PH .20 .50
66 Eddie Kennison PH .30 .75
67 Eric Swann PH .20 .50
68 Gus Frerotte PH .30 .75
69 Herman Moore PH .30 .75
70 Irving Fryar PH .30 .75
71 Jamal Anderson PH .50 1.25
72 Jeff Blake PH .50 1.25
73 Jim Harbaugh PH .30 .75
74 Joey Galloway PH .30 .75
75 Keenan McCardell PH .30 .75
76 Kevin Greene PH .30 .75
77 Keyshawn Johnson PH .50 1.25
78 Kordell Stewart PH .50 1.25
79 Marcus Allen PH .50 1.25
80 Mario Bates PH .20 .50
81 Mark Brunell PH .60 1.50
82 Michael Jackson PH .30 .75
83 Mike Alstott PH .50 1.25
84 Scott Mitchell PH .30 .75
85 Shannon Sharpe PH .30 .75
86 Steve McNair PH .60 1.50
87 Terrell Davis PH .60 1.50
88 Tim Brown PH .50 1.25
89 Ty Detmer PH .30 .75
90 Tyrone Wheatley PH .30 .75

1997 UD3 Generation Excitement

COMPLETE SET (15) 50.00 120.00
STATED ODDS 1:11
GE1 Jerry Rice 5.00 12.00
GE2 Carl Pickens 1.50 4.00
GE3 Curtis Conway 1.50 4.00
GE4 John Elway 10.00 25.00
GE5 Ike Hilliard 2.50 6.00
GE6 Marvin Harrison 2.50 6.00
GE7 Emmitt Smith 8.00 20.00
GE8 Barry Sanders 8.00 20.00
GE9 Deion Sanders 2.50 6.00
GE10 Rae Carruth .75 2.00
GE11 Curtis Martin 3.00 8.00
GE12 Terry Glenn 2.50 6.00
GE13 Napoleon Kaufman 2.50 6.00
GE14 Kordell Stewart 2.50 6.00
GE15 Jake Plummer 3.00 8.00

1997 UD3 Marquee Attraction

COMPLETE SET (15) 100.00 250.00
STATED ODDS 1:144
MA1 Steve Young 8.00 20.00
MA2 Troy Aikman 12.50 30.00
MA3 Keyshawn Johnson 6.00 15.00
MA4 Marcus Allen 6.00 15.00
MA5 Dan Marino 25.00 60.00
MA6 Mark Brunell 6.00 15.00
MA7 Eddie George 6.00 15.00
MA8 Brett Favre 25.00 60.00
MA9 Drew Bledsoe 8.00 20.00
MA10 Eddie Kennison 4.00 10.00
MA11 Terrell Davis 8.00 20.00
MA12 Warrick Dunn 6.00 15.00
MA13 Yatil Green 2.00 5.00
MA14 Troy Davis 2.00 5.00
MA15 Shawn Springs 2.00 5.00

1997 UD3 Signature Performers

COMPLETE SET (4) 100.00 200.00
STATED ODDS 1:1500
PF1 Curtis Martin 30.00 60.00
(issued via redemption)
PF2 Troy Aikman 60.00 120.00
PF3 Marcus Allen 25.00 60.00
PF4 Eddie George 15.00 40.00

1998 UD3

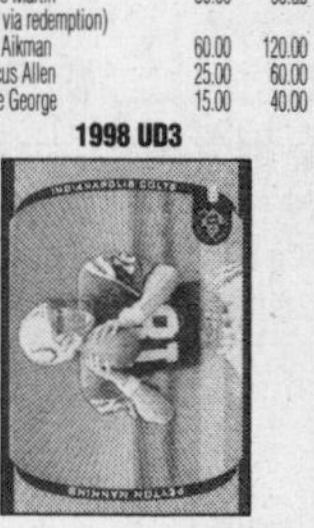

The 1998 UD Cubed set contains 270 standard size cards. The 3-card packs retail for $3.99 each. The set contains the subsets: Future Shock-Embossed (1-30; 1:6), Next Wave-Embossed (31-60; 1:4), Upper Realm-Embossed (61-90; 1:125), Future Shock-Light F/X (91-120; 1:12), Next Wave-Light F/X (121-150; 1:1.5), Upper Realm-Light F/X (151-180; 1:6), Future Shock-Rainbow (181-210; 1:1.33), Next Wave-Rainbow (211-240; 1:12), and Upper Realm-Rainbow (241-270; 1:24).

1 Peyton Manning FE 15.00 30.00
2 Ryan Leaf FE 2.00 5.00
3 Andre Wadsworth FE 1.25 3.00
4 Charles Woodson FE 2.00 5.00
5 Curtis Enis FE .75 2.00
6 Grant Wistrom FE 1.25 3.00
7 Greg Ellis FE .75 2.00
8 Fred Taylor FE 2.00 5.00
9 Duane Starks FE .75 2.00
10 Keith Brooking FE 2.00 5.00
11 Takeo Spikes FE 2.00 5.00
12 Jason Peter FE .75 2.00
13 Anthony Simmons FE 1.25 3.00
14 Kevin Dyson FE 2.00 5.00
15 Brian Simmons FE 1.25 3.00
16 Robert Edwards FE 1.25 3.00
17 Randy Moss FE 8.00 20.00
18 John Avery FE 1.25 3.00
19 Marcus Nash FE .75 2.00
20 Jerome Pathon FE 2.00 5.00
21 Jacquez Green FE 1.25 3.00
22 Robert Holcombe FE 1.25 3.00
23 Pat Johnson FE 1.25 3.00
24 Germane Crowell FE 1.25 3.00
25 Joe Jurevicius FE 2.00 5.00
26 Skip Hicks FE 1.25 3.00
27 Ahman Green FE 3.00 8.00
28 Brian Griese FE 2.50 6.00
29 Hines Ward FE 5.00 12.00
30 Tavian Banks FE 1.25 3.00
31 Warrick Dunn NE 1.50 4.00
32 Jake Plummer NE 1.50 4.00
33 Derrick Mayes NE 1.00 2.50
34 Napoleon Kaufman NE 1.50 4.00
35 Jamal Anderson NE 1.50 4.00
36 Marvin Harrison NE 1.50 4.00
37 Jermaine Lewis NE 1.00 2.50
38 Corey Dillon NE 1.50 4.00
39 Keyshawn Johnson NE 1.50 4.00
40 Mike Alstott NE 1.50 4.00
41 Bobby Hoying NE 1.00 2.50
42 Keenan McCardell NE 1.00 2.50
43 Will Blackwell NE .60 1.50
44 Peter Boulware NE .60 1.50
45 Tony Banks NE 1.00 2.50
46 Rod Smith WR NE 1.00 2.50
47 Tony Gonzalez NE 1.50 4.00
48 Antowain Smith NE 1.00 2.50
49 Rae Carruth NE .60 1.50
50 J.J. Stokes NE 1.00 2.50
51 Brad Johnson NE 1.50 4.00
52 Shawn Springs NE .60 1.50
53 Elvis Grbac NE .60 1.50
54 Jimmy Smith NE 1.00 2.50
55 Terry Glenn NE 1.50 4.00
56 Tiki Barber NE 1.50 4.00
57 Gus Frerotte NE .60 1.50
58 Danny Wuerffel NE 1.00 2.50
59 Fred Lane NE .60 1.50
60 Todd Collins NE .60 1.50
61 Barry Sanders UE 2.50 6.00
62 Troy Aikman UE 1.50 4.00
63 Dan Marino UE 3.00 8.00
64 Drew Bledsoe UE 1.25 3.00
65 Dorsey Levens UE .75 2.00
66 Jerome Bettis UE .75 2.00
67 John Elway UE 3.00 8.00
68 Steve Young UE 1.00 2.50
69 Terrell Davis UE .75 2.00
70 Kordell Stewart UE .50 1.25
71 Jeff George UE .50 1.25
72 Emmitt Smith UE 2.50 6.00
73 Irving Fryar UE .50 1.25
74 Brett Favre UE 3.00 8.00
75 Eddie George UE .75 2.00
76 Terry Allen UE .75 2.00
77 Warren Moon UE .75 2.00
78 Mark Brunell UE .75 2.00
79 Robert Smith UE .75 2.00
80 Jerry Rice UE 1.50 4.00
81 Tim Brown UE .75 2.00
82 Carl Pickens UE .50 1.25
83 Joey Galloway UE .50 1.25
84 Herman Moore UE .50 1.25
85 Adrian Murrell UE .50 1.25
86 Thurman Thomas UE .75 2.00
87 Robert Brooks UE .50 1.25
88 Michael Irvin UE .75 2.00
89 Andre Rison UE .50 1.25
90 Marshall Faulk UE 1.00 2.50
91 Peyton Manning FF 25.00 50.00
92 Ryan Leaf FF 3.00 8.00
93 Andre Wadsworth FF 2.00 5.00
94 Charles Woodson FF 3.00 8.00
95 Curtis Enis FF 1.25 3.00
96 Grant Wistrom FF 2.00 5.00
97 Greg Ellis FF 1.25 3.00
98 Fred Taylor FF 3.00 8.00
99 Duane Starks FF 1.25 3.00
100 Keith Brooking FF 3.00 8.00
101 Takeo Spikes FF 3.00 8.00
102 Jason Peter FF 1.25 3.00
103 Anthony Simmons FF 2.00 5.00
104 Kevin Dyson FF 3.00 8.00
105 Brian Simmons FF 2.00 5.00
106 Robert Edwards FF 2.00 5.00
107 Randy Moss FF 12.00 30.00
108 John Avery FF 2.00 5.00
109 Marcus Nash FF 1.25 3.00
110 Jerome Pathon FF 3.00 8.00
111 Jacquez Green FF 2.00 5.00
112 Robert Holcombe FF 2.00 5.00
113 Pat Johnson FF 2.00 5.00
114 Germane Crowell FF 2.00 5.00
115 Joe Jurevicius FF 3.00 8.00
116 Skip Hicks FF 2.00 5.00
117 Ahman Green FF 5.00 12.00
118 Brian Griese FF 4.00 10.00
119 Hines Ward FF 7.50 20.00
120 Tavian Banks FF 2.00 5.00
121 Warrick Dunn NF .75 2.00
122 Jake Plummer NF .75 2.00
123 Derrick Mayes NF .50 1.25
124 Napoleon Kaufman NF .75 2.00
125 Jamal Anderson NF .75 2.00
126 Marvin Harrison NF .75 2.00
127 Jermaine Lewis NF .50 1.25
128 Corey Dillon NF .75 2.00
129 Keyshawn Johnson NF .75 2.00
130 Mike Alstott NF .75 2.00
131 Bobby Hoying NF .50 1.25
132 Keenan McCardell NF .50 1.25
133 Will Blackwell NF .30 .75
134 Peter Boulware NF .30 .75
135 Tony Banks NF .50 1.25
136 Rod Smith NF .50 1.25
137 Tony Gonzalez NF .75 2.00
138 Antowain Smith NF .50 1.25
139 Rae Carruth NF .30 .75
140 J.J. Stokes NF .50 1.25
141 Brad Johnson NF .75 2.00
142 Shawn Springs NF .30 .75
143 Elvis Grbac NF .30 .75
144 Jimmy Smith NF .50 1.25
145 Terry Glenn NF .75 2.00
146 Tiki Barber NF .75 2.00
147 Gus Frerotte NF .30 .75
148 Danny Wuerffel NF .50 1.25
149 Fred Lane NF .30 .75
150 Todd Collins NF .30 .75
151 Barry Sanders UF 6.00 15.00
152 Troy Aikman UF 4.00 10.00
153 Dan Marino UF 7.50 20.00
154 Drew Bledsoe UF 3.00 8.00
155 Dorsey Levens UF 2.00 5.00
156 Jerome Bettis UF 2.00 5.00
157 John Elway UF 7.50 20.00
158 Steve Young UF 2.50 6.00
159 Terrell Davis UF 2.00 5.00
160 Kordell Stewart UF 1.25 3.00
161 Jeff George UF 1.25 3.00
162 Emmitt Smith UF 6.00 15.00
163 Irving Fryar UF 1.25 3.00
164 Brett Favre UF 7.50 20.00
165 Eddie George UF 2.00 5.00
166 Terry Allen UF 2.00 5.00
167 Warren Moon UF 2.00 5.00
168 Mark Brunell UF 2.00 5.00
169 Robert Smith UF 2.00 5.00
170 Jerry Rice UF 4.00 10.00
171 Tim Brown UF 2.00 5.00
172 Carl Pickens UF 1.25 3.00
173 Joey Galloway UF 1.25 3.00
174 Herman Moore UF 1.25 3.00
175 Adrian Murrell UF 1.25 3.00
176 Thurman Thomas UF 2.00 5.00
177 Robert Brooks UF 1.25 3.00
178 Michael Irvin UF 2.00 5.00
179 Andre Rison UF 1.25 3.00
180 Marshall Faulk UF 2.50 6.00
181 Peyton Manning FR RC 8.00 20.00
182 Ryan Leaf FR RC 1.00 2.50
183 Andre Wadsworth FR RC .60 1.50
184 Charles Woodson FR RC 1.00 2.50
185 Curtis Enis FR RC .40 1.00
186 Grant Wistrom FR RC .60 1.50
187 Greg Ellis FR RC .40 1.00
188 Fred Taylor FR RC 1.25 3.00
189 Duane Starks FR RC .40 1.00
190 Keith Brooking FR RC 1.00 2.50
191 Takeo Spikes FR RC 1.00 2.50
192 Jason Peter FR RC .40 1.00
193 Anthony Simmons FR RC .60 1.50
194 Kevin Dyson FR RC 1.00 2.50
195 Brian Simmons FR RC .60 1.50
196 Robert Edwards FR RC .60 1.50
197 Randy Moss FR RC 6.00 15.00
198 John Avery FR RC .60 1.50
199 Marcus Nash FR RC .40 1.00
200 Jerome Pathon FR RC 1.00 2.50
201 Jacquez Green FR RC .60 1.50
202 Robert Holcombe FR RC .60 1.50
203 Pat Johnson FR RC .60 1.50
204 Germane Crowell FR RC .60 1.50
205 Joe Jurevicius FR RC 1.00 2.50
206 Skip Hicks FR RC .60 1.50
207 Ahman Green FR RC 2.00 5.00
208 Brian Griese FR RC 1.50 4.00
209 Hines Ward FR RC 4.00 8.00
210 Tavian Banks FR RC .60 1.50
211 Warrick Dunn NR 3.00 8.00
212 Jake Plummer NR 3.00 8.00
213 Derrick Mayes NR 2.00 5.00
214 Napoleon Kaufman NR 3.00 8.00
215 Jamal Anderson NR 3.00 8.00
216 Marvin Harrison NR 3.00 8.00
217 Jermaine Lewis NR 2.00 5.00
218 Corey Dillon NR 3.00 8.00
219 Keyshawn Johnson NR 3.00 8.00
220 Mike Alstott NR 3.00 8.00
221 Bobby Hoying NR 2.00 5.00
222 Keenan McCardell NR 2.00 5.00
223 Will Blackwell NR 1.25 3.00
224 Peter Boulware NR 1.25 3.00
225 Tony Banks NR 2.00 5.00
226 Rod Smith NR 2.00 5.00
227 Tony Gonzalez NR 3.00 8.00
228 Antowain Smith NR 1.25 3.00
229 Rae Carruth NR 1.25 3.00
230 J.J. Stokes NR 2.00 5.00
231 Brad Johnson NR 3.00 8.00
232 Shawn Springs NR 1.25 3.00
233 Elvis Grbac NR 1.25 3.00
234 Jimmy Smith NR 2.00 5.00
235 Terry Glenn NR 3.00 8.00
236 Tiki Barber NR 2.00 5.00
237 Gus Frerotte NR 1.25 3.00
238 Danny Wuerffel NR 2.00 5.00
239 Fred Lane NR 1.25 3.00
240 Todd Collins NR 1.25 3.00
241 Barry Sanders UR 12.50 30.00
242 Troy Aikman UR 7.50 20.00
243 Dan Marino UR 15.00 40.00
244 Drew Bledsoe UR 6.00 15.00
245 Dorsey Levens UR 4.00 10.00
246 Jerome Bettis UR 4.00 10.00
247 John Elway UR 15.00 40.00
248 Steve Young UR 5.00 12.00
249 Terrell Davis UR 4.00 10.00
250 Kordell Stewart UR 2.50 6.00
251 Jeff George UR 2.50 6.00
252 Emmitt Smith UR 12.50 30.00
253 Irving Fryar UR 2.50 6.00
254 Brett Favre UR 15.00 40.00
255 Eddie George UR 4.00 10.00
256 Terry Allen UR 4.00 10.00
257 Warren Moon UR 4.00 10.00
258 Mark Brunell UR 4.00 10.00
259 Robert Smith UR 4.00 10.00
260 Jerry Rice UR 7.50 20.00
261 Tim Brown UR 4.00 10.00
262 Carl Pickens UR 2.50 6.00
263 Joey Galloway UR 2.50 6.00
264 Herman Moore UR 2.50 6.00
265 Adrian Murrell UR 2.50 6.00
266 Thurman Thomas UR 4.00 10.00
267 Robert Brooks UR 2.50 6.00
268 Michael Irvin UR 4.00 10.00
269 Andre Rison UR 2.50 6.00
270 Marshall Faulk UR 5.00 12.00
P243 Dan Marino UR Promo 1.25 3.00

1998 UD3 Die Cuts

COMP.EMB.DIE CUT (90) 200.00 400.00
*EMB.DIE CUT 1-30: SAME PRICE
EMB.DIE CUT 31-60: .5X TO 1.2X
EMB.DIE CUT 61-90: 1.2X TO 3X
EMBOSSED PRINT RUN 2000 SERIAL #'d SETS
*FX DIE CUT 91-120: .5X TO 1.2X
*FX DIE CUT 121-150: 2X TO 5X
*FX DIE CUT 151-180: .5X TO 1.2X
FX STATED PRINT RUN 1000 SETS
*RAINBOW DIE CUT 181-210: 6X TO 15X
*RAINBOW DIE CUT 211-240: 2X TO 5X
*RAINBOW DIE CUT 241-270: 1.5X TO 4X
RAINBOW PRINT RUN 100 SETS

2002 UD Authentics

Released in mid-September 2002, this set contains 90 veterans, 50 rookies, and 8 flashback cards. The flashback cards are serial #'d to either 1989 or 1990. Boxes contained 18 packs of 5 cards. SRP was $6.99 per pack.

COMP.SET w/o SP's (90) 10.00 25.00
1 Jake Plummer .30 .75
2 David Boston .25 .60
3 Thomas Jones .40 1.00
4 Michael Vick .60 1.50
5 Warrick Dunn .30 .75
6 Jamal Lewis .30 .75
7 Chris Redman .25 .60
8 Travis Taylor .25 .60
9 Drew Bledsoe .40 1.00
10 Eric Moulds .30 .75
11 Travis Henry .25 .60
12 Chris Weinke .25 .60
13 Muhsin Muhammad .30 .75
14 Anthony Thomas .30 .75
15 Jim Miller .25 .60
16 Marty Booker .30 .75
17 Corey Dillon .30 .75
18 Jon Kitna .30 .75
19 Peter Warrick .30 .75
20 Tim Couch .25 .60
21 Emmitt Smith 1.00 2.50
22 Joey Galloway .30 .75
23 Quincy Carter .25 .60
24 Brian Griese .30 .75
25 Terrell Davis .40 1.00
26 Shannon Sharpe .40 1.00
27 Germane Crowell .25 .60
28 James Stewart .25 .60
29 Az-Zahir Hakim .25 .60
30 Brett Favre 1.00 2.50
31 Ahman Green .30 .75
32 Terry Glenn .30 .75
33 Jermaine Lewis .25 .60
34 James Allen .25 .60
35 Corey Bradford .25 .60
36 Edgerrin James .30 .75
37 Marvin Harrison .40 1.00
38 Peyton Manning .75 2.00
39 Jimmy Smith .30 .75
40 Mark Brunell .30 .75
41 Trent Green .30 .75
42 Johnnie Morton .30 .75
43 Priest Holmes .40 1.00
44 Ricky Williams .30 .75
45 Chris Chambers .30 .75
46 Jay Fiedler .30 .75
47 Daunte Culpepper .30 .75
48 Randy Moss .40 1.00
49 Michael Bennett .30 .75
50 Troy Brown .30 .75
51 Antowain Smith .30 .75
52 Tom Brady 1.00 2.50
53 Aaron Brooks .30 .75
54 Deuce McAllister .30 .75
55 Joe Horn .30 .75
56 Amani Toomer .30 .75
57 Kerry Collins .30 .75
58 Ron Dayne .30 .75
59 Chad Pennington .40 1.00
60 Curtis Martin .40 1.00
61 Vinny Testaverde .30 .75
62 Jerry Rice .75 2.00
63 Rich Gannon .30 .75
64 Tim Brown .40 1.00
65 Donovan McNabb .40 1.00
66 Duce Staley .30 .75
67 James Thrash .30 .75
68 Plaxico Burress .30 .75
69 Jerome Bettis .40 1.00
70 Kordell Stewart .30 .75
71 Doug Flutie .40 1.00
72 Drew Brees .60 1.50
73 LaDainian Tomlinson .50 1.25
74 Garrison Hearst .30 .75
75 Jeff Garcia .30 .75
76 Terrell Owens .40 1.00
77 Ricky Watters .30 .75
78 Shaun Alexander .30 .75
79 Trent Dilfer .30 .75
80 Isaac Bruce .40 1.00
81 Kurt Warner .40 1.00
82 Marshall Faulk .40 1.00
83 Keyshawn Johnson .30 .75
84 Michael Pittman .30 .75
85 Brad Johnson .30 .75
86 Eddie George .30 .75
87 Jevon Kearse .30 .75
88 Steve McNair .40 1.00
89 Shane Matthews .25 .60
90 Stephen Davis .30 .75
91 Josh McCown RC 2.00 5.00
92 Kurt Kittner RC 1.25 3.00
93 T.J. Duckett RC 2.00 5.00
94 Wes Pate RC 1.25 3.00
95 Chester Taylor RC 2.00 5.00
96 Ron Johnson RC 1.50 4.00
97 Lamont Brightful RC 1.25 3.00
98 Josh Reed RC 1.50 4.00
99 Randy Fasani RC 1.50 4.00
100 DeShaun Foster RC 2.00 5.00
101 Julius Peppers RC 4.00 10.00
102 William Green RC 1.50 4.00
103 Andre Davis RC 1.50 4.00
104 Chad Hutchinson RC 1.25 3.00
105 Antonio Bryant RC 2.00 5.00
106 Roy Williams RC 2.00 5.00
107 Clinton Portis RC 2.50 6.00
108 Herb Haygood RC 1.25 3.00
109 Ashley Lelie RC 1.50 4.00
110 Joey Harrington RC 2.00 5.00
111 Luke Staley RC 1.25 3.00
112 Javon Walker RC 2.00 5.00
113 David Carr RC 2.00 5.00
114 Jonathan Wells RC 2.00 5.00
115 Jabar Gaffney RC 2.00 5.00
116 Brian Allen RC 1.25 3.00
117 David Garrard RC 2.50 6.00
118 Leonard Henry RC 1.25 3.00
119 Rohan Davey RC 2.00 5.00
120 Deion Branch RC 2.00 5.00
121 J.T. O'Sullivan RC 1.50 4.00
122 Donte Stallworth RC 2.00 5.00
123 Tim Carter RC 1.50 4.00
124 Daryl Jones RC 1.25 3.00
125 Ronald Curry RC 1.50 4.00
126 Napoleon Harris RC 1.50 4.00
127 Brian Westbrook RC 3.00 8.00
128 Antwaan Randle El RC 2.00 5.00
129 Reche Caldwell RC 2.00 5.00
130 Quentin Jammer RC 2.00 5.00
131 Brandon Doman RC 1.25 3.00
132 Maurice Morris RC 1.50 4.00
133 Eric Crouch RC 2.00 5.00
134 Lamar Gordon RC 1.50 4.00
135 Travis Stephens RC 1.25 3.00
136 Marquise Walker RC 1.25 3.00
137 Jake Schifino RC 1.25 3.00
138 Patrick Ramsey RC 2.00 5.00
139 Ladell Betts RC 2.00 5.00
140 Cliff Russell RC 1.25 3.00
141 Chris Chandler/1989 1.25 3.00
142 Tim Brown/1989 1.50 4.00
143 Wesley Walls/1989 1.25 3.00
144 Rod Woodson/1989 1.50 4.00
145 Rich Gannon/1990 1.25 3.00
146 Emmitt Smith/1990 4.00 10.00
147 Junior Seau/1990 1.50 4.00
148 Shannon Sharpe/1990 1.50 4.00

2002 UD Authentics Gold 25

*1-90 VETS: 8X TO 20X BASIC CARDS
*91-140 ROOKIES: 1X TO 2.5X BASIC CARDS
*141-149 FLASHBACK: 2X TO 5X
STATED PRINT RUN 25 SER.#'d SETS

2002 UD Authentics All-Star Authentics

STATED ODDS 1:18
*GOLD/25: 1.2X TO 3X BASIC JSY
GOLD PRINT RUN 25 SER.#'d SETS
AABL Drew Bledsoe 4.00 10.00
AABO David Boston 2.50 6.00
AACB Courtney Brown 2.50 6.00
AACM Curtis Martin 4.00 10.00
AACS Corey Simon 2.50 6.00
AADF Doug Flutie 4.00 10.00
AADW Darren Woodson 3.00 8.00
AAEJ Edgerrin James 3.00 8.00
AAEM Eric Moulds 3.00 8.00
AAJP Jake Plummer 3.00 8.00
AAJS Junior Seau 4.00 10.00
AAPH Priest Holmes 4.00 10.00
AAPP Peerless Price 2.50 6.00
AARG Rod Gardner 2.50 6.00
AASD Stephen Davis 3.00 8.00
AASM Steve McNair 4.00 10.00
AATC Tim Couch 2.50 6.00
AATJ Thomas Jones 4.00 10.00
AATW Terrence Wilkins 2.50 6.00

2002 UD Authentics American Authentics Level 1

STATED ODDS 1:216
UNPRICED LEVEL 1 GOLD SER.#'d OF 15
*LEVEL 2: .8X TO 2X LEVEL 1
LEVEL 2 PRINT RUN 25 SER.#'d SETS
UNPRICED LEVEL 2 GOLD SER.#'d OF 5
ST1AT Anthony Thomas 7.50 20.00
ST1DC Daunte Culpepper/56* 20.00 40.00
ST1LT LaDainian Tomlinson SP 30.00 80.00
ST1PM Peyton Manning 50.00 100.00
ST1TG Tony Gonzalez/56* 20.00 40.00

2002 UD Authentics Glory Bound Jerseys

STATED ODDDS 1:18
*GOLD/25: 1.2X TO 3X BASIC JSY
GOLD PRINT RUN 25 SER.#'d SETS
GBJAB Antonio Bryant 3.00 8.00
GBJAL Ashley Lelie 2.50 6.00
GBJCP Clinton Portis 4.00 10.00
GBJDC David Carr 3.00 8.00
GBJDF DeShaun Foster 3.00 8.00
GBJDG David Garrard 4.00 10.00
GBJDS Donte Stallworth 3.00 8.00
GBJJG Jabar Gaffney 3.00 8.00
GBJJH Joey Harrington 3.00 8.00
GBJJM Josh McCown 3.00 8.00
GBJJP Julius Peppers 6.00 15.00
GBJJR Josh Reed 2.50 6.00
GBJJW Javon Walker 3.00 8.00
GBJLB Ladell Betts 3.00 8.00
GBJMM Maurice Morris 2.50 6.00
GBJMW Marquise Walker 2.00 5.00
GBJPR Patrick Ramsey 3.00 8.00
GBJRD Rohan Davey 3.00 8.00
GBJRJ Ron Johnson 2.50 6.00
GBJRW Roy Williams 3.00 8.00
GBJTD T.J. Duckett 3.00 8.00
GBJTS Travis Stephens 2.00 5.00
GBJWG William Green 2.50 6.00

2002 UD Authentics Rumble Backs

COMPLETE SET (20) 20.00 50.00
STATED ODDS 1:18
RB1 Emmitt Smith 3.00 8.00
RB2 Marshall Faulk 1.25 3.00
RB3 Edgerrin James 1.00 2.50
RB4 Terrell Davis 1.25 3.00
RB5 Anthony Thomas 1.00 2.50
RB6 LaDainian Tomlinson 1.50 4.00
RB7 Curtis Martin 1.25 3.00
RB8 Jerome Bettis 1.25 3.00
RB9 Ricky Watters 1.00 2.50
RB10 Ricky Williams 1.00 2.50
RB11 Eddie George 1.00 2.50
RB12 Jamal Lewis 1.00 2.50
RB13 Corey Dillon 1.00 2.50
RB14 Warrick Dunn 1.00 2.50
RB15 Ahman Green 1.00 2.50
RB16 Priest Holmes 1.25 3.00
RB17 Duce Staley 1.00 2.50
RB18 Michael Bennett 1.00 2.50
RB19 Deuce McAllister 1.00 2.50
RB20 Ron Dayne 1.00 2.50

2009 UD Black

1-90 VETERAN PRINT RUN 250
91-131 ROOKIE AU PRINT RUN 199-399
1 Greg Jennings 8.00 20.00
2 Darrell Green 6.00 15.00
3 Larry Fitzgerald 8.00 20.00
4 Kurt Warner 8.00 20.00
5 Matt Ryan 8.00 20.00
6 Michael Turner 6.00 15.00
7 Bubba Smith 5.00 12.00
8 Ray Lewis 8.00 20.00
9 Thurman Thomas 8.00 20.00
10 Ed Reed 6.00 15.00
11 Jim Kelly 8.00 20.00
12 Jerry Kramer 6.00 15.00
13 Jonathan Stewart 6.00 15.00
14 Deacon Jones 6.00 15.00
15 Billy Sims 6.00 15.00
16 Anthony Munoz 6.00 15.00
17 Ken Anderson 6.00 15.00
18 Mike Ditka 6.00 15.00
19 Gale Sayers 8.00 20.00
20 Matt Forte 8.00 20.00
21 Jack Youngblood 5.00 12.00
22 Marshawn Lynch 6.00 15.00
23 Jerricho Cotchery 6.00 15.00
24 Roger Staubach 12.00 30.00
25 Emmitt Smith 12.00 30.00
26 Bob Lilly 6.00 15.00
27 Daryl Johnston 8.00 20.00
28 Randy White 8.00 20.00
29 Troy Aikman 10.00 25.00
30 Tony Romo 10.00 25.00
31 Merlin Olsen 6.00 15.00
32 Paul Hornung 8.00 20.00
33 Felix Jones 8.00 20.00
34 DeMarcus Ware 6.00 15.00
35 Brandon Marshall 6.00 15.00
36 Lem Barney 5.00 12.00
37 John Elway 12.00 30.00
38 Calvin Johnson 8.00 20.00
39 Barry Sanders 10.00 25.00
40 Kevin Smith 6.00 15.00
41 Aaron Rodgers 15.00 40.00
42 Andre Johnson 6.00 15.00
43 Steve Slaton 6.00 15.00
44 Peyton Manning 15.00 40.00
45 Earl Campbell 8.00 20.00
46 Reggie Wayne 6.00 15.00
47 Maurice Jones-Drew 6.00 15.00
48 Dwayne Bowe 6.00 15.00
49 Bob Griese 6.00 15.00
50 Joey Porter 6.00 15.00
51 Ron Yary 5.00 12.00
52 Adrian Peterson 12.00 30.00
53 Alan Page 6.00 15.00
54 Tom Brady 12.00 30.00
55 Matt Cassel 6.00 15.00
56 Drew Brees 8.00 20.00
57 Brandon Jacobs 6.00 15.00
58 Marques Colston 6.00 15.00
59 Lawrence Taylor 8.00 20.00
60 Eli Manning 8.00 20.00
61 Don Maynard 6.00 15.00
62 Brett Favre 20.00 50.00
63 Jason Campbell 5.00 12.00
64 Fred Biletnikoff 8.00 20.00
65 Kellen Winslow Sr. 6.00 15.00
66 Darren McFadden 8.00 20.00
67 Brian Dawkins 6.00 15.00
68 Brian Westbrook 6.00 15.00
69 Chuck Bednarik 6.00 15.00
70 L.C. Greenwood 6.00 15.00
71 Ronnie Brown 6.00 15.00
72 Ben Roethlisberger 12.00 30.00
73 Terry Bradshaw 10.00 25.00
74 Harry Carson 5.00 12.00
75 Franco Harris 8.00 20.00
76 Rocky Bleier 6.00 15.00
77 Jack Ham 6.00 15.00
78 Ronnie Lott 8.00 20.00
79 LaDainian Tomlinson 8.00 20.00
80 Antonio Gates 6.00 15.00
81 Steve Young 10.00 25.00
82 Jerry Rice 12.00 30.00
83 Roger Craig 6.00 15.00
84 Frank Gore 6.00 15.00
85 Tom Rathman 5.00 12.00
86 Jim Zorn 5.00 12.00
87 Derrick Brooks 6.00 15.00
88 Chris Johnson 8.00 20.00
89 Joe Theismann 8.00 20.00
90 Clinton Portis 6.00 15.00
91 Andre Smith AU/399 RC 6.00 15.00
92 Nate Davis AU/399 RC 6.00 15.00
93 Jason Smith AU/399 RC 6.00 15.00
94 B.J. Raji AU/399 RC 10.00 25.00
95 James Davis AU/399 RC 8.00 20.00
96 Donald Brown AU/199 RC 12.00 30.00
97 Mike Wallace AU/399 RC 25.00 50.00
98 Percy Harvin AU/399 RC 25.00 60.00
99 Glen Coffee AU/399 RC 6.00 15.00
100 Matthew Stafford AU/199 RC 75.00 150.00
101 Knowshon Moreno AU/199 RC 12.00 30.00
102 Mohamed Massaquoi AU/399 RC 6.00 15.00
103 Vontae Davis AU/399 RC 8.00 20.00
104 Shonn Greene AU/399 RC 12.00 30.00
105 Josh Freeman AU/199 RC 30.00 80.00
106 Mike Goodson AU/399 RC 8.00 20.00
107 Brandon Tate AU/399 RC 8.00 20.00
108 Darrius Heyward-Bey AU/399 RC 8.00 20.00
109 Javon Ringer AU/399 RC 8.00 20.00
110 Derrick Williams AU/399 RC 6.00 15.00
111 Clay Matthews AU/399 RC 40.00 80.00
112 Jeremy Maclin AU/199 RC 15.00 40.00
113 Patrick Turner AU/399 RC 6.00 15.00
114 Hakeem Nicks AU/399 RC 12.00 30.00
115 Chris Wells AU/199 RC 20.00 40.00
116 James Laurinaitis AU/399 RC 10.00 25.00
117 Malcolm Jenkins AU/399 RC 8.00 20.00
118 Brandon Pettigrew AU/399 RC 8.00 20.00
119 Juaquin Iglesias AU/399 RC 6.00 15.00
120 LeSean McCoy AU/199 RC 20.00 50.00
122 Ramses Barden AU/399 RC 5.00 12.00
123 Brian Orakpo AU/399 RC 8.00 20.00
124 Michael Crabtree AU/199 RC 30.00 60.00
125 Brian Cushing AU/399 RC 8.00 20.00
126 Mark Sanchez AU/399 RC 40.00 100.00
127 Rey Maualuga AU/399 RC 10.00 25.00
128 Stephen McGee AU/399 RC 8.00 20.00
129 Eugene Monroe AU/399 RC 5.00 12.00
130 Alphonso Smith AU/399 RC 6.00 15.00
131 Aaron Curry AU/399 RC 8.00 20.00
132 Pat White AU/399 RC 8.00 20.00

2009 UD Black Autographs

STATED PRINT RUN 10-75
SERIAL #'d UNDER 25 NOT PRICED
1 Greg Jennings/75 20.00 50.00
2 Darrell Green/25 30.00 60.00
7 Bubba Smith/75 15.00 40.00
8 Ray Lewis/25 50.00 100.00
9 Thurman Thomas/25 20.00 50.00
11 Jim Kelly/25 50.00 100.00
12 Jerry Kramer/75 15.00 40.00
13 Jonathan Stewart/25 15.00 40.00
14 Deacon Jones/75 15.00 40.00
15 Billy Sims/75 15.00 40.00
16 Anthony Munoz/25 20.00 50.00
17 Ken Anderson/75 12.00 30.00
19 Gale Sayers/25 30.00 60.00
20 Matt Forte/35 20.00 50.00
21 Jack Youngblood/75 12.00 30.00
22 Marshawn Lynch/25 12.00 30.00
26 Bob Lilly/50 15.00 40.00
27 Daryl Johnston/75 20.00 50.00
28 Randy White/25 20.00 50.00
31 Merlin Olsen/25 15.00 40.00
32 Paul Hornung/75 15.00 40.00
34 DeMarcus Ware/50 15.00 40.00
35 Brandon Marshall/25 15.00 40.00
36 Lem Barney/75 12.00 30.00
40 Kevin Smith/75 12.00 30.00
43 Steve Slaton/50 12.00 30.00
44 Peyton Manning/25 100.00 175.00
45 Earl Campbell/50 20.00 50.00
46 Reggie Wayne/25 20.00 50.00
47 Maurice Jones-Drew/50 15.00 40.00
48 Dwayne Bowe/35 15.00 40.00
49 Bob Griese/25 25.00 60.00
50 Joey Porter/75 12.00 30.00
51 Ron Yary/75 12.00 30.00
53 Alan Page/50 15.00 40.00
57 Brandon Jacobs/25 15.00 40.00
58 Marques Colston/75 15.00 40.00
59 Lawrence Taylor/25 30.00 60.00
60 Eli Manning/25 50.00 100.00
61 Don Maynard/50 12.00 30.00
63 Jason Campbell/25 12.00 30.00
64 Fred Biletnikoff/35 25.00 60.00
65 Kellen Winslow Sr./50 12.00 30.00
68 Brian Westbrook/25 15.00 40.00
70 L.C. Greenwood/75 20.00 50.00
71 Ronnie Brown/25 15.00 40.00
74 Harry Carson/75 12.00 30.00
76 Rocky Bleier/75 20.00 50.00
77 Jack Ham/25 30.00 80.00
78 Ronnie Lott/50 20.00 50.00
83 Roger Craig/75 15.00 40.00
85 Tom Rathman/75 15.00 40.00
86 Jim Zorn/75 12.00 30.00
87 Derrick Brooks/50 15.00 40.00
88 Chris Johnson/50 30.00 60.00
89 Joe Theismann/25 20.00 50.00
90 Clinton Portis/25 15.00 40.00

2009 UD Black Biography Plaque Autographs

STATED PRINT RUN 5-50
SERIAL #'d UNDER 25 NOT PRICED
BPSBL Bob Lilly/50 15.00 40.00
BPSDJ Deacon Jones/50 15.00 40.00
BPSGJ Greg Jennings/50 20.00 50.00
BPSGS Gale Sayers/25 30.00 60.00
BPSJA Jared Allen/50 30.00 60.00
BPSJK Jim Kelly/25 50.00 100.00
BPSJT Joe Theismann/25 20.00 50.00
BPSJY Jack Youngblood/50 12.00 30.00
BPSKA Ken Anderson/50 12.00 30.00
BPSKW Kurt Warner/25 40.00 80.00
BPSLA Steve Largent/25 25.00 60.00
BPSLT Lawrence Taylor/25 25.00 60.00
BPSMC Marques Colston/50 20.00 50.00
BPSMR Matt Ryan/25 40.00 80.00
BPSMT Michael Turner/25 15.00 40.00
BPSPA Alan Page/50 15.00 40.00
BPSPM Peyton Manning/25 100.00 200.00
BPSRB Rocky Bleier/25 25.00 60.00
BPSRW Randy White/50 15.00 40.00
BPSSL Steve Slaton/25 15.00 40.00

2009 UD Black Cut Autographs

CUT AUTO PRINT RUN 1-172
SERIAL #'d UNDER 20 NOT PRICED
BCBA Red Badgro/28 30.00 60.00
BCBB Bert Bell/32 30.00 60.00
BCCC Charley Conerly/172 25.00 50.00
BCDL Dick Lane/25 40.00 80.00
BCEH Elroy Hirsch/85 30.00 60.00
BCES Ernie Stautner/24 20.00 50.00
BCFG Frank Gatski/43 20.00 50.00
BCGC George Connor/81 20.00 50.00
BCGM George McAfee/88 20.00 50.00
BCGU Gene Upshaw/35 30.00 60.00
BCJP Jim Parker/24 30.00 60.00
BCLA Dante Lavelli/85 20.00 50.00
BCLC Lou Creekmur/34 40.00 80.00
BCLG Lou Groza/22 30.00 60.00
BCLN Leo Nomellini/21 30.00 60.00
BCMU George Musso/37 30.00 60.00
BCOG Otto Graham/20 40.00 80.00
BCSB Sammy Baugh/53 40.00 80.00
BCTC Tony Canadeo/34 20.00 50.00
BCTF Tom Fears/21 30.00 60.00
BCTL Tom Landry/26 125.00 250.00
BCWE Weeb Ewbank/42 20.00 50.00

2009 UD Black Dual Autographs

STATED PRINT RUN 5-35
BG Shonn Greene/25 25.00 60.00
Donald Brown
BM Drew Brees/25 100.00 200.00
Archie Manning
CJ Brandon Jacobs/35 20.00 50.00
Earl Campbell
CS Chris Johnson/35 30.00 60.00
Steve Slaton
FD Josh Freeman/25 40.00 80.00
Nate Davis
HB Darrius Heyward-Bey/35 30.00 60.00
Kenny Britt
HC Michael Crabtree/25 40.00 80.00
Graham Harrell
JD Javon Ringer/35 20.00 50.00
Devin Moore
JL James Laurinaitis/35 15.00 40.00
Malcolm Jenkins
JO Deacon Jones/35 30.00 60.00
Merlin Olsen
JW DeMarcus Ware/35 40.00 80.00
Ed Jones
LH Chuck Howley/35 30.00 60.00
Bob Lilly
MC Chase Coffman/35 25.00 50.00
Jeremy Maclin
MS Mark Sanchez/25 60.00 120.00
Rey Maualuga
MW Knowshon Moreno/25 50.00 80.00
Chris Wells
NF Brooks Foster/35 20.00 50.00
Hakeem Nicks
PC Brandon Pettigrew/35 10.00 25.00
Jared Cook
PK Alex Karras/25 25.00 50.00
Alan Page
PW Clinton Portis/25 15.00 40.00
Brian Westbrook
SF Matt Forte/35 25.00 50.00
Jonathan Stewart
SM Knowshon Moreno/25 60.00 120.00
Matthew Stafford
SS Matthew Stafford/25 100.00 200.00
Mark Sanchez
WR Chris Wells/25 25.00 50.00
Brian Robiskie

2009 UD Black Dual Player Autographs on Jersey

DUAL JSY AU PRINT RUN 15-25
SERIAL #'d UNDER 25 NOT PRICED
DPCS Earl Campbell/25 50.00 100.00
Steve Slaton
DPEL Lee Evans/25 20.00 40.00
Marshawn Lynch

2009 UD Black Film Slides Autographs

STATED PRINT RUN 9-75
SERIAL #'d UNDER 20 NOT PRICED
FSAP Adrian Peterson/28 125.00 250.00
FSBL Rocky Bleier/50 20.00 50.00
FSBS Barry Sanders/20 60.00 120.00
FSCP Clinton Portis/26 15.00 40.00
FSES Emmitt Smith/22 100.00 175.00
FSFB Fred Biletnikoff/50 20.00 50.00
FSFH Franco Harris/32 25.00 60.00
FSJT Joe Theismann/50 15.00 40.00
FSLB Lem Barney/75 12.00 30.00
FSMF Matt Forte/22 20.00 50.00
FSMR Matt Ryan/25 40.00 80.00
FSMT Michael Turner/25 15.00 40.00
FSRB Ronnie Brown/23 15.00 40.00
FSRY Ron Yary/75 12.00 30.00
FSSL Steve Largent/25 25.00 60.00
FSTO LaDainian Tomlinson/21 30.00 60.00

2009 UD Black Lustrous Materials Patch Autographs

STATED PRINT RUN 5-30
SERIAL #'d UNDER 25 NOT PRICED
LPAB Anquan Boldin/30 20.00 50.00
LPBJ Brandon Jacobs/50 12.00 30.00
LPBW Brian Westbrook/50 15.00 40.00
LPCP Clinton Portis/50 12.00 30.00
LPDB Dwayne Bowe/50 15.00 40.00
LPFG Frank Gore/30 20.00 50.00
LPGJ Greg Jennings/50 30.00 60.00
LPJO Chris Johnson/50 50.00 100.00
LPJT Joe Theismann/50 20.00 50.00
LPKS Kevin Smith/50 12.00 30.00
LPKW Kurt Warner/30 50.00 100.00
LPMC Marques Colston/50 30.00 60.00
LPMF Matt Forte/50 15.00 40.00
LPMJ Maurice Jones-Drew/50 15.00 40.00
LPMR Matt Ryan/30 40.00 80.00
LPMS Mike Singletary/50 30.00 60.00
LPPM Peyton Manning/50 100.00 175.00
LPTR Tony Romo/30 50.00 100.00

2009 UD Black Quad Autographs

STATED PRINT RUN 20
ROOKQB Josh Freeman/20 125.00 250.00
Mark Sanchez

Matthew Stafford
Nate Davis
ROOKRB Knowshon Moreno 50.00 120.00
Chris Wells
LeSean McCoy
Donald Brown
ROOKWR Hakeem Nicks/20 100.00 200.00
Michael Crabtree
Jeremy Maclin
Percy Harvin

2009 UD Black Quad Jersey Autographs

STATED PRINT RUN 5-75
UNPRICED 1/1 PATCHES EXIST
SERIAL #'d UNDER 25 NOT PRICED
1PQAH A.J. Hawk/75 12.00 30.00
1PQBJ Bo Jackson/34 50.00 100.00
1PQBY Billy Sims/75 15.00 40.00
1PQCP Clinton Portis/25 20.00 50.00
1PQFG Frank Gore/50 15.00 40.00
1PQJO Chris Johnson/75 40.00 80.00
1PQJS Jonathan Stewart/75 12.00 30.00
1PQKA Ken Anderson/25 20.00 50.00
1PQKW Kellen Winslow Sr./75 12.00 30.00
1PQML Marshawn Lynch/25 12.00 30.00
1PQMR Matt Ryan/25 40.00 80.00
1PQPS Phil Simms/75 15.00 40.00
1PQRB Ronnie Brown/25 15.00 40.00
1PQRC Roger Craig/75 15.00 40.00
1PQSS Steve Slaton/50 10.00 25.00
1PQTA Troy Aikman/25 50.00 100.00
1PQTR Tony Romo/25 40.00 80.00

2009 UD Black Quad Jersey Autographs Patch

QUAD PATCH AUTO PRINT RUN 5-50
SERIAL #'d UNDER 25 NOT PRICED
1PQAH A.J. Hawk/50 12.00 30.00
1PQBY Billy Sims/50 15.00 40.00
1PQDB Derrick Brooks/50 20.00 50.00
1PQFG Frank Gore/25 15.00 40.00
1PQGJ Greg Jennings/25 30.00 60.00
1PQJH Jack Ham/25 20.00 50.00
1PQJO Chris Johnson/50 50.00 100.00
1PQJS Jonathan Stewart/50 15.00 40.00
1PQKA Ken Anderson/25 20.00 50.00
1PQKW Kellen Winslow Sr./25 20.00 50.00
1PQMF Matt Forte/50 30.00 60.00
1PQML Marshawn Lynch/50 15.00 40.00
1PQMR Matt Ryan/25 50.00 100.00
1PQPS Phil Simms/35 20.00 50.00
1PQRB Ronnie Brown/25 20.00 50.00
1PQRC Roger Craig/50 15.00 40.00
1PQSS Steve Slaton/25 15.00 40.00
1PQTR Tony Romo/25 40.00 80.00

2009 UD Black Triple Autographs

TRIPLE AUTO PRINT RUN 5-25
HGW Shaun Hill/25 40.00 80.00
Patrick Willis
Frank Gore
PHI Donovan McNabb/15 50.00 100.00
Brian Westbrook
DeSean Jackson
RAM Merlin Olsen/25 40.00 80.00
Roman Gabriel
Deacon Jones
RBS Shonn Greene/25 40.00 80.00
Javon Ringer
Devin Moore
RUN Chris Wells/15 50.00 100.00
LeSean McCoy
Knowshon Moreno
NFCE Brian Westbrook/25 40.00 80.00
Clinton Portis
Brandon Jacobs
PASS Mark Sanchez/15 100.00 200.00
Graham Harrell
Matthew Stafford
CATCH Michael Crabtree/15 100.00 175.00
Jeremy Maclin
Percy Harvin
GENES Peyton Manning/15 250.00 400.00
Archie Manning
Eli Manning

1998 UD Choice Previews

The 1998 Upper Deck UD Choice Previews set was issued in one series totalling 55 cards. The cards were intended to give collectors a sneak preview of the "new" set that replaced Collector's Choice. The cards were packaged 6-cards per pack with 24-packs per box and no inserts.

COMPLETE SET (55) 4.00 10.00
2 Rob Moore .15 .40
4 Larry Centers .08 .25
7 Jamal Anderson .25 .60
12 Byron Hanspard .08 .25
15 Jermaine Lewis .15 .40
20 Eric Moulds .25 .60
22 Bruce Smith .15 .40
26 Rae Carruth .08 .25
28 Winslow Oliver .08 .25
32 Erik Kramer .08 .25
35 Curtis Conway .15 .40
39 Jeff Blake .15 .40
40 Carl Pickens .15 .40
49 Deion Sanders .25 .60
53 Ed McCaffrey .15 .40
55 John Mobley .08 .25
58 Scott Mitchell .15 .40
62 Bryant Westbrook .08 .25
67 Reggie White .25 .60
70 LeRoy Butler .08 .25
72 Marshall Faulk .30 .75
76 Quentin Coryatt .08 .25
77 Keenan McCardell .15 .40
80 Jimmy Smith .15 .40
84 Andre Rison .15 .40
86 Tony Gonzalez .25 .60
92 Yatil Green .08 .25
96 Brad Johnson .25 .60
98 Jake Reed .15 .40
103 Troy Davis .08 .25
104 Andre Hastings .08 .25
110 Terry Glenn .25 .60
111 Ben Coates .15 .40
115 Danny Kanell .15 .40
119 Tiki Barber .25 .60
122 Glenn Foley .15 .40
124 Kyle Brady .08 .25
129 Jeff George .15 .40
131 Darrell Russell .08 .25
136 Irving Fryar .15 .40
137 Mike Mamula .08 .25
143 Levon Kirkland .08 .25
147 Greg Lloyd .08 .25
150 Orlando Pace .08 .25
151 Isaac Bruce .25 .60
155 Natrone Means .15 .40
157 Tony Martin .15 .40
161 Merton Hanks .08 .25
165 J.J. Stokes .15 .40
168 Chad Brown .08 .25
173 Trent Dilfer .25 .60
175 Warren Sapp .15 .40
180 Steve McNair .25 .60
186 Gus Frerotte .08 .25
191 Cris Dishman .08 .25

1998 UD Choice

The 1998 UD Choice set consists of 438 standard size cards. The set is divided into Series One with 255 cards and Series Two with 183 cards. The 12-card packs retail for a suggested price of $1.29 each. The set contains the subsets: Rookie Class (193-222), DYOC Winners (223-252), and Domination Next (256-285). The Domination Next subset was randomly inserted in packs at a rate of 1:4. An SE parallel version was also produced and sequentially numbered to 2,000. The card fronts feature color action game photos within a white border. The Upper Deck logo is found in the bottom right corner with the featured player's name, number, and team in the opposite corner.

COMPLETE SET (438) 25.00 60.00
COMP.SERIES 1 (255) 12.50 30.00
COMP.SERIES 2 (183) 12.50 30.00
COMP.FACT.SER.1 (275) 20.00 40.00
1 Jake Plummer .20 .50
2 Rob Moore .10 .30
3 Simeon Rice .10 .30
4 Larry Centers .07 .20
5 Aeneas Williams .07 .20
6 Chris Gedney .07 .20
7 Jamal Anderson .20 .50
8 Michael Booker .07 .20
9 Ronnie Bradford RC .07 .20
10 Cornelius Bennett .07 .20
11 Terance Mathis .10 .30
12 Byron Hanspard .07 .20
13 Peter Boulware .07 .20
14 Jonathan Ogden .07 .20
15 Jermaine Lewis .10 .30
16 Tony Siragusa .07 .20
17 Brian Kinchen .07 .20
18 Michael Jackson .07 .20
19 Doug Flutie .20 .50
20 Eric Moulds .20 .50
21 Antowain Smith .20 .50
22 Bruce Smith .10 .30
23 Jay Riemersma .07 .20
24 Ruben Brown .07 .20
25 Fred Lane .07 .20
26 Rae Carruth .07 .20
27 Wesley Walls .10 .30
28 Winslow Oliver .07 .20
29 Tyrone Poole .07 .20
30 Lamar Lathon .07 .20
31 Anthony Johnson .07 .20
32 Erik Kramer .07 .20
33 Darnell Autry .07 .20
34 Bobby Engram .10 .30
35 Curtis Conway .10 .30
36 Jeff Jaeger .07 .20
37 Chris Penn .07 .20
38 Corey Dillon .20 .50
39 Jeff Blake .10 .30
40 Carl Pickens .10 .30
41 Ki-Jana Carter .07 .20
42 Reinard Wilson .07 .20
43 Tremain Mack .07 .20
44 Troy Aikman .40 1.00
45 Larry Allen .07 .20
46 Darren Woodson .07 .20
47 Anthony Miller .07 .20
48 Erik Williams .07 .20
49 Deion Sanders .20 .50
50 Richie Cunningham .07 .20
51 John Elway .75 2.00
52 Steve Atwater .07 .20
53 Ed McCaffrey .10 .30
54 Maa Tanuvasa .07 .20
55 John Mobley .07 .20
56 Bill Romanowski .07 .20
57 Shannon Sharpe .10 .30
58 Scott Mitchell .10 .30
59 Jason Hanson .07 .20
60 Herman Moore .10 .30
61 Luther Elliss .07 .20
62 Bryant Westbrook .07 .20
63 Kevin Abrams RC .10 .30
64 Brett Favre .75 2.00
65 Gilbert Brown .07 .20
66 Antonio Freeman .20 .50
67 Reggie White .20 .50
68 Mark Chmura .10 .30
69 Seth Joyner .07 .20
70 LeRoy Butler .07 .20
71 Marvin Harrison .20 .50
72 Marshall Faulk .25 .60
73 Ken Dilger .07 .20
74 Steve Morrison .07 .20
75 Zack Crockett .07 .20
76 Quentin Coryatt .07 .20
77 Keenan McCardell .10 .30
78 Mark Brunell .20 .50
79 Renaldo Wynn .07 .20
80 Jimmy Smith .10 .30
81 James O. Stewart .10 .30
82 Kevin Hardy .07 .20
83 Marcus Allen .20 .50
84 Andre Rison .10 .30
85 Pete Stoyanovich .07 .20
86 Tony Gonzalez .20 .50
87 Derrick Thomas .20 .50
88 Rich Gannon .20 .50
89 Elvis Grbac .10 .30
90 Dan Marino .75 2.00
91 Lawrence Phillips .07 .20
92 Yatil Green .07 .20
93 Zach Thomas .20 .50
94 Olindo Mare RC .07 .20
95 Charles Jordan .07 .20
96 Brad Johnson .20 .50
97 Cris Carter .20 .50
98 Jake Reed .10 .30
99 Ed McDaniel .07 .20
100 Dwayne Rudd .07 .20
101 Leroy Hoard .07 .20
102 Danny Wuerffel .10 .30
103 Troy Davis .07 .20
104 Andre Hastings .07 .20
105 Nicky Savoie .07 .20
106 Willie Roaf .07 .20
107 Ray Zellars .07 .20
108 Tedy Bruschi .40 1.00
109 Drew Bledsoe .30 .75
110 Terry Glenn .20 .50
111 Ben Coates .10 .30
112 Willie Clay .07 .20
113 Chris Slade .07 .20
114 Larry Whigham .07 .20
115 Danny Kanell .10 .30
116 Jessie Armstead .07 .20
117 Phillippi Sparks .07 .20
118 Michael Strahan .10 .30
119 Tiki Barber .20 .50
120 Charles Way .07 .20
121 Chris Calloway .07 .20
122 Glenn Foley .10 .30
123 Wayne Chrebet .20 .50
124 Kyle Brady .07 .20
125 Keyshawn Johnson .20 .50
126 Aaron Glenn .07 .20
127 Jomoo Forrior .07 .20
128 Victor Green .07 .20
129 Jeff George .10 .30
130 Rickey Dudley .07 .20
131 Darrell Russell .07 .20
132 Tim Brown .20 .50
133 James Trapp .07 .20
134 Napoleon Kaufman .20 .50
135 Bobby Hoying .10 .30
136 Irving Fryar .10 .30
137 Mike Mamula .07 .20
138 Troy Vincent .07 .20
139 Bobby Taylor .07 .20
140 Chris Boniol .07 .20
141 Jerome Bettis .20 .50
142 Charles Johnson .07 .20
143 Levon Kirkland .07 .20
144 Carnell Lake .07 .20
145 Will Blackwell .07 .20
146 Tim Lester .07 .20
147 Greg Lloyd .07 .20
148 Tony Banks .10 .30
149 Ryan McNeil .07 .20
150 Orlando Pace .07 .20
151 Isaac Bruce .20 .50
152 Eddie Kennison .10 .30
153 Leslie O'Neal .07 .20
154 Darren Bennett .07 .20
155 Natrone Means .10 .30
156 Junior Seau .20 .50
157 Tony Martin .10 .30
158 Rodney Harrison .10 .30
159 Freddie Jones .07 .20
160 Terrell Owens .20 .50
161 Merton Hanks .07 .20
162 Chris Doleman .07 .20
163 Steve Young .25 .60
164 Chuck Levy .07 .20
165 J.J. Stokes .10 .30
166 Ken Norton .07 .20
167 Bennie Blades .07 .20
168 Chad Brown .07 .20
169 Warren Moon .20 .50
170 Cortez Kennedy .07 .20
171 Darryl Williams .07 .20
172 Michael Sinclair .07 .20
173 Trent Dilfer .20 .50
174 Mike Alstott .20 .60
175 Warren Sapp .10 .30
176 Reidel Anthony .10 .30
177 Derrick Brooks .20 .50
178 Horace Copeland .07 .20
179 Hardy Nickerson .07 .20
180 Steve McNair .20 .50
181 Anthony Dorsett .07 .20
182 Chris Sanders .07 .20
183 Derrick Mason .10 .30
184 Eddie George .20 .50
185 Blaine Bishop .07 .20
186 Gus Frerotte .07 .20
187 Terry Allen .20 .50
188 Darrell Green .10 .30
189 Ken Harvey .07 .20
190 Matt Turk .07 .20
191 Cris Dishman .07 .20
192 Keith Thibodeaux RC .07 .20
193 Peyton Manning RC 5.00 12.00
194 Ryan Leaf RC .40 1.00
195 Charles Woodson RC .50 1.25
196 Andre Wadsworth RC .25 .60
197 Keith Brooking RC .40 1.00
198 Jason Peter RC .15 .40
199 Curtis Enis RC .15 .40
200 Randy Moss RC 3.00 8.00
201 Tra Thomas RC .15 .40
202 Robert Edwards RC .25 .60
203 Kevin Dyson RC .40 1.00
204 Fred Taylor RC .60 1.50
205 Corey Chavous RC .40 1.00
206 Grant Wistrom RC .25 .60
207 Vonnie Holliday RC .25 .60
208 Brian Simmons RC .25 .60
209 Jeremy Staat RC .15 .40
210 Alonzo Mayes RC .15 .40
211 Anthony Simmons RC .25 .60
212 Sam Cowart RC .25 .60
213 Flozell Adams RC .15 .40
214 Terry Fair RC .25 .60
215 Germane Crowell RC .25 .60
216 Robert Holcombe RC .25 .60
217 Jacquez Green RC .25 .60
218 Skip Hicks RC .25 .60
219 Takeo Spikes RC .40 1.00
220 Az-Zahir Hakim RC .40 1.00
221 Ahman Green RC 1.25 3.00
222 C.Fuamatu-Ma'afala RC .25 .60
223 Darnell Autry DYOC .07 .20
224 John Randle DYOC .10 .30
225 Scott Mitchell DYOC .07 .20
226 Troy Aikman DYOC .20 .50
227 Terrell Davis DYOC .20 .50
228 Kordell Stewart DYOC .20 .50
229 Warrick Dunn DYOC .20 .50
230 Craig Newsome DYOC .07 .20
231 Brett Favre DYOC .25 .60
232 Kordell Stewart DYOC .20 .50
233 Barry Sanders DYOC .25 .60
234 Dan Marino DYOC .25 .60
235 Dan Marino DYOC .25 .60
236 Tamarick Vanover DYOC .07 .20
237 Warrick Dunn DYOC .20 .50
238 Andre Rison DYOC .07 .20
239 Dan Marino DYOC .25 .60
240 Reggie White DYOC .20 .50
241 Tim Brown DYOC .20 .50
242 Joe Montana DYOC .25 .60
243 Robert Brooks DYOC .10 .30
244 Danny Kanell DYOC .07 .20
245 Emmitt Smith DYOC .25 .60
246 Barry Sanders DYOC .25 .60
247 Brett Favre DYOC .30 .75
248 Brett Favre DYOC .30 .75
249 Jerome Bettis DYOC .07 .20
250 Kordell Stewart DYOC .20 .50
251 Terrell Davis DYOC .20 .50
252 Drew Bledsoe DYOC .20 .50
253 Troy Aikman CL .20 .50
254 Dan Marino CL .30 .75
255 Warrick Dunn CL .20 .50
256 Peyton Manning DN 7.50 15.00
257 Ryan Leaf DN .75 2.00
258 Andre Wadsworth DN .60 1.50
259 Charles Woodson DN .75 2.00
260 Curtis Enis DN .40 1.00
261 Grant Wistrom DN .60 1.50
262 Greg Ellis DN RC .40 1.00
263 Fred Taylor DN .75 2.00
264 Duane Starks DN RC .40 1.00
265 Keith Brooking DN .75 2.00
266 Takeo Spikes DN .75 2.00
267 Anthony Simmons DN .60 1.50
268 Kevin Dyson DN .75 2.00
269 Robert Edwards DN .60 1.50
270 Randy Moss DN 4.00 10.00
271 John Avery DN RC .60 1.50
272 Marcus Nash DN RC .40 1.00
273 Jerome Pathon DN RC .75 2.00
274 Jacquez Green DN .60 1.50
275 Robert Holcombe DN .60 1.50
276 Pat Johnson DN RC .60 1.50
277 Germane Crowell DN .60 1.50
278 Tony Simmons DN RC .60 1.50
279 Joe Jurevicius DN RC .75 2.00
280 Skip Hicks DN .40 1.00
281 Sam Cowart DN .60 1.50
282 Rashaan Shehee DN RC .60 1.50
283 Brian Griese DN RC 1.50 4.00
284 Tim Dwight DN RC .75 2.00
285 Ahman Green DN 1.50 4.00
286 Adrian Murrell .10 .30
287 Corey Chavous .20 .50
288 Eric Swann .07 .20
289 Frank Sanders .10 .30
290 Eric Metcalf .07 .20
291 Jammi German RC .15 .40
292 Eugene Robinson .07 .20
293 Chris Chandler .10 .30
294 Tony Martin .10 .30
295 Jessie Tuggle .07 .20
296 Errict Rhett .10 .30
297 Jim Harbaugh .10 .30
298 Eric Green .10 .30
299 Ray Lewis .20 .50
300 Jamie Sharper .07 .20
301 Fred Coleman RC .15 .40
302 Rob Johnson .10 .30
303 Quinn Early .07 .20
304 Thurman Thomas .20 .50
305 Andre Reed .10 .30
306 Sean Gilbert .07 .20
307 Kerry Collins .10 .30
308 Jason Peter .07 .20
309 Michael Bates .07 .20
310 William Floyd .10 .30
311 Alonzo Mayes RC .15 .40
312 Tony Parrish RC .40 1.00
313 Walt Harris .07 .20
314 Edgar Bennett .07 .20
315 Jeff Jaeger .07 .20
316 Brian Simmons .10 .30
317 David Dunn .07 .20
318 Ashley Ambrose .07 .20
319 Darnay Scott .10 .30
320 Neil O'Donnell .10 .30
321 Flozell Adams .10 .30
322 Stepfret Williams .07 .20
323 Emmitt Smith .60 1.50
324 Michael Irvin .20 .50
325 Chris Warren .10 .30
326 Eric Brown RC .15 .40
327 Rod Smith WR .10 .30
328 Terrell Davis .20 .50
329 Neil Smith .10 .30
330 Darrien Gordon .07 .20
331 Curtis Alexander RC .15 .40
332 Barry Sanders .60 1.50
333 David Sloan .07 .20
334 Johnnie Morton .10 .30
335 Robert Porcher .07 .20
336 Tommy Vardell .07 .20
337 Vonnie Holliday .10 .30
338 Dorsey Levens .20 .50
339 Derrick Mayes .10 .30
340 Robert Brooks .10 .30
341 Raymont Harris .07 .20
342 E.G. Green RC .25 .60
343 Torrance Small .07 .20
344 Carlton Gray .07 .20
345 Aaron Bailey .07 .20
346 Jeff Burris .07 .20
347 Donovin Darius RC .25 .60
348 Tavian Banks RC .10 .30
349 Aaron Beasley .07 .20
350 Tony Brackens .07 .20
351 Bryce Paup .07 .20
352 Chester McGlockton .07 .20
353 Leslie O'Neal .07 .20
354 Derrick Alexander WR .10 .30
355 Kimble Anders .10 .30
356 Tamarick Vanover .07 .20
357 Brock Marion .07 .20
358 Larry Shannon RC .15 .40
359 Karim Abdul-Jabbar .20 .50
360 Troy Drayton .07 .20
361 O.J. McDuffie .10 .30
362 John Randle .10 .30
363 David Palmer .07 .20
364 Robert Smith .20 .50
365 Kailee Wong RC .15 .40
366 Duane Clemons .07 .20
367 Kyle Turley RC .40 1.00
368 Sean Dawkins .07 .20
369 Lamar Smith .10 .30
370 Cameron Cleeland RC .15 .40
371 Keith Poole .07 .20
372 Tebucky Jones RC .15 .40
373 Willie McGinest .07 .20
374 Ty Law .10 .30
375 Lawyer Milloy .10 .30
376 Tony Carter .07 .20
377 Shaun Williams RC .25 .60
378 Brian Alford RC .15 .40
379 Tyrone Wheatley .10 .30
380 Jason Sehorn .10 .30
381 David Patten RC .40 1.00
382 Scott Frost RC .15 .40
383 Mo Lewis .07 .20
384 Kevin Williams DB RC .15 .40
385 Curtis Martin .20 .50
386 Vinny Testaverde .10 .30
387 Mo Collins RC .15 .40
388 James Jett .10 .30
389 Eric Allen .07 .20
390 Jon Ritchie RC UER .25 .60
(John on back)
391 Harvey Williams .07 .20
392 Tra Thomas .07 .20
393 Rodney Peete .07 .20
394 Hugh Douglas UER .07 .20
(card #395 on back)
395 Charlie Garner .10 .30
396 Karl Hankton RC .25 .60
397 Kordell Stewart .20 .50
398 George Jones .07 .20
399 Earl Holmes .07 .20
400 Hines Ward RC 2.50 5.00
401 Jason Gildon .07 .20
402 Ricky Proehl .07 .20
403 Az-Zahir Hakim .07 .20
404 Amp Lee .07 .20
405 Eric Hill .07 .20
406 Leonard Little RC .40 1.00
407 Charlie Jones .07 .20
408 Craig Whelihan RC .07 .20
409 Terrell Fletcher .07 .20
410 Kenny Bynum RC .15 .40
411 Mikhael Ricks RC .25 .60
412 R.W. McQuarters RC .25 .60
413 Jerry Rice .40 1.00
414 Garrison Hearst .20 .50
415 Ty Detmer .10 .30
416 Gabe Wilkins .07 .20
417 Michael Black RC .40 1.00
418 James McKnight .20 .50
419 Darrin Smith .07 .20
420 Joey Galloway .10 .30
421 Ricky Watters .10 .30
422 Warrick Dunn .20 .50
423 Brian Kelly RC .25 .60
424 Bert Emanuel .10 .30
425 John Lynch .10 .30
426 Regan Upshaw .07 .20
427 Yancey Thigpen .07 .20
428 Kenny Holmes .07 .20
429 Frank Wycheck .07 .20
430 Samari Rolle RC .15 .40
431 Brian Mitchell .07 .20
432 Stephen Alexander RC .25 .60
433 Jamie Asher .07 .20
434 Michael Westbrook .10 .30
435 Dana Stubblefield .07 .20
436 Dan Wilkinson .07 .20
437 Dan Marino CL .25 .60
438 Jerry Rice CL .20 .50

1998 UD Choice Choice Reserve

COMP.CHOICE RES. (255) 400.00 800.00
*VETS: 3X TO 8X BASIC CARDS
*ROOKIES: 1.2X TO 3X BASIC CARDS
CHOICE RESERVE STATED ODDS 1:6

1998 UD Choice Domination Next SE

*DOM NEXT SE: 1.5X TO 3X BASE CARD HI

1998 UD Choice Prime Choice Reserve

*STARS: 20X TO 50X BASE CARD HI
*ROOKIES: 8X TO 20X BASE CARD HI
PRIME CHOICE RES. PRINT RUN 100 SETS
193 Peyton Manning 175.00 300.00
256 Peyton Manning DN 175.00 300.00

1998 UD Choice Mini Bobbing Head

COMPLETE SET (30) 12.50 25.00
STATED ODDS 1:4
M1 Jake Plummer .50 1.25
M2 Jamal Anderson .50 1.25
M3 Michael Jackson .20 .50
M4 Bruce Smith .30 .75
M5 Rae Carruth .20 .50
M6 Curtis Conway .30 .75
M7 Jeff Blake .30 .75
M8 Troy Aikman 1.00 2.50
M9 Michael Irvin .50 1.25
M10 Terrell Davis .50 1.25
M11 Barry Sanders 1.50 4.00
M12 Herman Moore .30 .75
M13 Reggie White .50 1.25
M14 Dorsey Levens .50 1.25
M15 Marvin Harrison .50 1.25
M16 Keenan McCardell .30 .75
M17 Andre Rison .30 .75
M18 Dan Marino 2.00 5.00
M19 Curtis Martin .50 1.25
M20 Keyshawn Johnson .50 1.25
M21 Tim Brown .50 1.25
M22 Kordell Stewart .50 1.25
M23 Greg Lloyd .20 .50
M24 Junior Seau .50 1.25
M25 Jerry Rice 1.00 2.50
M26 Merton Hanks .20 .50
M27 Joey Galloway .30 .75
M28 Warrick Dunn .50 1.25
M29 Warren Sapp .30 .75
M30 Darrell Green .30 .75

1998 UD Choice Starquest

COMPLETE BLUE SET (30) 7.50 15.00
BLUE STATED ODDS 1:1H, 20 PER FACT.SET
*GREENS: 1.2X TO 3X BASIC INSERTS
GREEN STATED ODDS 1:7
*REDS: 2.5X TO 6X BASIC INSERTS
RED STATED ODDS 1:23
*GOLDS: 20X TO 50X BASIC INSERTS
GOLD STATED PRINT RUN 100 SETS
1 Warren Moon .25 .60
2 Jerry Rice .50 1.25
3 Jeff George .15 .40
4 Brett Favre 1.00 2.50
5 Junior Seau .25 .60
6 Cris Carter .25 .60
7 John Elway 1.00 2.50
8 Troy Aikman .50 1.25
9 Steve Young .30 .75
10 Kordell Stewart .25 .60
11 Drew Bledsoe .40 1.00
12 Dorsey Levens .25 .60
13 Dan Marino 1.00 2.50
14 Joey Galloway .15 .40
15 Antonio Freeman .25 .60
16 Jake Plummer .25 .60
17 Corey Dillon .25 .60
18 Mark Brunell .25 .60
19 Andre Rison .15 .40
20 Barry Sanders .75 2.00
21 Deion Sanders .25 .60
22 Emmitt Smith .75 2.00
23 Antowain Smith .25 .60
24 Herman Moore .15 .40
25 Napoleon Kaufman .25 .60
26 Jerome Bettis .25 .60
27 Eddie George .25 .60
28 Warrick Dunn .25 .60
29 Adrian Murrell .15 .40
30 Terrell Davis .25 .60

1998 UD Choice Starquest/Rookquest Blue

COMPLETE SET (30) 15.00 30.00
BLUE STATED ODDS ONE PER PACK
*GREENS: 1.5X TO 3X
GREEN STATED ODDS 1:7
*REDS: 3.5X TO 7X
RED STATED ODDS 1:23
*GOLDS: 20X TO 40X
GOLD STATED PRINT RUN 100 SETS
SR1 John Elway 2.50 6.00
Peyton Manning
SR2 Drew Bledsoe .50 1.25
Ryan Leaf
SR3 Barry Sanders .75 2.00
Tavian Banks
SR4 Brett Favre 1.00 2.50
Vonnie Holliday
SR5 Junior Seau .30 .75
Takeo Spikes
SR6 Deion Sanders .40 1.00
Charles Woodson
SR7 Jerry Rice 2.50 6.00
Randy Moss
SR8 Reggie White .20 .50
Andre Wadsworth
SR9 Emmitt Smith .60 1.50
Fred Taylor
SR10 Michael Irvin .30 .75
Kevin Dyson
SR11 Troy Aikman .50 1.25
Shaun Williams
SR12 Jerome Bettis .30 .75
Curtis Enis
SR13 Dan Marino 1.25 3.00
Brian Griese
SR14 Steve Young .40 1.00
R.W.McQuarters
SR15 Dana Stubblefield .08 .25
Greg Ellis
SR16 Jake Plummer .30 .75
Pat Johnson
SR17 Corey Dillon .30 .75
Rashaan Shehee
SR18 Mark Brunell .30 .75
Jerome Pathon
SR19 Andre Rison .20 .50
Jacquez Green
SR20 Mike Alstott .20 .50
Jon Ritchie
SR21 Dorsey Levens .75 2.00
Ahman Green
SR22 Kordell Stewart 1.25 3.00
Hines Ward
SR23 Antowain Smith .20 .50
Skip Hicks
SR24 Herman Moore .20 .50
Germane Crowell
SR25 Kevin Greene .20 .50
Jason Peter
SR26 Keyshawn Johnson .20 .50
Marcus Nash
SR27 Eddie George .30 .75
Robert Holcombe
SR28 Warrick Dunn .08 .25
John Avery
SR29 Tamarick Vanover .30 .75
Tim Dwight
SR30 Terrell Davis .30 .75
Robert Edwards

2004 UD Diamond All-Star

UD Diamond All-Star was initially released in mid-July 2004 as a retail-only product. The base set consists of 120-cards including 30-short printed rookies. Retail boxes contained 24-packs of 6-cards and carried an S.R.P. of $2.99 per pack. Two parallel sets and a variety of inserts can be found seeded in packs highlighted by the Stars of 2004 Autographs inserts.

COMP.SET w/o SP's (90) 7.50 20.00
ROOKIE STATED ODDS 1:6
1 Michael Vick .25 .60
2 Julius Peppers .15 .40
3 Roy Williams S .15 .40
4 Ahman Green .15 .40
5 Trent Green .15 .40
6 Tom Brady .40 1.00
7 Rich Gannon .15 .40
8 Drew Brees .20 .50
9 Brad Johnson .15 .40
10 Todd Heap .15 .40
11 Chad Johnson .20 .50
12 Ashley Lelie .12 .30
13 Marvin Harrison .20 .50
14 Daunte Culpepper .15 .40
15 Amani Toomer .15 .40
16 Terrell Owens .20 .50
17 Shaun Alexander .15 .40
18 Mark Brunell .15 .40
19 Drew Bledsoe .20 .50
20 Rudi Johnson .15 .40
21 Charles Rogers .12 .30
22 Edgerrin James .15 .40
23 Randy Moss .20 .50
24 Tiki Barber .20 .50
25 Hines Ward .20 .50
26 Koren Robinson .12 .30
27 Laveranues Coles .12 .30
28 Travis Henry .12 .30
29 Carson Palmer .20 .50
30 Joey Harrington .15 .40
31 Byron Leftwich .15 .40
32 Moe Williams .12 .30
33 Chad Pennington .20 .50
34 Duce Staley .15 .40
35 Marshall Faulk .20 .50
36 Clinton Portis .20 .50
37 Marcel Shipp .12 .30
38 Eric Moulds .15 .40
39 Andre Davis .12 .30
40 Brett Favre .50 1.25
41 Fred Taylor .15 .40
42 Ty Law .15 .40
43 Santana Moss .15 .40
44 Tommy Maddox .15 .40
45 Torry Holt .15 .40
46 Peerless Price .12 .30
47 Stephen Davis .15 .40
48 Quincy Carter .12 .30
49 David Carr .12 .30
50 Dante Hall .15 .40
51 Deuce McAllister .15 .40
52 Jerry Rice .40 1.00
53 Tim Rattay .12 .30
54 Derrick Brooks .15 .40
55 Warrick Dunn .15 .40
56 Anthony Thomas .15 .40
57 Keyshawn Johnson .15 .40
58 Domanick Davis .12 .30
59 Ricky Williams .15 .40
60 Aaron Brooks .15 .40
61 Tim Brown .20 .50
62 Brandon Lloyd .15 .40
63 Steve McNair .20 .50
64 Kyle Boller .15 .40
65 Brian Urlacher .20 .50
66 Jake Plummer .15 .40
67 Peyton Manning .40 1.00
68 Chris Chambers .15 .40
69 Jeremy Shockey .15 .40
70 Brian Westbrook .20 .50
71 Matt Hasselbeck .15 .40
72 Derrick Mason .15 .40
73 Anquan Boldin .20 .50
74 Jake Delhomme .15 .40
75 Jeff Garcia .15 .40
76 Donald Driver .20 .50
77 Priest Holmes .20 .50
78 Corey Dillon .15 .40
79 Curtis Martin .20 .50
80 LaDainian Tomlinson .20 .50
81 Marc Bulger .15 .40
82 Jamal Lewis .15 .40
83 Marty Booker .15 .40
84 Quentin Griffin .12 .30
85 Andre Johnson .20 .50
86 Junior Seau .20 .50
87 Joe Horn .15 .40
88 Donovan McNabb .20 .50
89 Kevan Barlow .12 .30
90 Eddie George .15 .40
91 Eli Manning RC 6.00 15.00
92 Larry Fitzgerald RC 2.50 6.00
93 Ben Roethlisberger RC 6.00 15.00
94 Roy Williams RC 1.00 2.50
95 Derrick Hamilton RC .60 1.50
96 Kellen Winslow RC 1.00 2.50
97 Bernard Berrian RC 1.00 2.50
98 Steven Jackson RC 1.50 4.00
99 DeAngelo Hall RC 1.00 2.50
100 Kevin Jones RC .75 2.00
101 Reggie Williams RC .75 2.00
102 Michael Clayton RC .75 2.00
103 Rashaun Woods RC .60 1.50
104 Devery Henderson RC 1.00 2.50
105 Ben Troupe RC .75 2.00
106 Cedric Cobbs RC .60 1.50
107 Lee Evans RC 1.00 2.50
108 Luke McCown RC .75 2.00
109 Chris Perry RC .75 2.00
110 J.P. Losman RC .75 2.00
111 Philip Rivers RC 4.00 10.00
112 Michael Jenkins RC 1.00 2.50
113 Greg Jones RC .60 1.50
114 Darius Watts RC .60 1.50
115 Tatum Bell RC .75 2.00
116 Ben Watson RC 1.00 2.50
117 Drew Henson RC .60 1.50
118 Keary Colbert RC .60 1.50
119 Matt Schaub RC 2.00 5.00
120 Julius Jones RC .75 2.00

2004 UD Diamond All-Star Gold Honors

*GOLD VETS: 10X TO 25X BASIC CARDS
*GOLD ROOKIES: 2.5X TO 6X
STATED PRINT RUN 50 SER.#'d SETS

2004 UD Diamond All-Star Silver Honors

COMPLETE SET (12) 50.00 120.00
*SILVER VETS: 2X TO 5X BASIC CARDS
*SILVER ROOKIES: .6X TO 1.5X
OVERALL GOLD/SILVER ODDS 1:6

2004 UD Diamond All-Star Dean's List Jersey

OVERALL INSERT ODDS 1:24
DLAG Ahman Green 3.00 8.00
DLBF Brett Favre 10.00 25.00
DLBU Brian Urlacher 4.00 10.00
DLCP Clinton Portis SP 5.00 12.00
DLDC Daunte Culpepper 3.00 8.00
DLDM Donovan McNabb 4.00 10.00
DLLT LaDainian Tomlinson 4.00 10.00
DLMH Marvin Harrison 4.00 10.00
DLMV Michael Vick SP 6.00 15.00
DLPH Priest Holmes 4.00 10.00
DLPM Peyton Manning 8.00 20.00
DLRM Randy Moss 4.00 10.00
DLRW Ricky Williams 3.00 8.00
DLSM Steve McNair 4.00 10.00
DLTB Tom Brady 8.00 20.00
DLTH Torry Holt 3.00 8.00

2004 UD Diamond All-Star Future Gems Jersey

OVERALL INSERT ODDS 1:24
FGAB Anquan Boldin SP 4.00 10.00
FGAJ Andre Johnson SP 4.00 10.00
FGBJ Bethel Johnson 2.50 6.00
FGBL Byron Leftwich 3.00 8.00
FGCB Chris Brown 2.50 6.00
FGCP Carson Palmer 4.00 10.00
FGCR Charles Rogers SP 2.50 6.00
FGDC Dallas Clark 4.00 10.00
FGDD Domanick Davis SP 2.50 6.00
FGJF Justin Fargas 3.00 8.00
FGKB Kyle Boller 3.00 8.00
FGKW Kelley Washington 2.50 6.00
FGLJ Larry Johnson 3.00 8.00
FGLS Lee Suggs 3.00 8.00
FGOS Onterrio Smith 2.50 6.00
FGRG Rex Grossman 3.00 8.00
FGTC Tyrone Calico 3.00 8.00
FGTN Terence Newman 3.00 8.00
FGTS Terrell Suggs 3.00 8.00
FGWM Willis McGahee 4.00 10.00

2004 UD Diamond All-Star Premium Stars

OVERALL INSERT ODDS 1:24
PS1 Michael Vick 1.50 4.00
PS2 Brett Favre 3.00 8.00
PS3 Peyton Manning 2.50 6.00
PS4 Randy Moss 1.25 3.00
PS5 Clinton Portis 1.25 3.00
PS6 Donovan McNabb 1.25 3.00
PS7 LaDainian Tomlinson 1.25 3.00
PS8 Jerry Rice 2.50 6.00
PS9 Ricky Williams 1.00 2.50
PS10 Chad Pennington 1.25 3.00
PS11 Priest Holmes 1.25 3.00
PS12 Tom Brady 2.50 6.00
PS13 Deuce McAllister 1.00 2.50
PS14 Michael Strahan 1.25 3.00
PS15 Steve McNair 1.25 3.00

2004 UD Diamond All-Star Promo

ONE PER PACK

AS1 Eli Manning	4.00	10.00
AS2 Larry Fitzgerald	1.50	4.00
AS3 Ben Roethlisberger	4.00	10.00
AS4 Philip Rivers	2.50	6.00
AS5 Roy Williams WR	.60	1.50
AS6 Steven Jackson	1.00	2.50
AS7 Kellen Winslow Jr.	.60	1.50
AS8 Reggie Williams	.50	1.25
AS9 Sean Taylor	1.25	3.00
AS10 Chris Gamble	.50	1.25
AS11 DeAngelo Hall	.60	1.50
AS12 Kevin Jones	.50	1.25
AS13 Teddy Lehman	.40	1.00
AS14 Michael Clayton	.50	1.25
AS15 Rashaun Woods	.40	1.00
AS16 Karlos Dansby	.60	1.50
AS17 Ben Troupe	.50	1.25
AS18 Kenechi Udeze	.50	1.25
AS19 Lee Evans	.60	1.50
AS20 Jonathan Vilma	.60	1.50
AS21 J.P. Losman	.50	1.25
AS22 Michael Jenkins	.60	1.50
AS23 Greg Jones	.40	1.00
AS24 Carlos Francis	.40	1.00
AS25 Devery Henderson	.60	1.50
AS26 Michael Turner	.75	2.00
AS27 Chris Perry	.50	1.25
AS28 Keary Colbert	.40	1.00
AS29 Matt Schaub	1.25	3.00
AS30 Cody Pickett	.50	1.25
AS31 Julius Jones	.50	1.25
AS32 Tommie Harris	.60	1.50
AS33 Will Smith	.50	1.25
AS34 Vince Wilfork	.60	1.50
AS35 D.J. Williams	.60	1.50
AS36 Joey Thomas	.40	1.00
AS37 Antwan Odom	.50	1.25
AS38 Dunta Robinson	.40	1.00
AS39 Craig Krenzel	.50	1.25
AS40 Cedric Cobbs	.40	1.00
AS41 Tatum Bell	.50	1.25
AS42 B.J. Symons	.40	1.00
AS43 P.K. Sam	.40	1.00
AS44 Jerricho Cotchery	.50	1.25
AS45 John Navarre	.40	1.00
AS46 Josh Harris	.40	1.00
AS47 Will Poole	.60	1.50
AS48 Matt Ware	.60	1.50
AS49 Samie Parker	.40	1.00
AS50 Drew Henson	.40	1.00
AS51 Michael Boulware	.60	1.50
AS52 Jared Lorenzen	.50	1.25
AS53 Derrick Strait	.40	1.00
AS54 Ben Watson	.60	1.50
AS55 Ernest Wilford	.50	1.25
AS56 Darius Watts	.40	1.00
AS57 Devard Darling	.40	1.00
AS58 Bob Sanders	1.50	4.00
AS59 Stuart Schweigert	.50	1.25
AS60 Robert Gallery	.60	1.50
AS61 Mewelde Moore	.50	1.25
AS62 Johnnie Morant	.40	1.00
AS63 Bernard Berrian	.60	1.50
AS64 Kris Wilson	.50	1.25
AS65 Ben Hartsock	.40	1.00
AS66 Jeff Smoker	.50	1.25
AS67 Luke McCown	.50	1.25
AS68 Derrick Hamilton	.40	1.00
AS69 Wild Card	.60	1.50

2004 UD Diamond All-Star Stars of 2004 Autographs

STATED PRINT RUN 100 SER.#'d SETS

BL Brandon Lloyd	12.00	30.00
CC Chris Chambers	12.00	30.00
DD Domanick Davis	12.00	30.00
TG Tony Gonzalez	15.00	40.00

2004 UD Diamond Pro Sigs

UD Diamond Pro Sigs was initially released in early October 2004. The base set consists of 140-cards including 50-short printed rookie cards. Hobby boxes contained 24-packs of 6-cards and carried an S.R.P. of $2.99 per pack. One partial parallel set and a variety of inserts can be found seeded in packs highlighted by the multi-tiered Signature Collection inserts.

COMP.SET w/o SP's (90)	7.50	20.00
91-140 ROOKIE STATED ODDS 1:6		
1 Marcel Shipp	.15	.40
2 Anquan Boldin	.25	.60
3 Michael Vick	.30	.75
4 Peerless Price	.15	.40
5 Warrick Dunn	.20	.50
6 Todd Heap	.20	.50
7 Kyle Boller	.20	.50
8 Jamal Lewis	.20	.50
9 Drew Bledsoe	.25	.60
10 Travis Henry	.15	.40
11 Eric Moulds	.20	.50
12 Julius Peppers	.20	.50
13 Stephen Davis	.20	.50
14 Jake Delhomme	.20	.50
15 Anthony Thomas	.20	.50
16 Brian Urlacher	.25	.60
17 Marty Booker	.20	.50
18 Chad Johnson	.25	.60
19 Rudi Johnson	.20	.50
20 Carson Palmer	.25	.60
21 Andre Davis	.15	.40
22 Jeff Garcia	.20	.50
23 Eddie George	.20	.50
24 Vinny Testaverde	.20	.50
25 Keyshawn Johnson	.20	.50
26 Ashley Lelie	.15	.40
27 Jake Plummer	.20	.50
28 Quentin Griffin	.15	.40
29 Charles Rogers	.15	.40
30 Joey Harrington	.20	.50
31 Ahman Green	.20	.50
32 Brett Favre	.60	1.50
33 Donald Driver	.25	.60
34 David Carr	.15	.40
35 Domanick Davis	.15	.40
36 Andre Johnson	.25	.60
37 Marvin Harrison	.25	.60
38 Edgerrin James	.20	.50
39 Peyton Manning	.50	1.25
40 Byron Leftwich	.20	.50
41 Fred Taylor	.20	.50
42 Trent Green	.20	.50
43 Dante Hall	.20	.50
44 Priest Holmes	.25	.60
45 Ricky Williams	.20	.50
46 Chris Chambers	.20	.50
47 Junior Seau	.25	.60
48 Daunte Culpepper	.20	.50
49 Randy Moss	.25	.60
50 Moe Williams	.15	.40
51 Tom Brady	.50	1.25
52 Deion Branch	.20	.50
53 Corey Dillon	.20	.50
54 Deuce McAllister	.20	.50
55 Aaron Brooks	.20	.50
56 Joe Horn	.20	.50
57 Michael Strahan	.25	.60
58 Tiki Barber	.25	.60
59 Jeremy Shockey	.20	.50
60 Chad Pennington	.25	.60
61 Santana Moss	.20	.50
62 Curtis Martin	.25	.60
63 Rich Gannon	.20	.50
64 Jerry Rice	.50	1.25
65 Jerry Porter	.15	.40
66 Terrell Owens	.25	.60
67 Brian Westbrook	.25	.60
68 Donovan McNabb	.25	.60
69 Hines Ward	.25	.60
70 Duce Staley	.20	.50
71 Tommy Maddox	.20	.50
72 Drew Brees	.25	.60
73 LaDainian Tomlinson	.25	.60
74 Tim Rattay	.15	.40
75 Brandon Lloyd	.20	.50
76 Kevan Barlow	.15	.40
77 Shaun Alexander	.20	.50
78 Koren Robinson	.15	.40
79 Matt Hasselbeck	.20	.50
80 Marshall Faulk	.25	.60
81 Torry Holt	.20	.50
82 Marc Bulger	.20	.50
83 Brad Johnson	.20	.50
84 Derrick Brooks	.20	.50
85 Steve McNair	.25	.60
86 Derrick Mason	.20	.50
87 Chris Brown	.15	.40
88 Mark Brunell	.20	.50
89 Laveranues Coles	.15	.40
90 Clinton Portis	.25	.60
91 Eli Manning RC	8.00	20.00
92 Larry Fitzgerald RC	3.00	8.00
93 Ben Roethlisberger RC	8.00	20.00
94 Roy Williams RC	1.25	3.00
95 Sean Taylor RC	2.50	6.00
96 Kellen Winslow RC	1.25	3.00
97 Chris Gamble RC	1.00	2.50
98 Steven Jackson RC	2.00	5.00
99 DeAngelo Hall RC	1.25	3.00
100 Kevin Jones RC	1.00	2.50
101 Reggie Williams RC	1.00	2.50
102 Michael Clayton RC	1.00	2.50
103 Rashaun Woods RC	.75	2.00
104 D.J. Williams RC	1.25	3.00
105 Ben Troupe RC	1.00	2.50
106 Mewelde Moore RC	1.00	2.50
107 Lee Evans RC	1.25	3.00
108 Jonathan Vilma RC	1.25	3.00
109 Chris Perry RC	1.00	2.50
110 J.P. Losman RC	1.00	2.50
111 Philip Rivers RC	5.00	12.00
112 Michael Jenkins RC	1.25	3.00
113 Greg Jones RC	.75	2.00
114 John Navarre RC	.75	2.00
115 Jerricho Cotchery RC	1.00	2.50
116 Michael Turner RC	1.50	4.00
117 Drew Henson RC	.75	2.00
118 Keary Colbert RC	.75	2.00
119 Matt Schaub RC	2.50	6.00
120 Cody Pickett RC	1.00	2.50
121 Luke McCown RC	1.00	2.50
122 P.K. Sam RC	.75	2.00
123 Ernest Wilford RC	1.00	2.50
124 Will Smith RC	1.00	2.50
125 Bernard Berrian RC	1.25	3.00
126 Robert Gallery RC	1.25	3.00
127 Ben Watson RC	1.25	3.00
128 Devery Henderson RC	1.25	3.00
129 Jeff Smoker RC	1.00	2.50
130 Josh Harris RC	.75	2.00
131 Julius Jones RC	1.00	2.50
132 Dunta Robinson RC	.75	2.00
133 Tatum Bell RC	1.00	2.50
134 Cedric Cobbs RC	.75	2.00
135 Devard Darling RC	.75	2.00
136 Johnnie Morant RC	.75	2.00
137 Derrick Hamilton RC	.75	2.00
138 Darius Watts RC	.75	2.00
139 Tommie Harris RC	1.25	3.00
140 B.J. Symons RC	.75	2.00

2004 UD Diamond Pro Sigs Rookie Gold

*ROOKIES: .8X TO 2X BASIC CARDS
STATED PRINT RUN 349 SER.#'d SETS

2004 UD Diamond Pro Sigs Signature Collection

STATED ODDS 1:24
UNPRICED PLATINUM PRINT RUN 10

SCAR Antwaan Randle El	6.00	15.00
SCBB Bernard Berrian	8.00	20.00
SCBC Brandon Chillar	6.00	15.00
SCBF Brett Favre SP		
SCBH Ben Hartsock SP	5.00	12.00
SCBJ B.J. Symons	5.00	12.00
SCBL Brandon Lloyd	6.00	15.00
SCBR Ben Roethlisberger SP	100.00	200.00
SCBT Ben Troupe	6.00	15.00
SCBW Ben Watson	8.00	20.00
SCCB Chris Brown SP	5.00	12.00
SCCC Cedric Cobbs	5.00	12.00
SCCF Clarence Farmer	5.00	12.00
SCCJ Chad Johnson SP	8.00	20.00
SCCL Casey Clausen	6.00	15.00
SCCP Cody Pickett	6.00	15.00
SCDA Dante Hall SP		
SCDD Devard Darling	5.00	12.00
SCDE Derrick Mason SP	6.00	15.00
SCDH DeAngelo Hall	8.00	20.00
SCDV Devery Henderson SP		
SCDW Darius Watts SP	5.00	12.00
SCEM Eli Manning	100.00	200.00
SCEW Ernest Wilford	6.00	15.00
SCGJ Greg Jones	5.00	12.00
SCHE Todd Heap SP	6.00	15.00
SCJC Jerricho Cotchery	6.00	15.00
SCJE Jesse Palmer SP	5.00	12.00
SCJG Joey Galloway SP	6.00	15.00
SCJM Johnnie Morant	5.00	12.00
SCJN John Navarre	5.00	12.00
SCJP J.P. Losman	6.00	15.00
SCJS Jeff Smoker	6.00	15.00
SCJV Jonathan Vilma	8.00	20.00
SCKC Keary Colbert	5.00	12.00
SCKJ Kevin Jones	6.00	15.00
SCKU Kenechi Udeze	6.00	15.00
SCLE Lee Evans SP	8.00	20.00
SCLM Luke McCown	6.00	15.00
SCMC Michael Clayton	6.00	15.00
SCMJ Michael Jenkins	8.00	20.00
SCMS Matt Schaub	25.00	50.00
SCPE Chris Perry	6.00	15.00
SCPM Peyton Manning SP	40.00	80.00
SCQW Quincy Wilson	6.00	15.00
SCRA Rashaun Woods	5.00	12.00
SCRE Reggie Williams	6.00	15.00
SCRG Robert Gallery	8.00	20.00
SCRJ Rudi Johnson SP	6.00	15.00
SCRW Roy Williams WR SP	15.00	40.00
SCSJ Steven Jackson	30.00	60.00
SCSP Samie Parker	5.00	12.00
SCTH Tommie Harris	8.00	20.00
SCTR Travis Henry	5.00	12.00
SCVW Vince Wilfork	8.00	20.00
SCWM Willis McGahee SP	8.00	20.00
SCWS Will Smith	6.00	15.00
SCZT Zach Thomas SP	10.00	25.00

2004 UD Diamond Pro Sigs Signature Collection Gold

*GOLD/25: 1X TO 2.5X BASIC AU
STATED PRINT RUN 25 SER.#'d SETS

SCBF Brett Favre	125.00	250.00
SCBR Ben Roethlisberger	125.00	250.00
SCEM Eli Manning	150.00	250.00
SCPM Peyton Manning	75.00	150.00

2001 UD Game Gear

This 110 card set was issued in early fall, 2001. The set is broken down into a 90 card veteran base set and a 20-card rookie subset. The Rookie Card were numbered from 90 through 110 and had different print runs. Cards numbered 91 through 100 had a print run of 1000 sets while cards numbered 101 through 110 had a print run of 500 sets.

COMP.SET w/o SP's (90)	12.00	30.00
1 Jake Plummer	.30	.75
2 David Boston	.25	.60
3 Jamal Anderson	.30	.75
4 Shawn Jefferson	.25	.60
5 Jamal Lewis	.40	1.00
6 Elvis Grbac	.30	.75
7 Ray Lewis	.40	1.00
8 Rob Johnson	.30	.75
9 Shawn Bryson	.25	.60
10 Muhsin Muhammad	.30	.75
11 Jeff Lewis	.25	.60
12 Marcus Robinson	.30	.75
13 James Allen	.25	.60
14 Brian Urlacher	.50	1.25
15 Cade McNown	.30	.75
16 Peter Warrick	.30	.75
17 Akili Smith	.25	.60
18 Corey Dillon	.30	.75
19 Tim Couch	.25	.60
20 Kevin Johnson	.25	.60
21 Emmitt Smith	1.00	2.50
22 Rocket Ismail	.30	.75
23 Joey Galloway	.30	.75
24 Terrell Davis	.40	1.00
25 Brian Griese	.30	.75
26 Ed McCaffrey	.30	.75
27 Mike Anderson	.30	.75
28 Charlie Batch	.30	.75
29 Germane Crowell	.25	.60
30 James Stewart	.25	.60
31 Brett Favre	1.25	3.00
32 Dorsey Levens	.30	.75
33 Ahman Green	.40	1.00
34 Peyton Manning	1.00	2.50
35 Edgerrin James	.40	1.00
36 Marvin Harrison	.40	1.00
37 Mark Brunell	.30	.75
38 Jimmy Smith	.30	.75
39 Fred Taylor	.40	1.00
40 Tony Gonzalez	.40	1.00
41 Derrick Alexander	.25	.60
42 Trent Green	.40	1.00
43 Lamar Smith	.30	.75
44 Oronde Gadsden	.25	.60
45 Zach Thomas	.40	1.00
46 Randy Moss	.40	1.00
47 Daunte Culpepper	.30	.75
48 Doug Chapman	.25	.60
49 Cris Carter	.40	1.00
50 Drew Bledsoe	.40	1.00
51 Terry Glenn	.30	.75
52 Troy Brown	.30	.75
53 Ricky Williams	.40	1.00
54 Jeff Blake	.30	.75
55 Aaron Brooks	.30	.75
56 Joe Horn	.30	.75
57 Kerry Collins	.30	.75
58 Ron Dayne	.30	.75
59 Amani Toomer	.30	.75
60 Tiki Barber	.40	1.00
61 Vinny Testaverde	.30	.75
62 Curtis Martin	.40	1.00
63 Wayne Chrebet	.30	.75
64 Rich Gannon	.30	.75
65 Jerry Rice	.75	2.00
66 Tim Brown	.40	1.00
67 Duce Staley	.30	.75
68 Donovan McNabb	.40	1.00
69 Jerome Bettis	.40	1.00
70 Kordell Stewart	.30	.75
71 Marshall Faulk	.40	1.00
72 Kurt Warner	.60	1.50
73 Torry Holt	.30	.75
74 Isaac Bruce	.40	1.00
75 Doug Flutie	.40	1.00
76 Junior Seau	.40	1.00
77 Jeff Garcia	.30	.75
78 Terrell Owens	.40	1.00
79 Matt Hasselbeck	.40	1.00
80 Shaun Alexander	.40	1.00
81 Ricky Watters	.30	.75
82 Keyshawn Johnson	.30	.75
83 Brad Johnson	.30	.75
84 Warrick Dunn	.40	1.00
85 Mike Alstott	.30	.75
86 Eddie George	.40	1.00
87 Steve McNair	.40	1.00
88 Jeff George	.30	.75
89 Michael Westbrook	.25	.60
90 Stephen Davis	.30	.75
91 Mike McMahon RC	1.25	3.00
92 James Jackson RC	1.00	2.50
93 Quincy Morgan RC	1.25	3.00
94 Travis Minor RC	1.25	3.00
95 Chris Chambers RC	1.50	4.00
96 Jesse Palmer RC	1.25	3.00
97 Santana Moss RC	2.00	5.00
98 Marques Tuiasosopo RC	1.25	3.00
99 Freddie Mitchell RC	1.00	2.50
100 Kevan Barlow RC	1.25	3.00
101 Michael Vick RC	8.00	20.00
102 Chris Weinke RC	1.50	4.00
103 Reggie Wayne RC	4.00	10.00
104 Robert Ferguson RC	2.00	5.00
105 Michael Bennett RC	1.50	4.00
106 Deuce McAllister RC	2.00	5.00
107 Drew Brees RC	12.00	30.00
108 LaDainian Tomlinson RC	6.00	15.00
109 Koren Robinson RC	1.50	4.00
110 Rod Gardner RC	1.50	4.00
EJ Edgerrin James SAMPLE	.60	1.50

2001 UD Game Gear Rookie Jerseys

91-100 PRINT RUN 1000
101-110 PRINT RUN 500

91 Mike McMahon	3.00	8.00
92 James Jackson	2.50	6.00
93 Quincy Morgan	3.00	8.00
94 Travis Minor	3.00	8.00
95 Chris Chambers	4.00	10.00
96 Jesse Palmer	3.00	8.00
97 Santana Moss	5.00	12.00
98 Marques Tuiasosopo	3.00	8.00
99 Freddie Mitchell	2.50	6.00
100 Kevan Barlow	3.00	8.00
101 Michael Vick	15.00	40.00
102 Chris Weinke	3.00	8.00
103 Reggie Wayne	8.00	20.00
104 Robert Ferguson	4.00	10.00
105 Michael Bennett	3.00	8.00
106 Deuce McAllister	4.00	10.00
107 Drew Brees	25.00	50.00
108 LaDainian Tomlinson	15.00	40.00
109 Koren Robinson	3.00	8.00
110 Rod Gardner	3.00	8.00

2001 UD Game Gear Autographs

STATED ODDS 1:18

ATGS Anthony Thomas	8.00	20.00
AZGS Az-Zahir Hakim	5.00	12.00
CCGS Chris Chambers	8.00	20.00
CJGS Chad Johnson	12.00	30.00
CWGS Chris Weinke SP/390*	6.00	15.00
DBGS Drew Brees	90.00	150.00
DMGS Dan Morgan	6.00	15.00
DTGS David Terrell	6.00	15.00
DUGS Deuce McAllister	8.00	20.00
GAGS Rich Gannon SP/360*	8.00	20.00
GWGS Gerard Warren	6.00	15.00
JBGS Jim Brown SP/295*	30.00	80.00
JGGS Jeff Garcia	6.00	15.00
JLGS Jamal Lewis SP/295*	8.00	20.00
JNGS Joe Namath SP/295*	50.00	100.00
JRGS John Riggins SP/395*	20.00	50.00
KRGS Koren Robinson	6.00	15.00
KYGS Ken-Yon Rambo	5.00	12.00
LTGS LaDainian Tomlinson	25.00	60.00
MBGS Michael Bennett	6.00	15.00
MVGS Michael Vick SP/195*	40.00	100.00
PMGS Peyton Manning	50.00	100.00
RDGS Ron Dayne	6.00	15.00
RGGS Rod Gardner SP/150*	8.00	20.00
RMGS Randy Moss SP/95*	50.00	100.00
RWGS Reggie Wayne	15.00	40.00
SMGS Santana Moss	10.00	25.00
TDGS Terrell Davis	10.00	25.00
TGGS Tony Gonzalez	8.00	20.00

2001 UD Game Gear Helmets

STATED ODDS 1:108

ASH Akili Smith	5.00	12.00
ATH Amani Toomer	6.00	15.00
CDH Corey Dillon	6.00	15.00
CWH Chris Weinke	6.00	15.00
DMH Deuce McAllister	8.00	20.00
DTH David Terrell	6.00	15.00
ESH Emmitt Smith	20.00	50.00
FTH Fred Taylor	8.00	20.00
IBH Isaac Bruce	8.00	20.00
JRH Jerry Rice	15.00	40.00
JSH Jason Sehorn	6.00	15.00
KBH Kevan Barlow	6.00	15.00
KMH Keenan McCardell	6.00	15.00
KRH Koren Robinson	6.00	15.00
KWH Kurt Warner	12.00	30.00
LTH LaDainian Tomlinson	12.00	30.00
MFH Marshall Faulk	8.00	20.00
MVH Michael Vick	15.00	40.00
PWH Peter Warrick	6.00	15.00
RGH Rod Gardner	6.00	15.00
RWH Reggie Wayne	8.00	20.00
SMH Santana Moss	10.00	25.00
TAH Troy Aikman	12.00	30.00
TBH Tiki Barber	8.00	20.00
TJH Thomas Jones	6.00	15.00
DBOH David Boston	5.00	12.00
DBRH Drew Brees	25.00	60.00
MBEH Michael Bennett	6.00	15.00
MBRH Mark Brunell	6.00	15.00

2001 UD Game Gear Jerseys

STATED ODDS 1:18

AHJ Az-Zahir Hakim	3.00	8.00
BFJ Brett Favre	15.00	40.00
DBJ Drew Bledsoe	5.00	12.00
EGJ Eddie George	5.00	12.00
ESJ Emmitt Smith	12.00	30.00
JRJ Jerry Rice	10.00	25.00
MBJ Mark Brunell	4.00	10.00
MFJ Marshall Faulk	5.00	12.00
PMJ Peyton Manning	12.00	30.00
RDJ Ron Dayne	4.00	10.00
RGJ Rich Gannon	4.00	10.00
RWJ Ricky Williams	5.00	12.00
SMJ Steve McNair	5.00	12.00
TAJ Troy Aikman	8.00	20.00
TCJ Tim Couch	3.00	8.00
TGJ Terry Glenn	4.00	10.00
WCJ Wayne Chrebet	4.00	10.00
WDJ Warrick Dunn	5.00	12.00

2001 UD Game Gear Uniforms

STATED ODDS 1:18

CBU Courtney Brown	3.00	8.00
CCU Cris Carter	5.00	12.00
DCU Daunte Culpepper	4.00	10.00
DMU Dan Marino	12.00	30.00
FMU Freddie Mitchell	3.00	8.00
JAU Jessie Armstead	3.00	8.00
JBU Jim Brown	12.00	30.00
JLU Jamal Lewis	5.00	12.00
JPU Jim Plunkett	4.00	10.00
KCU Kerry Collins	4.00	10.00
RDU Ron Dayne	4.00	10.00
RLU Ray Lewis	5.00	12.00
RMU Randy Moss	5.00	12.00
THU Torry Holt	4.00	10.00
WPU Walter Payton	20.00	50.00

2000 UD Graded

Released in mid January 2001, this 160-card set features 90 base cards sequentially numbered to 1500, 45 rookie cards, numbers 91-135, sequentially numbered to 1325, the first 855 of which were graded and inserted at the rate of one in two packs, and 25 autographed rookie cards, numbers 136-165, where card numbers 136-155 are sequentially numbered to 500 and card numbers 156-165 are sequentially numbered to 250. Of the autographed rookie cards, a total of 1217 cards were not graded, and graded versions were inserted at the rate of one in six packs. Card numbers 138, 139, 147, 148, and 163 were not issued. Cards are white along the top and the bottom with grey stripes, vertical on base cards and horizontal on rookie subsets, silver foil highlights and color player photographs. Serial numbers are placed on all of the card fronts. Graded versions of this set were encased with a blue SGC label so as not to be confused with cards graded after the initial packout. Upper Deck Graded series was packaged in 6-pack boxes with packs containing three ungraded and one graded card and carried a suggested retial price of $49.99.

COMP.SET w/o RC's (90)	50.00	100.00
91-135 ROOKIE PRINT RUN 1325		
136-155 ROOKIE AU PRINT RUN 500		
156-165 ROOKIE AU PRINT RUN 250		
1 Jake Plummer	1.00	2.50
2 David Boston	.75	2.00
3 Jamal Anderson	1.00	2.50
4 Shawn Jefferson	.75	2.00
5 Qadry Ismail	1.00	2.50
6 Tony Banks	.75	2.00
7 Priest Holmes	1.25	3.00
8 Rob Johnson	1.00	2.50
9 Eric Moulds	1.00	2.50
10 Steve Beuerlein	1.00	2.50
11 Muhsin Muhammad	1.00	2.50
12 Donald Hayes	.75	2.00
13 Tim Biakabutuka	1.00	2.50
14 Cade McNown	.75	2.00
15 Marcus Robinson	1.00	2.50
16 James Allen	.75	2.00
17 Akili Smith	.75	2.00
18 Corey Dillon	1.00	2.50
19 Tim Couch	1.00	2.50
20 Kevin Johnson	.75	2.00
21 Troy Aikman	2.00	5.00
22 Emmitt Smith	3.00	8.00
23 Rocket Ismail	1.00	2.50
24 Terrell Davis	1.25	3.00
25 Rod Smith	1.00	2.50
26 Brian Griese	1.00	2.50
27 Charlie Batch	1.00	2.50
28 James Stewart	.75	2.00
29 Germane Crowell	.75	2.00
30 Brett Favre	4.00	10.00
31 Antonio Freeman	1.00	2.50
32 Dorsey Levens	1.00	2.50
33 Peyton Manning	3.00	8.00
34 Edgerrin James	1.25	3.00
35 Marvin Harrison	1.25	3.00
36 Mark Brunell	1.00	2.50
37 Jimmy Smith	1.00	2.50
38 Fred Taylor	1.25	3.00
39 Elvis Grbac	.75	2.00
40 Tony Gonzalez	1.25	3.00
41 Lamar Smith	.75	2.00
42 Jay Fiedler	1.00	2.50
43 Randy Moss	1.25	3.00
44 Daunte Culpepper	1.00	2.50
45 Robert Smith	1.00	2.50
46 Cris Carter	1.25	3.00
47 Drew Bledsoe	1.25	3.00
48 Kevin Faulk	1.00	2.50
49 Terry Glenn	1.00	2.50
50 Ricky Williams	1.25	3.00
51 Jeff Blake	1.00	2.50
52 Joe Horn	1.00	2.50
53 Kerry Collins	1.00	2.50
54 Amani Toomer	1.00	2.50
55 Tiki Barber	1.25	3.00
56 Wayne Chrebet	1.00	2.50
57 Curtis Martin	1.25	3.00
58 Vinny Testaverde	1.00	2.50
59 Tyrone Wheatley	.75	2.00
60 Tim Brown	1.25	3.00
61 Rich Gannon	1.00	2.50
62 Duce Staley	1.00	2.50
63 Charles Johnson	.75	2.00
64 Donovan McNabb	1.25	3.00
65 Bobby Shaw RC	1.00	2.50
66 Kordell Stewart	1.00	2.50
67 Jerome Bettis	1.25	3.00
68 Marshall Faulk	1.25	3.00
69 Isaac Bruce	1.25	3.00
70 Torry Holt	1.25	3.00
71 Kurt Warner	2.00	5.00
72 Neil Smith	.75	2.00
73 Ryan Leaf	1.00	2.50
74 Curtis Conway	1.00	2.50
75 Jeff Garcia	1.00	2.50
76 Charlie Garner	1.00	2.50
77 Jerry Rice	2.50	6.00
78 Ricky Watters	1.00	2.50
79 Brock Huard	.75	2.00
80 Jon Kitna	1.00	2.50
81 Keyshawn Johnson	1.00	2.50
82 Jacquez Green	.75	2.00
83 Mike Alstott	1.25	3.00
84 Shaun King	.75	2.00
85 Eddie George	1.00	2.50
86 Kevin Dyson	1.00	2.50
87 Steve McNair	1.25	3.00
88 Brad Johnson	1.00	2.50
89 Stephen Davis	1.00	2.50
90 Jeff George	1.00	2.50
91 Ron Dixon RC	2.00	5.00
92 Avion Black RC	2.00	5.00
93 Hank Poteat RC	2.00	5.00
94 Doug Chapman RC	2.00	5.00
95 Drew Haddad RC	2.00	5.00
96 Rondell Mealey RC	2.00	5.00
97 Spergon Wynn RC	2.50	6.00
98 Keith Bulluck RC	2.50	6.00
99 John Abraham RC	3.00	8.00
100 Rob Morris RC	2.50	6.00
101 Jerry Porter RC	3.00	8.00
102 Laveranues Coles RC	3.00	8.00
103 Jarious Jackson RC	2.50	6.00
104 Tom Brady RC	150.00	300.00
105 Jonas Lewis RC	2.00	5.00
106 Todd Husak RC	2.00	5.00
107 Shyrone Stith RC	2.00	5.00
108 Sammy Morris RC	2.50	6.00
109 Corey Simon RC	2.50	6.00
110 Chad Morton RC	3.00	8.00
111 Brian Urlacher RC	12.00	30.00
112 Anthony Becht RC	2.50	6.00
113 Chris Cole RC	2.50	6.00
114 Anthony Lucas RC	2.00	5.00
115 Charles Lee RC	2.00	5.00
116 JaJuan Dawson RC	2.00	5.00
117 Darrell Jackson RC	2.50	6.00
118 Gari Scott RC	2.00	5.00
119 Windrell Hayes RC	2.00	5.00
120 Paul Smith RC	2.00	5.00
121 Mareno Philyaw RC	2.00	5.00
122 Trevor Gaylor RC	2.00	5.00
123 Muneer Moore RC	2.00	5.00
124 Michael Wiley RC	2.00	5.00
125 Ronney Jenkins RC	2.00	5.00
126 Frank Moreau RC	2.00	5.00
127 Dante Hall RC	3.00	8.00
128 Darren Howard RC	2.00	5.00
129 Todd Pinkston RC	2.00	5.00
130 Mike Anderson RC	3.00	8.00
131 Doug Johnson RC	2.50	6.00
132 Shaun Ellis RC	3.00	8.00
133 James Williams RC	2.00	5.00
134 Ron Dugans RC	2.00	5.00
135 Frank Murphy RC	2.00	5.00
136 Dez White AU RC	8.00	20.00
137 Danny Farmer AU RC	6.00	15.00
140 Reuben Droughns AU RC	10.00	25.00
141 Jamal Lewis AU RC	10.00	25.00
142 J.R. Redmond AU RC	6.00	15.00
143 Tee Martin AU RC	10.00	25.00
144 Giovanni Carmazzi AU RC	6.00	15.00
145 Tim Rattay AU RC	8.00	20.00
146 Trung Canidate AU RC	8.00	20.00
149 Chris Coleman AU RC	6.00	15.00
150 Corey Moore AU RC	6.00	15.00
151 Troy Walters AU RC	6.00	15.00
152 Joe Hamilton AU RC	6.00	15.00
153 Kwame Cavil AU RC	6.00	15.00
154 Dennis Northcutt AU RC	8.00	20.00
155 Travis Taylor AU RC	8.00	20.00
156 Curtis Keaton AU RC	8.00	20.00
157 Shaun Alexander AU RC	15.00	40.00
158 Chad Pennington AU RC	20.00	50.00
159 Sylvester Morris AU RC	8.00	20.00
160 Plaxico Burress AU RC	25.00	50.00
161 Ron Dayne AU RC	12.00	30.00
162 Courtney Brown AU RC	10.00	25.00
164 Peter Warrick AU RC	12.00	30.00
165 Chris Redman AU RC	10.00	25.00

2000 UD Graded Jerseys

STATED PRINT RUN 2127 TOTAL CARDS

GBF Brett Favre	20.00	50.00
GCC Cris Carter	8.00	20.00
GDB Drew Bledsoe	8.00	20.00
GDM Dan Marino	25.00	60.00
GEJ Edgerrin James	10.00	25.00
GES Emmitt Smith	25.00	60.00
GIB Isaac Bruce	10.00	25.00
GJR Jerry Rice	15.00	40.00
GKJ Keyshawn Johnson	6.00	15.00
GKW Kurt Warner	15.00	40.00
GMB Mark Brunell	8.00	20.00
GPM Peyton Manning	20.00	50.00
GPW Peter Warrick	8.00	20.00
GRD Ron Dayne	8.00	20.00
GRJ Rob Johnson	6.00	15.00
GRM Randy Moss	8.00	20.00
GSK Shaun King	5.00	12.00
GSM Steve McNair	10.00	25.00
GTA Troy Aikman	12.50	30.00
GTH Torry Holt	8.00	20.00
GTJ Thomas Jones	10.00	25.00

2001 UD Graded

This 135 card set was issued in five card packs with a SRP of $49.99 per pack with six packs per box. The first 45 cards in the set feature leading NFL players while the other 90 cards are split with two different versions of 2001 NFL rookies. Each of these players have an action and a portrait shot. The rookies also have three different tiers of print runs: Cards numbered 46 to 55 have a print run of 500 serial numbered sets, cards numbered 56 to 65 have a print run of 750 serial numbered sets and cards numbered 66 through 90 have a print run of 900 serial numbered sets.

COMP.SET w/o SP's (45)	25.00	60.00
56-65: TWO VERSIONS SER.#'d TO 750 EACH		
1 Jake Plummer	.60	1.50
2 Jamal Anderson	.60	1.50
3 Jamal Lewis	.75	2.00
4 Rob Johnson	.60	1.50
5 Muhsin Muhammad	.60	1.50
6 Marcus Robinson	.60	1.50
7 Peter Warrick	.60	1.50
8 Corey Dillon	.60	1.50
9 Tim Couch	.50	1.25
10 Emmitt Smith	2.00	5.00
11 Terrell Davis	.75	2.00
12 Brian Griese	.60	1.50
13 Charlie Batch	.60	1.50
14 Brett Favre	2.50	6.00
15 Peyton Manning	2.00	5.00
16 Edgerrin James	.75	2.00
17 Mark Brunell	.60	1.50
18 Fred Taylor	.75	2.00
19 Tony Gonzalez	.75	2.00
20 Trent Green	.75	2.00
21 Lamar Smith	.60	1.50
22 Randy Moss	.75	2.00
23 Daunte Culpepper	.60	1.50
24 Drew Bledsoe	.75	2.00
25 Ricky Williams	.75	2.00
26 Kerry Collins	.60	1.50
27 Ron Dayne	.60	1.50
28 Vinny Testaverde	.60	1.50
29 Curtis Martin	.75	2.00
30 Rich Gannon	.60	1.50
31 Charlie Garner	.60	1.50
32 Duce Staley	.60	1.50
33 Donovan McNabb	.75	2.00
34 Jerome Bettis	.75	2.00
35 Marshall Faulk	.75	2.00
36 Kurt Warner	1.25	3.00
37 Doug Flutie	.75	2.00
38 Jeff Garcia	.60	1.50
39 Terrell Owens	.75	2.00
40 Matt Hasselbeck	.75	2.00
41 Keyshawn Johnson	.60	1.50
42 Mike Alstott	.60	1.50
43 Eddie George	.75	2.00
44 Steve McNair	.75	2.00
45 Stephen Davis	.60	1.50
46 Michael Bennett Action RC	2.50	6.00
46P Michael Bennett Portrait RC	2.50	6.00
47 Drew Brees Action RC	20.00	50.00
47P Drew Brees Portrait RC	20.00	50.00
48 Chad Johnson Action RC	5.00	12.00
48P Chad Johnson Portrait RC	5.00	12.00
49 Deuce McAllister Action RC	3.00	8.00
49P Deuce McAllister Portrait RC	3.00	8.00
50 Santana Moss Action RC	4.00	10.00
50P Santana Moss Portrait RC	4.00	10.00
51 Koren Robinson Action RC	2.50	6.00
51P Koren Robinson Portrait RC	2.50	6.00
52 David Terrell Action RC	2.50	6.00
52P David Terrell Portrait RC	2.50	6.00
53 LaDainian Tomlinson Act RC	10.00	25.00
53P LaDainian Tomlinson Port RC	10.00	25.00
54 Michael Vick Action RC	12.00	30.00
54P Michael Vick Portrait RC	12.00	30.00
55 Chris Weinke Action RC	2.50	6.00
55P Chris Weinke Portrait RC	2.50	6.00
56 Reggie Wayne Action RC	5.00	12.00
56P Reggie Wayne Portrait RC	5.00	12.00
57 Anthony Thomas Action RC	2.50	6.00
57P Anthony Thomas Portrait RC	2.50	6.00
58 Sage Rosenfels Action RC	2.50	6.00
58P Sage Rosenfels Portrait RC	2.50	6.00
59 Rod Gardner Action RC	2.00	5.00
59P Rod Gardner Portrait RC	2.00	5.00
60 Quincy Morgan Action RC	2.00	5.00
60P Quincy Morgan Portrait RC	2.00	5.00
61 Freddie Mitchell Action RC	1.50	4.00
61P Freddie Mitchell Portrait RC	1.50	4.00
62 Gerard Warren Action RC	2.00	5.00
62P Gerard Warren Portrait RC	2.00	5.00
63 James Jackson Action RC	1.50	4.00
63P James Jackson Portrait RC	1.50	4.00
64 Travis Henry Action RC	2.00	5.00
64P Travis Henry Portrait RC	2.00	5.00
65 Chris Chambers Action RC	2.50	6.00
65P Chris Chambers Portrait RC	2.50	6.00
66 Vinny Sutherland Action RC	1.50	4.00
66P Vinny Sutherland Portrait RC	1.50	4.00
67 Todd Heap Action RC	2.50	6.00
67P Todd Heap Portrait RC	2.50	6.00
68 Dan Morgan Action RC	2.00	5.00
68P Dan Morgan Portrait RC	2.00	5.00
69 Rudi Johnson Action RC	2.50	6.00
69P Rudi Johnson Portrait RC	2.50	6.00
70 Quincy Carter Action RC	2.00	5.00
70P Quincy Carter Portrait RC	2.00	5.00
71 Kevin Kasper Action RC	1.50	4.00
71P Kevin Kasper Portrait RC	1.50	4.00
72 Scotty Anderson Action RC	1.50	4.00
72P Scotty Anderson Portrait RC	1.50	4.00
73 Mike McMahon Action RC	2.00	5.00
73P Mike McMahon Portrait RC	2.00	5.00
74 Robert Ferguson Action RC	2.50	6.00
74P Robert Ferguson Portrait RC	2.50	6.00
75 Snoop Minnis Action RC	1.50	4.00
75P Snoop Minnis Portrait RC	1.50	4.00
76 Josh Heupel Action RC	2.50	6.00
76P Josh Heupel Portrait RC	2.50	6.00
77 Travis Minor Action RC	2.00	5.00
77P Travis Minor Portrait RC	2.00	5.00
78 Justin Smith Action RC	2.50	6.00
78P Justin Smith Portrait RC	2.50	6.00
79 Jesse Palmer Action RC	2.00	5.00
79P Jesse Palmer Portrait RC	2.00	5.00
80 Marques Tuiasosopo Act RC	2.00	5.00
80P Marques Tuiasosopo Port RC	2.00	5.00
81 A.J. Feeley Action RC	2.00	5.00
81P A.J. Feeley Portrait RC	2.00	5.00
82 Correll Buckhalter Act RC	2.50	6.00
82P Correll Buckhalter Portrait RC	2.50	6.00
83 Kevan Barlow Action RC	2.00	5.00
83P Kevan Barlow Portrait RC	2.00	5.00
84 Alex Bannister Action RC	1.50	4.00
84P Alex Bannister Portrait RC	1.50	4.00
85 Josh Booty Action RC	2.00	5.00
85P Josh Booty Portrait RC	2.00	5.00
86 Eddie Berlin Action RC	1.50	4.00
86P Eddie Berlin Portrait RC	1.50	4.00
87 Andre Carter Action RC	2.00	5.00
87P Andre Carter Portrait RC	2.00	5.00
88 LaMont Jordan Action RC	2.50	6.00
88P LaMont Jordan Portrait RC	2.50	6.00
89 Ken-Yon Rambo Action RC	1.50	4.00
89P Ken-Yon Rambo Portrait RC	1.50	4.00
90 Alge Crumpler Action RC	2.50	6.00
90P Alge Crumpler Portrait RC	2.50	6.00

2001 UD Graded Rookie Autographs

46-55 PRINT RUN 500
56-65 PRINT RUN 750

46 Michael Bennett	8.00	20.00
47 Drew Brees	90.00	150.00
48 Chad Johnson	30.00	60.00
49 Deuce McAllister	10.00	25.00
50 Santana Moss	12.00	30.00
51 Koren Robinson	8.00	20.00
52 David Terrell	8.00	20.00
53 LaDainian Tomlinson	60.00	120.00
54 Michael Vick	90.00	150.00
55 Chris Weinke	8.00	20.00
56 Reggie Wayne	30.00	60.00
57 Anthony Thomas	10.00	25.00
58 Sage Rosenfels	10.00	25.00
59 Rod Gardner	8.00	20.00
60 Quincy Morgan	8.00	20.00
61 Freddie Mitchell	6.00	15.00
62 Gerard Warren	8.00	20.00
63 James Jackson	6.00	15.00
64 Travis Henry	8.00	20.00
65 Chris Chambers	10.00	25.00

2001 UD Graded Rookie Jerseys

STATED PRINT RUN 500-750

46 Michael Bennett	5.00	12.00
47 Drew Brees	40.00	100.00
48 Chad Johnson	10.00	25.00
49 Deuce McAllister	6.00	15.00
50 Santana Moss	8.00	20.00

51 Koren Robinson 5.00 12.00
52 David Terrell 5.00 12.00
53 LaDainian Tomlinson 20.00 50.00
54 Michael Vick 25.00 60.00
55 Chris Weinke 5.00 12.00
56 Reggie Wayne 12.00 30.00
57 Anthony Thomas 6.00 15.00
58 Sage Rosenfels 6.00 15.00
59 Rod Gardner 5.00 12.00
60 Quincy Morgan 5.00 12.00
61 Freddie Mitchell 4.00 10.00
62 Gerard Warren 5.00 12.00
63 James Jackson 4.00 10.00
64 Travis Henry 5.00 12.00
65 Chris Chambers 6.00 15.00

2001 UD Graded Jerseys

STATED ODDS 1:2
*BLUE/125: .6X TO 1.5X BASIC JSY
BLUE STATED PRINT RUN 125
BF Brett Favre 15.00 40.00
CB Charlie Batch 4.00 10.00
CC Cris Carter 5.00 12.00
CH Chris Chandler 4.00 10.00
DB David Boston 3.00 8.00
DC Daunte Culpepper 4.00 10.00
JL Jamal Lewis 5.00 12.00
JR Jerry Rice 10.00 25.00
JS Jimmy Smith 4.00 10.00
KJ Keyshawn Johnson 4.00 10.00
KM Keenan McCardell 4.00 10.00
KW Kurt Warner 8.00 20.00
MB Mark Brunell 4.00 10.00
MF Marshall Faulk 5.00 12.00
PM Peyton Manning 12.00 30.00
PW Peter Warrick 4.00 10.00
RD Ron Dayne 4.00 10.00
RM Randy Moss 5.00 12.00
SS Shannon Sharpe 5.00 12.00
TB Tiki Barber 5.00 12.00

2002 UD Graded

This 200 card set consists of 90 veterans and 110 rookies. Cards 91-150 were serial #'d to 700, cards 151-180 were numbered to 550 and autographed, and cards 181-200 were numbered to 250 and autographed. Please note that some cards were only available as redemptions with an expiration date of 9/30/2005. Pack SRP was $49.99. Each pack contained one PSA graded rookie and 4 regular cards.

COMP.SET w/o SP's (90) 20.00 50.00
151-180 ROOKIE AUTO PRINT RUN 550
1 David Boston .30 .75
2 Frank Sanders .30 .75
3 Jake Plummer .40 1.00
4 Shawn Jefferson .30 .75
5 Michael Vick .75 2.00
6 Warrick Dunn .40 1.00
7 Chris Redman .30 .75
8 Ray Lewis .50 1.25
9 Travis Taylor .30 .75
10 Drew Bledsoe .50 1.25
11 Eric Moulds .40 1.00
12 Travis Henry .30 .75
13 Chris Weinke .30 .75
14 Muhsin Muhammad .40 1.00
15 Anthony Thomas .40 1.00
16 Brian Urlacher .50 1.25
17 Jim Miller .30 .75
18 Corey Dillon .40 1.00
19 Jon Kitna .40 1.00
20 Peter Warrick .40 1.00
21 James Jackson .30 .75
22 Kevin Johnson .30 .75
23 Tim Couch .30 .75
24 Emmitt Smith 1.25 3.00
25 Joey Galloway .40 1.00
26 Quincy Carter .30 .75
27 Brian Griese .40 1.00
28 Shannon Sharpe .50 1.25
29 Terrell Davis .50 1.25
30 Az-Zahir Hakim .30 .75
31 Germane Crowell .30 .75
32 Mike McMahon .30 .75
33 Ahman Green .40 1.00
34 Brett Favre 1.25 3.00
35 Terry Glenn .40 1.00
36 Jermaine Lewis .30 .75
37 James Allen .30 .75
38 Edgerrin James .40 1.00
39 Marvin Harrison .50 1.25
40 Peyton Manning 1.00 2.50
41 Fred Taylor .40 1.00
42 Jimmy Smith .40 1.00
43 Mark Brunell .40 1.00
44 Priest Holmes .50 1.25
45 Trent Green .40 1.00
46 Chris Chambers .40 1.00
47 Jay Fiedler .40 1.00
48 Ricky Williams .40 1.00
49 Daunte Culpepper .40 1.00
50 Michael Bennett .40 1.00
51 Randy Moss .50 1.25
52 Antowain Smith .40 1.00
53 Tom Brady 1.25 3.00
54 Troy Brown .40 1.00
55 Aaron Brooks .40 1.00
56 Deuce McAllister .40 1.00
57 Joe Horn .40 1.00
58 Kerry Collins .40 1.00
59 Ron Dayne .40 1.00
60 Chad Pennington .50 1.25
61 Curtis Martin .50 1.25
62 Vinny Testaverde .40 1.00
63 Jerry Rice 1.00 2.50
64 Rich Gannon .40 1.00
65 Tim Brown .50 1.25
66 Donovan McNabb .50 1.25
67 Duce Staley .40 1.00
68 Freddie Mitchell .30 .75
69 Hines Ward .50 1.25
70 Jerome Bettis .50 1.25
71 Kordell Stewart .40 1.00
72 Doug Flutie .50 1.25
73 Drew Brees .75 2.00
74 LaDainian Tomlinson .60 1.50
75 Garrison Hearst .40 1.00
76 Jeff Garcia .40 1.00
77 Terrell Owens .50 1.25
78 Koren Robinson .30 .75
79 Shaun Alexander .40 1.00
80 Trent Dilfer .40 1.00
81 Isaac Bruce .50 1.25
82 Kurt Warner .50 1.25
83 Marshall Faulk .50 1.25
84 Brad Johnson .40 1.00
85 Keyshawn Johnson .40 1.00
86 Rob Johnson .40 1.00
87 Eddie George .40 1.00
88 Steve McNair .50 1.25
89 Rod Gardner .30 .75
90 Stephen Davis .40 1.00
91 Daniel Graham A RC 1.50 4.00
92 Josh McCown A RC 2.00 5.00
93 Josh Scobey A RC 1.50 4.00
94 T.J. Duckett A RC 2.00 5.00
95 Ronald Curry A RC 1.50 4.00
96 Kalimba Edwards A RC 1.50 4.00
97 Chester Taylor A RC 2.00 5.00
98 Randy Fasani A RC 1.50 4.00
99 Adrian Peterson A RC 2.00 5.00
100 Chad Hutchinson A RC 1.25 3.00
101 Javon Walker A RC 2.00 5.00
102 Jonathan Wells A RC 2.00 5.00
103 David Garrard A RC 2.50 6.00
104 Leonard Henry A RC 1.25 3.00
105 Dusty Bonner A RC 1.25 3.00
106 Donte Stallworth A RC 2.00 5.00
107 J.T. O'Sullivan A RC 1.50 4.00
108 Mike Williams A RC 1.25 3.00
109 Tim Carter A RC 1.50 4.00
110 Larry Ned A RC 1.25 3.00
111 Brian Westbrook A RC 3.00 8.00
112 Freddie Milons A RC 1.25 3.00
113 Ed Reed A RC 8.00 20.00
114 Antwaan Randle El A RC 2.00 5.00
115 Julius Peppers A RC 4.00 10.00
116 Quentin Jammer A RC 2.00 5.00
117 John Henderson A RC 1.50 4.00
118 Travis Stephens A RC 1.25 3.00
119 Ladell Betts A RC 2.00 5.00
120 Cliff Russell A RC 1.25 3.00
121 Daniel Graham P RC 1.50 4.00
122 Josh McCown P RC 2.00 5.00
123 Josh Scobey P RC 1.50 4.00
124 T.J. Duckett P RC 2.00 5.00
125 Ronald Curry P RC 1.50 4.00
126 Kalimba Edwards P RC 1.50 4.00
127 Chester Taylor P RC 2.00 5.00
128 Randy Fasani P RC 1.50 4.00
129 Adrian Peterson P RC 2.00 5.00
130 Chad Hutchinson P RC 1.25 3.00
131 Javon Walker P RC 2.00 5.00
132 Jonathan Wells P RC 2.00 5.00
133 David Garrard P RC 2.50 6.00
134 Leonard Henry P RC 1.25 3.00
135 Dusty Bonner P RC 1.25 3.00
136 Donte Stallworth P RC 2.00 5.00
137 J.T. O'Sullivan P RC 1.50 4.00
138 Mike Williams P RC 1.25 3.00
139 Tim Carter P RC 1.50 4.00
140 Larry Ned P RC 1.25 3.00
141 Brian Westbrook P RC 3.00 8.00
142 Freddie Milons P RC 1.25 3.00
143 Ed Reed P RC 8.00 20.00
144 Antwaan Randle El P RC 2.00 5.00
145 Julius Peppers P RC 4.00 10.00
146 Quentin Jammer P RC 2.00 5.00
147 John Henderson P RC 1.50 4.00
148 Travis Stephens P RC 1.25 3.00
149 Ladell Betts P RC 2.00 5.00
150 Cliff Russell P RC 1.25 3.00
151 Ron Johnson A AU RC 6.00 15.00
152 Josh Reed A AU RC 6.00 15.00
153 DeShaun Foster A AU RC 8.00 20.00
154 Andre Davis A AU RC 6.00 15.00
155 Antonio Bryant A AU RC 8.00 20.00
156 Roy Williams A AU RC 8.00 20.00
157 Woody Dantzler A AU RC 6.00 15.00
158 Luke Staley A AU RC 5.00 12.00
159 Jabar Gaffney A AU RC 8.00 20.00
160 Rohan Davey A AU RC 8.00 20.00
161 Brandon Doman A AU RC 5.00 12.00
162 Napoleon Harris A AU RC 6.00 15.00
163 Reche Caldwell A AU RC 8.00 20.00
164 Kelly Campbell A AU RC 6.00 15.00
165 Eric Crouch A AU RC 8.00 20.00
166 Ron Johnson P AU RC 6.00 15.00
167 Josh Reed P AU RC 6.00 15.00
168 DeShaun Foster P AU RC 8.00 20.00
169 Andre Davis P AU RC 6.00 15.00
170 Antonio Bryant P AU RC 8.00 20.00
171 Roy Williams P AU RC 8.00 20.00
172 Woody Dantzler P AU RC 6.00 15.00
173 Luke Staley P AU RC 5.00 12.00
174 Jabar Gaffney P AU RC 8.00 20.00
175 Rohan Davey P AU RC 8.00 20.00
176 Brandon Doman P AU RC 5.00 12.00
177 Napoleon Harris P AU RC 6.00 15.00
178 Reche Caldwell P AU RC 8.00 20.00
179 Kelly Campbell P AU RC 6.00 15.00
180 Eric Crouch P AU RC 8.00 20.00
181 Kurt Kittner A AU RC 6.00 15.00
182 Jeremy Shockey A AU RC 15.00 40.00
183 William Green A AU RC 8.00 20.00
184 Clinton Portis A AU RC 12.00 30.00
185 Ashley Lelie A AU RC 8.00 20.00
186 Joey Harrington A AU RC 10.00 25.00
187 David Carr A AU RC 10.00 25.00
188 Maurice Morris A AU RC 8.00 20.00
189 Marquise Walker A AU RC 6.00 15.00
190 Patrick Ramsey A AU RC 10.00 25.00
191 Kurt Kittner P AU RC 6.00 15.00
192 Jeremy Shockey P AU RC 15.00 40.00
193 William Green P AU RC 8.00 20.00
194 Clinton Portis P AU RC 12.00 30.00
195 Ashley Lelie P AU RC 8.00 20.00
196 Joey Harrington P AU RC 10.00 25.00
197 David Carr P AU RC 10.00 25.00
198 Maurice Morris P AU RC 8.00 20.00
199 Marquise Walker P AU RC 6.00 15.00
200 Patrick Ramsey P AU RC 10.00 25.00

2002 UD Graded Gold

*1-90 VETS: 5X TO 12X BASIC CARDS
*91-150 ROOKIES: 1X TO 2.5X
*151-180 ROOKIES: .8X TO 2X
*181-200 ROOKIES: .6X TO 1.5X
GOLD PRINT RUN 75 SER.#'d SETS

2002 UD Graded Dual Game Jerseys

STATED PRINT RUN 100 SER.#'d SETS
BP100 Drew Bledsoe 8.00 20.00
Peerless Price
BS100 Mark Brunell 6.00 15.00
Jimmy Smith
BT100 Drew Brees 12.00 30.00
LaDainianTomlinson
CM100 Daunte Culpepper 8.00 20.00
Randy Moss
FC100 Jay Fiedler 6.00 15.00
Chris Chambers
FS100 Junior Seau 8.00 20.00
Doug Flutie
GR100 Rich Gannon 15.00 40.00
Jerry Rice
JC100 Tim Couch 5.00 12.00
Kevin Johnson
JP100 Michael Pittman 6.00 15.00
Keyshawn Johnson
MJ100 Peyton Manning 15.00 40.00
Edgerrin James
MT100 Curtis Martin 8.00 20.00
Vinny Testaverde
PB100 Jake Plummer 6.00 15.00
David Boston
SB100 Kordell Stewart 6.00 15.00
Kendrell Bell
SS100 Corey Simon 6.00 15.00
Duce Staley
TB100 Anthony Thomas 6.00 15.00
Marty Booker
WF100 Brett Favre 20.00 50.00
Kurt Warner
WH100 Kurt Warner 8.00 20.00
Torry Holt

2002 UD Graded Jerseys

STATED PRINT RUN 50-200
UNPRICED GOLD PRINT RUN 10-15
G1AN Mike Anderson/200 3.00 8.00
G1BA Brad Johnson/200 3.00 8.00
G1BL Drew Bledsoe/200 4.00 10.00
G1BO David Boston/200 2.50 6.00
G1BR Drew Brees/200 6.00 15.00
G1BU Brian Urlacher/200 4.00 10.00
G1CM Curtis Martin/200 4.00 10.00
G1CP Chad Pennington/200 4.00 10.00
G1CW Chris Weinke/200 2.50 6.00
G1DB Drew Bledsoe/200 4.00 10.00
G1DF Doug Flutie/200 4.00 10.00
G1EG Eddie George/200 3.00 8.00
G1EJ Edgerrin James/200 3.00 8.00
G1JJ J.J. Stokes/200 2.50 6.00
G1JS Junior Seau/200 4.00 10.00
G1KJ Keyshawn Johnson/200 3.00 8.00
G1KW Kurt Warner/200 4.00 10.00
G1LT LaDainian Tomlinson/200 5.00 12.00
G1MA Mike Alstott/200 3.00 8.00
G1MB Mark Brunell/200 3.00 8.00
G1MF Marshall Faulk/200 4.00 10.00
G1MN Peyton Manning/200 8.00 20.00
G1MO Johnnie Morton/200 3.00 8.00
G1MS Michael Strahan/200 4.00 10.00
G1PH Priest Holmes/200 4.00 10.00
G1PM Peyton Manning/200 8.00 20.00
G1RA Ron Dayne/200 3.00 8.00
G1RD Ron Dayne/200 3.00 8.00
G1RG Rich Gannon/200 3.00 8.00
G1RG Rod Gardner/200 2.50 6.00
G1RM Randy Moss/200 4.00 10.00
G1SD Stephen Davis/200 3.00 8.00
G1SE Junior Seau/200 4.00 10.00
G1SM Steve McNair/200 4.00 10.00
G1TC Tim Couch/200 2.50 6.00
G1TD Terrell Davis/200 4.00 10.00
G1TG Trent Green/200 3.00 8.00
G1TJ Thomas Jones/200 4.00 10.00
G1TO Terrell Owens/200 4.00 10.00
G1TT Travis Taylor/200 2.50 6.00
G1VT Vinny Testaverde/200 3.00 8.00
G1WE Chris Weinke/200 2.50 6.00
G2DB Drew Bledsoe/100 5.00 12.00
G2EJ Edgerrin James/100 4.00 10.00
G2JP Jake Plummer/100 4.00 10.00
G2JR Jerry Rice/100 10.00 25.00
G2KW Kurt Warner/100 5.00 12.00
G2RM Randy Moss/100 5.00 12.00
G2SD Stephen Davis/100 4.00 10.00
G2SM Steve McNair/100 5.00 12.00
G2TC Tim Couch/100 3.00 8.00
G2TO Terrell Owens/100 5.00 12.00
G3BO David Boston/50 4.00 10.00
G3CA David Carr/50 6.00 15.00
G3CB Champ Bailey/50 6.00 15.00
G3CM Curtis Martin/50 6.00 15.00
G3CO Courtney Brown/50 4.00 10.00
G3DS Duce Staley/50 5.00 12.00
G3EG Eddie George/50 5.00 12.00
G3EJ Edgerrin James/50 5.00 12.00
G3IB Isaac Bruce/50 6.00 15.00
G3KS Kordell Stewart/50 5.00 12.00
G3KW Kurt Warner/50 6.00 15.00
G3MB Mark Brunell/50 5.00 12.00
G3MH Marvin Harrison/50 6.00 15.00
G3PM Peyton Manning/50 12.00 30.00
G3RD Ron Dayne/50 5.00 12.00
G3RG Rich Gannon/50 5.00 12.00
G3RM Randy Moss/50 6.00 15.00
G3SM Steve McNair/50 6.00 15.00
G3TB Tim Brown/50 6.00 15.00
G3TC Tim Couch/50 4.00 10.00
G3TD Terrell Davis/50 6.00 15.00
G3TO Terrell Owens/50 6.00 15.00
G4AT Anthony Thomas/75 4.00 10.00
G4BF Brett Favre/75 12.00 30.00
G4BO David Boston/75 3.00 8.00
G4BR Drew Brees/75 8.00 20.00
G4CM Curtis Martin/75 5.00 12.00
G4DB Drew Bledsoe/75 5.00 12.00
G4DC Daunte Culpepper/75 4.00 10.00
G4DF Doug Flutie/75 5.00 12.00
G4DM Dan Marino/75 12.00 30.00
G4DS Duce Staley/75 4.00 10.00
G4EJ Edgerrin James/75 4.00 10.00
G4EM Eric Moulds/75 4.00 10.00
G4FO DeShaun Foster/75 5.00 12.00
G4IB Isaac Bruce/75 5.00 12.00
G4JE John Elway/75 10.00 25.00
G4JH Joey Harrington/75 5.00 12.00
G4JP Jake Plummer/75 4.00 10.00
G4JR Jerry Rice/75 10.00 25.00
G4JS James Stewart/75 3.00 8.00
G4KS Kordell Stewart/75 4.00 10.00
G4KW Kurt Warner/75 5.00 12.00
G4MB Mark Brunell/75 4.00 10.00
G4MH Marvin Harrison/75 5.00 12.00
G4PM Peyton Manning/75 10.00 25.00
G4PR Patrick Ramsey/75 5.00 12.00
G4RG Rich Gannon/75 4.00 10.00
G4SD Stephen Davis/75 4.00 10.00
G4SM Steve McNair/75 5.00 12.00
G4TH Torry Holt/75 5.00 12.00
G4WS Warren Sapp/75 4.00 10.00
G5AT Anthony Thomas/75 4.00 10.00
G5BF Brett Favre/75 12.00 30.00
G5BO David Boston/75 3.00 8.00
G5BU Brian Urlacher/75 5.00 12.00
G5CA David Carr/75 5.00 12.00
G5CM Curtis Martin/75 5.00 12.00
G5CP Chad Pennington/75 5.00 12.00
G5DC Daunte Culpepper/75 4.00 10.00
G5DF Doug Flutie/75 5.00 12.00
G5EM Eric Moulds/75 4.00 10.00
G5JH Joey Harrington/75 5.00 12.00
G5JL Jamal Lewis/75 4.00 10.00
G5JP Jake Plummer/75 4.00 10.00
G5JR Jerry Rice/75 10.00 25.00
G5JS James Stewart/75 3.00 8.00
G5KJ Keyshawn Johnson/75 4.00 10.00
G5KW Kurt Warner/75 5.00 12.00
G5LT LaDainian Tomlinson/75 6.00 15.00
G5MB Mark Brunell/75 4.00 10.00
G5PM Peyton Manning/75 10.00 25.00
G5RL Ray Lewis/75 5.00 12.00
G5WD Warrick Dunn/75 4.00 10.00
G6AT Anthony Thomas/50 5.00 12.00
G6BF Brett Favre/50 15.00 40.00
G6BO David Boston/50 4.00 10.00
G6CG Charlie Garner/50 5.00 12.00
G6DC David Carr/50 6.00 15.00
G6DF Doug Flutie/50 6.00 15.00
G6JR Jerry Rice/50 12.00 30.00
G6KW Kurt Warner/50 6.00 15.00
G6LT LaDainian Tomlinson/50 8.00 20.00
G6TJ Thomas Jones/50 6.00 15.00

2002 UD Graded Rookie Jerseys

STATED PRINT RUN 50-350
*GOLD/125: .5X TO 1.2X JSY/350
GOLD PRINT RUN 10-125
AB500 Antonio Bryant 4.00 10.00
AD500 Andre Davis 3.00 8.00
AL500 Ashley Lelie 3.00 8.00
CP500 Clinton Portis 5.00 12.00
CR500 Cliff Russell 2.50 6.00
DC500 David Carr 4.00 10.00
DF500 DeShaun Foster 4.00 10.00
DG500 Daniel Graham 3.00 8.00
DS500 Donte Stallworth 4.00 10.00
EC500 Eric Crouch 4.00 10.00
EL500 Antwaan Randle El 4.00 10.00
JG500 Jabar Gaffney 4.00 10.00
JH500 Joey Harrington/50 6.00 15.00
JM500 Josh McCown 4.00 10.00
JP500 Julius Peppers 8.00 20.00
JR500 Josh Reed 3.00 8.00
JS500 Jeremy Shockey 6.00 15.00
LB500 Ladell Betts 4.00 10.00
MM500 Maurice Morris 3.00 8.00
MW500 Marquise Walker 2.50 6.00
PR500 Patrick Ramsey 4.00 10.00
RC500 Reche Caldwell 4.00 10.00
RD500 Rohan Davey 4.00 10.00
RJ500 Ron Johnson 3.00 8.00
RW500 Roy Williams 4.00 10.00
TC500 Tim Carter 3.00 8.00
TJ500 T.J. Duckett 4.00 10.00
TS500 Travis Stephens 2.50 6.00
WA500 Javon Walker 4.00 10.00
WG500 William Green 3.00 8.00
RGDC David Carr/50 6.00 15.00
RGDS Donte Stallworth/50 6.00 15.00
RGJP Julius Peppers/50 12.00 30.00
RGWG William Green/50 5.00 12.00

1999 UD Ionix

The 1999 Upper Deck Ionix set was issued in one series for a total of 90 cards and was distributed in four-card packs with a suggested retail price of $4.99. The fronts feature action color photos of 60 veterans and 30 rookies printed on thick, double-laminated metalized cards.. The Rookie subset cards have an insertion rate of 1:4 packs.

COMPLETE SET (90) 40.00 100.00
COMP.SET w/o SP's (60) 12.50 25.00
1 Jake Plummer .30 .75
2 Adrian Murrell .30 .75
3 Jamal Anderson .30 .75
4 Chris Chandler .30 .75
5 Priest Holmes .40 1.00
6 Michael Jackson .25 .60
7 Antowain Smith .25 .60
8 Doug Flutie .40 1.00
9 Tim Biakabutuka .30 .75
10 Muhsin Muhammad .30 .75
11 Erik Kramer .30 .75
12 Curtis Enis .25 .60
13 Corey Dillon .30 .75
14 Ty Detmer .30 .75
15 Justin Armour .25 .60
16 Troy Aikman .60 1.50
17 Emmitt Smith 1.00 2.50
18 John Elway 1.25 3.00
19 Terrell Davis .40 1.00
20 Barry Sanders 1.00 2.50
21 Charlie Batch .30 .75
22 Brett Favre 1.25 3.00
23 Dorsey Levens .30 .75
24 Marshall Faulk .40 1.00
25 Peyton Manning 1.25 3.00
26 Mark Brunell .30 .75
27 Fred Taylor .30 .75
28 Elvis Grbac .25 .60
29 Andre Rison .30 .75
30 Dan Marino 1.25 3.00
31 Karim Abdul-Jabbar .30 .75
32 Randall Cunningham .40 1.00
33 Randy Moss .40 1.00
34 Drew Bledsoe .40 1.00
35 Terry Glenn .30 .75
36 Danny Wuerffel .30 .75
37 Kent Graham .25 .60
38 Gary Brown .25 .60
39 Vinny Testaverde .30 .75
40 Keyshawn Johnson .30 .75
41 Napoleon Kaufman .25 .60
42 Tim Brown .40 1.00
43 Koy Detmer .25 .60
44 Duce Staley .30 .75
45 Kordell Stewart .30 .75
46 Jerome Bettis .40 1.00
47 Isaac Bruce .40 1.00
48 Robert Holcombe .25 .60
49 Jim Harbaugh .30 .75
50 Natrone Means .30 .75
51 Steve Young .50 1.25
52 Jerry Rice .75 2.00
53 Jon Kitna .30 .75
54 Joey Galloway .30 .75
55 Warrick Dunn .30 .75
56 Trent Dilfer .30 .75
57 Steve McNair .40 1.00
58 Eddie George .30 .75
59 Skip Hicks .25 .60
60 Michael Westbrook .25 .60
61 Tim Couch RC .75 2.00
62 Ricky Williams RC 1.25 3.00
63 Daunte Culpepper RC .75 2.00
64 Akili Smith RC .60 1.50
65 Donovan McNabb RC 4.00 10.00
66 Michael Bishop RC .60 1.50
67 Brock Huard RC .60 1.50
68 Torry Holt RC 1.25 3.00
69 Cade McNown RC .60 1.50
70 Shaun King RC .60 1.50
71 Champ Bailey RC 1.50 4.00
72 Chris Claiborne RC .50 1.25
73 Jevon Kearse RC .75 2.00
74 D'Wayne Bates RC .50 1.25
75 David Boston RC .60 1.50
76 Edgerrin James RC 1.00 2.50
77 Sedrick Irvin RC .50 1.25
78 Dameane Douglas RC .50 1.25
79 Troy Edwards RC .60 1.50
80 Ebenezer Ekuban RC .50 1.25
81 Kevin Faulk RC .75 2.00
82 Joe Germaine RC .60 1.50
83 Kevin Johnson RC .60 1.50
84 Andy Katzenmoyer RC .60 1.50
85 Rob Konrad RC .50 1.25
86 Chris McAlister RC .60 1.50
87 Peerless Price RC .60 1.50
88 Tai Streets RC .60 1.50
89 Autry Denson RC .50 1.25
90 Amos Zereoue RC .60 1.50

1999 UD Ionix Reciprocal

COMPLETE SET (90) 200.00 400.00
*RECIP.STARS 1-60: 1.2X TO 3X
RECIP.1-60 STATED ODDS 1:6
*RECIPROCAL 61-90: .6X TO 1.5X
RECIP.61-90 STATED ODDS 1:19

1999 UD Ionix Astronomix

COMPLETE SET (25) 100.00 200.00
STATED ODDS 1:23
A1 Keyshawn Johnson 2.50 6.00
A2 Emmitt Smith 5.00 12.00
A3 Eddie George 2.50 6.00
A4 Fred Taylor 2.50 6.00
A5 Peyton Manning 8.00 20.00
A6 John Elway 8.00 20.00
A7 Brett Favre 8.00 20.00
A8 Terrell Davis 2.50 6.00
A9 Mark Brunell 2.50 6.00
A10 Dan Marino 8.00 20.00
A11 Randall Cunningham 2.50 6.00
A12 Steve McNair 2.50 6.00
A13 Jamal Anderson 2.50 6.00
A14 Barry Sanders 8.00 20.00
A15 Jake Plummer 1.50 4.00
A16 Drew Bledsoe 3.00 8.00
A17 Jerome Bettis 2.50 6.00
A18 Jerry Rice 5.00 12.00
A19 Warrick Dunn 2.50 6.00
A20 Steve Young 3.00 8.00
A21 Terrell Owens 2.50 6.00
A22 Ricky Williams 2.00 5.00
A23 Akili Smith .75 2.00
A24 Cade McNown .75 2.00
A25 David Boston 1.00 2.50

1999 UD Ionix Electric Forces

COMPLETE SET (20) 30.00 60.00
STATED ODDS 1:6
EF1 Ricky Williams .75 2.00
EF2 Tim Couch .40 1.00
EF3 Daunte Culpepper 1.50 4.00
EF4 Akili Smith .30 .75
EF5 Cade McNown .30 .75
EF6 Donovan McNabb 2.00 5.00
EF7 Brock Huard .40 1.00
EF8 Michael Bishop .40 1.00
EF9 Torry Holt 1.00 2.50
EF10 Peerless Price .40 1.00
EF11 Peyton Manning 2.50 6.00
EF12 Jake Plummer .50 1.25
EF13 John Elway 2.50 6.00
EF14 Mark Brunell .75 2.00
EF15 Steve Young 1.00 2.50
EF16 Jamal Anderson .75 2.00
EF17 Kordell Stewart .50 1.25
EF18 Eddie George .75 2.00
EF19 Fred Taylor .75 2.00
EF20 Brett Favre 2.50 6.00

1999 UD Ionix HoloGrFX

COMPLETE SET (10) 150.00 400.00
STATED ODDS 1:1500
H1 Ricky Williams 15.00 30.00
H2 Tim Couch 15.00 30.00
H3 Cade McNown 10.00 25.00
H4 Peyton Manning 30.00 80.00
H5 Jake Plummer 10.00 25.00
H6 Randy Moss 25.00 60.00
H7 Barry Sanders 30.00 80.00
H8 Jamal Anderson 15.00 30.00
H9 Terrell Davis 15.00 30.00
H10 Brett Favre 30.00 80.00

1999 UD Ionix Power F/X

COMPLETE SET (9) 20.00 40.00
STATED ODDS 1:11
P1 Peyton Manning 3.00 8.00
P2 Randy Moss 2.50 6.00
P3 Terrell Davis 1.00 2.50
P4 Steve Young 1.25 3.00
P5 Dan Marino 3.00 8.00
P6 Warrick Dunn 1.00 2.50
P7 Keyshawn Johnson 1.00 2.50
P8 Barry Sanders 3.00 8.00
P9 Tim Couch .60 1.50
P10 Ricky Williams 1.25 3.00

1999 UD Ionix UD Authentics

AS Akili Smith 25.00 50.00
BH Brock Huard 25.00 50.00
CM Cade McNown 25.00 50.00
DC Daunte Culpepper 40.00 80.00
DM Donovan McNabb 40.00 100.00
MB Michael Bishop 25.00 50.00
RW Ricky Williams 25.00 50.00
SK Shaun King 25.00 50.00
TC Tim Couch 25.00 50.00
TH Torry Holt 25.00 60.00

1999 UD Ionix Warp Zone

COMPLETE SET (15) 50.00 120.00
STATED ODDS 1:108
W1 Ricky Williams 3.00 8.00
W2 Tim Couch 1.50 4.00
W3 Cade McNown 1.25 3.00
W4 Daunte Culpepper 6.00 15.00
W5 Akili Smith 1.25 3.00
W6 Brock Huard 1.50 4.00
W7 Donovan McNabb 8.00 20.00
W8 Jake Plummer 1.50 4.00
W9 Jamal Anderson 2.50 6.00
W10 John Elway 8.00 20.00
W11 Randy Moss 6.00 15.00
W12 Terrell Davis 2.50 6.00
W13 Troy Aikman 5.00 12.00
W14 Barry Sanders 8.00 20.00
W15 Fred Taylor 2.50 6.00

2000 UD Ionix

Released as a 120-card set and a retail only product, UD Ionix features 60 base veteran cards and 60 Futuristic Rookie cards sequentially numbered to 2000. Base Issue cards are all foil and have colored backgrounds to match the featured player's team colors. Ionix was packaged in 24-pack boxes with packs containing four cards and carried a suggested retail price of $3.99.

COMPLETE SET (120) 150.00 300.00
COMP.SET w/o RC's (60) 5.00 12.00
61-120 ROOKIE PRINT RUN 2000
1 Jake Plummer .15 .40
2 Jamal Anderson .15 .40
3 Qadry Ismail .15 .40
4 Rob Johnson .15 .40
5 Eric Moulds .15 .40
6 Muhsin Muhammad .15 .40
7 Patrick Jeffers .15 .40
8 Cade McNown .12 .30
9 Marcus Robinson .15 .40
10 Akili Smith .12 .30
11 Corey Dillon .15 .40
12 Tim Couch .15 .40
13 Kevin Johnson .12 .30
14 Troy Aikman .30 .75
15 Emmitt Smith .50 1.25
16 Rocket Ismail .15 .40
17 Terrell Davis .20 .50
18 Olandis Gary .15 .40
19 Charlie Batch .15 .40
20 James Stewart .12 .30
21 Brett Favre .60 1.50
22 Antonio Freeman .15 .40
23 Peyton Manning .50 1.25
24 Edgerrin James .20 .50
25 Marvin Harrison .20 .50
26 Mark Brunell .15 .40
27 Fred Taylor .20 .50
28 Elvis Grbac .12 .30
29 Tony Gonzalez .20 .50
30 O.J. McDuffie .15 .40
31 Damon Huard .15 .40
32 Randy Moss .20 .50
33 Cris Carter .20 .50
34 Drew Bledsoe .20 .50
35 Terry Glenn .15 .40
36 Ricky Williams .20 .50
37 Kerry Collins .15 .40
38 Amani Toomer .15 .40
39 Keyshawn Johnson .15 .40
40 Vinny Testaverde .15 .40
41 Tim Brown .20 .50
42 Rich Gannon .15 .40
43 Duce Staley .15 .40
44 Donovan McNabb .20 .50
45 Troy Edwards .12 .30
46 Jerome Bettis .20 .50
47 Marshall Faulk .20 .50
48 Kurt Warner .30 .75
49 Junior Seau .20 .50
50 Jeff Graham .12 .30
51 Charlie Garner .15 .40
52 Jerry Rice .40 1.00
53 Ricky Watters .15 .40
54 Jon Kitna .15 .40
55 Mike Alstott .20 .50
56 Shaun King .12 .30
57 Eddie George .15 .40
58 Steve McNair .20 .50
59 Brad Johnson .15 .40
60 Stephen Davis .15 .40
61 Ahmed Plummer RC 1.25 3.00
62 Courtney Brown RC 1.50 4.00
63 Deltha O'Neal RC 1.50 4.00
64 Chad Morton RC 2.00 5.00
65 Corey Simon RC 1.50 4.00
66 Hank Poteat RC 1.25 3.00
67 Raynoch Thompson RC 1.25 3.00
68 Darren Howard RC 1.25 3.00
69 Rondell Mealey RC 1.25 3.00
70 Marcus Knight RC 1.25 3.00
71 Keith Bulluck RC UER 1.50 4.00
Name spelled Bullock on card
72 John Abraham RC 2.00 5.00
73 Rob Morris RC 1.50 4.00
74 Chris Redman RC 1.50 4.00
75 Joe Hamilton RC 1.25 3.00
76 Jarious Jackson RC 1.50 4.00
77 Tom Brady RC 60.00 120.00
78 Chad Pennington RC 3.00 8.00
79 Tee Martin RC 2.00 5.00
80 Giovanni Carmazzi RC 1.25 3.00
81 Tim Rattay RC 1.50 4.00
82 Marc Bulger RC 2.00 5.00
83 Todd Husak RC 1.25 3.00
84 Curtis Keaton RC 1.25 3.00
85 Ron Dayne RC 2.00 5.00
86 Shaun Alexander RC 2.50 6.00
87 Thomas Jones RC 2.50 6.00
88 Reuben Droughns RC 2.00 5.00
89 Jamal Lewis RC 2.00 5.00
90 J.R. Redmond RC 1.25 3.00
91 Travis Prentice RC 1.50 4.00
92 Shyrone Stith RC 1.25 3.00
93 Chris Hovan RC 1.50 4.00
94 Michael Wiley RC 1.25 3.00
95 Trung Canidate RC 1.50 4.00
96 Sebastian Janikowski RC 2.00 5.00
97 Brian Urlacher RC 8.00 20.00
98 Bubba Franks RC 2.00 5.00
99 Anthony Becht RC 1.50 4.00
100 Chris Cole RC 1.50 4.00
101 R.Jay Soward RC 1.25 3.00
102 Peter Warrick RC 2.00 5.00
103 Plaxico Burress RC 2.00 5.00
104 Sylvester Morris RC 1.25 3.00
105 Dez White RC 1.50 4.00
106 Travis Taylor RC 1.50 4.00
107 Trevor Gaylor RC 1.25 3.00
108 Anthony Lucas RC 1.25 3.00
109 Sherrod Gideon RC 1.25 3.00
110 Todd Pinkston RC 1.25 3.00
111 Dennis Northcutt RC 1.50 4.00
112 Jerry Porter RC 2.00 5.00
113 Ron Dugans RC 1.25 3.00
114 Laveranues Coles RC 2.00 5.00
115 Darrell Jackson RC 1.50 4.00
116 Danny Farmer RC 1.25 3.00
117 Gari Scott RC 1.25 3.00
118 JaJuan Dawson RC 1.25 3.00
119 Troy Walters RC 1.25 3.00
120 Quinton Spotwood RC 1.25 3.00

2000 UD Ionix High Voltage

COMPLETE SET (15) 4.00 10.00
STATED ODDS 1:4
HV1 Fred Taylor .50 1.25
HV2 Michael Westbrook .30 .75
HV3 James Stewart .30 .75
HV4 Keyshawn Johnson .40 1.00
HV5 Marcus Robinson .40 1.00
HV6 Charlie Batch .40 1.00
HV7 Marvin Harrison .50 1.25
HV8 Olandis Gary .40 1.00
HV9 Curtis Martin .50 1.25
HV10 Isaac Bruce .50 1.25
HV11 Jake Plummer .40 1.00
HV12 Shaun King .30 .75
HV13 Jimmy Smith .40 1.00
HV14 Muhsin Muhammad .40 1.00
HV15 Rocket Ismail .40 1.00

2000 UD Ionix Majestix

COMPLETE SET (15) 10.00 25.00
STATED ODDS 1:11
M1 Steve Young 1.00 2.50
M2 Jerry Rice 1.50 4.00
M3 Troy Aikman 1.25 3.00
M4 Emmitt Smith 2.00 5.00
M5 Vinny Testaverde .60 1.50
M6 Cris Carter .75 2.00
M7 Brett Favre 2.50 6.00
M8 Eddie George .60 1.50
M9 Herman Moore .60 1.50
M10 Drew Bledsoe .75 2.00
M11 Tim Brown .75 2.00
M12 Steve Beuerlein .60 1.50
M13 Brad Johnson .60 1.50
M14 Mark Brunell .60 1.50
M15 Randy Moss .75 2.00

2000 UD Ionix Rookie Xtreme

COMPLETE SET (15) 12.50 30.00
STATED ODDS 1:11
RX1 Trung Canidate .30 .75
RX2 Peter Warrick .40 1.00
RX3 Plaxico Burress .40 1.00
RX4 Jamal Lewis .40 1.00
RX5 Thomas Jones .50 1.25
RX6 Chad Pennington .60 1.50
RX7 Chris Redman .30 .75
RX8 Ron Dayne .40 1.00
RX9 Courtney Brown .30 .75
RX10 Corey Simon .30 .75
RX11 Shaun Alexander .50 1.25
RX12 Dez White .30 .75
RX13 J.R. Redmond .25 .60
RX14 Shyrone Stith .25 .60
RX15 Travis Taylor .30 .75

2000 UD Ionix Sunday Best

COMPLETE SET (15) 10.00 25.00
STATED ODDS 1:23
SB1 Stephen Davis .75 2.00
SB2 Brian Griese .75 2.00
SB3 Corey Dillon .75 2.00
SB4 Muhsin Muhammad .75 2.00
SB5 Charlie Batch .75 2.00
SB6 Shaun King .60 1.50
SB7 Germane Crowell .60 1.50
SB8 Drew Bledsoe 1.00 2.50
SB9 Jake Plummer .75 2.00
SB10 Torry Holt 1.00 2.50
SB11 Marcus Robinson .75 2.00
SB12 Ricky Williams 1.00 2.50
SB13 Tim Couch .75 2.00
SB14 Kevin Johnson .60 1.50
SB15 Warrick Dunn .75 2.00

2000 UD Ionix Super Trio

COMPLETE SET (15) 12.50 30.00
STATED ODDS 1:23
ST1 Peyton Manning 2.50 6.00
ST2 Edgerrin James 1.00 2.50
ST3 Marvin Harrison 1.00 2.50
ST4 Kurt Warner 1.50 4.00
ST5 Marshall Faulk 1.00 2.50
ST6 Isaac Bruce 1.00 2.50
ST7 Mark Brunell .75 2.00
ST8 Fred Taylor 1.00 2.50
ST9 Jimmy Smith .75 2.00
ST10 Troy Aikman 1.50 4.00
ST11 Emmitt Smith 2.50 6.00
ST12 Rocket Ismail .75 2.00
ST13 Brad Johnson .75 2.00
ST14 Stephen Davis .75 2.00
ST15 Michael Westbrook .60 1.50

2000 UD Ionix UD Authentics

BLUE STATED PRINT RUN 300
GOLD STATED PRINT RUN 100
*GREEN/25: 1X TO 2.5X BLUE AU/300
*GREEN/25: .6X TO 1.5X HI GOLD AU/100
GREEN STATED PRINT RUN 25
AF Antonio Freeman G 8.00 20.00
BG Brian Griese B 5.00 12.00
BJ Brad Johnson G 8.00 20.00
BU Brian Urlacher B 25.00 60.00
CA Champ Bailey B 5.00 12.00
CB Charlie Batch B 5.00 12.00
CC Cris Carter B 8.00 20.00
CN Chris Coleman B 4.00 10.00
CP Chad Pennington G 15.00 40.00
CR Chris Redman G 8.00 20.00
DA David Boston B 4.00 10.00
DF Danny Farmer B 4.00 10.00
DL Dorsey Levens G 8.00 20.00
DN Dennis Northcutt B 5.00 12.00
EJ Edgerrin James G 10.00 25.00
EM Eric Moulds G 8.00 20.00
FR Bubba Franks B 6.00 15.00
IB Isaac Bruce B 6.00 15.00
JH Joe Hamilton B 4.00 10.00
JL Jamal Lewis G 10.00 25.00
JP Jake Plummer G 8.00 20.00
KJ Keyshawn Johnson G 8.00 20.00
KW Kurt Warner G 20.00 50.00
MB Mark Brunell G 8.00 20.00
MC Cade McNown G 6.00 15.00
MF Marshall Faulk G 12.00 30.00
MH Marvin Harrison G 10.00 25.00
MW Michael Wiley B 4.00 10.00
OG Olandis Gary B 5.00 12.00
PM Peyton Manning G 50.00 100.00
PW Peter Warrick G 10.00 25.00
RD Ron Dayne G 10.00 25.00
RJ Rob Johnson B 5.00 12.00
RL Ray Lucas B 4.00 10.00
RM Randy Moss G 20.00 50.00
RS R.Jay Soward B 4.00 10.00
SA Shaun Alexander B 8.00 20.00
SG Sherrod Gideon B 4.00 10.00
SL Sylvester Morris G 6.00 15.00

TA Troy Aikman G	25.00	60.00
TB Tim Brown B	10.00	25.00
TC Tim Couch G	8.00	20.00
TD Terrell Davis G	10.00	25.00
TH Torry Holt G	10.00	25.00
TJ Thomas Jones G	12.00	30.00
TM Tee Martin B	6.00	15.00
TO Terrell Owens B	10.00	25.00
TP Travis Prentice B	5.00	12.00
TR Tim Rattay B	5.00	12.00
TW Troy Walters B	4.00	10.00
WC Wayne Chrebet B	5.00	12.00

2000 UD Ionix Warp Zone

COMPLETE SET (15)	60.00	150.00
STATED ODDS 1:239		
WZ1 Marshall Faulk	4.00	10.00
WZ2 Kurt Warner	6.00	15.00
WZ3 Peyton Manning	10.00	25.00
WZ4 Edgerrin James	4.00	10.00
WZ5 Brett Favre	12.00	30.00
WZ6 Tim Couch	3.00	8.00
WZ7 Ricky Williams	4.00	10.00
WZ8 Mark Brunell	3.00	8.00
WZ9 Fred Taylor	4.00	10.00
WZ10 Terrell Davis	4.00	10.00
WZ11 Dan Marino	12.00	30.00
WZ12 Randy Moss	4.00	10.00
WZ13 Emmitt Smith	10.00	25.00
WZ14 Eddie George	3.00	8.00
WZ15 Steve McNair	4.00	10.00

2008 UD Masterpieces

This set was released on November 4, 2008. The base set consists of 105 cards. Cards 1-99 feature veterans with several rookie cards mixed in, and cards 101-110 are short-printed rookies.

COMPLETE SET (105)	75.00	135.00
COMP.SET w/o SP's (86)	15.00	40.00
91-99 TW ODDS 1:12 HOBBY		
101-110 RC ODDS 1:6 HOBBY		
1 Donnie Avery RC	.60	1.50
2 Adrian Peterson	.75	2.00
3 David Tyree	.50	1.25
Eli Manning		
4 Alan Ameche	.30	.75
5 Barry Sanders	.75	2.00
6 Bart Starr	.75	2.00
7 Ben Roethlisberger	.50	1.25
8 Brett Favre	1.25	3.00
9 Bob Sanders	.40	1.00
10 Brett Favre	1.25	3.00
11 Brian Urlacher	.50	1.25
12 Earl Bennett RC	.75	2.00
13 Champ Bailey	.40	1.00
14 Chuck Bednarik	.40	1.00
15 Dan Marino	1.00	2.50
16 Brian Bosworth	.50	1.25
17 Devin Thomas RC	.60	1.50
18 Andre Caldwell RC	.60	1.50
19 Desmond Howard	.30	.75
20 Devin Hester	.50	1.25
21 Dick Butkus	.60	1.50
22 Harry Douglas RC	.60	1.50
23 Don Shula	.30	.75
24 Donovan McNabb	.50	1.25
25 Kevin O'Connell RC	.60	1.50
26 Doug Flutie	.40	1.00
27 Drew Pearson	.40	1.00
28 Dwight Clark	.40	1.00
29 Early Doucet RC	.60	1.50
30 Ed Podolak	.30	.75
31 Eli Manning	.50	1.25
32 Joe Flacco RC	2.50	6.00
33 James Hardy RC	.60	1.50
34 Franco Harris	.50	1.25
35 Frank Reich	.30	.75
36 Dexter Jackson RC	.60	1.50
37 Gale Sayers	.60	1.50
38 Chris Johnson RC	2.00	5.00
39 Herm Edwards	.30	.75
40 Howard Cosell	.40	1.00
41 Dustin Keller RC	.75	2.00
42 Jamaal Charles RC	1.25	3.00
43 Jim Brown	.60	1.50
44 Jim Thorpe	.60	1.50
46 Joe Montana	1.00	2.50
47 Joe Namath	.60	1.50
48 John David Booty RC	.60	1.50
49 John Elway	.75	2.00
50 Johnny Unitas	.75	2.00
51 Jordy Nelson RC	1.00	2.50
52 Kellen Winslow Sr.	.40	1.00
53 Eddie Royal RC	.75	2.00
54 Kevin Dyson	.30	.75
55 Kevin Dyson	.30	.75
56 Kevin Smith RC	1.00	2.50
57 LaDainian Tomlinson	.50	1.25
58 Limas Sweed RC	.75	2.00
60 Malcolm Kelly RC	.60	1.50
61 Mario Manningham RC	.75	2.00
62 Marvin Harrison	.50	1.25
63 Jerome Simpson RC	.75	2.00
64 Matt Forte RC	1.25	3.00
66 Chris Long RC	.75	2.00
67 Paul Hornung	.50	1.25
68 Peyton Manning	.75	2.00
69 Randy Moss	.50	1.25
71 Ray Rice RC	1.00	2.50
72 Red Grange	.60	1.50
73 Lester Hayes	.40	1.00
74 Sammy Baugh	.50	1.25
75 Adrian Peterson	.75	2.00
76 Steve Slaton RC	.75	2.00
77 Billy Sims	.40	1.00
78 Jack Lambert	.50	1.25
79 Scott Norwood	.30	.75
80 Snow Plow Game	.30	.75
81 Terrell Owens	.50	1.25
82 Terry Bradshaw	.75	2.00
83 Tom Brady	.75	2.00
84 Tom Brady	.75	2.00
85 Tony Romo	.60	1.50
86 Vince Lombardi	.75	2.00
87 Vince Young	.40	1.00
88 Walter Payton	1.00	2.50
89 Wes Welker	.50	1.25
90 Y.A. Tittle	.50	1.25
91 Adrian Peterson	4.00	10.00
Dick Butkus		
Time Warp		
92 Johnny Unitas	5.00	12.00
Peyton Manning		
Time Warp		
93 Brett Favre	4.00	10.00
Paul Hornung		
Time Warp		
94 Randy Moss	3.00	8.00
Mel Blount		
Time Warp		
95 Paul Hornung	5.00	12.00
Joe Montana		
Joe Theismann		
Brady Quinn		
Time Warp		
96 Bob Sanders	4.00	10.00
Lynn Swann		
Time Warp		
97 Paul Hornung	4.00	10.00
Brett Favre		
Time Warp		
98 Fran Tarkenton	4.00	10.00
Adrian Peterson		
Time Warp		
99 Eli Manning	4.00	10.00
Y.A. Tittle		
Time Warp		
101 Rashard Mendenhall SP RC	2.50	6.00
102 Brian Brohm SP RC	1.25	3.00
103 Chad Henne SP RC	1.25	3.00
104 Jake Long SP RC	1.25	3.00
105 Felix Jones SP RC	2.00	5.00
106 Darren McFadden SP RC	3.00	8.00
107 DeSean Jackson SP RC	2.50	6.00
108 Glenn Dorsey SP RC	1.25	3.00
109 Jonathan Stewart SP RC	2.00	5.00
110 Matt Ryan SP RC	5.00	12.00

2008 UD Masterpieces Framed Black

*VETS: 1X TO 2.5X BASIC CARDS
*ROOKIES: .6X TO 1.5X BASIC CARDS

2008 UD Masterpieces Framed Blue 150

*VETS:1.2 X TO 3X BASIC CARDS
*ROOKIES: .8X TO 2X BASIC CARDS
STATED PRINT RUN 150 SER.#'d SETS

2008 UD Masterpieces Framed Burgundy

*VETS 1-90: 3X TO 8X BASIC CARDS
*ROOKIES 1-90: 2X TO 5X BASIC CARDS
*TIME WARP 91-99: .8X TO 2X BASIC CARDS
*ROOKIES 101-110: 1.5X TO 4X BASIC CARDS
STATED PRINT RUN 10-25 SER.#'d SETS

2008 UD Masterpieces Framed Brown 99

*VETS: 1.5X TO 4X BASIC CARDS
*ROOKIES: 1X TO 2.5X BASIC CARDS
STATED PRINT RUN 99 SER.#'d SETS

2008 UD Masterpieces Framed Green 50

*VETS 1-90: 2X TO 5X BASIC CARDS
*ROOKIES 1-90: 1.2X TO 3X BASIC CARDS
*TIME WARP 91-99: .5X TO 1.2X BASIC CARDS
*ROOKIES 101-110: .8X TO 2X BASIC CARDS
STATED PRINT RUN 50 SER.#'d SETS

2008 UD Masterpieces Framed Green 75

*VETS 1-90: 2X TO 5X BASIC CARDS
*ROOKIES 1-90: 1.2X TO 3X BASIC CARDS
*TIME WARP 91-99: .5X TO 1.2X BASIC CARDS
*ROOKIES 101-110: .8X TO 2X BASIC CARDS
STATED PRINT RUN 75 SER.#'d SETS

2008 UD Masterpieces Framed Light Blue 10

*VETS 1-90: 4X TO 10X BASIC CARDS
*ROOKIES 1-90: 2.5X TO 6X BASIC CARDS
*TIME WARP 91-99: .8X TO 2X BASIC CARDS
*ROOKIES 101-110: 1.5X TO 4X BASIC CARDS
STATED PRINT RUN 10 SERIAL #'D SETS

2008 UD Masterpieces Framed Blue 50

*VETS 1-90: 2X TO 5X BASIC CARDS
*ROOKIES 1-90: 1.2X TO 3X BASIC CARDS
*TIME WARP 91-99: .5X TO 1.2X BASIC CARDS
*ROOKIES 101-110: .8X TO 2X BASIC CARDS
STATED PRINT RUN 50 SER.#'d SETS

2008 UD Masterpieces Framed Red 199

*VETS: 1.2X TO 3X BASIC CARDS
*ROOKIES: .8X TO 2X BASIC CARDS
STATED PRINT RUN 199 SER.#'d SETS

2008 UD Masterpieces Framed Silver

*VETS/RET/50-89: 2X TO 5X BASIC CARDS
*VETS/RET/30-49: 2.5X TO 6X BASIC CARDS
*VETS/RET/15-29: 3X TO 8X BASIC CARDS
*ROOKIES/50-89: 1.2X TO 3X BASIC CARDS
*ROOKIES/30-49: 1.5X TO 4X BASIC CARDS
*ROOKIES/15-29: 2X TO 5X BASIC CARDS
STATED PRINT RUN 1-89

2008 UD Masterpieces Captured on Canvas Jerseys

*PATCH/50: .6X TO 1.5X BASIC INSERTS		
PATCH PRINT RUN 50 SER.#'d SETS		
OVERALL JERSEY ODDS 1:6 HOBBY		
CC1 Tom Brady	6.00	15.00
CC2 Dexter Jackson	2.00	5.00
CC3 Anquan Boldin	3.00	8.00
CC4 Brian Brohm	2.50	6.00
CC5 Brian Westbrook	3.00	8.00
CC6 Calvin Johnson	4.00	10.00
CC7 Chad Henne	2.50	6.00
CC8 Chad Johnson	3.00	8.00
CC9 Chris Cooley	4.00	10.00
CC10 Chris Johnson	6.00	15.00
CC11 Brett Favre	10.00	25.00
CC12 Tony Romo	5.00	12.00
CC13 Dallas Clark	3.00	8.00
CC14 Darren McFadden	6.00	15.00
CC15 Devin Thomas	2.00	5.00
CC16 DeMarcus Ware	3.00	8.00
CC17 Harry Douglas	2.00	5.00
CC18 DeSean Jackson	5.00	12.00
CC19 Devin Hester	4.00	10.00
CC20 Kevin O'Connell	2.00	5.00
CC21 Braylon Edwards	3.00	8.00
CC22 Dwayne Bowe	3.00	8.00
CC23 Early Doucet	2.00	5.00
CC24 Ed Reed	3.00	8.00
CC25 Dustin Keller	2.50	6.00
CC26 Felix Jones	4.00	10.00
CC27 James Hardy	2.00	5.00
CC29 Roy Williams WR	3.00	8.00
CC30 Greg Olsen	3.00	8.00
CC31 Jamaal Charles	4.00	10.00
CC32 Jay Cutler	4.00	10.00
CC35 Joe Flacco	8.00	20.00
CC36 Glenn Dorsey	2.50	6.00
CC37 Joey Galloway	3.00	8.00
CC38 John David Booty	2.00	5.00
CC39 Jonathan Stewart	5.00	12.00
CC40 Jordy Nelson	3.00	8.00
CC41 LaDainian Tomlinson	4.00	10.00
CC42 Kevin Smith	2.50	6.00
CC43 JaMarcus Russell	3.00	8.00
CC44 Willis McGahee	3.00	8.00
CC45 Limas Sweed	2.50	6.00
CC46 Malcolm Kelly	2.00	5.00
CC47 Mario Manningham	2.50	6.00
CC48 Andre Caldwell	2.00	5.00
CC49 Matt Forte	4.00	10.00
CC50 Matt Leinart	4.00	10.00
CC51 Matt Ryan	8.00	20.00
CC52 Michael Clayton	2.50	6.00
CC53 Jake Long	2.50	6.00
CC54 Jerome Simpson	2.50	6.00
CC55 Rashard Mendenhall	5.00	12.00
CC56 Ray Rice	5.00	12.00
CC57 Ryan Grant	4.00	10.00
CC58 Steve Slaton	2.50	6.00
CC59 Steven Jackson	4.00	10.00
CC60 Reggie Bush	4.00	10.00

2008 UD Masterpieces Stroke Of Genius Autographs

UNPRICED FRAMED RED PRINT RUN 10		
SOG1 Adrian Arrington	4.00	10.00
SOG2 Andre Woodson	5.00	12.00
SOG3 Ben Roethlisberger SP		
SOG4 Ben Watson	5.00	12.00
SOG5 Billy Sims	10.00	25.00
SOG6 Bo Jackson SP	100.00	200.00
SOG7 Marc Bulger	8.00	20.00
SOG8 Dallas Clark	8.00	20.00
SOG10 Brian Bosworth	12.00	30.00
SOG11 Brian Brohm SP	5.00	12.00
SOG12 Calais Campbell	4.00	10.00
SOG13 Jamal Lewis	8.00	20.00
SOG14 Chad Henne	5.00	12.00
SOG15 Chad Johnson SP	10.00	25.00
SOG16 Chris Johnson	20.00	50.00
SOG17 Chris Long	5.00	12.00
SOG18 Jamaal Charles	8.00	20.00
SOG19 Colt Brennan SP	10.00	25.00
SOG21 Trent Edwards	6.00	15.00
SOG22 Darren McFadden SP	40.00	80.00
SOG23 Daryl Johnston	15.00	30.00
SOG24 Devin Thomas	4.00	10.00
SOG25 DeMarcus Ware	10.00	25.00
SOG26 Dennis Dixon	8.00	20.00
SOG27 Derek Anderson	6.00	15.00
SOG28 DeSean Jackson	10.00	25.00
SOG29 Y.A. Tittle	20.00	40.00
SOG30 Dick Butkus SP	60.00	100.00
SOG31 Kevin O'Connell	4.00	10.00
SOG33 Eli Manning SP	50.00	80.00
SOG34 Erik Ainge	5.00	12.00
SOG35 Felix Jones	12.00	30.00
SOG37 Fred Davis	4.00	10.00
SOG38 Glenn Dorsey	8.00	20.00
SOG40 Jack Ham SP	25.00	50.00
SOG42 Jake Long	5.00	12.00
SOG43 Jason Campbell SP	15.00	30.00
SOG45 Jeff Garcia SP	15.00	30.00
SOG46 Jerry Kramer	10.00	25.00
SOG48 Joe Flacco	25.00	50.00
SOG50 Joe Namath SP	200.00	400.00
SOG51 John David Booty SP	4.00	10.00
SOG52 John Elway SP	125.00	200.00
SOG53 Jonathan Stewart SP	15.00	40.00
SOG54 Jordy Nelson	10.00	25.00
SOG55 Ken Stabler SP	20.00	40.00
SOG56 Kenny Phillips	5.00	12.00
SOG58 Kevin Smith	5.00	12.00
SOG59 Kurt Warner SP	40.00	80.00
SOG60 LaDainian Tomlinson SP	30.00	60.00
SOG63 Leodis McKelvin	4.00	10.00
SOG64 Lester Hayes SP	10.00	25.00
SOG65 Limas Sweed	5.00	12.00
SOG66 Malcolm Kelly	4.00	10.00
SOG67 Jerome Simpson	5.00	12.00
SOG68 Matt Flynn	30.00	60.00
SOG69 Matt Forte	12.00	30.00
SOG70 Matt Ryan SP	60.00	120.00
SOG71 Dexter Jackson	4.00	10.00
SOG73 Michael Huff	5.00	12.00
SOG74 Mike Hart	5.00	12.00
SOG75 Mike Jenkins	5.00	12.00
SOG76 Owen Schmitt	5.00	12.00
SOG77 Patrick Willis	8.00	20.00
SOG78 Paul Hornung SP	15.00	30.00
SOG79 Peyton Manning SP	60.00	120.00
SOG80 Rashard Mendenhall	10.00	25.00
SOG81 Ray Rice	12.00	30.00
SOG82 Roger Craig	10.00	25.00
SOG83 Roman Gabriel	30.00	60.00
SOG84 Cadillac Williams SP	8.00	20.00
SOG85 Steve Slaton	5.00	12.00
SOG86 Tashard Choice	4.00	10.00
SOG87 Tom Rathman	10.00	25.00
SOG88 Tony Romo SP		

2005 UD Mini Jersey Collection

This 100-card set was released in December, 2005. This set was issued through Upper Deck's retail outlets and these cards were available in three-card packs with a $5.99 SRP which came 18 packs to a box. Cards numbered 1-70 feature veterans sequenced in team alphabetical order; while cards numbered 71-85 feature leading 2005 NFL rookies and the set concludes with a season review subset (cards 86-100).

COMPLETE SET (100)	20.00	50.00
1 Kurt Warner	.40	1.00
2 Anquan Boldin	.30	.75
3 Michael Vick	.40	1.00
4 Warrick Dunn	.30	.75
5 Kyle Boller	.30	.75
6 Ray Lewis	.40	1.00
7 Jake Delhomme	.30	.75
8 DeShaun Foster	.30	.75
9 Carson Palmer	.40	1.00
10 Chad Johnson	.30	.75
11 Rudi Johnson	.30	.75
12 Kellen Winslow	.30	.75
13 Lee Suggs	.25	.60
14 Julius Jones	.25	.60
15 Drew Bledsoe	.40	1.00
16 Tatum Bell	.25	.60
17 Jake Plummer	.30	.75
18 Roy Williams WR	.30	.75
19 Kevin Jones	.25	.60
20 Brett Favre	1.00	2.50
21 Ahman Green	.30	.75
22 David Carr	.25	.60
23 Andre Johnson	.40	1.00
24 Peyton Manning	.75	2.00
25 Edgerrin James	.30	.75
26 Marvin Harrison	.40	1.00
27 Byron Leftwich	.30	.75
28 Fred Taylor	.30	.75
29 Priest Holmes	.30	.75
30 Trent Green	.30	.75
31 Tony Gonzalez	.30	.75
32 A.J. Feeley	.25	.60
33 Randy McMichael	.25	.60
34 Daunte Culpepper	.30	.75
35 Nate Burleson	.25	.60
36 Tom Brady	.75	2.00
37 Corey Dillon	.30	.75
38 Aaron Brooks	.25	.60
39 Joe Horn	.30	.75
40 Deuce McAllister	.30	.75
41 Eli Manning	.60	1.50
42 Tiki Barber	.40	1.00
43 Jeremy Shockey	.40	1.00
44 Chad Pennington	.40	1.00
45 Curtis Martin	.40	1.00
46 Santana Moss	.30	.75
47 Randy Moss	.40	1.00
48 Kerry Collins	.30	.75
49 Donovan McNabb	.40	1.00
50 Terrell Owens	.40	1.00
51 Brian Westbrook	.30	.75
52 Ben Roethlisberger	.60	1.50
53 Jerome Bettis	.40	1.00
54 Drew Brees	.40	1.00
55 LaDainian Tomlinson	.40	1.00
56 Kevan Barlow	.25	.60
57 Tim Rattay	.25	.60
58 Matt Hasselbeck	.30	.75
59 Shaun Alexander	.30	.75
60 Darrell Jackson	.25	.60
61 Marc Bulger	.30	.75
62 Steven Jackson	.40	1.00
63 Torry Holt	.30	.75
64 Michael Pittman	.25	.60
65 Brian Griese	.30	.75
66 Michael Clayton	.25	.60
67 Steve McNair	.40	1.00
68 Drew Bennett	.30	.75
69 Clinton Portis	.30	.75
70 Patrick Ramsey	.30	.75
71 Alex Smith QB RC	1.25	3.00
72 Aaron Rodgers RC	8.00	20.00
73 Jason Campbell RC	1.00	2.50
74 Ronnie Brown RC	1.00	2.50
75 Cadillac Williams RC	.75	2.00
76 Cedric Benson RC	.75	2.00
77 J.J. Arrington RC	.60	1.50
78 Braylon Edwards RC	1.00	2.50
79 Troy Williamson RC	.60	1.50
80 Mike Williams	.75	2.00
81 Matt Jones RC	.60	1.50
82 Mark Clayton RC	.60	1.50
83 Roddy White RC	1.00	2.50
84 Reggie Brown RC	.50	1.25
85 Eric Shelton RC	.50	1.25
86 Peyton Manning SR	.75	2.00
87 Ben Roethlisberger SR	.60	1.50
88 Julius Jones SR	.25	.60
89 Michael Vick SR	.40	1.00
90 Tom Brady SR	.75	2.00
91 Corey Dillon SR	.30	.75
92 Terrell Owens SR	.40	1.00
93 Donovan McNabb SR	.40	1.00
94 Priest Holmes SR	.30	.75
95 Kevin Jones SR	.25	.60
96 Jerome Bettis SR	.40	1.00
97 Torry Holt SR	.30	.75
98 Clinton Portis SR	.30	.75
99 Drew Brees SR	.40	1.00
100 Tiki Barber SR	.40	1.00
NNO Checklist Card	.05	.15

2005 UD Mini Jersey Collection Replica Jerseys Autographs

STATED ODDS 1:360		
AW Andrew Walter	50.00	100.00
CF Charlie Frye	50.00	100.00
CR Carlos Rogers	50.00	100.00
DG David Greene	50.00	100.00
DO Dan Orlovsky	50.00	100.00
KO Kyle Orton	60.00	100.00
RW Roddy White	60.00	120.00
VM Vernand Morency	50.00	100.00

2005 UD Mini Jersey Collection Replica Jerseys White

ONE MINI JERSEY PER PACK		
*DARK: 1X TO 2.5X WHITE JERSEYS		
DARK STATED ODDS 1:18		
BF Brett Favre	8.00	20.00
BL Byron Leftwich	2.50	6.00
BR Ben Roethlisberger	5.00	12.00
BU Brian Urlacher	2.50	6.00
CP1 Chad Pennington	2.50	6.00
CP2 Carson Palmer	3.00	8.00
DB Drew Bledsoe	2.50	6.00
DC Daunte Culpepper	2.50	6.00
DM Donovan McNabb	3.00	8.00
EM Eli Manning	4.00	10.00
JJ Julius Jones	3.00	8.00
KJ Kevin Jones	2.50	6.00
LT LaDainian Tomlinson	2.50	6.00
MH Marvin Harrison	2.50	6.00
MV Michael Vick	4.00	10.00
PM Peyton Manning	5.00	12.00
RM Randy Moss	2.50	6.00
TB1 Tom Brady	5.00	12.00
TB2 Tedy Bruschi	2.50	6.00
TO Terrell Owens	2.50	6.00

2003 UD Patch Collection

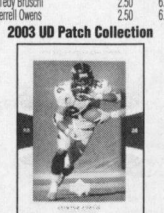

Released in October of 2003, this set consists of 162 cards, including 105 veterans and 57 rookies. Cards 1-90 are veterans. Rookies 91-120 were inserted at a rate of 1:4, rookies 121-132 were inserted at a rate of 1:20, and rookies 133-147 were inserted at a rate of 1:40. Cards 121-147 feature collectible patches on the card front. Cards 148-162 were inserted at a rate of 1:40 and also feature collectible patches on card front. A Peyton Manning sample card was produced to preview this set and that card can be located at the end of our checklist. Boxes contained 20 packs of 5 cards. SRP was $3.99.

COMP.SET w/o SP's (90)	7.50	20.00
1 Peyton Manning	.75	2.00
2 Aaron Brooks	.30	.75
3 Joey Harrington	.25	.60
4 Brett Favre	1.00	2.50
5 Donovan McNabb	.40	1.00
6 Jeff Garcia	.30	.75
7 Michael Vick	.50	1.25
8 David Carr	.30	.75
9 Drew Brees	.40	1.00
10 Chad Pennington	.40	1.00
11 Daunte Culpepper	.30	.75
12 Tom Brady	1.00	2.50
13 Kurt Warner	.40	1.00
14 Brad Johnson	.30	.75
15 Josh McCown	.30	.75
16 Drew Bledsoe	.40	1.00
17 Rich Gannon	.30	.75
18 Tim Couch	.25	.60
19 Keyshawn Johnson	.40	1.00
20 Travis Henry	.25	.60
21 LaDainian Tomlinson	.40	1.00
22 Emmitt Smith	1.00	2.50
23 Michael Bennett	.30	.75
24 Mark Brunell	.30	.75
25 Steve McNair	.40	1.00
26 Clinton Portis	.30	.75
27 Eddie George	.30	.75
28 Marshall Faulk	.40	1.00
29 Curtis Martin	.40	1.00
30 Ahman Green	.30	.75
31 Priest Holmes	.40	1.00
32 Edgerrin James	.40	1.00
33 Deuce McAllister	.30	.75
34 Ricky Williams	.30	.75
35 Anthony Thomas	.30	.75
36 Jerome Bettis	.40	1.00
37 Shaun Alexander	.30	.75
38 Jake Plummer	.30	.75
39 Patrick Ramsey	.30	.75
40 Laveranues Coles	.25	.60
41 David Boston	.25	.60
42 Jay Fiedler	.25	.60
43 Garrison Hearst	.30	.75
44 Corey Dillon	.30	.75
45 Charlie Garner	.30	.75
46 Fred Taylor	.30	.75
47 Chad Hutchinson	.25	.60
48 Quincy Carter	.25	.60
49 Kevan Barlow	.25	.60
50 Tommy Maddox	.30	.75
51 Kordell Stewart	.30	.75
52 Chris Redman	.25	.60
53 Jamal Lewis	.30	.75
54 Zach Thomas	.40	1.00
55 Junior Seau	.40	1.00
56 Chris Chambers	.30	.75
57 Matt Hasselbeck	.30	.75
58 Marc Bulger	.40	1.00
59 Isaac Bruce	.40	1.00
60 Torry Holt	.40	1.00
61 Kelly Holcomb	.25	.60
62 Plaxico Burress	.30	.75
63 Ray Lewis	.40	1.00
64 Brian Urlacher	.40	1.00
65 Tim Brown	.40	1.00
66 William Green	.25	.60
67 Kevin Johnson	.25	.60
68 Trent Green	.30	.75
69 Santana Moss	.30	.75
70 Tony Gonzalez	.40	1.00
71 Rod Smith	.30	.75
72 Ashley Lelie	.25	.60
73 Peerless Price	.25	.60
74 Antonio Bryant	.25	.60
75 Duce Staley	.30	.75
76 Darrell Jackson	.30	.75
77 Jeremy Shockey	.40	1.00
78 Kerry Collins	.30	.75
79 Koren Robinson	.30	.75
80 Jerry Rice	.75	2.00
81 Terrell Owens	.40	1.00
82 Antwaan Randle El	.30	.75
83 Donte Stallworth	.25	.60
84 Randy Moss	.40	1.00
85 Chad Johnson	.40	1.00
86 Hines Ward	.40	1.00
87 Rod Gardner	.25	.60
88 Marvin Harrison	.40	1.00
89 Eric Moulds	.30	.75
90 Julius Peppers	.40	1.00
91 Nate Hybl RC	1.00	2.50
92 Lon Sheriff RC	.75	2.00
93 Gerald Hayes RC	1.00	2.50
94 B.J. Askew RC	1.00	2.50
95 Artose Pinner RC	.75	2.00
96 Domanick Davis RC	1.00	2.50
97 LaBrandon Toefield RC	1.00	2.50
98 Lee Suggs RC	1.00	2.50
99 Cecil Sapp RC	.75	2.00
100 Kelley Washington RC	.75	2.00
101 Kevin Curtis RC	1.25	3.00
102 Zuriel Smith RC	.75	2.00
103 Carl Ford RC	.75	2.00
104 Travis Anglin RC	.75	2.00
105 Terrence Edwards RC	.75	2.00
106 Troy Polamalu RC	12.50	25.00
107 Nate Burleson RC	1.00	2.50
108 Cecil Moore RC	.75	2.00
109 Kassim Osgood RC	1.25	3.00
110 Teyo Johnson RC	1.00	2.50
111 Jason Witten RC	3.00	8.00
112 Vishante Shiancoe RC	1.25	3.00
113 Kevin Ware RC	.75	2.00
114 Mike Pinkard RC	.75	2.00
115 Donald Lee RC	1.00	2.50
116 Justin Gage RC	1.00	2.50
117 Adrian Madise RC	.75	2.00
118 Anthony Adams RC	1.00	2.50
119 Dan Curley RC	.75	2.00
120 Dallas Clark RC	2.00	5.00
121 Kyle Boller RI RC	2.50	6.00
122 Chris Simms RI RC	2.50	6.00
123 Dave Ragone RI RC	1.50	4.00
124 Kliff Kingsbury RI RC	2.00	5.00
125 Brad Banks RI RC	2.00	5.00
126 Gibran Hamdan RI RC	1.50	4.00
127 Ken Dorsey RI RC	2.00	5.00
128 Seneca Wallace RI RC	2.50	6.00
129 Brian St.Pierre RI RC	2.00	5.00
130 Rex Grossman RI RC	2.50	6.00
131 Brooks Bollinger RI RC	2.00	5.00
132 Jason Gesser RI RC	2.00	5.00
133 Carson Palmer RI RC	6.00	15.00
134 Byron Leftwich RI RC	3.00	8.00
135 Charles Rogers RI RC	2.50	6.00
136 Andre Johnson RI RC	8.00	20.00
137 Willis McGahee RI RC	4.00	10.00
138 Larry Johnson RI RC	3.00	8.00
139 Musa Smith RI RC	2.00	5.00
140 Chris Brown RI RC	2.00	5.00
141 Onterrio Smith RI RC	2.00	5.00
142 Justin Fargas RI RC	3.00	8.00
143 Bryant Johnson RI RC	3.00	8.00
144 Taylor Jacobs RI RC	2.00	5.00
145 Bethel Johnson RI RC	2.00	5.00
146 Tyrone Calico RI RC	2.50	6.00
147 Anquan Boldin RI RC	5.00	12.00
148 Michael Vick AP	3.00	8.00
149 Brett Favre AP	6.00	15.00
150 Chad Pennington AP	2.50	6.00
151 Kurt Warner AP	2.50	6.00
152 David Carr AP	2.00	5.00
153 Donovan McNabb AP	2.50	6.00
154 LaDainian Tomlinson AP	2.50	6.00
155 Marshall Faulk AP	2.50	6.00
156 Emmitt Smith AP	6.00	15.00
157 Jerry Rice AP	5.00	12.00
158 Terrell Owens AP	2.50	6.00
159 Brian Urlacher AP	2.50	6.00
160 Randy Moss AP	2.50	6.00
161 Ricky Williams AP	2.00	5.00
162 Peyton Manning AP	5.00	12.00
P162 Peyton Manning AP SAMPLE	1.50	4.00

2003 UD Patch Collection Gold Patches

*ROOKIES 121-132: 1.5X TO 4X BASE
*ROOKIES 133-147: 1.2X TO 3X BASE
*AP VETS 148-162: 2X TO 5X BASE
STATED PRINT RUN 25 SER.#'d SETS

2003 UD Patch Collection Jumbo Patches

STATED ODDS ONE PER BOX		
*GOLD/25: 1.2X TO 3X BASIC INSERTS		
GOLD PRINT RUN 25 SER.#'d SETS		
AJ Andre Johnson	5.00	12.00
BF Brett Favre	8.00	20.00
BL Byron Leftwich	2.00	5.00
BU Brian Urlacher	3.00	8.00
CP Chad Pennington	3.00	8.00
DB Drew Brees	3.00	8.00
DC David Carr	2.50	6.00
DM Donovan McNabb	3.00	8.00
ES Emmitt Smith	8.00	20.00
JH Joey Harrington	2.00	5.00
JR Jerry Rice	6.00	15.00
JS Jeremy Shockey	3.00	8.00
KB Kyle Boller	3.00	8.00
LJ Larry Johnson	2.00	5.00
LT LaDainian Tomlinson	3.00	8.00
MC Deuce McAllister	2.50	6.00
MF Marshall Faulk	3.00	8.00
MV Michael Vick	4.00	10.00
PM Peyton Manning	6.00	15.00
PO Clinton Portis	2.50	6.00
RM Randy Moss	3.00	8.00
RW Ricky Williams	2.50	6.00
SC Carson Palmer	4.00	10.00
TO Terrell Owens	3.00	8.00

2003 UD Patch Collection Jumbo Patches Autographs

PRINT RUN 50 SERIAL #'d SETS		
PM Peyton Manning	60.00	100.00
TO Terrell Owens		

2003 UD Patch Collection Signature Patches

STATED ODDS 1:410		
*GOLD/25: .8X TO 2X BASIC AUTO		
*GOLD/25: .6X TO 1.5X BASIC AU SP		
GOLD PRINT RUN 25 SER.#'d SETS		
SPAB Aaron Brooks	10.00	25.00
SPBL Byron Leftwich	12.00	30.00
SPCH Chad Pennington	12.00	30.00
SPCJ Chad Johnson	12.00	30.00
SPCP Carson Palmer SP	75.00	150.00
SPDB Drew Brees SP	30.00	60.00
SPJG Jeff Garcia	10.00	25.00
SPJJ James Jackson	8.00	20.00
SPKB Kevan Barlow	8.00	20.00
SPPM Peyton Manning	60.00	120.00
SPRG Rod Gardner	8.00	20.00
SPRJ Rudi Johnson	12.00	30.00
SPRW Reggie Wayne	12.00	30.00
SPTH Todd Heap	10.00	25.00
SPWM Willis McGahee SP	25.00	50.00

2003 UD Patch Collection All Upper Deck Patches

STATED ODDS 1:22		
*GOLD/25: 1.5X TO 4X BASIC INSERTS		
GOLD PRINT RUN 25 SER.#'d SETS		
UD1 Edgerrin James	2.50	6.00
UD2 Aaron Brooks	2.00	5.00
UD3 Steve McNair	2.50	6.00
UD4 Tim Couch	1.50	4.00
UD5 Tom Brady	6.00	15.00
UD6 Joey Harrington	1.50	4.00
UD7 Jeremy Shockey	2.50	6.00
UD8 Daunte Culpepper	2.00	5.00
UD9 Jeff Garcia	2.00	5.00
UD10 David Boston	1.50	4.00
UD11 Deuce McAllister	2.00	5.00
UD12 Ahman Green	2.00	5.00
UD13 Tim Brown	2.50	6.00
UD14 Shaun Alexander	2.00	5.00
UD15 Laveranues Coles	1.50	4.00
UD16 Priest Holmes	2.50	6.00
UD17 Clinton Portis	2.00	5.00
UD18 Marvin Harrison	2.50	6.00
UD19 Drew Bledsoe	2.50	6.00
UD20 Corey Dillon	2.00	5.00
UD21 Drew Brees	2.50	6.00

2002 UD Piece of History

Released in late May 2002, this 162 card set features 100 veterans and 62 rookies. Most rookies were serial #'d to 2002, with some being serial #'d to 500, and others being serial #'d to 500 and also containing a jersey swatch. Cards were issued in 24 pack boxes with 5 cards per pack. SRP was $2.99 per pack.

COMP.SET w/o SP's (100)	10.00	25.00
1 David Boston	.25	.60
2 Jake Plummer	.30	.75
3 Chris Chandler	.30	.75
4 Jamal Anderson	.30	.75
5 Michael Vick	.60	1.50
6 Elvis Grbac	.25	.60
7 Qadry Ismail	.30	.75
8 Ray Lewis	.40	1.00
9 Eric Moulds	.30	.75
10 Rob Johnson	.30	.75
11 Travis Henry	.25	.60
12 Chris Weinke	.25	.60
13 Donald Hayes	.25	.60
14 Muhsin Muhammad	.30	.75
15 Anthony Thomas	.30	.75
16 Brian Urlacher	.40	1.00
17 David Terrell	.25	.60
18 Jim Miller	.25	.60
19 Marty Booker	.30	.75
20 Corey Dillon	.30	.75
21 Jon Kitna	.30	.75
22 Peter Warrick	.30	.75
23 James Jackson	.25	.60
24 Kevin Johnson	.25	.60
25 Tim Couch	.25	.60
26 Emmitt Smith	1.00	2.50
27 Quincy Carter	.25	.60
28 Rocket Ismail	.30	.75
29 Brian Griese	.30	.75
30 Ed McCaffrey	.30	.75
31 Rod Smith	.30	.75
32 Terrell Davis	.40	1.00
33 Charlie Batch	.25	.60
34 James Stewart	.25	.60
35 Mike McMahon	.25	.60
36 Ahman Green	.30	.75
37 Antonio Freeman	.40	1.00
38 Bill Schroeder	.25	.60
39 Brett Favre	1.00	2.50
40 Dominic Rhodes	.30	.75
41 Edgerrin James	.30	.75
42 Marvin Harrison	.40	1.00
43 Peyton Manning	.75	2.00
44 Jimmy Smith	.30	.75
45 Mark Brunell	.30	.75
46 Priest Holmes	.40	1.00
47 Tony Gonzalez	.40	1.00
48 Trent Green	.30	.75
49 Chris Chambers	.30	.75
50 Jay Fiedler	.30	.75
51 Lamar Smith	.30	.75
52 Oronde Gadsden	.25	.60
53 Daunte Culpepper	.30	.75
54 Michael Bennett	.30	.75
55 Randy Moss	.40	1.00
56 Antowain Smith	.30	.75
57 Drew Bledsoe	.40	1.00
58 Tom Brady	1.00	2.50
59 Troy Brown	.30	.75
60 Aaron Brooks	.30	.75
61 Joe Horn	.30	.75
62 Michael Strahan	.40	1.00
63 Kerry Collins	.30	.75
64 Ron Dayne	.30	.75
65 Tiki Barber	.40	1.00
66 Curtis Martin	.40	1.00
67 Laveranues Coles	.30	.75
68 Santana Moss	.30	.75
69 Vinny Testaverde	.30	.75
70 Jerry Rice	.75	2.00
71 Rich Gannon	.30	.75
72 Tim Brown	.40	1.00
73 Donovan McNabb	.40	1.00
74 Duce Staley	.30	.75
75 Freddie Mitchell	.25	.60
76 James Thrash	.30	.75
77 Jerome Bettis	.40	1.00
78 Kendrell Bell	.25	.60
79 Kordell Stewart	.30	.75
80 Doug Flutie	.40	1.00
81 Junior Seau	.40	1.00
82 LaDainian Tomlinson	.50	1.25
83 Garrison Hearst	.30	.75
84 Jeff Garcia	.30	.75
85 Terrell Owens	.40	1.00
86 Matt Hasselbeck	.40	1.00
87 Ricky Watters	.30	.75
88 Shaun Alexander	.30	.75
89 Isaac Bruce	.40	1.00
90 Kurt Warner	.40	1.00
91 Marshall Faulk	.40	1.00
92 Torry Holt	.40	1.00
93 Brad Johnson	.30	.75
94 Keyshawn Johnson	.30	.75
95 Mike Alstott	.30	.75
96 Warrick Dunn	.30	.75
97 Eddie George	.30	.75
98 Steve McNair	.40	1.00
99 Stephen Davis	.30	.75
100 Tony Banks	.25	.60
101 Antonio Bryant RC	2.00	5.00
102 Adrian Peterson RC	2.00	5.00
103 Brian Poli-Dixon RC	1.25	3.00
104 Kyle Johnson RC	1.25	3.00
105 Clinton Portis RC	2.50	6.00
106 David Carr/500 RC	4.00	10.00
107 Rocky Calmus RC	1.50	4.00
108 Eric Crouch RC	2.00	5.00
109 Jeremy Shockey RC	3.00	8.00
110 Jabar Gaffney RC	2.00	5.00
111 Damien Anderson RC	1.25	3.00
112 Josh Reed RC	1.50	4.00
113 Lamar Gordon RC	1.50	4.00
114 Julius Peppers/500 RC	8.00	20.00
115 Kelly Campbell RC	1.50	4.00
116 Leonard Henry RC	1.25	3.00
117 Chad Hutchinson/500 RC	2.50	6.00
118 Luke Staley RC	1.25	3.00
119 Josh Scobey RC	1.50	4.00
120 Marquise Walker RC	1.25	3.00
121 Roy Williams RC	2.00	5.00
122 Patrick Ramsey RC	2.00	5.00
123 Ashley Lelie/500 RC	3.00	8.00
124 Rohan Davey RC	2.00	5.00
125 Ron Johnson RC	1.50	4.00
126 T.J. Duckett RC	2.00	5.00
127 Cliff Russell RC	1.25	3.00
128 William Green/500 RC	3.00	8.00
129 Reche Caldwell RC	2.00	5.00
130 Donte Stallworth RC	2.00	5.00
131 Javon Walker RC	2.00	5.00
132 David Garrard RC	2.50	6.00
133 Quentin Jammer RC	2.00	5.00
134 Ladell Betts RC	2.00	5.00
135 Freddie Milons RC	1.25	3.00
136 Brian Westbrook RC	3.00	8.00
137 John Henderson RC	1.50	4.00
138 Kalimba Edwards RC	1.50	4.00
139 Daniel Graham RC	1.50	4.00
140 Josh McCown RC	2.00	5.00
141 Joey Harrington/500 JSY RC	5.00	12.00
142 Phillip Buchanon/500 JSY RC	5.00	12.00
143 Maurice Morris/1500 JSY RC	3.00	8.00
144 George Godsey/1500 JSY RC	2.50	6.00

145 J.T. O'Sullivan/1500 JSY RC 3.00 8.00
146 Kurt Kittner/500 JSY RC 3.00 8.00
147 DeShaun Foster/500 JSY RC 5.00 12.00
148 Antwaan Randle El/1500 JSY RC 4.00 10.00
149 Woody Dantzler/1500 JSY RC 3.00 8.00
150 Randy Fasani/1500 JSY RC 3.00 8.00
151 Kahlil Hill/1500 JSY RC 2.50 6.00
152 Atrews Bell/1500 JSY RC 2.50 6.00
153 Eric McCoo/1500 JSY RC 2.50 6.00
154 Ricky Williams/1500 JSY RC 3.00 8.00
155 Albert Haynesworth/500 RC 5.00 12.00
156 Lamont Thompson/1500 JSY RC 3.00 8.00
157 Andre Davis/1500 JSY RC 3.00 8.00
158 Travis Stephens/500 JSY RC 3.00 8.00
159 Delvon Flowers/1500 JSY RC 2.50 6.00
160 Robert Thomas/1500 JSY RC 2.50 6.00
161 Marques Anderson/1500 JSY RC 3.00 8.00
162 Kenyon Coleman/1500 JSY RC 2.50 6.00

2002 UD Piece of History Hitmakers

COMPLETE SET (6) 4.00 10.00
STATED ODDS 1:30
HM1 Dan Morgan .60 1.50
HM2 Chris Claiborne .60 1.50
HM3 Marvin Jones .60 1.50
HM4 Andy Katzenmoyer .60 1.50
HM5 Rocky Calmus .75 2.00
HM6 Kevin Hardy .60 1.50

2002 UD Piece of History Hitmakers Jerseys

STATED ODDDS 1:336
HMJBU Brian Urlacher SP 10.00 25.00
HMJCC Chris Claiborne 4.00 10.00
HMJDM Dan Morgan 4.00 10.00
HMJJS Junior Seau 6.00 15.00
HMJRH Rodney Harrison 5.00 12.00
HMJRL Ray Lewis SP 10.00 25.00

2002 UD Piece of History National Honors

COMPLETE SET (11) 7.50 20.00
STATED ODDS 1:9
NH1 Doug Flutie 1.25 3.00
NH2 Chris Weinke .75 2.00
NH3 Desmond Howard 1.00 2.50
NH4 Ty Detmer 1.00 2.50
NH5 Eric Crouch 1.25 3.00
NH6 Ricky Williams 1.00 2.50
NH7 Ron Dayne 1.00 2.50
NH8 Vinny Testaverde 1.00 2.50
NH9 Charles Woodson 1.25 3.00
NH10 Tim Brown 1.25 3.00
NH11 Eddie George 1.00 2.50

2002 UD Piece of History National Honors Jerseys

STATED ODDS 1:168
NHJCWE Chris Weinke 4.00 10.00
NHJCWO Charles Woodson/52* 10.00 25.00
NHJDF Doug Flutie 6.00 15.00
NHJDH Desmond Howard 5.00 12.00
NHJEG Eddie George 5.00 12.00
NHJMA Marcus Allen 10.00 25.00
NHJRD Ron Dayne SP 5.00 12.00
NHJRW Ricky Williams/52* 8.00 20.00
NHJTB Tim Brown 6.00 15.00
NHJVT Vinny Testaverde 5.00 12.00

2002 UD Piece of History Rookie Glory

COMPLETE SET (13) 12.50 30.00
STATED ODDS 1:7
RG1 Brian Urlacher 1.25 3.00
RG2 Anthony Thomas 1.00 2.50
RG3 Emmitt Smith 3.00 8.00
RG4 Mike Anderson 1.00 2.50
RG5 Edgerrin James 1.00 2.50
RG6 Randy Moss 1.25 3.00
RG7 Curtis Martin 1.25 3.00
RG8 Charles Woodson 1.25 3.00
RG9 Hugh Douglas .75 2.00
RG10 Jerome Bettis 1.25 3.00
RG11 Kendrell Bell .75 2.00
RG12 Warrick Dunn 1.00 2.50
RG13 Jevon Kearse 1.00 2.50

2002 UD Piece of History Rookie Glory Jerseys

STATED ODDS 1:108
RGJAT Anthony Thomas 5.00 12.00
RGJBU Brian Urlacher 6.00 15.00
RGJCM Curtis Martin 6.00 15.00
RGJCW Charles Woodson/52* 10.00 25.00
RGJDC Daunte Culpepper/92* 6.00 15.00
RGJEJ Edgerrin James SP 6.00 15.00
RGJHD Hugh Douglas 4.00 10.00
RGJJK Jevon Kearse SP 6.00 15.00
RGJLT LaDainian Tomlinson 8.00 20.00
RGJMB Michael Bennett 5.00 12.00
RGJPM Peyton Manning 12.00 30.00
RGJRM Randy Moss SP 8.00 20.00
RGJWD Warrick Dunn 5.00 12.00

2002 UD Piece of History Run to History

COMPLETE SET (6) 7.50 20.00
STATED ODDS 1:30
RH1 Luke Staley 1.00 2.50
RH2 Ricky Williams 1.25 3.00
RH3 Ron Dayne 1.25 3.00
RH4 LaDainian Tomlinson 2.00 5.00
RH5 Garrison Hearst 1.25 3.00
RH6 Eddie George 1.25 3.00

2002 UD Piece of History Run to History Jerseys

STATED ODDS 1:336
RHJEG Eddie George 5.00 12.00
RHJEJ Edgerrin James 5.00 12.00
RHJJL Jamal Lewis 5.00 12.00
RHJLT LaDainian Tomlinson SP 8.00 20.00
RHJRD Ron Dayne 5.00 12.00
RHJRW Ricky Williams/82* 8.00 20.00

2002 UD Piece of History The Big Game

COMPLETE SET (30) 30.00 80.00
STATED ODDS 1:6
BG1 Chris Chandler 1.00 2.50
BG2 Trent Dilfer 1.00 2.50
BG3 Darren Sharper 1.00 2.50
BG4 Jamal Lewis 1.00 2.50
BG5 Ray Lewis 1.25 3.00
BG6 Rod Woodson 1.25 3.00
BG7 Bruce Smith 1.25 3.00
BG8 Emmitt Smith 3.00 8.00
BG9 Larry Allen .75 2.00
BG10 Ed McCaffrey 1.00 2.50
BG11 Rod Smith 1.00 2.50
BG12 Terrell Davis 1.25 3.00
BG13 John Elway 2.50 6.00
BG14 Brett Favre 3.00 8.00
BG15 Antonio Freeman 1.25 3.00
BG16 Dorsey Levens 1.00 2.50
BG17 Drew Bledsoe 1.25 3.00
BG18 Tom Brady 3.00 8.00
BG19 Troy Brown 1.00 2.50
BG20 Michael Strahan 1.25 3.00
BG21 Jessie Armstead .75 2.00
BG22 Junior Seau 1.25 3.00
BG23 Jerry Rice 2.50 6.00
BG24 Ricky Watters 1.00 2.50
BG25 Kurt Warner 1.25 3.00
BG26 Marshall Faulk 1.25 3.00
BG27 London Fletcher .75 2.00
BG28 Isaac Bruce 1.25 3.00
BG29 Steve McNair 1.25 3.00
BG30 Darrell Green 1.25 3.00

2002 UD Piece of History The Big Game Jerseys

STATED ODDS 1:48
*PATCH/25: 1.2X TO 3X BASIC JSY
*PATCH/25: 1X TO 2.5X BASIC JSY SP
PATCH PRINT RUN 25 SER.#'d SETS
BGJBF Brett Favre 12.00 30.00
BGJBS Bruce Smith 5.00 12.00
BGJCC Chris Chandler SP 5.00 12.00
BGJCM Curtis Martin SP 6.00 15.00
BGJDB Drew Bledsoe 5.00 12.00
BGJDG Darrell Green 5.00 12.00
BGJDM Dan Marino 20.00 50.00
BGJIB Isaac Bruce SP 6.00 15.00
BGJJA Jessie Armstead 3.00 8.00
BGJJE John Elway SP 15.00 40.00
BGJJK Jim Kelly 10.00 25.00
BGJJL Jamal Lewis SP 5.00 12.00
BGJJR Jerry Rice 10.00 25.00
BGJJS Junior Seau 5.00 12.00
BGJKW Kurt Warner 5.00 12.00
BGJLA Larry Allen 3.00 8.00
BGJLF London Fletcher 3.00 8.00
BGJMF Marshall Faulk 5.00 12.00
BGJMS Michael Strahan 5.00 12.00
BGJOP Orlando Pace 4.00 10.00
BGJRD Ron Dayne 4.00 10.00
BGJRL Ray Lewis 5.00 12.00
BGJRW Rod Woodson 5.00 12.00
BGJSM Steve McNair SP 6.00 15.00
BGJSY Steve Young SP 12.00 30.00
BGJTD Trent Dilfer 4.00 10.00
BGJTT Travis Taylor 3.00 8.00

2005 UD Portraits

This 200-card set was released in October, 2005. The set was issued in eight-card hobby packs with an $125 SRP. Cards numbered 1-100 feature veterans in team alphabetical order while cards 101-200 feature 2005 rookies and those cards were issued to a stated print run of 425 serial numbered sets.

DRAFT PICK PRINT RUN 425 SER.#'d SETS
1 Larry Fitzgerald 1.25 3.00
2 Anquan Boldin 1.00 2.50
3 Josh McCown 1.00 2.50
4 Michael Vick 1.25 3.00
5 Alge Crumpler 1.00 2.50
6 Peerless Price .75 2.00
7 Ray Lewis 1.25 3.00
8 Jamal Lewis 1.00 2.50
9 Todd Heap 1.00 2.50
10 Derrick Mason 1.00 2.50
11 J.P. Losman .75 2.00
12 Willis McGahee 1.25 3.00
13 Eric Moulds .75 2.00
14 Jake Delhomme 1.00 2.50
15 DeShaun Foster 1.00 2.50
16 Steve Smith 1.25 3.00
17 Brian Urlacher 1.25 3.00
18 Rex Grossman 1.00 2.50
19 Muhsin Muhammad 1.00 2.50
20 Carson Palmer 1.25 3.00
21 Rudi Johnson 1.00 2.50
22 Chad Johnson 1.00 2.50
23 Julius Jones .75 2.00
24 Keyshawn Johnson 1.00 2.50
25 Drew Bledsoe 1.25 3.00
26 Tatum Bell .75 2.00
27 Jake Plummer 1.00 2.50
28 Ashley Lelie .75 2.00
29 Roy Williams WR 1.00 2.50
30 Kevin Jones .75 2.00
31 Joey Harrington 1.00 2.50
32 Brett Favre 3.00 8.00
33 Ahman Green 1.00 2.50
34 Javon Walker .75 2.00
35 David Carr .75 2.00
36 Andre Johnson 1.25 3.00
37 Domanick Davis .75 2.00
38 Peyton Manning 2.50 6.00
39 Reggie Wayne 1.25 3.00
40 Edgerrin James 1.00 2.50
41 Marvin Harrison 1.25 3.00
42 Byron Leftwich 1.00 2.50
43 Fred Taylor 1.00 2.50
44 Jimmy Smith 1.00 2.50
45 Priest Holmes 1.00 2.50
46 Larry Johnson 1.00 2.50
47 Trent Green 1.00 2.50
48 A.J. Feeley .75 2.00
49 Chris Chambers 1.00 2.50
50 Randy McMichael .75 2.00
51 Daunte Culpepper 1.00 2.50
52 Onterrio Smith .75 2.00
53 Nate Burleson .75 2.00
54 Tom Brady 2.50 6.00
55 Corey Dillon 1.00 2.50
56 Deion Branch .75 2.00
57 David Givens .75 2.00
58 Aaron Brooks .75 2.00
59 Deuce McAllister 1.00 2.50
60 Joe Horn 1.00 2.50
61 Eli Manning 2.00 5.00
62 Jeremy Shockey 1.25 3.00
63 Tiki Barber 1.25 3.00
64 Chad Pennington 1.25 3.00
65 Curtis Martin 1.25 3.00
66 Jonathan Vilma 1.00 2.50
67 Kerry Collins 1.00 2.50
68 Jerry Porter .75 2.00
69 Randy Moss 1.25 3.00
70 Donovan McNabb 1.25 3.00
71 Terrell Owens 1.25 3.00
72 Brian Dawkins 1.00 2.50
73 Brian Westbrook 1.00 2.50
74 Ben Roethlisberger 2.00 5.00
75 Jerome Bettis 1.25 3.00
76 Hines Ward 1.25 3.00
77 Duce Staley 1.00 2.50
78 Drew Brees 1.25 3.00
79 LaDainian Tomlinson 1.25 3.00
80 Antonio Gates 1.25 3.00
81 Eric Parker .75 2.00
82 Tim Rattay .75 2.00
83 Kevan Barlow .75 2.00
84 Eric Johnson .75 2.00
85 Shaun Alexander 1.00 2.50
86 Darrell Jackson .75 2.00
87 Matt Hasselbeck 1.00 2.50
88 Marc Bulger 1.00 2.50
89 Steven Jackson 1.25 3.00
90 Marshall Faulk 1.25 3.00
91 Torry Holt 1.00 2.50
92 Michael Pittman .75 2.00
93 Brian Griese 1.00 2.50
94 Michael Clayton .75 2.00
95 Steve McNair 1.25 3.00
96 Billy Volek .75 2.00
97 Chris Brown .75 2.00
98 Clinton Portis 1.00 2.50
99 Patrick Ramsey 1.00 2.50
100 Santana Moss 1.00 2.50
101 Aaron Rodgers RC 20.00 50.00
102 Alex Smith QB RC 3.00 8.00
103 Charlie Frye RC 2.00 5.00
104 Andrew Walter RC 1.50 4.00
105 Jason Campbell RC 2.50 6.00
106 Dan Orlovsky RC 2.00 5.00
107 Derek Anderson RC 1.50 4.00
108 Kyle Orton RC 2.00 5.00
109 David Greene RC 1.25 3.00
110 James Kilian RC 1.25 3.00
111 Matt Jones RC 1.50 4.00
112 Cedric Benson RC 2.00 5.00
113 Ronnie Brown RC 2.50 6.00
114 Cadillac Williams RC 2.00 5.00
115 Ciatrick Fason RC 1.25 3.00
116 Vernand Morency RC 1.25 3.00
117 Eric Shelton RC 1.25 3.00
118 Maurice Clarett 1.25 3.00
119 Marion Barber RC 2.00 5.00
120 Anthony Davis RC 1.25 3.00
121 J.J. Arrington RC 1.50 4.00
122 Ryan Moats RC 1.50 4.00
123 Frank Gore RC 3.00 8.00
124 Alvin Pearman RC 1.25 3.00
125 Darren Sproles RC 2.00 5.00
126 Cedric Houston RC 2.00 5.00
127 Braylon Edwards RC 2.50 6.00
128 Troy Williamson RC 1.50 4.00
129 Mark Clayton RC 2.00 5.00
130 Chris Henry RC 2.00 5.00
131 Roddy White RC 2.50 6.00
132 Fred Gibson RC 1.50 4.00
133 Craphonso Thorpe RC 1.25 3.00
134 Terrence Murphy RC 1.25 3.00
135 Roydell Williams RC 1.50 4.00
136 Roscoe Parrish RC 1.25 3.00
137 Reggie Brown RC 1.25 3.00
138 Craig Bragg RC 1.25 3.00
139 Larry Brackins RC 1.25 3.00
140 Rasheed Marshall RC 1.50 4.00
141 J.R. Russell RC 1.25 3.00
142 Vincent Jackson RC 2.50 6.00
143 Dante Ridgeway RC 1.25 3.00
144 Chad Owens RC 1.50 4.00
145 Airese Currie RC 1.25 3.00
146 Marcus Maxwell RC 1.25 3.00
147 Paris Warren RC 1.50 4.00
148 Tab Perry RC 1.25 3.00
149 Jerome Mathis RC 2.00 5.00
150 Courtney Roby RC 1.50 4.00
151 Heath Miller RC 2.50 6.00
152 Alex Smith TE RC 1.25 3.00
153 Kevin Everett RC 2.00 5.00
154 Travis Johnson RC 1.25 3.00
155 Mike Patterson RC 1.25 3.00
156 DeMarcus Ware RC 4.00 10.00
157 Erasmus James RC 1.50 4.00
158 Dan Cody RC 1.50 4.00
159 David Pollack RC 1.50 4.00
160 Shaun Cody RC 1.50 4.00
161 Matt Roth RC 1.50 4.00
162 Marcus Spears RC 1.50 4.00
163 Jonathan Babineaux RC 1.50 4.00
164 Justin Tuck RC 2.50 6.00
165 Channing Crowder RC 1.50 4.00
166 Odell Thurman RC 2.00 5.00
167 Barrett Ruud RC 2.00 5.00
168 Lance Mitchell RC 1.50 4.00
169 Derrick Johnson RC 1.50 4.00
170 Shawne Merriman RC 2.00 5.00
171 Kevin Burnett RC 1.50 4.00
172 Darryl Blackstock RC 1.25 3.00
173 Antrel Rolle RC 2.00 5.00
174 Adam Jones RC 1.50 4.00
175 Fabian Washington RC 1.50 4.00
176 Carlos Rogers RC 2.00 5.00
177 Corey Webster RC 1.50 4.00
178 Justin Miller RC 1.50 4.00
179 Eric Green RC 1.25 3.00
180 Marlin Jackson RC 1.25 3.00
181 Luis Castillo RC 1.50 4.00
182 Thomas Davis RC 1.25 3.00
183 Kirk Morrison RC 2.00 5.00
184 Vincent Fuller RC 1.50 4.00
185 Donte Nicholson RC 1.25 3.00
186 Brodney Pool RC 2.00 5.00
187 Mike Nugent RC 1.50 4.00
188 Timmy Chang RC 1.50 4.00
189 Matt Cassel RC 4.00 10.00
190 Adrian McPherson RC 1.25 3.00
191 Gino Guidugli RC 1.25 3.00
192 Stefan LeFors RC 1.25 3.00
193 Marcus Randall RC 1.50 4.00
194 Brandon Jacobs RC 2.50 6.00
195 Walter Reyes RC 1.25 3.00
196 Mark Bradley RC 1.25 3.00
197 Josh Bullocks RC 1.50 4.00
198 Chase Lyman RC 1.25 3.00
199 Harry Williams RC 1.50 4.00
200 Mike Williams 2.00 5.00

2005 UD Portraits Gold

*VETERANS: 1X TO 2.5X BASIC CARDS
*ROOKIES: .8X TO 2X BASIC CARDS
GOLD PRINT RUN 75 SER.#'d SETS

2005 UD Portraits Platinum

*VETERANS: 2.5X TO 6X BASIC CARDS
*ROOKIES: 1.5X TO.4X BASIC CARDS
PLATINUM PRINT RUN 30 SER.#'d SETS

2005 UD Portraits Cut Signatures 8x10

UNPRICED CUT AUTOS SER.#'d 1-5

2005 UD Portraits Memorable Materials

TWO MEMORABLE MATERIALS PER BOX
UNPRICED AUTOS PRINT RUN 15 SETS
MMAB Anquan Boldin 2.50 6.00
MMAG Ahman Green 3.00 8.00
MMAN Antrel Rolle 3.00 8.00
MMAO Antonio Gates 2.50 6.00
MMAR Aaron Rodgers 20.00 40.00
MMAS Alex Smith QB 6.00 15.00
MMAW Andrew Walter 2.50 6.00
MMBD Brian Dawkins 3.00 8.00
MMBE Braylon Edwards 4.00 10.00
MMBL Byron Leftwich 2.50 6.00
MMBR Ben Roethlisberger 7.50 20.00
MMOA Carlos Rogers 2.50 6.00
MMCF Charlie Frye 2.50 6.00
MMCI Ciatrick Fason 2.50 6.00
MMCP Carson Palmer 3.00 8.00
MMCR Chris Brown 2.50 6.00
MMCW Cadillac Williams 5.00 12.00
MMDM Donovan McNabb 4.00 10.00
MMDS Deion Sanders 3.00 8.00
MMJA J.J. Arrington 2.50 6.00
MMJC Jason Campbell 3.00 8.00
MMJJ Julius Jones 4.00 10.00
MMJL J.P. Losman 3.00 8.00
MMKO Kyle Orton 2.50 6.00
MMLJ LaMont Jordan 3.00 8.00
MMMA Mark Clayton 2.50 6.00
MMMB Marc Bulger 2.50 6.00
MMMC Michael Clayton 2.50 6.00
MMMM Muhsin Muhammad 2.50 6.00
MMMO Maurice Clarett 2.50 6.00
MMMV Michael Vick 5.00 12.00
MMMY Mark Bradley 3.00 8.00
MMPM Peyton Manning 5.00 12.00
MMRB Ronnie Brown 6.00 15.00
MMRE Reggie Brown 2.50 6.00
MMRM Ryan Moats 3.00 8.00
MMRO Roddy White 3.00 8.00
MMRP Roscoe Parrish 2.50 6.00
MMRW Reggie Wayne 2.50 6.00
MMTW Troy Williamson 2.50 6.00
MMVM Vernand Morency 2.50 6.00

2005 UD Portraits Rookie Signature Portait Duals 8x10

STATED PRINT RUN 45 SER.#'d SETS
DRP1 Alex Smith QB 100.00 200.00
Aaron Rodgers
DRP2 Cadillac Williams 40.00 100.00
Ronnie Brown
DRP3 Mark Clayton 25.00 60.00
Braylon Edwards
DRP4 Roddy White 25.00 60.00
Troy Williamson
DRP5 Cedric Benson 25.00 60.00
Vernand Morency
DRP6 David Greene 25.00 60.00
David Pollack
DRP7 Antrel Rolle 20.00 50.00
Marlin Jackson
DRP8 Charlie Frye 25.00 60.00
Andrew Walter
DRP9 Ciatrick Fason 25.00 60.00
Ryan Moats
DRP10 Aaron Rodgers 100.00 175.00
J.J. Arrington
DRP11 Frank Gore 40.00 80.00
Roscoe Parrish
DRP12 Jason Campbell 40.00 100.00
Ronnie Brown
DRP13 Roscoe Parrish 20.00 50.00
Craphonso Thorpe
DRP14 Dan Orlovsky 25.00 60.00
Kyle Orton
DRP15 Erasmus James 15.00 40.00
Anttaj Hawthorne
DRP16 Braylon Edwards 25.00 60.00
Mike Williams
DRP17 Marion Barber 40.00 100.00
Frank Gore
DRP18 Mike Williams 25.00 60.00
Maurice Clarett

2005 UD Portraits Scrapbook Materials

ONE PER BOX
SBAB Anquan Boldin 3.00 8.00
SBAG Ahman Green 3.00 8.00
SBAN Antrel Rolle 4.00 10.00
SBAR Aaron Rodgers SP 20.00 50.00
SBAS Alex Smith QB 5.00 12.00
SBAW Andrew Walter 3.00 8.00
SBBE Braylon Edwards 3.00 8.00
SBBF Brett Favre 10.00 25.00
SBBR Ben Roethlisberger 6.00 15.00
SBCA Carlos Rogers 4.00 10.00
SBCB Cedric Benson 4.00 10.00
SBCF Charlie Frye 4.00 10.00
SBCI Ciatrick Fason 2.50 6.00
SBCP Carson Palmer SP 5.00 12.00
SBCW Cadillac Williams 2.50 6.00
SBDB Drew Bennett 3.00 8.00
SBDM Donovan McNabb 4.00 10.00
SBDR Drew Bledsoe 4.00 10.00
SBEM Eli Manning 6.00 15.00
SBFG Frank Gore 4.00 10.00
SBHM Heath Miller 3.00 8.00
SBJA J.J. Arrington 3.00 8.00
SBJC Jason Campbell 3.00 8.00
SBJJ Julius Jones 2.50 6.00
SBJL J.P. Losman SP 3.00 8.00
SBKO Kyle Orton 2.50 6.00
SBLE Lee Evans 3.00 8.00
SBMA Mark Clayton 4.00 10.00
SBMB Mark Bradley 2.50 6.00
SBMC Michael Clayton 2.50 6.00
SBMO Maurice Clarett 3.00 8.00
SBMV Michael Vick 4.00 10.00
SBMW Mike Williams 4.00 10.00
SBPM Peyton Manning 8.00 20.00
SBRB Ronnie Brown 3.00 8.00
SBRE Reggie Wayne 4.00 10.00
SBRW Roy Williams WR 3.00 8.00
SBSJ Steven Jackson 4.00 10.00
SBTB Tiki Barber 4.00 10.00
SBTW Troy Williamson 3.00 8.00
SBVJ Vincent Jackson 3.00 8.00
SBVM Vernand Morency 3.00 8.00

2005 UD Portraits Scrapbook Moments

STATED PRINT RUN 425 SER.#'d SETS
1 Aaron Brooks .75 2.00
2 Anthony Davis .75 2.00
3 Antonio Gates 1.25 3.00
4 Ahman Green 1.00 2.50
5 Antrel Rolle 1.00 2.50
6 Anquan Boldin 1.00 2.50
7 Aaron Rodgers 8.00 20.00
8 Alex Smith QB 1.50 4.00
9 Andrew Walter .75 2.00
10 Braylon Edwards 1.25 3.00
11 Brett Favre 3.00 8.00
12 Ben Roethlisberger 2.00 5.00
13 Cedric Benson 1.00 2.50
14 Charlie Frye 1.00 2.50
15 Ciatrick Fason .75 2.00
16 Carson Palmer 1.25 3.00
17 Cadillac Williams 1.00 2.50
18 Drew Bennett 1.00 2.50
19 Carlos Rogers 1.00 2.50
20 Donovan McNabb 1.25 3.00
21 Drew Bledsoe 1.25 3.00
22 Eli Manning 2.00 5.00
23 Frank Gore 1.50 4.00
24 Heath Miller 1.25 3.00
25 J.J. Arrington .75 2.00
26 Joe Horn 1.00 2.50
27 Julius Jones .75 2.00
28 Jack Lambert 1.50 4.00
29 J.P. Losman .75 2.00
30 Jason Campbell 1.25 3.00
31 Jason White 1.00 2.50
32 Kyle Orton 1.00 2.50
33 Lee Evans 1.00 2.50
34 Mark Clayton 1.00 2.50
35 Marc Bulger 1.00 2.50
36 Michael Clayton .60 1.50
37 David Greene .75 2.00
38 Maurice Clarett .75 2.00
39 Michael Vick 1.25 3.00
40 Mark Bradley .75 2.00
41 Paul Hornung 1.50 4.00
42 Peyton Manning 2.50 6.00
43 Ronnie Brown 1.25 3.00
44 Reggie Wayne 1.25 3.00
45 Roy Williams WR 1.00 2.50
46 Steven Jackson 1.25 3.00
47 Tiki Barber 1.25 3.00
48 Troy Williamson .75 2.00
49 Vincent Jackson 1.25 3.00
50 Vernand Morency .75 2.00

2005 UD Portraits Scrapbook Signatures

UNPRICED AUTO PRINT RUN 20 SETS
SSAB Aaron Brooks 10.00 25.00
SSAG Antonio Gates 15.00 40.00
SSAH Ahman Green 12.00 30.00
SSAQ Anquan Boldin 12.00 30.00
SSAR Aaron Rodgers 500.00 800.00
SSAS Alex Smith QB 100.00 175.00
SSAW Andrew Walter 12.00 30.00
SSBF Brett Favre 150.00 250.00
SSBR Ben Roethlisberger 75.00 125.00
SSCB Cedric Benson 15.00 40.00
SSCI Ciatrick Fason 10.00 25.00
SSCW Cadillac Williams 15.00 40.00
SSDG David Greene 10.00 25.00
SSDM Donovan McNabb 25.00 50.00
SSDR Drew Bledsoe 15.00 40.00
SSFG Frank Gore 15.00 40.00
SSJA J.J. Arrington 12.00 30.00
SSJJ Julius Jones 10.00 25.00
SSJK Jack Lambert 30.00 60.00
SSJL J.P. Losman 10.00 25.00
SSKO Kyle Orton 15.00 40.00
SSLE Lee Evans 12.00 30.00
SSMB Marc Bulger 12.00 30.00
SSMC Michael Clayton 10.00 25.00
SSMU Maurice Clarett 10.00 25.00
SSMY Mark Bradley 10.00 25.00
SSPH Paul Hornung 20.00 40.00
SSPM Peyton Manning 75.00 125.00
SSRE Reggie Wayne 15.00 40.00
SSRW Roy Williams WR 12.00 30.00
SSTB Tiki Barber 15.00 40.00
SSTW Troy Williamson 12.00 30.00
SSVJ Vincent Jackson 20.00 50.00

2005 UD Portraits Signature Portraits 8x10

ONE 8X10 AUTO PER BOX
SP1 Ahman Green 15.00 40.00
SP2 Byron Leftwich SP 25.00 50.00
SP3 Michael Vick SP 30.00 60.00
SP4 Peyton Manning 75.00 125.00
SP5 Antonio Gates 15.00 40.00
SP6 Lee Evans 10.00 25.00
SP7 Bob Griese 20.00 50.00
SP8 Michael Clayton 12.50 30.00
SP9 Archie Manning 20.00 50.00
SP10 Jack Lambert 40.00 80.00
SP11 Ben Roethlisberger SP 100.00 175.00
SP12 Steven Jackson 15.00 40.00
SP13 Marc Bulger 12.50 30.00
SP14 Drew Bledsoe SP 30.00 60.00
SP15 Rudi Johnson 15.00 40.00
SP16 Julius Jones 15.00 40.00
SP17 Carson Palmer SP 40.00 80.00
SP18 Roy Williams WR 15.00 40.00
SP19 Fred Taylor 12.50 30.00
SP20 Eli Manning SP 75.00 125.00
SP21 Donovan McNabb SP 60.00 100.00
SP22 Brett Favre SP 125.00 250.00
SP23 J.P. Losman 15.00 40.00
SP24 Domanick Davis 10.00 25.00
SP25 Joe Horn 10.00 25.00
SP26 Tiki Barber 15.00 40.00
SP27 Steve Largent 30.00 60.00
SP28 Bernie Kosar 15.00 40.00
SP29 Paul Hornung 25.00 60.00
SP30 Charlie Joiner 15.00 40.00
SP31 George Blanda 30.00 60.00
SP32 Gale Sayers SP 50.00 100.00
SP33 Fran Tarkenton 30.00 60.00
SP34 Dan Marino SP 125.00 250.00
SP35 John Elway SP 125.00 250.00
SP36 Joe Montana SP 125.00 250.00
SP37 Jack Ham 20.00 50.00
SP38 Raymond Berry 15.00 40.00
SP39 Don Maynard 15.00 40.00
SP40 LaDainian Tomlinson 40.00 80.00
SP41 Len Dawson 20.00 50.00
SP42 Joe Theismann 15.00 40.00
SP43 Joe Greene 30.00 60.00
SP44 Marcus Allen 25.00 50.00
SP45 Mike Singletary SP 30.00 60.00
SP46 Deion Sanders 50.00 100.00
SP47 Troy Aikman 60.00 120.00
SP48 Kyle Orton 15.00 40.00
SP49 Charlie Frye 10.00 25.00
SP50 Andrew Walter 10.00 25.00
SP51 Dan Orlovsky 10.00 25.00
SP52 David Greene 10.00 25.00
SP53 Heath Miller 12.00 30.00
SP54 Vernand Morency 12.50 30.00
SP55 Mike Williams 10.00 25.00
SP56 Ciatrick Fason 10.00 25.00
SP57 J.J. Arrington 10.00 25.00
SP58 Braylon Edwards 25.00 50.00
SP59 Art Donovan 12.50 30.00
SP60 Mark Clayton 10.00 25.00
SP61 Ronnie Brown 30.00 60.00
SP62 Cadillac Williams 25.00 60.00
SP63 Cedric Benson 10.00 25.00
SP64 Alex Smith QB 30.00 60.00
SP65 Aaron Rodgers 150.00 250.00
SP66 Jason Campbell 15.00 40.00
SP67 Roddy White 15.00 30.00
SP68 Roscoe Parrish 10.00 25.00
SP69 Troy Williamson 10.00 25.00
SP70 Maurice Clarett 10.00 25.00
SP71 Antrel Rolle 10.00 25.00
SP72 Reggie Brown 10.00 25.00

2005 UD Portraits Signature Portraits Dual 8x10

DUAL PRINT RUN 45 SER.#'D SETS
UNPRICED TRIPLE SIGS #'d TO 10
UNPRICED QUAD SIGS #'d TO 5
DSP1 Peyton Manning [illegible] 150.00
Reggie Wayne
DSP2 Michael Vick 40.00 80.00
Alge Crumpler
DSP3 Brett Favre 125.00 250.00
Ahman Green
DSP4 Lee Evans 20.00 50.00
J.P. Losman
DSP5 Deuce McAllister 20.00 50.00
Joe Horn
DSP6 Drew Bledsoe 90.00 150.00
Julius Jones
DSP7 Donovan McNabb 90.00 150.00
Brian Dawkins
DSP8 Carson Palmer 90.00 150.00
Chad Johnson
DSP9 Marc Bulger 50.00 100.00
Steven Jackson

2002-03 UD SuperStars

This 300 card set was released in March, 2003. This set was issued in five card packs with an $3 SRP. The packs were issued in 24 pack boxes which came 12 boxes to a case. The final 50 cards of the set featured two rookies from different sports.

COMPLETE SET (300) 30.00 80.00
10 Jake Plummer .20 .50
21 Michael Vick .40 1.00
38 Tom Brady .60 1.50
39 Antowain Smith .20 .50
40 Drew Bledsoe .40 1.00
52 Anthony Thomas .25 .60
60 Corey Dillon .25 .60
63 Tim Couch .15 .40
70 Brian Griese .25 .60
72 Dirk Nowitzki .50 1.25
73 Emmitt Smith .75 2.00
74 Quincy Carter .20 .50
90 Ricky Williams .25 .60
92 Ahman Green .30 .75
93 Brett Favre .75 2.00
105 Edgerrin James .40 1.00
106 Peyton Manning .60 1.50
107 Mark Brunell .25 .60
108 Jimmy Smith .15 .40
111 Priest Holmes .30 .75
125 Steve McNair .25 .60
126 Eddie George .25 .60
133 Daunte Culpepper .25 .60
134 Randy Moss .50 1.25
140 Aaron Brooks .25 .60
141 Deuce McAllister .40 1.00
163 Curtis Martin .30 .75
164 Chad Pennington .40 1.00
176 Jerry Rice .60 1.50
177 Rich Gannon .20 .50
189 Donovan McNabb .40 1.00
195 Jerome Bettis .30 .75
196 Kordell Stewart .15 .40
206 LaDainian Tomlinson .40 1.00
214 Jeff Garcia .25 .60
215 Terrell Owens .40 1.00
224 Shaun Alexander .15 .40
233 Kurt Warner .30 .75
234 Marshall Faulk .30 .75
248 Stephen Davis .15 .40
251 Josh McCown .30 .75
Jose Valverde
252 Doug Devore .20 .50
Wendell Bryant
253 T.J. Duckett .40 1.00
Ilya Kovalchuk
256 Freddy Sanchez .75 2.00
Rohan Davey
257 Julius Peppers .75 2.00
Eric Cole
259 Kyle Kane .20 .50
Roger Mason Jr.
260 Edwin Almonte .30 .75
Adrian Peterson
261 Andre Davis 1.50 4.00
Rick Nash
262 Dajuan Wagner .60 1.50
William Green
263 Cam Esslinger 1.50 4.00
Clinton Portis
264 Chad Hutchinson .50 1.25
Casey Jacobsen
265 Ashley Lelie .75 2.00
Rene Reyes
266 Nene Hilario .40 1.00
Nick Rolovich
267 Joey Harrington 1.25 3.00
Tayshaun Prince
268 Henrik Zetterberg 1.50 4.00
Kalimba Edwards
270 Mike Dunleavy .40 1.00
Phillip Buchanon
271 Brandon Puffer .20 .50
Jabar Gaffney
272 Bostjan Nachbar .20 .50
Jonathan Wells
273 David Carr 4.00 10.00
Yao Ming
274 Juan Brito .20 .50
Ryan Sims
275 Kazuhisa Ishii .30 .75
Kareem Rush
277 Luis Martinez .20 .50
Craig Nall
278 Marcus Haislip .60 1.50
Javon Walker
279 Kevin Frederick .50 1.25
Shaun Hill
280 Donte?ÇÖ Stallworth .60 1.50
Curtis Borchardt
281 Tyler Yates 1.00 2.50
Jeremy Shockey
282 Jaime Cerda .20 .50
Tim Carter
286 Adrian Burnside .60 1.50
Antwaan Randle El
287 Ben Howard .20 .50
Reche Caldwell
288 Oliver Perez .40 1.00
Quentin Jammer
289 Luis Ugueto .20 .50
Jerramy Stevens
290 Maurice Morris .20 .50
Matt Thornton
291 So Taguchi .30 .75
Lamar Gordon
292 Jason Simontacchi .20 .50
Robert Thomas
293 Felix Escalona .20 .50
Marquise Walker
294 Brandon Backe .30 .75
Travis Stephens
296 Patrick Ramsey .60 1.50
Juan Dixon

2002-03 UD SuperStars Gold

*GOLD 1-250: 2.5X TO 6X BASIC
*GOLD MATSUI: 6X TO 12X BASIC
*GOLD 251-300: 2X TO 5X BASIC

2002-03 UD SuperStars Benchmarks

B2 Barry Bonds 2.50 6.00
Jerry Rice
B3 Marshall Faulk 1.00 2.50
Tony Gwynn
B5 Allen Iverson 1.00 2.50
Donovan McNabb
B6 Nomar Garciaparra 2.00 5.00
Tom Brady
B7 Kevin Garnett 1.50 4.00
Randy Moss
B8 Sammy Sosa 1.25 3.00
Anthony Thomas
B9 Mark McGwire 2.50 6.00
Kurt Warner

2002-03 UD SuperStars City All-Stars Dual Jersey

ABBD Aaron Brooks 6.00 15.00
Baron Davis
ADDM Andre Davis 5.00 12.00
Darius Miles
ADPW Adam Dunn 4.00 10.00
Peter Warrick
BGJS Brian Griese 6.00 15.00
Joe Sakic
DBTH Drew Brees 6.00 15.00
Trevor Hoffman
DCTO Daunte Culpepper 8.00 20.00
Torii Hunter
ECRG Eric Chavez 6.00 15.00
Rich Gannon
EJJO Edgerrin James 5.00 12.00
Jermaine O'Neal
JBJF Jay Fiedler 4.00 10.00
Josh Beckett
JGCB Jabbar Gaffney 6.00 15.00
Craig Biggio
JGJS Jeff Garcia 6.00 15.00
J.T. Snow
JLDS John LeClair 6.00 15.00
Duce Staley
JPLG Jake Plummer 4.00 10.00
Luis Gonzalez
LTRK LaDainian Tomlinson 6.00 15.00
Ryan Klesko
MFJD Marshall Faulk 6.00 15.00
J.D. Drew
MVAJ Michael Vick 10.00 25.00
Andruw Jones
PHMS Priest Holmes 6.00 15.00
Mike Sweeney
PI AM Paul Lo Duca 6.00 15.00
Andre Miller
RACP Roberto Alomar 6.00 15.00
Chad Pennington
RDBW Ron Dayne 6.00 15.00
Bernie Williams
SAEM Shaun Alexander 6.00 15.00
Edgar Martinez
SDJS Stephen Davis 6.00 15.00
Jerry Stackhouse SP
SMPG Steve McNair 10.00 25.00
Pau Gasol
THJD Torry Holt 5.00 12.00
J.D. Drew
TORA Terrell Owens 6.00 15.00
Rich Aurilia
WSMB Wally Szczerbiak 5.00 12.00
Michael Bennett

2002-03 UD SuperStars City All-Stars Triple Jersey

CVT Chipper Jones 15.00 40.00
Michael Vick
Jason Terry
IGS Ichiro Suzuki 30.00 60.00
Gary Payton
Shaun Alexander
JCK Ken Griffey Jr. 10.00 25.00
Corey Dillon
Kenyon Martin
JDW Jacque Jones 10.00 25.00
Daunte Culpepper
Wally Szczerbiak
JDY Jeff Bagwell 40.00 80.00
David Carr
Yao Ming
JKA Jason Kendall 15.00 30.00
Kordell Stewart
Alexei Kovalev
JMK J.D. Drew 10.00 25.00
Marshall Faulk
Keith Tkachuk
JSB Joey Harrington 25.00 50.00
Steve Yzerman
Ben Wallace
MJA Mark Prior 5.00 12.00
Jay Williams
Anthony Thomas
MJC Mike Piazza 10.00 25.00
Jason Kidd
Curtis Martin
MJJ Miguel Tejada 10.00 25.00
Jason Richardson
Jerry Rice
OTD Omar Vizquel 10.00 25.00
Tim Couch
Dajuan Wagner
PTP Pedro Martinez 20.00 50.00
Tom Brady
Paul Pierce

2002-03 UD SuperStars Dual Legendary Cuts

MMJU Mickey Mantle
Johnny Unitas
WCWP Wilt Chamberlain
Walter Payton

2002-03 UD SuperStars Keys to the City

COMPLETE SET (10) 10.00 25.00
K3 Mark McGwire 1.50 4.00
Kurt Warner
K4 Brian Urlacher 1.00 2.50

Sammy Sosa
K5 Pedro Martinez 1.00 2.50
Tom Brady
K7 Mike Piazza .75 2.00
Curtis Martin
K8 Jeff Bagwell 1.50 4.00
David Carr
K9 Steve Yzerman 1.25 3.00
Joey Harrington
K10 Alex Rodriguez 1.25 3.00
Emmitt Smith

2002-03 UD SuperStars Legendary Leaders Dual Jersey

AIDM Allen Iverson 10.00 25.00
Donovan McNabb
DCJB David Carr 6.00 15.00
Jeff Bagwell
EJJO Edgerrin James 6.00 15.00
Jermaine O'Neal
ESAR Emmitt Smith 15.00 40.00
Alex Rodriguez
JGKC Jason Giambi 4.00 10.00
Kerry Collins
JKCP Jason Kidd 8.00 20.00
Chad Pennington
JRCD Ken Griffey Jr. 6.00 15.00
Corey Dillon
JRJR Jerry Rice 10.00 25.00
Jason Richardson
JSTG Junior Seau 6.00 15.00
Tony Gwynn
JWAT Jay Williams 6.00 15.00
Anthony Thomas
KGRM Kevin Garnett 15.00 30.00
Randy Moss
KWMM Kurt Warner 20.00 50.00
Mark McGwire
PMTB Pedro Martinez 12.50 30.00
Tom Brady
RMPM Reggie Miller 15.00 30.00
Peyton Manning
SSBU Sammy Sosa 8.00 20.00
Brian Urlacher
SYJH Steve Yzerman 10.00 25.00
Joey Harrington
TCOV Tim Couch 4.00 10.00
Omar Vizquel

2002-03 UD SuperStars Legendary Leaders Triple Jersey

ADJ Allen Iverson 20.00 50.00
Donovan McNabb
Jeremy Roenick
AEM Alex Rodriguez 20.00 50.00
Emmitt Smith
Mike Modano
CJS Cal Ripken 20.00 50.00
Jaromir Jagr
Stephen Davis
GMS Greg Maddux 12.50 30.00
Michael Vick
Shareef Abdur-Rahim
JDM Jason Giambi 10.00 25.00
Drew Bledsoe
Mark Messier
KJT Karl Malone 20.00 50.00
Jerry Rice
Tony Gwynn
LBP Larry Walker 15.00 40.00
Brian Griese
Patrick Roy
MCA Mike Piazza 10.00 25.00
Chad Pennington
Alexei Yashin
MPS Mark McGwire 30.00 80.00
Peyton Manning
Steve Yzerman
PPT Pedro Martinez 20.00 50.00
Paul Pierce
Tom Brady
RJM Roger Clemens 30.00 60.00
Jerry Rice
Mario Lemieux
SEB Sammy Sosa 10.00 25.00
Eric Daze
Brian Urlacher
SKM Sammy Sosa 25.00 60.00
Kobe Bryant
Marshall Faulk
TEM Tony Gwynn 30:00 60.00
Emmitt Smith
Mario Lemieux

2002-03 UD SuperStars Magic Moments

COMPLETE SET (20) 10.00 25.00
MM11 Kurt Warner .50 1.25
MM12 Brett Favre 1.25 3.00
MM13 Tom Brady 1.00 2.50

2002-03 UD SuperStars Rookie Review

R2 Ichiro Suzuki 2.00 5.00
Michael Vick
R4 Vince Carter 1.25 3.00
Peyton Manning
R5 Emmitt Smith 2.00 5.00
Sammy Sosa
R6 Mark Prior .75 2.00
Drew Brees
R10 Derek Jeter 1.50 4.00
Jerome Bettis

2002-03 UD SuperStars Spokesmen

*BLACK: 1.25X TO 3X BASIC SPOKESMEN
BLACK/GOLD INSERTS IN SPOKESMEN PACKS
BLACK PRINT RUN 250 SERIAL #'d SETS
*GOLD/25: 3X TO 8X BASIC INSERTS
GOLD PRINT RUN 25 SERIAL #'d SETS
UD11 Peyton Manning 1.25 3.00
UD26 Peyton Manning 1.25 3.00

2003 Ultimate Collection

Released in September of 2003, this set consists of 107 cards including 55 veterans and 52 rookies. Each veteran is serial numbered to 750. The non-autographed rookies are serial numbered to 750 or 250, and the autographed rookies are serial numbered to 250.

1 Peyton Manning 2.00 5.00
2 Aaron Brooks .75 2.00
3 Joey Harrington .60 1.50
4 Brett Favre 2.50 6.00
5 Donovan McNabb 1.00 2.50
6 Jeff Garcia .75 2.00
7 Michael Vick 1.25 3.00
8 David Carr .75 2.00
9 Drew Brees 1.00 2.50
10 Chad Pennington 1.00 2.50
11 Drew Bledsoe 1.00 2.50
12 Tom Brady 2.50 6.00
13 Kurt Warner 1.00 2.50
14 Brad Johnson .75 2.00
15 Jay Fiedler .60 1.50
16 Tim Couch .60 1.50
17 Trent Green .75 2.00
18 Daunte Culpepper .75 2.00
19 Keyshawn Johnson 1.00 2.50
20 Garrison Hearst .75 2.00
21 LaDainian Tomlinson 1.00 2.50
22 Emmitt Smith 2.50 6.00
23 Steve McNair 1.00 2.50
24 Chris Redman .60 1.50
25 Chad Hutchinson .60 1.50
26 Deuce McAllister .75 2.00
27 Eddie George .75 2.00
28 Marshall Faulk 1.00 2.50
29 Ahman Green .75 2.00
30 Julius Peppers 1.00 2.50
31 Priest Holmes 1.00 2.50
32 Edgerrin James 1.00 2.50
33 Jerry Rice 2.00 5.00
34 Ricky Williams .75 2.00
35 Anthony Thomas .75 2.00
36 Jerome Bettis 1.00 2.50
37 Shaun Alexander .75 2.00
38 Randy Moss 1.00 2.50
39 Jeremy Shockey 1.00 2.50
40 Patrick Ramsey .75 2.00
41 Clinton Portis .75 2.00
42 Terrell Owens 1.00 2.50
43 Corey Dillon .75 2.00
44 Mark Brunell .75 2.00
45 Rich Gannon .75 2.00
46 Curtis Martin 1.00 2.50
47 Josh McCown .75 2.00
48 Kerry Collins .75 2.00
49 Peerless Price .60 1.50
50 David Boston .60 1.50
51 Plaxico Burress .75 2.00
52 Marvin Harrison 1.00 2.50
53 Travis Henry .60 1.50
54 Brian Urlacher 1.00 2.50
55 Jake Plummer .75 2.00
56 Dave Ragone/750 RC 2.00 5.00
57 Brian St.Pierre AU/250 RC 10.00 25.00
58 Tony Romo/750 RC 20.00 50.00
59 Dallas Clark/750 RC 5.00 12.00
60 Kirk Farmer/750 RC 2.50 6.00
61 Juston Wood/750 RC 2.00 5.00
62 Justin Gage/750 RC 2.50 6.00
63 Sam Aiken/750 RC 2.50 6.00
64 LaBrandon Toefield/750 RC 2.50 6.00
65 L.J. Smith/750 RC 3.00 8.00
66 Domanick Davis/750 RC 2.50 6.00
67 Artose Pinner/750 RC 2.00 5.00
68 Dahrran Diedrick/750 RC 2.00 5.00
69 Lee Suggs/750 RC 2.50 6.00
70 Bethel Johnson/750 RC 2.00 5.00
71 Tyrone Calico/750 RC 2.50 6.00
72 Kevin Curtis/750 RC 3.00 8.00
73 Bobby Wade/750 RC 2.50 6.00
74 Brandon Lloyd/750 RC 5.00 12.00
75 Bryant Johnson/750 RC 3.00 8.00
76 J.R. Tolver/750 RC 2.50 6.00
77 Billy McMullen/750 RC 2.00 5.00
78 Nate Burleson/750 RC 2.50 6.00
79 Jason Johnson AU/250 RC 8.00 20.00
80 Talman Gardner/250 RC 5.00 12.00
81 Anquan Boldin/250 RC 12.00 30.00
82 Musa Smith/250 RC 5.00 12.00
83 Teyo Johnson/250 RC 6.00 15.00
84 Kyle Boller AU/250 RC 12.00 30.00
85 Carson Palmer AU/250 RC 50.00 100.00
86 Byron Leftwich AU/250 RC 12.00 30.00
87 Earnest Graham AU/250 RC 12.00 30.00
88 Chris Brown AU/250 RC 8.00 20.00
89 Chris Simms AU/250 RC 12.00 30.00
90 Kliff Kingsbury AU/250 RC 10.00 25.00
91 Jason Gesser/750 RC 2.50 6.00
92 Brad Banks AU/250 RC 10.00 25.00
93 Ken Dorsey AU/250 RC 10.00 25.00
94 Rex Grossman AU/250 RC 15.00 40.00
95 Willis McGahee AU/250 RC 20.00 50.00
96 Larry Johnson AU/250 RC 12.00 30.00
97 Quentin Griffin AU/250 RC 10.00 25.00
98 Onterrio Smith AU/250 RC 8.00 20.00
99 Justin Fargas AU/250 RC 12.00 30.00
100 Kareem Kelly AU/250 RC 8.00 20.00
101 Arnaz Battle AU/250 RC 12.00 30.00
102 Kelley Washington AU/250 RC 8.00 20.00
103 Seneca Wallace AU/250 RC 12.00 30.00
104 Taylor Jacobs AU/250 RC 8.00 20.00
105 Andre Johnson/750 RC 8.00 20.00
106 Charles Rogers/250 RC 6.00 15.00
107 Terrell Suggs AU/250 RC 20.00 40.00

2003 Ultimate Collection Gold

*VETS 1-55: 1X TO 2.5X BASIC CARDS
1-55 VETERAN PRINT RUN 75
*ROOKIES/75: .8X TO 2X RC/750
*ROOKIES/25: .8X TO 2X RC/250
*ROOK.AU/25: .6X TO 1.5X AU/250
56-107 ROOKIE PRINT RUN 25-75
58 Tony Romo/75 40.00 100.00
85 Carson Palmer AU/25 125.00 250.00
94 Rex Grossman AU/25 100.00 200.00
95 Willis McGahee AU/25 60.00 150.00
96 Larry Johnson AU/25 60.00 150.00

2003 Ultimate Collection Buy Back Autographs

STATED PRINT RUN 1-36
SER.#'d UNDER 25 NOT PRICED
1 Shaun Alexander 02SP/19 15.00 40.00
3 Shaun Alexander 02UDG/35 15.00 40.00
4 Shaun Alexander 02UDSS/36 15.00 40.00
13 Aaron Brooks 02UDG/20 15.00 40.00
15 Aaron Brooks 02UDSS/23 15.00 40.00
26 Tim Couch 02SP/24 15.00 40.00
27 Tim Couch 02UDA/19 15.00 40.00
28 Tim Couch 02UDG/28 15.00 40.00
35 Jeff Garcia 01UDPPJsy/29 15.00 40.00
37 Jeff Garcia 02UDSS/24 15.00 40.00
38 Rod Gardner 02SP/29 15.00 40.00
40 Rod Gardner 02UDSS/24 15.00 40.00
43 Peyton Manning 01UDPPJsy/29 50.00 100.00
44 Peyton Manning 02SPLC/25 50.00 100.00
48 Peyton Manning 02UDSS/24 50.00 100.00
54 Terrell Owens 02UDG/20 25.00 50.00
58 Anthony Thomas 02UDG/34 15.00 40.00
60 Anthony Thomas 02UDSS/35 15.00 40.00
62 LaDainian Tomlinson 02UDG/20 40.00 80.00

2003 Ultimate Collection Game Jerseys

STATED PRINT RUN 99-250
*GOLD/25: 1X TO 2.5X BASE JSY/250
*GOLD/25: .6X TO 1.5X BASE JSY/99
GOLD STATED PRINT RUN 25
UJAB Aaron Brooks/250 4.00 10.00
UJAG Ahman Green/250 4.00 10.00
UJBA Tom Brady/250 12.00 30.00
UJBF Brett Favre/250 12.00 30.00
UJBR Drew Brees/250 5.00 12.00
UJBS Barry Sanders/99 20.00 50.00
UJBU Brian Urlacher/250 5.00 12.00
UJCP1 Chad Pennington/250 5.00 12.00
UJCP2 Clinton Portis/250 4.00 10.00
UJDA Dan Marino/99 25.00 60.00
UJDB Drew Bledsoe/250 5.00 12.00
UJDC Daunte Culpepper/250 4.00 10.00
UJDM Donovan McNabb/250 5.00 12.00
UJEJ Edgerrin James/250 5.00 12.00
UJFT Fran Tarkenton/99 10.00 25.00
UJJE John Elway/99 25.00 60.00
UJJG Jeff Garcia/250 4.00 10.00
UJJK Jim Kelly/99 12.00 30.00
UJJM Joe Montana/99 25.00 60.00
UJJN Joe Namath/99 15.00 40.00
UJJR Jerry Rice/250 10.00 25.00
UJKJ Keyshawn Johnson/250 5.00 12.00
UJKW Kurt Warner/250 5.00 12.00
UJLT LaDainian Tomlinson/250 5.00 12.00
UJMA Marcus Allen/99 10.00 25.00
UJMC Deuce McAllister/250 4.00 10.00
UJMF Marshall Faulk/250 5.00 12.00
UJMV Michael Vick/250 6.00 15.00
UJPH Priest Holmes/250 5.00 12.00
UJPM Peyton Manning/250 10.00 25.00
UJRM Randy Moss/250 5.00 12.00
UJRW Ricky Williams/250 4.00 10.00
UJST Bart Starr/99 20.00 50.00
UJSY Steve Young/99 12.00 30.00
UJTA Troy Aikman/99 12.00 30.00
UJTC Tim Couch/250 3.00 8.00
UJTO Terrell Owens/250 5.00 12.00
UJWP Walter Payton/99 30.00 80.00

2003 Ultimate Collection Game Jersey Autographs

STATED PRINT RUN 25 SER.#'d SETS
GOLD/10 NOT PRICED DUE TO SCARCITY
UJSBS Bart Starr 150.00 250.00
UJSDM Dan Marino 125.00 250.00
UJSJM Joe Montana 125.00 250.00
UJSJN Joe Namath 100.00 175.00
UJSMV Michael Vick 60.00 100.00
UJSPM Peyton Manning 100.00 200.00

2003 Ultimate Collection Game Jersey Duals

STATED PRINT RUN 99-250
*GOLD/25: .8X TO 2X BASE DUAL/250
*GOLD/25: .5X TO 1.2X BASE DUAL/99-100
GOLD PRINT RUN 25 SER.#'d SETS
UDJAM Troy Aikman 20.00 50.00
Peyton Manning/99
UDJBC Aaron Brooks 5.00 12.00
Tim Couch/250
UDJCB David Carr 15.00 40.00
Tom Brady/250
UDJFM Marshall Faulk 6.00 15.00
Curtis Martin/250
UDJFR Brett Favre 12.00 30.00
Jerry Rice/250
UDJHB Joey Harrington 6.00 15.00
Drew Brees/250
UDJHW Priest Holmes 6.00 15.00
Ricky Williams/250
UDJKB Jim Kelly 10.00 25.00
Drew Bledsoe/250
UDJMC Dan Marino 25.00 60.00
David Carr/99
UDJMS Deuce McAllister 20.00 50.00
Barry Sanders/100
UDJMV Donovan McNabb 8.00 20.00
Michael Vick/250
UDJMG1 Donovan McNabb 6.00 15.00
Jeff Garcia/250
UDJMG2 Joe Montana 25.00 60.00
Jeff Garcia/99
UDJNP Joe Namath 10.00 25.00
Chad Pennington/99
UDJPD Clinton Portis 6.00 15.00
Terrell Davis/250
UDJPF Walter Payton 30.00 80.00
Marshall Faulk/99
UDJPM Chad Pennington 6.00 15.00
Randy Moss/250
UDJPT Walter Payton 20.00 50.00
Anthony Thomas/250
UDJPW Walter Payton 30.00 80.00
Ricky Williams/99
UDJRO Jerry Rice 12.00 30.00
Terrell Owens/250
UDJSF Bart Starr 40.00 100.00
Brett Favre/99
UDJST Barry Sanders 20.00 50.00
LaDainian Tomlinson/99
UDJTC Fran Tarkenton 10.00 25.00
Daunte Culpepper/99
UDJYV Steve Young 12.00 30.00
Michael Vick/99

2003 Ultimate Collection Game Jersey Duals Autographs

STATED PRINT RUN 25 SER.#'d SETS
GOLD/10 NOT PRICED DUE TO SCARCITY
DJSEM John Elway 200.00 400.00
Donovan McNabb
DJSMM Dan Marino 300.00 500.00
Peyton Manning
DJSNP Joe Namath 125.00 250.00
Chad Pennington
DJSSF Bart Starr 400.00 550.00
Brett Favre
DJSVM Michael Vick 75.00 150.00
Donovan McNabb
DJSYV Steve Young 100.00 200.00
Michael Vick

2003 Ultimate Collection Game Jersey Duals Patches

STATED PRINT RUN 25 SER.#'d SETS
UNPRICED PATCH GOLD PRINT RUN 3-10
DGPAM Troy Aikman 50.00 125.00
Peyton Manning/25
DGPBR Mark Brunell 20.00 50.00
Dave Ragone/25
DGPBW Terry Bradshaw 40.00 100.00
Kurt Warner/25
DGPJM Edgerrin James 20.00 50.00
Willis McGahee/25
DGPMC Randy Moss 25.00 60.00
Daunte Culpepper/25
DGPMF Dan Marino 60.00 150.00
Jay Fiedler/25
DGPMG Joe Montana 60.00 150.00
Jeff Garcia/25
DGPPT Walter Payton 50.00 120.00
Anthony Thomas/25
DGPRM Jerry Rice 50.00 125.00
Randy Moss/25
DGPRO Jerry Rice 50.00 125.00
Terrell Owens/25
DGPSF Bart Starr 80.00 200.00
Brett Favre/25
DGPVM Michael Vick 30.00 80.00
Donovan McNabb/25

2003 Ultimate Collection Game Jersey Patches

STATED PRINT RUN 25-175
*GOLD/25: 1X TO 2.5X BASE PATCH/141-175
*GOLD/25: .8X TO 2X BASE PATCH/99
GOLD PRINT RUN 10-25
GJPAB Aaron Brooks/175 6.00 15.00
GJPAG Ahman Green/175 6.00 15.00
GJPBA Barry Sanders/25 50.00 120.00
GJPBF Brett Favre/99 25.00 60.00
GJPBS Bart Starr/25 40.00 100.00
GJPBU Brian Urlacher/175 8.00 20.00
GJPCA David Carr/175 6.00 15.00
GJPCP1 Chad Pennington/99 10.00 25.00
GJPCP2 Clinton Portis/175 6.00 15.00
GJPDC Daunte Culpepper/175 6.00 15.00
GJPDB1 Drew Bledsoe/175 8.00 20.00
GJPDB2 Drew Brees/99 10.00 25.00
GJPDM1 Dan Marino/25 60.00 150.00
GJPDM2 Deuce McAllister/175 6.00 15.00
GJPDM3 Donovan McNabb/99 10.00 25.00
GJPEG Eddie George/175 6.00 15.00
GJPEJ Edgerrin James/99 10.00 25.00
GJPES Emmitt Smith/175 20.00 50.00
GJPFT Fran Tarkenton/99 12.00 30.00
GJPJE John Elway/99 30.00 80.00
GJPJG Jeff Garcia/175 6.00 15.00
GJPJM Joe Montana/25 60.00 150.00
GJPJN Joe Namath/25 40.00 100.00
GJPJR Jerry Rice/175 15.00 40.00
GJPKJ Keyshawn Johnson/175 8.00 20.00
GJPKW Kurt Warner/99 10.00 25.00
GJPLT LaDainian Tomlinson/175 8.00 20.00
GJPMF Marshall Faulk/175 8.00 20.00
GJPMV Michael Vick/99 12.00 30.00
GJPPH Priest Holmes/175 8.00 20.00
GJPPM Peyton Manning/175 15.00 40.00
GJPRM Randy Moss/175 8.00 20.00
GJPRW Ricky Williams/99 8.00 20.00
GJPSY Steve Young/25 30.00 80.00
GJPTA Troy Aikman/99 15.00 40.00
GJPTC Tim Couch/175 5.00 12.00
GJPTO Terrell Owens/175 8.00 20.00
GJPTB1 Terry Bradshaw/25 40.00 100.00
GJPTB2 Tom Brady/175 20.00 50.00
GJPWP Walter Payton/25 60.00 150.00

2003 Ultimate Collection Ultimate Signatures

*GOLD/50: .6X TO 1.5X BASE AUTO
GOLD STATED PRINT RUN 10-50
USAB Aaron Brooks 10.00 25.00
USBA Barry Sanders 90.00 150.00
USBB Brad Banks 8.00 20.00
USBF Brett Favre/25 175.00 300.00
USBL Byron Leftwich 10.00 25.00
USBS Bart Starr/25 100.00 200.00
USCH Chad Pennington 12.00 30.00
USCP Carson Palmer 75.00 125.00
USCS Chris Simms 12.00 30.00
USDB Drew Brees 30.00 60.00
USDC David Carr/25 12.00 30.00
USDE Deuce McAllister 10.00 25.00
USDM Dan Marino/25 125.00 250.00
USFT Fran Tarkenton/25 30.00 60.00
USJE John Elway/25 100.00 200.00
USJF Justin Fargas 10.00 25.00
USJK Jim Kelly 20.00 50.00
USJM Joe Montana/25 125.00 250.00
USJN Joe Namath/25 75.00 135.00
USJR Jerry Rice/25 100.00 200.00
USKK Kliff Kingsbury 8.00 20.00
USKS Ken Stabler 25.00 50.00
USLT LaDainian Tomlinson 50.00 80.00
USMA Marcus Allen 20.00 40.00
USPM Peyton Manning 75.00 125.00
USRG Rex Grossman 10.00 25.00
USSU Donovan McNabb 25.00 50.00
USSY Steve Young/25 90.00 150.00
USTA Troy Aikman/25 75.00 150.00
USTB Terry Bradshaw/25 75.00 150.00
USTC Tim Couch 8.00 20.00

2003 Ultimate Collection Ultimate Signatures Duals

DSBT Drew Brees 75.00 150.00
LaDainian Tomlinson/50
DSGM Jeff Garcia 100.00 200.00
Joe Montana/25
DSGY Jeff Garcia 75.00 150.00
Steve Young/25
DSMF Dan Marino 125.00 250.00
Jay Fiedler/25
DSMM Peyton Manning 100.00 200.00
Archie Manning/50
DSMP Peyton Manning 100.00 200.00
Carson Palmer/50
DSMY Joe Montana 200.00 400.00
Steve Young/25
DSNP Joe Namath 125.00 250.00
Chad Pennington/25
DSPL Carson Palmer 30.00 80.00
Byron Leftwich/50
DSSF Bart Starr 300.00 500.00
Brett Favre/25
DSSS Phil Simms 30.00 60.00
Chris Simms/50

2003 Ultimate Collection Ultimate Signatures Duals Gold

SER.#'d TO 10 NOT PRICED
DSBT Drew Brees 60.00 150.00
LaDainian Tomlinson/25
DSMM Peyton Manning 125.00 200.00
Archie Manning/25
DSMP Peyton Manning 125.00 250.00
Carson Palmer/25
DSPL Carson Palmer 50.00 120.00
Byron Leftwich/25
DSSS Phil Simms 40.00 100.00
Chris Simms/25

2004 Ultimate Collection

Ultimate Collection was initially released in late December 2004 and remained one of the hottest products of the year. The base set consists of 135-cards including 64-veterans serial numbered to 750 as well as multi-level numbered rookie cards and autographed rookie cards. Hobby boxes contained 4-packs of 4-cards and carried an S.R.P. of $100 per pack. Three parallel sets and a variety of inserts can be found seeded in packs highlighted by a huge checklist of Buy Back Autographs and the Ultimate Signatures inserts.

1-65 VETERAN PRINT RUN 750
66-91/99A/133-135 PRINT RUN 750
92-98 ROOKIE PRINT RUN 250
99B-124/131-132 AU RC PRINT RUN 250
125-130 AU RC PRINT RUN 150 SER.#'d SETS
UNPRICED PLATINUM PRINT RUN 10
1 Emmitt Smith 4.00 10.00
2 Anquan Boldin 1.50 4.00
3 Michael Vick 2.00 5.00
4 Peerless Price 1.00 2.50
5 Kyle Boller 1.25 3.00
6 Jamal Lewis 1.25 3.00
7 Drew Bledsoe 1.50 4.00
8 Travis Henry 1.00 2.50
9 Stephen Davis 1.25 3.00
10 Jake Delhomme 1.25 3.00
11 Rex Grossman 1.25 3.00
12 Brian Urlacher 1.50 4.00
13 Carson Palmer 1.50 4.00
14 Chad Johnson 1.50 4.00
15 Jeff Garcia 1.25 3.00
16 Keyshawn Johnson 1.25 3.00
17 Roy Williams S 1.25 3.00
18 Jake Plummer 1.25 3.00
19 Joey Harrington 1.25 3.00
20 Charles Rogers 1.00 2.50
21 Ahman Green 1.25 3.00
22 Brett Favre 4.00 10.00
23 David Carr 1.00 2.50
24 Domanick Davis 1.00 2.50
25 Andre Johnson 1.50 4.00
26 Edgerrin James 1.25 3.00
27 Peyton Manning 3.00 8.00
28 Marvin Harrison 1.50 4.00
29 Byron Leftwich 1.25 3.00
30 Fred Taylor 1.25 3.00
31 Priest Holmes 1.50 4.00
32 Tony Gonzalez 1.50 4.00
33 Trent Green 1.25 3.00
34 Ricky Williams 1.25 3.00
35 Chris Chambers 1.25 3.00
36 Jay Fiedler 1.00 2.50
37 Randy Moss 1.50 4.00
38 Daunte Culpepper 1.25 3.00
39 Tom Brady 3.00 8.00
40 Corey Dillon 1.25 3.00
41 Deuce McAllister 1.25 3.00
42 Aaron Brooks 1.25 3.00
43 Tiki Barber 1.50 4.00
44 Jeremy Shockey 1.25 3.00
45 Chad Pennington 1.50 4.00
46 Curtis Martin 1.50 4.00
47 Santana Moss 1.25 3.00
48 Jerry Rice 3.00 8.00
49 Rich Gannon 1.25 3.00
50 Donovan McNabb 1.50 4.00
51 Terrell Owens 1.50 4.00
52 Hines Ward 1.50 4.00
53 Plaxico Burress 1.25 3.00
54 LaDainian Tomlinson 1.50 4.00
55 Tim Rattay 1.00 2.50
56 Matt Hasselbeck 1.25 3.00
57 Shaun Alexander 1.25 3.00
58 Marc Bulger 1.25 3.00
59 Marshall Faulk 1.50 4.00
60 Torry Holt 1.25 3.00
61 Brad Johnson 1.25 3.00
62 Steve McNair 1.50 4.00
63 Chris Brown 1.00 2.50
64 Mark Brunell 1.25 3.00
65 Clinton Portis 1.50 4.00
66 Michael Turner RC 4.00 10.00
67 Kris Wilson RC 2.50 6.00
68 Jeff Smoker RC 2.50 6.00
69 Adimchinobe Echemandu RC 2.50 6.00
71 Thomas Tapeh RC 2.50 6.00
72 Chris Cooley RC 3.00 8.00
73 Cody Pickett RC 2.50 6.00
74 P.K. Sam RC 2.00 5.00
75 Ben Hartsock RC 2.00 5.00
76 Tim Euhus RC 2.00 5.00
77 Jammal Lord RC 2.00 5.00
78 Ricardo Colclough RC 2.50 6.00
79 D.J. Hackett RC 2.50 6.00
80 Ahmad Carroll RC 2.00 5.00
81 Troy Fleming RC 2.00 5.00
82 John Navarre RC 2.00 5.00
83 Craig Krenzel RC 2.50 6.00
84 Johnnie Morant RC 2.00 5.00
85 D.J. Williams RC 3.00 8.00
86 Jarrett Payton RC 2.50 6.00
87 Quincy Wilson RC 2.50 6.00
88 B.J. Symons RC 2.00 5.00
89 Tommie Harris RC 3.00 8.00
90 Jonathan Vilma RC 3.00 8.00
91 Karlos Dansby RC 3.00 8.00
92 Jerricho Cotchery RC 3.00 8.00
93 Samie Parker RC 2.50 6.00
94 Carlos Francis RC 2.50 6.00
95 Jim Sorgi RC 3.00 8.00
96 Derrick Hamilton RC 2.50 6.00
97 Dunta Robinson RC 2.50 6.00
98 Chris Gamble RC 3.00 8.00
99A Josh Harris RC 2.00 5.00
99B Devery Henderson AU RC 10.00 25.00
100 Julius Jones AU RC 10.00 25.00
101 Cedric Cobbs AU RC 6.00 15.00
102 Greg Jones AU RC 6.00 15.00
103 Tatum Bell AU RC 8.00 20.00
104 Michael Jenkins AU RC 10.00 25.00
105 Devard Darling AU RC 6.00 15.00
106 Lee Evans AU RC 10.00 25.00
107 Keary Colbert AU RC 6.00 15.00
108 Bernard Berrian AU RC 10.00 25.00
109 Ben Watson AU RC 10.00 25.00
110 Matt Schaub AU RC 50.00 100.00
111 Darius Watts AU RC 6.00 15.00
112 Kevin Jones AU RC 8.00 20.00
113 Luke McCown AU RC 8.00 20.00
114 DeAngelo Hall AU RC 10.00 25.00
115 Rashaun Woods AU RC 6.00 15.00
116 Michael Clayton AU RC 8.00 20.00
117 Ben Troupe AU RC 8.00 20.00
118 B.J. Sams AU RC 6.00 15.00
119 Reggie Williams AU RC 8.00 20.00
120 Chris Perry AU RC 8.00 20.00
121 Roy Williams AU RC 20.00 50.00
122 Robert Gallery AU RC 10.00 25.00
123 J.P. Losman AU RC 8.00 20.00
124 Steven Jackson AU RC 50.00 100.00
125 Drew Henson AU RC 6.00 15.00
126 Kellen Winslow AU RC 15.00 40.00
127 Ben Roethlisberger AU RC 250.00 400.00
128 Philip Rivers AU RC 75.00 150.00
129 Larry Fitzgerald AU RC 75.00 150.00
130 Eli Manning AU RC 250.00 400.00
131 Ernest Wilford AU RC 8.00 20.00
132 Mewelde Moore AU RC 8.00 20.00
133 Will Smith RC 2.50 6.00
134 Kenechi Udeze RC 2.50 6.00
135 Matt Mauck RC 2.00 5.00

2004 Ultimate Collection Gold

*VETS: .8X TO 2X BASIC CARDS
*ROOKIES/75: .8X TO 2X BASIC RC/750
1-91/99A/133-135 PRINT RUN 75 SETS
*ROOKIES/25: 1X TO 2.5X BASE RC/250
92-98 STATED PRINT RUN 25 SETS

2004 Ultimate Collection HoloGold

*VETS: 1.2X TO 3X BASE CARDS
*ROOKIES/30: 1.2X TO 3X BASIC RC/750
1-91/99A/133-135 PRINT RUN 30 SETS
UNPRICED 92-98 PRINT RUN 5 SETS

2004 Ultimate Collection Buy Back Autographs

SER.#'d UNDER 22 NOT PRICED
BBCC1 Chris Chambers 01UDRT/25 12.00 30.00
BBCC2 Chris Chambers 01UDORG/20 12.00 30.00
BBCJ1 Chad Johnson 03SPA/26 15.00 40.00
BBCJ2 Chad Johnson 03SPSIG/42 15.00 40.00
BBCJ3 Chad Johnson 03SS/45 15.00 40.00
BBCJ4 Chad Johnson 03UDGJ/33 15.00 40.00
BBDB1 Drew Bledsoe 00UDGJ/21
BBDE3 Deuce McAllister 03SPA/26 15.00 40.00
BBDK Derrick Mason 03SPA/40 12.50 30.00
BBFT Fran Tarkenton 03SPSIG/28 15.00 40.00
BBJO3 Josh McCown 03SPA/27 12.50 30.00
BBJO4 Josh McCown 03SPSIG/22 12.50 30.00
BBJO5 Josh McCown 03UDSOS/24 12.50 30.00
BBKS2 Ken Stabler 03SPSIG/26 25.00 60.00
BBRA Randy White 01UDLTT/33 15.00 40.00
BBRW3 Roy Williams S 03UDGJ/31 15.00 40.00
BBTH2 Travis Henry 03SPA/36 10.00 25.00
BBTH4 Travis Henry 03SPSIG/46 10.00 25.00
BBTH5 Travis Henry 03SS/39 10.00 25.00
BBTO Todd Heap 03SS/30 10.00 25.00
BBZT2 Zach Thomas 04SPxSS/50 12.50 30.00

2004 Ultimate Collection Game Jerseys

STATED PRINT RUN 175 SER.#'d SETS
*GOLD: 1X TO 2.5X BASIC JSY/175
GOLD PRINT RUN 25 SER.#'d SETS
UGJBF Brett Favre 10.00 25.00
UGJBL Byron Leftwich 3.00 8.00
UGJBS Barry Sanders 10.00 25.00
UGJCA Carson Palmer 4.00 10.00
UGJCL Clinton Portis 4.00 10.00
UGJCP Chad Pennington 4.00 10.00
UGJDA David Carr 2.50 6.00
UGJDC Daunte Culpepper 3.00 8.00
UGJDM Deuce McAllister 3.00 8.00
UGJDO Donovan McNabb 4.00 10.00
UGJED Eric Dickerson 5.00 12.00
UGJES Emmitt Smith 12.00 30.00
UGJFT Fran Tarkenton 5.00 12.00
UGJJE John Elway 12.00 30.00
UGJJM Joe Montana 12.00 30.00
UGJJN Joe Namath 8.00 20.00
UGJJR Jerry Rice 8.00 20.00
UGJJS Jeremy Shockey 3.00 8.00
UGJLS Lynn Swann 10.00 25.00
UGJLT LaDainian Tomlinson 4.00 10.00
UGJMA Dan Marino 12.00 30.00
UGJMF Marshall Faulk 4.00 10.00
UGJMH Marvin Harrison 4.00 10.00
UGJMV Michael Vick 5.00 12.00
UGJPH Priest Holmes 4.00 10.00
UGJPM Peyton Manning 8.00 20.00
UGJPS Phil Simms 4.00 10.00
UGJRM Randy Moss 4.00 10.00
UGJRS Roger Staubach 8.00 20.00
UGJRW Ricky Williams 3.00 8.00
UGJSM Steve McNair 4.00 10.00
UGJSY Steve Young 6.00 15.00
UGJTA Troy Aikman 8.00 20.00
UGJTB Tom Brady 8.00 20.00
UGJTE Terry Bradshaw 8.00 20.00
UGJTO Terrell Owens 4.00 10.00
UGJWP Walter Payton 20.00 50.00

2004 Ultimate Collection Game Jersey Autographs

STATED PRINT RUN 25 SER.#'d SETS
UGJSBF Brett Favre 175.00 300.00
UGJSCP Chad Pennington 25.00 60.00
UGJSDA Daunte Culpepper 20.00 50.00
UGJSDC David Carr 15.00 40.00
UGJSDM Deuce McAllister 20.00 50.00
UGJSDO Donovan McNabb 60.00 120.00
UGJSJE John Elway 125.00 250.00
UGJSJM Joe Montana 125.00 250.00
UGJSJN Joe Namath 100.00 175.00
UGJSJT Joe Theismann 25.00 60.00
UGJSLT LaDainian Tomlinson 25.00 60.00
UGJSMV Michael Vick 50.00 100.00
UGJSPM Peyton Manning 125.00 250.00
UGJSSM Steve McNair 25.00 60.00
UGJSTB Tom Brady 125.00 250.00

2004 Ultimate Collection Game Jersey Duals

STATED PRINT RUN 99 SER.#'d SETS
*GOLD/15: .8X TO 2X BASIC DUAL
GOLD STATED PRINT RUN 15
UNPRICED DUAL AU PRINT RUN 15 SETS
BP Tom Brady 15.00 40.00
Chad Pennington
CF David Carr 20.00 50.00
Brett Favre
CM Daunte Culpepper 8.00 20.00
Steve McNair
EM John Elway 25.00 60.00
Joe Montana
EP Eli Manning 25.00 60.00
Philip Rivers
FM Brett Favre 20.00 50.00
Peyton Manning
HJ Priest Holmes 8.00 20.00
Edgerrin James
LP Byron Leftwich 8.00 20.00
Carson Palmer
LR Larry Fitzgerald 10.00 25.00
Randy Moss
MB Joe Montana 30.00 80.00
Tom Brady
MM Dan Marino 25.00 60.00
Joe Montana
MO Randy Moss 8.00 20.00
Terrell Owens
MR Randy Moss 15.00 40.00
Jerry Rice
NU Joe Namath 20.00 50.00
Johnny Unitas
OM Terrell Owens 8.00 20.00
Donovan McNabb
PG Clinton Portis 8.00 20.00
Ahman Green
PM Chad Pennington 15.00 40.00
Peyton Manning
PS Walter Payton 30.00 80.00
Gale Sayers
RO Jerry Rice 15.00 40.00
Terrell Owens
SA Roger Staubach 12.00 30.00
Troy Aikman
SF Emmitt Smith 20.00 50.00
Marshall Faulk
SG Jeremy Shockey 8.00 20.00
Tony Gonzalez
SP Barry Sanders 30.00 80.00
Walter Payton
SW Jeremy Shockey 8.00 20.00
Kellen Winslow Jr.
TL Lawrence Taylor 8.00 20.00
Ronnie Lott
TM LaDainian Tomlinson 8.00 20.00
Deuce McAllister
UT Brian Urlacher 8.00 20.00
Zach Thomas
VB Michael Vick 15.00 40.00
Tom Brady
VM Michael Vick 10.00 25.00
Mark Brunell
WH Ricky Williams 8.00 20.00
Priest Holmes

2004 Ultimate Collection Game Jersey Dual Autographs

UNPRICED DUAL JSY AU PRINT RUN 15
UNPRICED DUAL PATCH AU PRINT RUN 5

2004 Ultimate Collection Game Jersey Dual Patches

STATED PRINT RUN 25 SER.#'d SETS
UNPRICED GOLD PRINT RUN 10
AE Troy Aikman 30.00 80.00
John Elway
BP Tom Brady 30.00 80.00
Chad Pennington
FV Brett Favre 40.00 100.00
Michael Vick
MC Randy Moss 20.00 50.00
Daunte Culpepper
MM Dan Marino 50.00 120.00
Joe Montana
NU Joe Namath 50.00 100.00
Johnny Unitas
PS Peyton Manning 30.00 80.00
Steve McNair
SM Barry Sanders 30.00 80.00
Deuce McAllister
VM Michael Vick 25.00 60.00
Donovan McNabb
WT Ricky Williams 20.00 50.00
LaDainian Tomlinson

2004 Ultimate Collection Game Jersey Logo Autographs

UNPRICED AU PRINT RUN 1 SET

2004 Ultimate Collection Game Jersey Patches

STATED PRINT RUN 150 SER.#'d SETS
*GOLD/25: .8X TO 2X BASIC PTCH/150
GOLD PRINT RUN 25 SER.#'d SETS
UNPRICED AUTO PRINT RUN 10 SETS
UPAG Ahman Green 6.00 15.00
UPBF Brett Favre 20.00 50.00
UPBL Byron Leftwich 6.00 15.00
UPBS Barry Sanders 20.00 50.00
UPBU Brian Urlacher 8.00 20.00
UPCA Carson Palmer 8.00 20.00
UPCC Cris Carter 8.00 20.00
UPCL Clinton Portis 8.00 20.00
UPCP Chad Pennington 8.00 20.00
UPDA David Carr 5.00 12.00
UPDB Drew Bledsoe 8.00 20.00
UPDC Daunte Culpepper 6.00 15.00
UPDE Deuce McAllister 6.00 15.00
UPDM Donovan McNabb 8.00 20.00
UPED Eric Dickerson 10.00 25.00
UPEJ Edgerrin James 6.00 15.00
UPES Emmitt Smith 20.00 50.00
UPFT Fran Tarkenton 10.00 25.00
UPGS Gale Sayers 12.00 30.00
UPJE John Elway 25.00 60.00
UPJM Joe Montana 25.00 60.00
UPJN Joe Namath 15.00 40.00
UPJR Jerry Rice 15.00 40.00
UPJS Jeremy Shockey 6.00 15.00
UPJU Johnny Unitas 25.00 60.00
UPLT LaDainian Tomlinson 8.00 20.00
UPMA Dan Marino 25.00 60.00
UPMB Mark Brunell 6.00 15.00
UPMF Marshall Faulk 8.00 20.00
UPMH Marvin Harrison 8.00 20.00
UPMV Michael Vick 10.00 25.00
UPPH Priest Holmes 8.00 20.00
UPPM Peyton Manning 15.00 40.00
UPRM Randy Moss 8.00 20.00
UPRS Roger Staubach 15.00 40.00
UPRW Ricky Williams 6.00 15.00
UPSM Steve McNair 8.00 20.00
UPTA Troy Aikman 15.00 40.00
UPTB Tom Brady 15.00 40.00
UPTO Terrell Owens 8.00 20.00
UPWP Walter Payton 40.00 100.00
UPZT Zach Thomas 8.00 20.00

2004 Ultimate Collection Game Jersey Patches Autographs

UNPRICED AU PRINT RUN 10 SER.#'d SETS

2004 Ultimate Collection Game Jersey Super Patches

SUPER PATCH PRINT RUN 15
USPBF Brett Favre 50.00 120.00
USPCP Chad Pennington 20.00 50.00
USPDE Deuce McAllister 15.00 40.00
USPDM Donovan McNabb 20.00 50.00
USPES Emmitt Smith 50.00 120.00
USPJR Jerry Rice 40.00 100.00
USPMV Michael Vick 25.00 60.00
USPPM Peyton Manning 40.00 100.00

USPRM Randy Moss 20.00 50.00
USPTB Tom Brady 40.00 100.00

2004 Ultimate Collection Rookie Jerseys

STATED PRINT RUN 199 SER.#'d SETS
*GOLD/25: .6X TO 1.5X BASIC JSY/199
GOLD PRINT RUN 25 SER.#'d SETS
UNPRICED AUTO PRINT RUN 1
URJBR Ben Roethlisberger 20.00 50.00
URJCC Cedric Cobbs 2.50 6.00
URJCP Chris Perry 3.00 8.00
URJDD Devard Darling 2.50 6.00
URJDE Devery Henderson 4.00 10.00
URJEM Eli Manning 20.00 50.00
URJGJ Greg Jones 2.50 6.00
URJJJ Julius Jones 3.00 8.00
URJJP J.P. Losman 3.00 8.00
URJKJ Kevin Jones 3.00 8.00
URJKW Kellen Winslow Jr. 4.00 10.00
URJLE Lee Evans 4.00 10.00
URJLF Larry Fitzgerald 10.00 25.00
URJMC Michael Clayton 3.00 8.00
URJMJ Michael Jenkins 4.00 10.00
URJPR Philip Rivers 12.00 30.00
URJRA Rashaun Woods 2.50 6.00
URJRO Roy Williams WR 4.00 10.00
URJRW Reggie Williams 3.00 8.00
URJSJ Steven Jackson 6.00 15.00
URJTB Tatum Bell 3.00 8.00

2004 Ultimate Collection Ultimate Signatures

UNPRICED QUAD AU PRINT RUN 5 SETS
USAG Ahman Green/100 10.00 25.00
USAR Andy Reid/100 10.00 25.00
USBF Brett Favre/25 175.00 300.00
USBL Byron Leftwich/275 8.00 20.00
USBP Bill Parcells/25 40.00 80.00
USBR Ben Roethlisberger/100 125.00 250.00
USBS Barry Sanders/25 100.00 200.00
USCC Chris Chambers/275 8.00 20.00
USCJ Chad Johnson/275 10.00 25.00
USDB Drew Bledsoe/275 10.00 25.00
USEC Earl Campbell/275 20.00 40.00
USEM Eli Manning/100 125.00 250.00
USFT Fran Tarkenton/275 20.00 40.00
USHL Howie Long/100 25.00 50.00
USJE John Elway/25 100.00 200.00
USJF John Fox/100 8.00 20.00
USJG Jon Gruden/100 10.00 25.00
USJJ Jimmy Johnson/100 10.00 25.00
USJM Joe Montana/25 100.00 200.00
USJN Joe Namath/25 75.00 150.00
USJP J.P. Losman/275 8.00 20.00
USJT Joe Theismann/275 10.00 25.00
USKB Kyle Boller/275 8.00 20.00
USKJ Kevin Jones/275 8.00 20.00
USKW Kellen Winslow Jr./100 12.00 30.00
USLD Len Dawson/275 10.00 25.00
USMB Mark Brunell/275 10.00 25.00
USMV Michael Vick/25 40.00 80.00
USPH Paul Hornung/275 15.00 40.00
USPM Peyton Manning/25 100.00 200.00
USPR Philip Rivers/275 50.00 100.00
USRG Rex Grossman/275 10.00 25.00
USRW Roy Williams WR/275 10.00 25.00
USTA Troy Aikman/25 50.00 100.00
USTB Tom Brady/25 200.00 350.00
USTH Travis Henry/275 6.00 15.00
USTS Tony Siragusa/275 8.00 20.00
USWI Kellen Winslow Sr./100 12.00 30.00

2004 Ultimate Collection Ultimate Signatures Duals

AS Troy Aikman/50 90.00 150.00
Roger Staubach
CV Daunte Culpepper/25 50.00 100.00
Michael Vick
EA John Elway/25 150.00 300.00
Troy Aikman
FM Brett Favre/25 250.00 400.00
Peyton Manning
JG Jimmy Johnson/25 25.00 60.00
Jon Gruden
MF Donovan McNabb/25 175.00 300.00
Brett Favre
MG Deuce McAllister/50 25.00 50.00
Ahman Green
MM Peyton Manning/50 250.00 400.00
Eli Manning
MN Joe Montana/25 250.00 400.00
Joe Namath
MT Deuce McAllister/50 40.00 100.00
LaDainian Tomlinson
PF Chad Pennington/50 125.00 250.00
Brett Favre
PR Bill Parcells/25 25.00 60.00
Andy Reid
SP Steve McNair/25 100.00 200.00
Peyton Manning
TB Joe Theismann/50 15.00 40.00
Mark Brunell
TG LaDainian Tomlinson/50 40.00 100.00
Ahman Green
TS Fran Tarkenton/25 50.00 100.00
Ken Stabler
WW Kellen Winslow Sr./50 25.00 60.00
Kellen Winslow Jr.

2004 Ultimate Collection Ultimate Signatures Quads

UNPRICED QUAD PRINT RUN 5

2005 Ultimate Collection

This 289-card set was released in January, 2006. The set was issued in the hobby in four-card packs with an $100 SRP which came four packs to a box. Cards numbered 1-100 feature veterans in alphabetical order by team while cards 101-269 feature rookies with cards numbered 200-249 all having autographs. All cards in this set are serial numbered, Cards numbered 1-100 and 270-289 were all issued to a stated print run of 550 serial numbered sets while cards numbered 101-200 and 250-269 were issued to a stated print run of 235 serial numbered sets. The signed rookies were issued to a stated print run of 225 serial numbered sets unless specifically notated in our checklist.

1-100/270-289 PRINT RUN 550 SER.#'d SETS
101-200/250-269 PRINT RUN 235 SETS
ROOKIE AUTO PRINT RUN 99-225
1 Larry Fitzgerald 1.50 4.00
2 Anquan Boldin 1.25 3.00
3 Kurt Warner 1.50 4.00
4 Michael Vick 1.50 4.00
5 Warrick Dunn 1.25 3.00
6 Alge Crumpler 1.25 3.00
7 Ray Lewis 1.50 4.00
8 Deion Sanders 2.00 5.00
9 Kyle Boller 1.25 3.00
10 Derrick Mason 1.25 3.00
11 J.P. Losman 1.00 2.50
12 Willis McGahee 1.50 4.00
13 Lee Evans 1.25 3.00
14 Eric Moulds 1.00 2.50
15 Jake Delhomme 1.25 3.00
16 Keary Colbert 1.00 2.50
17 DeShaun Foster 1.25 3.00
18 Brian Urlacher 1.50 4.00
19 Rex Grossman 1.25 3.00
20 Muhsin Muhammad 1.25 3.00
21 Carson Palmer 1.50 4.00
22 Rudi Johnson 1.25 3.00
23 Chad Johnson 1.25 3.00
24 Julius Jones 1.00 2.50
25 Keyshawn Johnson 1.25 3.00
26 Drew Bledsoe 1.50 4.00
27 Tatum Bell 1.00 2.50
28 Jake Plummer 1.25 3.00
29 Ashley Lelie 1.00 2.50
30 Roy Williams WR 1.25 3.00
31 Kevin Jones 1.00 2.50
32 Jeff Garcia 1.25 3.00
33 Brett Favre 4.00 10.00
34 Ahman Green 1.25 3.00
35 Javon Walker 1.00 2.50
36 David Carr 1.00 2.50
37 Andre Johnson 1.50 4.00
38 Domanick Davis 1.00 2.50
39 Peyton Manning 3.00 8.00
40 Reggie Wayne 1.50 4.00
41 Edgerrin James 1.25 3.00
42 Marvin Harrison 1.50 4.00
43 Byron Leftwich 1.25 3.00
44 Fred Taylor 1.25 3.00
45 Jimmy Smith 1.25 3.00
46 Priest Holmes 1.25 3.00
47 Larry Johnson 1.25 3.00
48 Trent Green 1.25 3.00
49 A.J. Feeley 1.00 2.50
50 Chris Chambers 1.25 3.00
51 Randy McMichael 1.00 2.50
52 Daunte Culpepper 1.25 3.00
53 Michael Bennett 1.25 3.00
54 Nate Burleson 1.00 2.50
55 Tom Brady 3.00 8.00
56 Corey Dillon 1.25 3.00
57 Deion Branch 1.00 2.50
58 David Givens 1.00 2.50
59 Aaron Brooks 1.00 2.50
60 Deuce McAllister 1.25 3.00
61 Joe Horn 1.25 3.00
62 Eli Manning 2.50 6.00
63 Jeremy Shockey 1.50 4.00
64 Tiki Barber 1.50 4.00
65 Chad Pennington 1.50 4.00
66 Curtis Martin 1.50 4.00
67 Laveranues Coles 1.00 2.50
68 Kerry Collins 1.25 3.00
69 LaMont Jordan 1.25 3.00
70 Randy Moss 1.50 4.00
71 Donovan McNabb 1.50 4.00
72 Terrell Owens 1.50 4.00
73 Brian Dawkins 1.25 3.00
74 Brian Westbrook 1.25 3.00
75 Ben Roethlisberger 2.50 6.00
76 Jerome Bettis 1.50 4.00
77 Hines Ward 1.50 4.00
78 Duce Staley 1.25 3.00
79 Drew Brees 1.50 4.00
80 LaDainian Tomlinson 1.50 4.00
81 Antonio Gates 1.50 4.00
82 Tim Rattay 1.00 2.50
83 Kevan Barlow 1.00 2.50
84 Eric Johnson 1.00 2.50
85 Shaun Alexander 1.25 3.00
86 Darrell Jackson 1.00 2.50
87 Matt Hasselbeck 1.25 3.00
88 Marc Bulger 1.25 3.00
89 Steven Jackson 1.50 4.00
90 Marshall Faulk 1.50 4.00
91 Torry Holt 1.25 3.00
92 Michael Pittman 1.00 2.50
93 Brian Griese 1.25 3.00
94 Michael Clayton 1.00 2.50
95 Steve McNair 1.50 4.00
96 Drew Bennett 1.25 3.00
97 Chris Brown 1.00 2.50
98 Clinton Portis 1.25 3.00
99 Patrick Ramsey 1.25 3.00
100 Santana Moss 1.25 3.00
101 James Kilian RC 2.50 6.00
102 Marlin Jackson RC 2.50 6.00
103 Corey Webster RC 3.00 8.00
104 Ryan Claridge RC 2.50 6.00
105 David Pollack RC 3.00 8.00
106 Deandra Cobb RC 2.50 6.00
107 Anttaj Hawthorne RC 2.50 6.00
108 Erasmus James RC 3.00 8.00
109 Dan Cody RC 3.00 8.00
110 Jerome Mathis RC 4.00 10.00
111 Barrett Ruud RC 4.00 10.00
112 Kevin Burnett RC 3.00 8.00
113 Jason White RC 4.00 10.00
114 Chase Lyman RC 2.50 6.00
115 Cedric Houston RC 4.00 10.00
116 Roydell Williams RC 3.00 8.00
117 Fred Gibson RC 3.00 8.00
118 Dustin Colquitt RC 3.00 8.00
119 Rasheed Marshall RC 3.00 8.00
120 Walter Reyes RC 2.50 6.00
121 Craig Bragg RC 2.50 6.00
122 Marcus Maxwell RC 2.50 6.00
123 LeRon McCoy RC 2.50 6.00
124 Harry Williams RC 3.00 8.00
125 Larry Brackins RC 2.50 6.00
126 J.R. Russell RC 2.50 6.00
127 Manuel White RC 3.00 8.00
128 Brandon Jones RC 3.00 8.00
129 Eric King RC 2.50 6.00
130 Travis Johnson RC 2.50 6.00
131 Mike Patterson RC 2.50 6.00
132 Marcus Spears RC 3.00 8.00
133 Darryl Blackstock RC 2.50 6.00
134 Michael Boley RC 4.00 10.00
135 Leroy Hill RC 4.00 10.00
136 Channing Crowder RC 3.00 8.00
137 Odell Thurman RC 4.00 10.00
138 Lance Mitchell RC 3.00 8.00
139 Jerome Collins RC 3.00 8.00
140 Stanford Routt RC 3.00 8.00
141 Justin Miller RC 3.00 8.00
142 Bryant McFadden RC 3.00 8.00
143 Eric Green RC 2.50 6.00
144 Fabian Washington RC 3.00 8.00
145 Antonio Perkins RC 3.00 8.00
146 Shaun Cody RC 3.00 8.00
147 Jonathan Babineaux RC 3.00 8.00
148 Ronald Bartell RC 3.00 8.00
149 Luis Castillo RC 3.00 8.00
150 Chris Carr RC 2.50 6.00
151 Justin Tuck RC 5.00 12.00
152 Brodney Pool RC 3.00 8.00
153 Matt Roth RC 3.00 8.00
154 DeMarcus Ware RC 8.00 20.00
155 Josh Bullocks RC 3.00 8.00
156 Vincent Fuller RC 3.00 8.00
157 Donte Nicholson RC 2.50 6.00
158 Rashied Davis RC 4.00 10.00
159 Nick Collins RC 4.00 10.00
160 Mike Nugent RC 3.00 8.00
161 Tyson Thompson RC 2.50 6.00
162 Darrent Williams RC 4.00 10.00
163 Kolvin Haydon RC 3.00 8.00
164 Oshiomogho Atogwe RC 4.00 10.00
165 Ryan Fitzpatrick RC 6.00 15.00
166 Stanley Wilson RC 3.00 8.00
167 Vonta Leach RC 3.00 8.00
168 Ellis Hobbs RC 4.00 10.00
169 Scott Starks RC 3.00 8.00
170 Lionel Gates RC 2.50 6.00
171 Alvin Pearman RC 2.50 6.00
172 Damien Nash RC 3.00 8.00
173 Noah Herron RC 2.50 6.00
174 Domonique Foxworth RC 3.00 8.00
175 Derrick Johnson CB RC 2.50 6.00
176 Lofa Tatupu RC 4.00 10.00
177 Daven Holly RC 2.50 6.00
178 Dante Ridgeway RC 2.50 6.00
179 Airese Currie RC 2.50 6.00
180 Adam Bergen RC 2.50 6.00
181 Kirk Morrison RC 4.00 10.00
182 Alfred Fincher RC 3.00 8.00
183 Jordan Beck RC 3.00 8.00
184 Sean Considine RC 2.50 6.00
185 Tab Perry RC 2.50 6.00
186 Travis Daniels RC 3.00 8.00
187 Paris Warren RC 3.00 8.00
188 Marviel Underwood RC 3.00 8.00
189 Jerome Carter RC 2.50 6.00
190 Kerry Rhodes RC 3.00 8.00
191 James Sanders RC 2.50 6.00
192 Stephen Spach RC 2.50 6.00
193 Bo Scaife RC 3.00 8.00
194 Andre Frazier RC 4.00 10.00
195 Alex Barron RC 2.50 6.00
196 Jammal Brown RC 4.00 10.00
197 Nehemiah Broughton RC 3.00 8.00
198 Elton Brown RC 2.50 6.00
199 David Baas RC 2.50 6.00
200 Joel Dreessen RC 3.00 8.00
201 Maurice Clarett AU/120 6.00 15.00
202 Craphonso Thorpe AU RC 5.00 12.00
203 Adam Jones AU RC 5.00 12.00
204 Mark Bradley AU RC 5.00 12.00
205 Vincent Jackson AU RC 12.50 30.00
206 Antrel Rolle AU RC 8.00 20.00
207 Heath Miller AU RC 10.00 25.00
208 Anthony Davis AU RC 5.00 12.00
209 Terrence Murphy AU RC 5.00 12.00
210 Chris Henry AU RC 8.00 20.00
211 Roscoe Parrish AU RC 5.00 12.00
212 Stefan LeFors AU RC 5.00 12.00
213 Derek Anderson AU RC 6.00 15.00
214 Darren Sproles AU RC 10.00 25.00
215 Adrian McPherson AU RC 5.00 12.00
216 Frank Gore AU RC 25.00 60.00
217 Marion Barber AU RC 12.00 30.00
218 Ryan Moats AU RC 5.00 12.00
219 Carlos Rogers AU RC 8.00 20.00
220 Vernand Morency AU RC 5.00 12.00
221 J.J. Arrington AU RC 6.00 15.00
222 Courtney Roby AU RC 6.00 15.00
223 Dan Orlovsky AU RC 8.00 20.00
224 Kyle Orton AU RC 15.00 40.00
225 David Greene AU RC 5.00 12.00
226 Roddy White AU/150 RC 20.00 40.00
227 Matt Jones AU/99 RC 8.00 20.00
228 Reggie Brown AU/150 RC 6.00 15.00
229 Mark Clayton AU/150 RC 8.00 20.00
230 Eric Shelton AU/150 RC 6.00 15.00
231 Ciatrick Fason AU/150 RC 6.00 15.00
232 Jason Campbell AU/150 RC 30.00 60.00
233 Charlie Frye AU/150 RC 10.00 25.00
234 Andrew Walter AU/150 RC 8.00 20.00
235 Troy Williamson AU/120 RC 8.00 20.00
236 Braylon Edwards AU/99 RC 25.00 60.00
237 Mike Williams AU/99 12.00 30.00
238 Cedric Benson AU/99 RC 10.00 25.00
239 Cadillac Williams AU/99 RC 10.00 25.00
240 Ronnie Brown AU/99 RC 12.00 30.00
241 Alex Smith QB AU/99 RC 75.00 135.00
242 Aaron Rodgers AU/99 RC 600.00 900.00
243 Matt Cassel AU RC 25.00 60.00
244 Brandon Jacobs AU RC 25.00 60.00
245 Alex Smith TE AU RC 5.00 12.00
246 Derrick Johnson AU RC 6.00 15.00
247 Chad Owens AU RC 6.00 15.00
248 Thomas Davis AU RC 5.00 12.00
249 Shawne Merriman AU RC 20.00 50.00
250 Gino Guidugli RC 2.50 6.00
251 Timmy Chang RC 3.00 8.00
252 Todd Mortensen RC 2.50 6.00
253 Bryan Randall RC 3.00 8.00
254 Brock Berlin RC 3.00 8.00
255 T.A. McLendon RC 2.50 6.00
256 Kay-Jay Harris RC 2.50 6.00
257 Bobby Purify RC 3.00 8.00
258 Steve Savoy RC 2.50 6.00
259 Keron Henry RC 2.50 6.00
260 Josh Davis RC 2.50 6.00
261 Chauncey Stovall RC 2.50 6.00
262 Efrem Hill RC 2.50 6.00
263 Sione Pouha RC 2.50 6.00
264 Jesse Lumsden RC 2.50 6.00
265 Vincent Burns RC 2.50 6.00
266 Brady Poppinga RC 4.00 10.00
267 Doomer Grigsby RC 4.00 10.00
268 Robert McCune RC 3.00 8.00
269 Fred Amey RC 2.50 6.00
270 T.J. Duckett 1.00 2.50
271 Jamal Lewis 1.25 3.00
272 Rod Gardner 1.00 2.50
273 Thomas Jones 1.50 4.00
274 Jason Witten 1.50 4.00
275 Roy Williams S 1.00 2.50
276 Mike Anderson 1.00 2.50
277 Joey Harrington 1.25 3.00
278 Charles Rogers 1.00 2.50
279 Donald Driver 1.50 4.00
280 Jabar Gaffney 1.00 2.50
281 Reggie Williams 1.00 2.50
282 Tony Gonzalez 1.25 3.00
283 Ricky Williams 1.25 3.00
284 Mewelde Moore 1.00 2.50
285 Plaxico Burress 1.25 3.00
286 Jerry Porter 1.00 2.50
287 Brandon Lloyd 1.00 2.50
288 Isaac Bruce 1.25 3.00
289 LaVar Arrington 1.25 3.00

2005 Ultimate Collection Gold Holofoil

*VETERANS: 1.2X TO 3X BASIC CARDS
*ROOKIES: .6X TO 1.5X BASIC CARDS
STATED PRINT RUN 40 SER.#'d SETS

2005 Ultimate Collection Game Jersey

STATED PRINT RUN 99 SER.#'d SETS
*GOLD: .5X TO 1.2X BASIC JERSEYS
GOLD PRINT RUN 50 SER.#'d SETS
*PLATINUM: .6X TO 1.5X BASIC JERSEYS
PLATINUM PRINT RUN 25 SER.#'d SETS
*PATCHES: .6X TO 1.5X BASIC JERSEYS
PATCH PRINT RUN 50 SER.#'d SETS
*GOLD PATCHES: .8X TO 2X BASIC JERSEYS
GOLD PATCH PRINT RUN 35 SER.#'d SETS
*PLAT.PATCHES: 1.2X TO 3X BASIC JERSEYS
PLATINUM PATCH PRINT RUN 20 SER.#'d SETS
UNPRICED PATCH AU PRINT RUN 15 SETS
GJAB Aaron Brooks 3.00 8.00
GJAG Ahman Green 4.00 10.00
GJAJ Andre Johnson 4.00 10.00
GJBE Tatum Bell 4.00 10.00
GJBF Brett Favre 12.50 30.00
GJBK Bernie Kosar 5.00 12.00
GJBL Byron Leftwich 4.00 10.00
GJBR Ben Roethlisberger 12.50 30.00
GJBS Barry Sanders 15.00 30.00
GJBU Brian Urlacher 4.00 10.00
GJBW Brian Westbrook 3.00 8.00
GJCD Corey Dillon 3.00 8.00
GJCH Chad Pennington 4.00 10.00
GJCL Clinton Portis 4.00 10.00
GJCM Curtis Martin 4.00 10.00
GJCP Carson Palmer 4.00 10.00
GJCU Daunte Culpepper 4.00 10.00
GJDA David Carr 3.00 8.00
GJDB Drew Bledsoe 4.00 10.00
GJDC Donovan McNabb 5.00 12.00
GJDD Domanick Davis 3.00 8.00
GJDE Derrick Mason 3.00 8.00
GJDE Deuce McAllister 3.00 8.00
GJDM Dan Marino 15.00 40.00
GJDR Drew Brees 3.00 8.00
GJDS Deion Sanders 6.00 15.00
GJEJ Edgerrin James 4.00 10.00
GJEM Eli Manning 10.00 25.00
GJFT Fred Taylor 3.00 8.00
GJJB Jerome Bettis 7.50 20.00
GJJE John Elway 12.50 30.00
GJJH Joey Harrington 4.00 10.00
GJJJ Julius Jones 5.00 12.00
GJJL Jamal Lewis 4.00 10.00
GJJM Joe Montana 20.00 40.00
GJJP J.P. Losman 3.00 8.00
GJJR Jerry Rice 7.50 20.00
GJJS Jeremy Shockey 4.00 10.00
GJJW Javon Walker 4.00 10.00
GJKJ Kevin Jones 4.00 10.00
GJKS Ken Stabler 6.00 15.00
GJLF Larry Fitzgerald 4.00 10.00
GJLT LaDainian Tomlinson 4.00 10.00
GJMA Marcus Allen 6.00 15.00
GJMB Marc Bulger 3.00 8.00
GJMF Marshall Faulk 4.00 10.00
GJMH Marvin Harrison 4.00 10.00
GJMS Mike Singletary 5.00 12.00
GJMV Michael Vick 6.00 15.00
GJON Ozzie Newsome 5.00 12.00
GJPH Priest Holmes 4.00 10.00
GJPM Peyton Manning 7.50 20.00
GJPR Philip Rivers 4.00 10.00
GJPS Phil Simms 6.00 15.00
GJRE Reggie Wayne 3.00 8.00
GJRI Ricky Williams 4.00 10.00
GJRL Ray Lewis 4.00 10.00
GJRM Randy Moss 4.00 10.00
GJRS Roger Staubach 7.50 20.00
GJRW Roy Williams WR 4.00 10.00
GJSA Shaun Alexander 5.00 12.00
GJSL Steve Largent 6.00 15.00
GJSM Steve McNair 4.00 10.00
GJSY Steve Young 7.50 20.00
GJTA Troy Aikman 7.50 20.00
GJTB Tom Brady 10.00 25.00
GJTD Tony Dorsett 5.00 12.00
GJTG Tony Gonzalez 3.00 8.00
GJTH Torry Holt 4.00 10.00
GJTO Terrell Owens 4.00 10.00
GJWD Warrick Dunn 3.00 8.00
GJWM Willis McGahee 3.00 8.00
GJWP Walter Payton 20.00 50.00

2005 Ultimate Collection Game Jersey Autographs

STATED PRINT RUN 25 SER.#'d SETS
UNPRICED LOGO AU PRINT RUN 1 SET
UNPRICED DUAL PRINT RUN 10 SETS
UNPRICED DUAL PATCH PRINT RUN 5 SETS
UNPRICED DUAL LOGO PRINT RUN 1 SET
AGJAG Ahman Green 20.00 50.00
AGJAR Aaron Rodgers 400.00 600.00
AGJAS Alex Smith QB 60.00 120.00
AGJBE Braylon Edwards 50.00 100.00
AGJBF Brett Favre 150.00 300.00
AGJBJ Bo Jackson 50.00 100.00
AGJBL Byron Leftwich 20.00 50.00
AGJBR Ben Roethlisberger 75.00 150.00
AGJBS Barry Sanders 100.00 200.00
AGJCB Cedric Benson 30.00 80.00
AGJCP Carson Palmer 40.00 80.00
AGJCW Cadillac Williams 25.00 60.00
AGJDE Deuce McAllister 12.50 30.00
AGJDM Dan Marino 150.00 300.00
AGJDS Deion Sanders 40.00 80.00
AGJEJ Edgerrin James 25.00 60.00
AGJEM Eli Manning 90.00 150.00
AGJJE John Elway 100.00 200.00
AGJJL J.P. Losman 12.50 30.00
AGJJM Joe Montana 125.00 250.00
AGJLT LaDainian Tomlinson 50.00 100.00
AGJMB Marc Bulger 20.00 50.00
AGJMC Michael Clayton 12.50 30.00
AGJMS Mike Singletary 25.00 60.00
AGJMV Michael Vick 50.00 100.00
AGJMW Mike Williams 20.00 50.00
AGJPM Peyton Manning 125.00 200.00
AGJRB Ronnie Brown 60.00 120.00
AGJRO Roy Williams WR 20.00 50.00
AGJRP Roscoe Parrish 12.50 30.00
AGJRS Roger Staubach 50.00 100.00
AGJRW Reggie Wayne 20.00 50.00
AGJSJ Steven Jackson 20.00 50.00
AGJTA Troy Aikman 60.00 100.00
AGJTB Tiki Barber 25.00 60.00
AGJTD Tony Dorsett 25.00 60.00
AGJTG Trent Green 20.00 50.00
AGJWH Roddy White 40.00 80.00

2005 Ultimate Collection Game Jersey Duals

STATED PRINT RUN 50 SER.#'d SETS
*PATCH/25: .6X TO 1.5X BASIC DUAL JSY
*GOLD/15: .8X TO 2X BASIC DUAL JSY
DJBB Cedric Benson 10.00 25.00
Ronnie Brown
DJBJ Marc Bulger 7.50 20.00
Steven Jackson
DJBS Drew Bledsoe 10.00 25.00
Roger Staubach
DJCB Mark Clayton 7.50 20.00
Reggie Brown
DJCW Jason Campbell 10.00 25.00
Cadillac Williams
DJDM Brian Dawkins 10.00 25.00
Donovan McNabb
DJEA Peyton Manning 25.00 50.00
Ben Roethlisberger
DJEM John Elway 35.00 60.00
Joe Montana
DJEW Braylon Edwards 10.00 25.00
Mike Williams
DJFG Brett Favre 20.00 40.00
Ahman Green
DJJA Julius Jones 12.50 30.00
Troy Aikman
DJJB Vincent Jackson 10.00 25.00
Mark Bradley
DJJD Julius Jones 10.00 25.00
Tony Dorsett
DJJM Edgerrin James 12.50 30.00
Peyton Manning
DJJP John Elway 25.00 50.00
Peyton Manning
DJJR Steven Jackson 10.00 25.00
Ronnie Brown
DJLP Byron Leftwich 7.50 20.00
Carson Palmer
DJLR J.P. Losman 12.50 30.00
Ben Roethlisberger
DJMA Eli Manning 15.00 40.00
Peyton Manning
DJMB Ryan Moats 7.50 20.00
Reggie Brown
DJMG Deuce McAllister 7.50 20.00
Ahman Green
DJMM Dan Marino 40.00 80.00
Joe Montana
DJMR Eli Manning 25.00 60.00
Aaron Rodgers
DJMV Donovan McNabb 10.00 25.00
Michael Vick
DJMW Michael Clayton 7.50 20.00
Roy Williams WR
DJOC Kyle Orton 10.00 25.00
Jason Campbell
DJPL Roscoe Parrish 6.00 15.00
J.P. Losman
DJPM Carson Palmer 12.50 30.00
Eli Manning
DJPW Roscoe Parrish 6.00 15.00
Roddy White
DJRA Aaron Rodgers 25.00 60.00
J.J. Arrington
DJRS Aaron Rodgers 25.00 60.00
Alex Smith QB
DJSF Eric Shelton 6.00 15.00
Ciatrick Fason
DJSM Alex Smith QB 25.00 50.00
Joe Montana
DJTM LaDainian Tomlinson 8.00 20.00
Deuce McAllister
DJTR Troy Williamson 7.50 20.00
Roddy White
DJWB Cadillac Williams 10.00 25.00
Ronnie Brown
DJWE Roy Williams WR 7.50 20.00
Braylon Edwards
DJWF Andrew Walter 7.50 20.00
Charlie Frye
DJWJ Cadillac Williams 12.50 30.00
Bo Jackson
DJWP Reggie Wayne 6.00 15.00
Roscoe Parrish
DJWW Mike Williams WR 7.50 20.00
Troy Williamson

2005 Ultimate Collection Rookie Jerseys

STATED PRINT RUN 99 SER.#'d SETS
*GOLD/50: .5X TO 1.2X BASIC JSY/99
GOLD PRINT RUN 50 SER.#'d SETS
*PLATINUM/25: .6X TO 1.5X BASIC JSY/99
PLATINUM PRINT RUN 25 SER.#'d SETS
*PATCH/50: .6X TO 1.5X BASIC JSY/99
PATCH PRINT RUN 50 SER.#'d SETS
*GOLD PATCH/20: 1.2X TO 3X BASIC JSY/99
GOLD PATCH PRINT RUN 20 SER.#'d SETS
RJAR Aaron Rodgers 40.00 80.00
RJAS Alex Smith QB 6.00 15.00
RJAW Andrew Walter 3.00 8.00
RJBE Braylon Edwards 5.00 12.00
RJCB Cedric Benson 4.00 10.00
RJCF Charlie Frye 4.00 10.00
RJCI Ciatrick Fason 2.50 6.00
RJCW Cadillac Williams 4.00 10.00
RJES Eric Shelton 2.50 6.00
RJHM Heath Miller 5.00 12.00
RJJC Jason Campbell 5.00 12.00
RJJJ J.J. Arrington 3.00 8.00
RJMB Mark Bradley 2.50 6.00
RJMC Mark Clayton 4.00 10.00
RJMJ Matt Jones 4.00 10.00
RJMO Maurice Clarett 3.00 8.00
RJMW Mike Williams 4.00 10.00
RJRB Reggie Brown 2.50 6.00
RJRO Ronnie Brown 5.00 12.00
RJRP Roscoe Parrish 2.50 6.00
RJRW Roddy White 5.00 12.00
RJSL Stefan LeFors 2.50 6.00
RJTW Troy Williamson 3.00 8.00
RJVJ Vincent Jackson 5.00 12.00
RJVM Vernand Morency 3.00 8.00

2005 Ultimate Collection Ultimate Signatures

OVERALL AUTO STATED ODDS 1:4
UNPRICED GOLD PRINT RUN 10 SER.#'d SETS
UNPRICED HOLOFOIL/5 ISSUED VIA MAIL
UNPRICED QUAD AU PRINT RUN 5 SETS
UNPRICED TRIPLE AU PRINT RUN 15 SETS
UNPRICED EIGHT AU PRINT RUN 1 SET
USAB Anquan Boldin/99 7.50 20.00
USAD Art Donovan/99 7.50 20.00
USAJ A.J. Feeley/99 6.00 15.00
USAM Adrian McPherson/99 6.00 15.00
USAN Antrel Rolle/99 7.50 20.00
USAR Aaron Rodgers/75 200.00 350.00
USAS Alex Smith QB/25 60.00 120.00
USAW Andrew Walter/99 12.50 30.00
USBE Braylon Edwards/75 20.00 50.00
USBJ Bo Jackson/75 40.00 80.00
USBK Bernie Kosar/99 12.50 30.00
USBS Barry Sanders/25 100.00 200.00
USCB Cedric Benson/75 12.50 30.00
USCF Charlie Frye/99 12.50 30.00
USCI Ciatrick Fason/99 6.00 15.00
USCL Maurice Clarett/75 6.00 15.00
USCP Carson Palmer/25 15.00 40.00
USCR Courtney Roby/99 6.00 15.00
USCW Cadillac Williams/75 20.00 50.00
USDD Domanick Davis/99 6.00 15.00
USDF Dan Fouts/25 25.00 60.00
USDJ Deacon Jones/99 12.50 30.00
USDM Dan Marino/25 125.00 250.00
USDO Don Maynard/99 6.00 15.00
USDS Deion Sanders/25 40.00 80.00
USEC Earl Campbell/75 20.00 40.00
USEJ Edgerrin James/25 20.00 50.00
USEM Eli Manning/25 90.00 150.00
USES Eric Shelton/99 6.00 15.00
USFH Franco Harris/75 40.00 80.00
USFR Fran Tarkenton/75 20.00 40.00
USGB George Blanda/75 25.00 50.00
USGS Gale Sayers/25 40.00 80.00
USJA J.J. Arrington/99 12.50 30.00
USJC Jason Campbell/99 25.00 50.00
USJH Joe Horn/99 6.00 15.00
USJJ Julius Jones/25 20.00 50.00
USJK Jim Kelly/25 40.00 80.00
USJL James Lofton/75 7.50 20.00
USJO Adam Jones/99 7.50 20.00
USJP Jim Plunkett/75 7.50 20.00
USJP J.P. Losman/99 7.50 20.00
USJT Joe Theismann/99 12.50 30.00
USKO Kyle Orton/99 15.00 40.00
USLA Larry Johnson/99 12.00 30.00
USLE Lee Evans/99 6.00 15.00
USLJ LaMont Jordan/99 6.00 15.00
USMA Marcus Allen/75 12.50 30.00
USMB Marc Bulger/75 6.00 15.00
USMC Mark Clayton/99 12.50 30.00
USMI Michael Clayton/99 7.50 20.00
USMS Mike Singletary/75 12.50 30.00
USMV Michael Vick/25 40.00 80.00
USMW Mike Williams/99 12.50 30.00
USNB Nate Burleson/99 6.00 15.00
USPM Peyton Manning/75 60.00 120.00
USRB Reggie Brown/99 12.50 30.00
USRD Andre Reed/99 7.50 20.00
USRE Reggie Wayne/99 15.00 30.00
USRO Ronnie Brown/99 30.00 80.00
USRP Roscoe Parrish/99 7.50 20.00
USRS Roger Staubach/25 60.00 100.00
USSJ Steven Jackson/75 12.50 30.00
USSL Steve Largent/75 12.50 30.00
USTA Troy Aikman/25 50.00 100.00
USTB Tiki Barber/99 20.00 40.00
USTD Tony Dorsett/25 20.00 50.00
USTG Trent Green/75 7.50 20.00
USTW Troy Williamson/99 12.50 30.00
USWH Roddy White/99 15.00 30.00

2005 Ultimate Collection Ultimate Signatures Duals

DUAL PRINT RUN 35 SER.#'d SETS
DSAB Troy Aikman 40.00 80.00
Drew Bledsoe
DSBJ Marc Bulger 25.00 50.00
Steven Jackson
DSBP George Blanda 40.00 80.00
Jim Plunkett
DSBS Cedric Benson 10.00 80.00
Gale Sayers
DSBW Cedric Benson 30.00 60.00
Roy Williams WR
DSCT Jason Campbell 30.00 60.00
Joe Theismann
DSEW Braylon Edwards 30.00 60.00
Mike Williams
DSFH Brett Favre 150.00 250.00
Paul Hornung
DSGM Ahman Green 20.00 40.00
Deuce McAllister
DSJC Steven Jackson 25.00 50.00
Earl Campbell
DSJS Julius Jones 60.00 120.00
Barry Sanders
DSKL Jim Kelly 30.00 60.00
J.P. Losman
DSLR Steve Largent 30.00 60.00
Andre Reed
DSMA Peyton Manning 100.00 200.00
Troy Aikman
DSPC Carson Palmer 30.00 60.00
Cris Collinsworth
DSPJ Jim Plunkett 60.00 120.00
Bo Jackson
DSRM Ben Roethlisberger 150.00 300.00
Dan Marino
DSRS Aaron Rodgers 175.00 300.00
Alex Smith QB
DSWB Cadillac Williams 60.00 120.00
Ronnie Brown
DSWC Troy Williamson 20.00 40.00
Mark Clayton

2006 Ultimate Collection

This 360-card set was released in November, 2006. The set was issued in the hobby in four-card packs, with an $100 SRP, which came four packs to a box. Cards numbered 1-200 feature veterans in alphabetical team order while cards 201-360 feature 2006 rookies. Within the rookie grouping: Cards numbered 201-260 were signed by the player to different serial numbered print runs, which information we have notated in our checklist. A few players did not return their signatures in time for pack out and the exchange deadline for those cards was November 15, 2009.

1-200 VET PRINT RUN 525
UNPRICED PRINT PLATE AUs #'d TO 1
1 Kurt Warner 2.00 5.00
2 Edgerrin James 1.50 4.00
3 Larry Fitzgerald 2.00 5.00
4 Anquan Boldin 1.50 4.00
5 Antrel Rolle 1.25 3.00
6 Karlos Dansby 1.25 3.00
7 Michael Vick 2.00 5.00
8 Warrick Dunn 1.50 4.00
9 DeAngelo Hall 1.50 4.00
10 Alge Crumpler 1.50 4.00
11 Roddy White 1.50 4.00
12 Michael Jenkins 1.50 4.00
13 Steve McNair 1.50 4.00
14 Jamal Lewis 1.50 4.00
15 Derrick Mason 1.50 4.00
16 Todd Heap 1.50 4.00
17 Mark Clayton 1.50 4.00
18 Ray Lewis 2.00 5.00
19 J.P. Losman 1.50 4.00
20 Willis McGahee 1.50 4.00
21 Lee Evans 1.50 4.00
22 Roscoe Parrish 1.25 3.00
23 Takeo Spikes 1.25 3.00
24 Nate Clements 1.25 3.00
25 Jake Delhomme 1.50 4.00
26 DeShaun Foster 1.50 4.00
27 Steve Smith 2.00 5.00
28 Keary Colbert 1.25 3.00
29 Julius Peppers 1.50 4.00
30 Chris Gamble 1.25 3.00
31 Rex Grossman 1.50 4.00
32 Thomas Jones 1.50 4.00
33 Cedric Benson 1.50 4.00
34 Muhsin Muhammad 1.50 4.00
35 Brian Urlacher 2.00 5.00
36 Nathan Vasher 1.25 3.00
37 Carson Palmer 2.00 5.00
38 Rudi Johnson 1.50 4.00
39 Chad Johnson 1.50 4.00
40 T.J. Houshmandzadeh 1.50 4.00
41 Odell Thurman 1.25 3.00
42 Deltha O'Neal 1.25 3.00
43 Charlie Frye 1.50 4.00
44 Reuben Droughns 1.50 4.00
45 Braylon Edwards 1.50 4.00
46 Joe Jurevicius 1.25 3.00
47 Kellen Winslow 1.50 4.00
48 Willie McGinest 1.25 3.00
49 Drew Bledsoe 2.00 5.00
50 Julius Jones 1.25 3.00
51 Terrell Owens 2.00 5.00
52 Terry Glenn 1.50 4.00
53 Jason Witten 2.00 5.00
54 DeMarcus Ware 1.50 4.00
55 Roy Williams S 1.50 4.00
56 Jake Plummer 1.50 4.00
57 Tatum Bell 1.25 3.00
58 Rod Smith 1.50 4.00
59 Javon Walker 1.50 4.00
60 Stephen Alexander 1.25 3.00
61 Champ Bailey 1.50 4.00
62 John Lynch 1.25 3.00
63 Jon Kitna 1.50 4.00
64 Kevin Jones 1.25 3.00
65 Roy Williams WR 1.50 4.00
66 Mike Williams 1.25 3.00
67 Marcus Pollard 1.25 3.00
68 Dre Bly 1.25 3.00
69 Brett Favre 4.00 10.00
70 Ahman Green 1.50 4.00
71 Donald Driver 2.00 5.00
72 Robert Ferguson 1.25 3.00
73 Charles Woodson 2.00 5.00
74 Kabeer Gbaja-Biamila 1.50 4.00
75 David Carr 1.25 3.00
76 Domanick Davis 1.25 3.00
77 Andre Johnson 2.00 5.00
78 Eric Moulds 1.25 3.00
79 Job Putzier 1.25 3.00
80 Dunta Robinson 1.25 3.00
81 Peyton Manning 3.00 8.00
82 Dominic Rhodes 1.50 4.00
83 Reggie Wayne 1.50 4.00
84 Marvin Harrison 2.00 5.00
85 Dallas Clark 1.50 4.00
86 Dwight Freeney 1.50 4.00
87 Bob Sanders 1.50 4.00
88 Byron Leftwich 1.50 4.00
89 Fred Taylor 1.50 4.00
90 Matt Jones 1.25 3.00
91 Ernest Wilford 1.25 3.00
92 Greg Jones 1.25 3.00
93 Mike Peterson 1.25 3.00
94 Trent Green 1.50 4.00
95 Larry Johnson 1.50 4.00
96 Samie Parker 1.25 3.00
97 Eddie Kennison 1.25 3.00
98 Tony Gonzalez 1.50 4.00
99 Patrick Surtain 1.25 3.00
100 Daunte Culpepper 1.50 4.00
101 Ronnie Brown 2.00 5.00
102 Chris Chambers 1.50 4.00
103 Marty Booker 1.25 3.00
104 Randy McMichael 1.25 3.00
105 Jason Taylor 1.50 4.00
106 Zach Thomas 2.00 5.00
107 Brad Johnson 1.50 4.00
108 Chester Taylor 1.50 4.00
109 Travis Taylor 1.25 3.00
110 Troy Williamson 1.25 3.00
111 Darren Sharper 1.50 4.00
112 Antoine Winfield 1.25 3.00
113 Tom Brady 3.00 8.00
114 Corey Dillon 1.50 4.00
115 Deion Branch 1.50 4.00
116 Ben Watson 1.25 3.00
117 Tedy Bruschi 2.00 5.00
118 Richard Seymour 1.25 3.00
119 Rodney Harrison 1.25 3.00
120 Drew Brees 2.00 5.00
121 Deuce McAllister 1.50 4.00
122 Joe Horn 1.50 4.00
123 Donte Stallworth 1.25 3.00
124 Will Smith 1.25 3.00
125 Fred Thomas 1.25 3.00
126 Eli Manning 2.50 6.00
127 Tiki Barber 2.00 5.00
128 Plaxico Burress 1.50 4.00
129 Jeremy Shockey 2.00 5.00
130 Osi Umenyiora 1.50 4.00
131 Michael Strahan 1.50 4.00
132 LaVar Arrington 1.50 4.00
133 Chad Pennington 2.00 5.00
134 Curtis Martin 2.00 5.00
135 Laveranues Coles 1.25 3.00
136 Justin McCareins 1.25 3.00
137 Jonathan Vilma 1.50 4.00
138 Shaun Ellis 1.25 3.00
139 Aaron Brooks 1.50 4.00
140 LaMont Jordan 1.50 4.00
141 Randy Moss 2.00 5.00
142 Doug Gabriel 1.25 3.00
143 Jerry Porter 1.25 3.00
144 Derrick Burgess 1.25 3.00
145 Donovan McNabb 2.00 5.00
146 Brian Westbrook 1.50 4.00
147 Reggie Brown 1.25 3.00
148 L.J. Smith 1.25 3.00
149 Jevon Kearse 1.50 4.00
150 Brian Dawkins 1.50 4.00
151 Ben Roethlisberger 2.50 6.00
152 Willie Parker 1.50 4.00
153 Hines Ward 2.00 5.00
154 Cedrick Wilson 1.25 3.00
155 Heath Miller 1.50 4.00

156 Joey Porter	1.25	3.00
157 Troy Polamalu	2.50	6.00
158 Philip Rivers	2.00	5.00
159 LaDainian Tomlinson	2.00	5.00
160 Keenan McCardell	1.50	4.00
161 Eric Parker	1.25	3.00
162 Antonio Gates	2.00	5.00
163 Shawne Merriman	1.50	4.00
164 Donnie Edwards	1.25	3.00
165 Alex Smith QB	2.00	5.00
166 Frank Gore	2.00	5.00
167 Antonio Bryant	1.25	3.00
168 Eric Johnson	1.25	3.00
169 Bryant Young	1.25	3.00
170 Shawntae Spencer	1.25	3.00
171 Matt Hasselbeck	1.50	4.00
172 Shaun Alexander	1.50	4.00
173 Darrell Jackson	1.50	4.00
174 Nate Burleson	1.25	3.00
175 Lofa Tatupu	1.50	4.00
176 Julian Peterson	1.25	3.00
177 Marc Bulger	1.50	4.00
178 Steven Jackson	2.00	5.00
179 Torry Holt	1.50	4.00
180 Kevin Curtis	1.50	4.00
181 Isaac Bruce	1.50	4.00
182 Leonard Little	1.25	3.00
183 Chris Simms	1.50	4.00
184 Cadillac Williams	1.50	4.00
185 Joey Galloway	1.50	4.00
186 Michael Clayton	1.25	3.00
187 Derrick Brooks	1.50	4.00
188 Ronde Barber	1.50	4.00
189 Billy Volek	1.25	3.00
190 Chris Brown	1.25	3.00
191 Drew Bennett	1.50	4.00
192 Travis Henry	1.25	3.00
193 Ben Troupe	1.25	3.00
194 Kyle Vanden Bosch	1.25	3.00
195 Sean Taylor	2.00	5.00
196 Mark Brunell	1.50	4.00
197 Clinton Portis	2.00	5.00
198 Santana Moss	1.50	4.00
199 Antwaan Randle El	1.50	4.00
200 Jason Campbell	1.50	4.00
201 Matt Leinart AU/99 RC	25.00	50.00
202 DeAngelo Williams AU/99 RC	25.00	50.00
203 Jay Cutler AU/99 RC	75.00	150.00
204 Joseph Addai AU/99 RC	15.00	40.00
205 Laurence Maroney AU/150 RC	8.00	20.00
206 Reggie Bush AU/99 RC	50.00	120.00
207 Santonio Holmes AU/99 RC	25.00	50.00
208 Vernon Davis AU/99 RC	25.00	50.00
209 Vince Young AU/99 RC	30.00	80.00
210 LenDale White AU/150 RC	8.00	20.00
211 Jerious Norwood AU/150 RC	8.00	20.00
212 Travis Wilson AU/150 RC	6.00	15.00
213 Brian Calhoun AU/150 RC	6.00	15.00
214 A.J. Hawk AU/99 RC	30.00	60.00
215 Greg Jennings AU/150 RC	30.00	60.00
216 Mario Williams AU/99 RC	20.00	50.00
217 Maurice Drew AU/150 RC	25.00	60.00
218 Marcedes Lewis AU/150 RC	10.00	25.00
219 Skyler Green AU/275 RC	5.00	12.00
220 Derek Hagan AU/150 RC	8.00	20.00
221 Tarvaris Jackson AU/150 RC	10.00	25.00
222 Chad Jackson AU/150 RC	6.00	15.00
223 Sinorice Moss AU/99 RC	15.00	40.00
224 Kellen Clemens AU/150 RC	8.00	20.00
225 Leon Washington AU/150 RC	8.00	20.00
226 Michael Huff AU/150 RC	8.00	20.00
227 Omar Jacobs AU/150 RC	6.00	15.00
228 Charlie Whitehurst AU/150 RC	10.00	25.00
229 Michael Robinson AU/150 RC	8.00	20.00
230 Brandon Williams AU/150 RC	6.00	15.00
231 Leonard Pope AU/275 RC	8.00	20.00
232 Greg Lee AU/275 RC	5.00	12.00
233 D.J. Shockley AU/275 RC	6.00	15.00
234 Demetrius Williams AU/275 RC	6.00	15.00
235 Reggie McNeal AU/275 RC	6.00	15.00
236 Jerome Harrison AU/275 RC	8.00	20.00
237 Anthony Fasano AU/275 RC	8.00	20.00
238 Brandon Marshall AU/275 RC	15.00	50.00
239 Ernie Sims AU/275 RC	6.00	15.00
240 Cory Rodgers AU/275 RC	6.00	15.00
241 Will Blackmon AU/275 RC	6.00	15.00
242 DeMeco Ryans AU/275 RC	8.00	20.00
243 Owen Daniels AU/275 RC	8.00	20.00
244 Josh Betts AU/275 RC	6.00	15.00
245 Chad Greenway AU/275 RC	8.00	20.00
246 Mike Hass AU/275 RC	6.00	15.00
247 Mathias Kiwanuka AU/275 RC	8.00	20.00
248 D'Brickashaw Ferguson AU/275 RC	8.00	20.00
249 Brad Smith AU/275 RC	8.00	20.00
250 Thomas Howard AU/275 RC	6.00	15.00
251 Jason Avant AU/275 RC	5.00	12.00
252 Brodrick Bunkley AU/275 RC	6.00	15.00
253 Willie Reid AU/275 RC	6.00	15.00
254 Kelly Jennings AU/275 RC	6.00	15.00
255 Jimmy Williams AU/275 RC	8.00	20.00
256 Joe Klopfenstein AU/275 RC	5.00	12.00
257 Tye Hill AU/275 RC	5.00	12.00
258 Dominique Byrd AU/275 RC	6.00	15.00
259 Maurice Stovall AU/150 RC	6.00	15.00
260 Bruce Gradkowski AU/275 RC	8.00	20.00
261 Abdul Hodge RC	2.50	6.00
262 Adam Jennings RC	3.00	8.00
263 Ahmad Brooks RC	4.00	10.00
264 Andrew Whitworth RC	2.50	6.00
265 Anthony Schlegel RC	3.00	8.00
266 Anthony Smith RC	4.00	10.00
267 Antonio Cromartie RC	4.00	10.00
268 Ashton Youboty RC	2.50	6.00
269 Ben Obomanu RC	4.00	10.00
270 Bennie Brazell RC	3.00	8.00
271 Bernard Pollard RC	3.00	8.00
272 Bobby Carpenter RC	2.50	6.00
273 Brett Basanez RC	4.00	10.00
274 Brett Elliott RC	4.00	10.00
275 Brodie Croyle RC	4.00	10.00
276 Calvin Lowry RC	4.00	10.00
277 Cedric Griffin RC	3.00	8.00
278 Cedric Humes RC	2.50	6.00
279 Charles Davis RC	3.00	8.00
280 Charles Gordon RC	3.00	8.00
281 Chris Gocong RC	3.00	8.00
282 Claude Wroten RC	2.50	6.00
283 Clint Ingram RC	4.00	10.00
284 Cody Hodges RC	3.00	8.00
285 Corey Bramlet RC	3.00	8.00
286 Cory Ross RC	4.00	10.00
287 Damien Rhodes RC	3.00	8.00
288 Danieal Manning RC	4.00	10.00
289 Daniel Bullocks RC	4.00	10.00
290 Darnell Bing RC	3.00	8.00
291 Darrell Hackney RC	3.00	8.00
292 Darryl Tapp RC	3.00	8.00
293 Daryn Colledge RC	4.00	10.00
294 David Anderson RC	3.00	8.00
295 David Kirtman RC	3.00	8.00
296 David Pittman RC	3.00	8.00
297 David Thomas RC	3.00	8.00
298 Davin Joseph RC	3.00	8.00
299 Andre Hall RC	3.00	8.00
300 Delanie Walker RC	4.00	10.00
301 Demetrius Summers RC	2.50	6.00
302 Devin Aromashodu RC	4.00	10.00
303 Devin Hester RC	8.00	20.00
304 Donte Whitner RC	4.00	10.00
305 D'Qwell Jackson RC	3.00	8.00
306 Dusty Dvoracek RC	4.00	10.00
307 Elvis Dumervil RC	4.00	10.00
308 Eric Smith RC	3.00	8.00
309 Freddie Keiaho RC	3.00	8.00
310 Frostee Rucker RC	3.00	8.00
311 Garrett Mills RC	4.00	10.00
312 Gerris Wilkinson RC	2.50	6.00
313 Haloti Ngata RC	4.00	10.00
314 Ingle Martin RC	3.00	8.00
315 J.D. Runnels RC	3.00	8.00
316 James Anderson RC	2.50	6.00
317 Jason Allen RC	3.00	8.00
318 Jason Pociask RC	3.00	8.00
319 Hank Baskett RC	4.00	10.00
320 Jeff King RC	3.00	8.00
321 Jeff Webb RC	3.00	8.00
322 Jeremy Bloom RC	3.00	8.00
323 Jeremy Trueblood RC	3.00	8.00
324 Joel Klatt RC	3.00	8.00
325 John McCargo RC	2.50	6.00
326 Johnathan Joseph RC	3.00	8.00
327 Jon Alston RC	2.50	6.00
328 Jonathan Orr RC	3.00	8.00
329 Kamerion Wimbley RC	4.00	10.00
330 Kent Smith RC	4.00	10.00
331 Kevin McMahan RC	3.00	8.00
332 Ko Simpson RC	3.00	8.00
333 Lawrence Vickers RC	3.00	8.00
334 Manny Lawson RC	3.00	8.00
335 Marcus Demps RC	2.00	5.00
336 Marcus McNeill RC	3.00	8.00
337 Marcus Vick RC	2.50	6.00
338 Marques Colston RC	8.00	20.00
339 Marques Hagans RC	2.50	6.00
340 Matt Shelton RC	4.00	10.00
341 Nick Mangold RC	3.00	8.00
342 P.J. Daniels RC	2.50	6.00
343 P.J. Pope RC	4.00	10.00
344 Miles Austin RC	15.00	30.00
345 Quinn Sypniewski RC	3.00	8.00
346 Richard Marshall RC	3.00	8.00
347 Richie Ross RC	3.00	8.00
348 Rocky McIntosh RC	3.00	8.00
349 Roman Harper RC	3.00	8.00
350 Ryan Cook RC	3.00	8.00
351 Mike Bell RC	4.00	10.00
352 Deuce Lutui RC	3.00	8.00
353 Tamba Hali RC	4.00	10.00
354 Tim Massaquoi RC	3.00	8.00
355 Todd Watkins RC	2.50	6.00
356 Tony Scheffler RC	4.00	10.00
357 Drew Olson RC	2.50	6.00
358 Wali Lundy RC	3.00	8.00
359 Wendell Mathis RC	3.00	8.00
360 Winston Justice RC	3.00	8.00

2006 Ultimate Collection Gold

*VETS 1-200: 1X TO 2.5X BASIC CARDS
*ROOKIES 261-360: .6X TO 1.5X BASIC CARDS
STATED PRINT RUN 50 SER.#'d SETS
UNPRICED GOLD AU PRINT RUN 10

2006 Ultimate Collection Achievements Signatures

STATED PRINT RUN 25 SER.#'d SETS

BF Brett Favre	125.00	200.00
BR Ben Roethlisberger	60.00	120.00
CW Cadillac Williams	25.00	50.00
LJ Larry Johnson	25.00	60.00
LT LaDainian Tomlinson	75.00	135.00
PM Peyton Manning	90.00	150.00
SY Steve Young	50.00	80.00
TB Tiki Barber	25.00	50.00

2006 Ultimate Collection Game Jersey Autographs

STATED PRINT RUN 30-35
UNPRICED AU COMBO PRINT RUN 1
UNPRICED LOGO PATCH PRINT RUN 1
UNPRICED AU PATCH PRINT RUN 15

ULTAC Alge Crumpler	12.00	30.00
ULTAD Tarvaris Jackson	15.00	40.00
ULTAG Antonio Gates	15.00	40.00
ULTAJ A.J. Hawk	15.00	40.00
ULTBC Brian Calhoun	10.00	25.00
ULTBF Brett Favre	125.00	200.00
ULTBL Byron Leftwich	12.00	30.00
ULTBM Brandon Marshall	15.00	40.00
ULTBR Ben Roethlisberger	60.00	120.00
ULTBU Reggie Bush	50.00	100.00
ULTBW Brandon Williams	10.00	25.00
ULTCA Cadillac Williams	12.00	30.00
ULTCF Charlie Frye	12.00	30.00
ULTCJ Chad Jackson	10.00	25.00
ULTCW Charlie Whitehurst	15.00	40.00
ULTDG David Givens	12.00	30.00
ULTDH Derek Hagan	12.00	30.00
ULTDW DeAngelo Williams	30.00	80.00
ULTEM Eli Manning	50.00	80.00
ULTFO DeShaun Foster	12.00	30.00
ULTJJ Julius Jones	10.00	25.00
ULTJK Joe Klopfenstein	10.00	25.00
ULTJN Jerious Norwood	12.00	30.00
ULTJO LaMont Jordan	12.00	30.00
ULTKC Kellen Clemens	12.00	30.00
ULTKJ Keyshawn Johnson	12.00	30.00
ULTLE Marcedes Lewis	15.00	40.00
ULTLJ Larry Johnson	12.00	30.00
ULTLM Laurence Maroney	12.00	30.00
ULTLT LaDainian Tomlinson	50.00	100.00
ULTLW LenDale White	12.00	30.00
ULTMB Marc Bulger	12.00	30.00
ULTMD Maurice Drew	25.00	60.00
ULTMH Michael Huff	12.00	30.00
ULTMI Mike Williams	10.00	25.00
ULTML Matt Leinart	15.00	40.00
ULTMR Michael Robinson	12.00	30.00
ULTMS Maurice Stovall	10.00	25.00
ULTMW Mario Williams	15.00	40.00
ULTNB Nate Burleson	10.00	25.00
ULTOJ Omar Jacobs	10.00	25.00
ULTPM Peyton Manning	90.00	150.00
ULTPR Philip Rivers	15.00	40.00
ULTRB Ronnie Brown	15.00	40.00
ULTRJ Rudi Johnson	12.00	30.00
ULTRW Reggie Wayne	12.00	30.00
ULTSH Santonio Holmes	20.00	50.00
ULTSM Sinorice Moss	15.00	40.00
ULTSS Steve Smith	15.00	40.00
ULTTA Lofa Tatupu	12.00	30.00
ULTTB Tiki Barber	15.00	40.00
ULTTH T.J. Houshmandzadeh/30	12.00	30.00
ULTTJ Thomas Jones	12.00	30.00
ULTVD Vernon Davis	20.00	50.00
ULTVY Vince Young	20.00	50.00
ULTWA Leon Washington	12.00	30.00
ULTWI Demetrius Williams	12.00	30.00

2006 Ultimate Collection Jerseys

STATED PRINT RUN 99 SER.#'d SETS
*PATCH SLVR/50 .6X TO 1.5X BASIC JSYs
PATCHES PRINT RUN 50 SER.#'d SETS
*PATCH GLD/30: .8X TO 2X BASIC JSYs
GOLD PATCH PRINT RUN 30
*SILVER/75: .4X TO 1X BASIC JSYs
SILVER PRINT RUN 75 SER.#'d SETS
*SPECTRUM/40: .6X TO 1.5X BASIC JSYs
SPECTRUM PRINT RUN 40 SER.#'d SETS

ULAB Anquan Boldin	3.00	8.00
ULAG Ahman Green	3.00	8.00
ULAS Alex Smith QB	4.00	10.00
ULBE Braylon Edwards	4.00	10.00
ULBF Brett Favre	8.00	20.00
ULBL Byron Leftwich	3.00	8.00
ULBR Ben Roethlisberger	6.00	15.00
ULBS Barry Sanders	10.00	25.00
ULBU Brian Urlacher	4.00	10.00
ULCJ Chad Johnson	3.00	8.00
ULCP Carson Palmer	4.00	10.00
ULCW Cadillac Williams	3.00	8.00
ULDB Drew Bledsoe	4.00	10.00
ULDC Daunte Culpepper	4.00	10.00
ULDD Domanick Davis	3.00	8.00
ULDF DeShaun Foster	3.00	8.00
ULDM Dan Marino	12.00	30.00
ULDO Donovan McNabb	4.00	10.00
ULDR Drew Brees	4.00	10.00
ULEJ Edgerrin James	4.00	10.00
ULEM Eli Manning	5.00	12.00
ULGA Antonio Gates	4.00	10.00
ULGR Trent Green	3.00	8.00
ULJD Jake Delhomme	3.00	8.00
ULJH Joe Horn	3.00	8.00
ULJJ Julius Jones	4.00	10.00
ULJK Jim Kelly	6.00	15.00
ULJL Jamal Lewis	3.00	8.00
ULJO LaMont Jordan	3.00	8.00
ULJP Jake Plummer	3.00	8.00
ULJS Jeremy Shockey	4.00	10.00
ULJT Jason Taylor	3.00	8.00
ULKS Ken Stabler	8.00	20.00
ULLF Larry Fitzgerald	4.00	10.00
ULLJ Larry Johnson	4.00	10.00
ULLT LaDainian Tomlinson	6.00	15.00
ULMC Deuce McAllister	3.00	8.00
ULMH Marvin Harrison	4.00	10.00
ULMV Michael Vick	4.00	10.00
ULPB Plaxico Burress	3.00	8.00
ULPH Priest Holmes	3.00	8.00
ULPM Peyton Manning	6.00	15.00
ULRB Ronnie Brown	4.00	10.00
ULRL Ray Lewis	4.00	10.00
ULRM Randy Moss	4.00	10.00
ULRS Rod Smith	3.00	8.00
ULRW Reggie Wayne	3.00	8.00
ULSA Shaun Alexander	4.00	10.00
ULSS Steve Smith	4.00	10.00
ULTB Tom Brady	6.00	15.00
ULTG Tony Gonzalez	3.00	8.00
ULTH Joe Theismann	6.00	15.00
ULTI Tiki Barber	4.00	10.00
ULTO Terrell Owens	4.00	10.00
ULTW Troy Williamson	3.00	8.00
ULWI Roy Williams WR	4.00	10.00
ULWM Willis McGahee	4.00	10.00
ULCB1 Champ Bailey	3.00	8.00
ULCB2 Cedric Benson	4.00	10.00

2006 Ultimate Collection Jerseys Dual

DUAL PRINT RUN 99 SER.#'d SETS
*PATCH/50: .5X TO 1.2X BASIC DUALS
PATCH PRINT RUN 50 SER.#'d SETS

UDBF Anquan Boldin	6.00	15.00
Larry Fitzgerald		
UDBH Champ Bailey	8.00	20.00
Michael Huff		
UDBL Reggie Bush	15.00	40.00
Matt Leinart		
UDBM Drew Brees	8.00	20.00
Deuce McAllister		
UDBO Drew Bledsoe	8.00	20.00
Terrell Owens		
UDBR Tom Brady	12.00	30.00
Ben Roethlisberger		
UDBW Ronnie Brown	6.00	15.00
LenDale White		
UDBY Cedric Benson	12.00	30.00
Vince Young		
UDCB Daunte Culpepper	6.00	15.00
Ronnie Brown		
UDCK Alge Crumpler	6.00	15.00
Joe Klopfenstein		
UDCS Chad Jackson	8.00	20.00
Santonio Holmes		
UDDC Jake Delhomme	8.00	20.00
Kellen Clemens		
UDDL DeAngelo Williams	10.00	25.00
Laurence Maroney		
UDEL Edgerrin James	6.00	15.00
Laurence Maroney		
UDFD DeShaun Foster	6.00	15.00
Maurice Drew		
UDFM Brett Favre	15.00	40.00
Peyton Manning		
UDGD Antonio Gates	8.00	20.00
Vernon Davis		
UDGG Tony Gonzalez	6.00	15.00
Antonio Gates		
UDHA Matt Hasselbeck	8.00	20.00
Shaun Alexander		
UDHH A.J. Hawk	8.00	20.00
Santonio Holmes		
UDJH Larry Johnson	6.00	15.00
Priest Holmes		
UDJM LaMont Jordan	6.00	15.00
Willis McGahee		
UDJS Julius Jones	8.00	20.00
Maurice Stovall		
UDJW Rudi Johnson	6.00	15.00
Cadillac Williams		
UDLD Marcedes Lewis	6.00	15.00
Maurice Drew		
UDLJ Byron Leftwich	8.00	20.00
Omar Jacobs		
UDME Dan Marino	20.00	50.00
John Elway		
UDMH Randy Moss	8.00	20.00
Marvin Harrison		
UDMM Peyton Manning	12.00	30.00
Eli Manning		
UDMY Donovan McNabb	12.00	30.00
Vince Young		
UDOJ Terrell Owens	5.00	12.00
Chad Jackson		
UDPB Jake Plummer	5.00	12.00
Tatum Bell		
UDPL Carson Palmer	12.00	30.00
Matt Leinart		
UDSB Barry Sanders	20.00	50.00
Reggie Bush		
UDSJ Steve Smith	8.00	20.00
Chad Johnson		
UDTD Tiki Barber	10.00	25.00
DeAngelo Williams		
UDTH Lofa Tatupu	8.00	20.00
A.J. Hawk		
UDTJ LaDainian Tomlinson	8.00	20.00
Larry Johnson		
UDTW Jason Taylor	5.00	12.00
Mario Williams		
UDVY Michael Vick	12.00	30.00
Vince Young		
UDWM Reggie Wayne	4.00	10.00
Sinorice Moss		

2006 Ultimate Collection Jerseys Triple

TRIPLE PRINT RUN 50 SER.#'d SETS
*TRI PATCH/25: .5X TO 1.2X BASIC TRIPLES
TRIPLE PATCH PRINT RUN 25

AJJ Shaun Alexander	10.00	25.00
Edgerrin James		
Larry Johnson		
BBS Tiki Barber	10.00	25.00
Plaxico Burress		
Jeremy Shockey		
BMH Drew Brees	10.00	25.00
Deuce McAllister		
Joe Horn		
BMS Drew Bledsoe	12.00	30.00
Peyton Manning		
Alex Smith QB		
BWM Reggie Bush	20.00	50.00
DeAngelo Williams		
Laurence Maroney		
DFP Jake Delhomme	6.00	15.00
DeShaun Foster		
Julius Peppers		
DLK Vernon Davis	8.00	20.00
Marcedes Lewis		
Joe Klopfenstein		
FBR Brett Favre	25.00	60.00
Tom Brady		
Ben Roethlisberger		
GHG Trent Green	6.00	15.00
Priest Holmes		
Tony Gonzalez		
JHM Chad Jackson	10.00	25.00
Santonio Holmes		
Sinorice Moss		
JWB Rudi Johnson	10.00	25.00
Cadillac Williams		
Ronnie Brown		
LYC Matt Leinart	15.00	40.00
Vince Young		
Kellen Clemens		
MCL Donovan McNabb	8.00	20.00
Daunte Culpepper		
Byron Leftwich		
PBS Jake Plummer	6.00	15.00
Tatum Bell		
Rod Smith		
RTG Philip Rivers	12.00	30.00
LaDainian Tomlinson		
Antonio Gates		
SJO Steve Smith	10.00	25.00
Chad Johnson		
Terrell Owens		
VPM Michael Vick	12.00	30.00
Carson Palmer		
Eli Manning		
WHH Mario Williams	10.00	25.00
A.J. Hawk		
Michael Huff		

2006 Ultimate Collection Jerseys Quad

QUAD PRINT RUN 25 SER.#'d SETS
*QUAD PATCH/20: .5X TO 1.2 X

BMWW Reggie Bush	25.00	60.00
Laurence Maroney		
DeAngelo Williams		
LenDale White		
HJMD Santonio Holmes	20.00	50.00
Chad Jackson		
Sinorice Moss		
Vernon Davis		
MSOJ Randy Moss	15.00	40.00
Steve Smith		
Terrell Owens		
Chad Johnson		
RMMB Ben Roethlisberger	30.00	80.00
Peyton Manning		
Donovan McNabb		
Tom Brady		
TAJJ LaDainian Tomlinson	20.00	50.00
Shaun Alexander		
Larry Johnson		
Edgerrin James		
YWCJ Vince Young	25.00	60.00
LenDale White		
Kellen Clemens		
Tarvaris Jackson		

2006 Ultimate Collection Rookie Jerseys

STATED PRINT RUN 99 SER.#'d SETS
*PATCH GLD/25: .8X TO 2X BASIC JSYs
PATCH GOLD PRINT RUN 25
*PATCH SLVR/50: .6X TO 1.5X BASIC JSYs
PATCH SILVER PRINT RUN 50
*SILVER/75: .4X TO 1X BASIC JSYs
SILVER PRINT RUN 75 SER.#'d SETS
*SPECTRUM/40: .6X TO 1.5X BASIC JSYs
SPECTRUM PRINT RUN 40 SER.#'d SETS

URAH A.J. Hawk	4.00	10.00
URBC Brian Calhoun	2.50	6.00
URBM Brandon Marshall	4.00	10.00
URBW Brandon Williams	2.50	6.00
URCJ Chad Jackson	2.50	6.00
URCW Charlie Whitehurst	4.00	10.00
URDH Derek Hagan	3.00	8.00
URDW DeAngelo Williams	5.00	12.00
URJA Jason Avant	2.50	6.00
URJK Joe Klopfenstein	2.50	6.00
URJN Jerious Norwood	3.00	8.00
URKC Kellen Clemens	3.00	8.00
URLE Matt Leinart	4.00	10.00
URLM Laurence Maroney	3.00	8.00
URLW LenDale White	3.00	8.00
URMD Maurice Drew	6.00	15.00
URMH Michael Huff	3.00	8.00
URML Marcedes Lewis	4.00	10.00
URMR Michael Robinson	3.00	8.00
URMS Maurice Stovall	2.50	6.00
URMW Mario Williams	4.00	10.00
UROJ Omar Jacobs	2.50	6.00
URRB Reggie Bush	8.00	20.00
URSH Santonio Holmes	5.00	12.00
URSM Sinorice Moss	4.00	10.00
URTJ Tarvaris Jackson	4.00	10.00
URTW Travis Wilson	2.50	6.00
URVD Vernon Davis	5.00	12.00
URVY Vince Young	5.00	12.00
URWA Leon Washington	3.00	8.00

2006 Ultimate Collection Stat Patches

STATED PRINT RUN 50 SER.#'d SETS

AB Anquan Boldin	6.00	15.00
AG Ahman Green	6.00	15.00
BA Tiki Barber	8.00	20.00
BF Brett Favre	15.00	40.00
BL Byron Leftwich	6.00	15.00
BR Ben Roethlisberger	12.00	30.00
BW Brian Westbrook	6.00	15.00
CB Champ Bailey	6.00	15.00
CC Chris Chambers	6.00	15.00
CD Corey Dillon	6.00	15.00
CJ Chad Johnson	6.00	15.00
CM Curtis Martin	8.00	20.00
CP Carson Palmer	8.00	20.00
DB Drew Bledsoe	8.00	20.00
DC Daunte Culpepper	8.00	20.00
DM Dan Marino	15.00	40.00
DO Donovan McNabb	8.00	20.00
DR Drew Brees	8.00	20.00
EJ Edgerrin James	8.00	20.00
EM Eli Manning	10.00	25.00
FT Fred Taylor	6.00	15.00
GA Antonio Gates	8.00	20.00
HA Matt Hasselbeck	6.00	15.00
JD Jake Delhomme	6.00	15.00
JS Jeremy Shockey	8.00	20.00
JW Javon Walker	6.00	15.00
LF Larry Fitzgerald	8.00	20.00
LJ Larry Johnson	8.00	20.00
LT LaDainian Tomlinson	8.00	20.00
MC Deuce McAllister	6.00	15.00
MH Marvin Harrison	8.00	20.00
MV Michael Vick	8.00	20.00
PB Plaxico Burress	6.00	15.00
PM Peyton Manning	12.00	30.00
PO Clinton Portis	8.00	20.00
RJ Rudi Johnson	6.00	15.00
RL Ray Lewis	8.00	20.00
RM Randy Moss	8.00	20.00
SS Steve Smith	8.00	20.00
TB Tom Brady	12.00	30.00
TG Trent Green	6.00	15.00
TH Torry Holt	6.00	15.00
TO Terrell Owens	8.00	20.00
PH1 Priest Holmes 27	6.00	15.00
PH2 Priest Holmes 86	6.00	15.00
RW1 Reggie Wayne 28	6.00	15.00
RW2 Reggie Wayne 83	6.00	15.00
SA1 Shaun Alexander 28	8.00	20.00
SA2 Shaun Alexander 89	8.00	20.00
TG1 Tony Gonzalez 56	6.00	15.00
TG2 Tony Gonzalez 78	6.00	15.00

2006 Ultimate Collection Super Jerseys

STATED PRINT RUN 50 SER.#'d SETS
UNPRICED PATCH PRINT RUN 10

SUPAG Antonio Gates	10.00	25.00
SUPAS Alex Smith QB	10.00	25.00
SUPBA Tiki Barber	10.00	25.00
SUPBF Brett Favre	20.00	50.00
SUPBR Ben Roethlisberger	15.00	40.00
SUPBU Reggie Bush	15.00	40.00
SUPCB Champ Bailey	8.00	20.00
SUPCJ Chad Johnson	8.00	20.00
SUPCP Carson Palmer	10.00	25.00
SUPCW Cadillac Williams	10.00	25.00
SUPDC Daunte Culpepper	10.00	25.00
SUPDF DeShaun Foster	8.00	20.00
SUPDM Donovan McNabb	10.00	25.00
SUPEJ Edgerrin James	10.00	25.00
SUPEM Eli Manning	12.00	30.00
SUPGR Trent Green	8.00	20.00
SUPJD Jake Delhomme	8.00	20.00
SUPJJ Julius Jones	10.00	25.00
SUPJO LaMont Jordan	8.00	20.00
SUPJP Jake Plummer	8.00	20.00
SUPJS Jeremy Shockey	10.00	25.00
SUPLJ Larry Johnson	10.00	25.00
SUPLT LaDainian Tomlinson	10.00	25.00
SUPMH Matt Hasselbeck	8.00	20.00
SUPML Matt Leinart	10.00	25.00
SUPMV Michael Vick	10.00	25.00
SUPPM Peyton Manning	15.00	40.00
SUPRB Ronnie Brown	10.00	25.00
SUPRM Randy Moss	10.00	25.00
SUPSA Shaun Alexander	10.00	25.00
SUPSS Steve Smith	10.00	25.00
SUPTB Tom Brady	15.00	40.00
SUPTG Tony Gonzalez	8.00	20.00
SUPTO Terrell Owens	10.00	25.00

2006 Ultimate Collection Ultimate Scripts

STATED PRINT RUN 35 SER.#'d SETS

USCAF Anthony Fasano	8.00	20.00
USCAG Antonio Gates	10.00	25.00
USCAH A.J. Hawk	20.00	50.00
USCAI Troy Aikman	50.00	100.00
USCAV Jason Avant	8.00	20.00
USCBB Brodrick Bunkley	6.00	15.00
USCBC Brian Calhoun	8.00	20.00
USCBE Braylon Edwards	10.00	25.00
USCBF Brett Favre	100.00	200.00
USCBG Bruce Gradkowski	10.00	25.00
USCBL Byron Leftwich	10.00	25.00
USCBM Brandon Marshall	10.00	30.00
USCBO Bob Griese	10.00	25.00
USCBR Ben Roethlisberger	60.00	100.00
USCBS Brad Smith	8.00	20.00
USCBU Reggie Bush	30.00	120.00
USCBW Brandon Williams	8.00	20.00
USCCG Chad Greenway	10.00	25.00
USCCJ Chad Jackson	8.00	20.00
USCCU Kevin Curtis	8.00	20.00
USCCW Charlie Whitehurst	8.00	20.00
USCDA Dan Fouts	12.00	30.00
USCDB Dominique Byrd	8.00	20.00
USCDE Demetrius Williams	8.00	20.00
USCDG David Givens	6.00	15.00
USCDH Derek Hagan	6.00	15.00
USCDM Dan Marino	100.00	200.00
USCDR Drew Bledsoe	10.00	25.00
USCDS D.J. Shockley	10.00	25.00
USCDW DeAngelo Williams	20.00	60.00
USCEM Eli Manning	50.00	80.00
USCES Ernie Sims	10.00	25.00
USCFO DeShaun Foster	8.00	20.00
USCGJ Greg Jennings	20.00	40.00
USCGL Greg Lee	6.00	15.00
USCHA Mike Hass	8.00	20.00
USCHI Tye Hill	6.00	15.00
USCHO T.J. Houshmandzadeh	8.00	20.00
USCJA Joseph Addai	12.00	60.00
USCJB Josh Betts	8.00	20.00
USCJC Jay Cutler	40.00	150.00
USCJE John Elway	75.00	150.00
USCJH Jerome Harrison	10.00	30.00
USCJJ Julius Jones	10.00	25.00
USCJK Joe Klopfenstein	6.00	15.00
USCJN Jerious Norwood	10.00	30.00
USCJO Keyshawn Johnson	10.00	25.00
USCJW Jimmy Williams	8.00	20.00
USCKC Kellen Clemens	10.00	25.00
USCKJ Kelly Jennings	8.00	20.00
USCLA LaMont Jordan	8.00	20.00
USCLE Matt Leinart	20.00	50.00
USCLJ Larry Johnson	10.00	30.00
USCLM Laurence Maroney	10.00	40.00
USCLO Lofa Tatupu	12.00	30.00
USCLP Leonard Pope	8.00	20.00
USCLT LaDainian Tomlinson	40.00	100.00
USCLW LenDale White	10.00	40.00
USCMA Derrick Mason	8.00	20.00
USCMD Maurice Drew	30.00	60.00
USCMH Michael Huff	10.00	25.00
USCMK Mathias Kiwanuka	10.00	25.00
USCML Marcedes Lewis	8.00	20.00
USCMM Muhsin Muhammad	8.00	20.00
USCMR Michael Robinson	8.00	20.00
USCMS Maurice Stovall	10.00	25.00
USCMV Michael Vick	30.00	60.00
USCMW Mario Williams	15.00	40.00
USCOD Owen Daniels	10.00	25.00
USCPH Paul Hornung	12.00	30.00
USCPM Peyton Manning	60.00	120.00
USCPR Philip Rivers	30.00	60.00
USCRB Ronnie Brown	10.00	30.00
USCRJ Rudi Johnson	10.00	25.00
USCRM Reggie McNeal	6.00	15.00
USCRO Cory Rodgers	6.00	15.00
USCRW Reggie Wayne	12.00	30.00
USCRY DeMeco Ryans	10.00	30.00
USCSH Santonio Holmes	20.00	50.00
USCSY Steve Young	50.00	100.00
USCTA Tarvaris Jackson	10.00	25.00
USCTB Tiki Barber	12.00	40.00
USCTH Thomas Howard	8.00	20.00
USCTJ Thomas Jones	10.00	25.00
USCTW Travis Wilson	10.00	25.00
USCVD Vernon Davis	12.00	30.00
USCVY Vince Young	25.00	100.00
USCWA Leon Washington	10.00	30.00
USCWB Will Blackmon	8.00	20.00
USCWI Cadillac Williams	10.00	25.00
USCWR Willie Reid	8.00	20.00

2006 Ultimate Collection Ultimate Signatures

STATED PRINT RUN 25-99
UNPRICED PRINT PLATES SER.#'d TO 1

USAH A.J. Hawk/99	20.00	50.00
USBA Ronde Barber/99	8.00	20.00
USBC Brian Calhoun/99	8.00	20.00
USBE Braylon Edwards/99	10.00	25.00
USBF Brett Favre/25	125.00	225.00
USBL Drew Bledsoe/25	15.00	40.00
USBR Reggie Brown/99	8.00	20.00
USBU Reggie Bush/25	75.00	150.00
USCJ Chad Jackson/99	10.00	25.00
USCP Carson Palmer/25		
USCS Chris Simms/99	8.00	20.00
USCU Kevin Curtis/99	6.00	15.00
USCW Cadillac Williams/25	15.00	40.00
USDB Drew Bennett/99	6.00	15.00
USDF D'Brickashaw Ferguson/99	6.00	15.00
USDG David Givens/99	6.00	15.00
USDM Deuce McAllister/75	8.00	20.00
USDW DeAngelo Williams/75	25.00	50.00
USEM Eli Manning/25	50.00	80.00
USFO DeShaun Foster/99	6.00	15.00
USGJ Greg Jennings/99	15.00	40.00
USHO T.J. Houshmandzadeh/99	8.00	20.00
USJA Joseph Addai/99	12.00	30.00
USJC Jay Cutler/25	100.00	175.00
USJO LaMont Jordan/75	6.00	15.00
USJW Jason Witten/99	20.00	40.00
USKC Kellen Clemens/99	10.00	25.00
USKO Kyle Orton/99	6.00	15.00
USLE Byron Leftwich/25	12.00	30.00
USLJ Larry Johnson/25	15.00	40.00
USLM Laurence Maroney/75	10.00	25.00
USLT LaDainian Tomlinson/25	50.00	100.00
USLW LenDale White/75	10.00	25.00
USMA Derrick Mason/99	6.00	15.00
USMB Marc Bulger/75	8.00	20.00
USMC Mark Clayton/75	8.00	20.00
USMD Maurice Drew/99	40.00	80.00
USMH Michael Huff/99	10.00	25.00
USML Matt Leinart/25	25.00	60.00
USMW Mario Williams/75	12.00	30.00
USNB Nate Burleson/99	6.00	15.00
USPM Peyton Manning/25	75.00	150.00
USRB Ronnie Brown/75	10.00	25.00
USRJ Rudi Johnson/99	10.00	25.00
USRO Ben Roethlisberger/25	60.00	120.00
USRW Reggie Wayne/99	12.00	30.00
USSH Santonio Holmes/75	20.00	40.00
USSM Sinorice Moss/99	10.00	25.00
USSS Steve Smith/75	10.00	25.00
USTA Lofa Tatupu/99	12.00	30.00
USTB Tiki Barber/25	20.00	50.00
USTH Thomas Jones/75	10.00	25.00
USTJ Tarvaris Jackson/99	10.00	25.00
USVD Vernon Davis/75	12.00	30.00
USVY Vince Young/25	60.00	120.00
USWH Charlie Whitehurst/99	10.00	25.00
USWI Mike Williams/99	6.00	15.00
USWP Willie Parker/99	10.00	25.00

2006 Ultimate Collection Ultimate Signatures Duals

STATED PRINT RUN 25 SER.#'d SETS

AS Troy Aikman	75.00	150.00
Roger Staubach		
BB Tiki Barber	60.00	120.00
Ronde Barber		
BG Drew Bennett	15.00	40.00
David Givens		
BJ Cedric Benson	30.00	80.00
Thomas Jones		
BM Reggie Bush	50.00	100.00
Deuce McAllister		
BS Reggie Bush	60.00	120.00
Gale Sayers		
CM Mark Clayton	30.00	60.00
Derrick Mason		
EC John Elway	250.00	400.00
Jay Cutler		
FW DeShaun Foster	25.00	60.00
DeAngelo Williams		
GD Antonio Gates	30.00	60.00
Vernon Davis		
GJ Trent Green	25.00	60.00
Larry Johnson		
HP Franco Harris	50.00	100.00
Willie Parker		
HR Santonio Holmes	25.00	60.00
Willie Reid		
HS A.J. Hawk	40.00	80.00
Ernie Sims		
JB LaMont Jordan	15.00	40.00
Aaron Brooks		
JH Rudi Johnson	25.00	50.00
T.J. Houshmandzadeh		
JM Chad Jackson	20.00	50.00
Laurence Maroney		
LD Marcedes Lewis	40.00	100.00
Maurice Drew		
LY Matt Leinart	50.00	120.00
Vince Young		
MF Dan Marino	200.00	350.00
Brett Favre		
MM Peyton Manning	150.00	250.00
Eli Manning		
OM Kyle Orton	15.00	40.00
Muhsin Muhammad		
SJ Steve Smith	20.00	50.00
Keyshawn Johnson		
ST Barry Sanders	150.00	300.00
LaDainian Tomlinson		
TE Tiki Barber	75.00	125.00
Eli Manning		
WA Reggie Wayne	40.00	100.00
Joseph Addai		
WB Cadillac Williams	25.00	60.00
Ronnie Brown		
WF Jason Witten	40.00	80.00
Anthony Fasano		
WG Mario Williams	25.00	60.00
L.C. Greenwood		
YW Vince Young	40.00	100.00
LenDale White		

2006 Ultimate Collection Ultimate Signatures Triples

TRIPLE SIGNATURE PRINT RUN 20

ADS Troy Aikman	75.00	150.00
Len Dawson		
Ken Stabler		
BWB Ronnie Brown	40.00	100.00
Cadillac Williams		
Cedric Benson		
HSG A.J. Hawk	40.00	100.00
Ernie Sims		
Chad Greenway		
JJP Rudi Johnson	30.00	60.00
LaMont Jordan		
Willie Parker		
JTB Larry Johnson	40.00	80.00
LaDainian Tomlinson		
Tiki Barber		
LBW Matt Leinart	50.00	100.00
Reggie Bush		
LenDale White		
SAB Roger Staubach	75.00	150.00
Troy Aikman		
Drew Bledsoe		
WMA DeAngelo Williams	40.00	80.00
Laurence Maroney		
Joseph Addai		
YLC Vince Young	50.00	120.00
Matt Leinart		
Jay Cutler		

2007 Ultimate Collection

This 160-card set was released in November, 2007. The set was issued into the hobby in four-card packs, with an $100 SRP, which came four packs to a box. Cards numbered 1-100 feature veterans issued to a stated print run of 400 serial numbered sets while cards number 101-160 were all signed by the player. Those Rookie Cards were broken down thusly: Cards numbered 101-110 were issued to a stated print run of 99 serial numbered sets, cards numbered 111-127 were issued to a stated print run of 150 serial numbered sets and cards numbered 128-160 were all issued to a stated print run of 250 serial numbered sets.

1-100 PRINT RUN 400 SER.#'d SETS
101-110 ROOKIE AU PRINT RUN 99
111-127 ROOKIE AU PRINT RUN 150
128-160 ROOKIE AU PRINT RUN 250

1 Matt Leinart	2.00	5.00
2 Edgerrin James	2.00	5.00
3 Larry Fitzgerald	2.50	6.00
4 Anquan Boldin	2.00	5.00
5 Marion Barber	2.50	6.00
6 Jerious Norwood	2.00	5.00
7 Alge Crumpler	2.00	5.00
8 Steve McNair	2.00	5.00
9 Willis McGahee	2.00	5.00
10 Mark Clayton	2.00	5.00
11 J.P. Losman	1.50	4.00
12 Anthony Thomas	1.50	4.00
13 Lee Evans	2.00	5.00
14 Jake Delhomme	2.00	5.00
15 DeAngelo Williams	2.50	6.00
16 Steve Smith	2.00	5.00
17 Rex Grossman	2.00	5.00
18 Cedric Benson	2.00	5.00
19 Brian Urlacher	2.50	6.00
20 Carson Palmer	2.00	5.00
21 Rudi Johnson	2.00	5.00
22 Chad Johnson	2.00	5.00
23 T.J. Houshmandzadeh	2.00	5.00
24 Charlie Frye	2.00	5.00
25 Kellen Winslow	2.00	5.00
26 Braylon Edwards	2.00	5.00
27 Tony Romo	3.00	8.00
28 Julius Jones	1.50	4.00
29 Terrell Owens	2.50	6.00
30 Jay Cutler	2.50	6.00
31 Travis Henry	2.00	5.00
32 Javon Walker	2.00	5.00
33 Jon Kitna	1.50	4.00
34 Roy Williams WR	2.00	5.00
35 Tatum Bell	1.50	4.00
36 Brett Favre	5.00	12.00
37 Donald Driver	2.50	6.00
38 Greg Jennings	2.50	6.00
39 Matt Schaub	2.00	5.00
40 Ahman Green	2.00	5.00
41 Andre Johnson	2.00	5.00
42 Peyton Manning	4.00	10.00
43 Joseph Addai	2.00	5.00
44 Marvin Harrison	2.50	6.00
45 Reggie Wayne	2.00	5.00
46 Byron Leftwich	2.00	5.00
47 Maurice Jones-Drew	2.50	6.00
48 Fred Taylor	2.00	5.00
49 Brodie Croyle	2.00	5.00
50 Larry Johnson	1.50	4.00
51 Tony Gonzalez	2.00	5.00
52 Trent Green	2.00	5.00
53 Ronnie Brown	2.00	5.00

54 Chris Chambers	2.00	5.00
55 Tarvaris Jackson	1.50	4.00
56 Chester Taylor	1.50	4.00
57 Troy Williamson	1.50	4.00
58 Tom Brady	4.00	10.00
59 Laurence Maroney	2.00	5.00
60 Randy Moss	2.50	6.00
61 Drew Brees	2.50	6.00
62 Reggie Bush	2.50	6.00
63 Deuce McAllister	2.00	5.00
64 Marques Colston	2.50	6.00
65 Eli Manning	2.50	6.00
66 Brandon Jacobs	2.00	5.00
67 Plaxico Burress	2.00	5.00
68 Chad Pennington	2.00	5.00
69 Thomas Jones	2.00	5.00
70 Laveranues Coles	1.50	4.00
71 LaMont Jordan	2.00	5.00
72 Dominic Rhodes	2.00	5.00
73 Ronald Curry	2.00	5.00
74 Donovan McNabb	2.50	6.00
75 Brian Westbrook	2.00	5.00
76 Reggie Brown	1.50	4.00
77 Ben Roethlisberger	2.50	6.00
78 Willie Parker	2.00	5.00
79 Hines Ward	2.50	6.00
80 Philip Rivers	2.50	6.00
81 LaDainian Tomlinson	2.50	6.00
82 Antonio Gates	2.50	6.00
83 Alex Smith QB	2.50	6.00
84 Frank Gore	2.50	6.00
85 Darrell Jackson	1.50	4.00
86 Matt Hasselbeck	2.00	5.00
87 Shaun Alexander	2.00	5.00
88 Deion Branch	2.00	5.00
89 Marc Bulger	2.00	5.00
90 Steven Jackson	2.50	6.00
91 Torry Holt	2.00	5.00
92 Jeff Garcia	2.00	5.00
93 Cadillac Williams	2.00	5.00
94 Joey Galloway	2.00	5.00
95 Vince Young	2.00	5.00
96 LenDale White	2.00	5.00
97 David Givens	1.50	4.00
98 Jason Campbell	2.00	5.00
99 Clinton Portis	2.00	5.00
100 Santana Moss	2.00	5.00
101 Adrian Peterson AU/99 RC	200.00	400.00
102 Brady Quinn AU/99 RC	15.00	40.00
103 Calvin Johnson AU/99 RC	100.00	175.00
104 Dwayne Bowe AU/99 RC	20.00	50.00
105 JaMarcus Russell AU/99 RC	10.00	25.00
106 Kevin Kolb AU/99 RC	40.00	80.00
107 Marshawn Lynch AU/99 RC	25.00	50.00
108 Robert Meachem AU/99 RC	15.00	40.00
109 Sidney Rice AU/99 RC	20.00	50.00
110 Ted Ginn AU/99 RC	12.00	30.00
111 Anthony Gonzalez AU/150 RC	10.00	25.00
112 Brian Leonard AU/150 RC	8.00	20.00
113 Chris Henry AU/150 RC	6.00	15.00
114 Chris Leak AU/150 RC	8.00	20.00
115 Drew Stanton AU/150 RC	6.00	15.00
116 Dwayne Jarrett AU/150 RC	8.00	20.00
117 Gaines Adams AU/150 RC	10.00	25.00
118 Greg Olsen AU/150 RC	12.00	30.00
119 Jason Hill AU/150 RC	10.00	25.00
120 Joe Thomas AU/150 RC	10.00	25.00
121 Kenny Irons AU/150 RC	6.00	15.00
122 LaRon Landry AU/150 RC	10.00	25.00
123 Leon Hall AU/150 RC	8.00	20.00
124 Lorenzo Booker AU/150 RC	8.00	20.00
125 Michael Bush AU/150 RC	10.00	25.00
126 Steve Smith AU/150 RC	10.00	25.00
127 Trent Edwards AU/150 RC	10.00	25.00
128 Amobi Okoye AU/250 RC	8.00	20.00
129 Antonio Pittman AU/250 RC	5.00	12.00
130 Aundrae Allison AU/250 RC	5.00	12.00
131 Brandon Jackson AU/250 RC	6.00	15.00
132 Brandon Meriweather AU/250 RC	8.00	20.00
133 Chansi Stuckey AU/250 RC	8.00	20.00
134 Craig Buster Davis AU/250 RC	6.00	15.00
135 Dallas Baker AU/250 RC	5.00	12.00
136 Darrelle Revis AU/250 RC	15.00	30.00
137 David Ball AU/250 RC	6.00	15.00
138 David Clowney AU/250 RC	6.00	15.00
139 Daymeion Hughes AU/250 RC	6.00	15.00
140 Dwayne Wright AU/250 RC	6.00	15.00
141 Eric Wright AU/250 RC	8.00	20.00
142 Garrett Wolfe AU/250 RC	5.00	12.00
143 John Beck AU/250 RC	8.00	20.00
144 Johnnie Lee Higgins AU/250 RC	6.00	15.00
145 Jordan Palmer AU/250 RC	6.00	15.00
146 Kenneth Darby AU/250 RC	6.00	15.00
147 Kolby Smith AU/250 RC	6.00	15.00
148 LaMarr Woodley AU/250 RC	15.00	30.00
149 Lawrence Timmons AU/250 RC	8.00	20.00
150 Legedu Naanee AU/250 RC	8.00	20.00
151 Matt Moore AU/250 RC	8.00	20.00
152 Paul Williams AU/250 RC	5.00	12.00
153 Quentin Moses AU/250 RC	6.00	15.00
154 Reggie Nelson AU/250 RC	6.00	15.00
155 Rhema McKnight AU/250 RC	5.00	12.00
156 Selvin Young AU/250 RC	6.00	15.00
157 Syvelle Newton AU/250 RC	6.00	15.00
158 Tony Hunt AU/250 RC	5.00	12.00
159 Tyler Palko AU/250 RC	6.00	15.00
160 Zach Miller AU/250 RC	8.00	20.00

2007 Ultimate Collection Achievement Patches

STATED PRINT RUN 99 SER.#'d SETS

UAPAG Anthony Gonzalez	4.00	10.00
UAPAP Adrian Peterson	15.00	40.00
UAPBF Brett Favre	15.00	40.00
UAPBO Dwayne Bowe	5.00	12.00
UAPBQ Brady Quinn	4.00	10.00
UAPCJ Chad Johnson	5.00	12.00
UAPCP Carson Palmer	5.00	12.00
UAPDB Drew Brees	6.00	15.00
UAPDJ Dwayne Jarrett	3.00	8.00
UAPDM Donovan McNabb	6.00	15.00
UAPEM Eli Manning	6.00	15.00
UAPGI Ted Ginn Jr.	3.00	8.00
UAPGR Trent Green	5.00	12.00
UAPHW Hines Ward	6.00	15.00
UAPJB John Beck	4.00	10.00
UAPJM Joe Montana	15.00	40.00
UAPJO Calvin Johnson	12.00	30.00
UAPJR JaMarcus Russell	2.50	6.00
UAPJT Jason Taylor	5.00	12.00
UAPKK Kevin Kolb	6.00	15.00
UAPLF Larry Fitzgerald	6.00	15.00
UAPLJ Larry Johnson	4.00	10.00
UAPLT LaDainian Tomlinson	6.00	15.00
UAPLY Marshawn Lynch	4.00	10.00
UAPMH Marvin Harrison	6.00	15.00
UAPML Matt Leinart	5.00	12.00
UAPPM Peyton Manning	10.00	25.00
UAPRB Reggie Bush	6.00	15.00
UAPRL Ray Lewis	6.00	15.00
UAPRM Robert Meachem	4.00	10.00
UAPRW Roy Williams WR	5.00	12.00
UAPSS Steve Smith	5.00	12.00
UAPSY Steve Young	12.00	30.00
UAPTB Tom Brady	15.00	40.00
UAPTG Tony Gonzalez	5.00	12.00
UAPTH Torry Holt	5.00	12.00
UAPTO Terrell Owens	6.00	15.00
UAPVY Vince Young	5.00	12.00
UAPWD Warrick Dunn	4.00	10.00

2007 Ultimate Collection Game Patches

STATED PRINT RUN 99 SER.#'d SETS

UGPAG Ahman Green	5.00	12.00
UGPAS Alex Smith QB	6.00	15.00
UGPBE Cedric Benson	5.00	12.00
UGPBF Brett Favre	15.00	40.00
UGPBF2 Brett Favre	15.00	40.00
UGPBL Byron Leftwich	5.00	12.00
UGPBR Ben Roethlisberger	6.00	15.00
UGPBW Brian Westbrook	5.00	12.00
UGPCB Champ Bailey	5.00	12.00
UGPCJ Chad Johnson	5.00	12.00
UGPCP Carson Palmer	5.00	12.00
UGPCW Cadillac Williams	5.00	12.00
UGPDB Drew Brees	6.00	16.00
UGPDD Donald Driver	6.00	15.00
UGPDM Donovan McNabb	6.00	15.00
UGPDW DeAngelo Williams	6.00	15.00
UGPEJ Edgerrin James	5.00	12.00
UGPEJ2 Edgerrin James	5.00	12.00
UGPES Emmitt Smith	15.00	40.00
UGPFG Frank Gore	6.00	15.00
UGPGA Antonio Gates	6.00	15.00
UGPHA Marvin Harrison	6.00	15.00
UGPHW Hines Ward	6.00	15.00
UGPJJ Julius Jones	4.00	10.00
UGPJT Jason Taylor	5.00	12.00
UGPLC Laveranues Coles	4.00	10.00
UGPLE Lee Evans	5.00	12.00
UGPLF Larry Fitzgerald	6.00	15.00
UGPLM Laurence Maroney	5.00	12.00
UGPLT LaDainian Tomlinson	6.00	15.00
UGPLT2 LaDainian Tomlinson	6.00	15.00
UGPMB Marc Bulger	5.00	12.00
UGPMH Matt Hasselbeck	5.00	12.00
UGPPM Peyton Manning	10.00	25.00
UGPPM2 Peyton Manning	10.00	25.00
UGPPO Clinton Portis	5.00	12.00
UGPPR Philip Rivers	6.00	15.00
UGPRB Reggie Bush	6.00	15.00
UGPRO Ronnie Brown	5.00	12.00
UGPRW Reggie Wayne	5.00	12.00
UGPSA Shaun Alexander	5.00	12.00
UGPSJ Steven Jackson	6.00	15.00
UGPSM Steve McNair	5.00	12.00
UGPTB Tom Brady	15.00	40.00
UGPTH T.J. Houshmandzadeh	5.00	12.00
UGPTR Tony Romo	8.00	20.00
UGPVY Vince Young	5.00	12.00
UGPWI Roy Williams WR	5.00	12.00
UGPWM Willis McGahee	5.00	12.00

2007 Ultimate Collection Materials Autographs

STATED PRINT RUN 1-25

UMAB Anquan Boldin	12.00	30.00
UMAD Joseph Addai		
UMAS Alex Smith QB	25.00	50.00
UMBF Brett Favre	150.00	250.00
UMDJ Brandon Jacobs	12.00	30.00
UMBU Reggie Bush	20.00	50.00
UMCL Mark Clayton	10.00	25.00
UMCT Chester Taylor	10.00	25.00
UMDR Drew Bennett		
UMEM Eli Manning	60.00	120.00
UMEM2 Eli Manning	60.00	120.00
UMFG Frank Gore	20.00	40.00
UMHO T.J. Houshmandzadeh	12.00	30.00
UMJT Joe Theismann	20.00	40.00
UMLE Lee Evans	10.00	25.00
UMLT LaDainian Tomlinson	40.00	80.00
UMMB Marc Bulger	10.00	25.00
UMML Matt Leinart	20.00	40.00
UMML2 Matt Leinart	20.00	40.00
UMMQ Marques Colston	10.00	25.00
UMTR Tony Romo		
UMWP Willie Parker	20.00	40.00

2007 Ultimate Collection Materials Dual

STATED PRINT RUN 75 SER.#'d SETS
*PATCH/25: .8X TO 2X BASIC DUAL/75
PATCH PRINT RUN 25 SER.#'d SETS

1 Peyton Manning	30.00	80.00
Tom Brady		
2 Reggie Bush	6.00	15.00
Deuce McAllister		
3 Shawne Merriman	6.00	15.00
Patrick Willis		
4 LaDainian Tomlinson	20.00	50.00
Adrian Peterson		
5 Tony Gonzalez	6.00	15.00
Antonio Gates		
6 Tony Romo	8.00	20.00
Terrell Owens		
7 Steve Smith	6.00	15.00
DeAngelo Williams		
8 Julius Jones	5.00	12.00
Thomas Jones		
9 Ronnie Brown	5.00	12.00
Cadillac Williams		
10 Maurice Jones-Drew	8.00	20.00
Marshawn Lynch		
11 Ted Ginn Jr.	10.00	25.00
Calvin Johnson		
12 Marvin Harrison	3.00	8.00
Anthony Gonzalez		
13 Peyton Manning	10.00	25.00
Eli Manning		
14 Chad Pennington	10.00	25.00
Tom Brady		
15 Brett Favre	25.00	60.00
Peyton Manning		
17 Brady Quinn	3.00	8.00
Matt Leinart		
18 Vince Young	6.00	15.00
Reggie Bush		
19 Edgerrin James	6.00	15.00
Frank Gore		
20 Steven Jackson	6.00	15.00
Shaun Alexander		
21 Leon Washington	5.00	12.00
Laveranues Coles		
22 Reggie Bush	6.00	15.00
Matt Leinart		
23 Torry Holt	4.00	10.00
Sidney Rice		
24 Michael Bush	3.00	8.00
JaMarcus Russell		
25 Matt Leinart	5.00	12.00
Carson Palmer		
26 Drew Stanton	10.00	25.00
Calvin Johnson		
27 Reggie Bush	6.00	15.00
Robert Meachem		
28 Philip Rivers	6.00	15.00
Ben Roethlisberger		
29 Hines Ward	6.00	15.00
Champ Bailey		
30 Laurence Maroney	5.00	12.00
Leon Washington		
31 Adrian Peterson	20.00	50.00
Marshawn Lynch		
32 Steve Smith USC	3.00	8.00
Dwayne Jarrett		
33 Willie Parker	5.00	12.00
Willis McGahee		
34 Chad Johnson	5.00	12.00
T.J. Houshmandzadeh		
35 Carson Palmer	5.00	12.00
Chad Johnson		
36 Peyton Manning	12.00	30.00
Marvin Harrison		
37 JaMarcus Russell	3.00	8.00
Brady Quinn		
38 Willis McGahee	6.00	15.00
Frank Gore		
39 Shaun Alexander	3.00	8.00
Michael Bush		
40 Anquan Boldin	6.00	15.00
Larry Fitzgerald		

2007 Ultimate Collection Materials Quad

QUAD PRINT RUN 25 SER.#'d SETS
UNPRICED PATCH PRINT RUN 10

1 Edgerrin James	15.00	40.00
Frank Gore		
Steven Jackson		
Shaun Alexander		
2 LaDainian Tomlinson	15.00	40.00
Frank Gore		
Steven Jackson		
Larry Johnson		
3 Reggie Bush	20.00	50.00
Matt Leinart		
Vince Young		
Maurice Jones-Drew		
4 Matt Hasselbeck	15.00	40.00
Shaun Alexander		
Ben Roethlisberger		
Willie Parker		
5 Peyton Manning	30.00	80.00
Marvin Harrison		
Reggie Wayne		
Joseph Addai		
6 Tony Romo	30.00	80.00
Drew Brees		
Carson Palmer		
Steve McNair		
7 Roy Williams WR	8.00	20.00
Robert Meachem		
Larry Fitzgerald		
Dwayne Bowe		
8 John Beck	20.00	50.00
Ted Ginn Jr.		
Drew Stanton		
Calvin Johnson		
9 Reggie Bush	15.00	40.00
Matt Leinart		
Carson Palmer		
Marcus Allen		
10 Steve Smith USC	8.00	20.00
Dwayne Jarrett		
Troy Smith		
Antonio Pittman		
11 Laveranues Coles	15.00	40.00
Javon Walker		
Hines Ward		
Lee Evans		
12 Reggie Wayne	12.00	30.00
Anquan Boldin		
Steve Smith		
Torry Holt		
13 Clinton Portis	15.00	40.00
Frank Gore		
Willis McGahee		
Edgerrin James		
14 Torry Holt	15.00	40.00
Isaac Bruce		
Larry Fitzgerald		
Anquan Boldin		
15 Roy Williams WR	15.00	40.00
Donald Driver		
Anquan Boldin		
Steve Smith		
16 Jason Hill	8.00	20.00
Patrick Willis		
Michael Bush		
Johnnie Lee Higgins		
18 JaMarcus Russell	12.00	30.00
Brady Quinn		
Kevin Kolb		
John Beck		
19 Laurence Maroney	15.00	40.00
LenDale White		
Leon Washington		
Maurice Jones-Drew		
20 Carson Palmer	15.00	40.00
Matt Leinart		
Reggie Bush		
LenDale White		
21 Marshawn Lynch	40.00	100.00
Adrian Peterson		
Brandon Jackson		
Kenny Irons		
22 Chad Johnson	15.00	40.00
Reggie Wayne		
Marvin Harrison		
Lee Evans		
23 Drew Stanton	8.00	20.00
Kevin Kolb		
Yamon Figurs		
Steve Smith USC		
24 Tom Brady	40.00	100.00
Peyton Manning		
Ben Roethlisberger		
Chad Pennington		
25 Warrick Dunn	15.00	40.00
Deuce McAllister		
Cadillac Williams		
DeAngelo Williams		
26 JaMarcus Russell	30.00	80.00
Adrian Peterson		
Ted Ginn Jr.		
Greg Olsen		
27 Brett Favre	75.00	150.00
Eli Manning		
Peyton Manning		
Tom Brady		
28 JaMarcus Russell	12.00	30.00
Brady Quinn		
Peyton Manning		
Donovan McNabb		
29 Calvin Johnson	8.00	20.00
Ted Ginn Jr.		
Dwayne Bowe		
Robert Meachem		
30 Troy Smith	10.00	25.00
Anthony Gonzalez		
Antonio Pittman		
Ted Ginn Jr.		

2007 Ultimate Collection Materials Silver

SILVER RUN 125 SER.#'d SETS
*GOLD/99: .5X TO 1.2X SILVER/125
GOLD PRINT RUN 99 SER.#'d SETS
*PATCH/35: 1X TO 2.5X SILVER/125
PATCHES PRINT RUN 35 SER.#'d SETS

UMAB Anquan Boldin	3.00	8.00
UMAC Alge Crumpler	3.00	8.00
UMAG Antonio Gates	4.00	10.00
UMAH A.J. Hawk	3.00	8.00
UMAJ Andre Johnson	3.00	8.00
UMAS Alex Smith QB	4.00	10.00
UMBD Brian Dawkins	3.00	8.00
UMBF Brett Favre	10.00	25.00
UMBJ Brandon Jacobs	3.00	8.00
UMBL Byron Leftwich	3.00	8.00
UMBM Marc Bulger	3.00	8.00
UMBR Ben Roethlisberger	4.00	10.00
UMTE2 Tedy Bruschi	4.00	10.00
UMBU Brian Urlacher	4.00	10.00
UMBW Brian Westbrook	3.00	8.00
UMCA Jason Campbell	3.00	8.00
UMCB Cedric Benson	3.00	8.00
UMCJ Chad Johnson	3.00	8.00
UMCL Michael Clayton	2.50	6.00
UMCO Marques Colston	4.00	10.00
UMCP Carson Palmer	3.00	8.00
UMCT Chester Taylor	2.50	6.00
UMDB Drew Bennett	2.50	6.00
UMDD Donald Driver	4.00	10.00
UMDE Deion Branch	3.00	8.00
UMDM Donovan McNabb	4.00	10.00
UMDM2 Donovan McNabb	4.00	10.00
UMDR Drew Brees	4.00	10.00
UMDW DeAngelo Williams	4.00	10.00
UMEJ Edgerrin James	3.00	8.00
UMEM Eli Manning	4.00	10.00
UMER Ed Reed	3.00	8.00
UMFG Frank Gore	4.00	10.00
UMFT Fred Taylor	3.00	8.00
UMGL Terry Glenn	3.00	8.00
UMHA Matt Hasselbeck	3.00	8.00
UMMH Marvin Harrison	4.00	10.00
UMHO T.J. Houshmandzadeh	3.00	8.00
UMHW Hines Ward	4.00	10.00
UMIB Isaac Bruce	3.00	8.00
UMJA Joseph Addai	3.00	8.00
UMJC Jay Cutler	4.00	10.00
UMJG Joey Galloway	3.00	8.00
UMJH Joe Horn	3.00	8.00
UMJL Jamal Lewis	3.00	8.00
UMJM Joe Montana	10.00	25.00
UMJN Jerious Norwood	3.00	8.00
UMJP Julius Peppers	3.00	8.00
UMJS Jeremy Shockey	3.00	8.00
UMJS2 Jeremy Shockey	3.00	8.00
UMJT Joe Theismann	4.00	10.00
UMJW Javon Walker	3.00	8.00
UMKW Kellen Winslow	3.00	8.00
UMLC Laveranues Coles	2.50	6.00
UMLE Lee Evans	3.00	8.00
UMLF Larry Fitzgerald	4.00	10.00
UMLJ Larry Johnson	2.50	6.00
UMLM Laurence Maroney	3.00	8.00
UMLT LaDainian Tomlinson	4.00	10.00
UMLW LenDale White	3.00	8.00
UMEM2 Eli Manning	4.00	10.00
UMMB Marion Barber	4.00	10.00
UMMC Mark Clayton	3.00	8.00
UMME Shawne Merriman	3.00	8.00
UMMH2 Marvin Harrison	4.00	10.00
UMMJ Maurice Jones-Drew	4.00	10.00
UMML Matt Leinart	3.00	8.00
UMML2 Matt Leinart	3.00	8.00
UMWM Willis McGahee	3.00	8.00
UMPB Plaxico Burress	3.00	8.00
UMPE Chad Pennington	3.00	8.00
UMPM Peyton Manning	8.00	20.00
UMPM2 Peyton Manning	8.00	20.00
UMPO Clinton Portis	3.00	8.00
UMPR Philip Rivers	4.00	10.00
UMRB Reggie Bush	4.00	10.00
UMRG Rex Grossman	3.00	8.00
UMRO Ronnie Brown	3.00	8.00
UMRW Reggie Wayne	3.00	8.00
UMSA Shaun Alexander	3.00	8.00
UMSH Santonio Holmes	3.00	8.00
UMSJ Steven Jackson	4.00	10.00
UMME2 Shawne Merriman	3.00	8.00
UMSS Steve Smith	3.00	8.00
UMST Steve McNair	3.00	8.00
UMTB Tom Brady	8.00	20.00
UMTB2 Tom Brady	8.00	20.00
UMTE Tedy Bruschi	4.00	10.00
UMTG Trent Green	3.00	8.00
UMTH Todd Heap	2.50	6.00
UMTO Terrell Owens	4.00	10.00
UMTR Tony Romo	5.00	12.00
UMTW Troy Williamson	2.50	6.00
UMVY Vince Young	3.00	8.00
UMWA Leon Washington	3.00	8.00
UMWD Warrick Dunn	3.00	8.00
UMWI Roy Williams WR	3.00	8.00
UMWM2 Willis McGahee	3.00	8.00
UMWP Willie Parker	3.00	8.00

2007 Ultimate Collection Materials Triple

TRIPLE PRINT RUN 50 SER.#'d SETS
*PATCH/15: .8X TO 2X BASIC TRIPLE/50
PATCH STATED PRINT RUN 15

1 Larry Johnson	10.00	25.00
Steven Jackson		
LaDainian Tomlinson		
2 Marc Bulger	8.00	20.00
Torry Holt		
Isaac Bruce		
3 Peyton Manning	15.00	40.00
Marvin Harrison		
Reggie Wayne		
4 Tom Brady	30.00	80.00
Peyton Manning		
Ben Roethlisberger		
5 Hines Ward	10.00	25.00
Willie Parker		
Ben Roethlisberger		
6 Calvin Johnson	15.00	40.00
Ted Ginn Jr.		
Dwayne Bowe		
7 Chad Johnson	8.00	20.00
T.J. Houshmandzadeh		
Carson Palmer		
8 Tony Hunt	6.00	15.00
Michael Bush		
Garrett Wolfe		
9 Adrian Peterson	25.00	60.00
Marshawn Lynch		
Kenny Irons		
10 Gaines Adams	5.00	12.00
Joe Thomas		
Patrick Willis		
11 Eli Manning	10.00	25.00
Jeremy Shockey		
Plaxico Burress		
12 JaMarcus Russell	8.00	20.00
Brady Quinn		
Kevin Kolb		
13 Frank Gore	10.00	25.00
Willis McGahee		
Edgerrin James		
14 Troy Smith	6.00	15.00
Antonio Pittman		
Anthony Gonzalez		
15 Anquan Boldin	10.00	25.00
Larry Fitzgerald		
Matt Leinart		
16 Robert Meachem	5.00	12.00
Anthony Gonzalez		
Calvin Johnson		
17 Drew Brees	20.00	50.00
Matt Hasselbeck		
Brett Favre		
18 Tony Romo	20.00	50.00
Eli Manning		
Donovan McNabb		
19 Brett Favre	20.00	50.00
Donald Driver		
Greg Jennings		
20 Drew Stanton	6.00	15.00
John Beck		
Trent Edwards		
21 JaMarcus Russell	6.00	15.00
Brady Quinn		
Troy Smith		
22 Sidney Rice	5.00	12.00
Dwayne Jarrett		
Steve Smith USC		
23 Reggie Bush	10.00	25.00
LaDainian Tomlinson		
Edgerrin James		
24 Cedric Benson	10.00	25.00
Brian Urlacher		
Rex Grossman		
25 JaMarcus Russell	25.00	60.00
Adrian Peterson		
Calvin Johnson		
26 Julius Jones	20.00	50.00
Tony Romo		
Terrell Owens		
27 Torry Holt	10.00	25.00
Anquan Boldin		
Terrell Owens		
29 DeAngelo Williams	10.00	25.00
Maurice Jones-Drew		
Leon Washington		
30 Chris Henry RB	10.00	25.00
Brian Leonard		
Steven Jackson		

2007 Ultimate Collection Rookie Materials Matchup

STATED PRINT RUN 99 SER.#'d SETS

AT Gaines Adams	3.00	8.00
Joe Thomas		
AW Patrick Willis	6.00	15.00
Gaines Adams		
BK Kevin Kolb	5.00	12.00
John Beck		
EB Trent Edwards	3.00	8.00
John Beck		
EL Marshawn Lynch	3.00	8.00
Trent Edwards		
FW Yamon Figurs	2.00	5.00
Paul Williams		
GB Anthony Gonzalez	4.00	10.00
Dwayne Bowe		
GG Ted Ginn Jr.	3.00	8.00
Anthony Gonzalez		
GM Robert Meachem	3.00	8.00
Ted Ginn Jr.		
HL Chris Henry RB	3.00	8.00
Marshawn Lynch		
HW Johnnie Lee Higgins	2.00	5.00
Paul Williams		
IJ Kenny Irons	2.50	6.00
Brandon Jackson		
JG Calvin Johnson	10.00	25.00
Ted Ginn Jr.		
JR Sidney Rice	4.00	10.00
Dwayne Jarrett		
JS Calvin Johnson	10.00	25.00
Drew Stanton		
KH Tony Hunt	5.00	12.00
Kevin Kolb		
LB Brian Leonard	3.00	8.00
Michael Bush		
MH Robert Meachem	3.00	8.00
Jason Hill		
PR Adrian Peterson	12.00	30.00
Sidney Rice		
QR JaMarcus Russell	3.00	8.00
Brady Quinn		
QT Brady Quinn	3.00	8.00
Joe Thomas		
RH Sidney Rice	4.00	10.00
Johnnie Lee Higgins		
SE Drew Stanton	3.00	8.00
Trent Edwards		
SH Steve Smith USC	3.00	8.00
Jason Hill		
SJ Dwayne Jarrett	3.00	8.00
Steve Smith USC		
SK Kevin Kolb	5.00	12.00
Drew Stanton		
SP Antonio Pittman	2.00	5.00
Troy Smith		
WA Patrick Willis	6.00	15.00
Gaines Adams		
WH Patrick Willis	6.00	15.00
Jason Hill		
WO Greg Olsen	2.50	6.00
Garrett Wolfe		

2007 Ultimate Collection Rookie Materials Matchup Autographs

STATED PRINT RUN 5-25

FW Paul Williams	20.00	50.00
Yamon Figurs		
GB Anthony Gonzalez	50.00	100.00
Dwayne Bowe		
GG Ted Ginn Jr.	50.00	100.00
Anthony Gonzalez		
GM Ted Ginn Jr.	25.00	60.00
Robert Meachem		
HW Johnnie Lee Higgins	20.00	50.00
Paul Williams		
LB Brian Leonard	25.00	60.00
Michael Bush		
MH Robert Meachem	20.00	50.00
Jason Hill		
QT Brady Quinn	60.00	120.00
Joe Thomas		
SK Drew Stanton	20.00	50.00
Kevin Kolb		

2007 Ultimate Collection Rookie Materials Silver

*BRONZE TRIPLE/25: 1X TO 2.5X BASIC SILVER
BRONZE TRIPLE SWATCH PRINT RUN 25
*GOLD/99: .5X TO 1.2X BASIC SILVER
GOLD PRINT RUN 50 SER.#'d SETS
*GREEN/50: .6X TO 1.5X BASIC SLVR
GREEN TRIPLE SWATCH PRINT RUN 50
*HOLOSILVER PATCH/50: .6X TO 1.5X BASIC SILVER
HOLOSILVER PATCH PRINT RUN 50 SER.#'d SETS

URMAG Anthony Gonzalez	2.50	6.00
URMAP Adrian Peterson	10.00	25.00
URMBJ Brandon Jackson	2.00	5.00
URMBL Brian Leonard	2.00	5.00
URMBQ Brady Quinn	2.50	6.00
URMCH Chris Henry RB	1.50	4.00
URMCJ Calvin Johnson	8.00	20.00
URMDB Dwayne Bowe	3.00	8.00
URMDJ Dwayne Jarrett	2.00	5.00
URMDS Drew Stanton	1.50	4.00
URMGA Gaines Adams	2.50	6.00
URMGO Greg Olsen	2.00	5.00
URMJB John Beck	2.50	6.00
URMJH Jason Hill	2.50	6.00
URMJR JaMarcus Russell	1.50	4.00
URMJT Joe Thomas	2.50	6.00
URMKI Kenny Irons	1.50	4.00
URMKK Kevin Kolb	4.00	10.00
URMMB Michael Bush	2.50	6.00
URMML Marshawn Lynch	2.50	6.00
URMPW Paul Williams	1.50	4.00
URMRM Robert Meachem	2.50	6.00
URMSR Sidney Rice	3.00	8.00
URMSS Steve Smith USC	2.50	6.00
URMTE Trent Edwards	2.50	6.00
URMTG Ted Ginn Jr.	2.00	5.00
URMTH Tony Hunt	1.50	4.00
URMTS Troy Smith	2.50	6.00
URMWI Patrick Willis	5.00	12.00
URMYF Yamon Figurs	1.50	4.00

2007 Ultimate Collection Rookie Rewind Super Patches

STATED PRINT RUN 99 SER.#'d SETS

AH A.J. Hawk	8.00	20.00
DW DeAngelo Williams	10.00	25.00
KC Kellen Clemens	8.00	20.00
LM Laurence Maroney	8.00	20.00
LW Leon Washington	8.00	20.00
MJ Maurice Jones-Drew	10.00	25.00
ML Matt Leinart	8.00	20.00
RB Reggie Bush	10.00	25.00
SH Santonio Holmes	8.00	20.00
VY Vince Young	8.00	20.00

2007 Ultimate Collection Rookie Signatures Gold

*GOLD/25: .6X TO 1.5X BASE RC/99
*GOLD/25: .6X TO 1.5X BASE RC/150
*GOLD/25: .8X TO 2X BASE RC/250
STATED PRINT RUN 25 SER.#'d SETS
UNPRICED NFL LOGO AU PRINT RUN 1
UNPRICED HOLOFOIL SER.#'d TO 10

101 Adrian Peterson	350.00	600.00
102 Brady Quinn	30.00	80.00
103 Calvin Johnson	100.00	200.00
106 Kevin Kolb	50.00	100.00
109 Sidney Rice	60.00	120.00

2007 Ultimate Collection Sunday Stars Signatures

*GOLD/50: .6X TO 1.5X BASIC AUTOS
GOLD PRINT RUN 50 SER.#'d SETS

SSAB Alan Branch	5.00	12.00
SSAG Anthony Gonzalez	6.00	15.00
SSAP Adrian Peterson SP	100.00	200.00
SSBR Bernard Berrian SP	5.00	12.00
SSCJ Chad Johnson SP	6.00	15.00
SSDB Dallas Baker	4.00	10.00
SSDJ Darrell Jackson	4.00	10.00
SSDS Drew Stanton	4.00	10.00
SSFG Frank Gore SP	6.00	15.00
SSGO Greg Olsen	5.00	12.00
SSJC Jerricho Cotchery	5.00	12.00
SSJF Joel Filani	5.00	12.00
SSLT LaDainian Tomlinson Blue Ink	30.00	60.00
SSLTR LaDainian Tomlinson Red Ink	40.00	80.00
SSMG Michael Griffin	6.00	15.00
SSML Marshawn Lynch SP	15.00	40.00
SSPH Paul Hornung SP	12.50	25.00
SSPP Paul Posluszny	6.00	15.00
SSSN Syvelle Newton	5.00	12.00
SSVJ Vincent Jackson	5.00	12.00
SSWP Willie Parker SP	8.00	20.00

2007 Ultimate Collection Ultimate Ink

STATED PRINT RUN 10-25

INKAB Alan Branch	8.00	20.00
INKAG Anthony Gonzalez	10.00	25.00
INKBL Brian Leonard	8.00	20.00
INKBS Barry Sanders	75.00	150.00
INKCJ Chad Johnson	8.00	20.00
INKCL Mark Clayton	8.00	20.00
INKCO Jerricho Cotchery	8.00	20.00
INKCT Chester Taylor	6.00	15.00
INKCW Cadillac Williams	8.00	20.00
INKDJ Dwayne Jarrett	8.00	20.00
INKDM Dan Marino	125.00	250.00
INKDP Drew Pearson	10.00	25.00
INKGJ Greg Jennings	10.00	25.00
INKGR Gary Russell	8.00	20.00
INKJA Joseph Addai	20.00	50.00
INKKD Kenneth Darby	8.00	20.00
INKKK Kevin Kolb	15.00	40.00
INKKS Kolby Smith	8.00	20.00
INKMB Marc Bulger	8.00	20.00
INKMC Marques Colston	10.00	25.00
INKMG Michael Griffin	10.00	25.00
INKML Marshawn Lynch	25.00	60.00
INKMS Matt Schaub	8.00	20.00
INKRC Roger Craig	10.00	25.00
INKSY Steve Young/10	90.00	150.00
INKTG Ted Ginn Jr.	8.00	20.00
INKTH T.J. Houshmandzadeh	8.00	20.00
INKTP Tyler Palko	8.00	20.00
INKVJ Vincent Jackson	8.00	20.00
INKWI Paul Williams	6.00	15.00
INKYO Selvin Young	15.00	40.00
INKZM Zach Miller	10.00	25.00

2007 Ultimate Collection Ultimate Inscriptions

STATED PRINT RUN 25 SER.#'d SETS

UIAA Aundrae Allison	6.00	15.00
UIAB Anquan Boldin	8.00	20.00
UIAG Anthony Gonzalez	10.00	25.00
UIBA David Ball	8.00	20.00
UIBE Drew Bennett	6.00	15.00
UIBJ Brandon Jacobs	8.00	20.00
UIBL Brian Leonard	8.00	20.00
UICJ Chad Johnson	8.00	20.00
UICS Chansi Stuckey	10.00	25.00
UIDB Dallas Baker	6.00	15.00
UIDJ Dwayne Jarrett	8.00	20.00
UIDP Drew Pearson	10.00	25.00
UIDT Drew Tate	8.00	20.00
UIFG Frank Gore	10.00	25.00
UIGJ Greg Jennings	10.00	25.00
UIGO Greg Olsen	8.00	20.00
UIGS Gale Sayers	40.00	80.00
UIIS Isaiah Stanback	6.00	15.00
UIJL John Lynch	25.00	50.00
UIJP Jordan Palmer	8.00	20.00
UIJR Jeff Rowe	6.00	15.00
UIJZ Jared Zabransky	8.00	20.00
UIKK Kevin Kolb	15.00	40.00
UIMC Mark Clayton	8.00	20.00
UIMG Michael Griffin	10.00	25.00
UIMM Marcus McCauley	8.00	20.00
UIMO Matt Moore	10.00	25.00
UIPH Paul Hornung	12.00	30.00
UIQM Quentin Moses	8.00	20.00
UIRB Reggie Bush	50.00	100.00
UIRC Roger Craig	10.00	25.00
UIRM Robert Meachem	10.00	25.00
UITG Ted Ginn Jr.	8.00	20.00
UIVJ Vincent Jackson	8.00	20.00
UIWI Paul Williams	6.00	15.00
UIWP Willie Parker	12.00	30.00
UIWY DeShawn Wynn	8.00	20.00
UIYF Yamon Figurs	6.00	15.00
UIZM Zach Miller	10.00	25.00

2007 Ultimate Collection Ultimate Signatures

*GOLD/50: .6X TO 1.5X BASIC AUTOS
GOLD PRINT RUN 5-50

USAB Alan Branch	5.00	12.00
USAG Anthony Gonzalez	6.00	15.00
USBJ Brandon Jacobs SP	20.00	40.00
USBL Brian Leonard	5.00	12.00
USBM Brandon Meriweather	6.00	15.00
USBO Anquan Boldin SP	6.00	15.00
USBQ Brady Quinn SP		
USCS Chansi Stuckey	6.00	15.00
USCT Courtney Taylor	5.00	12.00
USDJ Dwayne Jarrett SP	5.00	12.00
USDS Drew Stanton	4.00	10.00
USEW Eric Wright	6.00	15.00
USGJ Greg Jennings	6.00	15.00
USGO Greg Olsen	5.00	12.00
USGR Gary Russell	5.00	12.00
USIS Isaiah Stanback	4.00	10.00
USJA Jamaal Anderson	5.00	12.00
USJF Joel Filani	5.00	12.00
USJH Johnnie Lee Higgins	5.00	12.00
USJR JaMarcus Russell SP	30.00	80.00
USJT Joe Thomas	6.00	15.00
USJZ Jared Zabransky	5.00	12.00
USKK Kevin Kolb SP	10.00	25.00
USLB Lorenzo Booker	5.00	12.00
USLH Leon Hall SP	5.00	12.00
USLL LaRon Landry SP	6.00	15.00
USLN Legedu Naanee	6.00	15.00
USLT Lawrence Timmons	6.00	15.00
USMB Michael Bush	6.00	15.00
USMC Rhema McKnight	4.00	10.00
USMG Michael Griffin	6.00	15.00
USQM Quentin Moses	5.00	12.00
USRM Robert Meachem SP	6.00	15.00
USRN Reggie Nelson	5.00	12.00
USTG Ted Ginn Jr. SP	5.00	12.00
USTM Tyrone Moss	4.00	10.00
USWI Paul Williams	4.00	10.00
USYF Yamon Figurs	4.00	10.00
USZM Zach Miller	6.00	15.00

2007 Ultimate Collection Ultimate Signatures Duals

STATED PRINT RUN 35 SER.#'d SETS

DSBS Marc Bulger	12.00	30.00
Matt Schaub		
DSCG Roger Craig	15.00	40.00
Frank Gore		
DSFW Yamon Figurs	12.00	30.00
Paul Williams		
DSGG Ted Ginn Jr.	20.00	50.00
Anthony Gonzalez		
DSGH Michael Griffin	12.00	30.00
Leon Hall		
DSHM Johnnie Lee Higgins	12.00	30.00
Zach Miller		
DSJH Chad Johnson	15.00	40.00
T.J. Houshmandzadeh		
DSLN LaRon Landry	12.00	30.00
Reggie Nelson		
DSLO Brian Leonard	15.00	40.00
Greg Olsen		
DSPL Adrian Peterson	150.00	300.00
Marshawn Lynch		
DSPS Jordan Palmer	12.00	30.00
Isaiah Stanback		
DSSG Alex Smith QB	30.00	60.00
Frank Gore		
DSSJ Barry Sanders	125.00	250.00
Calvin Johnson		
DSSK Drew Stanton	15.00	40.00
Kevin Kolb		
DSTB LaDainian Tomlinson	40.00	80.00
Reggie Bush		

2007 Ultimate Collection Write of Passage Signatures

*GOLD/50: .5X TO 1.2X BASIC AUTOS
GOLD PRINT RUN 5-50

WPAA Aundrae Allison	4.00	10.00
WPAG Anthony Gonzalez	6.00	15.00
WPBL Brian Leonard	5.00	12.00
WPCT Chester Taylor	4.00	10.00
WPCW Cadillac Williams SP	10.00	25.00
WPDJ Dwayne Jarrett	5.00	12.00
WPDS Drew Stanton	4.00	10.00
WPDW DeShawn Wynn	5.00	12.00
WPGJ Greg Jennings	6.00	15.00
WPJA Joseph Addai SP	20.00	40.00
WPKK Kevin Kolb	10.00	25.00
WPML Marshawn Lynch SP	20.00	50.00
WPMM Marcus McCauley	5.00	12.00
WPQM Quentin Moses	5.00	12.00
WPRB Reggie Brown	4.00	10.00
WPRM Robert Meachem	6.00	15.00
WPRO Jeff Rowe	4.00	10.00
WPSY Selvin Young	8.00	20.00
WPTG Ted Ginn SP	5.00	12.00
WPTH Tony Hunt	4.00	10.00
WPTM Tyrone Moss	4.00	10.00
WPWI Paul Williams	4.00	10.00

2008 Ultimate Collection

This set was released on February 17, 2009. The base set consists of 214 cards. Cards 1-130 feature veterans serial numbered of 275, and cards 131-200 are rookies serial numbered of 275. Cards 201-221 are autographed jersey rookie cards serial numbered of 99-375. This product was released with 4 cards per pack and 1 pack per hobby box.

1-130 STATED PRINT RUN 275
131-200 ROOKIE PRINT RUN 275
201-221 JSY AU RC PRINT RUN 99-375

1 Jake Delhomme	2.00	5.00
2 Trent Edwards	1.50	4.00
3 Marshawn Lynch	2.00	5.00
4 Jason Taylor	2.00	5.00
5 Chad Pennington	2.00	5.00
6 Ronnie Brown	2.00	5.00
7 Thomas Jones	2.00	5.00
8 Brett Favre	6.00	15.00
9 Jerricho Cotchery	2.00	5.00
10 Tom Brady	4.00	10.00
11 Randy Moss	2.50	6.00
12 Laurence Maroney	2.00	5.00
13 Ed Reed	2.00	5.00
14 Ray Lewis	2.50	6.00
15 Willis McGahee	2.00	5.00
16 Carson Palmer	2.50	6.00
17 Chad Johnson	2.00	5.00
18 T.J. Houshmandzadeh	2.00	5.00
19 Derek Anderson	1.50	4.00
20 Braylon Edwards	2.00	5.00
21 Kellen Winslow	2.00	5.00
22 Ben Roethlisberger	2.50	6.00
23 Troy Polamalu	2.50	6.00
24 Santonio Holmes	2.00	5.00
25 DeMeco Ryans	2.00	5.00
26 Andre Johnson	2.00	5.00
27 Matt Schaub	2.00	5.00
28 Peyton Manning	4.00	10.00
29 Reggie Wayne	2.00	5.00
30 Dallas Clark	2.00	5.00
31 David Garrard	2.00	5.00
32 Fred Taylor	2.00	5.00
33 Maurice Jones-Drew	2.00	5.00
34 Vince Young	2.00	5.00
35 Alge Crumpler	2.00	5.00
36 LenDale White	2.00	5.00
37 Jay Cutler	2.50	6.00
38 Marvin Harrison	2.50	6.00
39 Brandon Marshall	2.00	5.00
40 Brodie Croyle	2.00	5.00
41 Dwayne Bowe	2.00	5.00
42 Larry Johnson	2.00	5.00
43 JaMarcus Russell	2.00	5.00
44 Ronald Curry	2.00	5.00
45 Jeremy Shockey	2.00	5.00
46 LaDainian Tomlinson	2.50	6.00
47 Antonio Cromartie	1.50	4.00
48 Antonio Gates	2.50	6.00
49 Shawne Merriman	2.00	5.00
50 Tony Romo	3.00	8.00
51 Terrell Owens	2.50	6.00
52 Marion Barber	2.00	5.00
53 Zach Thomas	2.00	5.00
54 Eli Manning	2.50	6.00
55 Plaxico Burress	2.00	5.00
56 Brandon Jacobs	2.00	5.00
57 Antonio Pierce	1.50	4.00
58 Donovan McNabb	2.50	6.00
59 Asante Samuel	1.50	4.00
60 Brian Westbrook	2.00	5.00
61 Jason Campbell	2.00	5.00
62 Clinton Portis	2.00	5.00
63 Chris Cooley	2.00	5.00
64 Kyle Orton	2.00	5.00
65 Brian Urlacher	2.50	6.00
66 Lance Briggs	1.50	4.00
67 Ernie Sims	1.50	4.00
68 Roy Williams	2.00	5.00
69 Calvin Johnson	2.50	6.00
70 Greg Jennings	2.50	6.00
71 Ryan Grant	2.50	6.00
72 Aaron Rodgers	5.00	12.00
73 A.J. Hawk	2.00	5.00
74 Tarvaris Jackson	2.00	5.00
75 Adrian Peterson	4.00	10.00
76 Bernard Berrian	2.00	5.00
77 Michael Turner	2.50	6.00
78 Jerious Norwood	2.00	5.00
79 Kurt Warner	2.50	6.00
80 DeAngelo Williams	2.00	5.00
81 Steve Smith	2.00	5.00
82 Dwayne Jarrett	2.00	5.00
83 Drew Brees	2.50	6.00
84 Reggie Bush	2.50	6.00
85 Marques Colston	2.00	5.00
86 Jeff Garcia	2.00	5.00
87 Joey Galloway	2.00	5.00
88 Hines Ward	2.00	5.00
89 Matt Leinart	2.50	6.00
90 Larry Fitzgerald	2.50	6.00
91 Edgerrin James	2.00	5.00
92 Marc Bulger	2.00	5.00
93 Torry Holt	2.00	5.00
94 Steven Jackson	2.50	6.00
95 Ricky Williams	2.00	5.00
96 Frank Gore	2.00	5.00
97 Vernon Davis	2.00	5.00
98 Matt Hasselbeck	2.00	5.00
99 Julius Jones	1.50	4.00
100 Deion Branch	2.00	5.00
101 Barry Sanders	4.00	10.00
102 Billy Sims	2.00	5.00
103 Bo Jackson	3.00	8.00
104 Brian Bosworth	2.50	6.00
105 Dan Marino	5.00	12.00
106 Daryl Johnston	2.50	6.00
107 Dick Butkus	3.00	8.00
108 Rod Woodson	2.50	6.00
109 Fran Tarkenton	2.50	6.00
110 Franco Harris	2.50	6.00
111 Herschel Walker	2.00	5.00
112 Jack Lambert	2.50	6.00
113 Jerry Kramer	2.00	5.00
114 Jim Brown	3.00	8.00
115 Jim Kelly	2.50	6.00
116 Joe Greene	2.50	6.00
117 Joe Montana	5.00	12.00
118 Joe Namath	3.00	8.00
119 John Elway	4.00	10.00
120 Ken Stabler	2.50	6.00
121 Ken Anderson	2.00	5.00
122 Emmitt Smith	5.00	12.00
123 Mel Blount	2.00	5.00
124 Paul Hornung	2.50	6.00
125 Roger Craig	2.00	5.00
126 Roman Gabriel	2.00	5.00
127 Bruce Smith	1.50	4.00
128 Terry Bradshaw	4.00	10.00
129 Tom Rathman	2.00	5.00
130 Y.A. Tittle	2.50	6.00
131 Kregg Lumpkin RC	3.00	8.00
132 Antoine Cason RC	3.00	8.00
133 Aqib Talib RC	3.00	8.00
134 Mike Tolbert RC	4.00	10.00
135 Chris Johnson RC	8.00	20.00
136 Bruce Davis RC	2.50	6.00
137 Calais Campbell RC	2.50	6.00
138 Jordy Nelson RC	4.00	10.00
139 Chevis Jackson RC	2.00	5.00
140 Chris Ellis RC	2.00	5.00
141 Brad Cottam RC	2.50	6.00
142 Will Franklin RC	2.50	6.00
143 Early Doucet RC	2.50	6.00
144 DaJuan Morgan RC	2.50	6.00
145 Mike Hart RC	3.00	8.00
146 Davone Bess RC	3.00	8.00
147 Tom Santi RC	2.50	6.00
148 Dennis Dixon RC	3.00	8.00
149 Dominique Rodgers-Cromartie RC	3.00	8.00
150 Jerod Mayo RC	3.00	8.00
151 Dexter Jackson RC	2.50	6.00
152 Fred Davis RC	3.00	8.00
153 Dwight Lowery RC	3.00	8.00
154 Colt Brennan RC	3.00	8.00
155 Erik Ainge RC	3.00	8.00
156 Frank Okam RC	2.00	5.00
157 Glenn Dorsey RC	3.00	8.00
158 Gosder Cherilus RC	2.50	6.00
159 Harry Douglas RC	2.50	6.00
160 Eddie Royal RC	3.00	8.00
161 Jacob Hester RC	3.00	8.00
162 Jacob Tamme RC	3.00	8.00
163 Chauncey Washington RC	2.50	6.00
164 Jermichael Finley RC	3.00	8.00
165 John Carlson RC	3.00	8.00
166 Jerome Simpson RC	3.00	8.00
167 Spencer Larsen RC	2.00	5.00
168 Josh Johnson RC	3.00	8.00
169 Keenan Burton RC	2.00	5.00
170 Keith Rivers RC	3.00	8.00
171 Kellen Davis RC	2.00	5.00
172 Kenny Phillips RC	3.00	8.00
173 Kevin O'Connell RC	2.50	6.00
174 Mike Cox RC	2.50	6.00
175 Lavelle Hawkins RC	2.00	5.00
176 Lawrence Jackson RC	2.50	6.00
177 Leodis McKelvin RC	2.50	6.00
178 Mario Manningham RC	3.00	8.00
179 Matt Flynn RC	8.00	20.00
180 Mike Jenkins RC	3.00	8.00
181 Owen Schmitt RC	3.00	8.00
182 Steve Johnson RC	6.00	15.00
183 Charles Godfrey RC	3.00	8.00
184 Peyton Hillis RC	10.00	25.00
185 Phillip Merling RC	2.50	6.00
186 Quentin Groves RC	2.50	6.00
187 Ryan Clady RC	3.00	8.00
188 Andre Caldwell RC	2.50	6.00
189 Ryan Torain RC	3.00	8.00
190 Sam Baker RC	2.00	5.00
191 Tracy Porter RC	3.00	8.00
192 Sedrick Ellis RC	3.00	8.00
193 Shawn Crable RC	2.00	5.00
194 Tashard Choice RC	2.50	6.00
195 Terrell Thomas RC	2.50	6.00
196 Tom Zbikowski RC	3.00	8.00
197 Trevor Laws RC	3.00	8.00
198 Vernon Gholston RC	2.50	6.00
199 Xavier Adibi RC	2.00	5.00
200 Chris Long RC	3.00	8.00
201 Darren McFadden JSY AU/99 RC	40.00	80.00
202 DeSean Jackson JSY AU/375 RC	20.00	50.00
203 Brian Brohm JSY AU/99 RC	15.00	40.00
204 Matt Ryan JSY AU/99 RC	75.00	150.00
205 Jonathan Stewart JSY AU/99 RC	20.00	50.00
206 Donnie Avery JSY AU/375 RC	8.00	20.00
207 Chad Henne JSY AU/375 RC	15.00	40.00
208 Jake Long JSY AU/375 RC	10.00	25.00
209 Rashard Mendenhall JSY AU/99 RC	25.00	60.00
210 Felix Jones JSY AU/375 RC	15.00	40.00
211 Dustin Keller JSY AU/375 RC	10.00	25.00
212 Jamaal Charles JSY AU/375 RC	20.00	50.00
215 Matt Forte JSY AU/375 RC	20.00	50.00
216 Kevin Smith JSY AU/375 RC	10.00	25.00
217 Ray Rice JSY AU/375 RC	25.00	50.00
218 Steve Slaton JSY AU/375 RC	10.00	25.00
219 Joe Flacco JSY AU/99 RC	50.00	120.00
220 Devin Thomas JSY AU/375 RC	8.00	20.00
221 John David Booty JSY AU/375 RC	8.00	20.00

2008 Ultimate Collection 1997 Legends Autographs

179 Steve Young	60.00	120.00
180 Emmitt Smith SP	500.00	800.00
181 Barry Sanders	350.00	500.00
182 Brett Favre SP	800.00	1,000.00
183 Rod Woodson	30.00	80.00
184 Jerry Rice SP	450.00	700.00
185 Jim Kelly	50.00	120.00
186 Troy Aikman	100.00	200.00
187 John Elway	300.00	450.00
189 Daryl Johnston SP	50.00	100.00
191 Marshall Faulk	30.00	80.00
193 Bo Jackson	50.00	100.00
194 Tom Rathman	30.00	80.00
195 Brian Bosworth	30.00	80.00

2008 Ultimate Collection Rookie Material Patch Autographs

ROOKIE PATCH PRINT RUN 10-15

202 DeSean Jackson/15	50.00	125.00
206 Donnie Avery/15	20.00	50.00
207 Chad Henne/15	25.00	60.00
208 Jake Long/15	25.00	60.00
209 Rashard Mendenhall/15	50.00	125.00
210 Felix Jones/15	40.00	100.00
211 Dustin Keller/15	25.00	60.00
212 Jamaal Charles/15	40.00	100.00
214 Malcolm Kelly/15	20.00	50.00
215 Matt Forte/15	40.00	100.00
216 Kevin Smith/15	25.00	60.00
217 Ray Rice/15	50.00	125.00
218 Steve Slaton/15	25.00	60.00
220 Devin Thomas/15	20.00	50.00
221 John David Booty/15	20.00	50.00

2008 Ultimate Collection Ultimate Signature Jerseys

STATED PRINT RUN 5-45

UAJ2 Jamal Lewis/30	10.00	25.00
UAJ5 Tony Romo/40	40.00	80.00
UAJ8 Eli Manning/35	40.00	80.00
UAJ9 Bob Sanders/40		
UAJ10 Eli Manning/35	40.00	80.00
UAJ11 Chad Johnson/35	10.00	25.00
UAJ12 Clinton Portis/25	20.00	50.00
UAJ16 Joseph Addai/30	20.00	50.00
UAJ17 Eli Manning/15	50.00	100.00
UAJ18 Peyton Manning/15	75.00	150.00
UAJ19 Kurt Warner/35	50.00	100.00
UAJ20 Peyton Manning/35	60.00	120.00
UAJ23 Larry Johnson/35	15.00	40.00
UAJ24 Marshawn Lynch/35	15.00	40.00
UAJ25 Peyton Manning/15	75.00	150.00
UAJ26 Peyton Manning/15	75.00	150.00
UAJ27 Roy Williams WR/20	15.00	40.00
UAJ28 Tony Romo/40	40.00	80.00
UAJ29 Marion Barber/30	20.00	50.00
UAJ30 Eli Manning/15	50.00	100.00

2008 Ultimate Collection Ultimate Dual Autograph Jerseys

DUAL AUTO JSY PRINT RUN 5-45
SERIAL #'d UNDER 15 NOT PRICED

5 DeSean Jackson	20.00	50.00
Malcolm Kelly/30		
6 Jonathan Stewart	25.00	60.00
Larry Johnson/15		
7 A.J. Hawk	20.00	50.00
DeMarcus Ware/35		
10 Marshawn Lynch	30.00	60.00
Rashard Mendenhall/25		
11 Jonathan Stewart	30.00	60.00
Rashard Mendenhall/25		
12 Dwayne Bowe	20.00	50.00
Roy Williams WR/25		
13 Bo Jackson	60.00	120.00
Rashard Mendenhall/25		
16 Devin Thomas EXCH	20.00	50.00
Limas Sweed/45		
17 Jason Campbell EXCH	20.00	50.00
David Garrard/30		
18 Adrian Peterson	100.00	200.00
Malcolm Kelly/15		
19 Fran Tarkenton	30.00	60.00
John David Booty/35		
20 Chad Henne		
Bob Griese/25		
21 Matt Forte	30.00	80.00
Kevin Smith/45		

2008 Ultimate Collection Ultimate Foursomes Jerseys Gold

STATED PRINT RUN 25-50
*PRIME/15: .5X TO 1.2X BASIC FOUR/50
PRIME PRINT RUN 15 SER.#'d SETS

1 LaDainian Tomlinson	15.00	40.00
Adrian Peterson		
Willie Parker		
Fred Taylor		
2 Tom Brady	20.00	50.00
Peyton Manning		
Tony Romo		
Ben Roethlisberger		
3 LaDainian Tomlinson	15.00	40.00
Adrian Peterson		
Edgerrin James		
Reggie Bush		
4 LaDainian Tomlinson	10.00	25.00
Drew Brees		
Philip Rivers		
Reggie Bush		
5 Marvin Harrison	10.00	25.00
Randy Moss		
Terrell Owens		
Chad Johnson		
6 Tom Brady	15.00	40.00
Eli Manning		
Randy Moss		
Plaxico Burress		
7 Brian Urlacher	10.00	25.00
A.J. Hawk		
Tedy Bruschi		
Shawne Merriman		
8 Jeremy Shockey/25	15.00	40.00
Eli Manning		
Ben Watson		
Tom Brady		
9 Eli Manning	15.00	40.00
Peyton Manning		
Tom Brady		
Tony Romo		
10 Donovan McNabb	10.00	25.00
Kurt Warner		
Vince Young		
Drew Brees		
11 Randy Moss	10.00	25.00
Steve Smith		
Reggie Wayne		
Larry Fitzgerald		
12 Carson Palmer	15.00	40.00
Derek Anderson		
David Garrard		
Peyton Manning		
13 Derek Anderson	15.00	40.00
Peyton Manning		
Marc Bulger		
Carson Palmer		
14 Ben Roethlisberger	15.00	40.00
Hines Ward		
Peyton Manning		
Marvin Harrison		
15 Tony Romo	12.00	30.00
Marion Barber		
Terrell Owens		
DeMarcus Ware		
16 Tony Gonzalez	10.00	25.00
Jeremy Shockey		
Antonio Gates		
Ben Watson		
17 Larry Johnson	10.00	25.00
LaDainian Tomlinson		
Jamal Lewis		
Clinton Portis		
18 Tom Brady	15.00	40.00
Carson Palmer		
Philip Rivers		
Jay Cutler		
20 Brian Westbrook	15.00	40.00
LaDainian Tomlinson		
Adrian Peterson		
Steven Jackson		
21 David Garrard	15.00	40.00
Eli Manning		
Ben Roethlisberger		
Aaron Rodgers		
22 Donovan McNabb	15.00	40.00
Brian Westbrook		
Peyton Manning		
Marvin Harrison		
23 Tom Brady	15.00	40.00
Laurence Maroney		
Wes Welker		
Randy Moss		
24 Matt Leinart	10.00	25.00
Reggie Bush		
Vince Young		
Brady Quinn		
25 Eli Manning	10.00	25.00
Ben Roethlisberger		
Donovan McNabb		
Kurt Warner		
26 Larry Johnson	10.00	25.00
LaDainian Tomlinson		
Ryan Grant		
Reggie Bush		
27 Ben Roethlisberger	10.00	25.00
Willie Parker		
Derek Anderson		
Jamal Lewis		
28 Bob Sanders	10.00	25.00
Charles Woodson		
Champ Bailey		
Ed Reed		
29 Tom Brady	15.00	40.00
Wes Welker		
Peyton Manning		
Reggie Wayne		

2008 Ultimate Collection Ultimate Foursomes Jerseys Patch Holofoil

*PATCH HOLO/20: .5X TO 1.2X JSY GOLD/50
STATED PRINT RUN 20 SER.#'d SETS

19 Donovan McNabb	12.00	30.00
Jason Campbell		
Vince Young		
JaMarcus Russell		
30 Larry Johnson	12.00	30.00
LaDainian Tomlinson		
Brian Westbrook		
Steven Jackson		

2008 Ultimate Collection Ultimate Futures Autograph Jerseys

STATED PRINT RUN 15-35

URAJ1 Devin Thomas/35	12.00	30.00
URAJ2 Brian Brohm/15	15.00	40.00
URAJ3 Chad Henne/35	15.00	40.00
URAJ4 Kevin Smith/35	12.00	30.00
URAJ6 DeSean Jackson/35	30.00	60.00
URAJ7 Felix Jones/35	30.00	80.00
URAJ8 Joe Flacco/35	50.00	120.00
URAJ9 John David Booty/35	12.00	30.00
URAJ10 Jonathan Stewart/15	40.00	80.00
URAJ13 Matt Ryan/15	75.00	150.00
URAJ14 Matt Forte/35	30.00	80.00

2008 Ultimate Collection Ultimate Futures Foursomes Jerseys Patch Holofoil

FUTURE FOUR PATCH PRINT RUN 25
*FUTURE FOUR JSY/50: .3X TO .8X PATCH/25
FUTURE FOUR JERSEY PRINT RUN 50
*FUT.FOUR PRIME/25: .4X TO 1X PATCH/25
FUTURE FOUR PRIME PRINT RUN 25

1 Darren McFadden	15.00	40.00
Felix Jones		
Jonathan Stewart		
Rashard Mendenhall		
2 Brian Brohm	25.00	60.00
Chad Henne		
Joe Flacco		
Matt Ryan		
3 Ray Rice	15.00	40.00
Steve Slaton		
Chris Johnson		
Kevin Smith		
4 Eddie Royal	15.00	40.00
Malcolm Kelly		
Ray Rice		
Chris Johnson		
5 Brian Brohm	6.00	15.00
Chad Henne		
Harry Douglas		
Mario Manningham		
6 Jonathan Stewart	12.00	30.00
Matt Forte		
Ray Rice		
Jamaal Charles		
7 Chad Henne	25.00	60.00
Joe Flacco		
Matt Ryan		
Kevin O'Connell		
8 DeSean Jackson	12.00	30.00
Early Doucet		
Malcolm Kelly		
Mario Manningham		
9 Brian Brohm	12.00	30.00
Limas Sweed		
Jordy Nelson		
Rashard Mendenhall		
10 Glenn Dorsey	15.00	40.00
Darren McFadden		
Early Doucet		
Felix Jones		
11 Matt Forte	15.00	40.00
Steve Slaton		
Chris Johnson		
Rashard Mendenhall		
12 Brian Brohm	5.00	12.00
Chad Henne		
John David Booty		
Kevin O'Connell		
13 Darren McFadden	15.00	40.00
Jonathan Stewart		
Matt Forte		
Chris Johnson		
14 Jonathan Stewart	15.00	40.00
Matt Forte		
Chris Johnson		
Rashard Mendenhall		
15 Darren McFadden	25.00	60.00
DeSean Jackson		
Dustin Keller		
Matt Ryan		

2008 Ultimate Collection Ultimate Generations Foursomes Jerseys Gold

STATED PRINT RUN 50 SER.#'d SETS
*SILVER/25: .5X TO 1.2X GOLD QUAD/50
PRIME SILVER PRINT RUN 25
UNPRICED PATCH PRINT RUN 10-20

2 Tom Brady	15.00	40.00
Chad Henne		
Randy Moss		
Jerry Rice		
4 Carson Palmer	20.00	50.00
Ken Anderson		
Ben Roethlisberger		
Terry Bradshaw		
5 Barry Sanders	25.00	60.00
LaDainian Tomlinson		
Darren McFadden		
Roger Craig		
8 Matt Ryan	25.00	60.00
Darren McFadden		
Peyton Manning		
LaDainian Tomlinson		
9 Dick Butkus	15.00	40.00
Jack Ham		
Shawne Merriman		
Patrick Willis		
11 Deion Sanders	10.00	25.00
Ed Reed		
Troy Polamalu		
Mel Blount		
12 Joe Flacco	20.00	50.00
Ben Roethlisberger		
Gale Sayers		
Matt Forte		
14 LaDainian Tomlinson	15.00	40.00
Chris Johnson		
Bo Jackson		
Matt Forte		
15 Peyton Manning	8.00	20.00
Carson Palmer		
Eli Manning		
John David Booty		
16 Kevin Smith	25.00	60.00
Barry Sanders		
Emmitt Smith		
Felix Jones		
17 Willie Parker	25.00	60.00
Rashard Mendenhall		
Walter Payton		
Matt Forte		
19 Reggie Bush	8.00	20.00
Vince Young		
John David Booty		
Jamaal Charles		
20 Roger Staubach	20.00	50.00
Troy Aikman		
Joe Theismann		
Jason Campbell		
21 Walter Payton	25.00	60.00
Gale Sayers		
Matt Forte		
Devin Hester		
22 John Elway	20.00	50.00
Jay Cutler		
Ben Roethlisberger		
Terry Bradshaw		
24 Carson Palmer	8.00	20.00
John David Booty		
Limas Sweed		
Roy Williams WR		
27 Fran Tarkenton		
Ken Anderson		
Peyton Manning		
Matt Ryan		
28 Emmitt Smith		
Felix Jones		
Ottis Anderson		
Brandon Jacobs		
30 Dick Butkus	15.00	40.00
Brian Urlacher		
Jack Ham		
A.J. Hawk		
31 Deion Sanders	12.00	30.00
Ed Reed		
Troy Polamalu		
Mel Blount		
32 Brett Favre	25.00	60.00
Eli Manning		
Aaron Rodgers		
Peyton Manning		
33 Kellen Winslow Jr.	10.00	25.00
Antonio Gates		
Tony Gonzalez		
Dustin Keller		
34 Chad Johnson	20.00	50.00
Eli Manning		
Joe Flacco		
Limas Sweed		
37 John Elway	30.00	80.00
Jay Cutler		
Brett Favre		
Aaron Rodgers		
39 Brian Bosworth	15.00	40.00
A.J. Hawk		
Dick Butkus		
DeMarcus Ware		

2008 Ultimate Collection Ultimate Highlight Signatures

STATED PRINT RUN 5-35
SERIAL #'d UNDER 15 NOT PRICED

UHA8 Paul Hornung/35	20.00	50.00
UHA10 Bo Jackson/30	40.00	100.00
UHA15 Matt Ryan/15	75.00	150.00
UHA17 Chad Johnson/35	10.00	25.00
UHA18 Tony Romo/20	40.00	80.00
UHA20 Roger Craig/35	15.00	40.00

2008 Ultimate Collection Ultimate Imagery Signatures

STATED PRINT RUN 5-15

UIA1 LaDainian Tomlinson/15	40.00	100.00
UIA2 Dan Marino		
UIA5 Peyton Manning/15	75.00	150.00
UIA6 Eli Manning/15	50.00	100.00
UIA10 Dick Butkus/20	30.00	60.00

2008 Ultimate Collection Ultimate Inscriptions

STATED PRINT RUN 10-45

UI1 Bo Jackson/15	40.00	100.00
UI2 Paul Hornung/35	20.00	50.00
UI3 Adrian Peterson/15	125.00	200.00
UI6 Daryl Johnston/35	25.00	50.00
UI9 Chad Johnson/25	15.00	40.00
UI11 Eli Manning/15	50.00	100.00
UI12 LaDainian Tomlinson/15	50.00	100.00
UI13 Steve Young/15	50.00	100.00
UI14 Don Maynard/45	10.00	25.00
UI16 Felix Jones/45	30.00	80.00
UI17 Peyton Manning/15	75.00	150.00
UI18 Marion Barber/25	20.00	50.00
UI19 Joe Greene/25	25.00	60.00
UI20 Brian Bosworth/35 EXCH	40.00	80.00

2008 Ultimate Collection Ultimate Inscriptions Dual

STATED PRINT RUN 5-25

1 Bo Jackson	50.00	100.00
Brian Bosworth/25		
3 Peyton Manning	150.00	300.00
Tony Romo/15		
6 Eli Manning	250.00	400.00
Peyton Manning/15		
8 Roy Williams WR	20.00	50.00
Chad Johnson/15		
9 Jack Ham	60.00	120.00
Joe Greene/15		
10 Franco Harris	60.00	120.00
Rashard Mendenhall/25		
11 Gale Sayers EXCH	60.00	120.00
Dick Butkus/15		
14 Marion Barber	40.00	80.00
Marshawn Lynch/15		
15 Paul Hornung EXCH		
Y.A. Tittle/15		

2008 Ultimate Collection Ultimate Legendary Signature Jerseys

STATED PRINT RUN 5-25
SERIAL #'d UNDER 15 NOT PRICED

ULAJ3 Bo Jackson/15	60.00	150.00
ULAJ4 Bo Jackson/15	60.00	150.00
ULAJ7 Dick Butkus/15 EXCH	40.00	100.00
ULAJ8 Brian Bosworth/15	40.00	80.00
ULAJ11 Fran Tarkenton/20	40.00	80.00
ULAJ12 Fran Tarkenton/20	40.00	80.00
ULAJ21 Joe Theismann/25	25.00	60.00
ULAJ22 Joe Theismann/25	25.00	60.00
ULAJ28 Ken Anderson/25 EXCH	12.00	30.00

2008 Ultimate Collection Ultimate Legendary Foursomes Jerseys Gold

STATED PRINT RUN 50 SER.#'d SETS
*PATCH/20: .5X TO 1.2X LEGEND.FOUR/50
PATCH PRINT RUN 10-20
*PRIME/15: .5X TO 1.2X LEGEND.FOUR/50
PRIME PRINT RUN 15 SER.#'d SETS

1 Roger Craig	30.00	80.00
Bo Jackson		
Barry Sanders		
Emmitt Smith		
5 Emmitt Smith	30.00	80.00
Gale Sayers		
Barry Sanders		
Billy Sims		
7 Dick Butkus	40.00	100.00
Gale Sayers		
Walter Payton		
Jim McMahon		
10 Jim Kelly		
Jim McMahon		
Fran Tarkenton		
John Elway		

2008 Ultimate Collection Ultimate Legendary Signatures

STATED PRINT RUN 10-30
SERIAL #'d UNDER 15 NOT PRICED

USL3 Bart Starr/20	75.00	150.00
USL4 Y.A. Tittle/30		
USL5 Franco Harris/15	40.00	80.00
USL6 Jerry Kramer/15	20.00	50.00
USL11 Paul Hornung/15	20.00	50.00
USL14 Bob Griese/15	30.00	60.00

2008 Ultimate Collection Ultimate Numbers Signatures

STATED PRINT RUN 4-85
SERIAL #'d UNDER 15 NOT PRICED

UNA1 Dick Butkus/51	40.00	80.00
UNA2 Darren McFadden/20		
UNA3 LaDainian Tomlinson/21	40.00	80.00
UNA7 Barry Sanders/20	60.00	120.00
UNA8 Chad Johnson/85	10.00	25.00
UNA10 Wes Welker/83	20.00	40.00
UNA13 Peyton Manning/18	75.00	150.00
UNA14 Marshawn Lynch/23	15.00	40.00
UNA16 Roger Craig/33	15.00	40.00
UNA17 Brian Bosworth/55	20.00	50.00
UNA19 Gale Sayers/40	30.00	80.00

2008 Ultimate Collection Ultimate Patch Gold

PATCH PRINT RUN 40 SER.#'d SETS

AH A.J. Hawk	10.00	25.00
AR Aaron Rodgers	15.00	40.00
BC Brodie Croyle	15.00	40.00
BS Bob Sanders	15.00	40.00
CH Chad Henne	20.00	50.00
CJ Chad Johnson	20.00	50.00
CP Clinton Portis	25.00	60.00
CW Cadillac Williams	10.00	25.00
DA Derek Anderson	12.00	30.00
JA Joseph Addai	10.00	25.00
JR Jerry Rice	15.00	40.00
JS Jonathan Stewart	10.00	25.00
KS Kevin Smith	8.00	20.00
LJ Larry Johnson	12.00	30.00
LT LaDainian Tomlinson	10.00	25.00
MB Marion Barber	25.00	60.00
RM Rashard Mendenhall	12.00	30.00
RW Roy Williams WR	15.00	40.00

2008 Ultimate Collection Ultimate Patch Autographs

STATED PRINT RUN 5-25
SERIAL #'d UNDER 15 NOT PRICED

UPAD Joseph Addai/15	25.00	50.00
UPAH A.J. Hawk/20	15.00	40.00
UPAR Aaron Rodgers/20		
UPBC Brodie Croyle/20	15.00	40.00
UPBS Bob Sanders/20		
UPCH Chad Henne/15	40.00	80.00
UPCP Clinton Portis/15	20.00	50.00
UPDA Derek Anderson/15	12.00	30.00
UPDB Dick Butkus/15	50.00	100.00
UPEM Eli Manning/15	50.00	100.00
UPFJ Felix Jones/15	40.00	100.00
UPGS Gale Sayers/20	40.00	80.00
UPJF Joe Flacco/25	75.00	150.00
UPJO Chad Johnson/15	12.00	30.00
UPJS Jonathan Stewart/25	30.00	80.00
UPKS Kevin Smith/25	15.00	40.00
UPKW Kurt Warner/20	35.00	60.00
UPLJ Larry Johnson/15	15.00	40.00
UPMB Marion Barber/20	25.00	50.00
UPME Rashard Mendenhall/20	30.00	60.00
UPML Marshawn Lynch/20	15.00	40.00
UPMR Matt Ryan/15	100.00	200.00
UPPM Peyton Manning/15	75.00	150.00
UPRW Roy Williams WR/20	15.00	40.00
UPTR Tony Romo/15	50.00	100.00
UPWI Kellen Winslow Sr./15	15.00	40.00

2008 Ultimate Collection Ultimate Patch Prime Silver

PRIME PRINT RUN 15 SER.#'d SETS

UPAP Adrian Peterson	25.00	60.00
UPBF Brett Favre	40.00	100.00
UPBJ Bo Jackson	20.00	50.00
UPDB Dick Butkus	20.00	50.00
UPEM Eli Manning	15.00	40.00
UPES Emmitt Smith	30.00	80.00
UPGS Gale Sayers	20.00	50.00
UPJF Joe Flacco	25.00	60.00
UPJK Jim Kelly	15.00	40.00
UPJR Jerry Rice	25.00	60.00
UPKW Kurt Warner	15.00	40.00
UPLT LaDainian Tomlinson	15.00	40.00
UPMC Darren McFadden	20.00	50.00
UPMR Matt Ryan	30.00	80.00
UPPM Peyton Manning	25.00	60.00
UPRM Randy Moss	15.00	40.00
UPSA Barry Sanders	25.00	60.00
UPSY Steve Young	20.00	50.00
UPTB Tom Brady	25.00	60.00
UPTR Tony Romo	20.00	50.00
UPWI Kellen Winslow Sr.	12.00	30.00

2008 Ultimate Collection Ultimate Rookie Autographs Trios

STATED PRINT RUN 15-35

1 Darren McFadden	75.00	150.00
Jonathan Stewart		
Rashard Mendenhall/15		
2 Devin Thomas	15.00	40.00
James Hardy		
Malcolm Kelly/25		
4 John David Booty	12.00	30.00
Sedrick Ellis		
Keith Rivers/25		
5 Joe Flacco	175.00	300.00
Matt Ryan		
Chad Henne/15		
6 John David Booty	15.00	40.00
Brian Brohm		
Andre Woodson/25		
7 DeSean Jackson	25.00	60.00
Early Doucet		
Malcolm Kelly/25		
9 Matt Forte	50.00	120.00
Kevin Smith		
Rashard Mendenhall/35		
11 Chris Johnson	60.00	120.00
Kevin Smith		
Matt Forte/25		
12 Ray Rice	40.00	100.00
Steve Slaton		
Jamaal Charles/35		
13 Frank Okam/25 EXCH	20.00	50.00
Jamaal Charles		
Limas Sweed		
14 Dustin Keller EXCH	15.00	40.00
Fred Davis		
John Carlson/25		
15 Jonathan Stewart	40.00	100.00
Kevin Smith		
Felix Jones/25		

2008 Ultimate Collection Ultimate Rookie Big Materials

STATED PRINT RUN 40 SER.#'d SETS

URBM3 Chad Henne	12.00	30.00
URBM4 Chris Johnson	30.00	80.00
URBM6 Darren McFadden	30.00	80.00
URBM7 DeSean Jackson	25.00	60.00
URBM9 Felix Jones	20.00	50.00
URBM12 Joe Flacco	30.00	80.00
URBM13 Jonathan Stewart	25.00	60.00
URBM14 Kevin Smith	12.00	30.00
URBM15 Malcolm Kelly		
URBM17 Matt Forte	20.00	50.00
URBM18 Matt Ryan	40.00	100.00
URBM19 Rashard Mendenhall	25.00	60.00
URBM21 Steve Slaton	12.00	30.00

2008 Ultimate Collection Ultimate Seasons Jerseys Autographs

STATED PRINT RUN 5-20
UNPRICED PATCH PRINT RUN 5-10
SERIAL #'d UNDER 15 NOT PRICED
*PLAYERS W/MULTIPLE CARDS: SAME PRICE

USEA5 Joe Flacco/20	75.00	125.00
USEA6 Joe Flacco/20	75.00	125.00
USEA7 Joe Flacco/20	75.00	125.00
USEA13 Felix Jones/15	40.00	100.00
USEA14 Felix Jones/15	40.00	100.00
USEA15 Felix Jones/15	40.00	100.00
USEA16 Felix Jones/15	40.00	100.00
USEA23 Chad Johnson/15	10.00	25.00
USEA24 Chad Johnson/15	10.00	25.00
USEA33 Rashard Mendenhall/15	25.00	60.00
USEA34 Rashard Mendenhall/15	25.00	60.00
USEA41 Jack Ham/15	50.00	100.00
USEA42 Jack Ham/15	50.00	100.00
USEA43 Jack Ham/15	50.00	100.00
USEA44 Jack Ham/15	50.00	100.00
USEA45 Fran Tarkenton/15	40.00	80.00
USEA46 Fran Tarkenton/15	40.00	80.00
USEA47 Fran Tarkenton/15	40.00	80.00
USEA48 Fran Tarkenton/15	40.00	80.00
USEA49 Matt Forte/15	50.00	100.00
USEA50 Matt Forte/15	50.00	100.00
USEA53 Tony Romo/15	50.00	100.00
USEA54 Tony Romo/15	50.00	100.00
USEA55 Tony Romo/15	50.00	100.00
USEA57 Brian Brohm/15	12.00	30.00
USEA65 Paul Hornung/15	20.00	50.00
USEA66 Paul Hornung/15	20.00	50.00
USEA67 Paul Hornung/15	20.00	50.00
USEA68 Paul Hornung/15	20.00	50.00
USEA69 Clinton Portis/15	20.00	50.00
USEA70 Clinton Portis/15	20.00	50.00
USEA71 Clinton Portis/15	20.00	50.00
USEA72 Clinton Portis/15	20.00	50.00
USEA73 Kurt Warner/15	50.00	100.00
USEA74 Kurt Warner/15	50.00	100.00
USEA75 Kurt Warner/15	50.00	100.00
USEA76 Kurt Warner/15	50.00	100.00
USEA81 Eli Manning/15	50.00	100.00
USEA82 Eli Manning/15	50.00	100.00
USEA83 Eli Manning/15	50.00	100.00
USEA84 Eli Manning/15	50.00	100.00
USEA95 Paul Hornung/15	20.00	50.00
USEA96 Paul Hornung/15	20.00	50.00
USEA97 Dick Butkus/15	40.00	100.00
USEA98 Dick Butkus/15	40.00	100.00
USEA99 Dick Butkus/15	40.00	100.00
USEA100 Dick Butkus/15	40.00	100.00

2008 Ultimate Collection Ultimate Signature Plays

STATED PRINT RUN 5-20
SERIAL #'d UNDER 15 NOT PRICED

USP4 Bert Jones/15	15.00	40.00
USP5 Billy Sims/15	20.00	50.00
USP6 Bo Jackson/15	40.00	100.00
USP9 Brian Bosworth/15	40.00	80.00
USP14 Rashard Mendenhall/15	40.00	80.00
USP17 Felix Jones/20	25.00	60.00
USP19 Don Maynard/15	12.00	30.00
USP27 Marshawn Lynch/15	12.00	30.00
USP34 Gale Sayers/15	40.00	80.00
USP35 Y.A. Tittle/15	15.00	40.00

2008 Ultimate Collection Ultimate Signatures

STATED PRINT RUN 15-35

US1 Adrian Peterson/15	125.00	200.00
US2 Roy Williams WR/20	15.00	40.00
US3 Eli Manning/20	50.00	100.00
US4 LaDainian Tomlinson/15	50.00	100.00
US5 Peyton Manning/20	75.00	150.00
US6 Peyton Manning/20	75.00	150.00

US7 Adrian Peterson/15 125.00 200.00
US8 LaDainian Tomlinson/15 50.00 100.00
US10 Larry Johnson/25 15.00 40.00
US11 Clinton Portis/30 15.00 40.00
US12 Tony Romo/35 40.00 80.00
US13 Eli Manning/20 50.00 100.00
US14 Tony Romo/35 40.00 80.00
US15 Chad Johnson/25 12.00 30.00

2008 Ultimate Collection Ultimate Signatures Duals

STATED PRINT RUN 10-35
SERIAL #'d UNDER 15 NOT PRICED
2 Chad Henne 20.00 50.00
Brian Brohm/25
6 Joe Flacco 60.00 120.00
Chad Henne/25
7 Dick Butkus 50.00 100.00
A.J. Hawk/25
8 Bart Starr 75.00 150.00
Brian Brohm/15
9 Archie Manning 60.00 120.00
Eli Manning/25
10 Peyton Manning 175.00 300.00
Matt Ryan/15
11 Jamal Lewis 20.00 50.00
Derek Anderson/25
12 Peyton Manning 150.00 250.00
Eli Manning/15
13 Trent Edwards 25.00 60.00
Marshawn Lynch/15
16 Jonathan Stewart 40.00 100.00
Felix Jones/25
17 Troy Aikman 125.00 200.00
Tony Romo/15
18 Jonathan Stewart 30.00 60.00
Rashard Mendenhall/25
19 Brian Brohm 40.00 80.00
Jordy Nelson/25
20 Don Maynard 30.00 60.00
Wes Welker/35

2008 Ultimate Collection Ultimate Signatures Triples

STATED PRINT RUN 5-35
SERIAL #'d UNDER 15 NOT PRICED
1 Chad Henne 60.00 120.00
Joe Flacco
John David Booty/25
2 Fran Tarkenton EXCH 40.00 80.00
Joe Theismann
Ken Anderson/25
3 Chad Johnson 25.00 60.00
(DeSean Jackson
Dwayne Bowe/35
5 Y.A. Tittle 50.00 100.00
Ottis Anderson
Eli Manning/25
7 Jeremy Shockey
Kellen Winslow Sr.
Dallas Clark/25

2008 Ultimate Collection Ultimate Six Jerseys

COMMON CARD 20.00 50.00
STATED PRINT RUN 20 SER.#'d SETS
UNPRICED PATCH PRINT RUN 5
1 Darren McFadden 40.00 100.00
LaDainian Tomlinson
Matt Ryan
Peyton Manning
Malcolm Kelly
Chad Johnson
2 Chad Johnson 20.00 50.00
DeSean Jackson
Early Doucet
Jerry Rice
Anquan Boldin
Malcolm Kelly
5 Jerry Rice 25.00 60.00
Randy Moss
Kellen Winslow Sr.
Kellen Winslow
Eli Manning
Peyton Manning
6 Paul Hornung 40.00 100.00
Brian Brohm
Brett Favre
Roger Staubach
Troy Aikman
Tony Romo
8 Barry Sanders 60.00 150.00
Kevin Smith
Walter Payton
Matt Forte
Emmitt Smith
Felix Jones
9 Franco Harris 30.00 80.00
Willie Parker
Rashard Mendenhall
Emmitt Smith
Marion Barber
Felix Jones
10 Tom Brady 12.00 30.00
Kevin O'Connell
Fran Tarkenton
John David Booty
Aaron Rodgers
Brian Brohm
13 Walter Payton 40.00 100.00
Billy Sims
Emmitt Smith
LaDainian Tomlinson
Adrian Peterson
Darren McFadden
16 Steve Young 25.00 60.00
Jerry Rice
Tom Brady
Randy Moss
Jason Campbell
Devin Thomas
18 Chad Johnson 15.00 40.00
Andre Caldwell
Hines Ward
Limas Sweed
Torry Holt
Donnie Avery
19 Jim Kelly 60.00 120.00
Trent Edwards
Brett Favre
Aaron Rodgers
Roger Staubach
Troy Aikman
22 Brian Westbrook 15.00 40.00
Felix Jones
Franco Harris
Willie Parker
Roger Craig
Frank Gore
23 Peyton Manning 30.00 80.00
Eli Manning
Terry Bradshaw
Ben Roethlisberger
Aaron Rodgers
Brian Brohm
24 Peyton Manning 40.00 100.00
Joe Flacco
Carson Palmer
Matt Ryan
Ben Roethlisberger
Brian Brohm
25 Brian Bosworth 20.00 50.00
Dick Butkus
Patrick Willis
A.J. Hawk
Jack Lambert
Ernie Cimo
26 Roger Staubach 50.00 120.00
Troy Aikman
Tony Romo
Bert Jones
Peyton Manning
Joe Flacco
27 Troy Aikman 30.00 80.00
Tony Romo
Carson Palmer
Ken Anderson
Randy Moss
Jerry Rice
28 Gale Sayers 25.00 60.00
Matt Forte
Billy Sims
Barry Sanders
Jack Lambert
A.J. Hawk
29 Barry Sanders 50.00 120.00
Kevin Smith
Bo Jackson
Darren McFadden
Walter Payton
Matt Forte
31 Franco Harris 30.00 80.00
Rashard Mendenhall
Barry Sanders
Kevin Smith
Marion Barber
Felix Jones
34 Dick Butkus 20.00 50.00
A.J. Hawk
Mike Singletary
Brian Urlacher
Mel Blount
Bob Sanders
35 Dick Butkus 20.00 50.00
Brian Bosworth
Jack Lambert
Shawne Merriman
A.J. Hawk
Patrick Willis
36 Peyton Manning 25.00 60.00
Brian Brohm
LaDainian Tomlinson
Matt Forte
Randy Moss
Limas Sweed
37 Steve Smith 30.00 80.00
DeSean Jackson
Randy Moss
Limas Sweed
Torry Holt
Devin Thomas
38 Adrian Peterson 25.00 60.00
Darren McFadden
Willie Parker
Rashard Mendenhall
Marion Barber
Felix Jones
39 Tom Brady 40.00 100.00
Chad Henne
Aaron Rodgers
Brian Brohm
Eli Manning
Matt Ryan
42 Rashard Mendenhall 30.00 80.00
Marion Barber
Matt Forte
Larry Johnson
Chris Johnson
Adrian Peterson

2009 Ultimate Collection

1-150 VET/LEGEND PRINT RUN 375
151-200 ROOKIE PRINT RUN 375
201-220 ROOKIE AU PRINT RUN 99-399
EXCH EXPIRATION: 2/3/2012
1 Larry Fitzgerald 2.00 5.00
2 Anquan Boldin 1.50 4.00
3 Steve Breaston 1.50 4.00
4 Adrian Wilson 1.25 3.00
5 Kurt Warner 2.00 5.00
6 Michael Turner 1.50 4.00
7 Roddy White 1.50 4.00
8 Tony Gonzalez 1.50 4.00
9 Matt Ryan 2.00 5.00
10 Ray Rice 2.00 5.00
11 Ed Reed 1.50 4.00
12 Joe Flacco 2.00 5.00
13 Marshawn Lynch 1.50 4.00
14 Terrell Owens 2.00 5.00
15 Lee Evans 1.50 4.00
16 Trent Edwards 1.25 3.00
17 DeAngelo Williams 2.00 5.00
18 Jonathan Stewart 1.50 4.00
19 Steve Smith 1.50 4.00
20 Julius Peppers 1.50 4.00
21 Jake Delhomme 1.50 4.00
22 Matt Forte 2.00 5.00
23 Devin Hester 2.00 5.00
24 Jay Cutler 2.00 5.00
25 Chad Johnson 1.50 4.00
26 Carson Palmer 2.00 5.00
27 Jamal Lewis 1.50 4.00
28 Braylon Edwards 1.50 4.00
29 Brady Quinn 1.50 4.00
30 Marion Barber 1.50 4.00
31 Jason Witten 2.00 5.00
32 DeMarcus Ware 1.50 4.00
33 Tony Romo 3.00 8.00
34 Brandon Marshall 1.50 4.00
35 Eddie Royal 1.50 4.00
36 Tony Scheffler 1.25 3.00
37 Brian Dawkins 1.50 4.00
38 Kyle Orton 1.50 4.00
39 Kevin Smith 1.50 4.00
40 Calvin Johnson 2.00 5.00
41 Ryan Grant 1.50 4.00
42 Greg Jennings 2.00 5.00
43 Donald Driver 1.50 4.00
44 Charles Woodson 2.00 5.00
45 Aaron Rodgers 4.00 10.00
46 Steve Slaton 1.50 4.00
47 Andre Johnson 1.50 4.00
48 Matt Schaub 1.50 4.00
49 Reggie Wayne 1.50 4.00
50 Anthony Gonzalez 1.25 3.00
51 Peyton Manning 3.00 8.00
52 Bob Sanders 1.50 4.00
53 Maurice Jones-Drew 1.50 4.00
54 David Garrard 1.50 4.00
55 Dwayne Bowe 1.50 4.00
56 Matt Cassel 1.50 4.00
57 Ronnie Brown 1.50 4.00
58 Ted Ginn Jr. 1.50 4.00
59 Chad Pennington 1.50 4.00
60 Adrian Peterson 3.00 8.00
61 Bernard Berrian 1.50 4.00
62 Brett Favre 12.00 30.00
63 Wes Welker 2.00 5.00
64 Randy Moss 2.00 5.00
65 Tom Brady 3.00 8.00
66 Pierre Thomas 1.50 4.00
67 Marques Colston 1.50 4.00
68 Drew Brees 2.00 5.00
69 Brandon Jacobs 1.50 4.00
70 Eli Manning 2.00 5.00
71 Thomas Jones 1.50 4.00
72 Darren McFadden 2.00 5.00
73 JaMarcus Russell 1.25 3.00
74 Brian Westbrook 1.50 4.00
75 DeSean Jackson 1.50 4.00
76 Donovan McNabb 2.00 5.00
77 Willie Parker 1.25 3.00
78 Hines Ward 1.50 4.00
79 Santonio Holmes 1.50 4.00
80 James Harrison 2.00 5.00
81 Ben Roethlisberger 2.00 5.00
82 Troy Polamalu 2.00 5.00
83 LaDainian Tomlinson 2.00 5.00
84 Vincent Jackson 1.50 4.00
85 Philip Rivers 2.00 5.00
86 Frank Gore 1.50 4.00
87 Patrick Willis 1.50 4.00
88 Shaun Hill 1.25 3.00
89 T.J. Houshmandzadeh 1.50 4.00
90 Matt Hasselbeck 1.50 4.00
91 Steven Jackson 1.50 4.00
92 Donnie Avery 1.50 4.00
93 Marc Bulger 1.50 4.00
94 Derrick Ward 1.25 3.00
95 Antonio Bryant 1.25 3.00
96 Chris Johnson 2.00 5.00
97 Clinton Portis 1.50 4.00
98 Santana Moss 1.50 4.00
99 Chris Cooley 1.50 4.00
100 Jason Campbell 1.25 3.00
101 Barry Sanders 4.00 10.00
102 Emmitt Smith 4.00 10.00
103 Dan Marino 5.00 12.00
104 Fred Biletnikoff 2.50 6.00
105 Jerry Rice 4.00 10.00
106 Bo Jackson 3.00 8.00
107 Earl Campbell 2.50 6.00
108 Paul Hornung 2.50 6.00
109 Roger Staubach 3.00 8.00
110 Bob Griese 2.50 6.00
111 Bob Lilly 2.00 5.00
112 Billy Sims 2.00 5.00
113 Steve Young 3.00 8.00
114 Alex Karras 2.00 5.00
115 Deacon Jones 2.00 5.00
116 Ken Anderson 2.00 5.00
117 Steve Largent 2.50 6.00
118 Don Maynard 2.00 5.00
119 Troy Aikman 3.00 8.00
120 Alan Page 2.00 5.00
121 Lawrence Taylor 2.50 6.00
122 Harry Carson 1.50 4.00
123 Roger Craig 2.00 5.00
124 Darrell Green 2.00 5.00
125 Randall Cunningham 2.50 6.00
126 Lem Barney 1.50 4.00
127 Donnie Shell 1.50 4.00
128 Daryl Johnston 2.50 6.00
129 Terry Bradshaw 3.00 8.00
130 Franco Harris 2.50 6.00
131 Roman Gabriel 2.00 5.00
132 Rocky Bleier 2.00 5.00
133 Joe Theismann 2.50 6.00
134 Phil Simms 2.00 5.00
135 Jim Kelly 2.50 6.00
136 Kellen Winslow Sr. 2.00 5.00
137 L.C. Greenwood 2.00 5.00
138 Warren Moon 2.50 6.00
139 Tim Brown 2.50 6.00
140 Doug Flutie 2.00 5.00
141 Thurman Thomas 2.50 6.00
142 Gale Sayers 3.00 8.00
143 Fran Tarkenton 2.50 6.00
144 Chuck Howley 1.50 4.00
145 Randy White 2.50 6.00
146 Archie Manning 2.50 6.00
147 Bubba Smith 1.50 4.00
148 Rod Woodson 2.00 5.00
149 Cliff Harris 2.00 5.00
150 Drew Bledsoe 2.00 5.00
151 Aaron Maybin RC 2.00 5.00
152 Julian Edelman RC 2.50 6.00
153 Tom Brandstater RC 2.50 6.00
154 Brian Cushing RC 2.50 6.00
155 Rey Maualuga RC 2.50 6.00
156 Clay Matthews RC 6.00 15.00
157 Brian Orakpo RC 2.50 6.00
158 B.J. Raji RC 2.50 6.00
159 Johnny Knox RC 4.00 10.00
160 Eugene Monroe RC 1.50 4.00
161 Louis Murphy RC 2.50 6.00
162 Tyson Jackson RC 2.00 5.00
163 Stephen McGee RC 2.50 6.00
164 Darius Butler RC 2.50 6.00
165 Brandon Tate RC 2.50 6.00
166 Derrick Williams RC 2.00 5.00
167 Mike Wallace RC 8.00 20.00
168 Mike Thomas RC 2.50 6.00
169 Glen Coffee RC 2.00 5.00
170 Jason Smith RC 2.00 5.00
171 Andre Brown RC 1.50 4.00
172 Robert Ayers RC 2.50 6.00
173 Malcolm Jenkins RC 2.50 6.00
174 Patrick Turner RC 2.00 5.00
175 Travis Beckum RC 2.00 5.00
176 Chase Coffman RC 2.00 5.00
177 James Laurinaitis RC 2.50 6.00
178 Curtis Painter RC 2.50 6.00
179 Duke Robinson RC 1.50 4.00
180 Andre Smith RC 2.00 5.00
181 Larry English RC 2.50 6.00
182 Michael Johnson RC 1.50 4.00
183 Patrick Chung RC 2.50 6.00
184 Vontae Davis RC 2.50 6.00
185 Brooks Foster RC 1.50 4.00
186 Rashad Jennings RC 2.50 6.00
187 William Moore RC 2.50 6.00
188 Evander Hood RC 3.00 8.00
189 Peria Jerry RC 2.00 5.00
190 Michael Oher RC 4.00 10.00
191 Alex Mack RC 2.00 5.00
192 Louis Delmas RC 2.50 6.00
193 Alphonso Smith RC 2.00 5.00
194 Richard Quinn RC 2.00 5.00
195 Fili Moala RC 2.00 5.00
196 Deon Butler RC 2.00 5.00
197 Brian Hartline RC 2.50 6.00
198 Mike Goodson RC 2.50 6.00
199 Austin Collie RC 2.50 6.00
200 Javon Ringer RC 2.50 6.00
201 Matthew Stafford AU/99 RC 125.00 200.00
202 Mark Sanchez AU/99 RC 50.00 100.00
203 Chris Wells AU/99 RC 20.00 50.00
204 Knowshon Moreno AU/99 RC 12.00 30.00
205 Michael Crabtree AU/99 RC 30.00 60.00
206 Darrius Heyward-Bey AU/99 RC 12.00 30.00
207 Donald Brown AU/99 RC 15.00 40.00
208 Percy Harvin AU/399 RC 20.00 50.00
209 Jeremy Maclin AU/300 RC 10.00 25.00
210 Josh Freeman AU/99 RC 30.00 80.00
211 Brandon Pettigrew AU/399 RC 6.00 15.00
212 Aaron Curry AU/399 RC 6.00 15.00
213 Kenny Britt AU/399 RC 8.00 20.00
214 LeSean McCoy AU/199 RC 30.00 80.00
215 Pat White AU/399 RC 6.00 15.00
216 Shonn Greene AU/399 RC 10.00 25.00
217 Hakeem Nicks AU/399 RC 15.00 40.00
219 Juaquin Iglesias AU/399 RC 5.00 12.00
220 Nate Davis AU/399 RC 5.00 12.00

2009 Ultimate Collection Ultimate Rookie Signatures Blue

*BLUE INK/35: .6X TO 1.5X BASE AU RC/399
*BLUE INK/35: .4X TO 1X BASE AU RC/99-199
*BLUE INK/15: .5X TO 1.2X BASE AU RC/99
BLUE INK PRINT RUN 15-35

2009 Ultimate Collection 1997 Legends Autographs

EXCH EXPIRATION: 2/3/2012
196 Bruce Smith 125.00 250.00
197 Tim Brown 40.00 80.00
198 Dan Marino 600.00 1,000.00
200 Darrell Green
201 Phil Simms 500.00 800.00
202 Lawrence Taylor EXCH 100.00 175.00
204 Harry Carson 20.00 50.00
205 Merlin Olsen 40.00 80.00
206 Earl Campbell 90.00 150.00
207 Randall Cunningham 40.00 80.00
208 Warren Moon 40.00 100.00
211 Doug Flutie 40.00 100.00
212 Drew Bledsoe 30.00 80.00
213 Herman Moore 25.00 60.00
214 Andre Reed 25.00 60.00
215 Mike Alstott 25.00 60.00
216 Christian Okoye 25.00 60.00

2009 Ultimate Collection Ultimate Dual Autograph Jerseys

DUAL JSY AU PRINT RUN 5-20
DSJBC Lance Briggs/20 20.00 40.00
Aaron Curry
DSJBP Derrick Brooks/20
Joey Porter
DSJFD Nate Davis/20 25.00 50.00
Josh Freeman

2009 Ultimate Collection Ultimate Enshrinement Signatures

ENSHRINEMENT AU PRINT RUN 10-25
EAP Alan Page/25 15.00 40.00
EDM Don Maynard/15 15.00 40.00
EEC Earl Campbell/15 20.00 50.00
EGS Gale Sayers/15 40.00 80.00
EHC Harry Carson/25 12.00 30.00
EKW Kellen Winslow Sr./15 20.00 50.00
ELB Lem Barney/25 12.00 30.00
EMS Mike Singletary/15 20.00 50.00
ESL Steve Largent/15 30.00 60.00

2009 Ultimate Collection Ultimate Enshrinements Dual Signatures

DUAL AU PRINT RUN 5-25
EDJO Merlin Olsen/15 60.00 100.00
Deacon Jones
EDLM Steve Largent/15 30.00 60.00
Don Maynard
EDPJ Alan Page/25 20.00 50.00
Deacon Jones

2009 Ultimate Collection Ultimate Future Six Jerseys

STATED PRINT RUN 99 SER.#'d SETS
*GOLD/25: .5X TO 1.2X BASIC SIX JSY
*PATCH/25: .8X TO 2X BASIC SIX JSY
1 Glen Coffee 6.00 15.00
LeSean McCoy
Shonn Greene
Chris Wells
Javon Ringer
Knowshon Moreno
2 Stephen McGee 15.00 40.00
Rhett Bomar
Matthew Stafford
Mark Sanchez
Josh Freeman
Nate Davis
3 Michael Crabtree 5.00 12.00
Percy Harvin
Jeremy Maclin
Darrius Heyward- Bey
Ramses Barden
Kenny Britt
4 Juaquin Iglesias 5.00 12.00
Darrius Heyward-Bey
Jeremy Maclin
Alohamed Massaquoi
Percy Harvin
Michael Crabtree
5 Aaron Curry 15.00 40.00
Mark Sanchez
Darrius Heyward-Bey
Matthew Stafford
Tyson Jackson
Jason Smith
6 Knowshon Moreno 6.00 15.00
Andre Brown
Chris Wells
Shonn Greene
LeSean McCoy
Donald Brown
7 Matthew Stafford 15.00 40.00
Brandon Pettigrew
Darrius Heyward-Bey
Knowshon Moreno
Tyson Jackson
Jason Smith
8 Rhett Bomar 6.00 15.00
Andre Brown
Ramses Barden
Michael Crabtree
Nate Davis
Glen Coffee
9 Michael Crabtree 12.00 30.00
Donald Brown
Percy Harvin
Chris Wells
Darrius Heyward-Bey
Knowshon Moreno
10 Derrick Williams 15.00 40.00
Brandon Pettigrew
Matthew Stafford
Michael Crabtree
Glen Coffee
Nate Davis
11 Matthew Stafford 15.00 40.00
Brandon Pettigrew
Derrick Williams
Rhett Bomar
Ramses Barden
Andre Brown
12 Ramses Barden 6.00 15.00
Derrick Williams
Michael Crabtree
Percy Harvin
Mohamed Massaquoi
Brian Robiskie
13 Brian Robiskie 8.00 20.00
Jeremy Maclin
Mike Wallace
Darrius Heyward-Bey
Juaquin Iglesias
Patrick Turner
14 Patrick Turner 6.00 15.00
Pat White
Mike Thomas
Darrius Heyward-Bey
Michael Crabtree
Brian Robiskie
15 Mark Sanchez 15.00 40.00
Nate Davis
Josh Freeman
Matthew Stafford
Rhett Bomar
Pat White

2009 Ultimate Collection Ultimate Futures Autograph Jerseys

STATED PRINT RUN 20 SER.#'d SETS
FSJAC Aaron Curry 10.00 25.00
FSJBP Brandon Pettigrew 10.00 25.00
FSJBR Brian Robiskie 10.00 25.00
FSJCW Chris Wells 15.00 40.00
FSJDB Donald Brown 10.00 25.00
FSJDH Darrius Heyward-Bey 10.00 25.00
FSJHN Hakeem Nicks 15.00 40.00
FSJJF Josh Freeman 40.00 80.00
FSJJI Juaquin Iglesias 8.00 20.00
FSJKB Kenny Britt 12.00 30.00
FSJKM Knowshon Moreno 30.00 80.00
FSJLM LeSean McCoy 25.00 60.00
FSJMC Michael Crabtree 30.00 80.00
FSJMS Matthew Stafford 75.00 150.00
FSJND Nate Davis 8.00 20.00
FSJPH Percy Harvin 40.00 80.00
FSJPT Patrick Turner 8.00 20.00
FSJSA Mark Sanchez 50.00 120.00
FSJSG Shonn Greene 15.00 40.00
FSJSM Stephen McGee 10.00 25.00

2009 Ultimate Collection Ultimate Generations Signature

STATED PRINT RUN 5-25
HHLB James Laurinaitis/25
A.J. Hawk
Jack Ham
Derrick Brooks
LWCT Aaron Curry/25
Lawrence Taylor
Ray Lewis
Patrick Willis
SJWJ Bruce Smith/25
Deacon Jones
Mario Williams
Tyson Jackson

2009 Ultimate Collection Ultimate Generations Six Jerseys

STATED PRINT RUN 35-75
*GOLD/25: .5X TO 1.2X BASIC SIX JSY
*PATCH/15: .6X TO 1.5X BASIC SIX JSY
1 Brett Favre 25.00 60.00
Jim Kelly
Mark Sanchez
Matthew Stafford
Peyton Manning
Terry Bradshaw
2 Adrian Peterson 20.00 50.00
Emmitt Smith
Franco Harris
Knowshon Moreno
Paul Hornung
Roger Craig
3 Andre Reed 15.00 40.00
Don Maynard
Fred Biletnikoff
Michael Crabtree
Randy Moss
Steve Largent
4 Alan Page 8.00 20.00
Albert Haynesworth
Bruce Smith
Deacon Jones
Randy White
Tyson Jackson
5 Aaron Curry 10.00 25.00
Dick Butkus
Jack Ham
Lawrence Taylor
Patrick Willis
Ray Lewis
6 Drew Brees 25.00 60.00
Eli Manning
Fran Tarkenton
Peyton Manning
Roger Staubach
Terry Bradshaw
7 Emmitt Smith 20.00 50.00
Roger Craig
LaDainian Tomlinson
Adrian Peterson
Brian Westbrook
Barry Sanders
8 Clinton Portis 15.00 40.00
Chris Wells
Adrian Peterson
Donald Brown
Marion Barber
Knowshon Moreno
9 Knowshon Moreno 15.00 40.00
Emmitt Smith
LeSean McCoy
Chris Wells
Thurman Thomas
Barry Sanders
10 Darrius Heyward-Bey/35 20.00 50.00
Anquan Boldin
Percy Harvin
Michael Crabtree
Randy Moss
Andre Johnson
11 Andre Johnson 10.00 25.00
Kenny Britt
Jeremy Maclin
Mohamed Massaquoi
Larry Fitzgerald
Calvin Johnson
12 Jim Kelly 15.00 40.00
Matthew Stafford
Peyton Manning
Phil Simms
Roger Staubach
Tom Brady
13 Patrick Turner 15.00 40.00
Andre Johnson
Michael Crabtree
Reggie Wayne
Brian Robiskie
Calvin Johnson
14 Phil Simms 12.00 30.00
Eli Manning
Rhett Bomar
Stephen McGee
Tony Romo
Troy Aikman
15 Bob Griese 15.00 40.00
Chad Pennington
Dan Marino
Roger Staubach
Tony Romo
Troy Aikman
16 Brian Piccolo 30.00 80.00
Emmitt Smith
Felix Jones
Marion Barber
Matt Forte
Walter Payton
17 Brett Favre 25.00 60.00
Dan Marino
Mark Sanchez
Matt Ryan
Matthew Stafford
Peyton Manning
18 Roger Craig 20.00 50.00
Steve Young
Jerry Rice
Michael Crabtree
Glen Coffee
Nate Davis
19 Andre Reed 8.00 20.00
Jim Kelly
Lee Evans
Marshawn Lynch
Thurman Thomas
Trent Edwards
20 Ben Roethlisberger 12.00 30.00
Franco Harris
Hines Ward
Lynn Swann
Terry Bradshaw
Willie Parker
21 Adrian Peterson 20.00 50.00
Barry Sanders
Chris Johnson
Knowshon Moreno
Paul Hornung
Walter Payton
22 Jack Ham UER 12.00 30.00
Lawrence Taylor
Mike Singletary
Ray Lewis
Derrick Brooks
A.J. Hawk
23 Josh Freeman 15.00 40.00
Mark Sanchez
Eli Manning
Kurt Warner
Matthew Stafford
Philip Rivers
25 Franco Harris
Hines Ward
Lynn Swann
Mike Wallace
Rashard Mendenhall
Willie Parker
26 Darrius Heyward-Bey
Fred Biletnikoff
Jerry Rice
Lynn Swann
Michael Crabtree
Mike Wallace
27 Emmitt Smith/35 20.00 50.00
Marion Barber
Bo Jackson
Darren McFadden
Barry Sanders
Kevin Smith
28 Barry Sanders 25.00 60.00
Billy Sims
Brian Piccolo
Kevin Smith
Matt Forte
Walter Payton
30 Mark Sanchez 20.00 50.00
Donovan McNabb
Josh Freeman
Ben Roethlisberger
Matthew Stafford
Tom Brady
31 Tony Romo 15.00 40.00
Troy Aikman
Jim Kelly
Trent Edwards
Donovan McNabb
Randall Cunningham
33 Barry Sanders 25.00 60.00
Chris Johnson
Earl Campbell
Kevin Smith
Matt Forte
Walter Payton
34 Barry Sanders 30.00 80.00
Brian Piccolo
Earl Campbell
Emmitt Smith
Gale Sayers
Paul Hornung
35 Andre Reed 12.00 30.00
Cris Carter
Don Maynard
Fred Biletnikoff
Jerry Rice
Steve Largent

2009 Ultimate Collection Ultimate Inscriptions

STATED PRINT RUN 20 SER.#'d SETS
EXCH EXPIRATION: 2/3/2012
IAC Aaron Curry 15.00 40.00
IAH Albert Haynesworth 10.00 25.00
IAP Alan Page 15.00 40.00
IBR Ben Roethlisberger 60.00 120.00
IBW Brian Westbrook 12.00 30.00
IDG Darrell Green
IDJ Deacon Jones 15.00 40.00
IEC Earl Campbell 40.00 80.00
IJK Jim Kelly 30.00 60.00
IKM Knowshon Moreno 30.00 60.00
ILB Lance Briggs 25.00 50.00
IMC Michael Crabtree 40.00 80.00
IMS Matthew Stafford 50.00 100.00
IPM Peyton Manning 125.00 250.00
IRC Randall Cunningham 25.00 50.00
IRL Ronnie Lott 40.00 80.00
ISA Mark Sanchez 50.00 100.00
ITB Tim Brown 20.00 50.00

2009 Ultimate Collection Ultimate Inscriptions Dual

DUAL AUTO PRINT RUN 5-35
HM Jeremy Maclin/35 40.00 100.00
Percy Harvin
LZ Steve Largent/35 60.00 120.00
Jim Zorn

2009 Ultimate Collection Ultimate Legendary Signatures

STATED PRINT RUN 10-45
LAK Alex Karras/35 EXCH 12.00 30.00
LAP Alan Page/40 12.00 30.00
LTB Tim Brown/35 15.00 40.00
LEC Earl Campbell/35 25.00 50.00
LJK Jim Kelly/20 30.00 60.00
LLB Lem Barney/50 10.00 25.00
LLT Lawrence Taylor/20
LRW Randy White/45 15.00 40.00
LWO Rod Woodson/35 EXCH 25.00 50.00

2009 Ultimate Collection Ultimate Legendary Six Jerseys

SIX JERSEY PRINT RUN 35-75
1 Dan Marino/75 30.00 60.00
Joe Theismann
John Elway
Roger Staubach
Terry Bradshaw
Warren Moon
2 Barry Sanders/35 30.00 60.00
Earl Campbell
Gale Sayers
LaDainian Tomlinson
Roger Craig
Walter Payton
5 Dan Marino/75 30.00 60.00
Fran Tarkenton
John Elway
Roger Staubach
Terry Bradshaw
Troy Aikman
6 Dan Marino/35 30.00 80.00
Jim Kelly
Joe Theismann
John Elway
Phil Simms
Randall Cunningham
7 Barry Sanders/30 30.00 80.00
John Elway
Paul Hornung
Roger Staubach
Troy Aikman
Walter Payton
15 Bob Lilly/35 30.00 60.00
Emmitt Smith
Jerry Rice
Roger Craig
Steve Young
Troy Aikman
17 Franco Harris 30.00 60.00
Thurman Thomas
Barry Sanders
Earl Campbell
Emmitt Smith
Roger Craig
20 Steve Young 30.00 60.00
Roger Craig
Emmitt Smith
Troy Aikman
Terry Bradshaw
Franco Harris

2009 Ultimate Collection Ultimate Loyality Signatures

STATED PRINT RUN 10-45
LYAK Alex Karras/25 15.00 40.00
LYBG Bob Griese/20 25.00 60.00
LYDJ Daryl Johnston/35
LYFB Fred Biletnikoff/25
LYGS Gale Sayers/25 30.00 60.00
LYHC Harry Carson/35 12.00 30.00
LYJH Jack Ham/20 15.00 40.00
LYJK Jim Kelly/15 30.00 80.00
LYJT Joe Theismann/45 20.00 50.00
LYKR Jerry Kramer/35 15.00 40.00
LYKW Kellen Winslow Sr./45 12.00 30.00
LYLB Lem Barney/35 12.00 30.00
LYLG L.C. Greenwood/25 15.00 40.00
LYLT Lawrence Taylor/25
LYMS Mike Singletary/25 20.00 50.00
LYPH Paul Hornung/35 15.00 40.00
LYPM Peyton Manning/25 75.00 150.00
LYRB Rocky Bleier/45 15.00 40.00
LYRL Ray Lewis/25 50.00 100.00
LYRW Reggie Wayne/25 12.00 30.00
LYSL Steve Largent/25 20.00 50.00
LYWH Randy White/25 20.00 50.00

2009 Ultimate Collection Ultimate Patch

STATED PRINT RUN 10-50
U1 Adrian Peterson 12.00 30.00
U2 LaDainian Tomlinson 8.00 20.00
U3 Randy Moss 8.00 20.00
U4 Peyton Manning 12.00 30.00
U5 Eli Manning 8.00 20.00
U6 Tony Romo 12.00 30.00
U7 Ben Roethlisberger 8.00 20.00
U8 Matt Ryan 10.00 25.00
U9 Pat White 5.00 12.00
U10 A.J. Hawk 6.00 15.00
U11 Tom Brady 12.00 30.00
U12 Donovan McNabb 8.00 20.00
U13 Patrick Willis 8.00 20.00
U14 Ray Lewis 8.00 20.00
U15 Brett Favre 20.00 50.00
U18 Brandon Jacobs 6.00 15.00
U19 Calvin Johnson 8.00 20.00
U20 Reggie Bush 8.00 20.00
U21 Drew Brees 8.00 20.00
U22 Matthew Stafford 25.00 60.00

U23 Knowshon Moreno 5.00 12.00
U24 Mark Sanchez 15.00 40.00
U25 Josh Freeman 10.00 25.00
U26 Darrius Heyward-Bey 5.00 12.00
U27 Michael Crabtree 10.00 25.00
U28 Donald Brown 5.00 12.00
U29 Chris Wells 8.00 20.00
U30 Jeremy Maclin 8.00 20.00
U31 Percy Harvin 8.00 20.00
U32 LeSean McCoy 10.00 25.00
U33 Aaron Curry 5.00 12.00
U34 Shonn Greene 8.00 20.00
U35 Chris Johnson 8.00 20.00
U36 Matt Forte 8.00 20.00
U37 Jonathan Stewart 6.00 15.00
U39 Brian Robiskie 5.00 12.00
U40 Walter Payton 25.00 60.00
U41 Fred Biletnikoff 12.00 30.00

2009 Ultimate Collection Ultimate Patch Autographs

STATED PRINT RUN 5-25
U9 Pat White/20 40.00 80.00
U13 Patrick Willis/15 30.00 60.00
U30 Jeremy Maclin/15 30.00 80.00
U31 Percy Harvin/20 100.00 175.00
U32 LeSean McCoy/20 60.00 120.00
U33 Aaron Curry/20 20.00 50.00
U34 Shonn Greene/15 30.00 80.00
U36 Matt Forte/20 30.00 80.00

2009 Ultimate Collection Ultimate Rookie Autographs Trios

STATED PRINT RUN 3-45
EXCH EXPIRATION: 2/3/2012
BBN Hakeem Nicks/25 12.00 30.00
Ramses Barden
Rhett Bomar
CCA Aaron Curry/45
Robert Ayers
Brian Cushing
HMB Percy Harvin/25 40.00 80.00
Jeremy Maclin
Kenny Britt
HMD Stephen McGee/25 15.00 40.00
Graham Harrell
Nate Davis
JDC Malcolm Jenkins/45 10.00 25.00
Patrick Chung
Vontae Davis
LCE Aaron Curry/15 15.00 40.00
James Laurinaitis
Larry English
MCM Clay Matthews/35 50.00 100.00
Brian Cushing
Rey Maualuga
PBC Chase Coffman/45 10.00 25.00
Brandon Pettigrew
Travis Beckum
RCH Darrius Heyward-Bey/15 25.00 60.00
Brian Robiskie
Michael Crabtree
RMG LeSean McCoy/25 25.00 60.00
Shonn Greene
Javon Ringer
SMH Knowshon Moreno/15 60.00 120.00
Darrius Heyward-Bey
Matthew Stafford
SSF Matthew Stafford/15 100.00 200.00
Mark Sanchez
Josh Freeman
SWP Matthew Stafford/15 75.00 150.00
Brandon Pettigrew
Derrick Williams
TTW Mike Wallace/25 25.00 60.00
Mike Thomas
Patrick Turner
WFD Pat White/25 20.00 50.00
Josh Freeman
Nate Davis

2009 Ultimate Collection Ultimate Rookie Big Materials

STATED PRINT RUN 99 SER.#'d SETS
B1 Mark Sanchez 20.00 50.00
B2 Matthew Stafford 30.00 80.00
B3 Josh Freeman 12.00 30.00
B4 Chris Wells 10.00 25.00
B5 Knowshon Moreno 8.00 20.00
B6 Donald Brown 6.00 15.00
B7 Shonn Greene 10.00 25.00
B8 Darrius Heyward-Bey 6.00 15.00
B9 Michael Crabtree 12.00 30.00
B10 Percy Harvin 10.00 25.00
B11 Jeremy Maclin 10.00 25.00
B12 Brandon Pettigrew 6.00 15.00
B13 Hakeem Nicks 10.00 25.00
B14 Aaron Curry 6.00 15.00
B15 Kenny Britt 8.00 20.00
B16 LeSean McCoy 12.00 30.00
B17 Brian Robiskie 6.00 15.00
B18 Nate Davis 5.00 12.00
B19 Pat White 8.00 20.00
B20 Javon Ringer 6.00 15.00
B21 Ramses Barden 6.00 15.00

2009 Ultimate Collection Ultimate Signatures Duals

DUAL AUTO PRINT RUN 5-65
EXCH EXPIRATION: 2/3/2012
DBG Bob Griese/15 50.00 100.00
Drew Brees
DBL Lance Briggs/25 40.00 80.00
Ray Lewis
DBW Pat White/35 15.00 40.00
Ronnie Brown
DCB Dwayne Bowe/25 12.00 30.00
Matt Cassel
DCH Darrius Heyward-Bey/25 20.00 50.00
Michael Crabtree
DGB Donald Brown/35 20.00 50.00
Shonn Greene
DHA Jared Allen/45 30.00 50.00
Albert Haynesworth
DHM Percy Harvin/35 50.00 100.00
Jeremy Maclin
DHW Albert Haynesworth/35 10.00 25.00
Mario Williams
DJR Chris Johnson/45 25.00 50.00
Javon Ringer
DSB Lance Briggs/25 30.00 60.00
Mike Singletary
DLM Steve Largent/35 25.00 50.00
Don Maynard
DMM Eli Manning/15 200.00 350.00
Peyton Manning
DRS Matt Ryan/15 75.00 150.00
Matthew Stafford
DTR Matt Ryan/15 50.00 100.00
Michael Turner
DWB Kurt Warner/25 30.00 60.00
Anquan Boldin
DWM Chris Wells/25 30.00 80.00
Knowshon Moreno

2009 Ultimate Collection Ultimate Signatures Quads

QUAD AUTO PRINT RUN 5-25
LBPW Joey Porter/15 100.00 200.00
Patrick Willis
Ray Lewis
Lance Briggs
LCCE Aaron Curry/25 30.00 80.00
James Laurinaitis
Larry English
Brian Cushing
PJOK Alan Page/25
Alex Karras
Deacon Jones
Merlin Olsen
SMCP Knowshon Moreno/15 60.00 120.00
Brandon Pettigrew
Matthew Stafford
Michael Crabtree
SSFD Nate Davis/15 100.00 175.00
Josh Freeman
Mark Sanchez
Matthew Stafford
WMMB Knowshon Moreno/15 30.00 80.00
Donald Brown
LeSean McCoy
Chris Wells

2009 Ultimate Collection Ultimate Signature Jerseys

STATED PRINT RUN 10-25
SJAB Anquan Boldin/15 12.00 30.00
SJAP Adrian Peterson/15 125.00 200.00
SJBJ Brandon Jacobs/25 12.00 30.00
SJBM Brandon Marshall/15 12.00 30.00
SJCJ Chris Johnson/15 40.00 80.00
SJDC Dallas Clark/25 15.00 40.00
SJDW DeMarcus Ware/25 15.00 40.00
SJFG Frank Gore/15 12.00 30.00
SJJA Jared Allen/25 40.00 80.00
SJKS Kevin Smith/15 12.00 30.00
SJKW Kurt Warner/15 50.00 100.00
SJLB Lance Briggs/15 25.00 50.00
SJLE Lee Evans/15 12.00 30.00
SJMF Matt Forte/25 15.00 40.00
SJMR Matt Ryan/15 50.00 100.00
SJPM Peyton Manning/15 100.00 175.00
SJPW Patrick Willis/15 25.00 50.00
SJRB Ronnie Brown/15 15.00 40.00
SJRL Ray Lewis/15 90.00 150.00
SJSS Steve Slaton/15 12.00 30.00

2009 Ultimate Collection Ultimate Six Jerseys

STATED PRINT RUN 50-99
*GOLD/25: .5X TO 1.2X BASIC SIX JSY
*PATCH/20: .6X TO 1.5X BASIC SIX JSY
1 Kurt Warner 15.00 40.00
Eli Manning
Peyton Manning
Drew Brees
Donovan McNabb
Tom Brady
2 Maurice Jones-Drew 15.00 40.00
LaDainian Tomlinson
Brian Westbrook
Michael Turner
Adrian Peterson
Clinton Portis
3 Calvin Johnson/99 10.00 25.00
Larry Fitzgerald
Reggie Wayne
Greg Jennings
Randy Moss
Andre Johnson
4 Tom Brady 12.00 30.00
Philip Rivers
Tony Romo
Ben Roethlisberger
Peyton Manning
Kurt Warner
5 Brian Urlacher 15.00 40.00
Albert Haynesworth
Jared Allen
Lofa Tatupu
Ray Lewis
Mario Williams
6 Peyton Manning/99 20.00 50.00
Dallas Clark
Marques Colston
Reggie Bush
Drew Brees
Reggie Wayne
7 Ben Roethlisberger 12.00 30.00
Santonio Holmes
Willie Parker
Kurt Warner
Larry Fitzgerald
Anquan Boldin
8 Matt Forte/99 10.00 25.00
Darren McFadden
Kevin Smith
Steve Slaton
Chris Johnson
Felix Jones
9 Marion Barber 12.00 30.00
Tony Romo
Drew Brees
Reggie Bush
Michael Turner
Matt Ryan
10 Matt Forte/99 15.00 40.00
Devin Hester
Brian Urlacher
A.J. Hawk
Greg Jennings
Aaron Rodgers
11 Tony Romo/99 12.00 30.00
Jay Cutler
Eli Manning
Matt Ryan
Donovan McNabb
Peyton Manning
12 Brian Westbrook/99 15.00 40.00
Adrian Peterson
Matt Forte
Marshawn Lynch
Chris Johnson
Steve Slaton
13 Tom Brady/99 15.00 40.00
Randy Moss
Wes Welker
Peyton Manning
Dallas Clark
Reggie Wayne
14 Darren McFadden/99 10.00 25.00
JaMarcus Russell
Darrius Heyward-Bey
Philip Rivers
Antonio Gates
LaDainian Tomlinson
15 Tony Romo 12.00 30.00
Marion Barber
Eli Manning
Brandon Jacobs
Brian Westbrook
Donovan McNabb
16 Michael Turner 15.00 40.00
Adrian Peterson
Reggie Bush
Matt Forte
Steve Slaton
DeAngelo Williams
17 Andre Johnson 10.00 25.00
Randy Moss
Brandon Marshall
Dwayne Bowe
Larry Fitzgerald
Anquan Boldin
18 Joseph Addai/99 10.00 25.00
Willie Parker
Maurice Jones-Drew
Ronnie Brown
Chris Johnson
LaDainian Tomlinson
19 Antonio Gates 10.00 25.00
Jason Witten
Heath Miller
Dallas Clark
Jeremy Shockey
Chris Cooley
20 Jason Campbell 12.00 30.00
Trent Edwards
Carson Palmer
Aaron Rodgers
Matt Schaub
Chad Pennington
21 Jason Witten 15.00 40.00
Marion Barber
Tony Romo
Hakeem Nicks
Brandon Jacobs
Eli Manning
22 Brandon Jacobs 10.00 25.00
Matt Forte
Clinton Portis
Frank Gore
Ryan Grant
Steve Slaton
23 Andre Johnson 10.00 25.00
Ed Reed
Ray Lewis
Reggie Wayne
Clinton Portis
Devin Hester
24 Carson Palmer 12.00 30.00
Ben Roethlisberger
Brady Quinn
Joe Flacco
Chad Pennington
David Garrard
25 Tom Brady/99 20.00 50.00
Joe Flacco
Matt Ryan
Mark Sanchez
Peyton Manning
Matthew Stafford
26 Albert Haynesworth 8.00 20.00
Aaron Curry
DeMarcus Ware
Jerod Mayo
Tyson Jackson
Mario Williams
27 Chris Johnson 15.00 40.00
DeAngelo Williams
Ronnie Brown
Adrian Peterson
Michael Turner
Reggie Bush
28 Hakeem Nicks 10.00 25.00
Steve Smith
Ramses Barden
Brandon Jacobs
Rhett Bomar
Eli Manning
29 Ramses Barden 10.00 25.00
Steve Smith
Hakeem Nicks
Mohamed Massaquoi
Brian Robiskie
Braylon Edwards
30 Peyton Manning/99 15.00 40.00
Joseph Addai
Dallas Clark
Antonio Gates
Philip Rivers
LaDainian Tomlinson

2012 Ultimate Collection

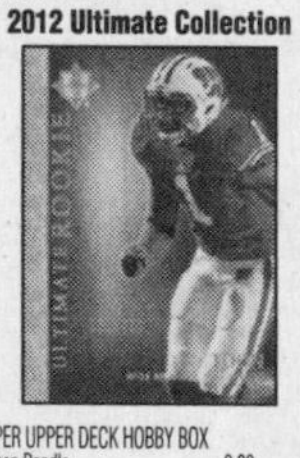

TWO PER UPPER DECK HOBBY BOX
1 Rueben Randle 2.00 5.00
2 Alfonzo Dennard 2.00 5.00
3 Alshon Jeffery 3.00 8.00
4 Brock Osweiler 2.50 6.00
5 B.J. Cunningham 1.50 4.00
6 Brandon Bolden 2.00 5.00
7 Brandon Thompson 1.50 4.00
8 Brandon Weeden 4.00 10.00
9 Brian Quick 2.50 6.00
10 Case Keenum 2.50 6.00
11 Chandler Harnish 2.00 5.00
12 Stephen Hill 2.00 5.00
13 Dwayne Allen 2.00 5.00
14 Courtney Upshaw 2.50 6.00
15 Cyrus Gray 2.00 5.00
16 Dan Herron 2.00 5.00
17 Davin Meggett 1.50 4.00
18 DeVier Posey 2.00 5.00
19 Doug Martin 3.00 8.00
20 Dwight Jones 1.50 4.00
21 Fozzy Whittaker 2.00 5.00
22 Gerell Robinson 2.00 5.00
23 Isaiah Pead 2.00 5.00
24 Dre Kirkpatrick 3.00 8.00
25 Jarius Wright 2.00 5.00
26 Jarrett Boykin 2.00 5.00
27 Bernard Pierce 2.00 5.00
28 Jeff Fuller 2.50 6.00
29 Jermaine Kearse 2.00 5.00
30 Joe Adams 2.00 5.00
31 Juron Criner 1.50 4.00
32 Justin Blackmon 4.00 10.00
33 Kellen Moore 3.00 8.00
34 Kendall Wright 2.50 6.00
35 Keshawn Martin 2.00 5.00
36 Kirk Cousins 3.00 8.00
37 LaMichael James 4.00 10.00
38 Chris Givens 1.50 4.00
39 Marc Tyler 2.00 5.00
40 Marquis Maze 2.00 5.00
41 Marvin McNutt 2.00 5.00
42 Ronnie Hillman 2.50 6.00
43 Melvin Ingram 2.50 6.00
44 Michael Egnew 1.50 4.00
45 Michael Floyd 4.00 10.00
46 Mohamed Sanu 2.00 5.00
47 Luke Kuechly 2.50 6.00
48 Nick Foles 3.00 8.00
49 Nick Toon 2.50 6.00
50 Quinton Coples 2.00 5.00
51 Rishard Matthews 2.00 5.00
52 Robert Griffin III 25.00 50.00
53 Russell Wilson 5.00 12.00
54 Ryan Broyles 2.00 5.00
55 Ryan Lindley 2.00 5.00
56 Ryan Tannehill 5.00 12.00
57 Tauren Poole 1.50 4.00
58 Tommy Streeter 2.00 5.00
59 Trent Richardson 10.00 20.00
60 T.J. Graham 2.00 5.00

2012 Ultimate Collection Rookie Autographs

2 Brandon Weeden 50.00 100.00
3 Robert Griffin III 400.00 600.00
6 Dan Herron 10.00 25.00
7 Doug Martin 20.00 40.00
8 Dwight Jones 8.00 20.00
9 Isaiah Pead 10.00 25.00
11 Jeff Fuller 12.00 30.00
12 Juron Criner 10.00 25.00
13 Kellen Moore 25.00 50.00
14 Kirk Cousins 25.00 50.00
15 Michael Floyd 60.00 120.00
16 Nick Foles 20.00 40.00
17 Nick Toon 15.00 30.00
18 Quinton Coples 10.00 25.00
19 Ryan Broyles 15.00 40.00
21 Ryan Tannehill 50.00 100.00

1991-92 Ultimate Promo Panel

1 Dmitri Starostenko 1.25 3.00
Popeye
Betty Boop
Bobby Hull
Larry Johnson BK
Pat Falloon
Stan Gelbaugh WLAF

2000 Ultimate Victory

Released as a 150-card set, Ultimate Victory features 90 veteran player cards and 60 rookie cards serial numbered to 2000. Base cards are all foil and have red foil highlights. Ultimate Victory was packaged in 24-pack boxes with five cards per pack and carried a suggested retail price of $2.99.

COMPLETE SET (150) 175.00 300.00
COMP.SET w/o SP's (90) 6.00 15.00
91-150 ROOKIE PRINT RUN 2000
1 Jake Plummer .15 .40
2 David Boston .12 .30
3 Frank Sanders .12 .30
4 Chris Chandler .15 .40
5 Jamal Anderson .15 .40
6 Shawn Jefferson .12 .30
7 Qadry Ismail .15 .40
8 Tony Banks .12 .30
9 Shannon Sharpe .20 .50
10 Peerless Price .15 .40
11 Rob Johnson .15 .40
12 Eric Moulds .15 .40
13 Muhsin Muhammad .15 .40
14 Steve Beuerlein .15 .40
15 Tim Biakabutuka .15 .40
16 Cade McNown .12 .30
17 Curtis Enis .12 .30
18 Marcus Robinson .15 .40
19 Akili Smith .12 .30
20 Corey Dillon .15 .40
21 Darnay Scott .15 .40
22 Tim Couch .15 .40
23 Kevin Johnson .12 .30
24 Errict Rhett .15 .40
25 Troy Aikman .30 .75
26 Emmitt Smith .50 1.25
27 Rocket Ismail .15 .40
28 Joey Galloway .15 .40
29 Terrell Davis .20 .50
30 Olandis Gary .15 .40
31 Ed McCaffrey .15 .40
32 Charlie Batch .15 .40
33 Germane Crowell .12 .30
34 James Stewart .12 .30
35 Brett Favre .60 1.50
36 Antonio Freeman .15 .40
37 Dorsey Levens .15 .40
38 Peyton Manning .50 1.25
39 Edgerrin James .20 .50
40 Marvin Harrison .20 .50
41 Mark Brunell .15 .40
42 Fred Taylor .20 .50
43 Jimmy Smith .15 .40
44 Elvis Grbac .12 .30
45 Tony Gonzalez .20 .50
46 Derrick Alexander .12 .30
47 Tony Martin .15 .40
48 Damon Huard .15 .40
49 O.J. McDuffie .15 .40
50 Randy Moss .20 .50
51 Robert Smith .15 .40
52 Daunte Culpepper .15 .40
53 Drew Bledsoe .20 .50
54 Terry Glenn .15 .40
55 Ricky Williams .20 .50
56 Jake Reed .15 .40
57 Jeff Blake .15 .40
58 Kerry Collins .15 .40
59 Amani Toomer .15 .40
60 Ike Hilliard .15 .40
61 Ray Lucas .12 .30
62 Curtis Martin .20 .50
63 Vinny Testaverde .15 .40
64 Tim Brown .20 .50
65 Rich Gannon .15 .40
66 Tyrone Wheatley .12 .30
67 Duce Staley .15 .40
68 Donovan McNabb .20 .50
69 Troy Edwards .12 .30
70 Jerome Bettis .20 .50
71 Marshall Faulk .20 .50
72 Kurt Warner .30 .75
73 Isaac Bruce .20 .50
74 Curtis Conway .15 .40
75 Freddie Jones .12 .30
76 Jeff Graham .12 .30
77 Jeff Garcia .15 .40
78 Jerry Rice .40 1.00
79 Ricky Watters .15 .40
80 Jon Kitna .15 .40
81 Derrick Mayes .12 .30
82 Keyshawn Johnson .15 .40
83 Shaun King .12 .30
84 Mike Alstott .20 .50
85 Eddie George .15 .40
86 Steve McNair .20 .50
87 Jevon Kearse .15 .40
88 Brad Johnson .15 .40
89 Stephen Davis .15 .40
90 Michael Westbrook .12 .30
91 Anthony Becht RC 1.25 3.00
92 Anthony Lucas RC 1.00 2.50
93 Bashir Yamini RC 1.00 2.50
94 Brian Urlacher RC 6.00 15.00
95 Chad Morton RC 1.50 4.00
96 Chad Pennington RC 2.50 6.00
97 Chris Cole RC 1.25 3.00
98 Chris Hovan RC 1.25 3.00
99 Tim Rattay RC 1.25 3.00
100 Chris Redman RC 1.25 3.00
101 Chris Samuels RC 1.25 3.00
102 Corey Simon RC 1.25 3.00
103 Courtney Brown RC 1.25 3.00
104 Curtis Keaton RC 1.00 2.50
105 Danny Farmer RC 1.00 2.50
106 Erron Kinney RC 1.00 2.50
107 Darren Howard RC 1.00 2.50
108 Deltha O'Neal RC 1.25 3.00
109 Dennis Northcutt RC 1.25 3.00
110 Demario Brown RC 1.00 2.50
111 Dez White RC 1.25 3.00
112 Frank Murphy RC 1.00 2.50
113 Gari Scott RC 1.00 2.50
114 Giovanni Carmazzi RC 1.00 2.50
115 J.R. Redmond RC 1.00 2.50
116 JaJuan Dawson RC 1.00 2.50
117 Jamal Lewis RC 1.50 4.00
118 Leon Murray RC 1.00 2.50
119 Jerry Porter RC 1.50 4.00
120 Joe Hamilton RC 1.00 2.50
121 John Abraham RC 1.50 4.00
122 John Engelberger RC 1.00 2.50
123 Keith Bulluck RC 1.25 3.00
124 Kwame Cavil RC 1,00 2.50
125 Laveranues Coles RC 1.50 4.00
126 Marc Bulger RC 1.50 4.00
127 Marcus Knight RC 1.00 2.50
128 Mareno Philyaw RC 1.00 2.50
129 Michael Wiley RC 1.00 2.50
130 Na'il Diggs RC 1.00 2.50
131 Peter Warrick RC 1.50 4.00
132 Plaxico Burress RC 1.50 4.00
133 Raynoch Thompson RC 1.00 2.50
134 Reuben Droughns RC 1.50 4.00
135 Rob Morris RC 1.25 3.00
136 Ron Dayne RC 1.50 4.00
137 Ron Dugans RC 1.00 2.50
138 Sebastian Janikowski RC 1.50 4.00
139 Shaun Alexander RC 2.00 5.00
140 Sherrod Gideon RC 1.00 2.50
141 Sylvester Morris RC 1.00 2.50
142 Tee Martin RC 1.50 4.00
143 Thomas Jones RC 2.00 5.00
144 Todd Husak RC 1.00 2.50
145 Todd Pinkston RC 1.00 2.50
146 Tom Brady RC 50.00 100.00
147 Travis Prentice RC 1.25 3.00
148 Travis Taylor RC 1.25 3.00
149 Trevor Gaylor RC 1.00 2.50
150 Trung Canidate RC 1.25 3.00

2000 Ultimate Victory Parallel

*VETS 1-90: 3X TO 8X BASIC CARDS
1-90 VETERAN ODDS 1:11
*ROOKIES 91-150: .4X TO 1X
91-150 ROOKIE ODDS 1:23

2000 Ultimate Victory Parallel 100

*VETS 1-90: 8X TO 20X BASIC CARDS
*ROOKIES 91-150: 1X TO 2.5X
STATED PRINT RUN 100 SER.#'d SETS
146 Tom Brady 150.00 250.00

2000 Ultimate Victory Parallel 25

*VETS 1-90: 20X TO 50X BASIC CARDS
*ROOKIES 91-150: 2.5X TO 6X
STATED PRINT RUN 25 SER.#'d SETS
146 Tom Brady 500.00 800.00

2000 Ultimate Victory Battle Ground

COMPLETE SET (10) 7.50 20.00
STATED ODDS 1:11
BG1 Eddie George .50 1.25
BG2 Edgerrin James .60 1.50
BG3 Terrell Davis .60 1.50
BG4 Jamal Anderson .50 1.25
BG5 Ricky Williams .60 1.50
BG6 Thomas Jones .75 2.00
BG7 Jamal Lewis .60 1.50
BG8 Ron Dayne .60 1.50
BG9 Shaun Alexander .75 2.00
BG10 Trung Canidate .50 1.25

2000 Ultimate Victory Competitors

COMPLETE SET (10) 6.00 15.00
STATED ODDS 1:11
UC1 Randy Moss 1.00 2.50
UC2 Peyton Manning 2.50 6.00
UC3 Stephen Davis .75 2.00
UC4 Cris Carter 1.00 2.50
UC5 Jevon Kearse .75 2.00
UC6 Peter Warrick 1.00 2.50
UC7 Plaxico Burress 1.00 2.50
UC8 Travis Taylor .75 2.00
UC9 Sylvester Morris .60 1.50
UC10 R.Jay Soward .60 1.50

2000 Ultimate Victory Crowning Glory

COMPLETE SET (10) 10.00 25.00
STATED ODDS 1:23
CG1 Peyton Manning 2.50 6.00
CG2 Edgerrin James 1.00 2.50
CG3 Randy Moss 1.00 2.50
CG4 Tim Couch .75 2.00
CG5 Eddie George .75 2.00
CG6 Terrell Davis 1.00 2.50
CG7 Marcus Robinson .75 2.00
CG8 Marvin Harrison 1.00 2.50
CG9 Charlie Batch .75 2.00
CG10 Shaun King .60 1.50

2000 Ultimate Victory Fabrics

SINGLE JERSEY ODDS 1:239
AZ Az-Zahir Hakim 6.00 15.00
IB Isaac Bruce 10.00 25.00
KC Kevin Carter 6.00 15.00
KW Kurt Warner 15.00 40.00
MF Marshall Faulk 10.00 25.00
TH Torry Holt 10.00 25.00
THIB Torry Holt 25.00 60.00
Isaac Bruce/100
MFKW Marshall Faulk 50.00 120.00
Kurt Warner 50
RAMS Kurt Warner
Marshall Faulk
Isaac Bruce
Torry Holt/10

2000 Ultimate Victory Legendary Fabrics

HL Howie Long/250 20.00 50.00
JM Joe Montana/250 30.00 80.00
RL Ronnie Lott/250 20.00 50.00
HOF Ronnie Lott 50.00 120.00
Howie Long
Joe Montana/100

1992 Ultimate WLAF Promos

This set of unnumbered cards was issued to promote the 1992 Ultimate WLAF release. The cards include the basic cardfront but the cardback has an advertisement for the set and rules for their "Win $1,000,000" game.

1 Tony Baker 1.50 4.00
2 Kerwin Bell 2.00 5.00
3 Stan Gelbaugh 2.00 5.00
4 Lee Morris 1.25 3.00
5 Pete Najarian 1.25 3.00
6 Mike Norseth 1.25 3.00
7 Eric Wilkerson 1.25 3.00

1992 Ultimate WLAF

The 1992 Ultimate WLAF football set consists of 200 standard-size cards. Twelve nine-card foil packs were packaged in each coliseum display box, and each box came with a mini-poster and one hologram card. There were ten different hologram cards produced, one for each WLAF team logo. In addition, each foil pack contained a giveaway game card, and the individual who collected all five letters to spell W-O-R-L-D would win one million dollars. The cards are checklisted alphabetically according to teams. The set closes with two topical subsets: How to Play the Game (180-192) and How To Collect Cards (193-200).

COMPLETE SET (200) 4.80 12.00
1 Barcelona Dragons/'91 Team Statistics .02 .10
Thomas Woods
2 Demetrius Davis .02 .10
3 Tim Egerton .01 .05
4 Scott Erney .01 .05
6 Anthony Greene .01 .05
7 Mike Hinnant UER .01 .05
(No position on front)
8 Erik Naposki .01 .05
9 Paul Palmer .07 .20
10 Gene Taylor .01 .05
11 Thomas Woods .01 .05
12 Tony Rice .40 1.00
13 Terry O'Shea .01 .05
14 Brett Wiese .01 .05
15 Phil Alexander .01 .05
Kicking Leader
16 Eric Wilkerson .01 .05
Rushing
Scoring Leader
17 Barcelona Dragons .01 .05
Team Picture
18 Barcelona Dragons .01 .05
Checklist
19 Birmingham Fire/'91 Team Statistics .01 .05
20 Eric Jones .01 .05
21 Steven Avery .01 .05
22 Willie Bouyer .01 .05
23 Anthony Parker/'91 Interception Leader .07 .20
24 Elroy Harris .01 .05
25 James Henry .01 .05
26 John Holland .02 .10
27 Mark Hopkins .01 .05
28 Arthur Hunter .01 .05
29 Danny Lockett/'91 Sacking Leader .01 .05
30 Kirk Maggio .01 .05
31 John Miller .01 .05
32 Ricky Shaw .01 .05
33 Phil Ross .01 .05
34 Mike Norseth .01 .05
35 Birmingham Fire .01 .05
Checklist
36 Frankfurt Galaxy/'91 Team Statistics .01 .05
37 Anthony Wallace .01 .05
38 Lew Barnes .01 .05
39 Richard Buchanan .01 .05
40 Yepi Pau'u .01 .05
41 Pat McGuirk UER .01 .05
(Played for Raleigh-Durham in 1991)
42 Tony Baker .20 .50
43 1992 TV Schedule 1 .01 .05
44 Tim Broady .01 .05
45 Lonnie Finch .01 .05
46 Chad Fortune .01 .05
47 Harry Jackson .01 .05
48 Jason Johnson .01 .05
49 Pat Moorer .01 .05
50 Mike Perez .02 .10
51 Mark Seals .01 .05
52 Cedric Stallworth .01 .05
53 Tom Whelihan .01 .05
54 Joe Johnson .10 .30
55 Frankfurt Galaxy .01 .05
Checklist
56 London Monarchs/'91 Team Statistics .02 .10
Stan Gelbaugh
57 Stan Gelbaugh .02 .10
58 Jeff Alexander .01 .05
59 Dana Brinson .01 .05
60 Marlon Brown .01 .05
61 Dedrick Dodge .01 .05
62 Judd Garrett .02 .10
63 Greg Horne .01 .05
64 Jon Horton .01 .05
65 Danny Lockett .01 .05
66 Andre Riley .01 .05
67 Charlie Young .01 .05
68 David Smith .01 .05
69 Irvin Smith .01 .05
70 Rickey Williams .01 .05
71 Roland Smith .01 .05
72 William Kirksey .01 .05
73 Phil Alexander .01 .05
74 London Monarchs .02 .10
Team Picture
75 London Monarchs .01 .05
Checklist
76 Montreal Machine/'91 Team Statistics .01 .05
77 Rollin Putzier .01 .05
78 Adam Bob .01 .05
79 K.D. Dunn .01 .05
80 Darryl Holmes .01 .05
81 Ricky Johnson .01 .05
82 Michael Finn .01 .05
83 Chris Mohr .02 .10
84 Don Murray .01 .05
85 Bjorn Nittmo .01 .05
86 Michael Proctor .01 .05
87 Broderick Sargent .01 .05
88 Richard Shelton .01 .05
89 Emanuel King .02 .10
90 Pete Mandley .02 .10
91 Kris McCall .01 .05
92 1992 TV Schedule 2 .01 .05
93 Montreal Machine .01 .05
Checklist
94 NY .01 .05
NJ Knights/'91 Team Statistics
95 Andre Alexander .01 .05
96 Pat Marlatt .01 .05
97 Cecil Fletcher .01 .05
98 Lonnie Turner .01 .05
99 Monty Gilbreath .01 .05
100 Tony Jones UER .01 .05
(Should be DB, not WR)
101 Kip Lewis .01 .05
102 Bobby Lilljedahl .01 .05
103 Mark Moore .01 .05
104 Falanda Newton .01 .05
105 Anthony Parker UER .07 .20
(Played for Chiefs in/1991, not Bears; was released by the Bears)
106 Kendall Trainor .01 .05
107 Eric Wilkerson .01 .05
108 Tony Woods .07 .20
109 Reggie Slack .01 .05
110 Joey Banes .01 .05
111 Ron Sancho .01 .05
112 Mike Husar .01 .05
113 NY .01 .05
NJ Knights
Checklist
114 Orlando Thunder/'91 Team Statistics .01 .05
115 Byron Williams UER .01 .05
(Waived by Orlando and picked up by NY-NJ)
116 Charlie Baumann .02 .10
117 Kerwin Bell .02 .10
118 Rodney Lossow .01 .05
119 Myron Jones .01 .05
120 Bruce Lasane .01 .05
121 Eric Mitchel .01 .05
122 Billy Owens .01 .05
123 1992 TV Schedule 3 .01 .05
124 Chris Roscoe .01 .05
125 Tommie Stowers .01 .05
126 Wayne Dickson UER .01 .05
(Not a rookie& he played for Orlando in 1991)
127 Scott Mitchell .50 1.25
128 Karl Dunbar .01 .05
129 Dana Brinson/'91 Punt Return Leader .01 .05
130 Orlando Thunder .01 .05
Checklist
131 Sacramento Surge .01 .05
Team Statistics
132 1992 TV Schedule 4 .01 .05
133 Mike Adams .01 .05
134 Greg Coauette .01 .05
135 Mel Farr Jr. .02 .10
(Should be TE; not FB)
136 Victor Floyd .01 .05
137 Paul Frazier .01 .05
138 Tom Gerhart .01 .05
139 Pete Najarian .01 .05
140 John Nies .01 .05
141 Carl Parker .01 .05
142 Saute Sapolu .01 .05
143 George Bethune .01 .05
144 David Archer .50 1.25
145 John Buddenberg .01 .05
146 Jon Horton UER .01 .05
(Incorrect stats on back)/'91 Receiving Yardage Leader
147 Sacramento Surge .01 .05
Checklist
148 San Antonio Riders/'91 Team Statistics .01 .05
149 Ricky Blake .02 .10
150 Jim Gallery .01 .05
151 Jason Garrett 1.25 3.00
152 John Garrett .01 .05
153 Broderick Graves .01 .05
154 Bill Hess .01 .05
155 Mike Johnson .02 .10
156 Lee Morris .01 .05
157 Dwight Pickens .01 .05
158 Kent Sullivan .01 .05
159 Ken Watson .01 .05
160 Ronnie Williams .01 .05
161 Titus Dixon .01 .05
162 Mike Kiselak .01 .05
163 Greg Lee .01 .05
164 Judd Garrett UER/'91 Receiving Leader .02 .10
(Had 71 receptions in/1991, not 18; game high was 12, not 13)
165 San Antonio Riders .01 .05
Checklist
166 Tenth Week Summaries .01 .05
167 Randy Bethel .01 .05
168 Melvin Patterson .01 .05
169 Eric Harmon .01 .05
170 Patrick Jackson .01 .05
171 Tim James .01 .05
172 George Koonce .07 .20
173 Babe Laufenberg .07 .20
174 Amir Rasul .01 .05
175 Stan Gelbaugh/'91 Passing Leader .08 .25
176 Jason Wallace .01 .05
177 Walter Wilson .01 .05
178 Power Meter Info .02 .10
179 Ohio Glory Checklist .01 .05
180 The Football Field .30 .75
Jim Kelly
181 Moving the Ball .30 .75
Jim Kelly

182 Defense	.10	.30
Back Field		
Cornerbacks and Safeties		
Lawrence Taylor		
183 Defense	.10	.30
Linebackers		
Lawrence Taylor		
184 Defense	.10	.30
Defensive Line		
Defensive Tackles		
and Ends		
Lawrence Taylor		
185 Offense	.30	.75
Offensive Line		
Centers, Guards,		
Tackles and Tight Ends		
Jim Kelly		
186 Offense	.10	.30
Receivers		
Lawrence Taylor		
187 Offense	.30	.75
Running Backs		
Jim Kelly		
188 Offensive	.30	.75
Quarterback		
Jim Kelly		
189 Special Teams	.01	.05
190 Rules and Regulations	.01	.05
WL Rules that differ		
from NFL 1990 Rules		
191 Defensive Overview	.01	.05
Scoring Touchdowns		
and Extra Points		
192 Offensive Overview	.01	.05
Scoring, Field Goals		
and Safeties		
193 How to Collect	.10	.30
What is a Set		
Lawrence Taylor		
194 How to Collect	.10	.30
What is a Wax Pack		
Lawrence Taylor		
195 How to Collect	.10	.30
Premier Editions		
Lawrence Taylor		
196 How to Collect	.10	.30
What Creates Value		
Lawrence Taylor		
197 How to Collect	.30	.75
Rookie Cards		
Jim Kelly		
198 How to Collect	.30	.75
Grading Your Cards		
Jim Kelly		
199 How to Collect	.30	.75
Storing Your Cards		
Jim Kelly		
200 How to Collect	.30	.75
Trading Your Cards		
Jim Kelly		

1992 Ultimate WLAF Logo Holograms

COMPLETE SET (10)	2.40	6.00
1 Barcelona Dragons	.30	.75
2 Birmingham Fire	.30	.75
3 Frankfurt Galaxy	.30	.75
4 London Monarchs	.30	.75
5 Montreal Machine	.30	.75
6 NY	.30	.75
NJ Knights		
7 Ohio Glory	.30	.75
8 Orlando Thunder	.30	.75
9 Sacramento Surge	.30	.75
10 San Antonio Riders	.30	.75

1991 Ultra

The 1991 Ultra football set contains 300 standard-size cards. Cards were issued in 14-card packs. The cards are alphabetically within and according to teams. The last subset included in this set was Rookie Prospects (279-298). Rookie Cards in this set include Mike Croel, Brett Favre, Randal Hill, Russell Maryland, Herman Moore, Mike Pritchard and Ricky Watters.

COMPLETE SET (300)	7.50	20.00
1 Don Beebe	.01	.05
2 Shane Conlan	.01	.05
3 Pete Metzelaars	.01	.05
4 Jamie Mueller	.01	.05
5 Scott Norwood	.01	.05
6 Andre Reed	.02	.10
7 Leon Seals	.01	.05
8 Bruce Smith	.08	.25
9 Leonard Smith	.01	.05
10 Thurman Thomas	.08	.25
11 Lewis Billups	.01	.05
12 Jim Breech	.01	.05
13 James Brooks	.02	.10
14 Eddie Brown	.01	.05
15 Boomer Esiason	.02	.10
16 David Fulcher	.01	.05
17 Rodney Holman	.01	.05
18 Bruce Kozerski	.01	.05
19 Tim Krumrie	.01	.05
20 Tim McGee	.01	.05
21 Anthony Munoz	.02	.10
22 Leon White	.01	.05
23 Ickey Woods	.01	.05
24 Carl Zander	.01	.05
25 Brian Brennan	.01	.05
26 Thane Gash	.01	.05
27 Leroy Hoard	.02	.10
28 Mike Johnson	.01	.05
29 Reggie Langhorne	.01	.05
30 Kevin Mack	.01	.05
31 Clay Matthews	.02	.10
32 Eric Metcalf	.02	.10
33 Steve Atwater	.01	.05
34 Melvin Bratton	.01	.05
35 John Elway	.50	1.25
36 Bobby Humphrey	.01	.05
37 Mark Jackson	.01	.05
38 Vance Johnson	.01	.05
39 Ricky Nattiel	.01	.05
40 Steve Sewell	.01	.05
41 Dennis Smith	.01	.05
42 David Treadwell	.01	.05
43 Michael Young	.01	.05
44 Ray Childress	.01	.05
45 Cris Dishman RC	.01	.05
46 William Fuller	.02	.10
47 Ernest Givins	.02	.10
48 John Grimsley UER	.01	.05
(Acquired line should		
be Trade '91, not		
Draft 6-'84)		
49 Drew Hill	.01	.05
50 Haywood Jeffires	.02	.10
51 Sean Jones	.02	.10
52 Johnny Meads	.01	.05
53 Warren Moon	.08	.25
54 Al Smith	.01	.05
55 Lorenzo White	.01	.05
56 Albert Bentley	.01	.05
57 Duane Bickett	.01	.05
58 Bill Brooks	.01	.05
59 Jeff George	.08	.25
60 Mike Prior	.01	.05
61 Rohn Stark	.01	.05
62 Jack Trudeau	.01	.05
63 Clarence Verdin	.01	.05
64 Steve DeBerg	.01	.05
65 Emile Harry	.01	.05
66 Albert Lewis	.01	.05
67 Nick Lowery UER	.01	.05
(NFL Exp. has 12		
years, should be 13)		
68 Todd McNair	.01	.05
69 Christian Okoye	.01	.05
70 Stephone Paige	.01	.05
71 Kevin Porter UER	.01	.05
(Front has traded		
logo, but he has been		
a Chief all career)		
72 Derrick Thomas	.08	.25
73 Robb Thomas	.01	.05
74 Barry Word	.01	.05
75 Marcus Allen	.08	.25
76 Eddie Anderson	.01	.05
77 Tim Brown	.08	.25
78 Mervyn Fernandez	.01	.05
79 Willie Gault	.02	.10
80 Ethan Horton	.01	.05
81 Howie Long	.08	.25
82 Vance Mueller	.01	.05
83 Jay Schroeder	.01	.05
84 Steve Smith	.01	.05
85 Greg Townsend	.01	.05
86 Mark Clayton	.02	.10
87 Jim C. Jensen	.01	.05
88 Dan Marino	.50	1.25
89 Tim McKyer UER	.01	.05
(Acquired line should		
be Trade '91, not		
Trade '90)		
90 John Offerdahl	.01	.05
91 Louis Oliver	.01	.05
92 Reggie Roby	.01	.05
93 Sammie Smith	.01	.05
94 Hart Lee Dykes	.01	.05
95 Irving Fryar	.02	.10
96 Tommy Hodson	.01	.05
97 Maurice Hurst	.01	.05
98 John Stephens	.01	.05
99 Andre Tippett	.01	.05
100 Mark Boyer	.01	.05
101 Kyle Clifton	.01	.05
102 James Hasty	.01	.05
103 Erik McMillan	.01	.05
104 Rob Moore	.08	.25
105 Joe Mott	.01	.05
106 Ken O'Brien	.01	.05
107 Ron Stallworth UER	.01	.05
(Acquired line should		
be Trade '91, not		
Draft 4-'89)		
108 Al Toon	.02	.10
109 Gary Anderson K	.01	.05
110 Bubby Brister	.01	.05
111 Thomas Everett	.01	.05
112 Merril Hoge	.01	.05
113 Louis Lipps	.01	.05
114 Greg Lloyd	.08	.25
115 Hardy Nickerson	.02	.10
116 Dwight Stone	.01	.05
117 Rod Woodson	.08	.25
118 Tim Worley	.01	.05
119 Rod Bernstine	.01	.05
120 Marion Butts	.02	.10
121 Gill Byrd	.01	.05
122 Arthur Cox	.01	.05
123 Burt Grossman	.01	.05
124 Ronnie Harmon	.01	.05
125 Anthony Miller	.02	.10
126 Leslie O'Neal	.02	.10
127 Gary Plummer	.01	.05
128 Sam Seale	.01	.05
129 Junior Seau	.08	.25
130 Broderick Thompson	.01	.05
131 Billy Joe Tolliver	.01	.05
132 Brian Blades	.02	.10
133 Jeff Bryant	.01	.05
134 Derrick Fenner	.01	.05
135 Jacob Green	.01	.05
136 Andy Heck	.01	.05
137 Patrick Hunter RC UER	.01	.05
(Photos on back		
show 23 and 27)		
138 Norm Johnson	.01	.05
139 Tommy Kane	.01	.05
140 Dave Krieg	.02	.10
141 John L. Williams	.01	.05
142 Terry Wooden	.01	.05
143 Steve Broussard	.01	.05
144 Keith Jones	.01	.05
145 Brian Jordan	.02	.10
146 Chris Miller	.02	.10
147 John Rade	.01	.05
148 Andre Rison	.02	.10
149 Mike Rozier	.01	.05
150 Deion Sanders	.15	.40
151 Neal Anderson	.02	.10
152 Trace Armstrong	.01	.05
153 Kevin Butler	.01	.05
154 Mark Carrier DB	.02	.10
155 Richard Dent	.02	.10
156 Dennis Gentry	.01	.05
157 Jim Harbaugh	.08	.25
158 Brad Muster	.01	.05
159 William Perry	.02	.10
160 Mike Singletary	.02	.10
161 Lemuel Stinson	.01	.05
162 Troy Aikman	.30	.75
163 Michael Irvin	.08	.25
164 Mike Saxon	.01	.05
165 Emmitt Smith	1.00	2.50
166 Jerry Ball	.01	.05
167 Michael Cofer	.01	.05
168 Rodney Peete	.02	.10
169 Barry Sanders	.50	1.25
170 Robert Brown	.01	.05
171 Anthony Dilweg	.01	.05
172 Tim Harris	.01	.05
173 Johnny Holland	.01	.05
174 Perry Kemp	.01	.05
175 Don Majkowski	.01	.05
176 Brian Noble	.01	.05
177 Jeff Query	.01	.05
178 Sterling Sharpe	.08	.25
179 Charles Wilson	.01	.05
180 Keith Woodside	.01	.05
181 Flipper Anderson UER	.01	.05
(Back photo not him)		
182 Bern Brostek	.01	.05
183 Pat Carter RC	.01	.05
184 Aaron Cox	.01	.05
185 Henry Ellard	.02	.10
186 Jim Everett	.02	.10
187 Cleveland Gary	.01	.05
188 Jerry Gray	.01	.05
189 Kevin Greene	.02	.10
190 Mike Wilcher	.01	.05
191 Alfred Anderson	.01	.05
192 Joey Browner	.01	.05
193 Anthony Carter	.02	.10
194 Chris Doleman	.01	.05
195 Rick Fenney	.01	.05
196 Darrell Fullington	.01	.05
197 Rich Gannon	.08	.25
198 Hassan Jones	.01	.05
199 Steve Jordan	.01	.05
200 Mike Merriweather	.01	.05
201 Al Noga	.01	.05
202 Herschel Walker	.02	.10
203 Wade Wilson	.02	.10
204 Morten Andersen	.01	.05
205 Gene Atkins	.01	.05
206 Toi Cook RC	.01	.05
207 Craig Heyward	.02	.10
208 Dalton Hilliard	.01	.05
209 Vaughan Johnson	.01	.05
210 Eric Martin	.01	.05
211 Brett Perriman	.08	.25
212 Pat Swilling	.02	.10
213 Steve Walsh	.01	.05
214 Ottis Anderson	.02	.10
215 Carl Banks	.01	.05
216 Maurice Carthon	.01	.05
217 Mark Collins	.01	.05
218 Rodney Hampton	.08	.25
219 Erik Howard	.01	.05
220 Mark Ingram	.02	.10
221 Pepper Johnson	.01	.05
222 Dave Meggett	.02	.10
223 Phil Simms	.02	.10
224 Lawrence Taylor	.08	.25
225 Lewis Tillman	.01	.05
226 Everson Walls	.01	.05
227 Fred Barnett	.08	.25
228 Jerome Brown	.01	.05
229 Keith Byars	.01	.05
230 Randall Cunningham	.08	.25
231 Byron Evans	.01	.05
232 Wes Hopkins	.01	.05
233 Keith Jackson	.02	.10
234 Heath Sherman	.01	.05
235 Anthony Toney	.01	.05
236 Reggie White	.08	.25
237 Rich Camarillo	.01	.05
238 Ken Harvey	.02	.10
239 Eric Hill	.01	.05
240 Johnny Johnson	.01	.05
241 Ernie Jones	.01	.05
242 Tim McDonald	.01	.05
243 Timm Rosenbach	.01	.05
244 Jay Taylor RC	.01	.05
245 Dexter Carter	.01	.05
246 Mike Cofer	.01	.05
247 Kevin Fagan	.01	.05
248 Don Griffin	.01	.05
249 Charles Haley	.02	.10
250 Brent Jones	.08	.25
251 Joe Montana UER	.50	1.25
(Born: Monongahela,		
not New Eagle)		
252 Darryl Pollard	.01	.05
253 Tom Rathman	.01	.05
254 Jerry Rice	.30	.75
255 John Taylor	.02	.10
256 Steve Young	.30	.75
257 Gary Anderson RB	.01	.05
258 Mark Carrier WR	.08	.25
259 Chris Chandler	.08	.25
260 Reggie Cobb	.01	.05
261 Reuben Davis	.01	.05
262 Willie Drewrey	.01	.05
263 Ron Hall	.01	.05
264 Eugene Marve	.01	.05
265 Winston Moss UER	.01	.05
(Acquired line should		
be Trade '91, not		
Draft 2-'87)		
266 Vinny Testaverde	.02	.10
267 Broderick Thomas	.01	.05
268 Jeff Bostic	.01	.05
269 Earnest Byner	.01	.05
270 Gary Clark	.08	.25
271 Darrell Green	.01	.05
272 Jim Lachey	.01	.05
273 Wilber Marshall	.01	.05
274 Art Monk	.02	.10
275 Gerald Riggs	.01	.05
276 Mark Rypien	.02	.10
277 Ricky Sanders	.01	.05
278 Alvin Walton	.01	.05
279 Nick Bell RC	.01	.05
280 Eric Bieniemy RC	.01	.05
281 Jarrod Bunch RC	.01	.05
282 Mike Croel RC	.01	.05
283 Brett Favre RC	5.00	10.00
284 Moe Gardner RC	.01	.05
285 Pat Harlow RC	.01	.05
286 Randal Hill RC	.01	.05
287 Todd Marinovich RC	.01	.05
288 Russell Maryland RC	.08	.25
289 Dan McGwire RC	.01	.05
290 Ernie Mills RC UER	.02	.10
(Patterns misspelled		
as patteran in		
first sentence)		
291 Herman Moore RC	.08	.25
292 Godfrey Myles RC	.01	.05
293 Browning Nagle RC	.01	.05
294 Mike Pritchard RC	.08	.25
295 Esera Tuaolo RC	.01	.05
296 Mark Vander Poel RC	.01	.05
297 Ricky Watters RC UER	.60	1.50
(Photo on back act-		
ually Ray Griggs)		
298 Chris Zorich RC	.08	.25
299 Checklist Card	.02	.10
300 Checklist Card	.02	.10

1991 Ultra All-Stars

COMPLETE SET (10)	6.00	12.00
RANDOM INSERTS IN HOBBY PACKS		
1 Barry Sanders	2.50	5.00
2 Keith Jackson	.15	.40
3 Bruce Smith	.40	1.00
4 Randall Cunningham	.40	1.00
5 Dan Marino	2.50	5.00
6 Charles Haley	.15	.40
7 John L. Williams	.07	.20
8 Darrell Green	.07	.20
9 Stephone Paige	.07	.20
10 Kevin Greene	.15	.40

1991 Ultra Performances

COMPLETE SET (10)	5.00	12.00
RANDOM INSERTS IN RETAIL PACKS		
1 Emmitt Smith	5.00	10.00
2 Andre Rison	.20	.50
3 Derrick Thomas	.60	1.25
4 Joe Montana	3.00	6.00
5 Warren Moon	.60	1.25
6 Mike Singletary	.20	.50
7 Thurman Thomas	.60	1.25
8 Rod Woodson	.60	1.25
9 Jerry Rice	2.00	4.00
10 Reggie White	.60	1.25

1991 Ultra Update

This 100-card standard-size set was produced by Fleer and featured some of the leading rookies and players who switched franchises during the 1991 season. Rookie Cards include Lawrence Dawsey, Ricky Ervins, Jeff Graham, Merton Hanks, Michael Jackson, Neil O'Donnell, Stanley Richard, Leonard Russell, Jon Vaughn and Harvey Williams. The cards are numbered with a "U" prefix.

COMP.FACT.SET (100)	10.00	25.00
U1 Brett Favre	7.50	15.00
U2 Moe Gardner	.02	.10
U3 Tim McKyer	.02	.10
U4 Bruce Pickens RC	.02	.10
U5 Mike Pritchard	.15	.40
U6 Cornelius Bennett	.07	.20
U7 Phil Hansen RC	.02	.10
U8 Henry Jones RC	.07	.20
U9 Mark Kelso	.02	.10
U10 James Lofton	.07	.20
U11 Anthony Morgan RC	.02	.10
U12 Stan Thomas	.02	.10
U13 Chris Zorich	.07	.20
U14 Reggie Rembert	.02	.10
U15 Alfred Williams RC	.02	.10
U16 Michael Jackson WR RC	.15	.40
U17 Ed King RC	.02	.10
U18 Joe Morris	.02	.10
U19 Vince Newsome	.02	.10
U20 Tony Casillas	.02	.10
U21 Russell Maryland	.15	.40
U22 Jay Novacek	.15	.40
U23 Mike Croel	.02	.10
U24 Gaston Green	.02	.10
U25 Kenny Walker RC	.02	.10
U26 Melvin Jenkins RC	.02	.10
U27 Herman Moore	.15	.40
U28 Kelvin Pritchett RC	.07	.20
U29 Chris Spielman	.07	.20
U30 Vinnie Clark RC	.02	.10
U31 Allen Rice	.02	.10
U32 Vai Sikahema	.02	.10
U33 Esera Tuaolo	.02	.10
U34 Mike Dumas RC	.02	.10
U35 John Flannery RC	.02	.10
U36 Allen Pinkett	.02	.10
U37 Tim Barnett RC	.02	.10
U38 Dan Saleaumua	.02	.10
U39 Harvey Williams RC	.15	.40
U40 Nick Bell	.02	.10
U41 Roger Craig	.07	.20
U42 Ronnie Lott	.07	.20
U43 Todd Marinovich	.02	.10
U44 Robert Delpino	.02	.10
U45 Todd Lyght RC	.02	.10
U46 Robert Young RC	.07	.20
U47 Aaron Craver RC	.02	.10
U48 Mark Higgs RC	.02	.10
U49 Vestee Jackson	.02	.10
U50 Carl Lee	.02	.10
U51 Felix Wright	.02	.10
U52 Darrell Fullington	.02	.10
U53 Pat Harlow	.02	.10
U54 Eugene Lockhart	.02	.10
U55 Hugh Millen RC	.02	.10
U56 Leonard Russell RC	.15	.40
U57 Jon Vaughn RC	.02	.10
U58 Quinn Early	.07	.20
U59 Bobby Hebert	.02	.10
U60 Rickey Jackson	.02	.10
U61 Sam Mills	.07	.20
U62 Jarrod Bunch	.02	.10
U63 John Elliott	.02	.10
U64 Jeff Hostetler	.07	.20
U65 Ed McCaffrey RC	2.50	6.00
U66 Kanavis McGhee RC	.02	.10
U67 Mo Lewis RC	.07	.20
U68 Browning Nagle	.02	.10
U69 Blair Thomas	.02	.10
U70 Antone Davis RC	.02	.10
U71 Brad Goebel RC	.02	.10
U72 Jim McMahon	.07	.20
U73 Clyde Simmons	.02	.10
U74 Randal Hill UER	.07	.20
(Card number on back		
U71 instead of U74)		
U75 Eric Swann RC	.15	.40
U76 Tom Tupa	.02	.10
U77 Jeff Graham RC	.15	.40
U78 Eric Green	.02	.10
U79 Neil O'Donnell RC	.15	.40
U80 Huey Richardson RC	.02	.10
U81 Eric Bieniemy	.02	.10
U82 John Friesz	.15	.40
U83 Eric Moten RC	.02	.10
U84 Stanley Richard RC	.02	.10
U85 Todd Bowles	.02	.10
U86 Merton Hanks RC	.15	.40
U87 Tim Harris	.02	.10
U88 Pierce Holt	.02	.10
U89 Ted Washington RC	.02	.10
U90 John Kasay RC	.07	.20
U91 Dan McGwire	.02	.10
U92 Lawrence Dawsey RC	.07	.20
U93 Charles McRae RC	.02	.10
U94 Jesse Solomon	.02	.10
U95 Robert Wilson RC	.02	.10
U96 Ricky Ervins RC	.07	.20
U97 Charles Mann	.02	.10
U98 Bobby Wilson RC	.02	.10
U99 Jerry Rice	.60	1.50
Pro-Visions		
U100 Checklist 1-100	.02	.10
(Nick Bell and		
Jim McMahon)		

1992 Ultra

This 450-card standard-size set features color action player photos. Cards were issued in 14-card packs. The cards are checklisted below alphabetically according to teams. The set closes with Draft Picks (417-446). Rookie Cards include Edgar Bennett, Steve Bono, Terrell Buckley, Amp Lee, Kevin Turner and Tommy Vardell.

COMPLETE SET (450)	6.00	15.00
1 Steve Broussard	.02	.10
2 Rick Bryan	.02	.10
3 Scott Case	.02	.10
4 Darion Conner	.02	.10
5 Bill Fralic	.02	.10
6 Moe Gardner	.02	.10
7 Tim Green	.02	.10
8 Michael Haynes	.07	.20
9 Chris Hinton	.02	.10
10 Mike Kenn	.02	.10
11 Tim McKyer	.02	.10
12 Chris Miller	.07	.20
13 Eric Pegram	.07	.20
14 Mike Pritchard	.07	.20
15 Andre Rison	.07	.20
16 Jessie Tuggle	.02	.10
17 Carlton Bailey RC	.02	.10
18 Howard Ballard	.02	.10
19 Cornelius Bennett	.07	.20
20 Shane Conlan	.02	.10
21 Kenneth Davis	.02	.10
22 Kent Hull	.02	.10
23 Mark Kelso	.02	.10
24 James Lofton	.07	.20
25 Keith McKeller	.02	.10
26 Nate Odomes	.02	.10
27 Jim Ritcher	.02	.10
28 Leon Seals	.02	.10
29 Darryl Talley	.02	.10
30 Steve Tasker	.07	.20
31 Thurman Thomas	.15	.40
32 Will Wolford	.02	.10
33 Jeff Wright	.02	.10
34 Neal Anderson	.02	.10
35 Trace Armstrong	.02	.10
36 Mark Carrier DB	.02	.10
37 Wendell Davis	.02	.10
38 Richard Dent	.07	.20
39 Shaun Gayle	.02	.10
40 Jim Harbaugh	.15	.40
41 Jay Hilgenberg	.02	.10
42 Darren Lewis	.02	.10
43 Steve McMichael	.07	.20
44 Anthony Morgan	.02	.10
45 Brad Muster	.02	.10
46 William Perry	.07	.20
47 John Roper	.02	.10
48 Lemuel Stinson	.02	.10
49 Tom Waddle	.02	.10
50 Donnell Woolford	.02	.10
51 Leo Barker RC	.02	.10
52 Eddie Brown	.02	.10
53 James Francis	.02	.10
54 David Fulcher UER	.02	.10
(Photo on back actually		
Eddie Brown)		
55 David Grant	.02	.10
56 Harold Green	.02	.10
57 Rodney Holman	.02	.10
58 Lee Johnson	.02	.10
59 Tim Krumrie	.02	.10
60 Tim McGee	.02	.10
61 Alonzo Mitz RC	.02	.10
62 Anthony Munoz	.07	.20
63 Alfred Williams	.02	.10
64 Stephen Braggs	.02	.10
65 Richard Brown RC	.02	.10
66 Randy Hilliard RC	.02	.10
67 Leroy Hoard	.07	.20
68 Michael Jackson	.07	.20
69 Mike Johnson	.02	.10
70 James Jones	.02	.10
71 Tony Jones	.02	.10
72 Ed King	.02	.10
73 Kevin Mack	.02	.10
74 Clay Matthews	.07	.20
75 Eric Metcalf	.07	.20
76 Vince Newsome	.02	.10
77 Steve Beuerlein	.07	.20
78 Larry Brown DB	.02	.10
79 Tony Casillas	.02	.10
80 Alvin Harper	.07	.20
81 Issiac Holt	.02	.10
82 Ray Horton	.02	.10
83 Michael Irvin	.15	.40
84 Daryl Johnston	.15	.40
85 Kelvin Martin	.02	.10
86 Ken Norton	.07	.20
87 Jay Novacek	.07	.20
88 Emmitt Smith	1.50	3.00
89 Vinson Smith RC	.02	.10
90 Mark Stepnoski	.07	.20
91 Tony Tolbert	.02	.10
92 Alexander Wright	.02	.10
93 Steve Atwater	.02	.10
94 Tyrone Braxton	.02	.10
95 Michael Brooks	.02	.10
96 Mike Croel	.02	.10
97 John Elway	1.00	2.50
98 Simon Fletcher	.02	.10
99 Gaston Green	.02	.10
100 Mark Jackson	.02	.10
101 Keith Kartz	.02	.10
102 Greg Kragen	.02	.10
103 Greg Lewis	.02	.10
104 Karl Mecklenburg	.02	.10
105 Derek Russell	.02	.10
106 Steve Sewell	.02	.10
107 Dennis Smith	.02	.10
108 David Treadwell	.02	.10
109 Kenny Walker	.02	.10
110 Michael Young	.02	.10
111 Jerry Ball	.02	.10
112 Bennie Blades	.02	.10
113 Lomas Brown	.02	.10
114 Scott Conover RC	.02	.10
115 Ray Crockett	.02	.10
116 Mel Gray	.07	.20
117 Willie Green	.02	.10
118 Erik Kramer	.07	.20
119 Dan Owens	.02	.10
120 Rodney Peete	.07	.20
121 Brett Perriman	.15	.40
122 Barry Sanders	1.00	2.50
123 Chris Spielman	.07	.20
124 Marc Spindler	.02	.10
125 William White	.02	.10
126 Tony Bennett	.02	.10
127 Matt Brock	.02	.10
128 LeRoy Butler	.02	.10
129 Chuck Cecil	.02	.10
130 Johnny Holland	.02	.10
131 Perry Kemp	.02	.10
132 Don Majkowski	.02	.10
133 Tony Mandarich	.02	.10
134 Brian Noble	.02	.10
135 Bryce Paup	.15	.40
136 Sterling Sharpe	.15	.40
137 Darrell Thompson	.02	.10
138 Mike Tomczak	.02	.10
139 Vince Workman	.02	.10
140 Ray Childress	.02	.10
141 Cris Dishman	.02	.10
142 Curtis Duncan	.02	.10
143 William Fuller	.07	.20
144 Ernest Givins	.07	.20
145 Haywood Jeffires	.07	.20
146 Sean Jones	.02	.10
147 Lamar Lathon	.02	.10
148 Bruce Matthews	.02	.10
149 Bubba McDowell	.02	.10
150 Johnny Meads	.02	.10
151 Warren Moon	.15	.40
152 Mike Munchak	.07	.20
153 Bo Orlando RC	.02	.10
154 Al Smith	.02	.10
155 Doug Smith	.02	.10
156 Lorenzo White	.02	.10
157 Chip Banks	.02	.10
158 Duane Bickett	.02	.10
159 Bill Brooks	.02	.10
160 Eugene Daniel	.02	.10
161 Jon Hand	.02	.10
162 Jeff Herrod	.02	.10
163 Jessie Hester	.02	.10
164 Scott Radecic	.02	.10
165 Rohn Stark	.02	.10
166 Clarence Verdin	.02	.10
167 John Alt	.02	.10
168 Tim Barnett	.02	.10
169 Tim Grunhard	.02	.10
170 Dino Hackett	.02	.10
171 Jonathan Hayes	.02	.10
172 Bill Maas	.02	.10
173 Chris Martin	.02	.10
174 Christian Okoye	.02	.10
175 Stephone Paige	.02	.10
176 Jayice Pearson RC	.02	.10
177 Kevin Porter	.02	.10
178 Kevin Ross	.02	.10
179 Dan Saleaumua	.02	.10
180 Tracy Simien RC	.02	.10
181 Neil Smith	.15	.40
182 Derrick Thomas	.15	.40
183 Robb Thomas	.02	.10
184 Barry Word	.02	.10
185 Marcus Allen	.15	.40
186 Eddie Anderson	.02	.10
187 Nick Bell	.02	.10
188 Tim Brown	.15	.40
189 Mervyn Fernandez	.02	.10
190 Willie Gault	.07	.20
191 Jeff Gossett	.02	.10
192 Ethan Horton	.02	.10
193 Jeff Jaeger	.02	.10
194 Howie Long	.15	.40
195 Ronnie Lott	.07	.20
196 Todd Marinovich	.02	.10
197 Don Mosebar	.02	.10
198 Jay Schroeder	.02	.10
199 Anthony Smith	.02	.10
200 Greg Townsend	.02	.10
201 Lionel Washington	.02	.10
202 Steve Wisniewski	.02	.10
203 Flipper Anderson	.02	.10
204 Robert Delpino	.02	.10
205 Henry Ellard	.07	.20
206 Jim Everett	.07	.20
207 Kevin Greene	.07	.20
208 Darryl Henley	.02	.10
209 Damone Johnson	.02	.10
210 Larry Kelm	.02	.10
211 Todd Lyght	.02	.10
212 Jackie Slater	.02	.10
213 Michael Stewart	.02	.10
214 Pat Terrell	.02	.10
215 Robert Young	.02	.10
216 Mark Clayton	.07	.20
217 Bryan Cox	.07	.20
218 Jeff Cross	.02	.10
219 Mark Duper	.07	.20
220 Harry Galbreath	.02	.10
221 David Griggs	.02	.10
222 Mark Higgs	.02	.10
223 Vestee Jackson	.02	.10
224 John Offerdahl	.02	.10
225 Louis Oliver	.02	.10
226 Tony Paige	.02	.10
227 Reggie Roby	.02	.10
228 Pete Stoyanovich	.02	.10
229 Richmond Webb	.02	.10
230 Terry Allen	.15	.40
231 Ray Berry	.02	.10
232 Anthony Carter	.07	.20
233 Cris Carter	.30	.75
234 Chris Doleman	.02	.10
235 Rich Gannon	.15	.40
236 Steve Jordan	.02	.10
237 Carl Lee	.02	.10
238 Randall McDaniel	.05	.15
239 Mike Merriweather	.02	.10
240 Harry Newsome	.02	.10
241 John Randle	.07	.20
242 Henry Thomas	.02	.10
243 Bruce Armstrong	.02	.10
244 Vincent Brown	.02	.10
245 Marv Cook	.02	.10
246 Irving Fryar	.07	.20
247 Pat Harlow	.02	.10
248 Maurice Hurst	.02	.10
249 Eugene Lockhart	.02	.10
250 Greg McMurtry	.02	.10
251 Hugh Millen	.02	.10
252 Leonard Russell	.07	.20
253 Chris Singleton	.02	.10
254 Andre Tippett	.02	.10
255 Jon Vaughn	.02	.10
256 Morten Andersen	.02	.10
257 Gene Atkins	.02	.10
258 Wesley Carroll	.02	.10
259 Jim Dombrowski	.02	.10
260 Quinn Early	.07	.20
261 Bobby Hebert	.02	.10
262 Joel Hilgenberg	.02	.10
263 Rickey Jackson	.02	.10
264 Vaughan Johnson	.02	.10
265 Eric Martin	.02	.10
266 Brett Maxie	.02	.10
267 Fred McAfee RC	.02	.10
268 Sam Mills	.02	.10
269 Pat Swilling	.02	.10
270 Floyd Turner	.02	.10
271 Steve Walsh	.02	.10
272 Stephen Baker	.02	.10
273 Jarrod Bunch	.02	.10
274 Mark Collins	.02	.10
275 John Elliott	.02	.10
276 Myron Guyton	.02	.10
277 Rodney Hampton	.07	.20
278 Jeff Hostetler	.07	.20
279 Mark Ingram	.02	.10
280 Pepper Johnson	.02	.10
281 Sean Landeta	.02	.10
282 Leonard Marshall	.02	.10
283 Kanavis McGhee	.02	.10
284 Dave Meggett	.07	.20
285 Bart Oates	.02	.10
286 Phil Simms	.07	.20
287 Reyna Thompson	.02	.10
288 Lewis Tillman	.02	.10
289 Brad Baxter	.02	.10
290 Mike Brim RC	.02	.10
291 Chris Burkett	.02	.10
292 Kyle Clifton	.02	.10
293 James Hasty	.02	.10
294 Joe Kelly	.02	.10
295 Jeff Lageman	.02	.10
296 Mo Lewis	.02	.10
297 Erik McMillan	.02	.10
298 Scott Mersereau	.02	.10
299 Rob Moore	.07	.20
300 Tony Stargell	.02	.10
301 Jim Sweeney	.02	.10
302 Marvin Washington	.02	.10
303 Lonnie Young	.02	.10
304 Eric Allen	.02	.10
305 Fred Barnett	.15	.40
306 Keith Byars	.02	.10
307 Byron Evans	.02	.10
308 Wes Hopkins	.02	.10
309 Keith Jackson	.07	.20
310 James Joseph	.02	.10
311 Seth Joyner	.02	.10
312 Roger Ruzek	.02	.10
313 Clyde Simmons	.02	.10
314 William Thomas	.02	.10
315 Reggie White	.15	.40
316 Calvin Williams	.07	.20
317 Rich Camarillo	.02	.10
318 Jeff Faulkner	.02	.10
319 Ken Harvey	.02	.10
320 Eric Hill	.02	.10
321 Johnny Johnson	.02	.10
322 Ernie Jones	.02	.10
323 Tim McDonald	.02	.10
324 Freddie Joe Nunn	.02	.10
325 Luis Sharpe	.02	.10
326 Eric Swann	.07	.20
327 Aeneas Williams	.07	.20
328 Michael Zordich RC	.02	.10
329 Gary Anderson K	.02	.10
330 Bubby Brister	.02	.10
331 Barry Foster	.07	.20
332 Eric Green	.02	.10
333 Bryan Hinkle	.02	.10
334 Tunch Ilkin	.02	.10
335 Carnell Lake	.02	.10
336 Louis Lipps	.02	.10
337 David Little	.02	.10
338 Greg Lloyd	.07	.20
339 Neil O'Donnell	.07	.20
340 Rod Woodson	.15	.40
341 Rod Bernstine	.02	.10
342 Marion Butts	.02	.10
343 Gill Byrd	.02	.10
344 John Friesz	.07	.20
345 Burt Grossman	.02	.10
346 Courtney Hall	.02	.10
347 Ronnie Harmon	.02	.10
348 Shawn Jefferson	.02	.10
349 Nate Lewis	.02	.10
350 Craig McEwen RC	.02	.10
351 Eric Moten	.02	.10
352 Gary Plummer	.02	.10
353 Henry Rolling	.02	.10
354 Broderick Thompson	.02	.10
355 Derrick Walker	.02	.10
356 Harris Barton	.02	.10
357 Steve Bono RC	.15	.40
358 Todd Bowles	.02	.10
359 Dexter Carter	.02	.10
360 Michael Carter	.02	.10
361 Keith DeLong	.02	.10
362 Charles Haley	.07	.20
363 Merton Hanks	.07	.20
364 Tim Harris	.02	.10
365 Brent Jones	.07	.20
366 Guy McIntyre	.02	.10
367 Tom Rathman	.02	.10
368 Bill Romanowski	.02	.10
369 Jesse Sapolu	.02	.10
370 John Taylor	.07	.20
371 Steve Young	.60	1.50
372 Robert Blackmon	.02	.10
373 Brian Blades	.07	.20
374 Jacob Green	.02	.10
375 Dwayne Harper	.02	.10
376 Andy Heck	.02	.10
377 Tommy Kane	.02	.10
378 John Kasay	.02	.10
379 Cortez Kennedy	.07	.20
380 Bryan Millard	.02	.10
381 Rufus Porter	.02	.10
382 Eugene Robinson	.02	.10
383 John L. Williams	.02	.10
384 Terry Wooden	.02	.10
385 Gary Anderson RB	.02	.10
386 Ian Beckles	.02	.10
387 Mark Carrier WR	.07	.20
388 Reggie Cobb	.02	.10
389 Tony Covington	.02	.10
390 Lawrence Dawsey	.07	.20
391 Ron Hall	.02	.10
392 Keith McCants	.02	.10
393 Charles McRae	.02	.10
394 Tim Newton	.02	.10
395 Jesse Solomon	.02	.10
396 Vinny Testaverde	.07	.20
397 Broderick Thomas	.02	.10
398 Robert Wilson	.02	.10
399 Earnest Byner	.02	.10
400 Gary Clark	.15	.40
401 Andre Collins	.02	.10
402 Brad Edwards	.02	.10
403 Kurt Gouveia	.02	.10
404 Darrell Green	.02	.10
405 Joe Jacoby	.02	.10
406 Jim Lachey	.02	.10

407 Chip Lohmiller .02 .10
408 Charles Mann .02 .10
409 Wilber Marshall .02 .10
410 Brian Mitchell .07 .20
411 Art Monk .07 .20
412 Mark Rypien .02 .10
413 Ricky Sanders .02 .10
414 Mark Schlereth RC .02 .10
415 Fred Stokes .02 .10
416 Bobby Wilson .02 .10
417 Corey Barlow RC .02 .10
418 Edgar Bennett RC .15 .40
419 Eddie Blake RC .02 .10
420 Terrell Buckley RC .02 .10
421 Willie Clay RC .02 .10
422 Rodney Culver RC .02 .10
423 Ed Cunningham RC .02 .10
424 Mark D'Onofrio RC .02 .10
425 Matt Darby RC .02 .10
426 Charles Davenport RC .02 .10
427 Will Furrer RC .02 .10
428 Keith Goganious RC .02 .10
429 Mario Bailey RC .02 .10
430 Chris Hakel RC .02 .10
431 Keith Hamilton RC .07 .20
432 Aaron Pierce RC .02 .10
433 Amp Lee RC .02 .10
434 Scott Lockwood RC .02 .10
435 Ricardo McDonald RC .02 .10
436 Dexter McNabb RC .02 .10
437 Chris Mims RC .02 .10
438 Mike Mooney RC .02 .10
439 Ray Roberts RC .02 .10
440 Patrick Rowe RC .02 .10
441 Leon Searcy RC .02 .10
442 Siran Stacy RC .02 .10
443 Kevin Turner RC .02 .10
444 Tommy Vardell RC .02 .10
445 Bob Whitfield RC .02 .10
446 Darryl Williams RC .02 .10
447 Checklist 1-110 .02 .10
448 Checklist 111-224 .02 .10
449 Checklist 230-340 UER .02 .10
(Missing 225-229)
450 Checklist 341-450 .02 .10
AD Super Bowl XXVII Strip .75 2.00
Mark Rypien
Reggie White
Chris Miller

1992 Ultra Award Winners

COMPLETE SET (10) 4.00 10.00
RANDOM INSERTS IN FOIL PACKS
1 Mark Rypien .10 .30
2 Cornelius Bennett .25 .60
UPI AFC Defensive POY
3 Anthony Munoz .25 .60
NFL Man of the Year
4 Lawrence Dawsey .25 .60
UPI NFC ROY
5 Thurman Thomas .60 1.25
Pro Football Weekly
NFL Offensive POY
6 Michael Irvin .60 1.25
Pro Bowl MVP
7 Mike Croel .10 .30
UPI AFC ROY
8 Barry Sanders 4.00 8.00
9 Pat Swilling .10 .30
AP Defensive POY
10 Leonard Russell .25 .60
Pro Football Weekly
NFL Offensive ROY

1992 Ultra Chris Miller

COMPLETE SET (10) 2.50 6.00
COMMON C.MILLER (1-10) .30 .75
COMMON SEND-OFF (11-12) .75 2.00
RANDOM INSERTS IN FOIL PACKS
AU Chris Miller AUTO 10.00 25.00
(Certified autograph)

1992 Ultra Reggie White

COMPLETE SET (10) 4.00 10.00
COMMON R.WHITE (1-10) .50 1.25
COMMON SEND-OFF (11-12) 1.00 2.50
RANDOM INSERTS IN FOIL PACKS

1992 Ultra Reggie White Autographs

COMMON CARD (1-10) 40.00 80.00

1993 Ultra

The 1993 Ultra set comprises 500 standard-size cards that were issued in 14 and 19-card packs. The cards are checklisted below alphabetically according to teams. Rookie Cards include Jerome Bettis, Drew Bledsoe, Vincent Brisby, Reggie Brooks, Curtis Conway, Troy Drayton, Garrison Hearst, Qadry Ismail, Terry Kirby, Leon Lett, O.J. McDuffie, Natrone Means, Glyn Milburn, Rick Mirer, Willie Roaf, Robert Smith and Dana Stubblefield.

COMPLETE SET (500) 7.50 20.00
1 Vinnie Clark .02 .10
2 Darion Conner .02 .10
3 Eric Dickerson .07 .20
4 Moe Gardner .02 .10
5 Tim Green .02 .10
6 Roger Harper RC .02 .10
7 Michael Haynes .07 .20
8 Bobby Hebert .02 .10
9 Chris Hinton .02 .10
10 Pierce Holt .02 .10
11 Mike Kenn .02 .10
12 Lincoln Kennedy RC .02 .10
13 Chris Miller .07 .20
14 Mike Pritchard .07 .20
15 Andre Rison .07 .20
16 Deion Sanders .30 .75
17 Tony Smith .02 .10
18 Jessie Tuggle .02 .10
19 Howard Ballard .02 .10
20 Don Beebe .02 .10
21 Cornelius Bennett .07 .20
22 Bill Brooks .02 .10
23 Kenneth Davis .02 .10
24 Phil Hansen .02 .10
25 Henry Jones .02 .10
26 Jim Kelly .15 .40
27 Nate Odomes .02 .10
28 John Parrella RC .02 .10
29 Andre Reed .07 .20
30 Frank Reich .07 .20
31 Jim Ritcher .02 .10
32 Bruce Smith .15 .40
33 Thomas Smith RC .07 .20
34 Darryl Talley .02 .10
35 Steve Tasker .07 .20
36 Thurman Thomas .15 .40
37 Jeff Wright .02 .10
38 Neal Anderson .02 .10
39 Trace Armstrong .02 .10
40 Mark Carrier DB .02 .10
41 Curtis Conway RC .30 .75
42 Wendell Davis .02 .10
43 Richard Dent .07 .20
44 Shaun Gayle .02 .10
45 Jim Harbaugh .15 .40
46 Craig Heyward .07 .20
47 Darren Lewis .02 .10
48 Steve McMichael .07 .20
49 William Perry .07 .20
50 Carl Simpson RC .02 .10
51 Alonzo Spellman .02 .10
52 Keith Van Horne .02 .10
53 Tom Waddle .02 .10
54 Donnell Woolford .02 .10
55 John Copeland RC .07 .20
56 Derrick Fenner .02 .10
57 James Francis .02 .10
58 Harold Green .02 .10
59 David Klingler .02 .10
60 Tim Krumrie .02 .10
61 Ricardo McDonald .02 .10
62 Tony McGee RC .07 .20
63 Carl Pickens .07 .20
64 Lamar Rogers .02 .10
65 Jay Schroeder .02 .10
66 Daniel Stubbs .02 .10
67 Steve Tovar RC .02 .10
68 Alfred Williams .02 .10
69 Darryl Williams .02 .10
70 Jerry Ball .02 .10
71 David Brandon .02 .10
72 Rob Burnett .02 .10
73 Mark Carrier WR .07 .20
74 Steve Everitt RC .02 .10
75 Dan Footman RC .02 .10
76 Leroy Hoard .07 .20
77 Michael Jackson .07 .20
78 Mike Johnson .02 .10
79 Bernie Kosar .07 .20
80 Clay Matthews .07 .20
81 Eric Metcalf .07 .20
82 Michael Dean Perry .07 .20
83 Vinny Testaverde .07 .20
84 Tommy Vardell .02 .10
85 Troy Aikman .60 1.50
86 Larry Brown DB .02 .10
87 Tony Casillas .02 .10
88 Thomas Everett .02 .10
89 Charles Haley .07 .20
90 Alvin Harper .07 .20
91 Michael Irvin .15 .40
92 Jim Jeffcoat .02 .10
93 Daryl Johnston .15 .40
94 Robert Jones .02 .10
95 Leon Lett RC .07 .20
96 Russell Maryland .02 .10
97 Nate Newton .07 .20
98 Ken Norton .07 .20
99 Jay Novacek .07 .20
100 Darrin Smith RC .07 .20
101 Emmitt Smith 1.25 3.00
102 Kevin Smith .07 .20
103 Mark Stepnoski .02 .10
104 Tony Tolbert .02 .10
105 Kevin Williams RC .15 .40
106 Steve Atwater .02 .10
107 Rod Bernstine .02 .10
108 Mike Croel .02 .10
109 Robert Delpino .02 .10
110 Shane Dronett .02 .10
111 John Elway 1.25 3.00
112 Simon Fletcher .02 .10
113 Greg Kragen .02 .10
114 Tommy Maddox .15 .40
115 Arthur Marshall RC .02 .10
116 Karl Mecklenburg .02 .10
117 Glyn Milburn RC .15 .40
118 Reggie Rivers RC .02 .10
119 Shannon Sharpe .15 .40
120 Dennis Smith .02 .10
121 Kenny Walker .02 .10
122 Dan Williams RC .02 .10
123 Bennie Blades .02 .10
124 Lomas Brown .02 .10
125 Bill Fralic .02 .10
126 Mel Gray .07 .20
127 Willie Green .02 .10
128 Jason Hanson .02 .10
129 Antonio London RC .02 .10
130 Ryan McNeil RC .15 .40
131 Herman Moore .15 .40
132 Rodney Peete .02 .10
133 Brett Perriman .15 .40
134 Kelvin Pritchett .02 .10
135 Barry Sanders 1.00 2.50
136 Tracy Scroggins .02 .10
137 Chris Spielman .07 .20
138 Pat Swilling .02 .10
139 Andre Ware .02 .10
140 Edgar Bennett .15 .40
141 Tony Bennett .02 .10
142 Matt Brock .02 .10
143 Terrell Buckley .02 .10
144 LeRoy Butler .02 .10
145 Mark Clayton .02 .10
146 Brett Favre 1.50 4.00
147 Jackie Harris .02 .10
148 Johnny Holland .02 .10
149 Bill Maas .02 .10
150 Brian Noble .02 .10
151 Bryce Paup .07 .20
152 Ken Ruettgers .02 .10
153 Sterling Sharpe .15 .40
154 Wayne Simmons RC .02 .10
155 John Stephens .02 .10
156 George Teague RC .07 .20
157 Reggie White .15 .40
158 Micheal Barrow RC .15 .40
159 Cody Carlson .02 .10
160 Ray Childress .02 .10
161 Cris Dishman .02 .10
162 Curtis Duncan .02 .10
163 William Fuller .02 .10
164 Ernest Givins .07 .20
165 Brad Hopkins RC .02 .10
166 Haywood Jeffires .07 .20
167 Lamar Lathon .02 .10
168 Wilber Marshall .02 .10
169 Bruce Matthews .02 .10
170 Bubba McDowell .02 .10
171 Warren Moon .15 .40
172 Mike Munchak .07 .20
173 Eddie Robinson .02 .10
174 Al Smith .02 .10
175 Lorenzo White .02 .10
176 Lee Williams .02 .10
177 Chip Banks .02 .10
178 John Baylor .02 .10
179 Duane Bickett .02 .10
180 Kerry Cash .02 .10
181 Quentin Coryatt .07 .20
182 Rodney Culver .02 .10
183 Steve Emtman .02 .10
184 Jeff George .15 .40
185 Jeff Herrod .02 .10
186 Jessie Hester .02 .10
187 Anthony Johnson .07 .20
188 Reggie Langhorne .02 .10
189 Roosevelt Potts RC .02 .10
190 Rohn Stark .02 .10
191 Clarence Verdin .02 .10
192 Will Wolford .02 .10
193 Marcus Allen .15 .40
194 John Alt .02 .10
195 Tim Barnett .02 .10
196 J.J.Birden .02 .10
197 Dale Carter .02 .10
198 Willie Davis .15 .40
199 Jaime Fields RC .02 .10
200 Dave Krieg .07 .20
201 Nick Lowery .02 .10
202 Charles Mincy RC .02 .10
203 Joe Montana 1.25 3.00
204 Christian Okoye .02 .10
205 Dan Saleaumua .02 .10
206 Will Shields RC .15 .40
207 Tracy Simien .02 .10
208 Neil Smith .15 .40
209 Derrick Thomas .15 .40
210 Harvey Williams .07 .20
211 Barry Word .02 .10
212 Eddie Anderson .02 .10
213 Patrick Bates RC .02 .10
214 Nick Bell .02 .10
215 Tim Brown .15 .40
216 Willie Gault .02 .10
217 Gaston Green .02 .10
218 Billy Joe Hobert RC .15 .40
219 Ethan Horton .02 .10
220 Jeff Hostetler .07 .20
221 James Lofton .07 .20
222 Howie Long .15 .40
223 Todd Marinovich .02 .10
224 Terry McDaniel .02 .10
225 Winston Moss .02 .10
226 Anthony Smith .02 .10
227 Greg Townsend .02 .10
228 Aaron Wallace .02 .10
229 Lionel Washington .02 .10
230 Steve Wisniewski .02 .10
231 Flipper Anderson .02 .10
232 Jerome Bettis RC 4.00 8.00
233 Marc Boutte .02 .10
234 Shane Conlan .02 .10
235 Troy Drayton RC .07 .20
236 Henry Ellard .07 .20
237 Jim Everett .07 .20
238 Cleveland Gary .02 .10
239 Sean Gilbert .07 .20
240 Darryl Henley .02 .10
241 David Lang .02 .10
242 Todd Lyght .02 .10
243 Anthony Newman .02 .10
244 Roman Phifer .02 .10
245 Gerald Robinson .02 .10
246 Henry Rolling .02 .10
247 Jackie Slater .02 .10
248 Keith Byars .02 .10
249 Marco Coleman .02 .10
250 Bryan Cox .02 .10
251 Jeff Cross .02 .10
252 Irving Fryar .07 .20
253 Mark Higgs .02 .10
254 Dwight Hollier RC .02 .10
255 Mark Ingram .02 .10
256 Keith Jackson .07 .20
257 Terry Kirby RC .15 .40
258 Dan Marino 1.25 3.00
259 O.J. McDuffie RC .15 .40
260 John Offerdahl .02 .10
261 Louis Oliver .02 .10
262 Pete Stoyanovich .02 .10
263 Troy Vincent .02 .10
264 Richmond Webb .02 .10
265 Jarvis Williams .02 .10
266 Terry Allen .15 .40
267 Anthony Carter .07 .20
268 Cris Carter .15 .40
269 Roger Craig .07 .20
270 Jack Del Rio .02 .10
271 Chris Doleman .02 .10
272 Qadry Ismail RC .15 .40
273 Steve Jordan .02 .10
274 Randall McDaniel .05 .15
275 Audray McMillian .02 .10
276 John Randle .07 .20
277 Sean Salisbury .02 .10
278 Todd Scott .02 .10
279 Robert Smith RC 1.00 2.50
280 Henry Thomas .02 .10
281 Ray Agnew .02 .10
282 Bruce Armstrong .02 .10
283 Drew Bledsoe RC 2.00 5.00
284 Vincent Brisby RC .15 .40
285 Vincent Brown .02 .10
286 Eugene Chung .02 .10
287 Marv Cook .02 .10
288 Pat Harlow .02 .10
289 Jerome Henderson .02 .10
290 Greg McMurtry .02 .10
291 Leonard Russell .07 .20
292 Chris Singleton .02 .10
293 Chris Slade RC .07 .20
294 Andre Tippett .02 .10
295 Brent Williams .02 .10
296 Scott Zolak .02 .10
297 Morten Andersen .02 .10
298 Gene Atkins .02 .10
299 Mike Buck .02 .10
300 Toi Cook .02 .10
301 Jim Dombrowski .02 .10
302 Vaughn Dunbar .02 .10
303 Quinn Early .07 .20
304 Joel Hilgenberg .02 .10
305 Dalton Hilliard .02 .10
306 Rickey Jackson .02 .10
307 Vaughan Johnson .02 .10
308 Reginald Jones .02 .10
309 Eric Martin .02 .10
310 Wayne Martin .02 .10
311 Sam Mills .02 .10
312 Brad Muster .02 .10
313 Willie Roaf RC .07 .20
314 Irv Smith RC .02 .10
315 Wade Wilson .02 .10
316 Carlton Bailey .02 .10
317 Michael Brooks .02 .10
318 Derek Brown TE .02 .10
319 Marcus Buckley RC .02 .10
320 Jarrod Bunch .02 .10
321 Mark Collins .02 .10
322 Eric Dorsey .02 .10
323 Rodney Hampton .07 .20
324 Mark Jackson .02 .10
325 Pepper Johnson .02 .10
326 Ed McCaffrey .15 .40
327 Dave Meggett .02 .10
328 Bart Oates .02 .10
329 Mike Sherrard .02 .10
330 Phil Simms .07 .20
331 Michael Strahan RC 1.25 3.00
332 Lawrence Taylor .15 .40
333 Brad Baxter .02 .10
334 Chris Burkett .02 .10
335 Kyle Clifton .02 .10
336 Boomer Esiason .07 .20
337 James Hasty .02 .10
338 Johnny Johnson .02 .10
339 Marvin Jones RC .02 .10
340 Jeff Lageman .02 .10
341 Mo Lewis .02 .10
342 Ronnie Lott .07 .20
343 Leonard Marshall .02 .10
344 Johnny Mitchell .02 .10
345 Rob Moore .07 .20
346 Browning Nagle .02 .10
347 Coleman Rudolph RC .02 .10
348 Blair Thomas .02 .10
349 Eric Thomas .02 .10
350 Brian Washington .02 .10
351 Marvin Washington .02 .10
352 Eric Allen .02 .10
353 Victor Bailey RC .02 .10
354 Fred Barnett .07 .20
355 Mark Bavaro .02 .10
356 Randall Cunningham .15 .40
357 Byron Evans .02 .10
358 Andy Harmon RC .07 .20
359 Tim Harris .02 .10
360 Lester Holmes .02 .10
361 Seth Joyner .02 .10
362 Keith Millard .02 .10
363 Leonard Renfro RC .02 .10
364 Heath Sherman .02 .10
365 Vai Sikahema .02 .10
366 Clyde Simmons .02 .10
367 William Thomas .02 .10
368 Herschel Walker .07 .20
369 Andre Waters .02 .10
370 Calvin Williams .07 .20
371 Johnny Bailey .02 .10
372 Steve Beuerlein .07 .20
373 Rich Camarillo .02 .10
374 Chuck Cecil .02 .10
375 Chris Chandler .07 .20
376 Gary Clark .07 .20
377 Ben Coleman RC .02 .10
378 Ernest Dye RC .02 .10
379 Ken Harvey .02 .10
380 Garrison Hearst RC .60 1.50
381 Randal Hill .02 .10
382 Robert Massey .02 .10
383 Freddie Joe Nunn .02 .10
384 Ricky Proehl .02 .10
385 Luis Sharpe .02 .10
386 Tyronne Stowe .02 .10
387 Eric Swann .07 .20
388 Aeneas Williams .02 .10
389 Chad Brown RC .07 .20
390 Dermontti Dawson .02 .10
391 Donald Evans .02 .10
392 Deon Figures RC .02 .10
393 Barry Foster .07 .20
394 Jeff Graham .07 .20
395 Eric Green .02 .10
396 Kevin Greene .07 .20
397 Carlton Haselrig .02 .10
398 Andre Hastings RC .07 .20
399 D.J. Johnson .02 .10
400 Carnell Lake .02 .10
401 Greg Lloyd .07 .20
402 Neil O'Donnell .15 .40
403 Darren Perry .02 .10
404 Mike Tomczak .02 .10
405 Rod Woodson .15 .40
406 Eric Bieniemy .02 .10
407 Marion Butts .02 .10
408 Gill Byrd .02 .10
409 Darren Carrington RC .02 .10
410 Darrien Gordon RC .02 .10
411 Burt Grossman .02 .10
412 Courtney Hall .02 .10
413 Ronnie Harmon .02 .10
414 Stan Humphries .07 .20
415 Nate Lewis .02 .10
416 Natrone Means RC .15 .40
417 Anthony Miller .07 .20
418 Chris Mims .02 .10
419 Leslie O'Neal .07 .20
420 Gary Plummer .02 .10
421 Stanley Richard .02 .10
422 Junior Seau .15 .40
423 Harry Swayne .02 .10
424 Jerrol Williams .02 .10
425 Harris Barton .02 .10
426 Steve Bono .07 .20
427 Kevin Fagan .02 .10
428 Don Griffin .02 .10
429 Dana Hall .02 .10
430 Adrian Hardy .02 .10
431 Brent Jones .07 .20
432 Todd Kelly RC .02 .10
433 Amp Lee .02 .10
434 Tim McDonald .02 .10
435 Guy McIntyre .02 .10
436 Tom Rathman .02 .10
437 Jerry Rice .75 2.00
438 Bill Romanowski .02 .10
439 Dana Stubblefield RC .15 .40
440 John Taylor .07 .20
441 Steve Wallace .02 .10
442 Michael Walter .02 .10
443 Ricky Watters .15 .40
444 Steve Young .60 1.50
445 Robert Blackmon .02 .10
446 Brian Blades .07 .20
447 Jeff Bryant .02 .10
448 Ferrell Edmunds .02 .10
449 Carlton Gray RC .02 .10
450 Dwayne Harper .02 .10
451 Andy Heck .02 .10
452 Tommy Kane .02 .10
453 Cortez Kennedy .07 .20
454 Kelvin Martin .02 .10
455 Dan McGwire .02 .10
456 Rick Mirer RC .15 .40
457 Rufus Porter .02 .10
458 Ray Roberts .02 .10
459 Eugene Robinson .02 .10
460 Chris Warren .07 .20
461 John L. Williams .02 .10
462 Gary Anderson RB .02 .10
463 Tyji Armstrong .02 .10
464 Reggie Cobb .02 .10
465 Eric Curry RC .02 .10
466 Lawrence Dawsey .02 .10
467 Steve DeBerg .02 .10
468 Santana Dotson .07 .20
469 Demetrius DuBose RC .02 .10
470 Paul Gruber .02 .10
471 Ron Hall .02 .10
472 Courtney Hawkins .02 .10
473 Hardy Nickerson .07 .20
474 Ricky Reynolds .02 .10
475 Broderick Thomas .02 .10
476 Mark Wheeler .02 .10
477 Jimmy Williams .02 .10
478 Carl Banks .02 .10
479 Reggie Brooks RC .07 .20
480 Earnest Byner .02 .10
481 Tom Carter RC .07 .20
482 Andre Collins .02 .10
483 Brad Edwards .02 .10
484 Ricky Ervins .02 .10
485 Kurt Gouveia .02 .10
486 Darrell Green .02 .10
487 Desmond Howard .07 .20
488 Jim Lachey .02 .10
489 Chip Lohmiller .02 .10
490 Charles Mann .02 .10
491 Tim McGee .02 .10
492 Brian Mitchell .07 .20
493 Art Monk .07 .20
494 Mark Rypien .02 .10
495 Ricky Sanders .02 .10
496 Checklist 1-126 .02 .10
Chip Lohmiller
497 Checklist 127-254 .02 .10
Ricky Proehl
498 Checklist 255-382 .02 .10
Randall Cunningham
499 Checklist 383-500 .02 .10
Dave Meggett
500 Inserts Checklist .02 .10

1993 Ultra All-Rookies

COMPLETE SET (10) 12.00 30.00
1 Patrick Bates .20 .50
2 Jerome Bettis 6.00 15.00
3 Drew Bledsoe 4.00 10.00
4 Curtis Conway 1.25 3.00
5 Garrison Hearst 2.50 6.00
6 Qadry Ismail .60 1.50
7 Marvin Jones .20 .50
8 Glyn Milburn .30 .75
9 Rick Mirer .60 1.50
10 Kevin Williams .30 .75

1993 Ultra Award Winners

COMPLETE SET (10) 15.00 40.00
1 Troy Aikman 6.00 15.00
2 Dale Carter .40 1.00
3 Chris Doleman .40 1.00
4 Santana Dotson .60 1.50
5 Barry Foster .75 2.00
6 Jason Hanson .40 1.00
7 Cortez Kennedy .60 1.50
8 Carl Pickens .75 2.00
9 Steve Tasker .75 2.00
10 Steve Young 6.00 15.00

1993 Ultra Michael Irvin

COMPLETE SET (10) 3.00 8.00
COMMON M.IRVIN (1-10) .40 1.00
STATED ODDS 1:12
COMMON SEND-OFF (11-12) .75 2.00
AU Michael Irvin AUTO 15.00 30.00
Certified Autograph

1993 Ultra League Leaders

COMPLETE SET (10) 20.00 50.00
1 Haywood Jeffires .75 2.00
2 Henry Jones .40 1.00
3 Audray McMillian .40 1.00
4 Warren Moon 1.50 4.00
5 Leslie O'Neal .75 2.00
6 Deion Sanders 3.00 8.00
7 Sterling Sharpe 1.50 4.00
8 Clyde Simmons .40 1.00
9 Emmitt Smith 12.50 30.00
10 Thurman Thomas 1.50 4.00

1993 Ultra Stars

COMPLETE SET (10) 20.00 50.00
RANDOM INSERTS IN JUMBO PACKS
1 Brett Favre 12.00 30.00
2 Barry Foster .60 1.50
3 Michael Irvin 2.00 5.00
4 Cortez Kennedy .60 1.50
5 Deion Sanders 2.50 6.00
6 Junior Seau 1.50 4.00
7 Derrick Thomas 1.50 4.00
8 Ricky Watters 1.00 2.50
9 Reggie White 1.50 4.00
10 Steve Young 5.00 12.00

1993 Ultra Touchdown Kings

COMPLETE SET (10) 15.00 40.00
1 Rodney Hampton .50 1.25
2 Dan Marino 4.00 10.00
3 Art Monk .75 2.00
4 Joe Montana 4.00 10.00
5 Jerry Rice 2.50 6.00
6 Andre Rison .75 2.00
7 Barry Sanders 3.00 8.00
8 Sterling Sharpe .75 2.00
9 Emmitt Smith 4.00 10.00
10 Thurman Thomas 1.50 4.00

1994 Ultra

Cards from this 525-card standard size set were issued in two series of 325 and 200. Cards were issued in 14, 17, and 20-card packs. Card fronts have full-bleed photos with the player's name, team, position and a helmet in gold foil at the bottom. The backs have three photos and statistics. The cards are grouped alphabetically within teams, and checklisted below alphabetically according to teams. Rookie Cards include Derrick Alexander, Mario Bates, Isaac Bruce, Lake Dawson, Trent Diller, Bert Emanuel, Marshall Faulk, William Floyd, Greg Hill, Charles Johnson, Bam Morris, Errict Rhett, Darnay Scott and Heath Shuler.

COMPLETE SET (525) 10.00 25.00
COMP.SERIES 1 (325) 5.00 12.00
COMP.SERIES 2 (200) 5.00 12.00
1 Steve Beuerlein .07 .20
2 Gary Clark .07 .20
3 Randal Hill .02 .10
4 Seth Joyner .02 .10
5 Jamir Miller RC .07 .20
6 Ronald Moore .02 .10
7 Luis Sharpe .02 .10
8 Clyde Simmons .02 .10
9 Eric Swann .07 .20
10 Aeneas Williams .02 .10
11 Chris Doleman .02 .10
12 Bert Emanuel RC .15 .40
13 Moe Gardner .02 .10
14 Jeff George .15 .40
15 Roger Harper .02 .10
16 Pierce Holt .02 .10
17 Lincoln Kennedy .02 .10
18 Erric Pegram .02 .10
19 Andre Rison .07 .20
20 Deion Sanders .30 .75
21 Jessie Tuggle .02 .10
22 Cornelius Bennett .07 .20
23 Bill Brooks .02 .10
24 Jeff Burris RC .07 .20
25 Kent Hull .02 .10
26 Henry Jones .02 .10
27 Jim Kelly .15 .40
28 Marvcus Patton .02 .10
29 Andre Reed .07 .20
30 Bruce Smith .15 .40
31 Thomas Smith .02 .10
32 Thurman Thomas .15 .40
33 Jeff Wright .02 .10
34 Trace Armstrong .02 .10
35 Mark Carrier DB .02 .10
36 Danle Jones .02 .10
37 Erik Kramer .07 .20
38 Terry Obee .02 .10
39 Alonzo Spellman .02 .10
40 John Thierry RC .02 .10
41 Tom Waddle .02 .10
42 Donnell Woolford .02 .10
43 Tim Worley .02 .10
44 Chris Zorich .02 .10
45 John Copeland .02 .10
46 Harold Green .02 .10
47 David Klingler .02 .10
48 Ricardo McDonald .02 .10
49 Tony McGee .02 .10
50 Louis Oliver .02 .10
51 Carl Pickens .07 .20
52 Darnay Scott RC .30 .75
53 Steve Tovar .02 .10
54 Dan Wilkinson RC .07 .20
55 Darryl Williams .02 .10
56 Derrick Alexander WR RC .15 .40
57 Michael Jackson .07 .20
58 Tony Jones .02 .10
59 Antonio Langham RC .07 .20
60 Eric Metcalf .07 .20
61 Stevon Moore .02 .10
62 Michael Dean Perry .07 .20
63 Anthony Pleasant .02 .10
64 Vinny Testaverde .07 .20
65 Eric Turner .02 .10
66 Tommy Vardell .02 .10
67 Troy Aikman .60 1.50
68 Larry Brown DB .02 .10
69 Shante Carver RC .02 .10
70 Charles Haley .07 .20
71 Michael Irvin .15 .40
72 Leon Lett .02 .10
73 Nate Newton .02 .10
74 Jay Novacek .07 .20
75 Darrin Smith .02 .10
76 Emmitt Smith 1.00 2.50
77 Tony Tolbert .02 .10
78 Erik Williams .02 .10
79 Kevin Williams WR .07 .20
80 Steve Atwater .02 .10
81 Rod Bernstine .02 .10
82 Ray Crockett .02 .10
83 Mike Croel .02 .10
84 Shane Dronett .02 .10
85 Jason Elam .07 .20
86 John Elway 1.25 3.00
87 Simon Fletcher .02 .10
88 Glyn Milburn .07 .20
89 Anthony Miller .07 .20
90 Shannon Sharpe .07 .20
91 Gary Zimmerman .02 .10
92 Bennie Blades .02 .10
93 Lomas Brown .02 .10
94 Mel Gray .02 .10
95 Jason Hanson .02 .10
96 Ryan McNeil .02 .10
97 Scott Mitchell .07 .20
98 Herman Moore .15 .40
99 Johnnie Morton RC .60 1.50
100 Robert Porcher .02 .10
101 Barry Sanders 1.00 2.50
102 Chris Spielman .07 .20
103 Pat Swilling .02 .10
104 Edgar Bennett .15 .40
105 Terrell Buckley .02 .10
106 Reggie Cobb .02 .10
107 Brett Favre 1.25 3.00
108 Sean Jones .02 .10
109 Ken Ruettgers .02 .10
110 Sterling Sharpe .07 .20
111 Wayne Simmons .02 .10
112 Aaron Taylor RC .02 .10
113 George Teague .02 .10
114 Reggie White .15 .40
115 Micheal Barrow .02 .10
116 Gary Brown .02 .10
117 Cody Carlson .02 .10
118 Ray Childress .02 .10
119 Cris Dishman .02 .10
120 Henry Ford RC .02 .10
121 Haywood Jeffires .07 .20
122 Bruce Matthews .02 .10
123 Bubba McDowell .02 .10
124 Marcus Robertson .02 .10
125 Eddie Robinson .02 .10
126 Webster Slaughter .02 .10
127 Trev Alberts RC .07 .20
128 Tony Bennett .02 .10
129 Ray Buchanan .02 .10
130 Quentin Coryatt .02 .10
131 Eugene Daniel .02 .10
132 Steve Emtman .02 .10
133 Marshall Faulk RC 2.50 6.00
134 Jim Harbaugh .15 .40
135 Roosevelt Potts .02 .10
136 Rohn Stark .02 .10
137 Marcus Allen .15 .40
138 Donnell Bennett RC .15 .40
139 Dale Carter .02 .10
140 Tony Casillas .02 .10
141 Mark Collins .02 .10
142 Willie Davis .07 .20
143 Tim Grunhard .02 .10
144 Greg Hill RC .15 .40
145 Joe Montana 1.25 3.00
146 Tracy Simien .02 .10
147 Neil Smith .07 .20
148 Derrick Thomas .15 .40
149 Tim Brown .15 .40
150 James Folston RC .02 .10
151 Rob Fredrickson RC .07 .20
152 Jeff Hostetler .07 .20
153 Rocket Ismail .07 .20
154 James Jett .02 .10
155 Terry McDaniel .02 .10
156 Winston Moss .02 .10
157 Greg Robinson .02 .10
158 Anthony Smith .02 .10
159 Steve Wisniewski .02 .10
160 Flipper Anderson .02 .10
161 Jerome Bettis .25 .60
162 Isaac Bruce RC 2.00 4.00
163 Shane Conlan .02 .10
164 Wayne Gandy RC .02 .10
165 Sean Gilbert .02 .10
166 Todd Lyght .02 .10
167 Chris Miller .02 .10
168 Anthony Newman .02 .10
169 Roman Phifer .02 .10
170 Jackie Slater .02 .10
171 Gene Atkins .02 .10
172 Aubrey Beavers RC .02 .10
173 Tim Bowens RC .07 .20
174 J.B. Brown .02 .10
175 Marco Coleman .02 .10
176 Bryan Cox .02 .10
177 Irving Fryar .07 .20
178 Terry Kirby .15 .40
179 Dan Marino 1.25 3.00
180 Troy Vincent .02 .10
181 Richmond Webb .02 .10
182 Terry Allen .07 .20
183 Cris Carter .30 .75
184 Jack Del Rio .02 .10
185 Vencie Glenn .02 .10
186 Randall McDaniel .05 .15
187 Warren Moon .15 .40
188 David Palmer RC .15 .40
189 John Randle .07 .20
190 Todd Scott .02 .10
191 Todd Steussie RC .07 .20
192 Henry Thomas .02 .10
193 Dewayne Washington RC .07 .20
194 Bruce Armstrong .02 .10
195 Harlon Barnett .02 .10
196 Drew Bledsoe .40 1.00
197 Vincent Brisby .07 .20
198 Vincent Brown .02 .10
199 Marion Butts .02 .10
200 Ben Coates .07 .20
201 Todd Collins .02 .10
202 Maurice Hurst .02 .10
203 Willie McGinest RC .15 .40
204 Ricky Reynolds .02 .10
205 Chris Slade .02 .10
206 Mario Bates RC .15 .40
207 Derek Brown RBK .02 .10
208 Vince Buck .02 .10
209 Quinn Early .07 .20
210 Jim Everett .07 .20
211 Michael Haynes .07 .20
212 Tyrone Hughes .07 .20
213 Joe Johnson RC .02 .10
214 Vaughan Johnson .02 .10
215 Willie Roaf .02 .10
216 Renaldo Turnbull .02 .10
217 Michael Brooks .02 .10
218 Dave Brown .07 .20
219 Howard Cross .02 .10
220 Stacey Dillard .02 .10
221 Jumbo Elliott .02 .10
222 Keith Hamilton .02 .10
223 Rodney Hampton .07 .20
224 Thomas Lewis RC .07 .20
225 Dave Meggett .02 .10
226 Corey Miller .02 .10
227 Thomas Randolph RC .02 .10
228 Mike Sherrard .02 .10
229 Kyle Clifton .02 .10
230 Boomer Esiason .07 .20
231 Aaron Glenn RC .15 .40
232 James Hasty .02 .10
233 Bobby Houston .02 .10
234 Johnny Johnson .02 .10
235 Mo Lewis .02 .10
236 Ronnie Lott .07 .20
237 Rob Moore .07 .20
238 Marvin Washington .02 .10
239 Ryan Yarborough RC .02 .10
240 Eric Allen .02 .10
241 Victor Bailey .02 .10
242 Fred Barnett .07 .20
243 Mark Bavaro .02 .10
244 Randall Cunningham .15 .40
245 Byron Evans .02 .10
246 William Fuller .02 .10
247 Andy Harmon .02 .10
248 William Perry .07 .20
249 Herschel Walker .07 .20
250 Bernard Williams RC .02 .10
251 Dermontti Dawson .02 .10
252 Deon Figures .02 .10
253 Barry Foster .02 .10
254 Kevin Greene .07 .20
255 Charles Johnson RC .15 .40
256 Levon Kirkland .02 .10
257 Greg Lloyd .07 .20
258 Neil O'Donnell .15 .40
259 Darren Perry .02 .10
260 Dwight Stone .02 .10
261 Rod Woodson .07 .20
262 John Carney .02 .10
263 Issac Davis RC .02 .10
264 Courtney Hall .02 .10
265 Ronnie Harmon .02 .10
266 Stan Humphries .07 .20
267 Vance Johnson .02 .10
268 Natrone Means .15 .40
269 Chris Mims .02 .10
270 Leslie O'Neal .02 .10
271 Stanley Richard .02 .10
272 Junior Seau .15 .40
273 Harris Barton .02 .10
274 Dennis Brown .02 .10
275 Eric Davis .02 .10
276 William Floyd RC .15 .40
277 John Johnson .02 .10
278 Tim McDonald .02 .10
279 Ken Norton Jr. .07 .20
280 Jerry Rice .60 1.50
281 Jesse Sapolu .02 .10
282 Dana Stubblefield .07 .20
283 Ricky Watters .07 .20
284 Bryant Young RC .25 .60
285 Steve Young .40 1.00
286 Sam Adams RC .07 .20

287 Brian Blades .07 .20
288 Ferrell Edmunds .02 .10
289 Patrick Hunter .02 .10
290 Cortez Kennedy .07 .20
291 Rick Mirer .15 .40
292 Nate Odomes .02 .10
293 Ray Roberts .02 .10
294 Eugene Robinson .02 .10
295 Rod Stephens .02 .10
296 Chris Warren .07 .20
297 Marty Carter .02 .10
298 Horace Copeland .02 .10
299 Eric Curry .02 .10
300 Santana Dotson .07 .20
301 Craig Erickson .02 .10
302 Paul Gruber .02 .10
303 Courtney Hawkins .02 .10
304 Martin Mayhew .02 .10
305 Hardy Nickerson .07 .20
306 Errict Rhett RC .15 .40
307 Vince Workman .02 .10
308 Reggie Brooks .07 .20
309 Tom Carter .02 .10
310 Andre Collins .02 .10
311 Brad Edwards .02 .10
312 Kurt Gouveia .02 .10
313 Darrell Green .02 .10
314 Ethan Horton .02 .10
315 Desmond Howard .07 .20
316 Tre Johnson RC .02 .10
317 Sterling Palmer RC .02 .10
318 Heath Shuler RC .15 .40
319 Tyronne Stowe .02 .10
320 NFL 75th Anniversary .02 .10
321 Checklist .02 .10
322 Checklist .02 .10
323 Checklist .02 .10
324 Checklist .02 .10
325 Checklist .02 .10
326 Garrison Hearst .15 .40
327 Eric Hill .02 .10
328 Seth Joyner .02 .10
329 Jim McMahon .07 .20
330 Jamir Miller .02 .10
331 Ricky Proehl .02 .10
332 Clyde Simmons .02 .10
333 Chris Doleman .02 .10
334 Bert Emanuel .15 .40
335 Jeff George .15 .40
336 D.J. Johnson .02 .10
337 Terance Mathis .07 .20
338 Clay Matthews .02 .10
339 Tony Smith .02 .10
340 Don Beebe .02 .10
341 Bucky Brooks RC .02 .10
342 Jeff Burris .07 .20
343 Kenneth Davis .02 .10
344 Phil Hansen .02 .10
345 Pete Metzelaars .02 .10
346 Darryl Talley .02 .10
347 Joe Cain .02 .10
348 Curtis Conway .15 .40
349 Shaun Gayle .02 .10
350 Chris Gedney .02 .10
351 Erik Kramer .07 .20
352 Vinson Smith .02 .10
353 John Thierry .02 .10
354 Lewis Tillman .02 .10
355 Mike Brim .02 .10
356 Derrick Fenner .02 .10
357 James Francis .02 .10
358 Louis Oliver .02 .10
359 Darnay Scott .15 .40
360 Dan Wilkinson .07 .20
361 Alfred Williams .02 .10
362 Derrick Alexander WR .15 .40
363 Rob Burnett .02 .10
364 Mark Carrier WR .07 .20
365 Steve Everitt .02 .10
366 Leroy Hoard .02 .10
367 Pepper Johnson .02 .10
368 Antonio Langham .07 .20
369 Shante Carver .02 .10
370 Alvin Harper .07 .20
371 Daryl Johnston .07 .20
372 Russell Maryland .02 .10
373 Kevin Smith .02 .10
374 Mark Stepnoski .02 .10
375 Darren Woodson .07 .20
376 Allen Aldridge RC .02 .10
377 Ray Crockett .02 .10
378 Karl Mecklenburg .02 .10
379 Anthony Miller .07 .20
380 Mike Pritchard .02 .10
381 Leonard Russell .02 .10
382 Dennis Smith .02 .10
383 Anthony Carter .07 .20
384 Van Malone RC .02 .10
385 Robert Massey .02 .10
386 Scott Mitchell .07 .20
387 Johnnie Morton .25 .60
388 Brett Perriman .07 .20
389 Tracy Scroggins .02 .10
390 Robert Brooks .15 .40
391 LeRoy Butler .02 .10
392 Reggie Cobb .02 .10
393 Sean Jones .02 .10
394 George Koonce .02 .10
395 Steve McMichael .07 .20
396 Bryce Paup .07 .20
397 Aaron Taylor .02 .10
398 Henry Ford .02 .10
399 Ernest Givins .07 .20
400 Jeremy Nunley RC .02 .10
401 Bo Orlando .02 .10
402 Al Smith .02 .10
403 Barron Wortham RC .02 .10
404 Trev Alberts .07 .20
405 Tony Bennett .02 .10
406 Kerry Cash .02 .10
407 Sean Dawkins RC .15 .40
408 Marshall Faulk .75 2.00
409 Jim Harbaugh .15 .40
410 Jeff Herrod .02 .10
411 Kimble Anders .07 .20
412 Donnell Bennett .07 .20
413 J.J. Birden .02 .10
414 Mark Collins .02 .10
415 Lake Dawson RC .07 .20
416 Greg Hill .15 .40
417 Charles Mincy .02 .10
418 Greg Biekert .02 .10
419 Rob Fredrickson .07 .20
420 Nolan Harrison .02 .10
421 Jeff Jaeger .02 .10
422 Albert Lewis .02 .10
423 Chester McGlockton .02 .10
424 Tom Rathman .02 .10
425 Harvey Williams .07 .20
426 Isaac Bruce .60 1.50
427 Troy Drayton .02 .10
428 Wayne Gandy .02 .10
429 Fred Stokes .02 .10
430 Robert Young .02 .10
431 Gene Atkins .02 .10
432 Aubrey Beavers .02 .10
433 Tim Bowens .07 .20
434 Keith Byars .02 .10
435 Jeff Cross .02 .10
436 Mark Ingram .02 .10
437 Keith Jackson .02 .10
438 Michael Stewart .02 .10
439 Chris Hinton .02 .10
440 Qadry Ismail .15 .40
441 Carlos Jenkins .02 .10
442 Warren Moon .15 .40
443 David Palmer .07 .20
444 John Reed .07 .20
445 Robert Smith .15 .40
446 Todd Steussie .07 .20
447 Dewayne Washington .07 .20
448 Marion Butts .02 .10
449 Tim Goad .02 .10
450 Myron Guyton .02 .10
451 Kevin Lee RC .02 .10
452 Willie McGinest .15 .40
453 Ricky Reynolds .02 .10
454 Michael Timpson .02 .10
455 Morten Andersen .02 .10
456 Jim Everett .07 .20
457 Michael Haynes .07 .20
458 Joe Johnson .02 .10
459 Wayne Martin .02 .10
460 Sam Mills .02 .10
461 Irv Smith .02 .10
462 Carlton Bailey .02 .10
463 Chris Calloway .02 .10
464 Mark Jackson .02 .10
465 Thomas Lewis .07 .20
466 Thomas Randolph .02 .10
467 Stevie Anderson RC .02 .10
468 Brad Baxter .02 .10
469 Aaron Glenn .07 .20
470 Jeff Lageman .02 .10
471 Johnny Mitchell .02 .10
472 Art Monk .07 .20
473 William Fuller .02 .10
474 Charlie Garner RC .50 1.25
475 Vaughn Hebron .02 .10
476 Bill Romanowski .02 .10
477 William Thomas .02 .10
478 Greg Townsend .02 .10
479 Bernard Williams .02 .10
480 Calvin Williams .07 .20
481 Eric Green .02 .10
482 Charles Johnson .15 .40
483 Carnell Lake .02 .10
484 Byron Bam Morris RC .07 .20
485 John L. Williams .02 .10
486 Darren Carrington .02 .10
487 Andre Coleman RC .02 .10
488 Isaac Davis .02 .10
489 Dwayne Harper .02 .10
490 Tony Martin .15 .40
491 Mark Seay RC .15 .40
492 Richard Dent .07 .20
493 William Floyd .15 .40
494 Rickey Jackson .02 .10
495 Brent Jones .07 .20
496 Ken Norton Jr. .07 .20
497 Gary Plummer .02 .10
498 Deion Sanders .30 .75
499 John Taylor .07 .20
500 Lee Woodall RC .02 .10
501 Bryant Young .25 .60
502 Sam Adams .07 .20
503 Howard Ballard .02 .10
504 Michael Bates .02 .10
505 Robert Blackmon .02 .10
506 John Kasay .02 .10
507 Kelvin Martin .02 .10
508 Kevin Mawae RC .15 .40
509 Rufus Porter .02 .10
510 Lawrence Dawsey .02 .10
511 Trent Dilfer RC .50 1.25
512 Thomas Everett .02 .10
513 Jackie Harris .02 .10
514 Errict Rhett .07 .20
515 Henry Ellard .07 .20
516 John Friesz .07 .20
517 Ken Harvey .02 .10
518 Ethan Horton .02 .10
519 Tre Johnson .02 .10
520 Jim Lachey .02 .10
521 Heath Shuler .15 .40
522 Tony Woods .02 .10
523 Checklist .02 .10
524 Checklist .02 .10
525 Checklist .02 .10

1994 Ultra Achievement Awards

COMPLETE SET (10) 4.00 10.00
COMPLETE JUMBO SET (10) 10.00 25.00
*JUMBOS: 1X TO 2.5X BASIC INSERT
ONE JUMBO SET PER HOBBY CASE
1 Marcus Allen .15 .40
2 John Elway 1.50 3.00
3 Dan Marino 1.50 3.00
4 Joe Montana 1.50 3.00
5 Jerry Rice .75 1.50
6 Barry Sanders 1.25 2.50
7 Sterling Sharpe .07 .20
8 Emmitt Smith 1.25 2.50
9 Thurman Thomas .15 .40
10 Reggie White .15 .40

1994 Ultra Award Winners

COMPLETE SET (5) 1.50 4.00
1 Jerome Bettis .30 .75
2 Rick Mirer .20 .50
3 Emmitt Smith 1.50 3.00
4 Dana Stubblefield .08 .25
5 Rod Woodson .08 .25

1994 Ultra First Rounders

COMPLETE SET (20) 2.50 6.00
1 Sam Adams .05 .15
2 Trev Alberts .05 .15
3 Shante Carver .02 .10
4 Marshall Faulk 2.50 5.00
5 William Floyd .10 .30
6 Rob Fredrickson .05 .15
7 Wayne Gandy .02 .10
8 Aaron Glenn .10 .30
9 Charles Johnson .10 .30
10 Joe Johnson .02 .10
11 Antonio Langham .05 .15
12 Willie McGinest .10 .30
13 Jamir Miller .05 .15
14 Johnnie Morton .60 1.25
15 Heath Shuler .10 .30
16 John Thierry .02 .10
17 Dewayne Washington .05 .15
18 Dan Wilkinson .05 .15
19 Bernard Williams .02 .10
20 Bryant Young .20 .50

1994 Ultra Flair Hot Numbers

COMPLETE SET (15) 7.50 20.00
RANDOM INSERTS IN SER.2 PACKS
1 Troy Aikman 1.00 2.00
2 Jerome Bettis .30 .75
3 Tim Brown .20 .50
4 John Elway 2.00 4.00
5 Rodney Hampton .08 .25
6 Michael Irvin .20 .50
7 Dan Marino 2.00 4.00
8 Joe Montana 2.00 4.00
9 Jerry Rice 1.00 2.00
10 Andre Rison .08 .25
11 Barry Sanders 1.50 3.00
12 Sterling Sharpe .08 .25
13 Emmitt Smith 1.50 3.00
14 Thurman Thomas .20 .50
15 Steve Young .60 1.25

1994 Ultra Flair Scoring Power

COMPLETE SET (6) 3.00 8.00
RANDOM INSERTS IN SER.2 PACKS
1 Marcus Allen .30 .75
2 Natrone Means .30 .75
3 Jerry Rice 1.50 3.00
4 Andre Rison .15 .40
5 Emmitt Smith 1.50 4.00
6 Ricky Watters .15 .40

1994 Ultra Flair Wave of the Future

COMPLETE SET (6) 1.50 4.00
RANDOM INSERTS IN SER.2 PACKS
1 Trent Dilfer .40 1.00
2 Marshall Faulk 1.25 3.00
3 Greg Hill .10 .30
4 Charles Johnson .10 .30
5 Heath Shuler .10 .30
6 Dan Wilkinson .05 .15

1994 Ultra Rick Mirer

COMPLETE SET (12) 1.50 4.00
COMMON MIRER (1-10) .20 .50
1-10: RANDOM INSERTS IN PACKS
COMMON SEND-OFF (11-12) .60 1.50
11-12 ISSUED VIA MAIL REDEMPTION
P1 Promo Sheet .40 1.00
base brand card and insert

1994 Ultra Rick Mirer Autographs

COMMON AUTO 12.50 30.00

1994 Ultra Second Year Standouts

COMPLETE SET (15) 2.00 5.00
1 Jerome Bettis .60 1.25
2 Drew Bledsoe 1.00 2.00
3 Reggie Brooks .15 .40
4 Tom Carter .07 .20
5 Eric Curry .07 .20
6 Jason Elam .15 .40
7 Tyrone Hughes .15 .40
8 James Jett .07 .20
9 Terry Kirby .30 .75
10 Natrone Means .30 .75
11 Rick Mirer .30 .75
12 Ronald Moore .07 .20
13 Willie Roaf .07 .20
14 Chris Slade .07 .20
15 Dana Stubblefield .15 .40

1994 Ultra Stars

COMPLETE SET (9) 25.00 60.00
RANDOM INSERTS IN 17-CARD PACK
1 Troy Aikman 4.00 10.00
2 Jerome Bettis 2.50 6.00
3 Tim Brown 1.50 4.00
4 Michael Irvin 1.50 4.00
5 Rick Mirer 1.00 2.50
6 Jerry Rice 5.00 12.00
7 Barry Sanders 6.00 15.00
8 Emmitt Smith 6.00 15.00
9 Rod Woodson 1.25 3.00

1994 Ultra Touchdown Kings

COMPLETE SET (9) 25.00 50.00
1 Marcus Allen .75 2.00
2 Dan Marino 6.00 15.00
3 Joe Montana 6.00 15.00
4 Jerry Rice 3.00 8.00
5 Andre Rison .40 1.00
6 Sterling Sharpe .40 1.00
7 Emmitt Smith 5.00 12.00
8 Ricky Watters .40 1.00
9 Steve Young 2.00 5.00

1995 Ultra

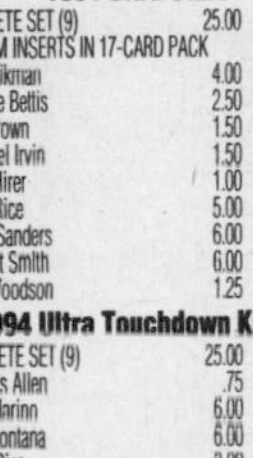

This standard-size set was printed in two series, which consisted of 550 standard-size cards. They were issued in 12 and 15 card packs with a suggested retail price of $2.29 and $2.99, respectively. Each pack comes with an insert card and a "Gold Medallion Edition" parallel set card. The series two set is also known as "Ultra Extra". Rookie cards include Ki-Jana Carter, Steve McNair, Michael Westbrook, Kerry Collins, Joey Galloway, J.J. Stokes, Tyrone Wheatley, Jeff Blake and Rashaan Salaam. The first series cards are grouped alphabetically within teams and checklisted below alphabetically according to teams. A Bam Morris prototype card was sent out as a promotion. It is very similar to the regular issue Morris, except that the prototype reads "1994 Steelers" instead of "1994 Pittsburgh" in the stat lines. A 4-card series two promo sheet was produced and priced below as an uncut sheet.

COMPLETE SET (550) 20.00 50.00
COMP.SERIES 1 (350) 10.00 25.00
COMP.SERIES 2 (200) 10.00 25.00
1 Michael Bankston .02 .10
2 Larry Centers .07 .20
3 Garrison Hearst .15 .40
4 Eric Hill .02 .10
5 Seth Joyner .02 .10
6 Lorenzo Lynch .02 .10
7 Jamir Miller .02 .10
8 Clyde Simmons .02 .10
9 Eric Swann .07 .20
10 Aeneas Williams .02 .10
11 Devin Bush RC .02 .10
12 Ron Davis RC .02 .10
13 Chris Doleman .02 .10
14 Bert Emanuel .15 .40
15 Jeff George .07 .20
16 Roger Harper .02 .10
17 Craig Heyward .07 .20
18 Pierce Holt .02 .10
19 D.J. Johnson .02 .10
20 Terance Mathis .07 .20
21 Chuck Smith .02 .10
22 Jessie Tuggle .02 .10
23 Cornelius Bennett .07 .20
24 Ruben Brown RC .15 .40
25 Jeff Burris .02 .10
26 Matt Darby .02 .10
27 Phil Hansen .02 .10
28 Henry Jones .02 .10
29 Jim Kelly .15 .40
30 Mark Maddox RC .02 .10
31 Andre Reed .07 .20
32 Bruce Smith .15 .40
33 Don Beebe .02 .10
34 Kerry Collins RC .75 2.00
35 Darion Conner .02 .10
36 Pete Metzelaars .02 .10
37 Sam Mills .07 .20
38 Tyrone Poole RC .15 .40
39 Joe Cain .02 .10
40 Mark Carrier DB .02 .10
41 Curtis Conway .15 .40
42 Jeff Graham .02 .10
43 Raymont Harris .02 .10
44 Erik Kramer .02 .10
45 Rashaan Salaam RC .07 .20
46 Lewis Tillman .02 .10
47 Donnell Woolford .02 .10
48 Chris Zorich .02 .10
49 Jeff Blake RC .30 .75
50 Mike Brim .02 .10
51 Ki-Jana Carter RC .15 .40
52 James Francis .02 .10
53 Carl Pickens .07 .20
54 Darnay Scott .07 .20
55 Steve Tovar .02 .10
56 Dan Wilkinson .07 .20
57 Alfred Williams .02 .10
58 Darryl Williams .02 .10
59 Derrick Alexander WR .15 .40
60 Rob Burnett .02 .10
61 Steve Everitt .02 .10
62 Leroy Hoard .02 .10
63 Michael Jackson .07 .20
64 Pepper Johnson .02 .10
65 Tony Jones .02 .10
66 Antonio Langham .02 .10
67 Anthony Pleasant .02 .10
68 Craig Powell RC .02 .10
69 Vinny Testaverde .07 .20
70 Eric Turner .02 .10
71 Troy Aikman .60 1.50
72 Charles Haley .07 .20
73 Michael Irvin .15 .40
74 Daryl Johnston .07 .20
75 Robert Jones .02 .10
76 Leon Lett .02 .10
77 Russell Maryland .02 .10
78 Jay Novacek .07 .20
79 Darrin Smith .02 .10
80 Emmitt Smith 1.25 2.50
81 Kevin Smith .02 .10
82 Erik Williams .02 .10
83 Kevin Williams WR .07 .20
84 Sherman Williams RC .02 .10
85 Darren Woodson .07 .20
86 Elijah Alexander RC .02 .10
87 Steve Atwater .02 .10
88 Ray Crockett .02 .10
89 Shane Dronett .02 .10
90 Jason Elam .07 .20
91 John Elway 1.25 3.00
92 Simon Fletcher .02 .10
93 Glyn Milburn .02 .10
94 Anthony Miller .07 .20
95 Leonard Russell .02 .10
96 Shannon Sharpe .07 .20
97 Bennie Blades .02 .10
98 Lomas Brown .02 .10
99 Willie Clay .02 .10
100 Luther Elliss RC .02 .10
101 Mike Johnson .02 .10
102 Robert Massey .02 .10
103 Scott Mitchell .07 .20
104 Herman Moore .15 .40
105 Brett Perriman .07 .20
106 Robert Porcher .02 .10
107 Barry Sanders 1.00 2.50
108 Chris Spielman .07 .20
109 Edgar Bennett .07 .20
110 Robert Brooks .15 .40
111 LeRoy Butler .02 .10
112 Brett Favre 1.50 3.00
113 Sean Jones .02 .10
114 John Jurkovic .02 .10
115 George Koonce .02 .10
116 Wayne Simmons .02 .10
117 George Teague .02 .10
118 Reggie White .15 .40
119 Micheal Barrow .02 .10
120 Gary Brown .02 .10
121 Cody Carlson .02 .10
122 Ray Childress .02 .10
123 Cris Dishman .02 .10
124 Bruce Matthews .02 .10
125 Steve McNair RC 1.25 3.00
126 Marcus Robertson .02 .10
127 Webster Slaughter .02 .10
128 Al Smith .02 .10
129 Tony Bennett .02 .10
130 Ray Buchanan .02 .10
131 Quentin Coryatt .07 .20
132 Sean Dawkins .07 .20
133 Marshall Faulk .75 2.00
134 Stephen Grant RC .02 .10
135 Jim Harbaugh .07 .20
136 Jeff Herrod .02 .10
137 Ellis Johnson RC .02 .10
138 Tony Siragusa .02 .10
139 Steve Beuerlein .07 .20
140 Tony Boselli RC .15 .40
141 Darren Carrington .02 .10
142 Reggie Cobb .02 .10
143 Kelvin Martin .02 .10
144 Kelvin Pritchett .02 .10
145 Joel Smeenge .02 .10
146 James O. Stewart RC .50 1.25
147 Marcus Allen .15 .40
148 Kimble Anders .07 .20
149 Dale Carter .07 .20
150 Mark Collins .02 .10
151 Willie Davis .07 .20
152 Lake Dawson .07 .20
153 Greg Hill .07 .20
154 Trezelle Jenkins RC .02 .10
155 Darren Mickell RC .02 .10
156 Tracy Simien .02 .10
157 Neil Smith .07 .20
158 William White .02 .10
159 Joe Aska RC .02 .10
160 Greg Biekert .02 .10
161 Tim Brown .15 .40
162 Rob Fredrickson .02 .10
163 Andrew Glover RC .02 .10
164 Jeff Hostetler .07 .20
165 Rocket Ismail .07 .20
166 Napoleon Kaufman RC .50 1.25
167 Terry McDaniel .02 .10
168 Chester McGlockton .07 .20
169 Anthony Smith .02 .10
170 Harvey Williams .02 .10
171 Steve Wisniewski .02 .10
172 Gene Atkins .02 .10
173 Aubrey Beavers .02 .10
174 Tim Bowens .02 .10
175 Bryan Cox .02 .10
176 Jeff Cross .02 .10
177 Irving Fryar .07 .20
178 Dan Marino 1.25 3.00
179 O.J. McDuffie .15 .40
180 Billy Milner .02 .10
181 Bernie Parmalee .07 .20
182 Troy Vincent .02 .10
183 Richmond Webb .02 .10
184 De. Alexander DE RC .02 .10
185 Cris Carter .15 .40
186 Jack Del Rio .02 .10
187 Qadry Ismail .07 .20
188 Ed McDaniel .02 .10
189 Randall McDaniel .05 .15
190 Warren Moon .07 .20
191 John Randle .07 .20
192 Jake Reed .07 .20
193 Fuad Reveiz .02 .10
194 Korey Stringer RC .10 .30
195 Dewayne Washington .07 .20
196 Bruce Armstrong .02 .10
197 Drew Bledsoe .40 1.00
198 Vincent Brisby .02 .10
199 Vincent Brown .02 .10
200 Marion Butts .02 .10
201 Ben Coates .07 .20
202 Myron Guyton .02 .10
203 Maurice Hurst .02 .10
204 Mike Jones .02 .10
205 Ty Law RC .60 1.50
206 Willie McGinest .07 .20
207 Chris Slade .02 .10
208 Mario Bates .07 .20
209 Quinn Early .07 .20
210 Jim Everett .02 .10
211 Mark Fields RC .15 .40
212 Michael Haynes .07 .20
213 Tyrone Hughes .07 .20
214 Joe Johnson .02 .10
215 Wayne Martin .02 .10
216 Willie Roaf .02 .10
217 Irv Smith .02 .10
218 Jimmy Spencer .02 .10
219 Winfred Tubbs .02 .10
220 Renaldo Turnbull .02 .10
221 Michael Brooks .02 .10
222 Dave Brown .07 .20
223 Chris Calloway .02 .10
224 Howard Cross .02 .10
225 John Elliott .02 .10
226 Keith Hamilton .02 .10
227 Rodney Hampton .07 .20
228 Thomas Lewis .07 .20
229 Thomas Randolph .02 .10
230 Mike Sherrard .02 .10
231 Michael Strahan .15 .40
232 Tyrone Wheatley RC .50 1.25
233 Brad Baxter .02 .10
234 Kyle Brady RC .15 .40
235 Kyle Clifton .02 .10
236 Hugh Douglas RC .15 .40
237 Boomer Esiason .07 .20
238 Aaron Glenn .02 .10
239 Bobby Houston .02 .10
240 Johnny Johnson .02 .10
241 Mo Lewis .02 .10
242 Johnny Mitchell .02 .10
243 Marvin Washington .02 .10
244 Fred Barnett .07 .20
245 Randall Cunningham .15 .40
246 William Fuller .02 .10
247 Charlie Garner .15 .40
248 Andy Harmon .02 .10
249 Greg Jackson .02 .10
250 Mike Mamula RC .02 .10
251 Bill Romanowski .02 .10
252 Bobby Taylor RC .15 .40
253 William Thomas .02 .10
254 Calvin Williams .07 .20
255 Michael Zordich .02 .10
256 Chad Brown .07 .20
257 Mark Bruener RC .07 .20
258 Dermontti Dawson .07 .20
259 Barry Foster .07 .20
260 Kevin Greene .07 .20
261 Charles Johnson .07 .20
262 Carnell Lake .02 .10
263 Greg Lloyd .07 .20
264 Byron Bam Morris .02 .10
265 Neil O'Donnell .07 .20
266 Darren Perry .02 .10
267 Ray Seals .02 .10
268 Kordell Stewart RC .60 1.50
269 John L. Williams .02 .10
270 Rod Woodson .07 .20
271 Jerome Bettis .15 .40
272 Isaac Bruce .30 .75
273 Kevin Carter RC .15 .40
274 Shane Conlan .02 .10
275 Troy Drayton .02 .10
276 Sean Gilbert .07 .20
277 Todd Lyght .02 .10
278 Chris Miller .02 .10
279 Anthony Newman .02 .10
280 Roman Phifer .02 .10
281 Robert Young .02 .10
282 John Carney .02 .10
283 Andre Coleman .02 .10
284 Courtney Hall .02 .10
285 Ronnie Harmon .02 .10
286 Dwayne Harper .02 .10
287 Stan Humphries .07 .20
288 Shawn Jefferson .02 .10
289 Tony Martin .07 .20
290 Natrone Means .07 .20
291 Chris Mims .02 .10
292 Leslie O'Neal .07 .20
293 Junior Seau .15 .40
294 Mark Seay .07 .20
295 Eric Davis .02 .10
296 William Floyd .07 .20
297 Merton Hanks .02 .10
298 Brent Jones .02 .10
299 Ken Norton Jr. .07 .20
300 Gary Plummer .02 .10
301 Jerry Rice .60 1.50
302 Deion Sanders .40 1.00
303 Jesse Sapolu .02 .10
304 J.J. Stokes RC .15 .40
305 Dana Stubblefield .07 .20
306 John Taylor .02 .10
307 Steve Wallace .02 .10
308 Lee Woodall .02 .10
309 Bryant Young .07 .20
310 Steve Young .50 1.25
311 Sam Adams .02 .10
312 Howard Ballard .02 .10
313 Robert Blackmon .02 .10
314 Brian Blades .07 .20
315 Joey Galloway RC .60 1.50
316 Carlton Gray .02 .10
317 Cortez Kennedy .07 .20
318 Rick Mirer .07 .20
319 Eugene Robinson .02 .10
320 Chris Warren .07 .20
321 Terry Wooden .02 .10
322 Derrick Brooks RC .60 1.50
323 Lawrence Dawsey .02 .10
324 Trent Dilfer .15 .40
325 Santana Dotson .02 .10
326 Thomas Everett .02 .10
327 Paul Gruber .02 .10
328 Jackie Harris .02 .10
329 Courtney Hawkins .02 .10
330 Martin Mayhew .02 .10
331 Hardy Nickerson .02 .10
332 Errict Rhett .07 .20
333 Warren Sapp RC .60 1.50
334 Charles Wilson .02 .10
335 Reggie Brooks .07 .20
336 Tom Carter .02 .10
337 Henry Ellard .07 .20
338 Ricky Ervins .02 .10
339 Darrell Green .02 .10
340 Ken Harvey .02 .10
341 Brian Mitchell .02 .10
342 Cory Raymer RC .02 .10
343 Heath Shuler .07 .20
344 Michael Westbrook RC .15 .40
345 Tony Woods .02 .10
346 Checklist .02 .10
347 Checklist .02 .10
348 Checklist .02 .10
349 Checklist .02 .10
350 Checklist .02 .10
351 Checklist .02 .10
352 Checklist .02 .10
353 Dave Krieg .02 .10
354 Rob Moore .07 .20
355 J.J. Birden .02 .10
356 Eric Metcalf .07 .20
357 Bryce Paup .07 .20
358 Willie Green .07 .20
359 Derrick Moore .02 .10
360 Michael Timpson .02 .10
361 Eric Bieniemy .02 .10
362 Keenan McCardell .15 .40
363 Andre Rison .07 .20
364 Lorenzo White .02 .10
365 Deion Sanders .40 1.00
366 Wade Wilson .02 .10
367 Aaron Craver .02 .10
368 Michael Dean Perry .02 .10
369 Rod Smith WR RC 5.00 12.00
370 Henry Thomas .02 .10
371 Mark Ingram .02 .10
372 Chris Chandler .07 .20
373 Mel Gray .02 .10
374 Flipper Anderson .02 .10
375 Craig Erickson .02 .10
376 Mark Brunell .40 1.00
377 Ernest Givins .02 .10
378 Randy Jordan .02 .10
379 Webster Slaughter .02 .10
380 Tamarick Vanover RC .15 .40
381 Gary Clark .02 .10
382 Steve Emtman .02 .10
383 Eric Green .02 .10
384 Louis Oliver .02 .10
385 Robert Smith .15 .40
386 Dave Meggett .02 .10
387 Eric Allen .02 .10
388 Wesley Walls .07 .20
389 Herschel Walker .07 .20
390 Ronald Moore .02 .10
391 Adrian Murrell .07 .20
392 Charles Wilson .02 .10
393 Derrick Fenner .02 .10
394 Pat Swilling .02 .10
395 Kelvin Martin .02 .10
396 Rodney Peete .02 .10
397 Ricky Watters .07 .20
398 Erric Pegram .07 .20
399 Leonard Russell .02 .10
400 Alexander Wright .02 .10
401 Darrien Gordon .02 .10
402 Alfred Pupunu .02 .10
403 Elvis Grbac .15 .40
404 Derek Loville .02 .10
405 Steve Broussard .02 .10
406 Ricky Proehl .02 .10
407 Bobby Joe Edmonds .02 .10
408 Alvin Harper .02 .10
409 Dave Moore RC .02 .10
410 Terry Allen .07 .20
411 Gus Frerotte .07 .20
412 Leslie Shepherd RC .07 .20
413 Stoney Case RC .02 .10
414 Frank Sanders RC .15 .40
415 Roell Preston RC .07 .20
416 Lorenzo Styles RC .02 .10
417 Justin Armour RC .02 .10
418 Todd Collins RC .50 1.25
419 Darick Holmes RC .07 .20
420 Kerry Collins .30 .75
421 Tyrone Poole .07 .20
422 Rashaan Salaam .07 .20
423 Todd Sauerbrun RC .02 .10
424 Ki-Jana Carter .15 .40
425 David Dunn RC .02 .10
426 Ernest Hunter RC .02 .10
427 Eric Zeier RC .15 .40
428 Eric Bjornson RC .02 .10
429 Sherman Williams .02 .10
430 Terrell Davis RC 1.00 2.50
431 Luther Elliss .02 .10
432 Kez McCorvey RC .02 .10
433 Antonio Freeman RC .50 1.25
434 Craig Newsome RC .02 .10
435 Steve McNair .60 1.50
436 Chris Sanders RC .07 .20
437 Zack Crockett RC .07 .20
438 Ellis Johnson .02 .10
439 Tony Boselli .15 .40
440 James O. Stewart .15 .40
441 Trezelle Jenkins .02 .10
442 Tamarick Vanover .15 .40
443 Derrick Alexander DE .02 .10
444 Chad May RC .02 .10
445 James A.Stewart RC .02 .10
446 Ty Law .15 .40
447 Curtis Martin RC 1.25 3.00
448 Will Moore RC .02 .10
449 Mark Fields .07 .20
450 Ray Zellars RC .07 .20
451 Charles Way RC .02 .10
452 Tyrone Wheatley .15 .40
453 Kyle Brady .15 .40
454 Wayne Chrebet RC 1.00 2.50
455 Hugh Douglas .07 .20
456 Chris T.Jones RC .02 .10
457 Mike Mamula .02 .10
458 Fred McCrary RC .02 .10
459 Bobby Taylor .15 .40
460 Mark Bruener .07 .20
461 Kordell Stewart .25 .60
462 Kevin Carter .07 .20
463 Lovell Pinkney RC .02 .10
464 Johnny Thomas RC .02 .10
465 Terrell Fletcher RC .02 .10
466 Jimmy Oliver RC .02 .10
467 J.J. Stokes .15 .40
468 Christian Fauria RC .07 .20
469 Joey Galloway .25 .60
470 Derrick Brooks .25 .60
471 Warren Sapp .15 .40
472 Michael Westbrook .15 .40
473 Garrison Hearst .15 .40
474 Jeff George .07 .20
475 Terance Mathis .07 .20
476 Andre Reed .07 .20
477 Bruce Smith .15 .40
478 Lamar Lathon .02 .10
479 Curtis Conway .15 .40
480 Jeff Blake .15 .40
481 Carl Pickens .07 .20
482 Eric Turner .02 .10
483 Troy Aikman .30 .75
484 Michael Irvin .15 .40
485 Emmitt Smith .50 1.25
486 John Elway .60 1.50
487 Shannon Sharpe .07 .20
488 Herman Moore .15 .40
489 Barry Sanders ES .50 1.25
490 Brett Favre ES .60 1.50
491 Reggie White .15 .40
492 Haywood Jeffires .02 .10
493 Sean Dawkins .02 .10
494 Marshall Faulk .40 1.00
495 Desmond Howard .07 .20
496 Steve Bono .07 .20
497 Derrick Thomas .15 .40
498 Irving Fryar .07 .20
499 Terry Kirby .07 .20
500 Dan Marino .60 1.50
501 O.J. McDuffie .15 .40
502 Cris Carter .15 .40
503 Warren Moon .07 .20
504 Jake Reed .07 .20
505 Drew Bledsoe .15 .40
506 Ben Coates .07 .20
507 Jim Everett .02 .10
508 Rodney Hampton .07 .20
509 Mo Lewis .02 .10
510 Tim Brown .15 .40
511 Jeff Hostetler .07 .20
512 Rocket Ismail .07 .20
513 Chester McGlockton .07 .20
514 Fred Barnett .07 .20
515 Greg Lloyd .07 .20
516 Byron Bam Morris .02 .10
517 Rod Woodson .07 .20
518 Jerome Bettis .15 .40
519 Isaac Bruce .15 .40
520 Stan Humphries .07 .20
521 Natrone Means .07 .20
522 Junior Seau .15 .40
523 William Floyd .07 .20
524 Jerry Rice .30 .75
525 Steve Young .25 .60
526 Cortez Kennedy .07 .20
527 Rick Mirer .07 .20
528 Chris Warren .07 .20
529 Trent Dilfer .15 .40
530 Errict Rhett .07 .20
531 Darrell Green .02 .10
532 Heath Shuler .07 .20
533 Stoney Case RO .02 .10
534 Eric Zeier RO .07 .20
535 Kerry Collins RO .15 .40
536 Steve McNair RO .50 1.25
537 Kordell Stewart RO .25 .60
538 Rob Johnson RO RC .40 1.00
539 Eric Ball EE .02 .10
540 Darrick Brownlow EE .02 .10
541 Paul Butcher EE .02 .10
542 Carlester Crumpler EE .02 .10
543 Maurice Douglas EE .02 .10
544 Keith Elias EE RC .02 .10
545 Kenneth Gant EE .02 .10
546 Corey Harris EE .02 .10
547 Andre Hastings EE .07 .20
548 Thomas Homco EE .02 .10
549 Lenny McGill EE .02 .10
550 Mark Pike EE .02 .10
P1 Promo Sheet .75 2.00
Dave Meggett
Justin Armour
Brett Favre
William Floyd
P264 Byron Bam Morris .40 1.00
Prototype Card
back includes '1994 Steelers'
in stat information

1995 Ultra Gold Medallion

COMPLETE SET (550) 100.00 250.00
COMP.SERIES 1 (350) 60.00 150.00
COMP.SERIES 2 (200) 40.00 100.00
*STARS: 3X TO 6X BASIC CARDS
*RCs: 1.2X TO 3X BASIC CARDS
ONE PER PACK

1995 Ultra Achievements

COMPLETE SET (10) 4.00 10.00
STATED ODDS 1:7
*GOLD MED.: .8X TO 2X BASIC INSERTS
1 Drew Bledsoe .60 1.50
2 Cris Carter .25 .60
3 Ben Coates .10 .30
4 Mel Gray .05 .15
5 Jerry Rice 1.00 2.50
6 Barry Sanders 1.50 4.00
7 Deion Sanders .60 1.50
8 Herschel Walker .10 .30
9 Dewayne Washington .10 .30
10 Steve Young .75 2.00

1995 Ultra All-Rookie Team

COMPLETE SET (10) 20.00 50.00
SER.2 STATED ODDS 1:55
*HOT PACK: .2X TO .5X BASIC INSERTS
HP SET: SER.2 STATED ODDS 1:360
1 Michael Westbrook .75 2.00
2 Terrell Davis 5.00 12.00
3 Curtis Martin 6.00 15.00
4 Joey Galloway 3.00 8.00
5 Rashaan Salaam .40 1.00
6 J.J. Stokes .75 2.00
7 Napoleon Kaufman 2.50 6.00

8 Mike Mamula	.20	.50
9 Kyle Brady	.75	2.00
10 Hugh Douglas	.75	2.00

1995 Ultra Award Winners

COMPLETE SET (6)	3.00	8.00
SER.1 STATED ODDS 1:5		
*GOLD MED.: .8X TO 2X BASIC INSERTS		
1 Tim Bowens	.02	.10
2 Marshall Faulk	.75	2.00
3 Dan Marino	1.25	3.00
4 Barry Sanders	1.00	2.50
5 Deion Sanders	.40	1.00
6 Steve Young	.50	1.25

1995 Ultra First Rounders

COMPLETE SET (20)	10.00	25.00
SER.1 STATED ODDS 1:7		
*GOLD MED: .8X TO 2X BASIC INSERTS		
1 Derrick Alexander DE	.05	.15
2 Tony Boselli	.25	.60
3 Kyle Brady	.25	.60
4 Mark Bruener	.10	.30
5 Devin Bush	.05	.15
6 Kevin Carter	.25	.60
7 Ki-Jana Carter	.25	.60
8 Kerry Collins	1.25	3.00
9 Mark Fields	.25	.60
10 Joey Galloway	1.00	2.50
11 Napoleon Kaufman	.75	2.00
12 Ty Law	1.00	2.50
13 Mike Mamula	.05	.15
14 Steve McNair	2.00	5.00
15 Rashaan Salaam	.10	.30
16 Warren Sapp	1.00	2.50
17 James O. Stewart	.75	2.00
18 J.J.Stokes	.25	.60
19 Michael Westbrook	.25	.60
20 Tyrone Wheatley	.75	2.00

1995 Ultra Magna Force

COMPLETE SET (20)	40.00	100.00
SER.2 STATED ODDS 1:20 HOBBY		
1 Emmitt Smith	10.00	20.00
2 Jerry Rice	5.00	10.00
3 Drew Bledsoe	4.00	8.00
4 Marshall Faulk	7.50	15.00
5 Heath Shuler	.75	1.50
6 Carl Pickens	.75	1.50
7 Ben Coates	.75	1.50
8 Terry Allen	.75	1.50
9 Terance Mathis	.75	1.50
10 Fred Barnett	.75	1.50
11 O.J. McDuffie	1.50	3.00
12 Garrison Hearst	1.50	3.00
13 Deion Sanders	4.00	8.00
14 Reggie White	1.50	3.00
15 Herman Moore	1.50	3.00
16 Brett Favre	10.00	20.00
17 William Floyd	.75	1.50
18 Curtis Martin	6.00	12.00
19 Joey Galloway	3.00	6.00
20 Tyrone Wheatley	2.50	5.00

1995 Ultra Overdrive

COMPLETE SET (20)	20.00	50.00
SER.2 STATED ODDS 1:20 RETAIL		
1 Barry Sanders	5.00	12.00
2 Troy Aikman	3.00	8.00
3 Natrone Means	.40	1.00
4 Steve Young	2.50	6.00
5 Errict Rhett	.40	1.00
6 Terrell Davis	2.00	5.00
7 Michael Westbrook	.20	.50
8 Michael Irvin	.75	2.00
9 Chris Warren	.40	1.00
10 Tim Brown	.75	2.00
11 Jerome Bettis	.75	2.00
12 Ricky Watters	.40	1.00
13 Derrick Thomas	.75	2.00
14 Bruce Smith	.75	2.00
15 Rashaan Salaam	.20	.50
16 Jeff Blake	.40	1.00
17 Alvin Harper	.20	.50
18 Shannon Sharpe	.40	1.00
19 Eric Swann	.40	1.00
20 Andre Rison	.40	1.00

1995 Ultra Rising Stars

COMPLETE SET (9)	15.00	40.00
SER.1 STATED ODDS 1:37		
*GOLD MED.: .6X TO 1.5X BASIC INSERTS		
1 Jerome Bettis	1.25	3.00
2 Jeff Blake	1.00	2.50
3 Drew Bledsoe	3.00	8.00
4 Ben Coates	.60	1.50
5 Marshall Faulk	6.00	15.00
6 Brett Favre	10.00	25.00
7 Natrone Means	.60	1.50
8 Byron Bam Morris	.30	.75
9 Eric Turner	.30	.75

1995 Ultra Second Year Standouts

COMPLETE SET (15)	4.00	8.00
SER.1 STATED ODDS 1:5		
*GOLD MED: .8X TO 2X BASIC INSERTS		
1 Derrick Alexander WR	.75	2.00
2 Mario Bates	.40	1.00
3 Tim Bowens	.20	.50
4 Bert Emanuel	.75	2.00
5 Marshall Faulk	4.00	10.00
6 William Floyd	.40	1.00
7 Rob Fredrickson	.20	.50
8 Antonio Langham	.20	.50
9 Byron Bam Morris	.20	.50
10 Errict Rhett	.40	1.00
11 Darnay Scott	.40	1.00
12 Heath Shuler	.40	1.00
13 Dewayne Washington	.40	1.00
14 Dan Wilkinson	.40	1.00
15 Bryant Young	.40	1.00

1995 Ultra Stars

COMPLETE SET (10)	7.50	15.00
SER.1 STATED ODDS 1:7 JUMBO		
*GOLD MED: .8X TO 2X BASIC INSERTS		
1 Tim Brown	.25	.60
2 Marshall Faulk	1.25	3.00
3 Irving Fryar	.10	.30
4 Dan Marino	2.00	5.00
5 Natrone Means	.10	.30
6 Jerry Rice	1.00	2.50
7 Barry Sanders	1.50	4.00
8 Deion Sanders	.60	1.50
9 Emmitt Smith	1.50	4.00
10 Rod Woodson	.10	.30

1995 Ultra Touchdown Kings

COMPLETE SET (10)	4.00	10.00
SER.1 STATED ODDS 1:7		
*GOLD MED: .8X TO 2X BASIC INSERTS		
1 Marshall Faulk	1.25	3.00
2 Terance Mathis	.10	.30
3 Natrone Means	.10	.30
4 Herman Moore	.25	.60
5 Carl Pickens	.10	.30
6 Jerry Rice	1.00	2.50
7 Andre Rison	.10	.30
8 Emmitt Smith	1.50	4.00
9 Chris Warren	.10	.30
10 Steve Young	.75	2.00

1995 Ultra Ultrabilities

COMPLETE SET (30)	25.00	50.00
SER.2 STATED ODDS 1:5		
1 Dan Marino	4.00	8.00
2 Steve Young	1.50	3.00
3 Drew Bledsoe	1.25	2.50
4 Jeff Blake	.60	1.25
5 Troy Aikman	2.00	4.00
6 John Elway	4.00	8.00
7 Trent Dilfer	.40	1.00
8 Steve Bono	.20	.50
9 Brett Favre	4.00	8.00
10 Kerry Collins	1.25	3.00
11 Barry Sanders	3.00	6.00
12 Errict Rhett	.20	.50
13 Emmitt Smith	3.00	6.00
14 Chris Warren	.20	.50
15 Irving Fryar	.20	.50
16 Charlie Garner	.40	1.00
17 Tim Brown	.40	1.00
18 Eric Metcalf	.20	.50
19 Herman Moore	.40	1.00
20 Robert Smith	.40	1.00
21 Natrone Means	.20	.50
22 Derrick Thomas	.40	1.00
23 Bruce Smith	.40	1.00
24 Hugh Douglas	.25	.60
25 Mike Mamula	.05	.15
26 Jerome Bettis	.40	1.00
27 Byron Bam Morris UER Rams helmet on back	.08	.25
28 Tim Bowens	.08	.25
29 William Floyd	.20	.50
30 Daryl Johnston	.20	.50

1996 Ultra

The 1996 Ultra set consists of 200 standard-size cards. The 12-card packs have a suggested retail priced of $2.49 each. Dealers had the option of purchasing either six, 12 or 30 box cases. Each case contained 24 packs per box with the 12 cards in the packs. The cards are grouped alphabetically within teams and checklisted below alphabetically according to teams. The following topical subsets are also part of the set: Rookies (164-178), First Impressions (179-188) and Secret Weapons (189-198). Rookie Cards include Tim Biakabutuka, Bobby Engram, Eddie George, Terry Glenn, Keyshawn Johnson, Leeland McElroy and Lawrence Phillips. A 3-card promo sheet was produced and priced below. Finally, some collectors have reported that the Ultra logo on the fronts can be found with either silver foil or bronze foil in addition to the intended gold foil.

COMPLETE SET (200)	10.00	25.00
1 Larry Centers	.08	.25
2 Garrison Hearst	.08	.25
3 Rob Moore	.08	.25
4 Eric Swann	.02	.10
5 Aeneas Williams	.02	.10
6 Bert Emanuel	.08	.25
7 Jeff George	.08	.25
8 Craig Heyward	.02	.10
9 Terance Mathis	.02	.10
10 Eric Metcalf	.02	.10
11 Cornelius Bennett	.02	.10
12 Darick Holmes	.02	.10
13 Jim Kelly	.20	.50
14 Bryce Paup	.02	.10
15 Bruce Smith	.08	.25
16 Mark Carrier WR	.02	.10
17 Kerry Collins	.20	.50
18 Lamar Lathon	.02	.10
19 Derrick Moore	.02	.10
20 Tyrone Poole	.02	.10
21 Curtis Conway	.20	.50
22 Jeff Graham	.02	.10
23 Raymont Harris	.08	.25
24 Erik Kramer	.02	.10
25 Rashaan Salaam	.08	.25
26 Jeff Blake	.20	.50
27 Ki-Jana Carter	.08	.25
28 Carl Pickens	.08	.25
29 Darnay Scott	.08	.25
30 Dan Wilkinson	.02	.10
31 Leroy Hoard	.02	.10
32 Michael Jackson	.08	.25
33 Andre Rison	.08	.25
34 Vinny Testaverde	.08	.25
35 Eric Turner	.02	.10
36 Troy Aikman	.50	1.25
37 Charles Haley	.08	.25
38 Michael Irvin	.20	.50
39 Daryl Johnston	.08	.25
40 Jay Novacek	.02	.10
41 Deion Sanders	.30	.75
42 Emmitt Smith	.75	2.00
43 Steve Atwater	.02	.10
44 Terrell Davis	.40	1.00
45 John Elway	1.00	2.50
46 Anthony Miller	.08	.25
47 Shannon Sharpe	.08	.25
48 Scott Mitchell	.08	.25
49 Herman Moore	.08	.25
50 Johnnie Morton	.08	.25
51 Brett Perriman	.02	.10
52 Barry Sanders	.75	2.00
53 Chris Spielman	.02	.10
54 Edgar Bennett	.08	.25
55 Robert Brooks	.20	.50
56 Mark Chmura	.08	.25
57 Brett Favre	1.00	2.50
58 Reggie White	.20	.50
59 Mel Gray	.02	.10
60 Haywood Jeffires	.02	.10
61 Steve McNair	.40	1.00
62 Chris Sanders	.08	.25
63 Rodney Thomas	.02	.10
64 Quentin Coryatt	.02	.10
65 Sean Dawkins	.02	.10
66 Ken Dilger	.08	.25
67 Marshall Faulk	.25	.60
68 Jim Harbaugh	.08	.25
69 Tony Boselli	.02	.10
70 Mark Brunell	.30	.75
71 Desmond Howard	.08	.25
72 Jimmy Smith	.20	.50
73 James O. Stewart	.08	.25
74 Marcus Allen	.20	.50
75 Steve Bono	.02	.10
76 Lake Dawson	.02	.10
77 Neil Smith	.08	.25
78 Derrick Thomas	.20	.50
79 Tamarick Vanover	.08	.25
80 Bryan Cox	.02	.10
81 Irving Fryar	.08	.25
82 Eric Green	.02	.10
83 Dan Marino	1.00	2.50
84 O.J. McDuffie	.08	.25
85 Bernie Parmalee	.02	.10
86 Cris Carter	.20	.50
87 Qadry Ismail	.08	.25
88 Warren Moon	.08	.25
89 Jake Reed	.08	.25
90 Robert Smith	.08	.25
91 Drew Bledsoe	.30	.75
92 Vincent Brisby	.02	.10
93 Ben Coates	.08	.25
94 Curtis Martin	.40	1.00
95 Willie McGinest	.02	.10
96 Dave Meggett	.02	.10
97 Mario Bates	.08	.25
98 Quinn Early	.02	.10
99 Jim Everett	.02	.10
100 Michael Haynes	.02	.10
101 Renaldo Turnbull	.02	.10
102 Dave Brown	.02	.10
103 Rodney Hampton	.08	.25
104 Mike Sherrard	.02	.10
105 Phillippi Sparks	.02	.10
106 Tyrone Wheatley	.08	.25
107 Hugh Douglas	.08	.25
108 Boomer Esiason	.08	.25
109 Aaron Glenn	.02	.10
110 Mo Lewis	.02	.10
111 Johnny Mitchell	.02	.10
112 Tim Brown	.20	.50
113 Jeff Hostetler	.02	.10
114 Rocket Ismail	.02	.10
115 Chester McGlockton	.02	.10
116 Harvey Williams	.02	.10
117 Fred Barnett	.02	.10
118 William Fuller	.02	.10
119 Charlie Garner	.08	.25
120 Ricky Watters	.08	.25
121 Calvin Williams	.02	.10
122 Kevin Greene	.08	.25
123 Greg Lloyd	.08	.25
124 Byron Bam Morris	.02	.10
125 Neil O'Donnell	.08	.25
126 Erric Pegram	.02	.10
127 Kordell Stewart	.20	.50
128 Yancey Thigpen	.08	.25
129 Rod Woodson	.08	.25
130 Jerome Bettis	.20	.50
131 Isaac Bruce	.20	.50
132 Troy Drayton	.02	.10
133 Sean Gilbert	.02	.10
134 Chris Miller	.02	.10
135 Andre Coleman	.02	.10
136 Ronnie Harmon	.02	.10
137 Aaron Hayden RC	.02	.10
138 Stan Humphries	.08	.25
139 Natrone Means	.08	.25
140 Junior Seau	.20	.50
141 William Floyd	.08	.25
142 Merton Hanks	.02	.10
143 Brent Jones	.02	.10
144 Derek Loville	.02	.10
145 Jerry Rice	.50	1.25
146 J.J. Stokes	.20	.50
147 Steve Young	.40	1.00
148 Brian Blades	.02	.10
149 Joey Galloway	.20	.50
150 Cortez Kennedy	.02	.10
151 Rick Mirer	.08	.25
152 Chris Warren	.08	.25
153 Derrick Brooks	.20	.50
154 Trent Dilfer	.20	.50
155 Alvin Harper	.02	.10
156 Jackie Harris	.02	.10
157 Hardy Nickerson	.02	.10
158 Errict Rhett	.08	.25
159 Terry Allen	.08	.25
160 Henry Ellard	.02	.10
161 Brian Mitchell	.02	.10
162 Heath Shuler	.08	.25
163 Michael Westbrook	.20	.50
164 Tim Biakabutuka RC	.20	.50
165 Tony Brackens RC	.20	.50
166 Rickey Dudley RC	.20	.50
167 Bobby Engram RC	.20	.50
168 Daryl Gardener RC	.02	.10
169 Eddie George RC	.60	1.50
170 Terry Glenn RC	.50	1.25
171 Kevin Hardy RC	.20	.50
172 Keyshawn Johnson RC	.50	1.25
173 Cedric Jones RC	.02	.10
174 Leeland McElroy RC	.08	.25
175 Jonathan Ogden RC	.20	.50
176 Lawrence Phillips RC	.20	.50
177 Simeon Rice RC	.50	1.25
178 Regan Upshaw RC	.02	.10
179 Justin Armour FI	.02	.10
180 Kyle Brady FI	.02	.10
181 Devin Bush FI	.02	.10
182 Kevin Carter FI	.02	.10
183 Wayne Chrebet FI	.30	.75
184 Napoleon Kaufman FI	.20	.50
185 Frank Sanders FI	.08	.25
186 Warren Sapp FI	.02	.10
187 Eric Zeier FI	.02	.10
188 Ray Zellars FI	.02	.10
189 Bill Brooks SW	.02	.10
190 Chris Calloway SW	.02	.10
191 Zack Crockett SW	.02	.10
192 Antonio Freeman SW	.20	.50
193 Tyrone Hughes SW	.02	.10
194 Daryl Johnston SW	.08	.25
195 Tony Martin SW	.02	.10
196 Keenan McCardell SW	.20	.50
197 Glyn Milburn SW	.02	.10
198 David Palmer SW	.02	.10
199 Checklist	.02	.10
200 Checklist	.02	.10
P1 Promo Sheet Trent Dilfer Brett Favre Mr.Momentum Daryl Johnston Secret Weapon	.75	2.00

1996 Ultra All-Rookie Die Cuts

COMPLETE SET (10)	15.00	40.00
STATED ODDS 1:180		
1 Bobby Engram	1.50	4.00
2 Daryl Gardener	.30	.75
3 Eddie George	5.00	12.00
4 Terry Glenn	4.00	10.00
5 Kevin Hardy	1.50	4.00
6 Keyshawn Johnson	4.00	10.00
7 Cedric Jones	.30	.75
8 Leeland McElroy	.75	2.00
9 Jonathan Ogden	1.50	4.00
10 Simeon Rice	4.00	10.00

1996 Ultra Mr. Momentum

COMPLETE SET (20)	15.00	40.00
STATED ODDS 1:10		
1 Robert Brooks	.75	1.50
2 Isaac Bruce	.75	1.50
3 Terrell Davis	1.50	3.00
4 John Elway	4.00	8.00
5 Marshall Faulk	1.00	2.00
6 Brett Favre	4.00	8.00
7 Joey Galloway	.75	1.50
8 Dan Marino	4.00	8.00
9 Curtis Martin	1.50	3.00
10 Herman Moore	.30	.75
11 Carl Pickens	.30	.75
12 Jerry Rice	2.00	4.00
13 Barry Sanders	3.00	6.00
14 Chris Sanders	.30	.75
15 Deion Sanders	1.25	2.50
16 Kordell Stewart	.75	1.50
17 Tamarick Vanover	.30	.75
18 Chris Warren	.30	.75
19 Ricky Watters	.30	.75
20 Steve Young	1.50	3.00

1996 Ultra Pulsating

COMPLETE SET (10)	12.50	30.00
STATED ODDS 1:20		
1 Isaac Bruce	.75	1.50
2 Brett Favre	4.00	8.00
3 Joey Galloway	.75	1.50
4 Curtis Martin	1.50	3.00
5 Rashaan Salaam	.30	.75
6 Barry Sanders	3.00	6.00
7 Deion Sanders	1.25	2.50
8 Emmitt Smith	3.00	6.00
9 Kordell Stewart	.75	1.50
10 Chris Warren	.30	.75

1996 Ultra Rookies

COMPLETE SET (30)	20.00	40.00
STATED ODDS 1:3		
1 Karim Abdul-Jabbar	1.00	2.50
2 Mike Alstott	1.25	3.00
3 Marco Battaglia	.30	.75
4 Tim Biakabutuka	1.00	2.50
5 Sean Boyd	.30	.75
6 Tony Brackens	.50	1.25
7 Duane Clemons	.30	.75
8 Bobby Engram	.50	1.25
9 Daryl Gardener	.30	.75
10 Eddie George	1.50	4.00
11 Terry Glenn	1.25	3.00
12 Kevin Hardy	.30	.75
13 Marvin Harrison	3.00	8.00
14 Dietrich Jells	.30	.75
15 Keyshawn Johnson	1.25	3.00
16 Lance Johnstone	.50	1.25
17 Cedric Jones	.30	.75
18 Marcus Jones	.30	.75
19 Danny Kanell	.50	1.25
20 Markco Maddox	.30	.75
21 Derrick Mayes	.50	1.25
22 Leeland McElroy	.50	1.25
23 Dell McGee	.30	.75
24 Alex Molden	.30	.75
25 Eric Moulds	1.50	4.00
26 Jonathan Ogden	1.00	2.50
27 Lawrence Phillips	1.00	2.50
28 Simeon Rice	1.25	3.00
29 Regan Upshaw	.30	.75
30 Jerome Woods	.30	.75

1996 Ultra Sledgehammer

COMPLETE SET (10)	7.50	20.00
STATED ODDS 1:15 HOBBY		
1 Jeff Blake	1.00	2.50
2 Terrell Davis	2.00	5.00
3 Hugh Douglas	.50	1.25
4 Marshall Faulk	1.25	3.00
5 Michael Irvin	1.00	2.50
6 Steve McNair	2.00	5.00
7 Natrone Means	.50	1.25
8 Erriet Rhett	.50	1.25
9 Emmitt Smith	4.00	10.00
10 Rodney Thomas	.20	.50

1997 Ultra

The 1997 Ultra set was released in two series totaling 350 cards with a large number of insert sets. Hobby packs of Series 1 and Series 2 also contained one Gold Medallion parallel card per pack with a Platinum Medallion parallel replacing the Gold version in 1:100 packs. The cardbacks were printed with a blue tinted back for NFC players and green for AFC players. An equally printed brown colored cardback variation was also produced for each series one veteran card. Series 2 packs also included randomly inserted "Lucky 13" redemptions (expirationdate 12/1/98) good for various Dan Marino signed collectibles including an embossed series 1 Ultra card as listed below. The cards were distributed in 24-pack hobby boxes with 10 cards per pack (2 inserts per pack) and a suggested retail price of $2.49.

COMPLETE SET (350)	40.00	80.00
COMP.SERIES 1 (200)	15.00	30.00
COMP.SERIES 2 (150)	25.00	50.00
*1-173 BROWN BACK: .4X TO 1X BASIC CARDS		
1 Brett Favre	1.25	2.50
2 Ricky Watters	.15	.40
3 Dan Marino	1.00	2.50
4 Bryan Still	.08	.25
5 Chester McGlockton	.08	.25
6 Tim Biakabutuka	.15	.40
7 Dave Brown	.08	.25
8 Mike Alstott	.25	.60
9 O.J. McDuffie	.15	.40
10 Mark Brunell	.30	.75
11 Michael Bates	.08	.25
12 Tyrone Wheatley	.15	.40
13 Eddie George	.25	.60
14 Kevin Greene	.15	.40
15 Jerris McPhail	.08	.25
16 Harvey Williams	.08	.25
17 Eric Swann	.08	.25
18 Carl Pickens	.15	.40
19 Terrell Davis	.30	.75
20 Charles Way	.08	.25
21 Jamie Asher	.08	.25
22 Qadry Ismail	.15	.40
23 Lawrence Phillips	.08	.25
24 John Friesz	.08	.25
25 Dorsey Levens	.25	.60
26 Willie McGinest	.08	.25
27 Chris T. Jones	.08	.25
28 Cortez Kennedy	.08	.25
29 Raymont Harris	.08	.25
30 William Roaf	.08	.25
31 Ted Johnson	.08	.25
32 Tony Martin	.15	.40
33 Jim Everett	.08	.25
34 Ray Zellars	.08	.25
35 Derrick Alexander WR	.15	.40
36 Leonard Russell	.08	.25
37 William Thomas	.08	.25
38 Karim Abdul-Jabbar	.15	.40
39 Kevin Turner	.08	.25
40 Robert Brooks	.15	.40
41 Kent Graham	.08	.25
42 Tony Brackens	.08	.25
43 Rodney Hampton	.15	.40
44 Drew Bledsoe	.30	.75
45 Barry Sanders	.75	2.00
46 Tim Brown	.25	.60
47 Reggie White	.25	.60
48 Terry Allen	.25	.60
49 Jim Harbaugh	.15	.40
50 John Elway	1.00	2.50
51 William Floyd	.15	.40
52 Michael Jackson	.15	.40
53 Larry Centers	.15	.40
54 Emmitt Smith	.75	2.00
55 Bruce Smith	.15	.40
56 Terrell Owens	.30	.75
57 Deion Sanders	.25	.60
58 Neil O'Donnell	.15	.40
59 Kordell Stewart	.25	.60
60 Bobby Engram	.15	.40
61 Keenan McCardell	.15	.40
62 Ben Coates	.15	.40
63 Curtis Martin	.30	.75
64 Hugh Douglas	.08	.25
65 Eric Moulds	.25	.60
66 Derrick Thomas	.25	.60
67 Byron Bam Morris	.08	.25
68 Bryan Cox	.08	.25
69 Rob Moore	.15	.40
70 Michael Haynes	.08	.25
71 Brian Mitchell	.08	.25
72 Alex Molden	.08	.25
73 Steve Young	.30	.75
74 Andre Reed	.15	.40
75 Michael Westbrook	.15	.40
76 Eric Metcalf	.15	.40
77 Tony Banks	.15	.40
78 Ken Dilger	.08	.25
79 John Henry Mills RC	.08	.25
80 Ashley Ambrose	.08	.25
81 Jason Dunn	.08	.25
82 Trent Dilfer	.25	.60
83 Wayne Chrebet	.25	.60
84 Ty Detmer	.15	.40
85 Aeneas Williams	.08	.25
86 Frank Wycheck	.08	.25
87 Jessie Tuggle	.08	.25
88 Steve McNair	.30	.75
89 Chris Slade	.08	.25
90 Anthony Johnson	.08	.25
91 Simeon Rice	.15	.40
92 Mike Tomczak	.08	.25
93 Sean Jones	.08	.25
94 Wesley Walls	.15	.40
95 Thurman Thomas	.25	.60
96 Scott Mitchell	.15	.40
97 Desmond Howard	.15	.40
98 Chris Warren	.15	.40
99 Glyn Milburn	.08	.25
100 Vinny Testaverde	.15	.40
101 James O.Stewart	.15	.40
102 Iheanyi Uwaezuoke	.08	.25
103 Stan Humphries	.15	.40
104 Terance Mathis	.15	.40
105 Thomas Lewis	.08	.25
106 Eddie Kennison	.15	.40
107 Rashaan Salaam	.08	.25
108 Curtis Conway	.15	.40
109 Chris Sanders	.08	.25
110 Marcus Allen	.25	.60
111 Gilbert Brown	.15	.40
112 Jason Sehorn	.15	.40
113 Zach Thomas	.25	.60
114 Bobby Hebert	.08	.25
115 Herman Moore	.15	.40
116 Ray Lewis	.40	1.00
117 Darnay Scott	.15	.40
118 Jamal Anderson	.25	.60
119 Keyshawn Johnson	.25	.60
120 Adrian Murrell	.15	.40
121 Sam Mills	.08	.25
122 Irving Fryar	.15	.40
123 Ki-Jana Carter	.08	.25
124 Gus Frerotte	.08	.25
125 Terry Glenn	.25	.60
126 Quentin Coryatt	.08	.25
127 Robert Smith	.15	.40
128 Jeff Blake	.15	.40
129 Natrone Means	.15	.40
130 Isaac Bruce	.25	.60
131 Lamar Lathon	.08	.25
132 Johnnie Morton	.15	.40
133 Jerry Rice	.50	1.25
134 Errict Rhett	.08	.25
135 Junior Seau	.25	.60
136 Joey Galloway	.15	.40
137 Napoleon Kaufman	.25	.60
138 Troy Aikman	.50	1.25
139 Kevin Hardy	.08	.25
140 Jimmy Smith	.15	.40
141 Edgar Bennett	.15	.40
142 Hardy Nickerson	.08	.25
143 Greg Lloyd	.08	.25
144 Dale Carter	.08	.25
145 Jake Reed	.15	.40
146 Cris Carter	.25	.60
147 Todd Collins	.08	.25
148 Mel Gray	.08	.25
149 Lawyer Milloy	.15	.40
150 Kimble Anders	.15	.40
151 Darick Holmes	.08	.25
152 Bert Emanuel	.15	.40
153 Marshall Faulk	.30	.75
154 Frank Sanders	.15	.40
155 Leeland McElroy	.08	.25
156 Rickey Dudley	.15	.40
157 Tamarick Vanover	.15	.40
158 Kerry Collins	.25	.60
159 Jeff Graham	.08	.25
160 Jerome Bettis	.25	.60
161 Greg Hill	.08	.25
162 John Mobley	.08	.25
163 Michael Irvin	.25	.60
164 Marvin Harrison	.25	.60
165 Jim Schwantz RC	.08	.25
166 Jermaine Lewis	.25	.60
167 Levon Kirkland	.08	.25
168 Nilo Silvan	.08	.25
169 Ken Norton	.08	.25
170 Yancey Thigpen	.15	.40
171 Antonio Freeman	.25	.60
172 Terry Kirby	.15	.40
173 Brad Johnson	.25	.60
174 Reidel Anthony RC	.25	.60
175 Tiki Barber RC	2.00	5.00
176 Pat Barnes RC	.25	.60
177 Michael Booker RC	.08	.25
178 Peter Boulware RC	.25	.60
179 Rae Carruth RC	.08	.25
180 Troy Davis RC	.15	.40
181 Corey Dillon RC	1.25	3.00
182 Jim Druckenmiller RC	.15	.40
183 Warrick Dunn RC	1.00	2.50
184 James Farrior RC	.25	.60
185 Yatil Green RC	.15	.40
186 Walter Jones RC	.25	.60
187 Tom Knight RC	.08	.25
188 Sam Madison RC	.25	.60
189 Tyrus McCloud RC	.08	.25
190 Orlando Pace RC	.25	.60
191 Jake Plummer RC	1.25	3.00
192 Dwayne Rudd RC	.25	.60
193 Darrell Russell RC	.08	.25
194 Sedrick Shaw RC	.15	.40
195 Shawn Springs RC	.15	.40
196 Bryant Westbrook RC	.08	.25
197 Danny Wuerffel RC	.25	.60
198 Reinard Wilson RC	.15	.40
199 Checklist Rodney Hampton	.08	.25
200 Checklist John Elway	.25	.60
201 Rick Mirer	.08	.25
202 Torrance Small	.08	.25
203 Ricky Proehl	.08	.25
204 Will Blackwell RC	.15	.40
205 Warrick Dunn	.50	1.25
206 Rob Johnson	.25	.60
207 Jim Schwantz	.08	.25
208 Ike Hilliard RC	.50	1.25
209 Chris Canty RC	.08	.25
210 Chris Boniol	.08	.25
211 Jim Druckenmiller	.08	.25
212 Tony Gonzalez RC	1.25	3.00
213 Scottie Graham	.08	.25
214 Byron Hanspard RC	.15	.40
215 Gary Brown	.08	.25
216 Darrell Russell	.08	.25
217 Sedrick Shaw	.15	.40
218 Boomer Esiason	.15	.40
219 Peter Boulware	.15	.40
220 Willie Green	.08	.25
221 Dietrich Jells	.08	.25
222 Freddie Jones RC	.15	.40
223 Eric Metcalf	.15	.40
224 John Henry Mills	.08	.25
225 Michael Timpson	.08	.25
226 Danny Wuerffel	.25	.60
227 Daimon Shelton RC	.08	.25
228 Henry Ellard	.08	.25
229 Flipper Anderson	.08	.25
230 Hunter Goodwin RC	.08	.25
231 Jay Graham RC	.15	.40
232 Duce Staley RC	2.50	6.00
233 Lamar Thomas	.08	.25
234 Rod Woodson	.15	.40
235 Zack Crockett	.08	.25
236 Ernie Mills	.08	.25
237 Kyle Brady	.08	.25
238 Jesse Campbell	.08	.25
239 Anthony Miller	.08	.25
240 Michael Haynes	.08	.25
241 Qadry Ismail	.15	.40
242 Tom Knight	.08	.25
243 Brian Manning RC	.08	.25
244 Derrick Mayes	.15	.40
245 Jamie Sharper RC	.15	.40
246 Sherman Williams	.08	.25
247 Yatil Green	.15	.40
248 Howard Griffith	.08	.25
249 Brian Blades	.08	.25
250 Mark Chmura	.15	.40
251 Chris Darkins	.08	.25
252 Willie Davis	.08	.25
253 Quinn Early	.08	.25
254 Marc Edwards RC	.08	.25
255 Charlie Jones	.08	.25
256 Jake Plummer	.60	1.50
257 Heath Shuler	.08	.25
258 Fred Barnett	.08	.25
259 William Henderson	.15	.40
260 Michael Booker	.08	.25
261 Chad Brown	.08	.25
262 Garrison Hearst	.15	.40
263 Leon Johnson RC	.15	.40
264 Antowain Smith RC	.75	2.00
265 Darnell Autry RC	.15	.40
266 Craig Heyward	.08	.25
267 Walter Jones	.08	.25
268 Dexter Coakley RC	.25	.60
269 Mercury Hayes	.08	.25
270 Brett Perriman	.08	.25
271 Chris Spielman	.08	.25
272 Kevin Greene	.15	.40
273 Kevin Lockett RC	.15	.40
274 Troy Davis	.15	.40
275 Brent Jones	.08	.25
276 Chris Chandler	.15	.40
277 Bryant Westbrook	.08	.25
278 Desmond Howard	.15	.40
279 Tyrone Hughes	.08	.25
280 Kez McCorvey	.08	.25
281 Stephen Davis	.25	.60
282 Steve Everitt	.08	.25
283 Andre Hastings	.08	.25
284 Marcus Robinson RC	2.00	5.00
285 Donnell Woolford	.08	.25
286 Mario Bates	.08	.25
287 Corey Dillon	.75	2.00
288 Jackie Harris	.08	.25
289 Lorenzo Neal	.08	.25
290 Anthony Pleasant	.08	.25
291 Andre Rison	.15	.40
292 Amani Toomer	.15	.40
293 Eric Turner	.08	.25
294 Elvis Grbac	.15	.40
295 Cris Dishman	.08	.25
296 Tom Carter	.08	.25
297 Mark Carrier DB	.08	.25
298 Orlando Pace	.15	.40
299 Jay Riemersma RC	.08	.25
300 Daryl Johnston	.15	.40
301 Joey Kent RC	.25	.60
302 Ronnie Harmon	.08	.25
303 Rocket Ismail	.15	.40
304 Terrell Davis	.30	.75
305 Sean Dawkins	.08	.25
306 Jeff George	.15	.40
307 David Palmer	.08	.25
308 Dwayne Rudd	.08	.25
309 J.J. Stokes	.15	.40
310 James Farrior	.15	.40
311 William Fuller	.08	.25
312 George Jones RC	.15	.40
313 John Allred RC	.08	.25
314 Tony Graziani RC	.25	.60
315 Jeff Hostetler	.08	.25
316 Keith Poole RC	.25	.60
317 Neil Smith	.15	.40
318 Steve Tasker	.08	.25
319 Mike Vrabel RC	6.00	15.00
320 Pat Barnes	.25	.60
321 James Hundon RC	.25	.60
322 O.J. Santiago RC	.15	.40
328 Billy Davis RC	.08	.25
324 Shawn Springs	.15	.40
325 Reinard Wilson	.08	.25
326 Charles Johnson	.15	.40
327 Micheal Barrow	.08	.25
328 Derrick Mason RC	1.25	3.00
329 Muhsin Muhammad	.15	.40
330 David LaFleur RC	.08	.25
331 Reidel Anthony	.15	.40
332 Tiki Barber	.75	2.00
333 Ray Buchanan	.08	.25
334 John Elway	1.00	2.50
335 Alvin Harper	.08	.25
336 Damon Jones RC	.08	.25
337 Dedric Ward RC	.15	.40
338 Jim Everett	.08	.25
339 Jon Harris	.08	.25
340 Warren Moon	.25	.60
341 Rae Carruth	.08	.25
342 John Mobley	.08	.25
343 Tyrone Poole	.08	.25
344 Mike Cherry RC	.08	.25
345 Horace Copeland	.08	.25
346 Deon Figures	.08	.25
347 Antwuan Wyatt RC	.08	.25
348 Tommy Vardell	.08	.25
349 Checklist (201-324)	.08	.25
350 Checklist/325-350 inserts	.08	.25
S1A Terrell Davis Sample AUTO	40.00	80.00
AU3 Dan Marino AUTO (reportedly 100 were signed)	40.00	100.00
S1 Terrell Davis Sample	1.25	3.00

1997 Ultra Gold Medallion

COMPLETE SET (346)	200.00	400.00
COMP.SERIES 1 (198)	75.00	150.00
COMP.SERIES 2 (148)	125.00	250.00
*STARS: 1.5X TO 3X BASIC CARDS		
*RCs: 1X TO 2X BASIC CARDS		
ONE PER HOBBY PACK		

1997 Ultra Platinum Medallion

*STARS: 25X TO 50X BASIC CARDS
*RCs: 8X TO 20X BASIC CARDS
STATED ODDS 1:100 HOBBY
STATED PRINT RUN LESS THAN 150 SETS

1997 Ultra All-Rookie Team

COMPLETE SET (12)	12.50	30.00
STATED ODDS 1:18 SER.2		
1 Antowain Smith	3.00	8.00
2 Jay Graham	.60	1.50
3 Ike Hilliard	2.00	5.00
4 Warrick Dunn	4.00	10.00
5 Tony Gonzalez	5.00	12.00
6 David LaFleur	.40	1.00
7 Reidel Anthony	1.00	2.50
8 Rae Carruth	.40	1.00
9 Byron Hanspard	.60	1.50
10 Joey Kent	1.00	2.50
11 Kevin Lockett	.60	1.50
12 Jake Plummer	5.00	12.00

1997 Ultra Blitzkrieg

COMPLETE SET (18)	20.00	50.00
STATED ODDS 1:6 SER.1		
*DIE CUTS: 1X TO 2.5X BASIC CARDS		
DIE CUT ODDS 1:36 SER.1		
1 Eddie George	.75	2.00
2 Terry Glenn	.75	2.00
3 Karim Abdul-Jabbar	.50	1.25
4 Emmitt Smith	2.50	6.00
5 Dan Marino	3.00	8.00
6 Brett Favre	3.00	8.00
7 Keyshawn Johnson	.75	2.00
8 Curtis Martin	1.00	2.50
9 Marvin Harrison	.75	2.00
10 Barry Sanders	2.50	6.00
11 Jerry Rice	1.50	4.00
12 Terrell Davis	1.00	2.50
13 Troy Aikman	1.50	4.00
14 Drew Bledsoe	1.00	2.50
15 John Elway	3.00	8.00
16 Kordell Stewart	.75	2.00
17 Kerry Collins	.75	2.00
18 Steve Young	1.00	2.50

1997 Ultra Comeback Kids

COMPLETE SET (10)	15.00	30.00
STATED ODDS 1:8 SER.2		
1 Dan Marino	3.00	8.00
2 Barry Sanders	2.50	6.00
3 Jerry Rice	1.50	4.00
4 John Elway	3.00	8.00
5 Steve Young	1.00	2.50
6 Deion Sanders	.75	2.00
7 Mark Brunell	1.00	2.50
8 Tim Biakabutuka	.50	1.25
9 Tony Banks	.50	1.25
10 Terry Allen	.75	2.00

1997 Ultra First Rounders

COMPLETE SET (12)	3.00	8.00
STATED ODDS 1:4 SER.2		
1 Antowain Smith	1.00	2.50
2 Rae Carruth	.10	.30
3 Peter Boulware	.30	.75
4 Shawn Springs	.20	.50
5 Bryant Westbrook	.10	.30
6 Orlando Pace	.30	.75
7 Jim Druckenmiller	.20	.50
8 Yatil Green	.20	.50
9 Reidel Anthony	.30	.75
10 Ike Hilliard	.60	1.50
11 Darrell Russell	.10	.30
12 Warrick Dunn	1.25	3.00

1997 Ultra Main Event

COMPLETE SET (10)	15.00	30.00
STATED ODDS 1:8 SER.2		
1 Dan Marino	3.00	8.00
2 Barry Sanders	2.50	6.00
3 Jerry Rice	1.50	4.00
4 Drew Bledsoe	1.00	2.50
5 John Elway	3.00	8.00
6 Troy Aikman	1.50	4.00
7 Deion Sanders	.75	2.00
8 Joey Galloway	.50	1.25

9 Steve McNair 1.00 2.50
10 Marshall Faulk 1.00 2.50

1997 Ultra Play of the Game

COMPLETE SET (10) 6.00 15.00
STATED ODDS 1:8 SER.1
1 Deion Sanders .75 2.00
2 Jerry Rice 1.50 4.00
3 Michael Westbrook .50 1.25
4 Steve McNair 1.00 2.50
5 Marshall Faulk 1.00 2.50
6 Terrell Davis 1.00 2.50
7 Mark Brunell 1.00 2.50
8 Isaac Bruce .75 2.00
9 Tony Banks .50 1.25
10 Jamal Anderson .75 2.00

1997 Ultra Reebok

COMP.REEBOK BRONZE (15) 1.50 4.00
*REEBOK GOLDS: 2X TO 5X BRONZES
*REEBOK GREENS: 25X TO 50X BRONZES
*REEBOK REDS: 12.5X TO 25X BRONZES
*REEBOK SILVERS: .75X TO 2X BRONZES
OVERALL REEBOK ODDS ONE PER PACK
202 Torrance Small .08 .25
207 Jim Schwantz .08 .25
210 Chris Boniol .08 .25
223 Eric Metcalf .15 .40
238 Jesse Campbell .08 .25
241 Qadry Ismail .15 .40
270 Brett Perriman .08 .25
271 Chris Spielman .08 .25
278 Desmond Howard .15 .40
282 Steve Everitt .08 .25
289 Lorenzo Neal .08 .25
317 Neil Smith .15 .40
318 Steve Tasker .15 .40
334 John Elway .50 1.25
343 Tyrone Poole .08 .25

1997 Ultra Rising Stars

COMPLETE SET (10) 6.00 12.00
STATED ODDS 1:4 SER.2
1 Keyshawn Johnson .60 1.50
2 Terrell Davis .75 2.00
3 Kordell Stewart .60 1.50
4 Kerry Collins .60 1.50
5 Joey Galloway .40 1.00
6 Steve McNair .75 2.00
7 Jamal Anderson .60 1.50
8 Michael Westbrook .40 1.00
9 Marshall Faulk .75 2.00
10 Isaac Bruce .60 1.50

1997 Ultra Rookies

COMPLETE SET (12) 4.00 10.00
STATED ODDS 1:4 SER.1
*GOLD EMBOSSED: 1.2X TO 3X BASIC INS.
GOLD EMBOSSED ODDS 1:18 SER.1
1 Darnell Autry .30 .75
2 Orlando Pace .20 .50
3 Peter Boulware .30 .75
4 Shawn Springs .30 .75
5 Bryant Westbrook .20 .50
6 Rae Carruth .20 .50
7 Jim Druckenmiller .60 1.50
8 Yatil Green .30 .75
9 James Farrior .20 .50
10 Dwayne Rudd .20 .50
11 Darrell Russell .20 .50
12 Warrick Dunn 2.00 5.00

1997 Ultra Specialists

COMPLETE SET (18) 35.00 80.00
STATED ODDS 1:6 SER.2
*ULTRA PARALL: .8X TO 2X BASIC INSERTS
ULTRA PARALLEL STATED ODDS 1:36 SER.2
1 Eddie George 1.25 3.00
2 Terry Glenn 1.25 3.00
3 Karim Abdul-Jabbar .75 2.00
4 Emmitt Smith 4.00 10.00
5 Brett Favre 5.00 12.00
6 Mark Brunell 1.50 4.00
7 Curtis Martin 1.50 4.00
8 Kerry Collins 1.25 3.00
9 Marvin Harrison 1.25 3.00
10 Jerry Rice 2.50 6.00
11 Tony Martin .75 2.00
12 Terrell Davis 1.50 4.00
13 Troy Aikman 2.50 6.00
14 Drew Bledsoe 1.50 4.00
15 John Elway 5.00 12.00
16 Kordell Stewart 1.25 3.00
17 Keyshawn Johnson 1.25 3.00
18 Steve Young 1.50 4.00

1997 Ultra Starring Role

COMPLETE SET (10) 60.00 150.00
STATED ODDS 1:288 SER.1
1 Emmitt Smith 8.00 20.00
2 Barry Sanders 8.00 20.00
3 Curtis Martin 3.00 8.00
4 Dan Marino 10.00 25.00
5 Keyshawn Johnson 2.50 6.00
6 Marvin Harrison 2.50 6.00
7 Terry Glenn 2.50 6.00
8 Eddie George 2.50 6.00
9 Brett Favre 10.00 25.00
10 Karim Abdul-Jabbar 1.50 4.00

1997 Ultra Stars

COMPLETE SET (10) 100.00 200.00
STATED ODDS 1:288 SER.1
1 Emmitt Smith 15.00 40.00
2 Barry Sanders 15.00 40.00
3 Curtis Martin 6.00 15.00
4 Dan Marino 20.00 50.00
5 Mark Brunell 6.00 15.00
6 Marvin Harrison 5.00 12.00
7 Terry Glenn 5.00 12.00
8 Eddie George 5.00 12.00
9 Brett Favre 20.00 50.00
10 Karim Abdul-Jabbar 3.00 8.00

1997 Ultra Sunday School

COMPLETE SET (10) 12.50 25.00
STATED ODDS 1:8 SER.1
1 Marvin Harrison 1.25 3.00
2 Barry Sanders 3.00 8.00
3 Troy Aikman 2.00 5.00
4 Drew Bledsoe 1.25 3.00
5 John Elway 4.00 10.00
6 Kordell Stewart 1.00 2.50
7 Kerry Collins 1.00 2.50
8 Steve Young 1.25 3.00
9 Deion Sanders 1.00 2.50
10 Joey Galloway .60 1.50

1997 Ultra Talent Show

COMPLETE SET (10) 4.00 8.00
STATED ODDS 1:4 SER.1
1 Joey Galloway .50 1.25
2 Steve McNair 1.00 2.50
3 Marshall Faulk 1.00 2.50
4 Isaac Bruce .75 2.00
5 Michael Westbrook .50 1.25
6 Zach Thomas .75 2.00
7 Jamal Anderson .75 2.00
8 Mike Alstott .75 2.00
9 Mark Brunell 1.00 2.50
10 Eddie Kennison .50 1.25

1998 Ultra

The 1998 Ultra set was issued in two series totalling 425 cards and was distributed in 10-card packs with a suggested retail price of $2.69. The fronts feature borderless color player photos. The backs carry player information and career statistics. Series 1 contains a limited 25-card subset of rookies (#201-225) with an insertion ratio of 1:3. Series 2 contains three subsets: Checklists (358-360), '98 Greats (361-385), and Rookies (386-425) with an insertion rate of 1:3. The basic hobby set includes a special card honoring the achievements of Reggie White. Also, 25-cards were randomly inserted in hobby packs which were redeemable for an autographed Reggie White mini-helmet.

COMPLETE SET (425) 50.00 120.00
COMP.SERIES 1 (225) 30.00 80.00
COMP.SERIES 2 (200) 25.00 50.00
1 Barry Sanders 1.00 2.50
2 Brett Favre 1.50 3.00
3 Napoleon Kaufman .30 .75
4 Robert Smith .30 .75
5 Terry Allen .30 .75
6 Vinny Testaverde .20 .50
7 William Floyd .10 .30
8 Carl Pickens .20 .50
9 Antonio Freeman .30 .75
10 Ben Coates .20 .50
11 Elvis Grbac .20 .50
12 Kerry Collins .20 .50
13 Orlando Pace .10 .30
14 Steve Broussard .10 .30
15 Terance Mathis .20 .50
16 Tiki Barber .30 .75
17 Cris Carter .30 .75
18 Eric Green .10 .30
19 Eric Metcalf .10 .30
20 Jeff George .20 .50
21 Leslie Shepherd .10 .30
22 Natrone Means .20 .50
23 Scott Mitchell .20 .50
24 Adrian Murrell .20 .50
25 Gilbert Brown .10 .30
26 Jimmy Smith .20 .50
27 Mark Bruener .10 .30
28 Troy Aikman .60 1.50
29 Warrick Dunn .30 .75
30 Jay Graham .10 .30
31 Craig Whelihan RC .10 .30
32 Ed McCaffrey .20 .50
33 Jamie Asher .10 .30
34 John Randle .20 .50
35 Michael Jackson .10 .30
36 Rickey Dudley .10 .30
37 Sean Dawkins .10 .30
38 Andre Rison .20 .50
39 Bert Emanuel .20 .50
40 Jeff Blake .20 .50
41 Curtis Conway .20 .50
42 Eddie Kennison .20 .50
43 James McKnight .30 .75
44 Rae Carruth .10 .30
45 Tito Wooten RC .10 .30
46 Cris Dishman .10 .30
47 Ernie Conwell .10 .30
48 Fred Lane .10 .30
49 Jamal Anderson .30 .75
50 Lake Dawson .10 .30
51 Michael Strahan .20 .50
52 Reggie White .30 .75
53 Trent Dilfer .30 .75
54 Troy Brown .20 .50
55 Wesley Walls .20 .50
56 Chidi Ahanotu .10 .30
57 Dwayne Rudd .10 .30
58 Jerry Rice .60 1.50
59 Johnnie Morton .20 .50
60 Sherman Williams .10 .30
61 Steve McNair .30 .75
62 Will Blackwell .10 .30
63 Chris Chandler .20 .50
64 Dexter Coakley .10 .30
65 Horace Copeland .10 .30
66 Jerald Moore .10 .30
67 Leon Johnson .10 .30
68 Mark Chmura .20 .50
69 Micheal Barrow .10 .30
70 Muhsin Muhammad .20 .50
71 Terry Glenn .30 .75
72 Tony Brackens .10 .30
73 Chad Scott .10 .30
74 Glenn Foley .20 .50
75 Keenan McCardell .20 .50
76 Peter Boulware .10 .30
77 Reidel Anthony .20 .50
78 William Henderson .20 .50
79 Tony Martin .20 .50
80 Tony Gonzalez .30 .75
81 Charlie Jones .10 .30
82 Chris Penn .10 .30
83 Chris Calloway .10 .30
84 Dale Carter .10 .30
85 Ki-Jana Carter .10 .30
86 Shawn Jefferson .10 .30
87 Antowain Smith .30 .75
88 Eric Turner .10 .30
89 John Mobley .10 .30
90 Ken Dilger .10 .30
91 Bobby Hoying .20 .50
92 Curtis Martin .30 .75
93 Drew Bledsoe .50 1.25
94 Gary Brown .10 .30
95 Marvin Harrison .30 .75
96 Todd Collins .10 .30
97 Chris Warren .20 .50
98 Danny Kanell .20 .50
99 Tony McGee .10 .30
100 Rod Smith .20 .50
101 Frank Sanders .20 .50
102 Irving Fryar .20 .50
103 Marcus Allen .30 .75
104 Marshall Faulk .40 1.00
105 Bruce Smith .20 .50
106 Charlie Garner .20 .50
107 Paul Justin .10 .30
108 Randal Hill .10 .30
109 Erik Kramer .10 .30
110 Rob Moore .20 .50
111 Shannon Sharpe .20 .50
112 Warren Moon .30 .75
113 Zach Thomas .30 .75
114 Dan Marino 1.50 3.00
115 Duce Staley .40 1.00
116 Eric Swann .10 .30
117 Kenny Holmes .10 .30
118 Merton Hanks .10 .30
119 Raymont Harris .10 .30
120 Terrell Davis .30 .75
121 Thurman Thomas .30 .75
122 Wayne Martin .10 .30
123 Charles Way .10 .30
124 Chuck Smith .10 .30
125 Corey Dillon .30 .75
126 Darnell Autry .10 .30
127 Isaac Bruce .30 .75
128 Joey Galloway .20 .50
129 Kimble Anders .20 .50
130 Aeneas Williams .10 .30
131 Andre Hastings .10 .30
132 Chad Lewis .20 .50
133 J.J. Stokes .20 .50
134 John Elway 1.25 3.00
135 Karim Abdul-Jabbar .30 .75
136 Ken Harvey .10 .30
137 Robert Brooks .20 .50
138 Rodney Thomas .10 .30
139 James Stewart .20 .50
140 Billy Joe Hobert .10 .30
141 Frank Wycheck .10 .30
142 Jake Plummer .30 .75
143 Jerris McPhail .10 .30
144 Kordell Stewart .30 .75
145 Terrell Owens .30 .75
146 Willie Green .10 .30
147 Anthony Miller .10 .30
148 Courtney Hawkins .10 .30
149 Larry Centers .10 .30
150 Gus Frerotte .10 .30
151 O.J. McDuffie .20 .50
152 Ray Zellars .10 .30
153 Terry Kirby .10 .30
154 Tommy Vardell .10 .30
155 Willie Davis .10 .30
156 Chris Canty .10 .30
157 Byron Hanspard .10 .30
158 Chris Penn .10 .30
159 Damon Jones .10 .30
160 Derrick Mayes .20 .50
161 Emmitt Smith 1.25 2.50
162 Keyshawn Johnson .30 .75
163 Mike Alstott .30 .75
164 Tom Carter .10 .30
165 Tony Banks .20 .50
166 Bryant Westbrook .10 .30
167 Chris Sanders .10 .30
168 Deion Sanders .30 .75
169 Garrison Hearst .30 .75
170 Jason Taylor .20 .50
171 Jerome Bettis .30 .75
172 John Lynch .20 .50
173 Troy Davis .10 .30
174 Freddie Jones .10 .30
175 Herman Moore .20 .50
176 Jake Reed .20 .50
177 Mark Brunell .30 .75
178 Ray Lewis .30 .75
179 Stephen Davis .10 .30
180 Tim Brown .30 .75
181 Willie McGinest .10 .30
182 Andre Reed .20 .50
183 Darrien Gordon .10 .30
184 David Palmer .10 .30
185 James Jett .20 .50
186 Junior Seau .30 .75
187 Zack Crockett .10 .30
188 Brad Johnson .30 .75
189 Charles Johnson .10 .30
190 Eddie George .30 .75
191 Jermaine Lewis .20 .50
192 Michael Irvin .30 .75
193 Reggie Brown LB .10 .30
194 Steve Young .40 1.00
195 Warren Sapp .20 .50
196 Wayne Chrebet .30 .75
197 David Dunn .10 .30
198 Dorsey Levens CL .20 .50
199 Troy Aikman CL .30 .75
200 John Elway CL .30 .75
201 Peyton Manning RC 12.00 30.00
202 Ryan Leaf RC 1.25 3.00
203 Charles Woodson RC 1.50 4.00
204 Andre Wadsworth RC 1.00 2.50
205 Brian Simmons RC 1.00 2.50
206 Curtis Enis RC .60 1.50
207 Randy Moss RC 6.00 15.00
208 Germane Crowell RC 1.00 2.50
209 Greg Ellis RC .60 1.50
210 Kevin Dyson RC 1.25 3.00
211 Skip Hicks RC 1.00 2.50
212 Alonzo Mayes RC .60 1.50
213 Robert Edwards RC 1.00 2.50
214 Fred Taylor RC 2.00 5.00
215 Robert Holcombe RC 1.00 2.50
216 John Dutton RC .60 1.50
217 Vonnie Holliday RC 1.00 2.50
218 Tim Dwight RC 1.25 3.00
219 Tavian Banks RC 1.00 2.50
220 Marcus Nash RC .60 1.50
221 Jason Peter RC .60 1.50
222 Michael Myers RC .60 1.50
223 Takeo Spikes RC 1.25 3.00
224 Kivuusama Mays RC .60 1.50
225 Jacquez Green RC 1.00 2.50
226 Doug Flutie .30 .75
227 Ike Hilliard .20 .50
228 Craig Heyward .10 .30
229 Kevin Hardy .10 .30
230 Jason Dunn .10 .30
231 Billy Davis .10 .30
232 Chester McGlockton .10 .30
233 Sean Gilbert .10 .30
234 Bert Emanuel .10 .30
235 Keith Byars .10 .30
236 Tyrone Wheatley .20 .50
237 Ricky Proehl .10 .30
238 Michael Bates .10 .30
239 Derrick Alexander .20 .50
240 Harvey Williams .10 .30
241 Mike Pritchard .10 .30
242 Paul Justin .10 .30
243 Jeff Hostetler .10 .30
244 Eric Moulds .30 .75
245 Jeff Burris .10 .30
246 Gary Brown .10 .30
247 Anthony Johnson .10 .30
248 Dan Wilkinson .10 .30
249 Chris Warren .20 .50
250 Chris Darkins .10 .30
251 Eric Metcalf .10 .30
252 Pat Swilling .10 .30
253 Lamar Smith .20 .50
254 Quinn Early .10 .30
255 Carlester Crumpler .10 .30
256 Eric Bieniemy .10 .30
257 Aaron Bailey .10 .30
258 Neil O'Donnell .20 .50
259 Rod Woodson .20 .50
260 Ricky Whittle .10 .30
261 Iheanyi Uwaezuoke .10 .30
262 Heath Shuler .10 .30
263 Darren Sharper .30 .75
264 John Henry Mills .10 .30
265 Marco Battaglia .10 .30
266 Yancey Thigpen .10 .30
267 Irv Smith .10 .30
268 Jamie Sharper .10 .30
269 Marcus Robinson 2.00 5.00
270 Dorsey Levens .30 .75
271 Qadry Ismail .20 .50
272 Desmond Howard .20 .50
273 Webster Slaughter .10 .30
274 Eugene Robinson .10 .30
275 Bill Romanowski .10 .30
276 Vincent Brisby .10 .30
277 Errict Rhett .20 .50
278 Albert Connell .10 .30
279 Thomas Lewis .10 .30
280 John Farquhar RC .10 .30
281 Marc Edwards .10 .30
282 Tyrone Davis .10 .30
283 Eric Allen .10 .30
284 Aaron Glenn .10 .30
285 Roosevelt Potts .10 .30
286 Kez McCorvey .10 .30
287 Joey Kent .20 .50
288 Jim Druckenmiller .10 .30
289 Sean Dawkins .10 .30
290 Edgar Bennett .10 .30
291 Vinny Testaverde .20 .50
292 Chris Slade .10 .30
293 Lamar Lathon .10 .30
294 Jackie Harris .10 .30
295 Jim Harbaugh .20 .50
296 Rob Fredrickson .10 .30
297 Ty Detmer .20 .50
298 Karl Williams .10 .30
299 Troy Drayton .10 .30
300 Curtis Martin .30 .75
301 Tamarick Vanover .10 .30
302 Lorenzo Neal .10 .30
303 John Hall .10 .30
304 Kevin Greene .20 .50
305 Bryan Still .10 .30
306 Neil Smith .20 .50
307 Greg Lloyd .10 .30
308 Shawn Jefferson .10 .30
309 Aaron Taylor .10 .30
310 Sedrick Shaw .10 .30
311 O.J. Santiago .10 .30
312 Kevin Abrams .10 .30
313 Dana Stubblefield .10 .30
314 Daryl Johnston .20 .50
315 Bryan Cox .10 .30
316 Jeff Graham .10 .30
317 Mario Bates .20 .50
318 Adrian Murrell .20 .50
319 Greg Hill .10 .30
320 Jahine Arnold .10 .30
321 Justin Armour .10 .30
322 Ricky Watters .20 .50
323 Lamont Warren .10 .30
324 Mack Strong .30 .75
325 Darnay Scott .20 .50
326 Brian Mitchell .10 .30
327 Rob Johnson .20 .50
328 Kent Graham .10 .30
329 Hugh Douglas .10 .30
330 Simeon Rice .20 .50
331 Rick Mirer .10 .30
332 Randall Cunningham .30 .75
333 Steve Atwater .10 .30
334 Latario Rachal .10 .30
335 Tony Martin .20 .50
336 Leroy Hoard .10 .30
337 Howard Griffith .10 .30
338 Kevin Lockett .10 .30
339 William Floyd .10 .30
340 Jerry Ellison .10 .30
341 Kyle Brady .10 .30
342 Michael Westbrook .20 .50
343 Kevin Turner .10 .30
344 David LaFleur .10 .30
345 Robert Jones .10 .30
346 Dave Brown .10 .30
347 Kevin Williams .10 .30
348 Amani Toomer .20 .50
349 Amp Lee .10 .30
350 Bryce Paup .10 .30
351 Dewayne Washington .10 .30
352 Mercury Hayes .10 .30
353 Tim Biakabutuka .20 .50
354 Ray Crockett .10 .30
355 Ted Washington .10 .30
356 Pete Mitchell .10 .30
357 Billy Jenkins RC .10 .30
358 Troy Aikman CL .30 .75
359 Drew Bledsoe CL .30 .75
360 Steve Young CL .30 .75
361 Antonio Freeman NG .20 .50
362 Antowain Smith NG .20 .50
363 Barry Sanders NG .60 1.50
364 Bobby Hoying NG .10 .30
365 Brett Favre NG .75 2.00
366 Corey Dillon NG .20 .50
367 Dan Marino NG .75 2.00
368 Drew Bledsoe NG .30 .75
369 Eddie George NG .20 .50
370 Emmitt Smith NG .60 1.50
371 Herman Moore NG .20 .50
372 Jake Plummer NG .20 .50
373 Jerome Bettis NG .20 .50
374 Jerry Rice NG .40 1.00
375 Joey Galloway NG .20 .50
376 John Elway NG .75 2.00
377 Kordell Stewart NG .20 .50
378 Mark Brunell NG .30 .75
379 Keyshawn Johnson NG .20 .50
380 Steve Young NG .30 .75
381 Steve McNair NG .20 .50
382 Terrell Davis NG .30 .75
383 Tim Brown NG .20 .50
384 Troy Aikman NG .40 1.00
385 Warrick Dunn NG .30 .75
386 Ryan Leaf 1.25 3.00
387 Tony Simmons RC .75 2.00
388 Rodney Williams RC .50 1.25
389 John Avery RC .75 2.00
390 Shaun Williams RC .75 2.00
391 Anthony Simmons RC .75 2.00
392 Rashaan Shehee RC .75 2.00
393 Robert Holcombe .75 2.00
394 Larry Shannon RC .50 1.25
395 Skip Hicks .75 2.00
396 Rod Rutledge RC .50 1.25
397 Donald Hayes RC .75 2.00
398 Curtis Enis .50 1.25
399 Mikhael Ricks RC .75 2.00
400 Brian Griese RC 2.50 6.00
401 Michael Pittman RC 1.50 4.00
402 Jacquez Green .75 2.00
403 Jerome Pathon RC 1.25 3.00
404 Ahman Green RC 3.00 8.00
405 Marcus Nash .50 1.25
406 Randy Moss 5.00 12.00
407 Terry Fair RC .75 2.00
408 Jammi German RC .50 1.25
409 Stephen Alexander RC .75 2.00
410 Grant Wistrom RC .75 2.00
411 Charlie Batch RC 1.25 3.00
412 Fred Taylor 1.50 4.00
413 Pat Johnson RC .75 2.00
414 Robert Edwards .75 2.00
415 Keith Brooking RC 1.25 3.00
416 Peyton Manning 10.00 25.00
417 Duane Starks RC .50 1.25
418 Andre Wadsworth .75 2.00
419 Brian Alford RC .50 1.25
420 Brian Kelly RC .75 2.00
421 Joe Jurevicius RC 1.25 3.00
422 Tebucky Jones RC .50 1.25
423 R.W. McQuarters RC .75 2.00
424 Kevin Dyson 1.00 2.50
425 Charles Woodson 1.25 3.00
R1 Reggie White COMM .25 .60
P20 Jeff George Promo .30 .75

1998 Ultra Gold Medallion

COMPLETE SET (425) 500.00 1,000.00
*GOLD MED.STARS: 1.2X TO 3X BASIC CARDS
*GOLD MED.RCs: .8X TO 2X BASIC CARDS
*GOLD MED.SER.2 DRAFT PICKS: 1.5X TO 4X
STATED ODDS 1:1 HOBBY

1998 Ultra Masterpiece

STATED PRINT RUN 1 SER.#'d SET

1998 Ultra Platinum Medallion

*PLAT.MED.STARS: 12X TO 30X
*PLAT.MED.SER.1 RCs: 3X TO 8X
*PLAT.MED.SER.2 DRAFT PICKS: 5X TO 10X
1-200/226-385 PRINT RUN 98 SER.#'d SETS
201-225/386-425 PRINT RUN 66 SER.#'d SETS
HOBBY ONLY INSERTS
201P Peyton Manning 200.00 350.00
416P Peyton Manning 200.00 350.00

1998 Ultra Sensational Sixty

COMPLETE SET (60) 15.00 40.00
ONE PER RETAIL PACK
1 Karim Abdul-Jabbar .40 1.00
2 Troy Aikman .75 2.00
3 Terry Allen .40 1.00
4 Mike Alstott .40 1.00
5 Tony Banks .25 .60
6 Jerome Bettis .40 1.00
7 Drew Bledsoe .60 1.50
8 Peter Boulware .15 .40
9 Robert Brooks .25 .60
10 Tim Brown .40 1.00
11 Isaac Bruce .40 1.00
12 Mark Brunell .40 1.00
13 Cris Carter .40 1.00
14 Kerry Collins .25 .60
15 Curtis Conway .25 .60
16 Terrell Davis .40 1.00
17 Troy Davis .15 .40
18 Trent Dilfer .40 1.00
19 Corey Dillon .40 1.00
20 Warrick Dunn .40 1.00
21 John Elway 1.50 4.00
22 Bert Emanuel .25 .60
23 Brett Favre 1.50 4.00
24 Antonio Freeman .40 1.00
25 Gus Frerotte .15 .40
26 Joey Galloway .25 .60
27 Eddie George .40 1.00
28 Jeff George .25 .60
29 Elvis Grbac .25 .60
30 Marvin Harrison .40 1.00
31 Bobby Hoying .25 .60
32 Michael Irvin .40 1.00
33 Brad Johnson .40 1.00
34 Keyshawn Johnson .40 1.00
35 Dan Marino 1.50 4.00
36 Curtis Martin .40 1.00
37 Tony Martin .25 .60
38 Keenan McCardell .25 .60
39 Steve McNair .40 1.00
40 Warren Moon .40 1.00
41 Herman Moore .25 .60
42 Johnnie Morton .25 .60
43 Terrell Owens .40 1.00
44 Carl Pickens .25 .60
45 Jake Plummer .40 1.00
46 Jerry Rice .75 2.00
47 Andre Rison .25 .60
48 Barry Sanders 1.25 3.00
49 Deion Sanders .40 1.00
50 Junior Seau .40 1.00
51 Shannon Sharpe .25 .60
52 Antowain Smith .40 1.00
53 Emmitt Smith 1.25 3.00
54 Jimmy Smith .25 .60
55 Robert Smith .40 1.00
56 Kordell Stewart .40 1.00
57 Jeff Blake .25 .60
58 Charles Way .15 .40
59 Reggie White .40 1.00
60 Steve Young .50 1.25

1998 Ultra Canton Classics

COMPLETE SET (10) 60.00 120.00
STATED ODDS 1:288
1 Terrell Davis 2.50 6.00
2 Brett Favre 10.00 25.00
3 John Elway 10.00 25.00
4 Barry Sanders 8.00 20.00
5 Eddie George 2.50 6.00
6 Jerry Rice 5.00 12.00
7 Emmitt Smith 8.00 20.00
8 Dan Marino 10.00 25.00
9 Troy Aikman 5.00 12.00
10 Marcus Allen 2.50 6.00

1998 Ultra Caught in the Draft

COMPLETE SET (15) 30.00 60.00
STATED ODDS 1:24
1 Andre Wadsworth .50 1.25
2 Curtis Enis .30 .75
3 Germane Crowell .50 1.25
4 Peyton Manning 7.50 15.00
5 Tavian Banks .30 .75
6 Fred Taylor 1.00 2.50
7 John Avery .30 .75
8 Randy Moss 4.00 10.00
9 Robert Edwards .50 1.25
10 Charles Woodson .75 2.00
11 Ryan Leaf .50 1.25
12 Ahman Green 1.50 4.00
13 Robert Holcombe .30 .75
14 Jacquez Green .50 1.25
15 Skip Hicks .50 1.25

1998 Ultra Damage, Inc.

COMPLETE SET (15) 50.00 100.00
STATED ODDS 1:72
1 Terrell Davis 2.00 5.00
2 Joey Galloway 1.25 3.00
3 Kordell Stewart 2.00 5.00
4 Troy Aikman 4.00 10.00
5 Barry Sanders 6.00 15.00
6 Ryan Leaf .60 1.50
7 Antonio Freeman 2.00 5.00
8 Keyshawn Johnson 2.00 5.00
9 Eddie George 2.00 5.00
10 Warrick Dunn 2.00 5.00
11 Drew Bledsoe 3.00 8.00
12 Peyton Manning 12.00 30.00
13 Antowain Smith 2.00 5.00
14 Brett Favre 8.00 20.00
15 Emmitt Smith 6.00 15.00

1998 Ultra Exclamation Points

COMPLETE SET (15) 150.00 300.00
STATED ODDS 1:288
1 Terrell Davis 5.00 12.00
2 Brett Favre 20.00 50.00
3 John Elway 20.00 50.00
4 Barry Sanders 15.00 40.00
5 Peyton Manning 25.00 50.00
6 Jerry Rice 10.00 25.00
7 Emmitt Smith 15.00 40.00
8 Dan Marino 20.00 50.00
9 Kordell Stewart 5.00 12.00
10 Mark Brunell 5.00 12.00
11 Ryan Leaf 2.00 5.00
12 Corey Dillon 5.00 12.00
13 Antowain Smith 5.00 12.00
14 Curtis Martin 5.00 12.00
15 Deion Sanders 5.00 12.00

1998 Ultra Flair Showcase Preview

COMPLETE SET (10) 75.00 150.00
STATED ODDS 1:144
1 Kordell Stewart 4.00 10.00
2 Mark Brunell 4.00 10.00
3 Terrell Davis 4.00 10.00
4 Brett Favre 15.00 40.00
5 Steve McNair 4.00 10.00
6 Curtis Martin 4.00 10.00
7 Warrick Dunn 4.00 10.00
8 Emmitt Smith 12.50 30.00
9 Dan Marino 15.00 40.00
10 Corey Dillon 4.00 10.00

1998 Ultra Indefensible

COMPLETE SET (10) 50.00 100.00
STATED ODDS 1:144
1 Jake Plummer 2.50 6.00
2 Mark Brunell 2.50 6.00
3 Terrell Davis 2.50 6.00
4 Jerry Rice 5.00 12.00
5 Barry Sanders 8.00 20.00
6 Curtis Martin 2.50 6.00
7 Warrick Dunn 2.50 6.00
8 Emmitt Smith 8.00 20.00
9 Dan Marino 10.00 25.00
10 Corey Dillon 2.50 6.00

1998 Ultra Next Century

COMPLETE SET (15) 40.00 80.00
STATED ODDS 1:72
1 Ryan Leaf 1.00 2.50
2 Peyton Manning 12.50 25.00
3 Charles Woodson 1.25 3.00
4 Randy Moss 6.00 15.00
5 Curtis Enis .50 1.25
6 Ahman Green 2.50 6.00
7 Skip Hicks .75 2.00
8 Andre Wadsworth .75 2.00
9 Germane Crowell .75 2.00
10 Robert Edwards .75 2.00
11 Tavian Banks .75 2.00
12 Takeo Spikes 1.00 2.50
13 Jacquez Green .75 2.00
14 Brian Simmons .75 2.00
15 Alonzo Mayes .50 1.25

1998 Ultra Rush Hour

COMPLETE SET (20) 20.00 40.00
STATED ODDS 1:6
1 Robert Edwards .50 1.25
2 John Elway 3.00 8.00
3 Mike Alstott .75 2.00
4 Robert Holcombe .50 1.25
5 Mark Brunell .75 2.00
6 Deion Sanders .75 2.00
7 Curtis Martin .75 2.00
8 Curtis Enis .30 .75
9 Dorsey Levens .75 2.00
10 Fred Taylor 1.00 2.50
11 John Avery .40 1.00
12 Eddie George .75 2.00
13 Jake Plummer .75 2.00
14 Andre Wadsworth .50 1.25
15 Fred Lane .30 .75
16 Corey Dillon .75 2.00
17 Brett Favre 3.00 8.00
18 Kordell Stewart .75 2.00
19 Steve McNair .75 2.00
20 Warrick Dunn .75 2.00

1998 Ultra Shots

COMPLETE SET (20) 15.00 35.00
STATED ODDS 1:6
1 Deion Sanders .75 2.00
2 Corey Dillon .75 2.00
3 Mike Alstott .75 2.00
4 Jake Plummer .75 2.00
5 Antowain Smith .75 2.00
6 Kordell Stewart .75 2.00
7 Curtis Martin .75 2.00
8 Bobby Hoying .50 1.25
9 Kerry Collins .50 1.25
10 Herman Moore .50 1.25
11 Terry Glenn .75 2.00
12 Eddie George .75 2.00
13 Drew Bledsoe 1.25 3.00
14 Steve McNair .75 2.00
15 Jerry Rice 1.50 4.00
16 Trent Dilfer .75 2.00
17 Joey Galloway .50 1.25
18 Dan Marino 3.00 8.00
19 Barry Sanders 2.50 6.00
20 Warrick Dunn .75 2.00

1998 Ultra Top 30

COMPLETE SET (30) 10.00 25.00
STATED ODDS: 1 PER RETAIL PACK
1 Warrick Dunn .30 .75
2 Troy Aikman .60 1.50
3 Trent Dilfer .30 .75
4 Tony Banks .20 .50
5 Tim Brown .30 .75
6 Terrell Davis .30 .75
7 Steve McNair .30 .75
8 Steve Young .40 1.00
9 Mark Brunell .30 .75
10 Kordell Stewart .30 .75
11 Keyshawn Johnson .30 .75
12 John Elway 1.25 3.00
13 Joey Galloway .20 .50
14 Jerry Rice .60 1.50
15 Jerome Bettis .30 .75
16 Jake Plummer .30 .75
17 Emmitt Smith 1.00 2.50
18 Eddie George .30 .75
19 Drew Bledsoe .50 1.25
20 Dan Marino 1.25 3.00
21 Curtis Martin .30 .75
22 Curtis Conway .20 .50
23 Cris Carter .30 .75
24 Corey Dillon .30 .75
25 Carl Pickens .20 .50
26 Brett Favre 1.25 3.00
27 Bobby Hoying .20 .50
28 Barry Sanders 1.00 2.50
29 Antowain Smith .30 .75
30 Antonio Freeman .30 .75

1998 Ultra Touchdown Kings

COMPLETE SET (15) 50.00 100.00
STATED ODDS 1:24
1 Terrell Davis 2.00 5.00
2 Joey Galloway 1.25 3.00
3 Kordell Stewart 2.00 5.00
4 Corey Dillon 2.00 5.00
5 Barry Sanders 6.00 15.00
6 Cris Carter 2.00 5.00
7 Antonio Freeman 2.00 5.00
8 Mike Alstott 2.00 5.00
9 Eddie George 2.00 5.00
10 Warrick Dunn 2.00 5.00
11 Drew Bledsoe 3.00 8.00
12 Karim Abdul-Jabbar 2.00 5.00
13 Mark Brunell 2.00 5.00
14 Brett Favre 8.00 20.00
15 Emmitt Smith 6.00 15.00

1999 Ultra

This 300 card set was released in July, 1999. The cards were issued in 10 card packs with a SRP of $2.69. Subsets include 3 Checklist card (248-250), Super Bowl Highlights (251-260) and a Rookie Subset (261-300). The Rookie subset were seeded one every 4 packs. Notable Rookie Cards include Tim Couch, Edgerrin James and Ricky Williams. A couple of weeks before the product's release, a promo card of Fred Taylor was released. It is listed at the end of the Ultra set.

COMPLETE SET (300) 30.00 80.00
COMP.SET w/o SP's (250) 8.00 20.00
1 Terrell Davis .25 .60
2 Courtney Hawkins .15 .40
3 Cris Carter .25 .60
4 Darnay Scott .15 .40
5 Darrell Green .25 .60
6 Jimmy Smith .20 .50
7 Doug Flutie .25 .60
8 Michael Jackson .15 .40
9 Warren Sapp .20 .50
10 Greg Hill .15 .40
11 Karim Abdul-Jabbar .20 .50
12 Greg Ellis .15 .40
13 Dan Marino .75 2.00
14 Napoleon Kaufman .15 .40
15 Peyton Manning .75 2.00
16 Simeon Rice .15 .40
17 Tony Simmons .15 .40
18 Carlester Crumpler .15 .40
19 Charles Johnson .15 .40
20 Derrick Alexander .15 .40
21 Kent Graham .15 .40
22 Randall Cunningham .25 .60
23 Trent Green .20 .50
24 Chris Spielman .20 .50
25 Carl Pickens .20 .50
26 Bill Romanowski .20 .50
27 Jermaine Lewis .15 .40
28 Ahman Green .20 .50
29 Bryan Still .15 .40
30 Dorsey Levens .20 .50
31 Frank Wycheck .20 .50
32 Jerome Bettis .25 .60
33 Reidel Anthony .15 .40
34 Robert Jones .15 .40
35 Terry Glenn .20 .50
36 Tim Brown .25 .60
37 Eric Metcalf .15 .40
38 Kevin Greene .20 .50
39 Takeo Spikes .15 .40
40 Brian Mitchell .20 .50
41 Duane Starks .15 .40
42 Eddie George .20 .50
43 Joe Jurevicius .15 .40
44 Kimble Anders .15 .40
45 Kordell Stewart .20 .50
46 Leroy Hoard .15 .40
47 Rod Smith .20 .50
48 Terrell Owens .25 .60
49 Ty Detmer .20 .50
50 Charles Woodson .25 .60
51 Andre Rison .20 .50
52 Chris Slade .15 .40
53 Frank Sanders .15 .40
54 Michael Irvin .25 .60
55 Jerome Pathon .15 .40
56 Desmond Howard .20 .50
57 Billy Davis .15 .40
58 Anthony Simmons .15 .40
59 James Jett .15 .40
60 Jake Plummer .20 .50
61 John Avery .15 .40
62 Marvin Harrison .25 .60
63 Merton Hanks .15 .40
64 Ricky Proehl .15 .40
65 Steve Beuerlein .20 .50
66 Willie McGinest .20 .50
67 Bryce Paup .15 .40
68 Brett Favre .75 2.00
69 Brian Griese .20 .50
70 Curtis Martin .25 .60
71 Drew Bledsoe .25 .60
72 Jim Harbaugh .20 .50
73 Joey Galloway .20 .50
74 Natrone Means .20 .50

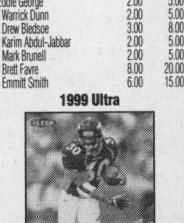

75 O.J. McDuffie	.20	.50
76 Tiki Barber	.25	.60
77 Wesley Walls	.20	.50
78 Will Blackwell	.15	.40
79 Bert Emanuel	.20	.50
80 J.J. Stokes	.15	.40
81 Steve McNair	.25	.60
82 Adrian Murrell	.20	.50
83 Dexter Coakley	.15	.40
84 Jeff George	.15	.40
85 Marshall Faulk	.25	.60
86 Tim Biakabutuka	.20	.50
87 Troy Drayton	.15	.40
88 Ty Law	.20	.50
89 Brian Simmons	.15	.40
90 Eric Allen	.20	.50
91 Jon Kitna	.20	.50
92 Junior Seau	.25	.60
93 Kevin Turner	.15	.40
94 Larry Centers	.20	.50
95 Robert Edwards	.15	.40
96 Rocket Ismail	.20	.50
97 Sam Madison	.15	.40
98 Stephen Alexander	.15	.40
99 Trent Dilfer	.20	.50
100 Vonnie Holliday	.15	.40
101 Charlie Garner	.20	.50
102 Deion Sanders	.25	.60
103 Jamal Anderson	.20	.50
104 Mike Vanderjagt	.15	.40
105 Aeneas Williams	.15	.40
106 Daryl Johnston	.25	.60
107 Hugh Douglas	.20	.50
108 Torrance Small	.15	.40
109 Amani Toomer	.20	.50
110 Amp Lee	.15	.40
111 Germane Crowell	.15	.40
112 Marco Battaglia	.15	.40
113 Michael Westbrook	.15	.40
114 Randy Moss	.25	.60
115 Ricky Watters	.20	.50
116 Rob Johnson	.20	.50
117 Tony Gonzalez	.25	.60
118 Charles Way	.15	.40
119 Chris Penn	.15	.40
120 Eddie Kennison	.20	.50
121 Elvis Grbac	.15	.40
122 Eric Moulds	.20	.50
123 Terry Fair	.15	.40
124 Tony Banks	.20	.50
125 Chris Chandler	.20	.50
126 Emmitt Smith	.60	1.50
127 Herman Moore	.20	.50
128 Irv Smith	.15	.40
129 Kyle Brady	.15	.40
130 Lamont Warren	.20	.50
131 Troy Davis	.15	.40
132 Andre Reed	.25	.60
133 Justin Armour	.15	.40
134 James Hasty	.15	.40
135 Johnnie Morton	.20	.50
136 Reggie Barlow	.15	.40
137 Robert Holcombe	.15	.40
138 Sean Dawkins	.15	.40
139 Steve Atwater	.20	.50
140 Tim Dwight	.20	.50
141 Wayne Chrebet	.20	.50
142 Alonzo Mayes	.15	.40
143 Mark Brunell	.20	.50
144 Antowain Smith	.15	.40
145 Byron Bam Morris	.15	.40
146 Isaac Bruce	.25	.60
147 Bryan Cox	.20	.50
148 Bryant Westbrook	.15	.40
149 Duce Staley	.20	.50
150 Barry Sanders	.60	1.50
151 La'Roi Glover RC	.25	.60
152 Ray Crockett	.15	.40
153 Tony Brackens	.15	.40
154 Roy Barker	.15	.40
155 Kerry Collins	.20	.50
156 Andre Wadsworth	.15	.40
157 Cameron Cleeland	.15	.40
158 Koy Detmer	.15	.40
159 Marcus Pollard	.15	.40
160 Patrick Jeffers RC	.30	.75
161 Aaron Glenn	.15	.40
162 Andre Hastings	.15	.40
163 Bruce Smith	.25	.60
164 David Palmer	.15	.40
165 Erik Kramer	.20	.50
166 Orlando Pace	.20	.50
167 Robert Brooks	.20	.50
168 Shawn Springs	.15	.40
169 Terance Mathis	.15	.40
170 Chris Calloway	.15	.40
171 Gilbert Brown	.20	.50
172 Charlie Jones	.15	.40
173 Curtis Enis	.15	.40
174 Eugene Robinson	.20	.50
175 Garrison Hearst	.20	.50
176 Jason Elam	.15	.40
177 John Randle	.20	.50
178 Keith Poole	.15	.40
179 Kevin Hardy	.15	.40
180 Keyshawn Johnson	.20	.50
181 O.J. Santiago	.15	.40
182 Jacquez Green	.15	.40
183 Bobby Engram	.20	.50
184 Damon Jones	.15	.40
185 Freddie Jones	.15	.40
186 Jake Reed	.20	.50
187 Jerry Rice	.50	1.25
188 Joey Kent	.15	.40
189 Lamar Smith	.15	.40
190 John Elway	.75	2.00
191 Leon Johnson	.15	.40
192 Mark Chmura	.15	.40
193 Peter Boulware	.15	.40
194 Zach Thomas	.25	.60
195 Marc Edwards	.20	.50
196 Mike Alstott	.25	.60
197 Yancey Thigpen	.15	.40
198 Oronde Gadsden	.15	.40
199 Rae Carruth	.15	.40
200 Troy Aikman	.40	1.00
201 Shawn Jefferson	.15	.40
202 Rob Moore	.15	.40
203 Rickey Dudley	.15	.40
204 Jason Taylor	.20	.50
205 Curtis Conway	.20	.50
206 Darrien Gordon	.15	.40
207 Eric Green	.15	.40
208 Jessie Armstead	.20	.50
209 Keenan McCardell	.20	.50
210 Robert Smith	.20	.50
211 Mo Lewis	.15	.40
212 Ryan Leaf	.20	.50
213 Steve Young	.30	.75
214 Tyrone Davis	.15	.40
215 Chad Brown	.15	.40
216 Ike Hilliard	.20	.50
217 Jimmy Hitchcock	.20	.50
218 Kevin Dyson	.15	.40
219 Levon Kirkland	.15	.40
220 Neil O'Donnell	.20	.50
221 Ray Lewis	.25	.60
222 Shannon Sharpe	.25	.60
223 Skip Hicks	.15	.40
224 Brad Johnson	.20	.50
225 Charlie Batch	.20	.50
226 Corey Dillon	.20	.50
227 Dale Carter	.15	.40
228 John Mobley	.15	.40
229 Hines Ward	.25	.60
230 Leslie Shepherd	.15	.40
231 Michael Strahan	.20	.50
232 R.W. McQuarters	.15	.40
233 Mike Pritchard	.15	.40
234 Antonio Freeman	.20	.50
235 Ben Coates	.20	.50
236 Michael Bates	.15	.40
237 Ed McCaffrey	.20	.50
238 Gary Brown	.15	.40
239 Mark Bruener	.15	.40
240 Mikhael Ricks	.15	.40
241 Muhsin Muhammad	.20	.50
242 Priest Holmes	.25	.60
243 Stephen Davis	.20	.50
244 Vinny Testaverde	.20	.50
245 Warrick Dunn	.20	.50
246 Derrick Mayes	.15	.40
247 Fred Taylor	.20	.50
248 Drew Bledsoe CL	.20	.50
249 Eddie George CL	.15	.40
250 Steve Young CL	.25	.60
251 Jamal Anderson BB	.25	.60
252 Darrien Gordon BB	.25	.60
Bill Romanowski BB		
253 Shannon Sharpe BB	.30	.75
254 Terrell Davis BB	.30	.75
255 Rod Smith BB	.25	.60
256 Rod Smith BB	.25	.60
257 John Elway BB	1.00	2.50
258 Tim Dwight BB	.25	.60
259 John Elway BB	1.00	2.50
Ed McCaffrey BB		
Howard Griffith BB		
Terrell Davis BB		
260 John Elway BB	1.00	2.50
261 Ricky Williams RC	1.50	4.00
262 Tim Couch RC	1.00	2.50
263 Chris Claiborne RC	.60	1.50
264 Champ Bailey RC	2.00	5.00
265 Torry Holt RC	1.50	4.00
266 Donovan McNabb RC	5.00	12.00
267 David Boston RC	.75	2.00
268 Chris McAlister RC	.75	2.00
269 Brock Huard RC	.75	2.00
270 Daunte Culpepper RC	1.00	2.50
271 Matt Stinchcomb RC	.60	1.50
272 Edgerrin James RC	1.25	3.00
273 Jevon Kearse RC	1.00	2.50
274 Ebenezer Ekuban RC	.60	1.50
275 Kris Farris RC	.60	1.50
276 Chris Terry RC	.60	1.50
277 Jerame Tuman RC	.60	1.50
278 Akili Smith RC	.75	2.00
279 Aaron Gibson RC	.60	1.50
280 Rahim Abdullah RC	.60	1.50
281 Peerless Price RC	.75	2.00
282 Antoine Winfield RC	.60	1.50
283 Antuan Edwards RC	.60	1.50
284 Rob Konrad RC	.60	1.50
285 Troy Edwards RC	.75	2.00
286 John Thornton RC	.60	1.50
287 James Johnson RC	.60	1.50
288 Gary Stills RC	.60	1.50
289 Mike Peterson RC	.75	2.00
290 Kevin Faulk RC	1.00	2.50
291 Jared DeVries RC	.60	1.50
292 Martin Gramatica RC	.60	1.50
293 Montae Reagor RC	.60	1.50
294 Andy Katzenmoyer RC	.75	2.00
295 Sedrick Irvin RC	.60	1.50
296 D'Wayne Bates RC	.60	1.50
297 Amos Zereoue RC	.75	2.00
298 Dre Bly RC	1.00	2.50
299 Kevin Johnson RC	.75	2.00
300 Cade McNown RC	.75	2.00
P247 Fred Taylor Promo	.75	2.00

1999 Ultra Gold Medallion

COMPLETE SET (300) 200.00 400.00
*GOLD MED.STARS: 1.2X TO 3X
*GOLD MED.RCs: .6X TO 1.5X
GOLD MED.VETERAN ODDS ONE PER PACK
GOLD MED.DRAFT PICK ODDS 1:25 PACKS
GOLD MED.BACK TO BACK ODDS 1:50
GOLD MED.DRAFT PICK ODDS 1:50

1999 Ultra Platinum Medallion

*PLAT.MED.STARS: 10X TO 25X
*PLAT.MED.RCs: 2.5X TO 6X
PM VETS PRINT RUN 99 SER.#'d SETS
PM DRAFT PICK PRINT RUN 65 SER.#'d SETS
PM BACK/BACK PRINT RUN 40 SER.#'d SETS

1999 Ultra As Good As It Gets

COMPLETE SET (15)	60.00	150.00
STATED ODDS 1:288		
1 Warrick Dunn	2.50	6.00
2 Terrell Davis	2.50	6.00
3 Robert Edwards	1.00	2.50
4 Randy Moss	6.00	15.00
5 Peyton Manning	8.00	20.00
6 Mark Brunell	2.50	6.00
7 John Elway	8.00	20.00
8 Jerry Rice	5.00	12.00
9 Jake Plummer	1.50	4.00
10 Fred Taylor	2.50	6.00
11 Emmitt Smith	5.00	12.00
12 Dan Marino	8.00	20.00
13 Charlie Batch	2.50	6.00
14 Brett Favre	8.00	20.00
15 Barry Sanders	8.00	20.00

1999 Ultra Caught In The Draft

COMPLETE SET (15)	25.00	50.00
STATED ODDS 1:18		
1 Ricky Williams	2.00	5.00
2 Tim Couch	1.00	2.50
3 Chris Claiborne	.50	1.25
4 Champ Bailey	1.50	4.00
5 Torry Holt	2.50	6.00
6 Donovan McNabb	5.00	12.00
7 David Boston	1.00	2.50
8 Andy Katzenmoyer	.75	2.00
9 Daunte Culpepper	4.00	10.00
10 Edgerrin James	4.00	10.00
11 Cade McNown	.75	2.00
12 Troy Edwards	.75	2.00
13 Akili Smith	.75	2.00
14 Peerless Price	1.00	2.50
15 Amos Zereoue	1.00	2.50

1999 Ultra Counterparts

COMPLETE SET (15)	40.00	80.00
STATED ODDS 1:36		
1 Troy Aikman	4.00	10.00
Michael Irvin		
2 Drew Bledsoe	2.50	6.00
Ben Coates		
3 Terrell Davis	2.00	5.00
Howard Griffith		
4 Warrick Dunn	2.00	5.00
Mike Alstott		
5 Brett Favre	6.00	15.00
Antonio Freeman		
6 Jake Plummer	1.25	3.00
Frank Sanders		
7 Randy Moss	5.00	12.00
Randall Cunningham		
8 Eddie George	2.00	5.00
Steve McNair		
9 Keyshawn Johnson	2.00	5.00
Wayne Chrebet		
10 Ryan Leaf	2.00	5.00
Mikhael Ricks		
11 Peyton Manning	6.00	15.00
Marshall Faulk		
12 Barry Sanders	6.00	15.00
Tommy Vardell		
13 Charlie Batch	2.00	5.00
Herman Moore		
14 Emmitt Smith	4.00	10.00
Daryl Johnston		
15 Kordell Stewart	2.00	5.00
Jerome Bettis		

1999 Ultra Damage, Inc.

COMPLETE SET (15)	50.00	120.00
STATED ODDS 1:72		
1 Brett Favre	8.00	20.00
2 Dan Marino	8.00	20.00
3 John Elway	8.00	20.00
4 Mark Brunell	2.50	6.00
5 Peyton Manning	8.00	20.00
6 Robert Edwards	1.00	2.50
7 Terrell Davis	2.50	6.00
8 Troy Aikman	5.00	12.00
9 Randy Moss	6.00	15.00
10 Kordell Stewart	1.50	4.00
11 Jerry Rice	5.00	12.00
12 Fred Taylor	2.50	6.00
13 Emmitt Smith	5.00	12.00
14 Charlie Batch	2.50	6.00
15 Barry Sanders	8.00	20.00

1999 Ultra Over The Top

COMPLETE SET (20)	10.00	20.00
STATED ODDS 1:6		
1 Troy Aikman	1.00	2.50
2 Drew Bledsoe	.60	1.50
3 Mark Brunell	.50	1.25
4 Randall Cunningham	.50	1.25
5 Jamal Anderson	.50	1.25
6 Warrick Dunn	.50	1.25
7 Robert Edwards	.20	.50
8 John Elway	1.50	4.00
9 Eddie George	.50	1.25
10 Eric Moulds	.50	1.25
11 Keyshawn Johnson	.50	1.25
12 Ryan Leaf	.50	1.25
13 Dan Marino	1.50	4.00
14 Steve McNair	.50	1.25
15 Jake Plummer	.30	.75
16 Jerry Rice	1.00	2.50
17 Deion Sanders	.50	1.25
18 Kordell Stewart	.30	.75
19 Fred Taylor	.50	1.25
20 Steve Young	.60	1.50

2000 Ultra

Released as a 249-card set, 2000 Ultra is composed of 220 veteran cards and 29 prospect cards found one in four packs. Base cards contain full-color action photography and rainbow holofoil stamping. Ultra was packaged in 24-pack boxes with packs that contained 10 cards and carried a suggested retail price of $2.99. It is thought that card #240 was released only in small quantities early in the print run.

COMPLETE SET (249)	40.00	100.00
COMP.SET w/o RC's (220)	7.50	20.00
220-250 ROOKIE ODDS 1:4		
1 Kurt Warner	.40	1.00
2 Derrick Alexander	.15	.40
3 Aaron Craver	.15	.40
4 Kevin Faulk	.20	.50
5 Marcus Robinson	.20	.50
6 Tony Banks	.15	.40
7 Jon Ritchie	.15	.40
8 Torry Holt	.25	.60
9 Joe Horn	.20	.50
10 Eddie George	.20	.50
11 Michael Westbrook	.15	.40
12 Gus Frerotte	.20	.50
13 Tim Brown	.25	.60
14 Tamarick Vanover	.15	.40
15 David Sloan	.15	.40
16 Darnay Scott	.20	.50
17 Junior Seau	.25	.60
18 Warren Sapp	.20	.50
19 Priest Holmes	.25	.60
20 Jerry Rice	.50	1.25
21 Cade McNown	.15	.40
22 Johnnie Morton	.20	.50
23 Vinny Testaverde	.20	.50
24 James Jett	.20	.50
25 Tony Gonzalez	.25	.60
26 Charlie Batch	.20	.50
27 Tony Simmons	.15	.40
28 James Stewart	.15	.40
29 Corey Dillon	.20	.50
30 Ricky Williams	.25	.60
31 Ryan Leaf	.20	.50
32 Terry Allen	.20	.50
33 Freddie Jones	.15	.40
34 Terry Kirby	.15	.40
35 Charles Johnson	.15	.40
36 William Henderson	.15	.40
37 Stephen Alexander	.15	.40
38 Moe Williams	.15	.40
39 David Boston	.15	.40
40 Emmitt Smith	.60	1.50
41 Ken Oxendine	.15	.40
42 Byron Hanspard	.15	.40
43 Dwight Stone	.15	.40
44 Jim Harbaugh	.20	.50
45 Curtis Enis	.15	.40
46 Peerless Price	.20	.50
47 Terance Mathis	.15	.40
48 Mike Alstott	.25	.60
49 Rod Smith	.20	.50
50 Marshall Faulk	.25	.60
51 Derrick Mayes	.15	.40
52 Keenan McCardell	.20	.50
53 Curtis Martin	.25	.60
54 Bobby Engram	.20	.50
55 Carl Pickens	.20	.50
56 Robert Smith	.20	.50
57 Ike Hilliard	.20	.50
58 Reidel Anthony	.15	.40
59 Jeff Graham	.15	.40
60 Mark Brunell	.20	.50
61 Joe Montgomery	.15	.40
62 Ed McCaffrey	.20	.50
63 Kenny Bynum	.15	.40
64 Curtis Conway	.20	.50
65 Trent Dilfer	.20	.50
66 Jake Reed	.20	.50
67 Jake Plummer	.20	.50
68 Tony Martin	.20	.50
69 Yatil Green	.15	.40
70 Keyshawn Johnson	.20	.50
71 Leroy Hoard	.15	.40
72 Skip Hicks	.15	.40
73 Marvin Harrison	.25	.60
74 Steve Beuerlein	.20	.50
75 Will Blackwell	.15	.40
76 Derek Loville	.15	.40
77 Warrick Dunn	.20	.50
78 Amos Zereoue	.15	.40
79 Ray Lucas	.15	.40
80 Randy Moss	.25	.60
81 Wesley Walls	.15	.40
82 Jimmy Smith	.20	.50
83 Kordell Stewart	.20	.50
84 Brian Griese	.20	.50
85 Martin Gramatica	.15	.40
86 Chris Chandler	.20	.50
87 Reggie Barlow	.15	.40
88 Jeff George	.20	.50
89 Tavian Banks	.15	.40
90 Mushin Muhammad	.20	.50
91 Steve McNair	.25	.60
92 Hines Ward	.25	.60
93 Brian Mitchell	.15	.40
94 Daunte Culpepper	.20	.50
95 Tim Dwight	.20	.50
96 Terrence Wilkins	.15	.40
97 Fred Lane	.15	.40
98 Brett Favre	.75	2.00
99 Richie Anderson	.15	.40
100 Jamal Anderson	.20	.50
101 Doug Flutie	.25	.60
102 Charles Woodson	.25	.60
103 Jacquez Green	.15	.40
104 Olandis Gary	.20	.50
105 Steve Young	.30	.75
106 Wayne Chrebet	.20	.50
107 Karim Abdul-Jabbar	.15	.40
108 Andre Rison	.20	.50
109 Eddie Kennison	.15	.40
110 Jevon Kearse	.20	.50
111 Tony Richardson RC	.20	.50
112 Jake Delhomme RC	.60	1.50
113 Errict Rhett	.20	.50
114 Akili Smith	.15	.40
115 Tyrone Wheatley	.15	.40
116 Corey Bradford	.15	.40
117 J.J. Stokes	.20	.50
118 Simeon Rice	.20	.50
119 Brad Johnson	.20	.50
120 Edgerrin James	.25	.60
121 Amani Toomer	.20	.50
122 O.J. McDuffie	.20	.50
123 Az-Zahir Hakim	.15	.40
124 Troy Edwards	.15	.40
125 Tim Biakabutuka	.20	.50
126 Jason Tucker	.15	.40
127 Charles Way	.15	.40
128 Terrell Davis	.25	.60
129 Garrison Hearst	.15	.40
130 Fred Taylor	.25	.60
131 Robert Holcombe	.15	.40
132 Frank Sanders	.15	.40
133 Morten Andersen	.15	.40
134 Cris Carter	.25	.60
135 Patrick Jeffers	.20	.50
136 Antonio Freeman	.20	.50
137 Jonathan Linton	.15	.40
138 Rashaan Shehee	.15	.40
139 Luther Broughton RC	.15	.40
140 Tim Couch	.20	.50
141 Keith Poole	.15	.40
142 Champ Bailey	.20	.50
143 Yancey Thigpen	.15	.40
144 Joey Galloway	.20	.50
145 Mac Cody	.15	.40
146 Damon Huard	.20	.50
147 Dorsey Levens	.20	.50
148 Donovan McNabb	.25	.60
149 Jamie Asher	.15	.40
150 Peyton Manning	.60	1.50
151 Leslie Shepherd	.15	.40
152 Charlie Rogers	.15	.40
153 Tony Horne	.15	.40
154 Jim Miller	.15	.40
155 Richard Huntley	.15	.40
156 Germane Crowell	.15	.40
157 Natrone Means	.20	.50
158 Justin Armour	.15	.40
159 Drew Bledsoe	.25	.60
160 Dedric Ward	.15	.40
161 Allen Rossum	.15	.40
162 Ricky Watters	.20	.50
163 Kerry Collins	.20	.50
164 James Johnson	.15	.40
165 Elvis Grbac	.15	.40
166 Larry Centers	.15	.40
167 Rob Moore	.15	.40
168 Jay Riemersma	.15	.40
169 Bill Schroeder	.20	.50
170 Deion Sanders	.25	.60
171 Jerome Bettis	.25	.60
172 Dan Marino	.75	2.00
173 Terrell Owens	.25	.60
174 Kevin Carter	.15	.40
175 Lamar Smith	.15	.40
176 Ken Dilger	.15	.40
177 Napoleon Kaufman	.20	.50
178 Kevin Williams	.15	.40
179 Tremain Mack	.15	.40
180 Troy Aikman	.40	1.00
181 Glyn Milburn	.15	.40
182 Pete Mitchell	.15	.40
183 Cameron Cleeland	.15	.40
184 Qadry Ismail	.20	.50
185 Michael Pittman	.15	.40
186 Kevin Dyson	.20	.50
187 Matt Hasselbeck	.25	.60
188 Kevin Johnson	.15	.40
189 Rich Gannon	.20	.50
190 Stephen Davis	.20	.50
191 Frank Wycheck	.20	.50
192 Eric Moulds	.20	.50
193 Jon Kitna	.20	.50
194 Mario Bates	.15	.40
195 Na Brown	.15	.40
196 Jeff Blake	.20	.50
197 Charles Evans	.15	.40
198 Oronde Gadsden	.20	.50
199 Donnell Bennett	.15	.40
200 Isaac Bruce	.25	.60
201 Olindo Mare	.15	.40
202 Darnell McDonald	.15	.40
203 Charlie Garner	.20	.50
204 Shawn Jefferson	.15	.40
205 Adrian Murrell	.15	.40
206 Peter Boulware	.15	.40
207 LeShon Johnson	.15	.40
208 Herman Moore	.20	.50
209 Duce Staley	.20	.50
210 Sean Dawkins	.15	.40
211 Antowain Smith	.20	.50
212 Albert Connell	.15	.40
213 Jeff Garcia	.20	.50
214 Kimble Anders	.15	.40
215 Shaun King	.15	.40
216 Rocket Ismail	.20	.50
217 Andrew Glover	.15	.40
218 Rickey Dudley	.15	.40
219 Michael Basnight	.15	.40
220 Terry Glenn	.20	.50
221 Peter Warrick RC	1.00	2.50
222 Ron Dayne RC	1.00	2.50
223 Thomas Jones RC	1.25	3.00
224 Joe Hamilton RC	.60	1.50
225 Tim Rattay RC	.75	2.00
226 Chad Pennington RC	1.50	4.00
227 Dennis Northcutt RC	.75	2.00
228 Troy Walters RC	.60	1.50
229 Travis Prentice RC	.75	2.00
230 Shaun Alexander RC	1.25	3.00
231 J.R. Redmond RC	.60	1.50
232 Chris Redman RC	.75	2.00
233 Tee Martin RC	1.00	2.50
234 Tom Brady RC	20.00	40.00
235 Travis Taylor RC	.75	2.00
236 R.Jay Soward RC	.60	1.50
237 Jamal Lewis RC	1.00	2.50
238 Giovanni Carmazzi RC	.60	1.50
239 Dez White RC	.75	2.00
240 LaVar Arrington RC SP	20.00	50.00
241 Laveranues Coles RC	1.00	2.50
242 Sherrod Gideon RC	.60	1.50
243 Trung Canidate RC	.75	2.00
244 Michael Wiley RC	.60	1.50
245 Anthony Lucas RC	.60	1.50
246 Darrell Jackson RC	.75	2.00
247 Plaxico Burress RC	1.00	2.50
248 Reuben Droughns RC	1.00	2.50
249 Marc Bulger RC	1.00	2.50
250 Danny Farmer RC	.60	1.50

2000 Ultra Gold Medallion

COMPLETE SET (249)	100.00	200.00
*VETS 1-220: 1.2X TO 3X BASIC CARDS		
1-220 STATED ODDS 1:1		
*ROOKIES 221-250: .6X TO 1.5X		
221-250 ROOKIE ODDS 1:4		
234 Tom Brady	25.00	60.00
240 LaVar Arrington SP	100.00	200.00

2000 Ultra Masterpiece

ONE SET PRODUCED

2000 Ultra Platinum Medallion

*VETS 1-220: 20X TO 50X BASIC CARDS		
1-220 VETERAN PRINT RUN 50		
*ROOKIES 221-250: 6X TO 15X		
221-250 ROOKIE PRINT RUN 25		
234 Tom Brady	800.00	1,200.00

2000 Ultra Dream Team

COMPLETE SET (10)	12.50	25.00
STATED ODDS 1:24		
1 Terrell Davis	.75	2.00
2 Brett Favre	2.50	6.00
3 Troy Aikman	1.25	3.00
4 Keyshawn Johnson	.60	1.50
5 Edgerrin James	.75	2.00
6 Randy Moss	.75	2.00
7 Marvin Harrison	.75	2.00
8 Kurt Warner	1.25	3.00
9 Fred Taylor	.75	2.00
10 Ricky Williams	.75	2.00

2000 Ultra Fast Lane

COMPLETE SET (15)	3.00	8.00
STATED ODDS 1:3		
1 Jimmy Smith	.30	.75
2 Cris Carter	.40	1.00
3 Marvin Harrison	.40	1.00
4 Tim Brown	.40	1.00
5 Mushin Muhammad	.30	.75
6 Isaac Bruce	.40	1.00
7 Bobby Engram	.30	.75
8 Terance Mathis	.25	.60
9 Randy Moss	.40	1.00
10 Rocket Ismail	.30	.75
11 Keyshawn Johnson	.30	.75
12 Terry Glenn	.30	.75
13 Jerry Rice	.75	2.00
14 Marcus Robinson	.30	.75
15 Antonio Freeman	.30	.75

2000 Ultra Head of the Class

COMPLETE SET (10)	5.00	12.00
STATED ODDS 1:6		
1 Peter Warrick	.30	.75
2 Ron Dayne	.30	.75
3 Thomas Jones	.40	1.00
4 Chad Pennington	.50	1.25
5 Joe Hamilton	.20	.50
6 Shaun Alexander	.40	1.00
7 J.R. Redmond	.20	.50
8 Troy Walters	.20	.50
9 Travis Prentice	.25	.60
10 Chris Redman	.25	.60

2000 Ultra Instant Three Play

COMPLETE SET (15)	3.00	8.00
STATED ODDS 1:3		
1 Peyton Manning	1.00	2.50
2 Curtis Enis	.25	.60
3 Charlie Batch	.30	.75
4 Fred Taylor	.40	1.00
5 Az-Zahir Hakim	.25	.60
6 Randy Moss	.40	1.00
7 Jacquez Green	.25	.60
8 Kevin Dyson	.30	.75
9 Brian Griese	.30	.75
10 Rashaan Shehee	.25	.60
11 Tony Simmons	.25	.60
12 Charles Woodson	.40	1.00
13 Hines Ward	.40	1.00
14 Skip Hicks	.25	.60
15 Tim Dwight	.30	.75

2000 Ultra Millennium Monsters

COMPLETE SET (10)	6.00	15.00
STATED ODDS 1:12		
1 Tim Couch	.40	1.00
2 Eddie George	.40	1.00
3 Brian Griese	.40	1.00
4 Keyshawn Johnson	.40	1.00
5 Peyton Manning	1.25	3.00
6 Randy Moss	.50	1.25
7 Ricky Williams	.50	1.25
8 Edgerrin James	.50	1.25
9 Cade McNown	.30	.75
10 Donovan McNabb	.50	1.25

2000 Ultra Won by One

COMPLETE SET (10)	25.00	50.00
STATED ODDS 1:72		
1 Peyton Manning	4.00	10.00
2 Randy Moss	1.50	4.00
3 Brett Favre	5.00	12.00
4 Terrell Davis	1.50	4.00
5 Dan Marino	5.00	12.00
6 Jake Plummer	1.25	3.00
7 Tim Couch	1.25	3.00
8 Eddie George	1.25	3.00
9 Brian Griese	1.25	3.00
10 Kurt Warner	2.50	6.00

2001 Ultra

Released as a 300-card set, 2001 Ultra is composed of 250 veteran cards and 60 rookie cards which are serial numbered to 2499. Base cards contain full-color action photography and rainbow holofoil stamping. Ultra was packaged in 24-pack boxes with packs that contained 10 cards and carried a suggested retail price of $2.99. Cards numbered U301 through U310 were issued later in the season and featured players who had an impact during the 2001 season.

COMP.SET w/o SP's (250)	10.00	25.00
251-310 ROOKIE PRINT RUN 2499		
1 Daunte Culpepper	.25	.60
2 Kurt Warner	.50	1.25
3 Emmitt Smith	.75	2.00
4 Eddie George	.30	.75
5 Ron Dayne	.25	.60
6 Zach Thomas	.30	.75
7 Itula Mili	.20	.50
8 Jake Reed	.25	.60
9 James Stewart	.20	.50
10 Terrence Wilkins	.20	.50
11 Jeff Blake	.25	.60
12 Kerry Collins	.25	.60
13 Christian Fauria	.20	.50
14 Jackie Harris	.25	.60
15 Kevin Johnson	.20	.50
16 Tony Martin	.25	.60
17 Joey Galloway	.25	.60
18 Junior Seau	.30	.75
19 Jason Tucker	.20	.50
20 Steve Beuerlein	.25	.60
21 Mike Cloud	.20	.50
22 Kevin Faulk	.25	.60
23 Az-Zahir Hakim	.20	.50
24 Charles Johnson	.20	.50
25 Curtis Martin	.30	.75
26 Eric Moulds	.25	.60
27 Bill Schroeder	.25	.60
28 Amani Toomer	.20	.50
29 Obafemi Ayanbadejo	.20	.50
30 Aaron Shea	.20	.50
31 Ken Dilger	.20	.50
32 Terry Glenn	.25	.60
33 Rocket Ismail	.20	.50
34 Dorsey Levens	.25	.60
35 Brian Mitchell	.20	.50
36 Tony Richardson	.20	.50
37 Sam Madison	.20	.50
38 Darren Sharper	.20	.50
39 Derrick Alexander	.20	.50
40 Aaron Brooks	.25	.60
41 Casey Crawford	.20	.50
42 Terrell Fletcher	.20	.50
43 William Henderson	.25	.60
44 Thomas Jones	.25	.60
45 Keenan McCardell	.25	.60
46 Chad Pennington	.30	.75
47 Akili Smith	.30	.75
48 Hines Ward	.30	.75
49 Champ Bailey	.30	.75
50 Cris Carter	.25	.60
51 Corey Dillon	.25	.60
52 Tony Gonzalez	.30	.75
53 Darrell Jackson	.25	.60
54 Chad Lewis	.20	.50
55 Dave Moore	.20	.50
56 Jay Riemersma	.20	.50
57 J.J. Stokes	.20	.50
58 Frank Wycheck	.25	.60
59 Tiki Barber	.30	.75
60 Tony Carter	.20	.50
61 Rickey Dudley	.25	.60
62 John Lynch	.25	.60
63 Larry Foster	.20	.50
64 Willie Jackson	.20	.50
65 Jamal Lewis	.30	.75
66 Herman Moore	.25	.60
67 Andre Rison	.25	.60
68 Michael Strahan	.30	.75
69 Charlie Batch	.25	.60
70 Larry Centers	.20	.50
71 Ron Dugans	.20	.50
72 Jeff Graham	.20	.50
73 Edgerrin James	.30	.75
74 Jermaine Lewis	.20	.50
75 Charles Woodson	.30	.75
76 Chris Redman	.30	.75
77 Jon Ritchie	.20	.50
78 Fred Taylor	.30	.75
79 Jamal Anderson	.25	.60
80 Isaac Bruce	.30	.75
81 Terrell Davis	.30	.75
82 Rich Gannon	.25	.60
83 Joe Horn	.25	.60
84 Eddie Kennison	.25	.60
85 Steve McNair	.30	.75
86 Travis Prentice	.20	.50
87 Rod Smith	.25	.60
88 Ricky Watters	.25	.60
89 Michael Bates	.20	.50
90 Byron Chamberlain	.20	.50
91 Warrick Dunn	.30	.75
92 Elvis Grbac	.25	.60
93 Patrick Jeffers	.20	.50
94 Ray Lewis	.30	.75
95 Sammy Morris	.25	.60
96 Marcus Robinson	.25	.60
97 Travis Taylor	.20	.50
98 Fred Beasley	.20	.50
99 Chris Chandler	.25	.60
100 Tim Dwight	.25	.60
101 Ahman Green	.30	.75
102 Shawn Jefferson	.20	.50
103 Jeremy McDaniel	.20	.50
104 Sylvester Morris	.20	.50
105 John Randle	.25	.60
106 Vinny Testaverde	.25	.60
107 Anthony Becht	.20	.50
108 Wayne Chrebet	.25	.60
109 Stephen Boyd	.20	.50
110 Jacquez Green	.20	.50
111 MarTay Jenkins	.20	.50
112 Jason Gildon	.20	.50
113 Chad Morton	.20	.50
114 Deion Sanders	.30	.75
115 Yancey Thigpen	.20	.50
116 Marty Booker	.25	.60
117 Curtis Conway	.25	.60
118 Jermaine Fazande	.20	.50
119 Matthew Hatchette	.20	.50
120 Pat Johnson	.20	.50
121 Terance Mathis	.20	.50
122 Terrell Owens	.30	.75
123 Corey Simon	.20	.50
124 Darrick Vaughn	.20	.50
125 Drew Bledsoe	.30	.75
126 Albert Connell	.20	.50
127 Brett Favre	1.00	2.50
128 Marvin Harrison	.30	.75
129 Keyshawn Johnson	.25	.60
130 Derrick Mason	.25	.60
131 Dennis Northcutt	.20	.50
132 Shannon Sharpe	.30	.75
133 Brian Urlacher	.40	1.00
134 Mike Anderson	.25	.60
135 Mark Bruener	.25	.60
136 Sean Dawkins	.20	.50
137 Jeff Garcia	.25	.60
138 Tony Horne	.20	.50
139 Shaun King	.20	.50
140 Cade McNown	.25	.60
141 Peerless Price	.20	.50
142 R.Jay Soward	.20	.50
143 Tyrone Wheatley	.25	.60
144 Richie Anderson	.20	.50
145 Mark Brunell	.25	.60
146 JaJuan Dawson	.20	.50
147 Charlie Garner	.25	.60
148 Desmond Howard	.25	.60
149 Jon Kitna	.25	.60
150 Duane Starks	.20	.50
151 J.R. Redmond	.20	.50
152 Duce Staley	.25	.60
153 Dez White	.25	.60
154 David Boston	.20	.50
155 Tim Couch	.20	.50
156 Jay Fiedler	.25	.60
157 Jessie Armstead	.20	.50
158 Rob Johnson	.25	.60
159 Brad Johnson	.25	.60
160 Derrick Mayes	.20	.50
161 Jerome Pathon	.20	.50
162 David Sloan	.20	.50
163 Wesley Walls	.20	.50
164 Shaun Alexander	.30	.75
165 Derrick Brooks	.30	.75
166 Germane Crowell	.20	.50
167 Doug Flutie	.30	.75
168 Ike Hilliard	.25	.60
169 Hugh Douglas	.20	.50
170 Wane McGarity	.20	.50
171 Michael Pittman	.25	.60
172 Shawn Bryson	.20	.50
173 Richard Huntley	.20	.50
174 Darnell Autry	.20	.50
175 Plaxico Burress	.25	.60
176 Trent Dilfer	.25	.60
177 Jeff George	.25	.60
178 Qadry Ismail	.25	.60
179 Ryan Leaf	.20	.50
180 Jim Miller	.25	.60
181 Jerry Rice	.60	1.50
182 Kordell Stewart	.25	.60
183 Ricky Williams	.30	.75
184 James Allen	.20	.50
185 Courtney Brown	.20	.50
186 Reidel Anthony	.20	.50
187 Bubba Franks	.25	.60
188 Priest Holmes	.30	.75
189 Napoleon Kaufman	.20	.50
190 Trevor Pryce	.20	.50
191 Jake Plummer	.25	.60
192 Jimmy Smith	.25	.60
193 Michael Wiley	.20	.50
194 Brock Huard	.20	.50
195 Troy Brown	.25	.60
196 Stephen Davis	.25	.60
197 Oronde Gadsden	.20	.50
198 Brad Hoover	.25	.60
199 La'Roi Glover	.20	.50
200 Donovan McNabb	.30	.75
201 Jerry Porter	.20	.50
202 Robert Smith	.25	.60
203 Justin Watson	.20	.50
204 Tim Biakabutuka	.20	.50
205 Laveranues Coles	.25	.60
206 Marshall Faulk	.30	.75
207 Jim Harbaugh	.25	.60
208 Doug Johnson	.20	.50
209 Tee Martin	.25	.60
210 Muhsin Muhammad	.25	.60
211 Darnay Scott	.25	.60
212 Jeremiah Trotter	.20	.50
213 Troy Aikman	.50	1.25
214 Kyle Brady	.20	.50
215 Sam Cowart	.20	.50
216 Darren Howard	.20	.50
217 Donald Hayes	.20	.50
218 Freddie Jones	.20	.50
219 Ed McCaffrey	.25	.60
220 David Patten	.20	.50
221 Brian Griese	.25	.60
222 Dedric Ward	.20	.50
223 Jerome Bettis	.30	.75
224 Greg Clark	.20	.50
225 Bobby Engram	.25	.60
226 Matt Hasselbeck	.30	.75
227 James Jett	.20	.50
228 Peyton Manning	.75	2.00
229 Randy Moss	.30	.75
230 Warren Sapp	.25	.60
231 James Thrash	.25	.60
232 Mike Alstott	.25	.60
233 Tim Brown	.30	.75

234 Randall Cunningham	.30	.75
235 Antonio Freeman	.30	.75
236 Torry Holt	.25	.60
237 Jevon Kearse	.25	.60
238 James McKnight	.20	.50
239 Marcus Pollard	.20	.50
240 Lamar Smith	.25	.60
241 Peter Warrick	.25	.60
242 Donnell Bennett	.20	.50
243 Joe Johnson	.20	.50
244 Troy Edwards	.20	.50
245 Trent Green	.30	.75
246 Jason Taylor	.30	.75
247 Aeneas Williams	.25	.60
248 Johnnie Morton	.25	.60
249 Frank Sanders	.20	.50
250 Jason Sehorn	.25	.60
251 Chris Weinke RC	1.50	4.00
252 Bobby Newcombe RC	1.50	4.00
253 LaDainian Tomlinson RC	6.00	15.00
254 Chad Johnson RC	3.00	8.00
255 Derrick Gibson RC	1.25	3.00
256 Sage Rosenfels RC	2.00	5.00
257 LaMont Jordan RC	2.00	5.00
258 Mike McMahon RC	1.50	4.00
259 Vinny Sutherland RC	1.25	3.00
260 Drew Brees RC	12.00	30.00
261 Deuce McAllister RC	2.00	5.00
262 Kevan Barlow RC	1.50	4.00
263 Jamar Fletcher RC	1.25	3.00
264 Gerard Warren RC	1.50	4.00
265 Todd Heap RC	2.00	5.00
266 Travis Henry RC	1.50	4.00
267 Quincy Morgan RC	1.50	4.00
268 Anthony Thomas RC	2.00	5.00
269 Andre Carter RC	1.50	4.00
270 Freddie Mitchell RC	1.25	3.00
271 Richard Seymour RC	2.00	5.00
272 Josh Booty RC	1.50	4.00
273 Robert Ferguson RC	2.00	5.00
274 Marques Tuiasosopo RC	1.50	4.00
275 Reggie Wayne RC	4.00	10.00
276 Jabari Holloway RC	1.25	3.00
277 Rudi Johnson RC	2.00	5.00
278 Michael Bennett RC	1.50	4.00
279 Snoop Minnis RC	1.25	3.00
280 Dan Morgan RC	1.50	4.00
281 Rod Gardner RC	1.50	4.00
282 Jesse Palmer RC	1.50	4.00
283 Michael Vick RC	8.00	20.00
284 Chris Chambers RC	2.00	5.00
285 James Jackson RC	1.25	3.00
286 David Terrell RC	1.50	4.00
287 Koren Robinson RC	1.50	4.00
288 Travis Minor RC	1.50	4.00
289 Santana Moss RC	2.50	6.00
290 Josh Heupel RC	2.00	5.00
291 Jamal Reynolds RC	1.25	3.00
292 Ken-Yon Rambo RC	1.25	3.00
293 Cedrick Wilson RC	1.50	4.00
294 Alge Crumpler RC	2.00	5.00
295 Fred Smoot RC	2.00	5.00
296 Dan Alexander RC	1.50	4.00
297 Tim Hasselbeck RC	1.50	4.00
298 Will Allen RC	2.00	5.00
299 Keith Adams RC	1.25	3.00
300 Heath Evans RC	1.50	4.00
U301 Quincy Carter RC	1.50	4.00
U302 Derrick Blaylock RC	1.50	4.00
U303 Correll Buckhalter RC	2.00	5.00
U304 A.J. Feeley RC	1.50	4.00
U305 Milton Wynn RC	1.25	3.00
U306 Kevin Kasper RC	1.25	3.00
U307 Justin McCareins RC	1.50	4.00
U308 Dave Dickenson RC	1.50	4.00
U309 Steve Smith RC	4.00	10.00
U310 Moran Norris RC	1.25	3.00

2001 Ultra Gold Medallion

*VETS 1-250: 4X TO 10X BASIC CARDS
VETERAN PRINT RUN 250
*ROOK.251-300: 1.2X TO 3X BASIC CARDS
ROOKIE PRINT RUN 100

2001 Ultra Platinum Medallion

*VETS 1-250: 12X TO 30X BASIC CARDS
1-250 VETERAN PRINT RUN 50
*ROOKIE 251-300: 3X TO 8X BASIC CARDS
251-300 ROOKIE PRINT RUN 25

253P LaDainian Tomlinson	125.00	250.00
260P Drew Brees	150.00	250.00
283P Michael Vick	125.00	250.00

2001 Ultra Ball Hawks

STATED ODDS 1:144

1 Troy Aikman	12.00	30.00
2 Derrick Alexander	5.00	12.00
3 Jamal Anderson	6.00	15.00
4 Charlie Batch	6.00	15.00
5 Courtney Brown	5.00	12.00
6 Mark Brunell	6.00	15.00
7 Tim Couch	5.00	12.00
8 Eddie George	8.00	20.00
9 Tony Gonzalez	8.00	20.00
10 Elvis Grbac	6.00	15.00
11 Marvin Harrison	8.00	20.00
12 Edgerrin James	8.00	20.00
13 Kevin Johnson	5.00	12.00
14 Jevon Kearse	6.00	15.00
15 Donovan McNabb	8.00	20.00
16 Steve McNair	8.00	20.00
17 Cade McNown	6.00	15.00
18 Herman Moore	6.00	15.00
19 Travis Prentice	5.00	12.00
20 Marcus Robinson	6.00	15.00
21 Emmitt Smith	20.00	50.00
22 Jimmy Smith	6.00	15.00
23 Duce Staley	6.00	15.00
24 Brian Urlacher	10.00	25.00

2001 Ultra College Greats Previews

COMPLETE SET (35)	40.00	80.00
STATED ODDS 1:22		
1 Marcus Allen	1.50	4.00
2 Drew Brees	6.00	15.00
3 Tim Brown	1.50	4.00
4 Earl Campbell	1.50	4.00
5 John Cappelletti	1.00	2.50
6 Ron Dayne	1.00	2.50
7 Tony Dorsett	1.50	4.00
8 Tim Dwight	1.00	2.50
9 Doug Flutie	1.50	4.00
10 Eddie George	1.25	3.00
11 Brian Griese	1.00	2.50
12 Archie Griffin	1.00	2.50
13 Franco Harris	1.50	4.00
14 Bob Hayes	1.25	3.00
15 Josh Heupel	1.00	2.50
16 Paul Hornung	1.50	4.00
17 Bo Jackson	2.00	5.00
18 Thomas Jones	1.00	2.50
19 Jamal Lewis	1.25	3.00
20 Bob Lilly	1.25	3.00
21 Johnny Lujack	1.25	3.00
22 Donovan McNabb	1.25	3.00
23 Santana Moss	1.25	3.00
24 Jim Plunkett	1.25	3.00
25 Billy Sims	1.25	3.00
26 Roger Staubach	2.50	6.00
27 Pat Sullivan	1.00	2.50
28 David Terrell	1.00	2.50
29 LaDainian Tomlinson	3.00	8.00
30 Amani Toomer	1.00	2.50
31 Michael Vick	4.00	10.00
32 Herschel Walker	1.25	3.00
33 Chris Weinke	1.00	2.50
34 Ricky Williams	1.25	3.00
35 Steve Young	2.00	5.00

2001 Ultra College Greats Previews Autographs

STATED ODDS 1:61

1 Marcus Allen	20.00	35.00
2 Drew Brees	75.00	125.00
3 Tim Brown	20.00	40.00
4 Earl Campbell	20.00	35.00
5 John Cappelletti	8.00	20.00
6 Ron Dayne	10.00	25.00
7 Tony Dorsett	25.00	50.00
8 Tim Dwight	8.00	20.00
9 Doug Flutie	20.00	40.00
10 Eddie George	10.00	25.00
12 Archie Griffin	12.00	30.00
13 Franco Harris	20.00	40.00
14 Bob Hayes	60.00	120.00
15 Josh Heupel	10.00	25.00
16 Paul Hornung	12.00	30.00
17 Bo Jackson	60.00	120.00
19 Jamal Lewis	10.00	25.00
20 Bob Lilly	10.00	25.00
22 Donovan McNabb	20.00	40.00
23 Santana Moss	10.00	25.00
24 Jim Plunkett	12.00	30.00
26 Roger Staubach	50.00	100.00
27 Pat Sullivan	8.00	20.00
28 David Terrell	8.00	20.00
29 LaDainian Tomlinson	75.00	150.00
30 Amani Toomer	8.00	20.00
31 Michael Vick	60.00	100.00
33 Chris Weinke	8.00	20.00

2001 Ultra College Greats Previews Autograph Redemptions

*SINGLES: .6X TO 1.5X UNSIGNED INSERTS

1 Marcus Allen	2.50	6.00
2 Drew Brees	10.00	25.00
3 Tim Brown	2.50	6.00
4 Earl Campbell	2.50	6.00
5 John Cappelletti	1.50	4.00
6 Ron Dayne	1.50	4.00
7 Tony Dorsett	2.50	6.00
8 Tim Dwight	1.50	4.00
9 Doug Flutie	2.50	6.00
10 Eddie George	2.00	5.00
12 Archie Griffin	1.50	4.00
13 Franco Harris	2.50	6.00
14 Bob Hayes	2.00	5.00
15 Josh Heupel	1.50	4.00
16 Paul Hornung	2.50	6.00
17 Bo Jackson	3.00	8.00
19 Jamal Lewis	2.00	5.00
20 Bob Lilly	2.00	5.00
22 Donovan McNabb	2.00	5.00
23 Santana Moss	2.00	5.00
24 Jim Plunkett	2.00	5.00
26 Roger Staubach	4.00	10.00
27 Pat Sullivan	1.50	4.00
28 David Terrell	1.25	3.00
29 LaDainian Tomlinson	5.00	12.00
30 Amani Toomer	1.50	4.00
31 Michael Vick	6.00	15.00
33 Chris Weinke	1.25	3.00

2001 Ultra Ground Command

COMPLETE SET (10)	7.50	20.00

STATED ODDS 1:22
*GOLD.MED/250: 1X TO 2.5X BASIC INSERT
GOLD MED.PRINT RUN 250 SER.#'d SETS
*PLAT.MED/50: 2.5X TO 6X BASIC INSERT
PLAT.MED.PRINT RUN 50 SER.#'d SETS

1 Emmitt Smith	1.50	4.00
2 Edgerrin James	.60	1.50
3 Marshall Faulk	.60	1.50
4 Jamal Lewis	.60	1.50
5 Mike Anderson	.50	1.25
6 Duce Staley	.50	1.25
7 Jamal Anderson	.50	1.25
8 Ricky Williams	.60	1.50
9 Corey Dillon	.50	1.25
10 Terrell Davis	.60	1.50

2001 Ultra Head of the Class

COMPLETE SET (25)	20.00	50.00
STATED ODDS 1:22		
1 Trung Canidate	.60	1.50
2 Thomas Jones	.75	2.00
3 Curtis Keaton	.60	1.50
4 Courtney Brown	.60	1.50
5 Chris Redman	1.00	2.50
6 Dennis Northcutt	.60	1.50
7 Sylvester Morris	.60	1.50
8 Shaun Alexander	1.00	2.50
9 Dez White	.75	2.00
10 Laveranues Coles	.75	2.00
11 R.Jay Soward	.60	1.50
12 Jamal Lewis	1.00	2.50
13 J.R. Redmond	.60	1.50
14 Travis Taylor	.60	1.50
15 Plaxico Burress	.75	2.00
16 Peter Warrick	.75	2.00
17 Joe Hamilton	.60	1.50
18 Ron Dugans	.60	1.50
19 Tee Martin	.75	2.00
20 Brian Urlacher	1.25	3.00
21 Ron Dayne	.75	2.00
22 Travis Prentice	.60	1.50
23 Chad Pennington	1.00	2.50
24 Corey Simon	.60	1.50
25 Mike Anderson	.75	2.00

2001 Ultra Head of the Class Player Worn Caps

STATED PRINT RUN 100 SER.#'d SETS

1 Trung Canidate	4.00	10.00
2 Thomas Jones	5.00	12.00
3 Curtis Keaton	4.00	10.00
4 Courtney Brown	4.00	10.00
5 Chris Redman	6.00	15.00
6 Dennis Northcutt	4.00	10.00
7 Sylvester Morris	4.00	10.00
8 Shaun Alexander	6.00	15.00
9 Dez White	5.00	12.00
10 Laveranues Coles	5.00	12.00
11 R.Jay Soward	4.00	10.00
12 Jamal Lewis	6.00	15.00
13 J.R. Redmond	4.00	10.00
14 Travis Taylor	4.00	10.00
15 Plaxico Burress	5.00	12.00
16 Peter Warrick	5.00	12.00
17 Joe Hamilton	4.00	10.00
18 Ron Dugans	4.00	10.00
19 Tee Martin	5.00	12.00
20 Brian Urlacher	8.00	20.00
21 Ron Dayne	5.00	12.00
22 Travis Prentice	4.00	10.00
23 Chad Pennington	6.00	15.00
24 Corey Simon	4.00	10.00
25 Mike Anderson	5.00	12.00

2001 Ultra Quick Strike

COMPLETE SET (20)	20.00	50.00

STATED ODDS 1:22
*GOLD.MED/250: .8X TO 2X BASIC INSERT
GOLD MED.PRINT RUN 250 SER.#'d SETS
*PLAT.MED/50: 2X TO 5X BASIC INSERT
PLAT.MED.PRINT RUN 50 SER.#'d SETS

1 Kurt Warner	1.50	4.00
2 Mark Brunell	.75	2.00
3 Fred Taylor	1.00	2.50
4 Emmitt Smith	2.50	6.00
5 Jerry Rice	2.00	5.00
6 Eddie George	1.00	2.50
7 Cade McNown	.75	2.00
8 Randy Moss	1.00	2.50
9 Donovan McNabb	1.00	2.50
10 Peyton Manning	2.50	6.00
11 Edgerrin James	1.00	2.50
12 Shaun King	.60	1.50
13 Troy Aikman	1.50	4.00
14 Tim Couch	.60	1.50
15 Jamal Lewis	1.00	2.50
16 Daunte Culpepper	.75	2.00
17 Brett Favre	3.00	8.00
18 Drew Bledsoe	1.00	2.50
19 Terrell Davis	1.00	2.50
20 Marshall Faulk	1.00	2.50

2001 Ultra Sunday's Best Jerseys

STATED ODDS 1:63 HOB, 1:96 RETAIL

1 Jamal Anderson	5.00	12.00
2 Jerome Bettis	6.00	15.00
3 Drew Bledsoe	6.00	15.00
4 Isaac Bruce	6.00	15.00
5 Mark Brunell	5.00	12.00
6 Trung Canidate	4.00	10.00
7 Tim Couch	4.00	10.00
8 Stephen Davis	5.00	12.00
9 Ron Dayne	5.00	12.00
10 Warrick Dunn	6.00	15.00
11 Marshall Faulk	6.00	15.00
12 Doug Flutie	6.00	15.00
13 Antonio Freeman	6.00	15.00
14 Brian Griese	5.00	12.00
15 Kevin Johnson	4.00	10.00
16 Thomas Jones	5.00	12.00
17 Napoleon Kaufman	4.00	10.00
18 Curtis Martin	6.00	15.00
19 Keenan McCardell	5.00	12.00
20 Terrell Owens	6.00	15.00
21 Jake Plummer	5.00	12.00
22 Jerry Rice	12.00	30.00
23 Jimmy Smith	5.00	12.00
24 Rod Smith	5.00	12.00
25 R.Jay Soward	4.00	10.00
26 Fred Taylor	6.00	15.00
27 Brian Urlacher	8.00	20.00
28 Kurt Warner	10.00	25.00

2001 Ultra Two Minute Thrill

COMPLETE SET (20)	15.00	40.00

STATED ODDS 1:22
*GOLD.MED/250: .8X TO 2X BASIC INSERT
GOLD MED.PRINT RUN 250 SER.#'d SETS
*PLAT.MED/50: 2X TO 5X BASIC INSERT
PLAT.MED.PRINT RUN 50 SER.#'d SETS

1 Troy Aikman	1.50	4.00
2 Terrell Davis	1.00	2.50
3 Keyshawn Johnson	.75	2.00
4 Peyton Manning	2.50	6.00
5 Donovan McNabb	1.00	2.50
6 Steve McNair	1.00	2.50
7 Cade McNown	.75	2.00
8 Ricky Williams	1.00	2.50
9 Brett Favre	3.00	8.00
10 Edgerrin James	1.00	2.50
11 Tim Couch	.60	1.50
12 Fred Taylor	1.00	2.50
13 Rich Gannon	.75	2.00
14 Kurt Warner	1.50	4.00
15 Randy Moss	1.00	2.50
16 Peter Warrick	.75	2.00
17 Ron Dayne	.75	2.00
18 Mark Brunell	.75	2.00
19 Daunte Culpepper	.75	2.00
20 Marshall Faulk	1.00	2.50

2001 Ultra White Rose Die Cast

White Rose Collectibles, a division of Fleer, released these 1:58 scale die-cast PT Cruiser cars in 2001. Each blister pack included one die-cast piece along with a 2001 Ultra card of the featured player. The cards are essentially a parallel to the player's base Ultra card but have been re-numbered and include the White Rose logo on the cardbacks. We've included pricing below on just the cards.

COMPLETE SET (38)	20.00	50.00
1 Michael Vick	1.50	4.00
2 Brian Urlacher	.60	1.50
3 Emmitt Smith	1.25	3.00
4 Charlie Batch	.40	1.00
5 Brett Favre	1.50	4.00
6 Kurt Warner	.75	2.00
7 Marshall Faulk	.50	1.25
8 Daunte Culpepper	.40	1.00
9 Randy Moss	.50	1.25
10 Ricky Williams	.50	1.25
11 Ron Dayne	.40	1.00
12 Tiki Barber	.50	1.25
13 Donovan McNabb	.50	1.25
14 Jake Plummer	.40	1.00
15 Jeff Garcia	.40	1.00
16 Keyshawn Johnson	.40	1.00
17 Stephen Davis	.40	1.00
18 Rod Gardner	.40	1.00
19 Eric Moulds	.40	1.00
20 Peter Warrick	.40	1.00
21 Jamal Lewis	.50	1.25
22 Terrell Davis	.50	1.25
23 Brian Griese	.40	1.00
24 Peyton Manning	1.25	3.00
25 Edgerrin James	.50	1.25
26 Eddie George	.50	1.25
27 Tony Gonzalez	.50	1.25
28 Rich Gannon	.40	1.00
29 Tim Brown	.50	1.25
30 Zach Thomas	.50	1.25
31 Drew Bledsoe	.50	1.25
32 Santana Moss	.50	1.25
33 Jerome Bettis	.50	1.25
34 LaDainian Tomlinson	1.25	3.00
35 Koren Robinson	.40	1.00
36 Fred Taylor	.50	1.25
37 Chris Weinke	.40	1.00
38 Tim Couch	.30	.75

2002 Ultra

This 240 card set was released in late July, 2002. It is composed of 200 veterans and 40 rookies. The rookies are seeded 1:4 packs. SRP for this product is $2.99. Boxes contain 24 packs, each with 10 cards per pack.

COMPLETE SET (240)	60.00	150.00
COMP.SET w/o SP's (200)	10.00	25.00
ROOKIE STATED ODDS 1:4		
1 Donovan McNabb	.30	.75
2 Chad Pennington	.30	.75
3 Shaun Alexander	.25	.60
4 Corey Dillon	.25	.60
5 Kurt Warner	.30	.75
6 Ed McCaffrey	.25	.60
7 Hugh Douglas	.20	.50
8 Tony Gonzalez	.30	.75
9 Travis Taylor	.20	.50
10 Tony Boselli	.25	.60
11 Chad Scott	.20	.50
12 Ernie Conwell	.20	.50
13 Brad Johnson	.25	.60
14 Donald Hayes	.20	.50
15 Emmitt Smith	.75	2.00
16 Jimmy Smith	.25	.60
17 Anthony Becht	.20	.50
18 Rod Gardner	.20	.50
19 Muhsin Muhammad	.25	.60
20 Troy Hambrick	.20	.50
21 Keenan McCardell	.25	.60
22 Laveranues Coles	.25	.60
23 Kevin Dyson	.25	.60
24 Grant Wistrom	.20	.50
25 Eric Moulds	.25	.60
26 Nate Clements	.20	.50
27 Terrell Davis	.30	.75
28 Aaron Glenn	.20	.50
29 Eric Hicks	.20	.50
30 Tiki Barber	.30	.75
31 Jake Plummer	.25	.60
32 Junior Seau	.30	.75
33 Marshall Faulk	.30	.75
34 Warrick Dunn	.25	.60
35 Bill Gramatica	.20	.50
36 Tim Couch	.20	.50
37 Kabeer Gbaja-Biamila	.25	.60
38 Kailee Wong	.20	.50
39 David Patten	.20	.50
40 Correll Buckhalter	.25	.60
41 Troy Brown	.25	.60
42 Drew Bledsoe	.30	.75
43 Travis Henry	.20	.50
44 Jim Miller	.20	.50
45 Rod Smith	.25	.60
46 Tai Streets	.20	.50
47 Snoop Minnis	.20	.50
48 Ron Dayne	.25	.60
49 Tyrone Wheatley	.25	.60
50 LaDainian Tomlinson	.40	1.00
51 Akili Smith	.25	.60
52 Warren Sapp	.25	.60
53 Adam Archuleta	.20	.50
54 Chris Fuamatu-Ma'afala	.20	.50
55 Marty Booker	.25	.60
56 Trevor Pryce	.20	.50
57 Peyton Manning	.60	1.50
58 Lamar Smith	.25	.60
59 Amani Toomer	.25	.60
60 Greg Biekert	.20	.50
61 Marcellus Wiley	.20	.50
62 Ahmed Plummer	.20	.50
63 Mike Alstott	.25	.60
64 Gary Walker	.20	.50
65 Champ Bailey	.30	.75
66 Chris Redman	.20	.50
67 David Terrell	.20	.50
68 Mike McMahon	.20	.50
69 Marvin Harrison	.30	.75
70 Jay Fiedler	.25	.60
71 JaJuan Dawson	.20	.50
72 Charlie Garner	.25	.60
73 Curtis Conway	.25	.60
74 J.J. Stokes	.20	.50
75 Ronde Barber	.25	.60
76 Alge Crumpler	.25	.60
77 Jamir Miller	.20	.50
78 Brett Favre	.75	2.00
79 Randy Moss	.30	.75
80 Joe Horn	.25	.60
81 Hines Ward	.30	.75
82 Lawyer Milloy	.20	.50
83 Aeneas Williams	.25	.60
84 Chris McAlister	.20	.50
85 Anthony Thomas	.25	.60
86 Johnnie Morton	.25	.60
87 Edgerrin James	.25	.60
88 Chris Chambers	.25	.60
89 Michael Strahan	.30	.75
90 Charles Woodson	.30	.75
91 Tim Dwight	.20	.50
92 Kevan Barlow	.20	.50
93 Donnie Abraham	.20	.50
94 Peter Boulware	.20	.50
95 Marcus Robinson	.25	.60
96 Shaun Rogers	.20	.50
97 Dominic Rhodes	.25	.60
98 Zach Thomas	.30	.75
99 Kerry Collins	.25	.60
100 Tim Brown	.30	.75
101 Garrison Hearst	.25	.60
102 Steve McNair	.30	.75
103 Fred Smoot	.25	.60
104 Isaac Bruce	.30	.75
105 Jamal Lewis	.25	.60
106 Brian Urlacher	.30	.75
107 Takeo Spikes	.20	.50
108 Marcus Pollard	.20	.50
109 Jason Taylor	.25	.60
110 Deuce McAllister	.25	.60
111 Jerry Rice	.60	1.50
112 Terrell Owens	.30	.75
113 Eddie George	.25	.60
114 Rob Morris	.20	.50
115 Mike Brown	.25	.60
116 Joey Galloway	.25	.60
117 Fred Taylor	.25	.60
118 Rich Gannon	.25	.60
119 Chris Chandler	.25	.60
120 Koren Robinson	.20	.50
121 Dan Morgan	.20	.50
122 Rocket Ismail	.25	.60
123 Mark Brunell	.25	.60
124 John Abraham	.25	.60
125 Stephen Davis	.25	.60
126 Patrick Kerney	.20	.50
127 Anthony Henry	.20	.50
128 Scotty Anderson	.20	.50
129 Oronde Gadsden	.20	.50
130 Willie Jackson	.20	.50
131 Kendrell Bell	.20	.50
132 Ray Lewis	.30	.75
133 Quincy Carter	.20	.50
134 James Stewart	.20	.50
135 Travis Minor	.20	.50
136 Kyle Turley	.20	.50
137 Jason Gildon	.25	.60
138 David Boston	.20	.50
139 Justin Smith	.20	.50
140 Jamie Sharper	.25	.60
141 Antowain Smith	.25	.60
142 Freddie Mitchell	.20	.50
143 Frank Sanders	.20	.50
144 Kevin Johnson	.20	.50
145 Darren Sharper	.25	.60
146 Eric Johnson	.20	.50
147 Ty Law	.25	.60
148 James Thrash	.25	.60
149 Matt Hasselbeck	.30	.75
150 Peerless Price	.20	.50
151 T.J. Houshmandzadeh	.30	.75
152 Mike Anderson	.25	.60
153 Jermaine Lewis	.20	.50
154 Trent Green	.25	.60
155 Ron Dixon	.20	.50
156 Duce Staley	.25	.60
157 Drew Brees	.50	1.25
158 Torry Holt	.30	.75
159 Keyshawn Johnson	.25	.60
160 Michael Vick	.50	1.25
161 Benjamin Gay	.20	.50
162 Bill Schroeder	.20	.50
163 Byron Chamberlain	.20	.50
164 Tedy Bruschi	.30	.75
165 Kordell Stewart	.25	.60
166 Deltha O'Neal	.20	.50
167 Quincy Morgan	.20	.50
168 Bubba Franks	.25	.60
169 Daunte Culpepper	.25	.60
170 Ricky Williams	.25	.60
171 Plaxico Burress	.25	.60
172 Trent Dilfer	.25	.60
173 Steve Smith	.30	.75
174 Greg Ellis	.20	.50
175 Tony Brackens	.20	.50
176 Santana Moss	.25	.60
177 Frank Wycheck	.20	.50
178 Michael Pittman	.25	.60
179 Peter Warrick	.25	.60
180 Antonio Freeman	.30	.75
181 Tom Brady	.75	2.00
182 Bobby Taylor	.25	.60
183 Jeff Garcia	.25	.60
184 Darrell Jackson	.25	.60
185 Chris Weinke	.20	.50
186 Darren Woodson	.25	.60
187 Hardy Nickerson	.20	.50
188 Wayne Chrebet	.25	.60
189 Samari Rolle	.20	.50
190 Jamal Anderson	.25	.60
191 James Jackson	.20	.50
192 Ahman Green	.25	.60
193 Michael Bennett	.25	.60
194 Aaron Brooks	.25	.60
195 Jerome Bettis	.30	.75
196 Jay Riemersma	.20	.50
197 Brian Griese	.25	.60
198 Priest Holmes	.30	.75
199 Curtis Martin	.30	.75
200 Derrick Mason	.25	.60
201 Antonio Bryant RC	1.50	4.00
202 David Carr RC	1.50	4.00
203 Eric Crouch RC	1.50	4.00
204 Freddie Milons RC	1.00	2.50
205 Najeh Davenport RC	1.50	4.00
206 Rohan Davey RC	1.50	4.00
207 T.J. Duckett RC	1.50	4.00
208 DeShaun Foster RC	1.50	4.00
209 Jabar Gaffney RC	1.50	4.00
210 William Green RC	1.25	3.00
211 Joey Harrington RC	1.50	4.00
212 Travis Stephens RC	1.00	2.50
213 Julius Peppers RC	3.00	8.00
214 Adrian Peterson RC	1.50	4.00
215 Josh Reed RC	1.25	3.00
216 Mike Williams RC	1.00	2.50
217 Javon Walker RC	1.50	4.00
218 Marquise Walker RC	1.00	2.50
219 Patrick Ramsey RC	1.50	4.00
220 Lamar Gordon RC	1.25	3.00
221 David Garrard RC	2.00	5.00
222 Major Applewhite RC	1.50	4.00
223 Andre Davis RC	1.25	3.00
224 Roy Williams RC	1.50	4.00
225 Tim Carter RC	1.25	3.00
226 Ron Johnson RC	1.25	3.00
227 Randy Fasani RC	1.25	3.00
228 Ashley Lelie RC	1.25	3.00
229 Ladell Betts RC	1.50	4.00
230 Antwaan Randle El RC	1.50	4.00
231 Jonathan Wells RC	1.50	4.00
232 Brian Westbrook RC	2.50	6.00
233 Clinton Portis RC	2.00	5.00
234 Luke Staley RC	1.00	2.50
235 Cliff Russell RC	1.00	2.50
236 Jeremy Shockey RC	2.50	6.00
237 Donte Stallworth RC	1.50	4.00
238 Daniel Graham RC	1.25	3.00
239 Reche Caldwell RC	1.50	4.00
240 Ryan Sims RC	1.50	4.00

2002 Ultra Gold Medallion

*VETS 1-200: 1.5X TO 4X BASIC CARDS
OVERALL ODDS ONE PER PACK
*ROOKIES 201-240: 1.2X TO 3X
201-240 ROOKIE PRINT RUN 100

2002 Ultra League Leaders

COMPLETE SET (27)	15.00	40.00
STATED ODDS 1:6		
1 Brett Favre	2.00	5.00
2 Kurt Warner	.75	2.00
3 Marshall Faulk	.75	2.00
4 Daunte Culpepper	.60	1.50
5 LaDainian Tomlinson	1.00	2.50
6 Jeff Garcia	.60	1.50
7 Terrell Owens	.75	2.00
8 Zach Thomas	.75	2.00
9 Brian Urlacher	.75	2.00
10 Corey Dillon	.60	1.50
11 David Boston	.50	1.25
12 Donovan McNabb	.75	2.00
13 Anthony Thomas	.60	1.50
14 Priest Holmes	.75	2.00
15 Torry Holt	.75	2.00
16 Marvin Harrison	.75	2.00
17 Stephen Davis	.60	1.50
18 Michael Strahan	.75	2.00
19 Rod Smith	.60	1.50
20 Ray Lewis	.75	2.00
21 Curtis Martin	.75	2.00
22 Aaron Brooks	.60	1.50
23 Antowain Smith	.60	1.50
24 Eddie George	.60	1.50
25 Emmitt Smith	2.00	5.00
26 Laveranues Coles	.60	1.50
27 Ricky Williams	.60	1.50

2002 Ultra League Leaders Memorabilia

STATED ODDS 1:20 HOB, 1:80 RET
*PLATINUM MED/25: 1.2X TO 3X BASIC JSY
PLATINUM MEDALLION PRINT RUN 25

1 Aaron Brooks	3.00	8.00
2 Laveranues Coles	3.00	8.00
3 Daunte Culpepper	3.00	8.00
4 Stephen Davis	3.00	8.00
5 Marshall Faulk	4.00	10.00
6 Jeff Garcia	3.00	8.00
7 Eddie George	3.00	8.00
8 Torry Holt	4.00	10.00
9 Curtis Martin	4.00	10.00
10 Donovan McNabb	4.00	10.00
11 Terrell Owens	4.00	10.00
12 Antowain Smith	3.00	8.00
13 Emmitt Smith	10.00	25.00
14 Anthony Thomas	3.00	8.00
15 LaDainian Tomlinson	5.00	12.00
16 Brian Urlacher	4.00	10.00
17 Kurt Warner	4.00	10.00
18 Ricky Williams	3.00	8.00

2002 Ultra LOGO Rhythm

COMPLETE SET (22)	15.00	40.00
STATED ODDS 1:12		
1 Brett Favre	2.50	6.00
2 Kurt Warner	1.00	2.50
3 Marshall Faulk	1.00	2.50
4 Daunte Culpepper	.75	2.00
5 LaDainian Tomlinson	1.25	3.00
6 Jeff Garcia	.75	2.00
7 Terrell Owens	1.00	2.50
8 Zach Thomas	1.00	2.50
9 Brian Urlacher	1.00	2.50
10 Drew Brees	1.50	4.00
11 Rich Gannon	.75	2.00
12 Germane Crowell	.60	1.50
13 Brian Griese	.75	2.00
14 Mark Brunell	.75	2.00
15 Ron Dayne	.75	2.00
16 Jake Plummer	.75	2.00
17 Ray Lewis	1.00	2.50
18 Corey Dillon	.75	2.00
19 Kordell Stewart	.75	2.00
20 Donovan McNabb	1.00	2.50
21 Michael Vick	1.50	4.00
22 Chad Pennington	1.00	2.50

2002 Ultra LOGO Rhythm Memorabilia

STATED ODDS 1:96 HOB, 1:192 RET

1 Germane Crowell	3.00	8.00
2 Daunte Culpepper	4.00	10.00
3 Marshall Faulk	5.00	12.00
4 Jeff Garcia	4.00	10.00
5 Brian Griese	4.00	10.00
6 Donovan McNabb	5.00	12.00
7 Terrell Owens	5.00	12.00
8 Chad Pennington	5.00	12.00
9 LaDainian Tomlinson	6.00	15.00
10 Brian Urlacher	5.00	12.00
11 Michael Vick	8.00	20.00
12 Kurt Warner	5.00	12.00

2002 Ultra San Diego Bound

COMPLETE SET (20)	40.00	100.00
STATED ODDS 1:72		
1 Brett Favre	5.00	12.00
2 Kurt Warner	2.00	5.00
3 Marshall Faulk	2.00	5.00
4 Daunte Culpepper	1.50	4.00
5 LaDainian Tomlinson	2.50	6.00
6 Jeff Garcia	1.50	4.00
7 Terrell Owens	2.00	5.00
8 Zach Thomas	2.00	5.00
9 Brian Urlacher	2.00	5.00
10 Drew Brees	3.00	8.00
11 Donovan McNabb	2.00	5.00
12 Brian Griese	1.50	4.00
13 Marvin Harrison	2.00	5.00
14 Tim Couch	1.25	3.00
15 Anthony Thomas	1.50	4.00
16 Tom Brady	5.00	12.00
17 Michael Vick	3.00	8.00
18 Fred Taylor	1.50	4.00
19 Chad Pennington	2.00	5.00
20 Trung Canidate	1.25	3.00

2002 Ultra San Diego Bound Memorabilia

STATED ODDS 1:48 HOB, 1:96 RET
*PLAT.MED/25: 1.2X TO 3X BASIC JSY
*PLAT.MED/25: .8X TO 2X BASIC JSY SP
PLATINAM MEDALLION PRINT RUN 25

1 Tom Brady	12.00	30.00
2 Tim Couch	3.00	8.00
3 Daunte Culpepper	4.00	10.00
4 Marshall Faulk SP	8.00	20.00
5 Jeff Garcia	4.00	10.00
6 Brian Griese	4.00	10.00
7 Donovan McNabb	5.00	12.00
8 Terrell Owens	5.00	12.00
9 Chad Pennington	5.00	12.00
10 Fred Taylor	4.00	10.00
11 Anthony Thomas	4.00	10.00
12 LaDainian Tomlinson	6.00	15.00
13 Brian Urlacher	5.00	12.00
14 Michael Vick	8.00	20.00
15 Kurt Warner	5.00	12.00

2003 Ultra

This 198-card set was released in May, 2003. The set was issued in eight-card packs with an SRP of $2.99 and those packs were issued 24 to a box. The first 160 cards are veterans, while the final 38 cards are rookies. Those rookie cards were issued at a stated rate of one in four.

COMP.SET w/o SP's (160)	12.50	30.00
ROOKIE 161-198 ODDS 1:4		
ROOKIE U199-U218 ODDS 1:4		
1 Rich Gannon	.25	.60
2 Warren Sapp	.25	.60
3 Steve McNair	.30	.75
4 Donovan McNabb	.30	.75
5 Chad Pennington	.30	.75
6 Michael Vick	.40	1.00
7 Hines Ward	.30	.75
8 Terrell Owens	.30	.75
9 Brett Favre	.75	2.00
10 Jeremy Shockey	.30	.75
11 William Green	.20	.50
12 Marvin Harrison	.30	.75
13 Mark Brunell	.25	.60
14 Todd Heap	.25	.60
15 Tim Couch	.20	.50
16 Javon Walker	.25	.60
17 Zach Thomas	.30	.75
18 Brian Westbrook	.30	.75
19 Matt Hasselbeck	.25	.60
20 Jevon Kearse	.25	.60
21 David Boston	.20	.50
22 Michael Bennett	.25	.60
23 James Mungro	.20	.50
24 Antowain Smith	.25	.60
25 Laveranues Coles	.20	.50
26 Curtis Conway	.20	.50
27 Peerless Price	.20	.50
28 Michael Strahan	.30	.75
29 Tommy Maddox	.25	.60
30 Dennis Northcutt	.20	.50
31 Rod Gardner	.20	.50
32 Marcel Shipp	.20	.50
33 Quincy Morgan	.20	.50
34 Reggie Wayne	.30	.75
35 Troy Brown	.25	.60
36 John Abraham	.25	.60
37 Tim Dwight	.20	.50
38 Jamal Lewis	.25	.60
39 Chad Hutchinson	.20	.50
40 Jerramy Stevens	.25	.60
41 Deion Branch	.25	.60
42 Jake Plummer	.25	.60
43 Junior Seau	.30	.75
44 T.J. Duckett	.25	.60
45 Emmitt Smith	.75	2.00
46 Edgerrin James	.30	.75
47 David Patten	.20	.50
48 Charlie Garner	.25	.60
49 Quentin Jammer	.20	.50
50 Corey Dillon	.25	.60
51 Rod Smith	.25	.60
52 Marc Boerigter	.20	.50
53 Michael Lewis	.20	.50
54 Kendrell Bell	.20	.50
55 Isaac Bruce	.30	.75
56 Warrick Dunn	.25	.60
57 Antonio Bryant	.20	.50
58 Peyton Manning	.60	1.50
59 Ty Law	.25	.60
60 Jerry Rice	.60	1.50
61 Jeff Garcia	.25	.60
62 Joey Galloway	.25	.60
63 Aaron Glenn	.20	.50
64 Aaron Brooks	.25	.60
65 Tim Brown	.30	.75
66 David Terrell	.20	.50
67 Fred Smoot	.20	.50
68 Brian Finneran	.20	.50
69 Roy Williams	.25	.60
70 Corey Bradford	.20	.50
71 Deuce McAllister	.25	.60
72 Jerry Porter	.20	.50
73 Kevan Barlow	.20	.50
74 Keith Brooking	.25	.60
75 Brian Urlacher	.30	.75
76 Jabar Gaffney	.20	.50
77 Randy Moss	.30	.75
78 Charles Woodson	.30	.75
79 Darrell Jackson	.25	.60
80 John Lynch	.25	.60
81 Chester Taylor	.25	.60
82 Anthony Thomas	.25	.60
83 Jonathan Wells	.20	.50
84 Daunte Culpepper	.25	.60
85 Phillip Buchanon	.20	.50
86 Koren Robinson	.25	.60
87 Ronde Barber	.25	.60
88 Julius Peppers	.30	.75
89 Clinton Portis	.25	.60
90 Jay Fiedler	.20	.50
91 Donte Stallworth	.20	.50
92 Marc Bulger	.30	.75
93 Joe Jurevicius	.25	.60
94 Jon Kitna	.25	.60
95 Ricky Williams	.25	.60
96 Joe Horn	.25	.60
97 Jerome Bettis	.30	.75
98 Kurt Warner	.30	.75
99 Travis Henry	.20	.50
100 Ahman Green	.25	.60
101 Jimmy Smith	.25	.60
102 Curtis Martin	.30	.75
103 Simeon Rice	.20	.50
104 Patrick Ramsey	.25	.60
105 Josh Reed	.20	.50
106 James Stewart	.20	.50
107 Trent Green	.25	.60
108 Randy McMichael	.20	.50
109 Amos Zereoue	.20	.50
110 Keyshawn Johnson	.30	.75
111 DeShaun Foster	.25	.60
112 Kevin Johnson	.20	.50
113 Dwight Freeney	.25	.60
114 Tom Brady	.75	2.00
115 Santana Moss	.25	.60
116 LaDainian Tomlinson	.30	.75
117 Joey Harrington	.20	.50
118 Priest Holmes	.30	.75
119 Amani Toomer	.25	.60
120 Plaxico Burress	.25	.60
121 Brad Johnson	.25	.60
122 Champ Bailey	.30	.75
123 Muhsin Muhammad	.25	.60
124 Ashley Lelie	.20	.50
125 Tony Gonzalez	.30	.75
126 Kerry Collins	.25	.60
127 Antwaan Randle El	.25	.60
128 Torry Holt	.30	.75
129 Ladell Betts	.20	.50
130 Travis Taylor	.20	.50
131 Marty Booker	.25	.60
132 Patrick Surtain	.20	.50
133 Duce Staley	.25	.60
134 Shaun Alexander	.25	.60
135 Eddie George	.25	.60
136 Eric Moulds	.25	.60
137 David Carr	.25	.60
138 Fred Taylor	.25	.60
139 Wayne Chrebet	.25	.60
140 Bobby Taylor	.25	.60
141 Derrick Brooks	.25	.60

142 Stephen Davis .25 .60
143 Ray Lewis .30 .75
144 Kelly Holcomb .20 .50
145 Terry Glenn .25 .60
146 Jason Taylor .25 .60
147 Todd Pinkston .20 .50
148 Derrick Mason .25 .60
149 Chad Johnson .30 .75
150 Ed McCaffrey .25 .60
151 Tiki Barber .30 .75
152 Drew Brees .30 .75
153 Marshall Faulk .30 .75
154 Drew Bledsoe .30 .75
155 Andre Davis .20 .50
156 Donald Driver .30 .75
157 Chris Chambers .25 .60
158 Brian Dawkins .25 .60
159 Garrison Hearst .25 .60
160 Frank Wycheck .20 .50
161 Carson Palmer RC 3.00 8.00
162 Byron Leftwich RC 1.50 4.00
163 Charles Rogers RC 1.25 3.00
164 Andre Johnson RC 4.00 10.00
165 Chris Simms RC 1.50 4.00
166 Rex Grossman RC 1.50 4.00
167 Brandon Lloyd RC 2.50 6.00
168 Lee Suggs RC 1.25 3.00
169 Larry Johnson RC 1.50 4.00
170 Onterrio Smith RC 1.00 2.50
171 Dave Ragone RC 1.00 2.50
172 Taylor Jacobs RC 1.00 2.50
173 Kelley Washington RC 1.00 2.50
174 Bryant Johnson RC 1.50 4.00
175 Kyle Boller RC 1.50 4.00
176 Ken Dorsey RC 1.25 3.00
177 Kliff Kingsbury RC 1.25 3.00
178 Jason Gesser RC 1.25 3.00
179 Brian St.Pierre RC 1.25 3.00
180 Brad Banks RC 1.25 3.00
181 Seneca Wallace RC 1.50 4.00
182 Tony Romo RC 12.00 30.00
183 Terrell Suggs RC 1.50 4.00
184 Terence Newman RC 1.25 3.00
185 Willis McGahee RC 2.00 5.00
186 Justin Fargas RC 1.50 4.00
187 Musa Smith RC 1.00 2.50
188 Earnest Graham RC 1.50 4.00
189 Chris Brown RC 1.00 2.50
190 LaBrandon Toefield RC 1.25 3.00
191 Bennie Joppru RC 1.00 2.50
192 Jason Witten RC 4.00 10.00
193 Anquan Boldin RC 2.50 6.00
194 Talman Gardner RC 1.00 2.50
195 Justin Gage RC 1.25 3.00
196 Sam Aiken RC 1.25 3.00
197 Kevin Curtis RC 1.50 4.00
198 Terrence Edwards RC 1.00 2.50
U199 DeWayne Robertson RC 1.25 3.00
U200 Kevin Williams RC 1.50 4.00
U201 Marcus Trufant RC 1.25 3.00
U202 Jimmy Kennedy RC 1.25 3.00
U203 Ty Warren RC 1.25 3.00
U204 Michael Haynes RC 1.00 2.50
U205 Jerome McDougle RC 1.00 2.50
U206 Dallas Clark RC 2.50 6.00
U207 William Joseph RC 1.00 2.50
U208 Andre Woolfolk RC 1.25 3.00
U209 Bethel Johnson RC 1.00 2.50
U210 Teyo Johnson RC 1.25 3.00
U211 Tyrone Calico RC 1.25 3.00
U212 L.J. Smith RC 1.50 4.00
U213 Nate Burleson RC 1.25 3.00
U214 B.J. Askew RC 1.25 3.00
U215 Billy McMullen RC 1.00 2.50
U216 Domanick Davis RC 1.25 3.00
U217 Doug Gabriel RC 1.25 3.00
U218 Quentin Griffin RC 1.25 3.00

2003 Ultra Gold Medallion

*VETS 1-160: 1.5X TO 4X BASIC CARDS
*ROOKIES 161-198: .5X TO 1.2X
ONE GOLD MEDALLION PER PACK
182 Tony Romo 20.00 50.00

2003 Ultra Platinum Medallion

*VETS 1-160: 6X TO 15X BASIC CARDS
*ROOKIES 161-98: 2X TO 5X
STATED PRINT RUN 100 SER.#'d SETS
182 Tony Romo 60.00 150.00

2003 Ultra Autographs

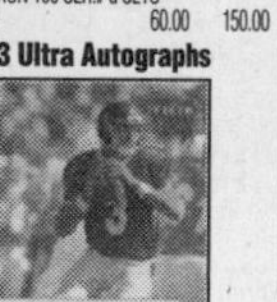

ANNOUNCED PRINT RUN 300-350
UAJ Andre Johnson/300* 25.00 60.00
UBL Byron Leftwich/300* 12.00 30.00
UCP Carson Palmer/300* 25.00 60.00
ULJ Larry Johnson/350* 12.00 30.00

2003 Ultra Award Winners

COMPLETE SET (10) 7.50 20.00
STATED ODDS 1:12
1 Priest Holmes 1.00 2.50
2 Clinton Portis .75 2.00
3 Rich Gannon .75 2.00
4 Derrick Brooks .75 2.00
5 Michael Vick 1.25 3.00
6 Jeremy Shockey 1.00 2.50
7 Ricky Williams .75 2.00
8 Marvin Harrison 1.00 2.50
9 Chad Pennington 1.00 2.50
10 Tommy Maddox .75 2.00

2003 Ultra Award Winners Memorabilia

STATED ODDS 1:25
*ULTRSWTCH/55-88: .8X TO 2X BASE JSY
*ULTRSWTCH/31-34: 1.2X TO 3X BASE JSY
*ULTRSWTCH/20-28: 1.5X TO 4X BASE JSY
ULTRASWATCH PRINT RUN 7-88
AWCP Clinton Portis 3.00 8.00
AWCP2 Chad Pennington 4.00 10.00
AWDB Derrick Brooks 3.00 8.00
AWDM Deuce McAllister 3.00 8.00
AWJS Jeremy Shockey 4.00 10.00
AWLT LaDainian Tomlinson 4.00 10.00
AWMF Marshall Faulk 4.00 10.00
AWMH Marvin Harrison 4.00 10.00
AWMV Michael Vick 5.00 12.00
AWPH Priest Holmes 4.00 10.00
AWRG Rich Gannon 3.00 8.00
AWRW Ricky Williams 3.00 8.00
AWTH Travis Henry 2.50 6.00
AWTO Terrell Owens 4.00 10.00

2003 Ultra Head of the Class

STATED PRINT RUN 599 SER.#'d SETS
1 Carson Palmer 3.00 8.00
2 Byron Leftwich 1.50 4.00
3 Charles Rogers 1.25 3.00
4 Andre Johnson 4.00 10.00
5 Chris Simms 1.50 4.00
6 Rex Grossman 1.50 4.00
7 Brandon Lloyd 2.50 6.00
8 Lee Suggs 1.25 3.00
9 Larry Johnson 1.50 4.00
10 Onterrio Smith 1.00 2.50
11 Dave Ragone 1.00 2.50
12 Taylor Jacobs 1.00 2.50
13 Kelley Washington 1.00 2.50
14 Bryant Johnson 1.50 4.00
15 Willis McGahee 2.00 5.00
NNO Carson Palmer JSY/1500 10.00 25.00

2003 Ultra Touchdown Kings

COMPLETE SET (15) 25.00 50.00
STATED ODDS 1:24
1 Jerry Rice 3.00 8.00
2 Peyton Manning 3.00 8.00
3 Randy Moss 1.50 4.00
4 Tom Brady 4.00 10.00
5 Brett Favre 4.00 10.00
6 Drew Bledsoe 1.50 4.00
7 Steve McNair 1.50 4.00
8 Emmitt Smith 4.00 10.00
9 Priest Holmes 1.50 4.00
10 Michael Vick 2.00 5.00
11 Chad Pennington 1.50 4.00
12 Donovan McNabb 1.50 4.00
13 Shaun Alexander 1.25 3.00
14 Ricky Williams 1.25 3.00
15 Clinton Portis 1.25 3.00

2003 Ultra Touchdown Kings Memorabilia

STATED ODDS 1:26
*CAREER/326: .5X TO 1.2X BASE JSY
*CAREER/147-202: .6X TO 1.5X BASE JSY
*CAREER/60-103: .8X TO 2X BASE JSY
*CAREER/35-47: 1.2X TO 3X BASE JSY
*CAREER26-27: 1.5X TO 4X BASE JSY
CAREER PRINT RUN 17-326
*ULTRSWTCH/31-34: 1.2X TO 3X BASE JSY
*ULTRSWTCH/20-28: 1.5X TO 4X BASE JSY
ULTRASWATCH PRINT RUN 2-37
TKBF Brett Favre 10.00 25.00
TKCP Clinton Portis 3.00 8.00
TKCP2 Chad Pennington 4.00 10.00
TKDB Drew Bledsoe 4.00 10.00
TKDM Donovan McNabb 4.00 10.00
TKES Emmitt Smith 10.00 25.00
TKJR Jerry Rice 8.00 20.00
TKMV Michael Vick 5.00 12.00
TKPH Priest Holmes 4.00 10.00
TKPM Peyton Manning 8.00 20.00
TKRM Randy Moss 4.00 10.00
TKRW Ricky Williams 3.00 8.00
TKSA Shaun Alexander 3.00 8.00
TKSM Steve McNair 4.00 10.00
TKTB Tom Brady 10.00 25.00

2004 Ultra

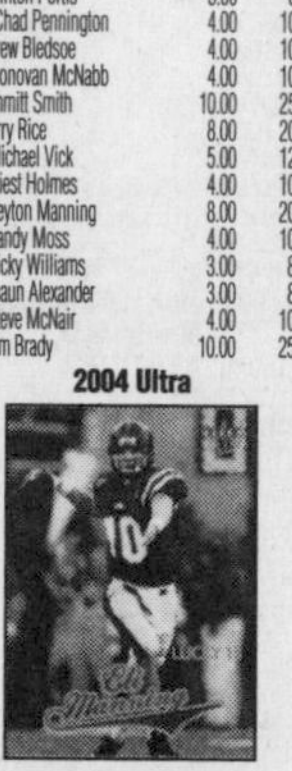

Ultra released in May of 2004 and was Fleer's first football product of the year. The base set consists of 232-cards including 200-veterans and 32-rookies. Thirteen of the rookies were designated as "Lucky 13" with only 500-copies produced of each card. Mike Williams is part of the Lucky 13 although he was declared ineligible for the NFL Draft. Hobby and retail boxes both contained 24-packs of 8-cards with an SRP of $2.99 for hobby and $1.99 for retail packs. Two parallel sets and a large section of inserts with a variety of game-used versions can be found seeded in packs. Insert highlights include Season Crowns Autographs and a triple signed Manning Family Passing Kings card. A 20-card Update set was included in packs of 2004 Fleer Tradition. Each of these cards was seeded two-per rookie hot pack in the product with one hot pack in every box on average. Some signed cards were issued via mail-in exchange or redemption cards with a number of those EXCH cards not yet appearing live on the secondary market as of the printing of this book.

COMP.SET w/o L13's (218) 25.00 60.00
COMP.SET w/o SP's (200) 12.50 30.00
COMP.UPDATE SET (21) 15.00 40.00
201-213 L13 ROOKIE/500 ODDS 1:100H,1:530R
214-232 ROOKIE ODDS 1:4H,1:6R
U234-U254 ODDS 2:1 TRADITION HOT PACK
1 Michael Vick .40 1.00
2 Kelley Washington .20 .50
3 Rex Grossman .25 .60
4 Boss Bailey .20 .50
5 Johnnie Morton .25 .60
6 Michael Strahan .30 .75
7 Joey Porter .25 .60
8 Keenan McCardell .20 .50
9 Quincy Carter .20 .50
10 Travis Henry .20 .50
11 Bertrand Berry .25 .60
12 Marvin Harrison .30 .75
13 Ty Law .25 .60
14 Phillip Buchanon .25 .60
15 Kevan Barlow .20 .50
16 Eddie George .25 .60
17 Drew Bledsoe .30 .75
18 Antonio Bryant .25 .60
19 Marcus Pollard .20 .50
20 Brian Russell RC .20 .50
21 Santana Moss .25 .60
22 Julian Peterson .25 .60
23 Justin McCareins .20 .50
24 Ed Reed .25 .60
25 Charles Tillman .25 .60
26 Dat Nguyen .20 .50
27 Ricky Manning .20 .50
28 Dwight Freeney .25 .60
29 Zach Thomas .30 .75
30 Tiki Barber .30 .75
31 Jay Riemersma .20 .50
32 Joe Jurevicius .20 .50
33 Marcel Shipp .20 .50
34 Justin Gage .25 .60
35 Charles Rogers .20 .50
36 Eddie Kennison .25 .60
37 Deion Branch .25 .60
38 Matt Hasselbeck .25 .60
39 L.J. Smith .25 .60
40 Jamal Lewis .25 .60
41 Muhsin Muhammad .25 .60
42 Terence Newman .25 .60
43 Jabar Gaffney .20 .50
44 Junior Seau .30 .75
45 Jeremy Shockey .25 .60
46 Hines Ward .30 .75
47 Brad Johnson .25 .60
48 Kyle Boller .25 .60
49 Steve Smith .30 .75
50 Quincy Morgan .20 .50
51 Corey Bradford .20 .50
52 Ricky Williams .25 .60
53 Amani Toomer .25 .60
54 Plaxico Burress .25 .60
55 Derrick Brooks .25 .60
56 Dre Bly .20 .50
57 Terrell Suggs .25 .60
58 DeShaun Foster .25 .60
59 Andre Davis .20 .50
60 Rod Smith .25 .60
61 Andre Johnson .30 .75
62 Randy McMichael .20 .50
63 Ike Hilliard .25 .60
64 Antwaan Randle El .25 .60
65 Warren Sapp .25 .60
66 LaBrandon Toefield .20 .50
67 Chad Johnson .30 .75
68 Javon Walker .20 .50
69 Jimmy Smith .25 .60
70 Donte Stallworth .20 .50
71 Brian Dawkins .25 .60
72 Leonard Little .20 .50
73 Ladell Betts .20 .50
74 Ray Lewis .30 .75
75 Stephen Davis .25 .60
76 Dennis Northcutt .20 .50
77 Ashley Lelie .20 .50
78 Billy Miller .20 .50
79 Chris Chambers .25 .60
80 John Abraham .20 .50
81 Quentin Jammer .20 .50
82 Isaac Bruce .25 .60
83 Peerless Price .20 .50
84 Jake Delhomme .25 .60
85 Lee Suggs .25 .60
86 Shannon Sharpe .30 .75
87 Domanick Davis .20 .50
88 Daunte Culpepper .25 .60
89 Shaun Ellis .20 .50
90 Drew Brees .30 .75
91 Torry Holt .25 .60
92 Alge Crumpler .25 .60
93 Mike Rucker .20 .50
94 Tim Couch .25 .60
95 Quentin Griffin .20 .50
96 David Carr .20 .50
97 Moe Williams .20 .50
98 Chad Pennington .30 .75
99 LaDainian Tomlinson .30 .75
100 Adam Archuleta .20 .50
101 Julius Peppers .25 .60
102 Clinton Portis .30 .75
103 Marcus Stroud .20 .50
104 Tom Brady .60 1.50
105 Teyo Johnson .20 .50
106 Terrell Owens .30 .75
107 Keith Bulluck .20 .50
108 Eric Moulds .25 .60
109 Jake Plummer .25 .60
110 Reggie Wayne .30 .75
111 Tedy Bruschi .30 .75
112 Rich Gannon .25 .60
113 Tony Parrish .20 .50
114 Steve McNair .30 .75
115 T.J. Duckett .25 .60
116 Peter Warrick .25 .60
117 Donald Driver .30 .75
118 Fred Taylor .25 .60
119 Joe Horn .25 .60
120 Jerry Porter .20 .50
121 Marc Bulger .25 .60
122 Trung Canidate .20 .50
123 Warrick Dunn .25 .60
124 Kelly Holcomb .20 .50
125 Robert Ferguson .20 .50
126 Byron Leftwich .25 .60
127 Michael Lewis .25 .60
128 Jerry Rice .60 1.50
129 Marshall Faulk .30 .75
130 Patrick Ramsey .25 .60
131 Josh McCown .25 .60
132 Anthony Thomas .25 .60
133 Joey Harrington .25 .60
134 Dante Hall .25 .60
135 Daniel Graham .20 .50
136 Richard Seymour .20 .50
137 Brandon Lloyd .25 .60
138 Anquan Boldin .30 .75
139 Jon Kitna .25 .60
140 Nick Barnett .25 .60
141 Priest Holmes .30 .75
142 Bethel Johnson .20 .50
143 Shaun Alexander .25 .60
144 Todd Heap .25 .60
145 Brian Urlacher .30 .75
146 Peyton Manning .60 1.50
147 Jason Taylor .25 .60
148 Kerry Collins .25 .60
149 Tommy Maddox .25 .60
150 Charles Lee .20 .50
151 Tim Rattay .20 .50
152 Carson Palmer .30 .75
153 Brett Favre .75 2.00
154 Trent Green .25 .60
155 Aaron Brooks .25 .60
156 Brian Westbrook .30 .75
157 Itula Mili .20 .50
158 Keith Brooking .20 .50
159 Rudi Johnson .25 .60
160 Najeh Davenport .25 .60
161 Kevin Johnson .20 .50
162 Boo Williams .20 .50
163 Corey Simon .25 .60
164 Darrell Jackson .25 .60
165 Darnerien McCants .20 .50
166 Willis McGahee .30 .75
167 Terry Glenn .25 .60
168 Dallas Clark .30 .75
169 Randy Moss .30 .75
170 Charles Woodson .30 .75
171 Jeff Garcia .25 .60
172 Chris Brown .20 .50
173 Emmitt Smith .75 2.00
174 Marty Booker .25 .60
175 Artose Pinner .20 .50
176 Tony Gonzalez .30 .75
177 Troy Brown .25 .60
178 Freddie Mitchell .20 .50
179 Marcus Trufant .20 .50
180 London Fletcher .20 .50
181 Roy Williams S .25 .60
182 Edgerrin James .25 .60
183 Michael Bennett .25 .60
184 Jerald Sowell .20 .50
185 David Boston .20 .50
186 Derrick Mason .25 .60
187 Bryant Johnson .20 .50
188 Corey Dillon .25 .60
189 Ahman Green .25 .60
190 Vonnie Holliday .20 .50
191 Deuce McAllister .25 .60
192 Donovan McNabb .30 .75
193 Koren Robinson .20 .50
194 Laveranues Coles .20 .50
195 Takeo Spikes .20 .50
196 Richie Anderson .20 .50
197 Onterrio Smith .20 .50
198 Curtis Martin .30 .75
199 Antonio Gates .30 .75
200 Champ Bailey .25 .60
201 Eli Manning L13 RC 30.00 60.00
202 Philip Rivers L13 RC 20.00 50.00
203 Roy Williams L13 RC 5.00 12.00
204 Drew Henson L13 RC 3.00 8.00
205 Chris Perry L13 RC 4.00 10.00
206 Larry Fitzgerald L13 RC 10.00 25.00
207 Rashaun Woods L13 RC 3.00 8.00
208 Reggie Williams L13 RC 4.00 10.00
209 Mike Williams L13 RC 4.00 10.00
210 Kellen Winslow L13 RC 5.00 12.00
211 Steven Jackson L13 RC 8.00 20.00
212 Kevin Jones L13 RC 4.00 10.00
213 Ben Roethlisberger L13 RC 30.00 60.00
214 Michael Turner RC 1.50 4.00
215 Tatum Bell RC 1.00 2.50
216 Quincy Wilson RC 1.00 2.50
217 Devery Henderson RC 1.25 3.00
218 Ernest Wilford RC 1.00 2.50
219 Cody Pickett RC 1.00 2.50
220 Ryan Dinwiddie RC .75 2.00
221 J.P. Losman RC 1.00 2.50
222 Derrick Knight RC .75 2.00
223 Michael Jenkins RC 1.25 3.00
224 Greg Jones RC .75 2.00
225 Cedric Cobbs RC .75 2.00
226 Will Poole RC 1.25 3.00
227 Michael Clayton RC 1.00 2.50
228 Sean Taylor RC 2.50 6.00
229 Will Smith RC 1.00 2.50
230 Jonathan Vilma RC 1.25 3.00
231 Lee Evans RC 1.25 3.00
232 Julius Jones RC 1.00 2.50
U234 D.J. Williams RC 1.25 3.00
U235 Mewelde Moore RC 1.00 2.50
U236 Ben Watson RC 1.25 3.00
U237 Robert Gallery RC 1.25 3.00
U238 DeAngelo Hall RC 1.25 3.00
U239 Luke McCown RC 1.00 2.50
U240 Ben Troupe RC 1.00 2.50
U241 Keary Colbert RC .75 2.00
U242 Matt Schaub RC 2.50 6.00
U243 Kenechi Udeze RC 1.00 2.50
U244 Jeff Smoker RC 1.00 2.50
U245 Derrick Hamilton RC .75 2.00
U246 Bernard Berrian RC 1.25 3.00
U247 Devard Darling RC .75 2.00
U248 Johnnie Morant RC .75 2.00
U249 Vince Wilfork RC 1.25 3.00
U250 Jerricho Cotchery RC 1.00 2.50
U251 Darius Watts RC .75 2.00
U252 Carlos Francis RC .75 2.00
U253 P.K. Sam RC .75 2.00

2004 Ultra Gold Medallion

*VETS: 1.5X TO 4X BASIC CARDS
*ROOKIES 201-213: .12X TO .3X
*ROOKIES 214-232: .4X TO 1X
OVERALL STATED ODDS 1:1H,1:3R
ROOKIE 201-232 ODDS 1:8H,1:12R
201 Eli Manning L13 12.00 30.00
213 Ben Roethlisberger L13 12.00 30.00

2004 Ultra Platinum Medallion

*VETS 1-200: 10X TO 25X BASIC CARDS
*ROOKIES 214-232: 2X TO 5X
1-200/214-232 PLAT/66 ODDS 1:45 HOB
1-200/214-232 PRINT RUN 66 #'d SETS
UNPRICED L13 201-213 ODDS 1:3650

2004 Ultra Update Draft Day

*DRAFT DAY/375: .6X TO 1.5X BASIC CARDS
STATED PRINT RUN 375 SER.#'d SETS

2004 Ultra Gridiron Producers

STATED ODDS 1:144H,1:288R
1GP Donovan McNabb 2.00 5.00
2GP Charles Rogers 1.25 3.00
3GP Daunte Culpepper 1.50 4.00
4GP Matt Hasselbeck 1.50 4.00
5GP Jerry Rice 4.00 10.00
6GP Tom Brady 4.00 10.00
7GP Byron Leftwich 1.50 4.00
8GP Ahman Green 1.50 4.00
9GP Stephen Davis 1.50 4.00
10GP LaDainian Tomlinson 2.00 5.00

2004 Ultra Gridiron Producers Game Used Copper

OVERALL GAME USED/AUTO ODDS 1:12
*GOLD/77: .6X TO 1.5X COPPER
GOLD PRINT RUN 77 SER.#'d SETS
UNPRICED PLATINUM PRINT RUN 9
*ULTRASWATCH/48-80: .6X TO 1.5X COPPER
*ULTRASWATCH/21-30: .8X TO 2X COPPER
*ULTRASWATCH/11-12: 1X TO 2.5X COPPER
ULTRASWATCH PRINT RUN 5-84
GPAG Ahman Green 4.00 10.00
GPBL Byron Leftwich 4.00 10.00
GPCR Charles Rogers 3.00 8.00
GPDC Daunte Culpepper 4.00 10.00
GPDM Donovan McNabb 5.00 12.00
GPJR Jerry Rice 10.00 25.00
GPLT LaDainian Tomlinson 5.00 12.00
GPMH Matt Hasselbeck 4.00 10.00
GPSD Stephen Davis 4.00 10.00
GPTB Tom Brady 10.00 25.00

2004 Ultra Hummer H2 In Package

*SINGLE CARDS: .3X TO .8X PACKAGE
201 Eli Manning 6.00 12.00
202 Philip Rivers 3.00 8.00
204 Drew Henson 1.50 4.00
206 Larry Fitzgerald 3.00 6.00
210 Kellen Winslow 2.00 5.00
213 Ben Roethlisberger 6.00 12.00

2004 Ultra Passing Kings

COMPLETE SET (10) 12.00 30.00
OVERALL KINGS ODDS 1:12H,1:24R
*GOLD/50: 1.5X TO 4X BASIC INSERTS
GOLD PRINT RUN 50 SER.#'d SETS
1PA Brett Favre 3.00 8.00
2PA Donovan McNabb 1.25 3.00
3PA Peyton Manning 2.50 6.00
4PA Steve McNair 1.25 3.00
5PA Daunte Culpepper 1.00 2.50
6PA Tom Brady 2.50 6.00
7PA Byron Leftwich 1.00 2.50
8PA Joey Harrington 1.00 2.50
9PA Matt Hasselbeck 1.00 2.50
10PA Marc Bulger 1.00 2.50
NNO Archie Manning AU/50 400.00 600.00
Eli Manning
Peyton Manning

2004 Ultra Performers

COMPLETE SET (15) 12.50 30.00
STATED ODDS 1:6H,1:8R
*GOLD DIE CUT: .4X TO 1X BASIC INSERTS
ONE GOLD PER RETAIL PACK
1UP Tom Brady 1.50 4.00
2UP Clinton Portis .75 2.00
3UP Priest Holmes .75 2.00
4UP Marshall Faulk .75 2.00
5UP Randy Moss .75 2.00
6UP Marvin Harrison .75 2.00
7UP Donovan McNabb .75 2.00
8UP Ricky Williams .60 1.50
9UP Brett Favre 2.00 5.00
10UP Steve McNair .75 2.00
11UP Peyton Manning 1.50 4.00
12UP Shaun Alexander .60 1.50
13UP Edgerrin James .60 1.50
14UP Chad Johnson .75 2.00
15UP Torry Holt .60 1.50

2004 Ultra Performers Game Used Copper

OVERALL GAME USED/AUTO ODDS 1:12
*GOLD/89: .6X TO 1.5X COPPER
GOLD PRINT RUN 88 SER.# SETS
*PLATINUM: 1.2X TO 3X COPPER
PLATINUM PRINT RUN 19 #'d SETS
*ULTRASWATCH/81-88: .6X TO 1.5X COP
*ULTRASWATCH/26-37: .8X TO 2X COP
*ULTRASWATCH/12-18: 1X TO 2.5X COP
ULTRASWATCH PRINT RUN 4-88
UPBF Brett Favre 12.00 30.00
UPCJ Chad Johnson 5.00 12.00
UPCP Clinton Portis 5.00 12.00
UPDM Donovan McNabb 5.00 12.00
UPEJ Edgerrin James 4.00 10.00
UPMF Marshall Faulk 5.00 12.00
UPMH Marvin Harrison 5.00 12.00
UPPH Priest Holmes 5.00 12.00
UPPM Peyton Manning 10.00 25.00
UPRM Randy Moss 5.00 12.00
UPRW Ricky Williams 4.00 10.00
UPSA Shaun Alexander 4.00 10.00
UPSM Steve McNair 5.00 12.00
UPTB Tom Brady 10.00 25.00
UPTH Torry Holt 4.00 10.00

2004 Ultra Receiving Kings

COMPLETE SET (10) 8.00 20.00
OVERALL KINGS ODDS 1:12H,1:24R
*GOLD/50: 2X TO 5X BASIC INSERTS
GOLD PRINT RUN 50 SER.#'d SETS
1RE Randy Moss 1.00 2.50
2RE Torry Holt .75 2.00
3RE Anquan Boldin 1.00 2.50
4RE Chad Johnson 1.00 2.50
5RE Derrick Mason .75 2.00
6RE Marvin Harrison 1.00 2.50
7RE Laveranues Coles .60 1.50
8RE Terrell Owens 1.00 2.50
9RE Charles Rogers .60 1.50
10RE Jerry Rice 2.00 5.00

2004 Ultra Rushing Kings

COMPLETE SET (10) 10.00 25.00
OVERALL KINGS ODDS 1:12H,1:24R
*GOLD/50: 2X TO 5X BASIC INSERTS
GOLD PRINT RUN 50 SER.#'d SETS
1RU Clinton Portis 1.00 2.50
2RU Priest Holmes 1.00 2.50
3RU Stephen Davis .75 2.00
4RU Marshall Faulk 1.00 2.50
5RU LaDainian Tomlinson 1.00 2.50
6RU Shaun Alexander .75 2.00
7RU Deuce McAllister .75 2.00
8RU Ricky Williams .75 2.00
9RU Jamal Lewis .75 2.00
10RU Ahman Green .75 2.00

2004 Ultra Season Crowns Autographs

STATED PRINT RUN 25-150
GOLD STATED PRINT RUN 25
1 Kyle Boller/150 6.00 15.00
2 Plaxico Burress/150 6.00 15.00
3 David Carr/150 5.00 12.00
4 LaDainian Tomlinson/150 30.00 60.00
6 Donovan McNabb/25 50.00 100.00
7 Matt Hasselbeck/70 10.00 25.00
8 Philip Rivers/150 30.00 60.00
9 Roy Williams WR/150 8.00 20.00
10 Eli Manning/150 75.00 135.00
11 Dante Hall/150 6.00 15.00
12 Brian Westbrook/150 8.00 20.00
13 Jake Delhomme/150 6.00 15.00
14 Kelley Washington/150 5.00 12.00
15 Joe Jurevicius/150 5.00 12.00
16 Byron Leftwich/150 8.00 20.00
17 Shaun Alexander/150 8.00 20.00
18 Drew Henson/150 5.00 12.00
19 Deuce McAllister/150 6.00 15.00
21 Steven Jackson/150 20.00 50.00
22 Will Poole/150 8.00 20.00

2004 Ultra Season Crowns Game Used Copper

COPPER PRINT RUN 349 SER.#'d SETS
*GOLD/99: .6X TO 1.5X COPPER
GOLD PRINT RUN 99 SER.#'d SETS
*PLATINUM/29: 1X TO 2.5X COPPER
PLATINUM PRINT RUN 29 SER.#'d SETS
*SILVER/149: .5X TO 1.2X COPPER
SILVER PRINT RUN 149 SER.#'d SETS
1 Rex Grossman 3.00 8.00
2 Julius Peppers 3.00 8.00
3 Antwaan Randle El 3.00 8.00
4 Charles Rogers 2.50 6.00
5 Brian Urlacher 4.00 10.00
6 Carson Palmer 4.00 10.00
7 Priest Holmes 4.00 10.00
8 Travis Henry 2.50 6.00
9 Andre Johnson 4.00 10.00
10 Marvin Harrison 4.00 10.00
11 Randy Moss 4.00 10.00
12 Corey Dillon 3.00 8.00
13 Ray Lewis 4.00 10.00
14 Ricky Williams 3.00 8.00
15 Peyton Manning Pants 8.00 20.00
16 Michael Bennett 3.00 8.00
17 Torry Holt 3.00 8.00
18 Deuce McAllister 3.00 8.00
19 Deion Branch 3.00 8.00
20 DeShaun Foster 3.00 8.00
21 Edgerrin James 3.00 8.00
22 Steve McNair 4.00 10.00
23 Brett Favre 10.00 25.00
24 Chad Pennington 4.00 10.00
25 Brad Johnson 3.00 8.00
26 Fred Taylor 3.00 8.00
27 Michael Vick 5.00 12.00
28 Derrick Brooks 3.00 8.00
29 LaDainian Tomlinson 4.00 10.00
30 Warren Sapp 3.00 8.00
31 Byron Leftwich 3.00 8.00
32 Donovan McNabb 4.00 10.00
33 Ahman Green 3.00 8.00
34 Emmitt Smith 10.00 25.00
35 Tommy Maddox 3.00 8.00
36 Shaun Alexander 3.00 8.00
37 Joey Harrington 3.00 8.00
38 Marshall Faulk 4.00 10.00
39 Jerry Rice 8.00 20.00
40 T.J. Duckett 3.00 8.00
41 Eric Moulds 3.00 8.00
42 Tom Brady 8.00 20.00
43 David Carr 2.50 6.00
44 Daunte Culpepper 3.00 8.00
45 Isaac Bruce 3.00 8.00
46 Chad Johnson 4.00 10.00
47 Jeremy Shockey 3.00 8.00
48 Eddie George 3.00 8.00
49 Quincy Carter 2.50 6.00
50 Aaron Brooks 3.00 8.00

2004 Ultra Three Kings Game Used

STATED PRINT RUN 33 SER.#'d SETS
FHB Marshall Faulk 15.00 40.00
Torry Holt
Marc Bulger
GMT Ahman Green 20.00 50.00
Deuce McAllister
LaDainianTomlinson
HHL Matt Hasselbeck 12.00 30.00
Joey Harrington
Byron Leftwich
HMR Marvin Harrison 40.00 80.00
Randy Moss
Jerry Rice
HWF Priest Holmes 20.00 50.00
Ricky Williams
Marshall Faulk
JRB Chad Johnson 12.00 30.00
Charles Rogers
Anquan Boldin
LAD Jamal Lewis 15.00 40.00
Shaun Alexander
Stephen Davis
MBF Peyton Manning 75.00 150.00
Tom Brady
Brett Favre
MMC Steve McNair 20.00 50.00
Donovan McNabb
Daunte Culpepper
ORM Terrell Owens 40.00 80.00
Jerry Rice
Randy Moss

2005 Ultra

This 248-card set was released in January, 2006. This set was issued in the hobby in eight-card packs with an $2.99 SRP which came 24 packs to a box. The first 200 cards in the set feature veterans while cards numbered 201-213 featured 13 leading 2005 NFL rookies with cards numbered 214-248 being other NFL rookies. The cards 201-213 were issued to a stated print run of 599 serial numbered sets. For all the rookies, the stated odds on those cards were in four hobby and one in five retail.

COMP.SET w/o RC's (200) 12.50 30.00
201-213 L13 PRINT RUN 599 SER.#'d SETS
OVERALL ROOKIE ODDS 1:4 HOB, 1:5 RET
1 Peyton Manning .60 1.50
2 Brian Westbrook .25 .60
3 Daunte Culpepper .25 .60
4 Marvin Harrison .30 .75
5 Edgerrin James .25 .60
6 Reggie Wayne .30 .75
7 Michael Vick .30 .75
8 Donte Stallworth .20 .50
9 Brian Urlacher .30 .75
10 Hines Ward .30 .75
11 Charles Rogers .20 .50
12 Roy Williams WR .25 .60
13 Julius Peppers .25 .60
14 Eric Moulds .20 .50
15 Ray Lewis .30 .75
16 Byron Leftwich .25 .60
17 Fred Taylor .25 .60
18 Andre Johnson .30 .75
19 Travis Henry .20 .50
20 Tom Brady .60 1.50
21 Drew Bledsoe .30 .75
22 Tiki Barber .30 .75
23 Larry Fitzgerald .30 .75
24 Jeff Garcia .25 .60
25 Rex Grossman .25 .60
26 Larry Johnson .25 .60
27 Curtis Martin .30 .75
28 Chad Pennington .30 .75
29 Dwight Freeney .25 .60
30 Peerless Price .20 .50
31 Rich Gannon .25 .60
32 Matt Hasselbeck .25 .60
33 Clinton Portis .25 .60
34 Jerry Rice .60 1.50
35 Jeremy Shockey .30 .75
36 Tony Gonzalez .25 .60
37 Deuce McAllister .25 .60
38 Shaun Alexander .25 .60
39 Peter Warrick .20 .50
40 Isaac Bruce .25 .60
41 Antonio Bryant .20 .50
42 Mike Alstott .25 .60
43 Domanick Davis .20 .50
44 Jake Delhomme .25 .60
45 Santana Moss .25 .60
46 Ahman Green .25 .60
47 David Carr .20 .50
48 Kyle Boller .25 .60
49 Chris Chambers .25 .60
50 Quentin Griffin .20 .50
51 Donovan McNabb .30 .75
52 Eli Manning .50 1.25
53 Julius Jones .20 .50
54 Sean Taylor .30 .75
55 Javon Walker .20 .50
56 Randy Moss .30 .75
57 Thomas Jones .30 .75
58 Joey Harrington .25 .60
59 Michael Boulware .20 .50
60 Marshall Faulk .30 .75
61 Tony Parrish .20 .50
62 Bertrand Berry .20 .50
63 Alge Crumpler .25 .60
64 Aaron Brooks .20 .50
65 Muhsin Muhammad .25 .60
66 Simeon Rice .20 .50
67 Corey Dillon .25 .60
68 Willis McGahee .30 .75
69 Ben Roethlisberger .50 1.25
70 Chad Johnson .25 .60
71 Jamal Lewis .25 .60
72 Drew Brees .30 .75
73 LaDainian Tomlinson .30 .75
74 Reuben Droughns .20 .50
75 Priest Holmes .25 .60
76 Jerry Porter .20 .50
77 Chris Brown .20 .50
78 Steve McNair .30 .75
79 Troy Brown .20 .50
80 Jerome Bettis .30 .75
81 Patrick Kerney .25 .60
82 Terrell Owens .30 .75
83 Brett Favre .75 2.00
84 Carson Palmer .30 .75
85 Jake Plummer .25 .60
86 Tedy Bruschi .30 .75
87 Plaxico Burress .25 .60
88 Jonathan Vilma .25 .60
89 Ed Reed .25 .60
90 Brian Dawkins .25 .60
91 Anquan Boldin .25 .60
92 Vinny Testaverde .25 .60
93 David Givens .20 .50
94 Rudi Johnson .25 .60
95 Philip Rivers .30 .75
96 Jimmy Smith .25 .60
97 Emmitt Smith .60 1.50
98 Eric Johnson .20 .50
99 Jeremiah Trotter .20 .50
100 Duce Staley .25 .60
101 Warrick Dunn .25 .60
102 Nate Burleson .20 .50
103 Marc Bulger .25 .60
104 Joe Horn .25 .60
105 Rodney Harrison .25 .60
106 Zach Thomas .30 .75
107 Michael Clayton .20 .50
108 Derrick Brooks .25 .60
109 Michael Lewis .20 .50
110 Kurt Warner .30 .75
111 Jason Witten .30 .75
112 Roy Williams S .20 .50
113 Kabeer Gbaja-Biamila .30 .75
114 Torry Holt .25 .60
115 Tim Rattay .20 .50
116 Josh McCown .25 .60
117 Brian Griese .25 .60
118 Patrick Ramsey .25 .60
119 A.J. Feeley .20 .50
120 Kerry Collins .25 .60
121 Trent Green .25 .60
122 Billy Volek .20 .50
123 Travis Taylor .20 .50
124 T.J. Houshmandzadeh .25 .60
125 James Farrior .20 .50
126 Bryan Scott .20 .50
127 Lito Sheppard .25 .60
128 David Patten .20 .50
129 Antwaan Randle El .25 .60
130 Antonio Gates .30 .75
131 Brandon Stokley .20 .50
132 Keyshawn Johnson .25 .60
133 Amani Toomer .25 .60
134 Shawn Springs .20 .50
135 Eddie George .25 .60
136 Kevin Jones .20 .50
137 Darrell Jackson .20 .50
138 Ricky Manning .20 .50
139 Laveranues Coles .20 .50
140 Champ Bailey .25 .60
141 Rod Smith .25 .60
142 Ashley Lelie .20 .50
143 Charles Woodson .30 .75
144 Drew Bennett .25 .60
145 Derrick Mason .25 .60
146 Donovin Darius .20 .50
147 Dennis Northcutt .20 .50
148 Jamie Sharper .20 .50
149 Steven Jackson .30 .75
150 David Terrell .20 .50
151 Onterrio Smith .20 .50
152 Donald Driver .30 .75
153 Antoine Winfield .25 .60
154 Michael Pittman .20 .50
155 Dan Morgan .20 .50
156 Troy Polamalu .40 1.00
157 Willie McGinest .25 .60
158 Justin McCareins .20 .50
159 Allen Rossum .20 .50
160 Deion Branch .20 .50
161 Deion Sanders .40 1.00
162 Josh Reed .20 .50
163 Lee Evans .25 .60
164 Lee Suggs .20 .50
165 Dante Hall .20 .50
166 Eddie Kennison .20 .50
167 Ken Dorsey .20 .50
168 Andre Dyson .20 .50
169 Keith Bulluck .20 .50
170 Todd Pinkston .20 .50
171 Jevon Kearse .25 .60
172 Dunta Robinson .20 .50
173 Steve Smith .30 .75
174 Koren Robinson .20 .50
175 Freddie Mitchell .20 .50
176 L.J. Smith .25 .60
177 Kevin Curtis .25 .60
178 Marcus Robinson .20 .50
179 Kellen Winslow .25 .60
180 Reggie Williams .20 .50
181 Bubba Franks .20 .50
182 J.P. Losman .20 .50
183 Chris Perry .20 .50
184 Michael Jenkins .25 .60
185 T.J. Duckett .20 .50
186 Rashaun Woods .20 .50
187 Ben Watson .25 .60
188 Bryant Johnson .20 .50
189 Dallas Clark .25 .60
190 William Green .20 .50
191 Daniel Graham .25 .60
192 Jerramy Stevens .25 .60
193 DeShaun Foster .25 .60
194 Nick Goings .20 .50
195 Ronald Curry .20 .50
196 Kevan Barlow .20 .50
197 Kevin Faulk .25 .60
198 Eric Parker .20 .50
199 Keenan McCardell .25 .60

200 LaMont Jordan	.25	.60
201 Alex Smith QB L13 RC	12.00	30.00
202 Aaron Rodgers L13 RC	60.00	120.00
203 Cedric Benson L13 RC	8.00	20.00
204 Braylon Edwards L13 RC	10.00	25.00
205 Ronnie Brown L13 RC	12.00	30.00
206 Cadillac Williams L13 RC	8.00	20.00
207 Troy Williamson L13 RC	6.00	15.00
208 Mark Clayton L13 RC	6.00	15.00
209 Charlie Frye L13 RC	8.00	20.00
210 Mike Williams L13	8.00	20.00
211 Marion Barber L13 RC	8.00	20.00
212 Eric Shelton L13 RC	5.00	12.00
213 Antrel Rolle L13 RC	8.00	20.00
214 Heath Miller RC	2.50	6.00
215 Dan Cody RC	1.50	4.00
216 Adam Jones RC	1.25	3.00
217 Derrick Johnson RC	1.50	4.00
218 Alex Smith TE RC	1.25	3.00
219 Kyle Orton RC	2.00	5.00
220 David Pollack RC	1.50	4.00
221 Erasmus James RC	1.50	4.00
222 Justin Tuck RC	2.50	6.00
223 Jason Campbell RC	2.50	6.00
224 Dan Orlovsky RC	2.00	5.00
225 Thomas Davis RC	1.25	3.00
226 J.J. Arrington RC	1.50	4.00
227 Roddy White RC	2.50	6.00
228 David Greene RC	1.25	3.00
229 Ciatrick Fason RC	1.25	3.00
230 Chris Henry RC	2.00	5.00
231 Reggie Brown RC	1.25	3.00
232 Vernand Morency RC	1.50	4.00
233 Carlos Rogers RC	2.00	5.00
234 Ryan Moats RC	1.50	4.00
235 Roscoe Parrish RC	1.25	3.00
236 Terrence Murphy RC	1.25	3.00
237 Shawne Merriman RC	2.00	5.00
238 Courtney Roby RC	1.50	4.00
239 Mark Bradley RC	1.25	3.00
240 Marcus Spears RC	1.50	4.00
241 Justin Miller RC	1.50	4.00
242 Matt Jones RC	1.50	4.00
243 DeMarcus Ware RC	4.00	10.00
244 Fabian Washington RC	1.50	4.00
245 Marlin Jackson RC	1.25	3.00
246 Corey Webster RC	1.50	4.00
247 Brandon Jacobs RC	2.50	6.00
248 Frank Gore RC	3.00	8.00

2005 Ultra Gold Medallion

*VETERANS: 1.2X TO 3X BASIC CARDS
*ROOKIES L13 201-213: .15X TO .4X
*ROOK.214-248: .4X TO 1X BASIC CARDS
OVERALL STATED ODDS 1:1 HOB, 1:3 RET
ROOKIE STATED ODDS 1:8 HOB, 1:12 RET

202 Aaron Rodgers L13	40.00	80.00

2005 Ultra Platinum Medallion

*VETERANS: 6X TO 15X BASIC CARDS
1-200 STATED PRINT RUN 50 SER.#'d SETS
UNPRICED L13 201-213 PRINT RUN 13 SETS
*ROOKIES 214-248: 2X TO 5X BASIC CARDS
214-248 STATED PRINT RUN 25 SER.#'d SETS

2005 Ultra All-Ultra Team Autographs Gold

OVERALL AUTO STATED ODDS 1:384
UNPRICED MASTERPIECES #'d TO 1

BB Bernard Berrian/49	7.50	20.00
BB1 Boss Bailey/66	7.50	20.00
CC Chris Chambers/26	12.50	30.00
DH Dante Hall/26	15.00	30.00
DS Donte Stallworth/27	15.00	30.00
JJ Julius Jones/26	30.00	60.00
JM Josh McCown/64	15.00	30.00
LF Larry Fitzgerald/21	30.00	60.00
LM Luke McCown/64	7.50	20.00
PR Philip Rivers/29	30.00	60.00
RB Ronde Barber/34	25.00	50.00
RW1 Reggie Williams/64	10.00	25.00
TB2 Troy Brown/26	15.00	40.00
WP Will Poole/51	7.50	20.00

2005 Ultra All-Ultra Team Autographs Platinum

PLATINUM PRINT RUN 25 SER.#'d SETS

BB Bernard Berrian	12.50	30.00
CC Chris Chambers	12.50	30.00
CP Chad Pennington	20.00	50.00
DF Doug Flutie	20.00	50.00
DH Dante Hall	12.50	30.00
EM Eli Manning	75.00	135.00
JJ Julius Jones	30.00	60.00
JM Josh McCown	10.00	25.00
LF Larry Fitzgerald	30.00	60.00
PB Plaxico Burress	12.50	30.00
PR Philip Rivers	20.00	50.00
RB Ronde Barber	25.00	60.00
RW1 Reggie Williams	20.00	50.00
RW2 Roy Williams WR	20.00	50.00
TB1 Tiki Barber	20.00	50.00
WP Will Poole	10.00	25.00

2005 Ultra All-Ultra Team Jerseys Gold

OVERALL JERSEY STATED ODDS 1:12
*PLATINUM: .8X TO 2X BASIC JERSEYS
PLATINUM PRINT RUN 50 SER.#'d SETS

AB Antonio Bryant	2.00	5.00
AJ Andre Johnson	2.50	6.00
BF Brett Favre	7.50	20.00
BL Byron Leftwich	3.00	8.00
BU Brian Urlacher	3.00	8.00
BW Brian Westbrook	2.50	6.00
CC Chris Chambers	2.50	6.00
CM Curtis Martin	3.00	8.00
CP1 Chad Pennington	3.00	8.00
CP2 Clinton Portis	3.00	8.00
CR Charles Rogers	2.50	6.00
DB Drew Bledsoe	3.00	8.00
DC1 David Carr	2.50	6.00
DC2 Daunte Culpepper	3.00	8.00
DD Domanick Davis	2.50	6.00
DF Dwight Freeney	2.50	6.00
DM Deuce McAllister	2.50	6.00
DS Donte Stallworth	2.50	6.00
EJ Edgerrin James	3.00	8.00
EM Eric Moulds	2.50	6.00
FT Fred Taylor	2.50	6.00
HW Hines Ward	3.00	8.00
JD Jake Delhomme	2.50	6.00
JG Jeff Garcia	2.50	6.00
JJ Julius Jones	4.00	10.00
JP Julius Peppers	2.50	6.00
JR Jerry Rice	5.00	12.00
JS Jeremy Shockey	3.00	8.00
KB Kyle Boller	2.50	6.00
LF Larry Fitzgerald	3.00	8.00
LJ Larry Johnson	3.00	8.00
MA Mike Alstott	2.50	6.00
MH1 Marvin Harrison	3.00	8.00
MH2 Matt Hasselbeck	3.00	8.00
MV Michael Vick	5.00	12.00
PM Peyton Manning	6.00	15.00
PP Peerless Price	2.50	6.00
PW Peter Warrick	2.50	6.00
QG Quentin Griffin	2.50	6.00
RG1 Rich Gannon	2.50	6.00
RG2 Rex Grossman	2.50	6.00
RL Ray Lewis	3.00	8.00
RW1 Reggie Wayne	2.50	6.00
RW2 Roy Williams WR	3.00	8.00
SA Shaun Alexander	4.00	10.00
SM Santana Moss	2.50	6.00
TB Tiki Barber	3.00	8.00
TG Tony Gonzalez	2.50	6.00
TH Travis Henry	2.00	5.00

2005 Ultra First Rounders

STATED ODDS 1:12 HOB, 1:15 RET

1 Michael Vick	1.50	4.00
2 LaDainian Tomlinson	1.50	4.00
3 Daunte Culpepper	1.25	3.00
4 Eli Manning	2.50	6.00
5 Randy Moss	1.50	4.00
6 Ben Roethlisberger	2.50	6.00
7 Carson Palmer	1.50	4.00
8 Joey Harrington	1.25	3.00
9 David Carr	1.00	2.50
10 Steve McNair	1.50	4.00
11 Edgerrin James	1.25	3.00
12 Philip Rivers	1.50	4.00
13 Willis McGahee	1.50	4.00
14 Kevin Jones	1.00	2.50
15 Larry Fitzgerald	1.50	4.00

2005 Ultra First Rounders Jerseys Copper

COPPER PRINT RUN 150 SER.#'d SETS
*PLATINUM: 1X TO 2.5X COPPER
PLATINUM PRINT RUN 25 SER.#'d SETS
UNPRICED ULTRASWATCH #'d TO DRAFT #

BR Ben Roethlisberger	10.00	25.00
CP Carson Palmer	4.00	10.00
DC Daunte Culpepper	4.00	10.00
DC David Carr	3.00	8.00
EM Eli Manning	7.50	20.00
JH Joey Harrington	4.00	10.00
LT LaDainian Tomlinson	5.00	12.00
MV Michael Vick	6.00	15.00
RM Randy Moss	4.00	10.00
SM Steve McNair	4.00	10.00

2005 Ultra Sensations

STATED ODDS 1:24 HOB, 1:48 RET

1 Drew Brees	2.00	5.00
2 Ben Roethlisberger	3.00	8.00
3 Aaron Brooks	1.25	3.00
4 Marc Bulger	1.50	4.00
5 Jerome Bettis	2.00	5.00
6 Santana Moss	1.50	4.00
7 Anquan Boldin	1.50	4.00
8 Michael Vick	2.00	5.00
9 Marvin Harrison	2.00	5.00
10 Randy Moss	2.00	5.00
11 Brian Westbrook	1.50	4.00
12 Julius Jones	1.25	3.00
13 Antonio Gates	2.00	5.00
14 Tom Brady	4.00	10.00
15 Donovan McNabb	2.00	5.00

2005 Ultra Sensations Jerseys Copper

COPPER PRINT RUN 150 SER.#'d SETS
*PLATINUM: 1X TO 2.5X COPPER
PLATINUM PRINT RUN 25 SER.#'d SETS
*ULTRASWATCH/81-88: .8X TO 2X COPPER
ULTRASWATCH SER.#'d TO JER.NUMBER

AB Anquan Boldin	3.00	8.00
AB Aaron Brooks	3.00	8.00
BR Ben Roethlisberger	10.00	25.00
DB Drew Brees	4.00	10.00
JB Jerome Bettis	4.00	10.00
MB Marc Bulger	3.00	8.00
MH Marvin Harrison	4.00	10.00
MV Michael Vick	6.00	15.00
RM Randy Moss	4.00	10.00
SM Santana Moss	3.00	8.00
TB Tom Brady	7.50	20.00

2005 Ultra TD Kings

STATED ODDS 1:6
*DIE CUTS: .3X TO .8X BASIC INSERTS
DIE CUTS TWO PER TARGET RETAIL

1 Shaun Alexander	1.00	2.50
2 Terrell Owens	1.25	3.00
3 Clinton Portis	1.00	2.50
4 Ahman Green	1.00	2.50
5 Torry Holt	1.00	2.50
6 Priest Holmes	1.00	2.50
7 Michael Vick	1.25	3.00
8 Peyton Manning	2.50	6.00
9 Donovan McNabb	1.25	3.00
10 Willis McGahee	1.25	3.00
11 Chad Johnson	1.00	2.50
12 Jamal Lewis	1.00	2.50
13 Marshall Faulk	1.25	3.00
14 Emmitt Smith	2.50	6.00
15 Brett Favre	3.00	8.00
16 Jerome Bettis	1.25	3.00
17 LaDainian Tomlinson	1.25	3.00
18 Muhsin Muhammad	1.00	2.50
19 Marvin Harrison	1.25	3.00
20 Corey Dillon	1.00	2.50

2005 Ultra TD Kings Jerseys Copper

OVERALL JERSEY STATED ODDS 1:12
*GOLD: .5X TO 1.2X COPPER
GOLD PRINT RUN 250 SER.#'d SETS
*PLATINUM: .6X TO 1.5X COPPER
PLATINUM PRINT RUN 99 SER.#'d SETS
RED STATED ODDS RETAIL
UNPRICED ULTRASWATCH #'d TO TD TOTAL

AG Ahman Green	3.00	8.00
BF Brett Favre	7.50	20.00
CJ Chad Johnson	3.00	8.00
CP Clinton Portis	3.00	8.00
DM Donovan McNabb	4.00	10.00
ES Emmitt Smith	7.50	20.00
JL Jamal Lewis	3.00	8.00
MF Marshall Faulk	3.00	8.00
MV Michael Vick	5.00	12.00
PH Priest Holmes	3.00	8.00
PM Peyton Manning	6.00	15.00
SA Shaun Alexander	4.00	10.00
TH Torry Holt	3.00	8.00
TO Terrell Owens	3.00	8.00
WM Willis McGahee	2.50	6.00

2006 Ultra

This 263-card set was released in June, 2006. The set was issued into the hobby in eight-card packs, with an $2.99 SRP, which came 24 packs to a box. The first 200 cards in the set feature veterans in alphabetical team order while cards numbered 201-263 all feature 2006 rookies. Cards numbered 201-213 were considered to be the most influential rookies in that crop and those cards were issued to a stated print run of 500 serial numbered sets. The overall odds of getting any rookie from a pack was stated to be one in four.

COMP.SET w/o RC's (200)	12.50	30.00

201-213 L13 PRINT RUN 500 SER.#'d SETS
OVERALL ROOKIE ODDS 1:4

1 Larry Fitzgerald	.30	.75
2 Anquan Boldin	.25	.60
3 Kurt Warner	.30	.75
4 Bryant Johnson	.20	.50
5 Marcel Shipp	.20	.50
6 J.J. Arrington	.20	.50
7 Michael Vick	.30	.75
8 Warrick Dunn	.25	.60
9 T.J. Duckett	.20	.50
10 Alge Crumpler	.25	.60
11 Michael Jenkins	.25	.60
12 DeAngelo Hall	.25	.60
13 Kyle Boller	.25	.60
14 Jamal Lewis	.25	.60
15 Todd Heap	.25	.60
16 Derrick Mason	.25	.60
17 Ray Lewis	.30	.75
18 Terrell Suggs	.25	.60
19 J.P. Losman	.25	.60
20 Willis McGahee	.25	.60
21 Eric Moulds	.20	.50
22 Lee Evans	.25	.60
23 Roscoe Parrish	.20	.50
24 Kelly Holcomb	.20	.50
25 Jake Delhomme	.25	.60
26 Steve Smith	.30	.75
27 Stephen Davis	.25	.60
28 Julius Peppers	.25	.60
29 DeShaun Foster	.25	.60
30 Keary Colbert	.20	.50
31 Chris Gamble	.20	.50
32 Kyle Orton	.30	.75
33 Thomas Jones	.25	.60
34 Rex Grossman	.25	.60
35 Muhsin Muhammad	.25	.60
36 Brian Urlacher	.30	.75
37 Adrian Peterson	.25	.60
38 Carson Palmer	.30	.75
39 Chad Johnson	.25	.60
40 Rudi Johnson	.25	.60
41 Chris Perry	.25	.60
42 T.J. Houshmandzadeh	.25	.60
43 Chris Henry	.20	.50
44 Deltha O'Neal	.20	.50
45 Trent Dilfer	.25	.60
46 Reuben Droughns	.25	.60
47 Antonio Bryant	.20	.50
48 Braylon Edwards	.25	.60
49 Charlie Frye	.25	.60
50 Dennis Northcutt	.20	.50
51 Drew Bledsoe	.30	.75
52 Julius Jones	.20	.50
53 Keyshawn Johnson	.25	.60
54 Jason Witten	.30	.75
55 Roy Williams S	.25	.60
56 Marion Barber	.30	.75
57 Terry Glenn	.25	.60
58 Jake Plummer	.25	.60
59 Mike Anderson	.25	.60
60 Champ Bailey	.25	.60
61 Tatum Bell	.20	.50
62 Rod Smith	.25	.60
63 Ashley Lelie	.20	.50
64 Joey Harrington	.20	.50
65 Kevin Jones	.20	.50
66 Roy Williams WR	.25	.60
67 Mike Williams	.20	.50
68 Marcus Pollard	.20	.50
69 Jeff Garcia	.25	.60
70 Brett Favre	.60	1.50
71 Javon Walker	.25	.60
72 Donald Driver	.30	.75
73 Samkon Gado	.25	.60
74 Najeh Davenport	.25	.60
75 Robert Ferguson	.20	.50
76 David Carr	.20	.50
77 Domanick Davis	.20	.50
78 Andre Johnson	.30	.75
79 Jabar Gaffney	.20	.50
80 Corey Bradford	.20	.50
81 Dunta Robinson	.20	.50
82 Peyton Manning	.50	1.25
83 Edgerrin James	.25	.60
84 Marvin Harrison	.30	.75
85 Reggie Wayne	.25	.60
86 Dallas Clark	.25	.60
87 Dwight Freeney	.25	.60
88 Cato June	.25	.60
89 Byron Leftwich	.25	.60
90 Fred Taylor	.25	.60
91 Jimmy Smith	.25	.60
92 Matt Jones	.20	.50
93 Ernest Wilford	.20	.50
94 Greg Jones	.20	.50
95 Trent Green	.25	.60
96 Priest Holmes	.25	.60
97 Larry Johnson	.25	.60
98 Tony Gonzalez	.25	.60
99 Dante Hall	.25	.60
100 Eddie Kennison	.20	.50
101 Gus Frerotte	.20	.50
102 Chris Chambers	.25	.60
103 Ronnie Brown	.30	.75
104 Ricky Williams	.20	.50
105 Randy McMichael	.20	.50
106 Zach Thomas	.30	.75
107 Daunte Culpepper	.25	.60
108 Nate Burleson	.20	.50
109 Michael Bennett	.20	.50
110 Mewelde Moore	.20	.50
111 Troy Williamson	.20	.50
112 Travis Taylor	.20	.50
113 Jermaine Wiggins	.20	.50
114 Tom Brady	.50	1.25
115 Corey Dillon	.25	.60
116 Deion Branch	.25	.60
117 Tedy Bruschi	.30	.75
118 David Givens	.25	.60
119 Patrick Pass	.20	.50
120 Aaron Brooks	.25	.60
121 Deuce McAllister	.25	.60
122 Joe Horn	.25	.60
123 Donte Stallworth	.20	.50
124 Antowain Smith	.20	.50
125 Devery Henderson	.20	.50
126 Eli Manning	.40	1.00
127 Tiki Barber	.30	.75
128 Jeremy Shockey	.30	.75
129 Plaxico Burress	.25	.60
130 Amani Toomer	.25	.60
131 Michael Strahan	.25	.60
132 Chad Pennington	.25	.60
133 Curtis Martin	.30	.75
134 Jonathan Vilma	.25	.60
135 Laveranues Coles	.20	.50
136 Justin McCareins	.20	.50
137 Ty Law	.20	.50
138 Korey Collins	.25	.60
139 LaMont Jordan	.25	.60
140 Randy Moss	.30	.75
141 Jerry Porter	.20	.50
142 Doug Gabriel	.20	.50
143 Zack Crockett	.20	.50
144 Donovan McNabb	.30	.75
145 Brian Westbrook	.25	.60
146 Terrell Owens	.30	.75
147 Jevon Kearse	.25	.60
148 L.J. Smith	.20	.50
149 Greg Lewis	.20	.50
150 Ben Roethlisberger	.40	1.00
151 Willie Parker	.25	.60
152 Hines Ward	.30	.75
153 Jerome Bettis	.30	.75
154 Antwaan Randle El	.25	.60
155 Heath Miller	.25	.60
156 Joey Porter	.20	.50
157 Drew Brees	.30	.75
158 LaDainian Tomlinson	.30	.75
159 Antonio Gates	.30	.75
160 Keenan McCardell	.25	.60
161 Donnie Edwards	.20	.50
162 Shawne Merriman	.25	.60
163 Eric Parker	.20	.50
164 Alex Smith	.30	.75
165 Kevan Barlow	.20	.50
166 Frank Gore	.30	.75
167 Brandon Lloyd	.20	.50
168 Eric Johnson	.20	.50
169 Julian Peterson	.20	.50
170 Matt Hasselbeck	.25	.60
171 Shaun Alexander	.25	.60
172 Darrell Jackson	.25	.60
173 Joe Jurevicius	.20	.50
174 Jerramy Stevens	.25	.60
175 D.J. Hackett	.20	.50
176 Marc Bulger	.25	.60
177 Steven Jackson	.30	.75
178 Torry Holt	.25	.60
179 Isaac Bruce	.25	.60
180 Kevin Curtis	.25	.60
181 Marshall Faulk	.25	.60
182 Chris Simms	.25	.60
183 Cadillac Williams	.25	.60
184 Michael Pittman	.20	.50
185 Michael Clayton	.20	.50
186 Joey Galloway	.25	.60
187 Brian Griese	.25	.60
188 Steve McNair	.25	.60
189 Chris Brown	.20	.50
190 Drew Bennett	.25	.60
191 Travis Henry	.20	.50
192 Ben Troupe	.20	.50
193 Billy Volek	.20	.50
194 Erron Kinney	.20	.50
195 Mark Brunell	.25	.60
196 Santana Moss	.25	.60
197 Clinton Portis	.30	.75
198 Chris Cooley	.25	.60
199 Ladell Betts	.20	.50
200 Sean Taylor	.30	.75
201 Matt Leinart L13 RC	10.00	25.00
202 Vince Young L13 RC	12.00	30.00
203 Reggie Bush L13 RC	25.00	60.00
204 D'Brickashaw Ferguson L13 RC	10.00	25.00
205 DeAngelo Williams L13 RC	12.00	30.00
206 Jay Cutler L13 RC	20.00	50.00
207 A.J. Hawk L13 RC	10.00	25.00
208 Mario Williams L13 RC	10.00	25.00
209 Santonio Holmes L13 RC	12.00	30.00
210 Chad Greenway L13 RC	10.00	25.00
211 Laurence Maroney L13 RC	8.00	20.00
212 LenDale White L13 RC	8.00	20.00
213 Sinorice Moss L13 RC	10.00	25.00
214 A.J. Nicholson RC	1.25	3.00
215 Abdul Hodge RC	1.25	3.00
216 Jeremy Bloom RC	1.50	4.00
217 Anthony Fasano RC	2.00	5.00
218 Bobby Carpenter RC	1.25	3.00
219 Brian Calhoun RC	1.25	3.00
220 Brodie Croyle RC	2.00	5.00
221 Chad Jackson RC	1.25	3.00
222 Charlie Whitehurst RC	2.00	5.00
223 Claude Wroten RC	1.25	3.00
224 Darnell Bing RC	1.50	4.00
225 Darrell Hackney RC	1.50	4.00
226 David Thomas RC	1.50	4.00
227 Demetrius Williams RC	1.50	4.00
228 Derek Hagan RC	1.50	4.00
229 Devin Hester RC	3.00	8.00
230 Dominique Byrd RC	1.50	4.00
231 D'Qwell Jackson RC	1.50	4.00
232 Elvis Dumervil RC	2.00	5.00
233 Haloti Ngata RC	2.00	5.00
234 Hank Baskett RC	2.00	5.00
235 Jason Avant RC	1.25	3.00
236 Jerome Harrison RC	2.00	5.00
237 Jimmy Williams RC	2.00	5.00
238 Joe Klopfenstein RC	1.25	3.00
239 Joseph Addai RC	2.00	5.00
240 Kellen Clemens RC	1.50	4.00
241 Cory Rodgers RC	1.50	4.00
242 Leon Washington RC	1.50	4.00
243 Leonard Pope RC	2.00	5.00
244 Marcedes Lewis RC	2.00	5.00
245 Martin Nance RC	1.50	4.00
246 Mathias Kiwanuka RC	2.00	5.00
247 Maurice Drew RC	3.00	8.00
248 Maurice Stovall RC	1.25	3.00
249 Michael Huff RC	1.50	4.00
250 Mike Hass RC	1.50	4.00
251 Omar Jacobs RC	1.25	3.00
252 Orien Harris RC	1.50	4.00
253 Owen Daniels RC	2.00	5.00
254 Reggie McNeal RC	1.50	4.00
255 DeMeco Ryans RC	2.00	5.00
256 Tamba Hali RC	2.00	5.00
257 Ernie Sims RC	1.50	4.00
258 Thomas Howard RC	1.50	4.00
259 Todd Watkins RC	1.25	3.00
260 Travis Wilson RC	1.25	3.00
261 Greg Lee RC	1.25	3.00
262 Tye Hill RC	1.25	3.00
263 Vernon Davis RC	2.50	6.00

2006 Ultra Gold Medallion

*VETS 1-200: 1.2X TO 3X BASIC CARDS
1-200 STATED ODDS 1:1
*ROOKIE L13: .25X TO .6X BASIC CARDS
201-213 L13 ROOKIE ODDS 1:288H,1:960R
*ROOKIE 214-263: .6X TO 1.5X BASIC CARDS
14-263 ROOKIE ODDS 1:24 H, 1:72 R

2006 Ultra Platinum Medallion

*VETS 1-200: 4X TO 10X BASIC CARDS
*ROOKIE 214-263: 1.5X TO 4X
1-200/214-263 PRINT 99 SER.#'d SETS
*ROOKIE L13: .6X TO 1.5X BASIC CARDS
201-213 ROOK.L13 PRINT 25 SER.#'d SETS

201 Matt Leinart L13	75.00	150.00
202 Vince Young L13	75.00	200.00
203 Reggie Bush L13	125.00	250.00
206 Jay Cutler L13	75.00	200.00
207 A.J. Hawk L13	60.00	120.00

2006 Ultra Achievements

COMPLETE SET (15)	6.00	15.00

STATED ODDS 1:6

UAAB Anquan Boldin	.75	2.00
UACD Corey Dillon	.75	2.00
UACM Curtis Martin	1.00	2.50
UADB Drew Bledsoe	1.00	2.50
UADC Daunte Culpepper	.75	2.00
UAHW Hines Ward	1.00	2.50
UALF Larry Fitzgerald	1.00	2.50
UALT LaDainian Tomlinson	1.00	2.50
UAMF Marshall Faulk	.75	2.00
UAMH Marvin Harrison	1.00	2.50
UAMV Michael Vick	1.00	2.50
UAPH Priest Holmes	.75	2.00
UASA Shaun Alexander	.75	2.00
UASM Steve McNair	.75	2.00
UATB Tom Brady	1.50	4.00

2006 Ultra Achievements Jerseys

STATED ODDS 1:72 HOB, 1:144 RET

UAAB Anquan Boldin	3.00	8.00
UACD Corey Dillon	3.00	8.00
UACM Curtis Martin	4.00	10.00
UADB Drew Bledsoe	4.00	10.00
UADC Daunte Culpepper	4.00	10.00
UAHW Hines Ward	4.00	10.00
UALF Larry Fitzgerald	3.00	8.00
UALT LaDainian Tomlinson	4.00	10.00
UAMF Marshall Faulk	3.00	8.00
UAMH Marvin Harrison	4.00	10.00
UAMV Michael Vick	4.00	10.00
UAPH Priest Holmes	3.00	8.00
UASA Shaun Alexander	5.00	12.00
UASM Steve McNair	4.00	10.00
UATB Tom Brady	6.00	15.00

2006 Ultra Autographics

STATED ODDS 1:288 HOB, 1:960 RET

ULAJ A.J. Hawk SP		
ULBF Brett Favre SP		
ULBG Brad Smith		
ULBQ Bruce Gradkowski	8.00	20.00
ULCG Chad Greenway	8.00	20.00
ULCP Carson Palmer SP		
ULCR Cory Rodgers	8.00	20.00
ULDE Demetrius Williams	8.00	20.00
ULDF D'Brickashaw Ferguson	8.00	20.00
ULDH Derek Hagan	8.00	20.00
ULDO Drew Olson	8.00	15.00
ULDR DeMeco Ryans SP		
ULDW DeAngelo Williams SP	25.00	60.00
ULEM Eli Manning SP	50.00	100.00
ULGR Gerald Riggs	8.00	20.00
ULHB Hank Baskett	8.00	20.00
ULJA Jason Avant	8.00	20.00
ULJN Jerious Norwood	12.00	30.00
ULKO Kyle Orton SP	8.00	20.00
ULLE LenDale White SP		
ULLT LaDainian Tomlinson SP	50.00	100.00
ULMI Mike Bell	8.00	20.00
ULMK Mathias Kiwanuka	10.00	25.00
ULML Matt Leinart SP	25.00	60.00
ULMN Martin Nance	8.00	20.00
ULMO DonTrell Moore	6.00	15.00
ULMV Michael Vick SP		
ULPH Paul Hornung SP	30.00	60.00
ULPM Peyton Manning SP		
ULRB Reggie Bush SP	60.00	120.00
ULRJ Rudi Johnson SP	10.00	25.00
ULRM Reggie McNeal	8.00	20.00
ULRW Reggie Wayne SP		
ULSI Sinorice Moss SP	10.00	25.00
ULTB Tiki Barber SP		
ULTJ T.J. Houshmandzadeh SP		
ULTR Travis Wilson	8.00	20.00
ULVD Vernon Davis SP		

2006 Ultra Award Winners

COMPLETE SET (15)	6.00	15.00

STATED ODDS 1:6

UAAAB Anquan Boldin	.75	2.00
UAABF Brett Favre	2.00	5.00
UAABR Ben Roethlisberger	1.25	3.00
UAACM Curtis Martin	1.00	2.50
UAACW Cadillac Williams	.75	2.00
UAAER Ed Reed	.75	2.00
UAAJV Jonathan Vilma	.75	2.00
UAAKW Kurt Warner	1.00	2.50
UAAMB Marc Bulger	.75	2.00
UAAMF Marshall Faulk	.75	2.00
UAAPH Priest Holmes	.75	2.00
UAARL Ray Lewis	1.00	2.50
UAARM Randy Moss	1.00	2.50
UAASM Steve McNair	.75	2.00
UAATS Terrell Suggs	.75	2.00

2006 Ultra Award Winners Jerseys

STATED ODDS 1:72 HOB, 1:144 RET

UAAAB Anquan Boldin	3.00	8.00
UAABF Brett Favre SP	10.00	25.00
UAABR Ben Roethlisberger	8.00	20.00
UAACM Curtis Martin	4.00	10.00
UAACW Cadillac Williams	3.00	8.00
UAAER Ed Reed	3.00	8.00
UAAJV Jonathan Vilma	3.00	8.00
UAAKW Kurt Warner	3.00	8.00
UAAMB Marc Bulger	3.00	8.00
UAAMF Marshall Faulk	3.00	8.00
UAAPH Priest Holmes	3.00	8.00
UAARL Ray Lewis	3.00	8.00
UAARM Randy Moss	4.00	10.00
UAASM Steve McNair	4.00	10.00
UAATS Terrell Suggs	3.00	8.00

2006 Ultra Campus Classics

STATED ODDS 1:12 HOB, 1:24 RET

CCAG Archie Griffin	1.00	2.50
CCBA Barry Sanders	2.50	6.00
CCBF Brett Favre	4.00	10.00
CCBO Bo Jackson	1.50	4.00
CCBS Billy Sims	1.00	2.50
CCCJ Chad Johnson	1.00	2.50
CCCP Carson Palmer	1.50	4.00
CCCW Charles White	1.00	2.50
CCDA Dan Fouts	1.00	2.50
CCDF Doug Flutie	1.00	2.50
CCDM Dan Marino	4.00	10.00
CCEC Earl Campbell	1.50	4.00
CCFT Fran Tarkenton	1.50	4.00
CCGR George Rogers	1.00	2.50
CCHW Herschel Walker	1.00	2.50
CCJH John Hannah	.75	2.00
CCJK Joe Klecko	.75	2.00
CCJP Jim Plunkett	1.00	2.50
CCJR Johnny Rodgers	1.50	4.00
CCJT Joe Theismann	1.50	4.00
CCKJ Keyshawn Johnson	1.00	2.50
CCKO Kyle Orton	1.00	2.50
CCLJ LaMont Jordan	1.00	2.50
CCMA Marcus Allen	1.50	4.00
CCMG Mike Garrett	.75	2.00
CCMV Michael Vick	1.50	4.00
CCNM Nat Moore	.75	2.00
CCPH Paul Hornung	1.00	2.50
CCPM Peyton Manning	3.00	8.00
CCRI Rocket Ismail	1.00	2.50
CCRJ Rudi Johnson	1.00	2.50
CCRS Roger Staubach	2.00	5.00
CCRW Reggie Wayne	1.00	2.50
CCSY Steve Young	2.00	5.00
CCTA Troy Aikman	2.00	5.00
CCTB Tiki Barber	1.00	2.50
CCTD Tony Dorsett	1.50	4.00
CCTJ T.J. Houshmandzadeh	.75	2.00

2006 Ultra Campus Classics Autographs

STATED PRINT RUN 25 SER.#'d SETS

CCBA Barry Sanders	75.00	150.00
CCBF Brett Favre	150.00	250.00
CCBS Billy Sims	15.00	40.00
CCCP Carson Palmer	20.00	50.00
CCCW Charles White	20.00	50.00
CCDA Dan Fouts	25.00	60.00
CCDF Doug Flutie	20.00	50.00
CCDM Dan Marino	150.00	250.00
CCFT Fran Tarkenton	20.00	50.00
CCHW Herschel Walker	30.00	60.00
CCJH John Hannah	15.00	40.00
CCJK Joe Klecko		
CCJR Johnny Rodgers	30.00	60.00
CCJT Joe Theismann	30.00	80.00
CCKJ Keyshawn Johnson		
CCKO Kyle Orton	15.00	40.00
CCMV Michael Vick	30.00	60.00
CCNM Nat Moore		
CCPH Paul Hornung		
CCPM Peyton Manning	90.00	150.00
CCRI Rocket Ismail	20.00	50.00
CCRJ Rudi Johnson	12.00	30.00
CCRS Roger Staubach	60.00	120.00
CCSY Steve Young	50.00	100.00
CCTJ T.J. Houshmandzadeh	12.00	30.00

2006 Ultra Dream Team

TWO PER JUMBO PACK

UDTAC Alge Crumpler	.60	1.50
UDTAG Antonio Gates	.75	2.00
UDTBA Tiki Barber	.75	2.00
UDTBD Brian Dawkins	.60	1.50
UDTBF Brett Favre	1.50	4.00
UDTBR Ben Roethlisberger	1.00	2.50
UDTBS Bob Sanders	.60	1.50
UDTBU Brian Urlacher	.75	2.00
UDTCB Champ Bailey	.60	1.50
UDTCJ Chad Johnson	.60	1.50
UDTCP Carson Palmer	.75	2.00
UDTDB Derrick Brooks	.60	1.50
UDTDF Dwight Freeney	.60	1.50
UDTDH DeAngelo Hall	.60	1.50
UDTEJ Edgerrin James	.60	1.50
UDTER Ed Reed	.60	1.50
UDTGL Terry Glenn	.60	1.50
UDTJP Joey Porter	.50	1.25
UDTJS Jeremy Shockey	.75	2.00
UDTJT Jason Taylor	.60	1.50
UDTJV Jonathan Vilma	.60	1.50
UDTLF Larry Fitzgerald	.75	2.00
UDTLJ Larry Johnson	.60	1.50
UDTLT LaDainian Tomlinson	.75	2.00
UDTMS Michael Strahan	.60	1.50
UDTMV Michael Vick	.75	2.00
UDTNR Neil Rackers	.50	1.25
UDTPE Julius Peppers	.60	1.50
UDTPM Peyton Manning	1.25	3.00
UDTPO Clinton Portis	.75	2.00
UDTRB Ronde Barber	.60	1.50
UDTRL Ray Lewis	.75	2.00
UDTRM Randy Moss	.75	2.00
UDTRW Roy Williams S	.60	1.50
UDTSA Shaun Alexander	.60	1.50
UDTSM Santana Moss	.60	1.50
UDTSS Steve Smith	.75	2.00
UDTTA Lofa Tatupu	.60	1.50
UDTTB Tom Brady	1.25	3.00
UDTTG Tony Gonzalez	.60	1.50
UDTTH Torry Holt	.60	1.50
UDTTP Troy Polamalu	1.00	2.50

2006 Ultra Head of the Class

STATED ODDS 1:4 WAL-MART PACKS

HCAF Anthony Fasano	1.25	3.00
HCAH A.J. Hawk	1.25	3.00
HCBC Brian Calhoun	.75	2.00
HCCJ Chad Jackson	.75	2.00
HCCR Brodie Croyle	1.25	3.00
HCCW Charlie Whitehurst	1.25	3.00
HCDA Devin Aromashodu	1.25	3.00
HCDB Dominique Byrd	1.00	2.50
HCDF D'Brickashaw Ferguson	1.25	3.00
HCDH Devin Hester	2.00	5.00
HCDW DeAngelo Williams	1.50	4.00
HCES Ernie Sims	1.00	2.50
HCGJ Greg Jennings	2.00	5.00
HCHA Mike Hass	1.00	2.50
HCHN Haloti Ngata	1.25	3.00
HCJA Joseph Addai	1.25	3.00
HCJB Jeremy Bloom	1.00	2.50
HCJC Jay Cutler	2.50	6.00
HCJH Jerome Harrison	1.25	3.00
HCJK Joe Klopfenstein	.75	2.00
HCLE Marcedes Lewis	1.25	3.00
HCLM Laurence Maroney	1.00	2.50
HCLP Leonard Pope	1.25	3.00
HCLW LenDale White	1.00	2.50
HCMD Maurice Drew	2.00	5.00
HCMH Michael Huff	1.00	2.50
HCML Matt Leinart	1.25	3.00
HCMS Maurice Stovall	.75	2.00
HCMV Marcus Vick	.75	2.00
HCMW Mario Williams	1.25	3.00
HCOJ Omar Jacobs	.75	2.00
HCRB Reggie Bush	2.50	6.00
HCRM Reggie McNeal	1.00	2.50
HCRO Cory Rodgers	1.00	2.50
HCSH Santonio Holmes	1.50	4.00
HCSM Sinorice Moss	1.25	3.00
HCTH Tye Hill	.75	2.00
HCTW Todd Watkins	.75	2.00
HCVD Vernon Davis	1.50	4.00
HCVY Vince Young	1.50	4.00
HCWA Leon Washington	1.00	2.50
HCWI Travis Wilson	.75	2.00

2006 Ultra Kings of Defense

COMPLETE SET (15)	6.00	15.00

STATED ODDS 1:6

KDBU Brian Urlacher	1.00	2.50
KDCB Champ Bailey	.75	2.00
KDDB Derrick Brooks	.75	2.00
KDDF Dwight Freeney	.75	2.00
KDJK Jevon Kearse	.75	2.00
KDJP Julius Peppers	.75	2.00
KDJT Jason Taylor	.75	2.00
KDJV Jonathan Vilma	.75	2.00
KDKB Kendrell Bell	.60	1.50
KDRL Ray Lewis	1.00	2.50
KDRW Roy Williams S	.75	2.00
KDTB Tedy Bruschi	1.00	2.50
KDTN Terence Newman	.60	1.50
KDTS Terrell Suggs	.75	2.00
KDWM Willie McGinest	.60	1.50

2006 Ultra Kings of Defense Jerseys

STATED ODDS 1:72 HOB, 1:144 RET

KDBU Brian Urlacher	4.00	10.00
KDCB Champ Bailey	3.00	8.00
KDDB Derrick Brooks	3.00	8.00
KDDF Dwight Freeney	2.50	6.00
KDJK Jevon Kearse	3.00	8.00
KDJP Julius Peppers	3.00	8.00
KDJT Jason Taylor	2.50	6.00
KDJV Jonathan Vilma	3.00	8.00
KDKB Kendrell Bell	2.50	6.00
KDRL Ray Lewis	3.00	8.00
KDRW Roy Williams S	3.00	8.00
KDTB Tedy Bruschi	6.00	15.00
KDTN Terence Newman	2.50	6.00
KDTS Terrell Suggs	3.00	8.00
KDWM Willie McGinest	2.50	6.00

2006 Ultra Lucky 13 Autographs

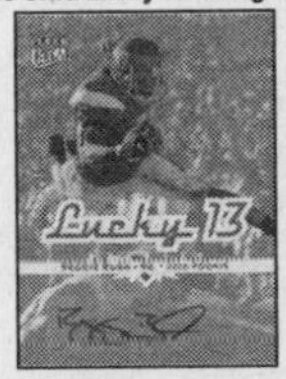

STATED PRINT RUN 25 SER.#'d SETS

201 Matt Leinart	75.00	150.00
202 Vince Young	125.00	250.00
203 Reggie Bush	200.00	400.00
204 D'Brickashaw Ferguson	40.00	100.00
205 DeAngelo Williams	50.00	125.00
206 Jay Cutler	200.00	400.00
209 Santonio Holmes	50.00	125.00
210 Chad Greenway	40.00	100.00
211 Laurence Maroney	30.00	80.00
212 LenDale White	30.00	80.00
213 Sinorice Moss	40.00	100.00

2006 Ultra Postseason Performers

COMPLETE SET (15)	6.00	15.00

STATED ODDS 1:6

UPPBR Ben Roethlisberger	1.25	3.00
UPPBU Brian Urlacher	1.00	2.50
UPPCP Chad Pennington	.75	2.00
UPPDB Drew Bledsoe	1.00	2.50
UPPDM Donovan McNabb	1.00	2.50
UPPEJ Edgerrin James	.75	2.00
UPPJD Jake Delhomme	.75	2.00
UPPJP Jake Plummer	.75	2.00
UPPKW Kurt Warner	1.00	2.50
UPPMF Marshall Faulk	.75	2.00
UPPMV Michael Vick	1.00	2.50
UPPRL Ray Lewis	1.00	2.50
UPPRM Randy Moss	1.00	2.50
UPPSM Steve McNair	.75	2.00
UPPTE Tedy Bruschi	1.00	2.50

2006 Ultra Postseason Performers Jerseys

STATED ODDS 1:72 HOB, 1:144 RET

UPPBR Ben Roethlisberger	8.00	20.00
UPPBU Brian Urlacher	4.00	10.00
UPPCP Chad Pennington	3.00	8.00
UPPDB Drew Bledsoe	4.00	10.00
UPPDM Donovan McNabb	4.00	10.00
UPPEJ Edgerrin James	4.00	10.00
UPPJD Jake Delhomme	4.00	10.00
UPPJP Jake Plummer	3.00	8.00
UPPKW Kurt Warner	3.00	8.00
UPPMF Marshall Faulk	3.00	8.00
UPPMV Michael Vick	4.00	10.00
UPPRL Ray Lewis	3.00	8.00
UPPRM Randy Moss	4.00	10.00
UPPSM Steve McNair	4.00	10.00
UPPTE Tedy Bruschi	6.00	15.00

2006 Ultra Scoring Kings

COMPLETE SET (15)	5.00	12.00

STATED ODDS 1:6

SKCJ Chad Johnson	.75	2.00
SKCP Carson Palmer	1.00	2.50
SKDC David Carr	.60	1.50
SKDM Deuce McAllister	.75	2.00
SKJH Joe Horn	.75	2.00
SKJS Jeremy Shockey	1.00	2.50
SKKM Keenan McCardell	.75	2.00
SKLJ LaMont Jordan	.75	2.00
SKMA Matt Hasselbeck	.75	2.00
SKPB Plaxico Burress	.75	2.00
SKPH Priest Holmes	.75	2.00
SKPO Clinton Portis	1.00	2.50
SKSS Steve Smith	1.00	2.50
SKTB Tiki Barber	1.00	2.50
SKWM Willis McGahee	.75	2.00

2006 Ultra Scoring Kings Jerseys

STATED ODDS 1:72 HOB, 1:144 RET

SKCJ Chad Johnson	3.00	8.00
SKCP Carson Palmer	4.00	10.00
SKDC David Carr	3.00	8.00
SKDM Deuce McAllister	3.00	8.00
SKJH Joe Horn	3.00	8.00
SKJS Jeremy Shockey	4.00	10.00
SKKM Keenan McCardell	3.00	8.00
SKLJ LaMont Jordan	3.00	8.00
SKMA Matt Hasselbeck	4.00	10.00
SKPB Plaxico Burress	3.00	8.00

SKPH Priest Holmes 3.00 8.00
SKPO Clinton Portis 4.00 10.00
SKSS Steve Smith 3.00 8.00
SKTB Tiki Barber 4.00 10.00
SKWM Willis McGahee 3.00 8.00

2006 Ultra Stars

COMPLETE SET (15) 6.00 15.00
STATED ODDS 1:6
USBE Tatum Bell .60 1.50
USBL Byron Leftwich .75 2.00
USBW Brian Westbrook .75 2.00
USCP Carson Palmer 1.00 2.50
USDC Daunte Culpepper .75 2.00
USDD Domanick Davis .60 1.50
USGR Trent Green .75 2.00
USJH Joey Harrington .60 1.50
USLF Larry Fitzgerald 1.00 2.50
USMA Mark Brunell .75 2.00
USMB Marc Bulger .75 2.00
USSA Shaun Alexander .75 2.00
USTB Tom Brady 1.50 4.00
USTE Tedy Bruschi 1.00 2.50
USTG Tony Gonzalez .75 2.00

2006 Ultra Stars Jerseys

STATED ODDS 1:72 HOB, 1:144 RET
USBE Tatum Bell 3.00 8.00
USBL Byron Leftwich 3.00 8.00
USBW Brian Westbrook 3.00 8.00
USCP Carson Palmer 4.00 10.00
USDC Daunte Culpepper 4.00 10.00
USDD Domanick Davis 3.00 8.00
USGR Trent Green 3.00 8.00
USJH Joey Harrington 3.00 8.00
USLF Larry Fitzgerald 3.00 8.00
USMA Mark Brunell 3.00 8.00
USMB Marc Bulger 3.00 8.00
USSA Shaun Alexander 5.00 12.00
USTB Tom Brady 6.00 15.00
USTE Tedy Bruschi 4.00 10.00
USTG Tony Gonzalez 3.00 8.00

2006 Ultra Target Exclusive Rookies

*201-213 L13: .1X TO .25X BASIC L13 RCs
*214-263: .4X TO 1X BASIC RCs
201-213 L13 ODDS ONE PER TARGET BOX
214-263 ODDS SEVEN PER TARGET BOX
PRINTED WITHOUT FOIL ON FRONT
201 Matt Leinart L13 3.00 8.00
203 Reggie Bush L13 15.00 40.00

2007 Ultra

This 300-card set was released in July, 2007. The set was issued into the hobby in five-card packs, with a $20 SRP, which came 15 packs to a box. Cards numbered 1-200 feature veterans in their 2006 team alphabetical order while cards numbered 201-300 feature 2007 NFL rookies. Cards numbered 201-213 feature the 13 players expected to have the biggest impact as rookies during the 2007 season.

COMP.SET w/o RCs (200) 15.00 40.00
HOBBY PRODUCED WITH SILVER HOLOFOIL
1 Bryant Johnson .30 .75
2 Matt Leinart .40 1.00
3 Edgerrin James .40 1.00
4 Larry Fitzgerald .50 1.25
5 Anquan Boldin .40 1.00
6 Jerious Norwood .40 1.00
7 Roddy White .40 1.00
8 Keith Brooking .30 .75
9 DeAngelo Hall .40 1.00
10 Michael Vick .50 1.25
11 Warrick Dunn .40 1.00
12 Alge Crumpler .40 1.00
13 Terrell Suggs .40 1.00
14 Derrick Mason .40 1.00
15 Todd Heap .30 .75
16 Ray Lewis .50 1.25
17 Steve McNair .40 1.00
18 Willis McGahee .40 1.00
19 Mark Clayton .40 1.00
20 Aaron Schobel .30 .75
21 Terrence McGee .30 .75
22 J.P. Losman .30 .75
23 Anthony Thomas .30 .75
24 Lee Evans .40 1.00
25 Keyshawn Johnson .40 1.00
26 DeAngelo Williams .50 1.25
27 Julius Peppers .40 1.00
28 Jake Delhomme .40 1.00
29 DeShaun Foster .40 1.00
30 Steve Smith .40 1.00
31 Mark Anderson .40 1.00
32 Devin Hester .50 1.25
33 Bernard Berrian .30 .75
34 Muhsin Muhammad .40 1.00
35 Rex Grossman .40 1.00
36 Cedric Benson .40 1.00
37 Brian Urlacher .50 1.25
38 Reggie Kelly .30 .75
39 Carson Palmer .40 1.00
40 Rudi Johnson .40 1.00
41 Chad Johnson .40 1.00
42 T.J. Houshmandzadeh .40 1.00
43 Jamal Lewis .40 1.00
44 Charlie Frye .40 1.00
45 Braylon Edwards .40 1.00
46 Kellen Winslow .40 1.00
47 DeMarcus Ware .40 1.00
48 Roy Williams S .40 1.00
49 Jason Witten .50 1.25
50 Marion Barber .40 1.00
51 Tony Romo .60 1.50
52 Julius Jones .30 .75
53 Terrell Owens .50 1.25
54 Terry Glenn .40 1.00
55 Rod Smith .40 1.00
56 Mike Bell .40 1.00
57 Jason Elam .30 .75
58 Jay Cutler .50 1.25
59 Champ Bailey .40 1.00
60 Javon Walker .40 1.00
61 Tatum Bell .30 .75
62 Jason Hanson .30 .75
63 Jon Kitna .30 .75
64 Kevin Jones .30 .75
65 Roy Williams WR .40 1.00
66 Mike Furrey .40 1.00
67 Charles Woodson .50 1.25
68 Aaron Kampman .40 1.00
69 Bubba Franks .30 .75
70 Brett Favre 1.00 2.50
71 Greg Jennings .50 1.25
72 Donald Driver .50 1.25
73 Ron Dayne .40 1.00
74 DeMeco Ryans .40 1.00
75 Jeb Putzier .30 .75
76 Matt Schaub .40 1.00
77 Ahman Green .40 1.00
78 Andre Johnson .40 1.00
79 Terrence Wilkins .30 .75
80 Bob Sanders .40 1.00
81 Dwight Freeney .40 1.00
82 Dallas Clark .30 .75
83 Adam Vinatieri .40 1.00
84 Peyton Manning .75 2.00
85 Joseph Addai .40 1.00
86 Marvin Harrison .50 1.25
87 Reggie Wayne .40 1.00
88 Rashean Mathis .30 .75
89 Matt Jones .40 1.00
90 Fred Taylor .40 1.00
91 Byron Leftwich .40 1.00
92 David Garrard .40 1.00
93 Reggie Williams .40 1.00
94 Maurice Jones-Drew .50 1.25
95 Damon Huard .40 1.00
96 Dante Hall .40 1.00
97 Eddie Kennison .30 .75
98 Trent Green .40 1.00
99 Larry Johnson .30 .75
100 Tony Gonzalez .40 1.00
101 Jason Taylor .40 1.00
102 Randy McMichael .30 .75
103 Zach Thomas .40 1.00
104 Daunte Culpepper .40 1.00
105 Ronnie Brown .40 1.00
106 Chris Chambers .40 1.00
107 Troy Williamson .30 .75
108 Tony Richardson .30 .75
109 Tarvaris Jackson .30 .75
110 Chester Taylor .30 .75
111 Travis Taylor .30 .75
112 Richard Seymour .30 .75
113 Reche Caldwell .30 .75
114 Tedy Bruschi .50 1.25
115 Ben Watson .30 .75
116 Tom Brady .75 2.00
117 Laurence Maroney .40 1.00
118 Asante Samuel .30 .75
119 Michael Lewis .30 .75
120 Devery Henderson .30 .75
121 Mike Karney .30 .75
122 Will Smith .30 .75
123 Drew Brees .50 1.25
124 Deuce McAllister .40 1.00
125 Reggie Bush .50 1.25
126 Marques Colston .50 1.25
127 Michael Strahan .40 1.00
128 Reuben Droughns .40 1.00
129 Jeremy Shockey .40 1.00
130 Eli Manning .50 1.25
131 Brandon Jacobs .40 1.00
132 Plaxico Burress .40 1.00
133 Jonathan Vilma .40 1.00
134 Jerricho Cotchery .40 1.00
135 Thomas Jones .40 1.00
136 Chad Pennington .40 1.00
137 Leon Washington .40 1.00
138 Laveranues Coles .30 .75
139 Dominic Rhodes .40 1.00
140 Andrew Walter .30 .75
141 Randy Moss .50 1.25
142 Ronald Curry .40 1.00
143 LaMont Jordan .40 1.00
144 Justin Fargas .30 .75
145 David Akers .30 .75
146 Correll Buckhalter .40 1.00
147 Brian Dawkins .40 1.00
148 L.J. Smith .30 .75
149 Donovan McNabb .50 1.25
150 Brian Westbrook .40 1.00
151 Reggie Brown .30 .75
152 Cedrick Wilson .30 .75
153 Aaron Smith .30 .75
154 Troy Polamalu .50 1.25
155 Ben Roethlisberger .50 1.25
156 Willie Parker .40 1.00
157 Hines Ward .50 1.25
158 Santonio Holmes .40 1.00
159 Eric Parker .30 .75
160 Leslie O'Neal .30 .75
161 Shawne Merriman .40 1.00
162 Philip Rivers .50 1.25
163 LaDainian Tomlinson .50 1.25
164 Antonio Gates .50 1.25
165 Walt Harris .30 .75
166 Vernon Davis .40 1.00
167 Alex Smith QB .50 1.25
168 Frank Gore .50 1.25
169 Arnaz Battle .30 .75
170 Maurice Morris .30 .75
171 Julian Peterson .30 .75
172 D.J. Hackett .30 .75
173 Lofa Tatupu .40 1.00
174 Darrell Jackson .30 .75
175 Matt Hasselbeck .40 1.00
176 Shaun Alexander .40 1.00
177 Deion Branch .40 1.00
178 Tye Hill .30 .75
179 Isaac Bruce .40 1.00
180 Marc Bulger .40 1.00
181 Steven Jackson .50 1.25
182 Torry Holt .40 1.00
183 Drew Bennett .30 .75
184 Jeff Garcia .40 1.00
185 Michael Clayton .30 .75
186 Derrick Brooks .40 1.00
187 Cadillac Williams .40 1.00
188 Joey Galloway .40 1.00
189 Ronde Barber .40 1.00
190 Chris Simms .30 .75
191 Keith Bulluck .30 .75
192 LenDale White .40 1.00
193 David Givens .30 .75
194 Vince Young .40 1.00
195 Ladell Betts .30 .75
196 Chris Cooley .40 1.00
197 Antwaan Randle El .30 .75
198 Jason Campbell .40 1.00
199 Clinton Portis .40 1.00
200 Santana Moss .40 1.00
201 JaMarcus Russell L13 RC 2.50 6.00
202 Brady Quinn L13 RC 4.00 10.00
203 Calvin Johnson L13 RC 12.00 30.00
204 Joe Thomas L13 RC 4.00 10.00
205 Adrian Peterson L13 RC 15.00 40.00
206 Marshawn Lynch L13 RC 4.00 10.00
207 Ted Ginn Jr. L13 RC 3.00 8.00
208 Leon Hall L13 RC 3.00 8.00
209 Dwayne Bowe L13 RC 5.00 12.00
210 Steve Smith USC L13 RC 4.00 10.00
211 Robert Meachem L13 RC 4.00 10.00
212 LaRon Landry L13 RC 4.00 10.00
213 Dwayne Jarrett L13 RC 3.00 8.00
214 Darius Walker RC 1.50 4.00
215 Chris Leak RC 2.00 5.00
216 Darrelle Revis RC 4.00 10.00
217 Paul Posluszny RC 2.50 6.00
218 Daymeion Hughes RC 2.00 5.00
219 LaMarr Woodley RC 2.50 6.00
220 Garrett Wolfe RC 1.50 4.00
221 DeShawn Wynn RC 2.00 5.00
222 Alan Branch RC 2.00 5.00
223 Greg Olsen RC 2.00 5.00
224 Tyler Palko RC 2.00 5.00
225 Jordan Palmer RC 2.00 5.00
226 Drew Stanton RC 1.50 4.00
227 Jamaal Anderson RC 2.00 5.00
228 Eric Wright RC 2.50 6.00
229 Quentin Moses RC 2.00 5.00
230 Patrick Willis RC 5.00 12.00
231 Troy Smith RC 2.50 6.00
232 Amobi Okoye RC 2.50 6.00
233 Lawrence Timmons RC 2.50 6.00
234 H.B. Blades RC 1.50 4.00
235 Jared Zabransky RC 2.00 5.00
236 John Beck RC 2.50 6.00
237 Kevin Kolb RC 4.00 10.00
238 Matt Moore RC 2.50 6.00
239 Trent Edwards RC 2.50 6.00
240 Antonio Pittman RC 1.50 4.00
241 Brandon Jackson RC 2.00 5.00
242 Chris Henry RC 1.50 4.00
243 Dwayne Wright RC 2.00 5.00
244 Brian Leonard RC 2.00 5.00
245 Kenneth Darby RC 2.00 5.00
246 Kenny Irons RC 1.50 4.00
247 Kolby Smith RC 2.00 5.00
248 Lorenzo Booker RC 2.00 5.00
249 Drew Tate RC 2.00 5.00
250 Tanard Jackson RC 1.50 4.00
251 Michael Bush RC 2.50 6.00
252 Selvin Young RC 2.00 5.00
253 Tony Hunt RC 1.50 4.00
254 Tyrone Moss RC 1.50 4.00
255 Reggie Nelson RC 2.00 5.00
256 Zach Miller RC 2.50 6.00
257 Anthony Gonzalez RC 2.50 6.00
258 Adam Carriker RC 2.00 5.00
259 Sidney Rice RC 3.00 8.00
260 Aundrae Allison RC 1.50 4.00
261 Chansi Stuckey RC 2.50 6.00
262 Courtney Taylor RC 2.00 5.00
263 Craig Buster Davis RC 2.00 5.00
264 Dallas Baker RC 1.50 4.00
265 David Clowney RC 2.00 5.00
266 David Ball RC 2.00 5.00
267 Jason Hill RC 2.50 6.00
268 Johnnie Lee Higgins RC 2.00 5.00
269 Rhema McKnight RC 1.50 4.00
270 Gaines Adams RC 2.50 6.00
271 Mike Walker RC 2.50 6.00
272 Steve Breaston RC 2.50 6.00
273 Gary Russell RC 2.00 5.00
274 Marcus McCauley RC 2.00 5.00
275 Jarvis Moss RC 2.00 5.00
276 Syvelle Newton RC 2.00 5.00
277 DeMarcus Tank Tyler RC 1.50 4.00
278 Alvin Banks RC 2.00 5.00
279 Joel Filani RC 2.00 5.00
280 Chris Davis RC 1.50 4.00
281 Matt Trannon RC 1.50 4.00
282 Ryan Kalil RC 2.00 5.00
283 Levi Brown RC 2.50 6.00
284 Anthony Spencer RC 2.50 6.00
285 Brandon Meriweather RC 2.50 6.00
286 Chris Houston RC 2.00 5.00
287 Michael Griffin RC 2.50 6.00
288 Jon Beason RC 2.00 5.00
289 Legedu Naanee RC 2.50 6.00
290 Eric Weddle RC 2.50 6.00
291 Isaiah Stanback RC 1.50 4.00
292 Aaron Ross RC 2.50 6.00
293 Sabby Piscitelli RC 2.50 6.00
294 Charles Johnson RC 1.50 4.00
295 Buster Davis RC 2.00 5.00
296 Justin Harrell RC 2.00 5.00
297 Stewart Bradley RC 2.00 5.00
298 A.J. Davis RC 1.50 4.00
299 David Irons RC 1.50 4.00
300 Scott Chandler RC 2.50 6.00

2007 Ultra Gold

*VETS: 1.5X TO 4X BASIC CARDS
*ROOKIE L13: .5X TO 1.2X BASIC CARDS
*ROOKIE 214-300: .5X TO 1.2X BASIC CARDS
ONE PER PACK

2007 Ultra Retail

COMPLETE SET (300) 25.00 50.00
*VETERANS 1-200: .25X TO .6X HOBBY
*ROOKIES 201-300: .3X TO .8X HOBBY
RETAIL PRODUCED WITH FLAT SILVER FOIL

2007 Ultra Autographics

STATED PRINT RUN 15-150
*RETAIL: .3X TO .8X BASIC AU/150
*RETAIL: .2X TO .5X BASIC AU/50
AB Anquan Boldin/50 8.00 20.00
BF Brett Favre/15 125.00 250.00
CH Chester Taylor/50 8.00 20.00
CJ Chad Johnson/50 8.00 20.00
CT Courtney Taylor/150 5.00 12.00
DB Drew Brees/50 40.00 80.00
DD Donald Driver/50 20.00 40.00
DH Daymeion Hughes/150 5.00 12.00
DR Darrelle Revis/150 12.50 25.00
EW Eric Wright/150 6.00 15.00
JT Joe Thomas/150 20.00 40.00
JT Joe Theismann/50 20.00 40.00
LE Lee Evans/50 8.00 20.00
MC Marques Colston/50 15.00 40.00
QM Quentin Moses/150 5.00 12.00
RB Ronnie Brown/50 10.00 25.00
TE Trent Edwards/150 6.00 15.00
TH Tony Hunt/150 4.00 10.00
ZM Zach Miller/150 6.00 15.00

2007 Ultra Comparisons

AP Gaines Adams 1.25 3.00
Julius Peppers
AT Jamaal Anderson 1.00 2.50
Jason Taylor
AW Aundrae Allison 1.25 3.00
Hines Ward
BH Dwayne Bowe 1.50 4.00
Marvin Harrison
BR John Beck 1.50 4.00
Tony Romo
CB David Clowney 1.00 2.50
Plaxico Burress
DC Craig Buster Davis 1.25 3.00
Marques Colston
ER Trent Edwards 1.25 3.00
Philip Rivers
GB Anthony Gonzalez 1.25 3.00
Anquan Boldin
GH Ted Ginn 1.00 2.50
Torry Holt
HB Leon Hall 1.00 2.50
Champ Bailey
HJ Tony Hunt .75 2.00
Larry Johnson
HS Chris Houston 1.00 2.50
Asante Samuel
IW Kenny Irons 1.00 2.50
Cadillac Williams
JF Dwayne Jarrett 1.25 3.00
Larry Fitzgerald
JG Brandon Jackson 1.00 2.50
Frank Gore
JO Calvin Johnson 4.00 10.00
Terrell Owens
KB Kevin Kolb 2.00 5.00
Marc Bulger
LJ Marshawn Lynch 1.25 3.00
Maurice Jones-Drew
LM Chris Leak 1.25 3.00
Donovan McNabb
LR LaRon Landry 1.25 3.00
Ed Reed
MG Zach Miller 1.25 3.00
Antonio Gates
MV Jarvis Moss 1.00 2.50
Jonathan Vilma
MW Robert Meachem 1.25 3.00
Roy Williams WR
NP Reggie Nelson 1.25 3.00
Troy Polamalu
OS Greg Olsen 1.00 2.50
Jeremy Shockey
OW Amobi Okoye 1.25 3.00
DeMarcus Ware
PA Antonio Pittman 1.25 3.00
Shaun Alexander
PL Paul Posluszny 1.25 3.00
Ray Lewis
PP Jordan Palmer 1.00 2.50
Carson Palmer
PT Adrian Peterson 5.00 12.00
LaDainian Tomlinson
QB Brady Quinn 2.00 5.00
Tom Brady
RJ Sidney Rice 1.50 4.00
Chad Johnson
RY JaMarcus Russell 1.00 2.50
Vince Young
SB Troy Smith 1.25 3.00
Drew Brees
SM Drew Stanton 2.50 6.00
Peyton Manning
SS Steve Smith WR 1.25 3.00
Steve Smith USC
SW Chansi Stuckey 1.25 3.00
Reggie Wayne
TF Joe Thomas 1.25 3.00
D'Brickashaw Ferguson
TM Lawrence Timmons 1.25 3.00
Shawne Merriman
WJ Darius Walker .75 2.00
Julius Jones
WU Patrick Willis 2.50 6.00
Brian Urlacher

2007 Ultra Dual Materials Gold

COMMON CARD/99 3.00 8.00
SEMISTARS/99 4.00 10.00
UNL.STARS/99 5.00 12.00
GOLD PRINT RUN 10-99
AG Ahman Green 4.00 10.00
AS Alex Smith QB 5.00 12.00
BF Brett Favre 10.00 25.00
BL Byron Leftwich 4.00 10.00
BR Ben Roethlisberger 5.00 12.00
BS Barry Sanders 12.00 30.00
CJ Chad Johnson 4.00 10.00
CP Carson Palmer 4.00 10.00
CP Clinton Portis 4.00 10.00
CS Chris Simms 3.00 8.00
DB Drew Brees 5.00 12.00
DM Dan Marino 15.00 40.00
EJ Edgerrin James 4.00 10.00
ES Emmitt Smith 15.00 40.00
HW Hines Ward 5.00 12.00
JH Joe Horn 4.00 10.00
JJ Julius Jones 3.00 8.00
JL Jamal Lewis 4.00 10.00
JN Joe Namath/25 25.00 60.00
JP Jake Plummer 4.00 10.00
JS Jeremy Shockey 4.00 10.00
JT Joe Theismann 8.00 20.00
LJ LaMont Jordan 4.00 10.00
LM Laurence Maroney 4.00 10.00
LT LaDainian Tomlinson 5.00 12.00
MA Marcus Allen 8.00 20.00
MB Marc Bulger/75 4.00 10.00
MF Marshall Faulk 4.00 10.00
ML Matt Leinart 4.00 10.00
MS Mike Singletary 8.00 20.00
MV Michael Vick 5.00 12.00
OW Terrell Owens/20 10.00 25.00
PA Carson Palmer 4.00 10.00
PE Chad Pennington/15 8.00 20.00
PM Priest Holmes 4.00 10.00
PM Peyton Manning 8.00 20.00
RG Rex Grossman/25 8.00 20.00
RJ Rudi Johnson/15 8.00 20.00
RL Ray Lewis/20 10.00 25.00
RS Rod Smith 4.00 10.00
RW Reggie Wayne 4.00 10.00
TG Trent Green 4.00 10.00
VY Vince Young 4.00 10.00
WM Willis McGahee 4.00 10.00
BF2 Brett Favre 10.00 25.00
CEB Cedric Benson 4.00 10.00
CHB Champ Bailey 4.00 10.00
CJ2 Chad Johnson 4.00 10.00
DEM Deuce McAllister 4.00 10.00
DM2 Donovan McNabb 5.00 12.00
DOM Donovan McNabb 5.00 12.00
LM2 Laurence Maroney 4.00 10.00
LT2 LaDainian Tomlinson 5.00 12.00
MH2 Marvin Harrison 5.00 12.00
MHK Matt Hasselbeck 4.00 10.00
MHN Marvin Harrison 5.00 12.00
MJ2 Maurice Jones-Drew 5.00 12.00
MJD Maurice Jones-Drew 5.00 12.00
ML2 Matt Leinart 4.00 10.00
PM2 Peyton Manning 8.00 20.00
RB2 Reggie Bush 5.00 12.00
REB Reggie Bush 5.00 12.00
RO2 Ben Roethlisberger 5.00 12.00
ROB Ronnie Brown 4.00 10.00
TB2 Tom Brady/50 10.00 25.00
TEB Tedy Bruschi 5.00 12.00
TOB Tom Brady 8.00 20.00
VY2 Vince Young 4.00 10.00

2007 Ultra Dual Materials Gold Patch

AB Anquan Boldin/30 10.00 25.00
AG Ahman Green 8.00 20.00
AL Marcus Allen 15.00 40.00
AS Alex Smith QB 10.00 25.00
BF1 Brett Favre 20.00 50.00
BL Byron Leftwich 8.00 20.00
BS Barry Sanders 25.00 60.00
CJ1 Chad Johnson 8.00 20.00
CP Clinton Portis 8.00 20.00
CP Carson Palmer 8.00 20.00
CS Chris Simms 6.00 15.00
DB Drew Brees 10.00 25.00
DM Dan Marino 30.00 80.00
EJ Edgerrin James 8.00 20.00
ES Emmitt Smith 30.00 80.00
GO Tony Gonzalez/20 10.00 25.00
HW Hines Ward 10.00 25.00
JH Joe Horn 8.00 20.00
JJ Julius Jones 6.00 15.00
JL Jamal Lewis 8.00 20.00
JP Jake Plummer 8.00 20.00
JS Jeremy Shockey 8.00 20.00
JT Joe Theismann 15.00 40.00
LJ LaMont Jordan 8.00 20.00
LM Laurence Maroney 8.00 20.00
LT LaDainian Tomlinson 10.00 25.00
MB Marc Bulger 8.00 20.00
MF Marshall Faulk 8.00 20.00
MH Marvin Harrison 10.00 25.00
ML Matt Leinart 8.00 20.00
MS Mike Singletary 15.00 40.00
MV Michael Vick 10.00 25.00
OW Terrell Owens/30 12.00 30.00
PA Carson Palmer 8.00 20.00
PE Chad Pennington 8.00 20.00
PH Priest Holmes 8.00 20.00
PM Peyton Manning 15.00 40.00
RG Rex Grossman 8.00 20.00
RJ Rudi Johnson 8.00 20.00
RL Ray Lewis 10.00 25.00
RM Randy Moss 10.00 25.00
RS Rod Smith 8.00 20.00
SA Shaun Alexander/30 10.00 25.00
SS Steve Smith 8.00 20.00
SY Steve Young 20.00 50.00
TE Tedy Bruschi 10.00 25.00
TG Trent Green 8.00 20.00
VY Vince Young 8.00 20.00
WA Reggie Wayne 8.00 20.00
WM Willis McGahee 8.00 20.00
WP Willie Parker/20 10.00 25.00
BF2 Brett Favre 20.00 50.00
CEB Cedric Benson 8.00 20.00
CHB Champ Bailey 8.00 20.00
CJ2 Chad Johnson 8.00 20.00
DEM Deuce McAllister 8.00 20.00
DM2 Donovan McNabb 10.00 25.00
DOM Donovan McNabb 10.00 25.00
HA2 Matt Hasselbeck/25 10.00 25.00
LM1 Laurence Maroney 8.00 20.00
LT2 LaDainian Tomlinson 10.00 25.00
MH2 Marvin Harrison 6.00 15.00
MJ2 Maurice Jones-Drew 10.00 25.00
MJD Maurice Jones-Drew 10.00 25.00
ML2 Matt Leinart 8.00 20.00
PM2 Peyton Manning 15.00 40.00
RB2 Reggie Bush 10.00 25.00
REB Reggie Bush 10.00 25.00
ROB Ronnie Brown 8.00 20.00
TAB Tatum Bell 6.00 15.00
TB2 Tom Brady 15.00 40.00
TOB Tom Brady 15.00 40.00
VY2 Vince Young 8.00 20.00

2007 Ultra Dual Materials Silver

AB Anquan Boldin/190 3.00 8.00
AG Ahman Green/199 3.00 8.00
AS Alex Smith QB/199 4.00 10.00
BF Brett Favre/199 8.00 20.00
BL Byron Leftwich/199 3.00 8.00
BS Barry Sanders/199 10.00 25.00
CP Carson Palmer/199 3.00 8.00
CP Clinton Portis/199 3.00 8.00
CS Chris Simms/199 2.50 6.00
DB Drew Brees/199 4.00 10.00
DM Dan Marino/199 12.00 30.00
EJ Edgerrin James/199 3.00 8.00
ES Emmitt Smith/199 12.00 30.00
GO Tony Gonzalez/40 5.00 12.00
HW Hines Ward/60 5.00 12.00
JH Joe Horn/199 3.00 8.00
JJ Julius Jones/199 2.50 6.00
JL Jamal Lewis/199 3.00 8.00
JN Joe Namath/50 12.00 30.00
JP Jake Plummer/199 3.00 8.00
JS Jeremy Shockey/199 3.00 8.00
JT Joe Theismann/199 6.00 15.00
LJ LaMont Jordan/199 3.00 8.00
MA Marcus Allen/199 6.00 15.00
MB Marc Bulger/90 4.00 10.00
MF Marshall Faulk/199 3.00 8.00
MS Mike Singletary/75 8.00 20.00
MV Michael Vick/199 4.00 10.00
OW Terrell Owens/30 6.00 15.00
PA Carson Palmer/199 3.00 8.00
PE Chad Pennington/199 3.00 8.00
PM Priest Holmes/199 3.00 8.00
RG Rex Grossman/199 3.00 8.00
RJ Rudi Johnson/60 4.00 10.00
RL Ray Lewis/75 5.00 12.00
RM Randy Moss/99 5.00 12.00
RS Rod Smith/199 3.00 8.00
RW Reggie Wayne/199 3.00 8.00
SA Shaun Alexander/40 5.00 12.00
SS Steve Smith/85 4.00 10.00
SY Steve Young/149 6.00 15.00
TG Trent Green/199 3.00 8.00
WM Willis McGahee/199 3.00 8.00
WP Willie Parker/20 6.00 15.00
BF2 Brett Favre/199 8.00 20.00
CEB Cedric Benson/199 3.00 8.00
CHB Champ Bailey/199 3.00 8.00
CJ1 Chad Johnson/199 3.00 8.00
CJ2 Chad Johnson/199 3.00 8.00
DEM Deuce McAllister/199 3.00 8.00
DM1 Donovan McNabb/60 5.00 12.00
DM2 Donovan McNabb/199 4.00 10.00
LM1 Laurence Maroney/199 3.00 8.00
LM2 Laurence Maroney/199 3.00 8.00
LT1 LaDainian Tomlinson/199 4.00 10.00
LT2 LaDainian Tomlinson/199 4.00 10.00
MH1 Marvin Harrison/199 4.00 10.00
MH2 Marvin Harrison/15 8.00 20.00
MHK Matt Hasselbeck/199 3.00 8.00
MJ1 Maurice Jones-Drew/199 4.00 10.00
MJ2 Maurice Jones-Drew/199 4.00 10.00
ML1 Matt Leinart/199 3.00 8.00
ML2 Matt Leinart/199 3.00 8.00
PM1 Peyton Manning/199 6.00 15.00
PM2 Peyton Manning/199 6.00 15.00
RB1 Reggie Bush/199 4.00 10.00
RB2 Reggie Bush/199 4.00 10.00
RO1 Ben Roethlisberger/199 4.00 10.00
RO2 Ben Roethlisberger/199 4.00 10.00
ROB Ronnie Brown/199 3.00 8.00
TAB Tatum Bell/55 3.00 8.00
TB1 Tom Brady/199 6.00 15.00
TB2 Tom Brady/199 6.00 15.00
TEB Tedy Bruschi/199 4.00 10.00
VY1 Vince Young/199 3.00 8.00
VY2 Vince Young/199 3.00 8.00

2007 Ultra Feel the Game

AG Ahman Green .75 2.00
AR Aaron Rodgers 2.50 6.00
AS Alex Smith QB 1.00 2.50
BD Brian Dawkins .75 2.00
BE Braylon Edwards .75 2.00
BL Byron Leftwich .75 2.00
BR Ben Roethlisberger 1.00 2.50
BW Brian Westbrook .75 2.00
CB Cedric Benson .75 2.00
CP Chad Pennington .75 2.00
CS Chris Simms .60 1.50
DM Donovan McNabb 1.00 2.50
EJ Edgerrin James .75 2.00
HW Hines Ward 1.00 2.50
JH Joe Horn .75 2.00
JJ Julius Jones .60 1.50
JL Jamal Lewis .75 2.00
JW Jason Witten 1.00 2.50
LT Lofa Tatupu .75 2.00
MV Michael Vick 1.00 2.50
RB Ronnie Brown .75 2.00
RG Rex Grossman .75 2.00
RL Ray Lewis 1.00 2.50
RW Roy Williams S .75 2.00
SJ Steven Jackson 1.00 2.50
TB Tedy Bruschi 1.00 2.50
JPE Julius Peppers .75 2.00
JPL Jake Plummer .75 2.00
LJN Larry Johnson .60 1.50
LJO LaMont Jordan .75 2.00

2007 Ultra Feel the Game Jerseys

AG Ahman Green 3.00 8.00
AR Aaron Rodgers 12.00 30.00
AS Alex Smith QB 4.00 10.00
BD Brian Dawkins 3.00 8.00
BE Braylon Edwards 3.00 8.00
BL Byron Leftwich 3.00 8.00
BR Ben Roethlisberger 4.00 10.00
BW Brian Westbrook 3.00 8.00
CB Cedric Benson 3.00 8.00
CP Chad Pennington 3.00 8.00
CS Chris Simms 2.50 6.00
DM Donovan McNabb 4.00 10.00
EJ Edgerrin James 3.00 8.00
HW Hines Ward 4.00 10.00
JH Joe Horn 3.00 8.00
JJ Julius Jones 2.50 6.00
JL Jamal Lewis 3.00 8.00
JW Jason Witten 4.00 10.00
LT Lofa Tatupu 3.00 8.00
MV Michael Vick 4.00 10.00
RB Ronnie Brown 3.00 8.00
RG Rex Grossman 3.00 8.00
RL Ray Lewis 4.00 10.00
RW Roy Williams S 3.00 8.00
SJ Steven Jackson 4.00 10.00
TB Tedy Bruschi 4.00 10.00
JPE Julius Peppers 3.00 8.00
JPL Jake Plummer 3.00 8.00
LJN Larry Johnson 2.50 6.00
LJO LaMont Jordan 3.00 8.00

2007 Ultra Field Generals

BF Brett Favre 2.00 5.00
BR Ben Roethlisberger 1.00 2.50
CP Carson Palmer .75 2.00
DB Drew Brees 1.00 2.50
DM Donovan McNabb 1.00 2.50
EM Eli Manning 1.00 2.50
JC Jay Cutler 1.00 2.50
JP Jake Plummer .75 2.00
MB Marc Bulger .75 2.00
ML Matt Leinart .75 2.00
MV Michael Vick 1.00 2.50
PM Peyton Manning 1.50 4.00
PR Philip Rivers 1.00 2.50
TB Tom Brady 1.50 4.00
VY Vince Young .75 2.00

2007 Ultra Field Generals Jerseys

BF Brett Favre 8.00 20.00
BR Ben Roethlisberger 4.00 10.00
CP Carson Palmer 3.00 8.00
DB Drew Brees 4.00 10.00
DM Donovan McNabb 4.00 10.00
EM Eli Manning 4.00 10.00
JC Jay Cutler 4.00 10.00
JP Jake Plummer 3.00 8.00
MB Marc Bulger 3.00 8.00
ML Matt Leinart 3.00 8.00
MV Michael Vick 4.00 10.00
PM Peyton Manning 6.00 15.00
PR Philip Rivers 4.00 10.00
TB Tom Brady 6.00 15.00
VY Vince Young 3.00 8.00

2007 Ultra Fresh Faces

TWO PER RETAIL FAT PACK
AB Alan Branch .75 2.00
AC Adam Carriker .75 2.00
AG Anthony Gonzalez 1.00 2.50
AR Aaron Ross 1.00 2.50
AS Anthony Spencer 1.00 2.50
BJ Brandon Jackson .75 2.00
BL Brian Leonard .75 2.00
BQ Brady Quinn 1.00 2.50
CH Chris Henry .60 1.50
CJ Calvin Johnson 3.00 8.00
CL Chris Leak .75 2.00
DB Dwayne Bowe 1.25 3.00
DH Daymeion Hughes .75 2.00
DJ Dwayne Jarrett .75 2.00
DR Darrelle Revis 1.50 4.00
DS Drew Stanton .60 1.50
DW Darius Walker .60 1.50
GA Gaines Adams 1.00 2.50
GO Greg Olsen .75 2.00
JA Jamaal Anderson .75 2.00
JP Jordan Palmer .75 2.00
JR JaMarcus Russell .60 1.50
JT Joe Thomas 1.00 2.50
LH Leon Hall .75 2.00
LL LaRon Landry 1.00 2.50
LT Lawrence Timmons 1.00 2.50
LW LaMarr Woodley 1.00 2.50
MB Michael Bush 1.00 2.50
ML Marshawn Lynch 1.00 2.50
PP Paul Posluszny 1.00 2.50
PW Patrick Willis 2.00 5.00
RM Robert Meachem 1.00 2.50
RN Reggie Nelson .75 2.00
SB Steve Breaston 1.00 2.50
SR Sidney Rice 1.25 3.00
SS Steve Smith USC 1.00 2.50
TG Ted Ginn Jr. .75 2.00
TS Troy Smith 1.00 2.50
APE Adrian Peterson 4.00 10.00
API Antonio Pittman .60 1.50
CHJ Charles Johnson .60 1.50
CHO Chris Houston .75 2.00

2007 Ultra Gridiron Legends

BJ Bo Jackson 3.00 8.00
BK Bernie Kosar 2.00 5.00
BS Barry Sanders 4.00 10.00
DM Dan Marino 5.00 12.00
ES Emmitt Smith 5.00 12.00
JN Joe Namath 3.00 8.00
JT Joe Theismann 2.50 6.00
MA Marcus Allen 2.50 6.00
MS Mike Singletary 2.50 6.00
SY Steve Young 3.00 8.00

2007 Ultra Gridiron Legends Autographs

*RETAIL UNNUMBERED: .3X TO .8X AU/99
BJ Bo Jackson/25 Red 75.00 150.00
DP Drew Pearson/99 20.00 40.00
JT Joe Theismann/99 15.00 30.00
LG L.C. Greenwood/99 15.00 30.00
PH Paul Hornung/99 20.00 40.00
RC Roger Craig/99 15.00 30.00

2007 Ultra Gridiron Legends Jerseys

BJ Bo Jackson 6.00 15.00
BS Barry Sanders 8.00 20.00
DM Dan Marino 10.00 25.00
ES Emmitt Smith 10.00 25.00
JN Joe Namath 8.00 20.00
JT Joe Theismann 5.00 12.00
MS Mike Singletary 5.00 12.00
SY Steve Young 6.00 15.00

2007 Ultra Paydirt

AG Antonio Gates 1.00 2.50
BW Brian Westbrook .75 2.00
CB Cedric Benson .75 2.00
CD Corey Dillon .75 2.00
CJ Chad Johnson .75 2.00
DM Deuce McAllister .75 2.00
LJ Larry Johnson .60 1.50
LT LaDainian Tomlinson 1.00 2.50
MH Marvin Harrison 1.00 2.50
RJ Rudi Johnson .75 2.00
SA Shaun Alexander .75 2.00
SJ Steven Jackson 1.00 2.50
TO Terrell Owens 1.00 2.50
WP Willie Parker .75 2.00
MJD Maurice Jones-Drew 1.00 2.50

2007 Ultra Paydirt Jerseys

AG Antonio Gates 4.00 10.00
BW Brian Westbrook 3.00 8.00
CB Cedric Benson 3.00 8.00
CD Corey Dillon 3.00 8.00
CJ Chad Johnson 3.00 8.00
DM Deuce McAllister 3.00 8.00
LJ Larry Johnson 2.50 6.00
LT LaDainian Tomlinson 4.00 10.00
MH Marvin Harrison 4.00 10.00
RJ Rudi Johnson 3.00 8.00
SA Shaun Alexander 3.00 8.00
SJ Steven Jackson 4.00 10.00
TO Terrell Owens 4.00 10.00
WP Willie Parker 3.00 8.00
MJD Maurice Jones-Drew 4.00 10.00

2007 Ultra Rookie Autographs

201 JaMarcus Russell L13/50 20.00 50.00
202 Brady Quinn L13/50 30.00 80.00
203 Calvin Johnson L13/50 75.00 150.00
204 Joe Thomas L13/150 15.00 40.00
205 Adrian Peterson L13/50 150.00 300.00
206 Marshawn Lynch L13/100 25.00 50.00
207 Ted Ginn Jr. L13/100 12.00 30.00
208 Leon Hall L13/150 12.00 30.00
209 Dwayne Bowe L13/150 30.00 60.00
210 Steve Smith USC L13/150 15.00 40.00
211 Robert Meachem L13/100 15.00 40.00
212 LaRon Landry L13/150 15.00 40.00
213 Dwayne Jarrett L13/150 12.00 30.00
214 Darius Walker 5.00 12.00
215 Chris Leak 6.00 15.00
216 Darrelle Revis 12.00 30.00
217 Paul Posluszny 8.00 20.00
218 Daymeion Hughes 6.00 15.00
219 LaMarr Woodley 10.00 25.00
220 Garrett Wolfe 5.00 12.00
221 DeShawn Wynn 6.00 15.00
222 Alan Branch 6.00 15.00
223 Greg Olsen 6.00 15.00
224 Tyler Palko 6.00 15.00
225 Jordan Palmer 6.00 15.00
226 Drew Stanton 5.00 12.00
227 Jamaal Anderson 6.00 15.00
228 Eric Wright 8.00 20.00
229 Quentin Moses 6.00 15.00
230 Patrick Willis 15.00 40.00
232 Amobi Okoye 8.00 20.00
233 Lawrence Timmons 8.00 20.00
234 H.B. Blades 5.00 12.00
235 Jared Zabransky 6.00 15.00
236 John Beck 8.00 20.00
237 Kevin Kolb 15.00 40.00
238 Matt Moore 12.00 30.00
239 Trent Edwards 8.00 20.00
240 Antonio Pittman 5.00 12.00
241 Brandon Jackson 6.00 15.00
242 Chris Henry 5.00 12.00
243 Dwayne Wright 6.00 15.00
244 Brian Leonard 6.00 15.00
245 Kenneth Darby 6.00 15.00
246 Kenny Irons 5.00 12.00
247 Kolby Smith 6.00 15.00
248 Lorenzo Booker 6.00 15.00
249 Drew Tate 6.00 15.00
251 Michael Bush 8.00 20.00
252 Selvin Young 10.00 25.00
253 Tony Hunt 5.00 12.00
254 Tyrone Moss 5.00 12.00
255 Reggie Nelson 6.00 15.00
256 Zach Miller 8.00 20.00
257 Anthony Gonzalez 12.00 30.00
258 Adam Carriker 6.00 15.00
259 Sidney Rice 10.00 25.00
260 Aundrae Allison 5.00 12.00
261 Chansi Stuckey 8.00 20.00
262 Courtney Taylor 6.00 15.00
263 Craig Buster Davis 6.00 15.00
264 Dallas Baker 5.00 12.00
265 David Clowney 6.00 15.00
266 David Ball 6.00 15.00
267 Jason Hill 8.00 20.00
268 Johnnie Lee Higgins 6.00 15.00
269 Rhema McKnight 5.00 12.00
270 Gaines Adams 8.00 20.00
273 Gary Russell 6.00 15.00
274 Marcus McCauley 6.00 15.00
279 Joel Filani 6.00 15.00

285 Brandon Meriweather	8.00	20.00
287 Michael Griffin	8.00	20.00
289 Legedu Naanee	8.00	20.00
291 Isaiah Stanback	5.00	12.00
295 Buster Davis	6.00	15.00
299 David Irons	5.00	12.00
300 Scott Chandler	8.00	20.00

2007 Ultra Signature Class Autographs

BQ Brady Quinn/25	30.00	80.00
DB Dallas Baker/150	8.00	20.00
DH Daymeion Hughes/150	6.00	15.00
GO Greg Olsen/150	10.00	25.00
GW Garrett Wolfe/250	8.00	20.00
HB H.B. Blades/150	6.00	15.00
JA Joseph Addai/50	10.00	25.00
JA Jamaal Anderson/150	8.00	20.00
JB John Beck/100	10.00	25.00
JC Jason Campbell/50	10.00	25.00
KK Kevin Kolb/50	20.00	50.00
KS Kolby Smith/250	8.00	20.00
LH Leon Hall/150	8.00	20.00
LJ Larry Johnson/50	12.00	30.00
LL LaRon Landry/100	10.00	25.00
LT LaDainian Tomlinson/25	40.00	100.00
LW LaMarr Woodley/250	10.00	25.00
MB Marc Bulger/50	8.00	20.00
MS Matt Schaub/150	8.00	20.00
PM Peyton Manning/50	60.00	120.00
PP Paul Posluszny/150	12.00	30.00
PR Philip Rivers/50	12.00	30.00
PW Patrick Willis/250	12.00	30.00
RB Ronnie Brown/50	10.00	25.00
RN Reggie Nelson/150	8.00	20.00
SC Scott Chandler/150	6.00	15.00
TH T.J. Houshmandzadeh/50	8.00	20.00
WP Willie Parker/50	10.00	25.00

2007 Ultra Signature Class Autographs Dual

BG Dwayne Bowe/50	20.00	50.00
Anthony Gonzalez		
BW Alan Branch/50	15.00	40.00
LaMarr Woodley		
HW Leon Hall/50	12.00	30.00
Eric Wright		
JP Brandon Jackson/25 EXCH	125.00	250.00
Adrian Peterson		
JR Jason Campbell/25		
Ronnie Brown		
JT LaDainian Tomlinson/25	40.00	100.00
Larry Johnson		
JW Brandon Jackson/75	12.00	30.00
Darius Walker		
LH Marshawn Lynch/75	15.00	40.00
Daymeion Hughes		
LN Chris Leak/75	15.00	40.00
Reggie Nelson		
MO Zach Miller/50	20.00	50.00
Greg Olsen		
QS Brady Quinn/50	25.00	60.00
Drew Stanton		
QW Brady Quinn/50	25.00	60.00
Darius Walker		
RJ Sidney Rice/25	25.00	60.00
Dwayne Jarrett		
RL JaMarcus Russell/25	20.00	50.00
LaRon Landry		
SA Chansi Stuckey/50	12.00	30.00
Gaines Adams		
WB Michael Bush/50	15.00	40.00
Garrett Wolfe		
WP Patrick Willis/50	20.00	50.00
Paul Posluszny		

2007 Ultra Signature Class Autographs Triple

ABP Joseph Addai/25	50.00	100.00
Ronnie Brown		
Willie Parker		
ATS Aundrae Allison/25	25.00	50.00
Courtney Taylor		
Chansi Stuckey		
CLR Philip Rivers/10	75.00	150.00
Jason Campbell		
Matt Leinart		
ELJ Trent Edwards/25	30.00	80.00
Marshawn Lynch		
Dwayne Jarrett		
HBW Leon Hall/25	30.00	60.00
Alan Branch		
LaMarr Woodley		
LBF Anquan Boldin/10	75.00	150.00
Larry Fitzgerald		
Matt Leinart		
NHL Reggie Nelson/25	25.00	60.00
Leon Hall		
LaRon Landry		
PWL Adrian Peterson/25	150.00	300.00
Darius Walker		
Marshawn Lynch		
QSR Brady Quinn/10	125.00	250.00
Drew Stanton		
JaMarcus Russell		
RLB JaMarcus Russell/10	125.00	250.00
LaRon Landry		
Dwayne Bowe		
SGJ Calvin Johnson/25	75.00	150.00
Ted Ginn Jr.		
Dwayne Jarrett		

2007 Ultra Stars

AB Anquan Boldin	.75	2.00
AC Alge Crumpler	.75	2.00
AG Antonio Gates	1.00	2.50
AJ Andre Johnson	.75	2.00
BU Brian Urlacher	1.00	2.50
CB Champ Bailey	.75	2.00
CJ Chad Johnson	.75	2.00
EM Eli Manning	1.00	2.50
JS Jeremy Shockey	.75	2.00
LE Lee Evans	.75	2.00
LF Larry Fitzgerald	1.00	2.50
LT LaDainian Tomlinson	1.00	2.50
MH Matt Hasselbeck	.75	2.00
ML Matt Leinart	.75	2.00
PH Priest Holmes	.75	2.00
RB Reggie Bush	1.00	2.50
RM Randy Moss	1.00	2.50
RS Rod Smith	.75	2.00
SA Shaun Alexander	.75	2.00
SJ Steven Jackson	1.00	2.50
SS Steve Smith	.75	2.00
VY Vince Young	.75	2.00
WM Willis McGahee	.75	2.00
CPA Carson Palmer	.75	2.00
CPO Clinton Portis	.75	2.00
RWA Reggie Wayne	.75	2.00
RWI Roy Williams WR	.75	2.00
TBE Tatum Bell	.60	1.50
TBR Tom Brady	1.50	4.00
TGO Tony Gonzalez	.75	2.00
TGR Trent Green	.75	2.00

2007 Ultra Stars Jerseys

AB Anquan Boldin	3.00	8.00
AC Alge Crumpler	3.00	8.00
AG Antonio Gates	4.00	10.00
AJ Andre Johnson	3.00	8.00
BU Brian Urlacher	4.00	10.00
CB Champ Bailey	3.00	8.00
CJ Chad Johnson	3.00	8.00
EM Eli Manning	4.00	10.00
JS Jeremy Shockey	3.00	8.00
LE Lee Evans	3.00	8.00
LF Larry Fitzgerald	4.00	10.00
LT LaDainian Tomlinson	4.00	10.00
MH Matt Hasselbeck	3.00	8.00
PH Priest Holmes	3.00	8.00
RB Reggie Bush	4.00	10.00
RM Randy Moss	4.00	10.00
RS Rod Smith	3.00	8.00
SA Shaun Alexander	3.00	8.00
SJ Steven Jackson	4.00	10.00
SS Steve Smith	3.00	8.00
VY Vince Young	3.00	8.00
WM Willis McGahee	3.00	8.00
CPA Carson Palmer	3.00	8.00
CPO Clinton Portis	3.00	8.00
RWA Reggie Wayne	3.00	8.00
RWI Roy Williams WR	3.00	8.00
TBE Tatum Bell	2.50	6.00
TBR Tom Brady	6.00	15.00
TGO Tony Gonzalez	3.00	8.00
TGR Trent Green	3.00	8.00

2007 Ultra Target Exclusive Rookies

*TARGET SILVER: .4X TO 1X BASIC CARDS
INSERTS IN SPECIAL TARGET RETAIL PACKS
TARGET VERSION FEATURES DIFFERENT PHOTOS

1996 Ultra Sensations

The 1996 Ultra Sensations set was issued in one series totalling 100 cards. The 12-card packs carried a suggested retail price of $2.49. Each card was produced in five different foil border colors with each inserted at various ratios. The Rainbow foil was the most difficult to pull (1% of total print run).

COMPLETE GOLD SET (101)	6.00	15.00
1 Leeland McElroy RC	.07	.20
2 Frank Sanders	.07	.20
3 Eric Swann	.02	.10
4 Jeff George	.07	.20
5 Terance Mathis	.02	.10
6 Eric Metcalf	.02	.10
7 Michael Jackson	.07	.20
8 Eric Turner	.02	.10
9 Jim Kelly	.15	.40
10 Bryce Paup	.02	.10
11 Bruce Smith	.07	.20
12 Thurman Thomas	.15	.40
13 Tim Biakabutuka RC	.15	.40
14 Kerry Collins	.15	.40
15 Muhsin Muhammad RC	.40	1.00
16 Winslow Oliver RC	.02	.10
17 Curtis Conway	.15	.40
18 Bryan Cox	.02	.10
19 Bobby Engram RC	.15	.40
20 Erik Kramer	.02	.10
21 Rashaan Salaam	.07	.20
22 Jeff Blake	.15	.40
23 Ki-Jana Carter	.07	.20
24 Carl Pickens	.07	.20
25 Troy Aikman	.40	1.00
26 Michael Irvin	.15	.40
27 Daryl Johnston	.07	.20
28 Deion Sanders	.30	.75
29 Emmitt Smith	.60	1.50
30 Terrell Davis	.30	.75
31 John Elway	.75	2.00
32 Anthony Miller	.07	.20
33 John Mobley RC	.02	.10
34 Scott Mitchell	.07	.20
35 Herman Moore	.07	.20
36 Barry Sanders	.60	1.50
37 Edgar Bennett	.07	.20
38 Robert Brooks	.15	.40
39 Brett Favre	.75	2.00
40 Reggie White	.15	.40
41 Eddie George RC	.50	1.25
42 Steve McNair	.30	.75
43 Chris Sanders	.07	.20
44 Quentin Coryatt	.02	.10
45 Marshall Faulk	.20	.50
46 Jim Harbaugh	.07	.20
47 Marvin Harrison RC	1.00	2.50
48 Mark Brunell	.25	.60
49 Natrone Means	.07	.20
50 Andre Rison	.07	.20
51 Marcus Allen	.15	.40
52 Steve Bono	.02	.10
53 Greg Hill	.07	.20
54 Tamarick Vanover	.07	.20
55 Karim Abdul-Jabbar RC	.15	.40
56 Dan Marino	.75	2.00
57 O.J. McDuffie	.07	.20
58 Zach Thomas RC	.30	.75
59 Cris Carter	.15	.40
60 Warren Moon	.07	.20
61 Jake Reed	.07	.20
62 Drew Bledsoe	.25	.60
63 Ben Coates	.07	.20
64 Terry Glenn RC	.40	1.00
65 Curtis Martin	.30	.75
66 Mario Bates	.07	.20
67 Michael Haynes	.02	.10
68 Dave Brown	.02	.10
69 Rodney Hampton	.07	.20
70 Amani Toomer RC	.40	1.00
71 Tyrone Wheatley	.07	.20
72 Keyshawn Johnson RC	.40	1.00
73 Neil O'Donnell	.07	.20
74 Tim Brown	.15	.40
75 Rickey Dudley RC	.15	.40
76 Napoleon Kaufman	.15	.40
77 Chester McGlockton	.02	.10
78 Charlie Garner	.07	.20
79 Chris T. Jones	.07	.20
80 Ricky Watters	.07	.20
81 Jerome Bettis	.15	.40
82 Kordell Stewart	.15	.40
83 Rod Woodson	.07	.20
84 Aaron Hayden	.02	.10
85 Stan Humphries	.07	.20
86 Junior Seau	.15	.40
87 Tony Banks RC	.15	.40
88 Isaac Bruce	.15	.40
89 Lawrence Phillips RC	.15	.40
90 Derek Loville	.02	.10
91 Jerry Rice	.40	1.00
92 J.J. Stokes	.15	.40
93 Steve Young	.30	.75
94 Joey Galloway	.15	.40
95 Rick Mirer	.07	.20
96 Chris Warren	.07	.20
97 Trent Dilfer	.15	.40
98 Errict Rhett	.07	.20
99 Terry Allen	.07	.20
100 Michael Westbrook	.15	.40
NNO Brett Favre OL	1.25	2.50
NNO Promo Sheet	1.00	2.50
Brett Favre Gold, Blue,		
and Marble Gold cards		

1996 Ultra Sensations Blue

*BLUE CARDS: .6X TO 1.5X BASIC CARDS

1996 Ultra Sensations Rainbow

*RAINBOW STARS: 6X TO 15X BASIC CARDS
*RAINBOW RCs: 3X TO 8X BASIC CARDS
RAINBOWS:RANDOM INS.IN PACKS

1996 Ultra Sensations Marble Gold

*STARS: .8X TO 2X BASIC CARDS
*RCs: .6X TO 1.5X BASIC CARDS

1996 Ultra Sensations Pewter

*PEWTER STARS: 1.5X TO 4X BASIC CARDS
*PEWTER RCs: 1.2X TO 3X BASIC CARDS
PEWTERS: RANDOM INS. IN PACKS

1996 Ultra Sensations Creative Chaos

COMPLETE SET (100)	400.00	800.00
STATED ODDS 1:12		
1A Emmitt Smith	6.00	15.00
Emmitt Smith		
1B Emmitt Smith	7.50	20.00
Brett Favre		
1C Emmitt Smith	5.00	12.00
Curtis Martin		
1D Emmitt Smith	5.00	12.00
Chris Warren		
1E Emmitt Smith	5.00	12.00
Deion Sanders		
1F Emmitt Smith	5.00	12.00
Steve Young		
1G Emmitt Smith	5.00	12.00
Jerry Rice		
1H Emmitt Smith	5.00	12.00
Terrell Davis		
1I Emmitt Smith	5.00	12.00
Carl Pickens		
1J Emmitt Smith	5.00	12.00
Marshall Faulk		
2A Brett Favre	7.50	20.00
Emmitt Smith		
2B Brett Favre	10.00	20.00
Brett Favre		
2C Brett Favre	6.00	15.00
Curtis Martin		
2D Brett Favre	5.00	12.00
Chris Warren		
2E Brett Favre	5.00	12.00
Deion Sanders		
2F Brett Favre	5.00	12.00
Steve Young		
2G Brett Favre	6.00	15.00
Jerry Rice		
2H Brett Favre	6.00	15.00
Terrell Davis		
2I Brett Favre	5.00	12.00
Carl Pickens		
2J Brett Favre	5.00	12.00
Marshall Faulk		
3A Curtis Martin	5.00	12.00
Emmitt Smith		
3B Curtis Martin	6.00	15.00
Brett Favre		
3C Curtis Martin	2.50	6.00
Curtis Martin		
3D Curtis Martin	4.00	10.00
Chris Warren		
3E Curtis Martin	4.00	10.00
Deion Sanders		
3F Curtis Martin	4.00	10.00
Steve Young		
3G Curtis Martin	4.00	10.00
Jerry Rice		
3H Curtis Martin	4.00	10.00
Terrell Davis		
3I Curtis Martin	4.00	10.00
Carl Pickens		
3J Curtis Martin	4.00	10.00
Marshall Faulk		
4A Chris Warren	5.00	12.00
Emmitt Smith		
4B Chris Warren	5.00	12.00
Brett Favre		
4C Chris Warren	4.00	10.00
Curtis Martin		
4D Chris Warren	1.50	4.00
Chris Warren		
4E Chris Warren	2.50	6.00
Deion Sanders		
4F Chris Warren	2.50	6.00
Steve Young		
4G Chris Warren	4.00	10.00
Jerry Rice		
4H Chris Warren	4.00	10.00
Terrell Davis		
4I Chris Warren	1.50	4.00
Carl Pickens		
4J Chris Warren	2.50	6.00
Marhsall Faulk		
5A Deion Sanders	5.00	12.00
Emmitt Smith		
5B Deion Sanders	5.00	12.00
Brett Favre		
5C Deion Sanders	4.00	10.00
Curtis Martin		
5D Deion Sanders	2.50	6.00
Chris Warren		
5E Deion Sanders	2.50	6.00
Deion Sanders		
5F Deion Sanders	2.50	6.00
Steve Young		
5G Deion Sanders	4.00	10.00
Jerry Rice		
5H Deion Sanders	4.00	10.00
Terrell Davis		
5I Deion Sanders	2.50	6.00
Carl Pickens		
5J Deion Sanders	2.50	6.00
Marshall Faulk		
6A Steve Young	5.00	12.00
Emmitt Smith		
6B Steve Young	5.00	12.00
Brett Favre		
6C Steve Young	4.00	10.00
Curtis Martin		
6D Steve Young	2.50	6.00
Chris Warren		
6E Steve Young	2.50	6.00
Deion Sanders		
6F Steve Young	2.50	6.00
Steve Young		
6G Steve Young	4.00	10.00
Jerry Rice		
6H Steve Young	4.00	10.00
Terrell Davis		
6I Steve Young	2.50	6.00
Carl Pickens		
6J Steve Young	2.50	6.00
Marshall Faulk		
7A Jerry Rice	5.00	12.00
Emmitt Smith		
7B Jerry Rice	6.00	15.00
Brett Favre		
7C Jerry Rice	4.00	10.00
Curtis Martin		
7D Jerry Rice	4.00	10.00
Chris Warren		
7E Jerry Rice	4.00	10.00
Deion Sanders		
7F Jerry Rice	4.00	10.00
Steve Young		
7G Jerry Rice	4.00	10.00
Jerry Rice		
7H Jerry Rice	4.00	10.00
Terrell Davis		
7I Jerry Rice	4.00	10.00
Carl Pickens		
7J Jerry Rice	4.00	10.00
Marshall Faulk		
8A Terrell Davis	7.50	20.00
Emmitt Smith		
8B Terrell Davis	6.00	15.00
Brett Favre		
8C Terrell Davis	4.00	10.00
Curtis Martin		
8D Terrell Davis	4.00	10.00
Chris Warren		
8E Terrell Davis	4.00	10.00
Deion Sanders		
8F Terrell Davis	4.00	10.00
Steve Young		
8G Terrell Davis	4.00	10.00
Jerry Rice		
8H Terrell Davis	4.00	10.00
Terrell Davis		
8I Terrell Davis	4.00	10.00
Carl Pickens		
8J Terrell Davis	4.00	10.00
Marshall Faulk		
9A Carl Pickens	5.00	12.00
Emmitt Smith		
9B Carl Pickens	5.00	12.00
Brett Favre		
9C Carl Pickens	4.00	10.00
Curtis Martin		
9D Carl Pickens	1.50	4.00
Chris Warren		
9E Carl Pickens	2.50	6.00
Deion Sanders		
9F Carl Pickens	2.50	6.00
Steve Young		
9G Carl Pickens	4.00	10.00
Jerry Rice		
9H Carl Pickens	4.00	10.00
Terrell Davis		
9I Carl Pickens	1.50	4.00
Carl Pickens		
9J Carl Pickens	2.50	6.00
Marshall Faulk		
10A Marshall Faulk	5.00	12.00
Emmitt Smith		
10B Marshall Faulk	6.00	12.00
Brett Favre		
10C Marshall Faulk	4.00	10.00
Curtis Martin		
10D Marshall Faulk	2.50	6.00
Chris Warren		
10E Marshall Faulk	2.50	6.00
Deion Sanders		
10F Marshall Faulk	2.50	6.00
Steve Young		
10G Marshall Faulk	4.00	10.00
Jerry Rice		
10H Marshall Faulk	4.00	10.00
Terrell Davis		
10I Marshall Faulk	2.50	6.00
Carl Pickens		
10J Marshall Faulk	2.50	6.00
Marshall Faulk		

1996 Ultra Sensations Random Rookies

COMPLETE SET (10)	40.00	100.00
COMP.HOBBY SER.1 (5)	20.00	50.00
COMP.RETAIL SER.2 (5)	20.00	50.00
CARDS 1-5 STATED ODDS 1:48 HOBBY		
CARDS 6-10 STATED ODDS 1:48 RETAIL		
*GOLDS: 1X TO 2.5X BASIC INSERTS		
GOLDS STATED 20% OF PRINT RUN		
1 Keyshawn Johnson	3.00	8.00
2 Eddie George	4.00	10.00
3 Leeland McElroy	2.00	5.00
4 Eric Moulds	4.00	10.00
5 Lawrence Phillips	2.50	6.00
6 Marvin Harrison	7.50	20.00
7 Tim Biakabutuka	2.50	6.00
8 Terry Glenn	3.00	8.00
9 Rickey Dudley	2.00	5.00
10 Tony Banks	2.50	6.00

1957-59 Union Oil Booklets

These booklets were distributed by Union Oil. The front cover of each booklet features a drawing of the subject player. The booklets are numbered and were issued over several years beginning in 1957. These are 12-page pamphlets and are approximately 4" by 5 1/2". The set is subtitled "Family Sports Fun." This was apparently primarily a Southern California promotion.

COMPLETE SET (44)	200.00	400.00
1 Elroy Hirsch FB 57	10.00	20.00
2 Les Richter FB 57	2.00	4.00
3 Frankie Albert FB 57	7.50	15.00
4 Y.A. Tittle FB 57	10.00	20.00
27 Bob Waterfield FB 58	10.00	20.00
28 Pete Elliott FB 58	5.00	10.00
29 Elroy Hirsch FB 58	7.50	15.00
30 Frank Gifford FB 58	10.00	20.00

1991 Upper Deck

This 700-card standard size set was the first football card set produced by Upper Deck. The set was released in two series. The first series contains 500 cards and the high-number series contains 200 additional cards numbered in continuation of the low series. Factory sets were produced for each series. Cards 72-99 feature team checklists with Vernon Wells drawings. Other subsets include Star Rookies (1-29), Aerial Threats (30-35), Season Leaders (401-406), Team MVP's (450-487), Rookie Force (AFC 601-626 and NFC 627-652) and an Arch Rivals subset with split-photo cards presenting one-on-one rivalries (653-658). Rookie Cards include Cody Carlson, Bryan Cox, Lawrence Dawsey, Ricky Ervins, Brett Favre, Jeff Graham, Alvin Harper, Randal Hill, Michael Jackson, Herman Moore, Bryce Paup, Erric Pegram, Mike Pritchard, Jake Reed, Leonard Russell, Ricky Watters and Harvey Williams. A Darrell Green insert (SP1) and an insert card commemorating Don Shula's historic 300th NFL victory (SP2) were randomly inserted in first and second series packs respectively. Two Promo cards were released to preview the set. We've listed them below, but they are not considered part of the complete set.

COMPLETE SET (700)	6.00	15.00
COMP.FACT.SET (700)	10.00	25.00
COMP.SERIES 1 SET (500)	4.00	10.00
COMP.SERIES 2 SET (200)	2.00	5.00
COMP.FACT.SERIES 2 (200)	2.50	6.00
1 Star Rookie Checklist	.01	.05
Dan McGwire		
2 Eric Bieniemy RC	.01	.05
3 Mike Dumas RC	.01	.05
4 Mike Croel RC	.01	.05
5 Russell Maryland RC	.08	.25
6 Charles McRae RC	.01	.05
7 Dan McGwire RC	.01	.05
8 Mike Pritchard RC	.08	.25
9 Ricky Watters RC	.60	1.50
10 Chris Zorich RC	.08	.25
11 Browning Nagle RC	.01	.05
12 Wesley Carroll RC	.01	.05
13 Brett Favre RC	5.00	10.00
14 Rob Carpenter RC	.01	.05
15 Eric Swann RC	.08	.25
16 Stanley Richard RC	.01	.05
17 Herman Moore RC	.08	.25
18 Todd Marinovich RC	.01	.05
19 Aaron Craver RC	.01	.05
20 Chuck Webb RC	.01	.05
21 Todd Lyght RC	.01	.05
22 Greg Lewis RC	.01	.05
23 Eric Turner RC	.02	.10
24 Alvin Harper RC	.08	.25
25 Jarrod Bunch RC	.01	.05
26 Bruce Pickens RC	.01	.05
27 Harvey Williams RC	.08	.25
28 Randal Hill RC	.02	.10
29 Nick Bell RC	.01	.05
30 Jim Everett AT	.02	.10
Henry Ellard		
31 Randall Cunningham AT	.01	.05
Keith Jackson		
32 Steve DeBerg AT	.01	.05
Stephone Paige		
33 Warren Moon AT	.02	.10
Drew Hill		
34 Dan Marino AT	.20	.50
Mark Clayton		
35 Joe Montana AT	.20	.50
Jerry Rice		
36 Percy Snow	.01	.05
37 Kelvin Martin	.01	.05
38 Scott Case	.01	.05
39 John Gesek RC	.01	.05
40 Barry Word	.01	.05
41 Cornelius Bennett	.02	.10
42 Mike Kenn	.01	.05
43 Andre Reed	.02	.10
44 Bobby Hebert	.01	.05
45 William Perry	.02	.10
46 Dennis Byrd	.01	.05
47 Martin Mayhew	.01	.05
48 Issiac Holt	.01	.05
49 William White	.01	.05
50 JoJo Townsell	.01	.05
51 Jarvis Williams	.01	.05
52 Joey Browner	.01	.05
53 Pat Terrell	.01	.05
54 Joe Montana UER	.50	1.25
(Born Monongahela,		
not New Eagle)		
55 Jeff Herrod	.01	.05
56 Cris Carter	.20	.50
57 Jerry Rice	.30	.75
58 Brett Perriman	.08	.25
59 Kevin Fagan	.01	.05
60 Wayne Haddix	.01	.05
61 Tommy Kane	.01	.05
62 Pat Beach	.01	.05
63 Jeff Lageman	.01	.05
64 Hassan Jones	.01	.05
65 Bennie Blades	.01	.05
66 Tim McGee	.01	.05
67 Robert Blackmon	.01	.05
68 Fred Stokes RC	.01	.05
69 Barney Bussey RC	.01	.05
70 Eric Metcalf	.02	.10
71 Mark Kelso	.01	.05
72 Neal Anderson TC	.01	.05
73 Boomer Esiason TC	.01	.05
74 Thurman Thomas TC	.08	.25
75 John Elway TC	.20	.50
76 Eric Metcalf TC	.02	.10
77 Vinny Testaverde TC	.02	.10
78 Johnny Johnson TC	.01	.05
79 Anthony Miller TC	.02	.10
80 Derrick Thomas TC	.02	.10
81 Jeff George TC	.02	.10
82 Troy Aikman TC	.15	.40
83 Dan Marino TC	.20	.50
84 Randall Cunningham TC	.02	.10
85 Deion Sanders TC	.01	.05
86 Jerry Rice TC	.15	.40
87 Lawrence Taylor TC	.02	.10
88 Al Toon TC	.01	.05
89 Barry Sanders TC	.20	.50
90 Warren Moon TC	.02	.10
91 Don Majkowski TC	.01	.05
92 Andre Tippett TC	.01	.05
93 Bo Jackson TC	.10	.30
94 Jim Everett TC	.02	.10
95 Art Monk TC	.02	.10
96 Morten Andersen TC	.01	.05
97 John L. Williams TC	.01	.05
98 Rod Woodson TC	.02	.10
99 Herschel Walker TC	.02	.10
100 Checklist 1-100	.01	.05
101 Steve Young	.30	.75
102 Jim Lachey	.01	.05
103 Tom Rathman	.01	.05
104 Earnest Byner	.01	.05
105 Karl Mecklenburg	.01	.05
106 Wes Hopkins	.01	.05
107 Michael Irvin	.08	.25
108 Burt Grossman	.01	.05
109 Jay Novacek UER	.08	.25
(Wearing 82, but card		
says he wears 84)		
110 Ben Smith	.01	.05
111 Rod Woodson	.08	.25
112 Ernie Jones	.01	.05
113 Bryan Hinkle	.01	.05
114 Vai Sikahema	.01	.05
115 Bubby Brister	.01	.05
116 Brian Blades	.02	.10
117 Don Majkowski	.01	.05
118 Rod Bernstine	.01	.05
119 Brian Noble	.01	.05
120 Eugene Robinson	.01	.05
121 John Taylor	.02	.10
122 Vance Johnson	.01	.05
123 Art Monk	.02	.10
124 John Elway	.50	1.25
125 Dexter Carter	.01	.05
126 Anthony Miller	.02	.10
127 Keith Jackson	.02	.10
128 Albert Lewis	.01	.05
129 Billy Ray Smith	.01	.05
130 Clyde Simmons	.01	.05
131 Merril Hoge	.01	.05
132 Ricky Proehl	.01	.05
133 Tim McDonald	.01	.05
134 Louis Lipps	.01	.05
135 Ken Harvey	.02	.10
136 Sterling Sharpe	.02	.10
137 Gill Byrd	.01	.05
138 Tim Harris	.01	.05
139 Derrick Fenner	.01	.05
140 Johnny Holland	.01	.05
141 Ricky Sanders	.01	.05
142 Bobby Humphrey	.01	.05
143 Roger Craig	.02	.10
144 Steve Atwater	.01	.05
145 Ickey Woods	.01	.05
146 Randall Cunningham	.08	.25
147 Marion Butts	.02	.10
148 Reggie White	.08	.25
149 Ronnie Harmon	.01	.05
150 Mike Saxon	.01	.05
151 Greg Townsend	.01	.05
152 Troy Aikman	.30	.75
153 Shane Conlan	.01	.05
154 Deion Sanders	.15	.40
155 Bo Jackson	.10	.30
156 Jeff Hostetler	.02	.10
157 Albert Bentley	.01	.05
158 James Williams	.01	.05
159 Bill Brooks	.01	.05
160 Nick Lowery	.01	.05
161 Ottis Anderson	.02	.10
162 Kevin Greene	.02	.10
163 Neil Smith	.08	.25
164 Jim Everett	.02	.10
165 Derrick Thomas	.08	.25
166 John L. Williams	.01	.05
167 Timm Rosenbach	.01	.05
168 Leslie O'Neal	.02	.10
169 Clarence Verdin	.01	.05
170 Dave Krieg	.02	.10
171 Steve Broussard	.01	.05
172 Emmitt Smith	1.00	2.50
173 Andre Rison	.02	.10
174 Bruce Smith	.08	.25
175 Mark Clayton	.02	.10
176 Christian Okoye	.01	.05
177 Duane Bickett	.01	.05
178 Stephone Paige	.01	.05
179 Fredd Young	.01	.05
180 Mervyn Fernandez	.01	.05
181 Phil Simms	.02	.10
182 Pete Holohan	.01	.05
183 Pepper Johnson	.01	.05
184 Jackie Slater	.01	.05
185 Stephen Baker	.01	.05
186 Frank Cornish	.01	.05
187 Dave Waymer	.01	.05
188 Terance Mathis	.02	.10
189 Darryl Talley	.01	.05
190 James Hasty	.01	.05
191 Jay Schroeder	.01	.05
192 Kenneth Davis	.01	.05
193 Chris Miller	.02	.10
194 Scott Davis	.01	.05
195 Tim Green	.01	.05
196 Dan Saleaumua	.01	.05
197 Rohn Stark	.01	.05
198 John Alt	.01	.05
199 Steve Tasker	.02	.10
200 Checklist 101-200	.01	.05
201 Freddie Joe Nunn	.01	.05
202 Jim Breech	.01	.05
203 Roy Green	.01	.05
204 Gary Anderson RB	.01	.05
205 Rich Camarillo	.01	.05
206 Mark Bortz	.01	.05
207 Eddie Brown	.01	.05
208 Brad Muster	.01	.05
209 Anthony Munoz	.02	.10
210 Dalton Hilliard	.01	.05
211 Erik McMillan	.01	.05
212 Perry Kemp	.01	.05
213 Jim Thornton	.01	.05
214 Anthony Dilweg	.01	.05
215 Cleveland Gary	.01	.05
216 Leo Goeas	.01	.05
217 Mike Merriweather	.01	.05
218 Courtney Hall	.01	.05
219 Wade Wilson	.02	.10
220 Billy Joe Tolliver	.01	.05
221 Harold Green	.02	.10
222 Al(Bubba) Baker	.02	.10
223 Carl Zander	.01	.05
224 Thane Gash	.01	.05
225 Kevin Mack	.01	.05
226 Morten Andersen	.01	.05
227 Dennis Gentry	.01	.05
228 Vince Buck	.01	.05
229 Mike Singletary	.02	.10
230 Rueben Mayes	.01	.05
231 Mark Carrier WR	.08	.25
232 Tony Mandarich	.01	.05
233 Al Toon	.02	.10
234 Renaldo Turnbull	.01	.05
235 Broderick Thomas	.01	.05
236 Anthony Carter	.02	.10
237 Flipper Anderson	.01	.05
238 Jerry Robinson	.01	.05
239 Vince Newsome	.01	.05
240 Keith Millard	.01	.05
241 Reggie Langhorne	.01	.05
242 James Francis	.01	.05
243 Felix Wright	.01	.05
244 Neal Anderson	.02	.10
245 Boomer Esiason	.02	.10
246 Pat Swilling	.02	.10
247 Richard Dent	.02	.10
248 Craig Heyward	.02	.10
249 Ron Morris	.01	.05
250 Eric Martin	.01	.05
251 Jim C. Jensen	.01	.05
252 Anthony Toney	.01	.05
253 Sammie Smith	.01	.05
254 Calvin Williams	.02	.10
255 Dan Marino	.50	1.25
256 Warren Moon	.08	.25
257 Tommie Agee	.01	.05
258 Haywood Jeffires	.02	.10
259 Eugene Lockhart	.01	.05
260 Drew Hill	.01	.05
261 Vinny Testaverde	.02	.10
262 Jim Arnold	.01	.05
263 Steve Christie	.01	.05
264 Chris Spielman	.02	.10
265 Reggie Cobb	.01	.05
266 John Stephens	.01	.05
267 Jay Hilgenberg	.01	.05
268 Brent Williams	.01	.05
269 Rodney Hampton	.08	.25
270 Irving Fryar	.02	.10
271 Terry McDaniel	.01	.05
272 Reggie Roby	.01	.05
273 Allen Pinkett	.01	.05
274 Tim McKyer	.01	.05
275 Bob Golic	.01	.05
276 Wilber Marshall	.01	.05
277 Ray Childress	.01	.05
278 Charles Mann	.01	.05
279 Cris Dishman RC	.01	.05
280 Mark Rypien	.02	.10
281 Michael Cofer	.01	.05
282 Keith Byars	.01	.05
283 Mike Rozier	.01	.05
284 Seth Joyner	.02	.10
285 Jessie Tuggle	.01	.05
286 Mark Bavaro	.01	.05
287 Eddie Anderson	.01	.05
288 Sean Landeta	.01	.05
289 Howie Long	.08	.25
(With George Brett)		
290 Reyna Thompson	.01	.05
291 Ferrell Edmunds	.01	.05
292 Willie Gault	.02	.10
293 John Offerdahl	.01	.05
294 Tim Brown	.08	.25
295 Bruce Matthews	.02	.10
296 Kevin Ross	.01	.05
297 Lorenzo White	.01	.05
298 Dino Hackett	.01	.05
299 Curtis Duncan	.01	.05
300 Checklist 201-300	.01	.05
301 Andre Ware	.02	.10
302 David Little	.01	.05
303 Jerry Ball	.01	.05
304 Dwight Stone UER	.01	.05
(He's a WR; not RB)		
305 Rodney Peete	.02	.10
306 Mike Baab	.01	.05
307 Tim Worley	.01	.05
308 Paul Farren	.01	.05
309 Carnell Lake	.01	.05
310 Clay Matthews	.02	.10
311 Alton Montgomery	.01	.05
312 Ernest Givins	.02	.10
313 Mike Horan	.01	.05
314 Sean Jones	.02	.10
315 Leonard Smith	.01	.05
316 Carl Banks	.01	.05
317 Jerome Brown	.01	.05
318 Everson Walls	.01	.05
319 Ron Heller	.01	.05
320 Mark Collins	.01	.05
321 Eddie Murray	.01	.05
322 Jim Harbaugh	.08	.25
323 Mel Gray	.02	.10
324 Keith Van Horne	.01	.05
325 Lomas Brown	.01	.05
326 Carl Lee	.01	.05
327 Ken O'Brien	.01	.05
328 Dermontti Dawson	.01	.05
329 Brad Baxter	.01	.05
330 Chris Doleman	.01	.05
331 Louis Oliver	.01	.05
332 Frank Stams	.01	.05
333 Mike Munchak	.02	.10
334 Fred Strickland	.01	.05
335 Mark Duper	.02	.10
336 Jacob Green	.01	.05
337 Tony Paige	.01	.05
338 Jeff Bryant	.01	.05
339 Lemuel Stinson	.01	.05
340 David Wyman	.01	.05
341 Lee Williams	.01	.05
342 Trace Armstrong	.01	.05
343 Junior Seau	.08	.25
344 John Roper	.01	.05
345 Jeff George	.08	.25
346 Herschel Walker	.02	.10
347 Sam Clancy	.01	.05
348 Steve Jordan	.01	.05
349 Nate Odomes	.01	.05
350 Martin Bayless	.01	.05
351 Brent Jones	.08	.25
352 Ray Agnew	.01	.05
353 Charles Haley	.02	.10
354 Andre Tippett	.01	.05
355 Ronnie Lott	.02	.10
356 Thurman Thomas	.08	.25
357 Fred Barnett	.08	.25
358 James Lofton	.02	.10
359 William Frizzell RC	.01	.05
360 Keith McKeller	.01	.05
361 Rodney Holman	.01	.05
362 Henry Ellard	.02	.10
363 David Fulcher	.01	.05
364 Jerry Gray	.01	.05
365 James Brooks	.02	.10
366 Tony Stargell	.01	.05
367 Keith McCants	.01	.05
368 Lewis Billups	.01	.05
369 Ervin Randle	.01	.05
370 Pat Leahy	.01	.05
371 Bruce Armstrong	.01	.05
372 Steve DeBerg	.01	.05
373 Guy McIntyre	.01	.05
374 Deron Cherry	.01	.05

375 Fred Marion .01 .05
376 Michael Haddix .01 .05
377 Kent Hull .01 .05
378 Jerry Holmes .01 .05
379 Jim Ritcher .01 .05
380 Ed West .01 .05
381 Richmond Webb .01 .05
382 Mark Jackson .01 .05
383 Tom Newberry .01 .05
384 Ricky Nattiel .01 .05
385 Keith Sims .01 .05
386 Ron Hall .01 .05
387 Ken Norton .02 .10
388 Paul Gruber .01 .05
389 Daniel Stubbs .01 .05
390 Ian Beckles .01 .05
391 Hoby Brenner .01 .05
392 Tory Epps .01 .05
393 Sam Mills .01 .05
394 Chris Hinton .01 .05
395 Steve Walsh .01 .05
396 Simon Fletcher .01 .05
397 Tony Bennett .02 .10
398 Aundray Bruce .01 .05
399 Mark Murphy .01 .05
400 Checklist 301-400 .01 .05
401 Barry Sanders SL .20 .50
402 Jerry Rice LL .15 .40
403 Warren Moon LL .02 .10
404 Derrick Thomas LL .02 .10
405 Nick Lowery LL .01 .05
406 Mark Carrier DB LL .02 .10
407 Michael Carter .01 .05
408 Chris Singleton .01 .05
409 Matt Millen .02 .10
410 Ronnie Lippett .01 .05
411 E.J. Junior .01 .05
412 Ray Donaldson .01 .05
413 Keith Willis .01 .05
414 Jessie Hester .01 .05
415 Jeff Cross .01 .05
416 Greg Jackson RC .01 .05
417 Alvin Walton .01 .05
418 Bart Oates .01 .05
419 Chip Lohmiller .01 .05
420 John Elliott .01 .05
421 Randall McDaniel .02 .10
422 Richard Johnson RC .01 .05
423 Al Noga .01 .05
424 Lamar Lathon .01 .05
425 Rick Fenney .01 .05
426 Jack Del Rio .02 .10
427 Don Mosebar .01 .05
428 Luis Sharpe .01 .05
429 Steve Wisniewski .01 .05
430 Jimmie Jones .01 .05
431 Freeman McNeil .01 .05
432 Ron Rivera .01 .05
433 Hart Lee Dykes .01 .05
434 Mark Carrier DB .02 .10
435 Rob Moore .08 .25
436 Gary Clark .08 .25
437 Heath Sherman .01 .05
438 Darrell Green .01 .05
439 Jessie Small .01 .05
440 Monte Coleman .01 .05
441 Leonard Marshall .01 .05
442 Richard Johnson .01 .05
443 Dave Meggett .02 .10
444 Barry Sanders .50 1.25
445 Lawrence Taylor .08 .25
446 Marcus Allen .08 .25
447 Johnny Johnson .01 .05
448 Aaron Wallace .01 .05
449 Anthony Thompson .01 .05
450 Steve DeBerg .15 .40
Dan Marino
Team MVP CL 453-473
451 Andre Rison MVP .02 .10
452 Thurman Thomas MVP .02 .10
453 Neal Anderson MVP .01 .05
454 Boomer Esiason MVP .01 .05
455 Eric Metcalf MVP .02 .10
456 Emmitt Smith TM .50 1.25
457 Bobby Humphrey MVP .01 .05
458 Barry Sanders TM .20 .50
459 Sterling Sharpe MVP .02 .10
460 Warren Moon MVP .02 .10
461 Albert Bentley MVP .01 .05
462 Steve DeBerg MVP .01 .05
463 Greg Townsend MVP .01 .05
464 Henry Ellard MVP .02 .10
465 Dan Marino MVP .20 .50
466 Anthony Carter MVP .02 .10
467 John Stephens MVP .01 .05
468 Pat Swilling MVP .01 .05
469 Ottis Anderson MVP .02 .10
470 Dennis Byrd MVP .01 .05
471 Randall Cunningham MVP .02 .10
472 Johnny Johnson MVP .01 .05
473 Rod Woodson MVP .02 .10
474 Anthony Miller MVP .02 .10
475 Jerry Rice MVP .15 .40
476 John L.Williams MVP .01 .05
477 Wayne Haddix MVP .01 .05
478 Earnest Byner MVP .01 .05
479 Doug Widell .01 .05
480 Tommy Hodson .01 .05
481 Shawn Collins .01 .05
482 Rickey Jackson .01 .05
483 Tony Casillas .01 .05
484 Vaughan Johnson .01 .05
485 Floyd Dixon .01 .05
486 Eric Green .01 .05
487 Harry Hamilton .01 .05
488 Gary Anderson K .01 .05
489 Bruce Hill .01 .05
490 Gerald Williams .01 .05
491 Cortez Kennedy .08 .25
492 Chet Brooks .01 .05
493 Dwayne Harper RC .01 .05
494 Don Griffin .01 .05
495 Andy Heck .01 .05
496 David Treadwell .01 .05
497 Irv Pankey .01 .05
498 Dennis Smith .01 .05
499 Marcus Dupree .08 .25
500 Checklist 401-500 .01 .05
501 Wendell Davis .01 .05
502 Matt Bahr .01 .05
503 Rob Burnett RC .02 .10
504 Maurice Carthon .01 .05
505 Donnell Woolford .01 .05
506 Howard Ballard .01 .05
507 Mark Boyer .01 .05
508 Eugene Marve .01 .05
509 Joe Kelly .01 .05
510 Will Wolford .01 .05
511 Robert Clark .01 .05
512 Matt Brock RC .01 .05
513 Chris Warren .08 .25
514 Ken Willis .01 .05
515 George Jamison RC .01 .05
516 Rufus Porter .01 .05
517 Mark Higgs RC .01 .05
518 Thomas Everett .01 .05
519 Robert Brown .01 .05
520 Gene Atkins .01 .05
521 Hardy Nickerson .02 .10
522 Johnny Bailey .01 .05
523 William Frizzell .01 .05
524 Steve McMichael .02 .10
525 Kevin Porter .01 .05
526 Carwell Gardner .01 .05
527 Eugene Daniel .01 .05
528 Vestee Jackson .01 .05
529 Chris Goode .01 .05
530 Leon Seals .01 .05
531 Darion Conner .01 .05
532 Stan Brock .01 .05
533 Kirby Jackson RC .01 .05
534 Marv Cook .01 .05
535 Bill Fralic .01 .05
536 Keith Woodside .01 .05
537 Hugh Green .01 .05
538 Grant Feasel .01 .05
539 Bubba McDowell .01 .05
540 Vai Sikahema .01 .05
541 Aaron Cox .01 .05
542 Roger Craig .02 .10
543 Robb Thomas .01 .05
544 Ronnie Lott .02 .10
545 Robert Delpino .01 .05
546 Greg McMurtry .01 .05
547 Jim Morrissey RC .01 .05
548 Johnny Rembert .01 .05
549 Markus Paul RC .01 .05
550 Karl Wilson RC .01 .05
551 Gaston Green .01 .05
552 Willie Drewrey .01 .05
553 Michael Young .01 .05
554 Tom Tupa .01 .05
555 John Friesz .08 .25
556 Cody Carlson RC .01 .05
557 Eric Allen .01 .05
558 Thomas Benson .01 .05
559 Scott Mersereau RC .01 .05
560 Lionel Washington .01 .05
561 Brian Brennan .01 .05
562 Jim Jeffcoat .01 .05
563 Jeff Jaeger .01 .05
564 D.J. Johnson .01 .05
565 Danny Villa .01 .05
566 Don Beebe .01 .05
567 Michael Haynes .08 .25
568 Brett Faryniarz RC .01 .05
569 Mike Prior .01 .05
570 John Davis RC .01 .05
571 Vernon Turner RC .01 .05
572 Michael Brooks .01 .05
573 Mike Gann .01 .05
574 Ron Holmes .01 .05
575 Gary Plummer .01 .05
576 Bill Romanowski .01 .05
577 Chris Jacke .01 .05
578 Gary Reasons .01 .05
579 Tim Jorden RC .01 .05
580 Tim McKyer .01 .05
581 Johnnie Jackson RC .01 .05
582 Ethan Horton .01 .05
583 Pete Stoyanovich .01 .05
584 Jeff Query .01 .05
585 Frank Reich .02 .10
586 Riki Ellison .01 .05
587 Eric Hill .01 .05
588 Anthony Shelton RC .01 .05
589 Steve Smith .01 .05
590 Garth Jax RC .01 .05
591 Greg Davis RC .01 .05
592 Bill Maas .01 .05
593 Henry Rolling RC .01 .05
594 Keith Jones .01 .05
595 Tootie Robbins .01 .05
596 Brian Jordan .02 .10
597 Derrick Walker RC .01 .05
598 Jonathan Hayes .01 .05
599 Nate Lewis RC .01 .05
600 Checklist 501-600 .01 .05
601 AFC Checklist RF .01 .05
Mike Croel
Greg Lewis
Keith Traylor
Kenny Walker
602 James Jones RC .01 .05
603 Tim Barnett RC .01 .05
604 Ed King RC .01 .05
605 Shane Curry RF .01 .05
606 Mike Croel RF .01 .05
607 Bryan Cox RC .08 .25
608 Shawn Jefferson RC .02 .10
609 Kenny Walker RC .01 .05
610 Michael Jackson WR RC .08 .25
611 Jon Vaughn RC .01 .05
612 Greg Lewis RF .01 .05
613 Joe Valerio RC .01 .05
614 Pat Harlow RF RC .01 .05
615 Henry Jones RC .02 .10
616 Jeff Graham RC .08 .25
617 Darryll Lewis RF RC .02 .10
618 Keith Traylor RF RC UER .01 .05
(Bronchos on back)
619 Scott Miller RF .01 .05
620 Nick Bell RF .01 .05
621 John Flannery RC .01 .05
622 Leonard Russell RC .02 .10
623 Alfred Williams RF RC .01 .05
624 Browning Nagle RF .01 .05
625 Harvey Williams RF .02 .10
626 Dan McGwire RF .01 .05
627 Favre .20 .50
Pritchard
Pegram CL
628 William Thomas RC .01 .05
629 Lawrence Dawsey RC .02 .10
630 Aeneas Williams RF RC .08 .25
631 Stan Thomas RF .01 .05
632 Randal Hill RF .01 .05
633 Moe Gardner RC .01 .05
634 Alvin Harper RF .02 .10
635 Esera Tuaolo RF RC .01 .05
636 Russell Maryland RF .02 .10
637 Anthony Morgan RC .01 .05
638 Erric Pegram RC .08 .25
639 Herman Moore RF .08 .25
640 Ricky Ervins RC .02 .10
641 Kelvin Pritchett RF RC .02 .10
642 Roman Phifer RC .01 .05
643 Antone Davis RC .01 .05
644 Mike Pritchard RF .02 .10
645 Vinnie Clark RC .01 .05
646 Jake Reed RC .20 .50
647 Brett Favre 1.50 4.00
648 Todd Lyght RF .01 .05
649 Bruce Pickens RF .01 .05
650 Darren Lewis RC .01 .05
651 Wesley Carroll RF .01 .05
652 James Joseph RC .02 .10
653 Robert Delpino AR .01 .05
Tim McDonald
654 Vencie Glenn AR .01 .05
Deion Sanders
655 Jerry Rice AR .10 .30
Terry McDaniel
656 Barry Sanders AR .20 .50
Derrick Thomas
657 Ken Tippins AR .01 .05
Lorenzo White
658 Christian Okoye AR .01 .05
Jacob Green
659 Rich Gannon .08 .25
660 Johnny Meads .01 .05
661 J.J. Birden RC .02 .10
662 Bruce Kozerski .01 .05
663 Felix Wright .01 .05
664 Al Smith .01 .05
665 Stan Humphries .08 .25
666 Alfred Anderson .01 .05
667 Nate Newton .02 .10
668 Vince Workman RC .02 .10
669 Ricky Reynolds .01 .05
670 Bryce Paup RC .08 .25
671 Gill Fenerty .01 .05
672 Darrell Thompson .01 .05
673 Anthony Smith .01 .05
674 Darryl Henley RC .01 .05
675 Brett Maxie .01 .05
676 Craig Taylor RC .01 .05
677 Steve Wallace .02 .10
678 Jeff Feagles RC .01 .05
679 James Washington RC .01 .05
680 Tim Harris .01 .05
681 Dennis Gibson .01 .05
682 Toi Cook RC .01 .05
683 Lorenzo Lynch .01 .05
684 Brad Edwards RC .01 .05
685 Ray Crockett RC .01 .05
686 Harris Barton .01 .05
687 Byron Evans .01 .05
688 Eric Thomas .01 .05
689 Jeff Criswell .01 .05
690 Eric Ball .01 .05
691 Brian Mitchell .02 .10
692 Quinn Early .02 .10
693 Aaron Jones .01 .05
694 Jim Dombrowski .01 .05
695 Jeff Bostic .01 .05
696 Tony Casillas .01 .05
697 Ken Lanier .01 .05
698 Henry Thomas .01 .05
699 Steve Beuerlein .02 .10
700 Checklist 601-700 .01 .05
1P Joe Montana Promo 1.00 2.50
Numbered 1
500P Barry Sanders Promo .75 2.00
Numbered 500 on back
SP1 Darrell Green .20 .50
(NFL's Fastest Man
SP2 Don Shula CO/300th Victory .75 2.00

1991 Upper Deck Game Breaker Holograms

COMPLETE SET (9) 3.00 8.00
GB1 Barry Sanders 1.00 2.50
GB2 Thurman Thomas .20 .50
GB3 Bobby Humphrey .07 .20
GB4 Earnest Byner .07 .20
GB5 Emmitt Smith 2.00 5.00
GB6 Neal Anderson .10 .30
GB7 Marion Butts .10 .30
GB8 James Brooks .10 .30
GB9 Marcus Allen .20 .50

1991 Upper Deck Joe Montana Heroes

COMPLETE SET (10) 4.00 10.00
COMMON MONTANA (1-9) .30 .75
RANDOM INSERTS IN LO SERIES
AU Joe Montana AUTO 40.00 100.00
(Certified Autograph)
NNO Title 4.00 8.00
Header Card SP

1991 Upper Deck Heroes Montana Box Bottoms

These eight oversized "cards" (approximately 5 1/4" by 7 1/4") were featured on the bottom of 1991 Upper Deck low series wax boxes. They are identical in design to the Montana Football Heroes insert cards, with the same color player photos in an oval frame. The backs are blank and the cards are unnumbered. We have checklisted them below according to their Heroes card numbering.

COMPLETE SET (8) 2.40 6.00
COMMON CARD (1-8) .40 1.00

1991 Upper Deck Joe Namath Heroes

COMPLETE SET (10) 4.00 10.00
COMMON NAMATH (10-18) .30 .75
RANDOM INSERTS IN HI SERIES
AU Joe Namath AUTO 60.00 120.00
(Certified Autograph)
NNO Title 4.00 8.00
Header Card SP

1991 Upper Deck Heroes Namath Box Bottoms

These eight oversized "cards" (approximately 5 1/4" by 7 1/4") were featured on the bottom of 1991 Upper Deck high series wax boxes. They are identical in design to the Namath Football Heroes insert cards, with the same color player photos in an oval frame. The backs are blank and the cards are unnumbered. We have checklisted them below according to the numbering of the Heroes cards.

COMPLETE SET (8) 2.40 6.00
COMMON CARD (10-17) .40 1.00

1991 Upper Deck Sheets

Upper Deck issued two football sheets in 1991. The 8 1/2" by 11" sheet to honor the Super Bowl XXV Champions features six Upper Deck Giants cards, which are listed as they appear counterclockwise beginning from the upper left corner. The background is a green football field design. At the top are the words, "Washington Redskins vs. New York Giants" and "The Upper Deck Company Salutes The Super Bowl XXV Champions" in yellow lettering. In the center are game highlights in red lettering. The sheet is bordered by two blue and one red stripe. The issue date appears in the lower right corner as do the production run and issue number, which appear in the Upper Deck gold foil stamp. The Rams sheet commemorated the 40th anniversary of the 1951 Rams championship team. 60,000 numbered Ram sheets were distributed. The backs of both sheets are blank.

COMPLETE SET (2) 4.00 10.00
1 Los Angeles Rams 2.00 5.00
Commemorative Sheet
October 1991 (60,000)
2 New York Giants 2.00 5.00
vs. Washington Redskins
October 27, 1991
(SB XXV Champions (72,000)
Rodney Hampton
Lawrence Taylor
Dave Meggett
Jeff Hostetler
Mark Collins
Ottis Anderson

1992 Upper Deck

The 1992 Upper Deck football set was issued in two series and totaled 620 standard-size cards. No low series cards were included in this year's second series packs. First series packs featured the following random insert sets: a ten-card Walter Payton "Football Heroes"; a 15-card Pro Bowl; and five Game Breaker holograms (GB1, GB3, GB4, GB6, and GB8). Randomly inserted throughout series II foil packs were a ten-card Dan Marino "Football Heroes" subset, special cards of James Lofton (SP3) and Art Monk (SP4), and three Game Breaker holograms (GB2, GB5, and GB7). A 20-card "Coach's Report" insert set was featured only in hobby packs while ten "Fanimation" cards were included only in retail packs. Members of both NFL Properties and the NFL Players Association are included in the second series.

COMPLETE SET (620) 6.00 15.00
COMP.SERIES 1 (400) 4.00 10.00
COMP.SERIES 2 (220) 2.50 5.00
1 Star Rookie Checklist .02 .10
Edgar Bennett
Terrell Buckley
Dexter McNabb
2 Edgar Bennett RC .08 .25
3 Eddie Blake RC .01 .05
4 Brian Bollinger RC .01 .05
5 Joe Bowden RC .01 .05
6 Terrell Buckley RC .01 .05
7 Willie Clay RC .01 .05
8 Ed Cunningham RC .01 .05
9 Matt Darby RC .01 .05
10 Will Furrer RC .01 .05
11 Chris Hakel RC .01 .05
12 Carlos Huerta .01 .05
13 Amp Lee RC .01 .05
14 Ricardo McDonald RC .01 .05
15 Dexter McNabb RC .01 .05
16 Chris Mims RC .01 .05
17 Derrick Moore RC .02 .10
18 Mark D'Onofrio RC .01 .05
19 Patrick Rowe RC .01 .05
20 Leon Searcy RC .01 .05
21 Torrance Small RC .02 .10
22 Jimmy Smith RC 1.25 3.00
23 Tony Smith WR RC .01 .05
24 Siran Stacy RC .01 .05
25 Kevin Turner RC .01 .05
26 Tommy Vardell RC .01 .05
27 Bob Whitfield RC .01 .05
28 Darryl Williams RC .01 .05
29 Jeff Sydner RC .01 .05
30 All-Rookie Checklist .01 .05
Mike Croel
Leonard Russell
31 Todd Marinovich AR .01 .05
32 Leonard Russell AR .01 .05
33 Nick Bell AR .01 .05
34 Alvin Harper AR .01 .05
35 Mike Pritchard AR .01 .05
36 Lawrence Dawsey AR .01 .05
37 Tim Barnett AR .01 .05
38 John Flannery AR .01 .05
39 Stan Thomas AR .01 .05
40 Ed King AR .01 .05
41 Charles McRae AR .01 .05
42 Eric Moten AR .01 .05
43 Moe Gardner AR .01 .05
44 Kenny Walker AR .01 .05
45 Esera Tuaolo AR .01 .05
46 Alfred Williams AR .01 .05
47 Bryan Cox AR .01 .05
48 Mo Lewis AR .01 .05
49 Mike Croel AR .01 .05
50 Stanley Richard AR .01 .05
51 Tony Covington AR .01 .05
52 Larry Brown DB AR .01 .05
53 Aeneas Williams AR .01 .05
54 John Kasay AR .01 .05
55 Jon Vaughn AR .01 .05
56 David Fulcher .01 .05
57 Barry Foster .02 .10
58 Terry Wooden .01 .05
59 Gary Anderson K .01 .05
60 Alfred Williams .01 .05
61 Robert Blackmon .01 .05
62 Brian Noble .01 .05
63 Terry Allen .08 .25
64 Darrell Green .01 .05
65 Darren Comeaux .01 .05
66 Rob Burnett .01 .05
67 Jarrod Bunch .01 .05
68 Michael Jackson .02 .10
69 Greg Lloyd .02 .10
70 Richard Brown RC .01 .05
71 Harold Green .01 .05
72 William Fuller .01 .05
73 Mark Carrier DB TC .01 .05
74 David Fulcher TC .01 .05
75 Cornelius Bennett TC .01 .05
76 Steve Atwater TC .01 .05
77 Kevin Mack TC .01 .05
78 Mark Carrier WR TC .01 .05
79 Tim McDonald TC .01 .05
80 Marion Butts TC .01 .05
81 Christian Okoye TC .01 .05
82 Jeff Herrod TC .01 .05
83 Emmitt Smith TC .25 .60
84 Mark Duper TC .01 .05
85 Keith Jackson TC .01 .05
86 Andre Rison TC .02 .10
87 John Taylor TC .01 .05
88 Rodney Hampton TC .02 .10
89 Rob Moore TC .01 .05
90 Chris Spielman TC .01 .05
91 Haywood Jeffires TC .01 .05
92 Sterling Sharpe TC .02 .10
93 Irving Fryar TC .01 .05
94 Marcus Allen TC .02 .10
95 Henry Ellard TC .01 .05
96 Mark Rypien TC .01 .05
97 Pat Swilling TC .01 .05
98 Brian Blades TC .01 .05
99 Eric Green TC .01 .05
100 Anthony Carter TC .01 .05
101 Burt Grossman .01 .05
102 Gary Anderson RB .01 .05
103 Neil Smith .08 .25
104 Jeff Feagles .01 .05
105 Shane Conlan .01 .05
106 Jay Novacek .02 .10
107 Bill Brooks .01 .05
108 Mark Ingram .01 .05
109 Anthony Munoz .02 .10
110 Wendell Davis .01 .05
111 Jim Everett .02 .10
112 Bruce Matthews .01 .05
113 Mark Higgs .01 .05
114 Chris Warren .02 .10
115 Brad Baxter .01 .05
116 Greg Townsend .01 .05
117 Al Smith .01 .05
118 Jeff Cross .01 .05
119 Terry McDaniel .01 .05
120 Ernest Givins .02 .10
121 Fred Barnett .02 .10
122 Flipper Anderson .01 .05
123 Floyd Turner .01 .05
124 Stephen Baker .01 .05
125 Tim Johnson .01 .05
126 Brent Jones .02 .10
127 Leonard Marshall .01 .05
128 Jim Price .01 .05
129 Jessie Hester .01 .05
130 Mark Carrier WR .02 .10
131 Bubba McDowell .01 .05
132 Andre Tippett .01 .05
133 James Hasty .01 .05
134 Mel Gray .02 .10
135 Christian Okoye .01 .05
136 Earnest Byner .01 .05
137 Ferrell Edmunds .01 .05
138 Henry Ellard .02 .10
139 Rob Moore .02 .10
140 Brian Jordan .02 .10
141 Clarence Verdin .01 .05
142 Cornelius Bennett .02 .10
143 John Taylor .02 .10
144 Derrick Thomas .08 .25
145 Thurman Thomas .08 .25
146 Warren Moon .08 .25
147 Vinny Testaverde .02 .10
148 Steve Bono RC .08 .25
149 Robb Thomas .01 .05
150 John Friesz .02 .10
151 Richard Dent .02 .10
152 Eddie Anderson .01 .05
153 Kevin Greene .02 .10
154 Marion Butts .01 .05
155 Barry Sanders .50 1.25
156 Andre Rison .02 .10
157 Ronnie Lott .02 .10
158 Eric Allen .01 .05
159 Mark Clayton .02 .10
160 Terance Mathis .02 .10
161 Darryl Talley .01 .05
162 Eric Metcalf .02 .10
163 Reggie Cobb .01 .05
164 Ernie Jones .01 .05
165 David Griggs .01 .05
166 Tom Rathman .01 .05
167 Bubby Brister .02 .10
168 Broderick Thomas .01 .05
169 Chris Doleman .01 .05
170 Charles Haley .02 .10
171 Michael Haynes .02 .10
172 Rodney Hampton .02 .10
173 Nick Bell .01 .05
174 Gene Atkins .01 .05
175 Mike Merriweather .01 .05
176 Reggie Roby .01 .05
177 Bennie Blades .01 .05
178 John L. Williams .01 .05
179 Rodney Peete .02 .10
180 Greg Montgomery .01 .05
181 Vince Newsome .01 .05
182 Andre Collins .01 .05
183 Erik Kramer .02 .10
184 Bryan Hinkle .01 .05
185 Reggie White .08 .25
186 Bruce Armstrong .01 .05
187 Anthony Carter .02 .10
188 Pat Swilling .01 .05
189 Robert Delpino .01 .05
190 Brent Williams .01 .05
191 Johnny Johnson .01 .05
192 Aaron Craver .01 .05
193 Vincent Brown .01 .05
194 Herschel Walker .02 .10
195 Tim McDonald .01 .05
196 Gaston Green .01 .05
197 Brian Blades .02 .10
198 Rod Bernstine .01 .05
199 Brett Perriman .02 .10
200 John Elway .50 1.25
201 Michael Carter .01 .05
202 Mark Carrier DB .01 .05
203 Cris Carter .20 .50
204 Kyle Clifton .01 .05
205 Alvin Wright .01 .05
206 Andre Ware .01 .05
207 Dave Waymer .01 .05
208 Darren Lewis .01 .05
209 Joey Browner .01 .05
210 Rich Miano .01 .05
211 Marcus Allen .08 .25
212 Steve Broussard .01 .05
213 Joel Hilgenberg .01 .05
214 Bo Orlando RC .01 .05
215 Clay Matthews .02 .10
216 Chris Hinton .01 .05
217 Al Edwards .01 .05
218 Tim Brown .08 .25
219 Sam Mills .01 .05
220 Don Majkowski .01 .05
221 James Francis .01 .05
222 Steve Hendrickson RC .01 .05
223 James Thornton .01 .05
224 Byron Evans .01 .05
225 Pepper Johnson .01 .05
226 Darryl Henley .01 .05
227 Simon Fletcher .01 .05
228 Hugh Millen .01 .05
229 Tim McGee .01 .05
230 Richmond Webb .01 .05
231 Tony Bennett .01 .05
232 Nate Odomes .01 .05
233 Scott Case .01 .05
234 Dalton Hilliard .01 .05
235 Paul Gruber .01 .05
236 Jeff Lageman .01 .05
237 Tony Mandarich .01 .05
238 Cris Dishman .01 .05
239 Steve Walsh .01 .05
240 Moe Gardner .01 .05
241 Bill Romanowski .01 .05
242 Chris Zorich .02 .10
243 Stephone Paige .01 .05
244 Mike Croel .01 .05
245 Leonard Russell .02 .10
246 Mark Rypien .01 .05
247 Aeneas Williams .02 .10
248 Steve Atwater .01 .05
249 Michael Stewart .01 .05
250 Pierce Holt .01 .05
251 Kevin Mack .01 .05
252 Sterling Sharpe .08 .25
253 Lawrence Dawsey .02 .10
254 Emmitt Smith .60 1.50
255 Todd Marinovich .01 .05
256 Neal Anderson .01 .05
257 Mo Lewis .01 .05
258 Vance Johnson .01 .05
259 Rickey Jackson .01 .05
260 Esera Tuaolo .01 .05
261 Wilber Marshall .01 .05
262 Keith Henderson .01 .05
263 William Thomas .01 .05
264 Rickey Dixon .01 .05
265 Dave Meggett .02 .10
266 Gerald Riggs .01 .05
267 Tim Harris .01 .05
268 Ken Harvey .01 .05
269 Clyde Simmons .01 .05
270 Irving Fryar .02 .10
271 Darion Conner .01 .05
272 Vince Workman .01 .05
273 Jim Harbaugh .08 .25
274 Lorenzo White .01 .05
275 Bobby Hebert .01 .05
276 Duane Bickett .01 .05
277 Jeff Bryant .01 .05
278 Scott Stephen .01 .05
279 Bob Golic .01 .05
280 Steve McMichael .02 .10
281 Jeff Graham .08 .25
282 Keith Jackson .02 .10
283 Howard Ballard .01 .05
284 Michael Brooks .01 .05
285 Freeman McNeil .02 .10
286 Rodney Holman .01 .05
287 Eric Bieniemy .01 .05
288 Seth Joyner .01 .05
289 Carwell Gardner .01 .05
290 Brian Mitchell .02 .10
291 Chris Miller .02 .10
292 Ray Berry .01 .05
293 Matt Brock .01 .05
294 Eric Thomas .01 .05
295 John Kasay .01 .05
296 Jay Hilgenberg .01 .05
297 Darrell Thompson .01 .05
298 Rich Gannon .08 .25
299 Steve Young .25 .60
300 Mike Kenn .01 .05
301 Emmitt Smith SL .25 .60
302 Haywood Jeffires SL .01 .05
303 Michael Irvin SL .08 .25
304 Warren Moon SL .02 .10
305 Chip Lohmiller SL .01 .05
306 Barry Sanders SL .20 .50
307 Ronnie Lott SL .02 .10
308 Pat Swilling SL .01 .05
309 Thurman Thomas SL .02 .10
310 Reggie Roby SL .01 .05
311 Season Leader CL .02 .10
Warren Moon
Michael Irvin
Thurman Thomas
312 Jacob Green .01 .05
313 Stephen Braggs .01 .05
314 Haywood Jeffires .02 .10
315 Freddie Joe Nunn .01 .05
316 Gary Clark .02 .10
317 Tim Barnett .01 .05
318 Mark Duper .01 .05
319 Eric Green .01 .05
320 Robert Wilson .01 .05
321 Michael Ball .01 .05
322 Eric Martin .01 .05
323 Alexander Wright .01 .05
324 Jessie Tuggle .01 .05
325 Ronnie Harmon .01 .05
326 Jeff Hostetler .02 .10
327 Eugene Daniel .01 .05
328 Ken Norton Jr. .02 .10
329 Reyna Thompson .01 .05
330 Jerry Ball .01 .05
331 Leroy Hoard .02 .10
332 Chris Martin .01 .05
333 Keith McKeller .01 .05
334 Brian Washington .01 .05
335 Eugene Robinson .01 .05
336 Maurice Hurst .01 .05
337 Dan Saleaumua .01 .05
338 Neil O'Donnell .02 .10
339 Dexter Davis .01 .05
340 Keith McCants .01 .05
341 Steve Beuerlein .02 .10
342 Roman Phifer .01 .05
343 Bryan Cox .02 .10
344 Art Monk .02 .10
345 Michael Irvin .08 .25
346 Vaughan Johnson .01 .05
347 Jeff Herrod .01 .05
348 Stanley Richard .01 .05
349 Michael Young .01 .05
350 Team MVP Checklist .02 .10
Rodney Hampton
Reggie Cobb
351 Jim Harbaugh MVP .02 .10
352 David Fulcher MVP .01 .05
353 Thurman Thomas MVP .02 .10
354 Gaston Green MVP .01 .05
355 Leroy Hoard MVP .01 .05
356 Reggie Cobb MVP .01 .05
357 Tim McDonald MVP .01 .05
358 R.Harmon MVP UER .01 .05
Bernstine misspelled
as Bernstein
359 Derrick Thomas MVP .02 .10
360 Jeff Herrod MVP .01 .05
361 Michael Irvin MVP .08 .25
362 Mark Higgs MVP .01 .05
363 Reggie White MVP .02 .10
364 Chris Miller MVP .01 .05
365 Steve Young MVP .10 .30
366 Rodney Hampton MVP .02 .10
367 Jeff Lageman MVP .01 .05
368 Barry Sanders MVP .20 .50
369 Haywood Jeffires MVP .01 .05
370 Tony Bennett MVP .01 .05
371 Leonard Russell MVP .01 .05
372 Jeff Jaeger MVP .01 .05
373 Robert Delpino MVP .01 .05
374 Mark Rypien MVP .01 .05
375 Pat Swilling MVP .01 .05
376 Cortez Kennedy MVP .02 .10
377 Eric Green MVP .01 .05
378 Cris Carter MVP .02 .10
379 John Roper .01 .05
380 Barry Word .01 .05
381 Shawn Jefferson .01 .05
382 Tony Casillas .01 .05
383 John Baylor RC .01 .05
384 Al Noga .01 .05
385 Charles Mann .01 .05
386 Gill Byrd .01 .05
387 Chris Singleton .01 .05
388 James Joseph .01 .05
389 Larry Brown DB .01 .05
390 Chris Spielman .02 .10
391 Anthony Thompson .01 .05
392 Karl Mecklenburg .01 .05
393 Joe Kelly .01 .05
394 Kanavis McGhee .01 .05
395 Bill Maas .01 .05
396 Marv Cook .01 .05
397 Louis Lipps .01 .05
398 Marty Carter RC .01 .05
399 Louis Oliver .01 .05
400 Eric Swann .02 .10
401 Troy Auzenne RC .01 .05
402 Kurt Barber .01 .05
403 Marc Boutte RC .01 .05
404 Dale Carter .02 .10
405 Marco Coleman .01 .05
406 Quentin Coryatt .01 .05
407 Shane Dronett RC .01 .05
408 Vaughn Dunbar .01 .05
409 Steve Emtman .01 .05
410 Dana Hall RC .01 .05
411 Jason Hansen RC .02 .10
412 Courtney Hawkins RC .02 .10
413 Terrell Buckley .01 .05
414 Robert Jones RC .01 .05
415 David Klingler .01 .05
416 Tommy Maddox .60 1.50
417 Johnny Mitchell RC .01 .05
418 Carl Pickens .02 .10
419 Tracy Scroggins .01 .05
420 Tony Sacca RC .01 .05
421 Kevin Smith .01 .05
422 Alonzo Spellman .02 .10
423 Troy Vincent RC .01 .05
424 Sean Gilbert RC .02 .10
425 Larry Webster RC .01 .05
426 Rookie Force Checklist .02 .10
Carl Pickens
David Klingler
427 Bill Fralic .01 .05
428 Kevin Murphy .01 .05
429 Lemuel Stinson .01 .05
430 Harris Barton .01 .05
431 Dino Hackett .01 .05
432 John Stephens .01 .05
433 Keith Jennings RC .01 .05
434 Derrick Fenner .01 .05
435 Kenneth Gant RC .01 .05
436 Willie Gault .02 .10
437 Steve Jordan .01 .05
438 Charles Haley .02 .10
439 Keith Kartz .01 .05
440 Nate Lewis .01 .05
441 Doug Widell .01 .05
442 William White .01 .05
443 Eric Hill .01 .05
444 Melvin Jenkins .01 .05
445 David Wyman .01 .05
446 Ed West .01 .05
447 Brad Muster .01 .05
448 Ray Childress .01 .05
449 Kevin Ross .01 .05
450 Johnnie Jackson .01 .05
451 Tracy Simien RC .01 .05
452 Don Mosebar .01 .05
453 Jay Hilgenberg .01 .05
454 Wes Hopkins .01 .05
455 Jay Schroeder .01 .05
456 Jeff Bostic .01 .05
457 Bryce Paup .08 .25
458 Dave Waymer .01 .05
459 Toi Cook .01 .05
460 Anthony Smith .01 .05
461 Don Griffin .01 .05
462 Bill Hawkins .01 .05
463 Courtney Hall .01 .05
464 Jeff Uhlenhake .01 .05
465 Mike Sherrard .01 .05
466 James Jones .01 .05
467 Jerrol Williams .01 .05
468 Eric Ball .01 .05
469 Randall McDaniel .02 .10
470 Alvin Harper .02 .10
471 Tom Waddle .01 .05
472 Tony Woods .01 .05
473 Kelvin Martin .01 .05
474 Jon Vaughn .01 .05
475 Gill Fenerty .01 .05
476 Aundray Bruce .01 .05
477 Morten Andersen .01 .05
478 Lamar Lathon .01 .05
479 Steve DeOssie .01 .05
480 Marvin Washington .01 .05
481 Herschel Walker .02 .10
482 Howie Long .08 .25
483 Calvin Williams .02 .10
484 Brett Favre 1.25 2.50
485 Johnny Bailey .01 .05
486 Jeff Gossett .01 .05
487 Carnell Lake .01 .05
488 Michael Zordich RC .01 .05
489 Henry Rolling .01 .05
490 Steve Smith .01 .05
491 Vestee Jackson .01 .05
492 Ray Crockett .01 .05
493 Dexter Carter .01 .05
494 Nick Lowery .01 .05
495 Cortez Kennedy .02 .10
496 Cleveland Gary .01 .05
497 Kelly Stouffer .01 .05
498 Carl Carter .01 .05
499 Shannon Sharpe .08 .25
500 Roger Craig .02 .10
501 Willie Drewrey .01 .05
502 Mark Schlereth RC .01 .05
503 Tony Martin .02 .10
504 Tom Newberry .01 .05
505 Ron Hall .01 .05
506 Scott Miller .01 .05
507 Donnell Woolford .01 .05
508 Dave Krieg .02 .10
509 Erric Pegram .02 .10
510 Checklist 401-510 .01 .05
511 Barry Sanders SBK .25 .60
512 Thurman Thomas SBK .02 .10
513 Warren Moon SBK .02 .10
514 John Elway SBK .20 .50
515 Ronnie Lott SBK .02 .10
516 Emmitt Smith SBK .25 .60
517 Andre Rison SBK .02 .10
518 Steve Atwater SBK .01 .05

519 Steve Young SBK	.10	.30
520 Mark Rypien SBK	.01	.05
521 Rich Camarillo	.01	.05
522 Mark Bavaro	.01	.05
523 Brad Edwards	.01	.05
524 Chad Hennings RC	.02	.10
525 Tony Paige	.01	.05
526 Shawn Moore	.01	.05
527 Sidney Johnson RC	.01	.05
528 Sanjay Beach RC	.01	.05
529 Kelvin Pritchett	.01	.05
530 Jerry Holmes	.01	.05
531 Al Del Greco	.01	.05
532 Bob Gagliano	.01	.05
533 Drew Hill	.01	.05
534 Donald Frank RC	.01	.05
535 Pio Sagapolutele RC	.01	.05
536 Jackie Slater	.01	.05
537 Vernon Turner	.01	.05
538 Bobby Humphrey	.01	.05
539 Audray McMillian	.01	.05
540 Gary Brown RC	.08	.25
541 Wesley Carroll	.01	.05
542 Nate Newton	.01	.05
543 Vai Sikahema	.01	.05
544 Chris Chandler	.08	.25
545 Nolan Harrison RC	.01	.05
546 Mark Green	.01	.05
547 Ricky Watters	.08	.25
548 J.J. Birden	.01	.05
549 Cody Carlson	.01	.05
550 Tim Green	.01	.05
551 Mark Jackson	.01	.05
552 Vince Buck	.01	.05
553 George Jamison	.01	.05
554 Anthony Pleasant	.01	.05
555 Reggie Johnson	.01	.05
556 John Jackson	.01	.05
557 Ian Beckles	.01	.05
558 Buford McGee	.01	.05
559 Fuad Reveiz UER	.01	.05
(Born in Colombia& not Columbia)		
560 Joe Montana	.50	1.25
561 Phil Simms	.02	.10
562 Greg McMurtry	.01	.05
563 Gerald Williams	.01	.05
564 Dave Cadigan	.01	.05
565 Rufus Porter	.01	.05
566 Jim Kelly	.08	.25
567 Deion Sanders	.20	.50
568 Mike Singletary	.02	.10
569 Boomer Esiason	.02	.10
570 Andre Reed	.02	.10
571 James Washington	.01	.05
572 Jack Del Rio	.01	.05
573 Gerald Perry	.01	.05
574 Vinnie Clark	.01	.05
575 Mike Piel	.01	.05
576 Michael Dean Perry	.02	.10
577 Ricky Proehl	.01	.05
578 Leslie O'Neal	.02	.10
579 Russell Maryland	.01	.05
580 Eric Dickerson	.02	.10
581 Fred Strickland	.01	.05
582 Nick Lowery	.01	.05
583 Joe Milinichik RC	.01	.05
584 Mark Vlasic	.01	.05
585 James Lofton	.02	.10
586 Bruce Smith	.08	.25
587 Harvey Williams	.02	.10
588 Bernie Kosar	.02	.10
589 Carl Banks	.01	.05
590 Jeff George	.08	.25
591 Fred Jones RC	.01	.05
592 Todd Scott	.01	.05
593 Keith Jones	.01	.05
594A Tootie Robbins ERR	.01	.05
(Card has him as a Denver Bronco)		
594B Tootie Robbins COR	.01	.05
595 Todd Philcox RC	.01	.05
596 Browning Nagle	.01	.05
597 Troy Aikman	.30	.75
598 Dan Marino	.50	1.25
599 Lawrence Taylor	.08	.25
600 Webster Slaughter	.01	.05
601 Aaron Cox	.01	.05
602 Matt Stover	.01	.05
603 Keith Sims	.01	.05
604 Dennis Smith	.01	.05
605 Kevin Porter	.01	.05
606 Anthony Miller	.02	.10
607 Ken O'Brien	.01	.05
608 Randall Cunningham	.08	.25
609 Timm Rosenbach	.01	.05
610 Junior Seau	.08	.25
611 Johnny Rembert	.01	.05
612 Rick Tuten	.01	.05
613 Willie Green	.01	.05
614 Sean Salisbury RC UER	.01	.05
(He is listed with Lions in 1990 and Chargers in 1991; he was with Vikings both years)		
615 Martin Bayless	.01	.05
616 Jerry Rice	.30	.75
617 Randal Hill	.01	.05
618 Dan McGwire	.01	.05
619 Merril Hoge	.01	.05
620 Checklist 571-620	.01	.05
A560 Joe Montana Blowup	6.00	15.00
Available only through Upper Deck Authenticated		
Card measures 8 1/2" by 11"		
A598 Dan Marino Blowup	6.00	15.00
Available only through Upper Deck Authenticated		
Card measures 8 1/2 x 11		
SP3 James Lofton Yardage	.30	.75
SP4 Art Monk Catches	.20	.50

1992 Upper Deck Gold

These 50 standard-size cards feature players licensed by NFL Properties. Each low series foil box contained one 15-card foil pack of these cards. Two Game Breaker holograms of Jerry Rice and Andre Reed were randomly inserted throughout these packs. On the Quarterback Club cards, the player's name is printed in a black stripe along the left edge, while the other cards have the player's name and position printed in different designs at the bottom. Though the backs of the Prospects cards feature a career summary, the backs of the remaining cards carry a color close-up photo as well as biography, statistics, or player profile. Two distinguishing features of the backs are a gold (instead of silver) Upper Deck hologram image and the NFL Properties logo. The cards are numbered on the back with a "G" prefix and subdivided into NFL Top Prospects (1-20), Quarterback Club (21-25), and veteran players (26-50). The key Rookie Cards in this set are Quentin Coryatt, Steve Emtman and Carl Pickens.

COMPLETE SET (50)	5.00	12.00
G1 Steve Emtman RC	.02	.10
G2 Carl Pickens RC	.10	.30
G3 Dale Carter RC	.10	.30
G4 Greg Skrepenak RC	.02	.10
G5 Kevin Smith RC	.05	.15
G6 Marco Coleman RC	.05	.15
G7 David Klingler RC	.05	.15
G8 Phillippi Sparks RC	.02	.10
G9 Tommy Maddox RC	.60	1.50
G10 Quentin Coryatt RC	.05	.15
G11 Ty Detmer	.10	.30
G12 Vaughn Dunbar RC	.02	.10
G13 Ashley Ambrose RC	.10	.30
G14 Kurt Barber RC	.02	.10
G15 Chester McGlockton RC	.10	.30
G16 Todd Collins RC	.02	.10
G17 Steve Israel RC	.02	.10
G18 Marquez Pope RC	.02	.10
G19 Alonzo Spellman RC	.05	.15
G20 Tracy Scroggins RC	.02	.10
G21 Jim Kelly QC	.10	.30
G22 Troy Aikman QC	.25	.60
G23 Randall Cunningham QC	.10	.30
G24 Bernie Kosar QC	.05	.15
G25 Dan Marino QC	.40	1.00
G26 Andre Reed	.05	.15
G27 Deion Sanders	.20	.50
G28 Randal Hill	.02	.10
G29 Eric Dickerson	.05	.15
G30 Jim Kelly	.10	.30
G31 Bernie Kosar	.05	.15
G32 Mike Singletary	.05	.15
G33 Anthony Miller	.05	.15
G34 Harvey Williams	.10	.30
G35 Randall Cunningham	.10	.30
G36 Joe Montana	.50	1.25
G37 Dan McGwire	.02	.10
G38 Al Toon	.05	.15
G39 Carl Banks	.02	.10
G40 Troy Aikman	.30	.75
G41 Junior Seau	.10	.30
G42 Jeff George	.10	.30
G43 Michael Dean Perry	.05	.15
G44 Lawrence Taylor	.10	.30
G45 Dan Marino	.50	1.25
G46 Jerry Rice	.30	.75
G47 Boomer Esiason	.05	.15
G48 Bruce Smith	.10	.30
G49 Leslie O'Neal	.05	.15
G50 Checklist Card	.02	.10

1992 Upper Deck Coach's Report

COMPLETE SET (20)	6.00	15.00
RANDOM INSERTS IN SER.2 HOBBY		
CR1 Mike Pritchard	.05	.15
CR2 Will Furrer	.05	.15
CR3 Alfred Williams	.05	.15
CR4 Tommy Vardell	.05	.15
CR5 Brett Favre	3.00	8.00
CR6 Alvin Harper	.10	.30
CR7 Mike Croel	.05	.15
CR8 Herman Moore	.10	.30
CR9 Edgar Bennett	.30	.75
CR10 Todd Marinovich	.05	.15
CR11 Aeneas Williams	.10	.30
CR12 Ricky Watters	.30	.75
CR13 Amp Lee	.05	.15
CR14 Terrell Buckley	.05	.15
CR15 Tim Barnett	.05	.15
CR16 Nick Bell	.05	.15
CR17 Leonard Russell	.10	.30
CR18 Lawrence Dawsey	.10	.30
CR19 Robert Porcher	.05	.15
CR20 Checklist	.10	.30
(Ricky Watters)		

1992 Upper Deck Fanimation

COMPLETE SET (10)	10.00	25.00
RANDOM INSERTS IN SER.2 RETAIL		
F1 Jim Kelly	.50	1.25
(Shotgun Kelly)		
F2 Dan Marino	4.00	8.00
(Machine Gun)		
F3 Lawrence Taylor	.50	1.25
(The Giant)		
F4 Deion Sanders	2.00	4.00
(Neon Deion)		
F5 Troy Aikman	0.00	0.00
(The Marshall)		
F6 Junior Seau	.50	1.25
(The Warrior)		
F7 Mike Singletary	.50	1.25
F8 Eric Dickerson	.50	1.25
(The Raider)		
F9 Jerry Rice	3.00	6.00
(Goldfinger)		
F10 Checklist Card	2.00	4.00
Jim Kelly		
Dan Marino		

1992 Upper Deck Game Breaker Holograms

COMPLETE SET (9)	2.50	6.00
STATED ODDS 1:30 PACKS		
GB2/GB5/GB7 ISSUED WITH SER.2		
GB1 Art Monk	.15	.40
GB2 Drew Hill	.07	.20
GB3 Haywood Jeffires	.15	.40
GB4 Andre Rison	.15	.40
GB5 Mark Clayton	.15	.40
GB6 Jerry Rice	1.50	3.00
GB7 Michael Haynes	.15	.40
GB8 Andre Reed	.15	.40
GB9 Michael Irvin	.40	1.00

1992 Upper Deck Dan Marino Heroes

COMPLETE SET (10)	10.00	25.00
COMMON MARINO (28-36)	1.25	3.00
MARINO HEADER (NNO)	2.00	5.00
RANDOM INSERTS IN SERIES 2 PACKS		
NNO Dan Marino AUTO	60.00	100.00
Header Card		
UDA #'d of 2800		

1992 Upper Deck Walter Payton Heroes

COMPLETE SET (10)	10.00	25.00
COMMON PAYTON (19-27)	1.25	3.00
PAYTON HEADER (NNO)	2.00	5.00
RANDOM INSERTS IN SER.1 PACKS		
NNO Walter Payton AUTO	175.00	300.00
Header Card, UDA/2800		

1992 Upper Deck Heroes Payton Box Bottoms

These eight oversized "cards" (approximately 5 1/4" by 7 1/4") were featured on the bottoms of 1992 Upper Deck first series waxboxes. They are identical in design to the Payton Football Heroes insert cards, with the same color player photos in an oval picture frame. The backs are blank and the cards are unnumbered. We have checklisted them below according to the numbering of the Heroes cards.

COMPLETE SET (8)	2.40	6.00
COMMON CARD (19-26)	.40	1.00

1992 Upper Deck Pro Bowl

COMPLETE SET (16)	7.50	20.00
STATED ODDS 1:30 SER.1 PACKS		
PB1 Haywood Jeffires	.75	2.00
Michael Irvin		
PB2 Mark Clayton	.40	1.00
Gary Clark		
PB3 Anthony Munoz	.60	1.50
Jim Lachey		
PB4 Warren Moon	.75	2.00
Mark Rypien		
PB5 Thurman Thomas	2.00	5.00
Barry Sanders		
PB6 Marion Butts	2.50	6.00
Emmitt Smith		
PB7 Greg Townsend	.75	2.00
Reggie White		
PB8 Cornelius Bennett	.40	1.00
Seth Joyner		
PB9 Derrick Thomas	.75	2.00
Pat Swilling		
PB10 Darryl Talley	.40	1.00
Chris Spielman		
PB11 Ronnie Lott	.60	1.50
Mark Carrier DB		
PB12 Steve Atwater	.40	1.00
Shaun Gayle		
PB13 Rod Woodson	.60	1.50
Darrell Green		
PB14 Jeff Gossett	.40	1.00
Chip Lohmiller		
PB15 Tim Brown	.75	2.00
Mel Gray		
PB16 Checklist Card	.75	2.00

1992 Upper Deck NFL Sheets

As an advertising promotion, Upper Deck released 8 1/2" by 11" commemorative sheets printed on card stock and picturing a series of Upper Deck cards. The fronts feature either captions indicating the event the sheet commemorates, or text advertising Upper Deck cards. The sheets have an Upper Deck stamp indicating the production run and serial number. The backs of the game sheets are blank. The backs of the advertising sheets are printed in black with the words "Upper Deck Limited Edition Commemorative Sheet." The AFC and NFC championship game commemorative sheets were distributed at Upper Deck's Super Bowl Card Show III and at the NFL Experience in Minneapolis. In the listing of sheets below, the players cards are listed beginning in the upper left corner of the sheet and moving toward the lower right corner. A sheet was also issued to promote Upper Deck's 1992 Comic Ball Comic Bowl IV cards. The front features a color photo of Lawrence Taylor, Jerry Rice, Thurman Thomas, Dan Marino, and various Looney Tunes characters set against a blue sky background. A green bottom border carries the issue number and production run in the Upper Deck gold foil stamp, the Looney Tunes logo, and product information. The Comic Ball logo overlaps the green border and the photo. The entire sheet is bordered by a thin black and wider white border.

COMPLETE SET (5)	10.00	25.00
1 AFC Championship	1.60	4.00
vs. Buffalo Bills		
Jan. 12, 1992 (30,000)		
Thurman Thomas		
Cornelius Bennett		
Andre Reed		
John Elway		
Steve Atwater		
Gaston Green		
2 NFC Championship	1.60	4.00
vs. Washington Redskins		
Jan. 12, 1992 (30,000)		
Mark Rypien		
Ricky Ervins		
Charles Mann		
Barry Sanders		
Chris Spielman		
Mel Gray		
3 Super Bowl XXVI Redskins	2.40	6.00
Jan. 26, 1992 (15,000)		
Mark Rypien		
Ricky Ervins		
Charles Mann		
Gary Clark		
Darrell Green		
Earnest Byner		
4 Super Bowl XXVI Bills	1.60	4.00
Jan. 26, 1992 (15,000)		
Thurman Thomas		
Bruce Smith		
Abdre Reed		
Darryl Talley		
James Lofton		
Cornelius Bennett		
5 Comic Ball IV	4.00	10.00
(15,000)		
Lawrence Taylor		
Jerry Rice		
Thurman Thomas		
Dan Marino		
Looney Tunes Characters		

1992 Upper Deck SCD Sheets

Upper Deck produced eight different sheets for insertion into the Sept. 18, 1992, issue of Sports Collector's Digest. Reportedly 8,000 of each sheet were produced, and one was inserted into each SCD issue. Each 11" by 8 1/2" sheet features two rows of three cards each, on a speckled granite background. The backs are covered by the phrase "Upper Deck Limited Edition Commemorative Sheet." The sheets are numbered at the lower left corner "Version X of 8."

COMPLETE SET (8)	24.00	60.00
1 Randall Cunningham	6.00	15.00
David Klingler		
Dan Marino		
Troy Aikman		
Jim Kelly		
Bernie Kosar		
2 Phillippi Sparks	1.60	4.00
Dale Carter		
Steve Emtman		
Kevin Smith		
Marco Coleman		
Carl Pickens		
3 Quentin Coryatt	1.60	4.00
Greg Skrepenak		
Chester McGlockton		
Kurt Barber		
Vaughn Dunbar		
Ashley Ambrose		
4 Ty Detmer	1.60	4.00
Steve Israel		
Tracy Scroggins		
Todd Collins		
Alonzo Spellman		
Marquez Pope		
5 Eric Dickerson	2.40	6.00
Randal Hill		
Jim Kelly		
Bernie Kosar		
Deion Sanders		
Andre Reed		
6 Joe Montana	6.00	15.00
Mike Singletary		
Randall Cunningham		
Anthony Miller		
Dan McGwire		
Harvey Williams		
7 Al Toon	4.00	10.00
Michael Dean Perry		
Troy Aikman		
Jeff George		
Carl Banks		
Junior Seau		
8 Dan Marino	6.00	15.00
Tommy Maddox		
Bruce Smith		
Leslie O'Neal		
Lawrence Taylor		
Jerry Rice		

1992-93 Upper Deck NFL Experience

This 50-card standard-size set commemorates the stars of previous Super Bowls and potential stars of tomorrow. The set was produced in conjunction with the NFL Experience, a theme park held January 28-31, 1993, at the Rose Bowl (Pasadena, California), the site of Super Bowl XXVII. The set was available only through hobby dealers and was introduced at the Super Bowl Card Show at the NFL Experience. The fronts of card numbers 1-20 have full-bleed color player photos that are edged on two sides by various border stripes, while the fronts of cards numbers 21-50 feature color player photos tilted slightly to the left and bordered in the remaining area by a ghosted background. Some cards are accented with silver foil highlights, with at least one set in every case having gold-foil highlights. The backs present a color close-up photo, player profile, game performance summary, or player quote. The set is subdivided as follows: Super Bowl MVPs (1-5), Super Bowl Moments (6-10), Future Champions (11-20), and Super Bowl Dreams (21-50).

COMP. FACT SET (50)	4.00	8.00
*GOLDS: 1.2X TO 3X SILVERS		
1 Joe Montana MVP	1.00	2.50
2 Roger Staubach MVP	.20	.50
3 Bart Starr MVP	.20	.50
4 Len Dawson MVP	.07	.20
5 Fred Biletnikoff MVP	.07	.20
6 Jim Plunkett	.07	.20
7 Terry Bradshaw	.20	.50
8 Jerry Rice	.40	1.00
9 Doug Williams	.02	.10
10 Dan Marino	.80	2.00
11 David Klingler	.07	.20
12 Steve Emtman	.02	.10
13 Dale Carter	.02	.10
14 Quentin Coryatt	.07	.20
15 Tommy Maddox	.10	.30
16 Vaughn Dunbar	.02	.10
17 Marco Coleman	.02	.10
18 Carl Pickens	.07	.20
19 Sean Gilbert	.07	.20
20 Tony Smith	.02	.10
21 Jim Kelly	.15	.40
22 Dan Marino	.80	2.00
23 Boomer Esiason	.07	.20
24 Bernie Kosar	.02	.10
25 Ken O'Brien	.02	.10
26 Deion Sanders	.30	.75
27 Mike Singletary	.07	.20
28 Andre Reed	.07	.20
29 Michael Dean Perry	.02	.10
30 Ricky Proehl	.02	.10
31 Leslie O'Neal	.02	.10
32 Jerry Rice	.40	1.00
33 Eric Dickerson	.07	.20
34 Troy Aikman	.40	1.00
35 Bruce Smith	.07	.20
36 Browning Nagle	.02	.10
37 Carl Banks	.02	.10
38 Harvey Williams	.07	.20
39 Jeff George	.07	.20
40 Lawrence Taylor	.08	.25
41 Webster Slaughter	.02	.10
42 Anthony Miller	.07	.20
43 Randall Cunningham	.07	.20
44 Timm Rosenbach	.02	.10
45 Russell Maryland	.02	.10
46 Randal Hill	.02	.10
47 Dan McGwire	.02	.10
48 Merril Hoge	.02	.10
49 Kevin Fagan	.02	.10
50 Junior Seau	.07	.20

1993 Upper Deck

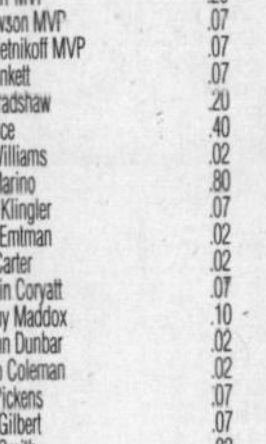

The 1993 Upper Deck football set was issued in a single series consisting of 530 standard-size cards. Cards were issued in 12-card hobby and retail packs and 22-card jumbo packs. Topical subsets featured are Star Rookies (1-29), All-Rookie Team (30-55), Hitmen (56-62), Team Checklists (63-90), Season Leaders (421-431), and Berman's Best (432-442). Rookie Cards include Jerome Bettis, Drew Bledsoe, Reggie Brooks, Curtis Conway, Garrison Hearst, Terry Kirby, O.J. McDuffie, Natrone Means and Rick Mirer. An Eric Dickerson Promo card was produced to preview the set. It can easily be differentiated from the regular issue card by the team (Raiders for the promo card, Falcons for the regular issue).

COMPLETE SET (530)	10.00	25.00
1 Star Rookie Checklist	.08	.25
Rick Mirer		
Garrison Hearst		
Curtis Conway		
Lincoln Kennedy		
2 Eric Curry RC	.01	.05
3 Rick Mirer RC	.08	.25
4 Dan Williams SR RC	.01	.05
5 Marvin Jones RC	.01	.05
6 Willie Roaf RC	.02	.10
7 Reggie Brooks SR RC	.02	.10
8 Horace Copeland RC	.02	.10
9 Lincoln Kennedy RC	.01	.05
10 Curtis Conway RC	.15	.40
11 Drew Bledsoe SR RC	1.00	2.50
12 Patrick Bates RC	.01	.05
13 Wayne Simmons RC	.01	.05
14 Irv Smith RC	.01	.05
15 Robert Smith SR RC	.50	1.25
16 O.J.McDuffie RC	.08	.25
17 Darrien Gordon SR RC	.01	.05
18 John Copeland RC	.02	.10
19 Derek Brown RBK RC	.01	.05
20 Jerome Bettis RC	2.50	5.00
21 Deon Figures RC	.01	.05
22 Glyn Milburn SR RC	.08	.25
23 Garrison Hearst SR RC	.30	.75
24 Qadry Ismail SR RC	.08	.25
25 Terry Kirby RC	.08	.25
26 Lamar Thomas RC	.01	.05
27 Tom Carter RC	.02	.10
28 Andre Hastings SR RC	.02	.10
29 George Teague RC	.02	.10
30 All-Rookie Team CL	.02	.10
Tommy Maddox		
31 David Klingler ART	.01	.05
32 Tommy Maddox ART	.02	.10
33 Vaughn Dunbar ART	.01	.05
34 Rodney Culver ART	.01	.05
35 Carl Pickens ART	.02	.10
36 Courtney Hawkins ART	.01	.05
37 Tyji Armstrong ART	.01	.05
38 Ray Roberts ART	.01	.05
39 Troy Auzenne ART	.01	.05
40 Shane Dronett ART	.01	.05
41 Chris Mims ART	.01	.05
42 Sean Gilbert ART	.01	.05
43 Steve Emtman ART	.01	.05
44 Robert Jones ART	.01	.05
45 Marco Coleman ART	.01	.05
46 Ricardo McDonald ART	.01	.05
47 Quentin Coryatt ART	.02	.10
48 Dana Hall ART	.01	.05
49 Darren Perry ART	.01	.05
50 Darryl Williams ART	.01	.05
51 Kevin Smith ART	.01	.05
52 Terrell Buckley ART	.01	.05
53 Troy Vincent ART	.01	.05
54 Lin Elliott ART	.01	.05
55 Dale Carter ART	.01	.05
56 Steve Atwater HIT	.01	.05
57 Junior Seau HIT	.02	.10
58 Ronnie Lott HIT	.01	.05
59 Louis Oliver HIT	.01	.05
60 Cortez Kennedy HIT	.01	.05
61 Pat Swilling HIT	.01	.05
62 Hitmen Checklist	.01	.05
63 Curtis Conway TC	.08	.25
64 Alfred Williams TC	.01	.05
65 Jim Kelly TC	.02	.10
66 Simon Fletcher TC	.01	.05
67 Eric Metcalf TC	.01	.05
68 Lawrence Dawsey TC	.01	.05
69 Garrison Hearst TC	.08	.25
70 Anthony Miller TC	.01	.05
71 Neil Smith TC	.01	.05
72 Jeff George TC	.02	.10
73 Emmitt Smith TC	.30	.75
74 Dan Marino TC	.30	.75
75 Clyde Simmons TC	.01	.05
76 Deion Sanders TC	.08	.25
77 Ricky Watters TC	.02	.10
78 Rodney Hampton TC	.02	.10
79 Brad Baxter TC	.01	.05
80 Barry Sanders TC	.25	.60
81 Warren Moon TC	.02	.10
82 Brett Favre TC	.40	1.00
83 Drew Bledsoe TC	.50	1.25
84 Tim Brown TC	.02	.10
85 Jim Everett TC	.01	.05
86 Earnest Byner TC	.01	.05
87 Wayne Martin TC	.01	.05
88 Rick Mirer TC	.08	.25
89 Barry Foster TC	.01	.05
90 Terry Allen TC	.02	.10
91 Vinnie Clark	.01	.05
92 Howard Ballard	.01	.05
93 Eric Ball	.01	.05
94 Marc Boutte	.01	.05
95 Larry Centers RC	.08	.25
96 Gary Brown	.01	.05
97 Hugh Millen	.01	.05
98 Anthony Newman RC	.01	.05
99 Darrell Thompson	.01	.05
100 George Jamison	.01	.05
101 James Francis	.01	.05
102 Leonard Harris	.01	.05
103 Lomas Brown	.01	.05
104 James Lofton	.02	.10
105 Jamie Dukes	.01	.05
106 Quinn Early	.02	.10
107 Ernie Jones	.01	.05
108 Torrance Small	.01	.05
109 Michael Carter	.01	.05
110 Aeneas Williams	.01	.05
111 Renaldo Turnbull	.01	.05
112 Al Smith	.01	.05
113 Troy Auzenne	.01	.05
114 Stephen Baker	.01	.05
115 Daniel Stubbs	.01	.05
116 Dana Hall	.01	.05
117 Lawrence Taylor	.08	.25
118 Ron Hall	.01	.05
119 Derrick Fenner	.01	.05
120 Martin Mayhew	.01	.05
121 Jay Schroeder	.01	.05
122 Michael Zordich	.01	.05
123 Ed McCaffrey	.08	.25
124 John Stephens	.01	.05
125 Brad Edwards	.01	.05
126 Don Griffin	.01	.05
127 Broderick Thomas	.01	.05
128 Ted Washington	.01	.05
129 Haywood Jeffires	.02	.10
130 Gary Plummer	.01	.05
131 Mark Wheeler	.01	.05
132 Ty Detmer	.08	.25
133 Derrick Walker	.01	.05
134 Henry Ellard	.02	.10
135 Neal Anderson	.01	.05
136 Bruce Smith	.08	.25
137 Cris Carter	.08	.25
138 Vaughn Dunbar	.01	.05
139 Dan Marino	.60	1.50
140 Troy Aikman	.30	.75
141 Randall Cunningham	.08	.25
142 Daryl Johnston	.08	.25
143 Mark Clayton	.01	.05
144 Rich Gannon	.08	.25
145 Nate Newton	.02	.10
146 Willie Gault	.01	.05
147 Brian Washington	.01	.05
148 Fred Barnett	.02	.10
149 Gill Byrd	.01	.05
150 Art Monk	.02	.10
151 Stan Humphries	.02	.10
152 Charles Mann	.01	.05
153 Greg Lloyd	.02	.10
154 Marvin Washington	.01	.05
155 Bernie Kosar	.02	.10
156 Pete Metzelaars	.01	.05
157 Chris Hinton	.01	.05
158 Jim Harbaugh	.08	.25
159 Willie Davis	.08	.25
160 Leroy Thompson	.01	.05
161 Scott Miller	.01	.05
162 Eugene Robinson	.01	.05
163 David Little	.01	.05
164 Pierce Holt	.01	.05
165 James Hasty	.01	.05
166 Dave Krieg	.02	.10
167 Gerald Williams	.01	.05
168 Kyle Clifton	.01	.05
169 Bill Brooks	.01	.05
170 Vance Johnson	.01	.05
171 Greg Townsend	.01	.05
172 Jason Belser	.01	.05
173 Brett Perriman	.08	.25
174 Steve Jordan	.01	.05
175 Kelvin Martin	.01	.05
176 Greg Kragen	.01	.05
177 Kerry Cash	.01	.05
178 Chester McGlockton	.02	.10
179 Jim Kelly	.08	.25
180 Todd McNair	.01	.05
181 Leroy Hoard	.02	.10
182 Seth Joyner	.01	.05
183 Sam Gash RC	.08	.25
184 Joe Nash	.01	.05
185 Lin Elliott RC	.01	.05
186 Robert Porcher	.01	.05
187 Tommy Hodson	.01	.05
188 Greg Lewis	.01	.05
189 Dan Saleaumua	.01	.05
190 Chris Goode	.01	.05
191 Henry Thomas	.01	.05
192 Bobby Hebert	.01	.05
193 Clay Matthews	.02	.10
194 Mark Carrier WR	.02	.10
195 Anthony Pleasant	.01	.05
196 Eric Dorsey	.01	.05
197 Clarence Verdin	.01	.05
198 Marc Spindler	.01	.05
199 Tommy Maddox	.08	.25
200 Wendell Davis	.01	.05
201 John Fina	.01	.05
202 Alonzo Spellman	.01	.05
203 Darryl Williams	.01	.05
204 Mike Croel	.01	.05
205 Ken Norton Jr.	.02	.10
206 Mel Gray	.02	.10
207 Chuck Cecil	.01	.05
208 John Flannery	.01	.05
209 Chip Banks	.01	.05
210 Chris Martin	.01	.05
211 Dennis Brown	.01	.05
212 Vinny Testaverde	.02	.10
213 Nick Bell	.01	.05
214 Robert Delpino	.01	.05
215 Mark Higgs	.01	.05
216 Al Noga	.01	.05
217 Andre Tippett	.01	.05
218 Pat Swilling	.01	.05
219 Phil Simms	.02	.10
220 Ricky Proehl	.01	.05
221 William Thomas	.01	.05
222 Jeff Graham	.02	.10
223 Darion Conner	.01	.05
224 Mark Carrier DB	.01	.05
225 Willie Green	.01	.05
226 Reggie Rivers RC	.01	.05
227 Andre Reed	.02	.10
228 Deion Sanders	.20	.50
229 Chris Doleman	.01	.05
230 Jerry Ball	.01	.05
231 Eric Dickerson	.02	.10
232 Carlos Jenkins	.01	.05
233 Mike Johnson	.01	.05
234 Marco Coleman	.01	.05
235 Leslie O'Neal	.02	.10
236 Browning Nagle	.01	.05
237 Carl Pickens	.02	.10
238 Steve Emtman	.01	.05
239 Alvin Harper	.02	.10
240 Keith Jackson	.02	.10
241 Jerry Rice	.40	1.00
242 Cortez Kennedy	.02	.10
243 Tyji Armstrong	.01	.05
244 Troy Vincent	.01	.05
245 Randal Hill	.01	.05
246 Robert Blackmon	.01	.05
247 Junior Seau	.08	.25
248 Sterling Sharpe	.08	.25
249 Thurman Thomas	.08	.25
250 David Klingler	.01	.05
251 Jeff George	.08	.25
252 Anthony Miller	.02	.10
253 Earnest Byner	.01	.05
254 Eric Swann	.02	.10
255 Jeff Herrod	.01	.05
256 Eddie Robinson	.01	.05
257 Eric Allen	.01	.05
258 John Taylor	.02	.10
259 Sean Gilbert	.02	.10
260 Ray Childress	.01	.05
261 Michael Haynes	.02	.10
262 Greg McMurtry	.01	.05
263 Bill Romanowski	.01	.05
264 Todd Lyght	.01	.05
265 Clyde Simmons	.01	.05
266 Webster Slaughter	.01	.05
267 J.J. Birden	.01	.05
268 Aaron Wallace	.01	.05
269 Carl Banks	.01	.05
270 Ricardo McDonald	.01	.05
271 Michael Brooks	.01	.05
272 Dale Carter	.01	.05
273 Mike Pritchard	.02	.10
274 Derek Brown TE	.01	.05
275 Burt Grossman	.01	.05
276 Mark Schlereth	.01	.05
277 Karl Mecklenburg	.01	.05
278 Rickey Jackson	.01	.05
279 Ricky Ervins	.01	.05
280 Jeff Bryant	.01	.05
281 Eric Martin	.01	.05
282 Carlton Haselrig	.01	.05
283 Kevin Mack	.01	.05
284 Brad Muster	.01	.05
285 Kelvin Pritchett	.01	.05
286 Courtney Hawkins	.01	.05
287 Levon Kirkland	.01	.05
288 Steve DeBerg	.01	.05
289 Edgar Bennett	.08	.25
290 Michael Dean Perry	.02	.10
291 Richard Dent	.02	.10
292 Howie Long	.08	.25
293 Chris Mims	.01	.05
294 Kurt Barber	.01	.05
295 Wilber Marshall	.01	.05
296 Ethan Horton	.01	.05
297 Tony Bennett	.01	.05
298 Johnny Johnson	.01	.05
299 Craig Heyward	.02	.10
300 Steve Israel	.01	.05
301 Kenneth Gant	.01	.05
302 Eugene Chung	.01	.05
303 Harvey Williams	.02	.10
304 Jarrod Bunch	.01	.05
305 Darren Perry	.01	.05
306 Steve Christie	.01	.05
307 John Randle	.02	.10
308 Warren Moon	.08	.25
309 Charles Haley	.02	.10
310 Tony Smith	.01	.05
311 Steve Broussard	.01	.05
312 Alfred Williams	.01	.05
313 Terrell Buckley	.01	.05
314 Trace Armstrong	.01	.05
315 Brian Mitchell	.02	.10
316 Steve Atwater	.01	.05
317 Nate Lewis	.01	.05
318 Richard Brown	.01	.05
319 Rufus Porter	.01	.05
320 Pat Harlow	.01	.05
321 Anthony Smith	.01	.05
322 Jack Del Rio	.01	.05
323 Darryl Talley	.01	.05
324 Sam Mills	.01	.05
325 Chris Miller	.02	.10
326 Ken Harvey	.01	.05
327 Rod Woodson	.08	.25
328 Tony Tolbert	.01	.05
329 Todd Kinchen	.01	.05
330 Brian Noble	.01	.05
331 Dave Meggett	.01	.05
332 Chris Spielman	.02	.10
333 Barry Word	.01	.05
334 Jessie Hester	.01	.05
335 Michael Jackson	.02	.10
336 Mitchell Price	.01	.05
337 Michael Irvin	.08	.25
338 Simon Fletcher	.01	.05
339 Keith Jennings	.01	.05
340 Vai Sikahema	.01	.05
341 Roger Craig	.02	.10
342 Ricky Watters	.08	.25
343 Reggie Cobb	.01	.05
344 Kanavis McGhee	.01	.05
345 Barry Foster	.02	.10
346 Marion Butts	.01	.05
347 Bryan Cox	.01	.05
348 Wayne Martin	.01	.05
349 Jim Everett	.02	.10
350 Nate Odomes	.01	.05
351 Anthony Johnson	.02	.10
352 Rodney Hampton	.02	.10
353 Terry Allen	.08	.25
354 Derrick Thomas	.08	.25
355 Calvin Williams	.02	.10
356 Pepper Johnson	.01	.05
357 John Elway	.60	1.50
358 Steve Young	.30	.75
359 Emmitt Smith	.60	1.50
360 Brett Favre	.75	2.00
361 Cody Carlson	.01	.05
362 Vincent Brown	.01	.05
363 Gary Anderson RB	.01	.05
364 Jon Vaughn	.01	.05
365 Todd Marinovich	.01	.05
366 Carnell Lake	.01	.05
367 Kurt Gouveia	.01	.05
368 Lawrence Dawsey	.01	.05
369 Neil O'Donnell	.08	.25
370 Duane Bickett	.01	.05
371 Ronnie Harmon	.01	.05
372 Rodney Peete	.01	.05
373 Cornelius Bennett	.02	.10
374 Brad Baxter	.01	.05
375 Ernest Givins	.02	.10
376 Keith Byars	.01	.05
377 Eric Bieniemy	.01	.05
378 Mike Brim	.01	.05
379 Darren Lewis	.01	.05
380 Heath Sherman	.01	.05
381 Leonard Russell	.02	.10
382 Brent Jones	.02	.10
383 David Whitmore	.01	.05
384 Ray Roberts	.01	.05
385 John Offerdahl	.01	.05
386 Keith McCants	.01	.05
387 John Baylor	.01	.05
388 Amp Lee	.01	.05
389 Chris Warren	.02	.10
390 Herman Moore	.08	.25
391 Johnny Bailey	.01	.05
392 Tim Johnson	.01	.05
393 Eric Metcalf	.02	.10
394 Chris Chandler	.02	.10
395 Mark Rypien	.01	.05
396 Christian Okoye	.01	.05
397 Shannon Sharpe	.08	.25
398 Eric Hill	.01	.05
399 David Lang	.01	.05
400 Bruce Matthews	.01	.05
401 Harold Green	.01	.05
402 Mo Lewis	.01	.05
403 Terry McDaniel	.01	.05
404 Wesley Carroll	.01	.05
405 Richmond Webb	.01	.05
406 Andre Rison	.02	.10
407 Lonnie Young	.01	.05
408 Tommy Vardell	.01	.05
409 Gene Atkins	.01	.05
410 Sean Salisbury	.01	.05
411 Kenneth Davis	.01	.05
412 John L. Williams	.01	.05
413 Roman Phifer	.01	.05
414 Bennie Blades	.01	.05
415 Tim Brown	.08	.25
416 Lorenzo White	.01	.05
417 Tony Casillas	.01	.05
418 Tom Waddle	.01	.05
419 David Fulcher	.01	.05
420 Jessie Tuggle	.01	.05
421 Emmitt Smith SL	.30	.75
422 Clyde Simmons SL	.01	.05
423 Sterling Sharpe SL	.02	.10
424 Sterling Sharpe SL	.02	.10
425 Emmitt Smith SL	.30	.75
426 Dan Marino SL	.30	.75
427 Henry Jones SL	.01	.05

Audray McMillian		
428 Thurman Thomas SL	.02	.10
429 Greg Montgomery SL	.01	.05
430 Pete Stoyanovich SL	.01	.05
431 Season Leaders CL	.15	.40
Emmitt Smith		
432 Steve Young BB	.15	.40
433 Jerry Rice BB	.20	.50
434 Ricky Watters BB	.02	.10
435 Barry Foster BB	.01	.05
436 Cortez Kennedy BB	.01	.05
437 Warren Moon BB	.02	.10
438 Thurman Thomas BB	.02	.10
439 Brett Favre BB	.40	1.00
440 Andre Rison BB	.02	.10
441 Barry Sanders BB	.25	.60
442 Chris Berman CL	.01	.05
443 Moe Gardner	.01	.05
444 Robert Jones	.01	.05
445 Reggie Langhorne	.01	.05
446 Flipper Anderson	.01	.05
447 James Washington	.01	.05
448 Aaron Craver	.01	.05
449 Jack Trudeau	.01	.05
450 Neil Smith	.08	.25
451 Chris Burkett	.01	.05
452 Russell Maryland	.01	.05
453 Drew Hill	.01	.05
454 Barry Sanders	.50	1.25
455 Jeff Cross	.01	.05
456 Bennie Thompson	.01	.05
457 Marcus Allen	.08	.25
458 Tracy Scroggins	.01	.05
459 LeRoy Butler	.01	.05
460 Joe Montana	.60	1.50
461 Eddie Anderson	.01	.05
462 Tim McDonald	.01	.05
463 Ronnie Lott	.02	.10
464 Gaston Green	.01	.05
465 Shane Conlan	.01	.05
466 Leonard Marshall	.01	.05
467 Melvin Jenkins	.01	.05
468 Don Beebe	.01	.05
469 Johnny Mitchell	.01	.05
470 Darryl Henley	.01	.05
471 Boomer Esiason	.02	.10
472 Mark Kelso	.01	.05
473 John Booty	.01	.05
474 Pete Stoyanovich	.01	.05
475 Thomas Smith RC	.02	.10
476 Carlton Gray RC	.01	.05
477 Dana Stubblefield RC	.08	.25
478 Ryan McNeil RC	.08	.25
479 Natrone Means RC	.08	.25
480 Carl Simpson RC	.01	.05
481 Robert O'Neal RC	.01	.05
482 Demetrius DuBose RC	.01	.05
483 Darrin Smith RC	.02	.10
484 Micheal Barrow RC	.08	.25
485 Chris Slade RC	.02	.10
486 Steve Tovar RC	.01	.05
487 Ron George RC	.01	.05
488 Steve Tasker	.02	.10
489 Will Furrer	.01	.05
490 Reggie White	.08	.25
491 Sean Jones	.01	.05
492 Gary Clark	.02	.10
493 Donnell Woolford	.01	.05
494 Steve Beuerlein	.02	.10
495 Anthony Carter	.02	.10
496 Louis Oliver	.01	.05
497 Chris Zorich	.01	.05
498 David Brandon	.01	.05
499 Bubba McDowell	.01	.05
500 Adrian Cooper	.01	.05
501 Bill Johnson	.01	.05
502 Shawn Jefferson	.01	.05
503 Siran Stacy	.01	.05
504 James Jones DT	.01	.05
505 Tom Rathman	.01	.05
506 Rob Moore	.02	.10
507 Kent Graham RC	.08	.25
508 Darren Carrington RC	.01	.05
509 Rickey Dixon	.01	.05
510 Toi Cook	.01	.05
511 Steve Smith	.01	.05
512 Eric Green	.01	.05
513 Phillippi Sparks	.01	.05
514 Lee Williams	.01	.05
515 Gary Reasons	.01	.05
516 Shane Dronett	.01	.05
517 Jay Novacek	.02	.10
518 Kevin Greene	.02	.10
519 Derek Russell	.01	.05
520 Quentin Coryatt	.02	.10
521 Santana Dotson	.02	.10
522 Donald Frank	.01	.05
523 Mike Prior	.01	.05
524 Dwight Hollier RC	.01	.05
525 Eric Davis	.01	.05
526 Dalton Hilliard	.01	.05
527 Rodney Culver	.01	.05
528 Jeff Hostetler	.02	.10
529 Ernie Mills	.01	.05
530 Craig Erickson	.02	.10
P231 Eric Dickerson Promo	.50	1.25

1993 Upper Deck America's Team

COMPLETE SET (15)	20.00	50.00
STATED ODDS 1:25 HOBBY		
JUMBOS:ONE PER SPEC.RETAIL BLISTER		
AT1 Roger Staubach	4.00	10.00
AT2 Chuck Howley	.75	2.00
AT3 Harvey Martin	.75	2.00
AT4 Randy White	1.25	3.00
AT5 Bob Lilly	1.25	3.00
AT6 Drew Pearson	1.25	3.00
AT7 Emmitt Smith	6.00	15.00
AT8 Troy Aikman	4.00	10.00
AT9 Ken Norton Jr.	1.25	3.00
AT10 Robert Jones	.75	2.00
AT11 Russell Maryland	.75	2.00
AT12 Jay Novacek	1.25	3.00
AT13 Michael Irvin	2.00	5.00
AT14 Troy Aikman CL	2.50	6.00
NNO Emmitt Smith HDR	4.00	10.00

1993 Upper Deck America's Team Jumbos

COMPLETE SET (15)	50.00	100.00
AT1 Roger Staubach	6.00	15.00
AT2 Chuck Howley	2.00	5.00
AT3 Harvey Martin	2.00	5.00
AT4 Randy White	2.50	6.00
AT5 Bob Lilly	2.50	6.00
AT6 Drew Pearson	2.50	6.00
AT7 Emmitt Smith	10.00	25.00
AT8 Bernie Kosar	2.00	5.00
AT9 Ken Norton Jr.	2.00	5.00
AT10 Robert Jones	2.00	5.00
AT11 Russell Maryland	2.00	5.00
AT12 Jay Novacek	3.00	8.00
AT13 Michael Irvin	4.00	10.00
AT14 Emmitt Smith CL	6.00	15.00
AT15 Emmitt Smith Header	6.00	15.00

1993 Upper Deck Future Heroes

COMPLETE SET (10)	6.00	15.00
STATED ODDS 1:20 HOB/JUM		
ONE PER SPECIAL RETAIL PACK		
37 Barry Foster	.10	.30
38 Junior Seau	.30	.75
39 Emmitt Smith	2.50	5.00
40 Troy Aikman	1.25	2.50
41 David Klingler	.05	.15
42 Ricky Watters	.30	.75
43 Barry Sanders	2.00	4.00
44 Brett Favre	3.00	6.00
45 Emmitt Smith CL	.60	1.25
NNO Ricky Watters Header	.30	.75

1993 Upper Deck Pro Bowl

COMPLETE SET (20)	20.00	50.00
STATED ODDS 1:25 RETAIL		
PB1 Andre Reed	.30	.75
PB2 Dan Marino	5.00	12.00
PB3 Warren Moon	.75	2.00
PB4 Anthony Miller	.30	.75
PB5 Barry Foster	.30	.75
PB6 Steve Atwater	.15	.40
PB7 Cortez Kennedy	.30	.75
PB8 Junior Seau	.75	2.00
PB9 Jerry Rice	3.00	8.00
PB10 Michael Irvin	.75	2.00
PB11 Sterling Sharpe	.75	2.00
PB12 Steve Young	2.50	6.00
PB13 Troy Aikman	2.50	6.00
PB14 Brett Favre	6.00	15.00
PB15 Emmitt Smith	5.00	12.00
PB16 Rodney Hampton	.30	.75
PB17 Barry Sanders	4.00	10.00
PB18 Ricky Watters	.75	2.00
PB19 Pat Swilling	.15	.40
PB20 Checklist Card	1.25	3.00

1993 Upper Deck Rookie Exchange

COMPLETE SET (6)	5.00	12.00
ONE SET PER TRADE CARD BY MAIL		
RE1 Trade Upper Deck Card Expired	.20	.50
RE1X Trade Upper Deck Card Punched	.20	.50
RE2 Drew Bledsoe	5.00	12.00
RE3 Rick Mirer	.20	.50
RE4 Garrison Hearst	.75	1.50
RE5 Marvin Jones	.02	.10
RE6 Curtis Conway	.30	.75
RE7 Jerome Bettis	5.00	10.00

1993 Upper Deck Team MVPs

COMPLETE SET (29)	12.50	25.00
ONE PER JUMBO PACK		
TM1 Neal Anderson	.07	.20
TM2 Harold Green	.07	.20
TM3 Thurman Thomas	.40	1.00
TM4 John Elway	3.00	6.00
TM5 Eric Metcalf	.15	.40
TM6 Reggie Cobb	.07	.20
TM7 Johnny Bailey	.07	.20
TM8 Junior Seau	.40	1.00
TM9 Derrick Thomas	.40	1.00
TM10 Steve Emtman	.07	.20
TM11 Troy Aikman	1.50	3.00
TM12 Dan Marino	3.00	6.00
TM13 Clyde Simmons	.07	.20
TM14 Andre Rison	.15	.40
TM15 Steve Young	1.50	3.00
TM16 Rodney Hampton	.15	.40
TM17 Rob Moore	.15	.40
TM18 Barry Sanders	2.50	5.00
TM19 Warren Moon	.40	1.00
TM20 Sterling Sharpe	.40	1.00
TM21 Jon Vaughn	.07	.20
TM22 Tim Brown	.40	1.00
TM23 Jim Everett	.15	.40
TM24 Gary Clark	.15	.40
TM25 Wayne Martin	.07	.20
TM26 Cortez Kennedy	.15	.40
TM27 Barry Foster	.15	.40
TM28 Terry Allen	.40	1.00
TM29 Checklist Card	.07	.20

1993 Upper Deck Team Chiefs

The 1993 Upper Deck Chiefs Team Set consists of 25 standard-size cards. The fronts display a color action player photo with white borders and two team color-coded stripes at the bottom. The player's name and position are printed in the top stripe. On the left side of the card, the team name is printed in a team color against a ghosted background. The backs carry a second photo alongside biographical and statistical information. The cards are numbered on the back with a "KC" prefix.

COMP.FACT SET (25)	3.20	8.00
KC1 Nick Lowery	.07	.20
KC2 Lonnie Marts	.07	.20
KC3 Marcus Allen	.30	.75
KC4 Bennie Thompson	.07	.20
KC5 Bryan Barker	.07	.20
KC6 Christian Okoye	.10	.30
KC7 Dale Carter	.10	.30
KC8 Dan Saleaumua	.07	.20
KC9 Dave Krieg	.10	.30
KC10 Derrick Thomas	.20	.50
KC11 Doug Terry	.07	.20
KC12 Fred Jones	.07	.20
KC13 Harvey Williams	.10	.30
KC14 J.J. Birden	.07	.20
KC15 Joe Montana	2.00	5.00
KC16 John Alt	.07	.20
KC17 Leonard Griffin	.07	.20
KC18 Matt Blundin	.07	.20
KC19 Neil Smith	.10	.30
KC20 Tim Barnett	.07	.20
KC21 Tim Grunhard	.07	.20
KC22 Todd McNair	.07	.20
KC23 Tracy Simien	.07	.20
KC24 Willie Davis	.10	.30
KC25 Joe Montana (Checklist back)	.60	1.50

1993 Upper Deck Team Cowboys

The 1993 Upper Deck Cowboys Team Set consists of 25 standard-size cards. The fronts display a color action player photo with white borders and two team color-coded stripes at the bottom. The player's name and position are printed in the top stripe. On the left side of the card, the team name is printed in a team color against a ghosted background. The backs carry a second photo alongside biographical and statistical information. The cards are numbered on the back with a "D" prefix.

COMP.FACT SET (25)	3.20	8.00
D1 Alvin Harper	.07	.20
D2 Charles Haley	.10	.30
D3 Jimmy Smith	.20	.50
D4 Darrin Smith	.07	.20
D5 Jim Jeffcoat	.07	.20
D6 Daryl Johnston	.15	.40
D7 Dixon Edwards	.07	.20
D8 Emmitt Smith	1.60	4.00
D9 James Washington	.07	.20
D10 Jay Novacek	.10	.30
D11 Ken Norton Jr.	.07	.20
D12 Kenneth Gant	.07	.20
D13 Larry Brown DB	.07	.20
D14 Leon Lett	.07	.20
D15 Lin Elliott	.07	.20
D16 Mark Tuinei	.07	.20
D17 Michael Irvin	.25	.60
D18 Nate Newton	.07	.20
D19 Robert Jones	.07	.20
D20 Thomas Everett UER (Photo actually Brock Marion)	.07	.20
D21 Tony Casillas	.07	.20
D22 Tony Tolbert	.07	.20
D23 Troy Aikman	.80	2.00
D24 Russell Maryland	.07	.20
D25 Troy Aikman (Checklist back)	.40	1.00

1993 Upper Deck Team 49ers

The 1993 Upper Deck 49ers Team Set consists of 25 standard-size cards. The fronts display a color action player photo with white borders and two team color-coded stripes at the bottom. The player's name and position are printed in the top stripe. On the left side of the card, the team name is printed in a team color against a ghosted background. The backs carry a second photo alongside biographical and statistical information. The cards are numbered on the back with an "SF" prefix.

COMP.FACT SET (25)	3.20	8.00
SF1 Amp Lee	.07	.20
SF2 Bill Romanowski	.07	.20
SF3 Brent Jones	.10	.30
SF4 Dana Hall	.07	.20
SF5 Dana Stubblefield	.25	.60
SF6 Dennis Brown	.07	.20
SF7 Dexter Carter	.07	.20
SF8 Don Griffin	.07	.20
SF9 Eric Davis	.07	.20
SF10 Guy McIntyre	.07	.20
SF11 Jamie Williams	.07	.20
SF12 Jerry Rice	.80	2.00
SF13 John Taylor	.10	.30
SF14 Keith DeLong	.07	.20
SF15 Marc Logan	.07	.20
SF16 Michael Walter	.07	.20
SF17 Mike Cofer	.07	.20
SF18 Odessa Turner	.07	.20
SF19 Ricky Watters	.25	.60
SF20 Steve Bono	.10	.30
SF21 Steve Young	.60	1.50
SF22 Ted Washington	.07	.20
SF23 Tom Rathman	.10	.30
SF24 Jesse Sapolu	.07	.20
SF25 Steve Young (Checklist back)	.30	.75

1993 Upper Deck 24K Gold

This eight card set was issued by Upper Deck only through their hobby channels. The black and gold fronts are horizontal and have the player's facsimile signature on the left with an etched portrait on the right. Although the cards are numbered on the back out of 2500, reportedly only 1500 of each card was produced. Six quarterbacks and two running backs are featured in this set.

COMPLETE SET (8)	100.00	200.00
1 Joe Montana	25.00	60.00
2 Emmitt Smith	20.00	50.00
3 Drew Bledsoe	15.00	40.00
4 Troy Aikman	12.50	30.00
5 Rick Mirer	4.00	10.00
6 Dan Marino	20.00	50.00
7 Steve Young	10.00	25.00
8 Thurman Thomas	6.00	15.00

1993-94 Upper Deck Miller Lite SB

Sponsored by Miller Lite Beer and Tombstone Pizza, the 1993 Upper Deck Super Bowl Showdown Series consists of five cards measuring approximately 5" by 3 1/2". One card was included in specially-marked half-cases of Miller Lite beer. Furthermore, the set could be obtained by mailing in the official certificate (included in each specially-marked case), along with three UPC symbols from three 24-packs (or case equivalents) of 12-ounce Miller Lite cans and the dated cash register receipt. All certificates must be received by March 18, 1994. All entries were entered in a random drawing for 1,000 sweepstakes prizes of a Joe Montana personally autographed collector sheet. The horizontal card fronts feature the starting quarterbacks from competing Super Bowl teams. On each side of the front is a color action player cut-out photo superimposed over a ghosted game photo. The quarterbacks' last names appear in the center of the card in white print above the Super Bowl depicted on the card, the final score, and the date all printed in gold foil lettering. A blue stripe intersects the lower portion of the left photo containing the words "Super Bowl," and "Showdowns" appears on a red stripe intersecting the right photo. A ghosted Super Bowl logo for the play-off depicted on the front, serves as a background for highlights of the quarterbacks' accomplishments during the game. The backs are bordered in team color-coded borders that fade to a metallic silver. Sponsor logos are printed on the lower edge. The cards are numbered on the front.

COMPLETE SET (5)	4.80	12.00
1 Troy Aikman Jim Kelly Super Bowl XXVII	1.20	3.00
2 Jim Kelly Mark Rypien Super Bowl XXVI	.80	2.00
3 John Elway Joe Montana Super Bowl XXIV	1.60	4.00
4 John Elway Phil Simms Super Bowl XXI	1.20	3.00
5 Joe Montana Dan Marino Super Bowl XIX	1.60	4.00

1994 Upper Deck Pro Bowl Samples

Measuring the standard-size, this six-card sample set spotlights players who participated in the Pro Bowl. The cards were originally passed out at the National Convention in Houston. On the left edge, the horizontal fronts have a purple stripe carrying the player's name, team name, and a holographic headshot framed by a black border. The rest of the front displays a full-bleed color action player photo with a metallic sheen. On a white screened background of a gray Upper Deck logos, the backs have the disclaimer "SAMPLE CARD" printed diagonally. The cards are unnumbered and checklisted below in alphabetical order.

COMPLETE SET (6)	14.00	35.00
1 Jerome Bettis	1.20	3.00
2 Brett Favre	4.80	12.00
3 John Elway	4.80	12.00
4 Thurman Thomas	1.20	3.00
5 Jerry Rice	2.40	6.00
6 Steve Young	2.00	5.00

1994 Upper Deck

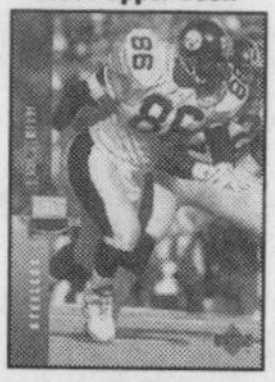

This 330-card standard-size set was released in one series. They were issued in 12-card packs with a suggested retail price of $1.99. The following subsets include Rookies (1-30) and Heavy Weights (31-40). Rookie Cards include Isaac Bruce, Trent Dilfer, Marshall Faulk, William Floyd, Errict Rhett, and Heath Shuler. A Joe Montana Promo card was produced and priced below.

COMPLETE SET (330)	12.50	25.00
1 Dan Wilkinson RC	.07	.20
2 Antonio Langham RC	.07	.20
3 Derrick Alexander WR RC	.15	.40
4 Charles Johnson RC	.15	.40
5 Bucky Brooks RC	.02	.10
6 Trev Alberts RC	.07	.20
7 Marshall Faulk RC	2.50	6.00
8 Willie McGinest RC	.15	.40
9 Aaron Glenn RC	.15	.40
10 Ryan Yarborough RC	.02	.10
11 Greg Hill RC	.15	.40
12 Sam Adams RC	.07	.20
13 John Thierry RC	.02	.10
14 Johnnie Morton RC	.30	.75
15 LeShon Johnson RC	.07	.20
16 David Palmer RC	.15	.40
17 Trent Dilfer RC	.50	1.25
18 Jamir Miller RC	.07	.20
19 Thomas Lewis RC	.07	.20
20 Heath Shuler RC	.15	.40
21 Wayne Gandy	.02	.10
22 Isaac Bruce RC	2.00	4.00
23 Joe Johnson RC	.02	.10
24 Mario Bates RC	.15	.40
25 Bryant Young RC	.25	.60
26 William Floyd RC	.15	.40
27 Errict Rhett RC	.15	.40
28 Chuck Levy RC	.02	.10
29 Darnay Scott RC	.30	.75
30 Rob Fredrickson RC	.07	.20
31 Jamir Miller HW	.02	.10
32 Thomas Lewis HW	.02	.10
33 John Thierry HW	.02	.10
34 Sam Adams HW	.02	.10
35 Joe Johnson HW	.02	.10
36 Bryant Young HW	.10	.30
37 Wayne Gandy HW	.02	.10
38 LeShon Johnson HW	.02	.10
39 Mario Bates HW	.07	.20
40 Greg Hill HW	.07	.20
41 Andy Heck	.02	.10
42 Warren Moon	.15	.40
43 Jim Everett	.07	.20
44 Bill Romanowski	.02	.10
45 Michael Haynes	.07	.20
46 Chris Doleman	.02	.10
47 Merril Hoge	.02	.10
48 Chris Miller	.02	.10
49 Clyde Simmons	.02	.10
50 Jeff George	.15	.40
51 Jeff Burris RC	.07	.20
52 Ethan Horton	.02	.10
53 Scott Mitchell	.07	.20
54 Howard Ballard	.02	.10
55 Lewis Tillman	.02	.10
56 Marion Butts	.02	.10
57 Erik Kramer	.07	.20
58 Ken Norton Jr.	.07	.20
59 Anthony Miller	.07	.20
60 Chris Hinton	.02	.10
61 Ricky Proehl	.02	.10
62 Craig Heyward	.07	.20
63 Darryl Talley	.02	.10
64 Tim Worley	.02	.10
65 Derrick Fenner	.02	.10
66 Jerry Ball	.02	.10
67 Darrin Smith	.02	.10
68 Mike Croel	.02	.10
69 Ray Crockett	.02	.10
70 Tony Bennett	.02	.10
71 Webster Slaughter	.02	.10
72 Anthony Johnson	.07	.20
73 Charles Mincy	.02	.10
74 Calvin Jones RC	.02	.10
75 Henry Ellard	.07	.20
76 Troy Vincent	.02	.10
77 Sean Salisbury	.02	.10
78 Pat Harlow	.02	.10
79 James Williams RC	.02	.10
80 Dave Brown	.07	.20
81 Kent Graham	.07	.20
82 Seth Joyner	.02	.10
83 Deon Figures	.02	.10
84 Stanley Richard	.02	.10
85 Tom Rathman	.02	.10
86 Rod Stephens	.02	.10
87 Ray Seals	.02	.10
88 Andre Collins	.02	.10
89 Cornelius Bennett	.07	.20
90 Richard Dent	.07	.20
91 Louis Oliver	.02	.10
92 Rodney Peete	.02	.10
93 Jackie Harris	.02	.10
94 Tracy Simien	.02	.10
95 Greg Townsend	.02	.10
96 Michael Stewart	.02	.10
97 Irving Fryar	.07	.20
98 Todd Collins	.02	.10
99 Irv Smith	.02	.10
100 Chris Calloway	.02	.10
101 Kevin Greene	.07	.20
102 John Friesz	.07	.20
103 Steve Bono	.07	.20
104 Brian Blades	.07	.20
105 Reggie Cobb	.02	.10
106 Eric Swann	.07	.20
107 Mike Pritchard	.02	.10
108 Bill Brooks	.02	.10
109 Jim Harbaugh	.15	.40
110 David Whitmore	.02	.10
111 Eddie Anderson	.02	.10
112 Ray Crittenden RC	.02	.10
113 Mark Collins	.02	.10
114 Brian Washington	.02	.10
115 Barry Foster	.02	.10
116 Gary Plummer	.02	.10
117 Marc Logan	.02	.10
118 John L. Williams	.02	.10
119 Marty Carter	.02	.10
120 Kurt Gouveia	.02	.10
121 Ronald Moore	.02	.10
122 Pierce Holt	.02	.10
123 Henry Jones	.02	.10
124 Donnell Woolford	.02	.10
125 Steve Tovar	.02	.10
126 Anthony Pleasant	.02	.10
127 Jay Novacek	.07	.20
128 Dan Williams	.02	.10
129 Barry Sanders	1.00	2.50
130 Robert Brooks	.15	.40
131 Lorenzo White	.02	.10
132 Kerry Cash	.02	.10
133 Joe Montana	1.25	3.00
134 Jeff Hostetler	.07	.20
135 Jerome Bettis	.25	.60
136 Dan Marino	1.25	3.00
137 Vencie Glenn	.02	.10
138 Vincent Brown	.02	.10
139 Rickey Jackson	.02	.10
140 Carlton Bailey	.02	.10
141 Jeff Lageman	.02	.10
142 William Thomas	.02	.10
143 Neil O'Donnell	.15	.40
144 Shawn Jefferson	.02	.10
145 Steve Young	.40	1.00
146 Chris Warren	.07	.20
147 Courtney Hawkins	.02	.10
148 Brad Edwards	.02	.10
149 O.J. McDuffie	.15	.40
150 David Lang	.02	.10
151 Chuck Cecil	.02	.10
152 Norm Johnson	.02	.10
153 Pete Metzelaars	.02	.10
154 Shaun Gayle	.02	.10
155 Alfred Williams	.02	.10
156 Eric Turner	.02	.10
157A Emmitt Smith ERR incorrect stat totals	1.00	2.50
157B Emmitt Smith COR corrected stats	1.00	2.50
158 Steve Atwater	.02	.10
159 Robert Porcher	.02	.10
160 Edgar Bennett	.15	.40
161 Bubba McDowell	.02	.10
162 Jeff Herrod	.02	.10
163 Keith Cash	.02	.10
164 Patrick Bates	.02	.10
165 Todd Lyght	.02	.10
166 Mark Higgs	.02	.10
167 Carlos Jenkins	.02	.10
168 Drew Bledsoe	.40	1.00
169 Wayne Martin	.02	.10
170 Mike Sherrard	.02	.10
171 Ronnie Lott	.07	.20
172 Fred Barnett	.07	.20
173 Eric Green	.02	.10
174 Leslie O'Neal	.02	.10
175 Brent Jones	.07	.20
176 Jon Vaughn	.02	.10
177 Vince Workman	.02	.10
178 Ron Middleton	.02	.10
179 Terry McDaniel	.02	.10
180 Willie Davis	.07	.20
181 Gary Clark	.07	.20
182 Bobby Hebert	.02	.10
183 Russell Copeland	.02	.10
184 Chris Gedney	.02	.10
185 Tony McGee	.02	.10
186 Rob Burnett	.02	.10
187 Charles Haley	.07	.20
188 Shannon Sharpe	.07	.20
189 Mel Gray	.02	.10
190 George Teague	.02	.10
191 Ernest Givins	.07	.20
192 Ray Buchanan	.02	.10
193 J.J. Birden	.02	.10
194 Tim Brown	.15	.40
195 Tim Lester	.02	.10
196 Marco Coleman	.02	.10
197 Randall McDaniel	.05	.15
198 Bruce Armstrong	.02	.10
199 Willie Roaf	.02	.10
200 Greg Jackson	.02	.10
201 Johnny Mitchell	.02	.10
202 Calvin Williams	.07	.20
203 Jeff Graham	.02	.10
204 Darren Carrington	.02	.10
205 Jerry Rice	.60	1.50
206 Cortez Kennedy	.07	.20
207 Charles Wilson	.02	.10
208 James Jenkins RC	.02	.10
209 Ray Childress	.02	.10
210 LeRoy Butler	.02	.10
211 Randal Hill	.02	.10
212 Lincoln Kennedy	.02	.10
213 Kenneth Davis	.02	.10
214 Terry Obee	.02	.10
215 Ricardo McDonald	.02	.10
216 Pepper Johnson	.02	.10
217 Alvin Harper	.07	.20
218 John Elway	1.25	3.00
219 Derrick Moore	.02	.10
220 Terrell Buckley	.02	.10
221 Haywood Jeffires	.07	.20
222 Jessie Hester	.02	.10
223 Kimble Anders	.07	.20
224 Rocket Ismail	.07	.20
225 Roman Phifer	.02	.10
226 Bryan Cox	.02	.10
227 Cris Carter	.30	.75
228 Sam Gash	.02	.10
229 Renaldo Turnbull	.02	.10
230 Rodney Hampton	.07	.20
231 Johnny Johnson	.02	.10
232 Tim Harris	.02	.10
233 Leroy Thompson	.02	.10
234 Junior Seau	.15	.40
235 Tim McDonald	.02	.10
236 Eugene Robinson	.02	.10
237 Lawrence Dawsey	.02	.10
238 Tim Johnson	.02	.10
239 Jason Elam	.07	.20
240 Willie Green	.02	.10
241 Larry Centers	.15	.40
242 Erric Pegram	.02	.10
243 Bruce Smith	.15	.40
244 Alonzo Spellman	.02	.10
245 Carl Pickens	.07	.20
246 Michael Jackson	.07	.20
247 Kevin Williams	.07	.20
248 Glyn Milburn	.07	.20
249 Herman Moore	.15	.40
250 Brett Favre	1.25	3.00
251 Al Smith	.02	.10
252 Roosevelt Potts	.02	.10
253 Marcus Allen	.15	.40
254 Anthony Smith	.02	.10
255 Sean Gilbert	.02	.10
256 Keith Byars	.02	.10
257 Scottie Graham RC	.07	.20
258 Leonard Russell	.02	.10
259 Eric Martin	.02	.10
260 Jarrod Bunch	.02	.10
261 Rob Moore	.07	.20
262 Herschel Walker	.07	.20
263 Levon Kirkland	.02	.10
264 Chris Mims	.02	.10
265 Ricky Watters	.07	.20
266 Rick Mirer	.15	.40
267 Santana Dotson	.07	.20
268 Reggie Brooks	.07	.20
269 Garrison Hearst	.15	.40
270 Thurman Thomas	.15	.40
271 Johnny Bailey	.02	.10
272 Andre Rison	.07	.20
273 Jim Kelly	.15	.40
274 Mark Carrier DB	.02	.10
275 David Klingler	.02	.10
276 Eric Metcalf	.07	.20
277 Troy Aikman	.60	1.50
278 Simon Fletcher	.02	.10
279 Pat Swilling	.02	.10
280 Sterling Sharpe	.07	.20
281 Cody Carlson	.02	.10
282 Steve Emtman	.02	.10
283 Neil Smith	.07	.20
284 James Jett	.02	.10
285 Shane Conlan	.02	.10
286 Keith Jackson	.02	.10
287 Qadry Ismail	.15	.40
288 Chris Slade	.02	.10
289 Derek Brown RBK	.02	.10
290 Phil Simms	.07	.20
291 Boomer Esiason	.07	.20
292 Eric Allen	.02	.10
293 Rod Woodson	.07	.20
294 Ronnie Harmon	.02	.10
295 John Taylor	.07	.20
296 Ferrell Edmunds	.02	.10
297 Craig Erickson	.02	.10
298 Brian Mitchell	.02	.10
299 Dante Jones	.02	.10
300 John Copeland	.02	.10
301 Steve Beuerlein	.07	.20
302 Deion Sanders	.30	.75
303 Andre Reed	.07	.20
304 Curtis Conway	.15	.40
305 Harold Green	.02	.10
306 Vinny Testaverde	.07	.20
307 Michael Irvin	.15	.40
308 Rod Bernstine	.02	.10
309 Chris Spielman	.07	.20
310 Reggie White	.15	.40
311 Gary Brown	.02	.10
312 Quentin Coryatt	.02	.10
313 Derrick Thomas	.15	.40
314 Greg Robinson	.02	.10
315 Troy Drayton	.02	.10
316 Terry Kirby	.15	.40
317 John Randle	.07	.20
318 Ben Coates	.07	.20
319 Tyrone Hughes	.07	.20
320 Corey Miller	.02	.10
321 Brad Baxter	.02	.10
322 Randall Cunningham	.15	.40
323 Greg Lloyd	.07	.20
324 Stan Humphries	.07	.20
325 Dana Stubblefield	.07	.20
326 Kelvin Martin	.02	.10
327 Hardy Nickerson	.07	.20
328 Desmond Howard	.07	.20
329 Mark Carrier WR	.07	.20
330 Daryl Johnston	.07	.20
P19 Joe Montana Promo	1.00	2.50

1994 Upper Deck Electric Gold

*STARS: 6X TO 15X BASIC CARDS
*RCs: 3X TO 8X BASIC CARDS
ONE PER HOBBY BOX

1994 Upper Deck Electric Silver

COMPLETE SET (330)	40.00	100.00
*STARS: 1.2X TO 3X BASIC CARDS		
*RCs: .8X TO 2X BASIC CARDS		
STATED OODS 1:1 HOB, 2:1 SPEC.RETAIL		

1994 Upper Deck Predictor Award Winners

COMPLETE SET (20)	20.00	50.00
STATED ODDS 1:20 HOBBY		
H PREFIX PRIZE SET (20)	12.50	30.00
*PRIZE CARDS: .15X TO .4X BASIC INSERTS		
HP1 Emmitt Smith	3.00	8.00
HP2 Barry Sanders W-2	3.00	8.00
HP3 Jerome Bettis	.75	2.00
HP4 Joe Montana	4.00	10.00
HP5 Dan Marino	4.00	10.00
HP6 Marshall Faulk	4.00	10.00
HP7 Dan Wilkinson	.10	.30
HP8 Sterling Sharpe	.25	.60
HP9 Thurman Thomas	.50	1.25
HP10 Longshot W-1 S.Young	.10	.30
HP11 Marshall Faulk W-1	4.00	10.00
HP12 Trent Dilfer	.75	2.00
HP13 Heath Shuler	.25	.60
HP14 David Palmer	.25	.60
HP15 Charles Johnson	.25	.60
HP16 Greg Hill	.25	.60
HP17 Johnnie Morton	.50	1.25
HP18 Errict Rhett	.25	.60
HP19 Darnay Scott	.50	1.25
HP20 ROY Longshot W-2	.10	.30

1994 Upper Deck Predictor League Leaders

COMPLETE SET (30)	20.00	50.00
STATED ODDS 1:20 RETAIL		
R PREFIX PRIZE SET (30)	12.50	30.00
*PRIZE CARDS: .15X to .4X BASIC INSERTS		
RP1 Troy Aikman	2.00	5.00
RP2 Steve Young	1.25	3.00
RP3 John Elway	4.00	10.00
RP4 Joe Montana	4.00	10.00
RP5 Brett Favre	4.00	10.00
RP6 Heath Shuler	.25	.60
RP7 Dan Marino W-2	4.00	10.00
RP8 Rick Mirer	.50	1.25
RP9 Drew Bledsoe W-1	1.25	3.00
RP10 The Longshot	.10	.30
RP11 Emmitt Smith	3.00	8.00
RP12 Barry Sanders W-1	3.00	8.00
RP13 Jerome Bettis	.75	2.00
RP14 Rodney Hampton	.25	.60
RP15 Thurman Thomas	.50	1.25
RP16 Marshall Faulk	4.00	10.00
RP17 Barry Foster	.10	.30
RP18 Reggie Brooks	.25	.60
RP19 Ricky Watters	.25	.60
RP20 Longshot W-2 Warren	.10	.30
RP21 Jerry Rice W-1	2.00	5.00
RP22 Sterling Sharpe	.25	.60
RP23 Andre Rison	.25	.60
RP24 Michael Irvin	.50	1.25
RP25 Tim Brown	.50	1.25
RP26 Shannon Sharpe	.25	.60
RP27 Andre Reed	.25	.60
RP28 Irving Fryar	.25	.60
RP29 Charles Johnson	.25	.60
RP30 Longshot W-2 Ellard	.10	.30

1994 Upper Deck Pro Bowl

COMPLETE SET (20)	25.00	60.00
STATED ODDS 1:20		
PB1 Jerome Bettis	1.50	4.00
PB2 Jay Novacek	.50	1.25
PB3 Shannon Sharpe	.50	1.25
PB4 Brent Jones	.50	1.25
PB5 Andre Rison	.50	1.25
PB6 Tim Brown	1.00	2.50
PB7 Anthony Miller	.50	1.25
PB8 Jerry Rice	4.00	10.00
PB9 Brett Favre	8.00	20.00
PB10 Emmitt Smith	6.00	15.00
PB11 Steve Young	2.50	6.00
PB12 John Elway	8.00	20.00
PB13 Warren Moon	1.00	2.50
PB14 Thurman Thomas	1.00	2.50
PB15 Ricky Watters	.50	1.25
PB16 Rod Woodson	.50	1.25
PB17 Reggie White	1.00	2.50
PB18 Tyrone Hughes	.50	1.25
PB19 Derrick Thomas	1.00	2.50
PB20 Checklist	.50	1.25

1994 Upper Deck Rookie Jumbos

1 Dan Wilkinson	.50	1.25
2 Antonio Langham	.50	1.25
3 Derrick Alexander WR RC	.60	1.50
4 Charles Johnson	.60	1.50
5 Bucky Brooks	.40	1.00
6 Trev Alberts	.50	1.25
7 Marshall Faulk	3.00	8.00
8 Willie McGinest	.60	1.50
9 Aaron Glenn	.60	1.50
10 Ryan Yarborough	.40	1.00
11 Greg Hill	.60	1.50
12 Sam Adams	.50	1.25
13 John Thierry	.40	1.00
14 Johnnie Morton	1.00	2.50
15 LeShon Johnson	.50	1.25
16 David Palmer	.60	1.50
17 Trent Dilfer	1.25	3.00
18 Jamir Miller	.50	1.25
19 Thomas Lewis	.50	1.25
20 Heath Shuler	.60	1.50
21 Wayne Gandy	.40	1.00
22 Isaac Bruce	2.50	6.00
23 Joe Johnson	.40	1.00
24 Mario Bates	.60	1.50
25 Bryant Young	.75	2.00
26 William Floyd	.60	1.50
27 Errict Rhett	.60	1.50
28 Chuck Levy	.40	1.00
29 Darnay Scott	1.00	2.50
30 Rob Fredrickson	.50	1.25

1994 Upper Deck Commemorative Cards

1 1994 Launch Tour/2000	2.00	5.00
Wayne Gretzky		
Reggie Jackson		
Michael Jordan		
Joe Montana		

1994-95 Upper Deck Sheets

These 11" by 8.5" sheets were issued by Upper Deck. The autograph sheet was given out during the 1995 Super Bowl Card Show VI for collectors to have signed by players appearing at the show. The Dan Marino was issued in 1995 to commemorate Marino's record breaking season.

COMPLETE SET (4)	12.00	30.00
NNO Rookie Class 1994	3.20	8.00
(numbered of 40,000)		
Dan Wilkinson		
Heath Shuler		
Trev Alberts		
Greg Hill		
Marshall Faulk		
Johnnie Morton		
NNO Super Bowl XXIX	1.60	4.00
Autograph Sheet		
Jan. 26-29, 1995		
NNO Upper Deck Salutes	3.20	8.00
St. Louis Rams		
Undated numbered of 30,000		
Sean Gilbert		
Kevin Carter		
Isaac Bruce		
Jerome Bettis		
Chris Miller		
Shane Conlan		
NNO Dan Marino/1995 Record Breaker	4.80	12.00
Numbered of 30,000		

1995 Upper Deck

This 300 card standard-size set was released in one series. They were issued in 12-card packs with a suggested retail price of $1.99. There is one subset, Rookies (1-30). Rookie Cards include Jeff Blake, Ki-Jana Carter, Kerry Collins, Joey Galloway, Curtis Martin, Steve McNair, Rashaan Salaam, J.J. Stokes, Michael Westbrook and Tyrone Wheatley. Joe Montana (#19) and Marshall Faulk (PB95) Promo cards were produced and listed at the end of our checklist.

COMPLETE SET (300) 12.50 30.00
1 Ki-Jana Carter RC .15 .40
2 Tony Boselli RC .15 .40
3 Steve McNair RC 1.50 4.00
4 Michael Westbrook RC .15 .40
5 Kerry Collins RC .75 2.00
6 Kevin Carter RC .15 .40
7 James A.Stewart RC .02 .10
8 Joey Galloway RC .75 2.00
9 Kyle Brady RC .15 .40
10 J.J. Stokes RC .15 .40
11 Derrick Alexander DE RC .02 .10
12 Warren Sapp RC .75 2.00
13 Mark Fields RC UER .15 .40
Linebacker on front, running back on back
14 Tyrone Wheatley RC .60 1.50
15 Napoleon Kaufman RC .60 1.50
16 James O. Stewart RC .60 1.50
17 Luther Elliss RC .02 .10
18 Rashaan Salaam RC .07 .20
19 Jimmy Oliver RC .02 .10
20 Mark Bruener RC .07 .20
21 Derrick Brooks RC .75 2.00
22 Christian Fauria RC .07 .20
23 Ray Zellars RC .07 .20
24 Todd Collins RC .50 1.25
25 Sherman Williams RC .02 .10
26 Frank Sanders RC .15 .40
27 Rodney Thomas RC .07 .20
28 Rob Johnson RC .50 1.25
29 Steve Stenstrom RC .02 .10
30 Curtis Martin RC 1.50 4.00
31 Gary Clark .02 .10
32 Troy Aikman .60 1.50
33 Mike Sherrard .02 .10
34 Fred Barnett .07 .20
35 Henry Ellard .07 .20
36 Terry Allen .07 .20
37 Jeff Graham .02 .10
38 Herman Moore .15 .40
39 Brett Favre 1.25 3.00
40 Trent Dilfer .15 .40
41 Derek Brown RBK .02 .10
42 Andre Rison .07 .20
43 Flipper Anderson .02 .10
44 Jerry Rice .60 1.50
45 Andre Reed .07 .20
46 Sean Dawkins .07 .20
47 Irving Fryar .07 .20
48 Vincent Brisby .02 .10
49 Rob Moore .07 .20
50 Carl Pickens .07 .20
51 Vinny Testaverde .07 .20
52 Ray Childress .02 .10
53 Eric Green .02 .10
54 Anthony Miller .07 .20
55 Lake Dawson .07 .20
56 Tim Brown .15 .40
57 Stan Humphries .07 .20
58 Rick Mirer .07 .20
59 Randal Hill .02 .10
60 Charles Haley .07 .20
61 Chris Calloway .02 .10
62 Calvin Williams .07 .20
63 Ethan Horton .02 .10
64 Cris Carter .15 .40
65 Curtis Conway .15 .40
66 Scott Mitchell .07 .20
67 Edgar Bennett .07 .20
68 Craig Erickson .02 .10
69 Jim Everett .02 .10
70 Terance Mathis .07 .20
71 Robert Young .02 .10
72 Brent Jones .02 .10
73 Bill Brooks .07 .20
74 Marshall Faulk .75 2.00
75 O.J. McDuffie .15 .40
76 Ben Coates .07 .20
77 Johnny Mitchell .02 .10
78 Darnay Scott .07 .20
79 Derrick Alexander WR .15 .40
80 Lorenzo White .02 .10
81 Charles Johnson .07 .20
82 John Elway 1.25 3.00
83 Willie Davis .07 .20
84 James Jett .07 .20
85 Mark Seay .07 .20
86 Brian Blades .07 .20
87 Ronald Moore .02 .10
88 Alvin Harper .02 .10
89 Dave Brown .07 .20
90 Randall Cunningham .15 .40
91 Heath Shuler .07 .20
92 Jake Reed .07 .20
93 Donnell Woolford .02 .10
94 Barry Sanders 1.00 2.50
95 Reggie White .15 .40
96 Lawrence Dawsey .02 .10
97 Michael Haynes .07 .20
98 Bert Emanuel .15 .40
99 Troy Drayton .02 .10
100 Steve Young .50 1.25
101 Bruce Smith .15 .40
102 Roosevelt Potts .02 .10
103 Dan Marino 1.25 3.00
104 Michael Timpson .02 .10
105 Boomer Esiason .07 .20
106 David Klingler .07 .20
107 Eric Metcalf .07 .20
108 Gary Brown .02 .10
109 Neil O'Donnell .07 .20
110 Shannon Sharpe .07 .20
111 Joe Montana 1.25 3.00
112 Jeff Hostetler .07 .20
113 Ronnie Harmon .02 .10
114 Chris Warren .07 .20
115 Larry Centers .07 .20
116 Michael Irvin .15 .40
117 Rodney Hampton .07 .20
118 Herschel Walker .07 .20
119 Reggie Brooks .07 .20
120 Qadry Ismail .07 .20
121 Chris Zorich .02 .10
122 Chris Spielman .07 .20
123 Sean Jones .02 .10
124 Errict Rhett .07 .20
125 Tyrone Hughes .07 .20
126 Jeff George .07 .20
127 Chris Miller .02 .10
128 Ricky Watters .07 .20
129 Jim Kelly .15 .40
130 Tony Bennett .02 .10
131 Terry Kirby .07 .20
132 Drew Bledsoe .40 1.00
133 Johnny Johnson .02 .10
134 Dan Wilkinson .07 .20
135 Leroy Hoard .02 .10
136 Darryll Lewis .02 .10
137 Barry Foster .07 .20
138 Shane Dronett .02 .10
139 Marcus Allen .15 .40
140 Harvey Williams .02 .10
141 Tony Martin .07 .20
142 Rod Stephens .02 .10
143 Eric Swann .07 .20
144 Daryl Johnston .07 .20
145 Dave Meggett .02 .10
146 Charlie Garner .15 .40
147 Ken Harvey .02 .10
148 Warren Moon .07 .20
149 Steve Walsh .02 .10
150 Pat Swilling .02 .10
151 Terrell Buckley .02 .10
152 Courtney Hawkins .02 .10
153 Willie Roaf .02 .10
154 Chris Doleman .02 .10
155 Jerome Bettis .15 .40
156 Dana Stubblefield .07 .20
157 Cornelius Bennett .07 .20
158 Quentin Coryatt .07 .20
159 Bryan Cox .02 .10
160 Marion Butts .02 .10
161 Aaron Glenn .02 .10
162 Louis Oliver .02 .10
163 Eric Turner .02 .10
164 Cris Dishman .02 .10
165 John L. Williams .02 .10
166 Simon Fletcher .02 .10
167 Neil Smith .07 .20
168 Chester McGlockton .07 .20
169 Natrone Means .07 .20
170 Sam Adams .02 .10
171 Clyde Simmons .02 .10
172 Jay Novacek .07 .20
173 Keith Hamilton .02 .10
174 William Fuller .02 .10
175 Tom Carter .02 .10
176 John Randle .07 .20
177 Lewis Tillman .02 .10
178 Mel Gray .02 .10
179 George Teague .02 .10
180 Hardy Nickerson .02 .10
181 Mario Bates .07 .20
182 D.J. Johnson .02 .10
183 Sean Gilbert .07 .20
184 Bryant Young .07 .20
185 Jeff Burris .02 .10
186 Floyd Turner .02 .10
187 Troy Vincent .02 .10
188 Willie McGinest .07 .20
189 James Hasty .02 .10
190 Jeff Blake RC .40 1.00
191 Stevon Moore .02 .10
192 Ernest Givins .02 .10
193 Byron Bam Morris .02 .10
194 Ray Crockett .02 .10
195 Dale Carter .07 .20
196 Terry McDaniel .02 .10
197 Leslie O'Neal .07 .20
198 Cortez Kennedy .07 .20
199 Seth Joyner .02 .10
200 Emmitt Smith 1.00 2.50
201 Thomas Lewis .07 .20
202 Andy Harmon .02 .10
203 Ricky Ervins .02 .10
204 Fuad Reveiz .02 .10
205 John Thierry .02 .10
206 Bennie Blades .02 .10
207 LeShon Johnson .07 .20
208 Charles Wilson .02 .10
209 Joe Johnson .02 .10
210 Chuck Smith .02 .10
211 Roman Phifer .02 .10
212 Ken Norton Jr. .07 .20
213 Bucky Brooks .02 .10
214 Ray Buchanan .02 .10
215 Tim Bowens .02 .10
216 Vincent Brown .02 .10
217 Marcus Turner .02 .10
218 Derrick Fenner .02 .10
219 Antonio Langham .02 .10
220 Cody Carlson .02 .10
221 Greg Lloyd .07 .20
222 Steve Atwater .02 .10
223 Donnell Bennett .07 .20
224 Rocket Ismail .07 .20
225 John Carney .02 .10
226 Eugene Robinson .02 .10
227 Aeneas Williams .02 .10
228 Darrin Smith .02 .10
229 Phillippi Sparks .02 .10
230 Eric Allen .02 .10
231 Brian Mitchell .02 .10
232 David Palmer .07 .20
233 Mark Carrier DB .02 .10
234 Dave Krieg .02 .10
235 Robert Brooks .15 .40
236 Eric Curry .02 .10
237 Wayne Martin .02 .10
238 Craig Heyward .07 .20
239 Isaac Bruce .30 .75
240 Deion Sanders .40 1.00
241 Steve Tasker .07 .20
242 Jim Harbaugh .07 .20
243 Aubrey Beavers .02 .10
244 Chris Slade .02 .10
245 Mo Lewis .02 .10
246 Alfred Williams .02 .10
247 Michael Dean Perry .02 .10
248 Marcus Robertson .02 .10
249 Kevin Greene .07 .20
250 Leonard Russell .02 .10
251 Greg Hill .07 .20
252 Rob Fredrickson .02 .10
253 Junior Seau .15 .40
254 Rick Tuten .02 .10
255 Garrison Hearst .15 .40
256 Russell Maryland .02 .10
257 Michael Brooks .02 .10
258 Bernard Williams .02 .10
259 Reggie Roby .02 .10
260 Dewayne Washington .07 .20
261 Raymont Harris .02 .10
262 Brett Perriman .07 .20
263 LeRoy Butler .02 .10
264 Santana Dotson .02 .10
265 Irv Smith .02 .10
266 Ron George .02 .10
267 Marquez Pope .02 .10
268 William Floyd .07 .20
269 Matt Darby .02 .10
270 Jeff Herrod .02 .10
271 Bernie Parmalee .07 .20
272 Leroy Thompson .02 .10
273 Ronnie Lott .07 .20
274 Steve Tovar .02 .10
275 Michael Jackson .07 .20
276 Al Smith .02 .10
277 Rod Woodson .07 .20
278 Glyn Milburn .02 .10
279 Kimble Anders .07 .20
280 Anthony Smith .02 .10
281 Andre Coleman .02 .10
282 Terry Wooden .02 .10
283 Mickey Washington .02 .10
284 Steve Beuerlein .07 .20
285 Mark Brunell .40 1.00
286 Keith Goganious .02 .10
287 Desmond Howard .07 .20
288 Darren Carrington .02 .10
289 Derek Brown TE .02 .10
290 Reggie Cobb .02 .10
291 Jeff Lageman .02 .10
292 Lamar Lathon .02 .10
293 Sam Mills .07 .20
294 Carlton Bailey .02 .10
295 Mark Carrier WR .07 .20
296 Willie Green .07 .20
297 Frank Reich .02 .10
298 Don Beebe .02 .10
299 Tim McKyer .02 .10
300 Pete Metzelaars .02 .10
A19 Joe Montana Blowup 6.00 15.00
Card Numbered #19
Card Measures 8 1/2 x 11
Upper Deck Authenticated
A103 Dan Marino Blowup 6.00 15.00
Card measures 8 1/2 x 11
Upper Deck Authenticated
P1 Joe Montana Promo .75 2.00
base brand card
Numbered 19
P2 Joe Montana Promo .75 2.00
Predictor card
Numbered 19
P3 Marshall Faulk Promo .40 1.00
Pro Bowl hologram card
Numbered PB95

1995 Upper Deck Electric Gold

*STARS: 4X TO 10X BASIC CARDS
*RCs: 1.5X TO 4X BASIC CARDS
STATED ODDS 1:35

1995 Upper Deck Electric Silver

COMPLETE SET (300) 40.00 100.00
*STARS: 1X TO 2.5X BASIC CARDS
*RCs: .6X TO 1.5X BASIC CARDS
ONE PER PACK

1995 Upper Deck Joe Montana Trilogy

COMPLETE SET (23) 20.00 50.00
COMMON CC 1.50 3.00
MT1-MT8: COL. CHOICE STATED ODDS 1:12
COMMON UD 2.00 4.00
MT9-MT16: UP. DECK STATED ODDS 1:12
COMMON SP 2.50 5.00
MT17-MT21: SP STATED ODDS 1:29
CCH Coll. Choice Header 1.50 3.00
SPH SP Header 2.00 4.00
UDH Upper Deck Header 2.50 5.00

1995 Upper Deck Predictor Award Winners

COMPLETE SET (20) 25.00 60.00
STATED ODDS 1:35 HOBBY
*PRIZE STARS: .6X TO 1.5X BASE CARD HI
*PRIZE ROOKIES: .3X TO .8X BASE CARD HI
HP1 Dan Marino 4.00 10.00
HP2 Steve Young 1.50 4.00
HP3 Drew Bledsoe 1.50 4.00
HP4 Troy Aikman 2.00 5.00
HP5 Barry Sanders 3.00 8.00
HP6 Emmitt Smith 3.00 8.00
HP7 Jerry Rice W2 2.00 5.00
HP8 Steve McNair 2.50 6.00
HP9 Natrone Means .30 .75
HP10 The Longshot W1 .20 .50
HP11 Ki-Jana Carter .30 .75
HP12 Steve McNair 2.50 6.00
HP13 Michael Westbrook .30 .75
HP14 Kerry Collins 1.25 3.00
HP15 Joey Galloway 1.25 3.00
HP16 Kyle Brady .30 .75
HP17 Napoleon Kaufman 1.00 2.50
HP18 Tyrone Wheatley 1.00 2.50
HP19 Rashaan Salaam .20 .50
HP20 The Longshot W1 .20 .50

1995 Upper Deck Predictor League Leaders

COMPLETE SET (30) 20.00 50.00
STATED ODDS 1:30 RET,1:17 SPEC.RET
*PRIZE STARS: .6X TO 1.5X BASE CARD HI
*PRIZE ROOKIES: .3X TO .8X BASE CARD HI
RP1 Dan Marino 4.00 10.00
RP2 Steve Young 1.50 4.00
RP3 Drew Bledsoe 1.50 4.00
RP4 Troy Aikman 2.00 5.00
RP5 John Elway 4.00 10.00
RP6 Brett Favre W2 4.00 10.00
RP7 Stan Humphries .30 .75
RP8 Jeff George .30 .75
RP9 Kerry Collins 1.25 3.00
RP10 The Longshot W1 .20 .50
RP11 Barry Sanders W2 3.00 8.00
RP12 Chris Warren .30 .75
RP13 Emmitt Smith W1 3.00 8.00
RP14 Natrone Means .30 .75
RP15 Rodney Hampton .30 .75
RP16 Marshall Faulk 3.00 8.00
RP17 Errict Rhett .30 .75
RP18 Napoleon Kaufman 1.00 2.50
RP19 Ki-Jana Carter .20 .50
RP20 The Longshot .20 .50
RP21 Jerry Rice W1 2.00 5.00
RP22 Ben Coates .30 .75
RP23 Cris Carter .60 1.50
RP24 Andre Reed .30 .75
RP25 Andre Rison .30 .75
RP26 Tim Brown .60 1.50
RP27 Michael Irvin .60 1.50
RP28 Irving Fryar .30 .75
RP29 Michael Westbrook .20 .50
RP30 The Longshot W2 .20 .50

1995 Upper Deck Pro Bowl

COMPLETE SET (25) 25.00 60.00
STATED ODDS 1:25
PB1 Barry Sanders 5.00 12.00
PB2 Brent Jones .20 .50
PB3 Cris Carter .75 2.00
PB4 Emmitt Smith 5.00 12.00
PB5 Jay Novacek .40 1.00
PB6 Jerome Bettis .75 2.00
PB7 Jerry Rice 3.00 8.00
PB8 Michael Irvin .75 2.00
PB9 Ricky Watters .40 1.00
PB10 Steve Young 2.50 6.00
PB11 Troy Aikman 3.00 8.00
PB12 Warren Moon .40 1.00
PB13 Terance Mathis .40 1.00
PB14 Ben Coates .40 1.00
PB15 Chris Warren .40 1.00
PB16 Dan Marino 6.00 15.00
PB17 Drew Bledsoe 2.00 5.00
PB18 Irving Fryar .40 1.00
PB19 Jeff Hostetler .40 1.00
PB20 John Elway 6.00 15.00
PB21 Leroy Hoard .20 .50
PB22 Marshall Faulk 4.00 10.00
PB23 Natrone Means .40 1.00
PB24 Tim Brown .75 2.00
PB25 Checklist .40 1.00

1995 Upper Deck Special Edition

COMPLETE SET (90) 12.50 30.00
ONE SILVER PER HOBBY PACK
*GOLD SE STARS: 3X TO 8X BASE CARD HI
*GOLD SE ROOKIES: 1.5X TO 4X BASE CARD HI
GOLD STATED ODDS 1:35 HOBBY
SE1 Terry Kirby .10 .30
SE2 Marcus Allen .25 .60
SE3 Bernie Parmalee .10 .30
SE4 Vernon Turner .05 .15
SE5 Dolphins Defense .05 .15
SE6 Kevin Turner .05 .15
SE7 Henry Thomas .05 .15
SE8 Barry Sanders 2.00 4.00
SE9 Marshall Faulk 1.50 3.00
SE10 Bill Bates .10 .30
SE11 Stan Humphries .10 .30
SE12 Barry Foster .10 .30
SE13 Shannon Sharpe .10 .30
SE14 Joe Montana 2.50 5.00
SE15 Bryan Cox .05 .15
SE16 Dale Carter .10 .30
SE17 Drew Bledsoe .75 1.50
SE18 Dan Marino 2.50 5.00
SE19 Ricky Watters .10 .30
SE20 Alvin Harper .05 .15
SE21 Harris Barton .05 .15
SE22 Dan Marino 2.50 5.00
SE23 Ronnie Harmon .05 .15
SE24 Michael Irvin .25 .60
SE25 Emmitt Smith 2.00 4.00
SE26 Jeff Christy .05 .15
SE27 Terry Allen .10 .30
SE28 Randall Cunningham .25 .60
SE29 Todd Steussie .05 .15
SE30 Warren Moon .10 .30
SE31 Robert Griffith .05 .15
SE32 Tony Tolbert .05 .15
SE33 William Fuller .05 .15
SE34 Bernard Williams .05 .15
SE35 Charlie Garner .25 .60
SE36 Troy Aikman 1.25 2.50
SE37 Alvin Harper .05 .15
SE38 Kenneth Gant .05 .15
SE39 Daryl Johnston .10 .30
SE40 Ben Coates .10 .30
SE41 Rickey Jackson .05 .15
SE42 O.J. McDuffie .25 .60
SE43 Marion Butts .05 .15
SE44 The Snap .05 .15
SE45 Kimble Anders .10 .30
SE46 Chiefs Defense .10 .30
SE47 Richmond Webb .05 .15
SE48 Carlos Jenkins .05 .15
SE49 James Harris DE .05 .15
SE50 Dexter Carter .05 .15
SE51 Qadry Ismail .10 .30
SE52 Jeff Herrod .05 .15
SE53 Sean Jones .05 .15
SE54 Keith Sims .05 .15
SE55 William Floyd .10 .30
SE56 Don Majkowski .05 .15
SE57 Chargers Defense .05 .15
SE58 Byron Evans .05 .15
SE59 Chad Hennings .05 .15
SE60 Eric Allen .05 .15
SE61 Curtis Martin 1.50 3.00
SE62 Napoleon Kaufman .60 1.25
SE63 Kevin Carter .25 .60
SE64 Luther Elliss .05 .15
SE65 Frank Sanders .10 .30
SE66 Rob Johnson .40 1.00
SE67 Christian Fauria .10 .30
SE68 Kyle Brady .25 .60
SE69 Ray Zellars .10 .30
SE70 James A.Stewart .05 .15
SE71 Ty Law .05 .15
SE72 Rodney Thomas .10 .30
SE73 Jimmy Oliver .05 .15
SE74 James O. Stewart .60 1.25
SE75 Dave Barr .05 .15
SE76 Kordell Stewart .75 2.00
SE77 Michael Westbrook .10 .30
SE78 Bobby Taylor .05 .15
SE79 Mark Fields .25 .60
SE80 Kerry Collins .75 1.50
SE81 Natrone Means .10 .30
SE82 Mark Seay .10 .30
SE83 Deion Sanders .75 1.50
SE84 Dana Stubblefield .10 .30
SE85 49ers Defense .10 .30
SE86 Alfred Pupunu .05 .15
SE87 Tim Harris .05 .15
SE88 Jerry Rice 1.25 2.50
SE89 Steve Young 1.00 2.00
SE90 Steve Young 1.25 2.50
Jerry Rice

1995 Upper Deck Gold Signature/Electric Gold

COMPLETE GOLD SET (300) 350.00 700.00
COMP.GOLD SIG.SET (150) 200.00 400.00
COMP. ELE.GOLD SET (150) 150.00 300.00
*GOLD STARS: 8X TO 20X BASE CARDS

1995 Upper Deck/GTE Phone Cards AFC

Upper Deck and GTE joined together to produce these 15 prepaid phone cards. Measuring approximately 3 3/8" by 2 1/8", the cards have rounded corners and carry 5 units of U.S. long distance calling. The fronts feature color action player photos of AFC football players, with the player's name, position and team in a team color-coded bar alongside the left. A red bar below the photo carries the words "Prepaid Calling Card, 5 Units". The backs have instructions on how to use the calling cards. The cards are unnumbered and checklisted below in alphabetical order. Just 2,500 of each card were produced, and they are individually numbered on the back. A special card with more detailed instructions was included with each set.

COMPLETE SET (15) 16.00 40.00
1 Marcus Allen 1.20 3.00
2 Drew Bledsoe 2.00 5.00
3 Gary Brown .40 1.00
4 Tim Brown 1.20 3.00
5 John Elway 4.80 12.00
6 Marshall Faulk 2.40 6.00
7 Barry Foster .40 1.00
8 Jim Kelly 1.20 3.00
9 Ronnie Lott .60 1.50
10 Dan Marino 4.80 12.00
11 Rick Mirer .60 1.50
12 Carl Pickens .60 1.50
13 Junior Seau .60 1.50
14 Vinny Testaverde .60 1.50
15 Title Card .40 1.00

1995 Upper Deck/GTE Phone Cards NFC

Upper Deck and GTE joined together to produce these 15 prepaid phone cards. Measuring approximately 3 3/8" by 2 1/8", the cards have rounded corners and carry five units of U.S. long distance calling. The fronts feature color action player photos of NFC football players, with the player's name, position and team in a team color-coded bar alongside the left. A blue bar below the photo carries the words "Prepaid Calling Card, 5 Units". The backs have instructions on how to use the calling cards. They are unnumbered and checklisted below in alphabetical order. Only 2,500 of each card were produced, and they are individually numbered on the back. A special card with more detailed instructions was included with each set.

COMPLETE SET (15) 12.00 30.00
1 Jerome Bettis 1.20 3.00
2 Gary Clark .40 1.00
3 Curtis Conway .80 2.00
4 Randall Cunningham 1.20 3.00
5 Rodney Hampton .40 1.00
6 Michael Haynes .40 1.00
7 Michael Irvin 1.20 3.00
8 Warren Moon 1.20 3.00
9 Hardy Nickerson .40 1.00
10 Jerry Rice 2.40 6.00
11 Andre Rison .80 2.00
12 Barry Sanders 4.80 12.00
13 Sterling Sharpe .80 2.00
14 Heath Shuler .80 2.00
15 Title Card .40 1.00

1995 Upper Deck Joe Montana Box Set

This 45-card, boxed set summarizes the career of Joe Montana from the Pennsylvania Pee-Wee Leagues through his NFL career. On the fronts, the full-bleed photos are edged by a gold foil design and a black-and-red bar. The backs feature a second color photo and commentary summarizing various facets of his career. The set is subdivided as follows: The Early Years (1-5), Montana's Dominance (6-25), The New Chief (26-30), Joe's Numbers (31-40), and Teammates (41-45). The set includes one of four oversized (8 1/8" by 3 3/8") cards commemorating Montana's Super Bowls. Each of these oversized cards was serial numbered and, apparently, also sold separately by Upper Deck Authenticated through the catalog.

COMP.FACTORY SET (46) 8.00 20.00
COMMON CARD (1-45) .24 .60
41 Bill Walsh CO .25 .60
42 Russ Francis .25 .60
43 Roger Craig .25 .60
44 Jerry Rice .50 1.25
45 Dwight Clark .25 .60
JM16 Joe Montana Promo .60 1.50
NNO1 Super Bowl XVI 2.00 5.00
(numbered of 24,000)
NNO2 Super Bowl XIX 1.60 4.00
(numbered of 38,000)
NNO3 Super Bowl XXIII 1.20 3.00
(numbered of 46,000)
NNO4 Super Bowl XXIV 2.40 6.00

1996 Upper Deck

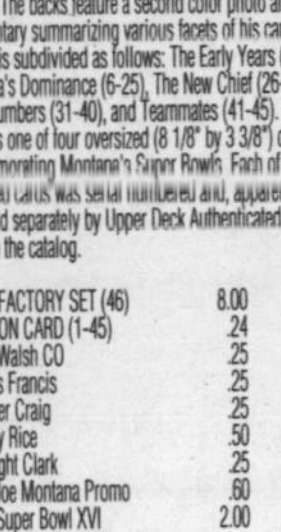

The 1996 Upper Deck set was issued in one series totalling 300-cards. The 12-card packs originally retailed for $2.99 each. The set contains a 33-card Star Rookies subset and numerous insert sets. Also included as an insert, in both Collector's Choice and Upper Deck packs (1:4 packs), was a game piece for the Meet the Stars promotion. Each game piece featured multiple choice trivia questions about football. A collector could scratch off the box next to the answer that they felt best matched the question to determine if they won. Instant win game pieces were also inserted one in 72 packs. Winning game pieces could be sent to Upper Deck for prize drawings. The Grand Prize was a chance to meet Dan Marino. Prizes for 2nd through 4th were for Upper Deck Authenticated shopping sprees. The 5th prize was two special Dan Marino Meet the Stars cards. The blankbacked die cut cards measure roughly 5" X 7" and are entitled Dynamic Debut and Magic Memories. These two cards are priced at the bottom of the base set below.

COMPLETE SET (300) 12.50 30.00
1 Keyshawn Johnson RC .50 1.25
2 Kevin Hardy RC .20 .50
3 Simeon Rice RC .50 1.25
4 Jonathan Ogden RC .20 .50
5 Cedric Jones RC .02 .10
6 Lawrence Phillips RC .20 .50
7 Tim Biakabutuka RC .20 .50
8 Terry Glenn RC .50 1.25
9 Rickey Dudley RC .20 .50
10 Willie Anderson RC .02 .10
11 Alex Molden RC .02 .10
12 Regan Upshaw RC .02 .10
13 Walt Harris RC .02 .10
14 Eddie George RC .60 1.50
15 John Mobley RC .02 .10
16 Duane Clemons RC .02 .10
17 Eddie Kennison RC .20 .50
18 Marvin Harrison RC 1.25 3.00
19 Daryl Gardener RC .02 .10
20 Leeland McElroy RC .08 .25
21 Eric Moulds RC .60 1.50
22 Alex Van Dyke RC .08 .25
23 Mike Alstott RC .50 1.25
24 Jeff Lewis RC .08 .25
25 Bobby Engram RC .20 .50
26 Derrick Mayes RC .20 .50
27 Karim Abdul-Jabbar RC .20 .50
28 Bobby Hoying RC .20 .50
29 Stepfret Williams RC .08 .25
30 Chris Darkins RC .02 .10
31 Stephen Davis RC .75 2.00
32 Danny Kanell RC .20 .50
33 Tony Brackens RC .20 .50
34 Leslie O'Neal .02 .10
35 Chris Doleman .02 .10
36 Larry Brown .02 .10
37 Ronnie Harmon .02 .10
38 Chris Spielman .02 .10
39 John Jurkovic .02 .10
40 Shawn Jefferson .02 .10
41 William Floyd .08 .25
42 Eric Davis .02 .10
43 Willie Clay .02 .10
44 Marco Coleman .02 .10
45 Lorenzo White .02 .10
46 Neil O'Donnell .08 .25
47 Natrone Means .08 .25
48 Cornelius Bennett .02 .10
49 Steve Walsh .02 .10
50 Jerome Bettis .20 .50
51 Boomer Esiason .08 .25
52 Glyn Milburn .02 .10
53 Kevin Greene .08 .25
54 Seth Joyner .02 .10
55 Jeff Graham .02 .10
56 Darren Woodson .08 .25
57 Dale Carter .02 .10
58 Lorenzo Lynch .02 .10
59 Tim Brown .20 .50
60 Jerry Rice .50 1.25
61 Garrison Hearst .08 .25
62 Eric Metcalf .08 .25
63 Leroy Hoard .02 .10
64 Thurman Thomas .20 .50
65 Sam Mills .02 .10
66 Curtis Conway .08 .25
67 Carl Pickens .08 .25
68 Deion Sanders .30 .75
69 Shannon Sharpe .08 .25
70 Herman Moore .20 .50
71 Robert Brooks .08 .25
72 Rodney Thomas .08 .25
73 Ken Dilger .08 .25
74 Mark Brunell .30 .75
75 Marcus Allen .20 .50
76 Dan Marino 1.00 2.50
77 Robert Smith .08 .25
78 Drew Bledsoe .30 .75
79 Jim Everett .02 .10
80 Rodney Hampton .08 .25
81 Adrian Murrell .08 .25
82 Daryl Hobbs RC .02 .10
83 Ricky Watters .08 .25
84 Yancey Thigpen .08 .25
85 Roman Phifer .02 .10
86 Tony Martin .08 .25
87 Dana Stubblefield .08 .25
88 Joey Galloway .20 .50
89 Errict Rhett .08 .25
90 Terry Allen .08 .25
91 Aeneas Williams .02 .10
92 Craig Heyward .02 .10
93 Vinny Testaverde .08 .25
94 Bryce Paup .02 .10
95 Kerry Collins .20 .50
96 Rashaan Salaam .08 .25
97 Dan Wilkinson .02 .10
98 Jay Novacek .02 .10
99 John Elway 1.00 2.50
100 Bennie Blades .02 .10
101 Edgar Bennett .08 .25
102 Darryll Lewis .02 .10
103 Marshall Faulk .25 .60
104 Bryan Schwartz .02 .10
105 Tamarick Vanover .08 .25
106 Terry Kirby .08 .25
107 John Randle .08 .25
108 Ted Johnson RC .20 .50
109 Mario Bates .08 .25
110 Phillippi Sparks .02 .10
111 Marvin Washington .02 .10
112 Terry McDaniel .02 .10
113 Bobby Taylor .02 .10
114 Carnell Lake .02 .10
115 Troy Drayton .02 .10
116 Darren Bennett .02 .10
117 J.J. Stokes .20 .50
118 Rick Mirer .08 .25
119 Jackie Harris .02 .10
120 Ken Harvey .02 .10
121 Rob Moore .08 .25
122 Jeff George .08 .25
123 Andre Rison .08 .25
124 Darick Holmes .02 .10
125 Tim McKyer .02 .10
126 Alonzo Spellman .02 .10
127 Jeff Blake .20 .50
128 Kevin Williams .02 .10
129 Anthony Miller .08 .25
130 Barry Sanders .75 2.00
131 Brett Favre 1.25 2.50
132 Steve McNair .40 1.00
133 Jim Harbaugh .08 .25
134 Desmond Howard .08 .25
135 Steve Bono .02 .10
136 Bernie Parmalee .02 .10
137 Warren Moon .08 .25
138 Curtis Martin .40 1.00
139 Irv Smith .02 .10
140 Thomas Lewis .02 .10
141 Kyle Brady .02 .10
142 Napoleon Kaufman .20 .50
143 Mike Mamula .02 .10
144 Erric Pegram .02 .10
145 Isaac Bruce .20 .50
146 Andre Coleman .02 .10
147 Merton Hanks .02 .10
148 Brian Blades .02 .10
149 Hardy Nickerson .02 .10
150 Michael Westbrook .20 .50
151 Larry Centers .08 .25
152 Morten Andersen .02 .10
153 Michael Jackson .08 .25
154 Bruce Smith .08 .25
155 Derrick Moore .02 .10
156 Mark Carrier DB .02 .10
157 John Copeland .02 .10
158 Emmitt Smith .75 2.00
159 Jason Elam .08 .25
160 Scott Mitchell .08 .25
161 Mark Chmura .08 .25
162 Blaine Bishop .02 .10
163 Tony Bennett .02 .10
164 Pete Mitchell .08 .25
165 Dan Saleaumua .02 .10
166 Pete Stoyanovich .02 .10
167 Cris Carter .20 .50
168 Vince Brisby .02 .10
169 Wayne Martin .02 .10
170 Tyrone Wheatley .08 .25
171 Mo Lewis .02 .10
172 Harvey Williams .02 .10
173 Calvin Williams .02 .10
174 Norm Johnson .02 .10
175 Mark Rypien .02 .10
176 Stan Humphries .08 .25
177 Derek Loville .02 .10
178 Christian Fauria .02 .10
179 Warren Sapp .02 .10
180 Henry Ellard .02 .10
181 Jamir Miller .02 .10
182 Jessie Tuggle .02 .10
183 Stevon Moore .02 .10
184 Jim Kelly .20 .50
185 Mark Carrier WR .02 .10
186 Chris Zorich .02 .10
187 Harold Green .02 .10
188 Chris Boniol .02 .10
189 Allen Aldridge .02 .10
190 Brett Perriman .02 .10
191 Chris Jacke .02 .10
192 Todd McNair .02 .10
193 Floyd Turner .02 .10
194 Jeff Lageman .02 .10
195 Derrick Thomas .20 .50
196 Eric Green .02 .10
197 Orlando Thomas .02 .10
198 Ben Coates .08 .25
199 Tyrone Hughes .02 .10
200 Dave Brown .02 .10
201 Brad Baxter .02 .10
202 Chester McGlockton .02 .10
203 Rodney Peete .02 .10
204 Willie Williams .02 .10
205 Kevin Carter .02 .10
206 Aaron Hayden RC .02 .10
207 Steve Young .40 1.00
208 Chris Warren .08 .25
209 Eric Curry .02 .10
210 Brian Mitchell .02 .10
211 Frank Sanders .08 .25
212 Terance Mathis UER .02 .10
name misspelled Terence
213 Eric Turner .02 .10
214 Bill Brooks .02 .10
215 John Kasay .02 .10
216 Erik Kramer .02 .10
217 Darnay Scott .08 .25
218 Charles Haley .08 .25
219 Steve Atwater .02 .10
220 Jason Hanson .02 .10
221 LeRoy Butler .02 .10
222 Cris Dishman .02 .10
223 Sean Dawkins .02 .10
224 James O. Stewart .08 .25
225 Greg Hill .08 .25
226 Jeff Cross .02 .10
227 Qadry Ismail .08 .25
228 Dave Meggett .02 .10
229 Eric Allen .02 .10
230 Chris Calloway .02 .10
231 Wayne Chrebet .30 .75
232 Jeff Hostetler .02 .10
233 Andy Harmon .02 .10
234 Greg Lloyd .08 .25
235 Toby Wright .02 .10
236 Junior Seau .20 .50
237 Bryant Young .08 .25
238 Robert Blackmon .02 .10
239 Trent Dilfer .20 .50
240 Leslie Shepherd .02 .10
241 Eric Swann .02 .10
242 Bert Emanuel .08 .25
243 Antonio Langham .02 .10
244 Steve Christie .02 .10
245 Tyrone Poole .02 .10
246 Jim Flanigan .02 .10
247 Tony McGee .02 .10
248 Michael Irvin .20 .50
249 Byron Bam Morris .02 .10
250 Terrell Davis .40 1.00
251 Johnnie Morton .08 .25
252 Sean Jones .02 .10
253 Chris Sanders .08 .25
254 Quentin Coryatt .02 .10
255 Willie Jackson .08 .25
256 Mark Collins .02 .10
257 Randal Hill .02 .10
258 David Palmer .02 .10
259 Will Moore .02 .10
260 Michael Haynes .02 .10
261 Mike Sherrard .02 .10
262 William Thomas .02 .10
263 Kordell Stewart .20 .50
264 D'Marco Farr .02 .10
265 Terrell Fletcher .02 .10
266 Lee Woodall .02 .10
267 Eugene Robinson .02 .10
268 Alvin Harper .02 .10
269 Gus Frerotte .08 .25
270 Antonio Freeman .20 .50
271 Clyde Simmons .02 .10
272 Chuck Smith .02 .10
273 Steve Tasker .02 .10
274 Kevin Butler .02 .10
275 Steve Tovar .02 .10
276 Troy Aikman .50 1.25
277 Aaron Craver .02 .10
278 Henry Thomas .02 .10
279 Craig Newsome .02 .10
280 Brent Jones .02 .10
281 Micheal Barrow .02 .10
282 Ray Buchanan .02 .10
283 Jimmy Smith .20 .50
284 Neil Smith .08 .25
285 O.J. McDuffie .08 .25
286 Jake Reed .08 .25
287 Ty Law .20 .50
288 Torrance Small .02 .10
289 Hugh Douglas .08 .25
290 Pat Swilling .02 .10

291 Charlie Garner .08 .25
292 Ernie Mills .02 .10
293 John Carney .02 .10
294 Ken Norton .02 .10
295 Cortez Kennedy .02 .10
296 Derrick Brooks .20 .50
297 Heath Shuler .08 .25
298 Reggie White .20 .50
299 Kimble Anders .08 .25
300 Willie McGinest .02 .10
P96 Dan Marino Promo .75 2.00
(Predictor Promo Card)
MS1 Dan Marino 2.00 5.00
Dynamic Debut
Meet the Stars Prize
MS2 Dan Marino 2.00 5.00
Magic Memories
Meet the Stars Prize
P13 Dan Marino Promo 1.00 2.50
(numbered 1996 on back)

1996 Upper Deck Game Face

COMPLETE SET (10) 4.00 10.00
ONE PER SPECIAL RETAIL PACK
GF1 Dan Marino 1.50 4.00
GF2 Barry Sanders 1.25 3.00
GF3 Jerry Rice .75 2.00
GF4 Stan Humphries .15 .40
GF5 Drew Bledsoe .50 1.25
GF6 Greg Lloyd .15 .40
GF7 Jim Harbaugh .15 .40
GF8 Rashaan Salaam .15 .40
GF9 Jeff Blake .30 .75
GF10 Reggie White .30 .75

1996 Upper Deck Game Jerseys

STATED ODDS 1:2500 80.00
GJ1 Dan Marino Teal 100.00 200.00
GJ2 Jerry Rice Red 75.00 150.00
GJ3 Joe Montana 100.00 200.00
GJ4R Jerry Rice Red 75.00 150.00
GJ4W Jerry Rice White 75.00 150.00
GJ5 Rashaan Salaam 25.00 60.00
GJ6 Marshall Faulk 40.00 100.00
GJ7 Dan Marino White 75.00 150.00
GJ8 Steve Young 60.00 120.00
GJ9 Barry Sanders 75.00 150.00
GJ10 Mark Brunell 30.00 80.00

1996 Upper Deck Hot Properties

COMPLETE SET (20) 40.00 100.00
STATED ODDS 1:11
*GOLD CARDS: 1X TO 2X REDS
GOLD STATED ODDS 1:71
HT1 Dan Marino 5.00 12.00
Drew Bledsoe
HT2 Jerry Rice 4.00 8.00
J.J. Stokes
HT3 Kordell Stewart 2.50 6.00
Deion Sanders
HT4 Brett Favre 7.50 15.00
Rick Mirer
HT5 Jeff Blake 2.50 6.00
Steve McNair
HT6 Emmitt Smith 6.00 12.00
Errict Rhett
HT7 John Elway 5.00 12.00
Warren Moon
HT8 Steve Young 4.00 8.00
Mark Brunell
HT9 Troy Aikman 3.00 8.00
Kerry Collins
HT10 Joey Galloway 2.50 6.00
Chris Sanders
HT11 Herman Moore 2.50 6.00
Cris Carter
HT12 Rodney Hampton 3.00 8.00
Terrell Davis
HT13 Carl Pickens 2.00 4.00
Isaac Bruce
HT14 Rashaan Salaam 2.00 4.00
Michael Westbrook
HT15 Marshall Faulk 3.00 8.00
Curtis Martin
HT16 Tamarick Vanover 1.00 2.50
Eric Metcalf
HT17 Keyshwan Johnson 2.50 6.00
Terry Glenn
HT18 Lawrence Phillips 2.50 6.00
Tim Biakabutuka
HT19 Kevin Hardy 3.00 8.00
Simeon Rice
HT20 Barry Sanders 5.00 12.00
Thurman Thomas

1996 Upper Deck Predictors

COMP.HOBBY SET (20) 30.00 60.00
COMP.RETAIL SET (20) 30.00 60.00
PH1-PH20: STATED ODDS 1:23 HOBBY
PR1-PR20: ODDS 1:23 RET, 1:14 SPEC.RET
PH1 Dan Marino/450 Yards Passing L 3.00 8.00
PH2 Steve Young/35 Completions L 1.25 3.00
PH3 Brett Favre/375 Yards Passing W 3.00 8.00
PH4 Drew Bledsoe/35 Completions W 1.00 2.50
PH5 Jeff George/380 Yards Passing L .30 .75
PH6 John Elway/30 Completions W 3.00 8.00
PH7 Barry Sanders/190 Total Yards W 2.50 6.00
PH8 Curtis Martin/58 Yard Play L 1.25 3.00
PH9 Marshall Faulk/195 Total Yards L .75 2.00
PH10 Emmitt Smith/75 Yard Play L 2.50 6.00
PH11 Terrell Davis/150 Yards Rushing W 1.25 3.00
PH12 Errict Rhett/50 Yard Play L .30 .75
PH13 Lawrence Phillips/55 Yard Play L .15 .40
PH14 Jerry Rice/14 Receptions L 1.50 4.00
PH15 Michael Irvin/130 Yards Receiving W.60 1.50
PH16 Joey Galloway/10 Receptions L .60 1.50
PH17 Herman Moore/190 Yards Receiving L .30 .75
PH18 Isaac Bruce/12 Receptions L .60 1.50
PH19 Carl Pickens/150 Yards Receiving W.30 .75
PH20 Keyshawn Johnson/11 Receptions L.60 1.50
PR1 Dan Marino/35 Completions L 3.00 8.00
PR2 Steve Young/435 Total Yards W 1.25 3.00
PR3 Brett Favre 30 COMP L 3.00 8.00
PR4 Drew Bledsoe/350 Yards Passing W 1.00 2.50
PR5 Jeff George/35 Completions L .30 .75
PR6 John Elway/350 Yards Passing W 3.00 8.00
PR7 Barry Sanders/70 Yard Play L 2.50 6.00
PR8 Curtis Martin/160 Yards Rushing W 1.25 3.00
PR9 Marshall Faulk/75 Yard Play L .75 2.00
PR10 Emmitt Smith/195 Total Yards L 2.50 6.00
PR11 Terrell Davis/59 Yard Play W 1.25 3.00
PR12 Errict Rhett/150 Yards Rushing L .30 .75
PR13 Lawrence Phillips/130 Yards Rushing L .15 .40
PR14 Jerry Rice/200 Yards Receiving L 1.50 4.00
PR15 Michael Irvin 12 REC W .60 1.50
PR16 Joey Galloway/250 Total Yards L .60 1.50
PR17 Herman Moore/12 Receptions W .30 .75
PR18 Isaac Bruce 200 YDS W .60 1.50
PR19 Carl Pickens/10 Receptions W .30 .75
PR20 Keyshawn Johnson/140 Yards Receiving L .60 1.50

1996 Upper Deck Pro Bowl

COMPLETE SET (20) 30.00 80.00
STATED ODDS 1:33
PB1 Warren Moon .75 2.00
PB2 Brett Favre 8.00 20.00
PB3 Steve Young 3.00 8.00
PB4 Barry Sanders 6.00 15.00
PB5 Emmitt Smith 6.00 15.00
PB6 Jerry Rice 4.00 10.00
PB7 Herman Moore .75 2.00
PB8 Michael Irvin 1.50 4.00
PB9 Mark Chmura .75 2.00
PB10 Reggie White 1.50 4.00
PB11 Jim Harbaugh .75 2.00
PB12 Jeff Blake 1.50 4.00
PB13 Curtis Martin 3.00 8.00
PB14 Marshall Faulk 2.00 5.00
PB15 Chris Warren .75 2.00
PB16 Bryan Cox .30 .75
PB17 Junior Seau 1.50 4.00
PB18 Carl Pickens .75 2.00
PB19 Yancey Thigpen .75 2.00
PB20 Ben Coates .75 2.00

1996 Upper Deck Proview

COMPLETE SET (40) 40.00 100.00
ONE PER UD TECH RETAIL PACK
*SILVERS: 1.2X TO 3X BASIC INSERTS
SILVER ODDS 1:35 UD TECH PACKS
*GOLDS: 3X TO 8X BASIC INSERTS
GOLD ODDS 1:143 UD TECH PACKS
PV1 Warren Moon .30 .75
PV2 Jerry Rice 1.50 4.00
PV3 Brett Favre 3.00 8.00
PV4 Jim Harbaugh .30 .75
PV5 Junior Seau .60 1.50
PV6 Jeff Blake .60 1.50
PV7 John Elway 3.00 8.00
PV8 Troy Aikman 1.50 4.00
PV9 Steve Young 1.25 3.00
PV10 Kordell Stewart .60 1.50
PV11 Drew Bledsoe 1.00 2.50
PV12 Jim Kelly .60 1.50
PV13 Dan Marino 3.00 8.00
PV14 Kerry Collins .60 1.50
PV15 Jeff Hostetler .15 .40
PV16 Terry Allen .30 .75
PV17 Carl Pickens .30 .75
PV18 Mark Brunell 1.00 2.50
PV19 Keyshawn Johnson .60 1.50
PV20 Barry Sanders 2.50 6.00
PV21 Deion Sanders 1.00 2.50
PV22 Emmitt Smith 2.50 6.00
PV23 Curtis Conway .60 1.50
PV24 Herman Moore .30 .75
PV25 Joey Galloway .60 1.50
PV26 Robert Smith .30 .75
PV27 Eddie George .75 2.00
PV28 Curtis Martin 1.25 3.00
PV29 Marshall Faulk .75 2.00
PV30 Terrell Davis 1.25 3.00
PV31 Rashaan Salaam .30 .75
PV32 Jamal Anderson .15 .40
PV33 Karim Abdul-Jabbar .15 .40
PV34 Edgar Bennett .30 .75
PV35 Thurman Thomas .60 1.50
PV36 Jerome Bettis .60 1.50
PV37 Tim Brown .60 1.50
PV38 Chris Sanders .30 .75
PV39 Eddie Kennison .15 .40
PV40 Shannon Sharpe .30 .75

1996 Upper Deck Rookie Jumbos

*SINGLES: .2X TO .5X BASIC CARDS

1996 Upper Deck Team Trio

COMPLETE SET (90) 40.00 80.00
STATED ODDS 1:4 HOB/RET, 1:2 SPEC.RET
TT1 Curtis Conway .50 1.25
TT2 Darnay Scott .25 .60
TT3 Bryce Paup .08 .25
TT4 Terrell Davis 1.00 2.50
TT5 Hardy Nickerson .08 .25
TT6 Frank Sanders .25 .60
TT7 Stan Humphries .25 .60
TT8 Tamarick Vanover .25 .60
TT9 Sean Dawkins .08 .25
TT10 Deion Sanders .75 2.00
TT11 Dan Marino 2.50 6.00
TT12 Charlie Garner .25 .60
TT13 Eric Metcalf .08 .25
TT14 J.J. Stokes .50 1.25
TT15 Chris Calloway .08 .25
TT16 Pete Mitchell .25 .60
TT17 Wayne Chrebet .75 2.00
TT18 Herman Moore .25 .60
TT19 Steve McNair 1.00 2.50
TT20 Edgar Bennett .25 .60
TT21 Kerry Collins .50 1.25
TT22 Vincent Brisby .08 .25
TT23 Jeff Hostetler .08 .25
TT24 Kevin Carter .08 .25
TT25 Michael Jackson .25 .60
TT26 Michael Westbrook .50 1.25
TT27 Tyrone Hughes .08 .25
TT28 Joey Galloway .50 1.25
TT29 Byron Bam Morris .08 .25
TT30 Warren Moon .25 .60
TT31 Rashaan Salaam .25 .60
TT32 Jeff Blake .50 1.25
TT33 Thurman Thomas .50 1.25
TT34 John Elway 2.50 6.00
TT35 Errict Rhett .25 .60
TT36 Garrison Hearst .25 .60
TT37 Andre Coleman .08 .25
TT38 Steve Bono .08 .25
TT39 Marshall Faulk .60 1.50
TT40 Troy Aikman 1.25 3.00
TT41 Terry Kirby .25 .60
TT42 Rodney Peete .08 .25
TT43 Craig Heyward .08 .25
TT44 Steve Young 1.00 2.50
TT45 Rodney Hampton .25 .60
TT46 Mark Brunell .75 2.00
TT47 Kyle Brady .08 .25
TT48 Scott Mitchell .25 .60
TT49 Chris Sanders .25 .60
TT50 Brett Favre 2.50 6.00
TT51 Mark Carrier WR .08 .25
TT52 Drew Bledsoe .75 2.00
TT53 Napoleon Kaufman .50 1.25
TT54 Mark Rypien .08 .25
TT55 Andre Rison .25 .60
TT56 Terry Allen .25 .60
TT57 Jim Everett .08 .25
TT58 Chris Warren .25 .60
TT59 Kordell Stewart .50 1.25
TT60 Jake Reed .25 .60
TT61 Erik Kramer .08 .25
TT62 Carl Pickens .25 .60
TT63 Jim Kelly .50 1.25
TT64 Anthony Miller .25 .60
TT65 Trent Dilfer .50 1.25
TT66 Larry Centers .25 .60
TT67 Junior Seau .50 1.25
TT68 Marcus Allen .50 1.25
TT69 Jim Harbaugh .25 .60
TT70 Emmitt Smith 2.00 5.00
TT71 O.J.McDuffie .25 .60
TT72 Ricky Watters .25 .60
TT73 Jeff George .25 .60
TT74 Jerry Rice 1.25 3.00
TT75 Dave Brown .08 .25
TT76 James O. Stewart .25 .60
TT77 Adrian Murrell .25 .60
TT78 Barry Sanders 2.00 5.00
TT79 Rodney Thomas .08 .25
TT80 Robert Brooks .50 1.25
TT81 Derrick Moore .08 .25
TT82 Curtis Martin 1.00 2.50
TT83 Tim Brown .50 1.25
TT84 Isaac Bruce .50 1.25
TT85 Vinny Testaverde .25 .60
TT86 Henry Ellard .08 .25
TT87 Mario Bates .25 .60
TT88 Rick Mirer .25 .60
TT89 Yancey Thigpen .25 .60
TT90 Cris Carter .50 1.25

1996 Upper Deck TV-Cels

COMPLETE SET (20) 60.00 150.00
1 Dan Marino 15.00 40.00
2 Steve Young 1W 2.00 5.00
3 Brett Favre 1W 5.00 12.00
4 Drew Bledsoe 2W 1.50 4.00
5 Jeff George 2W 1.25 3.00
6 John Elway 2W 4.00 10.00
7 Barry Sanders 1W 3.00 8.00
8 Curtis Martin 1W 2.50 6.00
9 Marshall Faulk 4.00 10.00
10 Emmitt Smith 15.00 40.00
11 Terrell Davis 1W 2.50 6.00
12 Errict Rhett 2.00 5.00
13 Lawrence Phillips 3.00 8.00
14 Jerry Rice 10.00 25.00
15 Michael Irvin 1W 1.50 4.00
16 Joey Galloway 3.00 8.00
17 Herman Moore 1W 1.25 3.00
18 Isaac Bruce 1W 1.50 4.00
19 Carl Pickens 1W 1.25 3.00
20 Keyshawn Johnson 3.00 8.00

1996 Upper Deck A Cut Above Jumbos

This set includes parallels of some of the ten 1997 Collector's Choice A Cut Above insert cards on oversized (3-1/2" by 5") stock. Two other players were switched from the original checklist. The sets were released in box set form through Upper Deck Authenticated and some retail outlets.

COMPLETE SET (10) 4.00 10.00
1 Terrell Davis 1.20 3.00
2 Tim Biakabutuka .20 .50
3 Drew Bledsoe .50 1.25
4 Emmitt Smith .80 2.00
5 Marshall Faulk
6 Brett Favre 1.20 3.00
7 Keyshawn Johnson .40 1.00
8 Deion Sanders .30 .75
9 Curtis Martin .40 1.00
10 Jerry Rice .60 1.50

1996 Upper Deck Troy Aikman A Cut Above Jumbos

This set was released through Upper Deck Authenticated and some retail outlets and sold in box set form. Each card is oversized (3-1/2" by 5") and die cut. The card numbering resumes where other A Cut Above sets left off.

COMPLETE SET (10) 4.00 10.00
COMMON CARD CA11-CA20) .40 1.00

1996 Upper Deck Troy Aikman Chronicles Jumbos

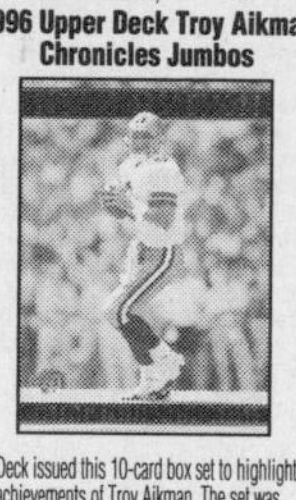

Upper Deck issued this 10-card box set to highlight the career achievements of Troy Aikman. The set was distributed primarily by UDA. A signed Aikman card from the set could also be purchased originally for $100.

COMP. FACT SET (10) 8.00 20.00
COMMON CARD (1-10) .80 2.00

1996 Upper Deck 22K Gold Dan Marino

1 Dan Marino 6.00 15.00
(50,000 Passing Yards)

1997 Upper Deck

The 1997 Upper Deck first series totals 300-cards and was distributed in 12-card packs with a suggested retail price of $2.49. The fronts feature color action player photos with player information on the backs. The set contains the topical subsets: Star Rookie (1-31), and Star Rookie Flashback (32-41).

COMPLETE SET (300) 20.00 40.00
1 Orlando Pace RC .25 .60
2 Darrell Russell RC .08 .25
3 Shawn Springs RC .15 .40
4 Bryant Westbrook RC .08 .25
5 Ike Hilliard RC .50 1.25
6 Peter Boulware RC .25 .60
7 Tom Knight RC .08 .25
8 Yatil Green RC .15 .40
9 Tony Gonzalez RC 1.25 3.00
10 Reidel Anthony RC .25 .60
11 Warrick Dunn RC 1.00 2.50
12 Kenny Holmes RC .25 .60
13 Jim Druckenmiller RC .15 .40
14 James Farrior RC .25 .60
15 David LaFleur RC .08 .25
16 Antowain Smith RC .75 2.00
17 Rae Carruth RC .08 .25
18 Dwayne Rudd RC .25 .60
19 Jake Plummer RC 1.25 3.00
20 Reinard Wilson RC .15 .40
21 Byron Hanspard RC .15 .40
22 Will Blackwell RC .15 .40
23 Troy Davis RC .15 .40
24 Corey Dillon RC 1.25 3.00
25 Joey Kent RC .25 .60
26 Renaldo Wynn RC .08 .25
27 Pat Barnes RC .25 .60
28 Kevin Lockett RC .15 .40
29 Darnell Autry RC .15 .40
30 Walter Jones RC .25 .60
31 Trevor Pryce RC .25 .60
32 Dan Marino SRF .50 1.25
33 Steve Young SRF .08 .25
34 John Elway SRF .50 1.25
35 Jerry Rice SRF .25 .60
36 Tim Brown SRF .25 .60
37 Deion Sanders SRF .25 .60
38 Troy Aikman SRF .25 .60
39 Barry Sanders SRF .40 1.00
40 Emmitt Smith SRF .40 1.00
41 Junior Seau SRF .25 .60
42 Neil Smith .15 .40
43 Brett Perriman .08 .25
44 Jim Everett .08 .25
45 Qadry Ismail .15 .40
46 Dana Stubblefield .08 .25
47 Bryant Young .08 .25
48 Ken Norton Jr. .08 .25
49 Terrell Owens .30 .75
50 Jerry Rice .50 1.25
51 Steve Young .30 .75
52 Terry Kirby .15 .40
53 Chris Doleman .08 .25
54 Lee Woodall .08 .25
55 Merton Hanks .08 .25
56 Garrison Hearst .15 .40
57 Rashaan Salaam .08 .25
58 Raymont Harris .08 .25
59 Curtis Conway .15 .40
60 Bobby Engram .15 .40
61 Bryan Cox .08 .25
62 Walt Harris .08 .25
63 Tyrone Hughes .08 .25
64 Rick Mirer .08 .25
65 Jeff Blake .15 .40
66 Carl Pickens .15 .40
67 Darnay Scott .15 .40
68 Tony McGee .08 .25
69 Ki-Jana Carter .08 .25
70 Ashley Ambrose .08 .25
71 Dan Wilkinson .08 .25
72 Chris Spielman .08 .25
73 Todd Collins .08 .25
74 Andre Reed .15 .40
75 Quinn Early .08 .25
76 Eric Moulds .25 .60
77 Darick Holmes .08 .25
78 Thurman Thomas .25 .60
79 Bruce Smith .15 .40
80 Bryce Paup .08 .25
81 John Elway 1.00 2.50
82 Terrell Davis .30 .75
83 Anthony Miller .08 .25
84 Shannon Sharpe .15 .40
85 Alfred Williams .08 .25
86 John Mobley .08 .25
87 Tory James .08 .25
88 Steve Atwater .08 .25
89 Darrien Gordon .08 .25
90 Mike Alstott .25 .60
91 Errict Rhett .08 .25
92 Trent Dilfer .25 .60
93 Courtney Hawkins .08 .25
94 Warren Sapp .15 .40
95 Regan Upshaw .08 .25
96 Hardy Nickerson .08 .25
97 Donnie Abraham RC .25 .60
98 Larry Centers .15 .40
99 Aeneas Williams .08 .25
100 Kent Graham UER .08 .25
(incorrect college name on back)
101 Rob Moore .15 .40
102 Frank Sanders .15 .40
103 Leeland McElroy .08 .25
104 Eric Swann .08 .25
105 Simeon Rice .15 .40
106 Seth Joyner .08 .25
107 Stan Humphries .15 .40
108 Tony Martin .15 .40
109 Charlie Jones .08 .25
110 Andre Coleman UER .08 .25
(card mistakenly #103)
111 Terrell Fletcher .08 .25
112 Junior Seau .25 .60
113 Eric Metcalf .15 .40
114 Chris Penn .08 .25
115 Marcus Allen .25 .60
116 Greg Hill .08 .25
117 Tamarick Vanover .15 .40
118 Lake Dawson .08 .25
119 Derrick Thomas .25 .60
120 Dale Carter .08 .25
121 Elvis Grbac .15 .40
122 Aaron Bailey .08 .25
123 Jim Harbaugh .15 .40
124 Marshall Faulk .30 .75
125 Sean Dawkins .08 .25
126 Marvin Harrison .25 .60
127 Ken Dilger .08 .25
128 Tony Bennett .08 .25
129 Jeff Herrod .08 .25
130 Chris Gardocki .08 .25
131 Cary Blanchard .08 .25
132 Troy Aikman .50 1.25
133 Emmitt Smith .75 2.00
134 Sherman Williams .08 .25
135 Michael Irvin .25 .60
136 Eric Bjornson .08 .25
137 Herschel Walker .15 .40
138 Tony Tolbert .08 .25
139 Deion Sanders .25 .60
140 Daryl Johnston .15 .40
141 Dan Marino 1.00 2.50
142 O.J. McDuffie .15 .40
143 Troy Drayton .08 .25
144 Karim Abdul-Jabbar .15 .40
145 Stanley Pritchett .08 .25
146 Fred Barnett .08 .25
147 Zach Thomas .25 .60
148 Shawn Wooden RC .08 .25
149 Ty Detmer .15 .40
150 Derrick Witherspoon .08 .25
151 Ricky Watters .15 .40
152 Charlie Garner .15 .40
153 Chris T. Jones .08 .25
154 Irving Fryar .15 .40
155 Mike Mamula .08 .25
156 Troy Vincent .08 .25
157 Bobby Taylor .08 .25
158 Chris Boniol .08 .25
159 Devin Bush .08 .25
160 Bert Emanuel .15 .40
161 Jamal Anderson .25 .60
162 Terance Mathis .15 .40
163 Cornelius Bennett .08 .25
164 Ray Buchanan .08 .25
165 Chris Chandler .15 .40
166 Dave Brown .08 .25
167 Danny Kanell .08 .25
168 Rodney Hampton .15 .40
169 Tyrone Wheatley .15 .40
170 Amani Toomer .15 .40
171 Chris Calloway .08 .25
172 Thomas Lewis .08 .25
173 Phillippi Sparks .08 .25
174 Mark Brunell .30 .75
175 Keenan McCardell .15 .40
176 Willie Jackson .08 .25
177 Jimmy Smith .15 .40
178 Pete Mitchell .08 .25
179 Natrone Means .15 .40
180 Kevin Hardy .08 .25
181 Tony Brackens .08 .25
182 James O. Stewart .15 .40
183 Wayne Chrebet .25 .60
184 Keyshawn Johnson .25 .60
185 Adrian Murrell .15 .40
186 Neil O'Donnell .15 .40
187 Hugh Douglas .08 .25
188 Mo Lewis .08 .25
189 Marvin Washington .08 .25
190 Aaron Glenn .08 .25
191 Barry Sanders .75 2.00
192 Scott Mitchell .15 .40
193 Herman Moore .15 .40
194 Johnnie Morton .15 .40
195 Glyn Milburn .08 .25
196 Reggie Brown LB .15 .40
197 Jason Hanson .08 .25
198 Steve McNair .30 .75
199 Eddie George .25 .60
200 Ronnie Harmon .08 .25
201 Chris Sanders .08 .25
202 Willie Davis .08 .25
203 Frank Wycheck .08 .25
204 Darryll Lewis .08 .25
205 Blaine Bishop .08 .25
206 Robert Brooks .15 .40
207 Brett Favre 1.25 2.50
208 Edgar Bennett .15 .40
209 Dorsey Levens .25 .60
210 Derrick Mayes .15 .40
211 Antonio Freeman .25 .60
212 Mark Chmura .15 .40
213 Reggie White .25 .60
214 Gilbert Brown .15 .40
215 LeRoy Butler .08 .25
216 Craig Newsome .08 .25
217 Kerry Collins .25 .60
218 Wesley Walls .15 .40
219 Muhsin Muhammad .15 .40
220 Anthony Johnson .08 .25
221 Tim Biakabutuka .15 .40
222 Kevin Greene .15 .40
223 Sam Mills .08 .25
224 John Kasay .08 .25
225 Micheal Barrow .08 .25
226 Drew Bledsoe .30 .75
227 Curtis Martin .30 .75
228 Terry Glenn .25 .60
229 Ben Coates .15 .40
230 Shawn Jefferson .08 .25
231 Willie McGinest .08 .25
232 Ted Johnson .08 .25
233 Lawyer Milloy .15 .40
234 Ty Law .15 .40
235 Willie Clay .08 .25
236 Tim Brown .25 .60
237 Rickey Dudley .15 .40
238 Napoleon Kaufman .25 .60
239 Chester McGlockton .08 .25
240 Rob Fredrickson .08 .25
241 Terry McDaniel .08 .25
242 Desmond Howard .15 .40
243 Jeff George .15 .40
244 Isaac Bruce .25 .60
245 Tony Banks .15 .40
246 Lawrence Phillips UER .08 .25
(card mistakenly #247)
247 Kevin Carter .08 .25
248 Roman Phifer .08 .25
249 Keith Lyle .08 .25
250 Eddie Kennison .15 .40
251 Craig Heyward .08 .25
252 Vinny Testaverde .15 .40
253 Derrick Alexander WR .15 .40
254 Michael Jackson .15 .40
255 Byron Bam Morris .08 .25
256 Eric Green .08 .25
257 Ray Lewis .40 1.00
258 Antonio Langham .08 .25
259 Michael McCrary .08 .25
260 Gus Frerotte .08 .25
261 Terry Allen .25 .60
262 Brian Mitchell .08 .25
263 Michael Westbrook .15 .40
264 Sean Gilbert .08 .25
265 Rich Owens .08 .25
266 Ken Harvey .08 .25
267 Jeff Hostetler .08 .25
268 Michael Haynes .08 .25
269 Mario Bates .08 .25
270 Renaldo Turnbull UER .08 .25
(card mistakenly #273)
271 Ray Zellars .08 .25
272 Joe Johnson .08 .25
273 Eric Allen .08 .25
274 Heath Shuler .08 .25
275 Daryl Hobbs .08 .25
276 John Friesz .08 .25
277 Brian Blades .08 .25
278 Joey Galloway .15 .40
279 Chris Warren .15 .40
280 Lamar Smith .25 .60
281 Cortez Kennedy .08 .25
282 Chad Brown .08 .25
283 Warren Moon .25 .60
284 Jerome Bettis .25 .60
285 Charles Johnson .15 .40
286 Kordell Stewart .25 .60
287 Erric Pegram .08 .25
288 Norm Johnson .08 .25
289 Levon Kirkland .08 .25
290 Greg Lloyd .08 .25
291 Carnell Lake .08 .25
292 Brad Johnson .25 .60
293 Cris Carter .25 .60
294 Jake Reed .15 .40
295 Robert Smith .15 .40
296 Derrick Alexander DE .08 .25
297 John Randle .15 .40
298 Dixon Edwards .08 .25
299 Orlando Thomas .08 .25
300 Dewayne Washington .08 .25

1997 Upper Deck Game Dated Moment Foils

STATED ODDS 1:1500
50 Jerry Rice 15.00 40.00
51 Steve Young 10.00 25.00
78 Thurman Thomas 8.00 20.00
81 John Elway 30.00 80.00
82 Terrell Davis 10.00 25.00
90 Mike Alstott 8.00 20.00
115 Marcus Allen 8.00 20.00
126 Marvin Harrison 8.00 20.00
132 Troy Aikman 15.00 40.00
133 Emmitt Smith 25.00 60.00
141 Dan Marino 30.00 80.00
151 Ricky Watters 5.00 12.00
154 Irving Fryar 5.00 12.00
174 Mark Brunell 10.00 25.00
184 Keyshawn Johnson 8.00 20.00
191 Barry Sanders 25.00 60.00
199 Eddie George 8.00 20.00
207 Brett Favre 30.00 80.00
217 Kerry Collins 8.00 20.00
224 John Kasay 3.00 8.00
226 Drew Bledsoe 10.00 25.00
227 Curtis Martin 10.00 25.00
228 Terry Glenn 8.00 20.00
236 Tim Brown 8.00 20.00
238 Napoleon Kaufman 8.00 20.00
250 Eddie Kennison 5.00 12.00
261 Terry Allen 8.00 20.00
278 Joey Galloway 5.00 12.00
284 Jerome Bettis 8.00 20.00
286 Kordell Stewart 8.00 20.00

1997 Upper Deck Game Jerseys

COMPLETE SET (10) 400.00 800.00
MULTI-COLORED PATCH: .6X TO 1.5X
STATED ODDS 1:2600
GJ1 Warren Moon 30.00 80.00
GJ2 Joey Galloway 20.00 50.00
GJ3 Terrell Davis 30.00 80.00
GJ4 Brett Favre GRN 100.00 200.00
GJ5 Brett Favre WHT 100.00 200.00
GJ6 Reggie White 60.00 100.00
GJ7 John Elway 100.00 200.00
GJ8 Troy Aikman 60.00 120.00
GJ9 Carl Pickens 15.00 40.00
GJ10 Herman Moore 15.00 40.00

1997 Upper Deck Memorable Moments

COMPLETE SET (10) 5.00 12.00
ONE PER SPECIAL RETAIL COLL.CHOICE
1 Steve Young .30 .75
2 Dan Marino 1.00 2.50
3 Terrell Davis .30 .75
4 Brett Favre 1.00 2.50
5 Ricky Watters .15 .40
6 Terry Glenn .25 .60
7 John Elway 1.00 2.50
8 Troy Aikman .50 1.25
9 Terry Allen .25 .60
10 Joey Galloway .15 .40

1997 Upper Deck MVPs

STATED PRINT RUN 100 SERIAL #'d SETS
1 Jerry Rice 20.00 50.00
2 Carl Pickens 6.00 15.00
3 Terrell Davis 12.50 30.00
4 Mike Alstott 10.00 25.00
5 Simeon Rice 6.00 15.00
6 Junior Seau 10.00 25.00
7 Marcus Allen 10.00 25.00
8 Troy Aikman 20.00 50.00
9 Dan Marino 40.00 100.00
10 Ricky Watters 6.00 15.00
11 Mark Brunell 12.50 30.00
12 Barry Sanders 30.00 80.00
13 Eddie George 10.00 25.00
14 Brett Favre 40.00 100.00
15 Kerry Collins 10.00 25.00
16 Drew Bledsoe 12.50 30.00
17 Napoleon Kaufman 10.00 25.00
18 Isaac Bruce 10.00 25.00
19 Terry Allen 10.00 25.00
20 Jerome Bettis 10.00 25.00

1997 Upper Deck Star Attractions

COMPLETE SET (20) 6.00 15.00
ONE PER COLL.CHOICE RETAIL JUMBO
*GOLD: .8X TO 2X BASIC INSERTS
GOLD ODDS 1:20 COLL.CHO.RET.JUMBO
SA1 Dan Marino 1.00 2.50
SA2 Emmitt Smith .75 2.00
SA3 John Elway 1.00 2.50
SA4 Kordell Stewart .25 .60
SA5 Napoleon Kaufman .25 .60
SA6 Curtis Martin .30 .75
SA7 Troy Aikman .50 1.25
SA8 Warrick Dunn 1.00 2.50
SA9 Antowain Smith .75 2.00
SA10 Reggie White .25 .60
SA11 Jeff George .15 .40
SA12 Brett Favre 1.00 2.50
SA13 Lawrence Phillips .08 .25
SA14 Rod Smith WR .15 .40
SA15 Steve Young .30 .75
SA16 Drew Bledsoe .30 .75
SA17 Barry Sanders .75 2.00
SA18 Terrell Davis .30 .75
SA19 Eddie George .25 .60
SA20 Deion Sanders .25 .60

1997 Upper Deck Star Crossed

COMPLETE SET (30) 12.50 30.00
SC1-SC9 STATED ODDS 1:23 HOBBY
SC10-SC18 STATED ODDS 1:27 SPEC.RETAIL
SC19-SC27 STATED ODDS 1:27 RETAIL
SC1 Dan Marino 2.00 5.00
SC2 Mark Brunell .60 1.50
SC3 Kerry Collins .50 1.25
SC4 Jerry Rice 1.00 2.50
SC5 Curtis Martin .60 1.50
SC6 Isaac Bruce .50 1.25
SC7 Eddie George .50 1.25
SC8 Kevin Greene .30 .75
SC9 Deion Sanders .50 1.25
SC10 Troy Aikman 1.00 2.50
SC11 John Elway 2.00 5.00
SC12 Steve Young .60 1.50
SC13 Barry Sanders 1.50 4.00
SC14 Jerome Bettis .50 1.25
SC15 Herman Moore .30 .75
SC16 Keyshawn Johnson .50 1.25
SC17 Simeon Rice .30 .75
SC18 Bruce Smith .30 .75
SC19 Drew Bledsoe .60 1.50
SC20 Kordell Stewart .50 1.25
SC21 Brett Favre 2.00 5.00
SC22 Emmitt Smith 1.50 4.00
SC23 Terrell Davis .60 1.50
SC24 Carl Pickens .30 .75
SC25 Terry Glenn .50 1.25
SC26 Reggie White .50 1.25
SC27 Rod Woodson .50 1.25
SC28 Trade Card .20 .50
SC29 Trade Card .20 .50
SC30 Trade Card .20 .50

1997 Upper Deck Team Mates

COMPLETE SET (60) 20.00 40.00
STATED ODDS 1:4 HOBBY, 1:2 RETAIL
TM1 Simeon Rice .25 .60
TM2 Eric Swann .15 .40
TM3 Terance Mathis .25 .60
TM4 Jamal Anderson .40 1.00
TM5 Vinny Testaverde .25 .60
TM6 Michael Jackson .25 .60
TM7 Thurman Thomas .40 1.00
TM8 Bruce Smith .25 .60
TM9 Kerry Collins .40 1.00
TM10 Anthony Johnson .15 .40
TM11 Bobby Engram .25 .60
TM12 Bryan Cox .15 .40
TM13 Carl Pickens .25 .60
TM14 Jeff Blake .25 .60
TM15 Troy Aikman .75 2.00
TM16 Emmitt Smith 1.25 3.00
TM17 John Elway 1.50 4.00
TM18 Terrell Davis .50 1.25
TM19 Herman Moore .25 .60
TM20 Barry Sanders 1.25 3.00
TM21 Brett Favre 1.50 4.00
TM22 Reggie White .40 1.00
TM23 Eddie George .40 1.00
TM24 Steve McNair .50 1.25
TM25 Marshall Faulk .50 1.25
TM26 Jim Harbaugh .25 .60
TM27 Mark Brunell .50 1.25
TM28 Keenan McCardell .25 .60
TM29 Marcus Allen .40 1.00
TM30 Derrick Thomas .40 1.00
TM31 Dan Marino 1.50 4.00
TM32 Karim Abdul-Jabbar .25 .60
TM33 Cris Carter .40 1.00
TM34 Jake Reed .25 .60
TM35 Curtis Martin .50 1.25
TM36 Drew Bledsoe .50 1.25
TM37 Mario Bates .15 .40
TM38 Ray Zellars .15 .40
TM39 Keyshawn Johnson .40 1.00
TM40 Adrian Murrell .25 .60
TM41 Tyrone Wheatley .25 .60
TM42 Rodney Hampton .25 .60
TM43 Napoleon Kaufman .40 1.00
TM44 Tim Brown .40 1.00
TM45 Ricky Watters .25 .60
TM46 Chris T. Jones .15 .40
TM47 Kordell Stewart .40 1.00
TM48 Jerome Bettis .40 1.00
TM49 Junior Seau .40 1.00
TM50 Tony Martin .25 .60
TM51 Steve Young .50 1.25
TM52 Jerry Rice .75 2.00
TM53 Joey Galloway .25 .60
TM54 Chris Warren .25 .60
TM55 Tony Banks .25 .60
TM56 Eddie Kennison .25 .60
TM57 Mike Alstott .40 1.00
TM58 Errict Rhett .15 .40
TM59 Terry Allen .40 1.00
TM60 Gus Frerotte .15 .40

1997 Upper Deck Crash the Game Super Bowl XXXI

COMPLETE SET (8) 3.00 8.00
COMP.FOIL PRIZE SET (9) 2.50 6.00
*FOIL PRIZES: .3X TO.8X
A1 Drew Bledsoe .60 1.50
A2 Curtis Martin .50 1.25
A3 Ben Coates .20 .50
A4 Terry Glenn .30 .75
N1 Brett Favre 1.20 3.00
N2 Edgar Bennett .20 .50
N3 Don Beebe .20 .50
N4 Antonio Freeman .50 1.25

1997 Upper Deck Mini

This set was issued in early 1998 by Upper Deck. The cards follow the basic set design and use the photos from the 1997 Collector's Choice football set but carry only the Upper Deck logo on the fronts. The backs have a 1998 copyright date and a unique numbering system that is different from 1997 Collector's Choice. Finally, the cards measure slightly smaller than standard size: roughly 2 5/16" by 3 5/8" and the first six cards in the set were created in a foil format similar to SP products.

COMPLETE SET (48) 30.00 60.00
1 Brett Favre FOIL SP 5.00 12.00
2 Drew Bledsoe FOIL SP 1.25 3.00
3 Emmitt Smith FOIL SP 3.00 8.00
4 Barry Sanders FOIL SP 2.50 6.00
5 Jerry Rice FOIL SP 2.50 6.00
6 Karim Abdul-Jabbar FOIL SP 1.00 2.50
7 Ken Norton .50 1.25
8 Curtis Conway .60 1.50
9 Rashaan Salaam .60 1.50
10 Jeff Blake .60 1.50
11 Jim Kelly 1.50 4.00
12 Bryce Paup .50 1.25
13 Terrell Davis 1.00 2.50
14 Errict Rhett .60 1.50
15 Simeon Rice .50 1.25
16 Junior Seau .75 2.00
17 Marcus Allen .75 2.00
18 Greg Hill .50 1.25
19 Jim Harbaugh .60 1.50
20 Deion Sanders 1.25 3.00
21 Michael Irvin 1.00 2.50
22 Zach Thomas .75 2.00
23 Bobby Taylor .60 1.50
24 Cornelius Bennett .60 1.50
25 Mark Brunell .60 1.50
26 Jimmy Smith .60 1.50
27 Keyshawn Johnson .60 1.50
28 Steve McNair .75 2.00
29 Frank Wycheck .60 1.50
30 Antonio Freeman .75 2.00
31 Reggie White 1.00 2.50
32 Kerry Collins .75 2.00
33 Kevin Greene .60 1.50
34 Terry Glenn .60 1.50
35 Ben Coates .60 1.50
36 Tim Brown 1.00 2.50
37 Chester McGlockton .50 1.25
38 Isaac Bruce .75 2.00
39 Vinny Testaverde .60 1.50
40 Antonio Langham .50 1.25
41 Michael Westbrook .50 1.25
42 Ken Harvey .50 1.25
43 Mario Bates .50 1.25
44 Joey Galloway .60 1.50
45 Jerome Bettis 1.00 2.50
46 Kordell Stewart .75 2.00
47 Greg Lloyd .50 1.25
48 Cris Carter 1.00 2.50

1998 Upper Deck

The 1998 Upper Deck set was issued with 255 standard size cards. The 10-card packs retail for $2.49 each. The set contains the subset: Star Rookie (1-42) with those cards seeded at the rate of 1:4. The card fronts feature color action photos with a black and grey three-sided border. A bronze foil parallel version of this set was also produced and serial-numbered to 100.

COMPLETE SET (255)	75.00	150.00
COMP.SET w/o SP's (213)	12.50	25.00
1 Peyton Manning RC	25.00	50.00
2 Ryan Leaf RC	2.00	5.00
3 Andre Wadsworth RC	1.25	3.00
4 Charles Woodson RC	3.00	8.00
5 Curtis Enis RC	1.00	2.50
6 Grant Wistrom RC	1.25	3.00
7 Greg Ellis RC	1.00	2.50
8 Fred Taylor RC	3.00	8.00
9 Duane Starks RC	1.00	2.50
10 Keith Brooking RC	2.00	5.00
11 Takeo Spikes RC	2.00	5.00
12 Jason Peter RC	1.00	2.50
13 Anthony Simmons RC	1.25	3.00
14 Kevin Dyson RC	2.00	5.00
15 Brian Simmons RC	1.25	3.00
16 Robert Edwards RC	1.25	3.00
17 Randy Moss RC	8.00	20.00
18 John Avery RC	1.25	3.00
19 Marcus Nash RC	1.00	2.50
20 Jerome Pathon RC	2.00	5.00
21 Jacquez Green RC	1.25	3.00
22 Robert Holcombe RC	1.25	3.00
23 Pat Johnson RC	1.25	3.00
24 Germane Crowell RC	1.25	3.00
25 Joe Jurevicius RC	2.00	5.00
26 Skip Hicks RC	1.25	3.00
27 Ahman Green RC	5.00	12.00
28 Brian Griese RC	4.00	10.00
29 Hines Ward RC	10.00	20.00
30 Tavian Banks RC	1.25	3.00
31 Tony Simmons RC	1.25	3.00
32 Victor Riley RC	1.00	2.50
33 Rashaan Shehee RC	1.25	3.00
34 R.W. McQuarters RC	1.25	3.00
35 Flozell Adams RC	1.00	2.50
36 Tra Thomas RC	1.00	2.50
37 Greg Favors RC	1.25	3.00
38 Jon Ritchie RC	1.25	3.00
39 Jesse Haynes RC	1.00	2.50
40 Ryan Sutter RC	1.00	2.50
41 Mo Collins RC	1.00	2.50
42 Tim Dwight RC	2.00	5.00
43 Chris Chandler	.15	.40
44 Byron Hanspard	.08	.25
45 Jessie Tuggle	.08	.25
46 Jamal Anderson	.25	.60
47 Terance Mathis	.15	.40
48 Morten Andersen	.08	.25
49 Jake Plummer	.25	.60
50 Mario Bates	.15	.40
51 Frank Sanders	.15	.40
52 Adrian Murrell	.15	.40
53 Simeon Rice	.15	.40
54 Aeneas Williams	.08	.25
55 Eric Swann UER	.08	.25
(number on back 98)		
56 Jim Harbaugh	.15	.40
57 Michael Jackson	.08	.25
58 Peter Boulware	.08	.25
59 Errict Rhett	.15	.40
60 Jermaine Lewis	.15	.40
61 Eric Zeier	.15	.40
62 Rod Woodson	.15	.40
63 Rob Johnson	.25	.60
64 Antowain Smith	.25	.60
65 Bruce Smith	.15	.40
66 Eric Moulds	.25	.60
67 Andre Reed	.15	.40
68 Thurman Thomas	.25	.60
69 Lonnie Johnson	.08	.25
70 Kerry Collins	.15	.40
71 Kevin Greene	.15	.40
72 Fred Lane	.08	.25
73 Rae Carruth	.08	.25
74 Michael Bates	.08	.25
75 William Floyd	.08	.25
76 Sean Gilbert	.08	.25
77 Erik Kramer	.08	.25
78 Edgar Bennett	.08	.25
79 Curtis Conway	.15	.40
80 Darnell Autry	.08	.25
81 Ryan Wetnight RC	.08	.25
82 Walt Harris	.08	.25
83 Bobby Engram	.15	.40
84 Jeff Blake	.15	.40
85 Carl Pickens	.15	.40
86 Darnay Scott	.15	.40
87 Corey Dillon	.25	.60
88 Reinard Wilson	.08	.25
89 Ashley Ambrose	.08	.25
90 Troy Aikman	.50	1.25
91 Michael Irvin	.25	.60
92 Emmitt Smith	.75	2.00
93 Deion Sanders	.25	.60
94 David LaFleur	.08	.25
95 Chris Warren	.15	.40
96 Darren Woodson	.08	.25
97 John Elway	1.00	2.50
98 Terrell Davis	.25	.60
99 Rod Smith	.15	.40
100 Shannon Sharpe	.15	.40
101 Ed McCaffrey	.15	.40
102 Steve Atwater	.08	.25
103 John Mobley	.08	.25
104 Darrien Gordon	.08	.25
105 Barry Sanders	.75	2.00
106 Scott Mitchell	.15	.40
107 Herman Moore	.15	.40
108 Johnnie Morton	.15	.40
109 Robert Porcher	.08	.25
110 Bryant Westbrook	.08	.25
111 Tommy Vardell	.08	.25
112 Brett Favre	1.00	2.50
113 Dorsey Levens	.25	.60
114 Reggie White	.25	.60
115 Antonio Freeman	.25	.60
116 Robert Brooks	.15	.40
117 Mark Chmura	.15	.40
118 Derrick Mayes	.15	.40
119 Gilbert Brown	.08	.25
120 Marshall Faulk	.30	.75
121 Jeff Burris	.08	.25
122 Marvin Harrison	.25	.60
123 Quentin Coryatt	.08	.25
124 Ken Dilger	.08	.25
125 Zack Crockett	.08	.25
126 Mark Brunell	.25	.60
127 Bryce Paup	.08	.25
128 Tony Brackens	.08	.25
129 Renaldo Wynn	.08	.25
130 Keenan McCardell	.15	.40
131 Jimmy Smith	.15	.40
132 Kevin Hardy	.08	.25
133 Elvis Grbac	.15	.40
134 Tamarick Vanover	.08	.25
135 Chester McGlockton	.08	.25
136 Andre Rison	.15	.40
137 Derrick Alexander	.15	.40
138 Tony Gonzalez	.25	.60
139 Derrick Thomas	.25	.60
140 Dan Marino	1.00	2.50
141 Karim Abdul-Jabbar	.25	.60
142 O.J. McDuffie	.15	.40
143 Yatil Green	.08	.25
144 Charles Jordan	.08	.25
145 Brock Marion	.08	.25
146 Zach Thomas	.25	.60
147 Brad Johnson	.25	.60
148 Cris Carter	.25	.60
149 Jake Reed	.15	.40
150 Robert Smith	.25	.60
151 John Randle	.15	.40
152 Dwayne Rudd	.08	.25
153 Randall Cunningham	.25	.60
154 Drew Bledsoe	.40	1.00
155 Terry Glenn	.25	.60
156 Ben Coates	.15	.40
157 Willie Clay	.08	.25
158 Chris Slade	.08	.25
159 Derrick Cullors RC	.08	.25
160 Ty Law	.15	.40
161 Danny Wuerffel	.15	.40
162 Andre Hastings	.08	.25
163 Troy Davis	.08	.25
164 Billy Joe Hobert	.08	.25
165 Eric Guliford	.08	.25
166 Mark Fields	.08	.25
167 Alex Molden	.08	.25
168 Danny Kanell	.15	.40
169 Tiki Barber	.25	.60
170 Charles Way	.08	.25
171 Amani Toomer	.15	.40
172 Michael Strahan	.15	.40
173 Jessie Armstead	.08	.25
174 Jason Sehorn	.15	.40
175 Glenn Foley	.15	.40
176 Curtis Martin	.25	.60
177 Aaron Glenn	.08	.25
178 Keyshawn Johnson	.25	.60
179 James Farrior	.08	.25
180 Wayne Chrebet	.25	.60
181 Keith Byars	.08	.25
182 Jeff George	.15	.40
183 Napoleon Kaufman	.25	.60
184 Tim Brown	.25	.60
185 Darrell Russell	.08	.25
186 Rickey Dudley	.08	.25
187 James Jett	.15	.40
188 Desmond Howard	.15	.40
189 Bobby Hoying	.15	.40
190 Charlie Garner	.15	.40
191 Irving Fryar	.15	.40
192 Chris T. Jones	.08	.25
193 Mike Mamula	.08	.25
194 Troy Vincent	.08	.25
195 Kordell Stewart	.25	.60
196 Jerome Bettis	.25	.60
197 Will Blackwell	.08	.25
198 Levon Kirkland	.08	.25
199 Carnell Lake	.08	.25
200 Charles Johnson	.08	.25
201 Greg Lloyd	.08	.25
202 Donnell Woolford	.08	.25
203 Tony Banks	.15	.40
204 Amp Lee	.08	.25
205 Isaac Bruce	.25	.60
206 Eddie Kennison	.15	.40
207 Ryan McNeil	.08	.25
208 Mike Jones	.08	.25
209 Ernie Conwell	.08	.25
210 Natrone Means	.15	.40
211 Junior Seau	.25	.60
212 Tony Martin	.15	.40
213 Freddie Jones	.08	.25
214 Bryan Still	.08	.25
215 Rodney Harrison	.15	.40
216 Steve Young	.30	.75
217 Jerry Rice	.50	1.25
218 Garrison Hearst	.25	.60
219 J.J. Stokes	.15	.40
220 Ken Norton	.08	.25
221 Greg Clark	.08	.25
222 Terrell Owens	.25	.60
223 Bryant Young	.08	.25
224 Warren Moon	.25	.60
225 Jon Kitna	.25	.60
226 Ricky Watters	.15	.40
227 Chad Brown	.08	.25
228 Joey Galloway	.15	.40
229 Shawn Springs	.08	.25
230 Cortez Kennedy	.08	.25
231 Trent Dilfer	.25	.60
232 Warrick Dunn	.25	.60
233 Mike Alstott	.25	.60
234 Warren Sapp	.15	.40
235 Bert Emanuel	.15	.40
236 Reidel Anthony	.15	.40
237 Hardy Nickerson	.08	.25
238 Derrick Brooks	.25	.60
239 Steve McNair	.25	.60
240 Yancey Thigpen	.08	.25
241 Anthony Dorsett	.08	.25
242 Blaine Bishop	.08	.25
243 Kenny Holmes	.08	.25
244 Eddie George	.25	.60
245 Chris Sanders	.08	.25
246 Gus Frerotte	.08	.25
247 Terry Allen	.25	.60
248 Dana Stubblefield	.08	.25
249 Michael Westbrook	.15	.40
250 Darrell Green	.15	.40
251 Brian Mitchell	.08	.25
252 Ken Harvey	.08	.25
CL1 Troy Aikman CL	.25	.60
CL2 Dan Marino CL	.30	.75
CL3 Herman Moore CL	.15	.40

1998 Upper Deck Bronze

*43-255 BRONZE VETS: 15X TO 40X BASIC CARDS
*1-42 BRONZE ROOKIES: 2X TO 4X
BRONZE PRINT RUN 100 SER.#'d SETS

1998 Upper Deck Constant Threat

COMPLETE SET (30)	50.00	100.00
STATED ODDS 1:12		
*BRNZ.DC VETS: 10X TO 25X BASIC INSERTS		
*BRONZE DC ROOKIES: 6X TO 15X		
BRONZE DIE CUT PRINT RUN 25		
*SILVER DC VETS: .8X TO 2X BAS.INSERTS		
*SILVER DC ROOKIE: .6X TO 1.5X BAS.INSERTS		
SILVER DIE CUT PRINT RUN 1000		
CT1 Dan Marino	4.00	10.00
CT2 Peyton Manning	7.50	15.00
CT3 Randy Moss	4.00	10.00
CT4 Brett Favre	4.00	10.00
CT5 Mark Brunell	1.00	2.50
CT6 Keyshawn Johnson	1.00	2.50
CT7 John Elway	4.00	10.00
CT8 Troy Aikman	2.00	5.00
CT9 Steve Young	1.25	3.00
CT10 Kordell Stewart	1.00	2.50
CT11 Drew Bledsoe	1.50	4.00
CT12 Joey Galloway	.60	1.50
CT13 Elvis Grbac	.60	1.50
CT14 Marvin Harrison	1.00	2.50
CT15 Napoleon Kaufman	1.00	2.50
CT16 Ryan Leaf	.60	1.50
CT17 Jake Plummer	1.00	2.50
CT18 Terrell Davis	1.00	2.50
CT19 Steve McNair	1.00	2.50
CT20 Barry Sanders	3.00	8.00
CT21 Deion Sanders	1.00	2.50
CT22 Emmitt Smith	3.00	8.00
CT23 Antowain Smith	1.00	2.50
CT24 Herman Moore	.60	1.50
CT25 Curtis Martin	1.00	2.50
CT26 Jerry Rice	2.00	5.00
CT27 Eddie George	1.00	2.50
CT28 Warrick Dunn	1.00	2.50
CT29 Curtis Enis	.60	1.50
CT30 Michael Irvin	1.00	2.50

1998 Upper Deck Define the Game

COMPLETE SET (30)	30.00	60.00
STATED ODDS 1:8		
*BRONZE DC VETS: 10X TO 25X BASIC INS.		
*BRONZE DC ROOKIES: 6X TO 15X BASIC INS.		
BRONZE DIE CUT PRINT RUN 50		
*SILVER DIE CUTS: .8X TO 2X BASIC INSERTS		
SILVER DIE CUT PRINT RUN 1500		
DG1 Dan Marino	3.00	8.00
DG2 Curtis Enis	.25	.60
DG3 Dorsey Levens	.75	2.00
DG4 Charles Woodson	.60	1.50
DG5 Junior Seau	.75	2.00
DG6 Tiki Barber	.75	2.00
DG7 Randy Moss	5.00	10.00
DG8 Troy Aikman	1.50	4.00
DG9 Jake Plummer	.75	2.00
DG10 Corey Dillon	.75	2.00
DG11 Jerry Rice	1.50	4.00
DG12 Emmitt Smith	2.50	6.00
DG13 Herman Moore	.50	1.25
DG14 Brad Johnson	.75	2.00
DG15 Gus Frerotte	.30	.75
DG16 Ryan Leaf	.50	1.25
DG17 Shannon Sharpe	.50	1.25
DG18 Jermaine Lewis	.50	1.25
DG19 Jerome Bettis	.75	2.00
DG20 Barry Sanders	2.50	6.00
DG21 Terry Allen	.75	2.00
DG22 Reidel Anthony	.50	1.25
DG23 Isaac Bruce	.75	2.00
DG24 Mike Alstott	.75	2.00
DG25 Rae Carruth	.30	.75
DG26 Tamarick Vanover	.30	.75
DG27 Eddie George	.75	2.00
DG28 Warrick Dunn	.75	2.00
DG29 Tony Gonzalez	.75	2.00
DG30 Keenan McCardell	.50	1.25

1998 Upper Deck Game Jerseys

1-10 STATED ODDS 1:2500		
11-20 STATED ODDS 1:288 HOBBY		
GJ1 Brett Favre	40.00	100.00
GJ2 Reggie White	30.00	80.00
GJ3 Barry Sanders	30.00	80.00
GJ4 John Elway	30.00	80.00
GJ5 Mark Brunell	15.00	40.00
GJ6 Mike Alstott	15.00	40.00
GJ7 Ryan Leaf	15.00	40.00
GJ8 Andre Wadsworth	12.00	30.00
GJ9 Robert Edwards	12.00	30.00
GJ10 Kevin Dyson	12.00	30.00
GJ11 Dan Marino	40.00	100.00
GJ12 Deion Sanders	15.00	40.00
GJ13 Steve Young	20.00	50.00
GJ14 Terrell Davis	12.00	30.00
GJ15 Tim Brown	12.00	30.00
GJ16 Peyton Manning	125.00	250.00
GJ17 Takeo Spikes	10.00	25.00
GJ18 Curtis Enis	8.00	20.00
GJ19 Fred Taylor	12.00	30.00
GJ20 John Avery	8.00	20.00

1998 Upper Deck Jumbos

COMPLETE SET (10)	6.00	15.00
ONE PER SPECIAL RETAIL BOX		
49 Jake Plummer	.60	1.50
64 Antowain Smith	.50	1.25
87 Corey Dillon	.60	1.50
98 Terrell Davis	.75	2.00
105 Barry Sanders	2.00	5.00
112 Brett Favre	2.00	5.00
126 Mark Brunell	.60	1.50
136 Andre Rison	.30	.75
195 Kordell Stewart	.60	1.50
232 Warrick Dunn	.50	1.25

1998 Upper Deck Super Powers

COMPLETE SET (30)	20.00	50.00
STATED ODDS 1:4 HOB, 1:2 RET		
*BRONZE DC/100: 8X TO 20X BASIC INSERTS		
BRONZE DIE CUT PRINT RUN 100 SETS		
*SILVER DC/2000: .8X TO 2X BASIC INSERTS		
SILVER DIE CUT PRINT RUN 2000		
S1 Dan Marino	2.50	6.00
S2 Jerry Rice	1.25	3.00
S3 Napoleon Kaufman	.60	1.50
S4 Brett Favre	2.50	6.00
S5 Andre Rison	.40	1.00
S6 Jerome Bettis	.60	1.50
S7 John Elway	2.50	6.00
S8 Troy Aikman	1.25	3.00
S9 Steve Young	.75	2.00
S10 Kordell Stewart	.60	1.50
S11 Drew Bledsoe	1.00	2.50
S12 Antonio Freeman	.60	1.50
S13 Mark Brunell	.60	1.50
S14 Shannon Sharpe	.40	1.00
S15 Trent Dilfer	.60	1.50
S16 Peyton Manning	5.00	10.00
S17 Cris Carter	.60	1.50
S18 Michael Irvin	.60	1.50
S19 Terry Glenn	.60	1.50
S20 Keyshawn Johnson	.60	1.50
S21 Deion Sanders	.60	1.50
S22 Emmitt Smith	2.00	5.00
S23 Marcus Allen	.60	1.50
S24 Dorsey Levens	.60	1.50
S25 Jake Plummer	.60	1.50
S26 Eddie George	.60	1.50
S27 Tim Brown	.60	1.50
S28 Warrick Dunn	.60	1.50
S29 Reggie White	.60	1.50
S30 Terrell Davis	.60	1.50

1999 Upper Deck

Released as a 270-card set, 1999 Upper Deck is comprised of 222 regular player cards, three checklists, and 45 star rookie cards seeded at one in four packs. Base cards have a bottom border that is enhanced with bronze foil and star rookies cards are bordered all the way around and are also enhanced with bronze foil. Packaged in 24 pack boxes, packs contained 10 cards and carried a suggested retail price of $2.99.

COMPLETE SET (270)	50.00	100.00
COMP.SET w/o SP's (225)	12.50	25.00
1 Jake Plummer	.20	.50
2 Adrian Murrell	.20	.50
3 Rob Moore	.15	.40
4 Larry Centers	.20	.50
5 Simeon Rice	.15	.40
6 Andre Wadsworth	.15	.40
7 Frank Sanders	.15	.40
8 Tim Dwight	.20	.50
9 Ray Buchanan	.15	.40
10 Chris Chandler	.20	.50
11 Jamal Anderson	.20	.50
12 O.J. Santiago	.15	.40
13 Danny Kanell	.15	.40
14 Terance Mathis	.15	.40
15 Priest Holmes	.25	.60
16 Tony Banks	.20	.50
17 Ray Lewis	.25	.60
18 Patrick Johnson	.15	.40
19 Michael Jackson	.15	.40
20 Michael McCrary	.15	.40
21 Jermaine Lewis	.15	.40
22 Eric Moulds	.20	.50
23 Doug Flutie	.25	.60
24 Antowain Smith	.15	.40
25 Rob Johnson	.20	.50
26 Bruce Smith	.25	.60
27 Andre Reed	.25	.60
28 Thurman Thomas	.25	.60
29 Fred Lane	.15	.40
30 Wesley Walls	.20	.50
31 Tim Biakabutuka	.20	.50
32 Kevin Greene	.20	.50
33 Steve Beuerlein	.20	.50
34 Muhsin Muhammad	.20	.50
35 Rae Carruth	.15	.40
36 Bobby Engram	.20	.50
37 Curtis Enis	.15	.40
38 Edgar Bennett	.20	.50
39 Erik Kramer	.20	.50
40 Steve Stenstrom	.15	.40
41 Alonzo Mayes	.15	.40
42 Curtis Conway	.20	.50
43 Tony McGee	.15	.40
44 Darnay Scott	.15	.40
45 Jeff Blake	.20	.50
46 Corey Dillon	.20	.50
47 Ki-Jana Carter	.15	.40
48 Takeo Spikes	.15	.40
49 Carl Pickens	.20	.50
50 Ty Detmer	.20	.50
51 Leslie Shepherd	.15	.40
52 Terry Kirby	.15	.40
53 Marquez Pope	.15	.40
54 Antonio Langham	.15	.40
55 Jamir Miller	.15	.40
56 Derrick Alexander DT	.15	.40
57 Troy Aikman	.40	1.00
58 Rocket Ismail	.20	.50
59 Emmitt Smith	.60	1.50
60 Michael Irvin	.25	.60
61 David LaFleur	.15	.40
62 Chris Warren	.20	.50
63 Deion Sanders	.25	.60
64 Greg Ellis	.15	.40
65 John Elway	.75	2.00
66 Bubby Brister	.15	.40
67 Terrell Davis	.25	.60
68 Ed McCaffrey	.20	.50
69 John Mobley	.15	.40
70 Bill Romanowski	.20	.50
71 Rod Smith	.20	.50
72 Shannon Sharpe	.25	.60
73 Charlie Batch	.20	.50
74 Germane Crowell	.15	.40
75 Johnnie Morton	.20	.50
76 Barry Sanders	.60	1.50
77 Robert Porcher	.15	.40
78 Stephen Boyd	.15	.40
79 Herman Moore	.20	.50
80 Brett Favre	.75	2.00
81 Mark Chmura	.15	.40
82 Antonio Freeman	.20	.50
83 Robert Brooks	.20	.50
84 Vonnie Holliday	.15	.40
85 Bill Schroeder	.20	.50
86 Dorsey Levens	.20	.50
87 Santana Dotson	.15	.40
88 Peyton Manning	.75	2.00
89 Jerome Pathon	.15	.40
90 Marvin Harrison	.25	.60
91 Ellis Johnson	.15	.40
92 Ken Dilger	.15	.40
93 E.G. Green	.15	.40
94 Jeff Burris	.15	.40
95 Mark Brunell	.20	.50
96 Fred Taylor	.20	.50
97 Jimmy Smith	.20	.50
98 James Stewart	.15	.40
99 Kyle Brady	.15	.40
100 Dave Thomas RC	.20	.50
101 Keenan McCardell	.20	.50
102 Elvis Grbac	.15	.40
103 Tony Gonzalez	.25	.60
104 Andre Rison	.20	.50
105 Donnell Bennett	.15	.40
106 Derrick Thomas	.25	.60
107 Warren Moon	.25	.60
108 Derrick Alexander WR	.15	.40
109 Dan Marino	.75	2.00
110 O.J. McDuffie	.20	.50
111 Karim Abdul-Jabbar	.20	.50
112 John Avery	.15	.40
113 Sam Madison	.15	.40
114 Jason Taylor	.20	.50
115 Zach Thomas	.25	.60
116 Randall Cunningham	.25	.60
117 Randy Moss	.25	.60
118 Cris Carter	.25	.60
119 Jake Reed	.20	.50
120 Matthew Hatchette	.20	.50
121 John Randle	.20	.50
122 Robert Smith	.20	.50
123 Drew Bledsoe	.25	.60
124 Ben Coates	.20	.50
125 Terry Glenn	.20	.50
126 Ty Law	.20	.50
127 Tony Simmons	.15	.40
128 Ted Johnson	.20	.50
129 Tony Carter	.15	.40
130 Willie McGinest	.20	.50
131 Danny Wuerffel	.20	.50
132 Cameron Cleeland	.15	.40
133 Eddie Kennison	.20	.50
134 Joe Johnson	.15	.40
135 Andre Hastings	.15	.40
136 La'Roi Glover RC	.25	.60
137 Kent Graham	.15	.40
138 Tiki Barber	.25	.60
139 Gary Brown	.15	.40
140 Ike Hilliard	.20	.50
141 Jason Sehorn	.20	.50
142 Michael Strahan	.20	.50
143 Amani Toomer	.20	.50
144 Kerry Collins	.20	.50
145 Vinny Testaverde	.20	.50
146 Wayne Chrebet	.20	.50
147 Curtis Martin	.25	.60
148 Mo Lewis	.15	.40
149 Aaron Glenn	.15	.40
150 Steve Atwater	.20	.50
151 Keyshawn Johnson	.20	.50
152 James Farrior	.20	.50
153 Rich Gannon	.20	.50
154 Tim Brown	.25	.60
155 Darrell Russell	.15	.40
156 Rickey Dudley	.15	.40
157 Charles Woodson	.25	.60
158 James Jett	.15	.40
159 Napoleon Kaufman	.15	.40
160 Duce Staley	.20	.50
161 Doug Pederson	.15	.40
162 Bobby Hoying	.15	.40
163 Koy Detmer	.15	.40
164 Kevin Turner	.15	.40
165 Charles Johnson	.15	.40
166 Mike Mamula	.15	.40
167 Jerome Bettis	.25	.60
168 Courtney Hawkins	.15	.40
169 Will Blackwell	.15	.40
170 Kordell Stewart	.20	.50
171 Richard Huntley	.15	.40
172 Levon Kirkland	.15	.40
173 Hines Ward	.25	.60
174 Trent Green	.20	.50
175 Marshall Faulk	.25	.60
176 Az-Zahir Hakim	.15	.40
177 Amp Lee	.15	.40
178 Robert Holcombe	.15	.40
179 Isaac Bruce	.25	.60
180 Kevin Carter	.15	.40
181 Jim Harbaugh	.20	.50
182 Junior Seau	.25	.60
183 Natrone Means	.20	.50
184 Ryan Leaf	.20	.50
185 Charlie Jones	.15	.40
186 Rodney Harrison	.20	.50
187 Mikhael Ricks	.15	.40
188 Steve Young	.30	.75
189 Terrell Owens	.25	.60
190 Jerry Rice	.50	1.25
191 J.J. Stokes	.15	.40
192 Irv Smith	.15	.40
193 Bryant Young	.20	.50
194 Garrison Hearst	.20	.50
195 Jon Kitna	.20	.50
196 Ahman Green	.20	.50
197 Joey Galloway	.20	.50
198 Ricky Watters	.20	.50
199 Chad Brown	.15	.40
200 Shawn Springs	.15	.40
201 Mike Pritchard	.15	.40
202 Trent Dilfer	.20	.50
203 Reidel Anthony	.15	.40
204 Bert Emanuel	.20	.50
205 Warrick Dunn	.20	.50
206 Jacquez Green	.15	.40
207 Hardy Nickerson	.15	.40
208 Mike Alstott	.25	.60
209 Eddie George	.20	.50
210 Steve McNair	.25	.60
211 Kevin Dyson	.15	.40
212 Frank Wycheck	.20	.50
213 Jackie Harris	.20	.50
214 Blaine Bishop	.15	.40
215 Yancey Thigpen	.15	.40
216 Brad Johnson	.20	.50
217 Rodney Peete	.20	.50
218 Michael Westbrook	.15	.40
219 Skip Hicks	.15	.40
220 Brian Mitchell	.20	.50
221 Dan Wilkinson	.20	.50
222 Dana Stubblefield	.15	.40
223 Kordell Stewart CL	.15	.40
224 Fred Taylor CL	.15	.40
225 Warrick Dunn CL	.15	.40
226 Champ Bailey RC	1.50	4.00
227 Chris McAlister RC	.60	1.50
228 Jevon Kearse RC	.75	2.00
229 Ebenezer Ekuban RC	.50	1.25
230 Chris Claiborne RC	.50	1.25
231 Andy Katzenmoyer RC	.60	1.50
232 Tim Couch RC	.75	2.00
233 Daunte Culpepper RC	.75	2.00
234 Akili Smith RC	.60	1.50
235 Donovan McNabb RC	4.00	10.00
236 Sean Bennett RC	.50	1.25
237 Brock Huard RC	.60	1.50
238 Cade McNown RC	.60	1.50
239 Shaun King RC	.60	1.50
240 Joe Germaine RC	.60	1.50
241 Ricky Williams RC	1.25	3.00
242 Edgerrin James RC	1.00	2.50
243 Sedrick Irvin RC	.50	1.25
244 Kevin Faulk RC	.75	2.00
245 Rob Konrad RC	.50	1.25
246 James Johnson RC	.50	1.25
247 Amos Zereoue RC	.60	1.50
248 Torry Holt RC	1.25	3.00
249 D'Wayne Bates RC	.50	1.25
250 David Boston RC	.60	1.50
251 Dameane Douglas RC	.50	1.25
252 Troy Edwards RC	.60	1.50
253 Kevin Johnson RC	.60	1.50
254 Peerless Price RC	.60	1.50
255 Antoine Winfield RC	.50	1.25
256 Mike Cloud RC	.50	1.25
257 Joe Montgomery RC	.50	1.25
258 Jermaine Fazande RC	.50	1.25
259 Scott Covington RC	.50	1.25
260 Aaron Brooks RC	.75	2.00
261 Patrick Kerney RC	.60	1.50
262 Cecil Collins RC	.50	1.25
263 Chris Greisen RC	.50	1.25
264 Craig Yeast RC	.50	1.25
265 Karsten Bailey RC	.50	1.25
266 Reginald Kelly RC	.50	1.25
267 Al Wilson RC	.75	2.00
268 Jeff Paulk RC	.50	1.25
269 Jim Kleinsasser RC	.75	2.00
270 Darrin Chiaverini RC	.50	1.25

1999 Upper Deck Exclusives Silver

*1-225 VETS/100: 8X TO 20X BASIC CARDS
*226-270 ROOKIE/100: 2.5X TO 6X BASIC RC
EXC.SILVER PRINT RUN 100 SER.#'d SETS

1999 Upper Deck 21 TD Salute

COMPLETE SET (10)	20.00	40.00
COMMON CARD (TD1-TD10)	2.00	5.00
STATED ODDS 1:23		
*SILVER/100: 3X TO 8X BASIC INSERTS		

1999 Upper Deck Game Jersey

HOBBY PACK (H) STATED ODDS 1:288		
HOBBY/RETAIL ODDS 1:2500		
BH Brock Huard H	10.00	25.00
BS Barry Sanders H	20.00	50.00
CM Cade McNown H	10.00	25.00
DB Drew Bledsoe H/R	25.00	60.00
DC Daunte Culpepper H	20.00	50.00
DF Doug Flutie H/R	15.00	40.00
DM Dan Marino H/R	40.00	100.00
DV David Boston H	10.00	25.00
EJ Edgerrin James H/R	20.00	50.00
EM Eric Moulds H	10.00	25.00
JA Jamal Anderson H/R	12.50	30.00
JE John Elway H	30.00	80.00
JR Jerry Rice H	25.00	60.00
KJ Keyshawn Johnson H/R	12.50	30.00
MC Donovan McNabb H	25.00	60.00
PM Peyton Manning H	25.00	60.00
RM Randy Moss H/R	25.00	60.00
SY Steve Young H/R	25.00	60.00
TA Troy Aikman H	15.00	40.00
TC Tim Couch H	12.50	30.00
TD Terrell Davis H/R	20.00	50.00
TDA T.Davis AUTO/30 H/R	125.00	250.00

1999 Upper Deck Game Jersey Patch

STATED ODDS 1:7500		
BHP Brock Huard	20.00	50.00
BSP Barry Sanders	60.00	150.00
CMP Cade McNown	25.00	60.00
DBP Drew Bledsoe	30.00	80.00
DCP Daunte Culpepper	30.00	80.00
DFP Doug Flutie	30.00	80.00
DMP Dan Marino	75.00	200.00
DVP David Boston	20.00	50.00
EJP Edgerrin James	50.00	100.00
JAP Jamal Anderson	30.00	80.00
JEP John Elway	60.00	150.00
JRP Jerry Rice	60.00	150.00
MCP Donovan McNabb	50.00	120.00
PMP Peyton Manning	75.00	200.00
RMP Randy Moss	50.00	120.00
SYP Steve Young	50.00	120.00
TAP Troy Aikman	50.00	120.00
TCP Tim Couch	25.00	60.00
TDP Terrell Davis	30.00	80.00

1999 Upper Deck Highlight Zone

COMPLETE SET (20)	60.00	120.00
STATED ODDS 1:23		
*SILVER/100: 2.5X TO 6X BASIC INSERTS		
Z1 Terrell Davis	1.50	4.00
Z2 Ricky Williams	4.00	10.00
Z3 Akili Smith	1.25	3.00
Z4 Charlie Batch	1.50	4.00
Z5 Jake Plummer	1.00	2.50
Z6 Emmitt Smith	3.00	8.00
Z7 Dan Marino	5.00	12.00
Z8 Tim Couch	1.50	4.00
Z9 Randy Moss	4.00	10.00
Z10 Troy Aikman	3.00	8.00
Z11 Barry Sanders	5.00	12.00
Z12 Jerry Rice	3.00	8.00
Z13 Mark Brunell	1.50	4.00
Z14 Jamal Anderson	1.50	4.00
Z15 Peyton Manning	5.00	12.00
Z16 Jerome Bettis	1.50	4.00
Z17 Donovan McNabb	10.00	25.00
Z18 Steve Young	2.00	5.00
Z19 Keyshawn Johnson	1.50	4.00
Z20 Brett Favre	5.00	12.00

1999 Upper Deck Live Wires

COMPLETE SET (15)	12.50	25.00
STATED ODDS 1:10		
*SILVER/100: 6X TO 15X BASIC INSERTS		
L1 Jake Plummer	.40	1.00
L2 Jamal Anderson	.60	1.50
L3 Emmitt Smith	1.25	3.00
L4 John Elway	2.00	5.00
L5 Barry Sanders	2.00	5.00
L6 Brett Favre	2.00	5.00
L7 Mark Brunell	.60	1.50
L8 Fred Taylor	.60	1.50
L9 Randy Moss	1.50	4.00
L10 Drew Bledsoe	.75	2.00
L11 Keyshawn Johnson	.60	1.50
L12 Jerome Bettis	.60	1.50
L13 Kordell Stewart	.40	1.00
L14 Terrell Owens	.60	1.50
L15 Eddie George	.60	1.50

1999 Upper Deck PowerDeck Inserts

COMPLETE SET (16)	125.00	250.00
STATED ODDS 1:24		
SP STATED ODDS 1:288		
1 Troy Aikman	3.00	8.00
2 Tim Couch SP	4.00	10.00
3 Daunte Culpepper SP	15.00	30.00
4 Terrell Davis	1.50	4.00
5 John Elway SP	20.00	40.00
6 Joe Germaine	1.00	2.50
7 Brock Huard	1.25	3.00
8 Shaun King	1.25	3.00
9 Dan Marino SP	20.00	40.00
10 Peyton Manning SP	15.00	40.00
11 Donovan McNabb	4.00	10.00
12 Cade McNown SP	6.00	15.00
13 Joe Montana	5.00	12.00
14 Randy Moss	4.00	10.00
15 Barry Sanders SP	20.00	40.00
16 Akili Smith SP	4.00	10.00

1999 Upper Deck Quarterback Class

COMPLETE SET (15)	15.00	30.00
STATED ODDS 1:10		
*SILVER/100: 6X TO 15X BASIC INSERTS		
QC1 Tim Couch	.25	.60
QC2 Akili Smith	.20	.50
QC3 Daunte Culpepper	1.25	3.00
QC4 Cade McNown	.20	.50
QC5 Donovan McNabb	1.50	4.00
QC6 Brock Huard	.25	.60
QC7 John Elway	2.00	5.00
QC8 Dan Marino	2.00	5.00
QC9 Brett Favre	2.00	5.00
QC10 Charlie Batch	.60	1.50
QC11 Steve Young	.75	2.00
QC12 Jake Plummer	.40	1.00
QC13 Peyton Manning	2.00	5.00
QC14 Mark Brunell	.60	1.50
QC15 Troy Aikman	1.25	3.00

1999 Upper Deck Strike Force

COMPLETE SET (30)	12.00	30.00
STATED ODDS 1:4		
*SILVER/100: 6X TO 15X BASIC INSERTS		
SF1 Jamal Anderson	.30	.75
SF2 Keyshawn Johnson	.30	.75
SF3 Eddie George	.30	.75
SF4 Steve Young	.50	1.25
SF5 Emmitt Smith	1.00	2.50
SF6 Karim Abdul-Jabbar	.30	.75
SF7 Kordell Stewart	.30	.75
SF8 Cade McNown	.30	.75
SF9 Tim Couch	.40	1.00
SF10 Corey Dillon	.30	.75
SF11 Peyton Manning	1.25	3.00
SF12 Curtis Martin	.40	1.00
SF13 Jerome Bettis	.40	1.00
SF14 Jon Kitna	.30	.75
SF15 Dan Marino	1.25	3.00
SF16 Eric Moulds	.30	.75
SF17 Charlie Batch	.30	.75
SF18 Ricky Williams	.50	1.25
SF19 Terrell Owens	.40	1.00
SF20 Ty Detmer	.30	.75
SF21 Curtis Enis	.25	.60
SF22 Doug Flutie	.40	1.00
SF23 Randall Cunningham	.40	1.00
SF24 Donovan McNabb	.75	2.00
SF25 Steve McNair	.40	1.00
SF26 Terrell Davis	.40	1.00
SF27 Daunte Culpepper	.30	.75
SF28 Warrick Dunn	.30	.75
SF29 Akili Smith	.30	.75
SF30 Barry Sanders	1.00	2.50

1999 Upper Deck Super Bowl XXXIII

This 25 card boxed set features color action photos of the top players from the Denver Broncos and the Atlanta Falcons, the two teams that played in the 1999 Super Bowl XXXIII. The backs carry player information. Cards 21-24 feature borderless color photos of four previous top Super Bowl players with facsimile autographs printed across the bottom half of the card.

COMP. FACT SET (25)	6.00	15.00
1 Jamal Anderson	.30	.75
2 Chris Chandler	.15	.40
3 Terance Mathis	.15	.40
4 Tony Martin	.15	.40
5 O.J. Santiago	.15	.40
6 Tim Dwight	.30	.75
7 Chuck Smith	.08	.25
8 Cornelius Bennett	.08	.25
9 Lester Archambeau	.08	.25
10 Ray Buchanan	.08	.25
11 Steve Atwater	.08	.25
12 Terrell Davis	.75	2.00
13 John Elway	1.20	3.00
14 Ed McCaffrey	.15	.40
15 John Mobley	.08	.25
16 Bill Romanowski	.08	.25
17 Shannon Sharpe UER	.15	.40
(photo is Rod Smith)		
18 Rod Smith	.15	.40
19 Neil Smith	.15	.40
20 Maa Tanuvasa	.08	.25
21 Troy Aikman	.75	2.00
22 Dan Marino	1.20	3.00
23 Jerry Rice	.75	2.00
24 Joe Montana	1.20	3.00
25 Super Bowl XXXIII Logo	.08	.25

2000 Upper Deck

Upper Deck features a 270-card base set comprised of 222 veteran cards 48 short-printed Rookie cards inserted in packs at the rate of one in four, and three checklist cards. Base cards feature a blue border along the right side of the card and bronze foil highlights. Upper Deck was packaged in 24-pack boxes with packs containing 10 cards and carried a suggested retail price of $2.99.

COMPLETE SET (1-270)	60.00	120.00
COMP.SET w/o RCs (225)	12.50	30.00
223-267 ROOKIE ODDS 1:4		

1 Jake Plummer .25 .60
2 Michael Pittman .20 .50
3 Rob Moore .20 .50
4 David Boston .20 .50
5 Frank Sanders .20 .50
6 Aeneas Williams .20 .50
7 Kwamie Lassiter .20 .50
8 Rob Fredrickson .20 .50
9 Tim Dwight .25 .60
10 Chris Chandler .25 .60
11 Jamal Anderson .25 .60
12 Shawn Jefferson .20 .50
13 Ken Oxendine .20 .50
14 Terance Mathis .20 .50
15 Bob Christian .20 .50
16 Qadry Ismail .25 .60
17 Jermaine Lewis .20 .50
18 Rod Woodson .30 .75
19 Michael McCrary .20 .50
20 Tony Banks .20 .50
21 Peter Boulware .20 .50
22 Shannon Sharpe .30 .75
23 Peerless Price .25 .60
24 Rob Johnson .25 .60
25 Eric Moulds .25 .60
26 Doug Flutie .30 .75
27 Jay Riemersma .20 .50
28 Antowain Smith .25 .60
29 Jonathan Linton .20 .50
30 Muhsin Muhammad .25 .60
31 Patrick Jeffers .25 .60
32 Steve Beuerlein .25 .60
33 Natrone Means .25 .60
34 Tim Biakabutuka .25 .60
35 Michael Bates .20 .50
36 Chuck Smith .20 .50
37 Wesley Walls .20 .50
38 Cade McNown .20 .50
39 Curtis Enis .20 .50
40 Marcus Robinson .25 .60
41 Eddie Kennison .20 .50
42 Bobby Engram .25 .60
43 Glyn Milburn .20 .50
44 Marty Booker .25 .60
45 Akili Smith .20 .50
46 Corey Dillon .25 .60
47 Darnay Scott .25 .60
48 Tremain Mack .20 .50
49 Damon Griffin .20 .50
50 Takeo Spikes .20 .50
51 Tony McGee .20 .50
52 Tim Couch .25 .60
53 Kevin Johnson .20 .50
54 Darrin Chiaverini .20 .50
55 Jamir Miller .20 .50
56 Errict Rhett .25 .60
57 Terry Kirby .20 .50
58 Marc Edwards .20 .50
59 Troy Aikman .50 1.25
60 Emmitt Smith .75 2.00
61 Rocket Ismail .25 .60
62 Jason Tucker .20 .50
63 Dexter Coakley .20 .50
64 Joey Galloway .25 .60
65 Wane McGarity .20 .50
66 Terrell Davis .30 .75
67 Olandis Gary .25 .60
68 Brian Griese .25 .60
69 Gus Frerotte .25 .60
70 Byron Chamberlain .20 .50
71 Ed McCaffrey .25 .60
72 Rod Smith .25 .60
73 Al Wilson .20 .50
74 Charlie Batch .25 .60
75 Germane Crowell .20 .50
76 Sedrick Irvin .20 .50
77 Johnnie Morton .25 .60
78 Robert Porcher .20 .50
79 Herman Moore .25 .60
80 James Stewart .20 .50
81 Brett Favre 1.00 2.50
82 Antonio Freeman .25 .60
83 Bill Schroeder .25 .60
84 Dorsey Levens .25 .60
85 Corey Bradford .20 .50
86 De'Mond Parker .20 .50
87 Vonnie Holliday .20 .50
88 Peyton Manning .75 2.00
89 Edgerrin James .30 .75
90 Marvin Harrison .30 .75
91 Ken Dilger .20 .50
92 Terrence Wilkins .20 .50
93 Marcus Pollard .20 .50
94 Fred Lane .20 .50
95 Mark Brunell .25 .60
96 Fred Taylor .30 .75
97 Jimmy Smith .25 .60
98 Keenan McCardell .25 .60
99 Carnell Lake .20 .50
100 Tavian Banks .20 .50
101 Kyle Brady .20 .50
102 Hardy Nickerson .20 .50
103 Elvis Grbac .20 .50
104 Tony Gonzalez .30 .75
105 Derrick Alexander WR .20 .50
106 Donnell Bennett .20 .50
107 Mike Cloud .20 .50
108 Donnie Edwards .20 .50
109 Jay Fiedler .25 .60
110 James Johnson .20 .50
111 Tony Martin .25 .60
112 Damon Huard .25 .60
113 O.J. McDuffie .25 .60
114 Thurman Thomas .30 .75
115 Zach Thomas .30 .75
116 Oronde Gadsden .25 .60
117 Randy Moss .30 .75
118 Robert Smith .25 .60
119 Cris Carter .30 .75
120 Matthew Hatchette .20 .50
121 Daunte Culpepper .25 .60
122 Leroy Hoard .20 .50
123 Drew Bledsoe .30 .75
124 Terry Glenn .25 .60
125 Troy Brown .25 .60
126 Kevin Faulk .25 .60
127 Lawyer Milloy .20 .50
128 Ricky Williams .30 .75
129 Keith Poole .20 .50
130 Jake Reed .25 .60
131 Cam Cleeland .20 .50
132 Jeff Blake .25 .60
133 Andrew Glover .20 .50
134 Kerry Collins .25 .60
135 Amani Toomer .25 .60
136 Joe Montgomery .20 .50
137 Ike Hilliard .25 .60
138 Tiki Barber .30 .75
139 Pete Mitchell .20 .50
140 Ray Lucas .20 .50
141 Mo Lewis .20 .50
142 Curtis Martin .30 .75
143 Vinny Testaverde .25 .60
144 Wayne Chrebet .25 .60
145 Dedric Ward .20 .50
146 Tim Brown .30 .75
147 Rich Gannon .25 .60
148 Tyrone Wheatley .20 .50
149 Napoleon Kaufman .25 .60
150 Charles Woodson .30 .75
151 Darrell Russell .20 .50
152 James Jett .25 .60
153 Rickey Dudley .20 .50
154 Jon Ritchie .20 .50
155 Duce Staley .25 .60
156 Donovan McNabb .30 .75
157 Torrance Small .20 .50
158 Allen Rossum .20 .50
159 Mike Mamula .20 .50
160 Na Brown .20 .50
161 Charles Johnson .20 .50
162 Kent Graham .20 .50
163 Troy Edwards .20 .50
164 Jerome Bettis .30 .75
165 Hines Ward .30 .75
166 Kordell Stewart .25 .60
167 Levon Kirkland .20 .50
168 Richard Huntley .20 .50
169 Marshall Faulk .30 .75
170 Kurt Warner .50 1.25
171 Torry Holt .30 .75
172 Isaac Bruce .30 .75
173 Kevin Carter .20 .50
174 Az-Zahir Hakim .20 .50
175 Ricky Proehl .20 .50
176 Jermaine Fazande .20 .50
177 Curtis Conway .25 .60
178 Freddie Jones .20 .50
179 Junior Seau .30 .75
180 Jeff Graham .20 .50
181 Jim Harbaugh .25 .60
182 Rodney Harrison .25 .60
183 Steve Young .40 1.00
184 Jerry Rice .60 1.50
185 Charlie Garner .25 .60
186 Terrell Owens .30 .75
187 Jeff Garcia .25 .60
188 Fred Beasley .20 .50
189 J.J. Stokes .25 .60
190 Ricky Watters .25 .60
191 Jon Kitna .25 .60
192 Derrick Mayes .20 .50
193 Sean Dawkins .20 .50
194 Charlie Rogers .20 .50
195 Mike Pritchard .20 .50
196 Cortez Kennedy .20 .50
197 Christian Fauria .20 .50
198 Warrick Dunn .25 .60
199 Shaun King .20 .50
200 Mike Alstott .30 .75
201 Warren Sapp .25 .60
202 Jacquez Green .20 .50
203 Reidel Anthony .20 .50
204 Dave Moore .20 .50
205 Keyshawn Johnson .25 .60
206 Eddie George .25 .60
207 Steve McNair .30 .75
208 Kevin Dyson .25 .60
209 Jevon Kearse .25 .60
210 Yancey Thigpen .20 .50
211 Frank Wycheck .25 .60
212 Isaac Byrd .20 .50
213 Neil O'Donnell .20 .50
214 Brad Johnson .25 .60
215 Stephen Davis .25 .60
216 Michael Westbrook .20 .50
217 Albert Connell .20 .50
218 Brian Mitchell .20 .50
219 Bruce Smith .30 .75
220 Stephen Alexander .20 .50
221 Jeff George .25 .60
222 Adrian Murrell .20 .50
223 Courtney Brown RC 1.25 3.00
224 John Engelberger RC 1.00 2.50
225 Deltha O'Neal RC 1.25 3.00
226 Corey Simon RC 1.25 3.00
227 R.Jay Soward RC 1.00 2.50
228 Marc Bulger RC 1.50 4.00
229 Raynoch Thompson RC 1.00 2.50
230 Deon Grant RC 1.00 2.50
231 Darrell Jackson RC 1.25 3.00
232 Chris Cole RC 1.25 3.00
233 Trevor Gaylor RC 1.00 2.50
234 John Abraham RC 1.50 4.00
235 Chris Redman RC 1.25 3.00
236 Joe Hamilton RC 1.00 2.50
237 Chad Pennington RC 2.50 6.00
238 Tee Martin RC 1.50 4.00
239 Giovanni Carmazzi RC 1.00 2.50
240 Tim Rattay RC 1.25 3.00
241 Ron Dayne RC 1.50 4.00
242 Shaun Alexander RC 2.00 5.00
243 Thomas Jones RC 2.00 5.00
244 Reuben Droughns RC 1.50 4.00
245 Jamal Lewis RC 1.50 4.00
246 Michael Wiley RC 1.00 2.50
247 J.R. Redmond RC 1.00 2.50
248 Travis Prentice RC 1.25 3.00
249 Todd Husak RC 1.00 2.50
250 Trung Canidate RC 1.25 3.00
251 Brian Urlacher RC 6.00 15.00
252 Anthony Becht RC 1.25 3.00
253 Bubba Franks RC 1.50 4.00
254 Tom Brady RC 20.00 50.00
255 Peter Warrick RC 1.50 4.00
256 Plaxico Burress RC 1.50 4.00
257 Sylvester Morris RC 1.00 2.50
258 Dez White RC 1.25 3.00
259 Travis Taylor RC 1.25 3.00
260 Todd Pinkston RC 1.00 2.50
261 Dennis Northcutt RC 1.25 3.00
262 Jerry Porter RC 1.50 4.00
263 Laveranues Coles RC 1.50 4.00
264 Danny Farmer RC 1.00 2.50
265 Curtis Keaton RC 1.00 2.50
266 Sherrod Gideon RC 1.00 2.50
267 Ron Dugans RC 1.00 2.50
268 Steve McNair CL .25 .60
269 Jake Plummer CL .20 .50
270 Antonio Freeman CL .20 .50

2000 Upper Deck Exclusives Gold

*VETS 1-222: 15X TO 40X BASIC CARDS
*ROOKIES 223-267: 3X TO 8X
GOLD PRINT RUN 25 SER.#'d SETS
254 Tom Brady 500.00 1,000.00

2000 Upper Deck Exclusives Silver

*VETS 1-222/268-270: 8X TO 20X
*ROOKIES 223-267: 1.5X TO 4X
SILVER PRINT RUN 100 SER.#'d SETS
254 Tom Brady 150.00 300.00

2000 Upper Deck e-Card

COMPLETE SET (6) 7.50 20.00
STATED ODDS TWO PER BOX
CP Chad Pennington 2.00 5.00
CR Chris Redman .50 1.25
JL Jamal Lewis 2.00 5.00
SA Shaun Alexander 2.50 6.00
TJ Thomas Jones 1.25 3.00
TT Travis Taylor .75 2.00

2000 Upper Deck e-Card Prizes

CPA Chad Pennington AU/200 20.00 50.00
CPB Chad Pennington (Ball/300 10.00 25.00
CPJ Chad Pennington Jsy AU/50 40.00 100.00
CRA Chris Redman (AU/200 7.50 20.00
CRB Chris Redman (Ball/300 6.00 15.00
CRJ Chris Redman (Jsy AU/50 20.00 50.00
JLA Jamal Lewis (AU/200 15.00 40.00
JLB Jamal Lewis (Ball/300 10.00 25.00
JLJ Jamal Lewis (Jsy AU/50 50.00 120.00
SAA Shaun Alexander (AU/200 20.00 50.00
SAB Shaun Alexander (Ball/300 10.00 25.00
SAJ Sha Alexander (Jsy AU/50 40.00 100.00
TJA Thomas Jones (AU/200 12.50 30.00
TJB Thomas Jones (Ball/300 7.50 20.00
TJJ Thomas Jones (Jsy AU/50 40.00 100.00
TTB Travis Taylor (Ball/300 6.00 15.00

2000 Upper Deck Game Jersey

STATED ODDS 1:287 HOBBY
AF Antonio Freeman 6.00 15.00
BF Brett Favre 25.00 60.00
BG Brian Griese 6.00 15.00
BO David Boston 5.00 12.00
CB Courtney Brown 6.00 15.00
CM Curtis Martin 8.00 20.00
CR Chris Redman 6.00 15.00
DA Daunte Culpepper 6.00 15.00
DL Dorsey Levens 6.00 15.00
DO Donovan McNabb 8.00 20.00
EM Eric Moulds 6.00 15.00
ES Emmitt Smith 20.00 50.00
FA Danny Farmer 5.00 12.00
FR Bubba Franks 8.00 20.00
HM Herman Moore 6.00 15.00
JA Jamal Anderson 6.00 15.00
JJ J.J. Stokes 6.00 15.00
JL Jamal Lewis 8.00 20.00
JR Jerry Rice 15.00 40.00
MA Mike Alstott 8.00 20.00
OG Olandis Gary 6.00 15.00
PB Plaxico Burress 8.00 20.00
RJ R.Jay Soward 5.00 12.00
RL Ray Lucas 5.00 12.00
RW Ricky Williams 8.00 20.00
SK Shaun King 5.00 12.00
SL Sylvester Morris 5.00 12.00
SM Steve McNair 8.00 20.00
SY Steve Young 12.00 30.00
TB Tim Brown 8.00 20.00
TH Torry Holt 8.00 20.00
TJ Thomas Jones 10.00 25.00
TM Tee Martin 8.00 20.00
TO Terrell Owens 8.00 20.00
TT Travis Taylor 6.00 15.00
KPGJ Brett Favre/60 Promo 40.00 100.00

2000 Upper Deck Game Jersey Autographs Gold

STATED ODDS 1:287 HOBBY
CPA Chad Pennington 30.00 60.00
DBA Drew Bledsoe 20.00 50.00
DMA Dan Marino 100.00 200.00
EGA Eddie George 15.00 40.00
EJA Edgerrin James 15.00 40.00
IBA Isaac Bruce 20.00 50.00
JOA Kevin Johnson 12.00 30.00
KJA Keyshawn Johnson 15.00 40.00
KWA Kurt Warner 30.00 60.00
MBA Mark Brunell 15.00 40.00
MCA Cade McNown 12.00 30.00
MFA Marshall Faulk 20.00 50.00
MHA Marvin Harrison 20.00 50.00
PMA Peyton Manning 75.00 150.00
PWA Peter Warrick 12.00 30.00
RDA Ron Dayne 12.00 30.00
RMA Randy Moss 50.00 100.00
SAA Shaun Alexander 15.00 40.00
TAA Troy Aikman 60.00 120.00
TCA Tim Couch 15.00 40.00
TDA Terrell Davis 20.00 50.00

2000 Upper Deck Game Jersey Autographs Silver Numbered

STATED PRINT RUN 8-92
SER.#'d UNDER 25 NOT PRICED
BOA David Boston/80 15.00 40.00
CBA Courtney Brown/92 15.00 40.00
DLA Dorsey Levens/25 30.00 80.00
EGA Eddie George/27 30.00 80.00
EJA Edgerrin James/32 30.00 80.00
IBA Isaac Bruce/80 25.00 60.00
JAA Jamal Anderson/32 25.00 60.00
JOA Kevin Johnson/85 15.00 40.00
MFA Marshall Faulk/28 75.00 150.00
MHA Marvin Harrison/88 25.00 60.00
PWA Peter Warrick/80 25.00 60.00
RDA Ron Dayne/27 30.00 80.00
SAA Shaun Alexander/37 30.00 80.00
TBA Tim Brown/81 40.00 80.00
TDA Terrell Davis/30 30.00 80.00

2000 Upper Deck Game Jersey Greats Autographs

STATED PRINT RUN 175-400
GJGBS1 Bart Starr/200 125.00 250.00
GJGBS2 Bart Starr/200 125.00 250.00
GJGDM Dan Marino/375 150.00 300.00
GJGJE John Elway/350 125.00 250.00
GJGJM Joe Montana 125.00 250.00
GJGJU Johnny Unitas/400 350.00 600.00
GJGJN1 Joe Namath/175 125.00 250.00
GJGJN2 Joe Namath/175 125.00 250.00
GJGRS Roger Staubach/400 75.00 150.00
GJGSY Steve Young/175 125.00 250.00
GJGTB Terry Bradshaw/400 100.00 200.00

2000 Upper Deck Game Jersey Patch

STATED ODDS 1:7500
*SERIAL #'d/25: .5X TO 1.2X BASIC JSY
SERIAL #'d STATED PRINT RUN 25
AFP Antonio Freeman 15.00 40.00
BFP Brett Favre 60.00 150.00
BGP Brian Griese 15.00 40.00
BOP David Boston 12.00 30.00
CMP Curtis Martin 20.00 50.00
DAP Daunte Culpepper 15.00 40.00
DBP Drew Bledsoe 20.00 50.00
DLP Dorsey Levens 15.00 40.00
DMP Dan Marino 60.00 150.00
EGP Eddie George 15.00 40.00
EJP Edgerrin James 20.00 50.00
ESP Emmitt Smith 50.00 125.00
FTP Fred Taylor 20.00 50.00
JAP Jamal Anderson 15.00 40.00
JOP Kevin Johnson 12.00 30.00
KJP Keyshawn Johnson 15.00 40.00
MBP Mark Brunell 15.00 40.00
MCP Cade McNown 12.00 30.00
MFP Marshall Faulk 20.00 50.00
MHP Marvin Harrison 20.00 50.00
OGP Olandis Gary 15.00 40.00
PMP Peyton Manning 50.00 125.00
RLP Ray Lucas 12.00 30.00
RMP Randy Moss 20.00 50.00
SKP Shaun King 12.00 30.00
TBP Tim Brown 20.00 50.00
TCP Tim Couch 15.00 40.00
TDP Terrell Davis 20.00 50.00
THP Torry Holt 20.00 50.00
TOP Terrell Owens 20.00 50.00

2000 Upper Deck Game Jersey Patch Autographs

STATED PRINT RUN 25 SERIAL #'d SETS
EGSP Eddie George 50.00 120.00
EJSP Edgerrin James 60.00 150.00
KWSP Kurt Warner 100.00 200.00
MFSP Marshall Faulk 60.00 150.00
RMSP Randy Moss EXCH 10.00 20.00
TCSP Tim Couch 50.00 120.00

2000 Upper Deck Headline Heroes

COMPLETE SET (15) 12.50 30.00
STATED ODDS 1:23
HH1 Mark Brunell .75 2.00
HH2 Damon Huard .75 2.00
HH3 Ricky Williams 1.00 2.50
HH4 Jevon Kearse .75 2.00
HH5 Keyshawn Johnson .75 2.00
HH6 Ricky Watters .75 2.00
HH7 Michael Westbrook .60 1.50
HH8 Charlie Batch .75 2.00
HH9 Warren Sapp .75 2.00
HH10 Muhsin Muhammad .75 2.00
HH11 Brett Favre 3.00 8.00
HH12 Jeff George .75 2.00
HH13 Germane Crowell .60 1.50
HH14 Troy Aikman 1.50 4.00
HH15 Jimmy Smith .75 2.00

2000 Upper Deck Highlight Zone

COMPLETE SET (10) 5.00 12.00
STATED ODDS 1:11
HZ1 Eddie George .50 1.25
HZ2 Steve McNair .60 1.50
HZ3 Kevin Dyson .50 1.25
HZ4 Kurt Warner 1.00 2.50
HZ5 Emmitt Smith 1.50 4.00
HZ6 Brad Johnson .50 1.25
HZ7 Curtis Martin .60 1.50
HZ8 Ray Lucas .40 1.00
HZ9 Akili Smith .40 1.00
HZ10 Jake Plummer .50 1.25

2000 Upper Deck New Guard

COMPLETE SET (15) 15.00 40.00
STATED ODDS 1:23
NG1 Tim Couch .75 2.00
NG2 Ricky Williams 1.00 2.50
NG3 Shaun King .60 1.50
NG4 Brian Griese .75 2.00
NG5 Rob Johnson .75 2.00
NG6 Marcus Robinson .75 2.00
NG7 Troy Edwards .60 1.50
NG8 Kevin Johnson .60 1.50
NG9 Cade McNown .60 1.50
NG10 Jon Kitna .75 2.00
NG11 Peyton Manning 2.50 6.00
NG12 Edgerrin James 1.00 2.50
NG13 Akili Smith .60 1.50
NG14 Donovan McNabb 1.00 2.50
NG15 Randy Moss 1.00 2.50

2000 Upper Deck Proving Ground

COMPLETE SET (10) 3.00 8.00
STATED ODDS 1:11
PG1 Marcus Robinson .50 1.25
PG2 Stephen Davis .50 1.25
PG3 Daunte Culpepper .50 1.25
PG4 Jevon Kearse .50 1.25
PG5 Marshall Faulk .60 1.50
PG6 Marvin Harrison .60 1.50
PG7 Germane Crowell .40 1.00
PG8 Darnay Scott .50 1.25
PG9 Duce Staley .50 1.25
PG10 Warrick Dunn .50 1.25

2000 Upper Deck Strike Force

COMPLETE SET (15) 3.00 6.00
STATED ODDS 1:4
SF1 Fred Taylor .40 1.00
SF2 Muhsin Muhammad .30 .75
SF3 Tony Gonzalez .40 1.00
SF4 Marcus Robinson .30 .75
SF5 Charlie Garner .30 .75
SF6 Torry Holt .40 1.00
SF7 Germane Crowell .25 .60
SF8 Amani Toomer .30 .75
SF9 Patrick Jeffers .30 .75
SF10 Albert Connell .25 .60
SF11 Olandis Gary .30 .75
SF12 Robert Smith .30 .75
SF13 Napoleon Kaufman .30 .75
SF14 Tim Biakabutuka .30 .75
SF15 Priest Holmes .40 1.00

2000 Upper Deck Wired

COMPLETE SET (15) 5.00 12.00
STATED ODDS 1:8
W1 Charlie Batch .50 1.25
W2 Terrell Davis .60 1.50
W3 Jake Plummer .50 1.25
W4 Cris Carter .60 1.50
W5 James Stewart .40 1.00
W6 Corey Dillon .50 1.25
W7 Ricky Watters .50 1.25
W8 Curtis Enis .40 1.00
W9 Errict Rhett .50 1.25
W10 Stephen Davis .50 1.25
W11 Mike Alstott .60 1.50
W12 Steve Beuerlein .50 1.25
W13 Michael Westbrook .40 1.00
W14 Terry Glenn .50 1.25
W15 Bill Schroeder .50 1.25

2000 Upper Deck 22K Gold John Elway

1 John Elway Commemorative die cut) 8.00 20.00

2001 Upper Deck

In July of 2001 Upper Deck released this base brand in both retail and hobby packs. The set consisted of 280 cards and cards 181-280 were short printed rookies. The stated odds for the rookies were 1:4 packs. The base set design had a border on only the bottom of the card where the player's name and team were represented. The cardfronts were full color action photos and were highlighted with silver-foil lettering and logo.

COMPLETE SET (280) 150.00 300.00
COMP.SET w/o SP's (180) 10.00 25.00
ROOKIE STATED ODDS 1:4
1 Jake Plummer .25 .60
2 David Boston .20 .50
3 Thomas Jones .25 .60
4 Frank Sanders .20 .50
5 Eric Zeier .20 .50
6 Jamal Anderson .25 .60
7 Chris Chandler .25 .60
8 Shawn Jefferson .20 .50
9 Darrick Vaughn .20 .50
10 Terance Mathis .20 .50
11 Jamal Lewis .30 .75
12 Shannon Sharpe .30 .75
13 Elvis Grbac .25 .60
14 Ray Lewis .30 .75
15 Qadry Ismail .25 .60
16 Chris Redman .30 .75
17 Rob Johnson .25 .60
18 Eric Moulds .25 .60
19 Sammy Morris .25 .60
20 Shawn Bryson .20 .50
21 Jeremy McDaniel .20 .50
22 Muhsin Muhammad .25 .60
23 Brad Hoover .25 .60
24 Tim Biakabutuka .20 .50
25 Steve Beuerlein .25 .60
26 Jeff Lewis .20 .50
27 Wesley Walls .20 .50
28 Cade McNown .25 .60
29 James Allen .20 .50
30 Marcus Robinson .25 .60
31 Brian Urlacher .40 1.00
32 Bobby Engram .25 .60
33 Peter Warrick .25 .60
34 Corey Dillon .25 .60
35 Akili Smith .20 .50
36 Danny Farmer .20 .50
37 Ron Dugans .20 .50
38 Jon Kitna .25 .60
39 Tim Couch .20 .50
40 Kevin Johnson .20 .50
41 Travis Prentice .20 .50
42 Spergon Wynn .20 .50
43 Errict Rhett .25 .60
44 Dennis Northcutt .20 .50
45 Courtney Brown .20 .50
46 Tony Banks .20 .50
47 Emmitt Smith .75 2.00
48 Joey Galloway .25 .60
49 Rocket Ismail .25 .60
50 Randall Cunningham .30 .75
51 James McKnight .20 .50
52 Terrell Davis .30 .75
53 Mike Anderson .25 .60
54 Brian Griese .25 .60
55 Rod Smith .25 .60
56 Ed McCaffrey .25 .60
57 Eddie Kennison .25 .60
58 Olandis Gary .20 .50
59 Charlie Batch .25 .60
60 Germane Crowell .20 .50
61 James O. Stewart .20 .50
62 Johnnie Morton .25 .60
63 Brett Favre 1.00 2.50
64 Antonio Freeman .30 .75
65 Dorsey Levens .25 .60
66 Ahman Green .30 .75
67 Bill Schroeder .25 .60
68 Peyton Manning .75 2.00
69 Edgerrin James .30 .75
70 Marvin Harrison .30 .75
71 Jerome Pathon .20 .50
72 Ken Dilger .20 .50
73 Mark Brunell .25 .60
74 Fred Taylor .30 .75
75 Jimmy Smith .25 .60
76 Keenan McCardell .25 .60
77 R.Jay Soward .20 .50
78 Todd Collins .20 .50
79 Tony Gonzalez .30 .75
80 Derrick Alexander .20 .50
81 Tony Richardson .20 .50
82 Sylvester Morris .20 .50
83 Oronde Gadsden .20 .50
84 Lamar Smith .25 .60
85 Jay Fiedler .25 .60
86 Jason Taylor .30 .75
87 Ray Lucas .20 .50
88 O.J. McDuffie .20 .50
89 Randy Moss .30 .75
90 Cris Carter .30 .75
91 Daunte Culpepper .25 .60
92 Moe Williams .20 .50
93 Troy Walters .20 .50
94 Drew Bledsoe .30 .75
95 Terry Glenn .25 .60
96 Kevin Faulk .25 .60
97 J.R. Redmond .20 .50
98 Troy Brown .25 .60
99 Ricky Williams .30 .75
100 Jeff Blake .25 .60
101 Joe Horn .25 .60
102 Albert Connell .20 .50
103 Aaron Brooks .25 .60
104 Chad Morton .20 .50
105 Kerry Collins .25 .60
106 Amani Toomer .25 .60
107 Ron Dayne .25 .60
108 Tiki Barber .30 .75
109 Ike Hilliard .25 .60
110 Ron Dixon .20 .50
111 Jason Sehorn .25 .60
112 Vinny Testaverde .25 .60
113 Wayne Chrebet .25 .60
114 Curtis Martin .30 .75
115 Dedric Ward .20 .50
116 Laveranues Coles .25 .60
117 Windrell Hayes .20 .50
118 Tim Brown .30 .75
119 Rich Gannon .25 .60
120 Tyrone Wheatley .25 .60
121 Charlie Garner .25 .60
122 Andre Rison .25 .60
123 Charles Woodson .30 .75
124 Trace Armstrong .20 .50
125 Duce Staley .25 .60
126 Donovan McNabb .30 .75
127 Darnell Autry .20 .50
128 Charles Johnson .20 .50
129 Torrance Small .20 .50
130 Kordell Stewart .25 .60
131 Jerome Bettis .30 .75
132 Plaxico Burress .25 .60
133 Bobby Shaw .20 .50
134 Troy Edwards .20 .50
135 Marshall Faulk .30 .75
136 Kurt Warner .50 1.25
137 Isaac Bruce .30 .75
138 Torry Holt .25 .60
139 Trent Green .30 .75
140 Az-Zahir Hakim .20 .50
141 Junior Seau .30 .75
142 Curtis Conway .25 .60
143 Doug Flutie .30 .75
144 Jeff Graham .20 .50
145 Freddie Jones .20 .50
146 Marcellus Wiley .20 .50
147 Jeff Garcia .25 .60
148 Jerry Rice .60 1.50
149 Fred Beasley .20 .50
150 Terrell Owens .30 .75
151 J.J. Stokes .20 .50
152 Garrison Hearst .25 .60
153 Ricky Watters .25 .60
154 Shaun Alexander .30 .75
155 Matt Hasselbeck .30 .75
156 Brock Huard .20 .50
157 Darrell Jackson .25 .60
158 John Randle .25 .60
159 Warrick Dunn .30 .75
160 Shaun King .20 .50
161 Ryan Leaf .20 .50
162 Mike Alstott .25 .60
163 Jacquez Green .20 .50
164 Brad Johnson .25 .60
165 Keyshawn Johnson .25 .60
166 Eddie George .30 .75
167 Steve McNair .30 .75
168 Neil O'Donnell .25 .60
169 Derrick Mason .25 .60
170 Frank Wycheck .20 .50
171 Kevin Dyson .20 .50
172 Jevon Kearse .25 .60
173 Jeff George .25 .60
174 Stephen Davis .25 .60
175 Larry Centers .25 .60
176 Michael Westbrook .20 .50
177 Stephen Alexander .20 .50
178 Ron Dayne .25 .60
179 Donovan McNabb .30 .75
180 Jimmy Smith .25 .60
181 Adam Archuleta RC 1.00 2.50
182 A.J. Feeley RC 1.00 2.50
183 Alex Bannister RC .75 2.00
184 Alge Crumpler RC 1.25 3.00
185 Andre Carter RC 1.00 2.50
186 Andre Dyson RC .75 2.00
187 Anthony Thomas RC 1.25 3.00
188 Arther Love RC .75 2.00
189 Bobby Newcombe RC 1.00 2.50
190 Brandon Spoon RC 1.00 2.50
191 Carlos Polk RC .75 2.00
192 Casey Hampton RC 1.25 3.00
193 Cedrick Wilson RC 1.00 2.50
194 Chad Johnson RC 2.00 5.00
195 Chris Chambers RC 1.25 3.00
196 Chris Taylor RC .75 2.00
197 Chris Weinke RC 1.00 2.50
198 Correll Buckhalter RC 1.25 3.00
199 Damione Lewis RC 1.00 2.50
200 Dan Alexander RC 1.00 2.50
201 Dan Morgan RC 1.00 2.50
202 Willie Middlebrooks RC 1.00 2.50
203 David Terrell RC 1.00 2.50
204 Derrick Gibson RC .75 2.00
205 Deuce McAllister RC 1.25 3.00
206 Drew Brees RC 12.50 25.00
207 Edgerton Hartwell RC .75 2.00
208 Fred Smoot RC 1.25 3.00
209 Freddie Mitchell RC .75 2.00
210 Gary Baxter RC .75 2.00
211 Gerard Warren RC 1.00 2.50
212 Hakim Akbar RC .75 2.00
213 Heath Evans RC 1.00 2.50
214 Jabari Holloway RC .75 2.00
215 Jamal Reynolds RC .75 2.00
216 Jamar Fletcher RC .75 2.00
217 James Jackson RC .75 2.00
218 Jamie Winborn RC 1.00 2.50
219 Jesse Palmer RC 1.00 2.50
220 Josh Booty RC 1.00 2.50
221 Josh Heupel RC 1.25 3.00
222 Justin Smith RC 1.25 3.00
223 Karon Riley RC .75 2.00
224 Ken Lucas RC 1.00 2.50
225 Kenyatta Walker RC .75 2.00
226 Ken-Yon Rambo RC .75 2.00
227 Kevan Barlow RC 1.00 2.50
228 Kevin Kasper RC .75 2.00
229 Koren Robinson RC 1.00 2.50
230 LaDainian Tomlinson RC 4.00 10.00
231 LaMont Jordan RC 1.25 3.00
232 Leonard Davis RC 1.25 3.00
233 Marcus Stroud RC 1.00 2.50
234 Marques Tuiasosopo RC 1.00 2.50
235 Snoop Minnis RC .75 2.00
236 Michael Bennett RC 1.00 2.50
237 Michael Stone RC .75 2.00
238 Mike McMahon RC 1.00 2.50
239 Michael Vick RC 5.00 12.00
240 Moran Norris RC .75 2.00
241 Morlon Greenwood RC .75 2.00
242 Nate Clements RC 1.00 2.50
243 Orlando Huff RC .75 2.00
244 Quincy Morgan RC 1.00 2.50
245 Reggie Wayne RC 2.50 6.00
246 Richard Seymour RC 1.25 3.00
247 Robert Ferguson RC 1.25 3.00
248 Rod Gardner RC 1.00 2.50
249 Rudi Johnson RC 1.25 3.00
250 Sage Rosenfels RC 1.25 3.00
251 Santana Moss RC 1.50 4.00
252 Scotty Anderson RC .75 2.00
253 Sedrick Hodge RC .75 2.00
254 Shaun Rogers RC 1.25 3.00
255 Steve Hutchinson RC 2.00 5.00
256 T.J. Houshmandzadeh RC 1.50 4.00
257 Tay Cody RC .75 2.00
258 George Layne RC .75 2.00
259 Todd Heap RC 1.25 3.00
260 Tommy Polley RC .75 2.00
261 Tony Dixon RC .75 2.00
262 Brian Allen RC .75 2.00
263 Torrance Marshall RC .75 2.00
264 Travis Henry RC 1.00 2.50
265 Travis Minor RC 1.00 2.50
266 Vinny Sutherland RC .75 2.00
267 Will Allen RC 1.25 3.00
268 Derrick Blaylock RC 1.00 2.50
269 Zeke Moreno RC 1.00 2.50
270 Chris Barnes RC .75 2.00
271 Dee Brown RC .75 2.00
272 Reggie White RC .75 2.00
273 Derek Combs RC .75 2.00
274 Steve Smith RC 2.50 6.00
275 John Capel RC .75 2.00
276 Justin McCareins RC 1.00 2.50
277 Damerien McCants RC 1.00 2.50
278 Eddie Berlin RC .75 2.00
279 Francis St. Paul RC .75 2.00
280 Quincy Carter RC 1.00 2.50

2001 Upper Deck Gold

*VETS 1-180: 4X TO 10X BASIC CARDS
1-180 VETERAN PRINT RUN 100
*ROOKIES 181-280: 2X TO 5X
181-280 ROOKIE PRINT RUN 50

2001 Upper Deck Championship Threads

STATED ODDS 1:144
CTAF Antonio Freeman 6.00 15.00
CTBF Brett Favre 20.00 50.00
CTDI Trent Dilfer 5.00 12.00
CTDL Dorsey Levens 5.00 12.00
CTEM Ed McCaffrey 5.00 12.00
CTIB Isaac Bruce 6.00 15.00
CTJL Jamal Lewis 6.00 15.00
CTJR Jerry Rice 12.00 30.00
CTKW Kurt Warner 10.00 25.00
CTMF Marshall Faulk 6.00 15.00
CTRL Ray Lewis 6.00 15.00
CTRS Rod Smith 5.00 12.00
CTSS Shannon Sharpe 6.00 15.00
CTTD Terrell Davis 6.00 15.00
CTTH Torry Holt 5.00 12.00

2001 Upper Deck Classic Drafts Jerseys

STATED ODDS 1:288
BGCD Brian Griese 6.00 15.00
DBCD Drew Bledsoe 8.00 20.00
DCCD Daunte Culpepper 6.00 15.00
DMCD Dan Marino 25.00 60.00
FTCD Fred Taylor 8.00 20.00
JECD John Elway 20.00 50.00
JKCD Jim Kelly 12.00 30.00
KECD Jevon Kearse 6.00 15.00
MBCD Mark Brunell 6.00 15.00
TCCD Tim Couch 5.00 12.00

2001 Upper Deck Constant Threat

COMPLETE SET (10) 5.00 12.00
STATED ODDS 1:36
CT1 Aaron Brooks .60 1.50
CT2 Charlie Batch .60 1.50
CT3 Donovan McNabb .75 2.00
CT4 Mark Brunell .60 1.50
CT5 Akili Smith .50 1.25
CT6 Ray Lucas .50 1.25
CT7 Jake Plummer .60 1.50
CT8 Steve McNair .75 2.00
CT9 Trent Green .75 2.00
CT10 Doug Flutie .75 2.00

2001 Upper Deck e-Card

COMPLETE SET (6) 10.00 25.00
STATED ODDS 1:12
ECW Chris Weinke .75 2.00
EDB Drew Brees 6.00 15.00
EFM Freddie Mitchell .60 1.50
ELT LaDainian Tomlinson 3.00 8.00
EMB Michael Bennett .75 2.00
EMV Michael Vick 4.00 10.00

2001 Upper Deck e-Card Prizes

JSY STATED PRINT RUN 300 SER.#'d SETS
AU STATED PRINT RUN 100 SER.#'d SETS
EACW Chris Weinke AU 10.00 25.00
EADB Drew Brees AU 100.00 200.00
EAFM Freddie Mitchell AU 8.00 20.00
EALT LaDainian Tomlinson AU 60.00 120.00
EAMB Michael Bennett AU 10.00 25.00
EAMV Michael Vick AU 75.00 150.00
EJCW Chris Weinke JSY 5.00 12.00
EJDB Drew Brees JSY 20.00 40.00
EJFM Freddie Mitchell JSY 4.00 10.00
EJLT LaDainian Tomlinson JSY 15.00 40.00
EJMB Michael Bennett JSY 5.00 12.00
EJMV Michael Vick JSY 15.00 40.00

2001 Upper Deck Game Jersey Autographs

STATED ODDS 1:288
BJAJ Brad Johnson 15.00 40.00
DCAJ Daunte Culpepper 15.00 40.00
IBAJ Isaac Bruce 20.00 50.00
JGAJ Jeff Garcia 15.00 40.00
JLAJ Jamal Lewis 20.00 50.00
JPAJ Jake Plummer 15.00 40.00
MAAJ Mike Alstott 15.00 40.00
PMAJ Peyton Manning 75.00 150.00
RMAJ Randy Moss 50.00 100.00

2001 Upper Deck Lettermen Patches

STATED PRINT RUN 50 SER.#'d SETS
CWLP Chris Weinke 12.00 30.00
DMLP Deuce McAllister 15.00 40.00
FMLP Freddie Mitchell 10.00 25.00
MBLP Michael Bennett 12.00 30.00
MTLP Marques Tuiasosopo 12.00 30.00
MVLP Michael Vick 50.00 120.00

2001 Upper Deck Power Surge

COMPLETE SET (10) 7.50 20.00
STATED ODDS 1:36
PS1 Eddie George 1.00 2.50
PS2 Cris Carter 1.00 2.50
PS3 Curtis Martin 1.00 2.50
PS4 Jerry Rice 2.00 5.00
PS5 Jamal Anderson .75 2.00
PS6 Keyshawn Johnson .75 2.00
PS7 Ricky Williams 1.00 2.50
PS8 Randy Moss 1.00 2.50
PS9 Marvin Harrison 1.00 2.50
PS10 Corey Dillon .75 2.00

2001 Upper Deck Premium Patches

STATED ODDS 1:5000
AFPP Drew Bledsoe 20.00 50.00
BFPP Brett Favre 60.00 150.00
BGPP Brian Griese 15.00 40.00
DLPP Dorsey Levens 15.00 40.00
EGPP Eddie George 20.00 50.00
EMPP Ed McCaffrey 15.00 40.00
FTPP Fred Taylor 20.00 50.00
IBPP Isaac Bruce 20.00 50.00

JLPP Jamal Lewis 20.00 50.00
JRPP Jerry Rice 40.00 100.00
KWPP Kurt Warner 30.00 80.00
MBPP Mark Brunell 15.00 40.00
MFPP Marshall Faulk 20.00 50.00
RSPP Rod Smith 15.00 40.00
SMPP Steve McNair 20.00 50.00
SSPP Shannon Sharpe 20.00 50.00
TAPP Troy Aikman 30.00 80.00
TCPP Tim Couch 12.00 30.00
THPP Torry Holt 15.00 40.00
TDPP Terrell Davis 20.00 50.00

2001 Upper Deck Proving Ground

COMPLETE SET (20) 6.00 15.00
STATED ODDS 1:9
PG1 Mike Anderson .40 1.00
PG2 Tim Couch .30 .75
PG3 Donovan McNabb .50 1.25
PG4 Aaron Brooks .40 1.00
PG5 Trent Dilfer .40 1.00
PG6 Brian Griese .40 1.00
PG7 Kevin Johnson .30 .75
PG8 Ahman Green .50 1.25
PG9 Sylvester Morris .30 .75
PG10 Peter Warrick .40 1.00
PG11 Tiki Barber .50 1.25
PG12 Torry Holt .40 1.00
PG13 Trent Green .50 1.25
PG14 Ed McCaffrey .40 1.00
PG15 Joe Horn .40 1.00
PG16 Muhsin Muhammad .40 1.00
PG17 Kerry Collins .40 1.00
PG18 Edgerrin James .50 1.25
PG19 Brad Hoover .40 1.00
PG20 Ron Dayne .40 1.00

2001 Upper Deck Rookie Threads

STATED ODDS 1:144
RTCC Chris Chambers 5.00 12.00
RTCJ Chad Johnson/102 SP 25.00 50.00
RTCW Chris Weinke 4.00 10.00
RTDB Drew Brees 15.00 40.00
RTDM Deuce McAllister 5.00 12.00
RTFM Freddie Mitchell 3.00 8.00
RTKB Kevan Barlow 4.00 10.00
RTKR Koren Robinson 4.00 10.00
RTLT LaDainian Tomlinson/50 SP 30.00 60.00
RTMB Michael Bennett 4.00 10.00
RTMV Michael Vick 20.00 50.00
RTRF Robert Ferguson 5.00 12.00
RTRG Rod Gardner 4.00 10.00
RTRW Reggie Wayne 10.00 25.00
RTTH Travis Henry 4.00 10.00

2001 Upper Deck Running Wild

COMPLETE SET (15) 10.00 25.00
STATED ODDS 1:24
RW1 Eddie George 1.00 2.50
RW2 Corey Dillon .75 2.00
RW3 Edgerrin James 1.00 2.50
RW4 Charlie Garner .75 2.00
RW5 Jamal Anderson .75 2.00
RW6 Emmitt Smith 2.50 6.00
RW7 Terrell Davis 1.00 2.50
RW8 Mike Anderson .75 2.00
RW9 James O. Stewart .60 1.50
RW10 Ricky Watters .75 2.00
RW11 Lamar Smith .75 2.00
RW12 Curtis Martin 1.00 2.50
RW13 Ricky Williams 1.00 2.50
RW14 Stephen Davis .75 2.00
RW15 Jerome Bettis 1.00 2.50

2001 Upper Deck Starstruck

COMPLETE SET (15) 7.50 20.00
STATED ODDS 1:24
S1 Curtis Martin .75 2.00
S2 Keyshawn Johnson .60 1.50
S3 Tim Brown .75 2.00
S4 Terrell Owens .75 2.00
S5 Duce Staley .60 1.50
S6 Rich Gannon .60 1.50
S7 Mike Anderson .60 1.50
S8 Stephen Davis .60 1.50
S9 Emmitt Smith 2.00 5.00
S10 Steve McNair .75 2.00
S11 Ricky Williams .75 2.00
S12 Marcus Robinson .60 1.50
S13 Vinny Testaverde .60 1.50
S14 Rod Smith .60 1.50
S15 Drew Bledsoe .75 2.00

2001 Upper Deck Teammates Jerseys

STATED ODDS 1:144
AST Troy Aikman / Emmitt Smith 30.00 80.00
BMT Charlie Batch / Herman Moore 8.00 20.00
CMT Daunte Culpepper / Randy Moss 10.00 25.00
DBT Ron Dayne / Tiki Barber 10.00 25.00
FLT Brett Favre / Dorsey Levens 20.00 50.00
GOT Jeff Garcia / Terrell Owens 10.00 25.00
KJT Shaun King / Keyshawn Johnson 8.00 20.00
MHT Peyton Manning / Marvin Harrison 20.00 50.00
MJT Peyton Manning / Edgerrin James 20.00 50.00
WFT Kurt Warner / Marshall Faulk 15.00 40.00

2002 Upper Deck

Released in September 2002, this set features 180 veterans, 30 Sunday Stars, and 100 rookies. Note that Ed Reed was intended to be card #222, but was misnumbered 310. Therefore, no cad #222 was produced and two #310 cards were issued. The Sunday Stars were inserted at a rate of 1:12, and the rookies were inserted at a rate of 1:4. Each box contained 24 packs of 8 cards. SRP was $2.99 per pack.

COMP.SET w/o SP's (180) 10.00 25.00
211-310 ROOKIE STATED ODDS 1:4
1 Jake Plummer .25 .60
2 Marcel Shipp .20 .50
3 David Boston .20 .50
4 Arnold Jackson .20 .50
5 Frank Sanders .20 .50
6 Freddie Jones .20 .50
7 Michael Vick .50 1.25
8 Jamal Anderson .25 .60
9 Warrick Dunn .25 .60
10 Maurice Smith .20 .50
11 Shawn Jefferson .20 .50
12 Chris Redman .20 .50
13 Jeff Blake .25 .60
14 Jamal Lewis .25 .60
15 Travis Taylor .20 .50
16 Ray Lewis .30 .75
17 Chris McAlister .20 .50
18 Drew Bledsoe .30 .75
19 Travis Henry .20 .60
20 Larry Centers .25 .60
21 Eric Moulds .25 .60
22 Reggie Germany .20 .50
23 Peerless Price .20 .50
24 Chris Weinke .20 .50
25 Lamar Smith .25 .60
26 Nick Goings .20 .50
27 Muhsin Muhammad .25 .60
28 Isaac Byrd .20 .50
29 Wesley Walls .25 .60
30 Jim Miller .20 .50
31 Anthony Thomas .25 .60
32 Dez White .20 .50
33 David Terrell .20 .50
34 Marty Booker .25 .60
35 Brian Urlacher .30 .75
36 Jon Kitna .25 .60
37 Corey Dillon .25 .60
38 Peter Warrick .25 .60
39 Darnay Scott .25 .60
40 Chad Johnson .30 .75
41 Tim Couch .20 .50
42 James Jackson .20 .50
43 JaJuan Dawson .20 .50
44 Kevin Johnson .20 .50
45 Quincy Morgan .20 .50
46 Courtney Brown .20 .50
47 Quincy Carter .20 .50
48 Emmitt Smith .75 2.00
49 Joey Galloway .25 .60
50 Rocket Ismail .25 .60
51 Ken-Yon Rambo .20 .50
52 Brian Griese .25 .60
53 Terrell Davis .30 .75
54 Mike Anderson .25 .60
55 Shannon Sharpe .30 .75
56 Ed McCaffrey .25 .60
57 Rod Smith .25 .60
58 Mike McMahon .20 .50
59 James Stewart .20 .50
60 Az-Zahir Hakim .20 .50
61 Desmond Howard .25 .60
62 Germane Crowell .20 .50
63 Brett Favre .75 2.00
64 Ahman Green .25 .60
65 Antonio Freeman .30 .75
66 Terry Glenn .25 .60
67 Kabeer Gbaja-Biamila .25 .60
68 Kent Graham .20 .50
69 James Allen .20 .50
70 Corey Bradford .20 .50
71 Jermaine Lewis .20 .50
72 Jamie Sharper .25 .60
73 Peyton Manning .60 1.50
74 Edgerrin James .25 .60
75 Dominic Rhodes .25 .60
76 Marvin Harrison .30 .75
77 Qadry Ismail .25 .60
78 Mark Brunell .25 .60
79 Fred Taylor .25 .60
80 Stacey Mack .20 .50
81 Jimmy Smith .25 .60
82 Keenan McCardell .25 .60
83 Trent Green .25 .60
84 Priest Holmes .30 .75
85 Derrick Alexander .20 .50
86 Johnnie Morton .25 .60
87 Snoop Minnis .20 .60
88 Tony Gonzalez .30 .75
89 Jay Fiedler .25 .60
90 Ricky Williams .25 .60
91 Chris Chambers .25 .60
92 Oronde Gadsden .20 .50
93 Zach Thomas .30 .75
94 Daunte Culpepper .25 .60
95 Michael Bennett .25 .60
96 Randy Moss .30 .75
97 Sean Dawkins .25 .60
98 Tom Brady .75 2.00
99 Antowain Smith .25 .60
100 David Patten .20 .50
101 Troy Brown .25 .60
102 Adam Vinatieri .30 .75
103 Aaron Brooks .25 .60
104 Deuce McAllister .25 .60
105 Jake Reed .25 .60
106 Jerome Pathon .20 .50
107 Joe Horn .25 .60
108 Kyle Turley .20 .50
109 Kerry Collins .25 .60
110 Ron Dayne .25 .60
111 Tiki Barber .30 .75
112 Amani Toomer .25 .60
113 Ike Hilliard .25 .60
114 Michael Strahan .30 .75
115 Vinny Testaverde .25 .60
116 Chad Pennington .30 .75
117 Curtis Martin .30 .75
118 Santana Moss .25 .60
119 Laveranues Coles .25 .60
120 Wayne Chrebet .25 .60
121 Rich Gannon .25 .60
122 Charlie Garner .25 .60
123 Jerry Rice .60 1.50
124 Tim Brown .30 .75
125 Charles Woodson .30 .75
126 Donovan McNabb .30 .75
127 Duce Staley .25 .60
128 Correll Buckhalter .25 .60
129 Freddie Mitchell .20 .50
130 James Thrash .25 .60
131 Todd Pinkston .20 .50
132 Kordell Stewart .25 .60
133 Jerome Bettis .30 .75
134 Chris Fuamatu-Ma'afala .20 .50
135 Hines Ward .30 .75
136 Plaxico Burress .25 .60
137 Kendrell Bell .20 .50
138 Doug Flutie .30 .75
139 Drew Brees .50 1.25
140 LaDainian Tomlinson .40 1.00
141 Curtis Conway .25 .60
142 Tim Dwight .20 .50
143 Junior Seau .30 .75
144 Jeff Garcia .25 .60
145 Garrison Hearst .25 .60
146 Kevan Barlow .20 .50
147 Terrell Owens .30 .75
148 J.J. Stokes .20 .50
149 Trent Dilfer .25 .60
150 Shaun Alexander .25 .60
151 Ricky Watters .25 .60
152 Bobby Engram .25 .60
153 Koren Robinson .20 .50
154 Kurt Warner .30 .75
155 Marshall Faulk .30 .75
156 Isaac Bruce .30 .75
157 Ricky Proehl .25 .60
158 Terrence Wilkins .20 .50
159 Torry Holt .30 .75
160 Brad Johnson .25 .60
161 Shaun King .20 .50
162 Rob Johnson .25 .60
163 Mike Alstott .25 .60
164 Michael Pittman .25 .60
165 Keyshawn Johnson .25 .60
166 Steve McNair .30 .75
167 Eddie George .25 .60
168 Derrick Mason .25 .60
169 Kevin Dyson .25 .60
170 Frank Wycheck .20 .50
171 Jevon Kearse .25 .60
172 Danny Wuerffel .25 .60
173 Stephen Davis .25 .60
174 Michael Westbrook .20 .50
175 Rod Gardner .20 .50
176 Champ Bailey .30 .75
177 Darrell Green .30 .75
178 Kurt Warner CL .25 .60
179 Brett Favre CL .60 1.50
180 Randy Moss CL .25 .60
181 David Boston SS .75 2.00
182 Jake Plummer SS 1.00 2.50
183 Michael Vick SS 2.00 5.00
184 Drew Bledsoe SS 1.25 3.00
185 Anthony Thomas SS 1.00 2.50
186 Tim Couch SS .75 2.00
187 Emmitt Smith SS 3.00 8.00
188 Ahman Green SS 1.00 2.50
189 Brett Favre SS 3.00 8.00
190 Edgerrin James SS 1.00 2.50
191 Peyton Manning SS 2.50 6.00
192 Mark Brunell SS 1.00 2.50
193 Daunte Culpepper SS 1.00 2.50
194 Randy Moss SS 1.25 3.00
195 Tom Brady SS 3.00 8.00
196 Aaron Brooks SS 1.00 2.50
197 Ricky Williams SS 1.00 2.50
198 Curtis Martin SS 1.25 3.00
199 Jerry Rice SS 2.50 6.00
200 Donovan McNabb SS 1.25 3.00
201 Jerome Bettis SS 1.25 3.00
202 Kordell Stewart SS 1.00 2.50
203 LaDainian Tomlinson SS 1.50 4.00
204 Jeff Garcia SS 1.00 2.50
205 Terrell Owens SS 1.25 3.00
206 Shaun Alexander SS 1.00 2.50
207 Kurt Warner SS 1.25 3.00
208 Marshall Faulk SS 1.25 3.00
209 Keyshawn Johnson SS 1.00 2.50
210 Steve McNair SS 1.25 3.00
211 Damien Anderson RC 1.25 3.00
212 Jason McAddley RC 1.50 4.00
213 Josh McCown RC 2.00 5.00
214 Josh Scobey RC 1.50 4.00
215 Preston Parsons RC 1.25 3.00
216 Dusty Bonner RC 1.25 3.00
217 Kahlil Hill RC 1.25 3.00
218 Kurt Kittner RC 1.25 3.00
219 T.J. Duckett RC 2.00 5.00
220 Chester Taylor RC 2.00 5.00
221 Kalimba Edwards RC 1.50 4.00
223 Ron Johnson RC 1.50 4.00
224 Tellis Redmon RC 1.25 3.00
225 Wes Pate RC 1.25 3.00
226 David Priestley RC 1.25 3.00
227 Josh Reed RC 1.50 4.00
228 Mike Williams RC 1.25 3.00
229 Ryan Denney RC 1.25 3.00
230 DeShaun Foster RC 2.00 5.00
231 Julius Peppers RC 4.00 10.00
232 Randy Fasani RC 1.50 4.00
233 Adrian Peterson RC 2.00 5.00
234 Alex Brown RC 2.00 5.00
235 Gavin Hoffman RC 1.25 3.00
236 Levi Jones RC 1.25 3.00
237 Andra Davis RC 1.25 3.00
238 Andre Davis RC 1.50 4.00
239 William Green RC 1.50 4.00
240 Antonio Bryant RC 2.00 5.00
241 Chad Hutchinson RC 1.25 3.00
242 Roy Williams RC 2.00 5.00
243 Woody Dantzler RC 1.50 4.00
244 Ashley Lelie RC 1.50 4.00
245 Clinton Portis RC 2.50 6.00
246 Lamont Thompson RC 1.50 4.00
247 James Mungro RC 2.00 5.00
248 Joey Harrington RC 2.00 5.00
249 Luke Staley RC 1.25 3.00
250 Craig Nall RC 1.50 4.00
251 Javon Walker RC 2.00 5.00
252 Najeh Davenport RC 2.00 5.00
253 David Carr RC 2.00 5.00
254 Saleem Rasheed RC 1.25 3.00
255 Mike Rumph RC 1.25 3.00
256 Jabar Gaffney RC 2.00 5.00
257 Jonathan Wells RC 2.00 5.00
258 Dwight Freeney RC 2.50 6.00
259 Larry Tripplett RC 1.25 3.00
260 David Garrard RC 2.50 6.00
261 John Henderson RC 1.50 4.00
262 Ryan Sims RC 2.00 5.00
263 Leonard Henry RC 1.25 3.00
264 Brian Allen RC 1.50 4.00
265 Atrews Bell RC 1.25 3.00
266 Bryant McKinnie RC 1.25 3.00
267 Kelly Campbell RC 1.50 4.00
268 Raonall Smith RC 1.25 3.00
269 Antwoine Womack RC 1.25 3.00
270 Daniel Graham RC 1.50 4.00
271 Deion Branch RC 2.00 5.00
272 Sam Simmons RC 1.25 3.00
273 Rohan Davey RC 2.00 5.00
274 Charles Grant RC 2.00 5.00
275 Derrick Lewis RC 1.25 3.00
276 Donte Stallworth RC 2.00 5.00
277 J.T. O'Sullivan RC 1.50 4.00
278 Keyuo Craver RC 1.25 3.00
279 Ricky Williams RC 1.50 4.00
280 Bryan Thomas RC 1.25 3.00
281 Jeremy Shockey RC 3.00 8.00
282 Tim Carter RC 1.50 4.00
283 Larry Ned RC 1.25 3.00
284 Napoleon Harris RC 1.50 4.00
285 Phillip Buchanon RC 2.00 5.00
286 Ronald Curry RC 1.50 4.00
287 Brian Westbrook RC 3.00 8.00
288 Freddie Milons RC 1.25 3.00
289 Lito Sheppard RC 2.00 5.00
290 Antwaan Randle El RC 2.00 5.00
291 Lee Mays RC 1.25 3.00
292 Daryl Jones RC 1.25 3.00
293 Justin Peelle RC 1.25 3.00
294 Quentin Jammer RC 2.00 5.00
295 Reche Caldwell RC 2.00 5.00
296 Seth Burford RC 1.25 3.00
297 Terry Charles RC 1.25 3.00
298 Brandon Doman RC 1.25 3.00
299 Maurice Morris RC 1.50 4.00
300 Eric Crouch RC 2.00 5.00
301 Lamar Gordon RC 1.50 4.00
302 Marquise Walker RC 1.25 3.00
303 Tracey Wistrom RC 1.50 4.00
304 Travis Stephens RC 1.25 3.00
305 Herb Haygood RC 1.25 3.00
306 Albert Haynesworth RC 2.00 5.00
307 Rocky Calmus RC 1.50 4.00
308 Cliff Russell RC 1.25 3.00
309 Ladell Betts RC 2.00 5.00
310A Patrick Ramsey RC 2.00 5.00
310B Ed Reed RC 8.00 20.00

2002 Upper Deck Battle-Worn

STATED ODDS 1:144
*GOLD/75: .8X TO 2X BASIC JSY
GOLD PRINT RUN 75 SER.#'d SETS
BWAT Anthony Thomas SP 4.00 10.00
BWBG Brian Griese SP 4.00 10.00
BWBU Brian Urlacher 4.00 10.00
BWJK Jevon Kearse 3.00 8.00
BWJS Junior Seau 4.00 10.00
BWMS Michael Strahan 4.00 10.00
BWRH Rodney Harrison 3.00 8.00
BWRL Ray Lewis 4.00 10.00
BWTB Tiki Barber 4.00 10.00
BWTD Terrell Davis 4.00 10.00

2002 Upper Deck Blitz Brigade

COMPLETE SET (14) 6.00 15.00
STATED ODDS 1:12 HOB/RET
BB1 Ray Lewis .75 2.00
BB2 Brian Urlacher .75 2.00
BB3 Kabeer Gbaja-Biamila .60 1.50
BB4 Zach Thomas .75 2.00
BB5 Michael Strahan .75 2.00
BB6 Charles Woodson .75 2.00
BB7 Kendrell Bell .50 1.25
BB8 Junior Seau .75 2.00
BB9 Rodney Harrison .60 1.50
BB10 Levon Kirkland .50 1.25
BB11 Warren Sapp .60 1.50
BB12 Jevon Kearse .60 1.50
BB13 Bruce Smith .75 2.00
BB14 Champ Bailey .75 2.00

2002 Upper Deck Buy Back Autographs

STATED PRINT RUN 1-100
SERIAL #'d UNDER 20 NOT PRICED
AG Ahman Green 01UDTT/22 15.00 40.00
JG Jeff Garcia 01UDTT/23 10.00 25.00
KS Kordell Stewart 99UD/33 8.00 20.00
BJ1 Brad Johnson 00UDL/48 8.00 20.00
PM1 Peyton Manning 99UDMVP/26 75.00 150.00
PM2 Peyton Manning 99UDPOH/25 75.00 150.00
PM3 Peyton Manning 99SPA/100 50.00 100.00
PM4 Peyton Manning 99UD/39 60.00 120.00
PM6 Peyton Manning 00UD/21 75.00 150.00
PM7 Peyton Manning 00UDMVP/32 75.00 150.00
PM11 Peyton Manning 01UDTT/39 60.00 120.00
TC1 Tim Couch 00UD/29 10.00 25.00
TC2 Tim Couch 01UDTT/27 10.00 25.00
TG2 Tony Gonzalez 01LEG/21 15.00 40.00

2002 Upper Deck First Team Fabrics

STATED ODDS 1:144 HOB/RET
*GOLD/150: .6X TO 1.5X BASIC JERSEY
GOLD PRINT RUN 150 SER.#'d SETS
FTCD Corey Dillon 3.00 8.00
FTDB David Boston 2.50 6.00
FTES Emmitt Smith 10.00 25.00
FTJP Jake Plummer 3.00 8.00
FTJS Jimmy Smith 3.00 8.00
FTKJ Keyshawn Johnson 3.00 8.00
FTMH Marvin Harrison 4.00 10.00
FTRS Rod Smith 3.00 8.00
FTTB Tom Brady 10.00 25.00
FTTC Tim Couch 2.50 6.00

2002 Upper Deck Flight Suits Jerseys

STATED ODDS 1:288
*GOLD/25: .8X TO 2X BASIC JERSEY
GOLD PRINT RUN 25 SER.#'d SETS
FSBF Brett Favre 12.00 30.00
FSDC Daunte Culpepper 4.00 10.00
FSDM Donovan McNabb 5.00 12.00
FSKS Kordell Stewart 4.00 10.00
FSMV Michael Vick 8.00 20.00
FSTB Tom Brady 12.00 30.00

2002 Upper Deck Fourth Quarter Fabrics

STATED ODDS 1:288 HOB/RET
*GOLD: .6X TO 1.5X BASIC JERSEYS
*GOLD/150: .4X TO 1X BASIC JSY SP
GOLD PRINT RUN 150 SER.#'d SETS
FQBF Brett Favre 12.00 30.00
FQBG Brian Griese 4.00 10.00
FQJR Jerry Rice SP 12.00 30.00
FQKW Kurt Warner 5.00 12.00
FQMF Marshall Faulk SP 6.00 15.00
FQPM Peyton Manning 10.00 25.00
FQRM Randy Moss 5.00 12.00

2002 Upper Deck Ground Shakers Jerseys

STATED ODDS 1:288
*GOLD/25: .8X TO 2X BASIC JERSEY
GOLD PRINT RUN 25 SER.#'d SETS
GSAT Anthony Thomas 4.00 10.00
GSCM Curtis Martin 5.00 12.00
GSES Emmitt Smith 12.00 30.00
GSLT LaDainian Tomlinson 6.00 15.00
GSTD Terrell Davis 5.00 12.00

2002 Upper Deck Kick-Off Classics Jerseys

STATED ODDS 1:288 HOB/RET
*GOLD/150: .5X TO 1.2X BASIC JSY
GOLD PRINT RUN 150 SER.#'d SETS
KOBF Brett Favre 15.00 40.00
KOCC Chris Chambers 5.00 12.00
KODM Donovan McNabb 6.00 15.00
KOEJ Edgerrin James 5.00 12.00
KOLT LaDainian Tomlinson 8.00 20.00

2002 Upper Deck NFL Patches

STATED PRINT RUN 1 SER.#'d SET

2002 Upper Deck Pigskin Patches

STATED ODDS 1:2500 HOB/RET
PPAB Aaron Brooks 15.00 40.00
PPAT Anthony Thomas H 15.00 40.00
PPBF Brett Favre 50.00 120.00
PPDC Daunte Culpepper H 15.00 40.00
PPDF Doug Flutie H 20.00 50.00
PPDM Donovan McNabb H 20.00 50.00
PPEJ Edgerrin James 15.00 40.00
PPES Emmitt Smith 50.00 120.00
PPJB Jerome Bettis 20.00 50.00
PPJG Jeff Garcia 15.00 40.00
PPJR Jerry Rice 40.00 100.00
PPKW Kurt Warner 20.00 50.00
PPLT LaDainian Tomlinson H
PPMF Marshall Faulk H 20.00 50.00
PPMV Michael Vick H 30.00 80.00
PPPM Peyton Manning 40.00 100.00
PPRG Rich Gannon H 15.00 40.00
PPRM Randy Moss 20.00 50.00
PPRW Ricky Williams H 15.00 40.00
PPTB Tom Brady H 50.00 120.00

2002 Upper Deck Playbooks Jerseys

PBAB Aaron Brooks 15.00 40.00
PBAG Ahman Green 15.00 40.00
PBAT Anthony Thomas 15.00 40.00
PBBF Brett Favre 50.00 125.00
PBBO David Boston 12.00 30.00
PBCM Curtis Martin 20.00 50.00
PBDC Daunte Culpepper 15.00 40.00
PBDM Donovan McNabb 20.00 50.00
PBJB Jerome Bettis 20.00 50.00
PBKW Kurt Warner 20.00 50.00
PBLT LaDainian Tomlinson 25.00 60.00
PBMF Marshall Faulk 20.00 50.00
PBPM Peyton Manning 40.00 100.00
PBRS Rod Smith 15.00 40.00
PBTB Tom Brady 50.00 125.00

2002 Upper Deck Power Surge

COMPLETE SET (14) 12.50 30.00
STATED ODDS 1:12 HOB/RET
PS1 Michael Vick 1.50 4.00
PS2 Anthony Thomas .75 2.00
PS3 Emmitt Smith 2.50 6.00
PS4 Terrell Davis 1.00 2.50
PS5 Brett Favre 2.50 6.00
PS6 Edgerrin James .75 2.00
PS7 Peyton Manning 2.00 5.00
PS8 Ricky Williams .75 2.00
PS9 Curtis Martin 1.00 2.50
PS10 Jerome Bettis 1.00 2.50
PS11 LaDainian Tomlinson 1.25 3.00
PS12 Shaun Alexander .75 2.00
PS13 Kurt Warner 1.00 2.50
PS14 Marshall Faulk 1.00 2.50

2002 Upper Deck Rookie Futures Jersey

STATED ODDS 1:72
*GOLD/150: .5X TO 1.5X BASIC JSY
GOLD PRINT RUN 150 SER.#'d SETS
RFAL Ashley Lelie 3.00 8.00
RFCP Clinton Portis 5.00 12.00
RFDC David Carr 4.00 10.00
RFDF DeShaun Foster 4.00 10.00
RFDS Donte Stallworth 4.00 10.00
RFEL Antwaan Randle El 4.00 10.00
RFJH Joey Harrington 4.00 10.00
RFJR Josh Reed 3.00 8.00
RFPR Patrick Ramsey 4.00 10.00
RFWG William Green 3.00 8.00

2002 Upper Deck Stadium Swatches

STATED ODDS 1:144
*GOLD/75: .6X TO 1.5X BASIC JSY
GOLD PRINT RUN 75 SER.#'d SETS
SSDF Doug Flutie 5.00 12.00
SSEG Eddie George 4.00 10.00
SSMB Michael Bennett 4.00 10.00
SSMB Mark Brunell SP 4.00 10.00
SSPW Peter Warrick 4.00 10.00
SSQC Quincy Carter SP 3.00 8.00

2002 Upper Deck Synchronicity

COMPLETE SET (14) 10.00 25.00
STATED ODDS 1:12 HOB/RET
SY1 Jake Plummer / David Boston .60 1.50
SY2 Michael Vick / Warrick Dunn 1.25 3.00
SY3 Drew Bledsoe / Josh Reed .75 2.00
SY4 Tim Couch / Andre Davis .60 1.50
SY5 Brett Favre / Javon Walker 2.00 5.00
SY6 Peyton Manning / Marvin Harrison 1.50 4.00
SY7 Mark Brunell / Jimmy Smith .60 1.50
SY8 Daunte Culpepper / Randy Moss .75 2.00
SY9 Tom Brady / Troy Brown 2.00 5.00
SY10 Aaron Brooks / Donte' Stallworth .75 2.00
SY11 Kurt Warner / Isaac Bruce .75 2.00
SY12 Donovan McNabb / Freddie Mitchell .75 2.00
SY13 Kordell Stewart / Plaxico Burress .60 1.50
SY14 Jeff Garcia / Terrell Owens .75 2.00

2002 Upper Deck Uniforms

STATED ODDS 1:72 HOB/RET
*GOLD/150: .6X TO 1.5X BASIC JSY
GOLD PRINT RUN 150 SER.#'d SETS
UDUBG Brian Griese 3.00 8.00
UDUBJ Brad Johnson 3.00 8.00
UDUCC Chris Chambers 3.00 8.00
UDUDB Drew Brees 6.00 15.00
UDUFT Fred Taylor 3.00 8.00
UDUIB Isaac Bruce 4.00 10.00
UDUJG Jeff Garcia 3.00 8.00
UDUJP Jerome Pathon 2.50 6.00
UDUMB Mark Brunell 3.00 8.00
UDUPM Peyton Manning 8.00 20.00
UDUQM Quincy Morgan 2.50 6.00
UDURD Ron Dayne 3.00 8.00
UDUSS Shannon Sharpe 4.00 10.00
UDUTB Tim Brown 4.00 10.00
UDUTH Travis Henry 2.50 6.00

2002 Upper Deck Wildcard Jerseys

STATED ODDS 1:144 HOB/RET
*GOLD/150: .5X TO 1.2X BASIC JSY
GOLD PRINT RUN 150 SER.#'d SETS
WCAG Ahman Green 4.00 10.00
WCCD Corey Dillon 4.00 10.00
WCDT David Terrell 3.00 8.00
WCIB Isaac Bruce 5.00 12.00
WCJP Jerome Pathon 3.00 8.00
WCMB Michael Bennett 4.00 10.00
WCMV Michael Vick 8.00 20.00
WCPW Peter Warrick 4.00 10.00
WCRM Randy Moss 5.00 12.00
WCTO Terrell Owens 5.00 12.00

2002 Upper Deck Twizzlers

7 Donovan McNabb 1.25 3.00
8 Donovan McNabb 1.25 3.00

2003 Upper Deck

Released in August of 2003, this set consists of 285 cards, including 180 veterans, 30 short prints (inserted 1:12), and 75 rookies. Rookies 211-240 were inserted at a rate of 1:4, and rookies 241-285 were inserted at a rate of 1:8. Boxes contained 24 packs of 8 cards, with an SRP of $2.99.

COMPLETE SET (285) 60.00 120.00
COMP.SET w/o SP's (180) 10.00 25.00
1 Brad Johnson .25 .60
2 Derrick Brooks .25 .60
3 Simeon Rice .20 .50
4 Warren Sapp .25 .60
5 Thomas Jones .30 .75
6 Mike Alstott .30 .75
7 Michael Pittman .20 .50
8 Tim Brown .30 .75
9 Rich Gannon .25 .60
10 Charlie Garner .25 .60
11 Jerry Porter .20 .50
12 Phillip Buchanon .20 .50
13 Charles Woodson .30 .75
14 James Thrash .20 .50
15 Duce Staley .25 .60
16 Brian Westbrook .30 .75
17 Correll Buckhalter .25 .60
18 Koy Detmer .20 .50
19 Brian Dawkins .25 .60
20 Jon Ritchie .20 .50
21 Ahman Green .25 .60
22 Donald Driver .30 .75
23 Bubba Franks .25 .60
24 Javon Walker .25 .60
25 Kabeer Gbaja-Biamila .25 .60
26 Robert Ferguson .20 .50
27 Eddie George .25 .60
28 Jevon Kearse .25 .60
29 Billy Volek .25 .60
30 Frank Wycheck .20 .50
31 Derrick Mason .25 .60
32 Tommy Maddox .25 .60
33 Jerome Bettis .30 .75
34 Antwaan Randle El .25 .60
35 Amos Zereoue .20 .50
36 Hines Ward .30 .75
37 Jeff Garcia .25 .60
38 Terrell Owens .30 .75
39 Tim Rattay .20 .50
40 Brandon Doman .20 .50
41 Tai Streets .20 .50
42 Garrison Hearst .25 .60
43 Kerry Collins .25 .60
44 Tiki Barber .30 .75
45 Amani Toomer .25 .60
46 Jesse Palmer .20 .50
47 Tim Carter .20 .50
48 Michael Strahan .30 .75
49 Ike Hilliard .20 .50
50 Marvin Harrison .30 .75
51 Peyton Manning .60 1.50
52 Marcus Pollard .20 .50
53 James Mungro .20 .50
54 Reggie Wayne .30 .75
55 Peerless Price .20 .50
56 Warrick Dunn .25 .60
57 T.J. Duckett .25 .60
58 Keith Brooking .25 .60
59 Doug Johnson .20 .50
60 Brian Finneran .20 .50
61 Chad Pennington .30 .75
62 Curtis Martin .30 .75
63 Marvin Jones .20 .50
64 Wayne Chrebet .25 .60
65 LaMont Jordan .25 .60
66 Curtis Conway .20 .50
67 Vinny Testaverde .25 .60
68 Tim Couch .20 .50
69 William Green .20 .50
70 Andre Davis .20 .50
71 Quincy Morgan .20 .50
72 Dennis Northcutt .20 .50
73 Kelly Holcomb .20 .50
74 Jake Plummer .25 .60
75 Mike Anderson .25 .60
76 Ashley Lelie .20 .50
77 Ed McCaffrey .25 .60
78 Shannon Sharpe .30 .75
79 Rod Smith .25 .60
80 Terrell Davis .30 .75
81 Antowain Smith .25 .60
82 Kevin Faulk .25 .60
83 David Patten .20 .50
84 Deion Branch .25 .60
85 Troy Brown .25 .60
86 Rohan Davey .20 .50
87 Jay Fiedler .20 .50
88 Randy McMichael .20 .50
89 Derrius Thompson .20 .50
90 Jason Taylor .25 .60
91 Zach Thomas .30 .75
92 Ricky Williams .25 .60
93 Deuce McAllister .25 .60
94 Donte Stallworth .20 .50
95 Jerome Pathon .20 .50
96 Michael Lewis .20 .50
97 Joe Horn .25 .60
98 Priest Holmes .30 .75
99 Johnnie Morton .25 .60
100 Eddie Kennison .20 .50
101 Dante Hall .25 .60
102 Tony Gonzalez .30 .75
103 Marc Boerigter .20 .50
104 Drew Brees .30 .75
105 David Boston .20 .50
106 Reche Caldwell .20 .50
107 Tim Dwight .20 .50
108 Doug Flutie .30 .75
109 Drew Bledsoe .30 .75
110 Eric Moulds .25 .60
111 Alex Van Pelt .20 .50
112 Charles Johnson .20 .50
113 Takeo Spikes .20 .50
114 Josh Reed .20 .50
115 Ladell Betts .20 .50
116 Laveranues Coles .20 .50
117 Champ Bailey .30 .75
118 Trung Canidate .20 .50
119 Kenny Watson .20 .50
120 Rod Gardner .20 .50
121 Kurt Warner .30 .75
122 Lamar Gordon .20 .50
123 Shaun McDonald RC .30 .75
124 Marc Bulger .30 .75
125 Isaac Bruce .30 .75
126 Torry Holt .30 .75
127 Matt Hasselbeck .25 .60
128 Maurice Morris .20 .50
129 Bobby Engram .20 .50
130 Darrell Jackson .25 .60
131 Koren Robinson .25 .60
132 Chris Redman .20 .50
133 Todd Heap .25 .60
134 Travis Taylor .20 .50
135 Ron Johnson .20 .50
136 Ray Lewis .30 .75
137 Jake Delhomme .30 .75
138 Muhsin Muhammad .25 .60
139 Stephen Davis .25 .60
140 Julius Peppers .30 .75
141 Rodney Peete .20 .50
142 Mark Brunell .25 .60
143 Jimmy Smith .25 .60
144 Kyle Brady .20 .50
145 Kevin Lockett .20 .50
146 David Garrard .30 .75
147 Fred Taylor .25 .60
148 Michael Bennett .25 .60
149 Ronald Bellamy RC .30 .75
150 Randy Moss .30 .75
151 D'Wayne Bates .20 .50
152 Josh McCown .25 .60
153 Marquise Walker .20 .50
154 Jeff Blake .25 .60
155 Freddie Jones .20 .50
156 Marcel Shipp .20 .50
157 Troy Hambrick .20 .50
158 Joey Galloway .25 .60
159 Terry Glenn .25 .60
160 Roy Williams .25 .60
161 Antonio Bryant .20 .50
162 Quincy Carter .20 .50
163 Anthony Thomas .25 .60
164 Marty Booker .25 .60
165 Dez White .20 .50
166 Adrian Peterson .20 .50
167 Kordell Stewart .25 .60
168 David Terrell .20 .50
169 Jabar Gaffney .20 .50
170 Bennie Joppru RC .25 .60
171 Corey Bradford .20 .50
172 David Carr .25 .60
173 James Stewart .20 .50
174 Ty Detmer .20 .50
175 Az-Zahir Hakim .20 .50
176 Bill Schroeder .20 .50
177 Jon Kitna .25 .60
178 Chad Johnson .30 .75
179 Ron Dugans .20 .50
180 Peter Warrick .25 .60
181 Brett Favre SS 3.00 8.00
182 Emmitt Smith SS 3.00 8.00
183 LaDainian Tomlinson SS 1.25 3.00
184 Joey Harrington SS .75 2.00
185 Brian Urlacher SS 1.25 3.00
186 Daunte Culpepper SS 1.00 2.50
187 Jamal Lewis SS 1.00 2.50
188 Shaun Alexander SS 1.00 2.50
189 Marshall Faulk SS 1.25 3.00
190 Travis Henry SS .75 2.00
191 Trent Green SS 1.00 2.50
192 Aaron Brooks SS 1.00 2.50
193 Chris Chambers SS 1.00 2.50
194 Tom Brady SS 3.00 8.00
195 Clinton Portis SS 1.00 2.50
196 Kevin Johnson SS .75 2.00
197 Santana Moss SS 1.00 2.50
198 Michael Vick SS 1.50 4.00
199 Edgerrin James SS 1.25 3.00
200 Jeremy Shockey SS 1.25 3.00
201 Kevan Barlow SS .75 2.00
202 Plaxico Burress SS 1.00 2.50
203 Steve McNair SS 1.25 3.00
204 Donovan McNabb SS 1.25 3.00
205 Jerry Rice SS 2.50 6.00
206 Keyshawn Johnson SS 1.25 3.00
207 Patrick Ramsey SS 1.00 2.50
208 Stephen Davis SS 1.00 2.50
209 Corey Dillon SS 1.00 2.50
210 Chad Hutchinson SS .75 2.00
211 Brad Banks RC 1.50 4.00
212 Kliff Kingsbury RC 1.50 4.00
213 Jason Gesser RC 1.50 4.00
214 Jason Johnson RC 1.25 3.00
215 Brian St.Pierre RC 1.50 4.00
216 Ken Dorsey RC 1.50 4.00
217 Seneca Wallace RC 2.00 5.00
218 Brooks Bollinger RC 1.50 4.00
219 Chris Brown RC 1.25 3.00
220 B.J Askew RC 1.50 4.00
221 Earnest Graham RC 2.00 5.00
222 Quentin Griffin RC 1.50 4.00
223 Musa Smith RC 1.25 3.00
224 Artose Pinner RC 1.25 3.00
225 Domanick Davis RC 1.50 4.00
226 Anquan Boldin RC 3.00 8.00
227 Talman Gardner RC 1.25 3.00
228 Brandon Lloyd RC 3.00 8.00
229 Bryant Johnson RC 2.00 5.00
230 Kareem Kelly RC 1.25 3.00
231 Arnaz Battle RC 2.00 5.00
232 Keenan Howry RC 1.25 3.00
233 Justin Gage RC 1.50 4.00
234 Tyrone Calico RC 1.50 4.00
235 Teyo Johnson RC 1.50 4.00
236 Malaefou MacKenzie RC 1.25 3.00
237 Terence Newman RC 1.50 4.00
238 Marcus Trufant RC 1.50 4.00
239 Mike Doss RC 2.00 5.00
240 Terrell Suggs RC 2.00 5.00
241 Carson Palmer RC 6.00 15.00
242 Byron Leftwich RC 3.00 8.00
243 Rex Grossman RC 3.00 8.00
244 Kyle Boller RC 3.00 8.00
245 Dave Ragone RC 2.00 5.00
246 Chris Simms RC 3.00 8.00
247 Larry Johnson RC 3.00 8.00
248 Lee Suggs RC 2.50 6.00
249 Justin Fargas RC 3.00 8.00
250 Onterrio Smith RC 2.00 5.00
251 Willis McGahee RC 4.00 10.00
252 Charles Rogers RC 2.50 6.00
253 Andre Johnson RC 8.00 20.00
254 Taylor Jacobs RC 2.00 5.00
255 Kelley Washington RC 2.00 5.00
256 Tony Romo RC 12.00 30.00
257 Jerel Myers RC 1.50 4.00
258 Kirk Farmer RC 2.00 5.00
259 Kevin Walter RC 4.00 10.00
260 Gibran Hamdan RC 1.50 4.00

261 Juston Wood RC 1.50 4.00
262 Travis Anglin RC 1.50 4.00
263 Marquel Blackwell RC 1.50 4.00
264 Jason Thomas RC 1.50 4.00
265 Carl Ford RC 1.50 4.00
266 Walter Young RC 1.50 4.00
267 Sultan McCullough RC 1.50 4.00
268 Dahrran Diedrick RC 1.50 4.00
269 Cecil Sapp RC 1.50 4.00
270 Doug Gabriel RC 2.00 5.00
271 LaBrandon Toefield RC 2.00 5.00
272 Adrian Madise RC 1.50 4.00
273 J.R. Tolver RC 2.00 5.00
274 Kevin Curtis RC 2.50 6.00
275 Bobby Wade RC 2.00 5.00
276 Sam Aiken RC 2.00 5.00
277 Mike Bush RC 1.50 4.00
278 Billy McMullen RC 1.50 4.00
279 Bethel Johnson RC 1.50 4.00
280 David Kircus RC 2.50 6.00
281 Zuriel Smith RC 1.50 4.00
282 LaTarence Dunbar RC 1.50 4.00
283 Nate Burleson RC 2.00 5.00
284 Antwone Savage RC 1.50 4.00
285 Terrence Edwards RC 1.50 4.00

2003 Upper Deck Gold

*VETS 1-180: 8X TO 20X BASIC CARDS
*SS 181-210: 2X TO 5X
*ROOKIES 211-240: 1.2X TO 3X
*ROOKIES 241-255: .8X TO 2X
*ROOKIES 256-285: 1X TO 2.5X
STATED PRINT RUN 50 SER.#'d SETS
256 Tony Romo 40.00 100.00

2003 Upper Deck Game Jerseys

GROUP 1 STATED ODDS 1:48HOB, 1:96RET
GROUP 2 STATED ODDS 1:72 HOB, 1:144 RET
*GOLD/99: .8X TO 2X BASIC JSY
GOLD PRINT RUN 99 SER.#'d SETS
GJAB Aaron Brooks 2 4.00 10.00
GJAL Ashley Lelie 1 3.00 8.00
GJAT Amani Toomer 1 4.00 10.00
GJBF Brett Favre 2 12.00 30.00
GJBG Brian Griese 1 4.00 10.00
GJBJ Brad Johnson 1 4.00 10.00
GJBR Antonio Bryant 2 3.00 8.00
GJCB1 Champ Bailey 1 5.00 12.00
GJCB2 Correll Buckhalter 1 4.00 10.00
GJCJ Chad Johnson 1 5.00 12.00
GJCP Clinton Portis 2 4.00 10.00
GJCW Charles Woodson 1 5.00 12.00
GJDC David Carr 2 4.00 10.00
GJDS Duce Staley 1 4.00 10.00
GJEM Eric Moulds 1 4.00 10.00
GJJB Jerome Bettis 2 5.00 12.00
GJJK Jevon Kearse 1 4.00 10.00
GJJL Jamal Lewis 2 4.00 10.00
GJJS Jeremy Shockey 2 5.00 12.00
GJKJ Kevin Johnson 2 3.00 8.00
GJKS Kordell Stewart 1 4.00 10.00
GJKW Kurt Warner 2 6.00 15.00
GJMA Mike Alstott 1 5.00 12.00
GJMB Mark Brunell 2 4.00 10.00
GJMF Marshall Faulk 2 5.00 12.00
GJMS Michael Strahan 1 5.00 12.00
GJMV Michael Vick 2 6.00 15.00
GJOG Olandis Gary 1 3.00 8.00
GJPM Peyton Manning 2 10.00 25.00
GJPW Peter Warrick 1 4.00 10.00
GJQJ Quentin Jammer 1 3.00 8.00
GJRG Rich Gannon 2 4.00 10.00
GJRL Ray Lewis 1 5.00 12.00
GJRM Randy Moss 2 5.00 12.00
GJRW Roy Williams 1 4.00 10.00
GJSE Junior Seau 2 5.00 12.00
GJSM Steve McNair 2 5.00 12.00
GJTH Torry Holt 2 5.00 12.00
GJWC Wayne Chrebet 1 4.00 10.00
GJWS Warren Sapp 1 4.00 10.00
GJZT Zach Thomas 1 5.00 12.00

2003 Upper Deck Game Jerseys Autographs

STATED PRINT RUN 5-99
GJAAB Antonio Bryant/99 12.00 30.00
GJAAL Ashley Lelie/99 12.00 30.00
GJACP Clinton Portis/26 30.00 80.00
GJADC David Carr/99 15.00 40.00
GJADF DeShaun Foster/99 15.00 40.00
GJAJS Jeremy Shockey/99 20.00 50.00
GJAKK Kurt Kittner/45 12.00 30.00
GJARW Roy Williams/99 15.00 40.00
GJAWD Woody Dantzler/99 12.00 30.00

2003 Upper Deck Game Jerseys Logos

STATED ODDS 1:5000 HOB, RET
PLODC David Carr/4*
PLOJG Jeff Garcia 25.00 60.00
PLOLT LaDainian Tomlinson 30.00 80.00
PLOMF Marshall Faulk 30.00 80.00
PLORW Ricky Williams/24*

2003 Upper Deck Game Jerseys Names

STATED ODDS 1:7500 HOB, RET
PNABF Brett Favre
PNACP Chad Pennington 25.00 60.00
PNADEM Deuce McAllister 20.00 50.00
PNADOM Donovan McNabb 25.00 60.00
PNAEJ Edgerrin James/18*
PNAKW Kurt Warner 30.00 80.00
PNAMV Michael Vick/11*
PNARM Randy Moss 25.00 60.00
PNATB Tom Brady 60.00 150.00
PNATO Terrell Owens 25.00 60.00

2003 Upper Deck Game Jerseys Numbers

STATED ODDS 1:2500 HOB, RET
PNUAG Ahman Green 15.00 40.00
PNUBR Drew Brees 20.00 50.00
PNUCP Clinton Portis 15.00 40.00
PNUDB Drew Bledsoe 20.00 50.00
PNUDC Daunte Culpepper 15.00 40.00
PNUEG Eddie George 15.00 40.00
PNUJB Jerome Bettis 20.00 50.00
PNUJS Jeremy Shockey 20.00 50.00
PNUMH Marvin Harrison 20.00 50.00
PNUTC Tim Couch 12.00 30.00

2003 Upper Deck Game Jerseys Duals

STATED ODDS 1:144HOB, 1:288RET
*GOLD/99: .6X TO 1.5X BASIC DUAL JSY
GOLD STATED PRINT RUN 99 SER.#'d SETS
DGJBM Drew Bledsoe 8.00 20.00
Willis McGahee
DGJBS Nate Burleson 4.00 10.00
Onterrio Smith
DGJBT Drew Brees 6.00 15.00
LaDainian Tomlinson
DGJCJ Tim Couch 6.00 15.00
Kevin Johnson
DGJCR David Carr 5.00 12.00
Dave Ragone
DGJCS Kerry Collins 6.00 15.00
Jeremy Shockey
DGJCW Carson Palmer 10.00 25.00
Kelley Washington
DGJDM Daunte Culpepper 6.00 15.00
Randy Moss
DGJFC Jay Fiedler 5.00 12.00
Chris Chambers
DGJFG Brett Favre 15.00 40.00
Ahman Green
DGJGR Rich Gannon 10.00 25.00
Jerry Rice
DGJJB Bryant Johnson 8.00 20.00
Anquan Boldin
DGJJG Taylor Jacobs 4.00 10.00
Rod Gardner
DGJKJ Keyshawn Johnson 6.00 15.00
Dual swatches
DGJMC Peyton Manning 12.00 30.00
Dallas Clark
DGJPC Chad Pennington 6.00 15.00
Wayne Chrebet
DGJWH Kurt Warner 6.00 15.00
Torry Holt

2003 Upper Deck Power Surge

COMPLETE SET (18) 12.50 30.00
STATED ODDS 1:8
PS1 Marshall Faulk 1.00 2.50
PS2 LaDainian Tomlinson 1.00 2.50
PS3 Ricky Williams .75 2.00
PS4 Edgerrin James 1.00 2.50
PS5 Deuce McAllister .75 2.00
PS6 Jerome Bettis 1.00 2.50
PS7 Ahman Green .75 2.00
PS8 Jeremy Shockey 1.00 2.50
PS9 Steve McNair 1.00 2.50
PS10 William Green .60 1.50
PS11 Daunte Culpepper .75 2.00
PS12 Terrell Owens 1.00 2.50
PS13 Jerry Rice 2.00 5.00
PS14 Brad Johnson .75 2.00
PS15 Priest Holmes 1.00 2.50
PS16 Clinton Portis .75 2.00
PS17 Brian Urlacher 1.00 2.50
PS18 Rod Gardner .60 1.50

2003 Upper Deck Rookie Future Jerseys

STATED ODDS 1:24 HOB, 1:48 RET
*GOLD/99: .8X TO 2X BASIC JSY
GOLD STATED PRINT RUN 99 SER.#'d SETS
RFAB Anquan Boldin 8.00 20.00
RFAJ Andre Johnson 6.00 15.00
RFAP Artose Pinner 2.50 6.00
RFBE Bethel Johnson 2.50 6.00
RFBJ Bryant Johnson 4.00 10.00
RFBL Byron Leftwich 4.00 10.00
RFBS Brian St.Pierre 3.00 8.00
RFCB Chris Brown 2.50 6.00
RFCP Carson Palmer 10.00 25.00
RFDC Dallas Clark 6.00 15.00
RFDR Dave Ragone 2.50 6.00
RFJF Justin Fargas 4.00 10.00
RFKB Kyle Boller 4.00 10.00
RFKC Kevin Curtis 4.00 10.00
RFKK Kliff Kingsbury 3.00 8.00
RFKW Kelley Washington 2.50 6.00
RFLJ Larry Johnson 4.00 10.00
RFMS Musa Smith 2.50 6.00
RFMT Marcus Trufant 3.00 8.00
RFNB Nate Burleson 3.00 8.00
RFOS Onterrio Smith 2.50 6.00
RFRG Rex Grossman 4.00 10.00
RFRM Ricky Manning 3.00 8.00
RFRO DeWayne Robertson EXCH 3.00 8.00
RFSW Seneca Wallace 4.00 10.00
RFTE Teyo Johnson 3.00 8.00
RFTG Tyrone Calico 3.00 8.00
RFTJ Taylor Jacobs 2.50 6.00
RFTN Terence Newman 3.00 8.00
RFTS Terrell Suggs 4.00 10.00
RFWM Willis McGahee 6.00 15.00
RFWP Willie Pile 2.50 6.00

2003 Upper Deck Rookie Future Jerseys Autographs

SERIAL #'d UNDER 21 NOT PRICED
RFAKW Kelley Washington/87 12.50 30.00
RFALJ Larry Johnson/34 20.00 50.00
RFARO DeWayne Robertson/63 15.00 40.00

2003 Upper Deck Rookie Premiere

COMPLETE SET (30) 15.00 40.00
STATED ODDS 1:1 RETAIL
RP1 Carson Palmer 1.25 3.00
RP2 Byron Leftwich .60 1.50
RP3 Kyle Boller .60 1.50
RP4 Rex Grossman .60 1.50
RP5 Dave Ragone .40 1.00
RP6 Kliff Kingsbury .50 1.25
RP7 Seneca Wallace .60 1.50
RP8 Brian St.Pierre .50 1.25
RP9 Dallas Clark 1.00 2.50
RP10 Willis McGahee .75 2.00
RP11 Larry Johnson .60 1.50
RP12 Musa Smith .40 1.00
RP13 Chris Brown .40 1.00
RP14 Justin Fargas .60 1.50
RP15 Artose Pinner .40 1.00
RP16 Onterrio Smith .40 1.00
RP17 Nate Burleson .50 1.25
RP18 Andre Johnson 1.50 4.00
RP19 Bryant Johnson .60 1.50
RP20 Taylor Jacobs .40 1.00
RP21 Bethel Johnson .40 1.00
RP22 Anquan Boldin 1.00 2.50
RP23 Tyrone Calico .50 1.25
RP24 Teyo Johnson .50 1.25
RP25 Kelley Washington .40 1.00
RP26 Kevin Curtis .60 1.50
RP27 Terence Newman .50 1.25
RP28 Marcus Trufant .50 1.25
RP29 Terrell Suggs .60 1.50
RP30 DeWayne Robertson .50 1.25

2003 Upper Deck Super Powers

COMPLETE SET (12) 10.00 25.00
STATED ODDS 1:12
SP1 Kurt Warner .75 2.00
SP2 Aaron Brooks .60 1.50
SP3 Joey Harrington .50 1.25
SP4 Brett Favre 2.00 5.00
SP5 Donovan McNabb .75 2.00
SP6 Emmitt Smith 2.00 5.00
SP7 Michael Vick 1.00 2.50
SP8 David Carr .60 1.50
SP9 Drew Brees .75 2.00
SP10 Chad Pennington .75 2.00
SP11 Drew Bledsoe .75 2.00
SP12 Tom Brady 2.00 5.00

2000 Upper Deck Plays of the Week

Released through Upper Deck's Collectors Club, this 38-card set was comprised of cards that measure 3 1/2"x5" and highlight 34 (2-per week) of the 1999 season's top plays. The cardfronts feature a "film cell" design showcasing full color action photos, while card backs contain a brief write-up of the featured play. The cards are not numbered, therefore they appear in order by week with the four tribute cards appearing in alphabetical order at the end of the set. NFL Plays of the Week was a mail-order set through the Upper Deck Collectors Club and was originally sold for $14.99.

COMPLETE SET (38) 7.50 20.00
1 Drew Bledsoe .30 .75
2 Troy Aikman .50 1.25
3 James Stewart .20 .50
4 Lance Schulters .20 .50
5 Brett Favre 1.00 2.50
6 Darryll Lewis .20 .50
7 Az-Zahir Hakim .20 .50
8 Neil O'Donnell .20 .50
9 Doug Pederson .20 .50
10 Dan Marino 1.00 2.50
11 Cade McNown .20 .50
12 Ed McCaffrey .25 .60
13 Kent Graham .20 .50
14 Tony Gonzalez .30 .75
15 Doug Flutie .30 .75
16 Marshall Faulk .30 .75
17 Kurt Warner .50 1.25
18 Keyshawn Johnson .25 .60
19 Jim Miller .20 .50
20 Peyton Manning .75 2.00
21 Donnie Abraham .20 .50
22 Edgerrin James .30 .75
23 Jake Plummer .25 .60
24 Cris Dishman .20 .50
25 Mike Vanderjagt .20 .50
26 Keith McKenzie .20 .50
27 Steve Beuerlein .25 .60
28 Jeff Blake .25 .60
29 Frank Wycheck .25 .60
30 Eric Bjornson .20 .50
31 Robert Smith .25 .60
32 Steve McNair .30 .75
33 Kenny Shedd .20 .50
34 Randy Moss .30 .75
35 John Elway .60 1.50
Gridiron Legends
36 Walter Payton GL 1.00 2.50
37 Frank Wycheck .25 .60
Kevin Dyson
38 Rams Super Bowl Champs .30 .75

2000 Upper Deck PowerDeck Super Bowl XXXIV

This Joe Montana card was distriubted at Super Bowl XXXIV in Atlanta. One card was inserted per seat cushion. The CD-ROM card was issued attached to a larger cardboard backer.

1 Joe Montana 10.00 20.00

2000 Upper Deck Super Bowl XXXIV Black Diamond

This 13-card set was released at the 2000 Super Bowl Card Show in Atlanta. Each card measures roughly 3 1/2" by 5" and features a top 1999 NFL rookie along with the Super Bowl XXXIV logo on the cardfronts. The #1 card was pulled from the set before its release, but there have been a few reports of some copies of the card in circulation.

COMPLETE SET (13) 10.00 25.00
1 Cecil Collins SP
2 Cade McNown .60 1.50
3 James Johnson .60 1.50
4 Champ Bailey .75 2.00
5 Tim Couch .75 2.00
6 Peerless Price .75 2.00
7 David Boston .60 1.50
8 Ricky Williams 1.00 2.50
9 Edgerrin James 1.00 2.50
10 Donovan McNabb 1.00 2.50
11 Torry Holt 1.00 2.50
12 Daunte Culpepper .75 2.00
13 Jevon Kearse .75 2.00
14 Akili Smith .60 1.50

2000 Upper Deck Super Bowl XXXIV Special Moments

These oversized cards (roughly 3 1/2" by 5") were distributed at the 2000 Super Bowl Card Show in Atlanta. Each features a special moment and player from a past Super Bowl with serial numbering of 2000-sets produced on the cardfronts.

COMPLETE SET (10) 8.00 20.00
1 Jerry Rice 1.25 3.00
2 Terrell Davis .60 1.50
3 Brett Favre 2.00 5.00
4 Joe Namath 1.25 3.00
5 Jamal Anderson .50 1.25
6 Chris Chandler .50 1.25
7 Steve Young .75 2.00
8 Joe Montana 2.00 5.00
9 Antonio Freeman .50 1.25
10 Emmitt Smith 1.50 4.00

2001 Upper Deck e-Card Manning

This single card was issued to attendees of the 2001 NFL Experience Super Bowl Card Show in Tampa, Florida through the Upper Deck corporate booth. The card features a scratch off area in which collector's would enter the revealed ID number at upperdeckdigital.com to have a chance to "digitize" the card into an autographed card or jersey card of Manning. The expiration date for enhancing the card on the website is July 1, 2002.

1 Peyton Manning 3.00 5.00
1J Peyton Manning JSY/200 12.50 30.00

2001 Upper Deck Super Bowl XXXV Black Diamond

These jumbo (roughly 3 1/2" by 5") cards were issued through the Upper Deck booth during the 2001 NFL Experience Super Bowl Card Show in Tampa, Florida. Each is essentially an enlarged version of the player's base 2000 Black Diamond Rookie Card along with a Super Bowl XXXV logo and a facsimile jersey swatch on the cardfronts. The cardbacks were re-written to reflect events from the 2000 season.

COMPLETE SET (10) 20.00 50.00
1 Courtney Brown 2.00 5.00
2 Ron Dayne 2.50 6.00
3 Shaun Alexander 3.00 8.00
4 Thomas Jones 2.50 6.00
5 Jamal Lewis 3.00 8.00
6 J.R. Redmond 2.00 5.00
7 Peter Warrick 2.50 6.00
8 Plaxico Burress 2.50 6.00
9 Sylvester Morris 2.00 5.00
10 Laveranues Coles 2.50 6.00

2001 Upper Deck Super Bowl XXXV Box Set

This 21-card set was issued to traditional retailers and the hobby to commemorate the Giants and Ravens in Super Bowl XXXV.

COMPLETE SET (21) 6.00 15.00
1 Trent Dilfer .50 1.25
2 Tony Banks .40 1.00
3 Rod Woodson .60 1.50
4 Jamal Lewis .60 1.50
5 Priest Holmes .60 1.50
6 Ray Lewis .60 1.50
7 Shannon Sharpe .60 1.50
8 Jermaine Lewis .40 1.00
9 Qadry Ismail .50 1.25
10 Travis Taylor .40 1.00
11 Tiki Barber .60 1.50
12 Kerry Collins .50 1.25
13 Ron Dayne .50 1.25
14 Ron Dixon .40 1.00
15 Ike Hilliard .50 1.25
16 Joe Jurevicious .40 1.00
17 Pete Mitchell .40 1.00
18 Amani Toomer .50 1.25
19 Jessie Armstead .40 1.00
20 Michael Strahan .60 1.50
NNO Jumbo Cover Card .40 1.00

2001 Upper Deck Super Bowl XXXV Box Set Game Jersey Jumbos

MF Marshall Faulk 12.00 30.00
PM Peyton Manning 30.00 80.00
RD Ron Dayne 10.00 25.00
RM Randy Moss 12.00 30.00
TB Tim Brown 12.00 30.00
WD Warrick Dunn 12.00 30.00

2001 Upper Deck Super Bowl XXXV Special Moments

Some attendees to the 2001 NFL Experience Super Bowl Card Show in Tampa, Florida could receive one-card from this set by visiting the Upper Deck booth. Each card is oversized (roughly 3 1/2" by 5") and highlights one player and his outstanding performance in a Super Bowl game. All were serial numbered of 2001-sets produced.

COMPLETE SET (6) 8.00 20.00
BF Brett Favre 3.00 8.00
EG Eddie George 1.00 2.50
JA Jamal Anderson .75 2.00
MF Marshall Faulk 1.00 2.50
TA Troy Aikman 1.50 4.00
TD Terrell Davis 1.00 2.50

2002 Upper Deck Super Bowl Card Show

These cards were available via a wrapper redemption contest at the 2002 Super Bowl Card Show in New Orleans. In order to receive a card one had to open a box of 2002 Upper Deck product at their booth to receive a pack which contained.one of the 6 cards in the set.

8 Archie Manning AU/100 15.00 40.00
8 Archie Manning/2002 .50 1.25
18 Peyton Manning/2002 1.50 4.00
18 Peyton Manning AU/500 50.00 100.00
SBAP Peyton Manning 1.50 4.00
Archie Manning/2002
SBAP Peyton Manning AU/36
Archie Manning AU

2003 Upper Deck Magazine

As a bonus to buyers of the Upper Deck magazine produced by Krause Publications late in 2003, a nine-card perforated sheet featuring players basically signed to Upper Deck exclusives was included. When the cards were perforated, these cards measured the standard size. Please note that all of these cards have a "UD" prefix.

COMPLETE SET (9) 8.00 20.00
UD6 Michael Vick 1.00 2.50

2003 Upper Deck Super Bowl Card Show

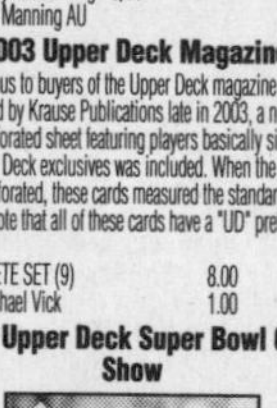

COMPLETE SET (10) 6.00 12.00
1 Tom Brady 1.00 2.50
2 Kurt Warner .40 1.00
3 Brett Favre 1.00 2.50
4 Drew Bledsoe .40 1.00
5 Joey Harrington .25 .60
6 Jeff Garcia .30 .75
7 Michael Vick .50 1.25
8 Peyton Manning .75 2.00
9 Donovan McNabb .40 1.00
10 David Carr .30 .75

2004 Upper Deck

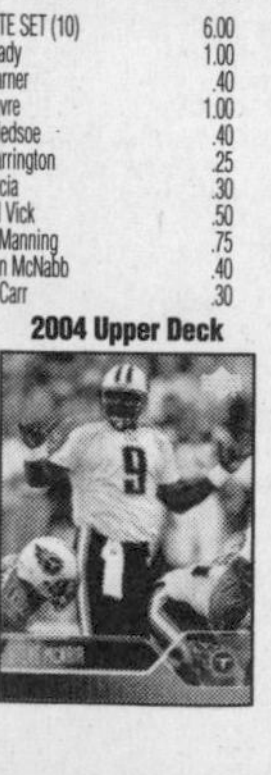

Upper Deck was initially released in mid-September 2004. The base set consists of 275-cards including 25-short printed rookies and 50-rookies issued one per pack. Hobby boxes contained 24-packs of 8-cards and carried an S.R.P. of $2.99 per pack. Two parallel sets and a variety of inserts can be found seeded in packs highlighted by the Signature Sensations autographed inserts.

COMPLETE SET (275) 75.00 135.00
COMP.SET w/o SP's (250) 30.00 60.00
COMP.SET w/o RC's (200) 10.00 25.00
201-225 ROOKIE STATED ODDS 1:8
226-275 ROOKIE STATED ODDS 1:1
UNPRICED PRINT PLATE PRINT RUN 1 SET
1 Anquan Boldin .30 .75
2 Josh McCown .25 .60
3 Emmitt Smith .75 2.00
4 Freddie Jones .20 .50
5 Marcel Shipp .20 .50
6 Shaun King .20 .50
7 Michael Vick .40 1.00
8 T.J. Duckett .25 .60
9 Peerless Price .20 .50
10 Warrick Dunn .25 .60
11 Keith Brooking .20 .50
12 Brian Finneran .20 .50
13 Anthony Wright .20 .50
14 Kyle Boller .25 .60
15 Jamal Lewis .25 .60
16 Todd Heap .25 .60
17 Ray Lewis .30 .75
18 Terrell Suggs .25 .60
19 Travis Taylor .20 .50
20 Drew Bledsoe .30 .75
21 Willis McGahee .30 .75
22 Eric Moulds .25 .60
23 Travis Henry .20 .50
24 Takeo Spikes .20 .50
25 Josh Reed .20 .50
26 Lawyer Milloy .20 .50
27 Stephen Davis .25 .60
28 Jake Delhomme .25 .60
29 Steve Smith .30 .75
30 DeShaun Foster .25 .60
31 Dan Morgan .25 .60
32 Julius Peppers .25 .60
33 Rod Smart .25 .60
34 Rex Grossman .25 .60
35 Thomas Jones .30 .75
36 Marty Booker .25 .60
37 Anthony Thomas .25 .60
38 Brian Urlacher .30 .75
39 Justin Gage .25 .60
40 Chad Johnson .30 .75
41 Carson Palmer .30 .75
42 Peter Warrick .25 .60
43 Jon Kitna .25 .60
44 Kelley Washington .20 .50
45 Rudi Johnson .25 .60
46 Jeff Garcia .25 .60
47 Dennis Northcutt .20 .50
48 Lee Suggs .25 .60
49 Andre Davis .20 .50
50 Quincy Morgan .20 .50
51 Kelly Holcomb .20 .50
52 Keyshawn Johnson .25 .60
53 Quincy Carter .20 .50
54 Antonio Bryant .25 .60
55 Terry Glenn .25 .60
56 Terence Newman .25 .60
57 Roy Williams S .25 .60
58 Champ Bailey .25 .60
59 Jake Plummer .25 .60
60 Quentin Griffin .20 .50
61 John Lynch .25 .60
62 Rod Smith .25 .60
63 Ashley Lelie .20 .50
64 Joey Harrington .25 .60
65 Az-Zahir Hakim .20 .50
66 Charles Rogers .20 .50
67 Tai Streets .20 .50
68 Shawn Bryson .20 .50
69 Artose Pinner .20 .50
70 Brett Favre .75 2.00
71 Nick Barnett .25 .60
72 Ahman Green .25 .60
73 Kabeer Gbaja-Biamila .25 .60
74 Javon Walker .20 .50
75 Donald Driver .30 .75
76 Tim Couch .25 .60
77 David Carr .20 .50
78 Corey Bradford .20 .50
79 J.J. Moses .20 .50
80 Domanick Davis .20 .50
81 Jabar Gaffney .20 .50
82 Andre Johnson .30 .75
83 Marvin Harrison .30 .75
84 Peyton Manning .60 1.50
85 Dallas Clark .30 .75
86 Edgerrin James .25 .60
87 Reggie Wayne .30 .75
88 Dwight Freeney .25 .60
89 Byron Leftwich .25 .60
90 LaBrandon Toefield .20 .50
91 Fred Taylor .25 .60
92 Troy Edwards .20 .50
93 Jimmy Smith .25 .60
94 Kyle Brady .25 .60
95 Trent Green .25 .60
96 Tony Gonzalez .30 .75
97 Dante Hall .25 .60
98 Priest Holmes .30 .75
99 Eddie Kennison .25 .60
100 Johnnie Morton .25 .60
101 Jay Fiedler .20 .50
102 Junior Seau .30 .75
103 Ricky Williams .25 .60
104 Chris Chambers .25 .60
105 Zach Thomas .30 .75
106 David Boston .20 .50
107 A.J. Feeley .20 .50
108 Daunte Culpepper .25 .60
109 Onterrio Smith .20 .50
110 Randy Moss .30 .75
111 Moe Williams .20 .50
112 Michael Bennett .25 .60
113 Jim Kleinsasser .20 .50
114 Tom Brady .60 1.50
115 Kevin Faulk .25 .60
116 Deion Branch .25 .60
117 Corey Dillon .25 .60
118 Troy Brown .25 .60
119 Adam Vinatieri .30 .75
120 Tedy Bruschi .30 .75
121 Aaron Brooks .25 .60
122 Deuce McAllister .25 .60
123 Donte' Stallworth .20 .50
124 Joe Horn .25 .60
125 Jerome Pathon .20 .50
126 Boo Williams .20 .50
127 Jeremy Shockey .25 .60
128 Kurt Warner .30 .75
129 Amani Toomer .25 .60
130 Tiki Barber .30 .75
131 Ike Hilliard .25 .60
132 Michael Strahan .30 .75
133 Chad Pennington .30 .75
134 Santana Moss .25 .60
135 Wayne Chrebet .25 .60
136 Curtis Martin .30 .75
137 LaMont Jordan .25 .60
138 Justin McCareins .20 .50
139 Jerry Rice .60 1.50
140 Rich Gannon .25 .60
141 Tim Brown .30 .75
142 Jerry Porter .20 .50
143 Warren Sapp .25 .60
144 Charles Woodson .30 .75
145 Donovan McNabb .30 .75
146 Brian Westbrook .30 .75
147 Todd Pinkston .20 .50
148 Jevon Kearse .25 .60
149 Freddie Mitchell .20 .50
150 Correll Buckhalter .25 .60
151 Terrell Owens .30 .75
152 Tommy Maddox .25 .60
153 Duce Staley .25 .60
154 Plaxico Burress .25 .60
155 Hines Ward .30 .75
156 Antwaan Randle El .25 .60
157 Jerome Bettis .30 .75
158 Kendrell Bell .20 .50
159 LaDainian Tomlinson .30 .75
160 Doug Flutie .30 .75
161 Quentin Jammer .20 .50
162 Drew Brees .30 .75
163 Reche Caldwell .25 .60
164 Tim Dwight .20 .50
165 Tim Rattay .20 .50
166 Kevan Barlow .20 .50
167 Brandon Lloyd .25 .60
168 Cedrick Wilson .20 .50
169 Julian Peterson .25 .60
170 Ahmed Plummer .20 .50
171 Matt Hasselbeck .25 .60
172 Koren Robinson .20 .50
173 Shaun Alexander .25 .60
174 Darrell Jackson .25 .60
175 Marcus Trufant .20 .50
176 Bobby Engram .25 .60
177 Marc Bulger .25 .60
178 Torry Holt .25 .60
179 Marshall Faulk .30 .75
180 Orlando Pace .25 .60
181 Isaac Bruce .25 .60
182 Kyle Turley .20 .50
183 Brad Johnson .25 .60
184 Charlie Garner .25 .60
185 Keenan McCardell .20 .50
186 Mike Alstott .25 .60
187 Derrick Brooks .25 .60
188 Brian Griese .25 .60
189 Steve McNair .30 .75
190 Chris Brown .20 .50
191 Eddie George .25 .60
192 Tyrone Calico .25 .60
193 Derrick Mason .25 .60
194 Drew Bennett .25 .60
195 Mark Brunell .25 .60
196 LaVar Arrington .25 .60
197 Clinton Portis .30 .75
198 Laveranues Coles .20 .50
199 Patrick Ramsey .25 .60
200 Rod Gardner .20 .50
201 Eli Manning RC 12.00 30.00
202 Larry Fitzgerald RC 5.00 12.00
203 Michael Jenkins RC 2.00 5.00
204 Ben Roethlisberger RC 12.00 30.00
205 Philip Rivers RC 8.00 20.00
206 Kellen Winslow RC 2.00 5.00
207 Kevin Jones RC 1.50 4.00
208 Steven Jackson RC 3.00 8.00
209 Reggie Williams RC 1.50 4.00
210 Chris Perry RC 1.50 4.00
211 Roy Williams RC 2.00 5.00
212 Rashaun Woods RC 1.25 3.00
213 Chris Gamble RC 1.50 4.00
214 Sean Taylor RC 4.00 10.00
215 Robert Gallery RC 2.00 5.00
216 Ben Troupe RC 1.50 4.00
217 Lee Evans RC 2.00 5.00
218 Michael Clayton RC 1.50 4.00
219 J.P. Losman RC 1.50 4.00
220 Devery Henderson RC 2.00 5.00
221 Drew Henson RC 1.25 3.00
222 DeAngelo Hall RC 2.00 5.00
223 Julius Jones RC 1.50 4.00
224 Ben Watson RC 2.00 5.00
225 Greg Jones RC 1.25 3.00
226 D.J. Williams RC .60 1.50
227 Tommie Harris RC .60 1.50
228 Shawn Andrews RC .50 1.25
229 Vince Wilfork RC .60 1.50
230 Dunta Robinson RC .40 1.00
231 Will Smith RC .50 1.25
232 Jonathan Vilma RC .60 1.50
233 Ricardo Colclough RC .50 1.25
234 Ahmad Carroll RC .40 1.00
235 Karlos Dansby RC .60 1.50
236 Matt Ware RC .60 1.50
237 Jim Sorgi RC .50 1.25
238 Will Poole RC .60 1.50
239 Derrick Strait RC .40 1.00
240 Andy Hall RC .40 1.00
241 Nathan Vasher RC .60 1.50
242 D.J. Hackett RC .50 1.25
243 Jason Babin RC .60 1.50
244 Derrick Hamilton RC .40 1.00
245 Michael Boulware RC .60 1.50
246 Michael Turner RC .75 2.00
247 Sean Jones RC .50 1.25
248 Ernest Wilford RC .50 1.25
249 Cedric Cobbs RC .40 1.00
250 Tatum Bell RC .50 1.25
251 Bernard Berrian RC .60 1.50
252 Vernon Carey RC .40 1.00
253 Kenechi Udeze RC .50 1.25
254 P.K. Sam RC .40 1.00
255 Ben Hartsock RC .40 1.00
256 Chris Cooley RC .60 1.50
257 Josh Harris RC .40 1.00
258 Cody Pickett RC .50 1.25
259 Carlos Francis RC .40 1.00
260 Devard Darling RC .40 1.00
261 Johnnie Morant RC .40 1.00
262 John Navarre RC .40 1.00
263 Kris Wilson RC .50 1.25
264 Jerricho Cotchery RC .50 1.25
265 Darius Watts RC .40 1.00
266 Quincy Wilson RC .50 1.25
267 Maurice Mann RC .40 1.00
268 Samie Parker RC .40 1.00
269 B.J. Symons RC .40 1.00
270 Matt Schaub RC 1.25 3.00
271 Jeff Smoker RC .50 1.25
272 Craig Krenzel RC .50 1.25
273 Luke McCown RC .50 1.25
274 Mewelde Moore RC .50 1.25
275 Keary Colbert RC .40 1.00

2004 Upper Deck UD Exclusive

*VETS 1-200: 6X TO 15X BASIC CARDS
*ROOKIES 201-225: 1X TO 2.5X
*ROOKIES 226-275: 3X TO 8X
STATED PRINT RUN 50 SER.#'d SETS
UNPRICED VINTAGE PRINT RUN 10 SET
UNPRICED VINT.PRINT PLATE PRINT RUN 1

2004 Upper Deck Game Jerseys

STATED ODDS 1:32 HOB, 1:28 RET
ABGJ Anquan Boldin 4.00 10.00
AJGJ Andre Johnson 4.00 10.00
BFGJ Brett Favre 10.00 25.00
CDGJ Corey Dillon 3.00 8.00
CJGJ Chad Johnson 4.00 10.00
CPGJ Clinton Portis 4.00 10.00
DCGJ Daunte Culpepper 3.00 8.00
DDGJ Domanick Davis 2.50 6.00
DMGJ Deuce McAllister 3.00 8.00
DOGJ Donovan McNabb 4.00 10.00
JDGJ Jake Delhomme 3.00 8.00
KBGJ Kyle Boller SP 4.00 10.00
LTGJ LaDainian Tomlinson 4.00 10.00
MVGJ Michael Vick 5.00 12.00
PHGJ Priest Holmes 4.00 10.00
PMGJ Peyton Manning 8.00 20.00
RMGJ Randy Moss 4.00 10.00
SAGJ Shaun Alexander 3.00 8.00
SMGJ Steve McNair 4.00 10.00
TBGJ Tom Brady 8.00 20.00
TSGJ Terrell Suggs SP 4.00 10.00

2004 Upper Deck Game Jersey Duals

STATED ODDS 1:480
BD2J Tom Brady 15.00 40.00
Jake Delhomme
FM2J Brett Favre 20.00 50.00
Peyton Manning
HF2J Priest Holmes 8.00 20.00
Marshall Faulk
MH2J Randy Moss 8.00 20.00
Marvin Harrison
SR2J Emmitt Smith 20.00 50.00
Jerry Rice
TP2J LaDainian Tomlinson 8.00 20.00
Clinton Portis
US2J Brian Urlacher 8.00 20.00
Junior Seau
VM2J Michael Vick 10.00 25.00
Donovan McNabb

2004 Upper Deck Game Jersey Patch Logos

PATCH LOGO STATED ODDS 1:2500
PLOAG Ahman Green 10.00 25.00
PLOBL Byron Leftwich 10.00 25.00
PLOBU Brian Urlacher 12.00 30.00
PLOCL Clinton Portis 12.00 30.00
PLOCP Chad Pennington 12.00 30.00
PLOHW Hines Ward 12.00 30.00
PLOJH Joe Horn 10.00 25.00
PLOMV Michael Vick 15.00 40.00
PLOPH Priest Holmes 12.00 30.00
PLORM Randy Moss 12.00 30.00
PLOTH Todd Heap 10.00 25.00

2004 Upper Deck Game Jersey Patch Names

PATCH NAMES ODDS 1:5000
PNAEJ Edgerrin James SP 15.00 40.00
PNALT LaDainian Tomlinson 15.00 40.00
PNAMS Michael Strahan 15.00 40.00
PNASA Santana Moss 12.00 30.00
PNASM Steve McNair 15.00 40.00
PNATB Tom Brady 30.00 80.00
PNATH Torry Holt 12.00 30.00
PNATO Terrell Owens 15.00 40.00

2004 Upper Deck Game Jersey Patch Numbers

PATCH NUMBER ODDS 1:1500
PNUBF Brett Favre 25.00 60.00
PNUCC Chris Chambers 8.00 20.00
PNUCJ Chad Johnson 10.00 25.00
PNUCP Clinton Portis 10.00 25.00
PNUDC Daunte Culpepper 8.00 20.00
PNUDH Dante Hall 8.00 20.00
PNUDM Deuce McAllister 8.00 20.00
PNUJL Jamal Lewis 8.00 20.00
PNUJR Jerry Rice 20.00 50.00
PNUMB Marc Bulger 8.00 20.00
PNUPM Peyton Manning 20.00 50.00
PNURG Rex Grossman 8.00 20.00

2004 Upper Deck Rewind to 1997 Jerseys

STATED ODDS 1:480
97BF Brett Favre 12.00 30.00
97CD Corey Dillon 4.00 10.00
97CM Curtis Martin 5.00 12.00
97DF Doug Flutie 5.00 12.00
97EM Eric Moulds 4.00 10.00
97ES Emmitt Smith SP 12.00 30.00
97JB Jerome Bettis 5.00 12.00
97JP Jake Plummer 4.00 10.00
97JR Jerry Rice SP 10.00 25.00
97JS Junior Seau 5.00 12.00
97MF Marshall Faulk 5.00 12.00
97TB Tim Brown SP 5.00 12.00
97TG Tony Gonzalez 5.00 12.00
97WD Warrick Dunn 4.00 10.00

2004 Upper Deck Rookie Futures Jerseys

STATED ODDS 1:24
RFBB Bernard Berrian 4.00 10.00
RFBR Ben Roethlisberger 20.00 50.00
RFBT Ben Troupe 3.00 8.00
RFBW Ben Watson 4.00 10.00
RFCC Cedric Cobbs 2.50 6.00
RFCP Chris Perry 3.00 8.00
RFDD Devard Darling 2.50 6.00
RFDE Devery Henderson 4.00 10.00
RFDK Derrick Hamilton 2.50 6.00
RFDR Dunta Robinson 2.50 6.00
RFDW Darius Watts 2.50 6.00
RFEM Eli Manning 20.00 50.00
RFGJ Greg Jones 2.50 6.00
RFHA DeAngelo Hall 4.00 10.00
RFJJ Julius Jones 3.00 8.00
RFJP J.P. Losman 3.00 8.00
RFKC Keary Colbert 2.50 6.00
RFKJ Kevin Jones 3.00 8.00
RFKW Kellen Winslow Jr. 4.00 10.00
RFLE Lee Evans 4.00 10.00
RFLF Larry Fitzgerald 8.00 20.00
RFLM Luke McCown 3.00 8.00
RFMI Michael Clayton 3.00 8.00
RFMJ Michael Jenkins 4.00 10.00
RFMM Mewelde Moore 3.00 8.00
RFMS Matt Schaub 8.00 20.00
RFPR Philip Rivers 12.00 30.00
RFRA Rashaun Woods 2.50 6.00

RFRG Robert Gallery	4.00	10.00
RFRO Roy Williams WR	4.00	10.00
RFRW Reggie Williams	3.00	8.00
RFSJ Steven Jackson	6.00	15.00
RFTB Tatum Bell	3.00	8.00

2004 Upper Deck Rookie Prospects

COMPLETE SET (30)	15.00	40.00
ONE PER RETAIL PACK		
RPBR Ben Roethlisberger	3.00	8.00
RPBT Ben Troupe	.40	1.00
RPBW Ben Watson	.50	1.25
RPCC Cedric Cobbs	.30	.75
RPCP Chris Perry	.40	1.00
RPDD Devard Darling	.30	.75
RPDE Devery Henderson	.50	1.25
RPDH Derrick Hamilton	.30	.75
RPDR Drew Henson	.30	.75
RPDW Darius Watts	.30	.75
RPEM Eli Manning	3.00	8.00
RPGJ Greg Jones	.30	.75
RPJJ Julius Jones	.40	1.00
RPJP J.P. Losman	.40	1.00
RPKC Keary Colbert	.30	.75
RPKJ Kevin Jones	.40	1.00
RPKW Kellen Winslow Jr.	.50	1.25
RPLE Lee Evans	.50	1.25
RPLF Larry Fitzgerald	1.25	3.00
RPLM Luke McCown	.40	1.00
RPMI Michael Clayton	.40	1.00
RPMJ Michael Jenkins	.50	1.25
RPMM Mewelde Moore	.40	1.00
RPMS Matt Schaub	1.00	2.50
RPPR Philip Rivers	2.00	5.00
RPRA Rashaun Woods	.30	.75
RPRO Roy Williams WR	.50	1.25
RPRW Reggie Williams	.40	1.00
RPSJ Steven Jackson	.75	2.00
RPTB Tatum Bell	.40	1.00

2004 Upper Deck Rookie Review Jerseys

STATED ODDS 1:480		
RRAB Anquan Boldin	4.00	10.00
RRAJ Andre Johnson	4.00	10.00
RRAP Artose Pinner	2.50	6.00
RRBJ Bethel Johnson	2.50	6.00
RRBL Byron Leftwich	3.00	8.00
RRCB Chris Brown	2.50	6.00
RRCP Carson Palmer	4.00	10.00
RRDC Dallas Clark	4.00	10.00
RRJF Justin Fargas	3.00	8.00
RRKB Kyle Boller	3.00	8.00
RRKW Kelley Washington	2.50	6.00
RRLJ Larry Johnson	3.00	8.00
RRMT Marcus Trufant	2.50	6.00
RROS Onterrio Smith	2.50	6.00
RRRG Rex Grossman	3.00	8.00
RRTC Tyrone Calico	3.00	8.00
RRTJ Teyo Johnson	2.50	6.00
RRTN Terence Newman	3.00	8.00
RRTS Terrell Suggs	3.00	8.00
RRWM Willis McGahee	4.00	10.00

2004 Upper Deck Signature Sensations

SIGN SENSATION PRINT RUN 4 88		
CARDS SER.#'d UNDER 20 NOT PRICED		
SSBE Ben Watson/84	12.50	30.00
SSBL Brandon Lloyd/85	10.00	25.00
SSBS Barry Sanders/20	100.00	175.00
SSBT Ben Troupe/86	15.00	40.00
SSBW Brian Westbrook/36		
SSCC Cedric Cobbs/34	15.00	40.00
SSCP Chris Perry/26	15.00	40.00
SSDD Domanick Davis/37		
SSDH DeAngelo Hall/21	15.00	40.00
SSDM Deuce McAllister/26	15.00	40.00
SSGJ Greg Jones/33	15.00	40.00
SSHA Dante Hall/82	12.50	30.00
SSJG Jon Gruden/60	12.00	30.00
SSJH Joe Horn/87	10.00	25.00
SSJJ Jimmy Johnson/60	15.00	40.00
SSJU Julius Jones/21		
SSKC Keary Colbert/85	12.50	30.00
SSKJ Kevin Jones/34	15.00	40.00
SSKW Kellen Winslow Jr./81	15.00	40.00
SSLE Lee Evans/83	12.00	30.00
SSLT LaDainian Tomlinson/21		
SSMI Michael Clayton/80	10.00	25.00
SSRA Rashaun Woods/81	10.00	25.00
SSRG Robert Gallery/74	12.00	30.00
SSRJ Rudi Johnson/32	12.00	30.00
SSRW Roy Williams S/31		
SSSJ Steven Jackson/39	75.00	135.00
SSTA Tatum Bell/26	15.00	40.00
SSTG Tony Gonzalez/88	10.00	25.00
SSWI Kellen Winslow Sr./80	12.00	30.00
SSWM Willis McGahee/21	15.00	40.00

2004 Upper Deck Earl Campbell Promo

This promo card was issued at the 2004 Super Bowl XXXVIII Card Show in Houston. It features Earl Campbell along with the notation "The Tyler Rose" on the cardfront as well as serial numbering of 1000-cards produced. Note that the copyright line on the back designates the year as 2003.

EC Earl Campbell	2.00	5.00

2004 Upper Deck Pepsi Get Out There and Play

NNO Donovan McNabb	1.25	3.00

2005 Upper Deck

This 275-card set was released in August, 2005. The set was issued into the hobby in eight-card packs with an $2.99 SRP which came 24 packs to a box. Cards numbered 1-193 were sequenced in team alphabetical order based on where the player pictured played in 2004. In addition, cards numbered 201-275 featured 2005 rookies. Cards numbered 201-225 were inserted at a stated rate of one in eight and cards numbered 226-275 were inserted at a stated rate of one per pack.

COMPLETE SET (275)	100.00	200.00
COMP.SET w/o SP's (250)	30.00	60.00
COMP.SET w/o RC's (200)	12.50	30.00
201-225 ROOKIE STATED ODDS 1:8		
226-275 ROOKIE STATED ODDS 1:1		
1 Larry Fitzgerald	.30	.75
2 Anquan Boldin	.25	.60
3 Kurt Warner	.30	.75
4 Josh McCown	.25	.60
5 Bryant Johnson	.20	.50
6 Duane Starks	.20	.50
7 Michael Vick	.30	.75
8 Warrick Dunn	.25	.60
9 T.J. Duckett	.20	.50
10 Peerless Price	.20	.50
11 Alge Crumpler	.25	.60
12 Patrick Kerney	.25	.60
13 Ed Reed	.25	.60
14 Ray Lewis	.30	.75
15 Kyle Boller	.25	.60
16 Ma'Ake Kemoeatu	.20	.50
17 Jamal Lewis	.25	.60
18 Derrick Mason	.25	.60
19 J.P. Losman	.20	.50
20 Willis McGahee	.30	.75
21 Lawyer Milloy	.25	.60
22 Lee Evans	.25	.60
23 Eric Moulds	.20	.50
24 Takeo Spikes	.20	.50
25 Jake Delhomme	.25	.60
26 DeShaun Foster	.25	.60
27 Keary Colbert	.20	.50
28 Stephen Davis	.25	.60
29 Nick Goings	.20	.50
30 Julius Peppers	.25	.60
31 Rex Grossman	.25	.60
32 Brian Urlacher	.30	.75
33 Thomas Jones	.30	.75
34 Muhsin Muhammad	.25	.60
35 Anthony Thomas	.20	.50
36 Bernard Berrian	.25	.60
37 Carson Palmer	.30	.75
38 Chad Johnson	.25	.60
39 Peter Warrick	.20	.50
40 T.J. Houshmandzadeh	.25	.60
41 Rudi Johnson	.25	.60
42 Justin Smith	.20	.50
43 Jeff Garcia	.25	.60
44 Lee Suggs	.20	.50
45 William Green	.20	.50
46 Kellen Winslow	.25	.60
47 Dennis Northcutt	.20	.50
48 Antonio Bryant	.20	.50
49 Julius Jones	.20	.50
50 Drew Bledsoe	.30	.75
51 Keyshawn Johnson	.25	.60
52 Al Johnson	.20	.50
53 Jason Witten	.30	.75
54 Roy Williams S	.20	.50
55 Jake Plummer	.25	.60
56 Champ Bailey	.25	.60
57 Tatum Bell	.20	.50
58 Reuben Droughns	.20	.50
59 Ashley Lelie	.20	.50
60 Rod Smith	.25	.60
61 Kevin Jones	.20	.50
62 Roy Williams WR	.25	.60
63 Charles Rogers	.20	.50
64 Joey Harrington	.25	.60
65 Az-Zahir Hakim	.20	.50
66 Dre Bly	.20	.50
67 Brett Favre	.75	2.00
68 Javon Walker	.20	.50
69 Ahman Green	.25	.60
70 Donald Driver	.30	.75
71 Robert Ferguson	.20	.50
72 Nick Barnett	.25	.60
73 David Carr	.20	.50
74 Domanick Davis	.20	.50
75 Andre Johnson	.30	.75
76 Jabar Gaffney	.20	.50
77 Dunta Robinson	.20	.50
78 Jamie Sharper	.20	.50
79 Peyton Manning	.60	1.50
80 Edgerrin James	.25	.60
81 Marvin Harrison	.30	.75
82 Reggie Wayne	.30	.75
83 Brandon Stokley	.20	.50
84 Dwight Freeney	.25	.60
85 Byron Leftwich	.25	.60
86 Fred Taylor	.25	.60
87 Jimmy Smith	.25	.60
88 Greg Jones	.20	.50
89 Donovin Darius	.20	.50
90 Reggie Williams	.20	.50
91 Priest Holmes	.25	.60
92 Larry Johnson	.25	.60
93 Tony Gonzalez	.25	.60
94 Trent Green	.25	.60
95 Eddie Kennison	.20	.50
96 Johnnie Morton	.25	.60
97 Jason Taylor	.25	.60
98 A.J. Feeley	.20	.50
99 Sammy Morris	.20	.50
100 Chris Chambers	.25	.60
101 Randy McMichael	.20	.50
102 Zach Thomas	.30	.75
103 Antoine Winfield	.25	.60
104 Daunte Culpepper	.25	.60
105 Michael Bennett	.25	.60
106 Nate Burleson	.20	.50
107 Onterrio Smith	.20	.50
108 Marcus Robinson	.20	.50
109 Tom Brady	.60	1.50
110 Corey Dillon	.25	.60
111 David Givens	.20	.50
112 David Patten	.20	.50
113 Adam Vinatieri	.30	.75
114 Troy Brown	.20	.50
115 Aaron Brooks	.20	.50
116 Deuce McAllister	.25	.60
117 Joe Horn	.25	.60
118 Donte Stallworth	.20	.50
119 Charles Grant	.20	.50
120 Jerome Pathon	.20	.50
121 Eli Manning	.50	1.25
122 Tiki Barber	.30	.75
123 Amani Toomer	.25	.60
124 Jeremy Shockey	.30	.75
125 Michael Strahan	.30	.75
126 Plaxico Burress	.25	.60
127 Chad Pennington	.30	.75
128 Curtis Martin	.30	.75
129 Laveranues Coles	.20	.50
130 Wayne Chrebet	.25	.60
131 Jonathan Vilma	.25	.60
132 Justin McCareins	.20	.50
133 Kerry Collins	.25	.60
134 Jerry Porter	.20	.50
135 LaMont Jordan	.25	.60
136 Randy Moss	.30	.75
137 Barry Sims	.20	.50
138 Warren Sapp	.25	.60
139 Donovan McNabb	.30	.75
140 Brian Westbrook	.25	.60
141 Terrell Owens	.30	.75
142 Jevon Kearse	.25	.60
143 Brian Dawkins	.25	.60
144 Ben Roethlisberger	.50	1.25
145 Jerome Bettis	.30	.75
146 Duce Staley	.25	.60
147 Cedrick Wilson	.20	.50
148 Hines Ward	.30	.75
149 Antwaan Randle El	.25	.60
150 Troy Polamalu	.40	1.00
151 Philip Rivers	.30	.75
152 Drew Brees	.30	.75
153 LaDainian Tomlinson	.30	.75
154 Antonio Gates	.30	.75
155 Reche Caldwell	.20	.50
156 Eric Parker	.20	.50
157 Kevan Barlow	.20	.50
158 Tim Rattay	.20	.50
159 Eric Johnson	.20	.50
160 Rashaun Woods	.20	.50
161 Brandon Lloyd	.20	.50
162 Julian Peterson	.20	.50
163 Matt Hasselbeck	.25	.60
164 Shaun Alexander	.25	.60
165 Michael Boulware	.20	.50
166 Darrell Jackson	.20	.50
167 Koren Robinson	.20	.50
168 Marcus Trufant	.20	.50
169 Marc Bulger	.25	.60
170 Steven Jackson	.30	.75
171 Marshall Faulk	.30	.75
172 Issac Bruce	.25	.60
173 Torry Holt	.25	.60
174 Michael Clayton	.20	.50
175 Michael Pittman	.20	.50
176 Brian Griese	.25	.60
177 Joey Galloway	.25	.60
178 Derrick Brooks	.25	.60
179 Josh Savage RC	.20	.50
180 Steve McNair	.30	.75
181 Chris Brown	.20	.50
182 Billy Volek	.20	.50
183 Ben Troupe	.20	.50
184 Drew Bennett	.25	.60
185 Clinton Portis	.25	.60
186 Mark Brunell	.25	.60
187 Patrick Ramsey	.25	.60
188 Sean Taylor	.30	.75
189 LaVar Arrington	.25	.60
190 Santana Moss	.25	.60
191 David Terrell	.20	.50
192 Deion Branch	.20	.50
193 Chester Taylor	.25	.60
194 Derrick Blaylock	.20	.50
195 Shaun Ellis	.20	.50
196 Terrell Suggs	.25	.60
197 Charles Woodson	.30	.75
198 Jason Elam	.20	.50
199 Lawrence Tynes RC	.25	.60
200 David Akers	.20	.50
201 Alex Smith QB RC	4.00	10.00
202 Aaron Rodgers RC	20.00	40.00
203 Ronnie Brown RC	3.00	8.00
204 Cadillac Williams RC	2.50	6.00
205 Braylon Edwards RC	3.00	8.00
206 Antrel Rolle RC	2.50	6.00
207 Cedric Benson RC	2.50	6.00
208 Troy Williamson RC	2.00	5.00
209 Mark Clayton RC	2.00	5.00
210 Matt Jones RC	2.00	5.00
211 Reggie Brown RC	1.50	4.00
212 Charlie Frye RC	2.50	6.00
213 Heath Miller RC	3.00	8.00
214 Vincent Jackson RC	3.00	8.00
215 Andrew Walter RC	2.00	5.00
216 Roddy White RC	3.00	8.00
217 Adam Jones RC	1.50	4.00
218 J.J. Arrington RC	2.00	5.00
219 Eric Shelton RC	1.50	4.00
220 Terrence Murphy RC	1.50	4.00
221 Frank Gore RC	4.00	10.00
222 Roscoe Parrish RC	1.50	4.00
223 Jason Campbell RC	3.00	8.00
224 Carlos Rogers RC	2.50	6.00
225 Mike Williams	2.50	6.00
226 Erasmus James RC	.60	1.50
227 Travis Johnson RC	.50	1.25
228 Dan Cody RC	.60	1.50
229 Thomas Davis RC	.50	1.25
230 David Pollack RC	.60	1.50
231 David Greene RC	.50	1.25
232 Alex Smith TE RC	.50	1.25
233 Ryan Moats RC	.60	1.50
234 Ciatrick Fason RC	.50	1.25
235 Vernand Morency RC	.60	1.50
236 Fred Gibson RC	.60	1.50
237 Craphonso Thorpe RC	.50	1.25
238 Kevin Everett RC	.75	2.00
239 Kyle Orton RC	.75	2.00
240 Derek Anderson RC	.60	1.50
241 Derrick Johnson RC	.60	1.50
242 Mark Bradley RC	.50	1.25
243 Chris Henry RC	.75	2.00
244 DeMarcus Ware RC	1.50	4.00
245 Luis Castillo RC	.60	1.50
246 Mike Patterson RC	.50	1.25
247 Brodney Pool RC	.75	2.00
248 Barrett Ruud RC	.75	2.00
249 Darren Sproles RC	.75	2.00
250 Stefan LeFors RC	.50	1.25
251 Josh Bullocks RC	.60	1.50
252 Kevin Burnett RC	.60	1.50
253 Lofa Tatupu RC	.75	2.00
254 Matt Roth RC	.60	1.50
255 Shaun Cody RC	.60	1.50
256 Shawne Merriman RC	.75	2.00
257 Corey Webster RC	.60	1.50
258 Channing Crowder RC	.60	1.50
259 Justin Miller RC	.60	1.50
260 Eric Green RC	.50	1.25
261 Marcus Spears RC	.60	1.50
262 Marlin Jackson RC	.50	1.25
263 Odell Thurman RC	.75	2.00
264 Mike Nugent RC	.60	1.50
265 Marion Barber RC	.75	2.00
266 Anttaj Hawthorne RC	.50	1.25
267 Dan Orlovsky RC	.75	2.00
268 Fabian Washington RC	.60	1.50
269 Justin Tuck RC	1.00	2.50
270 Jerome Mathis RC	.75	2.00
271 Ronald Bartell RC	.60	1.50
272 Kirk Morrison RC	.75	2.00
273 Adrian McPherson RC	.50	1.25
274 Matt Cassel RC	2.50	6.00
275 Maurice Clarett	.60	1.50

2005 Upper Deck UD Exclusive

*VETS: 5X TO 12X BASE CARD HI		
*ROOKIES 201-225: 1.2X TO 3X BASE CARD HI		
*ROOKIES 226-275: 4X TO 10X BASE CARD HI		
STATED PRINT RUN 50 SER.#'d SETS		
202 Aaron Rodgers	125.00	200.00

2005 Upper Deck UD Exclusive Spectrum

UNPRICED SPECTRUM PRINT RUN 10 SETS

2005 Upper Deck Barry Sanders Heroes

COMPLETE SET (10)	10.00	25.00
COMMON CARD	1.25	3.00
STATED ODDS 1:12 HOB, 1:24 RET		
UNPRICED AUTOGRAPH PRINT RUN 5		

2005 Upper Deck Barry Sanders Heroes Jerseys

COMMON CARD	40.00	80.00
STATED PRINT RUN 25 SER.#'d SETS		

2005 Upper Deck Game Jerseys

GAME JSY/ROOK.FUTURE JSY ODDS 1:8 H		
STATED ODDS 1:24 RETAIL		
*PATCHES: 1X TO 2.5X BASIC JERSEYS		
PATCH STATED ODDS 1:288H, 1:960R		
AH Ahman Green	3.00	8.00
BL Byron Leftwich	3.00	8.00
BR Ben Roethlisberger	8.00	20.00
DB Drew Bledsoe	4.00	10.00
DC Daunte Culpepper	3.00	8.00
DE Deuce McAllister	3.00	8.00
DM Donovan McNabb	4.00	10.00
DR David Carr	2.50	6.00
DS Duce Staley	3.00	8.00
EJ Edgerrin James	3.00	8.00
EM Eli Manning	6.00	15.00
ER Eric Moulds	2.50	6.00
JB Jerome Bettis	5.00	12.00
JH Joey Harrington	3.00	8.00
JJ Julius Jones	2.50	6.00
JL Jamal Lewis	3.00	8.00
JP Jake Plummer	3.00	8.00
JR Jerry Rice	8.00	20.00
JS Jeremy Shockey	4.00	10.00
JU Julius Peppers	3.00	8.00
KE Keyshawn Johnson	3.00	8.00
KJ Kevin Jones	2.50	6.00
LF Larry Fitzgerald	4.00	10.00
LT LaDainian Tomlinson	4.00	10.00
MB Marc Bulger	3.00	8.00
MF Marshall Faulk	4.00	10.00
MH Matt Hasselbeck	3.00	8.00
MS Michael Strahan	4.00	10.00
MV Michael Vick	4.00	10.00
OS Onterrio Smith	2.50	6.00
PM Peyton Manning	8.00	20.00
PR Philip Rivers	4.00	10.00
RG Rod Gardner	2.50	6.00
RL Ray Lewis	4.00	10.00
RM Randy Moss	4.00	10.00
SA Shaun Alexander	3.00	8.00
SM Steve McNair	4.00	10.00
TB Tom Brady	8.00	20.00
TG Trent Green	3.00	8.00
TI Tiki Barber	4.00	10.00
TY Tony Gonzalez	3.00	8.00
WM Willis McGahee	4.00	10.00

2005 Upper Deck MVP Predictors

STATED ODDS 1:12 HOB/RET		
MVP1 Anquan Boldin	1.50	4.00
MVP2 Larry Fitzgerald	1.50	4.00
MVP3 Michael Vick	2.50	5.00
MVP4 Warrick Dunn	1.50	4.00
MVP5 Jamal Lewis	1.50	4.00
MVP6 Kyle Boller	1.50	4.00
MVP7 Willis McGahee	1.50	4.00
MVP8 J.P. Losman	1.50	4.00
MVP9 Jake Delhomme	1.50	4.00
MVP10 Stephen Davis	1.25	3.00
MVP11 Mushin Muhammad	1.25	3.00
MVP12 Rex Grossman	1.00	2.50
MVP13 Carson Palmer	1.50	4.00
MVP14 Rudi Johnson	1.25	3.00
MVP15 Chad Johnson	1.50	4.00
MVP16 Jeff Garcia	1.25	3.00
MVP17 Lee Suggs	1.00	2.50
MVP18 Julius Jones	1.50	4.00
MVP19 Drew Bledsoe	1.50	4.00
MVP20 Jake Plummer	1.50	4.00
MVP21 Reuben Droughns	1.25	3.00
MVP22 Ashley Lelie	1.00	2.50
MVP23 Roy Williams WR	1.50	4.00
MVP24 Kevin Jones	1.50	4.00
MVP25 Joey Harrington	1.50	4.00
MVP26 Brett Favre	3.00	8.00
MVP27 Ahman Green	1.50	4.00
MVP28 Javon Walker	1.25	3.00
MVP29 David Carr	1.50	4.00
MVP30 Andre Johnson	1.00	2.50
MVP31 Domanick Davis	1.25	3.00
MVP32 Peyton Manning	2.50	6.00
MVP33 Edgerrin James	1.50	4.00
MVP34 Marvin Harrison	1.25	3.00
MVP35 Byron Leftwich	1.50	4.00
MVP36 Fred Taylor	1.25	3.00
MVP37 Trent Green	1.50	4.00
MVP38 Priest Holmes	1.50	4.00
MVP39 Chris Chambers	1.00	2.50
MVP40 Daunte Culpepper	1.50	4.00
MVP41 Randy Moss	1.50	4.00
MVP42 Tom Brady	3.00	8.00
MVP43 Corey Dillon	1.50	4.00
MVP44 Aaron Brooks	1.50	4.00
MVP45 Joe Horn	1.00	2.50
MVP46 Deuce McAllister	1.50	4.00
MVP47 Eli Manning	2.50	6.00
MVP48 Tiki Barber	1.50	4.00
MVP49 Chad Pennington	1.50	4.00
MVP50 Laveranues Coles	1.00	2.50
MVP51 Curtis Martin	1.50	4.00
MVP52 Jerry Porter	1.00	2.50
MVP53 Kerry Collins	1.50	4.00
MVP54 Donovan McNabb	2.00	5.00
MVP55 Terrell Owens	1.50	4.00
MVP56 Brian Westbrook	1.25	3.00
MVP57 Ben Roethlisberger	3.00	8.00
MVP58 Hines Ward	1.50	4.00
MVP59 Drew Brees	1.50	4.00
MVP60 LaDainian Tomlinson	1.50	4.00
MVP61 Kevan Barlow	1.00	2.50
MVP62 Shaun Alexander WIN	30.00	60.00
MVP63 Matt Hasselbeck	1.50	4.00
MVP64 Darrell Jackson	1.00	2.50
MVP65 Marc Bulger	1.50	4.00
MVP66 Torry Holt	1.25	3.00
MVP67 Marshall Faulk	1.50	4.00
MVP68 Michael Pittman	1.00	2.50
MVP69 Michael Clayton	1.25	3.00
MVP70 Brian Griese	1.50	4.00
MVP71 Steve McNair	1.50	4.00
MVP72 Chris Brown	1.25	3.00
MVP73 Clinton Portis	1.50	4.00
MVP74 Patrick Ramsey	1.25	3.00
MVP75 J.J. Arrington	1.50	4.00
MVP76 Alex Smith QB	2.00	5.00
MVP77 Ronnie Brown	2.00	5.00
MVP78 Cadillac Williams	1.25	3.00
MVP79 Ciatrick Fason	1.50	4.00
MVP80 Matt Jones	1.25	3.00
MVP81 Braylon Edwards	1.50	4.00
MVP82 Troy Williamson	1.50	4.00
MVP83 Mark Clayton	1.50	4.00
MVP84 Roddy White	1.25	3.00
MVP85 Reggie Brown	1.50	4.00
MVP86 Stefan LeFors	1.00	2.50
MVP87 Frank Gore	2.00	5.00
MVP88 Charlie Frye	1.50	4.00
MVP89 Jason Campbell	1.50	4.00
MVP90 Wild Card	1.25	3.00

2005 Upper Deck Rookie Futures Jerseys

GAME JSY/ROOKIE FUT.JSY ODDS 1:8 HOB		
STATED ODDS 1:24 RETAIL		
AJ Adam Jones	3.00	8.00
AN Antrel Rolle	3.00	8.00
AS Alex Smith QB	10.00	25.00
AW Andrew Walter	3.00	8.00
BE Braylon Edwards	7.50	20.00
CA Carlos Rogers	3.00	8.00
CF Charlie Frye	3.00	8.00
CI Ciatrick Fason	3.00	8.00
CR Courtney Roby	3.00	8.00
CW Cadillac Williams	8.00	20.00
ES Eric Shelton	3.00	8.00
FG Frank Gore	6.00	15.00
JC Jason Campbell	5.00	12.00
JJ J.J. Arrington	3.00	8.00
KO Kyle Orton	3.00	8.00
MB Mark Bradley	3.00	8.00
MC Mark Clayton	3.00	8.00
MJ Matt Jones	4.00	10.00
MO Maurice Clarett	3.00	8.00
RB Ronnie Brown	10.00	25.00
RE Reggie Brown	3.00	8.00
RM Ryan Moats	3.00	8.00
RP Roscoe Parrish	3.00	8.00
RW Roddy White	4.00	10.00
SL Stefan LeFors	3.00	8.00
TM Terrence Murphy	3.00	8.00
TW Troy Williamson	3.00	8.00
VJ Vincent Jackson	5.00	12.00
VM Vernand Morency	3.00	8.00

2005 Upper Deck Rookie Futures Dual Jerseys

STATED ODDS 1:288		
AR J.J. Arrington Antrel Rolle	10.00	25.00
CB Mark Clayton Mark Bradley	10.00	25.00
CW Jason Campbell Cadillac Williams	15.00	40.00
FE Braylon Edwards Charlie Frye	15.00	40.00
FO Charlie Frye Kyle Orton	8.00	20.00
GS Frank Gore Alex Smith QB	15.00	40.00
LS Stefan LeFors Eric Shelton	7.50	20.00
MM Vernand Morency Ryan Moats	7.50	20.00
RB Ronnie Brown Carlos Rogers	15.00	40.00
RP Antrel Rolle Roscoe Parrish	7.50	20.00
WB Ronnie Brown Cadillac Williams	15.00	40.00
WE Braylon Edwards Troy Williamson	15.00	40.00
WR Reggie Brown Roddy White	10.00	25.00

2005 Upper Deck Rookie Predictor Autographs

PRIZES FOR UD DEBUT ROY PREDICTOR		
202 Aaron Rodgers/25	250.00	400.00
204 Cadillac Williams/25	60.00	120.00
205 Braylon Edwards/25	50.00	100.00
206 Antrel Rolle/100		
207 Cedric Benson/25		
208 Troy Williamson/25		
209 Mark Clayton/25		
211 Reggie Brown/100		
212 Charlie Frye/100		
213 Heath Miller/100	20.00	40.00
214 Vincent Jackson/100		
215 Andrew Walter/100		
216 Roddy White/100		
217 Adam Jones/100		
218 J.J. Arrington/100	10.00	25.00
219 Eric Shelton/100	8.00	20.00
220 Terrence Murphy/50	8.00	20.00
221 Frank Gore/100	40.00	75.00
223 Jason Campbell/50	35.00	60.00
224 Carlos Rogers/40		
225 Mike Williams/25	15.00	40.00

2005 Upper Deck Rookie Prospects

COMPLETE SET (30)	15.00	30.00
ONE PER RETAIL PACK		
RPAJ Adam Jones	.40	1.00
RPAN Antrel Rolle	.60	1.50
RPAS Alex Smith QB	1.00	2.50
RPAW Andrew Walter	.50	1.25
RPBE Braylon Edwards	.75	2.00
RPCA Carlos Rogers	.60	1.50
RPCF Charlie Frye	.60	1.50
RPCR Courtney Roby	.50	1.25
RPCT Ciatrick Fason	.40	1.00
RPCW Cadillac Williams	.60	1.50
RPES Eric Shelton	.40	1.00
RPFG Frank Gore	1.00	2.50
RPJA J.J. Arrington	.50	1.25
RPJC Jason Campbell	.75	2.00
RPKO Kyle Orton	.60	1.50
RPMB Mark Bradley	.40	1.00
RPMC Mark Clayton	.50	1.25
RPMJ Matt Jones	.50	1.25
RPMO Maurice Clarett	.40	1.00
RPMW Mike Williams	.60	1.50
RPRB Ronnie Brown	.75	2.00
RPRE Reggie Brown	.40	1.00
RPRM Ryan Moats	.40	1.00
RPRP Roscoe Parrish	.40	1.00
RPRW Roddy White	.75	2.00
RPSL Stefan LeFors	.40	1.00
RPTM Terrence Murphy	.40	1.00
RPTW Troy Williamson	.50	1.25
RPVJ Vincent Jackson	.75	2.00
RPVM Vernand Morency	.40	1.00

2005 Upper Deck Signature Sensations

CARDS SER.#'d TO PLAYER'S JERSEY NO.		
AB Aaron Brooks		
AD Anthony Davis/28	12.50	30.00
AG Antonio Gates/85	12.50	30.00
AH Ahman Green/30	20.00	40.00
AN Anttaj Hawthorne/77	10.00	25.00
AQ Anquan Boldin/81	10.00	25.00
AR Antrel Rolle		
BA Barrett Ruud/38	20.00	40.00
BF Brett Favre		
BJ Brandon Jacobs/27	50.00	100.00
BL Byron Leftwich		
CB Chris Brown/27	12.50	30.00
CD Cedric Benson/32	25.00	60.00
CE Chris Berman/25	12.50	30.00
CJ Chad Johnson/85	10.00	25.00
CW Cadillac Williams/24		
DD Domanick Davis/37	12.50	30.00
DE Deuce McAllister/26	12.50	30.00
DI Deion Sanders/37	40.00	80.00
DO Dan Orlovsky		
DP David Pollack/47	25.00	50.00
DS Darren Sproles/47	25.00	50.00
EJ Erasmus James/90	12.50	30.00
ES Eric Shelton/32	12.50	30.00
FG Fred Gibson/82	10.00	25.00
FT Fred Taylor/28	12.50	30.00
HM Heath Miller/89	20.00	50.00
JA J.J. Arrington/30	15.00	40.00
JB James Butler/22		
JH Joe Horn/87	7.50	20.00
JJ Julius Jones/21	7.50	20.00
JO J.P. Losman		
KC Keary Colbert/83	10.00	25.00
LE Lee Evans/83	10.00	25.00
LJ Larry Johnson/34	12.00	30.00
MAO Marion Barber/21		
MB Marc Bulger		
MI Michael Clayton/80	10.00	25.00
MM Muhsin Muhammad/87	7.50	20.00
MV Michael Vick		
NB Nate Burleson/81	12.50	30.00
RB Ronnie Brown/23		
RJ Rudi Johnson/32	15.00	40.00
RM Ryan Moats/20		
RW Roy Williams WR		
RY Reggie Wayne/87	12.50	30.00
SJ Steven Jackson/39	30.00	60.00
TM T.A. McLendon/44	12.50	30.00
TS Taylor Stubblefield/21		
TW Troy Williamson/82	15.00	40.00
VJ Vincent Jackson/81	15.00	40.00
VM Vernand Morency/33	12.50	30.00
WR Walter Reyes/39	10.00	25.00

2005 Upper Deck Troy Aikman Heroes

COMPLETE SET (10)	10.00	25.00
COMMON CARD	1.25	3.00
STATED ODDS 1:12 HOB, 1:24 RET		
UNPRICED AUTOGRAPH PRINT RUN 5		

2005 Upper Deck Troy Aikman Heroes Jerseys

COMMON CARD	40.00	80.00
STATED PRINT RUN 25 SER.#'d SETS		

2005 Upper Deck LAPD

These cards were produced by Upper Deck but issued by the Los Angeles Police Department during the 2005 NFL season. Each card appears to be a standard issue 2005 Upper Deck card on the front but the cardback has been re-created to include a safety message, a new card number, and the LAPD logo. Each NFL team is represented in the set by one player.

COMPLETE SET (32)	12.50	25.00
1 Anquan Boldin	.30	.75
2 DeAngelo Hall	.30	.75
3 Eric Moulds	.30	.75
4 Steve Smith	.50	1.25
5 Rex Grossman	.30	.75
6 Chad Johnson	.30	.75
7 Roy Williams S	.50	1.25
8 John Lynch	.30	.75
9 Kevin Jones	.60	1.50
10 Javon Walker	.30	.75
11 Domanick Davis	.30	.75
12 Peyton Manning	1.00	2.50
13 Byron Leftwich	.50	1.25
14 Priest Holmes	.50	1.25
15 Ronnie Brown	1.50	4.00
16 Daunte Culpepper	.50	1.25
17 Adam Vinatieri	.50	1.25
18 Joe Horn	.30	.75
19 Jeremy Shockey	.50	1.25
20 Jevon Kearse	.30	.75
21 Jerome Bettis	.50	1.25
22 Torry Holt	.30	.75
23 Drew Brees	.30	.75
24 Alex Smith QB	1.50	4.00
25 Matt Hasselbeck	.30	.75
26 Joey Galloway	.30	.75
27 Clinton Portis	.50	1.25
28 Kyle Boller	.30	.75
29 Steve McNair	.50	1.25
30 Kerry Collins	.30	.75
31 Jonathan Vilma	.30	.75
32 Braylon Edwards	.75	2.00

2005 Upper Deck Rookies National Convention

Upper Deck produced this set and distributed it at the 2005 National Sport Collectors Convention in Chicago. The set includes the top-6 2005 NFL draft picks along with the title "The National" printed on the cardfronts. The company made the cards available to collectors via a wrapper redemption program at their show booth and each card was serial numbered to 750-copies. Each player also signed just 5-cards.

COMPLETE SET (6)	20.00	40.00
UNPRICED AUTOS SER.#'d TO 5		
NFL1 Alex Smith QB	4.00	10.00
NFL2 Braylon Edwards	4.00	10.00
NFL3 Cedric Benson	3.00	8.00
NFL4 Aaron Rodgers	6.00	15.00
NFL5 Ronnie Brown	4.00	10.00
NFL6 Cadillac Williams	3.00	8.00

2006 Upper Deck

This 275-card set was released in August, 2006. The set was issued into the hobby in eight card packs, with an $2.99 SRP, which came 24 packs to a box. Cards numbered 1-200 are veteran players sequenced in alphabetical team order while cards 201-275 are all rookies. The rookies are broken into two subsets, both of which are in first name alphabetical order: Cards numbered 201-225 were inserted at a stated rate of one in eight while cards numbered 226-275 were inserted at a stated rate of one per pack.

COMPLETE SET (275)	150.00	300.00
COMP.SET w/o SP's (250)	30.00	60.00
COMP.SET w/o RC's (200)	12.00	30.00
201-225 ROOKIE ODDS 1:8		
226-275 ROOKIE ODDS 1:1		
1 Larry Fitzgerald	.30	.75
2 Anquan Boldin	.25	.60
3 J.J. Arrington	.20	.50
4 Kurt Warner	.30	.75
5 Neil Rackers	.20	.50
6 Edgerrin James	.25	.60
7 Michael Vick	.30	.75
8 Alge Crumpler	.25	.60
9 Warrick Dunn	.25	.60
10 Michael Jenkins	.25	.60
11 Roddy White	.25	.60
12 DeAngelo Hall	.25	.60
13 Jamal Lewis	.25	.60
14 Derrick Mason	.25	.60
15 Todd Heap	.25	.60
16 Kyle Boller	.25	.60
17 Ray Lewis	.30	.75
18 Ed Reed	.25	.60
19 Willis McGahee	.25	.60
20 Lee Evans	.25	.60
21 J.P. Losman	.25	.60
22 Rashad Baker	.20	.50
23 Takeo Spikes	.20	.50
24 Aaron Schobel	.20	.50
25 Steve Smith	.30	.75
26 Jake Delhomme	.25	.60
27 DeShaun Foster	.25	.60
28 Keary Colbert	.20	.50
29 Julius Peppers	.25	.60
30 Ma'Ake Kemoeatu	.20	.50
31 Rex Grossman	.25	.60
32 Muhsin Muhammad	.25	.60
33 Brian Urlacher	.30	.75
34 Thomas Jones	.25	.60
35 Cedric Benson	.25	.60
36 Nathan Vasher	.20	.50
37 Rudi Johnson	.25	.60
38 Chad Johnson	.25	.60
39 T.J. Houshmandzadeh	.25	.60
40 Chris Henry	.20	.50
41 Deltha O'Neal	.20	.50
42 Odell Thurman	.20	.50
43 Carson Palmer	.30	.75
44 Charlie Frye	.25	.60
45 Reuben Droughns	.25	.60
46 Braylon Edwards	.25	.60
47 Kellen Winslow Jr.	.25	.60
48 Steve Heiden	.20	.50
49 Joe Jurevicius	.20	.50
50 Drew Bledsoe	.30	.75
51 Julius Jones	.20	.50
52 Terrell Owens	.30	.75
53 Terry Glenn	.25	.60
54 Jason Witten	.30	.75
55 DeMarcus Ware	.25	.60
56 Roy Williams S	.25	.60
57 Jake Plummer	.25	.60
58 Tatum Bell	.20	.50
59 Al Wilson	.20	.50
60 Rod Smith	.25	.60
61 Ashley Lelie	.20	.50
62 Champ Bailey	.25	.60
63 Javon Walker	.25	.60
64 Jon Kitna	.20	.50
65 Kevin Jones	.25	.60
66 Roy Williams WR	.25	.60
67 Mike Williams	.20	.50
68 Marcus Pollard	.20	.50
69 Dre Bly	.20	.50
70 Brett Favre	.60	1.50
71 Ahman Green	.25	.60
72 Donald Driver	.30	.75
73 Robert Ferguson	.20	.50
74 Bubba Franks	.20	.50
75 Kabeer Gbaja-Biamila	.25	.60
76 David Carr	.20	.50
77 Domanick Davis	.20	.50
78 Andre Johnson	.30	.75
79 Eric Moulds	.20	.50
80 Jeb Putzier	.20	.50
81 Dunta Robinson	.20	.50
82 Peyton Manning	.50	1.25
83 Dominic Rhodes	.25	.60
84 Reggie Wayne	.25	.60
85 Marvin Harrison	.30	.75
86 Dallas Clark	.25	.60
87 Dwight Freeney	.25	.60
88 Bob Sanders	.25	.60
89 Byron Leftwich	.25	.60
90 Fred Taylor	.25	.60
91 Greg Jones	.20	.50
92 Ernest Wilford	.20	.50
93 John Henderson	.20	.50
94 Matt Jones	.20	.50
95 Trent Green	.25	.60
96 Larry Johnson	.25	.60
97 Priest Holmes	.25	.60
98 Eddie Kennison	.20	.50
99 Tony Gonzalez	.25	.60
100 Dante Hall	.25	.60
101 Daunte Culpepper	.25	.60
102 Ronnie Brown	.30	.75
103 Marty Booker	.20	.50
104 Chris Chambers	.25	.60
105 Randy McMichael	.20	.50
106 Zach Thomas	.30	.75
107 Brad Johnson	.25	.60
108 Chester Taylor	.25	.60
109 Antoine Winfield	.20	.50
110 Koren Robinson	.20	.50

111 Travis Taylor .20 .50
112 Darren Sharper .25 .60
113 Tom Brady .50 1.25
114 Corey Dillon .25 .60
115 Deion Branch .25 .60
116 Reche Caldwell .20 .50
117 Ben Watson .20 .50
118 Tedy Bruschi .30 .75
119 Rodney Harrison .20 .50
120 Drew Brees .30 .75
121 Deuce McAllister .25 .60
122 Joe Horn .25 .60
123 Donte Stallworth .20 .50
124 Devery Henderson .20 .50
125 Will Smith .20 .50
126 Eli Manning .40 1.00
127 Tiki Barber .30 .75
128 Plaxico Burress .25 .60
129 Amani Toomer .25 .60
130 Jeremy Shockey .30 .75
131 Michael Strahan .25 .60
132 Osi Umenyiora .25 .60
133 Chad Pennington .25 .60
134 Curtis Martin .30 .75
135 Justin McCareins .20 .50
136 Laveranues Coles .20 .50
137 Jonathan Vilma .25 .60
138 Shaun Ellis .20 .50
139 Aaron Brooks .25 .60
140 LaMont Jordan .25 .60
141 Randy Moss .30 .75
142 Jerry Porter .20 .50
143 Doug Gabriel .20 .50
144 Derrick Burgess .20 .50
145 Donovan McNabb .30 .75
146 Brian Westbrook .25 .60
147 Jevon Kearse .25 .60
148 Reggie Brown .20 .50
149 L.J. Smith .20 .50
150 Brian Dawkins .25 .60
151 Ben Roethlisberger .40 1.00
152 Willie Parker .25 .60
153 Hines Ward .30 .75
154 Cedrick Wilson .20 .50
155 Heath Miller .25 .60
156 Joey Porter .20 .50
157 Troy Polamalu .40 1.00
158 Philip Rivers .30 .75
159 LaDainian Tomlinson .30 .75
160 Keenan McCardell .25 .60
161 Eric Parker .20 .50
162 Antonio Gates .30 .75
163 Shawne Merriman .25 .60
164 Donnie Edwards .20 .50
165 Alex Smith QB .30 .75
166 Frank Gore .30 .75
167 Antonio Bryant .20 .50
168 Eric Johnson .20 .50
169 Arnaz Battle .20 .50
170 Bryant Young .20 .50
171 Matt Hasselbeck .25 .60
172 Shaun Alexander .25 .60
173 Darrell Jackson .25 .60
174 Etric Pruitt .20 .50
175 Julian Peterson .20 .50
176 Lofa Tatupu .25 .60
177 Marc Bulger .25 .60
178 Steven Jackson .30 .75
179 Torry Holt .25 .60
180 Kevin Curtis .25 .60
181 Isaac Bruce .25 .60
182 Leonard Little .20 .50
183 Chris Simms .25 .60
184 Cadillac Williams .25 .60
185 Joey Galloway .25 .60
186 Michael Clayton .20 .50
187 Derrick Brooks .25 .60
188 Ronde Barber .25 .60
189 Billy Volek .20 .50
190 Chris Brown .20 .50
191 Drew Bennett .25 .60
192 Ben Troupe .20 .50
193 David Givens .25 .60
194 Adam Jones .20 .50
195 Mark Brunell .25 .60
196 Clinton Portis .30 .75
197 Santana Moss .25 .60
198 Chris Cooley .25 .60
199 Antwaan Randle El .25 .60
200 Sean Taylor .30 .75
201 A.J. Hawk RC 2.50 6.00
202 Anthony Fasano RC 2.50 6.00
203 Brian Calhoun RC 1.50 4.00
204 Chad Greenway RC 2.50 6.00
205 Chad Jackson RC 1.50 4.00
206 DeAngelo Williams RC 3.00 8.00
207 D'Brickashaw Ferguson RC 2.50 6.00
208 Brodie Croyle RC 2.50 6.00
209 Haloti Ngata RC 2.50 6.00
210 Jay Cutler RC 5.00 12.00
211 Joseph Addai RC 2.50 6.00
212 Laurence Maroney RC 2.00 5.00
213 LenDale White RC 2.00 5.00
214 Maurice Drew RC 4.00 10.00
215 Mario Williams RC 2.50 6.00
216 Matt Leinart RC 2.50 6.00
217 Maurice Stovall RC 1.50 4.00
218 Michael Huff RC 2.00 5.00
219 Reggie Bush RC 5.00 12.00
220 Santonio Holmes RC 3.00 8.00
221 Sinorice Moss RC 2.50 6.00
222 Kellen Clemens RC 2.00 5.00
223 Tarvaris Jackson RC 2.50 6.00
224 Vernon Davis RC 3.00 8.00
225 Vince Young RC 3.00 8.00
226 Donte Whitner RC 1.00 2.50
227 Antonio Cromartie RC 1.00 2.50
228 Ashton Youboty RC .60 1.50
229 Bobby Carpenter RC .60 1.50
230 Brad Smith RC 1.00 2.50
231 Brandon Williams RC .60 1.50
232 Dominique Byrd RC .75 2.00
233 Brodrick Bunkley RC .75 2.00
234 Charlie Whitehurst RC 1.00 2.50
235 Demetrius Williams RC .75 2.00
236 Cory Rodgers RC .75 2.00
237 Daniel Bullocks RC 1.00 2.50
238 Manny Lawson RC .75 2.00
239 Darrell Hackney RC .75 2.00
240 Darryl Tapp RC .75 2.00
241 David Thomas RC .75 2.00
242 DeMeco Ryans RC 1.00 2.50
243 Derek Hagan RC .75 2.00
244 Devin Hester RC 1.50 4.00
245 D'Qwell Jackson RC .75 2.00
246 Brandon Marshall RC 1.00 2.50
247 Ernie Sims RC .75 2.00
248 Gabe Watson RC .60 1.50
249 Jason Allen RC .75 2.00
250 Greg Jennings RC 1.50 4.00
251 Marcus Vick RC .60 1.50
252 Jason Avant RC .60 1.50
253 Jeremy Bloom RC .75 2.00
254 Jerome Harrison RC 1.00 2.50
255 Joe Klopfenstein RC .60 1.50
256 Johnathan Joseph RC .75 2.00
257 Jimmy Williams RC 1.00 2.50
258 Kamerion Wimbley RC 1.00 2.50
259 Leon Washington RC .75 2.00
260 Marcedes Lewis RC 1.00 2.50
261 Marcus McNeill RC .75 2.00
262 Mathias Kiwanuka RC 1.00 2.50
263 Leonard Pope RC 1.00 2.50
264 Tamba Hali RC 1.00 2.50
265 Mike Hass RC .75 2.00
266 Omar Jacobs RC .60 1.50
267 Jerious Norwood RC .75 2.00
268 Owen Daniels RC 1.00 2.50
269 P.J. Daniels RC .60 1.50
270 Ray Edwards RC 1.00 2.50
271 Michael Robinson RC .75 2.00
272 Rocky McIntosh RC .75 2.00
273 Travis Wilson RC .60 1.50
274 Tye Hill RC .60 1.50
275 Thomas Howard RC .75 2.00

2006 Upper Deck Exclusive Edition Rookies

*EXCLUSIVE EDITION: .1X TO .25X
30-PER ROOKIE EDITION FAT PACK

2006 Upper Deck Target Exclusive Rookies

*SINGLES: .25X TO .6X BASIC CARDS
TWO PER SPECIAL TARGET PACKS
TARGET VERSION PHOTOS DIFFER

2006 Upper Deck Target Exclusive Rookies Autographs

RANDOM INSERTS IN TARGET PACKS
GOLD FOIL PRINTED ON FRONT
202 Anthony Fasano
210 Jay Cutler 150.00 300.00
211 Joseph Addai 75.00 150.00
216 Matt Leinart SP
219 Reggie Bush SP
225 Vince Young SP
232 Dominique Byrd
234 Charlie Whitehurst
235 Demetrius Williams
236 Cory Rodgers
239 Darrell Hackney
242 DeMeco Ryans
243 Derek Hagan
246 Brandon Marshall
247 Ernie Sims
250 Greg Jennings
254 Jerome Harrison
257 Jimmy Williams
259 Leon Washington
263 Leonard Pope
268 Owen Daniels

2006 Upper Deck UD Exclusive Gold

*VETS 1-200: 4X TO 10X BASIC CARDS
*ROOKIES 201-225: 1X TO 2.5X BASIC CARDS
*ROOKIES 226-275: 2.5X TO 6X BASIC CARDS
STATED PRINT RUN 100 SER.#'d SETS
219 Reggie Bush 12.00 30.00

2006 Upper Deck UD Exclusive Silver

*VETERANS 1-200: 6X TO 15X BASIC CARDS
*ROOKIES 201-225: 1.5X TO 4X BASIC CARDS
*ROOKIES 226-275: 4X TO 10X BASIC CARDS
STATED PRINT RUN 50 SER.#'d SETS
219 Reggie Bush 20.00 50.00

2006 Upper Deck 10 Sack Club

COMPLETE SET (10) 2.50 6.00
STATED ODDS 1:6
10SDB Derrick Burgess .50 1.25
10SDF Dwight Freeney .60 1.50
10SJP Joey Porter .50 1.25
10SJT Jason Taylor .60 1.50
10SKG Kabeer Gbaja-Biamila .60 1.50
10SMS Michael Strahan .60 1.50
10SOU Osi Umenyiora .60 1.50
10SPE Julius Peppers .60 1.50
10SSM Shawne Merriman .60 1.50
10SSR Simeon Rice .50 1.25

2006 Upper Deck 1000 Yard Receiving Club

COMPLETE SET (15) 4.00 10.00
STATED ODDS 1:6
1KREAB Anquan Boldin .60 1.50
1KRECC Chris Chambers .60 1.50
1KRECJ Chad Johnson .60 1.50
1KREHW Hines Ward .75 2.00
1KREJG Joey Galloway .60 1.50
1KREJW Javon Walker .60 1.50
1KRELF Larry Fitzgerald .75 2.00
1KREMH Marvin Harrison .75 2.00
1KREPB Plaxico Burress .60 1.50
1KRERM Randy Moss .75 2.00
1KRERW Reggie Wayne .60 1.50
1KRESM Santana Moss .60 1.50
1KRESS Steve Smith .75 2.00
1KRETH Torry Holt .60 1.50
1KRETO Terrell Owens .75 2.00

2006 Upper Deck 1000 Yard Rushing Club

COMPLETE SET (20) 8.00 20.00
STATED ODDS 1:4.5
1KRAG Ahman Green .60 1.50
1KRCD Corey Dillon .60 1.50
1KRCM Curtis Martin .75 2.00
1KRCP Clinton Portis .75 2.00
1KRCW Cadillac Williams .60 1.50
1KRDM Deuce McAllister .60 1.50
1KREJ Edgerrin James .60 1.50
1KRJL Jamal Lewis .60 1.50
1KRJO LaMont Jordan .60 1.50
1KRKJ Kevin Jones .50 1.25
1KRLJ Larry Johnson .60 1.50
1KRLT LaDainian Tomlinson .75 2.00
1KRPH Priest Holmes .60 1.50
1KRRJ Rudi Johnson .60 1.50
1KRSA Shaun Alexander .60 1.50
1KRSJ Steven Jackson .75 2.00
1KRTB Tiki Barber .75 2.00
1KRWD Warrick Dunn .60 1.50
1KRWM Willis McGahee .60 1.50
1KRWP Willie Parker .60 1.50

2006 Upper Deck 3000 Yard Passing Club

COMPLETE SET (20) 8.00 20.00
STATED ODDS 1:4.5
3KPAB Aaron Brooks .60 1.50
3KPBF Brett Favre 1.50 4.00
3KPBR Drew Brees .75 2.00
3KPBU Marc Bulger .60 1.50
3KPCA David Carr .50 1.25
3KPCP Carson Palmer .75 2.00
3KPDB Drew Bledsoe .75 2.00
3KPDC Daunte Culpepper .60 1.50
3KPDM Donovan McNabb .75 2.00
3KPEM Eli Manning 1.00 2.50
3KPJD Jake Delhomme .60 1.50
3KPJH Joey Harrington .50 1.25
3KPJP Jake Plummer .60 1.50
3KPKW Kurt Warner .75 2.00
3KPMB Mark Brunell .60 1.50
3KPMH Matt Hasselbeck .60 1.50
3KPPM Peyton Manning 1.25 3.00
3KPSM Steve McNair .60 1.50
3KPTB Tom Brady 1.25 3.00
3KPTG Trent Green .60 1.50

2006 Upper Deck All Upper Deck Team

TWO PER RETAIL FAT PACK
AC Alge Crumpler .60 1.50
AG Antonio Gates .75 2.00
AW Al Wilson .50 1.25
BA Tiki Barber .75 2.00
BF Brett Favre 1.50 4.00
BR Ben Roethlisberger 1.00 2.50
BS Bob Sanders .60 1.50
BU Brian Urlacher .75 2.00
CB Champ Bailey .60 1.50
CJ Chad Johnson .60 1.50
CP Carson Palmer .75 2.00
DB Derrick Brooks .60 1.50
DF Dwight Freeney .60 1.50
DM Donovan McNabb .75 2.00
EJ Edgerrin James .60 1.50
JM Jerome Mathis .50 1.25
JP Julius Peppers .60 1.50
JS Jeremy Shockey .75 2.00
LB Lance Briggs .60 1.50
LF Larry Fitzgerald .75 2.00
LJ Larry Johnson .60 1.50
LT LaDainian Tomlinson .75 2.00
MS Mack Strong .40 1.00
MV Michael Vick .75 2.00
NR Neil Rackers .50 1.25
NV Nathan Vasher .50 1.25
OU Osi Umenyiora .60 1.50
OW Terrell Owens .75 2.00
PM Peyton Manning 1.25 3.00
PO Clinton Portis .75 2.00
RB Ronde Barber .60 1.50
RJ Rudi Johnson .60 1.50
RM Randy Moss .75 2.00
RS Richard Seymour .50 1.25
SA Shaun Alexander .60 1.50
SM Santana Moss .60 1.50
SS Steve Smith .75 2.00
ST Sean Taylor .75 2.00
TB Tom Brady 1.25 3.00
TG Tony Gonzalez .60 1.50
TH Torry Holt .60 1.50
TP Troy Polamalu 1.00 2.50

2006 Upper Deck Collect The Rookies Game

1 Reggie Bush .50 1.25
2 Jay Cutler .50 1.25
3 Santonio Holmes .30 .75
4 Matt Leinart .25 .60
5 DeAngelo Williams .30 .75
6 Vince Young .30 .75

2006 Upper Deck Fantasy Top 25

COMPLETE SET (25) 15.00 40.00
STATED ODDS 1:4
F25AB Anquan Boldin .75 2.00
F25BR Tom Brady 1.50 4.00
F25CJ Chad Johnson .75 2.00
F25CP Carson Palmer 1.00 2.50
F25CW Cadillac Williams .75 2.00
F25DM Donovan McNabb 1.00 2.50
F25DW DeAngelo Williams .75 2.00
F25EJ Edgerrin James .75 2.00
F25EM Eli Manning 1.25 3.00
F25HA Matt Hasselbeck .75 2.00
F25JO LaMont Jordan .75 2.00
F25LF Larry Fitzgerald 1.00 2.50
F25LJ Larry Johnson .75 2.00
F25LT LaDainian Tomlinson 1.00 2.50
F25MH Marvin Harrison 1.00 2.50
F25PM Peyton Manning 1.50 4.00
F25PO Clinton Portis 1.00 2.50
F25RB Reggie Bush 1.25 3.00
F25RJ Rudi Johnson .75 2.00
F25RM Randy Moss 1.00 2.50
F25SA Shaun Alexander .75 2.00
F25SS Steve Smith 1.00 2.50
F25TB Tiki Barber 1.00 2.50
F25TG Trent Green .75 2.00
F25TH Torry Holt .75 2.00

2006 Upper Deck Game Jerseys

STATED ODDS 1:24
GJAB Aaron Brooks 3.00 8.00
GJAC Alge Crumpler 3.00 8.00
GJBA Tiki Barber 4.00 10.00
GJBD Brian Dawkins 4.00 10.00
GJBE Braylon Edwards 4.00 10.00
GJBL Drew Bledsoe 4.00 10.00
GJBR Tom Brady 6.00 15.00
GJBU Brian Urlacher 4.00 10.00
GJCA David Carr 3.00 8.00
GJCD Corey Dillon 3.00 8.00
GJCF Charlie Frye 3.00 8.00
GJCW Cadillac Williams 3.00 8.00
GJDB Drew Brees 4.00 10.00
GJDC Daunte Culpepper 4.00 10.00
GJDM Deuce McAllister 4.00 10.00
GJEM Eli Manning 6.00 15.00
GJER Ed Reed 3.00 8.00
GJJJ Julius Jones 4.00 10.00
GJJO LaMont Jordan 3.00 8.00
GJJP Julius Peppers 3.00 8.00
GJJS Jeremy Shockey 4.00 10.00
GJKJ Kevin Jones 4.00 10.00
GJKO Kyle Orton 3.00 8.00
GJLE Byron Leftwich 4.00 10.00
GJLF Larry Fitzgerald 3.00 8.00
GJLJ Larry Johnson 5.00 12.00
GJMB Marc Bulger SP 10.00 25.00
GJMH Matt Hasselbeck 4.00 10.00
GJMW Mike Williams 3.00 8.00
GJPB Plaxico Burress 3.00 8.00
GJPH Priest Holmes 3.00 8.00
GJPL Jake Plummer 3.00 8.00
GJPM Peyton Manning 6.00 15.00
GJRB Ronnie Brown 4.00 10.00
GJRJ Rudi Johnson 3.00 8.00
GJSJ Steven Jackson 4.00 10.00
GJSS Steve Smith 4.00 10.00
GJTB Tatum Bell 3.00 8.00
GJTG Tony Gonzalez 3.00 8.00
GJTO Terrell Owens 4.00 10.00
GJTW Troy Williamson 3.00 8.00
GJWM Willis McGahee 4.00 10.00

2006 Upper Deck Gridiron Debut

RANDOM INSERTS IN WAL-MART PACKS
GDAF Anthony Fasano 1.00 2.50
GDAH A.J. Hawk 1.00 2.50
GDAV Jason Avant .60 1.50
GDBB Brodrick Bunkley .75 2.00
GDBC Brian Calhoun .60 1.50
GDBM Brandon Marshall 1.00 2.50
GDBW Brandon Williams .60 1.50
GDCJ Chad Jackson .60 1.50
GDCR Brodie Croyle 1.00 2.50
GDCW Charlie Whitehurst 1.00 2.50
GDDB Dominique Byrd .75 2.00
GDDF D'Brickashaw Ferguson 1.00 2.50
GDDW DeAngelo Williams 1.25 3.00
GDES Ernie Sims .75 2.00
GDHA Derek Hagan .75 2.00
GDHN Haloti Ngata 1.00 2.50
GDJA Joseph Addai 1.00 2.50
GDJC Jay Cutler 2.00 5.00
GDJK Joe Klopfenstein .60 1.50
GDJN Jerious Norwood .75 2.00
GDKC Kellen Clemens .75 2.00
GDKW Kamerion Wimbley 1.00 2.50
GDLE Marcedes Lewis 1.00 2.50
GDLM Laurence Maroney .75 2.00
GDLP Leonard Pope 1.00 2.50
GDLW LenDale White .75 2.00
GDMD Maurice Drew 1.50 4.00
GDMH Michael Huff .75 2.00
GDML Matt Leinart 1.00 2.50
GDMR Michael Robinson .75 2.00
GDMS Maurice Stovall .60 1.50
GDMW Mario Williams 1.00 2.50
GDOJ Omar Jacobs .60 1.50
GDRB Reggie Bush 2.00 5.00
GDSH Santonio Holmes 1.25 3.00
GDSM Sinorice Moss 1.00 2.50
GDTJ Tarvaris Jackson 1.00 2.50
GDTW Travis Wilson .60 1.50
GDVD Vernon Davis 1.25 3.00
GDVY Vince Young 1.25 3.00
GDWA Leon Washington .75 2.00
GDWI Demetrius Williams .75 2.00

2006 Upper Deck Joe Theismann Heroes

COMPLETE SET (10) 12.00 30.00
COMMON CARD 1.50 4.00
STATED ODDS 1:24
UNPRICED AUTOS SER.#'d TO 5

2006 Upper Deck Joe Theismann Heroes Jerseys

COMMON CARD 35.00 60.00
STATED PRINT RUN 25 SER.#'d SETS

2006 Upper Deck Roger Staubach Heroes

COMPLETE SET (10) 12.00 30.00
COMMON CARD 1.50 4.00
STATED ODDS 1:24
UNPRICED AUTOS SER.#'d TO 5

2006 Upper Deck Roger Staubach Heroes Jerseys

COMMON CARD 40.00 80.00
STATED PRINT RUN 25 SER.#'d SETS

2006 Upper Deck Rookie Exclusive Rookie Photo Shoot Flashback

AB Anquan Boldin .30 .75
AJ Adam Jones .25 .60
AR Antrel Rolle .25 .60
AW Andrew Walter .25 .60
BL Byron Leftwich .30 .75
BU Brian Urlacher .40 1.00
CJ Chad Johnson .30 .75
CP Carson Palmer .40 1.00
CR Carlos Rogers .25 .60
CW Cadillac Williams .30 .75
DB Drew Brees .40 1.00
DC Daunte Culpepper .30 .75
DM Donovan McNabb .40 1.00
EJ Edgerrin James .30 .75
EM Eli Manning .50 1.25
FG Frank Gore .40 1.00
HW Hines Ward .40 1.00
JC Jason Campbell .30 .75
JG Joey Galloway .30 .75
JJ Julius Jones .25 .60
JL Jamal Lewis .30 .75
JP Jake Plummer .30 .75
KJ Kevin Jones .25 .60
KW Kellen Winslow .30 .75
LE Lee Evans .30 .75
LF Larry Fitzgerald .40 1.00
LJ Larry Johnson .30 .75
LT LaDainian Tomlinson .40 1.00
MC Mark Clayton .30 .75
MH Marvin Harrison .40 1.00
MJ Michael Jenkins .30 .75
MJ Matt Jones .25 .60
MV Michael Vick .40 1.00
PB Plaxico Burress .30 .75
PM Peyton Manning .60 1.50
PR Philip Rivers .40 1.00
RB Reggie Brown .25 .60
RB Ronnie Brown .40 1.00
RJ Rudi Johnson .30 .75
RO Ben Roethlisberger .50 1.25
RW Reggie Wayne .30 .75
SA Shaun Alexander .30 .75
SJ Steven Jackson .40 1.00
SM Santana Moss .30 .75
TH Torry Holt .30 .75
TW Troy Williamson .25 .60
WD Warrick Dunn .30 .75
WH Roddy White .30 .75
WI Reggie Williams .30 .75
WM Willis McGahee .30 .75

2006 Upper Deck Rookie Futures Jerseys

STATED ODDS 1:24 HOB
RFAH A.J. Hawk 4.00 10.00
RFBC Brian Calhoun 2.50 6.00
RFBM Brandon Marshall 4.00 10.00
RFBW Brandon Williams 2.50 6.00
RFCJ Chad Jackson 2.50 6.00
RFCW Charlie Whitehurst 4.00 10.00
RFDH Derek Hagan 3.00 8.00
RFDW DeAngelo Williams 5.00 12.00
RFJA Jason Avant 2.50 6.00
RFJK Joe Klopfenstein 2.50 6.00
RFJN Jerious Norwood 3.00 8.00
RFKC Kellen Clemens 3.00 8.00
RFLE Marcedes Lewis 4.00 10.00
RFLM Laurence Maroney 3.00 8.00
RFLW LenDale White 3.00 8.00
RFMD Maurice Drew 6.00 15.00
RFML Matt Leinart 4.00 10.00
RFMR Michael Robinson 3.00 8.00
RFMS Maurice Stovall 2.50 6.00
RFMW Mario Williams 4.00 10.00
RFOJ Omar Jacobs 2.50 6.00
RFRB Reggie Bush 8.00 20.00
RFSH Santonio Holmes 5.00 12.00
RFSM Sinorice Moss 4.00 10.00
RFTJ Tarvaris Jackson 4.00 10.00
RFTW Travis Wilson 2.50 6.00
RFVD Vernon Davis 5.00 12.00
RFVY Vince Young 5.00 12.00
RFWA Leon Washington 3.00 8.00
RFWI Demetrius Williams 3.00 8.00

2006 Upper Deck Rookie Futures Jerseys Dual

BL Matt Leinart 15.00 40.00
Reggie Bush SP
BW LenDale White 20.00 50.00
Reggie Bush SP
CJ Kellen Clemens 8.00 20.00
Omar Jacobs
DL Marcedes Lewis 10.00 25.00
Maurice Drew
DR Michael Robinson 10.00 25.00
Vernon Davis
HH A.J. Hawk 12.00 30.00
Santonio Holmes
HW Derek Hagan 8.00 20.00
Travis Wilson
JM Chad Jackson 8.00 20.00
Sinorice Moss
LY Matt Leinart 10.00 25.00
Vince Young SP
MW Brandon Williams 8.00 20.00
Brandon Marshall
NC Brian Calhoun 8.00 20.00
Jerious Norwood
WM DeAngelo Williams 12.00 30.00
Laurence Maroney

2006 Upper Deck Rookie Futures Jersey Autographs

STATED PRINT RUN 10-100
RFAH A.J. Hawk/100 15.00 40.00
RFBC Brian Calhoun/100 10.00 25.00
RFBM Brandon Marshall/100 15.00 40.00
RFBW Brandon Williams/100 10.00 25.00
RFCJ Chad Jackson/100 10.00 25.00
RFCW Charlie Whitehurst/100 15.00 40.00
RFDH Derek Hagan/100 12.00 30.00
RFDW DeAngelo Williams/100 20.00 50.00
RFJA Jason Avant/100 10.00 25.00
RFJK Joe Klopfenstein/100 10.00 25.00
RFJN Jerious Norwood/100 12.00 30.00
RFKC Kellen Clemens/100 12.00 30.00
RFLE Marcedes Lewis/25 30.00 60.00
RFLM Laurence Maroney/100 12.00 30.00
RFLW LenDale White/100 12.00 30.00
RFMD Maurice Drew/100 25.00 60.00
RFML Matt Leinart/25 30.00 80.00
RFMR Michael Robinson/100 12.00 30.00
RFMS Maurice Stovall/100 10.00 25.00
RFMW Mario Williams/35 50.00 100.00
RFOJ Omar Jacobs/100 10.00 25.00
RFRB Reggie Bush/10
RFSH Santonio Holmes/100 30.00 60.00
RFSM Sinorice Moss/100 15.00 40.00
RFTJ Tarvaris Jackson/100 15.00 40.00
RFTW Travis Wilson/100
RFVD Vernon Davis/100 20.00 50.00
RFVY Vince Young/50 75.00 150.00
RFWA Leon Washington/100 20.00 50.00
RFWI Demetrius Williams/100 12.00 30.00

2006 Upper Deck Rookie Futures Jersey Dual Autographs

STATED PRINT RUN 10-50
SERIAL #'d UNDER 25 NOT PRICED
BW LenDale White/25 60.00 150.00
Reggie Bush
CJ Kellen Clemens/50 15.00 40.00
Omar Jacobs
DL Marcedes Lewis/25 30.00 80.00
Maurice Drew
DR Michael Robinson/50 30.00 80.00
Vernon Davis
HH A.J. Hawk/50 50.00 120.00
Santonio Holmes
HW Derek Hagan/50 15.00 40.00
Travis Wilson
JM Chad Jackson/50 20.00 50.00
Sinorice Moss
LY Matt Leinart/25 40.00 100.00
Vince Young
MW Brandon Williams/50 25.00 60.00
Brandon Marshall
NC Brian Calhoun/50 20.00 50.00
Jerious Norwood
WM DeAngelo Williams/50 40.00 100.00
Laurence Maroney

2006 Upper Deck XL Jerseys

RETAIL PACK STATED ODDS 1:288
AUTO PATCHES TOO SCARCE TO PRICE
XLAG Antonio Gates 10.00 25.00
XLBA Tiki Barber 10.00 25.00
XLBD Brian Dawkins 10.00 25.00
XLBE Braylon Edwards 10.00 25.00
XLBF Brett Favre 30.00 60.00
XLBL Drew Bledsoe 10.00 25.00
XLBR Ben Roethlisberger 30.00 60.00
XLCP Carson Palmer 10.00 25.00
XLCW Cadillac Williams 10.00 25.00
XLDB Drew Brees 10.00 25.00
XLDF DeShaun Foster 8.00 20.00
XLDG David Givens 6.00 15.00
XLEM Eli Manning 15.00 40.00
XLGJ Greg Jones 6.00 15.00
XLHO T.J. Houshmandzadeh 8.00 20.00
XLHW Hines Ward 10.00 25.00
XLJJ Julius Jones 10.00 25.00
XLJO LaMont Jordan 8.00 20.00
XLJP Julius Peppers 10.00 25.00
XLKC Kevin Curtis 6.00 15.00
XLKJ Keyshawn Johnson 8.00 20.00
XLKO Kyle Orton 8.00 20.00
XLKW Kurt Warner 8.00 20.00
XLLE Byron Leftwich 10.00 25.00
XLLJ Larry Johnson 10.00 25.00
XLLT LaDainian Tomlinson 12.00 30.00
XLMV Michael Vick 10.00 25.00
XLPL Jake Plummer 8.00 20.00
XLPM Peyton Manning 20.00 50.00
XLPR Philip Rivers 10.00 25.00
XLRB Ronnie Brown 10.00 25.00
XLRO Ronde Barber 8.00 20.00
XLRW Reggie Wayne 8.00 20.00
XLTB Tom Brady 15.00 40.00
XLTE Tedy Bruschi 10.00 25.00
XLTW Troy Williamson 8.00 20.00

2006 Upper Deck Employee Quad Jerseys

LJDJSCRB LeBron James 50.00 100.00
Derek Jeter
Sidney Crosby
Reggie Bush

2006 Upper Deck National NFL

COMPLETE SET (6) 5.00 10.00
NFL1 Peyton Manning 1.00 2.50
NFL2 Ben Roethlisberger .75 2.00
NFL3 Brett Favre 1.25 3.00
NFL4 Tom Brady 1.00 2.50
NFL5 Alex Smith QB .60 1.50
NFL6 Donovan McNabb .60 1.50

2006 Upper Deck National NFL VIP

COMPLETE SET (6) 6.00 12.00
1 Cedric Benson .75 2.00
2 Michael Vick 1.00 2.50
3 Tom Brady 1.50 4.00
4 Shaun Alexander .75 2.00
5 Cadillac Williams .75 2.00
6 Aaron Rodgers 2.00 5.00

2006 Upper Deck National Southern California

COMPLETE SET (6) 5.00 12.00
SoCal3 LaDainian Tomlinson .75 2.00
SoCal4 Philip Rivers .75 2.00

2006 Upper Deck Tuff Stuff

1 Reggie Bush 1.25 3.00
2 Matt Leinart .75 2.00
3 Vince Young 1.00 2.50
4 Jay Cutler .75 2.00
13 Tom Brady .60 1.50
14 Ben Roethlisberger .60 1.50
15 Peyton Manning .75 2.00
16 Brett Favre .75 2.00
17 Santonio Holmes .60 1.50
18 Mario Williams .40 1.00
19 DeAngelo Williams .75 2.00
20 Laurence Maroney .75 2.00
29 Kellen Clemens .40 1.00
30 Vernon Davis .60 1.50
31 Joseph Addai .75 2.00
32 Chad Jackson .50 1.25
33 Greg Jennings .40 1.00
34 A.J. Hawk .75 2.00
35 Maurice Drew .75 2.00
36 Devin Hester .60 1.50
41 LaDainian Tomlinson .50 1.25
42 Tony Romo 1.00 2.50
43 Drew Brees .40 1.00
44 Larry Johnson .40 1.00

2007 Upper Deck

This 300-card set was released in August, 2007. The set was issued into the hobby in fifteen-card packs, with an $2.99 SRP, which came 16 packs to a box. Cards numbered 1-200 feature veterans while cards 201-300 feature 2007 NFL rookies. Those Rookie Cards were inserted at stated rates of one per hobby pack and one per eight retail packs.

COMPLETE SET (300) 150.00 250.00
COMP.SET w/o RC's (200) 12.50 30.00
ROOKIE ODDS 1:1 HOB, 1:8 RET
1 Karlos Dansby .20 .50
2 Edgerrin James .25 .60
3 Matt Leinart .25 .60
4 Larry Fitzgerald .30 .75
5 Anquan Boldin .25 .60
6 Joe Horn .25 .60
7 Michael Jenkins .25 .60
8 Michael Vick .30 .75
9 Warrick Dunn .25 .60
10 Alge Crumpler .25 .60
11 Derrick Mason .25 .60
12 Ed Reed .25 .60
13 Willis McGahee .25 .60
14 Steve McNair .25 .60
15 Mark Clayton .25 .60
16 Todd Heap .20 .50
17 Ray Lewis .30 .75
18 J.P. Losman .20 .50
19 Peerless Price .20 .50
20 Lee Evans .25 .60
21 Anthony Thomas .20 .50
22 David Carr .25 .60
23 DeAngelo Williams .30 .75
24 Julius Peppers .25 .60
25 Jake Delhomme .25 .60
26 DeShaun Foster .25 .60
27 Steve Smith .25 .60
28 Muhsin Muhammad .25 .60
29 Rex Grossman .25 .60
30 Desmond Clark .20 .50
31 Devin Hester .30 .75
32 Cedric Benson .25 .60
33 Bernard Berrian .20 .50
34 Brian Urlacher .30 .75
35 Justin Smith .20 .50
36 T.J. Houshmandzadeh .25 .60
37 Carson Palmer .25 .60
38 Rudi Johnson .25 .60
39 Chad Johnson .25 .60
40 Kamerion Wimbley .20 .50
41 Charlie Frye .25 .60
42 Tim Carter .20 .50
43 Jamal Lewis .25 .60
44 Kellen Winslow .25 .60
45 Braylon Edwards .25 .60
46 Roy Williams S .25 .60
47 Marion Barber .30 .75
48 Jason Witten .30 .75
49 Terry Glenn .25 .60
50 Demarcus Ware .25 .60
51 Tony Romo .40 1.00
52 Julius Jones .20 .50
53 Terrell Owens .30 .75
54 Mike Bell .25 .60
55 John Lynch .25 .60
56 Rod Smith .25 .60
57 Travis Henry .25 .60
58 Jay Cutler .30 .75
59 Javon Walker .25 .60
60 Champ Bailey .25 .60
61 Tatum Bell .20 .50
62 Mike Furrey .25 .60
63 Jon Kitna .20 .50
64 Kevin Jones .20 .50
65 Roy Williams WR .25 .60
66 Bubba Franks .20 .50
67 Charles Woodson .30 .75
68 Brett Favre .60 1.50
69 Donald Driver .30 .75
70 A.J. Hawk .25 .60
71 Ahman Green .25 .60
72 DeMeco Ryans .25 .60
73 Matt Schaub .25 .60
74 Andre Johnson .25 .60
75 Mario Williams .25 .60
76 Ron Dayne .25 .60
77 Dwight Freeney .25 .60
78 Dallas Clark .20 .50
79 Peyton Manning .50 1.25
80 Marvin Harrison .30 .75
81 Reggie Wayne .25 .60
82 Joseph Addai .25 .60
83 Matt Jones .25 .60
84 David Garrard .25 .60
85 Ernest Wilford .20 .50
86 Reggie Williams .25 .60
87 Maurice Jones-Drew .30 .75
88 Fred Taylor .25 .60
89 Byron Leftwich .25 .60
90 Eddie Kennison .20 .50
91 Samie Parker .20 .50
92 Derrick Johnson .20 .50
93 Trent Green .25 .60
94 Larry Johnson .20 .50
95 Tony Gonzalez .25 .60
96 Damon Huard .25 .60
97 Zach Thomas .25 .60
98 Daunte Culpepper .25 .60
99 Ronnie Brown .25 .60
100 Jason Taylor .25 .60
101 Chris Chambers .25 .60
102 Antoine Winfield .20 .50
103 Ryan Longwell .20 .50
104 Chester Taylor .20 .50
105 Tarvaris Jackson .20 .50
106 Troy Williamson .20 .50
107 Rodney Harrison .20 .50
108 Randy Moss .30 .75
109 Stephen Gostkowski .20 .50
110 Donte Stallworth .25 .60
111 Tom Brady .50 1.25
112 Laurence Maroney .25 .60
113 Ben Watson .20 .50
114 Tedy Bruschi .30 .75
115 Charles Grant .20 .50
116 Michael Lewis .20 .50
117 Drew Brees .30 .75
118 Marques Colston .30 .75
119 Reggie Bush .30 .75
120 Deuce McAllister .25 .60
121 Amani Toomer .25 .60
122 Reuben Droughns .25 .60
123 Michael Strahan .25 .60
124 Plaxico Burress .25 .60
125 Osi Umenyiora .25 .60
126 Eli Manning .30 .75
127 Jeremy Shockey .25 .60
128 Brandon Jacobs .25 .60
129 Jonathan Vilma .25 .60
130 Jerricho Cotchery .25 .60
131 Chris Baker .20 .50
132 Chad Pennington .25 .60
133 Leon Washington .25 .60
134 Laveranues Coles .20 .50
135 Nnamdi Asomugha .30 .75
136 Dominic Rhodes .25 .60
137 Warren Sapp .25 .60
138 Justin Fargas .20 .50
139 Ronald Curry .25 .60
140 Brian Dawkins .25 .60
141 L.J. Smith .20 .50
142 Mike Patterson .20 .50
143 Brian Westbrook .25 .60
144 Reggie Brown .20 .50
145 Donovan McNabb .30 .75
146 Hines Ward .30 .75
147 James Farrior .20 .50
148 Ike Taylor .20 .50
149 Santonio Holmes .25 .60
150 Ben Roethlisberger .30 .75
151 Willie Parker .25 .60
152 Troy Polamalu .30 .75
153 Michael Turner .30 .75
154 Vincent Jackson .25 .60
155 Nate Kaeding .20 .50
156 Philip Rivers .30 .75
157 Antonio Gates .30 .75
158 Shawne Merriman .25 .60
159 LaDainian Tomlinson .30 .75
160 Arnaz Battle .20 .50
161 Nate Clements .20 .50
162 Ashley Lelie .25 .60
163 Alex Smith QB .30 .75
164 Frank Gore .30 .75
165 Vernon Davis .25 .60
166 Mack Strong .20 .50
167 Lofa Tatupu .25 .60
168 Maurice Morris .20 .50
169 Bobby Engram .20 .50
170 Matt Hasselbeck .25 .60
171 Shaun Alexander .25 .60
172 Deion Branch .25 .60
173 Leonard Little .20 .50
174 Pisa Tinoisamoa .20 .50
175 Drew Bennett .20 .50
176 Steven Jackson .30 .75
177 Marc Bulger .25 .60
178 Torry Holt .25 .60
179 Isaac Bruce .25 .60
180 Ronde Barber .25 .60
181 Chris Simms .20 .50
182 Mike Alstott .25 .60
183 Derrick Brooks .25 .60
184 Cadillac Williams .25 .60
185 Michael Clayton .20 .50
186 Joey Galloway .25 .60
187 Brandon Jones .20 .50
188 Keith Bulluck .20 .50
189 Nick Harper .20 .50
190 David Givens .20 .50
191 Vince Young .25 .60
192 LenDale White .25 .60
193 Mark Brunell .25 .60
194 Sean Taylor .30 .75
195 Chris Cooley .25 .60
196 Brandon Lloyd .25 .60
197 Jason Campbell .25 .60
198 Clinton Portis .25 .60

199 Santana Moss	.25	.60
200 Antwaan Randle El	.20	.50
201 Levi Brown RC	1.50	4.00
202 Alan Branch RC	1.25	3.00
203 Buster Davis RC	1.25	3.00
204 Steve Breaston RC	1.50	4.00
205 Justin Blalock RC	1.00	2.50
206 Chris Houston RC	1.25	3.00
207 Laurent Robinson RC	1.50	4.00
208 Ben Grubbs RC	1.25	3.00
209 Troy Smith RC	1.50	4.00
210 Yamon Figurs RC	1.00	2.50
211 Le'Ron McClain RC	1.50	4.00
212 Trent Edwards RC	1.50	4.00
213 Dwayne Wright RC	1.25	3.00
214 Jon Beason RC	1.25	3.00
215 Ryan Kalil RC	1.25	3.00
216 Dan Bazuin RC	1.25	3.00
217 Garrett Wolfe RC	1.00	2.50
218 Michael Okwo RC	1.25	3.00
219 Chris Leak RC	1.25	3.00
220 Leon Hall RC	1.25	3.00
221 Jeff Rowe RC	1.00	2.50
222 Eric Wright RC	1.50	4.00
223 Isaiah Stanback RC	1.00	2.50
224 Anthony Spencer RC	1.50	4.00
225 Jarvis Moss RC	1.25	3.00
226 Tim Crowder RC	1.50	4.00
227 Ikaika Alama-Francis RC	1.50	4.00
228 Justin Harrell RC	1.25	3.00
229 Brandon Jackson RC	1.25	3.00
230 James Jones RC	1.50	4.00
231 Jacoby Jones RC	1.50	4.00
232 Tony Ugoh RC	1.25	3.00
233 Daymeion Hughes RC	1.25	3.00
234 Reggie Nelson RC	1.25	3.00
235 Justin Durant RC	1.25	3.00
236 Turk McBride RC	1.25	3.00
237 DeMarcus Tank Tyler RC	1.00	2.50
238 Kolby Smith RC	1.25	3.00
239 Lorenzo Booker RC	1.25	3.00
240 Marcus McCauley RC	1.25	3.00
241 Brandon Meriweather RC	1.50	4.00
242 Antonio Pittman RC	1.00	2.50
243 Usama Young RC	1.25	3.00
244 Aaron Ross RC	1.50	4.00
245 Zak DeOssie RC	1.25	3.00
246 Darrelle Revis RC	2.50	6.00
247 David Harris RC	1.25	3.00
248 Zach Miller RC	1.50	4.00
249 Johnnie Lee Higgins RC	1.25	3.00
250 Michael Bush RC	1.50	4.00
251 Quentin Moses RC	1.25	3.00
252 Victor Abiamiri RC	1.50	4.00
253 Tony Hunt RC	1.00	2.50
254 Stewart Bradley RC	1.25	3.00
255 Lawrence Timmons RC	1.50	4.00
256 LaMarr Woodley RC	1.50	4.00
257 Matt Spaeth RC	1.50	4.00
258 Eric Weddle RC	1.50	4.00
259 Scott Chandler RC	1.50	4.00
260 Anthony Waters RC	1.25	3.00
261 Joe Staley RC	1.25	3.00
262 Jason Hill RC	1.50	4.00
263 Josh Wilson RC	1.25	3.00
264 Brandon Mebane RC	1.25	3.00
265 Adam Carriker RC	1.25	3.00
266 Jonathan Wade RC	1.25	3.00
267 Arron Sears RC	1.25	3.00
268 Sabby Piscitelli RC	1.50	4.00
269 Quincy Black RC	1.50	4.00
270 Michael Griffin RC	1.50	4.00
271 Chris Henry RB RC	1.00	2.50
272 Paul Williams RC	1.00	2.50
273 Chris Davis RC	1.00	2.50
274 H.B. Blades RC	1.00	2.50
275 Jordan Palmer RC	1.25	3.00
276 JaMarcus Russell RC	1.00	2.50
277 Calvin Johnson RC	5.00	12.00
278 Brady Quinn RC	1.50	4.00
279 Adrian Peterson RC	6.00	15.00
280 Marshawn Lynch RC	1.50	4.00
281 Ted Ginn Jr. RC	1.25	3.00
282 LaRon Landry RC	1.50	4.00
283 Jamaal Anderson RC	1.25	3.00
284 Amobi Okoye RC	1.50	4.00
285 Dwayne Bowe RC	2.00	5.00
286 Greg Olsen RC	1.25	3.00
287 Gaines Adams RC	1.50	4.00
288 Patrick Willis RC	3.00	8.00
289 Drew Stanton RC	1.00	2.50
290 Kevin Kolb RC	2.50	6.00
291 John Beck RC	1.50	4.00
292 Anthony Gonzalez RC	1.50	4.00
293 Sidney Rice RC	2.00	5.00
294 Robert Meachem RC	1.50	4.00
295 Joe Thomas RC	1.50	4.00
296 Dwayne Jarrett RC	1.25	3.00
297 Kenny Irons RC	1.00	2.50
298 Brian Leonard RC	1.25	3.00
299 Craig Buster Davis RC	1.25	3.00
300 Steve Smith USC RC	1.50	4.00

2007 Upper Deck Exclusive Edition Rookies

COMPLETE SET (100)	15.00	40.00

*SINGLES: .1X TO .25X BASIC CARDS
30-PER ROOKIE EDITION FAT PACK

2007 Upper Deck Gold Predictor Edition

COMPLETE SET (300)	100.00	200.00

*VETS: .4X TO 1X BASIC CARDS
*ROOKIES: .3X TO .8X BASIC CARDS
ISSUED AS PRIZE FOR PREDICTOR WINNERS

2007 Upper Deck Silver

*VETS 1-200: 4X TO 10X BASIC CARDS
*ROOKIES 201-300: .8X TO 2X BASIC CARDS
STATED PRINT RUN 99 SER.#'d SETS
STATED ODDS 1:16

2007 Upper Deck 1964 Philadelphia

OVERALL INSERT ODDS 1:4 H, 1:12 R
UNPRICED AUTO PRINT RUN 5
OVERALL AUTO ODDS 1:16 H, 1:2500 R

1 Matt Leinart	1.25	3.00
2 Larry Fitzgerald	1.50	4.00
3 Anquan Boldin	1.25	3.00
4 Edgerrin James	1.25	3.00
5 Jerious Norwood	1.25	3.00
6 Michael Vick	1.50	4.00
7 Alge Crumpler	1.25	3.00
8 Warrick Dunn	1.25	3.00
9 Steve McNair	1.25	3.00
10 Ray Lewis	1.50	4.00
11 Mark Clayton	1.25	3.00
12 Todd Heap	1.00	2.50
13 Jake Delhomme	1.25	3.00
14 Steve Smith	1.25	3.00
15 Julius Peppers	1.25	3.00
16 Brian Urlacher	1.50	4.00
17 Devin Hester	1.50	4.00
18 Bernard Berrian	1.00	2.50
19 Mike Singletary	2.50	6.00
20 Chad Johnson	1.25	3.00
21 T.J. Houshmandzadeh	1.25	3.00
22 Carson Palmer	1.25	3.00
23 Tony Romo	2.00	5.00
24 Terrell Owens	1.50	4.00
25 Roy Williams S	1.25	3.00
26 Marion Barber	1.50	4.00
27 Drew Pearson	2.00	5.00
28 Champ Bailey	1.25	3.00
29 Javon Walker	1.25	3.00
30 John Lynch	1.25	3.00
31 Jay Cutler	1.50	4.00
32 Brandon Marshall	1.25	3.00
33 Kevin Jones	1.00	2.50
34 Roy Williams WR	1.25	3.00
35 Brett Favre	3.00	8.00
36 Donald Driver	1.50	4.00
37 Paul Hornung	2.50	6.00
38 Andre Johnson	1.25	3.00
39 Matt Schaub	1.25	3.00
40 Ahman Green	1.25	3.00
41 Marvin Harrison	1.50	4.00
42 Joseph Addai	1.25	3.00
43 Peyton Manning	2.50	6.00
44 Reggie Wayne	1.25	3.00
45 Dwight Freeney	1.25	3.00
46 Maurice Jones-Drew	1.50	4.00
47 Fred Taylor	1.25	3.00
48 Larry Johnson	1.00	2.50
49 Tony Gonzalez	1.25	3.00
50 Ronnie Brown	1.25	3.00
51 Zach Thomas	1.25	3.00
52 Chester Taylor	1.00	2.50
53 Tarvaris Jackson	1.00	2.50
54 Tom Brady	2.50	6.00
55 Tedy Bruschi	1.50	4.00
56 Laurence Maroney	1.25	3.00
57 Drew Brees	1.50	4.00
58 Marques Colston	1.50	4.00
59 Reggie Bush	1.50	4.00
60 Eli Manning	1.50	4.00
61 Plaxico Burress	1.25	3.00
62 Jeremy Shockey	1.25	3.00
63 Michael Strahan	1.25	3.00
64 Curtis Martin	1.50	4.00
65 Chad Pennington	1.25	3.00
66 Laveranues Coles	1.00	2.50
67 Jerricho Cotchery	1.25	3.00
68 Ronald Curry	1.25	3.00
69 Marcus Allen	2.50	6.00
70 Donovan McNabb	1.50	4.00
71 Brian Westbrook	1.25	3.00
72 L.J. Smith	1.00	2.50
73 Willie Parker	1.25	3.00
74 Ben Roethlisberger	1.50	4.00
75 Santonio Holmes	1.25	3.00
76 L.C. Greenwood	2.00	5.00
77 Philip Rivers	1.50	4.00
78 LaDainian Tomlinson	1.50	4.00
79 Shawne Merriman	1.25	3.00
80 Frank Gore	1.50	4.00
81 Vernon Davis	1.25	3.00
82 Roger Craig	2.00	5.00
83 Alex Smith QB	1.50	4.00
84 Deion Branch	1.25	3.00
85 Matt Hasselbeck	1.25	3.00
86 Shaun Alexander	1.25	3.00
87 Lofa Tatupu	1.25	3.00
88 Marc Bulger	1.25	3.00
89 Steven Jackson	1.50	4.00
90 Torry Holt	1.25	3.00
91 Isaac Bruce	1.25	3.00
92 Cadillac Williams	1.25	3.00
93 Ronde Barber	1.25	3.00
94 Joey Galloway	1.25	3.00
95 Michael Clayton	1.00	2.50
96 Vince Young	1.25	3.00
97 Jason Campbell	1.25	3.00
98 Santana Moss	1.25	3.00
99 Antwaan Randle El	1.00	2.50
100 Joe Theismann	2.50	6.00

2007 Upper Deck College to Pros

OVERALL INSERT ODDS 1:4 H, 1:12 R

AJ Andre Johnson	1.00	2.50
BA Marion Barber	1.25	3.00
BE Braylon Edwards	1.00	2.50
BF Brett Favre	2.50	6.00
BR Ben Roethlisberger	1.25	3.00
CB Champ Bailey	1.00	2.50
CJ Chad Johnson	1.00	2.50
CP Carson Palmer	1.00	2.50
CW Charles Woodson	1.25	3.00
DB Drew Brees	1.25	3.00
DH Devin Hester	1.25	3.00
DM Donovan McNabb	1.25	3.00
EM Eli Manning	1.25	3.00
ES Emmitt Smith	3.00	8.00
FG Frank Gore	1.25	3.00
HW Hines Ward	1.25	3.00
JG Joey Galloway	1.00	2.50
JM Joe Montana	3.00	8.00
LF Larry Fitzgerald	1.25	3.00
LJ Larry Johnson	.75	2.00
LT LaDainian Tomlinson	1.25	3.00
MB Marc Bulger	1.00	2.50
MC Steve McNair	1.00	2.50
MH Matt Hasselbeck	1.00	2.50
ML Matt Leinart	1.00	2.50
MS Matt Schaub	1.00	2.50
MV Michael Vick	1.25	3.00
PE Chad Pennington	1.00	2.50
PM Peyton Manning	2.00	5.00
PO Clinton Portis	1.00	2.50
PR Philip Rivers	1.25	3.00
RB Reggie Bush	1.25	3.00
RM Randy Moss	1.25	3.00
RO Ronnie Brown	1.00	2.50
RW Roy Williams WR	1.00	2.50
SA Shaun Alexander	1.00	2.50
SJ Steven Jackson	1.25	3.00
SM Santana Moss	1.00	2.50
TB Tom Brady	2.00	5.00
TG Tony Gonzalez	1.00	2.50
TH T.J. Houshmandzadeh	1.00	2.50
VY Vince Young	1.00	2.50
WA Reggie Wayne	1.00	2.50
WD Warrick Dunn	1.00	2.50
WI Cadillac Williams	1.00	2.50

2007 Upper Deck College to Pros Autographs

STATED PRINT RUN 10-25

NTNBA Marion Barber/25	15.00	40.00
NTNDB Drew Brees	40.00	100.00
NTNLJ Larry Johnson/25	12.00	30.00
NTNMB Marc Bulger/25	15.00	40.00
NTNML Matt Leinart/25	15.00	40.00
NTNPM Peyton Manning/25	75.00	150.00
NTNPR Philip Rivers/25	20.00	50.00
NTNRO Ronnie Brown/25	15.00	40.00
NTNVY Vince Young/25	15.00	40.00
NTNWA Reggie Wayne	15.00	40.00

2007 Upper Deck Football Heroes

OVERALL INSERT ODDS 1:4 H, 1:12 R

FH73 JaMarcus Russell	.50	1.25
FH74 JaMarcus Russell	.50	1.25
FH75 JaMarcus Russell	.50	1.25
FH76 JaMarcus Russell	.50	1.25
FH77 JaMarcus Russell	.50	1.25
FH78 Calvin Johnson	2.50	6.00
FH79 Calvin Johnson	2.50	6.00
FH80 Calvin Johnson	2.50	6.00
FH81 Calvin Johnson	2.50	6.00
FH82 Calvin Johnson	2.50	6.00
FH83 Adrian Peterson	3.00	8.00
FH84 Adrian Peterson	3.00	8.00
FH85 Adrian Peterson	3.00	8.00
FH86 Adrian Peterson	3.00	8.00
FH87 Adrian Peterson	3.00	8.00
FH88 Brady Quinn	.75	2.00
FH89 Brady Quinn	.75	2.00
FH90 Brady Quinn	.75	2.00
FH91 Brady Quinn	.75	2.00
FH92 Brady Quinn	.75	2.00
FH93 Marshawn Lynch	.75	2.00
FH94 Marshawn Lynch	.75	2.00
FH95 Marshawn Lynch	.75	2.00
FH96 Marshawn Lynch	.75	2.00
FH97 Marshawn Lynch	.75	2.00
FH98 Ted Ginn Jr.	.60	1.50
FH99 Ted Ginn Jr.	.60	1.50
FH100 Ted Ginn Jr.	.60	1.50
FH101 Ted Ginn Jr.	.60	1.50
FH102 Ted Ginn Jr.	.60	1.50
FH103 Gaines Adams	.75	2.00
FH104 Gaines Adams	.75	2.00
FH105 Gaines Adams	.75	2.00
FH106 Gaines Adams	.75	2.00
FH107 Gaines Adams	.75	2.00
FH108 Joe Thomas	.75	2.00
FH109 Joe Thomas	.75	2.00
FH110 Joe Thomas	.75	2.00
FH111 Joe Thomas	.75	2.00
FH112 Joe Thomas	.75	2.00
FH113 Dwayne Bowe	1.00	2.50
FH114 Dwayne Bowe	1.00	2.50
FH115 Dwayne Bowe	1.00	2.50
FH116 Dwayne Bowe	1.00	2.50
FH117 Dwayne Bowe	1.00	2.50

2007 Upper Deck Game Jerseys

OVERALL MEMORABILIA ODDS 1:8H, 1:288R

BF Brett Favre	8.00	20.00
BL Byron Leftwich	3.00	8.00
CB Chris Brown	2.50	6.00
CE Cedric Benson	3.00	8.00
CF Charlie Frye	3.00	8.00
CJ Chad Johnson	3.00	8.00
CR Charles Rogers	2.50	6.00
CS Chris Simms	2.50	6.00
CW Cadillac Williams Red	3.00	8.00
CW2 Cadillac Williams Wht	3.00	8.00
DC Daunte Culpepper Teal	3.00	8.00
DC2 Daunte Culpepper Wht	3.00	8.00
DE Deuce McAllister	3.00	8.00
DM Dan Marino	12.00	30.00
DW Domanick Williams	2.50	6.00
EJ Edgerrin James	3.00	8.00
EJ2 Edgerrin James	3.00	8.00
ES Emmitt Smith		
FT Fred Taylor	3.00	8.00
HW Hines Ward	4.00	10.00
JS Jeremy Shockey	3.00	8.00
KB Kyle Boller	2.50	6.00
KO Kyle Orton	3.00	8.00
KW Kurt Warner	3.00	8.00
LA Larry Johnson	2.50	6.00
LJ LaMont Jordan	3.00	8.00
LT LaDainian Tomlinson		
MB Marc Bulger	3.00	8.00
MC Donovan McNabb	4.00	10.00
MH Marvin Harrison	4.00	10.00
MM Muhsin Muhammad	3.00	8.00
MV Michael Vick Red	4.00	10.00
MV2 Michael Vick Wht	4.00	10.00
MW Mike Williams	2.50	6.00
NB Nate Burleson	2.50	6.00
PM Peyton Manning	6.00	15.00
RW Reggie Wayne	3.00	8.00
SM Steve McNair	3.00	8.00
TG Trent Green	3.00	8.00
TH Torry Holt	3.00	8.00
WM Willis McGahee	3.00	8.00
WM2 Willis McGahee	3.00	8.00

2007 Upper Deck Inkredible

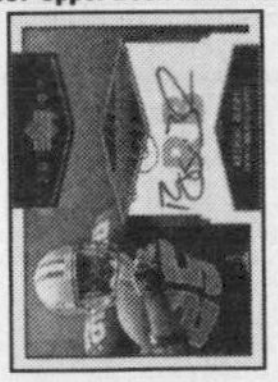

OVERALL AUTO ODDS 1:16 H, 1:2500 R
UNPRICED RED INK SER.#'d TO 10

INKAB Anquan Boldin	6.00	15.00
INKAD Joseph Addai	15.00	40.00
INKAO Amobi Okoye	6.00	15.00
INKCT Chester Taylor	6.00	15.00
INKFG Frank Gore	8.00	20.00
INKGA Gaines Adams	6.00	15.00
INKGR Gary Russell	6.00	15.00
INKJA Jamaal Anderson	6.00	15.00
INKJC Jason Campbell	8.00	20.00
INKKI Kenny Irons	6.00	15.00
INKKK Kevin Kolb	8.00	20.00
INKLE Lee Evans	6.00	15.00
INKLL LaRon Landry	8.00	20.00
INKMB Marc Bulger	8.00	20.00
INKRB Reggie Bush	75.00	150.00
INKRM Robert Meachem	8.00	20.00
INKSR Sidney Rice	12.50	25.00
INKZM Zach Miller	0.00	20.00

2007 Upper Deck MVP Predictor

OVERALL PREDICTOR ODDS 1:16H, 1:64R

MVPAJ Andre Johnson	1.50	4.00
MVPBF Brett Favre	4.00	10.00
MVPBU Reggie Bush	2.00	5.00
MVPCB Cedric Benson	1.50	4.00
MVPCJ Chad Johnson	1.50	4.00
MVPCP Carson Palmer	1.50	4.00
MVPCT Chester Taylor	1.25	3.00
MVPCW Cadillac Williams	1.50	4.00
MVPDB Drew Brees	2.00	5.00
MVPDM Donovan McNabb	2.00	5.00
MVPEJ Edgerrin James	1.50	4.00
MVPEM Eli Manning	2.00	5.00
MVPFG Frank Gore	2.00	5.00
MVPFT Fred Taylor	1.50	4.00
MVPJC Jay Cutler	2.00	5.00
MVPLE Lee Evans	1.50	4.00
MVPLJ Larry Johnson	1.25	3.00
MVPLT LaDainian Tomlinson	2.00	5.00
MVPMB Marc Bulger	1.50	4.00
MVPML Matt Leinart	1.50	4.00
MVPMO Santana Moss	1.50	4.00
MVPMV Michael Vick	2.00	5.00
MVPPE Chad Pennington	1.50	4.00
MVPPM Peyton Manning	3.00	8.00
MVPRB Ronnie Brown	1.50	4.00
MVPRW Roy Williams WR	1.50	4.00
MVPSA Shaun Alexander	1.50	4.00
MVPSJ Steven Jackson	2.00	5.00
MVPSM Steve McNair	1.50	4.00
MVPSS Steve Smith	1.50	4.00
MVPTB Tom Brady	50.00	100.00
MVPTR Tony Romo	2.50	6.00
MVPVY Vince Young	1.50	4.00
MVPWP Willie Parker	1.50	4.00

2007 Upper Deck NFL Ink

OVERALL AUTO ODDS 1:16H, 1:2500R
UNPRICED RED INK SER.#'d TO 10

AP Adrian Peterson		
BQ Brady Quinn	50.00	120.00
CD Craig Buster Davis	6.00	15.00
CJ Calvin Johnson	100.00	200.00
CW Cadillac Williams	8.00	20.00
DB Dwayne Bowe	12.00	30.00
DJ Dwayne Jarrett	8.00	20.00
EM Eli Manning		
EW Eric Wright	6.00	15.00
JF Joel Filani	6.00	15.00
JP Jordan Palmer	6.00	15.00
JT Joe Theismann		
LB Lorenzo Booker	8.00	20.00
LF Larry Fitzgerald	8.00	20.00
LJ Larry Johnson	15.00	40.00
LL LaRon Landry	8.00	20.00
MB Marion Barber	12.00	30.00
MG Michael Griffin	6.00	15.00
ML Matt Leinart	40.00	80.00
RB Ronnie Brown	8.00	20.00
RN Reggie Nelson	8.00	20.00
TG Ted Ginn Jr.		
TP Tyler Palko	6.00	15.00
TR Tony Romo		
WP Willie Parker	12.00	30.00

2007 Upper Deck Rookie Bonus

RELEASED IN RETAIL FACTORY SET

BC1 Adrian Peterson	1.25	3.00
BC2 Brady Quinn	.30	.75
BC6 JaMarcus Russell	.20	.50

2007 Upper Deck Rookie Exclusive Photo Shoot Flashback

RPS1 Alex Smith QB	.40	1.00
RPS2 Andre Johnson	.30	.75
RPS3 Anquan Boldin	.30	.75
RPS4 Ben Roethlisberger	.40	1.00
RPS5 Brian Urlacher	.40	1.00
RPS6 Cadillac Williams	.30	.75
RPS7 Carson Palmer	.30	.75
RPS8 Chad Johnson	.30	.75
RPS9 Donovan McNabb	.40	1.00
RPS10 Drew Brees	.40	1.00
RPS11 Eli Manning	.40	1.00
RPS12 Frank Gore	.40	1.00
RPS13 Julius Peppers	.30	.75
RPS14 LaDainian Tomlinson	.40	1.00
RPS15 Larry Fitzgerald	.40	1.00
RPS16 Larry Johnson	.25	.60
RPS17 Lee Evans	.30	.75
RPS18 Matt Leinart	.30	.75
RPS19 Maurice Jones-Drew	.40	1.00
RPS20 Peyton Manning	.60	1.50
RPS21 Philip Rivers	.40	1.00
RPS22 Hines Ward	.40	1.00
RPS23 Reggie Bush	.40	1.00
RPS24 Reggie Wayne	.30	.75
RPS25 Ronnie Brown	.30	.75
RPS26 Roy Williams WR	.30	.75
RPS27 Shaun Alexander	.30	.75
RPS28 Steven Jackson	.40	1.00
RPS29 Torry Holt	.30	.75
RPS30 Vince Young	.30	.75

2007 Upper Deck Rookie Fantasy Team

TWO PER TARGET RETAIL RACK PACKS

RFTAA Aundrae Allison	.50	1.25
RFTAG Anthony Gonzalez	.75	2.00
RFTAP Adrian Peterson	3.00	8.00
RFTBA Dallas Baker	.50	1.25
RFTBJ Brandon Jackson	.60	1.50
RFTBL Brian Leonard	.60	1.50
RFTBQ Brady Quinn	.75	2.00
RFTCD Chris Davis	.50	1.25
RFTCH Chris Henry RB	.50	1.25
RFTDA Craig Buster Davis	.60	1.50
RFTDB Dwayne Bowe	1.00	2.50
RFTDC David Clowney	.60	1.50
RFTDJ Dwayne Jarrett	.60	1.50
RFTDS Drew Stanton	.50	1.25
RFTDW Dwayne Wright	.60	1.50
RFTGO Greg Olsen	.60	1.50
RFTGW Garrett Wolfe	.50	1.25
RFTHI Johnnie Lee Higgins	.60	1.50
RFTIS Isaiah Stanback	.50	1.25
RFTJB John Beck	.75	2.00
RFTJH Jason Hill	.75	2.00
RFTJJ Jacoby Jones	.75	2.00
RFTJO James Jones	.75	2.00
RFTJP Jordan Palmer	.60	1.50
RFTJR JaMarcus Russell	.50	1.25
RFTKI Kenny Irons	.50	1.25
RFTKK Kevin Kolb	1.25	3.00
RFTKS Kolby Smith	.60	1.50
RFTLB Lorenzo Booker	.60	1.50
RFTLM Le'Ron McClain	.75	2.00
RFTLR Laurent Robinson	.75	2.00
RFTMB Michael Bush	.75	2.00
RFTML Marshawn Lynch	.75	2.00
RFTMM Martrez Milner	.50	1.25
RFTMS Matt Spaeth	.75	2.00
RFTMW Mike Walker	.75	2.00
RFTPI Antonio Pittman	.50	1.25
RFTPW Paul Williams	.50	1.25
RFTRM Robert Meachem	.75	2.00
RFTRR Ryne Robinson	.60	1.50
RFTSB Steve Breaston	.75	2.00
RFTSC Scott Chandler	.75	2.00
RFTSR Sidney Rice	1.00	2.50
RFTSS Steve Smith USC	.75	2.00
RFTTE Trent Edwards	.75	2.00
RFTTG Ted Ginn Jr.	.60	1.50
RFTTH Tony Hunt	.50	1.25
RFTTS Troy Smith	.75	2.00
RFTYF Yamon Figurs	.50	1.25
RFTZM Zach Miller	.75	2.00

2007 Upper Deck Rookie Ink

OVERALL AUTO ODDS 1:16H, 1:2500R
UNPRICED RED INK SER.#'d TO 10

RIAP Antonio Pittman	5.00	12.00
RIBL Brian Leonard	6.00	15.00
RICD Craig Buster Davis	6.00	15.00
RIDB Dwayne Bowe	10.00	25.00
RIDH Daymeion Hughes	6.00	15.00
RIDR Darrelle Revis	12.00	30.00
RIDS Drew Stanton	5.00	12.00
RIDW DeShawn Wynn	6.00	15.00
RIGO Greg Olsen	6.00	15.00
RIHB H.B. Blades	5.00	12.00
RIHI Johnnie Lee Higgins	6.00	15.00
RIJB John Beck	8.00	20.00
RIJH Jason Hill	8.00	20.00
RIJT Joe Thomas	8.00	20.00
RILH Leon Hall	6.00	15.00
RILT Lawrence Timmons	8.00	20.00
RIML Marshawn Lynch		
RIPP Paul Posluszny	8.00	20.00
RIPW Patrick Willis	15.00	40.00
RIRN Reggie Nelson	6.00	15.00
RISS Steve Smith USC	8.00	20.00
RITE Trent Edwards	8.00	20.00
RITG Ted Ginn Jr.	6.00	15.00
RITM Tyrone Moss	5.00	12.00
RIWR Dwayne Wright	6.00	15.00

2007 Upper Deck Rookie Jerseys

OVERALL MEMORABILIA ODDS 1:8H, 1:288R

AG Anthony Gonzalez	4.00	10.00
AP Adrian Peterson	15.00	40.00
BJ Brandon Jackson	3.00	8.00
BL Brian Leonard	3.00	8.00
BQ Brady Quinn	4.00	10.00
CH Chris Henry RB	2.50	6.00
CJ Calvin Johnson	12.00	30.00
DB Dwayne Bowe	6.00	15.00
DJ Dwayne Jarrett	3.00	8.00
DS Drew Stanton	2.50	6.00
GA Gaines Adams	4.00	10.00
GO Greg Olsen	3.00	8.00
GW Garrett Wolfe	2.50	6.00
JB John Beck	4.00	10.00
JH Jason Hill	4.00	10.00
JL Johnnie Lee Higgins	3.00	8.00
JR JaMarcus Russell	2.50	6.00
JT Joe Thomas	4.00	10.00
KI Kenny Irons	2.50	6.00
KK Kevin Kolb	6.00	15.00
MB Michael Bush	4.00	10.00
ML Marshawn Lynch	4.00	10.00
PW Patrick Willis	6.00	15.00
RM Robert Meachem	4.00	10.00
SR Sidney Rice	5.00	12.00
SS Steve Smith USC	4.00	10.00
TE Trent Edwards	4.00	10.00
TG Ted Ginn Jr.	3.00	8.00
TH Tony Hunt	2.50	6.00
TS Troy Smith	4.00	10.00
WI Paul Williams	2.50	6.00
YF Yamon Figurs	2.50	6.00

2007 Upper Deck Rookie Tandem Materials

OVERALL MEMORABILIA ODDS 1:8H, 1:288R

AT Gaines Adams	8.00	20.00
Joe Thomas		
BR JaMarcus Russell	15.00	40.00
Dwayne Bowe		
EL Trent Edwards	8.00	20.00
Marshawn Lynch		
GG Ted Ginn Jr.	8.00	20.00
Anthony Gonzalez		
GS Ted Ginn Jr.	8.00	20.00
Troy Smith		
HL Chris Henry RB	10.00	25.00
Marshawn Lynch		
IJ Brandon Jackson	8.00	20.00
Kenny Irons		
JR Calvin Johnson	15.00	40.00
JaMarcus Russell		
JS Dwayne Jarrett	8.00	20.00
Steve Smith USC		
KH Kevin Kolb	8.00	20.00
Tony Hunt		
LB Brian Leonard	10.00	25.00
Michael Bush		
PL Adrian Peterson	20.00	50.00
Marshawn Lynch		
PR Adrian Peterson	15.00	40.00
Sidney Rice		
QR Brady Quinn	15.00	40.00
JaMarcus Russell		
QT Brady Quinn	15.00	40.00
Joe Thomas		
SP Troy Smith	8.00	20.00
Antonio Pittman		

2007 Upper Deck ROY Predictor

OVERALL PREDICTOR ODDS 1:16H, 1:64R

ROYAG Anthony Gonzalez	2.00	5.00
ROYAO Amobi Okoye	2.00	5.00
ROYAP Adrian Peterson	40.00	80.00
ROYBJ Brandon Jackson	1.50	4.00
ROYBL Brian Leonard	1.50	4.00
ROYBQ Brady Quinn	2.00	5.00
ROYCD Craig Buster Davis	1.50	4.00
ROYCJ Calvin Johnson	6.00	15.00
ROYCL Chris Leak	1.50	4.00
ROYDB Dwayne Bowe	2.50	6.00
ROYDJ Dwayne Jarrett	1.50	4.00
ROYDR Darrelle Revis	3.00	8.00
ROYDS Drew Stanton	1.25	3.00
ROYGA Gaines Adams	2.00	5.00
ROYGO Greg Olsen	1.50	4.00
ROYJB John Beck	2.00	5.00
ROYJH Jason Hill	2.00	5.00
ROYJJ James Jones	2.00	5.00
ROYJR JaMarcus Russell	1.25	3.00
ROYKI Kenny Irons	1.25	3.00
ROYKK Kevin Kolb	3.00	8.00
ROYLB Lorenzo Booker	1.50	4.00
ROYLR Laurent Robinson	2.00	5.00
ROYMB Michael Bush	2.00	5.00
ROYML Marshawn Lynch	2.00	5.00
ROYPW Paul Williams	1.25	3.00
ROYRM Robert Meachem	2.00	5.00
ROYSB Steve Breaston	2.00	5.00
ROYSR Sidney Rice	2.50	6.00
ROYSS Steve Smith USC	2.00	5.00
ROYTE Trent Edwards	2.00	5.00
ROYTG Ted Ginn Jr.	1.50	4.00
ROYTH Tony Hunt	1.25	3.00
ROYZM Zach Miller	2.00	5.00

2007 Upper Deck Signature Sensations

OVERALL AUTO ODDS 1:16H, 1:2500R
UNPRICED RED INK SER.#'d TO 10

SSAB Alan Branch	5.00	12.00
SSBJ Brandon Jackson	8.00	20.00
SSBM Brandon Meriweather	6.00	15.00
SSCJ Chad Johnson	8.00	20.00
SSCL Chris Leak	12.00	30.00
SSCT Chester Taylor	6.00	15.00
SSGW Garrett Wolfe	8.00	20.00
SSHU Tony Hunt	5.00	12.00
SSIS Isaiah Stanback	8.00	20.00
SSJZ Jared Zabransky	6.00	15.00
SSLG L.C. Greenwood	20.00	40.00
SSLW LaMarr Woodley	10.00	25.00
SSMB Michael Bush	8.00	20.00
SSMM Marcus McCauley	6.00	15.00
SSRW Reggie Wayne	10.00	25.00
SSSN Syvelle Newton	5.00	12.00
SSTH T.J. Houshmandzadeh	6.00	15.00

2007 Upper Deck Super Bowl Predictor

OVERALL PREDICTOR ODDS 1:16H, 1:64R

SBP1 Edgerrin James	2.00	5.00
Larry Fitzgerald		
Matt Leinart		
SBP2 Michael Vick	1.25	3.00
Warrick Dunn		
Michael Jenkins		
SBP3 Ray Lewis	1.50	4.00
Steve McNair		
Mark Clayton		
SBP4 Anthony Thomas	1.25	3.00
Lee Evans		
J.P. Losman		
SBP5 Jake Delhomme	1.50	4.00
Julius Peppers		
Steve Smith		
SBP6 Brian Urlacher	2.00	5.00
Rex Grossman		
Devin Hester		
SBP7 Rudi Johnson	2.00	5.00
Chad Johnson		
Carson Palmer		
SBP8 Jamal Lewis	1.25	3.00
Braylon Edwards		
Kellen Winslow		
SBP9 Terry Glenn	5.00	12.00
Terrell Owens		
Tony Romo		
SBP10 Champ Bailey	2.00	5.00
Javon Walker		
Jay Cutler		
SBP11 Jon Kitna	1.25	3.00
Roy Williams WR		
Kevin Jones		
SBP12 Brett Favre	5.00	12.00
Donald Driver		
Greg Jennings		
SBP13 Ahman Green	1.25	3.00
Andre Johnson		
Matt Schaub		
SBP14 Marvin Harrison	3.00	8.00
Peyton Manning		
Joseph Addai		
SBP15 Fred Taylor	1.50	4.00
Byron Leftwich		
Maurice Jones-Drew		
SBP16 Larry Johnson	2.00	5.00
Tony Gonzalez		
Damon Huard		
SBP17 Chris Chambers	1.50	4.00
Jason Taylor		
Ronnie Brown		
SBP18 Chester Taylor	1.50	4.00
Troy Williamson		
Tarvaris Jackson		
SBP19 Tom Brady	4.00	10.00
Tedy Bruschi		
Laurence Maroney		
SBP20 Drew Brees	2.50	6.00
Deuce McAllister		
Reggie Bush		
SBP21 Plaxico Burress	40.00	80.00
Jeremy Shockey		
Eli Manning		
SBP22 Chad Pennington	1.60	4.00
Laveranues Coles		
Leon Washington		
SBP23 LaMont Jordan	1.25	3.00
Ronald Curry		
Nnamdi Asomugha		
SBP24 Donovan McNabb	2.00	5.00
Reggie Brown		
Brian Westbrook		
SBP25 Hines Ward	3.00	8.00
Ben Roethlisberger		
Willie Parker		
SBP26 LaDainian Tomlinson	3.00	8.00
Antonio Gates		
Philip Rivers		
SBP27 Frank Gore	2.00	5.00
Alex Smith QB		
Vernon Davis		
SBP28 Shaun Alexander	2.00	5.00
Matt Hasselbeck		
Deion Branch		
SBP29 Torry Holt	2.00	5.00
Marc Bulger		
Steven Jackson		
SBP30 Joey Galloway	1.50	4.00
Chris Simms		
Cadillac Williams		
SBP31 David Givens	2.50	6.00
LenDale White		
Vince Young		
SBP32 Santana Moss	1.50	4.00
Clinton Portis		
Jason Campbell		

2007 Upper Deck Target Exclusive Rookies

*ROOKIES: .4X TO 1X BASIC CARDS
FEATURES NEW PHOTO AND GRAY BORDER

2007 Upper Deck Target Exclusive Rookies Autographs

AUTO/5 TOO SCARCE TO PRICE

2007 Upper Deck Alumni Greats

These cards were packaged one at a time with a 1:64 die-cast car and offered at a retail price of $12.99. Each card follows the format of the base 2007 Upper Deck Football set but includes the player in his college uniform.

DCCU3 Julius Peppers	1.50	4.00
DCCU4 Lee Evans	1.50	4.00
DCCU5 Shawne Merriman	1.50	4.00
DCCU6 Jared Lorenzen	1.25	3.00
DCCU7 Shaun Alexander	1.50	4.00
DCCU8 Ronnie Brown	1.50	4.00
DCCU9 Warrick Dunn	1.50	4.00
DCCU10 Champ Bailey	1.50	4.00
DCCU11 Joseph Addai	1.50	4.00
DCCU12 Willis McGahee	1.50	4.00
DCCU13 Braylon Edwards	1.50	4.00
DCCU14 Ahman Green	1.50	4.00
DCCU15 Mark Clayton	1.50	4.00
DCCU16 Larry Johnson	1.25	3.00
DCCU17 Peyton Manning	3.00	8.00
DCCU18 Ryan Fowler	1.25	3.00

2007 Upper Deck Prilosec Brett Favre

This 6-card set was sponsored by Prilosec and produced by Upper Deck. It pays tribute to the career of Brett Favre from his high school days through to the NFL.

COMPLETE SET (6)	6.00	15.00
COMMON FAVRE	1.25	3.00

2008 Upper Deck

COMPLETE SET (325)	125.00	250.00
COMP.SET w/o SP's (300)	25.00	50.00
COMP.SET w/o RC's (200)	10.00	25.00

ROOKIE ODDS 4:1 HOB, 2:1 RET

1 Edgerrin James	.20	.50
2 Matt Leinart	.25	.60
3 Larry Fitzgerald	.25	.60
4 Anquan Boldin	.20	.50
5 Antrel Rolle	.15	.40
6 Joe Horn	.20	.50
7 Warrick Dunn	.20	.50
8 Alge Crumpler	.20	.50
9 Jerious Norwood	.20	.50
10 Michael Jenkins	.15	.40
11 Derrick Mason	.20	.50
12 Ed Reed	.20	.50
13 Willis McGahee	.20	.50
14 Steve McNair	.20	.50
15 Todd Heap	.15	.40
16 Ray Lewis	.25	.60
17 Terrell Suggs	.15	.40
18 Trent Edwards	.15	.40
19 Lee Evans	.20	.50
20 Roscoe Parrish	.15	.40
21 Marshawn Lynch	.20	.50
22 Stacy Andrews	.15	.40
23 DeAngelo Williams	.20	.50
24 Julius Peppers	.20	.50
25 Steve Smith	.20	.50
26 Jake Delhomme	.20	.50
27 Lance Briggs	.15	.40
28 Rex Grossman	.20	.50
29 Devin Hester	.25	.60
30 Bernard Berrian	.20	.50
31 Brian Urlacher	.25	.60
32 Cedric Benson	.20	.50
33 Greg Olsen	.20	.50
34 T.J. Houshmandzadeh	.20	.50
35 Carson Palmer	.25	.60
36 Rudi Johnson	.20	.50
37 Chad Johnson	.20	.50
38 Kurt Warner	.25	.60
39 Kamerion Wimbley	.15	.40
40 Josh Cribbs	.25	.60
41 Jamal Lewis	.20	.50
42 Kellen Winslow	.20	.50
43 Braylon Edwards	.20	.50
44 Eric Wright	.15	.40
45 Anthony Henry	.15	.40
46 Roy Williams S	.20	.50
47 Marion Barber	.20	.50
48 Jason Witten	.25	.60
49 DeMarcus Ware	.20	.50
50 Tony Romo	.30	.75
51 Julius Jones	.15	.40
52 Terrell Owens	.25	.60
53 Greg Ellis	.15	.40
54 Patrick Crayton	.20	.50
55 John Lynch	.20	.50
56 Brandon Marshall	.20	.50
57 Travis Henry	.15	.40
58 Jay Cutler	.25	.60
59 Dre Bly	.15	.40
60 Javon Walker	.20	.50
61 Champ Bailey	.20	.50
62 Tatum Bell	.15	.40
63 Calvin Johnson	.25	.60
64 Jon Kitna	.20	.50
65 Roy Williams WR	.20	.50
66 Ernie Sims	.15	.40
67 Aaron Kampman	.20	.50
68 Bubba Franks	.15	.40
69 Charles Woodson	.25	.60
70 Brett Favre	.60	1.50
71 Donald Driver	.20	.50
72 A.J. Hawk	.20	.50
73 Ahman Green	.20	.50
74 DeMeco Ryans	.20	.50
75 Andre Johnson	.20	.50
76 Mario Williams	.20	.50
77 Ron Dayne	.15	.40
78 Dwight Freeney	.20	.50
79 Dallas Clark	.20	.50
80 Peyton Manning	.40	1.00
81 Marvin Harrison	.25	.60
82 Reggie Wayne	.20	.50
83 Joseph Addai	.20	.50
84 Matt Jones	.20	.50
85 David Garrard	.20	.50
86 Ernest Wilford	.15	.40
87 Reggie Williams	.20	.50
88 Maurice Jones-Drew	.20	.50
89 Fred Taylor	.20	.50
90 Reggie Nelson	.15	.40
91 Dwayne Bowe	.20	.50
92 Samie Parker	.15	.40
93 Derrick Johnson	.15	.40
94 Larry Johnson	.20	.50
95 Brodie Croyle	.20	.50
96 Tony Gonzalez	.20	.50
97 Jared Allen	.25	.60
98 Zach Thomas	.20	.50
99 Ronnie Brown	.20	.50
100 Jason Taylor	.20	.50
101 Ted Ginn Jr.	.20	.50
102 John Beck	.15	.40
103 Antoine Winfield	.15	.40
104 Adrian Peterson	.40	1.00
105 Bob Sanders	.20	.50
106 Sidney Rice	.25	.60
107 Chester Taylor	.15	.40
108 Wes Welker	.25	.60
109 Rodney Harrison	.15	.40
110 Randy Moss	.25	.60
111 Donte Stallworth	.15	.40
112 Tom Brady	.40	1.00
113 Laurence Maroney	.20	.50
114 Ben Watson	.15	.40
115 Tedy Bruschi	.25	.60

116 Mike Vrabel .15 .40
117 Charles Grant .15 .40
118 Drew Brees .25 .60
119 Marques Colston .20 .50
120 Reggie Bush .25 .60
121 Deuce McAllister .20 .50
122 Mike McKenzie .15 .40
123 Amani Toomer .20 .50
124 Michael Strahan .20 .50
125 Plaxico Burress .20 .50
126 Osi Umenyiora .20 .50
127 Eli Manning .25 .60
128 Jeremy Shockey .20 .50
129 Brandon Jacobs .20 .50
130 Antonio Pierce .15 .40
131 Jonathan Vilma .20 .50
132 Jerricho Cotchery .20 .50
133 Kellen Clemens .20 .50
134 Leon Washington .20 .50
135 Thomas Jones .20 .50
136 Kirk Morrison .15 .40
137 Nnamdi Asomugha .20 .50
138 Derrick Burgess .15 .40
139 Justin Fargas .15 .40
140 Ronald Curry .20 .50
141 JaMarcus Russell .20 .50
142 Brian Dawkins .20 .50
143 Brian Westbrook .20 .50
144 Reggie Brown .15 .40
145 Donovan McNabb .25 .60
146 Hines Ward .20 .50
147 Santonio Holmes .20 .50
148 Ben Roethlisberger .25 .60
149 Willie Parker .20 .50
150 Troy Polamalu .25 .60
151 James Farrior .15 .40
152 Heath Miller .15 .40
153 Chris Chambers .20 .50
154 Philip Rivers .25 .60
155 Antonio Gates .25 .60
156 Shawne Merriman .20 .50
157 LaDainian Tomlinson .25 .60
158 Antonio Cromartie .15 .40
159 Shaun Phillips .15 .40
160 Jamal Williams .15 .40
161 Arnaz Battle .15 .40
162 Nate Clements .15 .40
163 Alex Smith QB .25 .60
164 Frank Gore .20 .50
165 Vernon Davis .20 .50
166 Patrick Willis .20 .50
167 Lofa Tatupu .20 .50
168 Patrick Kerney .15 .40
169 Bobby Engram .15 .40
170 Matt Hasselbeck .20 .50
171 Shawn Andrews .15 .40
172 Deion Branch .20 .50
173 D.J. Hackett .15 .40
174 Leonard Little .15 .40
175 Pisa Tinoisamoa .15 .40
176 Steven Jackson .25 .60
177 Marc Bulger .20 .50
178 Torry Holt .20 .50
179 Isaac Bruce .20 .50
180 Randy McMichael .15 .40
181 Ronde Barber .15 .40
182 Cadillac Williams .20 .50
183 Derrick Brooks .20 .50
184 Michael Clayton .15 .40
185 Jeff Garcia .20 .50
186 Joey Galloway .20 .50
187 Gaines Adams .15 .40
188 Keith Bulluck .15 .40
189 Nick Harper .15 .40
190 David Givens .15 .40
191 Vince Young .20 .50
192 LenDale White .20 .50
193 Eric Moulds .20 .50
194 Jason Campbell .20 .50
195 Randall Godfrey .15 .40
196 Chris Cooley .20 .50
197 Brandon Lloyd .15 .40
198 Clinton Portis .20 .50
199 Santana Moss .15 .40
200 London Fletcher .15 .40
201 Will Franklin RC .60 1.50
202 Jerome Felton RC .50 1.25
203 Adrian Arrington RC .60 1.50
204 Alex Brink RC .75 2.00
205 Allen Patrick RC .60 1.50
206 Andre Caldwell RC .60 1.50
207 Anthony Morelli RC .60 1.50
208 Antoine Cason RC .75 2.00
209 Aqib Talib RC .75 2.00
210 Ben Moffitt RC .50 1.25
211 Caleb Campbell RC .75 2.00
212 T.C. Ostrander RC .60 1.50
213 Bruce Davis RC .60 1.50
214 Calais Campbell RC .60 1.50
215 Chris Williams RC .60 1.50
216 Chad Henne RC .75 2.00
217 Chevis Jackson RC .50 1.25
218 Chris Ellis RC .50 1.25
219 Chris Johnson RC 2.00 5.00
220 Cory Boyd RC .50 1.25
221 Craig Steltz RC .60 1.50
222 DJ Hall RC .60 1.50
223 Chauncey Washington RC .60 1.50
224 Darius Reynaud RC .50 1.25
225 Davone Bess RC .75 2.00
226 DeJuan Tribble RC .50 1.25
227 DeMario Pressley RC .60 1.50
228 Dennis Keyes RC .50 1.25
229 Derrick Harvey RC .50 1.25
230 Donnie Avery RC .60 1.50
231 Xavier Omon RC .75 2.00
232 Dre Moore RC .60 1.50
233 Dustin Keller RC .75 2.00
234 Earl Bennett RC .75 2.00
235 Erik Ainge RC .75 2.00
236 Erin Henderson RC .75 2.00
237 Curtis Lofton RC .60 1.50
238 Felix Jones RC 1.25 3.00
239 Josh Barrett RC .50 1.25
240 Gosder Cherilus RC .60 1.50
241 Harry Douglas RC .60 1.50
242 Colt Brennan RC .75 2.00
243 J Leman RC .50 1.25
244 Jack Ikegwuonu RC .50 1.25
245 Jacob Hester RC .75 2.00
246 Jacob Tamme RC .75 2.00
247 Jamaal Charles RC 1.25 3.00
248 James Hardy RC .60 1.50
249 Jermichael Finley RC .75 2.00
250 Jerod Mayo RC .75 2.00
251 Joe Flacco RC 2.50 6.00
252 John Carlson RC .75 2.00
253 John David Booty RC .60 1.50
254 Jonathan Goff RC .50 1.25
255 Jonathan Hefney RC .60 1.50
256 Jordon Dizon RC .75 2.00
257 Jordy Nelson RC 1.00 2.50
258 Josh Johnson RC .75 2.00
259 Justin Forsett RC .75 2.00
260 Kalvin McRae RC .50 1.25
261 Keenan Burton RC .50 1.25
262 Kellen Davis RC .50 1.25
263 Kentwan Balmer RC .60 1.50
264 Keon Lattimore RC .60 1.50
265 Kevin O'Connell RC .60 1.50
266 Kevin Smith RC .75 2.00
267 Thomas DeCoud RC .50 1.25
268 Malcolm Kelly RC .60 1.50
269 Marcus Monk RC .60 1.50
270 Mario Manningham RC .75 2.00
271 Mario Urrutia RC .50 1.25
272 Martellus Bennett RC .60 1.50
273 Martin Rucker RC .60 1.50
274 Matt Flynn RC 1.50 4.00
275 Matt Forte RC 1.25 3.00
276 Owen Schmitt RC .75 2.00
277 Paul Hubbard RC .60 1.50
278 Paul Smith RC .75 2.00
279 Philip Wheeler RC .60 1.50
280 Quentin Groves RC .60 1.50
281 Quintin Demps RC .75 2.00
282 Rashard Mendenhall RC 1.50 4.00
283 Ray Rice RC 1.50 4.00
284 Ryan Clady RC .75 2.00
285 Ryan Grice-Mullen RC .50 1.25
286 Ryan Torain RC .75 2.00
287 Spencer Larsen RC .50 1.25
288 Marcus Thomas RC .60 1.50
289 Shawn Crable RC .50 1.25
290 Frank Okam RC .50 1.25
291 Tashard Choice RC .60 1.50
292 Terrell Thomas RC .60 1.50
293 Thomas Brown RC .60 1.50
294 Tom Zbikowski RC .75 2.00
295 Simeon Castille RC .60 1.50
296 Trevor Laws RC .75 2.00
297 Vernon Gholston RC .60 1.50
298 Vince Hall RC .50 1.25
299 Xavier Adibi RC .50 1.25
300 Yvenson Bernard RC .75 2.00
301 Andre Woodson SP RC 2.50 6.00
302 Brian Brohm SP RC 2.50 6.00
303 Devin Thomas SP RC 2.00 5.00
304 Dennis Dixon SP RC 2.50 6.00
305 Matt Ryan SP RC 10.00 25.00
306 Darren McFadden SP RC 6.00 15.00
307 Jonathan Stewart SP RC 4.00 10.00
308 Mike Hart SP RC 2.50 6.00
309 DeSean Jackson SP RC 5.00 12.00
310 Early Doucet SP RC 2.00 5.00
311 Lavelle Hawkins SP RC 1.50 4.00
312 Limas Sweed SP RC 2.50 6.00
313 Jake Long SP RC 2.50 6.00
314 Sam Baker SP RC 1.50 4.00
315 Glenn Dorsey SP RC 2.50 6.00
316 Sedrick Ellis SP RC 2.50 6.00
317 Chris Long SP RC 2.50 6.00
318 Lawrence Jackson SP RC 2.00 5.00
319 Ali Highsmith SP RC 1.50 4.00
320 Dan Connor SP RC 2.50 6.00
321 Kenny Phillips SP RC 2.50 6.00
322 Keith Rivers SP RC 2.50 6.00
323 Justin King SP RC 2.00 5.00
324 Mike Jenkins SP RC 2.50 6.00
325 Fred Davis SP RC 2.50 6.00

2008 Upper Deck College to Pros

UNPRICED AUTO PRINT RUN 5
CP1 Donnie Avery 1.00 2.50
CP2 Earl Bennett 1.25 3.00
CP3 John David Booty 1.00 2.50
CP4 Brian Brohm 1.25 3.00
CP5 Andre Caldwell 1.00 2.50
CP6 Jamaal Charles 2.00 5.00
CP7 Glenn Dorsey 1.25 3.00
CP8 Early Doucet 1.00 2.50
CP9 Harry Douglas 1.00 2.50
CP10 Joe Flacco 4.00 10.00
CP11 Matt Forte 2.00 5.00
CP12 James Hardy 1.00 2.50
CP13 Chad Henne 1.25 3.00
CP14 DeSean Jackson 2.50 6.00
CP15 Chris Johnson 3.00 8.00
CP16 Felix Jones 2.00 5.00
CP17 Devin Thomas 1.00 2.50
CP18 Dexter Jackson 1.00 2.50
CP19 Dustin Keller 1.25 3.00
CP20 Malcolm Kelly 1.00 2.50
CP21 Jake Long 1.25 3.00
CP22 Darren McFadden 3.00 8.00
CP23 Rashard Mendenhall 2.50 6.00
CP24 Kevin O'Connell 1.00 2.50
CP25 Mario Manningham 1.25 3.00
CP26 Ray Rice 2.50 6.00
CP27 Eddie Royal 1.25 3.00
CP28 Matt Ryan 5.00 12.00
CP29 Jerome Simpson 1.25 3.00
CP30 Steve Slaton 1.25 3.00
CP31 Kevin Smith 1.25 3.00
CP32 Jonathan Stewart 2.00 5.00
CP33 Limas Sweed 1.25 3.00
CP34 Jordy Nelson 1.50 4.00

2008 Upper Deck Excell Rookie Cards

ERCAC Andre Caldwell .75 2.00
ERCBB Brian Brohm 1.00 2.50
ERCCH Chad Henne 1.00 2.50
ERCDA Donnie Avery .75 2.00
ERCDJ DeSean Jackson 2.00 5.00
ERCDK Dustin Keller 1.00 2.50
ERCDM Darren McFadden 2.50 6.00
ERCDT Devin Thomas .75 2.00
ERCER Eddie Royal 1.00 2.50
ERCFJ Felix Jones 1.50 4.00
ERCHD Harry Douglas .75 2.00
ERCJA Dexter Jackson .75 2.00
ERCJB John David Booty .75 2.00
ERCJC Jamaal Charles 1.50 4.00
ERCJF Joe Flacco 3.00 8.00
ERCJH James Hardy .75 2.00
ERCJL Jake Long 1.00 2.50
ERCJN Jordy Nelson 1.25 3.00
ERCJS Jerome Simpson 1.00 2.50
ERCKO Kevin O'Connell .75 2.00
ERCKS Kevin Smith 1.00 2.50
ERCLS Limas Sweed 1.00 2.50
ERCMF Matt Forte 1.50 4.00
ERCMK Malcolm Kelly .75 2.00
ERCMM Mario Manningham 1.00 2.50
ERCMR Matt Ryan 4.00 10.00
ERCRM Rashard Mendenhall 2.00 5.00
ERCRR Ray Rice 2.00 5.00
ERCSS Steve Slaton 1.00 2.50
ERCST Jonathan Stewart 1.50 4.00

2008 Upper Deck Game Jerseys

*GOLD/200: .5X TO 1.2X SILVER JSY
GOLD/200 INSERTED IN HOT BOXES
OVERALL MEMORABILIA ODDS 1:8
UDGJAC Antonio Cromartie 2.50 6.00
UDGJAK Aaron Kampman 3.00 8.00
UDGJAS Alex Smith QB 4.00 10.00
UDGJBD Brian Dawkins 3.00 8.00
UDGJBE Braylon Edwards 3.00 8.00
UDGJBJ Brandon Jacobs 3.00 8.00
UDGJBR Ben Roethlisberger 4.00 10.00
UDGJBU Brian Urlacher 4.00 10.00
UDGJCJ Chad Johnson 3.00 8.00
UDGJCP Carson Palmer 4.00 10.00
UDGJDB Drew Brees 4.00 10.00
UDGJDG David Garrard 3.00 8.00
UDGJEM Eli Manning 4.00 10.00
UDGJFT Fred Taylor 3.00 8.00
UDGJGJ Greg Jennings 4.00 10.00
UDGJJA Joseph Addai 3.00 8.00
UDGJJC Jason Campbell 3.00 8.00
UDGJJG Jeff Garcia 3.00 8.00
UDGJJV Jonathan Vilma 3.00 8.00
UDGJLE Lee Evans 3.00 8.00
UDGJMB Marion Barber 5.00 12.00
UDGJMH Matt Hasselbeck 3.00 8.00
UDGJRL Ray Lewis 4.00 10.00
UDGJSJ Steven Jackson 4.00 10.00
UDGJSM Shawne Merriman 3.00 8.00
UDGJSR Sidney Rice 4.00 10.00
UDGJSS Steve Smith 3.00 8.00
UDGJTE Trent Edwards 2.50 6.00
UDGJTR Tony Romo 5.00 12.00
UDGJVY Vince Young 3.00 8.00

2008 Upper Deck Green Bay Gamers

1 A.J. Hawk 2.00 5.00
2 Greg Jennings 2.50 6.00
3 Brady Poppinga 1.50 4.00
4 Chad Clifton 1.50 4.00
5 Nick Collins 1.50 4.00
6 Mason Crosby 1.50 4.00
7 Ryan Grant 2.50 6.00
8 Aaron Rodgers 5.00 12.00
9 Mark Tauscher 1.50 4.00
10 Donald Lee 2.00 5.00
11 Will Blackmon 1.50 4.00
12 Scott Wells 1.50 4.00
13 Aaron Kampman 2.00 5.00
14 Al Harris 1.50 4.00
15 Donald Driver 2.00 5.00
16 Brian Brohm 2.50 6.00
17 Brandon Jackson 2.00 5.00
18 Ruvell Martin 1.50 4.00
19 Jordy Nelson 3.00 8.00
20 Matt Flynn 5.00 12.00
21 Charles Woodson 2.50 6.00
22 Nick Barnett 1.50 4.00
23 James Jones 1.50 4.00
24 Kabeer Gbaja-Biamila 1.50 4.00

2008 Upper Deck Masterpieces Preview

COMPLETE SET (10) 12.00 30.00
STATED ODDS 1:8
MPP1 Franco Harris 1.50 4.00
MPP2 Dwight Clark 1.25 3.00
MPP3 Alan Ameche 1.00 2.50
MPP4 Vince Lombardi 2.50 6.00
MPP5 Adrian Peterson 2.00 5.00
MPP6 Gale Sayers 2.00 5.00
MPP7 Walter Payton 3.00 8.00
MPP8 Tom Brady 2.00 5.00
MPP9 Red Grange 2.00 5.00
MPP10 Johnny Unitas 2.50 6.00

2008 Upper Deck Mystery Iconic Cuts Redemption

STATED PRINT RUN 1-66
SERIAL #'d UNDER 20 NOT PRICED
IC5 Arnie Weinmeister/26 40.00 80.00
IC14 Bill Willis/56 30.00 60.00
IC41 Dick Lane/24 75.00 150.00
IC44 Doak Walker/22 75.00 150.00
IC51 Dutch Clark/20 60.00 120.00
IC55 Eddie Arcaro/25 50.00 100.00
IC59 Eleanor Powell/26 20.00 50.00
IC60 Elizabeth Montgomery/43 50.00 100.00
IC61 Elroy Hirsch/55 30.00 60.00
IC63 Ernie Stautner/53 30.00 60.00
IC66 Frank Gatski/60 40.00 80.00
IC73 George Connor/70 20.00 50.00
IC75 George Musso/20 50.00 100.00
IC81 Glenn Ford/37 20.00 50.00
IC91 J. Paul Getty/28 50.00 100.00
IC93 Jack Haley/35 40.00 80.00
IC95 Jack Lord/34 40.00 80.00
IC100 Jim Parker/26 30.00 60.00
IC122 Lucille Ball/26 100.00 175.00
IC129 Mel Torme/66 40.00 80.00
IC131 Mike Webster/25 75.00 125.00
IC133 Red Badgro/30 80.00 80.00
IC136 Otto Graham/54 30.00 60.00
IC138 Paul Brown/62 50.00 100.00
IC143 Ray Nitschke/26 75.00 150.00
IC144 Red Buttons/30 40.00 80.00
IC154 Roosevelt Brown/66 20.00 50.00
IC162 Sid Gillman/22 50.00 100.00
IC173 Tony Canadeo/51 30.00 60.00
IC178 Vincent Price/38 60.00 100.00
IC182 Weeb Ewbank/30 40.00 80.00

2008 Upper Deck Potential Unlimited

TWO PER RACK PACK
PU1 John David Booty .60 1.50
PU2 Andre Woodson .75 2.00
PU3 Antoine Cason .75 2.00
PU4 Brady Quinn .60 1.50
PU5 Brian Brohm .75 2.00
PU6 Calais Campbell .60 1.50
PU7 Chris Ellis .50 1.25
PU8 Chris Long .75 2.00
PU9 Colt Brennan .75 2.00
PU10 Dan Connor .75 2.00
PU11 Darren McFadden 2.00 5.00
PU12 DeSean Jackson 1.50 4.00
PU13 Glenn Dorsey .75 2.00
PU14 Jake Long .75 2.00
PU15 JaMarcus Russell .60 1.50
PU16 Jonathan Stewart 1.25 3.00
PU17 Rashard Mendenhall 1.50 4.00
PU18 Joe Flacco 2.50 6.00
PU19 Jordy Nelson 1.00 2.50
PU20 Keith Rivers .75 2.00
PU21 Kenny Phillips .75 2.00
PU22 Limas Sweed .75 2.00
PU23 Justin King .60 1.50
PU24 Mario Manningham .75 2.00
PU25 Mario Urrutia .50 1.25
PU26 Martin Rucker .60 1.50
PU27 Matt Ryan 3.00 8.00
PU28 Mike Hart .75 2.00
PU29 Ray Rice 1.50 4.00
PU30 Sam Baker .50 1.25
PU31 Sedrick Ellis .75 2.00
PU32 Chris Johnson 2.00 5.00
PU33 Trent Edwards .50 1.25

2008 Upper Deck Record Breakers

COMPLETE SET (6) 6.00 15.00
ISSUED AT THE 2008 NFL EXPERIENCE IN AZ
RB1 Brett Favre 2.00 5.00
RB2 Tom Brady 1.25 3.00
RB3 Adrian Peterson 1.25 3.00
RB4 Tony Gonzalez .60 1.50
RB5 Randy Moss .75 2.00
RB6 Devin Hester .75 2.00

2008 Upper Deck Rookie Autographs

OVERALL AUTO ODDS 1:16
201-300 PRINT RUN 35 SER.#'d SETS
UNPRICED 301-325 PRINT RUN 10
201 Will Franklin 8.00 20.00
202 Jerome Felton 6.00 15.00
203 Adrian Arrington 8.00 20.00
204 Alex Brink 10.00 25.00
205 Allen Patrick 8.00 20.00
206 Andre Caldwell 8.00 20.00
207 Anthony Morelli 8.00 20.00
208 Antoine Cason 10.00 25.00
209 Aqib Talib 10.00 25.00
210 Ben Moffitt 6.00 15.00
213 Bruce Davis 8.00 20.00
214 Calais Campbell 8.00 20.00
215 Chris Williams 8.00 20.00
216 Chad Henne 30.00 80.00
217 Chevis Jackson 6.00 15.00
218 Chris Ellis 6.00 15.00
219 Chris Johnson 60.00 120.00
220 Cory Boyd 6.00 15.00
221 Craig Steltz 8.00 20.00
222 DJ Hall 8.00 20.00
224 Darius Reynaud 6.00 15.00
225 Davone Bess 10.00 25.00
226 DeJuan Tribble 6.00 15.00
227 DeMario Pressley 8.00 20.00
228 Dennis Keyes 6.00 15.00
229 Derrick Harvey 6.00 15.00
230 Donnie Avery 8.00 20.00
231 Xavier Omon 10.00 25.00
232 Dre Moore 8.00 20.00
233 Dustin Keller 12.00 30.00
235 Erik Ainge 10.00 25.00
236 Erin Henderson 10.00 25.00
237 Curtis Lofton 8.00 20.00
238 Felix Jones 30.00 80.00
239 Josh Barrett 6.00 15.00
240 Gosder Cherilus 8.00 20.00
241 Harry Douglas 8.00 20.00
242 Colt Brennan 15.00 40.00
243 J Leman 6.00 15.00
244 Jack Ikegwuonu 6.00 15.00
245 Jacob Hester 10.00 25.00
246 Jacob Tamme 10.00 25.00
247 Jamaal Charles 25.00 60.00
248 James Hardy 8.00 20.00
249 Jermichael Finley 15.00 40.00
251 Joe Flacco 50.00 120.00
252 John Carlson 10.00 25.00
253 John David Booty 8.00 20.00
255 Jonathan Hefney 8.00 20.00
256 Jordon Dizon 10.00 25.00
257 Jordy Nelson 20.00 40.00
258 Josh Johnson 10.00 25.00
259 Justin Forsett 10.00 25.00
260 Kalvin McRae 6.00 15.00
261 Keenan Burton 6.00 15.00
262 Kellen Davis 6.00 15.00
263 Kentwan Balmer 8.00 20.00
264 Keon Lattimore 8.00 20.00
265 Kevin O'Connell 8.00 20.00
267 Thomas DeCoud 6.00 15.00
268 Malcolm Kelly 8.00 20.00
269 Marcus Monk 8.00 20.00
270 Mario Manningham 15.00 30.00
271 Mario Urrutia 6.00 15.00
272 Martellus Bennett 8.00 20.00
273 Martin Rucker 8.00 20.00
274 Matt Flynn 30.00 60.00
275 Matt Forte 25.00 60.00
276 Owen Schmitt 10.00 25.00
277 Paul Hubbard 8.00 20.00
278 Paul Smith 10.00 25.00
279 Philip Wheeler 8.00 20.00
280 Quentin Groves 8.00 20.00
281 Quintin Demps 10.00 25.00
282 Rashard Mendenhall 40.00 80.00
283 Ray Rice 25.00 60.00
284 Ryan Clady 10.00 25.00
286 Ryan Torain 10.00 25.00
287 Spencer Larsen 6.00 15.00
288 Marcus Thomas 8.00 20.00
289 Shawn Crable 6.00 15.00
290 Frank Okam 6.00 15.00
291 Tashard Choice 8.00 20.00
292 Terrell Thomas 8.00 20.00
293 Thomas Brown 8.00 20.00
294 Tom Zbikowski 10.00 25.00
296 Trevor Laws 10.00 25.00
297 Vernon Gholston 8.00 20.00
298 Vince Hall 6.00 15.00
299 Xavier Adibi 6.00 15.00
300 Yvenson Bernard 10.00 25.00

2008 Upper Deck Rookie Jerseys

*GOLD/350: .5X TO 1.2X SILVER JSY
GOLD/350 INSERTED IN HOT BOXES
OVERALL MEMORABILIA ODDS 1:8
UDRJBB Brian Brohm 2.50 6.00
UDRJCH Chad Henne 2.50 6.00
UDRJCJ Chris Johnson 6.00 15.00
UDRJDA Donnie Avery 2.00 5.00
UDRJDJ Dexter Jackson 2.00 5.00
UDRJDK Dustin Keller 2.50 6.00
UDRJDM Darren McFadden 6.00 15.00
UDRJDT Devin Thomas 2.00 5.00
UDRJEB Earl Bennett 2.50 6.00
UDRJED Early Doucet 2.00 5.00
UDRJFJ Felix Jones 4.00 10.00
UDRJGD Glenn Dorsey 2.50 6.00
UDRJJA DeSean Jackson 5.00 12.00
UDRJJF Joe Flacco 6.00 15.00
UDRJJL Jake Long 2.50 6.00
UDRJJN Jordy Nelson 3.00 8.00
UDRJJS Jonathan Stewart 4.00 10.00
UDRJKO Kevin O'Connell 2.00 5.00
UDRJLS Limas Sweed 2.50 6.00
UDRJMF Matt Forte 4.00 10.00
UDRJMK Malcolm Kelly 2.00 5.00
UDRJMM Mario Manningham 2.50 6.00
UDRJMR Matt Ryan 8.00 20.00
UDRJRR Ray Rice 5.00 12.00
UDRJSS Steve Slaton 2.50 6.00

2008 Upper Deck Same Day Signatures

INSERTS IN VARIOUS UD BRANDS
SDS1 Donnie Avery 8.00 20.00
SDS2 Earl Bennett 10.00 25.00
SDS3 John David Booty
SDS4 Brian Brohm 10.00 25.00
SDS5 Andre Caldwell 8.00 20.00
SDS6 Jamaal Charles 15.00 40.00
SDS7 Glenn Dorsey
SDS8 Early Doucet
SDS9 Harry Douglas
SDS10 Joe Flacco 100.00 200.00
SDS11 Matt Forte 15.00 40.00
SDS12 James Hardy
SDS13 Chad Henne
SDS14 DeSean Jackson 20.00 50.00
SDS15 Dexter Jackson 8.00 20.00
SDS16 Chris Johnson 75.00 150.00
SDS17 Felix Jones
SDS18 Dustin Keller 25.00 50.00
SDS19 Malcolm Kelly
SDS20 Chris Long
SDS21 Jake Long
SDS22 Mario Manningham
SDS23 Darren McFadden 40.00 100.00
SDS24 Rashard Mendenhall 20.00 50.00
SDS25 Jordy Nelson 30.00 60.00
SDS26 Kevin O'Connell 8.00 20.00
SDS27 Ray Rice 20.00 50.00
SDS28 Eddie Royal 10.00 25.00
SDS29 Matt Ryan 100.00 200.00
SDS30 Jerome Simpson
SDS31 Steve Slaton
SDS32 Kevin Smith
SDS33 Jonathan Stewart 15.00 40.00
SDS34 Limas Sweed 12.00 30.00
SDS35 Devin Thomas 8.00 20.00
SDS36 Erik Ainge
SDS37 Martellus Bennett
SDS38 Colt Brennan
SDS39 Keenan Burton
SDS40 John Carlson
SDS41 Tashard Choice
SDS42 Fred Davis
SDS43 Dennis Dixon
SDS44 Jordon Dizon
SDS45 Vernon Gholston
SDS46 Mike Hart
SDS47 Derrick Harvey
SDS48 Lavelle Hawkins
SDS49 Jacob Hester
SDS50 Josh Johnson
SDS51 Jerod Mayo
SDS52 Leodis McKelvin
SDS53 Kenny Phillips
SDS54 Keith Rivers
SDS55 Andre Woodson
SDS56 Joe Flacco
Matt Ryan
SDS57 Chad Henne
Jake Long
SDS58 Darren McFadden
Felix Jones
SDS59 Jordy Nelson 25.00 50.00
Devin Thomas
SDS60 Rashard Mendenhall 20.00 50.00
Limas Sweed

2008 Upper Deck Signature Shots

OVERALL AUTO ODDS 1:16
SS1 Adrian Peterson 75.00 150.00
SS2 Andre Woodson 6.00 15.00
SS3 Dwayne Bowe 8.00 20.00
SS4 Antoine Cason 6.00 15.00
SS5 Aqib Talib 6.00 15.00
SS6 Paul Posluszny 6.00 15.00
SS7 Brandon Marshall 6.00 15.00
SS8 Brett Favre
SS9 John Beck 5.00 12.00
SS10 Michael Huff 5.00 12.00
SS11 Calais Campbell 5.00 12.00
SS12 Wes Welker 20.00 40.00
SS13 Jamal Lewis 8.00 20.00
SS14 Chris Long 6.00 15.00
SS15 Clinton Portis 12.00 30.00
SS16 Colt Brennan 15.00 40.00
SS17 Dan Connor 6.00 15.00
SS18 Sidney Rice 8.00 20.00
SS19 Darrell Jackson 5.00 12.00
SS20 Darren McFadden
SS21 Kolby Smith 5.00 12.00
SS22 DeSean Jackson 12.00 30.00
SS23 Early Doucet 5.00 12.00
SS24 Chad Henne 12.00 30.00
SS25 Frank Gore 20.00 40.00
SS26 Fred Davis 5.00 12.00
SS27 Glenn Dorsey 6.00 15.00
SS28 Tony Hunt 5.00 12.00
SS29 Jake Long 6.00 15.00
SS30 Shawn Crable 5.00 12.00
SS31 Jerious Norwood 5.00 12.00
SS32 Ben Watson 5.00 12.00
SS33 Joe Flacco 30.00 80.00
SS34 John Carlson 6.00 15.00
SS35 Jonathan Stewart 12.00 30.00
SS36 Joseph Addai 12.00 30.00
SS38 Brandon Jacobs 6.00 15.00
SS39 Lawrence Jackson 5.00 12.00
SS40 Limas Sweed 6.00 15.00
SS41 Justin King 5.00 12.00
SS42 Marion Barber 12.00 30.00
SS43 Mark Clayton 5.00 12.00
SS44 Matt Ryan 50.00 100.00
SS45 Jeff Garcia 6.00 15.00
SS46 Mike Hart 6.00 15.00
SS47 Dennis Dixon
SS48 Peyton Manning 60.00 120.00
SS49 Lorenzo Booker 5.00 12.00
SS50 Ray Rice 10.00 25.00
SS51 Sam Baker 4.00 10.00
SS52 Sedrick Ellis 6.00 15.00
SS53 Tashard Choice 5.00 12.00
SS54 Tom Zbikowski 6.00 15.00
SS55 Brandon Meriweather 5.00 12.00
SS56 Tony Romo 40.00 80.00
SS57 Marcus McCauley 5.00 12.00
SS58 Vince Hall
SS59 Dwayne Wright 4.00 10.00
SS60 Xavier Adibi 4.00 10.00

2008 Upper Deck Star Quest Silver Board

SILVER ANNOUNCED ODDS 1:2
*RAINBOW BLACK: .6X TO 1.5X SILVER
BLACK ANNOUNCED ODDS 1:16 HOB
*RAINBOW BLUE: .4X TO 1X SILVER
BLUE ANNOUNCED ODDS 1:4
*RAINBOW GOLD: .8X TO 2X SILVER
GOLD ANNOUNCED ODDS 1:24
*RAINBOW GREEN: .6X TO 1.5X SILVER
GREEN ANNOUNCED ODDS 1:16
*RAINBOW RED: .5X TO 1.2X SILVER
RED ANNOUNCED ODDS 1:6
OVERALL STAR QUEST ODDS 1:16
SQ1 Adrian Peterson 1.50 4.00
SQ2 Andre Woodson .75 2.00
SQ3 Antonio Cromartie .50 1.25
SQ4 Ben Roethlisberger 1.00 2.50
SQ5 Brian Westbrook .75 2.00
SQ6 Carson Palmer 1.00 2.50
SQ7 Chris Long .75 2.00
SQ8 Darren McFadden 2.00 5.00
SQ9 DeSean Jackson 1.50 4.00
SQ10 Drew Brees 1.00 2.50
SQ11 Early Doucet .60 1.50
SQ12 Ed Reed .75 2.00
SQ13 Ernie Sims .60 1.50
SQ14 Fred Taylor .75 2.00
SQ15 Glenn Dorsey .75 2.00
SQ16 Shawn Crable .50 1.25
SQ17 Joseph Addai .75 2.00
SQ18 Kenny Phillips .75 2.00
SQ19 LaDainian Tomlinson 1.00 2.50
SQ20 Larry Fitzgerald 1.00 2.50
SQ21 Matt Hasselbeck .75 2.00
SQ22 Matt Ryan 3.00 8.00
SQ23 Osi Umenyiora .75 2.00
SQ24 Patrick Willis .75 2.00
SQ25 Peyton Manning 1.50 4.00
SQ26 Randy Moss 1.00 2.50
SQ27 Sam Baker .50 1.25
SQ28 Terrell Owens 1.00 2.50
SQ29 Tom Brady 1.50 4.00
SQ30 Tony Romo 1.25 3.00

2008 Upper Deck Superstar

UNPRICED AUTO PRINT RUN 5
UDSSAP Adrian Peterson 2.00 5.00
UDSSBR Ben Roethlisberger 1.25 3.00
UDSSCP Clinton Portis 1.00 2.50
UDSSEM Eli Manning 1.25 3.00
UDSSLT LaDainian Tomlinson 1.25 3.00
UDSSML Marshawn Lynch 1.00 2.50
UDSSPM Peyton Manning 2.00 5.00
UDSSRM Randy Moss 1.25 3.00
UDSSTB Tom Brady 2.00 5.00
UDSSTR Tony Romo 1.50 4.00

2008 Upper Deck Superstar Autographs

UNPRICED AUTO PRINT RUN 5

2008 Upper Deck Target Exclusive Rookies

UNPRICED AUTO PRINT RUN 5
1 Alex Brink 1.50 4.00
2 Andre Woodson 1.50 4.00
3 Antoine Cason 1.50 4.00
4 Brian Brohm 1.50 4.00
5 Calais Campbell 1.25 3.00
6 Chris Ellis 1.00 2.50
7 Chris Long 1.50 4.00
8 Colt Brennan 1.50 4.00
9 Dan Connor 1.50 4.00
10 Darren McFadden 4.00 10.00
11 DeSean Jackson 3.00 8.00
12 Glenn Dorsey 1.50 4.00
13 Jake Long 1.50 4.00
14 Shawn Crable 1.00 2.50
15 J Leman 1.00 2.50
16 Joe Flacco 5.00 12.00
17 John Carlson 1.50 4.00
18 Jordy Nelson 2.00 5.00
19 Keith Rivers 1.50 4.00
20 Kenny Phillips 1.50 4.00
21 Limas Sweed 1.50 4.00
22 Justin King 1.25 3.00
23 Mario Manningham 1.50 4.00
24 Mario Urrutia 1.00 2.50
25 Martin Rucker 1.25 3.00
26 Matt Ryan 6.00 15.00
27 Mike Hart 1.50 4.00
28 Sam Baker 1.00 2.50
29 Sedrick Ellis 1.50 4.00
30 Chris Johnson 4.00 10.00

2008 Upper Deck Team Colors Jerseys

*GOLD/299: .5X TO 1.2X SILVER JSY
GOLD/299 INSERTED IN HOT BOXES
OVERALL MEMORABILIA ODDS 1:8
TCAP Adrian Peterson 5.00 12.00
TCBE Braylon Edwards 3.00 8.00
TCBF Brett Favre 8.00 20.00
TCCB Cedric Benson 2.50 6.00
TCCJ Calvin Johnson 3.00 8.00
TCCP Carson Palmer 3.00 8.00
TCDB Dwayne Bowe 2.50 6.00
TCDG David Garrard 2.50 6.00
TCEM Eli Manning 3.00 8.00
TCJC Jay Cutler 4.00 10.00
TCMB Marion Barber 5.00 12.00
TCML Marshawn Lynch 2.50 6.00
TCPM Peyton Manning 5.00 12.00
TCPR Philip Rivers 3.00 8.00
TCRB Reggie Bush 3.00 8.00
TCSA Shaun Alexander 2.50 6.00
TCTB Tedy Bruschi 3.00 8.00
TCTO Terrell Owens 4.00 10.00
TCWM Willis McGahee 2.50 6.00
TCWP Willie Parker 4.00 10.00

2008 Upper Deck 20th Anniversary

Upper Deck produced this 80-card set featuring past and present athletes from baseball, football, basketball and hockey and issued them through their Certified Diamond Dealers program. Eight cards were released every month from March through December 2008. By entering in all 80 unique codes from the back of the cards on the company's website by December 31, 2008, collectors had a chance to win a trip to four major sporting events.

UD16 Joe Montana .75 2.00
UD17 Brett Favre .75 2.00
UD18 Reggie Bush .40 1.00
UD19 Ben Roethlisberger .50 1.25
UD20 Tom Brady .60 1.50
UD21 Peyton Manning .60 1.50
UD22 Randy Moss .30 .75
UD23 Dan Marino 1.00 2.50
UD24 Walter Payton 1.25 3.00
UD25 LaDainian Tomlinson .40 1.00
UD26 Tony Romo .75 2.00
UD27 Joseph Addai .30 .75
UD28 Vince Young .30 .75
UD29 Matt Leinart .30 .75
UD30 Adrian Peterson .75 2.00
UD66 Darren McFadden .75 2.00
UD67 Matt Ryan 1.50 4.00
UD68 Brian Brohm .30 .75
UD69 Felix Jones .75 2.00
UD70 Rashard Mendenhall .60 1.50

2009 Upper Deck

COMPLETE SET (325) 90.00 150.00
COMP.SET w/o SP's (300) 25.00 50.00
COMP.SET w/o RC's (200) 10.00 25.00
FOUR ROOKIES PER HOBBY PACK
1 Kurt Warner .25 .60
2 Tim Hightower .15 .40
3 Larry Fitzgerald .25 .60
4 Anquan Boldin .20 .50
5 Steve Breaston .20 .50
6 Matt Leinart .20 .50
7 Adrian Wilson .15 .40
8 Michael Turner .20 .50
9 Jerious Norwood .20 .50
10 Roddy White .20 .50
11 Michael Jenkins .15 .40
12 Matt Ryan .25 .60
13 John Abraham .15 .40
14 Ed Reed .20 .50
15 Willis McGahee .20 .50
16 Ray Rice .25 .60
17 Le'Ron McClain .20 .50
18 Derrick Mason .20 .50
19 Joe Flacco .25 .60
20 Ray Lewis .25 .60
21 Mark Clayton .15 .40
22 Lee Evans .20 .50
23 Marshawn Lynch .20 .50
24 Leodis McKelvin .15 .40
25 Trent Edwards .15 .40
26 Terrell Owens .25 .60
27 Roscoe Parrish .15 .40
28 DeAngelo Williams .25 .60
29 Jonathan Stewart .20 .50
30 Steve Smith .20 .50
31 Muhsin Muhammad .20 .50
32 Jake Delhomme .20 .50
33 Jon Beason .15 .40
34 Julius Peppers .20 .50
35 Brian Urlacher .25 .60
37 Matt Forte .25 .60
38 Tommie Harris .15 .40
39 Lance Briggs .20 .50
40 Devin Hester .25 .60
41 Olin Kreutz .15 .40
42 Leon Hall .15 .40
43 Cedric Benson .20 .50
44 Reggie Kelly .15 .40
45 Carson Palmer .25 .60
46 Chad Johnson .20 .50
47 Laveranues Coles .15 .40
48 Jamal Lewis .20 .50
49 Braylon Edwards .20 .50
50 Derek Anderson .15 .40
51 Joe Thomas .20 .50
52 Brady Quinn .20 .50
53 Marion Barber .20 .50
54 Jason Witten .25 .60
55 Bradie James .15 .40
56 Tony Romo .40 1.00
57 DeMarcus Ware .20 .50
58 Felix Jones .25 .60
59 Roy Williams WR .20 .50
60 Brandon Marshall .20 .50
61 Eddie Royal .20 .50
62 Michael Pittman .15 .40
63A Jay Cutler .25 .60
63B Kyle Orton .20 .50
64 Champ Bailey .20 .50
65 Daunte Culpepper .20 .50
66 Kevin Smith .20 .50
67 Calvin Johnson .25 .60
68 Jason Hanson .15 .40
69 Rudi Johnson .15 .40
70 Ryan Grant .20 .50
71 Greg Jennings .25 .60
72 Donald Driver .20 .50
73 Aaron Rodgers .50 1.25
74 Aaron Kampman .20 .50
75 Charles Woodson .25 .60
76 Will Blackmon .15 .40
77 A.J. Hawk .20 .50
78 Steve Slaton .20 .50
79 Andre Johnson .20 .50
80 Kevin Walter .20 .50
81 Kris Brown .15 .40
82 Matt Schaub .20 .50
83 DeMeco Ryans .20 .50
84 Mario Williams .20 .50
85 Peyton Manning .40 1.00
86 Joseph Addai .25 .60
87 Reggie Wayne .20 .50
88 Anthony Gonzalez .15 .40
89 Dallas Clark .20 .50
90 Adam Vinatieri .20 .50
91 Dwight Freeney .20 .50
92 Bob Sanders .20 .50
93 Maurice Jones-Drew .20 .50
94 Marcedes Lewis .15 .40
95 Justin Durant .15 .40
96 Rashean Mathis .15 .40
97 David Garrard .20 .50
98 Tony Gonzalez .20 .50
99 Larry Johnson .20 .50
100 Dwayne Bowe .20 .50
101 Matt Cassel .20 .50
102 Tyler Thigpen .15 .40
103 Ronnie Brown .20 .50
104 Ricky Williams .20 .50
105 Greg Camarillo .20 .50
106 Ted Ginn Jr. .20 .50
107 Chad Pennington .20 .50
108 Joey Porter .20 .50
109 Adrian Peterson .40 1.00
110 Visanthe Shiancoe .20 .50
111 Bernard Berrian .20 .50
112A Sage Rosenfels .15 .40
112B Brett Favre holding jsy 125.00 200.00
112C Brett Favre passing 40.00 100.00
113 Jared Allen .25 .60
114 Chester Taylor .15 .40
115 Tom Brady .40 1.00
116 Wes Welker .25 .60
117 Stephen Gostkowski .15 .40
118 Randy Moss .25 .60
119 Kevin Faulk .15 .40
120 Sammy Morris .15 .40
121 Reggie Bush .25 .60
122 Drew Brees .25 .60
123 Pierre Thomas .20 .50
124 Lance Moore .20 .50
125 Marques Colston .20 .50
126 Jeremy Shockey .15 .40
127 Eli Manning .25 .60
128 Brandon Jacobs .20 .50
129 Domenik Hixon .15 .40
130 Ahmad Bradshaw .20 .50
131 Steve Smith USC .20 .50
132 Thomas Jones .20 .50
133 Bart Scott .15 .40
134 Dustin Keller .15 .40
135 Kellen Clemens .15 .40
136 Leon Washington .20 .50
137 Jerricho Cotchery .20 .50
138 Johnnie Lee Higgins .15 .40
139 Justin Fargas .15 .40
140 Darren McFadden .25 .60
141 JaMarcus Russell .15 .40
142 Kirk Morrison .15 .40
143 Brian Westbrook .20 .50
144 DeSean Jackson .20 .50
145 Donovan McNabb .25 .60
146 Shawn Andrews .15 .40
147 Asante Samuel .15 .40
148 Reggie Brown .15 .40

149 Willie Parker	.15	.40
150 Hines Ward	.20	.50
151 Santonio Holmes	.20	.50
152 Ben Roethlisberger	.25	.60
153 James Harrison	.25	.60
154 Troy Polamalu	.25	.60
155 Rashard Mendenhall	.20	.50
156 LaDainian Tomlinson	.25	.60
157 Vincent Jackson	.20	.50
158 Antonio Gates	.20	.50
159 Philip Rivers	.25	.60
160 Shawne Merriman	.20	.50
161 Antonio Cromartie	.15	.40
162 Chris Chambers	.20	.50
163 Darren Sproles	.20	.50
164 Frank Gore	.20	.50
165 Isaac Bruce	.20	.50
166 Alex Smith	.20	.50
167 Patrick Willis	.20	.50
168 Josh Morgan	.15	.40
169 Shaun Hill	.15	.40
170 Vernon Davis	.20	.50
171 Julius Jones	.15	.40
172 Matt Hasselbeck	.20	.50
173 Lofa Tatupu	.20	.50
174 Deion Branch	.20	.50
175 T.J. Houshmandzadeh	.20	.50
176 Steven Jackson	.20	.50
177 Antonio Pittman	.15	.40
178 Donnie Avery	.20	.50
179 Marc Bulger	.20	.50
180 Oshiomogho Atogwe	.15	.40
181 Warrick Dunn	.20	.50
182 Kellen Winslow	.20	.50
183 Barrett Ruud	.15	.40
184 Michael Clayton	.15	.40
185 Aqib Talib	.15	.40
186 Ronde Barber	.15	.40
187 Cadillac Williams	.20	.50
188 Chris Johnson	.25	.60
189 LenDale White	.20	.50
190 Bo Scaife	.15	.40
191 Kerry Collins	.20	.50
192 Cortland Finnegan	.15	.40
193 Vince Young	.20	.50
194 Clinton Portis	.20	.50
195 Santana Moss	.20	.50
196 Chris Cooley	.20	.50
197 Antwaan Randle El	.15	.40
198 Jason Campbell	.15	.40
199 London Fletcher	.15	.40
200 Albert Haynesworth	.15	.40
201 Morgan Trent RC	.60	1.50
202 Everette Brown RC	.60	1.50
203 Clay Matthews RC	2.00	5.00
204 Eben Britton RC	.60	1.50
205 Andre Brown RC	.50	1.25
206 DeAngelo Smith RC	.60	1.50
207 Glen Coffee RC	.60	1.50
208 Jairus Byrd RC	.75	2.00
209 Sherrod Martin RC	.60	1.50
210 Victor Harris RC	.75	2.00
211 Sen'Derrick Marks RC	.50	1.25
212 Shawn Nelson RC	.60	1.50
213 Captain Munnerlyn RC	.60	1.50
214 D.J. Moore RC	.60	1.50
215 Gerald McRath RC	.60	1.50
216 Alphonso Smith RC	.60	1.50
217 Darius Butler RC	.75	2.00
218 Chase Coffman RC	.60	1.50
219 Mike Goodson RC	.75	2.00
220 Ron Brace RC	.60	1.50
221 William Beatty RC	.50	1.25
222 Michael Hamlin RC	.60	1.50
223 Marcus Freeman RC	.75	2.00
224 Michael Oher RC	1.25	3.00
225 Patrick Chung RC	.75	2.00
226 Larry English RC	.75	2.00
227 Connor Barwin RC	.75	2.00
228 Eric Wood RC	.60	1.50
229 Peria Jerry RC	.60	1.50
230 Clint Sintim RC	.75	2.00
231 Fili Moala RC	.60	1.50
232 Keenan Lewis RC	.75	2.00
233 Derrick Williams RC	.60	1.50
234 Kaluka Maiava RC	.75	2.00
235 Rhett Bomar RC	.60	1.50
236 Sean Smith RC	.75	2.00
237 Antoine Caldwell RC	.50	1.25
238 Cody Brown RC	.50	1.25
239 Travis Beckum RC	.60	1.50
240 William Moore RC	.75	2.00
241 Brian Robiskie RC	.75	2.00
242 Curtis Painter RC	.75	2.00
243 Vontae Davis RC	.75	2.00
244 Richard Quinn RC	.60	1.50
245 Robert Ayers RC	.75	2.00
246 Brandon Gibson RC	.75	2.00
247 Alex Mack RC	.60	1.50
248 Asher Allen RC	.60	1.50
249 Max Unger RC	.60	1.50
250 Herman Johnson RC	.60	1.50
251 Jamon Meredith RC	.60	1.50
252 Jonathan Luigs RC	.50	1.25
253 Phil Loadholt RC	.60	1.50
254 Sebastian Vollmer RC	.60	1.50
255 Michael Mitchell RC	.60	1.50
256 Javon Ringer RC	.75	2.00
257 Nate Davis RC	.60	1.50
258 Rudy Carpenter RC	.60	1.50
259 Paul Kruger RC	.60	1.50
260 Stephen McGee RC	.75	2.00
261 Ian Johnson RC	.75	2.00
262 Mike Wallace RC	1.50	4.00
263 Brian Hartline RC	.75	2.00
264 Devin Moore RC	.60	1.50
265 Jared Cook RC	.75	2.00
266 Sammie Stroughter RC	.75	2.00
267 Quan Cosby RC	.60	1.50
268 Brooks Foster RC	.50	1.25
269 Anthony Hill RC	.50	1.25
270 Mike Thomas RC	.75	2.00
271 Eugene Monroe RC	.50	1.25
272 Rodney Ferguson RC	.60	1.50
273 Rey Maualuga RC	.75	2.00
274 Tony Fiammetta RC	.60	1.50
275 Michael Johnson RC	.50	1.25
276 Evander Hood RC	1.00	2.50
277 Austin Collie RC	.75	2.00
278 Jason Phillips RC	.60	1.50
279 Ramses Barden RC	.50	1.25
280 Louis Delmas RC	.75	2.00
281 James Davis RC	.75	2.00
282 Demetrius Byrd RC	.60	1.50
283 Frank Summers RC	.75	2.00
284 Juaquin Iglesias RC	.60	1.50
285 Jasper Brinkley RC	.60	1.50
286 Louis Murphy RC	.75	2.00
287 Kevin Barnes RC	.60	1.50
288 Gartrell Johnson RC	.50	1.25
289 Matt Shaughnessy RC	.60	1.50
290 Patrick Turner RC	.60	1.50
291 Cornelius Ingram RC	.50	1.25
292 Jarron Gilbert RC	.60	1.50
293 James Casey RC	.60	1.50
294 Rashad Jennings RC	.75	2.00
295 Deon Butler RC	.60	1.50
296 James Laurinaitis RC	.75	2.00
297 Brandon Tate RC	.75	2.00
298 Nic Harris RC	.60	1.50
299 Brian Cushing RC	.75	2.00
300 Alex Magee RC	.60	1.50
301 Andre Smith RC	1.50	4.00
302 Shonn Greene RC	3.00	8.00
303 Pat White RC	2.00	5.00
304 Malcolm Jenkins RC	2.00	5.00
305 Matthew Stafford RC	10.00	25.00
306 Michael Crabtree RC	4.00	10.00
307 Tyson Jackson RC	1.50	4.00
308 Brandon Pettigrew RC	2.00	5.00
309 Brian Orakpo RC	2.00	5.00
310 Jeremy Maclin RC	3.00	8.00
311 Jason Smith RC	1.50	4.00
312 Chris Wells RC	3.00	8.00
313 Aaron Curry RC	2.00	5.00
314 Mark Sanchez RC	6.00	15.00
315 Aaron Maybin RC	1.50	4.00
316 B.J. Raji RC	2.00	5.00
317 Kenny Britt RC	2.50	6.00
318 Mohamed Massaquoi RC	1.50	4.00
319 Knowshon Moreno RC	2.00	5.00
320 Percy Harvin RC	3.00	8.00
321 Hakeem Nicks RC	3.00	8.00
322 LeSean McCoy RC	4.00	10.00
323 Darrius Heyward-Bey RC	2.00	5.00
324 Josh Freeman RC	4.00	10.00
325 Donald Brown RC	2.00	5.00
0 Michael Vick SP	15.00	40.00

2009 Upper Deck 3D Stars

STATED ODDS 1:8		
3D1 Tom Brady	4.00	10.00
Randy Moss		
3D2 Adrian Peterson	4.00	10.00
3D3 Randy Moss	2.50	6.00
3D4 Devin Hester	2.50	6.00
3D5 Dallas Clark	4.00	10.00
Peyton Manning		
3D6 Chad Johnson	2.00	5.00
3D7 Michael Turner	2.00	5.00
3D8 Matt Ryan	2.50	6.00
3D9 Larry Fitzgerald	2.50	6.00
3D10 Kurt Warner	2.50	6.00
3D11 Tony Romo	4.00	10.00
3D12 Wes Welker	2.50	6.00
3D13 Andre Johnson	2.00	5.00
3D14 Reggie Wayne	2.00	5.00
3D15 Willie Parker	1.50	4.00
3D16 Carson Palmer	2.50	6.00
3D17 Calvin Johnson	2.50	6.00
3D18 Terrell Owens	2.50	6.00
3D19 Jake Delhomme	2.00	5.00
Steve Smith		
3D20 Marion Barber	2.00	5.00
3D21 Reggie Bush	2.50	6.00
3D22 Lee Evans	2.00	5.00
3D23 Maurice Jones-Drew	2.00	5.00
3D24 Frank Gore	2.00	5.00
3D25 Ben Roethlisberger	2.50	6.00
3D26 David Tyree	2.50	6.00
Eli Manning		
3D27 Brian Westbrook	2.00	5.00
3D28 Clinton Portis	2.00	5.00
3D29 Steven Jackson	2.00	5.00
3D30 Drew Brees	2.50	6.00
3D31 Philip Rivers	2.50	6.00
3D32 Michael Crabtree	3.00	8.00
3D33 Chris Wells	2.50	6.00
3D34 Mark Sanchez	5.00	12.00
3D35 LeSean McCoy	3.00	8.00
3D36 Josh Freeman	3.00	8.00
3D37 Hakeem Nicks	2.50	6.00
3D38 Shonn Greene	2.50	6.00
3D39 Matthew Stafford	8.00	20.00
3D40 Donald Brown	1.50	4.00
3D41 Kenny Britt	2.00	5.00
3D42 Aaron Curry	1.50	4.00
3D43 Pat White	1.50	4.00
3D44 Percy Harvin	2.50	6.00
3D45 Knowshon Moreno	1.50	4.00
3D46 Brandon Pettigrew	1.50	4.00
3D47 Darrius Heyward-Bey	1.50	4.00
3D48 Jeremy Maclin	2.50	6.00
3D49 Mohamed Massaquoi	1.25	3.00
3D50 Barack Obama	6.00	15.00

2009 Upper Deck America's Team

RANDOM INSERTS IN 2009 UD BOXES		
ONE FIVE CARD PACK PER SPECIAL BLASTER		
1 Miles Austin	2.50	6.00
2 Andre Gurode	1.00	2.50
3 Anthony Spencer	1.00	2.50
4 Benny Barnes	1.00	2.50
5 Bill Bates	1.25	3.00
6 Billy Joe Dupree	1.00	2.50
7 Bobby Carpenter	1.00	2.50
8 Bob Breunig	1.00	2.50
9 Marc Colombo	1.00	2.50
10 Bob Lilly	1.25	3.00
11 Leonard Davis	1.00	2.50
12 Martellus Bennett	1.00	2.50
13 Andre Gurode	1.00	2.50
14 Charlie Waters	1.25	3.00
15 Chuck Howley	1.25	3.00
16 Cliff Harris	1.25	3.00
17 Cornell Green	1.00	2.50
18 Benny Barnes	1.00	2.50
19 D.D. Lewis	1.00	2.50
20 Dan Reeves	1.25	3.00
21 Danny White	1.25	3.00
22 Bill Bates	1.25	3.00
23 Daryl Johnston	1.50	4.00
24 Billy Joe Dupree	1.00	2.50
25 Bob Breunig	1.00	2.50
26 Bob Lilly	1.25	3.00
27 DeMarcus Ware	1.25	3.00
28 Charlie Waters	1.25	3.00
29 Cliff Harris	1.25	3.00
30 Cornell Green	1.00	2.50
31 D.D. Lewis	1.00	2.50
32 Dan Reeves	1.25	3.00
33 Drew Pearson	1.25	3.00
34 Danny White	1.25	3.00
35 Ed Too Tall Jones	1.25	3.00
36 John Niland	1.00	2.50
37 Eddie LeBaron	1.50	4.00
38 Emmitt Smith	2.50	6.00
39 Drew Pearson	1.25	3.00
40 Everson Walls	1.00	2.50
41 Felix Jones	1.50	4.00
42 Flozell Adams	1.00	2.50
43 Ed Too Tall Jones	1.25	3.00
44 George Andrie	1.00	2.50
45 Miles Austin	2.50	6.00
46 Greg Ellis	1.00	2.50
47 Harvey Martin	1.00	2.50
48 Everson Walls	1.00	2.50
49 Felix Jones	1.50	4.00
50 Jackie Smith	1.00	2.50
51 Jason Witten	1.50	4.00
52 Jay Novacek	1.25	3.00
53 George Andrie	1.00	2.50
54 Jethro Pugh	1.00	2.50
55 Jim Jeffcoat	1.00	2.50
56 Jimmy Johnson	1.25	3.00
57 John Fitzgerald	1.00	2.50
58 Greg Ellis	1.00	2.50
59 Bobby Carpenter	1.00	2.50
60 Jason Witten	1.50	4.00
61 Jay Novacek	1.25	3.00
62 Larry Cole	1.00	2.50
63 Jethro Pugh	1.00	2.50
64 Jim Jeffcoat	1.00	2.50
65 Marion Barber	1.25	3.00
66 Mark Stepnoski	1.00	2.50
67 Mark Tuinei	1.00	2.50
68 Mel Renfro	1.25	3.00
69 Michael Downs	1.00	2.50
70 Marc Colombo	1.00	2.50
71 John Fitzgerald	1.00	2.50
72 Larry Cole	1.00	2.50
73 Marion Barber	1.25	3.00
74 Nick Folk	1.00	2.50
75 Pat Donovan	1.00	2.50
76 Mark Stepnoski	1.00	2.50
77 Patrick Crayton	1.00	2.50
78 Leonard Davis	1.00	2.50
79 Martellus Bennett	1.00	2.50
80 Mel Renfro	1.25	3.00
81 Randy White	1.50	4.00
82 Michael Downs	1.00	2.50
83 Nick Folk	1.00	2.50
84 Roger Staubach	2.00	5.00
85 Roy Williams WR	1.25	3.00
86 Pat Donovan	1.00	2.50
87 Scott Laidlaw	1.00	2.50
88 Terence Newman	1.00	2.50
89 Terrell Owens	1.50	4.00
90 Roger Staubach	2.00	5.00
91 Thomas Henderson	1.00	2.50
92 Troy Aikman	2.00	5.00
93 Tom Rafferty	1.00	2.50
94 Tony Romo	2.50	6.00
95 Roy Williams WR	1.25	3.00
96 Terence Newman	1.00	2.50
97 Tony Romo	2.50	6.00
98 Tony Tolbert	1.00	2.50
99 Troy Aikman	2.00	5.00
100 Thomas Henderson	1.00	2.50

2009 Upper Deck America's Team Autographs

RANDOM INSERTS IN 2009 UD BOXES		
ONE FIVE CARD PACK PER SPECIAL BLASTER		
4 Benny Barnes	20.00	40.00
5 Bill Bates	25.00	50.00
6 Billy Joe Dupree	25.00	50.00
8 Bob Breunig	25.00	50.00
10 Bob Lilly	50.00	100.00
14 Charlie Waters	25.00	50.00
15 Chuck Howley	40.00	80.00
16 Cliff Harris		
17 Cornell Green	25.00	50.00
19 D.D. Lewis	25.00	50.00
20 Dan Reeves	30.00	60.00
21 Danny White	30.00	60.00
23 Daryl Johnston	30.00	60.00
33 Drew Pearson	25.00	50.00
35 Ed Too Tall Jones	40.00	80.00
36 John Niland	25.00	50.00
37 Eddie LeBaron	50.00	100.00
38 Emmitt Smith	250.00	400.00
40 Everson Walls	25.00	50.00
44 George Andrie	25.00	50.00
50 Jackie Smith	20.00	40.00
52 Jay Novacek	25.00	50.00
54 Jethro Pugh	25.00	50.00
55 Jim Jeffcoat	25.00	50.00
56 Jimmy Johnson	30.00	80.00
57 John Fitzgerald	20.00	40.00
62 Larry Cole	25.00	50.00
66 Mark Stepnoski	25.00	50.00
68 Mel Renfro	25.00	50.00
69 Michael Downs	25.00	50.00
75 Pat Donovan	25.00	50.00
81 Randy White	50.00	100.00
84 Roger Staubach	125.00	200.00
87 Scott Laidlaw	25.00	50.00
91 Thomas Henderson	30.00	60.00
93 Tom Rafferty	25.00	50.00
94 Tony Romo	125.00	200.00
98 Tony Tolbert	25.00	50.00
99 Troy Aikman		

2009 Upper Deck America's Team Jerseys

23 Daryl Johnston	10.00	25.00
38 Emmitt Smith	15.00	40.00
41 Felix Jones	8.00	20.00
51 Jason Witten SP	30.00	60.00
65 Marion Barber	8.00	20.00
84 Roger Staubach	12.00	30.00
89 Terrell Owens	6.00	15.00
94 Tony Romo	12.00	30.00
97 Tony Romo		
99 Troy Aikman	12.00	30.00

2009 Upper Deck Game Day Gear

INSERTS IN VARIOUS 2009 UD PRODUCTS		
AC Andre Caldwell	2.50	6.00
AG Anthony Gonzalez	2.50	6.00
AJ Jason Avant	2.50	6.00
AR Aaron Ross	2.50	6.00
AS Aaron Schobel	2.50	6.00
AV Adam Vinatieri	3.00	8.00
BB Brian Brohm	2.50	6.00
BE Bernard Berrian	3.00	8.00
BJ Brandon Jacobs	3.00	8.00
BO John David Booty	3.00	8.00
BQ Brady Quinn	3.00	8.00
BR Deion Branch	3.00	8.00
BW Ben Watson	2.50	6.00
CC Chris Chambers	3.00	8.00
CH Chris Henry	2.50	6.00
CJ Chris Johnson	4.00	10.00
CR Antonio Cromartie	2.50	6.00
CT Chester Taylor	2.50	6.00
DA Donnie Avery	3.00	8.00
DB Dre Bly	2.50	6.00
DC Dexter Jackson	2.50	6.00
DE DeSean Jackson	3.00	8.00
DJ Dwayne Jarrett	2.50	6.00
DK Dustin Keller	2.50	6.00
DS Drew Stanton	2.50	6.00
DT Devin Thomas	2.50	6.00
EA Earl Bennett	3.00	8.00
ED Early Doucet	3.00	8.00
ER Eddie Royal	3.00	8.00
FJ Felix Jones	4.00	10.00
FO Matt Forte	4.00	10.00
GD Glenn Dorsey	2.50	6.00
GJ Greg Jones	2.50	6.00
HD Harry Douglas	2.50	6.00
HE Chad Henne	3.00	8.00
HM Heath Miller	3.00	8.00
IB Isaac Bruce	3.00	8.00
JA Jared Allen	4.00	10.00
JC Jamaal Charles	4.00	10.00
FL Joe Flacco	4.00	10.00
JG Jeff Garcia	3.00	8.00
JH James Hardy	3.00	8.00
JL Jake Long	2.50	6.00
JN Jerious Norwood	3.00	8.00
JS Jonathan Stewart	3.00	8.00
KO Kevin O'Connell	2.50	6.00
KS Kevin Smith	3.00	8.00
LE Marcedes Lewis	2.50	6.00
LM Laurence Maroney	3.00	8.00
LS Limas Sweed	3.00	8.00
ME Rashard Mendenhall	3.00	8.00
MH Michael Huff	2.50	6.00
MJ Michael Jenkins	2.50	6.00
MK Malcolm Kelly	2.50	6.00
ML Matt Leinart	3.00	8.00
MM Mario Manningham	3.00	8.00
MO Randy Moss	4.00	10.00
MR Matt Ryan	4.00	10.00
MS Matt Schaub	3.00	8.00
MV Mike Vrabel	3.00	8.00
NE Jordy Nelson	4.00	10.00
RJ Rudi Johnson	2.50	6.00
RM Robert Meachem	3.00	8.00
RR Ray Rice	4.00	10.00
RW Roy Williams WR	3.00	8.00
SA Asante Samuel	2.50	6.00
SI Jerome Simpson	2.50	6.00
SL Steve Slaton	3.00	8.00
SM Sinorice Moss	3.00	8.00
SR Sidney Rice	3.00	8.00
SU Terrell Suggs	2.50	6.00
TB Tedy Bruschi	3.00	8.00
TH Todd Heap	2.50	6.00
TS Troy Smith	3.00	8.00
TW Travis Wilson	2.50	6.00
VD Vernon Davis	3.00	8.00
VY Vince Young	3.00	8.00
WD Warrick Dunn	3.00	8.00

2009 Upper Deck Game Jersey

OVERALL MEMORABILIA ODDS 3:16		
GJAB Anquan Boldin	3.00	8.00
GJAG Antonio Gates	3.00	8.00
GJAJ Andre Johnson	3.00	8.00
GJAR Aaron Rodgers	12.00	30.00
GJAS Alex Smith	3.00	8.00
GJBQ Brady Quinn	3.00	8.00
GJBR Ben Roethlisberger	4.00	10.00
GJBU Brian Urlacher	4.00	10.00
GJCB Champ Bailey	3.00	8.00
GJCD Craig Davis	2.50	6.00
GJCP Carson Palmer	4.00	10.00
GJDB Drew Brees	4.00	10.00
GJDM Donovan McNabb	4.00	10.00
GJDW DeAngelo Williams	4.00	10.00
GJEJ Edgerrin James	3.00	8.00
GJFG Frank Gore	3.00	8.00
GJHW Hines Ward	3.00	8.00
GJJA Jared Allen	4.00	10.00
GJJC Jay Cutler	4.00	10.00
GJJP Julius Peppers	3.00	8.00
GJJW Javon Walker	2.50	6.00
GJLE Lee Evans	3.00	8.00
GJLT LaDainian Tomlinson	4.00	10.00
GJMC Marques Colston	3.00	8.00
GJMH Marvin Harrison	4.00	10.00
GJMJ Maurice Jones-Drew	3.00	8.00
GJML Marshawn Lynch	3.00	8.00
GJRB Ronnie Brown	3.00	8.00
GJRL Ray Lewis	4.00	10.00
GJRM Randy Moss	4.00	10.00

2009 Upper Deck Mystery Iconic Cuts Redemption

AUTOS ISSUED VIA EXCH CARD		
EXCH EXCH Card		
ICCB Cliff Battles/22	50.00	100.00
ICCC Charley Conerly/32	20.00	50.00
ICDL Dick Lane/21	40.00	80.00
ICDT Danny Thomas/41	30.00	60.00
ICDW Doak Walker/72	75.00	150.00
ICEH Elroy Hirsch/50	15.00	40.00
ICES Ernie Stautner/43	15.00	40.00
ICEW Weeb Ewbank/30	15.00	40.00
ICGC George Connor/45	15.00	40.00
ICGD Glenn Davis/75	20.00	50.00
ICGU Gene Upshaw/48	20.00	50.00
ICJP Jim Parker/31	20.00	50.00
ICLA Dante Lavelli/52	15.00	40.00
ICLG Lou Groza/26	40.00	80.00
ICLH Lamar Hunt/22	50.00	100.00
ICMM George McAfee/66	15.00	40.00
ICOG Otto Graham/31	20.00	50.00
ICRB Roosevelt Brown/62	15.00	40.00
ICSB Sammy Baugh/75	40.00	80.00
ICTC Tony Canadeo/28	40.00	80.00
ICTF Tom Fears/70	15.00	40.00

2009 Upper Deck Premier Rookie Jersey Autographs

ROOKIE JSY AUTO PRINT RUN 5-40		
RPAB Andre Brown/40	10.00	25.00
RPAC Aaron Curry/40	15.00	40.00
RPBO Rhett Bomar/40	12.00	30.00
RPBP Brandon Pettigrew/40	15.00	40.00
RPBR Brian Robiskie/40	15.00	40.00
RPBU Deon Butler/40	12.00	30.00
RPCW Chris Wells/40	25.00	60.00
RPDB Donald Brown/40	15.00	40.00
RPDH Darrius Heyward-Bey/40	15.00	40.00
RPDW Derrick Williams/40	12.00	30.00
RPGC Glen Coffee/40	12.00	30.00
RPHN Hakeem Nicks/40	25.00	60.00
RPJF Josh Freeman/40	30.00	80.00
RPJI Juaquin Iglesias/40	12.00	30.00
RPJM Jeremy Maclin/40	25.00	60.00
RPJR Javon Ringer/40	15.00	40.00
RPJS Jason Smith/40		
RPKB Kenny Britt/40	20.00	50.00
RPKM Knowshon Moreno/25	20.00	50.00
RPLM LeSean McCoy/40	30.00	80.00
RPMC Michael Crabtree/25	40.00	100.00
RPMM Mohamed Massaquoi/40	12.00	30.00
RPMW Mike Wallace/40	30.00	80.00
RPND Nate Davis/40	12.00	30.00
RPPH Percy Harvin/40	25.00	60.00
RPPT Patrick Turner/40	12.00	30.00
RPPW Pat White/40	15.00	40.00
RPRB Ramses Barden/40	10.00	25.00
RPSG Shonn Greene/40	25.00	60.00
RPSM Stephen McGee/40	15.00	40.00
RPTJ Tyson Jackson/40	12.00	30.00

2009 Upper Deck Rookie Jersey

OVERALL MEMORABILIA ODDS 3:16		
RJAC Aaron Curry	2.50	6.00
RJBO Rhett Bomar	2.00	5.00
RJBP Brandon Pettigrew	2.50	6.00
RJBR Brian Robiskie	2.50	6.00
RJCW Chris Wells	5.00	12.00
RJDB Donald Brown	2.50	6.00
RJDE Deon Butler	2.00	5.00
RJDH Darrius Heyward-Bey	2.50	6.00
RJDW Derrick Williams	2.00	5.00
RJGC Glen Coffee	2.00	5.00
RJHN Hakeem Nicks	4.00	10.00
RJJF Josh Freeman	5.00	12.00
RJJI Juaquin Iglesias	2.00	5.00
RJJM Jeremy Maclin	5.00	12.00
RJJR Javon Ringer	2.50	6.00
RJJS Jason Smith	2.00	5.00
RJKB Kenny Britt	3.00	8.00
RJKM Knowshon Moreno	5.00	12.00
RJLM LeSean McCoy	5.00	12.00
RJMC Michael Crabtree	5.00	12.00
RJMM Mohamed Massaquoi	2.00	5.00
RJMS Mark Sanchez	8.00	20.00
RJND Nate Davis	2.00	5.00
RJPH Percy Harvin	6.00	15.00
RJPT Patrick Turner	2.00	5.00
RJPW Pat White	2.50	6.00
RJRB Ramses Barden	1.50	4.00
RJSG Shonn Greene	4.00	10.00
RJST Matthew Stafford	6.00	15.00
RJTJ Tyson Jackson	2.00	5.00

2009 Upper Deck Rookie Sensations

TWO PER RETAIL RACK PACK		
RSAC Aaron Curry	.60	1.50
RSAM Aaron Maybin	.50	1.25
RSBC Brian Cushing	.60	1.50
RSBO Brian Orakpo	.60	1.50
RSBR Brian Robiskie	.60	1.50
RSBU Deon Butler	.50	1.25
RSCW Chris Wells	1.00	2.50
RSDB Donald Brown	.60	1.50
RSDH Darrius Heyward-Bey	.60	1.50
RSDW Derrick Williams	.50	1.25
RSEM Eugene Monroe	.40	1.00
RSGC Glen Coffee	.50	1.25
RSHN Hakeem Nicks	1.00	2.50
RSJF Josh Freeman	1.25	3.00
RSJI Juaquin Iglesias	.50	1.25
RSJM Jeremy Maclin	1.00	2.50
RSJR Javon Ringer	.60	1.50
RSJS Jason Smith	.50	1.25
RSKB Kenny Britt	.75	2.00
RSKM Knowshon Moreno	.60	1.50
RSLM LeSean McCoy	1.25	3.00
RSMC Michael Crabtree	1.25	3.00
RSMJ Malcolm Jenkins	.60	1.50
RSMM Mohamed Massaquoi	.50	1.25
RSMO Michael Oher	1.00	2.50
RSMS Mark Sanchez	2.00	5.00
RSND Nate Davis	.50	1.25
RSPH Percy Harvin	1.00	2.50
RSPW Pat White	.60	1.50
RSSG Shonn Greene	1.00	2.50
RSSM Andre Smith	.50	1.25
RSST Matthew Stafford	3.00	8.00
RSTJ Tyson Jackson	.50	1.25

2009 Upper Deck Same Day Signatures

OVERALL AUTO ODDS 1:16 HOB		
SDAB Andre Brown	6.00	15.00
SDAC Aaron Curry	10.00	25.00
SDDA Ramses Barden	6.00	15.00
SDBP Brandon Pettigrew	10.00	25.00
SDBU Deon Butler	8.00	20.00
SDCW Chris Wells	25.00	60.00
SDDB Donald Brown	10.00	25.00
SDDH Darrius Heyward-Bey	10.00	25.00
SDDW Derrick Williams	8.00	20.00
SDGC Glen Coffee	8.00	20.00
SDHN Hakeem Nicks	15.00	40.00
SDJF Josh Freeman	20.00	50.00
SDJI Juaquin Iglesias	8.00	20.00
SDJM Jeremy Maclin	30.00	60.00
SDJR Javon Ringer	10.00	25.00
SDJS Jason Smith	8.00	20.00
SDKB Kenny Britt	12.00	30.00
SDKM Knowshon Moreno	40.00	80.00
SDLM LeSean McCoy	25.00	60.00
SDMC Michael Crabtree	50.00	100.00
SDMM Mohamed Massaquoi	8.00	20.00
SDMS Mark Sanchez	75.00	150.00
SDMT Mike Thomas	10.00	25.00
SDMW Mike Wallace	20.00	50.00
SDND Nate Davis	8.00	20.00
SDPH Percy Harvin	50.00	120.00
SDPT Patrick Turner	8.00	20.00
SDPW Pat White	20.00	50.00
SDRB Rhett Bomar	8.00	20.00
SDRO Brian Robiskie	10.00	25.00
SDSG Shonn Greene	20.00	50.00
SDSM Stephen McGee	10.00	25.00
SDST Matthew Stafford	75.00	150.00
SDTJ Tyson Jackson	8.00	20.00

2009 Upper Deck Signature Shots

OVERALL AUTO ODDS 1:16 HOB		
SSAB Ahmad Bradshaw	8.00	20.00
SSAC Aaron Curry	6.00	15.00
SSAG Anthony Gonzalez	8.00	20.00
SSAH A.J. Hawk	6.00	15.00
SSAL Alex Smith	6.00	15.00
SSAN Derek Anderson	5.00	12.00
SSAP Adrian Peterson		
SSAR Aaron Rodgers	100.00	175.00
SSAS Andre Smith	5.00	12.00
SSAW Andre Woodson	5.00	12.00
SSBB Bernard Berrian	6.00	15.00
SSBC Brian Cushing	6.00	15.00
SSBE Braylon Edwards	8.00	20.00
SSBJ Brandon Jacobs	6.00	15.00
SSBM Brandon Marshall	6.00	15.00
SSBO Anquan Boldin	6.00	15.00
SSBR Brian Brohm	5.00	12.00
SSCB Colt Brennan	8.00	20.00
SSCC Chase Coffman	5.00	12.00
SSCD Craig Davis	5.00	12.00
SSCH Chad Henne	6.00	15.00
SSCJ Calvin Johnson	20.00	50.00
SSCL Chris Long	6.00	15.00
SSCP Clinton Portis	12.50	25.00
SSCS Chansi Stuckey	5.00	12.00
SSCW Chris Wells	10.00	25.00
SSDA Donnie Avery	6.00	15.00
SSDB Donald Brown	10.00	25.00
SSDH Darrius Heyward-Bey	6.00	15.00
SSDJ DeSean Jackson	6.00	15.00
SSDK Dustin Keller	5.00	12.00
SSDL Donald Lee	5.00	12.00
SSDM Darren McFadden	25.00	50.00
SSDW Dwayne Bowe	6.00	15.00
SSED Early Doucet	6.00	15.00
SSEM Eugene Monroe	4.00	10.00
SSER Eddie Royal	8.00	20.00
SSEW Eric Weddle	5.00	12.00
SSFG Frank Gore	6.00	15.00
SSFL Joe Flacco	25.00	50.00
SSFM Fili Moala	5.00	12.00
SSGH Graham Harrell	10.00	25.00
SSGM Gerald McRath	5.00	12.00
SSGW Garrett Wolfe	6.00	15.00
SSHA DJ Hall	5.00	12.00
SSHD Harry Douglas	5.00	12.00
SSHE Chris Henry	5.00	12.00
SSHN Hakeem Nicks	15.00	30.00
SSJA Joseph Addai	8.00	20.00
SSJB John David Booty	6.00	15.00
SSJC Chad Johnson	6.00	15.00
SSJE Malcolm Jenkins	6.00	15.00
SSJF Josh Freeman	10.00	25.00
SSJI Juaquin Iglesias	5.00	12.00
SSJJ Josh Johnson	5.00	12.00
SSJL James Laurinaitis	6.00	15.00
SSJM Jeremy Maclin	10.00	25.00
SSJN Jerious Norwood	6.00	15.00
SSJO Chris Johnson	8.00	20.00
SSJR JaMarcus Russell	5.00	12.00
SSJS Jonathan Stewart	8.00	20.00
SSKM Knowshon Moreno	6.00	15.00
SSKS Kevin Smith	6.00	15.00
SSLM LeSean McCoy	15.00	30.00
SSLT LaDainian Tomlinson		
SSLY Marshawn Lynch	6.00	15.00
SSMC Michael Crabtree	25.00	50.00
SSME Rashard Mendenhall	8.00	20.00
SSMF Matt Forte	8.00	20.00
SSMJ Michael Johnson	4.00	10.00
SSML Matt Leinart	6.00	15.00
SSMO Michael Oher	25.00	50.00
SSMR Matt Ryan	25.00	50.00
SSMS Matthew Stafford	50.00	100.00
SSMW Mike Walker	6.00	15.00
SSND Nate Davis	8.00	20.00
SSNE Jordy Nelson	8.00	20.00
SSOR Brian Orakpo	6.00	15.00
SSPH Percy Harvin	40.00	80.00
SSPW Patrick Willis	6.00	15.00
SSQD Quintin Demps	5.00	12.00
SSRI Javon Ringer	6.00	15.00
SSRM Rey Maualuga	6.00	15.00
SSRW Reggie Wayne	8.00	20.00
SSSA Mark Sanchez	50.00	100.00
SSSM Alphonso Smith	5.00	12.00
SSSS Sean Smith	6.00	15.00
SSST Steve Smith USC	6.00	15.00
SSTB Thomas Brown	5.00	12.00
SSTG Ted Ginn Jr.	6.00	15.00
SSTR Tony Romo	40.00	80.00
SSTT Tyler Thigpen	5.00	12.00
SSVD Vontae Davis	6.00	15.00
SSVH Victor Harris	6.00	15.00
SSVJ Vincent Jackson	6.00	15.00
SSVY Vince Young	8.00	20.00
SSWM William Moore	8.00	20.00

2009 Upper Deck Franchise Super Bowl XLIII

This set was issued at the Upper Deck booth during the 2009 Super Bowl Card Show in Tampa, Florida. A complete set was given to any collector that opened a specified number of football card packs at the booth during the show.

COMPLETE SET (6)	5.00	10.00
FRA1 Chris Johnson	.75	2.00
FRA2 Darren McFadden	.75	2.00
FRA3 Joe Flacco	.75	2.00
FRA4 Jonathan Stewart	.60	1.50
FRA5 Matt Forte	.75	2.00
FRA6 Matt Ryan	.75	2.00

2009 Upper Deck Limited Edition Brett Favre

ISSUED AS BONUS VIA MAIL REDEMPTION		
BF1 Brett Favre	8.00	20.00
BF2 Brett Favre	8.00	20.00
BF3 Brett Favre	8.00	20.00
BF4 Brett Favre	8.00	20.00
BF5 Brett Favre	8.00	20.00
BF6 Brett Favre	8.00	20.00

2010-11 Upper Deck College Colors

COMPLETE SET (15)	6.00	15.00
6 Barry Sanders	.50	1.25
7 Bo Jackson	.40	1.00
8 Peyton Manning	.50	1.25
9 Adrian Peterson	.60	1.50
10 Tim Tebow	1.50	4.00
11 Chris Wells	.30	.75
12 Shonn Greene	.30	.75
13 John Elway	.50	1.25

2011 Upper Deck

COMP.SET w/o ROOKIES (50)	5.00	12.00
201-209 RANDOM INSERTS IN HOBBY		
210-218 RANDOM INSERTS IN RETAIL		
1 Jack Youngblood	.20	.50
2 Thurman Thomas	.30	.75
3 Steve Young	.40	1.00
4 Jack Ham	.25	.60
5 Troy Aikman	.40	1.00
6 Herman Moore	.20	.50
7 Rocket Ismail	.25	.60
8 Roman Gabriel	.25	.60
9 Bob Griese	.30	.75
10 Mike Alstott	.20	.50
11 Alan Page	.25	.60
12 Bo Jackson	.40	1.00
13 Steve Largent	.30	.75
14 John Elway	.50	1.25
15 Paul Hornung	.30	.75
16 Craig Morton	.20	.50
17 Greg Pruitt	.20	.50
18 Jerry Rice	.50	1.25
19 Lee Roy Selmon	.20	.50
20 Lee Roy Jordan	.20	.50
21 George Rogers	.20	.50
22 Tim Brown	.30	.75
23 Thurman Thomas	.30	.75
24 Doug Flutie	.25	.60
25 Barry Sanders	.50	1.25
26 John Cappelletti	.20	.50
27 Kellen Winslow Sr.	.25	.60
28 Jim Kelly	.30	.75
29 Roger Craig	.25	.60
30 Floyd Little	.20	.50
31 Bernie Kosar	.25	.60
32 Rocky Bleier	.25	.60
33 Brian Bosworth	.25	.60
34 Charles White	.20	.50
35 Earl Campbell	.30	.75
36 Doug Flutie	.25	.60
37 Ron Yary	.20	.50
38 Keith Jackson	.20	.50
39 Billy Sims	.25	.60
40 Mike Singletary	.30	.75
41 Daryl Johnston	.30	.75
42 Bubba Smith	.20	.50
43 Steve Young	.40	1.00
44 Troy Aikman	.40	1.00
45 John Elway	.50	1.25
46 Jerry Rice	.50	1.25
47 Tim Brown	.30	.75
48 Barry Sanders	.50	1.25
49 Earl Campbell	.30	.75
50 Jim Kelly	.30	.75
51 Ronald Johnson SP	2.50	6.00
52 Adrian Clayborn SP	3.00	8.00
53 Niles Paul SP	4.00	10.00
54 Mark Herzlich SP	2.50	6.00
55 Stephen Paea SP	3.00	8.00
56 Colin Kaepernick SP	5.00	12.00
57 Allen Bailey SP	2.50	6.00
58 Torrey Smith SP	4.00	10.00
59 Evan Royster SP	3.00	8.00
60 DeMarco Murray SP	6.00	15.00
61 Titus Young SP	4.00	10.00
62 Noel Devine SP	3.00	8.00
63 Jeremy Beal SP	2.50	6.00
64 Pat Devlin SP	3.00	8.00
65 Greg Little SP	3.00	8.00
66 Cameron Heyward SP	3.00	8.00
67 Armon Binns SP	2.50	6.00
68 Greg Jones SP	2.50	6.00
69 Jake Locker SP	8.00	20.00
70 Vincent Brown SP	3.00	8.00
71 Andy Dalton SP	5.00	12.00
72 Jeremy Kerley SP	3.00	8.00
73 Jerrel Jernigan SP	2.50	6.00
74 Daniel Thomas SP	3.00	8.00
75 Prince Amukamara SP	3.00	8.00
76 Von Miller SP	4.00	10.00
77 Delone Carter SP	2.50	6.00
78 Graig Cooper SP	2.50	6.00
79 Deunta Williams	.75	2.00
80 Mike Pouncey SP	3.00	8.00
81 T.J. Yates SP	4.00	10.00
82 Jimmy Smith SP	3.00	8.00
83 Jamie Harper	1.00	2.50
84 Ras-I Dowling SP	3.00	8.00
85 Chimdi Chekwa	.75	2.00
86 Greg Salas	1.00	2.50
87 Anthony Allen SP	2.00	5.00
88 Kendall Hunter SP	3.00	8.00
89 Bruce Carter SP	3.00	8.00
90 Marvin Austin SP	2.50	6.00
91 Pierre Allen	1.00	2.50
92 Rashad Carmichael SP	2.50	6.00
93 Quan Sturdivant SP	3.00	8.00
94 Vai Taua	.75	2.00
95 Austin Pettis SP	2.50	6.00
96 Cecil Shorts SP	2.50	6.00
97 DeAndre McDaniel SP	2.50	6.00
98 Ross Homan	1.00	2.50
99 Anthony Castonzo SP	2.00	5.00
100 Nathan Enderle	1.00	2.50
101 Tandon Doss SP	2.50	6.00
102 Kelvin Sheppard SP	3.00	8.00
103 Ryan Kerrigan SP	3.00	8.00
104 Dane Sanzenbacher SP	3.00	8.00
105 D.J. Williams SP	3.00	8.00
106 Adrian Taylor SP	2.50	6.00
107 Sam Acho SP	2.50	6.00
108 Terrence Toliver	.75	2.00
109 Marcus Cannon SP	2.00	5.00
110 Colin McCarthy	.75	2.00
111 Roy Helu	2.00	5.00
112 Ricky Stanzi SP	5.00	12.00
113 Mason Foster SP	3.00	8.00
114 Brooks Reed	1.00	2.50
115 James Cleveland SP	2.00	5.00
116 Brandon Saine SP	3.00	8.00
117 Jabaal Sheard SP	3.00	8.00
118 Drake Nevis SP	3.00	8.00
119 Armando Allen SP	3.00	8.00
120 Corey Liuget SP	2.00	5.00
121 Luke Stocker	.75	2.00
122 Dwayne Harris SP	3.00	8.00
123 Ahmad Black	.75	2.00
124 Nate Solder	1.00	2.50
125 Jerrod Johnson SP	2.50	6.00
126 Cameron Jordan SP	2.50	6.00
127 Stefen Wisniewski SP	3.00	8.00
128 Tyrod Taylor SP	3.00	8.00
129 Lance Kendricks SP	2.50	6.00
130 Alex Wujciak SP	2.50	6.00
131 Christian Ponder SP	6.00	15.00
132 Jeff Maehl SP	3.00	8.00
133 Phil Taylor	.75	2.00
134 Eric Hagg	1.00	2.50
135 Darvin Adams	.75	2.00
136 Shaun Chapas	.75	2.00
137 Adam Weber	.75	2.00
138 Damien Berry	.75	2.00
139 Aldon Smith	1.50	4.00
140 Lawrence Wilson	.75	2.00
141 Lee Ziemba	.60	1.50
142 Bilal Powell	.60	1.50
143 Kendric Burney	.60	1.50
144 Taylor Potts	.75	2.00
145 Ryan Bartholomew	.60	1.50
146 Lester Jean	.75	2.00
147 Tyron Smith	1.25	3.00
148 Zack Pianalto	.75	2.00
149 Scott Lutrus	.60	1.50
150 Jason Pinkston	.60	1.50
151 Brandon Hogan	.60	1.50
152 Ryan Whalen	.75	2.00
153 Jarvis Williams	.60	1.50
154 Kyle Adams	.60	1.50
155 Chykie Brown	.60	1.50
156 Derrick Locke	.75	2.00
157 Davon House	.75	2.00
158 Stevan Ridley	1.00	2.50
159 Armand Robinson	.75	2.00
160 Mario Butler	.60	1.50
161 Charles Clay	.75	2.00
162 Jarvis Jenkins	.60	1.50
163 Kris Durham	.75	2.00
164 Joe Lefeged	.75	2.00
165 Chris Carter	.75	2.00
166 Korey Lindsey-Woods	.60	1.50
167 Allen Bradford	.75	2.00
168 Stephen Burton	.60	1.50
169 Virgil Green	.75	2.00
170 Jock Sanders	.75	2.00
171 Rob Housler	.75	2.00
172 Matt Szczur	2.00	5.00
173 Ian Williams	.75	2.00
174 Brandon Burton	.75	2.00
175 Orlando Franklin	.75	2.00
176 Ryan Mallett	2.00	5.00
177 Akeem Ayers	.75	2.00

178 Marcell Dareus 1.00 2.50
179 Jacquizz Rodgers 1.00 2.50
180 Blaine Gabbert 1.50 4.00
181 Shane Vereen 1.00 2.50
182 Casey Matthews 1.00 2.50
183 Jonathan Baldwin 1.00 2.50
184 Dion Lewis 1.00 2.50
185 John Clay 1.00 2.50
186 Justin Houston 1.00 2.50
187 Jordan Todman .60 1.50
188 J.J. Watt 1.25 3.00
189 Sione Fua .75 2.00
190 Randall Cobb 1.25 3.00
191 Nick Fairley 1.25 3.00
192 Mark Ingram 2.00 5.00
193 Da'Quan Bowers 1.00 2.50
194 Aaron Williams .75 2.00
195 Julio Jones 2.00 5.00
196 Rahim Moore .75 2.00
197 A.J. Green 2.00 5.00
198 Cam Newton 8.00 20.00
199 Ryan Williams 1.25 3.00
200 Kyle Rudolph 1.00 2.50
201 Blaine Gabbert 6.00 15.00
202 Courtney Smith 8.00 20.00
203 Daniel Thomas 10.00 20.00
204 Leonard Hankerson 10.00 25.00
205 Julio Jones 8.00 20.00
206 Mark Ingram 15.00 30.00
207 Ryan Mallett 12.00 30.00
208 Mario Fannin 5.00 12.00
209 Torrey Smith 8.00 20.00
210 A.J. Green 20.00 50.00
211 Cam Newton 40.00 80.00
212 DeMarco Murray 20.00 40.00
213 Jake Locker 30.00 60.00
214 Jonathan Baldwin 15.00 30.00
215 Mikel Leshoure 10.00 25.00
216 Ryan Williams 10.00 25.00
217 Edmond Gates 6.00 15.00
218 Von Miller 20.00 40.00

2011 Upper Deck 15 Stripe

*ROOKIES: 2.5X TO 6X BASIC CARDS
*ROOKIES: 1.2X TO 3X BASIC SP
EACH REDEEMABLE FOR 15 BASE CARDS

2011 Upper Deck 25 Stripe

*ROOKIES: 4X TO 10X BASIC CARDS
*ROOKIES: 2X TO 5X BASIC SP
EACH REDEEMABLE FOR 25 BASE CARDS

2011 Upper Deck 100 Stripe

*ROOKIES: 6X TO 15X BASIC CARDS
*ROOKIES: 3X TO 8X BASIC SP
EACH REDEEMABLE FOR 100 BASE CARDS

2011 Upper Deck 20th Anniversary

STATED ODDS 1:2 HOBBY
20A1 Jack Youngblood .75 2.00
20A2 Bubba Smith .75 2.00
20A3 Steve Young 1.50 4.00
20A4 Jack Ham 1.00 2.50
20A5 Troy Aikman 1.50 4.00
20A6 Herman Moore .75 2.00
20A7 Rocket Ismail 1.00 2.50
20A8 Roman Gabriel 1.00 2.50
20A9 Bob Griese 1.25 3.00
20A10 Mike Alstott .75 2.00
20A11 Alan Page 1.00 2.50
20A12 Bo Jackson 1.50 4.00
20A13 Steve Largent 1.25 3.00
20A14 John Elway 2.00 5.00
20A15 Paul Hornung 1.25 3.00
20A16 Craig Morton .75 2.00
20A17 Greg Pruitt .75 2.00
20A18 Jerry Rice 2.00 5.00
20A19 Lee Roy Selmon .75 2.00
20A20 Lee Roy Jordan .75 2.00
20A21 George Rogers .75 2.00
20A22 Tim Brown 1.25 3.00
20A23 Thurman Thomas 1.25 3.00
20A24 Doug Flutie 1.00 2.50
20A25 Barry Sanders 2.00 5.00
20A26 John Cappelletti .75 2.00
20A27 Kellen Winslow Sr. 1.00 2.50
20A28 Jim Kelly 1.25 3.00
20A29 Roger Craig 1.00 2.50
20A30 Floyd Little .75 2.00
20A31 Bernie Kosar 1.00 2.50
20A32 Rocky Bleier 1.00 2.50
20A33 Brian Bosworth 1.00 2.50
20A34 Charles White .75 2.00
20A35 Earl Campbell 1.25 3.00
20A36 Daryl Johnston 1.25 3.00
20A37 Ron Yary .75 2.00
20A38 Keith Jackson .75 2.00
20A39 Billy Sims 1.00 2.50
20A40 Mike Singletary 1.25 3.00
20A41 Mario Butler .75 2.00
20A42 Justin Houston 1.25 3.00
20A43 Marcell Dareus 1.25 3.00
20A44 Tandon Doss 1.00 2.50
20A45 Tyron Smith 1.50 4.00
20A46 Evan Royster 1.25 3.00
20A47 Charles Clay 1.00 2.50
20A48 Colin McCarthy 1.00 2.50
20A49 Adrian Taylor 1.00 2.50
20A50 Niles Paul 1.25 3.00
20A51 Chimdi Chekwa 1.00 2.50
20A52 Ricky Stanzi 2.50 6.00
20A53 Orlando Franklin 1.00 2.50
20A54 Von Miller 1.50 4.00
20A55 Jeff Maehl 1.25 3.00
20A56 Colin Kaepernick 3.00 8.00
20A57 Tyrod Taylor 1.25 3.00
20A58 Ahmad Black 1.00 2.50
20A59 Christian Ponder 3.00 8.00
20A60 Scott Lutrus .75 2.00
20A61 Armon Binns 1.00 2.50
20A62 Anthony Castonzo .75 2.00
20A63 Lawrence Wilson 1.00 2.50
20A64 Brooks Reed 1.25 3.00
20A65 Torrey Smith 1.50 4.00
20A66 Jarvis Williams .75 2.00
20A67 Delone Carter 1.00 2.50
20A68 Adam Weber 1.00 2.50
20A69 Daniel Thomas 1.00 2.50
20A70 Ross Homan 1.25 3.00
20A71 Sam Acho 1.00 2.50
20A72 Greg Little 1.25 3.00
20A73 Adrian Clayborn 1.25 3.00
20A74 Jeremy Kerley 1.25 3.00
20A75 Taylor Potts 1.00 2.50
20A76 Virgil Green 1.00 2.50
20A77 Damien Berry 1.00 2.50
20A78 Kyle Adams .75 2.00
20A79 Andy Dalton 3.00 8.00
20A80 Dane Sanzenbacher 1.25 3.00
20A81 Stevan Ridley 1.25 3.00
20A82 Sione Fua 1.00 2.50
20A83 Greg Salas 1.25 3.00
20A84 Vai Taua 1.00 2.50
20A85 Anthony Allen .75 2.00
20A86 James Cleveland .75 2.00
20A87 Jason Pinkston .75 2.00
20A88 Roy Helu 2.50 6.00
20A89 Ryan Bartholomew .75 2.00
20A90 Austin Pettis 1.00 2.50
20A91 Nate Solder 1.25 3.00
20A92 Bilal Powell .75 2.00
20A93 Stefen Wisniewski 1.25 3.00
20A94 Terrence Toliver 1.00 2.50
20A95 Jock Sanders 1.00 2.50
20A96 Zack Pianalto 1.00 2.50
20A97 Jake Locker 5.00 12.00
20A98 Korey Lindsey-Woods .75 2.00
20A99 Ras-I Dowling 1.25 3.00
20A100 Jeremy Beal 1.00 2.50
20A101 Luke Stocker 1.00 2.50
20A102 J.J. Watt 1.50 4.00
20A103 Stephen Paea 1.25 3.00
20A104 Greg Jones 1.25 3.00
20A105 Brandon Saine 1.25 3.00
20A106 Bruce Carter 1.25 3.00
20A107 Corey Liuget .75 2.00
20A108 Ian Williams 1.25 3.00
20A109 Pierre Allen 1.25 3.00
20A110 Titus Young 1.50 4.00
20A111 Jabaal Sheard 1.25 3.00
20A112 Nathan Enderle 1.25 3.00
20A113 Akeem Ayers 1.00 2.50
20A114 Jimmy Smith 1.25 3.00
20A115 Cameron Jordan 1.00 2.50
20A116 Pat Devlin 1.25 3.00
20A117 D.J. Williams 1.25 3.00
20A118 Quan Sturdivant 1.25 3.00
20A119 Jerrel Jernigan 1.00 2.50
20A120 Davon House 1.00 2.50
20A121 Allen Bailey 1.00 2.50
20A122 Rahim Moore 1.00 2.50
20A123 Alex Wujciak 1.00 2.50
20A124 Shaun Chapas 1.00 2.50
20A125 Kelvin Sheppard 1.25 3.00
20A126 Marvin Austin 1.00 2.50
20A127 Armando Allen 1.25 3.00
20A128 Jerrod Johnson 1.00 2.50
20A129 Mark Herzlich 1.00 2.50
20A130 Drake Nevis 1.00 2.50
20A131 Ronald Johnson 1.00 2.50
20A132 Ryan Kerrigan 1.25 3.00
20A133 Mike Pouncey 1.25 3.00
20A134 Noel Devine 1.25 3.00
20A135 Allen Bradford 1.00 2.50
20A136 Cameron Heyward 1.25 3.00
20A137 Dwayne Harris 1.25 3.00
20A138 Da'Quan Bowers 1.00 2.50
20A139 Joe Lefeged 1.00 2.50
20A140 Prince Amukamara 1.25 3.00
20A141 T.J. Yates 1.50 4.00
20A142 Kendall Hunter 1.25 3.00
20A143 Darvin Adams 1.00 2.50
20A144 DeMarco Murray 2.50 6.00
20A145 Randall Cobb 1.50 4.00
20A146 Vincent Brown 1.25 3.00
20A147 Cecil Shorts 1.00 2.50
20A148 DeAndre McDaniel 1.00 2.50
20A149 Kris Durham 1.00 2.50
20A150 Lance Kendricks 1.00 2.50
20A151 Derrick Locke 1.00 2.50
20A152 Matt Szczur 2.50 6.00
20A153 Chris Carter 1.00 2.50
20A154 Graig Cooper 1.00 2.50
20A155 Aaron Williams 1.00 2.50
20A156 Jamie Harper 1.00 2.50
20A157 Casey Matthews 1.25 3.00
20A158 Ryan Mallett 2.50 6.00
20A159 A.J. Green 2.50 6.00
20A160 Julio Jones 2.50 6.00
20A161 Jonathan Baldwin 1.25 3.00
20A162 Blaine Gabbert 2.00 5.00
20A163 Lee Ziemba .75 2.00
20A164 Cam Newton 6.00 15.00
20A165 Mark Ingram 2.50 6.00
20A166 Rob Housler 1.00 2.50
20A167 Dion Lewis 1.25 3.00
20A168 Nick Fairley 1.50 4.00
20A169 Shane Vereen 1.25 3.00
20A170 John Clay 1.25 3.00
20A171 Jacquizz Rodgers 1.25 3.00
20A172 Jordan Todman .75 2.00
20A173 Ryan Williams 1.50 4.00
20A174 Kyle Rudolph 1.25 3.00

2011 Upper Deck Class Of

COMPLETE SET (20) 6.00 15.00
RANDOM INSERTS IN PACKS
CO1 Tim Brown .60 1.50
CO2 Jerry Rice 1.00 2.50
CO3 Bo Jackson .75 2.00
CO4 Charles White .40 1.00
CO5 John Elway 1.00 2.50
CO6 Earl Campbell .60 1.50
CO7 Doug Flutie .50 1.25
CO8 Troy Aikman .75 2.00
CO9 George Rogers .40 1.00
CO10 Keith Jackson .40 1.00
CO11 John Cappelletti .40 1.00
CO12 Kellen Winslow Sr. .50 1.25
CO13 Paul Hornung .60 1.50
CO14 Thurman Thomas .60 1.50
CO15 Floyd Little .40 1.00
CO16 Lee Roy Selmon .40 1.00
CO17 Bob Griese .60 1.50
CO18 Jake Locker 1.50 4.00
CO19 Daniel Thomas .60 1.50
CO20 DeMarco Murray 1.25 3.00

2011 Upper Deck Conference Clashes

COMPLETE SET (20) 5.00 12.00
RANDOM INSERTS IN PACKS
CC1 Greg Pruitt 1.00 2.50
Barry Sanders
CC2 John Elway 1.00 2.50
Troy Aikman
CC3 Thurman Thomas .60 1.50
Greg Pruitt
CC4 Barry Sanders 1.00 2.50
Billy Sims
CC5 Charles White 1.00 2.50
John Elway
CC6 Mark Ingram 3.00 8.00
Cam Newton
CC7 Charles White .75 2.00
Troy Aikman
CC8 Roger Craig .50 1.25
Kellen Winslow Sr.
CC9 Ryan Williams .75 2.00
Torrey Smith
CC10 Blaine Gabbert 1.25 3.00
DeMarco Murray
CC11 Jake Locker 1.50 4.00
John Elway
CC12 Jonathan Baldwin .60 1.50
Noel Devine
CC13 Kendall Hunter 1.25 3.00
DeMarco Murray
CC14 DeMarco Murray 1.25 3.00
Daniel Thomas
CC15 A.J. Green 1.25 3.00
Mark Ingram
CC16 Mark Ingram 1.25 3.00
Bo Jackson
CC17 Jacquizz Rodgers 1.50 4.00
Jake Locker
CC18 Mark Ingram 1.25 3.00
Ryan Mallett
CC19 Julio Jones 1.25 3.00
A.J. Green
CC20 A.J. Green 3.00 8.00
Cam Newton

2011 Upper Deck Dream Tandems

COMPLETE SET (20) 6.00 15.00
RANDOM INSERTS IN PACKS
DT1 Tim Brown .75 2.00
Troy Aikman
DT2 John Elway 1.00 2.50
Jerry Rice
DT3 Lee Roy Selmon .50 1.25
Alan Page
DT4 Barry Sanders 1.00 2.50
Jerry Rice
DT5 Jerry Rice 1.00 2.50
Troy Aikman
DT6 Tim Brown .60 1.50
Rocket Ismail
DT7 Steve Largent .75 2.00
Steve Young
DT8 Tim Brown .60 1.50
Kellen Winslow Sr.
DT9 Bo Jackson .75 2.00
Doug Flutie
DT10 Bo Jackson 3.00 8.00
Cam Newton
DT11 Barry Sanders 1.00 2.50
John Elway
DT12 George Rogers .40 1.00
Floyd Little
DT13 Brian Bosworth .60 1.50
Mike Singletary
DT14 Mark Ingram 3.00 8.00
Cam Newton
DT15 Blaine Gabbert 1.25 3.00
A.J. Green
DT16 Barry Sanders 1.00 2.50
Troy Aikman
DT17 Brian Bosworth .50 1.25
Lee Roy Selmon
DT18 Jake Locker 1.50 4.00
Daniel Thomas
DT19 A.J. Green 1.25 3.00
Julio Jones
DT20 Mark Ingram 1.25 3.00
Blaine Gabbert

2011 Upper Deck Evolution Video Cards

ANNOUNCED ODDS 1:HOBBY CASE
UDVC1 Adrian Peterson red 25.00 60.00
UDVC2 Adrian Peterson wht 25.00 60.00
UDVC6 DeSean Jackson 15.00 40.00
UDVC7 Patrick Willis 20.00 50.00
UDVC9 Tony Romo 15.00 40.00

2011 Upper Deck Historical Programs

COMPLETE SET (25) 8.00 20.00
RANDOM INSERTS IN PACKS
HP1 Jack Youngblood .40 1.00
HP2 Steve Young .75 2.00
HP3 Troy Aikman .75 2.00
HP4 Herman Moore .40 1.00
HP5 Bob Griese .60 1.50
HP6 Bo Jackson .75 2.00
HP7 John Elway 1.00 2.50
HP8 Craig Morton .40 1.00
HP9 Lee Roy Jordan .40 1.00
HP10 Doug Flutie .50 1.25
HP11 Tim Brown .60 1.50
HP12 Kellen Winslow Sr. .50 1.25
HP13 Jim Kelly .60 1.50
HP14 Roger Craig .50 1.25
HP15 Barry Sanders 1.00 2.50
HP16 John Cappelletti .40 1.00
HP17 Floyd Little .40 1.00
HP18 Charles White .40 1.00
HP19 Earl Campbell .60 1.50
HP20 Billy Sims .50 1.25
HP21 Jake Locker 1.50 4.00
HP22 Ryan Williams .75 2.00
HP23 Christian Ponder 1.25 3.00
HP24 Ryan Mallett 1.25 3.00
HP25 A.J. Green 1.25 3.00

2011 Upper Deck Rookie Autographs

RANDOM INSERTS IN PACKS
EXCH EXPIRATION: 3/9/2013
51 Ronald Johnson 8.00 20.00
52 Adrian Clayborn 25.00 50.00
53 Niles Paul 10.00 25.00
54 Mark Herzlich 5.00 12.00
55 Stephen Paea 6.00 15.00
56 Colin Kaepernick 25.00 50.00
57 Allen Bailey 5.00 12.00
58 Torrey Smith 15.00 30.00
59 Evan Royster 8.00 20.00
60 DeMarco Murray 25.00 50.00
61 Titus Young 8.00 20.00
62 Noel Devine 6.00 15.00
63 Jeremy Beal 6.00 15.00
64 Pat Devlin 8.00 20.00
65 Greg Little 6.00 15.00
66 Cameron Heyward 6.00 15.00
67 Armon Binns 5.00 12.00
68 Greg Jones 5.00 12.00
69 Jake Locker 60.00 120.00
70 Vincent Brown 6.00 15.00
71 Andy Dalton 25.00 60.00
72 Jeremy Kerley 8.00 20.00
73 Jerrel Jernigan 6.00 15.00
74 Daniel Thomas 10.00 25.00
75 Prince Amukamara EXCH 15.00 30.00
76 Von Miller 15.00 40.00
77 Delone Carter 5.00 12.00
78 Graig Cooper 6.00 15.00
79 Deunta Williams 5.00 12.00
80 Mike Pouncey 12.00 30.00
81 T.J. Yates 8.00 20.00
82 Jimmy Smith 8.00 20.00
83 Jamie Harper 6.00 15.00
84 Ras-I Dowling 6.00 15.00
85 Chimdi Chekwa 5.00 12.00
86 Greg Salas 6.00 15.00
87 Anthony Allen 5.00 12.00
88 Kendall Hunter 10.00 25.00
89 Bruce Carter 12.00 30.00
90 Dane Sanzenbacher 6.00 15.00
91 Pierre Allen 6.00 15.00
92 Rashad Carmichael 5.00 12.00
93 Quan Sturdivant 6.00 15.00
94 Vai Taua 5.00 12.00
95 Austin Pettis 5.00 12.00
96 Cecil Shorts 5.00 12.00
97 DeAndre McDaniel 5.00 12.00
98 Ross Homan 6.00 15.00
99 Anthony Castonzo 4.00 10.00
100 Nathan Enderle 6.00 15.00
101 Tandon Doss 5.00 12.00
102 Kelvin Sheppard 8.00 20.00
103 Ryan Kerrigan 8.00 20.00
104 Dane Sanzenbacher 8.00 20.00
105 D.J. Williams 6.00 15.00
106 Adrian Taylor 8.00 20.00
107 Sam Acho 8.00 20.00
108 Terrence Toliver 5.00 12.00
109 Marcus Cannon 4.00 10.00
110 Colin McCarthy 5.00 12.00
111 Roy Helu 10.00 25.00
112 Ricky Stanzi 30.00 60.00
113 Mason Foster 8.00 20.00
114 Brooks Reed 8.00 20.00
115 James Cleveland 4.00 10.00
116 Brandon Saine 8.00 20.00
117 Jabaal Sheard 6.00 15.00
118 Drake Nevis 8.00 20.00
119 Armando Allen 8.00 20.00
120 Corey Liuget 8.00 20.00
121 Luke Stocker 6.00 15.00
122 Dwayne Harris 6.00 15.00
123 Ahmad Black 5.00 12.00
124 Nate Solder 5.00 12.00
125 Jerrod Johnson 5.00 12.00
126 Cameron Jordan 10.00 25.00
127 Stefen Wisniewski 5.00 12.00
128 Tyrod Taylor 6.00 15.00
129 Lance Kendricks 5.00 12.00
130 Alex Wujciak 6.00 15.00
131 Christian Ponder 25.00 50.00
132 Jeff Maehl 12.00 30.00
133 Phil Taylor 5.00 12.00
134 Eric Hagg 8.00 20.00
135 Darvin Adams 5.00 12.00
136 Shaun Chapas 5.00 12.00
137 Adam Weber 6.00 15.00
138 Damien Berry 5.00 12.00
139 Aldon Smith 15.00 40.00
140 Lawrence Wilson 5.00 12.00
141 Lee Ziemba 10.00 25.00
142 Bilal Powell 4.00 10.00
143 Kendric Burney 6.00 15.00
144 Taylor Potts 8.00 20.00
145 Ryan Bartholomew 4.00 10.00
146 Lester Jean 5.00 12.00
147 Tyron Smith 12.00 30.00
148 Zack Pianalto 8.00 20.00
149 Scott Lutrus 4.00 10.00
150 Jason Pinkston 8.00 20.00
151 Brandon Hogan 4.00 10.00
152 Ryan Whalen 5.00 12.00
153 Jarvis Williams 6.00 15.00
154 Kyle Adams 5.00 12.00
155 Chykie Brown 6.00 15.00
156 Derrick Locke 5.00 12.00
157 Davon House 6.00 15.00
158 Stevan Ridley 8.00 20.00
159 Armand Robinson 5.00 12.00
160 Mario Butler 5.00 12.00
161 Charles Clay 5.00 12.00
162 Jarvis Jenkins 6.00 15.00
163 Kris Durham 6.00 15.00
164 Joe Lefeged 5.00 12.00
165 Chris Carter 5.00 12.00
166 Korey Lindsey-Woods 4.00 10.00
167 Allen Bradford 6.00 15.00
168 Stephen Burton 4.00 10.00
169 Virgil Green 6.00 15.00
170 Jock Sanders 10.00 25.00
171 Rob Housler 6.00 15.00
172 Matt Szczur 15.00 30.00
173 Ian Williams 8.00 20.00
174 Brandon Burton 6.00 15.00
175 Orlando Franklin 6.00 15.00
176 Ryan Mallett 40.00 80.00
177 Akeem Ayers 8.00 20.00
178 Marcell Dareus 12.00 30.00
179 Jacquizz Rodgers 12.00 30.00
180 Blaine Gabbert 30.00 60.00
181 Shane Vereen 12.00 30.00
182 Casey Matthews 8.00 20.00
183 Jonathan Baldwin 8.00 20.00
184 Dion Lewis 8.00 20.00
185 John Clay 8.00 20.00
186 Justin Houston 15.00 30.00
187 Jordan Todman 8.00 20.00
188 J.J. Watt 12.00 30.00
189 Sione Fua 5.00 12.00
190 Randall Cobb 25.00 50.00
192 Mark Ingram 25.00 50.00
193 Da'Quan Bowers 8.00 20.00
194 Aaron Williams 5.00 12.00
195 Julio Jones 30.00 60.00
196 Rahim Moore 6.00 15.00
197 A.J. Green 25.00 50.00
198 Cam Newton 100.00 175.00
199 Ryan Williams 25.00 50.00
200 Kyle Rudolph 8.00 20.00

2011 Upper Deck Rookie Letterman Autographs

ANNOUNCED PRINT RUN 210-800
EXCH EXPIRATION: 3/9/2013
RSLAB Allen Bailey/500* 6.00 15.00
(serial #'d to 50, letters spell HURRICANES)
RSLAD Andy Dalton/550* 30.00 60.00
(serial #'d to 50, letters spell HORNED FROGS)
RSLAG A.J. Green/280* 30.00 60.00
(serial #'d to 35, letters spell BULLDOGS)
RSLAP Austin Pettis/700* 12.00 30.00
(serial #'d to 100, letters spell BRONCOS)
RSLBC Bruce Carter/600* 10.00 25.00
(serial #'d to 75, letters spell TAR HEELS)
RSLBE Jeremy Beal/700* 6.00 15.00
(serial #'d to 100, letters spell SOONERS)
RSLBG Blaine Gabbert/300* 25.00 50.00
(serial #'d to 50, letters spell TIGERS)
RSLBI Armon Binns/800* 6.00 15.00
(serial #'d to 100, letters spell BEARCATS)
RSLBS Brandon Saine/600* 10.00 25.00
(serial #'d to 75, letters spell BUCKEYES)
RSLCH Cameron Heyward/800* 10.00 25.00
(serial #'d to 100, letters spell BUCKEYES)
RSLCP Christian Ponder/315* 20.00 50.00
(serial #'d to 35, letters spell SEMINOLES)
RSLDH Dwayne Harris/700* 10.00 25.00
(serial #'d to 100, letters spell PIRATES)
RSLDM DeMarco Murray/350* 30.00 80.00
(serial #'d to 50, letters spell SOONERS)
RSLDT Daniel Thomas/400* 15.00 40.00
(serial #'d to 50, letters spell WILDCATS)
RSLER Evan Royster/420* 10.00 25.00
(serial #'d to 35, letters spell NITTANY LIONS)
RSLGC Graig Cooper/500* 8.00 20.00
(serial #'d to 50, letters spell HURRICANES)
RSLGL Greg Little/600* 8.00 20.00
(serial #'d to 75, letters spell TARHEELS)
RSLJB Jonathan Baldwin/280* 10.00 25.00
(serial #'d to 35, letters spell PANTHERS)
RSLJC John Clay/245* 10.00 25.00
(serial #'d to 35, letters spell BADGERS)
RSLJJ Jerrel Jernigan/700* 8.00 20.00
(serial #'d to 100, letters spell TROJANS)
RSLJK Jeremy Kerley/550* 10.00 20.00
(serial #'d to 50, letters spell HORNED FROGS)
RSLJL Jake Locker/245* 30.00 80.00
(serial #'d to 35, letters spell HUSKIES)
RSLJO Jerrod Johnson/600* 8.00 20.00
(serial #'d to 100, letters spell AGGIES)
RSLJU Julio Jones/275* 25.00 60.00
(serial #'d to 25, letters spell CRIMSON TIDE)
RSLKA Colin Kaepernick/600* 15.00 40.00
(serial #'d to 75, letters spell WOLF PACK)
RSLKH Kendall Hunter/700* 10.00 25.00
(serial #'d to 100, letters spell COWBOYS)
RSLLS Luke Stocker/750* 8.00 20.00
(serial #'d to 75, letters spell VOLUNTEERS)
RSLMH Mark Herzlich/600* 8.00 20.00
(serial #'d to 100, letters spell EAGLES)
RSLMI Mark Ingram/275* 30.00 80.00
(serial #'d to 25, letters spell CRIMSON TIDE)
RSLND Noel Devine/600* 12.00 30.00
(serial #'d to 50, letters spell MOUNTAINEERS)
RSLNE Nathan Enderle/700* 8.00 20.00
(serial #'d to 100, letters spell VANDALS)
RSLNP Niles Paul/550* 10.00 25.00
(serial #'d to 50, letters spell CORNHUSKERS)
RSLPD Pat Devlin/600* 10.00 25.00
(serial #'d to 75, letters spell BLUE HENS)
RSLRH Roy Helu/550* 20.00 50.00
(serial #'d to 50, letters spell CORNHUSKERS)
RSLRJ Ronald Johnson/700* 8.00 20.00
(serial #'d to 100, letters spell TROJANS)
RSLRK Ryan Kerrigan/600* 10.00 25.00
(serial #'d to 50, letters spell BOILERMAKERS)
RSLRM Ryan Mallett/250* 20.00 50.00
(serial #'d to 25, letters spell RAZORBACKS)
RSLRO Jacquizz Rodgers/245* 20.00 50.00
(serial #'d to 35, letters spell BEAVERS)
RSLRW Ryan Williams/210* 20.00 50.00
(serial #'d to 35, letters spell HOKIES)
RSLTT Terrence Toliver/600* 8.00 20.00
(serial #'d to 100, letters spell TIGERS)
RSLTY Titus Young/700* 12.00 30.00
(serial #'d to 100, letters spell BRONCOS)
RSLVB Vincent Brown/600* 10.00 25.00
(serial #'d to 100, letters spell AZTECS)
RSLVM Von Miller/600* 20.00 40.00
(serial #'d to 100, letters spell AGGIES)

2011 Upper Deck Saturday in Action

COMPLETE SET (15) 6.00 15.00
RANDOM INSERTS IN PACKS
SIA1 Troy Aikman .75 2.00
SIA2 John Elway 1.00 2.50
SIA3 Rocket Ismail .50 1.25
SIA4 Barry Sanders 1.00 2.50
SIA5 Bo Jackson .75 2.00
SIA6 Thurman Thomas .60 1.50
SIA7 Floyd Little .40 1.00
SIA8 Charles White .40 1.00
SIA9 Doug Flutie .50 1.25
SIA10 Jerry Rice 1.00 2.50
SIA11 Jim Kelly .60 1.50
SIA12 Steve Young .75 2.00
SIA13 Cam Newton 3.00 8.00
SIA14 Mark Ingram 1.25 3.00
SIA15 A.J. Green 1.25 3.00

2011 Upper Deck Ultimate Rookie Signatures

RANDOM INSERTS IN PACKS
EXCH EXPIRATION: 3/9/2013
1 Allen Bailey 10.00 25.00
2 Cameron Heyward 12.00 30.00
4 Mark Herzlich 12.00 30.00
5 Jake Locker 75.00 135.00
6 Von Miller 20.00 50.00
7 Christian Ponder 60.00 120.00
8 Pat Devlin 12.00 30.00
9 Daniel Thomas 12.00 30.00
10 DeMarco Murray 40.00 80.00
11 Evan Royster 12.00 30.00
12 Noel Devine 12.00 30.00
13 Kendall Hunter 12.00 30.00
14 Greg Little 12.00 30.00
15 Armon Binns 10.00 25.00
16 Terrence Toliver 10.00 25.00
17 Niles Paul 12.00 30.00
18 Ronald Johnson 10.00 25.00
19 Austin Pettis 10.00 25.00
20 Titus Young 15.00 40.00

2012 Upper Deck

COMP.SET w/o ROOK (50) 5.00 12.00
COMP.SET w/o SP's (150) 20.00 50.00
248-272 INSERTED IN HOBBY PACKS
273-297 INSERTED IN RETAIL PACKS
1 Adrian Peterson .30 .75
2 Alan Page .25 .60
3 Andre Ware .25 .60
4 Anthony Carter .20 .50
5 Archie Griffin .20 .50
6 Barry Sanders .50 1.25
7 Bernie Kosar .25 .60
8 Billy Cannon .20 .50
9 Billy Sims .25 .60
10 Bo Jackson .40 1.00
11 Brian Bosworth .25 .60
12 Charles White .20 .50
13 Dan Marino .60 1.50
14 Danny Wuerffel .25 .60
15 Dave Casper .20 .50
16 Doug Flutie .25 .60
17 Drew Bledsoe .25 .60
18 Drew Brees .30 .75
19 Earl Campbell .25 .60
20 Eddie George .25 .60
21 Gale Sayers .30 .75
22 Gary Beban .20 .50
23 George Rogers .20 .50
24 Gino Torretta .20 .50
25 Herschel Walker .25 .60
26 Jason White .20 .50
27 Jim McMahon .25 .60
28 Jim Plunkett .20 .50
29 John Cappelletti .20 .50
30 Johnny Rodgers .20 .50
31 Kellen Winslow Sr. .20 .50
32 Ken Stabler .30 .75
33 Lawrence Taylor .25 .60
34 Lee Roy Jordan .20 .50
35 Marques Colston .25 .60
36 Mike Singletary .30 .75
37 Paul Hornung .25 .60
38 Rocket Ismail .25 .60
39 Rod Woodson .25 .60
40 Roman Gabriel .25 .60
41 Ron Dayne .20 .50
42 Steve Young .40 1.00
43 Thurman Thomas .30 .75
44 Tim Brown .30 .75
45 Todd Marinovich .20 .50
46 Tony Dorsett .30 .75
47 Troy Aikman .40 1.00
48 Ty Detmer .20 .50
49 Warren Moon .30 .75
50 William Perry .20 .50
51 Bobby Massie .40 1.00
52 Alameda Ta'amu .75 2.00
53 Alfred Morris .50 1.25
54 Michael Brockers .60 1.50
55 Zach Brown .50 1.25
56 Antwon Bailey .50 1.25
57 Audie Cole .50 1.25
58 Emil Igwenagu .50 1.25
59 B.J. Cunningham .50 1.25
60 Tyler Hansen .50 1.25
61 Ryan Steed .40 1.00
62 Brandon Weeden 1.25 3.00
63 Brian Reader .50 1.25
64 Bryce Beall .40 1.00
65 David Molk .60 1.50
66 Cam Johnson .60 1.50
67 Case Keenum .75 2.00
68 Casey Hayward .60 1.50
69 Duane Bennett .60 1.50
70 Winston Guy .40 1.00
71 Cliff Harris .60 1.50
72 Cody Johnson .50 1.25
73 Coryell Judie .50 1.25
74 Courtney Upshaw .75 2.00
75 Tim Benford .40 1.00
76 Da'Jon McKnight .50 1.25
77 Dan Persa .50 1.25
78 Coby Fleener .75 2.00
79 David DeCastro .75 2.00
80 David Paulson .75 2.00
81 Amini Silatolu .40 1.00
82 Derek Moye .60 1.50
83 Devon Still .60 1.50
84 Devon Wylie .60 1.50
85 Evan Rodriguez .50 1.25
86 George Iloka .50 1.25
87 Greg Childs .60 1.50
88 Tyler Shoemaker .50 1.25
89 Harrison Smith .60 1.50
90 Jared Crick .60 1.50
91 Jarrett Lee .60 1.50
92 Jason Ford .50 1.25
93 Jeff Fuller .75 2.00
94 Jermaine Kearse .60 1.50
95 Jake Bequette .60 1.50
96 Josh Chapman .60 1.50
97 Junior Hemingway .60 1.50
98 Justin Blackmon 1.25 3.00
99 Keenan Robinson .60 1.50
100 Kellen Moore 1.00 2.50
101 Bobby Wagner .60 1.50
102 Kentrell Lockett .60 1.50
103 Keshawn Martin .60 1.50
104 Micanor Regis .40 1.00
105 Kirk Cousins 1.00 2.50
106 Brock Osweiler .75 2.00
107 LaMichael James 1.25 3.00
108 Lavasier Tuinei .50 1.25
109 Jeremy Ebert .50 1.25
110 Marc Tyler .60 1.50
111 Marcus Forston .50 1.25
112 Markelle Martin .50 1.25
113 Marquis Maze .50 1.25
114 Nelson Rosario .50 1.25
115 Matt Kalil .75 2.00
116 Rodney Stewart .50 1.25
117 Michael Egnew .50 1.25
118 Michael Floyd 1.25 3.00
119 Brandon Washington .40 1.00
120 Mike Harris .40 1.00
121 Mike Willie .60 1.50
122 Darrell Scott .50 1.25
123 Mychal Kendricks .60 1.50
124 Robert Blanton .50 1.25
125 Nick Foles 1.00 2.50
126 Nick Toon .75 2.00
127 Shea McClellin .75 2.00
128 Rhett Ellison .50 1.25
129 Quinton Coples .60 1.50
130 James-Michael Johnson .50 1.25
131 Darron Thomas 1.00 2.50
132 William Vlachos .50 1.25
133 Rueben Randle .60 1.50
134 Russell Wilson 1.00 2.50
135 Ryan Broyles .60 1.50
136 Fletcher Cox .60 1.50
137 Ryan Tannehill 1.50 4.00
138 Sean Spence .50 1.25
139 Stephfon Green .60 1.50
140 Brian Linthicum .50 1.25
141 Mike Martin .60 1.50
142 Tony Dye .40 1.00
143 Travis Benjamin .60 1.50
144 Trent Richardson 2.00 5.00
145 Trenton Robinson .50 1.25
146 Ladarius Green .50 1.25
147 Kelechi Osemele .60 1.50
148 Vinny Curry .60 1.50
149 Shaun Prater .60 1.50
150 Zebrie Sanders .50 1.25
151 A.J. Jenkins 4.00 10.00
152 Whitney Mercilus 3.00 8.00
153 Alfonzo Dennard 3.00 8.00
154 Andre Branch 2.50 6.00
155 Lucas Nix 2.00 5.00
156 Antonio Allen 2.50 6.00
157 Billy Winn 3.00 8.00
158 Brandon Bolden 3.00 8.00
159 Brandon Boykin 3.00 8.00
160 Thomas Mayo 2.00 5.00
161 Brandon Thompson 2.50 6.00
162 Joe Looney 2.50 6.00
163 Chandler Harnish 3.00 8.00
164 Olivier Vernon 3.00 8.00
165 Keith Tandy 2.50 6.00
166 Kevin Koger 2.50 6.00
167 Cordy Glenn 2.50 6.00
168 Cyrus Gray 3.00 8.00
169 Dan Herron 3.00 8.00
170 Darius Reynolds 2.50 6.00
171 Davin Meggett 2.50 6.00
172 Dominique Davis 2.50 6.00
173 Donnie Fletcher 2.00 5.00
174 Dont'a Hightower 5.00 12.00
175 Doug Martin 5.00 12.00
176 Dwayne Allen 3.00 8.00
177 Dwight Jones 2.50 6.00
178 Gerell Robinson 3.00 8.00
179 Isaiah Pead 3.00 8.00
180 Jarius Wright 3.00 8.00
181 Jarrett Boykin 3.00 8.00
182 Jayron Hosley 3.00 8.00
183 Jamell Fleming 3.00 8.00
184 Jermaine Thomas 2.50 6.00
185 Joe Adams 3.00 8.00
186 Kyle Wilber 3.00 8.00
187 Jordan Jefferson 3.00 8.00
188 Jordan White 2.50 6.00
189 Juron Criner 2.50 6.00
190 Kendall Reyes 2.50 6.00
191 Kendall Wright 4.00 10.00
192 Tommy Streeter 3.00 8.00
193 Laron Byrd 2.50 6.00
194 Lavonte David 4.00 10.00
195 Levy Adcock 2.50 6.00
196 Danius Hanks 3.00 8.00
197 Marvin Jones 2.50 6.00
198 Marvin McNutt 4.00 10.00
199 Melvin Ingram 4.00 10.00
200 Bradie Ewing 2.50 6.00
201 Nigel Bradham 2.50 6.00
202 Riley Reiff 5.00 12.00
203 Ronnell Lewis 3.00 8.00
204 Ryan Lindley 3.00 8.00
205 Stephon Gilmore 4.00 10.00
206 Tank Carder 3.00 8.00
207 Tauren Poole 2.50 6.00
208 Eric Page 2.50 6.00
209 Travis Lewis 2.50 6.00
210 Vontaze Burfict 2.50 6.00
211 Aaron Corp 2.50 6.00
212 Alshon Jeffery 6.00 15.00
213 Bernard Pierce 3.00 8.00
214 Bobby Rainey 3.00 8.00
215 Chris Galippo 2.50 6.00
216 Brian Quick 4.00 10.00
217 Mike Daniels 4.00 10.00
218 Eddie Whitley 2.50 6.00
219 DeVier Posey 3.00 8.00
220 Dontari Poe 3.00 8.00
221 Dre Kirkpatrick 5.00 12.00
222 Edwin Baker 2.50 6.00
223 Fozzy Whittaker 3.00 8.00
224 Trevor Guyton 2.50 6.00
225 Jacory Harris 2.50 6.00
226 Janoris Jenkins 3.00 8.00
227 Jerry Franklin 2.50 6.00
228 Jonathan Martin 2.50 6.00
229 Chris Givens 2.50 6.00
230 Lamar Miller 4.00 10.00
231 Lance Lewis 2.50 6.00
232 Brandon Carswell 2.50 6.00
233 Lennon Creer 2.50 6.00
234 Leonard Johnson 2.50 6.00
235 Luke Kuechly 4.00 10.00
236 Josh Norman 2.00 5.00
237 Marshall Lobbestael 2.50 6.00
238 Mohamed Sanu 3.00 8.00
239 T.Y. Hilton 3.00 8.00
240 T.J. Graham 3.00 8.00
241 Orson Charles 3.00 8.00
242 Patrick Edwards 3.00 8.00
243 Richard Matthews 3.00 8.00
244 Robert Griffin III 8.00 20.00
245 Ronnie Hillman 4.00 10.00
246 Stephen Garcia 3.00 8.00
247 Stephen Hill 3.00 8.00
248 Quinton Coples 5.00 12.00
249 Robert Griffin III 50.00 100.00
250 Trent Richardson 30.00 60.00
251 Alfonzo Dennard 5.00 12.00
252 Alshon Jeffery 8.00 20.00
253 Brandon Bolden 5.00 12.00
254 Brandon Thompson 4.00 10.00
255 Case Keenum 6.00 15.00
256 Stephen Hill 5.00 12.00
257 Cyrus Gray 5.00 12.00
258 DeVier Posey 5.00 12.00
259 Doug Martin 8.00 20.00
260 Isaiah Pead 8.00 20.00
261 Jarius Wright 5.00 12.00
262 Rueben Randle 5.00 12.00
263 Joe Adams 5.00 12.00
264 Kendall Wright 6.00 15.00
265 Kirk Cousins 8.00 20.00
266 Darron Thomas 8.00 20.00
267 Marc Tyler 5.00 12.00
268 Marquis Maze 5.00 12.00
269 Chris Givens 4.00 10.00
270 Michael Egnew 4.00 10.00
271 Mohamed Sanu 5.00 12.00
272 Nick Toon 6.00 15.00
273 Ryan Lindley 8.00 20.00
274 Ryan Tannehill 20.00 50.00
275 Tauren Poole 6.00 15.00
276 Lamar Miller 10.00 25.00
277 B.J. Cunningham 6.00 15.00
278 Brandon Weeden 15.00 40.00
279 Brian Quick 10.00 25.00
280 Dwayne Allen 8.00 20.00
281 Courtney Upshaw 10.00 25.00
282 Dan Herron 8.00 20.00
283 Dwight Jones 6.00 15.00
284 Gerell Robinson 8.00 20.00
285 Jarrett Boykin 8.00 20.00
286 Brock Osweiler 10.00 25.00
287 Jeff Fuller 10.00 25.00
288 Juron Criner 6.00 15.00
289 Justin Blackmon 15.00 40.00
290 Kellen Moore 12.00 30.00
291 LaMichael James 15.00 40.00
292 Marvin McNutt 8.00 20.00
293 Michael Floyd 15.00 40.00
294 Bernard Pierce 8.00 20.00
295 Nick Foles 12.00 30.00
296 Russell Wilson 12.00 30.00
297 Ryan Broyles 8.00 20.00
NNO QB Draft Trade 25.00 60.00

2012 Upper Deck 1993 SP Inserts

SP STATED ODDS 1:5
93SP1 Alameda Ta'amu 2.00 5.00
93SP2 Alfonzo Dennard 1.50 4.00
93SP3 Alshon Jeffery 2.50 6.00
93SP4 Lamar Miller 2.00 5.00
93SP5 B.J. Cunningham 1.25 3.00
93SP6 Brandon Bolden 1.50 4.00
93SP7 Brandon Thompson 1.25 3.00
93SP8 Brandon Weeden 3.00 8.00
93SP9 Brian Quick 2.00 5.00
93SP10 Brock Osweiler 2.50 6.00
93SP11 Case Keenum 2.00 5.00
93SP12 Chandler Harnish 1.50 4.00
93SP13 Marvin Jones 1.25 3.00
93SP14 Darron Thomas 1.50 4.00
93SP15 Bernard Pierce 1.50 4.00
93SP16 Dwayne Allen 1.50 4.00
93SP17 Courtney Upshaw 2.00 5.00
93SP18 Cyrus Gray 1.50 4.00
93SP19 Dan Herron 1.50 4.00
93SP20 Davin Meggett 1.25 3.00
93SP21 DeVier Posey 1.50 4.00
93SP22 Doug Martin 2.50 6.00
93SP23 Dwight Jones 1.25 3.00
93SP24 Rueben Randle 1.50 4.00
93SP25 Gerell Robinson 1.50 4.00
93SP26 Greg Childs 1.50 4.00
93SP27 Isaiah Pead 1.50 4.00
93SP28 Dre Kirkpatrick 2.50 6.00
93SP29 Jared Crick 1.50 4.00
93SP30 Jarius Wright 1.50 4.00

93SP31 Jarrett Boykin	1.50	4.00
93SP32 Eric Page	1.25	3.00
93SP33 Jeff Fuller	2.00	5.00
93SP34 Jermaine Kearse	1.50	4.00
93SP35 Joe Adams	1.50	4.00
93SP36 Juron Criner	1.25	3.00
93SP37 Justin Blackmon	3.00	8.00
93SP38 Kellen Moore	2.50	6.00
93SP39 Kendall Wright	2.00	5.00
93SP40 Keshawn Martin	1.50	4.00
93SP41 Kirk Cousins	2.50	6.00
93SP42 LaMichael James	4.00	10.00
93SP43 Chris Givens	1.25	3.00
93SP44 Marc Tyler	1.50	4.00
93SP45 Marquis Maze	1.50	4.00
93SP46 Marvin McNutt	2.00	5.00
93SP47 Ronnie Hillman	2.00	5.00
93SP48 Melvin Ingram	2.00	5.00
93SP49 Michael Egnew	1.25	3.00
93SP50 Michael Floyd	5.00	12.00
93SP51 Mohamed Sanu	1.50	4.00
93SP52 Luke Kuechly	2.00	5.00
93SP53 Nick Foles	2.50	6.00
93SP54 Nick Toon	2.00	5.00
93SP55 Quinton Coples	1.50	4.00
93SP56 Rishard Matthews	1.50	4.00
93SP57 Robert Griffin III	15.00	40.00
93SP58 Russell Wilson	2.50	6.00
93SP59 Ryan Broyles	1.50	4.00
93SP60 Ryan Lindley	1.50	4.00
93SP61 Ryan Tannehill	4.00	10.00
93SP62 Tauren Poole	1.25	3.00
93SP63 Tommy Streeter	1.50	4.00
93SP64 Trent Richardson	8.00	20.00
93SP65 Stephen Hill	1.50	4.00
93SP66 Thurman Thomas	1.25	3.00
93SP67 Antonio Freeman	.75	2.00
93SP68 Johnny Rodgers	.75	2.00
93SP69 Billy Cannon	.75	2.00
93SP70 Bo Jackson	1.50	4.00
93SP71 Bob Lilly	1.00	2.50
93SP72 Charles White	.75	2.00
93SP73 Chris Spielman	.75	2.00
93SP74 Danny Wuerffel	.75	2.00
93SP75 Dave Casper	.75	2.00
93SP76 Drew Brees	1.25	3.00
93SP77 Earl Campbell	1.25	3.00
93SP78 Eric Metcalf	.75	2.00
93SP79 Floyd Little	.75	2.00
93SP80 Gary Beban	.75	2.00
93SP81 Gino Torretta	.75	2.00
93SP82 Harry Carson	.75	2.00
93SP83 Herman Moore	.75	2.00
93SP84 Jason White	1.00	2.50
93SP85 Bernie Kosar	1.00	2.50
93SP86 Billy Sims	1.00	2.50
93SP87 Kellen Winslow Sr.	1.00	2.50
93SP88 Lawrence Taylor	1.00	2.50
93SP89 Marques Colston	1.00	2.50
93SP90 Ozzie Newsome	1.00	2.50
93SP91 Randy White	1.00	2.50
93SP92 Roger Staubach	1.50	4.00
93SP93 Roman Gabriel	1.00	2.50
93SP94 Ron Dayne	.75	2.00
93SP95 Ron Yary	.75	2.00
93SP96 Steve Young	1.50	4.00
93SP97 Todd Marinovich	.75	2.00
93SP98 Troy Aikman	1.50	4.00
93SP99 Ty Detmer	.75	2.00
93SP100 Warren Moon	1.25	3.00

2012 Upper Deck 1993 SP Inserts Autographs

93SP1 Alameda Ta'amu	15.00	40.00
93SP2 Alfonzo Dennard	12.00	30.00
93SP3 Alshon Jeffery	30.00	60.00
93SP5 B.J. Cunningham	10.00	25.00
93SP6 Brandon Bolden	12.00	30.00
93SP7 Brandon Thompson	10.00	25.00
93SP8 Brandon Weeden	40.00	80.00
93SP9 Brian Quick		
93SP10 Brock Osweiler	25.00	50.00
93SP11 Case Keenum	15.00	40.00
93SP12 Chandler Harnish	12.00	30.00
93SP13 Marvin Jones	10.00	25.00
93SP15 Bernard Pierce	12.00	30.00
93SP16 Dwayne Allen	12.00	30.00
93SP17 Courtney Upshaw	12.00	30.00
93SP18 Cyrus Gray	12.00	30.00
93SP19 Dan Herron	12.00	30.00
93SP20 Davin Meggett	10.00	25.00
93SP21 DeVier Posey	12.00	30.00
93SP22 Doug Martin	25.00	50.00
93SP23 Dwight Jones	10.00	25.00
93SP24 Rueben Randle		
93SP25 Gerell Robinson	12.00	30.00
93SP26 Greg Childs	12.00	30.00
93SP27 Isaiah Pead	12.00	30.00
93SP28 Dre Kirkpatrick	25.00	50.00
93SP29 Jared Crick	12.00	30.00
93SP30 Jarius Wright	12.00	30.00
93SP31 Jarrett Boykin	12.00	30.00
93SP32 Eric Page	10.00	25.00
93SP33 Jeff Fuller	15.00	40.00
93SP34 Jermaine Kearse	12.00	30.00
93SP35 Joe Adams	12.00	30.00
93SP37 Justin Blackmon	60.00	100.00
93SP38 Kellen Moore	30.00	60.00
93SP39 Kendall Wright	12.00	30.00
93SP40 Keshawn Martin	15.00	40.00
93SP41 Kirk Cousins	30.00	60.00
93SP42 LaMichael James	50.00	80.00
93SP44 Marc Tyler	8.00	20.00
93SP45 Marquis Maze	12.00	30.00
93SP46 Marvin McNutt	25.00	50.00
93SP47 Ronnie Hillman	15.00	40.00
93SP48 Melvin Ingram	15.00	30.00
93SP49 Michael Egnew	12.00	30.00
93SP50 Michael Floyd	60.00	100.00
93SP51 Mohamed Sanu	12.00	30.00
93SP52 Luke Kuechly	20.00	40.00
93SP53 Nick Foles	20.00	50.00
93SP54 Nick Toon	30.00	60.00
93SP55 Quinton Coples	12.00	30.00
93SP56 Rishard Matthews	8.00	20.00
93SP57 Robert Griffin III	250.00	400.00
93SP58 Russell Wilson	60.00	100.00
93SP59 Ryan Broyles	25.00	50.00
93SP60 Ryan Lindley	12.00	30.00
93SP61 Ryan Tannehill	50.00	100.00
93SP62 Tauren Poole	10.00	25.00
93SP64 Trent Richardson	100.00	175.00
93SP65 Stephen Hill	12.00	30.00
93SP66 Thurman Thomas	20.00	40.00
93SP67 Antonio Freeman	20.00	40.00
93SP68 Johnny Rodgers	15.00	30.00
93SP70 Bo Jackson		
93SP71 Bob Lilly	30.00	60.00
93SP74 Danny Wuerffel		
93SP75 Dave Casper		
93SP76 Drew Brees	60.00	120.00
93SP78 Eric Metcalf		
93SP79 Floyd Little	15.00	30.00
93SP81 Gino Torretta	10.00	25.00
93SP83 Herman Moore		
93SP84 Jason White		
93SP87 Kellen Winslow Sr.	10.00	25.00
93SP88 Lawrence Taylor	15.00	40.00
93SP89 Marques Colston	25.00	50.00
93SP90 Ozzie Newsome	12.00	30.00
93SP91 Randy White	30.00	60.00
93SP92 Roger Staubach		
93SP93 Roman Gabriel	12.00	30.00
93SP94 Ron Dayne	20.00	40.00
93SP96 Steve Young	40.00	80.00
93SP98 Troy Aikman		
93SP99 Ty Detmer	25.00	50.00
93SP100 Warren Moon		

2012 Upper Deck College Mascot Manufactured Patch

GROUP A ODDS 1:99 HOB
GROUP B ODDS 1:158 HOB
GROUP C ODDS 1:1752 HOB
GROUP D ODDS 1:7595 HOB
OVERALL STATED ODDS 1:40 HOBBY

CM1 Big Al A	15.00	40.00
CM2 Sparky B	6.00	15.00
CM3 Willie the Wildcat B	6.00	15.00
CM4 Tusk A	12.00	30.00
CM5 Black Jack C	50.00	100.00
CM6 War Eagle C	50.00	100.00
CM7 Aubie A	8.00	20.00
CM8 Bruiser B	8.00	20.00
CM9 Buster Bronco B	8.00	
CM10 Baldwin the Eagle B	6.00	15.00
CM11 Cosmo A	6.00	15.00
CM12 Oski A	6.00	15.00
CM13 Knightro B	6.00	15.00
CM14 Ralphie B	8.00	20.00
CM15 YoUDee C	15.00	40.00
CM16 PeeDee B	8.00	20.00
CM17 Albert E. Gator A	12.00	30.00
CM18 Uga D	250.00	350.00
CM19 Hairy Dawg A	10.00	25.00
CM20 Buzz A	6.00	15.00
CM21 Herky Hawk A	10.00	25.00
CM22 The Wildcat B	8.00	20.00
CM23 Mike the Tiger D	250.00	350.00
realistic tiger image		
CM24 Mike the Tiger A	12.00	30.00
tiger costume image		
CM25 Sebastian the Ibis C	40.00	80.00
CM26 Sparty A	10.00	25.00
CM27 Goldy Gopher B	6.00	15.00
CM28 Bully A	8.00	20.00
CM29 Truman the Tiger A	8.00	20.00
CM30 Monte B	6.00	15.00
CM31 Herbie Husker A	8.00	20.00
CM32 Lil Red D	100.00	175.00
CM33 Rameses B	10.00	25.00
CM34 The Leprechaun A	15.00	30.00
CM35 Brutus Buckeye A	20.00	50.00
CM36 Sooner Schooner A	10.00	25.00
CM37 Pistol Pete A	8.00	20.00
CM38 The Duck A	20.00	40.00
CM39 Benny Beaver C	25.00	50.00
CM40 Roc the Panther A	6.00	15.00
CM41 The Clemson Tiger A	10.00	25.00
CM42 Purdue Pete A	8.00	20.00
CM43 Cocky B	8.00	20.00
CM44 Rocky D. Bull B	6.00	15.00
CM45 Super Frog B	6.00	15.00
CM46 Smokey A	10.00	25.00
CM47 Reveille A	10.00	25.00
CM48 Bevo D	125.00	200.00
CM49 Hook Em A	8.00	20.00
CM50 Raider Red A	6.00	15.00
CM51 Joe and Josephine Bruin A	8.00	20.00
CM52 Traveler D	150.00	250.00
CM53 Trojan Warrior A	8.00	20.00
CM54 CavMan A	6.00	15.00
CM55 HokieBird A	6.00	15.00
CM56 Demon Deacon A	6.00	15.00
CM57 Harry the Husky A	8.00	20.00
CM58 Big Red A	8.00	20.00
CM59 Bucky Badger A	10.00	25.00
CM60 Handsome Dan A	8.00	20.00

2012 Upper Deck Rookie Autographs

51 Bobby Massie	4.00	10.00
52 Alameda Ta'amu	8.00	20.00
53 Alfred Morris	5.00	12.00
54 Michael Brockers	10.00	25.00
56 Antwon Bailey	5.00	12.00
57 Audie Cole	5.00	12.00
58 Emil Igwenagu	5.00	12.00
59 B.J. Cunningham	10.00	25.00
60 Tyler Hansen	5.00	12.00
61 Ryan Steed	4.00	10.00
62 Brandon Weeden	30.00	60.00
63 Brian Reader	5.00	12.00
64 Bryce Beall	4.00	10.00
65 David Molk	6.00	15.00
66 Cam Johnson	6.00	15.00
67 Case Keenum	12.00	30.00
68 Casey Hayward	6.00	15.00
69 Duane Bennett	5.00	12.00
70 Winston Guy	4.00	10.00
71 Cliff Harris	8.00	20.00
72 Cody Johnson	5.00	12.00
73 Coryell Judie	5.00	12.00
74 Courtney Upshaw	8.00	20.00
75 Tim Benford	4.00	10.00
76 Da'Jon McKnight	5.00	12.00
77 Dan Persa	5.00	12.00
78 Coby Fleener	8.00	20.00
80 David Paulson	8.00	20.00
81 Amini Silatolu	4.00	10.00
82 Derek Moye	8.00	20.00
84 Devon Wylie	6.00	15.00
85 Evan Rodriguez	5.00	12.00
86 George Iloka	5.00	12.00
87 Greg Childs	8.00	20.00
88 Tyler Shoemaker	5.00	12.00
89 Harrison Smith	6.00	15.00
90 Jared Crick	8.00	20.00
91 Jarrett Lee	8.00	20.00
92 Jason Ford	5.00	12.00
93 Jeff Fuller	8.00	20.00
94 Jermaine Kearse	6.00	15.00
95 Jake Bequette	6.00	15.00
96 Josh Chapman	6.00	15.00
97 Junior Hemingway	8.00	20.00
98 Justin Blackmon	25.00	50.00
99 Keenan Robinson	5.00	12.00
100 Kellen Moore	20.00	40.00
101 Bobby Wagner	6.00	15.00
102 Kentrell Lockett	4.00	10.00
103 Keshawn Martin	6.00	15.00
104 Micanor Regis	4.00	10.00
105 Kirk Cousins	12.00	30.00
106 Brock Osweiler	20.00	40.00
107 LaMichael James	25.00	50.00
108 Lavasier Tuinei	5.00	12.00
109 Jeremy Ebert	5.00	12.00
110 Marc Tyler	6.00	15.00
112 Markelle Martin	5.00	12.00
113 Marquis Maze	15.00	30.00
114 Nelson Rosario	5.00	12.00
115 Matt Kalil	8.00	20.00
116 Rodney Stewart	5.00	12.00
117 Michael Egnew	5.00	12.00
118 Michael Floyd	25.00	50.00
121 Mike Willie	6.00	15.00
123 Mychal Kendricks	6.00	15.00
124 Robert Blanton	5.00	12.00
125 Nick Foles	8.00	20.00
126 Nick Toon	15.00	30.00
127 Shea McClellin	8.00	20.00
128 Rhett Ellison	5.00	12.00
129 Quinton Coples	6.00	15.00
130 James-Michael Johnson	5.00	12.00
132 William Vlachos	5.00	12.00
133 Rueben Randle	10.00	25.00
134 Russell Wilson	25.00	50.00
135 Ryan Broyles	20.00	40.00
137 Ryan Tannehill	30.00	60.00
139 Stephfon Green	10.00	25.00
140 Brian Linthicum	5.00	12.00
141 Mike Martin	6.00	15.00
142 Tony Dye	4.00	10.00
143 Travis Benjamin	6.00	15.00
144 Trent Richardson	50.00	100.00
145 Trenton Robinson	5.00	12.00
146 Ladarius Green	6.00	15.00
147 Kelechi Osemele	6.00	15.00
149 Shaun Prater	6.00	15.00
151 A.J. Jenkins	12.00	30.00
152 Whitney Mercilus	6.00	15.00
153 Alfonzo Dennard	8.00	20.00
154 Andre Branch	5.00	12.00
155 Lucas Nix	4.00	10.00
157 Billy Winn	6.00	15.00
158 Brandon Bolden	6.00	15.00
160 Thomas Mayo	4.00	10.00
161 Brandon Thompson	5.00	12.00
162 Joe Looney	5.00	12.00
163 Chandler Harnish	6.00	15.00
165 Keith Tandy	5.00	12.00
166 Kevin Koger	6.00	15.00
168 Cyrus Gray	6.00	15.00
169 Dan Herron	8.00	20.00
171 Davin Meggett	6.00	15.00
172 Dominique Davis	5.00	12.00
173 Donnie Fletcher	4.00	10.00
174 Dont'a Hightower	15.00	30.00
175 Doug Martin	15.00	30.00
176 Dwayne Allen	6.00	15.00
177 Dwight Jones	5.00	12.00
178 Gerell Robinson	6.00	15.00
179 Isaiah Pead	6.00	15.00
180 Jarius Wright	8.00	20.00
181 Jarrett Boykin	8.00	20.00
182 Jayron Hosley	6.00	15.00
183 Jamell Fleming	6.00	15.00
184 Jermaine Thomas	5.00	12.00
185 Joe Adams	6.00	15.00
186 Kyle Wilber	6.00	15.00
187 Jordan Jefferson	6.00	15.00
188 Jordan White	6.00	15.00
190 Kendall Reyes	5.00	12.00
191 Kendall Wright	10.00	25.00
193 Laron Byrd	5.00	12.00
194 Lavonte David	6.00	15.00
195 Levy Adcock	5.00	12.00
196 Darius Hanks	8.00	20.00
197 Marvin Jones	5.00	12.00
198 Marvin McNutt	20.00	40.00
199 Melvin Ingram	8.00	20.00
200 Bradie Ewing	5.00	12.00
201 Nigel Bradham	5.00	12.00
202 Riley Reiff	20.00	40.00
203 Ronnell Lewis	10.00	25.00
204 Ryan Lindley	8.00	20.00
205 Stephon Gilmore	6.00	15.00
206 Tank Carder	6.00	15.00
207 Tauren Poole	8.00	20.00
208 Eric Page	5.00	12.00
209 Travis Lewis	5.00	12.00
210 Vontaze Burfict	5.00	12.00
212 Alshon Jeffery	20.00	40.00
213 Bernard Pierce	6.00	15.00
214 Bobby Rainey	6.00	15.00
215 Chris Galippo	5.00	12.00
216 Brian Quick	8.00	20.00
217 Mike Daniels	8.00	20.00
218 Eddie Whitley	6.00	15.00
219 DeVier Posey	8.00	20.00
220 Dontari Poe	6.00	15.00
221 Dre Kirkpatrick	12.00	30.00
222 Edwin Baker	8.00	20.00
223 Fozzy Whittaker	6.00	15.00
224 Trevor Guyton	5.00	12.00
226 Janoris Jenkins	6.00	15.00
227 Jerry Franklin	5.00	12.00
228 Jonathan Martin	5.00	12.00
232 Brandon Carswell	5.00	12.00
233 Lennon Creer	5.00	12.00
234 Leonard Johnson	5.00	12.00
235 Luke Kuechly	15.00	30.00
236 Josh Norman	4.00	10.00
237 Marshall Lobbestael	5.00	12.00
238 Mohamed Sanu	8.00	20.00
240 T.J. Graham	6.00	15.00
241 Orson Charles	8.00	20.00
242 Patrick Edwards	6.00	15.00
243 Rishard Matthews	6.00	15.00
244 Robert Griffin III	125.00	200.00
245 Ronnie Hillman	10.00	25.00
246 Stephen Garcia	6.00	15.00
247 Stephen Hill	20.00	40.00

2012 Upper Deck Rookie Exclusives

RANDOM INSERTS IN PACKS

REAJ Alshon Jeffery	1.25	3.00
REBW Brandon Weeden	1.50	4.00
REJB Justin Blackmon	1.50	4.00
REKW Kendall Wright	1.00	2.50
RELJ LaMichael James	1.50	4.00
RELM Lamar Miller	1.00	2.50
REMF Michael Floyd	1.50	4.00
RENF Nick Foles	1.25	3.00
RERG Robert Griffin III	4.00	10.00
RETR Trent Richardson	2.50	6.00

2012 Upper Deck Rookie Lettermen Autographs

SERIAL #'d 5-45, TOTAL PRINT RUNS 100-405

RLAD Alfonzo Dennard/275*	10.00	25.00
serial #'d to 25,		
letters spell CORNHUSKERS		
RLAJ1 Alshon Jeffery/200*	25.00	50.00
G,A,M,E,C,O,K,S serial #'d to 25,		
letters spell GAMECOCKS		
RLAJ2 Alshon Jeffery C/10	25.00	50.00
C serial #'d to 10,		
letters spell GAMECOCKS		
RLAT Alameda Ta'amu/315*	8.00	20.00
serial #'d to 45,		
letters spell HUSKIES		
RLBB Brandon Bolden/270*	8.00	20.00
serial #'d to 45,		
letters spell REBELS		
RLBC B.J. Cunningham/360*	8.00	20.00
serial #'d to 45,		
letters spell SPARTANS		
RLBO Jarrett Boykin/270*	10.00	25.00
serial #'d to 45,		
letters spell HOKIES		
RLBQ Brian Quick/300*	12.00	30.00
serial #'d to 25,		
letters spell MOUNTAINEERS		
RLBT Brandon Thompson/270*	8.00	20.00
serial #'d to 45;		
letters spell TIGERS		
RLBW Brandon Weeden/315*	30.00	60.00
serial #'d to 45,		
letters spell COWBOYS		
RLCG Cyrus Gray/270*	8.00	20.00
serial #'d to 45,		
letters spell AGGIES		
RLCH Chandler Harnish/315*	10.00	25.00
serial #'d to 45,		
letters spell HUSKIES		
RLCK Case Keenum/315*	12.00	30.00
serial #'d to 45,		
letters spell COUGARS		
RLCU Courtney Upshaw/275*	12.00	30.00
serial #'d to 25,		
letters spell CRIMSON TIDE		
RLDA Davin Meggett/405*	8.00	20.00
serial #'d to 45,		
letters spell TERRAPINS		
RLDH Dan Herron/360*	10.00	25.00
serial #'d to 45,		
letters spell BUCKEYES		
RLDJ Dwight Jones/360*	6.00	15.00
serial #'d to 45,		
letters spell TAR HEELS		
RLDM Doug Martin/315*	20.00	40.00
serial #'d to 45,		
letters spell BRONCOS		
RLDP DeVier Posey/360*	10.00	25.00
serial #'d to 45,		
letters spell BUCKEYES		
RLGC1 Greg Childs/315*	10.00	25.00
R,A,O,B,C,K,S serial #'d to 35,		
letters spell RAZORBACKS		
RLGC2 Greg Childs Z/15	15.00	40.00
Z serial #'d to 15,		
letters spell RAZORBACKS		
RLGR Gerell Robinson/405*	6.00	15.00
serial #'d to 45,		
letters spell SUN DEVILS		
RLIP Isaiah Pead/360*	8.00	20.00
serial #'d to 45,		
letters spell BEARCATS		
RLJA Joe Adams/350*	12.00	30.00
serial #'d to 35,		
letters spell RAZORBACKS		
RLJB1 Justin Blackmon/160*	40.00	80.00
serial #'d to 25,		
letters spell COWBOYS		
RLJB2 Justin Blackmon O/10	40.00	80.00
one O serial #'d to 10,		
letters spell COWBOYS		
RLJC Jared Crick/275*	12.00	30.00
serial #'d to 25,		
letters spell CORNHUSKERS		
RLJF1 Jeff Fuller/175*	8.00	20.00
serial #'d to 35,		
letters spell AGGIES		
RLJF2 Jeff Fuller G/15	10.00	25.00
one G serial #'d to 15,		
letters spell AGGIES		
RLJJ Janoris Jenkins/225*	8.00	20.00
serial #'d to 45,		
letters spell LIONS		
RLJK Jermaine Kearse/315*	8.00	20.00
serial #'d to 45,		
letters spell HUSKIES		
RLJU1 Juron Criner/245*	10.00	25.00
serial #'d to 35,		
letters spell WILDCATS		
RLJU2 Juron Criner C/15	15.00	30.00
C serial #'d to 15,		
letters spell WILDCATS		
RLKC1 Kirk Cousins/245*	20.00	40.00
C serial #'d to 35,		
letters spell SPARTANS		
RLKC2 Kirk Cousins S/15	20.00	40.00
one S serial #'d to 15,		
letters spell SPARTANS		
RLKM Keshawn Martin/360*	8.00	20.00
serial #'d to 45,		
letters spell SPARTANS		
RLLA1 LaMichael James/100*	90.00	150.00
serial #'d to 25,		
letters spell DUCKS		
RLLA2 LaMichael James U/10	175.00	300.00
U serial #'d to 10,		
letters spell DUCKS		
RLLK Luke Kuechly/270*	12.00	30.00
serial #'d to 45,		
letters spell EAGLES		
RLMC Marvin McNutt/360*	12.00	30.00
serial #'d to 45,		
letters spell HAWKEYES		
RLME Michael Egnew/270*	8.00	20.00
serial #'d to 45,		
letters spell TIGERS		
RLMF1 Michael Floyd/300*	30.00	60.00
serial #'d to 25,		
letters spell FIGHTING IRISH		
RLMF2 Michael Floyd I/10	40.00	80.00
one I serial #'d to 10,		
letters spell FIGHTING IRISH		
RLMI Melvin Ingram/405*	12.00	30.00
serial #'d to 45,		
letters spell GAMECOCKS		
RLMM Marquis Maze/385*	12.00	30.00
serial #'d to 35,		
letters spell CRIMSON TIDE		
RLMO1 Kellen Moore/210*	15.00	40.00
serial #'d to 35,		
letters spell BRONCOS		
RLMO2 Kellen Moore B/15	25.00	60.00
serial #'d to 15,		
letters spell BRONCOS		
RLMS Mohamed Sanu/210*	12.00	30.00
serial #'d to 15,		
letters spell SCARLET KNIGHTS		
RLMT Marc Tyler/315*	8.00	20.00
serial #'d to 45,		
letters spell TROJANS		
RLNF Nick Foles/280*	12.00	30.00
serial #'d to 35,		
letters spell WILDCATS		
RLNT Nick Toon/245*	15.00	40.00
serial #'d to 35,		
letters spell BADGERS		
RLQC Quinton Coples/360*	10.00	25.00
serial #'d to 45,		
letters spell TAR HEELS		
RLRB Ryan Broyles/315*	15.00	40.00
serial #'d to 45,		
letters spell SOONERS		
RLRG Robert Griffin III/225*	125.00	250.00
serial #'d to 45,		
letters spell BEARS		
RLRL Ryan Lindley/210*	8.00	20.00
serial #'d to 35,		
letters spell AZTECS		
RLRT Ryan Tannehill/210*	30.00	60.00
serial #'d to 35,		
letters spell AGGIES		
RLRW Russell Wilson/315*	20.00	40.00
serial #'d to 45,		
letters spell BADGERS		
RLTP Tauren Poole/350*	8.00	20.00
serial #'d to 35,		
letters spell VOLUNTEERS		
RLTR1 Trent Richardson/150*	75.00	150.00
serial #'d to 15,		
letters spell CRIMSON TIDE		
RLTR2 Trent Richardson T/5		
T serial #'d to 5,		
letters spell CRIMSON TIDE		

2012 Upper Deck Tim Tebow

COMPLETE SET (10)	15.00	40.00
COMMON TEBOW (TT1-TT10)	1.00	2.50
INSERTED IN UD RACK PACKS		
TT4 Tim Tebow	5.00	12.00
TT7 Tim Tebow	5.00	12.00

2009 Upper Deck 20th Anniversary

CARDS ISSUED IN FIVE CARD RUNS
EACH PRICED EQUALLY WITHIN RUNS

6 Notre Dame Fighting Irish	.20	.50
7 Notre Dame Fighting Irish	.20	.50
8 Notre Dame Fighting Irish	.20	.50
9 Notre Dame Fighting Irish	.20	.50
10 Notre Dame Fighting Irish	.20	.50
31 San Francisco 49ers	.20	.50
32 San Francisco 49ers	.20	.50
33 San Francisco 49ers	.20	.50
34 San Francisco 49ers	.20	.50
35 San Francisco 49ers	.20	.50
41 Dallas Cowboys	.40	1.00
42 Dallas Cowboys	.40	1.00
43 Dallas Cowboys	.40	1.00
44 Dallas Cowboys	.40	1.00
45 Dallas Cowboys	.40	1.00
141 Louisiana Super Bowl	.20	.50
142 Louisiana Super Bowl	.20	.50
143 Louisiana Super Bowl	.20	.50
144 Louisiana Super Bowl	.20	.50
145 Louisiana Super Bowl	.20	.50
221 Miami Hurricanes	.20	.50
222 Miami Hurricanes	.20	.50
223 Miami Hurricanes	.20	.50
224 Miami Hurricanes	.20	.50
225 Miami Hurricanes	.20	.60
311 Georgia Tech Yellow Jackets	.20	.50
Colorado Buffaloes		
College Football National Champions		
312 Georgia Tech Yellow Jackets	.20	.50
Colorado Buffaloes		
College Football National Champions		
313 Georgia Tech Yellow Jackets	.20	.50
Colorado Buffaloes		
College Football National Champions		
314 Georgia Tech Yellow Jackets	.20	.50
Colorado Buffaloes		
College Football National Champions		
315 Georgia Tech Yellow Jackets	.20	.50
Colorado Buffaloes		
College Football National Champions		
436 Washington Redskins	.20	.50
437 Washington Redskins	.20	.50
438 Washington Redskins	.20	.50
439 Washington Redskins	.20	.50
440 Washington Redskins	.20	.50
496 University of Washington Huskies	.20	.50
Miami Hurricanes		
College Football National Champions		
497 University of Washington Huskies	.20	.50
Miami Hurricanes		
College Football National Champions		
498 University of Washington Huskies	.20	.50
Miami Hurricanes		
College Football National Champions		
499 University of Washington Huskies	.20	.50
Miami Hurricanes		
College Football National Champions		
500 University of Washington Huskies	.20	.50
Miami Hurricanes		
College Football National Champions		
596 NCAA Football Champions	.20	.50
Alabama Crimson Tide		
597 NCAA Football Champions	.20	.50
Alabama Crimson Tide		
598 NCAA Football Champions	.20	.50
Alabama Crimson Tide		
599 NCAA Football Champions	.20	.50
Alabama Crimson Tide		
600 NCAA Football Champions	.20	.50
Alabama Crimson Tide		
611 Final Game in Cleveland Stadium	.20	.50
612 Final Game in Cleveland Stadium	.20	.50
613 Final Game in Cleveland Stadium	.20	.50
614 Final Game in Cleveland Stadium	.20	.50
615 Final Game in Cleveland Stadium	.20	.50
796 Carolina Panthers	.20	.50
Kerry Collins		
797 Carolina Panthers	.20	.50
798 Carolina Panthers	.20	.50
799 Carolina Panthers	.20	.50
800 Carolina Panthers	.20	.50
801 Jacksonville Jaguars	.20	.50
802 Jacksonville Jaguars	.20	.50
803 Jacksonville Jaguars	.20	.50
804 Jacksonville Jaguars	.20	.50
805 Jacksonville Jaguars	.20	.50
901 Dallas Cowboys	.40	1.00
902 Dallas Cowboys	.40	1.00
903 Dallas Cowboys	.40	1.00
904 Dallas Cowboys	.40	1.00
905 Dallas Cowboys	.40	1.00
961 NCAA Football Champions	.20	.50
Nebraska Cornhuskers		
962 NCAA Football Champions	.20	.50
Nebraska Cornhuskers		
963 NCAA Football Champions	.20	.50
Nebraska Cornhuskers		
964 NCAA Football Champions	.20	.50
Nebraska Cornhuskers		
965 NCAA Football Champions	.20	.50
Nebraska Cornhuskers		
1016 Green Bay Packers	.30	.75
1017 Green Bay Packers	.30	.75
1018 Green Bay Packers	.30	.75
1019 Green Bay Packers	.30	.75
1020 Green Bay Packers	.30	.75
1086 NCAA Football Champions	.20	.50
1087 NCAA Football Champions	.20	.50
1088 NCAA Football Champions	.20	.50
1089 NCAA Football Champions	.20	.50
1090 NCAA Football Champions	.20	.50
1136 Denver Broncos	.20	.50
1137 Denver Broncos	.20	.50
1138 Denver Broncos	.20	.50
1139 Denver Broncos	.20	.50
1140 Denver Broncos	.20	.50
1176 NCAA Football Champions	.20	.50
1177 NCAA Football Champions	.20	.50
1178 NCAA Football Champions	.20	.50
1179 NCAA Football Champions	.20	.50
1180 NCAA Football Champions	.20	.50
1181 Peyton Manning	.75	2.00
1182 Peyton Manning	.75	2.00
1183 Peyton Manning	.75	2.00
1184 Peyton Manning	.75	2.00
1185 Peyton Manning	.75	2.00
1261 Denver Broncos	.20	.50
1262 Denver Broncos	.20	.50
1263 Denver Broncos	.20	.50
1264 Denver Broncos	.20	.50
1265 Denver Broncos	.20	.50
1396 St. Louis Rams	.20	.50
1397 St. Louis Rams	.20	.50
1398 St. Louis Rams	.20	.50
1399 St. Louis Rams	.20	.50
1400 St. Louis Rams	.20	.50
1516 Baltimore Ravens	.20	.50
1517 Baltimore Ravens	.20	.50
1518 Baltimore Ravens	.20	.50
1519 Baltimore Ravens	.20	.50
1520 Baltimore Ravens	.20	.50
1626 New England Patriots	.20	.50
1627 New England Patriots	.20	.50
1628 New England Patriots	.20	.50
1629 New England Patriots	.20	.50
1630 New England Patriots	.20	.50
1656 Ed Reed	.25	.60
1657 Ed Reed	.25	.60
1658 Ed Reed	.25	.60
1659 Ed Reed	.25	.60
1660 Ed Reed	.25	.60
1686 Tom Brady	.75	2.00
1687 Tom Brady	.75	2.00
1688 Tom Brady	.75	2.00
1689 Tom Brady	.75	2.00
1690 Tom Brady	.75	2.00
1691 Brian Westbrook	.40	1.00
1692 Brian Westbrook	.40	1.00
1693 Brian Westbrook	.40	1.00
1694 Brian Westbrook	.40	1.00
1695 Brian Westbrook	.40	1.00
1706 Clinton Portis	.40	1.00
1707 Clinton Portis	.40	1.00
1708 Clinton Portis	.40	1.00
1709 Clinton Portis	.40	1.00
1710 Clinton Portis	.40	1.00
1716 Tuck Rule NFL Playoff Game	.20	.50
1717 Tuck Rule NFL Playoff Game	.20	.50
1718 Tuck Rule NFL Playoff Game	.20	.50
1719 Tuck Rule NFL Playoff Game	.20	.50
1720 Tuck Rule NFL Playoff Game	.20	.50
1751 Troy Polamalu	.40	1.00
1752 Troy Polamalu	.40	1.00
1753 Troy Polamalu	.40	1.00
1754 Troy Polamalu	.40	1.00
1755 Troy Polamalu	.40	1.00
1771 Tampa Bay Buccaneers	.20	.50
1772 Tampa Bay Buccaneers	.20	.50
1773 Tampa Bay Buccaneers	.20	.50
1774 Tampa Bay Buccaneers	.20	.50
1775 Tampa Bay Buccaneers	.20	.50
1856 Tony Romo	.75	2.00
1857 Tony Romo	.75	2.00
1858 Tony Romo	.75	2.00
1859 Tony Romo	.75	2.00
1860 Tony Romo	.75	2.00
1911 Eli Manning	.40	1.00
1912 Eli Manning	.40	1.00
1913 Eli Manning	.40	1.00
1914 Eli Manning	.40	1.00
1915 Eli Manning	.40	1.00
1916 New England Patriots	.20	.50
1917 New England Patriots	.20	.50
1918 New England Patriots	.20	.50
1919 New England Patriots	.20	.50
1920 New England Patriots	.20	.50
1971 Ben Roethlisberger	.50	1.25
1972 Ben Roethlisberger	.50	1.25
1973 Ben Roethlisberger	.50	1.25
1974 Ben Roethlisberger	.50	1.25
1975 Ben Roethlisberger	.50	1.25
1986 Peyton Manning	.75	2.00
1987 Peyton Manning	.75	2.00
1988 Peyton Manning	.75	2.00
1989 Peyton Manning	.75	2.00
1990 Peyton Manning	.75	2.00
2051 NFL Game Played in Mexico	.20	.50
2052 NFL Game Played in Mexico	.20	.50
2053 NFL Game Played in Mexico	.20	.50
2054 NFL Game Played in Mexico	.20	.50
2055 NFL Game Played in Mexico	.20	.50
2056 New England Patriots	.20	.50
2057 New England Patriots	.20	.50
2058 New England Patriots	.20	.50
2059 New England Patriots	.20	.50
2060 New England Patriots	.20	.50
2136 Pittsburgh Steelers	.20	.50
2137 Pittsburgh Steelers	.20	.50
2138 Pittsburgh Steelers	.20	.50
2139 Pittsburgh Steelers	.20	.50
2140 Pittsburgh Steelers	.20	.50
2321 Adrian Peterson	1.00	2.50
2322 Adrian Peterson	1.00	2.50
2323 Adrian Peterson	1.00	2.50
2324 Adrian Peterson	1.00	2.50
2325 Adrian Peterson	1.00	2.50
2341 Indianapolis Colts	.20	.50
2342 Indianapolis Colts	.20	.50
2343 Indianapolis Colts	.20	.50
2344 Indianapolis Colts	.20	.50
2345 Indianapolis Colts	.20	.50
2396 New York Giants	.20	.50
2397 New York Giants	.20	.50
2398 New York Giants	.20	.50
2399 New York Giants	.20	.50
2400 New York Giants	.20	.50
2406 Brett Favre	1.25	3.00
2407 Brett Favre	1.25	3.00
2408 Brett Favre	1.25	3.00
2409 Brett Favre	1.25	3.00
2410 Brett Favre	1.25	3.00
2461 Brett Favre	1.00	2.50
2462 Brett Favre	1.00	2.50
2463 Brett Favre	1.00	2.50
2464 Brett Favre	1.00	2.50
2465 Brett Favre	1.00	2.50
2466 Matt Ryan	.60	1.50
2467 Matt Ryan	.60	1.50
2468 Matt Ryan	.60	1.50
2469 Matt Ryan	.60	1.50
2470 Matt Ryan	.60	1.50
2496 Chris Johnson	.40	1.00
2497 Chris Johnson	.40	1.00
2498 Chris Johnson	.40	1.00
2499 Chris Johnson	.40	1.00
2500 Chris Johnson	.40	1.00

2009 Upper Deck 20th Anniversary Memorabilia

NFLAP Adrian Peterson	10.00	25.00
NFLBF Brett Favre	20.00	50.00
NFLBU Brian Urlacher	4.00	10.00
NFLCP Carson Palmer	5.00	12.00
NFLDG David Garrard	3.00	8.00
NFLDH Devin Hester	4.00	10.00
NFLDW DeAngelo Williams	3.00	8.00
NFLEJ Edgerrin James	4.00	10.00
NFLJP Julius Peppers	4.00	10.00
NFLMC Donovan McNabb	5.00	12.00
NFLPM Peyton Manning	8.00	20.00
NFLRM Randy Moss	6.00	15.00
NFLTR Tony Romo	8.00	20.00

2009 Upper Deck Hawaii Trade Conference Autographs

UNPRICED AU PRINT RUN 1-25

2009 Upper Deck Own the Rookies

This set was distributed directly to hobby shops and dealers in December 2009. Each features the top ten rookies of the 2009 season and was issued in a sealed cellophane wrapper as a set.

COMPLETE SET (10)	3.00	8.00
RW1 Mark Sanchez	.75	2.00
RW2 Donald Brown	.25	.60
RW3 Matthew Stafford	1.25	3.00
RW4 Mohamed Massaquoi	.20	.50
RW5 Jeremy Maclin	.40	1.00
RW6 Hakeem Nicks	.40	1.00
RW7 Shonn Greene	.40	1.00
RW8 Percy Harvin	.40	1.00
RW9 Josh Freeman	.50	1.25
RW10 Chris Wells	.40	1.00

2009 Upper Deck Prominent Cuts

COMPLETE SET (60)	30.00	60.00
14 Steve Largent	.40	1.00

2009 Upper Deck Prominent Cuts Cut Signatures

OVERALL CUT SIGN. ODDS ONE PER BOX
STATED PRINT RUN B/WN 1-118

PCDR Darrell Royal/3		
PCJT Jim Thorpe/1		
PCLU Johnny Lujack/47	30.00	60.00
PCOG Otto Graham/1		
PCSO Steve Owens/77	15.00	30.00
PCVD Vince Dooley/1		
PCBEB Gary Beban/23		
PCGMA George McAfee/1		
PCLAT Johnny Lattner/107	20.00	40.00
PCLOU Lou Creekmur/1		
PCSBA Sammy Baugh/1		
PCSEM Bobby Bowden/1		
PCSFJ John Cappelletti/25	15.00	30.00
PCBILL Bill Belichick/1		
PCHANK Hank Stram/5		
PCIRISH Lou Holtz/2		

2011 Upper Deck Signature Icons Las Vegas Summit Promos

UNPRICED AUTO PRINT RUN 4-15
LVBJ Bo Jackson/15
LVSY Steve Young/10

1993 Upper Deck Adventures in Toon World

NNO Joe Montana	1.00	2.50
Wayne Gretzky		
Reggie Jackson		
Michael Jordan		

2005 Upper Deck AFL

COMPLETE SET (90)	20.00	40.00
1 Hunkie Cooper	.30	.75
2 Siaha Burley	.30	.75
3 Sherdrick Bonner	.30	.75
4 Bo Kelly	.20	.50
5 Evan Hlavacek	.20	.50
6 Tacoma Fontaine	.20	.50
7 Troy Bergeron	.40	1.00
8 Darrin Chiaverini	.30	.75
9 Bobby Pesavento	.20	.50
10 Tom Pace	.20	.50
11 Raymond Philyaw	.30	.75
12 Bob McMillen	.30	.75
13 Etu Molden	.30	.75
14 Jeremy McDaniel	.30	.75
15 Todd Hammel	.30	.75
16 John Dutton	.30	.75
17 Damian Harrell	.40	1.00
18 Kevin McKenzie	.20	.50
19 Willis Marshall	.20	.50
20 Rashad Floyd	.20	.50
21 Andy McCullough	.20	.50
22 Damien Groce	.30	.75
23 Chad Salisbury	.20	.50
24 Sedrick Robinson	.20	.50
25 Cornelius White	.20	.50
26 Wilmont Perry	.20	.50
27 Clint Stoerner	.75	2.00
28 Will Pettis	.30	.75
29 Bobby Sippio	.30	.75
30 Jason Shelley	.20	.50
31 Duke Pettijohn	.20	.50
32 Robert Thomas	.20	.50
33 Jim Kubiak	.30	.75
34 Dialleo Burks	.30	.75
35 Matt Nagy	.60	1.50
36 Kevin Gaines	.20	.50
37 Josh Bush	.20	.50
38 Michael Bishop	.40	1.00
39 Anthony Hines	.20	.50
40 Chris Jackson	.30	.75
41 Jerome Riley	.20	.50
42 Josh Jeffries	.20	.50
43 Clint Dolezel	.40	.75
44 Marcus Nash	.40	1.00
45 Coco Blalock	.30	.75
46 Cornelius Bonner	.20	.50
47 Frank Carter	.20	.50

48 John Kaleo .30 .75
49 Kevin Ingram .20 .50
50 Greg Hopkins .30 .75
51 Lonnie Ford .20 .50
52 Brian Sump .20 .50
53 Leon Murray .20 .50
54 Darryl Hammond .20 .50
55 Fred Coleman .20 .50
56 Ahmad Hawkins .20 .50
57 Gabe Amey .20 .50
58 Andy Kelly .30 .75
59 Chris Pointer .20 .50
60 Aaron Bailey .30 .75
61 Dan Curran .20 .50
62 Lamont Moore .20 .50
63 Thabiti Davis .30 .75
64 Aaron Garcia .40 1.00
65 Lincoln DuPree .20 .50
66 William Holder .20 .50
67 Chris Anthony .20 .50
68 Markeith Cooper .20 .50
69 Cory Fleming .30 .75
70 Kenny McEntyre .30 .75
71 Bret Cooper .20 .50
72 Travis McGriff .30 .75
73 Joe Hamilton .30 .75
74 Tony Graziani .40 1.00
75 Takuya Furutani .20 .50
76 Chris Ryan .20 .50
77 Joseph Todd .20 .50
78 Sean Scott .30 .75
79 Mark Grieb .40 1.00
80 James Hundon .30 .75
81 James Roe .30 .75
82 Omarr Smith .30 .75
83 Rashied Davis .30 .75
84 Calvin Schexnayder .20 .50
85 Shane Stafford .40 .75
86 Lawrence Samuels .30 .75
87 T.T. Toliver .20 .50
88 Freddie Solomon .30 .75
89 Cliff Dell .20 .50
90 Rich Young .20 .50

2005 Upper Deck AFL Gold

*GOLD: 5X TO 12X BASIC CARDS
GOLD PRINT RUN 100 SER.#'d SETS

2005 Upper Deck AFL Arena Action

STATED ODDS 1:10
AA1 Kenny McEntyre 1.50 4.00
AA2 Cory Fleming 1.50 4.00
AA3 Marcus Nash 2.00 5.00
AA4 Hunkie Cooper 1.50 4.00
AA5 Tony Graziani 2.00 5.00
AA6 Kevin Ingram 1.00 2.50
AA7 Dan Curran 1.00 2.50
AA8 Mark Grieb 2.00 5.00
AA9 Joe Hamilton 1.50 4.00
AA10 Will Pettis 1.50 4.00
AA11 Damian Harrell 2.00 5.00
AA12 Rashad Floyd 1.00 2.50
AA13 Etu Molden 1.50 4.00
AA14 Lincoln DuPree 1.00 2.50
AA15 Kevin McKenzie 1.00 2.50
AA16 James Roe 1.50 4.00
AA17 T.T. Toliver 1.00 2.50
AA18 Sedrick Robinson 1.00 2.50
AA19 Rashied Davis 1.50 4.00
AA20 Clint Dolezel 1.50 4.00
AA21 Chris Jackson 1.50 4.00
AA22 Thabiti Davis 1.50 4.00
AA23 Aaron Bailey 1.50 4.00
AA24 Freddie Solomon 1.50 4.00
AA25 Bobby Sippio 1.50 4.00
AA26 Lawrence Samuels 1.50 4.00
AA27 Siaha Burley 1.50 4.00
AA28 Markeith Cooper 1.00 2.50
AA29 Aaron Garcia 2.00 5.00
AA30 Cornelius White 1.00 2.50

2005 Upper Deck AFL ArenaBowl Archives

COMPLETE SET (18) 12.50 25.00
STATED ODDS 1:20
AB1 Arena Bowl I .75 2.00
AB2 Arena Bowl II .75 2.00
AB3 Arena Bowl III .75 2.00
AB4 Arena Bowl IV .75 2.00
AB5 Arena Bowl V .75 2.00
AB6 Arena Bowl VI .75 2.00
AB7 Arena Bowl VII .75 2.00
AB8 Arena Bowl VIII .75 2.00
AB9 Arena Bowl IX .75 2.00
AB10 Arena Bowl X .75 2.00
AB11 Arena Bowl XI .75 2.00
AB12 Arena Bowl XII .75 2.00
AB13 Arena Bowl XIII .75 2.00
AB14 Arena Bowl XIV .75 2.00
AB15 Arena Bowl XV .75 2.00
AB16 Arena Bowl XVI .75 2.00
AB17 Arena Bowl XVII .75 2.00
AB18 Arena Bowl XVIII .75 2.00

2005 Upper Deck AFL Arenagraphs

STATED ODDS 1:24 HOB, 1:48 RET
ABA Aaron Bailey 10.00 25.00
AGA Aaron Garcia 12.50 30.00
AMA Adrian McPherson 30.00 80.00
BMA Bob McMillen 10.00 25.00
CDA Clint Dolezel 12.50 30.00
CFA Cory Fleming 12.50 30.00
CJA Chris Jackson 10.00 25.00
DBA David Baker 7.50 20.00
DHA Damian Harrell 12.50 30.00
EMA Etu Molden 10.00 25.00
HCA Hunkie Cooper 12.50 30.00
JEA John Elway SP 125.00 200.00
JHA James Hundon
JJA Jerry Jones
KEA Kevin McKenzie 7.50 20.00
KIA Kevin Ingram 7.50 20.00
KMA Kenny McEntyre 10.00 25.00
LSA Lawrence Samuels 10.00 25.00
MDA Mike Ditka SP 50.00 100.00
MGA Mark Grieb 12.50 30.00
MNA Marcus Nash 12.50 30.00
OSA Omarr Smith 10.00 25.00
RDA Rashied Davis 10.00 25.00
SBA Siaha Burley 7.50 20.00
SRA Sedrick Robinson 10.00 25.00
TFA Tacoma Fontaine 12.50 30.00
TGA Tony Graziani 12.50 30.00
TMA Tim McGraw SP 125.00 200.00
TTA T.T. Toliver 7.50 20.00
WPA Will Pettis 10.00 25.00

2005 Upper Deck AFL Arenagraphs Duals

STATED PRINT RUN 50 SER.#'d SETS
BBA2 Aaron Bailey 15.00 40.00
Coco Blalock
BFA2 Siaha Burley 15.00 40.00
Tacoma Fontaine
DNA2 Clint Dolezel 20.00 50.00
Marcus Nash
EHA2 John Elway/25 150.00 300.00
Damian Harrell
FMA2 Cory Fleming 15.00 40.00
Kenny McEntyre
GGA2 Tony Graziani 25.00 60.00
Aaron Garcia
GHA2 Mark Grieb
James Hundon
GIA2 Tony Graziani 20.00 50.00
Kevin Ingram
HMA2 Damian Harrell 15.00 40.00
Kevin McKenzie
MBA2 Tim McGraw/25 100.00 175.00
David Baker
MMA2 Bob McMillen 15.00 40.00
Etu Molden
RPA2 Sedrick Robinson 15.00 40.00
Will Pettis
SDA2 Omarr Smith 15.00 40.00
Rashied Davis
STA2 Lawrence Samuels 15.00 40.00
T.T. Toliver
TCA2 Robert Thomas 20.00 50.00
Hunkie Cooper

2005 Upper Deck AFL Dance Team Stars

COMPLETE SET (10) 15.00 40.00
STATED ODDS 1:36
DTS1 Crystal 2.00 5.00
DTS2 Gina 2.00 5.00
DTS3 Katie 2.00 5.00
DTS4 Christina 2.00 5.00
DTS5 Heather 2.00 5.00
DTS6 Lisa 2.00 5.00
DTS7 Gloria 2.00 5.00
DTS8 Kelli 2.00 5.00
DTS9 Bridget 2.00 5.00
DTS10 Katie 2.00 5.00

2005 Upper Deck AFL Jerseys

STATED ODDS 1:12
AGJ Aaron Garcia 8.00 20.00
BSJ Bobby Sippio 5.00 12.00
CAJ Chris Anthony 4.00 10.00
CDJ Clint Dolezel 5.00 12.00
CJJ Chris Jackson 5.00 12.00
CRJ Chris Ryan 4.00 10.00
CSJ Corey Sawyer
DHJ Damian Harrell 8.00 20.00
HCJ Hunkie Cooper 5.00 12.00
JHJ James Hundon 8.00 20.00
JRJ James Roe 5.00 12.00
KEJ Kevin McKenzie 4.00 10.00
KIJ Kevin Ingram 4.00 10.00
LSJ Lawrence Samuels 5.00 12.00
MGJ Mark Grieb 8.00 20.00
MNJ Marcus Nash 8.00 20.00
MRJ Mark Ricks
OSJ Omarr Smith 5.00 12.00
RDJ Rashied Davis 5.00 12.00
RRJ Ricky Ross 4.00 10.00
SBJ Siaha Burley 5.00 12.00
SRJ Sedrick Robinson 4.00 10.00
TFJ Tacoma Fontaine 4.00 10.00
TGJ Tony Graziani 8.00 20.00
THJ Todd Hammel 5.00 12.00
TTJ T.T. Toliver 4.00 10.00
WPJ Will Pettis 5.00 12.00

2005 Upper Deck AFL League Luminaries

STATED ODDS 1:24
LL1 Tommy Maddox 2.50 6.00
LL2 David Baker 2.00 5.00
LL3 Kurt Warner 2.50 6.00
LL4 John Elway OWN 5.00 12.00
LL5 Danny White CO 2.50 6.00
LL6 Tim McGraw OWN 4.00 10.00
LL7 Adrian McPherson 7.50 20.00
LL8 Marcus Nash 2.50 6.00
LL9 Tony Graziani 3.00 8.00
LL10 Cory Fleming 2.50 6.00
LL11 Mike Ditka OWN 5.00 12.00
LL12 Jay Gruden 2.00 5.00
LL13 Tim Marcum CO 2.00 5.00
LL14 Kevin Swayne 2.00 5.00
LL15 Barry Wagner 2.00 5.00

2005 Upper Deck AFL Timeline

STATED ODDS 1:30
AFL1 Barry Wagner 2.00 5.00
AFL2 Sherdrick Bonner 2.00 5.00
AFL3 Jerry Jones OWN 2.50 6.00
AFL4 Tim McGraw OWN 4.00 10.00
AFL5 John Elway OWN 5.00 12.00
AFL6 Jay Gruden 2.00 5.00
AFL7 Tim Marcum 2.00 5.00
AFL8 Mike Ditka OWN 5.00 12.00
AFL9 Jim Kubiak 2.50 6.00
AFL10 David Baker COM 2.00 5.00
AFL11 Aaron Garcia 2.50 6.00
AFL12 2004 Attendance Record 2.00 5.00

2006 Upper Deck AFL

This 190-card set was released in February, 2006. The set was issued into the hobby in eight-card packs which came 24 packs to a box.

COMPLETE SET (190) 30.00 60.00
1 Sherdrick Bonner .30 .75
2 Clarence Coleman .20 .50
3 Randy Gatewood .20 .50
4 Tom Pace .20 .50
5 Vince Amey .20 .50
6 Evan Hlavacek .20 .50
7 Josh Jeffries .20 .50
8 Gary Kral .20 .50
9 Bo Kelly .20 .50
10 Clarence Lawson .20 .50
11 Damien Groce .30 .75
12 John Fitzgerald .20 .50
13 Kevin Nickerson .30 .75
14 Tom Briggs .20 .50
15 Darrin Chiaverini .30 .75
16 Ira Gooch .20 .50
17 Tacoma Fontaine .30 .75
18 Lindsay Fleshman .20 .50
19 Tim Seder .20 .50
20 Henry Bryant .20 .50
21 Sedrick Robinson .20 .50
22 Damon Mason .20 .50
23 Raymond Philyaw .30 .75
24 John Moyer .20 .50
25 Etu Molden .30 .75
26 Henry Douglas .20 .50
27 Bob McMillen .30 .75
28 Todd Hammel .30 .75
29 Jeremy McDaniel .30 .75
30 Keith Gispert .20 .50
31 Russell Shaw .20 .50
32 C.J. Johnson .20 .50
33 Cornelius White .20 .50
34 John Dutton .30 .75
35 Damian Harrell .40 1.00
36 Willis Marshall .20 .50
37 Clay Rush .20 .50
38 Andy McCullough .30 .75
39 Kevin McKenzie .20 .50
40 Rich Young .20 .50
41 Ahmad Hawkins .20 .50
42 Rashad Floyd .20 .50
43 Delvin Hughley .20 .50
44 Saul Patu .20 .50
45 Matt D'Orazio .30 .75
46 Lenzie Jackson .20 .50
47 B.J. Barre .20 .50
48 Mike Sutton .20 .50
49 Gillis Wilson .20 .50
50 Randall Lane .20 .50
51 Frank Carter .20 .50
52 Bobby Olive .20 .50
53 Jamarr Ward .20 .50
54 Thabiti Davis .30 .75
55 John Kaleo .30 .75
56 Clint Dolezel .40 1.00
57 Jason Shelley .20 .50
58 Will Pettis .30 .75
59 Hamin Milligan .20 .50
60 Duke Pettijohn .20 .50
61 Carlos Martinez .20 .50
62 Lucas Yarnell .20 .50
63 Jermaine Lewis .20 .50
64 Joe Minucci .20 .50
65 Jermaine Jones .20 .50
66 Scottie Montgomery .20 .50
67 Jim Kubiak .30 .75
68 Matt Nagy .40 1.00
69 Troy Bergeron .40 1.00
70 Chris Jackson .30 .75
71 Derek Lee .40 1.00
72 Robert Thomas .20 .50
73 Kevin Aldridge .20 .50
74 Nelson Garner .20 .50
75 Nick Ward .20 .50
76 Ricky Parker .20 .50
77 Willie Gary .20 .50
78 Michael Bishop .40 1.00
79 Anthony Hines .30 .75
80 Chris Avery .30 .75
81 Josh Bush .20 .50
82 Rupert Grant .20 .50
83 Bryant Shaw .20 .50
84 Dennison Robinson .20 .50
85 Kahlil Carter .20 .50
86 Chris Ryan .20 .50
87 Marvin Taylor .20 .50
88 Timon Marshall .20 .50
89 Traco Rachal .20 .50
90 Marcus Nash .40 1.00
91 Coco Blalock .30 .75
92 Joe Douglass .20 .50
93 Ricky Ross .20 .50
94 Sunungura Rusununguko .20 .50
95 Marlion Jackson .20 .50
96 Jerome Riley .20 .50
97 Wilky Bazile .20 .50
98 Dameon Porter .20 .50
99 Rodney Filer .20 .50
100 Cornelius Bonner .20 .50
101 Brian Mann .20 .50
102 Silas Demary .30 .75
103 Tony Locke .20 .50
104 Kevin Ingram .20 .50
105 Lonnie Ford .20 .50
106 Greg Hopkins .30 .75
107 Remy Hamilton .20 .50
108 Brian Sump .20 .50
109 Antuan Simmons .20 .50
110 Jerald Brown .20 .50
111 Anthony Derricks .20 .50
112 Leon Murray .20 .50
113 James Baron .20 .50
114 Clint Stoerner .50 1.25
115 T.T. Toliver .30 .75
116 Jarrick Hillery .20 .50
117 Darryl Hammond .20 .50
118 Tony Dodson .20 .50
119 Hardy Mitchell .20 .50
120 Levelle Brown .20 .50
121 DeRon Jenkins .20 .50
122 Cory Fleming .30 .75
123 Andy Kelly .30 .75
124 Aaron Bailey .30 .75
125 B.J. Cohen .20 .50
126 Carl Bond .20 .50
127 Nyle Wiren .20 .50
128 Jermaine Miles .20 .50
129 Stacy Evans .20 .50
130 Terrance Joseph .20 .50
131 Nikia Adderson .20 .50
132 Calvin Spears .20 .50
133 Chris Pointer .20 .50
134 Steve Smith .20 .50
135 Aaron Garcia .40 1.00
136 Mike Horacek .30 .75
137 Chris Anthony .20 .50
138 Ernest Certain .20 .50
139 Josh White .20 .50
140 Rob Bironas .20 .50
141 Lynaris Elpheage .20 .50
142 Corey Johnson .20 .50
143 Marcus Owen .20 .50
144 Sir Mawn Wilson .20 .50
145 Chris Angel .20 .50
146 Billy Parker .20 .50
147 Joe Hamilton .30 .75
148 E.J. Burt .20 .50
149 Jimmy Fryzel .20 .50
150 Wes Ours .20 .50
151 Idris Price .20 .50
152 Kenny McEntyre .30 .75
153 Chris Sanders .20 .50
154 Jerrian James .20 .50
155 Jonathan Ordway .20 .50
156 Tony Graziani .40 1.00
157 Marcus Knight .30 .75
158 Sean Scott .30 .75
159 Kevin Gaines .20 .50
160 Tyronne Jones .20 .50
161 Rob Milanese .20 .50
162 Chris Brown .20 .50
163 Eddie Moten .20 .50
164 Calvin Coleman .20 .50
165 Mark Grieb .40 1.00
166 James Roe .30 .75
167 Rashied Davis .30 .75
168 James Hundon .30 .75
169 Barry Wagner .20 .50
170 Rodney Wright .20 .50
171 Shalon Baker .20 .50
172 Dan Frantz .20 .50
173 Calvin Schexnayder .20 .50
174 Clevan Thomas .20 .50
175 Fred Coleman .20 .50
176 Shane Stafford .40 1.00
177 Lawrence Samuels .30 .75
178 Freddie Solomon .30 .75
179 Ronney Daniels .20 .50
180 Bobby Sippio .30 .75
181 Matt George .20 .50
182 Jarrod Penright .20 .50
183 Demetris Bendross .20 .50
184 Tramain Jones .20 .50
185 Khori Ivy .20 .50
186 Kelvin Hunter .20 .50
187 Siaha Burley .30 .75
188 Justin Skaggs .20 .50
189 Orshawante Bryant .20 .50
190 Joe Germaine .30 .75

2006 Upper Deck AFL Gold

*GOLD: 5X TO 12X BASIC CARDS
GOLD PRINT RUN 100 SER.#'d SETS

2006 Upper Deck AFL Arena Action

AA1 Jarrick Hillery 1.00 2.50
AA2 Derek Lee 2.00 5.00
AA3 Troy Bergeron 2.00 5.00
AA4 Andy McCullough 1.50 4.00
AA5 Cliff Dell 1.50 4.00
AA6 Cornelius White 1.00 2.50
AA7 Anthony Derricks 1.00 2.50
AA8 Thabiti Davis 1.50 4.00
AA9 Ira Gooch 1.00 2.50
AA10 Rashad Floyd 1.00 2.50
Ahmad Hawkins
AA11 Chris Jackson 1.50 4.00
AA12 Tacoma Fontaine 1.00 2.50
AA13 Anthony Hines 1.50 4.00
AA14 Jimmy Fryzel 1.00 2.50
AA15 Kevin Ingram 1.00 2.50
AA16 Damian Harrell 2.00 5.00
AA17 Marcus Nash 2.00 5.00
AA18 Siaha Burley 1.50 4.00
AA19 Coco Blalock 1.50 4.00
AA20 Aaron Bailey 1.50 4.00
AA21 Dialleo Burks 1.50 4.00
AA22 Sean Scott 1.50 4.00
AA23 Darryl Hammond 1.00 2.50

2006 Upper Deck AFL Arena Award Winners

COMPLETE SET (10) 10.00 20.00
AAW1 Kevin Ingram .75 2.00
AAW2 Damian Harrell 1.50 4.00
AAW3 Silas Demary 1.25 3.00
AAW4 Doug Plank .75 2.00
AAW5 Troy Bergeron 1.50 4.00
AAW6 Silas Demary 1.25 3.00
AAW7 Remy Hamilton .75 2.00
AAW8 Cory Fleming 1.25 3.00
AAW9 Marcus Nash 1.50 4.00
AAW10 Kenny McEntyre 1.25 3.00

2006 Upper Deck AFL ArenaBowl Recap

COMPLETE SET (10) 8.00 20.00
AB1 ArenaBowl XIX Logo .75 2.00
Las Vegas
AB2 Siaha Burley 1.25 3.00
Arena Battle Skills Challenge
AB3 John Kaleo 1.25 3.00
Arena Battle Skills Challenge
AB4 Mike Dailey .75 2.00
Media Day
AB5 Kevin McKenzie .75 2.00
AB6 Derek Lee 1.50 4.00
AB7 Chris Jackson 1.25 3.00
AB8 Clay Rush .75 2.00
AB9 Colorado Crush .75 2.00
AB10 John Dutton 1.25 3.00

2006 Upper Deck AFL Arenagraphs

OVERALL AUTO ODDS 1:12
AB Aaron Bailey 10.00 25.00
AG Aaron Garcia 12.50 30.00
AK Andy Kelly 10.00 25.00
BM Bob McMillen 12.50 30.00
CB Coco Blalock 8.00 20.00
CD Clint Dolezel 12.50 30.00
CF Cory Fleming 10.00 25.00
CJ Chris Jackson 10.00 25.00
CS Clint Stoerner 25.00 50.00
DB David Baker SP 15.00 40.00
DG Damien Groce 8.00 20.00
DH Damian Harrell 12.50 30.00
DL Derek Lee 10.00 25.00
DP Doug Plank 8.00 20.00
EM Etu Molden 12.50 30.00
GR Jay Gruden 10.00 25.00
HC Hunkie Cooper 10.00 25.00
JD John Dutton 10.00 25.00
JF John Fitzgerald 8.00 20.00
JG Joe Germaine 12.50 30.00
JH Joe Hamilton 12.50 30.00
JK John Kaleo 10.00 25.00
JR James Roe 12.50 30.00
KE Kenny McEntyre 10.00 25.00
KI Kevin Ingram 8.00 20.00
KM Kevin McKenzie 8.00 20.00
LS Lawrence Samuels 8.00 20.00
MA Marcus Nash 12.50 30.00
MB Michael Bishop 12.50 30.00
MD Mike Ditka 40.00 80.00
MG Mark Grieb 12.50 30.00
MN Matt Nagy 12.50 30.00
OS Omarr Smith 10.00 25.00
RJ Ron Jaworski SP 15.00 40.00
RP Raymond Philyaw 10.00 25.00
RT Robert Thomas 8.00 20.00
SB Siaha Burley 10.00 25.00
SD Silas Demary 8.00 20.00
SH Shane Stafford 12.50 30.00
SS Sean Scott 10.00 25.00
TB Troy Bergeron 12.50 30.00
TF Tacoma Fontaine 10.00 25.00
TG Tony Graziani 12.50 30.00
TM Tim McGraw SP 75.00 150.00
TT T.T. Toliver 8.00 20.00
WP Will Pettis 8.00 20.00
DGI Dancer: Gina 12.50 30.00
DHE Dancer: Heidi 12.50 30.00
DHY Dancer: Holly 12.50 30.00
DJS Dancer: Jessica 12.50 30.00
DKR Dancer: Kara 12.50 30.00
DNI Dancer: Nikki 12.50 30.00
DRA Dancer: Rachel 12.50 30.00
DSU Dancer: Susan 12.50 30.00
DVI Dancer: Victoria 12.50 30.00

2006 Upper Deck AFL Arenagraphs Duals

BD Michael Bishop 30.00 60.00
Clint Dolezel
BG Siaha Burley
Joe Germaine
BK Aaron Bailey 30.00 60.00
Andy Kelly
BL Troy Bergeron 30.00 60.00
Derek Lee
BM David Baker 50.00 100.00
Mike Ditka
GG Aaron Garcia 40.00 80.00
Tony Graziani
GJ Tony Graziani 30.00 60.00
Ron Jaworski
HD Damian Harrell 30.00 60.00
John Dutton
HF Joe Hamilton
Cory Fleming
KI John Kaleo 30.00 60.00
Kevin Ingram
NB Marcus Nash 30.00 60.00
Coco Blalock
PG Doug Plank 30.00 60.00
Jay Gruden
PM Raymond Philyaw 30.00 60.00
Etu Molden
SP Clint Stoerner 40.00 80.00
Will Pettis
SS Shane Stafford 30.00 60.00
Lawrence Samuels

2006 Upper Deck AFL Arenagraphs Triples

UNPRICED TRIPLE SER.#'d TO 10

2006 Upper Deck AFL Dream Team Dancers

COMPLETE SET (16) 25.00 50.00
DT1 Erin 2.00 5.00
DT2 Kara 2.00 5.00
DT3 Gina 2.00 5.00
DT4 Heidi 2.00 5.00
DT5 Holly 2.00 5.00
DT6 Jessica 2.00 5.00
DT7 Susan 2.00 5.00
DT8 Karen 2.00 5.00
DT9 Meghan 2.00 5.00
DT10 Laverne 2.00 5.00
DT11 Layne 2.00 5.00
DT12 Michelle 2.00 5.00
DT13 Michelle 2.00 5.00
DT14 Nikki 2.00 5.00
DT15 Rachel 2.00 5.00
DT16 Victoria 2.00 5.00

2006 Upper Deck AFL Fabrics

STATED ODDS 1:12
FAAB Aaron Bailey 5.00 12.00
FAAG Aaron Garcia 8.00 20.00
FAAK Andy Kelly 8.00 20.00
FACD Clint Dolezel 8.00 20.00
FACH Charlie Davidson 4.00 10.00
FACR Clay Rush 4.00 10.00
FACS Clint Stoerner 10.00 25.00
FADB David Baker 10.00 25.00
FADG Damien Groce 5.00 12.00
FADH Damian Harrell 8.00 20.00
FAJD John Dutton 8.00 20.00
FAJK John Kaleo 5.00 12.00
FAJR James Roe 5.00 12.00
FAKI Kevin Ingram 4.00 10.00
FAKM Kevin McKenzie 4.00 10.00
FAKN Kevin Nickerson 4.00 10.00
FALM Leon Murray 5.00 12.00
FALS Lawrence Samuels 5.00 12.00
FAMA Marcus Nash 5.00 12.00
FAMG Mark Grieb 8.00 20.00
FAMH Mike Horacek 5.00 12.00
FAMK Marcus Knight 5.00 12.00
FARD Rashied Davis 8.00 20.00
FARP Raymond Philyaw 5.00 12.00
FASB Siaha Burley 5.00 12.00
FASD Silas Demary 4.00 10.00
FASH Shane Stafford 8.00 20.00
FASK Steve Konopka 4.00 10.00
FASS Sean Scott 5.00 12.00
FAST Steve Smith 4.00 10.00
FATB Tom Briggs 4.00 10.00
FATG Tony Graziani 8.00 20.00
FATT T.T. Toliver 4.00 10.00

2006 Upper Deck AFL League Leaders

COMPLETE SET (10) 15.00 40.00
LL1 Mark Grieb 2.50 6.00
LL2 Andy Kelly 2.00 5.00
LL3 Marcus Nash 2.50 6.00
LL4 Siaha Burley 2.00 5.00
LL5 Michael Bishop 2.50 6.00
LL6 Michael Bishop 2.50 6.00
LL7 Siaha Burley 2.00 5.00
LL8 Remy Hamilton 1.50 4.00
LL9 Silas Demary 2.00 5.00
LL10 Billy Parker 1.50 4.00

1993-97 Upper Deck Authenticated Commemorative Cards

Upper Deck Authenticated, in addition to its line of certified autograph products, produced a continuing series of over-sized (4" by 6") unsigned cards commemorating various events, players and teams. These are often referred to as "C-Cards." These cards typically are serially numbered and encased in clear plastic holders. The print number is noted at the end of the card description when known. Most of these cards are unnumbered but have been assigned numbers below for cataloging purposes.

1 Draft Picks 1993 3.00 8.00
Curtis Conway
Drew Bledsoe
Eric Curry
(serial numbered of 7500)
2 Joe Montana 4.00 10.00
Dan Marino 1993
Classic Confrontation
(numbered of 20,000)
3 Rookie Standouts 1994 3.00 8.00
Marshall Faulk
Heath Shuler
Darnay Scott
(serial numbered of 10,000)
4 Joe Montana 1995 5.00 12.00
Notre Dame Tradition
(numbered of 10,000)
5 Joe Montana 1995 5.00 12.00
Salute, SP Die-Cut
(numbered of 10,000)
6 Troy Aikman 1996/3-Time Champ 4.00 10.00
7 Dallas Cowboys 1996 2.50 6.00
Super Bowl 30
(numbered of 5000)
8 Jerry Rice 1996/1000 receptions 4.00 10.00
(numbered of 5000)
9 Troy Aikman 1997 4.00 10.00
Red Zone
(numbered of 2500)
10 Terrell Davis 1997 4.00 10.00
Red Zone
(numbered of 2500)
11 Reggie White 1997 1.50 4.00
Packers NFC Champs
(numbered of 5000)
A133 Joe Montana Blowup 1994 6.00 15.00
Upper Deck
Authenticated 8 1/2 x 11
A139 Dan Marino Blowup 1993 6.00 15.00
Upper Deck
Authenticated 8 1/2 x 11
A140 Troy Aikman Blowup 1993 5.00 12.00
Upper Deck
Authenticated 8 1/2-inch by 11-inch
A460 Joe Montana Blowup 1993 6.00 15.00
Upper Deck
Authenticated 8 1/2 x 11

1994-96 Upper Deck Authenticated Dan Marino Jumbos

These oversized (roughly 4" by 6") cards were issued only through Upper Deck Authenticated. UDA, through their contract with Dan Marino, was able to issue special cards to honor his record breaking career over a number of years. Each is generally serial numbered and was originally distributed within a plastic card holder.

COMPLETE SET (7) 30.00 60.00
COMMON CARD (1-7) 5.00 12.00
1 Dan Marino 1994 SP/300 Career TD Passes
A136 Dan Marino Blowup 1994 6.00 15.00
Upper Deck
Authenticated 8 1/2 x 11

1995 Upper Deck Authenticated Dan Marino 24K Gold

Upper Deck Authenticated issued these 24K Cards in 1995 to honor Dan Marino's record breaking season. The cards measures the standard size and are sculpted using the "Metaltech" process where 24K gold and a nickle-silver combination are embossed onto stainless steel. Each card comes with a screw-down lucite block and black jeweler's pouch.

COMPLETE SET (4) 40.00 100.00
COMMON MARINO (1-4) 12.00 30.00

1995 Upper Deck Authenticated Joe Montana Jumbos

Upper Deck released this 4-card set through it's Upper Deck Authenticated catalog. The cards of the 49ers' great quarterback measure approximately 5" by 3 1/2" and feature color action photos of Joe Montana playing in four Super Bowls. Each card came packaged in its own snap together plastic holder. The backs carry regular and post season statistics as well as the card's number.

COMPLETE SET (4) 16.00 40.00
COMMON CARD (1-4) 4.00 10.00

1999 Upper Deck Century Legends

This 173-card features color action photos of some of the league's all-time great players along with top rookies from the 1999 NFL Draft class. The set contains two subsets and two different Walter Payton signed inserts. Cards 4, 6, 14, 26, 31, 38, and 43 were never released. Two cards, #168B Eric Dickerson CM and #172B John Riggins, were inserted in packs with each featuring an embossed player image that was used to help identify the cards for removal during the pack-out process. Most copies of these two cards were pulled from production before pack-out.

COMPLETE SET (173) 20.00 50.00
1 Jim Brown .50 1.25
2 Jerry Rice .60 1.50
3 Joe Montana 1.00 2.50
5 Johnny Unitas .75 2.00
7 Otto Graham .25 .60
8 Walter Payton 1.25 3.00
9 Dick Butkus .50 1.25
10 Bob Lilly .25 .60
11 Sammy Baugh .30 .75
12 Barry Sanders .75 2.00
13 Deacon Jones .25 .60
15 Gino Marchetti .20 .50
16 John Elway 1.00 2.50
17 Anthony Munoz .25 .60
18 Ray Nitschke .40 1.00
19 Dick Lane .20 .50
20 John Hannah .20 .50
21 Gale Sayers .50 1.25
22 Reggie White .30 .75
23 Ronnie Lott .30 .75
24 Jim Parker .20 .50
25 Merlin Olsen .25 .60
27 Dan Marino 1.00 2.50
28 Forrest Gregg .20 .50
29 Roger Staubach .60 1.50
30 Jack Lambert .30 .75
32 Marion Motley .25 .60
33 Earl Campbell .30 .75
34 Alan Page .25 .60
35 Bronko Nagurski .30 .75
36 Mel Blount .25 .60
37 Deion Sanders .30 .75
39 Sid Luckman .25 .60
40 Raymond Berry .25 .60
41 Bart Starr .75 2.00
42 Willie Lanier .20 .50
44 Terry Bradshaw .75 2.00
45 Herb Adderley .25 .60
46 Steve Largent .30 .75
47 Jack Ham .30 .75
48 John Mackey .20 .50
49 Bill George .20 .50
50 Willie Brown .20 .50
51 Jerry Rice .60 1.50
52 Barry Sanders .75 2.00
53 John Elway 1.00 2.50
54 Reggie White .30 .75
55 Dan Marino 1.00 2.50
56 Deion Sanders .30 .75
57 Bruce Smith .30 .75
58 Steve Young .40 1.00
59 Emmitt Smith .75 2.00
60 Brett Favre 1.00 2.50
61 Rod Woodson .30 .75
62 Troy Aikman .50 1.25
63 Terrell Davis .30 .75
64 Michael Irvin .30 .75
65 Andre Rison .25 .60
66 Warren Moon .30 .75
67 Thurman Thomas .30 .75
68 Randall Cunningham .30 .75
69 Jerome Bettis .30 .75
70 Junior Seau .30 .75
71 Drew Bledsoe .30 .75
72 Andre Reed .30 .75
73 Tim Brown .30 .75
74 Derrick Thomas .30 .75
75 Jake Plummer .25 .60
76 Kordell Stewart .25 .60
77 Herman Moore .25 .60
78 Shannon Sharpe .30 .75
79 Antonio Freeman .25 .60
80 Ricky Watters .25 .60
81 Warrick Dunn .25 .60
82 Mark Brunell .25 .60
83 Randy Moss .30 .75
84 Fred Taylor .25 .60
85 Curtis Martin .30 .75
86 Keyshawn Johnson .25 .60
87 Eddie George .25 .60
88 Marshall Faulk .30 .75
89 Joey Galloway .25 .60
90 Vinny Testaverde .25 .60
91 Garrison Hearst .25 .60
92 Jimmy Smith .25 .60
93 Doug Flutie .30 .75
94 Napoleon Kaufman .20 .50
95 Natrone Means .25 .60
96 Peyton Manning 1.00 2.50
97 Steve McNair .30 .75
98 Corey Dillon .25 .60
99 Terrell Owens .30 .75
100 Charlie Batch .25 .60
101 Brett Favre APR .75 2.00
102 Terrell Davis APR .25 .60
103 Roger Staubach APR .50 1.25
104 Terry Bradshaw APR .60 1.50
105 Fran Tarkenton APR .30 .75
106 Walter Payton APR 1.00 2.50
107 Mark Brunell APR .20 .50
108 Jim Brown APR .40 1.00
109 Kordell Stewart APR .20 .50
110 Bart Starr APR .60 1.50
111 Steve Largent APR .25 .60
112 Raymond Berry APR .20 .50
113 Emmitt Smith APR .60 1.50
114 Forrest Gregg APR .15 .40
115 Drew Bledsoe APR .25 .60
116 Dick Butkus APR .40 1.00
117 Johnny Unitas APR .60 1.50
118 Joe Montana APR .75 2.00
119 Deacon Jones APR .20 .50
120 Steve Young APR .30 .75
121 Bob Lilly APR .20 .50
122 Troy Aikman APR .40 1.00
123 Alan Page APR .20 .50
124 Earl Campbell APR .25 .60
125 Deion Sanders APR .25 .60
126 Ronnie Lott APR .25 .60
127 Reggie White APR .25 .60
128 Marshall Faulk APR .25 .60
129 Gale Sayers APR .40 1.00
130 Dick Lane APR .15 .40
131 Ricky Williams RC .60 1.50
132 Tim Couch RC .40 1.00
133 Donovan McNabb RC 2.00 5.00
134 Daunte Culpepper RC .40 1.00
135 Edgerrin James RC .50 1.25
136 Cade McNown RC .30 .75
137 Torry Holt RC .60 1.50
138 David Boston RC .30 .75
139 Champ Bailey RC .75 2.00
140 Peerless Price RC .30 .75
141 D'Wayne Bates RC .25 .60
142 Joe Germaine RC .30 .75
143 Brock Huard RC .30 .75
144 Chris Claiborne RC .25 .60
145 Jevon Kearse RC .40 1.00
146 Troy Edwards RC .30 .75
147 Amos Zereoue RC .30 .75
148 Aaron Brooks RC .40 1.00
149 Andy Katzenmoyer RC .30 .75
150 Kevin Faulk RC .40 1.00
151 Shaun King RC .30 .75
152 Kevin Johnson RC .30 .75
153 Dameane Douglas RC .25 .60
154 Mike Cloud RC .25 .60
155 Sedrick Irvin RC .25 .60
156 Akili Smith RC .30 .75
157 Rob Konrad RC .25 .60
158 Scott Covington RC .25 .60
159 Jeff Paulk RC .25 .60
160 Shawn Bryson RC .25 .60
161 Joe Montana CM .75 2.00
162 John Elway CM .75 2.00
163 Joe Namath CM .50 1.25
164 Jerry Rice CM .50 1.25
165 Terry Bradshaw CM .60 1.50
166 Jim Brown CM .40 1.00
167 Paul Warfield CM .25 .60
168A Herman Moore CM .20 .50
168B Eric Dickerson CM ERR 25.00 50.00
(card is partially embossed)
169 Walter Payton CM 1.00 2.50
170 Roger Staubach CM .50 1.25
171 Ken Stabler CM .30 .75
172A Steve Young CM .30 .75
172B John Riggins CM ERR 20.00 50.00
(card is partially embossed)
173 Troy Aikman CM .40 1.00
174 Fran Tarkenton CM .30 .75
175 Doug Williams CM .20 .50
176 Steve Largent CM .25 .60
177 Marcus Allen CM .25 .60
178 Mike Singletary CM .25 .60
179 Earl Campbell CM .25 .60
180 Dan Fouts CM .25 .60
WPAC Walter Payton AU/50 400.00 600.00
WPCL W.Payton Jsy AU/34 1,000.00 1,500.00

1999 Upper Deck Century Legends Century Collection

*STARS: 10X TO 25X BASIC CARDS
*RCs: 3X TO 8X BASIC CARDS
STATED PRINT RUN 100 SER.#'d SETS

1999 Upper Deck Century Legends 20th Century Superstars

COMPLETE SET (10)	15.00	30.00
STATED ODDS 1:11		
S1 Tim Couch	.40	1.00
S2 Ricky Williams	1.00	2.50
S3 Akili Smith	.40	1.00
S4 Donovan McNabb	2.50	6.00
S5 Jake Plummer	.50	1.25
S6 Brett Favre	2.50	6.00
S7 Steve Young	1.00	2.50
S8 Randy Moss	2.00	5.00
S9 Kordell Stewart	.50	1.25
S10 Peyton Manning	2.50	6.00

1999 Upper Deck Century Legends Epic Milestones

COMPLETE SET (10)	20.00	40.00
STATED ODDS 1:11		
EM1 John Elway	2.50	6.00
EM2 Joe Montana	4.00	10.00
EM3 Randy Moss	2.00	5.00
EM4 Terrell Davis	.75	2.00
EM5 Dan Marino	2.50	6.00
EM6 Jamal Anderson	.75	2.00
EM7 Jerry Rice	1.50	4.00
EM8 Barry Sanders	2.50	6.00
EM9 Emmitt Smith	1.50	4.00
EM10 Walter Payton	4.00	10.00

1999 Upper Deck Century Legends Epic Signatures

STATED ODDS 1:23		
AM Art Monk	15.00	40.00
CC Cris Carter	15.00	40.00
CJ Charlie Joiner	10.00	25.00
DB Dick Butkus	30.00	60.00
DF Dan Fouts	12.00	30.00
DM Dan Marino	125.00	200.00
DR Dan Reeves	12.00	30.00
DW Doug Williams	12.00	30.00
EC Earl Campbell	20.00	50.00
FL Floyd Little	10.00	25.00
FT Fran Tarkenton	20.00	50.00
GS Gale Sayers	30.00	60.00
HC Harold Carmichael	10.00	25.00
JM Joe Montana	75.00	150.00
JN Joe Namath	60.00	120.00
JR Jerry Rice	125.00	200.00
JU Johnny Unitas	200.00	350.00
JY Jack Youngblood	10.00	25.00
LD Len Dawson	12.00	30.00
MS Mike Singletary	12.00	30.00
MY Don Maynard	10.00	25.00
ON Ozzie Newsome	10.00	25.00
PW Paul Warfield	10.00	25.00
RB Raymond Berry	10.00	25.00
RM Randy Moss	40.00	80.00
RS Roger Staubach	60.00	120.00
SL Steve Largent	15.00	40.00
TA Troy Aikman	75.00	125.00
TB Terry Bradshaw	60.00	120.00
TD Terrell Davis	12.00	30.00

1999 Upper Deck Century Legends Epic Signatures Century Gold

*GOLDS: .8X TO 2X BASIC INSERTS		
JRC Jerry Rice	100.00	200.00

1999 Upper Deck Century Legends Jerseys of the Century

STATED ODDS 1:418		
*MULTI-COLORED SWATCHES: .6X TO 1.2X		
GJ1 Jerry Rice	40.00	100.00
GJ2 Roger Staubach	30.00	80.00
GJ3 Warren Moon	15.00	40.00
GJ4 Ken Stabler	25.00	60.00
GJ5 Reggie White	25.00	60.00
GJ6 Dan Marino	50.00	120.00
GJ7 Doug Flutie	20.00	50.00
GJ8 Bob Lilly	15.00	40.00
GJ10 Jim Brown	30.00	80.00

1999 Upper Deck Century Legends Tour de Force

COMPLETE SET (10)	25.00	50.00
STATED ODDS 1:23		
A1 Tim Couch	.75	2.00
A2 Ricky Williams	1.50	4.00
A3 Peyton Manning	4.00	10.00
A4 Troy Aikman	2.50	6.00
A5 Jake Plummer	.75	2.00
A6 Jamal Anderson	1.25	3.00
A7 Terrell Davis	1.25	3.00
A8 Barry Sanders	4.00	10.00
A9 Fred Taylor	1.25	3.00
A10 Keyshawn Johnson	1.25	3.00

2009-10 Upper Deck Champ's Hall of Legends Memorabilia

STATED ODDS 1:160		
HLBO Bo Jackson	20.00	50.00
HLDM Dan Marino	25.00	60.00
HLEW John Elway	25.00	50.00
HLFH Franco Harris	12.00	30.00
HLJR Jerry Rice	15.00	40.00
HLWM Warren Moon	10.00	25.00

2009-10 Upper Deck Champ's Signatures

STATED ODDS 1:15		
CSDF Doug Flutie	25.00	60.00
CSES Emmitt Smith		
CSJR Jerry Rice	75.00	150.00
CSSA Barry Sanders		
CSWM Warren Moon	60.00	120.00

2002 Upper Deck Collector's Club

This set was issued directly to members of the Upper Deck Collector's Club. Each member could choose a set of cards from one sport only. The cards are highlighted with silver foil on the fronts along with the "club exclusive" notation on both front and back. One of two different jersey cards was issued with each set.

COMPLETE SET (20)	12.50	25.00
NFL1 Peyton Manning	1.00	2.50
NFL2 Aaron Brooks	.40	1.00
NFL3 Brett Favre	1.25	3.00
NFL4 Daunte Culpepper	.40	1.00
NFL5 Donovan McNabb	.50	1.25
NFL6 Eddie George	.40	1.00
NFL7 Edgerrin James	.40	1.00
NFL8 Emmitt Smith	1.25	3.00
NFL9 Jerome Bettis	.50	1.25
NFL10 Jerry Rice	1.00	2.50
NFL11 Kerry Collins	.40	1.00
NFL12 Kurt Warner	.50	1.25
NFL13 LaDainian Tomlinson	.60	1.50
NFL14 Marshall Faulk	.50	1.25
NFL15 Michael Vick	.75	2.00
NFL16 Ahman Green	.40	1.00
NFL17 Randy Moss	.50	1.25
NFL18 Ricky Williams	.40	1.00
NFL19 Shaun Alexander	.40	1.00
NFL20 Terrell Davis	.50	1.25
PMJ Peyton Manning JSY	12.00	30.00
MVJ Michael Vick JSY	10.00	25.00

2011 Upper Deck College Legends

COMPLETE SET (100)	8.00	20.00
1 Keith Jackson	.20	.50
2 Tommy McDonald	.25	.60
3 Willie Buchanon	.20	.50
4 Ron Yary	.20	.50
5 Tony Casillas	.20	.50
6 Steve Young	.40	1.00
7 Jason White	.20	.50
8 Daryl Johnston	.30	.75
9 Troy Aikman	.40	1.00
10 Rocket Ismail	.25	.60
11 Bubba Smith	.20	.50
12 Roman Gabriel	.25	.60
13 Bob Griese	.30	.75
14 Alan Page	.25	.60
15 Mike Alstott	.20	.50
16 Craig Morton	.20	.50
17 Bo Jackson	.40	1.00
18 John Elway	.50	1.25
19 Paul Hornung	.30	.75
20 Greg Pruitt	.20	.50
21 Jerry Rice	.50	1.25
22 Lee Roy Selmon	.20	.50
23 George Rogers	.20	.50
24 Lee Roy Jordan	.20	.50
25 Doug Flutie	.25	.60
26 Tim Brown	.30	.75
27 Barry Sanders	.50	1.25
28 Jim Kelly	.30	.75
29 Kellen Winslow Sr.	.25	.60
30 Bernie Kosar	.25	.60
31 John Cappelletti	.20	.50
32 Roger Craig	.25	.60
33 Rocky Bleier	.25	.60
34 Floyd Little	.20	.50
35 Brian Bosworth	.25	.60
36 Charles White	.20	.50
37 Earl Campbell	.30	.75
38 Mike Singletary	.30	.75
39 Thurman Thomas	.30	.75
40 Eddie George	.25	.60
41 Danny Wuerffel	.20	.50
42 Billy Cannon	.20	.50
43 Rod Woodson	.25	.60
44 Dave Casper	.20	.50
45 Ozzie Newsome	.25	.60
46 Archie Griffin	.25	.60
47 Andre Rison	.20	.50
48 Chris Spielman	.20	.50
49 Antonio Freeman	.20	.50
50 Tony Mandarich	.20	.50
51 Daryle Lamonica	.20	.50
52 Herman Moore	.20	.50
53 Cris Carter	.30	.75
54 Dwight Stephenson	.20	.50
55 Ken Stabler	.30	.75
56 Gary Beban	.20	.50
57 Gino Torretta	.20	.50
58 Anthony Carter	.20	.50
59 Ron Dayne	.20	.50
60 Andre Ware	.25	.60
61 Eric Metcalf	.20	.50
62 Steve Owens	.20	.50
63 Jim Plunkett	.25	.60
64 Ty Detmer	.20	.50
65 Herschel Walker	.25	.60
66 Todd Marinovich	.20	.50
67 Warren Moon	.25	.60
68 Gale Sayers	.30	.75
69 William Perry	.25	.60
70 Dan Marino	.60	1.50
71 Tom Rathman	.20	.50
72 Joe Theismann	.30	.75
73 Billy Sims	.25	.60
74 Jim McMahon	.25	.60
75 Johnny Rodgers	.20	.50
76 Tony Dorsett	.30	.75
77 Adrian Peterson	.40	1.00
78 Drew Brees	.30	.75
79 Aaron Rodgers	.50	1.25
80 Steven Jackson	.25	.60
81 Jake Locker	.75	2.00
82 Pat Devlin	.30	.75
83 Christian Ponder	.60	1.50
84 Colin Kaepernick	.40	1.00
85 Prince Amukamara	.30	.75
86 DeMarco Murray	.60	1.50
87 Kendall Hunter	.30	.75
88 Noel Devine	.30	.75
89 Daniel Thomas	.30	.75
90 Greg Little	.30	.75
91 Leonard Hankerson	.30	.75
92 Ronald Johnson	.25	.60
93 Titus Young	.40	1.00
94 Blaine Gabbert	.50	1.25
95 Cam Newton	1.50	4.00
96 Ryan Mallett	.60	1.50
97 Andy Dalton	.75	2.00
98 Mark Ingram	.60	1.50
99 A.J. Green	.60	1.50
100 Julio Jones	.60	1.50

2011 Upper Deck College Legends All-Americans

AAAC Anthony Carter	.40	1.00
AAAP Adrian Peterson	.75	2.00
AABB Brian Bosworth	.50	1.25
AABC Billy Cannon	.40	1.00
AABG Bob Griese	.60	1.50
AABJ Bo Jackson	.75	2.00
AABS Barry Sanders	1.00	2.50
AACN Cam Newton	3.00	8.00
AACS Chris Spielman	.40	1.00
AACW Charles White	.40	1.00
AADF Doug Flutie	.50	1.25
AADW Danny Wuerffel	.40	1.00
AAEC Earl Campbell	.60	1.50
AAGB Gary Beban	.40	1.00
AAGP Greg Pruitt	.40	1.00
AAGR George Rogers	.40	1.00
AAGS Gale Sayers	.60	1.50
AAJC John Cappelletti	.40	1.00
AAJE John Elway	1.00	2.50
AAJT Joe Theismann	.60	1.50
AAJW Jason White	.40	1.00
AAKW Kellen Winslow Sr.	.50	1.25
AALS Lee Roy Selmon	.40	1.00
AAMI Mark Ingram	1.25	3.00
AAPA Alan Page	.50	1.25
AAPH Paul Hornung	.60	1.50
AASI Billy Sims	.50	1.25
AASM Bubba Smith	.40	1.00
AASO Steve Owens	.40	1.00
AASY Steve Young	.75	2.00
AATA Troy Aikman	.75	2.00
AATB Tim Brown	.60	1.50
AATC Tony Casillas	.40	1.00
AATM Tommy McDonald	.50	1.25
AATT Thurman Thomas	.60	1.50

2011 Upper Deck College Legends All-Americans Autographs

STATED PRINT RUN 5-70		
AAAC Anthony Carter/70	10.00	25.00
AAAP Adrian Peterson		
AABB Brian Bosworth		
AABC Billy Cannon		
AABG Bob Griese		
AABJ Bo Jackson/5		
AABS Barry Sanders		
AACN Cam Newton		
AACS Chris Spielman		
AACW Charles White/70	10.00	25.00
AADF Doug Flutie		
AADW Danny Wuerffel/5		
AAEC Earl Campbell		
AAGB Gary Beban/5		
AAGP Greg Pruitt/70	10.00	25.00
AAGR George Rogers/70	10.00	25.00
AAGS Gale Sayers		
AAJC John Cappelletti/70	12.00	30.00
AAJE John Elway		
AAJT Joe Theismann		
AAJW Jason White/70	10.00	25.00
AAKW Kellen Winslow Sr.		
AAMI Mark Ingram		
AAPA Alan Page/25	15.00	40.00
AAPH Paul Hornung		
AASI Billy Sims/70	12.00	30.00
AASO Steve Owens/70	10.00	25.00
AASY Steve Young		
AATA Troy Aikman		
AATB Tim Brown		
AATC Tony Casillas/70	10.00	25.00
AATM Tommy McDonald/70	12.00	30.00
AATT Thurman Thomas/5		

2011 Upper Deck College Legends Autographs

OVERALL AUTO STATED ODDS 3:20		
EXCH EXPIRATION: 5/1/2014		
1 Keith Jackson	6.00	15.00
2 Tommy McDonald	8.00	20.00
3 Willie Buchanon	6.00	15.00
4 Ron Yary	6.00	15.00
5 Tony Casillas	6.00	15.00
6 Steve Young SP	100.00	200.00
7 Jason White	6.00	15.00
8 Daryl Johnston	8.00	20.00
9 Troy Aikman SP EXCH	100.00	175.00
10 Rocket Ismail	15.00	40.00
12 Roman Gabriel	8.00	20.00
13 Bob Griese SP		
14 Alan Page	8.00	20.00
15 Mike Alstott	8.00	20.00
16 Craig Morton	6.00	15.00
17 Bo Jackson SP	100.00	175.00
18 John Elway SP	250.00	400.00
19 Paul Hornung	12.00	30.00
20 Greg Pruitt	6.00	15.00
21 Jerry Rice SP		
23 George Rogers	6.00	15.00
24 Lee Roy Jordan	6.00	15.00
25 Doug Flutie SP	50.00	100.00
26 Tim Brown SP	40.00	80.00
27 Barry Sanders SP		
28 Jim Kelly SP	125.00	200.00
29 Kellen Winslow Sr. SP	20.00	40.00
30 Bernie Kosar SP	30.00	80.00
31 John Cappelletti	6.00	15.00
32 Roger Craig	8.00	20.00
33 Rocky Bleier	8.00	20.00
34 Floyd Little	6.00	15.00
35 Brian Bosworth	15.00	40.00
36 Charles White	6.00	15.00
37 Earl Campbell SP		
38 Mike Singletary	20.00	40.00
39 Thurman Thomas	40.00	80.00
40 Eddie George SP		
41 Danny Wuerffel SP	20.00	40.00
42 Billy Cannon SP	20.00	40.00
43 Rod Woodson SP		
44 Dave Casper SP	10.00	25.00
45 Ozzie Newsome SP	12.00	30.00
46 Archie Griffin SP		
48 Chris Spielman	20.00	40.00
49 Antonio Freeman	6.00	15.00
50 Tony Mandarich	10.00	25.00
51 Daryle Lamonica SP	40.00	80.00
52 Herman Moore	6.00	15.00
53 Cris Carter SP	30.00	60.00
54 Dwight Stephenson	8.00	20.00
55 Ken Stabler		
56 Gary Beban SP	10.00	25.00
57 Gino Torretta	8.00	20.00
58 Anthony Carter	6.00	15.00
59 Ron Dayne	8.00	20.00
60 Andre Ware SP	12.00	30.00
61 Eric Metcalf	8.00	20.00
62 Steve Owens	6.00	15.00
64 Ty Detmer SP	15.00	40.00
65 Herschel Walker SP	50.00	100.00
66 Todd Marinovich SP	20.00	40.00
67 Warren Moon SP		
68 Gale Sayers	20.00	40.00
69 William Perry	8.00	20.00
70 Dan Marino SP		
71 Tom Rathman	6.00	15.00
72 Joe Theismann	10.00	25.00
73 Billy Sims	8.00	20.00
74 Jim McMahon	125.00	200.00
75 Johnny Rodgers SP	12.00	30.00
76 Tony Dorsett SP	100.00	175.00
77 Adrian Peterson SP EXCH	250.00	400.00
78 Drew Brees SP		
79 Aaron Rodgers SP		
80 Steven Jackson SP	60.00	100.00
81 Jake Locker	30.00	60.00
82 Pat Devlin	5.00	12.00
83 Christian Ponder	15.00	40.00
84 Colin Kaepernick	6.00	15.00
85 Prince Amukamara	5.00	12.00
86 DeMarco Murray	15.00	40.00
87 Kendall Hunter	6.00	15.00
88 Noel Devine	5.00	12.00
89 Daniel Thomas	5.00	12.00
90 Greg Little	6.00	15.00
91 Leonard Hankerson	5.00	12.00
92 Ronald Johnson	5.00	12.00
93 Titus Young	5.00	12.00
94 Blaine Gabbert SP	20.00	40.00
95 Cam Newton SP	125.00	200.00
96 Ryan Mallett	15.00	40.00
97 Andy Dalton	20.00	50.00
98 Mark Ingram	25.00	50.00
99 A.J. Green SP	60.00	120.00
100 Julio Jones SP EXCH	40.00	80.00

2011 Upper Deck College Legends Bowl Game Heroes

BGHAC Anthony Carter	.40	1.00
BGHAP Adrian Peterson	.75	2.00
BGHAR Aaron Rodgers	1.00	2.50
BGHBB Brian Bosworth	.50	1.25
BGHBJ Bo Jackson	.75	2.00
BGHBK Bernie Kosar	.50	1.25
BGHBS Barry Sanders	1.00	2.50
BGHCN Cam Newton	3.00	8.00
BGHCW Charles White	.40	1.00
BGHDB Drew Brees	.60	1.50
BGHDF Doug Flutie	.50	1.25
BGHDJ Daryl Johnston	.60	1.50
BGHDM Dan Marino	1.25	3.00
BGHDW Danny Wuerffel	.40	1.00
BGHEC Earl Campbell	.60	1.50
BGHGB Gary Beban	.40	1.00
BGHGP Greg Pruitt	.40	1.00
BGHJK Jim Kelly	.60	1.50
BGHJM Jim McMahon	.50	1.25
BGHJP Jim Plunkett	.50	1.25
BGHMI Mark Ingram	1.25	3.00
BGHRD Ron Dayne	.40	1.00
BGHSI Billy Sims	.50	1.25
BGHTT Thurman Thomas	.60	1.50
BGHWM Warren Moon	.50	1.25

2011 Upper Deck College Legends Bowl Game Heroes Autographs

STATED PRINT RUN 5-75		
BGHAC Anthony Carter/75	10.00	25.00
BGHAP Adrian Peterson		
BGHAR Aaron Rodgers		
BGHBB Brian Bosworth/30	30.00	60.00
BGHBJ Bo Jackson		
BGHBK Bernie Kosar/5		
BGHBS Barry Sanders		
BGHCN Cam Newton/75	75.00	150.00
BGHCW Charles White/75	8.00	20.00
BGHDB Drew Brees		
BGHDF Doug Flutie		
BGHDJ Daryl Johnston/75	12.00	30.00
BGHDM Dan Marino		
BGHDW Danny Wuerffel/30	12.00	30.00
BGHEC Earl Campbell		
BGHGB Gary Beban/75	8.00	20.00
BGHGP Greg Pruitt/75	10.00	25.00
BGHJK Jim Kelly/5		
BGHJM Jim McMahon		
BGHMI Mark Ingram		
BGHRD Ron Dayne		
BGHSI Billy Sims/75	12.00	30.00
BGHTT Thurman Thomas		
BGHWM Warren Moon		

2011 Upper Deck College Legends Decades Best

DBAC Anthony Carter	.40	1.00
DBAG Archie Griffin	.50	1.25
DBAP Adrian Peterson	.75	2.00
DBBB Brian Bosworth	.50	1.25
DBBG Bob Griese	.60	1.50
DBBJ Bo Jackson	.75	2.00
DBBK Bernie Kosar	.50	1.25
DBBS Barry Sanders	1.00	2.50
DBCC Cris Carter	.60	1.50
DBCM Craig Morton	.40	1.00
DBCW Charles White	.40	1.00
DBDF Doug Flutie	.50	1.25
DBDM Dan Marino	1.25	3.00
DBEC Earl Campbell	.60	1.50
DBEG Eddie George	.50	1.25
DBFL Floyd Little	.40	1.00
DBGP Greg Pruitt	.40	1.00
DBGR George Rogers	.40	1.00
DBGS Gale Sayers	.60	1.50
DBJC John Cappelletti	.40	1.00
DBJE John Elway	1.00	2.50
DBJR Jerry Rice	1.00	2.50
DBJT Joe Theismann	.60	1.50
DBJW Jason White	.40	1.00
DBKW Kellen Winslow Sr.	.50	1.25
DBLS Lee Roy Selmon	.40	1.00
DBMS Mike Singletary	.60	1.50
DBPA Alan Page	.50	1.25
DBPH Paul Hornung	.60	1.50
DBRD Ron Dayne	.40	1.00
DBRG Roman Gabriel	.50	1.25
DBRY Ron Yary	.40	1.00
DBSI Billy Sims	.50	1.25
DBSM Bubba Smith	.40	1.00
DBSO Steve Owens	.40	1.00
DBSY Steve Young	.75	2.00
DBTA Troy Aikman	.75	2.00
DBTB Tim Brown	.60	1.50
DBTM Tommy McDonald	.50	1.25
DBTT Thurman Thomas	.60	1.50

2011 Upper Deck College Legends Decades Best Autographs

STATED PRINT RUN 5-80		
DBAC Anthony Carter		
DBAG Archie Griffin/15	15.00	40.00
DBAP Adrian Peterson		
DBBB Brian Bosworth/15	50.00	100.00
DBBG Bob Griese		
DBBJ Bo Jackson		
DBBK Bernie Kosar		
DBBS Barry Sanders		
DBCC Cris Carter		
DBCM Craig Morton/80	10.00	25.00
DBCW Charles White/80	8.00	20.00
DBDF Doug Flutie		
DBDM Dan Marino		
DBEC Earl Campbell/15	15.00	40.00
DBEG Eddie George/5		
DBFL Floyd Little/80	10.00	25.00
DBGP Greg Pruitt/80	10.00	25.00
DBGR George Rogers/80	10.00	25.00
DBGS Gale Sayers/5		
DBJC John Cappelletti/80	10.00	25.00
DBJE John Elway/5		
DBJR Jerry Rice		
DBJT Joe Theismann		
DBJW Jason White/80	12.00	30.00
DBKW Kellen Winslow Sr.		
DBMS Mike Singletary/15	40.00	80.00
DBPA Alan Page/15	12.00	30.00
DBPH Paul Hornung		
DBRD Ron Dayne		
DBRG Roman Gabriel/15	12.00	30.00
DBRY Ron Yary/80	10.00	25.00
DBSI Billy Sims/80	12.00	30.00
DBSO Steve Owens		
DBSY Steve Young/5		
DBTA Troy Aikman		
DBTB Tim Brown		
DBTM Tommy McDonald/80	12.00	30.00
DBTT Thurman Thomas		

2011 Upper Deck College Legends Inscriptions

STATED PRINT RUN 5-99		
CIAC Anthony Carter/25	30.00	60.00
CIAG Archie Griffin/5		
CIAM Prince Amukamara		
CIAP Adrian Peterson		
CIAW Andre Ware/25	15.00	40.00
CIBB Brian Bosworth/25	40.00	80.00
CIBC Billy Cannon		
CIBG Bob Griese		
CIBJ Bo Jackson		
CIBK Bernie Kosar		
CIBS Barry Sanders		
CICK Colin Kaepernick/99	12.00	30.00
CICM Craig Morton/99	10.00	25.00
CICN Cam Newton		
CICP Christian Ponder/25	25.00	60.00
CICS Chris Spielman/25	15.00	40.00
CICW Charles White/99	10.00	25.00
CIDF Doug Flutie/5		
CIDM DeMarco Murray/99	30.00	60.00
CIDW Danny Wuerffel/25	15.00	40.00
CIEC Earl Campbell		
CIEG Eddie George		
CIEM Eric Metcalf/25	12.00	30.00
CIFL Floyd Little/99	15.00	40.00
CIGA Blaine Gabbert/99	15.00	40.00
CIGB Gary Beban/25	12.00	30.00
CIGL Greg Little/99	10.00	25.00
CIGP Greg Pruitt/99	10.00	25.00
CIGR George Rogers/99	10.00	25.00
CIGS Gale Sayers		
CIJC John Cappelletti/99	10.00	25.00
CIJL Jake Locker/99	30.00	60.00
CIJR Johnny Rodgers		
CIJT Joe Theismann/99	15.00	40.00
CIJW Jason White/99	15.00	40.00
CIKH Kendall Hunter/99	10.00	25.00
CIKW Kellen Winslow Sr.		
CILH Leonard Hankerson/99	8.00	20.00
CIMA Tony Mandarich/25	15.00	40.00
CIMI Mark Ingram/25	25.00	60.00
CIND Noel Devine/99	8.00	20.00
CION Ozzie Newsome/25	15.00	40.00
CIPA Alan Page/99	12.00	30.00
CIPH Paul Hornung/99	15.00	40.00
CIRB Rocky Bleier/99	15.00	40.00
CIRD Ron Dayne/25	20.00	50.00
CIRG Roman Gabriel/25	15.00	40.00
CIRJ Ronald Johnson/99	6.00	15.00
CIRY Ron Yary/99	10.00	25.00
CISI Billy Sims/99	12.00	30.00
CISO Steve Owens		
CITB Tim Brown/5		
CITC Tony Casillas/99	10.00	25.00
CITM Tommy McDonald/99	12.00	30.00
CITR Tom Rathman/99	12.00	30.00
CITY Titus Young/99	10.00	25.00
CIWP William Perry/25	15.00	40.00

1992 Upper Deck Comic Ball 4

This 198-card set of Upper Deck's animation-style trading cards contains ten 18-card stories; 16 special cards featuring Marino, Taylor, Rice and Thomas with their Looney Toons teammates, and two checklist cards. We've listed below only the cards which feature NFL players. Packs also contained nine holograms featuring NFL standouts Dan Marino, Lawrence Taylor, Jerry Rice and Thurman Thomas with Looney Toons characters such as Bugs Bunny, Daffy Duck, Elmer Fudd, Porky Pig, The Tasmanian Devil, Sylvester and Tweety.

COMPLETE SET (198)	10.00	20.00
1 Pop Goes The Martian	.20	.50
Jerry Rice		
Lawrence Taylor		
Thurman Thomas		
Dan Marino		
5 Pop Goes The Martian	.08	.25
Lawrence Taylor		
6 Pop Goes The Martian	.08	.25
Lawrence Taylor		
10 Pop Goes The Martian	.30	.75
Jerry Rice		
Lawrence Taylor		
Thurman Thomas		
Dan Marino		
11 Pop Goes The Martian	.30	.75
Lawrence Taylor		
Dan Marino		
15 Pop Goes The Martian	.30	.75
Dan Marino		
16 Pop Goes The Martian	.30	.75
Dan Marino		
19 Hang Time	.20	.50
Jerry Rice		
Lawrence Taylor		
Thurman Thomas		
Dan Marino		
24 Hang Time	.08	.25
Lawrence Taylor		
25 Hang Time	.08	.25
Lawrence Taylor		
27 Hang Time	.30	.75
Dan Marino		
31 Hang Time	.30	.75
Dan Marino		
36 Hang Time	.30	.75
Lawrence Taylor		
Dan Marino		
37 Run and Shout	.20	.50
Jerry Rice		
Lawrence Taylor		
Thurman Thomas		
Dan Marino		
39 Run and Shout	.08	.25
Thurman Thomas		
44 Run and Shout	.08	.25
Thurman Thomas		
46 Run and Shout	.08	.25
Thurman Thomas		
47 Run and Shout	.08	.25
Thurman Thomas		
48 Run and Shout	.08	.25
Thurman Thomas		
49 Run and Shout	.08	.25
Lawrence Taylor		
50 Run and Shout	.08	.25
Lawrence Taylor		
Thurman Thomas		
51 Run and Shout	.08	.25
Thurman Thomas		
52 Run and Shout	.08	.25
Thurman Thomas		
55 I Get a Kick Out of You	.20	.50
Jerry Rice		
Lawrence Taylor		
Thurman Thomas		
Dan Marino		
57 I Get a Kick Out of You	.20	.50
Jerry Rice		
58 I Get a Kick Out of You	.20	.50
Jerry Rice		
59 I Get a Kick Out of You	.20	.50
Jerry Rice		
60 I Get a Kick Out of You	.30	.75
Jerry Rice		
Dan Marino		
72 I Get a Kick Out of You	.30	.75
Jerry Rice		
Dan Marino		
73 Zee Smell of Victory	.20	.50
Jerry Rice		
Lawrence Taylor		
Thurman Thomas		
Dan Marino		
74 Zee Smell of Victory	.08	.25
Thurman Thomas		
Lawrence Taylor		
75 Zee Smell of Victory	.08	.25
Thurman Thomas		
Lawrence Taylor		
80 Zee Smell of Victory	.08	.25
Thurman Thomas		
Lawrence Taylor		
82 Zee Smell of Victory	.08	.25
Thurman Thomas		
83 Zee Smell of Victory	.08	.25
Thurman Thomas		
Lawrence Taylor		
84 Zee Smell of Victory	.08	.25
Thurman Thomas		
85 Zee Smell of Victory	.08	.25
Thurman Thomas		
86 Zee Smell of Victory	.08	.25
Thurman Thomas		
91 Zee Smell of Victory	.30	.75
Dan Marino		
92 Zee Smell of Victory	.30	.75
Dan Marino		
93 Zee Smell of Victory	.20	.50
Jerry Rice		
94 Zee Smell of Victory	.20	.50
Jerry Rice		
95 Zee Smell of Victory	.20	.50
Jerry Rice		
96 Zee Smell of Victory	.08	.25
Thurman Thomas		
97 Zee Smell of Victory	.08	.25
Thurman Thomas		
98 Zee Smell of Victory	.08	.25
Lawrence Taylor		
100 Crowd Control	.20	.50
Jerry Rice		
Lawrence Taylor		
Thurman Thomas		
Dan Marino		
109 Crowd Control	.08	.25
Thurman Thomas		
110 Crowd Control	.00	.25
Thurman Thomas		
Lawrence Taylor		
111 Crowd Control	.08	.25
Thurman Thomas		
Lawrence Taylor		
112 Crowd Control	.08	.25
Thurman Thomas		
113 Crowd Control	.08	.25
Thurman Thomas		
116 Crowd Control	.08	.25
Thurman Thomas		
Lawrence Taylor		
117 Crowd Control	.08	.25
Thurman Thomas		
Lawrence Taylor		
118 Repeat Defender	.20	.50
Jerry Rice		
Lawrence Taylor		
Thurman Thomas		
Dan Marino		
120 Repeat Defender	.08	.25
Lawrence Taylor		
125 Repeat Defender	.08	.25
Lawrence Taylor		
126 Repeat Defender	.08	.25
Lawrence Taylor		
127 Repeat Defender	.08	.25
Lawrence Taylor		
129 Repeat Defender	.08	.25
Lawrence Taylor		
131 Repeat Defender	.08	.25
Lawrence Taylor		
132 Repeat Defender	.20	.50
Jerry Rice		
136 Hoppin' Half Time	.20	.50
Jerry Rice		
Lawrence Taylor		
Thurman Thomas		
Dan Marino		
137 Hoppin' Half Time	.30	.75
Jerry Rice		
Dan Marino		
142 Hoppin' Half Time	.30	.75
Jerry Rice		
Dan Marino		
147 Hoppin' Half Time	.30	.75
Jerry Rice		
Dan Marino		
149 Hoppin' Half Time	.30	.75
Jerry Rice		
Dan Marino		
151 Hoppin' Half Time	.30	.75
Jerry Rice		
Dan Marino		
152 Hoppin' Half Time	.20	.50
Jerry Rice		
153 Hoppin' Half Time	.30	.75
Dan Marino		
154 Martian Touchdown	.20	.50
Jerry Rice		
Lawrence Taylor		
Thurman Thomas		
Dan Marino		
155 Martian Touchdown	.08	.25
Lawrence Taylor		
159 Martian Touchdown	.08	.25
Lawrence Taylor		
160 Martian Touchdown	.08	.25
Lawrence Taylor		
169 Martian Touchdown	.30	.75
Dan Marino		
Lawrence Taylor		
170 Martian Touchdown	.30	.75
Dan Marino		
Lawrence Taylor		
171 Martian Touchdown	.30	.75
Dan Marino		
Lawrence Taylor		
172 Gut-Check Time	.20	.50
Jerry Rice		
Lawrence Taylor		
Thurman Thomas		
Dan Marino		
174 Gut-Check Time	.30	.75
Dan Marino		
175 Gut-Check Time	.30	.75
Thurman Thomas		
Jerry Rice		
Dan Marino		
176 Gut-Check Time	.30	.75
Jerry Rice		
Dan Marino		
177 Gut-Check Time	.30	.75
Dan Marino		
Thurman Thomas		
Jerry Rice		
178 Gut-Check Time	.30	.75
Dan Marino		
Jerry Rice		
179 Gut-Check Time	.30	.75
Dan Marino		
Jerry Rice		
Thurman Thomas		
180 Gut-Check Time	.30	.75
Dan Marino		
Jerry Rice		
Thurman Thomas		
190 Half Time	.08	.25
Thurman Thomas		
191 Half Time	.08	.25
Thurman Thomas		
192 Half Time	.20	.50
Jerry Rice		
193 Half Time	.20	.50
Jerry Rice		
194 Half Time	.30	.75
Dan Marino		
195 Half Time	.30	.75
Dan Marino		
196 Half Time	.08	.25
Lawrence Taylor		
197 Half Time	.30	.75
Dan Marino		
Lawrence Taylor		

1992 Upper Deck Comic Ball 4 Holograms

1A Dan Marino with Bugs and Porky	2.00	5.00
2 Jerry Rice with Daffy Duck	1.25	3.00
3 Lawrence Taylor with Daffy Duck	.75	2.00
4 Thurman Thomas with Wile E. Coyote	1.00	2.50

2008 Upper Deck Draft Edition

COMPLETE SET (250)	25.00	60.00
COMP.RC SET (100)	15.00	30.00
101-200: TWO PER PACK		
201-250: ONE PER PACK		
1 Anthony Morelli RC	.40	1.00
2 Adarius Bowman RC	.40	1.00
3 Ali Highsmith RC	.30	.75
4 Andre Woodson RC	.50	1.25
5 Allen Patrick RC	.40	1.00
6 Antoine Cason RC	.50	1.25
7 Aqib Talib RC	.50	1.25
8 Ben Moffitt RC	.30	.75
9 Gosder Cherilus RC	.40	1.00
10 Brian Brohm RC	.50	1.25
11 Calais Campbell RC	.40	1.00
12 Chad Henne RC	.50	1.25
13 Chevis Jackson RC	.30	.75
14 Davone Bess RC	.50	1.25
15 Justin Forsett RC	.50	1.25
16 Chris Ellis RC	.30	.75
17 Chris Long RC	.50	1.25
18 Colt Brennan RC	.50	1.25
19 Craig Steltz RC	.40	1.00
20 DJ Hall RC	.40	1.00
21 Dan Connor RC	.50	1.25
22 Darren McFadden RC	1.25	3.00
23 DeMario Pressley RC	.40	1.00
24 Dennis Dixon RC	.50	1.25
25 Derrick Harvey RC	.30	.75
26 DeSean Jackson RC	1.00	2.50
27 Dominique Rodgers-Cromartie RC	.50	1.25
28 Donnie Avery RC	.40	1.00
29 Dorien Bryant RC	.40	1.00
30 Dre Moore RC	.40	1.00
31 Kellen Davis RC	.30	.75
32 DaJuan Morgan RC	.40	1.00
33 Earl Bennett RC	.50	1.25
34 Early Doucet RC	.40	1.00
35 Kentwan Balmer RC	.40	1.00
36 Erik Ainge RC	.50	1.25
37 Felix Jones RC	.75	2.00
38 Frank Okam RC	.30	.75
39 Fred Davis RC	.50	1.25
40 Glenn Dorsey RC	.50	1.25
41 Harry Douglas RC	.40	1.00
42 Jack Ikegwuonu RC	.30	.75
43 Bruce Davis RC	.40	1.00
44 Jacob Tamme RC	.50	1.25
45 Jake Long RC	.50	1.25
46 Jamaal Charles RC	.75	2.00
47 James Hardy RC	.40	1.00
48 Erin Henderson RC	.50	1.25
49 J Leman RC	.30	.75
50 Joe Flacco RC	1.50	4.00
51 John Carlson RC	.50	1.25
52 John David Booty RC	.40	1.00
53 Jonathan Hefney RC	.40	1.00
54 Jonathan Stewart RC	.75	2.00
55 Jordy Nelson RC	.60	1.50
56 Josh Johnson RC	.50	1.25
57 Jacob Hester RC	.50	1.25
58 Keenan Burton RC	.30	.75
59 Keith Rivers RC	.50	1.25
60 Kenny Phillips RC	.50	1.25
61 Kevin Smith RC	.50	1.25
62 Lavelle Hawkins RC	.30	.75
63 Lawrence Jackson RC	.40	1.00
64 Limas Sweed RC	.50	1.25
65 Adrian Arrington RC	.40	1.00
66 Malcolm Kelly RC	.40	1.00
67 Martellus Bennett RC	.40	1.00
68 Marcus Monk RC	.40	1.00
69 Mario Manningham RC	.50	1.25
70 Mario Urrutia RC	.30	.75
71 Martin Rucker RC	.40	1.00

72 Matt Flynn RC 1.00 2.50
73 Matt Forte RC .75 2.00
74 Matt Ryan RC 2.00 5.00
75 Mike Hart RC .50 1.25
76 Mike Jenkins RC .50 1.25
77 Vernon Gholston RC .40 1.00
78 Owen Schmitt RC .50 1.25
79 Jonathan Goff RC .30 .75
80 Shawn Crable RC .30 .75
81 Justin King RC .40 1.00
82 Philip Wheeler RC .40 1.00
83 Paul Smith RC .50 1.25
84 Rashard Mendenhall RC 1.00 2.50
85 Ray Rice RC 1.00 2.50
86 Ryan Clady RC .50 1.25
87 Ryan Torain RC .50 1.25
88 Sam Baker RC .30 .75
89 Quintin Demps RC .50 1.25
90 Sam Keller RC .40 1.00
91 Phillip Merling RC .40 1.00
92 Steve Slaton RC .50 1.25
93 Tashard Choice RC .40 1.00
94 Terrell Thomas RC .40 1.00
95 Thomas Brown RC .40 1.00
96 Tom Zbikowski RC .50 1.25
97 DeJuan Tribble RC .30 .75
98 Trevor Laws RC .50 1.25
99 Vince Hall RC .30 .75
100 Xavier Adibi RC .30 .75
101 Edgerrin James .25 .60
102 Matt Leinart .30 .75
103 Larry Fitzgerald .30 .75
104 Joe Horn .25 .60
105 Warrick Dunn .25 .60
106 Jerious Norwood .25 .60
107 Ed Reed .25 .60
108 Willis McGahee .25 .60
109 Steve McNair .25 .60
110 Ray Lewis .30 .75
111 J.P. Losman .20 .50
112 Lee Evans .25 .60
113 Marshawn Lynch .25 .60
114 Eric Moulds .25 .60
115 Julius Peppers .25 .60
116 Steve Smith .25 .60
117 DeShaun Foster .25 .60
118 Devin Hester .30 .75
119 Bernard Berrian .25 .60
120 Cedric Benson .25 .60
121 Thomas Jones .25 .60
122 T.J. Houshmandzadeh .25 .60
123 Carson Palmer .30 .75
124 Chad Johnson .25 .60
125 Derek Anderson .20 .50
126 Kellen Winslow .25 .60
127 Braylon Edwards .25 .60
128 Anthony Henry .20 .50
129 Marion Barber .25 .60
130 DeMarcus Ware .25 .60
131 Tony Romo .40 1.00
132 Brandon Marshall .25 .60
133 Jay Cutler .30 .75
134 Champ Bailey .25 .60
135 Tatum Bell .20 .50
136 Calvin Johnson .30 .75
137 Jon Kitna .25 .60
138 Ernie Sims .20 .50
139 Aaron Kampman .25 .60
140 Charles Woodson .30 .75
141 A.J. Hawk .25 .60
142 DeMeco Ryans .25 .60
143 Andre Johnson .25 .60
144 Mario Williams .25 .60
145 Dwight Freeney .25 .60
146 Dallas Clark .25 .60
147 Joseph Addai .25 .60
148 David Garrard .25 .60
149 Reggie Nelson .20 .50
150 Maurice Jones-Drew .25 .60
151 Dwayne Bowe .25 .60
152 Derrick Johnson .20 .50
153 Brodie Croyle .25 .60
154 Ronnie Brown .25 .60
155 Ted Ginn .25 .60
156 Channing Crowder .20 .50
157 Antoine Winfield .20 .50
158 Adrian Peterson .50 1.25
159 Sidney Rice .30 .75
160 Wes Welker .30 .75
161 Laurence Maroney .25 .60
162 Ben Watson .20 .50
163 Drew Brees .30 .75
164 Reggie Bush .30 .75
165 Marques Colston .25 .60
166 Amani Toomer .25 .60
167 Osi Umenyiora .25 .60
168 Eli Manning .30 .75
169 Jonathan Vilma .25 .60
170 Kellen Clemens .25 .60
171 Kirk Morrison .20 .50
172 Nnamdi Asomugha .25 .60
173 JaMarcus Russell .25 .60
174 Brian Westbrook .25 .60
175 Reggie Brown .20 .50
176 Brian Dawkins .25 .60
177 Hines Ward .25 .60
178 Santonio Holmes .25 .60
179 Ben Roethlisberger .30 .75
180 Shawne Merriman .25 .60
181 LaDainian Tomlinson .30 .75
182 Antonio Cromartie .20 .50
183 Shaun Phillips .20 .50
184 Patrick Willis .25 .60
185 Alex Smith QB .30 .75
186 Frank Gore .25 .60
187 Lofa Tatupu .25 .60
188 Bobby Engram .20 .50
189 Deion Branch .25 .60
190 Steven Jackson .30 .75
191 Pisa Tinoisamoa .20 .50
192 Torry Holt .25 .60
193 Cadillac Williams .25 .60
194 Michael Clayton .20 .50
195 Gaines Adams .20 .50
196 Vince Young .25 .60
197 LenDale White .25 .60
198 Chris Cooley .25 .60
199 Clinton Portis .25 .60
200 Santana Moss .20 .50
201 Brian Brohm .60 1.50
Mario Urrutia
Alumni Association
202 Darren McFadden 1.50 4.00
Felix Jones
Alumni Association
203 DeJuan Tribble 2.50 6.00
Matt Ryan
Alumni Association
204 Early Doucet .60 1.50
Glenn Dorsey
Alumni Association
205 Jake Long .60 1.50
Mike Hart
Alumni Association
206 Colt Brennan .60 1.50
Davone Bess
Alumni Association
207 John David Booty .50 1.25
Fred Davis
Alumni Association
208 Derek Anderson .75 2.00
Steven Jackson
Alumni Association
209 Tom Brady 1.25 3.00
Braylon Edwards
Alumni Association
210 Reggie Bush .75 2.00
Matt Leinart
Alumni Association
211 Ali Highsmith .40 1.00
J Leman
Pigskin Pairings
212 Antoine Cason .60 1.50
DeJuan Tribble
Pigskin Pairings
213 Colt Brennan .60 1.50
Dennis Dixon
Pigskin Pairings
214 Darren McFadden 1.50 4.00
Mike Hart
Pigskin Pairings
215 Fred Davis .60 1.50
Martin Rucker
Pigskin Pairings
216 Jonathan Hefney .50 1.25
Craig Steltz
Pigskin Pairings
217 Limas Sweed .60 1.50
Mario Manningham
Pigskin Pairings
218 Sam Baker .60 1.50
Jake Long
Pigskin Pairings
219 Kentwan Balmer .60 1.50
Glenn Dorsey
Pigskin Pairings
220 Steve Slaton 1.25 3.00
Ray Rice
Pigskin Pairings
221 Ali Highsmith .60 1.50
Dan Connor
Franchise Foundations
222 Antoine Cason .60 1.50
Terrell Thomas
Franchise Foundations
223 Brian Brohm .60 1.50
Andre Woodson
Franchise Foundations
224 Chris Long .60 1.50
Quentin Groves
Franchise Foundations
225 Craig Steltz .60 1.50
Kenny Phillips
Franchise Foundations
226 Fred Davis .60 1.50
John Carlson
Franchise Foundations
227 Glenn Dorsey .60 1.50
Sedrick Ellis
Franchise Foundations
228 Jake Long .60 1.50
Sam Baker
Franchise Foundations
229 Limas Sweed .60 1.50
Early Doucet
Franchise Foundations
230 Tashard Choice 1.50 4.00
Darren McFadden
Franchise Foundations
231 Ali Highsmith .40 1.00
Chevis Jackson
Campus Combos
232 Chad Henne .60 1.50
Mario Manningham
Campus Combos
233 Lavelle Hawkins 1.25 3.00
DeSean Jackson
Campus Combos
234 Erin Henderson .60 1.50
Dre Moore
Campus Combos
235 Malcolm Kelly .50 1.25
Allen Patrick
Campus Combos
236 Mario Urrutia .50 1.25
Harry Douglas
Campus Combos
237 Martin Rucker .50 1.25
Adam Spieker
Campus Combos
238 Felix Jones 1.00 2.50
Peyton Hillis
Campus Combos
239 Jonathan Hefney .60 1.50
Erik Ainge
Campus Combos
240 Vince Hall .40 1.00
Xavier Adibi
Campus Combos
241 Colt Brennan .60 1.50
Dwight Lowery
Conference Clashes
242 Dennis Dixon .60 1.50
Keith Rivers
Conference Clashes
243 Harry Douglas .60 1.50
Mike Jenkins
Conference Clashes
244 Jacob Hester .60 1.50
Kenny Phillips
Conference Clashes
245 Jonathan Hefney .50 1.25
DJ Hall
Conference Clashes
246 Malcolm Kelly .50 1.25
Frank Okam
Conference Clashes
247 J Leman .60 1.50
Mario Manningham
Conference Clashes
248 Matt Ryan 2.50 6.00
Chris Long
Conference Clashes
249 John David Booty .50 1.25
Antoine Cason
Conference Clashes
250 Sam Keller .50 1.25
Allen Patrick
Conference Clashes

2008 Upper Deck Draft Edition Black

*ROOKIES 1-100: X TO X BASIC CARDS
*SINGLES 201-250: X TO X BASIC CARDS
STATED PRINT RUN 200 SER.#'d SETS

2008 Upper Deck Draft Edition Blue

*ROOKIES 1-100: .6X TO 1.5X BASIC CARDS
*SINGLES 201-250: .5X TO 1.2X BASIC CARDS
APPROXIMATE ODDS 1:8

2008 Upper Deck Draft Edition Bronze

*ROOKIES 1-100: 1X TO 2.5X BASIC CARDS
*SINGLES 201-250: .6X TO 1.5X BASIC CARDS
STATED PRINT RUN 175 SER.#'d SETS

2008 Upper Deck Draft Edition Gold

*ROOKIES 1-100: 4X TO 10X BASIC CARDS
*SINGLES 201-250: 2.5X TO 6X BASIC CARDS
STATED PRINT RUN 25 SER.#'d SETS

2008 Upper Deck Draft Edition Green

*ROOKIES 1-100: .6X TO 1.5X BASIC CARDS
*SINGLES 201-250: .4X TO 1X BASIC CARDS
RANDOM INSERTS IN RETAIL PACKS

2008 Upper Deck Draft Edition Platinum

UNPRICED PLATINUM PRINT RUN 1

2008 Upper Deck Draft Edition Red

*ROOKIES 1-100: .5X TO 1.2X BASIC CARDS
*SINGLES 201-250: .4X TO 1X BASIC CARDS
APPROXIMATE ODDS 1:2

2008 Upper Deck Draft Edition Silver

*ROOKIES 1-100: 1.2X TO 3X BASIC CARDS
*SINGLES 201-250: .8X TO 2X BASIC CARDS
STATED PRINT RUN 100 SER.#'d SETS

2008 Upper Deck Draft Edition Autographs

201-250 PRINT RUN 25
UNPRICED PLATINUM PRINT RUN 1
1 Anthony Morelli 4.00 10.00
2 Adarius Bowman 4.00 10.00
4 Andre Woodson 5.00 12.00
6 Antoine Cason 5.00 12.00
60C Antoine Cason on-card 10.00 25.00
(on-card autograph signed/ at hobby Trade Conference)
7 Aqib Talib 5.00 12.00
9 Gosder Cherilus 4.00 10.00
10 Brian Brohm 5.00 12.00
11 Calais Campbell 4.00 10.00
12 Chad Henne 5.00 12.00
13 Chevis Jackson 3.00 8.00
14 Davone Bess 5.00 12.00
15 Justin Forsett 5.00 12.00
16 Chris Ellis 3.00 8.00
17 Chris Long 5.00 12.00
18 Colt Brennan SP 5.00 12.00
19 Craig Steltz 4.00 10.00
20 DJ Hall 4.00 10.00
21 Dan Connor 5.00 12.00
22 Darren McFadden SP 30.00 60.00
23 DeMario Pressley 4.00 10.00
24 Dennis Dixon 5.00 12.00
25 Derrick Harvey 3.00 8.00
26 DeSean Jackson 12.00 30.00
27 Dominique Rodgers-Cromartie SP 8.00 20.00
28 Donnie Avery 4.00 10.00
29 Dorien Bryant 4.00 10.00
30 Dre Moore 4.00 10.00
31 Kellen Davis 3.00 8.00
32 DaJuan Morgan 4.00 10.00
34 Early Doucet 4.00 10.00
35 Kentwan Balmer 4.00 10.00
36 Erik Ainge 5.00 12.00
37 Felix Jones EXCH
38 Frank Okam 3.00 8.00
39 Fred Davis 5.00 12.00
40 Glenn Dorsey 5.00 12.00
42 Jack Ikegwuonu 3.00 8.00
43 Bruce Davis 4.00 10.00
44 Jacob Tamme 5.00 12.00
45 Jake Long 5.00 12.00
46 Jamaal Charles 8.00 20.00
47 James Hardy 4.00 10.00
48 Erin Henderson 5.00 12.00
49 J Leman 3.00 8.00
50 Joe Flacco 15.00 40.00
51 John Carlson 5.00 12.00
52 John David Booty 4.00 10.00
53 Jonathan Hefney 4.00 10.00
54 Jonathan Stewart 8.00 20.00
56 Josh Johnson 5.00 12.00
57 Jacob Hester 5.00 12.00
58 Keenan Burton 3.00 8.00
59 Keith Rivers 5.00 12.00
60 Kenny Phillips 5.00 12.00
61 Kevin Smith 5.00 12.00
62 Lavelle Hawkins 3.00 8.00
63 Lawrence Jackson 4.00 10.00
64 Limas Sweed 10.00 25.00
65 Adrian Arrington 4.00 10.00
66 Malcolm Kelly EXCH
70 Mario Urrutia 3.00 8.00
71 Martin Rucker 4.00 10.00
72 Matt Flynn 20.00 40.00
73 Matt Forte 15.00 40.00
74 Matt Ryan 25.00 60.00
75 Mike Hart 5.00 12.00
76 Mike Jenkins EXCH
77 Vernon Gholston 4.00 10.00
78 Owen Schmitt 5.00 12.00
80 Shawn Crable 3.00 8.00
81 Justin King EXCH
82 Philip Wheeler 4.00 10.00
83 Paul Smith 5.00 12.00
84 Rashard Mendenhall 20.00 50.00
85 Ray Rice 20.00 40.00
86 Ryan Clady 5.00 12.00
88 Sam Baker 3.00 8.00
89 Quintin Demps
90 Sam Keller 4.00 10.00
91 Phillip Merling 4.00 10.00
93 Tashard Choice 4.00 10.00
94 Terrell Thomas 4.00 10.00
95 Thomas Brown 4.00 10.00
96 Tom Zbikowski 5.00 12.00
97 DeJuan Tribble 3.00 8.00
98 Trevor Laws 5.00 12.00
100 Xavier Adibi 3.00 8.00
201 Brian Brohm 20.00 50.00
Mario Urrutia
Alumni Association
202 Darren McFadden 50.00 120.00
Felix Jones
Alumni Association
203 DeJuan Tribble 60.00 120.00
Matt Ryan
Alumni Association
204 Early Doucet 20.00 50.00
Glenn Dorsey
Alumni Association
205 Jake Long 20.00 50.00
Mike Hart
Alumni Association
206 Colt Brennan 12.00 30.00
Davone Bess
Alumni Association
207 John David Booty 8.00 20.00
Fred Davis
Alumni Association
212 Antoine Cason 12.00 30.00
DeJuan Tribble
Pigskin Pairings
213 Colt Brennan 25.00 60.00
Dennis Dixon
Pigskin Pairings
214 Darren McFadden 40.00 100.00
Mike Hart
Pigskin Pairings
215 Fred Davis 15.00 40.00
Martin Rucker
Pigskin Pairings
216 Jonathan Hefney 12.00 30.00
Craig Steltz
Pigskin Pairings
218 Sam Baker 20.00 50.00
Jake Long
Pigskin Pairings
219 Kentwan Balmer 20.00 50.00
Glenn Dorsey
Pigskin Pairings
222 Antoine Cason 12.00 30.00
Terrell Thomas
Franchise Foundations
223 Brian Brohm 12.00 30.00
Andre Woodson
Franchise Foundations
225 Craig Steltz 15.00 40.00
Kenny Phillips
Franchise Foundations
226 Fred Davis 12.00 30.00
John Carlson
Franchise Foundations
227 Glenn Dorsey 15.00 40.00
Sedrick Ellis
Franchise Foundations
228 Jake Long 20.00 50.00
Sam Baker
Franchise Foundations
229 Limas Sweed 20.00 50.00
Early Doucet
Franchise Foundations
230 Tashard Choice 40.00 100.00
Darren McFadden
Franchise Foundations
233 Lavelle Hawkins 15.00 40.00
DeSean Jackson
Campus Combos
234 Erin Henderson 12.00 30.00
Dre Moore
Campus Combos
238 Felix Jones 40.00 100.00
Peyton Hillis
Campus Combos
239 Jonathan Hefney 15.00 40.00
Erik Ainge
Campus Combos
242 Dennis Dixon 15.00 40.00
Keith Rivers
Conference Clashes
244 Jacob Hester 20.00 50.00
Kenny Phillips
Conference Clashes
245 Jonathan Hefney 12.00 30.00
DJ Hall
Conference Clashes
248 Matt Ryan 60.00 120.00
Chris Long
Conference Clashes
249 John David Booty 8.00 20.00
Antoine Cason
Conference Clashes

2008 Upper Deck Draft Edition Autographs Bronze

*BRONZE/50: .6X TO 1.5X BASIC AUTO
BRONZE PRINT RUN 50 SER.#'d SETS
50 Joe Flacco 25.00 60.00
66 Malcolm Kelly 6.00 15.00
74 Matt Ryan 40.00 100.00

2008 Upper Deck Draft Edition Autographs Blue

*BLUE/75: .6X TO 1.5X BASIC AUTO
BLUE PRINT RUN 75 SER.#'d SETS
50 Joe Flacco 25.00 60.00
74 Matt Ryan 40.00 100.00

2008 Upper Deck Draft Edition Autographs Gold

*GOLD/25: .8X TO 2X BASIC AUTO
1-100 GOLD PRINT RUN 25
UNPRICED 201-250 GOLD PRINT RUN 10
50 Joe Flacco 30.00 80.00
66 Malcolm Kelly 8.00 20.00
74 Matt Ryan 50.00 120.00

2008 Upper Deck Draft Edition Autographs Red

*RED/125: .5X TO 1.2X BASIC AUTO
RED PRINT RUN 125 SER.#'d SETS
50 Joe Flacco 20.00 50.00
74 Matt Ryan 30.00 80.00

2008 Upper Deck Draft Edition College Greats

COMPLETE SET (10) 6.00 15.00
RANDOM INSERTS IN RETAIL PACKS
CG1 Brian Brohm .50 1.25
CG2 Matt Ryan 2.00 5.00
CG3 Darren McFadden 1.25 3.00
CG4 DeSean Jackson 1.00 2.50
CG5 Early Doucet .40 1.00
CG6 Keith Rivers .50 1.25
CG7 Limas Sweed .50 1.25
CG8 Marcus Monk .40 1.00
CG9 Mike Hart .50 1.25
CG10 Antoine Cason .50 1.25

2008 Upper Deck Draft Edition Stars of the Draft

COMPLETE SET (10) 10.00 25.00
RANDOM INSERTS IN RETAIL PACKS
SOD1 Brian Brohm .75 2.00
SOD2 Matt Ryan 3.00 8.00
SOD3 Darren McFadden 2.00 5.00
SOD4 DeSean Jackson 1.50 4.00
SOD5 Early Doucet .60 1.50
SOD6 Limas Sweed .75 2.00
SOD7 Keith Rivers .75 2.00
SOD8 Antoine Cason .75 2.00
SOD9 Mike Hart .75 2.00
SOD10 Dan Connor .75 2.00

2009 Upper Deck Draft Edition

COMPLETE SET (295) 50.00 100.00
COMP.SET w/o SP's (200) 25.00 50.00
1 Curtis Painter RC .40 1.00
2 DeAngelo Smith RC .30 .75
3 Matthew Stafford RC 2.00 5.00
4 Chris Wells RC .60 1.50
5 Michael Johnson RC .25 .60
6 Percy Harvin RC .60 1.50
7 Michael Crabtree RC .75 2.00
8 Knowshon Moreno RC .40 1.00
9 Jason Smith RC .30 .75
10 James Laurinaitis RC .40 1.00
11 Rey Maualuga RC .40 1.00
12 Hunter Cantwell RC .40 1.00
13 Chase Daniel RC .40 1.00
14 Alphonso Smith RC .30 .75
15 Jason Phillips RC .30 .75
16 Pat White RC .40 1.00
17 Peria Jerry RC .30 .75
18 Graham Harrell RC .40 1.00
19 Sammie Stroughter RC .40 1.00
20 James Davis RC .40 1.00
21 Javon Ringer RC .40 1.00
22 D.J. Moore RC .30 .75
23 Nate Davis RC .30 .75
24 P.J. Hill RC .30 .75
25 Kevin Barnes RC .30 .75
26 Darrius Heyward-Bey RC .40 1.00
28 Glen Coffee RC .30 .75
29 Jaison Williams RC .30 .75
30 Brian Robiskie RC .40 1.00
31 Derrick Williams RC .30 .75
32 Darius Passmore RC .30 .75
33 Chase Coffman RC .30 .75
34 Cornelius Ingram RC .25 .60
35 Travis Beckum RC .30 .75
36 Brandon Pettigrew RC .40 1.00
37 Louis Delmas RC .40 1.00
38 Alex Mack RC .30 .75
39 Duke Robinson RC .25 .60
40 Jarett Dillard RC .40 1.00
41 Kraig Urbik RC .30 .75
42 Herman Johnson RC .30 .75
43 Otis Wiley RC .25 .60
44 Michael Oher RC .60 1.50
45 Phil Loadholt RC .30 .75
46 Alex Boone RC .40 1.00
47 Max Unger RC .30 .75
48 Andre Smith RC .30 .75
49 Fili Moala RC .30 .75
52 Terrance Taylor RC .30 .75
53 Sen'Derrick Marks RC .25 .60
54 Tyson Jackson RC .30 .75
55 Captain Munnerlyn RC .30 .75
56 Ian Campbell RC .30 .75
57 Asher Allen RC .30 .75
58 Brandon Tate RC .40 1.00
59 Darry Beckwith RC .30 .75
60 Jasper Brinkley RC .30 .75
61 Brian Cushing RC .40 1.00
62 Dannell Ellerbe RC .30 .75
63 Marcus Freeman RC .40 1.00
64 Maurice Crum RC .30 .75
65 Anthony Heygood RC .25 .60
66 Patrick Chung RC .40 1.00
67 Jeremy Maclin RC .60 1.50
68 Troy Kropog RC .25 .60
69 William Moore RC .40 1.00
70 Kevin Ellison RC .30 .75
71 Malcolm Jenkins RC .40 1.00
72 Victor Harris RC .40 1.00
73 Vontae Davis RC .40 1.00
74 Matt Shaughnessy RC .30 .75
75 Mike Mickens RC .30 .75
76 LeSean McCoy RC .75 2.00
77 Rudy Carpenter RC .30 .75
78 Arian Foster RC .75 2.00
79 Devin Moore RC .30 .75
80 Tyrell Sutton RC .30 .75
81 Ian Johnson RC .40 1.00
82 James Casey RC .30 .75
83 Paul Kruger RC .30 .75
84 Kenny Britt RC .50 1.25
85 Josh Freeman RC .75 2.00
86 Louis Murphy RC .40 1.00
87 Demetrius Byrd RC .30 .75
88 Brandon Gibson RC .40 1.00
89 Aaron Kelly RC .30 .75
90 Keenan Lewis RC .40 1.00
91 Nathan Brown RC .30 .75
92 Connor Barwin RC .40 1.00
93 B.J. Raji RC .40 1.00
94 Tom Brandstater RC .40 1.00
95 Shonn Greene RC .60 1.50
96 Brannan Southerland RC .30 .75
97 Eben Britton RC .30 .75
98 Jairus Byrd RC .40 1.00
99 Nic Harris RC .30 .75
100 Ryan Purvis RC .30 .75
101 Clay Matthews RC 1.00 2.50
102 Mark Sanchez RC 1.25 3.00
103 Brian Orakpo RC .40 1.00
104 Tim Jamison RC .30 .75
105 Jonathan Luigs RC .25 .60
106 Darius Butler RC .40 1.00
107 Eugene Monroe RC .25 .60
108 Xavier Fulton RC .25 .60
109 Andrew Gardner RC .25 .60
110 Jamon Meredith RC .30 .75
111 Jason Watkins RC .30 .75
112 Fenuki Tupou RC .25 .60
113 Juaquin Iglesias RC .30 .75
114 Marko Mitchell RC .30 .75
115 Kenny McKinley RC .40 1.00
116 Ramses Barden RC .25 .60
117 Jeremy Childs RC .30 .75
119 Tiquan Underwood RC .30 .75
120 Quan Cosby RC .30 .75
121 David Veikune RC .30 .75
122 Brennan Marion RC .30 .75
123 Morgan Trent RC .30 .75
124 Larry English RC .40 1.00
125 Mohamed Massaquoi RC .30 .75
126 Aaron Curry RC .40 1.00
127 Rashad Jennings RC .40 1.00
128 Jeremiah Johnson RC .40 1.00
129 Michael Hamlin RC .30 .75
130 Andre Brown RC .25 .60
132 Keegan Herring RC .30 .75
133 Willie Tuitama RC .30 .75
134 Cedric Peerman RC .30 .75
135 Gerald McRath RC .30 .75
136 Jared Cook RC .40 1.00
137 Austin Collie RC .40 1.00
138 Garrett Reynolds RC .30 .75
139 Cullen Harper RC .40 1.00
140 Donald Brown RC .40 1.00
141 John Parker Wilson RC .40 1.00
142 Derek Pegues RC .25 .60
143 Rhett Bomar RC .30 .75
144 Mike Reilly RC .30 .75
145 Clint Sintim RC .40 1.00
146 Courtney Greene RC .25 .60
147 Sean Smith RC .40 1.00
148 Shawn Nelson RC .30 .75
149 Hakeem Nicks RC .60 1.50
150 Bear Pascoe RC .30 .75
151 Clinton Portis .25 .60
152 Brett Favre .75 2.00
153 Drew Brees .30 .75
154 Peyton Manning .50 1.25
155 Eli Manning .30 .75
156 Tony Romo .50 1.25
157 Jay Cutler .30 .75
158 Brandon Marshall .25 .60
159 LaDainian Tomlinson .30 .75
160 Michael Turner .25 .60
161 Darren McFadden .30 .75
162 Devin Hester .30 .75
163 Marion Barber .25 .60
164 Troy Polamalu .30 .75
165 Ben Roethlisberger .30 .75
166 Chris Johnson .30 .75
167 Matt Forte .30 .75
168 Matt Ryan .30 .75
169 Aaron Rodgers .60 1.50
170 Greg Jennings .30 .75
171 Brian Westbrook .25 .60
172 Adrian Peterson .50 1.25
173 Larry Fitzgerald .30 .75
174 Reggie Wayne .25 .60
175 Trent Edwards .20 .50
176 Marshawn Lynch .25 .60
177 Brian Urlacher .30 .75
178 Jason Campbell .20 .50
179 Ronnie Brown .25 .60
180 Anquan Boldin .25 .60
181 Brady Quinn .25 .60
182 Roddy White .25 .60
183 Felix Jones .30 .75
184 Jason Witten .30 .75
185 Andre Johnson .25 .60
186 Calvin Johnson .30 .75
187 Tom Brady .50 1.25
188 A.J. Hawk .25 .60
189 Patrick Willis .25 .60
190 Philip Rivers .30 .75
191 Chris Cooley .25 .60
192 Dwayne Bowe .25 .60
193 Mario Williams .25 .60
194 DeMarcus Ware .25 .60
195 Joey Porter .25 .60
196 Hines Ward .25 .60
197 Lance Briggs .25 .60
198 Frank Gore .25 .60
199 Nnamdi Asomugha .25 .60
200 Donovan McNabb .30 .75
201 Chris Wells SR .60 1.50
202 Mark Sanchez SR 1.25 3.00
203 Curtis Painter SR .40 1.00
204 Michael Crabtree SR .75 2.00
205 Knowshon Moreno SR .40 1.00
206 LeSean McCoy SR .75 2.00
207 Shonn Greene SR .60 1.50
208 Matthew Stafford SR 2.00 5.00
209 Josh Freeman SR .75 2.00
210 Pat White SR .40 1.00
211 Aaron Curry SR .40 1.00
212 Alphonso Smith SR .30 .75
213 Darrius Heyward-Bey SR .40 1.00
214 Percy Harvin SR .60 1.50
215 James Laurinaitis SR .40 1.00
216 Brian Robiskie SR .40 1.00
217 Jeremy Maclin SR .60 1.50
218 William Moore SR .40 1.00
219 Chase Coffman SR .30 .75
220 Brandon Pettigrew SR .40 1.00
221 Hakeem Nicks SR .60 1.50
222 Michael Johnson SR .25 .60
223 Fili Moala SR .30 .75
224 Rey Maualuga SR .40 1.00
225 Brian Cushing SR .40 1.00
226 Donald Brown SR .40 1.00
227 Malcolm Jenkins SR .40 1.00
228 Vontae Davis SR .40 1.00
229 Patrick Chung SR .40 1.00
230 Sen'Derrick Marks SR .25 .60
231 Troy Polamalu .40 1.00
Rey Maualuga
Alumni Association
232 John Parker Wilson .40 1.00
Andre Smith
Alumni Association
233 Michael Crabtree .75 2.00
Wes Welker
Alumni Association
234 Hines Ward 2.00 5.00
Matthew Stafford
Alumni Association
235 Matthew Stafford 2.00 5.00
Knowshon Moreno
Alumni Association
236 James Laurinaitis .40 1.00
A.J. Hawk
Alumni Association
237 Cullen Harper .40 1.00
James Davis
Alumni Association
238 Adrian Peterson .60 1.50
Juaquin Iglesias
Alumni Association
239 Drew Brees .40 1.00
Curtis Painter
Alumni Association
240 Graham Harrell .75 2.00
Michael Crabtree
Alumni Association
241 Peria Jerry .30 .75
Patrick Willis
Alumni Association
242 Calvin Johnson .40 1.00
Michael Johnson
Alumni Association
243 Mark Sanchez 1.25 3.00
Anthony Munoz
Alumni Association
244 Everette Brown .30 .75
Anquan Boldin
Alumni Association
245 Rey Maualuga .40 1.00
Brian Cushing
Alumni Association
246 Clint Sintim .40 1.00
Eugene Monroe
Alumni Association
247 Percy Harvin .60 1.50
Louis Murphy
Alumni Association
248 LeSean McCoy .75 2.00
Larry Fitzgerald
Alumni Association
249 Jason Campbell .25 .60
Sen'Derrick Marks
Alumni Association
250 Mohamed Massaquoi .40 1.00
Knowshon Moreno
Alumni Association
251 John Parker Wilson 2.00 5.00
Matthew Stafford
Conference Clashes
252 Michael Johnson .30 .75
Everette Brown
Conference Clashes
253 William Moore .40 1.00
Graham Harrell
Conference Clashes
254 Javon Ringer .60 1.50
Chris Wells
Conference Clashes
255 Brian Robiskie .40 1.00
Derrick Williams
Conference Clashes
256 Darrius Heyward-Bey .40 1.00
Aaron Kelly
Conference Clashes
257 Demetrius Byrd .60 1.50
Percy Harvin
Conference Clashes
258 Sen'Derrick Marks .40 1.00
Knowshon Moreno
Conference Clashes
259 Malcolm Jenkins .40 1.00
Vontae Davis
Conference Clashes
260 Brandon Pettigrew .40 1.00
Chase Coffman
Conference Clashes
261 Brian Orakpo .40 1.00
Graham Harrell
Conference Clashes
262 Andre Smith .60 1.50
Michael Oher
Conference Clashes
263 James Laurinaitis .60 1.50
Shonn Greene
Conference Clashes
264 Tyson Jackson .30 .75
Andre Smith
Conference Clashes
265 Brandon Gibson .40 1.00
Rey Maualuga
Conference Clashes
266 Chris Wells .60 1.50
Shonn Greene
Conference Clashes
267 Michael Crabtree .60 1.50
Jeremy Maclin
Conference Clashes
268 Mark Sanchez 1.25 3.00
Rudy Carpenter
Conference Clashes
269 Quan Cosby .75 2.00
Michael Crabtree
Conference Clashes
270 P.J. Hill .40 1.00
Javon Ringer
Conference Clashes
271 Knowshon Moreno AA .40 1.00
272 Michael Crabtree AA .75 2.00
273 Herman Johnson AA .30 .75
274 Fili Moala AA .30 .75
275 James Laurinaitis AA .40 1.00
276 Jeremy Maclin AA .60 1.50
277 Chase Coffman AA .30 .75
278 Jarett Dillard AA .40 1.00
279 Michael Oher AA .60 1.50
280 Javon Ringer AA .40 1.00
281 Aaron Maybin AA .30 .75
282 Andre Smith AA .30 .75
283 Rey Maualuga AA .40 1.00
284 Malcolm Jenkins AA .40 1.00
285 Shonn Greene AA .60 1.50
286 Adrian Peterson AA .75 2.00
287 Peyton Manning AA .75 2.00
288 Calvin Johnson AA .50 1.25
289 Darren McFadden AA .50 1.25
290 A.J. Hawk AA .40 1.00
291 Ben Roethlisberger .50 1.25
Philip Rivers
Eli Manning
Draft Class
292 Matt Forte .50 1.25
Darren McFadden
Chris Johnson
Draft Class
293 LaDainian Tomlinson .50 1.25
Drew Brees
Reggie Wayne
Draft Class
294 Jim Kelly .50 1.25
Roger Craig
Darrell Green
Draft Class
295 Mario Williams .50 1.25
Vince Young
Reggie Bush
Draft Class
296 Jason Campbell 1.00 2.50
Aaron Rodgers
Marion Barber
Draft Class
297 Matt Ryan .50 1.25
Darren McFadden
Joe Flacco
Draft Class
298 Charles Woodson .75 2.00
Hines Ward
Peyton Manning
Draft Class
299 Devin Hester .50 1.25
A.J. Hawk
Jay Cutler
Draft Class
300 Chris Cooley .50 1.25
Larry Fitzgerald
Ben Roethlisberger
Draft Class

2009 Upper Deck Draft Edition Blue 50

*ROOKIES 1-150: 2.5X TO 6X BASIC CARDS
*VETS 151-200: 5X TO 12X BASIC CARDS
*SR 201-230: 2X TO 5X BASIC CARDS
*DUAL 231-270: 2X TO 5X BASIC CARDS
*AA 271-285: 2X TO 5X BASIC CARDS
*VETS 286-300: 3X TO 8X BASIC CARDS
BLUE PRINT RUN 50 SER.#'d SETS

2009 Upper Deck Draft Edition Burgundy 75

*ROOKIES 1-150: 2X TO 5X BASIC CARDS
*VETS 151-200: 4X TO 10X BASIC CARDS
*SR 201-230: 1.5X TO 4X BASIC CARDS
*DUAL 231-270: 1.5X TO 4X BASIC CARDS
*AA 271-285: 1.5X TO 4X BASIC CARDS

*VETS 286-300: 2.5X TO 6X BASIC CARDS
BURGUNDY PRINT RUN 75 SER.#'d SETS

2009 Upper Deck Draft Edition Copper 25

*ROOKIES 1-150: 4X TO 10X BASIC CARDS
*VETS 151-200: 8X TO 20X BASIC CARDS
*SR 201-230: 3X TO 8X BASIC CARDS
*DUAL 231-270: 3X TO 8X BASIC CARDS
*AA 271-285: 3X TO 8X BASIC CARDS
*VETS 286-300: 5X TO 12X BASIC CARDS
COPPER PRINT RUN 25 SER.#'d SETS

2009 Upper Deck Draft Edition Dark Green

*ROOKIES 1-150: .8X TO 2X BASIC CARDS
*VETS 151-200: 1.5X TO 4X BASIC CARDS
*SR 201-230: .4X TO 1.5X BASIC CARDS
*DUAL 231-270: .6X TO 1.5X BASIC CARDS
*AA 271-285: .6X TO 1.5X BASIC CARDS
*VETS 286-300: 1X TO 2.5X BASIC CARDS
RANDOM INSERTS IN RETAIL PACKS

2009 Upper Deck Draft Edition Green 350

*ROOKIES 1-150: 1.2X TO 3X BASIC CARDS
*VETS 151-200: 2.5X TO 6X BASIC CARDS
*SR 201-230: 1X TO 2.5X BASIC CARDS
*DUAL 231-270: 1X TO 2.5X BASIC CARDS
*AA 271-285: 1X TO 2.5X BASIC CARDS
*VETS 286-300: 1.5X TO 4X BASIC CARDS
GREEN PRINT RUN 350-351

2009 Upper Deck Draft Edition Bronze 125

*ROOKIES 1-150: 1.5X TO 4X BASIC CARDS
*VETS 151-200: 3X TO 8X BASIC CARDS
*SR 201-230: 1.2X TO 3X BASIC CARDS
*DUAL 231-270: 1.2X TO 3X BASIC CARDS
*AA 271-285: 1.2X TO 3X BASIC CARDS
*VETS 286-300: 2X TO 5X BASIC CARDS
BRONZE PRINT RUN 125 SER.#'d SETS

2009 Upper Deck Draft Edition Brown

*ROOKIES 1-150: .8X TO 2X BASIC CARDS
*VETS 151-200: 1.5X TO 4X BASIC CARDS
*SR 201-230: .4X TO 1.5X BASIC CARDS
*DUAL 231-270: .6X TO 1.5X BASIC CARDS
*AA 271-285: .6X TO 1.5X BASIC CARDS
*VETS 286-300: 1X TO 2.5X BASIC CARDS
RANDOM INSERTS IN HOBBY PACKS

2009 Upper Deck Draft Edition Autographs Blue

*1-150 BLUE/25: .5X TO 1.2X COPPER AU
1-150 BLUE ROOKIE PRINT RUN 25
151-200 BLUE UNPRICED VET PRINT RUN 3
3 Matthew Stafford 60.00 120.00
7 Michael Crabtree 30.00 80.00
8 Knowshon Moreno 30.00 80.00
102 Mark Sanchez 40.00 100.00

2009 Upper Deck Draft Edition Autographs Copper

1-150 COPPER PRINT RUN 50
151-198 UNPRICED COPPER PRINT RUN 5
201-230 COPPER SR PRINT RUN 25
232-270 COPPER DUAL PRINT RUN 50
271-290 COPPER AA PRINT RUN 25
291-295 UNPRICED COPPER PRINT RUN 10
OVERALL AUTO ODDS 5:16
1 Curtis Painter 8.00 20.00
3 Matthew Stafford 50.00 100.00
4 Chris Wells 12.00 30.00
5 Michael Johnson 5.00 12.00
6 Percy Harvin 12.00 30.00
7 Michael Crabtree 25.00 60.00
8 Knowshon Moreno 25.00 60.00
9 Jason Smith 6.00 15.00
10 James Laurinaitis 8.00 20.00
11 Rey Maualuga 8.00 20.00
12 Hunter Cantwell 8.00 20.00
14 Alphonso Smith 6.00 15.00
16 Pat White 8.00 20.00
17 Peria Jerry 6.00 15.00
18 Graham Harrell 12.00 30.00
20 James Davis 8.00 20.00
21 Javon Ringer 10.00 25.00
22 D.J. Moore 6.00 15.00
24 P.J. Hill 6.00 15.00
25 Kevin Barnes 6.00 15.00
26 Darrius Heyward-Bey 8.00 20.00
29 Jaison Williams 6.00 15.00
31 Derrick Williams 6.00 15.00
33 Chase Coffman 6.00 15.00
34 Cornelius Ingram 5.00 12.00
35 Travis Beckum 6.00 15.00
36 Brandon Pettigrew 8.00 20.00
39 Duke Robinson 5.00 12.00
40 Jarett Dillard 8.00 20.00
41 Kraig Urbik 6.00 15.00
42 Herman Johnson 6.00 15.00
43 Otis Wiley 5.00 12.00
44 Michael Oher 15.00 40.00
45 Phil Loadholt 6.00 15.00
46 Alex Boone 8.00 20.00
47 Max Unger 6.00 15.00
48 Andre Smith 6.00 15.00
49 Fili Moala 6.00 15.00
52 Terrance Taylor 6.00 15.00
53 Sen'Derrick Marks 5.00 12.00
54 Tyson Jackson 6.00 15.00
56 Ian Campbell 6.00 15.00
59 Darry Beckwith 6.00 15.00
60 Jasper Brinkley 6.00 15.00
61 Brian Cushing 8.00 20.00
63 Marcus Freeman 8.00 20.00
64 Maurice Crum 6.00 15.00
65 Anthony Heygood 5.00 12.00
67 Jeremy Maclin 12.00 30.00
68 Troy Kropog 5.00 12.00
69 William Moore 8.00 20.00
71 Malcolm Jenkins 8.00 20.00
72 Victor Harris 8.00 20.00
73 Vontae Davis 8.00 20.00
74 Matt Shaughnessy 6.00 15.00
75 Mike Mickens 6.00 15.00
76 LeSean McCoy 12.00 30.00
77 Rudy Carpenter EXCH 6.00 15.00
78 Arian Foster 30.00 60.00
79 Devin Moore 6.00 15.00
80 Tyrell Sutton 6.00 15.00
83 Paul Kruger 6.00 15.00
84 Kenny Britt 10.00 25.00
87 Demetrius Byrd 6.00 15.00
88 Brandon Gibson 8.00 20.00
89 Aaron Kelly 6.00 15.00
90 Keenan Lewis 8.00 20.00
91 Nathan Brown 6.00 15.00
93 B.J. Raji 8.00 20.00
94 Tom Brandstater 8.00 20.00
95 Shonn Greene 12.00 30.00
96 Brannan Southerland 6.00 15.00
99 Nic Harris 6.00 15.00
100 Ryan Purvis 6.00 15.00
102 Mark Sanchez 30.00 80.00
103 Brian Orakpo 8.00 20.00
104 Tim Jamison 6.00 15.00
105 Jonathan Luigs 5.00 12.00
107 Eugene Monroe 5.00 12.00
108 Xavier Fulton 5.00 12.00
109 Andrew Gardner 5.00 12.00
110 Jamon Meredith 6.00 15.00
111 Jason Watkins 6.00 15.00
112 Fenuki Tupou 5.00 12.00
113 Juaquin Iglesias 6.00 15.00
114 Marko Mitchell 6.00 15.00
115 Kenny McKinley 8.00 20.00
116 Ramses Barden 5.00 12.00
117 Mike Thomas 8.00 20.00
119 Tiquan Underwood 6.00 15.00
120 Quan Cosby 6.00 15.00
121 David Veikune 6.00 15.00
122 Brennan Marion 6.00 15.00
123 Morgan Trent 6.00 15.00
124 Deon Butler 6.00 15.00
125 Mohamed Massaquoi 6.00 15.00
126 Aaron Curry 8.00 20.00
127 Rashad Jennings 8.00 20.00
128 Jeremiah Johnson 8.00 20.00
129 Michael Hamlin 6.00 15.00
130 Andre Brown 5.00 12.00
131 Brad Lester 5.00 12.00
132 Keegan Herring 6.00 15.00
133 Willie Tuitama 6.00 15.00
135 Gerald McRath 6.00 15.00
136 Jared Cook 8.00 20.00
137 Austin Collie 10.00 25.00
138 Garrett Reynolds 6.00 15.00
140 Donald Brown 8.00 20.00
141 John Parker Wilson 8.00 20.00
142 Derek Pegues 5.00 12.00
143 Rhett Bomar 6.00 15.00
144 Mike Reilly 6.00 15.00
145 Clint Sintim 8.00 20.00
148 Shawn Nelson 6.00 15.00
149 Hakeem Nicks 12.00 30.00
150 Bear Pascoe 6.00 15.00
201 Chris Wells SR/25 15.00 40.00
202 Mark Sanchez SR/25 60.00 120.00
203 Curtis Painter SR/25 10.00 25.00
204 Michael Crabtree SR/25 50.00 100.00
205 Knowshon Moreno SR/25 25.00 60.00
206 LeSean McCoy SR/25 20.00 50.00
207 Shonn Greene SR/25 15.00 40.00
208 Matthew Stafford SR/25 60.00 120.00
210 Pat White SR/25 10.00 25.00
211 Aaron Curry SR/25 10.00 25.00
212 Alphonso Smith SR/25 8.00 20.00
213 Darrius Heyward-Bey SR/25 10.00 25.00
214 Percy Harvin SR/25 15.00 40.00
215 James Laurinaitis SR/25 10.00 25.00
217 Jeremy Maclin SR/25 15.00 40.00
218 William Moore SR/25 10.00 25.00
219 Chase Coffman SR/25 8.00 20.00
220 Brandon Pettigrew SR/25 10.00 25.00
221 Hakeem Nicks SR/25 15.00 40.00
222 Michael Johnson SR/25 6.00 15.00
223 Fili Moala SR/25 8.00 20.00
224 Rey Maualuga SR/25 10.00 25.00
225 Brian Cushing SR/25 10.00 25.00
226 Donald Brown SR/25 10.00 25.00
227 Malcolm Jenkins SR/25 10.00 25.00
228 Vontae Davis SR/25 10.00 25.00
229 Patrick Chung SR/25 10.00 25.00
230 Sen'Derrick Marks SR/25 6.00 15.00
232 John Parker Wilson EXCH 12.00 30.00
Andre Smith
Alumni Association
235 Matthew Stafford 75.00 135.00
Knowshon Moreno
Alumni Association
236 James Laurinaitis 20.00 50.00
A.J. Hawk
Alumni Association
237 Cullen Harper 12.00 30.00
James Davis
Alumni Association
238 Adrian Peterson 60.00 100.00
Juaquin Iglesias
Alumni Association
239 Drew Brees 30.00 60.00
Curtis Painter
Alumni Association
240 Graham Harrell 30.00 80.00
Michael Crabtree
Alumni Association
241 Peria Jerry 12.00 30.00
Patrick Willis
Alumni Association
242 Calvin Johnson 25.00 50.00
Michael Johnson
Alumni Association
243 Mark Sanchez 30.00 80.00
Anthony Munoz
Alumni Association
245 Rey Maualuga 12.00 30.00
Brian Cushing
Alumni Association
246 Clint Sintim 12.00 30.00
Eugene Monroe
Alumni Association
248 LeSean McCoy 40.00 80.00
Larry Fitzgerald
Alumni Association
249 Jason Campbell 12.00 30.00
Sen'Derrick Marks
Alumni Association
250 Mohamed Massaquoi 40.00 80.00
Knowshon Moreno
Alumni Association
251 John Parker Wilson 30.00 80.00
Matthew Stafford
Conference Clashes
253 William Moore 15.00 40.00
Graham Harrell
Conference Clashes
254 Javon Ringer 30.00 60.00
Chris Wells
Conference Clashes
256 Darrius Heyward-Bey 10.00 25.00
Aaron Kelly
Conference Clashes
257 Demetrius Byrd 20.00 50.00
Percy Harvin
Conference Clashes
258 Sen'Derrick Marks 30.00 80.00
Knowshon Moreno
Conference Clashes
259 Malcolm Jenkins 12.00 30.00
Vontae Davis
Conference Clashes
260 Brandon Pettigrew EXCH 12.00 30.00
Chase Coffman
Conference Clashes
261 Brian Orakpo EXCH 15.00 40.00
Graham Harrell
Conference Clashes
262 Andre Smith 20.00 50.00
Michael Oher
Conference Clashes
263 James Laurinaitis 20.00 50.00
Shonn Greene
Conference Clashes
264 Tyson Jackson 12.00 30.00
Andre Smith
Conference Clashes
265 Brandon Gibson 12.00 30.00
Rey Maualuga
Conference Clashes
266 Chris Wells 30.00 60.00
Shonn Greene
Conference Clashes
267 Michael Crabtree 40.00 80.00
Jeremy Maclin
Conference Clashes
268 Mark Sanchez 25.00 60.00
Rudy Carpenter
Conference Clashes
269 Quan Cosby 30.00 80.00
Michael Crabtree
Conference Clashes
270 P.J. Hill 12.00 30.00
Javon Ringer
Conference Clashes
271 Knowshon Moreno AA/25 50.00 100.00
272 Michael Crabtree AA/25 50.00 100.00
273 Herman Johnson AA/25 8.00 20.00
274 Fili Moala AA/25 8.00 20.00
275 James Laurinaitis AA/25 10.00 25.00
276 Jeremy Maclin AA/25 15.00 40.00
277 Chase Coffman AA/25 8.00 20.00
278 Jarett Dillard AA/25 10.00 25.00
279 Michael Oher AA/25 25.00 60.00
280 Javon Ringer AA/25 10.00 25.00
282 Andre Smith AA/25 8.00 20.00
283 Rey Maualuga AA/25 10.00 26.00
284 Malcolm Jenkins AA/25 10.00 25.00
285 Shonn Greene AA/25 25.00 60.00
286 Adrian Peterson AA/25
287 Peyton Manning AA/25 50.00 100.00
288 Calvin Johnson AA/25 30.00 60.00
289 Darren McFadden AA/25 30.00 60.00
290 A.J. Hawk AA/25 10.00 25.00

2009 Upper Deck Draft Edition Autographs Silver

*1-150 SILVER: .3X TO .8X COPPER AUTO
151-200 DRAFT HISTORY VETS NOT PRICED
201-230 SCOUTING REPORT/5 NOT PRICED
232-270 DUAL AUTO/15 NOT PRICED
271-285 ROOKIE ALL AMER/5 NOT PRICED
286-290 VETERAN AA/5 NOT PRICED
292-295 DRAFT CLASS/5 NOT PRICED

2009-10 Upper Deck Draft Edition Alma Mater

COMPLETE SET (24) 25.00 50.00
RANDOM INSERTS IN PACKS
UNPRICED BLACK PRINT RUN ONE SET
*BLUE: .6X TO 1.5X BASE HI
BLUE PRINT RUN 99 SER.#'d SETS
AMMR Matt Ryan 2.00 5.00
AMTB Terry Bradshaw 1.00 2.50

2009-10 Upper Deck Draft Edition Alma Mater Green

*GREEN: .75X TO 2X BASE HI
GREEN PRINT RUN 50 SER.#'d SETS

2009-10 Upper Deck Draft Edition Alma Mater Autographs

STATED PRINT RUN 10 TO 99 SER.#'d SETS
SOME UNPRICED DUE TO SCARCITY
AMMR Matt Ryan/25 50.00 100.00
AMTB Terry Bradshaw/10

2009-10 Upper Deck Draft Edition Alma Mater Red

*RED: 2X TO 5X BASE HI
RED PRINT RUN 25 SER.#'d SETS

1998 Upper Deck Encore

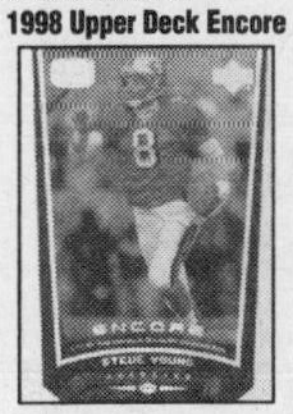

The 1998 Upper Deck Encore set was issued in one series totalling 150 cards and distributed in six-card packs with a suggested retail price of $3.99. The set features color player photos printed on cards with a special rainbow-foil treatment and contains the following subset with an insertion rate of 1:4 packs: Star Rookies (1-30).

COMPLETE SET (150) 75.00 150.00
1 Peyton Manning RC 20.00 40.00
2 Ryan Leaf RC 1.50 4.00
3 Andre Wadsworth RC 1.25 3.00
4 Charles Woodson RC 2.00 5.00
5 Curtis Enis RC .75 2.00
6 Fred Taylor RC 2.50 6.00
7 Duane Starks RC .75 2.00
8 Keith Brooking RC 1.50 4.00
9 Takeo Spikes RC 1.50 4.00
10 Kevin Dyson RC 1.50 4.00
11 Robert Edwards RC 1.25 3.00
12 Randy Moss RC 8.00 20.00
13 John Avery RC 1.25 3.00
14 Marcus Nash RC .75 2.00
15 Jerome Pathon RC 1.50 4.00
16 Jacquez Green RC 1.25 3.00
17 Robert Holcombe RC 1.25 3.00
18 Pat Johnson RC 1.25 3.00
19 Skip Hicks RC 1.25 3.00
20 Ahman Green RC 4.00 10.00
21 Brian Griese RC 3.00 8.00
22 Hines Ward RC 7.50 15.00
23 Tavian Banks RC 1.25 3.00
24 Tony Simmons RC 1.25 3.00
25 Rashaan Shehee RC 1.25 3.00
26 R.W. McQuarters RC 1.25 3.00
27 Jon Ritchie RC 1.25 3.00
28 Ryan Sutter RC .75 2.00
29 Tim Dwight RC 1.50 4.00
30 Charlie Batch RC 1.50 4.00
31 Chris Chandler .25 .60
32 Jamal Anderson .40 1.00
33 Terance Mathis .25 .60
34 Jake Plummer .40 1.00
35 Mario Bates .25 .60
36 Frank Sanders .25 .60
37 Adrian Murrell .25 .60
38 Jim Harbaugh .25 .60
39 Michael Jackson .15 .40
40 Jermaine Lewis .25 .60
41 Doug Flutie .40 1.00
42 Rob Johnson .25 .60
43 Antowain Smith .40 1.00
44 Eric Moulds .40 1.00
45 Thurman Thomas .40 1.00
46 Kevin Greene .15 .40
47 Fred Lane .15 .40
48 Rae Carruth .15 .40
49 William Floyd .15 .40
50 Erik Kramer .15 .40
51 Edgar Bennett .15 .40
52 Curtis Conway .25 .60
53 Bobby Engram .25 .60
54 Jeff Blake .25 .60
55 Carl Pickens .25 .60
56 Darnay Scott .15 .40
57 Corey Dillon .40 1.00
58 Troy Aikman .75 2.00
59 Michael Irvin .40 1.00
60 Emmitt Smith 1.25 3.00
61 Deion Sanders .40 1.00
62 John Elway 1.50 4.00
63 Terrell Davis .40 1.00
64 Rod Smith WR .25 .60
65 Shannon Sharpe .25 .60
66 Ed McCaffrey .25 .60
67 Barry Sanders 1.25 3.00
68 Scott Mitchell .15 .40
69 Herman Moore .25 .60
70 Johnnie Morton .25 .60
71 Brett Favre 1.50 4.00
72 Dorsey Levens .40 1.00
73 Reggie White .40 1.00
74 Antonio Freeman .40 1.00
75 Robert Brooks .25 .60
76 Marshall Faulk .50 1.25
77 Marvin Harrison .40 1.00
78 Mark Brunell .40 1.00
79 Keenan McCardell .25 .60
80 Jimmy Smith .25 .60
81 Elvis Grbac .25 .60
82 Andre Rison .25 .60
83 Tony Gonzalez .40 1.00
84 Derrick Thomas .40 1.00
85 Dan Marino 1.50 4.00
86 Karim Abdul-Jabbar .40 1.00
87 O.J. McDuffie .25 .60
88 Zach Thomas .40 1.00
89 Brad Johnson .40 1.00
90 Cris Carter .40 1.00
91 Jake Reed .25 .60
92 Robert Smith .40 1.00
93 John Randle .25 .60
94 Randall Cunningham .40 1.00
95 Drew Bledsoe .60 1.50
96 Terry Glenn .40 1.00
97 Ben Coates .25 .60
98 Danny Wuerffel .25 .60
99 Andre Hastings .15 .40
100 Troy Davis .15 .40
101 Danny Kanell .25 .60
102 Tiki Barber .40 1.00
103 Amani Toomer .25 .60
104 Vinny Testaverde .25 .60
105 Glenn Foley .25 .60
106 Curtis Martin .40 1.00
107 Keyshawn Johnson .40 1.00
108 Wayne Chrebet .40 1.00
109 Jeff George .25 .60
110 Napoleon Kaufman .40 1.00
111 Tim Brown .40 1.00
112 James Jett .15 .40
113 Bobby Hoying .25 .60
114 Charlie Garner .25 .60
115 Irving Fryar .25 .60
116 Kordell Stewart .40 1.00
117 Jerome Bettis .40 1.00
118 Will Blackwell .15 .40
119 Charles Johnson .15 .40
120 Tony Banks .25 .60
121 Amp Lee .15 .40
122 Isaac Bruce .40 1.00
123 Eddie Kennison .25 .60
124 Natrone Means .25 .60
125 Junior Seau .40 1.00
126 Bryan Still .15 .40
127 Steve Young .50 1.25
128 Jerry Rice .75 2.00
129 Garrison Hearst .40 1.00
130 J.J. Stokes .25 .60
131 Terrell Owens .40 1.00
132 Warren Moon .15 .40
133 Jon Kitna .40 1.00
134 Ricky Watters .25 .60
135 Joey Galloway .25 .60
136 Trent Dilfer .40 1.00
137 Warrick Dunn .40 1.00
138 Mike Alstott .40 1.00
139 Bert Emanuel .25 .60
140 Reidel Anthony .25 .60
141 Steve McNair .40 1.00
142 Yancey Thigpen .15 .40
143 Eddie George .40 1.00
144 Chris Sanders .15 .40
145 Gus Frerotte .15 .40
146 Terry Allen .40 1.00
147 Michael Westbrook .25 .60
148 Troy Aikman CL .40 1.00
149 Dan Marino CL .40 1.00
150 Randy Moss CL 1.50 6.00

1998 Upper Deck Encore F/X

*F/X VETS: 8X TO 20X BASIC CARDS
*F/X ROOKIES: 1.2X TO 3X BASIC CARDS
STATED PRINT RUN 125 SER.#'d SETS

1998 Upper Deck Encore Constant Threat

COMPLETE SET (15) 40.00 80.00
STATED ODDS 1:11
CT1 Dan Marino 4.00 10.00
CT2 Peyton Manning 10.00 20.00
CT3 Randy Moss 5.00 12.00
CT4 Brett Favre 4.00 10.00
CT5 Mark Brunell 1.00 2.50
CT6 John Elway 4.00 10.00
CT7 Ryan Leaf .75 2.00
CT8 Jake Plummer 1.00 2.50
CT9 Terrell Davis 1.00 2.50
CT10 Barry Sanders 3.00 8.00
CT11 Emmitt Smith 3.00 8.00
CT12 Curtis Martin 1.00 2.50
CT13 Eddie George 1.00 2.50
CT14 Warrick Dunn 1.00 2.50
CT15 Curtis Enis .40 1.00

1998 Upper Deck Encore Driving Forces

COMPLETE SET (14) 30.00 60.00
STATED ODDS 1:23
*F/X GOLD/1500: .8X TO 2X BASIC INSERTS
F1 Terrell Davis 1.50 4.00
F2 Barry Sanders 5.00 12.00
F3 Doug Flutie 1.50 4.00
F4 Mark Brunell 1.50 4.00
F5 Garrison Hearst 1.50 4.00
F6 Jamal Anderson 1.50 4.00
F7 Jerry Rice 3.00 8.00
F8 John Elway 6.00 15.00
F9 Robert Smith 1.50 4.00
F10 Kordell Stewart 1.50 4.00
F11 Eddie George 1.50 4.00
F12 Antonio Freeman 1.50 4.00
F13 Dan Marino 6.00 15.00
F14 Steve Young 2.00 5.00

1998 Upper Deck Encore Milestones

1 Peyton Manning/26 250.00 500.00
12 Randy Moss/17 125.00 250.00
60 Emmitt Smith/124 30.00 60.00
62 John Elway/60 60.00 100.00
63 Terrell Davis/30 15.00 40.00
67 Barry Sanders/100 40.00 80.00
85 Dan Marino/400 15.00 40.00
128 Jerry Rice/184 12.50 30.00

1998 Upper Deck Encore Rookie Encore

COMPLETE SET (10) 40.00 80.00
STATED ODDS 1:23
*F/X GOLD/500: 1.2X TO 3X BASIC INSERTS
RE1 Randy Moss 6.00 15.00
RE2 Peyton Manning 12.50 25.00
RE3 Charlie Batch .60 1.50
RE4 Fred Taylor 1.50 4.00
RE5 Robert Edwards .40 1.00
RE6 Curtis Enis .40 1.00
RE7 Robert Holcombe .40 1.00
RE8 Ryan Leaf .60 1.50
RE9 John Avery .40 1.00
RE10 Tim Dwight 1.00 2.50

1998 Upper Deck Encore Super Powers

COMPLETE SET (15) 40.00 80.00
STATED ODDS 1:11
S1 Dan Marino 4.00 10.00
S2 Napoleon Kaufman 1.00 2.50
S3 Brett Favre 4.00 10.00
S4 John Elway 4.00 10.00
S5 Randy Moss 5.00 12.00
S6 Kordell Stewart 1.00 2.50
S7 Mark Brunell 1.00 2.50
S8 Peyton Manning 10.00 20.00
S9 Emmitt Smith 3.00 8.00
S10 Jake Plummer 1.00 2.50
S11 Eddie George 1.00 2.50
S12 Warrick Dunn 1.00 2.50
S13 Jerome Bettis 1.00 2.50
S14 Terrell Davis 1.00 2.50
S15 Fred Taylor 1.25 3.00

1998 Upper Deck Encore Superstar Encore

COMPLETE SET (6) 20.00 50.00
STATED ODDS 1:23
*F/X VETS/25: 12X TO 30X BASIC INSERTS
*F/X ROOKIES/25: 6X TO 15X
RR1 Brett Favre 4.00 10.00
RR2 Barry Sanders 3.00 8.00
RR3 Mark Brunell 1.00 2.50
RR4 Emmitt Smith 3.00 8.00
RR5 Randy Moss 6.00 15.00
RR6 Terrell Davis 1.00 2.50

1998 Upper Deck Encore UD Authentics

COMPLETE SET (5) 250.00 500.00
STATED ODDS 1:288
DM2 Dan Marino 60.00 120.00
JM2 Joe Montana 50.00 100.00
(49ers photo)
MB2 Mark Brunell 15.00 40.00
RM Randy Moss 90.00 150.00
TD Terrell Davis 15.00 40.00

1999 Upper Deck Encore

Released as a 225-card set, the 1999 Upper Deck Encore set is comprised of 180 regular player cards and 45 short printed Star Rookies cards found one in every eight packs. The base set parallels the regular issue 1999 Upper Deck set with an enhanced rainbow holo-foil card stock. Encore was packaged in 24-pack boxes with six cards per pack and carried a suggested retail price of $3.99.

COMPLETE SET (225) 50.00 120.00
COMP.SET w/o SP's (180) 15.00 40.00
1 Jake Plummer .25 .60
2 Adrian Murrell .25 .60
3 Rob Moore .20 .50
4 Simeon Rice .20 .50
5 Andre Wadsworth .20 .50
6 Frank Sanders .20 .50
7 Tim Dwight .25 .60
8 Chris Chandler .25 .60
9 Jamal Anderson .25 .60
10 O.J. Santiago .20 .50
11 Tony Graziani .20 .50
12 Terance Mathis .20 .50
13 Priest Holmes .30 .75
14 Stoney Case .20 .50
15 Ray Lewis .30 .75
16 Peter Boulware .20 .50
17 Errict Rhett .20 .50
18 Jermaine Lewis .20 .50
19 Eric Moulds .25 .60
20 Doug Flutie .30 .75
21 Antowain Smith .20 .50
22 Rob Johnson .25 .60
23 Bruce Smith .30 .75
24 Andre Reed .30 .75
25 Wesley Walls .25 .60
26 Tim Biakabutuka .25 .60
27 Fred Lane .20 .50
28 Steve Beuerlein .25 .60
29 Muhsin Muhammad .25 .60
30 Rae Carruth .20 .50
31 Bobby Engram .25 .60
32 Curtis Enis .20 .50
33 Edgar Bennett .25 .60
34 Curtis Conway .25 .60
35 Shane Matthews .20 .50
36 Tony McGee .20 .50
37 Darnay Scott .20 .50
38 Jeff Blake .25 .60
39 Corey Dillon .25 .60
40 Ki-Jana Carter .20 .50
41 Ty Detmer .25 .60
42 Leslie Shepherd .20 .50
43 Terry Kirby .20 .50
44 Antonio Langham .20 .50
45 Jamir Miller .20 .50
46 Marc Edwards .25 .60
47 Troy Aikman .50 1.25
48 Rocket Ismail .25 .60
49 Emmitt Smith .75 2.00
50 Michael Irvin .30 .75
51 Deion Sanders .30 .75
52 Greg Ellis .20 .50
53 Bubby Brister .20 .50
54 Terrell Davis .30 .75
55 Ed McCaffrey .25 .60
56 Rod Smith .25 .60
57 Shannon Sharpe .30 .75
58 Brian Griese .25 .60
59 Charlie Batch .25 .60
60 Germane Crowell .20 .50
61 Johnnie Morton .25 .60
62 Robert Porcher .20 .50
63 Ron Rivers .20 .50
64 Herman Moore .25 .60
65 Brett Favre 1.00 2.50
66 Bill Schroeder .25 .60
67 Antonio Freeman .25 .60
68 Dorsey Levens .25 .60
69 Desmond Howard .25 .60
70 Vonnie Holliday .20 .50
71 Peyton Manning 1.00 2.50
72 Jerome Pathon .20 .50
73 Marvin Harrison .30 .75
74 Ken Dilger .20 .50
75 E.G. Green .20 .50
76 Cornelius Bennett .25 .60
77 Mark Brunell .25 .60
78 Fred Taylor .25 .60
79 Jimmy Smith .25 .60
80 James Stewart .20 .50
81 Keenan McCardell .25 .60
82 Carnell Lake .25 .60
83 Elvis Grbac .20 .50
84 Tony Gonzalez .30 .75
85 Andre Rison .25 .60
86 Derrick Thomas .30 .75
87 Warren Moon .30 .75
88 Derrick Alexander WR .20 .50
89 Dan Marino 1.00 2.50
90 O.J. McDuffie .25 .60
91 Karim Abdul-Jabbar .25 .60
92 Sam Madison .20 .50
93 Zach Thomas .30 .75
94 Tony Martin .25 .60
95 Randall Cunningham .30 .75
96 Randy Moss .30 .75
97 Cris Carter .30 .75
98 Jake Reed .25 .60
99 John Randle .25 .60
100 Robert Smith .25 .60
101 Drew Bledsoe .30 .75
102 Ben Coates .25 .60
103 Terry Glenn .25 .60
104 Tony Simmons .20 .50
105 Terry Allen .25 .60
106 Danny Wuerffel .25 .60
107 Cameron Cleeland .20 .50
108 Eddie Kennison .25 .60
109 Billy Joe Hobert .20 .50
110 Andre Hastings .20 .50
111 Kent Graham .20 .50
112 Tiki Barber .30 .75
113 Gary Brown .20 .50
114 Ike Hilliard .25 .60
115 Jason Sehorn .25 .60
116 Kerry Collins .25 .60
117 Vinny Testaverde .25 .60
118 Wayne Chrebet .25 .60
119 Curtis Martin .30 .75
120 Rick Mirer .25 .60
121 Aaron Glenn .20 .50
122 Keyshawn Johnson .25 .60
123 Rich Gannon .25 .60
124 Tim Brown .30 .75
125 Darrell Russell .20 .50
126 Tyrone Wheatley .25 .60
127 Charles Woodson .30 .75
128 Napoleon Kaufman .20 .50
129 Duce Staley .25 .60
130 Doug Pederson .20 .50
131 Kevin Turner .20 .50
132 Charles Johnson .20 .50
133 Jerome Bettis .30 .75
134 Courtney Hawkins .20 .50
135 Kordell Stewart .25 .60
136 Richard Huntley .20 .50
137 Levon Kirkland .20 .50
138 Hines Ward .30 .75
139 Kurt Warner RC 5.00 12.00
140 Marshall Faulk .30 .75
141 Az-Zahir Hakim .20 .50
142 Amp Lee .20 .50
143 Isaac Bruce .30 .75
144 Kevin Carter .20 .50
145 Jim Harbaugh .25 .60
146 Junior Seau .30 .75
147 Natrone Means .25 .60
148 Rodney Harrison .25 .60
149 Mikhael Ricks .20 .50
150 Erik Kramer .25 .60
151 Steve Young .40 1.00
152 Terrell Owens .30 .75
153 Jerry Rice .60 1.50
154 J.J. Stokes .20 .50
155 Jeff Garcia RC 3.00 8.00
156 Lawrence Phillips .25 .60
157 Jon Kitna .25 .60
158 Derrick Mayes .20 .50
159 Ricky Watters .25 .60
160 Chad Brown .20 .50
161 Shawn Springs .20 .50
162 Sean Dawkins .20 .50
163 Trent Dilfer .25 .60
164 Reidel Anthony .20 .50
165 Bert Emanuel .25 .60
166 Warrick Dunn .25 .60
167 Jacquez Green .20 .50
168 Mike Alstott .30 .75
169 Eddie George .25 .60
170 Steve McNair .30 .75
171 Kevin Dyson .20 .50
172 Frank Wycheck .25 .60
173 Blaine Bishop .20 .50
174 Yancey Thigpen .20 .50
175 Brad Johnson .25 .60
176 Michael Westbrook .20 .50
177 Skip Hicks .20 .50
178 Brian Mitchell .25 .60
179 Dana Stubblefield .20 .50
180 Stephen Davis .25 .60
181 Champ Bailey RC 2.50 6.00
182 Chris McAlister RC 1.00 2.50
183 Jevon Kearse RC 1.25 3.00
184 Ebenezer Ekuban RC .75 2.00
185 Chris Claiborne RC .75 2.00
186 Andy Katzenmoyer RC 1.00 2.50
187 Tim Couch RC 1.25 3.00
188 Daunte Culpepper RC 1.25 3.00
189 Akili Smith RC 1.00 2.50
190 Donovan McNabb RC 3.00 8.00
191 Sean Bennett RC .75 2.00
192 Brock Huard RC 1.00 2.50
193 Cade McNown RC 1.00 2.50
194 Shaun King RC 1.00 2.50
195 Joe Germaine RC 1.00 2.50
196 Ricky Williams RC 2.00 5.00
197 Edgerrin James RC 1.50 4.00
198 Sedrick Irvin RC .75 2.00
199 Kevin Faulk RC 1.25 3.00
200 Rob Konrad RC .75 2.00
201 James Johnson RC .75 2.00
202 Amos Zereoue RC 1.00 2.50
203 Torry Holt RC 2.00 5.00
204 D'Wayne Bates RC .75 2.00
205 David Boston RC 1.00 2.50
206 Dameane Douglas RC .75 2.00
207 Troy Edwards RC 1.00 2.50
208 Kevin Johnson RC 1.00 2.50
209 Peerless Price RC 1.00 2.50
210 Antoine Winfield RC .75 2.00
211 Mike Cloud RC .75 2.00
212 Joe Montgomery RC .75 2.00
213 Jermaine Fazande RC .75 2.00
214 Scott Covington RC .75 2.00
215 Aaron Brooks RC 1.25 3.00
216 Terry Jackson RC .75 2.00
217 Cecil Collins RC .75 2.00
218 Olandis Gary RC 1.25 3.00
219 Craig Yeast RC .75 2.00
220 Karsten Bailey RC .75 2.00
221 Reginald Kelly RC .75 2.00
222 Travis McGriff RC .75 2.00
223 Jeff Paulk RC .75 2.00
224 Jim Kleinsasser RC 1.25 3.00
225 Jason Tucker RC 1.00 2.50
WPE W.Payton Jsy AU/34 1,000.00 1,500.00

1999 Upper Deck Encore F/X

*STARS: 8X TO 20X BASIC CARDS
*RCs: 1X TO 2.5X
STATED PRINT RUN 100 SER.#'d SETS

1999 Upper Deck Encore F/X Gold

STATED PRINT RUN 1 SER.#'d SET

1999 Upper Deck Encore Electric Currents

COMPLETE SET (20) 10.00 20.00
STATED ODDS 1:6
EC1 Steve Young 1.00 2.50
EC2 Doug Flutie .75 2.00
EC3 Jon Kitna .75 2.00
EC4 Randall Cunningham .75 2.00
EC5 Curtis Enis .30 .75
EC6 Jerry Rice 1.50 4.00
EC7 Antonio Freeman .75 2.00
EC8 Keyshawn Johnson .75 2.00
EC9 Steve McNair .75 2.00
EC10 Kordell Stewart .50 1.25
EC11 Drew Bledsoe 1.00 2.50
EC12 Corey Dillon .75 2.00
EC13 Vinny Testaverde .50 1.25
EC14 Tim Brown .75 2.00
EC15 Antowain Smith .75 2.00
EC16 Charlie Batch .75 2.00
EC17 Stephen Davis .75 2.00
EC18 Isaac Bruce .75 2.00
EC19 Curtis Martin .75 2.00
EC20 Ricky Watters .50 1.25

1999 Upper Deck Encore Game Used Helmets

COMPLETE SET (20) 300.00 600.00
STATED ODDS 1:575
HAS Akili Smith 10.00 25.00
HBF Brett Favre 40.00 100.00
HBH Brock Huard 10.00 25.00
HCB Champ Bailey 12.50 30.00
HCC Cecil Collins 10.00 25.00
HCM Cade McNown 10.00 25.00
HDB David Boston 10.00 25.00
HDC Daunte Culpepper 30.00 80.00
HDM Dan Marino 40.00 100.00
HDW D'Wayne Bates 10.00 25.00
HEJ Edgerrin James 25.00 60.00
HJR Jerry Rice 25.00 60.00
HKF Kevin Faulk 10.00 25.00
HKJ Kevin Johnson 10.00 25.00
HMB Mark Brunell 10.00 25.00
HMC Donovan McNabb 30.00 80.00
HTC Tim Couch 10.00 25.00
HTD Terrell Davis 10.00 25.00
HTE Troy Edwards 10.00 25.00
HTH Torry Holt 20.00 50.00

1999 Upper Deck Encore Live Wires

COMPLETE SET (15) 20.00 40.00
STATED ODDS 1:11
L1 Jake Plummer .60 1.50
L2 Jamal Anderson 1.00 2.50
L3 Emmitt Smith 2.00 5.00
L4 John Elway 3.00 8.00
L5 Barry Sanders 3.00 8.00
L6 Brett Favre 3.00 8.00
L7 Mark Brunell 1.00 2.50
L8 Fred Taylor 1.00 2.50
L9 Randy Moss 2.00 5.00
L10 Drew Bledsoe 1.25 3.00
L11 Keyshawn Johnson 1.00 2.50
L12 Jerome Bettis 1.00 2.50
L13 Kordell Stewart .60 1.50
L14 Terrell Owens 1.00 2.50
L15 Eddie George 1.00 2.50

1999 Upper Deck Encore Seize the Game

COMPLETE SET (30) 50.00 100.00
SG1-SG20 STATED ODDS 1:20
SG21-SG30 STATED ODDS 1:23
*SG1-SG20 GOLD/250: 1X TO 2.5X
*SG21-SG30 GOLD/250: 1.2X TO 3X
SG1 Donovan McNabb 3.00 8.00
SG2 Keyshawn Johnson 1.50 4.00
SG3 Eddie George 1.50 4.00
SG4 Randall Cunningham 1.50 4.00
SG5 Charlie Batch 1.50 4.00
SG6 Curtis Martin 1.50 4.00
SG7 Edgerrin James 2.50 6.00
SG8 Jake Plummer 1.00 2.50
SG9 Drew Bledsoe 2.00 5.00
SG10 Marshall Faulk 2.00 5.00
SG11 Fred Taylor 1.50 4.00
SG12 Terrell Owens 1.50 4.00
SG13 Jerome Bettis 1.50 4.00
SG14 Antonio Freeman 1.50 4.00
SG15 Corey Dillon 1.50 4.00

SG16 Jerry Rice 3.00 8.00
SG17 Curtis Enis .60 1.50
SG18 Warrick Dunn 1.50 4.00
SG19 Kordell Stewart 1.00 2.50
SG20 Jamal Anderson 1.50 4.00
SG21 Terrell Davis 1.25 3.00
SG22 Randy Moss 2.50 6.00
SG23 Troy Aikman 2.50 6.00
SG24 Dan Marino 4.00 10.00
SG25 Ricky Williams 1.00 2.50
SG26 Peyton Manning 3.00 8.00
SG27 Steve Young 1.50 4.00
SG28 Tim Couch .60 1.50
SG29 Emmitt Smith 2.50 6.00
SG30 Brett Favre 4.00 10.00

1999 Upper Deck Encore UD Authentics

STATED ODDS 1:144
BH Brock Huard 7.50 20.00
CM Cade McNown 7.50 20.00
DB David Boston 7.50 20.00
EJ Edgerrin James 20.00 50.00
JN Joe Namath 50.00 120.00
KF Kevin Faulk 10.00 25.00
KW Kurt Warner 40.00 80.00
MB Mark Brunell 10.00 25.00
PM Peyton Manning 60.00 120.00
RM Randy Moss 30.00 80.00
SK Shaun King EXCH 1.25 3.00
TA Troy Aikman 30.00 80.00
TC Tim Couch 7.50 20.00
TE Troy Edwards 7.50 20.00
TH Torry Holt 12.50 30.00

1999 Upper Deck Encore Upper Realm

COMPLETE SET (10) 12.50 30.00
STATED ODDS 1:12
UR1 Randy Moss 1.50 4.00
UR2 Warrick Dunn .75 2.00
UR3 Stephen Davis .75 2.00
UR4 Peyton Manning 2.00 5.00
UR5 Tim Biakabutuka .50 1.25
UR6 Steve Young 1.00 2.50
UR7 Kurt Warner 4.00 10.00
UR8 Steve McNair .75 2.00
UR9 Dan Marino 2.50 6.00
UR10 Jake Plummer .50 1.25

2000 Upper Deck Encore

Released in early December 2000, Encore features a 270-card set consisting of 222 regular issue cards, 45 Star Rookie cards inserted at the rate of one in 6, and three checklist cards. The base card design parallels that of the regular issue Upper Deck set from earlier this year with cards enhanced with gold foil highlights and a rainbow holofoil card stock. Encore was packaged in 24-pack boxes with packs containing five cards each and carried a suggested retail price of $4.99. An Update set of 13-cards was issued in April 2001 as part of 3-card packs distributed directly to Upper Deck hobby accounts.

COMPLETE SET (270) 50.00 120.00
COMP.SET w/o SP's (225) 6.00 15.00
223-267 ROOKIE ODDS 1:6
1 Jake Plummer .20 .50
2 Michael Pittman .15 .40
3 Rob Moore .15 .40
4 David Boston .15 .40
5 Frank Sanders .15 .40
6 Aeneas Williams .15 .40
7 Kwamie Lassiter .15 .40
8 Rob Fredrickson .15 .40
9 Tim Dwight .20 .50
10 Chris Chandler .20 .50
11 Jamal Anderson .20 .50
12 Shawn Jefferson .15 .40
13 Brian Finneran RC .25 .60
14 Terance Mathis .15 .40
15 Bob Christian .15 .40
16 Qadry Ismail .20 .50
17 Jermaine Lewis .15 .40
18 Rod Woodson .25 .60
19 Michael McCrary .15 .40
20 Tony Banks .15 .40
21 Peter Boulware .15 .40
22 Shannon Sharpe .25 .60
23 Peerless Price .20 .50
24 Rob Johnson .20 .50
25 Eric Moulds .20 .50
26 Doug Flutie .25 .60
27 Jeremy McDaniel .15 .40
28 Antowain Smith .20 .50
29 Shawn Bryson .15 .40
30 Muhsin Muhammad .20 .50
31 Donald Hayes .15 .40
32 Steve Beuerlein .20 .50
33 Reggie White .25 .60
34 Tim Biakabutuka .20 .50
35 Michael Bates .15 .40
36 Chuck Smith .15 .40
37 Wesley Walls .15 .40
38 Cade McNown .15 .40
39 Curtis Enis .15 .40
40 Marcus Robinson .20 .50
41 Eddie Kennison .15 .40
42 Bobby Engram .20 .50
43 Glyn Milburn .15 .40
44 Marty Booker .20 .50
45 Akili Smith .15 .40
46 Corey Dillon .20 .50
47 James Allen .15 .40
48 Tremain Mack .15 .40
49 Damon Griffin .15 .40
50 Takeo Spikes .15 .40
51 Tony McGee .15 .40
52 Tim Couch .20 .50
53 Kevin Johnson .15 .40
54 Darrin Chiaverini .15 .40
55 Jamir Miller .15 .40
56 Errict Rhett .20 .50
57 Aaron Shea RC .20 .50
58 Kevin Thompson RC .15 .40
59 Troy Aikman .40 1.00
60 Emmitt Smith .60 1.50
61 Rocket Ismail .20 .50
62 Jason Tucker .15 .40
63 Chris Brazzell RC .15 .40
64 Joey Galloway .20 .50
65 Wane McGarity .15 .40
66 Terrell Davis .25 .60
67 Olandis Gary .20 .50
68 Brian Griese .20 .50
69 Gus Frerotte .20 .50
70 Byron Chamberlain .15 .40
71 Ed McCaffrey .20 .50
72 Rod Smith .20 .50
73 Al Wilson .15 .40
74 Charlie Batch .20 .50
75 Germane Crowell .15 .40
76 Sedrick Irvin .15 .40
77 Johnnie Morton .20 .50
78 Robert Porcher .15 .40
79 Herman Moore .20 .50
80 James Stewart .15 .40
81 Brett Favre .75 2.00
82 Antonio Freeman .20 .50
83 Bill Schroeder .20 .50
84 Dorsey Levens .20 .50
85 Herbert Goodman RC .15 .40
86 Ahman Green .20 .50
87 Matt Hasselbeck .25 .60
88 Peyton Manning .60 1.50
89 Edgerrin James .25 .60
90 Marvin Harrison .25 .60
91 Basil Mitchell .15 .40
92 Terrence Wilkins .15 .40
93 Karim Abdul-Jabbar .15 .40
94 Ken Dilger .15 .40
95 Mark Brunell .20 .50
96 Fred Taylor .25 .60
97 Jimmy Smith .20 .50
98 Keenan McCardell .20 .50
99 Stacey Mack .15 .40
100 Jonathan Quinn .15 .40
101 Kyle Brady .15 .40
102 Hardy Nickerson .15 .40
103 Elvis Grbac .15 .40
104 Tony Gonzalez .25 .60
105 Derrick Alexander WR .15 .40
106 Tony Richardson RC .20 .50
107 Michael Cloud .15 .40
108 Donnie Edwards .15 .40
109 Jay Fiedler .20 .50
110 James Johnson .15 .40
111 Tony Martin .20 .50
112 Damon Huard .20 .50
113 Lamar Smith .15 .40
114 Thurman Thomas .25 .60
115 Mike Quinn .15 .40
116 Oronde Gadsden .20 .50
117 Randy Moss .25 .60
118 Robert Smith .20 .50
119 Cris Carter .25 .60
120 Matthew Hatchette .15 .40
121 Daunte Culpepper .20 .50
122 Moe Williams .15 .40
123 Drew Bledsoe .25 .60
124 Terry Glenn .20 .50
125 Troy Brown .20 .50
126 Kevin Faulk .20 .50
127 Lawyer Milloy .15 .40
128 Ricky Williams .25 .60
129 Keith Poole .15 .40
130 Jake Reed .20 .50
131 Jake Delhomme RC .60 1.50
132 Jeff Blake .20 .50
133 Andrew Glover .15 .40
134 Kerry Collins .20 .50
135 Amani Toomer .20 .50
136 Joe Montgomery .15 .40
137 Ike Hilliard .20 .50
138 Tiki Barber .25 .60
139 Pete Mitchell .15 .40
140 Ray Lucas .15 .40
141 Mo Lewis .15 .40
142 Curtis Martin .25 .60
143 Vinny Testaverde .20 .50
144 Wayne Chrebet .20 .50
145 Dedric Ward .15 .40
146 Tim Brown .25 .60
147 Rich Gannon .20 .50
148 Tyrone Wheatley .15 .40
149 Napoleon Kaufman .20 .50
150 Charles Woodson .25 .60
151 Darrell Russell .15 .40
152 James Jett .20 .50
153 Rickey Dudley .15 .40
154 Jon Ritchie .15 .40
155 Duce Staley .20 .50
156 Donovan McNabb .25 .60
157 Torrance Small .15 .40
158 Ron Powlus RC .25 .60
159 Mike Mamula .15 .40
160 Dameane Douglas .15 .40
161 Charles Johnson .15 .40
162 Kent Graham .15 .40
163 Troy Edwards .15 .40
164 Jerome Bettis .25 .60
165 Hines Ward .25 .60
166 Kordell Stewart .20 .50
167 Levon Kirkland .15 .40
168 Bobby Shaw RC .20 .50
169 Marshall Faulk .25 .60
170 Kurt Warner .40 1.00
171 Torry Holt .25 .60
172 Isaac Bruce .25 .60
173 Kevin Carter .15 .40
174 Az-Zahir Hakim .15 .40
175 Ricky Proehl .15 .40
176 Robert Chancey .15 .40
177 Curtis Conway .20 .50
178 Freddie Jones .15 .40
179 Junior Seau .25 .60
180 Jeff Graham .15 .40
181 Reggie Jones RC .15 .40
182 Rodney Harrison .20 .50
183 Rick Mirer .15 .40
184 Jerry Rice .50 1.25
185 Charlie Garner .20 .50
186 Terrell Owens .25 .60
187 Jeff Garcia .20 .50
188 Fred Beasley .15 .40
189 J.J. Stokes .20 .50
190 Ricky Watters .20 .50
191 Jon Kitna .20 .50
192 Derrick Mayes .15 .40
193 Sean Dawkins .15 .40
194 Charlie Rogers .15 .40
195 Brock Huard .15 .40
196 Cortez Kennedy .15 .40
197 Christian Fauria .15 .40
198 Warrick Dunn .20 .50
199 Shaun King .15 .40
200 Mike Alstott .25 .60
201 Warren Sapp .20 .50
202 Jacquez Green .15 .40
203 Reidel Anthony .15 .40
204 Dave Moore .15 .40
205 Keyshawn Johnson .20 .50
206 Eddie George .20 .50
207 Steve McNair .25 .60
208 Billy Volek RC .25 .60
209 Jevon Kearse .20 .50
210 Yancey Thigpen .15 .40
211 Frank Wycheck .20 .50
212 Carl Pickens .20 .50
213 Neil O'Donnell .15 .40
214 Brad Johnson .20 .50
215 Stephen Davis .20 .50
216 Michael Westbrook .15 .40
217 Albert Connell .15 .40
218 Aaron Stecker RC .20 .50
219 Bruce Smith .25 .60
220 Stephen Alexander .15 .40
221 Jeff George .20 .50
222 Adrian Murrell .15 .40
223 Courtney Brown RC .75 2.00
224 John Engelberger RC .60 1.50
225 Deltha O'Neal RC .75 2.00
226 Corey Simon RC .75 2.00
227 R.Jay Soward RC .60 1.50
228 Chris Samuels RC .75 2.00
229 Avion Black RC .60 1.50
230 Doug Chapman RC .60 1.50
231 Darrell Jackson RC .75 2.00
232 Chris Cole RC .75 2.00
233 Trevor Gaylor RC .60 1.50
234 Chad Morton RC 1.00 2.50
235 Chris Redman RC .75 2.00
236 Joe Hamilton RC .60 1.50
237 Chad Pennington RC 1.50 4.00
238 Tee Martin RC 1.00 2.50
239 Giovanni Carmazzi RC .60 1.50
240 Tim Rattay RC .75 2.00
241 Ron Dayne RC 1.00 2.50
242 Shaun Alexander RC 1.25 3.00
243 Thomas Jones RC 1.25 3.00
244 Reuben Droughns RC 1.00 2.50
245 Jamal Lewis RC 1.00 2.50
246 Michael Wiley RC .60 1.50
247 J.R. Redmond RC .60 1.50
248 Travis Prentice RC .75 2.00
249 Todd Husak RC .60 1.50
250 Trung Canidate RC .75 2.00
251 Brian Urlacher RC 4.00 10.00
252 Anthony Becht RC .75 2.00
253 Bubba Franks RC 1.00 2.50
254 Tom Brady RC 25.00 50.00
255 Peter Warrick RC 1.00 2.50
256 Plaxico Burress RC 1.00 2.50
257 Sylvester Morris RC .60 1.50
258 Dez White RC .75 2.00
259 Travis Taylor RC .75 2.00
260 Todd Pinkston RC .60 1.50
261 Dennis Northcutt RC .75 2.00
262 Jerry Porter RC 1.00 2.50
263 Laveranues Coles RC 1.00 2.50
264 Danny Farmer RC .60 1.50
265 Curtis Keaton RC .60 1.50
266 Windrell Hayes RC .60 1.50
267 Ron Dugans RC .60 1.50
268 Steve McNair CL .20 .50
269 Jake Plummer CL .15 .40
270 Antonio Freeman CL .15 .40
271 Brad Hoover RC .75 2.00
272 Charles Lee RC .60 1.50
273 Deon Dyer RC .60 1.50
274 Doug Johnson RC .75 2.00
275 JaJuan Dawson RC .60 1.50
276 Jarious Jackson RC .75 2.00
277 Larry Foster RC .60 1.50
278 Mike Anderson RC 1.00 2.50
279 Ron Dixon RC .60 1.50
280 Sammy Morris RC .75 2.00
281 Shyrone Stith RC .60 1.50
282 Spergon Wynn RC .75 2.00
283 Troy Walters RC .60 1.50

2000 Upper Deck Encore Highlight Zone

COMPLETE SET (10) 3.00 8.00
STATED ODDS 1:7
HZ1 Eddie George .40 1.00
HZ2 Steve McNair .50 1.25
HZ3 Kevin Dyson .40 1.00
HZ4 Kurt Warner .75 2.00
HZ5 Emmitt Smith 1.25 3.00
HZ6 Brad Johnson .40 1.00
HZ7 Curtis Martin .50 1.25
HZ8 Ray Lucas .30 .75
HZ9 Akili Smith .30 .75
HZ10 Jake Plummer .40 1.00

2000 Upper Deck Encore Proving Ground

COMPLETE SET (10) 2.50 6.00
STATED ODDS 1:7
PG1 Marcus Robinson .40 1.00
PG2 Stephen Davis .40 1.00
PG3 Daunte Culpepper .40 1.00
PG4 Jevon Kearse .40 1.00
PG5 Marshall Faulk .50 1.25
PG6 Marvin Harrison .50 1.25
PG7 Germane Crowell .30 .75
PG8 Darnay Scott .40 1.00
PG9 Duce Staley .40 1.00
PG10 Warrick Dunn .40 1.00

2000 Upper Deck Encore Rookie Combo Jerseys

STATED ODDS 1:287
RC1 Dez White 40.00 80.00
Brian Urlacher
RC2 Tee Martin 10.00 25.00
Plaxico Burress
RC3 Jerry Porter 10.00 25.00
Sylvester Morris
RC4 Peter Warrick 10.00 25.00
Courtney Brown
RC5 Peter Warrick 6.00 15.00
Curtis Keaton
RC6 Travis Prentice 8.00 20.00
Dennis Northcutt
RC7 Travis Taylor 8.00 20.00
Jamal Lewis
Chris Redman
RC8 Ron Dayne 10.00 25.00
Thomas Jones
Shaun Alexander
RC9 Chad Pennington 10.00 25.00
Laveranues Coles
Anthony Becht

2000 Upper Deck Encore Rookie Helmets

STATED ODDS 1:287
HAS Shaun Alexander 8.00 20.00
HBF Bubba Franks 6.00 15.00
HBU Brian Urlacher 25.00 60.00
HCB Courtney Brown 5.00 12.00
HCK Curtis Keaton 4.00 10.00
HCP Chad Pennington 10.00 25.00
HCR Chris Redman 5.00 12.00
HCS Corey Simon 5.00 12.00
HDF Danny Farmer 4.00 10.00
HDN Dennis Northcutt 5.00 12.00
HDR Reuben Droughns 6.00 15.00
HDU Ron Dugans 4.00 10.00
HDW Dez White 5.00 12.00
HJL Jamal Lewis 6.00 15.00
HJP Jerry Porter 6.00 15.00
HJR J.R. Redmond 4.00 10.00
HLC Laveranues Coles 6.00 15.00
HPB Plaxico Burress 6.00 15.00
HPI Todd Pinkston 4.00 10.00
HPW Peter Warrick 6.00 15.00
HRD Ron Dayne 6.00 15.00
HRJ R.Jay Soward 4.00 10.00
HSM Sylvester Morris 4.00 10.00
HTJ Thomas Jones 8.00 20.00
HTM Tee Martin 6.00 15.00
HTP Travis Prentice 5.00 12.00
HTT Travis Taylor 5.00 12.00
HTW Anthony Becht 5.00 12.00

2000 Upper Deck Encore Rookie Helmets Autographs

STATED PRINT RUN 25 SER.#'d SETS
AHBU Brian Urlacher 100.00 200.00
AHCB Courtney Brown 15.00 40.00
AHCP Chad Pennington 50.00 100.00
AHCR Chris Redman 15.00 40.00
AHDF Danny Farmer 12.00 30.00
AHDN Dennis Northcutt 15.00 40.00
AHDU Ron Dugans 12.00 30.00
AHDW Dez White 15.00 40.00
AHLC Laveranues Coles 20.00 50.00
AHPB Plaxico Burress 40.00 80.00
AHRD Ron Dayne 20.00 50.00
AHSA Shaun Alexander 25.00 60.00
AHSM Sylvester Morris 12.00 30.00
AHTP Travis Prentice 15.00 40.00

2000 Upper Deck Encore UD Authentics

STATED ODDS 1:23
BU Brian Urlacher 25.00 60.00
CB Courtney Brown 5.00 12.00
CC Chris Coleman 4.00 10.00
CM Corey Moore 4.00 10.00
CP Chad Pennington 10.00 25.00
CR Chris Redman 5.00 12.00
DF Danny Farmer 4.00 10.00
DJ Darrell Jackson 5.00 12.00
DN Dennis Northcutt 5.00 12.00
DU Ron Dugans 4.00 10.00
DW Dez White 5.00 12.00
DX Ron Dixon 4.00 10.00
JO Doug Johnson 5.00 12.00
KC Kwame Cavil 4.00 10.00
LC Laveranues Coles 6.00 15.00
MA Mike Anderson 6.00 15.00
MW Michael Wiley 4.00 10.00
PB Plaxico Burress 8.00 20.00
RD Ron Dayne 6.00 15.00
SA Shaun Alexander 10.00 25.00
SG Sherrod Gideon 4.00 10.00
SM Sylvester Morris 4.00 10.00
TC Trung Canidate 5.00 12.00
TG Trevor Gaylor 4.00 10.00
TM Tee Martin 6.00 15.00
TP Travis Prentice 5.00 12.00
TR Tim Rattay 5.00 12.00
TW Troy Walters 4.00 10.00

2005 Upper Deck ESPN

This 160-card set was released through Upper Deck's retail channels in September, 2005. The set was issued in nine-card packs with an $2.99 SRP which came 24 packs to a box. Cards numbered 1-100 feature veterans in team alphabetical order while cards numbered 101-160 feature 2005 rookies. Those rookies were inserted into packs at a stated rate of one in four.

COMP.SET w/o RC's (100) 10.00 25.00
DRAFT PICK STATED ODDS 1:4
1 Larry Fitzgerald .30 .75
2 Josh McCown .25 .60
3 Anquan Boldin .25 .60
4 Michael Vick .30 .75
5 Warrick Dunn .25 .60
6 Peerless Price .20 .50
7 Alge Crumpler .25 .60
8 Jamal Lewis .25 .60
9 Kyle Boller .25 .60
10 Derrick Mason .25 .60
11 Willis McGahee .30 .75
12 J.P. Losman .20 .50
13 Eric Moulds .20 .50
14 Jake Delhomme .25 .60
15 Steve Smith .30 .75
16 DeShaun Foster .25 .60
17 Muhsin Muhammad .25 .60
18 Thomas Jones .30 .75
19 Rex Grossman .25 .60
20 Chad Johnson .25 .60
21 Carson Palmer .30 .75
22 Rudi Johnson .25 .60
23 Lee Suggs .20 .50
24 Kellen Winslow .25 .60
25 Luke McCown .20 .50
26 Julius Jones .20 .50
27 Keyshawn Johnson .25 .60
28 Drew Bledsoe .30 .75
29 Tatum Bell .20 .50
30 Jake Plummer .25 .60
31 Rod Smith .25 .60
32 Roy Williams WR .25 .60
33 Kevin Jones .20 .50
34 Joey Harrington .25 .60
35 Jeff Garcia .25 .60
36 Brett Favre .75 2.00
37 Javon Walker .20 .50
38 Ahman Green .25 .60
39 David Carr .20 .50
40 Andre Johnson .30 .75
41 Domanick Davis .20 .50
42 Peyton Manning .60 1.50
43 Edgerrin James .25 .60
44 Marvin Harrison .30 .75
45 Byron Leftwich .25 .60
46 Fred Taylor .25 .60
47 Jimmy Smith .25 .60
48 Priest Holmes .25 .60
49 Trent Green .25 .60
50 Tony Gonzalez .25 .60
51 Larry Johnson .25 .60
52 Chris Chambers .25 .60
53 A.J. Feeley .20 .50
54 Randy McMichael .20 .50
55 Daunte Culpepper .25 .60
56 Nate Burleson .20 .50
57 Michael Bennett .25 .60
58 Tom Brady .60 1.50
59 Deion Branch .20 .50
60 Corey Dillon .25 .60
61 Aaron Brooks .20 .50
62 Deuce McAllister .25 .60
63 Joe Horn .25 .60
64 Eli Manning .50 1.25
65 Jeremy Shockey .30 .75
66 Tiki Barber .30 .75
67 Plaxico Burress .25 .60
68 Chad Pennington .30 .75
69 Curtis Martin .30 .75
70 Laveranues Coles .20 .50
71 Jerry Porter .20 .50
72 Randy Moss .30 .75
73 Kerry Collins .25 .60
74 Donovan McNabb .30 .75
75 Brian Westbrook .25 .60
76 Terrell Owens .30 .75
77 Ben Roethlisberger .50 1.25
78 Jerome Bettis .30 .75
79 Hines Ward .30 .75
80 Drew Brees .30 .75
81 LaDainian Tomlinson .30 .75
82 Antonio Gates .30 .75
83 Tim Rattay .20 .50
84 Eric Johnson .20 .50
85 Rashaun Woods .20 .50
86 Matt Hasselbeck .25 .60
87 Shaun Alexander .25 .60
88 Darrell Jackson .20 .50
89 Marc Bulger .25 .60
90 Marshall Faulk .30 .75
91 Torry Holt .25 .60
92 Brian Griese .25 .60
93 Michael Pittman .20 .50
94 Michael Clayton .20 .50
95 Steve McNair .30 .75
96 Chris Brown .20 .50
97 Drew Bennett .25 .60
98 Clinton Portis .25 .60
99 Patrick Ramsey .25 .60
100 Santana Moss .25 .60
101 Aaron Rodgers RC 6.00 15.00
102 Alex Smith QB RC 1.25 3.00
103 Charlie Frye RC .75 2.00
104 Andrew Walter RC .60 1.50
105 David Greene RC .50 1.25
106 Dan Orlovsky RC .75 2.00
107 Derek Anderson RC .60 1.50
108 Cadillac Williams RC .75 2.00
109 Ronnie Brown RC 1.00 2.50
110 Ciatrick Fason RC .50 1.25
111 Cedric Benson RC .75 2.00
112 Vincent Jackson RC 1.00 2.50
113 Eric Shelton RC .50 1.25
114 Frank Gore RC 1.25 3.00
115 Braylon Edwards RC 1.00 2.50
116 Roddy White RC 1.00 2.50
117 Troy Williamson RC .60 1.50
118 Craphonso Thorpe RC .50 1.25
119 Mark Clayton RC .75 2.00
120 Fred Gibson RC .60 1.50
121 Reggie Brown RC .50 1.25
122 Matt Jones RC .75 2.00
123 David Pollack RC .60 1.50
124 Derrick Johnson RC .60 1.50
125 Erasmus James RC .60 1.50
126 Antrel Rolle RC .75 2.00
127 Thomas Davis RC .50 1.25
128 Adam Jones RC .60 1.50
129 Corey Webster RC .60 1.50
130 Marlin Jackson RC .50 1.25
131 Brodney Pool RC .75 2.00
132 Mark Bradley RC .50 1.25
133 Stefan LeFors RC .50 1.25
134 Alex Smith TE RC .50 1.25
135 Heath Miller RC 1.00 2.50
136 Jason Campbell RC 1.00 2.50
137 Kyle Orton RC .75 2.00
138 Vernand Morency RC .60 1.50
139 Carlos Rogers RC .75 2.00
140 J.J. Arrington RC .60 1.50
141 Ryan Moats RC .60 1.50
142 Chris Henry RC .75 2.00
143 Terrence Murphy RC .50 1.25
144 Fabian Washington RC .60 1.50
145 Roscoe Parrish RC .50 1.25
146 Kevin Everett RC .75 2.00
147 Travis Johnson RC .50 1.25
148 Mike Williams .75 2.00
149 Maurice Clarett .60 1.50
150 Channing Crowder RC .60 1.50
151 Odell Thurman RC .75 2.00
152 DeMarcus Ware RC 1.50 4.00
153 Shawne Merriman RC .75 2.00
154 Jerome Mathis RC .75 2.00
155 Marcus Spears RC .60 1.50
156 Luis Castillo RC .60 1.50
157 Darren Sproles RC .75 2.00
158 Marion Barber RC .75 2.00
159 Justin Tuck RC 1.00 2.50
160 Courtney Roby RC .60 1.50

2005 Upper Deck ESPN Holofoil

*VETERANS: 3X TO 8X BASIC CARDS
*ROOKIES: 1X TO 2.5X BASIC CARDS
STATED ODDS 1:24
STATED PRINT RUN 199 SER.#'d SETS

2005 Upper Deck ESPN ESPY Award Winners

COMPLETE SET (20) 12.50 30.00
BASIC INSERTS ONE PER PACK OVERALL
*HOLOFOIL: 3X TO 8X BASIC INSERTS
HOLOFOIL PRINT RUN 25 SER.#'d SETS
EA1 Michael Vick .75 2.00
EA2 Tom Brady 1.50 4.00
EA3 Daunte Culpepper .60 1.50
EA4 Kurt Warner .75 2.00
EA5 Randy Moss .75 2.00
EA6 Michael Vick .75 2.00
EA7 Marshall Faulk .75 2.00
EA8 Marshall Faulk .75 2.00
EA9 Brett Favre 2.00 5.00
EA10 Brett Favre 2.00 5.00
EA11 Peyton Manning 1.50 4.00
EA12 Peyton Manning 1.50 4.00
EA13 Barry Sanders 2.00 5.00
EA14 Jerry Rice 1.50 4.00
EA15 Brett Favre 2.00 5.00
EA16 Donte Stallworth .50 1.25
EA17 Brett Favre 2.00 5.00
EA18 Tommy Maddox .60 1.50
EA19 Steve McNair .75 2.00
EA20 Antonio Freeman .60 1.50

2005 Upper Deck ESPN Ink

AUTO OVERALL STATED ODDS 1:480
AN Antrel Rolle 10.00 25.00
AR Aaron Rodgers 125.00 200.00
AS Alex Smith QB 30.00 60.00
AW Andrew Walter 12.50 30.00
BE Braylon Edwards
BR Ben Roethlisberger 60.00 120.00
CB Chris Berman
CE Cedric Benson
DA David Pollack 12.50 30.00
DD Domanick Davis 7.50 20.00
DP Dan Patrick
JP J.P. Losman 12.50 30.00
JT Joe Theismann
JW Jason White 10.00 25.00
KM Kenny Mayne 10.00 25.00
KO Kyle Orton
LC Linda Cohn
MA Mark Clayton
MB Marc Bulger 10.00 25.00
MC Maurice Clarett
MI Michael Clayton 10.00 25.00
PM Peyton Manning
RB Ronnie Brown 40.00 80.00
RW Reggie Wayne
SS Stuart Scott 25.00 50.00
TD Thomas Davis 7.50 20.00
VM Vernand Morency
WR Walter Reyes 7.50 20.00

2005 Upper Deck ESPN Insider Playmakers

COMPLETE SET (8) 3.00 8.00
ONE PER PACK
BF Brett Favre 1.00 2.50
CD Corey Dillon .30 .75
DM Donovan McNabb .40 1.00
EJ Edgerrin James .30 .75
JS Jeremy Shockey .40 1.00
LT LaDainian Tomlinson .40 1.00
MV Michael Vick .40 1.00
TO Terrell Owens .40 1.00

2005 Upper Deck ESPN Magazine Covers

COMPLETE SET (20) 12.50 30.00
BASIC INSERTS ONE PER PACK OVERALL
*HOLOFOIL: 3X TO 8X BASIC INSERTS
HOLOFOIL PRINT RUN 25 SER.#'d SETS
TM1 LaDainian Tomlinson .75 2.00
TM2 Corey Dillon .60 1.50
TM3 Terrell Owens .75 2.00
Donovan McNabb
TM4 Randy Moss .75 2.00
TM5 Dante Hall .50 1.25
TM6 Tom Brady 1.50 4.00
TM7 Steve McNair .75 2.00
TM8 Mike Vanderjagt .50 1.25
TM9 Jeremy Shockey .75 2.00
TM10 Derrick Brooks .60 1.50
TM11 Michael Vick .75 2.00
TM12 Terrell Owens .75 2.00
TM13 Jerry Rice 1.50 4.00
Tim Brown
TM14 Donovan McNabb .75 2.00
TM15 Marshall Faulk .75 2.00
TM16 Ben Roethlisberger 1.25 3.00
TM17 Randy Moss .75 2.00
TM18 Daunte Culpepper .60 1.50
TM19 Edgerrin James .60 1.50
TM20 Brett Favre 2.00 5.00

2005 Upper Deck ESPN Plays of the Week

COMPLETE SET (30) 15.00 40.00
BASIC INSERTS ONE PER PACK OVERALL
*HOLOFOIL: 3X TO 8X BASIC INSERTS
HOLOFOIL PRINT RUN 25 SER.#'d SETS
PW1 Michael Vick .75 2.00
PW2 Donovan McNabb .75 2.00
PW3 Roy Williams S .50 1.25
PW4 Ben Roethlisberger 1.25 3.00
PW5 Brian Urlacher .75 2.00
PW6 Jerome Bettis .75 2.00
PW7 Julius Jones .50 1.25
PW8 Ed Reed .60 1.50
PW9 Randy Moss .75 2.00
PW10 Peyton Manning 1.50 4.00
PW11 Brett Favre 2.00 5.00
PW12 Santana Moss .60 1.50
PW13 Deion Branch .50 1.25
PW14 Dante Hall .50 1.25
PW15 Rodney Harrison .60 1.50
PW16 Byron Leftwich .60 1.50
PW17 Larry Fitzgerald .75 2.00
PW18 Chad Johnson .60 1.50
PW19 Kevin Jones .50 1.25
PW20 Willis McGahee .75 2.00
PW21 Steven Jackson .75 2.00
PW22 Eli Manning 1.25 3.00
PW23 Marvin Harrison .75 2.00
PW24 Terrell Owens .75 2.00
PW25 Daunte Culpepper .60 1.50
PW26 Joe Horn .60 1.50
PW27 Ahman Green .60 1.50
PW28 LaDainian Tomlinson .75 2.00
PW29 Carson Palmer .75 2.00
PW30 Marc Bulger .60 1.50

2005 Upper Deck ESPN Sports Center Swatches

STATED ODDS 1:12
AG Ahman Green 3.00 8.00
AJ Andre Johnson 2.50 6.00
BF Brett Favre 7.50 20.00
BR Ben Roethlisberger 7.50 20.00
BU Brian Urlacher 3.00 8.00
CP Chad Pennington 3.00 8.00
DA David Carr 3.00 8.00
DC Daunte Culpepper 3.00 8.00
DF DeShaun Foster 2.50 6.00
DR Drew Brees 2.50 6.00
DS Donte Stallworth 2.50 6.00
EJ Edgerrin James 3.00 8.00
EM Eli Manning 6.00 15.00
HW Hines Ward 3.00 8.00
JE Jerry Porter 2.50 6.00
JH Joey Harrington 3.00 8.00
JJ Julius Jones 4.00 10.00
JL Jamal Lewis 3.00 8.00
JR Jerry Rice 6.00 15.00
JS Jeremy Shockey 3.00 8.00
KJ Kevin Jones 3.00 8.00
LF Larry Fitzgerald 3.00 8.00
LS Lee Suggs 2.50 6.00
LT LaDainian Tomlinson 3.00 8.00
MB Marc Bulger 2.50 6.00
MF Marshall Faulk 3.00 8.00
MH Marvin Harrison 3.00 8.00
MV Michael Vick 4.00 10.00
PH Priest Holmes 3.00 8.00
PM Peyton Manning 5.00 12.00
PR Philip Rivers 3.00 8.00
RG Rex Grossman 3.00 8.00
SA Shaun Alexander 4.00 10.00
SM Steve McNair 2.50 6.00
TB Tom Brady 7.50 20.00
TG Trent Green 2.50 6.00
TH Todd Heap 2.00 5.00
TI Tiki Barber SP 6.00 15.00
TJ T.J. Duckett 2.50 6.00
TN Terrence Newman 2.50 6.00
TO Terrell Owens 3.00 8.00
TY Tony Gonzalez 2.50 6.00

2005 Upper Deck ESPN Sports Century

COMPLETE SET (10) 10.00 25.00
BASIC INSERTS ONE PER PACK OVERALL
*HOLOFOIL: 3X TO 8X BASIC INSERTS
HOLOFOIL PRINT RUN 25 SER.#'d SETS
SCBJ Bo Jackson 1.25 3.00
SCBS Barry Sanders 2.00 5.00
SCDB Dick Butkus 1.50 4.00
SCDM Dan Marino 2.50 6.00
SCDS Deion Sanders 1.25 3.00
SCGS Gale Sayers 1.25 3.00
SCJB Jim Brown 1.50 4.00
SCJM Joe Montana 3.00 8.00
SCLT Lawrence Taylor 1.25 3.00
SCWP Walter Payton 3.00 8.00

2005 Upper Deck ESPN Sports Century Signatures

AUTO OVERALL STATED ODDS 1:480
AD Art Donovan 15.00 40.00
CJ Charlie Joiner 10.00 25.00
CT Charley Taylor 10.00 25.00
DC Dave Casper 12.50 30.00
DD Dan Dierdorf 10.00 25.00
DM Don Maynard
HA Herb Adderley 12.50 30.00
JL James Lofton
LC L.C. Greenwood 15.00 30.00
MA Marcus Allen
MO Merlin Olsen 15.00 40.00
OA Ottis Anderson 10.00 25.00
ON Ozzie Newsome 15.00 40.00
RB Raymond Berry

2005 Upper Deck ESPN This Day in Football History

COMPLETE SET (20) 12.50 30.00
BASIC INSERTS ONE PER PACK OVERALL
*HOLOFOIL: 3X TO 8X BASIC INSERTS
HOLOFOIL PRINT RUN 25 SER.#'d SETS
1 Drew Bledsoe .75 2.00
2 Jerry Rice 1.25 3.00
3 Jamal Lewis .75 2.00
4 Jerry Rice 1.25 3.00
5 Johnny Unitas 1.50 4.00
6 Walter Payton 3.00 8.00
7 Corey Dillon .75 2.00
8 Eddie George .60 1.50
9 Tom Dempsey .50 1.25
10 Derrick Thomas .75 2.00
11 Dan Marino 2.50 6.00
12 Jim Brown 1.50 4.00
13 David Carr .75 2.00
14 Dan Marino 2.50 6.00
15 Eric Dickerson .60 1.50
16 Steve Largent .75 2.00
17 Marvin Harrison .75 2.00
18 Terrell Owens .75 2.00
19 Barry Sanders 2.00 5.00
20 Franco Harris .75 2.00

2003 Upper Deck Finite

Released in December of 2003, this set contains 300 cards, including 191 veterans and 109 rookies. Cards 1-100 are serial numbered to 2350. Cards 101-160 make up the Major Factors (MF) subset and are serial numbered to 750. Cards 161-185 make up the Prominent Powers (PP) subset and are serial numbered to 500. Cards 186-200 make up the First Class Finite (FCF) subset and are serial numbered to 100. FCF cards were inserted at a rate of 1:84. Finite Rookies Tier 1 (201-250) are serial numbered to 999, Rookies Tier 2 (251-285) are serial numbered to 500, and Rookies Tier 3 (286-300) are serial numbered to 100. Boxes contained 10 packs of 3 cards.

COMP.SET w/o SP's (100) 35.00 60.00
201-250 ROOKIE PRINT RUN 999
251-285 ROOKIE PRINT RUN 500
286-300 ROOKIE PRINT RUN 100
1 Peyton Manning 1.25 3.00
2 Aaron Brooks .50 1.25
3 Joey Harrington .40 1.00
4 Brett Favre 1.50 4.00
5 Donovan McNabb .60 1.50
6 Steve McNair .60 1.50
7 Michael Vick .75 2.00
8 David Carr .50 1.25
9 Drew Brees .60 1.50
10 Chad Pennington .60 1.50
11 Daunte Culpepper .50 1.25
12 Tom Brady 1.50 4.00
13 Kurt Warner .60 1.50
14 Brad Johnson .50 1.25
15 Drew Bledsoe .60 1.50
16 Jake Plummer .50 1.25
17 Jeff Garcia .50 1.25
18 Mark Brunell .50 1.25
19 Josh McCown .50 1.25
20 Travis Henry .40 1.00
21 LaDainian Tomlinson .60 1.50
22 Emmitt Smith 1.50 4.00
23 Michael Bennett .50 1.25
24 Brian Westbrook .60 1.50
25 Curtis Martin .60 1.50
26 Clinton Portis .50 1.25
27 Eddie George .50 1.25
28 Marshall Faulk .60 1.50
29 Deuce McAllister .50 1.25

30 Ahman Green .50 1.25
31 LaMont Jordan .50 1.25
32 Edgerrin James .60 1.50
33 Jamel White .40 1.00
34 Ricky Williams .50 1.25
35 Anthony Thomas .50 1.25
36 Amos Zereoue .40 1.00
37 Ladell Betts .40 1.00
38 Stephen Davis .50 1.25
39 T.J. Duckett .50 1.25
40 Troy Hambrick .40 1.00
41 Maurice Morris .40 1.00
42 James Jackson .40 1.00
43 Correll Buckhalter .50 1.25
44 Keith Brooking .50 1.25
45 Michael Strahan .60 1.50
46 Jason Taylor .50 1.25
47 Kendrell Bell .40 1.00
48 Jevon Kearse .50 1.25
49 Chris Horn RC .50 1.25
50 Quentin Jammer .40 1.00
51 Phillip Buchanon .40 1.00
52 Charles Woodson .60 1.50
53 Rod Woodson .60 1.50
54 Simeon Rice .40 1.00
55 Derrick Brooks .50 1.25
56 Warren Sapp .50 1.25
57 John Lynch .50 1.25
58 Champ Bailey .60 1.50
59 Reggie Wayne .60 1.50
60 Darrell Jackson .50 1.25
61 Derrick Mason .50 1.25
62 Travis Minor .40 1.00
63 Eric Parker RC .60 1.50
64 Ron Johnson .40 1.00
65 Dante Hall .50 1.25
66 David Terrell .40 1.00
67 Daniel Graham .40 1.00
68 Randy McMichael .40 1.00
69 Jeremy Shockey .60 1.50
70 J.J. Stokes .40 1.00
71 Johnnie Morton .50 1.25
72 Dennis Northcutt .40 1.00
73 Peter Warrick .50 1.25
74 Rod Smith .50 1.25
75 Javon Walker .50 1.25
76 Tim Carter .40 1.00
77 Wayne Chrebet .50 1.25
78 Corey Bradford .40 1.00
79 Deion Branch .50 1.25
80 Jerry Rice 1.25 3.00
81 Terrell Owens .60 1.50
82 Josh Reed .40 1.00
83 Ed McCaffrey .50 1.25
84 Randy Moss .60 1.50
85 Chad Johnson .60 1.50
86 Hines Ward .60 1.50
87 Rod Gardner .40 1.00
00 Tony Gonzalez .60 1.50
89 David Boston .40 1.00
90 Jerry Porter .40 1.00
91 Kevin Johnson .40 1.00
92 Rohan Davey .40 1.00
93 Tim Rattay .40 1.00
94 Jon Kitna .50 1.25
95 Jay Fiedler .40 1.00
96 Doug Flutie .60 1.50
97 Quincy Carter .40 1.00
98 Vinny Testaverde .50 1.25
99 Kelly Holcomb .40 1.00
100 Marc Bulger .60 1.50
101 Patrick Ramsey MF 1.25 3.00
102 Tim Couch MF 1.00 2.50
103 Tommy Maddox MF 1.25 3.00
104 Chad Hutchinson MF 1.00 2.50
105 Trent Green MF 1.25 3.00
106 Kerry Collins MF 1.25 3.00
107 Will Heller MF RC 1.50 4.00
108 Brian Griese MF 1.25 3.00
109 Kordell Stewart MF 1.25 3.00
110 Jake Delhomme MF 1.50 4.00
111 Chris Redman MF 1.00 2.50
112 Mike Anderson MF 1.25 3.00
113 Olandis Gary MF 1.00 2.50
114 Antonio Gates MF RC 20.00 40.00
115 Garrison Hearst MF 1.25 3.00
116 Fred Taylor MF 1.25 3.00
117 Casey Fitzsimmons MF RC 1.50 4.00
118 Tiki Barber MF 1.50 4.00
119 Mike Alstott MF 1.50 4.00
120 Kevan Barlow MF 1.00 2.50
121 Jamal Lewis MF 1.25 3.00
122 Mike Banks MF RC 1.25 3.00
123 Jimmy Farris MF RC 1.25 3.00
124 Warrick Dunn MF 1.25 3.00
125 Jerome Bettis MF 1.50 4.00
126 Antonio Chatman MF RC 2.00 5.00
127 Bubba Franks MF 1.25 3.00
128 Todd Heap MF 1.25 3.00
129 Shannon Sharpe MF 1.50 4.00
130 Donald Driver MF 1.50 4.00
131 Antonio Freeman MF 1.25 3.00
132 Joey Galloway MF 1.25 3.00
133 Marc Boerigter MF 1.00 2.50
134 Torry Holt MF 1.50 4.00
135 Amani Toomer MF 1.25 3.00
136 Marty Booker MF 1.25 3.00
137 Santana Moss MF 1.25 3.00
138 Jimmy Smith MF 1.25 3.00
139 Jabar Gaffney MF 1.00 2.50
140 Isaac Bruce MF 1.50 4.00
141 Laveranues Coles MF 1.00 2.50
142 Quincy Morgan MF 1.00 2.50
143 Peerless Price MF 1.00 2.50
144 Eric Moulds MF 1.25 3.00
145 Troy Brown MF 1.25 3.00
146 Plaxico Burress MF 1.25 3.00
147 Chris Chambers MF 1.25 3.00
148 Tim Brown MF 1.50 4.00
149 Antonio Brown MF RC 1.25 3.00
150 Koren Robinson MF 1.25 3.00
151 David Boston MF 1.00 2.50
152 C.J. Jones MF RC 1.25 3.00
153 Marvin Harrison MF 1.50 4.00
154 Keyshawn Johnson MF 1.50 4.00
155 J.J. Moses MF RC 1.25 3.00
156 Antwaan Randle El MF 1.25 3.00
157 Ashley Lelie MF 1.00 2.50
158 Andre Davis MF 1.00 2.50
159 Donte Stallworth MF 1.00 2.50
160 Antonio Bryant MF 1.00 2.50
161 Tom Brady PP 5.00 12.00
162 Drew Bledsoe PP 2.00 5.00
163 Rich Gannon PP 1.50 4.00
164 David Carr PP 1.50 4.00
165 Drew Brees PP 2.00 5.00
166 Aaron Brooks PP 1.50 4.00
167 Joey Harrington PP 1.25 3.00
168 Matt Hasselbeck PP 1.50 4.00
169 Jake Plummer PP 1.50 4.00
170 Edgerrin James PP 2.00 5.00
171 Ahman Green PP 1.50 4.00
172 Deuce McAllister PP 1.50 4.00
173 Priest Holmes PP 2.00 5.00
174 Travis Henry PP 1.25 3.00
175 William Green PP 1.25 3.00
176 Corey Dillon PP 1.50 4.00
177 Shaun Alexander PP 1.50 4.00
178 Jeremy Shockey PP 2.00 5.00
179 Brian Dawkins PP 1.50 4.00
180 Roy Williams PP 1.50 4.00
181 Julius Peppers PP 2.00 5.00
182 Ray Lewis PP 2.00 5.00
183 Junior Seau PP 2.00 5.00
184 Zach Thomas PP 2.00 5.00
185 Brian Urlacher PP 2.00 5.00
186 Michael Vick FCF 4.00 10.00
187 Jeff Garcia FCF 2.50 6.00
188 Daunte Culpepper FCF 2.50 6.00
189 Steve McNair FCF 3.00 8.00
190 Chad Pennington FCF 3.00 8.00
191 LaDainian Tomlinson FCF 3.00 8.00
192 Clinton Portis FCF 2.50 6.00
193 Ricky Williams FCF 2.50 6.00
194 Donovan McNabb FCF 3.00 8.00
195 Peyton Manning FCF 6.00 15.00
196 Marshall Faulk FCF 3.00 8.00
197 Kurt Warner FCF 3.00 8.00
198 Emmitt Smith FCF 8.00 20.00
199 Jerry Rice FCF 6.00 15.00
200 Brett Favre FCF 8.00 20.00
201 Carson Palmer RC 4.00 10.00
202 Kyle Boller RC 2.00 5.00
203 Kliff Kingsbury RC 1.50 4.00
204 Brooks Bollinger RC 1.50 4.00
205 Mike Doss RC 2.00 5.00
206 Dewayne White RC 1.25 3.00
207 Roderick Babers RC 1.25 3.00
208 Seneca Wallace RC 2.00 5.00
209 Nate Hybl RC 1.50 4.00
210 Jason Gesser RC 1.50 4.00
211 Willis McGahee RC 2.50 6.00
212 George Wrighster RC 1.25 3.00
213 Drayton Florence RC 2.00 5.00
214 L.J. Smith RC 2.00 5.00
215 B.J. Askew RC 1.50 4.00
216 Adewale Ogunleye RC 2.50 6.00
217 Ahmaad Galloway RC 1.50 4.00
218 Dwone Hicks RC 1.25 3.00
219 Travaris Robinson RC 1.25 3.00
220 William Joseph RC 1.25 3.00
221 Terrence Kiel RC 1.50 4.00
222 Marcus Trufant RC 1.50 4.00
223 Terence Newman RC 1.50 4.00
224 Nnamdi Asomugha RC 5.00 12.00
225 Troy Polamalu RC 15.00 30.00
226 Terrell Suggs RC 2.00 5.00
227 Boss Bailey RC 1.50 4.00
228 Dan Klecko RC 1.50 4.00
229 Jerome McDougle RC 1.25 3.00
230 Johnathan Sullivan RC 1.25 3.00
231 Mike Seidman RC 1.25 3.00
232 Dallas Clark RC 3.00 8.00
233 Tony Romo RC 15.00 40.00
234 Reggie Newhouse RC 1.25 3.00
235 David Tyree RC 2.00 5.00
236 Andre Woolfolk RC 1.50 4.00
237 Domanick Davis RC 1.50 4.00
238 Zuriel Smith RC 1.25 3.00
239 Tommy Jones RC 1.25 3.00
240 Arnaz Battle RC 2.00 5.00
241 Kassim Osgood RC 2.00 5.00
242 Gerald Hayes RC 1.50 4.00
243 Keenan Howry RC 1.25 3.00
244 Bobby Wade RC 1.50 4.00
245 Brock Forsey RC 1.50 4.00
246 Walter Young RC 1.25 3.00
247 Shaun McDonald RC 1.50 4.00
248 Nate Burleson RC 1.50 4.00
249 Anquan Boldin RC 3.00 8.00
250 Taylor Jacobs RC 1.25 3.00
251 Chris Simms RC 2.50 6.00
252 Rex Grossman RC 2.50 6.00
253 Arlen Harris RC 1.50 4.00
254 Dave Ragone RC 1.50 4.00
255 Chris Brown RC 1.50 4.00
256 Musa Smith RC 1.50 4.00
257 Artose Pinner RC 1.50 4.00
258 Sammy Davis RC 2.00 5.00
259 DeWayne Robertson RC 2.00 5.00
260 Tony Hollings RC 2.00 5.00
261 LaBrandon Toefield RC 2.00 5.00
262 Cortez Hankton RC 2.00 5.00
263 Justin Griffith RC 2.00 5.00
264 Jeremi Johnson RC 1.50 4.00
265 E.J. Henderson RC 2.00 5.00
266 Casey Moore RC 1.50 4.00
267 Ken Hamlin RC 2.50 6.00
268 Nick Barnett RC 2.50 6.00
269 Vishante Shiancoe RC 2.50 6.00
270 Aaron Walker RC 2.00 5.00
271 Bennie Joppru RC 1.50 4.00
272 Terrence Edwards RC 1.50 4.00
273 Willie Ponder RC 1.50 4.00
274 Pisa Tinoisamoa RC 2.50 6.00
275 Doug Gabriel RC 2.00 5.00
276 Kerry Carter RC 1.50 4.00
277 Avon Cobourne RC 1.50 4.00
278 Sam Aiken RC 2.00 5.00
279 Brandon Lloyd RC 4.00 10.00
280 LaTarence Dunbar RC 1.50 4.00
281 J.R. Tolver RC 2.00 5.00
282 Kevin Curtis RC 2.50 6.00
283 Tyrone Calico RC 2.00 5.00
284 Bryant Johnson RC 2.50 6.00
285 Charles Rogers RC 2.00 5.00
286 Teyo Johnson RC 6.00 15.00
287 Jason Witten RC 20.00 50.00
288 Kelley Washington RC 5.00 12.00
289 Billy McMullen RC 5.00 12.00
290 Adrian Madise RC 5.00 12.00
291 Justin Gage RC 6.00 15.00
292 Andre Johnson RC 20.00 50.00
293 Bethel Johnson RC 5.00 12.00
294 Lee Suggs RC 6.00 15.00
295 Larry Johnson RC 8.00 20.00
296 Justin Fargas RC 8.00 20.00
297 Onterrio Smith RC 5.00 12.00
298 Ken Dorsey RC 6.00 15.00
299 Brian St.Pierre RC 6.00 15.00
300 Byron Leftwich RC 8.00 20.00

2003 Upper Deck Finite Gold

*VETS 1-100: 2.5X TO 6X BASIC CARDS
*VET MF 101-160: 1.2X TO 3X
*ROOKIE MF 101-160: 1X TO 2.5X
*VET PP 161-185: 1X TO 2.5X
*VET FCF 186-200: .6X TO 1.5X
*ROOKIES 201-250: 1.2X TO 3X
*ROOKIES 251-285: 1X TO 2.5X
*ROOKIES 286-300: .3X TO .8X
GOLD/50 ODDS 1:10
STATED PRINT RUN 50 SER.#'d SETS
233 Tony Romo 50.00 120.00

2003 Upper Deck Finite Autographs

OVERALL AUTO STATED ODDS 1:10
AB Antonio Bryant/100 8.00 20.00
AD Andre Davis/263 6.00 15.00
AL Mike Alstott/175 15.00 40.00
AP Artose Pinner/396 6.00 15.00
AQ Anquan Boldin/396 20.00 50.00
AZ Az-Zahir Hakim/186 6.00 15.00
BB Brad Banks/1000 6.00 15.00
BD Brandon Doman/262 6.00 15.00
BR Bryant Johnson/396 10.00 25.00
BS Brian St.Pierre/720 6.00 15.00
CB Chris Brown/396 6.00 15.00
CJ Chad Johnson/815 8.00 20.00
CP Clinton Portis/70 30.00 80.00
CS Chris Simms/80 20.00 40.00
DC Dallas Clark/396 20.00 40.00
DF DeShaun Foster/207 8.00 20.00
DF2 DeShaun Foster/651 6.00 15.00
EC Eric Crouch/263 10.00 25.00
EG Earnest Graham/800 8.00 20.00
JA Jason Johnson/205 6.00 15.00
JB Jeff Blake/35 12.00 30.00
JF Justin Fargas/396 10.00 25.00
JG Jabar Gaffney/260 6.00 15.00
JJ James Jackson/300 6.00 15.00
JS Jeremy Shockey/93 15.00 40.00
KA Kareem Kelly/1300 5.00 12.00
KB Kevan Barlow/107 8.00 20.00
KC Kelly Campbell/262 6.00 15.00
KC Kevin Curtis/396 10.00 25.00
KK Kurt Kittner/55 10.00 25.00
KL Kliff Kingsbury/396 8.00 20.00
KM Keenan McCardell/30 12.00 30.00
KW Kelley Washington/1058 5.00 12.00
LJ Larry Johnson/396 10.00 25.00
LS Luke Staley/263 6.00 15.00
MB Marc Bulger/35 15.00 40.00
MS Musa Smith/396 6.00 15.00
MT Marcus Trufant/396 8.00 20.00
NB Nate Burleson/396 8.00 20.00
NH Napoleon Harris/262 6.00 15.00
PM1 Peyton Manning/1280 40.00 80.00
PM2 Peyton Manning/1254 40.00 80.00
PR Patrick Ramsey/190 8.00 20.00
QG Quentin Griffin/447 8.00 20.00
RC Reche Caldwell/261 6.00 15.00
RD Rohan Davey/262 6.00 15.00
RJ Ron Johnson/263 6.00 15.00
RW Roy Williams/151 25.00 50.00
SU Lee Suggs/30 12.00 30.00
SW Seneca Wallace/414 10.00 25.00
TA Taylor Jacobs/409 6.00 15.00
TG Tony Gonzalez/46 15.00 40.00
TH Todd Heap/63 12.00 30.00
TM Travis Minor/364 6.00 15.00
TS Terrell Suggs/950 10.00 25.00
VT Vinny Testaverde/212 8.00 20.00
WD Woody Dantzler/207 6.00 15.00

2003 Upper Deck Finite Autographs Gold

AB Antonio Bryant 12.00 30.00
AD Andre Davis 12.00 30.00
AL Mike Alstott 20.00 50.00
AL Ashley Lelie 12.00 30.00
AP Artose Pinner 12.00 30.00
AQ Anquan Boldin 40.00 100.00
AZ Az-Zahir Hakim 12.00 30.00
BB Brad Banks 15.00 40.00
BD Brandon Doman 12.00 30.00
BR Bryant Johnson 20.00 50.00
BS Brian St.Pierre 15.00 40.00
CB Chris Brown 12.00 30.00
CJ Chad Johnson 20.00 50.00
CP Clinton Portis 15.00 40.00
CS Chris Simms 20.00 50.00
DC Dallas Clark 30.00 80.00
DC David Carr 15.00 40.00
DF DeShaun Foster 15.00 40.00
DF2 DeShaun Foster 15.00 40.00
EC Eric Crouch 20.00 50.00
EG Earnest Graham 20.00 50.00
JA Jason Johnson
JB Jeff Blake
JF Justin Fargas 20.00 50.00
JG Jabar Gaffney 12.00 30.00
JJ James Jackson
JS Jeremy Shockey 20.00 50.00
KA Kareem Kelly
KB Kevan Barlow
KC Kelly Campbell
KC Kevin Curtis 20.00 50.00
KK Kurt Kittner 12.00 30.00
KL Kliff Kingsbury 15.00 40.00
KM Keenan McCardell 15.00 40.00
KW Kelley Washington
LJ Larry Johnson 20.00 50.00
LS Luke Staley 12.00 30.00
MB Marc Bulger
MM Maurice Morris 12.00 30.00
MS Musa Smith
MT Marcus Trufant 15.00 40.00
NB Nate Burleson 15.00 40.00
NH Napoleon Harris 12.00 30.00
PM1 Peyton Manning 60.00 120.00
PM2 Peyton Manning 60.00 120.00
PR Patrick Ramsey 15.00 40.00
QG Quentin Griffin 15.00 40.00
RC Reche Caldwell 12.00 30.00
RD Rohan Davey 12.00 30.00
RJ Ron Johnson
RW Roy Williams 15.00 40.00
SU Lee Suggs 15.00 40.00
SW Seneca Wallace 20.00 50.00
TA Taylor Jacobs 12.00 30.00
TG Tony Gonzalez 20.00 50.00
TH Todd Heap 15.00 40.00
TM Travis Minor 12.00 30.00
TS Terrell Suggs 30.00 60.00
VT Vinny Testaverde 15.00 40.00
WD Woody Dantzler

2003 Upper Deck Finite Jerseys

OVERALL JERSEY STATED ODDS 1:4
*BLACK/99: .8X TO 2X BASIC JSY
BLACK PRINT RUN 99 SER.#'d SETS
*GOLD/25: 1.2X TO 3X BASIC JSY
GOLD PRINT RUN 25 SER.#'d SETS
FJAB Anquan Boldin 4.00 10.00
FJAG Ahman Green 3.00 8.00
FJAJ Andre Johnson 6.00 15.00
FJAP Artose Pinner 2.50 6.00
FJBE Bethel Johnson 2.50 6.00
FJBF Brett Favre 10.00 25.00
FJBJ Bryant Johnson 4.00 10.00
FJBL Byron Leftwich 2.50 6.00
FJBS Brian St.Pierre 3.00 8.00
FJCB Chris Brown 2.50 6.00
FJCP Carson Palmer 5.00 12.00
FJCU Daunte Culpepper 3.00 8.00
FJDA Dallas Clark 6.00 15.00
FJDC David Carr 3.00 8.00
FJDR Dave Ragone 2.50 6.00
FJDR DeWayne Robertson 3.00 8.00
FJES Emmitt Smith 10.00 25.00
FJGA Rich Gannon 3.00 8.00
FJJF Justin Fargas 4.00 10.00
FJKB Kyle Boller 2.50 6.00
FJKC Kevin Curtis 2.50 6.00
FJKK Kliff Kingsbury 3.00 8.00
FJKW Kelley Washington 2.50 6.00
FJLJ Larry Johnson 2.50 6.00
FJMC Donovan McNabb 4.00 10.00
FJMS Musa Smith 2.50 6.00
FJMT Marcus Trufant 2.00 5.00
FJMV Michael Vick SP 8.00 20.00
FJNB Nate Burleson 3.00 8.00
FJOS Onterrio Smith 2.50 6.00
FJPC Chad Pennington 4.00 10.00
FJPH Priest Holmes 4.00 10.00
FJPM Peyton Manning 8.00 20.00
FJPO Clinton Portis 3.00 8.00
FJRG Rex Grossman 2.50 6.00
FJSW Seneca Wallace 4.00 10.00
FJTA Taylor Jacobs 2.50 6.00
FJTC Tyrone Calico 3.00 8.00
FJTJ Teyo Johnson 3.00 8.00
FJTN Terence Newman 2.00 5.00
FJTS Terrell Suggs 2.50 6.00
FJWM Willis McGahee 3.00 8.00

2004 Upper Deck Finite HG

Upper Deck Finite HG was initially released in late November 2004. The base set consists of 278-cards including 65-rookies serial numbered to 275 and 13-rookies numbered to 99. Hobby boxes contained 10-packs of 3-cards each. One parallel set and a variety of game jersey and autograph inserts can be found seeded in packs.

COMP.SET w/o SP's (100) 12.50 30.00
101-265 ROOKIE PRINT RUN 275
266-278 ROOKIE PRINT RUN 99
1 Emmitt Smith 1.25 3.00
2 Anquan Boldin .50 1.25
3 Josh McCown .40 1.00
4 Michael Vick .60 1.50
5 Peerless Price .30 .75
6 Warrick Dunn .40 1.00
7 Todd Heap .40 1.00
8 Jamal Lewis .40 1.00
9 Kyle Boller .40 1.00
10 Drew Bledsoe .50 1.25
11 Travis Henry .30 .75
12 Eric Moulds .40 1.00
13 Jake Delhomme .40 1.00
14 Steve Smith .50 1.25
15 Stephen Davis .40 1.00
16 Rex Grossman .40 1.00
17 Brian Urlacher .50 1.25
18 Thomas Jones .50 1.25
19 Rudi Johnson .40 1.00
20 Carson Palmer .50 1.25
21 Chad Johnson .50 1.25
22 Jeff Garcia .40 1.00
23 Andre Davis .30 .75
24 Lee Suggs .40 1.00
25 Keyshawn Johnson .40 1.00
26 Eddie George .40 1.00
27 Vinny Testaverde .40 1.00
28 Quentin Griffin .30 .75
29 Champ Bailey .40 1.00
30 Jake Plummer .40 1.00
31 Az-Zahir Hakim .30 .75
32 Joey Harrington .40 1.00
33 Charles Rogers .30 .75
34 Javon Walker .30 .75
35 Ahman Green .40 1.00
36 Brett Favre 1.25 3.00
37 Domanick Davis .30 .75
38 David Carr .30 .75
39 Andre Johnson .50 1.25
40 Edgerrin James .40 1.00
41 Marvin Harrison .50 1.25
42 Reggie Wayne .50 1.25
43 Peyton Manning 1.00 2.50
44 Fred Taylor .40 1.00
45 Jimmy Smith .40 1.00
46 Byron Leftwich .40 1.00
47 Dante Hall .40 1.00
48 Tony Gonzalez .50 1.25
49 Trent Green .40 1.00
50 Priest Holmes .50 1.25
51 Zach Thomas .50 1.25
52 A.J. Feeley .30 .75
53 Chris Chambers .40 1.00
54 Randy McMichael .30 .75
55 Randy Moss .50 1.25
56 Onterrio Smith .30 .75
57 Daunte Culpepper .40 1.00
58 Tom Brady 1.00 2.50
59 Deion Branch .40 1.00
60 Corey Dillon .40 1.00
61 Donte' Stallworth .30 .75
62 Deuce McAllister .40 1.00
63 Aaron Brooks .40 1.00
64 Amani Toomer .40 1.00
65 Jeremy Shockey .40 1.00
66 Kurt Warner .50 1.25
67 Curtis Martin .50 1.25
68 Chad Pennington .50 1.25
69 Santana Moss .40 1.00
70 Jerry Porter .30 .75
71 Jerry Rice 1.00 2.50
72 Rich Gannon .40 1.00
73 Justin Fargas .40 1.00
74 Terrell Owens .50 1.25
75 Brian Westbrook .50 1.25
76 Donovan McNabb .50 1.25
77 Tommy Maddox .40 1.00
78 Hines Ward .50 1.25
79 Plaxico Burress .40 1.00
80 Antonio Gates .50 1.25
81 LaDainian Tomlinson .50 1.25
82 Drew Brees .50 1.25
83 Brandon Lloyd .40 1.00
84 Tim Rattay .30 .75
85 Kevan Barlow .30 .75
86 Koren Robinson .30 .75
87 Shaun Alexander .40 1.00
88 Matt Hasselbeck .40 1.00
89 Torry Holt .40 1.00
90 Marc Bulger .40 1.00
91 Marshall Faulk .50 1.25
92 Chris Simms .40 1.00
93 Keenan McCardell .30 .75
94 Derrick Brooks .40 1.00
95 Steve McNair .50 1.25
96 Chris Brown .30 .75
97 Derrick Mason .40 1.00
98 Mark Brunell .40 1.00
99 Laveranues Coles .30 .75
100 Clinton Portis .50 1.25
101 Michael Jenkins RC 4.00 10.00
102 Ryan Krause RC 2.50 6.00
103 Darnell Dockett RC 2.50 6.00
104 Quincy Wilson RC 3.00 8.00
105 Nate Lawrie RC 2.50 6.00
106 Joey Thomas RC 2.50 6.00
107 Junior Siavii RC 2.50 6.00
108 Landon Johnson RC 2.50 6.00
109 Michael Waddell RC 2.50 6.00
110 Lee Evans RC 4.00 10.00
111 Jason David RC 2.50 6.00
112 Chris Collins RC 2.50 6.00
113 Troy Fleming RC 2.50 6.00
114 Tim Euhus RC 2.50 6.00
115 Sean Jones RC 3.00 8.00
116 Jason Babin RC 4.00 10.00
117 Jorge Cordova RC 2.50 6.00
118 Josh Scobee RC 3.00 8.00
119 Luke McCown RC 3.00 8.00
120 Darius Watts RC 2.50 6.00
121 Clarence Moore RC 2.50 6.00
122 Randy Starks RC 2.50 6.00
123 Brandon Miree RC 2.50 6.00
124 Gibril Wilson RC 4.00 10.00
125 Jeremy LeSueur RC 2.50 6.00
126 Dwan Edwards RC 2.50 6.00
127 Richard Seigler RC 2.50 6.00
128 Stanford Samuels RC 2.50 6.00
129 Casey Clausen RC 3.00 8.00
130 Erik Coleman RC 3.00 8.00
131 Donnell Washington RC 3.00 8.00
132 Jammal Lord RC 2.50 6.00
133 Chris Cooley RC 4.00 10.00
134 Shawntae Spencer RC 2.50 6.00
135 Marcus Tubbs RC 2.50 6.00
136 Caleb Miller RC 2.50 6.00
137 Jeff Shoate RC 2.50 6.00
138 Bradlee Van Pelt RC 3.00 8.00
139 D.J. Hackett RC 3.00 8.00
140 Greg Brooks RC 2.50 6.00
141 Thomas Tapeh RC 3.00 8.00
142 Ben Hartsock RC 2.50 6.00
143 Madieu Williams RC 2.50 6.00
144 Vince Wilfork RC 4.00 10.00
145 Marquis Cooper RC 2.50 6.00
146 Nate Kaeding RC 4.00 10.00
147 B.J. Symons RC 2.50 6.00
148 Maurice Mann RC 2.50 6.00
149 Tim Anderson RC 3.00 8.00
150 Michael Turner RC 5.00 12.00
151 Kris Wilson RC 3.00 8.00
152 Keiwan Ratliff RC 2.50 6.00
153 Kenechi Udeze RC 3.00 8.00
154 Courtney Watson RC 2.50 6.00
155 Stacy Andrews RC 2.50 6.00
156 Jeff Smoker RC 3.00 8.00
157 Carlos Francis RC 2.50 6.00
158 Derek Abney RC 2.50 6.00
159 Dexter Wynn RC 2.50 6.00
160 Jason Wright RC 2.50 6.00
161 Dunta Robinson RC 2.50 6.00
162 Nathan Vasher RC 4.00 10.00
163 Karlos Dansby RC 4.00 10.00
164 Jake Grove RC 2.50 6.00
165 Matt Mauck RC 2.50 6.00
166 Johnnie Morant RC 2.50 6.00
167 Justin Jenkins RC 2.50 6.00
168 Cedric Cobbs RC 2.50 6.00
169 Ben Troupe RC 3.00 8.00
170 Bob Sanders RC 10.00 25.00
171 Will Smith RC 3.00 8.00
172 Michael Boulware RC 4.00 10.00
173 Nat Dorsey RC 2.50 6.00
174 Casey Bramlet RC 2.50 6.00
175 Ernest Wilford RC 3.00 8.00
176 Kendrick Starling RC 2.50 6.00
177 Mewelde Moore RC 3.00 8.00
178 Ben Watson RC 4.00 10.00
179 Ricardo Colclough RC 3.00 8.00
180 Tommie Harris RC 4.00 10.00
181 Dontarrious Thomas RC 3.00 8.00
182 Keith Lewis RC 2.50 6.00
183 John Navarre RC 2.50 6.00
184 Samie Parker RC 2.50 6.00
185 B.J. Johnson RC 2.50 6.00
186 Tatum Bell RC 3.00 8.00
187 Mike Karney RC 3.00 8.00
188 Ahmad Carroll RC 2.50 6.00
189 Will Allen RC 3.00 8.00
190 Teddy Lehman RC 2.50 6.00
191 Justin Smiley RC 3.00 8.00
192 Cody Pickett RC 3.00 8.00
193 Jerricho Cotchery RC 3.00 8.00
194 Tramon Douglas RC 2.50 6.00
195 Greg Jones RC 2.50 6.00
196 Kellen Winslow RC 4.00 10.00
197 Chris Gamble RC 3.00 8.00
198 Dexter Reid RC 2.50 6.00
199 Daryl Smith RC 2.50 6.00
200 Max Starks RC 3.00 8.00
201 J.P. Losman RC 3.00 8.00
202 Rashaun Woods RC 2.50 6.00
203 Triandos Luke RC 2.50 6.00
204 Rashad Washington RC 2.50 6.00
205 Derrick Ward RC 4.00 10.00
206 Matt Kranchick RC 3.00 8.00
207 Keith Smith RC 2.50 6.00
208 Travis LaBoy RC 3.00 8.00
209 Demorrio Williams RC 4.00 10.00
210 Jason Shivers RC 2.50 6.00
211 Craig Krenzel RC 3.00 8.00
212 Keary Colbert RC 2.50 6.00
213 Mark Jones RC 2.50 6.00
214 Shawn Johnson RC 2.50 6.00
215 Jarrett Payton RC 3.00 8.00
216 Michael Gaines RC 2.50 6.00
217 Matt Ware RC 4.00 10.00
218 Antwan Odom RC 3.00 8.00
219 Brandon Chillar RC 3.00 8.00
220 Michael Clayton RC 3.00 8.00
221 Jamaar Taylor RC 2.50 6.00
222 George Wilson RC 3.00 8.00
223 Tony Hargrove RC 2.50 6.00
224 Sean Ryan RC 2.50 6.00
225 Stuart Schweigert RC 3.00 8.00
226 Igor Olshansky RC 3.00 8.00
227 Keyaron Fox RC 3.00 8.00
228 Glenn Earl RC 2.50 6.00
229 Bruce Thornton RC 2.50 6.00
230 Derrick Hamilton RC 2.50 6.00
231 Sloan Thomas RC 3.00 8.00
232 Matthias Askew RC 2.50 6.00
233 Ran Carthon RC 2.50 6.00
234 Ben Utecht RC 3.00 8.00
235 Kendyll Pope RC 2.50 6.00
236 Marquise Hill RC 2.50 6.00
237 Shawn Andrews RC 3.00 8.00
238 Jim Sorgi RC 3.00 8.00
239 Devard Darling RC 2.50 6.00
240 Patrick Crayton RC 4.00 10.00
241 Ryan McGuffey RC 2.50 6.00
242 Darrion Scott RC 3.00 8.00
243 DeAngelo Hall RC 4.00 10.00
244 Alex Lewis RC 2.50 6.00
245 D.J. Williams RC 4.00 10.00
246 Chris Snee RC 3.00 8.00
247 Matt Schaub RC 8.00 20.00
248 Devery Henderson RC 4.00 10.00
249 Jeris McIntyre RC 2.50 6.00
250 Wes Welker RC 15.00 40.00
251 Bruce Perry RC 2.50 6.00
252 Jeff Dugan RC 2.50 6.00
253 Derrick Strait RC 2.50 6.00
254 Terry Johnson RC 2.50 6.00
255 Niko Koutouvides RC 2.50 6.00
256 Von Hutchins RC 2.50 6.00
257 Josh Harris RC 2.50 6.00
258 Bernard Berrian RC 4.00 10.00
259 Roderick Green RC 2.50 6.00
260 Romar Crenshaw RC 2.50 6.00
261 Jacob Rogers RC 4.00 10.00
262 Sean Taylor RC 8.00 20.00
263 J.R. Reed RC 2.50 6.00
264 Jonathan Vilma RC 4.00 10.00
265 Stephen Peterman RC 4.00 10.00
266 Eli Manning RC 40.00 80.00
267 Philip Rivers RC 30.00 60.00
268 Larry Fitzgerald RC 12.00 30.00
269 Ben Roethlisberger RC 50.00 100.00
270 Kevin Jones RC 4.00 10.00
271 Steven Jackson RC 8.00 20.00
272 Roy Williams RC 5.00 12.00
273 Julius Jones RC 4.00 10.00
274 Reggie Williams RC 4.00 10.00
275 Chris Perry RC 4.00 10.00
276 Robert Gallery RC 5.00 12.00
277 Kellen Winslow RC 5.00 12.00
278 Drew Henson RC 3.00 8.00

2004 Upper Deck Finite HG Radiance

*VETS 1-100: 10X TO 25X BASIC CARDS
*ROOKIES 101-265: 5X TO 12X BASIC RC
*ROOKIES 266-278: 3X TO 8X BASIC RC
RADIANCE PRINT RUN 15 SETS

2004 Upper Deck Finite HG Fabrics

STATED ODDS 1:10
*RADIANCE/25: 1.2X TO 3X BASIC JSY
*RADIANCE/25: 1X TO 2.5X JSY SP
RADIANCE PRINT RUN 25 SER.#'d SETS
FFBA Barry Sanders SP 12.00 30.00
FFBF Brett Favre 10.00 25.00
FFBU Brian Urlacher 4.00 10.00
FFCP Clinton Portis 4.00 10.00
FFCR Charles Rogers 2.50 6.00
FFCW Charles Woodson 4.00 10.00
FFDA David Boston 2.50 6.00
FFDB Drew Bledsoe 4.00 10.00
FFDC Daunte Culpepper 3.00 8.00
FFDE Deuce McAllister 3.00 8.00
FFDM Dan Marino SP 15.00 40.00
FFEM Eric Moulds 3.00 8.00
FFES Emmitt Smith 10.00 25.00
FFFT Fred Taylor 3.00 8.00
FFIB Isaac Bruce 3.00 8.00
FFJB Jerome Bettis 4.00 10.00
FFJF John Elway 12.00 30.00
FFJK Jevon Kearse 3.00 8.00
FFJM Joe Montana SP 15.00 40.00
FFJP Jake Plummer 3.00 8.00
FFJU Johnny Unitas 12.00 30.00
FFKC Kerry Collins 3.00 8.00
FFKE Kellen Winslow Sr. SP 6.00 15.00
FFKW Kurt Warner 4.00 10.00
FFLA LaVar Arrington 4.00 10.00
FFLD Len Dawson SP 8.00 20.00
FFLT LaDainian Tomlinson 4.00 10.00
FFMA Mark Brunell 3.00 8.00
FFMB Marc Bulger 3.00 8.00
FFMV Michael Vick 5.00 12.00
FFPM Peyton Manning 8.00 20.00
FFRM Randy Moss 4.00 10.00
FFRS Roger Staubach SP 10.00 25.00
FFSM Santana Moss 3.00 8.00
FFST Steve McNair 4.00 10.00
FFTA Troy Aikman SP 10.00 25.00
FFTB Tom Brady 8.00 20.00
FFTG Tony Gonzalez 4.00 10.00
FFTM Tommy Maddox 3.00 8.00
FFTO Terrell Owens 4.00 10.00
FFWS Warren Sapp 3.00 8.00
FFZT Zach Thomas 4.00 10.00

2004 Upper Deck Finite HG Fabrics Duals

STATED ODDS 1:30
AS Troy Aikman SP 15.00 40.00
Roger Staubach
BB Marc Bulger 4.00 10.00
Isaac Bruce
BM David Boston 4.00 10.00
Eric Moulds
BP Mark Brunell 5.00 12.00
Clinton Portis
BW Tom Brady 10.00 25.00
Kurt Warner
EM John Elway SP 30.00 80.00
Dan Marino
FW Larry Fitzgerald 8.00 20.00
Roy Williams WR
JJ Julius Jones 2.50 6.00
Kevin Jones
LR J.P. Losman 20.00 50.00
Ben Roethlisberger
MB Tommy Maddox 8.00 20.00
Jerome Bettis
MM Peyton Manning 10.00 25.00
Steve McNair
PA Clinton Portis 5.00 12.00
LaVar Arrington
RM Philip Rivers 20.00 50.00
Eli Manning
UD Johnny Unitas SP 20.00 50.00
Len Dawson
WS Charles Woodson 5.00 12.00
Warren Sapp

2004 Upper Deck Finite HG Fabrics Triples

STATED ODDS 1:40
BRB Isaac Bruce 6.00 15.00
Charles Rogers
David Boston
BVB Marc Bulger 10.00 25.00
Michael Vick
Mark Brunell
JJJ Julius Jones 6.00 15.00
Greg Jones
Kevin Jones
MMF Eli Manning 40.00 80.00
Joe Montana
Brett Favre
MRR Eli Manning 30.00 80.00
Philip Rivers
Ben Roethlisberger
NAM Joe Namath SP 25.00 60.00
Troy Aikman
Dan Marino
OMM Terrell Owens SP 8.00 20.00
Randy Moss
Santana Moss
PBM Jake Plummer 8.00 20.00
Drew Bledsoe
Steve McNair
PST Clinton Portis 20.00 50.00
Emmitt Smith
LaDainian Tomlinson
SPT Barry Sanders 15.00 40.00
Chris Perry
LaDainian Tomlinson
UAT Brian Urlacher 8.00 20.00
Lavar Arrington
Zach Thomas
USE Johnny Unitas SP 30.00 80.00
Roger Staubach
John Elway
WFW Roy Williams WR 12.00 30.00
Larry Fitzgerald
Kellen Winslow Jr.
WMF Reggie Williams 12.00 30.00
Randy Moss
Larry Fitzgerald
WWG Kellen Winslow Jr. 8.00 20.00
Kellen Winslow Sr.
Tony Gonzalez

2004 Upper Deck Finite HG Rookie Fabrics

STATED ODDS 1:10
BB Bernard Berrian 4.00 10.00
BR Ben Roethlisberger 15.00 40.00
BT Ben Troupe 3.00 8.00
CP Chris Perry 3.00 8.00
DH Devery Henderson 4.00 10.00
DW Darius Watts 2.50 6.00
EM Eli Manning 12.00 30.00
GJ Greg Jones 2.50 6.00
JJ Julius Jones 3.00 8.00
JP J.P. Losman 3.00 8.00
KC Keary Colbert 2.50 6.00
KJ Kevin Jones 3.00 8.00
KW Kellen Winslow Jr. 4.00 10.00
LE Lee Evans 4.00 10.00
LF Larry Fitzgerald 8.00 20.00
LM Luke McCown 3.00 8.00
MC Michael Clayton 3.00 8.00
MJ Michael Jenkins 4.00 10.00
PR Philip Rivers 10.00 25.00
RA Rashaun Woods 2.50 6.00
RE Reggie Williams 3.00 8.00
RG Robert Gallery 4.00 10.00
RW Roy Williams WR 4.00 10.00
SJ Steven Jackson 6.00 15.00
TB Tatum Bell 3.00 8.00

2004 Upper Deck Finite HG Signatures

STATED ODDS 1:10
FSAN Andy Reid SP 20.00 50.00
FSAR Antwaan Randle El 6.00 15.00
FSBC Brandon Chillar 6.00 15.00
FSBE Ben Watson 8.00 20.00
FSBH Ben Hartsock 5.00 12.00
FSBL Brandon Lloyd 6.00 15.00
FSBR Ben Roethlisberger SP 100.00 175.00
FSBS Barry Sanders SP 60.00 120.00
FSBT Ben Troupe 6.00 15.00
FSBW Brian Westbrook 8.00 20.00
FSCC Casey Clausen 6.00 15.00
FSCE Cedric Cobbs 5.00 12.00
FSCF Clarence Farmer 5.00 12.00
FSCO Cody Pickett 6.00 15.00
FSCP Chad Pennington 8.00 20.00
FSDB Drew Bledsoe SP 10.00 25.00
FSDD Devard Darling 5.00 12.00
FSDE Deuce McAllister 6.00 15.00
FSDH Devery Henderson 8.00 20.00
FSDR Drew Henson SP 5.00 12.00
FSDW Darius Watts 5.00 12.00
FSEM Eli Manning 100.00 200.00
FSGA Robert Gallery 8.00 20.00
FSGR Jon Gruden SP 10.00 25.00
FSHA DeAngelo Hall 8.00 20.00
FSJC Jerricho Cotchery 6.00 15.00
FSJF John Fox SP 5.00 12.00
FSJG Joey Galloway 6.00 15.00
FSJJ Julius Jones 6.00 15.00
FSJM Johnnie Morant 5.00 12.00
FSJN John Navarre 5.00 12.00
FSJO Joe Montana SP 100.00 200.00
FSJP J.P. Losman 6.00 15.00
FSJS Josh McCown 6.00 15.00
FSJT Joe Theismann SP 10.00 25.00
FSJV Jonathan Vilma 8.00 20.00
FSKC Keary Colbert 5.00 12.00
FSKE Kelley Washington 5.00 12.00
FSKJ Kevin Jones 6.00 15.00
FSLE Lee Evans 8.00 20.00
FSMS Matt Schaub 15.00 40.00
FSMV Michael Vick SP 30.00 60.00
FSNA Joe Namath 50.00 100.00
FSPM Peyton Manning SP 50.00 100.00
FSPR Philip Rivers 40.00 80.00
FSQW Quincy Wilson 6.00 15.00
FSRE Reggie Williams 6.00 15.00
FSRG Rex Grossman 6.00 15.00
FSRJ Rudi Johnson 6.00 15.00
FSRW Roy Williams WR 8.00 20.00
FSSJ Steven Jackson 12.00 30.00
FSSP Samie Parker 5.00 12.00
FSTB Tatum Bell 6.00 15.00
FSTH Tommie Harris 8.00 20.00
FSTR Travis Henry 5.00 12.00
FSWM Willis McGahee 8.00 20.00

2004 Upper Deck Finite HG Signatures Radiance

*RADIANCE: .8X TO 2X BASIC SIGS
RADIANCE PRINT RUN 25 SER.#'d SETS
FSAN Andy Reid 30.00 80.00
FSBR Ben Roethlisberger 125.00 250.00
FSBS Barry Sanders 175.00 300.00
FSEM Eli Manning 175.00 300.00
FSJO Joe Montana 125.00 250.00
FSMV Michael Vick 50.00 100.00
FSPM Peyton Manning 125.00 200.00
FSPR Philip Rivers 75.00 150.00

2007 Upper Deck First Edition

This 200-card set was released in July, 2007. The set was issued through Upper Deck's retail channels and contained 10 cards with an 99 cent SRP which came 36 packs to a box. Cards numbered 1-100 feature veterans in team alphabetical order while cards numbered 101-200 feature 2007 NFL rookies.

COMPLETE SET (200)	20.00	40.00
COMP.SET w/o RCs (100)	8.00	20.00
1 Matt Leinart	.12	.30
2 Larry Fitzgerald	.15	.40
3 Anquan Boldin	.12	.30
4 Michael Vick	.15	.40
5 Warrick Dunn	.12	.30
6 Alge Crumpler	.12	.30
7 Steve McNair	.12	.30
8 Mark Clayton	.12	.30
9 Todd Heap	.10	.25
10 Ray Lewis	.15	.40
11 J.P. Losman	.10	.25
12 Lee Evans	.12	.30
13 Anthony Thomas	.10	.25
14 Jake Delhomme	.12	.30
15 DeShaun Foster	.12	.30
16 Steve Smith	.12	.30
17 Cedric Benson	.12	.30
18 Bernard Berrian	.10	.25
19 Brian Urlacher	.15	.40
20 Carson Palmer	.12	.30
21 Rudi Johnson	.12	.30
22 Chad Johnson	.12	.30
23 Kellen Winslow	.12	.30
24 Braylon Edwards	.12	.30
25 Tony Romo	.20	.50
26 Julius Jones	.10	.25
27 Terrell Owens	.15	.40
28 Jay Cutler	.15	.40
29 Javon Walker	.12	.30
30 Champ Bailey	.12	.30
31 Jon Kitna	.10	.25
32 Kevin Jones	.10	.25
33 Roy Williams WR	.12	.30
34 Brett Favre	.30	.75
35 Donald Driver	.15	.40
36 A.J. Hawk	.12	.30
37 Andre Johnson	.12	.30
38 Mario Williams	.12	.30
39 Ron Dayne	.12	.30
40 Peyton Manning	.25	.60
41 Marvin Harrison	.15	.40
42 Reggie Wayne	.12	.30
43 Joseph Addai	.12	.30
44 Maurice Jones-Drew	.15	.40
45 Fred Taylor	.12	.30
46 Byron Leftwich	.12	.30
47 Larry Johnson	.10	.25
48 Tony Gonzalez	.12	.30
49 Damon Huard	.12	.30
50 Ronnie Brown	.12	.30
51 Jason Taylor	.12	.30
52 Chris Chambers	.12	.30
53 Chester Taylor	.10	.25
54 Tarvaris Jackson	.10	.25
55 Troy Williamson	.10	.25
56 Tom Brady	.25	.60
57 Laurence Maroney	.12	.30
58 Ben Watson	.10	.25
59 Asante Samuel	.10	.25
60 Chad Pennington	.12	.30
61 Leon Washington	.12	.30
62 Laveranues Coles	.10	.25
63 Eli Manning	.15	.40
64 Jeremy Shockey	.12	.30
65 Brandon Jacobs	.12	.30
66 Drew Brees	.15	.40
67 Marques Colston	.15	.40
68 Reggie Bush	.15	.40
69 Deuce McAllister	.12	.30
70 Jerry Porter	.12	.30
71 Justin Fargas	.10	.25
72 Randy Moss	.15	.40
73 Brian Westbrook	.12	.30
74 Reggie Brown	.10	.25
75 Donovan McNabb	.15	.40
76 Ben Roethlisberger	.15	.40
77 Willie Parker	.12	.30
78 Troy Polamalu	.15	.40
79 Antonio Gates	.15	.40
80 Shawne Merriman	.12	.30
81 LaDainian Tomlinson	.15	.40
82 Alex Smith QB	.15	.40
83 Frank Gore	.15	.40
84 Vernon Davis	.12	.30
85 Steven Jackson	.15	.40
86 Marc Bulger	.12	.30
87 Torry Holt	.12	.30
88 Isaac Bruce	.12	.30
89 Matt Hasselbeck	.12	.30
90 Shaun Alexander	.12	.30
91 Deion Branch	.12	.30
92 Cadillac Williams	.12	.30
93 Michael Clayton	.10	.25
94 Joey Galloway	.12	.30
95 Vince Young	.12	.30
96 LenDale White	.12	.30
97 Jason Campbell	.12	.30
98 Clinton Portis	.12	.30
99 Santana Moss	.12	.30
100 Antwaan Randle El	.10	.25
101 JaMarcus Russell RC	.40	1.00
102 Brady Quinn RC	.60	1.50
103 Calvin Johnson RC	2.00	5.00
104 Adrian Peterson RC	2.50	6.00
105 Joe Thomas RC	.60	1.50
106 Levi Brown RC	.60	1.50
107 Gaines Adams RC	.60	1.50
108 Adam Carriker RC	.50	1.25
109 Ted Ginn Jr. RC	.50	1.25
110 Anthony Gonzalez RC	.60	1.50
111 Troy Smith RC	.60	1.50
112 Leon Hall RC	.50	1.25
113 LaMarr Woodley RC	.60	1.50
114 Alan Branch RC	.50	1.25
115 Patrick Willis RC	1.25	3.00
116 Reggie Nelson RC	.50	1.25
117 Paul Posluszny RC	.60	1.50
118 Dwayne Bowe RC	.75	2.00
119 Steve Smith RC	.60	1.50
120 Dwayne Jarrett RC	.50	1.25
121 Marshawn Lynch RC	.60	1.50
122 Darius Walker RC	.40	1.00
123 Daymeion Hughes RC	.50	1.25
124 LaRon Landry RC	.60	1.50
125 Jon Beason RC	.50	1.25
126 Lawrence Timmons RC	.60	1.50
127 Drew Stanton RC	.40	1.00
128 Trent Edwards RC	.60	1.50
129 John Beck RC	.60	1.50
130 Kevin Kolb RC	1.00	2.50
131 Amobi Okoye RC	.60	1.50
132 Michael Bush RC	.60	1.50
133 Darrelle Revis RC	1.00	2.50
134 H.B. Blades RC	.40	1.00
135 Jamaal Anderson RC	.50	1.25
136 Robert Meachem RC	.60	1.50
137 Sidney Rice RC	.75	2.00
138 Craig Davis RC	.50	1.25
139 Paul Williams RC	.40	1.00
140 Greg Olsen RC	.50	1.25
141 Jarvis Moss RC	.50	1.25
142 Justin Harrell RC	.50	1.25
143 DeMarcus Tank Tyler RC	.40	1.00
144 Aaron Ross RC	.60	1.50
145 Chris Houston RC	.50	1.25
146 Brandon Meriweather RC	.60	1.50
147 Eric Weddle RC	.60	1.50
148 Lorenzo Booker RC	.50	1.25
149 Buster Davis RC	.50	1.25
150 Antonio Pittman RC	.40	1.00
151 Chris Henry RC	.40	1.00
152 Kenny Irons RC	.40	1.00
153 Brandon Jackson RC	.50	1.25
154 Tony Hunt RC	.40	1.00
155 Brian Leonard RC	.50	1.25
156 Garrett Wolfe RC	.40	1.00
157 Yamon Figurs RC	.40	1.00
158 Johnnie Lee Higgins RC	.50	1.25
159 Jordan Palmer RC	.50	1.25
160 Chris Leak RC	.50	1.25
161 Rhema McKnight RC	.40	1.00
162 Dwayne Wright RC	.50	1.25
163 Matt Moore RC	.60	1.50
164 Jeff Rowe RC	.40	1.00
165 Zach Miller RC	.60	1.50
166 Ben Patrick RC	.50	1.25
167 Joe Staley RC	.50	1.25
168 Eric Wright RC	.60	1.50
169 Aundrae Allison RC	.40	1.00
170 Steve Breaston RC	.60	1.50
171 David Harris RC	.50	1.25
172 Brandon Siler RC	.40	1.00
173 Tim Shaw RC	.50	1.25
174 Selvin Young RC	.50	1.25
175 Michael Griffin RC	.60	1.50
176 Kenneth Darby RC	.50	1.25
177 Anthony Spencer RC	.60	1.50
178 Charles Johnson RC	.40	1.00
179 Quentin Moses RC	.50	1.25
180 DeShawn Wynn RC	.50	1.25
181 Scott Chandler RC	.60	1.50
182 Stewart Bradley RC	.50	1.25
183 Ahmad Bradshaw RC	1.00	2.50
184 Matt Spaeth RC	.60	1.50
185 Ray McDonald RC	.50	1.25
186 Ben Grubbs RC	.50	1.25
187 Jon Abbate RC	.40	1.00
188 Victor Abiamiri RC	.60	1.50
189 Courtney Taylor RC	.50	1.25
190 A.J. Davis RC	.40	1.00
191 Nate Harris RC	.50	1.25
192 Jonathan Wade RC	.50	1.25
193 Tim Crowder RC	.60	1.50
194 Legedu Naanee RC	.60	1.50
195 Quinn Pitcock RC	.50	1.25
196 Marcus McCauley RC	.50	1.25
197 Sabby Piscitelli RC	.60	1.50
198 Tanard Jackson RC	.40	1.00
199 Josh Gattis RC	.40	1.00
200 Rufus Alexander RC	.50	1.25

2007 Upper Deck First Edition Gold

*VETS: 1.5X TO 4X BASIC CARDS
*ROOKIES: .6X TO 1.5X BASIC CARDS

2007 Upper Deck First Edition 1st and Goal

FGBJ Brandon Jacobs	.60	1.50
FGBR Ronnie Brown	.60	1.50
FGCP Clinton Portis	.60	1.50
FGCT Chester Taylor	.50	1.25
FGCW Cadillac Williams	.60	1.50
FGDM Deuce McAllister	.60	1.50
FGEJ Edgerrin James	.60	1.50
FGFG Frank Gore	.75	2.00
FGJA Joseph Addai	.60	1.50
FGKJ Kevin Jones	.50	1.25
FGLJ Larry Johnson	.50	1.25
FGLT LaDainian Tomlinson	.75	2.00
FGMB Marion Barber	.60	1.50
FGMJ Maurice Jones-Drew	.75	2.00
FGRB Reggie Bush	.75	2.00
FGRJ Rudi Johnson	.60	1.50
FGSA Shaun Alexander	.60	1.50
FGSJ Steven Jackson	.75	2.00
FGTJ Thomas Jones	.60	1.50
FGWP Willie Parker	.60	1.50

2007 Upper Deck First Edition Autographs

RANDOM INSERTS IN PACKS

SEAO Amobi Okoye	5.00	12.00
SEBA Dallas Baker	5.00	12.00
SEBL Brian Leonard	4.00	10.00
SEBU Marc Bulger	4.00	10.00
SECD Craig Davis	5.00	12.00
SECT Chester Taylor	3.00	8.00
SEDB David Ball	4.00	10.00
SEDH Daymeion Hughes	3.00	8.00
SEDW Dwayne Wright	3.00	8.00
SEGA Gaines Adams	5.00	12.00
SEGW Garrett Wolfe	5.00	12.00
SEHB H.B. Blades	4.00	10.00
SEHI Johnnie Lee Higgins	4.00	10.00
SEHO T.J. Houshmandzadeh	4.00	10.00
SEJB John Beck	6.00	15.00
SEJH Jason Hill	5.00	12.00
SEJP Jordan Palmer	5.00	12.00
SEJT Joe Thomas	5.00	12.00
SEKD Kenneth Darby	5.00	12.00
SEKS Kolby Smith	4.00	10.00
SELH Leon Hall	5.00	12.00
SELN Legedu Naanee	4.00	10.00
SELT Lawrence Timmons	5.00	12.00
SELW LaMarr Woodley	8.00	20.00
SEMM Matt Moore	5.00	12.00
SEQM Quentin Moses	4.00	10.00
SERM Rhema McKnight	4.00	10.00
SERN Reggie Nelson	5.00	12.00
SESC Scott Chandler	4.00	10.00
SESY Selvin Young	8.00	20.00
SETP Tyler Palko	4.00	10.00
SEZM Zach Miller	4.00	10.00

2007 Upper Deck First Edition Freshman Phenoms

FPAO Amobi Okoye	.75	2.00
FPAP Adrian Peterson	3.00	8.00
FPBJ Brandon Jackson	.60	1.50
FPBQ Brady Quinn	.75	2.00
FPCJ Calvin Johnson	2.50	6.00
FPDB Dwayne Bowe	1.00	2.50
FPDJ Dwayne Jarrett	.60	1.50
FPDS Drew Stanton	.50	1.25
FPDW Darius Walker	.50	1.25
FPGA Gaines Adams	.75	2.00
FPGO Greg Olsen	.60	1.50
FPJR JaMarcus Russell	.50	1.25
FPLH Leon Hall	.60	1.50
FPLL LaRon Landry	.75	2.00
FPML Marshawn Lynch	.75	2.00
FPPP Paul Posluszny	.75	2.00
FPRM Robert Meachem	.75	2.00
FPRN Reggie Nelson	.60	1.50
FPSS Steve Smith USC	.75	2.00
FPTG Ted Ginn Jr.	.60	1.50

2007 Upper Deck First Edition Passing Grade

PGAS Alex Smith QB	.75	2.00
PGBF Brett Favre	1.50	4.00
PGBR Ben Roethlisberger	.75	2.00
PGCP Carson Palmer	.60	1.50
PGDB Drew Brees	.75	2.00
PGDM Donovan McNabb	.75	2.00
PGEM Eli Manning	.75	2.00
PGJD Jake Delhomme	.60	1.50
PGJL J.P. Losman	.50	1.25
PGMB Marc Bulger	.60	1.50
PGMH Matt Hasselbeck	.60	1.50
PGML Matt Leinart	.60	1.50
PGMV Michael Vick	.75	2.00
PGPE Chad Pennington	.60	1.50
PGPM Peyton Manning	1.25	3.00
PGRG Rex Grossman	.60	1.50
PGSM Steve McNair	.60	1.50
PGTB Tom Brady	1.25	3.00
PGTR Tony Romo	1.00	2.50
PGVY Vince Young	.60	1.50

2007 Upper Deck First Edition Sophomore Sensations

SSAF Anthony Fasano	.50	1.25
SSAH A.J. Hawk	.60	1.50
SSDH Devin Hester	.75	2.00
SSDW DeAngelo Williams	.75	2.00
SSJA Joseph Addai	.60	1.50
SSJC Jay Cutler	.75	2.00
SSJN Jerious Norwood	.60	1.50
SSLM Laurence Maroney	.60	1.50
SSLW Leon Washington	.60	1.50
SSMA Mark Anderson	.60	1.50
SSMC Marques Colston	.75	2.00
SSMH Michael Huff	.60	1.50
SSMJ Maurice Jones-Drew	.75	2.00
SSML Matt Leinart	.60	1.50
SSMW Mario Williams	.60	1.50
SSRB Reggie Bush	.75	2.00
SSSH Santonio Holmes	.60	1.50
SSTJ Tarvaris Jackson	.50	1.25
SSVD Vernon Davis	.60	1.50
SSVY Vince Young	.60	1.50

2007 Upper Deck First Edition Speed 2 Burn

SBBR Ronnie Brown	.60	1.50
SBBW Brian Westbrook	.60	1.50
SBCB Champ Bailey	.60	1.50
SBCJ Chad Johnson	.60	1.50
SBDH Devin Hester	.75	2.00
SBFG Frank Gore	.75	2.00
SBFT Fred Taylor	.60	1.50
SBLJ Larry Johnson	.50	1.25
SBLT LaDainian Tomlinson	.75	2.00
SBMV Michael Vick	.75	2.00
SBRB Reggie Bush	.75	2.00
SBRW Reggie Wayne	.60	1.50
SBSA Shaun Alexander	.60	1.50
SBSJ Steven Jackson	.75	2.00
SBSM Santana Moss	.60	1.50
SBSS Steve Smith	.60	1.50
SBTO Terrell Owens	.75	2.00
SBVY Vince Young	.60	1.50
SBWI Roy Williams WR	.60	1.50
SBWP Willie Parker	.60	1.50

2008 Upper Deck First Edition

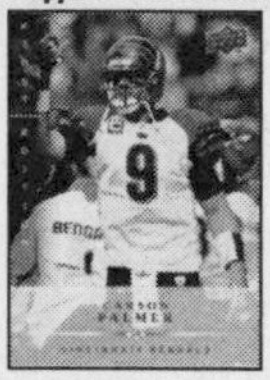

This set was released on September 8, 2008. The base set consists of 225 cards. Cards 1-150 feature veterans, and cards 151-225 are rookies.

COMPLETE SET (225)	20.00	40.00
COMP.FACT.SET (226)	25.00	40.00
1 Edgerrin James	.12	.30
2 Matt Leinart	.15	.40
3 Larry Fitzgerald	.15	.40
4 Anquan Boldin	.12	.30
5 Antrel Rolle	.10	.25
6 Joe Horn	.12	.30
7 Warrick Dunn	.12	.30
8 Jerious Norwood	.12	.30
9 Michael Jenkins	.10	.25
10 Ed Reed	.12	.30
11 Willis McGahee	.12	.30
12 Steve McNair	.12	.30
13 Todd Heap	.10	.25
14 Ray Lewis	.15	.40
15 Terrell Suggs	.10	.25
16 Trent Edwards	.10	.25
17 Lee Evans	.12	.30
18 Roscoe Parrish	.10	.25
19 Marshawn Lynch	.12	.30
20 DeAngelo Williams	.12	.30
21 Julius Peppers	.12	.30
22 Steve Smith	.12	.30
23 Cedric Benson	.12	.30
24 Greg Olsen	.12	.30
25 Lance Briggs	.12	.30
26 Rex Grossman	.12	.30
27 Devin Hester	.15	.40
28 Brian Urlacher	.15	.40
29 T.J. Houshmandzadeh	.12	.30
30 Carson Palmer	.15	.40
31 Rudi Johnson	.12	.30
32 Chad Johnson	.12	.30
33 Stacy Andrews	.12	.30
34 Kamerion Wimbley	.10	.25
35 Joshua Cribbs	.15	.40
36 Jamal Lewis	.12	.30
37 Kellen Winslow	.12	.30
38 Braylon Edwards	.12	.30
39 Marion Barber	.12	.30
40 Jason Witten	.15	.40
41 DeMarcus Ware	.12	.30
42 Tony Romo	.20	.50
43 Terrell Owens	.15	.40
44 John Lynch	.12	.30
45 Brandon Marshall	.12	.30
46 Jay Cutler	.15	.40
47 Dre Bly	.10	.25
48 Champ Bailey	.12	.30
49 Tatum Bell	.10	.25
50 Calvin Johnson	.15	.40
51 Jon Kitna	.12	.30
52 Roy Williams WR	.12	.30
53 Ernie Sims	.10	.25
54 Aaron Kampman	.12	.30
55 Charles Woodson	.15	.40
56 Brett Favre	.40	1.00
57 Donald Driver	.12	.30
58 A.J. Hawk	.12	.30
59 DeMeco Ryans	.12	.30
60 Andre Johnson	.12	.30
61 Mario Williams	.12	.30
62 Ron Dayne	.10	.25
63 Dwight Freeney	.12	.30
64 Dallas Clark	.12	.30
65 Peyton Manning	.25	.60
66 Marvin Harrison	.15	.40
67 Reggie Wayne	.12	.30
68 Matt Jones	.12	.30
69 David Garrard	.12	.30
70 Reggie Williams	.12	.30
71 Maurice Jones-Drew	.12	.30
72 Fred Taylor	.12	.30
73 Dwayne Bowe	.12	.30
74 Derrick Johnson	.10	.25
75 Larry Johnson	.12	.30
76 Tony Gonzalez	.12	.30
77 Ronnie Brown	.12	.30
78 Jason Taylor	.12	.30
79 Ted Ginn Jr.	.12	.30
80 John Beck	.10	.25
81 Adrian Peterson	.25	.60
82 Sidney Rice	.15	.40
83 Chester Taylor	.10	.25
84 Bernard Berrian	.12	.30
85 Wes Welker	.15	.40
86 Randy Moss	.15	.40
87 Tom Brady	.25	.60
88 Laurence Maroney	.12	.30
89 Mike Vrabel	.10	.25
90 Drew Brees	.15	.40
91 Marques Colston	.12	.30
92 Reggie Bush	.15	.40
93 Mike McKenzie	.10	.25
94 Michael Strahan	.12	.30
95 Plaxico Burress	.12	.30
96 Eli Manning	.15	.40
97 Jeremy Shockey	.12	.30
98 Brandon Jacobs	.12	.30
99 Jerricho Cotchery	.12	.30
100 Kellen Clemens	.12	.30
101 Leon Washington	.12	.30
102 Thomas Jones	.12	.30
103 Kirk Morrison	.10	.25
104 Nnamdi Asomugha	.12	.30
105 Derrick Burgess	.10	.25
106 Ronald Curry	.12	.30
107 JaMarcus Russell	.12	.30
108 Brian Dawkins	.12	.30
109 Brian Westbrook	.12	.30
110 Reggie Brown	.10	.25
111 Donovan McNabb	.15	.40
112 Hines Ward	.12	.30
113 Santonio Holmes	.12	.30
114 Ben Roethlisberger	.15	.40
115 Willie Parker	.12	.30
116 Troy Polamalu	.15	.40
117 Philip Rivers	.15	.40
118 Antonio Gates	.15	.40
119 Shawne Merriman	.12	.30
120 LaDainian Tomlinson	.15	.40
121 Antonio Cromartie	.10	.25
122 Alex Smith QB	.15	.40
123 Frank Gore	.12	.30
124 Vernon Davis	.12	.30
125 Patrick Willis	.12	.30
126 Lofa Tatupu	.12	.30
127 Patrick Kerney	.10	.25
128 Bobby Engram	.10	.25
129 Matt Hasselbeck	.12	.30
130 Deion Branch	.12	.30
131 Pisa Tinoisamoa	.10	.25
132 Steven Jackson	.15	.40
133 Marc Bulger	.12	.30
134 Torry Holt	.12	.30
135 Randy McMichael	.10	.25
136 Ronde Barber	.10	.25
137 Cadillac Williams	.12	.30
138 Joey Galloway	.12	.30
139 Jeff Garcia	.12	.30
140 Gaines Adams	.10	.25
141 Keith Bulluck	.10	.25
142 Nick Harper	.10	.25
143 Vince Young	.12	.30
144 LenDale White	.12	.30
145 Alge Crumpler	.12	.30
146 Jason Campbell	.12	.30
147 Chris Cooley	.12	.30
148 Brandon Lloyd	.10	.25
149 Clinton Portis	.12	.30
150 Santana Moss	.10	.25
151 Alex Brink RC	.60	1.50
152 Anthony Morelli RC	.50	1.25
153 Antoine Cason RC	.60	1.50
154 Aqib Talib RC	.60	1.50
155 Calais Campbell RC	.50	1.25
156 Erin Henderson RC	.60	1.50
157 Chris Johnson RC	1.50	4.00
158 DJ Hall RC	.50	1.25
159 DeJuan Tribble RC	.40	1.00
160 Derrick Harvey RC	.40	1.00
161 Mike Jenkins RC	.60	1.50
162 Dustin Keller RC	.60	1.50
163 Erik Ainge RC	.60	1.50
164 Felix Jones RC	1.00	2.50
165 Gosder Cherilus RC	.50	1.25
166 Jack Ikegwuonu RC	.40	1.00
167 Jacob Hester RC	.60	1.50
168 Chauncey Washington RC	.50	1.25
169 J Leman RC	.40	1.00
170 Joe Flacco RC	2.00	5.00
171 John David Booty RC	.50	1.25
172 Jordy Nelson RC	.75	2.00
173 Josh Johnson RC	.60	1.50
174 Kenny Phillips RC	.60	1.50
175 Malcolm Kelly RC	.50	1.25
176 Marcus Monk RC	.50	1.25
177 Mario Manningham RC	.60	1.50
178 Mario Urrutia RC	.40	1.00
179 Martin Rucker RC	.50	1.25
180 Matt Flynn RC	1.25	3.00
181 Matt Forte RC	1.00	2.50
182 Jerome Felton RC	.40	1.00
183 Owen Schmitt RC	.60	1.50
184 Ryan Grice-Mullen RC	.40	1.00
185 Paul Hubbard RC	.50	1.25
186 Quentin Groves RC	.50	1.25
187 Ray Rice RC	1.25	3.00
188 Ryan Clady RC	.60	1.50
189 Ryan Torain RC	.60	1.50
190 Adrian Arrington RC	.50	1.25
191 Shawn Crable RC	.40	1.00
192 Allen Patrick RC	.60	1.50
193 Tashard Choice RC	.50	1.25
194 Terrell Thomas RC	.50	1.25
195 Thomas Brown RC	.50	1.25
196 Tom Zbikowski RC	.60	1.50
197 Jermichael Finley RC	.60	1.50
198 Trevor Laws RC	.60	1.50
199 Vince Hall RC	.40	1.00
200 Xavier Adibi RC	.40	1.00
201 Ali Highsmith RC	.40	1.00
202 Andre Woodson RC	.60	1.50
203 Brian Brohm RC	.60	1.50
204 Chad Henne RC	.60	1.50
205 Chris Long RC	.60	1.50
206 Colt Brennan RC	.60	1.50
207 Dan Connor RC	.60	1.50
208 Darren McFadden RC	1.50	4.00
209 Dennis Dixon RC	.60	1.50
210 DeSean Jackson RC	1.25	3.00
211 Early Doucet RC	.50	1.25
212 Fred Davis RC	.60	1.50
213 Glenn Dorsey RC	.60	1.50
214 Jake Long RC	.60	1.50
215 Jonathan Stewart RC	1.00	2.50
216 Justin King RC	.50	1.25
217 Keith Rivers RC	.60	1.50
218 Lavelle Hawkins RC	.40	1.00
219 Lawrence Jackson RC	.50	1.25
220 Limas Sweed RC	.60	1.50
221 Matt Ryan RC	2.50	6.00
222 Mike Hart RC	.60	1.50
223 Earl Bennett RC	.60	1.50
224 Sam Baker RC	.40	1.00
225 Sedrick Ellis RC	.60	1.50

2008 Upper Deck First Edition Jerseys

ONE PER FACTORY SET

FGJAB Anquan Boldin	2.50	6.00
FGJAC Alge Crumpler	2.50	6.00
FGJAG Antonio Gates	3.00	8.00
FGJAJ Andre Johnson	2.50	6.00
FGJAL Shaun Alexander	2.50	6.00
FGJAP Adrian Peterson	5.00	12.00
FGJAR Aaron Rodgers	6.00	15.00
FGJAS Alex Smith QB	3.00	8.00
FGJBB Bernard Berrian	2.50	6.00
FGJBC Brodie Croyle	2.50	6.00
FGJBE Braylon Edwards	2.50	6.00
FGJBF Brett Favre	8.00	20.00
FGJBJ Brandon Jacobs	2.50	6.00
FGJBQ Brady Quinn	2.50	6.00
FGJBR Drew Brees	3.00	8.00
FGJBS Bob Sanders	2.50	6.00
FGJBW Ben Watson	2.00	5.00
FGJCA Jason Campbell	2.50	6.00
FGJCB Champ Bailey	2.50	6.00
FGJCJ Calvin Johnson	3.00	8.00
FGJCL Michael Clayton	2.00	5.00
FGJCO Jerricho Cotchery	2.50	6.00
FGJCP Carson Palmer	3.00	8.00
FGJCW Cadillac Williams	2.50	6.00
FGJDA Derek Anderson	2.00	5.00
FGJDB Dwayne Bowe	2.50	6.00
FGJDC Dallas Clark	2.50	6.00
FGJDD Donald Driver	2.50	6.00
FGJDF DeShaun Foster	2.50	6.00
FGJDG David Garrard	2.50	6.00
FGJDH Devin Hester	3.00	8.00
FGJDM Derrick Mason	2.50	6.00
FGJDO Donovan McNabb	3.00	8.00
FGJDW DeMarcus Ware	2.50	6.00
FGJEJ Edgerrin James	2.50	6.00
FGJEM Eli Manning	3.00	8.00
FGJER Ed Reed	2.50	6.00
FGJES Ernie Sims	2.00	5.00
FGJFG Frank Gore	2.50	6.00
FGJFT Fred Taylor	2.50	6.00
FGJGJ Greg Jennings	3.00	8.00
FGJGO Greg Olsen	2.50	6.00
FGJHM Heath Miller	3.00	8.00
FGJHO Torry Holt	2.50	6.00
FGJHU Michael Huff	2.00	5.00
FGJHW Hines Ward	2.50	6.00
FGJIB Isaac Bruce	2.50	6.00
FGJJA Jason Witten	3.00	8.00
FGJJC Jay Cutler	3.00	8.00
FGJJG Joey Galloway	2.50	6.00
FGJJN Jerious Norwood	2.50	6.00
FGJJP Julius Peppers	2.50	6.00
FGJJR JaMarcus Russell	2.50	6.00
FGJJT Jason Taylor	2.50	6.00
FGJJV Jonathan Vilma	2.50	6.00
FGJJW Javon Walker	2.50	6.00
FGJKJ Kevin Jones	2.00	5.00
FGJKM Kirk Morrison	2.00	5.00
FGJKW Kellen Winslow	2.50	6.00
FGJLE Lee Evans	2.50	6.00
FGJLF Larry Fitzgerald	3.00	8.00
FGJLJ Larry Johnson	2.50	6.00
FGJLM Laurence Maroney	2.50	6.00
FGJLT LaDainian Tomlinson	3.00	8.00
FGJLW LenDale White	2.50	6.00
FGJLY Marshawn Lynch	2.50	6.00
FGJMA Marques Colston	2.50	6.00
FGJMB Marc Bulger	2.50	6.00
FGJMC Deuce McAllister	2.50	6.00
FGJMH Marvin Harrison	3.00	8.00
FGJMJ Maurice Jones-Drew	2.50	6.00
FGJML Matt Leinart	3.00	8.00
FGJMS Matt Schaub	2.50	6.00
FGJMV Mike Vrabel	2.00	5.00
FGJPB Plaxico Burress	2.50	6.00
FGJPM Peyton Manning	5.00	12.00
FGJPO Clinton Portis	2.50	6.00
FGJPW Patrick Willis	2.50	6.00
FGJRB Reggie Bush	3.00	8.00
FGJRG Ryan Grant	3.00	8.00
FGJRJ Rudi Johnson	2.50	6.00
FGJRL Ray Lewis	3.00	8.00
FGJRM Randy Moss	3.00	8.00
FGJRO Ronnie Brown	2.50	6.00
FGJRW Roy Williams WR	2.50	6.00
FGJSA Asante Samuel	2.00	5.00
FGJSM Shawne Merriman	2.50	6.00
FGJSS Steve Smith	2.50	6.00
FGJTA Tatum Bell	2.00	5.00
FGJTB Tedy Bruschi	3.00	8.00
FGJTG Tony Gonzalez	2.50	6.00
FGJTH Todd Heap	2.00	5.00
FGJTS Terrell Suggs	2.00	5.00
FGJVY Vince Young	2.50	6.00
FGJWA Kurt Warner	3.00	8.00
FGJWE Brian Westbrook	2.50	6.00
FGJWI DeAngelo Williams	2.50	6.00
FGJWM Willis McGahee	2.50	6.00
FGJWO Charles Woodson	3.00	8.00
FGJZT Zach Thomas	2.50	6.00

2008 Upper Deck First Edition Star Quest

SQ1 Adrian Peterson	2.00	5.00
SQ2 Andre Woodson	.75	2.00
SQ3 Antonio Cromartie	.75	2.00
SQ4 Ben Roethlisberger	1.25	3.00
SQ5 Brian Westbrook	1.00	2.50
SQ6 Carson Palmer	1.25	3.00
SQ7 Chris Long	.75	2.00
SQ8 Darren McFadden	2.00	5.00
SQ9 DeSean Jackson	1.50	4.00
SQ10 Drew Brees	1.25	3.00
SQ11 Early Doucet	.60	1.50
SQ12 Ed Reed	1.00	2.50
SQ13 Ernie Sims	.75	2.00
SQ14 Fred Taylor	1.00	2.50
SQ15 Glenn Dorsey	.75	2.00
SQ16 Shawn Crable	.50	1.25
SQ17 Joseph Addai	1.00	2.50
SQ18 Kenny Phillips	.75	2.00
SQ19 LaDainian Tomlinson	1.25	3.00
SQ20 Larry Fitzgerald	1.25	3.00
SQ21 Matt Hasselbeck	1.25	3.00
SQ22 Matt Ryan	3.00	8.00
SQ23 Osi Umenyiora	1.00	2.50
SQ24 Patrick Willis	1.00	2.50
SQ25 Peyton Manning	2.00	5.00
SQ26 Randy Moss	1.25	3.00
SQ27 Sam Baker	.60	1.50
SQ28 Terrell Owens	1.25	3.00
SQ29 Tom Brady	2.00	5.00
SQ30 Tony Romo	1.50	4.00

2009 Upper Deck First Edition

COMPLETE SET (200)	20.00	40.00
1 Kurt Warner	.15	.40
2 Tim Hightower	.10	.25
3 Larry Fitzgerald	.15	.40
4 Anquan Boldin	.12	.30
5 Steve Breaston	.12	.30
6 Matt Ryan	.15	.40
7 Michael Jenkins	.10	.25
8 Jerious Norwood	.12	.30
9 Roddy White	.12	.30
10 Michael Turner	.12	.30
11 Ed Reed	.12	.30
12 Willis McGahee	.12	.30
13 Joe Flacco	.15	.40
14 Ray Lewis	.15	.40
15 Derrick Mason	.12	.30
16 Lee Evans	.12	.30
17 Marshawn Lynch	.12	.30
18 Trent Edwards	.10	.25
19 Leodis McKelvin	.10	.25
20 Terrell Owens	.15	.40
21 DeAngelo Williams	.15	.40
22 Steve Smith	.12	.30
23 Muhsin Muhammad	.12	.30
24 Jonathan Stewart	.12	.30
25 Jake Delhomme	.12	.30
26 Devin Hester	.15	.40
27 Matt Forte	.15	.40
28 Lance Briggs	.12	.30
29 Jay Cutler	.15	.40
30 Brian Urlacher	.15	.40
31 Carson Palmer	.15	.40
32 Chad Johnson	.12	.30
33 Laveranues Coles	.10	.25
34 Cedric Benson	.12	.30
35 Jamal Lewis	.12	.30
36 Derek Anderson	.10	.25
37 Brady Quinn	.12	.30
38 Braylon Edwards	.12	.30
39 Felix Jones	.15	.40
40 Jason Witten	.15	.40
41 Roy Williams WR	.12	.30
42 DeMarcus Ware	.12	.30
43 Tony Romo	.25	.60
44 Marion Barber	.12	.30
45 Kyle Orton	.12	.30
46 Eddie Royal	.12	.30
47 Champ Bailey	.12	.30
48 Brandon Marshall	.12	.30
49 Jason Hanson	.10	.25
50 Calvin Johnson	.15	.40
51 Kevin Smith	.12	.30
52 Daunte Culpepper	.12	.30
53 A.J. Hawk	.12	.30
54 Aaron Rodgers	.30	.75
55 Donald Driver	.12	.30
56 Greg Jennings	.15	.40
57 Ryan Grant	.12	.30
58 Matt Schaub	.12	.30
59 Andre Johnson	.12	.30
60 Steve Slaton	.12	.30
61 Mario Williams	.12	.30
62 DeMeco Ryans	.12	.30
63 Peyton Manning	.25	.60
64 Joseph Addai	.15	.40
65 Reggie Wayne	.12	.30
66 Anthony Gonzalez	.10	.25
67 Dallas Clark	.12	.30
68 Bob Sanders	.12	.30
69 Maurice Jones-Drew	.12	.30
70 David Garrard	.12	.30
71 Marcedes Lewis	.10	.25
72 Rashean Mathis	.10	.25
73 Justin Durant	.10	.25
74 Larry Johnson	.12	.30
75 Matt Cassel	.12	.30
76 Tyler Thigpen	.10	.25
77 Dwayne Bowe	.12	.30
78 Ronnie Brown	.12	.30
79 Greg Camarillo	.12	.30
80 Ted Ginn Jr.	.12	.30
81 Chad Pennington	.12	.30
82 Joey Porter	.12	.30
83 Adrian Peterson	.25	.60
84 Bernard Berrian	.12	.30
85 Jared Allen	.15	.40
86 Chester Taylor	.10	.25
87 Visanthe Shiancoe	.12	.30
88 Tom Brady	.25	.60
89 Wes Welker	.15	.40
90 Randy Moss	.15	.40
91 Kevin Faulk	.10	.25
92 Sammy Morris	.10	.25
93 Reggie Bush	.15	.40
94 Drew Brees	.15	.40
95 Lance Moore	.12	.30
96 Pierre Thomas	.12	.30
97 Marques Colston	.12	.30
98 Brandon Jacobs	.12	.30
99 Ahmad Bradshaw	.12	.30
100 Steve Smith USC	.12	.30
101 Eli Manning	.15	.40
102 Domenik Hixon	.10	.25
103 Thomas Jones	.12	.30
104 Jerricho Cotchery	.12	.30
105 Kellen Clemens	.10	.25
106 Dustin Keller	.10	.25
107 Leon Washington	.12	.30
108 Darren McFadden	.15	.40
109 JaMarcus Russell	.10	.25
110 Johnnie Lee Higgins	.10	.25
111 Justin Fargas	.10	.25
112 Asante Samuel	.10	.25
113 Brian Westbrook	.12	.30
114 DeSean Jackson	.12	.30
115 Donovan McNabb	.15	.40
116 Shawn Andrews	.10	.25
117 Troy Polamalu	.15	.40
118 Willie Parker	.10	.25
119 Ben Roethlisberger	.15	.40
120 Santonio Holmes	.12	.30
121 Hines Ward	.12	.30
122 James Harrison	.15	.40
123 Darren Sproles	.12	.30
124 LaDainian Tomlinson	.15	.40
125 Philip Rivers	.15	.40
126 Antonio Gates	.12	.30
127 Vincent Jackson	.12	.30
128 Patrick Willis	.12	.30
129 Frank Gore	.12	.30
130 Vernon Davis	.12	.30
131 Julius Jones	.10	.25
132 Matt Hasselbeck	.12	.30
133 Deion Branch	.12	.30
134 Lofa Tatupu	.12	.30
135 Marc Bulger	.12	.30
136 Donnie Avery	.12	.30
137 Steven Jackson	.12	.30
138 Kellen Winslow	.12	.30
139 Cadillac Williams	.12	.30
140 Michael Clayton	.10	.25
141 Ronde Barber	.10	.25
142 Kerry Collins	.12	.30
143 Chris Johnson	.15	.40
144 LenDale White	.12	.30
145 Bo Scaife	.10	.25
146 Clinton Portis	.12	.30
147 Jason Campbell	.10	.25
148 Santana Moss	.12	.30
149 Antwaan Randle El	.10	.25
150 Albert Haynesworth	.10	.25
151 Ramses Barden RC	.30	.75
152 Andre Brown RC	.30	.75
153 Patrick Turner RC	.40	1.00
154 Mike Wallace RC	1.00	2.50
155 Derrick Williams RC	.40	1.00
156 Deon Butler RC	.40	1.00
157 Juaquin Iglesias RC	.40	1.00
158 Stephen McGee RC	.50	1.25
159 Patrick Chung RC	.50	1.25
160 Darius Butler RC	.50	1.25
161 Alex Mack RC	.40	1.00
162 Glen Coffee RC	.40	1.00
163 Nate Davis RC	.40	1.00
164 Chase Coffman RC	.40	1.00
165 Evander Hood RC	.60	1.50
166 James Laurinaitis RC	.50	1.25
167 Vontae Davis RC	.50	1.25
168 Brian Robiskie RC	.50	1.25
169 Eugene Monroe RC	.30	.75
170 Javon Ringer RC	.50	1.25
171 Clay Matthews RC	1.25	3.00
172 Rey Maualuga RC	.50	1.25
173 Brian Cushing RC	.50	1.25
174 Michael Oher RC	.75	2.00
175 Brandon Tate RC	.50	1.25
176 Andre Smith RC	.40	1.00
177 Shonn Greene RC	.75	2.00
178 Pat White RC	.50	1.25
179 Malcolm Jenkins RC	.50	1.25
180 Matthew Stafford RC	3.00	8.00
181 Michael Crabtree RC	1.00	2.50
182 Tyson Jackson RC	.40	1.00
183 Brandon Pettigrew RC	.50	1.25
184 Brian Orakpo RC	.50	1.25
185 Jeremy Maclin RC	.75	2.00
186 Jason Smith RC	.40	1.00
187 Chris Wells RC	.75	2.00
188 Aaron Curry RC	.50	1.25
189 Mark Sanchez RC	1.50	4.00
190 Aaron Maybin RC	.40	1.00
191 B.J. Raji RC	.50	1.25
192 Kenny Britt RC	.60	1.50
193 Mohamed Massaquoi RC	.40	1.00
194 Knowshon Moreno RC	.50	1.25
195 Percy Harvin RC	.75	2.00
196 Hakeem Nicks RC	.75	2.00
197 LeSean McCoy RC	1.00	2.50
198 Darrius Heyward-Bey RC	.50	1.25
199 Josh Freeman RC	1.00	2.50
200 Donald Brown RC	.50	1.25

2009 Upper Deck First Edition Silver

*VETS: 1.5X TO 4X BASIC CARDS
*ROOKIES: .6X TO 1.5X BASIC CARDS
ONE SILVER PER PACK

2009 Upper Deck First Edition Bombs Away

OVERALL INSERT ODDS 1:1

BA1 Kurt Warner	.75	2.00
BA2 Drew Brees	.75	2.00
BA3 Carson Palmer	.75	2.00
BA4 Tom Brady	1.25	3.00
BA5 Ben Roethlisberger	.75	2.00
BA6 Marc Bulger	.60	1.50
BA7 Philip Rivers	.75	2.00
BA8 Jay Cutler	.75	2.00
BA9 Trent Edwards	.50	1.25
BA10 Joe Flacco	.75	2.00
BA11 Kyle Orton	.60	1.50
BA12 Peyton Manning	1.25	3.00
BA13 Jake Delhomme	.60	1.50
BA14 Chad Pennington	.60	1.50
BA15 David Garrard	.60	1.50
BA16 Kerry Collins	.60	1.50
BA17 Donovan McNabb	.75	2.00
BA18 Eli Manning	.75	2.00

BA19 Aaron Rodgers 1.50 4.00
BA20 Matt Schaub .60 1.50
BA21 Matt Ryan .75 2.00
BA22 Tony Romo 1.25 3.00
BA23 Matt Hasselbeck .60 1.50
BA24 Matt Cassel .60 1.50
BA25 Jason Campbell .50 1.25

2009 Upper Deck First Edition Crunch Time

OVERALL INSERT ODDS 1:1
CT1 Albert Haynesworth .50 1.25
CT2 Ray Lewis .75 2.00
CT3 Brian Urlacher .75 2.00
CT4 Asante Samuel .50 1.25
CT5 Ed Reed .60 1.50
CT6 Troy Polamalu .75 2.00
CT7 Shawne Merriman .60 1.50
CT8 James Harrison .75 2.00
CT9 Dwight Freeney .60 1.50
CT10 Lance Briggs .60 1.50
CT11 Nnamdi Asomugha .60 1.50
CT12 A.J. Hawk .60 1.50
CT13 Bob Sanders .60 1.50
CT14 Keith Bulluck .50 1.25
CT15 Antrel Rolle .50 1.25
CT16 Adrian Wilson .50 1.25
CT17 Julius Peppers .60 1.50
CT18 DeMarcus Ware .60 1.50
CT19 Patrick Willis .60 1.50
CT20 DeMeco Ryans .60 1.50
CT21 Jared Allen .75 2.00
CT22 Lofa Tatupu .60 1.50
CT23 Nick Collins .50 1.25
CT24 Chris Hope .50 1.25
CT25 Jerod Mayo .60 1.50

2009 Upper Deck First Edition Speed to Burn

OVERALL INSERT ODDS 1:1
SB1 Darren McFadden .75 2.00
SB2 Steven Jackson .60 1.50
SB3 Chris Johnson .75 2.00
SB4 Devin Hester .75 2.00
SB5 Reggie Wayne .60 1.50
SB6 Randy Moss .75 2.00
SB7 Ted Ginn Jr. .60 1.50
SB8 Darren Sproles .60 1.50
SB9 Reggie Bush .75 2.00
SB10 Steve Smith .60 1.50
SB11 Santana Moss .60 1.50
SB12 Larry Fitzgerald .75 2.00
SB13 Lee Evans .60 1.50
SB14 Chad Johnson .60 1.50
SB15 Willie Parker .50 1.25
SB16 Willis McGahee .60 1.50
SB17 DeSean Jackson .60 1.50
SB18 Santonio Holmes .60 1.50
SB19 Eddie Royal .60 1.50
SB20 Calvin Johnson .75 2.00
SB21 Roy Williams WR .60 1.50
SB22 Brian Dawkins .60 1.50
SB23 Ed Reed .60 1.50
SB24 Michael Turner .60 1.50
SB25 Terrell Owens .75 2.00

2009 Upper Deck First Edition Star Attractions

OVERALL INSERT ODDS 1:1
SA1 Matt Ryan .75 2.00
SA2 Adrian Peterson 1.25 3.00
SA3 Chris Johnson .75 2.00
SA4 Randy Moss .75 2.00
SA5 Kurt Warner .75 2.00
SA6 Michael Turner .60 1.50
SA7 Thomas Jones .60 1.50
SA8 Steve Smith .80 1.50
SA9 Peyton Manning 1.25 3.00
SA10 Anquan Boldin .60 1.50
SA11 DeAngelo Williams .75 2.00
SA12 Andre Johnson .60 1.50
SA13 Donovan McNabb .75 2.00
SA14 Brian Westbrook .60 1.50
SA15 Ben Roethlisberger .75 2.00
SA16 Larry Fitzgerald .75 2.00
SA17 Clinton Portis .60 1.50
SA18 Marion Barber .60 1.50
SA19 Eli Manning .75 2.00
SA20 Frank Gore .60 1.50
SA21 Ray Lewis .75 2.00
SA22 Tom Brady 1.25 3.00
SA23 Shawne Merriman .60 1.50
SA24 Calvin Johnson .75 2.00
SA25 Troy Polamalu .75 2.00

2004 Upper Deck Foundations

Upper Deck Foundations was initially released in late September 2004. The base set consists of 263-cards including 140-rookies serial numbered to 250, 17 rookie jersey cards numbered to 1299 and 6-rookie jersey cards numbered to 499. Hobby boxes contained 24-packs of 5-cards and carried an S.R.P. of $4.99 per pack. Two parallel sets and a variety of inserts can be found seeded in packs highlighted by the Dual Endorsements autograph and Signature Foundations inserts.

COMP.SET w/o SP's (100) 7.50 20.00
101-240 ROOKIE PRINT RUN 350
241-257 ROOKIE JSY PRINT RUN 1299
258-263 ROOKIE JSY PRINT RUN 499
1 Josh McCown .25 .60
2 Emmitt Smith .75 2.00
3 Anquan Boldin .30 .75
4 T.J. Duckett .25 .60
5 Peerless Price .20 .50
6 Michael Vick .40 1.00
7 Todd Heap .25 .60
8 Kyle Boller .25 .60
9 Jamal Lewis .25 .60
10 Travis Henry .20 .50
11 Eric Moulds .25 .60
12 Drew Bledsoe .30 .75
13 Steve Smith .30 .75
14 Stephen Davis .25 .60
15 Jake Delhomme .25 .60
16 Rex Grossman .25 .60
17 Brian Urlacher .30 .75
18 Anthony Thomas .25 .60
19 Rudi Johnson .25 .60
20 Chad Johnson .30 .75
21 Carson Palmer .30 .75
22 Quincy Morgan .20 .50
23 Jeff Garcia .25 .60
24 Andre Davis .20 .50
25 Roy Williams S .25 .60
26 Eddie George .25 .60
27 Keyshawn Johnson .25 .60
28 Jake Plummer .25 .60
29 Champ Bailey .25 .60
30 Ashley Lelie .20 .50
31 Joey Harrington .25 .60
32 Charles Rogers .20 .50
33 Az-Zahir Hakim .20 .50
34 Javon Walker .20 .50
35 Brett Favre .75 2.00
36 Ahman Green .25 .60
37 Domanick Davis .20 .50
38 David Carr .20 .50
39 Andre Johnson .30 .75
40 Peyton Manning .60 1.50
41 Marvin Harrison .30 .75
42 Edgerrin James .25 .60
43 Jimmy Smith .25 .60
44 Fred Taylor .25 .60
45 Byron Leftwich .25 .60
46 Trent Green .25 .60
47 Tony Gonzalez .30 .75
48 Priest Holmes .30 .75
49 Dante Hall .25 .60
50 Ricky Williams .25 .60
51 David Boston .20 .50
52 Chris Chambers .25 .60
53 A.J. Feeley .20 .50
54 Randy Moss .30 .75
55 Michael Bennett .25 .60
56 Daunte Culpepper .25 .60
57 Troy Brown .25 .60
58 Tom Brady .60 1.50
59 Corey Dillon .25 .60
60 Donte' Stallworth .20 .50
61 Deuce McAllister .25 .60
62 Aaron Brooks .25 .60
63 Kurt Warner .30 .75
64 Jeremy Shockey .25 .60
65 Santana Moss .25 .60
66 Curtis Martin .30 .75
67 Chad Pennington .30 .75
68 Amani Toomer .25 .60
69 Tim Brown .30 .75
70 Rich Gannon .25 .60
71 Jerry Rice .60 1.50
72 Jerry Porter .20 .50
73 Terrell Owens .30 .75
74 Jevon Kearse .25 .60
75 Donovan McNabb .30 .75
76 Tommy Maddox .25 .60
77 Plaxico Burress .25 .60
78 Hines Ward .30 .75
79 Duce Staley .25 .60
80 LaDainian Tomlinson .30 .75
81 Drew Brees .30 .75
82 Donnie Edwards .25 .60
83 Tim Rattay .20 .50
84 Kevan Barlow .20 .50
85 Brandon Lloyd .25 .60
86 Shaun Alexander .25 .60
87 Matt Hasselbeck .25 .60
88 Koren Robinson .20 .50
89 Torry Holt .25 .60
90 Marshall Faulk .30 .75
91 Marc Bulger .25 .60
92 Keenan McCardell .20 .50
93 Derrick Brooks .25 .60
94 Brad Johnson .25 .60
95 Steve McNair .30 .75
96 Derrick Mason .25 .60
97 Chris Brown .20 .50
98 Mark Brunell .25 .60
99 LaVar Arrington .25 .60
100 Clinton Portis .30 .75
101 Brandon Chillar RC 2.50 6.00
102 Mike Karney RC 2.50 6.00
103 Jamaar Taylor RC 2.00 5.00
104 Casey Clausen RC 2.50 6.00
105 Drew Carter RC 2.50 6.00
106 Travis LaBoy RC 2.50 6.00
107 Jonathan Vilma RC 3.00 8.00
108 Tramon Douglas RC 2.00 5.00
109 Bob Sanders RC 8.00 20.00
110 Mewelde Moore RC 2.50 6.00
111 Randy Starks RC 2.00 5.00
112 Tank Johnson RC 2.00 5.00
113 Triandos Luke RC 2.00 5.00
114 Dexter Reid RC 2.00 5.00
115 Cedric Cobbs RC 2.00 5.00
116 Darius Watts RC 2.00 5.00
117 Ryan Krause RC 2.00 5.00
118 Igor Olshansky RC 2.50 6.00
119 Adimchinobe Echemandu RC 2.50 6.00
120 Jason Fife RC 2.00 5.00
121 Justin Smiley RC 2.50 6.00
122 Marcus Tubbs RC 2.00 5.00
123 Nathan Vasher RC 3.00 8.00
124 Troy Fleming RC 2.00 5.00
125 Ben Troupe RC 2.50 6.00
126 Jammal Lord RC 2.00 5.00
127 Jared Lorenzen RC 2.50 6.00
128 Shawntae Spencer RC 2.00 5.00
129 Darnell Dockett RC 2.00 5.00
130 Derrick Strait RC 2.00 5.00
131 Clarence Moore RC 2.00 5.00
132 Jason Babin RC 3.00 8.00
133 Jerricho Cotchery RC 2.50 6.00
134 Karlos Dansby RC 3.00 8.00
135 Marquise Hill RC 2.00 5.00
136 Niko Koutouvides RC 2.00 5.00
137 Andy Hall RC 2.00 5.00
138 Teddy Lehman RC 2.00 5.00
139 Will Smith RC 2.50 6.00
140 Bernard Berrian RC 3.00 8.00
141 Chris Cooley RC 3.00 8.00
142 Landon Johnson RC 2.00 5.00
143 Devard Darling RC 2.00 5.00
144 Mark Jones RC 2.00 5.00
145 Jake Grove RC 2.00 5.00
146 John Navarre RC 2.00 5.00
147 Keary Colbert RC 2.00 5.00
148 Gilbert Gardner RC 2.00 5.00
149 P.K. Sam RC 2.00 5.00
150 Richard Seigler RC 2.00 5.00
151 Marquis Cooper RC 2.00 5.00
152 Tommie Harris RC 3.00 8.00
153 Thomas Tapeh RC 2.50 6.00
154 Ben Utecht RC 2.50 6.00
155 Chris Gamble RC 2.50 6.00
156 Daryl Smith RC 2.00 5.00
157 Sean Taylor RC 6.00 15.00
158 Caleb Miller RC 2.00 5.00
159 Johnnie Morant RC 2.00 5.00
160 Keith Smith RC 2.00 5.00
161 Matt Mauck RC 2.00 5.00
162 Matt Ware RC 3.00 8.00
163 Quincy Wilson RC 2.50 6.00
164 Samie Parker RC 2.00 5.00
165 Kendrick Starling RC 2.00 5.00
166 Antwan Odom RC 2.50 6.00
167 Brandon Miree RC 2.00 5.00
168 Casey Bramlet RC 2.00 5.00
169 Cody Pickett RC 2.50 6.00
170 Demorrio Williams RC 3.00 8.00
171 Dunta Robinson RC 2.00 5.00
172 D.J. Hackett RC 2.50 6.00
173 Josh Harris RC 2.00 5.00
174 Kenechi Udeze RC 2.50 6.00
175 Michael Boulware RC 3.00 8.00
176 Ricardo Colclough RC 2.50 6.00
177 Shawn Andrews RC 2.50 6.00
178 Jeris McIntyre RC 2.00 5.00
179 Jim Corgi RC 2.50 6.00
180 Clarence Farmer RC 2.00 5.00
181 Courtney Watson RC 2.00 5.00
182 Derek Abney RC 2.00 5.00
183 Dwan Edwards RC 2.00 5.00
184 Ryan Dinwiddie RC 2.00 5.00
185 B.J. Johnson RC 2.00 5.00
186 Ben Watson RC 3.00 8.00
187 Kris Wilson RC 2.50 6.00
188 Michael Turner RC 4.00 10.00
189 Derrick Ward RC 3.00 8.00
190 Jonathan Smith RC 2.50 6.00
191 Vernon Carey RC 2.00 5.00
192 Ben Hartsock RC 2.00 5.00
193 Rich Gardner RC 2.50 6.00
194 D.J. Williams RC 3.00 8.00
195 Derrick Hamilton RC 2.00 5.00
196 Drew Henson RC 2.00 5.00
197 Jeff Smoker RC 2.50 6.00
198 Joey Thomas RC 2.00 5.00
199 Keyaron Fox RC 2.50 6.00
200 Nate Lawrie RC 2.00 5.00
201 Sloan Thomas RC 2.50 6.00
202 Justin Jenkins RC 2.00 5.00
203 Stuart Schweigert RC 2.50 6.00
204 Ran Carthon RC 2.00 5.00
205 Ahmad Carroll RC 2.00 5.00
206 Bradlee Van Pelt RC 2.50 6.00
207 Patrick Crayton RC 3.00 8.00
208 Chris Snee RC 2.50 6.00
209 Fred Russell RC 2.50 6.00
210 Dontarrious Thomas RC 2.50 6.00
211 Will Poole RC 3.00 8.00
212 Jarrett Payton RC 2.50 6.00
213 Keiwan Ratliff RC 2.00 5.00
214 Nate Kaeding RC 3.00 8.00
215 Tim Euhus RC 2.00 5.00
216 Sean Jones RC 2.50 6.00
217 Will Allen RC 2.50 6.00
218 B.J. Symons RC 2.00 5.00
219 Carlos Francis RC 2.00 5.00
220 Craig Krenzel RC 2.50 6.00
221 Andrae Thurman RC 2.00 5.00
222 Ernest Wilford RC 2.50 6.00
223 Glenn Earl RC 2.00 5.00
224 Jeremy LeSueur RC 2.00 5.00
225 Junior Siavii RC 2.00 5.00
226 Maurice Mann RC 2.00 5.00
227 Michael Waddell RC 2.00 5.00
228 Jason Wright RC 2.00 5.00
229 Sean Ryan RC 2.00 5.00
230 Vince Wilfork RC 3.00 8.00
231 Matt Kegel RC 3.00 8.00
232 Chris Collins RC 2.00 5.00
233 Jonathan Smith RC 2.00 5.00
234 Renaldo Works RC 2.00 5.00
235 Matt Kranchick RC 2.50 6.00
236 J.R. Reed RC 2.00 5.00
237 Jason Shivers RC 2.00 5.00
238 Donnell Washington RC 2.50 6.00
239 Jorge Cordova RC 2.00 5.00
240 Wes Welker RC 12.00 30.00
241 Robert Gallery JSY RC 2.50 6.00
242 Luke McCown JSY RC 2.00 5.00
243 Roy Williams JSY RC 2.50 6.00
244 Julius Jones JSY RC 2.00 5.00
245 Tatum Bell JSY RC 2.00 5.00
246 Steven Jackson JSY RC 4.00 10.00
247 Reggie Williams JSY RC 2.00 5.00
248 Devery Henderson JSY RC 2.50 6.00
249 DeAngelo Hall JSY RC 2.50 6.00
250 Rashaun Woods JSY RC 1.50 4.00
251 Chris Perry JSY RC 2.00 5.00
252 Matt Schaub JSY RC 5.00 12.00
253 Lee Evans JSY RC 2.50 6.00
254 Michael Jenkins JSY RC 2.50 6.00
255 J.P. Losman JSY RC 2.00 5.00
256 Kevin Jones JSY RC 2.00 5.00
257 Michael Clayton JSY RC 2.00 5.00
258 Eli Manning JSY RC 12.00 30.00
259 Ben Roethlisberger JSY RC 12.00 30.00
260 Larry Fitzgerald JSY RC 6.00 15.00
261 Philip Rivers JSY RC 8.00 20.00
262 Greg Jones JSY RC 1.50 4.00
263 Kellen Winslow JSY RC 2.50 6.00

2004 Upper Deck Foundations Exclusive Gold

*STARS: 4X TO 10X BASE CARD HI
*ROOKIES 101-240: .5X TO 1.2X
STATED PRINT RUN 100 SER.#'d SETS

2004 Upper Deck Foundations Exclusive Rainbow Platinum

UNPRICED PLATINUM PRINT RUN 10

2004 Upper Deck Foundations Exclusive Rainbow Silver

*VETS: 5X TO 12X BASIC CARDS
*ROOKIES: .6X TO 1.5X BASIC CARDS
RAINBOW SILVER PRINT RUN 100 SETS

2004 Upper Deck Foundations Dual Endorsements

STATED ODDS 1:96
DEBH Tom Brady SP 100.00 200.00
Drew Henson
DEBL Drew Bledsoe 20.00 50.00
J.P. Losman
DEBR Kyle Boller 40.00 80.00
Philip Rivers
DEBW Tatum Bell 12.00 30.00
Darius Watts
DECH Michael Clayton 15.00 40.00
Devery Henderson
DEEW Lee Evans 20.00 50.00
J.P.Losman
DEFW Reggie Williams 20.00 50.00
Roy Williams WR
DEHJ DeAngelo Hall 20.00 50.00
Michael Jenkins
DEHW Joe Horn 20.00 50.00
Roy Williams WR
DEJH Julius Jones 15.00 40.00
Drew Henson/50*
DEJJ Kevin Jones 25.00 60.00
Steven Jackson
DEMM Peyton Manning 150.00 300.00
Eli Manning
DEMP Deuce McAllister 15.00 40.00
Chris Perry SP
DEMR Eli Manning 175.00 300.00
Ben Roethlisberger
DERR Ben Roethlisberger 100.00 200.00
Philip Rivers
DEVM Michael Vick 90.00 150.00
Eli Manning SP
DEWJ Roy Williams WR 20.00 50.00
Kevin Jones
DEWW Kellen Winslow Sr. SP 20.00 50.00
Kellen Winslow Jr.

2004 Upper Deck Foundations Patches

STATED PRINT RUN 50 SER.#'d SETS
FPAB Antonio Bryant 8.00 20.00
FPAL Ashley Lelie 6.00 15.00
FPAN Anthony Thomas 8.00 20.00
FPAT Amani Toomer 8.00 20.00
FPBF Brett Favre 25.00 60.00
FPBL Byron Leftwich 8.00 20.00
FPCB Champ Bailey 8.00 20.00
FPCC Chris Chambers 8.00 20.00
FPCD Corey Dillon 8.00 20.00
FPCJ Chad Johnson 10.00 25.00
FPCM Curtis Martin 10.00 25.00
FPCW Charles Woodson 10.00 25.00
FPDB David Boston 6.00 15.00
FPDC Daunte Culpepper 8.00 20.00
FPDS Duce Staley 8.00 20.00
FPEM Eric Moulds 8.00 20.00
FPFT Fred Taylor 8.00 20.00
FPIB Isaac Bruce 8.00 20.00
FPJG Jeff Garcia 8.00 20.00
FPJH Joey Harrington 8.00 20.00
FPJK Jevon Kearse 8.00 20.00
FPJL Jamal Lewis 8.00 20.00
FPJR Jerry Rice 20.00 50.00
FPJS Junior Seau 10.00 25.00
FPKB Kyle Boller 8.00 20.00
FPKJ Keyshawn Johnson 8.00 20.00
FPKM Keenan McCardell 6.00 15.00
FPMB Mark Brunell 8.00 20.00
FPMF Marshall Faulk 10.00 25.00
FPMH Marvin Harrison 10.00 25.00
FPPP Peerless Price 6.00 15.00
FPRL Ray Lewis 10.00 25.00
FPRM Randy Moss 10.00 25.00
FPRW Ricky Williams 8.00 20.00
FPTB Tiki Barber 10.00 25.00
FPTH Travis Henry 6.00 15.00
FPTI Tim Brown 10.00 25.00
FPTO Terrell Owens 10.00 25.00
FPWD Warrick Dunn 8.00 20.00
FPWS Warren Sapp 8.00 20.00
FPZT Zach Thomas 10.00 25.00

2004 Upper Deck Foundations Rookie Foundations Patch

*ROOKIE PATCH/25: 1.5X TO 4X BASIC JSY
STATED PRINT RUN 25 SER.#'d SETS

2004 Upper Deck Foundations Rookie Foundations Patch Autographs

STATED PRINT RUN 25 SER.#'d SETS
241AP Robert Gallery 30.00 80.00
242AP Luke McCown 25.00 60.00
243AP Roy Williams WR 30.00 80.00
244AP Julius Jones 25.00 60.00
245AP Tatum Bell 25.00 60.00
246AP Steven Jackson 75.00 150.00
248AP Devery Henderson 30.00 80.00
249AP DeAngelo Hall 30.00 80.00
250AP Rashaun Woods 20.00 50.00
251AP Chris Perry 25.00 60.00
252AP Matt Schaub 75.00 150.00
253AP Lee Evans 30.00 80.00
254AP Michael Jenkins 30.00 80.00
255AP J.P. Losman 25.00 60.00
256AP Kevin Jones 20.00 50.00
257AP Michael Clayton 20.00 50.00
258AP Eli Manning 350.00 500.00
259AP Ben Roethlisberger 250.00 400.00
260AP Larry Fitzgerald 100.00 200.00
261AP Philip Rivers 125.00 250.00
262AP Greg Jones 20.00 50.00
263AP Kellen Winslow Jr. 30.00 80.00

2004 Upper Deck Foundations Signature Foundations

STATED ODDS 1:12
SFBB Bernard Berrian 8.00 20.00
SFBC Brandon Chillar 6.00 15.00
SFBH Ben Hartsock SP 5.00 12.00
SFBJ B.J. Symons 5.00 12.00
SFBR Ben Roethlisberger SP 100.00 200.00
SFBW Ben Watson 8.00 20.00
SFCC Casey Clausen 6.00 15.00
SFCO Cody Pickett 6.00 15.00
SFCP Chris Perry SP 6.00 15.00
SFDA Devard Darling 5.00 12.00
SFDE DeAngelo Hall 8.00 20.00
SFDH Dante Hall SP 6.00 15.00
SFDR Drew Henson SP 5.00 12.00
SFDV Devery Henderson 8.00 20.00
SFDW Darius Watts 5.00 12.00
SFEM Eli Manning SP 100.00 200.00
SFEW Ernest Wilford 6.00 15.00
SFGJ Greg Jones 5.00 12.00
SFJC Jerricho Cotchery 6.00 15.00
SFJJ Julius Jones SP 6.00 15.00
SFJN John Navarre 5.00 12.00
SFJO Johnnie Morant 5.00 12.00
SFJP J.P. Losman SP 6.00 15.00
SFJS Jeff Smoker 6.00 15.00
SFJV Jonathan Vilma 8.00 20.00
SFKC Keary Colbert 5.00 12.00
SFKE Kellen Winslow Jr. SP 8.00 20.00
SFKJ Kevin Jones SP 6.00 15.00
SFKU Kenechi Udeze 6.00 15.00
SFLE Lee Evans SP 8.00 20.00
SFLM Luke McCown 6.00 15.00
SFLT LaDainian Tomlinson SP 40.00 80.00
SFMI Michael Clayton 6.00 15.00
SFMJ Michael Jenkins 8.00 20.00
SFMS Matt Schaub 15.00 40.00
SFMV Michael Vick/100* 30.00 60.00
SFPM Peyton Manning SP 50.00 100.00
SFPR Philip Rivers SP 30.00 80.00
SFQW Quincy Wilson 6.00 15.00
SFRE Reggie Williams 6.00 15.00
SFRG Robert Gallery 8.00 20.00
SFRO Roy Williams WR 8.00 20.00
SFRW Rashaun Woods SP 5.00 12.00
SFSJ Steven Jackson SP 12.00 30.00
SFTB Tatum Bell SP 6.00 15.00
SFTH Todd Heap SP 6.00 15.00
SFTO Tommie Harris 8.00 20.00
SFVW Vince Wilfork 8.00 20.00
SFWS Will Smith 6.00 15.00

2005 Upper Deck Foundations

This 258-card set was released in November, 2005. The set was issued through the hobby in five-card packs with an $4.99 SRP which came 24 packs to a box. Cards numbered 1-100 feature veterans sequenced by alphabetical team order while cards numbered 101-260 feature rookie. In the rookie grouping, cards numbered 201-260 were all autographed. Cards numbered 101-200 were issued to a stated print run of 399 serial numbered sets while cards numbered 201-260 were issued to stated print runs between 575 and 699 serial numbered copies. Those signed rookies were inserted into packs at a stated rate of one in 12. Please note that no cards number 233 or 257 were released.

COMP.SET w/o RCs (100) 7.50 20.00
101-200 RC PRINT RUN 399 SER.#'d SETS
ROOKIE AU STATED ODDS 1:12
UNPRICED ROOKIE FOUNDATIONS #'d TO 1
1 Larry Fitzgerald .30 .75
2 Anquan Boldin .25 .60
3 Kurt Warner .30 .75
4 Michael Vick .30 .75
5 T.J. Duckett .20 .50
6 Peerless Price .20 .50
7 Todd Heap .25 .60
8 Jamal Lewis .25 .60
9 Kyle Boller .25 .60
10 Derrick Mason .25 .60
11 J.P. Losman .20 .50
12 Willis McGahee .30 .75
13 Lee Evans .25 .60
14 Eric Moulds .20 .50
15 Jake Delhomme .25 .60
16 Keary Colbert .20 .50
17 DeShaun Foster .25 .60
18 Brian Urlacher .30 .75
19 Rex Grossman .25 .60
20 Muhsin Muhammad .25 .60
21 Carson Palmer .30 .75
22 Rudi Johnson .25 .60
23 Chad Johnson .25 .60
24 Julius Jones .20 .50
25 Keyshawn Johnson .25 .60
26 Drew Bledsoe .30 .75
27 Tatum Bell .20 .50
28 Jake Plummer .25 .60
29 Ashley Lelie .20 .50
30 Roy Williams WR .25 .60
31 Kevin Jones .20 .50
32 Jeff Garcia .25 .60
33 Brett Favre .75 2.00
34 Ahman Green .25 .60
35 Javon Walker .20 .50
36 David Carr .20 .50
37 Andre Johnson .30 .75
38 Domanick Davis .20 .50
39 Peyton Manning .60 1.50
40 Reggie Wayne .30 .75
41 Edgerrin James .25 .60
42 Marvin Harrison .30 .75
43 Byron Leftwich .25 .60
44 Fred Taylor .25 .60
45 Jimmy Smith .25 .60
46 Priest Holmes .25 .60
47 Tony Gonzalez .25 .60
48 Trent Green .25 .60
49 A.J. Feeley .20 .50
50 Chris Chambers .25 .60
51 Randy McMichael .20 .50
52 Daunte Culpepper .25 .60
53 Michael Bennett .25 .60
54 Nate Burleson .20 .50
55 Tom Brady .60 1.50
56 Corey Dillon .25 .60
57 Deion Branch .20 .50
58 Richard Seymour .20 .50
59 Aaron Brooks .20 .50
60 Deuce McAllister .25 .60
61 Joe Horn .25 .60
62 Eli Manning .50 1.25
63 Jeremy Shockey .30 .75
64 Tiki Barber .30 .75
65 Chad Pennington .30 .75
66 Curtis Martin .30 .75
67 Laveranues Coles .20 .50
68 Kerry Collins .25 .60
69 LaMont Jordan .25 .60
70 Randy Moss .30 .75
71 Donovan McNabb .30 .75
72 Terrell Owens .30 .75
73 Jeremiah Trotter .20 .50
74 Brian Westbrook .25 .60
75 Ben Roethlisberger .50 1.25
76 Jerome Bettis .30 .75
77 Hines Ward .30 .75
78 Antwaan Randle El .25 .60
79 Drew Brees .30 .75
80 LaDainian Tomlinson .30 .75
81 Antonio Gates .30 .75
82 Tim Rattay .20 .50
83 Brandon Lloyd .20 .50
84 Eric Johnson .20 .50
85 Shaun Alexander .25 .60
86 Darrell Jackson .20 .50
87 Matt Hasselbeck .25 .60
88 Marc Bulger .25 .60
89 Steven Jackson .30 .75
90 Marshall Faulk .30 .75
91 Torry Holt .25 .60
92 Joey Galloway .25 .60
93 Brian Griese .25 .60
94 Michael Clayton .20 .50
95 Steve McNair .30 .75
96 Drew Bennett .25 .60
97 Chris Brown .20 .50
98 Clinton Portis .25 .60
99 Patrick Ramsey .25 .60
100 Santana Moss .25 .60
101 Gino Guidugli RC 1.50 4.00
102 James Kilian RC 1.50 4.00
103 Matt Cassel RC 5.00 12.00
104 Adrian McPherson RC 1.50 4.00
105 Timmy Chang RC 2.00 5.00
106 Chris Rix RC 2.00 5.00
107 Lionel Gates RC 1.50 4.00
108 Alvin Pearman RC 1.50 4.00
109 Damien Nash RC 2.00 5.00
110 Noah Herron RC 1.50 4.00
111 Steve Savoy RC 1.50 4.00
112 Craig Bragg RC 1.50 4.00
113 Larry Brackins RC 1.50 4.00
114 Nick Collins RC 2.50 6.00
115 Josh Davis RC 1.50 4.00
116 Chad Owens RC 2.00 5.00
117 Dante Ridgeway RC 1.50 4.00
118 Airese Currie RC 1.50 4.00
119 Chauncey Stovall RC 1.50 4.00
120 Harry Williams RC 2.00 5.00
121 Alex Smith TE RC 1.50 4.00
122 Jerome Collins RC 2.00 5.00
123 Rick Razzano RC 1.50 4.00
124 Derrick Johnson RC 2.00 5.00
125 Mike Patterson RC 1.50 4.00
126 Jonathan Babineaux RC 2.00 5.00
127 Matt Roth RC 2.00 5.00
128 Shaun Cody RC 2.00 5.00
129 Justin Tuck RC 3.00 8.00
130 Vincent Burns RC 1.50 4.00
131 DeMarcus Ware RC 5.00 12.00
132 Jerome Mathis RC 2.50 6.00
133 Darryl Blackstock RC 1.50 4.00
134 Robert McCune RC 2.00 5.00
135 Channing Crowder RC 2.00 5.00
136 Odell Thurman RC 2.50 6.00
137 Marcus Maxwell RC 1.50 4.00
138 Lance Mitchell RC 2.00 5.00
139 Jordan Beck RC 2.00 5.00
140 Alfred Fincher RC 2.00 5.00
141 Kirk Morrison RC 2.50 6.00
142 Kelvin Hayden RC 2.00 5.00
143 Justin Miller RC 2.00 5.00
144 Bryant McFadden RC 2.00 5.00
145 Eric Green RC 1.50 4.00
146 Fabian Washington RC 2.00 5.00
147 Ellis Hobbs RC 2.50 6.00
148 Ronald Bartell RC 2.00 5.00
149 Brodney Pool RC 2.00 5.00
150 Josh Bullocks RC 2.00 5.00
151 Vincent Fuller RC 2.00 5.00
152 Donte Nicholson RC 1.50 4.00
153 Sean Considine RC 1.50 4.00
154 Oshiomogho Atogwe RC 2.50 6.00
155 Dustin Fox RC 2.00 5.00
156 Mike Nugent RC 2.00 5.00
157 Shane Boyd RC 1.50 4.00
158 Ryan Fitzpatrick RC 4.00 10.00
159 Brock Berlin RC 2.00 5.00
160 Bryan Randall RC 2.00 5.00
161 Matt Jones RC 2.00 5.00
162 Todd Mortensen RC 1.50 4.00
163 Darian Durant RC 1.50 4.00
164 Stanley Wilson RC 2.00 5.00
165 Nehemiah Broughton RC 2.00 5.00
166 Manuel White RC 2.00 5.00
167 Zach Tuiasosopo RC 1.50 4.00
168 Deandra Cobb RC 1.50 4.00
169 Charles Frederick 1.50 4.00
170 Efrom Hill RC 1.50 4.00
171 Jason Anderson RC 1.50 4.00
172 Rasheed Marshall RC 2.00 5.00
173 Tab Perry RC 1.50 4.00
174 Paris Warren RC 2.00 5.00
175 Roydell Williams RC 2.00 5.00
176 Fred Amey RC UER 1.50 4.00
(card #100 on back)
177 Kerry Wright RC 2.00 5.00
178 Joel Dreessen RC 2.00 5.00
179 Bo Scaife RC 2.00 5.00
180 Alex Barron RC 1.50 4.00
181 Jammal Brown RC 2.50 6.00
182 Michael Roos RC 1.50 4.00
183 Khalif Barnes RC 1.50 4.00
184 Logan Mankins RC 2.50 6.00
185 Elton Brown RC 1.50 4.00
186 David Baas RC 1.50 4.00
187 Chris Spencer RC 2.50 6.00
188 Marcus Spears RC 2.00 5.00
189 Trent Cole RC 2.50 6.00
190 Luis Castillo RC 2.00 5.00
191 Bill Swancutt RC 1.50 4.00
192 Jesse Lumsden RC 1.50 4.00
193 Lofa Tatupu RC 2.50 6.00
194 Boomer Grigsby RC 2.50 6.00
195 Domonique Foxworth RC 2.00 5.00
196 Travis Daniels RC 2.00 5.00
197 Darrent Williams RC 2.50 6.00
198 Kerry Rhodes RC 2.00 5.00
199 Mark Bradley RC 1.50 4.00
200 Bobby Purify RC 2.00 5.00
201 Dan Orlovsky AU/699 RC 5.00 12.00
202 David Greene AU/699 RC 3.00 8.00
203 Anthony Davis AU/699 RC 3.00 8.00
204 Taylor Stubblefield AU/699 RC 3.00 8.00
205 Walter Reyes AU/699 RC 3.00 8.00
206 Darren Sproles AU/699 RC 15.00 30.00
207 Courtney Roby AU/375 RC 5.00 12.00
208 Marlin Jackson AU/699 RC 3.00 8.00
209 Corey Webster AU/699 RC 4.00 10.00
210 Ryan Moats AU/699 RC 3.00 8.00
211 Marion Barber AU/375 RC 12.00 30.00
212 Frank Gore AU/699 RC 10.00 25.00
213 Kay-Jay Harris AU/699 RC 3.00 8.00
214 Anttaj Hawthorne AU/699 RC 3.00 8.00
215 Adam Jones AU/699 RC 3.00 8.00
216 Stefan LeFors AU/375 RC 4.00 10.00
217 Barrett Ruud AU/699 RC 5.00 12.00
218 Kevin Burnett AU/699 RC 4.00 10.00
219 T.A. McLendon AU/699 RC 3.00 8.00
220 James Butler AU/699 RC 4.00 10.00
221 J.R. Russell AU/699 RC 3.00 8.00
222 Vincent Jackson AU/300 RC 8.00 20.00
223 J.J. Arrington AU/699 RC 4.00 10.00
224 Maurice Clarett AU/175 6.00 15.00
225 Brandon Jacobs AU/699 RC 6.00 15.00
226 Craphonso Thorpe AU/699 RC 3.00 8.00
227 Fred Gibson AU/575 RC 4.00 10.00
228 Travis Johnson AU/699 RC 3.00 8.00
229 Kyle Orton AU/575 RC 8.00 20.00
230 Jason White AU/575 RC 5.00 12.00
231 Terrence Murphy AU/575 RC 3.00 8.00
232 Mark Clayton AU/375 RC 5.00 12.00
234 David Pollack AU/575 RC 4.00 10.00
235 Erasmus James AU/575 RC 4.00 10.00
236 Dan Cody AU/575 RC 4.00 10.00
237 Thomas Davis AU/575 RC 3.00 8.00
238 Carlos Rogers AU/575 RC 5.00 12.00
239 Derek Anderson AU/699 RC 4.00 10.00
240 Antrel Rolle AU/575 RC 5.00 12.00
241 Shawne Merriman AU/575 RC 5.00 12.00
242 Reggie Brown AU/699 RC 3.00 8.00
243 Heath Miller AU/699 RC 6.00 15.00
244 Roscoe Parrish AU/375 RC 4.00 10.00
245 Roddy White AU/375 RC 8.00 20.00
246 Eric Shelton AU/699 RC 3.00 8.00
247 Vernand Morency AU/575 RC 3.00 8.00
248 Ciatrick Fason AU/375 RC 4.00 10.00
249 Andrew Walter AU/375 RC 5.00 12.00
250 Jason Campbell AU/375 RC 20.00 40.00
251 Charles Frederick AU/699 RC 3.00 8.00
252 Troy Williamson AU/175 RC 8.00 20.00
253 Braylon Edwards AU/175 RC 12.00 30.00
254 Mike Williams AU/175 10.00 25.00
255 Cedric Benson AU/50 RC 30.00 50.00
256 Cadillac Williams AU/175 RC 10.00 25.00
258 Charlie Frye AU/175 RC 10.00 25.00
259 Alex Smith QB AU/175 RC 30.00 60.00
260 Aaron Rodgers AU/175 RC 250.00 400.00
P1 Ben Roethlisberger Promo 2.50 6.00

2005 Upper Deck Foundations Exclusive Gold

*VETERANS 1-100: 3X TO 8X BASIC CARDS
*ROOKIES 101-200: .5X TO 1.2X BASIC CARDS
1-200 PRINT RUN 99 SER.#'d SETS
*ROOKIE AU: 1.2X TO 3X BASE AU/575-699
*ROOKIE AU: 1X TO 2.5X BASE AU/300-375
*ROOK.AU/252-259: .6X TO 1.5X AU/175
*ROOK.AU/252-259: .4X TO 1X AU/50
ROOKIE AUTO PRINT RUN 25 SER.#'d SETS
OVERALL GOLD STATED ODDS 1:24
260 Aaron Rodgers AU 400.00 600.00

2005 Upper Deck Foundations Signature Foundations Silver

SILVER STATED ODDS 1:24
UNPRICED PLATINUM #'d TO 1
SFAA Aaron Brooks 3.00 8.00
SFAB Anquan Boldin SP 6.00 15.00
SFAD Anthony Davis 3.00 8.00
SFAG Ahman Green SP 7.50 20.00
SFAH Anttaj Hawthorne 3.00 8.00
SFAJ A.J. Feeley 4.00 10.00
SFAN Antrel Rolle 4.00 10.00
SFAP Alan Page SP 7.50 20.00
SFAR Aaron Rodgers SP 175.00 300.00
SFAS Alex Smith QB SP 40.00 80.00
SFAW Andrew Walter 4.00 10.00
SFBA Marion Barber 12.00 30.00
SFBD Brian Dawkins 15.00 30.00
SFBE Braylon Edwards SP 25.00 60.00
SFBJ Brandon Jacobs 6.00 15.00
SFBL Byron Leftwich SP 10.00 25.00
SFBR Barrett Ruud 6.00 15.00
SFBS Barry Sanders SP 60.00 120.00
SFCA Carlos Rogers 4.00 10.00
SFCC Cris Collinsworth SP 7.50 20.00
SFCF Charlie Frye SP 6.00 15.00
SFCI Ciatrick Fason SP
SFCJ Chad Johnson 12.50 25.00
SFCK Charles Frederick 3.00 8.00
SFCN Chuck Noll SP 12.50 30.00
SFCO Corey Webster 3.00 8.00
SFCR Chris Brown SP
SFCT Craphonso Thorpe 3.00 8.00
SFCW Cadillac Williams SP 30.00 60.00
SFDA Derek Anderson 6.00 15.00
SFDB Drew Bennett 3.00 8.00
SFDC Dave Casper SP
SFDD Domanick Davis SP
SFDG David Greene 4.00 10.00
SFDM Deuce McAllister SP 15.00 40.00
SFDO Dan Orlovsky 4.00 10.00
SFDP David Pollack 4.00 10.00
SFDS Darren Sproles 10.00 25.00
SFDW Dwight Clark SP 10.00 25.00
SFEJ Erasmus James 3.00 8.00
SFEM Eli Manning SP 60.00 100.00
SFFG Frank Gore 15.00 30.00
SFFR Fred Gibson 3.00 8.00
SFFT Fred Taylor 4.00 10.00
SFHM Heath Miller 6.00 15.00
SFJA J.J. Arrington 4.00 10.00
SFJB James Butler 3.00 8.00
SFJC Jason Campbell 15.00 30.00
SFJH Joe Horn SP 10.00 25.00
SFJW Jason White 4.00 10.00
SFKC Keary Colbert 3.00 8.00
SFKJ Kay-Jay Harris 3.00 8.00
SFKO Kyle Orton 6.00 15.00
SFKS Ken Stabler SP 30.00 60.00
SFLJ Larry Johnson 8.00 20.00
SFLT LaDainian Tomlinson SP 50.00 80.00
SFMA Dan Marino SP 60.00 120.00
SFMB Marc Bulger SP 10.00 25.00
SFMC Mark Clayton SP 6.00 15.00
SFMJ Marlin Jackson SP
SFMM Muhsin Muhammad 6.00 15.00
SFMW Mike Williams SP 6.00 15.00
SFNB Nate Burleson 6.00 15.00
SFPM Peyton Manning SP 60.00 100.00
SFRB Ronnie Brown SP 30.00 80.00
SFRC Roger Craig SP 7.50 20.00
SFRE Reggie Brown 5.00 12.00
SFRG Reggie Wayne 6.00 15.00
SFRJ Rudi Johnson 6.00 15.00
SFRM Ryan Moats 4.00 10.00
SFRW Roy Williams WR SP 20.00 40.00
SFTB Tiki Barber SP
SFTE Terrence Murphy 4.00 10.00
SFTM T.A. McLendon 3.00 8.00
SFTS Taylor Stubblefield 3.00 8.00
SFTW Troy Williamson SP
SFVM Vernand Morency 6.00 15.00
SFWR Walter Reyes 3.00 8.00

2005 Upper Deck Foundations Signature Foundations Gold

*GOLD/20: 1X TO 2.5X BASIC AU
*GOLD/20: .6X TO 1.5X BASIC AU SP
GOLD PRINT RUN 20 SETS
SFAR Aaron Rodgers 400.00 600.00

2005 Upper Deck Foundations Dual Endorsements

STATED ODDS 1:288
DEAG Derek Anderson/75 12.50 30.00
David Greene
DEBT Anquan Boldin/50 10.00 25.00
Craphonso Thorpe
DEBW Ronnie Brown/75 75.00 150.00
Cadillac Williams
DECD Chad Johnson/50 15.00 40.00
Derek Anderson
DECN Dave Casper/50 15.00 40.00
Ozzie Newsome
DECR Jason Campbell/75 15.00 40.00
Carlos Rogers
DECW Michael Clayton/50 20.00 50.00
Roy Williams WR
DEDH Anthony Davis/75 7.50 20.00
Kay-Jay Harris
DEEW Braylon Edwards/75 30.00 80.00
Mike Williams
DEGB Fred Gibson/75 12.50 30.00
Reggie Brown
DEGC Antonio Gates/50 20.00 50.00
Alge Crumpler
DEHF Chris Henry/75 12.50 30.00
Charles Frederick
DEHM Joe Horn/50 10.00 25.00
Deuce McAllister
DEJH Erasmus James/75 7.50 20.00
Anttaj Hawthorne
DEKB Keary Colbert/50 7.50 20.00
Anquan Boldin
DEMB Ryan Moats/50 15.00 40.00
Marion Barber

DEMH Terrence Murphy/50 12.50 30.00
Chris Henry
DEMO Jim McMahon/75 25.00 60.00
Kyle Orton
DEOD Merlin Olsen/50 15.00 40.00
Art Donovan
DEOS Kyle Orton/75 25.00 60.00
Taylor Stubblefield
DERA Ryan Moats/75 12.50 30.00
J.J. Arrington
DERD Carlos Rogers/75 7.50 20.00
Thomas Davis
DERT Courtney Roby/50
Craphonso Thorpe
DESM Eric Shelton/50 10.00 25.00
Vernand Morency
DETF Fred Taylor/50 12.50 30.00
Ciatrick Fason
DEWB Reggie Wayne/50 12.50 30.00
Drew Bennett
DEWG Jason White/50 12.50 30.00
David Greene
DEWM Troy Williamson/75 12.50 30.00
Mike Williams
DEWO Jason White/75 12.50 30.00
Dan Orlovsky
DEWP Roddy White/75 12.50 30.00
Roscoe Parrish

2005 Upper Deck Foundations Three Star Signatures

STATED PRINT RUN 75 SER.#'d SETS
CPJ Dan Cody 15.00 40.00
David Pollack
Travis Johnson
DHJ Anthony Davis 12.50 30.00
Anttaj Hawthorne
Erasmus James
EMC Braylon Edwards 30.00 80.00
Terrence Murphy
Mark Clayton
FWJ Ciatrick Fason 15.00 40.00
Troy Williamson
Erasmus James
HPT Chris Henry 15.00 40.00
Roscoe Parrish
Craphonso Thorpe
HWB Chris Henry 15.00 40.00
Roddy White
Mark Bradley
LEP J.P. Losman 15.00 40.00
Lee Evans
Roscoe Parrish
MBB Shawne Merriman 20.00 50.00
Kevin Burnett
Thomas Davis
MJW Peyton Manning 90.00 150.00
Marlin Jackson
Reggie Wayne
MSB Ryan Moats 30.00 50.00
Darren Sproles
Marion Barber
PJJ David Pollack 40.00 80.00
Rudi Johnson
Chad Johnson
RDJ Antrel Rolle 12.50 30.00
Adam Jones
Carlos Rogers
RGP Antrel Rolle 25.00 50.00
Frank Gore
Roscore Parrish
RSF Aaron Rodgers 175.00 300.00
Alex Smith QB
Jason Campbell

2005 Upper Deck Foundations Four Star Signatures

UNPRICED PRINT RUN 20 SER.#'d SETS

2005 Upper Deck Foundations Five Star Signatures

UNPRICED PRINT RUN 15 SER.#'d SETS

2005 Upper Deck Foundations Six Star Signatures

UNPRICED PRINT RUN 10 SER.#'d SETS

2005 Upper Deck Foundations Eight Star Signatures

UNPRICED PRINT RUN 5 SER.#'d SETS

2000 Upper Deck Gold Reserve

Released in Late November 2000 as a 222-card set, gold reserve features 177 veteran player cards and 41 rookie cards. Base card design is full-bleed color with player action photography and gold foil highlights. Shortly before it's release, card numbers 220, 221, and 222 were pulled from the set, therefore Gold Reserve is numbered up to 225. Gold Reserve was released primarily as a retail product and was packaged in 24-pack boxes with packs containing 10 cards and carried a suggested retail price of $2.99.

COMP.SET w/o RC's (180) 10.00 25.00
RC STATED PRINT RUN 2500 SER.#'d SETS
1 Jake Plummer .25 .60
2 Rob Moore .20 .50
3 David Boston .20 .50
4 Frank Sanders .20 .50
5 Chris Chandler .25 .60
6 Jamal Anderson .25 .60
7 Shawn Jefferson .20 .50
8 Terance Mathis .20 .50
9 Qadry Ismail .25 .60
10 Jermaine Lewis .20 .50
11 Tony Banks .20 .50
12 Peter Boulware .20 .50
13 Shannon Sharpe .30 .75
14 Peerless Price .25 .60
15 Rob Johnson .25 .60
16 Eric Moulds .25 .60
17 Doug Flutie .30 .75
18 Antowain Smith .25 .60
19 Muhsin Muhammad .25 .60
20 Patrick Jeffers .25 .60
21 Steve Beuerlein .25 .60
22 Natrone Means .25 .60
23 Tim Biakabutuka .25 .60
24 Wesley Walls .20 .50
25 Cade McNown .20 .50
26 Curtis Enis .20 .50
27 Marcus Robinson .25 .60
28 Eddie Kennison .20 .50
29 Bobby Engram .25 .60
30 Akili Smith .20 .50
31 Corey Dillon .25 .60
32 Damon Griffin .20 .50
33 Takeo Spikes .20 .50
34 Tony McGee .20 .50
35 Tim Couch .25 .60
36 Kevin Johnson .20 .50
37 Darrin Chiaverini .20 .50
38 Errict Rhett .25 .60
39 Troy Aikman .50 1.25
40 Emmitt Smith .75 2.00
41 Rocket Ismail .25 .60
42 Jason Tucker .20 .50
43 Joey Galloway .25 .60
44 Wane McGarity .20 .50
45 Terrell Davis .30 .75
46 Olandis Gary .25 .60
47 Brian Griese .25 .60
48 Gus Frerotte .25 .60
49 Ed McCaffrey .25 .60
50 Rod Smith .25 .60
51 Charlie Batch .25 .60
52 Germane Crowell .20 .50
53 Johnnie Morton .25 .60
54 Robert Porcher .20 .50
55 Herman Moore .25 .60
56 James Stewart .20 .50
57 Brett Favre 1.00 2.50
58 Antonio Freeman .25 .60
59 Bill Schroeder .25 .60
60 Dorsey Levens .25 .60
61 Corey Bradford .20 .50
62 Vonnie Holliday .20 .50
63 Peyton Manning .75 2.00
64 Edgerrin James .30 .75
65 Marvin Harrison .30 .75
66 Ken Dilger .20 .50
67 Terrence Wilkins .20 .50
68 Marcus Pollard .20 .50
69 Mark Brunell .25 .60
70 Fred Taylor .30 .75
71 Jimmy Smith .25 .60
72 Keenan McCardell .25 .60
73 Carnell Lake .20 .50
74 Kyle Brady .20 .50
75 Hardy Nickerson .20 .50
76 Elvis Grbac .20 .50
77 Tony Gonzalez .30 .75
78 Derrick Alexander .20 .50
79 Donnell Bennett .20 .50
80 Mike Cloud .20 .50
81 Donnie Edwards .20 .50
82 Jay Fiedler .25 .60
83 James Johnson .20 .50
84 Tony Martin .25 .60
85 Damon Huard .25 .60
86 O.J. McDuffie .25 .60
87 Thurman Thomas .30 .75
88 Oronde Gadsden .25 .60
89 Randy Moss .30 .75
90 Robert Smith .25 .60
91 Cris Carter .30 .75
92 Daunte Culpepper .25 .60
93 Matthew Hatchette .20 .50
94 Drew Bledsoe .30 .75
95 Terry Glenn .25 .60
96 Troy Brown .25 .60
97 Kevin Faulk .25 .60
98 Lawyer Milloy .20 .50
99 Ricky Williams .30 .75
100 Keith Poole .20 .50
101 Jake Reed .25 .60
102 Jeff Blake .25 .60
103 Andrew Glover .20 .50
104 Kerry Collins .25 .60
105 Amani Toomer .25 .60
106 Joe Montgomery .20 .50
107 Ike Hilliard .25 .60
108 Tiki Barber .30 .75
109 Ray Lucas .20 .50
110 Mo Lewis .20 .50
111 Curtis Martin .30 .75
112 Vinny Testaverde .25 .60
113 Wayne Chrebet .25 .60
114 Dedric Ward .20 .50
115 Tim Brown .30 .75
116 Rich Gannon .25 .60
117 Tyrone Wheatley .20 .50
118 Napoleon Kaufman .25 .60
119 Charles Woodson .30 .75
120 James Jett .25 .60
121 Rickey Dudley .20 .50
122 Duce Staley .25 .60
123 Donovan McNabb .30 .75
124 Torrance Small .20 .50
125 Allen Rossum .20 .50
126 Na Brown .20 .50
127 Charles Johnson .20 .50
128 Kent Graham .20 .50
129 Troy Edwards .20 .50
130 Jerome Bettis .30 .75
131 Hines Ward .30 .75
132 Kordell Stewart .25 .60
133 Richard Huntley .20 .50
134 Marshall Faulk .30 .75
135 Kurt Warner .50 1.25
136 Torry Holt .30 .75
137 Isaac Bruce .30 .75
138 Kevin Carter .20 .50
139 Az-Zahir Hakim .20 .50
140 Jermaine Fazande .20 .50
141 Curtis Conway .25 .60
142 Freddie Jones .20 .50
143 Junior Seau .30 .75
144 Jeff Graham .20 .50
145 Jim Harbaugh .25 .60
146 Jerry Rice .60 1.50
147 Charlie Garner .25 .60
148 Terrell Owens .30 .75
149 Jeff Garcia .25 .60
150 J.J. Stokes .25 .60
151 Ricky Watters .25 .60
152 Jon Kitna .25 .60
153 Derrick Mayes .20 .50
154 Sean Dawkins .20 .50
155 Charlie Rogers .20 .50
156 Cortez Kennedy .20 .50
157 Warrick Dunn .25 .60
158 Shaun King .20 .50
159 Mike Alstott .30 .75
160 Warren Sapp .25 .60
161 Jacquez Green .20 .50
162 Reidel Anthony .20 .50
163 Keyshawn Johnson .25 .60
164 Eddie George .25 .60
165 Steve McNair .30 .75
166 Kevin Dyson .25 .60
167 Jevon Kearse .25 .60
168 Yancey Thigpen .20 .50
169 Isaac Byrd .20 .50
170 Neil O'Donnell .20 .50
171 Brad Johnson .25 .60
172 Stephen Davis .25 .60
173 Michael Westbrook .20 .50
174 Albert Connell .20 .50
175 Bruce Smith .30 .75
176 Stephen Alexander .20 .50
177 Jeff George .25 .60
178 Bubba Franks RC 1.50 4.00
179 Brian Urlacher RC 6.00 15.00
180 Chad Pennington RC 2.50 6.00
181 Tim Rattay RC 1.25 3.00
182 Chris Redman RC 1.25 3.00
183 Corey Simon RC 1.25 3.00
184 Courtney Brown RC 1.25 3.00
185 Curtis Keaton RC 1.00 2.50
186 Danny Farmer RC 1.00 2.50
187 Erron Kinney RC 1.00 2.50
188 Deltha O'Neal RC 1.25 3.00
189 Dennis Northcutt RC 1.25 3.00
190 Dez White RC 1.25 3.00
191 Frank Murphy RC 1.00 2.50
192 Gari Scott RC 1.00 2.50
193 Giovanni Carmazzi RC 1.00 2.50
194 J.R. Redmond RC 1.00 2.50
195 JaJuan Dawson RC 1.00 2.50
196 Jamal Lewis RC 1.50 4.00
197 Jerry Porter RC 1.50 4.00
198 Joe Hamilton RC 1.00 2.50
199 Laveranues Coles RC 1.50 4.00
200 Michael Wiley RC 1.00 2.50
201 Peter Warrick RC 1.50 4.00
202 Plaxico Burress RC 1.50 4.00
203 R.Jay Soward RC 1.00 2.50
204 Reuben Droughns RC 1.50 4.00
205 Rob Morris RC 1.25 3.00
206 Ron Dayne RC 1.50 4.00
207 Ron Dugans RC 1.00 2.50
208 Sebastian Janikowski RC 1.50 4.00
209 Shaun Alexander RC 2.00 5.00
210 Sylvester Morris RC 1.00 2.50
211 Tee Martin RC 1.50 4.00
212 Thomas Jones RC 2.00 5.00
213 Todd Husak RC 1.00 2.50
214 Todd Pinkston RC 1.00 2.50
215 Tom Brady RC 60.00 120.00
216 Travis Prentice RC 1.25 3.00
217 Travis Taylor RC 1.25 3.00
218 Trevor Gaylor RC 1.00 2.50
219 Trung Canidate RC 1.25 3.00
223 Peyton Manning CL .60 1.50
224 Randy Moss CL .25 .60
225 Kurt Warner CL .40 1.00

2000 Upper Deck Gold Reserve Face Masks

STATED PRINT RUN 100 SER.#'d SETS
*GOLD/25: .6X TO 1.5X FACE MASK/100
GOLD STATED PRINT RUN 25 SETS
FMCB Courtney Brown 10.00 25.00
FMCK Curtis Keaton 8.00 20.00
FMCP Chad Pennington 20.00 50.00
FMCR Chris Redman 10.00 25.00
FMDR Reuben Droughns 12.00 30.00
FMJL Jamal Lewis 12.00 30.00
FMJR J.R. Redmond 8.00 20.00
FMPB Plaxico Burress 12.00 30.00
FMPW Peter Warrick 12.00 30.00
FMRD Ron Dayne 12.00 30.00
FMRJ R.Jay Soward 8.00 20.00
FMSA Shaun Alexander 15.00 40.00
FMSM Sylvester Morris 8.00 20.00
FMTJ Thomas Jones 15.00 40.00
FMTT Travis Taylor 10.00 25.00

2000 Upper Deck Gold Reserve Gold Mine

COMPLETE SET (12) 6.00 15.00
STATED ODDS 1:12
GM1 Dez White .50 1.25
GM2 Peter Warrick .60 1.50
GM3 Plaxico Burress .60 1.50
GM4 Bubba Franks .60 1.50
GM5 Jamal Lewis .60 1.50
GM6 Travis Taylor .50 1.25
GM7 Chris Redman .50 1.25
GM8 Sylvester Morris .40 1.00
GM9 Courtney Brown .50 1.25
GM10 Shaun Alexander .75 2.00
GM11 Trung Canidate .50 1.25
GM12 J.R. Redmond .40 1.00

2000 Upper Deck Gold Reserve Gold Strike

COMPLETE SET (12) 6.00 15.00
STATED ODDS 1:12
GS1 Eddie George .50 1.25
GS2 Edgerrin James .60 1.50
GS3 Terrell Davis .60 1.50
GS4 Jamal Anderson .50 1.25
GS5 Ricky Williams .60 1.50
GS6 Marshall Faulk .60 1.50
GS7 Keyshawn Johnson .50 1.25
GS8 Brett Favre 2.00 5.00
GS9 Cade McNown .40 1.00
GS10 Emmitt Smith 1.50 4.00
GS11 Peyton Manning 1.50 4.00
GS12 Kurt Warner 1.00 2.50

2000 Upper Deck Gold Reserve Setting the Standard

COMPLETE SET (12) 6.00 15.00
STATED ODDS 1:12
SS1 Randy Moss .60 1.50
SS2 Peyton Manning 1.50 4.00
SS3 Stephen Davis .50 1.25
SS4 Cris Carter .60 1.50
SS5 Jevon Kearse .50 1.25
SS6 Jerry Rice 1.25 3.00
SS7 Troy Aikman 1.00 2.50
SS8 Edgerrin James .60 1.50
SS9 Daunte Culpepper .50 1.25
SS10 Shaun King .40 1.00
SS11 Mark Brunell .50 1.25
SS12 Fred Taylor .60 1.50

2000 Upper Deck Gold Reserve Solid Gold Gallery

COMPLETE SET (6) 6.00 15.00
STATED ODDS 1:23
SG1 Jamal Lewis .75 2.00
SG2 Peter Warrick .75 2.00
SG3 Ron Dayne .75 2.00
SG4 Chad Pennington 1.25 3.00
SG5 Thomas Jones 1.00 2.50
SG6 Plaxico Burress .75 2.00

2000 Upper Deck Gold Reserve UD Authentics

STATED ODDS 1:160
*GOLD/25: 1.2X TO 3X BASIC AUTO
GOLD STATED PRINT RUN 25
CC Chris Coleman EXCH .40 1.00
CP Chad Pennington 12.00 30.00
CR Chris Redman 5.00 12.00
DF Doug Flutie 8.00 20.00
DU Ron Dugans EXCH .40 1.00
DW Dez White 5.00 12.00
FA Danny Farmer EXCH .40 1.00
JH Joe Hamilton EXCH .40 1.00
KC Kwame Cavil 4.00 10.00
MW Michael Wiley 4.00 10.00
RD Ron Dayne 8.00 20.00
SA Shaun Alexander 12.00 30.00
SG Sherrod Gideon 4.00 10.00
SJ Sebastian Janikowski EXCH .40 1.00
SK Shaun King EXCH .40 1.00
TA Troy Aikman 30.00 60.00
TJ Thomas Jones EXCH .40 1.00
TM Tee Martin 6.00 15.00
TR Tim Rattay 5.00 12.00
TW Troy Walters 4.00 10.00

2009 Upper Deck Goodwin Champions

COMMON CARD (1-150) .15 .40
COMMON NIGHT 5.00 12.00
COMMON SP (151-190) 1.25 3.00
151-190 STATED ODDS 1:2 HOBBY
COMMON SUPER SP (191-210) 1.50 4.00
191-210 STATED ODDS 1:10 HOBBY
PLATES RANDOMLY INSERTED
PLATE PRINT RUN 1 SET PER COLOR
BLACK-CYAN-MAGENTA-YELLOW ISSUED
NO PLATE PRICING DUE TO SCARCITY
45 Peyton Manning .50 1.25
57 Eli Manning .40 1.00
68 Matt Ryan .40 1.00
94 Adrian Peterson .60 1.50
99 Ben Roethlisberger .50 1.25
125 Chris Johnson .40 1.00

2009 Upper Deck Goodwin Champions Mini

COMPLETE SET (192) 75.00 150.00
*MINI 1-150: 1X TO 2.5X BASIC
APPX.MINI ODDS ONE PER PACK
PLATES RANDOMLY INSERTED
PLATE PRINT RUN 1 SET PER COLOR
BLACK-CYAN-MAGENTA-YELLOW ISSUED
NO PLATE PRICING DUE TO SCARCITY

2009 Upper Deck Goodwin Champions Mini Black Border

*MINI BLK 1-150: 1.5X TO 4X BASE
*MINI BLK 211-252: .75X TO 2X MINI
RANDOM INSERTS IN PACKS

2009 Upper Deck Goodwin Champions Mini Black Border Foil

RANDOM INSERTS IN PACKS
STATED PRINT RUN 8 SER.#'d SETS
NO PRICING DUE TO SCARCITY

2009 Upper Deck Goodwin Champions Mini Foil

*MINI FOIL 1-150: 3X TO 8X BASE
*MINI FOIL 211-252: 1.5X TO 4X MINI
RANDOM INSERTS IN PACKS
ANNCD PRINT RUN OF 88 TOTAL SETS

2011 Upper Deck Goodwin Champions

COMP.SET w/o VAR (210) 40.00 80.00
COMP.SET w/o SP's (150) 10.00 25.00
COMMON SP (151-190) 1.00 2.50
151-190 SP ODDS 1:3 HOBBY
COMMON SP (191-210) 1.50 4.00
191-210 SP ODDS 1:12 HOBBY
COMMON VARIATION SP 4.00 10.00
15 Bo Jackson .30 .75
20 Dan Marino .50 1.25
36 Jake Locker .40 1.00
40 Troy Aikman .30 .75
48 Drew Brees .25 .60
57 Barry Sanders .40 1.00
65 Mark Ingram .60 1.50
71A John Elway .40 1.00
71B John Elway Lightning SP 4.00 10.00
78 Cam Newton 1.00 2.50
80 Aaron Rodgers .30 .75
82 Earl Campbell .25 .60
83 Jerry Rice .40 1.00
86 Von Miller .30 .75
102 Billy Sims .20 .50
104 Steve Young .30 .75
109 Julio Jones .50 1.25
113A A.J. Green .50 1.25
113B A.J. Green Lightning SP 6.00 15.00
206 Walter Camp SP 1.50 4.00

2011 Upper Deck Goodwin Champions Mini

*1-150 MINI: 1X TO 2.5X BASIC
1-150 MINI ODDS 1:4 HOBBY
COMMON CARD (211-231) .60 1.50
211-231 MINI ODDS 1:13 HOBBY
PRINTING PLATES RANDOMLY INSERTED
PLATE PRINT RUN 1 SET PER COLOR
BLACK-CYAN-MAGENTA-YELLOW ISSUED
NO PLATE PRICING DUE TO SCARCITY

2011 Upper Deck Goodwin Champions Mini Black

*1-150 MINI BLACK: 1.2X TO 3X BASIC
1-150 MINI BLACK ODDS 1:13 HOBBY
*211-231 MINI BLK: .6X TO 1.5X BASIC MINI
211-231 MINI BLACK ODDS 1:46 HOBBY

2011 Upper Deck Goodwin Champions Mini Foil

*1-150 MINI FOIL: 2.5X TO 6X BASIC
1-150 ANNCD PRINT RUN OF 89
*211-231 MINI FOIL : 1X TO 2.5X BASIC MINI
211-231 ANNCD PRINT RUN OF 178
PRINT RUNS PROVIDED BY UD

2011 Upper Deck Goodwin Champions Mini Foil Black

RANDOM INSERTS IN PACKS
STATED PRINT RUN 9 SER.#'d SETS
NO PRICING DUE TO SCARCITY

2011 Upper Deck Goodwin Champions Mini Foil Presidential Gold

RANDOM INSERTS IN PACKS
STATED PRINT RUN 1 SER.#'d SET
NO PRICING DUE TO SCARCITY

2011 Upper Deck Goodwin Champions Autographs

GROUP A ODDS 1:1577 HOBBY
GROUP B ODDS 1:729 HOBBY
GROUP C ODDS 1:339 HOBBY
GROUP D ODDS 1:246 HOBBY
GROUP E ODDS 1:72 HOBBY
GROUP F ODDS 1:35 HOBBY
OVERALL AUTO ODDS 1:20 HOBBY
NO GROUP A PRICING DUE TO SCARCITY
EXCHANGE DEADLINE 6/7/2013
BS Billy Sims F 5.00 12.00
JA Bo Jackson B 50.00 100.00

2011 Upper Deck Goodwin Champions Figures of Sport

COMP.SET. w/o SP's (14) 10.00 25.00
COMMON CARD (1-14) .60 1.50
1-14 STATED ODDS 1:21 HOBBY
15-18 SP ODDS 1:300 HOBBY
FS2 Jerry Rice 1.50 4.00
FS8 Cam Newton 2.00 5.00

2011 Upper Deck Goodwin Champions Memorabilia

GROUP A ODDS 1:14,613 HOBBY
GROUP B ODDS 1:179 HOBBY
GROUP C ODDS 1:31 HOBBY
GROUP D ODDS 1:22 HOBBY
NO GROUP A PRICING AVAILABLE
AI Troy Aikman C 3.00 8.00
BJ Bo Jackson D 4.00 10.00
BS Barry Sanders C 6.00 15.00
EH Earl Campbell C 3.00 8.00
JE John Elway C 5.00 12.00
JR Jerry Rice C 4.00 10.00
YO Steve Young C 4.00 10.00

2011 Upper Deck Goodwin Champions Memorabilia Dual

GROUP A ODDS 1:87,680 HOBBY
GROUP B ODDS 1:8768 HOBBY
GROUP C ODDS 1:2923 HOBBY
GROUP D ODDS 1:877 HOBBY
GROUP E ODDS 1:585 HOBBY
NO GROUP A PRICING AVAILABLE
JE John Elway D 6.00 15.00

2011 Upper Deck Goodwin Champions Sport Royalty Autographs

RANDOM INSERTS IN PACKS
NO PRICING DUE TO SCARCITY
BG Bob Griese
CP Clinton Portis
JE John Elway
WP William Perry

2007 Upper Deck Goudey Sport Royalty

ONE PER HOBBY BOX LOADER
ES Emmitt Smith 4.00 10.00
JN Joe Namath 6.00 15.00
LT LaDainian Tomlinson 3.00 8.00
PM Peyton Manning 5.00 12.00

2007 Upper Deck Goudey Sport Royalty Autographs

STATED ODDS TWO PER CASE
FOUND IN HOBBY BOX LOADER PACKS
LT LaDainian Tomlinson 75.00 150.00
PM Peyton Manning 100.00 175.00

2008 Upper Deck Goudey

COMP.SET w/o HIGH #s (200) 20.00 50.00
COMMON CARD (1-200) .20 .50
COMMON ROOKIE (1-200) .30 .75
COMMON SP (201-230) 2.00 5.00
COMMON SP (231-250) 1.50 4.00
COMMON SP (251-270) 2.00 5.00
COMMON CARD (271-300) 2.00 5.00
COMMON CARD (301-330) 3.00 8.00
275 Brett Favre SR SP 4.00 10.00
278 Barry Sanders SR SP 3.00 8.00
289 Emmitt Smith SR SP 3.00 8.00
295 John Elway SR SP 3.00 8.00
302 Tom Brady SR SP 6.00 15.00
304 Dan Marino SR SP 6.00 15.00
327 Terry Bradshaw SR SP 4.00 10.00

2008 Upper Deck Goudey Mini Black Backs

*BLACK 1-200: .75X TO 2X GRN 1-200
*BLACK RC 1-200: .75X TO 2X GRN RC 1-200
*BLACK SP 201-250: .75X TO 2X GRN 201-250
*BLACK SP 251-270: .5X TO 1.2X GRN 251-270
*BLACK SR 271-330: .5X TO 1.2X GRN 271-330
RANDOM INSERTS IN PACKS
STATED PRINT RUN 34 SER.#'d SETS
278 Barry Sanders SR 10.00 25.00

2008 Upper Deck Goudey Mini Blue Backs

*BLUE 1-200: 1.5X TO 4X BASIC 1-200
*BLUE RC 1-200: 1X TO 2.5X BASIC RC 1-200
*BLUE 201-270: .6X TO 1.5X BASIC SP 201-270
*BLUE 271-330: .6X TO 1.5X BASIC SR 201-270
RANDOM INSERTS IN PACKS

2008 Upper Deck Goudey Mini Green Backs

RANDOM INSERTS IN PACKS
STATED PRINT RUN 88 SER.#'d SETS
275 Brett Favre SR 5.00 12.00
278 Barry Sanders SR 4.00 10.00
289 Emmitt Smith SR 4.00 10.00
295 John Elway SR 6.00 15.00
302 Tom Brady SR 10.00 25.00
304 Dan Marino SR 5.00 12.00
327 Terry Bradshaw SR 3.00 8.00

2008 Upper Deck Goudey Mini Red Backs

*RED 1-200: 1X TO 2.5X BASIC 1-200
*RED RC 1-200: .75X TO 2X BASIC RC 1-200
*RED 201-270: .5X TO 1.2X BASIC SP 201-270
*RED 271-330: .5X to 1.2X BASIC SR 271-330
RANDOM INSERTS IN PACKS

2008 Upper Deck Goudey Mini Taupe Backs

RANDOM INSERTS IN PACKS
STATED PRINT RUN 8 SER.#'d SETS
NO PRICING DUE TO SCARCITY

2008 Upper Deck Goudey Hit Parade of Champions

RANDOM INSERTS IN PACKS
3 Ben Roethlisberger .75 2.00
9 Emmitt Smith 1.25 3.00
11 Joe Montana 1.25 3.00
12 Joe Namath .75 2.00
15 LaDainian Tomlinson .75 2.00
24 Peyton Manning .75 2.00
27 Roger Staubach .75 2.00
29 Tom Brady 1.00 2.50

2008 Upper Deck Goudey Sport Royalty Autographs

OVERALL AUTO ODDS 1:18 HOBBY
ASTERISK EQUALS PARTIAL EXCHANGE
EXCHANGE DEADLINE 7/17/2010
TB Terry Bradshaw SP 125.00 250.00

2009 Upper Deck Goudey

COMPLETE SET (300) 200.00 300.00
COMP.SET w/o SP's (200) 20.00 50.00
COMMON CARD (1-200) .20 .50
COMMON RC (1-200) .40 1.00
COMMON SP (201-300) 2.00 5.00
APPX.SP ODDS 201-220 1:9 HOBBY
APPX.SP ODDS 221-260 1:6 HOBBY
APPX.SP ODDS 261-300 1:6 HOBBY
251 Adrian Peterson SR SP 4.00 10.00

2009 Upper Deck Goudey Mini Black Back

RANDOM INSERTS IN PACKS
STATED PRINT RUN 21 SER.#'d SETS
NO PRICING DUE TO SCARCITY

2009 Upper Deck Goudey Mini Green Back

*GREEN 1-200: 1.2X TO 3X BASIC
*GREEN RC 1-200: .6X TO 1.5X BASIC
COMMON CARD (201-300) .75 2.00
APPROX.ODDS 1:6 HOBBY
251 Adrian Peterson SR 4.00 10.00

2009 Upper Deck Goudey Mini Navy Blue Back

*BLUE 1-200: 1.5X TO 4X BASIC
*BLUE RC 1-200: .75X TO 2X BASIC
*BLUE: 201-300: .6X TO 1.5X MINI GREEN
APPROX.ODDS 1:9 HOBBY

2000 Upper Deck Hawaii

These cards were issued by Upper Deck and given away at the Kit Young annual conference in Hawaii in 2000. These cards feature autographs of four athletes Upper Deck brought over to the conference. Each player signed a card serial numbered to 500. The card featuring all four players signed was not included in the factory set, but 100 cards featuring all four players were also signed and distributed. Two Kit Young cards were also included with the factory sets.

COMPLETE SET (6) 160.00 400.00
JN Joe Namath AU 40.00 100.00
GAU Julius Erving AU/100 200.00 400.00
Gordie Howe AU
Joe Namath AU
Tom Seaver AU

2005 Upper Deck Hawaii Trade Conference Signature Supremacy

ISSUED AT '05 HAWAII TRADE SHOW
PRINT RUNS B/WN 5-10 COPIES PER
NO PRICING DUE TO SCARCITY

2006 Upper Deck Hawaii Trade Conference Signature Dual Jumbos

UNPRICED AUTO PRINT RUN 8-15

2006 Upper Deck Hawaii Trade Conference Signature Jumbos

UNPRICED AUTO PRINT RUN 9-15

2007 Upper Deck Hawaii Trade Conference

COMPLETE SET (13) 15.00 40.00
10 Peyton Manning 1.50 4.00

2007 Upper Deck Hawaii Trade Conference Autographs

10 Peyton Manning/35 75.00 150.00

2008 Upper Deck Hawaii Trade Conference Autographs

AUTOS TOO SCARCE TO PRICE

2008 Upper Deck Heroes

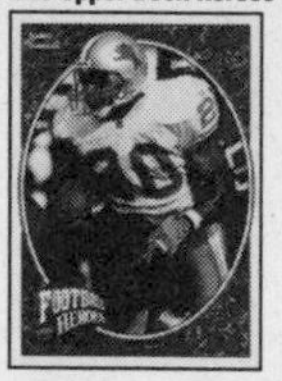

This set was released on July 8, 2008. The base set consists of 266 skip-numbered cards. Each subject in the set has between 2-4 different cards. Cards #1-100 feature veterans, cards 101-200 are rookies, cards 201-245 are legends, and cards 246-269 are miscellaneous subjects from track and field and famous guitarists.

COMPLETE SET (266) 25.00 60.00
UNPRICED PRINT PLATE PRINT RUN 1
UNPRICED BLACK PRINT RUN 1
EACH HAS MULTIPLE CARDS: EQUAL VALUE
1 Adrian Peterson .50 1.25
2 Adrian Peterson .50 1.25
3 Adrian Peterson .50 1.25
4 Adrian Peterson .50 1.25
5 Brett Favre .75 2.00
6 Brett Favre .75 2.00
7 Brett Favre .75 2.00
8 Brett Favre .75 2.00
9 Braylon Edwards .25 .60
10 Braylon Edwards .25 .60
11 Braylon Edwards .25 .60
12 Braylon Edwards .25 .60
13 Brodie Croyle .25 .60
14 Brodie Croyle .25 .60
15 Brodie Croyle .25 .60
16 Brodie Croyle .25 .60
17 Bob Sanders .25 .60
18 Bob Sanders .25 .60
19 Bob Sanders .25 .60
20 Bob Sanders .25 .60
21 Chad Johnson .25 .60
22 Chad Johnson .25 .60
23 Chad Johnson .25 .60
24 Chad Johnson .25 .60
25 DeMarcus Ware .25 .60
26 DeMarcus Ware .25 .60
27 DeMarcus Ware .25 .60
28 DeMarcus Ware .25 .60
29 Derek Anderson .20 .50
30 Derek Anderson .20 .50
31 Derek Anderson .20 .50
32 Derek Anderson .20 .50
33 Devin Hester .30 .75
34 Devin Hester .30 .75
35 Devin Hester .30 .75
36 Devin Hester .30 .75
37 Dwayne Bowe .25 .60
38 Dwayne Bowe .25 .60
39 Dwayne Bowe .25 .60
40 Dwayne Bowe .25 .60
41 Eli Manning .30 .75
42 Eli Manning .30 .75
43 Eli Manning .30 .75
44 Eli Manning .30 .75
45 Jason Campbell .25 .60
46 Jason Campbell .25 .60
47 Jason Campbell .25 .60
48 Jason Campbell .25 .60
49 Joseph Addai .25 .60
50 Joseph Addai .25 .60
51 Joseph Addai .25 .60
52 Joseph Addai .25 .60
53 LenDale White .25 .60
54 LenDale White .25 .60
55 LenDale White .25 .60
56 LenDale White .25 .60
57 LaDainian Tomlinson .30 .75
58 LaDainian Tomlinson .30 .75
59 LaDainian Tomlinson .30 .75
60 LaDainian Tomlinson .30 .75
61 Marion Barber .25 .60
62 Marion Barber .25 .60
63 Marion Barber .25 .60
64 Marion Barber .25 .60
65 Marshawn Lynch .25 .60
66 Marshawn Lynch .25 .60
67 Marshawn Lynch .25 .60
68 Marshawn Lynch .25 .60
69 Greg Jennings .30 .75
70 Greg Jennings .30 .75
71 Greg Jennings .30 .75
72 Greg Jennings .30 .75
73 Patrick Willis .25 .60
74 Patrick Willis .25 .60
75 Patrick Willis .25 .60
76 Patrick Willis .25 .60
77 Peyton Manning .50 1.25
78 Peyton Manning .50 1.25
79 Peyton Manning .50 1.25
80 Peyton Manning .50 1.25
81 David Garrard .25 .60
82 David Garrard .25 .60
83 David Garrard .25 .60
84 David Garrard .25 .60
85 Ryan Grant .30 .75
86 Ryan Grant .30 .75
87 Ryan Grant .30 .75
88 Ryan Grant .30 .75
89 Tony Romo .40 1.00
90 Tony Romo .40 1.00
91 Tony Romo .40 1.00
92 Tony Romo .40 1.00
93 Wes Welker .30 .75
94 Wes Welker .30 .75
95 Wes Welker .30 .75
96 Wes Welker .30 .75
97 Willie Parker .25 .60
98 Willie Parker .25 .60
99 Willie Parker .25 .60
100 Willie Parker .25 .60
101 Adarius Bowman RC .40 1.00
102 Adarius Bowman RC .40 1.00
103 Ali Highsmith RC .30 .75
104 Ali Highsmith RC .30 .75
105 Andre Woodson RC .50 1.25
106 Andre Woodson RC .50 1.25
107 Antoine Cason RC .50 1.25
108 Antoine Cason RC .50 1.25
109 Aqib Talib RC .50 1.25
110 Aqib Talib RC .50 1.25
111 Ben Moffitt RC .30 .75
112 Ben Moffitt RC .30 .75
113 Brian Brohm RC .50 1.25
114 Brian Brohm RC .50 1.25
115 Calais Campbell RC .40 1.00
116 Calais Campbell RC .40 1.00
117 Chad Henne RC .50 1.25
118 Chad Henne RC .50 1.25
119 Chevis Jackson RC .30 .75
120 Chevis Jackson RC .30 .75
121 Chris Long RC .50 1.25
122 Chris Long RC .50 1.25
123 Colt Brennan RC .50 1.25
124 Colt Brennan RC .50 1.25
125 Craig Steltz RC .40 1.00
126 Craig Steltz RC .40 1.00
127 DJ Hall RC .40 1.00
128 DJ Hall RC .40 1.00
129 Dan Connor RC .50 1.25
130 Dan Connor RC .50 1.25
131 Darren McFadden RC 1.25 3.00
132 Darren McFadden RC 1.25 3.00
133 Dennis Dixon RC .50 1.25
134 Dennis Dixon RC .50 1.25
135 Derrick Harvey RC .30 .75
136 Derrick Harvey RC .30 .75
137 DeSean Jackson RC 1.00 2.50
138 DeSean Jackson RC 1.00 2.50
139 Dwight Lowery RC .50 1.25
140 Dwight Lowery RC .50 1.25
141 Early Doucet RC .40 1.00
142 Early Doucet RC .40 1.00
143 Felix Jones RC .75 2.00
144 Felix Jones RC .75 2.00
145 Fred Davis RC .50 1.25
146 Fred Davis RC .50 1.25
147 Glenn Dorsey RC .50 1.25
148 Glenn Dorsey RC .50 1.25
149 Jacob Tamme RC .50 1.25
150 Jacob Tamme RC .50 1.25
151 Jake Long RC .50 1.25
152 Jake Long RC .50 1.25
153 Shawn Crable RC .30 .75
154 Shawn Crable RC .30 .75
155 J Leman RC .30 .75
156 J Leman RC .30 .75
157 Joe Flacco RC 1.50 4.00
158 Joe Flacco RC 1.50 4.00
159 John Carlson RC .50 1.25
160 John Carlson RC .50 1.25
161 Jonathan Hefney RC .40 1.00
162 Jonathan Hefney RC .40 1.00
163 Jonathan Stewart RC .75 2.00
164 Jonathan Stewart RC .75 2.00
165 Keith Rivers RC .50 1.25
166 Keith Rivers RC .50 1.25
167 Lavelle Hawkins RC .30 .75
168 Lavelle Hawkins RC .30 .75
169 Lawrence Jackson RC .40 1.00
170 Lawrence Jackson RC .40 1.00
171 Limas Sweed RC .50 1.25
172 Limas Sweed RC .50 1.25
173 Justin King RC .40 1.00
174 Justin King RC .40 1.00
175 Malcolm Kelly RC .40 1.00
176 Malcolm Kelly RC .40 1.00
177 Mario Manningham RC .50 1.25
178 Mario Manningham RC .50 1.25
179 Matt Ryan RC 2.00 5.00
180 Matt Ryan RC 2.00 5.00
181 Mike Hart RC .50 1.25

182 Mike Hart RC .50 1.25
183 Mike Jenkins RC .50 1.25
184 Mike Jenkins RC .50 1.25
185 Ray Rice RC 1.00 2.50
186 Ray Rice RC 1.00 2.50
187 Rashard Mendenhall RC 1.00 2.50
188 Rashard Mendenhall RC 1.00 2.50
189 Sam Baker RC .30 .75
190 Sam Baker RC .30 .75
191 Sedrick Ellis RC .50 1.25
192 Sedrick Ellis RC .50 1.25
193 Tashard Choice RC .40 1.00
194 Tashard Choice RC .40 1.00
195 Terrell Thomas RC .40 1.00
196 Terrell Thomas RC .40 1.00
197 Tom Zbikowski RC .50 1.25
198 Tom Zbikowski RC .50 1.25
199 Xavier Adibi RC .30 .75
200 Xavier Adibi RC .30 .75
201 Barry Sanders .75 2.00
202 Barry Sanders .75 2.00
203 Barry Sanders .75 2.00
204 Billy Sims .40 1.00
205 Billy Sims .40 1.00
206 Billy Sims .40 1.00
207 Bo Jackson .75 2.00
208 Bo Jackson .75 2.00
209 Bo Jackson .75 2.00
210 Dan Marino 1.00 2.50
211 Dan Marino 1.00 2.50
212 Dan Marino 1.00 2.50
213 Fran Tarkenton .50 1.25
214 Fran Tarkenton .50 1.25
215 Fran Tarkenton .50 1.25
216 Franco Harris .50 1.25
217 Franco Harris .50 1.25
218 Franco Harris .50 1.25
219 Mel Blount .40 1.00
220 Mel Blount .40 1.00
221 Mel Blount .40 1.00
222 Paul Hornung .50 1.25
223 Paul Hornung .50 1.25
224 Paul Hornung .50 1.25
225 Jim Brown .60 1.50
226 Jim Brown .60 1.50
227 Jim Brown .60 1.50
228 Jim McMahon .50 1.25
229 Jim McMahon .50 1.25
230 Jim McMahon .50 1.25
231 John Elway .75 2.00
232 John Elway .75 2.00
233 John Elway .75 2.00
234 Ken Stabler .50 1.25
235 Ken Stabler .50 1.25
236 Ken Stabler .50 1.25
237 Ken Anderson .40 1.00
238 Ken Anderson .40 1.00
239 Ken Anderson .40 1.00
240 Roger Craig .40 1.00
241 Roger Craig .40 1.00
242 Roger Craig .40 1.00
243 Gale Sayers .60 1.50
244 Gale Sayers .60 1.50
245 Gale Sayers .60 1.50
246 Michael Johnson .40 1.00
247 Michael Johnson .40 1.00
248 Michael Johnson .40 1.00
249 Steve Vai .40 1.00
250 Steve Vai .40 1.00
251 Steve Vai .40 1.00
252 Tom Morello .40 1.00
253 Tom Morello .40 1.00
254 Tom Morello .40 1.00
255 Justin Hayward .75 2.00
256 Justin Hayward .75 2.00
257 Justin Hayward .75 2.00
258 Rulon Gardner .40 1.00
259 Rulon Gardner .40 1.00
260 Rulon Gardner .40 1.00
264 Tony Iommi .40 1.00
265 Tony Iommi .40 1.00
266 Tony Iommi .40 1.00
267 Jackie Joyner-Kersee .40 1.00
268 Jackie Joyner-Kersee .40 1.00
269 Jackie Joyner-Kersee .40 1.00

2008 Upper Deck Heroes Blue

*VETS 1-100: 2.5X TO 6X BASIC CARDS
*ROOKIES 101-200: 1X TO 2.5X BASIC CARDS
*LEGENDS 201-269: 2X TO 5X BASIC CARDS
STATED PRINT RUN 125 SER.#'d SETS

2008 Upper Deck Heroes Bronze

*VETS 1-100: 3X TO 8X BASIC CARDS
*ROOKIES 101-200: 1.2X TO 3X BASIC CARDS
*LEGENDS 201-269: 2.5X TO 6X BASIC CARDS
STATED PRINT RUN 75 SER.#'d SETS

2008 Upper Deck Heroes Gold

*VETS 1-100: 4X TO 10X BASIC CARDS
*ROOKIES 101-200: 2X TO 5X BASIC CARDS
*LEGENDS 201-269: 3X TO 8X BASIC CARDS
STATED PRINT RUN 25 SER.#'d SETS

2008 Upper Deck Heroes Green

*VETS: 2X TO 5X BASIC CARDS
*ROOKIES: .8X TO 2X BASIC CARDS
*LEGENDS: 1.5X TO 4X BASIC CARDS
STATED PRINT RUN 350 SER.#'d SETS

2008 Upper Deck Heroes Platinum

*VETS 1-100: 8X TO 20X BASIC CARDS
*ROOKIES 101-200: 3X TO 8X BASIC CARDS
*LEGENDS/10 201-269: 6X TO 15X BASIC CARDS
PLATINUM PRINT RUN 1-10

2008 Upper Deck Heroes Autograph Jerseys

STATED PRINT RUN 15 SER.#'d SETS
UNPRICED PATCH AU PRINT RUN 5
1 Adrian Peterson 90.00 150.00
5 Brett Favre 125.00 200.00
17 Bob Sanders 40.00 80.00
41 Eli Manning 50.00 120.00
57 LaDainian Tomlinson 50.00 100.00
77 Peyton Manning 75.00 150.00
81 David Garrard 30.00 60.00
89 Tony Romo 60.00 120.00
93 Wes Welker 40.00 80.00

2008 Upper Deck Heroes Autographs Blue

COMMON CARD 3.00 8.00
SEMISTARS 4.00 10.00
UNLISTED STARS 5.00 12.00
BLUE PRINT RUN 150-350
UNPRICED BLACK PRINT RUN 1
UNPRICED CUT AUTO PRINT RUN 1
UNPRICED PLATINUM PRINT RUN 5-15
101 Adarius Bowman/250 4.00 10.00
103 Ali Highsmith/250 3.00 8.00
105 Andre Woodson/150 5.00 12.00
107 Antoine Cason/250 5.00 12.00
109 Aqib Talib/250 5.00 12.00
113 Brian Brohm/150 5.00 12.00
115 Calais Campbell/250 4.00 10.00
117 Chad Henne/250 5.00 12.00
119 Chevis Jackson/250 3.00 8.00
121 Chris Long/250 5.00 12.00
123 Colt Brennan/150 5.00 12.00
125 Craig Steltz/250 4.00 10.00
127 DJ Hall/250 4.00 10.00
129 Dan Connor/250 5.00 12.00
131 Darren McFadden/150 15.00 40.00
133 Dennis Dixon/250 5.00 12.00
135 Derrick Harvey/350 3.00 8.00
137 DeSean Jackson/150 10.00 25.00
139 Dwight Lowery/250 5.00 12.00
141 Early Doucet/250 4.00 10.00
143 Felix Jones/250 10.00 25.00
145 Fred Davis/250 5.00 12.00
147 Glenn Dorsey/250 5.00 12.00
149 Jacob Tamme/250 5.00 12.00
151 Jake Long/250 5.00 12.00
153 Shawn Crable/350 3.00 8.00
155 J Leman/250 3.00 8.00
157 Joe Flacco/250 25.00 60.00
159 John Carlson/250 5.00 12.00
161 Jonathan Hefney/250 4.00 10.00
163 Jonathan Stewart/250 8.00 20.00
165 Keith Rivers/250 5.00 12.00
167 Lavelle Hawkins/250 3.00 8.00
169 Lawrence Jackson/250 4.00 10.00
171 Limas Sweed/250 5.00 12.00
173 Justin King/250 4.00 10.00
175 Malcolm Kelly/250 4.00 10.00
179 Matt Ryan/150 30.00 80.00
181 Mike Hart/250 5.00 12.00
183 Mike Jenkins/250 5.00 12.00
185 Ray Rice/250 10.00 25.00
187 Rashard Mendenhall/350 12.00 30.00
189 Sam Baker/350 3.00 8.00
191 Sedrick Ellis/350 5.00 12.00
193 Tashard Choice/250 4.00 10.00
195 Terrell Thomas/250 4.00 10.00
199 Xavier Adibi/350 3.00 8.00

2008 Upper Deck Heroes Autographs Bronze

*BRONZE/50-75: .5X TO 1.2X BLUE AUTO
*BRONZE/25: .6X TO 1.5X BLUE AUTO
BRONZE STATED PRINT RUN 25-75
131 Darren McFadden/25 30.00 80.00
179 Matt Ryan/25 75.00 150.00

2008 Upper Deck Heroes Autographs Gold

*101-200 GOLD ROOKIES: .6X TO 1.5X BLUE AU
GOLD STATED PRINT RUN 10-40
SERIAL #'d OF 10 NOT PRICED
EACH HAS MULTIPLE CARDS: EQUAL VALUE
1 Adrian Peterson/25 90.00 150.00
5 Brett Favre/25 125.00 200.00
9 Braylon Edwards/25 12.00 30.00
13 Brodie Croyle/25 10.00 25.00
17 Bob Sanders/25 30.00 60.00
21 Chad Johnson/25 10.00 25.00
25 DeMarcus Ware/25 12.00 30.00
29 Derek Anderson/25 12.00 30.00
37 Dwayne Bowe/25 12.00 30.00
41 Eli Manning/25 40.00 80.00
45 Jason Campbell/25 10.00 25.00
49 Joseph Addai/25 15.00 40.00
57 LaDainian Tomlinson/25 EXCH 40.00 80.00
61 Marion Barber/25 15.00 40.00
65 Marshawn Lynch/25 10.00 25.00
73 Patrick Willis/25 12.00 30.00
77 Peyton Manning/25 60.00 120.00
81 David Garrard/25 20.00 50.00
89 Tony Romo/25 60.00 120.00
93 Wes Welker/25 25.00 60.00
204 Billy Sims/40 8.00 20.00
207 Bo Jackson/25 40.00 80.00
213 Fran Tarkenton/25 25.00 50.00
216 Franco Harris/25 25.00 50.00
219 Mel Blount/40 EXCH
222 Paul Hornung/40 15.00 40.00
234 Ken Stabler/25 30.00 60.00
237 Ken Anderson/40 8.00 20.00
240 Roger Craig/40 10.00 25.00
246 Michael Johnson/25 40.00 80.00
258 Rulon Gardner/25 EXCH
267 Jackie Joyner-Kersee/25 15.00 30.00

2008 Upper Deck Heroes Jerseys Blue

BLUE PRINT RUN 125-175
*BRONZE/75: .5X TO 1.2X BLUE
BRONZE PRINT RUN 75 SER.#'d SETS
*GREEN RETAIL: .4X TO 1X BLUE
UNPRICED BLACK PATCH PRINT RUN 5
EACH HAS MULTIPLE CARDS: EQUAL VALUE
1 Adrian Peterson/175 8.00 20.00
5 Brett Favre/175 8.00 20.00
9 Braylon Edwards/125 3.00 8.00
13 Brodie Croyle/125 3.00 8.00
17 Bob Sanders/125 4.00 10.00
21 Chad Johnson/175 3.00 8.00
25 DeMarcus Ware/175 3.00 8.00
29 Derek Anderson/175 2.50 6.00
33 Devin Hester/175 4.00 10.00
37 Dwayne Bowe/125 3.00 8.00
41 Eli Manning/125 4.00 10.00
45 Jason Campbell/175 3.00 8.00
49 Joseph Addai/175 3.00 8.00
53 LenDale White/175 3.00 8.00
57 LaDainian Tomlinson/175 4.00 10.00
61 Marion Barber/175 3.00 8.00
65 Marshawn Lynch/175 3.00 8.00
69 Greg Jennings/125 4.00 10.00
73 Patrick Willis/125 3.00 8.00
77 Peyton Manning/175 6.00 15.00
81 David Garrard/125 3.00 8.00
85 Ryan Grant/125 5.00 12.00
89 Tony Romo/175 6.00 15.00
93 Wes Welker/125 4.00 10.00
97 Willie Parker/125 3.00 8.00

2008 Upper Deck Heroes Jerseys Gold

*GOLD 1-100: .6X TO 1.5X BLUE
1-100 GOLD PRINT RUN 35
201-245 GOLD PRINT RUN 25
SUBJECTS HAVE MULTIPLE CARDS OF EQUAL VALUE
*PLAT.PATCH 1-100: .8X TO 2X BLUE
*PLAT.PATCH 201-245: .6X TO 1.5X GOLD
1-100 PLATINUM PATCH PRINT RUN 25
201-245 PLAT.PATCH PRINT RUN 10
201 Barry Sanders 15.00 40.00
204 Billy Sims 8.00 20.00
207 Bo Jackson 15.00 40.00
210 Dan Marino 20.00 50.00
213 Fran Tarkenton 10.00 25.00
216 Franco Harris 10.00 25.00
219 Mel Blount 10.00 25.00
222 Paul Hornung 10.00 25.00
225 Jim Brown 12.00 30.00
228 Jim McMahon 10.00 25.00
231 John Elway 15.00 40.00
234 Ken Stabler 12.00 30.00
237 Ken Anderson 10.00 25.00
240 Roger Craig 8.00 20.00
243 Gale Sayers 10.00 25.00

2009 Upper Deck Heroes

This set was released on June 16, 2009 and was issued in 8-card packs with 24-packs per box at an SRP of $1.59 per pack. The base set consists of 416 skip-numbered cards and each subject in the set has between 2-4 different cards. Cards #1-100 feature veterans, cards 101-198 are rookies, 201-300 are NFL legends, 301-340 feature miscellaneous subjects from track and field, tennis, volleyball and ice skating, 341-360 feature famous historical figures, 361-384 are famous guitarists, 401-470 are artist's renderings of various subjects in the set, and 471-489 feature dual player cards including some hockey players. Finally, cards #301-489 were short printed.

1 Brett Favre .75 2.00
2 Brett Favre .75 2.00
3 LaDainian Tomlinson .30 .75
4 LaDainian Tomlinson .30 .75
5 LaDainian Tomlinson .30 .75
6 LaDainian Tomlinson .30 .75
7 Jay Cutler .30 .75
8 Jay Cutler .30 .75
9 Jay Cutler .30 .75
10 Jay Cutler .30 .75
11 Drew Brees .30 .75
12 Drew Brees .30 .75
13 Drew Brees .30 .75
14 Drew Brees .30 .75
15 Matt Forte .30 .75
16 Matt Forte .30 .75
17 Matt Forte .30 .75
18 Matt Forte .30 .75
19 Darren McFadden .30 .75
20 Darren McFadden .30 .75
21 Darren McFadden .30 .75
22 Darren McFadden .30 .75
23 Ben Roethlisberger .30 .75
24 Ben Roethlisberger .30 .75
25 Ben Roethlisberger .30 .75
26 Ben Roethlisberger .30 .75
27 Brett Favre .75 2.00
28 Brett Favre .75 2.00
29 Peyton Manning .50 1.25
30 Peyton Manning .50 1.25
31 Peyton Manning .50 1.25
32 Peyton Manning .50 1.25
33 Tony Romo .50 1.25
34 Tony Romo .50 1.25
35 Tony Romo .50 1.25
36 Tony Romo .50 1.25
37 Devin Hester .30 .75
38 Devin Hester .30 .75
39 Devin Hester .30 .75
40 Devin Hester .30 .75
41 Eli Manning .30 .75
42 Eli Manning .30 .75
43 Eli Manning .30 .75
44 Eli Manning .30 .75
45 A.J. Hawk .25 .60
46 A.J. Hawk .25 .60
47 A.J. Hawk .25 .60
40 A.J. Hawk .25 .60
49 Adrian Peterson .50 1.25
50 Adrian Peterson .50 1.25
51 Adrian Peterson .50 1.25
52 Adrian Peterson .50 1.25
53 Dallas Clark .25 .60
54 Dallas Clark .25 .60
55 Dallas Clark .25 .60
56 Dallas Clark .25 .60
57 Larry Fitzgerald .30 .75
58 Larry Fitzgerald .30 .75
59 Larry Fitzgerald .30 .75
60 Larry Fitzgerald .30 .75
61 Philip Rivers .30 .75
62 Philip Rivers .30 .75
63 Philip Rivers .30 .75
64 Philip Rivers .30 .75
65 Brian Westbrook .25 .60
66 Brian Westbrook .25 .60
67 Brian Westbrook .25 .60
68 Brian Westbrook .25 .60
69 Tom Brady .50 1.25
70 Tom Brady .50 1.25
71 Tom Brady .50 1.25
72 Tom Brady .50 1.25
73 Clinton Portis .25 .60
74 Clinton Portis .25 .60
75 Clinton Portis .25 .60
76 Clinton Portis .25 .60
77 Marvin Harrison .30 .75
78 Marvin Harrison .30 .75
79 Marvin Harrison .30 .75
80 Marvin Harrison .30 .75
81 Aaron Rodgers .60 1.50
82 Aaron Rodgers .60 1.50
83 Aaron Rodgers .60 1.50
84 Aaron Rodgers .60 1.50
85 Kurt Warner .30 .75
86 Kurt Warner .30 .75
87 Kurt Warner .30 .75
88 Kurt Warner .30 .75
89 Steven Jackson .25 .60
90 Steven Jackson .25 .60
91 Steven Jackson .25 .60
92 Steven Jackson .25 .60
93 Reggie Wayne .25 .60
94 Reggie Wayne .25 .60
95 Reggie Wayne .25 .60
96 Reggie Wayne .25 .60
97 Calvin Johnson .30 .75
98 Calvin Johnson .30 .75
99 Calvin Johnson .30 .75
100 Calvin Johnson .30 .75
101 LeSean McCoy RC 1.00 2.50
102 LeSean McCoy RC 1.00 2.50
103 Michael Crabtree RC 1.00 2.50
104 Michael Crabtree RC 1.00 2.50
105 Jeremy Maclin RC .75 2.00
106 Jeremy Maclin RC .75 2.00
107 Chris Wells RC .75 2.00
108 Chris Wells RC .75 2.00
109 Nate Davis RC .40 1.00
110 Nate Davis RC .40 1.00
111 Percy Harvin RC .75 2.00
112 Percy Harvin RC .75 2.00
113 Knowshon Moreno RC .50 1.25
114 Knowshon Moreno RC .50 1.25
115 Curtis Painter RC .50 1.25
116 Curtis Painter RC .50 1.25
117 Matthew Stafford RC 2.50 6.00
118 Matthew Stafford RC 2.50 6.00
119 Chase Coffman RC .40 1.00
120 Chase Coffman RC .40 1.00
121 Shonn Greene RC .75 2.00
122 Shonn Greene RC .75 2.00
123 Marcus Freeman RC .50 1.25
124 Marcus Freeman RC .50 1.25
125 Brian Robiskie RC .50 1.25
126 Brian Robiskie RC .50 1.25
127 James Laurinaitis RC .50 1.25
128 James Laurinaitis RC .50 1.25
129 Pat White RC .50 1.25
130 Pat White RC .50 1.25
131 James Davis RC .50 1.25
132 James Davis RC .50 1.25
133 Darrius Heyward-Bey RC .50 1.25
134 Darrius Heyward-Bey RC .50 1.25
135 Everette Brown RC .40 1.00
136 Everette Brown RC .40 1.00
137 Sean Smith RC .50 1.25
138 Sean Smith RC .50 1.25
139 Fili Moala RC .40 1.00
140 Fili Moala RC .40 1.00
141 Juaquin Iglesias RC .40 1.00
142 Juaquin Iglesias RC .40 1.00
143 Mark Sanchez RC 1.50 4.00
144 Mark Sanchez RC 1.50 4.00
145 Derrick Williams RC .40 1.00
146 Derrick Williams RC .40 1.00
147 Brandon Gibson RC .50 1.25
148 Brandon Gibson RC .50 1.25
149 Brandon Pettigrew RC .50 1.25
150 Brandon Pettigrew RC .50 1.25
151 Donald Brown RC .50 1.25
152 Donald Brown RC .50 1.25
153 Josh Freeman RC 1.00 2.50
154 Josh Freeman RC 1.00 2.50
155 Andre Smith RC .40 1.00
156 Andre Smith RC .40 1.00
157 Hakeem Nicks RC .75 2.00
158 Hakeem Nicks RC .75 2.00
161 Keenan Lewis RC .50 1.25
162 Keenan Lewis RC .50 1.25
163 Louis Murphy RC .50 1.25
164 Louis Murphy RC .50 1.25
165 Demetrius Byrd RC .40 1.00
166 Demetrius Byrd RC .40 1.00
167 Malcolm Jenkins RC .50 1.25
168 Malcolm Jenkins RC .50 1.25
169 Brian Cushing RC .50 1.25
170 Brian Cushing RC .50 1.25
171 Vontae Davis RC .50 1.25
172 Vontae Davis RC .50 1.25
173 Rey Maualuga RC .50 1.25
174 Rey Maualuga RC .50 1.25
175 Michael Johnson RC .30 .75
176 Michael Johnson RC .30 .75
177 Jonathan Luigs RC .30 .75
178 Jonathan Luigs RC .30 .75
179 D.J. Moore RC .40 1.00
180 D.J. Moore RC .40 1.00
181 William Moore RC .50 1.25
182 William Moore RC .50 1.25
183 Brian Orakpo RC .50 1.25
184 Brian Orakpo RC .50 1.25
185 Aaron Curry RC .50 1.25
186 Aaron Curry RC .50 1.25
187 Michael Oher RC .75 2.00
188 Michael Oher RC .75 2.00
189 Darius Butler RC .50 1.25
190 Darius Butler RC .50 1.25
191 Sen'Derrick Marks RC .30 .75
192 Sen'Derrick Marks RC .30 .75
193 Javon Ringer RC .50 1.25
194 Javon Ringer RC .50 1.25
195 Tyson Jackson RC .40 1.00
196 Tyson Jackson RC .40 1.00
197 Graham Harrell RC .50 1.25
198 Graham Harrell RC .50 1.25
201 Paul Hornung .50 1.25
202 Paul Hornung .50 1.25
203 Paul Hornung .50 1.25
204 Paul Hornung .50 1.25
205 Paul Hornung .50 1.25
206 Bob Griese .50 1.25
207 Bob Griese .50 1.25
208 Bob Griese .50 1.25
209 Bob Griese .50 1.25
210 Bob Griese .50 1.25
211 Jerry Kramer .40 1.00
212 Jerry Kramer .40 1.00
213 Jerry Kramer .40 1.00
214 Jerry Kramer .40 1.00
215 Jerry Kramer .40 1.00
216 Merlin Olsen .40 1.00
217 Merlin Olsen .40 1.00
218 Merlin Olsen .40 1.00
219 Merlin Olsen .40 1.00
220 Mike Singletary .50 1.25
221 Mike Singletary .50 1.25
222 Mike Singletary .50 1.25
223 Mike Singletary .50 1.25
224 Don Maynard .40 1.00
225 Don Maynard .40 1.00
226 Don Maynard .40 1.00
227 Don Maynard .40 1.00
232 Terry Bradshaw .60 1.50
233 Terry Bradshaw .60 1.50
234 Emmitt Smith .75 2.00
235 Emmitt Smith .75 2.00
236 Bob Lilly .40 1.00
237 Bob Lilly .40 1.00
238 Bob Lilly .40 1.00
239 Bob Lilly .40 1.00
240 Thurman Thomas .50 1.25
241 Thurman Thomas .50 1.25
242 Thurman Thomas .50 1.25
243 Thurman Thomas .50 1.25
247 Jack Ham .40 1.00
248 Jack Ham .40 1.00
249 Jack Ham .40 1.00
250 Mike Ditka .40 1.00
251 Mike Ditka .40 1.00
252 Troy Aikman .60 1.50
253 Troy Aikman .60 1.50
254 Roger Staubach .60 1.50
255 Roger Staubach .60 1.50
261 Bart Starr .75 2.00
262 Bart Starr .75 2.00
266 Steve Young .60 1.50
267 Steve Young .60 1.50
268 Steve Young .60 1.50
269 Darrell Green .40 1.00
270 Darrell Green .40 1.00
271 Darrell Green .40 1.00
272 Earl Campbell .50 1.25
273 Earl Campbell .50 1.25
274 Earl Campbell .50 1.25
275 Fred Biletnikoff .50 1.25
276 Fred Biletnikoff .50 1.25
277 Fred Biletnikoff .50 1.25
278 Fred Biletnikoff .50 1.25
279 Alex Karras .40 1.00
280 Alex Karras .40 1.00
281 Alex Karras .40 1.00
282 Alex Karras .40 1.00
283 Lawrence Taylor .50 1.25
284 Lawrence Taylor .50 1.25
285 Lawrence Taylor .50 1.25
286 Jim Kelly .50 1.25
287 Jim Kelly .50 1.25
288 Jim Kelly .50 1.25
289 Phil Simms .40 1.00
290 Phil Simms .40 1.00
291 Phil Simms .40 1.00
292 Phil Simms .40 1.00
297 Alan Page .40 1.00
298 Alan Page .40 1.00
299 Alan Page .40 1.00
300 Alan Page .40 1.00
301 Kristi Yamaguchi .40 1.00
302 Kristi Yamaguchi .40 1.00
303 Kristi Yamaguchi .40 1.00
304 Kristi Yamaguchi .40 1.00
305 Peggy Fleming .40 1.00
306 Peggy Fleming .40 1.00
307 Peggy Fleming .40 1.00
308 Peggy Fleming .40 1.00
325 Michael Johnson Track .50 1.25
326 Michael Johnson Track .50 1.25
327 Michael Johnson Track .50 1.25
328 Michael Johnson Track .50 1.25
329 Laird Hamilton .40 1.00
330 Laird Hamilton .40 1.00
331 Laird Hamilton .40 1.00
332 Laird Hamilton .40 1.00
333 Lindsay Davenport .40 1.00
334 Lindsay Davenport .40 1.00
335 Lindsay Davenport .40 1.00
336 Lindsay Davenport .40 1.00
337 Phil Dalhausser .40 1.00
338 Phil Dalhausser .40 1.00
339 Phil Dalhausser .40 1.00
340 Phil Dalhausser .40 1.00
341 Pablo Picasso .40 1.00
342 Vincent Van Gogh .40 1.00
343 Thomas Edison .40 1.00
344 George Washington .40 1.00
345 Mount Rushmore .40 1.00
346 Paul Revere .40 1.00
347 Sitting Bull .40 1.00
348 Sir Isaac Newton .40 1.00
349 Wolfgang Mozart .40 1.00
350 Ludwig Beethoven .40 1.00
351 Woodstock Anniv. .40 1.00
352 Wyatt Earp .40 1.00
353 Benjamin Franklin .40 1.00
354 Christopher Columbus .40 1.00
355 Florence Nightingale .40 1.00
356 Johnny Appleseed .40 1.00
357 William Wallace .40 1.00
358 Frederick Douglass .40 1.00
359 Davy Crockett .40 1.00
360 Daniel Boone .40 1.00
361 Pete Best .50 1.25
362 Pete Best .50 1.25
363 Pete Best .50 1.25
364 Pete Best .50 1.25
373 Justin Hayward .50 1.25
374 Justin Hayward .50 1.25
375 Justin Hayward .50 1.25
376 Steve Vai .50 1.25
377 Steve Vai .50 1.25
378 Steve Vai .50 1.25
379 Tony Iommi .50 1.25
380 Tony Iommi .50 1.25
381 Tony Iommi .50 1.25
382 Tom Morello .50 1.25
383 Tom Morello .50 1.25
384 Tom Morello .50 1.25
401 Brett Favre ART 2.00 5.00
402 Peyton Manning ART 1.25 3.00
403 Tony Romo ART 1.25 3.00
404 Devin Hester ART .75 2.00
405 Eli Manning ART .75 2.00
406 Ben Roethlisberger ART .75 2.00
407 Calvin Johnson ART .75 2.00
408 LaDainian Tomlinson ART .75 2.00
409 Larry Fitzgerald ART .75 2.00
410 Philip Rivers ART .75 2.00
411 Brian Westbrook ART .60 1.50
412 Tom Brady ART 1.25 3.00
413 Plaxico Burress ART .60 1.50
414 Marvin Harrison ART .75 2.00
415 Aaron Rodgers ART 1.50 4.00
416 Carson Palmer ART .75 2.00
417 Jay Cutler ART .75 2.00
418 Drew Brees ART .75 2.00
419 Darren McFadden ART .75 2.00
420 Matt Forte ART .75 2.00
421 Paul Hornung ART .75 2.00
422 Bob Griese ART .75 2.00
423 Jerry Kramer ART .60 1.50
425 Mike Singletary ART .75 2.00
426 Don Maynard ART .60 1.50
429 Emmitt Smith ART 1.25 3.00
430 Bob Lilly ART .60 1.50
431 Thurman Thomas ART .75 2.00
432 Tony Dorsett ART .75 2.00
433 Jack Ham ART .60 1.50
434 Mike Ditka ART .60 1.50
436 Alex Karras ART .60 1.50
437 Troy Aikman ART 1.00 2.50
438 Alan Page ART .60 1.50
439 Fred Biletnikoff ART .75 2.00
440 Earl Campbell ART .75 2.00
441 Kristi Yamaguchi ART .60 1.50
442 Peggy Fleming ART .60 1.50
447 Laird Hamilton ART .60 1.50
448 Lindsay Davenport ART .60 1.50
449 Michael Johnson Trck ART .60 1.50
450 Phil Dalhausser ART .60 1.50
451 Pablo Picasso ART .60 1.50
452 Vincent Van Gogh ART .60 1.50
453 Thomas Edison ART .60 1.50
454 George Washington ART .60 1.50
455 Mount Rushmore ART .60 1.50
456 Paul Revere ART .60 1.50
457 Sitting Bull ART .60 1.50
458 Wolfgang Mozart ART .60 1.50
459 Ludwig Beethoven ART .60 1.50
460 Woodstock Anniv. ART .60 1.50
461 Wyatt Earp ART .60 1.50
462 Benjamin Franklin ART .60 1.50
463 Christopher Columbus ART .60 1.50
464 Florence Nightingale ART .60 1.50
465 Johnny Appleseed ART .60 1.50
466 William Wallace ART .60 1.50
467 Frederick Douglass ART .60 1.50
468 Davy Crockett ART .60 1.50
469 Daniel Boone ART .60 1.50
470 Sir Isaac Newton ART .60 1.50
471 Brett Favre HH 2.00 5.00
Joe Namath
472 Eli Manning HH 1.50 4.00
Peyton Manning
473 Don Maynard HH 1.00 2.50
Fred Biletnikoff
474 Eli Manning HH 1.50 4.00
Tom Brady
475 Marvin Harrison HH 1.00 2.50
Reggie Wayne
476 Tony Romo HH 1.50 4.00
Troy Aikman
478 Ben Roethlisberger HH 1.00 2.50
Carson Palmer
479 Eli Manning HH 1.50 4.00
Tony Romo
480 LaDainian Tomlinson HH 1.00 2.50
Philip Rivers
481 Barry Sanders HH 1.50 4.00
Gordie Howe
483 Ray Bourque HH 1.50 4.00
Tom Brady
484 Eli Manning HH 1.00 2.50
Mark Messier
485 Ben Roethlisberger HH 1.00 2.50
Evgeni Malkin
486 Mario Lemieux HH 1.25 3.00
Terry Bradshaw
488 Mike Modano HH 1.50 4.00
Tony Romo
489 Bobby Hull HH .75 2.00
Mike Ditka

2009 Upper Deck Heroes Blue

*1-100 VETS: 2.5X TO 6X BASIC INSERTS
*101-198 ROOKIES: 1X TO 2.5X
*201-300 LEGENDS: 1.5X TO 4X
*301-384 MISC: 1.5X TO 4X
*401-440 ART NFL: 1.2X TO 3X
*441-470 ART MISC: 1.2X TO 3X
*471-489 ART DUAL: 1X TO 2.5X
BLUE PRINT RUN 99 SER.#'d SETS

2009 Upper Deck Heroes Orange

*1-100 VETS: 4X TO 10X BASIC INSERTS
*101-198 ROOKIES: 1.5X TO 4X
*201-300 LEGENDS: 2.5X TO 6X
*301-384 MISC: 2.5X TO 6X
*401-440 ART NFL: 2X TO 5X
*441-470 ART MISC: 2X TO 5X
*471-489 ART DUAL: 1.5X TO 4X
STATED PRINT RUN 35 SER.#'d SETS

2009 Upper Deck Heroes Purple

*1-100 VETS: 8X TO 20X BASIC INSERTS
*101-198 ROOKIES: 4X TO 10X
*201-300 LEGENDS: 5X TO 12X
*301-384 MISC: 5X TO 12X
*401-440 ART NFL: 4X TO 10X
*441-470 ART MISC: 4X TO 10X
*471-489 ART DUAL: 3X TO 8X
STATED PRINT RUN 10 SER.#'d SETS

2009 Upper Deck Heroes Autographs Gold

*101-198 ROOK/25: .6X TO 1.5X SILVER/199
*101-198 ROOK/25: .5X TO 1.2X SILVER/99
101-198 ROOKIE PRINT RUN 10-25
402-440 ART NFL PRINT RUN 9-50
441-450 ART MISC PRINT RUN 25
472-488 ART DUAL PRINT RUN 40
420 Matt Forte ART/50 EXCH 12.00 30.00
421 Paul Hornung ART/25 15.00 40.00
426 Don Maynard ART/25 15.00 30.00
430 Bob Lilly ART/25 10.00 25.00
431 Thurman Thomas ART/25 20.00 40.00
436 Alex Karras ART/25 12.00 30.00
438 Alan Page ART/25 12.00 30.00
439 Fred Biletnikoff ART/25 20.00 40.00
440 Earl Campbell ART/25 20.00 40.00
442 Peggy Fleming ART/25 EXCH 10.00 25.00
450 Phil Dalhausser ART/25 EXCH 15.00 40.00
472 Eli Manning HH/20 75.00 150.00
Peyton Manning
473 Don Maynard HH/20 20.00 40.00
Fred Biletnikoff
479 Eli Manning HH 75.00 150.00
Tony Romo
481 Barry Sanders HH 150.00 250.00
Gordie Howe

2009 Upper Deck Heroes Autographs Silver

3-96 VET PRINT RUN 4-25
101-198 ROOKIE PRINT RUN 50-199
201-300 NFL LEGEND PRINT RUN 5-35
301-400 MISC LEGEND PRINT RUN 20-51
EACH HAS MULTIPLE CARDS EQUAL VALUE
SERIAL #'d UNDER 15 NOT PRICED
29 Peyton Manning/25 60.00 100.00
30 Peyton Manning/25 60.00 100.00
31 Peyton Manning/25 60.00 100.00
32 Peyton Manning/25 60.00 100.00
53 Dallas Clark/15 10.00 25.00
54 Dallas Clark/15 10.00 25.00
55 Dallas Clark/15 10.00 25.00
56 Dallas Clark/15 10.00 25.00
73 Clinton Portis/15 10.00 25.00
74 Clinton Portis/15 10.00 25.00
75 Clinton Portis/15 10.00 25.00
76 Clinton Portis/15 10.00 25.00
93 Reggie Wayne/25 10.00 25.00
94 Reggie Wayne/25 10.00 25.00
95 Reggie Wayne/25 10.00 25.00
96 Reggie Wayne/25 10.00 25.00
101 LeSean McCoy/199 10.00 25.00
102 LeSean McCoy/199 10.00 25.00
103 Michael Crabtree/50 30.00 80.00
104 Michael Crabtree/50 30.00 80.00
105 Jeremy Maclin/99 10.00 25.00
106 Jeremy Maclin/99 10.00 25.00
107 Chris Wells/50 20.00 50.00
108 Chris Wells/50 20.00 50.00
111 Percy Harvin/99 10.00 25.00
112 Percy Harvin/99 10.00 25.00
113 Knowshon Moreno/50 30.00 60.00
114 Knowshon Moreno/50 30.00 60.00
115 Curtis Painter/199 5.00 12.00
116 Curtis Painter/199 5.00 12.00
117 Matthew Stafford/50 50.00 100.00
118 Matthew Stafford/50 50.00 100.00
119 Chase Coffman/199 4.00 10.00
120 Chase Coffman/199 4.00 10.00
121 Shonn Greene/99 10.00 25.00
122 Shonn Greene/99 10.00 25.00
123 Marcus Freeman/199 5.00 12.00
124 Marcus Freeman/199 5.00 12.00
125 Brian Robiskie/199 5.00 12.00
126 Brian Robiskie/199 5.00 12.00
127 James Laurinaitis/199 5.00 12.00
128 James Laurinaitis/199 5.00 12.00
129 Pat White/199 5.00 12.00
130 Pat White/199 5.00 12.00
131 James Davis/199 5.00 12.00
132 James Davis/199 5.00 12.00
133 Darrius Heyward-Bey/199 5.00 12.00
134 Darrius Heyward-Bey/199 5.00 12.00
139 Fili Moala/199 4.00 10.00
140 Fili Moala/199 4.00 10.00
141 Juaquin Iglesias/199 4.00 10.00
142 Juaquin Iglesias/199 4.00 10.00
143 Mark Sanchez/50 30.00 80.00
144 Mark Sanchez/50 30.00 80.00
145 Derrick Williams/199 4.00 10.00
146 Derrick Williams/199 4.00 10.00
147 Brandon Gibson/199 5.00 12.00
148 Brandon Gibson/199 5.00 12.00
149 Brandon Pettigrew/199 5.00 12.00
150 Brandon Pettigrew/199 5.00 12.00
151 Donald Brown/199 5.00 12.00
152 Donald Brown/199 5.00 12.00
153 Josh Freeman/99 12.00 30.00
154 Josh Freeman/99 12.00 30.00
155 Andre Smith/199 4.00 10.00
161 Keenan Lewis/199 5.00 12.00
162 Keenan Lewis/199 5.00 12.00
165 Demetrius Byrd/199 4.00 10.00
166 Demetrius Byrd/199 4.00 10.00
167 Malcolm Jenkins/199 5.00 12.00
168 Malcolm Jenkins/199 5.00 12.00
169 Brian Cushing/199 5.00 12.00
170 Brian Cushing/199 5.00 12.00
171 Vontae Davis/199 5.00 12.00
172 Vontae Davis/199 5.00 12.00
173 Rey Maualuga/199 5.00 12.00
174 Rey Maualuga/199 5.00 12.00
175 Michael Johnson/199 3.00 8.00
176 Michael Johnson/199 3.00 8.00
177 Jonathan Luigs/199 3.00 8.00
178 Jonathan Luigs/199 3.00 8.00
179 D.J. Moore/199 4.00 10.00
180 D.J. Moore/199 4.00 10.00
181 William Moore/199 5.00 12.00
182 William Moore/199 5.00 12.00
183 Brian Orakpo/199 5.00 12.00
184 Brian Orakpo/199 5.00 12.00
185 Aaron Curry/199 5.00 12.00
186 Aaron Curry/199 5.00 12.00
189 Darius Butler/199 5.00 12.00
190 Darius Butler/199 5.00 12.00
191 Sen'Derrick Marks/199 3.00 8.00
192 Sen'Derrick Marks/199 3.00 8.00
195 Tyson Jackson/199 4.00 10.00
196 Tyson Jackson/199 4.00 10.00
197 Graham Harrell/199 8.00 20.00
198 Graham Harrell/199 8.00 20.00
201 Paul Hornung/25 12.50 30.00
202 Paul Hornung/25 12.50 30.00
203 Paul Hornung/25 12.50 30.00
204 Paul Hornung/25 12.50 30.00
205 Paul Hornung/25 12.50 30.00
211 Jerry Kramer/25 8.00 20.00
212 Jerry Kramer/25 8.00 20.00
213 Jerry Kramer/25 8.00 20.00
214 Jerry Kramer/25 8.00 20.00
215 Jerry Kramer/25 8.00 20.00
216 Merlin Olsen/25 15.00 30.00
217 Merlin Olsen/25 15.00 30.00
218 Merlin Olsen/25 15.00 30.00
219 Merlin Olsen/25 15.00 30.00
224 Don Maynard/25 8.00 20.00
225 Don Maynard/25 8.00 20.00
226 Don Maynard/25 8.00 20.00
227 Don Maynard/25 8.00 20.00
232 Terry Bradshaw/35 EXCH 60.00 120.00
233 Terry Bradshaw/35 EXCH 60.00 120.00
234 Emmitt Smith/35 EXCH 75.00 150.00
235 Emmitt Smith/35 EXCH 75.00 150.00
236 Bob Lilly/35 EXCH 8.00 20.00
237 Bob Lilly/35 EXCH 8.00 20.00
238 Bob Lilly/35 EXCH 8.00 20.00
239 Bob Lilly/35 EXCH 8.00 20.00
240 Thurman Thomas/25 12.00 30.00
241 Thurman Thomas/25 12.00 30.00
242 Thurman Thomas/25 12.00 30.00
243 Thurman Thomas/25 12.00 30.00
247 Jack Ham/25 15.00 40.00
248 Jack Ham/25 15.00 40.00
240 Jack Ham/25 15.00 40.00
275 Fred Biletnikoff/25 15.00 40.00
276 Fred Biletnikoff/25 15.00 40.00
277 Fred Biletnikoff/25 15.00 40.00
278 Fred Biletnikoff/25 15.00 40.00
279 Alex Karras/25 10.00 25.00
280 Alex Karras/25 10.00 25.00
281 Alex Karras/25 10.00 25.00
282 Alex Karras/25 10.00 25.00
297 Alan Page/25 10.00 25.00
298 Alan Page/25 10.00 25.00
299 Alan Page/25 10.00 25.00
300 Alan Page/25 10.00 25.00
301 Kristi Yamaguchi/10 25.00 50.00
302 Kristi Yamaguchi/10 25.00 50.00
303 Kristi Yamaguchi/10 25.00 50.00
304 Kristi Yamaguchi/10 25.00 50.00
305 Peggy Fleming/20 EXCH 10.00 25.00
306 Peggy Fleming/20 EXCH 10.00 25.00
307 Peggy Fleming/20 EXCH 10.00 25.00
308 Peggy Fleming/20 EXCH 10.00 25.00
325 Michael Johnson Track/20 EXCH 12.00 30.00
326 Michael Johnson Track/20 EXCH 12.00 30.00
327 Michael Johnson Track/20 EXCH 12.00 30.00
328 Michael Johnson Track/20 EXCH 12.00 30.00
329 Laird Hamilton/20 EXCH 20.00 40.00
330 Laird Hamilton/20 EXCH 20.00 40.00
331 Laird Hamilton/20 EXCH 20.00 40.00
332 Laird Hamilton/20 EXCH 20.00 40.00
337 Phil Dalhausser/20 EXCH 20.00 40.00
338 Phil Dalhausser/20 EXCH 20.00 40.00
339 Phil Dalhausser/20 EXCH 20.00 40.00
340 Phil Dalhausser/20 EXCH 20.00 40.00
373 Justin Hayward/48 20.00 50.00
374 Justin Hayward/51 20.00 50.00
375 Justin Hayward/51 20.00 50.00
376 Steve Vai/45 30.00 60.00
377 Steve Vai/50 30.00 60.00
378 Steve Vai/46 30.00 60.00
379 Tony Iommi/50 30.00 60.00
380 Tony Iommi/50 30.00 60.00
382 Tom Morello/40 20.00 50.00
384 Tom Morello/35 20.00 50.00

2009 Upper Deck Heroes Jerseys Gold Patch

*2-100 GOLD VET/15: .6X TO 1.5X PURP/50
2-100 GOLD PATCH VET PRINT RUN 15
201-292 UNPRICED GOLD LEG PRINT RUN 5
EACH HAS MULTIPLE CARDS EQUAL VALUE
49 Adrian Peterson/15 12.00 30.00

2009 Upper Deck Heroes Jerseys Purple

1-100 PURPLE VET PRINT RUN 50
402-420 UNPRICED VET ART PRINT RUN 15
421-440 UNPRICED LEG ART PRINT RUN 5
472-480 DUAL ART PRINT RUN 25
481-488 DUAL ART PRINT RUN 150
*7-98 GREEN VET/150: .3X TO .8X PURPLE/50
7-98 GREEN VET PRINT RUN 150
3-100 UNPRICED SILVER VET PRINT RUN 10
201-292 UNPRICED SILVER LEG PRINT RUN 15
PLAYERS HAVE MULTIPLE CARDS OF EQUAL VALUE
1 Brett Favre 12.00 30.00
2 Brett Favre 12.00 30.00
3 LaDainian Tomlinson 5.00 12.00
4 LaDainian Tomlinson 5.00 12.00
5 LaDainian Tomlinson 5.00 12.00
6 LaDainian Tomlinson 5.00 12.00
7 Jay Cutler 5.00 12.00
8 Jay Cutler 5.00 12.00
9 Jay Cutler 5.00 12.00
10 Jay Cutler 5.00 12.00
11 Drew Brees 5.00 12.00
12 Drew Brees 5.00 12.00
13 Drew Brees 5.00 12.00

14 Drew Brees 5.00 12.00
15 Matt Forte 5.00 12.00
16 Matt Forte 5.00 12.00
17 Matt Forte 5.00 12.00
18 Matt Forte 5.00 12.00
19 Darren McFadden 5.00 12.00
20 Darren McFadden 5.00 12.00
21 Darren McFadden 5.00 12.00
22 Darren McFadden 5.00 12.00
23 Ben Roethlisberger 5.00 12.00
24 Ben Roethlisberger 5.00 12.00
27 Brett Favre 12.00 30.00
29 Peyton Manning 8.00 20.00
30 Peyton Manning 8.00 20.00
31 Peyton Manning 8.00 20.00
32 Peyton Manning 8.00 20.00
33 Tony Romo 8.00 20.00
34 Tony Romo 8.00 20.00
35 Tony Romo 8.00 20.00
36 Tony Romo 8.00 20.00
37 Devin Hester 5.00 12.00
38 Devin Hester 5.00 12.00
39 Devin Hester 5.00 12.00
40 Devin Hester 5.00 12.00
41 Eli Manning 5.00 12.00
42 Eli Manning 5.00 12.00
43 Eli Manning 5.00 12.00
44 Eli Manning 5.00 12.00
45 A.J. Hawk 4.00 10.00
46 A.J. Hawk 4.00 10.00
47 A.J. Hawk 4.00 10.00
48 A.J. Hawk 4.00 10.00
53 Dallas Clark 4.00 10.00
54 Dallas Clark 4.00 10.00
55 Dallas Clark 4.00 10.00
56 Dallas Clark 4.00 10.00
57 Larry Fitzgerald 5.00 12.00
58 Larry Fitzgerald 5.00 12.00
59 Larry Fitzgerald 5.00 12.00
60 Larry Fitzgerald 5.00 12.00
61 Philip Rivers 5.00 12.00
62 Philip Rivers 5.00 12.00
63 Philip Rivers 5.00 12.00
64 Philip Rivers 5.00 12.00
65 Brian Westbrook 4.00 10.00
68 Brian Westbrook 4.00 10.00
69 Tom Brady 8.00 20.00
70 Tom Brady 8.00 20.00
71 Tom Brady 8.00 20.00
72 Tom Brady 8.00 20.00
76 Clinton Portis 4.00 10.00
77 Marvin Harrison 5.00 12.00
78 Marvin Harrison 5.00 12.00
79 Marvin Harrison 5.00 12.00
80 Marvin Harrison 5.00 12.00
81 Aaron Rodgers 10.00 25.00
82 Aaron Rodgers 10.00 25.00
83 Aaron Rodgers 10.00 25.00
84 Aaron Rodgers 10.00 25.00
89 Steven Jackson 4.00 10.00
90 Steven Jackson 4.00 10.00
91 Steven Jackson 4.00 10.00
92 Steven Jackson 4.00 10.00
93 Reggie Wayne 4.00 10.00
94 Reggie Wayne 4.00 10.00
95 Reggie Wayne 4.00 10.00
96 Reggie Wayne 4.00 10.00
97 Calvin Johnson 5.00 12.00
98 Calvin Johnson 5.00 12.00
99 Calvin Johnson 5.00 12.00
100 Calvin Johnson 5.00 12.00
402 Peyton Manning ART/15
404 Devin Hester ART/15
405 Eli Manning ART/15
407 Calvin Johnson ART/15
408 LaDainian Tomlinson ART/15
413 Plaxico Burress ART/15
417 Jay Cutler ART/15
418 Drew Brees ART/15
420 Matt Forte ART/15
421 Paul Hornung ART/5
423 Jerry Kramer ART/5
425 Mike Singletary ART/5
426 Don Maynard ART/5
429 Emmitt Smith ART/5
433 Jack Ham ART/5
437 Troy Aikman ART/5
440 Earl Campbell ART/5
471 Brett Favre/25 30.00 60.00
Joe Namath
472 Eli Manning/25 20.00 40.00
Peyton Manning
474 Eli Manning/25 15.00 40.00
Tom Brady
475 Marvin Harrison/25 8.00 20.00
Reggie Wayne
476 Tony Romo/25 15.00 40.00
Troy Aikman
479 Eli Manning/25 10.00 25.00
Tony Romo
480 LaDainian Tomlinson/25 8.00 20.00
Philip Rivers
481 Barry Sanders/150 12.00 30.00
Gordie Howe HH
483 Tom Brady/150 10.00 25.00
Ray Bourque HH
484 Eli Manning/150 10.00 25.00
Mark Messier HH
485 Ben Roethlisberger/150 12.00 30.00
Evgeni Malkin HH
486 Terry Bradshaw/150 15.00 40.00
Mario Lemieux HH
488 Tony Romo/150 8.00 20.00
Mike Modano HH

2009 Upper Deck Heroes Jerseys Retail Blue

RANDOM INSERTS IN RETAIL PACKS
RJAC Andre Caldwell 2.50 6.00
RJAG Anthony Gonzalez 2.50 6.00
RJAS Alex Smith 3.00 8.00
RJBE Braylon Edwards 3.00 8.00
RJBQ Brady Quinn 3.00 8.00
RJCH Chad Henne 3.00 8.00
RJCJ Chris Johnson 4.00 10.00
RJDA Donnie Avery 3.00 8.00
RJDC DeSean Jackson 3.00 8.00
RJDK Dustin Keller 2.50 6.00
RJDM Darren McFadden 4.00 10.00
RJDS Dexter Jackson 2.50 6.00
RJDT Devin Thomas 2.50 6.00
RJED Early Doucet 3.00 8.00
RJER Eddie Royal 3.00 8.00
RJGD Glenn Dorsey 2.50 6.00
RJJC Jamaal Charles 4.00 10.00
RJJF Joe Flacco 4.00 10.00
RJJH James Hardy 3.00 8.00
RJJL Jake Long 2.50 6.00
RJJN Jordy Nelson 4.00 10.00
RJJR JaMarcus Russell 2.50 6.00
RJJS Jerome Simpson 2.50 6.00
RJJT Jonathan Stewart 3.00 8.00
RJKK Kevin Kolb 2.50 6.00
RJKS Kevin Smith 3.00 8.00
RJLS Limas Sweed 3.00 8.00
RJMF Matt Forte 4.00 10.00
RJMK Malcolm Kelly 2.50 6.00
RJMM Mario Manningham 3.00 8.00
RJRR Ray Rice 4.00 10.00
RJSS Steve Slaton 3.00 8.00
RJTE Trent Edwards 2.50 6.00
RJTJ Tarvaris Jackson 3.00 8.00
RJTS Troy Smith 3.00 8.00
RJVY Vince Young 3.00 8.00

1999 Upper Deck HoloGrFX

Released as a 89-card set, 1999 Upper Deck HoloGrFX was comprised of 60-veteran cards and 29-rookies seeded one every two packs. Base cards are all-foil and feature a laser-etching effect in the background. Card #90 (Michael Bishop) was not released in packs, but at least one copy surfaced in the marketplace after the intitial release. It has an embossed image of a face that was added as part of the method used by the printer to identify cards to be pulled from the pack-out process.

COMPLETE SET (89) 12.50 30.00
1 Jake Plummer .20 .50
2 Jamal Anderson .20 .50
3 Priest Holmes .25 .60
4 Antowain Smith .15 .40
5 Doug Flutie .25 .60
6 Tim Biakabutuka .20 .50
7 Curtis Enis .15 .40
8 Corey Dillon .20 .50
9 Darnay Scott .15 .40
10 Leslie Shepherd .15 .40
11 Troy Aikman .40 1.00
12 Emmitt Smith .60 1.50
13 Michael Irvin .25 .60
14 Terrell Davis .25 .60
15 Shannon Sharpe .25 .60
16 Rod Smith .20 .50
17 Barry Sanders .60 1.50
18 Charlie Batch .20 .50
19 Herman Moore .20 .50
20 Brett Favre .75 2.00
21 Dorsey Levens .20 .50
22 Antonio Freeman .20 .50
23 Peyton Manning .75 2.00
24 Mark Brunell .20 .50
25 Fred Taylor .20 .50
26 Jimmy Smith .20 .50
27 Andre Rison .20 .50
28 Tony Gonzalez .25 .60
29 Dan Marino .75 2.00
30 Karim Abdul-Jabbar .20 .50
31 Randy Moss .25 .60
32 Randall Cunningham .25 .60
33 Drew Bledsoe .25 .60
34 Terry Glenn .20 .50
35 Cameron Cleeland .15 .40
36 Andre Hastings .15 .40
37 Amani Toomer .20 .50
38 Kent Graham .15 .40
39 Curtis Martin .25 .60
40 Keyshawn Johnson .20 .50
41 Vinny Testaverde .20 .50
42 Napoleon Kaufman .15 .40
43 Tim Brown .25 .60
44 Duce Staley .20 .50
45 Kordell Stewart .20 .50
46 Jerome Bettis .25 .60
47 Marshall Faulk .25 .60
48 Natrone Means .20 .50
49 Ryan Leaf .20 .50
50 Steve Young .30 .75
51 Jerry Rice .50 1.25
52 Terrell Owens .25 .60
53 Joey Galloway .20 .50
54 Ricky Watters .20 .50
55 Jon Kitna .20 .50
56 Warrick Dunn .20 .50
57 Trent Dilfer .20 .50
58 Steve McNair .25 .60
59 Eddie George .20 .50
60 Brad Johnson .20 .50
61 Tim Couch RC .60 1.50
62 Donovan McNabb RC 2.50 6.00
63 Akili Smith RC .50 1.25
64 Edgerrin James RC .75 2.00
65 Ricky Williams RC 1.00 2.50
66 Torry Holt RC 1.00 2.50
67 Champ Bailey RC 1.25 3.00
68 David Boston RC .50 1.25
69 Daunte Culpepper RC .60 1.50
70 Cade McNown RC .50 1.25
71 Troy Edwards RC .50 1.25
72 Kevin Johnson RC .50 1.25
73 James Johnson RC .40 1.00
74 Rob Konrad RC .40 1.00
75 Kevin Faulk RC .60 1.50
76 Shaun King RC .50 1.25
77 Peerless Price RC .50 1.25
78 Mike Cloud RC .40 1.00
79 Jermaine Fazande RC .40 1.00
80 D'Wayne Bates RC .40 1.00
81 Brock Huard RC .50 1.25
82 Marty Booker RC .50 1.25
83 Karsten Bailey RC .40 1.00
84 Al Wilson RC .60 1.50
85 Joe Germaine RC .50 1.25
86 Dameane Douglas RC .40 1.00
87 Sedrick Irvin RC .40 1.00
88 Aaron Brooks RC .60 1.50
89 Cecil Collins RC .40 1.00
90 Michael Bishop SP
(stamped with embossed face)

1999 Upper Deck HoloGrFX Ausome

COMPLETE SET (89) 75.00 150.00
*AUSOME STARS: 1.5X TO 4X BASIC CARDS
AUSOME VETERAN STATED ODDS 1:8
*AUSOME RCs: .6X TO 1.5X
AUSOME DRAFT PICK STATED ODDS 1:17

1999 Upper Deck HoloGrFX 24/7

COMPLETE SET (15) 12.50 30.00
STATED ODDS 1:3
*GOLD CARDS: 3X TO 8X BASIC INSERTS
GOLD STATED ODDS 1:105
N1 Jake Plummer .25 .60
N2 Emmitt Smith 1.25 3.00
N3 Terrell Davis .40 1.00
N4 Peyton Manning 2.00 5.00
N5 Drew Bledsoe .75 2.00
N6 Troy Aikman 1.25 3.00
N7 Ricky Williams 1.00 2.50
N8 Keyshawn Johnson .40 1.00
N9 Akili Smith .30 .75
N10 Eddie George .40 1.00
N11 Edgerrin James 2.00 5.00
N12 David Boston .40 1.00
N13 Cade McNown .30 .75
N14 Jerome Bettis .40 1.00
N15 Herman Moore .25 .60

1999 Upper Deck HoloGrFX Future Fame

COMPLETE SET (6) 15.00 40.00
STATED ODDS 1:34
*GOLD CARDS: 1.2X TO 3X BASIC INSERTS
GOLD STATED ODDS 1:431
FF1 John Elway 4.00 10.00
FF2 Dan Marino 4.00 10.00
FF3 Emmitt Smith 2.50 6.00
FF4 Randy Moss 3.00 8.00
FF5 Tim Brown .75 2.00
FF6 Barry Sanders 4.00 10.00

1999 Upper Deck HoloGrFX Star View

COMPLETE SET (9) 15.00 30.00
STATED ODDS 1:17
*GOLD: 1.2X TO 3X BASIC INSERTS
GOLD STATED ODDS 1:210
S1 Dan Marino 2.50 6.00
S2 Brett Favre 2.50 6.00
S3 Barry Sanders 2.50 6.00
S4 Terrell Davis .50 1.25
S5 Mark Brunell .50 1.25
S6 Eddie George .50 1.25
S7 Fred Taylor .50 1.25
S8 Tim Couch .50 1.25
S9 Randy Moss 2.00 5.00

1999 Upper Deck HoloGrFX UD Authentics

STATED ODDS 1:432
AS Akili Smith 10.00 25.00
BH Brock Huard 10.00 25.00
CM Cade McNown 12.00 30.00
DC Daunte Culpepper 15.00 40.00
DM Donovan McNabb 25.00 60.00
EG Eddie George 12.00 30.00
EJ Edgerrin James 15.00 40.00
EM Eric Moulds 10.00 25.00
JA Jamal Anderson 12.00 30.00
JP Jake Plummer 12.00 30.00
JR Jerry Rice 60.00 120.00
PM Peyton Manning 50.00 100.00
RW Ricky Williams 15.00 40.00
SK Shaun King 10.00 25.00
SY Steve Young 30.00 80.00
TA Troy Aikman 50.00 100.00
TC Tim Couch 12.00 30.00
TD Terrell Davis 15.00 40.00
TH Torry Holt 15.00 40.00

2002 Upper Deck Honor Roll

Released in late-October 2002 as a retail only product, this set contains 90 veterans and 150 rookies. The rookies were serial #'d to 1375.

COMP.SET w/o SP's (90) 10.00 25.00
91-180 ROOKIE PRINT RUN 1375
1 Jake Plummer .20 .50
2 David Boston .15 .40
3 Michael Vick .40 1.00
4 Warrick Dunn .20 .50
5 Jamal Lewis .20 .50
6 Chris Redman .15 .40
7 Drew Bledsoe .25 .60
8 Travis Henry .15 .40
9 Chris Weinke .15 .40
10 Anthony Thomas .20 .50
11 Marty Booker .20 .50
12 Corey Dillon .20 .50
13 Michael Westbrook .15 .40
14 Tim Couch .15 .40
15 Emmitt Smith .60 1.50
16 Quincy Carter .15 .40
17 Brian Griese .20 .50
18 Terrell Davis .25 .60
19 Az-Zahir Hakim .15 .40
20 Brett Favre .60 1.50
21 Ahman Green .20 .50
22 Corey Bradford .15 .40
23 Edgerrin James .20 .50
24 Peyton Manning .50 1.25
25 Stacey Mack .15 .40
26 Mark Brunell .20 .50
27 Trent Green .20 .50
28 Priest Holmes .25 .60
29 Ricky Williams .20 .50
30 Jay Fiedler .20 .50
31 Daunte Culpepper .20 .50
32 Randy Moss .25 .60
33 Antowain Smith .20 .50
34 Tom Brady .60 1.50
35 Aaron Brooks .20 .50
36 Deuce McAllister .20 .50
37 Kerry Collins .20 .50
38 Ron Dayne .20 .50
39 Curtis Martin .25 .60
40 Vinny Testaverde .20 .50
41 Jerry Rice .50 1.25
42 Rich Gannon .20 .50
43 Donovan McNabb .25 .60
44 Duce Staley .20 .50
45 Jerome Bettis .25 .60
46 Kordell Stewart .20 .50
47 Doug Flutie .25 .60
48 LaDainian Tomlinson .30 .75
49 Jeff Garcia .20 .50
50 Terrell Owens .25 .60
51 Darrell Jackson .20 .50
52 Shaun Alexander .20 .50
53 Kurt Warner .25 .60
54 Marshall Faulk .25 .60
55 Keyshawn Johnson .20 .50
56 Brad Johnson .20 .50
57 Eddie George .20 .50
58 Steve McNair .25 .60
59 Stephen Davis .20 .50
60 Rod Gardner .15 .40
61 Jake Plummer .20 .50
Thomas Jones
David Boston
62 Michael Vick .30 .75
Warrick Dunn
Shawn Jefferson
63 Chris Redman .15 .40
Jamal Lewis
Travis Taylor
64 Drew Bledsoe .20 .50
Travis Henry
Peerless Price
65 Jim Miller .15 .40
Anthony Thomas
Marty Booker
66 Jon Kitna .15 .40
Corey Dillon
Peter Warrick
67 Tim Couch .12 .30
Jamel White
Kevin Johnson
68 Quincy Carter .50 1.25
Emmitt Smith
Rocket Ismail
69 Brian Griese .20 .50
Terrell Davis
Rod Smith
70 Mike McMahon .12 .30
James Stewart
Az-Zahir Hakim
71 Brett Favre .50 1.25
Ahman Green
Terry Glenn
72 Peyton Manning .40 1.00
Edgerrin James
Marvin Harrison
73 Mark Brunell .15 .40
Fred Taylor
Jimmy Smith
74 Trent Green .20 .50
Priest Holmes
Johnnie Morton
75 Jay Fiedler .15 .40
Ricky Williams
Chris Chambers
76 Daunte Culpepper .20 .50
Michael Bennett
Randy Moss
77 Tom Brady .50 1.25
Antowain Smith
Troy Brown
78 Aaron Brooks .15 .40
Deuce McAllister
Joe Horn
79 Kerry Collins .15 .40
Ron Dayne
Amanti Toomer
80 Vinny Testaverde .20 .50
Curtis Martin
Laveranues Coles
81 Rich Gannon .40 1.00
Tim Brown
Jerry Rice
82 Donovan McNabb .20 .50
Duce Staley
James Thrash
83 Kordell Stewart .20 .50
Jerome Bettis
Hines Ward
84 Drew Brees .30 .75
LaDainian Tomlinson
Curtis Conway
85 Jeff Garcia .20 .50
Garrison Hearst
Terrell Owens
86 Trent Dilfer .15 .40
Shaun Alexander
Darrell Jackson
87 Kurt Warner .20 .50
Marshall Faulk
Isaac Bruce
88 Brad Johnson .15 .40
Michael Pittman
Keyshawn Johnson
89 Steve McNair .20 .50
Eddie George
Derrick Mason
90 Shane Matthews .15 .40
Stephen Davis
Rod Gardner
91 Adrian Peterson RC 2.00 5.00
92 Albert Haynesworth RC 2.00 5.00
93 Alex Brown RC 2.00 5.00
94 Andre Davis RC 1.50 4.00
95 Antwoine Womack RC 1.25 3.00
96 Antonio Bryant RC 2.00 5.00
97 Antwaan Randle El RC 2.00 5.00
98 Ashley Lelie RC 1.50 4.00
99 Ed Reed RC 5.00 12.00
100 Brandon Doman RC 1.25 3.00
101 Brian Allen RC 1.25 3.00
102 Najeh Davenport RC 2.00 5.00
103 Brian Westbrook RC 3.00 8.00
104 Chad Hutchinson RC 1.25 3.00
105 Chester Taylor RC 2.00 5.00
106 Cliff Russell RC 1.25 3.00
107 Clinton Portis RC 2.50 6.00
108 Craig Nall RC 1.50 4.00
109 Javin Hunter RC 1.25 3.00
110 Bryan Thomas RC 1.25 3.00
111 Daniel Graham RC 1.50 4.00
112 Daryl Jones RC 1.25 3.00
113 David Carr RC 2.00 5.00
114 David Garrard RC 2.50 6.00
115 Shaun Hill RC 2.50 6.00
116 Deion Branch RC 2.00 5.00
117 Derrick Lewis RC 1.25 3.00
118 DeShaun Foster RC 2.00 5.00
119 Jeff Kelly RC 1.25 3.00
120 Donte Stallworth RC 2.00 5.00
121 Levi Jones RC 1.25 3.00
122 Dwight Freeney RC 2.50 6.00
123 Eric Crouch RC 2.00 5.00
124 Freddie Milons RC 1.25 3.00
125 Jamin Elliott RC 1.25 3.00
126 Herb Haygood RC 1.25 3.00
127 J.T. O'Sullivan RC 1.50 4.00
128 Jabar Gaffney RC 2.00 5.00
129 Jake Schifino RC 1.25 3.00
130 Jason McAddley RC 1.50 4.00
131 Javon Walker RC 2.00 5.00
132 Jeremy Shockey RC 3.00 8.00
133 Jerramy Stevens RC 2.00 5.00
134 Joey Harrington RC 2.00 5.00
135 John Henderson RC 1.50 4.00
136 Jonathan Wells RC 2.00 5.00
137 Josh McCown RC 2.00 5.00
138 Josh Reed RC 1.50 4.00
139 Josh Scobey RC 1.50 4.00
140 Julius Peppers RC 4.00 10.00
141 Kalimba Edwards RC 1.50 4.00
142 Kelly Campbell RC 1.50 4.00
143 Keyuo Craver RC 1.25 3.00
144 Kurt Kittner RC 1.25 3.00
145 Ladell Betts RC 2.00 5.00
146 Lamar Gordon RC 1.50 4.00
147 Larry Ned RC 1.25 3.00
148 Lee Mays RC 1.25 3.00
149 Leonard Henry RC 1.25 3.00
150 Lito Sheppard RC 2.00 5.00
151 Luke Staley RC 1.25 3.00
152 Marquise Walker RC 1.25 3.00
153 Maurice Morris RC 1.50 4.00
154 Darrell Hill RC 1.25 3.00
155 Napoleon Harris RC 1.50 4.00
156 Patrick Ramsey RC 2.00 5.00
157 Kevin Curtis RC 1.25 3.00
158 Phillip Buchanon RC 2.00 5.00
159 Kendall Newson RC 1.25 3.00
160 Quentin Jammer RC 2.00 5.00
161 Randy Fasani RC 1.50 4.00
162 Reche Caldwell RC 2.00 5.00
163 Ricky Williams RC 1.50 4.00
164 Rocky Calmus RC 1.50 4.00
165 Rohan Davey RC 2.00 5.00
166 Ron Johnson RC 1.50 4.00
167 Ronald Curry RC 1.50 4.00
168 Roy Williams RC 2.00 5.00
169 Ryan Sims RC 2.00 5.00
170 Sam Simmons RC 1.25 3.00
171 Seth Burford RC 1.25 3.00
172 T.J. Duckett RC 2.00 5.00
173 Tellis Redmon RC 1.25 3.00
174 Tim Carter RC 1.50 4.00
175 Travis Stephens RC 1.25 3.00
176 Wendell Bryant RC 1.25 3.00
177 Lamont Thompson RC 1.50 4.00
178 William Green RC 1.50 4.00
179 Dennis Johnson RC 1.25 3.00
180 Michael Lewis RC 2.00 5.00

2002 Upper Deck Honor Roll Gold

*VETS 1-90: 15X TO 40X BASIC CARDS
*ROOKIES 91-180: 2.5X TO 6X
STATED PRINT RUN 25 SER.#'d SETS

2002 Upper Deck Honor Roll Clutch Performers Jerseys

STATED ODDS 1:72
CPBO David Boston 3.00 8.00
CPCC Cris Carter 5.00 12.00
CPCD Corey Dillon 4.00 10.00
CPEJ Edgerrin James 4.00 10.00
CPJP Jake Plummer 4.00 10.00
CPMH Marvin Harrison 5.00 12.00
CPPM Peyton Manning 10.00 25.00
CPRM Randy Moss 5.00 12.00
CPVT Vinny Testaverde 4.00 10.00

2002 Upper Deck Honor Roll Dean's List

COMPLETE SET (30) 25.00 60.00
*GOLD/25: 2X TO 5X BASIC INSERTS
GOLD PRINT RUN 25 SER.#'d SETS
DLQ1 Jake Plummer .75 2.00
DLQ2 Donovan McNabb 1.00 2.50
DLQ3 Kurt Warner 1.00 2.50
DLQ4 Brett Favre 2.50 6.00
DLQ5 Peyton Manning 2.00 5.00
DLQ6 Rich Gannon .75 2.00
DLQ7 Daunte Culpepper .75 2.00
DLQ8 Drew Bledsoe 1.00 2.50
DLQ9 Vinny Testaverde .75 2.00
DLQ10 Jeff Garcia .75 2.00
DLR1 Marshall Faulk 1.00 2.50
DLR2 Edgerrin James .75 2.00
DLR3 Curtis Martin 1.00 2.50
DLR4 Stephen Davis .75 2.00
DLR5 Eddie George .75 2.00
DLR6 Ricky Williams .75 2.00
DLR7 Jerome Bettis 1.00 2.50
DLR8 Terrell Davis 1.00 2.50
DLR9 Emmitt Smith 2.50 6.00
DLR10 Warrick Dunn .75 2.00
DLW1 Randy Moss 1.00 2.50
DLW2 Wayne Chrebet .75 2.00
DLW3 Marvin Harrison 1.00 2.50
DLW4 Jimmy Smith .75 2.00
DLW5 Jerry Rice 2.00 5.00
DLW6 Tim Brown 1.00 2.50
DLW7 Keyshawn Johnson .75 2.00
DLW8 David Boston .60 1.50
DLW9 Terrell Owens 1.00 2.50
DLW10 Isaac Bruce 1.00 2.50

2002 Upper Deck Honor Roll Field Generals Dual Jerseys

STATED ODDS 1:240
FGCH David Carr 5.00 12.00
Joey Harrington
FGDC Rohan Davey 5.00 12.00
David Carr
FGHM Joey Harrington 5.00 12.00
Josh McCown
FGHR Joey Harrington 5.00 12.00
Patrick Ramsey
FGMG Josh McCown 6.00 15.00
David Garrard

2002 Upper Deck Honor Roll Great Connections Dual Jerseys

STATED ODDS 1:240
GCBF Doug Flutie 8.00 20.00
Drew Brees
GCCJ LaMont Jordan 4.00 10.00
Wayne Chrebet
GCGM Johnnie Morton 4.00 10.00
Trent Green
GCRB Ladell Betts 5.00 12.00
Patrick Ramsey
GCSF Doug Flutie 5.00 12.00
Junior Seau

2002 Upper Deck Honor Roll Letterman Autographs

STATED ODDS 1:480
HRLAT Anthony Thomas 12.00 30.00
HRLBR Drew Brees 25.00 60.00
HRLCW Chris Weinke 10.00 25.00
HRLLT LaDainian Tomlinson 30.00 80.00
HRLLLP Luke Petitgout 10.00 25.00
HRLMV Michael Vick 30.00 50.00
HRLPM Peyton Manning 50.00 100.00
HRLRC Rosevelt Colvin 15.00 40.00
HRLRW Roy Williams 12.00 30.00

2002 Upper Deck Honor Roll Offensive Threats Dual Jerseys

STATED ODDS 1:240
OTBF Brett Favre 12.00 30.00
Mark Brunell
OTFC Curtis Conway 5.00 12.00
Doug Flutie
OTGS J.J. Stokes 4.00 10.00
Jeff Garcia
OTMB Mark Brunell 10.00 25.00
Peyton Manning
OTRW Charles Woodson 10.00 25.00
Jerry Rice

2002 Upper Deck Honor Roll Rookie Honor Roll Jerseys

STATED ODDS 1:72
RHRAL Ashley Lelie 3.00 8.00
RHRDC David Carr 4.00 10.00
RHRDG David Garrard 5.00 12.00
RHRDS Donte Stallworth 4.00 10.00
RHREL Antwaan Randle El 4.00 10.00
RHRJH Joey Harrington 4.00 10.00
RHRJM Josh McCown 4.00 10.00
RHRPR Patrick Ramsey 4.00 10.00
RHRRD Rohan Davey 4.00 10.00

2002 Upper Deck Honor Roll Sophomore Standouts

COMPLETE SET (30) 12.00 30.00
SSQ1-SSQ10 STATED ODDS 1:24
SSR1-SSR10 STATED ODDS 1:24
SSW1-SSW10 STATED ODDS 1:24
*GOLD/25: 2.5X TO 6X BASIC INSERTS
GOLD STATED PRINT RUN 25 SER.#'d SETS
SSQ1 Michael Vick 1.50 4.00
SSQ2 Tom Brady 2.50 6.00
SSQ3 Chris Redman .60 1.50
SSQ4 Quincy Carter .60 1.50
SSQ5 Mike McMahon .60 1.50
SSQ6 Chris Weinke .60 1.50
SSQ7 Aaron Brooks .75 2.00
SSQ8 Drew Brees 1.50 4.00
SSQ9 Chad Pennington 1.00 2.50
SSQ10 Sage Rosenfels .75 2.00
SSR1 LaDainian Tomlinson 1.25 3.00
SSR2 Anthony Thomas .75 2.00
SSR3 Shaun Alexander .75 2.00
SSR4 James Jackson .60 1.50
SSR5 Dominic Rhodes .75 2.00
SSR6 Thomas Jones 1.00 2.50
SSR7 Michael Bennett .75 2.00
SSR8 Elvis Joseph .60 1.50
SSR9 Travis Henry .60 1.50
SSR10 Kevan Barlow .60 1.50
SSW1 Chris Chambers .75 2.00
SSW2 Snoop Minnis .60 1.50
SSW3 Plaxico Burress .75 2.00
SSW4 Quincy Morgan .60 1.50
SSW5 Robert Ferguson .75 2.00
SSW6 Travis Taylor .60 1.50
SSW7 Santana Moss .75 2.00
SSW8 Rod Gardner .60 1.50
SSW9 David Terrell .60 1.50
SSW10 Freddie Mitchell .60 1.50

2002 Upper Deck Honor Roll Students of the Game

COMPLETE SET (30) 12.00 30.00
SGQ1-SGQ10 STATED ODDS 1:24
SGR1-SGR10 STATED ODDS 1:24
SGW1-SGW10 STATED ODDS 1:24
*GOLD/25: 2.5X TO 6X BASIC INSERTS
GOLD PRINT RUN 25 SER.#'d SETS
SGQ1 David Carr .75 2.00
SGQ2 Joey Harrington .75 2.00
SGQ3 Patrick Ramsey .75 2.00
SGQ4 Josh McCown .75 2.00
SGQ5 Kurt Kittner .50 1.25
SGQ6 Randy Fasani .60 1.50
SGQ7 J.T. O'Sullivan .60 1.50
SGQ8 Rohan Davey .75 2.00
SGQ9 Chad Hutchinson .50 1.25
SGQ10 David Garrard 1.00 2.50
SGR1 William Green .60 1.50
SGR2 T.J. Duckett .75 2.00
SGR3 DeShaun Foster .75 2.00
SGR4 Clinton Portis 1.00 2.50
SGR5 Maurice Morris .60 1.50
SGR6 Travis Stephens .50 1.25
SGR7 Jonathan Wells .75 2.00
SGR8 Lamar Gordon .60 1.50
SGR9 LaDell Betts .75 2.00
SGR10 Brian Westbrook 1.25 3.00
SGW1 Ashley Lelie .60 1.50
SGW2 Donte Stallworth .75 2.00
SGW3 Javon Walker .75 2.00
SGW4 Josh Reed .60 1.50
SGW5 Jabar Gaffney .75 2.00
SGW6 Reche Caldwell .75 2.00
SGW7 Antonio Bryant .75 2.00
SGW8 Tim Carter .60 1.50
SGW9 Marquise Walker .50 1.25
SGW10 Ron Johnson .60 1.50

2002 Upper Deck Honor Roll Up and Coming Jerseys

STATED ODDS 1:72
UCBO David Boston 2.50 6.00
UCBR Drew Brees 6.00 15.00
UCLC Laveranues Coles 3.00 8.00
UCRD Ron Dayne 3.00 8.00
UCRM Randy Moss 4.00 10.00
UCSM Santana Moss 3.00 8.00
UCTC Tim Couch 2.50 6.00
UCTJ Thomas Jones 4.00 10.00

2003 Upper Deck Honor Roll

Released in September of 2003, this set contains 190 cards including 100 base cards, 30 short prints, and 60 rookies. The short prints were inserted at a rate of 1:6. Please note that rookie cards can be found in both the base cards and the short prints. Rookies 131-190 are serial numbered to 2003. Boxes contained 24 packs of 5 cards. Pack SRP was $2.99.

COMP.SET w/o SP's (100) 10.00 25.00
131-190 ROOKIE/2003 ODDS 1:8
1 Corey Dillon .25 .60
2 Kelley Washington RC .25 .60
3 Peter Warrick .25 .60
4 Joey Harrington .20 .50
5 Az-Zahir Hakim .20 .50
6 David Kircus RC .40 1.00
7 Jabar Gaffney .20 .50
8 Domanick Davis RC .30 .75
9 Dave Ragone RC .25 .60
10 Kordell Stewart .25 .60
11 Justin Gage RC .30 .75
12 Bobby Wade RC .30 .75
13 Anthony Thomas .25 .60
14 Chad Hutchinson .20 .50
15 Antonio Bryant .20 .50
16 Bradie James RC .40 1.00
17 Josh McCown .25 .60
18 Jeff Blake .25 .60
19 Kenny King RC .30 .75
20 Daunte Culpepper .25 .60
21 Michael Bennett .25 .60
22 Randy Moss .30 .75
23 Onterrio Smith RC .25 .60
24 Mark Brunell .25 .60
25 George Wrighster RC .25 .60
26 Fred Taylor .25 .60
27 Jake Delhomme .30 .75
28 Mike Seidman RC .25 .60
29 Walter Young RC .25 .60
30 Chris Redman .20 .50
31 Jamal Lewis .25 .60
32 Ovie Mughelli RC .30 .75
33 Koren Robinson .25 .60
34 Shaun Alexander .25 .60
35 Taco Wallace RC .25 .60
36 Kurt Warner .30 .75
37 Kevin Curtis RC .40 1.00
38 Torry Holt .30 .75
39 Patrick Ramsey .25 .60
40 Laveranues Coles .20 .50
41 Gibran Hamdan RC .25 .60
42 Drew Bledsoe .30 .75
43 Jerel Myers RC .25 .60
44 Eric Moulds .25 .60
45 Drew Brees .30 .75
46 David Boston .20 .50
47 LaDainian Tomlinson .30 .75
48 Reche Caldwell .20 .50
49 Priest Holmes .30 .75
50 Tony Gonzalez .30 .75
51 Mike Pinkard RC .25 .60
52 Aaron Brooks .25 .60
53 Deuce McAllister .25 .60
54 Montrae Holland RC .30 .75
55 Jay Fiedler .20 .50
56 Junior Seau .30 .75
57 Chris Chambers .25 .60
58 Ricky Williams .25 .60
59 Tom Brady .75 2.00
60 Troy Brown .25 .60
61 Antowain Smith .25 .60
62 Jake Plummer .25 .60
63 Cecil Sapp RC .25 .60
64 Adrian Madise RC .25 .60
65 Tim Couch .20 .50
66 William Green .20 .50
67 Kelly Holcomb .20 .50
68 Chad Pennington .30 .75
69 Santana Moss .25 .60
70 Curtis Martin .30 .75
71 Michael Vick .40 1.00
72 LaTarence Dunbar RC .25 .60
73 Peerless Price .20 .50
74 Marvin Harrison .30 .75
75 Peyton Manning .60 1.50
76 Edgerrin James .30 .75
77 Jeremy Shockey .30 .75
78 Tiki Barber .30 .75
79 Kevin Walter RC .60 1.50
80 Jeff Garcia .25 .60
81 Terrell Owens .30 .75
82 Andrew Williams RC .25 .60
83 Tommy Maddox .25 .60
84 Plaxico Burress .25 .60
85 Brian St.Pierre RC .30 .75
86 Steve McNair .30 .75
87 Eddie George .25 .60
88 Derrick Mason .25 .60
89 Brett Favre .75 2.00
90 Ahman Green .25 .60
91 Donald Driver .30 .75
92 Donovan McNabb .30 .75
93 Brian Dawkins .25 .60
94 Norman LeJeune RC .25 .60
95 Jerry Rice .60 1.50
96 Rich Gannon .25 .60
97 Siddeeq Shabazz RC .25 .60
98 DeWayne White RC .25 .60
99 Brad Johnson .25 .60
100 Keyshawn Johnson .30 .75
101 Chad Johnson SP 1.00 2.50
102 Artose Pinner SP RC .75 2.00
103 David Carr SP .75 2.00
104 Brian Urlacher SP 1.00 2.50
105 Jason Witten SP RC 3.00 8.00
106 Emmitt Smith SP 2.50 6.00
107 Nate Burleson SP RC 1.00 2.50
108 LaBrandon Toefield SP RC 1.00 2.50
109 Julius Peppers SP 1.00 2.50
110 Musa Smith SP RC .75 2.00
111 Seneca Wallace SP RC 1.25 3.00
112 Marshall Faulk SP 1.00 2.50
113 Brad Banks SP RC 1.00 2.50
114 Travis Henry SP .60 1.50
115 Mike Scifres SP RC .75 2.00
116 J.R. Tolver SP RC 1.00 2.50
117 Kliff Kingsbury SP RC 1.00 2.50
118 Clinton Portis SP .75 2.00
119 Kevin Johnson SP .60 1.50
120 Brooks Bollinger SP RC 1.00 2.50
121 Terrence Edwards SP RC .75 2.00
122 Steve Sciullo SP RC .75 2.00
123 Ken Dorsey SP RC 1.00 2.50
124 Jerome Bettis SP 1.00 2.50
125 Chris Brown SP RC .75 2.00
126 Carl Ford SP RC .75 2.00
127 Billy McMullen SP RC .75 2.00
128 Doug Gabriel SP RC 1.00 2.50
129 Earnest Graham SP RC 1.25 3.00
130 Chris Simms SP RC 1.50 4.00
131 Carson Palmer RC 3.00 8.00
132 Charles Rogers RC 1.25 3.00
133 Andre Johnson RC 4.00 10.00
134 DeWayne Robertson RC 1.25 3.00
135 Terence Newman RC 1.25 3.00
136 Johnathan Sullivan RC 1.00 2.50
137 Byron Leftwich RC 1.50 4.00
138 Jordan Gross RC 1.00 2.50
139 Kevin Williams RC 1.50 4.00
140 Terrell Suggs RC 1.50 4.00
141 Marcus Trufant RC 1.25 3.00
142 Jimmy Kennedy RC 1.25 3.00
143 Ty Warren RC 1.25 3.00
144 Michael Haynes RC 1.00 2.50
145 Jerome McDougle RC 1.00 2.50
146 J.T. Wall RC 1.00 2.50
147 Bryant Johnson RC 1.50 4.00
148 Calvin Pace RC 1.25 3.00
149 Kyle Boller RC 1.50 4.00
150 Quentin Griffin RC 1.25 3.00
151 Lee Suggs RC 1.25 3.00
152 Rex Grossman RC 1.50 4.00
153 Willis McGahee RC 2.00 5.00
154 Dallas Clark RC 2.50 6.00
155 William Joseph RC 1.00 2.50
156 Kwame Harris RC 1.00 2.50
157 Larry Johnson RC 1.50 4.00
158 Andre Woolfolk RC 1.25 3.00
159 Nick Barnett RC 1.50 4.00
160 Dahrran Diedrick RC 1.00 2.50

161 Teyo Johnson RC 1.25 3.00
162 Justin Fargas RC 1.50 4.00
163 Eric Steinbach RC 1.00 2.50
164 Boss Bailey RC 1.25 3.00
165 Charles Tillman RC 2.00 5.00
166 Eugene Wilson RC 1.50 4.00
167 Jonathan Stinchcomb RC 1.25 3.00
168 Al Johnson RC 1.25 3.00
169 Rashean Mathis RC 1.25 3.00
170 Keenan Howry RC 1.00 2.50
171 Ben Joppru RC 1.00 2.50
172 Rashad Moore RC 1.00 2.50
173 Shaun McDonald RC 1.25 3.00
174 Taylor Jacobs RC 1.00 2.50
175 Bethel Johnson RC 1.00 2.50
176 Matt Wilhelm RC 1.25 3.00
177 Kawika Mitchell RC 1.50 4.00
178 Chris Kelsay RC 1.25 3.00
179 Lon Sheriff RC 1.00 2.50
180 Ricky Manning RC 1.25 3.00
181 Terry Pierce RC 1.00 2.50
182 Chaun Thompson RC 1.00 2.50
183 Victor Hobson RC 1.00 2.50
184 Anquan Boldin RC 2.50 6.00
185 Justin Griffith RC 1.25 3.00
186 Osi Umenyiora RC 2.00 5.00
187 Brandon Lloyd RC 2.50 6.00
188 Michael Doss RC 1.50 4.00
189 Alonzo Jackson RC 1.00 2.50
190 Tyrone Calico RC 1.25 3.00

2003 Upper Deck Honor Roll Gold

*VETS 1-100: 12X TO 30X BASIC CARDS
*ROOKIES 1-100: 10X TO 25X
*VETS 101-130: 4X TO 10X BASIC CARDS
*ROOKIES 101-130: 3X TO 8X
*ROOKIES 131-190: 2.5X TO 6X
STATED PRINT RUN 25 SERIAL #'d SETS

2003 Upper Deck Honor Roll Silver

*VETS 1-100: 3X TO 8X BASIC CARDS
*ROOKIES 1-100: 2.5X TO 6X
*VETS 101-130: 1X TO 2.5X BASIC CARDS
*ROOKIES 101-130: .8X TO 2X
*ROOKIES 131-190: .6X TO 1.5X
OVERALL PARALLEL ODDS 1:24
SILVER PRINT RUN 200 SER.#'d SETS

2003 Upper Deck Honor Roll Dean's List

STATED ODDS 1:13
*SILVER/200: .5X TO 1.2X BASIC JSY
SILVER PRINT RUN 200 SER.#'d SETS
*GOLD/25: 1X TO 2.5X BASIC JSY
GOLD PRINT RUN 25 SER.#'d SETS
DLAN Mike Anderson 3.00 8.00
DLBL Byron Leftwich 2.50 6.00
DLBO Kyle Boller 4.00 10.00
DLBS Brandon Stokley 3.00 8.00
DLCB Champ Bailey SP 4.00 10.00
DLCJ Chad Johnson 4.00 10.00
DLCM Chris McAlister 3.00 8.00
DLCS Chris Samuels 2.50 6.00
DLCU Curtis Martin 4.00 10.00
DLDC Dallas Clark 6.00 15.00
DLDM Damerian McCants 2.50 6.00
DLDR Dave Ragone 2.50 6.00
DLDW Dez White SP 2.50 6.00
DLJB Josh Booty 2.50 6.00
DLJK Jevon Kearse SP 3.00 8.00
DLKB Kendrell Bell 2.50 6.00
DLKC Kerry Collins 3.00 8.00
DLKW Kevin Ware 2.50 6.00
DLMA Mike Alstott 4.00 10.00
DLMB Marty Booker 3.00 8.00
DLMC Donovan McNabb SP 4.00 10.00
DLMM Michael McCrary 2.50 6.00
DLMR Marcus Robinson 3.00 8.00
DLMV Michael Vick SP 5.00 12.00
DLOG Olandis Gary 2.50 6.00
DLOP Orlando Pace 3.00 8.00
DLPB Plaxico Burress SP 3.00 8.00
DLPM Peyton Manning SP 8.00 20.00
DLQJ Quentin Jammer 2.50 6.00
DLRG Rex Grossman 2.50 6.00
DLRO DeWayne Robertson 3.00 8.00
DLRW Reggie Wayne 4.00 10.00
DLSA Shaun Alexander 3.00 8.00
DLSC Carson Palmer 5.00 12.00
DLSH Jeremy Shockey 4.00 10.00
DLSI Corey Simon 3.00 8.00
DLSM Sammy Morris 3.00 8.00
DLTB Tiki Barber 4.00 10.00
DLTH Torry Holt 4.00 10.00
DLZT Zach Thomas 4.00 10.00

2003 Upper Deck Honor Roll Letterman Autographs

OVERALL AUTOGRAPH ODDS 1:240
*GOLD/25: .8X TO 2X BASE AUTO
GOLD PRINT RUN 25 SER.#'d SETS
HRLCJ Chad Johnson 10.00 25.00
HRLDM Deuce McAllister 8.00 20.00
HRLHE Travis Henry 6.00 15.00
HRLJJ James Jackson 6.00 15.00
HRLKB Kevan Barlow 6.00 15.00
HRLMM Snoop Minnis 6.00 15.00
HRLPM Peyton Manning 40.00 80.00
HRLRJ Rudi Johnson 10.00 25.00
HRLTH Todd Heap 8.00 20.00
HRLTM Travis Minor 6.00 15.00

2008 Upper Deck Icons

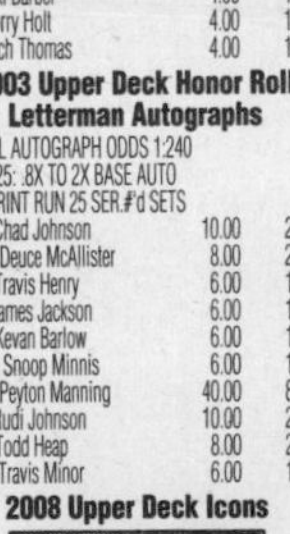

This set was released on August 27, 2008. The base set consists of 248 cards. Cards 1-100 feature veterans, while cards 101-200 are rookies serial numbered of 750 and cards 201-250 are rookies serial numbered of 999.

COMP.SET w/o RC's (100) 8.00 20.00
ROOKIE/750 PRINT RUN 750 SER.#'d SETS
ROOKIE/999 PRINT RUN 999 SER.#'d SETS
1 Edgerrin James .25 .60
2 Larry Fitzgerald .30 .75
3 Matt Leinart .30 .75
4 Jamal Lewis .25 .60
5 Aaron Rodgers .60 1.50
6 Steve McNair .25 .60
7 Ray Lewis .30 .75
8 Todd Heap .20 .50
9 Willis McGahee .25 .60
10 Marshawn Lynch .25 .60
11 Roscoe Parrish .20 .50
12 Trent Edwards .20 .50
13 DeShaun Foster .25 .60
14 Julius Peppers .25 .60
15 Thomas Jones .25 .60
16 Brian Urlacher .30 .75
17 Devin Hester .30 .75
18 Rex Grossman .25 .60
19 Carson Palmer .30 .75
20 T.J. Houshmandzadeh .25 .60
21 Rudi Johnson .25 .60
22 Derek Anderson .20 .50
23 Kellen Winslow .25 .60
24 Braylon Edwards .25 .60
25 Tony Romo .40 1.00
26 Terrell Owens .30 .75
27 Marion Barber .25 .60
28 Brandon Marshall .25 .60
29 Travis Henry .20 .50
30 Champ Bailey .25 .60
31 Calvin Johnson .30 .75
32 Joseph Addai .25 .60
33 Jon Kitna .25 .60
34 Brett Favre .75 2.00
35 Donald Driver .25 .60
36 Ryan Grant .30 .75
37 Greg Jennings .30 .75
38 DeMeco Ryans .25 .60
39 Andre Johnson .25 .60
40 Matt Schaub .25 .60
41 Peyton Manning .50 1.25
42 Reggie Wayne .25 .60
43 Bob Sanders .25 .60
44 David Garrard .25 .60
45 Maurice Jones-Drew .25 .60
46 Matt Jones .25 .60
47 Fred Taylor .25 .60
48 Tony Gonzalez .25 .60
49 Derrick Johnson .20 .50
50 Dwayne Bowe .25 .60
51 Larry Johnson .25 .60
52 Ronnie Brown .25 .60
53 Ted Ginn Jr. .25 .60
54 Jason Taylor .25 .60
55 Tarvaris Jackson .25 .60
56 Adrian Peterson .50 1.25
57 Ben Roethlisberger .30 .75
58 Tom Brady .50 1.25
59 Randy Moss .30 .75
60 Laurence Maroney .25 .60
61 Wes Welker .30 .75
62 Drew Brees .30 .75
63 Marques Colston .25 .60
64 Reggie Bush .30 .75
65 Eli Manning .30 .75
66 Antonio Pierce .20 .50
67 Plaxico Burress .25 .60
68 Jeremy Shockey .25 .60
69 Jonathan Vilma .25 .60
70 JaMarcus Russell .25 .60
71 Kirk Morrison .20 .50
72 Ronald Curry .25 .60
73 Brian Westbrook .25 .60
74 Brian Dawkins .25 .60
75 Donovan McNabb .30 .75
76 Santonio Holmes .25 .60
77 Willie Parker .25 .60
78 Troy Polamalu .30 .75
79 LaDainian Tomlinson .30 .75
80 Shawne Merriman .25 .60
81 Antonio Cromartie .20 .50
82 Antonio Gates .30 .75
83 Alex Smith QB .30 .75
84 Frank Gore .25 .60
85 Patrick Willis .25 .60
86 Matt Hasselbeck .25 .60
87 Shaun Alexander .25 .60
88 Deion Branch .25 .60
89 Steven Jackson .30 .75
90 Torry Holt .25 .60
91 Marc Bulger .25 .60
92 Jeff Garcia .25 .60
93 Cadillac Williams .25 .60
94 Joey Galloway .25 .60
95 Vince Young .25 .60
96 LenDale White .25 .60
97 Albert Haynesworth .20 .50
98 Jason Campbell .25 .60
99 Chris Cooley .25 .60
100 Clinton Portis .25 .60
101 Earl Bennett RC 1.25 3.00
102 Adrian Arrington RC 1.00 2.50
103 Ali Highsmith RC .75 2.00
104 Allen Patrick RC 1.00 2.50
105 Andre Caldwell RC 1.00 2.50
106 Andre Woodson RC 1.25 3.00
107 Antoine Cason RC 1.25 3.00
108 Aqib Talib RC 1.25 3.00
109 Ben Moffitt RC .75 2.00
110 Brian Brohm RC 1.25 3.00
111 Bruce Davis RC 1.00 2.50
112 Calais Campbell RC 1.00 2.50
113 Chad Henne RC 1.25 3.00
114 Chevis Jackson RC .75 2.00
115 Chris Ellis RC .75 2.00
116 Chris Johnson RC 3.00 8.00
117 Chris Long RC 1.25 3.00
118 Colt Brennan RC 1.25 3.00
119 Craig Steltz RC 1.00 2.50
120 DJ Hall RC 1.00 2.50
121 Dan Connor RC 1.25 3.00
122 Darren McFadden RC 3.00 8.00
123 Davone Bess RC 1.25 3.00
124 DeMario Pressley RC 1.00 2.50
125 Dennis Dixon RC 1.25 3.00
126 DeSean Jackson RC 2.50 6.00
127 Donnie Avery RC 1.00 2.50
128 Jerome Simpson RC 1.25 3.00
129 Dre Moore RC 1.00 2.50
130 Dwight Lowery RC 1.25 3.00
131 Early Doucet RC 1.00 2.50
132 Erik Ainge RC 1.25 3.00
133 Felix Jones RC 2.00 5.00
134 Fred Davis RC 1.25 3.00
135 Glenn Dorsey RC 1.25 3.00
136 Harry Douglas RC 1.00 2.50
137 Eddie Royal RC 1.25 3.00
138 Jack Ikegwuonu RC .75 2.00
139 Jacob Hester RC 1.25 3.00
140 Jacob Tamme RC 1.25 3.00
141 Jake Long RC 1.25 3.00
142 Jamaal Charles RC 2.00 5.00
143 James Hardy RC 1.00 2.50
144 J Leman RC .75 2.00
145 Joe Flacco RC 4.00 10.00
146 John Carlson RC 1.25 3.00
147 John David Booty RC 1.00 2.50
148 Jonathan Goff RC .75 2.00
149 Jonathan Hefney RC 1.00 2.50
150 Jonathan Stewart RC 2.00 5.00
151 Jordy Nelson RC 1.50 4.00
152 Josh Johnson RC 1.25 3.00
153 Justin Forsett RC 1.25 3.00
154 Justin King RC 1.00 2.50
155 Keenan Burton RC .75 2.00
156 Keith Rivers RC 1.25 3.00
157 Kenny Phillips RC 1.25 3.00
158 Kentwan Balmer RC 1.00 2.50
159 Kevin O'Connell RC 1.00 2.50
160 Kevin Smith RC 1.25 3.00
161 Alex Brink RC 1.25 3.00
162 Lavelle Hawkins RC .75 2.00
163 Lawrence Jackson RC 1.00 2.50
164 Limas Sweed RC 1.25 3.00
165 Malcolm Kelly RC 1.00 2.50
166 Marcus Monk RC 1.00 2.50
167 Mario Manningham RC 1.25 3.00
168 Mario Urrutia RC .75 2.00
169 Martellus Bennett RC 1.00 2.50
170 Martin Rucker RC 1.00 2.50
171 Matt Flynn RC 2.50 6.00
172 Matt Forte RC 2.00 5.00
173 Matt Ryan RC 5.00 12.00
174 Mike Hart RC 1.25 3.00
175 Mike Jenkins RC 1.25 3.00
176 Owen Schmitt RC 1.25 3.00
177 Paul Smith RC 1.25 3.00
178 Philip Wheeler RC 1.00 2.50
179 Quentin Groves RC 1.00 2.50
180 Quintin Demps RC 1.25 3.00
181 Rashard Mendenhall RC 2.50 6.00
182 Ray Rice RC 2.50 6.00
183 Ryan Clady RC 1.25 3.00
184 Ryan Torain RC 1.25 3.00
185 Sam Baker RC .75 2.00
186 Anthony Morelli RC 1.00 2.50
187 Sedrick Ellis RC 1.25 3.00
188 Dexter Jackson RC 1.00 2.50
189 Shawn Crable RC .75 2.00
190 Steve Slaton RC 1.25 3.00
191 Tashard Choice RC 1.00 2.50
192 Terrell Thomas RC 1.00 2.50
193 Thomas Brown RC 1.00 2.50
194 Tom Zbikowski RC 1.25 3.00
195 Gosder Cherilus RC 1.00 2.50
196 Trevor Laws RC 1.25 3.00
197 Vernon Gholston RC 1.00 2.50
198 Vince Hall RC .75 2.00
199 Xavier Adibi RC .75 2.00
200 Yvenson Bernard RC 1.25 3.00
201 Jerome Felton RC .75 2.00
202 Simeon Castille RC 1.00 2.50
203 Craig Stevens RC .75 2.00
204 Barry Richardson RC .75 2.00
205 Beau Bell RC 1.00 2.50
206 Caleb Campbell RC 1.25 3.00
207 T.C. Ostrander RC 1.00 2.50
208 Brad Cottam RC 1.00 2.50
209 Brandon Flowers RC 1.25 3.00
211 Chauncey Washington RC 1.00 2.50
212 Chris Williams RC 1.00 2.50
213 Cory Boyd RC .75 2.00
214 Will Franklin RC 1.00 2.50
215 Jo-Lonn Dunbar RC 1.00 2.50
216 Xavier Omon RC 1.25 3.00
217 Darius Reynaud RC .75 2.00
218 Dantrell Savage RC 1.00 2.50
219 DeJuan Tribble RC .75 2.00
220 Dennis Keyes RC .75 2.00
221 Devin Thomas RC 1.00 2.50
222 Marcus Griffin RC .75 2.00
223 Drew Radovich RC 1.00 2.50
224 Marcus Thomas RC 1.00 2.50
225 Frank Okam RC .75 2.00
226 Brian Bonner RC .75 2.00
227 Jamie Silva RC 1.00 2.50
228 Jehuu Caulcrick RC 1.00 2.50
229 Jermichael Finley RC 1.25 3.00
230 Jerod Mayo RC 1.25 3.00
231 Brandon McAnderson RC 1.00 2.50
232 Jordon Dizon RC 1.25 3.00
233 Josh Barrett RC .75 2.00
234 Kalvin McRae RC .75 2.00
235 Kellen Davis RC .75 2.00
236 Keon Lattimore RC 1.00 2.50
237 Leodis McKelvin RC 1.00 2.50
239 Curtis Lofton RC 1.00 2.50
240 Paul Hubbard RC 1.00 2.50
241 Titus Brown RC .75 2.00
242 Ryan Grice-Mullen RC .75 2.00
243 Spencer Larsen RC .75 2.00
244 Thomas DeCoud RC .75 2.00
245 Erin Henderson RC 1.25 3.00
246 Tracy Porter RC 1.25 3.00
247 Trae Williams RC .75 2.00
248 Trevor Scott RC 1.00 2.50
249 Wesley Woodyard RC 1.00 2.50
250 Xavier Lee RC 1.00 2.50

2008 Upper Deck Icons Blue Die Cut

*VETS/70-99: 4X TO 10X BASIC CARDS
*ROOKIES/70-99: .8X TO 2X BASIC CARDS
*VETS/45-69: 5X TO 12X BASIC CARDS
*ROOKIES/45-69: 1X TO 2.5X BASIC CARDS
*VETS/30-44: 6X TO 15X BASIC CARDS
*ROOKIES/30-44: 1.2X TO 3X BASIC CARDS
*VETS/20-29: 8X TO 20X BASIC CARDS
*ROOKIES/20-29: 1.5X TO 4X BASIC CARDS
*VETS/10-19: 10X TO 25X BASIC CARDS
*ROOKIES/10-19: 2X TO 5X BASIC CARDS
STATED PRINT RUN 1-98
122 Darren McFadden/20 12.00 30.00

2008 Upper Deck Icons Gold Die Cut

*VETS 1-100: 4X TO 10X BASIC CARDS
*ROOKIES 101-250: .8X TO 2X BASIC CARDS
STATED PRINT RUN 75 SER.#'d SETS

2008 Upper Deck Icons Rainbow Foil

*VETS: 1.5X TO 4X BASIC CARDS
RANDOM INSERTS IN RETAIL PACKS

2008 Upper Deck Icons Silver Die Cut

*VETS 1-100: 3X TO 8X BASIC CARDS
*ROOKIES 101-250: .6X TO 1.5X BASIC CARDS
STATED PRINT RUN 150 SER.#'d SETS

2008 Upper Deck Icons Class of 2008 Silver

SILVER PRINT RUN 750 SER.#'d SETS
*BLUE/250: .5X TO 1.2X SILVER/750
BLUE PRINT RUN 250 SER.#'d SETS
*GOLD/99: .6X TO 1.5X SILVER/750
GOLD PRINT RUN 99 SER.#'d SETS
C01 Darren McFadden 2.00 5.00
C02 DeSean Jackson 1.50 4.00
C03 Brian Brohm .75 2.00
C04 Matt Ryan 3.00 8.00
C05 Devin Thomas .60 1.50
C06 Jonathan Stewart 1.25 3.00
C07 Jake Long .75 2.00
C08 Chad Henne .75 2.00
C09 Chris Johnson 2.00 5.00
C010 Chris Long .75 2.00
C011 Earl Bennett .75 2.00
C012 Rashard Mendenhall 1.50 4.00
C013 Glenn Dorsey .75 2.00
C014 Early Doucet .60 1.50
C015 Andre Caldwell .60 1.50
C016 Felix Jones 1.25 3.00
C017 Dustin Keller .75 2.00
C018 Jamaal Charles 1.25 3.00
C019 Joe Flacco 2.50 6.00
C020 John David Booty .60 1.50
C021 Jordy Nelson 1.00 2.50
C022 Jerome Simpson .75 2.00
C023 Kevin Smith .75 2.00
C024 Limas Sweed .75 2.00
C025 Donnie Avery .60 1.50
C026 Malcolm Kelly .60 1.50
C027 Mario Manningham .75 2.00
C028 James Hardy .60 1.50
C029 Matt Forte 1.25 3.00
C030 Dexter Jackson .60 1.50
C031 Eddie Royal .75 2.00
C032 Ray Rice 1.50 4.00
C033 Steve Slaton .75 2.00
C034 Harry Douglas .60 1.50
C035 Kevin O'Connell .60 1.50

2008 Upper Deck Icons Class of 2008 Jersey Silver

STATED PRINT RUN 199 SER.#'d SETS
*GOLD/75: .5X TO 1.2X SILVER/199
GOLD PRINT RUN 75 SER.#'d SETS
C01 Darren McFadden 6.00 15.00
C02 DeSean Jackson 5.00 12.00
C03 Brian Brohm 2.50 6.00
C04 Matt Ryan 6.00 15.00
C05 Devin Thomas 2.00 5.00
C06 Jonathan Stewart 5.00 12.00
C07 Jake Long 2.50 6.00
C08 Chad Henne 5.00 12.00
C09 Chris Johnson 6.00 15.00
C010 Chris Long 2.50 6.00
C011 Earl Bennett 2.50 6.00
C012 Rashard Mendenhall 5.00 12.00
C013 Glenn Dorsey 2.50 6.00
C014 Early Doucet 2.00 5.00
C015 Andre Caldwell 2.00 5.00
C016 Felix Jones 4.00 10.00
C017 Dustin Keller 2.50 6.00
C018 Jamaal Charles 4.00 10.00
C019 Joe Flacco 8.00 20.00
C020 John David Booty 2.00 5.00
C021 Jordy Nelson 3.00 8.00
C022 Jerome Simpson 2.50 6.00
C023 Kevin Smith 2.50 6.00
C024 Limas Sweed 2.50 6.00
C025 Donnie Avery 2.00 5.00
C026 Malcolm Kelly 2.00 5.00
C027 Mario Manningham 2.50 6.00
C028 James Hardy 2.00 5.00
C029 Matt Forte 4.00 10.00
C030 Dexter Jackson 2.00 5.00
C031 Eddie Royal 2.50 6.00
C032 Ray Rice 5.00 12.00
C033 Steve Slaton 2.50 6.00
C034 Harry Douglas 2.00 5.00
C035 Kevin O'Connell 2.00 5.00

2008 Upper Deck Icons Future Foundations Silver

SILVER PRINT RUN 750 SER.#'d SETS
*BLUE/250: .5X TO 1.2X SILVER/750
BLUE PRINT RUN 250 SER.#'d SETS
*GOLD/99: .6X TO 1.5X SILVER/750
GOLD PRINT RUN 99 SER.#'d SETS
FF1 A.J. Hawk 1.25 3.00
FF2 Anquan Boldin 1.25 3.00
FF3 Ben Roethlisberger 1.50 4.00
FF4 Bob Sanders 1.25 3.00
FF5 Brady Quinn 1.25 3.00
FF6 Brian Brohm .75 2.00
FF7 Calvin Johnson 1.50 4.00
FF8 Chad Henne .75 2.00
FF9 Chad Johnson 1.25 3.00
FF10 Darren McFadden 2.00 5.00
FF11 Derek Anderson 1.00 2.50
FF12 Early Doucet .60 1.50
FF13 Felix Jones 1.25 3.00
FF14 Dustin Keller .75 2.00
FF15 JaMarcus Russell 1.25 3.00
FF16 Joe Flacco 2.50 6.00
FF17 Jonathan Stewart 1.25 3.00
FF18 Jerome Simpson .75 2.00
FF19 Kevin Smith .75 2.00
FF20 Malcolm Kelly .60 1.50
FF21 Marshawn Lynch 1.25 3.00
FF22 Matt Forte 1.25 3.00
FF23 Matt Ryan 3.00 8.00
FF24 Rashard Mendenhall 1.50 4.00
FF25 Vince Young 1.25 3.00

2008 Upper Deck Icons Future Foundations Jersey Silver

SILVER PRINT RUN 199 SER.#'d SETS
*GOLD/75: .5X TO 1.2X SILVER/199
GOLD PRINT RUN 75 SER.#'d SETS
FF1 A.J. Hawk 3.00 8.00
FF2 Anquan Boldin 3.00 8.00
FF3 Ben Roethlisberger 4.00 10.00
FF4 Bob Sanders 4.00 10.00
FF5 Brady Quinn 3.00 8.00
FF6 Brian Brohm 2.50 6.00
FF7 Calvin Johnson 4.00 10.00
FF8 Chad Henne 5.00 12.00
FF9 Chad Johnson 3.00 8.00
FF10 Darren McFadden 6.00 15.00
FF11 Derek Anderson 2.50 6.00
FF12 Early Doucet 2.00 5.00
FF13 Felix Jones 4.00 10.00
FF14 Dustin Keller 2.50 6.00
FF15 JaMarcus Russell 3.00 8.00
FF16 Joe Flacco 8.00 20.00
FF17 Jonathan Stewart 5.00 12.00
FF18 Jerome Simpson 2.50 6.00
FF19 Kevin Smith 2.50 6.00
FF20 Malcolm Kelly 2.00 5.00
FF21 Marshawn Lynch 3.00 8.00
FF22 Matt Forte 4.00 10.00
FF23 Matt Ryan 6.00 15.00
FF24 Rashard Mendenhall 5.00 12.00
FF25 Vince Young 3.00 8.00

2008 Upper Deck Icons Future Stars Materials

FSM1 Adrian Peterson 6.00 15.00
FSM2 Dwayne Bowe 3.00 8.00
FSM3 Brady Quinn 3.00 8.00
FSM4 Darren McFadden 6.00 15.00
FSM5 DeSean Jackson 5.00 12.00
FSM6 Brian Brohm 2.50 6.00
FSM7 Matt Ryan 6.00 15.00
FSM8 Earl Bennett 2.50 6.00
FSM9 Jonathan Stewart 5.00 12.00
FSM10 Kevin O'Connell 2.00 5.00
FSM11 Chad Henne 5.00 12.00
FSM12 Chris Johnson 6.00 15.00
FSM13 Glenn Dorsey 2.50 6.00
FSM14 Rashard Mendenhall 5.00 12.00
FSM15 Dexter Jackson 2.00 5.00
FSM16 Early Doucet 2.00 5.00
FSM17 Eddie Royal 2.50 6.00
FSM18 Felix Jones 4.00 10.00
FSM19 Dustin Keller 2.50 6.00
FSM20 Jamaal Charles 4.00 10.00
FSM21 Joe Flacco 8.00 20.00
FSM22 John David Booty 2.00 5.00
FSM23 Jerome Simpson 2.50 6.00
FSM24 Kevin Smith 2.50 6.00
FSM25 Limas Sweed 2.50 6.00
FSM26 Steve Slaton 2.50 6.00
FSM27 Malcolm Kelly 2.00 5.00
FSM28 Mario Manningham 2.50 6.00
FSM29 Matt Forte 4.00 10.00
FSM30 Jordy Nelson 3.00 8.00
FSM31 Devin Thomas 2.00 5.00
FSM32 Ray Rice 5.00 12.00
FSM33 Andre Caldwell 2.00 5.00

2008 Upper Deck Icons Immortal Lettermen

PRINT RUNS 20-97 PER LETTER
TOTAL PRINT RUNS 306-630
*PARALLEL: .4X TO 1X BASIC INSERTS
PARAL.PRINT RUNS 25-99 PER LETTER
PARALLEL TOTAL PRINT RUNS 306-636
AROY Chris Johnson/99 15.00 40.00
(Letters spell out AFC OFFENSIVE ROY
Total print run 1485)
BB19 Brian Bosworth/78 8.00 20.00
(Letters spell out BOSWORTH
Total print run 624)
BF1 Brett Favre/124 15.00 40.00
(Letters spell out BROADWAY BRETT
Total print run 1612)
BF2 Brett Favre/127 15.00 40.00
(Letters spell out NEW YORK JETS
Total print run 1397)
BJ18 Bo Jackson/78 12.00 30.00
(Letters spell out JACKSON
Total print run 546)
BN4 Bronko Nagurski/61 8.00 20.00
(Letters spell out NAGURSKI
Total print run 488)
BS16 Barry Sanders/71 15.00 40.00
(Letters spell out SANDERS
Total print run 497)
DB21 Dick Butkus/77 10.00 25.00
(Letters spell out BUTKUS
Total print run 462)
DM20 Dan Marino/61 25.00 60.00
(Letters spell out MARINO
Total print run 366)
FH23 Franco Harris/51 10.00 25.00
(Letters spell out HARRIS
Total print run 306)
FT22 Fran Tarkenton/38 10.00 25.00
(Letters spell out TARKENTON
Total print run 342)
GS3 Gale Sayers/88 10.00 25.00
(Letters spell out SAYERS
Total print run 528)
JB26 Jim Brown/97 10.00 25.00
(Letters spell out BROWN
Total print run 485)
JL25 Jack Lambert/90 10.00 25.00
(Letters spell out LAMBERT
Total print run 630)
JT7 Jim Thorpe/53 15.00 40.00
(Letters spell out THORPE
Total print run 318)
JU2 Johnny Unitas/88 15.00 40.00
(Letters spell out UNITAS
Total print run 528)
KS28 Ken Stabler/72 10.00 25.00
(Letters spell out STABLER
Total print run 504)
LA14 Lance Alworth/80 6.00 15.00
(Letters spell out ALWORTH
Total print run 560)
NROY Matt Ryan/99 12.00 30.00
(Letters spell out NFC OFFENSIVE ROY
Total print run 1485)
OG9 Otto Graham/80 6.00 15.00
(Letters spell out GRAHAM
Total print run 480)
RG1 Red Grange/51 10.00 25.00
(Letters spell out GRANGE
Total print run 306)
RS15 Roger Staubach/64 10.00 25.00
(Letters spell out STAUBACH
Total print run 512)
SI17 Billy Sims/80 5.00 12.00
(Letters spell out SIMS
Total print run 320)
SL10 Sid Luckman/80 6.00 15.00
(Letters spell out LUCKMAN
Total print run 560)
TL5 Tom Landry/88 10.00 25.00
(Letters spell out LANDRY
Total print run 528)
WE13 Weeb Ewbank/90 5.00 12.00
(Letters spell out EWBANK
Total print run 540)
WP8 Walter Payton/64 30.00 80.00
(Letters spell out PAYTON
Total print run 384)
YT12 Y.A. Tittle/80 6.00 15.00
(Letters spell out TITTLE
Total print run 480)

2008 Upper Deck Icons Immortal Lettermen Autographs

TOTAL AUTO PRINT RUNS 72-270
AUTO STATED PRINT RUNS 12-42
BB19 Brian Bosworth/27 25.00 50.00
(Letters spell out THE BOZ
Total print run 162)
BJ18 Bo Jackson/18 50.00 100.00
(Letters spell out BO KNOWS
Total print run 126)
BS16 Barry Sanders/20 90.00 175.00
(Letters spell out SANDERS
Total print run 140)
DB21 Dick Butkus/22 40.00 80.00
(Letters spell out BUTKUS
Total print run 132)
DM20 Dan Marino/16 125.00 250.00
(Letters spell out MARINO
Total print run 96)
FH23 Franco Harris/26 40.00 80.00
(Letters spell out HARRIS
Total print run 156)
FT22 Fran Tarkenton/30 30.00 60.00
(Letters spell out TARKENTON
Total print run 270)
JB26 Jim Brown/12 40.00 80.00
(Letters spell out BROWNS
Total print run 72)
JL25 Jack Lambert/20 40.00 80.00
(Letters spell out TEETH
Total print run 100)
KS28 Ken Stabler/16 40.00 80.00
(Letters spell out THE SNAKE
Total print run 128)
SI17 Billy Sims/42 15.00 30.00
(Letters spell out SIMS
Total print run 168)

2008 Upper Deck Icons Legendary Icons Silver

SILVER PRINT RUN 799 SER.#'d SETS
*BLUE/250: .5X TO 1.2X SILVER/799
BLUE PRINT RUN 250 SER.#'d SETS
*GOLD/99: .6X TO 1.5X SILVER/799
GOLD PRINT RUN 99 SER.#'d SETS
LI1 Barry Sanders 2.50 6.00
LI2 Billy Sims 1.25 3.00
LI3 Bo Jackson 2.00 5.00
LI4 Brian Bosworth 1.50 4.00
LI5 Dan Marino 3.00 8.00
LI6 Dick Butkus 2.00 5.00
LI7 Emmitt Smith 3.00 8.00
LI8 Bert Jones 1.00 2.50
LI9 Jack Lambert 1.50 4.00
LI10 Jim Brown 2.00 5.00
LI11 Joe Theismann 1.50 4.00
LI12 Ken Anderson 1.25 3.00
LI13 Lynn Swann 1.50 4.00
LI14 Roger Craig 1.25 3.00
LI15 Ottis Anderson 1.00 2.50

2008 Upper Deck Icons Legendary Icons Autographs

STATED PRINT RUN 25 SER.#'d SETS
LI1 Barry Sanders 60.00 120.00
LI2 Billy Sims 15.00 30.00
LI3 Bo Jackson 30.00 60.00
LI4 Brian Bosworth 20.00 40.00
LI5 Dan Marino 90.00 150.00
LI6 Dick Butkus EXCH 30.00 60.00
LI7 Emmitt Smith 90.00 150.00
LI8 Bert Jones
LI9 Jack Lambert 30.00 60.00
LI10 Jim Brown
LI11 Joe Theismann 15.00 30.00
LI12 Ken Anderson 20.00 40.00
LI13 Lynn Swann
LI14 Roger Craig 25.00 50.00
LI15 Ottis Anderson

2008 Upper Deck Icons Legendary Icons Jersey Silver

SILVER PRINT RUN 150 SER.#'d SETS
*GOLD/25: .6X TO 1.5X SILVER/150
GOLD PRINT RUN 25 SER.#'d SETS
*PATCH/15: 1.2X TO 3X SILVER/150
PATCH PRINT RUN 15 SER.#'d SETS
LI1 Barry Sanders 8.00 20.00
LI2 Billy Sims 4.00 10.00
LI3 Bo Jackson 8.00 20.00
LI4 Brian Bosworth 5.00 12.00
LI5 Dan Marino 10.00 25.00
LI6 Dick Butkus 6.00 15.00
LI7 Emmitt Smith 10.00 25.00
LI8 Bert Jones 3.00 8.00
LI9 Jack Lambert 5.00 12.00
LI10 Jim Brown 6.00 15.00
LI11 Joe Theismann 5.00 12.00
LI12 Ken Anderson 4.00 10.00
LI13 Lynn Swann 5.00 12.00
LI14 Roger Craig 4.00 10.00
LI15 Ottis Anderson 3.00 8.00

2008 Upper Deck Icons Movie Icons

STATED PRINT RUN 999 SER.#'d SETS
*SILVER DC/99: .6X TO 1.5X BASIC INSERTS
SILVER DIE CUT PRINT RUN 99 SER.#'d SETS
*GOLD DIE CUT/75: .8X TO 2X BASIC INSERTS
GOLD DIE CUT PRINT RUN 75 SER.#'d SETS
*BLUE DIE CUT/35: 1.2X TO 3X BASIC INSERTS
BLUE DIE CUT PRINT RUN 35 SER.#'d SETS
MI3 Billy Dee Williams .40 1.00
MI4 Burt Reynolds .40 1.00
MI9 Ed O'Neill .40 1.00

2008 Upper Deck Icons Movie Icons Lettermen

STATED PRINT RUN 47-68 EACH LETTER
TOTAL PRINT RUNS 272-378
*PARALLEL: .4X TO 1X BASIC INSERTS
PARALLEL PRINT RUNS 30-47 EACH LETTER
TOTAL PARALLEL PRINT RUNS 240-480
BR5 Burt Reynolds/47 5.00 12.00
(Letters spell out REYNOLDS
Total print run 376)
BW4 Billy Dee Williams/47 5.00 12.00
(Letters spell out WILLIAMS
Total print run 376)
EO11 Ed O'Neill/63 5.00 12.00
(Letters spell out O'NEILL
Total print run 378)
HA13 Goldie Hawn/68 5.00 12.00
(Letters spell out HAWN
Total print run 272)

2008 Upper Deck Icons Movie Icons Lettermen Autographs

TOTAL AUTO PRINT RUNS 63--120
BW Billy Dee Williams/12 15.00 40.00
(Letters spell out GALE SAYERS
Total print run 120)
BR Burt Reynolds/14 30.00 60.00
(Letters spell out PAUL CREWE
Total print run 63)
EO Ed O'Neill/12 30.00 60.00
(Letters spell out POLK HIGH
Total print run 96)

2008 Upper Deck Icons NFL Chronology Silver

SILVER PRINT RUN 750 SER.#'d SETS
*BLUE/250: .5X TO 1.2X SILVER/750
BLUE PRINT RUN 250 SER.#'d SETS
*GOLD/99: .6X TO 1.5X SILVER/750
GOLD PRINT RUN 99 SER.#'d SETS
CHR2 Jim Brown 2.00 5.00
CHR4 Joe Namath 2.00 5.00
CHR5 Franco Harris 1.50 4.00
CHR7 Jack Lambert 1.50 4.00
CHR8 Walter Payton 3.00 8.00
CHR9 Joe Montana 3.00 8.00
CHR10 Dan Marino 3.00 8.00
CHR13 Walter Payton 3.00 8.00
CHR14 Bo Jackson 2.00 5.00
CHR15 Barry Sanders 2.50 6.00
CHR16 Brett Favre 4.00 10.00
CHR17 Rod Woodson 1.50 4.00
CHR18 Jerry Rice 2.50 6.00
CHR19 Emmitt Smith 3.00 8.00
CHR20 Brett Favre 4.00 10.00
CHR21 Barry Sanders 2.50 6.00
CHR23 John Elway 2.50 6.00
CHR25 Terrell Owens 1.50 4.00
CHR26 Terrell Owens 1.50 4.00
CHR27 Jerry Rice 2.50 6.00
CHR28 Emmitt Smith 3.00 8.00
CHR29 Marvin Harrison 1.50 4.00
CHR30 Clinton Portis 1.25 3.00
CHR31 Jerry Rice 2.50 6.00
CHR32 Anquan Boldin 1.25 3.00
CHR33 Peyton Manning 2.50 6.00
CHR34 Devin Hester 1.50 4.00
CHR35 LaDainian Tomlinson 1.50 4.00
CHR36 Antonio Cromartie 1.00 2.50
CHR37 Tony Gonzalez 1.25 3.00
CHR38 Adrian Peterson 2.50 6.00
CHR39 Tom Brady 2.50 6.00
CHR40 Randy Moss 1.50 4.00

2008 Upper Deck Icons NFL Chronology Jersey Silver

SILVER PRINT RUN 150 SER.#'d SETS
*GOLD/50: .5X TO 1.2X SILVER/150
GOLD PRINT RUN 50 SER.#'d SETS
CHR2 Jim Brown 6.00 15.00
CHR4 Joe Namath 8.00 20.00
CHR5 Franco Harris 6.00 15.00
CHR7 Jack Lambert 5.00 12.00
CHR8 Walter Payton 10.00 25.00
CHR9 Joe Montana 10.00 25.00
CHR10 Dan Marino 10.00 25.00
CHR13 Walter Payton 10.00 25.00
CHR14 Bo Jackson 8.00 20.00
CHR15 Barry Sanders 8.00 20.00
CHR16 Brett Favre 10.00 25.00
CHR17 Rod Woodson 5.00 12.00
CHR18 Jerry Rice 8.00 20.00
CHR19 Emmitt Smith 10.00 25.00
CHR20 Brett Favre 10.00 25.00
CHR21 Barry Sanders 8.00 20.00
CHR23 John Elway 8.00 20.00
CHR25 Terrell Owens 4.00 10.00
CHR26 Terrell Owens 4.00 10.00
CHR27 Jerry Rice 8.00 20.00
CHR28 Emmitt Smith 10.00 25.00
CHR29 Marvin Harrison 4.00 10.00
CHR30 Clinton Portis/200 3.00 8.00
CHR31 Jerry Rice 8.00 20.00
CHR32 Anquan Boldin 3.00 8.00
CHR33 Peyton Manning 6.00 15.00
CHR34 Devin Hester 4.00 10.00
CHR35 LaDainian Tomlinson 4.00 10.00
CHR36 Antonio Cromartie/200 2.50 6.00
CHR37 Tony Gonzalez/200 3.00 8.00
CHR38 Adrian Peterson 6.00 15.00
CHR39 Tom Brady 6.00 15.00
CHR40 Randy Moss 4.00 10.00

2008 Upper Deck Icons NFL Icons Silver

SILVER PRINT RUN 799 SER.#'d SETS
*BLUE/250: .5X TO 1.2X SILVER/799
BLUE PRINT RUN 250 SER.#'d SETS
*GOLD/99: .6X TO 1.5X SILVER/799
GOLD PRINT RUN 99 SER.#'d SETS
NFL1 Adrian Peterson 2.50 6.00
NFL2 Aaron Schobel 1.00 2.50
NFL3 Brandon Marshall 1.25 3.00
NFL4 Ben Roethlisberger 1.50 4.00
NFL5 A.J. Hawk 1.25 3.00
NFL6 Bob Sanders 1.25 3.00
NFL7 DeMarcus Ware 1.25 3.00
NFL8 Brett Favre 4.00 10.00
NFL9 Jamal Lewis 1.25 3.00
NFL10 Brady Quinn 1.25 3.00
NFL11 Cadillac Williams 1.25 3.00
NFL12 Chad Johnson 1.25 3.00
NFL13 Aaron Rodgers 3.00 8.00
NFL14 Clinton Portis 1.25 3.00
NFL15 David Garrard 1.25 3.00
NFL16 Derek Anderson 1.00 2.50
NFL17 Dallas Clark 1.25 3.00
NFL18 Donald Lee 1.25 3.00
NFL19 Dwayne Bowe 1.25 3.00
NFL20 Roy Williams WR 1.25 3.00
NFL21 Eli Manning 1.50 4.00
NFL22 Frank Gore 1.25 3.00
NFL23 Marques Colston 1.25 3.00
NFL24 Brodie Croyle 1.25 3.00
NFL25 Jason Campbell 1.25 3.00
NFL26 Jeff Garcia 1.25 3.00
NFL27 Jeremy Shockey 1.25 3.00
NFL28 Joseph Addai 1.25 3.00
NFL29 Kellen Winslow 1.25 3.00
NFL30 LaDainian Tomlinson 1.50 4.00
NFL31 Larry Johnson 1.25 3.00
NFL32 Marc Bulger 1.25 3.00
NFL33 Marion Barber 1.25 3.00
NFL34 Marshawn Lynch 1.25 3.00
NFL35 Kurt Warner 1.50 4.00
NFL36 Matt Schaub 1.25 3.00
NFL37 Michael Huff 1.00 2.50
NFL38 Mike Vrabel 1.00 2.50
NFL39 Patrick Willis 1.25 3.00
NFL40 Peyton Manning 2.50 6.00
NFL41 Philip Rivers 1.50 4.00
NFL42 Randy Moss 1.50 4.00
NFL43 Jerricho Cotchery 1.25 3.00
NFL44 Tom Brady 2.50 6.00
NFL45 Ben Watson 1.00 2.50
NFL46 Tony Romo 2.00 5.00
NFL47 Troy Polamalu 1.50 4.00
NFL48 Trent Edwards 1.00 2.50
NFL49 Wes Welker 1.50 4.00
NFL50 Braylon Edwards 1.25 3.00

2008 Upper Deck Icons NFL Icons Autographs

STATED PRINT RUN 35-56
NFL1 Adrian Peterson 90.00 150.00
NFL2 Aaron Schobel 6.00 15.00
NFL3 Brandon Marshall
NFL4 Ben Roethlisberger 50.00 100.00
NFL5 A.J. Hawk 10.00 25.00
NFL6 Bob Sanders 30.00 80.00
NFL7 DeMarcus Ware 10.00 25.00
NFL8 Brett Favre 100.00 200.00
NFL9 Jamal Lewis
NFL10 Brady Quinn 25.00 50.00
NFL11 Cadillac Williams 8.00 20.00
NFL12 Chad Johnson 8.00 20.00
NFL13 Aaron Rodgers 125.00 200.00
NFL14 Clinton Portis 10.00 25.00
NFL15 David Garrard 10.00 25.00
NFL16 Derek Anderson 10.00 25.00
NFL17 Dallas Clark 10.00 25.00
NFL18 Donald Lee
NFL19 Dwayne Bowe 8.00 20.00
NFL20 Roy Williams WR
NFL21 Eli Manning 35.00 60.00
NFL22 Frank Gore 10.00 25.00
NFL23 Marques Colston 20.00 40.00
NFL24 Brodie Croyle 8.00 20.00
NFL25 Jason Campbell 10.00 25.00
NFL26 Jeff Garcia 8.00 20.00
NFL27 Jeremy Shockey EXCH 20.00 40.00
NFL28 Joseph Addai 15.00 30.00
NFL29 Kellen Winslow
NFL30 LaDainian Tomlinson 35.00 60.00
NFL31 Larry Johnson 10.00 25.00

NFL32 Marc Bulger
NFL33 Marion Barber 15.00 30.00
NFL34 Marshawn Lynch 10.00 25.00
NFL35 Kurt Warner 20.00 40.00
NFL36 Matt Schaub/56 10.00 25.00
NFL37 Michael Huff
NFL39 Patrick Willis/56 10.00 25.00
NFL40 Peyton Manning 60.00 100.00
NFL41 Philip Rivers 15.00 30.00
NFL43 Jerricho Cotchery 8.00 20.00
NFL44 Tom Brady 100.00 175.00
NFL45 Ben Watson 6.00 15.00
NFL46 Tony Romo 60.00 120.00
NFL48 Trent Edwards/56
NFL49 Wes Welker
NFL50 Braylon Edwards

2008 Upper Deck Icons NFL Icons Jersey Silver

SILVER PRINT RUN 150 SER.#'d SETS
*GOLD/50: .5X TO 1.2X SILVER/150
GOLD PRINT RUN 50 SER.#'d SETS
*PATCH/25: 1X TO 2.5X SILVER/150
PATCH PRINT RUN 25 SER.#'d SETS
NFL1 Adrian Peterson 6.00 15.00
NFL2 Aaron Schobel 2.50 6.00
NFL3 Brandon Marshall 3.00 8.00
NFL4 Ben Roethlisberger 4.00 10.00
NFL5 A.J. Hawk 3.00 8.00
NFL6 Bob Sanders 3.00 8.00
NFL7 DeMarcus Ware 3.00 8.00
NFL8 Brett Favre 10.00 25.00
NFL9 Jamal Lewis 3.00 8.00
NFL10 Brady Quinn 3.00 8.00
NFL11 Cadillac Williams 3.00 8.00
NFL12 Chad Johnson 3.00 8.00
NFL13 Aaron Rodgers 12.00 30.00
NFL14 Clinton Portis 3.00 8.00
NFL15 David Garrard 3.00 8.00
NFL16 Derek Anderson 2.50 6.00
NFL17 Dallas Clark 3.00 8.00
NFL18 Donald Lee 3.00 8.00
NFL19 Dwayne Bowe 3.00 8.00
NFL20 Roy Williams WR 3.00 8.00
NFL21 Eli Manning 4.00 10.00
NFL22 Frank Gore 3.00 8.00
NFL23 Marques Colston 3.00 8.00
NFL24 Brodie Croyle 3.00 8.00
NFL25 Jason Campbell 3.00 8.00
NFL26 Jeff Garcia 3.00 8.00
NFL27 Jeremy Shockey 3.00 8.00
NFL28 Joseph Addai 3.00 8.00
NFL29 Kellen Winslow 3.00 8.00
NFL30 LaDainian Tomlinson 4.00 10.00
NFL31 Larry Johnson 3.00 8.00
NFL32 Marc Bulger 3.00 8.00
NFL33 Marion Barber 3.00 8.00
NFL34 Marshawn Lynch 3.00 8.00
NFL35 Kurt Warner 4.00 10.00
NFL36 Matt Schaub 3.00 8.00
NFL37 Michael Huff 2.50 6.00
NFL38 Mike Vrabel 2.50 6.00
NFL39 Patrick Willis 3.00 8.00
NFL40 Peyton Manning 6.00 15.00
NFL41 Philip Rivers 4.00 10.00
NFL42 Randy Moss 4.00 10.00
NFL43 Jerricho Cotchery 3.00 8.00
NFL44 Tom Brady 6.00 15.00
NFL45 Ben Watson 2.50 6.00
NFL46 Tony Romo 5.00 12.00
NFL47 Troy Polamalu 6.00 15.00
NFL48 Trent Edwards 2.50 6.00
NFL49 Wes Welker 4.00 10.00
NFL50 Braylon Edwards 3.00 8.00

2008 Upper Deck Icons NFL Legends

STATED PRINT RUN 999 SER.#'d SETS
*SILVER DC/150: .6X TO 1.5X BASIC INSERTS
SILVER DIE CUT PRINT RUN 150 SER.#'d SETS
*GOLD DIE CUT/75: .8X TO 2X BASIC INSERTS
GOLD DIE CUT PRINT RUN 75 SER.#'d SETS
*BLUE DC/88: .6X TO 1.5X BASIC INSERTS
*BLUE DC/47-58: .8X TO 2X BASIC INSERTS
*BLUE DC/32-34: 1X TO 2.5X BASIC INSERTS
*BLUE DC/10-20: 1.5X TO 4X BASIC INSERTS
BLUE DIE CUT PRINT RUN 7-88
LEG1 Barry Sanders 2.50 6.00
LEG2 Billy Sims 1.25 3.00
LEG3 Bo Jackson 2.00 5.00
LEG4 Bob Griese 1.50 4.00
LEG5 Brian Bosworth 1.50 4.00
LEG6 Dan Marino 3.00 8.00
LEG7 Daryl Johnston 1.50 4.00
LEG8 Emmitt Smith 3.00 8.00
LEG9 Fran Tarkenton 1.50 4.00
LEG10 Herschel Walker 1.25 3.00
LEG11 Jack Lambert 1.50 4.00
LEG12 Jim Brown 2.00 5.00
LEG13 Jim McMahon 1.50 4.00
LEG14 Joe Montana 3.00 8.00
LEG15 Joe Namath 2.00 5.00
LEG16 Joe Theismann 1.50 4.00
LEG17 John Elway 2.50 6.00
LEG18 Ken Stabler 1.50 4.00
LEG20 Lynn Swann 1.50 4.00
LEG21 Mel Blount 1.25 3.00
LEG22 Roger Craig 1.25 3.00
LEG24 Sonny Jurgensen 1.25 3.00
LEG25 Y. A. Tittle 1.50 4.00

2008 Upper Deck Icons Presidential Icons Lettermen

PL1 Barack Obama/229 15.00 40.00
PL2 Barack Obama/127 15.00 40.00

2008 Upper Deck Icons Rookie Autographs Rainbow

STATED PRINT RUN 135-155
101 Earl Bennett 5.00 12.00
102 Adrian Arrington 4.00 10.00
103 Ali Highsmith 3.00 8.00
104 Allen Patrick 4.00 10.00
105 Andre Caldwell 4.00 10.00
106 Andre Woodson 5.00 12.00
107 Antoine Cason 5.00 12.00
108 Aqib Talib 5.00 12.00
109 Ben Moffitt 3.00 8.00
110 Brian Brohm/100 5.00 12.00
111 Bruce Davis 4.00 10.00
112 Calais Campbell 4.00 10.00
113 Chad Henne 5.00 12.00
114 Chevis Jackson 3.00 8.00
115 Chris Ellis 3.00 8.00
116 Chris Johnson 25.00 60.00
117 Chris Long 5.00 12.00
118 Colt Brennan/100 8.00 20.00
119 Craig Steltz 4.00 10.00
120 DJ Hall 4.00 10.00
121 Dan Connor 5.00 12.00
122 Darren McFadden/100 25.00 50.00
123 Davone Bess 5.00 12.00
124 DeMario Pressley/155 4.00 10.00
125 Dennis Dixon 8.00 20.00
126 DeSean Jackson 15.00 40.00
127 Donnie Avery 4.00 10.00
128 Jerome Simpson 5.00 12.00
129 Dre Moore/155 4.00 10.00
130 Dwight Lowery 5.00 12.00
131 Early Doucet 4.00 10.00
132 Erik Ainge 5.00 12.00
133 Felix Jones 15.00 40.00
134 Fred Davis 5.00 12.00
136 Harry Douglas 4.00 10.00
138 Jack Ikegwuonu 3.00 8.00
139 Jacob Hester 5.00 12.00
140 Jacob Tamme 5.00 12.00
141 Jake Long 5.00 12.00
142 Jamaal Charles 8.00 20.00
143 James Hardy 4.00 10.00
145 Joe Flacco 25.00 80.00
146 John Carlson 5.00 12.00
147 John David Booty 4.00 10.00
149 Jonathan Hefney/155 4.00 10.00
150 Jonathan Stewart/100 15.00 40.00
151 Jordy Nelson 10.00 25.00
152 Josh Johnson 5.00 12.00
153 Justin Forsett 5.00 12.00
154 Justin King 4.00 10.00
155 Keenan Burton 3.00 8.00
156 Keith Rivers 5.00 12.00
157 Kenny Phillips 5.00 12.00
159 Kevin O'Connell 4.00 10.00
160 Kevin Smith 5.00 12.00
161 Alex Brink 5.00 12.00
162 Lavelle Hawkins 3.00 8.00
163 Lawrence Jackson 4.00 10.00
164 Limas Sweed 5.00 12.00
165 Malcolm Kelly 4.00 10.00
166 Marcus Monk 4.00 10.00
167 Mario Manningham 5.00 12.00
168 Mario Urrutia 3.00 8.00
169 Martellus Bennett 4.00 10.00
170 Martin Rucker 4.00 10.00
171 Matt Flynn 25.00 60.00
172 Matt Forte 15.00 40.00
173 Matt Ryan/100 40.00 100.00
174 Mike Hart 5.00 12.00
175 Mike Jenkins/155 5.00 12.00
176 Owen Schmitt/155 5.00 12.00
177 Paul Smith 5.00 12.00
178 Philip Wheeler 4.00 10.00
179 Quentin Groves/155 4.00 10.00
180 Quintin Demps 5.00 12.00
181 Rashard Mendenhall 15.00 40.00
182 Ray Rice 15.00 40.00
183 Ryan Clady 5.00 12.00
184 Ryan Torain 5.00 12.00
185 Sam Baker 3.00 8.00
186 Anthony Morelli 4.00 10.00
187 Sedrick Ellis 5.00 12.00
188 Dexter Jackson 4.00 10.00
190 Steve Slaton 5.00 12.00
191 Tashard Choice 4.00 10.00
192 Terrell Thomas 4.00 10.00
193 Thomas Brown 4.00 10.00
194 Tom Zbikowski 5.00 12.00
195 Gosder Cherilus 4.00 10.00
196 Trevor Laws 5.00 12.00
197 Vernon Gholston 4.00 10.00
199 Xavier Adibi 3.00 8.00

2008 Upper Deck Icons Rookie Autographs Rainbow Die Cut

*DIE CUT/25: .6X TO 1.5X AU/135-155
DIE CUT PRINT RUN 25 SER.#'d SETS
145 Joe Flacco 60.00 120.00
173 Matt Ryan 125.00 200.00

2008 Upper Deck Icons Rookie Brilliance Silver

SILVER PRINT RUN 799 SER.#'d SETS
*BLUE/250: .5X TO 1.2X SILVER/799
BLUE PRINT RUN 250 SER.#'d SETS
*GOLD/99: .6X TO 1.5X SILVER/799
GOLD PRINT RUN 99 SER.#'d SETS
RB1 Donnie Avery .60 1.50
RB2 Jake Long .75 2.00
RB3 Brian Brohm .75 2.00
RB4 Chad Henne .75 2.00
RB5 Chris Johnson 2.00 5.00
RB6 Chris Long .75 2.00
RB7 Devin Thomas .60 1.50
RB8 Darren McFadden 2.00 5.00
RB9 Earl Bennett .75 2.00
RB10 Glenn Dorsey .75 2.00
RB11 DeSean Jackson 1.50 4.00
RB12 Harry Douglas .60 1.50
RB13 Early Doucet .60 1.50
RB14 Andre Caldwell .60 1.50
RB15 Felix Jones 1.25 3.00
RB16 Dustin Keller .75 2.00
RB17 Jamaal Charles 1.25 3.00
RB18 Joe Flacco 2.50 6.00
RB19 John David Booty .60 1.50
RB20 Jonathan Stewart 1.25 3.00
RB21 Jordy Nelson 1.00 2.50
RB22 Jerome Simpson .75 2.00
RB23 Kevin Smith .75 2.00
RB24 Limas Sweed .75 2.00
RB25 Malcolm Kelly .60 1.50
RB26 Mario Manningham .75 2.00
RB27 James Hardy .60 1.50
RB28 Matt Forte 1.25 3.00
RB29 Matt Ryan 3.00 8.00
RB30 Dexter Jackson .60 1.50
RB31 Eddie Royal .75 2.00
RB32 Rashard Mendenhall 1.50 4.00
RB33 Ray Rice 1.50 4.00
RB34 Steve Slaton .75 2.00
RB35 Kevin O'Connell .60 1.50

2008 Upper Deck Icons Rookie Brilliance Autographs

STATED PRINT RUN 125-199
RB1 Donnie Avery/165 4.00 10.00
RB2 Jake Long/199 5.00 12.00
RB3 Brian Brohm/125 5.00 12.00
RB4 Chad Henne/165 15.00 40.00
RB5 Chris Johnson/165 25.00 60.00
RB6 Chris Long/165 5.00 12.00
RB7 Devin Thomas/165 4.00 10.00
RB8 Darren McFadden/125 20.00 50.00
RB9 Earl Bennett/165 5.00 12.00
RB10 Glenn Dorsey/165 5.00 12.00
RB11 DeSean Jackson/165 15.00 40.00
RB12 Harry Douglas/199 4.00 10.00
RB13 Early Doucet/199 4.00 10.00
RB14 Andre Caldwell/165 4.00 10.00
RB15 Felix Jones/165 15.00 40.00
RB16 Dustin Keller/199 5.00 12.00
RB17 Jamaal Charles/165 12.00 30.00
RB18 Joe Flacco/165 30.00 80.00
RB19 John David Booty/165 4.00 10.00
RB20 Jonathan Stewart/125 15.00 40.00
RB21 Jordy Nelson/165 10.00 25.00
RB22 Jerome Simpson/165 5.00 12.00
RB23 Kevin Smith/165 5.00 12.00
RB24 Limas Sweed/165 5.00 12.00
RB25 Malcolm Kelly/165 4.00 10.00
RB26 Mario Manningham/166 5.00 12.00
RB27 James Hardy/165 4.00 10.00
RB28 Matt Forte/165 12.00 30.00
RB29 Matt Ryan/125 40.00 100.00
RB30 Dexter Jackson/165 4.00 10.00
RB31 Eddie Royal/165 5.00 12.00
RB32 Rashard Mendenhall/165 15.00 40.00
RB33 Ray Rice/165 15.00 40.00
RB34 Steve Slaton/165 5.00 12.00
RB35 Kevin O'Connell/165 4.00 10.00

2008 Upper Deck Icons Rookie Brilliance Jersey Silver

SILVER PRINT RUN 199 SER.#'d SETS
*GOLD/99: .5X TO 1.2X SILVER/199
GOLD PRINT RUN 99 SER.#'d SETS
*PATCH/35: 1X TO 2.5X SILVER/199
PATCH PRINT RUN 35 SER.#'d SETS
RB1 Donnie Avery 2.00 5.00
RB2 Jake Long 2.50 6.00
RB3 Brian Brohm 2.50 6.00
RB4 Chad Henne 5.00 12.00
RB5 Chris Johnson 6.00 15.00
RB6 Chris Long 2.50 6.00
RB7 Devin Thomas 2.00 5.00
RB8 Darren McFadden 6.00 15.00
RB9 Earl Bennett 2.50 6.00
RB10 Glenn Dorsey 2.50 6.00
RB11 DeSean Jackson 5.00 12.00
RB12 Harry Douglas 2.00 5.00
RB13 Early Doucet 2.00 5.00
RB14 Andre Caldwell 2.00 5.00
RB15 Felix Jones 4.00 10.00
RB16 Dustin Keller 2.50 6.00
RB17 Jamaal Charles 4.00 10.00
RB18 Joe Flacco 8.00 20.00
RB19 John David Booty 2.00 5.00
RB20 Jonathan Stewart 5.00 12.00
RB21 Jordy Nelson 3.00 8.00
RB22 Jerome Simpson 2.50 6.00
RB23 Kevin Smith 2.50 6.00
RB24 Limas Sweed 2.50 6.00
RB25 Malcolm Kelly 2.00 5.00
RB26 Mario Manningham 2.50 6.00
RB27 James Hardy 2.00 5.00
RB28 Matt Forte 4.00 10.00
RB29 Matt Ryan 6.00 15.00
RB30 Dexter Jackson 2.00 5.00
RB31 Eddie Royal 2.50 6.00
RB32 Rashard Mendenhall 5.00 12.00
RB33 Ray Rice 5.00 12.00
RB34 Steve Slaton 2.50 6.00
RB35 Kevin O'Connell 2.00 5.00

2009 Upper Deck Icons

COMP.SET w/o SP's (100) 8.00 20.00
101-170 ROOKIE PRINT RUN 599
171-200 LEGEND PRINT RUN 599
1 Tony Romo .50 1.25
2 Marion Barber .25 .60
3 Terrell Owens .30 .75
4 Jason Witten .30 .75
5 DeMarcus Ware .25 .60
6 Eli Manning .30 .75
7 Brandon Jacobs .25 .60
8 Antonio Pierce .20 .50
9 Donovan McNabb .30 .75
10 Brian Westbrook .25 .60
11 DeSean Jackson .25 .60
12 Chris Cooley .25 .60
13 Jason Campbell .20 .50
14 Clinton Portis .25 .60
15 Santana Moss .25 .60
16 Tim Hightower .20 .50
17 Larry Fitzgerald .30 .75
18 Anquan Boldin .25 .60
19 Kurt Warner .30 .75
20 Frank Gore .25 .60
21 Patrick Willis .25 .60
22 Isaac Bruce .25 .60
23 Julius Jones .20 .50
24 Steven Jackson .25 .60
25 Matt Forte .30 .75
26 Brian Urlacher .30 .75
27 Kyle Orton .25 .60
28 Calvin Johnson .30 .75
29 Aaron Rodgers .60 1.50
30 Ryan Grant .25 .60
31 Greg Jennings .30 .75
32 A.J. Hawk .25 .60
33 Aaron Kampman .25 .60
34 Adrian Peterson .50 1.25
35 Matt Ryan .30 .75
36 Michael Turner .25 .60
37 Jake Delhomme .25 .60
38 Steve Smith .25 .60
39 DeAngelo Williams .30 .75
40 Drew Brees .30 .75
41 Reggie Bush .30 .75
42 Marques Colston .25 .60
43 Jonathan Vilma .20 .50
44 Earnest Graham .20 .50
45 Jeff Garcia .25 .60
46 Trent Edwards .20 .50
47 Marshawn Lynch .25 .60
48 Lee Evans .25 .60
49 Chad Pennington .25 .60
50 Ronnie Brown .25 .60
51 Joey Porter .25 .60
52 Tom Brady .50 1.25
53 Randy Moss .30 .75
54 Wes Welker .30 .75
55 Bart Scott .20 .50
56 Thomas Jones .25 .60
57 Laveranues Coles .20 .50
58 Jerricho Cotchery .25 .60
59 Jay Cutler .30 .75
60 Brandon Marshall .25 .60
61 Eddie Royal .25 .60
62 Tyler Thigpen .20 .50
63 Larry Johnson .25 .60
64 Dwayne Bowe .25 .60
65 Tony Gonzalez .25 .60
66 JaMarcus Russell .20 .50
67 Darren McFadden .30 .75
68 Philip Rivers .30 .75
69 LaDainian Tomlinson .30 .75
70 Antonio Gates .25 .60
71 Vincent Jackson .25 .60
72 Derrick Mason .25 .60
73 Ray Lewis .30 .75
74 Joe Flacco .30 .75
75 Carson Palmer .30 .75
76 Chad Johnson .25 .60
77 T.J. Houshmandzadeh .25 .60
78 Keith Rivers .20 .50
79 Jamal Lewis .25 .60
80 Brady Quinn .25 .60
81 Braylon Edwards .25 .60
82 Ben Roethlisberger .30 .75
83 Willie Parker .20 .50
84 Hines Ward .25 .60
85 Troy Polamalu .30 .75
86 James Harrison .30 .75
87 Steve Slaton .25 .60
88 Matt Schaub .25 .60
89 Andre Johnson .25 .60
90 Peyton Manning .50 1.25
91 Joseph Addai .30 .75
92 Reggie Wayne .25 .60
93 Bob Sanders .25 .60
94 David Garrard .25 .60
95 John Henderson .20 .50
96 Maurice Jones-Drew .25 .60
97 LenDale White .25 .60
98 Chris Johnson .30 .75
99 Albert Haynesworth .20 .50
100 Roddy White .25 .60
101 Matthew Stafford RC 8.00 20.00
102 Mark Sanchez RC 5.00 12.00
103 Eben Britton RC 1.25 3.00
104 Josh Freeman RC 3.00 8.00
105 Chris Wells RC 2.50 6.00
106 Javon Ringer RC 1.50 4.00
107 Knowshon Moreno RC 1.50 4.00
108 James Davis RC 1.50 4.00
109 Victor Harris RC 1.50 4.00
110 P.J. Hill RC 1.25 3.00
111 Michael Crabtree RC 3.00 8.00
112 Darrius Heyward-Bey RC 1.50 4.00
113 Jeremy Maclin RC 2.50 6.00
114 Percy Harvin RC 2.50 6.00
115 Brian Robiskie RC 1.50 4.00
116 Aaron Kelly RC 1.25 3.00
117 Kenny Britt RC 2.00 5.00
118 Ramses Barden RC 1.00 2.50
119 Alphonso Smith RC 1.25 3.00
120 Demetrius Byrd RC 1.25 3.00
121 Chase Coffman RC 1.25 3.00
122 Brandon Pettigrew RC 1.50 4.00
123 Clay Matthews RC 4.00 10.00
124 Fili Moala RC 1.25 3.00
125 Michael Oher RC 2.50 6.00
126 Andre Smith RC 1.25 3.00
127 Derek Pegues RC 1.00 2.50
128 Jason Smith RC 1.25 3.00
129 Duke Robinson RC 1.00 2.50
130 Max Unger RC 1.25 3.00
131 Hakeem Nicks RC 2.50 6.00
132 Alex Mack RC 1.25 3.00
133 Nate Davis RC 1.25 3.00
134 Andre Brown RC 1.00 2.50
135 Eugene Monroe RC 1.00 2.50
136 Alex Boone RC 1.50 4.00
137 Graham Harrell RC 1.50 4.00
138 Jonathan Luigs RC 1.00 2.50
139 Brian Orakpo RC 1.50 4.00
140 Patrick Chung RC 1.50 4.00
141 Austin Collie RC 1.50 4.00
142 Tyson Jackson RC 1.25 3.00
143 Michael Johnson RC 1.00 2.50
144 Devin Moore RC 1.25 3.00
145 Juaquin Iglesias RC 1.25 3.00
146 Quan Cosby RC 1.25 3.00
147 D.J. Moore RC 1.25 3.00
148 LeSean McCoy RC 3.00 8.00
149 Sean Smith RC 1.50 4.00
150 B.J. Raji RC 1.50 4.00
151 Jared Cook RC 1.50 4.00
152 Everette Brown RC 1.25 3.00
153 Cedric Peerman RC 1.25 3.00
154 James Laurinaitis RC 1.50 4.00
155 Rey Maualuga RC 1.50 4.00
156 Brandon Tate RC 1.50 4.00
157 Aaron Curry RC 1.50 4.00
158 Brian Cushing RC 1.50 4.00
159 Rashad Jennings RC 1.50 4.00
160 Marcus Freeman RC 1.50 4.00
161 Malcolm Jenkins RC 1.50 4.00
162 Vontae Davis RC 1.50 4.00
163 Mike Mickens RC 1.25 3.00
164 Derrick Williams RC 1.25 3.00
165 William Moore RC 1.50 4.00
166 Shonn Greene RC 2.50 6.00
167 Mohamed Massaquoi RC 1.25 3.00
168 Aaron Maybin RC 1.25 3.00
169 Donald Brown RC 1.50 4.00
170 Darius Butler RC 1.50 4.00
171 Bob Griese 2.00 5.00
172 Jack Youngblood 1.25 3.00
173 Thurman Thomas 2.00 5.00
174 Rocky Bleier 1.50 4.00
175 Jack Ham 1.50 4.00
176 Darrell Green 1.50 4.00
177 Paul Hornung 2.00 5.00
178 Ken Anderson 1.50 4.00
179 Joe Theismann 2.00 5.00
180 Barry Sanders 3.00 8.00
181 Bob Lilly 1.50 4.00
182 Merlin Olsen UER 1.50 4.00
(name misspelled Olson)
183 Fred Biletnikoff 2.00 5.00
184 Earl Campbell 2.00 5.00
185 Jim Kelly 2.00 5.00
186 Daryl Johnston 2.00 5.00
187 Mike Ditka 1.50 4.00
188 Lem Barney 1.25 3.00
189 Mike Singletary 2.00 5.00
190 Don Maynard 1.50 4.00
191 Anthony Munoz 1.50 4.00
192 Ron Yary 1.25 3.00
193 John Elway 3.00 8.00
194 Terry Bradshaw 2.50 6.00
195 Billy Sims 1.50 4.00
196 Bubba Smith 1.25 3.00
197 Jerry Kramer 1.50 4.00
198 Alan Page 1.50 4.00
199 Tom Rathman 1.25 3.00
200 Alex Karras 1.50 4.00

2009 Upper Deck Icons Gold Holofoil Die Cut

*VETS 1-100: 4X TO 10X BASIC CARDS
1-100 STATED PRINT RUN 75
*ROOKIES 101-170: .8X TO 2X
101-170 STATED PRINT RUN 50
*LEGENDS 171-200: 1.2X TO 3X
171-200 STATED PRINT RUN 25

2009 Upper Deck Icons Gold Foil

*VETS 1-100: 3X TO 8X BASIC CARDS
1-100 STATED PRINT RUN 125
*ROOKIES 101-170: .6X TO 1.5X
*LEGENDS 171-200: .6X TO 1.5X
101-200 STATED PRINT RUN 99

2009 Upper Deck Icons Rainbow Foil

*VETS: 1.5X TO 4X BASIC CARDS
RANDOM INSERTS IN RETAIL PACKS

2009 Upper Deck Icons Autographs

101-170 ROOKIE PRINT RUN 75-150
171-200 LEGEND PRINT RUN 5-25
101 Matthew Stafford/75 50.00 100.00
102 Mark Sanchez/75 50.00 100.00
103 Eben Britton 4.00 10.00
104 Josh Freeman/75 12.00 30.00
105 Chris Wells/75 20.00 50.00
106 Javon Ringer 6.00 15.00
107 Knowshon Moreno/75 30.00 60.00
108 James Davis 5.00 12.00
109 Victor Harris 5.00 12.00
110 P.J. Hill 4.00 10.00
111 Michael Crabtree/75 30.00 60.00
112 Darrius Heyward-Bey 5.00 12.00
113 Jeremy Maclin 15.00 40.00
114 Percy Harvin 30.00 50.00
115 Brian Robiskie 5.00 12.00
116 Aaron Kelly 4.00 10.00
117 Kenny Britt 6.00 15.00
118 Ramses Barden 3.00 8.00
119 Alphonso Smith 4.00 10.00
120 Demetrius Byrd 4.00 10.00
121 Chase Coffman 4.00 10.00
122 Brandon Pettigrew 5.00 12.00
123 Clay Matthews 25.00 50.00
124 Fili Moala 4.00 10.00
125 Michael Oher 25.00 50.00
126 Andre Smith 6.00 15.00
127 Derek Pegues 3.00 8.00
128 Jason Smith 4.00 10.00
129 Duke Robinson 3.00 8.00
130 Max Unger 5.00 12.00
131 Hakeem Nicks 8.00 20.00
132 Alex Mack 5.00 12.00
133 Nate Davis 4.00 10.00
134 Andre Brown 3.00 8.00
135 Eugene Monroe 3.00 8.00
136 Alex Boone 5.00 12.00
137 Graham Harrell 8.00 20.00
138 Jonathan Luigs 3.00 8.00
139 Brian Orakpo 5.00 12.00
140 Patrick Chung 6.00 15.00
141 Austin Collie 5.00 12.00
142 Tyson Jackson 4.00 10.00
143 Michael Johnson 3.00 8.00
144 Devin Moore 4.00 10.00
145 Juaquin Iglesias 4.00 10.00
146 Quan Cosby 4.00 10.00
147 D.J. Moore 4.00 10.00
148 LeSean McCoy 10.00 25.00
149 Sean Smith 5.00 12.00
150 B.J. Raji 5.00 12.00
151 Jared Cook 5.00 12.00
153 Cedric Peerman 4.00 10.00
154 James Laurinaitis 5.00 12.00
155 Rey Maualuga 5.00 12.00
156 Brandon Tate 5.00 12.00
157 Aaron Curry 5.00 12.00
158 Brian Cushing 5.00 12.00
159 Rashad Jennings 5.00 12.00
160 Marcus Freeman 5.00 12.00
161 Malcolm Jenkins 5.00 12.00
162 Vontae Davis 5.00 12.00
163 Mike Mickens 4.00 10.00
164 Derrick Williams 4.00 10.00
165 William Moore 5.00 12.00
166 Shonn Greene 15.00 30.00
167 Mohamed Massaquoi 4.00 10.00
169 Donald Brown/75 10.00 25.00
170 Darius Butler 6.00 15.00
174 Rocky Bleier/25 20.00 40.00
178 Ken Anderson/25 20.00 40.00
181 Bob Lilly/25 12.00 30.00
188 Lem Barney/25 12.00 30.00
191 Anthony Munoz/25 12.00 30.00
198 Alan Page/25 12.00 30.00
199 Tom Rathman/25 12.00 30.00
200 Alex Karras/25 12.00 30.00

2009 Upper Deck Icons Class of 2009 Silver

SILVER PRINT RUN 450 SER.#'d SETS
*GOLD/130: .5X TO 1.2X SILVER/450
AC Aaron Curry 1.00 2.50
AS Andre Smith .75 2.00
BC Brian Cushing 1.00 2.50
BO Brian Orakpo 1.00 2.50
BP Brandon Pettigrew 1.00 2.50
BR Brian Robiskie 1.00 2.50
CC Chase Coffman .75 2.00
CM Clay Matthews 2.50 6.00
CW Chris Wells 1.50 4.00
DB Donald Brown 1.00 2.50
DH Darrius Heyward-Bey 1.00 2.50
DW Derrick Williams .75 2.00
EB Everette Brown .75 2.00
HN Hakeem Nicks 1.50 4.00
JD James Davis 1.00 2.50
JF Josh Freeman 2.00 5.00
JI Juaquin Iglesias .75 2.00
JL James Laurinaitis 1.00 2.50
JM Jeremy Maclin 1.50 4.00
JO Michael Johnson .60 1.50
JR Javon Ringer 1.00 2.50
KB Kenny Britt 1.25 3.00
KM Knowshon Moreno 1.00 2.50
LM LeSean McCoy 2.00 5.00
MC Michael Crabtree 2.00 5.00
MJ Malcolm Jenkins 1.00 2.50
MS Mark Sanchez 3.00 8.00
MU Louis Murphy 1.00 2.50
ND Nate Davis .75 2.00
PH Percy Harvin 1.50 4.00
RJ Rashad Jennings 1.00 2.50
RM Rey Maualuga 1.00 2.50
SG Shonn Greene 1.50 4.00
ST Matthew Stafford 5.00 12.00
VD Vontae Davis 1.00 2.50

2009 Upper Deck Icons Class of 2009 Autographs

STATED PRINT RUN 50-99
AC Aaron Curry/99 5.00 12.00
AS Andre Smith/99 4.00 10.00
BC Brian Cushing/99 5.00 12.00
BO Brian Orakpo/99 5.00 12.00
BP Brandon Pettigrew/99 5.00 12.00
BR Brian Robiskie/99 5.00 12.00
CC Chase Coffman/99 4.00 10.00
CM Clay Matthews/99 25.00 50.00
CW Chris Wells/50 15.00 40.00
DB Donald Brown/50 5.00 12.00
DH Darrius Heyward-Bey/50 5.00 12.00
DW Derrick Williams/99 4.00 10.00
HN Hakeem Nicks/99 8.00 20.00
JD James Davis/99 5.00 12.00
JF Josh Freeman/50 15.00 40.00
JI Juaquin Iglesias/99 4.00 10.00
JL James Laurinaitis/99 5.00 12.00
JM Jeremy Maclin/50 15.00 40.00
JO Michael Johnson/99 4.00 10.00
JR Javon Ringer/99 5.00 12.00
KB Kenny Britt/99 6.00 15.00
KM Knowshon Moreno/50 20.00 50.00
LM LeSean McCoy/99 10.00 25.00
MC Michael Crabtree/50 20.00 50.00
MJ Malcolm Jenkins/99 5.00 12.00
MS Mark Sanchez/50 50.00 100.00
ND Nate Davis/99 4.00 10.00
PH Percy Harvin/99 25.00 50.00
RJ Rashad Jennings/99 5.00 12.00
RM Rey Maualuga/99 5.00 12.00
SG Shonn Greene/99 8.00 20.00
ST Matthew Stafford/50 50.00 100.00
VD Vontae Davis/99 5.00 12.00

2009 Upper Deck Icons Decade of Dominance Silver

SILVER PRINT RUN 450 SER.#'d SETS
*GOLD/130: .6X TO 1.5X SILVER/450
DDAP Adrian Peterson 2.50 6.00
DDBR Ben Roethlisberger 1.50 4.00
DDBU Brian Urlacher 1.50 4.00
DDBW Brian Westbrook 1.25 3.00
DDCJ Calvin Johnson 1.50 4.00
DDCP Clinton Portis 1.25 3.00
DDCU Jay Cutler 1.50 4.00
DDDB Derrick Brooks 1.25 3.00
DDDC Dallas Clark 1.25 3.00
DDDF Dwight Freeney 1.25 3.00
DDDH Devin Hester 1.50 4.00
DDDS Darren Sharper 1.25 3.00
DDDW DeMarcus Ware 1.25 3.00
DDEM Eli Manning 1.50 4.00
DDER Ed Reed 1.25 3.00
DDFA Brett Favre 4.00 10.00
DDFG Frank Gore 1.25 3.00
DDGJ Greg Jennings 1.50 4.00
DDHO T.J. Houshmandzadeh 1.25 3.00
DDHW Hines Ward 1.25 3.00
DDJA Jared Allen 1.50 4.00
DDJH James Harrison 1.50 4.00
DDJP Joey Porter 1.25 3.00
DDJW Jason Witten 1.50 4.00
DDLB Lance Briggs 1.25 3.00
DDLF Larry Fitzgerald 1.50 4.00
DDMB Marion Barber 1.25 3.00
DDMJ Maurice Jones-Drew 1.25 3.00
DDMW Mario Williams 1.25 3.00
DDNA Nnamdi Asomugha 1.25 3.00
DDPM Peyton Manning 2.50 6.00
DDPR Philip Rivers 1.50 4.00
DDPW Patrick Willis 1.25 3.00
DDRW Reggie Wayne 1.25 3.00
DDSJ Steven Jackson 1.25 3.00
DDTB Tom Brady 2.50 6.00
DDTO LaDainian Tomlinson 1.50 4.00
DDTP Troy Polamalu 1.50 4.00
DDTR Tony Romo 2.50 6.00
DDWJ Walter Jones 1.00 2.50

2009 Upper Deck Icons Decade of Dominance Jerseys

STATED PRINT RUN 150-199
DDBR Ben Roethlisberger/199 4.00 10.00
DDBU Brian Urlacher/199 4.00 10.00
DDBW Brian Westbrook/199 3.00 8.00
DDCP Clinton Portis/199 3.00 8.00
DDCU Jay Cutler/199 4.00 10.00
DDDC Dallas Clark/199 3.00 8.00
DDDH Devin Hester/199 4.00 10.00
DDDW DeMarcus Ware/199 3.00 8.00
DDEM Eli Manning/199 4.00 10.00
DDFA Brett Favre/199 10.00 25.00
DDFG Frank Gore/199 3.00 8.00
DDHO T.J. Houshmandzadeh/199 3.00 8.00
DDHW Hines Ward/199 4.00 10.00
DDJA Jared Allen/199 4.00 10.00
DDJW Jason Witten/150 4.00 10.00
DDLF Larry Fitzgerald/199 4.00 10.00
DDMJ Maurice Jones-Drew/199 3.00 8.00
DDPM Peyton Manning/199 6.00 15.00
DDPR Philip Rivers/150 4.00 10.00
DDPW Patrick Willis/199 3.00 8.00
DDRW Reggie Wayne/199 3.00 8.00
DDSJ Steven Jackson/199 3.00 8.00
DDTB Tom Brady/199 8.00 20.00
DDTO LaDainian Tomlinson/199 4.00 10.00
DDTP Troy Polamalu/199 6.00 15.00
DDTR Tony Romo/199 6.00 15.00

2009 Upper Deck Icons Greats of the Game Silver

SILVER PRINT RUN 450 SER.#'d SETS
*DIE CUT/40: 1X TO 2.5X SILVER/450
*GOLD/199: .5X TO 1.2X SILVER/450
GGBG Bob Griese 1.50 4.00
GGBJ Bo Jackson 2.00 5.00
GGBS Barry Sanders 2.50 6.00
GGDB Dick Butkus 2.00 5.00
GGDJ Daryl Johnston 1.50 4.00
GGES Emmitt Smith 2.50 6.00
GGFH Franco Harris 1.50 4.00
GGGS Gale Sayers 2.00 5.00
GGJE John Elway 2.50 6.00
GGJH Jack Ham 1.25 3.00
GGJT Joe Theismann 1.50 4.00
GGKW Kellen Winslow Sr. 1.25 3.00
GGMD Mike Ditka 1.25 3.00
GGPH Paul Hornung 1.50 4.00
GGRS Roger Staubach 2.00 5.00
GGSI Billy Sims 1.25 3.00
GGST Bart Starr 2.50 6.00
GGSY Steve Young 2.00 5.00
GGTA Troy Aikman 2.00 5.00
GGTB Terry Bradshaw 2.00 5.00

2009 Upper Deck Icons Greats of the Game Jerseys

STATED PRINT RUN 99 SER.#'d SETS
GGBG Bob Griese 6.00 15.00
GGBJ Bo Jackson 8.00 20.00
GGBS Barry Sanders 10.00 25.00
GGDB Dick Butkus 8.00 20.00
GGDJ Daryl Johnston 10.00 25.00
GGES Emmitt Smith 10.00 25.00
GGFH Franco Harris 6.00 15.00
GGGS Gale Sayers 8.00 20.00
GGJE John Elway 10.00 25.00
GGJT Joe Theismann 6.00 15.00
GGKW Kellen Winslow Sr. 5.00 12.00
GGPH Paul Hornung 6.00 15.00
GGRS Roger Staubach 10.00 25.00
GGSI Billy Sims 5.00 12.00
GGSY Steve Young 8.00 20.00
GGTA Troy Aikman 8.00 20.00
GGTB Terry Bradshaw 8.00 20.00

2009 Upper Deck Icons Immortal Lettermen

TOTAL PRINT RUNS 430-630
STATED PRINT RUNS 62-150
ILAK Alex Karras/105 5.00 12.00
(Letters spell out LIONS
Total print run 525)
ILAP Alan Page/76 5.00 12.00
(Letters spell out VIKINGS
Total print run 532)
ILBG Bob Griese/75 8.00 20.00
(Letters spell out DOLPHINS
Total print run 600)
ILBL Bobby Layne/86 6.00 15.00
(Letters spell out LIONS
Total print run 430)
ILBP Brian Piccolo/125 6.00 15.00
(Letters spell out BEARS
Total print run 600)
ILBT Bulldog Turner/86 5.00 12.00
(Letters spell out BEARS
Total print run 430)
ILCB Chuck Bednarik/87/88 5.00 12.00
(Letters spell out EAGLES
Total print run 528)
ILCH Chuck Howley/75/76 5.00 12.00
(Letters spell out COWBOYS
Total print run 525)
ILCR Roger Craig/105 5.00 12.00
(Letters spell out 49ERS
Total print run 525)
ILDJ Deacon Jones/131 5.00 12.00
(Letters spell out RAMS
Total print run 524)
ILDM Don Maynard/131 5.00 12.00
(Letters spell out JETS
Total print run 524)
ILEC Earl Campbell/99/100 6.00 15.00
(Letters spell out OILERS
Total print run 594)
ILED Eric Dickerson/150 5.00 12.00
(Letters spell out RAMS
Total print run 600)
ILEJ Ed Jones/75/76 5.00 12.00
(Letters spell out
Total print run 525)
ILFB Fred Biletnikoff/86/87 10.00 25.00
(Letters spell out RAIDERS
Total print run 609)
ILFH Franco Harris/74/75 8.00 20.00
(Letters spell out STEELERS
Total print run 592)
ILGH George Halas/86 6.00 15.00
(Letters spell out BEARS
Total print run 430)
ILGS Gale Sayers/120 8.00 20.00
(Letters spell out BEARS
Total print run 600)
ILHC Harry Carson/87/88 5.00 12.00
(Letters spell out GIANTS
Total print run 522)
ILJG Joe Greene/74/75 8.00 20.00
(Letters spell out STEELERS
Total print run 592)
ILJK Jerry Kramer/76 5.00 12.00
(Letters spell out PACKERS
Total print run 532)
ILJR Jerry Rice/124 15.00 40.00
(Letters spell out 49ERS
Total print run 620)
ILJU Johnny Unitas/126 10.00 25.00
(Letters spell out COLTS
Total print run 630)
ILJZ Jim Zorn/65/66 5.00 12.00
(Letters spell out SEAHAWKS
Total print run 520)
ILKW Kellen Winslow Sr./71/72 5.00 12.00
(Letters spell out CHARGERS
Total print run 568)
ILMD Mike Ditka/120 6.00 15.00
(Letters spell out BEARS
Total print run 600)
ILMO Merlin Olsen/131 5.00 12.00
(Letters spell out RAMS
Total print run 524)
ILMS Mike Singletary/115 6.00 15.00
(Letters spell out BEARS
Total print run)
ILPS Phil Simms/99/100 5.00 12.00
(Letters spell out GIANTS
Total print run 600)
ILRB Rocky Bleier/65/66 6.00 15.00
(Letters spell out STEELERS
Total print run 520)
ILRC Randall Cunningham/99/100 8.00 20.00
(Letters spell out EAGLES
Total print run 594)
ILRG Roman Gabriel/131 6.00 15.00
(Letters spell out RAMS
Total print run 524)
ILTB Terry Bradshaw/75 10.00 25.00
(Letters spell out STEELERS
Total print run 600)
ILTT Thurman Thomas/120 6.00 15.00
(Letters spell out BILLS
Total print run 600)
ILVL Vince Lombardi/62 8.00 20.00
(Letters spell out PACKERS
Total print run 434)
ILYT Y.A. Tittle/104 5.00 12.00
(Letters spell out GIANTS
Total print run 624)
ILBL1 Bob Lilly/75/76 6.00 15.00
(Letters spell out COWBOYS
Total print run 525)
ILPH1 Paul Hornung/82/83 6.00 15.00
(Letters spell out PACKERS
Total print run 574)

2009 Upper Deck Icons Immortal Lettermen Autographs

TOTAL AUTO PRINT RUNS 24-104
AUTO STATED PRINT RUNS 3-25
ILAK Alex Karras/20 15.00 40.00
(Letters spell out LIONS
Total print run 100)
ILAP Alan Page/14 25.00 60.00
(Letters spell out VIKINGS
Total print run 98)
ILBL Bob Lilly/14 15.00 40.00
(Letters spell out COWBOYS
Total print run 98)
ILCH Chuck Howley/14/15 25.00 50.00
(Letters spell out COWBOYS
Total print run 98)
ILCR Roger Craig/20 12.00 30.00
(Letters spell out 49ERS
Total print run 100)
ILDJ Deacon Jones/25 12.00 30.00
(Letters spell out RAMS
Total print run 100)
ILDM Don Maynard/25 15.00 40.00
(Letters spell out JETS
Total print run 100)
ILEC Earl Campbell/4 25.00 50.00
(Letters spell out OILERS
Total print run 24)
ILEJ Ed Jones/14 15.00 40.00
Lettters spell out COWBOYS
Total print run 98)
ILFH Franco Harris/3 40.00 80.00
(Letters spell out STEELERS
Total print run 24)
ILHC Harry Carson/17 12.00 30.00
(Letters spell out GIANTS
Total print run 102)
ILJK Jerry Kramer/14 20.00 50.00
(Letters spell out PACKERS
Total print run 98)
ILJZ Jim Zorn/12 12.00 30.00
(Letters spell out SEAHAWKS

Total print run 96)
ILKW Kellen Winslow Sr./6 25.00 50.00
(Letters spell out CHARGERS
Total print run 48)
ILGS Gale Sayers/5 25.00 50.00
(Letters spell out BEARS
Total print run 25)
ILMO Merlin Olsen/25 15.00 40.00
(Letters spell out RAMS
Total print run 100)
ILPH Paul Hornung/7 20.00 50.00
(Letters spell out PACKERS
Total print run 49)
ILPS Phil Simms/4 40.00 80.00
(Letters spell out GIANTS
Total print run 24)
ILRB Rocky Bleier/13 30.00 60.00
(Letters spell out STEELERS
Total print run 104)
ILRC Randall Cunningham/5 30.00 60.00
Letters spell out EAGLES
Total print run 30)
ILRG Roman Gabriel/25 15.00 40.00
Letters spell out RAMS
Total print run 100)
ILTT Thurman Thomas/5 30.00 60.00
(Letters spell out BILLS
Total print run 25)

2009 Upper Deck Icons Movie Lettermen

TOTAL PRINT RUNS 216-555
STATED PRINT RUNS 20-111
MLAH Anthony Michael Hall/45/46 4.00 10.00
(Letters spell out JOHNNY WALKER
Total print run 540)
MLBB Beau Bridges/49/50 4.00 10.00
(Letters spell out MATT CUSHMAN
Total print run 539)
MLCH Corey Haim/111 4.00 10.00
(Letters spell out LUCAS
Total print run 555)
MLEB Ernest Borgnine/42/43 4.00 10.00
(Letters spell out VINCE LOMBARDI
Total print run 546)
MLHW Henry Winkler/22 4.00 10.00
(Letters spell out COACH KLEIN
Total print run 220)
MLLH Lauren Holley/20 5.00 12.00
(Letters spell out CINDY ROONEY
Total print run 220)
MLMR Mickey Rourke EXCH 4.00 10.00
MLSA Sean Astin/56 4.00 10.00
(Letters spell out RUDY
Total print run 224)
MLSB Scott Bakula/24/25 5.00 12.00
(Letters spell out PAUL BLAKE
Total print run 216)
MMBJ Bruce Jenner/22 4.00 10.00
(Letters spell out JIM GREGORY
Total print run 220)
MMCS Charlie Sheen/37/38 4.00 10.00
(Letters spell out CAPPIE
Total print run 222)

2009 Upper Deck Icons Movie Lettermen Autographs

TOTAL AUTO PRINT RUN 100
AUTO STATED PRINT RUNS 10-20
MLAH Anthony Michael Hall EXCH 12.50 25.00
(Letters spell out / Total print run)
MLCH Corey Haim 90.00 150.00
(Letters spell out / Total print run)
MLEB Ernest Borgnine 15.00 30.00
(Letters spell out / Total print run)
MLHW Henry Winkler/10 20.00 40.00
(Letters spell out / Total print run)
MLMR Mickey Rourke EXCH 15.00 30.00
(Letters spell out / Total print run)

2009 Upper Deck Icons NFL Icons Silver

SILVER PRINT RUN 450 SER.#'d SETS
*GOLD/199: .5X TO 1.2X SILVER/450
*DIE CUT/40: .8X TO 2X SILVER/450
ICAG Antonio Gates 1.25 3.00
ICAP Adrian Peterson 2.50 6.00
ICBA Brandon Jacobs 1.25 3.00
ICBD Brian Dawkins 1.25 3.00
ICBF Brett Favre 4.00 10.00
ICBH Braylon Edwards 1.25 3.00
ICBM Brandon Marshall 1.25 3.00
ICBR Drew Brees 1.50 4.00
ICCB Champ Bailey 1.25 3.00
ICCC Chris Cooley 1.25 3.00
ICCJ Chad Johnson 1.25 3.00
ICCP Clinton Portis 1.25 3.00
ICDB Deion Branch 1.25 3.00
ICDC Dallas Clark 1.25 3.00
ICDD Donald Driver 1.25 3.00
ICDG David Garrard 1.25 3.00
ICDI DeAngelo Williams 1.50 4.00
ICDM Donovan McNabb 1.50 4.00
ICDW DeMarcus Ware 1.25 3.00
ICEJ Edgerrin James 1.25 3.00
ICFG Frank Gore 1.25 3.00
ICHW Hines Ward 1.25 3.00
ICJA Joseph Addai 1.50 4.00
ICJC Jay Cutler 1.50 4.00
ICJL Jamal Lewis 1.25 3.00
ICJP Julius Peppers 1.25 3.00
ICJT Jason Taylor 1.25 3.00
ICKW Kellen Winslow Jr. 1.25 3.00
ICLE Lee Evans 1.25 3.00
ICLJ Larry Johnson 1.25 3.00
ICLT LaDainian Tomlinson 1.50 4.00
ICMB Marc Bulger 1.25 3.00
ICMC Marques Colston 1.25 3.00
ICMH Marvin Harrison 1.50 4.00
ICMJ Maurice Jones-Drew 1.25 3.00
ICMK Matt Hasselbeck 1.25 3.00
ICML Marshawn Lynch 1.25 3.00
ICPM Peyton Manning 2.50 6.00
ICPW Patrick Willis 1.25 3.00
ICRB Ronde Barber 1.00 2.50
ICRL Ray Lewis 1.50 4.00
ICRR Ronnie Brown 1.25 3.00
ICRU Reggie Bush 1.50 4.00
ICSH Santonio Holmes 1.25 3.00
ICSJ Steven Jackson 1.25 3.00
ICSS Steve Smith 1.25 3.00
ICTB Tom Brady 2.50 6.00
ICTG Tony Gonzalez 1.25 3.00
ICVJ Vincent Jackson 1.25 3.00
ICWP Willie Parker 1.00 2.50

2009 Upper Deck Icons NFL Icons Jerseys

STATED PRINT RUN 299 SER.#'d SETS
ICAG Antonio Gates 3.00 8.00
ICBA Brandon Jacobs 3.00 8.00
ICBD Brian Dawkins 3.00 8.00
ICBF Brett Favre 10.00 25.00
ICBH Braylon Edwards 3.00 8.00
ICBM Brandon Marshall 3.00 8.00
ICBR Drew Brees 4.00 10.00
ICCB Champ Bailey 3.00 8.00
ICCJ Chad Johnson 3.00 8.00
ICCP Clinton Portis 3.00 8.00
ICDB Deion Branch 3.00 8.00
ICDC Dallas Clark 3.00 8.00
ICDD Donald Driver 3.00 8.00
ICDG David Garrard 3.00 8.00
ICDI DeAngelo Williams 4.00 10.00
ICDM Donovan McNabb 4.00 10.00
ICDW DeMarcus Ware 3.00 8.00
ICEJ Edgerrin James 3.00 8.00
ICFG Frank Gore 3.00 8.00
ICHW Hines Ward 3.00 8.00
ICJA Joseph Addai 4.00 10.00
ICJC Jay Cutler 4.00 10.00
ICJL Jamal Lewis 3.00 8.00
ICJP Julius Peppers 3.00 8.00
ICJT Jason Taylor 3.00 8.00
ICKW Kellen Winslow Jr. 3.00 8.00
ICLE Lee Evans 3.00 8.00
ICLJ Larry Johnson 3.00 8.00
ICLT LaDainian Tomlinson 4.00 10.00
ICMB Marc Bulger 3.00 8.00
ICMC Marques Colston 3.00 8.00
ICMH Marvin Harrison 4.00 10.00
ICMJ Maurice Jones-Drew 3.00 8.00
ICMK Matt Hasselbeck 3.00 8.00
ICML Marshawn Lynch 3.00 8.00
ICPM Peyton Manning 6.00 15.00
ICPW Patrick Willis 3.00 8.00
ICRB Ronde Barber 2.50 6.00
ICRL Ray Lewis 4.00 10.00
ICRR Ronnie Brown 3.00 8.00
ICRU Reggie Bush 4.00 10.00
ICSH Santonio Holmes 3.00 8.00
ICSJ Steven Jackson 3.00 8.00
ICSS Steve Smith 3.00 8.00
ICTB Tom Brady 6.00 15.00
ICTG Tony Gonzalez 3.00 8.00
ICVJ Vincent Jackson 3.00 8.00
ICWP Willie Parker 2.50 6.00

2009 Upper Deck Icons NFL Reflections Silver

SILVER PRINT RUN 450 SER.#'d SETS
*GOLD/199: .5X TO 1.2X SILVER/450
*DIE CUT/40: .8X TO 2X SILVER/450
RFAP Joseph Addai 1.50 4.00
Willie Parker
RFBB Champ Bailey 1.25 3.00
Ronde Barber
RFBE Braylon Edwards 1.25 3.00
Deion Branch
RFBJ Maurice Jones-Drew 1.25 3.00
Ronnie Brown
RFBV Mike Vrabel 1.25 3.00
Tody Bruschi
RFCE Lee Evans 1.25 3.00
Marques Colston
RFDJ Andre Johnson 1.25 3.00
Donald Driver
RFDS Aaron Schobel 1.25 3.00
Vernon Davis
RFGC Antonio Gates 1.25 3.00
Dallas Clark
RFGH Jeff Garcia 1.25 3.00
Matt Hasselbeck
RFGY David Garrard 1.25 3.00
Vince Young
RFHH Devin Hester 1.50 4.00
Santonio Holmes
RFJC Michael Jenkins 1.00 2.50
Ronald Curry
RFJG Edgerrin James 1.25 3.00
Frank Gore
RFJL Brandon Jacobs 1.25 3.00
Jamal Lewis
RFJM Deuce McAllister 1.25 3.00
Larry Johnson
RFLW DeAngelo Williams 1.50 4.00
Marshawn Lynch
RFMC Donovan McNabb 1.50 4.00
Jay Cutler
RFMS Darren Sproles 1.25 3.00
Laurence Maroney
RFMW Ben Watson 1.25 3.00
Heath Miller
RFQS Brady Quinn 1.25 3.00
Matt Schaub
RFRH Aaron Ross 1.00 2.50
Michael Huff
RFSJ Steve Smith 1.25 3.00
Vincent Jackson
RFSP Alex Smith 1.50 4.00
Carson Palmer
RFTP Jason Taylor 1.25 3.00
Julius Peppers

2009 Upper Deck Icons NFL Reflections Jerseys

STATED PRINT RUN 99 SER.#'d SETS
RFAP Joseph Addai 6.00 15.00
Willie Parker
RFBB Champ Bailey 5.00 12.00
Ronde Barber
RFBE Braylon Edwards 5.00 12.00
Deion Branch
RFBJ Maurice Jones-Drew 5.00 12.00
Ronnie Brown
RFBV Mike Vrabel 5.00 12.00
Tedy Bruschi
RFCE Lee Evans 5.00 12.00
Marques Colston
RFDJ Andre Johnson 5.00 12.00
Donald Driver
RFDS Aaron Schobel 5.00 12.00
Vernon Davis
RFGC Antonio Gates 5.00 12.00
Dallas Clark
RFGH Jeff Garcia 5.00 12.00
Matt Hasselbeck
RFGY David Garrard 5.00 12.00
Vince Young
RFHH Devin Hester 6.00 15.00
Santonio Holmes
RFJC Michael Jenkins 4.00 10.00
Ronald Curry
RFJG Edgerrin James 5.00 12.00
Frank Gore
RFJL Brandon Jacobs 5.00 12.00
Jamal Lewis
RFJM Deuce McAllister 5.00 12.00
Larry Johnson
RFLW DeAngelo Williams 6.00 15.00
Marshawn Lynch
RFMC Donovan McNabb 6.00 15.00
Jay Cutler
RFMS Darren Sproles 5.00 12.00
Laurence Maroney
RFMW Ben Watson 5.00 12.00
Heath Miller
RFQS Brady Quinn 5.00 12.00
Matt Schaub
RFRH Aaron Ross 4.00 10.00
Michael Huff
RFSJ Steve Smith 5.00 12.00
Vincent Jackson
RFSP Alex Smith 6.00 15.00
Carson Palmer
RFTP Jason Taylor 5.00 12.00
Julius Peppers

2009 Upper Deck Icons Sophomore Sensations Silver

SILVER PRINT RUN 450 SER.#'d SETS
*GOLD/130: .5X TO 1.2X SILVER/450
SSBB Brian Brohm 1.00 2.50
SSCJ Chris Johnson 1.50 4.00
SSDA Donnie Avery 1.25 3.00
SSDJ DeSean Jackson 1.25 3.00
SSDK Dustin Keller 1.00 2.50
SSDM Darren McFadden 1.50 4.00
SSEB Earl Bennett 1.25 3.00
SSED Early Doucet 1.25 3.00
SSER Eddie Royal 1.25 3.00
SSFJ Felix Jones 1.50 4.00
SSHD Harry Douglas 1.00 2.50
SSJB John David Booty 1.25 3.00
SSJC Jamaal Charles 1.50 4.00
SSJF Joe Flacco 1.50 4.00
SSJH James Hardy 1.25 3.00
SSJN Jordy Nelson 1.50 4.00
SSJS Jonathan Stewart 1.25 3.00
SSKS Kevin Smith 1.25 3.00
SSLS Limas Sweed 1.25 3.00
SSMF Matt Forte 1.50 4.00
SSMK Malcolm Kelly 1.00 2.50
SSMR Matt Ryan 1.50 4.00

2009 Upper Deck Icons Sophomore Sensations Jerseys

STATED PRINT RUN 299 SER.#'d SETS
SSBB Brian Brohm 2.50 6.00
SSCJ Chris Johnson 4.00 10.00
SSDA Donnie Avery 3.00 8.00
SSDJ DeSean Jackson 3.00 8.00
SSDK Dustin Keller 2.50 6.00
SSDM Darren McFadden 4.00 10.00
SSEB Earl Bennett 3.00 8.00
SSER Eddie Royal 3.00 8.00
SSFJ Felix Jones 4.00 10.00
SSHD Harry Douglas 2.50 6.00
SSJB John David Booty 3.00 8.00
SSJC Jamaal Charles 4.00 10.00
SSJF Joe Flacco 4.00 10.00
SSJH James Hardy 3.00 8.00
SSJN Jordy Nelson 4.00 10.00
SSJS Jonathan Stewart 3.00 8.00
SSKS Kevin Smith 3.00 8.00
SSLS Limas Sweed 3.00 8.00
SSMF Matt Forte 4.00 10.00
SSMK Malcolm Kelly 2.50 6.00
SSMR Matt Ryan 4.00 10.00

2009 Upper Deck Icons Sophomore Sensations Autographs

STATED PRINT RUN 50 SER.#'d SETS
SSBB Brian Brohm/50 8.00 20.00
SSCJ Chris Johnson/50 12.00 30.00
SSDA Donnie Avery/50 10.00 25.00
SSDJ DeSean Jackson/50 10.00 25.00
SSDK Dustin Keller/50 8.00 20.00
SSEB Earl Bennett/50 10.00 25.00
SSED Early Doucet/50 10.00 25.00
SSER Eddie Royal/50 10.00 25.00
SSFJ Felix Jones/50 12.00 30.00
SSHD Harry Douglas/50 8.00 20.00
SSJB John David Booty/50 10.00 25.00
SSJC Jamaal Charles/50 12.00 30.00
SSJF Joe Flacco/50 12.00 30.00
SSJH James Hardy/50 10.00 25.00
SSJN Jordy Nelson/50 12.00 30.00
SSJS Jonathan Stewart/30 12.00 30.00
SSKS Kevin Smith/50 10.00 25.00
SSLS Limas Sweed/50 10.00 25.00
SSMF Matt Forte/50 12.00 30.00
SSMK Malcolm Kelly/50 8.00 20.00

2009 Upper Deck Icons Sports Lettermen

TOTAL PRINT RUNS 250-297
STATED PRINT RUNS 25-43
SLKY Kristi Yamaguchi 5.00 12.00
(Letters spell out / Total print run)
SLLD Lindsay Davenport/33 4.00 10.00
(Letters spell out DAVENPORT
Total print run 297)
SLLH Laird Hamilton/37 5.00 12.00
(Letters spell out / Total print run)
SLMJ Michael Johnson track 5.00 12.00
(Letters spell out / Total print run)
SLPD Phil Dalhausser 5.00 12.00
(Letters spell out / Total print run)
SLPF Peggy Fleming/42 4.00 10.00
(Letters spell out FLEMING
Total print run 294)

2009 Upper Deck Icons Sports Lettermen Autographs

SLKY Kristi Yamaguchi/3 50.00 100.00
(Letters spell out YAMAGUCHI/ Total print run 27)
SLMJ Michael Johnson track 20.00 40.00
(Letters spell out / Total print run)
SLPD Phil Dalhausser 15.00 30.00
(Letters spell out / Total print run)
SLPF Peggy Fleming 20.00 40.00
(Letters spell out / Total print run)

2009 Upper Deck Icons Sweet Spot Icons Autographs

SSIAH Anthony Michael Hall 15.00 30.00
SSIAM Archie Manning/98 30.00 60.00
SSIBS Billy Sims EXCH
SSICF Carrie Fisher EXCH
SSICH Corey Haim/120 60.00 100.00
SSIJP Jeremy Piven/50 40.00 80.00
SSIKA Ken Anderson/60 20.00 40.00
SSIKK Kim Kardashian/55 75.00 125.00
SSIPB Pete Best EXCH
SSIRC Roger Craig/60 20.00 40.00
SSIRK Mickey Rourke/50 25.00 50.00
SSISS Scottie Schwartz/100 12.50 25.00
SSITR Tom Rathman/100 20.00 40.00

2008 Upper Deck Kellogg's Autographs

JR Jerry Rice 30.00 60.00
JT Joe Theismann 8.00 20.00

2005 Upper Deck Kickoff

This 135-card set was released through Upper Deck retail channels in August, 2005. The set was issued in six-card packs which came 24 packs to a box. Cards numbered 1-100 feature veteran players in team alphabetical order while cards numbered 91-135 featured 2005 rookies. Those rookies were inserted at a stated rate of one per pack.

COMPLETE SET (135) 20.00 50.00
COMP.SET w/o RC's (90) 7.50 20.00
ONE DRAFT PICK PER PACK
1 Larry Fitzgerald .20 .50
2 Anquan Boldin .15 .40
3 Josh McCown .15 .40
4 Michael Vick .20 .50
5 Alge Crumpler .15 .40
6 Peerless Price .12 .30
7 Ray Lewis .20 .50
8 Kyle Boller .15 .40
9 Derrick Mason .15 .40
10 J.P. Losman .12 .30
11 Willis McGahee .20 .50
12 Eric Moulds .12 .30
13 Jake Delhomme .15 .40
14 DeShaun Foster .15 .40
15 Steve Smith .20 .50
16 Thomas Jones .20 .50
17 Rex Grossman .15 .40
18 Muhsin Muhammad .15 .40
19 Carson Palmer .20 .50
20 Rudi Johnson .15 .40
21 Chad Johnson .15 .40
22 Julius Jones .12 .30
23 Keyshawn Johnson .15 .40
24 Drew Bledsoe .20 .50
25 Tatum Bell .12 .30
26 Jake Plummer .15 .40
27 Ashley Lelie .12 .30
28 Roy Williams WR .15 .40
29 Kevin Jones .12 .30
30 Joey Harrington .15 .40
31 Brett Favre .50 1.25
32 Ahman Green .15 .40
33 Javon Walker .12 .30
34 David Carr .12 .30
35 Andre Johnson .20 .50
36 Domanick Davis .12 .30
37 Peyton Manning .40 1.00
38 Reggie Wayne .20 .50
39 Marvin Harrison .20 .50
40 Byron Leftwich .15 .40
41 Fred Taylor .15 .40
42 Jimmy Smith .15 .40
43 Priest Holmes .15 .40
44 Larry Johnson .15 .40
45 Trent Green .15 .40
46 A.J. Feeley .12 .30
47 Chris Chambers .15 .40
48 Randy McMichael .12 .30
49 Daunte Culpepper .15 .40
50 Michael Bennett .15 .40
51 Nate Burleson .12 .30
52 Tom Brady .40 1.00
53 Corey Dillon .15 .40
54 Deion Branch .12 .30
55 Aaron Brooks .12 .30
56 Deuce McAllister .15 .40
57 Joe Horn .15 .40
58 Eli Manning .30 .75
59 Jeremy Shockey .20 .50
60 Tiki Barber .20 .50
61 Chad Pennington .20 .50
62 Curtis Martin .20 .50
63 Kerry Collins .15 .40
64 Jerry Porter .12 .30
65 Randy Moss .20 .50
66 Donovan McNabb .20 .50
67 Terrell Owens .20 .50
68 Brian Westbrook .15 .40
69 Ben Roethlisberger .30 .75
70 Jerome Bettis .20 .50
71 Hines Ward .20 .50
72 Drew Brees .20 .50
73 LaDainian Tomlinson .20 .50
74 Antonio Gates .20 .50
75 Kevan Barlow .12 .30
76 Eric Johnson .12 .30
77 Shaun Alexander .15 .40
78 Matt Hasselbeck .15 .40
79 Marc Bulger .15 .40
80 Steven Jackson .20 .50
81 Torry Holt .15 .40
82 Michael Pittman .12 .30
83 Brian Griese .15 .40
84 Michael Clayton .12 .30
85 Steve McNair .20 .50
86 Drew Bennett .15 .40
87 Chris Brown .12 .30
88 Clinton Portis .15 .40
89 Patrick Ramsey .15 .40
90 Santana Moss .15 .40
91 Aaron Rodgers RC 7.50 15.00
92 Alex Smith QB RC .75 2.00
93 Charlie Frye RC .50 1.25
94 Andrew Walter RC .40 1.00
95 Jason Campbell RC .60 1.50
96 Derek Anderson RC .40 1.00
97 David Greene RC .30 .75
98 Ronnie Brown RC .60 1.50
99 Cadillac Williams RC .50 1.25
100 Cedric Benson RC .50 1.25
101 Ciatrick Fason RC .30 .75
102 Vernand Morency RC .40 1.00
103 Matt Jones RC .50 1.25
104 Maurice Clarett .40 1.00
105 Mike Williams .50 1.25
106 Braylon Edwards RC .60 1.50
107 Mark Clayton RC .50 1.25
108 Reggie Brown RC .30 .75
109 Troy Williamson RC .40 1.00
110 Roddy White RC .60 1.50
111 Jerome Mathis RC .50 1.25
112 Heath Miller RC .60 1.50
113 Antrel Rolle RC .50 1.25
114 Adam Jones RC .40 1.00
115 Vincent Jackson RC .60 1.50
116 Alex Smith TE RC .30 .75
117 Marcus Spears RC .40 1.00
118 Courtney Roby RC .40 1.00
119 Stefan LeFors RC .30 .75
120 Derrick Johnson RC .40 1.00
121 Shawne Merriman RC .50 1.25
122 Thomas Davis RC .30 .75
123 Marlin Jackson RC .30 .75
124 Ryan Moats RC .40 1.00
125 Dan Orlovsky RC .50 1.25
126 Kyle Orton RC .50 1.25
127 Adrian McPherson RC .30 .75
128 Eric Shelton RC .30 .75
129 Chris Henry RC .50 1.25
130 Carlos Rogers RC .50 1.25
131 Roscoe Parrish RC .30 .75
132 J.J. Arrington RC .40 1.00
133 Mark Bradley RC .30 .75
134 Frank Gore RC .75 2.00
135 Terrence Murphy RC .30 .75

2005 Upper Deck Kickoff Autographs

UNPRICED AUTO STATED ODDS 1:480
KSAW Andrew Walter 8.00 20.00
KSCF Ciatrick Fason 8.00 20.00
KSCJ Chad Johnson
KSCW Corey Webster
KSDA Derek Anderson 8.00 20.00
KSDD Domanick Davis
KSDO Dan Orlovsky 8.00 20.00
KSEJ Erasmus James
KSEM Eli Manning SP
KSFG Fred Gibson 6.00 15.00
KSJA J.J. Arrington 8.00 20.00
KSJB James Butler
KSJH Joe Horn
KSJJ Julius Jones SP
KSJW Jason White 8.00 20.00
KSKC Keary Colbert
KSKH Kay-Jay Harris
KSKO Kyle Orton
KSMB Marc Bulger SP
KSMC Michael Clayton SP
KSMJ Marlin Jackson
KSMM Muhsin Muhammad
KSNB Nate Burleson
KSRB Ronnie Brown SP
KSRJ Rudi Johnson 10.00 25.00
KSRP Roscoe Parrish
KSRW Reggie Wayne
KSTA T.A. McLendon
KSTM Terrence Murphy 8.00 20.00
KSVM Vernand Morency

2005 Upper Deck Kickoff Game Jerseys

STATED ODDS 1:24
KJAD Andre Davis 2.50 6.00
KJBL Byron Leftwich 4.00 10.00
KJBU Brian Urlacher 4.00 10.00
KJBW Brian Westbrook 3.00 8.00
KJCD Corey Dillon 4.00 10.00
KJCH Chad Pennington 4.00 10.00
KJCR Charles Rogers 3.00 8.00
KJDA David Carr 4.00 10.00
KJDB Drew Bledsoe 4.00 10.00
KJDC Daunte Culpepper 4.00 10.00
KJDM Derrick Mason 3.00 8.00
KJDS Donte Stallworth 3.00 8.00
KJEJ Edgerrin James 4.00 10.00
KJFM Freddie Mitchell 2.50 6.00
KJHW Hines Ward 4.00 10.00
KJIB Isaac Bruce 3.00 8.00
KJJH Joey Harrington 4.00 10.00
KJJL Jamal Lewis 4.00 10.00
KJJP Jerry Porter 3.00 8.00
KJJS Jeremy Shockey 4.00 10.00
KJJT Jason Taylor 2.50 6.00
KJKW Kelley Washington 2.50 6.00
KJMC Deuce McAllister 4.00 10.00
KJMS Michael Strahan 3.00 8.00
KJPP Peerless Price 2.50 6.00
KJRM Randy Moss 4.00 10.00
KJSM Jimmy Smith 3.00 8.00
KJST Steve McNair 3.00 8.00
KJTH Torry Holt 4.00 10.00
KJTP Todd Heap 2.50 6.00

1997 Upper Deck Legends

This 208-card set was distributed in packs with a suggested retail price of $4.99 and features color action photos of some of the league's all-time great players. The set contains the following two subsets: Legendary Leaders, which honors ten great coaches, and Super Bowl Memories, which features photographs by Walter Iooss, Jr., of behind the scenes of the Super Bowl.

COMPLETE SET (208) 30.00 80.00
1 Bart Starr 1.00 2.50
2 Jim Brown 1.00 2.50
3 Joe Namath 1.25 3.00
4 Walter Payton 2.00 5.00
5 Terry Bradshaw 1.25 3.00
6 Franco Harris .25 .60
7 Dan Fouts .25 .60
8 Steve Largent .25 .60
9 Johnny Unitas 1.00 2.50
10 Gale Sayers .60 1.50
11 Roger Staubach 1.25 3.00
12 Tony Dorsett .25 .60
13 Fran Tarkenton .60 1.50
14 Charley Taylor .15 .40
15 Ray Nitschke .25 .60
16 Jim Ringo .15 .40
17 Dick Butkus .60 1.50
18 Fred Biletnikoff .25 .60
19 Lenny Moore .15 .40
20 Len Dawson .25 .60
21 Lance Alworth .15 .40
22 Chuck Bednarik .15 .40
23 Raymond Berry .15 .40
24 Donnie Shell .10 .30
25 Mel Blount .15 .40
26 Willie Brown .15 .40
27 Ken Houston .10 .30
28 Larry Csonka .25 .60
29 Mike Ditka .50 1.25
30 Art Donovan .15 .40
31 Sam Huff .15 .40
32 Lem Barney .10 .30
33 Hugh McElhenny .15 .40
34 Otto Graham .30 .75
35 Joe Greene .25 .60
36 Mike Rozier .10 .30
37 Lou Groza .15 .40
38 Ted Hendricks .10 .30
39 Elroy Hirsch .15 .40
40 Paul Hornung .30 .75
41 Charlie Joiner .15 .40
42 Deacon Jones .15 .40
43 Bill Bradley .10 .30
44 Floyd Little .10 .30
45 Willie Lanier .10 .30
46 Bob Lilly .15 .40
47 Sid Luckman .15 .40
48 John Mackey .10 .30
49 Don Maynard .15 .40
50 Mike McCormack .10 .30
51 Bobby Mitchell .15 .40
52 Ron Mix .10 .30
53 Marion Motley .10 .30
54 Leo Nomellini .10 .30
55 Mark Duper .10 .30
56 Mel Renfro .10 .30
57 Jim Otto .15 .40
58 Alan Page .15 .40
59 Joe Perry .15 .40
60 Andy Robustelli .10 .30
61 Lee Roy Selmon .10 .30
62 Jackie Smith .15 .40
63 Art Shell .15 .40
64 Jan Stenerud .10 .30
65 Gene Upshaw .15 .40
66 Y.A. Tittle .25 .60
67 Paul Warfield .25 .60
68 Kellen Winslow .15 .40
69 Randy White .15 .40
70 Larry Wilson .10 .30
71 Willie Wood .15 .40
72 Jack Ham .15 .40
73 Jack Youngblood .10 .30
74 Dan Abramowicz .10 .30
75 Dick Anderson .10 .30
76 Ken Anderson .15 .40
77 Steve Bartkowski .10 .30
78 Bill Bergey .10 .30
79 Rocky Bleier .15 .40
80 Cliff Branch .15 .40
81 John Brodie .10 .30
82 Bobby Bell .10 .30
83 Billy Cannon .10 .30
84 Gino Cappelletti .10 .30
85 Harold Carmichael .10 .30
86 Dave Casper .10 .30
87 Wes Chandler .10 .30
88 Todd Christensen .10 .30
89 Dwight Clark .15 .40
90 Mark Clayton .10 .30
91 Cris Collinsworth .10 .30
92 Roger Craig .15 .40
93 Randy Cross .10 .30
94 Isaac Curtis .10 .30
95 Mike Curtis .10 .30
96 Ben Davidson .10 .30
97 Fred Dean .10 .30
98 Tom Dempsey .10 .30
99 Eric Dickerson .15 .40
100 Lynn Dickey .10 .30
101 John McKay LL .10 .30
102 Carl Eller .10 .30
103 Chuck Foreman .10 .30
104 Russ Francis .10 .30
105 Joe Gibbs LL .15 .40
106 Gary Garrison .10 .30
107 Randy Gradishar .10 .30
108 L.C. Greenwood .15 .40
109 Rosey Grier .10 .30
110 Steve Grogan .10 .30
111 Ray Guy .10 .30
112 John Hadl .10 .30
113 Jim Hart .10 .30
114 George Halas LL .15 .40
115 Mike Haynes .10 .30
116 Charlie Hennigan .10 .30
117 Chuck Howley .10 .30
118 Harold Jackson .10 .30
119 Tom Jackson .10 .30
120 Ron Jaworski .10 .30
121 John Jefferson .10 .30
122 Billy Johnson .10 .30
123 Ed Too Tall Jones .15 .40
124 Jack Kemp .60 1.50
125 Jim Kiick .10 .30
126 Billy Kilmer .15 .40
127 Jerry Kramer .15 .40
128 Paul Krause .10 .30
129 Daryle Lamonica .10 .30
130 Bill Walsh LL .15 .40
131 James Lofton .10 .30
132 Hank Stram LL .10 .30
133 Archie Manning .15 .40
134 Jim Marshall .10 .30
135 Harvey Martin .10 .30
136 Tommy McDonald .10 .30
137 Max McGee .15 .40
138 Reggie McKenzie .10 .30
139 Karl Mecklenburg .10 .30
140 Tom Landry LL .25 .60
141 Terry Metcalf .10 .30
142 Matt Millen .10 .30
143 Earl Morrall .10 .30
144 Mercury Morris .10 .30
145 Chuck Noll LL .15 .40
146 Joe Morris .10 .30
147 Mark Moseley .10 .30
148 Haven Moses .10 .30
149 Chuck Muncie .10 .30
150 Anthony Munoz .15 .40
151 Tommy Nobis .10 .30
152 Babe Parilli .10 .30
153 Drew Pearson .15 .40
154 Ozzie Newsome .10 .30
155 Jim Plunkett .15 .40
156 William Perry .10 .30
157 Johnny Robinson .10 .30
158 Ahmad Rashad .15 .40
159 George Rogers .10 .30
160 Sterling Sharpe .15 .40
161 Billy Sims .15 .40
162 Sid Gillman LL .10 .30
163 Mike Singletary .25 .60
164 Charlie Sanders .10 .30
165 Bubba Smith .10 .30
166 Ken Stabler .75 2.00
167 Freddie Solomon .10 .30
168 John Stallworth .15 .40
169 Dwight Stephenson .15 .40
170 Vince Lombardi LL .40 1.00
171 Weeb Ewbank LL .10 .30
172 Lionel Taylor .10 .30
173 Otis Taylor .10 .30
174 Joe Theismann .25 .60
175 Bob Trumpy .10 .30
176 Mike Webster .10 .30
177 Jim Zorn .10 .30
178 Joe Montana 2.00 5.00
179 Packers Superbowl SM .15 .40
180 Bart Starr SM .50 1.25
181 Max McGee SM .15 .40
182 Joe Namath SM .60 1.50
183 Johnny Unitas SM .50 1.25
184 Len Dawson SM .15 .40
185 Chuck Howley SM .10 .30
186 Roger Staubach SM .60 1.50
187 Paul Warfield SM .15 .40
188 Larry Csonka SM .15 .40
189 Fran Tarkenton SM .25 .60
190 Terry Bradshaw SM .60 1.50
191 Ken Stabler SM .30 .75
192 Fred Biletnikoff SM .15 .40
193 Chuck Foreman SM .10 .30
194 Harvey Martin SM .10 .30
195 Tony Dorsett SM .15 .40
196 Terry Bradshaw SM .60 1.50
197 John Stallworth SM .10 .30
198 Franco Harris SM .15 .40
199 Ken Anderson SM .10 .30
200 Joe Theismann SM .15 .40
201 Jim Plunkett SM .10 .30
202 Roger Craig SM .10 .30
203 William Perry SM .10 .30
204 Steve Grogan SM .10 .30
205 Joe Montana SM 1.00 2.50
206 Huss Francis SM .10 .30
207 Joe Montana SM 1.00 2.50
208 Joe Montana SM 1.00 2.50

1997 Upper Deck Legends Autographs

STATED ODDS 1:5H, 1:7 SPEC.RET,1:10R
AL1 Bart Starr SP 500.00 800.00
AL2 Jim Brown SP 800.00 1,200.00
AL3 Joe Namath SP 600.00 800.00
AL4 Walter Payton SP 1,500.00 2,000.00
AL5 Terry Bradshaw SP 500.00 800.00
AL6 Franco Harris SP 450.00 700.00
AL7 Dan Fouts 25.00 50.00
AL8 Steve Largent 15.00 40.00
AL9 Johnny Unitas SP 1,200.00 2,000.00
AL10 Gale Sayers 25.00 50.00
AL11 Roger Staubach 125.00 200.00
AL12 Tony Dorsett SP 250.00 350.00
AL13 Fran Tarkenton 25.00 60.00
AL14 Charley Taylor 10.00 25.00
AL15 Ray Nitschke 90.00 175.00
AL16 Jim Ringo 40.00 80.00
AL17 Dick Butkus SP 600.00 1,000.00
AL18 Fred Biletnikoff 20.00 50.00
AL19 Lenny Moore 12.50 30.00
AL20 Len Dawson 30.00 60.00
AL21 Lance Alworth SP 90.00 175.00
AL22 Chuck Bednarik 25.00 50.00
AL23 Raymond Berry 12.50 30.00
AL24 Donnie Shell 12.50 30.00
AL25 Mel Blount 15.00 40.00
AL26 Willie Brown 12.50 30.00
AL27 Ken Houston 10.00 25.00
AL28 Larry Csonka SP 175.00 300.00
AL29 Mike Ditka 25.00 50.00
AL30 Art Donovan 20.00 50.00
AL31 Sam Huff 30.00 60.00
AL32 Lem Barney 12.50 30.00
AL33 Hugh McElhenny 12.00 30.00
AL34 Otto Graham 35.00 60.00
AL35 Joe Greene SP 175.00 300.00
AL36 Mike Rozier 15.00 40.00
AL37 Lou Groza 25.00 50.00
AL38 Ted Hendricks 10.00 25.00
AL39 Elroy Hirsch 40.00 80.00
AL40 Paul Hornung 20.00 50.00
AL41 Charlie Joiner 10.00 25.00
AL42 Deacon Jones 15.00 40.00
AL43 Bill Bradley 10.00 25.00
AL44 Floyd Little 10.00 25.00
AL45 Willie Lanier 25.00 50.00
AL46 Bob Lilly 25.00 50.00
AL47 Sid Luckman EXCH 1.25 3.00
AL48 John Mackey 15.00 40.00
AL49 Don Maynard 12.00 30.00
AL50 Mike McCormack 15.00 40.00
AL51 Bobby Mitchell 10.00 25.00
AL52 Ron Mix 15.00 40.00
AL53 Marion Motley 30.00 60.00
AL54 Leo Nomellini 40.00 80.00
AL55 Mark Duper 15.00 40.00
AL56 Mel Renfro 15.00 40.00
AL57 Jim Otto 15.00 40.00
AL58 Alan Page 15.00 40.00
AL59 Joe Perry 25.00 50.00
AL60 Andy Robustelli 15.00 40.00
AL61 Lee Roy Selmon 25.00 50.00
AL62 Jackie Smith 10.00 25.00
AL63 Art Shell SP 75.00 150.00
AL64 Jan Stenerud 15.00 40.00
AL65 Gene Upshaw 25.00 50.00
AL66 Y.A. Tittle 25.00 50.00
AL67 Paul Warfield 15.00 40.00
AL68 Kellen Winslow 25.00 50.00
AL69 Randy White 25.00 50.00
AL70 Larry Wilson 12.50 30.00
AL71 Willie Wood EXCH 1.25 3.00
AL72 Jack Ham 25.00 60.00
AL73 Jack Youngblood 12.50 30.00
AL74 Danny Abramowicz 10.00 25.00
AL75 Dick Anderson 12.50 30.00
AL76 Ken Anderson 10.00 25.00
AL77 Steve Bartkowski 12.50 30.00
AL78 Bill Bergey 10.00 25.00
AL79 Rocky Bleier 15.00 40.00
AL80 Cliff Branch 12.50 30.00
AL81 John Brodie 25.00 50.00
AL82 Bobby Bell 12.50 30.00
AL83 Billy Cannon SP 60.00 120.00
AL84 Gino Cappelletti 10.00 25.00
AL85 Harold Carmichael 10.00 25.00
AL86 Dave Casper 12.50 30.00
AL87 Wes Chandler 12.50 30.00
AL88 Todd Christensen 12.50 30.00
AL89 Dwight Clark 12.50 30.00
AL90 Mark Clayton 12.50 30.00
AL91 Cris Collinsworth 10.00 25.00
AL92 Roger Craig 12.50 30.00
AL93 Randy Cross 12.50 30.00
AL94 Isaac Curtis 10.00 25.00
AL95 Mike Curtis 12.50 30.00
AL96 Ben Davidson 10.00 25.00

AL97 Fred Dean EXCH	1.25	3.00
AL98 Tom Dempsey	10.00	25.00
AL99 Eric Dickerson	15.00	40.00
AL100 Lynn Dickey	15.00	40.00
AL102 Carl Eller	30.00	60.00
AL103 Chuck Foreman	12.50	30.00
AL104 Russ Francis SP		
AL104X Russ Francis EXCH	1.25	3.00
AL106 Gary Garrison	10.00	25.00
AL107 Randy Gradishar	10.00	25.00
AL108 L.C. Greenwood	15.00	40.00
AL109 Rosey Grier	20.00	50.00
AL110 Steve Grogan	12.50	30.00
AL111 Ray Guy	12.50	30.00
AL112 John Hadl	12.50	30.00
AL113 Jim Hart	10.00	25.00
AL115 Mike Haynes	15.00	40.00
AL116 Charlie Hennigan	10.00	25.00
AL117 Chuck Howley	12.50	30.00
AL118 Harold Jackson	10.00	25.00
AL119 Tom Jackson	12.50	30.00
AL120 Ron Jaworski	12.50	30.00
AL121 John Jefferson	12.50	30.00
AL122 Billy Johnson EXCH	1.25	3.00
AL123 Ed Too Tall Jones	20.00	50.00
AL124 Jack Kemp	40.00	80.00
AL125 Jim Kiick	12.50	30.00
AL126 Billy Kilmer	10.00	25.00
AL127 Jerry Kramer	20.00	50.00
AL128 Paul Krause	12.50	30.00
AL129 Daryle Lamonica	25.00	50.00
AL131 James Lofton	12.50	30.00
AL133 Archie Manning	15.00	40.00
AL134 Jim Marshall	30.00	60.00
AL135 Harvey Martin	25.00	50.00
AL136 Tommy McDonald	12.50	30.00
AL137 Max McGee	25.00	60.00
AL138 Reggie McKenzie	10.00	25.00
AL139 Karl Mecklenburg	10.00	25.00
AL141 Terry Metcalf	12.50	30.00
AL142 Matt Millen SP	50.00	100.00
AL143 Earl Morrall	12.50	30.00
AL144 Mercury Morris	12.50	30.00
AL146 Joe Morris	12.50	30.00
AL147 Mark Moseley	10.00	25.00
AL148 Haven Moses	10.00	25.00
AL149 Chuck Muncie	10.00	25.00
AL150 Anthony Munoz	12.50	30.00
AL151 Tommy Nobis	10.00	25.00
AL152 Babe Parilli	10.00	25.00
AL153 Drew Pearson	15.00	40.00
AL154 Ozzie Newsome	12.50	30.00
AL155 Jim Plunkett	12.50	30.00
AL156 William Perry	12.50	30.00
AL157 Johnny Robinson	12.50	30.00
AL158 Ahmad Rashad	12.50	30.00
AL159 George Rogers	20.00	50.00
AL160 Sterling Sharpe	15.00	40.00
AL161 Billy Sims	15.00	40.00
AL163 Mike Singletary	15.00	40.00
AL164 Charlie Sanders	12.50	30.00
AL165 Bubba Smith SP	125.00	250.00
AL166 Ken Stabler	60.00	120.00
AL167 Freddie Solomon	10.00	25.00
AL168 John Stallworth	15.00	40.00
AL169 Dwight Stephenson	15.00	40.00
AL172 Lionel Taylor	10.00	25.00
AL173 Otis Taylor SP	60.00	120.00
AL174 Joe Theismann	12.00	30.00
AL175 Bob Trumpy EXCH	1.25	3.00
AL176 Mike Webster SP	100.00	200.00
AL177 Jim Zorn	15.00	40.00
AL178 Joe Montana	300.00	500.00

1997 Upper Deck Legends Big Game Hunters

COMPLETE SET (20)	125.00	250.00
STATED ODDS 1:75, 1:58 SPEC.RETAIL		
B1 Joe Montana	15.00	40.00
B2 Bart Starr	10.00	25.00
B3 Roger Staubach	12.50	30.00
B4 Johnny Unitas	10.00	25.00
B5 Terry Bradshaw	12.50	30.00
B6 Ken Stabler	7.50	20.00
B7 Jim Plunkett	3.00	8.00
B8 Len Dawson	6.00	15.00
B9 Fran Tarkenton	7.50	20.00
B10 Dan Fouts	6.00	15.00
B11 Daryle Lamonica	3.00	8.00
B12 Y.A. Tittle	4.00	10.00
B13 Joe Namath	12.50	30.00
B14 Ken Anderson	4.00	10.00
B15 John Brodie	3.00	8.00
B16 Billy Kilmer	4.00	10.00
B17 Earl Morrall	3.00	8.00
B18 Jack Kemp	7.50	20.00
B19 Steve Grogan	3.00	8.00
B20 Joe Theismann	6.00	15.00

1997 Upper Deck Legends Marquee Matchups

COMPLETE SET (30)	40.00	100.00
STATED ODDS 1:17, 1:8 SPEC.RETAIL		
MM1 Joe Namath / Dan Fouts	2.50	6.00
MM2 John Unitas / Joe Namath	3.00	8.00
MM3 Len Dawson / Bart Starr	2.50	6.00
MM4 Roger Staubach / Fran Tarkenton	2.50	6.00
MM5 Terry Bradshaw / Ken Stabler	2.50	6.00
MM6 Joe Montana / Ken Anderson	4.00	10.00
MM7 Bart Starr / John Unitas	3.00	8.00
MM8 Joe Greene / Jim Kiick	2.00	5.00
MM9 Franco Harris / Walter Payton	4.00	10.00
MM10 Ken Stabler / Dan Fouts	2.50	6.00
MM11 Charlie Joiner / Steve Largent	1.25	3.00
MM12 James Lofton / Drew Pearson	1.25	3.00
MM13 John Brodie / Deacon Jones	1.25	3.00
MM14 Fred Biletnikoff / Don Maynard	2.00	5.00
MM15 Jim Brown / Chuck Bednarik	2.50	6.00
MM16 Ray Nitschke / Gale Sayers	2.50	6.00
MM17 Paul Hornung / Dick Butkus	2.50	6.00
MM18 Joe Montana / Eric Dickerson	4.00	10.00
MM19 Tony Dorsett / Mike Singletary	2.00	5.00
MM20 Billy Sims / Chuck Foreman	.75	2.00
MM21 Len Dawson / Willie Brown	1.25	3.00
MM22 Johnny Robinson / Larry Wilson	.75	2.00
MM23 Marion Motley / Raymond Berry	1.25	3.00
MM24 Ron Mix / Jim Otto	.75	2.00
MM25 Roger Staubach / Terry Bradshaw	3.00	8.00
MM26 Bob Lilly / Billy Kilmer	2.00	5.00
MM27 Ted Hendricks / Russ Francis	.75	2.00
MM28 Babe Parilli / Jack Kemp	2.00	5.00
MM29 Deacon Jones / Alan Page	2.00	5.00
MM30 Dick Butkus / Ray Nitschke	2.50	6.00

1997 Upper Deck Legends Sign of the Times

STATED PRINT RUN 100 SETS		
ST1 Joe Montana	200.00	350.00
ST2 Fran Tarkenton	60.00	120.00
ST3 Johnny Unitas	350.00	600.00
ST3X Johnny Unitas EXCH	4.00	10.00
ST4 Joe Namath	150.00	250.00
ST5 Terry Bradshaw	125.00	250.00
ST6 Jim Brown	100.00	200.00
ST7 Franco Harris	75.00	125.00
ST8 Walter Payton	500.00	800.00
ST9 Steve Largent	75.00	125.00
ST10 Bart Starr	175.00	300.00

2000 Upper Deck Legends

Released in late September 2000, Upper Deck NFL Legends was comprised of 132 cards. The set was divided up into 90 Veteran Player cards, 12 20th Century Legends cards sequentially numbered to 2500, and 30 Generation Y2K Rookie cards. Base cards have a blue border along the bottom card edge and silver foil highlights. NFL Legends was packaged in 24-pack boxes with packs containing five cards and carried a suggested retail price of $4.99.

COMPLETE SET (132)	200.00	400.00
COMP.SET w/o SP's (90)	7.50	20.00
1 Jake Plummer	.20	.50
2 Jamal Anderson	.20	.50
3 Doug Flutie	.25	.60
4 Jim Kelly	.30	.75
5 Dick Butkus	.40	1.00
6 Mike Singletary	.25	.60
7 Gale Sayers	.40	1.00
8 Boomer Esiason	.25	.60
9 Anthony Munoz	.20	.50
10 Otto Graham	.20	.50
11 Jim Brown	.40	1.00
12 Ozzie Newsome	.15	.40
13 Bob Lilly	.20	.50
14 Troy Aikman	.40	1.00
15 Emmitt Smith	.60	1.50
16 Roger Staubach	.50	1.25
17 Deion Sanders	.25	.60
18 Tony Dorsett	.25	.60
19 Terrell Davis	.25	.60
20 John Elway	.60	1.50
21 Charlie Batch	.20	.50
22 Brett Favre	.75	2.00
23 Bart Starr	.60	1.50
24 Reggie White	.25	.60
25 Earl Campbell	.25	.60
26 Peyton Manning	.60	1.50
27 Edgerrin James	.25	.60
28 Johnny Unitas	.60	1.50
29 Marvin Harrison	.25	.60
30 Mark Brunell	.20	.50
31 Fred Taylor	.25	.60
32 Len Dawson	.25	.60
33 Dan Marino	.75	2.00
34 Bob Griese	.25	.60
35 Mark Duper	.20	.50
36 Thurman Thomas	.25	.60
37 Fran Tarkenton	.30	.75
38 Randy Moss	.25	.60
39 Cris Carter	.25	.60
40 Gary Anderson	.15	.40
41 John Randle	.20	.50
42 Drew Bledsoe	.25	.60
43 Archie Manning	.20	.50
44 Ricky Williams	.25	.60
45 Frank Gifford	.25	.60
46 Kerry Collins	.20	.50
47 Phil Simms	.25	.60
48 Vinny Testaverde	.20	.50
49 Curtis Martin	.25	.60
50 Keyshawn Johnson	.20	.50
51 Joe Namath	.50	1.25
52 Marcus Allen	.25	.60
53 Bruce Smith	.25	.60
54 Ken Stabler	.30	.75
55 Fred Biletnikoff	.25	.60
56 Howie Long	.25	.60
57 Ron Jaworski	.20	.50
58 Harold Carmichael	.15	.40
59 Kordell Stewart	.20	.50
60 Levon Kirkland	.15	.40
61 Mel Blount	.20	.50
62 Jerome Bettis	.25	.60
63 John Stallworth	.20	.50
64 Franco Harris	.25	.60
65 Jim Harbaugh	.20	.50
66 Kellen Winclow	.20	.50
67 Charlie Joiner	.15	.40
68 Junior Seau	.25	.60
69 Jerry Rice	.50	1.25
70 Steve Young	.30	.75
71 Joe Montana	.75	2.00
72 Roger Craig	.20	.50
73 Ronnie Lott	.25	.60
74 Jon Kitna	.20	.50
75 Steve Largent	.25	.60
76 Ricky Watters	.20	.50
77 Kurt Warner	.40	1.00
78 Marshall Faulk	.25	.60
79 Isaac Bruce	.25	.60
80 Merlin Olsen	.20	.50
81 Lee Roy Selmon	.20	.50
82 Tim Brown	.25	.60
83 Tim Couch	.20	.50
84 Mike Alstott	.25	.60
85 Eddie George	.20	.50
86 Steve McNair	.25	.60
87 Brad Johnson	.20	.50
88 Sonny Jurgensen	.25	.60
89 Art Monk	.20	.50
90 Joe Theismann	.25	.60
91 Ray Nitschke TCL	4.00	10.00
92 Doak Walker TCL	3.00	8.00
93 Thurman Thomas TCL	3.00	8.00
94 Jim Brown TCL	5.00	12.00
95 Sammy Baugh TCL	3.00	8.00
96 Reggie White TCL	3.00	8.00
97 Eric Dickerson TCL	2.50	6.00
98 Paul Hornung TCL	3.00	8.00
99 Deion Sanders TCL	3.00	8.00
100 Bronko Nagurski TCL	3.00	8.00
101 Walter Payton TCL	12.00	30.00
102 Jim Thorpe TCL	5.00	12.00
103 Ron Dayne RC	2.00	5.00
104 Tim Rattay RC	1.50	4.00
105 Brian Urlacher RC	8.00	20.00
106 Bubba Franks RC	2.00	5.00
107 Chad Pennington RC	3.00	8.00
108 Chris Cole RC	1.50	4.00
109 Chris Redman RC	1.50	4.00
110 Courtney Brown RC	1.50	4.00
111 Curtis Keaton RC	1.25	3.00
112 Dennis Northcutt RC	1.50	4.00
113 Dez White RC	1.50	4.00
114 Giovanni Carmazzi RC	1.25	3.00
115 J.R. Redmond RC	1.25	3.00
116 JaJuan Dawson RC	1.25	3.00
117 Jamal Lewis RC	2.00	5.00
118 Jerry Porter RC	2.00	5.00
119 Laveranues Coles RC	2.00	5.00
120 Peter Warrick RC	2.00	5.00
121 Plaxico Burress RC	2.00	5.00
122 R.Jay Soward RC	1.25	3.00
123 Reuben Droughns RC	2.00	5.00
124 Ron Dixon RC	1.25	3.00
125 Ron Dugans RC	1.25	3.00
126 Shaun Alexander RC	2.50	6.00
127 Sylvester Morris RC	1.25	3.00
128 Thomas Jones RC	2.50	6.00
129 Todd Pinkston RC	1.25	3.00
130 Travis Prentice RC	1.50	4.00
131 Travis Taylor RC	1.50	4.00
132 Trung Canidate RC	1.50	4.00

2000 Upper Deck Legends Autographs

STATED ODDS 1:47		
AM Archie Manning	10.00	25.00
AZ Anthony Munoz	10.00	25.00
BE Boomer Esiason	12.00	30.00
BG Bob Griese	12.00	30.00
BJ Brad Johnson	10.00	25.00
BL Drew Bledsoe	25.00	50.00
BL2 Bob Lilly	10.00	25.00
BR Mark Brunell	10.00	25.00
BS Bart Starr	75.00	150.00
CC Cris Carter	12.00	30.00
CJ Charlie Joiner	8.00	20.00
DA Terrell Davis	12.00	30.00
DB Dick Butkus	20.00	50.00
DF Doug Flutie	12.00	30.00
DM Dan Marino	125.00	250.00
EC Earl Campbell	25.00	50.00
EG Eddie George	12.00	30.00
EJ Edgerrin James	12.00	30.00
FB Fred Biletnikoff	12.00	30.00
FG Frank Gifford	30.00	60.00
FH Franco Harris	25.00	50.00
FT Fran Tarkenton	25.00	50.00
GS Gale Sayers	25.00	50.00
HC Harold Carmichael	8.00	20.00
HL Howie Long	25.00	60.00
IB Isaac Bruce	12.00	30.00
JA Jamal Anderson	10.00	25.00
JB Jerome Bettis	60.00	120.00
JB2 Jim Brown	60.00	120.00
JK Jim Kelly	40.00	80.00
JM Joe Montana	60.00	120.00
JN Joe Namath	50.00	100.00
JP Jake Plummer	10.00	25.00
JS John Stallworth	10.00	25.00
JT Joe Theismann	12.00	30.00
JU Johnny Unitas	250.00	400.00
KI Jon Kitna	10.00	25.00
KJ Keyshawn Johnson	10.00	25.00
KS Ken Stabler	25.00	50.00
KW Kellen Winslow	10.00	25.00
LD Len Dawson	20.00	50.00
LS Lee Roy Selmon	10.00	25.00
MA Marcus Allen	12.00	30.00
MB Mel Blount	10.00	25.00
MD Mark Duper	10.00	25.00
MH Marvin Harrison	25.00	50.00
MK Art Monk	15.00	40.00
MS Mike Singletary	12.00	30.00
OG Otto Graham	20.00	50.00
ON Ozzie Newsome	8.00	20.00
PM Peyton Manning	75.00	135.00
PS Phil Simms	15.00	40.00
RC Roger Craig	10.00	25.00
RI Ricky Watters	10.00	25.00
RJ Ron Jaworski	10.00	25.00
RL Ronnie Lott SP	300.00	450.00
RM Randy Moss	30.00	60.00
RS Roger Staubach	75.00	135.00
RW Ricky Williams EXCH	1.50	4.00
SJ Sonny Jurgensen	12.00	30.00
SL Steve Largent	12.00	30.00
SY Steve Young	30.00	60.00
TA Troy Aikman	50.00	100.00
TB Tim Brown	12.00	30.00
TC Tim Couch	10.00	25.00
TD Tony Dorsett	30.00	60.00
VT Vinny Testaverde	10.00	25.00
WA Kurt Warner	30.00	60.00

2000 Upper Deck Legends Autographs Gold

*GOLD/25: .8X TO 2X BASIC AUTO		
GOLD PRINT RUN 25 SER.#'d SETS		
BS Bart Starr	125.00	250.00
DM Dan Marino	250.00	400.00
JU Johnny Unitas	500.00	750.00
PM Peyton Manning	125.00	250.00
RL Ronnie Lott	200.00	400.00
RW Ricky Williams	4.00	8.00

2000 Upper Deck Legends Canton Calling

COMPLETE SET (6)	6.00	12.00
STATED ODDS 1:18		
CC1 Peyton Manning	2.00	5.00
CC2 Steve Young	1.00	2.50
CC3 Jerry Rice	1.50	4.00
CC4 Randy Moss	.75	2.00
CC5 Cris Carter	.75	2.00
CC6 Emmitt Smith	2.00	5.00

2000 Upper Deck Legends Defining Moments

COMPLETE SET (10)	7.50	20.00
STATED ODDS 1:9		
DM1 Terrell Davis	.50	1.25
DM2 Troy Aikman	.75	2.00
DM3 Jerry Rice	1.00	2.50
DM4 Walter Payton	2.00	5.00
DM5 Joe Namath	1.00	2.50
DM6 Emmitt Smith	1.25	3.00
DM7 Steve Young	.60	1.50
DM8 Franco Harris	.60	1.25
DM9 Kurt Warner	.75	2.00
DM10 Brett Favre	1.50	4.00

1997 Upper Deck Legends Jumbos

*JUMBOS: 3X TO 8X BASIC CARDS		
ONE PER SPECIAL RETAIL PACK		
101 John McKay LL	1.00	2.50

2000 Upper Deck Legends Legendary Jerseys

STATED ODDS 1:23		
LJBF Brett Favre	20.00	50.00
LJBL Bob Lilly	8.00	20.00
LJCB Cliff Branch	8.00	20.00
LJCH Charles Haley	8.00	20.00
LJDB Drew Bledsoe	10.00	25.00
LJDF Doug Flutie	10.00	25.00
LJDJ Daryl Johnston	10.00	25.00
LJDM Dan Marino	20.00	50.00
LJDS Deion Sanders	10.00	25.00
LJED Eric Dickerson	8.00	20.00
LJEM John Elway / Dan Marino	60.00	150.00
LJES Emmitt Smith	20.00	50.00
LJFB Fred Biletnikoff	10.00	25.00
LJFT Fran Tarkenton	15.00	40.00
LJGU Gene Upshaw	6.00	15.00
LJHL Howie Long	15.00	40.00
LJHW Herschel Walker	8.00	20.00
LJJA Jamal Anderson	8.00	20.00
LJJB John Brodie	10.00	30.00
LJJE John Elway	15.00	40.00
LJJM Joe Montana	20.00	50.00
LJJN Joe Namath	15.00	40.00
LJJP Jim Plunkett	8.00	20.00
LJJR Jerry Rice	15.00	40.00
LJKN Ken Norton Jr.	6.00	12.00
LJKS Ken Stabler	12.00	30.00
LJKW Kurt Warner	12.00	30.00
LJMA1 Marcus Allen	10.00	25.00
LJMA2 Marcus Allen SE	10.00	25.00
LJMB Mark Brunell	8.00	20.00
LJMF Marshall Faulk	10.00	25.00
LJMI Michael Irvin	10.00	25.00
LJNO Jay Novacek	8.00	20.00
LJOS Otis Sistrunk	6.00	15.00
LJPM Peyton Manning	20.00	50.00
LJRL Ronnie Lott	10.00	25.00
LJRM Randy Moss	8.00	20.00
LJRS Roger Staubach	15.00	40.00
LJRW Reggie White	10.00	25.00
LJSM Bruce Smith	10.00	25.00
LJSY Steve Young	12.00	30.00
LJTA Troy Aikman	15.00	40.00
LJTC Todd Christensen	6.00	15.00
LJTD Terrell Davis	10.00	25.00
LJTH1 Ted Hendricks	8.00	20.00
LJTH2 Ted Hendricks SE	8.00	20.00
LJVE Mark Van Eeghen	6.00	15.00
LJWM Warren Moon	10.00	25.00
LJWP Walter Payton	25.00	60.00

2000 Upper Deck Legends Millennium QBs

COMPLETE SET (10)	6.00	15.00
STATED ODDS 1:5		
M1 Joe Montana	1.25	3.00
M2 Dan Marino	1.25	3.00
M3 John Elway	1.00	2.50
M4 Fran Tarkenton	.50	1.25
M5 Sammy Baugh	.40	1.00
M6 Joe Namath	.75	2.00
M7 Warren Moon	.40	1.00
M8 Mark Brunell	.30	.75
M9 Brett Favre	1.25	3.00
M10 Drew Bledsoe	.40	1.00

2000 Upper Deck Legends Reflections in Time

COMPLETE SET (10)	6.00	15.00
STATED ODDS 1:11		
R1 Earl Campbell / Eddie George	.75	2.00
R2 Mike Singletary / Junior Seau	.75	2.00
R3 Doak Walker / Ricky Williams	.75	2.00
R4 Archie Manning / Peyton Manning	2.00	5.00
R5 Reggie White / Jevon Kearse	.75	2.00
R6 Harold Carmichael / Randy Moss	.75	2.00
R7 Gale Sayers / Edgerrin James	1.25	3.00
R8 Warren Moon / Daunte Culpepper	.75	2.00
R9 Roger Staubach / Troy Aikman	1.50	4.00
R10 Thurman Thomas / Marshall Faulk	.75	2.00

2000 Upper Deck Legends Rookie Gallery

COMPLETE SET (10)	10.00	25.00
STATED ODDS 1:21		
RG1 Peter Warrick	1.00	2.50
RG2 Chris Redman	.75	2.00
RG3 Courtney Brown	.75	2.00
RG4 Thomas Jones	1.25	3.00
RG5 Chad Pennington	1.50	4.00
RG6 Jamal Lewis	1.00	2.50
RG7 Plaxico Burress	1.00	2.50
RG8 Ron Dayne	1.00	2.50
RG9 Sylvester Morris	.60	1.50
RG10 Shaun Alexander	1.25	3.00

2001 Upper Deck Legends

This 180 card set featured a mix of veterans, retired players and 2001 NFL rookies. Cards numbered 91 through 180 were released in a lesser quantity than the other first 90 card in the set. Those cards were printed to a quantity of 750.

COMP.SET w/o SP's (90)	10.00	25.00
91-180 ROOKIE PRINT RUN 750		
1 Jake Plummer	.25	.60
2 Jamal Anderson	.25	.60
3 Ray Lewis	.30	.75
4 Johnny Unitas	.75	2.00
5 Jamal Lewis	.30	.75
6 Andre Reed	.30	.75
7 Jim Kelly	.50	1.25
8 Thurman Thomas	.30	.75
9 Rob Johnson	.25	.60
10 Brian Urlacher	.40	1.00
11 Dick Butkus	.50	1.25
12 Gale Sayers	.50	1.25
13 James Allen	.20	.50
14 Corey Dillon	.25	.60
15 Jim Brown	.60	1.50
16 Tim Couch	.20	.50
17 Joey Galloway	.25	.60
18 Emmitt Smith	.75	2.00
19 Randy White	.40	1.00
20 Roger Staubach	.60	1.50
21 Troy Aikman	.50	1.25
22 Tony Dorsett	.40	1.00
23 Brian Griese	.25	.60
24 Floyd Little	.25	.60
25 John Elway	1.00	2.50
26 Mike Anderson	.25	.60
27 Terrell Davis	.30	.75
28 Barry Sanders	.75	2.00
29 Charlie Batch	.25	.60
30 Bart Starr	.75	2.00
31 Paul Hornung	.40	1.00
32 Reggie White	.40	1.00
33 Warren Moon	.40	1.00
34 Edgerrin James	.30	.75
35 Peyton Manning	.75	2.00
36 Mark Brunell	.25	.60
37 Tony Gonzalez	.30	.75
38 Eric Dickerson	.30	.75
39 Jack Youngblood	.25	.60
40 Jay Fiedler	.25	.60
41 Lamar Smith	.25	.60
42 Dan Marino	1.00	2.50
43 Oronde Gadsden	.20	.50
44 Cris Carter	.30	.75
45 Fran Tarkenton	.50	1.25
46 Daunte Culpepper	.25	.60
47 Randy Moss	.30	.75
48 Robert Smith	.25	.60
49 Drew Bledsoe	.30	.75
50 Archie Manning	.30	.75
51 Jeff Blake	.25	.60
52 Ricky Williams	.30	.75
53 Kerry Collins	.25	.60
54 Ron Dayne	.25	.60
55 Lawrence Taylor	.40	1.00
56 Wayne Chrebet	.25	.60
57 Vinny Testaverde	.25	.60
58 Joe Namath	.60	1.50
59 Jim Plunkett	.30	.75
60 George Blanda	.40	1.00
61 Tim Brown	.30	.75
62 Jerry Rice	.60	1.50
63 Ken Stabler	.50	1.25
64 Marcus Allen	.40	1.00
65 Donovan McNabb	.30	.75
66 Harold Carmichael	.25	.60
67 Franco Harris	.40	1.00
68 Jerome Bettis	.30	.75
69 Terry Bradshaw	.60	1.50
70 Doug Flutie	.30	.75
71 Lance Alworth	.30	.75
72 Junior Seau	.30	.75
73 Kellen Winslow	.30	.75
74 Dan Fouts	.40	1.00
75 Joe Montana	1.00	2.50
76 Terrell Owens	.30	.75
77 Jeff Garcia	.25	.60
78 Steve Young	.50	1.25
79 Matt Hasselbeck	.30	.75
80 Kurt Warner	.50	1.25
81 Marshall Faulk	.30	.75
82 Brad Johnson	.25	.60
83 Eddie George	.30	.75
84 Charley Taylor	.30	.75
85 Stephen Davis	.25	.60
86 Jeff George	.25	.60
87 John Riggins	.40	1.00
88 Joe Theismann	.40	1.00
89 Michael Westbrook	.20	.50
90 Sonny Jurgensen	.40	1.00
91 Andre Carter RC	2.00	5.00
92 Cedrick Wilson RC	2.00	5.00
93 Kevan Barlow RC	2.00	5.00
94 Anthony Thomas RC	2.50	6.00
95 David Terrell RC	2.00	5.00
96 Chad Johnson RC	4.00	10.00
97 Justin Smith RC	2.50	6.00
98 Rudi Johnson RC	2.50	6.00
99 T.J. Houshmandzadeh RC	3.00	8.00
100 Brandon Spoon RC	2.00	5.00
101 Nate Clements RC	2.00	5.00
102 Travis Henry RC	2.00	5.00
103 Kevin Kasper RC	1.50	4.00
104 Willie Middlebrooks RC	2.00	5.00
105 Gerard Warren RC	2.00	5.00
106 James Jackson RC	1.50	4.00
107 Quincy Morgan RC	2.00	5.00
108 Bobby Newcombe RC	2.00	5.00
109 Arnold Jackson RC	1.50	4.00
110 Carlos Polk RC	1.50	4.00
111 Drew Brees RC	15.00	40.00
112 LaDainian Tomlinson RC	8.00	20.00
113 Tay Cody RC	1.50	4.00
114 Zeke Moreno RC	2.00	5.00
115 Snoop Minnis RC	1.50	4.00
116 George Layne RC	1.50	4.00
117 Derrick Blaylock RC	2.00	5.00
118 Reggie Wayne RC	5.00	12.00
119 Tony Dixon RC	1.50	4.00
120 Quincy Carter RC	2.00	5.00
121 Chris Chambers RC	2.50	6.00
122 Jamar Fletcher RC	1.50	4.00
123 Josh Heupel RC	2.50	6.00
124 Travis Minor RC	2.00	5.00
125 A.J. Feeley RC	2.00	5.00
126 Correll Buckhalter RC	2.50	6.00
127 Freddie Mitchell RC	1.50	4.00
128 Alge Crumpler RC	2.50	6.00
129 Michael Vick RC	10.00	25.00
130 Vinny Sutherland RC	1.50	4.00
131 Marcus Stroud RC	2.00	5.00
132 Mike McMahon RC	2.00	5.00
133 Scotty Anderson RC	1.50	4.00
134 Shaun Rogers RC	2.50	6.00
135 Jesse Palmer RC	2.00	5.00
136 Will Allen RC	2.50	6.00
137 LaMont Jordan RC	2.50	6.00
138 Santana Moss RC	3.00	8.00
139 Reggie White RC	1.50	4.00
140 Jamal Reynolds RC	1.50	4.00
141 Robert Ferguson RC	2.50	6.00
142 Torrance Marshall RC	1.50	4.00
143 Chris Weinke RC	2.00	5.00
144 Dan Morgan RC	2.00	5.00
145 Steve Smith RC	5.00	12.00
146 Dee Brown RC	1.50	4.00
147 Arther Love RC	1.50	4.00
148 Hakim Akbar RC	1.50	4.00
149 Jabari Holloway RC	1.50	4.00
150 Derek Combs RC	1.50	4.00
151 Derrick Gibson RC	1.50	4.00
152 Ken-Yon Rambo RC	1.50	4.00
153 Marques Tuiasosopo RC	2.00	5.00
154 Adam Archuleta RC	2.00	5.00
155 Tommy Polley RC	1.50	4.00
156 Brian Allen RC	1.50	4.00
157 Milton Wynn RC	1.50	4.00
158 Francis St.Paul RC	1.50	4.00
159 Edgerton Hartwell RC	1.50	4.00
160 Gary Baxter RC	1.50	4.00
161 Todd Heap RC	2.50	6.00
162 Chris Barnes RC	1.50	4.00
163 Fred Smoot RC	2.50	6.00
164 Rod Gardner RC	2.00	5.00
165 Sage Rosenfels RC	2.50	6.00
166 Damerien McCants RC	2.00	5.00
167 Deuce McAllister RC	2.50	6.00
168 Moran Norris RC	1.50	4.00
169 Sedrick Hodge RC	1.50	4.00
170 Alex Bannister RC	1.50	4.00
171 Heath Evans RC	2.00	5.00
172 Josh Booty RC	2.00	5.00
173 Ken Lucas RC	2.00	5.00
174 Koren Robinson RC	2.00	5.00
175 Chris Taylor RC	1.50	4.00
176 Andre Dyson RC	1.50	4.00
177 Dan Alexander RC	2.00	5.00
178 Justin McCareins RC	2.00	5.00
179 Eddie Berlin RC	1.50	4.00
180 Michael Bennett RC	2.00	5.00

2001 Upper Deck Legends Autographs

STATED ODDS 1:54		
PRINT RUNS ANNC'd BY UPPER DECK		
AM Archie Manning	15.00	40.00
AR Andre Reed	15.00	40.00
BS1 Barry Sanders	75.00	150.00
BS2 Bart Starr	75.00	135.00
BU Brian Urlacher	25.00	50.00
CT Charley Taylor	10.00	25.00
DB Dick Butkus	40.00	80.00
DC Daunte Culpepper SP/50*	40.00	80.00
DF1 Dan Fouts	15.00	40.00
DF2 Doug Flutie SP/50*	50.00	100.00
DM Dan Marino	125.00	200.00
ED Eric Dickerson	30.00	60.00
FH Franco Harris	30.00	60.00
FT Fran Tarkenton	25.00	50.00
GS Gale Sayers	30.00	60.00
HC Harold Carmichael	6.00	15.00
JB1 Jeff Blake	6.00	15.00
JB2 Jim Brown SP/50*	150.00	300.00
JE John Elway	100.00	200.00
JG1 Jeff Garcia SP/50*	30.00	60.00
JG2 Jeff George SP/50*	30.00	60.00
JK Jim Kelly SP/100*	150.00	250.00
JM Joe Montana	60.00	120.00
JN Joe Namath	50.00	100.00
JP1 Jake Plummer SP/50*	25.00	50.00
JP2 Jim Plunkett	15.00	40.00
JR John Riggins	20.00	50.00
JT Joe Theismann UER (name misspelled Theisman)	15.00	40.00
JU Johnny Unitas	250.00	400.00
JY Jack Youngblood	10.00	25.00
KS Ken Stabler	40.00	80.00
KW1 Kellen Winslow	15.00	40.00
KW2 Kurt Warner	25.00	50.00
LA Lance Alworth SP/100*	40.00	80.00
LT Lawrence Taylor SP/100*	50.00	100.00
MA Marcus Allen	25.00	50.00
PH Paul Hornung	20.00	50.00
PM Peyton Manning	90.00	150.00
RM Randy Moss SP/50*	60.00	120.00
RS Roger Staubach	60.00	120.00
RW Ricky Williams SP/50*	40.00	80.00
TA Troy Aikman	50.00	100.00
TB1 Terry Bradshaw	60.00	100.00
TB2 Tim Brown	25.00	50.00
TD Tony Dorsett SP/100*	60.00	120.00
TT Thurman Thomas	15.00	40.00
VT Vinny Testaverde	50.00	100.00
WC Wayne Chrebet	6.00	15.00
WM Warren Moon	25.00	60.00

2001 Upper Deck Legends Legendary Artwork

COMPLETE SET (15)	30.00	60.00
STATED ODDS 1:18		
LA1 Jim Thorpe	2.00	5.00
LA2 Jerry Rice	2.50	6.00
LA3 Bart Starr	3.00	8.00
LA4 Fran Tarkenton	2.00	5.00
LA5 Barry Sanders	3.00	8.00
LA6 Jim Brown	2.50	6.00
LA7 Joe Montana	4.00	10.00
LA8 Joe Namath	2.50	6.00
LA9 John Elway	3.00	8.00
LA10 Johnny Unitas	3.00	8.00
LA11 Roger Staubach	2.50	6.00
LA12 Terry Bradshaw	2.50	6.00
LA13 Walter Payton	4.00	10.00
LA14 Dan Marino	3.00	8.00
LA15 Dick Butkus	2.00	5.00

2001 Upper Deck Legends Legendary Cuts

STATED PRINT RUN 1-113		
330 TOTAL CARDS AVAILABLE		
LCBN Bronko Nagurski/28	250.00	450.00
LCEN Ernie Nevers/63	150.00	250.00
LCET Emlen Tunnell/22	100.00	200.00
LCGH George Halas/113	350.00	600.00

2001 Upper Deck Legends Memorable Materials

STATED ODDS 1:36		
MMBS Barry Sanders	15.00	40.00
MMCB Charlie Batch	5.00	12.00
MMDB Drew Bledsoe	6.00	15.00
MMDF Doug Flutie	6.00	15.00
MMDM Dan Marino	15.00	40.00
MMED Eric Dickerson SP/150*	6.00	15.00
MMIB Isaac Bruce UER (name misspelled Issac on front)	6.00	15.00
MMJE John Elway	15.00	40.00
MMMB Mark Brunell	5.00	12.00
MMMF Marshall Faulk	6.00	15.00
MMSM Steve McNair	6.00	15.00
MMWP Walter Payton SP/150*	40.00	100.00

2001 Upper Deck Legends Past Patterns Jerseys

STATED ODDS 1:18		
PPAM Archie Manning	8.00	20.00
PPAR Andre Reed	6.00	15.00
PPBF Brett Favre	15.00	40.00
PPCC Cris Carter	6.00	15.00
PPDF Doug Flutie	6.00	15.00
PPDM Dan Marino	15.00	40.00
PPES Emmitt Smith	15.00	40.00
PPFT Fred Taylor	5.00	12.00
PPGB George Blanda	6.00	15.00
PPJG Jeff George	4.00	10.00
PPJK Jim Kelly	8.00	20.00
PPJM Joe Montana SP/150	25.00	60.00
PPJN Joe Namath SP/150	15.00	40.00
PPJP Jim Plunkett	5.00	12.00
PPJR Jerry Rice	10.00	25.00
PPJS Junior Seau	5.00	12.00
PPJTA John Taylor	4.00	10.00
PPKC Kerry Collins	4.00	10.00
PPKN Ken Norton	4.00	8.00
PPLT Lawrence Taylor	6.00	15.00
PPMA Mike Alstott	4.00	10.00
PPPH Paul Hornung	10.00	25.00
PPPM Peyton Manning	12.00	30.00
PPRS Roger Staubach SP/95	25.00	50.00
PPRSM Robert Smith	4.00	10.00
PPRW1 Reggie White	8.00	20.00
PPRW2 Rod Woodson	5.00	12.00
PPSD Stephen Davis	4.00	10.00
PPSJ Sonny Jurgensen	6.00	15.00
PPSK Shaun King	4.00	10.00
PPSS Shannon Sharpe SP	6.00	15.00
PPSY Steve Young	8.00	20.00
PPTA Troy Aikman	8.00	20.00
PPTB Terry Bradshaw SP/150	25.00	50.00
PPTC Tim Couch	4.00	8.00
PPWD Warrick Dunn	5.00	12.00
PPWM Warren Moon	6.00	15.00

2001 Upper Deck Legends Timeless Tributes Jersey

STATED ODDS 1:36		
TTBS Bruce Smith	10.00	25.00
TTDG Darrell Green	10.00	25.00
TTDT Derrick Thomas	12.00	30.00
TTHM Harvey Martin	10.00	25.00
TTJB Jerome Bettis	15.00	40.00
TTJM Joe Montana	15.00	40.00
TTKN Ken Norton Jr.	6.00	15.00
TTLT Lawrence Taylor	10.00	25.00
TTRW Randy White	10.00	25.00
TTTT Thurman Thomas	10.00	25.00
TTWS Warren Sapp	8.00	20.00

2004 Upper Deck Legends

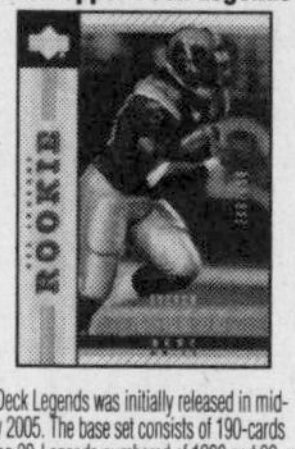

Upper Deck Legends was initially released in mid-January 2005. The base set consists of 190-cards including 20-Legends numbered of 1299 and 80-rookies serial numbered to 650. Hobby boxes contained 24-packs of 5-cards and carried an S.R.P. of $4.99 per pack. One parallel set and a variety of autograph and jersey inserts can be found seeded in packs highlighted by one of the more actively traded autographed inserts of the year in Legendary Signatures.

COMP.SET w/o SP's (90)	7.50	20.00
91-110 LEGENDS/1250 ODDS 1:24		
111-190 ROOKIE/650 ODDS 1:12		
UNPRICED PRINT PLATE PRINT RUN 1		
1 Josh McCown	.20	.50
2 Emmitt Smith	.60	1.50
3 Michael Vick	.30	.75
4 Peerless Price	.15	.40
5 Ray Lewis	.25	.60
6 Kyle Boller	.20	.50
7 Deion Sanders	.25	.60
8 Drew Bledsoe	.25	.60
9 Travis Henry	.15	.40
10 Eric Moulds	.20	.50
11 Steve Smith	.25	.60
12 Stephen Davis	.20	.50
13 Jake Delhomme	.20	.50
14 Rex Grossman	.20	.50
15 Brian Urlacher	.25	.60
16 Thomas Jones	.25	.60
17 Chad Johnson	.25	.60
18 Rudi Johnson	.20	.50
19 Carson Palmer	.25	.60
20 William Green	.15	.40
21 Andre Davis	.15	.40
22 Jeff Garcia	.20	.50
23 Roy Williams S	.20	.50
24 Eddie George	.20	.50
25 Keyshawn Johnson	.20	.50
26 Reuben Droughns	.20	.50
27 Jake Plummer	.20	.50
28 Champ Bailey	.20	.50
29 Charles Rogers	.15	.40
30 Joey Harrington	.20	.50
31 Ahman Green	.20	.50
32 Brett Favre	.60	1.50
33 Javon Walker	.15	.40
34 David Carr	.15	.40
35 Domanick Davis	.15	.40
36 Andre Johnson	.25	.60
37 Marvin Harrison	.25	.60
38 Edgerrin James	.20	.50
39 Peyton Manning	.50	1.25
40 Byron Leftwich	.20	.50
41 Fred Taylor	.20	.50
42 Trent Green	.20	.50

43 Tony Gonzalez	.25	.60
44 Priest Holmes	.25	.60
45 Zach Thomas	.25	.60
46 Chris Chambers	.20	.50
47 Jay Fiedler	.15	.40
48 Daunte Culpepper	.20	.50
49 Randy Moss	.25	.60
50 Onterrio Smith	.15	.40
51 Tom Brady	.50	1.25
52 Deion Branch	.20	.50
53 Corey Dillon	.20	.50
54 Deuce McAllister	.20	.50
55 Aaron Brooks	.20	.50
56 Joe Horn	.20	.50
57 Tiki Barber	.25	.60
58 Kurt Warner	.25	.60
59 Jeremy Shockey	.20	.50
60 Chad Pennington	.25	.60
61 Santana Moss	.20	.50
62 Curtis Martin	.25	.60
63 Kerry Collins	.20	.50
64 Jerry Rice	.50	1.25
65 Jerry Porter	.15	.40
66 Terrell Owens	.25	.60
67 Jevon Kearse	.20	.50
68 Donovan McNabb	.25	.60
69 Hines Ward	.25	.60
70 Plaxico Burress	.20	.50
71 Duce Staley	.20	.50
72 Drew Brees	.25	.60
73 LaDainian Tomlinson	.25	.60
74 Tim Rattay	.15	.40
75 Brandon Lloyd	.20	.50
76 Kevan Barlow	.15	.40
77 Shaun Alexander	.20	.50
78 Koren Robinson	.15	.40
79 Matt Hasselbeck	.20	.50
80 Marshall Faulk	.25	.60
81 Torry Holt	.20	.50
82 Marc Bulger	.20	.50
83 Brian Griese	.20	.50
84 Derrick Brooks	.20	.50
85 Steve McNair	.25	.60
86 Derrick Mason	.20	.50
87 Chris Brown	.15	.40
88 Mark Brunell	.20	.50
89 Laveranues Coles	.15	.40
90 Clinton Portis	.25	.60
91 Dick Butkus	2.50	6.00
92 Gale Sayers	2.00	5.00
93 Mike Ditka	1.50	4.00
94 Jim Brown	2.50	6.00
95 Roger Staubach	2.50	6.00
96 Troy Aikman	2.50	6.00
97 John Elway	4.00	10.00
98 Barry Sanders	3.00	8.00
99 Bart Starr	4.00	10.00
100 Paul Hornung	1.50	4.00
101 Len Dawson	1.50	4.00
102 Dan Marino	4.00	10.00
103 Fran Tarkenton	1.50	4.00
104 Archie Manning	1.50	4.00
105 Joe Namath	2.50	6.00
106 Ken Stabler	2.00	5.00
107 Lynn Swann	2.00	5.00
108 Terry Bradshaw	2.50	6.00
109 Joe Montana	4.00	10.00
110 Joe Theismann	1.50	4.00
111 Bernard Berrian RC	2.00	5.00
112 Ben Hartsock RC	1.25	3.00
113 Karlos Dansby RC	2.00	5.00
114 Thomas Tapeh RC	1.50	4.00
115 Keary Colbert RC	1.25	3.00
116 Ben Troupe RC	1.50	4.00
117 Jonathan Vilma RC	2.00	5.00
118 Jamaar Taylor RC	1.25	3.00
119 Ben Roethlisberger RC	12.00	30.00
120 Samie Parker RC	1.25	3.00
121 Dunta Robinson RC	1.25	3.00
122 Dontarrious Thomas RC	1.50	4.00
123 Adimchinobe Echemandu RC	1.50	4.00
124 Darius Watts RC	1.25	3.00
125 Ben Watson RC	2.00	5.00
126 Terry Johnson RC	1.25	3.00
127 D.J. Hackett RC	1.50	4.00
128 Devery Henderson RC	2.00	5.00
129 Kellen Winslow Jr. RC	2.00	5.00
130 Travis LaBoy RC	1.50	4.00
131 Maurice Mann RC	1.25	3.00
132 Rashaun Woods RC	1.25	3.00
133 Michael Turner RC	2.50	6.00
134 Junior Siavii RC	1.25	3.00
135 Johnnie Morant RC	1.25	3.00
136 Larry Fitzgerald RC	5.00	12.00
137 Kevin Jones RC	1.50	4.00
138 Will Smith RC	1.50	4.00
139 Robert Gallery RC	2.00	5.00
140 Michael Jenkins RC	2.00	5.00
141 Cedric Cobbs RC	1.25	3.00
142 Igor Olshansky RC	1.50	4.00
143 Josh Harris RC	1.25	3.00
144 Michael Clayton RC	1.50	4.00
145 Mewelde Moore RC	1.50	4.00
146 Jason Babin RC	2.00	5.00
147 Cody Pickett RC	1.50	4.00
148 Lee Evans RC	2.00	5.00
149 Greg Jones RC	1.25	3.00
150 Marcus Tubbs RC	1.25	3.00
151 Craig Krenzel RC	1.50	4.00
152 Roy Williams RC	2.00	5.00
153 Tatum Bell RC	1.50	4.00
154 Kenechi Udeze RC	1.50	4.00
155 Shawn Andrews RC	1.50	4.00
156 Reggie Williams RC	1.50	4.00
157 Julius Jones RC	1.50	4.00
158 Vince Wilfork RC	2.00	5.00
159 Vernon Carey RC	1.25	3.00
160 Eli Manning RC	12.00	30.00
161 Devard Darling RC	1.25	3.00
162 Sean Taylor RC	4.00	10.00
163 Teddy Lehman RC	1.25	3.00
164 Jammal Lord RC	1.25	3.00
165 J.P. Losman RC	1.50	4.00
166 Jerricho Cotchery RC	1.50	4.00
167 Ahmad Carroll RC	1.25	3.00
168 Michael Boulware RC	2.00	5.00
169 Quincy Wilson RC	1.50	4.00
170 Derrick Hamilton RC	1.25	3.00
171 Kris Wilson RC	1.50	4.00
172 D.J. Williams RC	2.00	5.00
173 P.K. Sam RC	1.25	3.00
174 Matt Schaub RC	4.00	10.00
175 Ernest Wilford RC	1.50	4.00
176 Chris Gamble RC	1.50	4.00
177 Courtney Watson RC	1.25	3.00
178 Drew Henson RC	1.25	3.00
179 Chris Perry RC	1.50	4.00
180 Tommie Harris RC	2.00	5.00
181 Marquis Cooper RC	1.25	3.00
182 Philip Rivers RC	8.00	20.00
183 Carlos Francis RC	1.25	3.00
184 DeAngelo Hall RC	2.00	5.00
185 Daryl Smith RC	1.25	3.00
186 Troy Fleming RC	1.25	3.00
187 Luke McCown RC	1.50	4.00
188 Steven Jackson RC	3.00	8.00
189 Ricardo Colclough RC	1.50	4.00
190 Gilbert Gardner RC	1.25	3.00

2004 Upper Deck Legends Gold

*GOLD VETS: 10X TO 25X BASIC CARDS
*GOLD LEGENDS: 25X TO 5X
*GOLD ROOKIES: 1.5X TO 4X
GOLD/25 STATED ODDS 1:192

2004 Upper Deck Legends Future Legends Jersey

STATED ODDS 1:24

FLBR Ben Roethlisberger	12.00	30.00
FLCP Chris Perry	2.50	6.00
FLEM Eli Manning	12.00	30.00
FLGJ Greg Jones	2.00	5.00
FLJJ Julius Jones	2.50	6.00
FLJP J.P. Losman	2.50	6.00
FLKJ Kevin Jones	2.50	6.00
FLKW Kellen Winslow Jr.	3.00	8.00
FLLE Lee Evans	3.00	8.00
FLLF Larry Fitzgerald	8.00	20.00
FLMC Michael Clayton	2.50	6.00
FLMJ Michael Jenkins	3.00	8.00
FLPR Philip Rivers	8.00	20.00
FLRE Reggie Williams	2.50	6.00
FLRG Robert Gallery	3.00	8.00
FLRW Roy Williams WR	3.00	8.00
FLSJ Steven Jackson	5.00	12.00
FLTB Tatum Bell	2.50	6.00

2004 Upper Deck Legends Future Legends Throwback Jersey

STATED ODDS 1:192

FLTBB Bernard Berrian	4.00	10.00
FLTBR Ben Roethlisberger	20.00	50.00
FLTBT Ben Troupe	3.00	8.00
FLTBW Ben Watson	4.00	10.00
FLTCC Cedric Cobbs	2.50	6.00
FLTCP Chris Perry	3.00	8.00
FLTDE Devery Henderson	4.00	10.00
FLTDH DeAngelo Hall	4.00	10.00
FLTDW Darius Watts	2.50	6.00
FLTEM Eli Manning	25.00	50.00
FLTGJ Greg Jones	2.50	6.00
FLTHA Derrick Hamilton	2.50	6.00
FLTJJ Julius Jones	3.00	8.00
FLTJP J.P. Losman	3.00	8.00
FLTKC Keary Colbert	2.50	6.00
FLTKJ Kevin Jones	3.00	8.00
FLTKW Kellen Winslow Jr.	4.00	10.00
FLTLE Lee Evans	4.00	10.00
FLTLF Larry Fitzgerald	10.00	25.00
FLTLM Luke McCown	3.00	8.00
FLTMC Michael Clayton	3.00	8.00
FLTMJ Michael Jenkins	4.00	10.00
FLTMS Matt Schaub	8.00	20.00
FLTPR Philip Rivers	12.00	30.00
FLTRA Rashaun Woods	2.50	6.00
FLTRE Reggie Williams	3.00	8.00
FLTRG Robert Gallery	4.00	10.00
FLTRW Roy Williams WR	4.00	10.00
FLTSJ Steven Jackson	6.00	15.00
FLTTB Tatum Bell	3.00	8.00

2004 Upper Deck Legends Immortal Inscriptions

STATED PRINT RUN 45 SER.#'d SETS

IIAM Archie Manning	20.00	50.00
IIBS Barry Sanders	75.00	150.00
IIDB Dick Butkus	60.00	120.00
IIDM Dan Marino	100.00	200.00
IIFH Franco Harris	30.00	80.00
IIFT Fran Tarkenton	25.00	80.00
IIGS Gale Sayers	50.00	100.00
IIHL Howie Long	50.00	100.00
IIJB Jim Brown	60.00	120.00
IIJE John Elway	100.00	200.00
IIJM Joe Montana	100.00	200.00
IIJN Joe Namath	60.00	120.00
IIJT Joe Theismann	20.00	50.00
IIKS Ken Stabler	30.00	80.00
IIKW Kellen Winslow Sr.	20.00	50.00
IIPH Paul Hornung	25.00	60.00
IIRS Roger Staubach	60.00	120.00
IITA Troy Aikman	60.00	100.00
IITB Terry Bradshaw	75.00	150.00

2004 Upper Deck Legends Legendary Jerseys

LEGENDARY JERSEY/99 ODDS 1:384

LJAM Archie Manning	10.00	25.00
LJBS Barry Sanders	20.00	50.00
LJDM Dan Marino	30.00	60.00
LJFT Fran Tarkenton	10.00	25.00
LJGS Gale Sayers	12.00	30.00
LJHL Howie Long	12.00	30.00
LJJE John Elway	20.00	50.00
LJJM Joe Montana	30.00	60.00
LJJN Joe Namath	15.00	40.00
LJJT Joe Theismann	10.00	25.00
LJJU Johnny Unitas	30.00	60.00
LJKS Ken Stabler	12.00	30.00
LJKW Kellen Winslow Sr.	10.00	25.00
LJLD Len Dawson	10.00	25.00
LJLS Lynn Swann	25.00	60.00
LJON Ozzie Newsome	8.00	20.00
LJRS Roger Staubach	15.00	40.00
LJTA Troy Aikman	12.00	30.00
LJTB Terry Bradshaw	15.00	40.00
LJWP Walter Payton	30.00	80.00

2004 Upper Deck Legends Legendary Lines of Defense Autographs

STATED PRINT RUN 75 SER.#'d SETS

HGL Jack Ham	125.00	250.00
Joe Greene		
Jack Lambert		
JGW Tom Jackson	30.00	60.00
Randy Gradishar		
Louis Wright		
PEM Alan Page	60.00	120.00
Carl Eller		
Jim Marshall		
SHD Mike Singletary	75.00	150.00
Dan Hampton		
Richard Dent		
YYJ Jim Youngblood	40.00	80.00
Jack Youngblood		
Deacon Jones		

2004 Upper Deck Legends Legendary Signatures

STATED ODDS 1:8

LSAK Alex Karras	10.00	25.00
LSAM Archie Manning SP	30.00	80.00
LSAN Andy Russell	6.00	15.00
LSAP Alan Page	6.00	15.00
LSBB Bill Bergey	5.00	12.00
LSBE Raymond Berry	8.00	20.00
LSBG Bob Griese	20.00	50.00
LSBI Billy Sims	6.00	15.00
LSBJ Bert Jones	6.00	15.00
LSBK Billy Kilmer	8.00	20.00
LSBL Bob Lilly	8.00	20.00
LSBS Barry Sanders SP	200.00	400.00
LSBY Billy Johnson	5.00	12.00
LSCB Cliff Branch	6.00	15.00
LSCE Carl Eller	5.00	12.00
LSCF Chuck Foreman	5.00	12.00
LSCJ Charlie Joiner	5.00	12.00
LSCM Craig Morton	6.00	15.00
LSCT Charley Taylor	6.00	15.00
LSDA Doug Atkins	6.00	15.00
LSDB Dick Butkus SP	125.00	250.00
LSDC Dave Casper	8.00	20.00
LSDF Dan Fouts SP	40.00	80.00
LSDH Dan Hampton	20.00	40.00
LSDI Dick Anderson SP	10.00	25.00
LSDJ Deacon Jones SP	25.00	50.00
LSDL Daryle Lamonica	8.00	20.00
LSDM Dan Marino SP	250.00	400.00
LSDO Don Maynard	6.00	15.00
LSDP Drew Pearson	6.00	15.00
LSEC Earl Campbell SP	40.00	80.00
LSED Eric Dickerson SP	15.00	40.00
LSEJ Ed Too Tall Jones	6.00	15.00
LSFG Frank Gifford SP	40.00	80.00
LSFT Fran Tarkenton SP	60.00	120.00
LSGA Roman Gabriel	10.00	25.00
LSGS Gale Sayers SP	60.00	120.00
LSHA Chris Hanburger	8.00	20.00
LSHC Harold Carmichael	5.00	12.00
LSHL Howie Long SP	40.00	80.00
LSHN John Hannah	5.00	12.00
LSHT Jim Hart	5.00	12.00
LSIC Isaac Curtis	5.00	12.00
LSJB Jim Brown SP	125.00	250.00
LSJE John Elway SP	125.00	250.00
LSJG Joe Greene SP	175.00	300.00
LSJH Jack Ham SP	125.00	200.00
LSJI Jim Marshall	6.00	15.00
LSJK Jerry Kramer	12.00	30.00
LSJL Jack Lambert SP	40.00	80.00
LSJM Joe Montana SP	125.00	250.00
LSJN Joe Namath SP	350.00	600.00
LSJO John Taylor	5.00	12.00
LSJP Jim Plunkett	6.00	15.00
LSJT Joe Theismann SP	25.00	50.00
LSJY Jim Youngblood	5.00	12.00
LSKA Ken Anderson	6.00	15.00
LSKI Jim Kiick	5.00	12.00
LSKS Ken Stabler SP	40.00	80.00
LSKW Kellen Winslow Sr. SP	12.00	30.00
LSLC L.C. Greenwood SP	25.00	50.00
LSLD Len Dawson SP	25.00	50.00
LSLW Louis Wright	5.00	12.00
LSMA Mark Duper	5.00	12.00
LSMC Mark Clayton	5.00	12.00
LSMD Mike Ditka SP	25.00	60.00
LSMF Manny Fernandez	5.00	12.00
LSMI Mike Curtis	5.00	12.00
LSMM Mercury Morris	5.00	12.00
LSMR Mel Renfro	6.00	15.00
LSMS Mike Singletary SP	60.00	120.00
LSMU Anthony Munoz	6.00	15.00
LSOM Ollie Matson	25.00	50.00
LSON Ozzie Newsome	6.00	15.00
LSPH Paul Hornung SP	60.00	120.00
LSPK Paul Krause	6.00	15.00
LSRA Ray Guy	6.00	15.00
LSRB Robert Brazile	5.00	12.00
LSRC Roger Craig	8.00	20.00
LSRD Richard Dent	12.00	30.00
LSRG Randy Gradishar	5.00	12.00
LSRJ Ron Jaworski	8.00	20.00
LSRO Roger Wehrli	6.00	15.00
LSRW Randy White	12.00	30.00
LSSB Steve Bartkowski	5.00	12.00
LSSH Sam Huff	12.00	30.00
LSSJ Sonny Jurgensen SP	15.00	40.00
LSSS Steve Spurrier SP	15.00	40.00
LSTA Troy Aikman SP	75.00	135.00
LSTB Terry Bradshaw/20*	200.00	400.00
LSTD Tony Dorsett/45*	150.00	300.00
LSVG Vencie Glenn	5.00	12.00
LSWB Willie Brown	6.00	15.00
LSWM Wilbert Montgomery	5.00	12.00
LSYO Jack Youngblood	6.00	15.00

2004 Upper Deck Legends Link to the Future Autographs

STATED PRINT RUN 25-50

LFBL Drew Bledsoe/50	20.00	50.00
J.P. Losman		
LFBM Kyle Boller/50	12.00	30.00
Luke McCown		
LFBR Drew Bledsoe	60.00	120.00
Philip Rivers/25		
LFCC Chris Chambers/25	15.00	40.00
Keary Colbert		
LFDK Deuce McAllister	25.00	60.00
Kevin Jones/25		
LFGB Ahman Green/50	12.00	30.00
Tatum Bell		
LFGC Joey Galloway/50	12.00	30.00
Michael Clayton		
LFGW Tony Gonzalez/50	15.00	40.00
Kellen Winslow Jr.		
LFHE Dante Hall/50	15.00	40.00
Lee Evans		
LFHH Joe Horn/50	12.00	30.00
Devery Henderson		
LFHT Todd Heap/50	12.00	30.00
Ben Troupe		
LFJW Chad Johnson/50	15.00	40.00
Reggie Williams		
LFMJ Deuce McAllister	40.00	100.00
Steven Jackson/25		
LFMM Peyton Manning	250.00	400.00
Eli Manning/25		
LFMW Derrick Mason/50	20.00	50.00
Roy Williams WR		
LFPS Chad Pennington	25.00	60.00
Matt Schaub/50		
LFRJ Roy Williams S/50	25.00	60.00
Julius Jones		
LFTE Tom Brady	250.00	400.00
Eli Manning/25		
LFTJ LaDainian Tomlinson	30.00	80.00
Julius Jones/25		
LFVR Michael Vick	200.00	400.00
Ben Roethlisberger/25		
LFWJ Brian Westbrook/50	15.00	40.00
Greg Jones		

2004 Upper Deck Legends Link to the Past Autographs

STATED PRINT RUN 25-50

LPBM Tom Brady/25	250.00	400.00
Joe Montana		
LPBS Mark Brunell/50	25.00	60.00
Ken Stabler		
LPCC Chris Chambers/50	20.00	50.00
Mark Clayton		
LPDC Domanick Davis/50	20.00	50.00
Earl Campbell		
LPDP Dan Marino	250.00	400.00
Peyton Manning/25		
LPFT Larry Fitzgerald/25	30.00	80.00
Charley Taylor		
LPGT Rex Grossman	25.00	60.00
Joe Theismann/50		
LPHH Tommie Harris/50	20.00	50.00
Dan Hampton		
LPHS Drew Henson/25	60.00	120.00
Roger Staubach		
LPJD Julius Jones/50	30.00	80.00
Tony Dorsett		
LPJE Steven Jackson	30.00	80.00
Eric Dickerson/50		
LPJH Greg Jones/50	25.00	60.00
Franco Harris		
LPJS Kevin Jones	100.00	200.00
Barry Sanders/25		
LPMJ Donovan McNabb/50	50.00	100.00
Ron Jaworski		
LPMM Eli Manning	175.00	300.00
Archie Manning/50		
LPPA Peyotn Manning	150.00	300.00
Archie Manning/25		
LPPN Chad Pennington/25	60.00	120.00
Joe Namath		
LPRB Ben Roethlisberger/25	200.00	350.00
Terry Bradshaw		
LPRF Philip Rivers	60.00	100.00
Dan Fouts/50		
LPUE Kenechi Udeze/50	15.00	40.00
Carl Eller		
LPVA Michael Vick	75.00	150.00
Troy Aikman/50		
LPWW Kellen Winslow Jr./50	25.00	60.00
Kellen Winslow Sr.		

2005 Upper Deck Legends

This 195-card set was released in August, 2005. The set was issued in five-card packs with an $4.99 SRP which also came 24 packs to a box. The set features mainly retired greats except for Brett Favre (card #7) and 2005 rookies (101-165, 191-195). In addition there are subsets featuring checklists (96-100) and Legends of the Hall (166-190). All of the rookies were issued to a stated print run of 725 serial numbered copies while the Legends of the Hall were issued to a stated print run of 1,025 copies.

COMP.SET w/o SP's (100)	7.50	20.00
ROOKIE PRINT RUN 725 SER.#'d SETS		
166-195 LEG.PRINT RUN 1025 SER.#'d SETS		
1 Charley Taylor	.25	.60
2 Roger Craig	.30	.75
3 Ozzie Newsome	.25	.60
4 Rocky Bleier	.30	.75
5 Russ Francis	.20	.50
6 Jerry Rice	.60	1.50
7 Pat Haden	.20	.50
8 Brett Favre	.75	2.00
9 Joe Ferguson	.20	.50
10 Ed Jones	.25	.60
11 Joe Washington	.20	.50
12 John Brodie	.20	.50
13 Peyton Manning	.60	1.50
14 Mark Van Eeghen	.20	.50
15 William Perry	.25	.60
16 Bob Brown	.20	.50
17 Herb Adderley	.25	.60
18 Deion Sanders	.40	1.00
19 Lenny Moore	.25	.60
20 Tom Mack	.20	.50
21 Jim McMahon	.30	.75
22 Bobby Mitchell	.25	.60
23 John Mackey	.20	.50
24 Curtis Martin	.30	.75
25 Junior Seau	.30	.75
26 Harold Jackson	.20	.50
27 Jim Zorn	.20	.50
28 Chuck Foreman	.20	.50
29 Willie Brown	.20	.50
30 Cliff Branch	.25	.60
31 Jerry Kramer	.25	.60
32 Harry Carson	.20	.50
33 Chuck Noll	.25	.60
34 Lon Hauss	.20	.50
35 Jim Plunkett	.25	.60
36 Ollie Matson	.25	.60
37 Billy Kilmer	.25	.60
38 Jim Marshall	.20	.50
39 Dan Dierdorf	.20	.50
40 Jim Kelly	.40	1.00
41 Vince Ferragamo	.20	.50
42 Ottis Anderson	.20	.50
43 Charlie Joiner	.20	.50
44 George Blanda	.30	.75
45 Drew Pearson	.25	.60
46 Andre Reed	.25	.60
47 Merlin Olsen	.25	.60
48 Paul Warfield	.25	.60
49 James Lofton	.20	.50
50 Art Donovan	.25	.60
51 Dwight Clark	.25	.60
52 Raymond Berry	.25	.60
53 L.C. Greenwood	.25	.60
54 Dave Casper	.25	.60
55 Don Maynard	.25	.60
56 Bud Grant	.20	.50
57 Roman Gabriel	.25	.60
58 Cris Collinsworth	.25	.60
59 Joe Theismann	.30	.75
60 Paul Hornung	.30	.75
61 Alan Page	.25	.60
62 Deacon Jones	.25	.60
63 Steve Largent	.30	.75
64 Phil Simms	.25	.60
65 Floyd Little	.20	.50
66 Archie Manning	.30	.75
67 Ken Stabler	.40	1.00
68 Fran Tarkenton	.30	.75
69 Len Dawson	.30	.75
70 Mike Ditka	.30	.75
71 Conrad Dobler	.20	.50
72 Jack Lambert	.30	.75
73 Marcus Allen	.30	.75
74 Bo Jackson	.40	1.00
75 Jerome Bettis	.30	.75
76 Jack Ham	.25	.60
77 Marshall Faulk	.30	.75
78 Mike Singletary	.30	.75
79 Bob Griese	.30	.75
80 Dick Butkus	.40	1.00
81 Gale Sayers	.40	1.00
82 Earl Campbell	.30	.75
83 Dan Fouts	.30	.75
84 Franco Harris	.30	.75
85 Steve Young	.40	1.00
86 Tony Dorsett	.25	.60
87 Jim Brown	.40	1.00
88 Roger Staubach	.50	1.25
89 Troy Aikman	.40	1.00
90 Barry Sanders	.50	1.25
91 Bernie Kosar	.25	.60
92 Dan Marino	.75	2.00
93 John Elway	.60	1.50
94 Randy Moss	.30	.75
95 Joe Montana	.75	2.00
96 Joe Montana CL	.50	1.25
97 Dan Marino CL	.50	1.25
98 John Elway CL	.40	1.00
99 Gale Sayers CL	.25	.60
100 Paul Hornung CL	.20	.50
101 Aaron Rodgers RC	25.00	50.00
102 Alex Smith QB RC	2.50	6.00
103 Cadillac Williams RC	1.50	4.00
104 Ronnie Brown RC	2.00	5.00
105 Ciatrick Fason RC	1.00	2.50
106 Charlie Frye RC	1.50	4.00
107 Derek Anderson RC	1.25	3.00
108 Braylon Edwards RC	2.00	5.00
109 Roddy White RC	2.00	5.00
110 Thomas Davis RC	1.00	2.50
111 Jason Campbell RC	2.00	5.00
112 Andrew Walter RC	1.25	3.00
113 Kyle Orton RC	1.50	4.00
114 David Greene RC	1.00	2.50
115 Cedric Benson RC	1.50	4.00
116 Vernand Morency RC	1.25	3.00
117 Eric Shelton RC	1.00	2.50
118 Maurice Clarett	1.25	3.00
119 Brandon Jacobs RC	2.00	5.00
120 Anthony Davis RC	1.00	2.50
121 Marion Barber RC	1.50	4.00
122 J.J. Arrington RC	1.25	3.00
123 Ryan Moats RC	1.25	3.00
124 Frank Gore RC	2.50	6.00
125 Stefan LeFors RC	1.00	2.50
126 Darren Sproles RC	1.50	4.00
127 Cedric Houston RC	1.50	4.00
128 Troy Williamson RC	1.25	3.00
129 Mark Clayton RC	1.50	4.00
130 Chris Henry RC	1.50	4.00
131 Fred Gibson RC	1.25	3.00
132 Craphonso Thorpe RC	1.00	2.50
133 Terrence Murphy RC	1.00	2.50
134 Dan Orlovsky RC	1.50	4.00
135 Roscoe Parrish RC	1.00	2.50
136 Reggie Brown RC	1.00	2.50
137 Craig Bragg RC	1.00	2.50
138 Larry Brackins RC	1.00	2.50
139 Adrian McPherson RC	1.00	2.50
140 Matt Jones RC	1.50	4.00
141 Heath Miller RC	2.00	5.00
142 Alex Smith TE RC	1.00	2.50
143 Kevin Everett RC	1.50	4.00
144 Jerome Mathis RC	1.50	4.00
145 Travis Johnson RC	1.00	2.50
146 Channing Crowder RC	1.25	3.00
147 Mike Williams	1.50	4.00
148 Barrett Ruud RC	1.50	4.00
149 Marcus Spears RC	1.25	3.00
150 Derrick Johnson RC	1.25	3.00
151 Shawne Merriman RC	1.50	4.00
152 Kevin Burnett RC	1.25	3.00
153 Erasmus James RC	1.25	3.00
154 Dan Cody RC	1.25	3.00
155 David Pollack RC	1.25	3.00
156 Antrel Rolle RC	1.50	4.00
157 Adam Jones RC	1.25	3.00
158 Mark Bradley RC	1.00	2.50
159 Carlos Rogers RC	1.50	4.00
160 Vincent Jackson RC	2.00	5.00
161 DeMarcus Ware RC	3.00	8.00
162 Corey Webster RC	1.25	3.00
163 Justin Miller RC	1.25	3.00
164 Eric Green RC	1.00	2.50
165 Marlin Jackson RC	1.00	2.50
166 Herb Adderley LH	1.50	4.00
167 Fran Tarkenton LH	2.00	5.00
168 Troy Aikman LH	2.50	6.00
169 Charlie Joiner LH	1.25	3.00
170 George Blanda LH	2.00	5.00
171 Jim Kelly LH	2.50	6.00
172 Joe Montana LH	5.00	12.00
173 Jack Ham LH	1.50	4.00
174 Marcus Allen LH	2.00	5.00
175 Tony Dorsett LH	1.50	4.00
176 Barry Sanders LH	3.00	8.00
177 Paul Warfield LH	1.50	4.00
178 Dan Marino LH	5.00	12.00
179 John Elway LH	4.00	10.00
180 Franco Harris LH	2.00	5.00
181 Mike Singletary LH	2.00	5.00
182 Gale Sayers LH	2.50	6.00
183 Bob Griese LH	2.00	5.00
184 Dan Fouts LH	2.00	5.00
185 Earl Campbell LH	2.00	5.00
186 Jim Brown LH	2.50	6.00
187 Dick Butkus LH	2.50	6.00
188 Paul Hornung LH	2.00	5.00
189 Roger Staubach LH	3.00	8.00
190 Steve Largent LH	2.00	5.00
191 Ryan Fitzpatrick RC	2.50	6.00
192 Alvin Pearman RC	1.00	2.50
193 Courtney Roby RC	1.25	3.00
194 Chase Lyman RC	1.00	2.50
195 Roydell Williams RC	1.25	3.00

2005 Upper Deck Legends Dream Teammates Autographs

UNPRICED PRINT RUN 10 SER.#'d SETS

2005 Upper Deck Legends Future Legends Jersey

STATED ODDS 1:24 HOB, 1:48 RET

AJ Adam Jones	3.00	8.00
AN Antrel Rolle	3.00	8.00
AS Alex Smith QB	10.00	25.00
AW Andrew Walter	3.00	8.00
BE Braylon Edwards	7.50	20.00
CA Carlos Rogers	3.00	8.00
CF Charlie Frye	3.00	8.00
CI Ciatrick Fason	3.00	8.00
CR Courtney Roby	3.00	8.00
CW Cadillac Williams	6.00	15.00
ES Eric Shelton	3.00	8.00
FG Frank Gore	5.00	12.00
JA J.J. Arrington	3.00	8.00
JC Jason Campbell	5.00	12.00
KO Kyle Orton	3.00	8.00
MB Mark Bradley	3.00	8.00
MC Mark Clayton	3.00	8.00
MJ Matt Jones	4.00	10.00
MO Maurice Clarett	3.00	8.00
RB Ronnie Brown	10.00	25.00
RE Reggie Brown	3.00	8.00
RM Ryan Moats	3.00	8.00
RP Roscoe Parrish	3.00	8.00
RW Roddy White	3.00	8.00
SL Stefan LeFors	3.00	8.00
TM Terrence Murphy	3.00	8.00
TW Troy Williamson	3.00	8.00
VJ Vincent Jackson	4.00	10.00
VM Vernand Morency	3.00	8.00

2005 Upper Deck Legends Legendary Cuts Timeless Tandems

NOT PRICED DUE TO SCARCITY

2005 Upper Deck Legends Legendary Heritage Autographs

UNPRICED HERITAGE SER.#'d TO 5

2005 Upper Deck Legends Legendary Jerseys

STATED PRINT RUN 60 SER.#'d SETS

BA Barry Sanders	25.00	50.00
BJ Bo Jackson	20.00	40.00
BK Bernie Kosar	7.50	20.00
DM Dan Marino	40.00	80.00
FT Fran Tarkenton	12.50	30.00
GS Gale Sayers	20.00	50.00
HA Herb Adderley UER	7.50	20.00
(name misspelled Adderly)		
JB John Brodie	12.50	30.00
JE John Elway	25.00	50.00
JI Jim Marshall	12.50	30.00
JK Jim Kelly	15.00	40.00
JM Joe Montana	40.00	80.00
JT Joe Theismann	12.50	30.00
JU Johnny Unitas	30.00	60.00
KS Ken Stabler	15.00	40.00
LT Lawrence Taylor	15.00	40.00
MA Marcus Allen	12.50	30.00
MO Merlin Olsen	12.50	30.00
ON Ozzie Newsome	7.50	20.00
PS Phil Simms	12.50	30.00
RL Ronnie Lott	15.00	40.00
RS Roger Staubach	15.00	40.00
SL Steve Largent	12.50	30.00
SY Steve Young	15.00	40.00
TA Troy Aikman	15.00	40.00
WP Walter Payton	40.00	100.00

2005 Upper Deck Legends Legendary Signatures

STATED ODDS 1:8 HOB, 1:24 RET

AD Art Donovan	8.00	20.00
AM Archie Manning SP	30.00	60.00
AP Alan Page	10.00	25.00
BB Bob Brown	8.00	20.00
BE Bob Griese SP	60.00	120.00
BG Bud Grant	30.00	80.00
BI Billy Kilmer	6.00	15.00
BJ Bo Jackson SP	50.00	100.00
BK Bernie Kosar SP	25.00	50.00
BM Bobby Mitchell	8.00	20.00
BS Barry Sanders SP	150.00	300.00
CB Cliff Branch	8.00	20.00
CC Cris Collinsworth	8.00	20.00
CD Conrad Dobler	5.00	12.00
CF Chuck Foreman	8.00	20.00
CJ Charlie Joiner	5.00	12.00
CN Chuck Noll	25.00	50.00
CT Charley Taylor	5.00	12.00
DA Dave Casper	8.00	20.00
DB Dick Butkus SP	75.00	150.00
DC Dwight Clark	8.00	20.00
DD Dan Dierdorf	8.00	20.00
DF Dan Fouts SP	50.00	100.00
DJ Deacon Jones SP	15.00	30.00
DM Don Maynard SP	30.00	50.00
DO Dan Marino SP	250.00	500.00
DR Drew Pearson SP	15.00	30.00
EC Earl Campbell SP	40.00	100.00
EJ Ed Jones	10.00	25.00
FH Franco Harris SP	50.00	100.00
FL Floyd Little	5.00	12.00
FT Fran Tarkenton SP	30.00	60.00
GB George Blanda SP	40.00	80.00
GS Gale Sayers SP	60.00	120.00
HA Herb Adderley	10.00	25.00
HC Harry Carson	8.00	20.00
HJ Harold Jackson	5.00	12.00
JB John Brodie	8.00	20.00
JC Jack Lambert SP	75.00	135.00
JE John Elway SP	100.00	200.00
JF Joe Ferguson	8.00	20.00
JH Jack Ham SP	40.00	80.00
JI Jim Brown	50.00	100.00
JK Jerry Kramer	8.00	20.00
JL James Lofton	8.00	20.00
JM Joe Montana SP	125.00	250.00
JP Jim Plunkett	10.00	25.00
JR Jim Marshall	8.00	20.00
JT Joe Theismann	10.00	25.00
JW Joe Washington	5.00	12.00
JY John Mackey	12.00	30.00
JZ Jim Zorn	8.00	20.00
KE Jim Kelly SP	40.00	80.00
KS Ken Stabler SP	40.00	80.00
LA Andre Reed	10.00	25.00
LD Len Dawson SP	50.00	80.00
LG L.C. Greenwood	15.00	30.00
LH Len Hauss	5.00	12.00
LM Lenny Moore	8.00	20.00
MA Marcus Allen SP	50.00	100.00
MC Jim McMahon	20.00	40.00
MD Mike Ditka SP	25.00	50.00
MO Merlin Olsen SP	30.00	60.00
MS Mike Singletary SP	30.00	60.00
MV Mark Van Eeghan	6.00	15.00
OA Ottis Anderson	8.00	20.00
OM Ollie Matson	20.00	40.00
ON Ozzie Newsome	5.00	12.00
PA Paul Hornung	15.00	40.00
PH Pat Haden	6.00	15.00
PW Paul Warfield	8.00	20.00
RB Rocky Bleier	15.00	40.00
RG Roger Craig	8.00	20.00
RO Roman Gabriel	10.00	25.00
RS Russ Francis	5.00	12.00
RU Roger Staubach SP	75.00	150.00
RY Raymond Berry	8.00	20.00
SL Steve Largent SP	20.00	40.00
TA Troy Aikman SP	40.00	100.00
TD Tony Dorsett SP	40.00	100.00
TM Tom Mack	6.00	15.00
VF Vince Ferragamo	8.00	20.00
WB Willie Brown	6.00	15.00
WP William Perry	8.00	20.00

2005 Upper Deck Legends Legends of the Hall Autographs

STATED PRINT RUN 25 SER.#'d SETS

BG Bob Griese	40.00	80.00
BS Barry Sanders	100.00	175.00
CJ Charlie Joiner	20.00	40.00
DB Dick Butkus	75.00	135.00
DF Dan Fouts	50.00	100.00
DM Dan Marino	150.00	300.00
EC Earl Campbell	25.00	50.00
FH Franco Harris	40.00	80.00
FT Fran Tarkenton	30.00	60.00
GB George Blanda	40.00	80.00
GS Gale Sayers	60.00	100.00
HA Herb Adderley	20.00	40.00
JB Jim Brown	75.00	135.00
JE John Elway	125.00	200.00
JH Jack Ham	35.00	60.00
JK Jim Kelly	60.00	100.00
JM Joe Montana	125.00	250.00
MA Marcus Allen	30.00	80.00
MS Mike Singletary	25.00	50.00
PH Paul Hornung	40.00	80.00
PW Paul Warfield	20.00	40.00
RS Roger Staubach	75.00	135.00
SL Steve Largent	30.00	60.00
TA Troy Aikman	75.00	135.00
TD Tony Dorsett	50.00	100.00

2005 Upper Deck Legends Link to the Future Autographs

UNPRICED PRINT RUN 20 SER.#'d SETS

2005 Upper Deck Legends Link to the Past Autographs

UNPRICED PRINT RUN 20 SER.#'d SETS

2005 Upper Deck Legends Touchdown Tandems Autographs

UNPRICED TANDEMS SER.#'d TO 20

2006 Upper Deck Legends

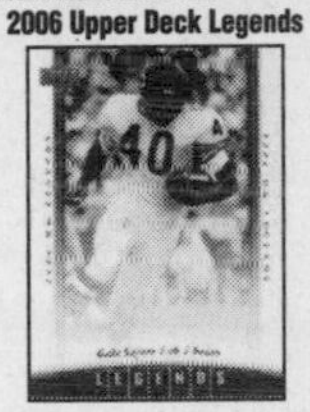

This 200-card set was released in August, 2006. The set was issued into the hobby in five-card packs with an $4.99 SRP which came 24 packs to a box. The first 100 cards (with a fex exceptions) featured retired greats while cards 101-200 featured rookies. Cards numbered 101-200 were issued to a stated print run of 750 serial numbered sets.

COMP.SET w/o RC's (100)	8.00	20.00
101-200 ROOKIE PRINT RUN 750		
1 Marshall Faulk	.25	.60
2 John Elway	.50	1.25
3 Barry Sanders	.50	1.25
4 Dan Marino	.60	1.50
5 Troy Aikman	.40	1.00
6 Roger Staubach	.50	1.25
7 Curtis Martin	.30	.75
8 O.J. McDuffie	.25	.60
9 Steve Young	.40	1.00
10 Jim Kelly	.40	1.00
11 Dan Fouts	.30	.75
12 Franco Harris	.30	.75
13 Christian Okoye	.25	.60
14 Craig Morton	.20	.50
15 Doug Flutie	.30	.75
16 Gale Sayers	.40	1.00
17 Bob Griese	.30	.75
18 Jim Plunkett	.25	.60
19 Marvin Harrison	.30	.75
20 L.C. Greenwood	.25	.60
21 Len Dawson	.30	.75
22 Ken Stabler	.40	1.00
23 Fran Tarkenton	.40	1.00
24 Herman Moore	.20	.50
25 Joe Theismann	.30	.75
26 Paul Hornung	.30	.75
27 Herschel Walker	.25	.60
28 Randy Moss	.30	.75
29 Drew Pearson	.25	.60
30 Don Maynard	.25	.60
31 Dwight Clark	.25	.60
32 Golden Richards	.20	.50
33 Wesley Walker	.25	.60
34 Greg Landry	.20	.50
35 Mick Tingelhoff	.20	.50
36 Ken O'Brien	.20	.50
37 Emerson Boozer	.20	.50
38 Reggie McKenzie	.20	.50
39 Wally Hilgenberg	.20	.50
40 Jan Stenerud	.20	.50
41 Roger Craig	.30	.75
42 Joe Cribbs	.25	.60
43 Reggie Rucker	.20	.50
44 Louis Lipps	.20	.50
45 Rick Upchurch	.20	.50
46 Ben Roethlisberger	.40	1.00
47 Rocket Ismail	.25	.60
48 Gary Clark	.25	.60
50 Dwight Stephenson	.20	.50
51 Joe Klecko	.20	.50
52 John Hannah	.20	.50
53 John Cappelletti	.20	.50
54 Tiki Barber	.30	.75
55 Coy Bacon	.20	.50
56 A.J. Duhe	.20	.50
57 Brett Favre	.60	1.50
58 Jon Kolb	.20	.50
59 Rich Saul	.20	.50
60B Diron Talbert	.20	.50

60A Antonio Freeman .25 .60
61 John Taylor .25 .60
62 Ron McDole .20 .50
63 Jethro Pugh .20 .50
64 Joe Jacoby .20 .50
65 Steve Smith .30 .75
66 Terrell Owens .30 .75
67 Charle Young .20 .50
68 Roy Jefferson .20 .50
69 Gary Fencik .20 .50
70 Terry Metcalf .20 .50
71 Johnny Rodgers .20 .50
72 Charles White .20 .50
73 Billy Sims .25 .60
74 Neal Anderson .20 .50
75 Marlin Briscoe .20 .50
76 Edgerrin James .25 .60
77 LaDainian Tomlinson .30 .75
78 Steve DeBerg .20 .50
79 Randy Grossman .20 .50
80 Ickey Woods .20 .50
81 Donovan McNabb .30 .75
82 Ron Mix .20 .50
83 Gerald Riggs Sr. .20 .50
84 Curt Warner .20 .50
85 Everson Walls .20 .50
86 Mike Quick .20 .50
87 Shaun Alexander .25 .60
88 Al Toon .20 .50
89 Nat Moore .20 .50
90 Michael Vick .30 .75
91 Carson Palmer .30 .75
92 Tom Brady .50 1.25
93 Gary Garrison .20 .50
94 Fred Dean .20 .50
95 Bob Trumpy .20 .50
96 Doug Cosbie .20 .50
97 Tommy Kramer .20 .50
98 Peyton Manning .50 1.25
99 John Brockington .20 .50
100 Stanley Morgan .25 .60
101 A.J. Hawk RC 2.50 6.00
102 Abdul Hodge RC 1.50 4.00
103 Antonio Cromartie RC 2.50 6.00
104 Anthony Fasano RC 2.50 6.00
105 Brandon Marshall RC 2.50 6.00
106 Ben Obomanu RC 2.50 6.00
107 Bobby Carpenter RC 1.50 4.00
108 Brad Smith RC 2.50 6.00
109 Erik Meyer RC 2.00 5.00
110 Brandon Williams RC 1.50 4.00
111 Brian Calhoun RC 1.50 4.00
112 Brodie Croyle RC 2.50 6.00
113 Frostee Rucker RC 2.00 5.00
114 Bruce Eugene RC 2.00 5.00
115 Bruce Gradkowski RC 2.50 6.00
116 Cedric Humes RC 1.50 4.00
117 Chad Greenway RC 2.50 6.00
118 Chad Jackson RC 1.50 4.00
119 Charles Davis RC 2.00 5.00
120 Charlie Whitehurst RC 2.50 6.00
121 Jason Allen RC 2.00 5.00
122 Cory Rodgers RC 2.00 5.00
123 Cory Ross RC 2.50 6.00
124 D.J. Shockley RC 2.00 5.00
125 Darnell Bing RC 2.00 5.00
126 Darrell Hackney RC 2.00 5.00
127 D'Brickashaw Ferguson RC 2.50 6.00
128 DeAngelo Williams RC 3.00 8.00
129 DeMeco Ryans RC 2.50 6.00
130 Demetrius Williams RC 2.00 5.00
131 Derek Hagan RC 2.00 5.00
132 Devin Aromashodu RC 2.50 6.00
133 Devin Hester RC 4.00 10.00
134 Dominique Byrd RC 2.00 5.00
135 Donte Whitner RC 2.50 6.00
136 DonTrell Moore RC 2.00 5.00
137 D'Qwell Jackson RC 2.00 5.00
138 Ernie Sims RC 2.00 5.00
139 John McCargo RC 1.50 4.00
140 Gerald Riggs Jr. RC 2.00 5.00
141 Greg Jennings RC 4.00 10.00
142 Greg Lee RC 1.50 4.00
143 Haloti Ngata RC 2.50 6.00
144 Johnathan Joseph RC 2.00 5.00
145 Jason Avant RC 1.50 4.00
146 Jay Cutler RC 5.00 12.00
147 Jeff King RC 2.00 5.00
148 Jeff Webb RC 2.00 5.00
149 Jeremy Bloom RC 2.00 5.00
150 Jerious Norwood RC 2.00 5.00
151 Jerome Harrison RC 2.50 6.00
152 Jimmy Williams RC 2.50 6.00
153 Joe Klopfenstein RC 1.50 4.00
154 Jonathan Orr RC 2.00 5.00
155 Joseph Addai RC 2.50 6.00
156 Josh Betts RC 2.00 5.00
157 Matt Baker RC 2.50 6.00
158 Kamerion Wimbley RC 2.50 6.00
159 Kellen Clemens RC 2.00 5.00
160 Ko Simpson RC 2.00 5.00
161 Laurence Maroney RC 2.00 5.00
162 Lawrence Vickers RC 2.00 5.00
163 LenDale White RC 2.00 5.00
164 Leon Washington RC 2.00 5.00
165 Leonard Pope RC 2.50 6.00
166 Marcedes Lewis RC 2.50 6.00
167 Marcus Vick RC 1.50 4.00
168 Mario Williams RC 2.50 6.00
169 Marques Hagans RC 1.50 4.00
170 Martin Nance RC 2.00 5.00
171 Mathias Kiwanuka RC 2.50 6.00
172 Matt Bernstein RC 1.50 4.00
173 Matt Leinart RC 2.50 6.00
174 Maurice Drew RC 4.00 10.00
175 Maurice Stovall RC 1.50 4.00
176 Michael Huff RC 2.00 5.00
177 Michael Robinson RC 2.00 5.00
178 Mike Hass RC 2.00 5.00
179 Miles Austin RC 6.00 15.00
180 Omar Jacobs RC 1.50 4.00
181 Owen Daniels RC 2.50 6.00
182 P.J. Daniels RC 1.50 4.00
183 Quinton Ganther RC 1.50 4.00
184 Reggie Bush RC 15.00 40.00
185 Reggie McNeal RC 2.00 5.00
186 Santonio Holmes RC 3.00 8.00
187 Sinorice Moss RC 2.50 6.00
188 Skyler Green RC 1.50 4.00
189 T.J. Williams RC 2.50 6.00
190 Tamba Hali RC 2.50 6.00
191 Manny Lawson RC 2.00 5.00
192 Tarvaris Jackson RC 2.50 6.00
193 Travis Wilson RC 1.50 4.00
194 Tye Hill RC 1.50 4.00
195 Vernon Davis RC 3.00 8.00
196 Vince Young RC 3.00 8.00
197 Wali Lundy RC 2.00 5.00
198 Wendell Mathis RC 2.00 5.00
199 Will Blackmon RC 2.00 5.00
200 Willie Reid RC 2.00 5.00

2006 Upper Deck Legends Canton Classics Autographs

UNPRICED CANTON AUTO SER.#'d TO 5

2006 Upper Deck Legends Franchise Signatures

UNPRICED FRANCHISE SIGS SER.#'d TO 5

2006 Upper Deck Legends Legendary Signatures

STATED ODDS 1:4
2 John Elway SP 100.00 200.00
3 Barry Sanders SP 125.00 250.00
4 Dan Marino SP 250.00 450.00
5 Troy Aikman SP 50.00 120.00
6 Roger Staubach SP 75.00 150.00
8 O.J. McDuffie 5.00 12.00
9 Steve Young SP 100.00 200.00
10 Jim Kelly SP 40.00 80.00
11 Dan Fouts SP 30.00 60.00
12 Franco Harris SP 50.00 100.00
13 Christian Okoye 6.00 15.00
14 Craig Morton 8.00 20.00
15 Doug Flutie SP 25.00 50.00
16 Gale Sayers SP 90.00 150.00
17 Bob Griese SP 40.00 80.00
18 Jim Plunkett 8.00 20.00
20 L.C. Greenwood SP 25.00 40.00
21 Len Dawson SP 25.00 50.00
22 Ken Stabler SP 30.00 60.00
23 Fran Tarkenton SP 30.00 50.00
24 Herman Moore 5.00 12.00
25 Joe Theismann 15.00 40.00
26 Paul Hornung 15.00 40.00
27 Herschel Walker SP 15.00 40.00
29 Drew Pearson 10.00 25.00
30 Don Maynard SP 20.00 40.00
31 Dwight Clark 8.00 20.00
32 Golden Richards 8.00 20.00
33 Wesley Walker 5.00 12.00
34 Greg Landry 6.00 15.00
35 Mick Tingelhoff 8.00 20.00
36 Ken O'Brien 5.00 12.00
37 Emerson Boozer 6.00 15.00
39 Wally Hilgenberg 5.00 12.00
40 Jan Stenerud 5.00 12.00
41 Roger Craig 5.00 12.00
42 Joe Cribbs 5.00 12.00
43 Reggie Rucker 5.00 12.00
44 Louis Lipps 6.00 15.00
45 Rick Upchurch 5.00 12.00
47 Rocket Ismail SP 8.00 20.00
48 Gary Clark 8.00 20.00
50 Dwight Stephenson 6.00 15.00
51 Joe Klecko 5.00 12.00
52 John Hannah 6.00 15.00
53 John Cappelletti 6.00 15.00
55 Coy Bacon 5.00 12.00
56 A.J. Duhe 5.00 12.00
59 Rich Saul 5.00 12.00
60 Antonio Freeman 6.00 15.00
60 Diron Talbert 5.00 12.00
61 John Taylor 6.00 15.00
62 Ron McDole 5.00 12.00
63 Jethro Pugh 6.00 15.00
64 Joe Jacoby 5.00 12.00
67 Charle Young 5.00 12.00
68 Roy Jefferson 6.00 15.00
69 Gary Fencik 6.00 15.00
70 Terry Metcalf 6.00 15.00
71 Johnny Rodgers 8.00 20.00
72 Charles White 6.00 15.00
73 Billy Sims 8.00 20.00
74 Neal Anderson 6.00 15.00
75 Marlin Briscoe 5.00 12.00
78 Steve DeBerg 5.00 12.00
79 Randy Grossman 6.00 15.00
80 Ickey Woods 6.00 15.00
82 Ron Mix 6.00 15.00
83 Gerald Riggs Sr. 5.00 12.00
84 Curt Warner 6.00 15.00
85 Everson Walls 8.00 20.00
86 Mike Quick 6.00 15.00
88 Al Toon 6.00 15.00
89 Nat Moore 6.00 15.00
93 Gary Garrison 5.00 12.00
94 Fred Dean 8.00 20.00
95 Bob Trumpy 5.00 12.00
96 Doug Cosbie 8.00 20.00
97 Tommy Kramer 6.00 15.00
99 John Brockington 8.00 20.00
100 Stanley Morgan 6.00 15.00

2006 Upper Deck Legends Signature Generations

UNPRICED SIG GENERATION SER.#'d TO 5

2006 Upper Deck Legends Time Passages Autographs

STATED PRINT RUN 5 SER.#'d SETS

2006 Upper Deck Legends Trophy Tandems Autographs

UNPRICED TROPHY TANDEM SER.#'d TO 5

1999 Upper Deck MVP Promos

These four cards were distributed at the 1998 Hawaii Trade Conference as well as other locations to promote the new Upper Deck brand. Dan Marino and Joe Montana signed a limited number of ProSign Promos.

COMPLETE SET (4) 80.00 200.00
54 Dan Marino 1.20 3.00
NNO Cover Card .02 .10
NNO Dan Marino AUTO 60.00 120.00
(ProSign card)
NNO Joe Montana AUTO 50.00 125.00
(ProSign card)

1999 Upper Deck MVP

The 1999 Upper Deck MVP set was issued in one series for a total of 220 cards and was distributed in packs with a suggested retail price of $1.59. The fronts feature color action player photos with player information on the backs.

COMPLETE SET (220) 10.00 25.00
1 Jake Plummer .15 .40
2 Adrian Murrell .15 .40
3 Larry Centers .15 .40
4 Frank Sanders .12 .30
5 Andre Wadsworth .12 .30
6 Rob Moore .12 .30
7 Simeon Rice .12 .30
8 Jamal Anderson .15 .40
9 Chris Chandler .15 .40
10 Chuck Smith .12 .30
11 Terance Mathis .12 .30
12 Tim Dwight .15 .40
13 Ray Buchanan .12 .30
14 O.J. Santiago .12 .30
15 Eric Zeier .12 .30
16 Priest Holmes .20 .50
17 Michael Jackson .12 .30
18 Jermaine Lewis .12 .30
19 Michael McCrary .12 .30
20 Rob Johnson .15 .40
21 Antowain Smith .12 .30
22 Thurman Thomas .20 .50
23 Doug Flutie .20 .50
24 Eric Moulds .15 .40
25 Bruce Smith .20 .50
26 Andre Reed UER .20 .50
((photo actually Kevin Williams)
27 Fred Lane .12 .30
28 Tim Biakabutuka .15 .40
29 Rae Carruth .12 .30
30 Wesley Walls .15 .40
31 Steve Beuerlein .15 .40
32 Muhsin Muhammad .15 .40
33 Erik Kramer .15 .40
34 Edgar Bennett .15 .40
35 Curtis Conway .15 .40
36 Curtis Enis .12 .30
37 Bobby Engram .15 .40
38 Alonzo Mayes .12 .30
39 Corey Dillon .15 .40
40 Jeff Blake .15 .40
41 Carl Pickens .15 .40
42 Darnay Scott .12 .30
43 Tony McGee .12 .30
44 Ki-Jana Carter .12 .30
45 Ty Detmer .15 .40
46 Terry Kirby .12 .30
47 Justin Armour .12 .30
48 Freddie Solomon .12 .30
49 Marquez Pope .12 .30
50 Antonio Langham .12 .30
51 Troy Aikman .30 .75
52 Emmitt Smith .50 1.25
53 Deion Sanders .20 .50
54 Rocket Ismail .15 .40
55 Michael Irvin .20 .50
56 Chris Warren .15 .40
57 Greg Ellis .12 .30
58 John Elway .60 1.50
59 Terrell Davis .20 .50
60 Rod Smith .15 .40
61 Shannon Sharpe .20 .50
62 Ed McCaffrey .15 .40
63 John Mobley .12 .30
64 Bill Romanowski .15 .40
65 Barry Sanders .50 1.25
66 Johnnie Morton .15 .40
67 Herman Moore .15 .40
68 Charlie Batch .15 .40
69 Germane Crowell .12 .30
70 Robert Porcher .12 .30
71 Brett Favre .60 1.50
72 Antonio Freeman .15 .40
73 Dorsey Levens .15 .40
74 Mark Chmura .12 .30
75 Vonnie Holliday .12 .30
76 Bill Schroeder .15 .40
77 Marshall Faulk .20 .50
78 Marvin Harrison .20 .50
79 Peyton Manning .60 1.50
80 Jerome Pathon .12 .30
81 E.G. Green .12 .30
82 Ellis Johnson .12 .30
83 Mark Brunell .15 .40
84 Jimmy Smith .15 .40
85 Keenan McCardell .15 .40
86 Fred Taylor .15 .40
87 James Stewart .12 .30
88 Kevin Hardy .12 .30
89 Elvis Grbac .12 .30
90 Andre Rison .15 .40
91 Derrick Alexander WR .12 .30
92 Tony Gonzalez .20 .50
93 Donnell Bennett .12 .30
94 Derrick Thomas .20 .50
95 Tamarick Vanover .15 .40
96 Dan Marino .60 1.50
97 Karim Abdul-Jabbar .15 .40
98 Zach Thomas .20 .50
99 O.J. McDuffie .15 .40
100 John Avery .12 .30
101 Sam Madison .12 .30
102 Randall Cunningham .20 .50
103 Cris Carter .20 .50
104 Robert Smith .15 .40
105 Randy Moss .20 .50
106 Jake Reed .15 .40
107 Matthew Hatchette .15 .40
108 John Randle .15 .40
109 Drew Bledsoe .20 .50
110 Terry Glenn .15 .40
111 Ben Coates .15 .40
112 Ty Law .15 .40
113 Tony Simmons .12 .30
114 Ted Johnson .15 .40
115 Danny Wuerffel .15 .40
116 Lamar Smith .12 .30
117 Sean Dawkins .12 .30
118 Cameron Cleeland .12 .30
119 Joe Johnson .12 .30
120 Andre Hastings .12 .30
121 Kent Graham .12 .30
122 Gary Brown .12 .30
123 Amani Toomer .15 .40
124 Tiki Barber .20 .50
125 Ike Hilliard .15 .40
126 Jason Sehorn .15 .40
127 Vinny Testaverde .15 .40
128 Curtis Martin .20 .50
129 Keyshawn Johnson .15 .40
130 Wayne Chrebot .15 .40
131 Mo Lewis .12 .30
132 Steve Atwater .15 .40
133 Donald Hollas .12 .30
134 Napoleon Kaufman .12 .30
135 Tim Brown .20 .50
136 Darrell Russell .12 .30
137 Rickey Dudley .12 .30
138 Charles Woodson .15 .40
139 Koy Detmer .12 .30
140 Duce Staley .15 .40
141 Charlie Garner .15 .40
142 Doug Pederson .12 .30
143 Jeff Graham .12 .30
144 Charles Johnson .12 .30
145 Kordell Stewart .15 .40
146 Jerome Bettis .20 .50
147 Hines Ward .20 .50
148 Courtney Hawkins .12 .30
149 Will Blackwell .12 .30
150 Richard Huntley .12 .30
151 Levon Kirkland .12 .30
152 Trent Green .15 .40
153 Tony Banks .15 .40
154 Isaac Bruce .20 .50
155 Eddie Kennison .15 .40
156 Az-Zahir Hakim .12 .30
157 Amp Lee .12 .30
158 Robert Holcombe .12 .30
159 Ryan Leaf .15 .40
160 Natrone Means .15 .40
161 Jim Harbaugh .15 .40
162 Junior Seau .20 .50
163 Charlie Jones .12 .30
164 Rodney Harrison .15 .40
165 Steve Young .25 .60
166 Jerry Rice .40 1.00
167 Garrison Hearst .15 .40
168 Terrell Owens .20 .50
169 J.J. Stokes .12 .30
170 Bryant Young .15 .40
171 Ricky Watters .15 .40
172 Joey Galloway .15 .40
173 Jon Kitna .15 .40
174 Ahman Green .15 .40
175 Mike Pritchard .12 .30
176 Chad Brown .12 .30
177 Warrick Dunn .15 .40
178 Trent Dilfer .15 .40
179 Mike Alstott .20 .50
180 Reidel Anthony .12 .30
181 Bert Emanuel .15 .40
182 Jacquez Green .12 .30
183 Hardy Nickerson .12 .30
184 Steve McNair .20 .50
185 Eddie George .15 .40
186 Yancey Thigpen .12 .30
187 Frank Wycheck .15 .40
188 Kevin Dyson .12 .30
189 Jackie Harris .15 .40
190 Blaine Bishop .12 .30
191 Skip Hicks .12 .30
192 Michael Westbrook .12 .30
193 Stephen Alexander .12 .30
194 Leslie Shepherd .12 .30
195 Jeff Hostetler .15 .40
196 Brian Mitchell .15 .40
197 Dan Wilkinson .15 .40
198 Terrell Davis CL .15 .40
199 Troy Aikman CL .25 .60
200 Tim Couch CL .15 .40
201 Ricky Williams RC .50 1.25
202 Tim Couch RC .30 .75
203 Akili Smith RC .25 .60
204 Daunte Culpepper RC .30 .75
205 Torry Holt RC .50 1.25
206 Edgerrin James RC .40 1.00
207 David Boston RC .25 .60
208 Peerless Price RC .25 .60
209 Chris Claiborne RC .20 .50
210 Champ Bailey RC .60 1.50
211 Cade McNown RC .25 .60
212 Jevon Kearse RC .30 .75
213 Joe Germaine RC .25 .60
214 D'Wayne Bates RC .20 .50
215 Dameane Douglas RC .20 .50
216 Troy Edwards RC .25 .60
217 Sedrick Irvin RC .20 .50
218 Brock Huard RC .25 .60
219 Amos Zereoue RC .25 .60
220 Donovan McNabb RC 1.25 3.00

1999 Upper Deck MVP Gold Script

*1-200 VETS/100: 15X TO 40X BASIC CARDS
*201-220 ROOKIES/100: 10X TO 25X BASIC RC
GOLD SCRIPT PRINT RUN 100 SER.#'d SETS

1999 Upper Deck MVP Silver Script

COMPLETE SET (217) 60.00 120.00
*1-200 VETS: 2X TO 5X BASIC CARDS
*201-220 ROOKIES: 1.2X TO 3X
STATED ODDS 1:2

1999 Upper Deck MVP Super Script

*1-200 VETS/25: 30X TO 80X BASIC CARDS
*201-220 ROOKIE/25: 20X TO 50X BASIC RC
STATED PRINT RUN 25 SERIAL #'d SETS

1999 Upper Deck MVP Draw Your Own Card

COMPLETE SET (30) 7.50 20.00
STATED ODDS 1:6
W1 Brett Favre .75 2.00
W2 Emmitt Smith .50 1.25
W3 John Elway .75 2.00
W4 Emmitt Smith .50 1.25
W5 Randy Moss .60 1.50
W6 Terrell Davis .25 .60
W7 Steve Young .30 .75
W8 Drew Bledsoe .30 .75
W9 Troy Aikman .50 1.25
W10 Terry Allen .08 .25
W11 Warrick Dunn .25 .60
W12 Kimble Anders .08 .25
W13 Joey Galloway .15 .40
W14 Barry Sanders .75 2.00
W15 Mark Brunell .25 .60
W16 Bruce Smith .15 .40
W17 Randy Moss .60 1.50
W18 Jerome Bettis .25 .60
W19 John Elway .75 2.00
W20 Jerome Bettis .25 .60
W21 Brett Favre .75 2.00
W22 Troy Aikman .50 1.25
W23 Cris Carter .25 .60
W24 Jason Gildon .08 .25
W25 Randall Cunningham .25 .60
W26 Thurman Thomas .15 .40
W27 Jerry Rice .50 1.25
W28 Jerome Bettis .25 .60
W29 Steve Young .30 .75
W30 Reggie White .25 .60

1999 Upper Deck MVP Drive Time

COMPLETE SET (14) 3.00 8.00
STATED ODDS 1:6
DT1 Steve Young .50 1.25
DT2 Kordell Stewart .25 .60
DT3 Eric Moulds .40 1.00
DT4 Corey Dillon .40 1.00
DT5 Doug Flutie .40 1.00
DT6 Charlie Batch .40 1.00
DT7 Curtis Martin .40 1.00
DT8 Marshall Faulk .50 1.25
DT9 Terrell Owens .40 1.00
DT10 Antowain Smith .40 1.00
DT11 Troy Aikman .75 2.00
DT12 Drew Bledsoe .50 1.25
DT13 Keyshawn Johnson .40 1.00
DT14 Steve McNair .40 1.00

1999 Upper Deck MVP Dynamics

COMPLETE SET (15) 30.00 60.00
STATED ODDS 1:28
D1 John Elway 5.00 12.00
D2 Steve Young 2.00 5.00
D3 Jake Plummer 1.00 2.50
D4 Fred Taylor 1.50 4.00
D5 Mark Brunell 1.50 4.00
D6 Joey Galloway 1.00 2.50
D7 Terrell Davis 1.50 4.00
D8 Randy Moss 4.00 10.00
D9 Charlie Batch 1.50 4.00
D10 Peyton Manning 5.00 12.00
D11 Barry Sanders 5.00 12.00
D12 Eddie George 1.50 4.00
D13 Warrick Dunn 1.50 4.00
D14 Jamal Anderson 1.50 4.00
D15 Brett Favre 5.00 12.00

1999 Upper Deck MVP Game Used Souvenirs

COMPLETE SET (22) 200.00 500.00
STATED ODDS 1:130
ASS Akili Smith 6.00 15.00
BFS Brett Favre 20.00 50.00
BHS Brock Huard 6.00 15.00
BSS Barry Sanders 15.00 40.00
CBS Champ Bailey 7.50 20.00
CMS Cade McNown 6.00 15.00
DBS David Boston 6.00 15.00
DCS Daunte Culpepper 12.50 30.00
DFS Doug Flutie 6.00 15.00
DMS Dan Marino 20.00 50.00
EJS Edgerrin James 12.50 30.00
ESS Emmitt Smith 15.00 40.00
JAS Jamal Anderson 6.00 15.00
JES John Elway 20.00 50.00
JPS Jake Plummer 6.00 15.00
KJS Keyshawn Johnson 6.00 15.00
MCS Donovan McNabb 15.00 40.00
PMS Peyton Manning 12.50 30.00
RMA Randy Moss AUTO/84 75.00 150.00
RMS Randy Moss 12.50 30.00
TCS Tim Couch 6.00 15.00
TDA Terrell Davis AUTO/30 50.00 120.00
TDS Terrell Davis 6.00 15.00
THS Torry Holt 6.00 15.00

1999 Upper Deck MVP Jumbos

COMPLETE SET (10) 20.00 40.00
ONE PER SPECIAL RETAIL BOX
201 Ricky Williams 1.00 2.50
202 Tim Couch .40 1.00
203 Akili Smith .30 .75
204 Daunte Culpepper 2.00 5.00
205 Torry Holt 1.25 3.00
206 Edgerrin James 2.00 5.00
207 David Boston .40 1.00
211 Cade McNown .30 .75
218 Brock Huard .40 1.00
220 Donovan McNabb 2.50 6.00

1999 Upper Deck MVP Power Surge

COMPLETE SET (15) 10.00 20.00
STATED ODDS 1:9
PS1 Jerome Bettis .75 2.00
PS2 Eddie George .75 2.00
PS3 Karim Abdul-Jabbar .50 1.25
PS4 Curtis Martin .75 2.00
PS5 Antowain Smith .75 2.00
PS6 Kordell Stewart .50 1.25
PS7 Curtis Enis .30 .75
PS8 Joey Galloway .50 1.25
PS9 Mark Brunell .75 2.00
PS10 Peyton Manning 2.50 6.00
PS11 Antonio Freeman .75 2.00
PS12 Jerry Rice 1.50 4.00
PS13 Eric Moulds .75 2.00
PS14 Drew Bledsoe 1.00 2.50
PS15 Fred Taylor .75 2.00

1999 Upper Deck MVP ProSign

STATED ODDS 1:216 RETAIL
AG Ahman Green 12.50 30.00
AM Adrian Murrell 5.00 12.00
AS Antowain Smith 12.50 30.00
AS Akili Smith 5.00 12.00
BH Brock Huard 7.50 20.00
CB Charlie Batch 5.00 12.00
CC Curtis Conway 7.50 20.00
CM Cade McNown SP 20.00 40.00
DC Daunte Culpepper SP
DM Donovan McNabb 40.00 80.00
EM Eric Moulds 7.50 20.00
EM Ed McCaffrey 7.50 20.00
FT Fred Taylor 20.00 50.00
GH Greg Hill 5.00 12.00
JA Jamal Anderson 7.50 20.00
JM John Mobley 5.00 12.00
JS Jimmy Smith 7.50 20.00
MB Michael Bishop 7.50 20.00
MF Marshall Faulk 20.00 40.00
MM Muhsin Muhammad 12.50 30.00
PH Priest Holmes 20.00 50.00
RE Robert Edwards 5.00 12.00
RL Ray Lewis 35.00 60.00
RM Randy Moss SP 150.00 300.00
RW Ricky Williams SP 100.00 200.00
RW Ricky Watters 7.50 20.00
SK Shaun King 5.00 12.00
SS Shannon Sharpe 12.50 30.00
TC Tim Couch 7.50 20.00
TD Terrell Davis 15.00 40.00
TG Trent Green 12.50 30.00
TH Torry Holt SP 15.00 40.00
TR Troy Drayton 5.00 12.00
KAJ Karim Abdul-Jabbar 5.00 12.00

1999 Upper Deck MVP Strictly Business

COMPLETE SET (13) 20.00 40.00
STATED ODDS 1:14
SB1 Eddie George 1.00 2.50
SB2 Curtis Martin 1.00 2.50
SB3 Fred Taylor 1.00 2.50
SB4 Steve Young 1.25 3.00
SB5 Kordell Stewart .60 1.50
SB6 Corey Dillon 1.00 2.50
SB7 Dan Marino 3.00 8.00
SB8 Jake Plummer .60 1.50
SB9 Jerry Rice 2.00 5.00
SB10 Warrick Dunn 1.00 2.50
SB11 Jerome Bettis 1.00 2.50
SB12 John Elway 3.00 8.00
SB13 Randy Moss 2.50 6.00

1999 Upper Deck MVP Theatre

COMPLETE SET (15) 12.50 25.00
STATED ODDS 1:9
M1 Terrell Davis .60 1.50
M2 Corey Dillon .60 1.50
M3 Brett Favre 2.00 5.00
M4 Jerry Rice 1.25 3.00
M5 Emmitt Smith 1.25 3.00
M6 Dan Marino 2.00 5.00
M7 Jerome Bettis .60 1.50
M8 Napoleon Kaufman .60 1.50
M9 Keyshawn Johnson .60 1.50
M10 Warrick Dunn .60 1.50
M11 Barry Sanders 2.00 5.00
M12 Troy Aikman 1.25 3.00
M13 Jamal Anderson .60 1.50
M14 Randall Cunningham .60 1.50
M15 Doug Flutie .60 1.50

2000 Upper Deck MVP

Released as both a Hobby and Retail product, Upper Deck MVP contains 187-veteran player cards, 29-prospect cards, and three checklists. Base cards are white-bordered and have gold foil highlights. Also inserted into this set was a Joe Montana tribute jersey card limited to just 350 copies. Card number 189 LaVar Arrington was not initially released as a full card, but instead packaged as a portion of a card with the center cut out. Card #220 Donovan Mcnabb CL was issued in two versions -- one with an embossed stamping on the front and one without. Like the Arrington, this card was supposed to have been pulled during the collation process but some copies did make the packout. MVP was packaged in boxes containing 28 packs of 10 cards each and carried a suggested retail price of $1.59.

COMPLETE SET (218) 10.00 25.00
1 Jake Plummer .12 .30
2 Michael Pittman .10 .25
3 Rob Moore .10 .25
4 David Boston .10 .25
5 Frank Sanders .10 .25
6 Aeneas Williams .10 .25
7 Kwamie Lassiter .10 .25
8 Tim Dwight .12 .30
9 Chris Chandler .12 .30
10 Jamal Anderson .12 .30
11 Shawn Jefferson .10 .25
12 Qadry Ismail .12 .30
13 Jermaine Lewis .10 .25
14 Rod Woodson .15 .40
15 Michael McCrary .10 .25
16 Tony Banks .10 .25
17 Peter Boulware .10 .25
18 Shannon Sharpe .15 .40
19 Peerless Price .12 .30
20 Rob Johnson .12 .30
21 Eric Moulds .12 .30
22 Doug Flutie .15 .40
23 Muhsin Muhammad .12 .30
24 Patrick Jeffers .12 .30
25 Steve Beuerlein .12 .30
26 Tim Biakabutuka .12 .30
27 Michael Bates .10 .25
28 Cade McNown .10 .25
29 Curtis Enis .10 .25
30 Marcus Robinson .12 .30
31 Shane Matthews .10 .25
32 Bobby Engram .12 .30
33 Glyn Milburn .10 .25
34 Akili Smith .10 .25
35 Corey Dillon .12 .30
36 Darnay Scott .12 .30
37 Tremain Mack .10 .25
38 Tim Couch .12 .30
39 Kevin Johnson .10 .25
40 Darrin Chiaverini .10 .25
41 Jamir Miller .10 .25
42 Errict Rhett .12 .30
43 Troy Aikman .25 .60
44 Emmitt Smith .40 1.00
45 Rocket Ismail .12 .30
46 Jason Tucker .10 .25
47 Dexter Coakley .10 .25
48 Joey Galloway .12 .30
49 Greg Ellis .10 .25
50 Terrell Davis .15 .40
51 Olandis Gary .12 .30
52 Brian Griese .12 .30
53 Ed McCaffrey .12 .30
54 Rod Smith .12 .30
55 Trevor Pryce .10 .25
56 Charlie Batch .12 .30
57 Germane Crowell .10 .25
58 Johnnie Morton .12 .30
59 Robert Porcher .10 .25
60 Luther Elliss .10 .25
61 James Stewart .10 .25
62 Brett Favre .50 1.25
63 Antonio Freeman .12 .30
64 Bill Schroeder .12 .30
65 Dorsey Levens .12 .30
66 Peyton Manning .40 1.00
67 Edgerrin James .15 .40
68 Marvin Harrison .12 .30
69 Ken Dilger .10 .25
70 Terrence Wilkins .10 .25
71 Mark Brunell .12 .30
72 Fred Taylor .12 .30
73 Jimmy Smith .12 .30
74 Keenan McCardell .10 .25
75 Carnell Lake .10 .25
76 Tony Brackens .10 .25
77 Kevin Hardy .10 .25
78 Hardy Nickerson .10 .25
79 Elvis Grbac .10 .25
80 Tony Gonzalez .12 .30
81 Derrick Alexander .12 .30
82 Donnell Bennett .10 .25
83 James Hasty .10 .25
84 Jay Fiedler .12 .30
85 James Johnson .10 .25
86 Tony Martin .10 .25
87 Damon Huard .12 .30
88 O.J. McDuffie .12 .30
89 Oronde Gadsden .12 .30
90 Zach Thomas .15 .40
91 Sam Madison .10 .25
92 Jeff George .12 .30
93 Randy Moss .15 .40
94 Robert Smith .12 .30
95 Cris Carter .15 .40
96 Matthew Hatchette .10 .25
97 Drew Bledsoe .15 .40
98 Terry Glenn .12 .30
99 Troy Brown .10 .25
100 Kevin Faulk .12 .30
101 Lawyer Milloy .10 .25
102 Ricky Williams .15 .40
103 Keith Poole .10 .25
104 Jake Reed .12 .30
105 Cam Cleeland .10 .25
106 Jeff Blake .12 .30
107 Andrew Glover .10 .25
108 Kerry Collins .12 .30
109 Amani Toomer .12 .30
110 Joe Montgomery .10 .25
111 Ike Hilliard .12 .30
112 Michael Strahan .12 .30
113 Jessie Armstead .10 .25
114 Ray Lucas .10 .25
115 Keyshawn Johnson .12 .30
116 Curtis Martin .15 .40
117 Vinny Testaverde .12 .30
118 Wayne Chrebet .12 .30
119 Dedric Ward .10 .25
120 Tim Brown .15 .40
121 Rich Gannon .12 .30
122 Tyrone Wheatley .10 .25
123 Napoleon Kaufman .12 .30
124 Charles Woodson .15 .40
125 Darrell Russell .10 .25
126 Duce Staley .12 .30
127 Donovan McNabb .15 .40
128 Torrance Small .10 .25
129 Allen Rossum .10 .25
130 Brian Dawkins .15 .40
131 Troy Vincent .10 .25
132 Troy Edwards .10 .25
133 Jerome Bettis .15 .40
134 Hines Ward .15 .40
135 Kordell Stewart .12 .30
136 Levon Kirkland .10 .25
137 Kent Graham .10 .25
138 Marshall Faulk .15 .40
139 Kurt Warner .25 .60
140 Torry Holt .15 .40
141 Isaac Bruce .15 .40
142 Kevin Carter .10 .25
143 Az-Zahir Hakim .10 .25
144 Todd Lyght .10 .25
145 Jermaine Fazande .10 .25
146 Curtis Conway .12 .30
147 Freddie Jones .10 .25
148 Junior Seau .15 .40
149 Jeff Graham .10 .25
150 Ryan Leaf .12 .30
151 Rodney Harrison .12 .30
152 Steve Young .20 .50
153 Jerry Rice .30 .75
154 Charlie Garner .12 .30
155 Terrell Owens .15 .40
156 Jeff Garcia .12 .30
157 Bryant Young .10 .25
158 Lance Schulters .10 .25
159 Ricky Watters .12 .30
160 Jon Kitna .12 .30
161 Derrick Mayes .10 .25
162 Sean Dawkins .10 .25
163 Cortez Kennedy .10 .25
164 Chad Brown .10 .25
165 Warrick Dunn .12 .30
166 Shaun King .10 .25
167 Mike Alstott .15 .40
168 Warren Sapp .12 .30
169 Jacquez Green .10 .25
170 Derrick Brooks .15 .40
171 John Lynch .12 .30
172 Donnie Abraham .10 .25
173 Eddie George .12 .30
174 Steve McNair .15 .40
175 Kevin Dyson .12 .30
176 Jevon Kearse .12 .30
177 Yancey Thigpen .10 .25
178 Frank Wycheck .12 .30
179 Eddie Robinson .10 .25
180 Samari Rolle .10 .25
181 Brad Johnson .12 .30
182 Stephen Davis .12 .30
183 Michael Westbrook .10 .25
184 Albert Connell .10 .25
185 Brian Mitchell .10 .25
186 Bruce Smith .15 .40
187 Stephen Alexander .10 .25
188 Peter Warrick RC .25 .60
189C Cutout Card 3.00 8.00
Arrington
190 Chris Redman RC .20 .50
191 Courtney Brown RC .20 .50
192 Brian Urlacher RC 1.00 2.50
193 Plaxico Burress RC .25 .60
194 Corey Simon RC .20 .50
195 Bubba Franks RC .25 .60
196 Deon Grant RC .15 .40
197 Michael Wiley RC .15 .40
198 Tim Rattay RC .20 .50
199 Ron Dayne RC .25 .60
200 Sylvester Morris RC .15 .40
201 Shaun Alexander RC .30 .75
202 Dez White RC .20 .50
203 Thomas Jones RC .30 .75
204 Reuben Droughns RC .25 .60
205 Travis Taylor RC .20 .50
206 Trevor Gaylor RC .15 .40
207 Jamal Lewis RC .25 .60
208 Chad Pennington RC .40 1.00
209 J.R. Redmond RC .15 .40
210 Laveranues Coles RC .25 .60
211 Travis Prentice RC .20 .50
212 R.Jay Soward RC .15 .40
213 Todd Pinkston RC .15 .40
214 Dennis Northcutt RC .20 .50
215 Shyrone Stith RC .15 .40
216 Tee Martin RC .25 .60
217 Giovanni Carmazzi RC .15 .40
218 Drew Bledsoe CL .12 .30
219 Steve Young CL .15 .40
220A Donovan McNabb CL SP 15.00 30.00
220B Donovan McNabb CL 15.00 30.00
(SP, embossed on front)

2000 Upper Deck MVP Gold Script

*VETS 1-220: 12X TO 30X BASIC CARDS
*ROOKIE 188-217: 8X TO 20X BASIC CARD
GOLD SCRIPT PRINT RUN 100 SER.#'d SETS

2000 Upper Deck MVP Silver Script

COMPLETE SET (218) 40.00 100.00
*VETS 1-220: 1.2X TO 3X BASIC CARDS
*ROOKIE 188-217: .8X TO 2X BASIC CARD
SILVER SCRIPT ODDS 1:2
189 LaVar Arrington 75.00 150.00
189C Cutout Card 12.00 30.00
Arrington
220 Donovan McNabb CL 50.00 100.00

2000 Upper Deck MVP Super Script

*VETS 1-220: 25X TO 60X BASIC CARDS
*ROOKIE 188-216: 15X TO 40X BASIC CARD
SUPER SCRIPT PRINT RUN 25 SER.#'d SETS

189 LaVar Arrington (full card; not cutout missing facsimile auto)	12.00	30.00

2000 Upper Deck MVP Air Show

COMPLETE SET (10)	5.00	12.00
STATED ODDS 1:14		
AS1 Brian Griese	.60	1.50
AS2 Drew Bledsoe	.75	2.00
AS3 Rob Johnson	.60	1.50
AS4 Jeff Garcia	.60	1.50
AS5 Ray Lucas	.50	1.25
AS6 Jon Kitna	.60	1.50
AS7 Jeff George	.60	1.50
AS8 Shaun King	.50	1.25
AS9 Troy Aikman	1.25	3.00
AS10 Steve Beuerlein	.60	1.50

2000 Upper Deck MVP Game Used Souvenirs

STATED ODDS 1:229 HOBBY		
AS Akili Smith	5.00	12.00
BF Brett Favre	25.00	60.00
BG Brian Griese	6.00	15.00
BJ Brad Johnson	6.00	15.00
CB Charlie Batch	6.00	15.00
CC Cris Carter	8.00	20.00
CM Cade McNown	5.00	12.00
DF Doug Flutie	8.00	20.00
DM Donovan McNabb	8.00	20.00
DM Dan Marino	25.00	60.00
EG Eddie George SB/40	60.00	100.00
EJ Edgerrin James	8.00	20.00
ES Emmitt Smith	20.00	50.00
FT Fred Taylor	8.00	20.00
JK Jon Kitna	6.00	15.00
JP Jake Plummer	6.00	15.00
JR Jerry Rice	15.00	40.00
KE Keyshawn Johnson	6.00	15.00
KJ Kevin Johnson	5.00	12.00
KW Kurt Warner SB/40	60.00	150.00
MA Mike Alstott	8.00	20.00
MB Mark Brunell	6.00	15.00
MF Marshall Faulk	8.00	20.00
PM Peyton Manning	20.00	50.00
RM Randy Moss	8.00	20.00
RW Ricky Williams	8.00	20.00
SD Stephen Davis	6.00	15.00
SK Shaun King	5.00	12.00
TA Troy Aikman	12.00	30.00
TC Tim Couch	6.00	15.00
TD Terrell Davis	8.00	20.00

2000 Upper Deck MVP Game Used Souvenirs Autographs

AUTO PRINT RUN 25 SER.#'d SETS		
ASA Akili Smith	20.00	50.00
BGA Brian Griese	25.00	60.00
BJA Brad Johnson	25.00	60.00
CDA Charlie Batch	25.00	60.00
CCA Cris Carter	30.00	80.00
DFA Doug Flutie	30.00	80.00
DMA Dan Marino	250.00	400.00
EJA Edgerrin James	30.00	80.00
JKA Jon Kitna	25.00	60.00
JPA Jake Plummer	25.00	60.00
KFA Keyshawn Johnson	25.00	60.00
KWA Kurt Warner	75.00	125.00
MBA Mark Brunell	25.00	60.00
MFA Marshall Faulk	30.00	80.00
PMA Peyton Manning	150.00	250.00
RMA Randy Moss	30.00	80.00
SDA Stephen Davis	25.00	60.00
TAA Troy Aikman	125.00	250.00
TCA Tim Couch	25.00	60.00
TDA Terrell Davis	30.00	80.00

2000 Upper Deck MVP Headliners

COMPLETE SET (10)	2.50	6.00
STATED ODDS 1:6		
H1 Isaac Bruce	.50	1.25
H2 Michael Westbrook	.30	.75
H3 James Stewart	.30	.75
H4 Keyshawn Johnson	.40	1.00
H5 Marcus Robinson	.40	1.00
H6 Charlie Batch	.40	1.00
H7 Marvin Harrison	.50	1.25
H8 Olandis Gary	.40	1.00
H9 Curtis Martin	.50	1.25
H10 Jevon Kearse	.40	1.00

2000 Upper Deck MVP Highlight Reel

COMPLETE SET (7)	5.00	12.00
STATED ODDS 1:28		
HR1 Marvin Harrison	1.25	3.00
HR2 Isaac Bruce	1.25	3.00
HR3 Cris Carter	1.25	3.00
HR4 Ray Lucas	.75	2.00
HR5 Muhsin Muhammad	1.00	2.50
HR6 Eddie George	1.00	2.50
HR7 Ricky Williams	1.25	3.00

2000 Upper Deck MVP Prolifics

COMPLETE SET (7)	10.00	25.00
STATED ODDS 1:28		
P1 Brett Favre	3.00	8.00
P2 Marshall Faulk	1.00	2.50
P3 Edgerrin James	1.00	2.50
P4 Peyton Manning	2.50	6.00
P5 Tim Couch	.75	2.00
P6 Dan Marino	3.00	8.00
P7 Kurt Warner	1.50	4.00

2000 Upper Deck MVP ProSign

STATED ODDS 1:215 RETAIL		
BG Brian Griese	10.00	25.00
CB Charlie Batch	10.00	25.00
CP Chad Pennington	15.00	40.00
CR Chris Redman	8.00	20.00
DW Dez White	8.00	20.00
EJ Edgerrin James	12.00	30.00
HT Ron Dayne	10.00	25.00
IB Isaac Bruce	12.00	30.00
JK Jon Kitna	10.00	25.00
JL Jamal Lewis	10.00	25.00
JP Jake Plummer	10.00	25.00
KC Kwame Cavil	8.00	20.00
KJ Keyshawn Johnson	10.00	25.00
KW Kurt Warner	20.00	50.00
MB Mark Brunell	10.00	25.00
MF Marshall Faulk	12.00	30.00
PM Peyton Manning	50.00	100.00
PW Peter Warrick EXCH	1.00	2.50
RD Ron Dugans	8.00	20.00
RM Randy Moss	30.00	60.00
SA Shaun Alexander	12.00	30.00
TC Tim Couch	10.00	25.00
TH Torry Holt	12.00	30.00
TJ Thomas Jones	12.00	30.00
TM Tee Martin	10.00	25.00
TT Travis Taylor	8.00	20.00

2000 Upper Deck MVP ProSign Gold

*GOLD/25: .8X TO 2X BASIC AUTO		
DM Dan Marino	175.00	300.00

2000 Upper Deck MVP Theatre

COMPLETE SET (10)	3.00	8.00
STATED ODDS 1:6		
M1 Troy Edwards	.30	.75
M2 Ed McCaffrey	.40	1.00
M3 Stephen Davis	.40	1.00
M4 Corey Dillon	.40	1.00
M5 Steve McNair	.50	1.25
M6 Jimmy Smith	.40	1.00
M7 Fred Taylor	.50	1.25
M8 Terrell Davis	.50	1.25
M9 Jon Kitna	.40	1.00
M10 Germane Crowell	.30	.75

2001 Upper Deck MVP

Released as both a Hobby and Retail product, Upper Deck MVP contains 280-veteran player cards, 45-prospect cards, and five checklists. Base cards are white-bordered with players team color trim and have silver foil highlights. MVP was packaged in boxes containing 24 packs of 8 cards each and carried a suggested retail price of $1.99.

COMPLETE SET (330)	20.00	50.00
1 Jake Plummer	.12	.30
2 David Boston	.10	.25
3 Thomas Jones	.12	.30
4 Michael Pittman	.12	.30
5 Frank Sanders	.10	.25
6 MarTay Jenkins	.10	.25
7 Pat Tillman RC	8.00	20.00
8 Tywan Mitchell	.10	.25
9 Jamal Anderson	.12	.30
10 Doug Johnson	.10	.25
11 Ephraim Salaam RC	.10	.25
12 Chris Chandler	.12	.30
13 Shawn Jefferson	.10	.25
14 Tim Dwight	.12	.30
15 Terance Mathis	.10	.25
16 Jamal Lewis	.15	.40
17 Shannon Sharpe	.15	.40
18 Trent Dilfer	.12	.30
19 Ray Lewis	.15	.40
20 Qadry Ismail	.12	.30
21 Travis Taylor	.10	.25
22 Chris Redman	.15	.40
23 Priest Holmes	.15	.40
24 Rod Woodson	.15	.40
25 Jamie Sharper	.10	.25
26 Doug Flutie	.15	.40
27 Rob Johnson	.12	.30
28 Eric Moulds	.12	.30
29 Sammy Morris	.12	.30
30 Shawn Bryson	.10	.25
31 Antowain Smith	.12	.30
32 Jeremy McDaniel	.10	.25
33 Sam Cowart	.10	.25
34 Muhsin Muhammad	.12	.30
35 Brad Hoover	.12	.30
36 Tim Biakabutuka	.10	.25
37 Steve Beuerlein	.12	.30
38 Donald Hayes	.10	.25
39 Jeff Lewis	.10	.25
40 Dameyune Craig	.10	.25
41 Wesley Walls	.10	.25
42 Isaac Byrd	.10	.25
43 Cade McNown	.12	.30
44 James Allen	.10	.25
45 Marcus Robinson	.12	.30
46 Brian Urlacher	.20	.50
47 Jim Miller	.12	.30
48 Curtis Enis	.10	.25
49 Eddie Kennison	.12	.30
50 Marty Booker	.12	.30
51 Bobby Engram	.12	.30
52 Peter Warrick	.12	.30
53 Corey Dillon	.12	.30
54 Akili Smith	.10	.25
55 Danny Farmer	.10	.25
56 Brandon Bennett	.10	.25
57 Curtis Keaton	.10	.25
58 Ron Dugans	.10	.25
59 Takeo Spikes	.10	.25
60 Scott Mitchell	.10	.25
61 Tim Couch	.10	.25
62 Kevin Johnson	.10	.25
63 Travis Prentice	.10	.25
64 Spergon Wynn	.10	.25
65 Errict Rhett	.12	.30
66 David Patten	.10	.25
67 Dennis Northcutt	.10	.25
68 Aaron Shea	.10	.25
69 Courtney Brown	.10	.25
70 Troy Aikman	.25	.60
71 Emmitt Smith	.40	1.00
72 Joey Galloway	.12	.30
73 Rocket Ismail	.12	.30
74 Randall Cunningham	.15	.40
75 Anthony Wright	.10	.25
76 James McKnight	.10	.25
77 Dexter Coakley	.10	.25
78 Terrell Davis	.15	.40
79 Mike Anderson	.12	.30
80 Brian Griese	.12	.30
81 Rod Smith	.12	.30
82 Ed McCaffrey	.12	.30
83 Olandis Gary	.10	.25
84 Trevor Pryce	.10	.25
85 John Mobley	.10	.25
86 Charlie Batch	.12	.30
87 Germane Crowell	.10	.25
88 James O. Stewart	.10	.25
89 Johnnie Morton	.12	.30
90 Herman Moore	.12	.30
91 Mario Bates	.10	.25
92 Desmond Howard	.12	.30
93 Stephen Boyd	.10	.25
94 Chris Claiborne	.10	.25
95 Kurt Schulz	.10	.25
96 Brett Favre	.50	1.25
97 Antonio Freeman	.15	.40
98 Dorsey Levens	.12	.30
99 Ahman Green	.15	.40
100 Matt Hasselbeck	.15	.40
101 De'Mond Parker	.10	.25
102 Bill Schroeder	.12	.30
103 Bubba Franks	.12	.30
104 Donald Driver	.15	.40
105 Darren Sharper	.12	.30
106 Peyton Manning	.40	1.00
107 Edgerrin James	.15	.40
108 Marvin Harrison	.15	.40
109 Jerome Pathon	.10	.25
110 Terrence Wilkins	.10	.25
111 Ken Dilger	.10	.25
112 Marcus Pollard	.10	.25
113 Brad Scioli RC	.10	.25
114 Mark Brunell	.12	.30
115 Fred Taylor	.15	.40
116 Jimmy Smith	.12	.30
117 Jamie Martin	.10	.25
118 Keenan McCardell	.12	.30
119 Kyle Brady	.10	.25
120 R.Jay Soward	.10	.25
121 Alvis Whitted	.10	.25
122 Brant Boyer RC	.10	.25
123 Elvis Grbac	.12	.30
124 Tony Gonzalez	.15	.40
125 Derrick Alexander	.10	.25
126 Tony Richardson	.10	.25
127 Frank Moreau	.10	.25
128 Sylvester Morris	.10	.25
129 Kevin Lockett	.10	.25
130 Donnie Edwards	.10	.25
131 Oronde Gadsden	.10	.25
132 Lamar Smith	.12	.30
133 Jay Fiedler	.12	.30
134 James Johnson	.10	.25
135 Thurman Thomas	.15	.40
136 Leslie Shepherd	.10	.25
137 Tony Martin	.12	.30
138 O.J. McDuffie	.10	.25
139 Zach Thomas	.15	.40
140 Randy Moss	.15	.40
141 Bubby Brister	.12	.30
142 Cris Carter	.15	.40
143 Daunte Culpepper	.12	.30
144 Moe Williams	.10	.25
145 Troy Walters	.10	.25
146 Chris Walsh RC	.10	.25
147 Matthew Hatchette	.10	.25
148 Kailee Wong	.10	.25
149 Robert Griffith	.10	.25
150 Drew Bledsoe	.15	.40
151 Terry Glenn	.12	.30
152 Kevin Faulk	.12	.30
153 J.R. Redmond	.10	.25
154 Tony Carter	.10	.25
155 Patrick Pass	.10	.25
156 Troy Brown	.12	.30
157 Tony Simmons	.10	.25
158 Michael Bishop	.12	.30
159 Lawyer Milloy	.12	.30
160 Ricky Williams	.15	.40
161 Jeff Blake	.12	.30
162 Joe Horn	.12	.30
163 Aaron Brooks	.12	.30
164 La'Roi Glover	.10	.25
165 Chad Morton	.10	.25
166 Keith Mitchell RC	.10	.26
167 Willie Jackson	.10	.25
168 Robert Wilson	.10	.25
169 Jake Reed	.12	.30
170 Kerry Collins	.12	.30
171 Amani Toomer	.12	.30
172 Ron Dayne	.12	.30
173 Tiki Barber	.15	.40
174 Greg Comella	.10	.25
175 Ike Hilliard	.12	.30
176 Joe Jurevicius	.10	.25
177 Ron Dixon	.10	.25
178 Jason Sehorn	.12	.30
179 Michael Strahan	.15	.40
180 Vinny Testaverde	.12	.30
181 Wayne Chrebet	.12	.30
182 Curtis Martin	.15	.40
183 Richie Anderson	.10	.25
184 Dedric Ward	.10	.25
185 Laveranues Coles	.12	.30
186 Windrell Hayes	.10	.25
187 Chad Pennington	.15	.40
188 Tim Brown	.15	.40
189 Rich Gannon	.12	.30
190 Tyrone Wheatley	.12	.30
191 Napoleon Kaufman	.10	.25
192 Jon Ritchie	.10	.25
193 James Jett	.10	.25
194 Rickey Dudley	.10	.25
195 Andre Rison	.12	.30
196 Eric Allen	.12	.30
197 Charles Woodson	.15	.40
198 Duce Staley	.12	.30
199 Donovan McNabb	.15	.40
200 Darnell Autry	.10	.25
201 Chad Lewis	.10	.25
202 Charles Johnson	.10	.25
203 Torrance Small	.10	.25
204 Todd Pinkston	.10	.25
205 Brian Mitchell	.12	.30
206 Hugh Douglas	.10	.25
207 David Akers RC	.10	.25
208 Kordell Stewart	.12	.30
209 Jerome Bettis	.15	.40
210 Bobby Shaw	.10	.25
211 Hines Ward	.15	.40
212 Plaxico Burress	.12	.30
213 Courtney Hawkins	.10	.25
214 Troy Edwards	.10	.25
215 Earl Holmes	.10	.25
216 Richard Huntley	.10	.25
217 Marshall Faulk	.15	.40
218 Kurt Warner	.25	.60
219 Isaac Bruce	.15	.40
220 Torry Holt	.12	.30
221 Trent Green	.15	.40
222 Justin Watson	.10	.25
223 Trung Canidate	.10	.25
224 Az-Zahir Hakim	.10	.25
225 Ricky Proehl	.10	.25
226 Dexter McCleon	.10	.25
227 London Fletcher	.10	.25
228 Junior Seau	.15	.40
229 Curtis Conway	.12	.30
230 Rodney Harrison	.12	.30
231 Jeff Graham	.10	.25
232 Freddie Jones	.10	.25
233 Reggie Jones	.10	.25
234 Ronney Jenkins	.10	.25
235 Trevor Gaylor	.10	.25
236 Jeff Garcia	.12	.30
237 Jerry Rice	.30	.75
238 Charlie Garner	.12	.30
239 Terrell Owens	.15	.40
240 J.J. Stokes	.10	.25
241 Fred Beasley	.10	.25
242 Tim Rattay	.10	.25
243 Garrison Hearst	.12	.30
244 Ricky Watters	.12	.30
245 Shaun Alexander	.15	.40
246 Jon Kitna	.12	.30
247 Brock Huard	.10	.25
248 Darrell Jackson	.12	.30
249 James Williams WR	.10	.25
250 Sean Dawkins	.10	.25
251 John Hilliard RC	.10	.25
252 Warrick Dunn	.15	.40
253 Shaun King	.10	.25
254 Ryan Leaf	.10	.25
255 Mike Alstott	.12	.30
256 Jacquez Green	.10	.25
257 Reidel Anthony	.10	.25
258 Derrick Brooks	.15	.40
259 John Lynch	.12	.30
260 Warren Sapp	.12	.30
261 Eddie George	.15	.40
262 Steve McNair	.15	.40
263 Rodney Thomas	.10	.25
264 Derrick Mason	.12	.30
265 Yancey Thigpen	.10	.25
266 Frank Wycheck	.10	.25
267 Chris Sanders	.10	.25
268 Carl Pickens	.12	.30
269 Kevin Dyson	.10	.25
270 Jevon Kearse	.12	.30
271 Jeff George	.12	.30
272 Stephen Davis	.12	.30
273 Brad Johnson	.12	.30
274 Albert Connell	.10	.25
275 James Thrash	.12	.30
276 Michael Westbrook	.10	.25
277 Stephen Alexander	.10	.25
278 Deion Sanders	.15	.40
279 Champ Bailey	.15	.40
280 Todd Husak	.10	.25
281 Dan Morgan RC	.30	.75
282 Josh Booty RC	.30	.75
283 Michael Vick RC	2.50	6.00
284 Mike McMahon RC	.30	.75
285 Reggie White RC	.25	.60
286 Chris Weinke RC	.30	.75
287 Drew Brees RC	3.00	8.00
288 Sage Rosenfels RC	.40	1.00
289 Marques Tuiasosopo RC	.30	.75
290 Josh Heupel RC	.40	1.00
291 David Rivers RC	.25	.60
292 Kevin Kasper RC	.25	.60
293 Jesse Palmer RC	.30	.75
294 LaDainian Tomlinson RC	2.50	6.00
295 Deuce McAllister RC	.40	1.00
296 Kevan Barlow RC	.30	.75
297 LaMont Jordan RC	.40	1.00
298 James Jackson RC	.25	.60
299 Anthony Thomas RC	.40	1.00
300 Correll Buckhalter RC	.40	1.00
301 Travis Henry RC	.30	.75
302 Dan Alexander RC	.30	.75
303 Travis Minor RC	.30	.75
304 Derrick Gibson RC	.25	.60
305 Rudi Johnson RC	.40	1.00
306 Michael Bennett RC	.30	.75
307 Alge Crumpler RC	.40	1.00
308 Todd Heap RC	.40	1.00
309 Snoop Minnis RC	.25	.60
310 Santana Moss RC	.50	1.25
311 Reggie Wayne RC	.75	2.00
312 Koren Robinson RC	.30	.75
313 Chris Chambers RC	.40	1.00
314 David Terrell RC	.30	.75
315 Rod Gardner RC	.30	.75
316 Quincy Morgan RC	.30	.75
317 Ken-Yon Rambo RC	.25	.60
318 Vinny Sutherland RC	.25	.60
319 David Allen RC	.25	.60
320 Bobby Newcombe RC	.30	.75
321 Ronney Daniels RC	.25	.60
322 T.J. Houshmandzadeh RC	.50	1.25
323 Chad Johnson RC	.60	1.50
324 Freddie Mitchell RC	.25	.60
325 Moran Norris RC	.25	.60
326 Ron Dayne CL	.10	.25
327 Mike Anderson CL	.10	.25
328 Jamal Lewis CL	.12	.30
329 Brian Urlacher CL	.15	.40
330 Darren Howard CL	.10	.25

2001 Upper Deck MVP Campus Classics Game Jerseys

STATED ODDS 1:144 HOB.		
CCAT Anthony Thomas	8.00	20.00
CCCM Cade McNown	6.00	15.00
CCCW Chris Weinke	6.00	15.00
CCDB Drew Brees	30.00	80.00
CCDM Deuce McAllister	8.00	20.00
CCFM Freddie Mitchell	5.00	12.00
CCJF Jamar Fletcher	5.00	12.00
CCKJ Keyshawn Johnson	6.00	15.00
CCLT LaDainian Tomlinson	15.00	40.00
CCMB Michael Bennett	6.00	15.00
CCMF Marshall Faulk	8.00	20.00
CCMT Marques Tuiasosopo	6.00	15.00
CCMV Michael Vick	20.00	50.00
CCPM Peyton Manning	25.00	60.00
CCRD Ron Dayne	6.00	15.00
CCTA Troy Aikman	15.00	40.00

2001 Upper Deck MVP Campus Classics Game Jerseys Autographs

STATED PRINT RUN 25 SER.#'d SETS		
CCSAT Anthony Thomas	30.00	80.00
CCSCM Cade McNown	25.00	60.00
CCSCW Chris Weinke	25.00	60.00
CCSDB Drew Brees	175.00	300.00
CCSDM Deuce McAllister	30.00	80.00
CCSFM Freddie Mitchell	20.00	50.00
CCSJF Jamar Fletcher	20.00	50.00
CCSLT LaDainian Tomlinson	150.00	300.00
CCSMB Michael Bennett	25.00	60.00
CCSMF Marshall Faulk	30.00	80.00
CCSMT Marques Tuiasosopo	25.00	60.00
CCSMV Michael Vick	125.00	300.00
CCSPM Peyton Manning	125.00	250.00
CCSRD Ron Dayne	25.00	60.00
CCSTA Troy Aikman	100.00	200.00

2001 Upper Deck MVP Souvenirs

STATED ODDS 1:48 HOB, 1:96 RET		
AB Aaron Brooks	4.00	10.00
BF Brett Favre	12.00	30.00
BU Brian Urlacher	6.00	15.00
BW Aaron Brooks Kurt Warner	10.00	25.00
CB Charlie Batch	4.00	10.00
CM Daunte Culpepper Randy Moss	6.00	15.00
DC Daunte Culpepper	4.00	10.00
DM Donovan McNabb	5.00	12.00
EJ Edgerrin James	5.00	12.00
FM Brett Favre Donovan McNabb	15.00	40.00
GB Rich Gannon Tim Brown	6.00	15.00
GD Jeff George Stephen Davis	5.00	12.00
GR Jeff Garcia Jerry Rice	12.00	30.00
JL Jamal Lewis	5.00	12.00
JR Jerry Rice	10.00	25.00
KJ Keyshawn Johnson	4.00	10.00
KW Kurt Warner	8.00	20.00
MC Donovan McNabb Daunte Culpepper	6.00	15.00
MJ Peyton Manning Edgerrin James	15.00	40.00
MR Cade McNown Marcus Robinson	5.00	12.00
PM Peyton Manning	12.00	30.00
PW Peter Warrick	4.00	10.00
RD Ron Dayne	4.00	10.00
RE J.R. Redmond	3.00	8.00
RM Randy Moss	5.00	12.00
SD Stephen Davis	4.00	10.00
TB Shaun King Keyshawn Johnson	5.00	12.00
TJ Thomas Jones	4.00	10.00
TM Vinny Testaverde Curtis Martin	6.00	15.00
WF Kurt Warner Marshall Faulk	10.00	25.00

2001 Upper Deck MVP Souvenirs Autographs

STATED PRINT RUN 25 SER.#'d SETS		
ABS Aaron Brooks	25.00	60.00
BUS Brian Urlacher	75.00	150.00
BWS Aaron Brooks Kurt Warner	40.00	100.00
CBS Charlie Batch	25.00	60.00
CMS Daunte Culpepper Randy Moss	75.00	150.00
DCS Daunte Culpepper	25.00	60.00
EJS Edgerrin James	30.00	80.00
GBS Rich Gannon Tim Brown	30.00	80.00
GDS Jeff George Stephen Davis	25.00	60.00
GRS Jeff Garcia Jerry Rice	175.00	300.00
JRS Jerry Rice	175.00	300.00
KWS Kurt Warner	40.00	100.00
MJS Peyton Manning Edgerrin James	150.00	250.00
MRS Cade McNown Marcus Robinson	25.00	60.00
PMS Peyton Manning	125.00	200.00
RDS Ron Dayne	25.00	60.00
RMS Randy Moss	75.00	150.00
SDS Stephen Davis	25.00	60.00
WFS Kurt Warner Marshall Faulk	75.00	150.00

2001 Upper Deck MVP Team MVP

COMPLETE SET (20)	5.00	12.00
STATED ODDS 1:6		
MVP1 Brian Griese	.50	1.25
MVP2 Rich Gannon	.50	1.25
MVP3 Marshall Faulk	.60	1.50
MVP4 Edgerrin James	.60	1.50
MVP5 Eddie George	.60	1.50
MVP6 Mike Anderson	.50	1.25
MVP7 Ed McCaffrey	.50	1.25
MVP8 Marvin Harrison	.60	1.50
MVP9 Isaac Bruce	.60	1.50
MVP10 Eric Moulds	.50	1.25
MVP11 Tony Gonzalez	.60	1.50
MVP12 Mike Alstott	.50	1.25
MVP13 Ray Lewis	.60	1.50
MVP14 Junior Seau	.60	1.50
MVP15 Warren Sapp	.50	1.25
MVP16 La'Roi Glover	.40	1.00
MVP17 Derrick Brooks	.60	1.50
MVP18 Charles Woodson	.60	1.50
MVP19 Champ Bailey	.60	1.50
MVP20 John Lynch	.50	1.25

2001 Upper Deck MVP Top 10 Performers

COMPLETE SET (10)	4.00	10.00
STATED ODDS 1:13		
TOP1 Mike Anderson	.50	1.25
TOP2 Vinny Testaverde	.50	1.25
TOP3 Terrell Owens	.60	1.50
TOP4 Aaron Brooks	.50	1.25
TOP5 Jamal Lewis	.60	1.50
TOP6 Fred Taylor	.60	1.50
TOP7 Randy Moss	.60	1.50
TOP8 Ricky Williams	.60	1.50
TOP9 Jason Sehorn	.50	1.25
TOP10 Shannon Sharpe	.60	1.50

2002 Upper Deck MVP

Released in July, 2002. There are 8 cards per pack and 24 packs per box. The set contains 255 veteran and 45 rookie cards.

COMPLETE SET (300)	20.00	50.00
1 Arnold Jackson	.12	.30
2 Dave Brown	.12	.30
3 David Boston	.12	.30
4 Frank Sanders	.12	.30
5 Jake Plummer	.15	.40
6 MarTay Jenkins	.12	.30
7 Freddie Jones	.12	.30
8 Jamal Anderson	.15	.40
9 Keith Brooking	.12	.30
10 Michael Vick	.30	.75
11 Rodney Thomas	.15	.40
12 Shawn Jefferson	.12	.30
13 Tony Martin	.15	.40
14 Warrick Dunn	.15	.40
15 Brandon Stokley	.15	.40
16 Chris McAlister	.12	.30
17 Chris Redman	.12	.30
18 Ray Lewis	.20	.50
19 Sam Gash	.12	.30
20 Travis Taylor	.12	.30
21 Terry Allen	.15	.40
22 Drew Bledsoe	.20	.50
23 Alex Van Pelt	.12	.30
24 Eric Moulds	.15	.40
25 Kenyatta Wright	.12	.30
26 Larry Centers	.15	.40
27 Peerless Price	.12	.30
28 Shawn Bryson	.12	.30
29 Travis Henry	.12	.30
30 Chris Weinke	.12	.30
31 Lamar Smith	.15	.40
32 Isaac Byrd	.12	.30
33 Muhsin Muhammad	.15	.40
34 Nick Goings	.12	.30
35 Richard Huntley	.12	.30
36 Tim Biakabutuka	.15	.40
37 Wesley Walls	.15	.40
38 Anthony Thomas	.15	.40
39 Brian Urlacher	.20	.50
40 David Terrell	.12	.30
41 Dez White	.12	.30
42 Jim Miller	.12	.30
43 Larry Whigham	.12	.30
44 Marty Booker	.15	.40
45 Chris Chandler	.15	.40
46 Corey Dillon	.15	.40
47 Darnay Scott	.15	.40
48 Jon Kitna	.15	.40
49 Peter Warrick	.15	.40
50 Ron Dugans	.12	.30
51 Scott Mitchell	.15	.40
52 Chad Johnson	.20	.50
53 Courtney Brown	.12	.30
54 JaJuan Dawson	.12	.30
55 James Jackson	.12	.30
56 Kevin Johnson	.12	.30
57 Quincy Morgan	.12	.30
58 Rickey Dudley	.12	.30
59 Tim Couch	.12	.30
60 Chris Sanders	.12	.30
61 Emmitt Smith	.50	1.25
62 Joey Galloway	.15	.40
63 Ken-Yon Rambo	.12	.30
64 La'Roi Glover	.12	.30
65 Quincy Carter	.12	.30
66 Rocket Ismail	.15	.40
67 Darren Woodson	.15	.40
68 Ryan Leaf	.12	.30
69 Chester McGlockton	.12	.30
70 Brian Griese	.15	.40
71 Shannon Sharpe	.20	.50
72 Kevin Kasper	.12	.30
73 Mike Anderson	.15	.40
74 Olandis Gary	.15	.40
75 Rod Smith	.15	.40
76 Terrell Davis	.20	.50
77 Anthony Carter	.15	.40
78 Az-Zahir Hakim	.12	.30
79 Charlie Batch	.12	.30
80 Chris Claiborne	.12	.30
81 Cory Schlesinger	.12	.30
82 Desmond Howard	.15	.40
83 Germane Crowell	.12	.30
84 James Stewart	.12	.30
85 Mike McMahon	.12	.30
86 Bill Schroeder	.12	.30
87 Ahman Green	.15	.40
88 Brett Favre	.50	1.25
89 Bubba Franks	.15	.40
90 Antonio Freeman	.20	.50
91 Donald Driver	.20	.50
92 Kabeer Gbaja-Biamila	.15	.40
93 William Henderson	.15	.40
94 Corey Bradford	.12	.30
95 Jamie Sharper	.15	.40
96 Jermaine Lewis	.12	.30
97 Kailee Wong	.12	.30
98 Matt Stevens	.12	.30
99 Tony Boselli	.15	.40
100 James Allen	.12	.30
101 Aaron Glenn	.12	.30
102 Edgerrin James	.15	.40
103 Dominic Rhodes	.15	.40
104 Marcus Pollard	.12	.30
105 Marvin Harrison	.20	.50
106 Peyton Manning	.40	1.00
107 Qadry Ismail	.15	.40
108 Reggie Wayne	.20	.50
109 Stacey Mack	.12	.30
110 Elvis Joseph	.12	.30
111 Fred Taylor	.15	.40
112 Jimmy Smith	.15	.40
113 Jonathan Quinn	.12	.30
114 Keenan McCardell	.15	.40
115 Mark Brunell	.15	.40
116 Trent Green	.15	.40
117 Derrick Alexander	.12	.30
118 Johnnie Morton	.15	.40
119 Snoop Minnis	.12	.30
120 Mike Cloud	.12	.30
121 Priest Holmes	.20	.50
122 Tony Gonzalez	.20	.50
123 Tony Richardson	.12	.30
124 Ricky Williams	.15	.40
125 Chris Chambers	.15	.40
126 James McKnight	.12	.30
127 Jay Fiedler	.15	.40
128 Zach Thomas	.20	.50
129 Oronde Gadsden	.12	.30
130 Ray Lucas	.12	.30
131 Randy Moss	.20	.50
132 Spergon Wynn	.12	.30
133 Cris Carter	.20	.50
134 Daunte Culpepper	.15	.40
135 Doug Chapman	.12	.30
136 Michael Bennett	.15	.40
137 Tom Brady	.50	1.25
138 Troy Brown	.15	.40
139 Adam Vinatieri	.20	.50
140 Antowain Smith	.15	.40
141 David Patten	.12	.30
142 Donald Hayes	.12	.30
143 J.R. Redmond	.12	.30
144 Willie Jackson	.12	.30
145 Jerome Pathon	.12	.30
146 Jake Reed	.15	.40
147 Aaron Brooks	.15	.40
148 John Carney	.12	.30
149 Deuce McAllister	.15	.40
150 Joe Horn	.15	.40
151 Kyle Turley	.12	.30
152 Robert Wilson	.12	.30
153 Tiki Barber	.20	.50
154 Amani Toomer	.15	.40
155 Ike Hilliard	.15	.40
156 Jason Sehorn	.15	.40
157 Joe Jurevicius	.12	.30
158 Kerry Collins	.15	.40
159 Michael Strahan	.20	.50
160 Ron Dayne	.15	.40
161 Wayne Chrebet	.15	.40
162 Chad Pennington	.20	.50
163 Curtis Martin	.20	.50
164 LaMont Jordan	.15	.40
165 Laveranues Coles	.15	.40
166 Marvin Jones	.12	.30
167 Santana Moss	.15	.40
168 Vinny Testaverde	.15	.40
169 Tyrone Wheatley	.15	.40
170 Charles Woodson	.20	.50
171 Charlie Garner	.15	.40
172 Jerry Rice	.40	1.00
173 John Parrella	.12	.30
174 Jon Ritchie	.12	.30
175 Rich Gannon	.15	.40
176 Tim Brown	.20	.50
177 Todd Pinkston	.12	.30
178 Correll Buckhalter	.15	.40
179 Donovan McNabb	.20	.50
180 Duce Staley	.15	.40
181 Freddie Mitchell	.12	.30
182 Hugh Douglas	.12	.30
183 James Thrash	.15	.40
184 Koy Detmer	.15	.40
185 Troy Edwards	.12	.30
186 Chris Fuamatu-Ma'afala	.12	.30
187 Hines Ward	.20	.50
188 Jerome Bettis	.20	.50
189 Kendrell Bell	.12	.30
190 Kordell Stewart	.15	.40
191 Mark Bruener	.15	.40
192 Plaxico Burress	.15	.40
193 Tim Dwight	.12	.30
194 Curtis Conway	.15	.40
195 Doug Flutie	.20	.50
196 Drew Brees	.30	.75
197 Junior Seau	.20	.50
198 LaDainian Tomlinson	.25	.60
199 Marcellus Wiley	.12	.30
200 Rodney Harrison	.15	.40
201 Stephen Alexander	.12	.30
202 Terrell Owens	.20	.50
203 Andre Carter	.12	.30
204 Cedrick Wilson	.15	.40
205 Fred Beasley	.12	.30
206 Garrison Hearst	.15	.40
207 J.J. Stokes	.12	.30
208 Jeff Garcia	.15	.40
209 Kevan Barlow	.12	.30
210 Tai Streets	.12	.30
211 Doug Evans	.12	.30
212 Bobby Engram	.15	.40
213 Darrell Jackson	.15	.40
214 James Williams	.12	.30
215 John Randle	.15	.40
216 Koren Robinson	.12	.30
217 Matt Hasselbeck	.20	.50
218 Shaun Alexander	.15	.40
219 Trent Dilfer	.15	.40
220 Aeneas Williams	.15	.40
221 Isaac Bruce	.20	.50
222 Kurt Warner	.20	.50
223 Marshall Faulk	.20	.50
224 Ricky Proehl	.15	.40
225 Torry Holt	.20	.50
226 Trung Canidate	.12	.30
227 Terrence Wilkins	.12	.30
228 John Lynch	.15	.40
229 Keyshawn Johnson	.15	.40
230 Michael Pittman	.15	.40
231 Mike Alstott	.15	.40
232 Rob Johnson	.15	.40
233 Shaun King	.12	.30
234 Warren Sapp	.15	.40
235 Brad Johnson	.15	.40
236 Derrick Mason	.15	.40
237 Eddie George	.15	.40
238 Frank Wycheck	.12	.30
239 Jevon Kearse	.15	.40
240 Kevin Dyson	.15	.40
241 Steve McNair	.20	.50
242 Chris Coleman	.12	.30
243 Darrell Green	.20	.50
244 Jacquez Green	.12	.30
245 Ki-Jana Carter	.15	.40
246 Michael Westbrook	.12	.30
247 Rod Gardner	.12	.30
248 Stephen Davis	.15	.40
249 Tony Banks	.12	.30
250 Champ Bailey	.20	.50
251 David Carr RC	.40	1.00
252 DeShaun Foster RC	.40	1.00
253 Antonio Bryant RC	.40	1.00
254 Joey Harrington RC	.40	1.00
255 William Green RC	.30	.75
256 Josh Reed RC	.30	.75
257 Patrick Ramsey RC	.40	1.00
258 Clinton Portis RC	.50	1.25
259 Jabar Gaffney RC	.40	1.00
260 Rohan Davey RC	.40	1.00
261 T.J. Duckett RC	.40	1.00
262 Ashley Lelie RC	.30	.75
263 Kurt Kittner RC	.25	.60
264 Luke Staley RC	.25	.60
265 Ron Johnson RC	.30	.75
266 Antwaan Randle El RC	.40	1.00
267 Travis Stephens RC	.25	.60
268 Marquise Walker RC	.25	.60
269 Julius Peppers RC	.75	2.00
270 Chad Hutchinson RC	.25	.60
271 Maurice Morris RC	.30	.75
272 Reche Caldwell RC	.40	1.00
273 Randy Fasani RC	.30	.75
274 Lamar Gordon RC	.30	.75
275 Donte Stallworth RC	.40	1.00
276 Brandon Doman RC	.25	.60
277 Damien Anderson RC	.25	.60
278 Roy Williams RC	.40	1.00
279 J.T. O'Sullivan RC	.30	.75
280 Leonard Henry RC	.25	.60
281 Javon Walker RC	.40	1.00
282 David Garrard RC	.50	1.25
283 Chester Taylor RC	.40	1.00
284 Andre Davis RC	.30	.75
285 Josh McCown RC	.40	1.00
286 Adrian Peterson RC	.40	1.00
287 Seth Burford RC	.25	.60
288 Deion Branch RC	.40	1.00
289 Jonathan Wells RC	.40	1.00
290 Ladell Betts RC	.40	1.00
291 Cliff Russell RC	.25	.60
292 Eric Crouch RC	.40	1.00
293 Dusty Bonner RC	.25	.60
294 Tim Carter RC	.30	.75
295 Brian Westbrook RC	.60	1.50
296 Quentin Jammer RC	.40	1.00
297 Brian Poli-Dixon RC	.25	.60
298 Donovan McNabb CL	.12	.30
299 Curtis Martin CL	.12	.30
300 Tom Brady CL	.30	.75

2002 Upper Deck MVP Gold

*VETS: 20X TO 50X BASIC CARDS
*ROOKIES: 10X TO 25X BASIC CARDS
STATED PRINT RUN 25 SER.#'d SETS

2002 Upper Deck MVP Silver

*VETS: 6X TO 15X BASIC CARDS
*ROOKIES: 3X TO 8X BASIC CARDS
STATED PRINT RUN 100 SER.#'d SETS

2002 Upper Deck MVP ProSign

STATED PRINT RUN 127 SER.#'d SETS		
PSAT Anthony Thomas	12.00	30.00
PSCC Chris Chambers	12.00	30.00
PSCW Chris Weinke	10.00	25.00
PSDB Drew Brees	30.00	60.00
PSEC Eric Crouch	15.00	40.00
PSFM Freddie Mitchell	10.00	25.00
PSJR Josh Reed	12.00	30.00
PSMMC Mike McMahon	10.00	25.00
PSMW Marquise Walker	10.00	25.00
PSPM Peyton Manning	50.00	100.00

PSRJ Ron Johnson	12.00	30.00
PSWG William Green	12.00	30.00

2002 Upper Deck MVP Souvenirs

STATED ODDS 1:48 HOB/RET

SSAB Anthony Becht	3.00	8.00
SSAT Anthony Thomas	4.00	10.00
SSBF Brett Favre	12.00	30.00
SSCB Champ Bailey	5.00	12.00
SSCC Curtis Conway	4.00	10.00
SSCG Charlie Garner	4.00	10.00
SSCP Chad Pennington	5.00	12.00
SSCW Charles Woodson	5.00	12.00
SSDB Drew Brees	8.00	20.00
SSDF Doug Flutie	5.00	12.00
SSDS Duce Staley	4.00	10.00
SSDT David Terrell	3.00	8.00
SSEM Eric Moulds	4.00	10.00
SSFS Frank Sanders	3.00	8.00
SSFT Fred Taylor	4.00	10.00
SSJA Jessie Armstead	3.00	8.00
SSJG Jeff Garcia	4.00	10.00
SSJJ J.J. Stokes	3.00	8.00
SSJS Junior Seau	5.00	12.00
SSMB Mark Brunell	4.00	10.00
SSRG Rod Gardner	3.00	8.00
SSSD Stephen Davis	4.00	10.00

2002 Upper Deck MVP Souvenirs Doubles

STATED ODDS 1:48

SDBB Mark Brunell	5.00	12.00
SDBG Champ Bailey Darrell Green	6.00	15.00
SDBT Drew Brees LaDainian Tomlinson	10.00	25.00
SDCH Kerry Collins Ike Hilliard	5.00	12.00
SDCJ Tim Couch Kevin Johnson	4.00	10.00
SDDA Warrick Dunn Mike Alstott	5.00	12.00
SDGF Jeff Garcia Doug Flutie	6.00	15.00
SDJF Freddie Jones Doug Flutie	6.00	15.00
SDLS Jermaine Lewis Jamie Sharper	5.00	12.00
SDMH Peyton Manning Marvin Harrison	12.00	30.00
SDMJ Quincy Morgan James Jackson	4.00	10.00
SDMT Jim Miller David Terrell	4.00	10.00
SDPJ LaMont Jordan Chad Pennington	6.00	15.00
SDPS Jake Plummer Frank Sanders	5.00	12.00
SDRR Jerry Rice	12.00	30.00
SDSM Duce Staley Donovan McNabb	6.00	15.00
SDTM Vinny Testaverde Curtis Martin	6.00	15.00
SDTT Anthony Thomas LaDainian Tomlinson	8.00	20.00
SDUS Brian Urlacher Junior Seau	6.00	15.00

2002 Upper Deck MVP Team MVP

COMPLETE SET (20)	10.00	25.00
STATED ODDS 1:6 HOB/RET		
TM1 Jake Plummer	.60	1.50
TM2 Michael Vick	1.25	3.00
TM3 Corey Dillon	.60	1.50
TM4 Tim Couch	.50	1.25
TM5 Rod Smith	.60	1.50
TM6 Brett Favre	2.00	5.00
TM7 Peyton Manning	1.50	4.00
TM8 Mark Brunell	.60	1.50
TM9 Randy Moss	.75	2.00
TM10 Ricky Williams	.60	1.50
TM11 Curtis Martin	.75	2.00
TM12 Donovan McNabb	.75	2.00
TM13 Kordell Stewart	.60	1.50
TM14 LaDainian Tomlinson	1.00	2.50
TM15 Jeff Garcia	.60	1.50
TM16 Terrell Owens	.75	2.00
TM17 Shaun Alexander	.60	1.50
TM18 Isaac Bruce	.75	2.00
TM19 Keyshawn Johnson	.60	1.50
TM20 Eddie George	.60	1.50

2002 Upper Deck MVP Top 10 Performers

COMPLETE SET (10)	7.50	20.00
STATED ODDS 1:12 HOB/RET		
TT1 Anthony Thomas	.60	1.50
TT2 Priest Holmes	.75	2.00
TT3 Tom Brady	2.00	5.00
TT4 Michael Strahan	.75	2.00
TT5 Jerry Rice	1.50	4.00
TT6 Rich Gannon	.60	1.50
TT7 Emmitt Smith	2.00	5.00
TT8 Jerome Bettis	.75	2.00
TT9 Kurt Warner	.75	2.00
TT10 Marshall Faulk	.75	2.00

2003 Upper Deck MVP

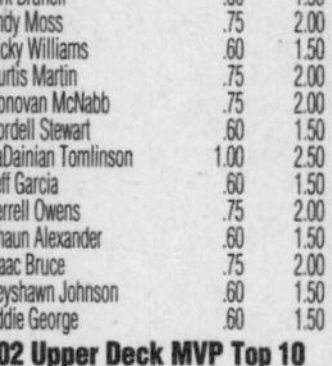

Issued in July of 2003, this set consists of 440 cards, including 330 veterans and 100 rookies. The rookie cards were issued approximately two per pack. Boxes featured 24 packs, each with 8 cards.

COMPLETE SET (440)	30.00	60.00
1 Brad Johnson	.15	.40
2 Dexter Jackson RC	.20	.50
3 Derrick Brooks	.15	.40
4 Simeon Rice	.12	.30
5 Warren Sapp	.15	.40
6 John Lynch	.15	.40
7 Joe Jurevicius	.15	.40
8 Ronde Barber	.15	.40
9 Mike Alstott	.20	.50
10 Michael Pittman	.12	.30
11 Keyshawn Johnson	.20	.50
12 Jerry Rice	.40	1.00
13 Tim Brown	.20	.50
14 Rich Gannon	.15	.40
15 Charlie Garner	.15	.40
16 Jerry Porter	.12	.30
17 Sebastian Janikowski	.15	.40
18 Zack Crockett	.15	.40
19 Tyrone Wheatley	.15	.40
20 Bill Romanowski	.15	.40
21 Charles Woodson	.20	.50
22 Rod Woodson	.20	.50
23 Donovan McNabb	.20	.50
24 James Thrash	.12	.30
25 Duce Staley	.15	.40
26 Brian Westbrook	.20	.50
27 A.J. Feeley	.12	.30
28 Koy Detmer	.12	.30
29 Brian Dawkins	.15	.40
30 Dorsey Levens	.15	.40
31 Jon Ritchie	.12	.30
32 Todd Pinkston	.12	.30
33 Chad Lewis	.15	.40
34 Brett Favre	.50	1.25
35 Ahman Green	.15	.40
36 Donald Driver	.20	.50
37 Bubba Franks	.15	.40
38 Javon Walker	.15	.40
39 Kabeer Gbaja-Biamila	.15	.40
40 Robert Ferguson	.12	.30
41 Tony Fisher	.12	.30
42 Marques Anderson	.12	.30
43 Ryan Longwell	.15	.40
44 Craig Nall	.12	.30
45 Steve McNair	.20	.50
46 Eddie George	.15	.40
47 Jevon Kearse	.15	.40
48 Kevin Carter	.15	.40
49 Samari Rolle	.15	.40
50 Keith Bulluck	.12	.30
51 Joe Nedney	.12	.30
52 Robert Holcombe	.12	.30
53 Drew Bennett	.15	.40
54 Frank Wycheck	.12	.30
55 Derrick Mason	.15	.40
56 Tommy Maddox	.15	.40
57 Jerome Bettis	.20	.50
58 Plaxico Burress	.15	.40
59 Antwaan Randle El	.15	.40
60 Amos Zereoue	.12	.30
61 Chris Fuamatu-Ma'afala	.15	.40
62 Jason Gildon	.15	.40
63 Kendrell Bell	.12	.30
64 Dewayne Washington	.12	.30
65 Jeff Reed RC	.40	1.00
66 Hines Ward	.20	.50
67 Jeff Garcia	.15	.40
68 Terrell Owens	.20	.50
69 Andre Carter	.12	.30
70 Tai Streets	.12	.30
71 Tim Rattay	.12	.30
72 Eric Johnson	.15	.40
73 Cedrick Wilson	.12	.30
74 Brandon Doman	.12	.30
75 Kevan Barlow	.12	.30
76 Bryant Young	.12	.30
77 Garrison Hearst	.15	.40
78 Kerry Collins	.15	.40
79 Daryl Jones	.12	.30
80 Tiki Barber	.20	.50
81 Amani Toomer	.15	.40
82 Tim Carter	.12	.30
83 Michael Strahan	.20	.50
84 Ike Hilliard	.12	.30
85 Brian Mitchell	.12	.30
86 Ron Dixon	.12	.30
87 Jeremy Shockey	.20	.50
88 Marvin Harrison	.20	.50
89 Peyton Manning	.40	1.00
90 Edgerrin James	.20	.50
91 Dominic Rhodes	.15	.40
92 Brock Huard	.12	.30
93 Marcus Pollard	.12	.30
94 James Mungro	.12	.30
95 Dwight Freeney	.15	.40
96 Reggie Wayne	.20	.50
97 Rob Morris	.12	.30
98 Michael Vick	.25	.60
99 Warrick Dunn	.15	.40
100 T.J. Duckett	.15	.40
101 Keith Brooking	.15	.40
102 Ray Buchanan	.12	.30
103 Alge Crumpler	.15	.40
104 Quentin McCord	.12	.30
105 Doug Johnson	.12	.30
106 Brian Finneran	.12	.30
107 Peerless Price	.12	.30
108 Chad Pennington	.20	.50
109 Curtis Martin	.20	.50
110 Laveranues Coles	.12	.30
111 Wayne Chrebet	.15	.40
112 LaMont Jordan	.15	.40
113 Anthony Becht	.12	.30
114 Marvin Jones	.12	.30
115 Mo Lewis	.12	.30
116 Sam Cowart	.12	.30
117 Vinnie Testaverde	.15	.40
118 Santana Moss	.15	.40
119 Tim Couch	.12	.30
120 William Green	.12	.30
121 Andre Davis	.12	.30
122 Quincy Morgan	.12	.30
123 Kevin Johnson	.12	.30
124 James Jackson	.12	.30
125 Jamel White	.12	.30
126 Robert Griffith	.12	.30
127 Dennis Northcutt	.12	.30
128 Josh Booty	.12	.30
129 Kelly Holcomb	.12	.30
130 Jake Plummer	.15	.40
131 Olandis Gary	.12	.30
132 Clinton Portis	.15	.40
133 Mike Anderson	.15	.40
134 Ashley Lelie	.12	.30
135 Ed McCaffrey	.15	.40
136 Shannon Sharpe	.20	.50
137 Rod Smith	.15	.40
138 John Mobley	.12	.30
139 Jason Elam	.15	.40
140 Terrell Davis	.20	.50
141 Tom Brady	.50	1.25
142 Christian Fauria	.12	.30
143 Antowain Smith	.15	.40
144 Kevin Faulk	.15	.40
145 Ty Law	.15	.40
146 Lawyer Milloy	.15	.40
147 David Patten	.12	.30
148 Deion Branch	.15	.40
149 Troy Brown	.15	.40
150 Rohan Davey	.12	.30
151 Adam Vinatieri	.20	.50
152 Jay Fiedler	.12	.30
153 Chris Chambers	.15	.40
154 Randy McMichael	.12	.30
155 Rob Konrad	.12	.30
156 Morlon Greenwood	.12	.30
157 Derrius Thompson	.12	.30
158 Travis Minor	.12	.30
159 Olindo Mare	.12	.30
160 Jason Taylor	.15	.40
161 Zach Thomas	.20	.50
162 Ricky Williams	.15	.40
163 Aaron Brooks	.15	.40
164 Deuce McAllister	.15	.40
165 Donte Stallworth	.12	.30
166 Jerome Pathon	.12	.30
167 J.T. O'Sullivan	.20	.50
168 Darrin Smith	.12	.30
169 Michael Lewis	.12	.30
170 John Carney	.12	.30
171 Kyle Turley	.12	.30
172 Joe Horn	.15	.40
173 Trent Green	.15	.40
174 Priest Holmes	.20	.50
175 Johnnie Morton	.15	.40
176 Eddie Kennison	.12	.30
177 Marvcus Patton	.12	.30
178 Omar Easy	.12	.30
179 Derrick Blaylock	.12	.30
180 Snoop Minnis	.12	.30
181 Dante Hall	.15	.40
182 Tony Gonzalez	.20	.50
183 Marc Boerigter	.12	.30
184 Drew Brees	.20	.50
185 David Boston	.12	.30
186 Stephen Alexander	.12	.30
187 Quentin Jammer	.12	.30
188 Donnie Edwards	.12	.30
189 LaDainian Tomlinson	.20	.50
190 Junior Seau	.20	.50
191 Reche Caldwell	.12	.30
192 Lorenzo Neal	.15	.40
193 Tim Dwight	.12	.30
194 Doug Flutie	.20	.50
195 Drew Bledsoe	.20	.50
196 Travis Henry	.12	.30
197 Eric Moulds	.15	.40
198 Alex Van Pelt	.12	.30
199 Charles Johnson	.12	.30
200 Nate Clements	.15	.40
201 Takeo Spikes	.12	.30
202 Bobby Shaw	.12	.30
203 London Fletcher	.12	.30
204 Sammy Morris	.15	.40
205 Josh Reed	.12	.30
206 Patrick Ramsey	.15	.40
207 Ladell Betts	.12	.30
208 Chad Morton	.12	.30
209 Trung Canidate	.12	.30
210 Kenny Watson	.12	.30
211 Jessie Armstead	.12	.30
212 Fred Smoot	.12	.30
213 Champ Bailey	.20	.50
214 Bruce Smith	.15	.40
215 Rod Gardner	.12	.30
216 Kurt Warner	.20	.50
217 Troy Edwards	.12	.30
218 Adam Archuleta	.12	.30
219 Grant Wistrom	.12	.30
220 Marshall Faulk	.20	.50
221 Jeff Wilkins	.12	.30
222 Aeneas Williams	.15	.40
223 Lamar Gordon	.12	.30
224 Marc Bulger	.20	.50
225 Isaac Bruce	.20	.50
226 Torry Holt	.20	.50
227 Matt Hasselbeck	.15	.40
228 Maurice Morris	.12	.30
229 Bobby Engram	.12	.30
230 Darrell Jackson	.15	.40
231 James Williams	.12	.30
232 Chad Brown	.12	.30
233 Anthony Simmons	.12	.30
234 Shaun Alexander	.15	.40
235 Koren Robinson	.15	.40
236 Chris Redman	.12	.30
237 Jamal Lewis	.15	.40
238 Brandon Stokley	.15	.40
239 Peter Boulware	.15	.40
240 Randy Hymes RC	.12	.30
241 Todd Heap	.15	.40
242 Travis Taylor	.12	.30
243 Ron Johnson	.12	.30
244 Ray Lewis	.20	.50
245 Jake Delhomme	.20	.50
246 DeShaun Foster	.15	.40
247 Dee Brown	.12	.30
248 Steve Smith	.20	.50
249 Kevin Dyson	.12	.30
250 Muhsin Muhammad	.15	.40
251 Stephen Davis	.15	.40
252 Julius Peppers	.20	.50
253 Rodney Peete	.12	.30
254 Mark Brunell	.15	.40
255 Jimmy Smith	.15	.40
256 Kyle Brady	.12	.30
257 Kevin Lockett	.12	.30
258 Quinn Gray	.15	.40
259 Tony Brackens	.12	.30
260 Marco Coleman	.12	.30
261 David Garrard	.20	.50
262 Fred Taylor	.15	.40
263 Daunte Culpepper	.15	.40
264 Michael Bennett	.15	.40
265 D'Wayne Bates	.12	.30
266 Cedric James	.12	.30
267 Kelly Campbell	.12	.30
268 Derrick Alexander	.12	.30
269 Byron Chamberlain	.12	.30
270 Shaun Hill	.20	.50
271 Randy Moss	.20	.50
272 Josh McCown	.15	.40
273 Thomas Jones	.20	.50
274 Wendell Bryant	.12	.30
275 Kevin Kasper	.12	.30
276 Jason McAddley	.12	.30
277 Emmitt Smith	.50	1.25
278 Preston Parsons	.12	.30
279 Freddie Jones	.12	.30
280 Marcel Shipp	.12	.30
281 Chad Hutchinson	.12	.30
282 Troy Hambrick	.12	.30
283 Dat Nguyen	.12	.30
284 Michael Wiley	.12	.30
285 Joey Galloway	.15	.40
286 Terry Glenn	.15	.40
287 La'Roi Glover	.12	.30
288 Roy Williams	.15	.40
289 Antonio Bryant	.12	.30
290 Quincy Carter	.12	.30
291 Anthony Thomas	.15	.40
292 Marty Booker	.15	.40
293 Dez White	.12	.30
294 Marcus Robinson	.15	.40
295 Kordell Stewart	.15	.40
296 David Terrell	.12	.30
297 John Davis	.12	.30
298 Mike Brown	.15	.40
299 Brian Urlacher	.20	.50
300 Jabar Gaffney	.12	.30
301 Jonathan Wells	.12	.30
302 JaJuan Dawson	.12	.30
303 Corey Bradford	.12	.30
304 Frank Murphy	.12	.30
305 Billy Miller	.12	.30
306 Aaron Glenn	.12	.30
307 Avion Black	.12	.30
308 David Carr	.15	.40
309 Joey Harrington	.12	.30
310 James Stewart	.12	.30
311 Ty Detmer	.12	.30
312 Jason Hanson	.12	.30
313 Bill Schroeder	.12	.30
314 Mikhael Ricks	.12	.30
315 Scotty Anderson	.12	.30
316 Robert Porcher	.12	.30
317 Az-Zahir Hakim	.12	.30
318 Jon Kitna	.15	.40
319 Ron Dugans	.12	.30
320 Chad Johnson	.20	.50
321 Brandon Bennett	.12	.30
322 T.J. Houshmandzadeh	.20	.50
323 Rudi Johnson	.20	.50
324 Kevin Hardy	.12	.30
325 Corey Dillon	.15	.40
326 Peter Warrick	.15	.40
327 Carson Palmer RC	.75	2.00
328 Byron Leftwich RC	.40	1.00
329 Rex Grossman RC	.40	1.00
330 Kyle Boller RC	.40	1.00
331 Dave Ragone RC	.25	.60
332 Chris Simms RC	.40	1.00
333 Brad Banks RC	.30	.75
334 Kliff Kingsbury RC	.30	.75
335 Jason Gesser RC	.30	.75
336 Jason Johnson RC	.25	.60
337 Brian St.Pierre RC	.30	.75
338 Ken Dorsey RC	.30	.75
339 Seneca Wallace RC	.40	1.00
340 Seth Marler RC	.25	.60
341 Tony Romo RC	8.00	20.00
342 J.T. Wall RC	.25	.60
343 Kirk Farmer RC	.30	.75
344 Ricky Manning RC	.30	.75
345 B.J. Askew RC	.30	.75
346 Juston Wood RC	.25	.60
347 Jeremi Johnson RC	.25	.60
348 Tom Lopienski RC	.25	.60
349 Justin Griffith RC	.30	.75
350 Ovie Mughelli RC	.30	.75
351 Bradie James RC	.40	1.00
352 Larry Johnson RC	.40	1.00
353 Lee Suggs RC	.30	.75
354 Justin Fargas RC	.40	1.00
355 Chris Brown RC	.25	.60
356 Onterrio Smith RC	.25	.60
357 Willis McGahee RC	.50	1.25
358 Claude Diggs RC	.25	.60
359 Lance Briggs RC	1.00	2.50
360 Earnest Graham RC	.40	1.00
361 Quentin Griffin RC	.30	.75
362 Michael Haynes RC	.25	.60
363 Musa Smith RC	.25	.60
364 Artose Pinner RC	.25	.60
365 Domanick Davis RC	.30	.75
366 LaBrandon Toefield RC	.30	.75
367 Bethel Johnson RC	.25	.60
368 Sultan McCullough RC	.25	.60
369 Dahrran Diedrick RC	.25	.60
370 Soloman Bates RC	.25	.60
371 Andrew Pinnock RC	.30	.75
372 Charles Rogers RC	.30	.75
373 Andre Johnson RC	1.00	2.50
374 Taylor Jacobs RC	.25	.60
375 Anquan Boldin RC	.60	1.50
376 Talman Gardner RC	.25	.60
377 Brandon Lloyd RC	.60	1.50
378 Bryant Johnson RC	.40	1.00
379 Kelley Washington RC	.25	.60
380 Kareem Kelly RC	.25	.60
381 Arnaz Battle RC	.40	1.00
382 Billy McMullen RC	.25	.60
383 Kennan Howry RC	.25	.60
384 Nate Burleson RC	.30	.75
385 Doug Gabriel RC	.30	.75
386 J.R. Tolver RC	.30	.75
387 Wayne Hunter RC	.25	.60
388 Teyo Johnson RC	.30	.75
389 Eric Steinbach RC	.25	.60
390 Kevin Curtis RC	.40	1.00
391 Bobby Wade RC	.30	.75
392 Sam Aiken RC	.30	.75
393 Willie Pile RC	.25	.60
394 Jerel Myers RC	.25	.60
395 Tyrone Calico RC	.30	.75
396 Terrence Edwards RC	.25	.60
397 Travis Anglin RC	.25	.60
398 Antwone Savage RC	.25	.60
399 Cato June RC	.50	1.25
400 Charles Drake RC	.25	.60
401 Ronald Bellamy RC	.30	.75
402 Justin Gage RC	.30	.75
403 Mat McBriar RC	.40	1.00
404 Kevin Garrett RC	.25	.60
405 Kenny Peterson RC	.30	.75
406 L.J. Smith RC	.40	1.00
407 Jason Witten RC	1.00	2.50
408 Dallas Clark RC	.60	1.50
409 DeWayne White RC	.25	.60
410 Mike Seidman RC	.25	.60
411 Aaron Walker RC	.30	.75
412 Bennie Joppru RC	.25	.60
413 Mike Pinkard RC	.25	.60
414 Danny Curley RC	.25	.60
415 Trent Smith RC	.30	.75
416 George Wrighster RC	.25	.60
417 Terrell Suggs RC	.40	1.00
418 Tully Banta-Cain RC	.40	1.00
419 Jerome McDougle RC	.25	.60
420 William Joseph RC	.25	.60
421 DeWayne Robertson RC	.30	.75
422 Jimmy Kennedy RC	.30	.75
423 Chris Kelsay RC	.30	.75
424 Kevin Williams RC	.40	1.00
425 Boss Bailey RC	.30	.75
426 Terry Pierce RC	.25	.60
427 Terence Newman RC	.30	.75
428 Marcus Trufant RC	.30	.75
429 Mike Doss RC	.40	1.00
430 Dennis Weathersby RC	.25	.60
431 Matt Wilhelm RC	.30	.75
432 Andre Woolfolk RC	.30	.75
433 Shane Walton RC	.25	.60
434 DeJuan Groce RC	.40	1.00
435 Antwoine Sanders RC	.25	.60
436 Julian Battle RC	.30	.75
437 Brett Favre CL	.30	.75
438 Chad Pennington CL	.12	.30
439 David Carr CL	.10	.25
440 Drew Brees CL	.12	.30

2003 Upper Deck MVP Silver

*VETS 1-326: 3X TO 8X BASIC CARDS
*ROOKIES 327-440: 1.5X TO 4X
STATED ODDS 1:12

341 Tony Romo	15.00	40.00

2003 Upper Deck MVP Future MVP

COMPLETE SET (42)	20.00	50.00
STATED ODDS 1:4		
QB1 Carson Palmer	1.00	2.50
QB2 Byron Leftwich	.50	1.25
QB3 Dave Ragone	.30	.75
QB4 Kyle Boller	.50	1.25
QB5 Chris Simms	.50	1.25
QB6 Kliff Kingsbury	.40	1.00
QB7 Jason Gesser	.40	1.00
QB8 Brad Banks	.40	1.00
QB9 Ken Dorsey	.40	1.00
QB10 Rex Grossman	.50	1.25
QB11 Jason Johnson	.30	.75
QB12 Tony Romo	5.00	12.00
QB13 Brian St.Pierre	.40	1.00
QB14 Seneca Wallace	.50	1.25
RB1 Larry Johnson	.50	1.25
RB2 Lee Suggs	.40	1.00
RB3 Onterrio Smith	.30	.75
RB4 Willis McGahee	.60	1.50
RB5 Justin Fargas	.50	1.25
RB6 Chris Brown	.30	.75
RB7 Domanick Davis	.40	1.00
RB8 LaBrandon Toefield	.40	1.00
RB9 Earnest Graham	.50	1.25
RB10 Musa Smith	.30	.75
RB11 Artose Pinner	.30	.75
RB12 Sultan McCullough	.30	.75
RB13 Dahrran Diedrick	.30	.75
RB14 Quentin Griffin	.40	1.00
WR1 Charles Rogers	.40	1.00
WR2 Andre Johnson	1.25	3.00
WR3 Taylor Jacobs	.30	.75
WR4 Anquan Boldin	.75	2.00
WR5 Brandon Lloyd	.75	2.00
WR6 Bryant Johnson	.50	1.25
WR7 Kelley Washington	.30	.75
WR8 Kareem Kelly	.30	.75
WR9 Talman Gardner	.30	.75
WR10 Arnaz Battle	.50	1.25
WR11 Tyrone Calico	.40	1.00
WR12 Billy McMullen	.30	.75
WR13 Keenan Howry	.30	.75
WR14 Teyo Johnson	.40	1.00

2003 Upper Deck MVP ProSign

STATED ODDS 1:480
SP ANNOUNCED PRINT RUN 40 OR LESS

PSBL Byron Leftwich SP	25.00	60.00
PSCP Carson Palmer SP	75.00	150.00
PSCS Chris Simms SP	15.00	40.00
PSEL Elvis Grbac		
PSJM Jim Miller	5.00	12.00
PSJT J.T. O'Sullivan	8.00	20.00
PSKD Ken Dorsey SP		
PSKK Kurt Kittner	5.00	12.00
PSKL Kliff Kingsbury SP	12.00	30.00
PSLP Luke Petitgout	5.00	12.00
PSPM Peyton Manning	60.00	120.00
PSQM Quincy Morgan	5.00	12.00
PSRC Reche Caldwell	5.00	12.00
PSRF Randy Fasani	5.00	12.00
PSRG Rex Grossman SP	25.00	60.00
PSRJ Ron Johnson	5.00	12.00
PSWM Willis McGahee SP	25.00	60.00
PSLJ Larry Johnson SP	15.00	40.00

2003 Upper Deck MVP Souvenirs

STATED ODDS 1:96

GBAG Ahman Green	5.00	12.00
GBBF Brett Favre	15.00	40.00
GBBU Brian Urlacher	6.00	15.00
GBCP Chad Pennington	6.00	15.00
GBCR Chris Redman	4.00	10.00
GBDA David Carr	5.00	12.00
GBDB Drew Brees	6.00	15.00
GBDC Daunte Culpepper	5.00	12.00
GBDM Deuce McAllister	5.00	12.00
GBEJ Edgerrin James	6.00	15.00
GBJH Joey Harrington	4.00	10.00
GBJL Jamal Lewis	5.00	12.00
GBJR Jerry Rice	12.00	30.00
GBKB Kevan Barlow	4.00	10.00
GBKJ Keyshawn Johnson	6.00	15.00
GBKW Kurt Warner	6.00	15.00
GBLC Laveranues Coles SP	4.00	10.00
GBLT LaDainian Tomlinson SP	6.00	15.00
GBMB Michael Bennett SP	5.00	12.00
GBMC Donovan McNabb	6.00	15.00
GBMO Santana Moss	5.00	12.00
GBMV Michael Vick	8.00	20.00
GBPB Plaxico Burress	5.00	12.00
GBPM Peyton Manning	12.00	30.00
GBPO Clinton Portis	5.00	12.00
GBRG Rich Gannon SP	5.00	12.00
GBRM Randy Moss	6.00	15.00
GBSA Shaun Alexander	5.00	12.00
GBSD Stephen Davis SP	5.00	12.00
GBSM Steve McNair SP	6.00	15.00
GBTB1 Tim Brown	6.00	15.00
GBTB2 Tom Brady SP	15.00	40.00
GBTC Tim Couch	4.00	10.00
GBTH Travis Henry	4.00	10.00
GBTO Terrell Owens	6.00	15.00

2003 Upper Deck MVP Talk of the Town

COMPLETE SET (90)	25.00	60.00
STATED ODDS 1:3		
TT1 Peyton Manning	1.50	4.00
TT2 Aaron Brooks	.60	1.50
TT3 Joey Harrington	.50	1.25
TT4 Brett Favre	2.00	5.00
TT5 Donovan McNabb	.75	2.00
TT6 Tim Couch	.50	1.25
TT7 Michael Vick	1.00	2.50
TT8 David Carr	.60	1.50
TT9 Drew Brees	.75	2.00
TT10 Chad Pennington	.75	2.00
TT11 Daunte Culpepper	.60	1.50
TT12 Tom Brady	2.00	5.00
TT13 Kurt Warner	.75	2.00
TT14 Brad Johnson	.60	1.50
TT15 Rich Gannon	.60	1.50
TT16 Jake Plummer	.60	1.50
TT17 Jeff Garcia	.60	1.50
TT18 Drew Bledsoe	.75	2.00
TT19 Steve McNair	.75	2.00
TT20 Mark Brunell	.60	1.50
TT21 Dave Ragone	.50	1.25
TT22 Kordell Stewart	.60	1.50
TT23 Jay Fiedler	.50	1.25
TT24 Tommy Maddox	.60	1.50
TT25 Chris Redman	.50	1.25
TT26 Jon Kitna	.60	1.50
TT27 Trent Green	.60	1.50
TT28 Kerry Collins	.60	1.50
TT29 Patrick Ramsey	.60	1.50
TT30 Chad Hutchinson	.50	1.25
TT31 Rodney Peete	.50	1.25
TT32 Josh McCown	.60	1.50
TT33 Matt Hasselbeck	.60	1.50
TT34 Kelly Holcomb	.50	1.25
TT35 Marc Bulger	.75	2.00
TT36 Carson Palmer	1.25	3.00
TT37 Byron Leftwich	.60	1.50
TT38 Kyle Boller	.75	2.00
TT39 Chris Simms	.60	1.50
TT40 Rex Grossman	.60	1.50
TT41 Marshall Faulk	.75	2.00
TT42 LaDainian Tomlinson	.75	2.00
TT43 Emmitt Smith	2.00	5.00
TT44 Ricky Williams	.60	1.50
TT45 Edgerrin James	.75	2.00
TT46 Deuce McAllister	.60	1.50
TT47 Eddie George	.60	1.50
TT48 Ahman Green	.60	1.50
TT49 Clinton Portis	.60	1.50
TT50 Anthony Thomas	.60	1.50
TT51 Priest Holmes	.75	2.00
TT52 Curtis Martin	.75	2.00
TT53 Michael Bennett	.60	1.50
TT54 Shaun Alexander	.60	1.50
TT55 Jerome Bettis	.75	2.00
TT56 Fred Taylor	.60	1.50
TT57 Travis Henry	.50	1.25
TT58 Garrison Hearst	.60	1.50
TT59 Charlie Garner	.60	1.50
TT60 Kevan Barlow	.50	1.25
TT61 Corey Dillon	.60	1.50
TT62 Duce Staley	.60	1.50
TT63 Jamal Lewis	.60	1.50
TT64 William Green	.50	1.25
TT65 Jerry Rice	1.50	4.00
TT66 Terrell Owens	.75	2.00
TT67 Randy Moss	.75	2.00
TT68 David Boston	.50	1.25
TT69 Marvin Harrison	.75	2.00
TT70 Isaac Bruce	.75	2.00
TT71 Torry Holt	.75	2.00
TT72 Plaxico Burress	.60	1.50
TT73 Keyshawn Johnson	.75	2.00
TT74 Chris Chambers	.60	1.50
TT75 Rod Smith	.60	1.50
TT76 Tim Brown	.75	2.00
TT77 Rod Gardner	.50	1.25
TT78 Peerless Price	.50	1.25
TT79 Jabar Gaffney	.50	1.25
TT80 Antonio Bryant	.50	1.25
TT81 Troy Brown	.60	1.50
TT82 Jimmy Smith	.60	1.50
TT83 Donald Driver	.75	2.00
TT84 Eric Moulds	.60	1.50
TT85 Kevin Johnson	.50	1.25
TT86 Charles Rogers	.60	1.50
TT87 Andre Johnson	1.50	4.00
TT88 Taylor Jacobs	.50	1.25
TT89 Tony Gonzalez	.75	2.00
TT90 Jeremy Shockey	.75	2.00

2002 Upper Deck National Convention

N6 Peyton Manning	.75	2.00
N7 Michael Vick	.60	1.50

2004 Upper Deck National Convention

STATED PRINT RUN 500 SER.#'d SETS

TN11 Tom Brady	1.50	4.00
TN12 Eli Manning	3.00	8.00
TN16 Michael Vick	.75	2.00

2005 Upper Deck National Convention

Upper Deck produced this set and distributed it at the 2005 National Sport Collectors Convention in Chicago. The set includes famous Chicago area athletes from a variety of sports with the title "The National" printed on the cardfronts. The company made the cards available to collectors via a wrapper redemption program at their show booth and each card was serial numbered to 750-copies. Some players also signed just 5-cards which are not priced due to scarcity.

STATED PRINT RUN 750 SER.#'d SETS
UNPRICED AUTO PRINT RUN 5

CL4 Walter Payton	3.00	8.00
CL5 Gale Sayers	2.00	5.00
CL6 Mike Ditka	2.00	5.00

2005 Upper Deck National Convention VIP

Upper Deck produced this set and distributed it to special VIP package members attending the 2005 National Sport Collectors Convention in Chicago. The set includes famous athletes from a variety of sports with the title "The National" printed on the cardfronts along with a "VIP" stamp.

VIP5 Peyton Manning	4.00	10.00
VIP6 Donovan McNabb	3.00	8.00

2007 Upper Deck National Convention

NTL8 Reggie Bush	1.00	2.50
NTL9 Vince Young	1.00	2.50
NTL10 Peyton Manning	1.25	3.00
NTL11 Matt Leinart	.60	1.50

2007 Upper Deck National Convention VIP

VIP8 Reggie Bush	1.25	3.00
VIP9 Vince Young	1.25	3.00
VIP10 Peyton Manning	2.00	5.00
VIP11 Matt Leinart	.75	2.00

2008 Upper Deck National Convention

NAT3 Devin Hester	.50	1.25
NAT7 Peyton Manning	.75	2.00
NAT12 Tom Brady	.75	2.00
NAT16 Brian Urlacher	.50	1.25
NAT18 LaDainian Tomlinson	.60	1.50
NAT19 Randy Moss	.50	1.25

2008 Upper Deck National Convention VIP

CARDS FEATURE VIP LOGO ON FRONT

NAT3 Devin Hester	1.50	4.00
NAT7 Peyton Manning	2.50	6.00
NAT12 Tom Brady	2.50	6.00
NAT16 Brian Urlacher	1.50	4.00
NAT18 LaDainian Tomlinson	2.00	5.00
NAT19 Randy Moss	1.50	4.00

2009 Upper Deck National Convention

NC2 Brady Quinn	.50	1.25
NC9 Adrian Peterson	1.00	2.50
NC11 Ben Roethlisberger	.60	1.50
NC19 Larry Fitzgerald	.50	1.25
NC20 Matt Ryan	.60	1.50
NC23 Peyton Manning	.75	2.00

2009 Upper Deck National Convention VIP

VIP9 Peyton Manning	2.50	6.00

2010 Upper Deck National Convention

COMPLETE SET (20)	15.00	40.00
NSC2 Anquan Boldin	1.25	3.00
NSC4 Joe Flacco	1.50	4.00
NSC8 Ray Rice	1.25	3.00
NSC12 Ray Lewis	1.25	3.00
NSC15 Vernon Davis	1.25	3.00
NSC18 Michael Oher	1.25	3.00

2010 Upper Deck National Convention Autographs

STATED PRINT RUN 9-90

NAJF Joe Flacco/54	30.00	60.00
NARR Ray Rice/90	25.00	50.00

2010 Upper Deck National Convention Million Pack March

MPM3 Roger Staubach	1.50	4.00
MPM6 Rocky Bleier	1.25	3.00

2010 Upper Deck National Convention VIP

COMPLETE SET (6)	6.00	15.00
VIP4 Joe Flacco	1.25	3.00

2011 Upper Deck National Convention

NSCC11 Mike Singletary	.75	2.00
NSCC18 Jake Locker	2.00	5.00

2011 Upper Deck National Convention Autographs

NSCCJL Jake Locker/18
NSCCMS Mike Singletary/10

2012 Upper Deck National Convention

NSCC4 Roger Staubach	1.25	3.00
NSCC7 Robert Griffin III	3.00	8.00
NSCC15 Trent Richardson	2.00	5.00

2012 Upper Deck National Convention Autographs

STATED PRINT RUN 1-35

1999 Upper Deck Ovation

The 1999 Upper Deck Ovation set was released in mid-September as a 90-card base set containing 60 veteran cards and a 30 card Rookie Ovation subset listed at one in four packs. Full color action photos are set against an embossed football background. Upper Deck Ovation was released in 20-pack boxes containing five cards each and carried a suggested retail price of $3.99 per pack.

COMPLETE SET (90)	50.00	120.00
COMP.SET w/o SP's (60)	10.00	20.00
1 Jake Plummer	.25	.60
2 Adrian Murrell	.25	.60
3 Jamal Anderson	.25	.60
4 Chris Chandler	.25	.60
5 Tony Banks	.25	.60
6 Antowain Smith	.20	.50
7 Doug Flutie	.30	.75
8 Tim Biakabutuka	.25	.60
9 Steve Beuerlein	.25	.60
10 Curtis Conway	.25	.60
11 Curtis Enis	.20	.50
12 Corey Dillon	.25	.60
13 Jeff Blake	.25	.60
14 Ty Detmer	.25	.60
15 Troy Aikman	.50	1.25
16 Emmitt Smith	.75	2.00
17 Terrell Davis	.30	.75
18 Bubby Brister	.20	.50
19 Barry Sanders	.75	2.00
20 Charlie Batch	.25	.60
21 Brett Favre	1.00	2.50
22 Dorsey Levens	.25	.60
23 Peyton Manning	1.00	2.50
24 Marvin Harrison	.30	.75
25 Mark Brunell	.25	.60
26 Fred Taylor	.25	.60
27 Elvis Grbac	.20	.50
28 Andre Rison	.25	.60
29 Dan Marino	1.00	2.50
30 Karim Abdul-Jabbar	.25	.60
31 Randall Cunningham	.30	.75
32 Randy Moss	.30	.75
33 Drew Bledsoe	.30	.75
34 Terry Glenn	.25	.60
35 Danny Wuerffel	.25	.60
36 Cam Cleeland	.20	.50
37 Kerry Collins	.25	.60
38 Amani Toomer	.25	.60
39 Curtis Martin	.30	.75
40 Keyshawn Johnson	.25	.60
41 Napoleon Kaufman	.20	.50
42 Tim Brown	.30	.75
43 Doug Pederson	.20	.50
44 Charles Johnson	.20	.50
45 Kordell Stewart	.25	.60
46 Jerome Bettis	.30	.75
47 Trent Green	.25	.60
48 Marshall Faulk	.30	.75
49 Natrone Means	.25	.60
50 Jim Harbaugh	.25	.60
51 Steve Young	.40	1.00
52 Jerry Rice	.60	1.50
53 Joey Galloway	.25	.60
54 Jon Kitna	.25	.60
55 Warrick Dunn	.25	.60
56 Trent Dilfer	.25	.60
57 Steve McNair	.30	.75
58 Eddie George	.25	.60
59 Brad Johnson	.25	.60
60 Skip Hicks	.20	.50
61 Tim Couch RC	1.00	2.50
62 Donovan McNabb RC	4.00	10.00
63 Akili Smith RC	.75	2.00
64 Edgerrin James RC	1.25	3.00
65 Ricky Williams RC	1.50	4.00
66 Torry Holt RC	1.50	4.00
67 Champ Bailey RC	2.00	5.00
68 David Boston RC	.75	2.00
69 Daunte Culpepper RC	1.00	2.50
70 Cade McNown RC	.75	2.00
71 Troy Edwards RC	.75	2.00
72 Kevin Johnson RC	.75	2.00
73 James Johnson RC	.60	1.50
74 Rob Konrad RC	.60	1.50
75 Kevin Faulk RC	1.00	2.50

76 Shaun King RC .75 2.00
77 Peerless Price RC .75 2.00
78 Mike Cloud RC .60 1.50
79 Jermaine Fazande RC .60 1.50
80 D'Wayne Bates RC .60 1.50
81 Brock Huard RC .75 2.00
82 Marty Booker RC .75 2.00
83 Karsten Bailey RC .60 1.50
84 Al Wilson RC 1.00 2.50
85 Joe Germaine RC .75 2.00
86 Dameane Douglas RC .60 1.50
87 Sedrick Irvin RC .60 1.50
88 Amos Zereoue RC .75 2.00
89 Cecil Collins RC .60 1.50
90 Ebenezer Ekuban RC .60 1.50
WPO W.Payton Jsy AU/34 1,000.00 1,500.00

1999 Upper Deck Ovation Standing Ovation

*STARS: 15X TO 40X BASE CARD HI
*ROOKIES: 5X TO 12X BASE CARD HI
STATED PRINT RUN 50 SER.#'d SETS

1999 Upper Deck Ovation A Piece of History

COMPLETE SET (13) 500.00 1,000.00
STATED PRINT RUN 4560 TOTAL CARDS
ASH Akili Smith 5.00 12.00
BFH Brett Favre 20.00 50.00
BHH Brock Huard 5.00 12.00
CMH Cade McNown 5.00 12.00
DCH Daunte Culpepper 15.00 40.00
DMH Dan Marino 25.00 60.00
EJH Edgerrin James 15.00 40.00
JGH Joe Germaine 5.00 12.00
JRH Jerry Rice 15.00 40.00
MCH Donovan McNabb 20.00 50.00
RWA R.Williams AUTO/34 100.00 200.00
RWH Ricky Williams 7.50 20.00
SYH Steve Young 10.00 25.00
THH Torry Holt 10.00 25.00

1999 Upper Deck Ovation Center Stage

COMPLETE SET (24) 100.00 200.00
CS1-CS8 STATED ODDS 1:9
CS9-CS16 STATED ODDS 1:25
CS17-CS24 STATED ODDS 1:99
CS1 Walter Payton 1.50 4.00
CS2 Barry Sanders 2.00 5.00
CS3 Emmitt Smith 1.25 3.00
CS4 Terrell Davis .60 1.50
CS5 Jamal Anderson .60 1.50
CS6 Fred Taylor .60 1.50
CS7 Ricky Williams 1.00 2.50
CS8 Edgerrin James 2.00 5.00
CS9 Walter Payton 3.00 8.00
CS10 Barry Sanders 4.00 10.00
CS11 Emmitt Smith 2.50 6.00
CS12 Terrell Davis 1.25 3.00
CS13 Jamal Anderson 1.25 3.00
CS14 Fred Taylor 1.25 3.00
CS15 Ricky Williams 2.00 5.00
CS16 Edgerrin James 4.00 10.00
CS17 Walter Payton 7.50 20.00
CS18 Barry Sanders 10.00 25.00
CS19 Emmitt Smith 6.00 15.00
CS20 Terrell Davis 3.00 8.00
CS21 Jamal Anderson 3.00 8.00
CS22 Fred Taylor 3.00 8.00
CS23 Ricky Williams 5.00 12.00
CS24 Edgerrin James 10.00 25.00

1999 Upper Deck Ovation Curtain Calls

COMPLETE SET (30) 40.00 80.00
STATED ODDS 1:4
CC1 Peyton Manning 3.00 8.00
CC2 Fred Taylor 1.00 2.50
CC3 Randy Moss 2.50 6.00
CC4 Cris Carter 1.00 2.50
CC5 Troy Aikman 2.00 5.00
CC6 Randall Cunningham 1.00 2.50
CC7 Mark Brunell 1.00 2.50
CC8 Jon Kitna 1.00 2.50
CC9 Steve McNair 1.00 2.50
CC10 Jake Plummer .60 1.50
CC11 Jerry Rice 2.00 5.00
CC12 Kordell Stewart .60 1.50
CC13 Warrick Dunn 1.00 2.50
CC14 Emmitt Smith 2.00 5.00
CC15 Jerome Bettis 1.00 2.50
CC16 Terrell Owens 1.00 2.50
CC17 Antonio Freeman 1.00 2.50
CC18 Joey Galloway .60 1.50
CC19 Curtis Martin 1.00 2.50
CC20 Tim Brown 1.00 2.50
CC21 Charlie Batch 1.00 2.50
CC22 Doug Flutie 1.00 2.50
CC23 Barry Sanders 3.00 8.00
CC24 Drew Bledsoe 1.25 3.00
CC25 Corey Dillon 1.00 2.50
CC26 Eddie George 1.00 2.50
CC27 Keyshawn Johnson 1.00 2.50
CC28 Steve Young 1.25 3.00
CC29 Brett Favre 3.00 8.00
CC30 Terrell Davis 1.00 2.50

1999 Upper Deck Ovation Spotlight

COMPLETE SET (15) 40.00 80.00
STATED ODDS 1:9
OS1 Tim Couch 1.00 2.50
OS2 Donovan McNabb 5.00 12.00
OS3 Akili Smith .75 2.00
OS4 Edgerrin James 4.00 10.00
OS5 Ricky Williams 2.00 5.00
OS6 Torry Holt 2.50 6.00
OS7 Champ Bailey 1.25 3.00
OS8 David Boston 1.00 2.50
OS9 Daunte Culpepper 4.00 10.00
OS10 Cade McNown .75 2.00
OS11 Troy Edwards .75 2.00
OS12 Kevin Johnson 1.00 2.50
OS13 Joe Germaine .75 2.00
OS14 Brock Huard 1.00 2.50
OS15 Kevin Faulk 1.00 2.50

1999 Upper Deck Ovation Star Performers

COMPLETE SET (15) 60.00 120.00
STATED ODDS 1:39
SP1 Terrell Davis 2.50 6.00
SP2 Peyton Manning 8.00 20.00
SP3 Brett Favre 8.00 20.00
SP4 Dan Marino 8.00 20.00
SP5 Barry Sanders 8.00 20.00
SP6 Jamal Anderson 2.50 6.00
SP7 Mark Brunell 2.50 6.00
SP8 Jerome Bettis 2.50 6.00
SP9 Charlie Batch 2.50 6.00
SP10 Antowain Smith 2.50 6.00
SP11 Jake Plummer 1.50 4.00
SP12 Joey Galloway 1.50 4.00
SP13 Randy Moss 6.00 15.00
SP14 Steve Young 3.00 8.00
SP15 Warrick Dunn 2.50 6.00

1999 Upper Deck Ovation Super Signatures Gold

GOLD PRINT RUN 150 SER.#'d SETS
JM Joe Montana 125.00 250.00
JN Joe Namath 100.00 200.00
WP Walter Payton 500.00 750.00

1999 Upper Deck Ovation Super Signatures Silver

SILVER PRINT RUN 300 SER.#'d SETS
JM Joe Montana 75.00 150.00
JN Joe Namath 50.00 120.00
WP Walter Payton 400.00 600.00

2000 Upper Deck Ovation

Released as a 90-card set, Upper Deck Ovation features 60 veteran players and 30 World Premier rookie cards sequentially numbered to 2500. Base cards have embossed white borders along the top, bottom and right side of the card in the texture of a football, and are enhanced with gold foil stamping. A special Joe Namath Autographed Jersey card sequentially numbered to 175 was also randomly inserted in packs. Ovation was packaged in 20-pack boxes with packs containing five cards and carried a suggested retail price of $3.99

COMPLETE SET (90) 125.00 250.00
COMP.SET w/o RC's (60) 7.50 20.00
61-90 ROOKIE PRINT RUN 2500
1 Jake Plummer .20 .50
2 Frank Sanders .15 .40
3 Chris Chandler .20 .50
4 Jamal Anderson .20 .50
5 Qadry Ismail .20 .50
6 Eric Moulds .20 .50
7 Muhsin Muhammad .20 .50
8 Steve Beuerlein .20 .50
9 Cade McNown .15 .40
10 Marcus Robinson .20 .50
11 Akili Smith .15 .40
12 Corey Dillon .20 .50
13 Tim Couch .20 .50
14 Kevin Johnson .15 .40
15 Troy Aikman .40 1.00
16 Emmitt Smith .60 1.50
17 Terrell Davis .25 .60
18 Olandis Gary .20 .50
19 Charlie Batch .20 .50
20 Germane Crowell .15 .40
21 Brett Favre .75 2.00
22 Antonio Freeman .20 .50
23 Peyton Manning .60 1.50
24 Edgerrin James .25 .60
25 Mark Brunell .20 .50
26 Fred Taylor .25 .60
27 Elvis Grbac .15 .40
28 Tony Gonzalez .25 .60
29 Tony Martin .20 .50
30 Damon Huard .20 .50
31 Randy Moss .25 .60
32 Daunte Culpepper .20 .50
33 Drew Bledsoe .25 .60
34 Terry Glenn .20 .50
35 Ricky Williams .25 .60
36 Jeff Blake .20 .50
37 Kerry Collins .20 .50
38 Amani Toomer .20 .50
39 Curtis Martin .25 .60
40 Vinny Testaverde .20 .50
41 Tim Brown .25 .60
42 Rickey Dudley .15 .40
43 Duce Staley .20 .50
44 Donovan McNabb .25 .60
45 Troy Edwards .15 .40
46 Jerome Bettis .25 .60
47 Marshall Faulk .25 .60
48 Kurt Warner .40 1.00
49 Freddie Jones .15 .40
50 Junior Seau .25 .60
51 Jerry Rice .50 1.25
52 Steve Young .30 .75
53 Ricky Watters .20 .50
54 Jon Kitna .20 .50
55 Shaun King .15 .40
56 Keyshawn Johnson .20 .50
57 Eddie George .20 .50
58 Steve McNair .25 .60
59 Brad Johnson .20 .50
60 Stephen Davis .20 .50
61 Courtney Brown RC 1.25 3.00
62 Corey Simon RC 1.25 3.00
63 R.Jay Soward RC 1.00 2.50
64 Anthony Becht RC 1.25 3.00
65 Chris Redman RC 1.25 3.00
66 Chad Pennington RC 2.50 6.00
67 Tee Martin RC 1.50 4.00
68 Giovanni Carmazzi RC 1.00 2.50
69 Ron Dayne RC 1.50 4.00
70 Shaun Alexander RC 2.00 5.00
71 Thomas Jones RC 2.00 5.00
72 Reuben Droughns RC 1.50 4.00
73 Jamal Lewis RC 1.50 4.00
74 J.R. Redmond RC 1.00 2.50
75 Travis Prentice RC 1.25 3.00
76 Trung Canidate RC 1.25 3.00
77 Brian Urlacher RC 6.00 15.00
78 Bubba Franks RC 1.50 4.00
79 Peter Warrick RC 1.50 4.00
80 Plaxico Burress RC 1.50 4.00
81 Sylvester Morris RC 1.00 2.50
82 Dez White RC 1.25 3.00
83 Travis Taylor RC 1.25 3.00
84 Todd Pinkston RC 1.00 2.50
85 Dennis Northcutt RC 1.25 3.00
86 Jerry Porter RC 1.50 4.00
87 Laveranues Coles RC 1.50 4.00
88 Danny Farmer RC 1.00 2.50
89 Curtis Keaton RC 1.00 2.50
90 Ron Dugans RC 1.00 2.50

2000 Upper Deck Ovation Standing Ovation

*VETS 1-60: 12X TO 30X BASIC CARDS
*ROOKIES 61-90: 2X TO 5X
STATED PRINT RUN 50 SER.#'d SETS

2000 Upper Deck Ovation A Piece of History

BFB Brett Favre 20.00 50.00
CPB Chad Pennington 10.00 25.00
CPH Chad Pennington Helmet 10.00 25.00
CRB Chris Redman 5.00 12.00
CRH Chris Redman Helmet 5.00 12.00
DCB Daunte Culpepper 5.00 12.00
DMB Dan Marino 20.00 50.00
EJB Edgerrin James 6.00 15.00
IBH Isaac Bruce Helmet 6.00 15.00
JRB Jerry Rice 12.00 30.00
KWH Kurt Warner Helmet 10.00 25.00
PMB Peyton Manning 15.00 40.00
PWB Peter Warrick 6.00 15.00
PWH Peter Warrick Helmet 6.00 15.00
RDB Ron Dayne 6.00 15.00
RDH Ron Dayne Helmet 6.00 15.00
RMB Randy Moss 6.00 15.00
SKH Shaun King Helmet 5.00 12.00
TCB Tim Couch 5.00 12.00
TJB Thomas Jones 6.00 15.00
TJH Thomas Jones Helmet 6.00 15.00

2000 Upper Deck Ovation A Piece of History Autographs

STATED PRINT RUN 25 SER.#'d SETS
CPA Chad Pennington Helmet 40.00 100.00
CRA Chris Redman Helmet 20.00 50.00
PMA Peyton Manning 125.00 225.00
PWA Peter Warrick 25.00 60.00
RMA Randy Moss 60.00 120.00
TJA Thomas Jones 30.00 80.00

2000 Upper Deck Ovation Center Stage

COMPLETE SET (10) 8.00 20.00
STATED ODDS 1:19
*ACT 2: .8X TO 2X BASIC INSERTS
ACT 2 STATED ODDS 1:79
*ACT 3/50: 3X TO 8X BASIC INSERTS
ACT 3 STATED PRINT RUN 50
CS1 Tim Couch .60 1.50
CS2 Fred Taylor .75 2.00
CS3 Kurt Warner 1.25 3.00
CS4 Edgerrin James .75 2.00
CS5 Ron Dayne .75 2.00
CS6 Jamal Lewis .75 2.00
CS7 Thomas Jones 1.00 2.50
CS8 Peter Warrick .75 2.00
CS9 Plaxico Burress .75 2.00
CS10 Chad Pennington 1.25 3.00

2000 Upper Deck Ovation Curtain Calls

COMPLETE SET (15) 3.00 8.00
STATED ODDS 1:3
CC1 Eddie George .40 1.00
CC2 Muhsin Muhammad .40 1.00
CC3 Marvin Harrison .50 1.25
CC4 Marcus Robinson .40 1.00
CC5 Duce Staley .40 1.00
CC6 Isaac Bruce .50 1.25
CC7 Germane Crowell .30 .75
CC8 Amani Toomer .40 1.00
CC9 Fred Taylor .50 1.25
CC10 Michael Westbrook .30 .75
CC11 Olandis Gary .40 1.00
CC12 Stephen Davis .40 1.00
CC13 Cade McNown .30 .75
CC14 Priest Holmes .50 1.25
CC15 Corey Dillon .40 1.00

2000 Upper Deck Ovation Spotlight

COMPLETE SET (15) 6.00 15.00
STATED ODDS 1:9
OS1 Edgerrin James .60 1.50
OS2 Rob Johnson .50 1.25
OS3 Jake Plummer .50 1.25
OS4 Jamal Anderson .50 1.25
OS5 James Stewart .40 1.00
OS6 Shaun King .40 1.00
OS7 Jon Kitna .50 1.25
OS8 Ricky Williams .60 1.50
OS9 Errict Rhett .50 1.25
OS10 Stephen Davis .50 1.25
OS11 Daunte Culpepper .50 1.25
OS12 Donovan McNabb .60 1.50
OS13 Kevin Johnson .40 1.00
OS14 Akili Smith .40 1.00
OS15 Cade McNown .40 1.00

2000 Upper Deck Ovation Star Performers

COMPLETE SET (15) 10.00 25.00
STATED ODDS 1:9
SP1 Mark Brunell .60 1.50
SP2 Eddie George .60 1.50
SP3 Brad Johnson .60 1.50
SP4 Vinny Testaverde .60 1.50
SP5 Marshall Faulk .75 2.00
SP6 Tim Couch .60 1.50
SP7 Brett Favre 2.50 6.00
SP8 Ricky Williams .75 2.00
SP9 Peyton Manning 2.00 5.00
SP10 Keyshawn Johnson .60 1.50
SP11 Emmitt Smith 2.00 5.00
SP12 Jerry Rice 1.50 4.00
SP13 Tim Brown .75 2.00
SP14 Randy Moss .75 2.00
SP15 Jamal Anderson .60 1.50

2000 Upper Deck Ovation Super Signatures Silver

SILVER PRINT RUN 10-100
*GOLD/50: .5X TO 1.2X SILVER/100
GOLD PRINT RUN 50
UNPRICED RAINBOW PRINT RUN 10
EG Eddie George 20.00 50.00
JB Jim Brown 75.00 150.00
JN Joe Namath 50.00 120.00
MB Mark Brunell 20.00 50.00
MF Marshall Faulk 25.00 60.00
PM Peyton Manning 75.00 150.00
RM Randy Moss 30.00 80.00
TD Terrell Davis 25.00 60.00

2001 Upper Deck Ovation

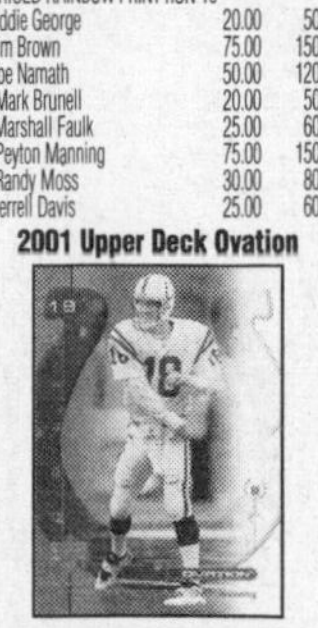

Issued in five card packs, this 150 card set features a mix of active players and 2001 NFL rookies. The first 90 cards are NFL vets while the final 60 cards were printed in lesser quantities. Cards numbered 91 through 115 had a stated print run of 700 sets, while card numbered from 116 through 135 had a stated print run of 425 sets and cards 136 through 150 had a stated print run of 250 sets.

COMP.SET w/o SP's (90) 10.00 25.00
91-115 ROOKIE PRINT RUN 700
135-150 ROOKIE PRINT RUN 250
1 Jake Plummer .20 .50
2 Thomas Jones .20 .50
3 Frank Sanders .15 .40
4 Jamal Anderson .20 .50
5 Chris Chandler .20 .50
6 Terance Mathis .15 .40
7 Jamal Lewis .25 .60
8 Elvis Grbac .20 .50
9 Travis Taylor .15 .40
10 Shawn Bryson .15 .40
11 Rob Johnson .20 .50
12 Eric Moulds .20 .50
13 Muhsin Muhammad .20 .50
14 Donald Hayes .15 .40
15 Tim Biakabutuka .15 .40
16 Cade McNown .20 .50
17 Marcus Robinson .20 .50
18 Brian Urlacher .30 .75
19 Akili Smith .15 .40
20 Peter Warrick .20 .50
21 Corey Dillon .20 .50
22 Kevin Johnson .15 .40
23 Spergon Wynn .15 .40
24 Tim Couch .15 .40
25 Tony Banks .15 .40
26 Emmitt Smith .60 1.50
27 Anthony Wright .15 .40
28 Terrell Davis .25 .60
29 Mike Anderson .20 .50
30 Brian Griese .20 .50
31 Ed McCaffrey .20 .50
32 Charlie Batch .20 .50
33 Germane Crowell .15 .40
34 Johnnie Morton .20 .50
35 Brett Favre .75 2.00
36 Antonio Freeman .25 .60
37 Dorsey Levens .20 .50
38 Ahman Green .25 .60
39 Peyton Manning .60 1.50
40 Edgerrin James .25 .60
41 Marvin Harrison .25 .60
42 Mark Brunell .20 .50
43 Fred Taylor .25 .60
44 Jimmy Smith .20 .50
45 Tony Gonzalez .25 .60
46 Trent Green .25 .60
47 Derrick Alexander .15 .40
48 Oronde Gadsden .15 .40
49 Tony Martin .20 .50
50 Lamar Smith .20 .50
51 Randy Moss .25 .60
52 Cris Carter .25 .60
53 Daunte Culpepper .20 .50
54 Drew Bledsoe .25 .60
55 Terry Glenn .20 .50
56 Ricky Williams .25 .60
57 Jeff Blake .20 .50
58 Aaron Brooks .20 .50
59 Kerry Collins .20 .50
60 Tiki Barber .25 .60
61 Ron Dayne .20 .50
62 Vinny Testaverde .20 .50
63 Wayne Chrebet .20 .50
64 Curtis Martin .25 .60
65 Tim Brown .25 .60
66 Rich Gannon .20 .50
67 Jerry Rice .50 1.25
68 Duce Staley .20 .50
69 Donovan McNabb .25 .60
70 Kordell Stewart .20 .50
71 Jerome Bettis .25 .60
72 Marshall Faulk .25 .60
73 Kurt Warner .40 1.00
74 Isaac Bruce .25 .60
75 Doug Flutie .25 .60
76 Junior Seau .25 .60
77 Jeff Garcia .20 .50
78 Garrison Hearst .20 .50
79 Terrell Owens .25 .60
80 Ricky Watters .20 .50
81 Matt Hasselbeck .25 .60
82 Keyshawn Johnson .20 .50
83 Warrick Dunn .25 .60
84 Mike Alstott .20 .50
85 Kevin Dyson .15 .40
86 Eddie George .25 .60
87 Steve McNair .25 .60
88 Jeff George .20 .50
89 Michael Westbrook .15 .40
90 Stephen Davis .20 .50
91 Milton Wynn RC 1.50 4.00
92 Dan Alexander RC 2.00 5.00
93 Rudi Johnson RC 2.50 6.00
94 Ken-Yon Rambo RC 1.50 4.00
95 Alex Bannister RC 1.50 4.00
96 Adam Archuleta RC 2.00 5.00
97 Andre Dyson RC 1.50 4.00
98 Cedrick Wilson RC 2.00 5.00
99 Chris Taylor RC 1.50 4.00
100 Eddie Berlin RC 1.50 4.00
101 Gary Baxter RC 1.50 4.00
102 Heath Evans RC 2.00 5.00
103 Jabari Holloway RC 1.50 4.00
104 Jamal Reynolds RC 1.50 4.00
105 Jamar Fletcher RC 1.50 4.00
106 Justin Smith RC 2.50 6.00
107 Kevin Kasper RC 1.50 4.00
108 Moran Norris RC 1.50 4.00
109 Nate Clements RC 2.00 5.00
110 Scotty Anderson RC 1.50 4.00
111 T.J. Houshmandzadeh RC 3.00 8.00
112 Travis Minor RC 2.00 5.00
113 Vinny Sutherland RC 1.50 4.00
114 Will Allen RC 2.50 6.00
115 Derrick Gibson RC 1.50 4.00
116 Kevan Barlow RC 2.50 6.00
117 LaMont Jordan RC 3.00 8.00
118 Todd Heap RC 3.00 8.00
119 Quincy Morgan RC 2.50 6.00
120 Dan Morgan RC 2.50 6.00
121 Gerard Warren RC 2.50 6.00
122 Mike McMahon RC 2.50 6.00
123 Sage Rosenfels RC 3.00 8.00
124 Marques Tuiasosopo RC 2.50 6.00
125 Josh Heupel RC 3.00 8.00
126 Jesse Palmer RC 2.50 6.00
127 Quincy Carter RC 2.50 6.00
128 Josh Booty RC 2.50 6.00
129 Correll Buckhalter RC 3.00 8.00
130 Travis Henry RC 2.50 6.00
131 Alge Crumpler RC 3.00 8.00
132 Snoop Minnis RC 2.00 5.00
133 Bobby Newcombe RC 2.50 6.00
134 Robert Ferguson RC 3.00 8.00
135 James Jackson RC 2.00 5.00
136 Michael Bennett RC 3.00 8.00
137 Drew Brees RC 25.00 60.00
138 Chris Chambers RC 4.00 10.00
139 Rod Gardner RC 3.00 8.00
140 Chad Johnson RC 6.00 15.00
141 Freddie Mitchell RC 2.50 6.00
142 Deuce McAllister RC 4.00 10.00
143 Santana Moss RC 5.00 12.00
144 Koren Robinson RC 3.00 8.00
145 David Terrell RC 3.00 8.00
146 LaDainian Tomlinson RC 12.00 30.00
147 Anthony Thomas RC 4.00 10.00
148 Reggie Wayne RC 8.00 20.00
149 Michael Vick RC 15.00 40.00
150 Chris Weinke RC 3.00 8.00

2001 Upper Deck Ovation Black and White Rookies

*ROOKIES: .3X TO .8X BASIC CARDS
91-115 ROOKIE PRINT RUN 700
116-135 ROOKIE PRINT RUN 425
136-150 ROOKIE PRINT RUN 250

2001 Upper Deck Ovation Embossed Rookies

*EMBOSSED: .4X TO 1X BASIC CARDS

2001 Upper Deck Ovation Rookie Autographs

STATED PRINT RUN 250 SER.#'d SETS
136 Michael Bennett 8.00 20.00
137 Drew Brees 100.00 200.00
138 Chris Chambers 10.00 25.00
139 Rod Gardner 8.00 20.00
140 Chad Johnson 15.00 40.00
141 Freddie Mitchell 6.00 15.00
142 Deuce McAllister 10.00 25.00
143 Santana Moss 12.00 30.00
145 David Terrell 8.00 20.00
146 LaDainian Tomlinson 75.00 150.00
147 Anthony Thomas 10.00 25.00
148 Reggie Wayne 20.00 50.00
149 Michael Vick 75.00 150.00
150 Chris Weinke 8.00 20.00

2001 Upper Deck Ovation Rookie Gear

STATED ODDS 1:20
RCC Chris Chambers 4.00 10.00
RCW Chris Weinke 3.00 8.00
RDB Drew Brees 12.00 30.00
RDM Deuce McAllister 4.00 10.00
RJJ James Jackson 2.50 6.00
RKB Kevan Barlow 3.00 8.00
RKR Koren Robinson 3.00 8.00
RMB Michael Bennett 3.00 8.00
RMV Michael Vick 12.00 30.00
RQM Quincy Morgan 3.00 8.00
RRF Robert Ferguson 4.00 10.00
RRG Rod Gardner 3.00 8.00
RSM Santana Moss 5.00 12.00

2001 Upper Deck Ovation Train for the Game Jerseys

STATED ODDS 1:120
TGBF Brett Favre 20.00 50.00
TGDF Doug Flutie SP 25.00 50.00
TGJA Jessie Armstead 6.00 15.00
TGJS Junior Seau 10.00 25.00
TGMB Mark Brunell 8.00 20.00
TGRD Ron Dayne 8.00 20.00

2001 Upper Deck Ovation Training Gear

STATED ODDS 1:20
TAS Akili Smith 4.00 10.00
TBF Brett Favre 15.00 40.00
TBO David Boston 4.00 10.00
TCC Curtis Conway 5.00 12.00
TCD Corey Dillon 5.00 12.00
TCG Charlie Garner 5.00 12.00
TCK Curtis Keaton 4.00 10.00
TCW Charles Woodson 6.00 15.00
TDB Drew Brees 12.00 30.00
TEG Elvis Grbac 5.00 12.00
TFS Frank Sanders 4.00 10.00
TFT Fred Taylor 6.00 15.00
TJG Jeff Garcia 5.00 12.00
TJJ J.J. Stokes 4.00 10.00
TJP Jake Plummer 5.00 12.00
TJR Jerry Rice 12.00 30.00
TJS Jason Sehorn 5.00 12.00
TKM Keenan McCardell 5.00 12.00
TMB Mark Brunell 5.00 12.00
TMP Michael Pittman 5.00 12.00
TPW Peter Warrick 5.00 12.00
TRD Ron Dayne 5.00 12.00
TRG Rich Gannon 5.00 12.00
TTB Tiki Barber 6.00 15.00
TTC Tim Couch 4.00 10.00
TTJ Thomas Jones 5.00 12.00
TTO Terrell Owens 6.00 15.00
TTW Tyrone Wheatley 5.00 12.00
TJRS Junior Seau 6.00 15.00

2001 Upper Deck Ovation Training Gear Trios

STATED ODDS 1:240
TTA Jake Plummer 10.00 25.00
Thomas Jones
David Boston
TTC Akili Smith 10.00 25.00
Corey Dillon
Peter Warrick
TTJ Mark Brunell 10.00 25.00
Fred Taylor
Keenan McCardell
TTO Rich Gannon 25.00 60.00
Tyrone Wheatley
Jerry Rice
TTGB Jeff Garcia 15.00 40.00
Terrell Owens
J.J. Stokes
TTNY Jessie Armstead 12.00 30.00
Tiki Barber
Ron Dayne
TTSD Junior Seau 20.00 50.00
Drew Brees
Doug Flutie

2002 Upper Deck Ovation

Released in August, 2002, this set contains 90 veterans and 30 rookies making a total of 120 cards. The rookie cards are sequentially #'d to 1985, and on average you get one rookie per box.

COMPLETE SET (120) 75.00 125.00
COMP.SET w/o SP's (90) 10.00 25.00
91-120 ROOKIE PRINT RUN 1985
1 David Boston .15 .40
2 Jake Plummer .20 .50
3 Warrick Dunn .20 .50
4 Michael Vick .40 1.00
5 Jamal Anderson .20 .50
6 Travis Taylor .15 .40
7 Ray Lewis .25 .60
8 Alex Van Pelt .15 .40
9 Travis Henry .15 .40
10 Drew Bledsoe .25 .60
11 Muhsin Muhammad .20 .50
12 Chris Weinke .15 .40
13 Lamar Smith .20 .50
14 Marty Booker .20 .50
15 Jim Miller .15 .40
16 Anthony Thomas .20 .50
17 Peter Warrick .20 .50
18 Jon Kitna .20 .50
19 Corey Dillon .20 .50
20 Quincy Morgan .15 .40
21 Tim Couch .15 .40
22 Rocket Ismail .20 .50
23 Quincy Carter .15 .40
24 Emmitt Smith .60 1.50
25 Shannon Sharpe .25 .60
26 Brian Griese .20 .50
27 Terrell Davis .25 .60
28 Mike McMahon .15 .40
29 James Stewart .15 .40
30 Az-Zahir Hakim .15 .40
31 Terry Glenn .20 .50
32 Brett Favre .60 1.50
33 Ahman Green .20 .50
34 James Allen .15 .40
35 Jermaine Lewis .15 .40
36 Marvin Harrison .25 .60
37 Peyton Manning .50 1.25
38 Edgerrin James .20 .50
39 Jimmy Smith .20 .50
40 Mark Brunell .20 .50
41 Johnnie Morton .20 .50
42 Trent Green .20 .50
43 Priest Holmes .25 .60
44 Jay Fiedler .20 .50
45 Chris Chambers .20 .50
46 Ricky Williams .20 .50
47 Randy Moss .25 .60
48 Michael Bennett .20 .50
49 Daunte Culpepper .20 .50
50 Troy Brown .20 .50
51 Tom Brady .60 1.50
52 Antowain Smith .20 .50
53 Joe Horn .20 .50
54 Aaron Brooks .20 .50
55 Deuce McAllister .20 .50
56 Amani Toomer .20 .50
57 Kerry Collins .20 .50
58 Ron Dayne .20 .50
59 Vinny Testaverde .20 .50
60 Curtis Martin .25 .60
61 Santana Moss .20 .50
62 Tim Brown .25 .60
63 Jerry Rice .50 1.25
64 Rich Gannon .20 .50
65 Donovan McNabb .25 .60
66 Duce Staley .20 .50
67 Freddie Mitchell .15 .40
68 Plaxico Burress .20 .50
69 Kordell Stewart .20 .50
70 Jerome Bettis .25 .60
71 Doug Flutie .25 .60
72 LaDainian Tomlinson .30 .75
73 Drew Brees .40 1.00
74 Terrell Owens .25 .60
75 Jeff Garcia .20 .50
76 Garrison Hearst .20 .50
77 Shaun Alexander .20 .50
78 Trent Dilfer .20 .50
79 Kurt Warner .25 .60
80 Marshall Faulk .25 .60
81 Isaac Bruce .25 .60
82 Keyshawn Johnson .20 .50
83 Brad Johnson .20 .50
84 Mike Alstott .20 .50
85 Rob Johnson .20 .50
86 Steve McNair .25 .60
87 Eddie George .20 .50
88 Jessie Armstead .15 .40
89 Rod Gardner .15 .40
90 Stephen Davis .20 .50
91 Andre Davis RC 1.50 4.00
92 Antonio Bryant RC 2.00 5.00
93 Antwaan Randle El RC 2.00 5.00
94 Ashley Lelie RC 1.50 4.00
95 Cliff Russell RC 1.25 3.00
96 Clinton Portis RC 2.50 6.00
97 Daniel Graham RC 1.50 4.00
98 David Carr RC 2.00 5.00
99 David Garrard RC 2.50 6.00
100 DeShaun Foster RC 2.00 5.00
101 Reche Caldwell RC 2.00 5.00
102 Donte Stallworth RC 2.00 5.00
103 Jabar Gaffney RC 2.00 5.00
104 Javon Walker RC 2.00 5.00
105 Jeremy Shockey RC 3.00 8.00
106 Joey Harrington RC 2.00 5.00
107 Josh McCown RC 2.00 5.00
108 Josh Reed RC 1.50 4.00
109 Julius Peppers RC 4.00 10.00
110 Marquise Walker RC 1.25 3.00
111 Maurice Morris RC 1.50 4.00
112 Patrick Ramsey RC 2.00 5.00
113 Quentin Jammer RC 2.00 5.00
114 Rohan Davey RC 2.00 5.00
115 Ron Johnson RC 1.50 4.00
116 Roy Williams RC 2.00 5.00
117 T.J. Duckett RC 2.00 5.00
118 Tim Carter RC 1.50 4.00
119 Travis Stephens RC 1.25 3.00
120 William Green RC 1.50 4.00

2002 Upper Deck Ovation Gold

*VETS: 15X TO 40X BASIC CARDS
STATED PRINT RUN 25 SER.#'d SETS

2002 Upper Deck Ovation Silver

*VETS: 5X TO 12X BASIC CARDS
STATED PRINT RUN 100 SER.#'d SETS

2002 Upper Deck Ovation Bound for Glory Jerseys

STATED ODDS 1:72 HOB/RET
*GOLD/25: 1X TO 2.5X BASIC JSY
GOLD PRINT RUN 25 SER.#'d SETS
BGCW Charles Woodson 5.00 12.00
BGDS Duce Staley 4.00 10.00
BGDT David Terrell 3.00 8.00
BGJH Joey Harrington 5.00 12.00
BGJJ James Jackson SP 3.00 8.00
BGLT LaDainian Tomlinson/75* 6.00 15.00
BGMB Michael Bennett 4.00 10.00
BGMW Michael Westbrook 3.00 8.00
BGPP Peerless Price 3.00 8.00
BGQM Quincy Morgan 3.00 8.00
BGRD Ron Dayne 4.00 10.00
BGRG Rod Gardner 3.00 8.00
BGTB Tom Brady 12.00 30.00
BGTB Tiki Barber 5.00 12.00
BGTH Travis Henry 3.00 8.00

2002 Upper Deck Ovation Jerseys

STATED ODDS 1:72 HOB/RET
*GOLD/25: 1X TO 2.5X BASIC JSY
GOLD PRINT RUN 25 SER.#'d SETS
OJAB Aaron Brooks 4.00 10.00
OJDC Daunte Culpepper 4.00 10.00
OJDF DeShaun Foster 5.00 12.00
OJDM Donovan McNabb SP 5.00 12.00
OJES Emmitt Smith 12.00 30.00
OJIB Isaac Bruce 5.00 12.00
OJJF Jay Fiedler 4.00 10.00
OJMB Mark Brunell SP 4.00 10.00
OJMF Marshall Faulk 5.00 12.00
OJPM Peyton Manning 10.00 25.00
OJRW Ricky Williams 4.00 10.00
OJTC Tim Couch 3.00 8.00
OJWS Warren Sapp 4.00 10.00

2002 Upper Deck Ovation Lead Performers

COMPLETE SET (30) 15.00 40.00
STATED ODDS 1:12 HOB/RET
LP1 Jake Plummer .60 1.50
LP2 Warrick Dunn .60 1.50
LP3 Michael Vick 1.25 3.00
LP4 Travis Henry .50 1.25
LP5 David Terrell .50 1.25
LP6 Brian Urlacher .75 2.00
LP7 Tim Couch .50 1.25
LP8 Brett Favre 2.00 5.00
LP9 Peyton Manning 1.50 4.00
LP10 Jimmy Smith .60 1.50
LP11 Mark Brunell .60 1.50
LP12 Trent Green .60 1.50
LP13 Chris Chambers .60 1.50
LP14 Jay Fiedler .60 1.50
LP15 Ricky Williams .60 1.50
LP16 Daunte Culpepper .60 1.50
LP17 Michael Bennett .60 1.50
LP18 Randy Moss .75 2.00
LP19 Antowain Smith .60 1.50
LP20 Tom Brady 2.00 5.00
LP21 Aaron Brooks .60 1.50
LP22 Deuce McAllister .60 1.50
LP23 Kerry Collins .60 1.50
LP24 Ron Dayne .60 1.50
LP25 Duce Staley .60 1.50
LP26 Kordell Stewart .60 1.50
LP27 Jerome Bettis .75 2.00
LP28 Drew Brees 1.25 3.00
LP29 Isaac Bruce .75 2.00
LP30 Steve McNair .75 2.00

2002 Upper Deck Ovation Milestones

COMPLETE SET (30) 15.00 40.00
STATED ODDS 1:12 HOB/RET
OM1 David Boston .50 1.25
OM2 Jamal Anderson .60 1.50
OM3 Tony Martin .60 1.50
OM4 Ray Lewis .75 2.00
OM5 Anthony Thomas .60 1.50
OM6 Corey Dillon .60 1.50
OM7 Emmitt Smith 2.00 5.00
OM8 Terrell Davis .75 2.00
OM9 Brett Favre 2.00 5.00
OM10 Edgerrin James .60 1.50
OM11 Peyton Manning 1.50 4.00
OM12 James Stewart .50 1.25
OM13 Mark Brunell .60 1.50
OM14 Priest Holmes .75 2.00
OM15 Randy Moss .75 2.00
OM16 Tom Brady 2.00 5.00
OM17 Drew Bledsoe .75 2.00
OM18 Curtis Martin .75 2.00
OM19 Michael Strahan .75 2.00
OM20 Vinny Testaverde .60 1.50
OM21 Jerry Rice 1.50 4.00
OM22 Rich Gannon .60 1.50
OM23 Tim Brown .75 2.00
OM24 Jerome Bettis .75 2.00
OM25 Kendrell Bell .50 1.25
OM26 Terrell Owens .75 2.00
OM27 Kurt Warner .75 2.00
OM28 Marshall Faulk .75 2.00
OM29 Eddie George .60 1.50
OM30 Darrell Green .75 2.00

2002 Upper Deck Ovation Standing O

COMPLETE SET (30) 15.00 40.00
STATED ODDS 1:12 HOB/RET
SO1 David Boston .50 1.25
SO2 Michael Vick 1.25 3.00
SO3 Jamal Lewis .60 1.50
SO4 Chris Weinke .50 1.25
SO5 Anthony Thomas .60 1.50
SO6 Jim Miller .50 1.25
SO7 Marty Booker .60 1.50
SO8 Peter Warrick .60 1.50
SO9 Emmitt Smith 2.00 5.00
SO10 Quincy Carter .50 1.25
SO11 Brian Griese .60 1.50
SO12 Mike Anderson .60 1.50
SO13 Rod Smith .60 1.50
SO14 Mike McMahon .50 1.25
SO15 Ahman Green .60 1.50
SO16 Edgerrin James .60 1.50
SO17 Marvin Harrison .75 2.00
SO18 Peyton Manning 1.50 4.00
SO19 Donovan McNabb .75 2.00
SO20 Freddie Mitchell .50 1.25
SO21 Jerome Bettis .75 2.00
SO22 Plaxico Burress .60 1.50
SO23 Doug Flutie .75 2.00
SO24 LaDainian Tomlinson 1.00 2.50
SO25 Garrison Hearst .60 1.50
SO26 Jeff Garcia .60 1.50
SO27 Terrell Owens .75 2.00
SO28 Shaun Alexander .60 1.50
SO29 Keyshawn Johnson .60 1.50
SO30 Rod Gardner .50 1.25

2002 Upper Deck Ovation Tried and True Jerseys

STATED ODDS 1:72 HOB/RET
*GOLD/25: 1X TO 2.5X BASIC JSY
GOLD PRINT RUN 25 SER.#'d SETS
TTAT Amani Toomer 4.00 10.00
TTBF Brett Favre 12.00 30.00
TTBS Bruce Smith 5.00 12.00
TTCD Corey Dillon/57* 4.00 10.00

TTDM Dan Marino 12.00 30.00
TTEJ Edgerrin James 4.00 10.00
TTJB Jerome Bettis 5.00 12.00
TTJE John Elway 10.00 25.00
TTJR Jerry Rice SP 10.00 25.00
TTKW Kurt Warner 5.00 12.00
TTMH Marvin Harrison 5.00 12.00
TTMW Michael Westbrook 3.00 8.00
TTRM Randy Moss 5.00 12.00
TTTH Torry Holt 5.00 12.00

1999 Upper Deck PowerDeck

Realeased in mid October of 1999, The Powerdeck set features 60 cards. 30 of the cards were made on an actual CD ROM which features audio and video footage of both stars and rookies. Also within the set were autographed CD ROM cards which were signed by each respective player and hand nubered to on 50 of each on the card front. Also available were the autographed Walter Payton Game Jersey cards which featured a game used jersey swatch and an authentic autograph on the card front and hand numbered to only 34 of each made exclusively for the Powerdeck Product. CD ROM cards were available at a rate of 1 per pack. Also included was a one of one gold auxillary power cards done in gold foil.

COMPLETE SET (30) 25.00 60.00
PD1 Troy Aikman 1.50 4.00
PD2 Drew Bledsoe 1.00 2.50
PD3 Randy Moss 1.00 2.50
PD4 Barry Sanders 2.50 6.00
PD5 Brett Favre 3.00 8.00
PD6 Terrell Davis 1.00 2.50
PD7 Peyton Manning 3.00 8.00
PD8 Emmitt Smith 2.50 6.00
PD9 Dan Marino 3.00 8.00
PD10 Jake Plummer .75 2.00
PD11 Eddie George .75 2.00
PD12 Jerry Rice 2.00 5.00
PD13 Steve Young 1.25 3.00
PD14 Mark Brunell .75 2.00
PD15 Kordell Stewart .75 2.00
PD16 Keyshawn Johnson .75 2.00
PD17 Fred Taylor .75 2.00
PD18 Jamal Anderson .75 2.00
PD19 Cecil Collins .60 1.50
PD20 Ricky Williams 1.50 4.00
PD21 Tim Couch 1.00 2.50
PD22 Donovan McNabb 2.50 6.00
PD23 Akili Smith .75 2.00
PD24 Edgerrin James 1.25 3.00
PD25 Daunte Culpepper 1.00 2.50
PD26 Brock Huard .75 2.00
PD27 Torry Holt 1.50 4.00
PD28 David Boston .75 2.00
PD29 Cade McNown .75 2.00
PD30 Champ Bailey 2.00 5.00
CHKL Checklist Card .08 .25
WPPD Walter Payton/ Jsy AU/34 1,000.00 1,500.00

1999 Upper Deck PowerDeck Auxiliary

Randomly inserted at a rate of aproximately two per pack, This is the parallel "paper card" set to the CD ROM set which features full color action shots with key rookies such as Tim Couch and Cade Mcnown.

COMPLETE SET (30) 10.00 25.00
AUX1 Troy Aikman .60 1.50
AUX2 Drew Bledsoe .40 1.00
AUX3 Randy Moss .40 1.00
AUX4 Barry Sanders 1.00 2.50
AUX5 Brett Favre 1.25 3.00
AUX6 Terrell Davis .40 1.00
AUX7 Peyton Manning 1.25 3.00
AUX8 Emmitt Smith 1.00 2.50
AUX9 Dan Marino 1.25 3.00
AUX10 Jake Plummer .30 .75
AUX11 Eddie George .30 .75
AUX12 Jerry Rice .75 2.00
AUX13 Steve Young .50 1.25
AUX14 Mark Brunell .30 .75
AUX15 Kordell Stewart .30 .75
AUX16 Keyshawn Johnson .30 .75
AUX17 Fred Taylor .30 .75
AUX18 Jamal Anderson .30 .75
AUX19 Cecil Collins .30 .75
AUX20 Ricky Williams .75 2.00
AUX21 Tim Couch .50 1.25
AUX22 Donovan McNabb 2.00 5.00
AUX23 Akili Smith .40 1.00
AUX24 Edgerrin James .60 1.50
AUX25 Daunte Culpepper .50 1.25
AUX26 Brock Huard .40 1.00
AUX27 Torry Holt .75 2.00
AUX28 David Boston .40 1.00
AUX29 Cade McNown .40 1.00
AUX30 Champ Bailey 1.00 2.50

1999 Upper Deck PowerDeck Auxiliary Gold

STATED PRINT RUN 1 SET

1999 Upper Deck PowerDeck Autographs

STATED PRINT RUN 50 SER.#'d SETS
AS Akili Smith 20.00 50.00
BH Brock Huard 20.00 50.00
CB Champ Bailey 50.00 100.00
CM Cade McNown 20.00 50.00
DC Daunte Culpepper 30.00 80.00
DM Dan Marino 100.00 200.00
EJ Edgerrin James 40.00 100.00
JP Jake Plummer 25.00 60.00
TA Troy Aikman 75.00 150.00
TC Tim Couch 25.00 60.00
TH Torry Holt 40.00 100.00

1999 Upper Deck PowerDeck Most Valuable Performances

COMPLETE SET (7) 60.00 150.00
STATED ODDS 1:287
*AUXILIARY CARDS: .25X TO .6X CD-ROMS
AUXILIARY STATED ODDS 1:287
M1 Brett Favre 20.00 50.00
M2 Joe Montana 25.00 60.00
M3 John Elway 20.00 50.00
M4 Emmitt Smith 12.50 30.00
M5 Jamal Anderson 6.00 15.00
M6 Randy Moss 15.00 40.00
M7 Terrell Davis 6.00 15.00

1999 Upper Deck PowerDeck Powerful Moments

COMPLETE SET (6) 25.00 60.00
STATED ODDS 1:23
*AUXILIARY CARDS: .25X TO .6X CD-ROMS
AUXILIARY STATED ODDS 1:23
P1 Joe Montana 7.50 20.00
P2 Terrell Davis 2.00 5.00
P3 John Elway 6.00 15.00
P4 Randy Moss 5.00 12.00
P5 Dan Marino 6.00 15.00
P6 Emmitt Smith 4.00 10.00

1999 Upper Deck PowerDeck Time Capsule

COMPLETE SET (6) 15.00 40.00
STATED ODDS 1:7
*AUXILIARY CARDS: .25X TO .6X CD's
AUXILIARY STATED ODDS 1:7
T1 Edgerrin James 6.00 15.00
T2 Barry Sanders 5.00 12.00
T3 Terrell Davis 1.50 4.00
T4 Emmitt Smith 3.00 8.00
T5 Dan Marino 5.00 12.00
T6 Tim Couch .75 2.00

1999 Upper Deck PowerDeck Athletes of the Century

These CD-Rom cards featuring four of the most prominent athletes of the 20th century were issued by Upper Deck in one boxed set. The cards are inserted into a computer and display various highlights of the player's career and his stats and other information.

COMPLETE SET (4) 8.00 20.00
3 Joe Montana 2.00 5.00

2004 Upper Deck Power Up

Upper Deck Power Up was initially released in mid-August 2004 as a retail-only product. The base set consists of 100-cards with no rookie cards. Boxes contained 24-packs of 6-cards and carried an S.R.P. of $1.99 per pack. Four parallel sets and two inserts can be found seeded in packs.

COMPLETE SET (100) 10.00 25.00
1 Emmitt Smith .60 1.50
2 Anquan Boldin .25 .60
3 Josh McCown .20 .50
4 Michael Vick .30 .75
5 Peerless Price .15 .40
6 Warrick Dunn .20 .50
7 Jamal Lewis .20 .50
8 Kyle Boller .20 .50
9 Ray Lewis .25 .60
10 Drew Bledsoe .25 .60
11 Travis Henry .15 .40
12 Eric Moulds .20 .50
13 Jake Delhomme .20 .50
14 Steve Smith .25 .60
15 Stephen Davis .20 .50
16 Anthony Thomas .20 .50
17 Marty Booker .20 .50
18 Rex Grossman .20 .50
19 Chad Johnson .25 .60
20 Rudi Johnson .20 .50
21 Jon Kitna .20 .50
22 Andre Davis .15 .40
23 Jeff Garcia .20 .50
24 William Green .15 .40
25 Antonio Bryant .20 .50
26 Quincy Carter .15 .40
27 Keyshawn Johnson .20 .50
28 Champ Bailey .20 .50
29 Jake Plummer .20 .50
30 Ashley Lelie .15 .40
31 Charles Rogers .15 .40
32 Joey Harrington .20 .50
33 Az-Zahir Hakim .15 .40
34 Brett Favre .60 1.50
35 Javon Walker .15 .40
36 Ahman Green .20 .50
37 David Carr .15 .40
38 Domanick Davis .15 .40
39 Andre Johnson .25 .60
40 Peyton Manning .50 1.25
41 Marvin Harrison .25 .60
42 Edgerrin James .20 .50
43 Byron Leftwich .20 .50
44 Fred Taylor .20 .50
45 Jimmy Smith .20 .50
46 Priest Holmes .25 .60
47 Trent Green .20 .50
48 Dante Hall .20 .50
49 Tony Gonzalez .25 .60
50 Ricky Williams .20 .50
51 Jay Fiedler .15 .40
52 Chris Chambers .20 .50
53 Daunte Culpepper .20 .50
54 Randy Moss .25 .60
55 Onterrio Smith .15 .40
56 Troy Brown .20 .50
57 Deion Branch .20 .50
58 Tom Brady .50 1.25
59 Deuce McAllister .20 .50
60 Aaron Brooks .20 .50
61 Joe Horn .20 .50
62 Jeremy Shockey .20 .50
63 Amani Toomer .20 .50
64 Tiki Barber .25 .60
65 Chad Pennington .25 .60
66 Santana Moss .20 .50
67 Curtis Martin .25 .60
68 Rich Gannon .20 .50
60 Jorry Rico .50 1.25
70 Tim Brown .25 .60
71 Jerry Porter .15 .40
72 Donovan McNabb .25 .60
73 Terrell Owens .25 .60
74 Jevon Kearse .20 .50
75 Hines Ward .25 .60
76 Jerome Bettis .25 .60
77 Tommy Maddox .20 .50
78 Plaxico Burress .20 .50
79 LaDainian Tomlinson .25 .60
80 Antonio Gates .25 .60
81 Drew Brees .25 .60
82 Tim Rattay .15 .40
83 Brandon Lloyd .20 .50
84 Kevan Barlow .15 .40
85 Matt Hasselbeck .20 .50
86 Shaun Alexander .20 .50
87 Koren Robinson .15 .40
88 Marshall Faulk .25 .60
89 Torry Holt .20 .50
90 Marc Bulger .20 .50
91 Isaac Bruce .20 .50
92 Brad Johnson .20 .50
93 Charlie Garner .20 .50
94 Keenan McCardell .15 .40
95 Steve McNair .25 .60
96 Eddie George .20 .50
97 Derrick Mason .20 .50
98 Mark Brunell .20 .50
99 Laveranues Coles .15 .40
100 Clinton Portis .25 .60

2004 Upper Deck Power Up Blue

*BLUE: 6X TO 15X BASIC CARDS
OVERALL PARALLEL STATED ODDS 1:4
BLUE WORTH 1000 POINTS EACH

2004 Upper Deck Power Up Green

*GREENS: 2X TO 5X BASIC CARDS
OVERALL PARALLEL STATED ODDS 1:4
GREEN WORTH 100 POINTS EACH

2004 Upper Deck Power Up Orange

*ORANGE: 3X TO 8X BASIC CARDS
OVERALL PARALLEL STATED ODDS 1:4
ORANGE WORTH 250 POINTS EACH

2004 Upper Deck Power Up Red

*REDS: 5X TO 12X BASIC CARDS
OVERALL PARALLEL STATED ODDS 1:4
RED WORTH 500 POINTS EACH

2004 Upper Deck Power Up Shining Through

COMPLETE SET (30) 7.50 20.00
STATED ODDS 1:1
ST1 Anquan Boldin .40 1.00
ST2 Michael Vick .50 1.25
ST3 Jamal Lewis .30 .75
ST4 Aaron Brooks .30 .75
ST5 DeShaun Foster .30 .75
ST6 Rex Grossman .30 .75
ST7 Rudi Johnson .30 .75
ST8 Andre Davis .25 .60
ST9 Antonio Bryant .30 .75
ST10 Clinton Portis .40 1.00
ST11 Brett Favre 1.00 2.50
ST12 David Carr .25 .60
ST13 Marvin Harrison .40 1.00
ST14 Byron Leftwich .30 .75
ST15 Priest Holmes .40 1.00
ST16 Dante Hall .30 .75
ST17 Chris Chambers .30 .75
ST18 Daunte Culpepper .30 .75
ST19 Tom Brady .75 2.00
ST20 Deuce McAllister .30 .75
ST21 Jeremy Shockey .30 .75
ST22 Santana Moss .30 .75
ST23 Jerry Rice .75 2.00
ST24 Donovan McNabb .40 1.00
ST25 Plaxico Burress .30 .75
ST26 LaDainian Tomlinson .40 1.00
ST27 Koren Robinson .25 .60
ST28 Ahman Green .30 .75
ST29 Steve McNair .40 1.00
ST30 Laveranues Coles .25 .60

2004 Upper Deck Power Up Stickers

COMPLETE SET (30) 20.00 50.00
STATED ODDS 1:6
PU1 Emmitt Smith 2.00 5.00
PU2 Michael Vick 1.00 2.50
PU3 Kyle Boller .60 1.50
PU4 Drew Bledsoe .75 2.00
PU5 Jake Delhomme .60 1.50
PU6 Brian Urlacher .75 2.00
PU7 Carson Palmer .75 2.00
PU8 Quincy Carter .50 1.25
PU9 Jake Plummer .60 1.50
PU10 Joey Harrington .60 1.50
PU11 Brett Favre 2.00 5.00
PU12 David Carr .50 1.25
PU13 Peyton Manning 1.50 4.00
PU14 Byron Leftwich .60 1.50
PU15 Priest Holmes .75 2.00
PU16 Ricky Williams .60 1.50
PU17 Randy Moss .75 2.00
PU18 Tom Brady 1.50 4.00
PU19 Deuce McAllister .60 1.50
PU20 Chad Pennington .75 2.00
PU21 Jeremy Shockey .60 1.50
PU22 Jerry Rice 1.50 4.00
PU23 Donovan McNabb .75 2.00
PU24 Hines Ward .75 2.00
PU25 LaDainian Tomlinson .75 2.00
PU26 Kevan Barlow .50 1.25
PU27 Matt Hasselbeck .60 1.50
PU28 Marshall Faulk .75 2.00
PU29 Steve McNair .75 2.00
PU30 Clinton Portis .75 2.00

2007 Upper Deck Premier

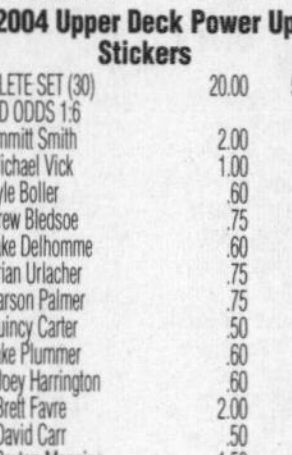

This 162-card set was released in September, 2007. The set was issued into the hobby in a pack (box) with a $300 SRP. Cards numbered 1-100 feature veterans which were issued to a stated print run of 225 serial numbered sets while cards numbered 101-163 feature 2007 NFL Rookies. Within that grouping, cards numbered 101-130 were signed and those cards were issued to a stated print run of 225 serial numbered sets and cards numbered 131-163 had both a signature and a player-worn jersey swatch and those cards were issued to a stated print run of 199 serial numbered sets. Card number 135 was not issued in this set.

STATED PRINT RUN 225 SER.#'d SETS
JSY AU RC PRINT RUN 55-199
1 Matt Leinart 2.50 6.00
2 Anquan Boldin 2.50 6.00
3 Larry Fitzgerald 3.00 8.00
4 Edgerrin James 2.50 6.00
5 Michael Vick 3.00 8.00
6 Warrick Dunn 2.50 6.00
7 Alge Crumpler 2.50 6.00
8 Steve McNair 2.50 6.00
9 Mark Clayton 2.50 6.00
10 Ray Lewis 3.00 8.00
11 J.P. Losman 2.00 5.00
12 Lee Evans 2.50 6.00
13 Anthony Thomas 2.00 5.00
14 Jake Delhomme 2.50 6.00
15 Steve Smith 2.50 6.00
16 Julius Peppers 2.50 6.00
17 Brian Urlacher 3.00 8.00
18 Cedric Benson 2.50 6.00
19 Rex Grossman 2.50 6.00
20 Carson Palmer 2.50 6.00
21 Chad Johnson 2.50 6.00
22 Rudi Johnson 2.50 6.00
23 Charlie Frye 2.50 6.00
24 Braylon Edwards 2.50 6.00
25 Jamal Lewis 2.50 6.00
26 Tony Romo 4.00 10.00
27 Terrell Owens 3.00 8.00
28 Julius Jones 2.00 5.00
29 Marion Barber 2.50 6.00
30 Jay Cutler 3.00 8.00
31 Javon Walker 2.50 6.00
32 Champ Bailey 2.50 6.00
33 Roy Williams WR 2.50 6.00
34 Jon Kitna 2.00 5.00
35 Tatum Bell 2.00 5.00
36 Greg Jennings 3.00 8.00
37 Brett Favre 6.00 15.00
38 Donald Driver 3.00 8.00
39 Matt Schaub 2.50 6.00
40 Andre Johnson 2.50 6.00
41 Ahman Green 2.50 6.00
42 Peyton Manning 5.00 12.00
43 Marvin Harrison 3.00 8.00
44 Reggie Wayne 2.50 6.00
45 Joseph Addai 2.50 6.00
46 Fred Taylor 2.50 6.00
47 Maurice Jones-Drew 3.00 8.00
48 Byron Leftwich 2.50 6.00
49 Damon Huard 2.50 6.00
50 Larry Johnson 2.00 5.00
51 Tony Gonzalez 2.50 6.00
52 Zach Thomas 2.50 6.00
53 Ronnie Brown 2.50 6.00
54 Chris Chambers 2.50 6.00
55 Tarvaris Jackson 2.00 5.00
56 Chester Taylor 2.00 5.00
57 Troy Williamson 2.00 5.00
58 Tom Brady 5.00 12.00
59 Donte Stallworth 2.50 6.00
60 Laurence Maroney 2.50 6.00
61 Reggie Bush 3.00 8.00
62 Deuce McAllister 2.50 6.00
63 Drew Brees 3.00 8.00
64 Marques Colston 3.00 8.00
65 Eli Manning 3.00 8.00
66 Plaxico Burress 2.50 6.00
67 Brandon Jacobs 2.50 6.00
68 Chad Pennington 2.50 6.00
69 Thomas Jones 2.50 6.00
70 Laveranues Coles 2.00 5.00
71 LaMont Jordan 2.50 6.00
72 Ronald Curry 2.50 6.00
73 Dominic Rhodes 2.50 6.00
74 Donovan McNabb 3.00 8.00
75 Brian Westbrook 2.50 6.00
76 Reggie Brown 2.00 5.00
77 Ben Roethlisberger 3.00 8.00
78 Hines Ward 3.00 8.00
79 Willie Parker 2.50 6.00
80 LaDainian Tomlinson 3.00 8.00
81 Philip Rivers 3.00 8.00
82 Antonio Gates 3.00 8.00
83 Frank Gore 3.00 8.00
84 Alex Smith QB 3.00 8.00
85 Ashley Lelie 2.50 6.00
86 Matt Hasselbeck 2.50 6.00
87 Shaun Alexander 2.50 6.00
88 Deion Branch 2.50 6.00
89 Marc Bulger 2.50 6.00
90 Torry Holt 2.50 6.00
91 Steven Jackson 3.00 8.00
92 Cadillac Williams 2.50 6.00
93 Chris Simms 2.00 5.00
94 Joey Galloway 2.50 6.00
95 Vince Young 2.50 6.00
96 David Givens 2.00 5.00
97 LenDale White 2.50 6.00
98 Jason Campbell 2.50 6.00
99 Santana Moss 2.50 6.00
100 Clinton Portis 2.50 6.00
101 Craig Buster Davis AU RC 6.00 15.00
102 Amobi Okoye AU RC 8.00 20.00
103 Aundrae Allison AU RC 5.00 12.00
104 Chansi Stuckey AU RC 8.00 20.00
105 LaRon Landry AU RC 8.00 20.00
106 Brandon Meriweather AU RC 8.00 20.00
107 Courtney Taylor AU RC 6.00 15.00
108 Dallas Baker AU RC 5.00 12.00
109 Darius Walker AU RC 5.00 12.00
110 David Ball AU RC 6.00 15.00
111 Darrelle Revis AU RC 12.00 30.00
112 David Clowney AU RC 6.00 15.00
113 David Irons AU RC 5.00 12.00
114 Daymeion Hughes AU RC 6.00 15.00
115 Jamaal Anderson AU RC 6.00 15.00
116 Dwayne Wright AU RC 6.00 15.00
117 Jordan Palmer AU RC 6.00 15.00
118 Eric Wright AU RC 8.00 20.00
119 Gary Russell AU RC 6.00 15.00
120 Joel Filani AU RC 6.00 15.00
121 Kenneth Darby AU RC 6.00 15.00
122 Legedu Naanee AU RC 8.00 20.00
123 Marcus McCauley AU RC 6.00 15.00
124 Paul Posluszny AU RC 8.00 20.00
125 Quentin Moses AU RC 6.00 15.00
126 Jeff Rowe AU RC 5.00 12.00
127 Matt Moore AU RC 8.00 20.00
128 Rhema McKnight AU RC 5.00 12.00
129 Scott Chandler AU RC 8.00 20.00
130 Tyrone Moss AU RC 5.00 12.00
131 Adrian Peterson JSY AU/55 RC 150.00 300.00
132 Patrick Willis JSY AU RC 20.00 50.00
133 Anthony Gonzalez JSY AU RC 10.00 25.00
134 Antonio Pittman JSY AU RC 6.00 15.00
136 Brady Quinn JSY AU RC 10.00 25.00
137 Brandon Jackson JSY AU RC 8.00 20.00
138 Brian Leonard JSY AU/125 RC 8.00 20.00
139 Calvin Johnson JSY AU RC 60.00 120.00
140 Paul Williams JSY AU RC 6.00 15.00
141 Johnnie Lee Higgins JSY AU RC 8.00 20.00
142 Trent Edwards JSY AU RC 10.00 25.00
143 Greg Olsen JSY AU RC 8.00 20.00
144 Drew Stanton JSY AU RC 6.00 15.00
145 Dwayne Bowe JSY AU RC 12.00 30.00
146 Dwayne Jarrett JSY AU RC 8.00 20.00
147 Yamon Figurs JSY AU RC 6.00 15.00
148 Chris Henry RB JSY AU RC 6.00 15.00
149 JaMarcus Russell JSY AU RC 6.00 15.00
150 Joe Thomas JSY AU RC 10.00 25.00
151 Gaines Adams JSY AU RC 10.00 25.00
152 Lorenzo Booker JSY AU RC 8.00 20.00
153 Kenny Irons JSY AU RC 6.00 15.00
154 Kevin Kolb JSY AU RC 15.00 40.00
155 John Beck JSY AU RC 10.00 25.00
156 Garrett Wolfe JSY AU RC 6.00 15.00
157 Marshawn Lynch JSY AU RC 10.00 25.00
158 Michael Bush JSY AU RC 10.00 25.00
159 Robert Meachem JSY AU RC 10.00 25.00
160 Sidney Rice JSY AU RC 12.00 30.00
161 Steve Smith JSY AU RC 10.00 25.00
162 Ted Ginn Jr. JSY AU RC 8.00 20.00
163 Tony Hunt JSY AU RC 6.00 15.00

2007 Upper Deck Premier Rookie Autographed Materials Blue

*BLUE/99: .5X TO 1.2X BASIC RCs
BLUE PRINT RUN 99 SER.#'d SETS
131 Adrian Peterson 125.00 250.00

2007 Upper Deck Premier Rookie Autographed Materials Bronze

*BRONZE/125: .4X TO 1X BASIC RCs
BRONZE PRINT RUN 125 SER.#'d SETS
131 Adrian Peterson 100.00 200.00

2007 Upper Deck Premier Rookie Autographed Materials Gold

GOLD PRINT RUN 175 SER.#'d SETS
UNPRICED NFL LOGO PRINT RUN 1
131 Adrian Peterson 125.00 250.00

2007 Upper Deck Premier Rookie Autographed Materials Green Patches

*PATCH/50: .5X TO 1.2X BASIC RCs
PATCHES PRINT RUN 50 SER.#'d SETS
131 Adrian Peterson 150.00 300.00

2007 Upper Deck Premier Foursomes Autographs

FOURSOME AUTO PRINT RUN 15
1 Anthony Gonzalez 15.00 40.00
Robert Meachem
Craig Buster Davis
Dwayne Bowe
2 Larry Johnson 150.00 300.00
LaDainian Tomlinson
Adrian Peterson
Marshawn Lynch
3 Mike Singletary 50.00 100.00
L.C. Greenwood
Patrick Willis
Lawrence Timmons
4 Peyton Manning 75.00 150.00
Philip Rivers
Brady Quinn
JaMarcus Russell
5 Chad Johnson
Marques Colston
Calvin Johnson
Dwayne Jarrett
6 Drew Brees 75.00 150.00
Eli Manning
Jason Campbell
Alex Smith QB
7 Joe Namath 200.00 350.00
Joe Montana
Dan Marino
Joe Theismann
8 Drew Stanton
John Beck
Kevin Kolb
Trent Edwards
9 Jamaal Anderson
Gaines Adams
Amobi Okoye
Adam Carriker
10 Reggie Nelson 12.00 30.00
Leon Hall
Darrelle Revis
Michael Griffin

2007 Upper Deck Premier Impressions Autographs Gold

GOLD PRINT RUN 25-99
*BRONZE/75: .5X TO 1.2X BASIC AU/99
*BRONZE/25: .5X TO 1.2X BASIC AU/50
BRONZE PRINT RUN 10-75
UNPRICED GOLD HOLOFOIL PRINT RUN 1
PIBF Brett Favre/25 125.00 200.00
PIBL Brian Leonard 6.00 15.00
PIBU Reggie Bush/50 12.00 30.00
PICW Cadillac Williams/50 10.00 25.00
PIDB David Ball 6.00 15.00
PIDC David Clowney 6.00 15.00
PIDS Drew Stanton 5.00 12.00
PIDW Dwayne Wright 6.00 15.00
PIES Emmitt Smith/25 100.00 200.00
PIGW Garrett Wolfe 5.00 12.00
PIJA Joseph Addai/50 10.00 25.00
PIJF Joel Filani 6.00 15.00
PIJP Jordan Palmer 6.00 15.00
PIJR JaMarcus Russell/50 8.00 20.00
PIKD Kenneth Darby 6.00 15.00
PILJ Larry Johnson/50 8.00 20.00
PILW LaMarr Woodley 8.00 20.00
PIMB Marc Bulger/50 10.00 25.00
PIPW Patrick Willis 15.00 40.00
PIRB Reggie Brown 5.00 12.00
PISY Selvin Young 6.00 15.00
PITE Trent Edwards 8.00 20.00
PITH Tony Hunt 5.00 12.00
PITP Tyler Palko 6.00 15.00
PIZM Zach Miller 8.00 20.00

2007 Upper Deck Premier Insignias Autographs Gold

GOLD PRINT RUN 10-99
*BRONZE/75: .5X TO 1.2X BASIC AU/99
*BRONZE/25: .5X TO 1.2X BASIC AU/50
BRONZE PRINT RUN 5-75
UNPRICED GOLD HOLOFOIL PRINT RUN 1
INAG Anthony Gonzalez 8.00 20.00
INBE Drew Bennett 5.00 12.00
INBJ Bo Jackson/25 60.00 120.00
INBR Drew Brees/25 40.00 80.00
INCJ Calvin Johnson/10 150.00 300.00
INCS Chansi Stuckey 8.00 20.00
INDB Dallas Baker 5.00 12.00
INDH Daymeion Hughes 6.00 15.00
INDW Darius Walker 5.00 12.00
INEM Eli Manning/25 50.00 80.00
INGA Gaines Adams 8.00 20.00
INIS Isaiah Stanback 5.00 12.00
INJA Jamaal Anderson 6.00 15.00
INJB John Beck 8.00 20.00
INJC Jerricho Cotchery 6.00 15.00
INJH Johnnie Lee Higgins 6.00 15.00
INMM Marcus McCauley 6.00 15.00
INMO Matt Moore 8.00 20.00
INMS Matt Schaub/50 12.00 30.00
INQM Quentin Moses 6.00 15.00
INRB Reggie Bush/50 50.00 120.00
INSC Scott Chandler 8.00 20.00
INSI Mike Singletary/50 15.00 40.00
INWY DeShawn Wynn 6.00 15.00

2007 Upper Deck Premier Noteworthy Autographs Gold

GOLD PRINT RUN 25-99
*BRONZE/75: .5X TO 1.2X GOLD AU/99
*BRONZE/25: .5X TO 1.2X GOLD AU/50
BRONZE PRINT RUN 15-75
UNPRICED GOLD HOLOFOIL PRINT RUN 1
NAA Aundrae Allison 6.00 15.00
NAB Alan Branch 6.00 15.00
NAP Adrian Peterson/25 125.00 250.00
NAS Alex Smith QB/25
NBM Brandon Meriweather 6.00 15.00
NCH Chris Henry RB 8.00 20.00
NCJ Chad Johnson/50 10.00 25.00
NCT Chester Taylor 6.00 15.00
NDB David Ball 5.00 12.00
NDD Donald Driver 15.00 30.00
NDP Drew Pearson 8.00 20.00
NEW Eric Wright 5.00 12.00
NJR Jeff Rowe 5.00 12.00
NJT Joe Thomas 8.00 20.00
NKK Kevin Kolb 10.00 25.00
NLL LaRon Landry 8.00 20.00
NLN Legedu Naanee 6.00 15.00
NLT LaDainian Tomlinson/50 25.00 60.00
NMG Michael Griffin 8.00 20.00
NML Matt Leinart/50 10.00 25.00
NRC Roger Craig 8.00 20.00
NSR Sidney Rice 10.00 25.00
NTH T.J. Houshmandzadeh/50 8.00 20.00
NTM Tyrone Moss 5.00 12.00
NWP Willie Parker/50 10.00 25.00

2007 Upper Deck Premier Octographs Autographs

UNPRICED OCTOGRAPHS PRINT RUN 5

2007 Upper Deck Premier Pairings Autographs

STATED PRINT RUN 25 SER.#'d SETS
1 Jamaal Anderson 12.00 30.00
Adam Carriker
2 Gaines Adams 12.00 30.00
Amobi Okoye
3 Aundrae Allison 12.00 30.00
Chansi Stuckey
4 Reggie Brown 12.00 30.00
Drew Bennett
6 Ronnie Brown 12.00 30.00
Brian Leonard
7 Drew Brees 60.00 120.00
Eli Manning
8 Marc Bulger 12.00 30.00
Jordan Palmer
9 Roger Craig 15.00 40.00
Frank Gore
10 David Clowney 12.00 30.00
Johnnie Lee Higgins
11 Marques Colston
Dwayne Jarrett
12 Jason Campbell 15.00 40.00
Courtney Taylor
13 Craig Buster Davis 20.00 50.00
Dwayne Bowe
14 Craig Buster Davis 15.00 40.00
Legedu Naanee
15 Kenneth Darby 15.00 40.00
Selvin Young
17 Ted Ginn Jr.
Troy Smith
18 L.C. Greenwood 15.00 40.00
Lawrence Timmons
19 Leon Hall 12.00 30.00
Alan Branch
20 T.J. Houshmandzadeh 12.00 30.00
Joel Filani
21 Leon Hall 15.00 40.00
Darrelle Revis
22 Kenny Irons 12.00 30.00
David Irons
23 Larry Johnson 20.00 50.00
Michael Bush
24 Darrell Jackson 20.00 50.00
Donald Driver
25 Chad Johnson 15.00 40.00
Robert Meachem
26 Dwayne Jarrett 20.00 50.00
Steve Smith USC
27 Kevin Kolb 15.00 40.00
Trent Edwards
28 Chris Leak 15.00 40.00
Dallas Baker
29 LaRon Landry 15.00 40.00
Michael Griffin
30 Chris Leak
Troy Smith
31 Robert Meachem 20.00 50.00
Sidney Rice
32 Reggie Nelson 10.00 25.00
Brandon Meriweather
33 Greg Olsen 15.00 40.00
Zach Miller
34 Willie Parker 15.00 40.00
Lorenzo Booker
35 Antonio Pittman 15.00 40.00
Anthony Gonzalez
36 Reggie Bush 30.00 80.00
Marshawn Lynch
37 Brady Quinn 40.00 100.00
JaMarcus Russell
38 Brady Quinn 40.00 100.00
Darius Walker
40 Drew Stanton 15.00 40.00
John Beck
43 Chester Taylor 12.00 30.00
Brandon Jackson
44 Lawrence Timmons 20.00 50.00
LaMarr Woodley
45 Reggie Wayne 25.00 60.00
Joseph Addai
46 Paul Williams 12.00 30.00
Yamon Figurs
47 Cadillac Williams 15.00 40.00
Tony Hunt
48 Eric Wright 10.00 25.00
Marcus McCauley
49 Patrick Willis 20.00 50.00
Paul Posluszny
50 Jared Zabransky 15.00 40.00
Legedu Naanee

2007 Upper Deck Premier Patches Dual

STATED PRINT RUN 35-99
*GOLD/75: .4X TO 1X BASIC INSERTS
GOLD PRINT RUN 15-75
*PLATINUM/15-25: .6X TO 15X BASIC INSERTS
PLATINUM PRINT RUN 15-25
UNPRICED MASTERPIECE PRINT RUN
PP2AB Anquan Boldin 6.00 15.00
PP2AG Ahman Green 6.00 15.00
PP2AP Adrian Peterson 15.00 40.00
PP2BF Brett Favre 15.00 40.00
PP2BL Brian Leonard 3.00 8.00
PP2BO Dwayne Bowe 5.00 12.00
PP2BQ Brady Quinn 4.00 10.00
PP2BU Brian Urlacher 10.00 25.00
PP2CJ Calvin Johnson 12.00 30.00
PP2CP Chad Pennington 6.00 15.00
PP2CT Chester Taylor 5.00 12.00
PP2DB Drew Brees 8.00 20.00
PP2DC David Carr 6.00 15.00
PP2DJ Dwayne Jarrett 3.00 8.00
PP2DM Deuce McAllister 6.00 15.00
PP2DS Drew Stanton 2.50 6.00
PP2DW DeAngelo Williams/35 10.00 25.00
PP2EJ Edgerrin James 6.00 15.00
PP2EV Lee Evans 6.00 15.00
PP2FT Fred Taylor 6.00 15.00
PP2GI Ted Ginn Jr. 3.00 8.00
PP2GO Anthony Gonzalez 4.00 10.00
PP2GR Trent Green 6.00 15.00
PP2HW Hines Ward 8.00 20.00
PP2JC Jay Cutler/35 10.00 25.00
PP2JH Joe Horn 6.00 15.00
PP2JO Chad Johnson 6.00 15.00
PP2JR JaMarcus Russell 2.50 6.00
PP2JS Jeremy Shockey 6.00 15.00
PP2LA LaMont Jordan 6.00 15.00
PP2LE Byron Leftwich 6.00 15.00
PP2LJ Larry Johnson 5.00 12.00
PP2LT LaDainian Tomlinson 8.00 20.00
PP2LY Marshawn Lynch 4.00 10.00
PP2MB Michael Bush 4.00 10.00
PP2MC Donovan McNabb 8.00 20.00
PP2MD Maurice Jones-Drew 8.00 20.00
PP2MH Matt Hasselbeck 6.00 15.00
PP2ML Matt Leinart 6.00 15.00
PP2PB Plaxico Burress 6.00 15.00
PP2PH Priest Holmes 6.00 15.00
PP2PR Philip Rivers 8.00 20.00
PP2RB Ronnie Brown 6.00 15.00
PP2RM Robert Meachem 4.00 10.00
PP2SJ Steven Jackson 8.00 20.00
PP2SR Sidney Rice 5.00 12.00
PP2TB Tom Brady 12.00 30.00
PP2TG Tony Gonzalez 6.00 15.00
PP2TH Tony Hunt 5.00 12.00
PP2TO Terrell Owens 8.00 20.00

2007 Upper Deck Premier Patches Dual Autographs

STATED PRINT RUN 25 SER.#'d SETS
PP2AB Anquan Boldin 15.00 40.00
PP2AP Adrian Peterson 125.00 250.00
PP2BF Brett Favre 125.00 250.00
PP2BL Brian Leonard 15.00 40.00
PP2BO Dwayne Bowe 25.00 60.00
PP2BQ Brady Quinn 20.00 50.00
PP2CJ Calvin Johnson 90.00 150.00
PP2CT Chester Taylor 12.00 30.00
PP2DB Drew Brees 50.00 100.00
PP2DJ Dwayne Jarrett 15.00 40.00
PP2DS Drew Stanton 12.00 30.00
PP2EV Lee Evans 15.00 40.00
PP2GI Ted Ginn Jr. 15.00 40.00
PP2GO Anthony Gonzalez 20.00 50.00
PP2JO Chad Johnson 15.00 40.00
PP2JR JaMarcus Russell 12.00 30.00
PP2LJ Larry Johnson 12.00 30.00
PP2LT LaDainian Tomlinson 40.00 80.00
PP2LY Marshawn Lynch 20.00 50.00
PP2MB Michael Bush 20.00 50.00
PP2MC Donovan McNabb
PP2ML Matt Leinart 15.00 40.00
PP2RB Ronnie Brown 15.00 40.00
PP2RM Robert Meachem 20.00 50.00
PP2SR Sidney Rice 40.00 80.00
PP2TB Tom Brady

2007 Upper Deck Premier Patches Triple

STATED PRINT RUN 99 SER.#'d SETS
*GOLD/75: .4X TO 1X BASIC INSERTS
GOLD PRINT RUN 75 SER.#'d SETS
*PLATINUM/10: .8X TO 2X BASIC INSERTS
PLATINUM PRINT RUN 10 SER.#'d SETS
UNPRICED MASTERPIECE PRINT RUN 1
PP3AP Adrian Peterson 15.00 40.00
PP3AS Alex Smith QB 8.00 20.00
PP3BJ Brandon Jackson 3.00 8.00
PP3BO Dwayne Bowe 5.00 12.00
PP3BQ Brady Quinn 4.00 10.00
PP3BR Ben Roethlisberger 8.00 20.00
PP3CB Champ Bailey 6.00 15.00
PP3CJ Chad Johnson 6.00 15.00
PP3CM Curtis Martin 8.00 20.00
PP3CP Carson Palmer 6.00 15.00
PP3DB Drew Brees 8.00 20.00
PP3DC Daunte Culpepper 6.00 15.00
PP3DJ Dwayne Jarrett 3.00 8.00
PP3DM Deuce McAllister 6.00 15.00
PP3EJ Edgerrin James 6.00 15.00
PP3EM Eli Manning 8.00 20.00
PP3FG Frank Gore 8.00 20.00
PP3GA Gaines Adams 5.00 12.00
PP3JA Joseph Addai 6.00 15.00
PP3JL Jamal Lewis 6.00 15.00
PP3JO Calvin Johnson 12.00 30.00
PP3JR JaMarcus Russell 2.50 6.00
PP3JS Jeremy Shockey 6.00 15.00
PP3LT LaDainian Tomlinson 8.00 20.00
PP3MB Marc Bulger 6.00 15.00
PP3MC Donovan McNabb 8.00 20.00
PP3MF Marshall Faulk 6.00 15.00
PP3MH Marvin Harrison 8.00 20.00
PP3ML Marshawn Lynch 4.00 10.00
PP3MV Michael Vick 8.00 20.00
PP3PE Chad Pennington 6.00 15.00
PP3PM Peyton Manning 12.00 30.00
PP3PO Clinton Portis 6.00 15.00
PP3RB Reggie Bush 8.00 20.00
PP3RJ Rudi Johnson 6.00 15.00
PP3RM Robert Meachem 4.00 10.00
PP3SA Shaun Alexander 6.00 15.00
PP3SH Santonio Holmes 6.00 15.00
PP3SM Shawne Merriman 6.00 15.00
PP3SR Sidney Rice 5.00 12.00
PP3SS Steve Smith USC 4.00 10.00
PP3TB Tom Brady 12.00 30.00
PP3TF Trent Edwards 4.00 10.00
PP3TG Ted Ginn Jr. 3.00 8.00
PP3TH Torry Holt 6.00 15.00
PP3TR Tony Romo 10.00 25.00
PP3TS Troy Smith 4.00 10.00
PP3VY Vince Young 6.00 15.00
PP3WM Willis McGahee 6.00 15.00
PP3WP Willie Parker 6.00 15.00

2007 Upper Deck Premier Patches Triple Autographs

TRIPLE PATCH AU PRINT RUN 5-15
PP3BQ Brady Quinn 20.00 50.00
PP3DB Drew Brees 50.00 100.00
PP3EM Eli Manning 50.00 100.00
PP3JA Joseph Addai 20.00 50.00
PP3JO Calvin Johnson 60.00 150.00

PP3JR JaMarcus Russell 12.00 30.00
PP3RB Reggie Bush 25.00 60.00

2007 Upper Deck Premier Penmanship Autographs Gold

GOLD PRINT RUN 99 SER.#'d SETS
*BRONZE/50-75: .5X TO 1.2X BASIC AU/99
*BRONZE/25: .5X TO 1.2X BASIC AU/50
*BRONZE/15: .5X TO 1.2X BASIC AU/25
BRONZE PRINT RUN 5-75
*GOLD HOLO/50: .6X TO 1.5X GOLD AU/99
*GOLD HOLO/25: .8X TO 2X GOLD AU/99
GOLD HOLOFOIL PRINT RUN 1-50
PPAA Aundrae Allison/99 5.00 12.00
PPAB Alan Branch/99 6.00 15.00
PPAD Joseph Addai/50 10.00 25.00
PPAG Anthony Gonzalez/99 8.00 20.00
PPAN Anquan Boldin/50 10.00 25.00
PPAO Amobi Okoye/99 8.00 20.00
PPAP Adrian Peterson/50 75.00 150.00
PPBA David Ball/99 6.00 15.00
PPBF Brett Favre/25 125.00 200.00
PPBJ Brandon Jackson/99 6.00 15.00
PPBL Brian Leonard/99 6.00 15.00
PPBQ Brady Quinn/25 20.00 50.00
PPBR Drew Brees/25
PPBU Marc Bulger/50 10.00 25.00
PPCB Champ Bailey/99 6.00 15.00
PPCD Craig Buster Davis/99 6.00 15.00
PPCH Chris Henry RB/99 5.00 12.00
PPCL Chris Leak/99 6.00 15.00
PPCM Curtis Martin/50
PPCS Chansi Stuckey/99 8.00 20.00
PPCT Courtney Taylor/99 6.00 15.00
PPCW Cadillac Williams/50
PPDB Dallas Baker/99 5.00 12.00
PPDC David Clowney/99 6.00 15.00
PPDD Donald Driver/99 15.00 30.00
PPDH Daymeion Hughes/99 6.00 15.00
PPDJ Dwayne Jarrett/99 6.00 15.00
PPDM Dan Marino/50 90.00 150.00
PPDP Drew Pearson/99 10.00 25.00
PPDR Darrelle Revis/99 10.00 25.00
PPDS Drew Stanton/99 5.00 12.00
PPDW Darius Walker/99 5.00 12.00
PPES Emmitt Smith/25 100.00 200.00
PPEW Eric Wright/99 8.00 20.00
PPFG Frank Gore/50 12.00 30.00
PPGA Gaines Adams/99 8.00 20.00
PPGO Greg Olsen/99 6.00 15.00
PPGW Garrett Wolfe/99 5.00 12.00
PPHI Johnnie Lee Higgins/99 6.00 15.00
PPHO T.J. Houshmandzadeh/50 10.00 25.00
PPIS Isaiah Stanback/99 5.00 12.00
PPJA Jamaal Anderson/99 6.00 15.00
PPJB John Beck/99 8.00 20.00
PPJC Jason Campbell/99 8.00 20.00
PPJF Joel Filani/99 6.00 15.00
PPJH Jason Hill/99 8.00 20.00
PPJO Chad Johnson/50 10.00 25.00
PPJP Jordan Palmer/99 6.00 15.00
PPJR Jeff Rowe/99 5.00 12.00
PPJT Joe Thomas/99 8.00 20.00
PPJZ Jared Zabransky/99 6.00 15.00
PPKD Kenneth Darby/99 6.00 15.00
PPKI Kenny Irons/99 5.00 12.00
PPKK Kevin Kolb/99 12.00 30.00
PPKS Kolby Smith/99 6.00 15.00
PPLB Lorenzo Booker/99 6.00 15.00
PPLE Lee Evans/50 10.00 25.00
PPLG L.C. Greenwood/99 10.00 25.00
PPLH Leon Hall/99 6.00 15.00
PPLJ Larry Johnson/50 8.00 20.00
PPLL LaRon Landry/99 8.00 20.00
PPLT Lawrence Timmons/99 8.00 20.00
PPLW LaMarr Woodley/99 8.00 20.00
PPMA Matt Leinart/50 10.00 25.00
PPMB Michael Bush/99 8.00 20.00
PPMC Marques Colston/99
PPME Robert Meachem/75 8.00 20.00
PPMG Michael Griffin/99 8.00 20.00
PPML Marshawn Lynch/50 12.00 30.00
PPMS Matt Schaub/50 10.00 25.00
PPPH Paul Hornung/50 12.00 30.00
PPPI Antonio Pittman/99 5.00 12.00
PPPM Peyton Manning/50 60.00 120.00
PPPP Paul Posluszny/99 8.00 20.00
PPPR Philip Rivers/50 12.00 30.00
PPPW Patrick Willis/99 15.00 40.00
PPRB Ronnie Brown/50 10.00 25.00
PPRC Roger Craig/99 6.00 15.00
PPRM Rhema McKnight/99 5.00 12.00
PPRN Reggie Nelson/99 6.00 15.00
PPSC Scott Chandler/99 8.00 20.00
PPSI Mike Singletary/50 15.00 40.00
PPSR Sidney Rice/99 10.00 25.00
PPSS Steve Smith USC/99 8.00 20.00
PPSY Steve Young/50 20.00 50.00
PPTA Chester Taylor/99 5.00 12.00
PPTE Trent Edwards/99 8.00 20.00
PPTH Tony Hunt/99 5.00 12.00
PPTJ Joe Theismann/99 8.00 20.00
PPTM Tyrone Moss/99 5.00 12.00
PPTS Troy Smith/50
PPVY Vince Young/50 10.00 25.00
PPWI Paul Williams/99 5.00 12.00
PPWR Dwayne Wright/99 6.00 15.00
PPWY DeShawn Wynn/99 6.00 15.00
PPYF Yamon Figurs/99 5.00 12.00
PPZM Zach Miller/99 8.00 20.00

2007 Upper Deck Premier Preeminence Autographs Gold

GOLD PRINT RUN 25-99
*BRONZE/75: .5X TO 1.2X BASIC AU/99
*BRONZE/25: .5X TO 1.2X BASIC AU/50
*BRONZE/15: .5X TO 1.2X BASIC AU/25
BRONZE PRINT RUN 15-75
UNPRICED GOLD HOLOFOIL PRINT RUN 1
PREAB Anquan Boldin/50 10.00 25.00
PREAC Adam Carriker 6.00 15.00
PREAO Amobi Okoye 8.00 20.00
PREAP Antonio Pittman 6.00 15.00
PREBJ Brandon Jackson 10.00 25.00
PRECL Chris Leak 6.00 15.00
PRECT Courtney Taylor 6.00 15.00
PREDR Darrelle Revis 10.00 25.00
PREDT Drew Tate 8.00 20.00
PREFG Frank Gore/50 12.00 30.00
PREGO Greg Olsen 8.00 20.00
PREJC Jason Campbell 12.00 30.00
PREJZ Jared Zabransky 8.00 20.00
PRELE Lee Evans/50 10.00 25.00
PRELG L.C. Greenwood 10.00 25.00
PRELT Lawrence Timmons 8.00 20.00
PREMC Marques Colston
PREPH Paul Hornung/50 12.00 30.00
PREPP Paul Posluszny 8.00 20.00
PREPR Philip Rivers/50 12.00 30.00
PRERM Rhema McKnight/50 8.00 20.00
PRERN Reggie Nelson 5.00 12.00
PRESN Syvelle Newton 6.00 15.00
PREVY Vince Young/25 30.00 80.00

2007 Upper Deck Premier Rare Patches Dual

STATED PRINT RUN 50 SER.#'d SETS
*GOLD/25: .5X TO 1.2X BASIC JSY/50
GOLD PRINT RUN 25 SER.#'d SETS
*PLAT.HOLOFOIL/10: .8X TO 2X BASIC JSY/50
PLATINUM HOLOFOIL PRINT RUN 10
UNPRICED GOLD HOLOFOIL PRINT RUN 1
AJ Shaun Alexander 10.00 25.00
Steven Jackson
BD Warrick Dunn 8.00 20.00
Lorenzo Booker
BM Peyton Manning 30.00 80.00
Tom Brady
BR Drew Brees 30.00 80.00
Tony Romo
CH Chris Chambers 8.00 20.00
T.J. Houshmandzadeh
CO Alge Crumpler 8.00 20.00
Greg Olsen
CP Clinton Portis 8.00 20.00
Jason Campbell
DD Donovan McNabb 10.00 25.00
Daunte Culpepper
DJ Donald Driver 10.00 25.00
Greg Jennings
DM Corey Dillon 8.00 20.00
Laurence Maroney
FB Anquan Boldin 10.00 25.00
Larry Fitzgerald
GG Ted Ginn Jr. 5.00 12.00
Anthony Gonzalez
HB Isaac Bruce 8.00 20.00
Torry Holt
JB Julius Jones 12.00 30.00
Marion Barber
JD Edgerrin James 10.00 25.00
Maurice Jones-Drew
JE Andre Johnson 8.00 20.00
Lee Evans
JJ Calvin Johnson 15.00 40.00
Dwayne Jarrett
JK Jeremy Shockey 8.00 20.00
Kellen Winslow
LT Jamal Lewis 8.00 20.00
Chester Taylor
MB Plaxico Burress 10.00 25.00
Eli Manning
MC Deuce McAllister 10.00 25.00
Marques Colston
ML Ray Lewis 10.00 25.00
Shawne Merriman
OG Terry Glenn 10.00 25.00
Terrell Owens
PC Chad Pennington 8.00 20.00
Laveranues Coles
PL Adrian Peterson 20.00 50.00
Marshawn Lynch
RB Sidney Rice 6.00 15.00
Dwayne Bowe
RG Antonio Gates 10.00 25.00
Philip Rivers
RP Ben Roethlisberger 15.00 40.00
Willie Parker
RQ Brady Quinn 5.00 12.00
JaMarcus Russell
RW Roy Williams S 8.00 20.00
Ed Reed
SG Frank Gore 10.00 25.00
Alex Smith QB
SJ Chad Johnson 8.00 20.00
Steve Smith
SU Mike Singletary 12.00 30.00
Brian Urlacher
SW Chris Simms 8.00 20.00
Cadillac Williams
TJ Larry Johnson 10.00 25.00
LaDainian Tomlinson
TP Jason Taylor 8.00 20.00
Julius Peppers
TT Trent Green 8.00 20.00
Tony Gonzalez
VT Zach Thomas 10.00 25.00
Jonathan Vilma
VY Michael Vick 10.00 25.00
Vince Young
WS Rod Smith 8.00 20.00
Javon Walker

2007 Upper Deck Premier Rare Patches Triple

STATED PRINT RUN 25 SER.#'d SETS
*GOLD/10: .5X TO 1.2X BASIC JSY/25
GOLD PRINT RUN 10 SER.#'d SETS
UNPRICED PLATINUM PRINT RUN 5
UNPRICED MASTERPIECE PRINT RUN
AHW Marvin Harrison 15.00 40.00
Reggie Wayne
Joseph Addai
BBC Drew Brees 15.00 40.00
Marc Bulger
Jay Cutler
BTB Derrick Brooks 15.00 40.00
Zach Thomas
Tedy Bruschi
FMB Brett Favre 30.00 80.00
Peyton Manning
Tom Brady
FST Michael Strahan 12.00 30.00
Jason Taylor
Dwight Freeney
IJL Brandon Jackson 6.00 15.00
Brian Leonard
Kenny Irons
JGJ Calvin Johnson 25.00 60.00
Ted Ginn Jr.
Dwayne Jarrett
JJG Larry Johnson 15.00 40.00
Steven Jackson
Frank Gore
JSB Emmitt Smith
Tiki Barber
Bo Jackson
LRS Ray Lewis 15.00 40.00
Ed Reed
Terrell Suggs
MNM Joe Namath
Joe Montana
Dan Marino
PLB Carson Palmer 15.00 40.00
Matt Leinart
Reggie Bush
PLH Adrian Peterson 30.00 80.00
Marshawn Lynch
Tony Hunt
PSA Barry Sanders 50.00 125.00
Marcus Allen
Walter Payton
RCB Tim Brown
Jerry Rice
Cris Carter
RQS Brady Quinn 8.00 20.00
JaMarcus Russell
Drew Stanton
SGP Troy Smith 5.00 12.00
Antonio Pittman
Anthony Gonzalez
TAF Shaun Alexander 15.00 40.00
Marshall Faulk
LaDainian Tomlinson
TSL Ronnie Lott
Lawrence Taylor
Mike Singletary

2007 Upper Deck Premier Rare Remnants Quad

STATED PRINT RUN 25 SER.#'d SETS
*GOLD/10: .5X TO 1.2X BASIC JSY/25
GOLD PRINT RUN 10 SER.#'d SETS
UNPRICED PLATINUM PRINT RUN 5
UNPRICED MASTERPIECE PRINT RUN 1
BDMB Tom Brady 30.00 80.00
Tedy Bruschi
Donte Stallworth
Laurence Maroney
BJHC Isaac Bruce 15.00 40.00
Torry Holt
Marc Bulger
Steven Jackson
BRDB Brian Dawkins 12.00 30.00
Champ Bailey
Ronde Barber
Ed Reed
BYLC Jay Cutler 20.00 50.00
Matt Leinart
Reggie Bush
Vince Young
CGBJ Frank Gore 15.00 40.00
Jason Campbell
Brandon Jacobs
Marion Barber
FHDJ Brett Favre 30.00 80.00
Donald Driver
A.J. Hawk
Greg Jennings
FMAT Shaun Alexander 30.00 80.00
Brett Favre
Peyton Manning
LaDainian Tomlinson
GGGG Terry Glenn 12.00 30.00
Joey Galloway
Ted Ginn Jr.
Anthony Gonzalez
JGJR Calvin Johnson 25.00 50.00
Ted Ginn Jr.
Dwayne Jarrett
Sidney Rice
LJFB Edgerrin James 15.00 40.00
Anquan Boldin
Larry Fitzgerald
Matt Leinart
MAWH Marvin Harrison 25.00 60.00
Peyton Manning
Reggie Wayne
Joseph Addai
MWWE Roy Williams WR 15.00 40.00
Lee Evans
Eli Manning
Kellen Winslow
PJMJ Larry Johnson 15.00 40.00
Andre Johnson
Carson Palmer
Willis McGahee
PLBH Adrian Peterson 60.00 150.00
Marshawn Lynch
Michael Bush
Tony Hunt
PMWC Chad Pennington 15.00 40.00
Curtis Martin
Laveranues Coles
Leon Washington
RQSS Brady Quinn 8.00 20.00
JaMarcus Russell
Drew Stanton
Troy Smith
RTGM LaDainian Tomlinson 20.00 50.00
Antonio Gates
Philip Rivers
Shawne Merriman
TMPA Jason Taylor 15.00 40.00
Julius Peppers
Shawne Merriman
Gaines Adams
TYSF Emmitt Smith 30.00 80.00
Marshall Faulk
Steve Young
Joe Theismann
YRBD Warrick Dunn 20.00 50.00
Anquan Boldin
Ben Roethlisberger
Vince Young

2007 Upper Deck Premier Rare Remnants Triple

STATED PRINT RUN 50 SER.#'d SETS
*GOLD/25: .5X TO 1.2X BASIC JSY/50
GOLD PRINT RUN 25 SER.#'d SETS
*PLATINUM/10: .8X TO 2X BASIC JSY/50
PLATINUM PRINT RUN 10 SER.#'d SETS
UNPRICED MASTERPIECE PRINT RUN 1
ARB Joseph Addai 12.00 30.00
JaMarcus Russell
Dwayne Bowe
AWM Peyton Manning 20.00 50.00
Reggie Wayne
Joseph Addai
BDS Drew Brees 10.00 25.00
Jake Delhomme
Chris Simms
BJH Torry Holt 12.00 30.00
Marc Bulger
Steven Jackson
BLW LenDale White 15.00 40.00
Matt Leinart
Reggie Bush
BRH Sidney Rice 10.00 25.00
Dwayne Bowe
Jason Hill
CBC Chris Chambers 10.00 25.00
Daunte Culpepper
Ronnie Brown
DNA Morten Andersen 10.00 25.00
Warrick Dunn
Jerious Norwood
DWS Jake Delhomme 12.00 30.00
DeAngelo Williams
Steve Smith
FAT Shaun Alexander 15.00 40.00
Marshall Faulk
LaDainian Tomlinson
FMT Brett Favre 25.00 60.00
Peyton Manning
LaDainian Tomlinson
FWH Johnnie Lee Higgins 8.00 20.00
Paul Williams
Yamon Figurs
HAB Shaun Alexander 10.00 25.00
Matt Hasselbeck
Deion Branch
HBL Brian Leonard 8.00 20.00
Lorenzo Booker
Tony Hunt
HJC Santonio Holmes 12.00 30.00
Greg Jennings
Marques Colston
JGJ Calvin Johnson 15.00 40.00
Ted Ginn Jr.
Dwayne Jarrett
JMB Calvin Johnson 15.00 40.00
Robert Meachem
Dwayne Bowe
JMG Edgerrin James 12.00 30.00
Willis McGahee
Frank Gore
JWW Reggie Wayne 10.00 25.00
Chad Johnson
Roy Williams WR
LIM Adrian Peterson 50.00 120.00
Marshawn Lynch
Kenny Irons
MGU Peyton Manning 20.00 50.00
Brian Urlacher
Rex Grossman
MJS Jeremy Shockey 12.00 30.00
Eli Manning
Brandon Jacobs
MRC Donovan McNabb 25.00 60.00
Tony Romo
Jason Campbell
MTG Ahman Green 10.00 25.00
Deuce McAllister
Chester Taylor
MWW DeAngelo Williams 12.00 30.00
Laurence Maroney
LenDale White
PJJ Rudi Johnson 12.00 30.00
Chad Johnson
Carson Palmer
PLJ Adrian Peterson 50.00 120.00
Brandon Jackson
Marshawn Lynch
PMW Chad Pennington 12.00 30.00
Curtis Martin
Leon Washington
PPC Alge Crumpler 12.00 30.00
Julius Peppers
Willie Parker
PRL Ray Lewis 12.00 30.00
Julius Peppers
Ed Reed
ROG Terry Glenn 25.00 60.00
Terrell Owens
Tony Romo
RQS Brady Quinn 6.00 15.00
JaMarcus Russell
Drew Stanton
RWH Hines Ward 15.00 40.00
Ben Roethlisberger
Santonio Holmes
SPG Troy Smith 10.00 25.00
Antonio Pittman
Anthony Gonzalez
SWO Bubba Franks 10.00 25.00
Jeremy Shockey
Kellen Winslow
TBM Champ Bailey 10.00 25.00
Jason Taylor
Shawne Merriman
TJG Larry Johnson 15.00 40.00
LaDainian Tomlinson
Frank Gore
VRL Michael Vick 15.00 40.00
Byron Leftwich
Ben Roethlisberger
WBC Laveranues Coles 10.00 25.00
Javon Walker
Anquan Boldin
WPJ Clinton Portis 10.00 25.00
Brian Westbrook
Brandon Jacobs

2007 Upper Deck Premier Remnants Quad

STATED PRINT RUN 99 SER.#'d SETS
*GOLD/75: .4X TO 1X BASIC JSY/99
GOLD PRINT RUN 75 SER.#'d SETS
*PLATINUM/10: .8X TO 2X BASIC JSY/99
PLATINUM PRINT RUN 10 SER.#'d SETS
UNPRICED MASTERPIECE PRINT RUN 1
UNPRICED QUAD AU PRINT RUN 15
PR4AC Alge Crumpler 8.00 20.00
PR4AP Adrian Peterson 20.00 50.00
PR4AS Alex Smith QB 10.00 25.00
PR4BF Brett Favre 20.00 50.00
PR4BJ Brandon Jacobs 8.00 20.00
PR4BQ Brady Quinn 5.00 12.00
PR4BR Ronnie Brown 8.00 20.00
PR4BU Brian Urlacher 10.00 25.00
PR4BW Brian Westbrook 8.00 20.00
PR4CJ Calvin Johnson 15.00 40.00
PR4CP Chad Pennington 8.00 20.00
PR4DB Dwayne Bowe 6.00 15.00
PR4DC David Carr 8.00 20.00
PR4DD Donald Driver 10.00 25.00
PR4DJ Dwayne Jarrett 4.00 10.00
PR4EJ Edgerrin James 8.00 20.00
PR4ER Ed Reed 8.00 20.00
PR4FG Frank Gore 10.00 25.00
PR4GO Tony Gonzalez 8.00 20.00
PR4HO Torry Holt 8.00 20.00
PR4HW Hines Ward 10.00 25.00
PR4JA Joseph Addai 8.00 20.00
PR4JN Jerious Norwood 8.00 20.00
PR4JP Julius Peppers 8.00 20.00
PR4JR JaMarcus Russell 3.00 8.00
PR4JT Jason Taylor 8.00 20.00
PR4KW Kellen Winslow 8.00 20.00
PR4LE Lee Evans 8.00 20.00
PR4LJ Larry Johnson 6.00 15.00
PR4LT LaDainian Tomlinson 10.00 25.00
PR4LW Leon Washington 8.00 20.00
PR4MB Marion Barber 10.00 25.00
PR4MD Maurice Jones-Drew 10.00 25.00
PR4MH Marvin Harrison 10.00 25.00
PR4ML Marshawn Lynch 5.00 12.00
PR4MV Michael Vick 10.00 25.00
PR4PB Plaxico Burress 8.00 20.00
PR4PM Peyton Manning 15.00 40.00
PR4RB Reggie Bush 10.00 25.00
PR4RL Ray Lewis 10.00 25.00
PR4RM Robert Meachem 5.00 12.00
PR4SH Santonio Holmes 8.00 20.00
PR4SJ Steven Jackson 10.00 25.00
PR4SR Sidney Rice 6.00 15.00
PR4TG Ted Ginn Jr. 4.00 10.00
PR4TH T.J. Houshmandzadeh 8.00 20.00
PR4TO Terrell Owens 10.00 25.00
PR4TR Tony Romo 12.00 30.00
PR4VY Vince Young 8.00 20.00
PR4WD Warrick Dunn 8.00 20.00

2007 Upper Deck Premier Remnants Quad Autographs

UNPRICED QUAD AU PRINT RUN 15

2007 Upper Deck Premier Remnants Triple

STATED PRINT RUN 99 SER.#'d SETS
*GOLD/75: .4X TO 1X BASIC JSY/99
GOLD PRINT RUN 75 SER.#'d SETS
*PLATINUM/25: .6X TO 1.5X BASIC JSY/99
PLATINUM PRINT RUN 25 SER.#'d SETS
UNPRICED MASTERPIECE PRINT RUN 1
PR3AB Anquan Boldin 6.00 15.00
PR3AG Antonio Gates 8.00 20.00
PR3AP Adrian Peterson 15.00 40.00
PR3AV Adam Vinatieri 6.00 15.00
PR3BF Brett Favre 15.00 40.00
PR3BQ Brady Quinn 4.00 10.00
PR3BR Ben Roethlisberger 8.00 20.00
PR3BW Brian Westbrook 6.00 15.00
PR3CB Champ Bailey 6.00 15.00
PR3CJ Chad Johnson 6.00 15.00
PR3CO Marques Colston 8.00 20.00
PR3CP Carson Palmer 6.00 15.00
PR3CT Chester Taylor 5.00 12.00
PR3CU Jay Cutler 8.00 20.00
PR3DB Drew Brees 8.00 20.00
PR3DJ Dwayne Jarrett 3.00 8.00
PR3DM Deuce McAllister 6.00 15.00
PR3EM Eli Manning 8.00 20.00
PR3EV Lee Evans 6.00 15.00
PR3FG Frank Gore 8.00 20.00
PR3JC Jason Campbell 6.00 15.00
PR3JO Calvin Johnson 12.00 30.00
PR3JR JaMarcus Russell 2.50 6.00
PR3LC Laveranues Coles 5.00 12.00
PR3LE Matt Leinart 6.00 15.00
PR3LF Larry Fitzgerald 8.00 20.00
PR3LJ Larry Johnson 5.00 12.00
PR3LM Laurence Maroney 6.00 15.00
PR3LT LaDainian Tomlinson 8.00 20.00
PR3MB Marc Bulger 6.00 15.00
PR3MC Donovan McNabb 8.00 20.00
PR3ML Marshawn Lynch 4.00 10.00
PR3MV Michael Vick 8.00 20.00
PR3PM Peyton Manning 12.00 30.00
PR3PR Philip Rivers 8.00 20.00
PR3RB Reggie Bush 8.00 20.00
PR3RG Rex Grossman 6.00 15.00
PR3RW Reggie Wayne 6.00 15.00
PR3SA Shaun Alexander 6.00 15.00
PR3SJ Steven Jackson 8.00 20.00
PR3SM Shawne Merriman 6.00 15.00
PR3SS Steve Smith 6.00 15.00
PR3TB Tom Brady 12.00 30.00
PR3TG Ted Ginn Jr. 3.00 8.00
PR3TO Terrell Owens 8.00 20.00
PR3TR Tony Romo 10.00 25.00
PR3VY Vince Young 6.00 15.00
PR3WI Roy Williams WR 6.00 15.00
PR3WM Willis McGahee 6.00 15.00
PR3WP Willie Parker 6.00 15.00

2007 Upper Deck Premier Remnants Triple Autographs

STATED PRINT RUN 25 SER.#'d SETS
PR3AB Anquan Boldin 20.00 50.00
PR3AG Antonio Gates 25.00 60.00
PR3AP Adrian Peterson 125.00 250.00
PR3BF Brett Favre 150.00 250.00
PR3CB Champ Bailey 20.00 50.00
PR3CJ Chad Johnson 20.00 50.00
PR3CO Marques Colston 25.00 60.00
PR3CT Chester Taylor 15.00 40.00
PR3DB Drew Brees 40.00 80.00
PR3DJ Dwayne Jarrett 20.00 50.00
PR3EM Eli Manning 50.00 100.00
PR3FG Frank Gore 25.00 60.00
PR3JC Jason Campbell 20.00 50.00
PR3JR JaMarcus Russell 15.00 40.00
PR3LE Matt Leinart 20.00 50.00
PR3LF Larry Fitzgerald 25.00 60.00
PR3LJ Larry Johnson 15.00 40.00
PR3LT LaDainian Tomlinson 40.00 80.00
PR3ML Marshawn Lynch 25.00 60.00
PR3PM Peyton Manning 100.00 200.00
PR3PR Philip Rivers 25.00 60.00
PR3SS Steve Smith 20.00 50.00
PR3TG Ted Ginn Jr. 20.00 50.00
PR3VY Vince Young 20.00 50.00
PR3WP Willie Parker 20.00 50.00

2007 Upper Deck Premier Six Autographs

UNPRICED SIX AU PRINT RUN 10

2007 Upper Deck Premier Stitchings Team Logo/NFL Draft

STATED PRINT RUN 75 SER.#'d SETS
*VARIATION/75: .4X TO 1X BASIC INSERTS
VARIATION PRINT RUN 75 SER.#'d SETS
*GOLD/40-50: .5X TO 1.2X BASIC INSERTS
*GOLD/20: .6X TO 1.5X BASIC INSERTS
GOLD PRINT RUN 20-50
*VARIATION PLAT.HOLO/40-50: .5X TO 1.2X
*VARIATION PLAT.HOLO/20: .6X TO 1.5X
VARIATION PLAT.HOLO.PRINT RUN 20-50
UNPRICED PLATINUM PRINT RUN 5
UNPRICED PLAT.VARIATION PRINT RUN 5
PS1 LaDainian Tomlinson 07MVP 8.00 20.00
PS2 Chris Leak 3.00 8.00
PS3 Adrian Peterson 15.00 40.00
PS4 Antonio Pittman 2.50 6.00
PS5 Brady Quinn 4.00 10.00
PS6 Brandon Jackson 3.00 8.00
PS7 Calvin Johnson 12.00 30.00
PS8 Jason Hill 4.00 10.00
PS9 Patrick Willis 8.00 20.00
PS10 Drew Stanton 2.50 6.00
PS11 Dwayne Bowe 5.00 12.00
PS12 Dwayne Jarrett 3.00 8.00
PS13 Lorenzo Booker 3.00 8.00
PS14 Garrett Wolfe 2.50 6.00
PS15 JaMarcus Russell 2.50 6.00
PS16 Kenny Irons 2.50 6.00
PS17 Marshawn Lynch 4.00 10.00
PS18 Michael Bush 4.00 10.00
PS19 Robert Meachem 4.00 10.00
PS20 Sidney Rice 5.00 12.00
PS21 Ted Ginn Jr. 3.00 8.00
PS22 Tony Hunt 2.50 6.00
PS23 Trent Edwards 4.00 10.00
PS24 Troy Smith 4.00 10.00
PS25 Chris Henry RB 2.50 6.00
PS26 Anthony Gonzalez 4.00 10.00
PS27 Brian Leonard 3.00 8.00
PS28 Greg Olsen 3.00 8.00
PS29 Yamon Figurs 2.50 6.00
PS30 Gaines Adams 4.00 10.00
PS31 Kevin Kolb 6.00 15.00
PS32 John Beck 4.00 10.00
PS33 Joe Thomas 4.00 10.00
PS34 Steve Smith USC 4.00 10.00
PS35 Frank Gore 8.00 20.00
PS36 Steve Young 10.00 25.00
PS37 Mike Singletary 8.00 20.00
PS38 Brian Urlacher 8.00 20.00
PS40 Gale Sayers 10.00 25.00
PS41 Walter Payton 15.00 40.00
PS42 Devin Hester 10.00 25.00
PS43 Carson Palmer 6.00 15.00
PS44 Chad Johnson 6.00 15.00
PS45 Jay Cutler 8.00 20.00
PS46 Champ Bailey 6.00 15.00
PS48 Kellen Winslow 6.00 15.00
PS49 Cadillac Williams 6.00 15.00
PS50 Larry Fitzgerald 8.00 20.00
PS51 Tony Gonzalez 6.00 15.00
PS52 Joseph Addai 6.00 15.00
PS53 Marvin Harrison 8.00 20.00
PS54 Marion Barber 8.00 20.00
PS55 Emmitt Smith 15.00 40.00
PS56 Tony Romo 10.00 25.00
PS58 Terrell Owens 8.00 20.00
PS59 Jason Taylor 6.00 15.00
PS60 Dan Marino 15.00 40.00
PS61 Donovan McNabb 8.00 20.00
PS62 Brian Westbrook 6.00 15.00
PS64 Jeremy Shockey 6.00 15.00
PS65 Eli Manning 8.00 20.00
PS66 Lawrence Taylor 8.00 20.00
PS67 Brett Favre 15.00 40.00
PS68 Vince Lombardi 12.00 30.00
PS69 Maurice Jones-Drew 8.00 20.00
PS70 Joe Namath 10.00 25.00
PS71 Barry Sanders 12.00 30.00
PS72 Roy Williams WR 6.00 15.00
PS74 Paul Hornung 8.00 20.00
PS75 Steve Smith 6.00 15.00
PS76 Bo Jackson 12.00 30.00
PS77 Marcus Allen 8.00 20.00
PS79 Steven Jackson 8.00 20.00
PS80 Torry Holt 6.00 15.00
PS81 Steve McNair 6.00 15.00
PS82 Willis McGahee 6.00 15.00
PS83 Reggie Bush 8.00 20.00
PS84 Marques Colston 8.00 20.00
PS85 Drew Brees 8.00 20.00
PS86 Shaun Alexander 6.00 15.00
PS87 L.C. Greenwood 6.00 15.00
PS88 Ben Roethlisberger 8.00 20.00
PS89 Willie Parker 6.00 15.00
PS90 Franco Harris 8.00 20.00
PS91 Hines Ward 8.00 20.00
PS92 Peyton Manning COLTS 15.00 40.00
PS93 Peyton Manning LOGO 15.00 40.00
PS94 Joe Montana SJ 15.00 40.00
PS96 Matt Leinart 6.00 15.00
PS97 Shawne Merriman 6.00 15.00
PS98 Larry Johnson 5.00 12.00
PS99 Tom Brady 15.00 40.00
PS100 Vince Young 6.00 15.00

2007 Upper Deck Premier Stitchings Autographs

STATED PRINT RUN 25 SER.#'d SETS
UNPRICED CUT AUTO PRINT RUN 1
PS1 LaDainian Tomlinson 60.00 120.00
PS2 Chris Leak 15.00 40.00
PS3 Adrian Peterson 175.00 300.00
PS5 Brady Quinn 40.00 100.00
PS6 Brandon Jackson 20.00 60.00
PS7 Calvin Johnson 75.00 150.00
PS8 Jason Hill 15.00 40.00
PS9 Patrick Willis 30.00 60.00
PS10 Drew Stanton 20.00 50.00
PS11 Dwayne Bowe 20.00 50.00
PS15 JaMarcus Russell 20.00 50.00
PS17 Marshawn Lynch 20.00 50.00
PS18 Michael Bush 20.00 50.00
PS19 Robert Meachem 20.00 50.00
PS20 Sidney Rice 50.00 100.00
PS21 Ted Ginn Jr. 20.00 50.00
PS22 Tony Hunt 15.00 40.00
PS23 Trent Edwards/20 20.00 50.00
PS27 Brian Leonard 20.00 50.00
PS28 Greg Olsen 20.00 50.00
PS29 Yamon Figurs/20 12.00 30.00
PS30 Gaines Adams 12.00 30.00
PS31 Kevin Kolb 30.00 80.00
PS33 Joe Thomas 15.00 40.00
PS35 Frank Gore 20.00 50.00
PS36 Steve Young 40.00 80.00
PS40 Gale Sayers 30.00 60.00
PS44 Chad Johnson 25.00 50.00
PS52 Joseph Addai 20.00 50.00
PS54 Marion Barber 20.00 50.00
PS65 Eli Manning 50.00 100.00
PS83 Reggie Bush 25.00 60.00
PS85 Drew Brees 40.00 80.00
PS94 Joe Montana 100.00 200.00
PS96 Matt Leinart 20.00 50.00
PS98 Larry Johnson 20.00 50.00
PS99 Tom Brady 200.00 400.00

2007 Upper Deck Premier Stitchings Cut Autographs

UNPRICED CUT AU PRINT RUN 1

2007 Upper Deck Premier Trios Autographs

STATED PRINT RUN 20 SER.#'d SETS
1 Jamaal Anderson 15.00 40.00
Gaines Adams
Amobi Okoye
2 Calvin Johnson 125.00 250.00
Joe Thomas
JaMarcus Russell
3 Patrick Willis 25.00 60.00
Paul Posluszny
Lawrence Timmons
4 Emmitt Smith 250.00 400.00
LaDainian Tomlinson
Adrian Peterson
5 Anthony Gonzalez 25.00 60.00
Craig Buster Davis
Steve Smith USC
6 Reggie Nelson 15.00 40.00
LaRon Landry
Brandon Meriweather
8 Eli Manning 50.00 100.00
Alex Smith QB
Matt Leinart
9 Marc Bulger 25.00 60.00
Matt Schaub
Jason Campbell
10 Champ Bailey 25.00 60.00
Leon Hall
Darrelle Revis
11 Chris Henry 15.00 40.00
Joel Filani
Paul Williams
12 Reggie Brown 40.00 80.00
Donald Driver
Lee Evans
13 Peyton Manning 75.00 150.00
Reggie Wayne
Joseph Addai
14 Drew Stanton 25.00 60.00
John Beck
Trent Edwards
15 Brandon Jackson 25.00 60.00
Marshawn Lynch
Kenny Irons
16 Frank Gore
Alex Smith QB
Jason Hill
18 Michael Bush 25.00 60.00
Zach Miller
Johnnie Lee Higgins
19 Chad Johnson 25.00 60.00
Drew Pearson
Dwayne Jarrett
20 Reggie Nelson 20.00 50.00
Chris Leak
Dallas Baker

2008 Upper Deck Premier

101-135 JSY AU PRINT RUN 199-375
136-160 ROOKIE AU PRINT RUN 199
UNPRICED GOLD PRINT RUN 1
1 Adrian Peterson 5.00 12.00
2 Hines Ward 2.50 6.00
3 Alex Smith QB 3.00 8.00
4 Andre Johnson 2.50 6.00
5 Anquan Boldin 2.50 6.00
6 Antonio Cromartie 2.00 5.00
7 Antonio Gates 3.00 8.00
8 Antonio Pierce 2.00 5.00
9 Barry Sanders 5.00 12.00
10 Ben Roethlisberger 3.00 8.00
11 Billy Sims 2.50 6.00
12 Bo Jackson 4.00 10.00
13 Bob Sanders 2.50 6.00
14 Brandon Marshall 2.50 6.00
15 Braylon Edwards 2.50 6.00
16 Brett Favre 8.00 20.00
17 Brian Bosworth 3.00 8.00
18 Brian Dawkins 2.50 6.00
19 Brian Urlacher 3.00 8.00
20 Brian Westbrook 2.50 6.00
21 Calvin Johnson 3.00 8.00
22 Cadillac Williams 2.50 6.00
23 Carson Palmer 3.00 8.00
24 Chad Johnson 2.50 6.00
25 Champ Bailey 2.50 6.00
26 Chris Cooley 2.50 6.00
27 Dallas Clark 2.50 6.00
28 David Garrard 2.50 6.00
29 Deion Branch 2.50 6.00
30 DeMarcus Ware 2.50 6.00
31 Tom Brady 5.00 12.00
32 Derek Anderson 2.00 5.00
33 Randy Moss 3.00 8.00
34 Devin Hester 3.00 8.00
35 Dick Butkus 4.00 10.00
36 Donovan McNabb 3.00 8.00
37 Drew Brees 3.00 8.00
38 Dwayne Bowe 2.50 6.00
39 Ed Reed 2.50 6.00
40 Edgerrin James 2.50 6.00
41 Eli Manning 3.00 8.00
42 Ernie Sims 2.00 5.00
43 Frank Gore 2.50 6.00
44 Fred Taylor 2.50 6.00
45 Greg Jennings 3.00 8.00
46 Jack Lambert 3.00 8.00
47 JaMarcus Russell 2.50 6.00
48 Jason Campbell 2.50 6.00
49 Jason Taylor 2.50 6.00
50 Jay Cutler 3.00 8.00
51 Jeff Garcia 2.50 6.00
52 Brandon Jacobs 2.50 6.00
53 Joey Galloway 2.50 6.00
54 John Elway 5.00 12.00
55 Jonathan Vilma 2.50 6.00
56 Chad Pennington 2.50 6.00
57 Kellen Winslow Jr. 2.50 6.00
58 Ken Stabler 3.00 8.00
59 Aaron Rodgers 6.00 15.00
60 LaDainian Tomlinson 3.00 8.00
61 LaRon Landry 2.50 6.00
62 Kellen Winslow Sr. 3.00 8.00
63 Larry Fitzgerald 3.00 8.00
64 Larry Johnson 2.50 6.00
65 LenDale White 2.50 6.00
66 Lofa Tatupu 2.50 6.00
67 Marc Bulger 2.50 6.00
68 Marion Barber 2.50 6.00
69 Marques Colston 2.50 6.00
70 Marshawn Lynch 2.50 6.00
71 Matt Hasselbeck 2.50 6.00
72 Matt Leinart 3.00 8.00
73 Maurice Jones-Drew 2.50 6.00
74 Patrick Willis 2.50 6.00
75 Peyton Manning 5.00 12.00
76 Philip Rivers 3.00 8.00
77 Plaxico Burress 2.50 6.00
78 Reggie Bush 3.00 8.00
79 Reggie Wayne 2.50 6.00
80 Ronnie Brown 2.50 6.00
81 Roscoe Parrish 2.00 5.00
82 Roy Williams WR 2.50 6.00
83 Ryan Grant 3.00 8.00
84 Santonio Holmes 2.50 6.00
85 Shawne Merriman 2.50 6.00
86 Sidney Rice 3.00 8.00
87 Steve McNair 2.50 6.00
88 Steve Smith 2.50 6.00
89 Steven Jackson 3.00 8.00
90 Tarvaris Jackson 2.50 6.00
91 Terrell Owens 3.00 8.00
92 Thomas Jones 2.50 6.00
93 Tony Gonzalez 2.50 6.00
94 Tony Romo 4.00 10.00
95 Torry Holt 2.50 6.00
96 Trent Edwards 2.00 5.00
97 Troy Polamalu 3.00 8.00
98 Vince Young 2.50 6.00
99 Warrick Dunn 2.50 6.00
100 Willis McGahee 2.50 6.00
101 Donnie Avery JSY AU/275 RC 6.00 15.00
102 Harry Douglas JSY AU/375 RC 6.00 15.00
103 Brian Brohm JSY AU/199 RC 8.00 20.00
104 Chad Henne JSY AU/275 RC 20.00 50.00
105 Chris Johnson JSY AU/275 RC 25.00 60.00
107 Devin Thomas JSY AU/275 RC 6.00 15.00
108 Darren McFadden JSY AU/199 RC 25.00 50.00
109 Earl Bennett JSY AU/275 RC 8.00 20.00

111 DeSean Jackson JSY AU/275 RC 20.00 50.00
112 Jake Long JSY AU/375 RC 8.00 20.00
113 Early Doucet JSY AU/375 RC 6.00 15.00
114 Andre Caldwell JSY AU/375 RC 6.00 15.00
115 Felix Jones JSY AU/275 RC 20.00 50.00
116 Dustin Keller JSY AU/375 RC 8.00 20.00
117 Jamaal Charles JSY AU/275 RC 12.00 30.00
118 Joe Flacco JSY AU/275 RC 40.00 80.00
119 John David Booty JSY AU/275 RC 6.00 15.00
120 Jonathan Stewart JSY AU/199 RC 20.00 50.00
121 Jordy Nelson JSY AU/275 RC 15.00 40.00
122 Jerome Simpson JSY AU/275 RC 8.00 20.00
123 Kevin Smith JSY AU/275 RC 8.00 20.00
124 Limas Sweed JSY AU/275 RC 8.00 20.00
125 Malcolm Kelly JSY AU/275 RC 6.00 15.00
126 Mario Manningham JSY AU/275 RC 15.00 30.00
127 James Hardy JSY AU/275 RC 6.00 15.00
128 Matt Forte JSY AU/375 RC 15.00 40.00
129 Matt Ryan JSY AU/199 RC 50.00 120.00
130 Dexter Jackson JSY AU/275 RC 6.00 15.00
131 Eddie Royal JSY AU/275 RC 8.00 20.00
132 Rashard Mendenhall JSY AU/275 RC 20.00 50.00
133 Ray Rice JSY AU/275 RC 20.00 50.00
134 Steve Slaton JSY AU/275 RC 8.00 20.00
135 Kevin O'Connell JSY AU/275 RC 6.00 15.00
137 Dennis Dixon AU RC 10.00 25.00
138 Ali Highsmith AU RC 4.00 10.00
139 Allen Patrick AU RC 5.00 12.00
140 Antoine Cason AU RC 6.00 15.00
141 Aqib Talib AU RC 6.00 15.00
142 Ben Moffitt AU RC 4.00 10.00
143 Anthony Morelli AU RC 5.00 12.00
144 Bruce Davis AU RC 5.00 12.00
145 Calais Campbell AU RC 5.00 12.00
146 Chevis Jackson AU RC 4.00 10.00
147 Chris Ellis AU RC 4.00 10.00
148 Craig Steltz AU RC 5.00 12.00
149 DJ Hall AU RC 5.00 12.00
150 Dan Connor AU RC 6.00 15.00
151 DeMario Pressley AU RC 5.00 12.00
152 Derrick Harvey AU RC 4.00 10.00
153 Dominique Rodgers-Cromartie AU RC 6.00 15.00
155 Fred Davis AU RC 6.00 15.00
156 Dwight Lowery RC 6.00 15.00
157 Chris Long AU RC 6.00 15.00
158 Leodis McKelvin AU RC 5.00 12.00
160 Keith Rivers AU RC 6.00 15.00

2008 Upper Deck Premier Silver

*VETS: .5X TO 1.2X BASIC CARDS
*RETIRED: .6X TO 1.5X BASIC CARDS
*ROOKIE JSY AU: .4X TO 1X BASIC CARDS
1-100 VETERAN PRINT RUN 35
101-135 ROOKIE JSY AU PRINT RUN 60

2008 Upper Deck Premier Emerging Stars Autographs Dual Gold

STATED PRINT RUN 10-100
UNPRICED SILVER SPECTRUM PRINT RUN 1
ES2 Colt Brennan 10.00 25.00
Davone Bess/50
ES3 Calais Campbell 6.00 15.00
Bruce Davis/100
ES4 Justin King 8.00 20.00
Antoine Cason/100
ES5 Joe Flacco 20.00 50.00
Derek Anderson/50
ES7 Chad Henne 12.00 30.00
Adrian Arrington/50
ES8 Dwayne Bowe 12.00 30.00
Early Doucet/50
ES10 Keith Rivers 10.00 25.00
A.J. Hawk/50
ES11 Brodie Croyle 10.00 25.00
Andre Woodson/50
ES12 Jamaal Charles 25.00 60.00
Chris Johnson/50
ES13 Jake Long 10.00 25.00
Chris Long/50
ES14 Jake Long 10.00 25.00
Sam Baker/50
ES15 Mike Hart 25.00 50.00
Ray Rice/25
ES16 Dennis Dixon 8.00 20.00
Josh Johnson/90
ES17 DeSean Jackson 25.00 50.00
Marshawn Lynch/50
ES18 DeSean Jackson 25.00 50.00
Lavelle Hawkins/50
ES19 Martin Rucker 8.00 20.00
Fred Davis/100
ES22 Erik Ainge 15.00 40.00
Matt Flynn/50
ES24 Jonathan Stewart 25.00 50.00
Dennis Dixon/50

2008 Upper Deck Premier Equipment 25

STATED PRINT RUN 25 SER.#'d SETS
PARALLELS #'d TO 10 AND 1/1 NOT PRICED
PEBF Brett Favre 25.00 60.00
PEBS Barry Sanders 25.00 60.00
PECJ Calvin Johnson 10.00 25.00
PEDB Dwayne Bowe 8.00 20.00
PEDM Dan Marino 30.00 80.00
PEEM Eli Manning 10.00 25.00
PEER Ed Reed 8.00 20.00
PEGJ Greg Jennings 10.00 25.00
PEJC Jay Cutler 10.00 25.00
PEJE John Elway 25.00 60.00
PEJO Chad Johnson 8.00 20.00
PEJR JaMarcus Russell 8.00 20.00
PEKW Kellen Winslow Jr. 8.00 20.00
PELM Laurence Maroney 8.00 20.00
PELT LaDainian Tomlinson 10.00 25.00
PEMJ Maurice Jones-Drew 8.00 20.00
PEPM Peyton Manning 15.00 40.00
PETB Tom Brady 15.00 40.00
PETR Tony Romo 12.00 30.00
PEWP Willie Parker 8.00 20.00

2008 Upper Deck Premier Five Jersey 30

STATED PRINT RUN 30 SER.#'d SETS
PARALLELS #'d TO 10 AND 1/1 NOT PRICED
BMJPR Eli Manning 12.00 30.00
Brandon Jacobs
Plaxico Burress
Antonio Pierce
Aaron Ross
BWEJB Wes Welker 12.00 30.00
Anquan Boldin
Braylon Edwards
Dwayne Bowe
Greg Jennings
EMMSM John Elway 40.00 100.00
Joe Montana
Jim McMahon
Ken Stabler
Dan Marino

FMBGP Carson Palmer 30.00 80.00
Brett Favre
Tom Brady
Peyton Manning
David Garrard
HBGSS Alex Smith QB 12.00 30.00
Matt Schaub
Matt Hasselbeck
David Garrard
Marc Bulger
HRPHS Lynn Swann 20.00 50.00
Franco Harris
Ben Roethlisberger
Santonio Holmes
Willie Parker
JTPJL LaDainian Tomlinson 12.00 30.00
Larry Johnson
Maurice Jones-Drew
Willie Parker
Marshawn Lynch
MBWVM Tom Brady 20.00 50.00
Randy Moss
Wes Welker
Mike Vrabel
Laurence Maroney
PHSMJ Willis McGahee 25.00 60.00
Maurice Jones-Drew
Gale Sayers
Walter Payton
Franco Harris
PTWLB Reggie Bush 12.00 30.00
LenDale White
Matt Leinart
Carson Palmer
Lofa Tatupu
SFTMP Barry Sanders 30.00 80.00
LaDainian Tomlinson
Dan Marino
Brett Favre
Adrian Peterson
SMTMH Emmitt Smith 25.00 60.00
LaDainian Tomlinson
Peyton Manning
Dan Marino
Paul Hornung
SORWB Tony Romo 30.00 80.00
Marion Barber
DeMarcus Ware
Terrell Owens
Emmitt Smith
SSPHS Gale Sayers 25.00 60.00
Barry Sanders
Walter Payton
Emmitt Smith
Franco Harris

2008 Upper Deck Premier Foursome Jersey 35

STATED PRINT RUN 35 SER.#'d SETS
PARALLELS #'d TO 15 AND 1/1 NOT PRICED
AHGS David Garrard 6.00 15.00
Derek Anderson
Matt Schaub
Matt Hasselbeck
EMFM Joe Montana 30.00 80.00
John Elway
Brett Favre
Peyton Manning
FCJM Jay Cutler 20.00 50.00
Brandon Marshall
Greg Jennings
Brett Favre
FYMN Brett Favre 20.00 50.00
Steve Young
Joe Montana
Joe Namath
GGPL Adrian Peterson 12.00 30.00
Marshawn Lynch
Ryan Grant
Frank Gore
JPBL Anquan Boldin 8.00 20.00
Chad Johnson
Matt Leinart
Carson Palmer
JTJB LaDainian Tomlinson 8.00 20.00
Reggie Bush
Larry Johnson
Maurice Jones-Drew
LWWB Patrick Willis 8.00 20.00
Jack Lambert
DeMarcus Ware
Brian Bosworth
MJJB Chad Johnson 8.00 20.00
Calvin Johnson
Dwayne Bowe
Randy Moss
MMBS Tom Brady 12.00 30.00
Randy Moss
Peyton Manning
Bob Sanders
STML Barry Sanders 12.00 30.00
Marshawn Lynch
Willis McGahee
LaDainian Tomlinson
VWSH AJ Hawk 6.00 15.00
Ernie Sims
DeMarcus Ware
Mike Vrabel
WWSJ Greg Jennings 8.00 20.00
Charles Woodson
Wes Welker
Asante Samuel

2008 Upper Deck Premier Foursome Patch 45

STATED PRINT RUN 45 SER.#'d SETS
*PATCH/15: .5X TO 1.2X PATCH/45
PARALLEL #'d 1/1 NOT PRICED
AJBG Brandon Jacobs 8.00 20.00
Ryan Grant
Marion Barber
Shaun Alexander
AJHJ Derek Anderson 8.00 20.00
Chad Johnson
Steven Jackson
T.J. Houshmandzadeh
CCJB Dwayne Bowe 8.00 20.00
Calvin Johnson
Jerricho Cotchery
Marques Colston
CHEH T.J. Houshmandzadeh 6.00 15.00
Santonio Holmes
Braylon Edwards
Mark Clayton
EMSM Dan Marino 30.00 80.00
Joe Montana
John Elway
Ken Stabler
FHRM Eli Manning 25.00 60.00
Brett Favre
Tony Romo
Matt Hasselbeck
FUJP Brett Favre 20.00 50.00
Adrian Peterson

Brian Urlacher
Calvin Johnson
GRPJ David Garrard 8.00 20.00
Ben Roethlisberger
Maurice Jones-Drew
Willie Parker
GSGW Ben Watson 8.00 20.00
Antonio Gates
Tony Gonzalez
Jeremy Shockey
GWYW Patrick Willis 6.00 15.00
Frank Gore
Vince Young
LenDale White
HBRB Deion Branch 10.00 25.00
Matt Hasselbeck
Tony Romo
Marion Barber
JBBS Chad Johnson 8.00 20.00
Lynn Swann
Deion Branch
Dwayne Bowe
JHJS Alex Smith QB 8.00 20.00
Matt Hasselbeck
Steven Jackson
Edgerrin James
JWMG Willis McGahee 6.00 15.00
Edgerrin James
Frank Gore
Reggie Wayne
MBGR Tom Brady 12.00 30.00
Philip Rivers
Peyton Manning
David Garrard
MFBP Tom Brady 20.00 50.00
Randy Moss
Brett Favre
Adrian Peterson
MMBM Tom Brady 30.00 80.00
Joe Montana
Peyton Manning
Dan Marino
MMGM Eli Manning 12.00 30.00
Peyton Manning
Ryan Grant
Laurence Maroney
MRRQ Philip Rivers 8.00 20.00
Eli Manning
Ben Roethlisberger
Brady Quinn
MTCW Randy Moss 8.00 20.00
Chris Chambers
Reggie Wayne
Fred Taylor
OBBJ Plaxico Burress 8.00 20.00
Greg Jennings
Terrell Owens
Deion Branch
PWRM Eli Manning 10.00 25.00
Tony Romo
Brian Westbrook
Clinton Portis
RCCR Jay Cutler 8.00 20.00
Philip Rivers
JaMarcus Russell
Brodie Croyle
RPSS Bob Sanders 8.00 20.00
Asante Samuel
Ed Reed
Troy Polamalu
SMTB Barry Sanders 20.00 50.00
LaDainian Tomlinson
Joe Montana
Tom Brady
SSFK Dwight Freeney 6.00 15.00
Aaron Schobel
Aaron Kampman
Michael Strahan
TAMJ Laurence Maroney 8.00 20.00
LaDainian Tomlinson
Joseph Addai
Maurice Jones-Drew
TGWC Antonio Cromartie 8.00 20.00
Tony Gonzalez
Fred Taylor
Wes Welker
WGAL Carnell Williams 6.00 15.00
Frank Gore
Joseph Addai
Marshawn Lynch
WHBY Vince Young 8.00 20.00
Michael Huff
Reggie Bush
LenDale White
WJBC Chad Johnson 8.00 20.00
Antonio Cromartie
Plaxico Burress
Charles Woodson
WMJB Wes Welker 8.00 20.00
Dwayne Bowe
Calvin Johnson
Brandon Marshall
WSWH Patrick Willis 6.00 15.00
DeMarcus Ware
A.J. Hawk
Ernie Sims

2008 Upper Deck Premier Foursomes Autographs

FOURSOME AUTO PRINT RUN 15
5 Derek Anderson 50.00 100.00
Jeff Garcia
Tony Romo
Marc Bulger
6 Joe Flacco 100.00 200.00
Chad Henne
Brian Brohm
Matt Ryan
9 Darren McFadden 75.00 150.00
Felix Jones
Jonathan Stewart
Rashard Mendenhall
10 Adrian Peterson 75.00 150.00
Ray Rice
Steve Slaton
Marshawn Lynch

2008 Upper Deck Premier Highlights Autographs Gold

GOLD PRINT RUN 25
UNPRICED SILVER SPECTRUM PRINT RUN 1
SH3 Jake Long 6.00 15.00
SH4 Adrian Peterson 75.00 150.00
SH5 Chad Johnson 10.00 25.00
SH6 Peyton Manning 50.00 100.00
SH7 Wes Welker 25.00 60.00
SH8 Kurt Warner 20.00 40.00
SH9 Eli Manning 30.00 60.00
SH10 Bob Sanders 20.00 50.00
SH11 Barry Sanders 75.00 150.00
SH12 Jeremy Shockey 10.00 25.00
SH13 LaDainianTomlinson 30.00 60.00
SH14 Jeff Garcia 10.00 25.00
SH15 Tom Brady 100.00 200.00

2008 Upper Deck Premier Inscriptions Autographs Gold

GOLD STATED PRINT RUN 15-35
UNPRICED GOLD SPECTRUM PRINT RUN 1
UNPRICED SILVER SPECTRUM PRINT RUN 5
INSCJ Chad Johnson/25 10.00 25.00
INSCL Chris Long/35 6.00 15.00
INSDB Dwayne Bowe/25 10.00 25.00
INSDJ Daryl Johnston/25 20.00 50.00
INSFJ Felix Jones/25 40.00 80.00
INSJL Jake Long/25 6.00 15.00
INSKS Ken Stabler/25 15.00 40.00
INSLT LaDainian Tomlinson/15 40.00 80.00
INSML Marshawn Lynch/25 10.00 25.00
INSPW Patrick Willis/35 10.00 25.00
INSWW Wes Welker/25 25.00 60.00

2008 Upper Deck Premier Legends Autographs Gold

UNPRICED GOLD SPECTRUM PRINT RUN 1
UNPRICED SILVER SPECTRUM PRINT RUN 5
SERIAL #'d UNDER 25 NOT PRICED
PLBG Bob Griese/25 15.00 40.00
PLBS Billy Sims25 12.00 30.00
PLDJ Daryl Johnston/25 15.00 40.00
PLDM Don Maynard/25 12.00 30.00
PLDM Dan Marino/25 75.00 150.00
PLFT Fran Tarkenton/25 20.00 50.00
PLJA Bo Jackson/25 30.00 60.00
PLJB Jim Brown/25 30.00 60.00
PLJT Joe Theismann/25 15.00 40.00
PLLH Lester Hayes/45 12.00 30.00
PLPH Paul Hornung/25 15.00 40.00
PLRC Roger Craig/50 10.00 25.00
PLSY Steve Young/25 30.00 60.00
PLYT Y.A. Tittle/25 15.00 40.00

2008 Upper Deck Premier Milestones Autographs Gold

GOLD STATED PRINT RUN 15-40
UNPRICED GOLD SPECTRUM PRINT RUN 1
UNPRICED SILVER SPECTRUM PRINT RUN 5
PMAP Adrian Peterson/25 75.00 150.00
PMBF Brett Favre/15 100.00 200.00
PMBS Bob Sanders/30 25.00 60.00
PMDM Dan Marino/15 100.00 200.00
PMEM Eli Manning/25 30.00 60.00
PMFA Brett Favre/15 100.00 200.00
PMJB Jim Brown/25 30.00 60.00
PMJE John Elway/15 100.00 200.00
PMLT LaDainian Tomlinson/25 30.00 60.00
PMPE Adrian Peterson/25 100.00 175.00
PMPH Paul Hornung/35 12.00 30.00
PMPM Peyton Manning/25 50.00 100.00
PMPW Patrick Willis/40 8.00 20.00
PMTB Tom Brady/25 100.00 200.00
PMWW Wes Welker/35 25.00 50.00

2008 Upper Deck Premier Octographs

UNPRICED OCTOGRAPHS PRINT RUN 8

2008 Upper Deck Premier Pairings Autographs

STATED PRINT RUN 30-50
1 Adrian Peterson 75.00 150.00
Joseph Addai/30
2 Dexter Jackson 20.00 50.00
DeSean Jackson
3 Aaron Schobel 10.00 25.00
Chris Long/42
4 DeMarcus Ware 6.00 15.00
Calais Campbell
5 Chevis Jackson 5.00 12.00
Antoine Cason
6 Devin Thomas 10.00 25.00
Jordy Nelson
7 Derek Anderson 25.00 60.00
Joe Flacco
8 Jeff Garcia 8.00 20.00
Brodie Croyle
10 Felix Jones 30.00 80.00
Chris Johnson
11 Larry Johnson 25.00 50.00
Matt Forte
12 Kenny Phillips 10.00 25.00
Frank Gore
13 Y.A. Tittle 40.00 80.00
Eli Manning
15 Ray Rice 25.00 50.00
Rashard Mendenhall
16 Owen Schmitt 5.00 12.00
Jacob Hester
17 Dennis Dixon 10.00 20.00
Josh Johnson
18 David Garrard 30.00 60.00
Chris Johnson
19 Brian Brohm 5.00 12.00
Mario Urrutia
20 Lawrence Jackson 5.00 12.00
Phillip Merling
22 Brian Brohm 15.00 40.00
Jordy Nelson
24 John Carlson 10.00 25.00
Tom Zbikowski
26 Bob Sanders 15.00 40.00
Kenny Phillips
27 Peyton Manning 60.00 120.00
Dallas Clark
28 Fred Davis 5.00 12.00
Martin Rucker
29 Sam Baker 5.00 12.00
Ryan Clady
30 Shawn Crable 15.00 40.00
Chad Henne
31 Cadillac Williams 15.00 30.00
Jason Campbell/30
32 Limas Sweed 15.00 40.00
Jamaal Charles
33 Dennis Dixon 50.00 100.00
Ben Roethlisberger/30
34 Leodis McKelvin 5.00 12.00
Dominique Rodgers-Cromartie

2008 Upper Deck Premier Penmanship Autographs Bronze

BRONZE PRINT RUN 30-65
*GOLD/25: .5X TO 1.2X BRONZE/30-65
GOLD PRINT RUN 25
UNPRICED GOLD SPECTRUM PRINT RUN 1
PP1 Aaron Schobel/65 6.00 15.00
PP2 Kurt Warner/40 15.00 40.00
PP3 Andre Caldwell/65 4.00 10.00
PP4 Andre Woodson/65 5.00 12.00
PP5 Trent Edwards/65 6.00 15.00
PP6 Reggie Wayne/65 8.00 20.00
PP7 Ben Roethlisberger/35 50.00 100.00
PP8 Ben Watson/65 6.00 15.00
PP10 Don Maynard/65 10.00 25.00
PP11 Bo Jackson/99 25.00 50.00
PP12 Derek Anderson/65 6.00 15.00
PP13 Brian Bosworth/65 EXCH
PP14 Brian Brohm/40 5.00 12.00
PP15 Paul Hornung/65 12.00 30.00
PP16 Brodie Croyle/65 8.00 20.00
PP17 Bruce Davis/99 4.00 10.00
PP18 Dan Marino/35 75.00 150.00
PP19 Y.A. Tittle/65 12.00 30.00
PP20 Cadillac Williams/40 8.00 20.00
PP21 Chad Henne/65 12.00 30.00
PP22 Chris Johnson/65 30.00 60.00
PP23 Chris Long/65 5.00 12.00
PP24 Clinton Portis/40 8.00 20.00
PP25 Colt Brennan/65 12.00 30.00
PP26 Dan Connor/65 5.00 12.00
PP27 Darren McFadden/35 25.00 60.00
PP28 Daryl Johnston/65 12.00 30.00
PP29 David Garrard/65 8.00 20.00
PP30 John Elway/35 75.00 150.00
PP31 DeMarcus Ware/65 8.00 20.00
PP32 Dennis Dixon/65 6.00 15.00
PP33 DeSean Jackson/65 15.00 40.00
PP34 Kolby Smith/32 6.00 15.00
PP36 Dallas Clark/99 8.00 20.00
PP37 Dwayne Bowe/65 8.00 20.00
PP38 Early Doucet/99 4.00 10.00
PP39 Aaron Rodgers/40 EXCH
PP40 Erik Ainge/65 5.00 12.00
PP41 Marion Barber/40 20.00 40.00
PP42 Felix Jones/65 15.00 40.00
PP43 Fran Tarkenton/40 15.00 40.00
PP44 Frank Gore/40 8.00 20.00
PP45 Fred Davis/99 5.00 12.00
PP47 Tom Rathman/65 10.00 25.00
PP48 Herschel Walker/65 EXCH
PP49 Jamaal Charles/65 8.00 20.00
PP50 Josh Johnson/99 5.00 12.00
PP51 John Beck/65 6.00 15.00
PP53 Jason Campbell/65 8.00 20.00
PP54 Joe Flacco/65 30.00 80.00
PP55 John David Booty/65 4.00 10.00
PP56 John Lynch/99 8.00 20.00
PP57 Jonathan Stewart/40 15.00 40.00
PP58 Jordy Nelson/65 10.00 25.00
PP59 Joseph Addai/35 8.00 20.00
PP60 Keith Rivers/65 5.00 12.00
PP61 Kellen Winslow Sr/65 10.00 25.00
PP62 Ken Stabler/40 12.00 30.00
PP63 Kenny Phillips/65 5.00 12.00
PP64 Kevin Smith/65 5.00 12.00
PP65 LaDainian Tomlinson/35 25.00 50.00
PP66 Larry Johnson/40 8.00 20.00
PP67 Lavelle Hawkins/99 3.00 8.00
PP68 Limas Sweed/99 5.00 12.00
PP69 Lawrence Jackson/65 4.00 10.00
PP70 Malcolm Kelly/65 4.00 10.00
PP71 Marc Bulger/40 8.00 20.00
PP72 Devin Thomas/65 4.00 10.00
PP73 Tom Brady/65 125.00 200.00
PP75 Matt Forte/99 15.00 40.00
PP77 Matt Ryan/35 50.00 120.00
PP78 Ottis Anderson/65 8.00 20.00
PP80 Mike Hart/65 5.00 12.00
PP81 Mike Jenkins/65 5.00 12.00
PP82 Sedrick Ellis/65 5.00 12.00
PP83 Patrick Willis/99 8.00 20.00
PP84 Paul Smith/119 5.00 12.00
PP85 Bob Griese/35 12.00 30.00
PP86 Philip Rivers/30 12.00 30.00
PP87 Ryan Torain/99 5.00 12.00
PP88 Rashard Mendenhall/65 12.00 30.00
PP89 Ray Rice/99 10.00 25.00
PP90 Roger Craig/65 10.00 25.00
PP91 Roman Gabriel/65 10.00 25.00
PP92 Sam Baker/65 3.00 8.00
PP93 Steve Slaton/65 5.00 12.00
PP94 Tashard Choice/65 4.00 10.00
PP95 Kevin Boss/65 8.00 20.00
PP96 Tony Romo/65 50.00 100.00
PP97 Leodis McKelvin/65 4.00 10.00
PP98 Marshawn Lynch/40 8.00 20.00
PP99 Wes Welker/65 20.00 40.00
PP100 Jerry Kramer/65 15.00 30.00

2008 Upper Deck Premier Rare Materials Dual 65

STATED PRINT RUN 65 SER.#'d SETS
*PATCH/25: .6X TO 1.5X DUAL/65
*TRIPLE/50: .5X TO 1.2X DUAL/65
*TRIPLE PATCH/15: .8X TO 2X DUAL/65
PP2AB Anquan Boldin 4.00 10.00
PP2AP Adrian Peterson 8.00 20.00
PP2AS Aaron Schobel 3.00 8.00
PP2BB Brian Bosworth 8.00 20.00
PP2BC Brodie Croyle 4.00 10.00
PP2BE Bernard Berrian 4.00 10.00
PP2BJ Bo Jackson 10.00 25.00
PP2BS Billy Sims 6.00 15.00
PP2BW Ben Watson 3.00 8.00
PP2CA Jason Campbell 4.00 10.00
PP2CB Champ Bailey 4.00 10.00
PP2CJ Chad Johnson 4.00 10.00
PP2CP Clinton Portis 4.00 10.00
PP2CW Cadillac Williams 4.00 10.00
PP2DB Dwayne Bowe 4.00 10.00
PP2DG David Garrard 4.00 10.00
PP2DH Devin Hester 5.00 12.00
PP2DM Dan Marino 15.00 40.00
PP2DW DeMarcus Ware 4.00 10.00
PP2ED Braylon Edwards 4.00 10.00
PP2EM Eli Manning 5.00 12.00
PP2ER Ed Reed 4.00 10.00
PP2ES Ernie Sims 3.00 8.00
PP2FG Frank Gore 4.00 10.00
PP2FT Fred Taylor 4.00 10.00
PP2HW Herschel Walker 6.00 15.00
PP2JA Joseph Addai 4.00 10.00
PP2JC Jay Cutler 5.00 12.00
PP2JM Joe Montana 15.00 40.00
PP2JN Jerious Norwood 4.00 10.00
PP2KS Ken Stabler 8.00 20.00
PP2KW Kellen Winslow Jr. 4.00 10.00
PP2LS Lynn Swann 10.00 25.00
PP2MB Marion Barber 4.00 10.00
PP2MC Jim McMahon 8.00 20.00
PP2MH Michael Huff 3.00 8.00
PP2ML Marshawn Lynch 4.00 10.00
PP2MS Matt Schaub 4.00 10.00
PP2MV Mike Vrabel 3.00 8.00
PP2PR Philip Rivers 5.00 12.00
PP2PW Patrick Willis 4.00 10.00
PP2RC Roger Craig 6.00 15.00
PP2RG Ryan Grant 5.00 12.00
PP2RW Roy Williams WR 4.00 10.00
PP2SA Asante Samuel 3.00 8.00
PP2SM Emmitt Smith 15.00 40.00
PP2SY Steve Young 10.00 25.00
PP2WE Brian Westbrook 4.00 10.00
PP2WI Kellen Winslow Sr. 6.00 15.00
PP2WM Willis McGahee 4.00 10.00

2008 Upper Deck Premier Remnants Quad 40

STATED PRINT RUN 40
UNPRICED AUTO PRINT RUN 9-15
PARALLELS #'d TO 10 AND 1/1 NOT PRICED
PR4AP Adrian Peterson 10.00 25.00
PR4AS Aaron Schobel 4.00 10.00
PR4BB Brian Bosworth 10.00 25.00
PR4BC Brodie Croyle 5.00 12.00
PR4BF Brett Favre 15.00 40.00
PR4BJ Bo Jackson 12.00 30.00
PR4BM Brian Brohm 4.00 10.00
PR4BR Ben Roethlisberger 6.00 15.00
PR4BS Bob Sanders 5.00 12.00
PR4BU Marc Bulger 5.00 12.00
PR4CA Jason Campbell 5.00 12.00
PR4CJ Chad Johnson 5.00 12.00
PR4CP Clinton Portis 5.00 12.00
PR4CW Cadillac Williams 5.00 12.00
PR4DA Darren McFadden 10.00 25.00
PR4DB Dwayne Bowe 5.00 12.00
PR4DC Dallas Clark 5.00 12.00
PR4DE Derek Anderson 4.00 10.00
PR4DG David Garrard 5.00 12.00
PR4DM Dan Marino 20.00 50.00
PR4DT Devin Thomas 3.00 8.00
PR4EM Eli Manning 6.00 15.00
PR4FG Frank Gore 5.00 12.00
PR4FJ Felix Jones 6.00 15.00
PR4JF Joe Flacco 12.00 30.00
PR4JG Jeff Garcia 5.00 12.00
PR4JI Jim McMahon 10.00 25.00
PR4JL Jack Lambert 10.00 25.00
PR4JM Joe Montana 20.00 50.00
PR4KS Ken Stabler 10.00 25.00
PR4KW Kellen Winslow Jr. 5.00 12.00
PR4LE Jamal Lewis 5.00 12.00
PR4LJ Larry Johnson 5.00 12.00
PR4LS Lynn Swann 10.00 25.00
PR4LT LaDainian Tomlinson 6.00 15.00
PR4MB Marion Barber 5.00 12.00
PR4MH Michael Huff 4.00 10.00
PR4ML Marshawn Lynch 5.00 12.00
PR4MR Matt Ryan 15.00 40.00
PR4PW Patrick Willis 5.00 12.00
PR4RC Roger Craig 8.00 20.00
PR4RM Rashard Mendenhall 8.00 20.00
PR4SI Billy Sims 8.00 20.00
PR4SM Kevin Smith 4.00 10.00
PR4WA Kurt Warner 6.00 15.00
PR4WI Kellen Winslow Sr. 8.00 20.00
PR4PM1 Peyton Manning 10.00 25.00
PR4PM2 Peyton Manning 10.00 25.00

2008 Upper Deck Premier Remnants Triple NFL

NFL STATED PRINT RUN 65
*JSY NO/25: .5X TO 1.2X NFL/65
JERSEY NUMBER PRINT RUN 25
UNPRICED HELMET DC PRINT RUN 1
PR3AD Joseph Addai 4.00 10.00
PR3AP Adrian Peterson 8.00 20.00
PR3AS Aaron Schobel 3.00 8.00
PR3BB Brian Bosworth 8.00 20.00
PR3BC Brodie Croyle 4.00 10.00
PR3BF Brett Favre 12.00 30.00
PR3BJ Bo Jackson 10.00 25.00
PR3BM Brian Brohm 3.00 8.00
PR3BO Bob Sanders 4.00 10.00
PR3BR Ben Roethlisberger 5.00 12.00
PR3BS Billy Sims 6.00 15.00
PR3BU Marc Bulger 4.00 10.00
PR3CJ Chad Johnson 4.00 10.00
PR3CP Clinton Portis 4.00 10.00
PR3CW Cadillac Williams 4.00 10.00
PR3DA Darren McFadden 8.00 20.00
PR3DB Dwayne Bowe 4.00 10.00
PR3DC Dallas Clark 4.00 10.00
PR3DE Derek Anderson 3.00 8.00
PR3DG David Garrard 4.00 10.00
PR3DK Dustin Keller 3.00 8.00
PR3DM Dan Marino 15.00 40.00
PR3DT Devin Thomas 2.50 6.00
PR3EM Eli Manning 5.00 12.00
PR3FG Frank Gore 4.00 10.00
PR3FJ Felix Jones 5.00 12.00
PR3JC Jason Campbell 4.00 10.00
PR3JF Joe Flacco 10.00 25.00
PR3JG Jeff Garcia 4.00 10.00
PR3JL Jack Lambert 8.00 20.00
PR3JM Joe Montana 15.00 40.00
PR3KS Ken Stabler 8.00 20.00
PR3LE Jamal Lewis 4.00 10.00
PR3LJ Larry Johnson 4.00 10.00
PR3LS Lynn Swann 8.00 20.00
PR3LT LaDainian Tomlinson 5.00 12.00
PR3MB Marion Barber 4.00 10.00
PR3MH Michael Huff 3.00 8.00
PR3ML Marshawn Lynch 4.00 10.00
PR3MR Matt Ryan 12.00 30.00
PR3MS Matt Schaub 4.00 10.00
PR3PW Patrick Willis 4.00 10.00
PR3RC Roger Craig 6.00 15.00
PR3RM Rashard Mendenhall 6.00 15.00
PR3SM Kevin Smith 3.00 8.00
PR3SY Steve Young 10.00 25.00
PR3WA Kurt Warner 5.00 12.00
PR3WI Kellen Winslow Sr. 6.00 15.00
PR3PM1 Peyton Manning 8.00 20.00
PR3PM2 Peyton Manning 8.00 20.00

2008 Upper Deck Premier Remnants Triple Autographs NFL

STATED PRINT RUN 15-45
UNPRICED QUAD AUTO PRINT RUN 9-15
AD Joseph Addai/25 12.00 30.00
AP Adrian Peterson/25 100.00 200.00
BC Brodie Croyle/25 12.00 30.00
BJ Bo Jackson/25 40.00 80.00
BM Brian Brohm/25 8.00 20.00
BO Bob Sanders/25 20.00 40.00
BR Ben Roethlisberger/25 60.00 120.00
BS Billy Sims/25 15.00 40.00
BU Marc Bulger/25 12.00 30.00
CJ Chad Johnson/25 12.00 30.00
CP Clinton Portis/25 12.00 30.00
CW Cadillac Williams/25 12.00 30.00
DA Darren McFadden/25 30.00 80.00
DB Dwayne Bowe/25 12.00 30.00
DC Dallas Clark/25 12.00 30.00
DE Derek Anderson/25 10.00 25.00
DG David Garrard/25 12.00 30.00
DK Dustin Keller/25 10.00 25.00
DM Dan Marino/25 100.00 200.00
DT Devin Thomas/35 6.00 15.00
EM Eli Manning/25 40.00 80.00
FG Frank Gore/25 12.00 30.00
FJ Felix Jones/45 15.00 40.00
JC Jason Campbell/25 12.00 30.00
JF Joe Flacco/25 60.00 120.00
JL Jack Lambert/25 40.00 80.00
JM Joe Montana/15 75.00 150.00
KS Ken Stabler/25 20.00 50.00
LJ Larry Johnson/25 12.00 30.00
LT LaDainian Tomlinson/25 40.00 80.00
MB Marion Barber/25 12.00 30.00
ML Marshawn Lynch/25 12.00 30.00
MR Matt Ryan/25 100.00 175.00
PW Patrick Willis/25 12.00 30.00
RC Roger Craig/25 15.00 40.00
RM Rashard Mendenhall/25 20.00 50.00
SM Kevin Smith/25 8.00 20.00
SY Steve Young/25 40.00 80.00
WA Kurt Warner/25 25.00 50.00
WI Kellen Winslow Sr./25 15.00 40.00
PM1 Peyton Manning/25 60.00 120.00
PM2 Peyton Manning/25 60.00 120.00

2008 Upper Deck Premier Rookie Autographed Patches Gold 30

*GOLD PATCH/30: .8X TO 2X BASIC CARD
GOLD PATCH PRINT RUN 30
GOLD PATCH 10 PARALLEL UNPRICED
GOLD PATCH 1/1 PARALLEL UNPRICED
105 Chris Johnson JSY AU 75.00 150.00
108 Darren McFadden JSY AU 50.00 120.00
115 Felix Jones JSY AU 50.00 120.00
118 Joe Flacco JSY AU 60.00 150.00
128 Matt Forte JSY AU 40.00 100.00
129 Matt Ryan JSY AU 100.00 200.00

2008 Upper Deck Premier Signatures Gold

GOLD PRINT RUN 15-99
UNPRICED GOLD SPECTRUM PRINT RUN 1
UNPRICED SILVER SPECTRUM PRINT RUN 5
SP1 A.J. Hawk/65 8.00 20.00
SP2 Aaron Schobel/65 6.00 15.00
SP5 Don Maynard/65 10.00 25.00
SP6 Ben Watson/99 6.00 15.00
SP7 Trent Edwards/35 6.00 15.00
SP8 Jason Campbell/65 8.00 20.00
SP9 Brodie Croyle/65 8.00 20.00
SP11 Chad Henne/99 12.00 30.00
SP12 Chad Johnson/35 8.00 20.00
SP13 Chris Johnson/99 40.00 80.00
SP14 Chris Long/65 5.00 12.00
SP15 Clinton Portis/35 8.00 20.00
SP16 Darren McFadden/15 40.00 80.00
SP17 David Garrard/35 8.00 20.00
SP18 Paul Hornung/65 12.00 30.00
SP19 Dennis Dixon/65 6.00 15.00
SP20 Derek Anderson/65 6.00 15.00
SP21 DeSean Jackson/99 15.00 40.00
SP22 Kurt Warner/35 15.00 40.00
SP23 DeMarcus Ware/65 8.00 20.00
SP24 Early Doucet/65 4.00 10.00
SP25 Erik Ainge/75 5.00 12.00
SP26 Felix Jones/99 20.00 50.00
SP27 Fred Davis/65 5.00 12.00
SP28 Jeremy Shockey/25 10.00 25.00
SP29 Jamaal Charles/65 12.00 30.00
SP30 Y.A. Tittle/65 12.00 30.00
SP31 Joe Flacco/65 40.00 80.00
SP32 John David Booty/65 4.00 10.00
SP33 Jordy Nelson/99 15.00 40.00
SP34 Kenny Phillips/65 5.00 12.00
SP35 Kevin Smith/99 5.00 12.00
SP36 Larry Johnson/35 8.00 20.00
SP37 Devin Thomas/80 4.00 10.00
SP38 Marshawn Lynch/20 10.00 25.00
SP39 Matt Flynn/65 15.00 40.00
SP40 Matt Forte/95 20.00 50.00
SP41 Matt Ryan/35 50.00 120.00
SP42 Mike Hart/99 5.00 12.00
SP43 Mike Jenkins/65 5.00 12.00
SP44 Rashard Mendenhall/65 15.00 40.00
SP45 Ray Rice/85 15.00 40.00
SP46 Eli Manning/65 25.00 50.00
SP47 Steve Slaton/99 5.00 12.00
SP48 Peyton Manning/65 40.00 80.00
SP49 Tony Romo/65 50.00 100.00
SP50 Bob Sanders/65 25.00 50.00

2008 Upper Deck Premier Significant Stars Autographs Dual Gold

GOLD DUAL PRINT RUN 15-35
UNPRICED SILVER SPECTRUM PRINT RUN 1
AP Adrian Peterson 75.00 150.00
Joseph Addai/25
BH Dick Butkus 50.00 100.00
A.J. Hawk/25
BL Dick Butkus 60.00 120.00
Jack Lambert/25
BW Marc Bulger 20.00 50.00
Kurt Warner/25
DJ David Garrard 20.00 50.00
Jason Campbell/25
EL Trent Edwards 15.00 40.00
Marshawn Lynch/25
HM Rashard Mendenhall 60.00 120.00
Franco Harris/25
JA Ken Anderson
Chad Johnson/25
JM Bo Jackson 60.00 150.00
Darren McFadden/15
LH Jake Long 25.00 60.00
Chad Henne/35
RB Marion Barber 40.00 100.00
Tony Romo/25
SC Bob Sanders 40.00 80.00
Dallas Clark/25
SR Barry Sanders 75.00 150.00
Roger Craig/15
TA Y.A. Tittle 15.00 40.00
Ottis Anderson/25
TS LaDainian Tomlinson 50.00 100.00
Gale Sayers/25

2008 Upper Deck Premier Six Autographs

UNPRICED SIX AUTO PRINT RUN 6

2008 Upper Deck Premier Stitchings Autographs

STATED PRINT RUN 20 SER.#'d SETS
PSAD Joseph Addai 12.00 30.00
PSAH A.J. Hawk 12.00 30.00
PSAP Adrian Peterson 100.00 175.00
PSAV Donnie Avery 5.00 12.00
PSAW Andre Woodson 6.00 15.00
PSBB Brian Brohm 6.00 15.00
PSBC Brodie Croyle 12.00 30.00
PSBF Brett Favre 3MVP 100.00 200.00
PSBO Dwayne Bowe 12.00 30.00
PSBS Barry Sanders 90.00 150.00
PSCH Chad Henne 12.00 30.00
PSCJ Chad Johnson 12.00 30.00
PSCL Chris Long 6.00 15.00
PSCO Colt Brennan 12.00 30.00
PSCP Clinton Portis 12.00 30.00
PSDA Derek Anderson 10.00 25.00
PSDB Dick Butkus 40.00 80.00
PSDD Dennis Dixon 10.00 25.00
PSDE DeSean Jackson 25.00 50.00
PSDG David Garrard 12.00 30.00
PSDJ Daryl Johnston 25.00 50.00
PSDM Dan Marino 100.00 200.00
PSDW DeMarcus Ware 12.00 30.00
PSEA Erik Ainge 6.00 15.00
PSED Early Doucet 5.00 12.00
PSEM Eli Manning 40.00 80.00
PSFA Brett Favre 100.00 200.00
PSFG Frank Gore 12.00 30.00
PSFH Franco Harris 30.00 60.00
PSFJ Felix Jones 30.00 80.00

PSFT Fran Tarkenton 25.00 50.00
PSGS Gale Sayers 25.00 60.00
PSHA Mike Hart 6.00 15.00
PSHE Jacob Hester 6.00 15.00
PSJA Bo Jackson 50.00 100.00
PSJB John David Booty 5.00 12.00
PSJC Jason Campbell 12.00 30.00
PSJE John Elway 100.00 175.00
PSJF Joe Flacco 50.00 100.00
PSJH Jack Ham 25.00 50.00
PSJK Jerry Kramer 20.00 40.00
PSJL Jack Lambert 30.00 60.00
PSJR Jerry Rice 100.00 175.00
PSJS Jonathan Stewart 25.00 50.00
PSJT Joe Theismann 20.00 50.00
PSKA Ken Anderson 15.00 40.00
PSKS Ken Stabler 20.00 50.00
PSLO Jake Long 6.00 15.00
PSLT LaDainian Tomlinson 30.00 60.00
PSMB Marion Barber 15.00 40.00
PSMC Darren McFadden 40.00 80.00
PSMF Matt Flynn 25.00 50.00
PSMK Malcolm Kelly 5.00 12.00
PSML Marshawn Lynch 12.00 30.00
PSMO Joe Montana 100.00 175.00
PSMR Matt Ryan 75.00 150.00
PSOA Ottis Anderson 12.00 30.00
PSPA Allen Patrick 5.00 12.00
PSPH Paul Hornung 20.00 50.00
PSPM Peyton Manning 90.00 150.00
PSPR Philip Rivers 15.00 40.00
PSPW Patrick Willis 12.00 30.00
PSRA Rashard Mendenhall 20.00 40.00
PSRC Roger Craig 15.00 40.00
PSRG Roman Gabriel 25.00 50.00
PSRO Tony Romo 75.00 150.00
PSRR Ray Rice 12.00 30.00
PSSA Bob Sanders 25.00 50.00
PSSI Billy Sims 15.00 40.00
PSSM Kevin Smith 6.00 15.00
PSSS Steve Slaton 6.00 15.00
PSTB Terry Bradshaw 60.00 120.00
PSTO Tom Brady 100.00 200.00
PSTR Tom Rathman 15.00 40.00
PSWE Wes Welker 25.00 50.00
PSWW Wes Welker 25.00 50.00
PSYT Y.A. Tittle 20.00 50.00

2008 Upper Deck Premier Stitchings Cut Signatures

STATED PRINT RUN 2-31
SER.#'d UNDER 14 NOT PRICED
PSCDS Dinah Shore/31 25.00 50.00
PSCGB George Burns/28 75.00 125.00
PSCLB1 Lucille Ball/16 175.00 300.00
PSCLB2 Lucille Ball/14 175.00 300.00

2008 Upper Deck Premier Stitchings Team Logo/NFL Draft Silver

SILVER PRINT RUN 30
*GOLD/15: .5X TO 1.2X SILVER/30
GOLD TEAM LOGO/DRAFT PRINT RUN 15
*COLL.LOGO/VAR GOLD/15: .5X TO 1.2X
GOLD COLL.LOGO/VAR PRINT RUN 15
*COLL.LOGO/VAR SLVR/30: .4X TO 1X
SILVER COLL.LOGO/VAR PRINT RUN 30
*GOLD VARIATION/15: .5X TO 1.2X SIL/30
GOLD VARIATION PRINT RUN 15
*SILVER VARIATION/30: .4X TO 1X SIL/30
SILVER VARIATION PRINT RUN 30
UNPRICED SILVER SPECTRUMS PRINT RUN 1
PSAD Joseph Addai 5.00 12.00
PSAH A.J. Hawk 5.00 12.00
PSAP Adrian Peterson 10.00 25.00
PSAV Donnie Avery 3.00 8.00
PSAW Andre Woodson 4.00 10.00
PSBB Brian Brohm 4.00 10.00
PSBC Brodie Croyle 5.00 12.00
PSBF Brett Favre 15.00 40.00
PSBJ Bert Jones 6.00 15.00
PSBL Mel Blount 8.00 20.00
PSBO Dwayne Bowe 5.00 12.00
PSBR Brandon Jacobs 5.00 12.00
PSBS Barry Sanders 15.00 40.00
PSBW Brian Bosworth BOZ 10.00 25.00
PSCB Champ Bailey 5.00 12.00
PSCH Chad Henne 4.00 10.00
PSCJ Chad Johnson 5.00 12.00
PSCL Chris Long 4.00 10.00
PSCO Colt Brennan 4.00 10.00
PSCP Clinton Portis 5.00 12.00
PSDA Derek Anderson 4.00 10.00
PSDB Dick Butkus 12.00 30.00
PSDD Dennis Dixon 4.00 10.00
PSDE DeSean Jackson 8.00 20.00
PSDG David Garrard 5.00 12.00
PSDJ Daryl Johnston 10.00 25.00
PSDM Dan Marino 20.00 50.00
PSDO Dorien Bryant 3.00 8.00
PSDW DeMarcus Ware 5.00 12.00
PSEA Erik Ainge 4.00 10.00
PSED Early Doucet 3.00 8.00
PSEM Eli Manning 6.00 15.00
PSER Ed Reed 5.00 12.00
PSFA Brett Favre MVP 15.00 40.00
PSFG Frank Gore 5.00 12.00
PSFH Franco Harris 10.00 25.00
PSFJ Felix Jones 6.00 15.00
PSFT Fran Tarkenton 10.00 25.00
PSGD Glenn Dorsey 4.00 10.00
PSGJ Greg Jennings 6.00 15.00
PSGS Gale Sayers 12.00 30.00
PSHA Mike Hart 4.00 10.00
PSHE Jacob Hester 4.00 10.00
PSJA Bo Jackson 12.00 30.00
PSJB John David Booty 3.00 8.00
PSJC Jason Campbell 5.00 12.00
PSJE John Elway 15.00 40.00
PSJF Joe Flacco 12.00 30.00
PSJH Jack Ham 8.00 20.00
PSJK Jerry Kramer 8.00 20.00
PSJL Jack Lambert 10.00 25.00
PSJM Jim McMahon 10.00 25.00
PSJR Jerry Rice 15.00 40.00
PSJS Jonathan Stewart 8.00 20.00
PSJT Joe Theismann 10.00 25.00
PSKA Ken Anderson 8.00 20.00
PSKS Ken Stabler 12.00 30.00
PSLE Matt Leinart 6.00 15.00
PSLO Jake Long 4.00 10.00
PSLS Lynn Swann 10.00 25.00
PSLT LaDainian Tomlinson 6.00 15.00
PSLY John Lynch 5.00 12.00
PSMB Marion Barber 5.00 12.00
PSMC Darren McFadden 10.00 25.00
PSME Don Meredith 10.00 25.00
PSMF Matt Flynn 8.00 20.00
PSMH Michael Huff 2.50 6.00
PSMK Malcolm Kelly 3.00 8.00
PSML Marshawn Lynch 5.00 12.00

PSMO Joe Montana 20.00 50.00
PSMR Matt Ryan 10.00 25.00
PSMS Matt Schaub 5.00 12.00
PSOA Ottis Anderson 6.00 15.00
PSPA Allen Patrick 3.00 8.00
PSPH Paul Hornung 10.00 25.00
PSPM Peyton Manning 10.00 25.00
PSPR Philip Rivers 6.00 15.00
PSPW Patrick Willis 5.00 12.00
PSRA Rashard Mendenhall 8.00 20.00
PSRC Roger Craig 8.00 20.00
PSRG Roman Gabriel 8.00 20.00
PSRM Randy Moss 6.00 15.00
PSRO Tony Romo 8.00 20.00
PSRR Ray Rice 8.00 20.00
PSRW Randy White 8.00 20.00
PSSA Bob Sanders 5.00 12.00
PSSB Sammy Baugh 10.00 25.00
PSSI Billy Sims 8.00 20.00
PSSJ Sonny Jurgensen 8.00 20.00
PSSM Kevin Smith 4.00 10.00
PSSS Steve Slaton 4.00 10.00
PSTB Terry Bradshaw 15.00 40.00
PSTG Tony Gonzalez 5.00 12.00
PSTO Tom Brady 10.00 25.00
PSTP Troy Polamalu 8.00 20.00
PSTR Tom Rathman 8.00 20.00
PSVY Vince Young 5.00 12.00
PSWE Wes Welker 112 REC 6.00 15.00
PSWW Wes Welker 6.00 15.00
PSYT Y.A. Tittle 10.00 25.00

2008 Upper Deck Premier Teams Jersey Team Logo

STATED PRINT RUN 65 SER.#'d SETS
*TEAM INITIAL/25: .5X TO 1.2X TEAM/65
TEAM INITIALS PRINT RUN 25
UNPRICED AFC/NFC PRINT RUN 1
AWE Braylon Edwards 5.00 12.00
Derek Anderson
Kellen Winslow Jr.
BBC Reggie Bush 6.00 15.00
Drew Brees
Marques Colston
BBL Terry Bradshaw 15.00 40.00
Mel Blount
Jack Lambert
BFL Matt Leinart 6.00 15.00
Larry Fitzgerald
Anquan Boldin
BMJ Eli Manning 6.00 15.00
Brandon Jacobs
Plaxico Burress
CBM Jay Cutler 6.00 15.00
Champ Bailey
Brandon Marshall
FJH Brett Favre 15.00 40.00
Greg Jennings
AJ Hawk
GSW Alex Smith 6.00 15.00
Frank Gore
Patrick Willis
HBT Matt Hasselbeck 5.00 12.00
Deion Branch
Lofa Tatupu
JGC Brodie Croyle 5.00 12.00
Larry Johnson
Tony Gonzalez
JHP Chad Johnson 6.00 15.00
Carson Palmer
T.J. Houshmandzadeh
LEW Jamal Lewis 5.00 12.00
Braylon Edwards
Kellen Winslow Jr.
MBW Randy Moss 10.00 25.00
Tom Brady
Wes Welker
MWS Peyton Manning 10.00 25.00
Reggie Wayne
Bob Sanders
PRP Willie Parker 6.00 15.00
Ben Roethlisberger
Troy Polamalu
RWB Tony Romo 8.00 20.00
Marion Barber III
DeMarcus Ware
TGC LaDainian Tomlinson 6.00 15.00
Antonio Cromartie
Antonio Gates
TGJ Fred Taylor 5.00 12.00
David Garrard
Maurice Jones-Drew
UBH Devin Hester 8.00 20.00
Matt Forte
Brian Urlacher
YWJ Vince Young 15.00 40.00
LenDale White
Chris Johnson

2008 Upper Deck Premier Trios Autographs

STATED PRINT RUN 15-25
2 DeSean Jackson
Jerome Simpson
Dexter Jackson
3 Leodis McKelvin
Dominique Rodgers-Cromartie
Mike Jenkins/25
4 Ben Watson 12.00 30.00
Dustin Keller
Fred Davis/25
6 Chad Johnson
Derek Anderson
Yvenson Bernard/25
8 Chris Johnson 75.00 150.00
Felix Jones
Kevin Smith
9 David Garrard 30.00 60.00
Joe Flacco
Chad Henne
10 DeMarcus Ware 12.00 30.00
Calais Campbell
Bruce Davis
11 Jason Campbell 25.00 60.00
David Garrard
Marc Bulger
12 Jake Long 15.00 40.00
Ryan Clady
Sam Baker
13 Brodie Croyle 30.00 60.00
Dwayne Bowe
Larry Johnson
16 Mike Hart 40.00 80.00
Chad Henne
Adrian Arrington
17 Peyton Manning 75.00 150.00
Joseph Addai
Dallas Clark
18 Sedrick Ellis
John David Booty
Terrell Thomas/25
19 Tom Brady 175.00 300.00
Joe Namath
John Elway/15

2008 Upper Deck Premier Trios Jersey 40

TRIOS JERSEY PRINT RUN 40
*TRIO JSY/25: .5X TO 1.2X TRIOS/40
TRIOS JERSEY 1/1 NOT PRICED
AJJ Steven Jackson 6.00 15.00
Chad Johnson
Derek Anderson
EMM John Elway 30.00 80.00
Dan Marino
Joe Montana
FMB Tom Brady 20.00 50.00
Peyton Manning
Brett Favre
FRR Ben Roethlisberger 15.00 40.00
Brett Favre
Philip Rivers
FWP Roy Williams WR 15.00 40.00
Brett Favre
Adrian Peterson
GGW Antonio Gates 6.00 15.00
Tony Gonzalez
Kellen Winslow Jr.
GPG Willie Parker 6.00 15.00
Ryan Grant
Frank Gore
HJL Devin Hester 6.00 15.00
Maurice Jones-Drew
Marshawn Lynch
HSL Matt Leinart 6.00 15.00
Matt Schaub
Matt Hasselbeck
JBJ Calvin Johnson 6.00 15.00
Chad Johnson
Anquan Boldin
JBL Edgerrin James 6.00 15.00
Anquan Boldin
Matt Leinart
JJB Greg Jennings 6.00 15.00
Calvin Johnson
Dwayne Bowe
JMG Frank Gore 5.00 12.00
Willis McGahee
Edgerrin James
JMJ Deuce McAllister 5.00 12.00
Brandon Jacobs
Larry Johnson
JMW Willis McGahee 5.00 12.00
LenDale White
Larry Johnson
JPL Marshawn Lynch 10.00 25.00
Larry Johnson
Adrian Peterson
JTM LaDainian Tomlinson 6.00 15.00
Larry Johnson
Laurence Maroney
MBC Deuce McAllister 6.00 15.00
Reggie Bush
Marques Colston
MMW Eli Manning 6.00 15.00
Patrick Willis
Deuce McAllister
MOJ Randy Moss 6.00 15.00
Terrell Owens
Chad Johnson
MPJ Willis McGahee 5.00 12.00
Jamal Lewis
Willie Parker
MRR Philip Rivers 6.00 15.00
Ben Roethlisberger
Eli Manning
PLB Matt Leinart 6.00 15.00
Carson Palmer
Reggie Bush
RBJ Daryl Johnston 8.00 20.00
Marion Barber
Tony Romo
RPS Bob Sanders 6.00 15.00
Ed Reed
Troy Polamalu
SCC Alex Smith QB 6.00 15.00
Jay Cutler
Brodie Croyle
SLS Lynn Swann 10.00 25.00
Limas Sweed
Santonio Holmes
SMR JaMarcus Russell 10.00 25.00
Ken Stabler
Darren McFadden
SRA Alex Smith QB 12.00 30.00
Aaron Rodgers
Derek Anderson
STS Barry Sanders 15.00 40.00
LaDainian Tomlinson
Gale Sayers
TBM Marion Barber 6.00 15.00
Laurence Maroney
LaDainian Tomlinson
WBE Tom Brady 10.00 25.00
Braylon Edwards
Charles Woodson
WBY Vince Young 6.00 15.00
LenDale White
Reggie Bush
WPL Charles Woodson 6.00 15.00
Matt Leinart
Carson Palmer
WSH A.J. Hawk 5.00 12.00
DeMarcus Ware
Ernie Sims

2008 Upper Deck Premier Trios Patch 75

TRIOS PATCH PRINT RUN 75
*TRIO PATCH/25: .5X TO 1.2X TRIO PATCH/75
TRIOS PATCH 1/1 NOT PRICED
AGC David Garrard 5.00 12.00
Derek Anderson
Brodie Croyle
AJJ Steven Jackson 6.00 15.00
Chad Johnson
Derek Anderson
AWE Braylon Edwards 5.00 12.00
Derek Anderson
Kellen Winslow Jr.
BBJ Greg Jennings 6.00 15.00
Plaxico Burress
Deion Branch
BGR David Garrard 15.00 40.00
Ben Roethlisberger
Terry Bradshaw
BMJ Eli Manning 6.00 15.00
Plaxico Burress
Brandon Jacobs
BMS Terry Bradshaw 15.00 40.00
Eli Manning
Alex Smith QB
BPP Willie Parker 15.00 40.00
Terry Bradshaw
Troy Polamalu

BRC Jay Cutler 6.00 15.00
Marc Bulger
Ben Roethlisberger
BVM Tom Brady 10.00 25.00
Mike Vrabel
Laurence Maroney
EBB John Elway 15.00 40.00
Terry Bradshaw
Tom Brady
EJB Greg Jennings 6.00 15.00
Braylon Edwards
Dwayne Bowe
FHM Brett Favre 15.00 40.00
Matt Hasselbeck
Eli Manning
FWG Brett Favre 15.00 40.00
Charles Woodson
Ryan Grant
GCB Brodie Croyle 5.00 12.00
Tony Gonzalez
Dwayne Bowe
GPR Carson Palmer 6.00 15.00
Ben Roethlisberger
David Garrard
GRC Philip Rivers 6.00 15.00
Antonio Gates
Antonio Cromartie
GSG Antonio Gates 6.00 15.00
Jeremy Shockey
Tony Gonzalez
GSW Ben Watson 5.00 12.00
Tony Gonzalez
Jeremy Shockey
HWP Brian Westbrook 10.00 25.00
Franco Harris
Willie Parker
JBW Chad Johnson 5.00 12.00
Champ Bailey
Cadillac Williams
JMB Brandon Marshall 6.00 15.00
Dwayne Bowe
Greg Jennings
JTJ LaDainian Tomlinson 6.00 15.00
Larry Johnson
Brandon Jacobs
MBM Tom Brady 10.00 25.00
Peyton Manning
Eli Manning
MBR Tom Brady 10.00 25.00
Philip Rivers
Peyton Manning
MCQ Randy Moss 6.00 15.00
Brodie Croyle
Brady Quinn
MFM Jim McMahon 25.00 60.00
Joe Montana
Brett Favre
MJJ Randy Moss 6.00 15.00
Chad Johnson
Calvin Johnson
MWA Peyton Manning 10.00 25.00
Reggie Wayne
Joseph Addai
OHB Santonio Holmes 6.00 15.00
Dwayne Bowe
Terrell Owens
PLB Carson Palmer 6.00 15.00
Matt Leinart
Reggie Bush
RSH Michael Huff 5.00 12.00
Ed Reed
Bob Sanders
SMR JaMarcus Russell 10.00 25.00
Darren McFadden
Ken Stabler
TGJ Fred Taylor 5.00 12.00
Maurice Jones-Drew
David Garrard
TJP Adrian Peterson 10.00 25.00
LaDainian Tomlinson
Maurice Jones-Drew
TSG LaDainian Tomlinson 12.00 30.00
Gale Sayers
Ryan Grant
VWH Mike Vrabel 5.00 12.00
DeMarcus Ware
A.J. Hawk
WAP Adrian Peterson 10.00 25.00
Brian Westbrook
Joseph Addai
WEH Wes Welker 6.00 15.00
Braylon Edwards
Santonio Holmes
WPJ Brian Westbrook 5.00 12.00
Maurice Jones-Drew
Willie Parker
WSC Asante Samuel 6.00 15.00
Charles Woodson
Antonio Cromartie
WSH A.J. Hawk 5.00 12.00
Ernie Sims
DeMarcus Ware

2008 Upper Deck Premier Vital Signs Autographs Gold

GOLD PRINT RUN 10-35
UNPRICED SILVER SPECTRUM PRINT RUN 1
SERIAL #'d UNDER 15 NOT PRICED
VT1 Ben Watson/35 6.00 15.00
VT2 Jerome Simpson/35 5.00 12.00
VT4 Devin Thomas/35 4.00 10.00
VT5 David Garrard/15 10.00 25.00
VT6 Brodie Croyle/35 8.00 20.00
VT7 Matt Flynn/35 40.00 80.00
VT8 DeSean Jackson/35 15.00 40.00
VT9 Jeff Garcia/35 8.00 20.00
VT10 Colt Brennan/35 15.00 40.00
VT11 Jonathan Stewart/15 25.00 60.00
VT12 Andre Woodson/35 5.00 12.00
VT13 Chad Henne/35 12.00 30.00
VT14 Chris Long/35 5.00 12.00
VT15 Rashard Mendenhall/35 12.00 30.00
VT16 Dennis Dixon/35 8.00 20.00
VT17 Early Doucet/35 4.00 10.00
VT18 Erik Ainge/35 5.00 12.00
VT19 Jamaal Charles/35 8.00 20.00
VT20 Joe Flacco/35 40.00 80.00
VT21 Felix Jones/50 25.00 60.00
VT22 Mike Hart/35 5.00 12.00
VT23 Steve Slaton/35 5.00 12.00
VT24 Harry Douglas/55 4.00 10.00
VT25 Mike Jenkins/55 5.00 12.00
VT26 Adrian Arrington/35 4.00 10.00
VT27 Calais Campbell/50 4.00 10.00
VT28 Dan Connor/35 5.00 12.00
VT29 Bruce Davis/35 4.00 10.00
VT30 Bob Sanders/35 25.00 60.00
VT31 Aaron Schobel/35 6.00 15.00
VT32 Ben Roethlisberger/15 50.00 100.00
VT35 Kenny Phillips/55 5.00 12.00

2000 Upper Deck Pros and Prospects

Released as a 126-card base set, the 2000 Upper Deck Pros and Prospects set is comprised of 84 regular cards and 42 draft picks-each sequentially numbered to 1000. Base cards have a white border that clouds into a full color action shot and card fronts are enhanced with bronze foil highlights. Pros and Prospects was packaged in 24-pack boxes containing five cards each pack and carried a suggested retail price of $4.99. An Update set of 26-cards was issued in April 2001 as part of 3-card packs distributed directly to Upper Deck hobby accounts.

COMPLETE SET (126) 300.00 600.00
COMP.SET w/o SP's (84) 7.50 20.00
85-152 ROOKIE PRINT RUN 1000
1 Jake Plummer .15 .40
2 Michael Pittman .12 .30
3 Tim Dwight .15 .40
4 Chris Chandler .15 .40
5 Qadry Ismail .15 .40
6 Shannon Sharpe .20 .50
7 Peerless Price .15 .40
8 Rob Johnson .15 .40
9 Eric Moulds .15 .40
10 Muhsin Muhammad .15 .40
11 Patrick Jeffers .15 .40
12 Steve Beuerlein .15 .40
13 Cade McNown .12 .30
14 Curtis Enis .12 .30
15 Marcus Robinson .15 .40
16 Akili Smith .12 .30
17 Corey Dillon .15 .40
18 Tim Couch .15 .40
19 Kevin Johnson .12 .30
20 Errict Rhett .15 .40
21 Troy Aikman .30 .75
22 Emmitt Smith .50 1.25
23 Rocket Ismail .15 .40
24 Terrell Davis .20 .50
25 Olandis Gary .15 .40
26 Brian Griese .15 .40
27 Ed McCaffrey .15 .40
28 Charlie Batch .15 .40
29 Germane Crowell .12 .30
30 James O. Stewart .12 .30
31 Brett Favre .60 1.50
32 Antonio Freeman .15 .40
33 Dorsey Levens .15 .40
34 Peyton Manning .50 1.25
35 Edgerrin James .20 .50
36 Marvin Harrison .20 .50
37 Mark Brunell .15 .40
38 Fred Taylor .20 .50
39 Jimmy Smith .15 .40
40 Elvis Grbac .12 .30
41 Tony Gonzalez .20 .50
42 Damon Huard .15 .40
43 James Johnson .12 .30
44 Jay Fiedler .15 .40
45 Randy Moss .20 .50
46 Robert Smith .15 .40
47 Cris Carter .20 .50
48 Drew Bledsoe .20 .50
49 Terry Glenn .15 .40
50 Ricky Williams .20 .50
51 Jeff Blake .15 .40
52 Keith Poole .12 .30
53 Kerry Collins .15 .40
54 Amani Toomer .15 .40
55 Vinny Testaverde .15 .40
56 Keyshawn Johnson .15 .40
57 Curtis Martin .20 .50
58 Tim Brown .20 .50
59 Rich Gannon .15 .40
60 Tyrone Wheatley .12 .30
61 Duce Staley .15 .40
62 Donovan McNabb .20 .50
63 Troy Edwards .12 .30
64 Jerome Bettis .20 .50
65 Marshall Faulk .20 .50
66 Kurt Warner .30 .75
67 Torry Holt .20 .50
68 Isaac Bruce .20 .50
69 Junior Seau .20 .50
70 Jeff Graham .12 .30
71 Steve Young .25 .60
72 Jerry Rice .40 1.00
73 Charlie Garner .15 .40
74 Ricky Watters .15 .40
75 Jon Kitna .15 .40
76 Warrick Dunn .15 .40
77 Shaun King .12 .30
78 Mike Alstott .20 .50
79 Eddie George .15 .40
80 Steve McNair .20 .50
81 Kevin Dyson .15 .40
82 Brad Johnson .15 .40
83 Stephen Davis .15 .40
84 Michael Westbrook .12 .30
85 Peter Warrick RC 4.00 10.00
86 LaVar Arrington RC 6.00 15.00
87 Chris Redman RC 3.00 8.00
88 Courtney Brown RC 3.00 8.00
89 Plaxico Burress RC 4.00 10.00
90 Corey Simon RC 3.00 8.00
91 Bubba Franks RC 4.00 10.00
92 Deon Grant RC 2.50 6.00
93 Brian Urlacher RC 15.00 40.00
94 Ron Dayne RC 4.00 10.00
95 Sylvester Morris RC 2.50 6.00
96 Shaun Alexander RC 5.00 12.00
97 Dez White RC 3.00 8.00
98 Thomas Jones RC 5.00 12.00
99 Travis Taylor RC 3.00 8.00
100 Kwame Cavil RC 2.50 6.00
101 Jamal Lewis RC 4.00 10.00
102 Chad Pennington RC 6.00 15.00
103 J.R. Redmond RC 2.50 6.00
104 Sebastian Janikowski RC 4.00 10.00
105 Anthony Lucas RC 2.50 6.00
106 Travis Prentice RC 3.00 8.00
107 Danny Farmer RC 2.50 6.00
108 Sherrod Gideon RC 2.50 6.00
109 Todd Pinkston RC 2.50 6.00
110 Dennis Northcutt RC 3.00 8.00
111 Tim Rattay RC 3.00 8.00
112 Troy Walters RC 2.50 6.00
113 Michael Wiley RC 2.50 6.00
114 R.Jay Soward RC 2.50 6.00
115 Trung Canidate RC 3.00 8.00
116 Reuben Droughns RC 4.00 10.00
117 Rondell Mealey RC 2.50 6.00
118 Chris Coleman RC 2.50 6.00
119 Giovanni Carmazzi RC 2.50 6.00
120 Trevor Insley RC 2.50 6.00
121 Shyrone Stith RC 2.50 6.00
122 Gari Scott RC 2.50 6.00
123 Tee Martin RC 4.00 10.00
124 Tom Brady RC 125.00 250.00
125 Marcus Knight RC 2.50 6.00
126 Jerry Porter RC 4.00 10.00
127 Brad Hoover RC 2.50 6.00
128 Chad Morton RC 3.00 8.00
129 Charles Lee RC 2.00 5.00
130 Damon Hodge RC 2.50 6.00
131 Darrell Jackson RC 2.50 6.00
132 Doug Johnson RC 2.50 6.00
133 Frank Moreau RC 2.00 5.00
134 JaJuan Dawson RC 2.00 5.00
135 Jake Delhomme RC 8.00 20.00
136 Jarious Jackson RC 2.50 6.00
137 Joe Hamilton RC 2.00 5.00
138 Larry Foster RC 2.00 5.00
139 Laveranues Coles RC 3.00 8.00
140 Aaron Shea RC 2.50 6.00
141 Matt Lytle RC 2.00 5.00
142 Mike Anderson RC 3.00 8.00
143 Ron Dixon RC 2.00 5.00
144 Ronney Jenkins RC 2.00 5.00
145 Sammy Morris RC 2.50 6.00
146 Shockmain Davis RC 2.00 5.00
147 Spergon Wynn RC 2.50 6.00
148 Todd Husak RC 2.00 5.00
149 Trevor Gaylor RC 2.00 5.00
150 Tywan Mitchell RC 2.00 5.00
151 Windrell Hayes RC 2.00 5.00
152 Bobby Shaw RC 2.50 6.00

2000 Upper Deck Pros and Prospects Future Fame

COMPLETE SET (10) 6.00 15.00
STATED ODDS 1:6
FF1 Peter Warrick .60 1.50
FF2 LaVar Arrington 1.00 2.50
FF3 Courtney Brown .50 1.25
FF4 Travis Taylor .50 1.25
FF5 Plaxico Burress .60 1.50
FF6 Ron Dayne .60 1.50
FF7 Jamal Lewis .60 1.50
FF8 Thomas Jones .75 2.00
FF9 Chad Pennington 1.00 2.50
FF10 Chris Redman .50 1.25

2000 Upper Deck Pros and Prospects Mirror Image

COMPLETE SET (10) 7.50 20.00
STATED ODDS 1:12
M1 Thomas Jones .75 2.00
Fred Taylor
M2 Ron Dayne .60 1.50
Jerome Bettis
M3 Plaxico Burress .60 1.50
Randy Moss
M4 Peter Warrick .60 1.50
Marvin Harrison
M5 Tee Martin .60 1.50
Peyton Manning
M6 Chris Redman .50 1.25
Brett Favre
M7 Lavar Arrington 1.00 2.50
Junior Seau
M8 Dez White .50 1.25
Jimmy Smith
M9 Chad Pennington 1.00 2.50
Kurt Warner
M10 Shaun Alexander .75 2.00
Marshall Faulk

2000 Upper Deck Pros and Prospects ProMotion

COMPLETE SET (10) 5.00 12.00
STATED ODDS 1:6
P1 Kurt Warner .75 2.00
P2 Eddie George .40 1.00
P3 Marshall Faulk .50 1.25
P4 Keyshawn Johnson .40 1.00
P5 Emmitt Smith 1.25 3.00
P6 Randy Moss .50 1.25
P7 Marvin Harrison .50 1.25
P8 Mark Brunell .40 1.00
P9 Curtis Martin .50 1.25
P10 Brett Favre 1.50 4.00

2000 Upper Deck Pros and Prospects Report Card

COMPLETE SET (12) 7.50 20.00
STATED ODDS 1:12
RC1 Edgerrin James .75 2.00
RC2 Tim Couch .60 1.50
RC3 Cade McNown .50 1.25
RC4 Champ Bailey .60 1.50
RC5 Donovan McNabb .75 2.00
RC6 Kevin Johnson .50 1.25
RC7 Shaun King .50 1.25
RC8 Peerless Price .60 1.50
RC9 David Boston .50 1.25
RC10 Ricky Williams .75 2.00
RC11 Akili Smith .50 1.25
RC12 Jevon Kearse .60 1.50

2000 Upper Deck Pros and Prospects Signature Piece 1

STATED ODDS 1:96
*SIG 2 BRONZE: .4X TO 1X SIG.PIECE 1
*GOLD/80-88: .6X TO 1.5X SIG.PIECE 1
*GOLD/32-50: .8X TO 2X SIG.PIECE 1
*GOLD/22-28: 1X TO 2.5X SIG.PIECE 1
GOLD STATED PRINT RUN 6-88
SPBG Brian Griese 15.00 40.00
SPCB Champ Bailey 15.00 40.00
SPCC Chris Claiborne 12.00 30.00
SPDB Drew Bledsoe 20.00 50.00
SPDF Danny Farmer 12.00 30.00
SPDL Dorsey Levens 15.00 40.00
SPDM Dan Marino 100.00 200.00
SPEG Edgerrin James 20.00 50.00
SPIB Isaac Bruce 20.00 50.00
SPKJ Kevin Johnson 12.00 30.00
SPKW Kurt Warner 30.00 60.00
SPMB Mark Brunell 15.00 40.00
SPMF Marshall Faulk 20.00 50.00
SPMH Marvin Harrison 20.00 50.00
SPOG Olandis Gary 15.00 40.00
SPPM Peyton Manning 75.00 150.00
SPRD Ron Dayne 20.00 50.00
SPRL Ray Lucas 12.00 30.00
SPRM Randy Moss 20.00 50.00
SPTA Troy Aikman 50.00 100.00
SPTH Torry Holt 20.00 50.00
SPTO Terrell Owens 20.00 50.00
SPWR Key. Johnson 12.00 30.00

2001 Upper Deck Pros and Prospects

Released as a 140-card base set, the 2001 Upper Deck Pros and Prospects set is comprised of 90 regular cards and 50 draft picks-each sequentially numbered to 1000. Base cards have a white border that clouds into a full color action shot and card fronts are enhanced with bronze foil highlights. Pros and Prospects were packaged in 24-pack boxes containing five cards each pack.

COMP.SET w/o SP's (90) 6.00 15.00
91-140 ROOKIE PRINT RUN 1000
1 Jake Plummer .15 .40
2 David Boston .12 .30
3 Jamal Anderson .15 .40
4 Doug Johnson .12 .30
5 Maurice Smith .12 .30
6 Jamal Lewis .20 .50
7 Shannon Sharpe .20 .50
8 Trent Dilfer .15 .40
9 Doug Flutie .20 .50
10 Rob Johnson .15 .40
11 Eric Moulds .15 .40
12 Muhsin Muhammad .15 .40
13 Brad Hoover .15 .40
14 Tim Biakabutuka .12 .30
15 Cade McNown .15 .40
16 James Allen .12 .30
17 Marcus Robinson .15 .40
18 Brian Urlacher .25 .60
19 Peter Warrick .15 .40
20 Corey Dillon .15 .40
21 Tim Couch .12 .30
22 Kevin Johnson .12 .30
23 Travis Prentice .12 .30
24 Troy Aikman .30 .75
25 Emmitt Smith .50 1.25
26 Terrell Davis .20 .50
27 Mike Anderson .15 .40
28 Brian Griese .15 .40
29 Charlie Batch .15 .40
30 Germane Crowell .12 .30
31 James Stewart .12 .30
32 Brett Favre .60 1.50
33 Antonio Freeman .20 .50
34 Dorsey Levens .15 .40
35 Ahman Green .20 .50
36 Peyton Manning .50 1.25
37 Edgerrin James .20 .50
38 Marvin Harrison .20 .50
39 Mark Brunell .15 .40
40 Fred Taylor .20 .50
41 Jimmy Smith .15 .40
42 Elvis Grbac .15 .40
43 Tony Gonzalez .20 .50
44 Derrick Alexander .12 .30
45 Oronde Gadsden .12 .30
46 Lamar Smith .15 .40
47 Jay Fiedler .15 .40
48 Randy Moss .20 .50
49 Moe Williams .12 .30
50 Cris Carter .20 .50
51 Daunte Culpepper .15 .40
52 Drew Bledsoe .20 .50
53 Terry Glenn .15 .40
54 Ricky Williams .20 .50
55 Jeff Blake .15 .40
56 Joe Horn .15 .40
57 Aaron Brooks .15 .40
58 La'Roi Glover .12 .30
59 Kerry Collins .16 .40
60 Amani Toomer .15 .40
61 Ron Dayne .15 .40
62 Vinny Testaverde .15 .40
63 Wayne Chrebet .15 .40
64 Curtis Martin .20 .50
65 Tim Brown .20 .50
66 Rich Gannon .15 .40
67 Tyrone Wheatley .15 .40
68 Duce Staley .15 .40
69 Donovan McNabb .20 .50
70 Kordell Stewart .15 .40
71 Jerome Bettis .20 .50
72 Marshall Faulk .20 .50
73 Kurt Warner .30 .75
74 Isaac Bruce .20 .50
75 Junior Seau .20 .50
76 Curtis Conway .15 .40
77 Jeff Garcia .15 .40
78 Jerry Rice .40 1.00
79 Charlie Garner .15 .40
80 Terrell Owens .20 .50
81 Ricky Watters .15 .40
82 Shaun Alexander .20 .50
83 Warrick Dunn .20 .50
84 Shaun King .12 .30
85 Derrick Brooks .20 .50
86 Eddie George .20 .50
87 Steve McNair .20 .50
88 Brad Johnson .15 .40
89 Jeff George .15 .40
90 Stephen Davis .15 .40
91 Jamal Reynolds RC 2.00 5.00
92 Justin Smith RC 3.00 8.00
93 Dan Morgan RC 2.50 6.00
94 Deuce McAllister RC 3.00 8.00
95 Drew Brees RC 20.00 50.00
96 Josh Booty RC 2.50 6.00
97 Mike McMahon RC 2.50 6.00
98 Sage Rosenfels RC 3.00 8.00
99 Marques Tuiasosopo RC 2.50 6.00
100 Josh Heupel RC 3.00 8.00
101 Heath Evans RC 2.50 6.00
102 Reggie White RC 2.00 5.00
103 Tim Hasselbeck RC 2.50 6.00
104 LaDainian Tomlinson RC 10.00 25.00
105 Kevan Barlow RC 2.50 6.00
106 LaMont Jordan RC 3.00 8.00
107 James Jackson RC 2.00 5.00
108 Anthony Thomas RC 3.00 8.00
109 Correll Buckhalter RC 3.00 8.00
110 Travis Henry RC 2.50 6.00
111 Dan Alexander RC 2.50 6.00
112 Travis Minor RC 2.50 6.00
113 Rudi Johnson RC 3.00 8.00
114 Michael Bennett RC 2.50 6.00
115 Todd Heap RC 3.00 8.00
116 Snoop Minnis RC 2.00 5.00
117 Santana Moss RC 4.00 10.00

118 Reggie Wayne RC 6.00 15.00
119 Koren Robinson RC 2.50 6.00
120 Chris Chambers RC 3.00 8.00
121 David Terrell RC 2.50 6.00
122 Rod Gardner RC 2.50 6.00
123 Quincy Morgan RC 2.50 6.00
124 Ken-Yon Rambo RC 2.00 5.00
125 Ronney Daniels RC 2.00 5.00
126 Ja'Mar Toombs RC 2.00 5.00
127 Bobby Newcombe RC 2.50 6.00
128 Cedrick Wilson RC 2.50 6.00
129 Chad Johnson RC 5.00 12.00
130 Shaun Rogers RC 3.00 8.00
131 Robert Ferguson RC 3.00 8.00
132 Kevin Kasper RC 2.00 5.00
133 Chris Weinke JSY RC 5.00 12.00
134 Freddie Mitchell JSY RC 4.00 10.00
135 Michael Vick JSY RC 20.00 50.00
136 Chris Taylor RC 2.00 5.00
137 Vinny Sutherland RC 2.00 5.00
138 Gerard Warren RC 2.50 6.00
139 Torrance Marshall RC 2.00 5.00
140 Jesse Palmer RC 2.50 6.00

2001 Upper Deck Pros and Prospects A Piece of History Autographs

STATED ODDS 1:192
BSAJ Bart Starr 75.00 150.00
CTAJ Charley Taylor 12.00 30.00
FTAJ Fran Tarkenton 30.00 60.00
JKAJ Jim Kelly 50.00 100.00
JTAJ Joe Theismann 15.00 40.00
JUAJ Johnny Unitas 300.00 450.00
JYAJ Jack Youngblood 12.00 30.00
RSAJ Roger Staubach 50.00 100.00
SYAJ Steve Young 60.00 120.00

2001 Upper Deck Pros and Prospects Centerpiece

COMPLETE SET (6) 6.00 15.00
STATED ODDS 1:22
C1 Randy Moss .75 2.00
C2 Donovan McNabb .75 2.00
C3 Kurt Warner 1.25 3.00
C4 Jamal Lewis .75 2.00
C5 Eddie George .75 2.00
C6 Mike Anderson .60 1.50

2001 Upper Deck Pros and Prospects Future Fame

COMPLETE SET (6) 10.00 25.00
STATED ODDS 1:22
F1 Michael Vick 3.00 8.00
F2 Deuce McAllister .75 2.00
F3 Drew Brees 5.00 12.00
F4 LaDainian Tomlinson 2.50 6.00
F5 Chris Weinke .60 1.50
F6 Santana Moss 1.00 2.50

2001 Upper Deck Pros and Prospects Game Jersey

STATED ODDS 1:23
*GOLD/50: .8X TO 2X BASIC JSY
GOLD/50 RANDOM INSERTS IN PACKS
GOLD PRINT RUN 50 SER.#'d SETS
BAJ Tiki Barber 6.00 15.00
BFJ Brett Favre 15.00 40.00
CDJ Corey Dillon 5.00 12.00
DCJ Daunte Culpepper 5.00 12.00
DLJ Dorsey Levens 5.00 12.00
EJJ Edgerrin James 6.00 15.00
ESJ Emmitt Smith 15.00 40.00
FTJ Fred Taylor 6.00 15.00
JEJ John Elway 15.00 40.00
JGJ Jeff Garcia 5.00 12.00
JMJ Joe Montana 15.00 40.00
JNJ Joe Namath 15.00 40.00
JPJ Jake Plummer 5.00 12.00
JRJ Jerry Rice 12.00 30.00
JSJ Junior Seau 6.00 15.00
KCJ Kerry Collins 5.00 12.00
KJJ Keyshawn Johnson 5.00 12.00
KMJ Keenan McCardell 5.00 12.00
KSJ Kordell Stewart 5.00 12.00
KWJ Kurt Warner 10.00 25.00
MAJ Marcus Allen 10.00 25.00
MBJ Mark Brunell 5.00 12.00
MFJ Marshall Faulk 6.00 15.00
PHJ Paul Hornung 10.00 25.00
PLJ Jim Plunkett 8.00 20.00
PMJ Peyton Manning 15.00 40.00
PSJ Phil Simms 8.00 20.00
RDJ Ron Dayne 5.00 12.00
RMJ Randy Moss 6.00 15.00
SKJ Shaun King 4.00 10.00
TAJ Troy Aikman 10.00 25.00
TBJ Terry Bradshaw 15.00 40.00
THJ Torry Holt 5.00 12.00
TJJ Thomas Jones 5.00 12.00
WDJ Warrick Dunn 6.00 15.00
WPJ Walter Payton 25.00 60.00

2001 Upper Deck Pros and Prospects A Piece of History Autographs Gold

*GOLD/50: 1X TO 2X BASIC JSY AU
JUAJ Johnny Unitas 400.00 700.00

2001 Upper Deck Pros and Prospects Game Jersey Combos

STATED PRINT RUN 25 SER.#'d SETS
ASC Troy Aikman 100.00 200.00
Emmitt Smith
FWC Marshall Faulk 40.00 100.00
Kurt Warner
JMC Edgerrin James 75.00 150.00
Peyton Manning
MCC Daunte Culpepper 40.00 100.00
Randy Moss
MYC Joe Montana 75.00 150.00
Steve Young
SBC Terry Bradshaw 75.00 150.00
Roger Staubach
SUC Bart Starr 125.00 250.00
Johnny Unitas

2001 Upper Deck Pros and Prospects ProActive

COMPLETE SET (9) 6.00 15.00
STATED ODDS 1:15
PA1 Kurt Warner 1.25 3.00
PA2 Eddie George .75 2.00
PA3 Marshall Faulk .75 2.00
PA4 Corey Dillon .60 1.50
PA5 Emmitt Smith 2.00 5.00
PA6 Randy Moss .75 2.00
PA7 Marvin Harrison .75 2.00
PA8 Rich Gannon .60 1.50
PA9 Brett Favre 2.50 6.00

2001 Upper Deck Pros and Prospects ProMotion

COMPLETE SET (9) 10.00 25.00
STATED ODDS 1:15
PM1 Michael Vick 3.00 8.00
PM2 Michael Bennett .60 1.50
PM3 Reggie Wayne 1.50 4.00
PM4 Chad Johnson 1.25 3.00
PM5 Chris Chambers .75 2.00
PM6 David Terrell .60 1.50
PM7 Snoop Minnis .50 1.25
PM8 Koren Robinson .60 1.50
PM9 Rod Gardner .60 1.50

2003 Upper Deck Pros and Prospects

This 190-card set was released in May, 2003. It was issued in five-card packs. The first 90 cards of this set featured veterans while cards 91 through 120 are veteran cards which were short printed at a stated rate of one in six. Cards numbered 121 through 190 feature rookies paired with a veteran player. Those cards were issued to a stated print run of 1800 serial numbered cards. A few of those cards were autographed and not every player returned their cards in time for pack-out. Those exchange cards could be redeemed until May 16, 2006.

COMP.SET w/o SP's (90) 7.50 20.00
ROOKIE PRINT RUN 1800
ROOKIE AU PRINT RUN 250-2000
1 Jake Plummer .25 .60
2 David Boston .20 .50
3 Warrick Dunn .25 .60
4 T.J. Duckett .25 .60
5 Chris Redman .20 .50
6 Jamal Lewis .25 .60
7 Drew Bledsoe .30 .75
8 Travis Henry .20 .50
9 Eric Moulds .25 .60
10 Peerless Price .20 .50
11 Rodney Peete .20 .50
12 Julius Peppers .30 .75
13 Anthony Thomas .25 .60
14 Brian Urlacher .30 .75
15 Marty Booker .25 .60
16 David Terrell .20 .50
17 Corey Dillon .25 .60
18 Peter Warrick .25 .60
19 Jon Kitna .25 .60
20 Tim Couch .20 .50
21 Andre Davis .20 .50
22 Quincy Morgan .20 .50
23 Dennis Northcutt .20 .50
24 Roy Williams .25 .60
25 Emmitt Smith .75 2.00
26 Joey Galloway .25 .60
27 Antonio Bryant .20 .50
28 Brian Griese .25 .60
29 Clinton Portis .25 .60
30 Shannon Sharpe .30 .75
31 Joey Harrington .20 .50
32 Az-Zahir Hakim .20 .50
33 Brett Favre .75 2.00
34 Robert Ferguson .20 .50
35 Donald Driver .30 .75
36 David Carr .25 .60
37 Jabar Gaffney .20 .50
38 Edgerrin James .30 .75
39 Marvin Harrison .30 .75
40 Reggie Wayne .30 .75
41 Mark Brunell .25 .60
42 Fred Taylor .25 .60
43 Priest Holmes .30 .75
44 Trent Green .25 .60
45 Marc Boerigter .20 .50
46 Jay Fiedler .20 .50
47 Chris Chambers .25 .60
48 Randy McMichael .20 .50
49 Randy Moss .30 .75
50 Daunte Culpepper .25 .60
51 Michael Bennett .25 .60
52 Antowain Smith .25 .60
53 David Patten .20 .50
54 Troy Brown .25 .60
55 Aaron Brooks .25 .60
56 Joe Horn .25 .60
57 Donte Stallworth .20 .50
58 Amani Toomer .25 .60
59 Kerry Collins .25 .60
60 Tiki Barber .30 .75
61 Santana Moss .25 .60
62 Curtis Martin .30 .75
63 Wayne Chrebet .25 .60
64 Rich Gannon .25 .60
65 Charlie Garner .25 .60
66 Tim Brown .30 .75
67 Donovan McNabb .30 .75
68 Duce Staley .25 .60
69 Hines Ward .30 .75
70 Antwaan Randle El .25 .60
71 Plaxico Burress .25 .60
72 Jerome Bettis .30 .75
73 Junior Seau .30 .75
74 LaDainian Tomlinson .30 .75
75 Tai Streets .20 .50
76 Kevan Barlow .20 .50
77 Garrison Hearst .25 .60
78 Jeff Garcia .25 .60
79 Shaun Alexander .25 .60
80 Matt Hasselbeck .25 .60
81 Marshall Faulk .30 .75
82 Marc Bulger .30 .75
83 Torry Holt .30 .75
84 Isaac Bruce .30 .75
85 Brad Johnson .25 .60
86 Keyshawn Johnson .30 .75
87 Steve McNair .30 .75
88 Kevin Dyson .20 .50
89 Patrick Ramsey .25 .60
90 Ladell Betts .20 .50
91 Marcel Shipp SP .60 1.50
92 Michael Vick SP 1.25 3.00
93 Ray Lewis SP 1.00 2.50
94 Josh Reed SP .60 1.50
95 Josh McCown SP .75 2.00
96 Kelly Holcomb SP .60 1.50
97 William Green SP .60 1.50
98 Chad Hutchinson SP .60 1.50
99 Rod Smith SP .75 2.00
100 James Stewart SP .60 1.50
101 Ahman Green SP .75 2.00
102 Peyton Manning SP 2.00 5.00
103 Jimmy Smith SP .75 2.00
104 Tony Gonzalez SP 1.00 2.50
105 Ricky Williams SP .75 2.00
106 Jason Taylor SP .75 2.00
107 Tom Brady SP 2.50 6.00
108 Deuce McAllister SP .75 2.00
109 Jeremy Shockey SP 1.00 2.50
110 Chad Pennington SP 1.00 2.50
111 Jerry Rice SP 2.00 5.00
112 A.J. Feeley SP .60 1.50
113 Tommy Maddox SP .75 2.00
114 Drew Brees SP 1.00 2.50
115 Terrell Owens SP 1.00 2.50
116 Maurice Morris SP .60 1.50
117 Kurt Warner SP 1.00 2.50
118 Derrick Brooks SP .75 2.00
119 Eddie George SP .75 2.00
120 Rod Gardner SP .60 1.50
121 Byron Leftwich AU RC 25.00 60.00
Chad Pennington AU/250
122 Ken Dorsey AU RC 8.00 20.00
Vinny Testaverde/2000
123 Carson Palmer AU RC 60.00 120.00
Peyton Manning AU/250
124 Chris Simms AU RC 25.00 50.00
Mark Brunell AU/250
125 Andre Johnson RC 5.00 12.00
Santana Moss
126 Brad Banks AU RC 8.00 20.00
Aaron Brooks AU/250
127 J.R. Tolver RC 1.50 4.00
Az-Zahir Hakim
128 Jerel Myers RC 1.25 3.00
Josh Reed
129 Ronald Bellamy RC 1.50 4.00
Amani Toomer
130 Jason Gesser RC 2.00 5.00
Drew Bledsoe
131 Kliff Kingsbury AU RC 10.00 25.00
Sammy Baugh/2000
132 Kyle Boller RC 40.00 80.00
Drew Brees AU/500
133 Larry Johnson RC 8.00 20.00
Anthony Thomas AU
134 Kareem Kelly AU RC 8.00 20.00
Johnnie Morton/2000
135 Bryant Johnson RC 10.00 25.00
Rod Gardner AU/500
136 Jason Johnson RC 6.00 15.00
Tim Couch AU/500
137 Terrell Suggs AU RC 12.00 30.00
Leo Nomellini/2000
138 Dave Ragone RC 8.00 20.00
Mark Brunell AU/500
139 Musa Smith RC 1.25 3.00
Charley Trippi
140 Juston Wood RC 1.25 3.00
Joey Harrington
141 Jason Thomas RC 2.00 5.00
Michael Vick
142 Earnest Graham AU RC 8.00 20.00
Emmitt Smith/2000
143 Willis McGahee AU RC 12.00 30.00
Edgerrin James/2000
144 ReShard Lee RC 10.00 25.00
Shaun Alexander AU/500
145 Anquan Boldin RC 3.00 8.00
Javon Walker
146 Taylor Jacobs AU RC 6.00 15.00
Reche Caldwell AU/250
147 Talman Gardner RC 1.25 3.00
Laveranues Coles
148 Bobby Wade RC 1.50 4.00
Dennis Northcutt
149 Billy McMullen RC 10.00 25.00
Isaac Bruce AU/500
150 Avon Cobourne RC 1.25 3.00
Amos Zereoue
151 Bradie James RC 2.00 5.00
Frank Kinard RC
152 Kelley Washington AU RC 6.00 15.00
Peerless Price/2000
153 Eric Steinbach RC 1.25 3.00
Jim Parker
154 Jimmy Kennedy RC 1.50 4.00
Ernie Stautner
155 Rien Long RC 1.25 3.00
Arnie Weinmeister
156 Chris Brown AU RC 8.00 20.00
Mike Anderson/2000
157 Teyo Johnson RC 2.00 5.00
Tony Gonzalez
158 Onterrio Smith RC 1.25 3.00
Maurice Morris
159 Justin Fargas AU RC 10.00 25.00
Clinton Portis/2000
160 Seneca Wallace RC 2.00 5.00
Antwaan Randle El
161 Brian St.Pierre RC 40.00 100.00
Peyton Manning AU/500
162 LaBrandon Toefield RC 40.00 80.00
LaDainian Tomlinson AU/500
163 Marquel Blackwell RC 1.50 4.00
Daunte Culpepper
164 Keenan Howry RC 1.25 3.00
A.J. Feeley
165 Justin Gage RC 1.50 4.00
Kirk Farmer RC
166 Shawn Witten RC 1.25 3.00
Andre Davis
167 Dennis Weathersby RC 1.50 4.00
Aeneas Williams
168 Boss Bailey RC 2.00 5.00
Champ Bailey
169 Brandon Lloyd RC 3.00 8.00
Kurt Kittner
170 Doug Gabriel RC 1.50 4.00
Chris Chambers
171 Akbar Gbaja-Biamila RC 1.50 4.00
K.Gbaja-Biamila
172 Dahrran Diedrick RC 1.50 4.00
Ahman Green
173 Kevin Curtis RC 2.00 5.00
Kevin Dyson
174 Sultan McCullough RC 8.00 20.00
Deuce McAllister AU/500
175 Mike Bush RC 1.50 4.00
Marcus Trufant RC
176 Zach Hilton RC 1.50 4.00
Sam Aiken RC
177 Terence Newman RC 1.50 4.00
Andre Woolfolk RC
178 Tyrone Calico RC 1.50 4.00
Kelly Holcomb
179 J.T. Wall RC 1.25 3.00
Terrence Edwards RC
180 Cory Paus RC 1.25 3.00
Mike Seidman RC
181 L.J. Smith RC 2.00 5.00
Marco Battaglia
182 Quentin Griffin AU RC 8.00 20.00
Antwone Savage RC/2000
183 Lee Suggs RC 2.00 5.00
Michael Vick
184 B.J. Askew RC 1.50 4.00
Ben Joppru RC
185 Mike Pinkard RC 1.50 4.00
Todd Heap
186 Arnaz Battle RC 2.00 5.00
Tim Brown
187 Charles Rogers RC 1.50 4.00
Plaxico Burress
188 Andrew Pinnock RC 1.50 4.00
Duce Staley
189 Rex Grossman RC 40.00 100.00
Peyton Manning AU/500
190 George Wrighster RC 1.25 3.00
Justin Peelle
KBBF Kyle Boller 100.00 200.00
Brett Favre AU/25
RGBF Rex Grossman 100.00 200.00
Brett Favre AU/25

2003 Upper Deck Pros and Prospects Gold

*UNSIGNED: 1.2X TO 3X BASIC CARDS
*AUTO/50: .8X TO 2X BASE AU/250
*AUTO/50: 1X TO 2.5X BASE AU/500
*AUTO/50: 1X TO 2.5X BASE AU/2000
STATED PRINT RUN 50 SER.#'d SETS

2003 Upper Deck Pros and Prospects Game Day Jerseys

STATED PRINT RUN 350 SER.#'d SETS
*GOLD/50: .8X TO 2X BASIC JSY
GOLD STATED PRINT RUN 50
*BRONZE/75: .6X TO 1.5X BASIC JSY
BRONZE STATED PRINT RUN 75
JCAC Avon Cobourne 2.50 6.00
JCAG Antonio Gilbert 2.50 6.00
JCAP Andrew Pinnock 3.00 8.00
JCBL Byron Leftwich 4.00 10.00
JCBS Brian St.Pierre 3.00 8.00
JCCP Carson Palmer 8.00 20.00
JCDR Dave Ragone 2.50 6.00
JCGA Justin Gage 3.00 8.00
JCJG Jason Gesser 3.00 8.00
JCJJ Jason Johnson 2.50 6.00
JCJS Jeremy Shockey 4.00 10.00
JCJT J.R. Tolver 3.00 8.00
JCJW Juston Wood 2.50 6.00
JCKD Ken Dorsey 3.00 8.00
JCKH Keenan Howry 2.50 6.00
JCKI Kliff Kingsbury 3.00 8.00
JCKJ Keyshawn Johnson 4.00 10.00
JCKK Kareem Kelly 2.50 6.00
JCLS Lee Suggs 3.00 8.00
JCMD Mike Doss 4.00 10.00
JCMF Marshall Faulk 4.00 10.00
JCPM Peyton Manning 8.00 20.00
JCRB Ronald Bellamy 3.00 8.00
JCSM Sultan McCullough 2.50 6.00
JCST J.J. Stokes 2.50 6.00
JCSW Seneca Wallace 4.00 10.00
JCTI Jason Thomas 2.50 6.00
JCTS Terrell Suggs 4.00 10.00
JCZH Zach Hilton 3.00 8.00

2003 Upper Deck Pros and Prospects Game Day Jersey Duals

STATED PRINT RUN 350 SER.#'d SETS
*GOLD/50: .8X TO 2X BASIC DUAL
GOLD STATED PRINT RUN 50
*BRONZE/75: .6X TO 1.5X BASIC DUAL
BRONZE STATED PRINT RUN 75
DJCBT Ronald Bellamy 4.00 10.00
Anthony Thomas
DJCCD Carson Palmer 10.00 25.00
Ken Dorsey
DJCDS Ken Dorsey 6.00 15.00
Jeremy Shockey
DJCDT Ken Dorsey 5.00 12.00
Vinny Testaverde
DJCGB Jason Gesser 6.00 15.00
Drew Bledsoe
DJCHH Keenan Howry 4.00 10.00
Joey Harrington
DJCJF J.J. Stokes 5.00 12.00
DeShaun Foster
DJCJT Jason Johnson 4.00 10.00
Jason Thomas
DJCKG Ken Dorsey 5.00 12.00
Jason Gesser
DJCKM Kareem Kelly 4.00 10.00
Sultan McCullough
DJCLD Byron Leftwich 6.00 15.00
Ken Dorsey
DJCLP Byron Leftwich 6.00 15.00
Chad Pennington
DJCPJ Carson Palmer 10.00 25.00
Keyshawn Johnson
DJCPK Carson Palmer 10.00 25.00
Kareem Kelly
DJCPL Carson Palmer 10.00 25.00
Byron Leftwich/255
DJCPW Brian St.Pierre 5.00 12.00
Juston Wood
DJCRK Dave Ragone 5.00 12.00
Kliff Kingsbury
DJCRU Dave Ragone 20.00 50.00
Johnny Unitas
DJCSB Terrell Suggs 6.00 15.00
Wendell Bryant
DJCSF Brian St.Pierre 6.00 15.00
Doug Flutie
DJCSS Terrell Suggs 6.00 15.00
Warren Sapp
DJCSV Lee Suggs 8.00 20.00
Michael Vick
DJCTD Marcus Trufant 6.00 15.00
Mike Doss
DJCTF J.R. Tolver 6.00 15.00
Marshall Faulk
DJCWJ Juston Wood 4.00 10.00
Jason Johnson
DJCWR Seneca Wallace 6.00 15.00
Antwaan Randle El

2003 Upper Deck Pros and Prospects The Power and the Potential

COMPLETE SET (30) 20.00 50.00
STATED PRINT RUN 1700 SER.#'d SETS
PP1 David Carr 2.00 5.00
Tom Brady
PP2 Joey Harrington 2.00 5.00
Brett Favre
PP3 Patrick Ramsey .60 1.50
Tim Couch
PP4 David Garrard .75 2.00
Steve McNair
PP5 Kurt Kittner 1.50 4.00
Peyton Manning
PP6 Josh McCown .75 2.00
Drew Bledsoe
PP7 Rohan Davey .60 1.50
Daunte Culpepper
PP8 Clinton Portis .75 2.00
Edgerrin James
PP9 William Green .60 1.50
Garrison Hearst
PP10 T.J. Duckett .75 2.00
Jerome Bettis
PP11 Maurice Morris .60 1.50
Shaun Alexander
PP12 Jonathan Wells .60 1.50
Eddie George
PP13 Lamar Gordon .75 2.00
Marshall Faulk
PP14 Ladell Betts .75 2.00
Mike Alstott
PP15 Brian Westbrook .75 2.00
Duce Staley
PP16 Donte Stallworth .60 1.50
Joe Horn
PP17 Antwaan Randle El .60 1.50
Plaxico Burress
PP18 Ashley Lelie .60 1.50
Rod Smith
PP19 Javon Walker .75 2.00
Donald Driver
PP20 Josh Reed .60 1.50
Eric Moulds
PP21 Jabar Gaffney .60 1.50
Jimmy Smith
PP22 Reche Caldwell .75 2.00
Marvin Harrison
PP23 Antonio Bryant .60 1.50
Joey Galloway
PP24 Deion Branch .60 1.50
Troy Brown
PP25 Marquise Walker .75 2.00
Keyshawn Johnson
PP26 Cliff Russell .50 1.25
Rod Gardner
PP27 Chad Hutchinson .75 2.00
Chad Pennington
PP28 Julius Peppers .75 2.00
Warren Sapp
PP29 Andre Davis .50 1.25
Quincy Morgan
PP30 Jeremy Shockey .75 2.00
Tony Gonzalez

1999 Upper Deck Retro

The 1999 Upper Deck Retro Set was issued in mid October and featured a 165 card set with a colored background with a white border. Set features the top players of the 1999 draft such as Edgerrin James and Tim Couch as well as past NFL superstars such as Joe Montana and Roger Staubach. Cards were distributed in a "lunchbox" style container which featured one Inkredible hand signed autographed card per sealed lunchbox of packs.

COMPLETE SET (165) 15.00 40.00
1 Jake Plummer .20 .50
2 Adrian Murrell .20 .50
3 Rob Moore .15 .40
4 Frank Sanders .15 .40
5 David Boston RC .30 .75
6 Tim Dwight .20 .50
7 Chris Chandler .20 .50
8 Jamal Anderson .20 .50
9 O.J. Santiago .15 .40
10 Terance Mathis .15 .40
11 Priest Holmes .25 .60
12 Tony Banks .20 .50
13 Patrick Johnson .15 .40
14 Scott Mitchell .15 .40
15 Jermaine Lewis .15 .40
16 Eric Moulds .20 .50
17 Doug Flutie .25 .60
18 Antowain Smith .15 .40
19 Thurman Thomas .25 .60
20 Peerless Price RC .30 .75
21 Fred Lane .15 .40
22 Tim Biakabutuka .20 .50
23 Steve Beuerlein .20 .50
24 Muhsin Muhammad .20 .50
25 Rae Carruth .15 .40
26 Curtis Enis .15 .40
27 Walter Payton 1.50 4.00
28 Bobby Engram .20 .50
29 Cade McNown RC .30 .75
30 Curtis Conway .20 .50
31 Darnay Scott .15 .40
32 Jeff Blake .20 .50
33 Corey Dillon .20 .50
34 Akili Smith RC .30 .75
35 Carl Pickens .20 .50
36 Tim Couch RC .40 1.00
37 Ty Detmer .20 .50
38 Jim Brown UER .60 1.50
(photo is Terry Kirby)
39 Kevin Johnson RC .30 .75
40 Ozzie Newsome .15 .40
41 Troy Aikman .40 1.00
42 Rocket Ismail .20 .50
43 Emmitt Smith .60 1.50
44 Michael Irvin .25 .60
45 Deion Sanders .25 .60
46 Roger Staubach .75 2.00
47 John Elway .75 2.00
48 Bubby Brister .15 .40
49 Terrell Davis .25 .60
50 Ed McCaffrey .20 .50
51 Rod Smith .20 .50
52 Shannon Sharpe .25 .60
53 Charlie Batch .20 .50
54 Johnnie Morton .20 .50
55 Barry Sanders .60 1.50
56 Sedrick Irvin RC .25 .60
57 Herman Moore .20 .50
58 Brett Favre .75 2.00
59 Mark Chmura .15 .40
60 Antonio Freeman .20 .50
61 Robert Brooks .20 .50
62 Dorsey Levens .20 .50
63 Peyton Manning .75 2.00
64 Jerome Pathon .15 .40
65 Marvin Harrison .25 .60
66 Edgerrin James RC .50 1.25
67 Ken Dilger .15 .40
68 Mark Brunell .20 .50
69 Fred Taylor .20 .50
70 Jimmy Smith .20 .50
71 James Stewart .15 .40
72 Keenan McCardell .20 .50
73 Elvis Grbac .15 .40
74 Mike Cloud RC .25 .60
75 Andre Rison .20 .50
76 Tony Gonzalez .25 .60
77 Warren Moon .25 .60
78 Derrick Alexander WR .15 .40
79 Dan Marino .75 2.00
80 O.J. McDuffie .20 .50
81 James Johnson RC .25 .60
82 Paul Warfield .40 1.00
83 Cecil Collins RC .25 .60
84 Randall Cunningham .40 1.00
85 Randy Moss .25 .60
86 Cris Carter .25 .60
87 Fran Tarkenton .50 1.25
88 Daunte Culpepper RC .40 1.00
89 Robert Smith .20 .50
90 Drew Bledsoe .25 .60
91 Terry Glenn .20 .50
92 Kevin Faulk RC .40 1.00
93 Tony Simmons .15 .40
94 Ben Coates .20 .50
95 Billy Joe Hobert .15 .40
96 Cameron Cleeland .15 .40
97 Eddie Kennison .20 .50
98 Andre Hastings .15 .40
99 Ricky Williams RC .60 1.50
100 Kerry Collins .20 .50
101 Joe Montgomery RC .25 .60
102 Gary Brown .15 .40
103 Ike Hilliard .20 .50
104 Amani Toomer .20 .50
105 Vinny Testaverde .20 .50
106 Wayne Chrebet .20 .50
107 Curtis Martin .25 .60
108 Joe Namath .75 2.00
109 Keyshawn Johnson .20 .50
110 Don Maynard .20 .50
111 Rich Gannon .20 .50
112 Tim Brown .25 .60
113 Charles Woodson .25 .60
114 Rickey Dudley .15 .40
115 Darrell Russell .15 .40
116 Napoleon Kaufman .15 .40
117 Donovan McNabb RC 2.00 5.00
118 Doug Pederson .15 .40
119 Duce Staley .20 .50
120 Torrance Small .15 .40
121 Charles Johnson .15 .40
122 Jerome Bettis .25 .60
123 Courtney Hawkins .15 .40
124 Kordell Stewart .20 .50
125 Troy Edwards RC .30 .75
126 Amos Zereoue RC .30 .75
127 Trent Green .20 .50
128 Marshall Faulk .25 .60
129 Az-Zahir Hakim .15 .40
130 Joe Germaine RC .30 .75
131 Torry Holt RC .60 1.50
132 Isaac Bruce .25 .60
133 Jim Harbaugh .20 .50
134 Junior Seau .25 .60
135 Natrone Means .20 .50
136 Ryan Leaf .20 .50
137 Dan Fouts .40 1.00
138 Mikhael Ricks .15 .40
139 Steve Young .30 .75
140 Terrell Owens .25 .60
141 Jerry Rice .50 1.25
142 J.J. Stokes .15 .40
143 Lawrence Phillips .20 .50
144 Joe Montana 1.25 3.00
145 Jon Kitna .20 .50
146 Ahman Green .20 .50
147 Joey Galloway .20 .50
148 Ricky Watters .20 .50
149 Brock Huard RC .30 .75
150 Steve Largent .40 1.00
151 Trent Dilfer .20 .50
152 Reidel Anthony .15 .40
153 Warrick Dunn .20 .50
154 Mike Alstott .25 .60
155 Shaun King RC .30 .75
156 Eddie George .20 .50
157 Steve McNair .25 .60
158 Kevin Dyson .15 .40
159 Frank Wycheck .20 .50
160 Yancey Thigpen .15 .40
161 Brad Johnson .20 .50
162 Rodney Peete .20 .50
163 Michael Westbrook .15 .40
164 Skip Hicks .15 .40
165 Champ Bailey RC .75 2.00
WP1 Walter Payton AU 400.00 600.00
WPR Walter Payton 1,000.00 1,500.00
Jersey AUTO/34

1999 Upper Deck Retro Gold

COMPLETE SET (165) 300.00 600.00
*GOLD STARS: 5X TO 12X BASIC CARDS
*GOLD RCs: 2.5X TO 6X
GOLD STATED PRINT RUN 175 SER.#'d SETS

1999 Upper Deck Retro Inkredible

ONE PER BOX
AK Akili Smith 5.00 12.00
AM Adrian Murrell 5.00 12.00
AS Antowain Smith 6.00 15.00
BH Brock Huard 5.00 12.00
CC Cris Carter 12.00 30.00
CM Cade McNown 5.00 12.00
DB David Boston 5.00 12.00
DC Daunte Culpepper 10.00 25.00
DF Dan Fouts 12.00 30.00
DL Dorsey Levens 7.50 20.00
FT Fran Tarkenton 15.00 40.00
GH Garrison Hearst 6.00 15.00
JK Jon Kitna 7.50 20.00
JM Joe Montana 60.00 120.00
JN Joe Namath 50.00 100.00
MC Donovan McNabb 20.00 50.00
OZ Ozzie Newsome 10.00 25.00
PW Paul Warfield 10.00 25.00
RG Roger Staubach 30.00 60.00
RM Randy Moss 30.00 80.00
RS Rod Smith 7.50 20.00
RW Ricky Williams 12.00 30.00
SK Shaun King 5.00 12.00
SL Steve Largent 12.00 30.00
TC Tim Couch 6.00 15.00
TD Terrell Davis 15.00 30.00
TH Torry Holt 12.00 30.00
TO Terrell Owens 15.00 40.00
WC Wayne Chrebet 7.50 20.00
WP Walter Payton 400.00 600.00

1999 Upper Deck Retro Inkredible Gold

STATED PRINT RUN 2-89
AM Adrian Murrell/29 12.00 30.00
AS Antowain Smith/23 15.00 40.00
CC Cris Carter/80 15.00 40.00
DB David Boston/89 8.00 20.00
DL Dorsey Levens/25 30.00 80.00
GH Garrison Hearst/20 15.00 40.00
OZ Ozzie Newsome/82 15.00 40.00
PW Paul Warfield/42 15.00 40.00
RM Randy Moss/84 50.00 120.00
RS Rod Smith/80 12.00 30.00
RW Ricky Williams/34 25.00 60.00
SL Steve Largent/80 15.00 40.00
TD Terrell Davis/30 30.00 80.00
TH Torry Holt/88 25.00 60.00
TO Terrell Owens/81 25.00 60.00
WC Wayne Chrebet/80 12.00 30.00
WP Walter Payton/34 800.00 1,200.00

1999 Upper Deck Retro Legends of the Fall

COMPLETE SET (30) 20.00 40.00
STATED ODDS 1:11
*SILVER CARDS: 7X TO 20X BASIC INSERTS
SILVER PRINT RUN 75 SER.#'d SETS
L1 Jake Plummer .40 1.00
L2 Corey Dillon .60 1.50
L3 Curtis Martin .60 1.50
L4 Vinny Testaverde .40 1.00
L5 Brett Favre 2.00 5.00
L6 Randy Moss 1.50 4.00
L7 John Elway 2.00 5.00
L8 Jerry Rice 1.25 3.00
L9 Troy Aikman 1.25 3.00
L10 Ricky Watters .40 1.00
L11 Keyshawn Johnson .60 1.50
L12 Mark Brunell .60 1.50
L13 Dorsey Levens .60 1.50
L14 Steve McNair .60 1.50
L15 Emmitt Smith 1.25 3.00
L16 Marshall Faulk .75 2.00
L17 Priest Holmes 1.00 2.50
L18 Steve Young .75 2.00
L19 Skip Hicks .25 .60
L20 Eddie George .60 1.50
L21 Garrison Hearst .40 1.00
L22 Drew Bledsoe .75 2.00
L23 Warrick Dunn .60 1.50
L24 Eric Moulds .60 1.50
L25 Joey Galloway .40 1.00
L26 Tim Brown .60 1.50
L27 Chris Chandler .40 1.00
L28 Peyton Manning 2.00 5.00
L29 Antonio Freeman .60 1.50
L30 Deion Sanders .60 1.50

1999 Upper Deck Retro Lunchboxes

COMPLETE SET (16) 150.00 250.00
ONE DUAL PLAYER BOX PER CASE
1 Joe Montana 12.50 25.00
2 Ricky Williams 3.00 8.00
3 Randy Moss 6.00 12.00
4 Barry Sanders 7.50 15.00
5 John Elway 7.50 15.00
6 Terrell Davis 4.00 10.00
7 Dan Marino 7.50 15.00
8 Joe Namath 7.50 15.00
9 Joe Montana 12.50 25.00
John Elway
10 Joe Montana 12.50 25.00
Dan Marino
11 John Elway 12.50 25.00
Dan Marino
12 Joe Montana 12.50 25.00
Joe Namath
13 Ricky Williams 4.00 10.00
Tim Couch
14 Joe Namath 12.50 25.00
Dan Marino
15 Tim Couch 12.50 25.00
Dan Marino
16 Barry Sanders 5.00 12.00
Terrell Davis

1999 Upper Deck Retro Old School/New School

STATED PRINT RUN 1000 SER.#'d SETS
*LEVEL 2 CARD/50: 3X TO 8X BASIC INSERT
ON1 Terrell Davis 2.00 5.00
Ricky Williams
ON2 Joe Montana 7.50 20.00
Jake Plummer
ON3 Cris Carter 4.00 10.00
Randy Moss
ON4 Randall Cunningham 3.00 8.00
Daunte Culpepper
ON5 Brett Favre 6.00 15.00
Jon Kitna
ON6 Emmitt Smith 2.50 6.00
Fred Taylor
ON7 Mark Brunell 1.50 4.00
Brock Huard
ON8 John Elway 6.00 15.00
Peyton Manning
ON9 Steve Young 3.00 8.00
Cade McNown
ON10 Don Maynard 1.50 4.00
Kevin Johnson
ON11 Dan Marino 7.50 20.00
Tim Couch
ON12 Jerry Rice 4.00 10.00
Terrell Owens
ON13 Marshall Faulk 3.00 8.00
Edgerrin James
ON14 Dan Fouts 1.50 4.00
Akili Smith
ON15 Barry Sanders 6.00 15.00
Jamal Anderson
ON16 Terry Glenn 1.50 4.00
David Boston
ON17 Deion Sanders 1.50 4.00
Champ Bailey
ON18 Andre Reed 1.00 2.50
Eric Moulds
ON19 Junior Seau 1.50 4.00
Chris Claiborne
ON20 Steve Largent 1.50 4.00
Joey Galloway
ON21 Kordell Stewart 1.50 4.00
Shaun King
ON22 Ricky Watters 1.50 4.00
Kevin Faulk
ON23 Thurman Thomas 1.50 4.00
Warrick Dunn
ON24 Tim Brown 1.50 4.00
Troy Edwards
ON25 Jerome Bettis 1.50 4.00
Cecil Collins
ON26 Isaac Bruce 2.50 6.00
Torry Holt
ON27 Fran Tarkenton 4.00 10.00
Donovan McNabb
ON28 Warren Moon 1.50 4.00
Charlie Batch
ON29 Herman Moore 1.50 4.00
D'Wayne Bates
ON30 Roger Staubach 5.00 12.00
Troy Aikman

1999 Upper Deck Retro Smashmouth

COMPLETE SET (15) 7.50 20.00
STATED ODDS 1:8

*LEVEL 2 CARDS: 5X TO 12X BASIC INSERTS
LEVEL 2 PRINT RUN 100 SER.#'d SETS

S1 Fred Taylor	.60	1.50
S2 Jamal Anderson	.60	1.50
S3 John Elway	2.00	5.00
S4 Brock Huard	.40	1.00
S5 Daunte Culpepper	1.50	4.00
S6 Charlie Batch	.60	1.50
S7 Steve McNair	.60	1.50
S8 Corey Dillon	.60	1.50
S9 Natrone Means	.40	1.00
S10 Randall Cunningham	.60	1.50
S11 Drew Bledsoe	.75	2.00
S12 Jerome Bettis	.60	1.50
S13 Antowain Smith	.60	1.50
S14 Steve Young	.75	2.00
S15 Eddie George	.60	1.50

1999 Upper Deck Retro Throwback Attack

COMPLETE SET (15) 10.00 25.00
STATED ODDS 1:5
*GOLD CARDS: 2X TO 5X BASIC INSERTS
GOLD PRINT RUN 500 SER.#'d SETS

T1 Brett Favre	1.50	4.00
T2 Herman Moore	.30	.75
T3 Troy Aikman	1.00	2.50
T4 Eric Moulds	.50	1.25
T5 Tim Couch	.40	1.00
T6 Terrell Owens	.50	1.25
T7 Champ Bailey	.50	1.25
T8 Kordell Stewart	.30	.75
T9 Mark Brunell	.50	1.25
T10 Curtis Martin	.50	1.25
T11 Torry Holt	1.00	2.50
T12 David Boston	.40	1.00
T13 Doug Flutie	.50	1.25
T14 Edgerrin James	1.50	4.00
T15 Akili Smith	.30	.75

2005 Upper Deck Rookie Debut

Upper Deck Rookie Debut was initially released in early-June 2005. The base set consists of 200-cards including 100-rookies inserted at the rate of 1:3 packs. Hobby boxes contained 28-packs of 6-cards and carried an S.R.P. of $2.99 per pack. Three parallel sets and a variety of inserts can be found seeded in packs highlighted by the Debut Ink and Draft Generations Autographs inserts.

COMP.SET w/o SP's (100) 10.00 20.00
ROOKIE STATED ODDS 1:3

1 Larry Fitzgerald	.30	.75
2 Kurt Warner	.30	.75
3 Anquan Boldin	.25	.60
4 Michael Vick	.30	.75
5 Warrick Dunn	.25	.60
6 Peerless Price	.20	.50
7 Jamal Lewis	.25	.60
8 Derrick Mason	.25	.60
9 Kyle Boller	.25	.60
10 Willis McGahee	.30	.75
11 J.P. Losman	.20	.50
12 Eric Moulds	.20	.50
13 Stephen Davis	.25	.60
14 Jake Delhomme	.25	.60
15 Steve Smith	.30	.75
16 Thomas Jones	.30	.75
17 Brian Urlacher	.30	.75
18 Rex Grossman	.25	.60
19 Carson Palmer	.30	.75
20 Rudi Johnson	.25	.60
21 Chad Johnson	.25	.60
22 Kellen Winslow	.25	.60
23 Luke McCown	.20	.50
24 Lee Suggs	.20	.50
25 Drew Bledsoe	.30	.75
26 Keyshawn Johnson	.25	.60
27 Julius Jones	.20	.50
28 Roy Williams S	.20	.50
29 Jake Plummer	.25	.60
30 Tatum Bell	.20	.50
31 Rod Smith	.25	.60
32 Roy Williams WR	.25	.60
33 Joey Harrington	.25	.60
34 Kevin Jones	.20	.50
35 Brett Favre	.75	2.00
36 Javon Walker	.20	.50
37 Ahman Green	.25	.60
38 David Carr	.20	.50
39 Andre Johnson	.30	.75
40 Domanick Davis	.20	.50
41 Peyton Manning	.60	1.50
42 Marvin Harrison	.30	.75
43 Edgerrin James	.25	.60
44 Reggie Wayne	.30	.75
45 Byron Leftwich	.25	.60
46 Jimmy Smith	.25	.60
47 Fred Taylor	.25	.60
48 Priest Holmes	.25	.60
49 Trent Green	.25	.60
50 Tony Gonzalez	.25	.60
51 Chris Chambers	.25	.60
52 Sammy Morris	.20	.50
53 A.J. Feeley	.20	.50
54 Daunte Culpepper	.25	.60
55 Nate Burleson	.20	.50
56 Michael Bennett	.25	.60
57 Tom Brady	.60	1.50
58 David Givens	.20	.50
59 Corey Dillon	.25	.60
60 Ty Law	.25	.60
61 Aaron Brooks	.20	.50
62 Joe Horn	.25	.60
63 Deuce McAllister	.25	.60
64 Eli Manning	.50	1.25
65 Tiki Barber	.30	.75
66 Amani Toomer	.25	.60
67 Chad Pennington	.30	.75
68 Curtis Martin	.30	.75
69 Santana Moss	.25	.60
70 Jerry Porter	.20	.50
71 Randy Moss	.30	.75
72 Kerry Collins	.25	.60
73 Donovan McNabb	.30	.75
74 Terrell Owens	.30	.75
75 Brian Westbrook	.25	.60
76 Ben Roethlisberger	.50	1.25
77 Hines Ward	.30	.75
78 Jerome Bettis	.30	.75
79 Duce Staley	.25	.60
80 Drew Brees	.30	.75
81 LaDainian Tomlinson	.30	.75
82 Antonio Gates	.30	.75
83 Tim Rattay	.20	.50
84 Kevan Barlow	.20	.50
85 Eric Johnson	.20	.50
86 Matt Hasselbeck	.25	.60
87 Shaun Alexander	.25	.60
88 Darrell Jackson	.20	.50
89 Marc Bulger	.25	.60
90 Marshall Faulk	.30	.75
91 Torry Holt	.25	.60
92 Chris Simms	.25	.60
93 Michael Clayton	.20	.50
94 Michael Pittman	.20	.50
95 Steve McNair	.30	.75
96 Drew Bennett	.25	.60
97 Chris Brown	.20	.50
98 Clinton Portis	.25	.60
99 Patrick Ramsey	.25	.60
100 Laveranues Coles	.20	.50
101 Gino Guidugli RC	.75	2.00
102 Kyle Orton RC	1.25	3.00
103 David Greene RC	.75	2.00
104 Charlie Frye RC	1.25	3.00
105 Andrew Walter RC	1.00	2.50
106 Dan Orlovsky RC	1.25	3.00
107 Jason White RC	1.25	3.00
108 Sonny Cumbie RC	.75	2.00
109 Ronnie Brown RC	1.50	4.00
110 Cadillac Williams RC	1.25	3.00
111 Anthony Davis RC	.75	2.00
112 Kay-Jay Harris RC	.75	2.00
113 Walter Reyes RC	.75	2.00
114 Darren Sproles RC	1.25	3.00
115 Mark Clayton RC	1.25	3.00
116 Braylon Edwards RC	1.50	4.00
117 Charles Frederick RC	.75	2.00
118 Fred Gibson RC	1.00	2.50
119 Craphonso Thorpe RC	.75	2.00
120 Terrence Murphy RC	.75	2.00
121 Antrel Rolle RC	1.25	3.00
122 Marlin Jackson RC	.75	2.00
123 Corey Webster RC	1.00	2.50
124 Travis Johnson RC	.75	2.00
125 Shawne Merriman RC	1.25	3.00
126 Aaron Rodgers RC	12.50	25.00
127 Alex Smith QB RC	2.00	5.00
128 T.A. McLendon RC	.75	2.00
129 Troy Williamson RC	1.00	2.50
130 Ryan Moats RC	1.00	2.50
131 Vernand Morency RC	1.00	2.50
132 Brock Berlin RC	1.00	2.50
133 J.J. Arrington RC	1.00	2.50
134 Frank Gore RC	2.00	5.00
135 Chris Henry RC	1.25	3.00
136 Roscoe Parrish RC	.75	2.00
137 Alex Smith TE RC	.75	2.00
138 Ciatrick Fason RC	.75	2.00
139 Marion Barber RC	1.25	3.00
140 J.R. Russell RC	.75	2.00
141 Heath Miller RC	1.50	4.00
142 Marcus Spears RC	1.00	2.50
143 Alvin Pearman RC	.75	2.00
144 David Pollack RC	1.00	2.50
145 Erasmus James RC	1.00	2.50
146 Noah Herron RC	.75	2.00
147 Dan Cody RC	1.00	2.50
148 Eric Shelton RC	.75	2.00
149 Anttaj Hawthorne RC	.75	2.00
150 Steve Savoy RC	.75	2.00
151 Mike Patterson RC	.75	2.00
152 Kirk Morrison RC	1.25	3.00
153 Airese Currie RC	.75	2.00
154 Derrick Johnson RC	1.00	2.50
155 Darryl Blackstock RC	.75	2.00
156 Mike Williams	1.25	3.00
157 Ernest Shazor RC	1.00	2.50
158 James Butler RC	1.00	2.50
159 Thomas Davis RC	.75	2.00
160 Carlos Rogers RC	1.25	3.00
161 Mark Bradley RC	.75	2.00
162 Jerome Mathis RC	1.25	3.00
163 Justin Miller RC	1.00	2.50
164 Donte Nicholson RC	.75	2.00
165 Derek Anderson RC	1.00	2.50
166 Brandon Browner RC	1.25	3.00
167 Domonique Foxworth RC	1.00	2.50
168 Kevin Burnett RC	1.00	2.50
169 Lorenzo Alexander RC	.75	2.00
170 Oshiomogho Atogwe RC	1.25	3.00
171 Dustin Fox RC	1.00	2.50
172 Jamaal Brimmer RC	.75	2.00
173 Ryan Fitzpatrick RC	2.00	5.00
174 Bill Swancutt RC	.75	2.00
175 Barrett Ruud RC	1.25	3.00
176 Channing Crowder RC	1.00	2.50
177 Timmy Chang RC	1.00	2.50
178 Chris Rix RC	1.00	2.50
179 Justin Tuck RC	1.50	4.00
180 Adam Jones RC	1.00	2.50
181 Bryant McFadden RC	1.00	2.50
182 Taylor Stubblefield RC	.75	2.00
183 Vincent Jackson RC	1.50	4.00
184 Craig Bragg RC	.75	2.00
185 Reggie Brown RC	.75	2.00
186 Roddy White RC	1.50	4.00
187 Jason Campbell RC	1.50	4.00
188 Derek Cameron Wake RC	2.50	6.00
189 Josh Davis RC	.75	2.00
190 Mike Nugent RC	1.00	2.50
191 Maurice Clarett	1.00	2.50
192 Brandon Jacobs RC	1.50	4.00
193 Matt Jones RC	1.25	3.00
194 Chad Owens RC	1.00	2.50
195 Paris Warren RC	1.00	2.50
196 Tab Perry RC	.75	2.00
197 Jovan Haye RC	.75	2.00
198 Cedric Benson RC	1.25	3.00
199 Bobby Purify RC	1.00	2.50
200 Stefan LeFors RC	.75	2.00

2005 Upper Deck Rookie Debut Blue

*VETERANS: 12X TO 30X BASIC CARDS
*ROOKIES: 3X TO 8X BASIC CARDS
BLUE STATED PRINT RUN 15 SETS

2005 Upper Deck Rookie Debut Gold 100

*VETERANS: 5X TO 12X BASIC CARDS
*ROOKIES: 1.2X TO 3X BASIC CARDS
GOLD/100 INSERTED IN HOBBY PACKS

2005 Upper Deck Rookie Debut Gold 150

*VETERANS: 5X TO 12X BASIC CARDS
*ROOKIES: 1.2X TO 3X BASIC CARDS
GOLD/150 INSERTED IN RETAIL PACKS

2005 Upper Deck Rookie Debut Gold Spectrum

*VETS: 8X TO 20X BASIC CARDS
*ROOKIES: 2X TO 5X BASIC CARDS
GOLD SPECTRUM PRINT RUN 50 SER.#'d SETS

2005 Upper Deck Rookie Debut All-Pros

COMPLETE SET (30) 12.50 30.00
STATED ODDS 1:4
*BLUE/15: 2.5X TO 6X BASIC INSERTS
BLUE PRINT RUN 15 SETS
*GOLD/100: .8X TO 2X BASIC INSERTS
GOLD PRINT RUN 100 SER.#'d SETS
*GOLD SPECT/50: 1.2X TO 3X BASIC INSERTS
GOLD SPECTRUM PRINT RUN 50 SETS

AP1 Peyton Manning	2.00	5.00
AP2 Donovan McNabb	1.00	2.50
AP3 Michael Vick	1.00	2.50
AP4 Tom Brady	2.00	5.00
AP5 Daunte Culpepper	.75	2.00
AP6 Drew Brees	1.00	2.50
AP7 Tiki Barber	1.00	2.50
AP8 Brian Westbrook	.75	2.00
AP9 Ahman Green	.75	2.00
AP10 Rudi Johnson	.75	2.00
AP11 LaDainian Tomlinson	1.00	2.50
AP12 Jerome Bettis	1.00	2.50
AP13 Hines Ward	1.00	2.50
AP14 Torry Holt	.75	2.00
AP15 Joe Horn	.75	2.00
AP16 Muhsin Muhammad	.75	2.00
AP17 Marvin Harrison	1.00	2.50
AP18 Antonio Gates	1.00	2.50
AP19 Tony Gonzalez	.75	2.00
AP20 Javon Walker	.60	1.50
AP21 Jason Witten	1.00	2.50
AP22 Alge Crumpler	.75	2.00
AP23 Andre Johnson	1.00	2.50
AP24 Ed Reed	.75	2.00
AP25 Champ Bailey	.75	2.00
AP26 Takeo Spikes	.60	1.50
AP27 Allen Rossum	.60	1.50
AP28 Terrence McGee	.75	2.00
AP29 Troy Polamalu	1.25	3.00
AP30 Roy Williams S	.60	1.50

2005 Upper Deck Rookie Debut Ink

STATED ODDS 1:28 HOB, 1:168 RET
*LIMITED: .6X TO 1.5X BASIC AU
*LIMITED: .5X TO 1.2X BASIC AU SP
LIMITEDD ODDS 6:1008 H, 6:3024 R

DIAD Anthony Davis	5.00	12.00
DIAH Anttaj Hawthorne SP	6.00	15.00
DIAN Antrel Rolle	8.00	20.00
DIAR Aaron Rodgers SP	175.00	300.00
DIAS Alex Smith QB SP	25.00	60.00
DIAW Andrew Walter	6.00	15.00
DIBE Braylon Edwards SP	15.00	40.00
DIBJ Brandon Jacobs	10.00	25.00
DIBR Barrett Ruud	8.00	20.00
DICB Cedric Benson SP	12.00	30.00
DICD Charles Frederick	5.00	12.00
DICF Charlie Frye	8.00	20.00
DICH Chris Henry SP	10.00	25.00
DICI Ciatrick Fason	5.00	12.00
DICO Corey Webster	6.00	15.00
DICR Carlos Rogers	8.00	20.00
DICT Craphonso Thorpe	5.00	12.00
DICW Cadillac Williams	12.00	30.00
DIDC Dan Cody	6.00	15.00
DIDG David Greene SP	6.00	15.00
DIDO Dan Orlovsky		
DIDP David Pollack SP	8.00	20.00
DIDS Darren Sproles SP	10.00	25.00
DIEJ Erasmus James	6.00	15.00
DIFG Fred Gibson	6.00	15.00
DIFR Frank Gore	12.00	30.00
DIJA J.J. Arrington	6.00	15.00
DIJB James Butler	6.00	15.00
DIJR J.R. Russell	5.00	12.00
DIJW Jason White	8.00	20.00
DIKH Kay-Jay Harris	5.00	12.00
DIKO Kyle Orton	8.00	20.00
DIMB Marion Barber	8.00	20.00
DIMC Mark Clayton	6.00	15.00
DIMJ Marlin Jackson	5.00	12.00
DIMW Mike Williams	8.00	20.00
DIRB Ronnie Brown SP	25.00	60.00
DIRM Ryan Moats	5.00	12.00
DIRP Roscoe Parrish		
DIRW Roddy White SP	12.00	30.00
DISC Sonny Cumbie	5.00	12.00
DITA T.A. McLendon	5.00	12.00
DITD Thomas Davis	5.00	12.00
DITM Terrence Murphy	5.00	12.00
DITS Taylor Stubblefield	5.00	12.00
DITW Troy Williamson SP	8.00	20.00
DIVM Vernand Morency	5.00	12.00
DIWR Walter Reyes	5.00	12.00

2005 Upper Deck Rookie Debut Draft Generations Autographs

UNPRICED PRINT RUN 10 SER.#'d SETS

2005 Upper Deck Rookie Debut Rookie of the Year Predictors

STATED ODDS 1:14

ROY1 Mike Williams	.60	1.50
ROY2 Jerome Mathis	.60	1.50
ROY3 Brandon Jacobs	.75	2.00
ROY4 Andrew Walter	.50	1.25
ROY5 Aaron Rodgers	7.50	15.00
ROY6 Cadillac Williams WIN	12.00	30.00
ROY7 Kyle Orton	.60	1.50
ROY8 Ronnie Brown	.75	2.00
ROY9 Troy Williamson	.50	1.25
ROY10 Craphonso Thorpe	.40	1.00
ROY11 Mark Clayton	.60	1.50
ROY12 Charlie Frye	.60	1.50
ROY13 David Greene	.40	1.00
ROY14 Vernand Morency	.50	1.25
ROY15 Chris Henry	.60	1.50
ROY16 Dan Orlovsky	.60	1.50
ROY17 Anthony Davis	.40	1.00
ROY18 Kay-Jay Harris	.40	1.00
ROY19 Walter Reyes	.40	1.00
ROY20 Darren Sproles	.60	1.50
ROY21 Fred Gibson	.50	1.25
ROY22 Terrence Murphy	.40	1.00
ROY23 Alex Smith QB	1.00	2.50
ROY24 Ryan Moats	.50	1.25
ROY25 Marion Barber	.60	1.50
ROY26 Frank Gore	1.00	2.50
ROY27 Taylor Stubblefield	.40	1.00
ROY28 Alex Smith TE	.40	1.00
ROY29 Charles Frederick	.40	1.00
ROY30 Roscoe Parrish	.40	1.00
ROY31 Roddy White	.75	2.00
ROY32 Ciatrick Fason	.40	1.00
ROY33 T.A. McLendon	.40	1.00
ROY34 J.J. Arrington	.50	1.25
ROY35 Derek Anderson	.50	1.25
ROY36 Stefan LeFors	.40	1.00
ROY37 Reggie Brown	.40	1.00
ROY38 Craig Bragg	.40	1.00
ROY39 J.R. Russell	.40	1.00
ROY40 Heath Miller	.75	2.00
ROY41 Jason Campbell	.75	2.00
ROY42 Offensive Field	.40	1.00

2005 Upper Deck Rookie Debut Saturday Swatches

STATED ODDS 1:28
*LIMITED: .5X TO 1.2X BASIC JERSEYS
LIMITED ODDS 4:168H, 4:504R
*PATCHES: 1.2X TO 3X BASIC JERSEYS
PATCHES PRINT RUN 50 SER.#'d SETS

SAAN Antrel Rolle	3.00	8.00
SABP Bobby Purify	3.00	8.00
SACO Chad Owens	3.00	8.00
SACR Carlos Rogers	3.00	8.00
SACW Cadillac Williams	5.00	12.00
SADA Derek Anderson	4.00	10.00
SADN Donte Nicholson	3.00	8.00
SADO Dan Orlovsky	3.00	8.00
SAES Ernest Shazor	3.00	8.00
SAFR Frank Gore	6.00	15.00
SAJR J.R. Russell	3.00	8.00
SAKO Kyle Orton	3.00	8.00
SAMC Mark Clayton	3.00	8.00
SAMS Marcus Spears	3.00	8.00
SAPW Paris Warren	3.00	8.00
SARB Ronnie Brown	10.00	25.00
SARM Ryan Moats	3.00	8.00
SARP Roscoe Parrish	3.00	8.00
SASL Stefan LeFors	3.00	8.00
SAST Santonio Thomas	3.00	8.00
SATC Timmy Chang	3.00	8.00
SATP Tab Perry	3.00	8.00
SATS Taylor Stubblefield	3.00	8.00
SAVM Vernand Morency	3.00	8.00

2005 Upper Deck Rookie Debut Sunday Swatches

STATED ODDS 1:28

SUAB Aaron Brooks	3.00	8.00
SUAL Ashley Lelie	3.00	8.00
SUAQ Anquan Boldin	3.00	8.00
SUBL Byron Leftwich	5.00	12.00
SUBR Ben Roethlisberger	10.00	25.00
SUCG Chad Pennington	5.00	12.00
SUCL Clinton Portis	5.00	12.00
SUCM Curtis Martin	5.00	12.00
SUCP Carson Palmer	5.00	12.00
SUCR Charles Rogers	3.00	8.00
SUDC David Carr	5.00	12.00
SUDM Derrick Mason	3.00	8.00
SUDU Daunte Culpepper	5.00	12.00
SUHW Hines Ward	5.00	12.00
SUJH Joey Harrington	5.00	12.00
SUJL Jamal Lewis	5.00	12.00
SUJS Jeremy Shockey	5.00	12.00
SUJW Javon Walker	3.00	8.00
SULT LaDainian Tomlinson	5.00	12.00
SUMA Matt Hasselbeck	3.00	8.00
SUMH Marvin Harrison	5.00	12.00
SUMV Michael Vick	6.00	15.00
SUPH Priest Holmes	5.00	12.00
SUPM Peyton Manning	6.00	15.00
SUPP Peerless Price	3.00	8.00
SURG Rex Grossman	3.00	8.00
SURW Roy Williams S	5.00	12.00
SUTB Tom Brady	7.50	20.00
SUTH Torry Holt	5.00	12.00
SUTO Terrell Owens	5.00	12.00

2006 Upper Deck Rookie Debut

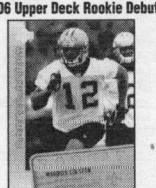

This 260-card set was released in October, 2006. The set was issued into the hobby in six-card packs which came 28 packs to a box. The first 100 cards in the set feature veterans in team alphabetical order while cards numbered 201-260 feature 2006 rookies. Within the rookie subset, cards numbered 101-200 were issued at a stated rate of one per pack, and cards numbered 201-260 were signed by the player and issued to a stated rate of one in 28. A few players in the autograph subset signed fewer cards than the rest of the players and those production numbers, for those specific players, which Upper Deck released are notated in our checklist.

COMP.SET w/o RC's (100) 10.00 25.00
101-200 ROOKIES ONE PER PACK
201-260 AU ROOKIE ODDS 1:28

1 Anquan Boldin	.25	.60
2 Larry Fitzgerald	.30	.75
3 Edgerrin James	.25	.60
4 Warrick Dunn	.25	.60
5 Alge Crumpler	.25	.60
6 Michael Vick	.30	.75
7 Jamal Lewis	.25	.60
8 Derrick Mason	.25	.60
9 Steve McNair	.25	.60
10 Willis McGahee	.25	.60
11 Lee Evans	.25	.60
12 J.P. Losman	.25	.60
13 Steve Smith	.30	.75
14 Jake Delhomme	.25	.60
15 DeShaun Foster	.25	.60
16 Rex Grossman	.25	.60
17 Brian Urlacher	.30	.75
18 Thomas Jones	.25	.60
19 Carson Palmer	.30	.75
20 Chad Johnson	.25	.60
21 T.J. Houshmandzadeh	.25	.60
22 Rudi Johnson	.25	.60
23 Charlie Frye	.25	.60
24 Reuben Droughns*	.25	.60
25 Braylon Edwards	.25	.60
26 Terrell Owens	.30	.75
27 Julius Jones	.20	.50
28 Drew Bledsoe	.30	.75
29 Terry Glenn	.25	.60
30 Jake Plummer	.25	.60
31 Tatum Bell	.20	.50
32 Javon Walker	.25	.60
33 Kevin Jones	.20	.50
34 Roy Williams WR	.25	.60
35 Jon Kitna	.25	.60
36 Brett Favre	.60	1.50
37 Donald Driver	.30	.75
38 Ahman Green	.25	.60
39 David Carr	.20	.50
40 Domanick Davis	.20	.50
41 Andre Johnson	.30	.75
42 Peyton Manning	.50	1.25
43 Reggie Wayne	.25	.60
44 Marvin Harrison	.30	.75
45 Byron Leftwich	.25	.60
46 Greg Jones	.20	.50
47 Ernest Wilford	.20	.50
48 Trent Green	.25	.60
49 Larry Johnson	.25	.60
50 Tony Gonzalez	.25	.60
51 Daunte Culpepper	.25	.60
52 Ronnie Brown	.30	.75
53 Chris Chambers	.25	.60
54 Brad Johnson	.25	.60
55 Chester Taylor	.25	.60
56 Troy Williamson	.20	.50
57 Tom Brady	.50	1.25
58 Deion Branch	.25	.60
59 Corey Dillon	.25	.60
60 Drew Brees	.30	.75
61 Deuce McAllister	.25	.60
62 Joe Horn	.25	.60
63 Eli Manning	.40	1.00
64 Tiki Barber	.30	.75
65 Plaxico Burress	.25	.60
66 Michael Strahan	.25	.60
67 Chad Pennington	.25	.60
68 Curtis Martin	.30	.75
69 Jonathan Vilma	.25	.60
70 Aaron Brooks	.25	.60
71 Randy Moss	.30	.75
72 LaMont Jordan	.25	.60
73 Donovan McNabb	.30	.75
74 Brian Westbrook	.25	.60
75 L.J. Smith	.20	.50
76 Ben Roethlisberger	.40	1.00
77 Hines Ward	.30	.75
78 Willie Parker	.25	.60
79 LaDainian Tomlinson	.30	.75
80 Philip Rivers	.30	.75
81 Antonio Gates	.30	.75
82 Alex Smith QB	.30	.75
83 Antonio Bryant	.20	.50
84 Frank Gore	.30	.75
85 Matt Hasselbeck	.25	.60
86 Shaun Alexander	.25	.60
87 Nate Burleson	.20	.50
88 Julian Peterson	.20	.50
89 Torry Holt	.25	.60
90 Marc Bulger	.25	.60
91 Steven Jackson	.30	.75
92 Cadillac Williams	.25	.60
93 Chris Simms	.25	.60
94 Joey Galloway	.25	.60
95 Drew Bennett	.25	.60
96 David Givens	.25	.60
97 Chris Brown	.20	.50
98 Clinton Portis	.30	.75
99 Santana Moss	.25	.60
100 Antwaan Randle El	.25	.60
101 Todd Watkins RC	1.00	2.50
102 Damarius Bilbo RC	1.25	3.00
103 Troy Bergeron RC	1.25	3.00
104 Jerious Norwood RC	1.25	3.00
105 Adam Jennings RC	1.25	3.00
106 Haloti Ngata RC	1.50	4.00
107 Ed Hinkel RC	1.50	4.00
108 P.J. Daniels RC	1.00	2.50
109 Quinn Sypniewski RC	1.25	3.00
110 Donte Whitner RC	1.50	4.00
111 John McCargo RC	1.00	2.50
112 Chris Denney RC	1.00	2.50
113 Richard Marshall RC	1.00	2.50
114 Brett Basanez RC	1.50	4.00
115 Nate Salley RC	1.25	3.00
116 Jeff King RC	1.25	3.00
117 Danieal Manning RC	1.50	4.00
118 Devin Hester RC	3.00	8.00
119 P.J. Pope RC	1.50	4.00
120 Johnathan Joseph RC	1.25	3.00
121 Andrew Whitworth RC	1.00	2.50
122 Ethan Kilmer RC	1.25	3.00
123 Bennie Brazell RC	1.25	3.00
124 Erik Meyer RC	1.25	3.00
125 J.D. Runnels RC	1.25	3.00
126 Kamerion Wimbley RC	1.50	4.00
127 D'Qwell Jackson RC	1.25	3.00
128 Lawrence Vickers RC	1.25	3.00
129 Bobby Carpenter RC	1.00	2.50
130 Demetrius Summers RC	1.00	2.50
131 Tony Scheffler RC	1.50	4.00
132 Domenik Hixon RC	1.50	4.00
133 Daniel Bullocks RC	1.50	4.00
134 Joe Klopfenstein RC	1.00	2.50
135 Joel Klatt RC	1.25	3.00
136 Daryn Colledge RC	1.50	4.00
137 Brandon Marshall RC	1.50	4.00
138 Brandon Williams RC	1.00	2.50
139 Ingle Martin RC	1.25	3.00
140 Matt Baker RC	1.50	4.00
141 David Anderson RC	1.25	3.00
142 Charles Spencer RC	1.00	2.50
143 Wali Lundy RC	1.25	3.00
144 Mario Williams RC	1.50	4.00
145 David Kirtman RC	1.25	3.00
146 Tamba Hali RC	1.50	4.00
147 Bernard Pollard RC	1.25	3.00
148 Derrick Ross RC	1.25	3.00
149 Jeff Webb RC	1.25	3.00
150 De'Arrius Howard RC	1.50	4.00
151 Chris Hannon RC	1.25	3.00
152 Jason Allen RC	1.25	3.00
153 Devin Aromashodu RC	1.50	4.00
154 Cedric Griffin RC	1.25	3.00
155 Ryan Cook RC	1.25	3.00
156 Jason Carter RC	1.25	3.00
157 Barrick Nealy RC	1.25	3.00
158 Wendell Mathis RC	1.25	3.00
159 David Thomas RC	1.25	3.00
160 Garrett Mills RC	1.50	4.00
161 Roman Harper RC	1.25	3.00
162 Marques Colston RC	3.00	8.00
163 Travis Wilson RC	1.00	2.50
164 Anthony Mix RC	1.25	3.00
165 Nick Mangold RC	1.25	3.00
166 Brett Elliott RC	1.50	4.00
167 Antonio Cromartie RC	1.50	4.00
168 Kevin McMahan RC	1.25	3.00
169 Derek Hagan RC	1.25	3.00
170 Marcedes Lewis RC	1.50	4.00
171 Kent Smith RC	1.50	4.00
172 John Madsen RC	1.50	4.00
173 Charlie Whitehurst RC	1.50	4.00
174 Deuce Lutui RC	1.25	3.00
175 Jeremy Bloom RC	1.25	3.00
176 Cedric Humes RC	1.00	2.50
177 Jason Avant RC	1.00	2.50
178 Brodie Croyle RC	1.50	4.00
179 Marcus McNeill RC	1.25	3.00
180 Manny Lawson RC	1.25	3.00
181 Delanie Walker RC	1.50	4.00
182 Kelly Jennings RC	1.25	3.00
183 Darryl Tapp RC	1.25	3.00
184 Ben Obomanu RC	1.50	4.00
185 Travis Lulay RC	1.25	3.00
186 Matt Henshaw RC	1.25	3.00
187 Clinton Solomon RC	1.25	3.00
188 Marques Hagans RC	1.00	2.50
189 Davin Joseph RC	1.25	3.00
190 Jeremy Trueblood RC	1.25	3.00
191 T.J. Williams RC	1.50	4.00
192 Alan Zemaitis RC	1.50	4.00
193 Quinton Ganther RC	1.00	2.50
194 Cody Hodges RC	1.25	3.00
195 Jesse Mahelona RC	1.25	3.00
196 Rocky McIntosh RC	1.25	3.00
197 Mike Espy RC	1.50	4.00
198 Willie Reid RC	1.25	3.00
199 Jonathan Orr RC	1.25	3.00
200 Joe Rubin RC	1.25	3.00
201 A.J. Hawk AU/200* RC	30.00	60.00
202 Anthony Fasano AU RC	6.00	15.00
203 Ashton Youboty AU RC	4.00	10.00
204 Brad Smith AU RC	5.00	12.00
205 Thomas Howard AU RC	4.00	10.00
206 Will Blackmon AU RC	4.00	10.00
207 Brian Calhoun AU/200* RC	8.00	20.00
208 Terrence Whitehead AU RC	4.00	10.00
209 Brodrick Bunkley AU RC	4.00	10.00
210 Bruce Gradkowski AU RC	6.00	15.00
211 Chad Greenway AU RC	6.00	15.00
212 Chad Jackson AU/200* RC	10.00	25.00
213 Miko Boll AU RC	8.00	20.00
214 Clint Ingram AU RC	6.00	15.00
215 Josh Betts AU RC	4.00	10.00
216 D.J. Shockley AU RC	6.00	15.00
217 D'Brickashaw Ferguson AU RC	5.00	12.00
218 DeAngelo Williams AU/25* RC	60.00	150.00
219 DeMeco Ryans AU RC	5.00	12.00
220 Demetrius Williams AU RC	4.00	10.00
221 Martin Nance AU RC	4.00	10.00
222 Dominique Byrd AU RC	5.00	12.00
223 Drew Olson AU RC	4.00	10.00
224 Ernie Sims AU RC	5.00	12.00
225 Gerald Riggs AU RC	5.00	12.00
226 Greg Jennings AU RC	20.00	40.00
227 Greg Lee AU RC	4.00	10.00
228 Hank Baskett AU RC	5.00	12.00
229 Jay Cutler AU/50* RC	125.00	250.00
230 DonTrell Moore AU RC	4.00	10.00
231 Jerome Harrison AU RC	8.00	20.00
232 Jimmy Williams AU RC	5.00	12.00
233 Darnell Bing AU RC	4.00	10.00
234 Joseph Addai AU RC	25.00	60.00
235 Kellen Clemens AU/200* RC	10.00	25.00
236 Laurence Maroney AU/50* RC	25.00	60.00
237 LenDale White AU/200* RC	15.00	40.00
238 Leon Washington AU RC	8.00	20.00
239 Leonard Pope AU RC	5.00	12.00
240 Cory Rodgers AU RC	4.00	10.00
241 Darrell Hackney AU RC	4.00	10.00
242 Mathias Kiwanuka AU RC	6.00	15.00
243 Matt Leinart AU/50* RC	50.00	120.00
244 Maurice Drew AU/300* RC	15.00	40.00
245 Maurice Stovall AU/300* RC	6.00	15.00
246 Michael Huff AU/300* RC	6.00	15.00
247 Michael Robinson AU RC	4.00	10.00
248 Mike Hass AU RC	4.00	10.00
249 Omar Jacobs AU RC	4.00	10.00
250 Owen Daniels AU RC	6.00	15.00
251 Reggie Bush AU/25* RC	150.00	300.00
252 Reggie McNeal AU RC	4.00	10.00
253 Santonio Holmes AU/120* RC	20.00	50.00
254 Sinorice Moss AU/240* RC	10.00	25.00
255 Tarvaris Jackson AU/300* RC	12.00	30.00
256 Andre Hall AU RC	5.00	12.00
257 Tye Hill AU RC	5.00	12.00
259 Vince Young AU/25* RC	150.00	300.00
260 Winston Justice AU RC	5.00	12.00

2006 Upper Deck Rookie Debut Holofoil

*VETERANS: 2.5X TO 6X BASIC CARDS
*ROOKIES: .8X TO 2X BASIC CARDS
HOLOFOIL/325 ODDS 1:28

2006 Upper Deck Rookie Debut Gold

*GOLD VETS: 5X TO 12X BASIC CARDS
*GOLD ROOKIES: 1.5X TO 4X BASIC CARDS
GOLD/99 INSERTED IN HOT BOXES
GOLD PRINT RUN 99 SER.#'d SETS

2006 Upper Deck Rookie Debut Draft Link

STATED ODDS 1:18 HOB, 1:36 RET

1 John Elway	4.00	10.00
Peyton Manning		
2 Barry Sanders	6.00	15.00
Reggie Bush		
3 Ben Roethlisberger	3.00	8.00
Jay Cutler		
4 Alge Crumpler	1.25	3.00
Joe Klopfenstein		
5 Ronde Barber	1.50	4.00
Ashton Youboty		
6 DeShaun Foster	1.50	4.00
LenDale White		
7 Chris Simms	1.25	3.00
Charlie Whitehurst		
8 Chris Chambers	1.25	3.00
Anthony Fasano		
9 Kevin Curtis	1.25	3.00
Brian Calhoun		
10 Derrick Mason	1.25	3.00
Brandon Marshall		
11 Drew Bledsoe	2.00	5.00
Eli Manning		
12 Keyshawn Johnson	1.50	4.00
Carson Palmer		
13 Greg Jones	1.50	4.00
Maurice Drew		
14 Jason Witten	1.25	3.00
Leonard Pope		
15 Thomas Jones	1.25	3.00
Byron Leftwich		
16 LaMont Jordan	1.50	4.00
Julius Jones		
17 Tom Brady	2.50	6.00
Marc Bulger		
18 Lofa Tatupu	1.50	4.00
DeMeco Ryans		
19 Larry Johnson	2.50	6.00
DeAngelo Williams		
20 Mike Williams	3.00	8.00
Matt Leinart		
21 Muhsin Muhammad	1.50	4.00
Chad Jackson		
22 Nate Burleson	1.25	3.00
Travis Wilson		
23 Reggie Wayne	1.50	4.00
Joseph Addai		
24 Reggie Brown	1.50	4.00
Sinorice Moss		
25 Ryan Moats	1.25	3.00
Brian Calhoun		
26 T.J. Houshmandzadeh	1.25	3.00
David Givens		
27 Philip Rivers	1.50	4.00
Cedric Benson		
28 LaDainian Tomlinson	1.50	4.00
Cadillac Williams		
29 Braylon Edwards	3.00	8.00
Vince Young		
30 Kyle Orton	1.50	4.00
Michael Robinson		
31 Muhsin Muhammad	1.50	4.00
LenDale White		
32 Brandon Lloyd	1.25	3.00
Demetrius Williams		
33 Michael Clayton	1.25	3.00
Tye Hill		
34 Ronnie Brown	5.00	12.00
Reggie Bush		
35 Dan Marino	3.00	8.00
DeAngelo Williams		
36 Tedy Bruschi	1.50	4.00
Clint Ingram		
37 Paul Hornung	1.50	4.00
Jim Plunkett		
38 Len Dawson	2.00	5.00
A.J. Hawk		
39 Gale Sayers	2.00	5.00
Bob Griese		
40 John Hannah	1.25	3.00
D'Brickashaw Ferguson		
41 Winston Justice	1.25	3.00
Dwight Stephenson		
42 Dan Fouts	1.50	4.00
Charlie Whitehurst		
43 Rocket Ismail	1.50	4.00
Jason Avant		
44 Ken Stabler	1.50	4.00
Kellen Clemens		
45 Roger Craig	1.50	4.00
LenDale White		
46 Brian Dawkins	1.50	4.00
Jimmy Williams		
47 Rudi Johnson	1.50	4.00
Leon Washington		
48 Tiki Barber	1.50	4.00
Maurice Drew		
49 Maurice Stovall	1.50	4.00
Steve Smith		
50 Peyton Manning	2.50	6.00
Michael Vick		
51 Lofa Tatupu	1.50	4.00
Darnell Bing		
52 Thomas Jones	1.50	4.00
Tiki Barber		
53 Reggie Wayne	1.50	4.00
Sinorice Moss		
54 Reggie Brown	1.25	3.00
Leonard Pope		
55 Michael Clayton	1.50	4.00
Joseph Addai		
56 Mark Clayton	1.25	3.00
Travis Wilson		
57 Larry Johnson	2.00	5.00
Franco Harris		
58 Muhsin Muhammad	1.25	3.00
Derrick Mason		
59 Chris Simms	3.00	8.00
Vince Young		
60 LaMont Jordan	2.00	5.00
Vernon Davis		
61 LaVar Arrington	1.50	4.00
Julius Peppers		
62 Marshall Faulk	1.50	4.00
Donovan McNabb		
63 David Carr	1.50	4.00
Alex Smith QB		
64 Kevin Jones	1.50	4.00
Heath Miller		
65 Andre Johnson	1.50	4.00
Larry Fitzgerald		
66 Troy Polamalu	2.00	5.00
Jason Allen		
67 J.P. Losman	1.25	3.00
Rex Grossman		
68 Jake Plummer	1.25	3.00
Drew Brees		
69 Clinton Portis	1.50	4.00
Tatum Bell		
70 Deuce McAllister	1.50	4.00
Willis McGahee		
71 Curtis Martin	1.50	4.00
Ahman Green		
72 Reuben Droughns	1.25	3.00
Brian Westbrook		
73 Edgerrin James	1.50	4.00
Charles Woodson		
74 Warrick Dunn	1.25	3.00
Keith Brooking		
75 Ed Reed	1.50	4.00
Steven Jackson		
76 Shaun Alexander	1.50	4.00
Marvin Harrison		
77 Junior Seau	1.50	4.00
Jamal Lewis		
78 Fred Taylor	1.50	4.00
Brian Urlacher		
79 Terry Glenn	1.50	4.00
Roy Williams WR		
80 Randy Moss	1.50	4.00
Matt Jones		
81 Torry Holt	1.25	3.00
Richard Seymour		
82 Hines Ward	1.50	4.00
Terrell Owens		
83 Joey Galloway	1.25	3.00
Plaxico Burress		
84 Donald Driver	1.25	3.00
Ronald Curry		
85 Santana Moss	1.25	3.00
Julian Peterson		
86 Chad Johnson	1.25	3.00
Anquan Boldin		
87 Bubba Franks	1.50	4.00
Jeremy Shockey		
88 Tony Gonzalez	1.25	3.00
Lee Evans		
89 Jonathan Vilma	1.25	3.00
Shawne Merriman		
90 Champ Bailey	1.25	3.00
Troy Williamson		
91 Daunte Culpepper	1.50	4.00
Dwight Freeney		
92 Roy Williams S	1.25	3.00
DeAngelo Hall		
93 Braylon Edwards	1.50	4.00
Jason Avant		
94 Matt Hasselbeck	2.50	6.00
Tom Brady		
95 Deion Branch	1.50	4.00
Greg Jennings		
96 Steve McNair	3.00	8.00
Vince Young		
97 Javon Walker	1.50	4.00
Willie Reid		
98 O.J. McDuffie	1.50	4.00
Santonio Holmes		
99 Chad Pennington	1.25	3.00
Eddie Kennison		
100 Philip Rivers	1.50	4.00
Mario Williams		

2006 Upper Deck Rookie Debut Draft Link Autographs

3 Ben Roethlisberger	90.00	150.00
Jay Cutler		
4 Alge Crumpler	10.00	25.00
Joe Klopfenstein		
5 Ronde Barber		
Ashton Youboty		
6 DeShaun Foster	15.00	40.00
LenDale White		
7 Chris Simms		
Charlie Whitehurst		
9 Kevin Curtis		
Brian Calhoun		
10 Derrick Mason	10.00	25.00
Brandon Marshall		
11 Drew Bledsoe	40.00	80.00
Eli Manning		
12 Keyshawn Johnson	20.00	40.00
Carson Palmer		
13 Greg Jones	20.00	40.00
Maurice Drew		
14 Jason Witten	15.00	30.00
Leonard Pope		
15 Thomas Jones	12.50	30.00
Byron Leftwich		
16 LaMont Jordan	12.50	30.00
Julius Jones		
18 Lofa Tatupu	10.00	25.00
DeMeco Ryans		
19 Larry Johnson	25.00	60.00
DeAngelo Williams		
20 Mike Williams	40.00	100.00
Matt Leinart		
21 Muhsin Muhammad	10.00	25.00
Chad Jackson		
22 Nate Burleson		
Travis Wilson		
23 Reggie Wayne	40.00	80.00
Joseph Addai		
24 Reggie Brown	10.00	25.00
Sinorice Moss		
25 Ryan Moats	10.00	25.00
Brian Calhoun		
27 Philip Rivers	20.00	50.00
Cedric Benson		
28 LaDainian Tomlinson	60.00	100.00
Cadillac Williams		
30 Kyle Orton	10.00	25.00
Michael Robinson		
31 Muhsin Muhammad	15.00	40.00
LenDale White		
33 Michael Clayton	8.00	20.00
Tye Hill		
34 Ronnie Brown	60.00	120.00
Reggie Bush		
46 Brian Dawkins	12.50	30.00
Jimmy Williams		
47 Rudi Johnson		
Leon Washington		
48 Tiki Barber	35.00	60.00
Maurice Drew		
49 Maurice Stovall	30.00	60.00
Steve Smith		
50 Peyton Manning	90.00	150.00
Michael Vick		
51 Lofa Tatupu		
Darnell Bing		
52 Thomas Jones	15.00	40.00
Tiki Barber		
53 Reggie Wayne		
Sinorice Moss		
54 Reggie Brown	10.00	25.00
Leonard Pope		
55 Michael Clayton	25.00	60.00
Joseph Addai		
56 Mark Clayton	20.00	50.00
Travis Wilson		
58 Muhsin Muhammad		
Derrick Mason		
59 Chris Simms	40.00	100.00
Vince Young		
60 LaMont Jordan		
Vernon Davis		
93 Braylon Edwards	15.00	40.00
Jason Avant		
100 Philip Rivers		
Mario Williams		

2006 Upper Deck Rookie Debut Future Star Materials Silver

SILVER STATED ODDS 1:28 HOBBY
*GOLD/125: .5X TO 1.2X SILVER JSYs
GOLD PRINT RUN 125 SER.#'d SETS

FSMBC Brian Calhoun	3.00	8.00
FSMBM Brandon Marshall	3.00	8.00
FSMBW Brandon Williams	3.00	8.00
FSMCJ Chad Jackson	3.00	8.00
FSMCW Charlie Whitehurst	3.00	8.00
FSMDH Derek Hagan	3.00	8.00
FSMDW Demetrius Williams	3.00	8.00
FSMJA Jason Avant	3.00	8.00
FSMJK Joe Klopfenstein	3.00	8.00
FSMJN Jerious Norwood	4.00	10.00
FSMKC Kellen Clemens	3.00	8.00
FSMLW Leon Washington	4.00	10.00
FSMML Matt Leinart	6.00	15.00
FSMMR Michael Robinson	3.00	8.00
FSMMS Maurice Stovall	3.00	8.00
FSMOJ Omar Jacobs	3.00	8.00
FSMRB Reggie Bush	10.00	25.00
FSMSM Sinorice Moss	3.00	8.00
FSMTJ Tarvaris Jackson	3.00	10.00
FSMTW Travis Wilson	3.00	8.00
FSMVY Vince Young	8.00	20.00

2006 Upper Deck Rookie Debut Game Dated

STATED ODDS 1:7 HOB, 1:14 RET

GDDAG Antonio Gates	1.50	4.00
GDDBA Ronde Barber	1.25	3.00
GDDBD Brian Dawkins	1.25	3.00
GDDBE Braylon Edwards	1.25	3.00
GDDBF Brett Favre	3.00	8.00
GDDBL Byron Leftwich	1.25	3.00
GDDBR Ben Roethlisberger	2.00	5.00
GDDCB Cedric Benson	1.25	3.00
GDDCF Charlie Frye	1.25	3.00
GDDCS Chris Simms	1.25	3.00
GDDDB Drew Bennett	1.25	3.00
GDDDF DeShaun Foster	1.25	3.00
GDDDG David Givens	1.25	3.00
GDDDM Derrick Mason	1.25	3.00
GDDEM Eli Manning	2.00	5.00
GDDJJ Julius Jones	1.00	2.50
GDDJO LaMont Jordan	1.25	3.00
GDDJW Jason Witten	1.50	4.00
GDDKC Kevin Curtis	1.25	3.00
GDDKJ Keyshawn Johnson	1.25	3.00
GDDKO Kyle Orton	1.50	4.00
GDDLJ Larry Johnson	1.25	3.00
GDDLT LaDainian Tomlinson	1.50	4.00
GDDMB Marc Bulger	1.25	3.00
GDDMM Muhsin Muhammad	1.25	3.00
GDDMO Ryan Moats	1.00	2.50
GDDMW Mike Williams	1.00	2.50
GDDNB Nate Burleson	1.00	2.50
GDDPM Peyton Manning	2.50	6.00
GDDPR Philip Rivers	1.50	4.00
GDDRB Reggie Brown	1.00	2.50
GDDRJ Rudi Johnson	1.25	3.00
GDDRM Randy Moss	1.50	4.00
GDDRO Ronnie Brown	1.50	4.00
GDDRW Reggie Wayne	1.25	3.00
GDDSS Steve Smith	1.50	4.00
GDDTA Lofa Tatupu	1.25	3.00
GDDTB Tedy Bruschi	1.50	4.00
GDDTH T.J. Houshmandzadeh	1.25	3.00
GDDTI Tiki Barber	1.50	4.00
GDDTJ Thomas Jones	1.25	3.00
GDDWP Willie Parker	1.25	3.00

2006 Upper Deck Rookie Debut Game Dated Autographs

STATED PRINT RUN 40 SER.#'d SETS

GDDAG Antonio Gates	15.00	40.00
GDDBA Ronde Barber	12.50	30.00
GDDBD Brian Dawkins	20.00	50.00
GDDBL Byron Leftwich	10.00	25.00
GDDBR Ben Roethlisberger	60.00	120.00
GDDCB Cedric Benson	12.50	30.00
GDDCF Charlie Frye	10.00	25.00
GDDCS Chris Simms	10.00	25.00
GDDDB Drew Bennett	8.00	20.00
GDDDF DeShaun Foster	10.00	25.00
GDDDG David Givens	12.50	30.00
GDDDM Derrick Mason	10.00	25.00
GDDEM Eli Manning	50.00	100.00
GDDJJ Julius Jones	12.50	30.00
GDDJO LaMont Jordan	10.00	25.00
GDDKC Kevin Curtis	10.00	25.00
GDDKJ Keyshawn Johnson	10.00	25.00
GDDKO Kyle Orton	10.00	25.00
GDDLJ Larry Johnson	12.50	30.00
GDDLT LaDainian Tomlinson	60.00	120.00
GDDMB Marc Bulger	10.00	25.00
GDDMM Muhsin Muhammad	8.00	20.00
GDDMO Ryan Moats	10.00	25.00
GDDMW Mike Williams	12.50	30.00
GDDNB Nate Burleson	10.00	25.00
GDDPM Peyton Manning	60.00	120.00
GDDPR Philip Rivers	20.00	40.00
GDDRB Reggie Brown	10.00	25.00
GDDRO Ronnie Brown	12.50	30.00
GDDRW Reggie Wayne	12.50	30.00
GDDTA Lofa Tatupu	12.50	30.00
GDDTJ Thomas Jones	10.00	25.00

2006 Upper Deck Rookie Debut Rookie Jerseys

INSERTS IN TARGET RETAIL PACKS

63TE A.J. Hawk	4.00	10.00
64TE Brian Calhoun	2.50	6.00
65TE Brandon Marshall	4.00	10.00
66TE Brandon Williams	2.50	6.00
67TE Chad Jackson	2.50	6.00
68TE Charlie Whitehurst	4.00	10.00
69TE Derek Hagan	3.00	8.00
70TE DeAngelo Williams	5.00	12.00
71TE Jason Avant	2.50	6.00
72TE Joe Klopfenstein	2.50	6.00
73TE Jerious Norwood	3.00	8.00
74TE Kellen Clemens	3.00	8.00
75TE Marcedes Lewis	4.00	10.00
76TE Laurence Maroney	3.00	8.00
77TE LenDale White	3.00	8.00
78TE Maurice Drew	6.00	15.00
79TE Michael Huff	3.00	8.00
80TE Matt Leinart	4.00	10.00
81TE Michael Robinson	3.00	8.00
82TE Maurice Stovall	2.50	6.00
83TE Mario Williams	4.00	10.00
84TE Omar Jacobs	2.50	6.00
85TE Reggie Bush	8.00	20.00
86TE Santonio Holmes	5.00	12.00
87TE Sinorice Moss	4.00	10.00
88TE Tarvaris Jackson	4.00	10.00
89TE Travis Wilson	2.50	6.00
90TE Vernon Davis	5.00	12.00
91TE Vince Young	5.00	12.00
92TE Leon Washington	3.00	8.00
93TE Demetrius Williams	3.00	8.00

2006 Upper Deck Rookie Debut Rookie Photo Shoot Flashback Silver

SILVER ODDS 1:4 HOB, 1:7 RET
*GOLD/99: .6X TO 1.5X SILVER INSERTS
GOLD/99 INSERTED IN HOT BOXES

RPF1 Ahman Green	1.00	2.50
RPF2 Alex Smith QB	1.25	3.00
RPF3 James Farrior	.75	2.00
RPF4 Andre Johnson	1.25	3.00
RPF5 Anquan Boldin	1.00	2.50
RPF6 Antonio Bryant	.75	2.00
RPF7 Antwaan Randle El	1.00	2.50
RPF8 Ben Roethlisberger	1.50	4.00
RPF9 Bobby Engram	.75	2.00
RPF10 Keith Brooking	.75	2.00
RPF11 Braylon Edwards	1.00	2.50
RPF12 Brian Urlacher	1.25	3.00
RPF13 Byron Leftwich	1.00	2.50
RPF14 Cadillac Williams	1.00	2.50
RPF15 Carson Palmer	1.25	3.00
RPF16 Chad Johnson	1.00	2.50
RPF17 Chad Pennington	1.00	2.50
RPF18 Champ Bailey	1.00	2.50
RPF19 Brian Griese	1.00	2.50
RPF20 Chris McAlister	.75	2.00
RPF21 Chris Chambers	1.00	2.50
RPF22 Takeo Spikes	.75	2.00
RPF23 Corey Dillon	1.00	2.50
RPF24 Curtis Martin	1.25	3.00
RPF25 Dallas Clark	1.00	2.50
RPF26 Bubba Franks	.75	2.00
RPF27 Daunte Culpepper	1.00	2.50
RPF28 Antoine Winfield	.75	2.00
RPF29 David Garrard	1.00	2.50
RPF30 DeAngelo Hall	1.00	2.50
RPF31 Dan Morgan	.75	2.00
RPF32 DeShaun Foster	1.00	2.50
RPF33 Deuce McAllister	1.00	2.50
RPF34 Dewayne Robertson	.75	2.00
RPF35 Kevan Barlow	.75	2.00
RPF36 Donovan McNabb	1.25	3.00
RPF37 Donte Stallworth	.75	2.00
RPF38 Drew Brees	1.25	3.00
RPF39 Eddie Kennison	.75	2.00
RPF40 Edgerrin James	1.00	2.50
RPF41 Eli Manning	1.50	4.00
RPF42 Eric Moulds	.75	2.00
RPF43 Fred Taylor	1.00	2.50
RPF44 Greg Jones	.75	2.00
RPF45 Hines Ward	1.25	3.00
RPF46 J.P. Losman	1.00	2.50
RPF47 Jake Plummer	1.00	2.50
RPF48 Jamal Lewis	1.00	2.50
RPF49 Javon Walker	1.00	2.50
RPF50 Jeremy Shockey	1.25	3.00
RPF51 Jerry Porter	.75	2.00
RPF52 Joey Galloway	1.00	2.50
RPF53 Jonathan Ogden	.75	2.00
RPF54 Julius Jones	.75	2.00
RPF55 Julius Peppers	1.00	2.50
RPF56 Kevin Curtis	1.00	2.50
RPF57 Kevin Jones	.75	2.00
RPF58 Kyle Boller	1.00	2.50
RPF59 LaDainian Tomlinson	1.25	3.00
RPF60 Corey Simon	.60	1.50
RPF61 Larry Fitzgerald	1.25	3.00
RPF62 Larry Johnson	1.00	2.50
RPF63 Jevon Kearse	1.00	2.50
RPF64 Laveranues Coles	.75	2.00
RPF65 Todd Pinkston	.75	2.00
RPF66 Marvin Harrison	1.25	3.00
RPF67 Michael Vick	1.25	3.00
RPF68 Mike Alstott	.75	2.00
RPF69 Nate Burleson	.75	2.00
RPF70 Orlando Pace	.75	2.00
RPF71 Peyton Manning	2.00	5.00
RPF72 Philip Rivers	1.25	3.00
RPF73 Plaxico Burress	1.00	2.50
RPF74 Kyle Orton	1.25	3.00
RPF75 Reggie Wayne	1.00	2.50
RPF76 Reuben Droughns	1.00	2.50
RPF77 Rex Grossman	1.00	2.50
RPF78 Richard Seymour	.75	2.00
RPF79 Ronnie Brown	1.25	3.00
RPF80 Roy Williams WR	1.00	2.50
RPF81 Roy Williams S	1.00	2.50
RPF82 Rudi Johnson	1.00	2.50
RPF83 Santana Moss	1.00	2.50
RPF84 Koren Robinson	.75	2.00
RPF85 Shaun Alexander	1.00	2.50
RPF86 Simeon Rice	.75	2.00
RPF87 Stephen Davis	1.00	2.50
RPF88 Joe Jurevicius	.75	2.00
RPF89 Steven Jackson	1.25	3.00
RPF90 T.J. Duckett	.75	2.00
RPF91 Tatum Bell	.75	2.00
RPF92 Terrell Suggs	1.00	2.50
RPF93 Terry Glenn	1.00	2.50
RPF94 Thomas Jones	1.00	2.50
RPF95 Todd Heap	1.00	2.50
RPF96 Tony Gonzalez	1.00	2.50
RPF97 Torry Holt	1.00	2.50
RPF98 Walter Jones	.75	2.00
RPF99 Warrick Dunn	1.00	2.50
RPF100 Willis McGahee	1.00	2.50

2006 Upper Deck Rookie Debut Star Materials Silver

SILVER ODDS 1:28 HOBBY
*GOLD/125: .5X TO 1.2X SILVER JSYs
GOLD/125 INSERTED IN HOT BOXES

SMBE Cedric Benson	3.00	8.00
SMBR Mark Brunell	3.00	8.00
SMCB Chris Brown	3.00	8.00
SMCJ Chad Johnson	3.00	8.00
SMCP Clinton Portis	4.00	10.00
SMCS Chris Simms	3.00	8.00
SMDC Daunte Culpepper	4.00	10.00
SMDD Domanick Davis	3.00	8.00
SMDM Donovan McNabb	4.00	10.00
SMDS Donte Stallworth	3.00	8.00
SMFT Fred Taylor	3.00	8.00
SMJH Joe Horn	3.00	8.00
SMJJ Julius Jones	4.00	10.00
SMJL Jamal Lewis	3.00	8.00
SMKB Kyle Boller	3.00	8.00
SMMB Marc Bulger	3.00	8.00
SMMH Marvin Harrison	4.00	10.00
SMRE Antwaan Randle El	3.00	8.00
SMRW Reggie Wayne	3.00	8.00
SMSH Jeremy Shockey	4.00	10.00
SMWM Willis McGahee	3.00	8.00

2008 Upper Deck Rookie Exclusives

COMPLETE SET (100)	12.50	30.00
RE1 Curtis Lofton	.12	.30
RE2 Ryan Clady	.15	.40
RE3 Allen Patrick	.12	.30
RE4 Kevin O'Connell	.12	.30
RE5 Aqib Talib	.15	.40
RE6 Davone Bess	.15	.40
RE7 Bruce Davis	.12	.30
RE8 Kalvin McRae	.10	.25
RE9 Chevis Jackson	.10	.25
RE10 Chris Johnson	.40	1.00
RE11 Craig Steltz	.12	.30
RE12 Alex Brink	.15	.40
RE13 DaJuan Morgan	.12	.30
RE14 DeMario Pressley	.12	.30
RE15 Chauncey Washington	.12	.30
RE16 Jacob Hester	.15	.40
RE17 Dustin Keller	.15	.40
RE18 Erik Ainge	.15	.40
RE19 Frank Okam	.10	.25
RE20 Kevin Smith	.15	.40
RE21 Harry Douglas	.12	.30
RE22 Kellen Davis	.10	.25
RE23 J Leman	.10	.25
RE24 Jamaal Charles	.25	.60
RE25 Jermichael Finley	.15	.40
RE26 Joe Flacco	.50	1.25
RE27 John David Booty	.12	.30
RE28 Jonathan Hefney	.12	.30
RE29 Jerome Felton	.10	.25
RE30 Justin Forsett	.15	.40
RE31 Keenan Burton	.10	.25
RE32 Geno Hayes	.10	.25
RE33 Keon Lattimore	.12	.30
RE34 Josh Johnson	.15	.40
RE35 Marcus Monk	.12	.30
RE36 Mario Urrutia	.10	.25
RE37 Martin Rucker	.12	.30
RE38 Matt Forte	.25	.60
RE39 Paul Hubbard	.12	.30
RE40 Phillip Merling	.12	.30
RE41 Quintin Demps	.15	.40
RE42 Ray Rice	.30	.75
RE43 Ryan Grice-Mullins	.10	.25
RE44 Anthony Morelli	.12	.30
RE45 Shawn Crable	.10	.25
RE46 Tashard Choice	.12	.30
RE47 Thomas Brown	.12	.30
RE48 Adrian Arrington	.12	.30
RE49 Quentin Groves	.12	.30
RE50 Xavier Adibi	.10	.25
RE51 Jordy Nelson	.20	.50
RE52 Derrick Harvey	.10	.25
RE53 Andre Caldwell	.12	.30
RE54 Antoine Cason	.15	.40
RE55 Dominique Rodgers-Cromartie	.15	.40
RE56 Leodis McKelvin	.12	.30
RE57 Calais Campbell	.12	.30
RE58 Chad Henne	.15	.40
RE59 Chris Ellis	.10	.25
RE60 Vernon Gholston	.12	.30
RE61 Jerome Simpson	.15	.40
RE62 Dexter Jackson	.12	.30
RE63 DeJuan Tribble	.10	.25
RE64 Dennis Keyes	.10	.25
RE65 Donnie Avery	.12	.30
RE66 Dre Moore	.12	.30
RE67 Earl Bennett	.15	.40
RE68 Eddie Royal	.15	.40
RE69 Felix Jones	.25	.60
RE70 Gosder Cherilus	.12	.30
RE71 Colt Brennan	.15	.40
RE72 Jack Ikegwuonu	.10	.25
RE73 Jacob Tamme	.15	.40
RE74 James Hardy	.12	.30
RE75 Jerod Mayo	.15	.40
RE76 Andre Woodson	.50	1.25
RE77 Brian Brohm	.50	1.25
RE78 Devin Thomas	.40	1.00
RE79 Mike Jenkins	.50	1.25
RE80 Matt Ryan	2.00	5.00
RE81 Darren McFadden	1.25	3.00
RE82 Jonathan Stewart	.75	2.00
RE83 Mike Hart	.50	1.25
RE84 DeSean Jackson	1.00	2.50
RE85 Early Doucet	.40	1.00
RE86 Lavelle Hawkins	.30	.75
RE87 Limas Sweed	.50	1.25
RE88 Jake Long	.50	1.25
RE89 Sam Baker	.30	.75
RE90 Glenn Dorsey	.50	1.25
RE91 Sedrick Ellis	.50	1.25
RE92 Chris Long	.50	1.25
RE93 Lawrence Jackson	.40	1.00
RE94 Ali Highsmith	.30	.75
RE95 Dan Connor	.50	1.25
RE96 Kenny Phillips	.50	1.25
RE97 Keith Rivers	.50	1.25
RE98 Justin King	.40	1.00
RE99 Dennis Dixon	.50	1.25
RE100 Fred Davis	.50	1.25

2008 Upper Deck Rookie Exclusives Photo Shoot Flashbacks

COMPLETE SET (30)	5.00	12.00
STATED ODDS 2:1		
1 Carson Palmer	.40	1.00
2 Matt Leinart	.40	1.00
3 Plaxico Burress	.30	.75
4 Brian Urlacher	.40	1.00
5 Drew Brees	.40	1.00
6 LaDainian Tomlinson	.40	1.00
7 Julius Peppers	.30	.75
8 Antwaan Randle El	.25	.60
9 Jeremy Shockey	.30	.75
10 Terrell Suggs	.25	.60
11 Dallas Clark	.30	.75
12 Willis McGahee	.30	.75
13 Larry Johnson	.30	.75
14 Anquan Boldin	.30	.75
15 Philip Rivers	.40	1.00
16 Steven Jackson	.40	1.00
17 Eli Manning	.40	1.00
18 Ben Roethlisberger	.40	1.00
19 Kellen Winslow	.30	.75
20 Ronnie Brown	.30	.75
21 Braylon Edwards	.30	.75
22 Adrian Peterson	.60	1.50
23 Frank Gore	.30	.75
24 Clinton Portis	.30	.75
25 Santonio Holmes	.30	.75
26 Reggie Bush	.40	1.00
27 Vince Young	.30	.75
28 Gaines Adams	.25	.60
29 Calvin Johnson	.40	1.00
30 JaMarcus Russell	.30	.75

2009 Upper Deck Rookie Exclusives

1 Alex Magee	.12	.30
2 Rashad Johnson	.12	.30
3 Cody Brown	.10	.25
4 Clint Sintim	.15	.40
5 Cornelius Ingram	.10	.25
6 Roy Miller	.12	.30
7 Kevin Barnes	.12	.30
8 DeAngelo Smith	.12	.30
9 Asher Allen	.12	.30
10 Bradley Fletcher	.12	.30
11 Patrick Turner	.12	.30
12 Travis Beckum	.12	.30
13 Sherrod Martin	.12	.30
14 Paul Kruger	.12	.30
15 Jairus Byrd	.15	.40
16 Alphonso Smith	.12	.30
17 Jason Williams	.15	.40
18 Larry English	.15	.40
19 David Veikune	.12	.30
20 Connor Barwin	.15	.40
21 B.J. Raji	.15	.40
22 Richard Quinn	.12	.30
23 Jarett Dillard	.15	.40
24 Johnny Knox	.25	.60
25 Austin Collie	.15	.40
26 Quinn Johnson	.12	.30
27 Gartrell Johnson	.10	.25
28 Andre Brown	.10	.25
29 Mike Goodson	.15	.40
30 Tom Brandstater	.15	.40
31 Louis Delmas	.15	.40
32 Stephen McGee	.15	.40
33 Ron Brace	.12	.30
34 Brian Hartline	.15	.40
35 Mike Wallace	.30	.75
36 Mike Thomas	.15	.40
37 Juaquin Iglesias	.12	.30
38 Nate Davis	.12	.30
39 Javon Ringer	.15	.40
40 Robert Ayers	.15	.40
41 Evander Hood	.20	.50
42 James Laurinaitis	.15	.40
43 Rey Maualuga	.15	.40
44 Eben Britton	.12	.30
45 Eric Wood	.12	.30
46 Louis Murphy	.15	.40
47 Mohamed Massaquoi	.12	.30
48 Kenny McKinley	.15	.40
49 Glen Coffee	.12	.30
50 Deon Butler	.12	.30
51 Vontae Davis	.15	.40
52 Tony Fiammetta	.12	.30
53 Fili Moala	.12	.30
54 Derrick Williams	.12	.30
55 Sean Smith	.15	.40
56 Peria Jerry	.12	.30
57 Chase Coffman	.12	.30
58 Brandon Tate	.15	.40
59 Everette Brown	.12	.30
60 Rhett Bomar	.12	.30
61 Max Unger	.12	.30
62 Alex Mack	.12	.30
63 D.J. Moore	.12	.30
64 Ramses Barden	.10	.25
65 Brandon Hughes	.10	.25
66 William Moore	.15	.40
67 Michael Johnson	.10	.25
68 Jared Cook	.15	.40
69 Jarron Gilbert	.12	.30
70 Brian Robiskie	.15	.40
71 Darius Butler	.15	.40
72 Anthony Hill	.10	.25
73 Malcolm Jenkins	.15	.40
74 Michael Oher	.25	.60
75 Patrick Chung	.15	.40
76 Knowshon Moreno SP	.50	1.25
77 Matthew Stafford SP	2.50	6.00
78 Michael Crabtree SP	1.00	2.50
79 Mark Sanchez SP	1.50	4.00
80 Aaron Curry SP	.50	1.25
81 Jeremy Maclin SP	.75	2.00
82 Chris Wells SP	.75	2.00
83 Donald Brown SP	.50	1.25
84 Josh Freeman SP	1.00	2.50
85 Jason Smith SP	.40	1.00
86 Eugene Monroe SP	.30	.75
87 Darrius Heyward-Bey SP	.50	1.25
88 Kenny Britt SP	.60	1.50
89 Hakeem Nicks SP	.75	2.00
90 Pat White SP	.50	1.25
91 Aaron Maybin SP	.40	1.00
92 Brian Cushing SP	.50	1.25
93 Brandon Pettigrew SP	.50	1.25
94 Brian Orakpo SP	.50	1.25
95 Percy Harvin SP	.75	2.00
96 Andre Smith SP	.40	1.00
97 Tyson Jackson SP	.40	1.00
98 Clay Matthews SP	1.25	3.00
99 LeSean McCoy SP	1.00	2.50
100 Shonn Greene SP	.75	2.00

2009 Upper Deck Rookie Exclusives College to Pros

AP Adrian Peterson	.60	1.50
AR Aaron Rodgers	.75	2.00
BR Ben Roethlisberger	.40	1.00
BU Brian Urlacher	.40	1.00
CB Champ Bailey	.30	.75
CJ Chris Johnson	.40	1.00
CP Carson Palmer	.40	1.00
DM Donovan McNabb	.40	1.00
EM Eli Manning	.40	1.00
FG Frank Gore	.30	.75
JC Jerricho Cotchery	.30	.75
JJ Julius Jones	.25	.60
JO Calvin Johnson	.40	1.00
JR JaMarcus Russell	.25	.60
LE Lee Evans	.30	.75
LF Larry Fitzgerald	.40	1.00
MJ Maurice Jones-Drew	.30	.75
MR Matt Ryan	.40	1.00
PM Peyton Manning	.60	1.50
PO Clinton Portis	.30	.75
PR Philip Rivers	.40	1.00
RB Reggie Bush	.40	1.00
RL Ray Lewis	.40	1.00
RO Ronnie Brown	.30	.75
SJ Steven Jackson	.30	.75
SL Steve Slaton	.30	.75
SS Steve Smith	.30	.75
TB Tom Brady	.60	1.50
TP Troy Polamalu	.40	1.00
TR Tony Romo	.60	1.50

2001 Upper Deck Rookie F/X

This 225 card set was issued in February, 2002. The cards were issued in five card packs which came 24 packs to a box and 16 boxes to a case. The SRP on the packs were $3.99. Rookie players were reproduced from earlier released products including Upper Deck Victory,Upper Deck Vintage, Upper Deck MVP, and base Upper Deck using a new foil card front and serial numbered to 750 of each brand reproduced. Rookie players were also featured on an all new F/X version also numbered to 750.

COMP.SET w/o SP's (225)	20.00	40.00
226-338 PRINT RUN 750 SER.#'d SETS		
1 Jake Plummer	.25	.60
2 Thomas Jones	.25	.60
3 David Boston	.20	.50
4 Jamal Anderson	.25	.60
5 Chris Chandler	.25	.60
6 Tony Martin	.25	.60
7 Jamal Lewis	.30	.75
8 Elvis Grbac	.25	.60
9 Ray Lewis	.30	.75
10 Rob Johnson	.25	.60
11 Eric Moulds	.25	.60
12 Muhsin Muhammad	.25	.60
13 Tim Biakabutuka	.20	.50
14 James Allen	.20	.50
15 Marcus Robinson	.25	.60
16 Brian Urlacher	.40	1.00
17 Jon Kitna	.25	.60
18 Peter Warrick	.25	.60
19 Corey Dillon	.25	.60
20 Kevin Johnson	.20	.50
21 Dennis Northcutt	.20	.50
22 Tim Couch	.20	.50
23 Rocket Ismail	.25	.60
24 Emmitt Smith	.75	2.00
25 Joey Galloway	.25	.60
26 Terrell Davis	.30	.75
27 Rod Smith	.25	.60
28 Brian Griese	.25	.60
29 Mike Anderson	.25	.60
30 Charlie Batch	.25	.60
31 James O. Stewart	.20	.50
32 Germane Crowell	.20	.50
33 Brett Favre	1.00	2.50
34 Antonio Freeman	.30	.75
35 Ahman Green	.30	.75
36 Peyton Manning	.75	2.00
37 Edgerrin James	.30	.75
38 Marvin Harrison	.30	.75
39 Jerome Pathon	.20	.50
40 Mark Brunell	.25	.60
41 Fred Taylor	.30	.75
42 Jimmy Smith	.25	.60
43 Tony Gonzalez	.30	.75
44 Priest Holmes	.30	.75
45 Trent Green	.30	.75
46 Oronde Gadsden	.20	.50
47 Jay Fiedler	.25	.60
48 Lamar Smith	.25	.60
49 Randy Moss	.30	.75
50 Cris Carter	.30	.75
51 Daunte Culpepper	.25	.60
52 Drew Bledsoe	.30	.75
53 Antowain Smith	.25	.60
54 Tom Brady	2.50	6.00
55 Ricky Williams	.30	.75
56 Joe Horn	.25	.60
57 Aaron Brooks	.25	.60
58 Kerry Collins	.25	.60
59 Tiki Barber	.30	.75
60 Ron Dayne	.25	.60
61 Vinny Testaverde	.25	.60
62 Wayne Chrebet	.25	.60
63 Curtis Martin	.30	.75
64 Tyrone Wheatley	.25	.60
65 Rich Gannon	.25	.60
66 Jerry Rice	.60	1.50
67 Duce Staley	.25	.60
68 Donovan McNabb	.30	.75
69 Kordell Stewart	.25	.60
70 Jerome Bettis	.30	.75
71 Marshall Faulk	.30	.75
72 Kurt Warner	.50	1.25
73 Torry Holt	.25	.60
74 Doug Flutie	.30	.75
75 Freddie Jones	.20	.50
76 Jeff Garcia	.25	.60
77 Garrison Hearst	.25	.60
78 Terrell Owens	.30	.75
79 Tai Streets	.20	.50
80 Ricky Watters	.25	.60
81 Matt Hasselbeck	.30	.75
82 Darrell Jackson	.25	.60
83 Brad Johnson	.25	.60
84 Warrick Dunn	.30	.75
85 Keyshawn Johnson	.30	.75
86 Eddie George	.30	.75
87 Steve McNair	.30	.75
88 Tony Banks	.20	.50
89 Michael Westbrook	.20	.50
90 Stephen Davis	.25	.60
91 Bob Christian	.20	.50
92 Brian Finneran	.20	.50
93 Brandon Stokley	.25	.60
94 Jeremy McDaniel	.20	.50
95 Brad Hoover	.25	.60
96 Donald Hayes	.20	.50
97 Jim Miller	.25	.60
98 Danny Farmer	.20	.50
99 Anthony Wright	.20	.50
100 Jackie Harris	.25	.60
101 Howard Griffith	.20	.50
102 Desmond Howard	.25	.60
103 Bill Schroeder	.25	.60
104 Terrence Wilkins	.20	.50
105 Todd Collins	.20	.50
106 Sylvester Morris	.20	.50
107 Zach Thomas	.30	.75
108 Robert Griffith	.20	.50
109 Kevin Faulk	.25	.60
110 Willie Jackson	.20	.50
111 Ron Dixon	.20	.50
112 Michael Strahan	.30	.75
113 Richie Anderson	.20	.50
114 Chad Pennington	.30	.75
115 Charles Woodson	.30	.75
116 Chad Lewis	.20	.50
117 Az-Zahir Hakim	.20	.50
118 Rodney Harrison	.25	.60
119 Mike Alstott	.25	.60
120 Jevon Kearse	.25	.60
121 Martay Jenkins	.20	.50
122 Pat Tillman RC	10.00	20.00
123 Rod Woodson	.30	.75
124 Marty Booker	.25	.60
125 Scott Mitchell	.20	.50
126 John Mobley	.20	.50
127 Stephen Boyd	.20	.50
128 Kurt Schulz	.20	.50
129 Kyle Brady	.20	.50
130 Donnie Edwards	.20	.50
131 J.J. Johnson	.20	.50
132 Chris Walsh RC	.20	.50
133 J.R. Redmond	.20	.50
134 Keith Mitchell	.20	.50
135 Joe Jurevicius	.20	.50
136 Eric Allen	.20	.50
137 Todd Pinkston	.20	.50
138 Bobby Shaw	.20	.50
139 Hines Ward	.30	.75
140 Ricky Proehl	.20	.50
141 London Fletcher	.20	.50
142 Jeff Graham	.20	.50
143 Tim Rattay	.20	.50
144 Fred Beasley	.20	.50
145 James Williams	.20	.50
146 Derrick Brooks	.30	.75
147 Warren Sapp	.25	.60
148 Derrick Mason	.25	.60
149 Kevin Dyson	.20	.50
150 Champ Bailey	.30	.75
151 Michael Pittman	.25	.60
152 Kwamie Lassiter	.20	.50
153 Maurice Smith	.20	.50
154 Keith Brooking	.20	.50
155 Travis Taylor	.20	.50
156 Tony Siragusa	.25	.60
157 Alex Van Pelt	.20	.50
158 Shane Matthews	.20	.50
159 Darnay Scott	.20	.50
160 Aaron Shea	.20	.50
161 JaJuan Dawson	.20	.50
162 Clint Stoerner	.25	.60
163 Dat Nguyen	.20	.50
164 Bill Romanowski	.25	.60
165 Robert Porcher	.20	.50
166 Bubba Franks	.25	.60
167 Rob Morris	.20	.50
168 Stacey Mack	.20	.50
169 Chris Hovan	.20	.50
170 Lawyer Milloy	.25	.60
171 La'Roi Glover	.20	.50
172 Jessie Armstead	.20	.50
173 Mo Lewis	.20	.50
174 Jon Ritchie	.20	.50
175 James Thrash	.25	.60
176 Trung Canidate	.20	.50
177 Grant Wistrom	.20	.50
178 Curtis Conway	.25	.60
179 Ronney Jenkins	.20	.50
180 John Lynch	.25	.60
181 Frank Sanders	.20	.50
182 Shawn Jefferson	.20	.50
183 Darrick Vaughn	.20	.50
184 Terance Mathis	.20	.50
185 Shannon Sharpe	.30	.75
186 Qadry Ismail	.25	.60
187 Sammy Morris	.20	.50
188 Shawn Bryson	.20	.50
189 Wesley Walls	.20	.50
190 Akili Smith	.20	.50
191 Ron Dugans	.20	.50
192 Travis Prentice	.20	.50
193 Courtney Brown	.20	.50
194 Ed McCaffrey	.25	.60
195 Olandis Gary	.20	.50
196 Johnnie Morton	.25	.60
197 Dorsey Levens	.25	.60
198 Ken Dilger	.20	.50
199 Keenan McCardell	.25	.60
200 Derrick Alexander	.20	.50
201 Tony Richardson	.20	.50
202 Jason Taylor	.30	.75
203 O.J. McDuffie	.20	.50
204 Troy Walters	.20	.50
205 Troy Brown	.25	.60
206 Jeff Blake	.25	.60
207 Albert Connell	.20	.50
208 Amani Toomer	.25	.60
209 Ike Hilliard	.25	.60
210 Jason Sehorn	.25	.60
211 Laveranues Coles	.25	.60
212 Tim Brown	.30	.75
213 Charlie Garner	.25	.60
214 Plaxico Burress	.25	.60
215 Troy Edwards	.20	.50
216 Isaac Bruce	.30	.75
217 Junior Seau	.30	.75
218 Marcellus Wiley	.20	.50
219 J.J. Stokes	.20	.50
220 Shaun Alexander	.30	.75
221 John Randle	.25	.60
222 Jacquez Green	.20	.50
223 Neil O'Donnell	.25	.60
224 Frank Wycheck	.20	.50
225 Stephen Alexander	.20	.50
226F A.J. Feeley F	1.00	2.50
X RC		
226U A.J. Feeley UD	.75	2.00
226VN A.J. Feeley VINT	.75	2.00
227U Adam Archuleta UD	.75	2.00
227VC Adam Archuleta VICT	.75	2.00
227VN Adam Archuleta VINT	.75	2.00
228U Willie Middlebrooks UD	.75	2.00
228VN Willie Middlebrooks VINT	.75	2.00
229U Alex Bannister UD	.60	1.50
229VC Alex Bannister VICT	.60	1.50
230M Alge Crumpler MVP	1.00	2.50
230U Alge Crumpler UD	1.00	2.50
230VC Alge Crumpler VICT	1.00	2.50
230VN Alge Crumpler VINT	1.00	2.50
231U Andre Carter UD	.75	2.00
231VN Andre Carter VINT	.75	2.00
232U Andre Dyson UD	.60	1.50
233F Anthony Thomas F/X RC	1.25	3.00
233M Anthony Thomas MVP	1.00	2.50
233U Anthony Thomas UD	1.00	2.50
233VC Anthony Thomas VICT	1.00	2.50
233VN Anthony Thomas VINT	1.00	2.50
234U Arther Love UD	.60	1.50
235M Bobby Newcombe MVP	.75	2.00
235U Bobby Newcombe UD	.75	2.00
235VC Bobby Newcombe VICT	.75	2.00
235VN Bobby Newcombe VINT	.75	2.00
236U Zeke Moreno UD	.75	2.00
237U Brandon Spoon UD	.75	2.00
238U Brian Allen UD	.60	1.50
239U Carlos Polk UD	.60	1.50
240U Casey Hampton UD	1.00	2.50
241F Cedrick Wilson F/X RC	1.00	2.50
241U Cedrick Wilson UD	.75	2.00
241VC Cedrick Wilson VICT	.75	2.00
242F Chad Johnson F/X RC	2.00	5.00
242M Chad Johnson MVP	1.50	4.00
242U Chad Johnson UD	1.50*	4.00
242VC Chad Johnson VICT	1.50	4.00
242VN Chad Johnson VINT	1.50	4.00
243U Chris Barnes UD	.60	1.50
243VC Chris Barnes VICT	.60	1.50
243VN Chris Barnes VINT	.60	1.50
244F Chris Chambers F/X RC	1.25	3.00
244M Chris Chambers MVP	1.00	2.50
244U Chris Chambers UD	1.00	2.50
244VC Chris Chambers VICT	1.00	2.50
244VN Chris Chambers VINT	1.00	2.50
245U Chris Taylor UD	.60	1.50
246F Chris Weinke F/X RC	1.00	2.50
246M Chris Weinke MVP	.75	2.00
246U Chris Weinke UD	.75	2.00
246VC Chris Weinke VICT	.75	2.00
246VN Chris Weinke VINT	.75	2.00
247F Correll Buckhalter F/X RC	1.25	3.00
247M Correll Buckhalter MVP	1.00	2.50
247U Correll Buckhalter UD	1.00	2.50
247VC Correll Buckhalter VICT	1.00	2.50
247VN Correll Buckhalter VINT	1.00	2.50
248U Damione Lewis UD	.75	2.00
249M Dan Alexander MVP	.75	2.00
249U Dan Alexander UD	.75	2.00
249VC Dan Alexander VICT	.75	2.00
250F Dan Morgan F/X RC	1.00	2.50
250M Dan Morgan MVP	.75	2.00
250U Dan Morgan UD	.75	2.00
250VC Dan Morgan VICT	.75	2.00
250VN Dan Morgan VINT	.75	2.00
251U Darnerien McCants UD	.75	2.00
252VN Dave Dickenson VINT	.75	2.00
253M David Allen MVP	.60	1.50
253VN David Allen VINT	.60	1.50
254M David Rivers MVP	.60	1.50
255F David Terrell F/X RC	1.00	2.50
255M David Terrell MVP	.75	2.00
255U David Terrell UD	.75	2.00
255VC David Terrell VICT	.75	2.00
255VN David Terrell VINT	.75	2.00
256U Dee Brown UD	.60	1.50
257U Derek Combs UD	.60	1.50
258U Derrick Blaylock UD	.75	2.00
259M Derrick Gibson MVP	.60	1.50
259U Derrick Gibson UD	.60	1.50
259VC Derrick Gibson VICT	.60	1.50
260F Deuce McAllister F/X RC	1.25	3.00
260M Deuce McAllister MVP	1.00	2.50
260U Deuce McAllister UD	1.00	2.50
260VC Deuce McAllister VICT	1.00	2.50
260VN Deuce McAllister VINT	1.00	2.50
261F Dominic Rhodes F/X RC	1.25	3.00
262F Drew Bennett F/X RC	2.00	5.00
263F Drew Brees F/X RC	8.00	20.00
263M Drew Brees MVP	6.00*	15.00
263U Drew Brees UD	6.00	15.00
263VC Drew Brees VICT	6.00	15.00
263VN Drew Brees VINT	6.00	15.00
264VN Dustin McClintock VINT	.75	2.00
265U Eddie Berlin UD	.60	1.50
265VC Eddie Berlin VICT	.60	1.50
266U Edgerton Hartwell UD	.60	1.50
267U Francis St.Paul UD	.60	1.50
268U Fred Smoot UD	1.00	2.50
269F Freddie Mitchell F/X RC	.75	2.00
269M Freddie Mitchell MVP	.60	1.50
269U Freddie Mitchell UD	.60	1.50
269VC Freddie Mitchell VICT	.60	1.50
269VN Freddie Mitchell VINT	.60	1.50
270U Gary Baxter UD	.60	1.50
270VC Gary Baxter VICT	.60	1.50
271U George Layne UD	.60	1.50
272U Gerard Warren UD	.75	2.00
272VC Gerard Warren VICT	.75	2.00
272VN Gerard Warren VINT	.75	2.00
273U Hakim Akbar UD	.60	1.50
273VN Hakim Akbar VINT	.60	1.50
274U Heath Evans UD	.75	2.00
274VC Heath Evans VICT	.75	2.00
275U Jabari Holloway UD	.60	1.50
275VC Jabari Holloway VICT	.60	1.50
276U Jamal Reynolds UD	.60	1.50
276VC Jamal Reynolds VICT	.60	1.50
276VN Jamal Reynolds VINT	.60	1.50
277U Jamar Fletcher UD	.60	1.50
277VC Jamar Fletcher VICT	.60	1.50
278F James Jackson F/X RC	.75	2.00

278M James Jackson MVP .60 1.50
278U James Jackson UD .60 1.50
278VC James Jackson VICT .60 1.50
278VN James Jackson VINT .60 1.50
279U Jamie Winborn UD .75 2.00
280F Jesse Palmer F/X RC 1.00 2.50
280M Jesse Palmer MVP .75 2.00
280U Jesse Palmer UD .75 2.00
280VC Jesse Palmer VICT .75 2.00
280VN Jesse Palmer VINT .75 2.00
281U John Capel UD .60 1.50
282F Josh Booty F/X RC 1.00 2.50
282M Josh Booty MVP .75 2.00
282U Josh Booty UD .75 2.00
282VC Josh Booty VICT .75 2.00
282VN Josh Booty VINT .75 2.00
283M Josh Heupel MVP 1.00 2.50
283U Josh Heupel UD 1.00 2.50
283VC Josh Heupel VICT 1.00 2.50
283VN Josh Heupel VINT 1.00 2.50
284F Justin McCareins F/X RC 1.00 2.50
284U Justin McCareins UD .75 2.00
285U Justin Smith UD 1.00 2.50
285VC Justin Smith VICT 1.00 2.50
285VN Justin Smith VINT 1.00 2.50
286U Karon Riley UD .60 1.50
287U Ken Lucas UD .75 2.00
288M Ken-Yon Rambo MVP .60 1.50
288U Ken-Yon Rambo UD .60 1.50
288VC Ken-Yon Rambo VICT .60 1.50
289U Kenyatta Walker UD .60 1.50
290F Kevan Barlow F/X RC 1.00 2.50
290M Kevan Barlow MVP .75 2.00
290U Kevan Barlow UD .75 2.00
290VC Kevan Barlow VICT .75 2.00
290VN Kevan Barlow VINT .75 2.00
291F Kevin Kasper F/X RC .75 2.00
291M Kevin Kasper MVP .60 1.50
291U Kevin Kasper UD .60 1.50
291VC Kevin Kasper VICT .60 1.50
291VN Kevin Kasper VINT .60 1.50
292F Koren Robinson F/X RC 1.00 2.50
292M Koren Robinson MVP .75 2.00
292U Koren Robinson UD .75 2.00
292VC Koren Robinson VICT .75 2.00
292VN Koren Robinson VINT .75 2.00
293F LaDainian Tomlinson F/X RC 4.00 10.00
293M LaDainian Tomlinson MVP 3.00 8.00
293U LaDainian Tomlinson UD 3.00 8.00
293VC LaDainian Tomlinson VICT 3.00 8.00
293VN LaDainian Tomlinson VINT 3.00 8.00
294F LaMont Jordan F/X RC 1.25 3.00
294M LaMont Jordan MVP 1.00 2.50
294U LaMont Jordan UD 1.00 2.50
294VC LaMont Jordan VICT 1.00 2.50
294VN LaMont Jordan VINT 1.00 2.50
295U Leonard Davis UD 1.00 2.50
295VN Leonard Davis VINT 1.00 2.50
296U Marcus Stroud UD .75 2.00
296VN Marcus Stroud VINT .75 2.00
297F Marques Tuiasosopo F/X RC 1.00 2.50
297M Marques Tuiasosopo MVP .75 2.00
297U Marques Tuiasosopo UD .75 2.00
297VC Marques Tuiasosopo VICT .75 2.00
297VN Marques Tuiasosopo VINT .75 2.00
298F Snoop Minnis F/X RC .75 2.00
298M Snoop Minnis MVP .60 1.50
298U Snoop Minnis UD .60 1.50
298VC Snoop Minnis VICT .60 1.50
298VN Snoop Minnis VINT .60 1.50
299F Michael Bennett F/X RC 1.00 2.50
299M Michael Bennett MVP .75 2.00
299U Michael Bennett UD .75 2.00
299VC Michael Bennett VICT .75 2.00
299VN Michael Bennett VINT .75 2.00
300U Michael Stone UD .60 1.50
301F Michael Vick F/X RC 5.00 12.00
301M Michael Vick MVP 4.00 10.00
301U Michael Vick UD 4.00 10.00
301VN Michael Vick VINT 4.00 10.00
302F Mike McMahon F/X RC 1.00 2.50
302M Mike McMahon MVP .75 2.00
302U Mike McMahon UD .75 2.00
302VC Mike McMahon VICT .75 2.00
302VN Mike McMahon VINT .75 2.00
303M Moran Norris MVP .60 1.50
303U Moran Norris UD .60 1.50
303VC Moran Norris VICT .60 1.50
303VN Moran Norris VINT .60 1.50
304U Morlon Greenwood UD .60 1.50
305U Nate Clements UD .75 2.00
305VC Nate Clements VICT .75 2.00
305VN Nate Clements VINT .75 2.00
306F Nick Goings F/X RC 1.25 3.00
307U Orlando Huff UD .60 1.50
308F Quincy Carter F/X RC 1.00 2.50
308U Quincy Carter UD .75 2.00
308VC Quincy Carter VICT .75 2.00
308VN Quincy Carter VINT .75 2.00
309F Quincy Morgan F/X RC 1.00 2.50
309M Quincy Morgan MVP .75 2.00
309U Quincy Morgan UD .75 2.00
309VC Quincy Morgan VICT .75 2.00
309VN Quincy Morgan VINT .75 2.00
310F Reggie Wayne F/X RC 2.50 6.00
310M Reggie Wayne MVP 2.00 5.00
310U Reggie Wayne UD 2.00 5.00
310VC Reggie Wayne VICT 2.00 5.00
310VN Reggie Wayne VINT 2.00 5.00
311M Reggie White MVP .60 1.50
311U Reggie White UD .60 1.50
312U Richard Seymour UD 1.00 2.50
312VN Richard Seymour VINT 1.00 2.50
313F Robert Ferguson F/X RC 1.25 3.00
313U Robert Ferguson UD 1.00 2.50
313VC Robert Ferguson VICT 1.00 2.50
313VN Robert Ferguson VINT 1.00 2.50
314F Rod Gardner F/X RC 1.00 2.50
314M Rod Gardner MVP .75 2.00
314U Rod Gardner UD .75 2.00
314VC Rod Gardner VICT .75 2.00
314VN Rod Gardner VINT .75 2.00
315M Ronney Daniels MVP .60 1.50
316F Rudi Johnson F/X RC 1.25 3.00
316M Rudi Johnson MVP 1.00 2.50
316U Rudi Johnson UD 1.00 2.50
316VC Rudi Johnson VICT 1.00 2.50
316VN Rudi Johnson VINT 1.00 2.50
317M Sage Rosenfels MVP 1.00 2.50
317U Sage Rosenfels UD 1.00 2.50
317VC Sage Rosenfels VICT 1.00 2.50
317VN Sage Rosenfels VINT 1.00 2.50
318F Santana Moss F/X RC 1.50 4.00
318M Santana Moss MVP 1.25 3.00
318U Santana Moss UD 1.25 3.00
318VC Santana Moss VICT 1.25 3.00
318VN Santana Moss VINT 1.25 3.00
319U Scotty Anderson UD .60 1.50
319VC Scotty Anderson VICT .60 1.50
320U Sedrick Hodge UD .60 1.50
321U Shaun Rogers UD 1.00 2.50
321VN Shaun Rogers VINT 1.00 2.50
322U Steve Hutchinson UD 1.00 2.50
323F Steve Smith F/X RC 2.50 6.00
323U Steve Smith UD 2.00 5.00
323VC Steve Smith VICT 2.00 5.00
324M T.J. Houshmandzadeh MVP 1.25 3.00
324U T.J. Houshmandzadeh UD 1.25 3.00
324VC T.J. Houshmandzadeh VICT 1.25 3.00
324VN T.J. Houshmandzadeh VINT 1.25 3.00
325U Tay Cody UD .60 1.50
326VC Tim Hasselbeck VICT .75 2.00
326VN Tim Hasselbeck VINT .75 2.00
327F Todd Heap F/X RC 1.25 3.00
327M Todd Heap MVP 1.00 2.50
327U Todd Heap UD 1.00 2.50
327VC Todd Heap VICT 1.00 2.50
327VN Todd Heap VINT 1.00 2.50
328U Tommy Polley UD .60 1.50
329U Tony Dixon UD .60 1.50
329VN Tony Dixon VINT .60 1.50
330U Torrance Marshall UD .60 1.50
331F Travis Henry F/X RC 1.00 2.50
331M Travis Henry MVP .75 2.00
331U Travis Henry UD .75 2.00
331VC Travis Henry VICT .75 2.00
331VN Travis Henry VINT .75 2.00
332F Travis Minor F/X RC 1.00 2.50
332M Travis Minor MVP .75 2.00
332U Travis Minor UD .75 2.00
332VC Travis Minor VICT .75 2.00
332VN Travis Minor VINT .75 2.00
333M Vinny Sutherland MVP .60 1.50
333U Vinny Sutherland UD .60 1.50
333VC Vinny Sutherland VICT .60 1.50
333VN Vinny Sutherland VINT .60 1.50
334U Will Allen UD 1.00 2.50
334VC Will Allen VICT 1.00 2.50
334VN Will Allen VINT 1.00 2.50
335VN Jason Brookins VINT RC 1.25 3.00
336VN Dominic Rhodes VINT RC 1.25 3.00
337VN Benjamin Gay VINT RC 1.00 2.50
338VC Troy Hambrick VICT RC 1.00 2.50
338VN Troy Hambrick VINT RC 1.00 2.50

2001 Upper Deck Rookie F/X Heroes of Football Jerseys

STATED ODDS 1:48
HFDM Dan Marino 15.00 40.00
HFDW Danny White 8.00 20.00
HFHA Herb Adderley 8.00 20.00
HFJE John Elway 15.00 40.00
HFJK Jim Kelly 10.00 25.00
HFJR John Riggins 12.00 30.00
HFJT Jim Taylor 12.00 30.00
HFMA Jim Marshall 8.00 20.00
HFON Ozzie Newsome 6.00 15.00
HFRL Ronnie Lott 8.00 20.00
HFRW Reggie White 8.00 20.00
HFSY Steve Young 10.00 25.00
HFTM Tom Mack 5.00 12.00
HFTT Thurman Thomas 8.00 20.00
HFWM Warren Moon 8.00 20.00

2001 Upper Deck Rookie F/X Legendary Combos Jerseys

STATED PRINT RUN 100 SER.#'d SETS
LCDB Ron Dayne 10.00 25.00
Tiki Barber
LCFG Brett Favre 30.00 80.00
Ahman Green
LCGM Brian Griese 8.00 20.00
Ed McCaffrey
LCMH Peyton Manning 25.00 60.00
Marvin Harrison
LCTB LaDainian Tomlinson 40.00 100.00
Drew Brees
LCWF Kurt Warner 15.00 40.00
Marshall Faulk
LCYR Steve Young 20.00 50.00
Jerry Rice

2001 Upper Deck Rookie F/X Legendary Cuts

STATED ODDS 1:788
LCBN Bronko Nagurski/50 200.00 300.00
LCDT Derrick Thomas/37 400.00 600.00
LCRB Red Badgro/65 75.00 135.00
LCVL Vince Lombardi/221 350.00 600.00
LCWE Weeb Ewbank/38 125.00 200.00

2001 Upper Deck Rookie F/X Legends In The Making Jerseys

STATED ODDS 1:48
LMBF Brett Favre 15.00 40.00
LMDB Drew Bledsoe 5.00 12.00
LMDBR Drew Brees 12.00 30.00
LMEG1 Eddie George 5.00 12.00
LMEG2 Elvis Grbac 4.00 10.00
LMJA Jamal Anderson 4.00 10.00
LMJR Jerry Rice 10.00 25.00
LMJRS Junior Seau 5.00 12.00
LMJS Jimmy Smith 4.00 10.00
LMKC Kerry Collins 4.00 10.00
LMLT LaDainian Tomlinson 6.00 15.00
LMPM Peyton Manning 12.00 30.00
LMTB Tim Brown 5.00 12.00
LMTC Tim Couch 3.00 8.00
LMTD Terrell Davis 5.00 12.00
LMWS Warren Sapp 4.00 10.00

2001 Upper Deck Rookie F/X PatchPlay Combos

STATED PRINT RUN 45 SER.#'d SETS
ABP Brett Favre 50.00 100.00
Antonio Freeman
BHP Isaac Bruce 15.00 40.00
Torry Holt
BSP Kordell Stewart 15.00 40.00
Jerome Bettis
BTP Mark Brunell 15.00 40.00
Fred Taylor
CHP Kerry Collins 12.00 30.00
Ike Hilliard
CMP Cris Carter 15.00 40.00
Randy Moss
FHP Marshall Faulk 15.00 40.00
Az-Zahir Hakim
GMP Brian Griese 12.00 30.00
Ed McCaffrey
GOP Terrell Owens 15.00 40.00
Jeff Garcia
GPP Drew Bledsoe 15.00 40.00
Terry Glenn
MHP Peyton Manning 40.00 80.00
Marvin Harrison
SBP Frank Sanders 10.00 25.00
David Boston
TUP Brian Urlacher 20.00 50.00
David Terrell
WBP Kurt Warner 25.00 60.00
Isaac Bruce
WFP Kurt Warner 25.00 60.00
Marshall Faulk

2005 Upper Deck Rookie Materials

This 130-card set was released through Upper Deck's retail outlets in September, 2005. The set was issued in nine-card packs which came 24 packs to a box. Cards numbered 1-90 feature veterans in team alphabetical order while cards numbered 91-130 feature 2005 rookies. Those rookies were issued at a stated rate of one in three.

COMP.SET w/o RC's (90) 10.00 - 25.00
DRAFT PICK STATED ODDS 1:3
1 Larry Fitzgerald .30 .75
2 Kurt Warner .30 .75
3 Michael Vick .30 .75
4 Peerless Price .20 .50
5 Todd Heap .25 .60
6 Jamal Lewis .25 .60
7 Kyle Boller .25 .60
8 J.P. Losman .20 .50
9 Willis McGahee .30 .75
10 Lee Evans .25 .60
11 Eric Moulds .20 .50
12 Jake Delhomme .25 .60
13 Keary Colbert .20 .50
14 DeShaun Foster .25 .60
15 Brian Urlacher .30 .75
16 Rex Grossman .25 .60
17 Muhsin Muhammad .25 .60
18 Carson Palmer .30 .75
19 Rudi Johnson .25 .60
20 Chad Johnson .25 .60
21 Julius Jones .20 .50
22 Keyshawn Johnson .25 .60
23 Drew Bledsoe .30 .75
24 Tatum Bell .20 .50
25 Jake Plummer .25 .60
26 Ashley Lelie .20 .50
27 Roy Williams WR .25 .60
28 Kevin Jones .20 .50
29 Jeff Garcia .25 .60
30 Brett Favre .75 2.00
31 Ahman Green .25 .60
32 Javon Walker .20 .50
33 David Carr .20 .50
34 Andre Johnson .30 .75
35 Domanick Davis .20 .50
36 Peyton Manning .60 1.50
37 Edgerrin James .25 .60
38 Marvin Harrison .30 .75
39 Byron Leftwich .25 .60
40 Fred Taylor .25 .60
41 Jimmy Smith .25 .60
42 Priest Holmes .25 .60
43 Tony Gonzalez .25 .60
44 Trent Green .25 .60
45 A.J. Feeley .20 .50
46 Chris Chambers .25 .60
47 Randy McMichael .20 .50
48 Daunte Culpepper .25 .60
49 Michael Bennett .25 .60
50 Nate Burleson .20 .50
51 Tom Brady .60 1.50
52 Corey Dillon .25 .60
53 Deion Branch .20 .50
54 Aaron Brooks .20 .50
55 Deuce McAllister .25 .60
56 Joe Horn .25 .60
57 Eli Manning .50 1.25
58 Jeremy Shockey .30 .75
59 Tiki Barber .30 .75
60 Chad Pennington .30 .75
61 Curtis Martin .30 .75
62 Laveranues Coles .20 .50
63 Kerry Collins .25 .60
64 LaMont Jordan .25 .60
65 Randy Moss .30 .75
66 Donovan McNabb .30 .75
67 Terrell Owens .30 .75
68 Brian Westbrook .25 .60
69 Ben Roethlisberger .50 1.25
70 Jerome Bettis .30 .75
71 Hines Ward .30 .75
72 Drew Brees .30 .75
73 LaDainian Tomlinson .30 .75
74 Antonio Gates .30 .75
75 Tim Rattay .20 .50
76 Eric Johnson .20 .50
77 Shaun Alexander .25 .60
78 Darrell Jackson .20 .50
79 Matt Hasselbeck .25 .60
80 Marc Bulger .25 .60
81 Steven Jackson .30 .75
82 Torry Holt .25 .60
83 Joey Galloway .25 .60
84 Brian Griese .25 .60
85 Michael Clayton .20 .50
86 Steve McNair .30 .75
87 Chris Brown .20 .50
88 Clinton Portis .25 .60
89 Patrick Ramsey .25 .60
90 Santana Moss .25 .60
91 Aaron Rodgers RC 12.50 25.00
92 Alex Smith QB RC 2.00 5.00
93 Jason Campbell RC 1.50 4.00
94 Charlie Frye RC 1.25 3.00
95 David Greene RC .75 2.00
96 Dan Orlovsky RC 1.25 3.00
97 Adrian McPherson RC .75 2.00
98 Kyle Orton RC 1.25 3.00
99 Andrew Walter RC 1.00 2.50
100 Cedric Benson RC 1.25 3.00
101 Cadillac Williams RC 1.25 3.00
102 Ronnie Brown RC 1.50 4.00
103 Vernand Morency RC 1.00 2.50
104 Ciatrick Fason RC .75 2.00
105 Maurice Clarett 1.00 2.50
106 Eric Shelton RC .75 2.00
107 J.J. Arrington RC 1.00 2.50
108 Frank Gore RC 2.00 5.00
109 Stefan LeFors RC .75 2.00
110 Troy Williamson RC 1.00 2.50
111 Braylon Edwards RC 1.50 4.00
112 Mike Williams 1.25 3.00
113 Vincent Jackson RC 1.50 4.00
114 Courtney Roby RC 1.00 2.50
115 Roddy White RC 1.50 4.00
116 Matt Jones RC 1.25 3.00
117 Ryan Moats RC 1.00 2.50
118 Mark Bradley RC .75 2.00
119 Mark Clayton RC 1.25 3.00
120 Terrence Murphy RC .75 2.00
121 Roscoe Parrish RC .75 2.00
122 Carlos Rogers RC 1.25 3.00
123 Antrel Rolle RC 1.25 3.00
124 Adam Jones RC 1.00 2.50
125 Heath Miller RC 1.50 4.00
126 Reggie Brown RC .75 2.00
127 Shawne Merriman RC 1.25 3.00
128 Marcus Spears RC 1.00 2.50
129 DeMarcus Ware RC 2.50 6.00
130 Mike Nugent RC 1.00 2.50

2005 Upper Deck Rookie Materials Icons

COMPLETE SET (15) 10.00 25.00
STATED ODDS 1:4
IC1 Brett Favre 2.50 6.00
IC2 Peyton Manning 2.00 5.00
IC3 Michael Vick 1.00 2.50
IC4 Donovan McNabb 1.00 2.50
IC5 Tom Brady 2.00 5.00
IC6 LaDainian Tomlinson 1.00 2.50
IC7 Priest Holmes .75 2.00
IC8 Clinton Portis .75 2.00
IC9 Ahman Green .75 2.00
IC10 Shaun Alexander .75 2.00
IC11 Randy Moss 1.00 2.50
IC12 Terrell Owens 1.00 2.50
IC13 Marvin Harrison 1.00 2.50
IC14 Torry Holt .75 2.00
IC15 Tony Gonzalez .75 2.00

2005 Upper Deck Rookie Materials Rookie Jerseys

STATED ODDS 1:8
R10 Braylon Edwards 6.00 15.00
R11 Cadillac Williams 8.00 20.00
R12 Courtney Roby 2.50 6.00
R13 Adam Jones 2.50 6.00
R14 J.J. Arrington 2.50 6.00
R15 Stefan LeFors 2.50 6.00
R16 Eric Shelton 2.50 6.00
R17 Frank Gore 5.00 12.00
R18 Andrew Walter 2.50 6.00
R19 Ryan Moats 2.50 6.00

2005 Upper Deck Rookie Materials Stars of Tomorrow

COMPLETE SET (15) 12.50 30.00
STATED ODDS 1:4
ST1 Alex Smith QB 1.00 2.50
ST2 Aaron Rodgers 8.00 20.00
ST3 Jason Campbell .75 2.00
ST4 Charlie Frye .60 1.50
ST5 David Greene .40 1.00
ST6 Ronnie Brown .75 2.00
ST7 Cedric Benson .60 1.50
ST8 Cadillac Williams .60 1.50
ST9 Eric Shelton .40 1.00
ST10 Ciatrick Fason .40 1.00
ST11 J.J. Arrington .50 1.25
ST12 Braylon Edwards .75 2.00
ST13 Troy Williamson .50 1.25
ST14 Mike Williams .60 1.50
ST15 Matt Jones .60 1.50

2004 Upper Deck Rookie Premiere

This set was issued as a 30-card factory box set in August 2004. Each factory set also included one gold foil parallel card. Each card includes front and back photos of the player taken at the NFL Rookie Premiere photo shoot.

COMPLETE SET (30) 15.00 30.00
1 Eli Manning 2.50 6.00
2 Ben Roethlisberger 2.50 6.00
3 Philip Rivers 1.50 4.00
4 Roy Williams WR .40 1.00
5 Larry Fitzgerald 1.00 2.50
6 Tatum Bell .30 .75
7 J.P. Losman .30 .75
8 Steven Jackson .60 1.50
9 Ben Watson .40 1.00
10 Devery Henderson .40 1.00
11 Kevin Jones .30 .75
12 Chris Perry .30 .75
13 Kellen Winslow Jr. .40 1.00
14 Lee Evans .40 1.00
15 Reggie Williams .30 .75
16 Ben Troupe .30 .75
17 Michael Clayton .30 .75
18 Michael Jenkins .40 1.00
19 Rashaun Woods .25 .60
20 DeAngelo Hall .40 1.00
21 Cedric Cobbs .25 .60
22 Luke McCown .30 .75
23 Robert Gallery .40 1.00
24 Julius Jones .30 .75
25 Matt Schaub .75 2.00
26 Keary Colbert .25 .60
27 Bernard Berrian .40 1.00
28 Greg Jones .25 .60
29 Darius Watts .25 .60
30 Checklist Card .25 .60

2004 Upper Deck Rookie Premiere Gold

COMPLETE SET (30) 20.00 50.00
*GOLD: 1X TO 2.5X BASIC CARDS
ONE GOLD PER FACTORY SET

2004 Upper Deck Rookie Premiere Autographs

BB Bernard Berrian 15.00 40.00
BR Ben Roethlisberger 175.00 300.00
BT Ben Troupe 12.00 30.00
BW Ben Watson 15.00 40.00
CC Cedric Cobbs 10.00 25.00
CP Chris Perry 12.00 30.00
DD Devard Darling 10.00 25.00
DH DeAngelo Hall 15.00 40.00
DH2 Devery Henderson 15.00 40.00
DW Darius Watts 10.00 25.00
EM Eli Manning 175.00 300.00
GJ Greg Jones 10.00 25.00
JJ Julius Jones 12.00 30.00
KC Keary Colbert 10.00 25.00
KJ Kevin Jones 12.00 30.00
LE Lee Evans 15.00 40.00
LF Larry Fitzgerald 60.00 100.00
LM Luke McCown 12.00 30.00
MC Michael Clayton 12.00 30.00
MJ Michael Jenkins 15.00 40.00
MS Matt Schaub 30.00 80.00
PR Philip Rivers 60.00 120.00
RG Robert Gallery 15.00 40.00
RW Rashaun Woods 10.00 25.00
RW2 Reggie Williams 12.00 30.00
RW3 Roy Williams WR 15.00 40.00
JL J.P. Losman 12.00 30.00

2005 Upper Deck Rookie Premiere

This set was issued as a 30-card factory box set with an $9.99 SRP in August 2005. Each factory set included one gold foil parallel card. Each base set card includes front and back photos of the player taken at the NFL Rookie Premiere photo shoot.

COMPLETE SET (30) 10.00 20.00
1 Ciatrick Fason .20 .50
2 Alex Smith QB .50 1.25
3 Antrel Rolle .30 .75
4 Cadillac Williams .30 .75
5 Ronnie Brown .40 1.00
6 Charlie Frye .30 .75
7 Roddy White .40 1.00
8 Braylon Edwards .40 1.00
9 Mark Bradley .20 .50
10 Vincent Jackson .40 1.00
11 Matt Jones .30 .75
12 Stefan LeFors .20 .50
13 Kyle Orton .30 .75
14 Troy Williamson .25 .60
15 Mark Clayton .30 .75
16 Aaron Rodgers 4.00 10.00
17 Cedric Benson .30 .75
18 Mike Williams .30 .75
19 Adam Jones .25 .60
20 Reggie Brown .20 .50
21 J.J. Arrington .25 .60
22 Andrew Walter .25 .60
23 David Greene .20 .50
24 Roscoe Parrish .20 .50
25 Terrence Murphy .20 .50
26 Jason Campbell .40 1.00
27 Maurice Clarett .25 .60
28 Frank Gore .50 1.25
29 Ryan Moats .25 .60
30 Checklist Card .30 .75

2005 Upper Deck Rookie Premiere Gold

COMPLETE SET (30) 30.00 80.00
*SINGLES: 1.2X TO 3X BASIC CARDS
ONE GOLD OR PLATINUM PER FACT.SET

2005 Upper Deck Rookie Premiere Platinum

COMPLETE SET (30) 30.00 80.00
*SINGLES: 1.2X TO 3X BASIC CARDS
ONE GOLD OR PLATINUM PER FACT.SET

2005 Upper Deck Rookie Premiere Autographs

STATED ODDS 1:24 FACTORY SETS
RSAJ Adam Jones 8.00 20.00
RSAN Antrel Rolle 12.00 30.00
RSAR Aaron Rodgers 250.00 400.00
RSAS Alex Smith QB 75.00 150.00
RSAW Andrew Walter 10.00 25.00
RSBE Braylon Edwards 40.00 100.00
RSCB Cedric Benson 20.00 40.00
RSCF Charlie Frye 12.00 30.00
RSCI Ciatrick Fason 8.00 20.00
RSCW Cadillac Williams 40.00 120.00
RSDG David Greene 8.00 20.00
RSFG Frank Gore 40.00 80.00
RSJA J.J. Arrington 10.00 25.00
RSJC Jason Campbell 20.00 50.00
RSKO Kyle Orton 15.00 40.00
RSMD Mark Bradley 8.00 20.00
RSMC Mark Clayton 10.00 25.00
RSMJ Matt Jones
RSMO Maurice Clarett
RSMW Mike Williams 12.00 30.00
RSRB Ronnie Brown 60.00 120.00
RSRE Reggie Brown 8.00 20.00
RSRM Ryan Moats 8.00 20.00
RSRP Roscoe Parrish 8.00 20.00
RSRW Roddy White 20.00 40.00
RSSL Stefan LeFors 8.00 20.00
RSTM Terrence Murphy 8.00 20.00
RSTW Troy Williamson 10.00 25.00
RSVJ Vincent Jackson 15.00 40.00

2005 Upper Deck Rookie Premiere Match-Ups

STATED ODDS 1:24 FACTORY SETS
RM1 Cadillac Williams 5.00 12.00
Ronnie Brown
RM2 Alex Smith QB 4.00 10.00
Stefan LeFors
RM3 Vincent Jackson 3.00 8.00
Mark Bradley
RM4 Braylon Edwards 4.00 10.00
Charlie Frye
RM5 Roscoe Parrish 2.50 6.00
Antrel Rolle
RM6 Reggie Brown 2.50 6.00
Ryan Moats
RM7 Aaron Rodgers 6.00 15.00
Terrence Murphy
RM8 Cedric Benson 2.50 6.00
Kyle Orton
RM9 Matt Jones 2.00 5.00
Troy Williamson
RM10 Braylon Edwards 4.00 10.00
Mike Williams

2006 Upper Deck Rookie Premiere

This 30-card set was released in factory set form in August, 2006. This set featured the leading 30 players who particpated in the yearly NFL rookie photo shoot. The set is sequenced in alphabetical order.

COMPLETE SET (30) 10.00 20.00
1 Jason Avant .25 .60
2 Reggie Bush .75 2.00
3 Brian Calhoun .25 .60
4 Kellen Clemens .30 .75
5 Vernon Davis .50 1.25
6 Maurice Drew .60 1.50
7 Derek Hagan .30 .75
8 A.J. Hawk .40 1.00
9 Santonio Holmes .50 1.25
10 Michael Huff .30 .75
11 Chad Jackson .25 .60
12 Tarvaris Jackson .40 1.00
13 Omar Jacobs .25 .60
14 Joe Klopfenstein .25 .60
15 Matt Leinart .40 1.00
16 Marcedes Lewis .40 1.00
17 Laurence Maroney .30 .75
18 Brandon Marshall .40 1.00
19 Sinorice Moss .40 1.00
20 Jerious Norwood .30 .75
21 Maurice Stovall .25 .60
22 Leon Washington .30 .75
23 LenDale White .30 .75
24 Charlie Whitehurst .40 1.00
25 Brandon Williams .25 .60
26 DeAngelo Williams .50 1.25
27 Demetrius Williams .30 .75
28 Mario Williams .40 1.00
29 Travis Wilson .25 .60
30 Vince Young .50 1.25

2006 Upper Deck Rookie Premiere Autographs

ONE AUTO PER 24-SET CASE
1 Jason Avant 5.00 12.00
2 Reggie Bush SP 100.00 200.00
3 Brian Calhoun 5.00 12.00
4 Kellen Clemens 6.00 15.00
5 Vernon Davis 12.00 30.00
6 Maurice Drew 50.00 80.00
7 Derek Hagan 6.00 15.00
8 A.J. Hawk SP
9 Santonio Holmes 20.00 50.00
10 Michael Huff 6.00 15.00
11 Chad Jackson 5.00 12.00
12 Tarvaris Jackson 10.00 25.00
13 Omar Jacobs 5.00 12.00
14 Joe Klopfenstein 5.00 12.00
15 Matt Leinart SP 50.00 120.00
16 Marcedes Lewis
17 Laurence Maroney 6.00 15.00
18 Brandon Marshall 20.00 40.00
19 Sinorice Moss 8.00 20.00
20 Jerious Norwood 6.00 15.00
21 Maurice Stovall 5.00 12.00
22 Leon Washington 6.00 15.00
23 LenDale White 6.00 15.00
24 Charlie Whitehurst 8.00 20.00
25 Brandon Williams 5.00 12.00
26 DeAngelo Williams SP 50.00 120.00
27 Demetrius Williams 6.00 15.00
28 Mario Williams 30.00 60.00
29 Travis Wilson 5.00 12.00
30 Vince Young SP 100.00 200.00

2007 Upper Deck Rookie Premiere

This 30-card set was released in factory set form in August, 2007. This set featured players who attended the 2007 NFL rookie photo shoot and the set is sequenced in alphabetical order.

COMPLETE SET (30) 7.50 15.00
1 Gaines Adams .30 .75
2 John Beck .30 .75
3 Lorenzo Booker .25 .60
4 Dwayne Bowe .40 1.00
5 Michael Bush .30 .75
6 Yamon Figurs .20 .50
7 Ted Ginn .25 .60
8 Anthony Gonzalez .30 .75
9 Chris Henry .20 .50
10 Jason Hill .30 .75
11 Tony Hunt .20 .50
12 Kenny Irons .20 .50
13 Brandon Jackson .25 .60
14 Dwayne Jarrett .25 .60
15 Calvin Johnson 1.00 2.50
16 Kevin Kolb .50 1.25
17 Brian Leonard .25 .60
18 Marshawn Lynch .30 .75
19 Robert Meachem .30 .75
20 Greg Olsen .25 .60
21 Adrian Peterson 3.00 8.00
22 Antonio Pittman .20 .50
23 Brady Quinn .30 .75
24 Sidney Rice .40 1.00
25 JaMarcus Russell .20 .50
26 Joe Thomas .20 .50
27 Steve Smith .30 .75
28 Troy Smith .30 .75
29 Drew Stanton .20 .50
30 Patrick Willis .60 1.50

2007 Upper Deck Rookie Premiere Autographs

1 Gaines Adams 20.00 50.00
2 John Beck 20.00 50.00
3 Lorenzo Booker 15.00 40.00
4 Dwayne Bowe 25.00 60.00
5 Michael Bush 20.00 50.00
6 Yamon Figurs 12.00 30.00
7 Ted Ginn
8 Anthony Gonzalez 20.00 50.00
9 Chris Henry 12.00 30.00
10 Jason Hill 20.00 50.00
11 Tony Hunt
12 Kenny Irons 12.00 30.00
13 Brandon Jackson 15.00 40.00
14 Dwayne Jarrett 15.00 40.00
15 Calvin Johnson 100.00 200.00
16 Kevin Kolb 30.00 80.00
17 Brian Leonard 15.00 40.00
18 Marshawn Lynch 20.00 50.00
19 Robert Meachem 20.00 50.00
20 Greg Olsen 15.00 40.00
21 Adrian Peterson 250.00 400.00
22 Antonio Pittman 12.00 30.00
23 Brady Quinn 50.00 120.00
24 Sidney Rice 25.00 60.00
25 JaMarcus Russell
26 Joe Thomas 20.00 50.00
27 Steve Smith 20.00 50.00
28 Troy Smith
29 Drew Stanton 12.00 30.00
30 Patrick Willis 40.00 100.00

2008 Upper Deck Rookie Premiere

COMPLETE SET (30) 7.50 15.00
1 Darren McFadden .75 2.00
2 DeSean Jackson .60 1.50
3 Brian Brohm .30 .75
4 Matt Ryan 1.25 3.00
5 Jonathan Stewart .50 1.25
6 Jerome Simpson .30 .75
7 Chad Henne .30 .75
8 Chris Johnson .75 2.00
9 Team Photo Checklist 1.25 3.00
10 Rashard Mendenhall .60 1.50
11 Earl Bennett .30 .75
12 Early Doucet .25 .60
13 Kevin O'Connell .25 .60
14 Felix Jones .50 1.25
15 Dustin Keller .30 .75
16 Jamaal Charles .50 1.25
17 Joe Flacco 1.00 2.50
18 John David Booty .25 .60
19 Jordy Nelson .40 1.00
20 Kevin Smith .30 .75
21 Limas Sweed .30 .75
22 Dexter Jackson .25 .60
23 Malcolm Kelly .25 .60
24 Jake Long .30 .75
25 Eddie Royal .30 .75
26 Matt Forte .50 1.25
27 Donnie Avery .25 .60
28 Ray Rice .60 1.50
29 Harry Douglas .25 .60
30 Devin Thomas .25 .60

2008 Upper Deck Rookie Premiere Autographs

1 Darren McFadden 30.00 60.00
2 DeSean Jackson 25.00 50.00
3 Brian Brohm 0.00 20.00
4 Matt Ryan 60.00 120.00
5 Jonathan Stewart 12.00 30.00
6 Jerome Simpson 8.00 20.00
7 Chad Henne 8.00 20.00
8 Chris Johnson 50.00 100.00
10 Rashard Mendenhall
11 Earl Bennett 8.00 20.00
12 Early Doucet 6.00 15.00
13 Kevin O'Connell 6.00 15.00
14 Felix Jones 30.00 60.00
15 Dustin Keller 8.00 20.00
16 Jamaal Charles 12.00 30.00
17 Joe Flacco 50.00 100.00
18 John David Booty 6.00 15.00
19 Jordy Nelson 20.00 40.00
20 Kevin Smith 8.00 20.00
21 Limas Sweed 8.00 20.00
22 Dexter Jackson 6.00 15.00
23 Malcolm Kelly 6.00 15.00
24 Jake Long 8.00 20.00
25 Eddie Royal 8.00 20.00
26 Matt Forte 30.00 60.00
27 Donnie Avery
28 Ray Rice 30.00 60.00
29 Harry Douglas 6.00 15.00
30 Devin Thomas 6.00 15.00

2009 Upper Deck Rookie Premiere

COMPLETE SET (30) 7.50 15.00
1 Aaron Curry .30 .75
2 Brandon Pettigrew .30 .75
3 Brian Robiskie .30 .75
4 Chris Wells .50 1.25
5 Darrius Heyward-Bey .30 .75
6 Deon Butler .25 .60
7 Derrick Williams .25 .60
8 Donald Brown .30 .75
9 Hakeem Nicks .50 1.25
10 Jason Smith .25 .60
11 Javon Ringer .30 .75
12 Jeremy Maclin .50 1.25
13 Josh Freeman .60 1.50
14 Juaquin Iglesias .25 .60
15 Kenny Britt .40 1.00
16 Knowshon Moreno .30 .75
17 LeSean McCoy .60 1.50
18 Mark Sanchez 1.00 2.50
19 Matthew Stafford 1.50 4.00
20 Michael Crabtree .60 1.50
21 Mohamed Massaquoi .25 .60
22 Nate Davis .25 .60
23 Pat White .30 .75
24 Patrick Turner .25 .60
25 Percy Harvin .50 1.25
26 Ramses Barden .20 .50
27 Rhett Bomar .25 .60
28 Shonn Greene .50 1.25
29 Tyson Jackson .25 .60
30 Checklist Card .25 .60

2009 Upper Deck Rookie Premiere Autographs

RANDOM INSERTS IN FACTORY SETS
1 Aaron Curry
2 Brandon Pettigrew 8.00 20.00
3 Brian Robiskie 8.00 20.00
4 Chris Wells 12.00 30.00
5 Darrius Heyward-Bey
6 Deon Butler 6.00 15.00
7 Derrick Williams 6.00 15.00
8 Donald Brown 8.00 20.00
9 Hakeem Nicks 12.00 30.00
10 Jason Smith 6.00 15.00
11 Javon Ringer 8.00 20.00
12 Jeremy Maclin 12.00 30.00
13 Josh Freeman 30.00 60.00
14 Juaquin Iglesias 6.00 15.00
15 Kenny Britt 10.00 25.00
16 Knowshon Moreno 20.00 50.00
17 LeSean McCoy 15.00 40.00
18 Mark Sanchez 75.00 150.00
19 Matthew Stafford
20 Michael Crabtree

21 Mohamed Massaquoi	6.00	15.00
22 Nate Davis	6.00	15.00
23 Pat White	8.00	20.00
24 Patrick Turner	6.00	15.00
25 Percy Harvin	40.00	80.00
26 Ramses Barden	5.00	12.00
27 Rhett Bomar		
28 Shonn Greene	12.00	30.00
29 Tyson Jackson	6.00	15.00

1996 Upper Deck Silver

The 1996 Upper Deck Silver set was issued only through Upper Deck's hobby channels. The set was issued in one series totalling 225 standard-size cards. The 10-card packs had a suggested retail price of $2.49 each. 28 packs were in a box and 20 boxes made up a case. The set contains the topical subset Season Leaders (211-225).

COMPLETE SET (225)	7.50	20.00
1 Larry Centers	.07	.20
2 Terance Mathis	.02	.10
3 Justin Armour	.02	.10
4 Kerry Collins	.15	.40
5 Jim Flanigan UER	.02	.10
Mike on front		
6 Dan Wilkinson	.02	.10
7 Eric Zeier	.02	.10
8 Deion Sanders	.20	.50
9 Steve Atwater	.02	.10
10 Johnnie Morton	.07	.20
11 Craig Newsome	.02	.10
12 Broncos Offensive Line	.02	.10
13 Ken Dilger	.07	.20
14 Mark Brunell	.25	.60
15 Tamarick Vanover	.07	.20
16 Bernie Parmalee	.02	.10
17 Orlando Thomas	.02	.10
18 Will Moore	.02	.10
19 Mark Fields	.02	.10
20 Tyrone Wheatley	.07	.20
21 Kyle Brady	.02	.10
22 Napoleon Kaufman	.15	.40
23 Mike Mamula	.02	.10
24 Erric Pegram	.02	.10
25 Brent Jones	.02	.10
26 Aaron Hayden RC	.02	.10
27 Christian Fauria	.02	.10
28 Cowboys Offensive Line	.07	.20
with Troy Aikman		
29 Derrick Brooks	.15	.40
30 Brian Mitchell	.02	.10
31 Garrison Hearst	.07	.20
32 Devin Bush	.02	.10
33 Andre Reed	.07	.20
34 Derrick Moore	.02	.10
35 Erik Kramer	.02	.10
36 Jeff Blake	.15	.40
37 Andre Rison	.07	.20
38 Troy Aikman	.40	1.00
39 Anthony Miller	.07	.20
40 Scott Mitchell	.07	.20
41 Reggie White	.15	.40
42 Chris Sanders	.07	.20
43 Ellis Johnson	.02	.10
44 Willie Jackson	.07	.20
45 Steve Bono	.02	.10
46 Terry Kirby	.07	.20
47 Jake Reed	.07	.20
48 Vincent Brisby	.02	.10
49 Quinn Early	.02	.10
50 Thomas Lewis	.02	.10
51 Wayne Chrebet	.25	.60
52 Pat Swilling	.02	.10
53 Bobby Taylor	.02	.10
54 Mark Bruener	.02	.10
55 Jerry Rice	.40	1.00
56 Natrone Means	.07	.20
57 Rick Mirer	.07	.20
58 Kevin Carter	.02	.10
59 Hardy Nickerson	.02	.10
60 Lions Offensive Line	.02	.10
with Scott Mitchell		
61 Eric Swann	.02	.10
62 Eric Metcalf	.02	.10
63 Russell Copeland	.02	.10
64 Pete Metzelaars	.02	.10
65 Curtis Conway	.15	.40
66 Darnay Scott	.07	.20
67 Leroy Hoard	.02	.10
68 Darren Woodson	.07	.20
69 John Elway	.75	2.00
70 Brett Perriman	.02	.10
71 Mark Chmura	.07	.20
72 Chris Chandler	.07	.20
73 Marshall Faulk	.20	.50
74 Pete Mitchell	.07	.20
75 Willie Davis	.02	.10
76 Irving Fryar	.07	.20
77 Robert Smith	.07	.20
78 Drew Bledsoe	.25	.60
79 Mario Bates	.07	.20
80 Chris Calloway	.02	.10
81 Boomer Esiason	.07	.20
82 Harvey Williams	.02	.10
83 Fred Barnett	.02	.10
84 Neil O'Donnell	.07	.20
85 Lee Woodall	.02	.10
86 Junior Seau	.15	.40
87 Brian Blades	.02	.10
88 Chris Miller	.02	.10
89 Warren Sapp	.02	.10
90 Terry Allen	.07	.20
91 Dave Krieg	.02	.10
92 Bert Emanuel	.07	.20
93 Jim Kelly	.15	.40
94 Mark Carrier WR	.02	.10
95 Jeff Graham	.02	.10
96 Tony McGee	.02	.10
97 Vinny Testaverde	.07	.20
98 Michael Irvin	.15	.40
99 Shannon Sharpe	.07	.20
100 Chris Spielman	.02	.10
101 Edgar Bennett	.07	.20
102 Haywood Jeffires	.02	.10
103 Quentin Coryatt	.02	.10
104 Jeff Lageman	.02	.10
105 Neil Smith	.07	.20
106 O.J. McDuffie	.07	.20
107 Warren Moon	.07	.20
108 Ben Coates	.07	.20
109 Michael Haynes	.02	.10
110 Mike Sherrard	.02	.10
111 Adrian Murrell	.07	.20
112 Jeff Hostetler	.02	.10
113 Charlie Garner	.07	.20
114 Yancey Thigpen	.07	.20
115 Steve Young	.25	.60
116 Tony Martin	.07	.20
117 49ers Offensive Line	.02	.10
118 Jerome Bettis	.15	.40
119 Alvin Harper	.02	.10
120 Heath Shuler	.07	.20
121 Rob Moore	.07	.20
122 Chris Doleman	.02	.10
123 Bruce Smith	.07	.20
124 Sam Mills	.02	.10
125 Donnell Woolford	.02	.10
126 Harold Green	.02	.10
127 Antonio Langham	.02	.10
128 Charles Haley	.07	.20
129 Aaron Craver	.02	.10
130 Barry Sanders	.60	1.50
131 Sean Jones	.02	.10
132 Steve McNair	.30	.75
133 Tony Bennett	.02	.10
134 Dolphins Offensive Line	.15	.40
with Dan Marino		
135 Greg Hill	.07	.20
136 Eric Green	.02	.10
137 John Randle	.07	.20
138 Dave Meggett	.02	.10
139 Irv Smith	.02	.10
140 Dave Brown	.02	.10
141 Raiders Offensive Line	.02	.10
142 Rocket Ismail	.02	.10
143 Rodney Peete	.02	.10
144 Kevin Greene	.07	.20
145 Derek Loville	.02	.10
146 Leslie O'Neal	.02	.10
147 Cortez Kennedy	.02	.10
148 Sean Gilbert	.02	.10
149 Jackie Harris	.02	.10
150 Henry Ellard	.02	.10
151 Frank Sanders	.07	.20
152 Jeff George	.07	.20
153 Darick Holmes	.02	.10
154 Tyrone Poole	.02	.10
155 Rashaan Salaam	.07	.20
156 Carl Pickens	.07	.20
157 Eric Turner	.02	.10
158 Jay Novacek	.02	.10
159 Terrell Davis	.30	.75
160 Herman Moore	.07	.20
161 Robert Brooks	.15	.40
162 Rodney Thomas	.02	.10
163 Sean Dawkins	.02	.10
164 James O. Stewart	.07	.20
165 Marcus Allen	.15	.40
166 Dan Marino	.75	2.00
167 Cris Carter	.15	.40
168 Curtis Martin	.30	.75
169 Tyrone Hughes	.02	.10
170 Rodney Hampton	.07	.20
171 Hugh Douglas	.07	.20
172 Tim Brown	.15	.40
173 Ricky Watters	.07	.20
174 Kordell Stewart	.15	.40
175 Stan Humphries	.07	.20
176 J.J. Stokes	.15	.40
177 Joey Galloway	.15	.40
178 Isaac Bruce	.15	.40
179 Errict Rhett	.07	.20
180 Michael Westbrook	.15	.40
181 Steelers Offensive Line	.02	.10
182 Craig Heyward	.02	.10
183 Bryce Paup	.02	.10
184 Brett Maxie	.02	.10
185 Kevin Butler	.02	.10
186 John Copeland	.02	.10
187 Keenan McCardell	.15	.40
188 Emmitt Smith	.60	1.50
189 Glyn Milburn	.02	.10
190 Jason Hanson	.02	.10
191 Brett Favre	.75	2.00
192 Darryll Lewis UER	.02	.10
name spelled Darryl on front		
193 Jim Harbaugh	.07	.20
194 Desmond Howard	.07	.20
195 Derrick Thomas	.15	.40
196 Bryan Cox	.02	.10
197 Amp Lee	.02	.10
198 Ty Law	.15	.40
199 Jim Everett	.02	.10
200 Vencie Glenn	.02	.10
201 Charles Wilson	.02	.10
202 Terry McDaniel	.02	.10
203 Calvin Williams	.02	.10
204 Greg Lloyd	.07	.20
205 Merton Hanks	.02	.10
206 Andre Coleman	.02	.10
207 Chris Warren	.07	.20
208 D'Marco Farr	.02	.10
209 Trent Dilfer	.15	.40
210 Ken Harvey	.02	.10
211 Jim Harbaugh SL	.07	.20
212 Brett Favre SL	.40	1.00
213 Curtis Martin SL	.15	.40
214 Carl Pickens SL	.07	.20
215 Norm Johnson SL	.02	.10
216 Bryce Paup SL	.02	.10
217 Herman Moore SL	.07	.20
218 Jerry Rice SL	.20	.50
219 Orlando Thomas SL	.02	.10
220 Emmitt Smith SL	.30	.75
221 Tyrone Hughes SL	.02	.10
222 Tamarick Vanover SL	.07	.20
223 Rick Tuten SL	.02	.10
224 49ers Defense SL	.02	.10
225 Lions Offensive Line SL	.02	.10
DM1 Dan Marino Promo	1.00	2.50

1996 Upper Deck Silver All-NFL

COMPLETE SET (20)	12.50	30.00
STATED ODDS 1:5		
AN1 Herman Moore	.40	1.00
AN2 Isaac Bruce	.75	2.00
AN3 Jerry Rice	2.00	5.00
AN4 Michael Irvin	.75	2.00
AN5 Eric Metcalf	.20	.50
AN6 Ben Coates	.40	1.00
AN7 Brett Favre	4.00	10.00
AN8 Jim Harbaugh	.40	1.00
AN9 Emmitt Smith	3.00	8.00
AN10 Barry Sanders	3.00	8.00
AN11 Chris Warren	.40	1.00
AN12 Curtis Martin	1.50	4.00
AN13 Hugh Douglas	.40	1.00
AN14 Neil Smith	.40	1.00
AN15 Reggie White	.75	2.00
AN16 Bryce Paup	.20	.50
AN17 Greg Lloyd	.40	1.00
AN18 Carnell Lake	.20	.50
AN19 Merton Hanks	.20	.50
AN20 Tamarick Vanover	.40	1.00

1996 Upper Deck Silver All-Rookie Team

COMPLETE SET (20)	50.00	100.00
STATED ODDS 1:18		
AR1 Joey Galloway	2.00	5.00
AR2 Chris Sanders	1.00	2.50
AR3 J.J. Stokes	2.00	5.00
AR4 Ken Dilger	1.00	2.50
AR5 Pete Mitchell	1.00	2.50
AR6 Kordell Stewart	2.00	5.00
AR7 Kerry Collins	2.00	5.00
AR8 Tony Boselli	.50	1.25
AR9 Terrell Davis	4.00	10.00
AR10 Rodney Thomas	.50	1.25
AR11 Rashaan Salaam	1.00	2.50
AR12 Curtis Martin	4.00	10.00
AR13 Napoleon Kaufman	2.00	5.00
AR14 Hugh Douglas	1.00	2.50
AR15 Ellis Johnson	.50	1.25
AR16 Kevin Carter	.50	1.25
AR17 Derrick Brooks	2.00	5.00
AR18 Craig Newsome	.50	1.25
AR19 Orlando Thomas	.50	1.25
AR20 Tamarick Vanover	1.00	2.50

1996 Upper Deck Silver Helmet Cards

COMPLETE SET (30)	100.00	200.00
STATED ODDS 1:23		
AC1 Jeff Blake	1.50	4.00
David Dunn		
AC2 Vinny Testaverde	1.25	3.00
Eric Zeier		
AC3 Rodney Thomas	1.25	3.00
Chris Sanders		
AC4 Mark Brunell	4.00	10.00
James O.Stewart		
AC5 Greg Lloyd	2.50	6.00
Kordell Stewart		
AE1 Marshall Faulk	3.00	8.00
Ken Dilger		
AE2 Wayne Chrebet	4.00	10.00
Hugh Douglas		
AE3 Dan Marino	15.00	30.00
Billy Milner		
AE4 Jim Kelly	2.50	6.00
Darick Holmes		
AE5 Drew Bledsoe	7.50	20.00
Curtis Martin		
AW1 Steve Bono	1.50	4.00
Tamarick Vanover UER		
name spelled Tamerick on front		
AW2 Chris Warren	2.50	6.00
Joey Galloway		
AW3 Natrone Means	1.50	4.00
Aaron Hayden		
AW4 Tim Brown	2.50	6.00
Napoleon Kaufman		
AW5 John Elway	20.00	40.00
Terrell Davis		
NC1 Erik Kramer	1.50	4.00
Rashaan Salaam		
NC2 Herman Moore	1.50	4.00
Luther Elliss		
NC3 Cris Carter	2.50	6.00
Orlando Thomas		
NC4 Errict Rhett	2.50	6.00
Derrick Brooks		
NC5 Robert Brooks	2.50	6.00
Craig Newsome		
NE1 Garrison Hearst	1.50	4.00
Frank Sanders		
NE2 Rodney Hampton	1.25	3.00
Tyrone Wheatley		
NE3 Ricky Watters	1.50	4.00
Mike Mamula		
NE4 Terry Allen	2.50	6.00
Michael Westbrook		
NE5 Emmitt Smith	15.00	30.00
Sherman Williams		
NW1 Jeff George	1.50	4.00
Devin Bush		
NW2 Sam Mills	2.50	6.00
Kerry Collins		
NW3 Mario Bates	1.25	3.00
Mark Fields		
NW4 Isaac Bruce	1.50	4.00
Kevin Carter		
NW5 Jerry Rice	10.00	20.00
J.J.Stokes		

1996 Upper Deck Silver Dan Marino

COMPLETE SET (4)	25.00	60.00
COMMON CARD (RS1-RS4)	6.00	15.00
STATED ODDS 1:81		

1996 Upper Deck Silver Prime Choice Rookies

COMPLETE SET (20)	20.00	40.00
SET AVAILABLE VIA MAIL REDEMPTION		
REDEMPT.CARD STATED ODDS 1:103		
1 Keyshawn Johnson	2.00	5.00
2 Kevin Hardy	.20	.50
3 Simeon Rice	.60	1.50
4 Tim Biakabutuka	.50	1.25
5 Terry Glenn	2.00	5.00
6 Rickey Dudley	.30	.75
7 Alex Molden	.20	.50
8 Regan Upshaw	.20	.50
9 Eddie George	2.50	6.00
10 John Mobley	.20	.50
11 Eddie Kennison	.50	1.25
12 Marvin Harrison	5.00	12.00
13 Leeland McElroy	.30	.75
14 Eric Moulds	2.50	6.00
15 Mike Alstott	2.00	5.00
16 Bobby Engram	.30	.75
17 Derrick Mayes	.30	.75
18 Karim Abdul-Jabbar	.50	1.25
19 Stepfret Williams	.20	.50
20 Jeff Lewis	.30	.75

2004 Upper Deck Sportsfest

These cards were issued in groups of five over the course of three days at the 2004 Sportsfest card show in Chicago. Collectors would receive a group of 5 each day in exchange for 10 Upper Deck card wrappers that carried and SRP valued of $2.99 or higher. A 16th card was issued as an exchange card good for the first pick in the 2004 NBA draft.

STATED PRINT RUN 500 SER.#'d SETS		
SF11 Tom Brady	1.00	2.50
SF12 Eli Manning	2.50	6.00

2005 Upper Deck Sportsfest

These cards were issued at the 2005 Sportsfest card show in Chicago. Collectors would receive a group of cards in exchange for a variety of Upper Deck card wrappers opened at Upper Deck's booth. Each card was serial numbered of 750.

COMPLETE SET (6)	12.50	25.00
NFL1 Michael Vick	1.00	2.50
NFL2 Tom Brady	2.50	6.00
NFL3 Eli Manning	3.00	8.00
NFL4 Peyton Manning	2.00	5.00
NFL5 Donovan McNabb	1.25	3.00
NFL6 Rex Grossman	1.00	2.50

2006 Upper Deck Sportsfest

UNPRICED AUTOS SER.#'d TO 5		
NFL1 Peyton Manning	1.50	4.00
NFL2 Ben Roethlisberger	1.25	3.00
NFL4 Tom Brady	1.50	4.00
NFL5 Cedric Benson	.75	2.00
NFL6 Shaun Alexander	.75	2.00

2008 Upper Deck Sportsfest

COMPLETE SET (12)	15.00	40.00
UNPRICED AUTO PRINT RUN 5 SETS		
SF3 Peyton Manning	1.00	2.50
SF6 Brian Urlacher	.60	1.50
SF10 Devin Hester	.60	1.50

2003 Upper Deck Standing O

Released in October of 2003, this retail only set consists of 84 cards, all of them veterans. Boxes contained 24 packs of 4 cards.

COMPLETE SET (84)	10.00	25.00
1 Michael Vick	.40	1.00
2 Tim Couch	.20	.50
3 Joey Harrington	.20	.50
4 Brett Favre	.75	2.00
5 Donovan McNabb	.30	.75
6 Jeff Garcia	.25	.60
7 Chris Redman	.20	.50
8 David Carr	.25	.60
9 Steve McNair	.30	.75
10 Chad Pennington	.30	.75
11 Daunte Culpepper	.25	.60
12 Tom Brady	.75	2.00
13 Kurt Warner	.30	.75
14 Brad Johnson	.25	.60
15 Aaron Brooks	.25	.60
16 Mark Brunell	.25	.60
17 Drew Brees	.30	.75
18 Peyton Manning	.60	1.50
19 Drew Bledsoe	.30	.75
20 Rich Gannon	.25	.60
21 Kordell Stewart	.25	.60
22 Josh McCown	.25	.60
23 Chad Hutchinson	.20	.50
24 Jake Delhomme	.30	.75
25 Patrick Ramsey	.25	.60
26 Jay Fiedler	.20	.50
27 Trent Green	.25	.60
28 Jake Plummer	.25	.60
29 Tommy Maddox	.25	.60
30 Matt Hasselbeck	.25	.60
31 Kerry Collins	.25	.60
32 Marshall Faulk	.30	.75
33 Edgerrin James	.30	.75
34 Ricky Williams	.25	.60
35 Emmitt Smith	.75	2.00
36 Deuce McAllister	.25	.60
37 Ahman Green	.25	.60
38 LaDainian Tomlinson	.30	.75
39 Priest Holmes	.30	.75
40 Curtis Martin	.30	.75
41 Travis Henry	.20	.50
42 Anthony Thomas	.25	.60
43 Fred Taylor	.25	.60
44 Jamal Lewis	.25	.60
45 Michael Bennett	.25	.60
46 Shaun Alexander	.25	.60
47 Garrison Hearst	.25	.60
48 Kevan Barlow	.20	.50
49 Charlie Garner	.25	.60
50 Clinton Portis	.25	.60
51 Eddie George	.25	.60
52 Corey Dillon	.25	.60
53 Jerome Bettis	.30	.75
54 Jeremy Shockey	.30	.75
55 Tony Gonzalez	.30	.75
56 Jerry Rice	.60	1.50
57 Tim Brown	.30	.75
58 Terrell Owens	.30	.75
59 Randy Moss	.30	.75
60 Keyshawn Johnson	.30	.75
61 Marvin Harrison	.30	.75
62 Peerless Price	.20	.50
63 Chris Chambers	.25	.60
64 David Boston	.20	.50
65 Laveranues Coles	.20	.50
66 Rod Gardner	.20	.50
67 Isaac Bruce	.30	.75
68 Torry Holt	.30	.75
69 Troy Brown	.25	.60
70 Antonio Bryant	.20	.50
71 Plaxico Burress	.25	.60
72 Antwaan Randle El	.25	.60
73 Rod Smith	.25	.60
74 Ashley Lelie	.20	.50
75 Eric Moulds	.25	.60
76 Chad Johnson	.30	.75
77 Kevin Johnson	.20	.50
78 Jevon Kearse	.25	.60
79 Zach Thomas	.30	.75
80 Roy Williams	.25	.60
81 Julius Peppers	.30	.75
82 Junior Seau	.30	.75
83 Ray Lewis	.30	.75
84 Brian Urlacher	.30	.75

2003 Upper Deck Standing O Die Cuts

COMPLETE SET (84)	25.00	60.00
*DIE CUTS: 1X TO 2.5X BASIC CARDS		
ONE PER PACK		

2003 Upper Deck Standing O Rookies

COMPLETE SET (42)	60.00	150.00
STATED ODDS 1:4		
*EMBOSSED: .8X TO 2X BASIC INSERTS		
EMBOSSED STATED ODDS 1:24		
*EMBOSSED DIE CUT: 2X TO 5X		
EMBOSSED DIE CUT ODDS 1:480		
1 Carson Palmer	2.50	6.00
2 Byron Leftwich	1.25	3.00
3 Kyle Boller	1.25	3.00
4 Rex Grossman	1.25	3.00
5 Dave Ragone	.75	2.00
6 Chris Simms	1.25	3.00
7 Seneca Wallace	1.25	3.00
8 Brian St.Pierre	1.00	2.50
9 Brooks Bollinger	1.00	2.50
10 Kliff Kingsbury	1.00	2.50
11 Gibran Hamdan	.75	2.00
12 Ken Dorsey	1.00	2.50
13 Willis McGahee	1.50	4.00
14 Larry Johnson	1.25	3.00
15 Musa Smith	.75	2.00
16 B.J. Askew	1.00	2.50
17 Chris Brown	.75	2.00
18 Justin Fargas	1.25	3.00
19 Artose Pinner	.75	2.00
20 Domanick Davis	1.00	2.50
21 Onterrio Smith	.75	2.00
22 Quentin Griffin	1.00	2.50
23 Charles Rogers	1.00	2.50
24 Andre Johnson	3.00	8.00
25 Bryant Johnson	1.25	3.00
26 Taylor Jacobs	.75	2.00
27 Bethel Johnson	.75	2.00
28 Anquan Boldin	2.00	5.00
29 Tyrone Calico	1.00	2.50
30 Teyo Johnson	1.00	2.50
31 Kelley Washington	.75	2.00
32 Nate Burleson	1.00	2.50
33 Kevin Curtis	1.25	3.00
34 Billy McMullen	.75	2.00
35 Dallas Clark	2.00	5.00
36 Ben Joppru	.75	2.00
37 L.J. Smith	1.25	3.00
38 DeWayne Robertson	1.00	2.50
39 Marcus Trufant	1.00	2.50
40 Boss Bailey	1.00	2.50
41 Troy Polamalu	8.00	20.00
42 Terence Newman	1.00	2.50

2003 Upper Deck Standing O Signatures

STATED ODDS 1:480		
SIAB Antonio Bryant/164*	6.00	15.00
SIAD Andre Davis/141*	6.00	15.00
SIAL Ashley Lelie/86*	6.00	15.00
SIAM Archie Manning/95*	15.00	30.00
SIBD Brandon Doman/141*	6.00	15.00
SIDC David Carr/86*	8.00	20.00
SIDF DeShaun Foster/95*	8.00	20.00
SIEC Eric Crouch/141*	10.00	25.00
SIJG Jabar Gaffney/141*	6.00	15.00
SIKC Kelly Campbell/141*	6.00	15.00
SIKK Kurt Kittner/86*	6.00	15.00
SILS Luke Staley/85*	6.00	15.00
SINH Napoleon Harris/141*	6.00	15.00
SIPM Peyton Manning/95*	60.00	100.00
SIRC Reche Caldwell/141*	6.00	15.00
SIRD Rohan Davey/141*	6.00	15.00
SIRJ Ron Johnson/141*	6.00	15.00
SIRW Roy Williams/149*	8.00	20.00

2003 Upper Deck Standing O Swatches

STATED ODDS 1:72		
SWAB Antonio Bryant	3.00	8.00
SWAD Andre Davis	3.00	8.00
SWAR Antwaan Randle El	4.00	10.00
SWBJ Brad Johnson	4.00	10.00
SWBU Marc Bulger	5.00	12.00
SWCP Clinton Portis	4.00	10.00
SWIB Isaac Bruce	5.00	12.00
SWJB Jeff Blake	4.00	10.00
SWJG Jeff Garcia	4.00	10.00
SWJH Joey Harrington	3.00	8.00
SWJM Josh McCown	4.00	10.00
SWJP Jerry Porter	3.00	8.00
SWJS Jeremy Shockey	5.00	12.00
SWKM Keenan McCardell	4.00	10.00
SWMB Mark Brunell	4.00	10.00
SWMH Matt Hasselbeck	4.00	10.00
SWMV Michael Vick	6.00	15.00
SWPE Julius Peppers	5.00	12.00
SWPR Patrick Ramsey	4.00	10.00
SWRS Rod Smith	4.00	10.00
SWTB Tom Brady	12.00	30.00

2003 Upper Deck Star Rookie Sportsfest

This 6-card set was distributed by Upper Deck at the 2003 Sportsfest in Chicago. Collectors were required to open specific boxes of Upper Deck product at the booth in order to receive the set.

COMPLETE SET (6)	5.00	12.00
AJ Andre Johnson	1.25	3.00
BL Byron Leftwich	.50	1.25
CP Carson Palmer	1.00	2.50
KB Kyle Boller	.50	1.25
RG Rex Grossman	.50	1.25
WM Willis McGahee	.60	1.50

2001 Upper Deck Top Tier

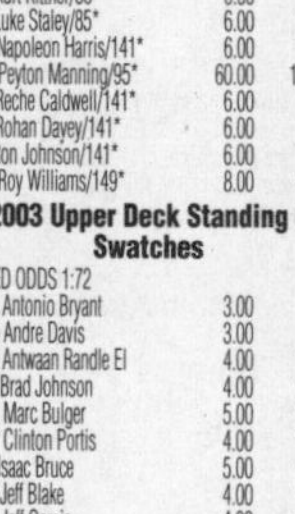

This 280 card set was issued in five-card packs. The first 180 cards in the set are NFL veterans while cards 181 through 280 feature Rookie Cards. The Rookie Cards were issued either in a stated print run of 1500, 2000 or 2500.

COMP.SET w/o SP's (180)	20.00	40.00
1 Jake Plummer	.30	.75
2 David Boston	.25	.60
3 Thomas Jones	.30	.75
4 Frank Sanders	.25	.60
5 Tony Martin	.30	.75
6 Jamal Anderson	.30	.75
7 Chris Chandler	.30	.75
8 Shawn Jefferson	.25	.60
9 Jammi German	.25	.60
10 Terance Mathis	.25	.60
11 Jamal Lewis	.40	1.00
12 Shannon Sharpe	.40	1.00
13 Elvis Grbac	.30	.75
14 Ray Lewis	.40	1.00
15 Qadry Ismail	.30	.75
16 Sam Gash	.25	.60
17 Rob Johnson	.30	.75
18 Eric Moulds	.30	.75
19 Sammy Morris	.30	.75
20 Shawn Bryson	.25	.60
21 Jeremy McDaniel	.25	.60
22 Muhsin Muhammad	.30	.75
23 Brad Hoover	.30	.75
24 Tim Biakabutuka	.25	.60
25 Donald Hayes	.25	.60
26 Dameyune Craig	.25	.60
27 Wesley Walls	.25	.60
28 Cade McNown	.30	.75
29 James Allen	.25	.60
30 Marcus Robinson	.30	.75
31 Brian Urlacher	.50	1.25
32 Bobby Engram	.30	.75
33 Shane Matthews	.25	.60
34 Peter Warrick	.30	.75
35 Corey Dillon	.30	.75
36 Akili Smith	.25	.60
37 Scott Mitchell	.25	.60
38 Jon Kitna	.30	.75
39 Tim Couch	.25	.60
40 Kevin Johnson	.25	.60
41 Travis Prentice	.25	.60
42 Spergon Wynn	.25	.60
43 Jamel White	.25	.60
44 JaJuan Dawson	.25	.60
45 Courtney Brown	.25	.60
46 Tony Banks	.25	.60
47 Emmitt Smith	1.00	2.50
48 Joey Galloway	.30	.75
49 Rocket Ismail	.30	.75
50 Anthony Wright	.25	.60
51 Darren Woodson	.30	.75
52 Terrell Davis	.40	1.00
53 Mike Anderson	.30	.75
54 Brian Griese	.30	.75
55 Rod Smith	.30	.75
56 Ed McCaffrey	.30	.75
57 Eddie Kennison	.30	.75
58 Olandis Gary	.25	.60
59 Charlie Batch	.30	.75
60 Germane Crowell	.25	.60
61 James O. Stewart	.25	.60
62 Johnnie Morton	.30	.75
63 Desmond Howard	.30	.75
64 Brett Favre	1.25	3.00
65 Antonio Freeman	.40	1.00
66 Dorsey Levens	.30	.75
67 Ahman Green	.40	1.00
68 Bill Schroeder	.30	.75
69 Bubba Franks	.30	.75
70 Peyton Manning	1.00	2.50
71 Edgerrin James	.40	1.00
72 Marvin Harrison	.40	1.00
73 Jerome Pathon	.25	.60
74 Lennox Gordon	.25	.60
75 Terrence Wilkins	.25	.60
76 Mark Brunell	.30	.75
77 Fred Taylor	.40	1.00
78 Jimmy Smith	.30	.75
79 Keenan McCardell	.30	.75
80 Kevin Hardy	.25	.60
81 Stacey Mack	.25	.60
82 Tony Gonzalez	.40	1.00
83 Derrick Alexander	.25	.60
84 Priest Holmes	.40	1.00
85 Trent Green	.40	1.00
86 Tony Horne	.25	.60
87 Oronde Gadsden	.25	.60
88 Lamar Smith	.30	.75
89 Jay Fiedler	.30	.75
90 Zach Thomas	.40	1.00
91 Ray Lucas	.25	.60
92 O.J. McDuffie	.25	.60
93 Randy Moss	.40	1.00
94 Cris Carter	.40	1.00
95 Daunte Culpepper	.30	.75
96 Robert Griffith	.25	.60
97 Jake Reed	.30	.75
98 Drew Bledsoe	.40	1.00
99 Terry Glenn	.30	.75
100 Kevin Faulk	.30	.75
101 Michael Bishop	.30	.75
102 Troy Brown	.30	.75
103 Ricky Williams	.40	1.00
104 Jeff Blake	.30	.75
105 Joe Horn	.30	.75
106 Willie Jackson	.25	.60
107 Aaron Brooks	.30	.75
108 Albert Connell	.25	.60
109 Kerry Collins	.30	.75
110 Amani Toomer	.30	.75
111 Ron Dayne	.30	.75
112 Tiki Barber	.40	1.00
113 Ike Hilliard	.30	.75
114 Ron Dixon	.25	.60
115 Michael Strahan	.40	1.00
116 Vinny Testaverde	.30	.75
117 Wayne Chrebet	.30	.75
118 Curtis Martin	.40	1.00
119 Richie Anderson	.25	.60
120 Laveranues Coles	.30	.75
121 Chad Pennington	.40	1.00
122 Tim Brown	.40	1.00
123 Rich Gannon	.30	.75
124 Tyrone Wheatley	.30	.75
125 Charlie Garner	.30	.75
126 Jerry Rice	.75	2.00
127 Charles Woodson	.40	1.00
128 Duce Staley	.30	.75
129 Donovan McNabb	.40	1.00
130 Todd Pinkston	.25	.60
131 Chad Lewis	.25	.60
132 Brian Mitchell	.30	.75
133 Kordell Stewart	.30	.75
134 Jerome Bettis	.40	1.00
135 Plaxico Burress	.30	.75
136 Bobby Shaw	.25	.60
137 Hines Ward	.40	1.00
138 Marshall Faulk	.40	1.00
139 Kurt Warner	.60	1.50
140 Isaac Bruce	.40	1.00
141 Torry Holt	.30	.75
142 Justin Watson	.25	.60
143 Az-Zahir Hakim	.25	.60
144 Junior Seau	.40	1.00
145 Curtis Conway	.30	.75
146 Doug Flutie	.40	1.00
147 Jeff Graham	.25	.60
148 Freddie Jones	.25	.60
149 Rodney Harrison	.30	.75
150 Jeff Garcia	.30	.75
151 Tai Streets	.25	.60
152 Terrell Owens	.40	1.00
153 J.J. Stokes	.25	.60
154 Garrison Hearst	.30	.75
155 Paul Smith	.25	.60
156 Ricky Watters	.30	.75
157 Shaun Alexander	.40	1.00
158 Matt Hasselbeck	.40	1.00
159 Brock Huard	.25	.60
160 Darrell Jackson	.30	.75
161 Karsten Bailey	.25	.60
162 Warrick Dunn	.40	1.00
163 Shaun King	.25	.60
164 Reidel Anthony	.25	.60
165 Mike Alstott	.30	.75
166 Jacquez Green	.25	.60
167 Brad Johnson	.30	.75
168 Keyshawn Johnson	.30	.75
169 Eddie George	.40	1.00
170 Steve McNair	.40	1.00
171 Neil O'Donnell	.30	.75
172 Derrick Mason	.30	.75
173 Frank Wycheck	.25	.60
174 Chris Sanders	.25	.60
175 Jevon Kearse	.30	.75
176 Jeff George	.30	.75
177 Stephen Davis	.30	.75
178 Kevin Lockett	.25	.60
179 Michael Westbrook	.25	.60
180 Stephen Alexander	.25	.60
181 Arnold Jackson/2000 RC	1.00	2.50
182 Bobby Newcombe/2000 RC	1.25	3.00
183 Vinny Sutherland/2000 RC	1.00	2.50
184 Michael Vick/1500 RC	8.00	20.00
185 Quentin McCord/2500 RC	1.00	2.50
186 Todd Heap/1500 RC	2.00	5.00
187 Chris Barnes/2000 RC	1.00	2.50
188 Travis Henry/1500 RC	1.50	4.00
189 Reggie Germany/2500 RC	.75	2.00
190 Tim Hasselbeck/2000 RC	1.25	3.00
191 Dan Morgan/2500 RC	1.00	2.50
192 Dee Brown/2000 RC	1.00	2.50
193 Chris Weinke/2000 RC	1.25	3.00
194 David Terrell/1500 RC	1.50	4.00
195 Anthony Thomas/1500 RC	2.00	5.00
196 Rudi Johnson/2500 RC	1.25	3.00
197 Chad Johnson/1500 RC	3.00	8.00
198 Quincy Morgan/2500 RC	1.00	2.50
199 James Jackson/1500 RC	1.25	3.00
200 Quincy Carter/2000 RC	1.25	3.00
201 Kevin Kasper/2500 RC	.75	2.00
202 Scotty Anderson/2000 RC	1.00	2.50
203 Mike McMahon/1500 RC	1.50	4.00
204 Robert Ferguson/1500 RC	2.00	5.00
205 David Martin/2000 RC	1.00	2.50
206 Reggie Wayne/2000 RC	3.00	8.00
207 Kabeer Gbaja-Biamila/2500 RC	1.25	3.00
208 Snoop Minnis/2000 RC	1.00	2.50
209 Derrick Blaylock/1500 RC	1.50	4.00
210 Josh Heupel/2500 RC	1.25	3.00
211 Travis Minor/2000 RC	1.25	3.00
212 Chris Chambers/2000 RC	1.50	4.00
213 Michael Bennett/1500 RC	1.50	4.00
214 Justin Smith/1500 RC	2.00	5.00
215 Deuce McAllister/2000 RC	1.50	4.00
216 Moran Norris/2500 RC	.75	2.00
217 Onome Ojo/2500 RC	.75	2.00
218 Jesse Palmer/1500 RC	1.50	4.00
219 Santana Moss/2000 RC	2.00	5.00
220 LaMont Jordan/2000 RC	1.50	4.00
221 Marques Tuiasosopo/2000 RC	1.25	3.00
222 A.J. Feeley/1500 RC	1.50	4.00
223 Correll Buckhalter/1500 RC	2.00	5.00
224 Freddie Mitchell/2000 RC	1.00	2.50
225 Chris Taylor/2500 RC	.75	2.00
226 Drew Brees/1500 RC	12.00	30.00
227 LaDainian Tomlinson/1500 RC	6.00	15.00
228 Dave Dickenson/2000 RC	1.25	3.00
229 Kevan Barlow/2000 RC	1.25	3.00
230 Andre Carter/2000 RC	1.25	3.00
231 Cedrick Wilson/2000 RC	1.25	3.00
232 David Allen/2500 RC	.75	2.00
233 Alex Bannister/1500 RC	1.25	3.00
234 Josh Booty/2000 RC	1.25	3.00
235 Koren Robinson/2500 RC	1.00	2.50
236 Damione Lewis/2000 RC	1.25	3.00
237 Eddie Berlin/2500 RC	.75	2.00
238 Darnerien McCants/1500 RC	1.50	4.00
239 Sage Rosenfels/2500 RC	1.25	3.00
240 Rod Gardner/1500 RC	1.50	4.00
241 Billy Baber/2500 RC	.75	2.00
242 Dan Alexander/2000 RC	1.25	3.00
243 Reggie White/2500 RC	.75	2.00
244 Adam Archuleta/2000 RC	1.25	3.00
245 Derrick Gibson/2500 RC	.75	2.00
246 Hakim Akbar/2000 RC	1.00	2.50
247 Brandon Manumaleuna/2500 RC	1.00	2.50
248 Andre King/2500 RC	.75	2.00
249 Corey Alston/2500 RC	.75	2.00
250 Fred Smoot/1500 RC	2.00	5.00
251 Kyle Vanden Bosch/2500 RC	1.25	3.00
252 Richard Seymour/1500 RC	2.00	5.00
253 Derek Combs/2000 RC	1.00	2.50
254 Ken-Yon Rambo/2500 RC	.75	2.00
255 Joey Getherall/2000 RC	1.00	2.50
256 Jonathan Carter/1500 RC	1.25	3.00
257 Gerard Warren/1500 RC	1.50	4.00
258 Carlos Polk/2000 RC	1.00	2.50
259 Milton Wynn/2500 RC	.75	2.00
260 Ronney Daniels/2000 RC	1.00	2.50
261 Edgerton Hartwell/1500 RC	1.25	3.00
262 Steve Smith/2000 RC	3.00	8.00
263 T.J. Houshmandzadeh/1500 RC	2.50	6.00
264 Alge Crumpler/2000 RC	1.50	4.00
265 Torrance Marshall/1500 RC	1.25	3.00
266 Tommy Polley/2000 RC	1.00	2.50
267 Sedrick Hodge/2000 RC	1.00	2.50
268 Kendrell Bell/2500 RC	1.25	3.00
269 Jamie Winborn/1500 RC	1.50	4.00
270 Brian Allen/2000 RC	1.00	2.50
271 Brandon Spoon/1500 RC	1.50	4.00
272 Paul Toviessa/2000 RC	1.00	2.50
273 Aaron Schobel/2500 RC	1.25	3.00
274 Will Allen/2500 RC	1.25	3.00
275 Jamar Fletcher/1500 RC	1.25	3.00
276 Andre Dyson/2000 RC	1.00	2.50
277 Nate Clements/2500 RC	1.00	2.50
278 Willie Middlebrooks/2500 RC	1.00	2.50
279 Ken Lucas/2500 RC	1.00	2.50
280 Jamal Reynolds/2000 RC	1.00	2.50

2001 Upper Deck Top Tier Home and Away Jerseys

OVERALL JSY or BALL ODDS 1:239		
HACC Chris Chambers	6.00	15.00
HADB Drew Brees	20.00	50.00
HADM Dan Morgan	5.00	12.00
HAFM Freddie Mitchell	4.00	10.00

HAJH Josh Heupel	6.00	15.00
HAJJ James Jackson	4.00	10.00
HAJP Jesse Palmer	5.00	12.00
HAKB Kevan Barlow	5.00	12.00
HAKR Koren Robinson	5.00	12.00
HAMB Michael Bennett	5.00	12.00
HAMC Deuce McAllister	6.00	15.00
HAMM Mike McMahon	5.00	12.00
HAMT Marques Tuiasosopo	5.00	12.00
HAMV Michael Vick	15.00	30.00
HAQM Quincy Morgan	5.00	12.00
HARF Robert Ferguson	6.00	15.00
HARG Rod Gardner	5.00	12.00
HARJ Rudi Johnson	6.00	15.00
HARW Reggie Wayne	10.00	25.00
HASM Santana Moss	8.00	20.00
HATH Travis Henry	5.00	12.00
HATM Travis Minor	5.00	12.00

2001 Upper Deck Top Tier Rookie Duos Footballs

OVERALL JSY or BALL ODDS 1:239

RDBT Drew Brees —	15.00	40.00
LaDainian Tomlinson		
RDHC Josh Heupel	4.00	10.00
Chris Chambers		
RDJJ Chad Johnson	6.00	15.00
Rudi Johnson		
RDMJ Quincy Morgan	3.00	8.00
James Jackson		
RDMW Reggie Wayne	8.00	20.00
Santana Moss		
RDRG Koren Robinson	4.00	10.00
Rod Gardner		
RDTT Anthony Thomas		10.00
David Terrell		
RDVB Michael Vick	15.00	40.00
Drew Brees		
RDWM Chris Weinke	3.00	8.00
Dan Morgan		

2001 Upper Deck Top Tier Then and Now Jerseys

OVERALL JSY or BALL ODDS 1:239

TNDM Deuce McAllister	8.00	20.00
TNFM Freddie Mitchell	5.00	12.00
TNJJ J.J. Stokes	5.00	12.00
TNJS Junior Seau	8.00	20.00
TNRD Ron Dayne	6.00	15.00
TNTA Troy Aikman	15.00	40.00

2001 Upper Deck Top Tier Tri-Stars Footballs

OVERALL JSY or BALL ODDS 1:239

3SCH Cade McNown	8.00	20.00
Brian Urlacher		
David Terrell		
3SGB Brett Favre	20.00	50.00
Ahman Green		
Antonio Freeman		
3SIC Edgerrin James	15.00	40.00
Peyton Manning		
Marvin Harrison		
3SMD Josh Heupel	6.00	15.00
Travis Minor		
Chris Chambers		
3SMV Daunte Culpepper	6.00	15.00
Randy Moss		
Cris Carter		
3SNO Aaron Brooks	6.00	15.00
Ricky Williams		
Joe Horn		
3SSF Jeff Garcia	6.00	15.00
Terrell Owens		
J.J. Stokes		
3STB Warrick Dunn	6.00	15.00
Mike Alstott		
Keyshawn Johnson		

2001 Upper Deck Top Tier Two of a Kind Footballs

OVERALL JSY or BALL ODDS 1:239

2KCV Daunte Culpepper	15.00	40.00
Michael Vick		
2KDB Ron Dayne	4.00	10.00
Michael Bennett		
2KFF Brett Favre	15.00	40.00
Robert Ferguson		
2KJJ Keyshawn Johnson	6.00	15.00
Chad Johnson		
2KJT Edgerrin James	12.00	30.00
LaDainian Tomlinson		
2KMT Randy Moss	5.00	12.00
David Terrell		
2KNO Ricky Williams	5.00	12.00
Deuce McAllister		
2KUM Brian Urlacher	6.00	15.00
Dan Morgan		
2KWM Peter Warrick	4.00	10.00
Snoop Minnis		

2007 Upper Deck Trilogy

This 184-card set was released in October, 2007. The set was issued into the hobby in three-card packs, with a $30 SRP, which came nine packs to a box. Cards number 1-100 feature veterans in alphabetical team order while cards number 101-184 feature 2007 NFL rookies that were issued to a stated print run of 399 serial numbered sets.

1 Matt Leinart	.60	1.50
2 Anquan Boldin	.60	1.50
3 Larry Fitzgerald	.75	2.00
4 Edgerrin James	.60	1.50
5 Michael Vick	.75	2.00
6 Warrick Dunn	.60	1.50
7 Joe Horn	.60	1.50
8 Steve McNair	.60	1.50
9 Willis McGahee	.60	1.50
10 Mark Clayton	.60	1.50
11 J.P. Losman	.50	1.25
12 Lee Evans	.60	1.50
13 Anthony Thomas	.50	1.25
14 Jake Delhomme	.60	1.50
15 DeAngelo Williams	.75	2.00
16 Steve Smith	.60	1.50
17 Rex Grossman	.60	1.50
18 Cedric Benson	.60	1.50
19 Brian Urlacher	.75	2.00
20 Carson Palmer	.60	1.50
21 Rudi Johnson	.60	1.50
22 Chad Johnson	.60	1.50
23 Charlie Frye	.60	1.50
24 Braylon Edwards	.60	1.50
25 Kellen Winslow	.60	1.50
26 Tony Romo	1.00	2.50
27 Julius Jones	.50	1.25
28 Terrell Owens	.75	2.00
29 Jay Cutler	.75	2.00
30 Travis Henry	.60	1.50
31 Javon Walker	.60	1.50
32 Jon Kitna	.50	1.25
33 Roy Williams WR	.60	1.50
34 Tatum Bell	.50	1.25
35 Brett Favre	1.50	4.00
36 Donald Driver	.75	2.00
37 Greg Jennings	.75	2.00
38 Matt Schaub	.60	1.50
39 Ahman Green	.60	1.50
40 Andre Johnson	.60	1.50
41 Peyton Manning	1.25	3.00
42 Joseph Addai	.60	1.50
43 Marvin Harrison	.75	2.00
44 Reggie Wayne	.60	1.50
45 Byron Leftwich	.60	1.50
46 Maurice Jones-Drew	.75	2.00
47 Fred Taylor	.60	1.50
48 Damon Huard	.60	1.50
49 Larry Johnson	.50	1.25
50 Tony Gonzalez	.60	1.50
51 Daunte Culpepper	.60	1.50
52 Ronnie Brown	.60	1.50
53 Chris Chambers	.60	1.50
54 Tarvaris Jackson	.50	1.25
55 Chester Taylor	.50	1.25
56 Troy Williamson	.50	1.25
57 Tom Brady	1.25	3.00
58 Laurence Maroney	.60	1.50
59 Randy Moss	.75	2.00
60 Drew Brees	.75	2.00
61 Reggie Bush	.75	2.00
62 Deuce McAllister	.60	1.50
63 Marques Colston	.75	2.00
64 Eli Manning	.75	2.00
65 Brandon Jacobs	.60	1.50
66 Plaxico Burress	.60	1.50
67 Chad Pennington	.60	1.50
68 Thomas Jones	.60	1.50
69 Laveranues Coles	.50	1.25
70 Nnamdi Asomugha	.75	2.00
71 LaMont Jordan	.60	1.50
72 Ronald Curry	.60	1.50
73 Donovan McNabb	.75	2.00
74 Brian Westbrook	.60	1.50
75 Reggie Brown	.50	1.25
76 Ben Roethlisberger	.75	2.00
77 Willie Parker	.60	1.50
78 Hines Ward	.75	2.00
79 Philip Rivers	.75	2.00
80 LaDainian Tomlinson	.75	2.00
81 Antonio Gates	.75	2.00
82 Shawne Merriman	.60	1.50
83 Alex Smith QB	.75	2.00
84 Frank Gore	.75	2.00
85 Vernon Davis	.60	1.50
86 Matt Hasselbeck	.60	1.50
87 Shaun Alexander	.60	1.50
88 Deion Branch	.60	1.50
89 Marc Bulger	.60	1.50
90 Steven Jackson	.75	2.00
91 Torry Holt	.60	1.50
92 Chris Simms	.50	1.25
93 Cadillac Williams	.60	1.50
94 Joey Galloway	.60	1.50
95 Vince Young	.60	1.50
96 LenDale White	.60	1.50
97 David Givens	.50	1.25
98 Jason Campbell	.60	1.50
99 Clinton Portis	.60	1.50
100 Ladell Betts	.50	1.25
101 JaMarcus Russell RC	1.50	4.00
102 Brady Quinn RC	2.50	6.00
103 Adrian Peterson RC	30.00	60.00
104 Marshawn Lynch RC	2.50	6.00
105 Anthony Gonzalez RC	2.50	6.00
106 Brian Leonard RC	2.00	5.00
107 Calvin Johnson RC	8.00	20.00
108 Darrelle Revis RC	4.00	10.00
109 Drew Stanton RC	1.50	4.00
110 Dwayne Bowe RC	3.00	8.00
111 Dwayne Jarrett RC	2.00	5.00
112 Kenny Irons RC	1.50	4.00
113 Kevin Kolb RC	4.00	10.00
114 LaRon Landry RC	2.50	6.00
115 Leon Hall RC	2.00	5.00
116 Robert Meachem RC	2.50	6.00
117 Sidney Rice RC	3.00	8.00
118 Steve Smith USC RC	2.50	6.00
119 Ted Ginn Jr. RC	2.00	5.00
120 Troy Smith RC	2.50	6.00
121 Adam Carriker RC	2.00	5.00
122 Alan Branch RC	2.00	5.00
123 Amobi Okoye RC	2.50	6.00
124 Antonio Pittman RC	1.50	4.00
125 Aundrae Allison RC	1.50	4.00
126 Brandon Jackson RC	2.00	5.00
127 Brandon Meriweather RC	2.50	6.00
128 Chansi Stuckey RC	2.50	6.00
129 Chris Henry RB RC	1.50	4.00
130 Chris Leak RC	2.00	5.00
131 Courtney Taylor RC	2.00	5.00
132 Craig Buster Davis RC	2.00	5.00
133 Dallas Baker RC	1.50	4.00
134 Darius Walker RC	1.50	4.00
135 David Ball RC	2.00	5.00
136 David Clowney RC	2.00	5.00
137 David Irons RC	1.50	4.00
138 Daymeion Hughes RC	2.00	5.00
139 DeShawn Wynn RC	2.00	5.00
140 Drew Tate RC	2.00	5.00
141 Dwayne Wright RC	2.00	5.00
142 Eric Wright RC	2.50	6.00
143 Gaines Adams RC	2.50	6.00
144 Garrett Wolfe RC	1.50	4.00
145 Gary Russell RC	2.00	5.00
146 Greg Olsen RC	2.00	5.00
147 H.B. Blades RC	1.50	4.00
148 Isaiah Stanback RC	1.50	4.00
149 Jamaal Anderson RC	2.00	5.00
150 Jared Zabransky RC	2.00	5.00
151 Jason Hill RC	2.50	6.00
152 Jeff Rowe RC	1.50	4.00
153 Joe Thomas RC	2.50	6.00
154 Joel Filani RC	2.00	5.00
155 John Beck RC	2.50	6.00
156 Johnnie Lee Higgins RC	2.00	5.00
157 Jordan Palmer RC	2.00	5.00
158 Kenneth Darby RC	2.00	5.00
159 Kolby Smith RC	2.00	5.00
160 LaMarr Woodley RC	2.50	6.00
161 Lawrence Timmons RC	2.50	6.00
162 Legedu Naanee RC	2.50	6.00
163 Lorenzo Booker RC	2.00	5.00
164 Marcus McCauley RC	2.00	5.00
165 Matt Moore RC	2.50	6.00
166 Michael Bush RC	2.50	6.00
167 Michael Griffin RC	2.50	6.00
168 Patrick Willis RC	5.00	12.00
169 Paul Posluszny RC	2.50	6.00
170 Paul Williams RC	1.50	4.00
171 Quentin Moses RC	2.00	5.00
172 Reggie Nelson RC	2.00	5.00
173 Rhema McKnight RC	1.50	4.00
174 Scott Chandler RC	2.50	6.00
175 Selvin Young RC	2.00	5.00
176 Syvelle Newton RC	2.00	5.00
177 Tony Hunt RC	1.50	4.00
178 Trent Edwards RC	2.50	6.00
179 Tyler Palko RC	2.00	5.00
180 Tyrone Moss RC	1.50	4.00
181 Yamon Figurs RC	1.50	4.00
182 Zach Miller RC	2.50	6.00
183 Laurent Robinson RC	2.50	6.00
184 James Jones RC	2.50	6.00

2007 Upper Deck Trilogy Gold

*VETS 1-100: 2X TO 5X BASIC CARDS
VETERAN PRINT RUN 99 SER.#'d SETS
*ROOKIES 101-184: 1X TO 2.5X BASIC CARDS
ROOKIE PRINT RUN 33 SER.#'d SETS

103 Adrian Peterson	100.00	200.00

2007 Upper Deck Trilogy Platinum

UNPRICED PLATINUM PRINT RUN 3

2007 Upper Deck Trilogy America's Game Signatures

STATED PRINT RUN 33-199

AA Aundrae Allison/199	3.00	8.00
AB Alan Branch/199	4.00	10.00
AG Anthony Gonzalez/133	5.00	12.00
BM Brandon Meriweather/199	5.00	12.00
DB Dallas Baker/199	3.00	8.00
DJ Dwayne Jarrett/199	4.00	10.00
DT Drew Tate/199	4.00	10.00
GR Gary Russell/199	4.00	10.00
IS Isaiah Stanback/199	3.00	8.00
JF Joel Filani/199	4.00	10.00
JH Jason Hill/133	5.00	12.00
JR Jeff Rowe/199	3.00	8.00
JZ Jared Zabransky/199	4.00	10.00
KK Kevin Kolb/199	8.00	20.00
MM Marcus McCauley/199	4.00	10.00
PM Peyton Manning/33	75.00	150.00
RC Roger Craig/169	8.00	20.00
RM Robert Meachem/199	5.00	12.00
SN Syvelle Newton/199	4.00	10.00
TM Tyrone Moss/199	3.00	8.00
WI Paul Williams/199	3.00	8.00
YF Yamon Figurs/199	3.00	8.00

2007 Upper Deck Trilogy Auto Focus Autographs

STATED PRINT RUN 9-99
SERIAL #'d UNDER 25 NOT PRICED

AB Anquan Boldin/33	10.00	25.00
BF Brett Favre/33	125.00	250.00
BQ Brady Quinn/33	30.00	80.00
CL Chris Leak/99	6.00	15.00
GJ Greg Jennings/33	10.00	25.00
JA Joseph Addai/33	15.00	40.00
JH Johnnie Lee Higgins/99	6.00	15.00
JO Chad Johnson/33	10.00	25.00
JR JaMarcus Russell/33	12.00	30.00
JZ Jared Zabransky/99	6.00	15.00
MB Marc Bulger/33	10.00	25.00
ML Marshawn Lynch/33	12.00	30.00
PP Paul Posluszny/99	10.00	25.00
RB Reggie Brown/33	10.00	25.00
TE Trent Edwards/99	10.00	25.00
TG Ted Ginn/33	12.00	30.00
TH T.J. Houshmandzadeh/33	10.00	25.00
VY Vince Young/33	15.00	40.00

2007 Upper Deck Trilogy Crystal Clear Combos Autographs

STATED PRINT RUN 99 SER.#'d SETS

HB Leon Hall	6.00	15.00
Alan Branch		
LB Chris Leak	6.00	15.00
Dallas Baker		

2007 Upper Deck Trilogy Crystal Clear Trios Autographs

UNPRICED TRIO AU PRINT RUN 9

2007 Upper Deck Trilogy Graphiti Autographs

STATED PRINT RUN 10-199

AA Aundrae Allison/199	3.00	8.00
AB Alan Branch/199	4.00	10.00
AG Anthony Gonzalez/199	5.00	12.00
AO Amobi Okoye/33	10.00	25.00
BA David Ball/199	4.00	10.00
CH Chris Henry RB/199	3.00	8.00
CS Chansi Stuckey/199	5.00	12.00
DA Darius Walker/199	3.00	8.00
DB Dallas Baker/199	3.00	8.00
DC David Clowney/199	4.00	10.00
DT Drew Tate/199	4.00	10.00
DW DeShawn Wynn/199	4.00	10.00
GR Gary Russell/199	4.00	10.00
IS Isaiah Stanback/199	3.00	8.00
JF Joel Filani/199	4.00	10.00
JR Jeff Rowe/199	3.00	8.00
JS Jared Zabransky/199	4.00	10.00
KD Kenneth Darby/199	4.00	10.00
KK Kevin Kolb/199	15.00	30.00
MM Marcus McCauley/199	4.00	10.00
PP Paul Posluszny/199	5.00	12.00
PW Paul Williams/199	3.00	8.00
QM Quentin Moses/199	4.00	10.00
SN Syvelle Newton/199	4.00	10.00
TM Tyrone Moss/199	3.00	8.00
YF Yamon Figurs/199	3.00	8.00
ZM Zach Miller/199	5.00	12.00

2007 Upper Deck Trilogy Materials Silver

STATED PRINT RUN 199 SER.#'d SETS
*GOLD/33: .6X TO 1.5X SILVER/199
GOLD PRINT RUN 33 SER.#'d SETS
UNPRICED PLATINUM PRINT RUN 3
*PATCH/79: .6X TO 1.5X SILVER/199
PATCH PRINT RUN 79 SER.#'d SETS
*PATCH HOLOGOLD/33: .8X TO 2X SLV/199
PATCH HOLOGOLD PRINT RUN 33 SER.#'d SETS

AB Anquan Boldin	3.00	8.00
AP Adrian Peterson	20.00	50.00
BJ Brandon Jacobs	3.00	8.00
BL Byron Leftwich	3.00	8.00
BQ Brady Quinn	2.50	6.00
CH Chris Henry RB	1.50	4.00
CJ Chad Johnson	3.00	8.00
CP Chad Pennington	3.00	8.00
DB Drew Bennett	2.50	6.00
DD Donald Driver	4.00	10.00
DF DeShaun Foster	3.00	8.00
JB John Beck	2.50	6.00
JC Jay Cutler	4.00	10.00
JP Julius Peppers	3.00	8.00
JR JaMarcus Russell	1.50	4.00
JS Jeremy Shockey	3.00	8.00
LF Larry Fitzgerald	4.00	10.00
MB Marion Barber	5.00	12.00
ML Marshawn Lynch	2.50	6.00
PB Plaxico Burress	3.00	8.00
PM Peyton Manning	6.00	15.00
RG Rex Grossman	3.00	8.00
RM Robert Meachem	2.50	6.00
RW Roy Williams WR	3.00	8.00
SH Santonio Holmes	3.00	8.00
SR Sidney Rice	3.00	8.00
TG Ted Ginn Jr.	2.00	5.00
VY Vince Young	3.00	8.00
WD Warrick Dunn	3.00	8.00
WM Willis McGahee	3.00	8.00

2007 Upper Deck Trilogy Rookie Autographed Patches

STATED PRINT RUN 33 SER.#'d SETS

AG Anthony Gonzalez	20.00	50.00
AP Adrian Peterson	200.00	400.00
BJ Brandon Jackson	15.00	40.00
BL Brian Leonard	15.00	40.00
BQ Brady Quinn	40.00	100.00
CH Chris Henry RB	12.00	30.00
CJ Calvin Johnson	100.00	200.00
DB Dwayne Bowe	25.00	60.00
DJ Dwayne Jarrett	15.00	40.00
DS Drew Stanton	12.00	30.00
GO Greg Olsen	15.00	40.00
GW Garrett Wolfe	12.00	30.00
HI Johnnie Lee Higgins	15.00	40.00
JB John Beck	20.00	50.00
JH Jason Hill	20.00	50.00
JR JaMarcus Russell	15.00	40.00
JT Joe Thomas	20.00	50.00
KI Kenny Irons	12.00	30.00
KK Kevin Kolb	30.00	80.00
LB Lorenzo Booker	15.00	40.00
MB Michael Bush	20.00	50.00
ML Marshawn Lynch	25.00	60.00
PI Antonio Pittman	12.00	30.00
PW Patrick Willis	40.00	80.00
RM Robert Meachem	20.00	50.00
SR Sidney Rice	25.00	60.00
SS Steve Smith USC	20.00	50.00
TE Trent Edwards	25.00	60.00
TG Ted Ginn Jr.	15.00	40.00
TH Tony Hunt	12.00	30.00
WI Paul Williams	12.00	30.00
YF Yamon Figurs	12.00	30.00

2007 Upper Deck Trilogy Rookie Autographs

STATED PRINT RUN 99-133

101 JaMarcus Russell/99	8.00	20.00
102 Brady Quinn/99	15.00	40.00
104 Marshawn Lynch/99	12.00	30.00
105 Anthony Gonzalez/99	8.00	20.00
106 Brian Leonard/99	6.00	15.00
107 Calvin Johnson/99	50.00	120.00
109 Drew Stanton/99	5.00	12.00
110 Dwayne Bowe/99	10.00	25.00
111 Dwayne Jarrett/99	6.00	15.00
113 Kevin Kolb/99	12.00	30.00
114 LaRon Landry/99	8.00	20.00
115 Leon Hall/99	6.00	15.00
116 Robert Meachem/99	8.00	20.00
117 Sidney Rice/99	10.00	25.00
118 Steve Smith USC/99	8.00	20.00
119 Ted Ginn Jr./99	6.00	15.00
122 Alan Branch/133	5.00	12.00
123 Amobi Okoye/132	6.00	15.00
124 Antonio Pittman/133	4.00	10.00
125 Aundrae Allison/133	4.00	10.00
127 Brandon Meriweather/133	6.00	15.00
128 Chansi Stuckey/133	6.00	15.00
129 Chris Henry RB/133	4.00	10.00
130 Chris Leak/133	5.00	12.00
131 Courtney Taylor/133	5.00	12.00
133 Dallas Baker/133	4.00	10.00
134 Darius Walker/133	4.00	10.00
135 David Ball/133	5.00	12.00
136 David Clowney/133	5.00	12.00
137 David Irons/133	4.00	10.00
139 DeShawn Wynn/133	5.00	12.00
140 Drew Tate/133	5.00	12.00
141 Dwayne Wright/99	6.00	15.00
142 Eric Wright/133	6.00	15.00
144 Garrett Wolfe/133	4.00	10.00
145 Gary Russell/133	5.00	12.00
146 Greg Olsen/133	5.00	12.00
148 Isaiah Stanback/133	4.00	10.00
150 Jared Zabransky/133	5.00	12.00
151 Jason Hill/133	6.00	15.00
152 Jeff Rowe/133	4.00	10.00
153 Joe Thomas/133	6.00	15.00
154 Joel Filani/133	5.00	12.00
156 Johnnie Lee Higgins/133	5.00	12.00
158 Kenneth Darby/133	5.00	12.00
159 Kolby Smith/133	5.00	12.00
160 LaMarr Woodley/133	8.00	20.00
161 Lawrence Timmons/133	6.00	15.00
162 Legedu Naanee/133	6.00	15.00
163 Lorenzo Booker/133	5.00	12.00
164 Marcus McCauley/133	5.00	12.00
165 Matt Moore/133	6.00	15.00
169 Paul Posluszny/133	6.00	15.00
170 Paul Williams/133	4.00	10.00
171 Quentin Moses/133	5.00	12.00
172 Reggie Nelson/133	5.00	12.00
173 Rhema McKnight/133	4.00	10.00
174 Scott Chandler/133	6.00	15.00
175 Selvin Young/133	5.00	12.00
176 Syvelle Newton/133	5.00	12.00
178 Trent Edwards/133	6.00	15.00
179 Tyler Palko/133	5.00	12.00
180 Tyrone Moss/133	4.00	10.00
181 Yamon Figurs/133	4.00	10.00
182 Zach Miller/133	6.00	15.00

2007 Upper Deck Trilogy Signature Future Autographs

STATED PRINT RUN 9-99
SERIAL #'d UNDER 33 NOT PRICED

AA Aundrae Allison/99	4.00	10.00
AB Alan Branch/99	5.00	12.00
AO Amobi Okoye/33	10.00	25.00
AP Adrian Peterson/99	125.00	250.00
BA David Ball/99	5.00	12.00
BM Brandon Meriweather/99	6.00	15.00
BQ Brady Quinn/99	25.00	60.00
CH Chris Henry RB/99	4.00	10.00
CS Chansi Stuckey/99	6.00	15.00
CT Courtney Taylor/99	5.00	12.00
DB Dallas Baker/99	4.00	10.00
DC David Clowney/99	5.00	12.00
DI David Irons/99	4.00	10.00
DT Drew Tate/99	5.00	12.00
DW DeShawn Wynn/99	5.00	12.00
GR Gary Russell/99	5.00	12.00
IS Isaiah Stanback/99	4.00	10.00
JF Joel Filani/99	5.00	12.00
JH Jason Hill/80	6.00	15.00
JR JaMarcus Russell/99	10.00	25.00
JZ Jared Zabransky/99	5.00	12.00
KS Kolby Smith/99	5.00	12.00
ML Marshawn Lynch/99	20.00	50.00
MM Marcus McCauley/99	5.00	12.00
MO Matt Moore/99	6.00	15.00
PP Paul Posluszny/99 Red Ink	6.00	15.00
QM Quentin Moses/99	5.00	12.00
RM Robert Meachem/99	6.00	15.00
RN Reggie Nelson/90	5.00	12.00
RO Jeff Rowe/99	4.00	10.00
SN Syvelle Newton/99	5.00	12.00
SY Selvin Young/99	5.00	12.00
TG Ted Ginn/99	5.00	12.00
TM Tyrone Moss/99	4.00	10.00
TP Tyler Palko/99	5.00	12.00
WA Darius Walker/99	4.00	10.00
WI Paul Williams/99	4.00	10.00
YF Yamon Figurs/99	4.00	10.00

2007 Upper Deck Trilogy Signature Numbers Autographs

STATED PRINT RUN 4-89
SERIAL #'d UNDER 20 NOT PRICED

BJ Brandon Jacobs/32	12.00	30.00
CW Cadillac Williams/24		
ES Emmitt Smith/22	125.00	250.00
FG Frank Gore/21	15.00	40.00
JA Joseph Addai/29	30.00	60.00
JC Jerricho Cotchery/89	5.00	12.00
LE Lee Evans/83	6.00	15.00
LT LaDainian Tomlinson/21		
WP Willie Parker/39	12.00	30.00

2007 Upper Deck Trilogy Signature Past Autographs

UNPRICED PRINT RUN 9 SER.#'d SETS

2007 Upper Deck Trilogy Signature Present Autographs

STATED PRINT RUN 33 SER.#'d SETS

BB Bernard Berrian	8.00	20.00
BJ Brandon Jacobs	10.00	25.00
BR Ronnie Brown	10.00	25.00
CB Champ Bailey	10.00	25.00
CJ Chad Johnson	10.00	25.00
CL Mark Clayton	10.00	25.00
CO Jerricho Cotchery	8.00	20.00
CT Chester Taylor	8.00	20.00
DJ Darrell Jackson	10.00	25.00
EM Eli Manning	35.00	60.00
FG Frank Gore	12.00	30.00
GJ Greg Jennings	10.00	25.00
JA Joseph Addai	30.00	60.00
JC Jason Campbell	10.00	25.00
JL John Lynch	10.00	25.00
LF Larry Fitzgerald	15.00	40.00
PM Peyton Manning	75.00	150.00
PR Philip Rivers	12.00	30.00
RB Reggie Brown	8.00	20.00
TH T.J. Houshmandzadeh	10.00	25.00
VJ Vincent Jackson Red Ink	8.00	20.00
WP Willie Parker	10.00	25.00

2007 Upper Deck Trilogy Sunday Best Jersey Silver

SILVER PRINT RUN 199 SER.#'d SETS
*GOLD/33: .6X TO 1.5X SILVER/199
GOLD PRINT RUN 33 SER.#'d SETS
UNPRICED PLATINUM PRINT RUN 3
*PATCH/79: .6X TO 1.5X SILVER/199
PATCH PRINT RUN 79 SER.#'d SETS
*PATCH HOLOGOLD/33: .8X TO 2X SILVER/199
PATCH HOLOGOLD PRINT RUN 33 SER.#'d SETS

AG Anthony Gonzalez	2.50	6.00
AJ Andre Johnson	3.00	8.00
BJ Brandon Jackson	3.00	8.00
BR Ben Roethlisberger	4.00	10.00
BU Brian Urlacher	4.00	10.00
CJ Calvin Johnson	8.00	20.00
CP Carson Palmer	3.00	8.00
DB Dwayne Bowe	3.00	8.00
DS Drew Stanton	1.50	4.00
EM Eli Manning	4.00	10.00
FG Frank Gore	4.00	10.00
HW Hines Ward	4.00	10.00
JA Joseph Addai	3.00	8.00
JR JaMarcus Russell	1.50	4.00
KK Kevin Kolb	4.00	10.00
LE Lee Evans	3.00	8.00
LJ Larry Johnson	2.50	6.00
LT LaDainian Tomlinson	4.00	10.00
MH Marvin Harrison	4.00	10.00
MJ Maurice Jones-Drew	4.00	10.00
ML Matt Leinart	3.00	8.00
PM Peyton Manning	6.00	15.00
PR Philip Rivers	4.00	10.00
SJ Steven Jackson	4.00	10.00
SM Shawne Merriman	3.00	8.00
SS Steve Smith	3.00	8.00
TB Tom Brady	6.00	15.00
TE Trent Edwards	2.50	6.00
TO Terrell Owens	4.00	10.00
TS Troy Smith	2.50	6.00

2007 Upper Deck Trilogy Supernova Swatches Silver

SILVER PRINT RUN 199 SER.#'d SETS
*GOLD/33: .6X TO 1.5X SILVER/199
GOLD PRINT RUN 33 SER.#'d SETS
UNPRICED PLATINUM PRINT RUN 3
*PATCH/79: .6X TO 1.5X SILVER/199
PATCH PRINT RUN 79 SER.#'d SETS
*PATCH HOLOGOLD/33: .8X TO 2X SLV/199
PATCH HOLOGOLD PRINT RUN 33 SER.#'d SETS

AC Alge Crumpler	3.00	8.00
AG Antonio Gates	4.00	10.00
AP Adrian Peterson	20.00	50.00
BL Brian Leonard	2.00	5.00
BO Dwayne Bowe	3.00	8.00
BQ Brady Quinn	2.50	6.00
BW Brian Westbrook	3.00	8.00
CJ Calvin Johnson	8.00	20.00
CT Chester Taylor	2.50	6.00
DB Drew Brees	4.00	10.00
DJ Dwayne Jarrett	2.00	5.00
ER Ed Reed	3.00	8.00
GJ Greg Jennings	4.00	10.00
JC Jason Campbell	3.00	8.00
KI Kenny Irons	1.50	4.00
KW Kellen Winslow	3.00	8.00
LC Laveranues Coles	2.50	6.00
LM Laurence Maroney	3.00	8.00
LT LaDainian Tomlinson	4.00	10.00
MB Marc Bulger	3.00	8.00
MC Marques Colston	4.00	10.00
ML Marshawn Lynch	2.50	6.00
RB Reggie Bush	4.00	10.00
RL Ray Lewis	4.00	10.00
RM Robert Meachem	2.50	6.00
SA Shaun Alexander	3.00	8.00
SS Steve Smith USC	2.50	6.00
TG Trent Green	3.00	8.00
TR Tony Romo	5.00	12.00
WP Willie Parker	3.00	8.00

2007 Upper Deck Trilogy Trilojerseys

STATED PRINT RUN 33 SER.#'d SETS

BBC Drew Brees	10.00	25.00
Reggie Bush		
Marques Colston		
BGB Ted Ginn Jr.	10.00	25.00
John Beck		
Lorenzo Booker		
BJH Torry Holt	10.00	25.00
Marc Bulger		
Steven Jackson		
CEJ Laveranues Coles	8.00	20.00
Andre Johnson		
Lee Evans		
ELE Lee Evans	10.00	25.00
Trent Edwards		
Marshawn Lynch		
FMB Brett Favre	40.00	100.00
Peyton Manning		
Tom Brady		
GBW Cedric Benson	8.00	20.00
Rex Grossman		
Garrett Wolfe		
GSW Jeremy Shockey	10.00	25.00
Antonio Gates		
Kellen Winslow		
HSB Torry Holt	8.00	20.00
Anquan Boldin		
Steve Smith		
JGB Calvin Johnson	15.00	40.00
Ted Ginn Jr.		
Dwayne Bowe		
LBF Anquan Boldin	10.00	25.00
Larry Fitzgerald		
Matt Leinart		
LBS Matt Leinart	10.00	25.00
Reggie Bush		
Troy Smith		
LTW Ray Lewis	10.00	25.00
Zach Thomas		
Patrick Willis		
MAJ Joseph Addai	10.00	25.00
Laurence Maroney		
Maurice Jones-Drew		
MAW Peyton Manning	15.00	40.00
Reggie Wayne		
Joseph Addai		
MFB Joe Montana	40.00	100.00
Brett Favre		
Tom Brady		
MJB Plaxico Burress	10.00	25.00
Eli Manning		
Brandon Jacobs		
MLS Ray Lewis	10.00	25.00
Willis McGahee		
Troy Smith		
MLY Peyton Manning	20.00	50.00
Byron Leftwich		
Vince Young		
MPR Peyton Manning	15.00	40.00
Carson Palmer		
JaMarcus Russell		
MRR Eli Manning	10.00	25.00
Ben Roethlisberger		
Philip Rivers		
PCV Chad Pennington	8.00	20.00
Laveranues Coles		
Jonathan Vilma		
PJI Chad Johnson	8.00	20.00
Carson Palmer		
Kenny Irons		
PLI Adrian Peterson	30.00	80.00
Marshawn Lynch		
Kenny Irons		
PMA Julius Peppers	10.00	25.00
Shawne Merriman		
Gaines Adams		
PTR Chester Taylor	30.00	80.00
Adrian Peterson		
Sidney Rice		
QWT Kellen Winslow	10.00	25.00
Brady Quinn		
Joe Thomas		
RBO Terrell Owens	20.00	50.00
Tony Romo		
Marion Barber		
RHB JaMarcus Russell	10.00	25.00
Michael Bush		
Johnnie Lee Higgins		
RPW Hines Ward	10.00	25.00
Ben Roethlisberger		
Willie Parker		
RQK Brady Quinn	10.00	25.00
JaMarcus Russell		
Kevin Kolb		
RTG LaDainian Tomlinson	10.00	25.00
Antonio Gates		
Philip Rivers		
SBP Gale Sayers	40.00	100.00
Reggie Bush		
Adrian Peterson		
SGG Ted Ginn Jr.	10.00	25.00
Troy Smith		
Anthony Gonzalez		
SJF DeShaun Foster	8.00	20.00
Steve Smith		
Dwayne Jarrett		
SJH Marvin Harrison	10.00	25.00
Chad Johnson		
Steve Smith		
SSS Emmitt Smith	30.00	80.00
Barry Sanders		
Gale Sayers		
SUG Brian Urlacher	12.00	30.00
Gale Sayers		
Rex Grossman		
TJG Larry Johnson	10.00	25.00
LaDainian Tomlinson		
Frank Gore		
VDC Alge Crumpler	10.00	25.00
Michael Vick		
Warrick Dunn		
WJB Roy Williams WR	15.00	40.00
Tatum Bell		
Calvin Johnson		
YLC Jay Cutler	10.00	25.00
Matt Leinart		
Vince Young		

1999 Upper Deck UD Authentics

Not much is known about the official release of these cards, but it is thought that they were issued as replacements for other redemption cards that could not be fulfilled. There are no brand logos present on the cards at all and look very much like the UD Ionix pack inserts.

DM Dan Marino	60.00	120.00
JM Joe Montana	50.00	100.00

1999 Upper Deck Victory

This 440 card set was issued in 12 card packs with a SRP of 99 cents and was released in August, 1999. Subsets include All-Victory (281 through 310), Season Leaders (311 through 340), Victory Parade (341 through 360), Rookie Flasback (361 through 380) and a shortprinted 99 Rookie Class subset (381-440). The Rookie Subset cards were issued one per pack.

COMPLETE SET (440)	30.00	60.00
COMP. SET w/o SP's (380)	5.00	10.00
1 Checklist Card	.07	.20
2 Jake Plummer	.12	.30
3 Adrian Murrell	.12	.30
4 Michael Pittman	.10	.25
5 Frank Sanders	.10	.25
6 Andre Wadsworth	.10	.25
7 Rob Moore	.10	.25
8 Simeon Rice	.10	.25
9 Kwamie Lassiter RC	.10	.25
10 Mario Bates	.10	.25
11 Checklist Card	.07	.20
12 Jamal Anderson	.12	.30
13 Chris Chandler	.12	.30
14 Chuck Smith	.10	.25
15 Terance Mathis	.10	.25
16 Tim Dwight	.12	.30
17 Ray Buchanan	.10	.25
18 O.J. Santiago	.10	.25
19 Lester Archambeau	.10	.25
20 Checklist Card	.07	.20
21 Tony Banks	.12	.30
22 Priest Holmes	.15	.40
23 Michael Jackson	.10	.25
24 Jermaine Lewis	.10	.25
25 Michael McCrary	.10	.25
26 Rod Woodson	.15	.40
27 Checklist Card	.07	.20
28 Rob Johnson	.12	.30
29 Antowain Smith	.10	.25
30 Thurman Thomas	.15	.40
31 Doug Flutie	.15	.40
32 Eric Moulds	.12	.30
33 Bruce Smith	.15	.40
34 Andre Reed	.15	.40
35 Phil Hansen	.10	.25
36 Checklist Card	.07	.20
37 Fred Lane	.10	.25
38 Tim Biakabutuka	.12	.30
39 Rae Carruth	.10	.25
40 Wesley Walls	.12	.30
41 Steve Beuerlein	.12	.30
42 Muhsin Muhammad	.12	.30
43 Kevin Greene	.12	.30
44 Checklist Card	.07	.20
45 Erik Kramer	.12	.30
46 Edgar Bennett	.12	.30
47 Curtis Conway	.12	.30
48 Curtis Enis	.10	.25
49 Bobby Engram	.12	.30
50 Alonzo Mayes	.10	.25
51 Tony Parrish	.10	.25
52 Glyn Milburn	.10	.25
53 Checklist Card	.07	.20
54 Corey Dillon	.12	.30
55 Jeff Blake	.12	.30
56 Carl Pickens	.12	.30
57 Darnay Scott	.10	.25
58 Tony McGee	.10	.25
59 Ki-Jana Carter	.10	.25
60 Takeo Spikes	.10	.25
61 Checklist Card	.07	.20
62 Ty Detmer	.12	.30
63 Terry Kirby	.10	.25
64 Derrick Alexander DT	.10	.25
65 Leslie Shepherd	.10	.25
66 Marquez Pope	.10	.25
67 Antonio Langham	.10	.25
68 Marc Edwards	.12	.30
69 Checklist Card	.07	.20
70 Troy Aikman	.25	.60
71 Emmitt Smith	.40	1.00
72 Deion Sanders	.15	.40
73 Rocket Ismail	.12	.30
74 Michael Irvin	.15	.40
75 Chris Warren	.12	.30
76 Greg Ellis	.10	.25
77 Kavika Pittman	.10	.25
78 David LaFleur	.10	.25
79 Checklist Card	.07	.20
80 John Elway	.50	1.25
81 Terrell Davis	.15	.40
82 Rod Smith	.12	.30
83 Shannon Sharpe	.15	.40
84 Ed McCaffrey	.12	.30
85 John Mobley	.10	.25
86 Bill Romanowski	.12	.30
87 Jason Elam	.10	.25
88 Howard Griffith	.10	.25
89 Checklist Card	.07	.20
90 Barry Sanders	.40	1.00
91 Johnnie Morton	.12	.30
92 Herman Moore	.12	.30
93 Charlie Batch	.12	.30
94 Germane Crowell	.10	.25
95 Robert Porcher	.10	.25
96 Stephen Boyd	.10	.25
97 Checklist Card	.07	.20
98 Brett Favre	.50	1.25
99 Antonio Freeman	.12	.30
100 Dorsey Levens	.12	.30
101 Mark Chmura	.10	.25
102 Vonnie Holliday	.10	.25
103 Bill Schroeder	.12	.30
104 LeRoy Butler	.12	.30
105 William Henderson	.12	.30
106 Checklist Card	.07	.20
107 Peyton Manning	.50	1.25
108 Marvin Harrison	.15	.40
109 Ken Dilger	.10	.25
110 Jerome Pathon	.10	.25
111 E.G. Green	.10	.25
112 Ellis Johnson	.10	.25
113 Jeff Burris	.10	.25
114 Checklist Card	.07	.20
115 Mark Brunell	.12	.30
116 Jimmy Smith	.12	.30
117 Keenan McCardell	.12	.30
118 Fred Taylor	.12	.30

119 James Stewart .10 .25
120 Dave Thomas .12 .30
121 Kyle Brady .10 .25
122 Bryce Paup .10 .25
123 Checklist Card .07 .20
124 Elvis Grbac .10 .25
125 Andre Rison .12 .30
126 Derrick Alexander WR .10 .25
127 Tony Gonzalez .15 .40
128 Donnell Bennett .10 .25
129 Derrick Thomas .15 .40
130 Tamarick Vanover .12 .30
131 Donnie Edwards .10 .25
132 Checklist Card .07 .20
133 Dan Marino .50 1.25
134 Karim Abdul-Jabbar .12 .30
135 Zach Thomas .15 .40
136 O.J. McDuffie .12 .30
137 John Avery .10 .25
138 Sam Madison .10 .25
139 Terrell Buckley .12 .30
140 Jason Taylor .12 .30
141 Oronde Gadsden .10 .25
142 Checklist Card .07 .20
143 Randall Cunningham .15 .40
144 Cris Carter .15 .40
145 Robert Smith .12 .30
146 Randy Moss .15 .40
147 Jake Reed .12 .30
148 Leroy Hoard .10 .25
149 Matthew Hatchette .12 .30
150 John Randle .12 .30
151 Gary Anderson .10 .25
152 Checklist Card .07 .20
153 Drew Bledsoe .15 .40
154 Terry Glenn .12 .30
155 Ben Coates .12 .30
156 Ty Law .12 .30
157 Tony Simmons .10 .25
158 Ted Johnson .12 .30
159 Willie McGinest .12 .30
160 Tony Carter .10 .25
161 Shawn Jefferson .10 .25
162 Checklist Card .07 .20
163 Danny Wuerffel .12 .30
164 Lamar Smith .10 .25
165 Keith Poole .10 .25
166 Cameron Cleeland .10 .25
167 Joe Johnson .10 .25
168 Andre Hastings .10 .25
169 La'Roi Glover RC .15 .40
170 Aaron Craver .10 .25
171 Checklist Card .07 .20
172 Kent Graham .10 .25
173 Gary Brown .10 .25
174 Amani Toomer .12 .30
175 Tiki Barber .15 .40
176 Ike Hilliard .12 .30
177 Jason Sehorn .12 .30
178 Michael Strahan .12 .30
179 Charles Way .10 .25
180 Checklist Card .07 .20
181 Vinny Testaverde .12 .30
182 Curtis Martin .15 .40
183 Keyshawn Johnson .12 .30
184 Wayne Chrebet .12 .30
185 Mo Lewis .10 .25
186 Steve Atwater .12 .30
187 Leon Johnson .10 .25
188 Bryan Cox .12 .30
189 Checklist Card .07 .20
190 Rich Gannon .12 .30
191 Napoleon Kaufman .10 .25
192 Tim Brown .15 .40
193 Darrell Russell .10 .25
194 Rickey Dudley .10 .25
195 Charles Woodson .15 .40
196 Harvey Williams .10 .25
197 James Jett .10 .25
198 Checklist Card .07 .20
199 Koy Detmer .10 .25
200 Duce Staley .12 .30
201 Bobby Taylor .12 .30
202 Doug Pederson .10 .25
203 Karl Hankton .10 .25
204 Charles Johnson .10 .25
205 Kevin Turner .10 .25
206 Hugh Douglas .12 .30
207 Checklist Card .07 .20
208 Kordell Stewart .12 .30
209 Jerome Bettis .15 .40
210 Hines Ward .15 .40
211 Courtney Hawkins .10 .25
212 Will Blackwell .10 .25
213 Richard Huntley .10 .25
214 Levon Kirkland .10 .25
215 Jason Gildon .12 .30
216 Checklist Card .07 .20
217 Trent Green .12 .30
218 Isaac Bruce .15 .40
219 Az-Zahir Hakim .10 .25
220 Amp Lee .10 .25
221 Robert Holcombe .10 .25
222 Ricky Proehl .10 .25
223 Kevin Carter .10 .25
224 Marshall Faulk .15 .40
225 Checklist Card .07 .20
226 Ryan Leaf .12 .30
227 Natrone Means .12 .30
228 Jim Harbaugh .12 .30
229 Junior Seau .15 .40
230 Charlie Jones .10 .25
231 Rodney Harrison .12 .30
232 Terrell Fletcher .10 .25
233 Tremayne Stephens .10 .25
234 Checklist Card .07 .20
235 Steve Young .20 .50
236 Jerry Rice .30 .75
237 Garrison Hearst .12 .30
238 Terrell Owens .15 .40
239 J.J. Stokes .10 .25
240 Bryant Young .12 .30
241 Tim McDonald .10 .25
242 Merton Hanks .10 .25
243 Travis Jervey .12 .30
244 Checklist Card .07 .20
245 Ricky Watters .12 .30
246 Joey Galloway .12 .30
247 Jon Kitna .12 .30
248 Ahman Green .12 .30
249 Mike Pritchard .10 .25
250 Chad Brown .10 .25
251 Christian Fauria .10 .25
252 Michael Sinclair .10 .25
253 Checklist Card .07 .20
254 Warrick Dunn .12 .30
255 Trent Dilfer .12 .30
256 Mike Alstott .15 .40
257 Reidel Anthony .10 .25
258 Bert Emanuel .12 .30
259 Jacquez Green .10 .25
260 Hardy Nickerson .10 .25
261 Derrick Brooks .15 .40
262 Dave Moore .10 .25
263 Checklist Card .07 .20
264 Steve McNair .15 .40
265 Eddie George .12 .30
266 Yancey Thigpen .10 .25
267 Frank Wycheck .12 .30
268 Kevin Dyson .10 .25
269 Jackie Harris .12 .30
270 Blaine Bishop .10 .25
271 Willie Davis .10 .25
272 Checklist Card .07 .20
273 Skip Hicks .10 .25
274 Michael Westbrook .10 .25
275 Stephen Alexander .10 .25
276 Dana Stubblefield .10 .25
277 Brad Johnson .12 .30
278 Brian Mitchell .12 .30
279 Dan Wilkinson .12 .30
280 Stephen Davis .12 .30
281 John Elway AV .40 1.00
282 Dan Marino AV .40 1.00
283 Troy Aikman AV .20 .50
284 Vinny Testaverde AV .10 .25
285 Corey Dillon AV .10 .25
286 Steve Young AV .15 .40
287 Randy Moss AV .12 .30
288 Drew Bledsoe AV .12 .30
289 Jerome Bettis AV .12 .30
290 Antonio Freeman AV .10 .25
291 Fred Taylor AV .10 .25
292 Doug Flutie AV .12 .30
293 Jerry Rice AV .25 .60
294 Peyton Manning AV .40 1.00
295 Brett Favre AV .40 1.00
296 Barry Sanders AV .30 .75
297 Keyshawn Johnson AV .10 .25
298 Mark Brunell AV .10 .25
299 Jamal Anderson AV .10 .25
300 Terrell Davis AV .12 .30
301 Randall Cunningham AV .12 .30
302 Kordell Stewart AV .10 .25
303 Warrick Dunn AV .10 .25
304 Jake Plummer AV .10 .25
305 Junior Seau AV .12 .30
306 Antowain Smith AV .07 .20
307 Charlie Batch AV .10 .25
308 Eddie George AV .10 .25
309 Michael Irvin AV .12 .30
310 Joey Galloway AV .10 .25
311 Randall Cunningham SL .12 .30
312 Vinny Testaverde SL .10 .25
313 Steve Young SL .15 .40
314 Chris Chandler SL .10 .25
315 John Elway SL .40 1.00
316 Steve Young SL .15 .40
317 Randall Cunningham SL .12 .30
318 Brett Favre SL .40 1.00
319 Vinny Testaverde SL .10 .25
320 Peyton Manning SL .40 1.00
321 Terrell Davis SL .12 .30
322 Jamal Anderson SL .10 .25
323 Garrison Hearst SL .10 .25
324 Barry Sanders SL .30 .75
325 Emmitt Smith SL .30 .75
326 Terrell Davis SL .12 .30
327 Fred Taylor SL .10 .25
328 Jamal Anderson SL .10 .25
329 Emmitt Smith SL .30 .75
330 Ricky Watters SL .10 .25
331 O.J. McDuffie SL .10 .25
332 Frank Sanders SL .07 .20
333 Rod Smith SL .10 .25
334 Marshall Faulk SL .12 .30
335 Antonio Freeman SL .10 .25
336 Randy Moss SL .12 .30
337 Antonio Freeman SL .10 .25
338 Terrell Owens SL .12 .30
339 Cris Carter SL .12 .30
340 Terance Mathis SL .07 .20
341 Jake Plummer VP .10 .25
342 Steve McNair VP .12 .30
343 Randy Moss VP .12 .30
344 Peyton Manning VP .40 1.00
345 Mark Brunell VP .10 .25
346 Terrell Owens VP .12 .30
347 Antowain Smith VP .07 .20
348 Jerry Rice VP .25 .60
349 Troy Aikman VP .20 .50
350 Fred Taylor VP .10 .25
351 Charlie Batch VP .10 .25
352 Dan Marino VP .40 1.00
353 Eddie George VP .10 .25
354 Drew Bledsoe VP .12 .30
355 Kordell Stewart VP .10 .25
356 Doug Flutie VP .12 .30
357 Deion Sanders VP .12 .30
358 Keyshawn Johnson VP .10 .25
359 Jerome Bettis VP .12 .30
360 Warrick Dunn VP .10 .25
361 John Elway RF .40 1.00
362 Dan Marino RF .40 1.00
363 Brett Favre RF .40 1.00
364 Andre Rison RF .10 .25
365 Rod Woodson RF .12 .30
366 Jerry Rice RF .25 .60
367 Barry Sanders RF .30 .75
368 Thurman Thomas RF .12 .30
369 Troy Aikman RF .20 .50
370 Ricky Watters RF .10 .25
371 Jerome Bettis RF .12 .30
372 Reggie White RF .12 .30
373 Junior Seau RF .12 .30
374 Deion Sanders RF .12 .30
375 Chris Chandler RF .10 .25
376 Curtis Martin RF .12 .30
377 Kordell Stewart RF .10 .25
378 Mark Brunell RF .10 .25
379 Cris Carter RF .12 .30
380 Emmitt Smith RF .30 .75
381 Tim Couch RC .50 1.25
382 Donovan McNabb RC 2.00 5.00
383 Akili Smith RC .40 1.00
384 Edgerrin James RC .60 1.50
385 Ricky Williams RC .75 2.00
386 Torry Holt RC .75 2.00
387 Champ Bailey RC 1.00 2.50
388 David Boston RC .40 1.00
389 Chris Claiborne RC .30 .75
390 Chris McAlister RC .40 1.00
391 Daunte Culpepper RC .50 1.25
392 Cade McNown RC .40 1.00
393 Troy Edwards RC .40 1.00
394 John Tait RC .30 .75
395 Anthony McFarland RC .40 1.00
396 Jevon Kearse RC .50 1.25
397 Damien Woody RC .30 .75
398 Matt Stinchcomb RC .30 .75
399 Luke Petitgout RC .30 .75
400 Ebenezer Ekuban RC .30 .75
401 L.J. Shelton RC .30 .75
402 Daylon McCutcheon RC .30 .75
403 Antoine Winfield RC .30 .75
404 Scott Covington RC .30 .75
405 Antuan Edwards RC .30 .75
406 Fernando Bryant RC .30 .75
407 Aaron Gibson RC .30 .75
408 Andy Katzenmoyer RC .40 1.00
409 Dimitrius Underwood RC .30 .75
410 Patrick Kerney RC .40 1.00
411 Al Wilson RC .50 1.25
412 Kevin Johnson RC .40 1.00
413 Joel Makovicka RC .30 .75
414 Reginald Kelly RC UER .30 .75
Card has the wrong birthdate
415 Jeff Paulk RC .30 .75
416 Brandon Stokley RC .50 1.25
417 Peerless Price RC .40 1.00
418 D'Wayne Bates RC .30 .75
419 Travis McGriff RC .30 .75
420 Sedrick Irvin RC .30 .75
421 Aaron Brooks RC .50 1.25
422 Mike Cloud RC .30 .75
423 Joe Montgomery RC .30 .75
424 Shaun King RC .40 1.00
425 Dameane Douglas RC .30 .75
426 Joe Germaine RC .40 1.00
427 James Johnson RC .30 .75
428 Michael Bishop RC .40 1.00
429 Karsten Bailey RC .30 .75
430 Craig Yeast RC .30 .75
431 Jim Kleinsasser RC .50 1.25
432 Martin Gramatica RC .30 .75
433 Jermaine Fazande RC .30 .75
434 Dre Bly RC .50 1.25
435 Brock Huard RC .40 1.00
436 Rob Konrad RC .30 .75
437 Tony Bryant RC .30 .75
438 Sean Bennett RC .30 .75
439 Kevin Faulk RC .50 1.25
440 Amos Zereoue RC .40 1.00

2000 Upper Deck Victory

Released as a 330-card set, Victory contains 195 base veteran cards, 20 Season Leaders, 25 All Victory Team Checklists, 30 Big Play Makers, 60 short printed Rookie Cards inserted at the rate of one in one, and a special Web Card inserted in every pack. Each Web Card has a number that can be checked on the Upper Deck Web site to see if it is a winner of one of 100 Peyton Manning autographed jerseys. Victory was packaged in 36-pack boxes with packs containing 12 cards each and carried a suggested retail price of $.99.

COMPLETE SET (330) 25.00 50.00
COMP.SET w/o RCs (270) 5.00 10.00
271-330 ROOKIE ODDS 1:1
1 Jake Plummer .12 .30
2 Michael Pittman .10 .25
3 Rob Moore .10 .25
4 David Boston .10 .25
5 Frank Sanders .10 .25
6 Aeneas Williams .10 .25
7 Tim Dwight .12 .30
8 Chris Chandler .12 .30
9 Jamal Anderson .12 .30
10 Shawn Jefferson .10 .25
11 Ken Oxendine .10 .25
12 Terance Mathis .10 .25
13 Qadry Ismail .12 .30
14 Jermaine Lewis .10 .25
15 Rod Woodson .15 .40
16 Michael McCrary .10 .25
17 Tony Banks .10 .25
18 Peter Boulware .10 .25
19 Shannon Sharpe .15 .40
20 Peerless Price .12 .30
21 Rob Johnson .12 .30
22 Eric Moulds .12 .30
23 Doug Flutie .15 .40
24 Jay Riemersma .10 .25
25 Antowain Smith .12 .30
26 Sam Cowart .10 .25
27 Muhsin Muhammad .12 .30
28 Patrick Jeffers .12 .30
29 Steve Beuerlein .12 .30
30 Natrone Means .12 .30
31 Tim Biakabutuka .12 .30
32 Michael Bates .10 .25
33 Wesley Walls .10 .25
34 Cade McNown .10 .25
35 Curtis Enis .10 .25
36 Marcus Robinson .12 .30
37 Bobby Engram .12 .30
38 Glyn Milburn .10 .25
39 Marty Booker .12 .30
40 Akili Smith .10 .25
41 Corey Dillon .12 .30
42 Darnay Scott .12 .30
43 Tremain Mack .10 .25
44 Michael Bankston .10 .25
45 Tony McGee .10 .25
46 Tim Couch .12 .30
47 Kevin Johnson .10 .25
48 Darrin Chiaverini .10 .25
49 Jamir Miller .10 .25
50 Errict Rhett .12 .30
51 Ty Detmer .12 .30
52 Terry Kirby .10 .25
53 Troy Aikman .25 .60
54 Emmitt Smith .40 1.00
55 Rocket Ismail .12 .30
56 Chris Warren .10 .25
57 Joey Galloway .12 .30
58 Terrell Davis .15 .40
59 Olandis Gary .12 .30
60 Brian Griese .12 .30
61 Gus Frerotte .12 .30
62 Glenn Cadrez .10 .25
63 Ed McCaffrey .12 .30
64 Rod Smith .12 .30
65 Charlie Batch .12 .30
66 Germane Crowell .10 .25
67 Stephen Boyd .10 .25
68 Johnnie Morton .12 .30
69 Robert Porcher .10 .25
70 James Stewart .10 .25
71 Brett Favre .50 1.25
72 Antonio Freeman .12 .30
73 Bill Schroeder .12 .30
74 Dorsey Levens .12 .30
75 Darren Sharper .12 .30
76 Peyton Manning .40 1.00
77 Edgerrin James .15 .40
78 Marvin Harrison .15 .40
79 Ken Dilger .10 .25
80 Terrence Wilkins .10 .25
81 Cornelius Bennett .10 .25
82 E.G. Green .10 .25
83 Mark Brunell .12 .30
84 Fred Taylor .15 .40
85 Jimmy Smith .12 .30
86 Keenan McCardell .12 .30
87 Carnell Lake .10 .25
88 Kevin Hardy .10 .25
89 Elvis Grbac .10 .25
90 Tony Gonzalez .15 .40
91 Derrick Alexander .10 .25
92 Donnell Bennett .10 .25
93 James Hasty .10 .25
94 Kevin Lockett .10 .25
95 Trace Armstrong .10 .25
96 Terrell Buckley .10 .25
97 Tony Martin .12 .30
98 Damon Huard .12 .30
99 O.J. McDuffie .12 .30
100 Brock Marion .10 .25
101 Zach Thomas .15 .40
102 Randy Moss .15 .40
103 Robert Smith .12 .30
104 Cris Carter .15 .40
105 Bubby Brister .12 .30
106 Daunte Culpepper .12 .30
107 John Randle .12 .30
108 Drew Bledsoe .15 .40
109 Terry Glenn .12 .30
110 Willie McGinest .12 .30
111 Kevin Faulk .12 .30
112 Tedy Bruschi .25 .60
113 Ricky Williams .15 .40
114 Keith Poole .10 .25
115 Jake Reed .12 .30
116 Mark Fields .10 .25
117 Jeff Blake .12 .30
118 Andrew Glover .10 .25
119 Kerry Collins .12 .30
120 Amani Toomer .12 .30
121 Jessie Armstead .10 .25
122 Ike Hilliard .12 .30
123 Ray Lucas .10 .25
124 Curtis Martin .15 .40
125 Vinny Testaverde .12 .30
126 Wayne Chrebet .12 .30
127 Dedric Ward .10 .25
128 Tim Brown .15 .40
129 Rich Gannon .12 .30
130 Tyrone Wheatley .10 .25
131 Napoleon Kaufman .12 .30
132 Charles Woodson .15 .40
133 Greg Biekert .10 .25
134 Rickey Dudley .10 .25
135 Duce Staley .12 .30
136 Donovan McNabb .15 .40
137 Torrance Small .10 .25
138 Mike Mamula .10 .25
139 Brian Dawkins .15 .40
140 Troy Vincent .10 .25
141 Kent Graham .10 .25
142 Troy Edwards .10 .25
143 Jerome Bettis .15 .40
144 Hines Ward .15 .40
145 Kordell Stewart .12 .30
146 Levon Kirkland .10 .25
147 Richard Huntley .10 .25
148 Marshall Faulk .15 .40
149 Kurt Warner .25 .60
150 Torry Holt .15 .40
151 Isaac Bruce .15 .40
152 Kevin Carter .10 .25
153 Az-Zahir Hakim .10 .25
154 Todd Lyght .10 .25
155 Jermaine Fazande .10 .25
156 Curtis Conway .12 .30
157 Freddie Jones .10 .25
158 Junior Seau .15 .40
159 Jeff Graham .10 .25
160 Moses Moreno .10 .25
161 Rodney Harrison .12 .30
162 Steve Young .20 .50
163 Jerry Rice .30 .75
164 Ken Norton .10 .25
165 Terrell Owens .15 .40
166 Jeff Garcia .12 .30
167 Ricky Watters .12 .30
168 Jon Kitna .12 .30
169 Derrick Mayes .10 .25
170 Sean Dawkins .10 .25
171 Chad Brown .10 .25
172 Warrick Dunn .12 .30
173 Keyshawn Johnson .12 .30
174 Shaun King .10 .25
175 Mike Alstott .15 .40
176 Warren Sapp .12 .30
177 Jacquez Green .10 .25
178 Derrick Brooks .15 .40
179 John Lynch .12 .30
180 Eddie George .12 .30
181 Steve McNair .15 .40
182 Kevin Dyson .12 .30
183 Jevon Kearse .12 .30
184 Yancey Thigpen .10 .25
185 Frank Wycheck .12 .30
186 Eddie Robinson .10 .25
187 Jeff George .12 .30
188 Brad Johnson .12 .30
189 Stephen Davis .12 .30
190 Michael Westbrook .10 .25
191 Albert Connell .10 .25
192 Brian Mitchell .10 .25
193 Bruce Smith .15 .40
194 Champ Bailey .12 .30
195 Sam Shade .10 .25
196 Marvin Harrison SL .12 .30
197 Jimmy Smith SL .10 .25
198 Randy Moss SL .12 .30
199 Marcus Robinson SL .10 .25
200 Tim Brown SL .12 .30
201 Jimmy Smith SL .10 .25
202 Marvin Harrison SL .12 .30
203 Muhsin Muhammad SL .10 .25
204 Tim Brown SL .12 .30
205 Cris Carter SL .12 .30
206 Edgerrin James SL .12 .30
207 Curtis Martin SL .12 .30
208 Stephen Davis SL .10 .25
209 Emmitt Smith SL .30 .75
210 Marshall Faulk SL .12 .30
211 Kurt Warner SL .20 .50
212 Steve Beuerlein SL .10 .25
213 Jeff George SL .10 .25
214 Peyton Manning SL .30 .75
215 Brad Johnson SL .10 .25
216 Kurt Warner CL .20 .50
217 Peyton Manning CL .30 .75
218 Edgerrin James CL .12 .30
219 Marshall Faulk CL .12 .30
220 Randy Moss CL .12 .30
221 Jimmy Smith CL .10 .25
222 Tony Gonzalez CL .12 .30
223 Tony Boselli CL .10 .25
224 Orlando Pace CL .10 .25
225 Larry Allen CL .10 .25
226 Randall McDaniel CL .10 .25
227 Tom Nalen CL .07 .20
228 Kevin Carter CL .07 .20
229 Jevon Kearse CL .10 .25
230 Warren Sapp CL .10 .25
231 Darrell Russell CL .07 .20
232 Derrick Brooks CL .12 .30
233 Peter Boulware CL .07 .20
234 Junior Seau CL .12 .30
235 Sam Madison CL .07 .20
236 Charles Woodson CL .12 .30
237 John Lynch CL .10 .25
238 Carnell Lake CL .07 .20
239 Mitch Berger CL RC .10 .25
240 Jason Hanson CL .07 .20
241 Randy Moss PM .12 .30
242 Kurt Warner PM .20 .50
243 Peyton Manning PM .30 .75
244 Marshall Faulk PM .12 .30
245 Edgerrin James PM .12 .30
246 Eddie George PM .10 .25
247 Stephen Davis PM .10 .25
248 Keyshawn Johnson PM .10 .25
249 Brad Johnson PM .10 .25
250 Ricky Williams PM .12 .30
251 Jimmy Smith PM .10 .25
252 Isaac Bruce PM .12 .30
253 Muhsin Muhammad PM .10 .25
254 Marcus Robinson PM .10 .25
255 Kevin Johnson PM .07 .20
256 Tim Couch PM .10 .25
257 Curtis Martin PM .12 .30
258 Charlie Batch PM .10 .25
259 Tim Brown PM .12 .30
260 Jerry Rice PM .25 .60
261 Drew Bledsoe PM .12 .30
262 Brett Favre PM .40 1.00
263 Mark Brunell PM .10 .25
264 Fred Taylor PM .12 .30
265 Troy Edwards PM .07 .20
266 Marvin Harrison PM .12 .30
267 Germane Crowell PM .07 .20
268 Terry Glenn PM .10 .25
269 Qadry Ismail PM .10 .25
270 Jake Plummer PM .10 .25
271 Anthony Becht RC .25 .60
272 Anthony Lucas RC .20 .50
273 Bashir Yamini RC .20 .50
274 Brian Urlacher RC 1.25 3.00
275 Chad Morton RC .30 .75
276 Chad Pennington RC .50 1.25
277 Chris Cole RC .25 .60
278 Chris Hovan RC .25 .60
279 Tim Rattay RC .25 .60
280 Chris Redman RC .25 .60
281 Chris Samuels RC .25 .60
282 Corey Simon RC .25 .60
283 Courtney Brown RC .25 .60
284 Curtis Keaton RC .20 .50
285 Danny Farmer RC .20 .50
286 Erron Kinney RC .20 .50
287 Darren Howard RC .20 .50
288 Deltha O'Neal RC .25 .60
289 Dennis Northcutt RC .25 .60
290 Demario Brown RC .20 .50
291 Dez White RC .25 .60
292 Frank Murphy RC .20 .50
293 Gari Scott RC .20 .50
294 Giovanni Carmazzi RC .20 .50
295 J.R. Redmond RC .20 .50
296 JaJuan Dawson RC .20 .50
297 Jamal Lewis RC .30 .75
298 Leon Murray RC .20 .50
299 Jerry Porter RC .30 .75
300 Joe Hamilton RC .20 .50
301 John Abraham RC .30 .75
302 John Engelberger RC .20 .50
303 Keith Bulluck RC .25 .60
304 Kwame Cavil RC .20 .50
305 Laveranues Coles RC .30 .75
306 Marc Bulger RC .30 .75
307 Marcus Knight RC .20 .50
308 Mareno Philyaw RC .20 .50
309 Michael Wiley RC .20 .50
310 Na'il Diggs RC .20 .50
311 Peter Warrick RC .30 .75
312 Plaxico Burress RC .30 .75
313 Raynoch Thompson RC .20 .50
314 Reuben Droughns RC .30 .75
315 Rob Morris RC .25 .60
316 Ron Dayne RC .30 .75
317 Ron Dugans RC .20 .50
318 Sebastian Janikowski RC .30 .75
319 Shaun Alexander RC .40 1.00
320 Sherrod Gideon RC .20 .50
321 Sylvester Morris RC .20 .50
322 Tee Martin RC .30 .75
323 Thomas Jones RC .40 1.00
324 Todd Husak RC .20 .50
325 Todd Pinkston RC .20 .50
326 Tom Brady RC 20.00 40.00
327 Travis Prentice RC .25 .60
328 Travis Taylor RC .25 .60
329 Trevor Gaylor RC .20 .50
330 Trung Canidate RC .25 .60

2001 Upper Deck Victory

This set was issued as a 440-card set including 370 veterans, 60 rookies, and 10 checklist cards. Each card features a full color photo with white borders. There were 10 cards per pack, 36 packs per box.

COMPLETE SET (440) 30.00 60.00
1 Jake Plummer .12 .30
2 David Boston .10 .25
3 Thomas Jones .12 .30
4 Michael Pittman .12 .30
5 Frank Sanders .10 .25
6 Joel Makovicka .10 .25
7 Corey Chavous .10 .25
8 Kwamie Lassiter .10 .25
9 Rob Moore .10 .25
10 Jamal Anderson .12 .30
11 Tony Martin .12 .30
12 Travis Jervey .10 .25
13 Chris Chandler .12 .30
14 Shawn Jefferson .10 .25
15 Rodney Thomas .10 .25
16 Terance Mathis .10 .25
17 Jessie Tuggle .10 .25
18 Ashley Ambrose .10 .25
19 Brian Finneran .12 .30
20 Maurice Smith .10 .25
21 Keith Brooking .12 .30
22 Jamal Lewis .15 .40
23 Shannon Sharpe .15 .40
24 Brandon Stokley .12 .30
25 Ray Lewis .15 .40
26 Qadry Ismail .12 .30
27 Travis Taylor .10 .25
28 Chris Redman .15 .40
29 Rod Woodson .15 .40
30 Pat Johnson .10 .25
31 Jermaine Lewis .10 .25
32 Elvis Grbac .12 .30
33 Tony Siragusa .12 .30
34 Larry Centers .12 .30
35 Rob Johnson .12 .30
36 Eric Moulds .12 .30
37 Sammy Morris .12 .30
38 Shawn Bryson .10 .25
39 Alex Van Pelt .10 .25
40 Jeremy McDaniel .10 .25
41 Sam Cowart .10 .25
42 Peerless Price .10 .25
43 Avion Black .10 .25
44 Phil Hansen .10 .25
45 Muhsin Muhammad .12 .30
46 Brad Hoover .12 .30
47 Tim Biakabutuka .10 .25
48 Wesley Walls .10 .25
49 Donald Hayes .10 .25
50 Jeff Lewis .10 .25
51 Dameyune Craig .10 .25
52 Mike Minter RC .12 .30
53 Isaac Byrd .10 .25
54 Patrick Jeffers .10 .25
55 Cade McNown .12 .30
56 James Allen .10 .25
57 Marcus Robinson .12 .30
58 Brian Urlacher .20 .50
59 Shane Matthews .10 .25
60 Glyn Milburn .10 .25
61 Scott Dragos RC .10 .25
62 Marty Booker .12 .30
63 Bobby Engram .12 .30
64 Kaseem Sinceno .10 .25
65 Ted Washington .10 .25
66 Peter Warrick .12 .30
67 Corey Dillon .12 .30
68 Akili Smith UER .10 .25
(stats line is for receivers)
69 Danny Farmer .10 .25
70 Scott Mitchell .10 .25
71 Darryl Williams .10 .25
72 Ron Dugans .10 .25
73 Takeo Spikes .10 .25
74 Jon Kitna .12 .30
75 Darnay Scott .12 .30
76 Tony McGee .10 .25
77 Tim Couch .10 .25
78 Kevin Johnson .10 .25
79 Travis Prentice .10 .25
80 Spergon Wynn .10 .25
81 Errict Rhett .12 .30
82 Ty Detmer .12 .30
83 Dennis Northcutt .10 .25
84 Aaron Shea .10 .25
85 Courtney Brown .10 .25
86 JaJuan Dawson .10 .25
87 Rickey Dudley .10 .25
88 Jamir Miller .10 .25
89 Clint Stoerner .12 .30
90 Emmitt Smith .40 1.00
91 Joey Galloway .12 .30
92 Rocket Ismail .12 .30
93 Ebenezer Ekuban .10 .25
94 Anthony Wright .10 .25
95 David LaFleur .10 .25
96 Dexter Coakley .10 .25
97 Jackie Harris .12 .30
98 Michael Wiley .10 .25
99 Wane McGarity .10 .25
100 Dat Nguyen .10 .25
101 Terrell Davis .15 .40
102 Mike Anderson .12 .30
103 Brian Griese .12 .30
104 Rod Smith .12 .30
105 Ed McCaffrey .12 .30
106 Olandis Gary .10 .25
107 Kavika Pittman .10 .25
108 Bill Romanowski .12 .30
109 Gus Frerotte .12 .30
110 Howard Griffith .10 .25
111 Eddie Kennison .12 .30
112 Charlie Batch .12 .30
113 Germane Crowell .10 .25
114 James O. Stewart .10 .25
115 Johnnie Morton .12 .30
116 Herman Moore .12 .30
117 Larry Foster .10 .25
118 Desmond Howard .12 .30
119 Cory Schlesinger .10 .25
120 Robert Porcher .10 .25
121 Sedrick Irvin .10 .25
122 David Sloan .10 .25
123 Jim Harbaugh .12 .30
124 Brett Favre .50 1.25
125 Antonio Freeman .15 .40
126 Dorsey Levens .12 .30
127 Ahman Green .15 .40
128 LeRoy Butler .12 .30
129 De'Mond Parker .10 .25
130 Bill Schroeder .12 .30
131 Bubba Franks .12 .30
132 Donald Driver .15 .40
133 Darren Sharper .12 .30
134 Corey Bradford .10 .25
135 Charles Lee .10 .25
136 Peyton Manning .40 1.00
137 Edgerrin James .15 .40
138 Marvin Harrison .15 .40
139 E.G. Green .10 .25
140 Terrence Wilkins .10 .25
141 Ken Dilger .10 .25
142 Jerome Pathon .10 .25
143 Rob Morris .10 .25
144 Lennox Gordon .10 .25
145 Chad Bratzke .10 .25
146 Mark Brunell .12 .30
147 Fred Taylor .15 .40
148 Jimmy Smith .12 .30
149 Jamie Martin .10 .25
150 Keenan McCardell .12 .30
151 Kyle Brady .10 .25
152 R.Jay Soward .10 .25
153 Alvis Whitted .10 .25
154 Stacey Mack .10 .25
155 Damon Jones .10 .25
156 Carnell Lake .10 .25
157 Kevin Hardy .10 .25
158 Trent Green .15 .40
159 Tony Gonzalez .15 .40
160 Derrick Alexander .10 .25
161 Tony Richardson .10 .25
162 Frank Moreau .10 .25
163 Sylvester Morris .10 .25
164 Priest Holmes .15 .40
165 Donnie Edwards .10 .25
166 Marvcus Patton .10 .25
167 Larry Parker .10 .25
168 Tony Horne .10 .25
169 Bubby Brister .12 .30
170 Oronde Gadsden .10 .25
171 Lamar Smith .12 .30
172 Jay Fiedler .12 .30
173 James Johnson .10 .25
174 Rob Konrad .10 .25
175 James McKnight .10 .25
176 Dedric Ward .10 .25
177 O.J. McDuffie .10 .25
178 Zach Thomas .15 .40
179 Ray Lucas .10 .25
180 Sam Madison .10 .25
181 Randy Moss .15 .40
182 Jake Reed .12 .30
183 Cris Carter .15 .40
184 Daunte Culpepper .12 .30
185 Moe Williams .10 .25
186 Troy Walters .10 .25
187 Todd Bouman .10 .25
188 Jim Kleinsasser .12 .30
189 Ed McDaniel .10 .25
190 Robert Griffith .10 .25
191 Byron Chamberlain .10 .25
192 Chris Hovan .10 .25
193 Drew Bledsoe .15 .40
194 Terry Glenn .12 .30
195 Kevin Faulk .12 .30
196 J.R. Redmond .10 .25
197 Antowain Smith .12 .30
198 Bert Emanuel .10 .25
199 Troy Brown .12 .30
200 Tony Simmons .10 .25
201 Michael Bishop .12 .30
202 Lawyer Milloy .12 .30
203 Torrance Small .10 .25
204 Ty Law .12 .30
205 Charles Johnson .10 .25
206 Willie McGinest .10 .25
207 Ricky Williams .15 .40
208 Jeff Blake .12 .30
209 Joe Horn .12 .30
210 Aaron Brooks .12 .30
211 La'Roi Glover .10 .25
212 Chad Morton .10 .25
213 Keith Mitchell .10 .25
214 Willie Jackson .10 .25
215 Robert Wilson .10 .25
216 Norman Hand .10 .25
217 Albert Connell .10 .25
218 Joe Johnson .10 .25
219 Kerry Collins .12 .30
220 Amani Toomer .12 .30
221 Ron Dayne .12 .30
222 Tiki Barber .15 .40
223 Greg Comella .10 .25
224 Ike Hilliard .12 .30
225 Joe Jurevicius .10 .25
226 Ron Dixon .10 .25
227 Jason Sehorn .12 .30
228 Michael Strahan .15 .40
229 Jessie Armstead .10 .25
230 Michael Barrow .10 .25
231 Jason Garrett .15 .40
232 Vinny Testaverde .12 .30
233 Wayne Chrebet .12 .30
234 Curtis Martin .15 .40
235 Richie Anderson .10 .25
236 Mo Lewis .10 .25
237 Laveranues Coles .12 .30
238 Windrell Hayes .10 .25
239 Chad Pennington .15 .40
240 Matthew Hatchette .10 .25
241 Anthony Becht .10 .25
242 Marvin Jones .10 .25
243 Tim Brown .15 .40
244 Rich Gannon .12 .30
245 Tyrone Wheatley .12 .30
246 Charlie Garner .12 .30
247 Jon Ritchie .10 .25
248 James Jett .10 .25
249 Roland Williams .10 .25
250 Jerry Porter .10 .25
251 Darrell Russell .10 .25
252 Charles Woodson .15 .40
253 Jerry Rice .30 .75
254 Greg Biekert .10 .25
255 Duce Staley .12 .30
256 Donovan McNabb .15 .40
257 Darnell Autry .10 .25
258 Chad Lewis .10 .25
259 Na Brown .10 .25
260 Koy Detmer .10 .25
261 Todd Pinkston .10 .25
262 Brian Mitchell .12 .30
263 Hugh Douglas .10 .25
264 James Thrash .12 .30
265 Ron Powlus .12 .30
266 Corey Simon .10 .25
267 Kordell Stewart .12 .30
268 Jerome Bettis .15 .40
269 Bobby Shaw .10 .25
270 Hines Ward .15 .40
271 Plaxico Burress .12 .30
272 Courtney Hawkins .10 .25
273 Troy Edwards .10 .25
274 Earl Holmes .10 .25
275 Richard Huntley .10 .25
276 Kent Graham .12 .30
277 Tee Martin .12 .30
278 Jon Witman .10 .25
279 Marshall Faulk .15 .40
280 Kurt Warner .25 .60
281 Isaac Bruce .15 .40
282 Torry Holt .12 .30
283 Joe Germaine .10 .25
284 Ernie Conwell .10 .25
285 Trung Canidate .10 .25
286 Az-Zahir Hakim .10 .25
287 Ricky Proehl .10 .25
288 Grant Wistrom .10 .25
289 London Fletcher .10 .25
290 Paul Justin .10 .25
291 Robert Holcombe .10 .25
292 Junior Seau .15 .40
293 Curtis Conway .12 .30
294 Rodney Harrison .12 .30
295 Jeff Graham .10 .25
296 Freddie Jones .10 .25
297 Reggie Jones .10 .25
298 Ronney Jenkins .10 .25
299 Trevor Gaylor .10 .25
300 Tim Dwight .12 .30
301 Fred McCrary .10 .25
302 Terrell Fletcher .10 .25

303 Doug Flutie	.15	.40
304 Dave Dickenson RC	.12	.30
305 Marcellus Wiley	.10	.25
306 Jeff Garcia	.12	.30
307 Jonas Lewis	.10	.25
308 Tai Streets	.10	.25
309 Terrell Owens	.15	.40
310 J.J. Stokes	.10	.25
311 Fred Beasley	.10	.25
312 Tim Rattay	.10	.25
313 Garrison Hearst	.12	.30
314 Giovanni Carmazzi	.10	.25
315 Bryant Young	.12	.30
316 Ricky Watters	.12	.30
317 Shaun Alexander	.15	.40
318 Matt Hasselbeck	.15	.40
319 Brock Huard	.10	.25
320 Darrell Jackson	.12	.30
321 James Williams	.10	.25
322 Charlie Rogers UER	.10	.25
(name misspelled on back Rodgers)		
323 Christian Fauria	.10	.25
324 Karsten Bailey	.10	.25
325 Travis Brown RC	.10	.25
326 Chad Brown	.10	.25
327 John Randle	.12	.30
328 Warrick Dunn	.15	.40
329 Shaun King	.10	.25
330 Rabih Abdullah	.10	.25
331 Mike Alstott	.12	.30
332 Jacquez Green	.10	.25
333 Reidel Anthony	.10	.25
334 Derrick Brooks	.15	.40
335 John Lynch	.12	.30
336 Warren Sapp	.12	.30
337 Brad Johnson	.12	.30
338 Keyshawn Johnson	.12	.30
339 Mark Royals	.10	.25
340 Dave Moore	.10	.25
341 Simeon Rice	.12	.30
342 Ronde Barber	.12	.30
343 Eddie George	.15	.40
344 Steve McNair	.15	.40
345 Samari Rolle	.10	.25
346 Derrick Mason	.12	.30
347 Randall Godfrey	.10	.25
348 Frank Wycheck	.10	.25
349 Chris Sanders	.10	.25
350 Neil O'Donnell	.12	.30
351 Kevin Dyson	.10	.25
352 Jevon Kearse	.12	.30
353 Chris Coleman	.10	.25
354 Mike Green	.10	.25
355 Blaine Bishop	.10	.25
356 Eddie Robinson	.10	.25
357 Jeff George	.12	.30
358 Stephen Davis	.12	.30
359 Donnell Bennett	.10	.25
360 Kevin Lockett	.10	.25
361 Derrius Thompson	.10	.25
362 Michael Westbrook	.10	.25
363 Stephen Alexander	.10	.25
364 Ki-Jana Carter	.10	.25
365 Champ Bailey	.15	.40
366 Todd Husak	.10	.25
367 Dan Wilkinson	.10	.25
368 Darrell Green	.15	.40
369 Sam Shade	.10	.25
370 Bruce Smith	.15	.40
371 Bobby Newcombe RC	.25	.60
372 Vinny Sutherland RC	.20	.50
373 Alge Crumpler RC	.30	.75
374 Michael Vick RC	3.00	8.00
375 Gary Baxter RC	.20	.50
376 Todd Heap RC	.30	.75
377 Nate Clements RC	.25	.60
378 Travis Henry RC	.25	.60
379 Dan Morgan RC	.25	.60
380 Chris Weinke RC	.25	.60
381 David Terrell RC	.25	.60
382 Anthony Thomas RC	.30	.75
383 Rudi Johnson RC	.30	.75
384 Justin Smith RC	.30	.75
385 T.J. Houshmandzadeh RC	.40	1.00
386 Chad Johnson RC	.50	1.25
387 Quincy Morgan RC	.25	.60
388 Gerard Warren RC	.25	.60
389 James Jackson RC	.20	.50
390 Quincy Carter RC	.25	.60
391 Kevin Kasper RC	.20	.50
392 Scotty Anderson RC	.20	.50
393 Mike McMahon RC	.25	.60
394 Jamal Reynolds RC	.20	.50
395 Robert Ferguson RC	.30	.75
396 Reggie Wayne RC	.60	1.50
397 Snoop Minnis RC	.20	.50
398 Chris Chambers RC	.30	.75
399 Jamar Fletcher RC	.20	.50
400 Travis Minor RC	.25	.60
401 Josh Heupel RC	.30	.75
402 Michael Bennett RC	.25	.60
403 Jabari Holloway RC	.20	.50
404 Moran Norris RC	.20	.50
405 Deuce McAllister RC	.30	.75
406 Will Allen RC	.30	.75
407 Jesse Palmer RC	.25	.60
408 LaMont Jordan RC	.30	.75
409 Santana Moss RC	.40	1.00
410 Ken-Yon Rambo RC	.20	.50
411 Derrick Gibson RC	.20	.50
412 Marques Tuiasosopo RC	.25	.60
413 Correll Buckhalter RC	.30	.75
414 Freddie Mitchell RC	.20	.50
415 Drew Brees RC	3.00	8.00
416 LaDainian Tomlinson RC	3.00	8.00
417 Cedrick Wilson RC	.25	.60
418 Kevan Barlow RC	.25	.60
419 Alex Bannister RC	.20	.50
420 Heath Evans RC	.25	.60
421 Josh Booty RC	.25	.60
422 Koren Robinson RC	.25	.60
423 Adam Archuleta RC	.25	.60
424 Dan Alexander RC	.25	.60
425 Eddie Berlin RC	.20	.50
426 Rod Gardner RC	.25	.60
427 Sage Rosenfels RC	.30	.75
428 Steve Smith RC	.60	1.50
429 Chris Barnes RC	.20	.50
430 Tim Hasselbeck RC	.25	.60
431 Peyton Manning CL	.25	.60
432 Mike Anderson CL	.10	.25
433 Jamal Lewis CL	.10	.25
434 Randy Moss CL	.10	.25
435 Donovan McNabb CL	.10	.25
436 Daunte Culpepper CL	.07	.20
437 Kurt Warner CL	.15	.40
438 Eddie George CL	.10	.25
439 Marshall Faulk CL	.10	.25
440 Brett Favre CL	.30	.75

2001 Upper Deck Victory Gold

*1-440 VETS: 2X TO 5X BASIC CARDS
*371-440 ROOKIES: 1X TO 2.5X
GOLD STATED ODDS 1:2

2000 Upper Deck Vintage Previews

Sent out as a bonus to those redeeming autographed redemption cards, these two card preview packs contain serial numberd versions of the Upper Deck Vintage football set. The packs contain one regular card, numbered to 900 and one rookie card numbered to 1,500, 1,000 or 500. The regular cards and rookie cards make up a 90-card set.

21-40 ROOKIE TRIO PRINT RUN 1500

1 Jamal Lewis	5.00	12.00
2 Sammy Morris	4.00	10.00
3 Peter Warrick	5.00	12.00
4 Travis Prentice	4.00	10.00
5 Mike Anderson	5.00	12.00
6 Sylvester Morris	3.00	8.00
7 Ron Dayne	5.00	12.00
8 Chad Pennington	8.00	20.00
9 Plaxico Burress	5.00	12.00
10 Laveranues Coles	5.00	12.00
11 Spergon Wynn	2.00	5.00
Dennis Northcutt		
12 Courtney Brown	2.00	5.00
JaJuan Dawson		
13 Raynoch Thompson	1.50	4.00
Thomas Jones		
14 Tom Brady	40.00	80.00
J.R. Redmond		
15 John Abraham	2.50	6.00
Windrell Hayes		
16 Todd Husak	2.00	5.00
Chris Samuels		
17 Giovanni Carmazzi	2.00	5.00
Tim Rattay		
18 Shaun Alexander	3.00	8.00
Darrell Jackson		
19 Rob Morris	2.00	5.00
Kevin McDougle		
20 Brian Urlacher	2.00	5.00
Dez White		
21 Doug Johnson	1.50	4.00
Darrick Vaughn		
Mark Simoneau		
22 Chris Redman	1.50	4.00
John Jones		
Travis Taylor		
23 Kwame Cavil	1.25	3.00
Corey Moore		
Erik Flowers		
24 Ray Green	1.50	4.00
Lester Towns		
Brad Hoover		
25 Curtis Keaton	1.25	3.00
Danny Farmer		
Ron Dugans		
26 Scottie Montgomery	1.50	4.00
KaRon Coleman		
Deltha O'Neal		
27 Bubba Franks	2.00	5.00
Na'il Diggs		
Charles Lee		
28 Troy Walters	1.25	3.00
Chris Hovan		
Doug Chapman		
29 Chad Morton	1.25	3.00
Darren Howard		
Terrelle Smith		
30 Gari Scott	1.25	3.00
Todd Pinkston		
Corey Simon		
31 Chris Coleman	1.50	4.00
Keith Bulluck		
Erron Kinney		
32 Peter Sirmon	1.50	4.00
Billy Volek		
Bashir Yamini		
33 Jason Webster	1.25	3.00
Ahmed Plummer		
Julian Peterson		
34 Shockmain Davis	1.50	4.00
Patrick Pass		
Antwan Harris		
35 R.Jay Soward	1.25	3.00
Shyrone Stith		
T.J. Slaughter		
36 Trevor Gaylor	1.25	3.00
Ronney Jenkins		
Rogers Beckett		
37 Tee Martin	2.00	5.00
Joe Hamilton		
Jarious Jackson		
38 Chris Cole	1.50	4.00
Ron Dixon		
James Williams		
39 Reuben Droughns	2.00	5.00
Trung Canidate		
Frank Moreau		
40 Mike Brown	2.00	5.00
Jerry Porter		
Michael Wiley		
41 Jake Plummer	.60	1.50
42 Jamal Anderson	.60	1.50
43 Qadry Ismail	.60	1.50
44 Doug Flutie	.75	2.00
45 Rob Johnson	.60	1.50
46 Steve Beuerlein	.60	1.50
47 Marcus Robinson	.60	1.50
48 Cade McNown	.50	1.25
49 Tim Couch	.60	1.50
50 Corey Dillon	.60	1.50
51 Troy Aikman	1.25	3.00
52 Emmitt Smith	2.00	5.00
53 Charlie Batch	.60	1.50
54 Brian Griese	.60	1.50
55 Terrell Davis	.75	2.00
56 Brett Favre	2.50	6.00
57 Antonio Freeman	.60	1.50
58 Peyton Manning	2.00	5.00
59 Edgerrin James	.75	2.00
60 Marvin Harrison	.75	2.00
61 Mark Brunell	.60	1.50
62 Fred Taylor	.75	2.00
63 Elvis Grbac	.50	1.25
64 Derrick Alexander	.50	1.25
65 Lamar Smith	.50	1.25
66 Daunte Culpepper	.60	1.50
67 Randy Moss	.75	2.00
68 Drew Bledsoe	.75	2.00
69 Vinny Testaverde	.60	1.50
70 Curtis Martin	.75	2.00
71 Kerry Collins	.60	1.50
72 Amani Toomer	.60	1.50
73 Jeff Blake	.60	1.50
74 Ricky Williams	.75	2.00
75 Rich Gannon	.60	1.50
76 Tim Brown	.75	2.00
77 Jerome Bettis	.75	2.00
78 Kurt Warner	1.25	3.00
79 Marshall Faulk	.75	2.00
80 Junior Seau	.75	2.00
81 Jeff Garcia	.60	1.50
82 Terrell Owens	.75	2.00
83 Jerry Rice	1.50	4.00
84 Ricky Watters	.60	1.50
85 Shaun King	.50	1.25
86 Keyshawn Johnson	.60	1.50
87 Steve McNair	.75	2.00
88 Eddie George	.60	1.50
89 Stephen Davis	.60	1.50
90 Brad Johnson	.60	1.50

2001 Upper Deck Vintage

Upper Deck released its Vintage set in August of 2001. The card design in that of the 2000 Upper Deck Vintage Preview set but this set is missing the serial numbers. The cards have either blue, red, or split blue and red borders, with the exception of the 10 season leader cards which had a white border. The cards are on greyback cardstock to give this set the vintage look. The rookies were on the split blue and red borders.

COMPLETE SET (290)	20.00	40.00
1 Jake Plummer	.15	.40
2 David Boston	.12	.30
3 Thomas Jones	.15	.40
4 Frank Sanders	.12	.30
5 Bob Christian	.12	.30
6 Jamal Anderson	.15	.40
7 Chris Chandler	.15	.40
8 Shawn Jefferson	.12	.30
9 Brian Finneran	.15	.40
10 Terance Mathis	.12	.30
11 Jamal Lewis	.20	.50
12 Shannon Sharpe	.20	.50
13 Elvis Grbac	.15	.40
14 Ray Lewis	.20	.50
15 Qadry Ismail	.15	.40
16 Brandon Stokley	.15	.40
17 Rob Johnson	.15	.40
18 Eric Moulds	.15	.40
19 Sammy Morris	.15	.40
20 Shawn Bryson	.12	.30
21 Jeremy McDaniel	.12	.30
22 Muhsin Muhammad	.15	.40
23 Brad Hoover	.15	.40
24 Tim Biakabutuka	.12	.30
25 Donald Hayes	.12	.30
26 Jeff Lewis	.12	.30
27 Wesley Walls	.12	.30
28 Cade McNown	.15	.40
29 James Allen	.12	.30
30 Marcus Robinson	.15	.40
31 Brian Urlacher	.25	.60
32 Jim Miller	.15	.40
33 Peter Warrick	.15	.40
34 Corey Dillon	.15	.40
35 Akili Smith	.12	.30
36 Danny Farmer	.12	.30
37 Ron Dugans	.12	.30
38 Jon Kitna	.15	.40
39 Tim Couch	.12	.30
40 Kevin Johnson	.12	.30
41 Travis Prentice	.12	.30
42 Spergon Wynn	.12	.30
43 Errict Rhett	.15	.40
44 Dennis Northcutt	.12	.30
45 Courtney Brown	.12	.30
46 Tony Banks	.12	.30
47 Emmitt Smith	.50	1.25
48 Joey Galloway	.15	.40
49 Rocket Ismail	.15	.40
50 Anthony Wright	.12	.30
51 Jackie Harris	.15	.40
52 Terrell Davis	.20	.50
53 Mike Anderson	.15	.40
54 Brian Griese	.15	.40
55 Rod Smith	.15	.40
56 Ed McCaffrey	.15	.40
57 Howard Griffith	.12	.30
58 Olandis Gary	.12	.30
59 Charlie Batch	.15	.40
60 Germane Crowell	.12	.30
61 James O. Stewart	.12	.30
62 Johnnie Morton	.15	.40
63 Desmond Howard	.15	.40
64 Brett Favre	.60	1.50
65 Antonio Freeman	.20	.50
66 Dorsey Levens	.15	.40
67 Ahman Green	.20	.50
68 Bill Schroeder	.15	.40
69 Bubba Franks	.15	.40
70 Peyton Manning	.50	1.25
71 Edgerrin James	.20	.50
72 Marvin Harrison	.20	.50
73 Jerome Pathon	.12	.30
74 Ken Dilger	.12	.30
75 Terrence Wilkins	.12	.30
76 Mark Brunell	.15	.40
77 Fred Taylor	.20	.50
78 Jimmy Smith	.15	.40
79 Keenan McCardell	.15	.40
80 R. Jay Soward	.12	.30
81 Todd Collins	.12	.30
82 Tony Gonzalez	.20	.50
83 Derrick Alexander	.12	.30
84 Trent Green	.20	.50
85 Sylvester Morris	.12	.30
86 Oronde Gadsden	.12	.30
87 Lamar Smith	.15	.40
88 Jay Fiedler	.15	.40
89 Zach Thomas	.20	.50
90 Ray Lucas	.12	.30
91 O.J. McDuffie	.12	.30
92 Randy Moss	.20	.50
93 Cris Carter	.20	.50
94 Daunte Culpepper	.15	.40
95 Robert Griffith	.12	.30
96 Jake Reed	.15	.40
97 Drew Bledsoe	.20	.50
98 Terry Glenn	.15	.40
99 Kevin Faulk	.15	.40
100 Michael Bishop	.15	.40
101 Troy Brown	.15	.40
102 Ricky Williams	.20	.50
103 Jeff Blake	.15	.40
104 Joe Horn	.15	.40
105 Willie Jackson	.12	.30
106 Aaron Brooks	.15	.40
107 Keith Poole	.12	.30
108 Kerry Collins	.15	.40
109 Amani Toomer	.15	.40
110 Ron Dayne	.15	.40
111 Tiki Barber	.20	.50
112 Ike Hilliard	.15	.40
113 Ron Dixon	.12	.30
114 Michael Strahan	.20	.50
115 Vinny Testaverde	.15	.40
116 Wayne Chrebet	.15	.40
117 Curtis Martin	.20	.50
118 Richie Anderson	.12	.30
119 Laveranues Coles	.15	.40
120 Chad Pennington	.20	.50
121 Tim Brown	.20	.50
122 Rich Gannon	.15	.40
123 Tyrone Wheatley	.15	.40
124 Charlie Garner	.15	.40
125 Andre Rison	.15	.40
126 Charles Woodson	.20	.50
127 Jon Ritchie	.12	.30
128 Duce Staley	.15	.40
129 Donovan McNabb	.20	.50
130 Darnell Autry	.12	.30
131 Chad Lewis	.12	.30
132 Brian Mitchell	.15	.40
133 Kordell Stewart	.15	.40
134 Jerome Bettis	.20	.50
135 Plaxico Burress	.15	.40
136 Bobby Shaw	.12	.30
137 Hines Ward	.20	.50
138 Marshall Faulk	.20	.50
139 Kurt Warner	.30	.75
140 Isaac Bruce	.20	.50
141 Torry Holt	.15	.40
142 Justin Watson	.12	.30
143 Az-ZahirHakim	.12	.30
144 Junior Seau	.20	.50
145 Curtis Conway	.15	.40
146 Doug Flutie	.20	.50
147 Jeff Graham	.12	.30
148 Freddie Jones	.12	.30
149 Rodney Harrison	.15	.40
150 Jeff Garcia	.15	.40
151 Jerry Rice	.40	1.00
152 Jonas Lewis	.12	.30
153 Terrell Owens	.20	.50
154 J.J. Stokes	.12	.30
155 Garrison Hearst	.15	.40
156 Ricky Watters	.15	.40
157 Shaun Alexander	.20	.50
158 Matt Hasselbeck	.20	.50
159 Brock Huard	.12	.30
160 Darrell Jackson	.15	.40
161 Itula Mili	.12	.30
162 Warrick Dunn	.20	.50
163 Shaun King	.12	.30
164 Reidel Anthony	.12	.30
165 Mike Alstott	.15	.40
166 Jacquez Green	.12	.30
167 Brad Johnson	.15	.40
168 Keyshawn Johnson	.15	.40
169 Eddie George	.20	.50
170 Steve McNair	.20	.50
171 Neil O'Donnell	.15	.40
172 Derrick Mason	.15	.40
173 Frank Wycheck	.12	.30
174 Chris Sanders	.12	.30
175 Jevon Kearse	.15	.40
176 Jeff George	.15	.40
177 Stephen Davis	.15	.40
178 Skip Hicks	.12	.30
179 Michael Westbrook	.12	.30
180 Stephen Alexander	.12	.30
181 Vinny Testaverde SH	.15	.40
182 Trent Green SH	.20	.50
183 Brian Griese SH	.15	.40
184 Kerry Collins SH	.15	.40
185 Aaron Brooks SH	.15	.40
186 Jamal Lewis SH	.20	.50
187 Jeff Garcia SH	.15	.40
188 Warrick Dunn SH	.20	.50
189 Mike Anderson SH	.15	.40
190 Lamar Smith SH	.15	.40
191 Daunte Culpepper SL	.15	.40
192 Darren Sharper SL	.15	.40
193 Marvin Harrison SL	.20	.50
194 Torry Holt SL	.15	.40
195 Trent Green SL	.20	.50
196 Peyton Manning SL	.50	1.25
197 Muhsin Muhammad SL	.15	.40
198 La'Roi Glover SL	.12	.30
199 Brian Griese SL	.15	.40
200 Darrick Vaughn SL	.12	.30
201 Bobby Newcombe RC	.40	1.00
202 Leonard Davis RC	.50	1.25
203 Alge Crumpler RC	.50	1.25
204 Michael Vick RC	2.00	5.00
205 Vinny Sutherland RC	.30	.75
206 Chris Barnes RC	.30	.75
207 Todd Heap RC	.50	1.25
208 Travis Henry RC	.40	1.00
209 Tim Hasselbeck RC	.40	1.00
210 Nate Clements RC	.40	1.00
211 Chris Weinke RC	.40	1.00
212 Dan Morgan RC	.40	1.00
213 Anthony Thomas RC	.50	1.25
214 David Terrell RC	.40	1.00
215 Chad Johnson RC	.75	2.00
216 Justin Smith RC	.50	1.25
217 Rudi Johnson RC	.50	1.25
218 T.J. Houshmandzadeh RC	.60	1.50
219 Gerard Warren RC	.40	1.00
220 James Jackson RC	.30	.75
221 Quincy Morgan RC	.40	1.00
222 Quincy Carter RC	.40	1.00
223 Tony Dixon RC	.30	.75
224 Kevin Kasper RC	.30	.75
225 Willie Middlebrooks RC	.40	1.00
226 Mike McMahon RC	.40	1.00
227 Shaun Rogers RC	.50	1.25
228 Jamal Reynolds RC	.30	.75
229 Robert Ferguson RC	.50	1.25
230 Reggie Wayne RC	1.00	2.50
231 Marcus Stroud RC	.40	1.00
232 Dustin McClintock RC	.40	1.00
233 Snoop Minnis RC	.30	.75
234 Chris Chambers RC	.50	1.25
235 Josh Heupel RC	.50	1.25
236 Travis Minor RC	.40	1.00
237 Michael Bennett RC	.40	1.00
238 Richard Seymour RC	.50	1.25
239 Hakim Akbar RC	.30	.75
240 Deuce McAllister RC	.50	1.25
241 Moran Norris RC	.30	.75
242 Jesse Palmer RC	.40	1.00
243 Will Allen RC	.50	1.25
244 LaMont Jordan RC	.50	1.25
245 Santana Moss RC	.60	1.50
246 Marques Tuiasosopo RC	.40	1.00
247 Correll Buckhalter RC	.50	1.25
248 Freddie Mitchell RC	.30	.75
249 A.J. Feeley RC	.40	1.00
250 Dave Dickenson RC	.40	1.00
251 Drew Brees RC	5.00	12.00
252 LaDainian Tomlinson RC	4.00	10.00
253 David Allen RC	.30	.75
254 Andre Carter RC	.40	1.00
255 Kevan Barlow RC	.40	1.00
256 Josh Booty RC	.40	1.00
257 Koren Robinson RC	.40	1.00
258 Adam Archuleta RC	.40	1.00
259 Rod Gardner RC	.40	1.00
260 Sage Rosenfels RC	.50	1.25
261 Reggie Germany	.30	.75
Ken-Yon Rambo RC		
262 Edgerton Hartwell	.30	.75
Gary Baxter RC		
263 Aaron Schobel	.50	1.25
Brandon Spoon RC		
264 John Capel	.30	.75
Karon Riley RC		
265 Billy Baber	.40	1.00
Derrick Blaylock RC		
266 Jamar Fletcher	.30	.75
Morlon Greenwood RC		
267 Andre King	.30	.75
Ronney Daniels RC		
268 Arther Love	.30	.75
Jabari Holloway RC		
269 Jonas Jennings	.30	.75
Kenyatta Walker RC		
270 Ben Hamilton	.30	.75
Paul Toviessa RC		
271 Chris Taylor	.30	.75
Jocy Getherall RC		
272 Casey Hampton RC	.50	1.25
Kendrell Bell RC		
273 Cedrick Wilson	.40	1.00
Jamie Winborn RC		
274 Alex Bannister	.40	1.00
Heath Evans RC		
275 Damione Lewis	.40	1.00
Ryan Pickett RC		
276 Tommy Polley	.30	.75
Brian Allen RC		
277 Jamie Henderson	.40	1.00
Reggie White RC		
278 Eddie Berlin	.40	1.00
Justin McCareins RC		
279 Andre Dyson	.40	1.00
Dan Alexander RC		
280 Quentin McCord	.40	1.00
Robert Garza RC		
281 Scotty Anderson	.30	.75
Eric Kelly		
Willie Howard RC		
282 Bhawoh Jue	.40	1.00
David Martin		
Torrance Marshall RC		
283 Steve Smith	1.00	2.50
Dee Brown		
Jarrod Cooper RC		
284 DeLawrence Grant	.30	.75
Derek Combs		
Derrick Gibson RC		
285 Carlos Polk	.40	1.00
Tay Cody		
Zeke Moreno RC		
286 David Rivers	.30	.75
Francis St. Paul		
Milton Wynn RC		
287 Ennis Davis	.30	.75
Kenny Smith		
Sedrick Hodge RC		
288 Ken Lucas	.50	1.25
Orlando Huff		
Steve Hutchinson RC		
289 Marcellus Rivers	.50	1.25
Derrick Burgess		
Tony Driver RC		
290 Damerien McCants	.50	1.25
Fred Smoot		
Mike Cerimele RC		

2001 Upper Deck Vintage Franchise Players

COMPLETE SET (7)	6.00	15.00
STATED ODDS 1:24		
FP1 Charlie Batch	.75	2.00
FP2 Ricky Williams	1.00	2.50
FP3 Brett Favre	3.00	8.00
FP4 Emmitt Smith	2.50	6.00
FP5 Terrell Davis	1.00	2.50
FP6 Jerome Bettis	1.00	2.50
FP7 Eddie George	1.00	2.50

2001 Upper Deck Vintage Matinee Idols

COMPLETE SET (10)	6.00	15.00
STATED ODDS 1:18		
M1 Stephen Davis	.75	2.00
M2 Mike Alstott	.75	2.00
M3 Ricky Williams	1.00	2.50
M4 Ricky Watters	.75	2.00
M5 Donovan McNabb	1.00	2.50
M6 Charlie Batch	.75	2.00
M7 Jamal Lewis	1.00	2.50
M8 Drew Bledsoe	1.00	2.50
M9 Aaron Brooks	.75	2.00
M10 Vinny Testaverde	.75	2.00

2001 Upper Deck Vintage Old School Attitude

COMPLETE SET (10)	6.00	15.00
STATED ODDS 1:18		
OS1 Tim Brown	1.00	2.50
OS2 Peyton Manning	2.50	6.00
OS3 Jamal Anderson	.75	2.00
OS4 Doug Flutie	1.00	2.50
OS5 Emmitt Smith	2.50	6.00
OS6 Cris Carter	1.00	2.50
OS7 Ed McCaffrey	.75	2.00
OS8 Fred Taylor	1.00	2.50
OS9 Curtis Martin	1.00	2.50
OS10 Tim Couch	.60	1.50

2001 Upper Deck Vintage Signatures

STATED ODDS 1:144 HOBBY		
ABVS Aaron Brooks	8.00	20.00
CBVS Charlie Batch	8.00	20.00
CDVS Corey Dillon	8.00	20.00
DFVS Doug Flutie	10.00	25.00
DIVS Trent Dilfer	8.00	20.00
EJVS Edgerrin James	10.00	25.00
IBVS Isaac Bruce	10.00	25.00
JBVS Jim Brown	75.00	150.00
JNVS Joe Namath	60.00	120.00
JRVS John Riggins	50.00	120.00
JSVS Junior Seau	25.00	50.00
MAVS Mike Anderson	8.00	20.00
MBVS Mark Brunell	8.00	20.00
MFVS Marshall Faulk	12.00	30.00
MRVS Marcus Robinson	8.00	20.00
NOVS Jeff Blake	8.00	20.00
PHVS Paul Hornung	15.00	30.00
PMVS Peyton Manning	50.00	100.00
TBVS Terry Bradshaw	50.00	120.00
TCVS Tim Couch	6.00	15.00
TDVS Terrell Davis	10.00	25.00
TGVS Tony Gonzalez	10.00	25.00
TOVS Terrell Owens	15.00	40.00
VTVS Vinny Testaverde	8.00	20.00
WCVS Wayne Chrebet	8.00	20.00

2001 Upper Deck Vintage Smashmouth

COMPLETE SET (15)	6.00	15.00
STATED ODDS 1:12		
S1 Ray Lewis	1.00	2.50
S2 Junior Seau	1.00	2.50
S3 Eddie George	1.00	2.50
S4 Jerome Bettis	1.00	2.50
S5 Ricky Williams	1.00	2.50
S6 Terrell Owens	1.00	2.50
S7 Warren Sapp	.75	2.00
S8 John Lynch	.75	2.00
S9 Brian Urlacher	1.25	3.00
S10 Zach Thomas	1.00	2.50
S11 Tyrone Wheatley	.75	2.00
S12 Stephen Davis	.75	2.00
S13 Mike Alstott	.75	2.00
S14 Fred Taylor	1.00	2.50
S15 Cris Carter	1.00	2.50

2001 Upper Deck Vintage Threads

STATED ODDS 1:144		
ASVT Akili Smith	3.00	8.00
BEVT Michael Bennett	4.00	10.00
BFVT Brett Favre	12.00	30.00
CDVT Corey Dillon	4.00	10.00
CJVT Chad Johnson	6.00	15.00
CWVT Chris Weinke	4.00	10.00
DMVT Deuce McAllister	5.00	12.00
DRVT Drew Brees	20.00	40.00
FMVT Freddie Mitchell	3.00	8.00
IHVT Ike Hilliard	4.00	10.00
JGVT Jeff Garcia	4.00	10.00
JJVT James Jackson	3.00	8.00
JRVT Jerry Rice	10.00	25.00
KBVT Kevan Barlow	4.00	10.00
KRVT Koren Robinson	4.00	10.00
KWVT Kurt Warner	8.00	20.00
LTVT LaDainian Tomlinson	10.00	25.00
MBVT Mark Brunell	4.00	10.00
MVVT Michael Vick	12.00	30.00
PWVT Peter Warrick	4.00	10.00
QMVT Quincy Morgan	4.00	10.00
RDVT Ron Dayne	4.00	10.00
RGVT Rod Gardner	4.00	10.00
RLVT Ray Lewis	5.00	12.00
RMVT Randy Moss	8.00	20.00
RWVT Reggie Wayne	8.00	20.00
SMVT Santana Moss	5.00	12.00
TAVT Troy Aikman	8.00	20.00
WSVT Warren Sapp	4.00	10.00
ZTVT Zach Thomas	5.00	12.00

2001 Upper Deck Vintage Threads Autographs

STATED PRINT RUN 100 SER.#'d SETS		
CDSVT Corey Dillon	20.00	50.00
DBSVT Drew Bledsoe	25.00	60.00
DCSVT Daunte Culpepper	20.00	50.00
JGSVT Jeff Garcia	20.00	50.00
JMSVT Joe Montana	150.00	300.00
JRSVT Jerry Rice	75.00	150.00
KWSVT Kurt Warner	40.00	100.00
MASVT Mike Alstott	20.00	50.00
MBSVT Mark Brunell	20.00	50.00
PMSVT Peyton Manning	60.00	120.00
RMSVT Randy Moss	50.00	100.00
SDSVT Stephen Davis	20.00	50.00
TASVT Troy Aikman	50.00	100.00
TCSVT Tim Couch	15.00	40.00

2001 Upper Deck Vintage Threads Combos

STATED PRINT RUN 50 SER.#'d SETS		
AMVTC Troy Aikman	20.00	50.00
Cade McNown		
BDVTC Tiki Barber		
Ron Dayne		
BFVTC Mark Brunell	40.00	100.00
Brett Favre		
DBVTC Ron Dayne	10.00	25.00
Michael Bennett		
FJVTC Marshall Faulk	12.00	30.00
Edgerrin James		
FMVTC Marshall Faulk	12.00	30.00
Deuce McAllister		
GSVTC Darrell Green	30.00	80.00
Deion Sanders		
MCVTC Donovan McNabb	12.00	30.00
Daunte Culpepper		
MJVTC Peyton Manning	30.00	80.00
Edgerrin James		
MRVTC Randy Moss	40.00	100.00
Jerry Rice		
WHVTC Kurt Warner	20.00	50.00
Torry Holt		

2011 Upper Deck World of Sports

COMPLETE SET (400)	75.00	150.00
COMP.SET w/o SPs (300)	25.00	60.00
89 Adrian Peterson	.40	1.00
90 Armon Binns	.15	.40
91 Rocket Ismail	.15	.40
92 Floyd Little	.25	.60
93 Greg Pruitt	.15	.40
94 Mikel Leshoure	.15	.40
95 Tim Brown	.15	.40
96 Kendall Hunter	.40	1.00
97 Doug Flutie	.15	.40
98 John Cappelletti	.15	.40
99 Bernie Kosar	.15	.40
100 Leonard Hankerson	.15	.40
101 Brian Bosworth	.15	.40
102 Andy Dalton	.75	2.00
103 Eric Metcalf	.15	.40
104 Christian Ponder	.60	1.50
105 Aaron Williams	.15	.40
106 Aldon Smith	.15	.40
107 Randall Cobb	.25	.60
108 Nick Fairley	.15	.40
109 Prince Amukamara	.25	.60
110 Ryan Mallett	.60	1.50
111 Titus Young	.15	.40
112 Daniel Thomas	.25	.60
113 Jonathan Baldwin	.15	.40
114 DeMarco Murray	.60	1.50
115 Colin Kaepernick	.40	1.00
116 Noel Devine	.25	.60
117 Kyle Rudolph	.40	1.00
118 Ryan Kerrigan	.40	1.00
119 Torrey Smith	.40	1.00
120 Adrian Clayborn	.15	.40
121 Justin Houston	.15	.40
122 Akeem Ayers	.15	.40
123 Ryan Williams	.15	.40
124 Greg Little	.15	.40
125 Charles White	.15	.40
126 Evan Royster	.15	.40
127 Allen Bradford	.15	.40
128 Rahim Moore	.15	.40
129 Da'Quan Bowers	.25	.60
130 Corey Liuget	.15	.40
131 Terrelle Pryor	.15	.40
132 Vincent Brown	.15	.40
133 Bo Jackson	.40	1.00
134 Terrence Toliver	.15	.40
135 Ricky Stanzi	.40	1.00
136 Jaiquawn Jarrett	.15	.40
137 Adam Weber	.15	.40
138 Bruce Carter	.15	.40
139 Rod Woodson	.25	.60
140 Drew Brees	.40	1.00
141 Dan Marino	.40	1.00
142 Greg Salas	.40	1.00
310 Bo Jackson SP	1.50	4.00
330 Archie Griffin SP	1.00	2.50
331 Blaine Gabbert SP	2.00	5.00
332 Von Miller SP	1.00	2.50
333 Aaron Rodgers SP	1.50	4.00
334 Tony Dorsett SP	1.00	2.50
335 John Elway SP	1.25	3.00
336 Bubba Smith SP	1.00	2.50
337 Barry Sanders SP	1.00	2.50
338 Earl Campbell SP	1.00	2.50
339 Gale Sayers SP	1.00	2.50
340 Troy Aikman SP	1.00	2.50
341 A.J. Green SP	1.00	2.50
342 Cam Newton SP	1.50	4.00
343 Jake Locker SP	1.25	3.00
344 Julio Jones SP	1.00	2.50
345 Billy Sims SP	1.00	2.50
346 Mark Ingram SP	1.00	2.50
347 Herschel Walker SP	1.00	2.50

2011 Upper Deck World of Sports All-Sport Apparel Memorabilia

OVERALL AUTO/MEM ODDS 3 PER BOX		
ASAG A.J. Green	4.00	10.00
ASBG Blaine Gabbert	3.00	8.00
ASCK Colin Kaepernick	3.00	8.00
ASCN Cam Newton	10.00	25.00
ASJL Jake Locker	5.00	12.00
ASMI Mark Ingram	6.00	15.00
ASPO Christian Ponder	4.00	10.00
ASTS Torrey Smith	3.00	8.00
ASTT Terrence Toliver	3.00	8.00
AWJJ Julio Jones	8.00	20.00

2011 Upper Deck World of Sports All-Sport Apparel Memorabilia Autographs

ASAG A.J. Green/10		
ASBG Blaine Gabbert/10		
ASCK Colin Kaepernick/15	12.00	30.00
ASCN Cam Newton/5		
ASMI Mark Ingram/15	40.00	80.00
ASPO Christian Ponder/20		
ASTS Torrey Smith/10		
ASTT Terrence Toliver/20		
AWJJ Julio Jones/10		

2011 Upper Deck World of Sports Athletes of the World Autographs

OVERALL AUTO/MEM ODDS 3 PER BOX		
AWDM Darren McFadden	8.00	20.00
AWFL Joe Flacco	10.00	25.00
AWMR Ryan Mathews	6.00	15.00
AWRM Rashard Mendenhall	6.00	15.00
AWST Jonathan Stewart		

2011 Upper Deck World of Sports Autographs

89 Adrian Peterson A		
90 Armon Binns B	4.00	10.00
91 Rocket Ismail B		
92 Floyd Little B	8.00	20.00
93 Greg Pruitt A		
94 Mikel Leshoure B		
95 Tim Brown B		
96 Kendall Hunter C	6.00	15.00
99 Bernie Kosar B		
100 Leonard Hankerson D	4.00	10.00
101 Brian Bosworth B		
102 Andy Dalton C	15.00	40.00
104 Christian Ponder B	12.00	30.00
105 Aaron Williams B	4.00	10.00
107 Randall Cobb B		
109 Prince Amukamara C	5.00	12.00
110 Ryan Mallett B	12.00	30.00
111 Titus Young B	4.00	10.00
112 Daniel Thomas C	5.00	12.00
114 DeMarco Murray B		
115 Colin Kaepernick C	6.00	15.00
116 Noel Devine B		
117 Kyle Rudolph C	6.00	15.00
118 Ryan Kerrigan C	6.00	15.00
119 Torrey Smith B	6.00	15.00
121 Justin Houston C	4.00	10.00
123 Ryan Williams B		
124 Greg Little C	4.00	10.00
125 Charles White C		
126 Evan Royster B		
127 Allen Bradford C	4.00	10.00
128 Rahim Moore C	4.00	10.00
129 Da'Quan Bowers C	5.00	12.00
130 Corey Liuget C	4.00	10.00
131 Terrelle Pryor A		
132 Vincent Brown C	4.00	10.00
133 Bo Jackson B	30.00	60.00
134 Terrence Toliver C	4.00	10.00
135 Ricky Stanzi C	12.00	30.00
136 Jaiquawn Jarrett C		
137 Adam Weber C	4.00	10.00
138 Bruce Carter B		
139 Rod Woodson B	20.00	40.00
140 Drew Brees A	30.00	60.00
141 Dan Marino A		
142 Greg Salas B	6.00	15.00
310 Bo Jackson A	30.00	60.00
331 Blaine Gabbert A		
332 Von Miller B	8.00	20.00
334 Tony Dorsett A		
335 John Elway A		
336 Bubba Smith A	15.00	30.00
337 Barry Sanders A		
338 Earl Campbell A		
339 Gale Sayers A		
341 A.J. Green A		
342 Cam Newton A	75.00	125.00
343 Jake Locker A		
344 Julio Jones A	25.00	50.00
345 Billy Sims A		
346 Mark Ingram A	25.00	50.00

2011 Upper Deck World of Sports Sports Nation Autographs Quad

STATED PRINT RUN 6 SER. #'d SETS
UNPRICED DUE TO SCARCITY
SNFBQB Y. A. Tittle
Fran Tarkenton
Archie Manning
Bart Starr
SNFBRB Barry Sanders
Franco Harris
Gale Sayers
Earl Campbell

2011 Upper Deck World of Sports SPx Shadow Box

STATED ODDS 1:360
SBAJ A.J. Green
SBAR Aaron Rodgers
SBBJ Bo Jackson
SBBR Drew Brees
SBBS Barry Sanders
SBCN Cam Newton
SBJE John Elway
SBJJ Julio Jones
SBTD Tony Dorsett

2002 Upper Deck XL

Released in June, 2002, this set contains 100-rookies and 500-veterans making a total of 600-cards. This was one of the most ambitious efforts in recent years from any card company in terms of player selection, hence the name "XL." The rookie cards were inserted at a stated rate of one every two packs.

COMPLETE SET (600)	75.00	150.00
COMP.SET w/o SP's (500)	25.00	60.00
ROOKIE STATED ODDS 1:2		
1 David Boston	.15	.40
2 Dave Brown	.15	.40
3 Frank Sanders	.15	.40
4 Jake Plummer	.20	.50
5 Joel Makovicka	.15	.40
6 Kwamie Lassiter	.15	.40
7 MarTay Jenkins	.15	.40
8 Michael Pittman	.20	.50
9 Raynoch Thompson	.15	.40
10 Rob Fredrickson	.15	.40
11 Ronald McKinnon	.15	.40
12 Steve Bush	.15	.40
13 Thomas Jones	.25	.60
14 Tywan Mitchell	.15	.40
15 Alvis Whitted	.15	.40
16 Ashley Ambrose	.15	.40
17 Bob Christian	.15	.40
18 Brady Smith	.15	.40
19 Brian Finneran	.15	.40
20 Chris Chandler	.20	.50
21 Chris Draft RC	.15	.40
22 Darrien Gordon	.15	.40
23 Doug Johnson	.15	.40
24 Ephraim Salaam	.15	.40
25 Jamal Anderson	.20	.50
26 Keith Brooking	.15	.40
27 Maurice Smith	.15	.40
28 Michael Vick	.40	1.00
29 Ray Buchanan	.15	.40
30 Shawn Jefferson	.15	.40
31 Terance Mathis	.15	.40
32 Tony Martin	.20	.50
33 Brandon Stokley	.20	.50
34 Chris McAlister	.15	.40
35 Chris Redman	.15	.40
36 Elvis Grbac	.15	.40
37 Jonathan Ogden	.20	.50
38 Moe Williams	.15	.40
39 Obafemi Ayanbadejo	.15	.40
40 Peter Boulware	.15	.40
41 Qadry Ismail	.20	.50
42 Randall Cunningham	.25	.60
43 Ray Lewis	.25	.60
44 Rod Woodson	.25	.60
45 Sam Adams	.15	.40
46 Shannon Sharpe	.25	.60
47 Terry Allen	.20	.50
48 Todd Heap	.20	.50
49 Tony Siragusa	.20	.50
50 Travis Taylor	.15	.40
51 Alex Van Pelt	.15	.40
52 Antoine Winfield	.15	.40
53 Eric Moulds	.20	.50
54 Jay Foreman RC	.15	.40
55 Jay Riemersma	.15	.40
56 Jeremy McDaniel	.15	.40
57 Keith Newman	.15	.40
58 Kenyatta Wright	.15	.40
59 Larry Centers	.20	.50
60 Peerless Price	.15	.40
61 Rob Johnson	.20	.50
62 Ruben Brown	.15	.40
63 Shawn Bryson	.15	.40
64 Travis Brown	.15	.40
65 Travis Henry	.15	.40
66 Brad Hoover	.15	.40
67 Brentson Buckner	.15	.40
68 Chris Weinke	.15	.40
69 Dameyune Craig	.15	.40
70 Deon Grant	.15	.40
71 Donald Hayes	.15	.40
72 Doug Evans	.15	.40
73 Isaac Byrd	.15	.40
74 Jay Williams RC	.15	.40
75 Lester Towns	.15	.40
76 Muhsin Muhammad	.20	.50
77 Richard Huntley	.15	.40
78 Steve Smith	.25	.60
79 Tim Biakabutuka	.20	.50
80 Todd Sauerbrun	.15	.40
81 Wesley Walls	.20	.50
82 Anthony Thomas	.20	.50
83 Brian Urlacher	.25	.60
84 Daimon Shelton	.15	.40
85 David Terrell	.15	.40
86 Dez White	.15	.40
87 Fred Baxter	.15	.40
88 James Allen	.15	.40
89 James Williams	.15	.40
90 Jim Miller	.15	.40
91 Keith Traylor	.15	.40
92 Larry Whigham	.15	.40
93 Marcus Robinson	.20	.50
94 Marty Booker	.20	.50
95 Mike Brown	.20	.50
96 Olin Kreutz RC	.30	.75
97 R.W. McQuarters	.15	.40
98 Rosevelt Colvin RC	.30	.75
99 Shane Matthews	.15	.40
100 Ted Washington	.15	.40
101 Akili Smith	.20	.50
102 Brandon Bennett	.15	.40
103 Brian Simmons	.15	.40
104 Chad Johnson	.25	.60
105 Corey Dillon	.20	.50
106 Darnay Scott	.20	.50
107 Jon Kitna	.20	.50
108 Lorenzo Neal	.20	.50
109 Peter Warrick	.20	.50
110 Ron Dugans	.15	.40
111 Scott Mitchell	.20	.50
112 Takeo Spikes	.15	.40
113 Tony McGee	.20	.50
114 Brant Boyer	.15	.40
115 Corey Fuller	.15	.40
116 Courtney Brown	.15	.40
117 Dwayne Rudd	.15	.40
118 JaJuan Dawson	.15	.40
119 Jamel White	.15	.40
120 James Jackson	.15	.40
121 Jamir Miller	.15	.40
122 Josh Booty	.15	.40
123 Kelly Holcomb	.20	.50
124 Kevin Johnson	.15	.40
125 Lenoy Jones RC	.15	.40
126 Quincy Morgan	.15	.40
127 Raymond Jackson RC	.15	.40
128 Rickey Dudley	.15	.40
129 Tim Couch	.15	.40
130 Darren Woodson	.20	.50
131 Dat Nguyen	.15	.40
132 Dexter Coakley	.15	.40
133 Duane Hawthorne	.15	.40
134 Emmitt Smith	.60	1.50
135 Jackie Harris	.20	.50
136 Joey Galloway	.20	.50
137 Ken-Yon Rambo	.15	.40
138 Larry Allen	.15	.40
139 Mike Lucky	.15	.40
140 Quincy Carter	.15	.40
141 Rocket Ismail	.20	.50
142 Reggie Swinton	.15	.40
143 Robert Thomas	.15	.40
144 Ryan Leaf	.15	.40
145 Troy Hambrick	.15	.40
146 Al Wilson	.20	.50
147 Bill Romanowski	.20	.50
148 Brian Griese	.20	.50
149 Chester McGlockton	.15	.40
150 Chris Cole	.15	.40
151 Deltha.O'Neal	.15	.40
152 Desmond Clark	.20	.50
153 Dwayne Carswell	.15	.40
154 Ian Gold	.15	.40
155 Jarious Jackson	.15	.40
156 Jason Elam	.20	.50
157 Keith Burns	.15	.40
158 Mike Anderson	.20	.50
159 Olandis Gary	.20	.50
160 Rod Smith	.20	.50
161 Scottie Montgomery	.15	.40
162 Terrell Davis	.25	.60
163 Trevor Pryce	.15	.40
164 Charlie Batch	.15	.40
165 Chris Claiborne	.15	.40
166 Cory Schlesinger	.15	.40
167 David Sloan	.15	.40
168 Desmond Howard	.20	.50
169 Germane Crowell	.15	.40
170 James Stewart	.15	.40
171 Johnnie Morton	.20	.50
172 Lamont Warren	.15	.40
173 Larry Foster	.15	.40
174 Mike McMahon	.15	.40
175 Robert Porcher	.15	.40
176 Shaun Rogers	.15	.40
177 Todd Lyght	.15	.40
178 Ty Detmer	.20	.50
179 Ahman Green	.20	.50
180 Antonio Freeman	.25	.60
181 Bhawoh Jue	.15	.40
182 Bill Schroeder	.15	.40
183 Brett Favre	.60	1.50
184 Bubba Franks	.20	.50
185 Corey Bradford	.15	.40
186 Darren Sharper	.20	.50
187 Donald Driver	.25	.60
188 Dorsey Levens	.20	.50
189 Doug Pederson	.15	.40
190 Kabeer Gbaja-Biamila	.20	.50
191 William Henderson	.20	.50
192 Aaron Glenn	.15	.40
193 Danny Wuerffel	.20	.50
194 Gary Walker	.15	.40
195 Jamie Sharper	.20	.50
196 Jermaine Lewis	.15	.40
197 Matt Stevens	.15	.40
198 Seth Payne RC	.15	.40
199 Tony Boselli	.20	.50
200 Dominic Rhodes	.20	.50
201 Edgerrin James	.20	.50
202 Jerome Pathon	.15	.40
203 Ken Dilger	.20	.50
204 Kevin McDougal	.15	.40
205 Marcus Pollard	.15	.40
206 Mark Rypien	.20	.50
207 Marvin Harrison	.25	.60
208 Peyton Manning	.50	1.25
209 Reggie Wayne	.25	.60
210 Terrence Wilkins	.15	.40
211 Donovin Darius	.15	.40
212 Elvis Joseph	.15	.40
213 Fred Taylor	.20	.50
214 Hardy Nickerson	.15	.40
215 Jimmy Smith	.20	.50
216 Jonathan Quinn	.15	.40
217 Keenan McCardell	.20	.50
218 Kevin Hardy	.15	.40
219 Kyle Brady	.15	.40
220 Mark Brunell	.20	.50
221 Patrick Washington	.15	.40
222 Sean Dawkins	.20	.50
223 Stacey Mack	.15	.40
224 Tony Brackens	.15	.40
225 Derrick Alexander	.15	.40
226 Donnie Edwards	.15	.40
227 Eric Hicks	.15	.40
228 Kendall Gammon RC	.15	.40
229 Snoop Minnis	.15	.40
230 Mike Cloud	.15	.40
231 Priest Holmes	.25	.60
232 Todd Collins	.20	.50
233 Tony Gonzalez	.25	.60
234 Tony Richardson	.15	.40
235 Trent Green	.20	.50
236 Will Shields	.15	.40
237 Brock Marion	.15	.40
238 Chris Chambers	.20	.50
239 Dedric Ward	.15	.40
240 Hunter Goodwin	.15	.40
241 James McKnight	.15	.40
242 Jay Fiedler	.20	.50
243 Kenny Mixon	.15	.40
244 Lamar Smith	.20	.50
245 Oronde Gadsden	.15	.40
246 Patrick Surtain	.15	.40
247 Ray Lucas	.15	.40
248 Sam Madison	.15	.40
249 Travis Minor	.15	.40
250 Zach Thomas	.25	.60
251 Byron Chamberlain	.15	.40
252 Chris Walsh	.15	.40
253 Cris Carter	.25	.60
254 Daunte Culpepper	.20	.50
255 Doug Chapman	.15	.40
256 Gary Anderson	.15	.40
257 Jake Reed	.20	.50
258 Jim Kleinsasser	.25	.60
259 Kailee Wong	.15	.40
260 Matt Birk	.15	.40
261 Michael Bennett	.20	.50
262 Randy Moss	.25	.60
263 Robert Tate	.15	.40
264 Spergon Wynn	.15	.40
265 Antowain Smith	.20	.50
266 Bryan Cox	.20	.50
267 David Patten	.15	.40
268 Drew Bledsoe	.25	.60
269 Adam Vinatieri	.25	.60
270 J.R. Redmond	.15	.40
271 Jermaine Wiggins	.15	.40
272 Kevin Faulk	.20	.50
273 Lawyer Milloy	.15	.40
274 Marc Edwards	.15	.40
275 Tedy Bruschi	.25	.60
276 Tom Brady	.60	1.50
277 Troy Brown	.20	.50
278 Ty Law	.20	.50
279 Willie McGinest	.20	.50
280 Aaron Brooks	.20	.50
281 Albert Connell	.15	.40
282 Boo Williams	.15	.40
283 Charlie Clemons RC	.15	.40
284 Deuce McAllister	.20	.50
285 Jay Bellamy	.15	.40
286 Jeff Blake	.20	.50
287 Joe Horn	.20	.50
288 John Carney	.15	.40
289 Kyle Turley	.15	.40
290 La'Roi Glover	.15	.40
291 Norman Hand	.15	.40
292 Ricky Williams	.20	.50
293 Robert Wilson	.15	.40
294 Sammy Knight	.15	.40
295 Terrelle Smith	.15	.40
296 Willie Jackson	.15	.40
297 Amani Toomer	.20	.50
298 Anthony Becht	.15	.40
299 Chad Pennington	.25	.60
300 Curtis Martin	.25	.60
301 Dan Campbell	.15	.40
302 Dave Thomas	.15	.40
303 Greg Comella	.15	.40
304 Ike Hilliard	.20	.50
305 James Farrior	.20	.50
306 Jason Garrett	.20	.50
307 Jason Sehorn	.20	.50
308 Jessie Armstead	.15	.40
309 Joe Jurevicius	.15	.40
310 John Abraham	.20	.50
311 Kerry Collins	.20	.50
312 Kevin Mawae	.15	.40
313 LaMont Jordan	.20	.50
314 Laveranues Coles	.20	.50
315 Marvin Jones	.15	.40
316 Matthew Hatchette	.15	.40
317 Michael Strahan	.25	.60
318 Michael Barrow	.15	.40
319 Morten Andersen	.15	.40
320 Richie Anderson	.15	.40
321 Ron Dayne	.20	.50
322 Ron Dixon	.15	.40
323 Ron Stone RC	.15	.40
324 Santana Moss	.20	.50
325 Tiki Barber	.25	.60
326 Vinny Testaverde	.20	.50
327 Wayne Chrebet	.20	.50
328 Anthony Dorsett	.15	.40
329 Charles Woodson	.25	.60
330 Charlie Garner	.20	.50
331 Regan Upshaw	.15	.40
332 Jerry Porter	.15	.40
333 Jerry Rice	.50	1.25
334 Jon Ritchie	.15	.40
335 Lincoln Kennedy	.15	.40
336 Marques Tuiasosopo	.15	.40
337 Rich Gannon	.20	.50
338 Roland Williams	.15	.40
339 Sebastian Janikowski	.15	.40
340 Barry Sims RC	.15	.40
341 Terry Kirby	.15	.40
342 Tim Brown	.25	.60
343 Tyrone Wheatley	.20	.50
344 Zack Crockett	.15	.40
345 A.J. Feeley	.15	.40
346 Brian Dawkins	.20	.50
347 Cecil Martin	.15	.40
348 Chad Lewis	.15	.40
349 Corey Simon	.15	.40
350 Correll Buckhalter	.20	.50
351 David Akers	.15	.40
352 Donovan McNabb	.25	.60
353 Duce Staley	.20	.50
354 Freddie Mitchell	.15	.40
355 Hugh Douglas	.15	.40
356 James Thrash	.20	.50
357 Brian Mitchell	.20	.50
358 Koy Detmer	.20	.50
359 Todd Pinkston	.15	.40
360 Tra Thomas	.15	.40
361 Troy Vincent	.20	.50
362 Alan Faneca RC	15.00	30.00
363 Amos Zereoue	.15	.40
364 Bobby Shaw	.15	.40
365 Chris Fuamatu-Ma'afala	.15	.40
366 Dan Kreider RC	3.00	8.00
367 Hines Ward	.25	.60
368 Jason Gildon	.20	.50
369 Jerome Bettis	.25	.60
370 Jon Witman	.15	.40
371 Kendrell Bell	.15	.40
372 Kordell Stewart	.20	.50
373 Mark Bruener	.20	.50
374 Plaxico Burress	.20	.50
375 Tommy Maddox	.20	.50
376 Troy Edwards	.15	.40
377 Curtis Conway	.20	.50
378 Darren Bennett	.15	.40
379 Doug Flutie	.25	.60
380 Drew Brees	.40	1.00
381 Fred McCrary	.15	.40
382 Freddie Jones	.15	.40
383 Jeff Graham	.15	.40
384 John Parrella	.15	.40
385 Junior Seau	.25	.60
386 LaDainian Tomlinson	.30	.75
387 Marcellus Wiley	.15	.40
388 Tay Cody	.15	.40
389 Raylee Johnson	.15	.40
390 Rodney Harrison	.20	.50
391 Ronney Jenkins	.15	.40
392 Ryan McNeil	.15	.40
393 Orlando Ruff	.15	.40
394 Terrell Fletcher	.15	.40
395 Tim Dwight	.15	.40
396 Ahmed Plummer	.15	.40
397 Andre Carter	.15	.40
398 Bryant Young	.15	.40
399 Dana Stubblefield	.15	.40
400 Eric Johnson	.15	.40
401 Fred Beasley	.15	.40
402 Garrison Hearst	.20	.50
403 J.J. Stokes	.15	.40
404 Jeff Garcia	.20	.50
405 Jeremy Newberry RC	.15	.40
406 Junior Bryant	.15	.40
407 Justin Swift	.15	.40
408 Kevan Barlow	.15	.40
409 Ray Brown	.15	.40
410 Tai Streets	.15	.40
411 Terrell Owens	.25	.60
412 Terry Jackson	.15	.40
413 Tim Rattay	.20	.50
414 Bobby Engram	.20	.50
415 Chad Brown	.15	.40
416 Christian Fauria	.15	.40
417 Darrell Jackson	.20	.50
418 James Williams	.15	.40
419 John Randle	.20	.50
420 Koren Robinson	.15	.40
421 Levon Kirkland	.15	.40
422 Mack Strong	.15	.40
423 Matt Hasselbeck	.25	.60
424 Ricky Watters	.20	.50
425 Shaun Alexander	.20	.50
426 Shawn Springs	.15	.40
427 Trent Dilfer	.20	.50
428 Walter Jones	.15	.40
429 Adam Timmerman	.20	.50
430 Aeneas Williams	.20	.50
431 Az-Zahir Hakim	.15	.40
432 Dre Bly	.15	.40
433 Ernie Conwell	.15	.40
434 Isaac Bruce	.25	.60
435 James Hodgins	.15	.40
436 Jamie Martin	.20	.50
437 Kurt Warner	.25	.60
438 Leonard Little	.20	.50
439 London Fletcher	.15	.40
440 Marshall Faulk	.25	.60
441 O.J. Brigance	.15	.40
442 Orlando Pace	.20	.50
443 Ricky Proehl	.20	.50
444 Torry Holt	.25	.60
445 Trung Canidate	.15	.40
446 Aaron Stecker	.15	.40
447 Brad Johnson	.20	.50
448 Dave Moore	.15	.40
449 Derrick Brooks	.25	.60
450 Jacquez Green	.15	.40
451 John Lynch	.20	.50
452 Karl Williams	.15	.40
453 Kenyatta Walker	.15	.40
454 Keyshawn Johnson	.20	.50
455 Mark Royals	.15	.40
456 Mike Alstott	.20	.50
457 Rabih Abdullah	.15	.40
458 Reidel Anthony	.15	.40
459 Ronde Barber	.20	.50
460 Shaun King	.15	.40
461 Simeon Rice	.15	.40
462 Warren Sapp	.20	.50
463 Warrick Dunn	.20	.50
464 Bruce Matthews	.20	.50
465 Chris Sanders	.15	.40
466 Derrick Mason	.20	.50
467 Eddie George	.20	.50
468 Erron Kinney	.15	.40
469 Frank Wycheck	.15	.40
470 Jevon Kearse	.20	.50
471 Kevin Dyson	.20	.50
472 Mike Green	.15	.40
473 Neil O'Donnell	.20	.50
474 Perry Phenix RC	.15	.40
475 Skip Hicks	.15	.40
476 Steve McNair	.25	.60
477 Champ Bailey	.25	.60
478 Chris Samuels	.15	.40
479 Dan Wilkinson	.15	.40
480 Darrell Green	.25	.60
481 Donnell Bennett	.15	.40
482 Donovan Greer RC	.15	.40
483 Ethan Albright RC	.15	.40
484 Fred Smoot	.20	.50
485 Kent Graham	.15	.40
486 Kevin Lockett	.15	.40
487 Ki-Jana Carter	.20	.50
488 Michael Bates	.15	.40
489 Michael Westbrook	.15	.40
490 Rod Gardner	.15	.40
491 Shawn Barber	.15	.40
492 Stephen Alexander	.15	.40
493 Stephen Davis	.20	.50
494 Tony Banks	.15	.40
495 Jeremiah Trotter	.15	.40
496 Jerome Bettis	.25	.60
497 Kurt Warner	.25	.60
498 Marshall Faulk	.25	.60
499 Randy Moss	.25	.60
500 Tom Brady	.60	1.50
501 Joey Harrington RC	.75	2.00
502 David Carr RC	.75	2.00
503 Rohan Davey RC	.75	2.00
504 Brandon Doman RC	.50	1.25
505 Woody Dantzler RC	.60	1.50
506 Kurt Kittner RC	.50	1.25
507 Donte Stallworth RC	.75	2.00
508 Major Applewhite RC	.75	2.00
509 Eric Crouch RC	.75	2.00
510 Justin Peelle RC	.50	1.25
511 J.T. O'Sullivan RC	.60	1.50
512 Jason McAddley RC	.60	1.50
513 Patrick Ramsey RC	.75	2.00
514 Randy Fasani RC	.60	1.50
515 Antwaan Randle El RC	.75	2.00
516 DeShaun Foster RC	.75	2.00
517 T.J. Duckett RC	.75	2.00
518 William Green RC	.60	1.50
519 Travis Stephens RC	.50	1.25
520 Luke Staley RC	.50	1.25
521 Leonard Henry RC	.50	1.25
522 Najeh Davenport RC	.75	2.00
523 Ricky Williams RC	.60	1.50
524 Maurice Morris RC	.60	1.50
525 Anthony Weaver RC	.50	1.25
526 Jeremy Allen RC	.50	1.25
527 Chester Taylor RC	.75	2.00
528 Clinton Portis RC	1.00	2.50
529 Damien Anderson RC	.50	1.25
530 Larry Ned RC	.50	1.25
531 Jonathan Wells RC	.75	2.00
532 Antwoine Womack RC	.50	1.25
533 Adrian Peterson RC	.75	2.00
534 Lamar Gordon RC	.60	1.50
535 Chad Hutchinson RC	.50	1.25
536 Antonio Bryant RC	.75	2.00
537 Josh Reed RC	.60	1.50
538 Jabar Gaffney RC	.75	2.00
539 Ashley Lelie RC	.60	1.50
540 Ron Johnson RC	.60	1.50
541 Marquise Walker RC	.50	1.25
542 Kelly Campbell RC	.60	1.50
543 Andre Davis RC	.60	1.50
544 Deion Branch RC	.75	2.00
545 James Mungro RC	.75	2.00
546 Brian Poli-Dixon RC	.50	1.25
547 Kahlil Hill RC	.50	1.25
548 Reche Caldwell RC	.75	2.00
549 Jeremy Shockey RC	1.25	3.00
550 Julius Peppers RC	1.50	4.00
551 Wendell Bryant RC	.50	1.25
552 John Henderson RC	.60	1.50
553 Quentin Jammer RC	.75	2.00
554 Roy Williams RC	.75	2.00
555 Daniel Graham RC	.60	1.50
556 Charles Grant RC	.75	2.00
557 Verron Haynes RC	.50	1.25
558 Ed Reed RC	3.00	8.00
559 Pete Rebstock RC	.50	1.25
560 Tellis Redmon RC	.50	1.25
561 Javon Walker RC	.75	2.00
562 Larry Tripplett RC	.50	1.25
563 Cliff Russell RC	.50	1.25
564 Rocky Calmus RC	.60	1.50
565 Tim Carter RC	.60	1.50
566 Josh Scobey RC	.60	1.50
567 Kyle Johnson RC	.50	1.25
568 Brian Westbrook RC	1.25	3.00
569 Zak Kustok RC	.50	1.25
570 Ronald Curry RC	.60	1.50
571 Atrews Bell RC	.50	1.25
572 Levar Fisher RC	.50	1.25
573 Dicenzo Miller RC	.50	1.25
574 Phillip Buchanon RC	.75	2.00
575 Freddie Milons RC	.50	1.25
576 Kalimba Edwards RC	.60	1.50
577 Raonall Smith RC	.50	1.25
578 Dameon Hunter RC	.50	1.25
579 Lee Mays RC	.50	1.25
580 Mike Rumph RC	.50	1.25
581 Josh McCown RC	.75	2.00
582 Napoleon Harris RC	.60	1.50
583 David Garrard RC	1.00	2.50
584 Wes Pate RC	.50	1.25
585 Lito Sheppard RC	.75	2.00
586 Gavin Hoffman RC	.50	1.25
587 David Priestley RC	.50	1.25
588 Dwight Freeney RC	1.00	2.50
589 Dusty Bonner RC	.50	1.25
590 Eric McCoo RC	.50	1.25
591 Robert Thomas RC	.50	1.25
592 Delvon Flowers RC	.50	1.25
593 LaDell Betts RC	.75	2.00
594 Jamar Martin RC	.60	1.50
595 Seth Burford RC	.50	1.25
596 Mike Williams RC	.50	1.25
597 Bryant McKinnie RC	.50	1.25
598 Ryan Sims RC	.75	2.00
599 Albert Haynesworth RC	.75	2.00
600 Craig Nall RC	.60	1.50

2002 Upper Deck XL Holofoil

*VETS 1-500: 12X TO 30X BASIC CARDS
*ROOKIES 501-600: 4X TO 10X
STATED PRINT RUN 65 SER.#'d SETS

366 Dan Kreider	20.00	50.00

2002 Upper Deck XL Big Time Jerseys

STATED PRINT RUN 250-500
*GREY BACKGROUND/50-100: .6X TO 1.5X

BTBG Brian Griese/500	3.00	8.00
BTBJ Brad Johnson/500	3.00	8.00
BTCC Curtis Conway/500	3.00	8.00
BTDB Drew Brees/500	6.00	15.00
BTDG Darrell Green/500	4.00	10.00
BTDM Donovan McNabb/500	4.00	10.00
BTDS Duce Staley/500	3.00	8.00
BTDT David Terrell/250	3.00	8.00
BTEM Eric Moulds/250	4.00	10.00
BTFJ Freddie Jones/500	2.50	6.00
BTGA Rod Gardner/500	2.50	6.00
BTIK Ike Hilliard/500	3.00	8.00
BTJA Jamal Anderson/250	4.00	10.00
BTJD JaJuan Dawson/500	2.50	6.00
BTJF Jay Fiedler/500	3.00	8.00
BTJG Jeff Graham/500	2.50	6.00
BTJH Joey Harrington/500	4.00	10.00
BTKC Kerry Collins/500	3.00	8.00
BTKK Kurt Kittner/500	2.50	6.00
BTKW Kurt Warner/250	5.00	12.00
BTMF Marshall Faulk/500	4.00	10.00
BTMP Michael Pittman/250	4.00	10.00
BTPM Peyton Manning/500	8.00	20.00
BTPW Peter Warrick/250	4.00	10.00
BTRG Rich Gannon/250	4.00	10.00
BTRW Ricky Williams/500	3.00	8.00
BTSM Santana Moss/500	3.00	8.00
BTWS Warren Sapp/250	4.00	10.00
BTZT Zach Thomas/250	5.00	12.00

2002 Upper Deck XL Super Swatch Jerseys

STATED PRINT RUN 75-800
*GREY BACKGROUND/400: .5X TO 1.2X
*GREY BACKGROUND/25: .6X TO 1.5X

SSAB Anthony Becht/800	2.50	6.00
SSAR Antwaan Randle El/800	4.00	10.00
SSAT Anthony Thomas/75	6.00	15.00
SSBR Mark Brunell/800	3.00	8.00
SSCM Curtis Martin/75	8.00	20.00
SSDB Drew Bledsoe/800	4.00	10.00
SSDC Daunte Culpepper/75	6.00	15.00
SSBF Doug Flutie/800	4.00	10.00
SSDR Drew Brees/800	6.00	15.00
SSDS DeShaun Foster/800	4.00	10.00
SSEM Eric Moulds/800	3.00	8.00
SSJJ James Jackson/800	2.50	6.00
SSJO Kevin Johnson/800	2.50	6.00
SSJP Jake Plummer/75	6.00	15.00
SSJR Jerry Rice/75	15.00	40.00
SSJS Junior Seau/800	4.00	10.00
SSKJ Keyshawn Johnson/800	3.00	8.00
SSLT LaDainian Tomlinson/800	5.00	12.00
SSMA Mike Alstott/800	3.00	8.00
SSMB Marty Booker/75	6.00	15.00
SSMM Maurice Morris/800	3.00	8.00
SSPM Peyton Manning/800	8.00	20.00
SSRD Ron Dayne/75	6.00	15.00
SSRM Randy Moss/75	8.00	20.00
SSSA Stephen Alexander/800	2.50	6.00
SSSD Stephen Davis/800	3.00	8.00
SSTB Tony Banks/800	2.50	6.00
SSTC Tim Couch/75	5.00	12.00
SSTH Travis Henry/800	2.50	6.00
SSWC Wayne Chrebet/800	3.00	8.00

2008 Upper Deck Yankee Stadium Legacy Collection Historical Moments

473 Notre Dame v. Army	1.50	4.00
2835 1958 NFL Championship	1.50	4.00

1990 U-Seal-It Stickers

This set was released in 1990 by U-Seal-It. Each NFL team was represented by a package of three-stickers measuring 2 standard card size. One blankbacked sticker (1989 copyright date) contained an assortment of metallic helmet stickers and a small team name banner. Another blankbacked sticker (1988 copyright date) featured a comical team mascot called a Hot Shot. Finally, the third sticker (1983 copyright date) featured the NFL Properties Huddle character with a UPC and team checklist on the cardback.

COMPLETE SET (84)	50.00	125.00
1 Atlanta Falcons Helmets	.60	1.50
2 Atlanta Falcons Hot Shot	.60	1.50
3 Atlanta Falcons Huddle	.60	1.50
4 Buffalo Bills Helmets	.80	2.00
5 Buffalo Bills Hot Shot	.80	2.00
6 Buffalo Bills Huddle	.80	2.00
7 Chicago Bears Helmets	.80	2.00
8 Chicago Bears Hot Shot	.80	2.00
9 Chicago Bears Huddle	.80	2.00
10 Cleveland Browns Helmets	.80	2.00
11 Cleveland Browns Hot Shot	.80	2.00
12 Cleveland Browns Huddle	.80	2.00
13 Cincinnati Bengals Helmets	.60	1.50
14 Cincinnati Bengals Hot Shot	.60	1.50
15 Cincinnati Bengals Huddle	.60	1.50
16 Dallas Cowboys Helmets	1.20	3.00
17 Dallas Cowboys Hot Shot	1.20	3.00
18 Dallas Cowboys Huddle	1.20	3.00
19 Denver Broncos Helmets	.80	2.00
20 Denver Broncos Hot Shot	.80	2.00
21 Denver Broncos Huddle	.80	2.00
22 Detroit Lions Helmets	.60	1.50
23 Detroit Lions Hot Shot	.60	1.50
24 Detroit Lions Huddle	.60	1.50
25 Green Bay Packers Helmets	1.20	3.00
26 Green Bay Packers Hot Shot	1.20	3.00
27 Green Bay Packers Huddle	1.20	3.00
28 Houston Oilers Helmets	.60	1.50
29 Houston Oilers Hot Shot	.60	1.50
30 Houston Oilers Huddle	.60	1.50
31 Indianapolis Colts Helmets	.60	1.50
32 Indianapolis Colts Hot Shot	.60	1.50
33 Indianapolis Colts Huddle	.60	1.50
34 Kansas City Chiefs Helmets	.60	1.50
35 Kansas City Chiefs Hot Shot	.60	1.50
36 Kansas City Chiefs Huddle	.60	1.50
37 Los Angeles Raiders Helmets	1.20	3.00
38 Los Angeles Raiders Hot Shot	1.20	3.00
39 Los Angeles Raiders Huddle	1.20	3.00
40 Los Angeles Rams Helmets	.60	1.50
41 Los Angeles Rams Hot Shot	.60	1.50
42 Los Angeles Rams Huddle	.60	1.50
43 Miami Dolphins Helmets	1.20	3.00
44 Miami Dolphins Hot Shot	1.20	3.00
45 Miami Dolphins Huddle	1.20	3.00
46 Minnesota Vikings Helmets	.80	2.00
47 Minnesota Vikings Hot Shot	.80	2.00
48 Minnesota Vikings Huddle	.80	2.00
49 New England Patriots Helmets	.60	1.50
50 New England Patriots Hot Shot	.60	1.50
51 New England Patriots Huddle	.60	1.50
52 New Orleans Saints Helmets	.60	1.50
53 New Orleans Saints Hot Shot	.60	1.50
54 New Orleans Saints Huddle	.60	1.50
55 New York Giants Helmets	.80	2.00
56 New York Giants Hot Shot	.80	2.00
57 New York Giants Huddle	.80	2.00
58 New York Jets Helmets	.80	2.00
59 New York Jets Hot Shot	.80	2.00
60 New York Jets Huddle	.80	2.00
61 Philadelphia Eagles Helmets	.60	1.50
62 Philadelphia Eagles Hot Shot	.60	1.50
63 Philadelphia Eagles Huddle	.60	1.50
64 Phoenix Cardinals Helmets	.60	1.50
65 Phoenix Cardinals Hot Shot	.60	1.50
66 Phoenix Cardinals Huddle	.60	1.50
67 Pittsburgh Steelers Helmets	1.20	3.00
68 Pittsburgh Steelers Hot Shot	1.20	3.00
69 Pittsburgh Steelers Huddle	1.20	3.00
70 San Diego Chargers Helmets	.60	1.50
71 San Diego Chargers Hot Shot	.60	1.50
72 San Diego Chargers Huddle	.60	1.50
73 San Francisco 49ers Helmets	1.20	3.00
74 San Francisco 49ers Hot Shot	1.20	3.00
75 San Francisco 49ers Huddle	1.20	3.00
76 Seattle Seahawks Helmets	.60	1.50
77 Seattle Seahawks Hot Shot	.60	1.50
78 Seattle Seahawks Huddle	.60	1.50
79 Tampa Bay Bucs Helmets	.60	1.50
80 Tampa Bay Bucs Hot Shot	.60	1.50
81 Tampa Bay Bucs Huddle	.60	1.50
82 Washington Redskins Helmets	.80	2.00
83 Washington Redskins Hot Shot	.80	2.00
84 Washington Redskins Huddle	.80	2.00

1993 U.S. Playing Cards Ditka's Picks

Part of the Bicycle Sports Collection, these 56 playing cards, featuring Mike Ditka's NFL player picks, measure the standard-size and have rounded corners. The set is checklisted below in playing card order by suits and assigned numbers to Aces (1), Jacks (11), Queens (12), and Kings (13).

COMP. FACT SET (56)	2.00	5.00
1C Steve Young	.20	.50
1D Joe Montana	.60	1.50
1H Dan Marino	.50	1.25
1S Troy Aikman	.30	.75
2C Jim Lachey	.01	.05
2D Richmond Webb	.01	.05
2H Wilber Marshall	.01	.05
2S Ronnie Lott	.02	.10
3C Sean Gilbert	.01	.05
3D Clay Matthews	.02	.10
3H Jeff Lageman	.01	.05
3S Audray McMillian	.01	.05
4C Morten Andersen	.01	.05
4D Pete Stoyanovich	.01	.05
4H Rohn Stark	.01	.05
4S Sean Landeta	.01	.05
5C Broderick Thomas	.01	.05
5D James Francis	.01	.05
5H Derrick Thomas	.07	.20
5S Tony Bennett	.01	.05
6C Seth Joyner	.01	.05
6D Percy Snow	.01	.05
6H Junior Seau	.07	.20
6S Chris Spielman	.01	.05
7C Pierce Holt	.01	.05
7D Rod Woodson	.07	.20
7H Ray Childress	.01	.05
7S Deion Sanders	.15	.40
8C Jay Novacek	.02	.10
8D Eric Green	.01	.05
8H Marv Cook	.01	.05
8S Brent Jones	.01	.05
9C Randall McDaniel	.02	.10
9D Mike Munchak	.02	.10
9H Bruce Matthews	.01	.05
9S Mark Stepnoski	.01	.05
10C Harris Barton	.01	.05
10D Steve Atwater	.01	.05
10H Henry Jones	.01	.05
10S Chuck Cecil	.01	.05
11C Sterling Sharpe	.07	.20
11D Anthony Miller	.02	.10
11H Haywood Jeffires	.02	.10
11S Jerry Rice	.30	.75
12C Reggie White	.07	.20
12D Howie Long	.02	.10
12H Cortez Kennedy	.02	.10
12S Chris Doleman	.01	.05
13C Emmitt Smith	.40	1.00
13D Thurman Thomas	.07	.20
13H Barry Foster	.01	.05
13S Barry Sanders	.50	1.25
WILD Tom Waddle	.01	.05
WILD Steve Wisniewski	.01	.05
NNO Ditka's AFC Picks	.02	.10
NNO Ditka's NFC Picks	.02	.10

1994 U.S. Playing Cards Ditka's Picks

Part of the Bicycle Sports Collection, these 56 playing cards, featuring Mike Ditka's NFL player picks, measure the standard size and have rounded corners. The set is checklisted below in playing card order by suits, with numbers assigned to Aces (1), Jacks (11), Queens (12), and Kings (13).

COMP. FACT SET (56)	1.60	4.00
1C Sterling Sharpe	.02	.10
1D Rickey Jackson	.01	.05
1H Emmitt Smith	.50	1.25
1S Rod Woodson	.02	.10
2C Marcus Robertson	.01	.05
2D Rohn Stark	.01	.05
2H Dave Cadigan	.01	.05
2S Kevin Williams	.02	.10
3C John Kasay	.01	.05
3D Carlton Haselrig	.01	.05
3H Donnell Woolford	.01	.05
3S Dan Wilkinson	.02	.10
4C Marshall Faulk	.80	2.00
4D Greg Montgomery	.01	.05
4H Leslie O'Neal	.01	.05
4S Eric Curry	.01	.05
5C Eric Turner	.01	.05
5D Rick Mirer	.02	.10
5H Kevin Smith	.01	.05
5S Troy Vincent	.01	.05
6C Cornelius Bennett	.02	.10
6D Seth Joyner	.02	.10
6H Gary Zimmerman	.01	.05
6S LeRoy Butler	.01	.05
7C Tommy Vardell	.01	.05
7D Richmond Webb	.01	.05
7H Ben Coates	.02	.10
7S Steve Everitt	.01	.05
8C Tom Rathman	.01	.05
8D Ray Childress	.01	.05
8H Tim Brown	.07	.20
8S Mark Bavaro	.01	.05
9C Bennie Blades	.01	.05
9D John(Jumbo) Elliott	.01	.05
9H Jim Lachey	.01	.05
9S Neil Smith	.02	.10
10C Sean Gilbert	.01	.05
10D Steve Tasker	.01	.05
10H Chris Zorich	.01	.05
10S Haywood Jeffires	.02	.10
11C Troy Aikman	.30	.75
11D Jeff Hostetler	.02	.10
11H Junior Seau	.02	.10
11S Mark Stepnoski	.01	.05
12C Chris Spielman	.01	.05
12D Marcus Allen	.07	.20
12H Reggie White	.07	.20
12S Harris Barton	.01	.05
13C Andre Rison	.02	.10
13D Randall McDaniel	.02	.10
13H Cortez Kennedy	.01	.05
13S Norm Johnson	.01	.05
WILD Heath Shuler	.15	.40
WILD Shannon Sharpe	.02	.10
NNO Ditka's AFC Picks	.02	.10
NNO Ditka's NFC Picks	.02	.10

1995 U.S. Playing Cards Ditka's Picks

Part of the Bicycle Sports Collection, these 56 playing cards, featuring Mike Ditka's NFL player picks, measure the standard size and have rounded corners. The set is checklisted below in playing card order by suits with numbers assigned to Aces (1), Jacks (11), Queens (12), and Kings (13).

COMP. FACT SET (56)	1.60	4.00
1C Randall McDaniel	.02	.10
1D Dan Marino	.50	1.25
1H Drew Bledsoe	.30	.75
1S Steve Young	.20	.50
2C Renaldo Turnbull	.01	.05
2D Tony Boselli	.01	.05

2H Ki-Jana Carter	.02	.10
2S Todd Sauerbrun	.01	.05
3C Aeneas Williams	.01	.05
3D Bruce Smith	.02	.10
3H Shawn Jefferson	.01	.05
3S Andy Harmon	.01	.05
4C Donnell Woolford	.01	.05
4D Ronnie Lott	.02	.10
4H Tim Brown	.07	.20
4S Charles Haley	.01	.05
5C Merton Hanks	.01	.05
5D Eric Turner	.01	.05
5H Ben Coates	.01	.05
5S Brian Williams OL	.01	.05
6C Eric Metcalf	.01	.05
6D Dave Meggett	.01	.05
6H Neil Smith	.02	.10
6S Ian Beckles	.01	.05
7C Herman Moore	.02	.10
7D Mel Gray	.01	.05
7H Ray Childress	.01	.05
7S Jim Lachey	.01	.05
8C Bennie Blades	.01	.05
8D Kevin Greene	.01	.05
8H Gary Zimmerman	.01	.05
8S William Roaf	.01	.05
9C Bryant Young	.01	.05
9D Bruce Matthews	.01	.05
9H Richmond Webb	.01	.05
9S Howard Cross	.01	.05
10C Seth Joyner	.01	.05
10D Marshall Faulk	.30	.75
10H Jeff Dellenbach	.01	.05
10S Cris Carter	.07	.20
11C Sean Gilbert	.01	.05
11D John Carney	.01	.05
11H Rohn Stark	.01	.05
11S Jerry Rice	.30	.75
12C Reggie White	.02	.10
12D Terry McDaniel	.01	.05
12H Rod Woodson	.02	.10
12S Daryl Johnston	.02	.10
13C Norm Johnson	.01	.05
13D Cortez Kennedy	.01	.05
13H Cornelius Bennett	.02	.10
13S Barry Sanders	.50	1.25
WILD Chris Spielman	.01	.05
WILD Junior Seau	.02	.10
NNO Ditka's NFC Picks	.02	.10
NNO Ditka's AFC Picks	.02	.10

2006 Utah Blaze AFL

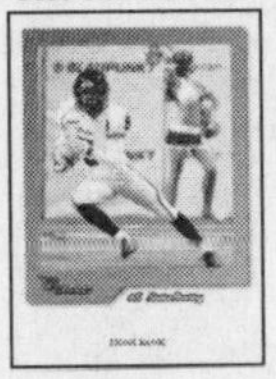

These blankbacked cards were sponsored by Zions Bank and issued by the team to fill fan requests for photos and for use at player signings. Each measures roughly 5" by 7" and includes a black and white image of the player on the front with the team logo and player name below the image. The backs are blank.

COMPLETE SET (23)	10.00	20.00
1 Orshaswante Bryant	.40	1.00
2 Siaha Burley	.40	1.00
3 Kevin Clemens	.40	1.00
4 John Culp	.40	1.00
5 Ryan Dennard	.40	1.00
6 Joe Germaine	.50	1.25
7 Jason Gesser	.60	1.50
8 Ernest Grant	.40	1.00
9 Aaron Hamilton	.40	1.00
10 Kelvin Hunter	.40	1.00
11 Craig Kobel	.40	1.00
12 Kautai Oleveo	.40	1.00
13 Hans Olsen	.40	1.00
14 Tom Pace	.50	1.25
15 Scott Pospisal	.40	1.00
16 Lewis Powell	.40	1.00
17 Chris Robinson	.40	1.00
18 Justin Skaggs	.40	1.00
19 Garrett Smith	.40	1.00
20 Justin Taplin	.40	1.00
21 Steve Videtich	.40	1.00
22 Ronnie Washburn	.40	1.00
23 Thal Woods	.40	1.00

2007 Utah Blaze AFL

COMPLETE SET (28)	6.00	12.00
1 Aaron Boone	.20	.50
2 Manaia Brown	.20	.50
3 Orshawante Bryant	.20	.50
4 Thaddeus Bullard	.20	.50
5 Siaha Burley	.30	.75
6 Frank Carter	.20	.50
7 Valentine Chude	.20	.50
8 John Culp	.20	.50
9 Ryan Dennard	.20	.50
10 Joe Germaine	.40	1.00
11 Jason Gesser	.40	1.00
12 Ernest Grant	.20	.50
13 Chris Janek	.20	.50
14 Steve Konopka	.20	.50
15 Clarence Lawson	.20	.50
16 Kautai Olevao	.20	.50
17 Hans Olsen	.20	.50
18 Tom Pace	.20	.50
19 Chris Robinson	.20	.50
20 Jacoby Shepherd	.20	.50
21 Dahnel Singfield	.20	.50
22 Justin Skaggs	.20	.50
23 Garrett Smith	.20	.50
24 Leroy Smith	.20	.50
25 Myniya Smith	.20	.50
26 Steve Videtich	.20	.50
27 Danny White CO	.30	.75
28 Big Budah (Emcee)	.20	.50

2008 Utah Blaze afl

COMPLETE SET (38)	7.50	15.00
1 Aaron Boone	.20	.50
2 E.J. Burt	.20	.50
3 Eddie Canonico	.20	.50
4 Corey Dodds	.20	.50
5 Rodney Filer	.20	.50
6 Rob Gatrell	.20	.50
7 Joe Germaine	.30	.75
8 Chris Janek	.20	.50
9 J'Shatlon Jones	.20	.50
10 Vaka Manupuna	.20	.50
11 Damorl Mason	.20	.50
12 J.J. McKolvoy	.20	.50
13 Dwayne Missouri	.20	.50
14 Kelvin Morris	.20	.50
15 Kautai Olevao	.20	.50
16 Tom Pace	.20	.50
17 Tupe Peko	.20	.50
18 Myniya Smith	.20	.50
19 Steve Videtich	.20	.50
20 Danny White CO	.40	1.00
21 Huey Whittaker	.20	.50
22 Devin Wyman	.20	.50
23 Big Budah ANN.	.20	.50
24 Chief - Mascot	.20	.50
25 Blaze Dancer: Alecia	.20	.50
26 Blaze Dancer: Ami	.20	.50
27 Blaze Dancer: Brittany	.20	.50
28 Blaze Dancer: Caitlin	.20	.50
29 Blaze Dancer: Chanelle	.20	.50
30 Blaze Dancer: Juliet	.20	.50
31 Blaze Dancer: Kate	.20	.50
32 Blaze Dancer: Kristina	.20	.50
33 Blaze Dancer: Melissa	.20	.50
34 Blaze Dancer: Nichole	.20	.50
35 Blaze Dancer: Nicole	.20	.50
36 Blaze Dancer: Randi	.20	.50
37 Blaze Dancer: Stephanie	.20	.50
38 Blaze Dancer: Tamy	.20	.50

2000 Vanguard

Issued as a 150-card set, Vanguard is comprised of 125 veteran player cards and 25 rookie cards which are sequentially numbered to 762. Base cards feature a red background with a black player name plate and white border along the bottom of the card. Player action photos are surrounded by a holofoil outline that fades into the red background. Rookie cards feature the same card design set against a green background. Vanguard was packaged in 24-pack boxes with packs containing four cards each.

COMP.SET w/o RCs (125)	15.00	30.00
UNPRICED PROOF PRINT RUN 1		
1 Tony Banks	.25	.60
2 Priest Holmes	.40	1.00
3 Qadry Ismail	.30	.75
4 Doug Flutie	.40	1.00
5 Rob Johnson	.30	.75
6 Eric Moulds	.30	.75
7 Peerless Price	.30	.75
8 Antowain Smith	.30	.75
9 Corey Dillon	.30	.75
10 Darnay Scott	.30	.75
11 Akili Smith	.25	.60
12 Tim Couch	.30	.75
13 Kevin Johnson	.25	.60
14 Terry Kirby	.25	.60
15 Terrell Davis	.40	1.00
16 Olandis Gary	.30	.75
17 Brian Griese	.30	.75
18 Ed McCaffrey	.30	.75
19 Rod Smith	.30	.75
20 Marvin Harrison	.40	1.00
21 Edgerrin James	.40	1.00
22 Peyton Manning	1.00	2.50
23 Terrence Wilkins	.25	.60
24 Mark Brunell	.30	.75
25 Keenan McCardell	.30	.75
26 Jimmy Smith	.30	.75
27 Fred Taylor	.40	1.00
28 Derrick Alexander	.25	.60
29 Donnell Bennett	.25	.60
30 Tony Gonzalez	.40	1.00
31 Elvis Grbac	.25	.60
32 Damon Huard	.30	.75
33 James Johnson	.25	.60
34 Dan Marino	1.25	3.00
35 Tony Martin	.30	.75
36 O.J. McDuffie	.30	.75
37 Drew Bledsoe	.40	1.00
38 Kevin Faulk	.30	.75
39 Terry Glenn	.30	.75
40 Wayne Chrebet	.30	.75
41 Ray Lucas	.25	.60
42 Curtis Martin	.40	1.00
43 Vinny Testaverde	.30	.75
44 Tim Brown	.40	1.00
45 Rich Gannon	.30	.75
46 Napoleon Kaufman	.30	.75
47 Tyrone Wheatley	.25	.60
48 Jerome Bettis	.40	1.00
49 Troy Edwards	.25	.60
50 Richard Huntley	.25	.60
51 Kordell Stewart	.30	.75
52 Jermaine Fazande	.25	.60
53 Jim Harbaugh	.30	.75
54 Mikhael Ricks	.25	.60
55 Junior Seau	.40	1.00
56 Brock Huard	.25	.60
57 Jon Kitna	.30	.75
58 Derrick Mayes	.25	.60
59 Ricky Watters	.30	.75
60 Eddie George	.30	.75
61 Jevon Kearse	.30	.75
62 Steve McNair	.40	1.00
63 Yancey Thigpen	.25	.60
64 David Boston	.25	.60
65 Rob Moore	.25	.60
66 Jake Plummer	.30	.75
67 Frank Sanders	.25	.60
68 Jamal Anderson	.30	.75
69 Chris Chandler	.30	.75
70 Tim Dwight	.30	.75
71 Terance Mathis	.25	.60
72 Steve Beuerlein	.30	.75
73 Tim Biakabutuka	.30	.75
74 Patrick Jeffers	.30	.75
75 Muhsin Muhammad	.30	.75
76 Bobby Engram	.30	.75
77 Curtis Enis	.25	.60
78 Cade McNown	.25	.60
79 Marcus Robinson	.30	.75
80 Troy Aikman	.60	1.50
81 Rocket Ismail	.30	.75
82 Emmitt Smith	1.00	2.50
83 Jason Tucker	.25	.60
84 Chris Warren	.25	.60
85 Charlie Batch	.30	.75
86 Germane Crowell	.25	.60
87 Herman Moore	.30	.75
88 Johnnie Morton	.30	.75
89 Barry Sanders	.75	2.00
90 Brett Favre	1.25	3.00
91 Antonio Freeman	.30	.75
92 Dorsey Levens	.30	.75
93 Bill Schroeder	.30	.75
94 Cris Carter	.40	1.00
95 Daunte Culpepper	.30	.75
96 Randy Moss	.40	1.00
97 Robert Smith	.30	.75
98 Cam Cleeland	.25	.60
99 Keith Poole	.25	.60
100 Ricky Williams	.40	1.00
101 Tiki Barber	.40	1.00
102 Kerry Collins	.30	.75
103 Ike Hilliard	.30	.75
104 Amani Toomer	.30	.75
105 Charles Johnson	.25	.60
106 Donovan McNabb	.40	1.00
107 Torrance Small	.25	.60
108 Duce Staley	.30	.75
109 Isaac Bruce	.40	1.00
110 Marshall Faulk	.40	1.00
111 Torry Holt	.40	1.00
112 Kurt Warner	.60	1.50
113 Charlie Garner	.30	.75
114 Terrell Owens	.40	1.00
115 Jerry Rice	.75	2.00
116 J.J. Stokes	.30	.75
117 Steve Young	.50	1.25
118 Mike Alstott	.40	1.00
119 Reidel Anthony	.25	.60
120 Warrick Dunn	.30	.75
121 Jacquez Green	.25	.60
122 Shaun King	.25	.60
123 Stephen Davis	.30	.75
124 Brad Johnson	.30	.75
125 Michael Westbrook	.25	.60
126 Thomas Jones RC	4.00	10.00
127 Jamal Lewis RC	3.00	8.00
128 Chris Redman RC	2.50	6.00
129 Travis Taylor RC	2.50	6.00
130 Dez White RC	2.50	6.00
131 Ron Dugans RC	2.00	5.00
132 Peter Warrick RC	3.00	8.00
133 Dennis Northcutt RC	2.50	6.00
134 Travis Prentice RC	2.50	6.00
135 Reuben Droughns RC	3.00	8.00
136 R.Jay Soward RC	2.00	5.00
137 Sylvester Morris RC	2.00	5.00
138 Troy Walters RC	2.00	5.00
139 Tom Brady RC	75.00	135.00
140 J.R. Redmond RC	2.00	5.00
141 Marc Bulger RC	3.00	8.00
142 Ron Dayne RC	3.00	8.00
143 Laveranues Coles RC	3.00	8.00
144 Chad Pennington RC	5.00	12.00
145 Jerry Porter RC	3.00	8.00
146 Plaxico Burress RC	3.00	8.00
147 Trung Canidate RC	2.50	6.00
148 Giovanni Carmazzi RC	2.00	5.00
149 Shaun Alexander RC	4.00	10.00
150 Todd Husak RC	2.00	5.00
S1 Jon Kitna Sample	1.00	2.50

2000 Vanguard Gold

*GOLD/122: 5X TO 12X BASIC CARDS
GOLD RETAIL PRINT RUN 122 SER.#'d SETS

2000 Vanguard Premiere Date

*PREM.DATE/138: 5X TO 12X BASIC CARDS
PREMIERE DATE PRINT RUN 138

2000 Vanguard Purple

*PURPLE/138: 5X TO 12X BASIC CARDS
PURPLE HOBBY PRINT RUN 138 SER.#'d SETS

2000 Vanguard Cosmic Force

COMPLETE SET (10)	20.00	50.00
STATED ODDS 1:73		
1 Tim Couch	1.00	2.50
2 Troy Aikman	2.00	5.00
3 Emmitt Smith	3.00	8.00
4 Terrell Davis	1.25	3.00
5 Barry Sanders	2.50	6.00
6 Brett Favre	4.00	10.00
7 Edgerrin James	1.25	3.00
8 Peyton Manning	3.00	8.00
9 Randy Moss	1.25	3.00
10 Kurt Warner	2.00	5.00

2000 Vanguard Game Worn Jerseys

1 Cris Carter	8.00	20.00
2 Randall Cunningham	8.00	20.00
3 Randy Moss	8.00	20.00
4 Ricky Williams	8.00	20.00
5 Wayne Chrebet	6.00	15.00
6 Koy Detmer	5.00	12.00
7 Donovan McNabb	8.00	20.00
8 Torrance Small	5.00	12.00
9 Duce Staley	6.00	15.00
10 Jerome Bettis	8.00	20.00
11 Kordell Stewart	6.00	15.00
12 Jerry Rice	15.00	40.00
13 Steve Young	12.00	30.00
14 Steve McNair	8.00	20.00

2000 Vanguard Game Worn Jersey Duals

STATED PRINT RUN 200 SER.#'d SETS		
1 Cris Carter Randy Moss	20.00	50.00
2 Ricky Williams Jerome Bettis	12.00	30.00
3 Duce Staley Donovan McNabb	12.00	30.00
4 Jerome Bettis Kordell Stewart	12.00	30.00
5 Jerry Rice Randy Moss	25.00	60.00
6 Steve Young Steve McNair	15.00	40.00

2000 Vanguard Game Worn Jersey Dual Patches

1 Olandis Gary/12 Ricky Williams	50.00	100.00
2 Mark Brunell/15 Steve Young	50.00	120.00
3 Cris Carter/25 Randy Moss	60.00	150.00
4 Jerome Bettis/35 Kordell Stewart	50.00	120.00
5 Jerry Rice/19 Randy Moss	75.00	150.00
6 Steve McNair/25 Donovan McNabb	50.00	120.00

2000 Vanguard Gridiron Architects

COMPLETE SET (20)	20.00	50.00
STATED ODDS 1:25		
1 Jake Plummer	.75	2.00
2 Cade McNown	.60	1.50
3 Tim Couch	.75	2.00
4 Troy Aikman	1.50	4.00
5 Emmitt Smith	2.50	6.00
6 Terrell Davis	1.00	2.50
7 Brett Favre	3.00	8.00
8 Edgerrin James	1.00	2.50
9 Peyton Manning	2.50	6.00
10 Fred Taylor	1.00	2.50
11 Dan Marino	3.00	8.00
12 Randy Moss	1.00	2.50
13 Drew Bledsoe	1.00	2.50
14 Curtis Martin	1.00	2.50
15 Terrell Owens	1.00	2.50
16 Marshall Faulk	1.00	2.50
17 Kurt Warner	1.50	4.00
18 Shaun King	.60	1.50
19 Eddie George	.75	2.00
20 Stephen Davis	.75	2.00

2000 Vanguard High Voltage

COMPLETE SET (36)	10.00	20.00
OVERALL ODDS ONE PER PACK		
*GOLD/199: 3X TO 8X BASIC INSERTS		
GOLD STATED PRINT RUN 199		
*GREEN/99: 4X TO 10X BASIC INSERTS		
GREEN STATED PRINT RUN 99		
*HOLOGRAPHIC SILVER/10: 20X TO 50X		
HOLOGRAPHIC SILVER PRINT RUN 10		
*RED/299: 2X TO 5X BASIC INSERTS		
RED STATED PRINT RUN 299		
1 Thomas Jones	.30	.75
2 Jamal Lewis	.25	.60
3 Eric Moulds	.20	.50
4 Marcus Robinson	.20	.50
5 Corey Dillon	.20	.50
6 Peter Warrick	.25	.60
7 Tim Couch	.20	.50
8 Kevin Johnson	.15	.40
9 Emmitt Smith	.60	1.50
10 Olandis Gary	.20	.50
11 Brian Griese	.20	.50
12 Charlie Batch	.20	.50
13 Antonio Freeman	.20	.50
14 Marvin Harrison	.25	.60
15 Edgerrin James	.25	.60
16 Mark Brunell	.20	.50
17 Fred Taylor	.25	.60
18 Damon Huard	.20	.50
19 Cris Carter	.25	.60
20 Daunte Culpepper	.20	.50
21 Randy Moss	.25	.60
22 Ron Dayne	.25	.60
23 Curtis Martin	.25	.60
24 Chad Pennington	.40	1.00
25 Jerome Bettis	.25	.60
26 Plaxico Burress	.25	.60
27 Isaac Bruce	.25	.60
28 Marshall Faulk	.25	.60
29 Kurt Warner	.40	1.00
30 Giovanni Carmazzi	.15	.40
31 Shaun Alexander	.30	.75
32 Jon Kitna	.20	.50
33 Eddie George	.20	.50
34 Warrick Dunn	.20	.50
35 Shaun King	.15	.40
36 Stephen Davis	.20	.50

2000 Vanguard Press Hobby

COMPLETE SET (10)	4.00	10.00
STATED ODDS 2:25 HOBBY		
1 Peter Warrick	.30	.75
2 Tim Couch	.30	.75
3 Terrell Davis	.40	1.00
4 Edgerrin James	.40	1.00
5 Peyton Manning	1.00	2.50
6 Fred Taylor	.40	1.00
7 Drew Bledsoe	.40	1.00
8 Chad Pennington	.50	1.25
9 Jon Kitna	.30	.75
10 Eddie George	.30	.75

2000 Vanguard Press Retail

COMPLETE SET (10)	6.00	15.00
STATED ODDS 2:25 RETAIL		
1 Thomas Jones	.50	1.25
2 Cade McNown	.30	.75
3 Troy Aikman	.75	2.00
4 Emmitt Smith	1.25	3.00
5 Brett Favre	1.50	4.00
6 Ron Dayne	.40	1.00
7 Randy Moss	.50	1.25
8 Marshall Faulk	.50	1.25
9 Kurt Warner	.75	2.00
10 Stephen Davis	.40	1.00

2001 Vanguard

This 150 card set was issued in October, 2001. The cards were issued in four card packs which had an SRP of $3.99 per pack and there were 24 packs in a box. The last 50 cards in the set are all Rookie Cards with a stated print run of 450 cards. A highlight of these cards featured Pacific's "Vision-Glow" Technology which utilized chromium stryene card stock.

COMP.SET w/o SP's (100)	12.50	30.00
1 David Boston	.25	.60
2 Thomas Jones	.30	.75
3 Jake Plummer	.30	.75
4 Jamal Anderson	.30	.75
5 Chris Chandler	.30	.75
6 Elvis Grbac	.30	.75
7 Jamal Lewis	.40	1.00
8 Shannon Sharpe	.40	1.00
9 Rob Johnson	.30	.75
10 Eric Moulds	.30	.75
11 Peerless Price	.25	.60
12 Tim Biakabutuka	.25	.60
13 Muhsin Muhammad	.30	.75
14 James Allen	.25	.60
15 Cade McNown	.30	.75
16 Marcus Robinson	.30	.75
17 Corey Dillon	.30	.75
18 Akili Smith	.25	.60
19 Peter Warrick	.30	.75
20 Tim Couch	.25	.60
21 Kevin Johnson	.25	.60
22 Travis Prentice	.25	.60
23 Rocket Ismail	.30	.75
24 Emmitt Smith	1.00	2.50
25 Mike Anderson	.30	.75
26 Terrell Davis	.40	1.00
27 Brian Griese	.30	.75
28 Ed McCaffrey	.30	.75
29 Rod Smith	.30	.75
30 Charlie Batch	.30	.75
31 Johnnie Morton	.30	.75
32 James Stewart	.25	.60
33 Brett Favre	1.25	3.00
34 Antonio Freeman	.40	1.00
35 Ahman Green	.40	1.00
36 Bill Schroeder	.30	.75
37 Marvin Harrison	.40	1.00
38 Edgerrin James	.40	1.00
39 Peyton Manning	1.00	2.50
40 Terrence Wilkins	.25	.60
41 Mark Brunell	.30	.75
42 Keenan McCardell	.30	.75
43 Jimmy Smith	.30	.75
44 Fred Taylor	.40	1.00
45 Derrick Alexander	.25	.60
46 Tony Gonzalez	.40	1.00
47 Sylvester Morris	.25	.60
48 Jay Fiedler	.30	.75
49 Oronde Gadsden	.25	.60
50 Lamar Smith	.30	.75
51 Cris Carter	.40	1.00
52 Daunte Culpepper	.30	.75
53 Randy Moss	.40	1.00
54 Drew Bledsoe	.40	1.00
55 Terry Glenn	.30	.75
56 Charles Johnson	.25	.60
57 J.R. Redmond	.25	.60
58 Jeff Blake	.30	.75
59 Joe Horn	.30	.75
60 Ricky Williams	.40	1.00
61 Tiki Barber	.40	1.00
62 Kerry Collins	.30	.75
63 Ron Dayne	.30	.75
64 Amani Toomer	.30	.75
65 Wayne Chrebet	.30	.75
66 Curtis Martin	.40	1.00
67 Vinny Testaverde	.30	.75
68 Tim Brown	.40	1.00
69 Rich Gannon	.30	.75
70 Jerry Rice	.75	2.00
71 Tyrone Wheatley	.30	.75
72 Donovan McNabb	.40	1.00
73 Duce Staley	.30	.75
74 Jerome Bettis	.40	1.00
75 Kordell Stewart	.30	.75
76 Hines Ward	.40	1.00
77 Isaac Bruce	.40	1.00
78 Marshall Faulk	.40	1.00
79 Torry Holt	.30	.75
80 Kurt Warner	.60	1.50
81 Curtis Conway	.30	.75
82 Tim Dwight	.30	.75
83 Doug Flutie	.40	1.00
84 Junior Seau	.40	1.00
85 Jeff Garcia	.30	.75
86 Terrell Owens	.40	1.00
87 Shaun Alexander	.40	1.00
88 Matt Hasselbeck	.40	1.00
89 Darrell Jackson	.30	.75
90 Mike Alstott	.30	.75
91 Warrick Dunn	.40	1.00
92 Keyshawn Johnson	.30	.75
93 Brad Johnson	.30	.75
94 Kevin Dyson	.25	.60
95 Eddie George	.40	1.00
96 Derrick Mason	.30	.75
97 Steve McNair	.40	1.00
98 Stephen Davis	.30	.75
99 Jeff George	.30	.75
100 Michael Westbrook	.25	.60
101 Bobby Newcombe RC	2.00	5.00
102 Alge Crumpler RC	2.50	6.00
103 Vinny Sutherland RC	1.50	4.00
104 Michael Vick RC	10.00	25.00
105 Todd Heap RC	2.50	6.00
106 Nate Clements RC	2.00	5.00
107 Travis Henry RC	2.00	5.00
108 Dan Morgan RC	2.00	5.00
109 Chris Weinke RC	2.00	5.00
110 David Terrell RC	2.00	5.00
111 Anthony Thomas RC	2.50	6.00
112 T.J. Houshmandzadeh RC	3.00	8.00
113 Chad Johnson RC	4.00	10.00
114 Rudi Johnson RC	2.50	6.00
115 James Jackson RC	1.50	4.00
116 Quincy Morgan RC	2.00	5.00
117 Quincy Carter RC	2.00	5.00
118 Scotty Anderson RC	1.50	4.00
119 Mike McMahon RC	2.00	5.00
120 Robert Ferguson RC	2.50	6.00
121 Reggie Wayne RC	5.00	12.00
122 Snoop Minnis RC	1.50	4.00
123 Chris Chambers RC	2.50	6.00
124 Jamar Fletcher RC	1.50	4.00
125 Josh Heupel RC	2.50	6.00
126 Travis Minor RC	2.00	5.00
127 Michael Bennett RC	2.00	5.00
128 Deuce McAllister RC	2.50	6.00
129 Will Allen RC	2.50	6.00
130 Jesse Palmer RC	2.00	5.00
131 LaMont Jordan RC	2.50	6.00
132 Santana Moss RC	3.00	8.00
133 Ken-Yon Rambo RC	1.50	4.00
134 Marques Tuiasosopo RC	2.00	5.00
135 Correll Buckhalter RC	2.50	6.00
136 A.J. Feeley RC	2.00	5.00
137 Freddie Mitchell RC	1.50	4.00
138 Chris Taylor RC	1.50	4.00
139 Adam Archuleta RC	2.00	5.00
140 Drew Brees RC	15.00	40.00
141 LaDainian Tomlinson RC	8.00	20.00
142 Kevan Barlow RC	2.00	5.00
143 Cedrick Wilson RC	2.00	5.00
144 Alex Bannister RC	1.50	4.00
145 Josh Booty RC	2.00	5.00
146 Heath Evans RC	2.00	5.00
147 Koren Robinson RC	2.00	5.00
148 Dan Alexander RC	2.00	5.00
149 Rod Gardner RC	2.00	5.00
150 Sage Rosenfels RC	2.50	6.00

2001 Vanguard Blue

*1-100 VETS: 3X TO 8X BASIC CARDS
*101-150 ROOKIES: .3X TO .8X
STATED PRINT RUN 299 SER.#'d SETS

2001 Vanguard Gold

*1-100 VETS: 5X TO 12X BASIC CARDS
*101-150 ROOKIES: .5X TO 1.2X
STATED PRINT RUN 99 SER.#'d SETS

2001 Vanguard Premiere Date

*1-100 VETS: 5X TO 12X BASIC CARDS
*101-150 ROOKIES: .5X TO 1.2X
STATED PRINT RUN 115 SER.#'d SETS

2001 Vanguard Red

*VETS/80-89: 5X TO 12X BASIC CARDS
*VETS/40-55: 6X TO 15X BASIC CARDS
*VETS/30-38: 8X TO 20X BASIC CARDS
*VETS/20-29: 10X TO 35X BASIC CARDS
*VETS/10-19: 12X TO 30X BASIC CARDS
1-100 VETERANS PRINT RUN 2-89
UNPRICED 101-150 ROOKIE PRINT RUN 10

2001 Vanguard Bombs Away

COMPLETE SET (30)	30.00	80.00
STATED PRINT RUN 999 SER.#'d SETS		
QUARTERBACKS FOUND IN HOBBY PACKS		
RECEIVERS FOUND IN RETAIL PACKS		
1 Michael Vick	4.00	10.00
2 Chris Weinke	1.00	2.50
3 Tim Couch	.75	2.00
4 Brian Griese	1.00	2.50
5 Brett Favre	4.00	10.00
6 Peyton Manning	3.00	8.00
7 Mark Brunell	1.00	2.50
8 Daunte Culpepper	1.00	2.50
9 Drew Bledsoe	1.25	3.00
10 Rich Gannon	1.00	2.50
11 Donovan McNabb	1.25	3.00
12 Kurt Warner	2.00	5.00
13 Drew Brees	6.00	15.00
14 Jeff Garcia	1.00	2.50
15 Steve McNair	1.25	3.00
16 Eric Moulds	1.00	2.50
17 David Terrell	1.00	2.50
18 Peter Warrick	1.00	2.50
19 Marvin Harrison	1.25	3.00
20 Jimmy Smith	1.00	2.50
21 Cris Carter	1.25	3.00
22 Santana Moss	1.25	3.00
23 Tim Brown	1.25	3.00
24 Jerry Rice	2.50	6.00
25 Freddie Mitchell	.75	2.00
26 Isaac Bruce	1.25	3.00
27 Torry Holt	1.00	2.50
28 Terrell Owens	1.25	3.00
29 Koren Robinson	1.00	2.50
30 Rod Gardner	1.00	2.50

2001 Vanguard Double Sided Jerseys

STATED ODDS 2:25 HOB, 1:49 RET		
*PATCH/50: .6X TO 1.5X BASIC INSERTS		
*PATCH/25: .8X TO 2X BASIC INSERTS		
1 Jake Plummer/270 David Boston	6.00	15.00
2 Rob Moore Frank Sanders	5.00	12.00
3 Thomas Jones Michael Pittman	6.00	15.00
4 Chris Gedney Ernie Conwell	5.00	12.00
5 Chris Griesen Neil O'Donnell	6.00	15.00
6 Chris Chandler Terance Mathis	6.00	15.00
7 Randall Cunningham Anthony Wright	8.00	20.00
8 Tim Biakabutuka Steve Beuerlein	6.00	15.00
9 Brad Hoover Moe Williams	6.00	15.00
10 Chris Weinke/270 Freddie Mitchell (college jersey swatches)	6.00	15.00
11 Patrick Jeffers Tim Dwight	6.00	15.00
12 Reggie White Jevon Kearse	8.00	20.00
13 Wesley Walls Frank Wycheck	5.00	12.00
14 Bobby Engram Dez White	6.00	15.00
15 Cade McNown James Allen	6.00	15.00
16 Shane Matthews Jim Miller	6.00	15.00
17 Brian Urlacher Zach Thomas	10.00	25.00
18 Anthony Thomas/270 LaDainian Tomlinson (college jersey swatches)	12.00	30.00
19 Corey Dillon/255 Peter Warrick	6.00	15.00
20 Ron Dugans Danny Farmer	5.00	12.00
21 Troy Aikman/265 Emmitt Smith	30.00	60.00
22 Wane McGarity James McKnight	5.00	12.00
23 Jason Tucker Ricky Proehl	5.00	12.00
24 Carl Pickens Kevin Dyson	6.00	15.00
25 Brian Griese/265 Olandis Gary	6.00	15.00
26 Dwayne Carswell Byron Chamberlain	5.00	12.00
27 Mike Anderson/260 Terrell Davis	8.00	20.00
28 Gus Frerotte Matt Hasselbeck	8.00	20.00
29 Herman Moore Johnnie Morton	6.00	15.00
30 James Stewart Larry Foster	5.00	12.00
31 Desmond Howard Tony Martin	6.00	15.00
32 Ahman Green Herbert Goodman	8.00	20.00
33 Brett Favre/260 Antonio Freeman	25.00	50.00
34 Dorsey Levens De'Mond Parker	6.00	15.00
35 Tyrone Davis Bubba Franks	6.00	15.00
36 William Henderson Greg Comella	6.00	15.00
37 Autry Denson James Johnson	5.00	12.00
38 Chris Walsh Troy Walters	5.00	12.00
39 Cris Carter/265 Robert Smith	8.00	20.00
40 Daunte Culpepper/265 Randy Moss	8.00	20.00
41 Damon Huard Bert Emanuel	6.00	15.00
42 Jeff Blake Willie Jackson	6.00	15.00
43 Kerry Collins Joe Jurevicius	6.00	15.00
44 Tiki Barber/275 Ron Dayne	8.00	20.00
45 Jason Sehorn Aeneas Williams	6.00	15.00
46 Amani Toomer Chris Sanders	6.00	15.00
47 Tyrone Wheatley Napoleon Kaufman	6.00	15.00
48 Marques Tuiasosopo/265 Drew Brees	15.00	30.00
49 Kurt Warner/265 Marshall Faulk	12.00	30.00
50 Eddie George/265 Steve McNair	8.00	20.00

2001 Vanguard In Focus

COMPLETE SET (15)	60.00	120.00
STATED PRINT RUN 99 SER. #'d SETS		
1 Jamal Lewis	3.00	8.00
2 Emmitt Smith	8.00	20.00
3 Mike Anderson	2.50	6.00
4 Terrell Davis	3.00	8.00
5 Brett Favre	10.00	25.00
6 Edgerrin James	3.00	8.00
7 Peyton Manning	8.00	20.00
8 Mark Brunell	2.50	6.00
9 Daunte Culpepper	2.50	6.00
10 Randy Moss	3.00	8.00
11 Ricky Williams	3.00	8.00
12 Jerry Rice	6.00	15.00
13 Donovan McNabb	3.00	8.00
14 Marshall Faulk	3.00	8.00
15 Kurt Warner	5.00	12.00

2001 Vanguard Prime Prospects Bronze

COMPLETE SET (36)	12.00	30.00
ONE BRONZE PER HOBBY PACK		
*SILVER/300: .8X TO 2X BRONZE		
SILVER STATED PRINT RUN 300		
1 Michael Vick	2.00	5.00
2 Travis Henry	.40	1.00
3 Dan Morgan	.40	1.00
4 Chris Weinke	.40	1.00
5 David Terrell	.40	1.00
6 Anthony Thomas	.50	1.25
7 Chad Johnson	.75	2.00
8 James Jackson	.30	.75
9 Quincy Morgan	.40	1.00
10 Quincy Carter	.40	1.00
11 Mike McMahon	.40	1.00
12 Robert Ferguson	.50	1.25
13 Reggie Wayne	1.00	2.50
14 Snoop Minnis	.30	.75
15 Chris Chambers	.50	1.25
16 Josh Heupel	.50	1.25
17 Travis Minor	.40	1.00
18 Michael Bennett	.40	1.00
19 Deuce McAllister	.50	1.25
20 Jesse Palmer	.40	1.00
21 LaMont Jordan	.50	1.25
22 Santana Moss	.60	1.50
23 Ken-Yon Rambo	.30	.75
24 Marques Tuiasosopo	.40	1.00
25 Correll Buckhalter	.50	1.25
26 Freddie Mitchell	.30	.75
27 Adam Archuleta	.40	1.00
28 Drew Brees	3.00	8.00
29 LaDainian Tomlinson	1.50	4.00
30 Kevan Barlow	.40	1.00
31 Cedrick Wilson	.40	1.00
32 Alex Bannister	.30	.75
33 Koren Robinson	.40	1.00
34 Dan Alexander	.40	1.00
35 Rod Gardner	.40	1.00
36 Sage Rosenfels	.50	1.25

2001 Vanguard V-Team

COMPLETE SET (25)	40.00	80.00
STATED PRINT RUN 1499 SER. #'d SETS		
1 Jamal Lewis	1.50	4.00
2 Corey Dillon	1.25	3.00
3 Peter Warrick	1.25	3.00
4 Tim Couch	1.00	2.50
5 Emmitt Smith	4.00	10.00
6 Mike Anderson	1.25	3.00
7 Terrell Davis	1.50	4.00
8 Brian Griese	1.25	3.00
9 Marvin Harrison	1.50	4.00
10 Edgerrin James	1.50	4.00
11 Peyton Manning	4.00	10.00
12 Mark Brunell	1.25	3.00
13 Fred Taylor	1.50	4.00
14 Cris Carter	1.50	4.00
15 Randy Moss	1.50	4.00
16 Drew Bledsoe	1.50	4.00
17 Ricky Williams	1.50	4.00
18 Ron Dayne	1.25	3.00
19 Jerry Rice	3.00	8.00
20 Donovan McNabb	1.50	4.00
21 Kurt Warner	2.50	6.00
22 Marshall Faulk	1.50	4.00
23 Jeff Garcia	1.25	3.00
24 Eddie George	1.50	4.00
25 Steve McNair	1.50	4.00

2001 Vanguard V-Team Rookies

COMPLETE SET (30)	50.00	100.00
STATED PRINT RUN 999 SER. #'d SETS		
1 Michael Vick	4.00	10.00
2 Travis Henry	.75	2.00
3 Chris Weinke	.75	2.00
4 David Terrell	.75	2.00
5 Anthony Thomas	1.00	2.50
6 Chad Johnson	1.50	4.00
7 James Jackson	.60	1.50
8 Quincy Morgan	.75	2.00
9 Quincy Carter	.75	2.00
10 Mike McMahon	.75	2.00
11 Robert Ferguson	1.00	2.50
12 Reggie Wayne	2.00	5.00
13 Snoop Minnis	.60	1.50
14 Chris Chambers	1.00	2.50
15 Josh Heupel	1.00	2.50
16 Travis Minor	.75	2.00
17 Michael Bennett	.75	2.00
18 Deuce McAllister	1.00	2.50
19 Jesse Palmer	.75	2.00
20 LaMont Jordan	1.00	2.50
21 Santana Moss	1.25	3.00
22 Marques Tuiasosopo	.75	2.00
23 Correll Buckhalter	1.00	2.50
24 A.J. Feeley	.75	2.00
25 Freddie Mitchell	.60	1.50
26 Drew Brees	6.00	15.00
27 LaDainian Tomlinson	3.00	8.00
28 Koren Robinson	.75	2.00
29 Rod Gardner	.75	2.00
30 Sage Rosenfels	1.00	2.50

1961 Vikings Team Issue

These large photos measure approximately 5" by 7" and feature black-and-white player photos. The set was issued in "Picture Pak" form in its own envelope by the team. Each has a large white border below the player photo with his position (initials), name, and team (Minnesota) printed in the border. The player photos carry a brief bio on the backs with stats when applicable; the coaches photos are blankbacked. The cards are unnumbered and checklisted below in alphabetical order.

COMPLETE SET (48)	300.00	500.00
1 Grady Alderman	6.00	12.00
2 Bill Bishop	6.00	12.00
3 Darrel Brewster CO	6.00	12.00
4 Jamie Caleb	6.00	12.00
5 Ed Culpepper	6.00	12.00
6 Bob Denton	6.00	12.00
7 Paul Dickson	6.00	12.00
8 Billy Gault	6.00	12.00
9 Harry Gilmer CO	7.50	15.00
10 Dick Grecni	6.00	12.00
11 Dick Haley	6.00	12.00
12 Rip Hawkins	6.00	12.00
13 Raymond Hayes	6.00	12.00
14 Gerry Huth	6.00	12.00
15 Gene Johnson	6.00	12.00
16 Don Joyce	6.00	12.00
17 Bill Lapham	6.00	12.00
18 Jim Leo	6.00	12.00
19 Jim Marshall	10.00	20.00
20 Tommy Mason	7.50	15.00
21 Doug Mayberry	6.00	12.00
22 Hugh McElhenny	10.00	20.00
23 Mike Mercer	6.00	12.00
24 Dave Middleton	6.00	12.00
25 Jack Morris	6.00	12.00
26 Rich Mostardo	6.00	12.00
27 Fred Murphy	6.00	12.00
28 Clancy Osborne	6.00	12.00
29 Dick Pesonen	6.00	12.00
30 Ken Petersen	6.00	12.00
31 Jim Prestel	6.00	12.00
32 Mike Rabold	6.00	12.00
33 Jerry Reichow	6.00	12.00
34 Karl Rubke	6.00	12.00
35 Bob Schnelker	6.00	12.00
36 Ed Sharockman	6.00	12.00
37 George Shaw	7.50	15.00
38 Willard Sherman	6.00	12.00
39 Lebron Shields	6.00	12.00
40 Gordon Smith	6.00	12.00
41 Charlie Sumner	6.00	12.00
42 Fran Tarkenton	20.00	40.00
43 Mel Triplett	6.00	12.00
44 Norm Van Brocklin CO	7.50	15.00
45 Stan West CO	6.00	12.00
46 A.D. Wiliams	6.00	12.00
47 Frank Youso	6.00	12.00
48 Walt Yowarsky CO	6.00	12.00

1963-64 Vikings Team Issue

This 20-card set of the Minnesota Vikings measures approximately 5" by 7" and features black-and-white borderless player portraits with the players position, name and team in a bar at the card bottom. The photos were likely issued over a number of years. Either a Vikings or Minnesota name can be found on the cardfronts.The backs are blank. The cards are unnumbered and checklisted below in alphabetical order.

COMPLETE SET (20)	100.00	200.00
1 Jim Battle	6.00	12.00
2 Larry Bowie	6.00	12.00
3 Bill Butler	6.00	12.00
4 Lee Calland	6.00	12.00
5 John Campbell	6.00	12.00
6 Leon Clarke	6.00	12.00
7 Paul Dickson	6.00	12.00
8 Terry Dillon	6.00	12.00
9 Paul Flatley	6.00	12.00
10 Tom Franckhauser	6.00	12.00
11 Rip Hawkins	6.00	12.00
12 Don Hultz	6.00	12.00
13 Errol Linden	6.00	12.00
14 Mike Mercer	6.00	12.00
15 Ray Poage	6.00	12.00
16 Jim Prestel	6.00	12.00
17 Jerry Reichow	6.00	12.00
18 Ed Sharockman	6.00	12.00
19 Gordon Smith	6.00	12.00
20 Tom Wilson	6.00	12.00

1965 Vikings Team Issue

This set of photos from the Minnesota Vikings measures approximately 4 1/4" by 5 1/2" and features black-and-white player portraits with the players position (appreviated), name and team "Vikings" in a bar at the card bottom. Most of the players in the set are shown wearing their white jersey and most include a facsimile autograph. Some photos were issued with variations on the placement of the facsimilie signature on the front. The photos were likely issued over a number of years and vary slightly in text style and size. The cardbacks are blank; each is unnumbered and checklisted below in alphabetical order.

COMPLETE SET (25)	150.00	300.00
1 Larry Bowie	6.00	12.00
2 Bill Brown	7.50	15.00
3 Fred Cox	10.00	20.00
(with Fran Tarkenton holding)		
4 Doug Davis	6.00	12.00
(facsimile sig in upper right)		
5 Paul Dickson	6.00	12.00
6 Carl Eller	7.50	15.00
8 Paul Flatley	6.00	12.00
(facsimile sig in upper right)		
8 Dale Hackbart	6.00	12.00
9 Rip Hawkins	6.00	12.00
10 Karl Kassulke	6.00	12.00
(no facsimilie sig)		
11 Phil King	6.00	12.00
(facsimile sig in upper left)		
12 John Kirby	6.00	12.00
(facsimile sig in upper right)		
13 Gary Larsen	6.00	12.00
(facsimile sig in upper left)		
14 Jim Lindsey	6.00	12.00
(facsimile sig in upper right)		
15 Jim Marshall	7.50	15.00
(facsimile sig in upper left)		
16 Tommy Mason	6.00	12.00
17A Jim Phillips	6.00	12.00
(facsimile sig in upper right)		
17B Jim Phillips	6.00	12.00
(facsimile sig in upper left)		
18 Ed Sharockman	6.00	12.00
19 Fran Tarkenton	12.50	25.00
20 Mick Tingelhoff	7.50	15.00
21 Norm Van Brocklin CO	7.50	15.00
22 Ron Vanderkelen	6.00	12.00
23 Bobby Walden	6.00	12.00
24 Lonnie Warwick	6.00	12.00
25 Roy Winston	6.00	12.00

1966 Vikings Team Issue

These large photo cards are approximately 8" by 10" and feature black-and-white player photos. Each has a white border and was printed on thick glossy stock. The cards are unnumbered and checklisted below in alphabetical order. They are very similar to the 1967 and 1968 issues, but can be differentiated by the player's position, name, and then team name spread out across the border below the photo. Any additions to the checklist below are appreciated.

COMPLETE SET (3)	15.00	30.00
1 Larry Bowie	6.00	12.00
2 Dave Tobey	6.00	12.00
3 Ron Vanderkelen	6.00	12.00

1967 Vikings Team Issue

These large photo cards are approximately 8" by 10" and feature black-and-white player photos. Each has a white border and was printed on thick glossy stock. The cards are unnumbered and checklisted below in alphabetical order. They are very similar to the 1966 and 1968 issues, but can be differentiated by the player's name, postion, and team name tightly arranged in the border below the photo.

COMPLETE SET (23)	100.00	200.00
1 Grady Alderman	7.50	15.00
(Offensive lineman)		
2 John Beasley	6.00	12.00
3 Bob Berry	6.00	12.00
4 Doug Davis	6.00	12.00
5 Paul Dickson	6.00	12.00
6 Paul Flatley	6.00	12.00
7 Bob Grim	6.00	12.00
8 Dale Hackbart	6.00	12.00
9 Don Hansen	6.00	12.00
10 Jim Hargrove	6.00	12.00
11 Clint Jones	6.00	12.00
12 Jeff Jordan	6.00	12.00
13 Joe Kapp	7.50	15.00
14 John Kirby	6.00	12.00
15 Gary Larsen	6.00	12.00
16 Earsell Mackbee	6.00	12.00
17 Marlin McKeever	6.00	12.00
18 Milt Sunde	6.00	12.00
19 Jim Vellone	6.00	12.00
20 Bobby Walden	6.00	12.00
21 Lonnie Warwick	6.00	12.00
22 Gene Washington	6.00	12.00
(End)		
23 Roy Winston	6.00	12.00

1968 Vikings Team Issue

These large photo cards are approximately 8" by 10" and feature black-and-white player photos. Each has a white border and was printed on thick glossy stock. The cards are unnumbered and checklisted below in alphabetical order. They are very similar to the 1966 and 1967 issues, but can be differentiated by the player's name, postion (initial), and team name loosely arranged in the border below the photo.

COMPLETE SET (3)	15.00	30.00
1 Grady Alderman	6.00	12.00
Tackle		
2 Gary Cuozzo	6.00	12.00
3 Gene Washington	6.00	12.00
Wide receiver		

1969 Vikings Team Issue

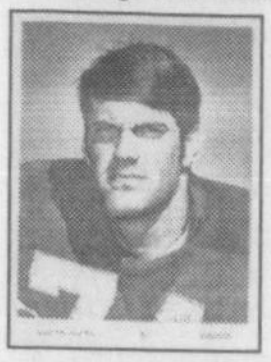

This 27-card set of the Minnesota Vikings measures approximately 5" by 6 7/8" and features black-and-white borderless player portraits with the players name, position and team in a wide bar at the bottom. The backs are blank. Although similar to earlier Vikings' team issues, these photos can be differentiated by the order in which the player details are listed at the bottom of the card. The cards are unnumbered and checklisted below in alphabetical order.

COMPLETE SET (27)	100.00	200.00
1 Bookie Bolin	5.00	10.00
2 Bobby Bryant	5.00	10.00
3 John Beasley	5.00	10.00
4 Gary Cuozzo	6.00	12.00
5 Doug Davis	5.00	10.00
6 Paul Dickson	5.00	10.00
7 Bob Grim	5.00	10.00
8 Dale Hackbart	5.00	10.00
9 Jim Hargrove	5.00	10.00
10 John Henderson	5.00	10.00
11 Wally Hilgenberg	5.00	10.00
12 Clinton Jones	5.00	10.00
13 Karl Kassulke	5.00	10.00
14 Kent Kramer	5.00	10.00
15 Gary Larsen	5.00	10.00
16 Bob Lee	5.00	10.00
17 Jim Lindsey	5.00	10.00
18 Earsell Mackbee	5.00	10.00
19 Mike McGill	5.00	10.00
20 Oscar Reed	5.00	10.00
21 Ed Sharockman	5.00	10.00
22 Steve Smith	5.00	10.00
23 Milt Sunde	5.00	10.00
24 Jim Vellone	5.00	10.00
25 Lonnie Warwick	5.00	10.00
26 Gene Washington	5.00	10.00
27 Charlie West	5.00	10.00

1970-71 Vikings Team Issue

This 17-card set of the Minnesota Vikings measures approximately 5" by 7" and features black-and-white borderless player portraits with the players name and team name only in a wide bar at the bottom. The backs are blank. The photos were likely issued over a number of years due to the different type styles used on the photo's text. The cards are unnumbered and checklisted below in alphabetical order. Any additions to this checklist would be greatly appreciated.

COMPLETE SET (17)	60.00	120.00
1 John Beasley	5.00	10.00
2 Doug Davis	5.00	10.00
3 Paul Dickson	5.00	10.00
4 Bob Grim	5.00	10.00
5 Jim Hargrove	5.00	10.00
6 John Henderson	5.00	10.00
7 Clint Jones	5.00	10.00
8 Bob Lee	5.00	10.00
9 Jim Lindsey	5.00	10.00
10 Oscar Reed	5.00	10.00
11 Ed Sharockman	5.00	10.00
12 Steve Smith	5.00	10.00
13 Milt Sunde	5.00	10.00
14 Dave Tobey	5.00	10.00
15 Jim Vellone	5.00	10.00
16 John Ward	5.00	10.00
17 Charlie West	5.00	10.00

1971 Vikings Color Photos

Issued in the late summer of 1971 (preseason), this team-issued set consists of 49 four-color close-up photos printed on thin paper stock. Each photo measures approximately 5" by 7 7/16". The player's name, position, and team name appear in a white bottom border. The backs are blank. The cards are unnumbered and checklisted below in alphabetical order.

COMPLETE SET (52)	175.00	300.00
1 Grady Alderman	4.00	8.00
2 Neill Armstrong CO	3.00	6.00
3 John Beasley	3.00	6.00
4 Bill Brown	4.00	8.00
5 Bob Brown	3.00	6.00
6 Bobby Bryant	4.00	8.00
7 Jerry Burns CO	3.00	6.00
8 Fred Cox	4.00	8.00
9 Gary Cuozzo	4.00	8.00
10 Doug Davis	3.00	6.00
11 Al Denson	3.00	6.00
12 Paul Dickson	3.00	6.00
13 Carl Eller	5.00	10.00
14 Bud Grant CO	7.50	15.00
15 Bob Grim	3.00	6.00
16 Leo Hayden	3.00	6.00
17 John Henderson	3.00	6.00
18 Wally Hilgenberg	4.00	8.00
19 Noel Jenke	3.00	6.00
20 Clint Jones	3.00	6.00
21 Karl Kassulke	3.00	6.00
22 Paul Krause	5.00	10.00
23 Gary Larsen	4.00	8.00
24 Bob Lee	3.00	6.00
25 Jim Lindsey	3.00	6.00
26 Jim Marshall	5.00	10.00
27 Bus Mertes CO	3.00	6.00
28 John Michels CO	3.00	6.00
29 Jocko Nelson CO	3.00	6.00
30 Dave Osborn	4.00	8.00
31 Alan Page	7.50	15.00
32 Jack Patera CO	3.00	6.00
33 Jerry Patton	3.00	6.00
34 Pete Perreault	3.00	6.00
35 Oscar Reed	3.00	6.00
36 Ed Sharockman	3.00	6.00
37 Norm Snead	4.00	8.00
38 Milt Sunde	3.00	6.00
39 Doug Sutherland	3.00	6.00
40 Mick Tingelhoff	4.00	8.00
41 Stu Voigt	3.00	6.00
42 John Ward	3.00	6.00
43 Lonnie Warwick	3.00	6.00
44 Gene Washington	4.00	8.00
45 Charlie West	3.00	6.00
46 Ed White	4.00	8.00
47 Carl Winfrey	3.00	6.00
48 Roy Winston	4.00	8.00
49 Jeff Wright	3.00	6.00
50 Nate Wright	4.00	8.00
51 Ron Yary	4.00	8.00
52 Godfrey Zaunbrecher	3.00	6.00

1971 Vikings Color Postcards

This 19-card set measures roughly 5" by 7 1/2" and features posed color close-up photos on the fronts. These cards were issued after the season had begun and may have been sold at the stadium. The player's name, position, and team name appear in a white bottom border. As with a postcard, the horizontal backs are divided into two sections by a thin black stripe. Brief biographical information is given at the upper left corner, while a box for the stamp is printed at the upper right corner. The cards are unnumbered and checklisted below in alphabetical order.

COMPLETE SET (19)	75.00	125.00
1 Grady Alderman	4.00	8.00
2 Neill Armstrong CO	3.00	6.00
3 John Beasley	3.00	6.00
4 Paul Dickson	3.00	6.00
5 Bud Grant CO	7.50	15.00
6 Wally Hilgenberg	4.00	8.00
7 Noel Jenke	3.00	6.00
8 Paul Krause	5.00	10.00
9 Gary Larsen	4.00	8.00
10 Dave Osborn	4.00	8.00
11 Alan Page	7.50	15.00
12 Jerry Patton	3.00	6.00
13 Doug Sutherland	4.00	8.00
14 Mick Tingelhoff	5.00	10.00
15 Lonnie Warwick	3.00	6.00
16 Charlie West	3.00	6.00
17 Jeff Wright	3.00	6.00
18 Nate Wright	4.00	8.00
19 Godfrey Zaunbrecher	3.00	6.00

1972 Vikings Color Postcards

Cards in this set measure roughly 4" by 5 7/8" and feature color close-up player photos. These cards were issued after the season had begun and likely were sold at the stadium. The player's name, position, and team name appear in a white bottom border. The backs included a typical postcard format although some have been found without the postcard format. The cards are unnumbered and checklisted below in alphabetical order.

COMPLETE SET ()		
1 John Beasley	3.00	6.00
2 Fran Tarkenton	7.50	15.00
3 Godfrey Zaunbrecher	3.00	6.00
(blank backed)		

1973 Vikings Team Issue

This 17-card set of the Minnesota Vikings measures roughly 5" by 7". The fronts feature white bordered black-and-white player portraits with the player's name and team in the bottom wide margin. The backs are blank. The photos can be differentiated from previous Vikings Team Issues by the distinctive white borders and scripted team name on the card fronts. The cards are unnumbered and checklisted below in alphabetical order.

COMPLETE SET (17)	50.00	100.00
1 John Beasley	4.00	8.00
2 Bob Berry	4.00	8.00
3 Terry Brown	4.00	8.00
4 Bobby Bryant	4.00	8.00
5 Larry Dibbles	4.00	8.00
6 Mike Eischeid	4.00	8.00
7 Charles Goodrum	4.00	8.00
8 Neil Graff	4.00	8.00
9 Wally Hilgenberg	4.00	8.00
10 Amos Martin	4.00	8.00
11 Brent McClanahan	4.00	8.00
12 John Michels	4.00	8.00
13 Oscar Reed	4.00	8.00
14 John Ward	4.00	8.00
15 Charlie West	4.00	8.00
16 Jeff Wright	4.00	8.00
17 Nate Wright	4.00	8.00

1974 Vikings Team Issue

These all-color blankbacked photos were released by the Vikings around 1974 presumably to fans via mail. Each includes the player's name and team name below the photo.

COMPLETE SET (11)	50.00	100.00
1 Bobby Bryant	4.00	8.00
2 Carl Eller	5.00	10.00
3 Chuck Foreman	5.00	10.00
4 John Gilliam	4.00	8.00
5 Paul Krause	5.00	10.00
6 Jim Marshall	5.00	10.00
7 Alan Page	6.00	12.00
8 Fran Tarkenton	7.50	15.00
9 Mick Tingelhoff	4.00	8.00
10 Ed White	4.00	8.00
11 Ron Yary	5.00	10.00

1975 Vikings Team Sheets

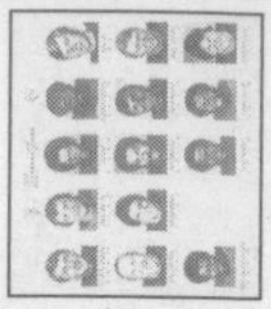

The Vikings issued these black and white player photo sheets for use in publicity opportunities. Each sheet features a number of small player images along with vital information about the player. Each sheet measures roughly 8" by 10" and is blankbacked.

COMPLETE SET (4)	20.00	40.00
1 Bud Grant CO	5.00	10.00
Autry Beamon		
Bob Berry		
Matt Blair		
Terry Brown		
Bobby Bryant		
Neil Clabo		
Fred Cox		
Steve Craig		
Carl Eller		
Chuck Foreman		
John Gilliam		
Charles Goodrum		
Wally Hilgenberg		
2 Wes Hamilton	5.00	10.00
Wally Hilgenberg		
Mark Kellar		
Paul Krause		
Bob Lee QB		
Jim Marshall		
Amos Martin		
Brent McClanahan		
Fred McNeill		
Robert Miller		
Mark Mullaney		
Alan Page		
Ahmad Rashad		
Steve Riley		
3 Doug Kingsriter	5.00	10.00
Paul Krause		
Jim Lash		
Steve Lawson		
Bob Lee QB		
Bob Lurtsema		
Ed Marinaro		
Jim Marshall		
Amos Martin		
Andy Maurer		
Brent McClanahan		
Fred McNeill		
Robert Miller		
Mark Mullaney		
4 Dave Osborn	7.50	15.00
Alan Page		
Steve Riley		
Jeff Siemon		
Doug Sutherland		
Fran Tarkenton		
Mick Tingelhoff		
Stu Voigt		
Ed White		
Roy Winston		
Jeff Wright		
Nate Wright		
Ron Yary		

1976 Vikings Team Sheets

The Vikings issued these black and white player photo sheets for use in publicity opportunities and to fill media requests. Each sheet features a group of small player/coach images along with vital information about the player below the image. Each sheet measures roughly 8" by 10" and is blankbacked.

COMPLETE SET (3)	20.00	35.00
1 Bud Grant CO	5.00	10.00
Nate Allen		
Scott Anderson		
Autry Beamon		
Bob Berry		
Matt Blair		
Bobby Bryant		
Neil Clabo		
Fred Cox		
Steve Craig		
Doug Dumler		
Carl Eller		
Chuck Foreman		
Charles Goodrum		
Windlan Hill		
2 Wes Hamilton	5.00	10.00
Wally Hilgenberg		
Mark Kellar		
Paul Krause		
Bob Lee		
Jim Marshall		
Amos Martin		
Brent McClanahan		
Fred McNeill		
Robert Miller		
Mark Mullaney		
Alan Page		
Ahmad Rashad		
Steve Riley		
3 Jeff Siemon	7.50	15.00
Doug Sutherland		
Fran Tarkenton		
Mick Tingelhoff		
Stu Voight		
Ed White		
James White		
Sammy White		
Leonard Willis		
Roy Winston		
Jeff Wright		
Nate Wright		
Ron Yary		

1978 Vikings Country Kitchen

This seven-card set was sponsored by Country Kitchen Restaurants and measures approximately 5" by 7". The front features a black and white head shot of the player. The card backs have biographical and statistical information. The cards are unnumbered and hence are listed alphabetically below.

COMPLETE SET (7)	25.00	50.00
1 Bobby Bryant	3.00	6.00
2 Tommy Kramer	5.00	10.00
3 Paul Krause	5.00	10.00
4 Ahmad Rashad	7.50	15.00
5 Jeff Siemon	3.00	6.00
6 Mick Tingelhoff	4.00	8.00
7 Sammie White	4.00	8.00

1979 Vikings SuperAmerica

The 1979 SuperAmerica Vikings set was distributed through the SuperAmerica convenience stores with a fill-up of gasoline. These 10" by 12" unnumbered sepia posters display watercolor art of the player in action, with a write-up about his career in the top third of the poster. The bottom third of the poster shows a watercolor close-up of the particular player along with a descriptive cutline for the poster. The posters are cataloged in alphabetical order below. There are seven known posters.

COMPLETE SET (7)	40.00	80.00
1 Bill Brown	5.00	10.00
2 Karl Kassulke	4.00	8.00
3 Jim Marshall	7.50	15.00
4 Hugh McElhenny	10.00	20.00
5 Dave Osborn	4.00	8.00
6 Fran Tarkenton	15.00	30.00
7 Gene Washington	5.00	10.00

1983 Vikings Police

The 1983 Minnesota Vikings set contains 17 numbered cards. The cards measure approximately 2 5/8" by 4 1/8". This first Viking police set is sponsored by Pillsbury, Minnesota Crime Prevention Officers Association, Green Giant, and Burger King. In addition to the Vikings' logo, logos of all five organizations appear on the backs. The fronts contain a Vikings logo.

COMPLETE SET (17)	4.00	10.00
1 Checklist Card	.30	.75
2 Tommy Kramer	.40	1.00
3 Ted Brown	.20	.50
4 Joe Senser	.20	.50
5 Sammie White	.40	1.00
6 Doug Martin	.20	.50
7 Matt Blair	.30	.75
8 Bud Grant CO	.75	2.00
9 Scott Studwell	.30	.75
10 Greg Coleman	.20	.50
11 John Turner	.20	.50
12 Jim Hough	.20	.50
13 Joey Browner	.40	1.00
14 Dennis Swilley	.20	.50
15 Darrin Nelson	.30	.75
16 Mark Mullaney	.20	.50
17 Fran Tarkenton	1.50	4.00
(All-Time Great)		

1984 Vikings Police

This numbered 18-card set features the Minnesota Vikings. Cards measure approximately 2 5/8" by 4 1/8" and are dated in the lower right corner of the reverse. The set was printed on thick card stock. Logos on the card backs are printed in color. The set was sponsored by Pillsbury, Burger King, and the Minnesota Crime Prevention Officers Association.

COMPLETE SET (18)	3.00	8.00
1 Checklist Card	.25	.60
2 Keith Nord	.15	.40
3 Joe Senser	.15	.40
4 Tommy Kramer	.30	.75
5 Darrin Nelson	.25	.60
6 Tim Irwin	.15	.40
7 Mark Mullaney	.15	.40
8 Les Steckel CO	.15	.40
9 Greg Coleman	.15	.40
10 Tommy Hannon	.15	.40
11 Curtis Rouse	.15	.40
12 Scott Studwell	.25	.60
13 Steve Jordan	.30	.75
14 Willie Teal	.15	.40
15 Ted Brown	.25	.60
16 Sammie White	.30	.75
17 Matt Blair	.25	.60
18 Jim Marshall	.75	2.00
(All Time Great)		

1985 Vikings Police

This 16-card set of Minnesota Vikings is numbered on the back. Cards measure approximately 2 5/8" by 4 1/8" and the backs contain a "Crime Prevention Tip". The set was sponsored by Frito-Lay, Pepsi-Cola, KS95-FM, and local area law enforcement agencies. Card backs are written in red and blue on white card stock. The set commemorates the 25th (Silver) Anniversary Season for the Vikings. The checklist card tells which week each card was available.

COMPLETE SET (16)	3.00	8.00
1 Checklist Card	.25	.60
2 Bud Grant CO	.50	1.25
3 Matt Blair	.25	.60
4 Alfred Anderson	.15	.40
5 Fred McNeill	.15	.40
6 Tommy Kramer	.30	.75
7 Jan Stenerud	.40	1.00
8 Sammie White	.30	.75
9 Doug Martin	.15	.40
10 Greg Coleman	.15	.40
11 Steve Riley	.15	.40
12 Walker Lee Ashley	.15	.40
13 Tim Irwin	.15	.40
14 Scott Studwell	.15	.40
15 Darrin Nelson	.25	.60
16 Mick Tingelhoff	.30	.75
(All-Time Great)		

1986 Vikings Police

This 14-card set of Minnesota Vikings is numbered on the back. Cards measure approximately 2 5/8" by 4 1/8" and the backs contain a "Crime Prevention Tip". The checklist for the set is on the back of the head coach card.

COMPLETE SET (14)	3.00	8.00
1 Jerry Burns CO	.15	.40
(Checklist back)		
2 Darrin Nelson	.25	.60
3 Tommy Kramer	.30	.75
4 Anthony Carter	.60	1.50
5 Scott Studwell	.15	.40
6 Chris Doleman	.60	1.50
7 Joey Browner	.30	.75
8 Steve Jordan	.30	.75
9 David Howard	.15	.40
10 Tim Newton	.15	.40
11 Leo Lewis	.15	.40
12 Keith Millard	.30	.75
13 Doug Martin	.15	.40
14 Bill Brown	.25	.60
(All-Time Great)		

1987 Vikings Police

This 14-card set of Minnesota Vikings is numbered on the back. Cards measure approximately 2 5/8" by 4 1/8" and are in full color on the front. The backs contain a "Crime Prevention Tip". The checklist for the set is on the back of the first card. Purple Power '87 is actually an action montage by artist Cliff Spohn. Reportedly 2.1 million cards were distributed during the 14-week promotion. The set was sponsored by the Vikings, Frito-Lay, Campbell's Soup, and KSTP-FM in cooperation with the Minnesota Crime Prevention Officers Association.

COMPLETE SET (14)	3.00	8.00
1 Vikings Theme Art	.25	.60
(checklist back)		
2 Jerry Burns CO	.25	.60
3 Scott Studwell	.15	.40
4 Tommy Kramer	.30	.75
5 Gerald Robinson	.15	.40
6 Wade Wilson	.40	1.00
7 Anthony Carter	.60	1.50
8 Terry Tausch	.15	.40
9 Leo Lewis	.15	.40
10 Keith Millard	.30	.75
11 Carl Lee	.15	.40
12 Steve Jordan	.25	.60
13 D.J. Dozier	.25	.60
14 Alan Page ATG	.60	1.50

1988 Vikings Police

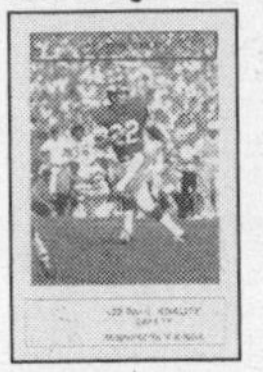

The 1988 Police Minnesota Vikings set contains 12 numbered cards measuring approximately 2 5/8" by 4 1/8". There are nine cards of current players, plus one checklist card, one "Vikings Defense" card, and one of "All-Time Great" Paul Krause.

COMPLETE SET (12)	2.50	6.00
1 Vikings Offense (Checklist on back)	.25	.60
2 Jesse Solomon	.15	.40
3 Kirk Lowdermilk	.15	.40
4 Darrin Nelson	.25	.60
5 Chris Doleman	.30	.75
6 D.J. Dozier	.25	.60
7 Gary Zimmerman	.40	1.00
8 Allen Rice	.15	.40
9 Joey Browner	.25	.60
10 Anthony Carter	.40	1.00
11 Vikings Defense	.25	.60
12 Paul Krause (All-Time Great)	.40	1.00

1989 Vikings Police

The 1989 Police Minnesota Vikings set contains ten standard-size cards. The fronts have gray borders and color action photos; the horizontally oriented backs have safety tips, bios, and career highlights. It has been reported that 175,000 cards of each player were given away by the police officers in the state of Minnesota.

COMPLETE SET (10)	2.50	6.00
1 Team Card (schedule on back)	.25	.60
2 Henry Thomas	.40	1.00
3 Rick Fenney	.15	.40
4 Chuck Nelson	.15	.40
5 Jim Gustafson	.15	.40
6 Wade Wilson	.30	.75
7 Randall McDaniel	.50	1.25
8 Jesse Solomon	.15	.40
9 Anthony Carter	.40	1.00
10 Joe Kapp (All-Time Great)	.30	.75

1989 Vikings Taystee Discs

The 1989 Taystee Minnesota Vikings set contains 12 white-bordered, approximately 2 3/4" diameter discs. The fronts have helmetless color mug shots; the backs are white and have sparse bio and stats. One disc was included in each specially-marked Taystee product, distributed only in the Minnesota area.

COMPLETE SET (12)	5.00	10.00
1 Chris Doleman	.50	1.25
2 Joey Browner	.40	1.00
3 Anthony Carter	.50	1.25
4 Steve Jordan	.30	.75
5 Scott Studwell	.30	.75
6 Wade Wilson	.40	1.00
7 Kirk Lowdermilk	.30	.75
8 Tommy Kramer	.40	1.00
9 Keith Millard	.30	.75
10 Rick Fenney	.30	.75
11 Gary Zimmerman	.40	1.00
12 Darrin Nelson	.30	.75

1990 Vikings Police

This ten-card standard-size set was issued to promote safety in the Minneapolis area by using members of the 1990 Minnesota Vikings. The card photos have posed action shots on the front along with an advertisement for Gatorade on the front and a crime prevention tip on the back. We have checklisted the cards in this set in alphabetical order.

COMPLETE SET (10)	2.00	5.00
1 Chris Doleman	.30	.75
2 Ray Berry	.14	.35
3 Mike Merriweather	.20	.50
4 Rick Fenney	.14	.35
5 Wade Wilson	.30	.75
6 Carl Lee	.14	.35
7 Hassan Jones	.20	.50
8 Scott Studwell	.14	.35
9 Anthony Carter	.40	1.00
10 Herschel Walker	.50	1.25

1991 Vikings Police

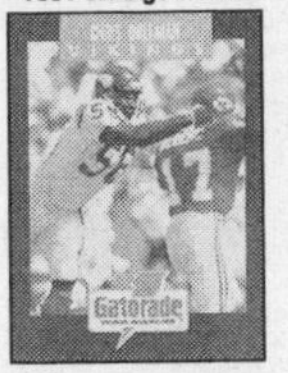

This ten-card standard-size set was sponsored by Gatorade. The cards were distributed by participating Minnesota police departments, one per week, beginning on Aug. 23 with Rick Fenney, and concluding on Oct. 27 with Chris Doleman. Card fronts display an action player photo enclosed in a purple border, while player's name is printed at the top in a gray rectangle. Gatorade's logo appears at the bottom of the picture. The first card's back lists the Vikings' game schedule. The horizontally oriented backs of the remaining cards feature a black and white close-up of the player and a biographical sketch on the left portion. Player's name, position, and jersey number appear in a black box at the top right, while the Vikadontis Rex mascot appears below. A crime prevention tip appears under the card number, while sponsor logos of Super Bowl XXVI, KFAN Sports Radio, and K102 Radio round out the back design.

COMPLETE SET (10)	2.00	5.00
1 Rick Fenney	.14	.35
2 Wade Wilson	.30	.75
3 Mike Merriweather	.20	.50
4 Hassan Jones	.14	.35
5 Rich Gannon	.40	1.00
6 Mark Dusbabek	.14	.35
7 Sean Salisbury	.20	.50
8 Reggie Rutland	.20	.50
9 Tim Irwin	.14	.35
10 Chris Doleman	.30	.75

1992 Vikings Police

This ten-card standard size set was primarily sponsored by Gatorade. The card fronts display an action color player photo framed by a purple border, while the player's name and team name appear in a gray rectangle at the top. The Gatorade logo appears at the bottom of the picture. The horizontally oriented backs carry a black-and-white close-up of the player and biographical information within a black outline box on the left side of the card. The player's name and position appear in a black bar at the top. Below are Vikadontis Rex (the team mascot), a crime prevention tip, and other sponsor logos (KFAN Sports Radio AM 1130 and K102).

COMPLETE SET (10)	2.40	6.00
1 Dennis Green CO (Schedule on back)	.20	.50
2 John Randle	.20	.50
3 Todd Scott	.14	.35
4 Anthony Carter	.30	.75
5 Steve Jordan	.20	.50
6 Terry Allen	.80	2.00
7 Brian Habib	.14	.35
8 Fuad Reveiz	.14	.35
9 Roger Craig	.20	.50
10 Cris Carter	.80	2.00

1993 Vikings Police

This ten-card standard-size set was primarily sponsored by Gatorade, and the cards feature on their fronts purple-bordered color player photos. The player's name and team name appear within a gray rectangle at the top, and the Gatorade logo is displayed at the bottom. The white and horizontal back carries a black-and-white player headshot in the upper left, with his biography shown below. His name, position, and uniform number appear in the black stripe at the top. Below are Vikadontis Rex (the team mascot), a crime prevention tip, and other sponsor logos (KFAN Sports Radio and K102).

COMPLETE SET (10)	2.00	5.00
1 Dennis Green CO (CL schedule on back)	.20	.50
2 Henry Thomas	.20	.50
3 Todd Scott	.10	.30
4 Jack Del Rio	.20	.50
5 Vencie Glenn	.10	.30
6 Fuad Reveiz	.10	.30
7 Cris Carter	.60	1.50
8 Terry Allen	.40	1.00
9 Roger Craig	.30	.75
10 Carlos Jenkins	.10	.30

1994 Vikings Police

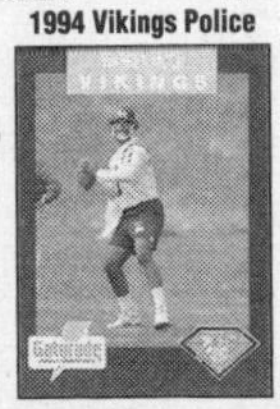

This ten-card set was primarily sponsored by Gatorade. Each standard sized card featured a purple border and full color player photos on glossy card stock. The player's and team name appear within a gray rectangle at the top of the card, and the Gatorade logo, as well as the NFL 75th team anniversary logo are positioned near the bottom corners of the card. The cardbacks contain a player bio and are numbered directly over a crime prevention tip.

COMPLETE SET (10)	2.00	5.00
1 Dennis Green CO CL	.10	.30
2 Randall McDaniel	.20	.50
3 Vencie Glenn	.10	.30
4 Jack Del Rio	.20	.50
5 Cris Carter	.50	1.25
6 Bernard Dafney	.10	.30
7 Scottie Graham	.20	.50
8 John Randle	.30	.75
9 Warren Moon	.40	1.00
10 Bud Grant CO	.30	.75

1995 Vikings Police

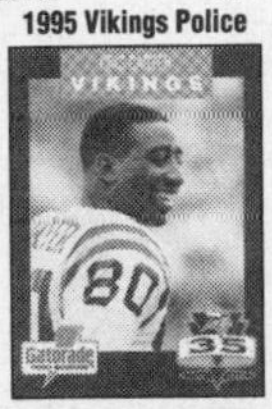

This ten-card set was primarily sponsered by Gatorade, and these standard sized cards feature on the front purple-bordered player photos. The player's and team name appear within a gray rectangle at the top of the card, and the Gatorade logo, as well as an 35th team anniversary logo are positioned at the bottom corners of the card. The white and horizontal back features a black and white headshot with the players biography below the photo. The players name, position, and number are in a black stripe on the top of the back of the card. Below are Vikadontis Rex (the team mascot), a crime prevention tip, and other sponsor logos (KFAN Sports Radio and K102) The cards are numbered on the back directly over the crime prevention tip.

COMPLETE SET (10)	2.40	6.00
1 Warren Moon CL	.40	1.00
2 Randall McDaniel	.20	.50
3 Jake Reed	.30	.75
4 Jack Del Rio	.20	.50
5 Cris Carter	.50	1.25
6 Fuad Reveiz	.10	.30
7 Amp Lee	.10	.30
8 John Randle	.30	.75
9 Andrew Jordan	.10	.30
10 DeWayne Washington	.20	.50

1996 Vikings Police

This ten-card set was primarily sponsered by EF Johnson. The standard-sized cards feature a purple and yellow border with full-color player photos on the fronts The player's name and team logo appear at the top of the card. The horizontal back features a black and white headshot with the player's biography below the photo. The cards are numbered on the back directly over a crime prevention tip.

COMPLETE SET (10)	2.00	5.00
1 Randall McDaniel	.20	.50
2 Qadry Ismail	.20	.50
3 Andrew Jordan	.10	.30
4 Cris Carter	.50	1.25
5 Vikadontis Rex Mascot	.10	.30
6 Jake Reed	.30	.75
7 Ed McDaniel	.10	.30
8 Mike Morris	.10	.30
9 Dixon Edwards	.10	.30
10 John Randle	.30	.75

1997 Vikings Police

This set of Vikings cards was distributed one game at a time during the 1997 NFL season. Each card was produced with a distinctive purple cardfront and sponsored by General Security Services Corp.

COMPLETE SET (8)	2.40	6.00
1 Cris Carter Jake Reed	.60	1.50
2 Robert Smith	.40	1.00
3 Jeff Brady	.30	.75
4 Brad Johnson	.60	1.50
5 Robert Griffith	.30	.75
6 Randall McDaniel	.30	.75
7 Leroy Hoard	.30	.75
8 John Randle	.40	1.00

1998 Vikings Pizza Hut

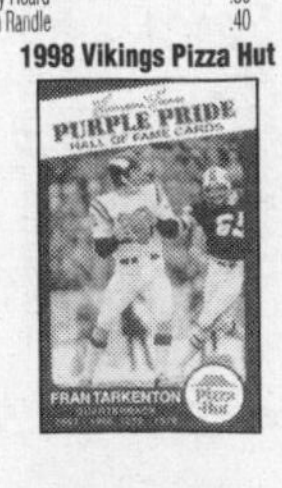

This set of unnumbered cards was distributed through participating Pizza Hut stores during the 1998 NFL season. Each card was printed on light plastic coated stock, featured rounded corners, and measured roughly 2 1/8" by 3 3/8".

COMPLETE SET (3)	10.00	18.00
1 Bud Grant CO	2.00	5.00
2 Paul Krause	2.00	5.00
3 Fran Tarkenton	3.00	8.00

1998 Vikings Police

This set of Vikings cards was sponsored by GSSC and produced with a yellow border and color player photo on the cardfronts. Each card measures standard size.

COMPLETE SET (8)	2.40	6.00
1 Brad Johnson	.60	1.50
2 Todd Steussie	.30	.75
3 Dwayne Rudd	.30	.75
4 Cris Carter	.60	1.50
5 Randall Cunningham	.60	1.50
6 Stalin Colinet	.30	.75
7 Robert Smith	.40	1.00
8 John Randle	.40	1.00

1999 Vikings Burger King

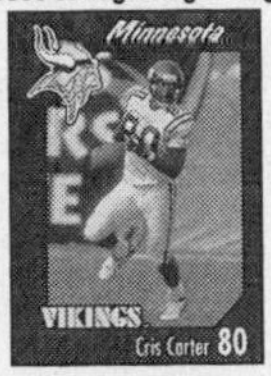

This set was sponsored and distributed by Burger King stores in the Minneapolis area during the 1999 NFL season. The cards were distributed in 4-card packs over 9-weeks of the season. Each pack contained three-player cards and one coupon/checklist card. Each card features a full-color front and back player photo with a purple border.

COMPLETE SET (36)	4.80	12.00
1 Cris Carter	.60	1.50
2 Stalin Colinet	.08	.25
3 Tony Williams DT	.08	.25
4 Gary Anderson K	.08	.25
5 Mike Morris	.08	.25
6 Randall McDaniel	.15	.40
7 Randall Cunningham	.50	1.25
8 Matthew Hatchette	.08	.25
9 Mitch Berger	.08	.25
10 Ed McDaniel	.08	.25
11 David Palmer	.15	.40
12 Kailee Wong	.08	.25
13 Randy Moss	1.60	4.00
14 Todd Steussie	.08	.25
15 Jeff Christy	.08	.25
16 John Randle	.30	.75
17 Jimmy Hitchcock	.08	.25
18 Chris Walsh	.08	.25
19 Jake Reed	.08	.25
20 Andrew Glover	.08	.25
21 Orlando Thomas	.08	.25
22 Dwayne Rudd	.08	.25
23 Leroy Hoard	.08	.25
24 Korey Stringer	.08	.25
25 Robert Smith	.30	.75
26 Daunte Culpepper	1.60	4.00
27 Robert Griffith	.08	.25
CL1 Checklist Week 1	.08	.25
CL2 Checklist Week 2	.08	.25
CL3 Checklist Week 3	.08	.25
CL4 Checklist Week 4	.08	.25
CL5 Checklist Week 5	.08	.25
CL6 Checklist Week 6	.08	.25
CL7 Checklist Week 7	.08	.25
CL8 Checklist Week 8	.08	.25
CL9 Checklist Week 9	.08	.25

1999 Vikings Police

This set of Vikings cards was produced with a purple border and color player photo on the cardfronts. Randy Moss was included for the first time in the, now traditional, Vikings Police issue. Each card measures standard size.

COMPLETE SET (8)	3.20	8.00
1 Randall Cunningham	.50	1.25
2 Cris Carter	.60	1.50
3 John Randle	.40	1.00
4 Randy Moss	1.60	4.00
5 Jeff Christy	.20	.50
6 Robert Smith	.40	1.00
7 Gary Anderson K	.20	.50
8 Robert Griffith	.20	.50

2000 Vikings Police

This set was sponsered by Card Connection, the American Society for Industrial Security and the MCPA. Each measures roughly 2 5/8" by 3 5/8." The Vikings 40th team anniversary logo is positioned at the upper right hand corner of the card. The cardbacks feature a crime prevention tip along with a black and white player photo. The cards are numbered by the crime prevention tip on the backs.

COMPLETE SET (9)	3.00	8.00
1 Daunte Culpepper	1.00	2.50
2 Mitch Berger	.20	.50
3 Robert Smith	.40	1.00
4 Randy Moss	1.25	3.00
5 John Randle	.40	1.00
6 Ed McDaniel	.20	.50
7 Dwayne Rudd	.20	.50
8 Cris Carter	.60	1.50
NNO Cover Card Fran Tarkenton Randy Moss	.60	1.50

2001 Vikings Police

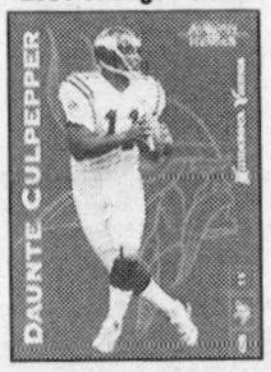

This set of Vikings cards was produced in standard card size with the typical color player photo on the cardfronts. The set featured the title "Autumn Heroes" at the top of the cards. This marked the 19th consecutive year for a Vikings Police-sponsored card set.

COMPLETE SET (10)	3.00	8.00
1 Kailee Wong	.20	.50
2 Mitch Berger	.20	.50
3 Cris Carter	.60	1.50
4 Robert Griffith	.20	.50
5 Randy Moss	1.25	3.00
6 Michael Bennett	.75	2.00
7 Matt Birk	.20	.50
8 Daunte Culpepper	.75	2.00
9 Jake Reed	.40	1.00
NNO Cover Card Daunte Culpepper	.40	1.00

2001 Vikings Upper Deck

This set was given away to the first 50,000 fans who attended the August 16, 2001 Vikings game. Each card includes a color photo player on front with the Upper Deck logo and a typical cardback.

COMPLETE SET (12)	4.00	10.00
1 Cris Carter	.50	1.25
2 Daunte Culpepper	.60	1.50
3 Randy Moss	1.00	2.50
4 Michael Bennett	1.00	2.50
5 Gary Anderson	.20	.50
6 Robert Griffith	.20	.50
7 Talance Sawyer	.20	.50
8 Lance Johnstone	.20	.50
9 Eric Kelly	.20	.50
10 Matt Birk	.20	.50
11 Todd Bouman	.30	.75
12 Mick Tingelhoff	.30	.75

2002 Vikings Police

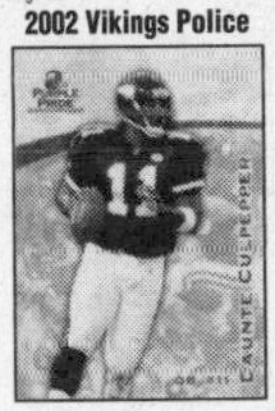

This set of Vikings cards was produced in standard card size with the typical color player photo on the cardfronts. The set featured the "Purple Pride" Vikings logo at the top of the cards. The cards are numbered by the safety tip on the back beginning with card #9.

COMPLETE SET (8)	4.00	8.00
9 Michael Bennett	.75	2.00
10 Mike Tice CO	.40	1.00
11 Chris Hovan	.50	1.25
12 Daunte Culpepper	1.00	2.50
13 Randy Moss	1.25	3.00
14 Matt Birk	.40	1.00
15 Jim Kleinsasser	.50	1.25
16 Byron Chamberlain	.50	1.25

2002 Vikings Score

This six-card set was given away at a Vikings home game during the 2002 season. Each card follows the design of the 200 Score set, but has been re-numbered 1-6. An additional Carl Eller card sponsored by US Link was issued at a later date.

COMPLETE SET (6)	3.00	8.00
1 Chris Hovan	.50	1.25
2 Moe Williams	.50	1.25
3 Michael Bennett	.75	2.00
4 Daunte Culpepper	1.00	2.50
5 Jim Kleinsasser	.50	1.25
6 Matt Birk	.40	1.00
CE Carl Eller	.75	2.00

2005 Vikings Activa Medallions

COMPLETE SET (22)	30.00	60.00
1 Fran Tarkenton	1.50	4.00
2 Alan Page	1.25	3.00
3 Scott Studwell	1.25	3.00
4 Carl Eller	1.25	3.00
5 Bill Brown	1.25	3.00
6 Cris Carter	1.50	4.00
7 Bud Grant	1.25	3.00
8 Chris Doleman	1.25	3.00
9 Mick Tingelhoff	1.25	3.00
10 Chuck Forman	1.25	3.00
11 Steve Jordan	1.25	3.00
12 Paul Krause	1.25	3.00
13 Carl Lee	1.25	3.00
14 45th Anniversary Logo	1.00	2.50
15 Randall McDaniel	1.25	3.00
16 Matt Blair	1.25	3.00
17 John Randle	1.25	3.00
18 Ahmad Rashad	1.25	3.00
19 Joey Browner	1.25	3.00
20 Ron Yary	1.25	3.00
21 Jerry Burns	1.25	3.00
22 Jim Marshall	1.25	3.00

2006 Vikings Topps

COMPLETE SET (12)	3.00	5.00
MIN1 Travis Taylor	.20	.50
MIN2 Troy Williamson	.20	.50
MIN3 Mewelde Moore	.20	.50
MIN4 Marcus Robinson	.20	.50
MIN5 Fred Smoot	.20	.50
MIN6 Darren Sharper	.25	.60
MIN7 Koren Robinson	.20	.50
MIN8 Chester Taylor	.25	.60
MIN9 Brad Johnson	.25	.60
MIN10 Erasmus James	.20	.50
MIN11 Chad Greenway	.30	.75
MIN12 Steve Hutchinson	.25	.60

2007 Vikings Topps

COMPLETE SET (12)	4.00	10.00
1 Chester Taylor	.20	.50
2 Tarvaris Jackson	.20	.50
3 Troy Williamson	.20	.50
4 Mewelde Moore	.20	.50
5 Adrian Peterson	1.50	4.00
6 Antoine Winfield	.20	.50
7 Steve Hutchinson	.25	.60
8 Darren Sharper	.25	.60
9 Kevin Williams	.20	.50
10 E.J. Henderson	.20	.50
11 Ryan Longwell	.20	.50
12 Sidney Rice	.40	1.00

2008 Vikings Topps

COMPLETE SET (12)	2.50	5.00
1 Chester Taylor	.20	.50
2 Adrian Peterson	.50	1.25
3 Tarvaris Jackson	.25	.60
4 Bernard Berrian	.25	.60
5 Sidney Rice	.30	.75
6 Bobby Wade	.20	.50
7 Kevin Williams	.20	.50
8 Pat Williams	.20	.50
9 Darren Sharper	.25	.60
10 Jared Allen	.30	.75
11 John David Booty	.30	.75
12 Tyrell Johnson	.40	1.00

1925-31 W590 Athletes

Issued over a period of years, this set (which measure approximately 1 3/8" by 2 1/2") features some of the leading athletes from the 1920's. The fronts have a photo with the players name, position and team on the bottom for the baseball players and sport and additional short bio info on the other athletes. The backs are blank and as these cards are unnumbered we have sequenced them in alphabetical order within sport. They were initally issued in strips and panels and can often be found intact. A number of the baseball players were re-issued from year-to-year with updated team information.

59 Walter Koppisch FB

1986 Waddingtons Game

This boxed set of 40 oversized (3 1/2" by 5 11/16") playing cards was produced in England and comes complete with a plastic tray and game rules. The object of the game is to play all of one's cards onto a central pattern based on typical movements in an American Football Game. The fronts feature colorful illustrations of five of the most famous teams in the NFL. Each team is portrayed on seven cards; moreover, there are five interception cards, which show merely the NFL logo. The backs of all the cards are printed in two colors of blue and have an oversized NFL logo. The cards have been checklisted below alphabetically according to teams, with the interception cards listed at the end. We've included the names of recognizable but unidentified players on the card fronts. Most of the art was apparently produced in the early 1980s based on the players featured.

COMPLETE SET (40)	50.00	80.00
1 Bears 10 Walter Payton	3.00	5.00
2 Bears 20 Walter Payton	3.00	5.00
3 Bears 40 Walter Payton	3.00	5.00
4 Bears 50 Walter Payton	3.00	5.00
5 Bears First Down Walter Payton	3.00	5.00
6 Bears Punt Walter Payton	3.00	5.00
7 Bears Touchdown Walter Payton	3.00	5.00
8 Cowboys 10 Danny White Tony Dorsett	.50	1.25
9 Cowboys 20 Danny White Tony Dorsett	.50	1.25
10 Cowboys 40 Danny White Tony Dorsett	.50	1.25
11 Cowboys 50 Danny White Tony Dorsett	.50	1.25
12 Cowboys First Down Danny White Tony Dorsett	.50	1.25
13 Cowboys Punt Danny White Tony Dorsett	.50	1.25
14 Cowboys Touchdown Danny White Tony Dorsett	.50	1.25
15 Dolphins 10 Lorenzo Hampton Eric Laakso	.30	.75
16 Dolphins 20 Lorenzo Hampton Eric Laakso	.30	.75
17 Dolphins 40 Lorenzo Hampton Eric Laakso	.30	.75
18 Dolphins 50 Lorenzo Hampton Eric Laakso	.30	.75
19 Dolphins First Down Lorenzo Hampton Eric Laakso	.30	.75
20 Dolphins Punt Lorenzo Hampton Eric Laakso	.30	.75
21 Dolphins Touchdown Lorenzo Hampton Eric Laakso	.30	.75
22 Redskins 10 John Riggins Joe Theismann	.50	1.25
23 Redskins 20 John Riggins Joe Theismann	.50	1.25
24 Redskins 40 John Riggins Joe Theismann	.50	1.25
25 Redskins 50 John Riggins Joe Theismann	.50	1.25
26 Redskins First Down John Riggins Joe Theismann	.50	1.25
27 Redskins Punt John Riggins Joe Theismann	.50	1.25
28 Redskins Touchdown John Riggins Joe Theismann	.50	1.25
29 Steelers 10 Terry Bradshaw Lynn Swann	1.25	2.50
30 Steelers 20 Terry Bradshaw Lynn Swann	1.25	2.50
31 Steelers 40 Terry Bradshaw Lynn Swann	1.25	2.50
32 Steelers 50 Terry Bradshaw Lynn Swann	1.25	2.50
33 Steelers First Down Terry Bradshaw Lynn Swann	1.25	2.50
34 Steelers Punt Terry Bradshaw Lynn Swann	1.25	2.50
35 Steelers Touchdown Terry Bradshaw Lynn Swann	1.25	2.50
36 Interception Card	.30	.75
37 Interception Card	.30	.75
38 Interception Card	.30	.75
39 Interception Card	.30	.75
40 Interception Card	.30	.75

1988 Wagon Wheel

This attractive set of eight large cards was issued in the United Kingdom by Burtons as an insert in a box of Chocolate Biscuits (cookies). Players in the set are recognizable but not explicitly identified on the card. The theme of the set is the explanation of American football to the British. The cards measure approximately 6 5/16" by 4 5/16" and are unnumbered. The card backs provide information on related mail order products available until May 31, 1988.

COMPLETE SET (8)	40.00	100.00
1 Defensive Back (Todd Bowles covering Mark Bavaro	5.00	10.00
2 Defensive Lineman (Ed Too Tall Jones and Neil Lomax)	6.00	12.00
3 Kicker (Kevin Butler)	3.00	8.00
4 Linebacker (Bob Brudzinski)	3.00	8.00
5 Offensive Lineman (Keith Van Horne leading Walter Payton)	20.00	50.00
6 Quarterback (John Elway)	15.00	40.00
7 Receiver (Steve Largent between Vann McElroy and Mike Haynes)	8.00	20.00
8 Running Back (Frank Pollard of the Steelers)	5.00	12.00

1988 Walter Payton Commemorative

Each of the 132 standard-size cards in this set pictures and features Walter Payton in some aspect of his great career. Cards listed below are generally listed by the title on the card back. Each set was packaged inside its own numbered (of 16,726) dark blue plastic box. Card fronts carry the NFL logo in the upper left corner and the Bears logo in the lower right corner. The set was issued in conjunction with a soft-cover book, "Sweetness".

COMP. FACT SET (132)	16.00	40.00
COMMON CARD (1-132)	.20	.50
1 Leading Scorer in NCAA History	.40	1.00
89 Ditka On Payton	.60	1.50
132 Last Few Moments	.40	1.00

1935 Wheaties All-Americans of 1934

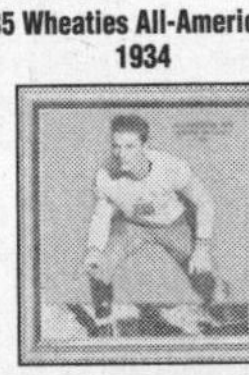

This set of cards is very similar to the 1934 Fancy Frames issue and is often referred to as "Wheaties FB2." They are differentiated by the printed "All American...1934" title line. Each features a blue and white photo of the player surrounded by a blue frame" border design which is often referred to as "fancy frames." The cardbacks are blank and each measures roughly 6" by 6 1/4" when cut around the frame border. The George Barclay and William Shepherd cards are thought to be the toughest to find.

COMPLETE SET (12)	1,500.00	2,500.00
1 George Barclay	100.00	175.00
2 Charles Hartwig	100.00	175.00
3 Dixie Howell	175.00	300.00
4 Don Hutson	350.00	600.00
5 Stan Kostka	100.00	175.00
6 Frank Larson	100.00	175.00
7 Bill Lee	100.00	175.00
8 George Maddox	100.00	175.00
9 Regis Monahan	100.00	175.00
10 John J. Robinson	100.00	175.00
11 William Shepherd	100.00	175.00
12 Cotton Warburton	100.00	175.00

1935 Wheaties Fancy Frames

Cards from this set could be cut from boxes of Wheaties cereals in the 1930s and are commonly found mis-cut. Each features a blue and white photo of a famous player or coach surrounded by a blue frame border design. The cards are often called "Wheaties FB1" as well as "Fancy Frames." In appearance they are very similar to the 1935 All-Americans issue, except for the player's name written in script on the cardfront. The cardbacks are blank and each measures roughly 6" by 6 1/4" when cut around the frame border. The Benny Friedman and Pop Warner cards are thought to be slightly tougher to find.

COMPLETE SET (8)	1,500.00	2,200.00
1 Jack Armstrong	75.00	150.00
(fictitious player)		
2 Chris Cagle	100.00	175.00
3 Benny Friedman	175.00	300.00
4 Red Grange	500.00	800.00
5 Howard Jones CO	100.00	175.00
6 Harry Kipke	100.00	175.00
7 Ernie Nevers	250.00	400.00
8 Pop Warner CO	175.00	300.00

1936 Wheaties All-Americans of 1935

This set is often referred to as "Wheaties FB3" or the "All American of 1935" set due to that title line appearing on the cardfronts. As was the case with most Wheaties cards, the fronts were printed in blue and white on an orange background. Bernie Bierman is thought to be tougher to find than the rest.

COMPLETE SET (12)	1,800.00	2,800.00
1 Sheldon Beise	150.00	250.00
2 Bernie Bierman SP	175.00	300.00
3 Darrell Lester	150.00	250.00
4 Eddie Michaels	150.00	250.00
5 Wayne Millner	250.00	400.00
6 Monk Moscrip	150.00	250.00
7 Andy Pilney	150.00	250.00
8 Dick Smith	150.00	250.00
9 Riley Smith	150.00	250.00
10 Truman Spain	150.00	250.00
11 Charles Wasicek	150.00	250.00
12 Bobby Wilson	150.00	250.00

1936 Wheaties Coaches

These cards are actually advertising panels cut from the backs of Wheaties cereal boxes. Unlike many of the other Wheaties cards from the era, they do not offer instructions on how or where to cut the cards from the boxes. Each includes a famous coach's picture along with a short quote and measures roughly 6" by 8 1/4" when cut cleanly. The Harry Stuhldreher is thought to be the toughest panel to find.

COMPLETE SET (7)	600.00	1,200.00
1 Bernie Bierman	100.00	175.00
2 Jim Crowley	125.00	200.00
3 Red Dawson	100.00	175.00
4 Andy Kerr	100.00	175.00
5 Bo McMillin	100.00	175.00
6 Harry Stuhldreher	150.00	250.00
7 Lynn Waldorf	100.00	175.00

1936 Wheaties Six-Man

Famous coaches are featured on this set of Wheaties box panels discussing the unique rules and strategy involved with 6-man football. Each measures roughly 6" by 8 1/4" when cut from the box and was printed with the familiar blue and orange color scheme. The Red Dawson and Ossie Solem cards are thought to be the toughest to find.

COMPLETE SET (6)	800.00	1,200.00
1 Bernie Bierman	150.00	250.00
2 Red Dawson	125.00	200.00
3 Tiny Hollingsberry	125.00	200.00
4 Andy Kerr	125.00	200.00
5 Ossie Solem	125.00	200.00
6 Tiny Thornhill	150.00	250.00

1937 Wheaties Big Ten Football

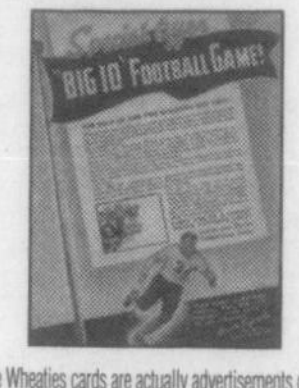

These Wheaties cards are actually advertisements cut from the backs of Wheaties cereal boxes. Each features a popular pro football player touting the "Big Ten Football Game" offered for sale on the box back. There was also a football field game board as part of the set that could be used to play a form of game with a football radio broadcast. The cards were printed in blue, white, and orange and each measures roughly 6" by 8 1/4" when cut cleanly from the box.

COMPLETE SET (5)	1,200.00	1,800.00
1 Ed Danowski	125.00	200.00
2 Arnie Herber	175.00	300.00
3 Ralph Kercheval	125.00	200.00
4 Ed Manske	125.00	200.00
5 Bronko Nagurski	600.00	1,000.00
6 Football Game Board	175.00	300.00

1940 Wheaties M4

This set is referred to as the "Champs in the USA" The cards measure about 6" 8 1'4" and are numbered. The drawing portion (inside the dotted lines) measures approximately 6" X 6". There is a Baseball player on each card and they are joined by football players, football coaches, race car drivers, airline pilots, a circus clown, ice skater, hockey star and golfers. Each athlete appears in what looks like a stamp with a serrated edge. The stamps appear one above the other with a brief block of copy describing his or her achievements. There appears to have been three printings, resulting in some variation panels. The full panels tell the cereal buyer to look for either 27, 39, or 63 champ stamps. The first nine panels apparently were printed more than once, since all the unknown variations occur with those numbers.

COMPLETE SET (20)	400.00	800.00
3 Jimmie Foxx	35.00	60.00
Bernie Bierman		
Bill Dickey		
4 Morris Arnovich	15.00	25.00
Earl Dutch Clark		
Capt R.L. Baker		
5 Joe Medwick	15.00	25.00
Matty Bell		
Ab Jenkins		
6A John Mize	15.00	25.00
Davey O'Brien		
Ralph Guldahl		
(27 stamp series)		
6C Gabby Hartnett	15.00	25.00
Davey O'Brien		
Ralph Guldahl		
(unknown series)		
7A Joe Cronin	15.00	25.00
Cecil Isbell		
Byron Nelson		
(27 stamp series)		
7C Paul Derringer	15.00	25.00
Cecil Isbell		
Byron Nelson		
(unknown series)		
8A Jack Manders	15.00	25.00
Ernie Lombardi		
George I. Myers		
(27 stamp series)		
10 Adele Inge	15.00	25.00
Lowell Red Dawson		
Billy Herman		
11 Dolph Camilli	15.00	25.00
Antoinette Concello		
Wallace Wade		

1941 Wheaties M5

This set is also referred to as "Champs of the U.S.A." These numbered cards made up the back of the Wheaties box; the whole panel measures 6" X 8 1/4" but the drawing portion (inside the dotted lines) is apparently 6" X 6". Each athlete appears in what looks like a stamp with a serrated edge. The stamps appear one above the other with a brief block of copy describing his or her achievements. The format is the same as the previous M4 set -- even the numbering system continues where the M4 set stops.

COMPLETE SET (8)	175.00	350.00
15 Bernie Bierman	20.00	40.00
Bob Feller		
Jessie McLeod		
16 Hank Greenberg	20.00	40.00
Lowell Red Dawson		
J.W. Stoker		

1951 Wheaties

The cards in this six-card set measure approximately 2 1/2" by 3 1/4". Cards of the 1951 Wheaties set are actually the backs of small individual boxes of Wheaties. The cards are waxed and depict three baseball players, one football player, one basketball player, and one golfer. They are occasionally found as complete boxes, which are worth 50 percent more than the prices listed below. The catalog designation for this set is F272-3. The cards are blank-backed and unnumbered; they are numbered below in alphabetical order for convenience.

COMPLETE SET (6)	300.00	600.00
2 Johnny Lujack FB	40.00	80.00

1952 Wheaties

The cards in this 60-card set measure 2" by 2 3/4". The 1952 Wheaties set of orange, blue and white, unnumbered cards was issued in panels of eight or ten cards on the backs of Wheaties cereal boxes. Each player appears in an action pose, designated in the checklist with an "A", and as a portrait, listed in the checklist with a "B". The catalog designation is F272-4. The cards are blank-backed and unnumbered, but have been assigned numbers below using a sport prefix (BB- baseball, BK- basketball, FB- football, G-Golf, OT- other).

COMPLETE SET (60)	600.00	1,000.00
FB1A Glenn Davis	4.00	8.00
FB1B Glenn Davis	4.00	8.00
FB2A Tom Fears	4.00	8.00
FB2B Tom Fears	4.00	8.00
FB3A Otto Graham	10.00	20.00
FB3B Otto Graham	10.00	20.00
FB4A Johnny Lujack	4.00	8.00
FB4B Johnny Lujack	4.00	8.00
FB5A Doak Walker	7.50	15.00
FB5B Doak Walker	7.50	15.00
FB6A Bob Waterfield	12.50	25.00
FB6B Bob Waterfield	12.50	25.00

1964 Wheaties Stamps

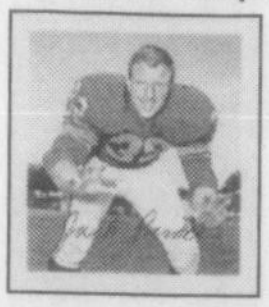

This set of 74 stamps was issued perforated within a 48-page album. There were 70 players and four team logo stamps bound into the album as six pages of 12 stamps each plus two stamps attached to the inside front cover. In fact, they are typically found this way, still bound into the album. The stamps measure approximately 2 1/2" by 2 3/4" and are unnumbered. The album itself measures approximately 8 1/8" by 11" and is entitled "Pro Bowl Football Player Stamp Album". The stamp list below has been alphabetized for convenience. Each player stamp has a facsimile autograph on the front. Note that there are no spaces in the album for Joe Schmidt, Y.A.Tittle, or the four team emblem stamps.

COMPLETE SET (74)	175.00	300.00
1 Herb Adderley	5.00	10.00
2 Grady Alderman	1.50	3.00
3 Doug Atkins	4.00	8.00
4 Sam Baker	1.50	3.00
(In Cowboys' uniform)		
5 Erich Barnes	1.50	3.00
(In Bears' jersey)		
6 Terry Barr	1.50	3.00
7 Dick Bass	2.00	4.00
8 Maxie Baughan	1.50	3.00
9 Raymond Berry	5.00	10.00
10 Charley Bradshaw	1.50	3.00
(In Rams' jersey)		
11 Jim Brown	20.00	40.00
12 Roger Brown	1.50	3.00
13 Timmy Brown	2.00	4.00
14 Gail Cogdill	1.50	3.00
15 Tommy Davis	1.50	3.00
16 Willie Davis	5.00	10.00
17 Bob DeMarco	1.50	3.00
18 Darrell Dess	1.50	3.00
19 Buddy Dial	1.50	3.00
(In Steelers' jersey)		
20 Mike Ditka	10.00	20.00
21 Galen Fiss	1.50	3.00
22 Lee Folkins	1.50	3.00
23 Joe Fortunato	1.50	3.00
24 Bill Glass	1.50	3.00
25 John Gordy	1.50	3.00
26 Ken Gray	1.50	3.00
27 Forrest Gregg	4.00	8.00
28 Rip Hawkins	1.50	3.00
29 Charley Johnson	2.00	4.00
30 John Henry Johnson	4.00	8.00
31 Hank Jordan	4.00	8.00
32 Jim Katcavage	1.50	3.00
33 Jerry Kramer	4.00	8.00
34 Joe Krupa	1.50	3.00
35 John LoVetere	1.50	3.00
(In Rams' jersey)		
36 Dick Lynch	1.50	3.00
37 Gino Marchetti	4.00	8.00
38 Joe Marconi	1.50	3.00
39 Tommy Mason	2.00	4.00
40 Dale Meinert	1.50	3.00
41 Lou Michaels	2.00	4.00
42 Minnesota Vikings	1.50	3.00
Emblem		
43 Bobby Mitchell	4.00	8.00
44 John Morrow	1.50	3.00
45 New York Giants	1.50	3.00
Emblem		
46 Merlin Olsen	6.00	12.00
47 Jack Pardee	2.00	4.00
48 Jim Parker	3.00	6.00
49 Bernie Parrish	1.50	3.00
50 Don Perkins	3.00	6.00
51 Richie Petitbon	1.50	3.00
52 Vince Promuto	1.50	3.00
53 Myron Pottios	1.50	3.00
54 Mike Pyle	1.50	3.00
55 Pete Retzlaff	2.00	4.00
56 Jim Ringo	4.00	8.00
(In Packers' jersey)		
57 Joe Rutgens	1.50	3.00
58 St. Louis Cardinals	1.50	3.00
Emblem		
59 San Francisco 49ers	1.50	3.00
Emblem		
60 Dick Schafrath	1.50	3.00
61 Joe Schmidt	4.00	8.00
62 Del Shofner	2.00	4.00
63 Norm Snead	2.00	4.00
64 Bart Starr	18.00	30.00
65 Jim Taylor	10.00	20.00
66 Roosevelt Taylor	2.00	4.00
67 Clendon Thomas	1.50	3.00
(In Rams' jersey)		
68 Y.A. Tittle	7.50	15.00
(In 49ers' jersey)		
69 Johnny Unitas	20.00	35.00
70 Bill Wade	2.00	4.00
71 Wayne Walker	1.50	3.00
72 Jesse Whittenton	1.50	3.00
73 Larry Wilson	3.00	6.00
74 Abe Woodson	1.50	3.00
NNO Stamp Album	10.00	20.00

1987 Wheaties Mini Posters

This set was distributed one per box in specially marked packages of Wheaties cereal in 1987. Each mini poster (measuring roughly 5" by 7") came folded inside a thin cellophane wrapper. Individual player information and statistics are printed in black and white on the card backs. The cards are numbered on the back in the upper left corner. This project was organized by Mike Schechter Associates and produced by Starline Inc. in conjunction with the NFL Players Association. Bernie Kosar and Lawrence Taylor are difficult to find and were not listed in the set the checklist Wheaties provided on the cereal box.

COMPLETE SET (26)	60.00	150.00
1 Tony Dorsett	5.00	12.00
2 Herschel Walker	1.25	3.00
3 Marcus Allen	5.00	12.00
4 Eric Dickerson	1.50	4.00
5 Walter Payton	15.00	25.00
6 Phil Simms	2.00	5.00
7 Tommy Kramer	1.00	2.50
8 Joe Morris	1.00	2.50
9 Roger Craig	2.00	5.00
10 Curt Warner	1.25	3.00
11 Andre Tippett	1.25	3.00
12 Joe Montana	15.00	25.00
13 Jim McMahon	2.00	5.00
14 Bernie Kosar SP	7.50	15.00
15 Jay Schroeder	1.00	2.50
16 Al Toon	1.00	2.50
17 Mark Gastineau	1.00	2.50
18 Kenny Easley	1.00	2.50
19 Howie Long	4.00	10.00
20 Dan Marino	15.00	25.00
21 Karl Mecklenburg	1.00	2.50
22 John Elway	15.00	25.00
23 Boomer Esiason	1.50	4.00
24 Dan Fouts	2.00	5.00
25 Jim Kelly	7.50	15.00
26 Louis Lipps	1.00	2.50
27 Lawrence Taylor SP	20.00	40.00

1991 Wild Card NFL Prototypes

This six-card Wild Card Prototype set measures the standard-size. The front design features glossy color action player photos, on a black card face with yellow highlighting around the picture and different color numbers appearing in the top and right borders. A football icon with the words "NFL Premier Edition" overlays the lower left corner of the picture. The backs shade from black to yellow and have a color headshot, biography, and statistics for the last three years. The cards are numbered in the upper right corner.

COMPLETE SET (6)	2.40	6.00
1 Troy Aikman	.40	1.00
2 Barry Sanders	.80	2.00
3 Thurman Thomas	.20	.50
4 Emmitt Smith	1.00	2.50
5 Jerry Rice	.40	1.00
6 Lawrence Taylor	.20	.50

1991 Wild Card

The Wild Card NFL contains 160 standard-size cards. Reportedly, production quantities were limited to 30,000 numbered ten-box cases. The series included three bonus cards (Wild Card Case Card, Wild Card Box Card, and Wild Card Hot Card) that were redeemable for the item pictured. Surprise wild card number 126 could be exchanged for a ten-card NFL Experience set, featuring five players each from the Washington Redskins and the Buffalo Bills. This set resembles that given away at the Super Bowl Show, except that the cards bear no date. The secondary market value of the striped cards did not prove to be as strong as Wild Card anticipated. Rookie Cards in this set include Ricky Ervins, Alvin Harper, Randal Hill, Michael Jackson, Herman Moore, Neil O'Donnell, Mike Pritchard, and Leonard Russell.

COMPLETE SET (160)	2.50	6.00
*5 STRIPES: 1.2X TO 3X BASIC CARDS		
*10 STRIPES: 2X TO 5X		
*20 STRIPES: 3X TO 8X		
*50 STRIPES: 6X TO 15X		
*100 STRIPE: 15X TO 40X		
*1000 STRIPE: 50X TO 120X		
1 Jeff George	.02	.10
2 Sean Jones	.02	.10
3 Duane Bickett	.01	.05
4 John Elway	.40	1.00
5 Christian Okoye	.02	.10
6 Steve Atwater	.01	.05
7 Anthony Munoz	.02	.10
8 Dave Krieg	.02	.10
9 Nick Lowery	.01	.05
10 Albert Bentley	.01	.05
11 Mark Jackson	.01	.05
12 Jeff Bryant	.01	.05
13 Johnny Hector	.01	.05
14 John L. Williams	.01	.05
15 Jim Everett	.02	.10
16 Mark Duper	.02	.10
17 Drew Hill UER	.02	.10
(Reversed negative		
on card front)		
18 Randal Hill RC	.02	.10
19 Ernest Givins	.02	.10
20 Ken O'Brien	.01	.05
21 Blair Thomas UER	.02	.10
(Says he caught 204		
passes in 1990)		
22 Derrick Thomas	.07	.20
23 Harvey Williams RC	.02	.10
24 Simon Fletcher	.01	.05
25 Stephone Paige	.01	.05
26 Barry Word	.01	.05
27 Warren Moon	.02	.10
28 Derrick Fenner	.01	.05
29 Shane Conlan	.01	.05
30 Karl Mecklenburg	.01	.05
31 Gary Anderson RB	.01	.05
32 Sammie Smith	.01	.05
33 Steve DeBerg	.02	.10
34 Dan McGwire RC UER	.01	.05
(TD stats say 29,		
should be 27)		
35 Roger Craig	.02	.10
36 Tom Tupa	.01	.05
37 Rod Woodson	.07	.20
38 Junior Seau	.07	.20
39 Bruce Pickens RC	.01	.05
40 Greg Townsend	.01	.05
41 Gary Clark	.02	.10
42 Broderick Thomas	.01	.05
43 Charles Mann	.02	.10
44 Browning Nagle RC	.01	.05
45 James Joseph RC	.02	.10
46 Emmitt Smith UER	.75	2.00
47 Cornelius Bennett	.02	.10
48 Maurice Hurst	.01	.05
49 Art Monk	.02	.10
50 Louis Lipps	.02	.10
51 Mark Rypien	.02	.10
52 Bubby Brister	.02	.10
53 John Stephens	.01	.05
54 Merril Hoge	.01	.05
55 Kevin Mack	.01	.05
56 Al Toon	.02	.10
57 Ronnie Lott	.02	.10
58 Eric Metcalf	.02	.10
59 Vinny Testaverde	.02	.10
60 Darrell Green	.01	.05
61 Randall Cunningham	.07	.20
62 Charles Haley	.02	.10
63 Mark Carrier	.02	.10
64 Jim Harbaugh	.02	.10
65 Richard Dent	.02	.10
66 Stan Thomas	.01	.05
67 Neal Anderson	.02	.10
68 Troy Aikman	.20	.50
69 Mike Pritchard RC	.02	.10
70 Deion Sanders	.10	.30
71 Andre Rison	.02	.10
72 Keith Millard	.01	.05
73 Jerry Rice	.20	.50
74 Johnny Johnson	.01	.05
75 Tim McDonald	.01	.05
76 Leonard Russell RC	.02	.10
77 Keith Jackson	.02	.10
78 Keith Byars	.02	.10
79 Ricky Proehl	.01	.05
80 Dexter Carter	.01	.05
81 Alvin Harper RC	.02	.10
82 Irving Fryar	.02	.10
83 Marion Butts	.02	.10
84 Alfred Williams RC	.01	.05
85 Timm Rosenbach	.01	.05
86 Steve Young	.20	.50
87 Albert Lewis	.01	.05
88 Rodney Peete	.02	.10
89 Barry Sanders	.40	1.00
90 Bennie Blades	.01	.05
91 Chris Spielman	.02	.10
92 John Friesz	.01	.05
93 Jerome Brown	.01	.05
94 Reggie White	.07	.20
95 Michael Irvin	.07	.20
96 Keith McCants	.01	.05
97 Vinnie Clark RC	.02	.10
98 Louis Oliver	.01	.05
99 Mark Clayton	.02	.10
100 John Offerdahl	.01	.05
101 Michael Carter	.01	.05
102 John Taylor	.02	.10
103 William Perry	.02	.10
104 Gill Byrd	.01	.05
105 Burt Grossman	.01	.05
106 Herman Moore RC	.07	.20
107 Howie Long	.07	.20
108 Bo Jackson	.08	.25
109 Kelvin Pritchett RC	.01	.05
110 Jacob Green	.01	.05
111 Chris Doleman	.02	.10
112 Herschel Walker	.02	.10
113 Russell Maryland RC	.02	.10
114 Anthony Carter	.02	.10
115 Joey Browner	.01	.05
116 Tony Mandarich	.01	.05
117 Don Majkowski	.01	.05
118 Ricky Ervins RC	.02	.10
119 Sterling Sharpe	.02	.10
120 Tim Harris	.01	.05
121 Hugh Millen RC	.01	.05
122 Mike Rozier	.01	.05
123 Chris Miller	.02	.10
124 Morten Andersen	.01	.05
125 Neil O'Donnell RC	.07	.20
126 Surprise Wild Card	.01	.05
(Exchangeable for		
ten-card NFL		
Experience set)		
127 Eddie Brown	.01	.05
128 James Francis	.01	.05
129 James Brooks	.01	.05
130 David Fulcher	.01	.05
131 Michael Jackson WR RC	.07	.20
132 Clay Matthews	.02	.10
133 Scott Norwood	.01	.05
134 Wesley Carroll RC	.01	.05
135 Thurman Thomas	.07	.20
136 Mark Ingram	.02	.10
137 Bobby Hebert	.02	.10
138 Bobby Wilson RC	.01	.05
139 Craig Heyward	.01	.05
140 Dalton Hilliard	.01	.05
141 Jeff Hostetler	.02	.10
142 Dave Meggett	.02	.10
143 Cris Dishman RC	.01	.05
144 Lawrence Taylor	.02	.10
145 Leonard Marshall	.01	.05
146 Pepper Johnson	.01	.05
147 Todd Marinovich RC	.01	.05
148 Mike Croel RC	.01	.05
149 Erik McMillan	.01	.05
150 Flipper Anderson	.01	.05
151 Cleveland Gary	.01	.05
152 Henry Ellard	.02	.10
153 Kevin Greene	.02	.10
154 Michael Cofer	.01	.05
155 Todd Lyght RC	.02	.10
156 Bruce Smith	.02	.10
157 Checklist 1	.01	.05
158 Checklist 2	.01	.05
159 Checklist 3	.01	.05
160 Checklist 4	.01	.05

1991 Wild Card NFL Redemption Cards

This ten-card standard-size set commemorates Super Bowl XXVI and features five players from each team. These cards were exchanged for Wild Card surprise card number 126, and thus they are numbered 126A-J. Cards 126A-126E feature Washington Redskins, whereas cards 126F-126J feature Buffalo Bills. In design, these redemption cards are identical to the 1991 Wild Card NFL Super Bowl Promos/NFL Experience set. The only detectible difference is that the Super Bowl promos have the date and location of the Super Bowl Card Show III on the back, while these redemption cards do not carry that information and are numbered differently.

COMPLETE SET (10)	1.20	3.00
126A Mark Rypien	.05	.15
126B Ricky Ervins	.05	.15
126C Darrell Green	.05	.15
126D Charles Mann	.05	.15
126E Art Monk	.08	.25
126F Thurman Thomas	.25	.60
126G Bruce Smith	.08	.25
126H Cornelius Bennett	.08	.25
126I Scott Norwood	.05	.15
126J Shane Conlan	.05	.15

1991 Wild Card NFL Super Bowl Promos

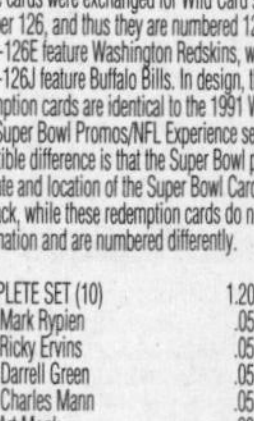

This ten-card standard-size set commemorates Super Bowl XXVI and features five players from each team. The cards were given away during the SuperBowl Card Show III by Wild Card, a corporate sponsor of the show. Prominently displayed on the card front is the "NFL Experience" logo. Cards 1-5 feature Washington Redskins, whereas cards 6-10 feature Buffalo Bills.

COMPLETE SET (10)	1.20	3.00
1 Mark Rypien	.08	.25
2 Ricky Ervins	.08	.25
3 Darrell Green	.08	.25
4 Charles Mann	.08	.25
5 Art Monk	.15	.40
6 Thurman Thomas	.40	1.00
7 Bruce Smith	.15	.40
8 Cornelius Bennett	.15	.40
9 Scott Norwood	.08	.25
10 Shane Conlan	.08	.25

1992 Wild Card NFL Prototypes

This 12-card Wild Card Prototype set features cards measuring the standard-size. The front design is the samer as the regular issue 1992 Wild Card NFL cards. The cards are numbered in the upper right corner of the reverse with a "P" prefix. The set numbering starts where the 1991 Wild Card Prototypes set left off.

COMPLETE SET (12)	2.00	5.00
P7 Barry Sanders	.60	1.50
P8 John Taylor	.07	.20
P9 John Elway	.60	1.50
P10 Erik Kramer	.07	.20
P11 Christian Okoye	.07	.20
P12 Leonard Russell	.07	.20
P13 Barry Sanders	.60	1.50
P14 Earnest Byner	.07	.20
P15 Warren Moon	.20	.50
P16 Ronnie Lott	.10	.30
P17 Michael Irvin	.20	.50
P18 Haywood Jeffires	.07	.20

1992 Wild Card

The 1992 Wild Card NFL set contains 460 standard-size cards issued in two series of 250 and 210 cards, respectively. It is reported that the first series production run was limited to 30,000 ten-box numbered foil cases. One hundred "case cards" and one thousand box cards were randomly inserted into the foil packs. Also cards from the Red Hot Rookie set were inserted in the packs. The first series is checklisted by teams. Subsets include Draft Picks (223-239) and League Leaders (240-245). Through a mail-in offer, the surprise card could be exchanged for a four-card cello pack featuring a P1 Barry Sanders (with first series Surprise Card 1) or P2 Emmitt Smith (with second series Surprise Card 251) Stat Smasher foil card, a Red Hot Rookie card, a Field Force card, and either a silver or gold Field Force card. Every jumbo pack included ten Series I cards, ten Series II cards, one Stat Smasher, one gold or silver foil Red Hot Rookie, and one gold or silver foil Running Wild. Rookie Cards include Edgar Bennett, Steve Bono, Terrell Buckley and Rob Johnson (his only Rookie Card). A Barry Sanders promo card was produced and distributed at the 1992 National Sports Collectors Convention. The card contains The National logo and was issued in striped values of 5, 10, 20, 50 and 100.

COMPLETE SET (460)	6.00	15.00
COMP.SERIES 1 (250)	2.00	5.00
COMP.SERIES 2 (210)	5.00	12.00
1 Surprise Card	.01	.05
2 Marcus Dupree	.08	.25
3 Jackie Slater	.01	.05
4 Robert Delpino	.01	.05
5 Jerry Gray	.01	.05
6 Jim Everett	.02	.10
7 Roman Phifer	.01	.05
8 Alvin Wright	.01	.05
9 Todd Lyght	.01	.05
10 Reggie White	.08	.25
11 Randal Hill	.01	.05
12 Keith Byars	.01	.05
13 Clyde Simmons	.01	.05
14 Keith Jackson	.02	.10
15 Seth Joyner	.01	.05
16 James Joseph	.01	.05
17 Eric Allen	.01	.05
18 Sammie Smith	.01	.05
19 Mark Clayton	.01	.05
20 Aaron Craver	.01	.05
21 Hugh Green	.01	.05
22 John Offerdahl	.01	.05
23 Jeff Cross	.01	.05
24 Ferrell Edmunds	.01	.05
25 Mark Duper	.01	.05
26 Ronnie Harmon	.01	.05
27 Derrick Walker	.01	.05
28 Gary Plummer	.01	.05
29 Rod Bernstine	.01	.05
30 Burt Grossman	.01	.05
31 Donnie Elder	.01	.05
32 John Friesz	.02	.10
33 Billy Ray Smith	.01	.05
34 Luis Sharpe	.01	.05
35 Aeneas Williams	.02	.10
36 Ken Harvey	.01	.05
37 Johnny Johnson UER	.01	.05
(1990 rushing stats		
are wrong)		
38 Eric Swann	.02	.10
39 Tom Tupa	.01	.05
40 Anthony Thompson	.01	.05
41 Broderick Thomas	.01	.05
42 Vinny Testaverde	.02	.10
43 Mark Carrier WR	.02	.10
44 Gary Anderson RB	.01	.05
45 Keith McCants	.01	.05
46 Reggie Cobb	.01	.05
47 Lawrence Dawsey	.01	.05
48 Kevin Murphy	.01	.05
49 Keith Woodside	.01	.05
50 Darrell Thompson	.01	.05
51 Vinnie Clark	.01	.05
52 Sterling Sharpe	.08	.25
53 Mike Tomczak	.01	.05
54A Don Majkowski ERR	.02	.10
(Listed as Dan)		
54B Don Majikowski COR	.02	.10
55 Tony Mandarich	.01	.05
56 Mark Murphy	.01	.05
57 Dexter McNabb RC	.01	.05
58 Rick Fenney	.01	.05
59 Cris Carter	.08	.25
60 Wade Wilson	.01	.05
61 Mike Merriweather	.01	.05
62 Rich Gannon	.08	.25
63 Herschel Walker	.02	.10
64 Chris Doleman	.02	.10
65 Al Noga UER	.01	.05
(On front, he's a DE;/(on back, he's a DT)		
66 Chris Mims RC	.01	.05
67 Ed Cunningham RC	.01	.05
68 Marcus Allen	.08	.25
69 Kevin Turner RC	.01	.05
70 Howie Long	.08	.25
71 Tim Brown	.08	.25
72 Nick Bell	.01	.05
73 Todd Marinovich	.01	.05
74 Jay Schroeder	.01	.05
75 Mervyn Fernandez	.01	.05
76 Tony Smith WR RC	.01	.05
77 John Alt	.01	.05
78 Christian Okoye	.01	.05
79 Nick Lowery	.01	.05
80 Derrick Thomas	.02	.10
81 Bill Maas	.01	.05
82 Dino Hackett	.01	.05
83 Deron Cherry	.01	.05
84 Barry Word	.01	.05
85 Mike Mooney RC	.01	.05
86 Cris Dishman	.01	.05
87 Bruce Matthews	.01	.05
88 Tony Jones	.01	.05
89 William Fuller	.01	.05
90 Ray Childress	.01	.05
91 Warren Moon	.08	.25
92 Lorenzo White	.01	.05
93 Joe Bowden RC	.01	.05
94 Tom Rathman	.01	.05
95 Keith Henderson	.01	.05
96 Jesse Sapolu	.01	.05
97 Charles Haley	.02	.10
98 Steve Young	.25	.60
99 John Taylor	.02	.10
100 Tim Harris	.01	.05
101 Scott Davis	.01	.05
102 Steve Bono RC	.08	.25
103 Mike Kenn	.01	.05
104 Mike Farr	.01	.05
105 Rodney Peete	.02	.10
106 Jerry Ball	.01	.05
107 Chris Spielman	.02	.10
108 Barry Sanders	.50	1.25
109 Bennie Blades	.01	.05
110 Herman Moore	.08	.25
111 Erik Kramer	.02	.10
112 Vance Johnson	.01	.05
113 Mike Croel	.01	.05
114 Mark Jackson	.01	.05
115 Steve Atwater	.01	.05
116 Gaston Green	.01	.05
117 John Elway	.50	1.25
118 Simon Fletcher	.01	.05
119 Karl Mecklenburg	.01	.05
120 Hart Lee Dykes	.01	.05
121 Jerome Henderson	.01	.05
122 Chris Singleton	.01	.05
123 Marv Cook	.01	.05
124 Leonard Russell	.01	.05
125 Hugh Millen	.01	.05
126 Pat Harlow	.01	.05
127 Andre Tippett	.01	.05
128 Bruce Armstrong	.01	.05
129 Gary Clark	.02	.10
130 Art Monk	.02	.10
131 Darrell Green	.01	.05
132 Wilber Marshall	.01	.05
133 Jim Lachey	.01	.05
134 Earnest Byner	.01	.05
135 Chip Lohmiller	.01	.05
136 Mark Rypien	.01	.05
137 Ricky Sanders	.01	.05
138 Stan Thomas	.01	.05
139 Neal Anderson	.01	.05
140 Trace Armstrong	.01	.05
141 Kevin Butler	.01	.05
142 Mark Carrier DB	.01	.05
143 Dennis Gentry	.01	.05
144 Jim Harbaugh	.02	.10
145 Richard Dent	.02	.10
146 Andre Rison	.02	.10
147 Bruce Pickens	.01	.05
148 Chris Hinton UER	.01	.05
(Dealt to Falcons in/1990, not 1989)		
149 Brian Jordan	.02	.10
150 Chris Miller	.01	.05
151 Moe Gardner	.01	.05
152 Bill Fralic	.01	.05
153 Michael Haynes	.02	.10
154 Mike Pritchard	.02	.10
155 Dean Biasucci	.01	.05
156 Clarence Verdin	.01	.05
157 Donnell Thompson	.01	.05
158 Duane Bickett	.01	.05
159 Jon Hand	.01	.05
160 Sam Graddy RC	.01	.05
161 Emmitt Smith	.60	1.50
162 Michael Irvin	.08	.25
163 Danny Noonan	.01	.05
164 Jack Del Rio	.01	.05
165 Jim Jeffcoat	.01	.05
166 Alexander Wright	.01	.05
167 Frank Minnifield	.01	.05
168 Ed King	.01	.05
169 Reggie Langhorne	.01	.05
170 Mike Baab	.01	.05
171 Eric Metcalf	.02	.10
172 Clay Matthews	.01	.05
173 Kevin Mack	.01	.05
174 Mike Johnson	.01	.05
175 Jeff Lageman	.01	.05
176 Freeman McNeil	.02	.10
177 Erik McMillan	.01	.05
178 James Hasty	.01	.05
179 Kyle Clifton	.01	.05
180 Joe Kelly	.01	.05
181 Phil Simms	.02	.10
182 Everson Walls	.01	.05
183 Jeff Hostetler	.02	.10
184 Dave Meggett	.02	.10
185 Matt Bahr	.01	.05
186 Mark Ingram	.01	.05
187 Rodney Hampton	.02	.10
188 Kanavis McGhee	.01	.05
189 Tim McGee	.01	.05
190 Eddie Brown	.01	.05
191 Rodney Holman	.01	.05
192 Harold Green	.01	.05
193 James Francis	.01	.05
194 Anthony Munoz	.02	.10
195 David Fulcher	.01	.05
196 Tim Krumrie	.01	.05
197 Bubby Brister	.02	.10
198 Rod Woodson	.08	.25
199 Louis Lipps	.01	.05
200 Carnell Lake	.01	.05

201 Don Beebe .01 .05
202 Thurman Thomas .08 .25
203 Cornelius Bennett .02 .10
204 Mark Kelso .01 .05
205 James Lofton .02 .10
206 Darryl Talley .01 .05
207 Morten Andersen .01 .05
208 Vince Buck .01 .05
209 Wesley Carroll .01 .05
210 Bobby Hebert .01 .05
211 Craig Heyward .02 .10
212 Dalton Hilliard .01 .05
213 Rickey Jackson .01 .05
214 Eric Martin .01 .05
215 Pat Swilling .01 .05
216 Steve Walsh .01 .05
217 Torrance Small RC .02 .10
218 Jacob Green .01 .05
219 Cortez Kennedy .02 .10
220 John L. Williams .01 .05
221 Terry Wooden .01 .05
222 Grant Feasel .01 .05
223 Siran Stacy RC .01 .05
224 Chris Hakel RC .01 .05
225 Todd Harrison RC .01 .05
226 Bob Whitfield RC .01 .05
227 Eddie Blake RC .01 .05
228 Keith Hamilton RC .02 .10
229 Darryl Williams RC .01 .05
230 Ricardo McDonald RC .01 .05
231 Alan Haller RC .01 .05
232 Leon Searcy RC .01 .05
233 Patrick Rowe RC .01 .05
234 Edgar Bennett RC .08 .25
235 Terrell Buckley RC .01 .05
236 Will Furrer RC .01 .05
237 Amp Lee RC UER .01 .05
(Front photo actually Edgar Bennett)
238 Jimmy Smith RC 1.00 2.50
239 Tommy Vardell RC .01 .05
240 Leonard Russell/'91 Offensive ROY .01 .05
241 Mike Croel/'91 Defensive ROY .01 .05
242 Warren Moon/'91 AFC Passing Leader.02 .10
243 Mark Rypien/'91 NFC Passing Leader.01 .05
244 Thurman Thomas/'91 AFC Rushing Leader .02 .10
245 Emmitt Smith/'91 NFC Rushing Leader.30 .75
246 Checklist 1-50 .01 .05
247 Checklist 51-100 .01 .05
248 Checklist 101-150 .01 .05
249 Checklist 151-200 .01 .05
250 Checklist 201-250 .01 .05
251 Surprise Card .01 .05
252 Erric Pegram .02 .10
253 Anthony Carter .02 .10
254 Roger Craig .02 .10
255 Hassan Jones .01 .05
256 Steve Jordan .01 .05
257 Randall McDaniel .02 .10
258 Henry Thomas .01 .05
259 Carl Lee .01 .05
260 Ray Agnew .01 .05
261 Irving Fryar .02 .10
262 Tom Waddle .01 .05
263 Greg McMurtry .01 .05
264 Stephen Baker .01 .05
265 Mark Collins .01 .05
266 Howard Cross .01 .05
267 Pepper Johnson .01 .05
268 Fred Barnett .02 .10
269 Heath Sherman .01 .05
270 William Thomas .01 .05
271 Bill Bates .02 .10
272 Issiac Holt .01 .05
273 Emmitt Smith .60 1.50
274 Eric Bieniemy .01 .05
275 Marion Butts .01 .05
276 Gill Byrd .01 .05
277 Robert Blackmon .01 .05
278 Brian Blades .02 .10
279 Joe Nash .01 .05
280 Bill Brooks .01 .05
281 Mel Gray .01 .05
282 Andre Ware .02 .10
283 Steve McMichael .01 .05
284 Brad Muster .01 .05
285 Ron Rivera .01 .05
286 Chris Zorich .02 .10
287 Chris Burkett .01 .05
288 Irv Eatman .01 .05
289 Rob Moore .02 .10
290 Joe Mott .01 .05
291 Brian Washington .01 .05
292 Michael Carter .01 .05
293 Dexter Carter .01 .05
294 Don Griffin .01 .05
295 John Taylor .02 .10
296 Ted Washington .01 .05
297 Monte Coleman .01 .05
298 Andre Collins .01 .05
299 Charles Mann .01 .05
300 Shane Conlan .01 .05
301 Keith McKeller .01 .05
302 Nate Odomes .01 .05
303 Riki Ellison .01 .05
304 Willie Gault .02 .10
305 Bob Golic .01 .05
306 Ethan Horton .01 .05
307 Ronnie Lott .02 .10
308 Don Mosebar .01 .05
309 Aaron Wallace .01 .05
310 Wymon Henderson .01 .05
311 Vance Johnson .01 .05
312 Ken Lanier .01 .05
313 Steve Sewell .01 .05
314 Dennis Smith .01 .05
315 Kenny Walker .01 .05
316 Chris Martin .01 .05
317 Albert Lewis .01 .05
318 Todd McNair .01 .05
319 Tracy Simien RC .01 .05
320 Percy Snow .01 .05
321 Mark Rypien .01 .05
322 Bryan Hinkle .01 .05
323 David Little .01 .05
324 Dwight Stone .01 .05
325 Van Waiters RC .01 .05
326 Pio Sagapolutele RC .01 .05
327 Michael Jackson .02 .10
328 Vestee Jackson .01 .05
329 Tony Paige .01 .05
330 Reggie Roby .01 .05
331 Haywood Jeffires .02 .10
332 Lamar Lathon .01 .05
333 Bubba McDowell .01 .05
334 Doug Smith .01 .05
335 Dean Steinkuhler .01 .05
336 Jessie Tuggle .01 .05
337 Freddie Joe Nunn .01 .05
338 Pat Terrell .01 .05
339 Tom McHale RC .01 .05
340 Sam Mills .01 .05
341 John Tice .01 .05
342 Brent Jones .02 .10
343 Robert Porcher RC .08 .25
344 Mark D'Onofrio RC .01 .05
345 David Tate .01 .05
346 Courtney Hawkins RC .02 .10
347 Ricky Watters .08 .25
348 Amp Lee .01 .05
349 Steve Young .25 .60
350 Natu Tuatagaloa RC .01 .05
351 Alfred Williams .01 .05
352 Derek Brown TE RC .01 .05
353 Marco Coleman RC UER .01 .05
(Back photo actually a Denver Bronco)
354 Tommy Maddox RC .60 1.50
355 Siran Stacy .01 .05
356 Greg Lewis .01 .05
357 Paul Gruber .01 .05
358 Troy Vincent RC .01 .05
359 Robert Wilson .01 .05
360 Jessie Hester .01 .05
361 Shaun Gayle .01 .05
362 Deron Cherry .01 .05
363 Wendell Davis .01 .05
364 David Klingler RC UER .01 .05
(Bio misspells his name as Klinger)
365 Jason Hanson RC .02 .10
366 Marquez Pope RC .01 .05
367 Robert Williams RC .01 .05
368 Kelvin Pritchett .01 .05
369 Dana Hall RC .01 .05
370 David Brandon RC .01 .05
371 Tim McKyer .01 .05
372 Darion Conner .01 .05
373 Derrick Fenner .01 .05
374 Hugh Millen .01 .05
375 Bill Jones RC .01 .05
376 J.J. Birden .01 .05
377 Ty Detmer .08 .25
378 Alonzo Spellman RC .02 .10
379 Sammie Smith .01 .05
380 Al Smith .01 .05
381 Louis Clark RC .01 .05
382 Vernice Smith RC .01 .05
383 Tony Martin .02 .10
384 Willie Green .01 .05
385 Sean Gilbert RC .02 .10
386 Eugene Chung RC .01 .05
387 Toi Cook .01 .05
388 Brett Maxie .01 .05
389 Steve Israel RC .01 .05
390 Mike Mularkey .01 .05
391 Barry Foster .02 .10
392 Hardy Nickerson .02 .10
393 Johnny Mitchell RC .01 .05
394 Thurman Thomas .08 .25
395 Tony Smith RC .01 .05
396 Keith Goganious RC .01 .05
397 Matt Darby RC .01 .05
398 Nate Turner RC .01 .05
399 Keith Jennings RC .01 .05
400 Mitchell Benson RC .01 .05
401 Kurt Barber RC .01 .05
402 Tony Sacca RC .01 .05
403 Steve Hendrickson RC .01 .05
404 Johnny Johnson .01 .05
405 Lorenzo Lynch .01 .05
406 Luis Sharpe .01 .05
407 Jim Everett .02 .10
408 Neal Anderson .01 .05
409 Ashley Ambrose RC .08 .25
410 George Williams RC .01 .05
411 Clarence Kay .01 .05
412 Dave Krieg .02 .10
413 Terrell Buckley .01 .05
414 Ricardo McDonald .01 .05
415 Kelly Stouffer .01 .05
416 Barney Bussey .01 .05
417 Ray Roberts RC .01 .05
418 Fred McAfee RC .01 .05
419 Fred Banks .01 .05
420 Tim McDonald .01 .05
421 Darryl Williams .01 .05
422 Bobby Abrams RC .01 .05
423 Tommy Vardell .01 .05
424 William White .01 .05
425 Billy Ray Smith .01 .05
426 Lemuel Stinson .01 .05
427 Brad Johnson RC 2.50 6.00
428 Herschel Walker .02 .10
429 Eric Thomas .01 .05
430 Anthony Thompson .01 .05
431 Ed West .01 .05
432 Edgar Bennett .08 .25
433 Warren Powers .01 .05
434 Byron Evans .01 .05
435 Rodney Culver RC .01 .05
436 Ray Horton .01 .05
437 Richmond Webb .01 .05
438 Mark McMillian RC .01 .05
439 Subset Checklist .01 .05
440 Lawrence Pete RC .01 .05
441 Rod Smith DB RC .01 .05
442 Mark Rodenhauser RC .01 .05
443 Scott Lockwood RC .01 .05
444 Charles Davenport RC .01 .05
445 Terry McDaniel .01 .05
446 Darren Perry RC .01 .05
447 Darrick Owens RC .01 .05
448 Alvin Wright .01 .05
449 Frank Stams .01 .05
450 Santana Dotson RC .02 .10
451 Mark Carrier DB .01 .05
452 Kevin Murphy .01 .05
453 Jeff Bryant .01 .05
454 Eric Allen .01 .05
455 Brian Bollinger RC .01 .05
456 Elston Ridgle RC .01 .05
457 Jim Riggs RC .01 .05
458 Checklist 251-320 .01 .05
459 Checklist 321-391 .01 .05
460 Checklist 392-460 .01 .05
P1 Barry Sanders Promo .40 1.00
P2 Barry Sanders Promo Sheet .75 2.00

1992 Wild Card 5 Stripe
*5 STRIPE: 1.2X TO 3X BASIC CARDS

1992 Wild Card 10 Stripe
*10 STRIPE: 2X TO 5X BASIC CARDS

1992 Wild Card 20 Stripe
*20 STRIPE: 3X TO 8X BASIC CARDS

1992 Wild Card 50 Stripe
*50 STRIPE: 6X TO 15X BASIC CARDS

1992 Wild Card 100 Stripe
*100 STRIPE: 15X TO 40X BASIC CARDS
427 Brad Johnson 60.00 150.00

1992 Wild Card 1000 Stripe
*1000 STRIPE: 50X TO 120X BASIC CARDS
238 Jimmy Smith 60.00 150.00
427 Brad Johnson 60.00 150.00

1992 Wild Card Class Back Attack
COMPLETE SET (5) 2.80 7.00
SP1 Vaughn Dunbar .20 .50
SP2 Barry Sanders 1.20 3.00
SP3 Emmitt Smith 1.20 3.00
SP4 Thurman Thomas .40 1.00
SP5 David Klingler .20 .50
(Red Hot Rookie; Surprise Card Redemption)

1992 Wild Card Field Force
COMPLETE SET (30) 6.00 15.00
*5 STRIPES: .8X to 2X BASIC INSERTS
*10 STRIPES: 1X to 2.5X BASIC INSERTS
*20 STRIPES: 1.5X to 4X BASIC INSERTS
*50 STRIPES: 2.5X to 6X BASIC INSERTS
*100 STRIPES: 4X to 10X BASIC INSERTS
*1000 STRIPES: 30X to 80X BASIC INSERTS
*SILVERS: .8X to 2X BASIC INSERTS
*GOLDS: 1.2X to 3X BASIC INSERTS
RANDOM INSERTS IN SER.2 PACKS
1 Joe Montana 1.00 2.50
2 Quentin Coryatt .10 .30
3 Tommy Vardell .10 .30
4 Jim Kelly .20 .50
5 John Elway 1.00 2.50
6 Ricky Watters .15 .40
7 Vinny Testaverde .15 .40
8 Randal Hill .10 .30
9 Amp Lee .10 .30
10 Vaughn Dunbar .10 .30
11 Troy Aikman .50 1.25
12 Deion Sanders .30 .75
13 Rodney Hampton .10 .30
14 Brett Favre 1.00 2.50
15 Warren Moon .20 .50
16 Browning Nagle .10 .30
17 Terrell Buckley .10 .30
18 Barry Sanders .75 2.00
19 Dan Marino 1.00 2.50
20 Carl Pickens .15 .40
21 Herschel Walker .15 .40
22 Ronnie Lott .20 .50
23 Steve Emtman .10 .30
24 Mark Rypien .10 .30
25 Bobby Hebert .10 .30
26 Dan McGwire .10 .30
27 Neil O'Donnell .10 .30
28 Cris Carter .20 .50
29 Randall Cunningham .20 .50
30 Jerry Rice .60 1.50

1992 Wild Card Pro Picks
COMPLETE SET (8) 3.00 8.00
ONE PER RETAIL JUMBO PACK
1 Emmitt Smith 1.00 2.50
2 Mark Rypien .02 .10
3 Warren Moon .15 .40
4 Leonard Russell .02 .10
5 Thurman Thomas .15 .40
6 John Elway .75 2.00
7 Barry Sanders .75 2.00
8 Steve Young .40 1.00

1992 Wild Card Red Hot Rookies
COMPLETE SET (30) 5.00 12.00
COMP.SERIES 1 (10) 2.00 4.00
COMP.SERIES 2 (20) 3.00 6.00
*5 STRIPES: .6X to 1.5X BASIC INSERTS
*10 STRIPES: .8X to 2X BASIC INSERTS
*20 STRIPES: 1.2X to 3X BASIC INSERTS
*50 STRIPES: 2.5X to 6X BASIC INSERTS
*100 STRIPES: 4X to 10X BASIC INSERTS
*1000 STRIPES: 25X to 60X BASIC INSERTS
*GOLDS: .4X to 1X BASIC INSERTS
*SILVERS: .3X to .8X BASIC INSERTS
RANDOM INSERTS IN FOIL PACKS
ONE GOLD OR SILVER CARD PER JU
1 Darryl Williams .10 .30
2 Amp Lee .10 .30
3 Will Furrer .10 .30
4 Edgar Bennett .25 .60
5 Terrell Buckley .15 .40
6 Bob Whitfield .10 .30
7 Siran Stacy .10 .30
8 Jimmy Smith 1.25 3.00
9 Kevin Turner .10 .30
10 Tommy Vardell .15 .40
11 Surprise Card .10 .30
12 Derek Brown TE .10 .30
13 Marco Coleman .10 .30
14 Quentin Coryatt .10 .30
15 Rodney Culver .10 .30
16 Ty Detmer .25 .60
17 Vaughn Dunbar .10 .30
18 Steve Emtman .15 .40
19 Sean Gilbert .15 .40
20 Courtney Hawkins .15 .40
21 David Klingler .15 .40
22 Amp Lee .10 .30
23 Tommy Maddox .75 2.00
24 Johnny Mitchell .10 .30
25 Darren Perry .10 .30
26 Carl Pickens .25 .60
27 Robert Porcher .15 .40
28 Tony Smith .10 .30
29 Alonzo Spellman .15 .40
30 Troy Vincent .10 .30

1992 Wild Card Running Wild
COMPLETE SET (40) 6.00 15.00
*5 STRIPES: .6X TO 1.5X BASIC INSERTS
*10 STRIPES: .8X TO 2X BASIC INSERTS
*20 STRIPES: 1.2X TO 3X BASIC INSERTS
*50 STRIPES: 2.5X TO 6X BASIC INSERTS
*100 STRIPES: 4X TO 10X BASIC INSERTS
*1000 STRIPES: 25X TO 60X BASIC INSERTS
*GOLDS: .6X to 1.5X SILVERS
ONE PER SERIES 2 JUMBO
1 Terry Allen .15 .40
2 Neal Anderson .07 .20
3 Eric Ball .07 .20
4 Nick Bell .07 .20
5 Edgar Bennett .40 1.00
6 Rod Bernstine .07 .20
7 Marion Butts .07 .20
8 Keith Byars .07 .20
9 Earnest Byner .07 .20
10 Roggio Cobb .07 .20
11 Roger Craig .15 .40
12 Rodney Culver .07 .20
13 Barry Foster .15 .40
14 Cleveland Gary .07 .20
15 Harold Green .07 .20
16 Gaston Green .07 .20
17 Rodney Hampton .15 .40
18 Mark Higgs .07 .20
19 Dalton Hilliard .07 .20
20 Bobby Humphrey UER .07 .20
(Misspelled Humphries)
21 Amp Lee .07 .20
22 Kevin Mack .07 .20
23 Eric Metcalf .15 .40
24 Brad Muster .07 .20
25 Christian Okoye .07 .20
26 Tom Rathman .07 .20
27 Leonard Russell .07 .20
28 Barry Sanders 2.00 5.00
29 Heath Sherman .07 .20
30 Emmitt Smith 2.50 6.00
31 Blair Thomas .07 .20
32 Thurman Thomas .40 1.00
33 Tommy Vardell .07 .20
34 Herschel Walker .15 .40
35 Chris Warren .15 .40
36 Ricky Watters .40 1.00
37 Lorenzo White .07 .20
38 John L. Williams .07 .20
39 Barry Word .07 .20
40 Vince Workman .07 .20

1992 Wild Card Stat Smashers
COMPLETE SET (52) 12.00 30.00
COMP.SERIES 1 (16) 6.00 15.00
COMP.SERIES 2 (36) 6.00 15.00
*5 STRIPES: .8X to 2X BASIC INSERTS
*10 STRIPES: 1X to 2.5X BASIC INSERTS
*20 STRIPES: 1.5X to 4X BASIC INSERTS
*50 STRIPES: 3X to 8X BASIC INSERTS
*100 STRIPES: 6X to 15X BASIC INSERTS
*1000 STRIPES: 20X to 50X BASIC INSERTS
SS1 Barry Sanders 1.25 3.00
SS2 Leonard Russell .10 .30
SS3 Thurman Thomas .20 .50
SS4 John Elway 1.50 4.00
SS5 Steve Young .60 1.50
SS6 Warren Moon .30 .75
SS7 Terrell Buckley .10 .30
SS8 Randall Cunningham .30 .75
SS9 Steve Emtman .10 .30
SS10 Dan Marino 1.50 4.00
SS11 Joe Montana 1.50 4.00
SS12 Carl Pickens .20 .50
SS13 Jerry Rice .75 2.00
SS14 Deion Sanders .40 1.00
SS15 Tommy Vardell .10 .30
SS16 Ricky Watters .20 .50
SS17 Troy Aikman .75 2.00
SS18 Dale Carter .10 .30
SS19 Quentin Coryatt .10 .30
SS20 Vaughn Dunbar .10 .30
SS21 Mark Duper .10 .30
SS22 Eric Metcalf .10 .30
SS23 Brett Favre 1.50 4.00
SS24 Barry Foster .10 .30
SS25 Jeff George .20 .50
SS26 Sean Gilbert UER .10 .30
(Stan on front)
SS27 Jim Harbaugh .20 .50
SS28 Courtney Hawkins .10 .30
SS29 Charles Haley .10 .30
SS30 Bobby Hebert .10 .30
SS31 Stan Humphries .20 .50
SS32 Michael Irvin .30 .75
SS33 Jim Kelly .30 .75
SS34 David Klingler .10 .30
SS35 Ronnie Lott .20 .50
SS36 Tommy Maddox .30 .75
SS37 Todd Marinovich .10 .30
SS38 Hugh Millen .10 .30
SS39 Art Monk .20 .50
SS40 Browning Nagle .10 .30
SS41 Neil O'Donnell .10 .30
SS42 Tom Rathman .10 .30
SS43 Andre Rison .20 .50
SS44 Mike Singletary .20 .50
SS45 Tony Smith .10 .30
SS46 Emmitt Smith 1.50 4.00
SS47 Pete Stoyanovich .10 .30
SS48 John Taylor .10 .30
SS49 Troy Vincent .10 .30
SS50 Herschel Walker .20 .50
SS51 Lorenzo White .10 .30
SS52 Rodney Culver .10 .30
P1 Barry Sanders PROMO 1.25 3.00
P2 Emmitt Smith PROMO 1.25 3.00

1992 Wild Card NASDAM

These five promo standard-size cards were given away at the NASDAM trade show in Orlando in the spring of 1992. Team color-coded stripes form a right angle at the lower left corner, while the customary series of colored numbers (1000, 100, 50, 20, 10, and 5) form a right angle at the upper right corner of the photo.

COMPLETE SET (5) .80 2.00
1 Edgar Bennett .30 .75
2 Amp Lee .10 .30
3 Terrell Buckley .20 .50
4 Tony Smith .10 .30
5 Will Furrer UER .10 .30
(Misspelled Furer)

1992 Wild Card NASDAM/SCAI Miami
Exclusively featuring Miami Dolphins, this six-card standard-size set was given out at the NASDAM/SCAI annual conference in Miami during November, 1992. The team color-coded stripes form a right angle at the lower left corner, while the customary series of colored numbers (1000, 100, 50, 20, 10, and 5) form a right angle at the upper right corner of the photo.

COMPLETE SET (6) 1.20 3.00
1 Mark Clayton .30 .75
2 Aaron Craver .20 .50
3 Tony Paige .20 .50
4 Mark Duper .30 .75
5 Tony Martin .30 .75
6 Reggie Roby .20 .50

1992 Wild Card Sacramento CardFest
This six-card standard-size set (of San Francisco 49ers) features color action player photos with thin black borders. A Sacramento CardFest icon is superimposed on the photo at the lower left. The player's name and position appear in the lower right corner.

COMPLETE SET (6) .80 2.00
1 Tom Rathman .10 .30
2 Steve Young .40 1.00
3 Steve Bono .20 .50
4 Brent Jones .10 .30
5 Ricky Watters .20 .50
6 Amp Lee .10 .30

1992 Wild Card WLAF

The Wild Card WLAF Football set contains 150 standard-size cards. It is reported that the production run was limited to 6,000 numbered ten-box cases, and that no factory sets were produced. The cards are checklisted according to teams.

COMPLETE SET (150) 2.40 6.00
*5 STRIPES: .6X TO 1.5X BASIC CARDS
*10 STRIPES: .8X TO 2X BASIC CARDS
*20 STRIPES: 1X TO 2.5X BASIC CARDS
*50 STRIPES: 2X TO 5X BASIC CARDS
*100 STRIPES: 4X TO 10X BASIC CARDS
*1000 STRIPES: 30X TO 80X BASIC CARDS
1 World Bowl Champs .02 .10
2 Pete Mandley .01 .05
3 Steve Williams .01 .05
4 Dee Thomas .01 .05
5 Emanuel King .01 .05
6 Anthony Dilweg .02 .10
7 Ben Brown .01 .05
8 Darryl Harris .01 .05
9 Aaron Emanuel .01 .05
10 Andre Brown .01 .05
11 Reggie McKenzie .02 .10
12 Darryl Holmes .01 .05
13 Michael Proctor .01 .05
14 Ricky Johnson .01 .05
15 Ray Savage .01 .05
16 George Searcy .01 .05
17 Titus Dixon .01 .05
18 Willie Fears .01 .05
19 Terrence Cooks .01 .05
20 Ivory Lee Brown .01 .05
21 Mike Johnson .01 .05
22 Doug Williams T .01 .05
23 Brad Goebel .02 .10
24 Tony Boles .01 .05
25 Cisco Richard .01 .05
26 Robb White .01 .05
27 Darrell Colbert .01 .05
28 Wayne Walker .01 .05
29 Ronnie Williams .01 .05
30 Erik Norgard .01 .05
31 Darren Willis .01 .05
32 Kent Wells .01 .05
33 Phil Logan .01 .05
34 Pat O'Hara .01 .05
35 Melvin Patterson .01 .05
36 Amir Rasul .01 .05
37 Tom Rouen .01 .05
38 Chris Cochrane .01 .05
39 Randy Bethel .01 .05
40 Eric Harmon .01 .05
41 Archie Herring .01 .05
42 Tim James .01 .05
43 Babe Laufenberg .02 .10
44 Herb Welch .01 .05
45 Stefon Adams .01 .05
46 Tony Burse .01 .05
47 Carl Parker .01 .05
48 Mike Prugle .01 .05
49 Mike Jones .02 .10
50 David Archer .30 .75
51 Corian Freeman .01 .05
52 Eddie Brown .01 .05
53 Paul Green .01 .05
54 Basil Proctor .01 .05
55 Michael Sinclair .02 .10
56 Louis Riddick .01 .05
57 Roman Matuez .01 .05
58 Darryl Clack .01 .05
59 Willie Davis .20 .50
60 Glen Rodgers .01 .05
61 Grantis Bell .01 .05
62 Joe Howard-Johnson .01 .05
63 Rocen Keeton .01 .05
64 Dean Witkowski .01 .05
65 Stacey Simmons .01 .05
66 Roger Vick .01 .05
67 Scott Mitchell .40 1.00
68 Todd Krumm .01 .05
69 Kerwin Bell .07 .20
70 Richard Carey .01 .05
71 Kip Lewis .01 .05
72 Andre Alexander .01 .05
73 Reggie Slack .01 .05
74 Falanda Newton .01 .05
75 Tony Woods .07 .20
76 Chris McLemore .01 .05
77 Eric Wilkerson .01 .05
78 Cornell Burbage .01 .05
79 Doug Pederson 1.20 3.00
80 Brent Pease .01 .05
81 Monty Gilbreath .01 .05
82 Wes Pritchett .01 .05
83 Byron Williams .01 .05
84 Ron Sancho .01 .05
85 Tony Jones .07 .20
86 Anthony Wallace .01 .05
87 Mike Perez .01 .05
88 Steve Bartalo .01 .05
89 Teddy Garcia .01 .05
90 Joe Greenwood .01 .05
91 Tony Baker .07 .20
92 Glenn Cobb .01 .05
93 Mark Tucker .01 .05
94 Lyneil Mayo .01 .05
95 Alex Espinoza .01 .05
96 Mike Norseth .01 .05
97 Steven Avery .01 .05
98 John Brantley .01 .05
99 Eddie Britton .01 .05
100 Philip Doyle .01 .05
101 Elroy Harris .01 .05
102 John R. Holland .01 .05
103 Mark Hopkins .01 .05
104 Arthur Hunter .01 .05
105 Paul McGowan .01 .05
106 John Miller .01 .05
107 Shawn Moore .01 .05
108 Phil Ross .01 .05
109 Eugene Rowell .01 .05
110 Joe Valerio .01 .05
111 Harvey Wilson .01 .05
112 Irvin Smith .01 .05
113 Tony Sargent .01 .05
114 Ricky Shaw .01 .05
115 Curtis Moore .01 .05
116 Fred McNair .01 .05
117 Danny Lockett .01 .05
118 William Kirksey .01 .05
119 Stan Gelbaugh .07 .20
120 Judd Garrett .02 .10
121 Dedrick Dodge .01 .05
122 Dan Crossman .01 .05
123 Jeff Alexander .01 .05
124 Lew Barnes .01 .05
125 Willie Don Wright .01 .05
126 Johnny Thomas .01 .05
127 Richard Buchanan .01 .05
128 Chad Fortune .01 .05
129 Eric Lindstrom .01 .05
130 Ron Goetz .01 .05
131 Bruce Clark .01 .05
132 Anthony Greene .01 .05
133 Demetrius Davis .01 .05
134 Mike Roth .01 .05
135 Tony Moss .01 .05
136 Scott Erney .01 .05
137 Brad Henke .01 .05
138 Malcolm Frank .01 .05
139 Sean Foster .01 .05
140 Michael Titley .01 .05
141 Rickey Williams .01 .05
142 Karl Dunbar .01 .05
143 Carl Bax .01 .05
144 Willie Bouyer .01 .05
145 Howard Feggins .01 .05
146 David Smith .01 .05
147 Bernard Ford .01 .05
148 Checklist 1 .01 .05
149 Checklist 2 .01 .05
150 Checklist 3 .01 .05
NNO Box Card .01 .05
(Redeemable for box of WLAF; inserted in various Wild Card products)

1992-93 Wild Card San Francisco
Exclusively featuring San Francisco 49ers, this six-card, standard-size set was originally given out at the Sports Collectors Card Expo held in San Francisco in September, 1992 and then reissued (with a slightly different show logo, different individual card numbers, and two replacement players) at the Spring National Sports Collectors Convention in San Francisco in March 1993. The two sets are indistinguishable except for the different show logo in the lower left corner of each obverse and the card numbering. The two sets are valued equally. The team color-coded stripes form a right angle at the lower left corner, while the customary series of colored numbers (1000, 100, 50, 20, 10, and 5) form a right angle at the upper right corner of the photo. The cards are numbered on the back; cards designated below as A are from the original 1992 set, whereas the B versions are from the 1993 reissue set. The complete set below applies to either set.

COMPLETE SET (6) 1.00 4.00
1A John Taylor .10 .30
1B Tom Rathman .10 .30
2A Amp Lee .10 .30
2B Steve Young .30 .75
3A Steve Bono .20 .50
3B Steve Bono .20 .50
4A Steve Young .30 .75
4B Brent Jones .10 .30
5A Tom Rathman .10 .30
5B Ricky Watters .20 .50
6A Don Griffin .10 .30
6B Amp Lee .10 .30

1993 Wild Card Prototypes
These six promo cards were given away at the 1993 National Sports Collectors Convention in Chicago, Ill. The cards are numbered on the back with a "P" prefix. The set numbering starts where the 1992 Wild Card Prototypes left off. A Superchrome version was also produced of each card. These were actually re-numbered (#SCP1-SCP6) but have been priced below using a multiplier.

COMPLETE SET (6) 1.60 4.00
P19 Emmitt Smith .80 2.00
P20 Ricky Watters .15 .40
P21 Drew Bledsoe .60 1.50
P22 Garrison Hearst .30 .75
P23 Barry Foster .15 .40
P24 Rick Mirer .30 .75

1993 Wild Card Prototypes Superchrome
These six standard-size promo cards feature on their fronts borderless metallic color player action shots, with the player's name, team, and position appearing within the jagged gold stripe at the bottom. The borderless horizontal back carries the player's name, team, and position at the top, followed by biography, statistics, and, on the right, another color player action shot. The cards are numbered on the back with an "SCP" prefix. Each card was also produced in a "Hobby Reserve" parallel version and distributed directly to dealer accounts. These cards are marked "Hobby Reserve" on the fronts.

COMPLETE SET (6) 3.00 7.50
*HOBBY RESERVE CARDS: .6X TO 1.5X
SCP1 Emmitt Smith 1.20 3.00
SCP2 Ricky Watters .30 .75
SCP3 Drew Bledsoe 1.00 2.50
SCP4 Garrison Hearst .20 .50
SCP5 Barry Foster .20 .50
SCP6 Rick Mirer .40 1.00

1993 Wild Card

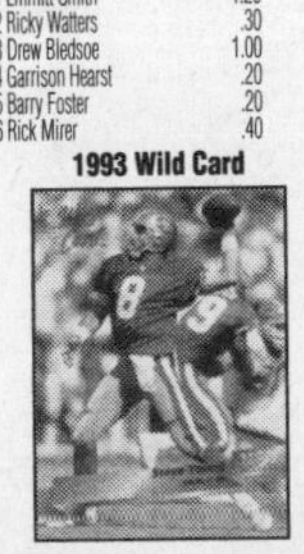

The 1993 Wild Card NFL football set consists of 260 standard-size cards. The first series cards are checklisted according to teams. Randomly inserted in early 1993 Wild Card packs were cards from the 1993 Stat Smashers, Field Force, and Red Hot Rookies sets. A different packaging scheme begun early in 1994 featured six Superchrome counterparts to the regular cards inserted in special Superchrome 15-card low-series and 13-card high-series hobby packs, and are valued at four to nine times the value of the regular issue cards. One of ten Superchrome Back-to-Back inserts, featuring a Field Force player on the front and a Red Hot Rookie on the back, was inserted in each 18-pack box. Also, special striped cards were randomly inserted into regular Wild Card packs. These cards came in varying "denominations" of stripes, ranging from five to 1,000, and the corresponding values for them are noted in the header below. Rookie Cards include Jerome Bettis, Drew Bledsoe, Reggie Brooks, Derek Brown, Garrison Hearst, O.J. McDuffie and Rick Mirer.

COMPLETE SET (260) 5.00 10.00
COMP.SERIES 1 (200) 3.00 6.00
COMP.SERIES 2 (60) 2.00 4.00
*5 STRIPES: 1X TO 2.5X BASIC CARDS
*10 STRIPES: 1.5X TO 3.5X BASIC CARDS
*20 STRIPES: 2X TO 5X BASIC CARDS
*50 STRIPE VETS: 5X TO 12X BASIC CARDS
*50 STRIPE RCs: 3X TO 8X BASIC CARDS
*100 STRIPES: 10X TO 25X BASIC CARDS
*100 STRIPE RCs: 8X TO 20X BASIC CARDS
*1000 STRIPE VETS: 50X TO 120X BASIC CARDS
*1000 STRIPE RCs: 50X TO 120X BASIC CARDS
1 Surprise Card .01 .05
2 Steve Young .30 .75
3 John Taylor .02 .10
4 Jerry Rice .40 1.00
5 Brent Jones .02 .10
6 Ricky Watters .02 .10
7 Elvis Grbac RC .60 1.50
8 Amp Lee .01 .05
9 Steve Bono .02 .10
10 Wendell Davis .01 .05
11 Mark Carrier DB .01 .05
12 Jim Harbaugh .02 .10
13 Curtis Conway RC .15 .40
14 Neal Anderson .01 .05
15 Tom Waddle .01 .05
16 Jeff Query .01 .05
17 David Klingler .01 .05
18 Eric Ball .01 .05
19 Derrick Fenner .01 .05
20 Steve Tovar RC .01 .05
21 Carl Pickens .02 .10
22 Ricardo McDonald .01 .05
23 Harold Green .01 .05
24 Keith McKeller .01 .05
25 Steve Christie .01 .05
26 Andre Reed .02 .10
27 Kenneth Davis .01 .05
28 Frank Reich .01 .05
29 Jim Kelly .08 .25
30 Bruce Smith .02 .10
31 Thurman Thomas .08 .25
32 Glyn Milburn RC .02 .10
33 John Elway .60 1.50
34 Vance Johnson .01 .05
35 Greg Lewis .01 .05
36 Steve Atwater .01 .05
37 Shannon Sharpe .02 .10
38 Mike Croel .01 .05
39 Kevin Mack .01 .05
40 Lawyer Tillman .01 .05
41 Tommy Vardell .01 .05
42 Bernie Kosar .02 .10
43 Eric Metcalf .02 .10
44 Clay Matthews .01 .05
45 Keith McCants .01 .05
46 Broderick Thomas .01 .05
47 Lawrence Dawsey .01 .05
48 Reggie Cobb .01 .05
49 Lamar Thomas RC .01 .05
50 Courtney Hawkins .02 .10
51 Ivory Lee Brown RC .01 .05
52 Ernie Jones .01 .05
53 Freddie Joe Nunn .01 .05
54 Chris Chandler .02 .10
55 Randal Hill .01 .05
56 Lorenzo Lynch .01 .05
57 Garrison Hearst RC .30 .75
58 Marion Butts .01 .05
59 Anthony Miller .02 .10
60 Eric Bieniemy .01 .05
61 Ronnie Harmon .01 .05
62 Junior Seau .08 .25
63 Gill Byrd .01 .05
64 Stan Humphries .02 .10
65 John Friesz .01 .05
66 J.J. Birden .02 .10
67 Joe Montana .60 1.50
68 Christian Okoye .02 .10
69 Dale Carter .01 .05
70 Barry Word .01 .05
71 Derrick Thomas .08 .25
72 Todd McNair .01 .05
73 Harvey Williams .01 .05
74 Jack Trudeau .01 .05
75 Rodney Culver .01 .05
76 Anthony Johnson .01 .05
77 Steve Emtman .01 .05
78 Quentin Coryatt .02 .10
79 Kerry Cash .01 .05
80 Jeff George .02 .10
81 Darrin Smith RC .01 .05
82 Jay Novacek .02 .10
83 Michael Irvin .08 .25
84 Alvin Harper .02 .10
85 Kevin Williams RC .02 .10
86 Troy Aikman .30 .75
87 Emmitt Smith .60 1.50
88 O.J. McDuffie RC .08 .25
89 Mike Williams WR RC .01 .05
90 Dan Marino .60 1.50
91 Aaron Craver .01 .05
92 Troy Vincent .01 .05
93 Keith Jackson .02 .10
94 Marco Coleman .01 .05
95 Mark Higgs .01 .05
96 Fred Barnett .02 .10
97 Wes Hopkins .01 .05
98 Randall Cunningham .08 .25
99 Heath Sherman .01 .05
100 Vai Sikahema .01 .05
101 Tony Smith .01 .05
102 Andre Rison .02 .10
103 Chris Miller .01 .05
104 Deion Sanders .20 .50
105 Mike Pritchard .02 .10
106 Steve Broussard .01 .05
107 Stephen Baker .01 .05
108 Carl Banks .01 .05
109 Jarrod Bunch .01 .05
110 Phil Simms .02 .10
111 Rodney Hampton .02 .10
112 Dave Meggett .01 .05
113 Pepper Johnson .01 .05
114 Coleman Rudolph RC .01 .05
115 Boomer Esiason .02 .10
116 Browning Nagle .01 .05
117 Rob Moore .02 .10
118 Marvin Jones RC .01 .05
119 Herman Moore .08 .25
120 Bennie Blades .01 .05
121 Erik Kramer .01 .05
122 Mel Gray .01 .05
123 Rodney Peete .01 .05
124 Barry Sanders .50 1.25
125 Chris Spielman .01 .05
126 Lamar Lathon .01 .05

127 Ernest Givins .02 .10
128 Lorenzo White .02 .10
129 Micheal Barrow RC .08 .25
130 Warren Moon .02 .10
131 Cody Carlson .01 .05
132 Reggie White .08 .25
133 Terrell Buckley .01 .05
134 Ed West .01 .05
135 Mark Brunell RC .60 1.50
136 Brett Favre .75 2.00
137 Edgar Bennett .02 .10
138 Sterling Sharpe .02 .10
139 George Teague RC .01 .05
140 Leonard Russell .02 .10
141 Drew Bledsoe RC 1.00 2.50
142 Eugene Chung .01 .05
143 Walter Stanley .01 .05
144 Scott Zolak .01 .05
145 Jon Vaughn .01 .05
146A Andre Tippett ERR .02 .10
name spelled Tippet on front
146B Andre Tippett COR .02 .10
name spelled Tippett on front
147 Alexander Wright .01 .05
148 Billy Joe Hobert RC .08 .25
149 Terry McDaniel .01 .05
150 Tim Brown .08 .25
151 Willie Gault .01 .05
152 Howie Long .08 .25
153 Todd Marinovich .01 .05
154 Jim Everett .02 .10
155 David Lang .01 .05
156 Henry Ellard .02 .10
157 Cleveland Gary .01 .05
158 Steve Israel .01 .05
159 Jerome Bettis RC 1.50 4.00
160 Jackie Slater .01 .05
161 Art Monk .02 .10
162 Ricky Sanders .01 .05
163 Brian Mitchell .01 .05
164 Reggie Brooks RC .01 .05
165 Mark Rypien .01 .05
166 Earnest Byner .01 .05
167 Andre Collins .01 .05
168 Quinn Early .02 .10
169 Fred McAfee .01 .05
170 Wesley Carroll .01 .05
171 Gene Atkins .01 .05
172 Derek Brown RBK RC .02 .10
UER, Name spelled Derrek)
173 Vaughn Dunbar .01 .05
174A Rickey Jackson ERR .01 .05
(Ricky on front)
174B Rickey Jackson COR .01 .05
(Rickey on front)
175 John L. Williams .01 .05
176 Carlton Gray RC .01 .05
177 Cortez Kennedy .02 .10
178 Kelly Stouffer .01 .05
179 Rick Mirer RC .08 .25
180 Dan McGwire .01 .05
181 Chris Warren .02 .10
182 Barry Foster .02 .10
183 Merril Hoge .01 .05
184 Darren Perry .01 .05
185 Deon Figures RC .01 .05
186A Jeff Graham ERR .02 .10
(Grahm on front)
186B Jeff Graham COR .02 .10
(Graham on front)
187 Dwight Stone .01 .05
188 Neil O'Donnell .02 .10
189 Rod Woodson .08 .25
190 Alex Van Pelt RC 1.00 2.50
191 Steve Jordan .01 .05
192 Roger Craig .02 .10
193 Qadry Ismail RC UER .08 .25
(Misspelled Quadry
on card front)
194 Robert Smith RC .50 1.25
195 Gino Torretta RC .02 .10
196 Anthony Carter .02 .10
197 Terry Allen .02 .10
198 Rich Gannon .08 .25
199 Checklist 1-100 .01 .05
200 Checklist 101-200 .01 .05
201 Victor Bailey RC .01 .05
202 Micheal Barrow .01 .05
203 Patrick Bates RC .01 .05
204 Jerome Bettis .75 2.00
205 Drew Bledsoe .50 1.25
206 Vincent Brisby RC .08 .25
207 Reggie Brooks .02 .10
208 Derek Brown RBK .02 .10
209 Keith Byars .01 .05
210 Tom Carter RC .01 .05
211 Curtis Conway .08 .25
212 Russell Copeland RC .02 .10
213 John Copeland RC .02 .10
214 Eric Curry RC .02 .10
215 Troy Drayton RC .02 .10
216 Jason Elam RC .08 .25
217 Steve Everitt RC .01 .05
218 Deon Figures .01 .05
219 Irving Fryar .02 .10
220 Darrien Gordon RC .01 .05
221 Carlton Gray .01 .05
222 Kevin Greene .02 .10
223 Andre Hastings RC .02 .10
224 Michael Haynes .02 .10
225 Garrison Hearst .15 .40
226 Bobby Hebert .01 .05
227 Lester Holmes .01 .05
228 Jeff Hostetler .02 .10
229 Desmond Howard .02 .10
230 Tyrone Hughes RC .02 .10
231 Qadry Ismail .02 .10
232 Rocket Ismail .02 .10
233 James Jett RC .08 .25
234 Marvin Jones .01 .05
235 Todd Kelly RC .01 .05
236 Lincoln Kennedy RC .01 .05
237 Terry Kirby RC .02 .10
238 Bernie Kosar .02 .10
239 Derrick Lassic RC .01 .05
240 Wilber Marshall .01 .05
241 O.J. McDuffie .08 .25
242 Ryan McNeil RC .08 .25
243 Natrone Means RC .08 .25
244 Glyn Milburn .02 .10
245 Rick Mirer .08 .25
246 Scott Mitchell .08 .25
247 Ronald Moore RC .02 .10
248 Lorenzo Neal RC .01 .05
249 Erric Pegram .02 .10
250 Roosevelt Potts RC .01 .05
251 Leonard Renfro RC .01 .05
252 Greg Robinson RC .01 .05
253 Wayne Simmons RC .01 .05
254 Chris Slade RC .02 .10
255 Irv Smith RC .02 .10
256 Robert Smith .20 .50
257 Dana Stubblefield RC .08 .25
258 George Teague .01 .05
259 Kevin Williams WR .02 .10
260 Checklist 201-260 .01 .05

1993 Wild Card Bomb Squad

COMPLETE SET (30) 3.00 8.00
ONE PER JUMBO PACK
1 Jerry Rice 1.00 2.50
2 John Taylor .08 .25
3 J.J. Birden .08 .25
4 Stephen Baker .05 .15
5 Victor Bailey .05 .15
6 O.J. McDuffie .25 .60
7 Haywood Jeffires .05 .15
8 Eric Green .05 .15
9 Johnny Mitchell .05 .15
10 Art Monk .08 .25
11 Quinn Early .08 .25
12 Troy Drayton .08 .25
13 Vincent Brisby .25 .60
14 Courtney Hawkins .08 .25
15 Tom Waddle .05 .15
16 Curtis Conway .25 .60
17 Andre Reed .08 .25
18 Carl Pickens .08 .25
19 Sterling Sharpe .08 .25
20 Shannon Sharpe .08 .25
21 Qadry Ismail .08 .25
22 Rocket Ismail .08 .25
23 Andre Rison .08 .25
24 Michael Haynes .08 .25
25 Alvin Harper .08 .25
26 Michael Irvin .25 .60
27 Michael Jackson .05 .15
28 Herman Moore .25 .60
29 Anthony Miller .08 .25
30 Gary Clark .08 .25

1993 Wild Card Bomb Squad Back to Back

COMPLETE SET (15) 6.00 15.00
RANDOM INSERTS IN JUMBO PACKS
1 Jerry Rice 2.50 6.00
John Taylor
2 Tom Waddle .60 1.50
Curtis Conway
3 Andre Reed .25 .60
Carl Pickens
4 Sterling Sharpe .25 .60
Shannon Sharpe
5 Qadry Ismail .25 .60
Rocket Ismail
6 Andre Rison .25 .60
Michael Haynes
7 Alvin Harper .60 1.50
Michael Irvin
8 Michael Jackson .60 1.50
Herman Moore
9 Anthony Miller .25 .60
Gary Clark
10 J.J. Birden .25 .60
Stephen Baker
11 Victor Bailey .60 1.50
O.J. McDuffie
12 Haywood Jeffires .10 .30
Eric Green
13 Johnny Mitchell .25 .60
Art Monk
14 Quinn Early .25 .60
Troy Drayton
15 Vincent Brisby .10 .30
Courtney Hawkins

1993 Wild Card Field Force

COMPLETE SET (90) 12.00 30.00
COMPLETE WEST SET (30) 4.00 10.00
COMPLETE EAST SET (30) 4.00 10.00
*SILVERS: .5X to 1.2X BASIC INSERTS
*GOLDS: .6X to 1.5X BASIC INSERTS
31-60: RANDOM INSERTS IN WEST
61-90: RANDOM INSERTS IN EAST
91-120: RANDOM INS.IN CENTRAL
31 Jerry Rice .75 2.00
32 Ricky Watters .07 .20
33 Steve Bono .07 .20
34 Amp Lee .02 .10
35 Steve Young .60 1.50
36 Tommy Maddox .02 .10
37 Cleveland Gary .02 .10
38 John Elway 1.25 3.00
39 Glyn Milburn .07 .20
40 Stan Humphries .07 .20
41 Junior Seau .20 .50
42 Natrone Means .20 .50
43 Dale Carter .02 .10
44 Joe Montana 1.25 3.00
45 Christian Okoye .07 .20
46 Deion Sanders .40 1.00
47 Roger Harper .02 .10
48 Steve Broussard .02 .10
49 Todd Marinovich .02 .10
50 Billy Joe Hobert .20 .50
51 Patrick Bates .02 .10
52 Jerome Bettis 1.50 4.00
53 Flipper Anderson .02 .10
54 Irv Smith .07 .20
55 Quinn Early .07 .20
56 Vaughn Dunbar .02 .10
57 Rick Mirer .20 .50
58 Carlton Gray .02 .10
59 Chris Warren .07 .20
60 Dan McGwire .02 .10
61 Pete Metzelaars .02 .10
62 Kenneth Davis .02 .10
63 Thurman Thomas .20 .50
64 Chris Chandler .07 .20
65 Garrison Hearst .30 .75
66 Ricky Proehl .02 .10
67 Steve Emtman .02 .10
68 Jeff George .07 .20
69 Clarence Verdin .02 .10
70 Troy Aikman .60 1.50
71 Emmitt Smith 1.25 3.00
72 Alvin Harper .07 .20
73 Michael Irvin .20 .50
74 O.J. McDuffie .20 .50
75 Troy Vincent .02 .10
76 Keith Jackson .07 .20
77 Dan Marino 1.25 3.00
78 Leonard Renfro .02 .10
79 Heath Sherman .02 .10
80 Derek Brown TE .02 .10
81 Rodney Hampton .07 .20
82 James Hasty .02 .10
83 Johnny Mitchell .02 .10
84 Brad Baxter .02 .10
85 Leonard Russell .07 .20
86 Marv Cook .02 .10
87 Drew Bledsoe 1.00 2.50
88 Ricky Ervins .02 .10
89 Art Monk .07 .20
90 Earnest Byner .02 .10
91 Tom Waddle .02 .10
92 Neal Anderson .02 .10
93 Curtis Conway .20 .50
94 Harold Green .02 .10
95 Jeff Query .02 .10
96 Carl Pickens .07 .20
97 David Klingler .02 .10
98 Michael Jackson .07 .20
99 Eric Metcalf .07 .20
100 Courtney Hawkins .07 .20
101 Eric Curry .07 .20
102 Reggie Cobb .02 .10
103 Mel Gray .02 .10
104 Barry Sanders 1.00 2.50
105 Rodney Peete .02 .10
106 Haywood Jeffires .07 .20
107 Cody Carlson .02 .10
108 Curtis Duncan .02 .10
109 Edgar Bennett .07 .20
110 George Teague .02 .10
111 Terrell Buckley .02 .10
112 Brett Favre 1.50 4.00
113 Deon Figures .02 .10
114 Rod Woodson .20 .50
115 Neil O'Donnell .07 .20
116 Barry Foster .07 .20
117 Cris Carter .20 .50
118 Gino Torretta .07 .20
119 Terry Allen .07 .20
120 Qadry Ismail .07 .20

1993 Wild Card Red Hot Rookies

COMPLETE SET (30) 4.00 10.00
COMPLETE WEST SET (10) 2.00 5.00
COMPLETE EAST SET (10) 2.00 5.00
31-40: RANDOM INSERTS IN WEST
41-50: RANDOM INSERTS IN EAST
51-60: RANDOM INS.IN CENTRAL P
31 Dana Stubblefield .15 .40
32 Todd Kelly .02 .10
33 Dan Williams .02 .10
34 Glyn Milburn .05 .15
35 Natrone Means .15 .40
36 Lincoln Kennedy .02 .10
37 Patrick Bates .02 .10
38 Jerome Bettis 2.50 6.00
39 Irv Smith .05 .15
40 Rick Mirer .15 .40
41 Garrison Hearst .50 1.25
42 Kevin Williams .05 .15
43 Terry Kirby .05 .15
44 O.J. McDuffie .15 .40
45 Leonard Renfro .02 .10
46 Victor Bailey .02 .10
47 Marvin Jones .02 .10
48 Drew Bledsoe 1.50 4.00
49 Reggie Brooks UER .02 .10
(Missing career college stats)
50 Tom Carter .02 .10
51 Curtis Conway .25 .60
52 Dan Footman .02 .10
53 Lamar Thomas .02 .10
54 Eric Curry .05 .15
55 Ryan McNeil .15 .40
56 Micheal Barrow .15 .40
57 Wayne Simmons .02 .10
58 George Teague .02 .10
59 Robert Smith .75 2.00
60 Qadry Ismail .15 .40

1993 Wild Card Stat Smashers

COMPLETE SET (60) 12.00 30.00
COMP.WEST SET (20) 4.00 10.00
53-72: RANDOM INSERTS IN WEST
73-92: RANDOM INSERTS IN EAST
93-112: RANDOM INS.IN CENTRAL
*GOLD CARDS: SAME PRICE
GOLD CARDS INSERTED IN RETAIL
53 Ricky Watters .07 .20
54 Jerry Rice .75 2.00
55 Steve Young .60 1.50
56 Shannon Sharpe .07 .20
57 John Elway 1.25 3.00
58 Glyn Milburn .07 .20
59 Marion Butts .02 .10
60 Junior Seau .20 .50
61 Natrone Means .20 .50
62 Joe Montana 1.25 3.00
63 J.J. Birden .07 .20
64 Michael Haynes .07 .20
65 Deion Sanders .40 1.00
66 Billy Joe Hobert .20 .50
67 Nick Bell .02 .10
68 Jerome Bettis 1.50 4.00
69 Vaughn Dunbar .02 .10
70 Quinn Early .07 .20
71 Dan McGwire .02 .10
72 Rick Mirer .20 .50
73 Kenneth Davis .02 .10
74 Thurman Thomas .20 .50
75 Garrison Hearst .30 .75
76 Ricky Proehl .02 .10
77 Jeff George .07 .20
78 Rodney Culver .02 .10
79 Troy Aikman .60 1.50
80 Emmitt Smith 1.25 3.00
81 Michael Irvin .20 .50
82 O.J. McDuffie .20 .50
83 Keith Jackson .07 .20
84 Dan Marino 1.25 3.00
85 Heath Sherman .02 .10
86 Fred Barnett .07 .20
87 Rodney Hampton .07 .20
88 Marvin Jones .02 .10
89 Brad Baxter .02 .10
90 Drew Bledsoe 1.00 2.50
91 Ricky Ervins .02 .10
92 Art Monk .07 .20
93 Neal Anderson .02 .10
94 Curtis Conway .20 .50
95 John Copeland .07 .20
96 Carl Pickens .07 .20
97 David Klingler .02 .10
98 Michael Jackson .07 .20
99 Kevin Mack .02 .10
100 Eric Curry .07 .20
101 Reggie Cobb .02 .10
102 Willie Green .02 .10
103 Barry Sanders 1.00 2.50
104 Haywood Jeffires .02 .10
105 Lorenzo White .07 .20
106 Sterling Sharpe .07 .20
107 Brett Favre 1.50 4.00
108 Neil O'Donnell .07 .20
109 Barry Foster .07 .20
110 Rich Gannon .20 .50
111 Robert Smith .40 1.00
112 Qadry Ismail .07 .20

1993 Wild Card Stat Smashers Rookies

COMPLETE SET (52) 6.00 15.00
*GOLDS: .6X to 1.5X BASIC INSERTS
ONE GOLD OR SILVER PER JUMBO P
1 Todd Kelly .05 .15
2 Dana Stubblefield .30 .75
3 Curtis Conway .30 .75
4 John Copeland .10 .30
5 Russell Copeland .10 .30
6 Thomas Smith .05 .15
7 Glyn Milburn .10 .30
8 Jason Elam .30 .75
9 Steve Everitt .05 .15
10 Eric Curry .10 .30
11 Horace Copeland .05 .15
12 Ronald Moore .10 .30
13 Garrison Hearst .50 1.25
14 Natrone Means .30 .75
15 Darrien Gordon .05 .15
16 Roosevelt Potts .05 .15
17 Kevin Williams .10 .30
18 Derrick Lassic .05 .15
19 O.J. McDuffie .30 .75
20 Terry Kirby .10 .30
21 Scott Mitchell .30 .75
22 Victor Bailey .05 .15
23 Vaughn Hebron .05 .15
24 Lincoln Kennedy .05 .15
25 Michael Strahan .10 .30
26 Marvin Jones .05 .15
27 Tony McGee .05 .15
28 Ryan McNeil .30 .75
29 Micheal Barrow .05 .15
30 Wayne Simmons .05 .15
31 George Teague .05 .15
32 Vincent Brisby .30 .75
33 Drew Bledsoe 1.50 4.00
34 Rocket Ismail .10 .30
35 Patrick Bates .05 .15
36 James Jett .30 .75
37 Jerome Bettis 2.50 6.00
38 Troy Drayton .10 .30
39 Tom Carter .05 .15
40 Reggie Brooks .10 .30
41 Lorenzo Neal .05 .15
42 Derek Brown RBK .10 .30
43 Tyrone Hughes .10 .30
44 Rick Mirer .30 .75
45 Carlton Gray .05 .15
46 Andre Hastings .10 .30
47 Deon Figures .05 .15
48 Qadry Ismail .10 .30
49 Robert Smith .60 1.50
50 Irv Smith .10 .30
51 Chris Slade .10 .30
52 Willie Roaf .05 .15

1993 Wild Card Superchrome

The Superchrome set was distributed in its own packaging, but is essentially a parallel to the base 1993 Wild Card set. The cards feature a metallized foil look and included many of the same inserts as the base product.

COMPLETE SET (260) 8.00 20.00
COMP.SERIES 1 (200) 4.00 10.00
COMP.SERIES 2 (60) 4.00 10.00
1 Surprise Card .02 .10
2 Steve Young .40 1.00
3 John Taylor .05 .15
4 Jerry Rice .50 1.25
5 Brent Jones .05 .15
6 Ricky Watters .05 .15
7 Elvis Grbac RC .75 2.00
8 Amp Lee .02 .10
9 Steve Bono .05 .15
10 Wendell Davis .02 .10
11 Mark Carrier DB .02 .10
12 Jim Harbaugh .05 .15
13 Curtis Conway RC .20 .50
14 Neal Anderson .02 .10
15 Tom Waddle .02 .10
16 Jeff Query .02 .10
17 David Klingler .02 .10
18 Eric Ball .02 .10
19 Derrick Fenner .02 .10
20 Steve Tovar RC .02 .10
21 Carl Pickens .05 .15
22 Ricardo McDonald .02 .10
23 Harold Green .02 .10
24 Keith McKeller .02 .10
25 Steve Christie .02 .10
26 Andre Reed .05 .15
27 Kenneth Davis .02 .10
28 Frank Reich .02 .10
29 Jim Kelly .10 .30
30 Bruce Smith .05 .15
31 Thurman Thomas .10 .30
32 Glyn Milburn RC .05 .15
33 John Elway .75 2.00
34 Vance Johnson .02 .10
35 Greg Lewis .02 .10
36 Steve Atwater .02 .10
37 Shannon Sharpe .05 .15
38 Mike Croel .02 .10
39 Kevin Mack .02 .10
40 Lawyer Tillman .02 .10
41 Tommy Vardell .02 .10
42 Bernie Kosar .05 .15
43 Eric Metcalf .05 .15
44 Clay Matthews .02 .10
45 Keith McCants .02 .10
46 Broderick Thomas .02 .10
47 Lawrence Dawsey .02 .10
48 Reggie Cobb .02 .10
49 Lamar Thomas RC .02 .10
50 Courtney Hawkins .05 .15
51 Ivory Lee Brown RC .02 .10
52 Ernie Jones .02 .10
53 Freddie Joe Nunn .02 .10
54 Chris Chandler .05 .15
55 Randal Hill .02 .10
56 Lorenzo Lynch .02 .10
57 Garrison Hearst RC .40 1.00
58 Marion Butts .02 .10
59 Anthony Miller .05 .15
60 Eric Bieniemy .02 .10
61 Ronnie Harmon .02 .10
62 Junior Seau .10 .30
63 Gill Byrd .02 .10
64 Stan Humphries .05 .15
65 John Friesz .02 .10
66 J.J. Birden .05 .15
67 Joe Montana .75 2.00
68 Christian Okoye .05 .15
69 Dale Carter .02 .10
70 Barry Word .02 .10
71 Derrick Thomas .10 .30
72 Todd McNair .02 .10
73 Harvey Williams .02 .10
74 Jack Trudeau .02 .10
75 Rodney Culver .02 .10
76 Anthony Johnson .02 .10
77 Steve Emtman .02 .10
78 Quentin Coryatt .05 .15
79 Kerry Cash .02 .10
80 Jeff George .05 .15
81 Darrin Smith RC .02 .10
82 Jay Novacek .05 .15
83 Michael Irvin .10 .30
84 Alvin Harper .05 .15
85 Kevin Williams RC .05 .15
86 Troy Aikman .40 1.00
87 Emmitt Smith .75 2.00
88 O.J. McDuffie RC .10 .30
89 Mike Williams WR RC .02 .10
90 Dan Marino .75 2.00
91 Aaron Craver .02 .10
92 Troy Vincent .02 .10
93 Keith Jackson .05 .15
94 Marco Coleman .02 .10
95 Mark Higgs .02 .10
96 Fred Barnett .05 .15
97 Wes Hopkins .02 .10
98 Randall Cunningham .10 .30
99 Heath Sherman .02 .10
100 Vai Sikahema .02 .10
101 Tony Smith .02 .10
102 Andre Rison .05 .15
103 Chris Miller .02 .10
104 Deion Sanders .25 .60
105 Mike Pritchard .05 .15
106 Steve Broussard .02 .10
107 Stephen Baker .02 .10
108 Carl Banks .02 .10
109 Jarrod Bunch .02 .10
110 Phil Simms .05 .15
111 Rodney Hampton .05 .15
112 Dave Meggett .02 .10
113 Pepper Johnson .02 .10
114 Coleman Rudolph RC .02 .10
115 Boomer Esiason .05 .15
116 Browning Nagle .02 .10
117 Rob Moore .05 .15
118 Marvin Jones RC .02 .10
119 Herman Moore .10 .30
120 Bennie Blades .02 .10
121 Erik Kramer .02 .10
122 Mel Gray .02 .10
123 Rodney Peete .02 .10
124 Barry Sanders .60 1.50
125 Chris Spielman .02 .10
126 Lamar Lathon .02 .10
127 Ernest Givins .05 .15
128 Lorenzo White .05 .15
129 Micheal Barrow RC .10 .30
130 Warren Moon .05 .15
131 Cody Carlson .02 .10
132 Reggie White .10 .30
133 Terrell Buckley .02 .10
134 Ed West .02 .10
135 Mark Brunell RC .75 2.00
136 Brett Favre 1.00 2.50
137 Edgar Bennett .05 .15
138 Sterling Sharpe .05 .15
139 George Teague RC .02 .10
140 Leonard Russell .05 .15
141 Drew Bledsoe RC 1.25 3.00
142 Eugene Chung .02 .10
143 Walter Stanley .02 .10
144 Scott Zolak .02 .10
145 Jon Vaughn .02 .10
146 Andre Tippett .02 .10
147 Alexander Wright .02 .10
148 Billy Joe Hobert RC .10 .30
149 Terry McDaniel .02 .10
150 Tim Brown .10 .30
151 Willie Gault .02 .10
152 Howie Long .05 .15
153 Todd Marinovich .02 .10
154 Jim Everett .05 .15
155 David Lang .02 .10
156 Henry Ellard .05 .15
157 Cleveland Gary .02 .10
158 Steve Israel .02 .10
159 Jerome Bettis RC 2.00 5.00
160 Jackie Slater .02 .10
161 Art Monk .05 .15
162 Ricky Sanders .02 .10
163 Brian Mitchell .02 .10
164 Reggie Brooks RC .02 .10
165 Mark Rypien .02 .10
166 Earnest Byner .02 .10
167 Andre Collins .02 .10
168 Quinn Early .05 .15
169 Fred McAfee .02 .10
170 Wesley Carroll .02 .10
171 Gene Atkins .02 .10
172 Derek Brown RBK RC UER .05 .15
(Name spelled Derrek on front)
173 Vaughn Dunbar .02 .10
174 Rickey Jackson UER .02 .10
(Name spelled Ricky on front)
175 John L. Williams .02 .10
176 Carlton Gray RC .02 .10
177 Cortez Kennedy .05 .15
178 Kelly Stouffer .02 .10
179 Rick Mirer RC .10 .30
180 Dan McGwire .02 .10
181 Chris Warren .05 .15
182 Barry Foster .05 .15
183 Merril Hoge .02 .10
184 Darren Perry .02 .10
185 Deon Figures RC .05 .15
186A Jeff Graham ERR .05 .15
(Name misspelled
Grahm on front)
186B Jeff Graham COR .05 .15
(Name spelled correctly)
187 Dwight Stone .02 .10
188 Neil O'Donnell .05 .15
189 Rod Woodson .10 .30
190 Alex Van Pelt RC 1.25 3.00
191 Steve Jordan .02 .10
192 Roger Craig .05 .15
193 Qadry Ismail RC UER .10 .30
(Misspelled Quadry
on card front)
194 Robert Smith RC .60 1.50
195 Gino Torretta RC .05 .15
196 Anthony Carter .05 .15
197 Terry Allen .05 .15
198 Rich Gannon .10 .30
199 Checklist 1-100 .02 .10
200 Checklist 101-200 .02 .10
201 Victor Bailey RC .02 .10
202 Micheal Barrow .10 .30
203 Patrick Bates RC .02 .10
204 Jerome Bettis 1.00 2.50
205 Drew Bledsoe .60 1.50
206 Vincent Brisby RC .10 .30
207 Reggie Brooks .05 .15
208 Derek Brown RBK .05 .15
209 Keith Byars .02 .10
210 Tom Carter RC .02 .10
211 Curtis Conway .10 .30
212 Russell Copeland RC .05 .15
213 John Copeland RC .05 .15
214 Eric Curry RC .05 .15
215 Troy Drayton RC .05 .15
216 Jason Elam RC .10 .30
217 Steve Everitt RC .02 .10
218 Deon Figures .05 .15
219 Irving Fryar .05 .15
220 Darrien Gordon RC .02 .10
221 Carlton Gray .02 .10
222 Kevin Greene .05 .15
223 Andre Hastings RC .05 .15
224 Michael Haynes .05 .15
225 Garrison Hearst .10 .30
226 Bobby Hebert .02 .10
227 Lester Holmes .02 .10
228 Jeff Hostetler .05 .15
229 Desmond Howard .05 .15
230 Tyrone Hughes RC .05 .15
231 Qadry Ismail .05 .15
232 Rocket Ismail .05 .15
233 James Jett RC .25 .60
234 Marvin Jones .02 .10
235 Todd Kelly RC .02 .10
236 Lincoln Kennedy RC .02 .10
237 Terry Kirby RC .05 .15
238 Bernie Kosar .05 .15
239 Derrick Lassic RC .02 .10
240 Wilber Marshall .02 .10
241 O.J. McDuffie .10 .30
242 Ryan McNeil RC .10 .30
243 Natrone Means RC .10 .30
244 Glyn Milburn .05 .15
245 Rick Mirer .10 .30
246 Scott Mitchell .10 .30
247 Ronald Moore RC .05 .15
248 Lorenzo Neal RC .02 .10
249 Eric Pegram .05 .15
250 Roosevelt Potts RC .02 .10
251 Leonard Renfro RC .02 .10
252 Greg Robinson RC .02 .10
253 Wayne Simmons RC .02 .10
254 Chris Slade RC .05 .15
255 Irv Smith RC .05 .15
256 Robert Smith .25 .60
257 Dana Stubblefield RC .10 .30
258 George Teague .02 .10
259 Kevin Williams WR .05 .15
260 Checklist 201-260 .02 .10

1993 Wild Card Superchrome Field Force

COMPLETE SET (10) 5.00 12.00
SCF1 Jerry Rice .60 1.50
SCF2 Glyn Milburn .07 .20
SCF3 Joe Montana 1.00 2.50
SCF4 Rick Mirer .15 .40
SCF5 Troy Aikman .50 1.25
SCF6 Emmitt Smith 1.00 2.50
SCF7 Dan Marino 1.00 2.50
SCF8 Drew Bledsoe .75 2.00
SCF9 Barry Sanders .75 2.00
SCF10 Brett Favre 1.25 3.00

1993 Wild Card Superchrome FF/RHR Back to Back

COMPLETE SET (10) 6.00 15.00
RANDOM INS.IN SUPERCHROME SER.
ONE FIELD FORCE/RED HOT ROOKIE
1 Troy Aikman .50 1.25
Dana Stubblefield
2 Drew Bledsoe .75 2.00
Drew Bledsoe
3 Brett Favre 1.25 3.00
Terry Kirby
4 Dan Marino 1.00 2.50
Reggie Brooks
5 Glyn Milburn .15 .40
Rick Mirer
6 Rick Mirer .15 .40
Glyn Milburn
7 Joe Montana 1.00 2.50
Jerome Bettis
8 Jerry Rice .60 1.50
Garrison Hearst
9 Barry Sanders .75 2.00
Victor Bailey
10 Emmitt Smith 1.00 2.50
Qadry Ismail UER
(Misspelled Quadry)

1993 Wild Card Superchrome Red Hot Rookies

COMPLETE SET (10) 5.00 12.00
1 Dana Stubblefield .30 .75
2 Glyn Milburn .15 .40
3 Jerome Bettis 5.00 12.00
4 Rick Mirer .30 .75
5 Garrison Hearst 1.00 2.50
6 Terry Kirby .15 .40
7 Victor Bailey .08 .25
8 Drew Bledsoe 3.00 8.00
9 Reggie Brooks .08 .25
10 Qadry Ismail .30 .75

1993 Wild Card Superchrome Rookies Promos

These five standard-size promo cards feature on their fronts metallic purple-bordered color player action shots set within gold elliptical inner borders. The cards are numbered on the back with a "P" prefix.

COMPLETE SET (6) 2.00 5.00
P1 Rick Mirer .30 .75
P2 Reggie Brooks .20 .50
P3 Glyn Milburn .20 .50
P4 Drew Bledsoe 1.00 2.50
P5 Jerome Bettis .60 1.50
P6 O.J. McDuffie .30 .75

1993 Wild Card Superchrome Rookies

COMPLETE SET (50) 5.00 12.00
1 Dana Stubblefield .20 .50
2 Todd Kelly .05 .15
3 Curtis Conway .20 .50
4 John Copeland .08 .25
5 Tony McGee .05 .15
6 Russell Copeland .08 .25
7 Thomas Smith .05 .15
8 Jason Elam .20 .50
9 Glyn Milburn .08 .25
10 Steve Everitt .05 .15
11 Demetrius DuBose .05 .15
12 Eric Curry .08 .25
13 Garrison Hearst .20 .50
14 Ronald Moore .08 .25
15 Darrien Gordon .05 .15
16 Natrone Means .20 .50
17 Roosevelt Potts .05 .15
18 Derrick Lassic .05 .15
19 Kevin Williams .08 .25
20 Scott Mitchell UER .20 .50
(Text indicates drafted in '91;
should be '90)
21 O.J. McDuffie .20 .50
22 Terry Kirby .08 .25
23 Vaughn Hebron .05 .15
24 Victor Bailey .05 .15
25 Lincoln Kennedy .05 .15
26 Michael Strahan .05 .15
27 Marvin Jones .05 .15
28 Will Shields .05 .15
29 Ryan McNeil .20 .50
30 Micheal Barrow .20 .50
31 George Teague .05 .15
32 Wayne Simmons .05 .15
33 Vincent Brisby .20 .50
34 Drew Bledsoe 1.00 2.50
35 Patrick Bates .05 .15
36 James Jett .40 1.00
37 Rocket Ismail .08 .25
38 Troy Drayton .08 .25
39 Jerome Bettis 1.50 4.00
40 Tom Carter .05 .15
41 Reggie Brooks .08 .25
42 Tyrone Hughes .08 .25
43 Derek Brown RBK .08 .25
44 Willie Roaf .05 .15
45 Carlton Gray .05 .15
46 Rick Mirer .20 .50
47 Andre Hastings .08 .25
48 Deon Figures .08 .25
49 Qadry Ismail .08 .25
50 Robert Smith .40 1.00

1993 Wild Card Superchrome Rookies Back to Back

COMPLETE SET (25) 8.00 20.00
RANDOM INS.IN SUPERCHROME ROOK
1 Victor Bailey .08 .25
Vaughn Hebron
2 Micheal Barrow .30 .75
Ryan McNeil
3 Patrick Bates .30 .75
Vincent Brisby
4 Jerome Bettis .30 .75
Natrone Means
5 Drew Bledsoe 3.00 8.00
Rick Mirer
6 Reggie Brooks .15 .40
Glyn Milburn
7 Derek Brown RBK .15 .40
Tyrone Hughes
8 Tom Carter .30 .75
Jason Elam
9 Curtis Conway .50 1.25
Steve Everitt
10 John Copeland .15 .40
Tony McGee
11 Russell Copeland .08 .25
Thomas Smith
12 Eric Curry .15 .40
Demetrius DuBose
13 Troy Drayton .08 .25
Darrien Gordon
14 Deon Figures .15 .40
Andre Hastings
15 Carlton Gray .08 .25
Willie Roaf
16 Garrison Hearst 1.00 2.50
Ronald Moore
17 Qadry Ismail .30 .75
Rocket Ismail
18 James Jett 1.50 4.00
Robert Smith
19 Marvin Jones .08 .25
Will Shields
20 Todd Kelly .30 .75
Dana Stubblefield
21 Lincoln Kennedy .10 .25
Michael Strahan
22 Terry Kirby .30 .75
O.J. McDuffie
23 Derrick Lassic .15 .40
Kevin Williams
24 Scott Mitchell .08 .25
Roosevelt Potts
25 Wayne Simmons .08 .25
George Teague

1966 Williams Portraits Packers

This set consists of charcoal portraits of Green Bay Packers players with each portrait measuring approximately 8" by 10" This set preceded the complete NFL Williams Portraits released in 1967. The prints look very similar to the 1967 set, with each including the player's name and position beneath the charcoal portrait with blankbacks. The 1966 set is distinguished primarily by the lack of a year on the copyright line. The portraits are unnumbered and have been checklisted below alphabetically. An album was also produced to house the complete set.

COMPLETE SET (34) 175.00 300.00
1 Herb Adderley 10.00 15.00
2 Lionel Aldridge 5.00 8.00
3 Donny Anderson 6.00 10.00
4 Ken Bowman 5.00 8.00
5 Zeke Bratkowski 6.00 10.00
6 Bob Brown SP 6.00 10.00
7 Tom Brown 5.00 8.00
8 Lee Roy Caffey 5.00 8.00
9 Don Chandler 5.00 8.00
10 Tommy Crutcher 5.00 8.00
11 Bill Curry SP
12 Carroll Dale 6.00 10.00
13 Willie Davis 8.00 12.00
14 Boyd Dowler 6.00 10.00
15 Marv Fleming 6.00 10.00
16 Gale Gillingham SP 5.00 8.00
17 Jim Grabowski 5.00 8.00
18 Forrest Gregg 8.00 12.00
19 Doug Hart SP 5.00 8.00
20 Paul Hornung 15.00 25.00
21 Bob Jeter 5.00 8.00
22 Hank Jordan 8.00 12.00
23 Ron Kostelnik 5.00 8.00
24 Jerry Kramer 8.00 12.00
25 Bob Long 5.00 8.00
26 Max McGee 6.00 10.00
27 Ray Nitschke 15.00 25.00
28 Elijah Pitts 5.00 8.00
29 Dave Robinson 6.00 10.00
30 Bob Skoronski 5.00 8.00
31 Bart Starr 25.00 40.00
32 Jim Taylor 12.00 20.00
33 Fuzzy Thurston 8.00 12.00
34 Steve Wright SP 5.00 8.00
35 Willie Wood 8.00 12.00

1967 Williams Portraits

This set consists of charcoal art portraits of NFL players. Each portrait measures approximately 8" by 10", and they were sold in sets of eight for $1 along with the end flap from Velveeta, or a front label from Kraft Deluxe Slices or Singles, Cracker Barrel Cheddar or Kraft Sliced Natural Cheese. There were four eight-portrait groups for each of the 16 NFL teams. Moreover, an official NFL portrait album which would hold 32 portraits was offered for $2. The player's name and position were printed beneath the charcoal portrait. The backs are blank. The portraits are unnumbered and have been checklisted below alphabetically according to team. A checklist sheet (8" by 10") was produced, but is not considered a card. The Redskins and Packers sets appear to be the easiest to find. Popular players issued in their Rookie Card year include Leroy Kelly, Tommy Nobis, Dan Reeves and Jackie Smith. Players issued before their Rookie Card year include Lem Barney, Brian Piccolo, Bubba Smith and Steve Spurrier. It is believed that six players on this checklist did not have portraits produced while several other player listed are incorrect. Several players apparently were switched out for new players in their respective sets: Chuck Walton replaced Mike Alford and Bob Pickens replaced Bob Jones as examples. Lastly, a Vince Lombardi Williams Portrait was issued for a Downtown Businessman's function for the Green Bay Chamber of Commerce on August 7, 1968. We price this photo below as well although it is not considered part of the complete set.

COMPLETE SET (512)	5,000.00	8,000.00
1 Taz Anderson	10.00	20.00
2 Gary Barnes	10.00	20.00
3 Lee Calland	10.00	20.00
4 Junior Coffey	10.00	20.00
5 Ed Cook	10.00	20.00
6 Perry Lee Dunn	10.00	20.00
7 Dan Grimm	10.00	20.00
8 Alex Hawkins	12.50	25.00
9 Randy Johnson	10.00	20.00
10 Lou Kirouac	10.00	20.00
11 Errol Linden	10.00	20.00
12 Billy Lothridge	10.00	20.00
13 Frank Marchlewski	10.00	20.00
14 Rich Marshall	10.00	20.00
15 Billy Martin E	10.00	20.00
16 Tom Moore	12.50	25.00
17 Tommy Nobis	15.00	30.00
18 Jim Norton	10.00	20.00
19 Nick Rassas	10.00	20.00
20 Ken Reaves	10.00	20.00
21 Bobby Richards	10.00	20.00
22 Jerry Richardson	10.00	20.00
23 Bob Riggle	10.00	20.00
24 Karl Rubke	10.00	20.00
25 Marion Rushing	10.00	20.00
26 Chuck Sieminski	10.00	20.00
27 Steve Sloan	10.00	20.00
28 Ron Smith	10.00	20.00
29 Don Talbert	10.00	20.00
30 Ernie Wheelwright	10.00	20.00
31 Sam Williams	10.00	20.00
32 Jim Wilson	10.00	20.00
33 Sam Ball	10.00	20.00
34 Raymond Berry	20.00	40.00
35 Bob Boyd DB	10.00	20.00
36 Ordell Braase	10.00	20.00
37 Barry Brown	10.00	20.00
38 Bill Curry	10.00	20.00
39 Mike Curtis	12.50	25.00
40 Alvin Haymond	10.00	20.00
41 Jerry Hill	10.00	20.00
42 David Lee	10.00	20.00
43 Jerry Logan	10.00	20.00
44 Tony Lorick	10.00	20.00
45 Lenny Lyles	10.00	20.00
46 John Mackey	15.00	30.00
47 Tom Matte	12.50	25.00
48 Lou Michaels	12.50	25.00
49 Fred Miller	10.00	20.00
50 Lenny Moore	20.00	40.00
51 Jimmy Orr	10.00	20.00
52 Jim Parker	15.00	30.00
53 Glenn Ressler	10.00	20.00
54 Willie Richardson	10.00	20.00
55 Don Shinnick	10.00	20.00
56 Billy Ray Smith	10.00	20.00
57 Bubba Smith	15.00	30.00
58 Dan Sullivan	10.00	20.00
59 Dick Szymanski	10.00	20.00
60 Johnny Unitas	60.00	100.00
61 Bob Vogel	10.00	20.00
62 Rick Volk	10.00	20.00
63 Jim Welch	10.00	20.00
64 Butch Wilson	10.00	20.00
65 Charlie Bivins	12.50	25.00
66 Charlie Brown DB	12.50	25.00
67 Doug Buffone	12.50	25.00
68 Rudy Bukich	12.50	25.00
69 Ronnie Bull	12.50	25.00
70 Dick Butkus	40.00	75.00
71 Jim Cadile	12.50	25.00
72 Jack Concannon	12.50	25.00
73 Frank Cornish DT	12.50	25.00
74 Don Croftcheck	12.50	25.00
75 Dick Evey	12.50	25.00
76 Joe Fortunato	12.50	25.00
77 Curtis Gentry	12.50	25.00
78 Bobby Joe Green	12.50	25.00
79 John Johnson DT	12.50	25.00
80 Jimmy Jones	12.50	25.00
81 Ralph Kurek	12.50	25.00
82 Roger LeClerc	12.50	25.00
83 Andy Livingston	12.50	25.00
84 Bennie McRae	12.50	25.00
85 Johnny Morris	12.50	25.00
86 Richie Petitbon	12.50	25.00
87 Loyd Phillips	12.50	25.00
88 Brian Piccolo	40.00	75.00
89 Bob Pickens	12.50	25.00
90 Jim Purnell	12.50	25.00
91 Mike Pyle	12.50	25.00
92 Mike Reilly	12.50	25.00
93 Gale Sayers	40.00	75.00
94 George Seals	12.50	25.00
95 Roosevelt Taylor	15.00	30.00
96 Bob Wetoska	12.50	25.00
97 Erich Barnes	10.00	20.00
98 Johnny Brewer	10.00	20.00
99 Monte Clark	10.00	20.00
100 Gary Collins	12.50	25.00
101 Larry Conjar	10.00	20.00
102 Vince Costello	10.00	20.00
103 Ross Fichtner	10.00	20.00
104 Bill Glass	10.00	20.00
105 Ernie Green	10.00	20.00
106 Jack Gregory	10.00	20.00
107 Charlie Harraway	10.00	20.00
108 Gene Hickerson	10.00	20.00
109 Fred Hoaglin	10.00	20.00
110 Jim Houston	10.00	20.00
111 Mike Howell	10.00	20.00
112 Joe Bob Isbell	10.00	20.00
113 Walter Johnson	10.00	20.00
114 Jim Kanicki	10.00	20.00
115 Ernie Kellerman	10.00	20.00
116 Leroy Kelly	15.00	30.00
117 Dale Lindsey	10.00	20.00
118 Clifton McNeil	10.00	20.00
119 Milt Morin	10.00	20.00
120 Nick Pietrosante	10.00	20.00
121 Frank Ryan	12.50	25.00
122 Dick Schafrath	10.00	20.00
123 Randy Schultz	10.00	20.00
124 Ralph Smith	10.00	20.00
125 Carl Ward	10.00	20.00
126 Paul Warfield	15.00	30.00
127 Paul Wiggin	10.00	20.00
128 John Wooten	10.00	20.00
129 George Andrie	12.50	25.00
130 Jim Boeke	12.50	25.00
131 Frank Clarke	15.00	30.00
132 Mike Connelly	12.50	25.00
133 Buddy Dial	12.50	25.00
134 Leon Donohue	12.50	25.00
135 Dave Edwards	12.50	25.00
136 Mike Gaechter	12.50	25.00
137 Walt Garrison	15.00	30.00
138 Pete Gent	12.50	25.00
139 Cornell Green	15.00	30.00
140 Bob Hayes	20.00	40.00
141 Chuck Howley	20.00	40.00
142 Lee Roy Jordan	20.00	40.00
143 Bob Lilly	35.00	60.00
144 Tony Liscio	12.50	25.00
145 Warren Livingston	12.50	25.00
146 Dave Manders	12.50	25.00
147 Don Meredith	40.00	75.00
148 Ralph Neely	12.50	25.00
149 John Niland	12.50	25.00
150 Pettis Norman	12.50	25.00
151 Don Perkins	15.00	30.00
152 Jethro Pugh	12.50	25.00
153 Dan Reeves	25.00	50.00
154 Mel Renfro	20.00	40.00
155 Jerry Rhome	12.50	25.00
156 Les Shy	12.50	25.00
157 J.D. Smith	12.50	25.00
158 Willie Townes	12.50	25.00
159 Danny Villanueva	12.50	25.00
160 John Wilbur	12.50	25.00
161 Lem Barney	15.00	30.00
162 Charley Bradshaw	10.00	20.00
163 Roger Brown	12.50	25.00
164 Ernie Clark	10.00	20.00
165 Gail Cogdill	10.00	20.00
166 Nick Eddy	10.00	20.00
167 Mel Farr	10.00	20.00
168 Bobby Felts	10.00	20.00
169 Ed Flanagan	10.00	20.00
170 Jim Gibbons	12.50	25.00
171 John Gordy	10.00	20.00
172 Larry Hand	10.00	20.00
173 Wally Hilgenberg	10.00	20.00
174 Alex Karras	20.00	40.00
175 Bob Kowalkowski	10.00	20.00
176 Ron Kramer	10.00	20.00
177 Mike Lucci	10.00	20.00
178 Bruce Maher	10.00	20.00
179 Amos Marsh	10.00	20.00
180 Darris McCord	10.00	20.00
181 Tom Nowatzke	10.00	20.00
182 Milt Plum	12.50	25.00
183 Wayne Rasmussen	10.00	20.00
184 Roger Shoals	10.00	20.00
185 Pat Studstill	10.00	20.00
186 Karl Sweetan	10.00	20.00
187 Bobby Thompson DB	10.00	20.00
188 Doug Van Horn	10.00	20.00
189 Wayne Walker	10.00	20.00
190 Tommy Watkins	10.00	20.00
191 Chuck Walton	10.00	20.00
192 Garo Yepremian	12.50	25.00
193 Herb Adderley	10.00	20.00
194 Lionel Aldridge	5.00	10.00
195 Donny Anderson	6.00	12.00
196 Ken Bowman	5.00	10.00
197 Zeke Bratkowski	6.00	12.00
198 Bob Brown DT	5.00	10.00
199 Tom Brown	5.00	10.00
200 Lee Roy Caffey	5.00	10.00
201 Don Chandler	6.00	12.00
202 Tommy Crutcher	5.00	10.00
203 Carroll Dale	6.00	12.00
204 Willie Davis	7.50	15.00
205 Boyd Dowler	6.00	12.00
206 Marv Fleming	6.00	12.00
207 Gale Gillingham	5.00	10.00
208 Jim Grabowski	5.00	10.00
209 Forrest Gregg	10.00	20.00
210 Doug Hart	5.00	10.00
211 Bob Jeter	5.00	10.00
212 Hank Jordan	7.50	15.00
213 Ron Kostelnik	5.00	10.00
214 Jerry Kramer	7.50	15.00
215 Bob Long	5.00	10.00
216 Max McGee	6.00	12.00
217 Ray Nitschke	12.50	25.00
218 Elijah Pitts	6.00	12.00
219 Dave Robinson	5.00	10.00
220 Bob Skoronski	5.00	10.00
221 Bart Starr	25.00	50.00
222 Fred Thurston	7.50	15.00
223 Willie Wood	10.00	20.00
224 Steve Wright	5.00	10.00
225 Dick Bass	12.50	25.00
226 Maxie Baughan	10.00	20.00
227 Joe Carollo	10.00	20.00
228 Bernie Casey	10.00	20.00
229 Don Chuy	10.00	20.00
230 Charlie Cowan	10.00	20.00
231 Irv Cross	10.00	20.00
232 Willie Ellison	10.00	20.00
233 Roman Gabriel	15.00	30.00
234 Bruce Gossett	10.00	20.00
235 Roosevelt Grier	12.50	25.00
236 Tony Guillory	10.00	20.00
237 Ken Iman	10.00	20.00
238 Deacon Jones	20.00	40.00
239 Les Josephson	10.00	20.00
240 Jon Kilgore	10.00	20.00
241 Chuck Lamson	10.00	20.00
242 Lamar Lundy	12.50	25.00
243 Tom Mack	15.00	30.00
244 Tommy Mason	12.50	25.00
245 Tommy McDonald	12.50	25.00
246 Ed Meador	10.00	20.00
247 Bill Munson	10.00	20.00
248 Bob Nichols	10.00	20.00
249 Merlin Olsen	20.00	40.00
250 Jack Pardee	12.50	25.00
251 Bucky Pope	10.00	20.00
252 Joe Scibelli	10.00	20.00
253 Jack Snow	12.50	25.00
254 Billy Truax	10.00	20.00
255 Clancy Williams	10.00	20.00
256 Doug Woodlief	10.00	20.00
257 Grady Alderman	12.50	25.00
258 John Beasley	10.00	20.00
259 Bob Berry	10.00	20.00
260 Larry Bowie	10.00	20.00
261 Bill Brown	12.50	25.00
262 Fred Cox	12.50	25.00
263 Doug Davis	10.00	20.00
264 Paul Dickson	10.00	20.00
265 Carl Eller	15.00	30.00
266 Paul Flatley	10.00	20.00
267 Dale Hackbart	10.00	20.00
268 Don Hansen	10.00	20.00
269 Clint Jones	10.00	20.00
270 Jeff Jordan	10.00	20.00
271 Karl Kassulke	10.00	20.00
272 John Kirby	10.00	20.00
273 Gary Larsen	10.00	20.00
274 Jim Lindsey	10.00	20.00
275 Earsell Mackbee	10.00	20.00
276 Jim Marshall	15.00	30.00
277 Marlin McKeever	10.00	20.00
278 Dave Osborn	10.00	20.00
279 Jim Phillips	10.00	20.00
280 Ed Sharockman	10.00	20.00
281 Jerry Shay	10.00	20.00
282 Milt Sunde	10.00	20.00
283 Archie Sutton	10.00	20.00
284 Mick Tingelhoff	12.50	25.00
285 Ron VanderKelen	10.00	20.00
286 Jim Vellone	10.00	20.00
287 Lonnie Warwick	10.00	20.00
288 Roy Winston	10.00	20.00
289 Doug Atkins	15.00	30.00
290 Vern Burke	10.00	20.00
291 Bruce Cortez	10.00	20.00
292 Gary Cuozzo	12.50	25.00
293 Ted Davis	10.00	20.00
294 John Douglas	10.00	20.00
295 Jim Garcia	10.00	20.00
296 Tom Hall	10.00	20.00
297 Jim Heidel	10.00	20.00
298 Leslie Kelley	10.00	20.00
299 Billy Kilmer	12.50	25.00
300 Kent Kramer	10.00	20.00
301 Jake Kupp	10.00	20.00
302 Earl Leggett	10.00	20.00
303 Obert Logan	10.00	20.00
304 Tom McNeill	10.00	20.00
305 John Morrow	10.00	20.00
306 Ray Ogden	10.00	20.00
307 Ray Rissmiller	10.00	20.00
308 George Rose	10.00	20.00
309 Dave Rowe	10.00	20.00
310 Brian Schweda	10.00	20.00
311 Dave Simmons	10.00	20.00
312 Jerry Simmons	10.00	20.00
313 Steve Stonebreaker	10.00	20.00
314 Jim Taylor	20.00	40.00
315 Mike Tilleman	10.00	20.00
316 Phil Vandersea	10.00	20.00
317 Joe Wendryhoski	10.00	20.00
318 Dave Whitsell	10.00	20.00
319 Fred Whittingham	10.00	20.00
320 Gary Wood	10.00	20.00
321 Ken Avery	10.00	20.00
322 Bookie Bolin	10.00	20.00
323 Henry Carr	12.50	25.00
324 Pete Case	10.00	20.00
325 Clarence Childs	10.00	20.00
326 Mike Ciccolella	10.00	20.00
327 Glen Condren	10.00	20.00
328 Bob Crespino	10.00	20.00
329 Don Davis	10.00	20.00
330 Tucker Frederickson	12.50	25.00
331 Charlie Harper	10.00	20.00
332 Phil Harris	10.00	20.00
333 Allen Jacobs	10.00	20.00
334 Homer Jones	10.00	20.00
335 Jim Katcavage	10.00	20.00
336 Tom Kennedy	10.00	20.00
337 Ernie Koy	10.00	20.00
338 Greg Larson	10.00	20.00
339 Spider Lockhart	10.00	20.00
340 Chuck Mercein	10.00	20.00
341 Jim Moran	10.00	20.00
342 Earl Morrall	12.50	25.00
343 Joe Morrison	10.00	20.00
344 Francis Peay	10.00	20.00
345 Del Shofner	12.50	25.00
346 Jeff Smith LB	10.00	20.00
347 Fran Tarkenton	30.00	60.00
348 Aaron Thomas	10.00	20.00
349 Larry Vargo	10.00	20.00
350 Freeman White	10.00	20.00
351 Sidney Williams	10.00	20.00
352 Willie Young	10.00	20.00
353 Sam Baker	10.00	20.00
354 Gary Ballman	10.00	20.00
355 Randy Beisler	10.00	20.00
356 Bob Brown OT	12.50	25.00
357 Timmy Brown	12.50	25.00
358 Mike Ditka	40.00	75.00
359 Dave Graham	10.00	20.00
360 Ben Hawkins	10.00	20.00
361 Fred Hill	10.00	20.00
362 King Hill	10.00	20.00
363 Lynn Hoyem	10.00	20.00
364 Don Hultz	10.00	20.00
365 Dwight Kelley	10.00	20.00
366 Israel Lang	10.00	20.00
367 Dave Lloyd	10.00	20.00
368 Aaron Martin	10.00	20.00
369 Ron Medved	10.00	20.00
370 John Meyers	10.00	20.00
371 Mike Morgan LB	10.00	20.00
372 Al Nelson	10.00	20.00
373 Jim Nettles	10.00	20.00
374 Floyd Peters	10.00	20.00
375 Gary Pettigrew	10.00	20.00
376 Ray Poage	10.00	20.00
377 Nate Ramsey	10.00	20.00
378 Dave Recher	10.00	20.00
379 Jim Ringo	10.00	20.00
380 Joe Scarpati	10.00	20.00
381 Jim Skaggs	10.00	20.00
382 Norm Snead	12.50	25.00
383 Harold Wells	10.00	20.00
384 Tom Woodeshick	10.00	20.00
385 Bill Asbury	12.50	25.00
386 John Baker	12.50	25.00
387 Jim Bradshaw	12.50	25.00
388 Rod Breedlove	12.50	25.00
389 John Brown	12.50	25.00
390 Amos Bullocks	12.50	25.00
391 Jim Butler	12.50	25.00
392 John Campbell	12.50	25.00
393 Mike Clark	12.50	25.00
394 Larry Gagner	12.50	25.00
395 Earl Gros	12.50	25.00
396 John Hilton	12.50	25.00
397 Dick Hoak	12.50	25.00
398 Roy Jefferson	12.50	25.00
399 Tony Jeter	12.50	25.00
400 Brady Keys	12.50	25.00
401 Ken Kortas	12.50	25.00
402 Ray Mansfield	12.50	25.00
403 Paul Martha	12.50	25.00
404 Ben McGee	12.50	25.00
405 Bill Nelsen	15.00	30.00
406 Kent Nix	12.50	25.00
407 Fran O'Brien	12.50	25.00
408 Andy Russell	15.00	30.00
409 Bill Saul	12.50	25.00
410 Don Shy	12.50	25.00
411 Clendon Thomas	12.50	25.00
412 Bruce Van Dyke	12.50	25.00
413 Lloyd Voss	12.50	25.00
414 Ralph Wenzel	12.50	25.00
415 J.R. Wilburn	12.50	25.00
416 Marv Woodson	12.50	25.00
417 Jim Bakken	10.00	20.00
418 Don Brumm	10.00	20.00
419 Vidal Carlin	10.00	20.00
420 Bobby Joe Conrad	10.00	20.00
421 Willis Crenshaw	10.00	20.00
422 Bob DeMarco	10.00	20.00
423 Pat Fischer	12.50	25.00
424 Billy Gambrell	10.00	20.00
425 Prentice Gautt	10.00	20.00
426 Ken Gray	10.00	20.00
427 Jerry Hillebrand	10.00	20.00
428 Charley Johnson	12.50	25.00
429 Bill Koman	10.00	20.00
430 Dave Long	10.00	20.00
431 Ernie McMillan	10.00	20.00
432 Dave Meggysey	10.00	20.00
433 Dale Meinert	10.00	20.00
434 Mike Melinkovich	10.00	20.00
435 Dave O'Brien	10.00	20.00
436 Sonny Randle	10.00	20.00
437 Bob Reynolds	10.00	20.00
438 Joe Robb	10.00	20.00
439 Johnny Roland	10.00	20.00
440 Roy Shivers	10.00	20.00
441 Sam Silas	10.00	20.00
442 Jackie Smith	15.00	30.00
443 Rick Sortun	10.00	20.00
444 Jerry Stovall	10.00	20.00
445 Chuck Walker	10.00	20.00
446 Bobby Williams	10.00	20.00
447 Dave Williams	10.00	20.00
448 Larry Wilson	15.00	30.00
449 Kermit Alexander	10.00	20.00
450 Cas Banaszek	10.00	20.00
451 Bruce Bosley	10.00	20.00
452 John Brodie	20.00	40.00
453 Joe Cerne	10.00	20.00
454 John David Crow	12.50	25.00
455 Tommy Davis	10.00	20.00
456 Bob Harrison	10.00	20.00
457 Matt Hazeltine	10.00	20.00
458 Stan Hindman	10.00	20.00
459 Charlie Johnson DT	10.00	20.00
460 Jim Johnson	12.50	25.00
461 Dave Kopay	10.00	20.00
462 Charlie Krueger	10.00	20.00
463 Roland Lakes	10.00	20.00
464 Cary Lewis	10.00	20.00
465 Dave McCormick	10.00	20.00
466 Kay McFarland	10.00	20.00
467 Clark Miller	10.00	20.00
468 George Mira	10.00	20.00
469 Howard Mudd	10.00	20.00
470 Frank Nunley	10.00	20.00
471 Dave Parks	10.00	20.00
472 Walter Rock	10.00	20.00
473 Len Rohde	10.00	20.00
474 Steve Spurrier	30.00	60.00
475 Monty Stickles	10.00	20.00
476 John Thomas	10.00	20.00
477 Bill Tucker	10.00	20.00
478 Dave Wilcox	12.50	25.00
479 Ken Willard	10.00	20.00
480 Dick Witcher	10.00	20.00
481 Willie Adams	6.00	12.00
482 Walt Barnes DL	6.00	12.00
483 Jim Carroll	6.00	12.00
484 Dave Crossan	6.00	12.00
485 Charlie Gogolak	6.00	12.00
486 Tom Goosby	6.00	12.00
487 Chris Hanburger	7.50	15.00
488 Rickie Harris	6.00	12.00
489 Len Hauss	6.00	12.00
490 Sam Huff	12.50	25.00
491 Steve Jackson LB	6.00	12.00
492 Mitch Johnson	6.00	12.00
493 Sonny Jurgensen	12.50	25.00
494 Carl Kammerer	6.00	12.00
495 Paul Krause	10.00	20.00
496 Joe Don Looney	7.50	15.00
497 Ray McDonald	6.00	12.00
498 Bobby Mitchell	10.00	20.00
499 Jim Ninowski	6.00	12.00
500 Brig Owens	6.00	12.00
501 Vince Promuto	6.00	12.00
502 Pat Richter	6.00	12.00
503 Joe Rutgens	6.00	12.00
504 Lonnie Sanders	6.00	12.00
505 Ray Schoenke	6.00	12.00
506 Jim Shorter	6.00	12.00
507 Jerry Smith	6.00	12.00
508 Ron Snidow	6.00	12.00
509 Jim Snowden	6.00	12.00
510 Charley Taylor	10.00	20.00
511 Steve Thurlow	6.00	12.00
512 A.D. Whitfield	6.00	12.00
513 Vince Lombardi CO	60.00	100.00
514 Portrait Album	30.00	50.00

1948 Wilson Advisory Staff

These glossy black and white photos measure roughly 8 1/8" by 10" and were likely issued over a number of years. Each features a top player or coach photo with the Wilson advisory staff line of text below the picture. They also include facsimile autographs.

COMPLETE SET (5)	100.00	200.00
1 Paul Christman	20.00	40.00
2 Johnny Lujack	37.50	75.00
3 Clark Shaughnessy	15.00	30.00
4 Charley Trippi	25.00	50.00
5 Lynn Waldorf	15.00	30.00

1962-66 Wilson Advisory Staff

These 8X10 glossy photos were likely issued over a number of years in the 1960s. Each features a top player or coach photo printed in black and white with the Wilson advisory staff line of text below the picture. Some also include facsimile autographs.

COMPLETE SET (4)	45.00	90.00
1 Bernie Bierman	7.50	15.00
2 Boyd Dowler	10.00	20.00
3 Hugh McElhenny	12.50	25.00
4 Gale Sayers	20.00	40.00

1999 Winner's Circle Die Cast

Hasbro and Winner's Circle released these die cast pieces featuring NFL players. Each package includes a die cast 1999 Mustang (NFC players) or 1999 Corvette (AFC players) along with an oversized cardboard stand-featuring a photo of the player. The player's photo is also included on the hood of the die cast car. Prices below reflect that of unopened blister packs.

COMPLETE SET (14)	25.00	50.00
1 Troy Aikman	2.50	5.00
2 Drew Bledsoe	2.00	4.00
3 Mark Brunell	2.00	4.00
4 Randall Cunningham	2.00	4.00
5 Terrell Davis	2.50	5.00
6 Warrick Dunn	2.00	4.00
7 John Elway	3.00	6.00
8 Brett Favre	3.00	6.00
9 Doug Flutie	2.00	4.00
10 Keyshawn Johnson	2.00	4.00
11 Dan Marino	3.00	6.00
12 Randy Moss	2.50	5.00
13 Barry Sanders	2.50	5.00
14 Deion Sanders	2.00	4.00

1974 Wonder Bread

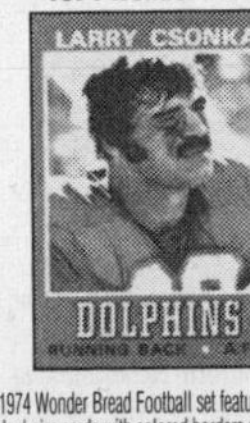

The 1974 Wonder Bread Football set features 30 standard-size cards with colored borders and color photographs of the players on the front. Season by season records are given on the back of the cards as well as a particular football technique. A "Topps Chewing Gum, Inc." copyright appears on the reverse. A parallel version of the cards was also distributed by Town Talk Bread

COMPLETE SET (30)	25.00	50.00
1 Jim Bakken	.60	1.50
2 Forrest Blue	.60	1.50
3 Bill Bradley	.60	1.50
4 Willie Brown	1.00	2.50
5 Larry Csonka	3.00	6.00
6 Ken Ellis	.60	1.50
7 Bruce Gossett	.60	1.50
8 Bob Griese	3.00	6.00
9 Chris Hanburger	.60	1.50
10 Winston Hill	.60	1.50
11 Jim Johnson	.75	2.00
12 Paul Krause	.75	2.00
13 Ted Kwalick	.60	1.50
14 Willie Lanier	1.00	2.50
15 Tom Mack	.75	2.00
16 Jim Otto	1.00	2.50
17 Alan Page	1.00	2.50
18 Frank Pitts	.60	1.50
19 Jim Plunkett	1.00	2.50
20 Mike Reid	.75	2.00
21 Paul Smith	.60	1.50
22 Bob Tucker	.60	1.50
23 Jim Tyrer	.60	1.50
24 Gene Upshaw	1.00	2.50
25 Phil Villapiano	.60	1.50
26 Paul Warfield	1.50	4.00
27 Dwight White	.75	2.00
28 Steve Owens	.75	2.00
29 Jerrel Wilson	.60	1.50
30 Ron Yary	.75	2.00

1974 Wonder Bread/Town Talk

The 1974 Town Talk Bread set features 30 standard-size cards with colored borders and color photographs of the players on the front. The cards are essentially a parallel version of the 1974 Wonder Bread release, but were distributed through Town Talk Bread products. A "Topps Chewing Gum, Inc." copyright appears on the reverse. These Town Talk cards are more difficult to find and are priced using the multiplier line given below. They are distinguished from the Wonder Bread issue by the absence of a credit line at the top of the cardback.

COMPLETE SET (30)	125.00	250.00
*TOWN TALK: 3X TO 6X BASIC CARDS		

1975 Wonder Bread

The 1975 Wonder Bread Football card set contains 24 standard-size cards with either blue (7-18) or red (1-6 and 19-24) borders. The backs feature several questions (about the player and the game of football) whose answers could be determined by turning the card upside down and reading the answers to the corresponding questions. The words "Topps Chewing Gum, Inc." appears at the bottom of the reverse of the card. Wonder Bread also produced a saver sheet and album for this set. A parallel version of the cards was also produced by Town Talk Bread.

COMPLETE SET (24)	20.00	40.00
1 Alan Page	.75	2.00
2 Emmitt Thomas	.60	1.50
3 John Mendenhall	.50	1.25
4 Ken Houston	.60	1.50
5 Jack Ham	1.50	4.00
6 L.C. Greenwood	.75	2.00
7 Tom Mack	.60	1.50
8 Winston Hill	.50	1.25
9 Isaac Curtis	.50	1.25
10 Terry Owens	.50	1.25
11 Drew Pearson	1.25	3.00
12 Don Cockroft	.50	1.25
13 Bob Griese	2.00	5.00
14 Riley Odoms	.50	1.25
15 Chuck Foreman	.60	1.50
16 Forrest Blue	.50	1.25
17 Franco Harris	2.50	6.00
18 Larry Little	.60	1.50
19 Bill Bergey	.50	1.25
20 Ray Guy	.60	1.50
21 Ted Hendricks	.75	2.00
22 Levi Johnson	.50	1.25
23 Jack Mildren	.50	1.25
24 Mel Tom	.50	1.25

1975 Wonder Bread/Town Talk

The 1975 Town Talk Bread card set contains 24 standard-size cards with either blue (7-18) or red (1-6 and 19-24) borders. The cards are essentially a parallel to the Wonder Bread issue. The words "Topps Chewing Gum, Inc." appears at the bottom of the cardback. These Town Talk cards are more difficult to find and are priced using the multiplier line given below. They are distinguished by the different "Town Talk" credit line at the top of the cardback.

COMPLETE SET (24)	125.00	250.00
*TOWN TALK: 4X TO 8X BASIC CARDS		

1976 Wonder Bread

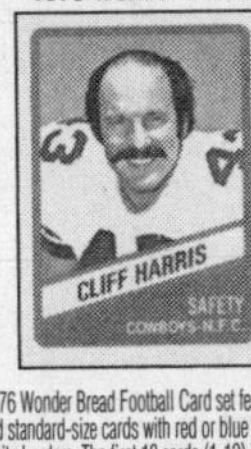

The 1976 Wonder Bread Football Card set features 24 colored standard-size cards with red or blue frame lines and white borders. The first 12 cards (1-12) in the set feature offensive players with a blue frame and the last 12 cards (13-24) feature defensive players with a red frame. The backs feature one of coach Hank Stram's favorite plays, with a football diagram and a text listing each offensive player's assignments of the particular play. The "Topps Chewing Gum, Inc." copyright appears at the bottom on the cardback. A parallel version of the cards was also produced by Town Talk Bread.

COMPLETE SET (24)	2.50	5.00
1 Craig Morton	.25	.50
2 Chuck Foreman	.15	.40
3 Franco Harris	.50	1.25
4 Mel Gray	.15	.40
5 Charley Taylor	.30	.75
6 Richard Caster	.10	.30
7 George Kunz	.10	.30
8 Rayfield Wright	.10	.30
9 Gene Upshaw	.25	.50
10 Tom Mack	.15	.40
11 Len Hauss	.10	.30
12 Garo Yepremian	.10	.30
13 Cedrick Hardman	.10	.30
14 Jack Youngblood	.25	.50
15 Wally Chambers	.10	.30
16 Jerry Sherk	.10	.30
17 Bill Bergey	.10	.30
18 Jack Ham	.30	.75
19 Fred Carr	.10	.30
20 Jack Tatum	.15	.40
21 Cliff Harris	.25	.50
22 Emmitt Thomas	.10	.30
23 Ken Riley	.10	.30
24 Ray Guy	.25	.50

1976 Wonder Bread/Town Talk

The 1976 Town Talk Bread football card set features 24 colored standard-size cards with red or blue frame lines and white borders. The cards are essentially a parallel version to the Wonder Bread release. The "Topps Chewing Gum, Inc." copyright appears at the bottom on the cardback. These Town Talk cards are more difficult to find than the Wonder Bread issue and are priced using the multiplier line given below. They are distinguished by the different credit line at the top of the cardback.

COMPLETE SET (24)	50.00	100.00
*TOWN TALK: 6X TO 12X BASIC CARDS		

1964 Yuban Coffee Canvas Premiums

These large portraits were issued by Yuban Coffee around 1964. Each features a current NFL star in a painting format printed on canvas. The backs are blank. Any additions to this list are appreciated.

COMPLETE SET (17)	2,000.00	3,500.00
1 Gary Ballman	90.00	150.00
2 Jim Brown	250.00	400.00
3 Gail Cogdill	90.00	150.00
4 Bill George	100.00	175.00
5 Frank Gifford	125.00	200.00
6 Matt Hazeltine	90.00	150.00
7 Paul Hornung	150.00	300.00
8 Charley Johnson	90.00	150.00
9 Don Meredith	125.00	250.00
10 Bobby Mitchell	100.00	175.00
11 Earl Morrall	100.00	175.00
12 Jack Pardee	90.00	150.00
13 Nick Pietrosante	90.00	150.00
14 Pete Retzlaff	100.00	175.00
15 Fran Tarkenton	125.00	250.00
16 Y.A. Tittle	125.00	250.00
17 Johnny Unitas	250.00	400.00

1995 Zenith Promos

Commemorating the 1994 achievements of three Future Hall of Famers, this 4-card promo set was issued to herald the release of the 1995 Pinnacle Zenith series. Measuring the standard size, the cards are printed on 24-point card stock utilizing Pinnacle's all-foil metalized printing technology. The fronts display color action cutouts on a brown geometric design and bronze metallized brick design. The horizontal backs carry a color closeup photo and 1994 statistics presented on a football field graphic. The disclaimer "PROMO" is printed diagonally across the backs.

COMPLETE SET (4)	5.00	12.00
1 Emmitt Smith	2.00	5.00
94 Steve Young	1.20	3.00
97 Dan Marino	2.40	6.00
NNO Title Card	.10	.30

1995 Zenith

This 150-card standard-size set was issued by Pinnacle to honor some of the top NFL players. The cards are printed on 24-point card stock untilizing Pinnacle's all-foil metalized printing technology. The fronts display color action photos superimposed over a brown geometric design and bronze metalized printing technology. The horizontal backs carry a color close-up and 1994 statistics presented on a football field graphic. The only key Rookie Card is Jeff Blake.

COMPLETE SET (150)	7.50	20.00
Z1 Emmitt Smith	.75	2.00
Z2 Chris Spielman	.08	.25
Z3 Johnny Mitchell	.05	.15
Z4 Boomer Esiason	.08	.25
Z5 Jackie Harris	.05	.15
Z6 Warren Moon	.08	.25
Z7 Harvey Williams	.05	.15
Z8 Steve Walsh	.05	.15
Z9 Cris Carter	.15	.40
Z10 Natrone Means	.08	.25
Z11 Art Monk	.08	.25
Z12 Leslie O'Neal	.08	.25
Z13 Adrian Murrell	.08	.25
Z14 John Elway	1.00	2.50
Z15 Larry Centers	.08	.25
Z16 Ricky Ervins	.05	.15
Z17 Jeff Graham	.05	.15
Z18 Ricky Watters	.08	.25
Z19 Eric Green	.05	.15
Z20 Curtis Conway	.15	.40
Z21 Jake Reed	.08	.25
Z22 Michael Timpson	.05	.15
Z23 Marcus Allen	.15	.40
Z24 Andre Rison	.08	.25
Z25 Terry Kirby	.08	.25
Z26 Reggie White	.15	.40
Z27 Randall Cunningham	.15	.40
Z28 Jim Kelly	.15	.40
Z29 Robert Brooks	.15	.40
Z30 Terance Mathis	.08	.25
Z31 Anthony Miller	.08	.25
Z32 Neil O'Donnell	.08	.25
Z33 Jeff Hostetler	.08	.25
Z34 Drew Bledsoe	.30	.75
Z35 Irving Spikes	.08	.25
Z36 Keith Byars	.05	.15
Z37 Rod Woodson	.08	.25
Z38 Rob Moore	.08	.25
Z39 Scott Mitchell	.08	.25
Z40 Cody Carlson	.05	.15
Z41 Alvin Harper	.05	.15
Z42 Chris Warren	.08	.25
Z43 Ben Coates	.08	.25
Z44 Jim Everett	.05	.15
Z45 Vinny Testaverde	.08	.25
Z46 Glyn Milburn	.05	.15
Z47 Calvin Williams	.08	.25
Z48 Fred Barnett	.08	.25
Z49 Tim Brown	.15	.40
Z50 Lorenzo White	.05	.15
Z51 Brent Jones	.05	.15
Z52 Henry Ellard	.08	.25
Z53 Rick Mirer	.08	.25
Z54 Junior Seau	.15	.40
Z55 Jeff Blake RC	.40	1.00
Z56 Desmond Howard	.08	.25
Z57 Jerry Rice	.50	1.25
Z58 Lewis Tillman	.05	.15
Z59 Roosevelt Potts	.05	.15
Z60 Rocket Ismail	.08	.25
Z61 Eric Hill	.05	.15
Z62 Brett Favre	1.00	2.50
Z63 Haywood Jeffires	.05	.15
Z64 Barry Foster	.08	.25
Z65 Flipper Anderson	.05	.15
Z66 Troy Aikman	.50	1.25
Z67 Herschel Walker	.08	.25
Z68 Sean Dawkins	.08	.25
Z69 Erric Pegram	.08	.25
Z70 Irving Fryar	.08	.25
Z71 Thurman Thomas	.15	.40
Z72 Eric Metcalf	.08	.25
Z73 John Taylor	.05	.15
Z74 Jeff George	.08	.25
Z75 Courtney Hawkins	.05	.15
Z76 Carl Pickens	.08	.25
Z77 Mike Sherrard	.05	.15
Z78 Rodney Hampton	.08	.25
Z79 Joe Montana	1.00	2.50
Z80 Willie Davis	.08	.25
Z81 Chris Penn	.05	.15
Z82 Dave Brown	.08	.25
Z83 Gary Brown	.05	.15
Z84 Andre Reed	.08	.25
Z85 Michael Irvin	.15	.40
Z86 Vincent Brisby	.05	.15
Z87 Barry Sanders	.75	2.00
Z88 Qadry Ismail	.08	.25
Z89 Reggie Brooks	.08	.25
Z90 Bruce Smith	.15	.40
Z91 David Klingler	.08	.25
Z92 Michael Haynes	.08	.25
Z93 Derek Russell	.05	.15
Z94 Steve Young	.40	1.00
Z95 Terry Allen	.08	.25
Z96 Mark Seay	.08	.25
Z97 Dan Marino	1.00	2.50
Z98 Jerry Rice/1994 Record Wrecker	.50	1.25
Z99 Cris Carter/1994 Record Wrecker	.15	.40
Z100 Art Monk Record Wrecker	.08	.25
Z101 Cortez Kennedy	.08	.25
Z102 Stan Humphries	.08	.25
Z103 Herman Moore	.15	.40
Z104 Ronald Moore	.05	.15
Z105 Greg Lloyd	.08	.25
Z106 Jerome Bettis	.15	.40
Z107 Craig Erickson	.05	.15

Z108 Keith Jackson	.05	.15
Z109 Sterling Sharpe	.08	.25
Z110 Ronnie Harmon	.05	.15
Z111 Deion Sanders	.30	.75
Z112 Charles Haley	.08	.25
Z113 Bernie Parmalee	.08	.25
Z114 Leroy Hoard	.05	.15
Z115 O.J. McDuffie	.15	.40
Z116 Garrison Hearst	.15	.40
Z117 Kevin Greene	.08	.25
Z118 Derek Brown	.05	.15
Z119 Mark Brunell	.30	.75
Z120 Kevin Williams	.08	.25
Z121 Dan Wilkinson	.08	.25
Z122 Chuck Levy	.05	.15
Z123 Derrick Alexander	.15	.40
Z124 Aaron Bailey RC	.05	.15
Z125 Thomas Lewis	.08	.25
Z126 Antonio Langham	.05	.15
Z127 Bryan Reeves	.05	.15
Z128 William Floyd	.08	.25
Z129 Lake Dawson	.08	.25
Z130 Bert Emanuel	.15	.40
Z131 Marshall Faulk	.60	1.50
Z132 Heath Shuler	.08	.25
Z133 David Palmer	.08	.25
Z134 Willie McGinest	.08	.25
Z135 Mario Bates	.08	.25
Z136 Byron Bam Morris	.05	.15
Z137 Tim Bowens	.05	.15
Z138 Errict Rhett	.08	.25
Z139 Charlie Garner	.15	.40
Z140 Darnay Scott	.08	.25
Z141 Greg Hill	.08	.25
Z142 LeShon Johnson	.08	.25
Z143 Charles Johnson	.08	.25
Z144 Trent Dilfer	.15	.40
Z145 Gus Frerotte	.08	.25
Z146 Johnnie Morton	.08	.25
Z147 Glenn Foley	.05	.15
Z148 Perry Klein	.05	.15
Z149 Ryan Yarborough	.08	.25
Z150 Tydus Winans	.05	.15

1995 Zenith Rookie Roll Call

COMPLETE SET (18)	75.00	150.00
STATED ODDS 1:72		
RC1 Marshall Faulk	20.00	50.00
RC2 Charlie Garner	5.00	12.00
RC3 Derrick Alexander WR	5.00	12.00
RC4 Heath Shuler	3.00	8.00
RC5 Glenn Foley	2.00	5.00
RC6 Trent Dilfer	5.00	12.00
RC7 David Palmer	3.00	8.00
RC8 Gus Frerotte	3.00	8.00
RC9 Byron Bam Morris	2.00	5.00
RC10 Mario Bates	3.00	8.00
RC11 Greg Hill	3.00	8.00
RC12 Errict Rhett	3.00	8.00
RC13 Darnay Scott	3.00	8.00
RC14 Lake Dawson	3.00	8.00
RC15 Bert Emanuel	5.00	12.00
RC16 LeShon Johnson	3.00	8.00
RC17 William Floyd	3.00	8.00
RC18 Charles Johnson	3.00	8.00

1995 Zenith Second Season

COMPLETE SET (25)	12.50	30.00
STATED ODDS 1:6		
SS1 Brett Favre	1.50	4.00
SS2 Dan Marino	1.50	4.00
SS3 Marcus Allen	.25	.60
SS4 Joe Montana	1.50	4.00
SS5 Vinny Testaverde	.15	.40
SS6 Emmitt Smith	1.25	3.00
SS7 Troy Aikman	.75	2.00
SS8 Steve Young	.60	1.50
SS9 William Floyd	.15	.40
SS10 Yancey Thigpen	.25	.60
SS11 Barry Foster	.15	.40
SS12 Natrone Means	.15	.40
SS13 Mark Seay	.15	.40
SS14 Stan Humphries	.15	.40
SS15 Tony Martin	.25	.60
SS16 Jerry Rice	.75	2.00
SS17 Deion Sanders	.50	1.25
SS18 Steve Young	.60	1.50
SS19 Steve Young	.60	1.50
SS20 Emmitt Smith	1.25	3.00
SS21 Troy Aikman	.75	2.00
SS22 Jerry Rice	.75	2.00
SS23 Ricky Watters	.15	.40
SS24 Steve Young	.60	1.50
SS25 Jerry Rice	.75	2.00
Steve Young		

1995 Zenith Z-Team

COMPLETE SET (18)	50.00	100.00
STATED ODDS 1:24		
ZT1 Dan Marino	8.00	20.00
ZT2 Troy Aikman	4.00	10.00
ZT3 Emmitt Smith	6.00	15.00
ZT4 Barry Sanders	6.00	15.00
ZT5 Joe Montana	8.00	20.00
ZT6 Jerry Rice	4.00	10.00
ZT7 John Elway	8.00	20.00
ZT8 Marshall Faulk	5.00	12.00
ZT9 Brett Favre	8.00	20.00
ZT10 Steve Young	3.00	8.00
ZT11 Sterling Sharpe	.75	2.00
ZT12 Drew Bledsoe	2.50	6.00
ZT13 Ricky Watters	.75	2.00
ZT14 Cris Carter	1.25	3.00
ZT15 Warren Moon	.75	2.00
ZT16 Natrone Means	.75	2.00
ZT17 Michael Irvin	1.25	3.00
ZT18 Chris Warren	.75	2.00

1996 Zenith Promos

This four-card set was issued by Pinnacle to preview its 1996 Zenith release. The cards are identical to their regular issue and Z-Team issue counterparts, except for the word "Promo" printed on the back of the card.

COMPLETE SET (4)	15.00	30.00
4 Emmitt Smith	6.00	15.00
Z-Team		
32 Jerry Rice	3.00	8.00
36 John Elway	4.00	10.00
NNO Title Card	.10	.30

1996 Zenith

The 1996 Zenith set was issued in one series totaling 150 standard-size cards. This was the second year Pinnacle Brands used the Zenith line to produce a high end football set during the off-season. The six card packs had a suggested retail price of $2.59 each. They were issued in 16 box cases with 24 packs in each box. Topical subsets in the set include 1995 Rookies (97-131), Proof Positive (132-146) and Checklist Cards (148-150). The Dallas Cowboy Triplets: Troy Aikman, Michael Irvin and Emmitt Smith are featured on card #147. There are no key Rookie Cards in this set.

COMPLETE SET (150)	10.00	25.00
1 Dan Marino	1.25	3.00
2 Yancey Thigpen	.08	.25
3 Marcus Allen	.20	.50
4 Curtis Conway	.20	.50
5 Troy Aikman	.60	1.50
6 William Floyd	.08	.25
7 Ricky Watters	.08	.25
8 Herman Moore	.08	.25
9 Jim Harbaugh	.08	.25
10 Isaac Bruce	.20	.50
11 Drew Bledsoe	.40	1.00
12 Jeff Blake	.20	.50
13 Tim Brown	.20	.50
14 Deion Sanders	.40	1.00
15 Greg Hill	.08	.25
16 Ben Coates	.08	.25
17 Errict Rhett	.08	.25
18 Barry Sanders	1.00	2.50
19 Erik Kramer	.02	.10
20 Emmitt Smith	1.00	2.50
21 Brett Favre	1.25	3.00
22 Jerome Bettis	.20	.50
23 Garrison Hearst	.08	.25
24 Michael Irvin	.20	.50
25 Chris Warren	.08	.25
26 Steve Young	.50	1.25
27 Cris Carter	.20	.50
28 Carl Pickens	.08	.25
29 Lake Dawson	.02	.10
30 Marshall Faulk	.25	.60
31 Vincent Brisby	.02	.10
32 Jerry Rice	.60	1.50
33 Eric Metcalf	.02	.10
34 Natrone Means	.08	.25
35 Steve Bono	.02	.10
36 John Elway	1.25	3.00
37 Jeff Hostetler	.02	.10
38 Scott Mitchell	.08	.25
39 Andre Rison	.08	.25
40 Daryl Johnston	.08	.25
41 Mark Brunell	.40	1.00
42 Jeff George	.08	.25
43 Mario Bates	.08	.25
44 Erric Pegram	.02	.10
45 Brent Jones	.02	.10
46 Trent Dilfer	.20	.50
47 Larry Centers	.08	.25
48 Anthony Miller	.08	.25
49 Reggie White	.20	.50
50 Bill Brooks	.02	.10
51 Chris Zorich	.02	.10
52 Jim Kelly	.20	.50
53 Junior Seau	.20	.50
54 Chris Miller	.02	.10
55 Gus Frerotte	.08	.25
56 Andre Reed	.08	.25
57 Darnay Scott	.08	.25
58 Brett Perriman	.02	.10
59 Edgar Bennett	.08	.25
60 Warren Moon	.08	.25
61 Neil O'Donnell	.08	.25
62 Jay Novacek	.02	.10
63 Byron Bam Morris	.02	.10
64 Jim Everett	.02	.10
65 Ken Norton, Jr.	.02	.10
66 Tony Martin	.08	.25
67 Steve Atwater	.02	.10
68 Henry Ellard	.02	.10
69 Rodney Hampton	.08	.25
70 Derrick Thomas	.20	.50
71 Stan Humphries	.08	.25
72 Harvey Williams	.02	.10
73 Greg Lloyd	.08	.25
74 Jake Reed	.08	.25
75 Charles Haley	.08	.25
76 Quinn Early	.02	.10
77 Rodney Peete	.02	.10
78 Brian Blades	.02	.10
79 Robert Brooks	.20	.50
80 Terry Allen	.08	.25
81 Dave Brown	.02	.10
82 Derrick Alexander WR	.08	.25
83 Terance Mathis	.02	.10
84 Rick Mirer	.08	.25
85 Herschel Walker	.08	.25
86 Charlie Garner	.08	.25
87 Jeff Graham	.02	.10
88 Bruce Smith	.08	.25
89 Terry Kirby	.08	.25
90 Craig Heyward	.02	.10
91 Bernie Parmalee	.02	.10
92 Adrian Murrell	.08	.25
93 Derek Loville	.02	.10
94 Heath Shuler	.08	.25
95 Shannon Sharpe	.08	.25
96 Bert Emanuel	.08	.25
97 Hugh Douglas	.08	.25
98 Lovell Pinkney	.02	.10
99 Sherman Williams	.02	.10
100 Tony Boselli	.02	.10
101 Wayne Chrebet	.20	.50
102 Orlando Thomas	.02	.10
103 Darick Holmes	.02	.10
104 Tyrone Wheatley	.08	.25
105 Christian Fauria	.02	.10
106 Frank Sanders	.08	.25
107 Chad May	.02	.10
108 James O. Stewart	.08	.25
109 Ken Dilger	.08	.25
110 Kyle Brady	.02	.10
111 Todd Collins	.08	.25
112 Terrell Fletcher	.02	.10
113 Eric Bjornson	.02	.10
114 Justin Armour	.02	.10
115 Rob Johnson	.20	.50
116 Terrell Davis	.40	1.00
117 J.J. Stokes	.20	.50
118 Rashaan Salaam	.08	.25
119 Chris Sanders	.08	.25
120 Kerry Collins	.20	.50
121 Michael Westbrook	.20	.50
122 Eric Zeier	.02	.10
123 Curtis Martin	.40	1.00
124 Rodney Thomas	.02	.10
125 Kordell Stewart	.20	.50
126 Joey Galloway	.20	.50
127 Steve McNair	.40	1.00
128 Napoleon Kaufman	.20	.50
129 Tamarick Vanover	.08	.25
130 Stoney Case	.02	.10
131 James A. Stewart	.02	.10
132 Carl Pickens PP	.08	.25
133 Jim Harbaugh PP	.08	.25
134 Yancey Thigpen PP	.08	.25
135 Ricky Watters PP	.08	.25
136 Isaac Bruce PP	.20	.50
137 Kordell Stewart PP	.20	.50
138 Jeff Blake PP	.08	.25
139 Terrell Davis PP	.20	.50
140 Scott Mitchell PP	.02	.10
141 Rodney Thomas PP	.02	.10
142 Robert Brooks PP	.20	.50
143 Joey Galloway PP	.20	.50
144 Brett Favre PP	.60	1.50
145 Kerry Collins PP	.20	.50
146 Herman Moore PP	.08	.25
147 Michael Irvin	.60	1.50
Emmitt Smith		
Troy Aikman		
148 Dan Marino	.20	.50
Checklist		
149 Jerry Rice	.20	.50
Checklist		
150 Emmitt Smith	.20	.50
Checklist		

1996 Zenith Artist's Proofs

COMPLETE SET (150)	200.00	400.00
*ARTIST PROOFS: 3X TO 8X BASIC CARDS		
STATED ODDS 1:23		

1996 Zenith Noteworthy '95

COMPLETE SET (18)	15.00	40.00
STATED ODDS: 1:12		
1 Dan Marino	3.00	8.00
2 Jerry Rice	1.50	4.00
3 Michael Irvin	.50	1.25
4 Emmitt Smith	2.50	6.00
5 Michael Irvin	2.50	6.00
Emmitt Smith		
6 Herman Moore	.25	.60
7 Brett Favre	3.00	8.00
8 Barry Sanders	2.50	6.00
9 Marcus Allen	.50	1.25
10 Steve Young	1.25	3.00
11 John Elway	3.00	8.00
12 Warren Moon	.25	.60
13 Jim Kelly	.50	1.25
14 Jim Everett	.08	.25
15 Charles Haley	.25	.60
16 Emmitt Smith	2.50	6.00
17 Troy Aikman	1.50	4.00
18 Larry Brown	.08	.25

1996 Zenith Rookie Rising

COMPLETE SET (18)	20.00	40.00
STATED ODDS: 1:24		
1 Sherman Williams	.30	.75
2 Curtis Martin	3.00	8.00
3 Michael Westbrook	1.50	4.00
4 Darick Holmes	.30	.75
5 James O.Stewart	.75	2.00
6 Eric Zeier	.30	.75
7 Tamarick Vanover	.75	2.00
8 J.J. Stokes	1.50	4.00
9 Kordell Stewart	1.50	4.00
10 Rodney Thomas	.30	.75
11 Kerry Collins	1.50	4.00
12 Terrell Davis	3.00	8.00
13 Steve McNair	3.00	8.00
14 Rashaan Salaam	.75	2.00
15 Joey Galloway	1.50	4.00
16 Wayne Chrebet	1.50	4.00
17 Chris Sanders	.75	2.00
18 Frank Sanders	.75	2.00

1996 Zenith Z-Team

COMPLETE SET (18)	50.00	120.00
STATED ODDS: 1:72		
1 Troy Aikman	4.00	10.00
2 Drew Bledsoe	2.50	6.00
3 Errict Rhett	.60	1.50
4 Emmitt Smith	6.00	15.00
5 Jerry Rice	4.00	10.00
6 Cris Carter	1.25	3.00
7 Curtis Martin	2.50	6.00
8 Deion Sanders	2.50	6.00
9 Brett Favre	8.00	20.00
10 Michael Irvin	1.25	3.00
11 Chris Warren	.60	1.50
12 Dan Marino	8.00	20.00
13 Steve Young	3.00	8.00
14 Marshall Faulk	1.50	4.00
15 Barry Sanders	6.00	15.00
16 John Elway	8.00	20.00
17 Isaac Bruce	1.25	3.00
18 Carl Pickens	.60	1.50

1997 Zenith

The 1997 Zenith set was issued in one series totaling 150 cards and was distributed in six-card packs with a suggested retail of $3.99. The fronts feature color player photos printed on 24 point card stock. The backs carry player information.

COMPLETE SET (150)	10.00	25.00
1 Brett Favre	1.25	3.00
2 Jerry Rice	.60	1.50
3 Shannon Sharpe	.20	.50
4 Dan Marino	1.25	3.00
5 James O.Stewart	.20	.50
6 Warren Moon	.30	.75
7 Emmitt Smith	1.00	2.50
8 Kordell Stewart	.30	.75
9 Kerry Collins	.30	.75
10 Ricky Watters	.20	.50
11 Gus Frerotte	.10	.30
12 Barry Sanders	1.00	2.50
13 Joey Galloway	.20	.50
14 Marshall Faulk	.40	1.00
15 Todd Collins	.10	.30
16 Steve McNair	.40	1.00
17 Tyrone Wheatley	.20	.50
18 Isaac Bruce	.30	.75
19 Troy Aikman	.60	1.50
20 Larry Centers	.20	.50
21 Alvin Harper	.10	.30
22 Rashaan Salaam	.10	.30
23 Eric Metcalf	.20	.50
24 Jim Everett	.10	.30
25 Ken Dilger	.10	.30
26 Curtis Martin	.40	1.00
27 Neil O'Donnell	.20	.50
28 Thurman Thomas	.30	.75
29 Andre Rison	.20	.50
30 Steve Bono	.20	.50
31 Garrison Hearst	.20	.50
32 Junior Seau	.30	.75
33 Napoleon Kaufman	.30	.75
34 Jerome Bettis	.30	.75
35 Frank Wycheck	.10	.30
36 Lamar Smith	.30	.75
37 Derrick Alexander WR	.20	.50
38 Steve Young	.40	1.00
39 Cris Carter	.30	.75
40 O.J. McDuffie	.20	.50
41 Deion Sanders	.30	.75
42 Robert Brooks	.20	.50
43 Jeff Blake	.20	.50
44 Marcus Allen	.30	.75
45 Herman Moore	.20	.50
46 Ray Zellars	.10	.30
47 Tim Brown	.30	.75
48 John Elway	1.25	3.00
49 Charles Johnson	.20	.50
50 Rodney Peete	.10	.30
51 Curtis Conway	.20	.50
52 Kevin Greene	.20	.50
53 Andre Reed	.20	.50
54 Mark Brunell	.40	1.00
55 Tony Martin	.20	.50
56 Elvis Grbac	.20	.50
57 Wayne Chrebet	.30	.75
58 Vinny Testaverde	.20	.50
59 Terry Allen	.30	.75
60 Dave Brown	.10	.30
61 LeShon Johnson	.10	.30
62 Trent Dilfer	.30	.75
63 Chris Warren	.20	.50
64 Chris Sanders	.10	.30
65 Kevin Carter	.10	.30
66 Jim Harbaugh	.20	.50
67 Terance Mathis	.20	.50
68 Ben Coates	.20	.50
69 Robert Smith	.20	.50
70 Drew Bledsoe	.40	1.00
71 Henry Ellard	.10	.30
72 Scott Mitchell	.20	.50
73 Andre Hastings	.10	.30
74 Rodney Hampton	.20	.50
75 Michael Jackson	.20	.50
76 Jeff Hostetler	.10	.30
77 Reggie White	.30	.75
78 Desmond Howard	.20	.50
79 Adrian Murrell	.20	.50
80 Carl Pickens	.20	.50
81 Erik Kramer	.10	.30
82 Terrell Davis	.40	1.00
83 Sean Dawkins	.10	.30
84 Jamal Anderson	.30	.75
85 Stan Humphries	.20	.50
86 Chris T. Jones	.10	.30
87 Hardy Nickerson	.10	.30
88 Anthony Johnson	.10	.30
89 Michael Haynes	.10	.30
90 Irving Spikes	.10	.30
91 Bruce Smith	.20	.50
92 Keenan McCardell	.20	.50
93 Chris Chandler	.20	.50
94 Tamarick Vanover	.20	.50
95 Dorsey Levens	.30	.75
96 Roman Phifer	.10	.30
97 Michael Irvin	.30	.75
98 Tim Biakabutuka	.20	.50
99 Stepfret Williams	.10	.30
100 Eddie George	.30	.75
101 Karim Abdul-Jabbar	.30	.75
102 Amani Toomer	.20	.50
103 Tony Banks	.20	.50
104 Regan Upshaw	.10	.30
105 Leeland McElroy	.10	.30
106 Jason Dunn	.10	.30
107 Keyshawn Johnson	.30	.75
108 Winslow Oliver	.10	.30
109 Walt Harris	.10	.30
110 Stanley Pritchett	.10	.30
111 Eddie Kennison	.20	.50
112 Terrell Owens	.40	1.00
113 Duane Clemons	.10	.30
114 John Mobley	.10	.30
115 Simeon Rice	.20	.50
116 Tony Brackens	.10	.30
117 Eric Moulds	.30	.75
118 Marvin Harrison	.30	.75
119 Rickey Dudley	.20	.50
120 Mike Alstott	.30	.75
121 Terry Glenn	.30	.75
122 Brian Dawkins	.30	.75
123 Kevin Hardy	.10	.30
124 Bobby Engram	.20	.50
125 Alex Van Dyke	.10	.30
126 Zach Thomas	.30	.75
127 Bryan Still	.10	.30
128 Detron Smith	.10	.30
129 Jerome Woods	.10	.30
130 Muhsin Muhammad	.20	.50
131 Lawrence Phillips	.10	.30
132 Alex Molden	.10	.30
133 Steve Young SH	.10	.30
134 Troy Aikman SH	.30	.75
135 Junior Seau SH	.10	.30
136 John Elway SH	.60	1.50
137 Dan Marino SH	.60	1.50
138 Desmond Howard SH	.20	.50
139 Brett Favre SH	.60	1.50
140 Jerry Rice SH	.30	.75
141 Kerry Collins SH	.20	.50
142 Barry Sanders SH	.50	1.25
143 Mark Brunell SH	.30	.75
144 Drew Bledsoe SH	.30	.75
145 Eddie Kennison SH	.20	.50
146 Marvin Harrison SH	.30	.75
147 Emmitt Smith SH	.50	1.25
148 Eddie George	.30	.75
Terry Glenn		
Rickey Dudley		
Bobby Hoying		
Awesome Foursome		
149 Emmitt Smith	.30	.75
Checklist back		
150 Dan Marino	.30	.75
Checklist back		

1997 Zenith Artist's Proofs

COMPLETE SET (150)	75.00	200.00
*SINGLES: 2.5X TO 6X BASIC CARDS		
AP STATED ODDS 1:47		

1997 Zenith Rookie Rising

COMPLETE SET (24)	20.00	50.00
STATED ODDS 1:11		
1 Eddie Kennison	1.00	2.50
2 Marvin Harrison	4.00	10.00
3 Keyshawn Johnson	3.00	8.00
4 Leeland McElroy	.60	1.50
5 Terrell Owens	4.00	10.00
6 Terry Glenn	2.50	6.00
7 Bobby Engram	.60	1.50
8 Karim Abdul-Jabbar	1.00	2.50
9 Lawrence Phillips	.60	1.50
10 Amani Toomer	1.50	4.00
11 Eric Moulds	3.00	8.00
12 Jason Dunn	.60	1.50
13 Stanley Pritchett	.60	1.50
14 Eddie George	2.50	6.00
15 Muhsin Muhammad	2.00	5.00
16 Rickey Dudley	1.50	4.00
17 Tony Banks	1.50	4.00
18 Bryan Still	.60	1.50
19 Tim Biakabutuka	1.50	4.00
20 Simeon Rice	1.00	2.50
21 Zach Thomas	2.00	5.00
22 Kevin Hardy	.60	1.50
23 Jerris McPhail	.60	1.50
24 Mike Alstott	2.50	6.00

1997 Zenith V2

COMPLETE SET (18)	100.00	200.00
STATED ODDS 1:18		
V1 Troy Aikman	5.00	12.00
V2 John Elway	10.00	25.00
V3 Jim Harbaugh	1.50	4.00
V4 Barry Sanders	8.00	20.00
V5 Deion Sanders	2.50	6.00
V6 Drew Bledsoe	3.00	8.00
V7 Dan Marino	10.00	25.00
V8 Terrell Davis	3.00	8.00
V9 Isaac Bruce	2.50	6.00
V10 Jerome Bettis	2.50	6.00
V11 Emmitt Smith	8.00	20.00
V12 Brett Favre	10.00	25.00
V13 Steve Young	3.00	8.00
V14 Mark Brunell	3.00	8.00
V15 Joey Galloway	1.50	4.00
V16 Kordell Stewart	2.50	6.00
V17 Jerry Rice	5.00	12.00
V18 Curtis Martin	3.00	8.00

1997 Zenith Z-Team Promos

This set of Promo cards was produced to promote the 1997 Zenith release. The cards are essentially parallels of the base insert set except for the word "Promo" clearly printed on the cardbacks. A Mirror Gold version of each Promo was also produced. We've added the "M" card number suffix below to the Mirrors to help with cataloging.

COMPLETE SET (6)	16.00	40.00
ZT2 Dan Marino	2.00	5.00
ZT2M Dan Marino	4.00	10.00
(Mirror Gold)		
ZT11 Brett Favre	2.00	5.00
ZT11M Brett Favre	4.00	10.00
ZT14 Barry Sanders	2.00	5.00
ZT14M Barry Sanders	4.00	10.00

1997 Zenith Z-Team

COMPLETE SET (18)	125.00	250.00
STATED ODDS 1:71		
*MIRROR GOLDS: .6X TO 1.5X BASIC INS.		
MIRROR GOLD STATED ODDS 1:191		
ZT1 Emmitt Smith	10.00	25.00
ZT2 Dan Marino	12.50	30.00
ZT3 Jerry Rice	6.00	15.00
ZT4 John Elway	12.50	30.00
ZT5 Curtis Martin	4.00	10.00
ZT6 Deion Sanders	3.00	8.00
ZT7 Tony Banks	2.00	5.00
ZT8 Jim Harbaugh	2.00	5.00
ZT9 Joey Galloway	2.00	5.00
ZT10 Troy Aikman	6.00	15.00
ZT11 Brett Favre	12.50	30.00
ZT12 Keyshawn Johnson	3.00	8.00
ZT13 Eddie George	3.00	8.00
ZT14 Barry Sanders	10.00	25.00
ZT15 Kordell Stewart	3.00	8.00
ZT16 Steve Young	4.00	10.00
ZT17 Terrell Davis	4.00	10.00
ZT18 Drew Bledsoe	4.00	10.00

1998 Zenith Dare to Tear Promos

Z1 Brett Favre	3.00	8.00
Z2 John Elway	2.50	6.00
Z5 Kordell Stewart	.75	2.00
Z8 Mark Brunell	1.00	2.50
Z20 Barry Sanders	2.50	6.00
Z21 Dan Marino	3.00	8.00
Z22 Drew Bledsoe	1.00	2.50
Z35 Steve Young	1.25	3.00
Z45 Emmitt Smith	2.50	6.00

2005 Zenith

This 181-card set was released in November, 2005. The set was issued in five-card packs with an $5 SRP which came 18 packs to a box. Cards numbered 1-100 feature veterans in team alphabetical order while cards 101-181 are all rookies. There are two distinct groupings of rookies, both of which are basically sequenced in first name alphabetical order. Cards numbered 1-150 are unsigned while cards 151-181 are all autographed. Please note that the unsigned Rookie Cards are nearly identical to the Museum Collection parallel cards with the Museum cards also being serial numberied to 999. The Rookie Cards also have the word "Rookie" printed repeatedly in the background of the photo on the cardfronts.

COMP.SET w/o RCs (100)	10.00	25.00
ROOKIE/999 STATED ODDS 1:24 RETAIL		
101-150 AU PRINT RUN 99 SER.#'d SETS		
1 Larry Fitzgerald	.30	.75
2 Anquan Boldin	.25	.60
3 Kurt Warner	.30	.75
4 Alge Crumpler	.25	.60
5 Michael Vick	.30	.75
6 Warrick Dunn	.25	.60
7 Jamal Lewis	.25	.60
8 Kyle Boller	.25	.60
9 Derrick Mason	.25	.60
10 Ray Lewis	.30	.75
11 Willis McGahee	.30	.75
12 J.P. Losman	.20	.50
13 Lee Evans	.25	.60
14 Eric Moulds	.20	.50
15 Jake Delhomme	.25	.60
16 Steve Smith	.30	.75
17 DeShaun Foster	.25	.60
18 Rex Grossman	.25	.60
19 Muhsin Muhammad	.25	.60
20 Brian Urlacher	.30	.75
21 Carson Palmer	.30	.75
22 Chad Johnson	.25	.60
23 Rudi Johnson	.25	.60
24 Lee Suggs	.20	.50
25 Reuben Droughns	.20	.50
26 Trent Dilfer	.25	.60
27 Drew Bledsoe	.30	.75
28 Julius Jones	.20	.50
29 Keyshawn Johnson	.25	.60
30 Roy Williams S	.20	.50
31 Ashley Lelie	.20	.50
32 Jake Plummer	.25	.60
33 Tatum Bell	.20	.50
34 Joey Harrington	.25	.60
35 Roy Williams WR	.25	.60
36 Kevin Jones	.20	.50
37 Ahman Green	.25	.60
38 Brett Favre	.75	2.00
39 Javon Walker	.20	.50
40 David Carr	.20	.50
41 Domanick Davis	.20	.50
42 Andre Johnson	.30	.75
43 Marvin Harrison	.30	.75
44 Edgerrin James	.25	.60
45 Peyton Manning	.60	1.50
46 Fred Taylor	.25	.60
47 Byron Leftwich	.25	.60
48 Jimmy Smith	.25	.60
49 Priest Holmes	.25	.60
50 Trent Green	.25	.60
51 Tony Gonzalez	.25	.60
52 Chris Chambers	.25	.60
53 A.J. Feeley	.20	.50
54 Daunte Culpepper	.25	.60
55 Michael Bennett	.25	.60
56 Nate Burleson	.20	.50
57 Tom Brady	.60	1.50
58 Deion Branch	.20	.50
59 Tedy Bruschi	.30	.75
60 Corey Dillon	.25	.60
61 Aaron Brooks	.20	.50
62 Deuce McAllister	.25	.60
63 Joe Horn	.25	.60
64 Eli Manning	.50	1.25
65 Tiki Barber	.30	.75
66 Plaxico Burress	.25	.60
67 Jeremy Shockey	.30	.75
68 Chad Pennington	.30	.75
69 Curtis Martin	.30	.75
70 Laveranues Coles	.20	.50
71 Kerry Collins	.25	.60
72 LaMont Jordan	.25	.60
73 Randy Moss	.30	.75
74 Brian Westbrook	.25	.60
75 Terrell Owens	.30	.75
76 Donovan McNabb	.30	.75
77 Ben Roethlisberger	.50	1.25
78 Duce Staley	.25	.60
79 Jerome Bettis	.30	.75
80 Hines Ward	.30	.75
81 Drew Brees	.30	.75
82 Antonio Gates	.30	.75
83 LaDainian Tomlinson	.30	.75
84 Kevan Barlow	.20	.50
85 Brandon Lloyd	.20	.50
86 Matt Hasselbeck	.25	.60
87 Shaun Alexander	.25	.60
88 Darrell Jackson	.20	.50
89 Torry Holt	.25	.60
90 Marc Bulger	.25	.60
91 Steven Jackson	.30	.75
92 Brian Griese	.25	.60
93 Michael Clayton	.20	.50
94 Steve McNair	.30	.75
95 Chris Brown	.20	.50
96 Drew Bennett	.25	.60
97 Patrick Ramsey	.25	.60
98 Clinton Portis	.25	.60
99 Santana Moss	.25	.60
100 LaVar Arrington	.25	.60
101 Adrian McPherson RC	1.00	2.50
102 Airese Currie RC	1.00	2.50
103 Alvin Pearman RC	1.00	2.50
104 Anthony Davis RC	1.00	2.50
105 Brandon Jacobs RC	2.00	5.00
106 Brandon Jones RC	1.25	3.00
107 Bryant McFadden RC	1.25	3.00
108 Cedric Houston RC	1.50	4.00
109 Chad Owens RC	1.25	3.00
110 Chris Henry RC	1.50	4.00
111 Craig Bragg RC	1.00	2.50
112 Craphonso Thorpe RC	1.00	2.50
113 Damien Nash RC	1.25	3.00
114 Dan Cody RC	1.25	3.00
115 Dan Orlovsky RC	1.50	4.00
116 Dante Ridgeway RC	1.00	2.50
117 Darren Sproles RC	1.50	4.00
118 David Greene RC	1.00	2.50
119 David Pollack RC	1.25	3.00
120 Deandra Cobb RC	1.00	2.50
121 DeMarcus Ware RC	3.00	8.00
122 Derek Anderson RC	1.25	3.00
123 Derrick Johnson RC	1.25	3.00
124 Erasmus James RC	1.25	3.00
125 Fabian Washington RC	1.25	3.00
126 Fred Gibson RC	1.25	3.00
127 Harry Williams RC	1.25	3.00
128 Heath Miller RC	2.00	5.00
129 J.R. Russell RC	1.00	2.50
130 James Kilian RC	1.00	2.50
131 Jerome Mathis RC	1.50	4.00
132 Larry Brackins RC	1.00	2.50
133 LeRon McCoy RC	1.00	2.50
134 Lionel Gates RC	1.00	2.50
135 Marcus Maxwell RC	1.00	2.50
136 Marcus Spears RC	1.25	3.00
137 Marion Barber RC	1.50	4.00
138 Marlin Jackson RC	1.00	2.50
139 Matt Cassel RC	3.00	8.00
140 Matt Roth RC	1.25	3.00
141 Mike Williams	1.50	4.00
142 Noah Herron RC	1.00	2.50
143 Paris Warren RC	1.25	3.00
144 Rasheed Marshall RC	1.25	3.00
145 Roydell Williams RC	1.25	3.00
146 Ryan Fitzpatrick RC	2.50	6.00
147 Shaun Cody RC	1.25	3.00
148 Shawne Merriman RC	1.50	4.00
149 Tab Perry RC	1.00	2.50
150 Thomas Davis RC	1.00	2.50
151 Adam Jones AU RC	12.00	30.00
152 Alex Smith QB AU RC	40.00	80.00
153 Antrel Rolle AU RC	20.00	50.00
154 Andrew Walter AU RC	15.00	40.00
155 Braylon Edwards AU RC	25.00	60.00
156 Cadillac Williams AU RC	20.00	50.00
157 Carlos Rogers AU RC	20.00	50.00
158 Charlie Frye AU RC	20.00	50.00
159 Ciatrick Fason AU RC	12.00	30.00
160 Courtney Roby AU RC	15.00	40.00
161 Eric Shelton AU RC	12.00	30.00
162 Frank Gore AU RC	25.00	60.00
163 J.J. Arrington AU RC	15.00	40.00
164 Kyle Orton AU RC	20.00	50.00
165 Jason Campbell AU RC	25.00	60.00
166 Mark Bradley AU RC	12.00	30.00
167 Mark Clayton AU RC	15.00	40.00
168 Matt Jones AU RC	15.00	40.00
169 Maurice Clarett AU	12.00	30.00
170 Reggie Brown AU RC	12.00	30.00
171 Ronnie Brown AU RC	40.00	80.00
172 Roddy White AU RC	25.00	60.00
173 Ryan Moats AU RC	12.00	30.00
174 Roscoe Parrish AU RC	12.00	30.00
175 Stefan LeFors AU RC	12.00	30.00
176 Terrence Murphy AU RC	12.00	30.00
177 Troy Williamson AU RC	15.00	40.00
178 Vernand Morency AU RC	12.00	30.00
179 Vincent Jackson AU RC	25.00	60.00
180 Aaron Rodgers AU RC	250.00	400.00
181 Cedric Benson AU RC	30.00	60.00

2005 Zenith Artist's Proofs

*VETERANS: 2X TO 5X BASIC CARDS
*ROOKIES: .5X TO 1.2X BASIC CARDS
STATED ODDS 1:18 HOB, 1:48 RET

2005 Zenith Artist's Proofs Gold

*VETERANS 1-100: 6X TO 15X BASIC CARDS
1-100 VET PRINT RUN 50 SER.#'d SETS
*ROOKIES 101-150: 1.5X TO 4X BASIC CARDS
101-150 ROOKIE PRINT RUN 25 SER.#'d SETS
OVERALL STATED ODDS 1:70 HOBBY

2005 Zenith Museum Collection

*VETERANS: 1.2X TO 3X BASIC CARDS
*ROOKIES: .4X TO 1X BASIC CARDS
STATED ODDS 1:4 HOB, 1:24 RET

2005 Zenith Z-Gold

*VETERANS: 2X TO 5X BASIC CARDS
STATED ODDS 1:12 RETAIL

2005 Zenith Z-Silver

*VETERANS: 1.2X TO 3X BASIC CARDS
STATED ODDS 1:3 RETAIL

2005 Zenith Z-Titanium

*VETERANS: 3X TO 8X BASIC CARDS
STATED PRINT RUN 99 SER.#'d SETS

2005 Zenith Aerial Assault Silver

STATED ODDS 1:18 HOB, 1:24 RET		
*GOLD: 1.2X TO 3X BASIC INSERTS		
GOLD PRINT RUN 100 SER.#'d SETS		
AA1 Aaron Brooks	.60	1.50
AA2 Ben Roethlisberger	1.50	4.00
AA3 Brett Favre	2.50	6.00
AA4 Byron Leftwich	.75	2.00
AA5 Carson Palmer	1.00	2.50
AA6 Chad Pennington	1.00	2.50
AA7 David Carr	.60	1.50
AA8 J.P. Losman	.60	1.50
AA9 Jake Plummer	.75	2.00
AA10 Kyle Boller	.75	2.00
AA11 Michael Vick	1.00	2.50
AA12 Peyton Manning	2.00	5.00
AA13 Rex Grossman	.75	2.00
AA14 Eli Manning	1.50	4.00
AA15 Drew Brees	1.00	2.50
AA16 Drew Bledsoe	1.00	2.50
AA17 Jake Delhomme	.75	2.00
AA18 Joey Harrington	.75	2.00
AA19 Daunte Culpepper	.75	2.00
AA20 Donovan McNabb	1.00	2.50
AA21 Matt Hasselbeck	.75	2.00
AA22 Marc Bulger	.75	2.00
AA23 Steve McNair	1.00	2.50
AA24 Trent Green	.75	2.00
AA25 Tom Brady	2.00	5.00

2005 Zenith Aerial Assault Jerseys

STATED PRINT RUN 250 SER.#'d SETS		
*PRIME: .8X TO 2X BASIC JERSEYS		
PRIME PRINT RUN 25 SER.#'d SETS		
AA1 Aaron Brooks	3.00	8.00
AA2 Ben Roethlisberger	10.00	25.00
AA3 Brett Favre	10.00	25.00
AA4 Byron Leftwich	4.00	10.00
AA5 Carson Palmer	4.00	10.00
AA6 Chad Pennington	4.00	10.00
AA7 David Carr	4.00	10.00
AA8 J.P. Losman	4.00	10.00
AA9 Jake Plummer	3.00	8.00
AA10 Kyle Boller	3.00	8.00
AA11 Michael Vick	6.00	15.00
AA12 Peyton Manning	7.50	20.00
AA13 Rex Grossman	3.00	8.00
AA14 Eli Manning	10.00	25.00
AA15 Drew Brees	4.00	10.00
AA16 Drew Bledsoe	4.00	10.00
AA17 Jake Delhomme	4.00	10.00
AA18 Joey Harrington	4.00	10.00
AA19 Daunte Culpepper	4.00	10.00
AA20 Donovan McNabb	5.00	12.00
AA21 Matt Hasselbeck	3.00	8.00
AA22 Marc Bulger	4.00	10.00
AA23 Steve McNair	4.00	10.00
AA24 Trent Green	3.00	8.00
AA25 Tom Brady	7.50	20.00

2005 Zenith Autumn Warriors Silver

STATED ODDS 1:18 HOB, 1:24 RET		
*GOLD: .8X TO 2X BASIC INSERTS		
GOLD PRINT RUN 100 SER.#'d SETS		
AW1 Ben Roethlisberger	3.00	8.00
Chad Pennington		
AW2 Walter Payton	5.00	12.00
Barry Sanders		
AW3 Marcus Allen	2.00	5.00
Bo Jackson		
AW4 Ray Lewis	1.25	3.00
Brian Urlacher		
AW5 Brett Favre	3.00	8.00
David Carr		
AW6 Corey Dillon	1.25	3.00
Clinton Portis		
AW7 Donovan McNabb	1.25	3.00
Daunte Culpepper		
AW8 Dan Marino	5.00	12.00
Peyton Manning		
AW9 Jerry Rice	2.00	5.00
Marvin Harrison		
AW10 Joe Montana	5.00	12.00
Tom Brady		
AW11 Joe Namath	2.50	6.00
Eli Manning		
AW12 Julius Jones	1.25	3.00
Kevin Jones		
AW13 Priest Holmes	1.25	3.00
LaDainian Tomlinson		
AW14 Michael Vick	1.25	3.00
Byron Leftwich		
AW15 Javon Walker	1.25	3.00
Roy Williams WR		
AW16 Terrell Owens	1.25	3.00
Andre Johnson		
AW17 Hines Ward	1.25	3.00
Chad Johnson		
AW18 Shaun Alexander	1.25	3.00

Deuce McAllister		
AW19 Edgerrin James	1.25	3.00
Jamal Lewis		
AW20 Marc Bulger	1.25	3.00
Matt Hasselbeck		

2005 Zenith Autumn Warriors Materials

STATED PRINT RUN 250 SER.#'d SETS
*PRIME: 1X TO 2.5X BASIC JERSEYS
PRIME PRINT RUN 25 SER.#'d SETS

AW1 Ben Roethlisberger	7.50	20.00
Chad Pennington		
AW2 Walter Payton	15.00	40.00
Barry Sanders		
AW3 Marcus Allen	7.50	20.00
Bo Jackson		
AW4 Ray Lewis	7.50	20.00
Brian Urlacher		
AW5 Brett Favre	10.00	25.00
David Carr		
AW6 Corey Dillon	4.00	10.00
Clinton Portis		
AW7 Donovan McNabb	5.00	12.00
Daunte Culpepper		
AW8 Dan Marino	15.00	40.00
Peyton Manning		
AW9 Jerry Rice	6.00	20.00
Marvin Harrison		
AW10 Joe Montana	15.00	40.00
Tom Brady		
AW11 Joe Namath	7.50	20.00
Eli Manning		
AW12 Julius Jones	3.00	8.00
Kevin Jones		
AW13 Priest Holmes	5.00	12.00
LaDainian Tomlinson		
AW14 Michael Vick	5.00	12.00
Byron Leftwich		
AW15 Javon Walker	4.00	10.00
Roy Williams WR		
AW16 Terrell Owens	5.00	12.00
Andre Johnson		
AW17 Hines Ward	5.00	12.00
Chad Johnson		
AW18 Shaun Alexander	4.00	10.00
Deuce McAllister		
AW19 Edgerrin James	4.00	10.00
Jamal Lewis		
AW20 Marc Bulger	4.00	10.00
Matt Hasselbeck		

2005 Zenith Black 'N Blue Silver

*GOLD: .8X TO 2X BASIC INSERTS
GOLD PRINT RUN 100 SER.#'d SETS

BB1 Ben Roethlisberger	2.50	6.00
BB2 Brett Favre	4.00	10.00
BB3 Brian Urlacher	1.50	4.00
BB4 Clinton Portis	1.25	3.00
BB5 Corey Dillon	1.25	3.00
BB6 Daunte Culpepper	1.25	3.00
BB7 Domanick Davis	1.00	2.50
BB8 Donovan McNabb	1.50	4.00
BB9 Edgerrin James	1.25	3.00
BB10 Eli Manning	2.50	6.00
BB11 Hines Ward	1.50	4.00
BB12 Jake Delhomme	1.25	3.00
BB13 Jamal Lewis	1.25	3.00
BB14 Jerome Bettis	1.50	4.00
BB15 Kevin Jones	1.00	2.50
BB16 LaDainian Tomlinson	1.50	4.00
BB17 Michael Vick	1.50	4.00
BB18 Peyton Manning	3.00	8.00
BB19 Priest Holmes	1.25	3.00
BB20 Shaun Alexander	1.25	3.00
BB21 Steven Jackson	1.50	4.00
BB22 Tedy Bruschi	1.50	4.00
BB23 Terrell Owens	1.50	4.00
BB24 Tiki Barber	1.50	4.00
BB25 Willis McGahee	1.50	4.00

2005 Zenith Canton Bound Silver

*GOLD: 1X TO 2.5X BASIC INSERTS
GOLD PRINT RUN 100 SER.#'d SETS

CB1 Brett Favre	3.00	8.00
CB2 Daunte Culpepper	1.00	2.50
CB3 Peyton Manning	2.50	6.00
CB4 Jerry Rice	2.50	6.00
CB5 Dan Marino	4.00	10.00
CB6 Michael Vick	1.25	3.00
CB7 Randy Moss	1.25	3.00
CB8 Priest Holmes	1.00	2.50
CB9 Tom Brady	2.50	6.00
CB10 LaDainian Tomlinson	1.25	3.00
CB11 Walter Payton	4.00	10.00
CB12 Terrell Owens	1.25	3.00
CB13 Donovan McNabb	1.25	3.00
CB14 Larry Fitzgerald	1.25	3.00
CB15 Carson Palmer	1.25	3.00
CB16 Brian Urlacher	1.25	3.00
CB17 Ben Roethlisberger	2.00	5.00
CB18 Edgerrin James	1.00	2.50
CB19 Willis McGahee	1.25	3.00
CB20 Julius Jones	.75	2.00
CB21 Kevin Jones	.75	2.00
CB22 Joe Montana	4.00	10.00
CB23 Earl Campbell	1.50	4.00
CB24 Eli Manning	2.00	5.00
CB25 Steve Young	2.00	5.00

2005 Zenith Canton Bound Materials

STATED PRINT RUN 199 SER.#'d SETS
*PRIME: .8X TO 2X BASIC JERSEYS
PRIME PRINT RUN 25 SER.#'d SETS

CB1 Brett Favre	10.00	25.00
CB2 Daunte Culpepper	4.00	10.00
CB3 Peyton Manning	7.50	20.00
CB4 Jerry Rice	6.00	15.00
CB5 Dan Marino	12.50	30.00
CB6 Michael Vick	6.00	15.00
CB7 Randy Moss	4.00	10.00
CB8 Priest Holmes	4.00	10.00
CB9 Tom Brady	7.50	20.00
CB10 LaDainian Tomlinson	4.00	10.00
CB11 Walter Payton	15.00	40.00
CB12 Terrell Owens	4.00	10.00
CB13 Donovan McNabb	5.00	12.00
CB14 Larry Fitzgerald	4.00	10.00
CB15 Carson Palmer	4.00	10.00
CB16 Brian Urlacher	4.00	10.00
CB17 Ben Roethlisberger	10.00	25.00
CB18 Edgerrin James	4.00	10.00
CB19 Willis McGahee	4.00	10.00
CB20 Julius Jones	5.00	12.00
CB21 Kevin Jones	4.00	10.00
CB22 Joe Montana	12.50	30.00
CB23 Earl Campbell	6.00	15.00
CB24 Eli Manning	10.00	25.00
CB25 Steve Young	6.00	15.00

2005 Zenith Epix Black 1st Down

*BLACK 1st/100: 1X TO 2.5X ORANGE 1
BLACK 1 PRINT RUN 100 SER.#'d SETS
*BLACK 2nd/50: 1.2X TO 3X ORANGE 1
BLACK 2 PRINT RUN 50 SER.#'d SETS
*BLACK 3rd/25: 2X TO 5X ORANGE 1
BLACK 3 PRINT RUN 25 SER.#'d SETS
*BLACK 4th/10: 3X TO 8X ORANGE 1
UNPRICED BLACK 4 PRINT RUN 10 SETS

2005 Zenith Epix Blue 1st Down

*BLUE 1st/600: .4X TO 1X ORANGE 1
BLUE 1 PRINT RUN 600 SER.#'d SETS
*BLUE 2nd/400: .5X TO 1.2X ORANGE 1
BLUE 2 PRINT RUN 400 SER.#'d SETS
*BLUE 3rd/250: .6X TO 1.5X ORANGE 1
BLUE 3 PRINT RUN 250 SER.#'d SETS
*BLUE 4th/150: .8X TO 2X ORANGE 1
BLUE 4 PRINT RUN 150 SER.#'d SETS

2005 Zenith Epix Emerald 1st Down

*EMERALD 1st/150: .8X TO 2X ORANGE 1
EMERALD 1 PRINT RUN 150 SER.#'d SETS
*EMERALD 2nd/100: 1X TO 2.5X ORANGE 1
EMERALD 2 PRINT RUN 100 SER.#'d SETS
*EMERALD 3rd/50: 1.2X TO 3X ORANGE 1
EMERALD 3 PRINT RUN 50 SER.#'d SETS
*EMERALD 4th/25: 2X TO 5X ORANGE 1
EMERALD 4 PRINT RUN 25 SER.#'d SETS

2005 Zenith Epix Orange 1st Down

ORANGE 1 PRINT RUN 1000 SER.#'d SETS
*ORANGE 2nd/600: .4X TO 1X ORANGE 1
ORANGE 2 PRINT RUN 600 SER.#'d SETS
*ORANGE 3rd/400: .5X TO 1.2X ORANGE 1
ORANGE 3 PRINT RUN 400 SER.#'d SETS
*ORANGE 4th/250: .6X TO 1.5X ORANGE 1
ORANGE 4 PRINT RUN 250 SER.#'d SETS

1 Alex Smith QB	1.50	4.00
2 Ben Roethlisberger	1.50	4.00
3 Brett Favre	2.50	6.00
4 Brian Urlacher	1.00	2.50
5 Cadillac Williams	1.00	2.50
6 Carson Palmer	1.00	2.50
7 Troy Williamson	.75	2.00
8 Chad Pennington	1.00	2.50
9 Michael Vick	1.00	2.50
10 David Carr	.60	1.50
11 Donovan McNabb	1.00	2.50
12 Edgerrin James	.75	2.00
13 Eli Manning	1.50	4.00
14 J.P. Losman	.60	1.50
15 Steven Jackson	1.00	2.50
16 Daunte Culpepper	.75	2.00
17 Julius Jones	.60	1.50
18 Kevin Jones	.60	1.50
19 LaDainian Tomlinson	1.00	2.50
20 Peyton Manning	2.00	5.00
21 Randy Moss	1.00	2.50
22 Ronnie Brown	1.25	3.00
23 Clinton Portis	.75	2.00
24 Tom Brady	2.00	5.00
25 Willis McGahee	1.00	2.50

2005 Zenith Epix Purple 1st Down

*PURPLE 1st/500: .4X TO 1X ORANGE 1
PURPLE 1 PRINT RUN 500 SER.#'d SETS
*PURPLE 2nd/250: .6X TO 1.5X ORANGE 1
PURPLE 2 PRINT RUN 250 SER.#'d SETS
*PURPLE 3rd/150: .8X TO 2X ORANGE 1
PURPLE 3 PRINT RUN 150 SER.#'d SETS
*PURPLE 4th/100: 1X TO 2.5X ORANGE 1
PURPLE 4 PRINT RUN 100 SER.#'d SETS

2005 Zenith Epix Red 1st Down

*RED 1st/250: .6X TO 1.5X ORANGE 1
RED 1 PRINT RUN 250 SER.#'d SETS
*RED 2nd/150: .8X TO 2X ORANGE 1
RED 2 PRINT RUN 150 SER.#'d SETS
*RED 3rd/100: 1X TO 2.5X ORANGE 1
RED 3 PRINT RUN 100 SER.#'d SETS
*RED 4th/50: 1.2X TO 3X ORANGE 1
RED 4 PRINT RUN 50 SER.#'d SETS

2005 Zenith Mozaics Silver

*GOLD: 1X TO 2.5X BASIC INSERTS
GOLD PRINT RUN 100 SER.#'d SETS

M1 Michael Vick	1.25	3.00
Warrick Dunn		
Alge Crumpler		
M2 Kyle Boller	1.00	2.50
Jamal Lewis		
Todd Heap		
M3 J.P. Losman	1.25	3.00
Willis McGahee		
Lee Evans		
M4 Carson Palmer	1.25	3.00
Rudi Johnson		
Chad Johnson		
M5 Joey Harrington	1.00	2.50
Kevin Jones		
Roy Williams WR		
M6 Brett Favre	3.00	8.00
Ahman Green		
Javon Walker		
M7 David Carr	1.25	3.00
Domanick Davis		
Andre Johnson		
M8 Peyton Manning	2.50	6.00
Edgerrin James		
Marvin Harrison		
M9 Tom Brady	2.50	6.00
Corey Dillon		
Deion Branch		
M10 Jake Delhomme	1.00	2.50
Julius Peppers		
DeShaun Foster		
M11 Donovan McNabb	1.00	2.50
Brian Westbrook		
Terrell Owens		
M12 Ben Roethlisberger	2.00	5.00
Jerome Bettis		
Hines Ward		
M13 Drew Brees	1.25	3.00
LaDainian Tomlinson		
Antonio Gates		
M14 Marc Bulger	1.25	3.00
Steven Jackson		
Torry Holt		
M15 Steve McNair	1.25	3.00
Chris Brown		
Drew Bennett		

2005 Zenith Mozaics Materials

STATED PRINT RUN 100 SER.#'d SETS
UNPRICED PRIME PRINT RUN 10 SETS

M1 Michael Vick	6.00	15.00
Warrick Dunn		
Alge Crumpler		
M2 Kyle Boller	5.00	12.00
Jamal Lewis		
Todd Heap		
M3 J.P. Losman	5.00	12.00
Willis McGahee		
Lee Evans		
M4 Carson Palmer	5.00	12.00
Rudi Johnson		
Chad Johnson		
M5 Joey Harrington	5.00	12.00
Kevin Jones		
Roy Williams WR		
M6 Brett Favre	15.00	40.00
Ahman Green		
Javon Walker		
M7 David Carr	4.00	10.00
Domanick Davis		
Andre Johnson		
M8 Peyton Manning	12.50	30.00
Edgerrin James		
Marvin Harrison		
M9 Tom Brady	10.00	25.00
Corey Dillon		
Deion Branch		
M10 Jake Delhomme	5.00	12.00
Julius Peppers		
DeShaun Foster		
M11 Donovan McNabb	6.00	15.00
Brian Westbrook		
Terrell Owens		
M12 Ben Roethlisberger	12.50	30.00
Jerome Bettis		
Hines Ward		
M13 Drew Brees	6.00	15.00
LaDainian Tomlinson		
Antonio Gates		
M14 Marc Bulger	5.00	12.00
Steven Jackson		
Torry Holt		
M15 Steve McNair	5.00	12.00
Chris Brown		
Drew Bennett		

2005 Zenith Prime Signature Cuts Gold

UNPRICED PRIME SIGS GOLD #'d TO 5

2005 Zenith Prime Signature Cuts Platinum

UNPRICED PRIME SIGS PLATINUM #'d TO 1

2005 Zenith Rookie Roll Call Silver

STATED ODDS 1:18 HOB, 1:24 RET
*GOLD: .8X TO 2X BASIC INSERTS
GOLD PRINT RUN 100 SER.#'d SETS

RC1 Adam Jones	.75	2.00
RC2 Alex Smith QB	1.50	4.00
RC3 Antrel Rolle	1.00	2.50
RC4 Andrew Walter	.75	2.00
RC5 Braylon Edwards	1.25	3.00
RC6 Cadillac Williams	1.00	2.50
RC7 Carlos Rogers	1.00	2.50
RC8 Charlie Frye	1.00	2.50
RC9 Ciatrick Fason	.60	1.50
RC10 Courtney Roby	.75	2.00
RC11 Eric Shelton	.60	1.50
RC12 Frank Gore	1.50	4.00
RC13 J.J. Arrington	.75	2.00
RC14 Kyle Orton	1.00	2.50
RC15 Jason Campbell	1.25	3.00
RC16 Mark Bradley	.60	1.50
RC17 Mark Clayton	1.00	2.50
RC18 Matt Jones	1.00	2.50
RC19 Maurice Clarett	.75	2.00
RC20 Reggie Brown	.60	1.50
RC21 Ronnie Brown	1.25	3.00
RC22 Roddy White	1.25	3.00
RC23 Ryan Moats	.75	2.00
RC24 Roscoe Parrish	.60	1.50
RC25 Stefan LeFors	.60	1.50
RC26 Terrence Murphy	.60	1.50
RC27 Troy Williamson	.75	2.00
RC28 Vernand Morency	.75	2.00
RC29 Vincent Jackson	1.25	3.00

2005 Zenith Rookie Roll Call Autographs

STATED PRINT RUN 25-300

RC1 Adam Jones/200	5.00	12.00
RC2 Alex Smith QB/25	40.00	80.00
RC3 Antrel Rolle/100	8.00	20.00
RC5 Braylon Edwards/50	25.00	60.00
RC6 Cadillac Williams/25	30.00	80.00
RC7 Carlos Rogers/250	8.00	20.00
RC8 Charlie Frye/200	8.00	20.00
RC9 Ciatrick Fason/150	5.00	12.00
RC10 Courtney Roby/150	6.00	15.00
RC11 Eric Shelton/250	5.00	12.00
RC12 Frank Gore/150	12.00	30.00
RC13 J.J. Arrington/25	12.00	30.00
RC14 Kyle Orton/150	8.00	20.00
RC15 Jason Campbell/25	30.00	60.00
RC16 Mark Bradley/100	5.00	12.00
RC17 Mark Clayton/25	12.00	30.00
RC18 Matt Jones/25	12.00	30.00
RC20 Reggie Brown/100	5.00	12.00
RC21 Ronnie Brown/25	50.00	120.00
RC22 Roddy White/25		
RC23 Ryan Moats/300	5.00	12.00
RC24 Roscoe Parrish/25	10.00	25.00
RC25 Stefan LeFors/125	5.00	12.00
RC26 Terrence Murphy/250	5.00	12.00
RC27 Troy Williamson/25	12.00	30.00
RC28 Vernand Morency/50	6.00	15.00
RC29 Vincent Jackson/175	10.00	25.00

2005 Zenith Rookie Roll Call Jerseys

*PRIME: .8X TO 2X BASIC JERSEYS
PRIME PRINT RUN 25 SER.#'d SETS

RC1 Adam Jones	3.00	8.00
RC2 Alex Smith QB	7.50	20.00
RC3 Antrel Rolle	3.00	8.00
RC4 Andrew Walter	3.00	8.00
RC5 Braylon Edwards	5.00	12.00
RC6 Cadillac Williams	5.00	12.00
RC7 Carlos Rogers	3.00	8.00
RC8 Charlie Frye	3.00	8.00
RC9 Ciatrick Fason	3.00	8.00
RC10 Courtney Roby	3.00	8.00
RC11 Eric Shelton	3.00	8.00
RC12 Frank Gore	5.00	12.00
RC13 J.J. Arrington	3.00	8.00
RC14 Kyle Orton	3.00	8.00
RC15 Jason Campbell	4.00	10.00
RC16 Mark Bradley	3.00	8.00
RC17 Mark Clayton	3.00	8.00
RC18 Matt Jones	3.00	8.00
RC19 Maurice Clarett	3.00	8.00
RC20 Reggie Brown	3.00	8.00
RC21 Ronnie Brown	7.50	20.00
RC22 Roddy White	4.00	10.00
RC23 Ryan Moats	3.00	8.00
RC24 Roscoe Parrish	3.00	8.00
RC25 Stefan LeFors	3.00	8.00
RC26 Terrence Murphy	3.00	8.00
RC27 Troy Williamson	3.00	8.00
RC28 Vernand Morency	3.00	8.00
RC29 Vincent Jackson	4.00	10.00

2005 Zenith Spellbound Silver

*GOLD: .8X TO 2X BASIC INSERTS
GOLD PRINT RUN 100 SER.#'d SETS

S1 Tom Brady T	3.00	8.00
S2 Tom Brady O	3.00	8.00
S3 Tom Brady M	3.00	8.00
S4 Ben Roethlisberger B	2.50	6.00
S5 Ben Roethlisberger E	2.50	6.00
S6 Ben Roethlisberger N	2.50	6.00
S7 Dan Marino D	5.00	12.00
S8 Dan Marino A	5.00	12.00
S9 Dan Marino N	5.00	12.00
S10 Eli Manning E	2.50	6.00
S11 Eli Manning L	2.50	6.00
S12 Eli Manning I	2.50	6.00
S13 Joe Montana J	5.00	12.00
S14 Joe Montana O	5.00	12.00
S15 Joe Montana E	5.00	12.00
S16 Jerry Rice J	3.00	8.00
S17 Jerry Rice E	3.00	8.00
S18 Jerry Rice R	3.00	8.00
S19 Jerry Rice R	3.00	8.00
S20 Jerry Rice Y	3.00	8.00
S21 Steve Young S	2.50	6.00
S22 Steve Young T	2.50	6.00
S23 Steve Young E	2.50	6.00
S24 Steve Young V	2.50	6.00
S25 Steve Young E	2.50	6.00

2005 Zenith Spellbound Jerseys

STATED PRINT RUN 250 SER.#'d SETS
*PRIME: 1.2X TO 3X BASIC JERSEYS
PRIME PRINT RUN 25 SER.#'d SETS

S1 Tom Brady T	8.00	20.00
S2 Tom Brady O	8.00	20.00
S3 Tom Brady M	8.00	20.00
S4 Ben Roethlisberger B	10.00	25.00
S5 Ben Roethlisberger E	10.00	25.00
S6 Ben Roethlisberger N	10.00	25.00
S7 Dan Marino D	12.50	30.00
S8 Dan Marino A	12.50	30.00
S9 Dan Marino N	12.50	30.00
S10 Eli Manning E	10.00	25.00
S11 Eli Manning L	10.00	25.00
S12 Eli Manning I	10.00	25.00
S13 Joe Montana J	12.50	30.00
S14 Joe Montana O	12.50	30.00
S15 Joe Montana E	12.50	30.00
S16 Jerry Rice J	6.00	15.00
S17 Jerry Rice E	6.00	15.00
S18 Jerry Rice R	6.00	15.00
S19 Jerry Rice R	6.00	15.00
S20 Jerry Rice Y	6.00	15.00
S21 Steve Young S	6.00	15.00
S22 Steve Young T	6.00	15.00
S23 Steve Young E	6.00	15.00
S24 Steve Young V	6.00	15.00
S25 Steve Young E	6.00	15.00

2005 Zenith Team Zenith Silver

STATED ODDS 1:18 HOB, 1:24 RET
*GOLD: 1.2X TO 3X BASIC INSERTS
GOLD PRINT RUN 100 SER.#'d SETS

TZ1 Ben Roethlisberger	1.50	4.00
TZ2 Brett Favre	2.50	6.00
TZ3 Michael Vick	1.00	2.50
TZ4 Julius Jones	.60	1.50
TZ5 Peyton Manning	2.00	5.00
TZ6 Tom Brady	2.00	5.00
TZ7 Kevin Jones	.60	1.50
TZ8 Willis McGahee	1.00	2.50
TZ9 Daunte Culpepper	.75	2.00
TZ10 Donovan McNabb	1.00	2.50

2005 Zenith Team Zenith Jerseys

STATED PRINT RUN 100 SER.#'d SETS
*PRIME: .6X TO 1.5X BASIC JERSEYS
PRIME PRINT RUN 25 SER.#'d SETS

TZ1 Ben Roethlisberger	12.50	30.00
TZ2 Brett Favre	12.50	30.00
TZ3 Michael Vick	7.50	20.00
TZ4 Julius Jones	6.00	15.00
TZ5 Peyton Manning	10.00	25.00
TZ6 Tom Brady	10.00	25.00
TZ7 Kevin Jones	5.00	12.00
TZ8 Willis McGahee	5.00	12.00
TZ9 Daunte Culpepper	5.00	12.00
TZ10 Donovan McNabb	6.00	15.00

2005 Zenith Z-Graphs

1 Anquan Boldin	8.00	20.00
5 Michael Vick	25.00	50.00
7 Jake Delhomme	8.00	20.00
10 Steve Smith	10.00	25.00
11 Brian Urlacher	10.00	25.00
12 Rex Grossman	10.00	25.00
14 Chad Johnson	8.00	20.00
15 Rudi Johnson	8.00	20.00
17 Drew Bledsoe	10.00	25.00
18 Julius Jones	10.00	25.00
19 Keyshawn Johnson	8.00	20.00
20 Roy Williams S	6.00	15.00
22 Ashley Lelie	6.00	15.00
26 Joey Harrington	8.00	20.00
28 Roy Williams WR	8.00	20.00
29 Ahman Green	8.00	20.00
32 Andre Johnson	10.00	25.00
33 David Carr	6.00	15.00
34 Domanick Davis	6.00	15.00
36 Marvin Harrison	15.00	40.00
39 Byron Leftwich	8.00	20.00
41 Jimmy Smith	8.00	20.00
43 Priest Holmes	8.00	20.00
56 Aaron Brooks	6.00	15.00
57 Deuce McAllister	8.00	20.00
58 Eli Manning	50.00	100.00
63 Chad Pennington	10.00	25.00
75 Donovan McNabb	15.00	40.00
80 Duce Staley	8.00	20.00
81 Hines Ward	20.00	40.00
89 Matt Hasselbeck	10.00	25.00
93 Michael Clayton	6.00	15.00
97 Clinton Portis	8.00	20.00
98 Patrick Ramsey	8.00	20.00

2005 Zenith Z-Jerseys

STATED ODDS 1:215 RET
*PRIME/75-100: .6X TO 1.5X BASIC JERSEYS
*PRIME/50-55: .6X TO 1.5X BASIC JERSEYS
*PRIME/25-30: .8X TO 2X BASIC JERSEYS
PRIME SER.#'d UNDER 25 NOT PRICED

1 Anquan Boldin	3.00	8.00
2 Bryant Johnson		
3 Josh McCown	3.00	8.00
4 Larry Fitzgerald		
5 Michael Vick	4.00	10.00
6 Warrick Dunn	3.00	8.00
7 Jake Delhomme	3.00	8.00
8 Julius Peppers	3.00	0.00
9 Stephen Davis	3.00	8.00
10 Steve Smith	4.00	10.00
11 Brian Urlacher	4.00	10.00
12 Rex Grossman	3.00	8.00
13 Carson Palmer	4.00	10.00
14 Chad Johnson	3.00	8.00
15 Rudi Johnson	3.00	8.00
16 Kellen Winslow Jr.	3.00	8.00
17 Drew Bledsoe	4.00	10.00
18 Julius Jones	2.50	6.00
19 Keyshawn Johnson	3.00	8.00
20 Roy Williams S	2.50	6.00
21 Troy Aikman	7.50	20.00
22 Ashley Lelie	2.50	6.00
23 Jake Plummer	3.00	8.00
24 Quentin Griffin	2.50	6.00
25 Tatum Bell	2.50	6.00
26 Joey Harrington		
27 Kevin Jones	2.50	6.00
28 Roy Williams WR	3.00	8.00
29 Ahman Green	3.00	8.00
30 Brett Favre	10.00	25.00
31 Javon Walker	2.50	6.00
32 Andre Johnson	4.00	10.00
33 David Carr	2.50	6.00
34 Domanick Davis	2.50	6.00
35 Edgerrin James	3.00	8.00
36 Marvin Harrison	4.00	10.00
37 Peyton Manning	8.00	20.00
38 Reggie Wayne	4.00	10.00
39 Byron Leftwich	3.00	8.00
40 Fred Taylor	3.00	8.00
41 Jimmy Smith	3.00	8.00
42 Reggie Williams	2.50	6.00
43 Priest Holmes	3.00	8.00
44 Tony Gonzalez	3.00	8.00
45 Trent Green	3.00	8.00
46 Chris Chambers	3.00	8.00
47 Jason Taylor	3.00	8.00
48 Dan Marino	12.50	30.00
49 Junior Seau	4.00	10.00
50 Daunte Culpepper	3.00	8.00
51 Michael Bennett	3.00	8.00
52 Bethel Johnson	2.50	6.00
53 Corey Dillon	3.00	8.00
54 Tom Brady	8.00	20.00
55 Ty Law	3.00	8.00
56 Aaron Brooks	2.50	6.00
57 Deuce McAllister	3.00	8.00
58 Eli Manning	6.00	15.00
59 Jeremy Shockey	4.00	10.00
60 Michael Strahan	4.00	10.00
61 Aaron Glenn	2.50	6.00
62 Anthony Becht	2.50	6.00
63 Chad Pennington	4.00	10.00
64 Curtis Martin	4.00	10.00
65 Charles Woodson	4.00	10.00
66 Jerry Rice	6.00	15.00
67 Rich Gannon	3.00	8.00
68 Sebastian Janikowski	2.50	6.00
69 Tyrone Wheatley	2.50	6.00
70 Kerry Collins	3.00	8.00
71 A.J. Feeley	2.50	6.00
72 Brian Westbrook	3.00	8.00
73 Corey Simon	2.50	6.00
74 Correll Buckhalter	3.00	8.00
75 Donovan McNabb	4.00	10.00
76 Hugh Douglas	2.50	6.00
77 Terrell Owens	4.00	10.00
78 Todd Pinkston	2.50	6.00
79 Ben Roethlisberger	6.00	15.00
80 Duce Staley	3.00	8.00
81 Hines Ward	4.00	10.00
82 Jerome Bettis	6.00	15.00
83 Drew Brees	4.00	10.00
84 LaDainian Tomlinson	4.00	10.00
85 Bryant Young	2.50	6.00
86 Jerry Rice	6.00	15.00
87 Steve Young	6.00	15.00
88 Koren Robinson	2.50	6.00
89 Matt Hasselbeck	3.00	8.00
90 Shaun Alexander	3.00	8.00
91 Marc Bulger	3.00	8.00
92 Torry Holt	3.00	8.00
93 Michael Clayton	2.50	6.00
94 Mike Alstott	3.00	8.00
95 Chris Brown	2.50	6.00
96 Steve McNair	4.00	10.00
97 Clinton Portis	3.00	8.00
98 Patrick Ramsey	3.00	8.00
99 Sean Taylor	12.00	30.00
100 LaVar Arrington	3.00	8.00

2005 Zenith Z-Team Silver

*GOLD: 1.2X TO 3X BASIC INSERTS
GOLD PRINT RUN 100 SER.#'d SETS

ZT1 Larry Fitzgerald	1.00	2.50
ZT2 Michael Vick	1.00	2.50
ZT3 Willis McGahee	1.00	2.50
ZT4 Cedric Benson	1.00	2.50
ZT5 Brian Urlacher	1.00	2.50
ZT6 Carson Palmer	1.00	2.50
ZT7 Braylon Edwards	1.25	3.00
ZT8 Julius Jones	.60	1.50
ZT9 Kevin Jones	.60	1.50
ZT10 Brett Favre	2.50	6.00
ZT11 David Carr	.60	1.50
ZT12 Peyton Manning	2.00	5.00
ZT13 Byron Leftwich	.75	2.00
ZT14 Priest Holmes	.75	2.00
ZT15 Ronnie Brown	1.25	3.00
ZT16 Daunte Culpepper	.75	2.00
ZT17 Tom Brady	2.00	5.00
ZT18 Eli Manning	1.50	4.00
ZT19 Chad Pennington	1.00	2.50
ZT20 Randy Moss	1.00	2.50
ZT21 Donovan McNabb	1.00	2.50
ZT22 Ben Roethlisberger	1.50	4.00
ZT23 LaDainian Tomlinson	1.00	2.50
ZT24 Alex Smith QB	1.50	4.00
ZT25 Steven Jackson	1.00	2.50

Draft Picks

2006 Aspire

This 36-card set was released in May, 2006. The set was issued into the hobby in four-card packs with an $4.99 SRP which came 24 packs to a box.

COMPLETE SET (36)	10.00	25.00
1 Reggie Bush	.75	2.00
2 Matt Leinart	.40	1.00
3 Vince Young	.50	1.25
4 Mario Williams	.40	1.00
5 Michael Huff	.30	.75
6 Vernon Davis	.50	1.25
7 LenDale White	.30	.75
8 Brodie Croyle	.40	1.00
9 Drew Olson	.25	.60
10 Maurice Drew	.60	1.50
11 Tye Hill	.25	.60
12 Michael Robinson	.30	.75
13 Joseph Addai	.40	1.00
14 Paul Pinegar	.25	.60
15 Jimmy Williams	.40	1.00
16 D.J. Shockley	.30	.75
17 Mike Hass	.30	.75
18 Demetrius Williams	.30	.75
19 Reggie McNeal	.30	.75
20 Charlie Whitehurst	.40	1.00
21 Maurice Stovall	.25	.60
22 Sinorice Moss	.40	1.00
23 Jason Avant	.25	.60
24 Omar Jacobs	.25	.60
25 Laurence Maroney	.30	.75
26 Martin Nance	.30	.75
27 Leonard Pope	.40	1.00
28 Rodrique Wright	.25	.60
29 David Thomas	.30	.75
30 Will Blackmon	.30	.75
31 Dominique Byrd	.30	.75
32 D'Brickashaw Ferguson	.40	1.00
33 Reggie Bush	.75	2.00
34 Matt Leinart	.40	1.00
35 Vince Young	.50	1.25
36 Jay Cutler	.75	2.00

2006 Aspire Autographs

OVERALL AUTO ODDS 1:8 H, 1:24 R

1A Reggie Bush	30.00	80.00
2A Matt Leinart	12.00	30.00
3A Vince Young	20.00	50.00
4A Mario Williams	4.00	10.00
5A Michael Huff		
6A Vernon Davis	5.00	12.00
7A LenDale White	3.00	8.00
8A Brodie Croyle	4.00	10.00
9A Drew Olson	2.50	6.00
10A Maurice Drew	6.00	15.00
11A Tye Hill	2.50	6.00
12A Michael Robinson	3.00	8.00
13A Joseph Addai	10.00	25.00
14A Paul Pinegar	2.50	6.00
15A Jimmy Williams	4.00	10.00
16A D.J. Shockley	3.00	8.00
17A Mike Hass	3.00	8.00
18A Demetrius Williams	3.00	8.00
19A Reggie McNeal	3.00	8.00
20A Charlie Whitehurst	4.00	10.00
21A Maurice Stovall	2.50	6.00
22A Sinorice Moss	4.00	10.00
23A Jason Avant	2.50	6.00
24A Omar Jacobs	2.50	6.00
26A Martin Nance	3.00	8.00
27A Leonard Pope	4.00	10.00
28A Rodrique Wright	2.50	6.00
29A David Thomas	3.00	8.00
30A Will Blackmon	3.00	8.00
31A Dominique Byrd	3.00	8.00
32A D'Brickashaw Ferguson	4.00	10.00
36A Jay Cutler	40.00	80.00

2006 Aspire Century Club Autographs

CENT.CLUB/100 ODDS 1:69 H, 1:207 R

1A Reggie Bush	40.00	100.00
2A Matt Leinart	15.00	40.00
3A Vince Young	25.00	60.00
4A Mario Williams	6.00	15.00
5A Michael Huff	5.00	12.00
6A Vernon Davis	8.00	20.00
7A LenDale White	5.00	12.00
8A Brodie Croyle	6.00	15.00
9A Drew Olson	4.00	10.00
10A Maurice Drew	10.00	25.00
11A Tye Hill	4.00	10.00
12A Michael Robinson	5.00	12.00
13A Joseph Addai	12.00	30.00
14A Paul Pinegar	4.00	10.00
15A Jimmy Williams	6.00	15.00
16A D.J. Shockley	5.00	12.00
17A Mike Hass	5.00	12.00
18A Demetrius Williams	5.00	12.00
19A Reggie McNeal	5.00	12.00
20A Charlie Whitehurst	6.00	15.00
21A Maurice Stovall	4.00	10.00
22A Sinorice Moss	6.00	15.00
23A Jason Avant	4.00	10.00
24A Omar Jacobs	4.00	10.00
26A Martin Nance	5.00	12.00
27A Leonard Pope	6.00	15.00
28A Rodrique Wright	4.00	10.00
29A David Thomas	5.00	12.00
30A Will Blackmon	5.00	12.00
31A Dominique Byrd	5.00	12.00
32A D'Brickashaw Ferguson	6.00	15.00
36A Jay Cutler	50.00	100.00

2006 Aspire Combo Autographs

UNPRICED AU/5 ODDS 1:4800H,1:14,400R

2006 Aspire 5 Star

COMPLETE SET (25)	12.50	30.00

5 CARDS PER PLAYER OF EQUAL VALUE
STATED ODDS 1:6 HOB, 1:18 RET

FS1 Reggie Bush	.60	1.50
FS6 Jay Cutler	.60	1.50
FS11 Matt Leinart	.30	.75
FS16 LenDale White	.25	.60
FS21 Vince Young	.40	1.00

2006 Aspire 5 Star Autographs

AUTO/25 ODDS 1:384 H/R
5 CARDS PER PLAYER OF EQUAL VALUE

FS1 Reggie Bush	25.00	60.00
FS6 Jay Cutler	30.00	80.00
FS11 Matt Leinart	20.00	50.00
FS16 LenDale White	12.00	30.00
FS21 Vince Young	30.00	80.00

2006 Aspire Hype

COMPLETE SET (7)	10.00	25.00
1 Vernon Davis	.60	1.50
2 Reggie Bush	1.00	2.50
3 Joseph Addai	.50	1.25
4 Matt Leinart	.50	1.25
5 Vince Young	.60	1.50
6 Jay Cutler	1.00	2.50
7 Laurence Maroney	.40	1.00

2006 Aspire School Pride

STATED ODDS 1:100 HOB. 1:300 RET

SPRB Reggie Bush 1	30.00	80.00
SPBC1 Bobby Carpenter 1	6.00	15.00
SPBC2 Bobby Carpenter 2	8.00	20.00
SPJC1 Jay Cutler 1	12.50	30.00
SPJC2 Jay Cutler 2	15.00	40.00
SPJC3 Jay Cutler 3	20.00	50.00
SPTH1 Tye Hill 1	5.00	12.00
SPTH2 Tye Hill 2	5.00	12.00
SPTH3 Tye Hill 3	8.00	20.00
SPOJ1 Omar Jacobs 1	8.00	20.00
SPOJ2 Omar Jacobs 2	10.00	25.00
SPOJ3 Omar Jacobs 3	10.00	25.00
SPLP1 Leonard Pope 2	6.00	15.00
SPLP2 Leonard Pope 3	8.00	20.00
SPDS1 D.J. Shockley 2	5.00	12.00
SPDS2 D.J. Shockley 3	6.00	15.00
SPCW1 Charlie Whitehurst 1	5.00	12.00
SPCW2 Charlie Whitehurst 2	6.00	15.00
SPCW3 Charlie Whitehurst 3		
SPMW1 Mario Williams 1	12.50	25.00
SPMW2 Mario Williams 2	15.00	30.00
SPAY1 Ashton Youboty 1	8.00	20.00
SPAY2 Ashton Youboty 2	10.00	25.00

2006 Aspire Title Ticket

TITLE TICKET/50 ODDS 1:1920H, 1:5760R
UNPRICED AUTO/10 ODDS 1:4800

1 Vince Young	25.00	60.00
2 Michael Huff	12.00	30.00
3 David Thomas	12.00	30.00
4 Reggie Bush	30.00	80.00
5 Matt Leinart	20.00	50.00
6 LenDale White	15.00	40.00

2006 Aspire Title Ticket Autographs

UNPRICED AU/10 ODDS 1:4800H,1:14,400R

2006 Aspire National Promos

These cards were issued at the 2006 National Sports Collector Convention. Each card appears to be from the base Aspire set but for the addition of "/5" after the card number on the backs.

1 Matt Leinart	.50	1.25
2 Vince Young	.60	1.50
3 Jay Cutler	1.00	2.50
4 LenDale White	.40	1.00
5 Reggie Bush	1.00	2.50

2006 Aspire National VIP Promos

COMPLETE SET (3)	6.00	15.00
1 Reggie Bush	1.50	4.00
2 Matt Leinart	.75	2.00
3 Vince Young	1.00	2.50

2007 Aspire

This 33-card set was released in May, 2007. The set was issued to the hobby in four-card packs, with an $4.99 SRP, which came 24 packs to a box.

COMPLETE SET (34)	8.00	20.00
1 JaMarcus Russell	.25	.60
2 Brady Quinn	.40	1.00
3 Drew Stanton	.25	.60
4 John Beck	.40	1.00
5 Trent Edwards	.40	1.00
6 Troy Smith	.40	1.00
7 Kevin Kolb	.60	1.50
8 Jared Zabransky	.30	.75
9 Jordan Palmer	.30	.75
10 Chris Leak	.30	.75
11 Adrian Peterson	1.50	4.00
12 Marshawn Lynch	.40	1.00
13 Brian Leonard	.30	.75
14 Antonio Pittman	.25	.60
15 Kenny Irons	.25	.60
16 Michael Bush	.40	1.00
17 Darius Walker	.25	.60
18 Calvin Johnson	1.25	3.00
19 Robert Meachem	.40	1.00
20 Dwayne Bowe	.50	1.25
21 Sidney Rice	.50	1.25
22 Craig Buster Davis	.30	.75
23 Steve Smith USC	.40	1.00
24 Anthony Gonzalez	.40	1.00
25 Greg Olsen	.30	.75
26 Zach Miller	.40	1.00
27 Levi Brown	.40	1.00
28 Gaines Adams	.40	1.00
29 Leon Hall	.30	.75
30 Ted Ginn Jr.	.30	.75
31 Patrick Willis	.75	2.00
32 Adam Carriker	.30	.75
33 Aaron Ross	.40	1.00
34 Matt Leinart CL	.30	.75
Vince Young		
Reggie Bush		

2007 Aspire 5 Star

STATED ODDS 1:6
5 CARDS PER PLAYER OF EQUAL VALUE

FS1 Calvin Johnson	1.00	2.50
FS2 Calvin Johnson	1.00	2.50
FS3 Calvin Johnson	1.00	2.50
FS4 Calvin Johnson	1.00	2.50
FS5 Calvin Johnson	1.00	2.50
FS6 Marshawn Lynch	.30	.75
FS7 Marshawn Lynch	.30	.75
FS8 Marshawn Lynch	.30	.75
FS9 Marshawn Lynch	.30	.75
FS10 Marshawn Lynch	.30	.75
FS11 Adrian Peterson	1.25	3.00
FS12 Adrian Peterson	1.25	3.00
FS13 Adrian Peterson	1.25	3.00
FS14 Adrian Peterson	1.25	3.00
FS15 Adrian Peterson	1.25	3.00
FS16 Brady Quinn	.30	.75
FS17 Brady Quinn	.30	.75
FS18 Brady Quinn	.30	.75
FS19 Brady Quinn	.30	.75
FS20 Brady Quinn	.30	.75
FS21 JaMarcus Russell	.20	.50
FS22 JaMarcus Russell	.20	.50
FS23 JaMarcus Russell	.20	.50
FS24 JaMarcus Russell	.20	.50
FS25 JaMarcus Russell	.20	.50

2007 Aspire 5 Star Autographs

AUTOGRAPH/25 ODDS 1:538
5 CARDS PER PLAYER OF EQUAL VALUE

FS6 Marshawn Lynch	12.00	30.00
FS7 Marshawn Lynch	12.00	30.00
FS8 Marshawn Lynch	12.00	30.00
FS9 Marshawn Lynch	12.00	30.00
FS10 Marshawn Lynch	12.00	30.00
FS11 Adrian Peterson	100.00	200.00
FS12 Adrian Peterson	100.00	200.00
FS13 Adrian Peterson	100.00	200.00
FS14 Adrian Peterson	100.00	200.00
FS15 Adrian Peterson	100.00	200.00
FS16 Brady Quinn	20.00	50.00
FS17 Brady Quinn	20.00	50.00
FS18 Brady Quinn	20.00	50.00
FS19 Brady Quinn	20.00	50.00
FS20 Brady Quinn	20.00	50.00
FS21 JaMarcus Russell	15.00	40.00
FS22 JaMarcus Russell	15.00	40.00
FS23 JaMarcus Russell	15.00	40.00
FS24 JaMarcus Russell	15.00	40.00
FS25 JaMarcus Russell	15.00	40.00

2007 Aspire Autographs

OVERALL AUTO ODDS 1:8
*CENTURY CLUB: .5X TO 1.2X BASIC AUTOS
CENTURY CLUB/100 ODDS 1:112

1 JaMarcus Russell	3.00	8.00
2 Brady Quinn	8.00	20.00
3 Drew Stanton	3.00	8.00
4 John Beck	5.00	12.00
5 Trent Edwards	5.00	12.00
6 Troy Smith SP	10.00	25.00
7 Kevin Kolb	8.00	20.00
8 Jared Zabransky	4.00	10.00
9 Jordan Palmer	4.00	10.00
10 Chris Leak SP	10.00	25.00
11 Adrian Peterson	60.00	120.00
12 Marshawn Lynch	5.00	12.00
13 Brian Leonard	4.00	10.00
14 Antonio Pittman	3.00	8.00
15 Kenny Irons	3.00	8.00
16 Michael Bush	5.00	12.00
17 Darius Walker	3.00	8.00
19 Robert Meachem	5.00	12.00
20 Dwayne Bowe	6.00	15.00
21 Sidney Rice	6.00	15.00
22 Craig Buster Davis	4.00	10.00
23 Steve Smith USC	5.00	12.00
24 Anthony Gonzalez	5.00	12.00
25 Greg Olsen	4.00	10.00
26 Zach Miller	5.00	12.00
27 Levi Brown	5.00	12.00
28 Gaines Adams	5.00	12.00
29 Leon Hall	4.00	10.00
31 Patrick Willis	10.00	25.00
32 Adam Carriker	4.00	10.00
33 Aaron Ross	5.00	12.00

2007 Aspire Autographs Dual

UNPRICED DUAL AUTO/5 ODDS 1:6720

2007 Aspire Century Club

COMPLETE SET (33)	12.50	30.00
STATED ODDS 1:2		
C1 JaMarcus Russell	.40	1.00
C2 Brady Quinn	.60	1.50
C3 Drew Stanton	.40	1.00
C4 John Beck	.60	1.50
C5 Trent Edwards	.60	1.50
C6 Troy Smith	.60	1.50
C7 Kevin Kolb	1.00	2.50
C8 Jared Zabransky	.50	1.25
C9 Jordan Palmer	.50	1.25
C10 Chris Leak	.50	1.25
C11 Adrian Peterson	2.50	6.00
C12 Marshawn Lynch	.60	1.50
C13 Brian Leonard	.50	1.25
C14 Antonio Pittman	.40	1.00
C15 Kenny Irons	.40	1.00
C16 Michael Bush	.60	1.50
C17 Darius Walker	.40	1.00
C18 Calvin Johnson	2.00	5.00
C19 Robert Meachem	.60	1.50
C20 Dwayne Bowe	.75	2.00
C21 Sidney Rice	.75	2.00
C22 Craig Buster Davis	.50	1.25
C23 Steve Smith USC	.60	1.50
C24 Anthony Gonzalez	.60	1.50
C25 Greg Olsen	.50	1.25
C26 Zach Miller	.60	1.50
C27 Levi Brown	.60	1.50
C28 Gaines Adams	.60	1.50
C29 Leon Hall	.50	1.25
C30 Ted Ginn Jr.	.50	1.25
C31 Patrick Willis	1.25	3.00
C32 Adam Carriker	.50	1.25
C33 Aaron Ross	.60	1.50

2007 Aspire Date and Place Ticket Swatches

TICKET PRINT RUN 50 SER.#'d SETS
*PROGRAM: .2X TO .5X TICKET
*PROGM/TICK/20: .5X TO 1.2X TICKET
PROGRAM/TICKET PRINT RUN 20
UNPRICED AUTO/10 ODDS 1:1244

DP1 Chris Leak	10.00	25.00
DP2 Dallas Baker	10.00	25.00
DP3 Jarvis Moss	12.00	30.00
DP4 Earl Everett	8.00	20.00
DP5 Troy Smith	12.00	30.00
DP6 Antonio Pittman	12.00	30.00
DP7 Anthony Gonzalez	15.00	40.00
DP8 Ted Ginn Jr.	12.00	30.00
DP9 Steve Smith USC	10.00	25.00
DP10 Leon Hall	10.00	25.00
DP11 LaMarr Woodley	10.00	25.00
DP12 Steve Breaston	8.00	20.00
DP13 JaMarcus Russell	20.00	50.00
DP14 Dwayne Bowe	10.00	25.00
DP15 Craig Buster Davis	12.00	30.00
DP16 Brady Quinn	15.00	40.00
DP17 Darius Walker	12.00	30.00
DP18 Adrian Peterson	30.00	80.00

2007 Aspire School Pride

STATED ODDS 1:40

SP1 Gaines Adams	5.00	12.00
SP2 Aundrae Allison SP	10.00	25.00
SP3 John Beck	5.00	12.00
SP4 Ted Ginn Jr.	6.00	15.00
SP5 Anthony Gonzalez	8.00	20.00
SP6 Antonio Pittman	8.00	20.00
SP7 Troy Smith	6.00	15.00
SP9A DeMarcus Tank Tyler 1	4.00	10.00
SP9B DeMarcus Tank Tyler 2	5.00	12.00

2007 Aspire Hype Orange

*BRONZE/550: .4X TO 1X ORANGE
*GOLD/220: .5X TO 1.2X ORANGE
*SILVER/480: .4X TO 1X ORANGE

1 JaMarcus Russell	.20	.50
2 Adrian Peterson	1.25	3.00
3 Calvin Johnson	1.00	2.50
4 Brady Quinn	.30	.75
5 Ted Ginn	.25	.60
6 Marshawn Lynch	.30	.75
7 John Beck	.30	.75

2008 Aspire

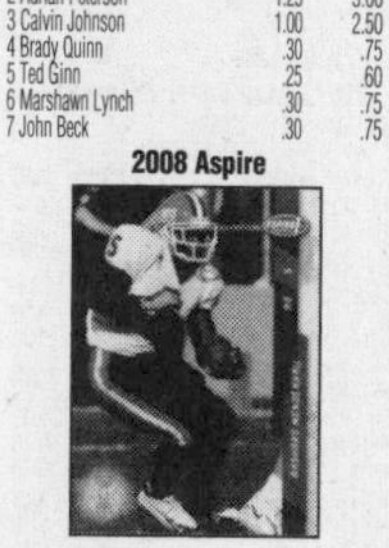

COMPLETE SET (33)	8.00	20.00
1 Matt Ryan	1.50	4.00
2 Brian Brohm	.40	1.00
3 Chad Henne	.40	1.00
4 Joe Flacco	1.25	3.00
5 John David Booty	.30	.75
6 Josh Johnson	.40	1.00
7 Erik Ainge	.40	1.00
8 Dennis Dixon	.40	1.00
9 Darren McFadden	1.00	2.50
10 Rashard Mendenhall	.75	2.00
11 Jonathan Stewart	.60	1.50
12 Jamaal Charles	.60	1.50
13 Felix Jones	.60	1.50
14 Ray Rice	.75	2.00
15 Kevin Smith	.40	1.00
16 Steve Slaton	.40	1.00
17 Mike Hart	.40	1.00
18 Malcolm Kelly	.30	.75
19 DeSean Jackson	.75	2.00
20 Limas Sweed	.40	1.00
21 Early Doucet	.30	.75
22 Andre Caldwell	.30	.75
23 Devin Thomas	.30	.75
24 James Hardy	.30	.75
25 Fred Davis	.40	1.00
26 Jake Long	.40	1.00
27 Sedrick Ellis	.40	1.00
28 Vernon Gholston	.30	.75
29 Keith Rivers	.40	1.00
30 Mike Jenkins	.40	1.00
31 Derrick Harvey	.25	.60
32 Dan Connor	.40	1.00
33 Leodis McKelvin	.30	.75

2008 Aspire 5 Star

STATED ODDS 1:6
5 CARDS PER PLAYER OF EQUAL VALUE

F1 Brian Brohm	.40	1.00
F6 Chad Henne	.40	1.00
F11 Darren McFadden	1.00	2.50
F16 Rashard Mendenhall	.75	2.00
F21 Matt Ryan	1.50	4.00

2008 Aspire 5 Star Autographs

5 STAR AUTO/25 ODDS 1:307
5 CARDS PER PLAYER OF EQUAL VALUE

F1 Brian Brohm	10.00	25.00
F6 Chad Henne	10.00	25.00
F11 Darren McFadden	25.00	60.00
F16 Rashard Mendenhall	25.00	60.00
F21 Matt Ryan	30.00	80.00

2008 Aspire Autographs

OVERALL AUTO ODDS 1:4
UNPRICED COMBO AU/5 ODDS 1:6720

A1 Matt Ryan	30.00	60.00
A2 Brian Brohm	5.00	12.00
A3 Chad Henne	5.00	12.00
A4 Joe Flacco	20.00	40.00
A5 John David Booty	4.00	10.00
A6 Josh Johnson	5.00	12.00
A7 Erik Ainge	5.00	12.00
A8 Dennis Dixon	5.00	12.00
A9A Darren McFadden BLK	20.00	40.00
A9B Darren McFadden BLUE	20.00	40.00
A9C Darren McFadden RED	25.00	50.00
A10 Rashard Mendenhall	15.00	40.00
A11 Jonathan Stewart	8.00	20.00
A12 Jamaal Charles	8.00	20.00
A13 Felix Jones	8.00	20.00
A14 Ray Rice	10.00	25.00
A15 Kevin Smith	5.00	12.00
A16 Steve Slaton	5.00	12.00
A17 Mike Hart	5.00	12.00
A18 Malcolm Kelly	4.00	10.00
A20 Limas Sweed	5.00	12.00
A22 Andre Caldwell	4.00	10.00
A23 Devin Thomas	4.00	10.00
A24 James Hardy	4.00	10.00
A25 Fred Davis	5.00	12.00
A26 Jake Long	5.00	12.00
A27 Sedrick Ellis	5.00	12.00
A28 Vernon Gholston	4.00	10.00
A29 Keith Rivers	5.00	12.00
A30 Mike Jenkins	5.00	12.00
A31 Derrick Harvey	3.00	8.00
A32 Dan Connor	5.00	12.00
A33 Leodis McKelvin	4.00	10.00

2008 Aspire Century Club

COMPLETE SET (33) 12.00 30.00
*SINGLES: .6X TO 1.5X BASIC CARDS
STATED ODDS 1:2

2008 Aspire Century Club Autographs

*CENTURY CLUB: .5X TO 1.2X BASIC AUTOS
CENTURY CLUB/100 ODDS 1:64

2008 Aspire Autographs Dual

UNPRICED COMBO AU/5 ODDS 1:6720

2008 Aspire Date and Place Ticket Swatches

DATE AND PLACE/50 ODDS 1:210
UNPRICED AUTOS SER.#'d TO 10

DP1 Early Doucet BCS Championship	6.00	15.00
DP2 Matt Flynn BCS Championship	15.00	40.00
DP3 Jacob Hester BCS Championship	8.00	20.00
DP4 Vernon Gholston BCS Championship	6.00	15.00
DP5 John David Booty Rose Bowl	6.00	15.00
DP6 Fred Davis Rose Bowl	10.00	25.00
DP7 Sedrick Ellis Rose Bowl	10.00	25.00
DP8 Lawrence Jackson Rose Bowl	8.00	20.00
DP9 Keith Rivers Rose Bowl	8.00	20.00
DP10 Rashard Mendenhall Rose Bowl	15.00	40.00
DP11 Darius Reynaud Fiesta Bowl	5.00	12.00
DP12 Owen Schmitt Fiesta Bowl	12.00	30.00
DP13 Steve Slaton Fiesta Bowl	8.00	20.00
DP14 Malcolm Kelly Fiesta Bowl	6.00	15.00
DP15 Marcus Howard Sugar Bowl	8.00	20.00
DP16 Jason Rivers Sugar Bowl	6.00	15.00
DP17 Xavier Adibi Orange Bowl	10.00	25.00
DP18 Brandon Flowers Orange Bowl	10.00	25.00

2008 Aspire Hula Bowl Autographs

*SILVER/250: .5X TO 1.2X BASIC AUTOS
SILVER PRINT RUN 250 SER.#'d SETS
*GOLD/50: .6X TO 1.5X BASIC AUTOS
GOLD PRINT RUN 50 SER.#'d SETS
OVERALL HULA BOWL AUTO ODDS 1:12

H1 Jabari Arthur	3.00	8.00
H2 Yvenson Bernard	4.00	10.00
H3 Alex Brink	4.00	10.00
H4 Andre Callender	4.00	10.00
H5 Jordon Dizon	4.00	10.00
H6 Marcus Fitzgerald	3.00	8.00
H7 Bruce Hocker	4.00	10.00
H8 Marcus Howard	4.00	10.00
H9 Tyrell Johnson	4.00	10.00
H10 Robert Jordan	3.00	8.00
H11 Keon Lattimore	3.00	8.00
H12 Gerard Lawson	3.00	8.00
H13 Justin McKinney	3.00	8.00
H14 Kalvin McRae	2.50	6.00
H15 Brent Miller	3.00	8.00
H16 Bernard Morris	3.00	8.00
H17 Kevin O'Connell	3.00	8.00
H18 T.C. Ostrander	3.00	8.00
H19 Maurice Purify	4.00	10.00
H20 Paul Raymond	3.00	8.00
H21 Jason Rivers	3.00	8.00
H22 Ricky Santos	4.00	10.00
H23 Paul Smith	4.00	10.00
H24 Darrell Strong	3.00	8.00
H25 Marcus Thomas	3.00	8.00
H26 Danny Woodhead	20.00	50.00

2008 Aspire School Pride

STATED ODDS 1:24

SP1 Marcus Howard	5.00	12.00
SP2 Keenan Burton	3.00	8.00
SP3 Bernard Morris	4.00	10.00
SP4 Devin Thomas	4.00	10.00
SP5 Vernon Gholston	4.00	10.00
SP6 Dustin Keller	5.00	12.00
SP7 Mike Jenkins	5.00	12.00

2009 Aspire Autographs

These cards were issued directly to dealers in May 2009 since SAGE suspended the Aspire brand for that year. No base cards were issued, just these ten autographed cards.

A1 Nick Reed	5.00	12.00
A2 Ryan Mouton	5.00	12.00
A3 Brandon Hughes	4.00	10.00
A4 Jerome Johnson	.5.00	12.00
A5 Andy Kemp	4.00	10.00
A6 Jaimie Thomas	4.00	10.00
A7 Anthony Felder	5.00	12.00
A8 Ray Feinga	4.00	10.00
A9 John Faletoese	5.00	12.00
A10 Bret Lockett	5.00	12.00

2011 Aspire Autographs

UNPRICED AUTO PRINT RUN 5

1994-95 Assets

Produced by Classic, the 1994 Assets set features stars from basketball, hockey, football, baseball, and auto racing. The set was released in two series of 50 cards each. 1,994 cases were produced of each series. This standard-sized card set features a player photo with his name in silver letters on the lower left corner and the Assets logo on the upper right. The back has a color photo on the left side along with a biography on the right side of the card. A Sprint phone card is randomly inserted in each five-card pack.

COMPLETE SET (100)	6.00	15.00
3 Troy Aikman	.20	.50
7 Marshall Faulk	.40	1.00
9 Drew Bledsoe	.20	.50
11 Steve Young	.15	.40
12 Dan Wilkinson	.05	.15
15 Charlie Garner	.08	.25
16 Derrick Alexander	.05	.15
23 Antonio Langham	.05	.15
24 Greg Hill	.05	.15
25 Marshall Faulk CL	.20	.50
28 Troy Aikman	.20	.50
32 Marshall Faulk	.40	1.00
34 Drew Bledsoe	.20	.50
36 Steve Young	.15	.40
37 Dan Wilkinson	.05	.15
40 Charlie Garner	.08	.25
41 Derrick Alexander	.05	.15
48 Antonio Langham	.05	.15
49 Greg Hill	.05	.15
52 Rashaan Salaam	.05	.15
55 Emmitt Smith	.40	1.00
59 Byron Bam Morris	.05	.15
61 Errict Rhett	.05	.15
63 Heath Shuler	.05	.15
66 William Floyd	.07	.20
67 Willie McGinest	.08	.25
70 Steve McNair	.30	.75
71 Ki-Jana Carter	.05	.15
74 Drew Bledsoe	.20	.50
77 Rashaan Salaam	.05	.15
80 Emmitt Smith	.40	1.00
84 Byron Bam Morris	.05	.15
86 Errict Rhett	.05	.15
88 Heath Shuler	.05	.15
91 William Floyd	.07	.20
92 Willie McGinest	.08	.25
95 Steve McNair	.30	.75
96 Ki-Jana Carter	.05	.15
99 Drew Bledsoe	.20	.50
100 Steve Young CL	.07	.20

1994-95 Assets Silver Signature

*SILVER SIGS: 1.2X TO 3X BASIC CARDS

1994-95 Assets Die Cuts

COMPLETE SET (25)	30.00	80.00
DC3 Troy Aikman	2.50	6.00
DC7 Marshall Faulk	4.00	10.00
DC8 Steve Young	1.25	3.00
DC14 Heath Shuler	.60	1.50
DC16 Byron Bam Morris	.60	1.50
DC21 Steve McNair	2.50	6.00
DC23 Errict Rhett	.60	1.50
DC25 Emmitt Smith	3.00	8.00

1994-95 Assets Phone Cards One Minute

COMPLETE SET (48) 7.50 20.00
*PIN NUMB.REVEALED: .2X to .5X BASIC INS.
*TWO DOLLAR: .5X TO 1.2X BASIC INSERTS

1 Troy Aikman	.50	1.25
2 Derrick Alexander	.15	.40
3 Drew Bledsoe	.20	.50
6 Marshall Faulk	.60	1.50
7 Charlie Garner	.15	.40
9 Greg Hill	.15	.40
12 Antonio Langham	.15	.40
22 Dan Wilkinson	.15	.40
24 Steve Young	.40	1.00
25 Drew Bledsoe	.40	1.00
27 Ki-Jana Carter	.15	.40
29 William Floyd	.15	.40
35 Willie McGinest	.15	.40
36 Steve McNair	.40	1.00
38 Byron Bam Morris	.15	.40
43 Errict Rhett	.15	.40
45 Rashaan Salaam	.15	.40
46 Heath Shuler	.15	.40
47 Emmitt Smith	.60	1.50

1994-95 Assets Phone Cards $5

COMPLETE SET (15) 8.00 20.00
*PIN NUMBER REVEALED: .2X TO .5X

1 Troy Aikman	.75	2.00
2 Drew Bledsoe	.50	1.25
6 Drew Bledsoe	.50	1.25
8 Ki-Jana Carter	.30	.75
11 Byron Bam Morris	.30	.75
12 Rashaan Salaam	.30	.75
13 Emmitt Smith	1.00	2.50

1994-95 Assets Phone Cards $100

COMPLETE SET (5) 15.00 40.00
*PIN NUMBER REVEALED: .2X TO .5X

1 Troy Aikman	5.00	12.00
2 Drew Bledsoe	4.00	10.00

1994-95 Assets Phone Cards $200

COMPLETE SET (5) 25.00 50.00
*PIN NUMBER REVEALED: .2X TO .5X

1 Drew Bledsoe	6.00	15.00
3 Ki-Jana Carter	4.00	10.00
5 Rashaan Salaam	4.00	10.00

1995 Assets Gold

COMPLETE SET (49)	6.00	15.00
15 Rashaan Salaam	.05	.15
16 Kyle Brady	.05	.15
17 J.J. Stokes	.10	.30
18 James O. Stewart	.20	.50
19 Michael Westbrook	.10	.30
20 Ki-Jana Carter	.07	.20
21 Steve McNair	.40	1.00
22 Kerry Collins	.30	.75
23 Byron Bam Morris	.05	.15
24 Errict Rhett	.08	.25
25 William Floyd	.07	.20
26 Drew Bledsoe	.08	.25
27 Marshall Faulk	.40	1.00
28 Troy Aikman	.25	.60
29 Steve Young	.15	.40
30 Trent Dilfer	.08	.25
31 Emmitt Smith	.40	1.00
50 Ki-Jana Carter CL	.05	.15

1995 Assets Gold Die Cuts Silver

COMPLETE SET (20) 10.00 25.00
*GOLDS: 1.2X to 3X SILVERS
STATED ODDS 1:72

SDC3 Kyle Brady	.40	1.00
SDC5 Marshall Faulk	.75	2.00
SDC11 Ki-Jana Carter	.50	1.25
SDC12 Rashaan Salaam	.50	1.25
SDC15 Emmitt Smith	1.50	4.00
SDC16 Drew Bledsoe	.75	2.00
SDC17 Kerry Collins	1.00	2.50
SDC19 Michael Westbrook	.40	1.00
SDC20 Heath Shuler	.50	1.25

1995 Assets Gold Printer's Proofs

*PRINT PROOF: 2X TO 5X BASIC CARDS

1995 Assets Gold Silver Signatures

COMP. SILVER SIG SET (50) 15.00 40.00
*SILVER SIGS: .8X TO 2X BASIC CARDS

1995 Assets Gold Phone Cards $2

COMPLETE SET (47) 15.00 40.00
*PIN NUMBER REVEALED: HALF VALUE

15 Rashaan Salaam	.30	.75
16 Kyle Brady	.30	.75
17 J.J. Stokes	.30	.75
18 James O. Stewart	.30	.75
19 Michael Westbrook	.30	.75
20 Ki-Jana Carter	.30	.75
21 Steve McNair	1.50	4.00
22 Kerry Collins	.75	2.00
23 Byron Bam Morris	.30	.75
24 Errict Rhett	.30	.75
25 William Floyd	.30	.75
26 Drew Bledsoe	.60	1.50
27 Marshall Faulk	.60	1.50
28 Troy Aikman	1.00	2.50
29 Steve Young	.75	2.00
30 Trent Dilfer	.30	.75
31 Emmitt Smith	1.25	3.00

1995 Assets Gold Phone Cards $5

COMPLETE SET (16) 25.00 60.00
*MICROLINED: .6X TO 1.5X BASIC INSERTS
STATED ODDS 1:18
*PIN NUMBER REVEALED: HALF VALUE

1 Drew Bledsoe	.75	2.00
2 Marshall Faulk	.75	2.00
5 Emmitt Smith	1.50	4.00
6 J.J. Stokes	.50	1.25
8 Michael Westbrook	.50	1.25
9 Troy Aikman	1.25	3.00
11 Ki-Jana Carter	.50	1.25

1995 Assets Gold Phone Cards $25

COMPLETE SET (5) 20.00 50.00
*PIN NUMBER REVEALED: HALF VALUE

1 Marshall Faulk Ki-Jana Carter	5.00	12.00
2 Steve McNair Kerry Collins	5.00	12.00

1995 Assets Gold Phone Cards $100

*PIN NUMBER REVEALED: HALF VALUE

1 Kerry Collins	6.00	15.00
3 Emmitt Smith	20.00	50.00
5 Steve Young	10.00	25.00

1995 Assets Gold Phone Cards $1000

UNNUMBERED RANDOM INSERTS IN PACKS

1996 Assets

The 1996 Classic Assets was issued in one set totalling 50 cards. This 50-card premium set has a tremendous selection of the top athletes in the world headlines. Each card features action photos, up-to-date statistics and is printed on high-quality, foil-stamped stock. Hot Print cards are parallel cards randomly inserted in Hot Packs and are valued at a multiple of the regular cards below.

COMPLETE SET (50)	5.00	10.00
1 Troy Aikman	.25	.60
2 Drew Bledsoe	.10	.30
5 Isaac Bruce	.08	.25
6 Kerry Collins	.08	.25
7 Trent Dilfer	.05	.15
10 Marshall Faulk	.20	.50
11 William Floyd	.05	.15
12 Joey Galloway	.05	.15
24 Steve McNair	.20	.50
25 Byron Bam Morris	.05	.15
35 Errict Rhett	.05	.15
36 Curtis Martin	.10	.30
40 Darnay Scott	.05	.15
41 Emmitt Smith	.40	1.00
49 Steve Young	.20	.50
50 Eric Zeier	.05	.15

1996 Assets Hot Prints

*HOT PRINTS: .8X TO 2X BASIC CARDS

1996 Assets A Cut Above

COMPLETE SET (20)	20.00	50.00
CA1 Keyshawn Johnson	1.25	3.00
CA2 Troy Aikman	1.50	4.00
CA7 Kevin Hardy	.50	1.25
CA8 Emmitt Smith	2.00	5.00
CA11 Marshall Faulk	1.00	2.50
CA13 Drew Bledsoe	1.00	2.50
CA19 Kerry Collins	.60	1.50

1996 Assets A Cut Above Phone Cards

COMPLETE SET (10) 12.50 30.00
*PIN NUMBER REVEALED: HALF VALUE

6 Marshall Faulk	1.25	3.00
7 Drew Bledsoe	1.25	3.00
10 Kerry Collins	.60	1.50

1996 Assets Crystal Phone Cards

COMPLETE SET (10) 20.00 50.00
*PIN NUMBER REVEALED: HALF VALUE

1 Troy Aikman	1.50	4.00
2 Drew Bledsoe	1.00	2.50
4 Marshall Faulk	1.25	3.00

1996 Assets Crystal Phone Cards $20

1 Troy Aikman	4.00	10.00
2 Drew Bledsoe	2.50	6.00
4 Marshall Faulk	3.00	8.00

1996 Assets Phone Cards $2

This 30-card set was inserted in retail packs at a rate of 1 per pack with a minimum value of $2 per phone card. The cards measure approximately 2 1/8" by 3 3/8" with rounded corners. The fronts display color aciton player photos with the player's name in a red bar below. The backs carry the instructions on how to use the cards and the expiration date of 1/31/97. Hot Print Cards parallel cards were randomly inserted in Hot Packs. These cards are valued as a mulitple of the cards below.

COMPLETE SET (30) 12.50 30.00
*$2 CARDS: .6X TO 1.5X $1 CARDS
*PIN NUMBER REVEALED: HALF VALUE

1996 Assets Phone Cards $5

COMPLETE SET (20) 30.00 80.00
*PIN NUMBER REVEALED: HALF VALUE

1 Troy Aikman	1.50	4.00
2 Drew Bledsoe	1.00	2.50
4 Isaac Bruce	.60	1.50
5 Kerry Collins	.60	1.50
7 Marshall Faulk	1.25	3.00
16 Emmitt Smith	2.00	5.00
20 Steve Young	1.25	3.00

1996 Assets Phone Cards $10

COMPLETE SET (10) 25.00 60.00
*PIN NUMBER REVEALED: HALF VALUE

1 Troy Aikman	2.50	6.00
2 Drew Bledsoe	2.00	5.00
4 Marshall Faulk	2.00	5.00
8 Emmitt Smith	3.00	8.00

1996 Assets Phone Cards $20

COMPLETE SET (5) 25.00 60.00
*PIN NUMBER REVEALED: HALF VALUE

3 Emmitt Smith	5.00	12.00

1996 Assets Phone Cards $100

COMPLETE SET (5) 40.00 80.00
*PIN NUMBER REVEALED: HALF VALUE

2 Marshall Faulk	6.00	15.00

1996 Assets Phone Cards $1000

NOT PRICED DUE TO SCARCITY
3 Marshall Faulk

1996 Assets Phone Cards $2000

NOT PRICED DUE TO SCARCITY
1 Emmitt Smith

1996 Assets Silksations

COMPLETE SET (10)	40.00	80.00
2 Kerry Collins	3.00	8.00
4 Marshall Faulk	5.00	12.00
8 Emmitt Smith	8.00	20.00

1997 Best Heroes of the Gridiron Promos

This set was produced to promote a football figurines product by the Best Card Company. Each card in this series was printed with a different design on the front presumably to represent a basic issue card and two insert sets that were never produced. The players are all pictured in their college uniforms. The unnumbered cardbacks include the Players Inc. and Collegiate Licensing Company logos within a larger "Heroes of the Gridiron" logo.

COMPLETE SET (3)	2.50	6.00
1 Mike Alstott (College Yearbook)	.75	2.00
2 Warrick Dunn (base set design)	1.00	2.50
3 Curtis Martin (Bragging Rights)	.75	2.00

1991 Classic Promos

These 1991 Classic Football Draft Pick promos measure the standard size. The front features an action color photo on a two-toned spotted gray background of the player with his name below in aqua or black print. The borders are a white and gray spotty pattern, with "Premiere Classic Edition" in the upper left hand corner and "91" in the upper right hand corner. The back states that these cards are for promotional purposes only. These five player cards (minus the "B" variations) were also issued as an unperforated promo sheet that measures approximately 7 1/2" by 7 1/8". The sheets were given away during the 1991 12th National Sports Collectors Convention in Anaheim (July 2nd-7th). The promo sheets bear a unique serial number("X of 10,000"). The backs have the warning "For Promotional Use Only" plastered over the Premier Classic Edition logo.

COMPLETE SET (7)	1.20	3.00
1 Antone Davis Black print on front	.20	.50
2A Rocket Ismail Black print on front	.40	1.00
2B Rocket Ismail Blue print on front	.40	1.00
3A Todd Lyght Black print on front	.20	.50
3B Todd Lyght Blue print on front	.20	.50
4 Russell Maryland Black print on front	.20	.50
5 Eric Turner Black print on front	.20	.50

1991 Classic

This 50-card set was distributed by Classic Games in factory set form. Top players from the 1991 NFL Draft are featured, including early cards of Brett Favre and Ricky Watters. Neither NFL team nor college team names are mentioned on the cards.

COMP. FACT SET (50)	1.50	4.00
1 Rocket Ismail	.15	.40
2 Russell Maryland	.01	.05
3 Eric Turner	.02	.10
4 Bruce Pickens	.01	.05
5 Mike Croel	.01	.05
6 Todd Lyght	.01	.05
7 Eric Swann	.02	.10
8 Antone Davis	.01	.05
9 Stanley Richard	.01	.05
10 Pat Harlow	.01	.05
11 Alvin Harper	.01	.05
12 Mike Pritchard	.02	.10
13 Leonard Russell	.02	.10
14 Dan McGwire	.01	.05
15 Bobby Wilson	.01	.05
16 Alfred Williams	.01	.05
17 Vinnie Clark	.01	.05
18 Kelvin Pritchett	.01	.05
19 Harvey Williams	.02	.10
20 Stan Thomas	.01	.05
21 Randal Hill	.02	.10
22 Todd Marinovich	.01	.05
23 Henry Jones	.01	.05
24 Jarrod Bunch	.02	.10
25 Mike Dumas	.01	.05
26 Ed King	.01	.05
27 Reggie Johnson	.01	.05
28 Roman Phifer	.01	.05
29 Mike Jones	.01	.05
30 Brett Favre	2.00	5.00
31 Browning Nagle	.01	.05
32 Esera Tuaolo	.01	.05
33 George Thornton	.01	.05
34 Dixon Edwards	.01	.05
35 Darryl Lewis	.01	.05
36 Eric Bieniemy	.01	.05
37 Shane Curry	.01	.05
38 Jerome Henderson	.01	.05
39 Wesley Carroll	.02	.10
40 Nick Bell	.01	.05
41 John Flannery	.01	.05
42 Ricky Watters	.25	.60
43 Jeff Graham	.08	.25
44 Eric Moten	.01	.05
45 Jesse Campbell	.01	.05
46 Chris Zorich	.02	.10
47 Doug Thomas	.01	.05
48 Phil Hansen	.02	.10
49 Kanavis McGhee	.02	.10
50 Reggie Barrett	.01	.05
P1 National Promo Sheet/10,00	1.00	2.50
NNO Rocket Ismail AU/1500	10.00	20.00

1992 Classic Promos

This six-card standard-size set was issued by Classic to preview the forthcoming draft pick issue. As with the regular issue foil and blister pack cards, the fronts have glossy color player photos enclosed by thin black borders. However, the color player photos on these promo cards differ from those used in the regular issue set. The Classic logo in the lower left corner is superimposed over a blue bottom stripe that includes player information. For background, the backs display the same unfocused image of a ball carrier breaking through the line in the deep, rich purple and maroon of the blister-pack cards. The backs present biography, but only the headings of the college stat categories appear. Further, the color close-up photos are also different, and the career summary has been replaced by a "News Flash" in the form of an advertisement for the draft pick set. Finally, the disclaimer "For Promotional Purposes Only" is stamped where the statistics would have been listed.

COMPLETE SET (6)	1.25	3.00
1 Desmond Howard	.30	.75
2 David Klingler	.20	.50
3 Quentin Coryatt	.20	.50
4 Carl Pickens	.50	1.25
5 Derek Brown	.20	.50
6 Casey Weldon	.20	.50

1992 Classic

The 1992 Classic Draft Picks Foil set contains 100 standard-size cards featuring the highest rated football players eligible for the 1992 NFL draft. The production run of the foil was limited to 14,000 ten-box cases, and to 40,000 of each bonus card. The fronts have glossy color player photos enclosed by thin black borders. A Classic logo in the lower left corner is superimposed over a blue bottom stripe that includes player information. Against the background of an unfocused image of a ball carrier breaking through the line, the backs have biography, college statistics, and career summary, with a color head shot in the lower left corner. This 100-card set needs to be distinguished from the 60-card set sold in blister packs only, which essentially was a re-package of the first 60-cards in the set. Though both sets are identical in design, the photos displayed on the fronts are different, as are the head shots on the backs. On some of the cards, the career summary also differs. However, the most distinctive feature is that background on the backs of the foil-pack cards are ghosted, whereas the same background on the blister-pack cards exhibits a deep, rich purple and maroon. Cards #30 and #54 are different in both versions. Key cards include Edgar Bennett, Marco Coleman, Quentin Coryatt, Sean Gilbert, Desmond Howard, David Klingler, Johnny Mitchell and Carl Pickens.

COMP.BLISTER SET (60)	2.00	5.00
COMPLETE FOIL SET (100)	4.00	10.00
1 Desmond Howard	.20	.50
2 David Klingler	.02	.10
3 Quentin Coryatt	.02	.10
4 Bill Johnson	.01	.05
5 Eugene Chung	.01	.05
6 Derek Brown TE	.01	.05
7 Carl Pickens	.30	.75
8 Chris Mims	.01	.05
9 Charles Davenport	.01	.05
10 Ray Roberts	.01	.05
11 Chuck Smith	.01	.05
12 Joe Bowden	.01	.05
13 Mirko Jurkovic	.01	.05
14 Tony Smith	.01	.05
15 Ken Swilling	.01	.05
16 Greg Skrepenak	.01	.05
17 Phillippi Sparks	.02	.10
18 Alonzo Spellman	.02	.10
19 Bernard Dafney	.01	.05
20 Edgar Bennett	.15	.40
21 Shane Dronett	.01	.05
22 Jeremy Lincoln	.01	.05
23 Dion Lambert	.01	.05
24 Siran Stacy	.01	.05
25 Tony Sacca	.01	.05
26 Sean Lumpkin	.01	.05
27 Tommy Vardell	.02	.10
28 Keith Hamilton	.08	.25
29 Ashley Ambrose	.02	.10
30 Sean Gilbert	.08	.25
31 Casey Weldon	.02	.10
32 Marc Boutte	.01	.05
33 Santana Dotson	.02	.10
34 Ronnie West	.01	.05
35 Michael Bankston	.01	.05
36 Mike Pawlawski	.02	.10
37 Dale Carter	.02	.10
38 Carlos Snow	.01	.05
39 Corey Barlow	.01	.05
40 Mark D'Onofrio	.01	.05
41 Matt Blundin	.01	.05
42 George Rooks	.01	.05
43 Patrick Rowe	.01	.05
44 Dwight Hollier	.01	.05
45 Joel Steed	.01	.05
46 Erick Anderson	.01	.05
47 Rodney Culver	.01	.05
48 Chris Hakel	.01	.05
49 Luke Fisher	.01	.05
50 Kevin Smith	.02	.10
51 Robert Brooks	.20	.50
52 Bucky Richardson	.01	.05
53 Steve Israel	.01	.05
54 Marco Coleman	.08	.25
55 Johnny Mitchell	.02	.10
56 Scottie Graham	.02	.10
57 Keith Goganious	.01	.05
58 Tommy Maddox	.50	1.25
59 Terrell Buckley	.02	.10
60 Dana Hall	.01	.05
61 Ty Detmer	.08	.25
62 Darryl Williams	.01	.05
63 Jason Hanson	.02	.10
64 Leon Searcy	.01	.05
65 Gene McGuire	.01	.05
66 Will Furrer	.01	.05
67 Darren Woodson	.08	.25
68 Tracy Scroggins	.01	.05
69 Corey Widmer	.01	.05
70 Robert Harris	.01	.05
71 Larry Tharpe	.01	.05
72 Lance Olberding	.01	.05
73 Stacey Dillard	.01	.05
74 Troy Auzenne	.01	.05
75 Tommy Jeter	.01	.05
76 Mike Evans	.01	.05
77 Shane Collins	.01	.05
78 Mark Thomas	.01	.05
79 Chester McGlockton	.02	.10
80 Robert Porcher	.08	.25
81 Marquez Pope	.02	.10
82 Rico Smith	.01	.05
83 Tyrone Williams	.02	.10
84 Rod Smith DB	.02	.10
85 Tyrone Legette	.01	.05
86 Wayne Hawkins	.01	.05
87 Derrick Moore	.01	.05
88 Tim Lester	.01	.05
89 Calvin Holmes	.01	.05
90 Reggie Dwight	.01	.05
91 Eddie Robinson	.01	.05
92 Robert Jones	.01	.05
93 Ricardo McDonald	.01	.05
94 Howard Dinkins	.01	.05
95 Todd Collins LB	.01	.05
96 Eddie Blake	.01	.05
97 Classic Quarterbacks Matt Blundin David Klingler Tommy Maddox Mike Pawlawski Tony Sacca Casey Weldon	.02	.10
98 Back-to-Back Ty Detmer Desmond Howard	.08	.25
NNO Checklist Card 2	.01	.05
NNO Checklist Card 1	.01	.05

1992 Classic Gold

COMP.FACT.GOLD (101) 20.00 50.00
*GOLDS: 1.5X TO 4X BASIC CARDS

AU1 Desmond Howard AUTO	10.00	25.00

1992 Classic Blister

COMP.BLISTER SET (60) 2.50 6.00
*BLISTER CARDS: .4X TO 1X BASIC CARDS

30 John Ray UER (name misspelled Rays)	.08	.25
54 Tyrone Ashley	.08	.25

1992 Classic Autographs

1 Alonzo Spellman	5.00	12.00
2 Erick Anderson	4.00	10.00
3 Troy Auzenne	4.00	10.00
4 Michael Bankston	4.00	10.00
5 Corey Barlow	4.00	10.00
6 Matt Blundin	4.00	10.00
7 Robert Brooks	7.50	20.00
8 Derek Brown TE	4.00	10.00
9 Terrell Buckley	5.00	12.00
10 Eugene Chung	4.00	10.00
11 Marco Coleman	6.00	15.00
12 Shane Collins	4.00	10.00
13 Todd Collins LB	4.00	10.00
14 Quentin Coryatt	5.00	12.00
15 Rodney Culver	10.00	25.00
16 Stacey Dillard	4.00	10.00
17 Howard Dinkins	4.00	10.00
18 Shane Dronett	4.00	10.00
19 Reggie Dwight	4.00	10.00
20 Mike Evans	4.00	10.00

21 Luke Fisher	4.00	10.00
22 Keith Goganious	4.00	10.00
23 Chris Hakel	4.00	10.00
24 Dana Hall	4.00	10.00
25 Jason Hanson	5.00	12.00
26 Robert Harris	4.00	10.00
27 Wayne Hawkins	4.00	10.00
28 Calvin Holmes	4.00	10.00
29 Desmond Howard	7.50	20.00
30 Steve Israel	4.00	10.00
31 Tommy Jeter	4.00	10.00
32 Bill Johnson	4.00	10.00
33 Dion Lambert	4.00	10.00
34 David Klingler	5.00	12.00
35 Tyrone Legette	4.00	10.00
36 Jeremy Lincoln	4.00	10.00
37 Sean Lumpkin	4.00	10.00
38 Gene McGuire	4.00	10.00
39 Derrick Moore	4.00	10.00
40 Mike Pawlawski	5.00	12.00
41 Robert Porcher	6.00	15.00
42 Bucky Richardson	4.00	10.00
43 Eddie Robinson	4.00	10.00
44 Tony Sacca	4.00	10.00
45 Greg Skrepenak	4.00	10.00
46 Kevin Smith	5.00	12.00
47 Rod Smith DB	5.00	12.00
48 Tony Smith	4.00	10.00
49 Carlos Snow	4.00	10.00
50 Phillippi Sparks	5.00	12.00
51 Larry Tharpe	4.00	10.00
52 Mark Thomas	4.00	10.00
53 Tommy Vardell	5.00	12.00
54 Casey Weldon	5.00	12.00
55 Ronnie West	4.00	10.00
56 Darryl Williams	4.00	10.00
57 Tyrone Williams	5.00	12.00

1992 Classic LPs

COMPLETE SET (10)	1.50	4.00
STATED PRINT RUN 40,000 SETS		
LP1 Desmond Howard	1.25	3.00
LP2 David Klingler	.25	.60
LP3 Siran Stacy	.10	.30
LP4 Casey Weldon	.25	.60
LP5 Sean Gilbert	.60	1.50
LP6 Matt Blundin	.10	.30
LP7 Tommy Maddox	3.00	8.00
LP8 Derek Brown TE	.10	.30
LP9 Tony Smith RB	.10	.30
LP10 Tony Sacca	.10	.30

1992-93 Classic C3

COMP.FACT SET (30)	6.00	15.00
14 Desmond Howard	.30	.75
15 David Klingler	.20	.50
16 Quentin Coryatt	.20	.50
17 Carl Pickens	.20	.50
18 Tony Smith	.20	.50
19 Rocket Ismail	.30	.75
20 Terrell Buckley	.20	.50

1993 Classic Gold Promos

These standard-size promo cards were sent to Classic Collectors Club members. The fronts feature color action player photos. The player's name, the word "Gold," and his position are gold foil stamped in a black stripe at the bottom. The production run "1 of 5,000" is gold foil stamped above this black stripe. The gold foil Classic logo at the upper left rounds out the front. On a blue-gray variegated background, the horizontal back has a narrowly cropped action photo, biography, and player profile. A tan pebble-grain panel designed for college statistics carries the disclaimer "For Promotional Purposes Only." The card is numbered on the back with a "PR" prefix.

COMPLETE SET (2)	1.60	4.00
PR1 Terry Kirby	.60	1.50
PR2 Jerome Bettis	1.20	3.00

1993 Classic

The 1993 Classic Football Draft Picks set consists of 100 standard-size cards. Randomly inserted throughout the foil packs were ten limited-print foil stamped cards, 1993 Classic Basketball Draft Pick Preview cards, 1993 Classic NFL Pro Line Preview cards, and 1,000 autographed cards by Super Bowl MVP Troy Aikman. Cards of number one pick Drew Bledsoe and number two pick Rick Mirer were exclusive to Classic until these players signed their NFL contracts. The production figures were 15,000 ten-box sequentially numbered cases, with 36 ten-card packs per box. The fronts feature color action player photos with blue stone-textured borders. The player's name and position is printed in a mustard bar at the bottom of the picture. The Classic Draft Picks logo overlaps the bar and the photo slightly to the right of center. The horizontal backs carry a small action photo, biographical information, statistics, and a player profile. Key cards include Jerome Bettis, Drew Bledsoe, Terry Kirby and Rick Mirer. Classic also issued 5,000 Gold Factory sets which include autographed cards of Drew Bledsoe and Rick Mirer.

COMPLETE SET (100)	2.50	6.00
1 Drew Bledsoe	.50	1.25
2 Rick Mirer	.08	.25
3 Garrison Hearst	.20	.50
4 Marvin Jones	.01	.05
5 John Copeland	.01	.05
6 Eric Curry	.01	.05
7 Curtis Conway	.08	.25
8 Willie Roaf	.02	.10
9 Lincoln Kennedy	.01	.05
10 Jerome Bettis	.75	2.00
11 Mike Compton	.01	.06
12 John Gerak	.01	.05
13 Will Shields	.02	.10
14 Ben Coleman	.01	.05
15 Ernest Dye	.01	.05
16 Lester Holmes	.01	.05
17 Brad Hopkins	.01	.05
18 Everett Lindsay	.01	.05
19 Todd Rucci	.01	.05
20 Lance Gunn	.01	.05
21 Elvis Grbac	.60	1.50
22 Shane Matthews	.25	.60
23 Rudy Harris	.01	.05
24 Richie Anderson	.08	.25
25 Derek Brown RB	.01	.05
26 Roger Harper	.01	.05
27 Terry Kirby	.08	.25
28 Natrone Means	.08	.25
29 Glyn Milburn	.02	.10
30 Adrian Murrell	.08	.25
31 Lorenzo Neal	.01	.05
32 Roosevelt Potts	.01	.05
33 Kevin Williams RBK	.01	.05
34 Russell Copeland	.01	.05
35 Fred Baxter	.01	.05
36 Troy Drayton	.02	.10
37 Chris Gedney	.01	.05
38 Irv Smith	.01	.05
39 Olanda Truitt	.01	.05
40 Victor Bailey	.01	.05
41 Horace Copeland	.01	.05
42 Ron Dickerson Jr.	.01	.05
43 Willie Harris	.01	.05
44 Tyrone Hughes	.01	.05
45 Qadry Ismail	.08	.25
46 Reggie Brooks	.02	.10
47 Sean LaChapelle	.01	.05
48 O.J.McDuffie UER	.20	.50
49 Larry Ryans	.01	.05
50 Kenny Shedd	.02	.10
51 Brian Stablein	.01	.05
52 Lamar Thomas	.01	.05
53 Kevin Williams WR	.02	.10
54 Othello Henderson	.01	.05
55 Kevin Henry	.01	.05
56 Todd Kelly	.01	.05
57 Devon McDonald	.01	.05
58 Michael Strahan	.75	2.00
59 Dan Williams	.01	.05
60 Gilbert Brown	.08	.25
61 Mark Caesar	.01	.05
62 Ronnie Dixon	.01	.05
63 John Parrella	.01	.05
64 Leonard Renfro	.01	.05
65 Coleman Rudolph	.01	.05
66 Ronnie Bradford	.01	.05
67 Tom Carter	.01	.05
68 Deon Figures	.01	.05
69 Derrick Frazier	.01	.05
70 Darrien Gordon	.02	.10
71 Carlton Gray	.01	.05
72 Adrian Hardy	.01	.05
73 Mike Reid	.01	.05
74 Thomas Smith	.01	.05
75 Robert O'Neal	.01	.05
76 Chad Brown	.01	.05
77 Demetrius DuBose	.01	.05
78 Reggie Givens	.01	.05
79 Travis Hill	.01	.05
80 Rich McKenzie	.01	.05
81 Barry Minter	.01	.05
82 Darrin Smith	.01	.05
83 Steve Tovar	.01	.05
84 Patrick Bates	.01	.05
85 Dan Footman	.01	.05
86 Ryan McNeil	.08	.25
87 Danan Hughes	.01	.05
88 Mark Brunell	.75	2.00
89 Ron Moore	.02	.10
90 Antonio London	.01	.05
91 Steve Everitt	.01	.05
92 Wayne Simmons	.01	.05
93 Robert Smith	.30	.75
94 Dana Stubblefield	.02	.10
95 George Teague	.02	.10
96 Carl Simpson	.01	.05
97 Billy Joe Hobert	.02	.10
98 Gino Torretta	.02	.10
99 Checklist 1	.01	.05
100 Checklist 2	.01	.05
POY1 Troy Aikman POY/17,500	2.00	5.00
AU1 Troy Aikman AU/1000	25.00	60.00
AU2 Drew Bledsoe AU/5000	20.00	40.00
AU3 Rick Mirer AU/5000	10.00	25.00
PR1A Drew Bledsoe Promo	1.00	2.50
PR1B Drew Bledsoe Promo	.75	2.00
P2 Rick Mirer Promo	.60	1.50

1993 Classic Gold

COMPLETE SET (100)	20.00	40.00
COMP.FACT.GOLD (102)	50.00	100.00
*GOLDS: 1.5X TO 4X BASIC CARDS		
STATED PRINT RUN 5000 SETS		

1993 Classic Autographs

13 Will Shields	3.00	8.00
70 Darrien Gordon	3.00	8.00

1993 Classic Draft Stars

COMPLETE SET (20)	7.50	20.00
ONE PER JUMBO PACK		
STATED PRINT RUN 20,000 SETS		
DS1 Drew Bledsoe	1.25	3.00
DS2 Rick Mirer	.25	.60
DS3 Garrison Hearst	.50	1.25
DS4 Marvin Jones	.05	.15
DS5 John Copeland	.05	.15
DS6 Eric Curry	.05	.15
DS7 Curtis Conway	.25	.60
DS8 Jerome Bettis	2.00	5.00
DS9 Patrick Bates	.05	.15
DS10 Tom Carter	.05	.15
DS11 Irv Smith	.05	.15
DS12 Robert Smith	.75	2.00
DS13 O.J.McDuffie	.50	1.25
DS14 Roosevelt Potts	.05	.15
DS15 Natrone Means	.25	.60
DS16 Glyn Milburn	.08	.25
DS17 Reggie Brooks	.08	.25
DS18 Kevin Williams WR	.08	.25
DS19 Qadry Ismail	.25	.60
DS20 Billy Joe Hobert	.08	.25
NNO Drew Bledsoe Rick Mirer Jumbo Card	4.00	10.00

1993 Classic LPs

COMPLETE SET (10)	7.50	20.00
STATED PRINT RUN 45,000 SETS		
LP1 Drew Bledsoe	3.00	8.00
LP2 Rick Mirer	.60	1.50
LP3 Garrison Hearst	1.25	3.00
LP4 Marvin Jones	.10	.30
LP5 John Copeland	.10	.30
LP6 Eric Curry	.10	.30
LP7 Curtis Conway	.60	1.50
LP8 Jerome Bettis	5.00	12.00
LP9 Reggie Brooks	.25	.60
LP10 Qadry Ismail	.60	1.50

1993 Classic Superhero Comics

COMPLETE SET (4)	10.00	25.00
STATED PRINT RUN 15,000 SETS		
SH1 Troy Aikman	10.00	12.00
SH2 Drew Bledsoe	4.00	10.00
SH3 Rick Mirer	.75	2.00
SH4 Garrison Hearst	1.50	4.00

1994 Classic Previews

Randomly inserted in Images packs, this five-card standard-size set features color player action shots on the fronts. These photos are borderless, except for the blue triangle in a lower corner that carries the player's position in white lettering. The player's name appears in the other corner. The back carries a borderless color player action shot, which is ghosted, except for the area around the player's head. A congratulatory message at the bottom gives the number of sets produced: 1,950. The cards are numbered on the back with a "PR" prefix.

COMPLETE SET (5)	4.00	7.00
PR1 Heath Shuler	.60	1.50
PR2 Trent Dilfer	1.25	3.00
PR3 Dan Wilkinson	.40	1.00
PR4 David Palmer	.40	1.00
PR5 Johnnie Morton	.40	1.00

1994 Classic Promos

These standard-size cards were issued to preview the design of the 1994 Classic Football Draft Picks series. The fronts feature color action shots of the players in their college uniforms. The photos are borderless, except for a royal blue lower corner that carries the player's position. The player's name is printed in the other lower corner. The borderless back carries a player action shot that is ghosted, with the exception of the area around the player's head. Player biography, statistics, and career highlights round out the back. Along the bottom are the words, "For promotional purposes only." The cards are numbered on the back with a "PR" prefix.

COMPLETE SET (3)	2.00	5.00
PR1 Marshall Faulk	1.20	3.00
PR2 Heath Shuler	.40	1.00
PR3 Heath Shuler	.40	1.00

1994 Classic

This 105-card standard-size set features color player action shots on the fronts. These photos are borderless, except for the blue triangle in a lower corner that carries the player's position in white lettering. The draftee's name and his new NFL team helmet logo appear in the other corner. The back carries a borderless color player action shot, which is ghosted, except for the area around the player's head. The player's statistics, brief biography, and career highlights round out the back. A parallel gold set was issued one per pack. The cards are valued as a multiple of the regular cards. Key players in this set include Isaac Bruce, Marshall Faulk and Errict Rhett. Two special inserts (one signed) featuring Jerry Rice were randomly inserted into packs, both in honor of Rice becoming the all-time TD reception leader. Signed versions of the Jerry Rice were hand signed on card front in silver and hand numbered to 1994 of each.

COMPLETE SET (105)	2.50	6.00
1 Heath Shuler	.02	.10
2 Trent Dilfer	.30	.75
3 Marshall Faulk	.75	2.00
4 Errict Rhett	.08	.25
5 Charlie Garner	.25	.60
6 Sam Adams	.01	.05
7 Shante Carver	.01	.05
8 Dwayne Chandler	.01	.05
9 Andre Coleman	.01	.05
10 Carlester Crumpler	.01	.05
11 Charles Johnson	.08	.25
12 David Palmer	.02	.10
13 Dan Wilkinson	.02	.10
14 LeShon Johnson	.01	.05
15 Mario Bates	.02	.10
16 Glenn Foley	.01	.05
17 William Gaines	.01	.05
18 Wayne Gandy	.01	.05
19 Jason Gildon	.02	.10
20 Eric Gant	.01	.05
21 Tre Johnson	.01	.05
22 Calvin Jones	.01	.05
23 Jake Kelchner	.01	.05
24 Perry Klein	.01	.05
25 Chuck Levy	.01	.05
26 Corey Louchiey	.01	.05
27 Chris Maumalanga	.01	.05
28 Jamir Miller	.02	.10
29 Jim Miller	.50	1.25
30 Johnnie Morton	.25	.60
31 Doug Nussmeier	.02	.10
32 Vaughn Parker	.01	.05
33 Darnay Scott	.15	.40
34 Fernando Smith	.01	.05
35 Lamar Smith	.40	1.00
36 Marcus Spears	.01	.05
37 Irving Spikes	.01	.05
38 Todd Steussie	.01	.05
39 Aaron Taylor	.01	.05
40 John Thierry	.01	.05
41 Dewayne Washington	.01	.05
42 Jason Winrow	.01	.05
43 Ronnie Woolfork	.01	.05
44 Bryant Young	.15	.40
45 Arthur Bussie	.01	.05
46 Derrick Alexander WR	.08	.25
47 Larry Allen	.08	.25
48 Aubrey Beavers	.01	.05
49 James Bostic	.01	.05
50 Jeff Burris	.01	.05
51 Lindsey Chapman	.01	.05
52 Isaac Davis	.01	.05
53 Lake Dawson	.02	.10
54 Tyronne Drakeford	.01	.05
55 William Floyd	.02	.10
56 Henry Ford	.01	.05
57 Rob Fredrickson	.02	.10
58 Aaron Glenn	.08	.25
59 Shelby Hill	.01	.05
60 Willie Jackson	.08	.25
61 Joe Johnson	.01	.05
62 Aaron Laing	.01	.05
63 Kevin Lee	.01	.05
64 Eric Mahlum	.01	.05
65 Steve Matthews	.01	.05
66 Willie McGinest	.08	.25
67 Kevin Mitchell	.01	.05
68 Byron Bam Morris	.02	.10
69 Thomas Randolph	.01	.05
70 Tony Richardson	.01	.05
71 Corey Sawyer	.02	.10
72 Jason Sehorn	.08	.25
73 Rob Waldrop	.01	.05
74 Jay Walker	.01	.05
75 Bernard Williams	.01	.05
76 Marvin Goodwin	.01	.05
77 Romeo Bandison	.01	.05
78 Bucky Brooks	.01	.05
79 James Folston	.01	.05
80 Donnell Bennett	.02	.10
81 Charlie Ward	.08	.25
82 Antonio Langham	.01	.05
83 Greg Hill	.02	.10
84 Anthony Phillips	.01	.05
85 Winfred Tubbs	.01	.05
86 Trev Alberts	.01	.05
87 Tim Bowens	.01	.05
88 Thomas Lewis	.01	.05
89 Allen Aldridge	.01	.05
90 Bert Emanuel	.08	.25
91 Ryan Yarborough	.01	.05
92 Lonnie Johnson	.01	.05
93 Isaac Bruce	.75	2.00
94 Checklist 1	.01	.05
95 Checklist 2	.01	.05
96 Troy Aikman FLB	.30	.75
97 Steve Young FLB	.08	.25
98 Rick Mirer FLB	.02	.10
99 Drew Bledsoe FLB	.20	.50
100 Jerry Rice FLB	.30	.75
101 Heath Shuler COMIC SP	.02	.10
102 M.Faulk COMIC SP	.30	.75
103 Trent Dilfer COMIC SP	.15	.40
104 D.Wilkinson COMIC SP	.02	.10
105 David Palmer COMIC SP	.02	.10
FD2 Marshall Faulk AUTO/10,000 (1994 Draft Day card)	10.00	25.00
JR1 Jerry Rice Special	6.00	15.00
NNO Marshall Faulk Promo (International Expo back)	.50	1.25
NNO Jerry Rice AUTO/1994	30.00	80.00

1994 Classic Gold

COMPLETE SET (105)	15.00	30.00
*GOLDS: 1.5X TO 4X BASIC CARDS		
ONE PER PACK		

1994 Classic Draft Stars

COMPLETE SET (20)	4.00	10.00
ONE DRAFT STARS PER MAGAZINE PACK		
MIRER SPECIAL RANDOM INSERT IN MAG		
1 Trev Alberts	.05	.15
2 Jeff Burris	.05	.15
3 Shante Carver	.05	.15
4 Trent Dilfer	.75	2.00
5 Marshall Faulk	2.00	5.00
6 William Floyd	.08	.25
7 Aaron Glenn	.25	.60
8 Greg Hill	.08	.25
9 Charles Johnson	.25	.60
10 Calvin Jones	.05	.15
11 Antonio Langham	.05	.15
12 Thomas Lewis	.05	.15
13 Willie McGinest	.25	.60
14 Jamir Miller	.08	.25
15 Johnnie Morton	.60	1.50
16 David Palmer	.08	.25
17 Darnay Scott	.40	1.00
18 Heath Shuler	.08	.25
19 Dan Wilkinson	.08	.25
20 Bryant Young	.40	1.00
NNO Rick Mirer Special	.40	1.00

1994 Classic Game Cards

COMPLETE SET (10)	3.00	6.00
ONE PER JUMBO PACK		
DB1 BLEDSOE INSERTED IN JUMBOS		
*PRIZE BOX SCRATCHED: .2X TO .5X		
GC1 Trent Dilfer	.60	1.50
GC2 Marshall Faulk	1.50	4.00
GC3 Heath Shuler	.07	.20
GC4 Dan Wilkinson	.07	.20
GC5 Antonio Langham	.02	.10
GC6 Willie McGinest	.20	.50
GC7 Greg Hill	.07	.20
GC8 Trev Alberts	.02	.10
GC9 Charles Johnson	.20	.50
GC10 Errict Rhett	.20	.50
DB1 Drew Bledsoe Special	5.00	12.00

1994 Classic Picks

COMPLETE SET (5)	6.00	15.00
STATED ODDS 1:36 HOBBY		
1 Heath Shuler	.20	.50
2 Trent Dilfer	1.50	4.00
3 Johnnie Morton	1.25	3.00
4 David Palmer	.20	.50
5 Marshall Faulk	4.00	10.00

1994 Classic ROY Sweepstakes

COMPLETE SET (20)	20.00	50.00
STATED ODDS 1:73		
ROY1 Trent Dilfer	3.00	8.00
ROY2 Mario Bates	.40	1.00
ROY3 Darnay Scott	1.50	4.00
ROY4 Johnnie Morton	2.50	6.00
ROY5 William Floyd	.40	1.00
ROY6 Errict Rhett	1.00	2.50
ROY7 Greg Hill	.40	1.00
ROY8 Lake Dawson	.40	1.00
ROY9 Charlie Garner	2.50	6.00
ROY10 Heath Shuler	.40	1.00
ROY11 Derrick Alexander WR	1.00	2.50
ROY12 LeShon Johnson	.20	.50
ROY13 Kevin Lee	.20	.50
ROY14 David Palmer	.40	1.00
ROY15 Charles Johnson	1.00	2.50
ROY16 Chuck Levy	.20	.50
ROY17 Calvin Jones	.20	.50
ROY18 Thomas Lewis	.20	.50
ROY19 Marshall Faulk WIN	8.00	20.00
ROY20 Field Card	.20	.50

1995 Classic Five Sport

The 1995 Classic Five Sport set was issued in one series of 200 standard-size cards. Cards were issued in 10-card regular packs (SRP $1.99). Boxes contained 36 packs. One autographed card was guaranteed in each pack and one certified autographed card (with an embossed logo) appeared in each box. There were also memorabilia redemption cards included in some packs and were guaranteed in at least one pack per box. The cards are numbered and divided into the five sports as follows: Basketball (1-42), Football (43-92), Baseball (93-122), Hockey (123-160), Racing (161-180), Alma Maters (181-190), Picture Perfect (191-200).

COMPLETE SET (200)	6.00	15.00
43 Ki-Jana Carter	.08	.25
44 Tony Boselli	.07	.20
45 Steve McNair	.40	1.00
46 Michael Westbrook	.08	.25
47 Kerry Collins	.40	1.00
48 Kevin Carter	.05	.15
49 Mike Mamula	.05	.15
50 Joey Galloway	.20	.50
51 Kyle Brady	.07	.20
52 J.J. Stokes	.08	.25
53 Derrick Alexander	.07	.20
54 Warren Sapp	.20	.50
55 Mark Fields	.05	.15
56 Ruben Brown	.05	.15
57 Ellis Johnson	.05	.15
58 Hugh Douglas	.08	.25
59 Tyrone Wheatley	.08	.25
60 Napoleon Kaufman	.15	.40
61 James O. Stewart	.08	.25
62 Luther Elliss	.05	.15
63 Rashaan Salaam	.08	.25
64 Tyrone Poole	.07	.20
65 Ty Law	.08	.25
66 Korey Stringer	.15	.40
67 Devin Bush	.05	.15
68 Mark Bruener	.05	.15
69 Derrick Brooks	.20	.50
70 Craig Powell	.05	.15
71 Craig Newsome	.05	.15
72 Anthony Cook	.05	.15
73 Ray Zellars	.05	.15
74 Todd Collins	.20	.50
75 Sherman Williams	.05	.15
76 Frank Sanders	.08	.25
77 Corey Fuller	.05	.15
78 Kordell Stewart	.20	.50
79 Curtis Martin	.60	1.50
80 Lorenzo Styles	.05	.15
81 Chris T. Jones	.05	.15
82 Zack Crockett	.05	.15
83 Stoney Case	.05	.15
84 Eric Zeier	.08	.25
85 Jimmy Hitchcock	.05	.15
86 Rodney Thomas	.07	.20
87 Rob Johnson	.20	.50
88 Tyrone Davis	.05	.15
89 Chad May	.05	.15
90 Ed Hervey	.05	.15
91 Terrell Davis	.50	1.25
92 John Walsh	.05	.15
181 Jerry Stackhouse Jimmy Hitchcock	.15	.40
182 Antonio McDyess Sherman Williams	.10	.30
184 Andrew DeClercq Ki-Jana Carter	.07	.20
185 Tyrone Wheatley Jimmy King	.10	.30
186 J.J. Stokes Ed O'Bannon	.10	.30
187 Warren Sapp Constantin Popa	.10	.30
188 Paul Wilson Derrick Brooks	.40	1.00
190 Bob Sura Derrick Alexander	.05	.15
191 Steve Young	.25	.60
194 Marshall Faulk	.20	.50
195 Troy Aikman	.30	.75
196 Drew Bledsoe	.20	.50
197 Emmitt Smith	.40	1.00

1995 Classic Five Sport Printer's Proofs

*PRINTER PROOF/75: 4X TO 10X BASIC CARDS
STATED PRINT RUN 795 SETS

1995 Classic Five Sport Red Die Cuts

*RED DIE CUT: 1.2X TO 3X BASIC CARDS
RED DIE CUT STATED ODDS 1:8

1995 Classic Five Sport Silver Die Cuts

COMPLETE SET (200)	12.00	30.00
*SILVER DC: .8X TO 2X BASIC CARDS		

1995 Classic Five Sport Autographs

*SIGNINGS VERSION: .4X TO 1X		
45 Steve McNair	12.00	30.00
47 Kerry Collins	6.00	15.00
49 Mike Mamula	2.00	5.00
50 Joey Galloway	5.00	12.00
51 Kyle Brady	2.50	6.00
55 Mark Fields	2.00	5.00
58 Hugh Douglas	2.00	5.00
60 Napoleon Kaufman SP	3.00	8.00
64 Tyrone Poole	2.00	5.00
77 Corey Fuller	2.00	5.00
84 Eric Zeier	2.50	6.00
87 Rob Johnson	3.00	8.00
89 Chad May	2.50	6.00
92 John Walsh	2.00	5.00

1995 Classic Five Sport Autographs Numbered

47 Kerry Collins/225	8.00	20.00
50 Joey Galloway/225	8.00	20.00
60 Napoleon Kaufman/225	6.00	15.00
191 Steve Young/225	25.00	60.00
196 Drew Bledsoe/225	15.00	40.00

1995 Classic Five Sport Classic Standouts

COMPLETE SET (10)	15.00	40.00
CS4 Rashaan Salaam	.75	2.00
CS7 Kerry Collins	1.50	4.00
CS9 Michael Westbrook	1.00	2.50
CS10 Emmitt Smith	3.00	8.00
NNO Kerry Collins Sample	1.00	2.50

1995 Classic Five Sport Fast Track

COMPLETE SET (20)	15.00	40.00
FT2 Michael Westbrook	.50	1.25
FT4 Kyle Brady	.40	1.00
FT8 Napoleon Kaufman	.50	1.25
FT11 J.J. Stokes	.40	1.00
FT15 Tyrone Wheatley	.60	1.50
FT17 Rashaan Salaam	.50	1.25
FT19 Steve McNair	1.50	4.00

1995 Classic Five Sport Hot Box Autographs

2 Kerry Collins/625	10.00	25.00
5 Steve McNair/630	12.00	30.00

1995 Classic Five Sport NFL Experience Previews

COMPLETE SET (5)	12.00	30.00
EP1 Emmitt Smith	6.00	15.00
EP2 Drew Bledsoe	2.00	5.00
EP3 Steve Young	4.00	8.00
EP4 Rashaan Salaam	1.50	4.00
EP5 Marshall Faulk	2.50	6.00

1995 Classic Five Sport On Fire

COMPLETE SET (20)	30.00	80.00
H1 Drew Bledsoe	2.50	6.00
H4 Ki-Jana Carter	1.50	4.00
H5 Michael Westbrook	1.50	4.00
H8 Tyrone Wheatley	2.00	5.00
R4 Steve McNair	2.50	6.00
R5 Rashaan Salaam	2.00	5.00
R7 J.J. Stokes	1.50	4.00
R8 Kyle Brady	1.50	4.00
R10 Napoleon Kaufman	2.00	5.00

1995 Classic Five Sport Phone Cards $3

COMPLETE SET (5)	4.00	8.00
4 Rashaan Salaam	.40	1.00

1995 Classic Five Sport Phone Cards $4

COMPLETE SET (5)	6.00	15.00
5 Michael Westbrook	.50	1.25

1995 Classic Five Sport Previews

COMPLETE SET (5)	3.00	8.00
SP3 Michael Westbrook	.40	1.00

1995 Classic Five Sport Record Setters

COMPLETE SET (10)	12.00	30.00
RS1 Kerry Collins	1.25	3.00
RS8 Rashaan Salaam	.60	1.50

1995 Classic Five Sport Strive For Five

COMPLETE SET (65)	12.00	30.00
FB1 Ki-Jana Carter	.20	.50
FB2 Rashaan Salaam	.25	.60
FB3 Napoleon Kaufman	.20	.50
FB4 Tyrone Wheatley	.20	.50
FB5 J.J. Stokes	.20	.50
FB6 Joey Galloway	.40	.75
FB7 Kerry Collins	.50	1.25
FB8 Michael Westbrook	.20	.50
FB9 Steve McNair	.75	2.00
FB10 Drew Bledsoe	.40	1.00
FB11 Marshall Faulk	.40	1.00
FB12 Troy Aikman	.75	2.00
FB13 Steve Young	.60	1.50

1995-96 Classic Five Sport Signings

COMPLETE SET (100)	6.00	15.00
31 Ki-Jana Carter	.10	.30
32 Tony Boselli	.08	.25
33 Steve McNair	.50	1.25
34 Michael Westbrook	.10	.30
35 Kerry Collins	.40	1.00
36 Kevin Carter	.07	.20
37 Mike Mamula	.07	.20
38 Joey Galloway	.25	.60
39 Kyle Brady	.08	.25
40 J.J. Stokes	.10	.30
41 Derrick Alexander	.08	.25
42 Warren Sapp	.25	.60
43 Hugh Douglas	.10	.30
44 Tyrone Wheatley	.10	.30
45 Napoleon Kaufman	.20	.50
46 James O. Stewart	.10	.30
47 Rashaan Salaam	.10	.30
48 Ty Law	.10	.30
49 Mark Bruener	.07	.20
50 Derrick Brooks	.25	.60
51 Curtis Martin	.75	2.00
52 Todd Collins	.25	.60
53 Sherman Williams	.07	.20
54 Frank Sanders	.10	.30
55 Eric Zeier	.10	.30
56 Rob Johnson	.25	.60
57 Chad May	.07	.20
58 Terrell Davis	.60	1.50
59 Stoney Case	.07	.20
91 Steve Young	.30	.75
94 Marshall Faulk	.25	.60
95 Troy Aikman	.40	1.00
96 Drew Bledsoe	.25	.60
97 Emmitt Smith	.50	1.25

1995-96 Classic Five Sport Signings Blue Signature

*BLUE SIGN: 1.5X TO 4X BASIC CARDS

1995-96 Classic Five Sport Signings Die Cuts

*DIE CUT: .8X TO 2X BASIC CARDS
STATED ODDS 1:4

1995-96 Classic Five Sport Signings Red Signature

*RED SIGN: 1.5X TO 4X BASIC CARDS

1995-96 Classic Five Sport Signings Etched in Stone

5 Emmitt Smith	4.00	10.00
6 Troy Aikman	3.00	8.00
7 Steve Young	2.50	6.00

1995-96 Classic Five Sport Signings Freshly Inked

COMPLETE SET (30)	12.00	30.00
STATED ODDS 1:10		
FS11 Hugh Douglas	.60	1.50
FS12 Curtis Martin	2.50	6.00
FS13 Michael Westbrook	.60	1.50
FS14 Kerry Collins	1.25	3.00
FS15 Kevin Carter	.40	1.00
FS16 Joey Galloway	1.00	2.50
FS17 Eric Zeier	.60	1.50
FS18 Terrell Davis	1.50	4.00
FS19 Napoleon Kaufman	.75	2.00
FS20 Rashaan Salaam	.60	1.50

1991 Classic Four Sport

This 230-card multi-sport standard-size set includes all 200 draft picks players from the four Classic Draft Picks sets (football, basketball, baseball, and hockey), plus an additional 30 draft picks not previously found in these other sets. A subset within the 230 cards consists of five cards highlighting the publicized one-on-one game between Billy Owens and Larry Johnson. As an additional incentive to collectors, Classic randomly inserted over 60,000 autographed cards into the 15-card foil packs; it is claimed that each case should contain two or more autographed cards. The autographed cards feature 61 different players, approximately two-thirds of whom were hockey players. The production run for the English version was 25,000 cases, and a bilingual (French) version of the set was also produced at 20 percent of the English production. The major subdivisions of set are according to sport: hockey (2-50), baseball (51-101), football (102-148), and basketball (149-202).

COMPLETE SET (230)	5.00	12.00
1 Larry Johnson Brien Taylor Russell Maryland Eric Lindros	.15	.40
102 Rocket Ismail	.20	.50
103 Russell Maryland	.05	.15
104 Eric Turner	.05	.15
105 Bruce Pickens	.05	.15
106 Mike Croel	.05	.15
107 Todd Lyght	.05	.15
108 Eric Swann	.05	.15
109 Antone Davis	.05	.15
110 Stanley Richard	.05	.15
111 Pat Harlow	.05	.15
112 Alvin Harper	.05	.15
113 Mike Pritchard	.05	.15
114 Leonard Russell	.05	.15
115 Dan McGwire	.05	.15
117 Vinnie Clark	.05	.15
118 Kelvin Pritchett	.05	.15
119 Harvey Williams	.05	.15
120 Stan Thomas	.05	.15
121 Randal Hill	.05	.15
122 Todd Marinovich	.05	.15
123 Henry Jones	.05	.15
124 Mike Dumas	.05	.15
125 Ed King	.05	.15
126 Reggie Johnson	.05	.15
127 Roman Phifer	.05	.15
128 Mike Jones	.05	.15
129 Brett Favre	1.25	3.00
130 Browning Nagle	.05	.15
131 Esera Tuaolo	.05	.15
132 George Thornton	.05	.15
133 Dixon Edwards	.05	.15
135 Eric Bieniemy	.05	.15
136 Shane Curry	.05	.15
137 Jerome Henderson	.05	.15
138 Wesley Carroll	.05	.15
139 Nick Bell	.05	.15
140 John Flannery	.05	.15
141 Ricky Watters	.20	.50
142 Jeff Graham	.05	.15
143 Eric Moten	.05	.15
144 Jesse Campbell	.05	.15
145 Chris Zorich	.05	.15
146 Doug Thomas	.05	.15
147 Phil Hansen	.05	.15
148 Reggie Barrett	.05	.15
203 Gary Brown	.05	.15
204 Rob Carpenter	.05	.15
205 Ricky Ervins	.05	.15
206 Donald Hollas	.05	.15
207 Greg Lewis	.05	.15
208 Darren Lewis	.05	.15
209 Anthony Morgan	.05	.15
211 Perry Carter	.05	.15
212 Melvin Cheatum	.05	.15
213 Jerome Harmon	.05	.15
217 Ed McCaffrey	.30	.75
220 Moe Gardner	.05	.15
221 Jon Vaughn	.05	.15
222 Lawrence Dawsey	.05	.15
223 Michael Stonebreaker	.05	.15
224 Shawn Moore	.05	.15

1991 Classic Four Sport French

COMPLETE SET (230)	6.00	15.00
*FRENCH VERSION: .4X TO 1X		

1991 Classic Four Sport Autographs

102A Rocket Ismail/2000	8.00	20.00
103A Russell Maryland/1000	3.00	8.00

1991 Classic Four Sport LPs

COMPLETE SET (10)	5.00	12.00
*FRENCH: SAME VALUE		
RANDOM INSERTS IN PACKS	.40	1.00
LP1 Rocket Ismail	.60	1.50
LP2 Rocket Ismail	.60	1.50
LP3 Rocket Ismail	.60	1.50
LP4 Rocket Ismail	.60	1.50
LP5 Rocket Ismail	.60	1.50
LP10 Russell Maryland Number One Pick	.50	1.25

1992 Classic Four Sport

The 1992 Classic Draft Picks Collection consists of 325 standard-size cards, featuring the top picks from football, basketball, baseball, and hockey drafts. According to Classic, 40,000 12 box foil cases were produced. Randomly inserted in the 12-card packs were over 100,000 autograph cards from over 50 of the top draft picks from basketball, football, baseball, and hockey, including cards autographed by Shaquille O'Neal, Desmond Howard, Roman Hamrlik, and Phil Nevin. Also inserted in the packs were "Instant Win Giveway Cards" that entitled the collector to the 500,000.00 sports memorabilia giveway that Classic offered in this contest. There was also a factory set produced with gold parallel cards.

COMPLETE SET (325)	6.00	15.00
76 Desmond Howard	.15	.40
77 David Klingler	.05	.15
78 Quentin Coryatt	.05	.15
79 Bill Johnson	.05	.15
80 Eugene Chung	.05	.15
81 Derek Brown	.05	.15
82 Carl Pickens	.08	.25
83 Chris Mims	.05	.15
84 Charles Davenport	.05	.15
85 Ray Roberts	.05	.15
86 Chuck Smith	.05	.15
87 Tony Smith RB	.05	.15
88 Ken Swilling	.05	.15
89 Greg Skrepenak	.05	.15
90 Phillippi Sparks	.05	.15
91 Alonzo Spellman	.05	.15
92 Bernard Dafney	.05	.15
93 Edgar Bennett	.08	.25
94 Shane Dronett	.05	.15
95 Jeremy Lincoln	.05	.15
96 Dion Lambert	.05	.15
97 Siran Stacy	.05	.15
98 Tony Sacca	.05	.15
99 Sean Lumpkin	.05	.15
100 Tommy Vardell	.05	.15
101 Keith Hamilton	.05	.15
102 Sean Gilbert	.05	.15
103 Casey Weldon	.05	.15
104 Marc Boutte	.05	.15
105 Arthur Marshall	.05	.15
106 Santana Dotson	.05	.15
107 Ronnie West	.05	.15
108 Mike Pawlawski	.05	.15
109 Dale Carter	.05	.15
110 Carlos Snow	.05	.15
111 Mark D'Onofrio	.05	.15
112 Matt Blundin	.05	.15
113 Patrick Rowe	.05	.15
114 Joel Steed	.05	.15
115 Erick Anderson	.05	.15
116 Rodney Culver	.05	.15
117 Chris Hakel	.05	.15
118 Kevin Smith	.05	.15
119 Robert Brooks	.07	.20
120 Bucky Richardson	.05	.15
121 Steve Israel	.05	.15
122 Marco Coleman	.05	.15
123 Johnny Mitchell	.05	.15
124 Scottie Graham	.05	.15
125 Keith Goganious	.05	.15
126 Tommy Maddox	.05	.15
127 Terrell Buckley	.05	.15
128 Dana Hall	.05	.15
129 Ty Detmer	.15	.40
130 Darryl Williams	.05	.15
131 Jason Hanson	.15	.40
132 Leon Searcy	.05	.15
133 Will Furrer	.05	.15

134 Darren Woodson .20 .50
135 Corey Widmer .05 .15
136 Larry Tharpe .05 .15
137 Lance Olberding .05 .15
138 Stacey Dillard .05 .15
139 Anthony Hamlet .05 .15
140 Mike Evans .05 .15
141 Chester McGlockton .05 .15
142 Marquez Pope .05 .15
143 Tyrone Legette .05 .15
144 Derrick Moore .05 .15
145 Calvin Holmes .05 .15
146 Eddie Robinson Jr. .05 .15
147 Robert Jones .05 .15
148 Ricardo McDonald .05 .15
149 Howard Dinkins .05 .15
150 Todd Collins .05 .15
310 Rocket Ismail FLB .05 .15
313 Ty Detmer and .15 .40
Desmond Howard

1992 Classic Four Sport Gold

COMP.FACT.SET (326) 60.00 120.00
*GOLD: 1.2X TO 3X BASIC CARDS
AU Future Superstars AU 30.00 60.00
Phil Nevin
Shaquille O'Neal
Desmond Howard
Roman Hamrlik
(Certified AUTO/9500)

1992 Classic Four Sport Autographs

76 Desmond Howard/975 4.00 10.00
77 David Klingler/1125 2.00 5.00
78A Quentin Coryatt/3500 2.50 6.00
82 Carl Pickens/1475 4.00 10.00
87 Tony Smith/3450 2.00 5.00
97 Siran Stacy/4325 2.00 5.00
98 Tony Sacca/1575 2.00 5.00
103 Casey Weldon/4350 2.00 5.00
108 Mike Pawlawski/1475 2.00 5.00
112 Matt Blundin/1575 2.00 5.00
126 Tommy Maddox/4575 6.00 15.00
127 Terrell Buckley/1475 2.00 5.00
129 Ty Detmer/1475 3.00 8.00
144 Derrick Moore/1575 2.00 5.00
301 Dave Brown/1575 2.00 5.00

1992 Classic Four Sport BCs

COMPLETE SET (20) 3.00 8.00
BC13 Desmond Howard .15 .40
BC14 David Klingler .08 .25
BC15 Terrell Buckley .08 .25
BC16 Quentin Coryatt .08 .25
BC17 Carl Pickens .08 .25

1992 Classic Four Sport LPs

LP1 Desmond Howard .20 .50
LP2 David Klingler .15 .40
LP3 Tommy Maddox .20 .50
LP4 Casey Weldon .15 .40
LP5 Tony Smith RB .20 .50
LP6 Terrell Buckley .15 .40
LP7 Carl Pickens .20 .50
LP15 Phil Nevin 1.50 4.00
Shaquille O'Neal
Roman Hamrlik
Desmond Howard
LP16 Matt Blundin .20 .50
David Klingler
Tommy Maddox
Mike Pawlawski
Tony Sacca
Casey Weldon

1992 Classic Four Sport Previews

COMPLETE SET (5) 6.00 15.00
CC2 Desmond Howard .60 1.50

1992 Classic Four Sport Promos

These five promo cards were packaged in a cello pack and distributed to dealers. The cards measure the standard size (2 1/2" by 3 1/2"). The fronts display the same full-bleed glossy color player photos as the above-mentioned preview cards. They differ in that the Classic logo at the upper left corner is not surmounted by the word Preview." The promo backs have a different design than the preview backs, displaying a second color player photo on the right side as well as biography and player profile in black print on a silver background. The cards are numbered on the back.

COMPLETE SET (5) 6.00 15.00
PR2 Desmond Howard .60 1.50

1993 Classic Four Sport

The 1993 Classic Four-Sport Draft Pick Collection set consists of 325 standard-size cards of the top 1993 draft picks from football, basketball, baseball, and hockey. Just 49,500 sequentially numbered 12-box cases were produced. The set includes two topical subsets: John R. Wooden Award (310-314) and All-Rookie Basketball Team (315-319).

COMPLETE SET (325) 4.00 10.00
91 Drew Bledsoe .50 1.25
92 Rick Mirer .08 .25
93 Garrison Hearst .20 .50
94 Marvin Jones .05 .15
95 John Copeland .05 .15
96 Eric Curry .05 .15
97 Curtis Conway .05 .15
98 Willie Roaf .05 .15
99 Lincoln Kennedy .05 .15
100 Jerome Bettis .60 1.50
101 Mike Compton .05 .15
102 John Gerak .05 .15
103 Will Shields .05 .15
104 Ben Coleman .05 .15
105 Ernest Dye .05 .15
106 Lester Holmes .05 .15
107 Brad Hopkins .05 .15
108 Everett Lindsay .05 .15
109 Todd Rucci .05 .15
110 Lance Gunn .05 .15
111 Elvis Grbac .07 .20
112 Shane Matthews .05 .15
113 Rudy Harris .05 .15
114 Richie Anderson .05 .15
115 Derek Brown .05 .15
116 Roger Harper .05 .15
117 Terry Kirby .07 .20
118 Natrone Means .08 .25
119 Glyn Milburn .05 .15
120 Adrian Murrell .08 .25
121 Lorenzo Neal .05 .15
122 Roosevelt Potts .05 .15
123 Kevin Williams WR .05 .15
124 Fred Baxter .05 .15
125 Troy Drayton .05 .15
126 Chris Gedney .05 .15
127 Irv Smith .05 .15
128 Olanda Truitt .05 .15
129 Victor Bailey .05 .15
130 Horace Copeland .05 .15
131 Ron Dickerson Jr. .05 .15
132 Willie Harris .05 .15
133 Tyrone Hughes .05 .15
134 Qadry Ismail .08 .25
135 Reggie Brooks .08 .25
136 Sean LaChapelle .05 .15
137 O.J.McDuffie .08 .25
138 Kenny Shedd .05 .15
139 Brian Stablein .05 .15
140 Lamar Thomas .05 .15
141 Kevin Williams RB .05 .15
142 Othello Henderson .05 .15
143 Kevin Henry .05 .15
144 Todd Kelly .05 .15
145 Devon McDonald .05 .15
146 Michael Strahan .40 1.00
147 Dan Williams .05 .15
148 Gilbert Brown .05 .15
149 Mark Caesar .05 .15
150 John Parrella .05 .15
151 Leonard Renfro .05 .15
152 Coleman Rudolph .05 .15
153 Ronnie Bradford .05 .15
154 Tom Carter .05 .15
155 Deon Figures .05 .15
156 Derrick Frazier .05 .15
157 Darrien Gordon .05 .15
158 Carlton Gray .05 .15
159 Adrian Hardy .05 .15
160 Mike Reid .05 .15
161 Thomas Smith .05 .15
162 Robert O'Neal .05 .15
163 Chad Brown .08 .25
164 Demetrius DuBose .05 .15
165 Reggie Givens .05 .15
166 Travis Hill .05 .15
167 Rich McKenzie .05 .15
168 Darrin Smith .05 .15
169 Steve Tovar .05 .15
170 Patrick Bates .05 .15
171 Dan Footman .05 .15
172 Ryan McNeil .05 .15
173 Danan Hughes .05 .15
174 Mark Brunell .30 .75
175 Ron Moore .05 .15
176 Antonio London .05 .15
177 Steve Everitt .05 .15
178 Wayne Simmons .05 .15
179 Robert Smith .20 .50
180 Dana Stubblefield .08 .25
181 George Teague .05 .15
182 Carl Simpson .05 .15
183 Billy Joe Hobert .05 .15
184 Gino Torretta .05 .15
PR1 Drew Bledsoe Promo 1.25 3.00

1993 Classic Four Sport Gold

COMP.FACT.SET (332) 150.00 250.00
*GOLD: 1.5X TO 4X BASIC CARDS
AU1 Jerome Bettis AU/3900 8.00 20.00

1993 Classic Four Sport Acetates

COMPLETE SET (12) 6.00 15.00
6 Drew Bledsoe 1.25 3.00
7 Rick Mirer .40 1.00
8 Garrison Hearst .75 2.00

1993 Classic Four Sport Autographs

91A Drew Bledsoe/275 50.00 100.00
92A Rick Mirer/375 5.00 12.00
93A Garrison Hearst/650 8.00 20.00
94A Marvin Jones/3650 1.50 4.00
184A Gino Torretta/3200 3.00 8.00
NNO Garrison Hearst Promo 10.00 25.00
(signed in gold ink
Phoenix card show promo)

1993 Classic Four Sport Chromium Draft Stars

COMPLETE SET (20) 8.00 20.00
DS48 Drew Bledsoe .75 2.00
DS49 Rick Mirer .40 1.00
DS50 Garrison Hearst .75 2.00
DS51 Jerome Bettis .75 2.00
DS52 Terry Kirby .30 .75
DS53 Glyn Milburn .30 .75
DS54 Reggie Brooks .30 .75

1993 Classic Four Sport LP Jumbos

COMPLETE SET (5) 12.00 30.00
1 Drew Bledsoe 2.50 6.00

1993 Classic Four Sport LPs

COMPLETE SET (25) 20.00 40.00
LP1 Four-in-One Card 1.50 4.00
Chris Webber
Drew Bledsoe
Alex Rodriguez
Alexandre Daigle
LP10 Drew Bledsoe 1.50 4.00
LP11 Rick Mirer .40 1.00
LP12 Garrison Hearst .75 2.00
LP13 Jerome Bettis 1.50 4.00
LP14 Marvin Jones .30 .75
LP15 Terry Kirby .40 1.00
LP16 Glyn Milburn .30 .75
LP17 Reggie Brooks .40 1.00

1993 Classic Four Sport MBNA Promos

This two-card set uses Classic's designs from its Four-Sport LPs "Four in One" insert number LP1. Card number 1 reproduces the Chris Webber/Alex Rodriguez side of LP1, card number 2 reproduces the Drew Bledsoe/Alexandre Daigle side. This set was issued exclusively to cardholders of the MBNA/ScoreBoard VISA. The backs contain congratulatory messages, information about the players depicted, and a notation than 10,000 sets were issued. Although the design and copyright reads 1993, these cards probably were first issued in 1994.

2 Drew Bledsoe 2.00 5.00
Alexander Daigle

1993 Classic Four Sport Power Pick Bonus

COMPLETE SET (20) 10.00 25.00
PP8 Drew Bledsoe .75 2.00
PP9 Rick Mirer .40 1.00
PP10 Garrison Hearst .75 2.00
PP11 Jerome Bettis .75 2.00
PP12 Terry Kirby .40 1.00
PP13 Glyn Milburn .40 1.00
PP14 Reggie Brooks .40 1.00
NNO Four in One Special 1.50 4.00

1993 Classic Four Sport Previews

COMPLETE SET (5) 2.50 6.00
CC3 Rick Mirer .30 .75

1993 Classic Four Sport Tri-Cards

COMPLETE SET (5) 10.00 25.00
TC2 Drew Bledsoe 2.00 5.00
TC7 Rick Mirer
TC12 Garrison Hearst
TC5 Drew Bledsoe 3.00 8.00
TC10 Chris Webber
TC15 Alex Rodriguez

1993 Classic Four Sport McDonald's

COMPLETE SET (35) 4.00 10.00
1 Troy Aikman .60 1.50
2 Drew Bledsoe .40 1.00
3 Eric Curry .05 .15
4 Garrison Hearst .20 .50
5 Lester Holmes .05 .15
6 Marvin Jones .05 .15
7 O.J. McDuffie .08 .25
8 Rick Mirer .08 .25
9 Leonard Renfro .05 .15
10 Jerry Rice .60 1.50
35 Leonard Renfro .05 .15
Lester Holmes
AU1 Troy Aikman/5000 40.00 80.00

1993 Classic Four Sport McDonald's LPs

COMPLETE SET (5) 3.00 8.00
LP2 Trench Warfare .20 .50
Leonard Renfro
Lester Holmes
LP5 Steve Young 1.25 3.00

1994 Classic Four Sport

Featuring top rookies from basketball, baseball, football and hockey, the 1994 Classic Four-Sport set consists of 200 standard-size cards. No more than 25,000 cases were produced. Over 100 players signed 100,000 cards that were randomly inserted four per case. Collectors who found one of 100 Glenn Robinson Instant Winner Cards received a complete Classic Four-Sport autographed card set. Also inserted on an average of one in every five cases were 4,695 hand-numbered 4-in-1 cards featuring all four number 1 picks. Classic's wrapper redemption program offered four levels of participation: 1) bronze-collect 20 wrappers and receive a 4-card Classic Player of the Year set, featuring Grant Hill, Shaquille O'Neal, Emmitt Smith, and Steve Young; 2) silver-collect 30 wrappers and receive the Classic Player of the Year set and a random autograph card; 3) gold-collect 144 wrappers and receive the Classic Player of the Year set and an autograph card by Muhammad Ali; and 4) platinum-collect 216 wrappers and receive the Classic Player of the Year set plus an autograph card by Shaquille O'Neal. The cards are numbered on the back and checklisted below by sport as follows: basketball (1-50), football (51-114), hockey (115-160), baseball (161-188), and Wooden Award Contenders (189-197).

COMPLETE SET (200) 6.00 15.00
51 Dan Wilkinson .07 .20
52 Marshall Faulk .75 2.00
53 Heath Shuler .08 .25
54 Willie McGinest .07 .20
55 Trev Alberts .05 .15
56 Trent Dilfer .20 .50
57 Bryant Young .08 .25
58 Sam Adams .07 .20
59 Antonio Langham .05 .15
60 Jamir Miller .05 .15
61 John Thierry .05 .15
62 Aaron Glenn .08 .25
63 Joe Johnson .05 .15
64 Bernard Williams .05 .15
65 Wayne Gandy .05 .15
66 Aaron Taylor .05 .15
67 Charles Johnson .15 .40
68 Dewayne Washington .05 .15
69 Todd Steussie .08 .25
70 Tim Bowens .05 .15
71 Johnnie Morton .08 .25
72 Rob Fredrickson .05 .15
73 Shante Carver .05 .15
74 Thomas Lewis .05 .15
75 Calvin Jones .05 .15
76 Henry Ford .05 .15
77 Jeff Burris .05 .15
78 William Floyd .15 .40
79 Derrick Alexander .08 .25
80 Darnay Scott .15 .40
81 Tre Johnson .05 .15
82 Eric Mahlum .05 .15
83 Errict Rhett .10 .30
84 Kevin Lee .05 .15
85 Andre Coleman .05 .15
86 Corey Sawyer .05 .15
87 Chuck Levy .07 .20
88 Greg Hill .05 .15
89 David Palmer .05 .15
90 Ryan Yarborough .05 .15
91 Charlie Garner .20 .50
92 Mario Bates .05 .15
93 Bert Emanuel .08 .25
94 Thomas Randolph .05 .15
95 Bucky Brooks .05 .15
96 Rob Waldrop .05 .15
97 Charlie Ward .20 .50
98 Winfred Tubbs .05 .15
99 James Folston .05 .15
100 Kevin Mitchell .05 .15
101 Aubrey Beavers .05 .15
102 Fernando Smith .05 .15
103 Jim Miller .10 .30
104 Byron Bam Morris .07 .20
105 Donnell Bennett .05 .15
106 Jason Sehorn .10 .30
107 Glenn Foley .05 .15
108 Lonnie Johnson .05 .15
109 Tyronne Drakeford .05 .15
110 Vaughn Parker .05 .15
111 Doug Nussmeier .05 .15
112 Perry Klein .05 .15
113 Jason Gildon .10 .30
114 Lake Dawson .05 .15
FO1 4-in-1 1.00 2.50
Glenn Robinson
Dan Wilkinson
Paul Wilson
Ed Jovanovski
Number One Draft Picks

1994 Classic Four Sport Gold

COMPLETE SET (200) 12.00 30.00
*GOLD: .8X TO 2X BASIC CARDS

1994 Classic Four Sport Printer's Proofs

*PRINT PROOFS: 2.5X TO 6X BASIC CARDS

1994 Classic Four Sport Autographs

53A Heath Shuler/1330 4.00 10.00
55A Trev Alberts/2520 2.00 5.00
56A Trent Dilfer/1495 8.00 20.00
81A Tre Johnson/1000 2.00 5.00
82A Eric Mahlum/1090 2.00 5.00
90A Ryan Yarborough/1020 2.00 5.00
93A Bert Emanuel/1100 2.50 6.00
96A Rob Waldrop/1095 2.00 5.00
97A Charlie Ward/1520 4.00 10.00
99A James Folston/1100 2.00 5.00
100A Kevin Mitchell/1090 2.00 5.00
103A Jim Miller/1030 4.00 10.00
108A Lonnie Johnson/1050 2.00 5.00
110A Vaughn Parker/750 2.00 5.00

1994 Classic Four Sport BCs

COMPLETE SET (20) 6.00 15.00
BC1 Marshall Faulk 1.00 2.50
BC2 Heath Shuler .30 .75
BC3 Antonio Langham .20 .50
BC4 Derrick Alexander .30 .75
BC5 Byron Bam Morris .20 .50

1994 Classic Four Sport C3 Collector's Club

The cards were issued to members of the 1995 Classic Collectors Club. Each is numbered 1 of 10,000 on the cardbacks and carries a 1995 copyright line. However, the cards are in the design of the 1994 Classic Four Sport set.

C1 Marshall Faulk 1.50 4.00
C3 Antonio Langham .40 1.00

1994 Classic Four Sport Classic Picks

COMPLETE SET (10) 6.00 15.00
21 Dan Wilkinson .40 1.00
22 Willie McGinest .40 1.00

1994 Classic Four Sport High Voltage

COMPLETE SET (20) 40.00 100.00
COMMON CARD (HV1-HV20) .75 2.00
COMMON SP (HV1-HV20)
HV1 Dan Wilkinson .75 2.00
HV5 Marshall Faulk 3.00 8.00
HV9 Heath Shuler 1.00 2.50
HV13 Trent Dilfer 1.50 4.00
HV17 Willie McGinest .75 2.00

1994 Classic Four Sport Phone Cards $1

COMPLETE SET (8) 3.00 8.00
*TWO DOLLAR: .5X TO 1.2X $1 CARDS
*THREE DOLLAR: .6X TO 1.5X $1 CARDS
*FOUR DOLLAR: .8X TO 2X $1 CARDS
*FIVE DOLLAR: 1X TO 2.5X $1 CARDS
*PIN NUMBER REVEALED: HALF VALUE
1 Trent Dilfer .40 1.00
2 Marshall Faulk 1.00 2.50

1994 Classic Four Sport Previews

COMPLETE SET (5) 6.00 15.00
P2 Marshall Faulk 2.00 5.00

1994 Classic Four Sport Tri-Cards

COMPLETE SET (5) 4.00 10.00
TC1 Marshall Faulk 2.00 5.00
Calvin Jones
Errict Rhett
TC2 Willie McGinest .75 2.00
Trev Alberts
Jamir Miller

1995 Classic NFL Rookies

This 110-card standard-size set features first-year NFL players. The cards were issued in 10-card packs, with 36 packs in a box and 12 boxes per case. For the card hobby, 2,950 sequentially numbered cases were produced. This set includes all 32 first round draft choices as well as many prominent later round picks. The set closes with an "Award Winner" subset at cards (101-105) as well as a flashback set of leading NFL players (106-110). Printed in 18-point stock, the full-bleed fronts feature color action photos. The player is identified in white lettering near the bottom. His position is in red lettering directly underneath his name. The backs contain biographical information, collegiate states and a player profile. The bottom right is dedicated to another player photo. All of this information is set against a white background. Key players in this set include Kerry Collins, Terrell Davis, Joey Galloway, Curtis Martin, Rashaan Salaam, Kordell Stewart, J.J. Stokes and Michael Westbrook.

COMPLETE SET (110) 5.00 12.00
1 Ki-Jana Carter .08 .25
2 Tony Boselli .02 .10
3 Steve McNair .60 1.50
4 Michael Westbrook .08 .25
5 Kerry Collins .50 1.25
6 Kevin Carter .08 .25
7 Mike Mamula .01 .05
8 Joey Galloway .30 .75
9 Kyle Brady .01 .05
10 J.J. Stokes .08 .25
11 Derrick Alexander .01 .05
12 Warren Sapp .02 .10
13 Mark Fields .08 .25
14 Ruben Brown .08 .25
15 Ellis Johnson .01 .05
16 Hugh Douglas .08 .25
17 Tyrone Wheatley .30 .75
18 Napoleon Kaufman .15 .40
19 James O. Stewart .30 .75
20 Luther Elliss .01 .05
21 Rashaan Salaam .02 .10
22 Tyrone Poole .08 .25
23 Ty Law .30 .75
24 Korey Stringer .07 .20
25 Billy Milner .01 .05
26 Devin Bush .01 .05
27 Mark Bruener .01 .05
28 Derrick Brooks .08 .25
29 Blake Brockermeyer .01 .05
30 Craig Powell .01 .05
31 Trezelle Jenkins .01 .05
32 Craig Newsome .01 .05
33 Thomas Bailey .01 .05
34 Chad May .01 .05
35 J.J. Smith .01 .05
36 Lorenzo Styles .01 .05
37 Brian Williams .01 .05
38 Damien Covington .01 .05
39 Steve Stenstrom .01 .05
40 Darius Holland .01 .05
41 Pete Mitchell .01 .05
42 Todd Collins .30 .75
43 Kordell Stewart .50 1.25
44 Eric Zeier .02 .10
45 Frank Sanders .08 .25
46 Ben Talley .01 .05
47 Billy Williams .01 .05
48 Chris T. Jones .01 .05
49 Tamarick Vanover .02 .10
50 Jimmy Hitchcock .01 .05
51 Chris Hudson .01 .05
52 Terrell Fletcher .02 .10
53 Brent Moss .01 .05
54 Terrell Davis .60 1.50
55 Rodney Thomas .02 .10
56 Larry Jones .01 .05
57 Ray Zellars .02 .10
58 David Sloan .01 .05
59 Brandon Bennett .01 .05
60 Brian DeMarco .01 .05
61 Bryan Schwartz .01 .05
62 Jack Jackson .01 .05
63 Bobby Taylor .08 .25
64 Kevin Hickman .01 .05
65 Matt O'Dwyer .01 .05
66 Patrick Riley .01 .05
67 Ki-Jana Carter .08 .25
68 Kerry Collins .50 1.25
69 Steve McNair .60 1.50
70 Tyrone Wheatley .30 .75
71 Antonio Freeman .30 .75
72 Clifton Abraham .01 .05
73 Kez McCorvey .01 .05
74 Lovell Pinkney .01 .05
75 Lee DeRamus .01 .05
76 John Walsh .01 .05
77 Cory Raymer .01 .05
78 Corey Fuller .01 .05
79 Tyrone Davis .01 .05
80 David Dunn .01 .05
81 Dana Howard .01 .05
82 Melvin Johnson .01 .05
83 Robert Baldwin .01 .05
84 Curtis Martin .60 1.50
85 Zack Crockett .02 .10
86 Jay Barker .01 .05
87 Christian Fauria .01 .05
88 Zach Wiegert .01 .05
89 Barrett Brooks .01 .05
90 Ken Dilger .02 .10
91 James A. Stewart .01 .05
92 Ed Hervey .01 .05
93 Torey Hunter .01 .05
94 Sherman Williams .01 .05
95 Shawn King .01 .05
96 Dave Barr .01 .05
97 Rob Johnson .15 .40
98 Stoney Case .02 .10
99 Ki-Jana Carter CL .01 .05
100 Steve McNair CL .08 .25
101 Rashaan Salaam AW .01 .05
102 Kerry Collins AW .15 .40
103 Rashaan Salaam AW .01 .05
104 Kerry Collins AW .15 .40
105 Jay Barker AW .01 .05
106 Drew Bledsoe .15 .40
107 Marshall Faulk .30 .75
108 Steve Young .08 .25
109 Troy Aikman .20 .50
110 Emmitt Smith .40 1.00
MF1 Marshall Faulk 5.00 12.00

1995 Classic NFL Rookies Printer's Proofs

COMPLETE SET (110) 60.00 120.00
*SINGLES: 3X TO 8X BASIC CARDS
STATED PRINT RUN 595 SETS

1995 Classic NFL Rookies Printer's Proofs Silver

COMPLETE SET (110) 100.00 200.00
*SINGLES: 5X TO 12X BASIC CARDS
STATED PRINT RUN 297 SETS

1995 Classic NFL Rookies Silver

COMPLETE SET (110) 16.00 40.00
*SINGLES: 1.2X TO 3X BASIC CARDS
ONE PER PACK

1995 Classic NFL Rookies Die Cuts

COMPLETE SET (32) 15.00 40.00
STATED PRINT RUN 4500 SER.#'d SETS
*PRINT.PROOF: 4X TO 10X BASIC INSERTS
PP STATED PRINT RUN 97 SETS
RANDOM INSERTS IN HOBBY PACKS
*SILVER SIG: 1X TO 2.5X BASIC INSERTS
SS STATED ODDS 1:48 RETAIL
SS STATED PRINT RUN 1750 SER.#'d SETS
1 Ki-Jana Carter .75 2.00
2 Tony Boselli .30 .75
3 Steve McNair 5.00 12.00
4 Michael Westbrook .75 2.00
5 Kerry Collins 4.00 10.00
6 Kevin Carter .75 2.00
7 Mike Mamula .15 .40
8 Joey Galloway 2.50 6.00
9 Kyle Brady .15 .40
10 J.J. Stokes .75 2.00
11 Derrick Alexander DE .15 .40
12 Warren Sapp .30 .75
13 Mark Fields .75 2.00
14 Ruben Brown .75 2.00
15 Ellis Johnson .15 .40
16 Hugh Douglas .75 2.00
17 Tyrone Wheatley 2.50 6.00
18 Napoleon Kaufman 1.25 3.00
19 James O. Stewart 2.50 6.00
20 Luther Elliss .15 .40
21 Rashaan Salaam .30 .75
22 Tyrone Poole .75 2.00
23 Ty Law 2.50 6.00
24 Korey Stringer .60 1.50
25 Billy Milner .15 .40
26 Devin Bush .15 .40
27 Mark Bruener .15 .40
28 Derrick Brooks .75 2.00
29 Blake Brockermeyer .15 .40
30 Craig Powell .15 .40
31 Trezelle Jenkins .15 .40
32 Craig Newsome .15 .40

1995 Classic NFL Rookies Draft Review

The first fourteen cards of this standard-size set was originally handed out to the media on NFL Draft Day (April 22) but were later reissued at a rate of one per three Classic NFL Rookies Retail rack packs. Eight additional cards that updated team selections where issued in packs only to complete the 22-card set. The original 14-card set also came with a certificate numbered out of 19,995 sets. The fronts feature full-bleed color action photos except at the bottom, where a red foil stripe edges the picture and displays the team logo, player's name and position, and a 1995 NFL Draft emblem. Since a player could be drafted by several different teams, the players are pictured in different pro uniforms. The backs carry biography, complete collegiate statistics, player profile, and a color player cutout.

COMPLETE SET (23) 12.50 15.00
1 Steve McNair-Oilers 1.25 3.00
2 Steve McNair-Vikings .40 2.00
3 Steve McNair-Jaguars .40 2.00
4 Ki-Jana Carter-Panthers .20 .50
5 Ki-Jana Carter-Jaguars .20 .50
6 Kerry Collins-Bills .40 1.00
7 Kerry Collins-Colts .40 1.00
8 Kerry Collins-Cardinals .40 1.00
9 John Walsh-Panthers .08 .25
10 John Walsh-Vikings .08 .25
11 John Walsh-Dolphins .08 .25
12 J.J. Stokes-Seahawks .20 .50
13 J.J. Stokes-Rams .20 .50
14 Emmitt Smith 1.00 2.50
15 Steve Young .60 1.25
16 Marshall Faulk .60 1.50
17 Troy Aikman .60 1.50
18 Ki-Jana Carter .20 .50
19 Kerry Collins .40 1.00
20 J.J. Stokes .20 .50
21 Michael Westbrook .20 .50
22 Kyle Brady .08 .25
NNO Checklist .20 .50
John Walsh
Steve McNair
Kerry Collins
NNO Draft Cover Card .08 .25
(Classic NFL Draft ad on back)

1995 Classic NFL Rookies Draft

D1 Ki-Jana Carter .60 1.50
D2 Kerry Collins .75 2.00
D2S Kerry Collins Sample .75 2.00

1995 Classic NFL Rookies Instant Energy

COMPLETE SET (20) 6.00 15.00
ONE PER RETAIL RACK PACK
IE1 Ki-Jana Carter .25 .60
IE2 Steve McNair 1.50 4.00
IE3 Michael Westbrook .25 .60
IE4 Joey Galloway .75 2.00
IE5 Tyrone Wheatley .75 2.00
IE6 Napoleon Kaufman .40 1.00
IE7 Warren Sapp .08 .25
IE8 Kevin Carter .25 .60
IE9 Todd Collins .40 1.00
IE10 Rob Johnson .40 1.00
IE11 Chad May .05 .15
IE12 Mike Mamula .05 .15
IE13 Sherman Williams .05 .15
IE14 Tony Boselli .08 .25
IE15 Kerry Collins 1.25 3.00
IE16 J.J. Stokes .25 .60
IE17 Rashaan Salaam .08 .25
IE18 Kordell Stewart 1.25 3.00
IE19 Derrick Brooks .25 .60
IE20 Frank Sanders .25 .60

1995 Classic NFL Rookies ROY Redemption

COMPLETE SET (20) 25.00 60.00
STATED ODDS 1:108 HOBBY
STATED PRINT RUN 2500 SETS
1 Ki-Jana Carter 1.00 2.50
2 Tony Boselli .40 1.00
3 Steve McNair 6.00 15.00
4 Michael Westbrook 1.00 2.50
5 Kerry Collins 4.00 10.00
6 Joey Galloway 3.00 8.00
7 Kyle Brady .20 .50
8 J.J. Stokes 1.00 2.50
9 Tyrone Wheatley 3.00 8.00
10 Napoleon Kaufman 1.50 4.00
11 Rashaan Salaam .40 1.00
12 James O. Stewart 3.00 8.00
13 Kordell Stewart 5.00 12.00
14 Frank Sanders 1.00 2.50
15 Ray Zellars .40 1.00
16 Zack Crockett .40 1.00
17 Tamarick Vanover .40 1.00
18 Chad May .20 .50
19 Eric Zeier .40 1.00
20 Field Card-C.Martin .20 .50
HP1 Ki-Jana Carter Sample .50 1.25
ROY1 Curtis Martin $50 PC 7.50 20.00

1995 Classic NFL Rookies Rookie Spotlight

COMPLETE SET (30) 6.00 15.00
ONE PER JUMBO
*HOLOFOILS: 2X TO 5X BASIC INSERTS
HOLOFOIL STATED ODDS 1:30 JUMBO
RS1 Ki-Jana Carter .20 .50
RS2 Steve McNair 1.25 3.00
RS3 Michael Westbrook .20 .50
RS4 Joey Galloway .60 1.50
RS5 Tyrone Wheatley .60 1.50
RS6 Napoleon Kaufman .30 .75
RS7 Kordell Stewart 1.00 2.50
RS8 Frank Sanders .20 .50
RS9 Zack Crockett .07 .20
RS10 Tamarick Vanover .07 .20
RS11 Chad May .02 .10
RS12 Eric Zeier .07 .20
RS13 Mike Mamula .02 .10
RS14 Warren Sapp .07 .20
RS15 Kevin Carter .20 .50
RS16 Derrick Brooks .20 .50
RS17 Todd Collins .40 1.00
RS18 Rob Johnson .30 .75
RS19 Chris T. Jones .02 .10
RS20 Terrell Fletcher .07 .20
RS21 Sherman Williams .02 .10
RS22 Tony Boselli .07 .20
RS23 Kerry Collins 1.00 2.50
RS24 J.J. Stokes .20 .50
RS25 Rashaan Salaam .07 .20
RS26 James O. Stewart .60 1.50
RS27 Rodney Thomas .07 .20
RS28 Jack Jackson .02 .10
RS29 Lovell Pinkney .02 .10
RS30 Ruben Brown .20 .50

1996 Classic NFL Rookies

The 1996 Classic NFL Rookies set was issued in one series totaling 100 standard-size cards. The set was issued in 10-card packs with 36 packs in a box and 12 boxes in a case. Among the topical subsets are: All-Americans (65-74), NFL Greats (75-79) and Checklists (99-100). There is also a gold parallel set that was issued one per special retail jumbo pack. The key players in this set are Terry Glenn, Keyshawn Johnson and Lawrence Phillips.

COMPLETE SET (100) 3.00 8.00
1 Keyshawn Johnson .40 1.00
2 Jonathan Ogden .15 .40
3 Kevin Hardy .15 .40
4 Leeland McElroy .07 .20
5 Terry Glenn .30 .75
6 Tim Biakabutuka .15 .40
7 Torly Brackens .15 .40
8 Duane Clemons .01 .05
9 Willie Anderson .01 .05
10 Karim Abdul-Jabbar .15 .40
11 Daryl Gardener .01 .05
12 Simeon Rice .20 .50
13 Eddie George .60 1.50
14 Andre Johnson .01 .05
15 Jon Runyan .01 .05
16 Jevon Langford .01 .05
17 Derrick Mayes .15 .40
18 Stephen Davis .50 1.25
19 Ray Farmer .01 .05
20 Chris Doering .01 .05
21 Jimmy Herndon .01 .05
22 Jerome Woods .01 .05
23 Scott Greene .01 .05
24 Jamain Stephens .01 .05
25 Tommie Frazier .15 .40
26 Dusty Zeigler .01 .05
27 Alex Molden .01 .05
28 Dietrich Jells .01 .05
29 Brian Roche .01 .05
30 Danny Kanell .15 .40
31 Roman Oben .01 .05
32 Chris Darkins .01 .05
33 Christian Peter .01 .05
34 Jeff Hartings .15 .40
35 Bobby Hoying .15 .40
36 Steve Taneyhill .01 .05
37 Lance Johnstone .07 .20
38 Zach Thomas .30 .75
39 Donnie Edwards .15 .40
40 Eric Moulds .40 1.00
41 Amani Toomer .30 .75
42 Scott Slutzker .01 .05
43 Matt Stevens .01 .05
44 Randall Godfrey .01 .05
45 Orpheus Roye .01 .05
46 Jason Odom .01 .05
47 Je'Rod Cherry .01 .05
48 Jeff Lewis .07 .20
49 Mike Alstott .40 1.00
50 Tony Banks .15 .40
51 Stepfret Williams .07 .20
52 Michael Cheever .01 .05
53 Bryant Mix .01 .05
54 James Ritchey .01 .05
55 Marcus Coleman .01 .05
56 Sedric Clark .01 .05
57 Kyle Wachholtz .01 .05
58 Johnny McWilliams .01 .05
59 Lawyer Milloy .20 .50
60 Alex Van Dyke .07 .20
61 Stanley Pritchett .01 .05
62 Ray Mickens .01 .05
63 Toraino Singleton .01 .05
64 Richard Huntley .07 .20
65 Eddie George AA .40 1.00
66 Terry Glenn AA .15 .40
67 Keyshawn Johnson AA .15 .40
68 Jonathan Ogden AA .07 .20
69 Tommie Frazier AA .07 .20
70 Kevin Hardy AA .01 .05
71 Zach Thomas AA .20 .50
72 Tony Brackens AA .07 .20
73 Lawyer Milloy AA .15 .40
74 Leeland McElroy AA .01 .05
75 Emmitt Smith .40 1.00
76 Steve McNair .15 .40
77 Kerry Collins .15 .40
78 Drew Bledsoe .15 .40
79 Marshall Faulk .30 .75
80 Pete Kendall .01 .05
81 Regan Upshaw .01 .05
82 Mercury Hayes .01 .05
83 Dou Innocent .01 .05
84 DeRon Jenkins .01 .05
85 Marco Battaglia .01 .05
86 John Mobley .01 .05
87 Cedric Jones .01 .05
88 Marvin Harrison .75 2.00
89 Israel Ifeanyi .01 .05
90 Reggie Brown .01 .05
91 Jermane Mayberry .01 .05
92 Brian Dawkins .40 1.00
93 Tedy Bruschi 1.00 2.50
94 Terrell Owens .75 2.00
95 Jermaine Lewis .07 .20
96 Sean Boyd .01 .05
97 Phillip Daniels .15 .40
98 Lawrence Phillips .01 .05
99 Keyshawn Johnson CL .15 .40
100 Terry Glenn CL .15 .40
P1 Keyshawn Johnson .50 1.25
Promo

1996 Classic NFL Rookies Gold

COMPLETE SET (90) 15.00 40.00
*GOLD CARDS: 1.5X TO 4X BASIC CARDS
ONE PER RETAIL PACK

1996 Classic NFL Rookies Autographs

ONE PER SPECIAL RETAIL BOX
2 Jonathan Ogden 6.00 15.00
6 Tim Biakabutuka 6.00 15.00
11 Daryl Gardener 5.00 12.00
17 Derrick Mayes 6.00 15.00
22 Jerome Woods 5.00 12.00
34 Jeff Hartings 4.00 10.00
37 Lance Johnstone 6.00 15.00
44 Randall Godfrey 4.00 10.00
48 Jeff Lewis 6.00 15.00
49 Mike Alstott 15.00 40.00
51 Stepfret Williams 4.00 10.00
57 Kyle Wachholtz 4.00 10.00
58 Johnny McWilliams 4.00 10.00
80 Pete Kendall 5.00 12.00
85 Marco Battaglia 5.00 12.00

1996 Classic NFL Rookies Die Cuts

COMPLETE SET (30) 30.00 80.00
STATED ODDS 1:100 RETAIL
1 Keyshawn Johnson 4.00 10.00
2 Kevin Hardy .75 2.00
3 Simeon Rice 1.25 3.00
4 Jonathan Ogden 1.25 3.00
5 Cedric Jones .75 2.00
6 Lawrence Phillips .75 2.00
7 Terry Glenn 2.50 6.00
8 Tim Biakabutuka 1.25 3.00
9 Emmitt Smith 6.00 15.00

10 Willie Anderson	.75	2.00
11 Alex Molden	.75	2.00
12 Regan Upshaw	.75	2.00
13 Kerry Collins	2.50	6.00
14 Eddie George	4.00	10.00
15 John Mobley	.75	2.00
16 Duane Clemons	.75	2.00
17 Reggie Brown	.75	2.00
18 Marshall Faulk	3.00	8.00
19 Marvin Harrison	6.00	15.00
20 Daryl Gardener	.75	2.00
21 Pete Kendall	.75	2.00
22 Joey Galloway	2.00	5.00
23 Jeff Hartings	1.25	3.00
24 Eric Moulds	3.00	8.00
25 Jermane Mayberry	.75	2.00
26 Steve McNair	2.00	5.00
27 Kyle Brady	.75	2.00
28 Jerome Woods	.75	2.00
29 Jamain Stephens	.75	2.00
30 Andre Johnson	.75	2.00

1996 Classic NFL Rookies Home Jersey Image

COMPLETE SET (30)	40.00	80.00
STATED ODDS 1:15 RETAIL PACKS		
HJ1 Keyshawn Johnson	4.00	8.00
HJ2 Kevin Hardy	1.50	3.00
HJ3 Jonathan Ogden	1.50	3.00
HJ4 Terry Glenn	3.00	6.00
HJ5 Tim Biakabutuka	1.50	3.00
HJ6 Karim Abdul-Jabbar	1.50	3.00
HJ7 Simeon Rice	2.00	4.00
HJ8 Eric Moulds	4.00	8.00
HJ9 Mike Alstott	4.00	8.00
HJ10 Leeland McElroy	.75	1.50
HJ11 Daryl Gardener	.15	.40
HJ12 Eddie George	6.00	12.00
HJ13 Amani Toomer	3.00	6.00
HJ14 Johnny McWilliams	.15	.40
HJ15 Derrick Mayes	1.50	3.00
HJ16 Duane Clemons	.15	.40
HJ17 Chris Darkins	.15	.40
HJ18 Ray Farmer	.15	.40
HJ19 Danny Kanell	1.50	3.00
HJ20 Bobby Hoying	1.50	3.00
HJ21 Zach Thomas	3.00	6.00
HJ22 Tony Banks	1.50	3.00
HJ23 Alex Van Dyke	.75	1.50
HJ24 Stepfret Williams	.75	1.50
HJ25 Chris Doering	.15	.40
HJ26 Lance Johnstone	.75	1.50
HJ27 Stephen Davis	5.00	10.00
HJ28 Scott Greene	.15	.40
HJ29 Tony Brackens	1.50	3.00
HJ30 Jevon Langford	.15	.40

1996 Classic NFL Rookies Road Jersey Images

COMPLETE SET (30)	40.00	80.00
ROAD JERSEY STATED ODDS 1:15 HOBBY		
RJ1 Keyshawn Johnson	4.00	8.00
RJ2 Kevin Hardy	1.50	3.00
RJ3 Jonathan Ogden	1.50	3.00
RJ4 Terry Glenn	3.00	6.00
RJ5 Tim Biakabutuka	1.50	3.00
RJ6 Karim Abdul-Jabbar	1.50	3.00
RJ7 Simeon Rice	2.00	4.00
RJ8 Eric Moulds	4.00	8.00
RJ9 Mike Alstott	4.00	8.00
RJ10 Leeland McElroy	.75	1.50
RJ11 Daryl Gardener	.15	.40
RJ12 Eddie George	6.00	12.00
RJ13 Amani Toomer	3.00	6.00
RJ14 Marvin Harrison	8.00	15.00
RJ15 Derrick Mayes	1.50	3.00
RJ16 Dietrich Jells	.15	.40
RJ17 Chris Darkins	.15	.40
RJ18 Ray Farmer	.15	.40
RJ19 Danny Kanell	1.50	3.00
RJ20 Bobby Hoying	1.50	3.00
RJ21 Zach Thomas	3.00	6.00
RJ22 Kyle Wachholtz	.15	.40
RJ23 Alex Van Dyke	.75	1.50
RJ24 Stepfret Williams	.75	1.50
RJ25 Chris Doering	.15	.40
RJ26 Lance Johnstone	.75	1.50
RJ27 Stephen Davis	5.00	10.00
RJ28 Scott Greene	.15	.40
RJ29 Tony Brackens	1.50	3.00
RJ30 Jevon Langford	.15	.40

1996 Classic NFL Rookies Rookie Lasers

COMPLETE SET (10)	25.00	60.00
STATED ODDS 1:100 HOBBY		
RL1 Keyshawn Johnson	8.00	20.00
RL2 Jonathan Ogden	3.00	8.00
RL3 Eddie George	12.50	30.00
RL4 Terry Glenn	6.00	15.00
RL5 Tommie Frazier	3.00	8.00
RL6 Karim Abdul-Jabbar	3.00	8.00
RL7 Duane Clemons	.40	1.00
RL8 Leeland McElroy	1.50	4.00
RL9 Tim Biakabutuka	3.00	8.00
RL10 Kevin Hardy	3.00	8.00

1996 Classic NFL Rookies ROY Contenders

COMPLETE SET (10)	15.00	40.00
STATED ODDS 1:20 SPECIAL RETAIL		
C1 Keyshawn Johnson	3.00	8.00
C2 Jonathan Ogden	1.25	3.00
C3 Eddie George	5.00	12.00
C4 Terry Glenn	2.50	6.00
C5 Eric Moulds	3.00	8.00
C6 Karim Abdul-Jabbar	1.25	3.00
C7 Leeland McElroy	.60	1.50
C8 Tim Biakabutuka	1.25	3.00
C9 Bobby Hoying	1.25	3.00
C10 Stephen Davis	4.00	10.00

1996 Classic NFL Rookies ROY Interactive

COMPLETE SET (20)	40.00	80.00
STATED ODDS 1:35		
RY1 Keyshawn Johnson	4.00	10.00
RY2 Jonathan Ogden	1.50	4.00
RY3 Steve Taneyhill	.20	.50
RY4 Leeland McElroy	.75	2.00
RY5 Terry Glenn	3.00	8.00
RY6 Tim Biakabutuka	1.50	4.00
RY7 Karim Abdul-Jabbar	1.50	4.00
RY8 Eddie George	6.00	15.00
RY9 Johnny McWilliams	.20	.50
RY10 Eric Moulds	4.00	10.00
RY11 Bobby Hoying	1.50	4.00
RY12 Chris Darkins	.20	.50
RY13 Derrick Mayes	1.50	4.00
RY14 Mike Alstott	4.00	10.00
RY15 Chris Doering	.20	.50
RY16 Danny Kanell	1.50	4.00
RY17 Stephen Davis	5.00	12.00
RY18 Amani Toomer	3.00	8.00
RY19 Dietrich Jells	.20	.50
RY20 Field Card	.20	.50

1996 Clear Assets

The 1996 Clear Assets set was issued in one series totaling 70 cards. The set features 75 upscale acetate cards of the most collectible athletes from baseball, basketball, football, hockey and auto racing. Also included is the debut appearance by many of the top players entering the 1996 football draft. Release date was April 1996.

COMPLETE SET (70)	6.00	15.00
29 Emmitt Smith	.60	1.50
30 Jeff Lewis	.08	.25
31 Joey Galloway	.15	.40
32 Steve McNair	.25	.60
33 Eric Moulds	.30	.75
34 Steve Young	.30	.75
35 Mike Alstott	.30	.75
36 Marshall Faulk	.20	.50
37 Kerry Collins	.15	.40
38 Kyle Brady	.10	.30
39 Drew Bledsoe	.20	.50
40 Troy Aikman	.40	1.00
41 Duane Clemons	.08	.25
42 Napoleon Kaufman	.10	.30
43 Stanley Pritchett	.08	.25
44 Marcus Coleman	.08	.25
45 Amani Toomer	.25	.60
46 Richard Huntley	.08	.25
47 Tony Banks	.10	.30
48 Keyshawn Johnson	.40	1.00
49 Kevin Hardy	.08	.25
50 Karim Abdul-Jabbar	.10	.30

1996 Clear Assets 3X

COMPLETE SET (10)	40.00	100.00
X5 Emmitt Smith	10.00	25.00
X8 Keyshawn Johnson	5.00	12.00
X10 Troy Aikman	6.00	15.00

1996 Clear Assets Phone Cards $1

COMPLETE SET (30)	5.00	12.00
*PIN NUMBER REVEALED: HALF VALUE		
$1 CARDS ONE PER RETAIL PACK		
*$2 CARDS: .6X TO 1.5X $1 CARDS		
ONE PER HOBBY PACK		
CARDS EXPIRED 10/1/97		
2 Marshall Faulk	.25	.60
7 Troy Aikman	.40	1.00
10 Jeff Lewis	.10	.30
12 Drew Bledsoe	.25	.60
14 Eric Moulds	.25	.60
18 Joey Galloway	.15	.40
21 Kerry Collins	.20	.50
23 Mike Alstott	.30	.75
24 Duane Clemons	.10	.30
26 Stanley Pritchett	.10	.30
27 Steve Young	.30	.75

1996 Clear Assets Phone Cards $5

COMPLETE SET (20)	12.00	30.00
*PIN NUMBER REVEALED:HALF VALUE		
2 Emmitt Smith	2.00	5.00
6 Troy Aikman	1.25	3.00
7 Keyshawn Johnson	1.00	2.50
10 Drew Bledsoe	.75	2.00
15 Kerry Collins	.50	1.25
17 Mike Alstott	.75	2.00
19 Steve Young	1.00	2.50
20 Marshall Faulk	.75	2.00

1996 Clear Assets Phone Cards $10

COMPLETE SET (10)	20.00	50.00
*PIN NUMBER REVEALED:HALF VALUE		
2 Troy Aikman	.50	6.00
4 Keyshawn Johnson	1.50	4.00
7 Napoleon Kaufman	1.00	2.50

1996 Clear Assets Phone Cards $1000

NOT PRICED DUE TO SCARCITY
2 Troy Aikman
3 Kerry Collins
4 Keyshawn Johnson

1992 Courtside Promos

The 1992 Courtside Draft Pix Promos include cards released at different times through different channels. Many are sometimes found with red overprint stamps on the back commemorating the card show where they were available as give-aways. The style of these promo and sample cards is very similar to that of the 1992 Courtside regular issue cards on the fronts with many different variations of cardbacks. Most of these promos are marked on the back clearly with "Promotion Not For Sale" or "Sample" or other similar line of type. Most of the cards contain a card number, while a few have been assigned card numbers based on their position in the regular issue set.

COMPLETE SET (12)	2.00	5.00
20A Tony Brooks	.08	.25
20B Amp Lee	.08	.25
22 Terrell Buckley	.20	.50
30 Tommy Vardell	.20	.50
40 Carl Pickens	.80	2.00
44 Quentin Coryatt	.20	.50
50 Mike Gaddis	.08	.25
60 Steve Emtman	.20	.50
(No statistics or bio on card back)		
66 Bucky Richardson	.08	.25
(unnumbered card; Jan.15-17, 1993 Tri-Star Show)		
70A Dana Hall	.08	.25
(issued for Jan.15-17, 1993 Bellevue, Wash. card show)		
70B Dana Hall	.08	.25
(issued for 1992 Sports Coll. Expo in San Francisco, CA)		
75 Johnny Mitchell	.08	.25
(noted as sample on back)		
NNO Steve Emtman	.08	.25
(Silver Foil, no stats on back)		

1992 Courtside

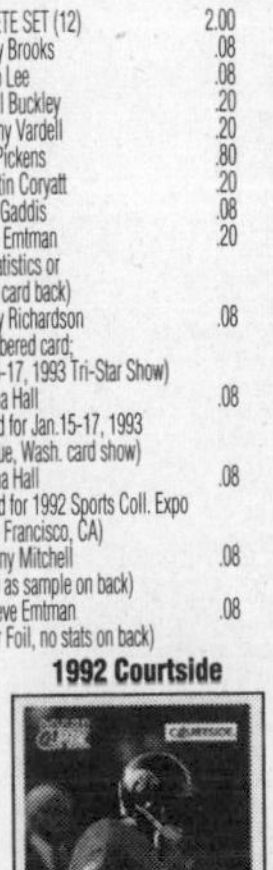

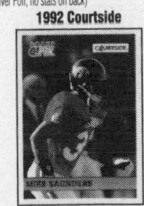

The 1992 Courtside Draft Pix football set contains 140 player cards. Ten short printed insert cards (five Award Winner and five All-America) were randomly inserted in the foil packs. This set also includes a foilgram card featuring Steve Emtman. Fifty thousand foilgram cards were printed, and collectors could receive one by sending in ten foil pack wrappers. Moreover, one set of foilgram cards and 20 free promo cards were offered to dealers for each case order. It has been reported that the production run was limited to 7,500 numbered cases, and that no factory sets were issued. Gold, silver, and bronze foil versions of the regular cards were randomly inserted within the foil cases in quantities of 1,000, 2,000, and 3,000 respectively. Reportedly more than 70,000 autographed cards were also inserted. The standard-size cards feature on the fronts glossy color action photos bordered in white (some of the cards are oriented horizontally). The player's name and position appear in a gold stripe cutting across the bottom. On the backs, the upper half has a color close-up photo, with biography and collegiate statistics below. Key cards include Quentin Coryatt, Amp Lee, Johnny Mitchell, Carl Pickens and Tommy Vardell.

COMPLETE SET (140)	2.00	5.00
1 Steve Emtman	.05	.15
2 Quentin Coryatt	.05	.15
3 Ken Swilling	.01	.05
4 Jay Leeuwenburg	.01	.05
5 Mazio Royster	.01	.05
6 Matt Veatch	.01	.05
7A Scott Lockwood ERR	.01	.05
No career totals		
7B Scott Lockwood COR	.01	.05
8 Todd Collins	.01	.05
9 Gene McGuire	.01	.05
10 Dale Carter	.05	.15
11 Michael Bankston	.01	.05
12 Jeremy Lincoln	.01	.05
13A Troy Auzenne ERR	.01	.05
Misspelled Auzene		
13B Troy Auzenne COR	.01	.05
14 Rod Smith DB	.01	.05
15 Andy Kelly	.10	.30
16 Chris Holder	.01	.05
17 Rico Smith	.01	.05
18 Chris Pedersen	.01	.05
19 Brian Treggs	.01	.05
20 Eugene Chung	.01	.05
21 Joel Steed	.01	.05
22 Ricardo McDonald	.01	.05
23 Nate Turner	.01	.05
24 Sean Lumpkin	.01	.05
25 Ty Detmer	.10	.30
26 Matt Darby	.01	.05
27 Michael Warfield	.01	.05
28 Tracy Scroggins	.01	.05
29 Carl Pickens	.30	.75
30 Chris Mims	.01	.05
31 Mark D'Onofrio	.01	.05
32 Dwight Hollier	.01	.05
33 Siupeli Malamala	.01	.05
34A Mark Barsotti ERR	.01	.05
Back stats jumbled with no career totals		
34B Mark Barsotti COR	.01	.05
35 Charles Davenport	.01	.05
36 Brian Bollinger	.01	.05
37 Willie McClendon	.01	.05
38 Calvin Holmes	.01	.05
39 Phillippi Sparks	.05	.15
40 Darryl Williams	.01	.05
41 Greg Skrepenak	.01	.05
42 Larry Webster	.01	.05
43 Dion Lambert	.01	.05
44 Sam Gash	.10	.30
45 Patrick Rowe	.01	.05
46 Scottie Graham	.05	.15
47 Darian Hagan	.01	.05
48 Arthur Marshall	.01	.05
49 Amp Lee	.05	.15
50 Tommy Vardell	.05	.15
51 Robert Porcher	.10	.30
52 Reggie Dwight	.01	.05
53 Torrance Small	.01	.05
54 Ronnie West	.01	.05
55 Tony Brooks	.01	.05
56 Anthony McDowell	.01	.05
57 Chris Hakel	.01	.05
58 Ed Cunningham	.01	.05
59 Ashley Ambrose	.10	.30
60 Alonzo Spellman	.05	.15
61 Harold Heath	.01	.05
62 Ron Lopez	.05	.15
63 Bill Johnson	.01	.05
64 Kent Graham	.05	.15
65 Aaron Pierce	.01	.05
66 Bucky Richardson	.01	.05
67A Todd Kinchen ERR	.01	.05
Long reception for '91 is on a different line		
67B Todd Kinchen COR	.01	.05
68 Ken Ealy	.01	.05
69 Carlos Snow	.01	.05
70 Dana Hall	.01	.05
71 Matt Rodgers	.01	.05
72 Howard Dinkins	.01	.05
73 Tim Lester	.01	.05
74 Mark Chmura	.10	.30
75 Johnny Mitchell	.05	.15
76 Mirko Jurkovic	.01	.05
77 Anthony Lynn	.01	.05
78 Roosevelt Collins	.01	.05
79 Tony Sands	.01	.05
80 Kevin Smith	.01	.05
81 Tony Brown	.01	.05
82 Bobby Fuller	.01	.05
83 Darryl Ashmore	.01	.05
84 Tyrone Legette	.01	.05
85 Mike Gaddis	.01	.05
86A Cal Dixon ERR	.01	.05
Should be number 101		
86B Gerald Dixon COR	.01	.05
87 T.J. Rubley	.01	.05
88 Mark Thomas	.01	.05
89 Corey Widmer	.01	.05
90 Robert Jones	.01	.05
91 Eddie Robinson	.01	.05
92 Rob Tomlinson	.01	.05
93 Russ Campbell	.01	.05
94 Keith Goganious	.01	.05
95 Rod Moore	.01	.05
96 Jerry Ostroski	.01	.05
97 Tyji Armstrong	.01	.05
98 Ronald Humphrey	.01	.05
99 Corey Harris	.01	.05
100 Terrell Buckley	.05	.15
101 Cal Dixon	.01	.05
See card number 86A		
102 Tyrone Williams	.05	.15
103 Joe Bowden	.01	.05
104 Santana Dotson	.05	.15
105 Jeff Blake	.60	1.50
106 Erick Anderson	.01	.05
107 Steve Israel	.01	.05
108 Chad Roghair	.01	.05
109 Todd Harrison	.01	.05
110 Chester McGlockton	.01	.05
111 Marquez Pope	.01	.05
112 George Rooks	.01	.05
113 Dion Johnson	.01	.05
114 Tim Simpson	.01	.05
115 Chris Walsh	.01	.05
116 Marc Boutte	.01	.05
117 Jamie Gill	.01	.05
118 Willie Clay	.01	.05
119 Tim Paulk	.01	.05
120 Ray Roberts	.01	.05
121 Jeff Thomason	.01	.05
122 Leodis Flowers	.01	.05
123 Robert Brooks	.30	.75
124 Jeff Ellis	.01	.05
125 John Fina	.01	.05
126A Michael Smith ERR	.01	.05
Back stats jumbled with no career totals		
126B Michael Smith COR	.01	.05
127 Mike Saunders	.20	.50
128 John Brown III	.01	.05
129 Reggie Yarbrough	.01	.05
130 Leon Searcy	.01	.05
131 Marcus Woods	.01	.05
132 Shane Collins	.01	.05
133 Chuck Smith	.01	.05
134 Keith Hamilton	.05	.15
135 Rodney Blackshear	.01	.05
136 Corey Barlow	.01	.05
137 Robert Harris	.01	.05
138 Tony Smith WR	.01	.05
139 Checklist 1	.01	.05
Some have 139 Auzenne spelled Auzene		
140 Checklist 2	.01	.05

1992 Courtside Bronze

COMPLETE SET (140)	4.00	10.00
*BRONZES: .8X TO 2X BASIC CARDS		

1992 Courtside Gold

COMPLETE SET (140)	4.00	10.00
*GOLDS: .8X TO 2X BASIC CARDS		

1992 Courtside Silver

COMPLETE SET (140)	4.00	10.00
*SILVERS: .8X TO 2X BASIC CARDS		

1992 Courtside Autographs

COMMON AUTOGRAPH	1.25	3.00
SEMISTARS	2.00	5.00
UNLISTED STARS	4.00	10.00
29 Carl Pickens	8.00	20.00
105 Jeff Blake	10.00	25.00
123 Robert Brooks	10.00	25.00
127 Mike Saunders	6.00	15.00

1992 Courtside Foilgrams

These five special foilgram standard-size cards were redeemable by mail via a wrapper offer. They feature some leading prospects of the 1992 draft.

COMPLETE SET (5)	1.60	4.00
1 Steve Emtman	.30	.75
2 Tommy Vardell	.30	.75
3 Terrell Buckley	.30	.75
4 Ty Detmer	.60	1.50
5 Amp Lee	.30	.75

1992 Courtside Inserts

COMPLETE SET (10)	2.50	6.00
AA1 Carl Pickens	1.25	3.00
AA2 Dale Carter	.25	.60
AA3 Tommy Vardell	.25	.60
AA4 Amp Lee	.25	.60
AA5 Leon Searcy	.07	.20
AW1 Steve Emtman	.25	.60
AW2 Ty Detmer	.50	1.25
Heisman		
AW3 Steve Emtman	.25	.60
AW4 Terrell Buckley	.25	.60
AW5 Erick Anderson	.07	.20

1993 Courtside Sean Dawkins

Sean Dawkins, who was drafted in the first round by the Indianapolis Colts, is showcased in this five-card, standard-size set. Only 20,000 sets of each player were produced, and Dawkins personally autographed 5,000 cards for random insertion within the sets. The fronts display full-bleed glossy action photos, with the backgrounds blurred to highlight the player. Each card has a color bar carrying a gold foil football icon, the words "Draft Pix," and the player's name in gold foil lettering. On a background reflecting the same color as the front bar, the backs have a second color action photo and either biography, statistics, player profile, or highlights. The complete set price below is a sealed price since it is not known if there is an autograph sealed inside. The cards were also issued as promos with the disclaimer "Promotional Not for Sale" stamped on the front in a circular format. The promos also included the words "Authentic Signature" printed in silver lettering toward the bottom of the front even though they were not signed.

COMPLETE SET (5)	2.00	5.00
COMMON CARD (1-5)	.40	1.00
*PROMOS: .6X TO 1.5X BASIC CARDS		
AU1 Sean Dawkins AU/5000	4.00	10.00
(Certified autograph)		

1993 Courtside Russell White

Russell White, who was drafted in the third round by the Los Angeles Rams, is showcased in this five-card, standard-size set. Just 20,000 sets of each player were produced, and White personally autographed 5,000 cards for random insertion within the sets. The fronts display full-bleed glossy action photos, with the backgrounds blurred to highlight the player. Each card has a color bar carrying a gold foil football icon, the words "Draft Pix," and the player's name in gold foil lettering. On a background reflecting the same color as the front bar, the backs have a second color action photo and either biography, statistics, player profile, or highlights. The complete set price below is a sealed price since it is not known if there is an autograph sealed inside. The cards were also issued as promos and those are identical to the regular issue except for "Promotional Not for Sale" stamped on the fronts in a circular format. These promos also include the words "Authentic Signature" printed in silver lettering toward the bottom of the front even though the cards were not signed.

COMPLETE SET (5)	1.00	2.50
COMMON CARD (1-5)	.20	.50
*PROMOS: .6X TO 1.5X BASIC INSERTS		
AU1 Russell White AU/5000	2.00	5.00
(Certified autograph)		

1993 Front Row Gold Collection Promos

Along with an 11" by 8 1/2" promo sheet (listed below), these five standard sized cards were issued in honor of Spectrum Holdings Group's purchase of the Front Row trademark. The set's title, "The Gold Collection" is stamped in gold foil and runs down the left edge of the cardfront. The cardbacks carry a disclaimer, "For Promotional Purposes Only." The unnumbered cards have been assigned numbers below alphabetically. The promo sheet features all five players and contains a gold foil seal bearing the sheet number (of 5000) produced.

COMPLETE SET (5)	2.00	5.00
1 Eric Curry	.30	.75
2 Andre Hastings	.30	.75
3 Qadry Ismail	.50	1.25
4 Lincoln Kennedy	.30	.75
5 O.J.McDuffie	.80	2.00
NNO Promo Sheet	.40	1.00
Eric Curry		
Andre Hastings		
Qadry Ismail		
Lincoln Kennedy		
O.J.McDuffie		

1993 Front Row Gold Collection

These ten cards were issued with the set title "The Gold Collection" printed in gold foil down the left side of the cardfront. On the back of the even-numbered cards appears player biographical and statistical information. The back of the odd-numbered cards features a player profile within a gray box. The cards were issued in factory set form with a certificate of authenticity numbered of 5000 sets produced.

COMPLETE SET (10)	2.40	6.00
1 Eric Curry	.20	.50
2 Eric Curry	.20	.50
3 Lincoln Kennedy	.20	.50
4 Lincoln Kennedy	.20	.50
5 O.J.McDuffie	.50	1.25
6 O.J.McDuffie	.50	1.25
7 Qadry Ismail	.30	.75
8 Qadry Ismail	.30	.75
9 Andre Hastings	.20	.50
10 Andre Hastings	.20	.50

1997 Genuine Article

The Genuine Article base set is divided into three series with either a B, an M or R prefix on the card numbers. The B prefix cards feature potential 1997 NFL Draft picks. The M prefix cards feature four different cards of 12-players while the R prefix cards include 6-players with four cards each. Genuine Article presumably had these 28-players under contract since no licensing notation is made on the cardbacks. The card photo quality varies from good to poor with very brief write-ups on the cardbacks. There also is a gold foil GA logo and/or Dream Picks set title on the cardfronts.

COMPLETE SET (82)	4.00	10.00
B1 Ronde Barber	.08	.25
B2 Steve Bush	.01	.05
B3 William Carr	.01	.05
B4 James Cunningham	.01	.05
B5 Pat Fitzgerland	.01	.05
B6 Mike Jenkins	.01	.05
B7 Damon Jones	.01	.05
B8 Nathan Perryman	.01	.05
B9 Tarek Saleh	.01	.05
B10 Damond Wilkins	.01	.05
M1 James Allen	.30	.75
M2 Terry Battle	.01	.05
M3 Tiki Barber	.40	1.00
M4 Michael Booker	.01	.05
M5 Troy Davis	.01	.05
M6 Jim Druckenmiller	.02	.10
M7 Yatil Green	.02	.10
M8 Derrick Mason	.30	.75
M9 Chris Miller WR	.01	.05
M10 Sedrick Shaw	.01	.05
M11 Antowain Smith	.20	.50
M12 Shawn Springs	.01	.05
M13 James Allen	.30	.75
M14 Terry Battle	.01	.05
M15 Tiki Barber	.40	1.00
M16 Michael Booker	.01	.05
M17 Troy Davis	.01	.05
M18 Jim Druckenmiller	.02	.10
M19 Yatil Green	.02	.10
M20 Derrick Mason	.30	.75
M21 Chris Miller WR	.01	.05
M22 Sedrick Shaw	.01	.05
M23 Antowain Smith	.20	.50
M24 Shawn Springs	.01	.05
M25 James Allen	.30	.75
M26 Terry Battle	.01	.05
M27 Tiki Barber	.40	1.00
M28 Michael Booker	.01	.05
M29 Troy Davis	.01	.05
M30 Jim Druckenmiller	.02	.10
M31 Yatil Green	.02	.10
M32 Derrick Mason	.30	.75
M33 Chris Miller WR	.01	.05
M34 Sedrick Shaw	.01	.05
M35 Antowain Smith	.20	.50
M36 Shawn Springs	.01	.05
M37 James Allen	.30	.75
M38 Terry Battle	.01	.05
M39 Tiki Barber	.40	1.00
M40 Michael Booker	.01	.05
M41 Troy Davis	.01	.05
M42 Jim Druckenmiller	.02	.10
M43 Yatil Green	.02	.10
M44 Derrick Mason	.30	.75
M45 Chris Miller WR	.01	.05
M46 Sedrick Shaw	.01	.05
M47 Antowain Smith UER	.20	.50
(name spelled Antowaine)		
M48 Shawn Springs	.01	.05
R1 Mike Alstott	.30	.75
R2 Tony Banks	.08	.25
R3 Tim Biakabutuka	.08	.25
R4 Terry Glenn	.15	.40
R5 Leeland McElroy	.01	.05
R6 Sherman Williams	.01	.05
R7 Mike Alstott	.30	.75
R8 Tony Banks	.08	.25
R9 Tim Biakabutuka UER	.08	.25
(name spelled Biakabutuk)		
R10 Terry Glenn	.15	.40
R11 Leeland McElroy	.01	.05
R12 Sherman Williams	.01	.05
R13 Mike Alstott	.30	.75
R14 Tony Banks	.08	.25
R15 Tim Biakabutuka UER	.08	.25
(name spelled Biakabutuk)		
R16 Terry Glenn	.15	.40
R17 Leeland McElroy	.01	.05
R18 Sherman Williams	.01	.05
R19 Mike Alstott	.30	.75
R20 Tony Banks	.08	.25
R21 Tim Biakabutuka	.08	.25
R22 Terry Glenn	.15	.40
R23 Leeland McElroy	.01	.05
R24 Sherman Williams	.01	.05

1997 Genuine Article Autographs

B1 Ronde Barber	2.00	5.00
B2 Steve Bush	.75	2.00
B3 William Carr	.75	2.00
B4 James Cunningham	.75	2.00
B5 Pat Fitzgerland	.75	2.00
B6 Mike Jenkins	.75	2.00
B7 Damon Jones	.75	2.00
B8 Nathan Perryman	.75	2.00
B9 Tarek Saleh	.75	2.00
B10 Damond Wilkins	.75	2.00
M1 James Allen	2.00	5.00
M2 Terry Battle	.75	2.00
M3 Tiki Barber	10.00	25.00
M4 Michael Booker	.75	2.00
M5 Troy Davis	1.25	3.00
M6 Jim Druckenmiller	1.25	3.00
M7 Yatil Green	1.25	3.00
M8 Derrick Mason	4.00	10.00
M9 Chris Miller WR	.75	2.00
M10 Sedrick Shaw	.75	2.00
M11 Antowain Smith	3.00	8.00
M12 Shawn Springs	1.25	3.00
R1 Mike Alstott	3.00	8.00
R2 Tony Banks	2.00	5.00
R3 Tim Biakabutuka	1.25	3.00
R4 Terry Glenn	2.00	5.00
R5 Leeland McElroy	1.25	3.00
R6 Sherman Williams	.75	2.00
GA3 Eddie George/100	.75	2.00

1997 Genuine Article Checklists

COMPLETE SET (4)	2.00	5.00
CK1 Terrell Davis	.60	1.50
CK2 Terrell Davis	.60	1.50
CK3 Eddie George	.40	1.00
(inserts checklist back)		
CK4 Eddie George	.40	1.00

1997 Genuine Article Duo-Sport Preview

COMPLETE SET (5)	2.50	6.00
DS1 Eddie George	.75	2.00
DS2 Karim Abdul-Jabbar	.50	1.25
DS3 Jim Druckenmiller	.50	1.25
DS4 Orlando Pace	.60	1.50
DS5 Yatil Green	.40	1.00

1997 Genuine Article Grand Achievements

COMPLETE SET (5)	3.00	8.00
GA1 Terrell Davis	2.50	6.00
GA2 Troy Davis	.40	1.00
GA3 Eddie George	1.25	3.00
GA4 Karim Abdul-Jabbar	.60	1.50
GA5 Troy Davis	.40	1.00

1997 Genuine Article Orlando Pace

COMPLETE SET (4)	.40	1.00
COMMON CARD (P1-P4)	.10	.30

1993-94 Images Four Sport

These 150 standard-size cards feature on their borderless fronts color player action shots with backgrounds that have been thrown out of focus. On the white background to the left, career highlights, biography and statistics are displayed. Just 6,500 of each card were produced. The set closes with Classic Headlines (128-147) and checklists (148-150). A redemption card inserted one per case entitled the collector to one set of basketball draft preview cards. This offered expired 9/30/94.

COMPLETE SET (150)	6.00	15.00
1 Drew Bledsoe	.40	1.00
5 Rick Mirer	.15	.40
9 Robert Smith	.20	.50
25 Lincoln Kennedy	.08	.25
26 Jerome Bettis	.40	1.00
29 Deon Figures	.08	.25
33 George Teague	.08	.25
39 Glyn Milburn	.10	.30
44 Gino Torretta	.15	.40
45 Roger Harper	.08	.25
48 Victor Bailey	.08	.25
53 Thomas Smith	.08	.25
55 Andre King	.08	.25
57 Reggie Brooks	.10	.30
58 Ron Moore	.08	.25
61 Dan Footman	.08	.25
64 Tom Carter	.08	.25
65 Qadry Ismail	.15	.40
70 Marvin Jones	.08	.25
71 Garrison Hearst	.20	.50
72 John Copeland	.08	.25
73 Darrien Gordon	.08	.25
78 Chad Brown	.08	.25
82 Irv Smith	.08	.25
83 Troy Drayton	.08	.25
87 Carlton Gray	.08	.25
88 Billy Joe Hobert	.08	.25
91 Carl Simpson	.08	.25
95 Roosevelt Potts	.08	.25
97 Derek Brown RB	.08	.25
102 Curtis Conway	.15	.40
103 Lamar Thomas	.08	.25
104 Willie Roaf	.08	.25
107 Eric Curry	.08	.25
108 Todd Kelly	.08	.25
114 Horace Copeland	.08	.25
116 Terry Kirby	.15	.40
117 Demetrius DuBose	.08	.25
118 Will Shields	.08	.25
119 Natrone Means	.15	.40
120 O.J. McDuffie	.10	.30
126 Kevin Williams WR	.08	.25
127 Lorenzo Neal	.08	.25
129 Drew Bledsoe B W	.30	.75
133 Rick Mirer B W	.08	.25
137 Jerome Bettis B W	.25	.60
140 Terry Kirby BW	.10	.30
144 Derek Brown RB BW	.08	.25

1993-94 Images Four Sport Acetates

COMPLETE SET (4)	12.00	30.00
2 Jerome Bettis	3.00	8.00
3 Steve Young	4.00	10.00

1993-94 Images Four Sport Chrome

COMPLETE SET (20)	15.00	40.00
CC7 Drew Bledsoe	1.50	4.00
CC8 Jerome Bettis	1.50	4.00
CC9 Terry Kirby	.40	1.00
CC10 Dana Stubblefield	.40	1.00
CC11 Rick Mirer	.60	1.50
NNO Uncut Sheet	30.00	80.00

1993-94 Images Four Sport Sudden Impact

COMPLETE SET (20)	4.00	10.00
SI15 Drew Bledsoe	.40	1.00
SI16 Rick Mirer	.25	.60
SI17 Derek Brown RB	.15	.40
SI18 Ron Moore	.15	.40
SI19 Jerome Bettis	.40	1.00

1995 Images Four Sport

Printed on 18-point micro-lined foil board, the 1995 Classic Images set consists of 120 standard-size cards, featuring the top draft picks from the four major sports. Classic produced 1,995 sequentially-numbered 16-box hobby cases. This series also features one "Hot Box" in every four cases; each pack in it included at least one card from five insert sets, plus the special Clear Excitement chase cards not found anywhere else, for a total of 24 inserts per Hot Box. There was a promotional card issued, not inserted into '94-95 Assets packs, for Grant Hill numbered HP1. The front is the same as the card in the set, but the back has an orange background and describes the product's features.

COMPLETE SET (120)	6.00	15.00
38 Dan Wilkinson	.15	.40
39 Marshall Faulk	.30	.75
40 Heath Shuler	.20	.50
41 Willie McGinest	.15	.40
42 Trev Alberts	.10	.30
43 Trent Dilfer	.20	.50
44 Bryant Young	.15	.40
45 Sam Adams	.10	.30
46 Antonio Langham	.10	.30
47 Jamir Miller	.10	.30
48 Aaron Glenn	.15	.40
49 Bernard Williams	.10	.30
50 Charles Johnson	.10	.30
51 Dewayne Washington	.10	.30
52 Tim Bowens	.10	.30
53 Johnnie Morton	.20	.50
54 Rob Fredrickson	.10	.30
55 Shante Carver	.10	.30
56 Henry Ford	.10	.30
57 Jeff Burris	.10	.30
58 William Floyd	.15	.40
59 Derrick Alexander	.15	.40
60 Darnay Scott	.20	.50
61 Errict Rhett	.20	.50
62 Greg Hill	.10	.30
63 David Palmer	.15	.40
64 Charlie Garner	.15	.40
65 Mario Bates	.10	.30
66 Bert Emanuel	.10	.30
67 Thomas Randolph	.10	.30
68 Aubrey Beavers	.10	.30
69 Byron Bam Morris	.10	.30
70 Lake Dawson	.10	.30
71 Todd Steussie	.15	.40
72 Aaron Taylor	.10	.30
73 Corey Sawyer	.10	.30
74 Kevin Mitchell	.10	.30
75 Emmitt Smith	.60	1.50

1995 Images Four Sport Classic Performances

COMPLETE SET (20)	20.00	50.00
CP8 Steve Young	1.50	4.00
CP9 Marshall Faulk	1.50	4.00
CP10 Derrick Alexander	.40	1.00
CP11 William Floyd	.40	1.00
CP12 Errict Rhett	.60	1.50
CP13 Byron Bam Morris	.40	1.00
CP14 Heath Shuler	.60	1.50
CP15 Emmitt Smith	3.00	8.00

1995 Images Four Sport Clear Excitement

COMPLETE SET (10)	60.00	150.00
C2 Emmitt Smith	12.50	30.00
C3 Troy Aikman	8.00	20.00
C4 Steve Young	6.00	15.00
E2 Marshall Faulk	6.00	15.00
E3 Drew Bledsoe	5.00	12.00

1995 Images Four Sport Draft Challenge

COMPLETE SET (25)	15.00	40.00
DC1 Rashaan Salaam	.50	1.25
DC2 Rashaan Salaam	.50	1.25
DC3 Rashaan Salaam	1.25	3.00
Bears		
DC4 Rashaan Salaam	.50	1.25
DC5 Rashaan Salaam	.50	1.25
DC6 Ki-Jana Carter	.50	1.25
DC7 Ki-Jana Carter	.50	1.25
DC8 Ki-Jana Carter	.50	1.25
DC9 Ki-Jana Carter	1.25	3.00
Bengals		
DC10 Ki-Jana Carter	.50	1.25
DC11 John Walsh	.40	1.00
DC12 John Walsh	.40	1.00
DC13 John Walsh	.40	1.00
DC14 John Walsh	.40	1.00
DC15 John Walsh	.40	1.00
Field Card		
DC16 Steve McNair	1.25	3.00
DC17 Steve McNair	1.25	3.00
DC18 Steve McNair	3.00	8.00
Oilers		
DC19 Steve McNair	1.25	3.00
DC20 Steve McNair	1.25	3.00
DC21 Kerry Collins	.75	2.00
DC22 Kerry Collins	.75	2.00
DC23 Kerry Collins	.75	2.00
DC24 Kerry Collins	.75	2.00
DC25 Kerry Collins	2.50	6.00
Field Card		

1995 Images Four Sport Draft Challenge Acetates

COMPLETE SET (5)	5.00	12.00
1 Rashaan Salaam	1.00	2.50
2 Ki-Jana Carter	1.00	2.50
3 John Walsh	.75	2.00
4 Steve McNair	2.00	5.00
5 Kerry Collins	1.25	3.00

1995 Images Four Sport Draft Challenge Acetates Autographs

1 Rashaan Salaam	10.00	25.00
2 Ki-Jana Carter	10.00	25.00
3 John Walsh	8.00	20.00
4 Steve McNair	15.00	40.00
5 Kerry Collins	12.00	30.00

1995 Images Four Sport EP

EP1 Drew Bledsoe	1.00	2.50
EP4 Marshall Faulk	1.00	2.50

1995 Images Four Sport Player of the Year

COMPLETE SET (4)	4.00	10.00
POY1 Steve Young	.75	2.00
POY2 Emmitt Smith	1.50	4.00

1995 Images Four Sport Previews

COMPLETE SET (5)	6.00	15.00
IP3 Marshall Faulk	1.00	2.50
IP5 Emmitt Smith	2.00	5.00

2011 Leaf Draft Draft Day Edition

COMPLETE SET (20)	6.00	15.00
RELEASED DIRECTLY TO DEALERS		
*BLACK: 2.5X TO 6X BASIC CARDS		
DD1 A.J. Green	.50	1.25
DD2 Andy Dalton	.60	1.50
DD3A Blaine Gabbert	.40	1.00
DD3B Blaine Gabbert	.40	1.00
DD4A Cam Newton	1.25	3.00
DD4B Cam Newton	1.25	3.00
DD5 Christian Ponder	.50	1.25
DD6 Colin Kaepernick	.30	.75
DD7 Daniel Thomas	.25	.60
DD8 DeMarco Murray	.50	1.25
DD9 Jake Locker	.60	1.50
DD10 Julio Jones	.50	1.25
DD11 Kendall Hunter	.25	.60
DD12 Mark Ingram	.50	1.25
DD13 Mikel Leshoure	.25	.60
DD14 Pat Devlin	.25	.60
DD15 Ricky Stanzi	.30	.75
DD16 Ryan Mallett	.50	1.25
DD17 Ryan Williams	.30	.75
DD18 Tyrod Taylor	.25	.60

2011 Leaf Draft Las Vegas Summit Promos

COMPLETE SET (3)	8.00	20.00
IS1 Cam Newton AA	3.00	8.00
IS2 Mark Ingram	2.00	5.00
IS3 A.J. Green Ultimate	2.00	5.00

2011 Leaf Draft Limited Edition

COMPLETE SET (20)	6.00	15.00
RELEASED DIRECTLY TO DEALERS		
*BLACK: 2.5X TO 6X BASIC CARDS		
1 A.J. Green	.50	1.25
2 Andy Dalton	.60	1.50
3A Blaine Gabbert	.40	1.00
3A Blaine Gabbert	.40	1.00
4A Cam Newton	1.25	3.00
4B Cam Newton	1.25	3.00
5 Christian Ponder	.50	1.25
6 Colin Kaepernick	.30	.75
7 Daniel Thomas	.25	.60
8 DeMarco Murray	.50	1.25
9 Jake Locker	.60	1.50
10 Julio Jones	.50	1.25
11 Kendall Hunter	.25	.60
12 Mark Ingram	.50	1.25
13 Mikel Leshoure	.25	.60
14 Pat Devlin	.25	.60
15 Ricky Stanzi	.30	.75
16 Ryan Mallett	.50	1.25
17 Ryan Williams	.30	.75
18 Tyrod Taylor	.25	.60

2012 Leaf Draft

COMPLETE SET (50)	6.00	15.00
COMP.FACT.SET (54)	15.00	40.00
*BLUE BORDER: .4X TO 1X RED		
*GOLD BORDER: 2X TO 5X RED		
1 A.J. Jenkins	.25	.60
2 Alshon Jeffery	.30	.75
3 Andre Branch	.15	.40
4 B.J. Cunningham	.15	.40
5 Bernard Pierce	.20	.50
6 Brandon Weeden	.40	1.00
7 Brock Osweiler	.25	.60
8 Chris Polk	.25	.60
9 Courtney Upshaw	.25	.60
10 Cyrus Gray	.20	.50
11 Darron Thomas	.30	.75
12 Devier Posey	.20	.50
13 Devon Still	.20	.50
14 Dont'a Hightower	.30	.75
15 Dontari Poe	.20	.50
16 Doug Martin	.30	.75
17 Dre Kirkpatrick	.30	.75
18 Dwayne Allen	.20	.50
19 Dwight Jones	.15	.40
20 Fletcher Cox	.20	.50
21 Isaiah Pead	.20	.50
22 Jacory Harris	.15	.40
23 Jeff Fuller	.25	.60
24 Joe Adams	.20	.50
25 Justin Blackmon	.40	1.00
26 Kellen Moore	.30	.75
27 Kirk Cousins	.30	.75
28 Lamar Miller	.25	.60
29 Luke Kuechly	.25	.60
30 Marc Tyler	.20	.50
31 Mark Barron	.30	.75
32 Marquis Maze	.20	.50
33 Matt Kalil	.25	.60
34 Melvin Ingram	.25	.60
35 Michael Floyd	.40	1.00
36 Mohamed Sanu	.20	.50
37 Nick Foles	.30	.75
38 Nick Perry	.20	.50
39 Nick Toon	.25	.60
40 Robert Griffin III	1.00	2.50
41 Robert Turbin	.20	.50
42 Ryan Broyles	.20	.50
43 Ryan Tannehill	.50	1.25
44 Stephen Hill	.20	.50
45 Stephon Gilmore	.20	.50
46 T.Y. Hilton	.20	.50
47 Tauren Poole	.15	.40
48 Terrance Ganaway	.15	.40
49 Trent Richardson	.60	1.50
50 Whitney Mercilus	.20	.50

2012 Leaf Draft Army All-American Bowl

AABAL1 Andrew Luck	1.50	4.00

2012 Leaf Draft Autographs Red

TWO RED BORDER AU PER RETAIL BOX		
*BLUE BORDER: .5X TO 1.2X RED BRDR		
ONE BLUE BORDER AU PER FACTORY SET		
AB1 Andre Branch SP	3.00	8.00
AB2 Antwon Bailey	3.00	8.00
AC2 Audie Cole	3.00	8.00
AD1 Alfonzo Dennard	4.00	10.00
AJJ A.J. Jenkins SP	5.00	12.00
AS1 Amini Silatolu	2.50	6.00
AT1 Alameda Ta'amu	5.00	12.00
BJC B.J. Cunningham SP	3.00	8.00
BM1 Bobby Massie	2.50	6.00
BM2 Brandon Mosley	2.50	6.00
BO1 Brock Osweiler SP	5.00	12.00
BP1 Bernard Pierce SP	4.00	10.00
BQ1 Brian Quick	5.00	12.00
BR1 Bobby Rainey	4.00	10.00
BT1 Brandon Thompson	3.00	8.00
BW1 Brandon Weeden SP	12.00	30.00
BW2 Bobby Wagner	4.00	10.00
CG1 Chris Givens	3.00	8.00
CG2 Cyrus Gray SP	4.00	10.00
CG3 Chris Galippo	3.00	8.00
CH2 Casey Hayward	4.00	10.00
CH3 Cliff Harris	4.00	10.00
CJ1 Chandler Jones	4.00	10.00
CJ2 Coryell Judie	3.00	8.00
CP1 Chris Polk SP	5.00	12.00
CU1 Courtney Upshaw SP	5.00	12.00
DA1 Dwayne Allen SP	4.00	10.00
DAL D'Anton Lynn	4.00	10.00
DDC David DeCastro	5.00	12.00
DF1 Donnie Fletcher	2.50	6.00
DH1 Dan Herron	4.00	10.00
DH2 Dont'a Hightower SP		
DI1 Duke Ihenacho	2.50	6.00
DK1 Dre Kirkpatrick	6.00	15.00
DM2 Doug Martin SP	6.00	15.00
DM3 Derek Moye	4.00	10.00
DP1 Dan Persa	3.00	8.00
DP2 DeVier Posey SP	4.00	10.00
DS1 Devon Still SP	4.00	10.00
DT1 Darron Thomas SP	6.00	15.00
DW1 Devon Wylie	4.00	10.00
FW1 Fozzy Whittaker	4.00	10.00
GC1 Greg Childs	4.00	10.00
GI1 George Iloka	3.00	8.00
GR1 Gerell Robinson	4.00	10.00
HS1 Harrison Smith	4.00	10.00
IP1 Isaiah Pead SP	4.00	10.00
JA1 Joe Adams SP	4.00	10.00
JB2 Justin Blackmon SP	25.00	50.00
JC1 Jared Crick	4.00	10.00
JF1 Jeff Fuller SP	5.00	12.00
JH1 Jacory Harris SP	3.00	8.00
JH2 Jerrell Harris	3.00	8.00
JJ1 Janoris Jenkins	4.00	10.00
JK1 Josh Kaddu	3.00	8.00
JM1 Jonathan Martin	3.00	8.00
JMJ James-Michael Johnson	3.00	8.00
JN1 Josh Norman	2.50	6.00
JW1 Jarius Wright	4.00	10.00
KC1 Kirk Cousins SP	6.00	15.00
KK1 Kevin Koger	4.00	10.00
KM1 Kellen Moore SP	6.00	15.00
KM2 Keshawn Martin	4.00	10.00
KR1 Keenan Robinson	3.00	8.00
KR2 Kendall Reyes	3.00	8.00
LD1 Lavonte David	5.00	12.00
LJ1 LaMichael James	8.00	20.00
LJ2 Leonard Johnson	3.00	8.00
LK1 Luke Kuechly SP	5.00	12.00
LN1 Lucas Nix	2.50	6.00
MB1 Mark Barron SP	6.00	15.00
ME1 Michael Egnew	3.00	8.00
MF1 Michael Floyd SP	12.00	30.00
MF1 Marcus Forston	3.00	8.00
MI1 Melvin Ingram SP	5.00	12.00
MJ1 Marvin Jones	3.00	8.00
MM1 Marquis Maze SP	4.00	10.00
MM2 Markelle Martin	3.00	8.00
MM3 Mike Martin	4.00	10.00
MS1 Mohamed Sanu SP	4.00	10.00
MT1 Marc Tyler SP	4.00	10.00
NB1 Nigel Bradham	3.00	8.00
NF1 Nick Foles SP	6.00	15.00
NP1 Nick Perry SP	4.00	10.00
NT1 Nick Toon SP	5.00	12.00
OC1 Orson Charles	4.00	10.00
PK1 Peter Konz	2.50	6.00
PW1 Patrick Witt	3.00	8.00
RB1 Ryan Broyles SP		
RB2 Robert Blanton	3.00	8.00
RE1 Rhett Ellison	3.00	8.00
RG3 Robert Griffin III SP	60.00	120.00
RS1 Ryan Steed	2.50	6.00
RT1 Robert Turbin SP	4.00	10.00
RT2 Ryan Tannehill SP	10.00	25.00
SG1 Stephon Gilmore SP	4.00	10.00
SH1 Stephen Hill SP	4.00	10.00
SM1 Shea McClellin	5.00	12.00
SP1 Shaun Prater	4.00	10.00
SS1 Sean Spence	3.00	8.00
TB1 Tim Benford	2.50	6.00
TG1 Terrance Ganaway SP	3.00	8.00
TG2 Trevor Guyton	3.00	8.00
TH1 Tyler Hansen	3.00	8.00
TL1 Travis Lewis	3.00	8.00
TM1 Thomas Mayo	2.50	6.00
TP1 Tauren Poole SP	3.00	8.00
TP2 Tydreke Powell	2.50	6.00
TR1 Trent Richardson SP	25.00	50.00
TR2 Trenton Robinson	3.00	8.00
TYH T.Y. Hilton SP	4.00	10.00
WM1 Whitney Mercilus SP	4.00	10.00
ZB1 Zach Brown	3.00	8.00
ZS1 Zebrie Sanders	2.50	6.00

2012 Leaf Draft Garden State Promos

NJPR1 Robert Griffin III	8.00	20.00
NJPR3 Trent Richardson	5.00	12.00

2012 Leaf Draft Robert Griffin

COMPLETE SET (3)	3.00	8.00
COMMON GRIFFIN (1-3)	1.00	2.50
ONE SET PER FACTORY SET		

2011 Leaf Metal Draft

UNPRICED GOLD PRINT RUN 1		
UNPRICED RED PRINT RUN 5		
RCAA1 Anthony Allen	3.00	8.00
RCAB1 Armon Binns	4.00	10.00
RCAD1 Andy Dalton	20.00	40.00
RCAJG A.J. Green	20.00	50.00
RCAP1 Austin Pettis	4.00	10.00
RCAS1 Aldon Smith	6.00	15.00
RCAW1 Aaron Williams	4.00	10.00
RCBG1 Blaine Gabbert	20.00	50.00
RCBP1 Bilal Powell	3.00	8.00
RCCH1 Cameron Heyward	5.00	12.00
RCCK1 Colin Kaepernick	15.00	40.00
RCCM1 Casey Matthews	5.00	12.00
RCCN1 Cam Newton	75.00	150.00
RCCP1 Christian Ponder	15.00	40.00
RCDA1 Darvin Adams	4.00	10.00
RCDB1 Damien Berry	4.00	10.00
RCDC1 Delone Carter	4.00	10.00
RCDH1 Dwayne Harris	5.00	12.00
RCDJW D.J. Williams	5.00	12.00
RCDL1 Derrick Locke	4.00	10.00
RCDL2 Dion Lewis	5.00	12.00
RCDM1 DeMarco Murray	20.00	40.00
RCDQB Da'Quan Bowers	5.00	12.00
RCDT1 Daniel Thomas	8.00	20.00
RCER1 Evan Royster	5.00	12.00
RCGC1 Graig Cooper	4.00	10.00
RCGL1 Greg Little	5.00	12.00
RCGM1 Greg McElroy	8.00	20.00
RCGS1 Greg Salas	5.00	12.00
RCJB1 Jonathan Baldwin	5.00	12.00
RCJC1 John Clay	5.00	12.00
RCJH1 Jamie Harper	5.00	12.00
RCJH2 Justin Houston	5.00	12.00
RCJJ1 Jerrel Jernigan	4.00	10.00
RCJJ2 Julio Jones	25.00	50.00
RCJJW J.J. Watt	6.00	15.00
RCJL1 Jake Locker	30.00	60.00
RCJT1 Jordan Todman	3.00	8.00
RCKH1 Kendall Hunter	5.00	12.00
RCKR1 Kyle Rudolph	5.00	12.00
RCLH1 Leonard Hankerson	5.00	12.00
RCLS1 Luke Stocker	4.00	10.00
RCMD1 Marcell Dareus	5.00	12.00
RCMH1 Mark Herzlich	4.00	10.00
RCMI1 Mark Ingram	25.00	50.00
RCML1 Mikel Leshoure	5.00	12.00
RCNE1 Nathan Enderle	5.00	12.00
RCNF1 Nick Fairley	6.00	15.00
RCNP1 Niles Paul	5.00	12.00
RCPA1 Prince Amukamara	5.00	12.00
RCPD1 Pat Devlin	5.00	12.00
RCRC1 Randall Cobb	10.00	25.00
RCRH1 Roy Helu	10.00	25.00
RCRJ1 Ronald Johnson	6.00	15.00
RCRM1 Ryan Mallett SP	20.00	40.00
RCRQ1 Robert Quinn	6.00	15.00
RCRS1 Ricky Stanzi	12.00	30.00
RCRW1 Ryan Williams	10.00	25.00
RCSR1 Stevan Ridley	5.00	12.00
RCSV1 Shane Vereen	5.00	12.00
RCTD1 Tandon Doss	4.00	10.00
RCTJY T.J. Yates	6.00	15.00
RCTS1 Torrey Smith	6.00	15.00
RCTT1 Terrence Toliver	4.00	10.00
RCTT2 Tyrod Taylor	5.00	12.00
RCTY1 Titus Young	6.00	15.00
RCVB1 Vincent Brown	5.00	12.00
RCVM1 Von Miller	8.00	20.00
RCWB1 Wes Bynum	10.00	25.00

2011 Leaf Metal Draft Prismatic Blue

*BLUE/25: .6X TO 1.5X BASIC AUTO
BLUE STATED PRINT RUN 25

2011 Leaf Metal Draft Prismatic Silver

*SILVER/50: .5X TO 1.2X BASIC AUTO
SILVER STATED PRINT RUN 50

2011 Leaf Metal Draft All-Americans

STATED PRINT RUN 50 SER.#'d SETS		
UNPRICED BLUE PRINT RUN 10		
UNPRICED GOLD PRINT RUN 1		
UNPRICED RED PRINT RUN 5		
*SILVER/25: .5X TO 1.2X BASIC INSERTS		
AAAJG A.J. Green	20.00	50.00
AADM1 DeMarco Murray	25.00	50.00
AADQB Da'Quan Bowers	6.00	15.00
AAJJ2 Julio Jones	25.00	60.00
AAJL1 Jake Locker	40.00	80.00
AAMD1 Marcell Dareus	6.00	15.00
AAMI1 Mark Ingram	30.00	60.00
AAML1 Mikel Leshoure	6.00	15.00
AANF1 Nick Fairley	8.00	20.00
AARM1 Ryan Mallett	25.00	60.00

2011 Leaf Metal Draft Touchdown Kings

STATED PRINT RUN 50 SER.#'d SETS		
UNPRICED BLUE PRINT RUN 10		
UNPRICED GOLD PRINT RUN 1		
UNPRICED RED PRINT RUN 5		
*SILVER/25: .5X TO 1.2X BASIC INSERTS		
TKAJG A.J. Green	25.00	50.00
TKDM1 DeMarco Murray	25.00	50.00
TKJB1 Jonathan Baldwin	6.00	15.00
TKJC1 John Clay	6.00	15.00
TKJJ2 Julio Jones	25.00	50.00
TKJT1 Jordan Todman	4.00	10.00
TKLH1 Leonard Hankerson	6.00	15.00
TKMI1 Mark Ingram	30.00	60.00
TKML1 Mikel Leshoure	6.00	15.00
TKSV1 Shane Vereen	6.00	15.00
TKTS1 Torrey Smith	8.00	20.00

2011 Leaf Metal Draft Young Guns

STATED PRINT RUN 50 SER.#'d SETS		
UNPRICED BLUE PRINT RUN 10		
UNPRICED GOLD PRINT RUN 1		
UNPRICED RED PRINT RUN 5		
*SILVER/25: .5X TO 1.2X BASIC INSERTS		
YGAD1 Andy Dalton	25.00	50.00
YGBG1 Blaine Gabbert	25.00	50.00
YGCK1 Colin Kaepernick	20.00	40.00
YGCN1 Cam Newton	100.00	200.00
YGCP1 Christian Ponder	25.00	50.00
YGJL1 Jake Locker	30.00	60.00
YGNE1 Nathan Enderle	6.00	15.00
YGPD1 Pat Devlin	6.00	15.00
YGRM1 Ryan Mallett	25.00	50.00

2012 Leaf Metal Draft

AB1 Andre Branch	4.00	10.00
AC1 Aaron Corp	4.00	10.00
AD1 Alfonzo Dennard	5.00	12.00
AJ1 Alshon Jeffery	8.00	20.00
AJJ A.J. Jenkins	6.00	15.00
BJC B.J. Cunningham	4.00	10.00
BO1 Brock Osweiler	6.00	15.00
BP1 Bernard Pierce	5.00	12.00
BQ1 Brian Quick	6.00	15.00
BT1 Brandon Thompson	4.00	10.00
BW1 Brandon Weeden	15.00	30.00
CF1 Coby Fleener	6.00	15.00
CG1 Chris Givens	4.00	10.00
CG2 Cyrus Gray	5.00	12.00
CH1 Chandler Harnish	5.00	12.00
CJ1 Chandler Jones	5.00	12.00
CK1 Case Keenum	6.00	15.00
CP1 Chris Polk	6.00	15.00
CU1 Courtney Upshaw	6.00	15.00
DA1 Dwayne Allen	5.00	12.00
DH1 Dan Herron	5.00	12.00
DH2 Dont'a Hightower	8.00	20.00
DK1 Dre Kirkpatrick	8.00	20.00
DM2 Doug Martin	8.00	20.00
DP1 Dan Persa	4.00	10.00
DP2 DeVier Posey	5.00	12.00
DS1 Devon Still	5.00	12.00
DT1 Darron Thomas	8.00	20.00
GR1 Gerell Robinson	5.00	12.00
IP1 Isaiah Pead	5.00	12.00
JA1 Joe Adams	5.00	12.00
JB2 Justin Blackmon	15.00	40.00
JC1 Jared Crick	5.00	12.00
JC2 Juron Criner	4.00	10.00
JF1 Jeff Fuller	6.00	15.00
JH1 Jacory Harris	4.00	10.00
JW1 Jarius Wright	5.00	12.00
KC1 Kirk Cousins	8.00	20.00
KM1 Kellen Moore	8.00	20.00
KM2 Keshawn Martin	5.00	12.00
KR1 Keenan Robinson	4.00	10.00
KW1 Kendall Wright	6.00	15.00
LD1 Lavonte David	6.00	15.00
LJ1 LaMichael James	12.00	30.00
LK1 Luke Kuechly	6.00	15.00
LM1 Lamar Miller	8.00	20.00
MB1 Mark Barron	8.00	20.00
ME1 Michael Egnew	4.00	10.00
MF1 Michael Floyd	10.00	25.00
MI1 Melvin Ingram	6.00	15.00
MJ1 Marvin Jones	4.00	10.00
MK1 Matt Kalil	6.00	15.00
MM1 Marquis Maze	5.00	12.00
MS1 Mohamed Sanu	5.00	12.00
MT1 Marc Tyler	5.00	12.00
NF1 Nick Foles	8.00	20.00
NP1 Nick Perry	5.00	12.00
NT1 Nick Toon	6.00	15.00
OC1 Orson Charles	5.00	12.00
QC1 Quinton Coples	5.00	12.00
RB1 Ryan Broyles	5.00	12.00
RG3 Robert Griffin III	60.00	120.00
RL2 Ryan Lindley	5.00	12.00
RR1 Rueben Randle	5.00	12.00
RT1 Robert Turbin	5.00	12.00
RT2 Ryan Tannehill	15.00	40.00
RW1 Russell Wilson	8.00	20.00
SG1 Stephon Gilmore	5.00	12.00
SH1 Stephen Hill	5.00	12.00
TG1 Terrance Ganaway	4.00	10.00
TL1 Travis Lewis	4.00	10.00
TP1 Tauren Poole	4.00	10.00
TR1 Trent Richardson	30.00	60.00
TS1 Tommy Streeter	5.00	12.00
TYH T.Y. Hilton	5.00	12.00
WM1 Whitney Mercilus	5.00	12.00
ZB1 Zach Brown	4.00	10.00

2012 Leaf Metal Draft Prismatic Blue

*PRISM BLUE/25: .6X TO 1.5X BASIC AU		
RG3 Robert Griffin III	200.00	400.00
RT2 Ryan Tannehill	60.00	120.00
TR1 Trent Richardson	60.00	120.00

2012 Leaf Metal Draft Prismatic Purple

*PRISM PURPLE/25: .6X TO 1.5X BASIC AU		
RG3 Robert Griffin III	200.00	400.00
RT2 Ryan Tannehill	60.00	120.00
TR1 Trent Richardson	60.00	120.00

2012 Leaf Metal Draft Prismatic Silver

*PRISM SILVER/99: .5X TO 1.2X BASIC AU		
RG3 Robert Griffin III	100.00	200.00

2012 Leaf Metal Draft Army All-American Bowl Prismatic Silver

AUTO STATED PRINT RUN 50		
*BASE LUCK: .1X TO .3X SLVR/99		
*PRISM PRPL LUCK/25: 1X TO 2.5X SLVR/99		
*PRISM BLUE LUCK/25: 1X TO 2.5X SLVR/99		
*PRISM GREEN AU/25: .5X TO 1.2X SLVR/50		
ATAAA1 Anthony Alford AU	8.00	20.00
ATAAA2 Arik Armstead AU	10.00	25.00
ATAAL1 Andrew Luck/99	40.00	80.00
ATABM1 Byron Marshall AU	8.00	20.00
ATABS1 Barry Sanders Jr. AU	50.00	100.00
ATACM1 Cyler Miles AU	10.00	25.00
ATADF1 Devin Fuller AU	6.00	15.00
ATADGB Dorial Green-Beckham AU	30.00	60.00
ATADN1 Durron Neal AU	10.00	25.00
ATADS1 Dwayne Stanford AU	8.00	20.00
ATADW2 Derrick Woods AU	8.00	20.00
ATAGH1 Germone Hopper AU	8.00	20.00
ATAGK1 Gunner Kiel AU	40.00	80.00
ATAJC1 Joel Caleb AU	10.00	25.00
ATAJP1 Jordan Payton AU	10.00	25.00
ATAKR1 Kei'Varae Russell AU	10.00	25.00
ATAKT1 Kent Taylor AU	10.00	25.00
ATASD1 Stefon Diggs AU	12.00	30.00
ATATJY T.J. Yeldon AU	15.00	40.00
ATATM1 Tyler Matthews AU	10.00	25.00

2011 Leaf Ultimate Draft

STATED PRINT RUN 49 SER.#'d SETS		
*GOLD/20: .5X TO 1.2X BASIC CARDS		
UNPRICED PURPLE PRINT RUN 5		
UNPRICED RED PRINT RUN 1		
UAA1 Anthony Allen	4.00	10.00
UAB1 Armon Binns	5.00	12.00
UAD1 Andy Dalton	25.00	50.00
UAJG A.J. Green	25.00	50.00
UAP1 Austin Pettis	5.00	12.00
UAS1 Aldon Smith	8.00	20.00
UAW1 Aaron Williams	5.00	12.00
UBG1 Blaine Gabbert	20.00	40.00
UBP1 Bilal Powell	4.00	10.00
UCH1 Cameron Heyward	6.00	15.00
UCK1 Colin Kaepernick	12.00	30.00
UCM1 Casey Matthews	6.00	15.00
UCN1 Cam Newton	90.00	150.00
UCP1 Christian Ponder	25.00	50.00
UDA1 Darvin Adams	5.00	12.00
UDB1 Damien Berry	5.00	12.00
UDC1 Delone Carter	5.00	12.00
UDH1 Dwayne Harris	6.00	15.00
UDJW D.J. Williams	6.00	15.00
UDL1 Derrick Locke	5.00	12.00
UDL2 Dion Lewis	6.00	15.00
UDM1 DeMarco Murray	25.00	50.00
UDQB Da'Quan Bowers	6.00	15.00
UER1 Evan Royster	6.00	15.00
UGC1 Graig Cooper	5.00	12.00
UGL1 Greg Little	6.00	15.00
UGM1 Greg McElroy	12.00	30.00
UGS1 Gregory Salas	6.00	15.00
UJB1 Jonathan Baldwin	6.00	15.00
UJC1 John Clay	6.00	15.00
UJH1 Jamie Harper	6.00	15.00
UJH2 Justin Houston	6.00	15.00
UJJ1 Jerrel Jernigan	5.00	12.00
UJJ2 Julio Jones	25.00	50.00
UJJW J.J. Watt	8.00	20.00
UJL1 Jake Locker	30.00	60.00
UJT1 Jordan Todman	4.00	10.00
UKH1 Kendall Hunter	8.00	20.00
UKR1 Kyle Rudolph	6.00	15.00
ULH1 Leonard Hankerson	6.00	15.00
ULS1 Luke Stocker	5.00	12.00
UMD1 Marcell Dareus	6.00	15.00
UMH1 Mark Herzlich	5.00	12.00
UMI1 Mark Ingram	25.00	50.00
UML1 Mikel Leshoure	6.00	15.00
UNE1 Nathan Enderle	6.00	15.00
UNF1 Nick Fairley	8.00	20.00
UNP1 Niles Paul	6.00	15.00
UPA1 Prince Amukamara	6.00	15.00
UPD1 Pat Devlin	6.00	15.00
UPP1 Patrick Peterson	30.00	60.00
URC1 Randall Cobb	12.00	30.00
URH1 Roy Helu	12.00	30.00
URJ1 Ronald Johnson	8.00	20.00
URM1 Ryan Mallett	20.00	40.00
URQ1 Robert Quinn	6.00	15.00
URS1 Ricky Stanzi	15.00	40.00
URW1 Ryan Williams	12.00	30.00
USR1 Stevan Ridley	6.00	15.00
USV1 Shane Vereen	6.00	15.00
UTD1 Tandon Doss	5.00	12.00
UTS1 Torrey Smith	8.00	20.00
UTT1 Terrence Toliver	5.00	12.00
UTT2 Tyrod Taylor	6.00	15.00
UTY1 Titus Young	8.00	20.00
UTYY T.J. Yates	8.00	20.00
UVB1 Vincent Brown	6.00	15.00
UVM1 Von Miller	8.00	20.00
UWB1 Wes Bynum	6.00	15.00

2011 Leaf Ultimate Draft Football Die Cuts

*FB DIE CUT/49: .4X TO 1X BASIC CARD/49		
STATED PRINT RUN 49 SER.#'d SETS		
*GOLD FB/20: .5X TO 1.2X BASIC CARD/49		
UNPRICED PURPLE PRINT RUN 5		
UNPRICED RED PRINT RUN 1		
FBCN1 Cam Newton	60.00	120.00

2011 Leaf Ultimate Draft Helmet Die Cuts

*HELMET DC/49: .4X TO 1X BASIC CARD/49		
STATED PRINT RUN 49 SER.#'d SETS		
*GOLD HEL/20: .5X TO 1.2X BASIC CARD/49		
UNPRICED PURPLE PRINT RUN 5		
UNPRICED RED PRINT RUN 1		
HCN1 Cam Newton	60.00	120.00

2011 Leaf Ultimate Draft Metal

*METAL/49: .4X TO 1X BASIC CARD/49		
STATED PRINT RUN 49 SER.#'d SETS		
*BLUE/20: .5X TO 1.2X BASIC CARD/49		
UNPRICED PRISM RED PRINT RUN 5		
UNPRICED PRISM SLVR PRINT RUN 1		
UCN1 Cam Newton	90.00	150.00

2012 Leaf Ultimate Draft

AJ1 Alshon Jeffery	8.00	20.00
BO1 Brock Osweiler	8.00	20.00
BP1 Bernard Pierce	5.00	12.00
BQ1 Brian Quick	6.00	15.00
BW1 Brandon Weeden	15.00	40.00
CF1 Coby Fleener	6.00	15.00
CG1 Chris Givens	4.00	10.00
CP1 Chris Polk	6.00	15.00
CU1 Courtney Upshaw	6.00	15.00
DA1 Dwayne Allen	5.00	12.00
DDC David DeCastro	6.00	15.00
DM2 Doug Martin	8.00	20.00
DP3 Dontari Poe	5.00	12.00
DS1 Devon Still	5.00	12.00
FC1 Fletcher Cox	5.00	12.00
IP1 Isaiah Pead	6.00	15.00
JA1 Joe Adams	5.00	12.00
JB2 Justin Blackmon	15.00	40.00
JC2 Juron Criner	4.00	10.00
JJ1 Janoris Jenkins	5.00	12.00
JM1 Jonathan Martin	4.00	10.00
KC1 Kirk Cousins	8.00	20.00
KW1 Kendall Wright	6.00	15.00
LJ1 LaMichael James	10.00	25.00
LK1 Luke Kuechly	6.00	15.00
LM1 Lamar Miller	8.00	20.00
MB1 Mark Barron EXCH	8.00	20.00
MF1 Michael Floyd	10.00	25.00
MI1 Melvin Ingram	6.00	15.00
MJ1 Marvin Jones	4.00	10.00
MS1 Mohamed Sanu	5.00	12.00
NF1 Nick Foles	8.00	20.00
NP1 Nick Perry	5.00	12.00
NT1 Nick Toon	6.00	15.00
OC1 Orson Charles	5.00	12.00
QC1 Quinton Coples	5.00	12.00
RG3 Robert Griffin III	75.00	150.00
RR1 Rueben Randle	5.00	12.00
RT1 Robert Turbin	5.00	12.00
RT2 Ryan Tannehill	12.00	30.00
RW1 Russell Wilson	8.00	20.00
SG1 Stephon Gilmore	5.00	12.00
SH1 Stephen Hill	5.00	12.00
TR1 Trent Richardson	30.00	60.00
WM1 Whitney Mercilus	5.00	12.00

2012 Leaf Ultimate Draft Silver

*SILVER/25: .6X TO 1.5X BASIC CARDS		
STATED PRINT RUN 25 SER.#'d SETS		
RG3 Robert Griffin III	100.00	200.00

2012 Leaf Ultimate Draft Inscriptions

*INSCRIPTION/25: .8X TO 2X BASIC CARDS		
STATED PRINT RUN 25 SER.#'d SETS		
RG3 Robert Griffin III	175.00	300.00
TR1 Trent Richardson	75.00	150.00

2012 Leaf Ultimate Draft Numeration

STATED PRINT RUN 6-41		
NUBO1 Brock Osweiler/17	15.00	40.00
NUBP1 Bernard Pierce/30	10.00	25.00
NUCU1 Courtney Upshaw/41	12.00	30.00
NUDM2 Doug Martin/22	25.00	50.00
NUIP1 Isaiah Pead/23	12.00	30.00
NULJ1 LaMichael James/21	30.00	60.00
NULK1 Luke Kuechly/40	12.00	30.00
NURT2 Ryan Tannehill/17	30.00	80.00
NURW1 Russell Wilson/16	20.00	50.00

2012 Leaf Ultimate Draft TD Countdown

STATED PRINT RUN 8-37		
TDCBP1 Bernard Pierce/27	12.00	30.00
TDCBW1 Brandon Weeden/37	20.00	50.00
TDCDM2 Doug Martin/16	20.00	50.00
TDCIP1 Isaiah Pead/15	12.00	30.00
TDCJB2 Justin Blackmon/18	25.00	60.00
TDCKC1 Kirk Cousins/25	20.00	50.00
TDCLJ1 LaMichael James/18	25.00	60.00
TDCNF1 Nick Foles/28	20.00	50.00
TDCRT1 Robert Turbin/19	12.00	30.00
TDCRW1 Russell Wilson/33	15.00	40.00
TDCTR1 Trent Richardson/24	50.00	100.00

2012 Leaf Valiant Draft

AB1 Andre Branch	4.00	10.00
AC1 Aaron Corp	4.00	10.00
AD1 Alfonzo Dennard	5.00	12.00
AJ1 Alshon Jeffery	8.00	20.00
AJJ A.J. Jenkins	6.00	15.00
BJC B.J. Cunningham	4.00	10.00
BO1 Brock Osweiler	6.00	15.00
BP1 Bernard Pierce	5.00	12.00
BQ1 Brian Quick	6.00	15.00
BR1 Bobby Rainey	5.00	12.00
BT1 Brandon Thompson	4.00	10.00
BW1 Brandon Weeden	12.00	30.00
CF1 Coby Fleener	6.00	15.00
CG1 Chris Givens	4.00	10.00
CG2 Cyrus Gray	5.00	12.00
CH1 Chandler Harnish	5.00	12.00
CJ1 Chandler Jones	5.00	12.00
CK1 Case Keenum	6.00	15.00
CP1 Chris Polk	6.00	15.00
CU1 Courtney Upshaw	6.00	15.00
DA1 Dwayne Allen	5.00	12.00
DH1 Dan Herron	5.00	12.00
DH2 Dont'a Hightower	8.00	20.00
DJ1 Dwight Jones	4.00	10.00
DK1 Dre Kirkpatrick	8.00	20.00
DM2 Doug Martin	8.00	20.00
DP1 Dan Persa	4.00	10.00
DP2 DeVier Posey	5.00	12.00
DP3 Dontari Poe	5.00	12.00
DS1 Devon Still	5.00	12.00
DT1 Darron Thomas	8.00	20.00
FC1 Fletcher Cox	5.00	12.00
GC1 Greg Childs	5.00	12.00
GR1 Gerell Robinson	5.00	12.00
IP1 Isaiah Pead	5.00	12.00
JA1 Joe Adams	5.00	12.00
JB2 Justin Blackmon	15.00	30.00
JC2 Juron Criner	4.00	10.00
JF1 Jeff Fuller	6.00	15.00
JH1 Jacory Harris	4.00	10.00
JJ1 Janoris Jenkins	5.00	12.00
JW1 Jarius Wright	5.00	12.00
KC1 Kirk Cousins	8.00	20.00
KM1 Kellen Moore	8.00	20.00
KM2 Keshawn Martin	5.00	12.00
KR1 Keenan Robinson	4.00	10.00
KW1 Kendall Wright	6.00	15.00
LD1 Lavonte David	6.00	15.00
LJ1 LaMichael James	8.00	20.00
LK1 Luke Kuechly	6.00	15.00
LM1 Lamar Miller	8.00	20.00
MB1 Mark Barron	8.00	20.00
ME1 Michael Egnew	4.00	10.00
MF1 Michael Floyd	10.00	25.00
MI1 Melvin Ingram	6.00	15.00
MJ1 Marvin Jones	4.00	10.00
MM1 Marquis Maze	5.00	12.00
MS1 Mohamed Sanu	5.00	12.00
MT1 Marc Tyler	5.00	12.00
NF1 Nick Foles	8.00	20.00
NP1 Nick Perry	5.00	12.00
NT1 Nick Toon	6.00	15.00
OC1 Orson Charles	5.00	12.00
QC1 Quinton Coples	5.00	12.00
RB1 Ryan Broyles	6.00	15.00
RG3 Robert Griffin III	75.00	150.00
RL2 Ryan Lindley	5.00	12.00
RR1 Rueben Randle	5.00	12.00
RT1 Robert Turbin	5.00	12.00
RT2 Ryan Tannehill	15.00	40.00
RW1 Russell Wilson	8.00	20.00
SG1 Stephon Gilmore	5.00	12.00
SH1 Stephen Hill	5.00	12.00
TG1 Terrance Ganaway	4.00	10.00
TL1 Travis Lewis	4.00	10.00
TP1 Tauren Poole	4.00	10.00
TR1 Trent Richardson	30.00	60.00
TS1 Tommy Streeter	5.00	12.00
TYH T.Y. Hilton	5.00	12.00
WM1 Whitney Mercilus	5.00	12.00
ZB1 Zach Brown	4.00	10.00

2012 Leaf Valiant Draft Blue

*BLUE/99: .5X TO 1.2X BASIC CARDS		
BLUE STATED PRINT RUN 99		
RG3 Robert Griffin III	75.00	150.00

2012 Leaf Valiant Draft Purple

*PURPLE/25: .6X TO 1.5X BASIC CARD		
PURPLE STATED PRINT RUN 25		
RG3 Robert Griffin III	150.00	250.00
RT2 Ryan Tannehill	40.00	80.00
TR1 Trent Richardson	50.00	100.00

2012 Leaf Valiant Draft Army All-American Bowl Black

*BLACK/20-25: 1.5X TO 4X BASIC GREEN		
AL1 Andrew Luck/25	100.00	175.00

2012 Leaf Valiant Draft Army All-American Bowl Green

RANDOM INSERTS IN PACKS		
*BLUE: .5X TO 1.2X BASIC GREEN		
*PURPLE/100-125: .8X TO 2X BASIC GREEN		
*YELLOW/40-50: 1.2X TO 3X BASIC GREEN		
AL1 Andrew Luck	10.00	25.00
BS1 Barry Sanders Jr.	3.00	8.00
GK1 Gunner Kiel	2.50	6.00

2012 Leaf Young Stars Draft

COMPLETE SET (100)	10.00	25.00
1 A.J. Jenkins	.30	.75
2 Alameda Ta'amu	.30	.75
3 Alfonzo Dennard	.25	.60
4 Alshon Jeffery	.40	1.00
5 Amini Silatolu	.15	.40
6 Andre Branch	.20	.50
7 Audie Cole	.20	.50
8 B.J. Cunningham	.20	.50
9 Bernard Pierce	.25	.60
10 Bobby Massie	.15	.40
11 Bobby Wagner	.25	.60
12 Brandon Mosley	.15	.40
13 Brandon Thompson	.20	.50
14 Brandon Weeden	.50	1.25
15 Brian Quick	.30	.75
16 Casey Hayward	.25	.60
17 Chandler Jones	.25	.60
18 Chris Givens	.20	.50
19 Chris Polk	.30	.75
20 Cliff Harris	.25	.60
21 Coby Fleener	.30	.75
22 Coryell Judie	.20	.50
23 Courtney Upshaw	.30	.75
24 Cyrus Gray	.25	.60
25 D'Anton Lynn	.25	.60
26 Dan Herron	.25	.60
27 David DeCastro	.30	.75
28 DeVier Posey	.25	.60
29 Devon Still	.25	.60
30 Devon Wylie	.25	.60
31 Dont'a Hightower	.40	1.00
32 Donnie Fletcher	.15	.40
33 Dontari Poe	.25	.60
34 Doug Martin	.40	1.00
35 Dre Kirkpatrick	.40	1.00
36 Duke Ihenacho	.15	.40
37 Dwight Jones	.20	.50
38 George Iloka	.20	.50
39 Greg Childs	.25	.60
40 Harrison Smith	.25	.60
41 Janoris Jenkins	.25	.60
42 Jared Crick	.25	.60
43 Jarius Wright	.25	.60
44 Jerrell Harris	.20	.50
45 Joe Adams	.25	.60
46 Jonathan Martin	.20	.50
47 Juron Criner	.20	.50
48 Justin Blackmon	.50	1.25
49 Keenan Robinson	.20	.50
50 Kendall Wright	.30	.75
51 Kirk Cousins	.40	1.00
52 Lamar Miller	.30	.75
53 LaMichael James	.50	1.25
54 Lavonte David	.30	.75
55 Lucas Nix	.15	.40
56 Luke Kuechly	.30	.75
57 Marcus Forston	.20	.50
58 Mark Barron	.40	1.00
59 Markelle Martin	.20	.50
60 Marvin Jones	.20	.50
61 Matt Kalil	.30	.75
62 Melvin Ingram	.30	.75
63 Michael Egnew	.20	.50
64 Michael Floyd	.50	1.25
65 Mike Martin	.25	.60
66 Mohamed Sanu	.25	.60
67 Nick Perry	.25	.60
68 Nick Toon	.30	.75
69 Nigel Bradham	.20	.50
70 Orson Charles	.25	.60
71 Peter Konz	.15	.40
72 Quinton Coples	.25	.60
73 Rhett Ellison	.20	.50
74 Robert Blanton	.20	.50
75 Robert Griffin III	2.00	5.00
76 Rueben Randle	.25	.60
77 Russell Wilson	.40	1.00
78 Ryan Broyles	.25	.60
79 Ryan Tannehill	.60	1.50
80 Sean Spence	.20	.50
81 Shea McClellin	.30	.75
82 Stephen Hill	.20	.50
83 Thomas Mayo	.15	.40
84 Tommy Streeter	.25	.60
85 Travis Lewis	.20	.50
86 Trent Richardson	.75	2.00
87 Trenton Robinson	.20	.50
88 Tydreke Powell	.15	.40
89 Whitney Mercilus	.25	.60
90 Zach Brown	.20	.50
91 Zebrie Sanders	.15	.40
92 Antwon Bailey	.20	.50
93 Bobby Rainey	.25	.60
94 Chris Galippo	.20	.50
95 Dwayne Allen	.25	.60
96 Gerell Robinson	.25	.60
97 Keshawn Martin	.25	.60
98 Kevin Koger	.25	.60
99 Tim Benford	.15	.40
100 Tyler Hansen	.20	.50

2012 Leaf Young Stars Draft Autographs

TWO AUTOS PER RETAIL BOX		
AB1 Andre Branch	2.50	6.00
AC2 Audie Cole	2.50	6.00
AD1 Alfonzo Dennard	3.00	8.00
AJ1 Alshon Jeffery SP		
AJJ A.J. Jenkins SP		
AS1 Amini Silatolu	2.00	5.00
AT1 Alameda Ta'amu	4.00	10.00
BJC B.J. Cunningham SP		
BM1 Bobby Massie	2.00	5.00
BM2 Brandon Mosley	2.00	5.00
BP1 Bernard Pierce SP		
BQ1 Brian Quick SP		
BR1 Bobby Rainey	3.00	8.00
BT1 Brandon Thompson	2.50	6.00
BW1 Brandon Weeden SP		
BW2 Bobby Wagner	3.00	8.00
CF1 Coby Fleener SP		
CG1 Chris Givens SP		
CG2 Cyrus Gray SP		
CH2 Casey Hayward	3.00	8.00
CH3 Cliff Harris	3.00	8.00
CJ1 Chandler Jones SP	4.00	10.00
CJ2 Coryell Judie	2.50	6.00
CP1 Chris Polk SP		
DA1 Dwayne Allen	3.00	8.00
DAL D'Anton Lynn	3.00	8.00
DDC David DeCastro	4.00	10.00
DF1 Donnie Fletcher	2.00	5.00
DH1 Dan Herron	3.00	8.00
DH2 Dont'a Hightower SP		
DI1 Duke Ihenacho	2.00	5.00
DJ1 Dwight Jones SP		
DK1 Dre Kirkpatrick	5.00	12.00
DM2 Doug Martin SP		
DP1 Dan Persa	2.50	6.00
DP2 DeVier Posey SP		
DP3 Dontari Poe SP		
DS1 Devon Still SP		
DW1 Devon Wylie	3.00	8.00
FW1 Fozzy Whittaker	3.00	8.00
GC1 Greg Childs	3.00	8.00
GI1 George Iloka	2.50	6.00
GR1 Gerell Robinson	3.00	8.00
HS1 Harrison Smith	3.00	8.00
JA1 Joe Adams SP		
JB2 Justin Blackmon SP		
JC2 Juron Criner SP		
JH1 Jerrell Harris	2.50	6.00
JJ1 Janoris Jenkins SP		
JM1 Jonathan Martin	2.50	6.00
JW1 Jarius Wright	3.00	8.00
KC1 Kirk Cousins SP		
KK1 Kevin Koger	3.00	8.00
KM2 Keshawn Martin	3.00	8.00
KR1 Keenan Robinson	2.50	6.00
KW1 Kendall Wright SP		
LD1 Lavonte David	4.00	10.00
LJ1 LaMichael James	8.00	20.00
LK1 Luke Kuechly SP		
LM1 Lamar Miller SP		
LN1 Lucas Nix	2.00	5.00
ME1 Michael Egnew SP		
MF2 Marcus Forston	2.50	6.00
MI1 Melvin Ingram SP		
MJ1 Marvin Jones	2.50	6.00
MK1 Matt Kalil SP		
MM2 Markelle Martin	2.50	6.00
MM3 Mike Martin	3.00	8.00
MS1 Mohamed Sanu SP		
NB1 Nigel Bradham	2.50	6.00
NP1 Nick Perry SP		
NT1 Nick Toon SP		
OC1 Orson Charles	3.00	8.00
PK1 Peter Konz	2.00	5.00
QC1 Quinton Coples SP		
RB1 Ryan Broyles SP		
RB2 Robert Blanton	2.50	6.00
RE1 Rhett Ellison	2.50	6.00
RG3 Robert Griffin III SP	60.00	120.00
RR1 Rueben Randle SP		
RT2 Ryan Tannehill SP		
RW1 Russell Wilson SP		
SG1 Stephon Gilmore SP		
SH1 Stephen Hill SP		
SM1 Shea McClellin	4.00	10.00
SS1 Sean Spence	2.50	6.00
TB1 Tim Benford	2.00	5.00
TH1 Tyler Hansen	2.50	6.00
TM1 Thomas Mayo	2.00	5.00

TP2 Tydreke Powell	2.00	5.00
TR2 Trenton Robinson	2.50	6.00
WM1 Whitney Mercilus SP		
ZB1 Zach Brown	2.50	6.00
ZS1 Zebrie Sanders	2.00	5.00

1996 Press Pass

The Press Pass set was issued in one series totalling 55 standard-size cards. The set was issued in three card packs. The fronts have two photos as well as the player's name and position on the bottom. The "96 Press Pass Draft Pick" logo is in the upper left. The backs include vital statistics, statistical information and some career information.

COMPLETE SET (55)	7.50	20.00
1 Keyshawn Johnson	.60	1.50
2 Jonathan Ogden	.25	.60
3 Duane Clemons	.07	.20
4 Kevin Hardy	.07	.20
5 Eddie George	1.00	2.50
6 Karim Abdul-Jabbar	.25	.60
7 Terry Glenn	.25	.60
8 Leeland McElroy	.15	.40
9 Simeon Rice	.30	.75
10 Roman Oben	.07	.20
11 Daryl Gardener	.07	.20
12 Marcus Coleman	.07	.20
13 Christian Peter	.07	.20
14 Tim Biakabutuka	.25	.60
15 Eric Moulds	.60	1.50
16 Chris Darkins	.07	.20
17 Andre Johnson	.07	.20
18 Lawyer Milloy	.25	.60
19 Jon Runyan	.07	.20
20 Mike Alstott	.60	1.50
21 Jeff Hartings	.25	.60
22 Amani Toomer	.50	1.25
23 Danny Kanell	.25	.60
24 Marco Battaglia	.07	.20
25 Stephen Davis	.60	1.50
26 Johnny McWilliams	.07	.20
27 Israel Ifeanyi	.07	.20
28 Scott Slutzker	.07	.20
29 Bryant Mix	.07	.20
30 Brian Roche	.07	.20
31 Stanley Pritchett	.07	.20
32 Jerome Woods	.07	.20
33 Tommie Frazier	.15	.40
34 Stepfret Williams	.07	.20
35 Ray Mickens	.07	.20
36 Alex Van Dyke	.07	.20
37 Bobby Hoying	.25	.60
38 Tony Brackens	.25	.60
39 Dietrich Jells	.07	.20
40 Jason Odom	.07	.20
41 Randall Godfrey	.07	.20
42 Willie Anderson	.07	.20
43 Tony Banks	.25	.60
44 Michael Cheever	.07	.20
45 Je'Rod Cherry	.07	.20
46 Chris Doering	.07	.20
47 Steve Taneyhill	.07	.20
48 Kyle Wachholtz	.07	.20
49 Dusty Zeigler	.07	.20
50 Derrick Mayes	.15	.40
51 Orpheus Roye	.07	.20
52 Sedric Clark	.07	.20
53 Richard Huntley	.15	.40
54 Donnie Edwards	.25	.60
55 Zach Thomas CL	.25	.60
RED Lawrence Phillips	2.50	6.00
P1 Tim Biakabutuka Promo	.40	1.00

1996 Press Pass Holofoil

COMPLETE SET (55)	20.00	50.00
*HOLOFOILS: 1.2X TO 3X BASIC CARDS		
ONE PER PACK		

1996 Press Pass Holofoil Emerald Proofs

*EMERALDS: 8X TO 20X BASIC CARDS
STATED ODDS 1:36

1996 Press Pass Autographs

COMPLETE SET (12)	100.00	200.00
STATED ODDS 1:72		
1 Karim Abdul-Jabbar	10.00	25.00
2 Tony Banks	10.00	25.00
3 Tim Biakabutuka	10.00	25.00
4 Duane Clemons	3.00	8.00
5 Stephen Davis	12.50	30.00
6 Chris Doering	3.00	8.00
7 Bobby Hoying	6.00	15.00
8 Keyshawn Johnson	15.00	40.00
9 Danny Kanell	6.00	15.00
10 Leeland McElroy	6.00	15.00
11 Jonathan Ogden	10.00	25.00
12 Steve Taneyhill	3.00	8.00

1996 Press Pass Crystal Ball

COMPLETE SET (12)	20.00	40.00
RANDOM INSERTS IN PACKS		
CB1 Lawyer Milloy	1.50	3.00
CB2 Terry Glenn	1.50	3.00
CB3 Duane Clemons	.40	1.00
CB4 Kevin Hardy	.40	1.00
CB5 Eddie George	6.00	12.00
CB6 Jonathan Ogden	1.50	3.00
CB7 Karim Abdul-Jabbar	1.50	3.00
CB8 Tim Biakabutuka	1.50	3.00
CB9 Eric Moulds	4.00	8.00
CB10 Danny Kanell	1.50	3.00
CB11 Leeland McElroy	1.00	2.00
CB12 Keyshawn Johnson	4.00	8.00

1996 Press Pass Phone Cards $5

COMPLETE SET (9)	6.00	15.00
STATED ODDS 1:36		
*$10 CARDS: .6X TO 1.5X BASIC INSERTS		
STATED ODDS 1:216		
*$20 CARDS: 1.2X TO 3X BASIC INSERTS		
STATED ODDS 1:864		
1 Keyshawn Johnson	1.25	3.00
2 Jonathan Ogden	.50	1.25
3 Tommie Frazier	.30	.75
4 Eddie George	2.00	5.00
5 Karim Abdul-Jabbar	.50	1.25
6 Terry Glenn	.50	1.25
7 Leeland McElroy	.30	.75
8 Tim Biakabutuka	.50	1.25
9 Kevin Hardy	.15	.40

1996 Press Pass Paydirt

These 75 standard-size cards were issued in five-card packs. This set is the retail version of Press Pass and also features various insert cards. This set features players projected to be among the leading rookies of the 1996 NFL season. The RED Lawrence Phillips card was the prize for an expired mail order pack redemption.

COMPLETE SET (75)	12.50	25.00
1 Keyshawn Johnson	.75	2.00
2 Jonathan Ogden	.30	.75
3 Duane Clemons	.02	.10
4 Kevin Hardy	.10	.30
5 Eddie George	1.00	2.50
6 Karim Abdul-Jabbar	.30	.75
7 Terry Glenn	.60	1.50
8 Leeland McElroy	.10	.30
9 Simeon Rice	.40	1.00
10 Roman Oben	.02	.10
11 Daryl Gardener	.02	.10
12 Marcus Coleman	.02	.10
13 Christian Peter UER Chris Doering stamp on front	.02	.10
14 Tim Biakabutuka	.30	.75
15 Eric Moulds	.30	.75
16 Chris Darkins	.02	.10
17 Andre Johnson	.02	.10
18 Lawyer Milloy	.30	.75
19 Jon Runyan	.02	.10
20 Mike Alstott	.60	1.50
21 Jeff Hartings	.30	.75
22 Amani Toomer	.50	1.25
23 Danny Kanell	.30	.75
24 Marco Battaglia	.02	.10
25 Stephen Davis	.60	1.50
26 Johnny McWilliams	.02	.10
27 Israel Ifeanyi	.02	.10
28 Scott Slutzker	.02	.10
29 Bryant Mix	.02	.10
30 Brian Roche	.02	.10
31 Stanley Pritchett	.02	.10
32 Jerome Woods	.02	.10
33 Tommie Frazier	.10	.30
34 Stepfret Williams	.02	.10
35 Ray Mickens	.02	.10
36 Alex Van Dyke	.02	.10
37 Bobby Hoying	.30	.75
38 Tony Brackens	.30	.75
39 Dietrich Jells	.02	.10
40 Jason Odom	.02	.10
41 Randall Godfrey	.02	.10
42 Willie Anderson	.02	.10
43 Tony Banks	.30	.75
44 Michael Cheever	.02	.10
45 Je'Rod Cherry	.02	.10
46 Chris Doering	.02	.10
47 Steve Taneyhill	.02	.10
48 Kyle Wachholtz	.02	.10
49 Dusty Zeigler	.02	.10
50 Derrick Mayes	.10	.30
51 Orpheus Roye	.02	.10
52 Sedric Clark	.02	.10
53 Richard Huntley	.10	.30
54 Donnie Edwards	.30	.75
55 Zach Thomas	.50	1.25
56 Alex Molden	.02	.10
57 Jimmy Herndon	.02	.10
58 Mike Alstott	.60	1.50
59 Scott Greene	.02	.10
60 Danny Kanell	.30	.75
61 Jonathan Ogden	.30	.75
62 Simeon Rice	.40	1.00
63 Kevin Hardy	.10	.30
64 Jon Runyan	.02	.10
65 Stephen Davis	.60	1.50
66 Tim Biakabutuka	.30	.75
67 Terry Glenn	.60	1.50
68 Leeland McElroy	.10	.30
69 Eric Moulds	.75	2.00
70 Karim Abdul-Jabbar	.30	.75
71 Lawyer Milloy	.10	.30
72 Derrick Mayes	.30	.75
73 Tommie Frazier	.10	.30
74 Bobby Hoying	.30	.75
75 Kyle Wachholtz CL	.02	.10
RED Lawrence Phillips	2.50	6.00

1996 Press Pass Paydirt Holofoil

COMPLETE SET (75)	30.00	80.00
*HOLOFOILS: 1.5X TO 4X BASIC CARDS		
STATED ODDS 1:4		

1996 Press Pass Paydirt Red

COMPLETE SET (75)	20.00	50.00
*REDS: .8X TO 2X BASIC CARDS		
ONE PER PACK		

1996 Press Pass Paydirt Autographs

COMPLETE SET (16)	100.00	200.00
STATED ODDS 1:72		
1 Karim Abdul-Jabbar	7.50	20.00
2 Tony Banks	7.50	20.00
3 Tim Biakabutuka	7.50	20.00
4 Duane Clemons	3.00	8.00
5 Stephen Davis	15.00	40.00
6 Chris Doering	3.00	8.00
7 Bobby Hoying	7.50	20.00
8 Keyshawn Johnson	15.00	40.00
9 Danny Kanell	6.00	15.00
10 Derrick Mayes	6.00	15.00
11 Leeland McElroy	3.00	8.00
12 Lawyer Milloy	7.50	20.00
13 Eric Moulds	15.00	40.00
14 Jonathan Ogden	7.50	20.00
15 Steve Taneyhill	3.00	8.00
16 Alex Van Dyke	3.00	8.00

1996 Press Pass Paydirt Game Breakers

COMPLETE SET (12)	20.00	40.00
STATED ODDS 1:18		
GB1 Lawyer Milloy	2.00	4.00
GB2 Terry Glenn	4.00	8.00
GB3 Duane Clemons	.20	.50
GB4 Kevin Hardy	.75	1.50
GB5 Eddie George	6.00	12.00
GB6 Jonathan Ogden	2.00	4.00
GB7 Karim Abdul-Jabbar	2.00	4.00
GB8 Tim Biakabutuka	2.00	4.00
GB9 Eric Moulds	2.00	4.00
GB10 Danny Kanell	2.00	4.00
GB11 Leeland McElroy	.75	1.50
GB12 Keyshawn Johnson	5.00	10.00

1996 Press Pass Paydirt Eddie George

COMPLETE SET (4)	75.00	125.00
EG1 Eddie George	2.50	6.00
EG2 Eddie George	5.00	10.00
EG3 Eddie George	15.00	30.00
EG4 Eddie George	45.00	90.00

1997 Press Pass

This 49-card set features some leading NFL prospects entering the 1997 season. The borderless full color shots feature an action photo on the front with the players name and position on the bottom. The backs feature biographical information, a brief blurb as well as collegiate stats for these players. Card #48, Joe Paterno, was pulled at the last minute due to licensing problems. However, a very small amount of cards did make it into packs. Card #48 is not considered part of the base set.

COMPLETE SET (49)	7.50	20.00
1 Orlando Pace	.20	.50
2 Warrick Dunn	.50	1.25
3 Danny Wuerffel	.20	.50
4 Darnell Autry	.07	.20
5 Troy Davis	.07	.20
6 Jake Plummer	.60	1.50
7 Corey Dillon	.60	1.50
8 Reidel Anthony	.20	.50
9 Byron Hanspard	.10	.30
10 Tiki Barber	1.00	2.50
11 Ike Hilliard	.20	.50
12 Rae Carruth	.07	.20
13 Yatil Green	.10	.30
14 Peter Boulware	.20	.50
15 Jim Druckenmiller	.10	.30
16 Pat Barnes	.07	.20
17 Trevor Pryce	.20	.50
18 Kevin Lockett	.07	.20
19 Koy Detmer	.20	.50
20 Bryant Westbrook	.07	.20
21 Darrell Russell	.07	.20
22 Tony Gonzalez	.60	1.50
23 Shawn Springs	.10	.30
24 Chris Canty	.07	.20
25 David LaFleur	.07	.20
26 Dwayne Rudd	.07	.20
27 Bob Sapp	.20	.50
28 Mike Vrabel	.75	2.00
29 Antowain Smith	.40	1.00
30 Keith Poole	.07	.20
31 Sedrick Shaw	.10	.30
32 Tremain Mack	.07	.20
33 Matt Russell	.07	.20
34 Reinard Wilson	.10	.30
35 Marc Edwards	.10	.30
36 Greg Jones	.07	.20
37 Michael Booker	.07	.20
38 James Farrior	.20	.50
39 Danny Wuerffel HL	.10	.30
40 Troy Davis HL	.07	.20
41 Corey Dillon HL	.40	1.00
42 Jake Plummer HL	.30	.75
43 Peter Boulware HL	.10	.30
44 Eddie Robinson CO	.20	.50
45 Bobby Bowden CO	.30	.75
46 Steve Spurrier CO	.50	1.25
47 Gary Barnett CO	.07	.20
48 Joe Paterno CO SP	30.00	50.00
49 Tom Osborne CO	.50	1.25
50 Jarrett Irons CL	.07	.20

1997 Press Pass Combine

COMPLETE SET (45)	10.00	25.00
*STARS: .6X TO 1.5X BASIC CARDS		
ONE PER PACK		
P1 Warrick Dunn Promo	.60	1.50

1997 Press Pass Red Zone

COMPLETE SET (49)	10.00	25.00
*STARS: .6X to 1.5X BASIC CARDS		
ONE PER HOBBY PACK		
48 Joe Paterno CO SP	50.00	100.00

1997 Press Pass Torquers Blue

COMPLETE SET (49)	10.00	25.00
*STARS: .6X to 1.5X BASIC CARDS		
ONE PER RETAIL PACK		
48 Joe Paterno CO SP	30.00	80.00

1997 Press Pass Autographs

COMPLETE SET (31)	200.00	400.00
STATED ODDS 1:72		
1 Reidel Anthony	7.50	20.00
2 Michael Booker	3.00	8.00
3 Peter Boulware	7.50	20.00
4 Bobby Bowden CO	20.00	40.00
5 Chris Canty	3.00	8.00
6 Rae Carruth	5.00	12.00
7 Troy Davis	5.00	12.00
8 Koy Detmer	7.50	20.00
9 Corey Dillon	12.00	30.00
10 Jim Druckenmiller	5.00	12.00
11 Warrick Dunn	12.00	30.00
12 James Farrior	15.00	30.00
13 Tony Gonzalez	15.00	30.00
14 Yatil Green	5.00	12.00
15 Byron Hanspard	5.00	12.00
16 Ike Hilliard	10.00	25.00
17 Greg Jones	3.00	8.00
18 David LaFleur	3.00	8.00
19 Kevin Lockett	3.00	8.00
20 Tom Osborne CO	30.00	60.00
21 Orlando Pace	7.50	20.00
22 Keith Poole	3.00	8.00
23 Darrell Russell	3.00	8.00
24 Matt Russell	3.00	8.00
25 Bob Sapp	3.00	8.00
26 Steve Spurrier CO	12.50	30.00
27 Gene Stallings CO	10.00	25.00
28 Mike Vrabel	25.00	50.00
29 Bryant Westbrook	3.00	8.00
30 Reinard Wilson	3.00	8.00
31 Danny Wuerffel	7.50	20.00

1997 Press Pass Big 12

COMPLETE SET (12)	10.00	20.00
STATED ODDS 1:12		
B1 Orlando Pace	1.00	2.50
B2 Peter Boulware	1.00	2.50
B3 Shawn Springs	.60	1.50
B4 Warrick Dunn	2.50	6.00
B5 Dwayne Rudd	.40	1.00
B6 Rae Carruth	.40	1.00
B7 Bryant Westbrook	.40	1.00
B8 Darrell Russell	.40	1.00
B9 Yatil Green	.60	1.50
B10 David LaFleur	.40	1.00
B11 Jim Druckenmiller	.60	1.50
B12 Reidel Anthony	1.00	2.50

1997 Press Pass Can't Miss

COMPLETE SET (6)	30.00	60.00
CM1 Warrick Dunn	12.00	30.00
CM2 Jim Druckenmiller	6.00	15.00
CM3 Yatil Green	3.00	8.00
CM4 Orlando Pace	3.00	8.00
CM5 Rae Carruth	2.50	6.00
CM6 Peter Boulware	3.00	8.00

1997 Press Pass Head Butt

COMPLETE SET (9)	12.50	30.00
STATED ODDS 1:18		
*DIE CUTS: .6X TO 1.5X BASIC INSERTS		
DIE CUT STATED ODDS 1:36		
HB1 Warrick Dunn	4.00	10.00
HB2 Orlando Pace	1.50	4.00
HB3 Troy Davis	.60	1.50
HB4 Reidel Anthony	1.50	4.00
HB5 Rae Carruth	.60	1.50
HB6 Yatil Green	1.00	2.50
HB7 Corey Dillon	5.00	12.00
HB8 Danny Wuerffel	1.50	4.00
HB9 Darnell Autry	.60	1.50

1997 Press Pass Marquee Matchups

COMPLETE SET (9)	15.00	30.00
STATED ODDS 1:18		
MM1 Jim Druckenmiller Danny Wuerffel	1.50	4.00
MM2 Warrick Dunn Corey Dillon	4.00	10.00
MM3 Darnell Autry Troy Davis	.75	2.00
MM4 Byron Hanspard Tiki Barber	3.00	8.00
MM5 Reidel Anthony Bryant Westbrook	1.50	4.00
MM6 Peter Boulware Orlando Pace	2.00	5.00
MM7 Rae Carruth Ike Hilliard	1.50	4.00
MM8 Yatil Green Shawn Springs	.75	2.00
MM9 David LaFleur Tony Gonzalez	2.50	6.00

1998 Press Pass

This 50-card set features some leading NFL prospects entering the 1998 season. The borderless full color shots feature an action photo on the front with the players name and position on the bottom. The backs feature biographical information, a brief blurb as well as collegiate stats for these players.

COMPLETE SET (50)	7.50	20.00
1 Peyton Manning	3.00	8.00
2 Ryan Leaf	.20	.50
3 Charles Woodson	.30	.75
4 Andre Wadsworth	.10	.30
5 Randy Moss	2.00	5.00
6 Curtis Enis	.08	.25
7 Tra Thomas	.08	.25
8 Flozell Adams	.08	.25
9 Jason Peter	.08	.25
10 Brian Simmons	.10	.30
11 Takeo Spikes	.20	.50
12 Michael Myers	.08	.25
13 Kevin Dyson	.20	.50
14 Grant Wistrom	.10	.30
15 Fred Taylor	.50	1.25
16 Germane Crowell	.10	.30
17 Sam Cowart	.10	.30
18 Anthony Simmons LB	.10	.30
19 Robert Edwards	.10	.30
20 Shaun Williams	.10	.30
21 Phil Savoy	.08	.25
22 Leonard Little	.20	.50
23 Saladin McCullough	.08	.25
24 Duane Starks	.08	.25
25 John Avery	.10	.30
26 Vonnie Holliday	.20	.50
27 Tim Dwight	.20	.50
28 Donovin Darius	.10	.30
29 Alonzo Mayes	.08	.25
30 Jerome Pathon	.20	.50
31 Brian Kelly	.10	.30
32 Hines Ward	1.25	2.50
33 Jacquez Green	.10	.30
34 Marcus Nash	.08	.25
35 Ahman Green	.60	1.50
36 Joe Jurevicius	.20	.50
37 Tavian Banks	.10	.30
38 Donald Hayes	.10	.30
39 Robert Holcombe	.10	.30
40 E.G. Green	.10	.30
41 John Dutton	.08	.25
42 Skip Hicks	.10	.30
43 Pat Johnson	.10	.30
44 Keith Brooking	.20	.50
45 Alan Faneca	.40	1.00
46 Steve Spurrier CO	.40	1.00
47 Mike Price CO	.08	.25
48 Bobby Bowden CO	.10	.30
49 Tom Osborne CO	.40	1.00
50 Peyton Manning CL	.60	1.50
P1 Randy Moss Promo	1.50	4.00

1998 Press Pass Paydirt Red

COMPLETE SET (50)	10.00	25.00
*PAYDIRT STARS: .6X TO 1.5X BASIC CARDS		
ONE PER HOBBY PACK		

1998 Press Pass Pick Offs Blue

COMPLETE SET (50)	10.00	25.00
*BLUE: .6X TO 1.5X BASIC CARDS		
ONE PER RETAIL PACK		

1998 Press Pass Reflectors

*REFLECTORS: 10X TO 25X BASIC CARDS		
STATED ODDS 1:180 PACKS		
R1 Peyton Manning	150.00	250.00

1998 Press Pass Autographs

STATED ODDS 1:18 HOB/1:36 RET		
1 Peyton Manning	100.00	200.00
2 Ryan Leaf	6.00	15.00
4 Andre Wadsworth	4.00	10.00
5 Randy Moss	75.00	150.00
6 Curtis Enis	3.00	8.00
9 Jason Peter	3.00	8.00
10 Brian Simmons	4.00	10.00
11 Takeo Spikes	6.00	15.00
12 Michael Myers	3.00	8.00
13 Kevin Dyson	6.00	15.00
14 Grant Wistrom	6.00	15.00
15 Fred Taylor	20.00	40.00
16 Germane Crowell	4.00	10.00
18 Anthony Simmons LB	4.00	10.00
19 Robert Edwards	4.00	10.00
20 Shaun Williams	6.00	15.00
21 Phil Savoy	3.00	8.00
25 John Avery	4.00	10.00
26 Vonnie Holliday	6.00	15.00
27 Tim Dwight	6.00	15.00
28 Donovin Darius	4.00	10.00
29 Alonzo Mayes	3.00	8.00
31 Brian Kelly	4.00	10.00
32 Hines Ward	35.00	60.00
33 Jacquez Green	4.00	10.00
34 Marcus Nash	3.00	8.00
35 Ahman Green	20.00	40.00
36 Joe Jurevicius	6.00	15.00
37 Tavian Banks	6.00	15.00
38 Donald Hayes	4.00	10.00
39 Robert Holcombe	4.00	10.00
42 Skip Hicks	4.00	10.00
43 Pat Johnson	4.00	10.00
45 Alan Faneca	12.00	30.00
46 Steve Spurrier CO	12.00	30.00
47 Mike Price CO	3.00	8.00
48 Bobby Bowden CO	20.00	40.00
49 Tom Osborne CO	15.00	30.00
NNO P.Manning SportsFest	100.00	175.00

1998 Press Pass Fields of Fury

COMPLETE SET (9)	30.00	60.00
STATED ODDS 1:36		
FF1 Peyton Manning	15.00	40.00
FF2 Marcus Nash	.60	1.50
FF3 Ryan Leaf	1.25	3.00
FF4 Randy Moss	10.00	25.00
FF5 Robert Edwards	.75	2.00
FF6 Curtis Enis	.60	1.50
FF7 Kevin Dyson	1.25	3.00
FF8 Fred Taylor	3.00	8.00
FF9 Jacquez Green	.75	2.00

1998 Press Pass Game Jerseys

COMPLETE SET (4)	125.00	250.00
STATED ODDS 1:720		
STATED PRINT RUN 425 SERIAL #'d SETS		
JC1 Peyton Manning	60.00	120.00
JC2 Ryan Leaf	10.00	25.00
JC3 Kevin Dyson	10.00	25.00
JC4 Tavian Banks	7.50	20.00
JCTB Tavian Banks Promo	4.00	10.00

1998 Press Pass Head Butt

COMPLETE SET (9)	15.00	30.00
STATED ODDS 1:18		
*DIE CUTS: .6X TO 1.5X BASIC INSERTS		
DIE CUT STATED ODDS 1:36		
HB1 Peyton Manning	8.00	20.00
HB2 Charles Woodson	1.00	2.50
HB3 Ryan Leaf	.60	1.50
HB4 Curtis Enis	.30	.75
HB5 Jacquez Green	.40	1.00
HB6 Ahman Green	2.00	5.00
HB7 Randy Moss	5.00	12.00
HB8 Tavian Banks	.40	1.00
HB9 Robert Edwards	.40	1.00

1998 Press Pass Kick-Off

COMPLETE SET (36)	10.00	25.00
ONE PER PACK		
KO1 Peyton Manning	3.00	8.00
KO2 Ryan Leaf	.25	.60
KO3 Charles Woodson	.40	1.00
KO4 Andre Wadsworth	.15	.40
KO5 Randy Moss	2.00	5.00
KO6 Curtis Enis	.10	.30
KO7 Donald Hayes	.15	.40
KO8 Flozell Adams	.10	.30
KO9 Jason Peter	.10	.30
KO10 Brian Simmons	.15	.40
KO11 Takeo Spikes	.25	.60
KO12 Germane Crowell	.15	.40
KO13 Donovin Darius	.15	.40
KO14 Grant Wistrom	.15	.40
KO15 Alonzo Mayes	.10	.30
KO16 Kevin Dyson	.25	.60
KO17 John Avery	.15	.40
KO18 Anthony Simmons LB	.15	.40
KO19 Robert Edwards	.15	.40
KO20 Shaun Williams	.15	.40
KO21 Leonard Little	.25	.60
KO22 Skip Hicks	.15	.40
KO23 Phil Savoy	.10	.30
KO24 Tavian Banks	.15	.40
KO25 Robert Holcombe	.15	.40
KO26 E.G. Green	.15	.40
KO27 Tim Dwight	.25	.60
KO28 Saladin McCullough	.10	.30
KO29 Fred Taylor	.60	1.50
KO30 Jerome Pathon	.25	.60
KO31 Brian Kelly	.15	.40
KO32 Hines Ward	1.25	3.00
KO33 Jacquez Green	.15	.40
KO34 Marcus Nash	.10	.30
KO35 Ahman Green	.75	2.00
KO36 Joe Jurevicius CL	.25	.60

1998 Press Pass Triple Threat

COMPLETE SET (9)	15.00	30.00
STATED ODDS 1:12		
TT1 Peyton Manning	4.00	10.00
TT2 Peyton Manning	4.00	10.00
TT3 Peyton Manning	4.00	10.00
TT4 Ryan Leaf	2.00	5.00
TT5 Ryan Leaf	2.00	5.00
TT6 Ryan Leaf	2.00	5.00
TT7 Charles Woodson	1.00	2.50
TT8 Charles Woodson	1.00	2.50
TT9 Charles Woodson	1.00	2.50

1998 Press Pass Trophy Case

COMPLETE SET (12)	20.00	40.00
STATED ODDS 1:9		
TC1 Peyton Manning	6.00	15.00
TC2 Ryan Leaf	.50	1.25
TC3 Charles Woodson	.75	2.00
TC4 Randy Moss	4.00	10.00
TC5 Curtis Enis	.25	.60
TC6 Grant Wistrom	.30	.75
TC7 Kevin Dyson	.50	1.25
TC8 Fred Taylor	1.25	3.00
TC9 Tavian Banks	.30	.75
TC10 Ahman Green	1.50	4.00
TC11 Skip Hicks	.30	.75
TC12 Andre Wadsworth	.30	.75

1999 Press Pass

The 1999 Press Pass set was issued in one series totalling 45 cards. The fronts feature color action photos of the newest rookies of the NFL. The backs carry player information.

COMPLETE SET (45)	6.00	15.00
1 Ricky Williams	.50	1.25
2 Tim Couch	.30	.75
3 Champ Bailey	.60	1.50
4 Chris Claiborne	.20	.50
5 Donovan McNabb	.75	2.00
6 Edgerrin James	.40	1.00
7 Akili Smith	.25	.60
8 John Tait	.20	.50
9 Jevon Kearse	.30	.75
10 Torry Holt	.50	1.25
11 Troy Edwards	.25	.60
12 Chris McAlister	.25	.60
13 Daunte Culpepper	.30	.75
14 Andy Katzenmoyer	.25	.60
15 David Boston	.25	.60
16 Ebenezer Ekuban	.20	.50
17 Peerless Price	.25	.60
18 Shaun King	.25	.60
19 Joe Germaine	.25	.60
20 Brock Huard	.25	.60
21 Michael Bishop	.25	.60
22 Amos Zereoue	.25	.60
23 Sedrick Irvin	.20	.50
24 Autry Denson	.20	.50
25 Kevin Faulk	.30	.75
26 James Johnson	.20	.50
27 D'Wayne Bates	.20	.50
28 Kevin Johnson	.25	.60
29 Tai Streets	.25	.60
30 Craig Yeast	.20	.50
31 Dre Bly	.30	.75
32 Anthony Poindexter	.20	.50
33 Jared DeVries	.20	.50
34 Rob Konrad	.20	.50
35 Dat Nguyen	.30	.75
36 Cade McNown	.25	.60
37 Scott Covington	.20	.50
38 Jon Jansen	.20	.50
39 Rufus French	.20	.50
40 Mike Rucker	.20	.50
41 Aaron Gibson	.20	.50
42 Kris Farris	.20	.50
43 Anthony McFarland	.25	.60
44 Matt Stinchcomb	.20	.50
45 Dee Miller CL	.20	.50

1999 Press Pass Paydirt Silver

COMPLETE SET (45)	10.00	25.00
*PAYDIRTS: .5X TO 1.2X BASIC CARDS		
STATED ODDS 1 PER HOBBY PACK		

1999 Press Pass Reflectors

*REFLECTORS: 8X TO 20X BASIC CARDS
STATED ODDS 1:180

1999 Press Pass Reflectors Solos

STATED PRINT RUN 1 SET

1999 Press Pass Torquers Blue

COMPLETE SET (45)	12.50	30.00
*TORQUERS: .6X TO 1.5X BASIC CARDS		
STATED ODDS 1 PER RETAIL PACK		

1999 Press Pass Autographs

COMPLETE SET (50)	300.00	600.00
STATED ODDS 1:16		
1 Ricky Williams	7.50	20.00
2 Tim Couch	6.00	15.00
3 Champ Bailey	7.50	20.00
4 Chris Claiborne	4.00	10.00
5 Donovan McNabb	15.00	40.00
6 Edgerrin James	12.00	30.00
7 Akili Smith	6.00	15.00
8 John Tait	5.00	12.00
9 Jevon Kearse	7.50	20.00
10 Torry Holt	10.00	25.00
11 Troy Edwards	5.00	12.00
12 Chris McAlister	5.00	12.00
13 Daunte Culpepper	7.50	20.00
14 Andy Katzenmoyer	10.00	25.00
15 David Boston	5.00	12.00
16 Ebenezer Ekuban	4.00	10.00
17 Peerless Price	5.00	12.00
18 Shaun King	5.00	12.00
19 Joe Germaine	5.00	12.00
20 Brock Huard	6.00	15.00
21 Michael Bishop	5.00	12.00
22 Amos Zereoue	5.00	12.00
23 Sedrick Irvin	4.00	10.00
24 Autry Denson	4.00	10.00
25 Kevin Faulk	6.00	15.00
26 James Johnson	4.00	10.00
27 D'Wayne Bates	4.00	10.00
28 Kevin Johnson	5.00	12.00
29 Tai Streets	5.00	12.00
30 Craig Yeast	4.00	10.00
31 Dre Bly	5.00	12.00
32 Anthony Poindexter	4.00	10.00
33 Jared DeVries	4.00	10.00
34 Rob Konrad	5.00	12.00
35 Dat Nguyen	6.00	15.00
36 Cade McNown	5.00	12.00
37 Scott Covington	5.00	12.00
38 Jon Jansen	4.00	10.00
39 Rufus French	4.00	10.00
40 Mike Rucker	6.00	15.00
41 Aaron Gibson	4.00	10.00
42 Kris Farris	4.00	10.00
43 Anthony McFarland	6.00	15.00
44 Matt Stinchcomb	5.00	12.00
45 Dee Miller CL	4.00	10.00
46 Antuan Edwards	5.00	12.00
47 Mike Peterson	4.00	10.00
48 Mike Cloud	4.00	10.00
49 Darnell McDonald	4.00	10.00
50 Jerame Tuman	6.00	15.00

1999 Press Pass Big Numbers

COMPLETE SET (9)	15.00	30.00
STATED ODDS 1:16		
*DIE CUTS: .6X TO 1.5X BASIC INSERTS		
DIE CUT STATED ODDS: 1:32		
BN1 Tim Couch	.50	1.25
BN2 Ricky Williams	1.00	2.50
BN3 Donovan McNabb	2.50	6.00
BN4 Edgerrin James	2.00	5.00
BN5 Peerless Price	.50	1.25
BN6 Amos Zereoue	.50	1.25
BN7 Daunte Culpepper	2.00	5.00
BN8 Tai Streets	.50	1.25
BN9 Akili Smith	.75	2.00

1999 Press Pass Game Jerseys

COMPLETE SET (6)	125.00	250.00
STATED ODDS 1:640		
JCAS Akili Smith	10.00	25.00
JCCM Cade McNown	10.00	25.00
JCDC Daunte Culpepper	40.00	80.00
JCPP Peerless Price	12.00	30.00
JCTC Tim Couch	12.00	30.00
JCTH Torry Holt	20.00	50.00

1999 Press Pass Goldenarm

COMPLETE SET (9)	10.00	20.00
STATED ODDS 1:10		
GA1 Tim Couch	.50	1.25
GA2 Donovan McNabb	2.50	6.00
GA3 Akili Smith	.75	2.00
GA4 Daunte Culpepper	2.00	5.00
GA5 Cade McNown	.30	.75
GA6 Brock Huard	.50	1.25
GA7 Joe Germaine	.30	.75
GA8 Shaun King	.30	.75
GA9 Michael Bishop	.50	1.25

1999 Press Pass Gridiron

COMPLETE SET (3)	2.00	5.00
ONE PER SPECIAL RETAIL BOX		
1 Tim Couch	.60	1.50
2 Akili Smith	.60	1.50
3 Ricky Williams	.75	2.00

1999 Press Pass Hardware

COMPLETE SET (12)	10.00	25.00
STATED ODDS 1:8		
H1 Cade McNown	.30	.75
H2 Ricky Williams	1.00	2.50
H3 Torry Holt	1.25	3.00
H4 Tim Couch	.50	1.25
H5 David Boston	.50	1.25
H6 Troy Edwards	.30	.75
H7 Michael Bishop	.50	1.25
H8 Champ Bailey	.75	2.00
H9 Mike Cloud	.30	.75
H10 Kevin Faulk	.50	1.25
H11 Autry Denson	.30	.75
H12 Donovan McNabb	2.50	6.00

1999 Press Pass X's and O's

COMPLETE SET (36)	7.50	20.00
ONE PER PACK		
P1 Daunte Culpepper X's PROMO	1.00	2.50
XO1 Ricky Williams	.60	1.50
XO2 Tim Couch	.30	.75
XO3 Champ Bailey	.50	1.25
XO4 Donovan McNabb	1.50	4.00
XO5 Edgerrin James	1.25	3.00
XO6 Akili Smith	.50	1.25
XO7 Torry Holt	.75	2.00
XO8 Troy Edwards	.20	.50
XO9 Daunte Culpepper	1.25	3.00
XO10 Andy Katzenmoyer	.20	.50
XO11 David Boston	.30	.75
XO12 Peerless Price	.30	.75
XO13 Shaun King	.20	.50
XO14 Joe Germaine	.20	.50
XO15 Brock Huard	.30	.75
XO16 Michael Bishop	.30	.75
XO17 Amos Zereoue	.30	.75
XO18 Sedrick Irvin	.15	.40
XO19 Autry Denson	.20	.50
XO20 Kevin Faulk	.30	.75
XO21 James Johnson	.20	.50
XO22 D'Wayne Bates	.20	.50
XO23 Kevin Johnson	.50	1.25
XO24 Tai Streets	.30	.75
XO25 Cade McNown	.20	.50
XO26 Scott Covington	.30	.75
XO27 Chris Claiborne	.15	.40
XO28 Jevon Kearse	.60	1.50
XO29 Rob Konrad	.30	.75
XO30 Dat Nguyen	.30	.75
XO31 Chris McAlister	.20	.50
XO32 Craig Yeast	.20	.50
XO33 Anthony Poindexter	.15	.40
XO34 Dre Bly	.30	.75
XO35 Mike Rucker	.30	.75
XO36 Tim Couch CL	.30	.75

2000 Press Pass

Press Pass was released as a 45-card set featuring top NCAA draft picks. Card backs carry college statistics and pertinent information highlighting each players most impressive skills. Press Pass was released in both Hobby and Retail form. Hobby was packaged in boxes of 24-packs containing five cards each and carried a suggested retail price of $3.59. Retail was packaged in boxes of 36-packs containing four cards each and carried a suggested retail price of $2.99.

COMPLETE SET (45)	10.00	25.00
1 Peter Warrick	.20	.50
2 Travis Claridge	.12	.30
3 Courtney Brown	.15	.40
4 Plaxico Burress	.20	.50
5 Chad Pennington	.30	.75
6 Thomas Jones	.25	.60
7 Ron Dayne	.20	.50
8 Brian Urlacher	.75	2.00
9 Corey Simon	.15	.40
10 Chris Samuels	.15	.40
11 Stockar McDougle	.12	.30
12 Deon Grant	.12	.30
13 Cosey Coleman	.12	.30
14 Sylvester Morris	.12	.30
15 Shyrone Stith	.12	.30
16 Shaun Alexander	.25	.60
17 Dez White	.15	.40
18 John Engelberger	.12	.30
19 Tim Rattay	.15	.40
20 Todd Pinkston	.12	.30
21 John Abraham	.20	.50
22 R.Jay Soward	.12	.30
23 Shaun Ellis	.20	.50
24 Keith Bulluck	.15	.40
25 Jerry Porter	.20	.50
26 Darren Howard	.12	.30

27 Joe Hamilton .12 .30
28 Deltha O'Neal .15 .40
29 Chris Redman .15 .40
30 Deon Dyer .12 .30
31 Jamal Lewis .20 .50
32 Chris Hovan .15 .40
33 Raynoch Thompson .12 .30
34 Travis Taylor .15 .40
35 Sebastian Janikowski .20 .50
36 Travis Prentice .15 .40
37 Tom Brady 8.00 20.00
38 Tee Martin .20 .50
39 J.R. Redmond .12 .30
40 Dennis Northcutt .15 .40
41 Laveranues Coles .20 .50
42 Danny Farmer .12 .30
43 Darrell Jackson .15 .40
44 Chris McIntosh .12 .30
45 Peter Warrick CL .15 .40
P1 Peter Warrick Promo .75 2.00

2000 Press Pass Gold Zone

COMPLETE SET (45) 10.00 25.00
*GOLD ZONE: .6X TO 1.5X BASIC CARDS
ONE GOLD PER HOBBY PACK

2000 Press Pass Reflectors

COMPLETE SET (45) 150.00 300.00
*REFLECTOR: 5X TO 12X BASIC CARDS
REFLECTOR/500 ODDS 1:72
UNPRICED REF.SOLO PRINT RUN 1
37 Tom Brady 100.00 200.00

2000 Press Pass Torquers

COMPLETE SET (45) 15.00 30.00
*TORQUERS: .6X TO 1.5X BASIC CARDS
ONE PER RETAIL PACK

2000 Press Pass Autographs

STATED ODDS 1:8 HOB, 1:36 RET
1 John Abraham 6.00 15.00
2 Shaun Alexander 6.00 15.00
3 Tom Brady 150.00 300.00
4 Courtney Brown 4.00 10.00
5 Keith Bulluck 4.00 10.00
6 Plaxico Burress 12.00 30.00
7 Giovanni Carmazzi 3.00 8.00
8 Kwame Cavil 3.00 8.00
9 Travis Claridge 3.00 8.00
10 Cosey Coleman 3.00 8.00
11 Laveranues Coles 5.00 12.00
12 Ron Dayne 5.00 12.00
13 Na'il Diggs 3.00 8.00
14 Ron Dugans 3.00 8.00
15 Deon Dyer 3.00 8.00
16 Shaun Ellis 5.00 12.00
17 John Engelberger 3.00 8.00
18 Danny Farmer 3.00 8.00
19 Deon Grant 3.00 8.00
20 Joe Hamilton 3.00 8.00
21 Darren Howard 3.00 8.00
22 Chris Hovan 4.00 10.00
23 Darrell Jackson 4.00 10.00
24 Sebastian Janikowski 6.00 15.00
25 Thomas Jones 6.00 15.00
26 Jamal Lewis 5.00 12.00
27 Tee Martin 5.00 12.00
28 Stockar McDougle 3.00 8.00
29 Chris McIntosh 3.00 8.00
30 Corey Moore 3.00 8.00
31 Rob Morris 4.00 10.00
32 Sylvester Morris 3.00 8.00
33 Dennis Northcutt 4.00 10.00
34 Deltha O'Neal 4.00 10.00
35 Chad Pennington 8.00 20.00
36 Todd Pinkston 3.00 8.00
37 Jerry Porter 5.00 12.00
38 Travis Prentice 4.00 10.00
39 Tim Rattay 4.00 10.00
40 Chris Redman 4.00 10.00
41 J.R. Redmond 3.00 8.00
42 Chris Samuels 4.00 10.00
43 Corey Simon 4.00 10.00
44 Marvel Smith 5.00 12.00
45 Shyrone Stith 3.00 8.00
46 Travis Taylor 4.00 10.00
47 Raynoch Thompson 3.00 8.00
48 Brian Urlacher 20.00 40.00
49 Todd Wade 3.00 8.00
50 Peter Warrick 5.00 12.00
50C Peter Warrick Clear/50 20.00 50.00
51 Dez White 4.00 10.00

2000 Press Pass Autographs Gold Standout Signatures

*GOLD STANDOUT/100: .6X TO 1.5X BASIC AU
*GOLD STANDOUT/50: 1X TO 2.5X BASIC AU
STATED PRINT RUN 100 SETS
3 Tom Brady 300.00 500.00

2000 Press Pass Big Numbers

COMPLETE SET (8) 4.00 10.00
STATED ODDS 1:12
*DIE CUTS: .6X TO 1.5X BASIC INSERTS
DIE CUT STATED ODDS 1:24
BN1 Peter Warrick .50 1.25
BN2 Ron Dayne .50 1.25
BN3 Courtney Brown .40 1.00
BN4 Plaxico Burress .50 1.25
BN5 Shaun Alexander .60 1.50
BN6 Thomas Jones .60 1.50
BN7 Chad Pennington .75 2.00
BN8 Chris Redman .40 1.00

2000 Press Pass Breakout

COMPLETE SET (35) 6.00 15.00
ONE PER PACK
BO1 Peter Warrick .25 .60
BO2 Sebastian Janikowski .25 .60
BO3 Courtney Brown .20 .50
BO4 Plaxico Burress .25 .60
BO5 Chad Pennington .40 1.00
BO6 Thomas Jones .30 .75
BO7 Ron Dayne .25 .60
BO8 Brian Urlacher 1.00 2.50
BO9 Deon Dyer .15 .40
BO10 Chris Samuels .20 .50
BO11 Stockar McDougle .15 .40
BO12 Deon Grant .15 .40
BO13 Cosey Coleman .15 .40
BO14 Shyrone Stith .15 .40
BO15 Tim Rattay .20 .50
BO16 Shaun Alexander .30 .75
BO17 Dez White .20 .50
BO18 John Engelberger .15 .40
BO19 Laveranues Coles .25 .60
BO20 J.R. Redmond .15 .40
BO21 R.Jay Soward .15 .40
BO22 Chris McIntosh .15 .40
BO23 Shaun Ellis .25 .60
BO24 Keith Bulluck .20 .50
BO25 Jerry Porter .25 .60
BO26 Darren Howard .15 .40
BO27 Tee Martin .25 .60
BO28 Deltha O'Neal .20 .50
BO29 Chris Redman .20 .50
BO30 Danny Farmer .15 .40
BO31 Jamal Lewis .25 .60
BO32 Chris Hovan .20 .50
BO33 Corey Simon .20 .50
BO34 Travis Taylor .20 .50
BO35 Ron Dayne CL .20 .50

2000 Press Pass Game Jerseys

HOBBY STATED ODDS 1:380
RETAIL STATED ODDS 1:720
STATED PRINT RUN 325-475
JC1 Ron Dayne 6.00 15.00
JC2 Thomas Jones 8.00 20.00
JC3 Chad Pennington 10.00 25.00
JC4 Chris Redman 5.00 12.00
JC5 Corey Simon 5.00 12.00
JC6 Peter Warrick AU/325 12.50 30.00

2000 Press Pass Gridiron

COMPLETE SET (3) 2.50 6.00
ONE PER SPECIAL RETAIL BOX
1 Peter Warrick .75 2.00
2 Chad Pennington 1.25 3.00
3 Ron Dayne .75 2.00

2000 Press Pass Paydirt

COMPLETE SET (12) 6.00 15.00
STATED ODDS 1:16
PD1 Peter Warrick .50 1.25
PD2 Plaxico Burress .50 1.25
PD3 Chad Pennington .75 2.00
PD4 Thomas Jones .60 1.50
PD5 Ron Dayne .50 1.25
PD6 Shyrone Stith .30 .75
PD7 Shaun Alexander .60 1.50
PD8 Chris Redman .40 1.00
PD9 Dez White .40 1.00
PD10 Jamal Lewis .50 1.25
PD11 J.R. Redmond .30 .75
PD12 Travis Taylor .40 1.00

2000 Press Pass Power Picks

COMPLETE SET (10) 6.00 15.00
STATED ODDS 1:12
PP1 Peter Warrick .40 1.00
PP2 Courtney Brown .30 .75
PP3 Plaxico Burress .40 1.00
PP4 Chad Pennington .60 1.50
PP5 Thomas Jones .50 1.25
PP6 Ron Dayne .40 1.00
PP7 Corey Simon .30 .75
PP8 Shaun Alexander .50 1.25
PP9 Brian Urlacher 1.50 4.00
PP10 Chris Samuels .30 .75

2000 Press Pass Showbound

COMPLETE SET (8) 3.00 8.00
STATED ODDS 1:8
SB1 Peter Warrick .40 1.00
SB2 Dez White .30 .75
SB3 Courtney Brown .30 .75
SB4 Plaxico Burress .40 1.00
SB5 Chad Pennington .60 1.50
SB6 Thomas Jones .50 1.25
SB7 Ron Dayne .40 1.00
SB8 Shaun Alexander .50 1.25

2001 Press Pass

Press Pass was released as a 50-card set featuring top NFL draft picks. The cardbacks carry college statistics and pertinent information highlighting each player's most impressive skills. The final four Power Picks subset cards were seeded at the rate of 1:16 packs. Press Pass was released in both hobby and retail pack form. Hobby was packaged in boxes of 24-packs containing five cards each and carried a suggested retail price of $3.49. Retail was packaged in boxes of 36-packs containing four cards each and carried a suggested retail price of $2.99.

COMPLETE SET (50) 10.00 25.00
COMP.FACT.SET (46) 10.00 25.00
COMP.SET w/o SP's (45) 7.50 20.00
UNPRICED SOLOS PRINT RUN 1/1
1 Michael Vick CL .75 2.00
2 Drew Brees 2.00 5.00
3 Michael Vick 1.25 3.00
4 Chris Weinke .25 .60
5 Marques Tuiasosopo .25 .60
6 Josh Booty .25 .60
7 Josh Heupel .30 .75
8 Sage Rosenfels .30 .75
9 Mike McMahon .25 .60
10 Deuce McAllister .30 .75
11 LaDainian Tomlinson 1.00 2.50
12 LaMont Jordan .30 .75
13 James Jackson .20 .50
14 Travis Henry .25 .60
15 Anthony Thomas .30 .75
16 Travis Minor .25 .60
17 Michael Bennett .25 .60
18 Kevan Barlow .25 .60
19 Rudi Johnson .30 .75
20 Santana Moss .40 1.00
21 Quincy Morgan .25 .60
22 Rod Gardner .25 .60
23 David Terrell .25 .60
24 Chris Chambers .30 .75
25 Reggie Wayne .60 1.50
26 Ken-Yon Rambo .20 .50
27 Chad Johnson .50 1.25
28 Snoop Minnis .20 .50
29 Freddie Mitchell .20 .50
30 Koren Robinson .25 .60
31 Bobby Newcombe .25 .60
32 Robert Ferguson .30 .75
33 Todd Heap .30 .75
34 Steve Hutchinson .30 .75
35 Leonard Davis .30 .75
36 Kenyatta Walker .20 .50
37 Justin Smith .30 .75
38 Jamal Reynolds .20 .50
39 Richard Seymour .30 .75
40 Shaun Rogers .30 .75
41 Gerard Warren .25 .60
42 Jamar Fletcher .20 .50
43 Gary Baxter .20 .50
44 Nate Clements .25 .60
45 Derrick Gibson .20 .50
46 Drew Brees PP 4.00 10.00
47 Michael Vick PP 2.50 6.00
48 Deuce McAllister PP .60 1.50
49 LaDainian Tomlinson PP 2.00 5.00
50 David Terrell PP .50 1.25

2001 Press Pass Gold Zone

COMPLETE SET (45) 15.00 30.00
*GOLD ZONE 1-45: .65X TO 1.5X BASIC CARDS
*GOLD ZONE PP 46-50: .5X TO 1.2X BASIC PP
STATED ODDS 1:1 HOBBY

2001 Press Pass Reflectors

*REFLECTOR 1-45: 2.5X TO 6X BASIC CARDS
*REFLECTOR PP 46-50: 1.5X TO 4X BASIC PP
REFLECTOR/500 ODDS 1:60
STATED PRINT RUN 500 SERIAL #'d SETS

2001 Press Pass Torquers

COMPLETE SET (45) 20.00 40.00
*TORQUERS 1-45: .6X TO 1.5X BASIC CARDS
*TORQUER PP 46-50: .5X TO 1.2X BASIC PP
STATED ODDS 1:1 RETAIL

2001 Press Pass Autographs

STATED ODDS 1:8 HOB, 1:36 RET
1 Dan Alexander 5.00 12.00
2 Brian Allen 4.00 10.00
3 Jeff Backus 4.00 10.00
4 Kevan Barlow 5.00 12.00
5 Michael Bennett 5.00 12.00
6 Drew Brees 50.00 80.00
7 Josh Booty 5.00 12.00
8 Chris Chambers 8.00 20.00
9 Nate Clements 5.00 12.00
10 Ennis Davis 3.00 8.00
11 Robert Ferguson 5.00 12.00
12 Jamar Fletcher 5.00 12.00
13 Rod Gardner 5.00 12.00
14 Casey Hampton 6.00 15.00
15 Todd Heap 8.00 20.00
16 Travis Henry 5.00 12.00
17 Jabari Holloway 4.00 10.00
19 Steve Hutchinson 6.00 15.00
20 James Jackson 5.00 12.00
21 Chad Johnson 12.50 30.00
22 Rudi Johnson 6.00 15.00
23 LaMont Jordan 6.00 15.00
24 Ben Leard 5.00 12.00
25 Torrance Marshall 5.00 12.00
26 Deuce McAllister 8.00 20.00
27 Mike McMahon 5.00 12.00
28 Snoop Minnis 4.00 10.00
29 Quincy Morgan 5.00 12.00
30 Santana Moss 8.00 20.00
31 Bobby Newcombe 5.00 12.00
32 Moran Norris 3.00 8.00
33 Jesse Palmer 5.00 12.00
34 Tommy Polley 5.00 12.00
35 Dominic Raiola 5.00 12.00
36 Ken-Yon Rambo 4.00 10.00
37 Jamal Reynolds 5.00 12.00
38 Koren Robinson 5.00 12.00
39 Sage Rosenfels 5.00 12.00
40 Justin Smith 5.00 12.00
41 David Terrell 5.00 12.00
42 Anthony Thomas 5.00 12.00
43 LaDainian Tomlinson 40.00 80.00
44 Marques Tuiasosopo 5.00 12.00
45 Michael Vick 40.00 80.00
46 Kenyatta Walker 3.00 8.00
47 Chad Ward 3.00 8.00
48 Gerard Warren 5.00 12.00
49 Reggie Wayne 15.00 30.00
50 Chris Weinke 5.00 12.00
18 Willie Howard 4.00 10.00
(not issued in packs)

2001 Press Pass Autograph Power Picks

STATED PRINT RUN 250 SERIAL #'d SETS
STATED ODDS 1:320 HOBBY
1 Michael Vick/100 60.00 120.00
2 LaDainian Tomlinson 50.00 100.00
3 David Terrell 6.00 15.00
4 Koren Robinson 6.00 15.00
5 Santana Moss 10.00 25.00
7 Michael Bennett 6.00 15.00
8 Drew Brees 50.00 100.00
9 Chris Weinke 6.00 15.00

2001 Press Pass Big Numbers

COMPLETE SET (9) 6.00 15.00
STATED ODDS 1:12
*DIE CUTS: .6X TO 1.5X BASIC INSERTS
DIE CUT STATED ODDS 1:24
BN1 Drew Brees 2.00 5.00
BN2 Michael Vick 1.25 3.00
BN3 Deuce McAllister .30 .75
BN4 LaDainian Tomlinson 1.00 2.50
BN5 Santana Moss .40 1.00
BN6 David Terrell .25 .60
BN7 Freddie Mitchell .20 .50
BN8 Koren Robinson .25 .60
BN9 Chad Johnson .50 1.25

2001 Press Pass Breakout

COMPLETE SET (36) 12.50 30.00
ONE PER PACK
B1 Drew Brees 2.00 5.00
B2 Michael Vick 1.25 3.00
B3 Chris Weinke .25 .60
B4 Marques Tuiasosopo .25 .60
B5 Josh Heupel .30 .75
B6 Sage Rosenfels .30 .75
B7 Mike McMahon .25 .60
B8 Deuce McAllister .30 .75
B9 LaDainian Tomlinson 1.00 2.50
B10 LaMont Jordan .30 .75
B11 James Jackson .20 .50
B12 Travis Henry .25 .60
B13 Anthony Thomas .30 .75
B14 Michael Bennett .25 .60
B15 Kevan Barlow .25 .60
B16 Rudi Johnson .30 .75
B17 Travis Minor .25 .60
B18 Ken-Yon Rambo .20 .50
B19 Santana Moss .40 1.00
B20 Quincy Morgan .25 .60
B21 Rod Gardner .25 .60
B22 David Terrell .25 .60
B23 Chris Chambers .30 .75
B24 Reggie Wayne .60 1.50
B25 Chad Johnson .50 1.25
B26 Snoop Minnis .20 .50
B27 Freddie Mitchell .20 .50
B28 Koren Robinson .25 .60
B29 Todd Heap .30 .75
B30 Leonard Davis .30 .75
B31 Kenyatta Walker .20 .50
B32 Jamal Reynolds .20 .50
B33 Richard Seymour .30 .75
B34 Justin Smith .30 .75
B35 Jamar Fletcher .20 .50
B36 David Terrell CL .20 .50

2001 Press Pass Game Jerseys

STATED ODDS 1:320 HOB, 1:720 RET
STATED PRINT RUN 400 SER.#'d SETS
JCCW Chris Weinke 8.00 20.00
JCDB Drew Brees 12.50 30.00
JCJS Justin Smith 8.00 20.00
JCLT LaDainian Tomlinson 12.50 30.00
JCMB Michael Bennett 8.00 20.00
JCMV Michael Vick 12.50 30.00
JCMVDB Michael Vick 15.00 40.00
Drew Brees

2001 Press Pass Paydirt

COMPLETE SET (6) 7.50 20.00
STATED ODDS 1:24
PD1 Drew Brees 4.00 10.00
PD2 Michael Vick 2.50 6.00
PD3 Deuce McAllister .60 1.50
PD4 LaDainian Tomlinson 2.00 5.00
PD5 Santana Moss .75 2.00
PD6 David Terrell .50 1.25

2001 Press Pass Showbound

COMPLETE SET (12) 8.00 20.00
STATED ODDS 1:8
SB1 Drew Brees 2.50 6.00
SB2 Michael Vick 1.50 4.00
SB3 Chris Weinke .30 .75
SB4 Koren Robinson .30 .75
SB5 Deuce McAllister .40 1.00
SB6 Michael Bennett .30 .75
SB7 LaDainian Tomlinson 1.25 3.00
SB8 Santana Moss .50 1.25
SB9 Rod Gardner .30 .75
SB10 David Terrell .30 .75
SB11 Chris Chambers .40 1.00
SB12 Chad Johnson .60 1.50

2002 Press Pass

Press Pass was released as a 50-card set featuring the top 2002 NFL draft picks with each card printed with silver foil highlights. The cardbacks carry college statistics and pertinent information highlighting each player's most impressive skills. Press Pass was released in both Hobby and Retail form. Hobby boxes included 24-packs containing five cards each and carried a suggested retail price of $3.59. Retail was issued in boxes of 36-packs containing four cards each and carried a suggested retail price of $2.99. Five short-printed (1:14 packs overall) Power Picks cards were included at the end of the set.

COMPLETE SET (50) 15.00 40.00
COMP.SET w/o SP's (45) 10.00 25.00
1 David Carr .40 1.00
2 Eric Crouch .40 1.00
3 Rohan Davey .40 1.00
4 David Garrard .50 1.25
5 Joey Harrington .40 1.00
6 Kurt Kittner .25 .60
7 David Neill .25 .60
8 Patrick Ramsey .40 1.00
9 Antwaan Randle El .40 1.00
10 Damien Anderson .25 .60
11 T.J. Duckett .40 1.00
12 DeShaun Foster .40 1.00
13 Lamar Gordon .30 .75
14 William Green .30 .75
15 Leonard Henry .25 .60
16 Adrian Peterson .40 1.00
17 Clinton Portis .50 1.25
18 Jonathan Wells .40 1.00
19 Brian Westbrook .60 1.50
20 Antonio Bryant .40 1.00
21 Reche Caldwell .40 1.00
22 Kelly Campbell .30 .75
23 Andre Davis .30 .75
24 Jabar Gaffney .40 1.00
25 Ron Johnson .30 .75
26 Ashley Lelie .30 .75
27 Josh Reed .30 .75
28 Cliff Russell .25 .60
29 Donte Stallworth .40 1.00
30 Javon Walker .40 1.00
31 Marquise Walker .25 .60
32 Daniel Graham .30 .75
33 Jeremy Shockey .60 1.50
34 Bryant McKinnie .25 .60
35 Mike Pearson .25 .60
36 Mike Williams .25 .60
37 Phillip Buchanon .40 1.00
38 Quentin Jammer .40 1.00
39 Kalimba Edwards .30 .75
40 Julius Peppers .75 2.00
41 Wendell Bryant .25 .60
42 John Henderson .30 .75
43 Ryan Sims .40 1.00
44 Roy Williams .40 1.00
45 David Carr CL .30 .75
46 David Carr PP 1.25 3.00
47 Joey Harrington PP 1.25 3.00
48 T.J. Duckett PP 1.25 3.00
49 Donte Stallworth PP 1.25 3.00
50 William Green PP 1.00 2.50

2002 Press Pass Gold Zone

*1-45 SINGLES: .5X TO 1.2X BASIC CARDS
*46-50 POWER PICK: .15X TO .4X BASIC PP
ONE PER HOBBY PACK

2002 Press Pass Reflectors

*SINGLES: 3X TO 8X BASIC CARDS
STATED PRINT RUN 500 SER.#'d SETS

2002 Press Pass Torquers

*1-45 SINGLES: .8X TO 2X BASIC CARDS
*46-50 POWER PICK: .25X TO .6X BASIC CARDS
ONE PER RETAIL PACK

2002 Press Pass Autographs

STATED ODDS 1:8 HOB, 1:36 RET
1 Damien Anderson 3.00 8.00
2 Antonio Bryant 5.00 12.00
3 Phillip Buchanon 5.00 12.00
4 Reche Caldwell 5.00 12.00
5 Rocky Calmus 4.00 10.00
6 Kelly Campbell 4.00 10.00
7 David Carr 5.00 12.00
8 Eric Crouch 5.00 12.00
9 Rohan Davey 5.00 12.00
10 Andre Davis 4.00 10.00
11 T.J. Duckett 5.00 12.00
12 Kalimba Edwards 4.00 10.00
13 DeShaun Foster 5.00 12.00
14 Jabar Gaffney 5.00 12.00
15 David Garrard 10.00 25.00
16 Lamar Gordon 4.00 10.00
17 Daniel Graham 4.00 10.00
18 William Green 4.00 10.00
19 Joey Harrington 5.00 12.00
20 John Henderson 4.00 10.00
21 Leonard Henry 3.00 8.00
22 Kyle Johnson 3.00 8.00
23 Ron Johnson 4.00 10.00
24 Levi Jones 3.00 8.00
25 Kurt Kittner 3.00 8.00
26 Ashley Lelie 4.00 10.00
27 Josh McCown 5.00 12.00
28 Freddie Milons 3.00 8.00
29 Maurice Morris 4.00 10.00
30 David Neill 3.00 8.00
31 Mike Pearson 3.00 8.00
32 Adrian Peterson 5.00 12.00
33 Patrick Ramsey 5.00 12.00
34 Antwaan Randle El 5.00 12.00
35 Josh Reed 4.00 10.00
36 Cliff Russell 3.00 8.00
37 Ryan Sims 5.00 12.00
38 Luke Staley 3.00 8.00
39 Donte Stallworth 5.00 12.00
40 Javon Walker 5.00 12.00
41 Marquise Walker 3.00 8.00
42 Anthony Weaver 3.00 8.00
43 Jonathan Wells 5.00 12.00
44 Brian Westbrook 20.00 40.00
45 Roy Williams 6.00 15.00

2002 Press Pass Autograph Power Picks

STATED PRINT RUN 250 SER.#'d SETS
1 Antonio Bryant 8.00 20.00
2 David Carr 8.00 20.00
3 Eric Crouch 8.00 20.00
4 Andre Davis 6.00 15.00
5 T.J. Duckett 8.00 20.00
6 DeShaun Foster 8.00 20.00
7 William Green 6.00 15.00
8 Joey Harrington 8.00 20.00
9 Kurt Kittner 5.00 12.00
10 Ashley Lelie 6.00 15.00
11 Josh Reed 6.00 15.00
12 Marquise Walker 5.00 12.00

2002 Press Pass Big Numbers

COMPLETE SET (36) 12.50 30.00
ONE PER PACK
BN1 David Carr .50 1.25
BN2 Eric Crouch .50 1.25
BN3 Rohan Davey .50 1.25
BN4 Joey Harrington .50 1.25
BN5 Kurt Kittner .30 .75
BN6 Patrick Ramsey .50 1.25
BN7 Antwaan Randle El .50 1.25
BN8 T.J. Duckett .50 1.25
BN9 DeShaun Foster .50 1.25
BN10 Lamar Gordon .40 1.00
BN11 William Green .40 1.00
BN12 Adrian Peterson .50 1.25
BN13 Clinton Portis .60 1.50
BN14 Javon Walker .50 1.25
BN15 Brian Westbrook .75 2.00
BN16 Antonio Bryant .50 1.25
BN17 Reche Caldwell .50 1.25
BN18 Kelly Campbell .40 1.00
BN19 Andre Davis .40 1.00
BN20 Jabar Gaffney .50 1.25
BN21 Ashley Lelie .40 1.00
BN22 Josh Reed .40 1.00
BN23 Donte Stallworth .50 1.25
BN24 Marquise Walker .30 .75
BN25 Daniel Graham .40 1.00
BN26 Jeremy Shockey .75 2.00
BN27 Bryant McKinnie .30 .75
BN28 Mike Pearson .30 .75
BN29 Phillip Buchanon .50 1.25
BN30 Quentin Jammer .50 1.25
BN31 Kalimba Edwards .40 1.00
BN32 Julius Peppers 1.00 2.50
BN33 Wendell Bryant .30 .75
BN34 John Henderson .40 1.00
BN35 Roy Williams .50 1.25
BN36 Joey Harrington CL .40 1.00

2002 Press Pass Game Used Jerseys

JERSEY/225 ODDS 1:160H, 1:720R
STATED PRINT RUN 225 SER.#'d SETS
JCAP Adrian Peterson 6.00 15.00
JCDC David Carr 6.00 15.00
JCDF DeShaun Foster 6.00 15.00
JCDG David Garrard 8.00 20.00
JCEC Eric Crouch 6.00 15.00
JCJH Joey Harrington 6.00 15.00
JCJM Josh McCown 6.00 15.00
JCJR Josh Reed 5.00 12.00
JCKK Kurt Kittner 4.00 10.00
JCLH Leonard Henry 4.00 10.00
JCLS Luke Staley 4.00 10.00
JCRW Roy Williams 6.00 15.00
JCWG William Green 5.00 12.00

2002 Press Pass Paydirt

COMPLETE SET (9) 6.00 15.00
STATED ODDS 1:12
*DIE CUT: .6X TO 1.5X BASIC INSERTS
PD1 David Carr .60 1.50
PD2 Joey Harrington .60 1.50
PD3 Kurt Kittner .40 1.00
PD4 T.J. Duckett .60 1.50
PD5 William Green .50 1.25
PD6 Clinton Portis .75 2.00
PD7 Antonio Bryant .60 1.50
PD8 DeShaun Foster .60 1.50
PD9 Donte Stallworth .60 1.50

2002 Press Pass Primetime

COMPLETE SET (12) 7.50 20.00
STATED ODDS 1:8
PT1 David Carr .60 1.50
PT2 Joey Harrington .60 1.50
PT3 T.J. Duckett .60 1.50
PT4 William Green .50 1.25
PT5 DeShaun Foster .60 1.50
PT6 Clinton Portis .75 2.00
PT7 Antonio Bryant .60 1.50
PT8 Jabar Gaffney .60 1.50
PT9 Ashley Lelie .50 1.25
PT10 Josh Reed .50 1.25
PT11 Donte Stallworth .60 1.50
PT12 Julius Peppers 1.25 3.00

2002 Press Pass Rookie Chase

COMPLETE SET (12) 15.00 40.00
STATED ODDS 1:24
RC1 David Carr 1.50 4.00
RC2 Joey Harrington 1.50 4.00
RC3 William Green 1.25 3.00
RC4 T.J. Duckett 1.50 4.00
RC5 Jabar Gaffney 1.50 4.00
RC6 Donte Stallworth 1.50 4.00
RC7 Antonio Bryant 1.50 4.00
RC8 Jeremy Shockey 2.50 6.00
RC9 Julius Peppers WIN 3.00 8.00
RC10 Josh Reed 1.25 3.00
RC11 DeShaun Foster 1.50 4.00
RC12 Field Card WIN 1.50 4.00

2002 Press Pass Showbound

COMPLETE SET (6) 4.00 10.00
STATED ODDS 1:24
SB1 David Carr .75 2.00
SB2 Joey Harrington .75 2.00
SB3 William Green .60 1.50
SB4 T.J. Duckett .75 2.00
SB5 Antonio Bryant .75 2.00
SB6 Julius Peppers 1.50 4.00

2003 Press Pass

Released in April 2003, this set features 45 draft pick players, and five power pick subset cards, which were inserted 1:14 packs. Boxes contained 28 packs of 5 cards. SRP was $3.99.

COMPLETE SET (50) 20.00 50.00
COMP.SET w/o SP's (45) 10.00 25.00
1 Brad Banks .30 .75
2 Kyle Boller .40 1.00
3 Ken Dorsey .30 .75
4 Jason Gesser .30 .75
5 Rex Grossman .40 1.00
6 Kliff Kingsbury .30 .75
7 Byron Leftwich .40 1.00
8 Carson Palmer .75 2.00
9 Dave Ragone .25 .60
10 Chris Simms .40 1.00
11 Brian St.Pierre .30 .75
12 Chris Brown .25 .60
13 Avon Cobourne .25 .60
14 Dahrran Diedrick .25 .60
15 Justin Fargas .40 1.00
16 Earnest Graham .40 1.00
17 Larry Johnson .40 1.00
18 Willis McGahee .50 1.25
19 Musa Smith .25 .60
20 Onterrio Smith .25 .60
21 Lee Suggs .30 .75
22 Anquan Boldin .60 1.50
23 Talman Gardner .25 .60
24 Taylor Jacobs .25 .60
25 Andre Johnson 1.00 2.50
26 Bryant Johnson .40 1.00
27 Brandon Lloyd .60 1.50
28 Charles Rogers .30 .75
29 Kelley Washington .25 .60
30 Teyo Johnson .30 .75
31 Bennie Joppru .25 .60
32 Jason Witten 1.00 2.50
33 Andrew Pinnock .30 .75
34 Jordan Gross .25 .60
35 Kwame Harris .25 .60
36 Eric Steinbach .25 .60
37 Brett Williams .25 .60
38 Terence Newman .30 .75
39 Marcus Trufant .30 .75
40 Andre Woolfolk .30 .75
41 Terrell Suggs .40 1.00
42 Jimmy Kennedy .30 .75
43 Boss Bailey .30 .75
44 Mike Doss .40 1.00
45 Carson Palmer CL .30 .75
46 Carson Palmer PP 1.50 4.00
47 Byron Leftwich PP .75 2.00
48 Charles Rogers PP .60 1.50
49 Kyle Boller PP .75 2.00
50 Andre Johnson PP 2.00 5.00

2003 Press Pass Retail

*RETAIL: .4X TO 1X HOBBY
RETAIL PRINTED WITH SILVER FOIL

2003 Press Pass Gold Zone

COMPLETE SET (45) 15.00 40.00
*GOLD: .6X TO 1.5X BASIC CARDS
ONE GOLD PER PACK

2003 Press Pass Reflectors

*REFLEC/500: 2.5X TO 6X BASIC CARDS
STATED PRINT RUN 500 SER.#'d SETS

2003 Press Pass Reflectors Proofs

*PROOF/100: 5X TO 12X BASIC CARDS
STATED PRINT RUN 100 SER.#'d SETS

2003 Press Pass Torquers

ONE PER RETAIL PACK

2003 Press Pass Autographed Footballs

ONE PER HOBBY CASE
PRICES ARE FOR SIGNED BALL AND COA
1 Byron Leftwich 30.00 80.00
2 Carson Palmer 50.00 100.00
3 Dave Ragone 12.50 30.00

2003 Press Pass Autographs Bronze

OVERALL AUTO ODDS 1:7 HOB, 1:56 RET
*GOLD/100: .6X TO 1.5X BRONZE AU
GOLD PRINT RUN 100 SER.#'d SETS
*SILVER/200: .5X TO 1.2X BRONZE AU
SILVER PRINT RUN 200 SER.#'d SETS
1 Boss Bailey 5.00 12.00
2 Brad Banks 5.00 12.00
3 Anquan Boldin 10.00 25.00
4 Kyle Boller 6.00 15.00
5 Chris Brown 4.00 10.00
6 Mike Bush 4.00 10.00
7 Tyrone Calico 5.00 12.00
8 Avon Cobourne 4.00 10.00
9 Angelo Crowell 5.00 12.00
10 Chris Davis 5.00 12.00
11 Domanick Davis 5.00 12.00
12 Dahrran Diedrick 4.00 10.00
13 Ken Dorsey 5.00 12.00
14 Mike Doss 6.00 15.00
15 Justin Fargas 6.00 15.00
16 Talman Gardner 4.00 10.00
17 Jason Gesser 5.00 12.00
18 Earnest Graham 6.00 15.00
19 Justin Griffith 5.00 12.00
20 DeJuan Groce 6.00 15.00
21 Jordan Gross 4.00 10.00
22 Kwame Harris 4.00 10.00
23 Michael Haynes 4.00 10.00
24 Wayne Hunter 4.00 10.00
25 Taylor Jacobs 4.00 10.00
26 Larry Johnson 6.00 15.00
27 Teyo Johnson 5.00 12.00
28 Ben Johnson 4.00 10.00
29 Bryant Johnson 6.00 15.00
30 Bennie Joppru 4.00 10.00
31 Kareem Kelly 4.00 10.00
32 Chris Kelsay 5.00 12.00
33 Jimmy Kennedy 5.00 12.00
34 Kliff Kingsbury 5.00 12.00
35 Byron Leftwich 6.00 15.00
36 Brandon Lloyd 10.00 25.00
37 Vincent Manuwai 4.00 10.00
38 Rashean Mathis 5.00 12.00
39 Sultan McCullough 4.00 10.00
40 Jerome McDougle 4.00 10.00
41 Willis McGahee 8.00 20.00
42 Terence Newman 5.00 12.00
43 Tony Pashos 4.00 10.00
44 Carson Palmer
45 Andrew Pinnock 5.00 12.00
46 Dave Ragone 4.00 10.00
47 DeWayne Robertson 5.00 12.00
48 Steve Sciullo 4.00 10.00
49 Musa Smith 4.00 10.00
50 Brian St.Pierre 5.00 12.00
51 Eric Steinbach 4.00 10.00
52 Jon Stinchcomb 5.00 12.00
53 Terrell Suggs 8.00 20.00
54 LaBrandon Toefield 5.00 12.00
55 Marcus Trufant 5.00 12.00
56 Bobby Wade 5.00 12.00
57 Seneca Wallace 6.00 15.00
58 Shane Walton 4.00 10.00
59 Kelley Washington 4.00 10.00
60 Dennis Weathersby 4.00 10.00
61 DeWayne White 4.00 10.00
62 Brett Williams 4.00 10.00
63 Juston Wood 4.00 10.00
64 Andre Woolfolk 5.00 12.00

2003 Press Pass Autograph Power Picks

STATED PRINT RUN 250 SER.#'d SETS
1 Brad Banks 5.00 12.00
2 Anquan Boldin 10.00 25.00
3 Kyle Boller 6.00 15.00
4 Taylor Jacobs 4.00 10.00
5 Larry Johnson 6.00 15.00
6 Byron Leftwich 6.00 15.00
7 Brandon Lloyd 10.00 25.00
8 Carson Palmer 40.00 80.00
9 Dave Ragone 4.00 10.00

2003 Press Pass Big Numbers

COMPLETE SET (36) 10.00 25.00
STATED ODDS ONE PER PACK
BN1 Brad Banks .40 1.00
BN2 Anquan Boldin .75 2.00
BN3 Kyle Boller
BN4 Chris Brown .30 .75
BN5 Avon Cobourne .30 .75
BN6 Ken Dorsey .40 1.00
BN7 Mike Doss .50 1.25
BN8 Justin Fargas .50 1.25
BN9 Talman Gardner .30 .75
BN10 Earnest Graham .50 1.25
BN11 Rex Grossman .50 1.25
BN12 Taylor Jacobs .30 .75
BN13 Andre Johnson 1.25 3.00
BN14 Bryant Johnson .50 1.25
BN15 Larry Johnson .50 1.25
BN16 Teyo Johnson .40 1.00
BN17 Bennie Joppru .30 .75
BN18 Jimmy Kennedy .40 1.00
BN19 Byron Leftwich .50 1.25
BN20 Brandon Lloyd .75 2.00
BN21 Jerome McDougle .30 .75
BN22 Willis McGahee .60 1.50
BN23 Terence Newman
BN24 Carson Palmer 1.00 2.50
BN25 Dave Ragone .30 .75
BN26 Charles Rogers .40 1.00
BN27 Chris Simms .50 1.25
BN28 Musa Smith .30 .75
BN29 Onterrio Smith .30 .75
BN30 Brian St.Pierre .40 1.00
BN31 Lee Suggs .40 1.00
BN32 Terrell Suggs .50 1.25
BN33 Kelley Washington .30 .75
BN34 Jason Witten 1.25 3.00
BN35 Andre Woolfolk .40 1.00
BN36 Byron Leftwich .50 1.25

2003 Press Pass Game Used Jerseys Gold

GOLD PRINT RUN 475 SER.#'d SETS
*HOLOFOIL/150: .6X TO 1.5X GOLD/475
HOLOFOIL PRINT RUN 150 SER.#'d SETS
*SILVER/225: .5X TO 1.2X GOLD/475
SILVER PRINT RUN 225 SER.#'d SETS
OVERALL JERSEY ODDS 1:84 HOB, 1:280 RET
JCBJ Bennie Joppru 3.00 8.00
JCBL Byron Leftwich 5.00 12.00
JCCP Carson Palmer 10.00 25.00
JCEG Earnest Graham 5.00 12.00
JCKD Ken Dorsey 4.00 10.00
JCKK Kareem Kelly 3.00 8.00
JCSW Seneca Wallace 5.00 12.00
JCTJ Teyo Johnson 4.00 10.00

2003 Press Pass Paydirt

COMPLETE SET (7) 10.00 25.00
STATED ODDS 1:14
PD1 Kyle Boller .75 2.00
PD2 Andre Johnson 2.00 5.00
PD3 Larry Johnson .75 2.00
PD4 Byron Leftwich .75 2.00
PD5 Carson Palmer 1.50 4.00
PD6 Rex Grossman .75 2.00
PD7 Charles Rogers .60 1.50

2003 Press Pass Primetime

COMPLETE SET (10) 10.00 25.00
STATED ODDS 1:9
PT1 Kyle Boller .75 2.00
PT2 Rex Grossman .75 2.00
PT3 Larry Johnson .75 2.00
PT4 Andre Johnson 2.00 5.00
PT5 Byron Leftwich .75 2.00
PT6 Carson Palmer 1.50 4.00
PT7 Dave Ragone .50 1.25
PT8 Charles Rogers .60 1.50
PT9 Chris Simms .75 2.00
PT10 Onterrio Smith .50 1.25

2003 Press Pass Rookie Chase

STATED ODDS 1:28
RC1 Taylor Jacobs .75 2.00
RC2 Larry Johnson 1.25 3.00
RC3 Andre Johnson 3.00 8.00
RC4 Byron Leftwich 1.25 3.00
RC5 Carson Palmer 2.50 6.00
RC6 Dave Ragone .75 2.00
RC7 Charles Rogers 1.00 2.50
RC8 Onterrio Smith .75 2.00
RC9 Terrell Suggs 1.25 3.00

2003 Press Pass Showbound

COMPLETE SET (7) 12.00 30.00
STATED ODDS 1:28

SB1 Byron Leftwich	1.25	3.00
SB2 Carson Palmer	2.50	6.00
SB3 Dave Ragone	.75	2.00
SB4 Larry Johnson	1.25	3.00
SB5 Charles Rogers	1.00	2.50
SB6 Andre Johnson	3.00	8.00
SB7 Kyle Boller	1.25	3.00

2004 Press Pass

The basic Press Pass product released in late April 2004. The base set consists of 50-cards including 5-Power Pick short prints at the end of the set. Mike Williams made an appearance in this product although he was declared ineligible for the NFL Draft. Hobby boxes contained 24-packs of 5-cards. Four parallel sets and a variety of inserts can be found seeded in hobby and retail packs highlighted by the Game Used Jerseys and the Autograph Inserts.

COMPLETE SET (50)	20.00	50.00
COMP.SET w/o SP's (45)	12.50	30.00
1 Casey Clausen	.30	.75
2 Craig Krenzel	.30	.75
3 J.P. Losman	.30	.75
4 Eli Manning	2.50	6.00
5 Luke McCown	.30	.75
6 John Navarre	.25	.60
7 Cody Pickett	.30	.75
8 Philip Rivers	1.50	4.00
9 Ben Roethlisberger	2.50	6.00
10 Matt Schaub	.75	2.00
11 Cedric Cobbs	.25	.60
12 Steven Jackson	.60	1.50
13 Kevin Jones	.30	.75
14 Greg Jones	.25	.60
15 Julius Jones	.30	.75
16 Jarrett Payton	.30	.75
17 Chris Perry	.30	.75
18 Michael Turner	.50	1.25
19 Quincy Wilson	.30	.75
20 Jason Wright	.25	.60
21 Bernard Berrian	.40	1.00
22 Michael Clayton	.30	.75
23 Devard Darling	.25	.60
24 Lee Evans	.40	1.00
25 Larry Fitzgerald	1.00	2.50
26 Devery Henderson	.40	1.00
27 Michael Jenkins	.40	1.00
28 Darius Watts	.25	.60
29 Mike Williams	.30	.75
30 Roy Williams WR	.40	1.00
31 Rashaun Woods	.25	.60
32 Ben Troupe	.30	.75
33 Shawn Andrews	.30	.75
34 Robert Gallery	.40	1.00
35 Tommie Harris	.40	1.00
36 Vince Wilfork	.40	1.00
37 Will Smith	.30	.75
38 Teddy Lehman	.25	.60
39 Jonathan Vilma	.40	1.00
40 D.J. Williams	.40	1.00
41 DeAngelo Hall	.40	1.00
42 Dunta Robinson	.25	.60
43 Derrick Strait	.25	.60
44 Keith Smith	.25	.60
45 Eli Manning CL	1.25	3.00
46 Eli Manning PP	4.00	10.00
47 Ben Roethlisberger PP	4.00	10.00
48 Larry Fitzgerald PP	1.50	4.00
49 Roy Williams PP	.60	1.50
50 Philip Rivers PP	2.50	6.00

2004 Press Pass Blue

COMPLETE SET (45)	30.00	60.00

*BLUES: .8X TO 2X BASIC CARDS
ONE PER RETAIL PACK

2004 Press Pass Gold

COMPLETE SET (45)	20.00	50.00

*GOLDS: .6X TO 1.5X BASIC CARDS
ONE GOLD PER HOBBY PACK

2004 Press Pass Reflectors

*REFLECTORS: 2.5X TO 6X BASIC CARDS
STATED PRINT RUN 500 SER.#'d SETS

2004 Press Pass Reflectors Proof

*REF.PROOFS: 5X TO 12X BASIC CARDS
STATED PRINT RUN 100 SER.#'d SETS

2004 Press Pass Autographs Bronze

OVERALL AUTO ODDS 1:7 PP PACKS
ALL ALSO INSERTED IN PRESS PASS SE

1 Bernard Berrian	5.00	12.00
2 Casey Clausen	4.00	10.00
2R Casey Clausen Red	5.00	12.00
3 Michael Clayton	4.00	10.00
3R Michael Clayton Red	5.00	12.00
4 Cedric Cobbs	3.00	8.00
5 Ricardo Colclough	4.00	10.00
6 Devard Darling	3.00	8.00
6R Devard Darling Red	4.00	10.00
7 Dwan Edwards	3.00	8.00
7R Dwan Edwards Red	4.00	10.00
8 Lee Evans	5.00	12.00
8R Lee Evans Red	6.00	15.00
9 Larry Fitzgerald	25.00	60.00
10 Robert Gallery	5.00	12.00
10R Robert Gallery Red	6.00	15.00
11 Jermaine Green	3.00	8.00
12 DeAngelo Hall	5.00	12.00
13 Tommie Harris	5.00	12.00
14 Ben Hartsock	3.00	8.00
15 Devery Henderson	5.00	12.00
16 Steven Jackson SP	15.00	40.00
17 Michael Jenkins	5.00	12.00
17R Michael Jenkins Red	6.00	15.00
18 Greg Jones	3.00	8.00
18R Greg Jones Red	4.00	10.00
19 Julius Jones	6.00	15.00
21 Sean Jones	4.00	10.00
22 Nate Kaeding	5.00	12.00
22R Nate Kaeding Red	6.00	15.00
23 Robert Kent	3.00	8.00
23R Robert Kent Red	4.00	10.00
24 Teddy Lehman	3.00	8.00
24R Teddy Lehman Red	4.00	10.00
25 Jared Lorenzen	4.00	10.00
25R Jared Lorenzen Red	5.00	12.00
26 Eli Manning	60.00	120.00
27 Luke McCown	4.00	10.00
28 Mewelde Moore	4.00	10.00
29 John Navarre	3.00	8.00
29R John Navarre Red	4.00	10.00
30 James Newson	5.00	12.00
30R James Newson Red	6.00	15.00
31 Tony Pape		
31R Tony Pape Red		
32 Jarrett Payton	4.00	10.00
33 Chris Perry	4.00	10.00
34 Cody Pickett	4.00	10.00
35 Philip Rivers	25.00	50.00
35R Philip Rivers Red	30.00	60.00
36 Ben Roethlisberger SP	75.00	150.00
36R Ben Roethlisberger Red	100.00	175.00
37 P.K. Sam	3.00	8.00
38 Matt Schaub	12.00	30.00
38R Matt Schaub Red	15.00	40.00
39 Justin Smiley	4.00	10.00
40 Keith Smith	3.00	8.00
40R Keith Smith Red	4.00	10.00
41 Will Smith	4.00	10.00
41R Will Smith Red	5.00	12.00
42 Jeff Smoker	4.00	10.00
42R Jeff Smoker Red	5.00	12.00
43 Derrick Strait	3.00	8.00
44 Andrae Thurman	3.00	8.00
44R Andrae Thurman Red	4.00	10.00
45 Ben Troupe	4.00	10.00
45R Ben Troupe Red	5.00	12.00
46 Michael Turner	8.00	20.00
47 Jonathan Vilma	5.00	12.00
47R Jonathan Vilma Red	6.00	15.00
48 Ben Watson	5.00	12.00
49 Darius Watts	3.00	8.00
49R Darius Watts Red	4.00	10.00
50 Vince Wilfork	5.00	12.00
51 D.J. Williams	5.00	12.00
51R D.J. Williams Red	6.00	15.00
52 Mike Williams	4.00	10.00
53 Quincy Wilson	4.00	10.00
53R Quincy Wilson Red	5.00	12.00
54 Kellen Winslow	8.00	20.00
54R Kellen Winslow Red	10.00	25.00
55 Rashaun Woods	3.00	8.00
56 Jason Wright	3.00	8.00

2004 Press Pass Autographs Blue

*BLUE: .6X TO 1.5X BRONZE AU
BLUE STATED PRINT RUN 25-50
BLUES INSERTED IN PRESS PASS SE

9 Larry Fitzgerald/25	60.00	120.00
20 Kevin Jones	6.00	15.00
26 Eli Manning	100.00	175.00
35 Philip Rivers	40.00	100.00
36 Ben Roethlisberger	100.00	200.00
36R Ben Roethlisberger Red	125.00	250.00

2004 Press Pass Autographs Gold

*GOLD: .6X TO 1.5X BRONZE AU
STATED PRINT RUN 50-100

20 Kevin Jones	6.00	15.00
26 Eli Manning	90.00	150.00
20R Eli Manning Red	100.00	175.00
35 Philip Rivers	40.00	80.00
36 Ben Roethlisberger	100.00	200.00
36R Ben Roethlisberger Red	125.00	225.00

2004 Press Pass Autographs Silver

*SILVER: .5X TO 1.2X BRONZE AU
SILVER STATED PRINT RUN 75-200

20 Kevin Jones	15.00	40.00
26 Eli Manning	90.00	150.00
35 Philip Rivers	25.00	60.00
36 Ben Roethlisberger	50.00	120.00

2004 Press Pass Big Numbers

COMPLETE SET (33)	12.50	30.00

ONE PER PACK
*COLLECTOR SERIES: .3X TO .8X

BN1 Casey Clausen	.40	1.00
BN2 Michael Clayton	.40	1.00
BN3 Cedric Cobbs	.30	.75
BN4 Devard Darling	.30	.75
BN5 Lee Evans	.50	1.25
BN6 Larry Fitzgerald	1.25	3.00
BN7 Robert Gallery	.50	1.25
BN8 DeAngelo Hall	.50	1.25
BN9 Steven Jackson	.75	2.00
BN10 Michael Jenkins	.50	1.25
BN11 Greg Jones	.30	.75
BN12 Kevin Jones	.40	1.00
BN13 Craig Krenzel	.40	1.00
BN14 J.P. Losman	.40	1.00
BN15 Eli Manning	3.00	8.00
BN16 John Navarre	.30	.75
BN17 Jarrett Payton	.40	1.00
BN18 Chris Perry	.40	1.00
BN19 Cody Pickett	.40	1.00
BN20 Philip Rivers	2.00	5.00
BN21 Ben Roethlisberger	3.00	8.00
BN22 Matt Schaub	1.00	2.50
BN23 Will Smith	.40	1.00
BN24 Ben Troupe	.40	1.00
BN25 Michael Turner	.60	1.50
BN26 Jonathan Vilma	.50	1.25
BN27 Vince Wilfork	.50	1.25
BN28 Quincy Wilson	.40	1.00
BN29 D.J. Williams	.50	1.25
BN30 Mike Williams	.40	1.00
BN31 Roy Williams WR	.50	1.25
BN32 Rashaun Woods	.30	.75
BN33 Eli Manning CL	3.00	8.00

2004 Press Pass Game Used Jerseys Silver

SILVER PRINT RUN 300 SER.#'d SETS
*GOLD/100: .6X TO 1.5X SILVER/300
GOLD PRINT RUN 100 SER.#'d SETS
*HOLOFOIL/50: .8X TO 2X SILVER/300
HOLOFOIL PRINT RUN 50 SER.#'d SETS
OVERALL JERSEY ODDS 1:72 H

JCBR Ben Roethlisberger	15.00	40.00
JCCP Cody Pickett	3.00	8.00
JCDD Devard Darling	2.50	6.00
JCDW Darius Watts	2.50	6.00
JCEM Eli Manning	20.00	40.00
JCJG Jermaine Green	2.50	6.00
JCJL Jared Lorenzen	3.00	8.00
JCJP Jarrett Payton	3.00	8.00
JCLM Luke McCown	3.00	8.00
JCMM Mewelde Moore	3.00	8.00
JCMS Matt Schaub	10.00	25.00
JCSJ Steven Jackson	10.00	25.00

2004 Press Pass Paydirt

COMPLETE SET (12)	12.50	30.00

STATED ODDS 1:6

PD1 Eli Manning	4.00	10.00
PD2 Roy Williams WR	.60	1.50
PD3 Kevin Jones	.50	1.25
PD4 Philip Rivers	2.50	6.00
PD5 Rashaun Woods	.40	1.00
PD6 Ben Roethlisberger	4.00	10.00
PD7 Ben Troupe	.50	1.25
PD8 Steven Jackson	1.00	2.50
PD9 Michael Clayton	.50	1.25
PD10 Chris Perry	.50	1.25
PD11 Larry Fitzgerald	1.50	4.00
PD12 Greg Jones	.40	1.00

2004 Press Pass Showbound

COMPLETE SET (9)	12.50	30.00

STATED ODDS 1:12

SB1 Steven Jackson	1.25	3.00
SB2 Larry Fitzgerald	2.00	5.00
SB3 Eli Manning	5.00	12.00
SB4 Kevin Jones	.60	1.50
SB5 Roy Williams WR	.75	2.00
SB6 Ben Roethlisberger	5.00	12.00
SB7 Philip Rivers	3.00	8.00
SB8 Chris Perry	.60	1.50
SB9 J.P. Losman	.60	1.50

2005 Press Pass

Press Pass was initially released in late April 2005. The base set consists of 50-cards with 5-short printed Power Picks. Hobby boxes contained 24-packs of 5-cards and carried an S.R.P. of $3.99 per pack. Four parallel sets and a variety of inserts can be found seeded in packs highlighted by the popular multi-tiered Autograph inserts. Red ink versions of many autographed cards were also created adding another level of collectibility.

COMPLETE SET (50)	25.00	50.00
COMP.SET w/o PP'S (45)	12.50	30.00

POWER PICK STATED ODDS 1:14 H/R
UNPRICED HOBBY SOLO PRINT RUN 1 SET

1 Derek Anderson	.30	.75
2 Brock Berlin	.30	.75
3 Charlie Frye	.40	1.00
4 Gino Guidugli	.25	.60
5 David Greene	.25	.60
6 Stefan LeFors	.25	.60
7 Dan Orlovsky	.40	1.00
8 Kyle Orton	.40	1.00
9 Aaron Rodgers	3.00	8.00
10 Alex Smith QB	.60	1.50
11 Andrew Walter	.30	.75
12 Jason White	.40	1.00
13 J.J. Arrington	.30	.75
14 Ronnie Brown	.50	1.25
15 Anthony Davis	.25	.60
16 Kay-Jay Harris	.25	.60
17 T.A. McLendon	.25	.60
18 Ryan Moats	.30	.75
19 Vernand Morency	.30	.75
20 Cadillac Williams	.40	1.00
21 Mark Bradley	.25	.60
22 Reggie Brown	.25	.60
23 Mark Clayton	.40	1.00
24 Braylon Edwards	.50	1.25
25 Fred Gibson	.30	.75
26 Terrence Murphy	.25	.60
27 J.R. Russell	.25	.60
28 Craphonso Thorpe	.25	.60
29 Roddy White	.50	1.25
30 Mike Williams	.40	1.00
31 Troy Williamson	.30	.75
32 Heath Miller	.50	1.25
33 Alex Smith TE	.25	.60
34 Khalif Barnes	.25	.60
35 Jammal Brown	.40	1.00
36 Brandon Browner	.40	1.00
37 Marlin Jackson	.25	.60
38 Carlos Rogers	.40	1.00
39 Antrel Rolle	.40	1.00
40 Dan Cody	.30	.75
41 Erasmus James	.30	.75
42 David Pollack	.30	.75
43 Anttaj Hawthorne	.25	.60
44 Derrick Johnson	.30	.75
45 Ronnie Brown CL	.25	.60
46 Cadillac Williams PP	.75	2.00
47 Aaron Rodgers PP	6.00	15.00
48 Alex Smith QB PP	1.25	3.00
49 Braylon Edwards PP	1.00	2.50
50 Mike Williams PP	.75	2.00

2005 Press Pass Blue

COMPLETE SET (45)	25.00	60.00

*SINGLES: .8X TO 2X BASIC CARDS
ONE PER RETAIL PACK

2005 Press Pass Reflectors

*SINGLES: 2.5X TO 6X BASIC CARDS
STATED PRINT RUN 500 SER.#'d SETS

2005 Press Pass Reflectors Proof

*SINGLES: 4X TO 10X BASIC CARDS
REFLECTORS/100 INSERTS IN HOBBY ONLY

2005 Press Pass Autograph Power Picks

STATED PRINT RUN 50-250

1 Ronnie Brown/76*	30.00	80.00
1R Ronnie Brown/24* Red	40.00	100.00
2 Braylon Edwards/40*	40.00	100.00
3 Charlie Frye/240*	12.00	30.00
4 Heath Miller/40*	15.00	40.00
5 Aaron Rodgers/246*	150.00	250.00
6 Andrew Walter/240*	10.00	25.00
7 Mike Williams/59*	15.00	40.00
7R Mike Williams/41* Red	20.00	50.00
8 Troy Williamson/250	12.00	30.00

2005 Press Pass Autographs Bronze

AUTO OVERALL ODDS 1:7

1 Derek Anderson	5.00	12.00
2 J.J. Arrington	5.00	12.00
3 Marion Barber	6.00	15.00
4 Khalif Barnes	4.00	10.00
5 Brock Berlin	5.00	12.00
6 Mark Bradley	4.00	10.00
7 Elton Brown	4.00	10.00
8 Jammal Brown	6.00	15.00
9 Reggie Brown	4.00	10.00
10 Ronnie Brown SP	20.00	50.00
11 Brandon Browner	6.00	15.00
12 Luis Castillo	5.00	12.00
13 Mark Clayton	5.00	12.00
14 Dan Cody	5.00	12.00
15 Jerome Collins	5.00	12.00
16 Sean Considine	4.00	10.00
17 Anthony Davis	4.00	10.00
18 Thomas Davis	4.00	10.00
19 Braylon Edwards SP	20.00	50.00
20 Ciatrick Fason	4.00	10.00
21 Diamond Ferri	4.00	10.00
22 Charlie Frye SP	8.00	20.00
23 Fred Gibson	5.00	12.00
24 David Greene	4.00	10.00
25 Gino Guidugli	4.00	10.00
26 Kay-Jay Harris	4.00	10.00
27 Anttaj Hawthorne	4.00	10.00
28 Chris Henry	6.00	15.00
29 Keron Henry	4.00	10.00
30 Noah Herron	4.00	10.00
31 Marlin Jackson	4.00	10.00
32 Erasmus James	5.00	12.00
33 Derrick Johnson	5.00	12.00
34 Stefan LeFors	4.00	10.00
35 T.A. McLendon	4.00	10.00
36 Heath Miller	10.00	25.00
37 Ryan Moats	4.00	10.00
38 Vernand Morency	4.00	10.00
39 Terrence Murphy	4.00	10.00
40 Dan Orlovsky	6.00	15.00
41 Kyle Orton	6.00	15.00
42 David Pollack	5.00	12.00
43 Walter Reyes	4.00	10.00
44 Aaron Rodgers SP	125.00	200.00
45 Carlos Rogers	6.00	15.00
46 Antrel Rolle	6.00	15.00
47 J.R. Russell	4.00	10.00
48 Barrett Ruud	6.00	15.00
49 Eric Shelton	4.00	10.00
50 Alex Smith TE	4.00	10.00
51 Craphonso Thorpe	4.00	10.00
52 Andrew Walter	5.00	12.00
53 Jason White	6.00	15.00
54 Roddy White	8.00	20.00
55 Cadillac Williams SP	8.00	20.00
56 Mike Williams SP	6.00	15.00
57 Troy Williamson	5.00	12.00
58 Stanley Wilson	5.00	12.00

2005 Press Pass Autographs Bronze Red Ink

*UNLISTED RED INK: .6X TO 1.5X
CARDS W/PRINT RUNS UNDER 20 NOT PRICED

1 Derek Anderson/50*	8.00	20.00
3 Marion Barber/20*	10.00	25.00
5 Brock Berlin/50*	8.00	20.00
6 Mark Bradley/11*		
7 Elton Brown/17*		
8 Jammal Brown/43*	10.00	25.00
9 Reggie Brown/50*	6.00	15.00
10 Ronnie Brown/10*		
11 Brandon Browner/25*	10.00	25.00
12 Luis Castillo/9*		
13 Mark Clayton/50*	8.00	20.00
14 Dan Cody/55*	8.00	20.00
15 Jerome Collins/49*	8.00	20.00
16 Sean Considine/45*	6.00	15.00
17 Anthony Davis/7*		
18 Thomas Davis/277*	6.00	15.00
20 Ciatrick Fason/12*		
21 Diamond Ferri/65*	6.00	15.00
22 Charlie Frye/9*		
23 Fred Gibson/50*	8.00	20.00
24 David Greene/50*	6.00	15.00
25 Gino Guidugli/199*	6.00	15.00
27 Anttaj Hawthorne/25*	6.00	15.00
28 Chris Henry/50*	10.00	25.00
29 Keron Henry/33*	6.00	15.00
30 Noah Herron/49*	6.00	15.00
31 Marlin Jackson/50*	6.00	15.00
32 Erasmus James/34*	8.00	20.00
33 Derrick Johnson/50*	8.00	20.00
34 Stefan LeFors/50*	6.00	15.00
35 T.A. McLendon/2*		
36 Heath Miller/10*		
37 Ryan Moats/194*	6.00	15.00
38 Vernand Morency/29*	6.00	15.00
39 Terrence Murphy/27*	6.00	15.00
40 Dan Orlovsky/130*	10.00	25.00
41 Kyle Orton/50*	10.00	25.00
42 David Pollack/25*	8.00	20.00
43 Walter Reyes/50*	6.00	15.00
45 Carlos Rogers/45*	10.00	25.00
46 Antrel Rolle/50*	10.00	25.00
47 J.R. Russell/34*	6.00	15.00
48 Barrett Ruud/290*	10.00	25.00
49 Eric Shelton/50*	6.00	15.00
50 Alex Smith TE/112*	6.00	15.00
51 Craphonso Thorpe/100* Red	6.00	15.00
52 Andrew Walter/10*		
53 Jason White/266*	10.00	25.00
54 Roddy White/138*	12.00	30.00
55 Cadillac Williams/10*		
57 Troy Williamson	8.00	20.00
58 Stanley Wilson/49*	8.00	20.00

2005 Press Pass Autographs Blue

*BLUE: .8X TO 2X BRONZE AUTOS
*BLUE: .6X TO 1.5X BRONZE SP AUTOS
BLUES WERE INSERTED IN PRESS PASS SE
BLUE PRINT RUN 50 SER.#'d SETS
SOME PRINT RUNS ADJUSTED FOR RED INKS

10 Ronnie Brown/25	40.00	100.00
19 Braylon Edwards/20*	30.00	80.00
44 Aaron Rodgers/50	175.00	300.00
55 Cadillac Williams/15*	20.00	50.00
56 Mike Williams/25	10.00	25.00

2005 Press Pass Autographs Blue Red Ink

*RED INK: .5X TO 1.2X BASIC BLUE AUTOS
CARDS W/PRINT RUNS UNDER 20 NOT PRICED

3 Marion Barber/25*	20.00	50.00
21 Diamond Ferri/36*	10.00	25.00
37 Ryan Moats/21*	12.00	30.00

2005 Press Pass Autographs Gold

*GOLD: .6X TO 1.5X BRONZE AUTOS
*GOLD: .5X TO 1.2X BRONZE SP AUTOS
GOLD HOBBY PRINT RUN 100 SER.#'d SETS
SOME PRINT RUNS ADJUSTED FOR RED INKS

10 Ronnie Brown/50	40.00	100.00
19 Braylon Edwards/40*	25.00	60.00
44 Aaron Rodgers/95*	125.00	200.00
55 Cadillac Williams/40*	25.00	60.00
56 Mike Williams/50	10.00	25.00

2005 Press Pass Autographs Gold Red Ink

*RED INK: .5X TO 1.2X BASE GOLD AUs
CARDS W/PRINT RUNS UNDER 20 NOT PRICED

2 J.J. Arrington/50*	10.00	25.00
17 Anthony Davis/50*	8.00	20.00
37 Ryan Moats/28*	8.00	20.00

2005 Press Pass Autographs Silver

*SILVER: .5X TO 1.2X BRONZE AUTOS
SILVER PRINT RUN 200 SER.#'d SETS

10 Ronnie Brown/75	40.00	80.00
19 Braylon Edwards/81*	20.00	50.00
44 Aaron Rodgers/186*	125.00	200.00
55 Cadillac Williams/90*	15.00	40.00
56 Mike Williams/75	10.00	25.00

2005 Press Pass Autographs Silver Red Ink

*UNLISTED RED INK: .6X TO 1.5X SILVER AU
PRINT RUNS UNDER 20 NOT PRICED

4 Khalif Barnes/50*	8.00	20.00
21 Diamond Ferri/22*	8.00	20.00
37 Ryan Moats/22*	8.00	20.00

2005 Press Pass Big Numbers

COMPLETE SET (25)	12.50	30.00

ONE PER PACK

BN1 Reggie Brown	.30	.75
BN2 Ronnie Brown	.60	1.50
BN3 Mark Clayton	.50	1.25
BN4 Dan Cody	.40	1.00
BN5 Anthony Davis	.30	.75
BN6 Braylon Edwards	.60	1.50
BN7 Charlie Frye	.50	1.25
BN8 Fred Gibson	.40	1.00
BN9 David Greene	.30	.75
BN10 Gino Guidugli	.30	.75
BN11 Derrick Johnson	.40	1.00
BN12 T.A. McLendon	.30	.75
BN13 Heath Miller	.60	1.50
BN14 Vernand Morency	.40	1.00
BN15 Dan Orlovsky	.50	1.25
BN16 Kyle Orton	.50	1.25
BN17 Aaron Rodgers	4.00	10.00
BN18 J.R. Russell	.30	.75
BN19 Alex Smith QB	.75	2.00
BN20 Andrew Walter	.40	1.00
BN21 Jason White	.50	1.25
BN22 Cadillac Williams	.50	1.25
BN23 Mike Williams	.50	1.25
BN24 Troy Williamson	.40	1.00
BN25 Aaron Rodgers CL	4.00	10.00

2005 Press Pass Game Used Jerseys Silver

OVERALL JERSEY ODDS 1:72H, 1:280R
SILVER PRINT RUN 300 SER.#'d SETS
*GOLD: .5X TO 1.2X SILVER JSYs
GOLD PRINT RUN 125 SER.#'d SETS
*HOLOFOIL: .8X TO 2X SILVER JSYs
HOLOFOIL PRINT RUN 50 SER.#'d SETS

JCAS Alex Smith TE	3.00	8.00
JCCT Craphonso Thorpe	3.00	8.00
JCDO Dan Orlovsky	5.00	12.00
JCJC Jerome Collins	4.00	10.00
JCJW Jason White	5.00	12.00
JCKO Kyle Orton	5.00	12.00
JCMB Mark Bradley	3.00	8.00
JCMJ Marlin Jackson	3.00	8.00
JCRW Roddy White	6.00	15.00
JCSL Stefan LeFors	3.00	8.00
JCTM Terrence Murphy	3.00	8.00

2005 Press Pass Paydirt

COMPLETE SET (12)	15.00	30.00

STATED ODDS 1:6 H/R

PD1 Cadillac Williams	.75	2.00
PD2 Charlie Frye	.75	2.00
PD3 Mike Williams	.75	2.00
PD4 Braylon Edwards	1.00	2.50
PD5 Alex Smith QB	1.25	3.00
PD6 Dan Orlovsky	.75	2.00
PD7 Andrew Walter	.60	1.50
PD8 Ronnie Brown	1.00	2.50
PD9 Heath Miller	1.00	2.50
PD10 Troy Williamson	.60	1.50
PD11 Aaron Rodgers	6.00	15.00
PD12 Mark Clayton	.75	2.00

2005 Press Pass Showbound

COMPLETE SET (9)	15.00	30.00

STATED ODDS 1:12 H/R

SB1 Alex Smith QB	1.25	3.00
SB2 Ronnie Brown	1.00	2.50
SB3 Aaron Rodgers	6.00	15.00
SB4 Cadillac Williams	.75	2.00
SB5 Heath Miller	1.00	2.50
SB6 Braylon Edwards	1.00	2.50
SB7 Mark Clayton	.75	2.00
SB8 Mike Williams	.75	2.00
SB9 Troy Williamson	.60	1.50

2006 Press Pass

This 50-card set was released in April, 2006. The set was issued in four-card packs into both hobby and retail channels. The hobby packs had an $3.99 SRP and came 28 to a box while the retails packs had an $2.99 SRP and came 24 to a box. Cards numbered 46-50 were "power pick" cards and those cards were inserted into packs at a stated rate of one in 14.

COMPLETE SET (50)	20.00	50.00
COMP.SET w/o SP's (45)	10.00	25.00

POWER PICK ODDS 1:14
UNPRICED SOLO SER.#'d TO 1

1 Brodie Croyle	.40	1.00
2 Jay Cutler	.75	2.00
3 Omar Jacobs	.25	.60
4 Matt Leinart	.40	1.00
5 Drew Olson	.25	.60
6 Michael Robinson	.30	.75
7 D.J. Shockley	.30	.75
8 Brad Smith	.40	1.00
9 Marcus Vick	.25	.60
10 Charlie Whitehurst	.40	1.00
11 Vince Young	.50	1.25
12 Joseph Addai	.40	1.00
13 Reggie Bush	.75	2.00
14 Jerome Harrison	.40	1.00
15 Laurence Maroney	.30	.75
16 Leon Washington	.30	.75
17 LenDale White	.30	.75
18 DeAngelo Williams	.50	1.25
19 Jason Avant	.25	.60
20 Derek Hagan	.30	.75
21 Chris Hannon	.30	.75
22 Santonio Holmes	.50	1.25
23 Chad Jackson	.25	.60
24 Greg Lee	.25	.60
25 Sinorice Moss	.40	1.00
26 Martin Nance	.30	.75
27 Maurice Stovall	.25	.60
28 Travis Wilson	.25	.60
29 Dominique Byrd	.30	.75
30 Vernon Davis	.50	1.25
31 Marcedes Lewis	.40	1.00
32 Leonard Pope	.40	1.00
33 Jimmy Williams	.40	1.00
34 Darnell Bing	.30	.75
35 Michael Huff	.30	.75
36 Mathias Kiwanuka	.40	1.00
37 Mario Williams	.40	1.00
38 Haloti Ngata	.40	1.00
39 Gabe Watson	.25	.60
40 Rodrique Wright	.25	.60
41 D'Brickashaw Ferguson	.40	1.00
42 Chad Greenway	.40	1.00
43 A.J. Hawk	.40	1.00
44 DeMeco Ryans	.40	1.00
45 Reggie Bush CL	.40	1.00
46 Reggie Bush PP	1.50	4.00
47 Matt Leinart PP	.75	2.00
48 Vince Young PP	1.00	2.50
49 A.J. Hawk PP	.75	2.00
50 DeAngelo Williams PP	1.00	2.50

2006 Press Pass Blue

*BLUE: .8X TO 2X BASIC CARDS
STATED ODDS 1:1 RETAIL

2006 Press Pass Reflectors

*SINGLES: 2X TO 5X BASIC CARDS
STATED PRINT RUN 500 SER.#'d SETS

2006 Press Pass Reflectors Proof

*SINGLES: 3X TO 8X BASIC CARDS
STATED PRINT RUN 100 SER.#'d SETS

2006 Press Pass Autographed 8X10 Redemption

1 Reggie Bush	75.00	150.00
2 Matt Leinart	30.00	80.00
3 Vince Young	60.00	120.00

2006 Press Pass Autographs Blue

*BLUE: .8X TO 2X BRONZE AUTOs
BLUE PRINT RUN 40-50 SER.#'d SETS

7 Reggie Bush/50	40.00	100.00
41 Matt Leinart/50	20.00	50.00
76 Vince Young/22*	30.00	80.00

2006 Press Pass Autographs Blue Red Ink

*RED INK: .5X TO 1.2X BASE BLUE AU
ANNCD PRINT RUNS UNDER 20 NOT PRICED

12 Jay Cutler/50	30.00	80.00
30 A.J. Hawk/35*	40.00	100.00
76 Vince Young/28*	40.00	100.00

2006 Press Pass Autographs Bronze

OVERALL AUTO ODDS 1:7

1 Joseph Addai	6.00	15.00
2 Devin Aromashodu	6.00	15.00
3 Jason Avant	4.00	10.00
4 Brett Basanez	6.00	15.00
5 Darnell Bing	5.00	12.00
6 Will Blackmon	5.00	12.00
7 Reggie Bush SP	50.00	100.00
8 Dominique Byrd	5.00	12.00
9 Bobby Carpenter	4.00	10.00
10 Barry Cofield	6.00	15.00
11 Brodie Croyle	6.00	15.00
12 Jay Cutler	25.00	60.00
13 Vernon Davis	8.00	20.00
14 Mike DeGory	4.00	10.00
15 Maurice Drew	10.00	25.00
16 Ray Edwards	6.00	15.00
17 Anthony Fasano	6.00	15.00
18 D'Brickashaw Ferguson	6.00	15.00
19 Charles Gordon	5.00	12.00
20 Bruce Gradkowski	6.00	15.00
21 Skyler Green	4.00	10.00
22 Chad Greenway	6.00	15.00
23 Darrell Hackney	5.00	12.00
24 Derek Hagan	5.00	12.00
25 Tamba Hali	6.00	15.00
26 Chris Hannon	5.00	12.00
27 Orien Harris	5.00	12.00
28 Jerome Harrison	6.00	15.00
29 Mike Hass	5.00	12.00
30 A.J. Hawk	12.00	30.00
31 Devin Hester	12.00	30.00
32 Tye Hill	4.00	10.00
33 Michael Huff	5.00	12.00
34 Chad Jackson	4.00	10.00
35 Tarvaris Jackson	6.00	15.00
36 Omar Jacobs SP	4.00	10.00
37 Jeff King	5.00	12.00
38 Mathias Kiwanuka	6.00	15.00
39 Joe Klopfenstein	4.00	10.00
40 Greg Lee	4.00	10.00
41 Matt Leinart SP	20.00	50.00
42 J.R. Lemon	4.00	10.00
43 Marcedes Lewis	6.00	15.00
44 John Madsen	4.00	10.00
45 Laurence Maroney	5.00	12.00
46 Reggie McNeal	5.00	12.00
47 DonTrell Moore	5.00	12.00
48 Martin Nance	5.00	12.00
49 Haloti Ngata	6.00	15.00
50 Drew Olson	4.00	10.00
51 Jonathan Orr	5.00	12.00
52 Paul Pinegar	4.00	10.00
53 Leonard Pope	6.00	15.00
54 Gerald Riggs	5.00	12.00
55 Michael Robinson	5.00	12.00
56 Cory Rodgers	5.00	12.00
57 DeMeco Ryans	6.00	15.00
58 D.J. Shockley	5.00	12.00
59 Ernie Sims	5.00	12.00
60 Brad Smith	6.00	15.00
61 Maurice Stovall	4.00	10.00
62 Marcus Vick SP	4.00	10.00
63 Leon Washington	5.00	12.00
64 Gabe Watson	4.00	10.00
65 LenDale White	5.00	12.00
66 Charlie Whitehurst	6.00	15.00
67 Gerris Wilkinson	4.00	10.00
68 Demetrius Williams	5.00	12.00
69 Jimmy Williams	6.00	15.00
70 Mario Williams	6.00	15.00
71 Travis Wilson	4.00	10.00
72 Eric Winston	4.00	10.00
73 Rodrique Wright	4.00	10.00
74 Claude Wroten	4.00	10.00
75 Ashton Youboty	4.00	10.00
76 Vince Young SP	40.00	80.00

2006 Press Pass Autographs Bronze Red Ink

*RED INK: .6X TO 1.5X BRNZ BLU INK

12 Jay Cutler/82*	25.00	60.00
20 Bruce Gradkowski/25*	10.00	25.00
30 A.J. Hawk/36*	30.00	80.00
45 Laurence Maroney/49*	8.00	20.00
63 Leon Washington/49*	8.00	20.00
76 Vince Young/23*	30.00	80.00

2006 Press Pass Autographs Gold

*GOLD: .6X TO 1.5X BRONZE AUTOS
GOLD PRINT RUN 63-100 CARDS

7 Reggie Bush/100	50.00	120.00
30 A.J. Hawk/62*	30.00	80.00
41 Matt Leinart/100	20.00	50.00
76 Vince Young/43*	40.00	100.00

2006 Press Pass Autographs Gold Red Ink

*RED INK: .5X TO 1.2X GOLD BLU INK

12 Jay Cutler/100	25.00	60.00
30 A.J. Hawk/38*	30.00	80.00
62 Marcus Vick/100	15.00	40.00
76 Vince Young/57*	30.00	80.00

2006 Press Pass Autographs Silver

*SILVER: .5X TO 1.2X BRONZE AUTOS
SILVER PRINT RUN 200 UNLESS NOTED

7 Reggie Bush	40.00	100.00
30 A.J. Hawk	15.00	40.00
41 Matt Leinart	15.00	40.00
76 Vince Young/104*	30.00	80.00

2006 Press Pass Autographs Silver Red Ink

*RED INK: .5X TO 1.2X SILVER BLU INK

12 Jay Cutler/200	40.00	100.00
62 Marcus Vick/200	12.00	30.00
76 Vince Young/96*	30.00	80.00

2006 Press Pass Autograph Power Picks

0

1 A.J. Hawk/250	10.00	25.00
2 Brodie Croyle/161*	10.00	25.00
3 Omar Jacobs/244*	6.00	15.00
4 Matt Leinart/150	12.00	30.00
5 Brad Smith/243*	10.00	25.00
6 Vince Young/82*	20.00	50.00
7 Reggie Bush/150	30.00	60.00
8 LenDale White/250	8.00	20.00
9 Marcus Vick/100	6.00	15.00

2006 Press Pass Big Numbers

COMPLETE SET (33)	8.00	20.00

STATED ODDS 1:1

BN1 Brodie Croyle	.50	1.25
BN2 Mathias Kiwanuka	.50	1.25
BN3 Omar Jacobs	.30	.75
BN4 Charlie Whitehurst	.50	1.25
BN5 Chad Jackson	.30	.75
BN6 D.J. Shockley	.40	1.00
BN7 Leonard Pope	.50	1.25
BN8 Vernon Davis	.60	1.50
BN9 DeAngelo Williams	.60	1.50
BN10 Sinorice Moss	.50	1.25
BN11 Jason Avant	.30	.75
BN12 Laurence Maroney	.40	1.00
BN13 Brad Smith	.50	1.25
BN14 Mario Williams	.50	1.25
BN15 Maurice Stovall	.30	.75
BN16 A.J. Hawk	.50	1.25
BN17 Santonio Holmes	.60	1.50
BN18 Travis Wilson	.30	.75
BN19 Haloti Ngata	.50	1.25
BN20 Michael Robinson	.40	1.00
BN21 Vince Young	.60	1.50
BN22 Michael Huff	.40	1.00
BN23 Drew Olson	.30	.75
BN24 Marcedes Lewis	.50	1.25
BN25 Matt Leinart	.50	1.25
BN26 Reggie Bush	1.00	2.50
BN27 LenDale White	.40	1.00
BN28 Jay Cutler	1.00	2.50
BN29 D'Brickashaw Ferguson	.50	1.25
BN30 Jimmy Williams	.50	1.25
BN31 Marcus Vick	.30	.75
BN32 Jerome Harrison	.50	1.25
BN33 Matt Leinart CL	.25	.60

2006 Press Pass Game Used Jerseys Blue

*BLUE/150: .5X TO 1.2X RED JSYs
BLUE INSERTED IN COLLECTOR TIN SETS
BLUE PRINT RUN 150 SER.#'d SETS

JCCH Chris Hannon	5.00	12.00

2006 Press Pass Game Used Jerseys Green

*GREEN/25: .8X TO 2X RED JSYs
GREEN INSERTED IN COLLECTOR TIN SETS

JCCH Chris Hannon	8.00	20.00

2006 Press Pass Game Used Jerseys Red

RED/BLUE/GREEN ISSUED IN COLLECTOR TINS

JCAF Anthony Fasano	5.00	12.00
JCAH A.J. Hawk	8.00	20.00
JCBB Brett Basanez	4.00	10.00
JCBC Brodie Croyle	6.00	15.00
JCBS Brad Smith	4.00	10.00
JCCR Cory Rodgers	4.00	10.00
JCDA Devin Aromashodu	4.00	10.00
JCDH Darrell Hackney	4.00	10.00
JCDO Drew Olson	4.00	10.00
JCDR DeMeco Ryans	5.00	12.00
JCDS D.J. Shockley	5.00	12.00
JCDW1 DeAngelo Williams	6.00	15.00
JCDW2 Demetrius Williams	5.00	12.00
JCGL Greg Lee	4.00	10.00
JCJH Jerome Harrison	4.00	10.00
JCJK Joe Klopfenstein	4.00	10.00
JCMD Maurice Drew	8.00	20.00
JCMH Mike Hass	5.00	12.00
JCML Marcedes Lewis	5.00	12.00
JCML Matt Leinart Shirt	5.00	12.00
JCMR Michael Robinson	5.00	12.00
JCOJ Omar Jacobs	5.00	12.00
JCPP Paul Pinegar	5.00	12.00
JCRB Reggie Bush Shirt	10.00	25.00
JCTJ Tarvaris Jackson	6.00	15.00
JCVD Vernon Davis	6.00	15.00

2006 Press Pass Game Used Jerseys Silver

SILVER RETAIL PRINT RUN 299 SETS
*GOLD: .5X TO 1.2X SILVER JERSEYS
GOLD HOBBY PRINT RUN 199 SETS
*HOLOFOIL: .8X TO 2X SILVER JERSEYS
HOLOFOIL PRINT RUN 50 SETS

JCAH A.J. Hawk	15.00	40.00
JCBB Brett Basanez	4.00	10.00
JCBS Brad Smith	4.00	10.00
JCCH Chris Hannon	4.00	10.00
JCCR Cory Rodgers	4.00	10.00
JCCW Charlie Whitehurst	5.00	12.00
JCDA Devin Aromashodu	4.00	10.00
JCDH Darrell Hackney	4.00	10.00
JCDO Drew Olson	4.00	10.00
JCDS D.J. Shockley	4.00	10.00
JCDW Demetrius Williams	5.00	12.00
JCGL Greg Lee	4.00	10.00
JCHN Haloti Ngata	5.00	12.00
JCJH Jerome Harrison	4.00	10.00
JCJK Joe Klopfenstein	4.00	10.00
JCMD Maurice Drew	8.00	20.00
JCMN Martin Nance	4.00	10.00
JCOJ Omar Jacobs	5.00	12.00

2006 Press Pass Paydirt

COMPLETE SET (12)	10.00	25.00
STATED ODDS 1:4		
PD1 Vince Young	.75	2.00
PD2 Matt Leinart	.60	1.50
PD3 Omar Jacobs	.40	1.00
PD4 LenDale White	.50	1.25
PD5 Jay Cutler	1.25	3.00
PD6 Reggie Bush	1.25	3.00
PD7 DeAngelo Williams	.75	2.00
PD8 Brodie Croyle	.60	1.50
PD9 Santonio Holmes	.75	2.00
PD10 Marcedes Lewis	.60	1.50
PD11 Maurice Stovall	.40	1.00
PD12 Sinorice Moss	.60	1.50

2006 Press Pass Target Exclusive

FOUR PER TARGET RETAIL BOX

1B Reggie Bush	1.25	3.00
2B Brodie Croyle	.60	1.50
3B A.J. Hawk	.60	1.50
4B Santonio Holmes	.75	2.00
5B Omar Jacobs	.40	1.00
6B Matt Leinart	.60	1.50
7B LenDale White	.50	1.25
8B DeAngelo Williams	.75	2.00
9B Vince Young	.75	2.00

2006 Press Pass Target Exclusive Autographs

STATED PRINT RUN 50 SER.#'d SETS

1 Reggie Bush	40.00	100.00
2 Brodie Croyle	15.00	40.00
3 A.J. Hawk	20.00	50.00
4 Omar Jacobs/45*	12.00	30.00
5 Matt Leinart	30.00	80.00
6 Brad Smith	15.00	40.00
8 LenDale White	20.00	50.00
9 Vince Young/30*	30.00	80.00

2006 Press Pass Target Exclusive Autographs Red Ink

7 Marcus Vick/50	15.00	40.00
9 Vince Young/20*	40.00	100.00

2006 Press Pass Teammates Autographs

1 Reggie Bush LenDale White	100.00	200.00
2 Reggie Bush Matt Leinart	50.00	120.00
3 Reggie Bush LenDale White Matt Leinart	100.00	200.00
4 LenDale White Matt Leinart	40.00	100.00

2006 Press Pass Wal-Mart Exclusive

FOUR PER WAL-MART RETAIL BOX

1A Reggie Bush UER defensive stats on back	1.25	3.00
2A Brodie Croyle	.60	1.50
3A A.J. Hawk	.60	1.50
4A Matt Leinart	.60	1.50
5A Sinorice Moss	.60	1.50
6A LenDale White	.50	1.25
7A DeAngelo Williams ERR (defensive stats on back)	.75	2.00
8A Marcus Vick	.40	1.00
9A Vince Young	.75	2.00

2006 Press Pass Wal-Mart Exclusive Autographs

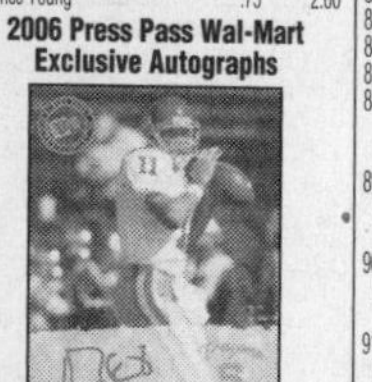

STATED PRINT RUN 50 SER.#'d SETS

1 Reggie Bush	50.00	120.00
2 Brodie Croyle	15.00	40.00
3 A.J. Hawk	50.00	100.00
4 Omar Jacobs/45*	12.00	30.00
5 Matt Leinart	25.00	60.00
6 Brad Smith	15.00	40.00
8 LenDale White	20.00	50.00
9 Vince Young/26*	40.00	100.00

2006 Press Pass Wal-Mart Exclusive Autographs Red Ink

8 Marcus Vick/50	25.00	50.00
9 Vince Young/24*	50.00	120.00

2007 Press Pass

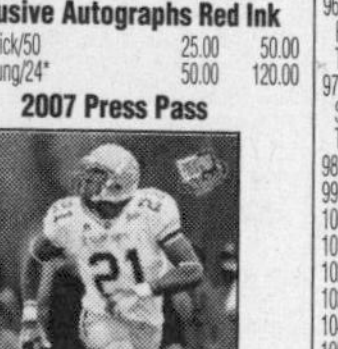

This 105-card set was released in April, 2007. The set was issued into the hobby in four-card packs, with an $3.99 SRP which came 28 packs to a box. The set has the following subsets: Leaders (57-67), Trophy Club (68-74), All-Americans (75-87), Teammates (88-97), Sophmore Sensations (98-100) and Power Picks (101-105). The Power Pick cards were inserted into packs at a stated rate of one in 14.

COMPLETE SET (105)	25.00	60.00
COMP.SET w/o SP's (100)	15.00	40.00
101-105 POWER PICK ODDS 1:14		
UNPRICED SOLO SER.#'d TO 1		
1 Chris Leak	.25	.60
2 Brady Quinn	.30	.75
3 JaMarcus Russell	.20	.50
4 Troy Smith	.30	.75
5 Drew Stanton	.20	.50
6 Michael Bush	.30	.75
7 Tony Hunt	.20	.50
8 Kenny Irons	.20	.50
9 Brandon Jackson	.25	.60
10 Marshawn Lynch	.30	.75
11 Adrian Peterson	1.25	3.00
12 Antonio Pittman	.20	.50
13 Brian Leonard	.25	.60
14 Dwayne Bowe	.40	1.00
15 Ted Ginn Jr.	.25	.60
16 Anthony Gonzalez	.30	.75
17 Dwayne Jarrett	.25	.60
18 Calvin Johnson	1.00	2.50
19 Robert Meachem	.30	.75
20 Sidney Rice	.40	1.00
21 Garrett Wolfe	.20	.50
22 Leon Hall	.25	.60
23 Gaines Adams	.30	.75
24 Jamaal Anderson	.25	.60
25 Alan Branch	.25	.60
26 Amobi Okoye	.30	.75
27 Paul Posluszny	.30	.75
28 Lawrence Timmons	.30	.75
29 LaRon Landry	.30	.75
30 Reggie Nelson	.25	.60
31 John Beck	.30	.75
32 Trent Edwards	.30	.75
33 Kevin Kolb	.50	1.25
34 Jordan Palmer	.25	.60
35 Lorenzo Booker	.25	.60
36 Darius Walker	.20	.50
37 Dwayne Wright	.25	.60
38 DeShawn Wynn	.25	.60
39 Zach Miller	.30	.75
40 Greg Olsen	.25	.60
41 Aundrae Allison	.20	.50
42 Dallas Baker	.20	.50
43 Jason Hill	.30	.75
44 Steve Smith USC	.30	.75
45 Darrelle Revis	.50	1.25
46 Aaron Ross	.30	.75
47 Adam Carriker	.25	.60
48 Charles Johnson	.20	.50
49 Jarvis Moss	.25	.60
50 Patrick Willis	.60	1.50
51 John Beck LDR	.30	.75
52 JaMarcus Russell LDR	.20	.50
53 Troy Smith LDR	.30	.75
54 Jordan Palmer LDR	.25	.60
55 Kevin Kolb LDR	.50	1.25
56 Brady Quinn LDR	.30	.75
57 Garrett Wolfe LDR	.20	.50
58 Dwayne Wright LDR	.25	.60
59 Ahmad Bradshaw LDR	.50	1.25
60 Johnnie Lee Higgins LDR	.25	.60
61 Robert Meachem LDR	.30	.75
62 Rhema McKnight LDR	.20	.50
63 Calvin Johnson LDR	1.00	2.50
64 Joel Filani LDR	.25	.60
65 Dwayne Bowe LDR	.40	1.00
66 Daymeion Hughes LDR	.25	.60
67 Reggie Nelson LDR	.25	.60
68 LaMarr Woodley TC	.30	.75
69 Troy Smith TC	.30	.75
70 Brady Quinn TC	.30	.75
71 Calvin Johnson TC	1.00	2.50
72 Paul Posluszny TC	.30	.75
73 Aaron Ross TC	.30	.75
74 Patrick Willis TC	.60	1.50
75 Troy Smith AA	.30	.75
76 Marshawn Lynch AA	.30	.75
77 Johnnie Lee Higgins AA	.25	.60
78 Dwayne Jarrett AA	.25	.60
79 Calvin Johnson AA	1.00	2.50
80 Robert Meachem AA	.30	.75
81 Zach Miller AA	.30	.75
82 Gaines Adams AA	.30	.75
83 Paul Posluszny AA	.30	.75
84 Leon Hall AA	.25	.60
85 LaRon Landry AA	.30	.75
86 Reggie Nelson AA	.25	.60
87 Aaron Ross AA	.30	.75
88 Marshawn Lynch Daymeion Hughes Teammates	.30	.75
89 Chris Leak Reggie Nelson Teammates	.25	.60
90 Lorenzo Booker Lawrence Timmons Teammates	.30	.75
91 JaMarcus Russell Dwayne Bowe Teammates	.40	1.00
92 Brandon Jackson Adam Carriker Teammates	.25	.60
93 Brady Quinn Darius Walker Teammates	.30	.75
94 Troy Smith Antonio Pittman Teammates	.20	.50
95 Ted Ginn Jr. Anthony Gonzalez Teammates	.30	.75
96 Tony Hunt Paul Posluszny Teammates	.30	.75
97 Dwayne Jarrett Steve Smith USC Teammates	.30	.75
98 Joseph Addai SS	.50	1.25
99 Reggie Bush SS	.60	1.50
100 Vince Young SS	.50	1.25
101 Brady Quinn PP	.75	2.00
102 JaMarcus Russell PP	.50	1.25
103 Adrian Peterson PP	3.00	8.00
104 Calvin Johnson PP	2.50	6.00
105 Ted Ginn Jr. PP	.60	1.50

2007 Press Pass Reflectors

*REFLECT.1-97: 2.5X TO 6X BASIC CARDS
*REFLECT. 98-100: 2X TO 5X BASIC CARDS
STATED PRINT RUN 500 SER.#'d SETS

2007 Press Pass Reflectors Blue

*BLUE 1-97: 1.5X TO 4X BASIC CARDS
*BLUE 98-100: 1.2X TO 3X BASIC CARDS
ONE BLUE PER RETAIL PACK

2007 Press Pass Reflectors Proof

*SINGLES 1-97: 4X TO 10X BASIC CARDS
*SINGLES 98-100: 3X TO 8X BASIC CARDS
STATED PRINT RUN 100 SER.#'d SETS

2007 Press Pass Autograph Power Picks

STATED PRINT RUN 25-250

AP Adrian Peterson/50	125.00	200.00
BJ Brandon Jackson/250	10.00	25.00
BQ Brady Quinn/99*	30.00	80.00
CJ Calvin Johnson/17*	100.00	200.00
DW Darius Walker/240*	8.00	20.00
JR JaMarcus Russell/90*	15.00	40.00
KI Kenny Irons/250	10.00	25.00
RM Robert Meachem/250	10.00	25.00
SR Sidney Rice/250	12.00	30.00
TG Ted Ginn Jr./101*	15.00	40.00
TS Troy Smith/20*	25.00	60.00

2007 Press Pass Autograph Power Picks Red Ink

TG Ted Ginn Jr./149*	20.00	50.00

2007 Press Pass Autographs Blue

*BLUE/40-50: .8X TO 2X BRONZE AUs
BLUE/40-50 INSERTED IN PRESS PASS SE
BLUE PRINT RUN 50 UNLESS NOTED

20 Ted Ginn Jr.	20.00	50.00
24 Chris Henry/25	15.00	40.00
47 Adrian Peterson/25	175.00	300.00
50 Brady Quinn/25	40.00	100.00
55 JaMarcus Russell/25	15.00	40.00

2007 Press Pass Autographs Blue Red Ink

*RED INK: .5X TO 1.2X BASIC BLUE AU

21 Anthony Gonzalez/47*	12.00	30.00
26 Jason Hill/46*	12.00	30.00
29 Brandon Jackson/50	10.00	25.00
69 LaMarr Woodley/50	12.00	30.00

2007 Press Pass Autographs Bronze

OVERALL AUTO ODDS 1:7 PP
UNPRICED PRINTING PLATES #'d TO 1

1 Gaines Adams	6.00	15.00
2 Joseph Addai SP	20.00	50.00
3 Aundrae Allison	4.00	10.00
4 Jamaal Anderson	5.00	12.00
5 Dallas Baker	4.00	10.00
6 John Beck	6.00	15.00
7 Lorenzo Booker	5.00	12.00
8 Dwayne Bowe	8.00	20.00
9 Ahmad Bradshaw	10.00	25.00
10 Alan Branch	5.00	12.00
11 Michael Bush	6.00	15.00
12 Adam Carriker	5.00	12.00
13 Scott Chandler	6.00	15.00
14 David Clowney	5.00	12.00
15 Tim Crowder	6.00	15.00
16 Kenneth Darby	5.00	12.00
17 Buster Davis	5.00	12.00
18 Craig Buster Davis	5.00	12.00
19 Joel Filani	5.00	12.00
20 Ted Ginn Jr. SP	15.00	40.00
21 Anthony Gonzalez	6.00	15.00
22 Michael Griffin	6.00	15.00
23 Leon Hall	5.00	12.00
24 Chris Henry	4.00	10.00
25 Johnnie Lee Higgins	5.00	12.00
26 Jason Hill	6.00	15.00
27 Daymeion Hughes	5.00	12.00
28 Kenny Irons		
29 Brandon Jackson	5.00	12.00
30 Tanard Jackson	4.00	10.00
31 Calvin Johnson SP	60.00	120.00
32 Charles Johnson	4.00	10.00
33 Kevin Kolb	10.00	25.00
34 LaRon Landry	6.00	15.00
35 Chris Leak	5.00	12.00
36 Brian Leonard	5.00	12.00
37 Marcus McCauley	5.00	12.00
38 Rhema McKnight	4.00	10.00
39 Robert Meachem		
40 Zach Miller	6.00	15.00
41 Matt Moore	6.00	15.00
42 Quentin Moses	5.00	12.00
43 Reggie Nelson	5.00	12.00
44 Amobi Okoye	6.00	15.00
45 Greg Olsen	5.00	12.00
46 Jordan Palmer	5.00	12.00
47 Adrian Peterson SP	100.00	200.00
48 Antonio Pittman SP	12.00	30.00
49 Paul Posluszny	6.00	15.00
50 Brady Quinn SP	30.00	80.00
51 Darrelle Revis	10.00	25.00
52 Sidney Rice	8.00	20.00
53 Aaron Ross	6.00	15.00
54 Jeff Rowe	4.00	10.00
55 JaMarcus Russell SP	10.00	25.00
56 Kolby Smith	5.00	12.00
57 Steve Smith USC	6.00	15.00
58 Troy Smith SP	15.00	40.00
59 Drew Stanton	4.00	10.00
60 Chansi Stuckey	6.00	15.00
61 Courtney Taylor	5.00	12.00
62 Zac Taylor	5.00	12.00
63 Lawrence Timmons	6.00	15.00
64 DeMarcus Tank Tyler	4.00	10.00
65 Darius Walker	4.00	10.00
66 Paul Williams	4.00	10.00
67 Patrick Willis	12.00	30.00
68 Garrett Wolfe	4.00	10.00
69 LaMarr Woodley	6.00	15.00
70 Dwayne Wright	5.00	12.00
71 DeShawn Wynn	5.00	12.00
72 Selvin Young	5.00	12.00
73 Vince Young SP	40.00	80.00

2007 Press Pass Autographs Bronze Red Ink

*RED INK: .6X TO 1.5X BRONZE BLUE INK
PRESS PASS ANNOUNCED PRINT RUNS BELOW

28 Kenny Irons/73*	6.00	15.00

2007 Press Pass Autographs Gold

*GOLD: .6X TO 1.5X BRONZE AUTOS
GOLD PRINT RUN 100 UNLESS NOTED

20 Ted Ginn Jr.	20.00	50.00
28 Kenny Irons	6.00	15.00
47 Adrian Peterson/40	100.00	200.00
48 Antonio Pittman	6.00	15.00
50 Brady Quinn/45*	20.00	50.00
55 JaMarcus Russell/34*	10.00	25.00

2007 Press Pass Autographs Gold Red Ink

*RED INK: .6X TO 1.5X GOLD BLUE INK

55 JaMarcus Russell/16*	20.00	50.00

2007 Press Pass Autographs Green

GREEN/RED PRINT RUN 25 SER.#'d SETS

21 Anthony Gonzalez	15.00	40.00
31 Calvin Johnson/18*	75.00	150.00
45 Greg Olsen	12.00	30.00
47 Adrian Peterson/10*	150.00	300.00
50 Brady Quinn	40.00	100.00
55 JaMarcus Russell	25.00	60.00
59 Drew Stanton/15*	10.00	25.00

2007 Press Pass Autographs Green Red Ink

20 Ted Ginn Jr./25	15.00	40.00
31 Calvin Johnson/7*	100.00	200.00
47 Adrian Peterson/15*	125.00	250.00

2007 Press Pass Autographs Silver

*SILVER: .5X TO 1.2X BRONZE AUTOS
SILVER PRINT RUN 200 UNLESS NOTED

20 Ted Ginn Jr.	15.00	40.00
28 Kenny Irons	5.00	12.00
47 Adrian Peterson/43	125.00	250.00
48 Antonio Pittman	5.00	12.00
50 Brady Quinn/76*	30.00	80.00
55 JaMarcus Russell/67*	10.00	25.00

2007 Press Pass Autographs Silver Red Ink

*RED INK: .6X TO 1.5X SILVER BLUE INK
PRESS PASS ANNOUNCED PRINT RUNS BELOW

29 Brandon Jackson/200*	6.00	15.00
50 Brady Quinn/24*	40.00	100.00
55 JaMarcus Russell/33*	25.00	60.00

2007 Press Pass Gridiron Gamers Jerseys Red

RANDOM INSERTS IN RETAIL PACKS

GGBB Brett Basanez	3.00	8.00
GGCS Chansi Stuckey	5.00	12.00
GGDR DeMeco Ryans	4.00	10.00
GGJJ Brandon Jackson	4.00	10.00
GGJR JaMarcus Russell	3.00	8.00
GGLH Leon Hall	4.00	10.00
GGMH Mike Hass	3.00	8.00
GGMJD Maurice Jones-Drew	5.00	12.00
GGML Marshawn Lynch	5.00	12.00

2007 Press Pass Gridiron Gamers Jerseys Silver

SILVER PRINT RUN 199-299
*GOLD/100: .5X TO 1.2X SILVER JSYs
GOLD PRINT RUN 100 SER.#'d SETS
*HOLOFOIL/50: .8X TO 2X SILVER JSYs
HOLOFOIL PRINT RUN 50 SER.#'d SETS

GGBL Brian Leonard/275	6.00	15.00
GGBQ Brady Quinn/250	12.00	30.00
GGCD Craig Buster Davis/275	5.00	12.00
GGCL Chris Leak/299	8.00	20.00
GGDJ Dwayne Jarrett/275	6.00	15.00
GGDS Drew Stanton/275	6.00	15.00
GGDW Darius Walker/299	5.00	12.00
GGGO Greg Olsen/275	8.00	20.00
GGGW Garrett Wolfe/299	6.00	15.00
GGKD Kenneth Darby/299	6.00	15.00
GGKI Kenny Irons/275	6.00	15.00
GGKK Kevin Kolb/275	3.00	8.00
GGLB Lorenzo Booker/275	5.00	12.00
GGLL LaRon Landry/299	6.00	15.00
GGML Marshawn Lynch/275	6.00	15.00
GGRB Reggie Bush/199	12.00	30.00
GGZM Zach Miller/299	6.00	15.00
GGDB2 Dwayne Bowe/250	6.00	15.00
GGJR1 JaMarcus Russell/199	6.00	15.00
GGJR2 Jeff Rowe/299	4.00	10.00

2007 Press Pass Primetime Players

COMPLETE SET (15)	10.00	25.00
STATED ODDS 1:4		
1 Brady Quinn	1.00	2.50
2 JaMarcus Russell	.60	1.50
3 Troy Smith	1.00	2.50
4 Drew Stanton	.60	1.50
5 Brandon Jackson	.75	2.00
6 Marshawn Lynch	1.00	2.50
7 Adrian Peterson	4.00	10.00
8 Antonio Pittman	.60	1.50
9 Dwayne Bowe	1.25	3.00
10 Dwayne Jarrett	.75	2.00
11 Calvin Johnson	3.00	8.00
12 Ted Ginn Jr.	.75	2.00
13 Robert Meachem	1.00	2.50
14 Sidney Rice	1.25	3.00
15 Darius Walker	.60	1.50

2007 Press Pass Sophomore Sensations Autographs

SSJA Joseph Addai	15.00	40.00
SSVY Vince Young	60.00	120.00
SSVYR Vince Young Red Ink/30*	75.00	150.00

2007 Press Pass Target Exclusive

COMPLETE SET (10)	10.00	25.00
STATED ODDS 4:1 TARGET BOXES		
TAR1 Brady Quinn	.60	1.50
TAR2 JaMarcus Russell	.40	1.00
TAR3 Troy Smith	.60	1.50
TAR4 Marshawn Lynch	.60	1.50
TAR5 Adrian Peterson	2.50	6.00
TAR6 Darius Walker	.40	1.00
TAR7 Dwayne Jarrett	.50	1.25
TAR8 Calvin Johnson	2.00	5.00
TAR9 Sidney Rice	.75	2.00
TAR10 Ted Ginn Jr.	.50	1.25

2007 Press Pass Target Exclusive Autographs

STATED PRINT RUN 25-50
RED INK TOO SCARCE TO PRICE

AP Adrian Peterson/50	100.00	200.00
BQ Brady Quinn/50	30.00	80.00
CJ Calvin Johnson/17*	75.00	150.00
DW Darius Walker/14*	12.00	30.00
JR JaMarcus Russell/45*	25.00	60.00
SR Sidney Rice/15*	25.00	50.00
TG Ted Ginn Jr./50	20.00	50.00
TS Troy Smith/20*	25.00	60.00

2007 Press Pass Wal-Mart Exclusive

COMPLETE SET (10)	10.00	25.00
WM1 Brady Quinn	.60	1.50
WM2 JaMarcus Russell	.40	1.00
WM3 Troy Smith	.60	1.50
WM4 Kenny Irons	.40	1.00
WM5 Marshawn Lynch	.60	1.50
WM6 Adrian Peterson	2.50	6.00
WM7 Dwayne Jarrett	.50	1.25
WM8 Calvin Johnson	2.00	5.00
WM9 Robert Meachem	.60	1.50
WM10 Ted Ginn Jr.	.50	1.25

2007 Press Pass Wal-Mart Exclusive Autographs

STATED PRINT RUN 25-50
RED INK TOO SCARCE TO PRICE

AP Adrian Peterson/49	100.00	200.00
BQ Brady Quinn/49*	30.00	80.00
CJ Calvin Johnson/18*	75.00	150.00
JR JaMarcus Russell/41*	25.00	60.00
KI Kenny Irons/30		
RM Robert Meachem/25	40.00	80.00
TG Ted Ginn Jr./49	20.00	50.00
TS Troy Smith/20*	25.00	60.00

2008 Press Pass

COMPLETE SET (105)	20.00	50.00
COMP.SET w/o SP's (100)	12.00	30.00
101-105 POWER PICK ODDS 1:14		
1 Glenn Dorsey	.30	.75
2 Chris Long	.30	.75
3 Dan Connor	.30	.75
4 Aqib Talib	.30	.75
5 Kenny Phillips	.30	.75
6 Erik Ainge	.30	.75
7 John David Booty	.25	.60
8 Colt Brennan	.30	.75
9 Brian Brohm	.30	.75
10 Joe Flacco	1.00	2.50
11 Chad Henne	.30	.75
12 Matt Ryan	1.25	3.00
13 Andre Woodson	.30	.75
14 Jamaal Charles	.50	1.25
15 Matt Forte	.50	1.25
16 Mike Hart	.30	.75
17 Jacob Hester	.30	.75
18 Chris Johnson	.75	2.00
19 Felix Jones	.50	1.25
20 Darren McFadden	.75	2.00
21 Rashard Mendenhall	.60	1.50
22 Ray Rice	.60	1.50
23 Steve Slaton	.30	.75
24 Kevin Smith	.30	.75
25 Jonathan Stewart	.50	1.25
26 Fred Davis	.30	.75
27 Adrian Arrington	.25	.60
28 Earl Bennett	.30	.75
29 Adarius Bowman	.25	.60
30 Early Doucet	.25	.60
31 James Hardy	.25	.60
32 DJ Hall	.25	.60
33 DeSean Jackson	.60	1.50
34 Malcolm Kelly	.25	.60
35 Mario Manningham	.30	.75
36 Limas Sweed	.30	.75
37 Devin Thomas	.25	.60
38 Lavelle Hawkins	.20	.50
39 Andre Caldwell	.25	.60
40 Vernon Gholston	.25	.60
41 Derrick Harvey	.20	.50
42 Keith Rivers	.30	.75
43 Mike Jenkins	.30	.75
44 Leodis McKelvin	.25	.60
45 Dennis Dixon	.30	.75
46 Josh Johnson	.30	.75
47 Tashard Choice	.25	.60
48 Chauncey Washington	.25	.60
49 John Carlson	.30	.75
50 Donnie Avery	.25	.60
51 Darren McFadden TC	.60	1.50
52 Matt Ryan TC	1.00	2.50
53 Glenn Dorsey TC	.25	.60
54 Dan Connor TC	.25	.60
55 Fred Davis TC	.25	.60
56 Chris Long TC	.25	.60
57 Dennis Dixon COL	.25	.60
58 Colt Brennan COL	.25	.60
59 Matt Ryan COL	1.00	2.50
60 Brian Brohm COL	.25	.60
61 Andre Woodson COL	.25	.60
62 Erik Ainge COL	.25	.60
63 Kevin Smith COL	.25	.60
64 Matt Forte COL	.40	1.00
65 Darren McFadden COL	.60	1.50
66 Jonathan Stewart COL	.40	1.00
67 Rashard Mendenhall COL	.50	1.25
68 Ray Rice COL	.50	1.25
69 Jamaal Charles COL	.40	1.00
70 Chris Johnson COL	.60	1.50
71 Jordy Nelson COL	.30	.75
72 Davone Bess COL	.25	.60
73 Donnie Avery COL	.20	.50
74 Devin Thomas COL	.20	.50
75 Mario Manningham COL	.25	.60
76 Dan Connor AA	.25	.60
77 Glenn Dorsey AA	.25	.60
78 Mike Jenkins AA	.25	.60
79 J Leman AA	.15	.40
80 Chris Long AA	.25	.60
81 Darren McFadden AA	.60	1.50
82 Jordy Nelson AA	.30	.75
83 Martin Rucker AA	.20	.50
84 Matt Ryan AA	1.00	2.50
85 Kevin Smith AA	.25	.60
86 Aqib Talib AA	.25	.60
87 Steve Slaton AA	.25	.60
88 Jonathan Stewart AA	.40	1.00
89 DeSean Jackson AA	.50	1.25
90 Andre Woodson TM Keenan Burton	.20	.50
91 Glenn Dorsey TM Jacob Hester	.20	.50
92 Brian Brohm TM Harry Douglas	.20	.50
93 Chad Henne TM Mario Manningham	.20	.50
94 Jamaal Charles TM Limas Sweed	.30	.75
95 John David Booty TM Chauncey Washington	.15	.40
96 Justin Forsett TM DeSean Jackson	.40	1.00
97 Matt Flynn TM Early Doucet	.40	1.00
98 Mike Hart TM Adrian Arrington	.20	.50
99 Dennis Dixon TM Jonathan Stewart	.30	.75
100 Darren McFadden TM Felix Jones	.50	1.25
101 Darren McFadden PP	1.50	4.00
102 Matt Ryan PP	2.50	6.00
103 Brian Brohm PP	.60	1.50
104 Jonathan Stewart PP	1.00	2.50
105 Malcolm Kelly PP	.50	1.25

2008 Press Pass Black and White

*B&W: 4X TO 10X BASIC CARDS
ANNOUNCED ODDS 1:144

2008 Press Pass Reflectors

*REFLECTORS: 2X TO 5X BASIC CARDS
STATED PRINT RUN 500 SER.#'d SETS

2008 Press Pass Reflectors Blue

*BLUE: 1.5X TO 4X BASIC CARDS
ONE BLUE PER RETAIL PACK

2008 Press Pass Reflectors Gold

*REFL GOLD: 3X TO 8X BASIC CARDS
STATED PRINT RUN 100 SER.#'d SETS

2008 Press Pass Reflectors Solo

UNPRICED SOLO PRINT RUN 1

2008 Press Pass Autograph Power Picks

STATED PRINT RUN 100-250
M.KELLY INSERTED IN PP SE
ANNC'D PRINT RUN ON CARDS W/RED INK VERSION

PPAW Andre Woodson/208*	8.00	20.00
PPBB Brian Brohm/100	8.00	20.00
PPCL Chris Long/100	12.00	30.00
PPDJ DeSean Jackson/154*	15.00	40.00
PPDM Darren McFadden/100	20.00	50.00
PPJS Jonathan Stewart/243*	15.00	40.00
PPLS Limas Sweed/237	8.00	20.00
PPMH Mike Hart/245*	8.00	20.00
PPMK Malcolm Kelly/250	6.00	15.00
PPMR Matt Ryan/80*	30.00	80.00
PPRM Rashard Mendenhall/230*	15.00	40.00

2008 Press Pass Autograph Power Picks Red Ink

*RED INK/20-76: .6X TO 1.5X BASIC AUTOS

PPAW Andre Woodson/10*		
PPDJ DeSean Jackson/76*	25.00	60.00
PPJS Jonathan Stewart/7*		
PPMH Mike Hart/5*		
PPMR Matt Ryan/20*	50.00	120.00
PPRM Rashard Mendenhall/20*	25.00	60.00

2008 Press Pass Autographs Blue

*BLUE/35-50: .8X TO 2X BRONZE AU
BLUE AUTO PRINT RUN 10-50
BLUES INSERTED IN PRESS PASS SE
ANNC'D PRINT RUN ON CARDS W/RED INK VERSION

PPSBB Brian Brohm/25	10.00	25.00
PPSDM Darren McFadden/35*	20.00	50.00
PPSFJ Felix Jones/25	20.00	50.00
PPSJF Joe Flacco/16*	40.00	80.00
PPSLS Limas Sweed/24		
PPSMR Matt Ryan/50	50.00	100.00

2008 Press Pass Autographs Blue Red Ink

*RED INK: .6X TO 1.5X BASE BLUE AU
RED INK ANNOUNCED PRINT RUN 1-50

2008 Press Pass Autographs Bronze

FIVE AUTOS PER HOBBY BOX
INSERTS IN SE: BOWMAN, PATRICK
MAR.SMITH, TALIB, TRAE WILLIAMS
UNPRICED PRINT PLATES PRINT RUN 1

PPSAA Adrian Arrington	4.00	10.00
PPSAB Adarius Bowman	4.00	10.00
PPSAC Andre Caldwell	4.00	10.00
PPSAC2 Antoine Cason	5.00	12.00
PPSAP Allen Patrick	4.00	10.00
PPSAT Aqib Talib	5.00	12.00
PPSAW Andre Woodson	5.00	12.00
PPSBB Brian Brohm SP	5.00	12.00
PPSCB Colt Brennan SP	12.00	30.00
PPSCC Calais Campbell	4.00	10.00
PPSCH Chad Henne	12.00	30.00
PPSCJ2 Chris Johnson	12.00	30.00
PPSCL Chris Long	5.00	12.00
PPSCW Chauncey Washington	4.00	10.00
PPSDA Donnie Avery	4.00	10.00
PPSDB Dorien Bryant	4.00	10.00
PPSDB2 Davone Bess	5.00	12.00
PPSDC Dan Connor	5.00	12.00
PPSDD Dennis Dixon	5.00	12.00
PPSDH DJ Hall	4.00	10.00
PPSDJ DeSean Jackson	10.00	25.00
PPSDM Darren McFadden SP	15.00	40.00
PPSDR Darius Reynaud	3.00	8.00
PPSDR2 Darrell Robertson	3.00	8.00
PPSDS Dantrell Savage	4.00	10.00
PPSDT Devin Thomas	4.00	10.00
PPSEA Erik Ainge	5.00	12.00
PPSEB Earl Bennett	5.00	12.00
PPSED Early Doucet	4.00	10.00
PPSER Eddie Royal	5.00	12.00
PPSFD Fred Davis SP	5.00	12.00
PPSFJ Felix Jones SP	15.00	40.00
PPSHD Harry Douglas	4.00	10.00
PPSJC Jamaal Charles	8.00	20.00
PPSJC2 John Carlson	5.00	12.00
PPSJDB John David Booty	4.00	10.00
PPSJF Joe Flacco	15.00	40.00
PPSJF2 Justin Forsett	5.00	12.00
PPSJH Jacob Hester	5.00	12.00
PPSJJ Josh Johnson	5.00	12.00
PPSJL J Leman	3.00	8.00
PPSJM Josh Morgan	5.00	12.00
PPSJN Jordy Nelson	8.00	20.00
PPSJS Jonathan Stewart SP	15.00	40.00
PPSJS2 Jamie Silva	4.00	10.00
PPSJT Jacob Tamme	5.00	12.00
PPSKB Keenan Burton	3.00	8.00
PPSKP Kenny Phillips	5.00	12.00
PPSKR Keith Rivers	5.00	12.00
PPSKS Kevin Smith	5.00	12.00
PPSLH Lavelle Hawkins	3.00	8.00
PPSLM Leodis McKelvin	4.00	10.00
PPSLS Limas Sweed SP	8.00	20.00
PPSMF Matt Flynn	12.00	30.00
PPSMF2 Matt Forte	8.00	20.00
PPSMG Marcus Griffin	3.00	8.00
PPSMH Mike Hart SP	8.00	20.00
PPSMH2 Marcus Henry	4.00	10.00
PPSMK Malcolm Kelly	4.00	10.00
PPSMM2 Mario Manningham	5.00	12.00
PPSMR Matt Ryan SP	50.00	100.00
PPSMR2 Martin Rucker	4.00	10.00
PPSMS Marcus Smith	4.00	10.00
PPSOS Owen Schmitt	5.00	12.00
PPSPS Paul Smith	5.00	12.00
PPSRL Rafael Little	4.00	10.00
PPSRM Rashard Mendenhall SP	15.00	40.00
PPSRR Ray Rice	10.00	25.00
PPSSS Steve Slaton	5.00	12.00
PPSTC Tashard Choice	4.00	10.00
PPSTW Trae Williams	3.00	8.00
PPSVG Vernon Gholston	4.00	10.00

2008 Press Pass Autographs Bronze Red Ink

*RED INK: .6X TO 1.5X BRONZE BLUE INK
*RED INK: .5X TO 1.2X BRONZE BLUE INK SPs

2008 Press Pass Autographs Green

*GREEN/25: 1X TO 2.5X BRONZE AUTO
GREEN AUTO PRINT RUN 25
GREENS INSERTED IN PRESS PASS SE

PPSAW Andre Woodson	12.00	30.00
PPSBB Brian Brohm	12.00	30.00
PPSCL Chris Long	12.00	30.00
PPSDJ DeSean Jackson	20.00	50.00
PPSDM Darren McFadden	30.00	80.00
PPSFJ Felix Jones	30.00	80.00
PPSJC Jamaal Charles	20.00	50.00
PPSJDB John David Booty	10.00	25.00
PPSJS Jonathan Stewart	20.00	50.00
PPSMK Malcolm Kelly	10.00	25.00
PPSMR Matt Ryan		

2008 Press Pass Autographs Gold

*GOLD: .6X TO 1.5X BRONZE AUs
*GOLD: .5X TO 1.2X BRONZE SP AUs
GOLD PRINT RUN 25-99

PPSBB Brian Brohm/50	10.00	25.00
PPSCB Colt Brennan/25	20.00	50.00
PPSCH Chad Henne	20.00	50.00
PPSDM Darren McFadden	20.00	50.00
PPSFJ Felix Jones/50	25.00	60.00
PPSMR Matt Ryan	50.00	100.00

2008 Press Pass Autographs Gold Red Ink

*RED INK: .6X TO 1.5X BASIC GOLD AU

PPSDM Darren McFadden/53*	25.00	60.00

2008 Press Pass Autographs Red

*RED/25: 1X TO 2.5X BRONZE AUTO
RED AUTO PRINT RUN 25 SETS
REDS INSERTED IN PRESS PASS SE
ANNC'D PRINT RUN ON CARDS W/RED INK VERSION

PPSAW Andre Woodson	12.00	30.00
PPSCL Chris Long	12.00	30.00
PPSDJ DeSean Jackson	20.00	50.00
PPSDM Darren McFadden	30.00	80.00
PPSJC Jamaal Charles	20.00	50.00
PPSJDB John David Booty		
PPSJS Jonathan Stewart	20.00	50.00
PPSLS Limas Sweed	12.00	30.00
PPSMK Malcolm Kelly	10.00	25.00

2008 Press Pass Autographs Red Red Ink

RED INK ANNOUNCED PRINT RUN 10-20

PPSBB Brian Brohm/18*	12.00	30.00
PPSFJ Felix Jones/20*	20.00	50.00

2008 Press Pass Autographs Silver

*SILVER: .5X TO 1.2X BRONZE AUs
*SILVER: .4X TO 1X BRONZE SP AUs
SILVER PRINT RUN 50-199

PPSBB Brian Brohm/100	8.00	20.00
PPSCB Colt Brennan/50	15.00	40.00
PPSDM Darren McFadden	15.00	40.00
PPSMR Matt Ryan	50.00	100.00

2008 Press Pass Autographs Silver Red Ink

*RED INK: .6X TO 1.5X BASIC SILVER AU

2008 Press Pass Gridiron Gamers Jerseys Silver

SILVER PRINT RUN 150-299
*GOLD/100: .6X TO 1.5X SLVR JSY/299
*GOLD/100: .5X TO 1.2X SLVR JSY/150-199
GOLD PRINT RUN 100 SER.#'d SETS
*HOLO/50: .8X TO 2X SLVR JSY/299
*HOLO/50: .6X TO 1.5X SLVR JSY/150-199
HOLOFOIL PRINT RUN 50 SER.#'d SETS
GRID GAMERS OVERALL ODDS 1:72 HOB

GGBB Brian Brohm/150	4.00	10.00
GGCB Colt Brennan/199	6.00	15.00
GGDB Davone Bess/299	4.00	10.00
GGDD Dennis Dixon/199	6.00	15.00
GGDH DJ Hall/299	4.00	10.00
GGED Early Doucet/199	4.00	10.00
GGJDB John David Booty/199	5.00	12.00
GGJF Justin Forsett/299	3.00	8.00
GGJH Jacob Hester/299	4.00	10.00
GGJS Jonathan Stewart/150	8.00	20.00
GGLH Lavelle Hawkins/299	3.00	8.00
GGMF Matt Forte/299	3.00	8.00
GGMH Mike Hart/199	6.00	15.00
GGMK Malcolm Kelly/150	6.00	15.00
GGMR Matt Ryan/150	10.00	25.00
GGRR Ray Rice/199	4.00	10.00
GGTC Tashard Choice/299	4.00	10.00
GGVG Vernon Gholston/299	4.00	10.00

2008 Press Pass Primetime Players

COMPLETE SET (15)	10.00	25.00
STATED ODDS 1:4		
PP1 Glenn Dorsey	.75	2.00
PP2 Chris Long	.75	2.00
PP3 Matt Ryan	3.00	8.00
PP4 Darren McFadden	2.00	5.00
PP5 Brian Brohm	.75	2.00
PP6 DeSean Jackson	1.50	4.00
PP7 Andre Woodson	.75	2.00
PP8 Malcolm Kelly	.60	1.50
PP9 Jonathan Stewart	1.25	3.00
PP10 Limas Sweed	.75	2.00
PP11 Rashard Mendenhall	1.50	4.00
PP12 Early Doucet	.60	1.50
PP13 Chad Henne	.75	2.00
PP14 Mario Manningham	.75	2.00
PP15 Felix Jones	1.25	3.00

2008 Press Pass Target Exclusive

RANDOM INSERTS IN TARGET STORE PACKS

TAR1 Glenn Dorsey	.75	2.00
TAR2 Chris Long	.75	2.00
TAR3 Matt Ryan	3.00	8.00
TAR4 Brian Brohm	.75	2.00
TAR5 Andre Woodson	.75	2.00
TAR6 Darren McFadden	2.00	5.00
TAR7 Jonathan Stewart	1.25	3.00
TAR8 DeSean Jackson	1.50	4.00
TAR9 Malcolm Kelly	.60	1.50
TAR10 Limas Sweed	.75	2.00

2008 Press Pass Target Exclusive Autographs

STATED PRINT RUN 25 SER.#'d SETS
MALCOLM KELLY INSERTED IN PP SE

TARAW Andre Woodson	15.00	40.00
TARCL Chris Long		
TARDJ DeSean Jackson/16*	20.00	50.00
TARDM Darren McFadden		
TARED Early Doucet	15.00	40.00
TARJS Jonathan Stewart/24*	30.00	60.00
TARMK Malcolm Kelly		
TARMR Matt Ryan/24*	75.00	135.00

2008 Press Pass Target Exclusive Autographs Red Ink

TARBB Brian Brohm/22*	12.00	30.00
TARDJ DeSean Jackson/9*		
TARJS Jonathan Stewart/1*		
TARLS Limas Sweed/23*		
TARMR Matt Ryan/1*		

2008 Press Pass Wal-Mart Exclusive

RANDOM INSERTS IN WAL-MART PACKS

WM1 Glenn Dorsey	.75	2.00
WM2 Chris Long	.75	2.00

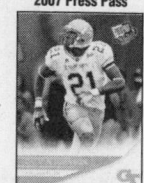

WM3 Matt Ryan 3.00 8.00
WM4 Brian Brohm .75 2.00
WM5 Andre Woodson .75 2.00
WM6 Darren McFadden 2.00 5.00
WM7 Jonathan Stewart 1.25 3.00
WM8 DeSean Jackson 1.50 4.00
WM9 Malcolm Kelly .60 1.50
WM10 Limas Sweed .75 2.00

2008 Press Pass Wal-Mart Exclusive Autographs

STATED PRINT RUN 21-25
MALCOLM KELLY INSERTED IN PP SE
WMBB Brian Brohm
WMCL Chris Long 20.00 50.00
WMDJ DeSean Jackson/21* 20.00 50.00
WMDM Darren McFadden 30.00 80.00
WMJS Jonathan Stewart 30.00 60.00
WMLS Limas Sweed 20.00 50.00
WMMH Mike Hart/23* 20.00 50.00
WMMK Malcolm Kelly
WMMR Matt Ryan/21* 75.00 135.00

2008 Press Pass Game Breakers

This product was released as a separate boxed set at major retail outlets. Each sealed set included either one previously issued 2008 Press Pass autographed card and memorabilia card.

COMP.FACT.SET (26) 10.00 20.00
COMPLETE SET (25) 6.00 15.00

2009 Press Pass

This set was released on April 10, 2009. The base set consists of 105 cards. This product was released with 4 cards per pack and 28 packs per hobby box.

COMPLETE SET (105) 20.00 50.00
COMP.SET w/o PP's (100) 12.00 30.00
101-105 POWER PICK ODDS 1:14 HOB
1 Rhett Bomar .25 .60
2 Chase Daniel .30 .75
3 Nate Davis .25 .60
4 Josh Freeman .60 1.50
5 Graham Harrell .30 .75
6 Mark Sanchez 1.00 2.50
7 Matthew Stafford 1.50 4.00
8 Pat White .30 .75
9 Andre Brown .20 .50
10 Donald Brown .30 .75
11 Glen Coffee .25 .60
12 James Davis .30 .75
13 Mike Goodson .30 .75
14 Shonn Greene .50 1.25
15 P.J. Hill .25 .60
16 Ian Johnson .30 .75
17 Jeremiah Johnson .30 .75
18 LeSean McCoy .60 1.50
19 Knowshon Moreno .30 .75
20 Javon Ringer .30 .75
21 Chris Wells .50 1.25
22 Ramses Barden .20 .50
23 Konny Britt .40 1.00
24 Michael Crabtree .60 1.50
25 Percy Harvin .50 1.25
26 Darrius Heyward-Bey .30 .75
27 Juaquin Iglesias .25 .60
28 Jeremy Maclin .50 1.25
29 Mohamed Massaquoi .25 .60
30 Louis Murphy .30 .75
31 Hakeem Nicks .50 1.25
32 Brian Robiskie .30 .75
33 Brandon Tate .30 .75
34 Derrick Williams .25 .60
35 Chase Coffman .25 .60
36 Brandon Pettigrew .30 .75
37 Everette Brown .25 .60
38 Tyson Jackson .25 .60
39 Kenny McKinley .30 .75
40 Aaron Maybin .25 .60
41 Brian Orakpo .30 .75
42 Aaron Curry .30 .75
43 Brian Cushing .30 .75
44 James Laurinaitis .30 .75
45 Rey Maualuga .30 .75
46 Vontae Davis .30 .75
47 Victor Harris .30 .75
48 Malcolm Jenkins .30 .75
49 D.J. Moore .25 .60
50 Alphonso Smith .25 .60
51 Chase Coffman TC .20 .50
52 Michael Crabtree TC .50 1.25
53 Shonn Greene TC .40 1.00
54 Graham Harrell TC .25 .60
55 Malcolm Jenkins TC .25 .60
56 James Laurinaitis TC .25 .60
57 Rey Maualuga TC .25 .60
58 Brian Orakpo TC .25 .60
59 Konny Britt LL .30 .75
60 Donald Brown LL .25 .60
61 Glen Coffee LL .20 .50
62 Quan Cosby LL .20 .50
63 Michael Crabtree LL .50 1.25
64 Chase Daniel LL .25 .60
65 Nate Davis LL .20 .50
66 Jarett Dillard LL .25 .60
67 Shonn Greene LL .40 1.00
68 Graham Harrell LL .25 .60
69 Austin Collie LL .25 .60
70 Gartrell Johnson LL .15 .40
71 Jeremy Maclin LL .40 1.00
72 LeSean McCoy LL .50 1.25
73 Knowshon Moreno LL .25 .60
74 Hakeem Nicks LL .40 1.00
75 Javon Ringer LL .25 .60
76 Mark Sanchez LL .75 2.00
77 Matthew Stafford LL 1.25 3.00
78 Donald Brown AA .25 .60
79 Chase Coffman AA .20 .50
80 Michael Crabtree AA .50 1.25
81 Aaron Curry AA .25 .60
82 Jarett Dillard AA .25 .60
83 Shonn Greene AA .40 1.00
84 Malcolm Jenkins AA .25 .60
85 James Laurinaitis AA .25 .60
86 Jeremy Maclin AA .40 1.00
87 Rey Maualuga AA .25 .60
88 Brian Orakpo AA .25 .60
89 Javon Ringer AA .25 .60
90 Alphonso Smith AA .20 .50
91 Matthew Stafford 1.00 2.50
Knowshon Moreno TM
92 Mark Sanchez .60 1.50
Rey Maualuga TM
93 Graham Harrell .40 1.00
Michael Crabtree TM
94 Chase Daniel .30 .75
Jeremy Maclin TM
95 Chris Wells .30 .75
Brian Robiskie TM
96 Percy Harvin .30 .75
Louis Murphy TM
97 Hakeem Nicks .30 .75
Brandon Tate TM
98 Aaron Maybin .15 .40
Derrick Williams TM
99 Malcolm Jenkins .20 .50
James Laurinaitis TM
100 Javon Ringer .20 .50
Brian Hoyer TM
101 Matthew Stafford PP 3.00 8.00
102 Mark Sanchez PP 2.00 5.00
103 Michael Crabtree PP 1.25 3.00
104 Chris Wells PP 1.00 2.50
105 Jeremy Maclin PP 1.00 2.50

2009 Press Pass Black and White

*B&W: 4X TO 10X BASIC CARDS
ANNOUNCED ODDS 1:140

2009 Press Pass Blue

*BLUE: 1.2X TO 3X BASIC CARDS
ONE BLUE PER RETAIL PACK

2009 Press Pass Reflectors

*REFLECT/500: 2X TO 5X BASIC CARDS
REFLECTORS PRINT RUN 500

2009 Press Pass Reflectors Gold

*REFLECT.GOLD/100: 3X TO 8X BASIC CARDS
REFLECTORS GOLD PRINT RUN 100

2009 Press Pass Autographs Bronze

*SILVER/199: .5X TO 1.2X BRONZE AU
*SILVER/54-199: .4X TO 1X BRONZE AU SP
SILVER PRINT RUN 54-199
*GOLD/99: .6X TO 1.5X BRONZE AU
*GOLD/75-99: .5X TO 1.2X BRONZE AU SP
GOLD PRINT RUN 75-99
OVERALL AUTO ODDS 1:6
*BLUE/40-50: .6X TO 1.5X BRONZE AU
*BLUE/50: .5X TO 1.2X BRONZE AU SP
BLUE PRINT RUN 50
*RED INK: .5X TO 1.2X BASIC AU
PRESS PASS ANNC'D RED INK PRINT RUNS
ANNC'D PRINT RUN UNDER 20 NOT PRICED
AB Andre Brown 3.00 8.00
AC Aaron Curry 5.00 12.00
AC2 Austin Collie 6.00 15.00
AF Arian Foster 20.00 40.00
BC Brian Cushing 5.00 12.00
BG Brandon Gibson 5.00 12.00
BH Brian Hoyer 5.00 12.00
BO Brian Orakpo 5.00 12.00
BP Brandon Pettigrew 5.00 12.00
BR Brian Robiskie 5.00 12.00
BR2 B.J. Raji 5.00 12.00
BT Brandon Tate 5.00 12.00
BU Brandon Underwood 5.00 12.00
CC Chase Coffman 4.00 10.00
CD Chase Daniel 5.00 12.00
CH Cullen Harper 5.00 12.00
CP Cedric Peerman 4.00 10.00
CW Chris Wells SP 15.00 40.00
DB Donald Brown 5.00 12.00
DB Darius Butler 5.00 12.00
DHB Darrius Heyward-Bey 5.00 12.00
DM D.J. Moore 4.00 10.00
DM2 Devin Moore 4.00 10.00
DW Derrick Williams 4.00 10.00
EB Everette Brown 4.00 10.00
GC Glen Coffee 4.00 10.00
GH Graham Harrell 8.00 20.00
GJ Gartrell Johnson 3.00 8.00
HC Hunter Cantwell 5.00 12.00
HN Hakeem Nicks 8.00 20.00
IJ Ian Johnson 5.00 12.00
JC3 James Casey 4.00 10.00
JC Jared Cook 5.00 12.00
JC2 Jeremy Childs 4.00 10.00
JD James Davis 5.00 12.00
JD2 Jarett Dillard 5.00 12.00
JF Josh Freeman 10.00 25.00
JI Juaquin Iglesias 4.00 10.00
JJ Jeremiah Johnson 5.00 12.00
JL James Laurinaitis 5.00 12.00
JM Jeremy Maclin SP 15.00 40.00
JR Javon Ringer 5.00 12.00
JW John Parker Wilson 5.00 12.00
KB Kenny Britt 6.00 15.00
KM Knowshon Moreno SP 30.00 60.00
KM2 Kenny McKinley 5.00 12.00
KO Kevin Ogletree 5.00 12.00
LM LeSean McCoy 10.00 25.00
LM2 Louis Murphy 5.00 12.00
MC Michael Crabtree 15.00 40.00
MG Mike Goodson 5.00 12.00
MJ Malcolm Jenkins 5.00 12.00
ML Marlon Lucky 4.00 10.00
MM Mohamed Massaquoi 4.00 10.00
MR Mike Reilly 4.00 10.00
MS Matthew Stafford SP 40.00 80.00
MS2 Mark Sanchez SP 30.00 80.00
MT Mike Thomas 5.00 12.00
ND Nate Davis 4.00 10.00
PH2 Percy Harvin 25.00 50.00
PH P.J. Hill 4.00 10.00
PW Pat White 5.00 12.00
QC Quan Cosby 4.00 10.00
RB Rhett Bomar 4.00 10.00
RB2 Ramses Barden 3.00 8.00
RJ Rashad Jennings 5.00 12.00
RM Rey Maualuga 5.00 12.00
SG Shonn Greene SP 12.00 30.00
SM Stephen McGee 5.00 12.00
TJ Tyson Jackson 4.00 10.00
VD Vontae Davis 5.00 12.00
VH Victor Harris 5.00 12.00
WM William Moore 5.00 12.00

2009 Press Pass Autographs Blue Red Ink

*RED INK: .5X TO 1.2X BASIC AU
PRESS PASS ANNC'D RED INK PRINT RUNS
ANNC'D PRINT RUN UNDER 20 NOT PRICED
BU Brandon Underwood/50 8.00 20.00

2009 Press Pass Autographs Green

*GREEN AU/25: .6X TO 1.5X BRONZE AU
GREEN/25 INSERTS IN WAL-MART PACKS
MC Michael Crabtree 20.00 50.00
MS Matthew Stafford 50.00 120.00
MS2 Mark Sanchez
PH2 Percy Harvin 40.00 80.00

2009 Press Pass Autographs Red

*RED/25: .6X TO 1.5X BRONZE AU
RED/25 INSERTS IN TARGET PACKS
MC Michael Crabtree 20.00 50.00
MS Matthew Stafford 50.00 120.00
MS2 Mark Sanchez Red Ink 40.00 100.00
PH2 Percy Harvin 40.00 80.00

2009 Press Pass Banner Season

COMPLETE SET (15) 8.00 20.00
STATED ODDS 1:4
BS1 Donald Brown .50 1.25
BS2 Michael Crabtree 1.00 2.50
BS3 Nate Davis .40 1.00
BS4 Josh Freeman 1.00 2.50
BS5 Shonn Greene .75 2.00
BS6 Graham Harrell .50 1.25
BS7 Percy Harvin .75 2.00
BS8 Darrius Heyward-Bey .50 1.25
BS9 Jeremy Maclin .75 2.00
BS10 LeSean McCoy 1.00 2.50
BS11 Knowshon Moreno .50 1.25
BS12 Hakeem Nicks .75 2.00
BS13 Mark Sanchez 1.50 4.00
BS14 Matthew Stafford 2.50 6.00
BS15 Chris Wells .75 2.00

2009 Press Pass Gridiron Gamers Jerseys Silver

SILVER PRINT RUN 199-299
*GOLD/100: .5X TO 1.2X SILVER JSY
GOLD PRINT RUN 100 SER.#'d SETS
*HOLOFOIL/50: .6X TO 1.5X SILVER JSY
HOLOFOIL PRINT RUN 50 SER.#'d SETS
OVERALL GAMERS ODDS 1:72
GGAF Arian Foster/299 8.00 20.00
GGBG Brandon Gibson/299 4.00 10.00
GGCD Chase Daniel/299 4.00 10.00
GGCH Cullen Harper/299 4.00 10.00
GGDHB Darrius Heyward-Bey/299 4.00 10.00
GGGJ Gartrell Johnson/299 2.50 6.00
GGJF Josh Freeman/299 6.00 15.00
GGJJ Jeremiah Johnson/299 4.00 10.00
GGJM Jeremy Maclin/199 8.00 20.00
GGJW John Parker Wilson/299 6.00 15.00
GGKB Kenny Britt/299 5.00 12.00
GGKM Kenny McKinley/299 4.00 10.00
GGLM LeSean McCoy/250 5.00 12.00
GGML Marlon Lucky/299 6.00 15.00
GGMS Mark Sanchez/299 10.00 25.00
GGRM Rey Maualuga/299 4.00 10.00

2009 Press Pass Gridiron Gamers Jerseys Green

GREEN/75-100 IN RETAIL BLASTER BOXES
*BRONZE RETAIL: .3X TO .8X GREEN RETAIL
*RED RETAIL/25: .6X TO 1.5X GREEN RETAIL
BB Brian Brohm/75 3.00 8.00
BG Brandon Gibson/99 5.00 12.00
CB Colt Brennan/99 4.00 10.00
CH Chad Henne/82 4.00 10.00
DA Donnie Avery/99 4.00 10.00
DB Davone Bess/75 3.00 8.00
DC Dan Connor/75 3.00 8.00
DD Dennis Dixon/75 4.00 10.00
DT Devin Thomas/99 3.00 8.00
DW Derrick Williams/82 4.00 10.00
EA Erik Ainge/75 4.00 10.00
ED Early Doucet/75 4.00 10.00
GJ Gartrell Johnson/99 3.00 8.00
IJ Ian Johnson/99 5.00 12.00
JC Jamaal Charles/75 5.00 12.00
KM Kenny McKinley/99 5.00 12.00
KP Kenny Phillips/75 3.00 8.00
LM Louis Murphy/99 5.00 12.00
LS Limas Sweed/99 4.00 10.00
MH Mike Hart/99 4.00 10.00
MK Malcolm Kelly/95 3.00 8.00
ND Nate Davis/75 4.00 10.00
QC Quan Cosby/75 4.00 10.00
SM Stephen McGee/99 5.00 12.00
TC Tashard Choice/75 3.00 8.00
VG Vernon Gholston/100 3.00 8.00
JDB John David Booty/75 4.00 10.00
JPW John Parker Wilson/99 5.00 12.00
RB1 Ramses Barden/75 3.00 8.00
RB2 Rhett Bomar/99 4.00 10.00

2009 Press Pass Power Pick Autographs

STATED PRINT RUN 150-250
*SHOWBOUND/25: .8X TO 2X BASIC AUTO
SHOWBOUND PRINT RUN 5-25
PPDB Donald Brown/250 6.00 15.00
PPDHB Darrius Heyward-Bey/250 6.00 15.00
PPDW Derrick Williams/250 5.00 12.00
PPJM Jeremy Maclin/197 12.00 30.00
PPKM Knowshon Moreno/238* 12.00 30.00
PPLM LeSean McCoy/250 12.00 30.00
PPMC Michael Crabtree/250 20.00 40.00
PPMS Matthew Stafford/140* 40.00 80.00
PPMS2 Mark Sanchez/140* 40.00 80.00
PPPH Percy Harvin/250 15.00 40.00
PPSG Shonn Greene/250 12.00 30.00

2009 Press Pass Power Pick Autographs Red Ink

PRESS PASS ANNC'D RED INK PRINT RUNS
ANNC'D PRINT RUN UNDER 20 NOT PRICED
PPCW Chris Wells/199 25.00 50.00

2009 Press Pass Target Exclusive Autographs

STATED PRINT RUN 25 SER.#'d SETS
TARCW Chris Wells 50.00 100.00
TARDB Donald Brown/15* 20.00 50.00
TARDW Derrick Williams
TARJM Jeremy Maclin/21*
TARKM Knowshon Moreno
TARLM LeSean McCoy
TARMC Michael Crabtree 25.00 60.00
TARMS Matthew Stafford 60.00 120.00
TARMS2 Mark Sanchez 60.00 120.00
TARPH Percy Harvin
TARSG Shonn Greene/20*

2009 Press Pass Wal-Mart Exclusive Autographs

STATED PRINT RUN 25 SER.#'d SETS
WMCW Chris Wells
WMDB Donald Brown
WMDW Derrick Williams 10.00 25.00
WMJM Jeremy Maclin 20.00 50.00
WMKM Knowshon Moreno
WMLM LeSean McCoy
WMMC Michael Crabtree 25.00 60.00
WMMS Matthew Stafford
WMMS2 Mark Sanchez 60.00 120.00
WMPH Percy Harvin
WMSG Shonn Greene

2009 Press Pass Game Breakers

This product was released as a separate boxed set at major retail outlets. Each sealed set included either one previously issued 2009 Press Pass autographed card and memorabilia card.

COMPLETE SET (25) 5.00 12.00
COMP.FACT.SET (26) 10.00 20.00
GB1 Matthew Stafford 1.25 3.00
GB2 Tyson Jackson .20 .50
GB3 Aaron Curry .25 .60
GB4 Mark Sanchez .75 2.00
GB5 Darrius Heyward-Bey .25 .60
GB6 B.J. Raji .25 .60
GB7 Michael Crabtree .50 1.25
GB8 Knowshon Moreno .25 .60
GB9 Brian Orakpo .25 .60
GB10 Josh Freeman .50 1.25
GB11 Jeremy Maclin .40 1.00
GB12 Brandon Pettigrew .25 .60
GB13 Percy Harvin .40 1.00
GB14 Donald Brown .25 .60
GB15 Hakeem Nicks .40 1.00
GB16 Kenny Britt .30 .75
GB17 Chris Wells .40 1.00
GB18 James Laurinaitis .25 .60
GB19 Brian Robiskie .25 .60
GB20 Pat White .25 .60
GB21 Mohamed Massaquoi .20 .50
GB22 LeSean McCoy .50 1.25
GB23 Shonn Greene .40 1.00
GB24 Glen Coffee .20 .50
GB25 Juaquin Iglesias .20 .50

2010 Press Pass

COMPLETE SET (105) 20.00 50.00
COMP.SET w/o PP's (100) 12.00 30.00
101-105 POWER PICK ODDS 1:14
1 Rolando McClain .30 .75
2 James Starks .50 1.25
3 Jahvid Best .50 1.25
4 Dan LeFevour .30 .75
5 Mardy Gilyard .30 .75
6 Tony Pike .30 .75
7 C.J. Spiller .50 1.25
8 Jacoby Ford .30 .75
9 Antonio Brown .50 1.25
10 Aaron Hernandez .50 1.25
11 Andre Roberts .30 .75
12 Tim Tebow 1.25 3.00
13 Ryan Mathews .60 1.50
14 Mike Kafka .30 .75
15 Jonathan Dwyer .30 .75
16 Derrick Morgan .25 .60
17 Demaryius Thomas .40 1.00
18 Arrelious Benn .30 .75
19 Dezmon Briscoe .25 .60
20 Brandon LaFell .30 .75
21 Charles Scott .25 .60
22 Donovan Warren .30 .75
23 Eric Decker .40 1.00
24 Anthony Dixon .30 .75
25 Danario Alexander .30 .75
26 Ndamukong Suh .60 1.50
27 Jimmy Clausen .30 .75
28 Golden Tate .30 .75
29 Dez Bryant 1.00 2.50
30 Sam Bradford 1.25 3.00
31 Jermaine Gresham .40 1.00
32 Gerald McCoy .30 .75
33 Dexter McCluster .30 .75
34 Jevan Snead .30 .75
35 Sean Canfield .25 .60
36 NaVorro Bowman .30 .75
37 Jason Pierre-Paul .50 1.25
38 Toby Gerhart .30 .75
39 Mike Williams .50 1.25
40 Zac Robinson .25 .60
41 Montario Hardesty .30 .75
42 Jerry Hughes .30 .75
43 Joe Haden .30 .75
44 Jordan Shipley .30 .75
45 Daryll Clark .30 .75
46 Anthony McCoy .25 .60
47 Joe McKnight .30 .75
48 Damian Williams .30 .75
49 Earl Thomas .30 .75
50 Jarrett Brown .30 .75
51 Tim Tebow TC .75 2.00
52 Toby Gerhart TC .20 .50
53 Golden Tate TC .20 .50
54 Aaron Hernandez TC .30 .75
55 Rolando McClain TC .20 .50
56 Sam Bradford TC .75 2.00
57 Jerry Hughes TC .20 .50
58 Tim Tebow TC .75 2.00
59 Sam Bradford TC .75 2.00
60 Ndamukong Suh TC .40 1.00
61 Tim Tebow CL .75 2.00
62 Jimmy Clausen CL .20 .50
63 Joe Webb CL .20 .50
64 Dan LeFevour CL .20 .50
65 Sean Canfield CL .15 .40
66 Ndamukong Suh CL .40 1.00
67 Tony Pike CL .20 .50
68 Toby Gerhart CL .20 .50
69 Ryan Mathews CL .40 1.00
70 Danario Alexander CL .20 .50
71 Dezmon Briscoe CL .15 .40
72 Mardy Gilyard CL .20 .50
73 Freddie Barnes CL .15 .40
74 Jordan Shipley CL .20 .50
75 Golden Tate CL .20 .50
76 Brandon LaFell CL .20 .50
77 Sean Canfield AC .15 .40
78 Toby Gerhart AC .20 .50
79 Damian Williams AC .20 .50
80 Dez Bryant AC .60 1.50
81 Eric Decker AC .25 .60
82 Jonathan Dwyer AC .20 .50
83 Demaryius Thomas AC .25 .60
84 C.J. Spiller AC .30 .75
85 Tim Tebow AC .75 2.00
86 Anthony Dixon AC .20 .50
87 Tony Pike AC .20 .50
88 Mardy Gilyard AC .20 .50
89 Dorin Dickerson AC .12 .30
90 Danario Alexander AC .20 .50
91 Dezmon Briscoe AC .15 .40
92 Jordan Shipley AC .20 .50
93 Dez Bryant TM .60 1.50
Zac Robinson
94 Tim Tebow TM .75 2.00
Aaron Hernandez
95 Jimmy Clausen TM .20 .50
Golden Tate
96 Sam Bradford TM .75 2.00
Gerald McCoy
97 Jevan Snead TM .20 .50
Dexter McCluster
98 Mardy Gilyard TM .20 .50
Tony Pike
99 Jonathan Dwyer TM .20 .50
Derrick Morgan
100 Joe McKnight TM .20 .50
Damian Williams
101 Tim Tebow PP 2.50 6.00
102 Jimmy Clausen PP .60 1.50
103 Dez Bryant PP 2.00 5.00
104 Sam Bradford PP 2.50 6.00
105 C.J. Spiller PP 1.00 2.50

2010 Press Pass Black and White

*SINGLES: 3X TO 8X BASIC CARDS
ANNOUNCED B&W ODDS 1:140 HOB

2010 Press Pass Blue

*BLUE: 1X TO 2.5X BASIC CARDS
ONE BLUE PER RETAIL PACK

2010 Press Pass Reflectors

*SINGLES: 1.5X TO 4X BASIC CARDS
STATED PRINT RUN 500 SER.#'d SETS

2010 Press Pass Reflectors Gold

*SINGLES: 2.5X TO 6X BASIC CARDS
STATED PRINT RUN 100 SER.#'d SETS

2010 Press Pass All American Autographs

RANDOM INSERTS IN SPECIAL BOXES
STATED PRINT RUN 50-397
*RED INK: .5X TO 1.2X BASIC AU
AH Aaron Hernandez/100 12.00 30.00
CS2 C.J. Spiller/97* 12.00 30.00
DD Dorin Dickerson/100 5.00 12.00
DM2 Derrick Morgan/100 6.00 15.00
FB Freddie Barnes/397 5.00 12.00
GM Gerald McCoy/50 10.00 25.00
GT Golden Tate/178* 6.00 15.00
JG Jermaine Gresham/245 8.00 20.00
JH1 Joe Haden/139* 8.00 20.00
JH2 Jerry Hughes/48* 10.00 25.00
JS1 Jordan Shipley/293* 6.00 15.00
MG Mardy Gilyard/297 6.00 15.00
NS Ndamukong Suh/99* 25.00 50.00
RM2 Rolando McClain/50 6.00 15.00
SB Sam Bradford/100 40.00 100.00
TG Toby Gerhart/194* 6.00 15.00
TT Tim Tebow/125* 75.00 125.00

2010 Press Pass All American Autographs Platinum

ANNOUNCED PLATINUM PRINT RUN 14-25
AH Aaron Hernandez/25 20.00 50.00
CS2 C.J. Spiller/25 20.00 50.00
DM2 Derrick Morgan/25 10.00 25.00
FB Freddie Barnes/25 10.00 25.00
GM Gerald McCoy/25 12.00 30.00
GT Golden Tate/14* 12.00 30.00
JG Jermaine Gresham/24 15.00 40.00
JH1 Joe Haden/25 12.00 30.00
JH2 Jerry Hughes/20* 12.00 30.00
JS1 Jordan Shipley/20* 12.00 30.00
MG Mardy Gilyard/21* 12.00 30.00
NS Ndamukong Suh/25 30.00 80.00
RM2 Rolando McClain/25 12.00 30.00
SB Sam Bradford/25 50.00 120.00
TG Toby Gerhart/23* 12.00 30.00
TT Tim Tebow/25 60.00 120.00

2010 Press Pass Autograph Power Picks

STATED PRINT RUN 74-250
*SHOWBOUND/25: .6X TO 1.5X AUTO/150-250
*SHOWBOUND/25: .5X TO 1.2X AUTO/75
SHOWBOUND PRINT RUN 25 SER.#'d SETS
*RED INK: .5X TO 1.2X BASIC AUTO
PPAB Arrelious Benn/173* 5.00 12.00
PPBL Brandon LaFell/246* 5.00 12.00
PPCS C.J. Spiller/149* 15.00 40.00
PPDB Dez Bryant/150 25.00 50.00
PPGT Golden Tate/235* 5.00 12.00
PPJB Jahvid Best/249* 15.00 40.00
PPJC Jimmy Clausen/75 8.00 20.00
PPRM Ryan Mathews/250 10.00 25.00
PPSB Sam Bradford/175 40.00 100.00
PPTG Toby Gerhart/247* 8.00 20.00
PPTT Tim Tebow/260 50.00 100.00

2010 Press Pass Autographs Bronze

OVERALL AUTO ODDS 1:5.6 HOB
*RED INK: .5X TO 1.2X BASIC AUTO
PPSAB Arrelious Benn 5.00 12.00
PPSAB2 Antonio Brown 8.00 20.00
PPSAD Anthony Dixon 5.00 12.00
PPSAH Aaron Hernandez 8.00 20.00
PPSAM Anthony McCoy 4.00 10.00
PPSAR Andre Roberts 5.00 12.00
PPSAV Alterraun Verner 5.00 12.00
PPSBG Brandon Ghee 4.00 10.00
PPSBL Brandon LaFell 5.00 12.00
PPSCM Chris McGaha 3.00 8.00
PPSCS C.J. Spiller SP 25.00 50.00
PPSCS2 Charles Scott 4.00 10.00
PPSCW Corey Wootton 4.00 10.00
PPSDA Danario Alexander 5.00 12.00
PPSDB Dezmon Briscoe 4.00 10.00
PPSDB2 Dez Bryant SP 25.00 50.00
PPSDC Daryll Clark 5.00 12.00
PPSDD Dorin Dickerson 3.00 8.00
PPSDL Dan LeFevour 5.00 12.00
PPSDM Dexter McCluster 5.00 12.00
PPSDM2 Derrick Morgan 4.00 10.00
PPSDT Demaryius Thomas 6.00 15.00
PPSDW Damian Williams 5.00 12.00
PPSDW2 Donovan Warren 5.00 12.00
PPSED Eric Decker 6.00 15.00
PPSET Earl Thomas 5.00 12.00
PPSFB Freddie Barnes 4.00 10.00
PPSGM Gerald McCoy 5.00 12.00
PPSGS George Selvie 4.00 10.00
PPSGT Golden Tate 5.00 12.00
PPSJB Jahvid Best 8.00 20.00
PPSJB2 Jarrett Brown 5.00 12.00
PPSJC Jimmy Clausen SP 5.00 12.00
PPSJD Jonathan Dwyer 5.00 12.00
PPSJF Jacoby Ford 8.00 20.00
PPSJG Jermaine Gresham 6.00 15.00
PPSJH Joe Haden 5.00 12.00
PPSJH2 Jerry Hughes 5.00 12.00
PPSJJ Javarris James 5.00 12.00
PPSJM Joe McKnight 5.00 12.00
PPSJPP Jason Pierre-Paul 8.00 20.00
PPSJS Jordan Shipley 5.00 12.00
PPSJS2 Jevan Snead 5.00 12.00
PPSJST James Starks 10.00 25.00
PPSJW Joe Webb 5.00 12.00
PPSJW2 Juice Williams 4.00 10.00
PPSMH Montario Hardesty 5.00 12.00
PPSMK Mike Kafka 5.00 12.00
PPSMW Mike Williams 8.00 20.00
PPSNB NaVorro Bowman 5.00 12.00
PPSNG Mardy Gilyard 5.00 12.00
PPSNS Ndamukong Suh 15.00 40.00
PPSRG Rob Gronkowski 12.00 30.00
PPSRM Ryan Mathews 10.00 25.00
PPSRM2 Rolando McClain 5.00 12.00
PPSSB Sam Bradford SP 50.00 120.00
PPSSC Sean Canfield 4.00 10.00
PPSSL Sean Lee 5.00 12.00
PPSTG Toby Gerhart 5.00 12.00
PPSTP Tony Pike 5.00 12.00
PPSTT Tim Tebow 60.00 120.00
PPSZR Zac Robinson 4.00 10.00

2010 Press Pass Autographs Blue

*BLUE/50: .6X TO 1.5X BRONZE AU
*BLUE/30: .6X TO 2X BRONZE AU
*BLUE/25-50: .5X TO 1.2X BRONZE AU SP
BLUE STATED PRINT RUN 25-50
PPSCS C.J. Spiller/23* 40.00 80.00
PPSJC Jimmy Clausen/25 8.00 20.00
PPSNS Ndamukong Suh/50 25.00 60.00
PPSSB Sam Bradford/45* 50.00 120.00
PPSTT Tim Tebow/50 75.00 150.00

2010 Press Pass Autographs Blue Red Ink

PRESS PASS ANNC'D RED INK PRINT RUNS
PPSAB Arrelious Benn/49* 8.00 20.00
PPSDM Dexter McCluster/50* 8.00 20.00
PPSJD Jonathan Dwyer/47* 8.00 20.00
PPSJF Jacoby Ford/50* 12.00 30.00
PPSJG Jermaine Gresham/21* 10.00 25.00
PPSRM Rolando McClain/50* 8.00 20.00

2010 Press Pass Autographs Gold

*GOLD/85-99: .6X TO 1.5X BRONZE AU
*GOLD/50-75: .5X TO 1.2X BRONZE AU SP
GOLD STATED PRINT RUN 50-99
*RED INK: .5X TO 1.2X BASIC AUTO
PPSJC Jimmy Clausen/50 8.00 20.00
PPSNS Ndamukong Suh/99 20.00 50.00
PPSSB Sam Bradford/70* 50.00 120.00
PPSTT Tim Tebow/99 50.00 120.00

2010 Press Pass Autographs Green

RANDOM INSERTS IN WAL-MART BLASTERS
STATED PRINT RUN 25 SER.#'d SETS
PPSCS C.J. Spiller/22* 50.00 100.00
PPSDB Dez Bryant EXCH
PPSGT Golden Tate/15* 15.00 40.00
PPSJB Jahvid Best
PPSJC Jimmy Clausen 12.00 30.00
PPSNS Ndamukong Suh
PPSSB Sam Bradford/20* 100.00 200.00
PPSTT Tim-Tebow 150.00 250.00

2010 Press Pass Autographs Red

RANDOM INSERTS IN TARGET BLASTERS
STATED PRINT RUN 25 SER.#'d SETS
PPSCS C.J. Spiller/22* 50.00 100.00
PPSDB Dez Bryant
PPSGT Golden Tate 15.00 40.00
PPSJB Jahvid Best/24*
PPSJC Jimmy Clausen 12.00 30.00
PPSNS Ndamukong Suh
PPSSB Sam Bradford/20* 100.00 200.00
PPSTT Tim Tebow 150.00 250.00

2010 Press Pass Autographs Silver

*SILVER/150-199: .5X TO 1.2X BRONZE AU
*SILVER/75-100: .4X TO 1X BRONZE AU SP
SILVER PRINT RUN 75-199
*RED INK: .5X TO 1.2X BASIC SLVR AU
PPSSB Sam Bradford/95* 50.00 120.00
PPSTT Tim Tebow/149* 60.00 120.00

2010 Press Pass Banner Season

COMPLETE SET (15) 8.00 20.00
STATED ODDS 1:4 HOB
BS1 Jahvid Best .75 2.00
BS2 C.J. Spiller .75 2.00
BS3 Tim Tebow 2.00 5.00
BS4 Ryan Mathews 1.00 2.50
BS5 Jonathan Dwyer .50 1.25
BS6 Arrelious Benn .50 1.25
BS7 Brandon LaFell .50 1.25
BS8 Ndamukong Suh 1.00 2.50
BS9 Jimmy Clausen .50 1.25
BS10 Golden Tate .60 1.25
BS11 Dez Bryant 1.50 4.00
BS12 Sam Bradford 2.00 5.00
BS13 Toby Gerhart .50 1.25
BS14 Gerald McCoy .50 1.25
BS15 Rolando McClain .50 1.25

2010 Press Pass Gridiron Gamers Jerseys Silver

SILVER PRINT RUN 199-299
*GOLD/99: .5X TO 1.2X SILVER
GOLD PRINT RUN 99 SER.#'d SETS
*HOLOFOIL/50: .6X TO 1.5X SILVER
HOLOFOIL PRINT RUN 50 SER.#'d SETS
GGAB Arrelious Benn/299 4.00 10.00
GGBL Brandon LaFell/299 4.00 10.00
GGDA Danario Alexander/299 4.00 10.00
GGDW Damian Williams/299 4.00 10.00
GGGT Golden Tate/199 4.00 10.00
GGJB Jahvid Best/199 6.00 15.00
GGJC Jimmy Clausen/199 6.00 15.00
GGJM Joe McKnight/299 4.00 10.00
GGJS Jevan Snead/299 5.00 12.00
GGMH Montario Hardesty/275 4.00 10.00
GGMW Mike Williams/299 5.00 12.00
GGSB Sam Bradford/199 10.00 25.00
GGSC Sean Canfield/299 4.00 10.00
GGTG Toby Gerhart/199 5.00 12.00

2010 Press Pass Saturday Signatures

RANDOM INSERTS IN SPECIAL BOXES
*PLATINUM: .8X TO 2X BASIC AUTO
AB Arrelious Benn 4.00 10.00
AD Anthony Dixon 4.00 10.00
AH Aaron Hernandez 6.00 15.00
AM Anthony McCoy
AR Andre Roberts 4.00 10.00
BL Brandon LaFell 4.00 10.00
CM Chris McGaha 2.50 6.00
CS1 Charles Scott 3.00 8.00
CS2 C.J. Spiller 6.00 15.00
DA Danario Alexander 4.00 10.00
DB Dezmon Briscoe 3.00 8.00
DC Daryll Clark 4.00 10.00
DL Dan LeFevour 4.00 10.00
DM1 Dexter McCluster 4.00 10.00
DM2 Derrick Morgan 3.00 8.00
DT Demaryius Thomas 5.00 12.00
DW Damian Williams 4.00 10.00
ED Eric Decker 5.00 12.00
ET Earl Thomas 4.00 10.00
FB Freddie Barnes 3.00 8.00
GM Gerald McCoy 4.00 10.00
GT Golden Tate 4.00 10.00
JB1 Jahvid Best 6.00 15.00
JB2 Jarrett Brown 4.00 10.00
JC Jimmy Clausen 4.00 10.00
JD Jonathan Dwyer 4.00 10.00
JF Jacoby Ford 4.00 10.00
JG Jermaine Gresham 5.00 12.00
JH1 Joe Haden 4.00 10.00
JH2 Jerry Hughes
JJ Javarris James 4.00 10.00
JM Joe McKnight 4.00 10.00
JP Jason Pierre-Paul 6.00 15.00
JS1 Jordan Shipley 4.00 10.00
JS2 Jevan Snead 4.00 10.00
JS3 James Starks 10.00 25.00
MG Mardy Gilyard 4.00 10.00
MH Montario Hardesty 4.00 10.00
MK Mike Kafka 4.00 10.00
MW Mike Williams 6.00 15.00
NB NaVorro Bowman 4.00 10.00
NS Ndamukong Suh
RG Rob Gronkowski 25.00 50.00
RM1 Ryan Mathews 8.00 20.00
RM2 Rolando McClain
SB Sam Bradford 40.00 80.00
SC Sean Canfield 3.00 8.00
TG Toby Gerhart 4.00 10.00
TP Tony Pike 4.00 10.00
TT Tim Tebow 80.00 100.00
ZR Zac Robinson

2010 Press Pass Saturday Signatures Platinum

*PLATINUM/15-25: .8X TO 2X BASIC AU
ANNOUNCED PRINT RUN 8-25
SB Sam Bradford/24 40.00 100.00

2010 Press Pass Saturday Signatures Platinum Red Ink

*RED INK: X TO X BASIC PLAT.AU
RED INK ANNOUNCED PRINT RUN 1-25
JG Jermaine Gresham/25
JM Joe McKnight/17*
TT Tim Tebow/25 75.00 125.00

2010 Press Pass Saturday Signatures Red Ink

*RED INK: X TO X BASIC AUTO
RED INK ANNOUNCED PRINT RUN 2-65
DC Daryll Clark/24*
DL Dan LeFevour/39*
DM1 Dexter McCluster/50*
DT Demaryius Thomas/50*
ED Eric Decker/58*
GT Golden Tate/14*
JB1 Jahvid Best/20* 10.00 25.00
JC Jimmy Clausen/24*
JD Jonathan Dwyer/65*
JF Jacoby Ford/47*
JM Joe McKnight/23*
MH Montario Hardesty/14*

2010 Press Pass Target Exclusive

RANDOM INSERTS IN TARGET PACKS
TAR1 Tim Tebow 4.00 10.00
TAR2 Jimmy Clausen 1.00 2.50
TAR3 Sam Bradford 4.00 10.00
TAR4 Jahvid Best 1.50 4.00
TAR5 Dez Bryant 3.00 8.00
TAR6 C.J. Spiller 1.50 4.00

2010 Press Pass Target Exclusive Autographs

STATED PRINT RUN 25 SER.#'d SETS
TARAB Arrelious Benn/1*
TARCS C.J. Spiller/20* 15.00 40.00
TARDB Dez Bryant/25 50.00 100.00
TARGT Golden Tate/19* 10.00 25.00
TARJB Jahvid Best/25 15.00 40.00
TARJC Jimmy Clausen/25 15.00 40.00
TARSB Sam Bradford/25 75.00 150.00
TARTG Toby Gerhart/22*
TARTT Tim Tebow/25 100.00 200.00

2010 Press Pass Wal-Mart Exclusive

RANDOM INSERTS IN WAL-MART PACKS
WM1 Tim Tebow 4.00 10.00
WM2 Jimmy Clausen 1.00 2.50
WM3 Sam Bradford 4.00 10.00
WM4 Jahvid Best 1.50 4.00
WM5 Dez Bryant 3.00 8.00
WM6 C.J. Spiller 1.50 4.00

2010 Press Pass Wal-Mart Exclusive Autographs

STATED PRINT RUN 25 SER.#'d SETS
WMBL Brandon LaFell/21*
WMCS C.J. Spiller/24* 15.00 40.00
WMDB Dez Bryant/18 50.00 100.00
WMGT Golden Tate/19* 10.00 25.00
WMJB Jahvid Best/22*
WMJC Jimmy Clausen/25 15.00 40.00
WMSB Sam Bradford/25 75.00 150.00
WMTG Toby Gerhart/22*
WMTT Tim Tebow/25 100.00 200.00

2011 Press Pass

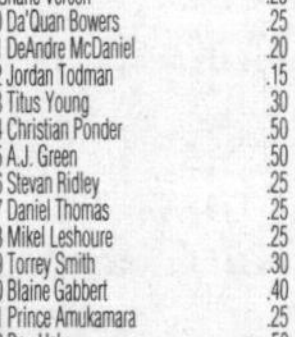

COMPLETE SET (105) 25.00 50.00
COMP.SET w/o PP's (100) 12.00 30.00
101-105 POWER PICK ODDS 1:14 HOB
UNPRICED SOLO PRINT RUN 1
1 Marcell Dareus .25 .60
2 Mark Ingram .50 1.25
3 Julio Jones .50 1.25
4 Ryan Mallett .50 1.25
5 Nick Fairley .30 .75
6 Cam Newton 1.25 3.00
7 Austin Pettis .20 .50
8 Darvin Adams .20 .50
9 Shane Vereen .25 .60
10 Da'Quan Bowers .25 .60
11 DeAndre McDaniel .20 .50
12 Jordan Todman .15 .40
13 Titus Young .30 .75
14 Christian Ponder .50 1.25
15 A.J. Green .50 1.25
16 Stevan Ridley .25 .60
17 Daniel Thomas .25 .60
18 Mikel Leshoure .25 .60
19 Torrey Smith .30 .75
20 Blaine Gabbert .40 1.00
21 Prince Amukamara .25 .60
22 Roy Helu .50 1.25
23 Niles Paul .25 .60
24 Colin Kaepernick .30 .75
25 Greg Little .25 .60
26 Ryan Williams .30 .75
27 Delone Carter .20 .50
28 Kyle Rudolph .25 .60
29 Cameron Heyward .25 .60
30 Dane Sanzenbacher .25 .60
31 Dion Lewis .25 .60
32 Kendall Hunter .25 .60
33 DeMarco Murray .50 1.25
34 Stephen Paea .25 .60
35 Evan Royster .25 .60
36 Jonathan Baldwin .25 .60
37 Ryan Kerrigan .25 .60
38 Andy Dalton .60 1.50
39 Von Miller .30 .75
40 Akeem Ayers .20 .50
41 Tyrod Taylor .25 .60
42 Jake Locker .60 1.50
43 John Clay .25 .60
44 Tandon Doss .20 .50
45 Derrick Locke .20 .50
46 Greg Salas .25 .60
47 Rahim Moore .20 .50
48 Randall Cobb .30 .75
49 Terrence Toliver .20 .50
50 Aldon Smith .40 1.00
51 Aaron Williams .20 .50

52 J.J. Watt .30 .75
53 Luke Stocker .20 .50
54 Cam Newton TC 1.25 3.00
55 Nick Fairley TC .30 .75
56 Da'Quan Bowers TC .25 .60
57 Cam Newton TC 1.25 3.00
58 Mark Ingram TC .50 1.25
59 Von Miller TC .30 .75
60 Cam Newton NL 1.25 3.00
61 Andy Dalton NL .60 1.50
62 Tyrod Taylor NL .25 .60
63 Dane Sanzenbacher NL .25 .60
64 Ryan Mallett NL .50 1.25
65 Colin Kaepernick NL .30 .75
66 Daniel Thomas NL .25 .60
67 DeMarco Murray NL .50 1.25
68 Jordan Todman NL .15 .40
69 Kendall Hunter NL .25 .60
70 Titus Young NL .30 .75
71 Julio Jones NL .50 1.25
72 Jerrel Jernigan NL .20 .50
73 Torrey Smith NL .30 .75
74 Da'Quan Bowers NL .25 .60
75 Ryan Kerrigan NL .25 .60
76 Nick Fairley NL .30 .75
77 Tandon Doss BS .20 .50
78 Randall Cobb BS .30 .75
79 Ryan Williams BS .30 .75
80 Torrey Smith BS .30 .75
81 Blaine Gabbert BS .40 1.00
82 A.J. Green BS .50 1.25
83 Jonathan Baldwin BS .25 .60
84 Mark Ingram BS .50 1.25
85 Julio Jones BS .50 1.25
86 Jake Locker BS .60 1.50
87 Ryan Mallett BS .50 1.25
88 Cam Newton BS 1.25 3.00
89 Daniel Thomas BS .25 .60
90 Mikel Leshoure BS .25 .60
91 Jordan Todman BS .15 .40
92 Da'Quan Bowers GC .30 .75
Nick Fairley
93 Blaine Gabbert GC .50 1.25
Ryan Mallett
94 A.J. Green GC .50 1.25
Julio Jones
95 Cam Newton GC 1.25 3.00
Tyrod Taylor
96 Mark Ingram GC .50 1.25
Daniel Thomas
97 Jake Locker GC .60 1.50
Christian Ponder
98 Jonathan Baldwin GC .30 .75
Torrey Smith
99 Mikel Leshoure GC .30 .75
Ryan Williams
100 DeMarco Murray GC .50 1.25
Kendall Hunter
101 Blaine Gabbert PP 1.00 2.50
102 A.J. Green PP 1.25 3.00
103 Cam Newton PP 3.00 8.00
104 Mark Ingram PP 1.25 3.00
105 Nick Fairley PP 1.25 3.00

2011 Press Pass Black and White
*BLACK/WHITE: 3X TO 8X BASIC CARDS
ANNOUNCED B&W ODDS 1:140 HOB

2011 Press Pass Reflectors
*REFLECTOR/299: 2X TO 5X BASIC INSERTS
REFLECTOR STATED PRINT RUN 299

2011 Press Pass Reflectors Blue
*BLUE: 1.2X TO 3X BASIC CARDS
ONE REFLECTOR BLUE PER RETAIL PACK

2011 Press Pass Reflectors Gold
*GOLD/100: 2.5X TO 6X BASIC INSERTS
GOLD STATED PRINT RUN 100

2011 Press Pass Reflectors Purple
*PURPLE/25: 5X TO 12X BASIC INSERTS
PURPLE STATED PRINT RUN 25

2011 Press Pass Autograph Power Picks
STATED PRINT RUN 35-250
*RED INK/16-53: .5X TO 1.2X BASIC AU
*SHOWBOUND/25: .6X TO 1.5X AU/125-250
*SHOWBOUND/25: .5X TO 1.2X AU/35-105
PPAG A.J. Green/52 25.00 50.00
PPBG Blaine Gabbert/95* 20.00 50.00
PPCN Cam Newton/230* 40.00 80.00
PPDB Da'Quan Bowers/125 8.00 20.00
PPDM DeMarco Murray/100 15.00 30.00
PPDT Daniel Thomas/234* 8.00 20.00
PPJB Jonathan Baldwin/197* 6.00 15.00
PPJJ Julio Jones/228* 12.00 30.00
PPJL Jake Locker/68* 30.00 60.00
PPMI Mark Ingram/246* 20.00 50.00
PPML Mikel Leshoure/55* 10.00 25.00
PPNF Nick Fairley/35 12.00 30.00
PPPA Prince Amukamara/150 10.00 25.00
PPRM Ryan Mallett/65* 25.00 50.00

2011 Press Pass Autographs Blue
*BLUE/50: .6X TO 1.5X BRONZE
*BLUE/50: .5X TO 1.2X BRONZE SP
*BLUE/25: .6X TO 1.5X BRONZE
BLUE STATED PRINT RUN 25-50
*RED INK/15-25: .5X TO 1.2X BASIC AU
PPSCN Cam Newton/50 50.00 120.00

2011 Press Pass Autographs Bronze
OVERALL AUTO ODDS 1:7 HOB
EXCH EXPIRATION: 3/31/2012
*RED INK/15-99: .5X TO 1.2X BASIC AU
PPSAA Akeem Ayers EXCH 3.00 8.00
PPSAB Armon Binns 3.00 8.00
PPSAB2 Ahmad Black 3.00 8.00
PPSAD Andy Dalton 10.00 25.00
PPSAG A.J. Green SP 12.00 30.00
PPSAP Austin Pettis 3.00 8.00
PPSAS Aldon Smith 6.00 15.00
PPSAW Aaron Williams 3.00 8.00
PPSBB Brandon Burton 3.00 8.00
PPSBG Blaine Gabbert SP 20.00 40.00
PPSCH Cameron Heyward 4.00 10.00
PPSCK Colin Kaepernick 10.00 25.00
PPSCN Cam Newton 30.00 80.00
PPSCP Christian Ponder 10.00 25.00
PPSDA Darvin Adams 3.00 8.00
PPSDB Da'Quan Bowers SP 10.00 25.00
PPSDC Delone Carter 3.00 8.00
PPSDL Dion Lewis 4.00 10.00
PPSDL2 Derrick Locke 3.00 8.00
PPSDM DeMarco Murray SP 10.00 25.00
PPSDM2 DeAndre McDaniel 3.00 8.00
PPSDN Drake Nevis 4.00 10.00
PPSDS Dane Sanzenbacher 4.00 10.00
PPSDT Daniel Thomas 4.00 10.00
PPSDW D.J. Williams 4.00 10.00
PPSER Evan Royster 4.00 10.00
PPSGL Greg Little 4.00 10.00
PPSGS Greg Salas 4.00 10.00
PPSJB Jonathan Baldwin SP 5.00 12.00
PPSJC John Clay 4.00 10.00
PPSJJ Julio Jones SP 15.00 40.00
PPSJJ2 Jerrel Jernigan 3.00 8.00
PPSJL Jake Locker SP 20.00 50.00
PPSJR Jacquizz Rodgers 4.00 10.00
PPSJT Jordan Todman 2.50 6.00
PPSJW J.J. Watt 5.00 12.00
PPSKH Kendall Hunter 4.00 10.00
PPSKR Kyle Rudolph 4.00 10.00
PPSLS Luke Stocker 3.00 8.00
PPSMD Marcell Dareus 8.00 20.00
PPSMH Mark Herzlich 3.00 8.00
PPSMI Mark Ingram 12.00 30.00
PPSML Mikel Leshoure SP 8.00 20.00
PPSNF Nick Fairley SP 10.00 25.00
PPSNP Niles Paul 4.00 10.00
PPSPA Prince Amukamara SP 8.00 20.00
PPSRC Randall Cobb 5.00 12.00
PPSRH Roy Helu 8.00 20.00
PPSRK Ryan Kerrigan 4.00 10.00
PPSRM Ryan Mallett SP 20.00 40.00
PPSRM2 Rahim Moore SP 4.00 10.00
PPSRW Ryan Williams 5.00 12.00
PPSSP Stephen Paea 4.00 10.00
PPSSR Stevan Ridley 4.00 10.00
PPSSV Shane Vereen 4.00 10.00
PPSTD Tandon Doss 3.00 8.00
PPSTS Torrey Smith 5.00 12.00
PPSTT Tyrod Taylor 4.00 10.00
PPSTT2 Terrence Toliver 3.00 8.00
PPSTY Titus Young 5.00 12.00
PPSVM Von Miller 6.00 15.00

2011 Press Pass Autographs Gold
*GOLD/99: .6X TO 1.5X BRONZE
*GOLD/75: .5X TO 1.2X BRONZE SP
*GOLD/35-50: .6X TO 1.5X BRONZE
GOLD STATED PRINT RUN 35-99
*RED INK/15-50: .5X TO 1.2X BASIC AU
PPSCN Cam Newton/90* 40.00 100.00

2011 Press Pass Autographs Green
*GREEN/25: .8X TO 2X BRONZE AU
RANDOM INSERTS IN WAL-MART BLASTER

2011 Press Pass Autographs Red
*RED/25: .8X TO 2X BRONZE AU
RANDOM INSERTS IN TARGET BLASTER

2011 Press Pass Autographs Silver
*SILVER/69-199: .5X TO 1.2X BRONZE
*SILVER/50-199: .4X TO 1X BRONZE SP
SILVER STATED PRINT RUN 50-199
*RED INK/19-50: .5X TO 1.2X BASIC AU
PPSCN Cam Newton/199 40.00 80.00

2011 Press Pass Class of 2011
COMPLETE SET (10) 8.00 20.00
STATED ODDS 1:7
CL1 Blaine Gabbert 1.00 2.50
CL2 Jake Locker 1.50 4.00
CL3 Ryan Mallett 1.25 3.00
CL4 Cam Newton 3.00 8.00
CL5 Jonathan Baldwin .60 1.50
CL6 Da'Quan Bowers .60 1.50
CL7 Nick Fairley .75 2.00
CL8 A.J. Green 1.25 3.00
CL9 Julio Jones 1.25 3.00
CL10 Mark Ingram 1.25 3.00

2011 Press Pass Class of 2011 Autographs
STATED PRINT RUN 35-199
*HOC/25: .6X TO 1.5X BASIC AU/199
*HOC/25: .5X TO 1.2X BASIC AU/35-110
*RED INK/22-35: .5X TO 1.2X BASIC AU
CLAG A.J. Green/50 20.00 50.00
CLBG Blaine Gabbert/90* 12.00 30.00
CLCN Cam Newton/194* 30.00 60.00
CLDB Da'Quan Bowers/100 8.00 20.00
CLDM DeMarco Murray/100 12.00 30.00
CLDT Daniel Thomas/164* 8.00 20.00
CLJB Jonathan Baldwin/199 6.00 15.00
CLJJ Julio Jones/177* 20.00 40.00
CLJL Jake Locker/77 20.00 50.00
CLMI Mark Ingram/189* 15.00 40.00
CLML Mikel Leshoure/75* 10.00 25.00
CLNF Nick Fairley/35 12.00 30.00
CLPA Prince Amukamara/110 10.00 25.00
CLRM Ryan Mallett/65* 15.00 40.00

2011 Press Pass Face to Face
STATED ODDS 1:4
FF1 Blaine Gabbert 1.00 2.50
DeMarco Murray
FF2 A.J. Green 1.00 2.50
Julio Jones
FF3 Cam Newton 2.50 6.00
Ryan Mallett
FF4 Jordan Todman .50 1.25
Dion Lewis
FF5 Jonathan Baldwin .50 1.25
Kyle Rudolph
FF6 Da'Quan Bowers .60 1.50
Nick Fairley
FF7 Jake Locker 1.25 3.00
Shane Vereen
FF8 Niles Paul .50 1.25
Kendall Hunter
FF9 Daniel Thomas .50 1.25
Delone Carter
FF10 Mikel Leshoure .50 1.25
Tandon Doss
FF11 Marcell Dareus .50 1.25
Stevan Ridley
FF12 Ryan Williams .60 1.50
Austin Pettis
FF13 Torrey Smith 1.00 2.50
Christian Ponder
FF14 Colin Kaepernick .60 1.50
Titus Young
FF15 Andy Dalton 1.25 3.00
John Clay

2011 Press Pass Gridiron Gamers Jerseys Silver
SILVER STATED PRINT RUN 225
*GOLD/99: .5X TO 1.2X SILVER/225
*HOLOFOIL/50: .6X TO 1.5X SILVER/225
*PURPLE/60: .6X TO 1.5X SILVER/225
JSY OVERALL ODDS 1:84 HOB
GGAD Andy Dalton 4.00 10.00
GGAG A.J. Green 5.00 12.00
GGBG Blaine Gabbert 6.00 15.00
GGDB Da'Quan Bowers 4.00 10.00
GGJB Jonathan Baldwin 4.00 10.00
GGJJ Julio Jones 8.00 20.00
GGJL Jake Locker 10.00 25.00
GGJR Jacquizz Rodgers 5.00 12.00
GGKR Kyle Rudolph 5.00 12.00
GGNP Niles Paul 8.00 20.00
GGPA Prince Amukamara 6.00 15.00
GGRH Roy Helu 6.00 15.00
GGRM Ryan Mallett 6.00 15.00
GGSR Stevan Ridley 4.00 10.00
GGSV Shane Vereen 4.00 10.00
GGTS Torrey Smith 5.00 12.00
GGTT Terrence Toliver 4.00 10.00

2011 Press Pass Target Exclusive
RANDOM INSERTS IN TARGET PACKS
TAR1 Blaine Gabbert 1.50 4.00
TAR2 Cam Newton 5.00 12.00
TAR3 Ryan Mallett 2.00 5.00
TAR4 Jake Locker 2.50 6.00
TAR5 A.J. Green 2.00 5.00
TAR6 Mark Ingram 2.00 5.00

2011 Press Pass Wal-Mart Exclusive
RANDOM INSERTS IN WAL-MART PACKS
WM1 Blaine Gabbert 1.50 4.00
WM2 Cam Newton 5.00 12.00
WM3 Ryan Mallett 2.00 5.00
WM4 Jake Locker 2.50 6.00
WM5 A.J. Green 2.00 5.00
WM6 Mark Ingram 2.00 5.00

2012 Press Pass
COMPLETE SET (50) 6.00 15.00
1 Dwayne Allen .25 .60
2 Mark Barron .40 1.00
3 Justin Blackmon .50 1.25
4 Andre Branch .20 .50
5 Ryan Broyles .25 .60
6 Orson Charles .25 .60
7 Quinton Coples .25 .60
8 Kirk Cousins .40 1.00
9 Jared Crick .25 .60
10 Alfonzo Dennard .25 .60
11 Jeremy Ebert .20 .50
12 Michael Egnew .20 .50
13 Michael Floyd .50 1.25
14 Nick Foles .40 1.00
15 Jeff Fuller .30 .75
16 Stephon Gilmore .25 .60
17 Chris Givens .20 .50
18 T.J. Graham .25 .60
19 Cyrus Gray .25 .60
20 Robert Griffin III 1.25 3.00
21 Dan Herron .25 .60
22 Stephen Hill .25 .60
23 LaMichael James .50 1.25
24 Alshon Jeffery .40 1.00
25 Marvin Jones .20 .50
26 Case Keenum .30 .75
27 Luke Kuechly .30 .75
28 Travis Lewis .20 .50
29 Ryan Lindley .25 .60
30 Andrew Luck 1.50 4.00
31 Doug Martin .40 1.00
32 Marquis Maze .25 .60
33 Whitney Mercilus .25 .60
34 Lamar Miller .30 .75
35 Kellen Moore .40 1.00
36 Brock Osweiler .30 .75
37 Isaiah Pead .25 .60
38 Dan Persa .20 .50
39 Dontari Poe .25 .60
40 DeVier Posey .25 .60
41 Trent Richardson .75 2.00
42 Gerell Robinson .25 .60
43 Mohamed Sanu .25 .60
44 Devon Still .25 .60
45 Tommy Streeter .25 .60
46 Ryan Tannehill .60 1.50
47 Courtney Upshaw .30 .75
48 Brandon Weeden .50 1.25
49 Jarius Wright .25 .60
50 Kendall Wright .30 .75

2012 Press Pass Blue
*BLUE: 1X TO 2.5X BASIC CARDS
BLUE STATED ODDS 1:1 RETAIL

2012 Press Pass Gold
*GOLD: 1X TO 2.5X BASIC CARDS
GOLD STATED ODDS 1:1 HOBBY

2012 Press Pass Reflectors
*REFLECTOR/299: 1.5X TO 4X BASIC CARDS
REFLECTOR STATED PRINT RUN 299
20 Robert Griffin III 8.00 20.00
30 Andrew Luck 8.00 20.00

2012 Press Pass Reflectors Proof
*PROOF/100: 2.5X TO 6X BASIC CARDS
HOBBY ONLY PROOF PRINT RUN 100
20 Robert Griffin III 12.00 30.00
30 Andrew Luck 12.00 30.00

2012 Press Pass All American Autographs Silver
SILVER PRINT RUN 99 SER.#'d SETS
*BLUE/50: .5X TO 1.2X SILVER/99
*RED/25: .6X TO 1.5X SILVER/99
AL Andrew Luck/98* 75.00 150.00
CF Coby Fleener/97* 6.00 15.00
CK Case Keenum 6.00 15.00
JB Justin Blackmon/95* 10.00 25.00
KM Kellen Moore/93* 8.00 20.00
LJ LaMichael James/89* 10.00 25.00
MF Michael Floyd 10.00 25.00
RG Robert Griffin III 75.00 150.00
TR Trent Richardson/97* 25.00 50.00

2012 Press Pass Autographs Blue
BLUE STATED PRINT RUN 50-99
PPSAB Andre Branch/50 4.00 10.00
PPSAC Audie Cole/47* 4.00 10.00
PPSAD Alfonzo Dennard/50 5.00 12.00
PPSAJ A.J. Jenkins/50 6.00 15.00
PPSAJ2 Alshon Jeffery/50 8.00 20.00
PPSAL Andrew Luck/50 100.00 200.00
PPSBO Brock Osweiler/47* 6.00 15.00
PPSBQ Brian Quick/99 6.00 15.00
PPSBT Brandon Thompson/34* 4.00 10.00
PPSBW Brandon Weeden/50 12.00 30.00
PPSBW2 Billy Winn/35* 5.00 12.00
PPSCF Coby Fleener/48* 8.00 20.00
PPSCG Cyrus Gray/30* 5.00 12.00
PPSCG2 Chris Givens/45* 4.00 10.00
PPSCH Casey Hayward/45* 5.00 12.00
PPSCJ Coryell Judie/45* 4.00 10.00
PPSCK Case Keenum/50 6.00 15.00
PPSCU Courtney Upshaw/50 6.00 15.00
PPSDA Dwayne Allen/50 5.00 12.00
PPSDH Dont'a Hightower/50 8.00 20.00
PPSDH2 Dan Herron/50 5.00 12.00
PPSDM Doug Martin/50 8.00 20.00
PPSDP Dan Persa/50 4.00 10.00
PPSDP2 Dontari Poe/50 5.00 12.00
PPSDP3 DeVier Posey/50 5.00 12.00
PPSDS Devon Still/50 5.00 12.00
PPSEA Emmanuel Acho/50 5.00 12.00
PPSFC Fletcher Cox/40* 5.00 12.00
PPSGR Gerell Robinson/50 5.00 12.00
PPSHS Harrison Smith/50 5.00 12.00
PPSIP Isaiah Pead/50 5.00 12.00
PPSJA Joe Adams/42* 5.00 12.00
PPSJB Justin Blackmon/50 20.00 50.00
PPSJC Jared Crick/50 5.00 12.00
PPSJE Jeremy Ebert/50 4.00 10.00
PPSJF Jeff Fuller/50 6.00 15.00
PPSJH Jayron Hosley/50 5.00 12.00
PPSJJ Janoris Jenkins/45* 5.00 12.00
PPSJW Jarius Wright/45* 5.00 12.00
PPSKC Kirk Cousins/50 10.00 25.00
PPSKK Kevin Koger/50 5.00 12.00
PPSKM Kellen Moore/50 12.00 30.00
PPSKR Kendall Reyes/50 4.00 10.00
PPSKW Kendall Wright/50 10.00 25.00
PPSLD Lavonte David/50 6.00 15.00
PPSLJ LaMichael James/50 12.00 30.00
PPSLK Luke Kuechly/50 6.00 15.00
PPSLM Lamar Miller/50 8.00 20.00
PPSMB Mark Barron/50 8.00 20.00
PPSME Michael Egnew/50 4.00 10.00
PPSMF Michael Floyd/50 20.00 40.00
PPSMI Melvin Ingram/40* 6.00 15.00
PPSMJ Marvin Jones/50 4.00 10.00
PPSMM Marquis Maze/50 5.00 12.00
PPSMS Mohamed Sanu/50 5.00 12.00
PPSNF Nick Foles/50 8.00 20.00
PPSNT Nick Toon/50 6.00 15.00
PPSOC Orson Charles/3*
PPSQC Quinton Coples/50 6.00 15.00
PPSRB Ryan Broyles/31* 8.00 20.00
PPSRG Robert Griffin III/49* 100.00 200.00
PPSRL Ryan Lindley/47* 5.00 12.00
PPSRT Ryan Tannehill/50 20.00 50.00
PPSRW Russell Wilson/50 8.00 20.00
PPSSG Stephon Gilmore/32* 5.00 12.00
PPSSH Stephen Hill/32* 8.00 20.00
PPSTG T.J. Graham/41* 5.00 12.00
PPSTH T.Y. Hilton/50 5.00 12.00
PPSTL Travis Lewis/46* 4.00 10.00
PPSTR Trent Richardson/41* 30.00 60.00
PPSTS Tommy Streeter/50
PPSVB Vick Ballard/50 4.00 10.00
PPSWM Whitney Mercilus/46* 5.00 12.00
PPSZB Zach Brown/50 4.00 10.00

2012 Press Pass Autographs Blue Red Ink
RED INK/15-20*: .5X TO 1.2X BLUE AUTO/50
ANNOUNCED RED INK PRINT RUN 1-47
PPSOC Orson Charles/47* 5.00 12.00

2012 Press Pass Autographs Bronze
*BRONZE AU/99-149: .3X TO .8X BLUE AU/50-99
BRONZE STATED PRINT RUN 25-149
PPSAL Andrew Luck/24* 250.00 400.00
PPSCK Case Keenum/25 8.00 20.00
PPSJB Justin Blackmon/23* 50.00 100.00
PPSKM Kellen Moore/25 15.00 40.00
PPSKW Kendall Wright/20* 12.00 30.00
PPSLJ LaMichael James/25 25.00 50.00
PPSLM Lamar Miller/24* 10.00 25.00
PPSMF Michael Floyd/25 25.00 50.00
PPSQC Quinton Coples/25 8.00 20.00
PPSRG Robert Griffin III/23* 125.00 250.00
PPSTR Trent Richardson/25 50.00 100.00

2012 Press Pass Autographs Bronze Red Ink
RED INK/15-49*: .5X TO 1.2X GOLD AU
ANNOUNCED RED INK PRINT RUN 1-49

2012 Press Pass Autographs Gold
*GOLD AU/175-249: .25X TO .6X BLUE/50-99
GOLD STATED PRINT RUN 25-249
PPSAL Andrew Luck/24* 150.00 300.00
PPSCK Case Keenum/25 8.00 20.00
PPSJB Justin Blackmon/25 25.00 60.00
PPSKM Kellen Moore/24* 15.00 40.00
PPSKW Kendall Wright/20* 12.00 30.00
PPSLJ LaMichael James/25 25.00 50.00
PPSLM Lamar Miller/25 10.00 25.00
PPSMF Michael Floyd/25 25.00 50.00
PPSQC Quinton Coples/25 8.00 20.00
PPSRG Robert Griffin III/22* 100.00 200.00
PPSTR Trent Richardson/19* 30.00 80.00

2012 Press Pass Autographs Gold Red Ink
RED INK/15-50*: .5X TO 1.2X GOLD AU
ANNOUNCED RED INK PRINT RUN 1-50

2012 Press Pass Autographs Silver
*SILVER AU: .25X TO .6X BLUE AU/50-99
OVERALL AUTO ODDS 1:5 HOB
PPSAJ2 Alshon Jeffery SP 8.00 20.00
PPSAL Andrew Luck 60.00 120.00
PPSBW Brandon Weeden SP 12.00 30.00
PPSCK Case Keenum SP 8.00 20.00
PPSJB Justin Blackmon SP 15.00 40.00
PPSKM Kellen Moore SP 8.00 20.00
PPSKW Kendall Wright SP 8.00 20.00
PPSLJ LaMichael James SP 15.00 30.00
PPSLM Lamar Miller SP 6.00 15.00
PPSMF Michael Floyd SP 12.00 30.00
PPSQC Quinton Coples SP 6.00 15.00
PPSRG Robert Griffin III SP 60.00 120.00
PPSRW Russell Wilson SP 8.00 20.00
PPSTR Trent Richardson SP 25.00 50.00

2012 Press Pass Autographs Silver Red Ink
RED INK/15-218*: .5X TO 1.2X SLVR AU
ANNOUNCED RED INK PRINT RUN 1-218

2012 Press Pass Autographs Target Red
*RED/15: .6X TO 1.5X BLUE AU/50-99
RED/4-15 INSERTS IN TARGET PACKS
PPSTR Trent Richardson/15 75.00 150.00

2012 Press Pass Autographs Target Red Red Ink
PPSRB Ryan Broyles/14* 20.00 40.00
PPSSH Stephen Hill/15 12.00 30.00
PPSWM Whitney Mercilus/15

2012 Press Pass Autographs Wal-Mart Green
*GREEN/15: .6X TO 1.5X BLUE AU/50-99
GREEN/3-15 INSERTS IN WAL-MART PACKS
PPSTR Trent Richardson/15 75.00 150.00
PPSWM Whitney Mercilus/1*

2012 Press Pass Autographs Wal-Mart Green Red Ink
PPSRB Ryan Broyles/15 20.00 40.00
PPSSH Stephen Hill/15 12.00 30.00
PPSWM Whitney Mercilus/14* 8.00 20.00

2012 Press Pass Power Pick Autographs Blue
STATED PRINT RUN 50 SER.#'d SETS
*RED/25: .5X TO 1.2X BLUE/45-50
*SILVER/99: .3X TO .8X BLUE/45-50
AJ Alshon Jeffery 10.00 25.00
AL Andrew Luck/49* 100.00 200.00
JB Justin Blackmon 12.00 30.00
KW Kendall Wright/45* 12.00 30.00
LJ LaMichael James 15.00 40.00
LM Lamar Miller/48* 8.00 20.00
MF Michael Floyd/3*
NF Nick Foles 10.00 25.00
QC Quinton Coples/3*
RG Robert Griffin III 75.00 150.00
RT Ryan Tannehill 25.00 50.00
TR Trent Richardson/46* 40.00 80.00

2012 Press Pass Power Pick Autographs Blue Red Ink
MF Michael Floyd/47* 15.00 40.00
QC Quinton Coples/47* 6.00 15.00

2012 Press Pass Fanfare
*BASE AU: .3X TO .8X BRONZE/59-99
RED INK/20-95: .5X TO 1.2X BASIC AU
FFAL Andrew Luck AU SP 60.00 120.00

2012 Press Pass Fanfare Blue
*BLUE/189-199: .4X TO 1X BRONZE/59-99
RED INK/25-50: .5X TO 1.2X BLUE/189-199

2012 Press Pass Fanfare Bronze
COMMON CARD/59-99 3.00 8.00
SEMISTARS/59-99 4.00 10.00
UNL.STARS/59-99 5.00 12.00
BRONZE STATED PRINT RUN 59-99
FFAB Andre Branch AU/69* 4.00 10.00
FFAC Audie Cole AU/99 4.00 10.00
FFAD Alfonzo Dennard AU/99 5.00 12.00
FFAJ1 Alshon Jeffery AU/99 8.00 20.00
FFAJ2 A.J. Jenkins AU/46* 6.00 15.00
FFAL Andrew Luck AU/98* 75.00 135.00
FFBO Brock Osweiler AU/99 8.00 20.00
FFBQ Brian Quick AU/99 6.00 15.00
FFBT Brandon Thompson AU/99 4.00 10.00
FFBW1 Brandon Weeden AU/99 10.00 25.00
FFBW2 Billy Winn AU/83* 5.00 12.00
FFCF Coby Fleener AU/94* 8.00 20.00
FFCG1 Chris Givens AU/90* 4.00 10.00
FFCG2 Cyrus Gray AU/99 5.00 12.00
FFCH Casey Hayward AU/87* 5.00 12.00
FFCJ Coryell Judie AU/99 4.00 10.00
FFCK Case Keenum AU/99 6.00 15.00
FFCU Courtney Upshaw AU/99 6.00 15.00
FFDA Dwayne Allen AU/97* 5.00 12.00
FFDH1 Dan Herron AU/99 5.00 12.00
FFDH2 Dont'a Hightower AU/99 8.00 20.00
FFDM Doug Martin AU/99 8.00 20.00
FFDP Dontari Poe AU/75* 5.00 12.00
FFDP1 Dan Persa AU/94*
FFDP2 DeVier Posey AU/88* 5.00 12.00
FFDS Devon Still AU/99 5.00 12.00
FFEA Emmanuel Acho AU/99 5.00 12.00
FFFC Fletcher Cox AU/82* 6.00 15.00
FFGR Gerell Robinson AU/75 5.00 12.00
FFHS Harrison Smith AU/99 5.00 12.00
FFIP Isaiah Pead AU/64* 5.00 12.00
FFJA Joe Adams AU/84* 5.00 12.00
FFJC Jared Crick AU/99 5.00 12.00
FFJE Jeremy Ebert AU/95* 4.00 10.00
FFJF Jeff Fuller AU/75* 6.00 15.00
FFJH Jayron Hosley AU/99 5.00 12.00
FFJJ Janoris Jenkins AU/88* 5.00 12.00
FFKC Kirk Cousins AU/99 8.00 20.00
FFKK Kevin Koger AU/97*
FFKM Kellen Moore AU/97* 8.00 20.00
FFKR Kendall Reyes AU/91* 4.00 10.00
FFKW Kendall Wright AU/97* 6.00 15.00
FFLD Lavonte David AU/99 6.00 15.00
FFLK Luke Kuechly AU/81* 6.00 15.00
FFLM Lamar Miller AU/97* 8.00 20.00
FFMB Mark Barron AU/49* 8.00 20.00
FFME Michael Egnew AU/99 4.00 10.00
FFMF Michael Floyd AU/99 10.00 25.00
FFMI Melvin Ingram AU/94* 6.00 15.00
FFMJ Marvin Jones AU/88* 4.00 10.00
FFMM Marquis Maze AU/99 5.00 12.00
FFMS Mohamed Sanu AU/88* 5.00 12.00
FFNF Nick Foles AU/85* 8.00 20.00
FFNT Nick Toon AU/99 6.00 15.00
FFOC Orson Charles AU/50* 5.00 12.00
FFQC Quinton Coples AU/99 5.00 12.00
FFRB Ryan Broyles AU/55* 5.00 12.00
FFRL Ryan Lindley AU/84* 5.00 12.00
FFRR Rueben Randle AU/75* 6.00 15.00
FFRT Ryan Tannehill AU/99 15.00 30.00
FFRW Russell Wilson AU/99 8.00 20.00
FFSG Stephon Gilmore AU/99 5.00 12.00
FFSH Stephen Hill AU/51* 5.00 12.00
FFTG T.J. Graham AU/99 5.00 12.00
FFTH T.Y. Hilton AU/59 5.00 12.00
FFTL Travis Lewis AU/78* 4.00 10.00
FFTS Tommy Streeter AU/99 5.00 12.00
FFVB Vick Ballard AU/98* 4.00 10.00
FFWM Whitney Mercilus AU/99 5.00 12.00
FFZB Zach Brown AU/93* 4.00 10.00

2012 Press Pass Fanfare Purple
*PURPLE/20-25: .8X TO 2X BRONZE/59-99
FFAL Andrew Luck AU/24* 125.00 200.00
FFJB Justin Blackmon AU/23* 30.00 60.00
FFJW Jarius Wright AU/25 UER 10.00 25.00
(wrong player on front)
FFLJ LaMichael James AU/15* 30.00 60.00
FFRG Robert Griffin III AU/25 125.00 250.00
FFTR Trent Richardson AU/25 40.00 80.00

2012 Press Pass Fanfare Gridiron Graphs Blue
BLUE STATED PRINT RUN 50
*RED/25: .5X TO 1.2X BLUE/50
*SILVER/99: .3X TO .8X BLUE/50
AJ Alshon Jeffery 12.00 30.00
AL Andrew Luck 75.00 135.00
JB Justin Blackmon/48* 25.00 50.00
KW Kendall Wright/45* 10.00 25.00
LJ LaMichael James 15.00 40.00
LM Lamar Miller 10.00 25.00
MF Michael Floyd 15.00 40.00
NF Nick Foles 12.00 30.00
NT Nick Toon 10.00 25.00
QC Quinton Coples 8.00 20.00
RG Robert Griffin III 75.00 150.00
TR Trent Richardson/47* 40.00 80.00

2012 Press Pass Fanfare Next Level Ink Blue
BLUE STATED PRINT RUN 50
*RED/25: .5X TO 1.2X BLUE/50
*SILVER/99: .3X TO .8X BLUE/50
AJ Alshon Jeffery 12.00 30.00
AL Andrew Luck 75.00 135.00
JB Justin Blackmon/49* 20.00 50.00
LJ LaMichael James 15.00 40.00
LM Lamar Miller/47* 10.00 25.00
MF Michael Floyd 15.00 40.00
QC Quinton Coples 8.00 20.00
RG Robert Griffin III/48* 75.00 150.00
TR Trent Richardson/49* 30.00 80.00

2012 Press Pass Fanfare Paydirt Autographs Blue
BLUE STATED PRINT RUN 50
*RED/25: .5X TO 1.2X BLUE/50
*SILVER/99: .3X TO .8X BLUE/50
AL Andrew Luck 60.00 120.00
BW Brandon Weeden 15.00 40.00
CK Case Keenum 10.00 25.00
JB Justin Blackmon/49* 20.00 50.00
KM Kellen Moore/49* 12.00 30.00
KW Kendall Wright/46* 10.00 25.00
LJ LaMichael James 15.00 40.00
RG Robert Griffin III 60.00 120.00
RW Russell Wilson 12.00 30.00
TR Trent Richardson/47* 30.00 80.00

2009 Press Pass Fusion
COMPLETE SET (90) 15.00 40.00
37 Mike Alstott .15 .40
38 Kenny Britt .30 .75
39 Donald Brown .30 .75
40 Michael Crabtree .75 2.00
41 Matt Forte .30 .75
42 Josh Freeman .50 1.25
43 Frank Gifford .15 .40
44 Shonn Greene .30 .75
45 Darrius Heyward-Bey .25 .60
46 James Laurinaitis .30 .75
47 Jeremy Maclin .50 1.25
48 LeSean McCoy .50 1.25
49 Darren McFadden .15 .40
50 Joe Montana .75 2.00
51 Matt Ryan .30 .75
52 Mark Sanchez 1.00 2.50
53 Deion Sanders .30 .75
54 Steve Slaton .15 .40
55 Kevin Smith .15 .40
56 Matthew Stafford 1.00 2.50
57 Jonathan Stewart .15 .40
58 Doug Williams .15 .40
59 Don Maynard .15 .40
61 Joe Flacco .30 .75
62 John Elway .75 2.00

2009 Press Pass Fusion Bronze
*BRONZE: 1X TO 2.5X BASE
STATED PRINT RUN 150 SER. #'d SETS

2009 Press Pass Fusion Gold
*GOLD: 2X TO 5X BASE
STATED PRINT RUN 50 SER. #'d SETS

2009 Press Pass Fusion Green
*GREEN: 3X TO 8X BASE
STATED PRINT RUN 25 SER. #'d SETS

2009 Press Pass Fusion Onyx
STATED PRINT RUN 1 SER. #'d SET
UNPRICED DUE TO SCARCITY

2009 Press Pass Fusion Silver
*SILVER: 1.25X TO 3X BASE
STATED PRINT RUN 99 SER. #'d SETS

2009 Press Pass Fusion Autographs Gold
STATED PRINT RUN 10-199
EXCHANGE DEADLINE 12/1/10
SSDM Don Maynard/199 7.50 15.00
SSDS2 Deion Sanders/50
SSDW Doug Williams/15
SSFG Frank Gifford/16
SSJE John Elway/49 75.00 125.00
SSJM Joe Montana/26 75.00 125.00

2009 Press Pass Fusion Autographs Green
STATED PRINT RUN 5-100
EXCHANGE DEADLINE 12/1/2010
SSDM Don Maynard/100 10.00 20.00
SSDS2 Deion Sanders/24
SSDW Doug Williams/10
SSFG Frank Gifford/5
SSJE John Elway/25 100.00 150.00
SSJM Joe Montana/15

2009 Press Pass Fusion Autographs Onyx
STATED PRINT RUN 1-25
EXCHANGE DEADLINE 12/1/10

2009 Press Pass Fusion Autographs Silver
RANDOM INSERT IN PACKS
EXCHANGE DEADLINE 12/1/2010
SSDM Don Maynard 7.50 15.00
SSDS2 Deion Sanders 25.00 50.00
SSDW Doug Williams
SSFG Frank Gifford 25.00 50.00
SSJE John Elway
SSJM Joe Montana 50.00 100.00

2009 Press Pass Fusion Classic Champions
COMPLETE SET (10) 6.00 15.00
STATED ODDS 1:10
CCH2 Doug Williams .60 1.50
CCH10 Deion Sanders 1.00 2.50

2009 Press Pass Fusion Classic Champions Autographs Gold
STATED PRINT RUN 15-99
CCHDW Doug Williams/50 10.00 20.00

2009 Press Pass Fusion Classic Champions Autographs Green
STATED PRINT RUN 10-50
CCHDW Doug Williams/25

2009 Press Pass Fusion Classic Champions Autographs Onyx
STATED PRINT RUN 5-25

2009 Press Pass Fusion Classic Champions Autographs Silver
STATED PRINT RUN 25-199
CCHDW Doug Williams/80 7.50 15.00

2009 Press Pass Fusion Collegiate Connections
COMPLETE SET (10) 6.00 15.00
STATED ODDS 1:10
CCN2 Joe Montana 2.50 6.00
Carl Yastrzemski
CCN4 Frank Gifford 1.00 2.50
Tom Seaver
CCN6 Willis Reed .60 1.50
Doug Williams
CCN7 Don Maynard .60 1.50
Nate Archibald

2009 Press Pass Fusion Collegiate Connections Autographs Gold
STATED PRINT RUN 10-94
CCNDMNA Don Maynard 15.00 30.00
Nate Archibald/94
CCNWRDW Willis Reed
Doug Williams/25

2009 Press Pass Fusion Collegiate Connections Autographs Onyx
STATED PRINT RUN 5-25
EXCHANGE DEADLINE 12/1/10
CCNDMNA Don Maynard
Nate Archibald/25
CCNFGTS Frank Gifford
Tom Seaver/5
CCNJMCY Joe Montana
Carl Yastrzemski/5
CCNWRDW Willis Reed
Doug Williams/15

2009 Press Pass Fusion Cross Training
COMPLETE SET (10) 6.00 15.00
STATED ODDS 1:10
CT3 Derrick Rose 1.00 2.50
Deion Sanders
CT9 John Elway 2.50 6.00
Matthew Stafford

2009 Press Pass Fusion Renowned Rivals
COMPLETE SET (10) 6.00 15.00
STATED ODDS 1:10
RR5 Joe Montana 2.50 6.00
John Elway

2009 Press Pass Fusion Renowned Rivals Autographs Gold
STATED PRINT RUN 10-50
EXCHANGE DEADLINE 12/1/2010
RRJMJE Joe Montana
John Elway

2009 Press Pass Fusion Renowned Rivals Autographs Onyx
STATED PRINT RUN 5-25
EXCHANGE DEADLINE 12/1/10
RRJMJE Joe Montana
John Elway/6

2009 Press Pass Fusion Revered Relics Gold
STATED PRINT RUN 5-50
*HOLOFOIL/25: .5X TO 1.2X BASIC RELIC
RRDB Donald Brown 4.00 10.00
RRDM Darren McFadden/30
RRJF Josh Freeman 6.00 15.00
RRJL1 James Laurinaitis
RRKS Kevin Smith
RRLM LeSean McCoy 6.00 15.00
RRMA Mike Alstott
RRMC Michael Crabtree 6.00 15.00
RRMS Mark Sanchez 8.00 20.00
RRSG Shonn Greene
RRSS Steve Slaton 6.00 15.00
RRMS2 Matthew Stafford 6.00 15.00
RRMFJS Matt Forte
Jonathan Stewart/5
RRDHBKB Darrius Heyward-Bey
Kenny Britt/15

2009 Press Pass Fusion Revered Relics Silver
STATED PRINT RUN 15-299
RRDB Donald Brown/35
RRJF Josh Freeman/35 6.00 15.00
RRJL1 James Laurinaitis/99 4.00 10.00
RRKS Kevin Smith/15
RRLM LeSean McCoy/75 4.00 10.00
RRMA Mike Alstott/150 4.00 10.00
RRMC Michael Crabtree/65 6.00 15.00
RRMS Mark Sanchez/299 6.00 15.00
RRSG Shonn Greene/99
RRSS Steve Slaton/55 4.00 10.00
RRMS2 Matthew Stafford/199 6.00 15.00

2009 Press Pass Fusion Timeless Talent
COMPLETE SET (10) 6.00 15.00
STATED ODDS 1:10
TT3 Frank Gifford .60 1.50
TT9 Matt Ryan 1.00 2.50
TT10 Mark Sanchez 2.50 6.00

2009 Press Pass Fusion Timeless Talent Autographs Gold
STATED PRINT RUN 15-99
TTFG Frank Gifford/15

2009 Press Pass Fusion Timeless Talent Autographs Green
STATED PRINT RUN 10-50
TTFG Frank Gifford/10

2009 Press Pass Fusion Timeless Talent Autographs Onyx
STATED PRINT RUN 5-25

2009 Press Pass Fusion Timeless Talent Autographs Silver
STATED PRINT RUN 26-193
TTFG Frank Gifford/28 25.00 50.00

2002 Press Pass JE

Press Pass JE was released as a 45-card set featuring top NFL draft picks. The standard sized cards were printed on premium 24 pt.stock. The card fronts feature a colored three-sided border with a full color action shot of the player. The Press Pass logo is in the upper left hand corner. The player's name and position is printed in silver lettering along the bottom half of the card. The card backs carry college statistics and pertinent information highlighting each players most impressive skills. Press Pass JE cards were released in both Hobby and Retail form.

COMPLETE SET (45) 10.00 25.00
1 David Carr .40 1.00
2 Julius Peppers .75 2.00
3 Joey Harrington .40 1.00
4 Mike Williams .25 .60
5 Quentin Jammer .40 1.00
6 Ryan Sims .40 1.00
7 Bryant McKinnie .25 .60
8 Roy Williams .40 1.00
9 John Henderson .30 .75
10 Wendell Bryant .25 .60
11 Donte Stallworth .40 1.00
12 Jeremy Shockey .60 1.50
13 William Green .30 .75
14 Phillip Buchanon .40 1.00
15 T.J. Duckett .40 1.00
16 Ashley Lelie .30 .75
17 Javon Walker .40 1.00
18 Daniel Graham .30 .75

19 Jerramy Stevens	.40	1.00
20 Patrick Ramsey	.40	1.00
21 Jabar Gaffney	.40	1.00
22 DeShaun Foster	.40	1.00
23 Kalimba Edwards	.30	.75
24 Josh Reed	.30	.75
25 Mike Pearson	.25	.60
26 Andre Davis	.30	.75
27 Reche Caldwell	.40	1.00
28 Clinton Portis	.50	1.25
29 Maurice Morris	.30	.75
30 Ladell Betts	.40	1.00
31 Antwaan Randle El	.40	1.00
32 Antonio Bryant	.40	1.00
33 Josh McCown	.40	1.00
34 Lamar Gordon	.30	.75
35 Marquise Walker	.25	.60
36 Cliff Russell	.25	.60
37 Brian Westbrook	.60	1.50
38 Eric Crouch	.40	1.00
39 Jonathan Wells	.40	1.00
40 David Garrard	.50	1.25
41 Rohan Davey	.40	1.00
42 Ron Johnson	.30	.75
43 Kurt Kittner	.25	.60
44 Adrian Peterson	.40	1.00
45 David Carr CL	.30	.75

2002 Press Pass JE Autographs

STATED ODDS 1:6 HOBBY
*SILVER AU/50: .8X TO 2X BASIC AUTO
SILVER AUTO PRINT RUN 50

1 Damien Anderson	2.50	6.00
2 Antonio Bryant	4.00	10.00
3 Phillip Buchanon	4.00	10.00
4 Reche Caldwell	4.00	10.00
5 Rocky Calmus	3.00	8.00
6 David Carr	4.00	10.00
7 Terry Charles	2.50	6.00
8 Eric Crouch	4.00	10.00
9 Najeh Davenport	4.00	10.00
10 Rohan Davey	4.00	10.00
11 Andre Davis	3.00	8.00
12 Kalimba Edwards	3.00	8.00
13 Jabar Gaffney	4.00	10.00
14 David Garrard	10.00	25.00
15 Lamar Gordon	3.00	8.00
16 Daniel Graham	3.00	8.00
17 William Green	3.00	8.00
18 Joey Harrington	4.00	10.00
19 John Henderson	3.00	8.00
20 Leonard Henry	2.50	6.00
21 Quentin Jammer	4.00	10.00
22 Ron Johnson	3.00	8.00
23 Kyle Johnson	2.50	6.00
24 Levi Jones	2.50	6.00
25 Kurt Kittner	2.50	6.00
26 Josh McCown	4.00	10.00
27 Freddie Milons	2.50	6.00
28 Maurice Morris	3.00	8.00
29 Mike Pearson	2.50	6.00
30 Adrian Peterson	4.00	10.00
31 Patrick Ramsey	4.00	10.00
32 Antwaan Randle El	4.00	10.00
33 Josh Reed	3.00	8.00
34 Cliff Russell	2.50	6.00
35 Josh Scobey	3.00	8.00
36 Ryan Sims	4.00	10.00
37 Luke Staley	2.50	6.00
38 Donte Stallworth	4.00	10.00
39 Marquise Walker	2.50	6.00
40 Anthony Weaver	2.50	6.00
41 Jonathan Wells	4.00	10.00
42 Brian Westbrook	12.00	30.00
43 Roy Williams	6.00	15.00

2002 Press Pass JE Class of 2002

COMPLETE SET (9)	5.00	12.00
STATED ODDS 1:8		
CL1 David Carr	.60	1.50
CL2 T.J. Duckett	.60	1.50
CL3 Jabar Gaffney	.60	1.50
CL4 William Green	.50	1.25
CL5 Joey Harrington	.60	1.50
CL6 Ashley Lelie	.50	1.25
CL7 Julius Peppers	1.25	3.00
CL8 Jeremy Shockey	1.00	2.50
CL9 Donte Stallworth	.60	1.50

2002 Press Pass JE Class of 2002 Autographs

STATED PRINT RUN 200 SER.#'d SETS

AB Antonio Bryant	5.00	12.00
AD Andre Davis	4.00	10.00
DC David Carr	5.00	12.00
DS Donte Stallworth	5.00	12.00
JH Joey Harrington	5.00	12.00
JR Josh Reed	4.00	10.00
KK Kurt Kittner	3.00	8.00
WG William Green	4.00	10.00

2002 Press Pass JE Game Used Jerseys

JERSEY/500 ODDS 1:24 HOBBY
STATED PRINT RUN 500 SER.#'d SETS
*NAMES/25: 1X TO 2.5X BASIC JSY
NAMES PRINT RUN 25 SER.#'d SETS
UNPRICED PATCH PRINT RUN 10

JEAD Andre Davis	4.00	10.00
JEAL Ashley Lelie	4.00	10.00
JEAP Adrian Peterson	5.00	12.00
JEBW Brian Westbrook	8.00	20.00
JEDC David Carr	5.00	12.00
JEDF DeShaun Foster	5.00	12.00
JEDGA David Garrard	6.00	15.00
JEDN David Neill	3.00	8.00
JEEC Eric Crouch	5.00	12.00
JEJH Joey Harrington	5.00	12.00
JEJM Josh McCown	5.00	12.00
JEJR Josh Reed	4.00	10.00
JEKK Kurt Kittner	3.00	8.00
JELH Leonard Henry	3.00	8.00
JELS Luke Staley	3.00	8.00
JEMM Maurice Morris	4.00	10.00
JEPR Patrick Ramsey	5.00	12.00
JERW Roy Williams	5.00	12.00
JEWG William Green	4.00	10.00

2002 Press Pass JE Game Used Jersey Autographs

STATED PRINT RUN 25 SER.#'d SETS

AJEDC David Carr	25.00	60.00
AJEJM Josh McCown	25.00	60.00
AJEJR Josh Reed	20.00	50.00
AJERW Roy Williams	25.00	60.00
AJEWG William Green	20.00	50.00

2002 Press Pass JE Old School

COMPLETE SET (27)	12.00	30.00
ONE PER PACK		
OS1 David Carr	.50	1.25
OS2 Julius Peppers	1.00	2.50
OS3 Joey Harrington	.50	1.25
OS4 Mike Williams	.30	.75
OS5 Quentin Jammer	.50	1.25
OS6 Ryan Sims	.50	1.25
OS7 Bryant McKinnie	.30	.75
OS8 Roy Williams	.50	1.25
OS9 Donte Stallworth	.50	1.25
OS10 Jeremy Shockey	.75	2.00
OS11 William Green	.40	1.00
OS12 T.J. Duckett	.50	1.25
OS13 Ashley Lelie	.40	1.00
OS14 Javon Walker	.50	1.25
OS15 Daniel Graham	.40	1.00
OS16 Patrick Ramsey	.50	1.25
OS17 Jabar Gaffney	.50	1.25
OS18 DeShaun Foster	.50	1.25
OS19 Josh Reed	.40	1.00
OS20 Andre Davis	.40	1.00
OS21 Reche Caldwell	.50	1.25
OS22 Clinton Portis	.60	1.50
OS23 Antwaan Randle El	.50	1.25
OS24 Antonio Bryant	.50	1.25
OS25 Marquise Walker	.30	.75
OS26 Eric Crouch	.50	1.25
OS27 Joey Harrington CL	.40	1.00

2002 Press Pass JE Rookie Vision

COMPLETE SET (12)	5.00	12.00
STATED ODDS 1:4		
RV1 David Carr	.50	1.25
RV2 T.J. Duckett	.50	1.25
RV3 DeShaun Foster	.50	1.25
RV4 Jabar Gaffney	.50	1.25
RV5 William Green	.40	1.00
RV6 Joey Harrington	.50	1.25
RV7 Ashley Lelie	.40	1.00
RV8 Julius Peppers	1.00	2.50
RV9 Patrick Ramsey	.50	1.25
RV10 Jeremy Shockey	.75	2.00
RV11 Donte Stallworth	.50	1.25
RV12 Javon Walker	.50	1.25

2002 Press Pass JE Up Close

COMPLETE SET (6)	3.00	8.00
STATED ODDS 1:12		
UC1 David Carr	.60	1.50
UC2 Jabar Gaffney	.60	1.50
UC3 William Green	.50	1.25
UC4 Joey Harrington	.60	1.50
UC5 Julius Peppers	1.25	3.00
UC6 T.J. Duckett	.60	1.50

2003 Press Pass JE

This 45-card set was released in May, 2003. The set was issued in four card packs which came 28 per box and 20 boxes per case. The hobby packs which included some exclusive inserts were available at $5.99 SRP and the retail packs were available at a $2.99 SRP.

COMPLETE SET (45)	10.00	25.00
1 Boss Bailey	.30	.75
2 Brad Banks	.30	.75
3 Anquan Boldin	.60	1.50
4 Kyle Boller	.40	1.00
5 Chris Brown	.25	.60
6 Avon Cobourne	.25	.60
7 Ken Dorsey	.30	.75
8 Justin Fargas	.40	1.00
9 Talman Gardner	.25	.60
10 Jason Gesser	.30	.75
11 Earnest Graham	.40	1.00
12 Jordon Gross	.25	.60
13 Rex Grossman	.40	1.00
14 Kwame Harris	.25	.60
15 Taylor Jacobs	.25	.60
16 Larry Johnson	.40	1.00
17 Bryant Johnson	.40	1.00
18 Andre Johnson	1.00	2.50
19 Teyo Johnson	.30	.75
20 William Joseph	.25	.60
21 Bennie Joppru	.25	.60
22 Jimmy Kennedy	.30	.75
23 Kliff Kingsbury	.30	.75
24 Byron Leftwich	.40	1.00
25 Brandon Lloyd	.60	1.50
26 Jerome McDougle	.25	.60
27 Willie McGahee	.50	1.25
28 Terence Newman	.30	.75
29 Carson Palmer	.75	2.00
30 Terry Pierce	.25	.60
31 Dave Ragone	.25	.60
32 DeWayne Robertson	.30	.75
33 Charles Rogers	.30	.75
34 Chris Simms	.40	1.00
35 Musa Smith	.25	.60
36 Onterrio Smith	.25	.60
37 Brian St.Pierre	.30	.75
38 Lee Suggs	.30	.75
39 Terrell Suggs	.40	1.00
40 Marcus Trufant	.30	.75
41 Seneca Wallace	.40	1.00
42 Kelley Washington	.25	.60
43 Jason Witten	1.00	2.50
44 Andre Woolfolk	.30	.75
45 Byron Leftwich CL	.15	.40

2003 Press Pass JE Old School

COMPLETE SET (27)	12.50	30.00
STATED ODDS ONE PER PACK		
OS1 Brad Banks	.40	1.00
OS2 Anquan Boldin	.75	2.00
OS3 Kyle Boller	.50	1.25
OS4 Chris Brown	.30	.75
OS5 Avon Cobourne	.30	.75
OS6 Ken Dorsey	.40	1.00
OS7 Rex Grossman	.50	1.25
OS8 Taylor Jacobs	.30	.75
OS9 Andre Johnson	1.25	3.00
OS10 Bryant Johnson	.50	1.25
OS11 Larry Johnson	.50	1.25
OS12 Jimmy Kennedy	.40	1.00
OS13 Byron Leftwich	.50	1.25
OS14 Brandon Lloyd	.75	2.00
OS15 Willis McGahee	.60	1.50
OS16 Terence Newman	.40	1.00
OS17 Carson Palmer	1.00	2.50
OS18 Dave Ragone	.30	.75
OS19 Charles Rogers	.40	1.00
OS20 Chris Simms	.50	1.25
OS21 Musa Smith	.30	.75
OS22 Onterrio Smith	.30	.75
OS23 Terrell Suggs	.50	1.25
OS24 Lee Suggs	.40	1.00
OS25 Kelley Washington	.30	.75
OS26 Andre Woolfolk	.40	1.00
OS27 Carson Palmer CL	.40	1.00

2003 Press Pass JE Retail

*RETAIL: .4X TO 1X HOBBY

2003 Press Pass JE Tin

COMP.FACT.SET (46)	10.00	20.00
COMPLETE SET (45)	6.00	15.00
*SINGLES: .3X TO .8X BASIC JE		

2003 Press Pass JE Class of 2003

COMPLETE SET (9)	8.00	20.00
STATED ODDS 1:9		
CL1 Kyle Boller	.60	1.50
CL2 Rex Grossman	.60	1.50
CL3 Larry Johnson	.60	1.50
CL4 Andre Johnson	1.50	4.00
CL5 Byron Leftwich	.60	1.50
CL6 Carson Palmer	1.25	3.00
CL7 Dave Ragone	.40	1.00
CL8 Charles Rogers	.50	1.25
CL9 Chris Simms	.60	1.50

2003 Press Pass JE Class of 2003 Autographs

STATED PRINT RUN 200 SER.#'d SETS

1 Brad Banks	6.00	15.00
2 Anquan Boldin	12.00	30.00
3 Kyle Boller	8.00	20.00
4 Chris Brown	5.00	12.00
5 Justin Fargas	8.00	20.00
6 Taylor Jacobs	5.00	12.00
7 Byron Leftwich	8.00	20.00
8 Carson Palmer	15.00	40.00
9 Dave Ragone	5.00	12.00

2003 Press Pass JE Game Used Jerseys Autographs

STATED PRINT RUN 25 SER.#'d SETS

AJCBL Byron Leftwich	30.00	80.00
AJCCP Carson Palmer	60.00	120.00

2003 Press Pass JE Game Used Jerseys Silver

SILVER PRINT RUN 200-375
*GOLD/450-575: .3X TO.8X SILVER
GOLD/450-575 ODDS 1:28
*HOLOFOIL/100-150: .6X TO 1.5X SILV
HOLOFOIL PRINT RUN 100-150
*NAMES/25: 1.2X TO 3X SILVER
NAMES STATED PRINT RUN 25
UNPRICED PATCH PRINT RUN 2-10

JCAC Avon Cobourne/375	3.00	8.00
JCAW Andre Woolfolk/375	4.00	10.00
JCBJ Bennie Joppru/250	3.00	8.00
JCBL Byron Leftwich/250	5.00	12.00
JCBL1 Brandon Lloyd/375	8.00	20.00
JCCP Carson Palmer/200	10.00	25.00
JCDD Dahrran Diedrick/375	3.00	8.00
JCEG Earnest Graham/250	5.00	12.00
JCJM Jerome McDougle/375	3.00	8.00
JCJW Jason Witten/375	20.00	40.00
JCKD Ken Dorsey/250	4.00	10.00
JCKK Kareem Kelly/250	3.00	8.00
JCSW Seneca Wallace/250	5.00	12.00
JCTJ Teyo Johnson/250	4.00	10.00

2003 Press Pass JE Rookie Vision

COMPLETE SET (12)	8.00	20.00
STATED ODDS 1:4		
RV1 Kyle Boller	.50	1.25
RV2 Justin Fargas	.50	1.25
RV3 Rex Grossman	.50	1.25
RV4 Taylor Jacobs	.30	.75
RV5 Larry Johnson	.50	1.25
RV6 Andre Johnson	1.25	3.00
RV7 Byron Leftwich	.50	1.25
RV8 Carson Palmer	1.00	2.50
RV9 Dave Ragone	.30	.75
RV10 Charles Rogers	.40	1.00
RV11 Chris Simms	.50	1.25
RV12 Lee Suggs	.40	1.00

2003 Press Pass JE Up Close

COMPLETE SET (6)	6.00	15.00
STATED ODDS 1:14		
UC1 Carson Palmer	1.25	3.00
UC2 Byron Leftwich	.60	1.50
UC3 Chris Simms	.60	1.50
UC4 Charles Rogers	.50	1.25
UC5 Dave Ragone	.40	1.00
UC6 Larry Johnson	.60	1.50

2006 Press Pass Legends

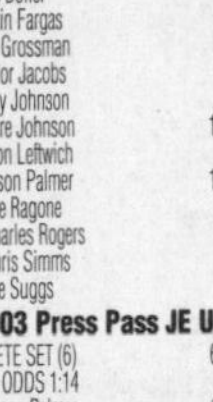

This 92-card set was released in July, 2006. The set featured a mix of 2006 NFL rookies and retired greats (both players and coaches). The set was issued into the hobby in six-card mini boxes which came three boxes to a full box. Cards numbered 1-55 feature 2006 NFL rookies while cards numbered 57-92 feature the retired greats.

COMP.SET w/o SP's (90)	20.00	40.00
UNPRICED PLATINUM PRINT RUN 1		
UNPRICED PRINT PLATES SER.#'d TO 1		
1 Brodie Croyle	.50	1.25
2 Tarvaris Jackson	.50	1.25
3 Derek Hagan	.40	1.00
4 Devin Aromashodu	.50	1.25
5 Mathias Kiwanuka	.50	1.25
6 Omar Jacobs	.30	.75
7 Tye Hill	.30	.75
8 Charlie Whitehurst	.50	1.25
9 Joe Klopfenstein	.30	.75
10 Chad Jackson	.30	.75
11 Leon Washington	.40	1.00
12 Ernie Sims	.40	1.00
13 Leonard Pope	.50	1.25
14 D.J. Shockley	.40	1.00
15 Joseph Addai	.50	1.25
16 Vernon Davis	.60	1.50
17 DeAngelo Williams	.60	1.50
18 Sinorice Moss	.50	1.25
19 Martin Nance	.40	1.00
20 Jason Avant	.30	.75
21 Laurence Maroney	.40	1.00
22 Brad Smith	.50	1.25
23 Mario Williams	.50	1.25
24 Brett Basanez	.50	1.25
25 Anthony Fasano	.50	1.25
26 Maurice Stovall	.30	.75
27 Bobby Carpenter	.30	.75
28 A.J. Hawk	.50	1.25
29 Santonio Holmes	.60	1.50
30 Ashton Youboty	.30	.75
31 Travis Wilson	.30	.75
32 Haloti Ngata	.50	1.25
33 Demetrius Williams	.40	1.00
34 Mike Hass	.40	1.00
35 Michael Robinson	.40	1.00
36 Greg Lee	.30	.75
37 Cory Rodgers	.40	1.00
38 Michael Huff	.40	1.00
39A Vince Young Clr	.60	1.50
39B Vince Young B&W	1.00	2.50
40 Reggie McNeal	.40	1.00
41 Bruce Gradkowski	.50	1.25
42 Darrell Hackney	.40	1.00
43 Maurice Drew	.75	2.00
44 Marcedes Lewis	.50	1.25
45 Drew Olson	.30	.75
46 Darnell Bing	.40	1.00
47A Reggie Bush Clr	1.00	2.50
47B Reggie Bush B&W	1.50	4.00
48 Dominique Byrd	.40	1.00
49A Matt Leinart Clr	.50	1.25
49B Matt Leinart B&W	.75	2.00
50 LenDale White	.40	1.00
51A Jay Cutler Clr	1.00	2.50
51B Jay Cutler B&W	1.50	4.00
52 D'Brickashaw Ferguson	.50	1.25
53 Marcus Vick	.30	.75
54 Jimmy Williams	.50	1.25
55 Jerome Harrison	.50	1.25
56 Ozzie Newsome	.50	1.25
57 Ken Stabler	.75	2.00
58A Bo Jackson B&W	.75	2.00
58B Bo Jackson Clr	1.25	3.00
59 Steve Spurrier	.75	2.00
60 Charlie Ward	.50	1.25
61 Fran Tarkenton	.75	2.00
62 Herschel Walker	.50	1.25
63 Billy Cannon	.50	1.25
64 Y.A. Tittle	.60	1.50
65 Roger Craig	.60	1.50
66 Tommie Frazier	.50	1.25
67 Rocky Bleier	.60	1.50
68B Tim Brown Clr	1.00	2.50
68A Tim Brown B&W	.60	1.50
69 Paul Hornung	.60	1.50
70 Joe Theismann	.60	1.50
71 Howard Cassady	.50	1.25
72 Archie Griffin	.40	1.00
73 Jack Tatum	.40	1.00
74 Paul Warfield	.50	1.25
75 Brian Bosworth	.60	1.50
76 Billy Sims	.50	1.25
77A Barry Sanders B&W	1.00	2.50
77B Barry Sanders Clr	1.50	4.00
78 Thurman Thomas	.50	1.25
79 Jack Ham	.50	1.25
80 Franco Harris	.60	1.50
81A Dan Marino B&W	1.25	3.00
81B Dan Marino Clr	2.00	5.00
82 Len Dawson	.60	1.50
83 Jim Plunkett	.50	1.25
84 Bob Lilly	.50	1.25
85 Steve Largent	.60	1.50
86 Ronnie Lott	.50	1.25
87 Bobby Bowden	.60	1.50
88 Bo Schembechler	.40	1.00
89 Darrell Royal	.50	1.25
90 Ara Parseghian	.50	1.25
91 Johnny Lattner SP	2.00	5.00
92 Desmond Howard SP	2.50	6.00

2006 Press Pass Legends Bronze

*BRONZE ROOKIE: .6X TO 1.5X BASIC CARDS
*BRNZ ROOK.B VERSION: .4X TO 1X
*BRONZE RETIRED: 1X TO 2.5X BASIC CARDS
*BRNZ RETIRED B VERSION: .6X TO 1.5X
BRONZE PRINT RUN 999 SER.#'d SETS

B91 Johnny Lattner	1.00	2.50
B92 Desmond Howard	1.25	3.00

2006 Press Pass Legends Emerald

*EMER.ROOKIE: 2.5X TO 6X BASIC CARDS
*EMER.ROOKIE B VERSION: 1.5X TO 4X
*EMER.RETIRED: 8X TO 20X BASIC CARDS
*EMER.RETIRED B VERSION: 5X TO 12X
EMERALD PRINT RUN 25 SER.#'d SETS

E91 Johnny Lattner	6.00	15.00
E92 Desmond Howard	8.00	20.00

2006 Press Pass Legends Gold

*GOLD ROOKIE: 1.5X TO 4X BASIC CARDS
*GOLD ROOKIE B VERSION: 1X TO 2.5X
*GOLD RETIRED: 3X TO 8X BASIC CARDS
*GOLD RETIRED B VERSION: 2X TO 5X
GOLD PRINT RUN 99 SER.#'d SETS

G91 Johnny Lattner	3.00	8.00
G92 Desmond Howard	4.00	10.00

2006 Press Pass Legends Platinum

UNPRICED PLATINUM PRINT RUN 1

2006 Press Pass Legends Red

UNPRICED RED PRINT RUN 5

2006 Press Pass Legends Silver

*SILVER ROOKIE: .8X TO 2X BASIC CARDS
*SILVER ROOKIE B VERSION: .5X TO 1.2X
*SILVER RETIRED: 1.5X TO 4X BASIC CARDS
*SILVER RETIRED B VERSION: 1X TO 2.5X
SILVER PRINT RUN 499 SER.#'d SETS

S91 Johnny Lattner	1.50	4.00
S92 Desmond Howard	2.00	5.00

2006 Press Pass Legends All Conference

STATED ODDS 1:15

AC1 Derek Hagan	.60	1.50
AC2 Mathias Kiwanuka	.75	2.00
AC3 D.J. Shockley	.60	1.50
AC4 Vernon Davis	1.00	2.50
AC5 Jason Avant	.50	1.25
AC6 Laurence Maroney	.60	1.50
AC7 A.J. Hawk	.75	2.00
AC8 Marcedes Lewis	.75	2.00
AC9 Darnell Bing	.60	1.50
AC10 Michael Robinson	.60	1.50
AC11 Greg Lee	.50	1.25
AC12 Michael Huff	.60	1.50
AC13 Vince Young	1.00	2.50
AC14 Darrell Hackney	.60	1.50
AC15 Reggie Bush	1.50	4.00
AC16 Matt Leinart	.75	2.00
AC17 Jay Cutler	1.50	4.00
AC18 D'Brickashaw Ferguson	.75	2.00
AC19 Mario Williams	.75	2.00
AC20 Jerome Harrison	.75	2.00

2006 Press Pass Legends All Conference Autographs Gold

1 Jason Avant/290	6.00	15.00
2 Darnell Bing/255	6.00	15.00
3 Reggie Bush/25	40.00	100.00
4 Jay Cutler/25	50.00	120.00
5 Vernon Davis/50	10.00	25.00
6 D'Brickashaw Ferguson/340	6.00	15.00
7 Darrell Hackney/225	5.00	12.00
7R Darrell Hackney/225 Red	6.00	15.00
8 A.J. Hawk/260	20.00	50.00
9 Michael Huff/250	6.00	15.00
10 Mathias Kiwanuka/250	6.00	15.00
10R Mathias Kiwanuka/250 Red	8.00	20.00
11 Greg Lee/310	5.00	12.00
12 Matt Leinart/25	20.00	50.00
13 Marcedes Lewis/310	6.00	15.00
14 Laurence Maroney/122	6.00	15.00
15 Michael Robinson/350	6.00	15.00
16 D.J. Shockley/365	5.00	12.00
16R D.J. Shockley/365 Red	6.00	15.00
17 Mario Williams/260	10.00	25.00
17R Mario Williams/260 Red	12.00	30.00
18 Vince Young/25	30.00	80.00

2006 Press Pass Legends All Conference Autographs Platinum

PLATINUM PRINT RUN 25 SER.#'d SETS

1 Jason Avant		
1R Jason Avant Red	10.00	25.00
2 Darnell Bing	10.00	25.00
3 Reggie Bush	40.00	100.00
4 Jay Cutler	50.00	120.00
5 Vernon Davis	15.00	40.00
6 D'Brickashaw Ferguson	10.00	25.00
7 Darrell Hackney	8.00	20.00
8 A.J. Hawk	30.00	80.00
9 Michael Huff	10.00	25.00
10 Mathias Kiwanuka Red	12.00	30.00
11 Greg Lee	8.00	20.00
12 Matt Leinart	20.00	50.00
13 Marcedes Lewis	10.00	25.00
14 Laurence Maroney	10.00	25.00
15 Michael Robinson Red	20.00	50.00
16 D.J. Shockley	10.00	25.00
17 Mario Williams	20.00	50.00
18 Vince Young	30.00	80.00

2006 Press Pass Legends Alumni Association

STATED ODDS 1:30

AA1 Ken Stabler / Brodie Croyle	3.00	8.00
AA2 Fran Tarkenton / Herschel Walker	1.50	4.00
AA3 LenDale White / Reggie Bush	4.00	10.00
AA4 Johnny Lattner / Paul Hornung	2.00	5.00
AA5 Paul Warfield / A.J. Hawk	2.00	5.00
AA6 Brian Bosworth / Billy Sims	2.50	6.00
AA7 Thurman Thomas / Barry Sanders	3.00	8.00
AA8 Dan Marino / Greg Lee	4.00	10.00
AA9 Ronnie Lott / Matt Leinart	2.00	5.00

2006 Press Pass Legends Alumni Association Autographs

1C Ken Stabler Blue / Brodie Croyle Blue/33*	100.00	175.00
2 Fran Tarkenton / Herschel Walker/50 Red	60.00	120.00
3 LenDale White / Reggie Bush/35 Red	100.00	200.00
4 Johnny Lattner / Paul Hornung/50	60.00	100.00
5 Paul Warfield / A.J. Hawk/50	50.00	80.00
6 Brian Bosworth / Billy Sims/50	60.00	100.00
7 Thurman Thomas / Barry Sanders/35	175.00	300.00
8 Dan Marino / Greg Lee/50	75.00	150.00
9 Ronnie Lott / Matt Leinart/35	40.00	100.00

2006 Press Pass Legends Autographs

STATED ODDS 1:5

1 Joseph Addai	6.00	15.00
2 Devin Aromashodu	4.00	10.00
3 Jason Avant	5.00	12.00
4 Brett Basanez	4.00	10.00
4R Brett Basanez Red	8.00	20.00
5 Darnell Bing	5.00	12.00
6 Rocky Bleier	12.00	30.00
7 Brian Bosworth SP	25.00	50.00
7R Brian Bosworth SP Red	30.00	60.00
8 Bobby Bowden	15.00	30.00
8R Bobby Bowden Red	30.00	60.00
9 Tim Brown SP		
10 Reggie Bush SP	40.00	100.00
11 Dominique Byrd	4.00	10.00
12 Billy Cannon	10.00	25.00
13 Bobby Carpenter	5.00	12.00
13R Bobby Carpenter Red	10.00	25.00
14 Howard Cassady	8.00	20.00
15 Roger Craig Red	6.00	15.00
16 Brodie Croyle Red	8.00	20.00
17 Jay Cutler	40.00	80.00
17R Jay Cutler Red	40.00	80.00
18 Vernon Davis	6.00	15.00
19 Len Dawson SP	40.00	80.00
20 Maurice Drew	12.00	30.00
20R Maurice Drew Red	15.00	40.00
21 Anthony Fasano	5.00	12.00
21R Anthony Fasano Red	6.00	15.00
22 D'Brickashaw Ferguson	6.00	15.00
23 Tommie Frazier	6.00	15.00
23R Tommie Frazier Red	6.00	15.00
24 Bruce Gradkowski	6.00	15.00
25 Archie Griffin	8.00	20.00
25R Archie Griffin Red	8.00	20.00
26 Darrell Hackney	4.00	10.00
27 Jack Ham	15.00	30.00
28 Franco Harris SP	25.00	50.00
29 Mike Hass	4.00	10.00
29R Mike Hass Red	10.00	25.00
30 A.J. Hawk	12.00	30.00
31 Tye Hill	5.00	12.00
32 Paul Hornung	15.00	30.00
33 Desmond Howard SP		
34 Michael Huff	5.00	12.00
34R Michael Huff Red	6.00	15.00
35 Bo Jackson SP		
36 Chad Jackson	6.00	15.00
37 Tarvaris Jackson	6.00	15.00
37R Tarvaris Jackson Red	8.00	20.00
38 Omar Jacobs	5.00	12.00
39 Mathias Kiwanuka	6.00	15.00
40 Joe Klopfenstein	4.00	10.00
41 Steve Largent SP	15.00	30.00
42 Johnny Lattner	8.00	20.00
42R Johnny Lattner Red	10.00	25.00
43 Greg Lee	4.00	10.00
44 Matt Leinart SP	20.00	50.00
45 Marcedes Lewis	4.00	10.00
46 Bob Lilly	8.00	15.00
46R Bob Lilly Red	10.00	20.00
47 Ronnie Lott SP	40.00	80.00
48 Dan Marino SP	75.00	150.00
48R Dan Marino SP Red	100.00	200.00
49 Laurence Maroney	5.00	12.00
50 Reggie McNeal	5.00	12.00
51 Martin Nance	5.00	12.00
51R Martin Nance Red	10.00	20.00
52 Ozzie Newsome SP	15.00	30.00
53 Haloti Ngata	6.00	15.00
54 Drew Olson	4.00	10.00
55 Ara Parseghian	12.50	30.00
55R Ara Parseghian Red	15.00	40.00
56 Jim Plunkett	6.00	15.00
56R Jim Plunkett Red	8.00	20.00
57 Leonard Pope	5.00	12.00
58 Michael Robinson	6.00	15.00
59 Cory Rodgers	4.00	10.00
59R Cory Rodgers Red	5.00	12.00
60 Darrell Royal	8.00	25.00
60R Darrell Royal Red	10.00	30.00
61 Barry Sanders SP	125.00	200.00
62 Bo Schembechler	40.00	80.00
63 D.J. Shockley	5.00	12.00
64 Billy Sims	6.00	15.00
64R Billy Sims Red	10.00	25.00
65 Brad Smith	5.00	12.00
66 Steve Spurrier	15.00	40.00
67 Ken Stabler Red SP	90.00	150.00
68 Fran Tarkenton SP		
69 Jack Tatum SP	30.00	60.00
70 Joe Theismann	10.00	25.00
70R Joe Theismann Red	30.00	80.00
71 Thurman Thomas	10.00	25.00
72 Y.A. Tittle SP		
73 Herschel Walker SP	15.00	40.00
74 Charlie Ward	6.00	15.00
75 Paul Warfield	8.00	20.00
76 Leon Washington	6.00	20.00
77 LenDale White	6.00	15.00
78 Charlie Whitehurst	6.00	15.00
78R Charlie Whitehurst Red	10.00	25.00
79 Demetrius Williams	6.00	15.00
80 Mario Williams	8.00	20.00
80R Mario Williams Red	10.00	25.00
81 Vince Young SP	30.00	80.00

2006 Press Pass Legends Legendary Legacy

STATED ODDS 1:15

1 Ken Stabler	3.00	8.00
2 Ozzie Newsome	2.00	5.00
3 Bo Jackson	3.00	8.00
4 Fran Tarkenton	3.00	8.00
5 Herschel Walker	2.00	5.00
6 Y.A. Tittle	2.50	6.00
7 Desmond Howard	2.00	5.00
8 Roger Craig	2.50	6.00
9 Tim Brown	2.50	6.00
10 Paul Hornung	2.50	6.00
11 Joe Theismann	2.50	6.00
12 Howard Cassady	2.00	5.00
13 Archie Griffin	1.50	4.00
14 Jack Tatum	1.50	4.00
15 Brian Bosworth	2.50	6.00
16 Steve Largent	2.50	6.00
17 Billy Sims	2.00	5.00
18 Franco Harris	2.50	6.00
19 Len Dawson	2.50	6.00
20 Ronnie Lott	2.00	5.00

2006 Press Pass Legends Legendary Legacy Autographs Gold

STATED PRINT RUN 100-400

1 Brian Bosworth/275	25.00	50.00
1R Brian Bosworth/275 Red	25.00	60.00
2 Tim Brown/125	25.00	60.00
3 Howard Cassady/400	8.00	20.00
4 Roger Craig/400	8.00	20.00
5 Len Dawson/130	10.00	25.00
5R Len Dawson/130 Red	12.50	30.00
6R Archie Griffin/255 Red	15.00	30.00
7R Franco Harris/105 Red	25.00	50.00
8 Paul Hornung/310	15.00	40.00
9 Desmond Howard/320	12.00	30.00
9R Desmond Howard/320 Red	15.00	40.00
10 Bo Jackson/115	40.00	80.00
10R Bo Jackson/115 Red	40.00	100.00
11 Steve Largent/120	15.00	40.00
12 Ronnie Lott/100	20.00	40.00
13 Ozzie Newsome/258	12.50	30.00
14 Billy Sims/320 Red	8.00	20.00
15 Ken Stabler/100	30.00	60.00
16 Fran Tarkenton/106	20.00	40.00
16R Fran Tarkenton/106 Red	25.00	50.00
17 Jack Tatum/175 Red	15.00	40.00
18 Joe Theismann/130	15.00	40.00
19 Y.A. Tittle/155	15.00	40.00
20 Herschel Walker/300	25.00	50.00
20R Herschel Walker/300 Red	30.00	60.00

2006 Press Pass Legends Legendary Legacy Autographs Platinum

PLATINUM PRINT RUN 25 SER.#'d SETS

1 Ken Stabler Red	60.00	120.00
2 Ozzie Newsome Red	25.00	50.00
3 Bo Jackson	75.00	150.00
4 Fran Tarkenton Red	25.00	50.00
5 Herschel Walker		
6 Y.A. Tittle	30.00	60.00
7 Desmond Howard Red	25.00	50.00
8 Roger Craig Red	20.00	40.00
9 Tim Brown	40.00	80.00
10 Paul Hornung	40.00	80.00
11 Joe Theismann	30.00	60.00
12 Howard Cassady	20.00	40.00
13 Archie Griffin	30.00	60.00
14 Jack Tatum	40.00	80.00
15 Brian Bosworth Red	30.00	80.00
16 Steve Largent	25.00	50.00
17 Billy Sims Red	20.00	40.00
18 Franco Harris Red	40.00	80.00
19 Len Dawson Red	30.00	60.00
20 Ronnie Lott	30.00	60.00

2006 Press Pass Legends Rookie Autographs 50

STATED PRINT RUN 50 SER.#'d SETS

1 Reggie Bush	40.00	100.00
2 Brodie Croyle	15.00	40.00
3 A.J. Hawk	30.00	80.00
4 Omar Jacobs	10.00	25.00
5 Matt Leinart	15.00	40.00
6 Brad Smith	15.00	40.00
6R Brad Smith Red	20.00	50.00
7 Marcus Vick Red	12.00	30.00
8 LenDale White	12.00	30.00
9 Vince Young	30.00	80.00
9R Vince Young Red	40.00	100.00

2006 Press Pass Legends Saturday Swatches

STATED ODDS 1:18
*PLATINUM: .8X TO 2X BASIC JSYs
PLATINUM PRINT RUN 50 SER.#'d SETS

AF Anthony Fasano SP	5.00	12.00
AH A.J. Hawk	10.00	25.00
BC Brodie Croyle	6.00	15.00
BS Brad Smith SP	4.00	10.00
CR Cory Rodgers SP	6.00	15.00
CW Charlie Whitehurst	4.00	10.00
DA Devin Aromashodu SP	4.00	10.00
DS D.J. Shockley SP	5.00	12.00
DW Demetrius Williams SP	4.00	10.00
JH Jerome Harrison	4.00	10.00
LW LenDale White	6.00	15.00
MD Maurice Drew SP	6.00	15.00
MH Mike Hass SP	6.00	15.00
ML Marcedes Lewis	3.00	8.00
MR Michael Robinson	4.00	10.00
OJ Omar Jacobs SP	5.00	12.00
TJ Tarvaris Jackson	3.00	8.00
VD Vernon Davis	4.00	10.00
DAW DeAngelo Williams	8.00	20.00
MHU Michael Huff	3.00	8.00

2007 Press Pass Legends

This 100-card set was released in July, 2007. The set was issued into the hobby in five card packs which came 18 to a box. Cards numbered 1-65 feature 2007 NFL rookies while cards numbered 66-100 feature retired greats.

COMPLETE SET (100)	20.00	40.00
UNPRICED PRINTING PLATES PRINT RUN 1		
1 Kenneth Darby	.40	1.00
2 Chris Henry	.30	.75
3 Zach Miller	.50	1.25
4 Jamaal Anderson	.40	1.00
5 Kenny Irons	.30	.75
6 Courtney Taylor	.40	1.00
7 John Beck	.50	1.25
8 Daymeion Hughes	.40	1.00
9 Marshawn Lynch	.50	1.25
10 Gaines Adams	.50	1.25
11 Chansi Stuckey	.50	1.25
12 Aundrae Allison	.30	.75
13 Dallas Baker	.30	.75
14 Chris Leak	.40	1.00
15 Jarvis Moss	.40	1.00
16 Reggie Nelson	.40	1.00
17 DeShawn Wynn	.40	1.00
18 Paul Williams	.30	.75
19 Dwayne Wright	.40	1.00
20 Lorenzo Booker	.40	1.00
21 Buster Davis	.40	1.00
22 Lawrence Timmons	.50	1.25
23 Quentin Moses	.40	1.00
24 Calvin Johnson	1.50	4.00
25 Kevin Kolb	.75	2.00
26 Michael Bush	.50	1.25
27 Amobi Okoye	.50	1.25
28 Kolby Smith	.40	1.00
29 Joseph Addai	.40	1.00
30 Dwayne Bowe	.60	1.50
31 Craig Buster Davis	.40	1.00
32 LaRon Landry	.50	1.25
33 JaMarcus Russell	.30	.75
34 Greg Olsen	.40	1.00
35 Alan Branch	.40	1.00
36 Leon Hall	.40	1.00
37 Drew Stanton	.30	.75
38 Adam Carriker	.40	1.00
39 Brandon Jackson	.40	1.00
40 Jeff Rowe	.30	.75
41 Garrett Wolfe	.30	.75
42 Brady Quinn	.50	1.25
43 Ted Ginn Jr.	.40	1.00
44 Anthony Gonzalez	.50	1.25
45 Antonio Pittman	.30	.75
46 Troy Smith	.50	1.25
47 Adrian Peterson	2.00	5.00
48 Patrick Willis	1.00	2.50
49 Tony Hunt	.30	.75
50 Paul Posluszny	.50	1.25
51 Darrelle Revis	.75	2.00
52 Brian Leonard	.40	1.00
53 Sidney Rice	.60	1.50
54 Trent Edwards	.50	1.25
55 Robert Meachem	.50	1.25
56 Michael Griffin	.50	1.25
57 Aaron Ross	.50	1.25
58 Vince Young	.40	1.00
59 Joel Filani	.40	1.00
60 Dwayne Jarrett	.40	1.00
61 Steve Smith USC	.50	1.25
62 Johnnie Lee Higgins	.40	1.00
63 Jordan Palmer	.40	1.00
64 David Clowney	.40	1.00
65 Jason Hill	.50	1.25
66 Ozzie Newsome	.50	1.25
67 Ken Stabler	.75	2.00
68 Bart Starr	1.00	2.50
69 Pat Sullivan	.40	1.00
70 Doug Flutie	.60	1.50
71 Ty Detmer	.40	1.00
72 Danny Wuerffel	.40	1.00
73 Jack Youngblood	.50	1.25
74 Fred Biletnikoff	.60	1.50
75 Herschel Walker	.50	1.25
76 Dick Butkus	.75	2.00
77 Y.A. Tittle	.60	1.50
78 Randy White	.50	1.25
79 Jerry Rice	1.00	2.50
80 Joe Bellino	.40	1.00
81 Tommie Frazier	.50	1.25
82 Tom Osborne	.50	1.25
83 Tom Rathman	.40	1.00
84 Johnny Rodgers	.40	1.00
85 Mike Rozier	.40	1.00
86 Jerome Bettis	.60	1.50
87 Paul Hornung	.60	1.50
88 Alan Page	.40	1.00
89 Rudy Ruettiger	.60	1.50
90 Joe Theismann	.60	1.50
91 Archie Griffin	.40	1.00
92 Brian Bosworth	.60	1.50
93 Steve Owens	.40	1.00
94 Billy Sims	.50	1.25

95 Archie Manning .60 1.50
96 Raymond Berry .50 1.25
97 James Lofton .40 1.00
98 Marcus Allen .60 1.50
99 John Hannah .40 1.00
100 Dick Butkus CL .50 1.25

2007 Press Pass Legends Bronze
*BRONZE ROOKIE: .8X TO 2X BASIC CARDS
*BRONZE RETIRED: 1X TO 2.5X BASIC CARDS
STATED PRINT RUN 999 SER.#'d SETS

2007 Press Pass Legends Emerald
*EMERALD ROOKIE: 3X TO 8X BASIC CARDS
*EMER.RETIRED: 4X TO 10X BASIC CARDS
STATED PRINT RUN 25 SER.#'d SETS

2007 Press Pass Legends Gold
*GOLD ROOKIE: 1.5X TO 4X BASIC CARDS
*GOLD RETIRED: 2X TO 5X BASIC CARDS
STATED PRINT RUN 99 SER.#'d SETS

2007 Press Pass Legends Platinum
UNPRICED PLATINUM PRINT RUN 1

2007 Press Pass Legends Red
UNPRICED RED PRINT RUN 10

2007 Press Pass Legends Silver
*SILVER ROOKIE: 1X TO 2.5X BASIC CARDS
*SILVER RETIRED: 1.2X TO 3X BASIC CARDS
STATED PRINT RUN 499 SER.#'d SETS

2007 Press Pass Legends All Conference
STATED ODDS 1:7
1 Jamaal Anderson .60 1.50
2 Kenny Irons .50 1.25
3 John Beck .75 2.00
4 Marshawn Lynch .75 2.00
5 Gaines Adams .75 2.00
6 Calvin Johnson 2.50 6.00
7 Kevin Kolb 1.25 3.00
8 Dwayne Bowe 1.00 2.50
9 LaRon Landry .75 2.00
10 JaMarcus Russell .50 1.25
11 Leon Hall .60 1.50
12 Adam Carriker .60 1.50
13 Ted Ginn Jr. .60 1.50
14 Anthony Gonzalez .75 2.00
15 Troy Smith .75 2.00
16 Adrian Peterson 3.00 8.00
17 Paul Posluszny .75 2.00
18 Robert Meachem .75 2.00
19 Dwayne Jarrett .60 1.50
20 Steve Smith USC .75 2.00

2007 Press Pass Legends All Conference Autographs Gold
STATED PRINT RUN 25-400
UNPRICED PRINTING PLATES PRINT RUN 1
ACAB Alan Branch/262* 5.00 12.00
ACABR Alan Branch Red Ink/50* 6.00 15.00
ACAC Adam Carriker/290 6.00 15.00
ACAG Anthony Gonzalez/285 6.00 15.00
ACAP Adrian Peterson/27* 100.00 200.00
ACAPR Adrian Peterson Red Ink/20* 100.00 200.00
ACAR Aaron Ross/235* 5.00 12.00
ACARR Aaron Ross Red Ink/50* 6.00 15.00
ACBD Buster Davis/160
ACCJ Calvin Johnson/17 75.00 150.00
ACCJR Calvin Johnson Red Ink/8* 100.00 200.00
ACCS Chansi Stuckey/50 6.00 15.00
ACDB Dallas Baker/392 5.00 12.00
ACDB2 Dwayne Bowe/378* 8.00 20.00
ACDB2R Dwayne Bowe Red Ink/22* 8.00 20.00
ACDH Daymeion Hughes/267* 4.00 10.00
ACDHR Daymeion Hughes Red Ink/45* 5.00 12.00
ACGA Gaines Adams/303* 5.00 12.00
ACJA Jamaal Anderson/310 5.00 12.00
ACJB John Beck/349* 5.00 12.00
ACJBR John Beck Red Ink/51* 6.00 15.00
ACJH Johnnie Lee Higgins/235 5.00 12.00
ACJR JaMarcus Russell/75 15.00 40.00
ACKI Kenny Irons/400 4.00 10.00
ACKK Kevin Kolb/353* 8.00 20.00
ACKKR Kevin Kolb Red Ink/47* 10.00 25.00
ACLH Leon Hall/307 5.00 12.00
ACLL LaRon Landry/249* 5.00 12.00
ACLLR LaRon Landry Red Ink/50* 6.00 15.00
ACMG Michael Griffin/262 5.00 12.00
ACPP Paul Posluszny/240* 8.00 20.00
ACRM Robert Meachem/360* 8.00 20.00
ACRMR Robert Meachem Red Ink/40* 10.00 25.00
ACSS Steve Smith USC/328* 6.00 15.00
ACSSR Steve Smith USC Red Ink/72* 8.00 20.00
ACTGR Ted Ginn Red Ink/68* 15.00 40.00
ACTS Troy Smith/20* 30.00 60.00
ACZM Zach Miller/353* 6.00 15.00
ACZMR Zach Miller/47* 8.00 20.00

2007 Press Pass Legends All Conference Autographs Platinum
PLATINUM PRINT RUN 25 SER.#'d SETS
ACAB Alan Branch 10.00 25.00
ACAC Adam Carriker 12.00 30.00
ACAG Anthony Gonzalez 10.00 25.00
ACAR Aaron Ross 10.00 25.00
ACBD Buster Davis 8.00 20.00
ACCJ Calvin Johnson 100.00 200.00
ACCS Chansi Stuckey 8.00 20.00
ACDB Dallas Baker 10.00 25.00
ACDB Dwayne Bowe 15.00 40.00
ACDH Daymeion Hughes 6.00 15.00
ACGA Gaines Adams/15* 10.00 25.00
ACGAR Gaines Adams Red Ink/10* 12.00 30.00
ACJA Jamaal Anderson 10.00 25.00
ACJB John Beck 10.00 25.00
ACJH Johnnie Lee Higgins 8.00 20.00
ACJR JaMarcus Russell 25.00 60.00
ACKI Kenny Irons 10.00 25.00
ACKK Kevin Kolb/18* 12.00 30.00
ACLH Leon Hall 10.00 25.00
ACLL LaRon Landry 12.00 30.00
ACMG Michael Griffin 10.00 25.00
ACPP Paul Posluszny/23* 12.00 30.00
ACRMR Robert Meachem Red Ink/24* 10.00 25.00
ACSS Steve Smith USC 10.00 25.00
ACTG Ted Ginn Jr./23* 12.00 30.00
ACTS Troy Smith/20* 15.00 40.00
ACZM Zach Miller/24* 8.00 20.00

2007 Press Pass Legends Alumni Association
STATED ODDS 1:14
1 Danny Wuerffel 1.50 4.00
Chris Leak
2 Y.A. Tittle 1.50 4.00
JaMarcus Russell
3 Joe Theismann 3.00 8.00
Brady Quinn
4 Paul Hornung 2.50 6.00
Jerome Bettis
5 Archie Griffin 2.00 5.00
Troy Smith
6 Billy Sims 3.00 8.00
Adrian Peterson
7 Archie Manning 2.00 5.00
Patrick Willis
8 Marcus Allen 2.00 5.00
Steve Smith USC
9 Johnny Rodgers 2.50 6.00
Mike Rozier
10 Ty Detmer 1.50 4.00
John Beck

2007 Press Pass Legends Alumni Association Autographs
STATED PRINT RUN 50 SER.#'d SETS
AMPW Archie Manning
Patrick Willis No Auto
AWKK Andre Ware 15.00 40.00
Kevin Kolb
BSAPR1 Billy Sims Red Ink/44* 100.00 200.00
Adrian Peterson Blue Ink
DWCL Danny Wuerffel 25.00 60.00
Chris Leak
JRMR Johnny Rodgers 60.00 100.00
Mike Rozier
JTBQ Joe Theismann 75.00 150.00
Brady Quinn
MASS Marcus Allen Blue Ink/25* 40.00 80.00
Steve Smith USC Blue Ink
MASSR Marcus Allen Blue Ink/25* 40.00 80.00
Steve Smith USC Red Ink
PHJB Paul Hornung 60.00 120.00
Jerome Bettis
RCTR Roger Craig 40.00 80.00
Tom Rathman
TDJB Ty Detmer 20.00 50.00
John Beck
TFBJ Tommie Frazier 25.00 50.00
Brandon Jackson
YTJR Y.A. Tittle Blue Ink/10* 40.00 80.00
JaMarcus Russell Blue Ink
YTJRR1 Y.A. Tittle Red Ink/15* 40.00 80.00
JaMarcus Russell Red Ink
YTJRR2 Y.A. Tittle Blue Ink/25* 40.00 80.00
JaMarcus Russell Red Ink JR
YTJRR3 Y.A. Tittle Blue Ink/10* 40.00 80.00
JaMarcus Russell Red Ink

2007 Press Pass Legends Autographs
*RED INK/19-181: .5X TO 1.2X BLUE INK
RED INK PRINT RUNS ANNCD BY PRESS PASS
UNPRICED PRINTING PLATES PRINT RUN 1
OVERALL AUTO ODDS 5:18
1 Gaines Adams
2 Joseph Addai 5.00 12.00
3 Marcus Allen
4 Aundrae Allison 4.00 10.00
5 Jamaal Anderson 6.00 15.00
6 Dallas Baker 4.00 10.00
7 John Beck 6.00 15.00
8 Joe Bellino 8.00 20.00
9 Raymond Berry 6.00 15.00
10 Jerome Bettis 40.00 80.00
11 Fred Biletnikoff 8.00 20.00
12 Lorenzo Booker 5.00 12.00
13 Brian Bosworth 15.00 40.00
14 Dwayne Bowe 8.00 20.00
15 Alan Branch 5.00 12.00
16 Michael Bush 6.00 15.00
17 Dick Butkus 35.00 60.00
18 Adam Carriker 5.00 12.00
19 David Clowney 5.00 12.00
20 Kenneth Darby 5.00 12.00
21 Buster Davis 5.00 12.00
22 Craig Buster Davis 5.00 12.00
23 Ty Detmer 5.00 12.00
24 Joel Filani 5.00 12.00
25 Doug Flutie 10.00 25.00
26 Tommie Frazier 10.00 25.00
27 Ted Ginn Jr. 5.00 12.00
28 Anthony Gonzalez 6.00 15.00
29 Archie Griffin 8.00 20.00
30 Michael Griffin 6.00 15.00
31 Leon Hall
32 John Hannah 6.00 15.00
33 Johnnie Lee Higgins 5.00 12.00
34 Jason Hill 6.00 15.00
35 Paul Hornung 12.50 30.00
36 Daymeion Hughes 5.00 12.00
37 Kenny Irons 4.00 10.00
38 Brandon Jackson 5.00 12.00
39 Calvin Johnson SP 50.00 100.00
40 Charles Johnson 4.00 10.00
41 Kevin Kolb 10.00 25.00
42 LaRon Landry 6.00 15.00
43 Chris Leak 5.00 12.00
44 Brian Leonard 5.00 12.00
45 James Lofton 8.00 20.00
46 Archie Manning 15.00 40.00
47 Rhema McKnight 4.00 10.00
48 Robert Meachem 6.00 15.00
49 Zach Miller 6.00 15.00
50 Matt Moore 6.00 15.00
51 Quentin Moses 5.00 12.00
52 Reggie Nelson 5.00 12.00
53 Ozzie Newsome 6.00 15.00
54 Amobi Okoye 6.00 15.00
55 Greg Olsen 5.00 12.00
56 Tom Osborne 15.00 30.00
57 Steve Owens 8.00 20.00
58 Alan Page 8.00 20.00
59 Jordan Palmer 5.00 12.00
60 William Perry 6.00 15.00
61 Adrian Peterson SP 60.00 120.00
62 Antonio Pittman 4.00 10.00
63 Paul Posluszny 6.00 15.00
64 Brady Quinn 15.00 40.00
65 Tom Rathman 8.00 20.00
66 Darrelle Revis 10.00 25.00
67 Jerry Rice
68 Sidney Rice 8.00 20.00
69 Johnny Rodgers 8.00 20.00
70 Aaron Ross 6.00 15.00
71 Mike Rozier 10.00 25.00
72 Rudy Ruettiger 25.00 50.00
73 JaMarcus Russell 4.00 10.00
74 Lee Roy Selmon 10.00 25.00
75 Billy Sims 8.00 20.00
76 Kolby Smith 5.00 12.00
77 Steve Smith USC 6.00 15.00
78 Troy Smith SP 8.00 20.00
79 Ken Stabler 35.00 60.00
80 Drew Stanton 4.00 10.00
81 Bart Starr 90.00 150.00
82 Chansi Stuckey 6.00 15.00
83 Pat Sullivan 6.00 15.00
84 Joe Theismann 10.00 25.00
85 Lawrence Timmons 6.00 15.00
86 Y.A. Tittle 15.00 30.00
87 Darius Walker 4.00 10.00
88 Herschel Walker 10.00 25.00
89 Andre Ware 10.00 25.00
90 Randy White 8.00 20.00
91 Paul Williams 4.00 10.00
92 Patrick Willis 12.50 30.00
93 Garrett Wolfe 4.00 10.00
94 Dwayne Wright 5.00 12.00
95 Danny Wuerffel 8.00 20.00
96 DeShawn Wynn 5.00 12.00
97 Selvin Young 5.00 12.00
98 Vince Young SP 20.00 50.00
99 Jack Youngblood 6.00 15.00

2007 Press Pass Legends Legendary Legacy
STATED ODDS 1:7
1 Ken Stabler 2.50 6.00
2 Doug Flutie 2.00 5.00
3 Herschel Walker 1.50 4.00
4 Dick Butkus 2.50 6.00
5 Y.A. Tittle 2.00 5.00
6 Jerry Rice 3.00 8.00
7 Joe Bellino 1.25 3.00
8 Tommie Frazier 1.50 4.00
9 Mike Rozier 1.25 3.00
10 Jerome Bettis 2.00 5.00
11 Paul Hornung 2.00 5.00
12 Alan Page 1.25 3.00
13 Joe Theismann 2.00 5.00
14 Archie Griffin 1.25 3.00
15 Brian Bosworth 2.00 5.00
16 Billy Sims 1.50 4.00
17 Archie Manning 2.00 5.00
18 Raymond Berry 1.50 4.00
19 James Lofton 1.25 3.00
20 Marcus Allen 2.00 5.00

2007 Press Pass Legends Legendary Legacy Autographs Gold
STATED PRINT RUN 50-400 SER.#'d SETS
AG Archie Griffin/175 12.50 30.00
AM Archie Manning/75 12.50 30.00
AP Alan Page/85 10.00 25.00
AW Andre Ware/400 6.00 15.00
BB Brian Bosworth/75* 25.00 50.00
BBR Brian Bosworth Red Ink/25* 30.00 60.00
BS Billy Sims/382* 6.00 15.00
DB Dick Butkus/33* 40.00 80.00
DBR Dick Butkus Red Ink/20* 50.00 100.00
DF Doug Flutie/125 12.00 30.00
DW Danny Wuerffel/400 6.00 15.00
HW Herschel Walker/100 10.00 25.00
JB1 Joe Bellino/396 6.00 15.00
JB2 Jerome Bettis/80 35.00 60.00
JL James Lofton/150 8.00 20.00
JR1 Jerry Rice/53 60.00 120.00
JR2 Johnny Rodgers/184* 12.50 30.00
JR2R Johnny Rodgers Red Ink/193* 12.50 30.00
JT Joe Theismann/100 15.00 40.00
MA Marcus Allen/55 15.00 40.00
MR Mike Rozier/400 6.00 15.00
PH Paul Hornung/153 15.00 40.00
PS Pat Sullivan/73* 8.00 20.00
RB Raymond Berry/345* 6.00 15.00
RBR Raymond Berry Red Ink/25* 10.00 25.00
TF Tommie Frazier/349* 6.00 15.00
TFR Tommie Frazier Red Ink/51* 8.00 20.00
YT Y.A. Tittle/40* 20.00 40.00

2007 Press Pass Legends Legendary Legacy Autographs Platinum
PLATINUM PRINT RUN 25 SER.#'d SETS
AG Archie Griffin 20.00 40.00
AM Archie Manning 25.00 50.00
AP Alan Page 12.50 30.00
AW Andre Ware 12.00 30.00
BS Billy Sims/22* 15.00 40.00
DB Dick Butkus/15* 25.00 60.00
DBR Dick Butkus Red Ink/10* 25.00 60.00
DF Doug Flutie 20.00 50.00
DW Danny Wuerffel 12.50 30.00
HW Herschel Walker 15.00 40.00
JB1 Joe Bellino 12.50 30.00
JB2 Jerome Bettis 40.00 80.00
JL James Lofton 12.50 30.00
JR1 Jerry Rice 90.00 150.00
JR2 Johnny Rodgers/22* 20.00 40.00
JT Joe Theismann 25.00 50.00
KS Ken Stabler 25.00 60.00
MA Marcus Allen 25.00 50.00
MR Mike Rozier 12.00 30.00
PH Paul Hornung 20.00 40.00
PSR Pat Sullivan Red Ink/23* 12.50 30.00
RB Raymond Berry 12.50 30.00
TF Tommie Frazier 25.00 50.00
YT Y.A. Tittle/15* 30.00 60.00
YTR Y.A. Tittle Red Ink/10* 30.00 60.00

2007 Press Pass Legends Saturday Swatches Silver
*PREMIUM/30-50: .8X TO 2X BASIC JSYs
PREMIUM PRINT RUN 10-50 SER.#'d SETS
UNPRICED PATCH PRINT RUN 5-10SETS
OVERALL SWATCH ODDS 1:18
SSAC Adam Carriker 3.00 8.00
SSAH A.J. Hawk 10.00 25.00
SSAP Adrian Peterson 10.00 25.00
SSBC Brodie Croyle 5.00 12.00
SSBJ Brandon Jackson 4.00 10.00
SSBQ Brady Quinn 8.00 20.00
SSCS Chansi Stuckey 3.00 8.00
SSDB2 Dwayne Bowe 4.00 10.00
SSDJ Dwayne Jarrett 3.00 8.00
SSDR DeMeco Ryans 4.00 10.00
SSDW Darius Walker 4.00 10.00
SSDW2 Dwayne Wright 3.00 8.00
SSDW3 DeShawn Wynn 3.00 8.00
SSGW Garrett Wolfe 3.00 8.00
SSJF Joel Filani 3.00 8.00
SSJP Jordan Palmer 3.00 8.00
SSJR JaMarcus Russell 3.00 8.00
SSKD Kenneth Darby 5.00 12.00
SSKI Kenny Irons 4.00 10.00
SSKK Kevin Kolb 4.00 10.00
SSKS Kolby Smith 4.00 10.00
SSLB Lorenzo Booker
SSMA Marcus Allen 6.00 15.00
SSMB Michael Bush 3.00 8.00
SSMJD Maurice Jones-Drew 4.00 10.00
SSML Marshawn Lynch 5.00 12.00
SSML2 Marcedes Lewis 3.00 8.00
SSSS Steve Smith USC 3.00 8.00
SSZM Zach Miller

2007 Press Pass Legends Student and Teacher Autographs
TOTF Tom Osborne 40.00 80.00
Tommie Frazier

2008 Press Pass Legends

COMPLETE SET (100) 25.00 50.00
UNPRICED PRINT PLATE PRINT RUN 1
1 Felix Jones .75 2.00
2 Darren McFadden 1.25 3.00
3 Matt Ryan 2.00 5.00
4 Lavelle Hawkins .30 .75
5 DeSean Jackson 1.00 2.50
6 Kevin Smith .50 1.25
7 Joe Flacco 1.50 4.00
8 Chris Johnson 1.25 3.00
9 Andre Caldwell .40 1.00
10 Derrick Harvey .30 .75
11 Tashard Choice .40 1.00
12 Colt Brennan .50 1.25
13 Donnie Avery .40 1.00
14 Rashard Mendenhall 1.00 2.50
15 Aqib Talib .50 1.25
16 Jordy Nelson .60 1.50
17 Andre Woodson .50 1.25
18 Brian Brohm .50 1.25
19 Harry Douglas .40 1.00
20 Glenn Dorsey .50 1.25
21 Early Doucet .40 1.00
22 Matt Flynn 1.00 2.50
23 Jacob Hester .50 1.25
24 Kenny Phillips .50 1.25
25 Mike Hart .50 1.25
26 Chad Henne .50 1.25
27 Mario Manningham .50 1.25
28 Devin Thomas .40 1.00
29 John Carlson .50 1.25
30 Vernon Gholston .40 1.00
31 Malcolm Kelly .40 1.00
32 Dennis Dixon .50 1.25
33 Jonathan Stewart .75 2.00
34 Dan Connor .50 1.25
35 Ray Rice 1.00 2.50
36 Josh Johnson .50 1.25
37 Mike Jenkins .50 1.25
38 Erik Ainge .50 1.25
39 Jamaal Charles .75 2.00
40 Limas Sweed .50 1.25
41 Leodis McKelvin .40 1.00
42 Matt Forte .75 2.00
43 John David Booty .40 1.00
44 Fred Davis .50 1.25
45 Sedrick Ellis .50 1.25
46 Keith Rivers .50 1.25
47 Eddie Royal .50 1.25
48 Earl Bennett .50 1.25
49 Chris Long .50 1.25
50 Steve Slaton .50 1.25
51 Ken Stabler .60 1.50
52 Gene Stallings .40 1.00
53 John Jefferson .40 1.00
54 Mike Singletary .60 1.50
55 Doug Flutie .50 1.25
56 Steve Young .75 2.00
57 Craig Morton .40 1.00
58 Cris Collinsworth .50 1.25
59 Steve Spurrier .60 1.50
60 Charlie Ward .40 1.00
61 Vince Dooley .40 1.00
62 Herschel Walker .50 1.25
63 Alex Karras .50 1.25
64A Gale Sayers dark jsy .75 2.00
64B Gale Sayers light jsy .75 2.00
65A Jack Lambert .60 1.50
(standing alone)
65B Jack Lambert .60 1.50
(pictured with teammates)
66 George Blanda .60 1.50
67 Leonard Marshall .40 1.00
68 Jimmy Johnson .50 1.25
69 Jim Kelly .60 1.50
70 Anthony Carter .40 1.00
71 Dan Dierdorf .40 1.00
72 Roger Craig .50 1.25
73 Tommie Frazier .50 1.25
74 Paul Hornung .60 1.50
75 Joe Montana 1.25 3.00
(running in photo)
75B Joe Montana 1.25 3.00
(pitching the ball)
76 Randy Gradishar .40 1.00
77 Chris Spielman .50 1.25
78 Brian Bosworth .60 1.50
79 Tommy McDonald .50 1.25
80 Barry Switzer .60 1.50
81 Eric Dickerson .50 1.25
82 Craig James .50 1.25
83 Brett Favre B&W 1.50 4.00
(black and white photo)
83B Brett Favre Clr 1.50 4.00
(color photo)
84 John Brodie .40 1.00
85 Floyd Little .40 1.00
86 Earl Campbell dark jsy .60 1.50
86B Earl Campbell light jsy .60 1.50
87 Tommy Nobis .40 1.00
88 Don Maynard .50 1.25
89 Troy Aikman .75 2.00
90 Billy Kilmer .50 1.25
91 Marcus Allen .60 1.50
92 Charles White .40 1.00
93 Hugh McElhenny .40 1.00
94 Warren Moon .60 1.50
95 Ollie Matson .50 1.25

2008 Press Pass Legends Bronze
*BRONZE ROOKIES: .6X TO 1.5X
*BRONZE RETIRED: 1X TO 2.5X
BRONZE PRINT RUN 999 SER.#'d SETS

2008 Press Pass Legends Emerald
*EMERALD ROOKIES: 3X TO 8X
*EMERALD RETIRED: 5X TO 12X
EMERALD PRINT RUN 25 SER.#'d SETS

2008 Press Pass Legends Gold
*GOLD ROOKIES: 1.2X TO 3X
*GOLD RETIRED: 2X TO 5X
GOLD PRINT RUN 99 SER.#'d SETS

2008 Press Pass Legends Silver Holofoil
*SILVER ROOKIES: .8X TO 2X
*SLVR RETIRED: 1.2X TO 3X
SILVER HOLO.PRINT RUN 499 SER.#'d SETS

2008 Press Pass Legends All Conference
COMPLETE SET (20) 10.00 25.00
STATED ODDS 1:7
AC1 Colt Brennan .60 1.50
AC2 Brian Brohm .60 1.50
AC3 Matt Ryan 2.50 6.00
AC4 Chris Long .60 1.50
AC5 Felix Jones 1.00 2.50
AC6 Darren McFadden 1.50 4.00
AC7 Jonathan Stewart 1.00 2.50
AC8 Rashard Mendenhall 1.25 3.00
AC9 Mike Hart .60 1.50
AC10 Chad Henne .60 1.50
AC11 DeSean Jackson 1.25 3.00
AC12 Mario Manningham .60 1.50
AC13 Limas Sweed .60 1.50
AC14 John David Booty .50 1.25
AC15 Ray Rice 1.25 3.00
AC16 Steve Slaton .60 1.50
AC17 Earl Bennett .60 1.50
AG18 Kevin Smith .60 1.50
AC19 Matt Forte 1.00 2.50
AC20 Jordy Nelson .75 2.00

2008 Press Pass Legends All Conference Autographs Gold
GOLD PRINT RUN 50-400
*PLAT/25: .6X TO 1.5X BASIC AU/100-400
*PLAT/25: .5X TO 1.2X BASIC AU/50
PLATINUM PRINT RUN 25 SER.#'d SETS
*RED INK/17-50: .5X TO 1.2X BASIC AUTO
ACAB Adarius Bowman/251 4.00 10.00
ACBB Brian Brohm/50 12.00 30.00
ACCB Colt Brennan/50 12.00 30.00
ACCH Chad Henne/150 10.00 25.00
ACCL Chris Long/99 8.00 20.00
ACDC Dan Connor/251 5.00 12.00
ACDD Dennis Dixon/245 5.00 12.00
ACDJ DeSean Jackson/150 10.00 25.00
ACDM Darren McFadden/100 15.00 40.00
ACEB Earl Bennett/250 5.00 12.00
ACFD Fred Davis/150 5.00 12.00
ACFJ Felix Jones/100 15.00 40.00
ACJDB John David Booty/200 4.00 10.00
ACJF Justin Forsett/400 5.00 12.00
ACJN Jordy Nelson/400 8.00 20.00
ACJS Jonathan Stewart/100 15.00 30.00
ACKS Kevin Smith/245 5.00 12.00
ACLS Limas Sweed/150 5.00 12.00
ACMF Matt Forte/399 12.00 30.00
ACMH Mike Hart/150 5.00 12.00
ACMM Mario Manningham/150 6.00 15.00
ACMR Matt Ryan/50 60.00 100.00
ACRM Rashard Mendenhall/147 20.00 40.00
ACRR Ray Rice/245 10.00 25.00
ACSS Steve Slaton/245 5.00 12.00
ACTC Tashard Choice/400 4.00 10.00

2008 Press Pass Legends Alumni Association
COMPLETE SET (10) 8.00 20.00
STATED ODDS 1:14
AA1 Felix Jones 1.50 4.00
Darren McFadden
AA2 Doug Flutie 2.50 6.00
Matt Ryan
AA3 Roger Craig 1.25 3.00
Tommie Frazier
AA4 Hugh McElhenny 1.50 4.00
Warren Moon
AA5 Paul Hornung 3.00 8.00
Joe Montana
AA6 Randy Gradishar 1.25 3.00
Chris Spielman
AA7 Cris Collinsworth 1.50 4.00
Steve Spurrier
AA8 Tommy McDonald 1.50 4.00
Brian Bosworth
AA9 Earl Campbell 1.50 4.00
Tommy Nobis
AA10 Eric Dickerson 1.25 3.00
Craig James

2008 Press Pass Legends Alumni Association Autographs
STATED PRINT RUN 25-50
TMBBR Tommy McDonald/28* 40.00 80.00
Brian Bosworth Red
DFMR Doug Flutie/50 50.00 100.00
Matt Ryan
DMFJ Darren McFadden/25 40.00 100.00
Felix Jones
ECTN Earl Campbell/50 EXCH
Tommy Nobis
EDCJ Eric Dickerson/50 EXCH
Craig James
HMWM Hugh McElhenny/50 20.00 40.00
Warren Moon
PHJM Paul Hornung/25 100.00 175.00
Joe Montana
RCTF Roger Craig/50 20.00 40.00
Tommie Frazier
RGCS Randy Gradishar/50 20.00 40.00
Chris Spielman
SSCC Steve Spurrier/50 30.00 60.00
Cris Collinsworth Red Ink
TMBB Tommy McDonald/22* 40.00 80.00
Brian Bosworth

2008 Press Pass Legends Legendary Legacy
COMPLETE SET (20) 12.00 30.00
STATED ODDS 1:7
LL1 Gale Sayers 2.00 5.00
LL2 Craig Morton 1.00 2.50
LL3 Charlie Ward 1.00 2.50
LL4 Warren Moon 1.50 4.00
LL5 Brett Favre 3.00 8.00
LL6 Joe Montana 3.00 8.00
LL7 Mike Singletary 1.50 4.00
LL8 Troy Aikman 2.00 5.00
LL9 Eric Dickerson 1.25 3.00
LL10 Steve Young 2.00 5.00
LL11 John Jefferson 1.00 2.50
LL12 Jack Lambert 1.50 4.00
LL13 Earl Campbell 1.50 4.00
LL14 Jim Kelly 1.50 4.00
LL15 Tommy McDonald 1.25 3.00
LL16 Craig James 1.25 3.00
LL17 Tommy Nobis 1.00 2.50
LL18 George Blanda 1.50 4.00
LL19 Chris Spielman 1.25 3.00
LL20 Cris Collinsworth 1.25 3.00

2008 Press Pass Legends Legendary Legacy Autographs Gold
GOLD PRINT RUN 25-392
*PLAT/21-25: .6X TO 1.5X GOLD AU/150-392
*PLAT/21-25: .5X TO 1.2X GOLD AU/50-130
*PLAT/21-25: .4X TO 1X GOLD AU/25
PLATINUM PRINT RUN 21-25
*RED INK: .5X TO 1.2X BASIC AUTO
LLBF Brett Favre/50 100.00 175.00
LLCJ Craig James/150 6.00 15.00
LLCM Craig Morton/392 5.00 12.00
LLCW Charlie Ward/311 5.00 12.00
LLEC Earl Campbell/100 EXCH
LLED Eric Dickerson/50 25.00 50.00
LLGB George Blanda/105 15.00 40.00
LLGS Gale Sayers/53 30.00 60.00
LLJJ John Jefferson/372 5.00 12.00
LLJK Jim Kelly/72 20.00 50.00
LLJL Jack Lambert/100 20.00 40.00
LLJM Joe Montana/25 75.00 150.00
LLMS Mike Singletary/130 10.00 25.00
LLSY Steve Young/75 25.00 60.00
LLTA Troy Aikman/50 40.00 80.00
LLTM Tommy McDonald/250 8.00 20.00
LLWM Warren Moon/100 10.00 25.00

2008 Press Pass Legends Saturday Signatures
*RED INK/20-82: .5X TO 1.2X BASIC AUTO
SSAA Adrian Arrington SP 8.00 20.00
SSAC Andre Caldwell 4.00 10.00
SSAC2 Antoine Cason SP
SSAC3 Anthony Carter 6.00 15.00
SSAD Adarius Bowman SP
SSAK Alex Karras 6.00 15.00
SSAP Allen Patrick 4.00 10.00
SSAT Aqib Talib SP
SSAW Andre Woodson 5.00 12.00
SSBB Brian Brohm 6.00 15.00
SSBB2 Brian Bosworth 12.00 30.00
SSBF Brett Favre 90.00 150.00
SSBK Billy Kilmer 5.00 12.00
SSBS Barry Switzer 30.00 60.00
SSCB Colt Brennan SP 15.00 40.00
SSCC Calais Campbell SP
SSCC2 Cris Collinsworth 5.00 12.00
SSCH Chad Henne 10.00 25.00
SSCJ Chris Johnson 12.00 30.00
SSCJ2 Craig James 5.00 12.00
SSCL Chris Long 5.00 12.00
SSCM Craig Morton 5.00 12.00
SSCS Chris Spielman 10.00 25.00
SSCW Chauncey Washington 5.00 12.00
SSCW2 Charlie Ward 8.00 20.00
SSCW3 Charles White 6.00 15.00
SSDA Donnie Avery 6.00 15.00
SSDB Dorien Bryant 4.00 10.00
SSDB2 Davone Bess 5.00 12.00
SSDC Dan Connor 5.00 12.00
SSDD Dennis Dixon 6.00 15.00
SSDD2 Dan Dierdorf 6.00 15.00
SSDF Doug Flutie 10.00 25.00
SSDH DJ Hall 5.00 12.00
SSDH2 Derrick Harvey 4.00 10.00
SSDJ DeSean Jackson 8.00 20.00
SSDM Darren McFadden 12.00 30.00
SSDM2 Don Maynard 5.00 12.00
SSDR Darius Reynaud 4.00 10.00
SSDS Dantrell Savage SP 4.00 10.00
SSDT Devin Thomas 5.00 12.00
SSEA Erik Ainge 6.00 15.00
SSEB Earl Bennett 5.00 12.00
SSEC Earl Campbell 20.00 40.00
SSED Early Doucet 5.00 12.00
SSED2 Eric Dickerson SP 25.00 50.00
SSER Eddie Royal 5.00 12.00
SSFD Fred Davis 5.00 12.00
SSFJ Felix Jones 10.00 30.00
SSFL Floyd Little 5.00 12.00
SSGB George Blanda 15.00 40.00
SSGS Gale Sayers SP 25.00 50.00
SSGS2 Gene Stallings 8.00 20.00
SSHM Hugh McElhenny 6.00 15.00
SSJB John Brodie 6.00 15.00
SSJC Jamaal Charles 8.00 25.00
SSJC2 John Carlson SP
SSJDB John David Booty 4.00 10.00
SSJF Joe Flacco 15.00 40.00
SSJF2 Justin Forsett 5.00 12.00
SSJH2 Jacob Hester 5.00 12.00
SSJJ Josh Johnson 4.00 10.00
SSJJ2 Jimmy Johnson 12.00 30.00
SSJJ3 John Jefferson 6.00 15.00
SSJK Jim Kelly 25.00 50.00
SSJL Jack Lambert SP 30.00 60.00
SSJM Joe Montana SP 50.00 100.00
SSJN Jordy Nelson 10.00 25.00
SSJS Jonathan Stewart 10.00 25.00
SSKB Keenan Burton SP 3.00 8.00
SSKP Kenny Phillips SP
SSKR Keith Rivers 5.00 12.00
SSKS Kevin Smith 6.00 15.00
SSKS2 Ken Stabler 20.00 40.00
SSLH Lavelle Hawkins 4.00 10.00
SSLM Leodis McKelvin SP 4.00 10.00
SSLM2 Leonard Marshall 4.00 10.00
SSLS Limas Sweed 5.00 12.00
SSMA Marcus Allen 20.00 40.00
SSMF Matt Forte 10.00 25.00
SSMH Mike Hart 6.00 15.00
SSMK Malcolm Kelly 6.00 15.00
SSMM Mario Manningham/162* 5.00 12.00
SSMR Matt Ryan 25.00 60.00
SSMS Mike Singletary SP 12.00 30.00
SSOS Owen Schmitt 5.00 12.00
SSPH Paul Hornung 10.00 25.00
SSRC Roger Craig 6.00 15.00
SSRG Randy Gradishar 5.00 12.00
SSRM Rashard Mendenhall 15.00 30.00
SSRR Ray Rice 8.00 20.00
SSSE Sedrick Ellis SP
SSSS Steve Slaton 6.00 15.00
SSSS2 Steve Spurrier 12.00 30.00
SSSY Steve Young 25.00 50.00
SSTA Troy Aikman SP 40.00 80.00
SSTC Tashard Choice 6.00 15.00
SSTF Tommie Frazier 6.00 15.00
SSTM Tommy McDonald 10.00 25.00
SSTN Tommy Nobis 5.00 12.00
SSVD Vince Dooley 6.00 15.00
SSVG Vernon Gholston 5.00 12.00
SSWM Warren Moon 10.00 25.00

2008 Press Pass Legends Saturday Swatches Silver
*PREMIUM/40-50: .8X TO 2X SLVR JSY
*PREMIUM/40-50: .5X TO 1.2X SLVR JSY SP
PREMIUM PRINT RUN 40-50
UNPRICED PATCH PRINT RUN 10
SSWAA Adrian Arrington 3.00 8.00
SSWBB Brian Brohm 4.00 10.00
SSWCB Colt Brennan 5.00 12.00
SSWCH Chad Henne 5.00 12.00
SSWDA Donnie Avery SP 3.00 8.00
SSWDC Dan Connor SP 6.00 15.00
SSWDM Darren McFadden 10.00 25.00
SSWDT Devin Thomas 4.00 10.00
SSWEA Erik Ainge SP 10.00 25.00
SSWED Early Doucet 4.00 10.00
SSWJC Jamaal Charles 4.00 10.00
SSWJH Jacob Hester 4.00 10.00
SSWJS Jonathan Stewart 6.00 15.00
SSWKS Kevin Smith 4.00 10.00
SSWLS Limas Sweed 4.00 10.00
SSWMA Marcus Allen 4.00 10.00
SSWMF Matt Forte 5.00 12.00
SSWMK Malcolm Kelly 5.00 12.00
SSWMR Matt Ryan 6.00 15.00
SSWSS Steve Slaton 4.00 10.00
SSWVG Vernon Gholston 4.00 10.00
SSWJDB John David Booty 3.00 8.00

2008 Press Pass Legends Student and Teacher Autographs
STATED PRINT RUN 25 SER.#'d SETS
BBBS Brian Bosworth 60.00 120.00
Barry Switzer
HWVD Herschel Walker EXCH
Vince Dooley

2009 Press Pass Legends
COMPLETE SET (100) 25.00 50.00
1 Glen Coffee .40 1.00
2 Mike Thomas .50 1.25
3 Nate Davis .40 1.00
4 Ian Johnson SP .75 2.00
5 B.J. Raji .50 1.25
6 Austin Collie .50 1.25
7 Ramses Barden .30 .75
8 James Davis .50 1.25
9 Gartrell Johnson .30 .75
10 Donald Brown .50 1.25
11 Darius Butler .50 1.25
12 Percy Harvin .75 2.00
13 Louis Murphy .50 1.25
14 Everette Brown .40 1.00
15 Mohamed Massaquoi .40 1.00
16 Knowshon Moreno .50 1.25
17 Matthew Stafford 2.50 6.00
18 Vontae Davis .50 1.25
19 Shonn Greene .75 2.00
20 Josh Freeman 1.00 2.50
21 Rashad Jennings .50 1.25
22 Tyson Jackson .40 1.00
23 Darrius Heyward-Bey .50 1.25
24 Javon Ringer .50 1.25
25 Chase Coffman .40 1.00
26 Jeremy Maclin .75 2.00
27 William Moore .50 1.25
28 Andre Brown .30 .75
29 Hakeem Nicks .75 2.00
30 Brandon Tate .50 1.25
31 Malcolm Jenkins .50 1.25
32 James Laurinaitis .50 1.25
33 Brian Robiskie .50 1.25
34 Chris Wells .75 2.00
35 Brandon Pettigrew .50 1.25
36 Juaquin Iglesias SP .60 1.50
37 Aaron Maybin .40 1.00
38 Derrick Williams .40 1.00
39 LeSean McCoy 1.00 2.50
40 James Casey .40 1.00
41 Jarett Dillard SP .75 2.00
42 Kenny Britt .60 1.50
43 Rhett Bomar .40 1.00
44 Jared Cook .50 1.25
45 Kenny McKinley .50 1.25
46 Brian Orakpo .50 1.25
47 Mike Goodson .50 1.25
48 Stephen McGee .50 1.25
49 Graham Harrell SP .75 2.00
50 Michael Crabtree 1.00 2.50
51 Brian Cushing .50 1.25
52 Rey Maualuga .50 1.25
53 Mark Sanchez 1.50 4.00
54 D.J. Moore .40 1.00
55 Cedric Peerman .40 1.00
56 Victor Harris .50 1.25
57 Aaron Curry .50 1.25
58 Alphonso Smith .40 1.00
59 Brandon Gibson .50 1.25
60 Pat White .50 1.25
61 Ozzie Newsome .50 1.25
62 Dick Anderson .40 1.00
63 Cliff Branch .50 1.25
64 Bruce Smith SP .75 2.00
65 Deion Sanders .60 1.50
66 Fran Tarkenton .60 1.50
67 Doug Williams .50 1.25
68 Frank Gifford SP 1.00 2.50
69 Lee Corso .50 1.25
70 Tom Jackson .50 1.25
71 Boomer Esiason .50 1.25
72 Kellen Winslow .50 1.25
73 Bill Cowher .50 1.25
74 Tommie Frazier .50 1.25
75 Lawrence Taylor .60 1.50
76 Rocky Bleier .50 1.25
77 Dave Casper .40 1.00
78 Paul Hornung .60 1.50
79 Joe Theismann .60 1.50
80 Ricky Watters .40 1.00
81 Howard Cassady .40 1.00
82 Kirk Herbstreit .50 1.25
83 Paul Warfield SP .75 2.00
84 Billy Sims .50 1.25
85 Dan Fouts .60 1.50
86 Bruce Smith SP .75 2.00
87 Tony Dorsett .60 1.50
88 Mike Alstott .40 1.00
89 Rod Woodson .50 1.25
90 Bob Lilly .50 1.25
91 Gary Beban .40 1.00
92 Sam Huff .50 1.25
93 Jim Kiick .40 1.00
94 Charley Taylor .40 1.00
95 John Brodie .40 1.00
96 John Elway 1.00 2.50
97 Randall Cunningham .60 1.50
98 Bernie Kosar SP .75 2.00
99 Rod Woodson SP .75 2.00
100 John Elway CL .60 1.50

2009 Press Pass Legends Bronze
*ROOKIES 1-60: .6X TO 1.5X BASIC CARDS
*ROOKIE SP: .4X TO 1X BASIC CARDS
*LEGENDS 61-100: 1X TO 2.5X BASIC CARDS
*LEGEND SP: .6X TO 1.5X BASIC CARDS
BRONZE PRINT RUN 899 SER.#'d SETS

2009 Press Pass Legends Emerald
*ROOKIES 1-60: 3X TO 8X BASIC CARDS
*ROOKIE SP: 2X TO 5X BASIC CARDS
*LEGENDS 61-100: 5X TO 12X BASIC CARDS
*LEGEND SP: 3X TO 8X BASIC CARDS
EMERALD PRINT RUN 25 SER.#'d SETS

2009 Press Pass Legends Gold
*ROOKIES 1-60: 1.2X TO 3X BASIC CARDS
*ROOKIE SP: .8X TO 2X BASIC CARDS
*LEGENDS 61-100: 2X TO 5X BASIC CARDS
*LEGEND SP: 1.2X TO 3X BASIC CARDS
GOLD PRINT RUN 99 SER.#'d SETS

2009 Press Pass Legends Red
ISSUED AT 2009 NATIONAL CONVENTION

2009 Press Pass Legends Silver Holofoil

*ROOKIES 1-100: 1X TO 2.5X BASIC CARDS
*ROOKIE SP: .6X TO 1.5X BASIC CARDS
*LEGENDS 61-100: 1.5X TO 4X BASIC CARDS
*LEGEND SP: 1X TO 2.5X BASIC CARDS
SILVER HOLOFOIL PRINT RUN 299 SER.#'d SETS

2009 Press Pass Legends All Conference

STATED ODDS 1:7

AC1 Matthew Stafford	3.00	8.00
AC2 Glen Coffee	.50	1.25
AC3 Knowshon Moreno	.60	1.50
AC4 Percy Harvin	1.00	2.50
AC5 Mohamed Massaquoi	.50	1.25
AC6 Hakeem Nicks	1.00	2.50
AC7 Darrius Heyward-Bey	.60	1.50
AC8 Aaron Curry	.60	1.50
AC9 Shonn Greene	1.00	2.50
AC10 Javon Ringer	.60	1.50
AC11 Chris Wells	1.00	2.50
AC12 Derrick Williams	.50	1.25
AC13 James Laurinaitis	.60	1.50
AC14 Mark Sanchez	2.00	5.00
AC15 Pat White	.60	1.50
AC16 Kenny Britt	.75	2.00
AC17 LeSean McCoy	1.25	3.00
AC18 Donald Brown	.60	1.50
AC19 Jeremy Maclin	1.00	2.50
AC20 Michael Crabtree	1.25	3.00

2009 Press Pass Legends All Conference Autographs

STATED PRINT RUN 99-299
*RED INK/49: .5X TO 1.2X BASIC AU
*PLATINUM/25: .6X TO 1.5X BASIC AUTO
PLAT.RED INK ANNC'D PRINT RUN 4-25

ACAC1 Aaron Curry/100	5.00	12.00
ACAC2 Austin Collie/299	6.00	15.00
ACBO Brian Orakpo/99	8.00	20.00
ACCW Chris Wells/141	10.00	25.00
ACDB Donald Brown/199	8.00	20.00
ACDHB Darrius Heyward-Bey/199	5.00	12.00
ACDM Mohamed Massaquoi/287	4.00	10.00
ACDW Derrick Williams/299	4.00	10.00
ACGC Glen Coffee/299	4.00	10.00
ACHN Hakeem Nicks/199	8.00	20.00
ACIJ Ian Johnson/299	5.00	12.00
ACJD Jarett Dillard/299	5.00	12.00
ACJL James Laurinaitis/150	8.00	20.00
ACJM Jeremy Maclin/199	8.00	20.00
ACJR Javon Ringer/299	5.00	12.00
ACKB Kenny Britt/299	6.00	15.00
ACKM Knowshon Moreno/150	12.00	30.00
ACLM LeSean McCoy/199	10.00	25.00
ACMC Michael Crabtree/150	15.00	40.00
ACMJ Malcolm Jenkins/150	5.00	12.00
ACMS1 Mark Sanchez/100	25.00	50.00
ACMS2 Matthew Stafford/150	30.00	60.00
ACND Nate Davis/138	4.00	10.00
ACPH Percy Harvin/199	15.00	40.00
ACPW Pat White/150	5.00	12.00
ACRB Rhett Bomar/299	4.00	10.00
ACRM Rey Maualuga/150	5.00	12.00
ACSG Shonn Greene/199	8.00	20.00

2009 Press Pass Legends Alumni Association

STATED ODDS 1:14

AA1 Lawrence Taylor	1.25	3.00
Hakeem Nicks		
AA2 Rod Woodson	1.25	3.00
Mike Alstott		
AA3 Lee Corso	1.50	4.00
Deion Sanders		
AA4 Fran Tarkenton	4.00	10.00
Matthew Stafford		
AA5 Tony Dorsett	1.50	4.00
LeSean McCoy		
AA6 Kellen Winslow	1.25	3.00
Jeremy Maclin		
AA7 Howard Cassady	1.25	3.00
Chris Wells		
AA8 John Brodie	3.00	8.00
John Elway		
AA9 Sam Huff	.75	2.00
Pat White		
AA10 Frank Gifford	2.50	6.00
Mark Sanchez		

2009 Press Pass Legends Alumni Association Autographs

STATED PRINT RUN 24-50

FTMS Fran Tarkenton/50 EXCH	40.00	80.00
Matthew Stafford		
HCCW Howard Cassady/50	20.00	50.00
Chris Wells		
JBJE John Brodie/25	100.00	200.00
John Elway		
KWJM Kellen Winslow/50	25.00	50.00
Jeremy Maclin		
LCDS Lee Corso/25	40.00	80.00
Deion Sanders		
LTHN Lawrence Taylor/25 EXCH		
Hakeem Nicks		
RWMA Rod Woodson/49	30.00	60.00
Mike Alstott		
TDLM Tony Dorsett/24	30.00	60.00
LeSean McCoy		
BEDHB Boomer Esiason/50 EXCH		
Darrius Heyward-Bey		

2009 Press Pass Legends Legends of the Fall

STATED ODDS 1:7

LOF1 Mike Alstott	1.00	2.50
LOF2 Tony Dorsett	1.50	4.00
LOF3 Paul Hornung	1.50	4.00
LOF4 Ozzie Newsome	1.25	3.00
LOF5 Deion Sanders	1.50	4.00
LOF6 Billy Sims	1.25	3.00
LOF7 Lawrence Taylor	1.50	4.00
LOF8 Rod Woodson	1.25	3.00
LOF9 Howard Cassady	1.00	2.50
LOF10 Kellen Winslow	1.25	3.00
LOF11 Boomer Esiason	1.25	3.00
LOF12 Dan Fouts	1.50	4.00
LOF13 Sam Huff	1.25	3.00
LOF14 Dave Casper	1.00	2.50
LOF15 Bruce Smith	1.25	3.00
LOF16 Doug Williams	1.25	3.00
LOF17 John Elway	2.50	6.00
LOF18 Matt Ryan	1.50	4.00
LOF19 Frank Gifford	1.50	4.00
LOF20 Bernie Kosar	1.25	3.00

2009 Press Pass Legends Legends of the Fall Autographs

STATED PRINT RUN 25-355
*RED INK/20-35: .5X TO 1.2X BASIC AU
RED INK ANNC'D PRINT RUN 5-35
*PLAT/24-25: .5X TO 1.2X GOLD AU/71-355
*PLAT/25: .4X TO 1X GOLD AU/25-50
PLATINUM PRINT RUN 8-25
UNPRICED RED INK PLAT.ANNC'D PR 5-16

LOFBK Bernie Kosar/150	8.00	20.00
LOFDF Dan Fouts/50	25.00	50.00
LOFDS Deion Sanders/35	25.00	50.00
LOFDW Doug Williams/150	8.00	20.00
LOFHC Howard Cassady/280	10.00	25.00
LOFJE John Elway/25	75.00	150.00
LOFKW Kellen Winslow/150	8.00	20.00
LOFLT Lawrence Taylor/50	25.00	50.00
LOFMA Mike Alstott/150	10.00	25.00
LOFON Ozzie Newsome/199	6.00	15.00
LOFPH Paul Hornung/71	20.00	40.00
LOFSH Sam Huff/150	8.00	20.00
LOFTD Tony Dorsett/25	25.00	50.00
LOFBS1 Billy Sims/355	6.00	15.00
LOFBS2 Bruce Smith/50	20.00	40.00
LOFLBE Boomer Esiason/50	8.00	20.00

2009 Press Pass Legends Saturday Signatures

*RED INK/20-138: .5X TO 1.2X BASIC AU
ANNOUNCED RED INK PRINT RUN 3-138
*PLATINUM/18-25: .6X TO 1.5X BASIC AUTO
PLATINUM PRINT RUN 18-25
SIX AUTOS PER HOBBY BOX

SSAB Andre Brown	3.00	8.00
SSAC1 Aaron Curry	5.00	12.00
SSAC2 Austin Collie	6.00	15.00
SSAF Arian Foster	25.00	50.00
SSAS Alphonso Smith	4.00	10.00
SSBC1 Bill Cowher	20.00	40.00
SSBC2 Brian Cushing	5.00	12.00
SSBE Boomer Esiason	6.00	15.00
SSBG Brandon Gibson	5.00	12.00
SSBH Brian Hoyer	5.00	12.00
SSBK Bernie Kosar	8.00	20.00
SSBL Bob Lilly	8.00	20.00
SSBO Brian Orakpo	8.00	20.00
SSBP Brandon Pettigrew	5.00	12.00
SSBR Brian Robiskie	5.00	12.00
SSBS1 Billy Sims	6.00	15.00
SSBS2 Bruce Smith	20.00	40.00
SSBT Brandon Tate	5.00	12.00
SSCB Cliff Branch	5.00	12.00
SSCC Chase Coffman	4.00	10.00
SSCH Cullen Harper	5.00	12.00
SSCP Cedric Peerman	4.00	10.00
SSCT Charley Taylor	5.00	12.00
SSCW Chris Wells	10.00	25.00
SSDA Dick Anderson	5.00	12.00
SSDB Donald Brown	8.00	20.00
SSDC Dave Casper	5.00	12.00
SSDF Dan Fouts	20.00	40.00
SSDHB Darrius Heyward-Bey	5.00	12.00
SSDM Devin Moore	4.00	10.00
SSDW1 Derrick Williams	4.00	10.00
SSDW2 Doug Williams	10.00	25.00
SSEB Everette Brown	4.00	10.00
SSFG Frank Gifford	12.00	30.00
SSFT Fran Tarkenton	12.00	30.00
SSGB Gary Beban	5.00	12.00
SSGC Glen Coffee	4.00	10.00
SSGH Graham Harrell	10.00	25.00
SSGJ Gartrell Johnson	3.00	8.00
SSHC1 Hunter Cantwell	5.00	12.00
SSHC2 Howard Cassady SP	15.00	40.00
SSHN Hakeem Nicks	8.00	20.00
SSIJ Ian Johnson	5.00	12.00
SSJB John Brodie	6.00	15.00
SSJC Jared Cook	5.00	12.00
SSJD1 James Davis	5.00	12.00
SSJD2 Jarett Dillard	5.00	12.00
SSJE John Elway	60.00	100.00
SSJF Josh Freeman	10.00	25.00
SSJI Juaquin Iglesias	4.00	10.00
SSJJ Jeremiah Johnson	5.00	12.00
SSJK Jim Kiick	5.00	12.00
SSJL James Laurinaitis	5.00	12.00
SSJM Jeremy Maclin	10.00	25.00
SSJR Javon Ringer	6.00	15.00
SSJT Joe Theismann	10.00	25.00
SSJW John Parker Wilson	8.00	20.00
SSKB Kenny Britt	6.00	15.00
SSKH Kirk Herbstreit	8.00	20.00
SSKM Knowshon Moreno	5.00	12.00
SSKW Kellen Winslow	8.00	20.00
SSLC Lee Corso	6.00	15.00
SSLM1 LeSean McCoy	8.00	20.00
SSLM2 Louis Murphy	5.00	12.00
SSMA Mike Alstott	15.00	30.00
SSMC Michael Crabtree	12.00	30.00
SSMG Mike Goodson	5.00	12.00
SSMM Mohamed Massaquoi	4.00	10.00
SSMS1 Mark Sanchez	25.00	60.00
SSMS2 Matthew Stafford	25.00	60.00
SSMT Mike Thomas	5.00	12.00
SSND Nate Davis	4.00	10.00
SSON Ozzie Newsome	6.00	15.00
SSPH1 Percy Harvin	20.00	50.00
SSPH2 P.J. Hill	4.00	10.00
SSPH3 Paul Hornung	15.00	30.00
SSPW1 Paul Warfield	8.00	20.00
SSPW2 Pat White	5.00	12.00
SSQC Quan Cosby	4.00	10.00
SSRB Rocky Bleier	8.00	20.00
SSRB1 Ramses Barden	3.00	8.00
SSRB2 Rhett Bomar	4.00	10.00
SSRC Randall Cunningham	8.00	20.00
SSRJ Rashad Jennings	5.00	12.00
SSRW1 Ricky Watters	6.00	15.00
SSRW2 Rod Woodson	20.00	40.00
SSSG Shonn Greene	8.00	20.00
SSSH Sam Huff	8.00	20.00
SSTF Tommie Frazier	8.00	20.00
SSTJ1 Tom Jackson	6.00	15.00
SSTJ2 Tyson Jackson	4.00	10.00
SSVD Vontae Davis	5.00	12.00

2009 Press Pass Legends Saturday Swatches Premium

PREMIUM PRINT RUN 30-99
*PATCH/17-25: .8X TO 2X PREMIUM JSY
PATCHES PRINT RUN 2-25
*SILVER/125-199: .3X TO .8X PREMIUM/80-99
*SILVER/125-199: .25X TO .6X PREMIUM/50
*SILVER/125-199: .2X TO .5X PREMIUM/30
*SILVER/70-99: .4X TO 1X PREMIUM/70-99
*SILVER/70-99: .3X TO .8X PREMIUM/50
*SILVER/50: .5X TO 1.2X PREMIUM/99
*SILVER/50: .4X TO 1X PREMIUM/50
*SILVER/25: .6X TO 1.5X PREMIUM/99
SILVER PRINT RUN 25-199

SSWAF Arian Foster/99	10.00	25.00
SSWBG Brandon Gibson/99	6.00	15.00
SSWBR Brian Robiskie/75	6.00	15.00
SSWCD Chase Daniel/99	5.00	12.00
SSWCH Cullen Harper/99		
SSWDB Donald Brown/99	8.00	20.00
SSWDM Darren McFadden/30		
SSWDW Derrick Williams/99	4.00	10.00
SSWGJ Gartrell Johnson/50	4.00	10.00
SSWIJ Ian Johnson/99		
SSWJF Josh Freeman/50	8.00	20.00
SSWJL James Laurinaitis/99	5.00	12.00
SSWJM Jeremy Maclin/35	12.00	30.00
SSWJS Jonathan Stewart/50	6.00	15.00
SSWJW John Parker Wilson/99	10.00	25.00
SSWKB Kenny Britt/99	5.00	12.00
SSWKM Kenny McKinley/99	5.00	12.00
SSWKS Kevin Smith/70	5.00	12.00
SSWLM LeSean McCoy/99	8.00	20.00
SSWMA Mike Alstott/99	10.00	25.00
SSWMC Michael Crabtree/99	12.00	30.00
SSWMF Matt Forte/50	6.00	15.00
SSWMG Mike Goodson/99	5.00	12.00
SSWMR Matt Ryan/80	6.00	15.00
SSWMS Mark Sanchez/99	12.00	30.00
SSWND Nate Davis/99	4.00	10.00
SSWQC Quan Cosby/99	6.00	15.00
SSWRB Ramses Barden/50	4.00	10.00
SSWRM Rey Maualuga/99	5.00	12.00
SSWSG Shonn Greene/99	8.00	20.00
SSWSM Stephen McGee/50	6.00	15.00
SSWSS Steve Slaton/99	6.00	15.00
SSWDHB Darrius Heyward-Bey/99	5.00	12.00
SSWLM2 Louis Murphy/99	6.00	15.00
SSWMS2 Matthew Stafford/50	12.00	30.00
SSWRB2 Rhett Bomar/50	5.00	12.00

2011 Press Pass Legends

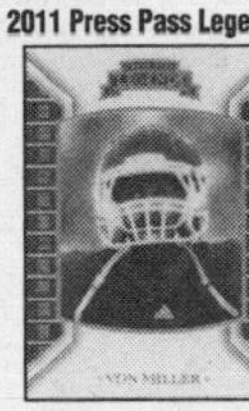

COMP.SET w/o SPs (90)	15.00	30.00
91-100 SP ODDS 1:18 HOB		
UNPRICED PLATINUM PRINT RUN 1		
UNPRICED PRINT PLATE PRINT RUN 1		
1 Blaine Gabbert	.50	1.25
2 Cam Newton	1.50	4.00
3 Ryan Mallett	.60	1.50
4 Jake Locker	.75	2.00
5 Andy Dalton	.75	2.00
6 Christian Ponder	.60	1.50
7 Colin Kaepernick	.40	1.00
8 Tyrod Taylor	.30	.75
9 Mark Ingram	.60	1.50
10 Daniel Thomas	.30	.75
11 Mikel Leshoure	.30	.75
12 Jacquizz Rodgers	.30	.75
13 Ryan Williams	.40	1.00
14 Shane Vereen	.30	.75
15 Jordan Todman	.20	.50
16 Dion Lewis	.30	.75
17 DeMarco Murray	.60	1.50
18 Stevan Ridley	.30	.75
19 Evan Royster	.30	.75
20 Kendall Hunter	.30	.75
21 Delone Carter	.25	.60
22 Derrick Locke	.25	.60
23 Roy Helu	.60	1.50
24 John Clay	.30	.75
25 Jonathan Baldwin	.30	.75
26 A.J. Green	.60	1.50
27 Julio Jones	.60	1.50
28 Torrey Smith	.40	1.00
29 Greg Little	.30	.75
30 Austin Pettis	.25	.60
31 Tandon Doss	.25	.60
32 Niles Paul	.30	.75
33 Terrence Toliver	.25	.60
34 Jerrel Jernigan	.25	.60
35 Titus Young	.40	1.00
36 Armon Binns	.25	.60
37 Greg Salas	.30	.75
38 Dane Sanzenbacher	.30	.75
39 Darvin Adams	.25	.60
40 Randall Cobb	.40	1.00
41 Kyle Rudolph	.30	.75
42 Luke Stocker	.25	.60
43 D.J. Williams	.30	.75
44 Da'Quan Bowers	.30	.75
45 Aldon Smith	.50	1.25
46 J.J. Watt	.40	1.00
47 Cameron Heyward	.30	.75
48 Ryan Kerrigan	.30	.75
49 Nick Fairley	.40	1.00
50 Marcell Dareus	.30	.75
51 Drake Nevis	.30	.75
52 Stephen Paea	.30	.75
53 Akeem Ayers	.25	.60
54 Mark Herzlich	.25	.60
55 Von Miller	.40	1.00
56 Prince Amukamara	.30	.75
57 Aaron Williams	.25	.60
58 Brandon Burton	.25	.60
59 DeAndre McDaniel	.25	.60
60 Rahim Moore	.25	.60
61 Ahmad Black	.25	.60
62 Dan Hampton	.30	.75
63 Karl Mecklenburg	.30	.75
64 Ickey Woods	.30	.75
65 Antonio Freeman	.30	.75
66 Bo Jackson	.60	1.50
67 Jim Plunkett	.40	1.00
68 Steve Young	.60	1.50
69 Hines Ward	.40	1.00
70 Michael Irvin	.50	1.25
71 Ed McCaffrey	.30	.75
72 Emmitt Smith	.75	2.00
73 Tommie Frazier	.40	1.00
74 Tony Rice	.30	.75
75 Willie Brown	.30	.75
76 Cris Carter	.50	1.25
77 Paul Hornung	.50	1.25
78 Tedy Bruschi	.50	1.25
79 Gino Cappelletti	.30	.75
80 Jim Otto	.30	.75
81 Paul Krause	.30	.75
82 Bob Griese	.50	1.25
83 Dan Marino	1.00	2.50
84 Warren Sapp	.40	1.00
85 Johnny Rodgers	.30	.75
86 Willie Davis	.30	.75
87 Mike Rozier	.30	.75
88 Major Harris	.30	.75
89 Dick LeBeau	.30	.75
90 Franco Harris	.50	1.25
91 Cam Newton SP	4.00	10.00
92 Mark Ingram SP	1.50	4.00
93 A.J. Green SP	1.50	4.00
94 Blaine Gabbert SP	1.25	3.00
95 Julio Jones SP	1.50	4.00
96 Emmitt Smith SP	1.50	4.00
97 Hines Ward SP	.75	2.00
98 Michael Irvin SP	1.00	2.50
99 Steve Young SP	1.25	3.00
100 Bo Jackson SP	1.25	3.00

2011 Press Pass Legends Bronze

*1-61 ROOKIES: 1.5X TO 4X BASIC CARDS
*62-90 LEGENDS: 1.2X TO 3X BASIC CARDS
*91-95 ROOKIES: 1X TO 2.5X BASIC SP
*96-100 LEGENDS: .8X TO 2X BASIC SP
STATED PRINT RUN 250 SER.#'d SETS

2011 Press Pass Legends Emerald

*1-61 ROOKIES: 4X TO 10X BASIC CARDS
*62-90 LEGENDS: 3X TO 8X BASIC CARDS
*91-95 ROOKIES: 2.5X TO 6X BASIC SP
*96-100 LEGENDS: 2X TO 5X BASIC SP
STATED PRINT RUN 25 SER.#'d SETS

2011 Press Pass Legends Gold

*1-61 ROOKIES: 2.5X TO 6X BASIC CARDS
*62-90 LEGENDS: 2X TO 5X BASIC CARDS
*91-95 ROOKIES: 1.5X TO 4X BASIC SP
*96-100 LEGENDS: 1.2X TO 3X BASIC SP
STATED PRINT RUN 99 SER.#'d SETS

2011 Press Pass Legends Silver Holofoil

*1-61 ROOKIES: 2X TO 5X BASIC CARDS
*62-90 LEGENDS: 1.5X TO 4X BASIC CARDS
*91-95 ROOKIES: 1.2X TO 3X BASIC SP
*96-100 LEGENDS: 1X TO 2.5X BASIC SP
STATED PRINT RUN 175 SER.#'d SETS

2011 Press Pass Legends All Americans

COMPLETE SET (13)	6.00	15.00
STATED ODDS 1:10		
AA1 Prince Amukamara	.60	1.50
AA2 Da'Quan Bowers	.60	1.50
AA3 Randall Cobb	.75	2.00
AA4 Nick Fairley	.75	2.00
AA5 Kendall Hunter	.60	1.50
AA6 Mark Ingram	1.25	3.00
AA7 Ryan Kerrigan	.60	1.50
AA8 Von Miller	.75	2.00
AA9 Drake Nevis	.60	1.50
AA10 Cam Newton	3.00	8.00
AA11 Stephen Paea	.60	1.50
AA12 Jordan Todman	.40	1.00
AA13 J.J. Watt	.75	2.00

2011 Press Pass Legends All Americans Autographs

STATED PRINT RUN 75-305
*RED INK: .5X TO 1.2X BASIC AUTO
*PLATINUM/25: .6X TO 1.5X BASIC AUTO
EXCH EXPIRATION: 5/31/2012

ACCN Cam Newton/230*	40.00	80.00
ACDB Da'Quan Bowers/100*	5.00	12.00
ACDN Drake Nevis/167*	5.00	12.00
ACJT Jordan Todman/305	3.00	8.00
ACJW J.J. Watt/195*	8.00	20.00
ACKH Kendall Hunter/305	5.00	12.00
ACMI Mark Ingram/245*	15.00	40.00
ACNF Nick Fairley/58*	6.00	15.00
ACPA Prince Amukamara/124*	5.00	12.00
ACRC Randall Cobb/195*	6.00	15.00
ACRK Ryan Kerrigan/155*	5.00	12.00
ACSP Stephen Paea/191*	5.00	12.00
ACVM Von Miller/199	8.00	20.00

2011 Press Pass Legends All-Americans Autographs Platinum Red Ink

ACDN Drake Nevis/25

2011 Press Pass Legends Legends of the Fall

COMPLETE SET (17)	8.00	20.00
STATED ODDS 1:7		
UNPRICED PRINT PLATE PRINT RUN 1		
LOF1 Bo Jackson	1.50	4.00
LOF2 Ickey Woods	.75	2.00
LOF3 Antonio Freeman	.75	2.00
LOF4 Jim Plunkett	1.00	2.50
LOF5 Tommie Frazier	1.00	2.50
LOF6 Michael Irvin	1.25	3.00
LOF7 Ed McCaffrey	.75	2.00
LOF8 Emmitt Smith	2.00	5.00
LOF9 Steve Young	1.50	4.00
LOF10 Hines Ward	1.00	2.50
LOF11 Tony Rice	.75	2.00
LOF12 Cris Carter	1.25	3.00
LOF13 Paul Hornung	1.25	3.00
LOF14 Tedy Bruschi	1.25	3.00
LOF15 Bob Griese	1.25	3.00
LOF16 Warren Sapp	1.00	2.50
LOF17 Franco Harris	1.25	3.00

2011 Press Pass Legends Legends of the Fall Autographs

STATED PRINT RUN 25-399
*PLAT15-25: .5X TO 1.2X BASIC AU/75-399
*PLAT/15-25: .4X TO 1X BASIC AU/25-50

LOFBG Bob Griese/65*	15.00	30.00
LOFBJ Bo Jackson/17*		
LOFEM Ed McCaffrey/274*	6.00	15.00
LOFES Emmitt Smith/10*	100.00	175.00
LOFFH Franco Harris/25	20.00	40.00
LOFHW Hines Ward/75	25.00	50.00
LOFIW Ickey Woods/375	5.00	12.00
LOFJP Jim Plunkett/135*	8.00	20.00
LOFLAF Antonio Freeman/369*	5.00	12.00
LOFMI Michael Irvin/49	20.00	40.00
LOFPH Paul Hornung/75*	15.00	40.00
LOFSY Steve Young/25	30.00	60.00
LOFTB Tedy Bruschi/13*	20.00	40.00
LOFTF Tommie Frazier/299	6.00	15.00
LOFTR Tony Rice/399	5.00	12.00
LOFWS Warren Sapp/150	8.00	20.00

2011 Press Pass Legends Legends of the Fall Autographs Red Ink

*RED INK: .5X TO 1.2X BASIC AU
RED INK ANNOUNCED PRINT RUN 8-87

LOFCC Cris Carter/25	20.00	40.00
LOFTB Tedy Bruschi/37*	20.00	40.00

2011 Press Pass Legends Past and Present

COMPLETE SET (10)	8.00	20.00
STATED ODDS 1:14		
PP1 Bo Jackson	4.00	10.00
Cam Newton		
PP2 Hines Ward	1.50	4.00
A.J. Green		
PP3 Emmitt Smith	1.50	4.00
Mark Ingram		
PP4 Steve Young	2.00	5.00
Jake Locker		
PP5 Michael Irvin	1.50	4.00
Julio Jones		
PP6 Cris Carter	.75	2.00
Jonathan Baldwin		
PP7 Dan Marino	1.50	4.00
Ryan Mallett		
PP8 Bob Griese	1.25	3.00
Blaine Gabbert		
PP9 Warren Sapp	1.00	2.50
Nick Fairley		
PP10 Franco Harris	.75	2.00
Evan Royster		

2011 Press Pass Legends Past and Present Autographs

STATED PRINT RUN 25-50

BGBG Bob Griese/50	20.00	50.00
Blaine Gabbert		
BJCN Bo Jackson/30*	125.00	200.00
Cam Newton		
BJCNR Bo Jackson/14*	125.00	200.00
Cam Newton Red Ink		
CCJD Cris Carter/50	20.00	40.00
Jonathan Baldwin		
DMRM Dan Marino/50	75.00	150.00
Ryan Mallett		
ESMI Emmitt Smith/50	100.00	175.00
Mark Ingram		
FHER Franco Harris/50	25.00	50.00
Evan Royster		
HWAG Hines Ward/25	40.00	80.00
A.J. Green		
MIJJ Michael Irvin/26*	30.00	60.00
Julio Jones		
MIJJR Michael Irvin Red Ink/24*	30.00	80.00
Julio Jones Red Ink		
SYJL Steve Young/50	40.00	80.00
Jake Locker		
WSNF Warren Sapp/25	30.00	60.00
Nick Fairley		

2011 Press Pass Legends Saturday Signatures

RANDOM INSERTS IN PACKS
*EMERALD/39-99: .5X TO 1.2X BASIC AU
*EMERALD/20-25: .6X TO 1.5X BASIC AU
*PLATINUM/20-25: .6X TO 1.5X BASIC AU
*RED INK: .5X TO 1.2X BASIC AU
UNPRICED PRINT PLATE PRINT RUN 1

SSAA Akeem Ayers		
SSAB Ahmad Black	4.00	10.00
SSAB2 Armon Binns	4.00	10.00
SSAD Andy Dalton	12.00	30.00
SSAF Antonio Freeman	5.00	12.00
SSAG A.J. Green	10.00	25.00
SSAP Austin Pettis	4.00	10.00
SSAS Aldon Smith	8.00	20.00
SSAW Aaron Williams	4.00	10.00
SSBB Brandon Burton	4.00	10.00
SSBG Blaine Gabbert	15.00	30.00
SSBJ Bo Jackson SP		
SSCC Cris Carter SP		
SSCH Cameron Heyward	5.00	12.00
SSCK Colin Kaepernick	6.00	15.00
SSCN Cam Newton	30.00	60.00
SSCP Christian Ponder	12.00	30.00
SSDA Darvin Adams	4.00	10.00
SSDB Da'Quan Bowers	5.00	12.00
SSDC Delone Carter	4.00	10.00
SSDH Dan Hampton	6.00	15.00
SSDL Dick LeBeau	15.00	30.00
SSDL2 Dion Lewis	5.00	12.00
SSDL3 Derrick Locke	4.00	10.00
SSDM Dan Marino SP	60.00	120.00
SSDM2 DeMarco Murray	10.00	25.00
SSDM3 DeAndre McDaniel	4.00	10.00
SSDN Drake Nevis	5.00	12.00
SSDS Dane Sanzenbacher	5.00	12.00
SSDT Daniel Thomas	5.00	12.00
(issued via wrapper redemption)		
SSDW D.J. Williams	5.00	12.00
SSEM Ed McCaffrey		
SSER Evan Royster	5.00	12.00
SSES Emmitt Smith SP		
SSFH Franco Harris SP	20.00	40.00
SSGC Gino Cappelletti	5.00	12.00
SSGL Greg Little	5.00	12.00
SSGS Greg Salas	5.00	12.00
SSHW Hines Ward SP	20.00	40.00
SSIW Ickey Woods	5.00	12.00
SSJB Jonathan Baldwin	5.00	12.00
SSJC John Clay	5.00	12.00
SSJJ Julio Jones	12.00	30.00
SSJJ2 Jerrel Jernigan	4.00	10.00
SSJL Jake Locker	20.00	40.00
SSJO Jim Otto	8.00	20.00
SSJP Jim Plunkett SP	8.00	20.00
SSJR Johnny Rodgers	5.00	12.00
SSJR2 Jacquizz Rodgers	6.00	15.00
SSJT Jordan Todman	3.00	8.00
SSJW J.J. Watt	6.00	15.00
SSKH Kendall Hunter	5.00	12.00
SSKM Karl Mecklenburg	5.00	12.00
SSKR Kyle Rudolph	5.00	12.00
SSLS Luke Stocker	4.00	10.00
SSMD Marcell Dareus	5.00	12.00
SSMH Major Harris	6.00	15.00
SSMH2 Mark Herzlich	4.00	10.00
SSMI Michael Irvin SP	20.00	40.00
SSMI2 Mark Ingram	15.00	40.00
SSML Mikel Leshoure	5.00	12.00
SSMR Mike Rozier	5.00	12.00
SSNF Nick Fairley	6.00	15.00
SSNP Niles Paul	5.00	12.00
SSPA Prince Amukamara	5.00	12.00
SSPH Paul Hornung SP	10.00	25.00
SSPK Paul Krause	6.00	15.00
SSRC Randall Cobb	6.00	15.00
SSRH Roy Helu	6.00	15.00
SSRK Ryan Kerrigan	6.00	15.00
SSRM Ryan Mallett	12.00	30.00
SSRM2 Rahim Moore	4.00	10.00
SSRW Ryan Williams	6.00	15.00
SSSP Stephen Paea	5.00	12.00
SSSR Stevan Ridley	5.00	12.00
SSSV Shane Vereen	5.00	12.00
SSSY Steve Young SP	25.00	50.00
SSTB Tedy Bruschi SP	20.00	40.00
SSTD Tandon Doss	4.00	10.00
SSTF Tommie Frazier	6.00	15.00
SSTR Tony Rice	5.00	12.00
SSTS Torrey Smith	5.00	12.00
SSTT Tyrod Taylor	5.00	12.00
SSTT2 Terrence Tolivor	4.00	10.00
SSTY Titus Young	5.00	12.00
SSVM Von Miller	6.00	15.00
SSWB Willie Brown	5.00	12.00
SSWD Warrick Dunn	8.00	20.00
SSWD2 Willie Davis	6.00	15.00
SSWS Warren Sapp SP	15.00	30.00

2011 Press Pass Legends Saturday Swatches Silver

OVERALL JSY STATED ODDS 1:18
*PREMIUM/99: .6X TO 1.5X SILVER JSY
UNPRICED PATCH PRINT RUN 5-10

SSWAD Andy Dalton	5.00	12.00
SSWAG A.J. Green	5.00	12.00
SSWBG Blaine Gabbert	6.00	15.00
SSWDB Da'Quan Bowers	4.00	10.00
SSWDL Derrick Locke	3.00	8.00
SSWJB Jonathan Baldwin	4.00	10.00
SSWJJ Julio Jones	6.00	15.00
SSWJL Jake Locker	8.00	20.00
SSWJR Jacquizz Rodgers	5.00	12.00
SSWKR Kyle Rudolph	5.00	12.00
SSWNP Niles Paul	5.00	12.00
SSWPA Prince Amukamara	5.00	12.00
SSWRH Roy Helu	5.00	12.00
SSWRM Ryan Mallett	6.00	15.00
SSWSR Stevan Ridley	4.00	10.00
SSWSV Shane Vereen	3.00	8.00
SSWTS Torrey Smith	4.00	10.00
SSWTT Terrence Toliver	3.00	8.00

2008 Press Pass Legends Bowl Edition

This set was released on December 26, 2008. The base set consists of 100 cards.

STATED PRINT RUN 299 SER.#'d SETS
UNPRICED PRINT PLATE PRINT RUN 1

1 Troy Aikman	2.50	6.00
2 Tedy Bruschi	1.50	4.00
3 Earl Campbell	2.00	5.00
4 Cris Collinsworth	1.50	4.00
5 Bill Cowher	2.00	5.00
6 Eric Dickerson	1.50	4.00
7 Glenn Dorsey	1.00	2.50
8 Brett Favre	4.00	10.00
9 Joe Flacco	3.00	8.00
10 Matt Forte	1.50	4.00
11 Tommie Frazier	1.50	4.00
12 DeSean Jackson	2.00	5.00
13 Chris Johnson	2.50	6.00
14 Jimmy Johnson	1.50	4.00
15 Felix Jones	1.50	4.00
16 Lee Roy Jordan	1.50	4.00
17 Jim Kelly	2.00	5.00
18 Jack Lambert	2.00	5.00
19 Chris Long	1.00	2.50
20 Darren McFadden	2.50	6.00
21 Rashard Mendenhall	2.00	5.00
22 Joe Montana	5.00	12.00
23 Warren Moon	2.50	6.00
24 Ray Rice	2.00	5.00
25 Eddie Royal	1.00	2.50
26 Matt Ryan	4.00	10.00
27 Gale Sayers	2.50	6.00
28 Mike Singletary	2.00	5.00
29 Steve Slaton	1.00	2.50
30 Kevin Smith	1.00	2.50
31 Chris Spielman	1.50	4.00
32 Ken Stabler	2.00	5.00
33 Jonathan Stewart	1.50	4.00
34 Barry Switzer	2.00	5.00
35 Herschel Walker	1.50	4.00
36 Steve Young	2.50	6.00
37 Derrick Brooks	1.25	3.00
38 Joey Galloway	1.25	3.00
39 Frank Gore	1.25	3.00
40 Paul Hornung	2.00	5.00
41 Sonny Jurgensen	1.50	4.00
42 Ray Lewis	1.50	4.00
43 George Rogers	1.25	3.00
44 Dick Butkus	2.50	6.00
45 Cris Carter	2.00	5.00
46 Bob Griese	2.00	5.00
47 Bo Jackson	2.50	6.00
48 Billy Kilmer	1.50	4.00
49 Floyd Little	1.25	3.00
50 Tommy McDonald	1.50	4.00
51 Tom Rathman	1.50	4.00
52 Billy Sims	1.50	4.00
53 Steve Spurrier	2.00	5.00
54 Aaron Kampman	1.25	3.00
55 Mike Rozier	1.25	3.00
56 Y.A. Tittle	2.00	5.00
57 Craig Morton	1.25	3.00
58 Hugh McElhenny	1.25	3.00
59 Roger Craig	1.50	4.00
60 Ty Detmer	1.25	3.00
61 Craig James	1.50	4.00
62 Tommy Nobis	1.25	3.00
63 Pat Sullivan	1.25	3.00
64 Joe Theismann	2.00	5.00
65 Zach Thomas	1.25	3.00
66 Danny Wuerffel	1.25	3.00
67 Raymond Berry	1.50	4.00
68 Rocky Bleier	1.50	4.00
69 Billy Cannon	1.25	3.00
70 Anthony Carter	1.25	3.00
71 John Jefferson	1.25	3.00
72 Johnny Rodgers	1.25	3.00
73 Charles White	1.25	3.00
74 Sam Huff	1.50	4.00
75 Paul Warfield	1.50	4.00
76 Donnie Avery	.75	2.00
77 Davone Bess	1.00	2.50
78 John David Booty	.75	2.00
79 Colt Brennan	1.00	2.50
80 Jamaal Charles	1.50	4.00
81 Harry Douglas	.75	2.00
82 Chad Henne	1.00	2.50
83 Malcolm Kelly	.75	2.00
84 Josh Morgan	1.00	2.50
85 Jordy Nelson	1.25	3.00
86 Limas Sweed	1.00	2.50
87 Devin Thomas	.75	2.00
88 James Lofton	1.25	3.00
89 Donnie Avery	.75	2.00
90 Joe Flacco	3.00	8.00
91 Matt Forte	1.50	4.00
92 DeSean Jackson	2.00	5.00
93 Chris Johnson	2.50	6.00
94 Felix Jones	1.50	4.00
95 Darren McFadden	2.50	6.00
96 Eddie Royal	1.00	2.50
97 Matt Ryan	4.00	10.00
98 Steve Slaton	1.00	2.50
99 Kevin Smith	1.00	2.50
100 Jonathan Stewart	1.50	4.00

2008 Press Pass Legends Bowl Edition 20 Yard Line Red

*VETS: .5X TO 1.2X BASIC CARDS
*ROOKIES: .4X TO 1X BASIC CARDS
*RETIRED: .5X TO 1.2X BASIC CARDS
STATED PRINT RUN 150 SER.#'d SETS

2008 Press Pass Legends Bowl Edition 15 Yard Line Blue

*ACTIVE: .6X TO 1.5X BASIC CARDS
*ROOKIES: .5X TO 1.2X BASIC CARDS
*RETIRED: .6X TO 1.5X BASIC CARDS
STATED PRINT RUN 99 SER.#'d SETS

2008 Press Pass Legends Bowl Edition 10 Yard Line Holofoil

*ACTIVE: .6X TO 1.5X BASIC CARDS
*ROOKIES: .5X TO 1.2X BASIC CARDS
*RETIRED: .6X TO 1.5X BASIC CARDS
STATED PRINT RUN 75 SER.#'d SETS

2008 Press Pass Legends Bowl Edition 5 Yard Line Gold

*ACTIVE: .8X TO 2X BASIC CARDS
*ROOKIES: .6X TO 1.5X BASIC CARDS
*RETIRED: .8X TO 2X BASIC CARDS
STATED PRINT RUN 50 SER.#'d SETS

2008 Press Pass Legends Bowl Edition Goal Line Emerald

*ACTIVE: 1X TO 2.5X BASIC CARDS
*ROOKIES: .8X TO 2X BASIC CARDS
*RETIRED: 1X TO 2.5X BASIC CARDS
STATED PRINT RUN 25 SER.#'d SETS

2008 Press Pass Legends Bowl Edition Touchdown Platinum

UNPRICED PLATINUM PRINT RUN 1

2008 Press Pass Legends Bowl Edition Autographs

STATED PRINT RUN 15-296
UNPRICED PRINT PLATE PRINT RUN 1
SERIAL #'d UNDER 19 NOT PRICED

AC Anthony Carter/100	6.00	15.00
AK Aaron Kampman/150	15.00	40.00
BC Bill Cowher/50	15.00	30.00
BC2 Billy Cannon/185	12.00	30.00
BF Brett Favre/19	100.00	200.00
BG Bob Griese/35	12.00	30.00
BK Billy Kilmer/199	5.00	12.00
BS Billy Sims/48	10.00	25.00
BS2 Barry Switzer/75	25.00	50.00
CC2 Cris Collinsworth/50	8.00	20.00
CJ Craig James/160	5.00	12.00
CM Craig Morton/244	6.00	15.00
CS Chris Spielman/125	10.00	25.00
CW Charles White/100	6.00	15.00
DB Derrick Brooks/235	6.00	15.00
DB2 Dick Butkus/25	30.00	60.00
DM Darren McFadden/225	12.00	30.00
DW Danny Wuerffel/68	12.00	30.00
EC Earl Campbell/175 EXCH		
ED Eric Dickerson/71	20.00	40.00
FG Frank Gore/100	8.00	20.00
FL Floyd Little/85	6.00	15.00
GR George Rogers/100	8.00	20.00
HM Hugh McElhenny/150	8.00	20.00
JG Joey Galloway/296	5.00	12.00
JJ Jimmy Johnson/100	8.00	20.00
JJ John Jefferson/145	5.00	12.00
JK Jack Lambert/46	25.00	50.00
JL James Lofton/55	6.00	15.00
JM Joe Montana/40	60.00	120.00
JP Jim Plunkett/125	8.00	20.00
JR Johnny Rodgers/29	8.00	20.00
JT Joe Theismann/65	10.00	25.00
LJ Lee Roy Jordan/150	8.00	20.00
MR Mike Rozier/91	10.00	25.00
MS Mike Singletary/25	12.00	30.00
PH Paul Hornung/60	10.00	25.00
PS Pat Sullivan/30	8.00	20.00
PW Paul Warfield/150	8.00	20.00
RB Raymond Berry/95	6.00	15.00
RB2 Rocky Bleier/150	8.00	20.00
RC Roger Craig/98	8.00	20.00
RL Ray Lewis/110	40.00	80.00
SH Sam Huff/100	10.00	25.00
TB Tedy Bruschi/25		
TD Ty Detmer/148	5.00	12.00
TF Tommie Frazier/100	10.00	25.00
TM Tommy McDonald/50	10.00	25.00
TN Tommy Nobis/99	6.00	15.00
TR Tom Rathman/150	10.00	25.00
WM Warren Moon/25	15.00	40.00
ZT Zach Thomas/97	10.00	25.00

2008 Press Pass Legends Bowl Edition Autographs Emerald

*EMERALD: .5X TO 1.2X BASIC AUTOS
EMERALD PRINT RUN 4-99
SERIAL #'d UNDER 20 NOT PRICED

JP Jim Plunkett/25	15.00	30.00
RL Ray Lewis/25	75.00	125.00

2008 Press Pass Legends Bowl Edition Autographs Onyx

*ONYX: .6X TO 1.5X BASIC AUTOS
ONYX PRINT RUN 1-25
SERIAL #'d UNDER 10 NOT PRICED

2008 Press Pass Legends Bowl Edition Autographs Sapphire

*SAPPHIRE: .5X TO 1.2X BASIC AUTOS
SAPPHIRE PRINT RUN 10-170
SERIAL #'d UNDER 20 NOT PRICED

DB2 Dick Butkus/25	30.00	60.00
JM Joe Montana/20	60.00	120.00
RL Ray Lewis/50	40.00	100.00

2008 Press Pass Legends Bowl Edition Bowl Busters

STATED PRINT RUN 250 SER.#'d SETS
UNPRICED PRINT PLATE PRINT RUN 1

BB1 Tommie Frazier	2.00	5.00
BB2 John Jefferson	1.50	4.00
BB4 Herschel Walker	2.00	5.00
BB5 Bob Griese	2.50	6.00
BB6 Cris Carter	2.50	6.00
BB7 Bo Jackson	3.00	8.00
BB8 Billy Sims	2.00	5.00
BB9 Steve Spurrier	2.50	6.00
BB10 Joe Theismann	2.50	6.00
BB11 Anthony Carter	1.50	4.00
BB12 Johnny Rodgers	1.50	4.00

2008 Press Pass Legends Bowl Edition Bowl Busters Autographs

STATED PRINT RUN 15-150
*SAPPHIRE: .5X TO 1.2X BASIC AUTOS
SAPPHIRE PRINT RUN 25-75
*EMERALD: .5X TO 1.2X BASIC AUTOS
EMERALD PRINT RUN 5-50
*ONYX: .6X TO 1.5X BASIC AUTOS
ONYX PRINT RUN 1-25
SERIAL #'d UNDER 20 NOT PRICED

AC Anthony Carter/150	6.00	15.00
BG Bob Griese/50	12.00	30.00
BS Billy Sims/100	8.00	20.00
CC Cris Carter/75	35.00	60.00
EC Earl Campbell/50	20.00	40.00
JJ John Jefferson/100	5.00	12.00
JR Johnny Rodgers/100	8.00	20.00

JT Joe Theismann/124 8.00 20.00
SS Steve Spurrier/50 25.00 50.00

2008 Press Pass Legends Bowl Edition Bringing Down the Goal Posts

STATED PRINT RUN 250 SER.#'d SETS
UNPRICED PRINT PLATE PRINT RUN 1
BDGP1 Jim Kelly 2.50 6.00
BDGP2 Lee Roy Jordan 2.00 5.00
BDGP3 Bill Cowher 2.00 5.00
BDGP4 Tom Rathman 2.00 5.00
BDGP5 Tommy McDonald 2.00 5.00
BDGP6 Tommy Nobis 1.50 4.00
BDGP7 Roger Craig 2.00 5.00
BDGP8 Charles White 1.50 4.00
BDGP9 Troy Aikman 3.00 8.00

2008 Press Pass Legends Bowl Edition Bringing Down the Goal Posts Autographs

STATED PRINT RUN 10-299
*SAPPHIRE/20-199: .5X TO 1.2X BASIC AUTOS
SAPPHIRE PRINT RUN 8-199
*EMERALD/20-99: .5X TO 1.2X BASIC AUTOS
EMERALD PRINT RUN 5-99
*ONYX/25: .6X TO 1.5X BASIC AUTOS
ONYX PRINT RUN 1-25
SERIAL #'d UNDER 20 NOT PRICED
BC Bill Cowher/50 15.00 30.00
CW Charles White/150 6.00 15.00
JL James Lofton/120 5.00 12.00
LJ Lee Roy Jordan/299 8.00 20.00
RC Roger Craig/120 8.00 20.00
TM Tommy McDonald/90 6.00 15.00
TN Tommy Nobis/125 6.00 15.00
TR Tom Rathman/175 10.00 25.00

2008 Press Pass Legends Bowl Edition Dream Matchup

STATED PRINT RUN 250 SER.#'d SETS
UNPRICED PRINT PLATE PRINT RUN 1
DM1 Joe Montana 6.00 15.00
Brett Favre
DM2 Steve Young 3.00 8.00
Troy Aikman
DM3 Barry Switzer 3.00 8.00
Jimmy Johnson
DM4 Warren Moon 3.00 8.00
Jim Kelly
DM5 Jack Lambert 2.50 6.00
Bill Cowher
DM6 Gale Sayers 3.00 8.00
Darren McFadden
DM7 Chris Spielman 2.00 5.00
Tedy Bruschi
DM8 Eric Dickerson 3.00 8.00
Bo Jackson
DM9 Earl Campbell 2.50 6.00
Billy Sims
DM10 Dick Butkus 3.00 8.00
Mike Singletary
DM11 Y.A. Tittle 2.50 6.00
Ken Stabler

2008 Press Pass Legends Bowl Edition Dream Matchup Autographs

STATED PRINT RUN 12-50
*ONYX/25: .5X TO 1.2X BASIC DUAL AU
ONYX PRINT RUN 10-25
SERIAL #'d UNDER 20 NOT PRICED
BSJJ Barry Switzer/24 Red Ink 60.00 100.00
Jimmy Johnson Blue Ink
ECBS Earl Campbell/25 Red Ink 40.00 80.00
Billy Sims Red Ink
JLBC Jack Lambert/25
Bill Cowher
YTKS Y.A. Tittle/50 25.00 50.00
Ken Stabler Red Ink

2008 Press Pass Legends Bowl Edition Institutional Icons

STATED PRINT RUN 250 SER.#'d SETS
UNPRICED PRINT PLATE PRINT RUN 1
II1 Jimmy Johnson 2.50 6.00
Jim Kelly
II2 Lee Roy Jordan 2.50 6.00
Ken Stabler
II3 Roger Craig 2.50 6.00
Tommie Frazier
Mike Rozier
Johnny Rodgers
II4 Tommy McDonald 2.50 6.00
Billy Sims
Barry Switzer
II5 Bo Jackson 3.00 8.00
Pat Sullivan
II6 Steve Spurrier 2.50 6.00
Danny Wuerffel
II7 Steve Young 3.00 8.00
Ty Detmer
II8 Y.A. Tittle 2.50 6.00
Billy Cannon
II9 Billy Kilmer 3.00 8.00
Troy Aikman

2008 Press Pass Legends Bowl Edition Institutional Icons Autographs

STATED PRINT RUN 10-50
*ONYX/25: .5X TO 1.2X BASIC DUAL AU
ONYX PRINT RUN 10-25
SERIAL #'d UNDER 20 NOT PRICED
BKTA Billy Kilmer/15 40.00 80.00
Troy Aikman
CFRR Roger Craig/48 Red 50.00 100.00
Tommie Frazier
Mike Rozier Red
Johnny Rodgers
LJKS Lee Roy Jordan/50 25.00 60.00
Ken Stabler
MSS Tommy McDonald/50 40.00 80.00
Billy Sims
Barry Switzer
SSDW Steve Spurrier/50 40.00 80.00
Danny Wuerffel
SYTD Steve Young/25 30.00 60.00
Ty Detmer
YTBC Y.A. Tittle/50 Blue 40.00 80.00
Billy Cannon Blue
YTBCR Y.A. Tittle/50 Red 50.00 100.00
Billy Cannon Red

2008 Press Pass Legends Bowl Edition MVP

STATED PRINT RUN 250 SER.#'d SETS
UNPRICED PRINT PLATE PRINT RUN 1
MVP1 Chris Spielman 2.00 5.00
MVP2 Tedy Bruschi 2.00 5.00
MVP3 Steve Young 3.00 8.00
MVP4 Tommie Frazier 2.00 5.00
MVP5 Jim Kelly 2.50 6.00
MVP6 Warren Moon 2.50 6.00
MVP7 Ken Stabler 2.50 6.00
MVP8 Cris Collinsworth 2.00 5.00
MVP9 Bo Jackson 3.00 8.00
MVP10 Steve Spurrier 2.50 6.00
MVP11 Y.A. Tittle 2.50 6.00
MVP12 Pat Sullivan 1.50 4.00
MVP13 Danny Wuerffel 1.50 4.00
MVP14 Charles White 1.50 4.00
MVP15 John Jefferson 1.50 4.00

2008 Press Pass Legends Bowl Edition MVP Autographs

STATED PRINT RUN 15-150
*SAPPHIRE/15-100: .5X TO 1.2X BASIC AUTO
SAPPHIRE PRINT RUN 10-100
*EMERALD/20-60: .5X TO 1.2X BASIC AUTOS
EMERALD PRINT RUN 5-60
*ONYX/25: .6X TO 1.5X BASIC AUTOS
ONYX PRINT RUN 1-25
SERIAL #'d UNDER 20 NOT PRICED
CC Cris Collinsworth/75 6.00 15.00
CS Chris Spielman/150 10.00 25.00
CW Charles White/148 5.00 12.00
DW Danny Wuerffel/150 10.00 25.00
JJ John Jefferson/100 6.00 15.00
KS Ken Stabler/24 20.00 40.00
PS Pat Sullivan/150 5.00 12.00
SS Steve Spurrier/50 50.00 80.00
SY Steve Young/50 35.00 60.00
TB Tedy Bruschi/25 30.00 50.00
TF Tommie Frazier/115 10.00 25.00
WM Warren Moon/25 20.00 50.00
YT Y.A. Tittle/20 20.00 40.00

2008 Press Pass Legends Bowl Edition Top 25

STATED PRINT RUN 250 SER.#'d SETS
UNPRICED PRINT PLATE PRINT RUN 1
TT1 Brett Favre 6.00 15.00
TT2 Herschel Walker 2.00 5.00
TT3 Steve Young 3.00 8.00
TT4 Jim Kelly 2.50 6.00
TT5 Warren Moon 3.00 8.00
TT6 George Rogers 1.50 4.00
TT7 Paul Hornung 2.50 6.00
TT8 Bo Jackson 3.00 8.00
TT9 Billy Sims 2.00 5.00
TT10 Dick Butkus 3.00 8.00
TT11 Floyd Little 1.50 4.00
TT12 Mike Rozier 1.50 4.00
TT13 Ty Detmer 1.50 4.00
TT14 Anthony Carter 1.50 4.00
TT15 Johnny Rodgers 1.50 4.00
TT16 Darren McFadden 3.00 8.00
TT17 Matt Ryan 4.00 10.00
TT18 Felix Jones 2.00 5.00
TT19 Mike Singletary 1.25 3.00
TT20 Troy Aikman 3.00 8.00
TT23 Gale Sayers 3.00 8.00

2008 Press Pass Legends Bowl Edition Top 25 Autographs

STATED PRINT RUN 15-174
*SAPPHIRE/20-84: .5X TO 1.2X BASIC AUTO
SAPPHIRE PRINT RUN 8-84
*EMERALD/20-52: .5X TO 1.2X BASIC AUTOS
EMERALD PRINT RUN 1-52
*ONYX/25: .6X TO 1.5X BASIC AUTOS
ONYX PRINT RUN 1-25
SERIAL #'d UNDER 18 NOT PRICED
AC Anthony Carter/155 5.00 12.00
BF Brett Favre/18 100.00 200.00
BS Billy Sims/100 8.00 20.00
DB Dick Butkus/25 30.00 60.00
EC Earl Campbell/75 15.00 30.00
FL Floyd Little/174 6.00 15.00
GR George Rogers/115 8.00 20.00
GS Gale Sayers/25 25.00 50.00
JK Jim Kelly/15 25.00 50.00
JR Johnny Rodgers/100 6.00 15.00
MR Mike Rozier/145 8.00 20.00
MS Mike Singletary/68 10.00 25.00
PH Paul Hornung/100 10.00 25.00
SY Steve Young/46 35.00 60.00
TD Ty Detmer/150 5.00 12.00
WM Warren Moon/35 15.00 40.00

2010 Press Pass Legends National Convention Silver

SILVER PRINT RUN 99 SER.#'d SETS
*GOLD/25: .6X TO 1.5X SILVER/99
NE1 Tim Tebow 15.00 40.00
NE2 Sam Bradford 15.00 40.00
NE3 C.J. Spiller 6.00 15.00
NE4 Jimmy Clausen 4.00 10.00

2010 Press Pass PE

COMPLETE SET (50) 7.50 20.00
1 Danario Alexander .30 .75
2 Arrelious Benn .30 .75
3 Jahvid Best .50 1.25
4 NaVorro Bowman .30 .75
5 Sam Bradford 1.25 3.00
6 Dezmon Briscoe .25 .60
7 Antonio Brown .50 1.25
8 Jarrett Brown .30 .75
9 Dez Bryant 1.00 2.50
10 Sean Canfield .25 .60
11 Daryll Clark .30 .75
12 Jimmy Clausen .30 .75
13 Eric Decker .40 1.00
14 Dorin Dickerson .20 .50
15 Anthony Dixon .30 .75
16 Jonathan Dwyer .30 .75
17 Jacoby Ford .30 .75
18 Toby Gerhart .30 .75
19 Mardy Gilyard .30 .75
20 Jermaine Gresham .40 1.00
21 Rob Gronkowski .75 2.00
22 Joe Haden .30 .75
23 Montario Hardesty .30 .75
24 Aaron Hernandez .50 1.25
25 Mike Kafka .30 .75
26 Brandon LaFell .30 .75
27 Dan LeFevour .30 .75
28 Ryan Mathews .60 1.50
29 Rolando McClain .30 .75
30 Dexter McCluster .30 .75
31 Anthony McCoy .25 .60
32 Gerald McCoy .30 .75
33 Joe McKnight .30 .75
34 Derrick Morgan .25 .60
35 Jason Pierre-Paul .50 1.25
36 Tony Pike .30 .75
37 Andre Roberts .30 .75
38 Zac Robinson .25 .60
39 Charles Scott .25 .60
40 Jordan Shipley .30 .75
41 Jevan Snead .30 .75
42 C.J. Spiller .50 1.25
43 Ndamukong Suh .60 1.50
44 Golden Tate .30 .75
45 Tim Tebow 1.25 3.00
46 Demaryius Thomas .40 1.00
47 Earl Thomas .30 .75
48 Donovan Warren .30 .75
49 Damian Williams .30 .75
50 Mike Williams .50 1.25

2010 Press Pass PE Blue

*BLUE: 1X TO 2.5X BASIC CARDS
ONE BLUE PER RETAIL PACK

2010 Press Pass PE Gold

*GOLD: 1.2X TO 3X BASIC CARDS
STATED ODDS 1:4 HOBBY

2010 Press Pass PE Class of 2010

COMPLETE SET (10) 6.00 15.00
STATED ODDS 1:4 HOB
CL1 Jahvid Best 1.00 2.50
CL2 C.J. Spiller 1.00 2.50
CL3 Tim Tebow 2.50 6.00
CL4 Ryan Mathews 1.25 3.00
CL5 Arrelious Benn .60 1.50
CL6 Jimmy Clausen .60 1.50
CL7 Golden Tate .60 1.50
CL8 Dez Bryant 2.00 5.00
CL9 Sam Bradford 2.50 6.00
CL10 Toby Gerhart .60 1.50

2010 Press Pass PE Class of 2010 Autographs

STATED PRINT RUN 49-199
*HOC RED/25: .6X TO 1.5X BASIC AU/100-199
*HOC RED/25: .5X TO 1.2X BASIC AU/49
HOC PRINT RUN 25 SER.#'d SETS
CLAB Arrelious Benn/150 5.00 12.00
CLBL Brandon LaFell/199 5.00 12.00
CLCS C.J. Spiller/100 20.00 50.00
CLDB Dez Bryant/100 25.00 50.00
CLGT Golden Tate/199 5.00 12.00
CLJC Jimmy Clausen/49 10.00 25.00
CLRM Ryan Mathews/199 10.00 25.00
CLSB Sam Bradford/150 40.00 100.00
CLTG Toby Gerhart/199 10.00 25.00
CLTT Tim Tebow/199 60.00 120.00

2010 Press Pass PE Face To Face

COMPLETE SET (20) 8.00 20.00
STATED ODDS 1:2 HOB
FF1 Jahvid Best .75 2.00
Joe McKnight
FF2 Golden Tate .50 1.25
Damian Williams
FF3 Jimmy Clausen .50 1.25
Toby Gerhart
FF4 C.J. Spiller .75 2.00
Andre Roberts
FF5 Tony Pike 1.00 2.50
Ryan Mathews
FF6 Mardy Gilyard .50 1.25
Arrelious Benn
FF7 Dezmon Briscoe .50 1.25
Danario Alexander
FF8 Brandon LaFell .75 2.00
Aaron Hernandez
FF9 Tim Tebow 2.00 5.00
Jevan Snead
FF10 Freddie Barnes .75 2.00
Antonio Brown
FF11 Zac Robinson 2.00 5.00
Sam Bradford
FF12 Jonathan Dwyer .50 1.25
Javarris James
FF13 Demaryius Thomas .60 1.50
Jacoby Ford
FF14 Anthony Dixon .50 1.25
Dexter McCluster
FF15 Dez Bryant 1.50 4.00
Jordan Shipley
FF16 Sean Canfield .40 1.00
Chris McGaha
FF17 Rolando McClain .50 1.25
Montario Hardesty
FF18 Eric Decker .75 2.00
Mike Williams
FF19 James Starks .75 2.00
Dan LeFevour
FF20 Ndamukong Suh 1.00 2.50
Gerald McCoy

2010 Press Pass PE Game Day Gear Jerseys Silver

OVERALL JSY ODDS 1:6.7 HOB
*GOLD/199: .5X TO 1.2X SILVER JSY
GOLD PRINT RUN 199 SER.#'d SETS
*PREMIUM/25: 1X TO 2.5X SILVER JSY
PREMIUM PRINT RUN 25 SER.#'d SETS
*SILVER HOLO/99: .6X TO 1.5X SILVER JSY
SILVER HOLOFOIL PRINT RUN 99
GDGAB Arrelious Benn 4.00 10.00
GDGBL Brandon LaFell 4.00 10.00
GDGDA Danario Alexander 4.00 10.00
GDGDB Dezmon Briscoe 4.00 10.00
GDGDM Dexter McCluster 4.00 10.00
GDGDW Damian Williams 3.00 8.00
GDGED Eric Decker 4.00 10.00
GDGGT Golden Tate 4.00 10.00
GDGJB Jahvid Best 5.00 12.00
GDGJC Jimmy Clausen 6.00 15.00
GDGJF Jacoby Ford 4.00 10.00
GDGJJ Javarris James 3.00 8.00
GDGJM Joe McKnight 4.00 10.00
GDGJS Jevan Snead 4.00 10.00
GDGMH Montario Hardesty 4.00 10.00
GDGMK Mike Kafka 3.00 8.00
GDGMW Mike Williams 4.00 10.00
GDGNB NaVorro Bowman 4.00 10.00
GDGNS Ndamukong Suh 6.00 15.00
GDGSB Sam Bradford 6.00 15.00
GDGSC Sean Canfield 3.00 8.00
GDGSJ Stafon Johnson 4.00 10.00
GDGTG Toby Gerhart 4.00 10.00
GDGTT Tim Tebow 10.00 25.00
GDGZR Zac Robinson 4.00 10.00

2010 Press Pass PE Game Day Gear Jerseys Autographs

STATED PRINT RUN 25 SER.#'d SETS
GDGAB Arrelious Benn 25.00 50.00
GDGBL Brandon LaFell 25.00 50.00
GDGGT Golden Tate 30.00 80.00
GDGJB Jahvid Best 50.00 100.00
GDGJJ Javarris James 25.00 50.00
GDGJS Jevan Snead 25.00 50.00
GDGMH Montario Hardesty 30.00 60.00
GDGSB Sam Bradford 150.00 300.00
GDGSC Sean Canfield 20.00 40.00
GDGTG Toby Gerhart 30.00 60.00
GDGTT Tim Tebow 200.00 400.00

2010 Press Pass PE Graduating Class Autographs

STATED PRINT RUN 25 SER.#'d SETS
CSJB C.J. Spiller 60.00 120.00
Jahvid Best
DBAB Dez Bryant EXCH 50.00 100.00
Arrelious Benn
DTBL DeMaryius Thomas/20* 15.00 40.00
Brandon LaFell
JCGT Jimmy Clausen 20.00 50.00
Golden Tate
TTRM Tim Tebow 75.00 150.00
Ryan Mathews
DTBL2 DeMaryius Thomas Red/5*
Brandon LaFell Red

2010 Press Pass PE Headliners

COMPLETE SET (34) 10.00 25.00
ONE PER HOBBY PACK
HL1 Rolando McClain .50 1.25
HL2 Jahvid Best .75 2.00
HL3 Dan LeFevour .50 1.25
HL4 Mardy Gilyard .50 1.25
HL5 Tony Pike .50 1.25
HL6 C.J. Spiller .75 2.00
HL7 Joe Haden .50 1.25
HL8 Tim Tebow 2.00 5.00
HL9 Ryan Mathews 1.00 2.50
HL10 Jonathan Dwyer .50 1.25
HL11 Derrick Morgan .40 1.00
HL12 Demaryius Thomas .60 1.50
HL13 Arrelious Benn .50 1.25
HL14 Dezmon Briscoe .40 1.00
HL15 Brandon LaFell .50 1.25
HL16 Eric Decker .60 1.50
HL17 Anthony Dixon .50 1.25
HL18 Ndamukong Suh 1.00 2.50
HL19 Jimmy Clausen .50 1.25
HL20 Golden Tate .50 1.25
HL21 Dez Bryant 1.50 4.00
HL22 Sam Bradford 2.00 5.00
HL23 Jermaine Gresham .60 1.50
HL24 Gerald McCoy .50 1.25
HL25 Dexter McCluster .50 1.25
HL26 Jason Pierre-Paul .75 2.00
HL27 Toby Gerhart .50 1.25
HL28 Mike Williams .75 2.00
HL29 Montario Hardesty .50 1.25
HL30 Jordan Shipley .50 1.25
HL31 Joe McKnight .50 1.25
HL32 Damian Williams .50 1.25
HL33 Jarrett Brown .50 1.25
HL34 Tim Tebow CL 1.50 4.00

2010 Press Pass PE Sideline Signatures Gold

OVERALL AUTO ODDS 1:2.9 HOB
*GOLD RED INK/20-346: .5X TO 1.2X GOLD AU
GOLD RED INK ANNC'D PRINT RUN 2-346
*EMERALD/20-25: .8X TO 2X GOLD AUTO
EMERALD PRINT RUN 9-25
*EMER.RED INK/19--25: .5X TO 1.2X EMER.AU
EMERALD RED INK ANNC'D PRINT RUN 1-25
SSAB Arrelious Benn 4.00 10.00
SSAB2 Antonio Brown 6.00 15.00
SSAD Anthony Dixon 4.00 10.00
SSAH Aaron Hernandez 6.00 15.00
SSAM Anthony McCoy 3.00 8.00
SSAR Andre Roberts 4.00 10.00
SSAV Alterraun Verner 4.00 10.00
SSBG Brandon Ghee 3.00 8.00
SSBL Brandon LaFell 4.00 10.00
SSBS Bill Stull 3.00 8.00
SSCM Chris McGaha 2.50 6.00
SSCS C.J. Spiller 25.00 50.00
SSCS2 Charles Scott 3.00 8.00
SSCW Corey Wootton 3.00 8.00
SSDA Danario Alexander 4.00 10.00
SSDB Dez Bryant EXCH 20.00 50.00
SSDB2 Dezmon Briscoe 3.00 8.00
SSDC Daryll Clark 4.00 10.00
SSDD Dorin Dickerson 2.50 6.00
SSDL Dan LeFevour 4.00 10.00
SSDM Dexter McCluster 4.00 10.00
SSDM2 Derrick Morgan 3.00 8.00
SSDT Demaryius Thomas 5.00 12.00
SSDW Damian Williams 4.00 10.00
SSDW2 Donovan Warren 4.00 10.00
SSED Eric Decker 5.00 12.00
SSED2 Ed Dickson 4.00 10.00
SSET Earl Thomas 4.00 10.00
SSFB Freddie Barnes 3.00 8.00
SSGH Greg Hardy 3.00 8.00
SSGM Gerald McCoy 4.00 10.00
SSGS George Selvie 3.00 8.00
SSGT Golden Tate 4.00 10.00
SSJB Jahvid Best 15.00 40.00
SSJB2 Jarrett Brown 4.00 10.00
SSJC Jimmy Clausen
SSJD Jonathan Dwyer 4.00 10.00
SSJF Jacoby Ford 6.00 15.00
SSJG Jermaine Gresham 5.00 12.00
SSJH Joe Haden 4.00 10.00
SSJH2 Jerry Hughes 4.00 10.00
SSJJ Javarris James 4.00 10.00
SSJM Joe McKnight 4.00 10.00
SSJPP Jason Pierre-Paul 6.00 15.00
SSJS Jordan Shipley 4.00 10.00
SSJS2 James Starks 10.00 25.00
SSJS3 Jevan Snead 4.00 10.00
SSJW Joe Webb 4.00 10.00
SSJW2 Jeremy Williams 2.50 6.00
SSJW3 Juice Williams 3.00 8.00
SSLB LeGarrette Blount 6.00 15.00
SSMG Mardy Gilyard 4.00 10.00
SSMH Montario Hardesty 4.00 10.00
SSMK Mike Kafka 4.00 10.00
SSMW Mike Williams 6.00 15.00
SSNB NaVorro Bowman 4.00 10.00
SSNR Naaman Roosevelt 4.00 10.00
SSNS Ndamukong Suh 15.00 40.00
SSRG Rob Gronkowski 8.00 20.00
SSRM Ryan Mathews 15.00 40.00
SSRM2 Rolando McClain 4.00 10.00
SSRS Rusty Smith 8.00 20.00
SSSB Sam Bradford 40.00 100.00
SSSC Sean Canfield 3.00 8.00
SSSH Shay Hodge 3.00 8.00
SSSJ Stafon Johnson 4.00 10.00
SSSL Sean Lee 4.00 10.00
SSSW Sean Weatherspoon 4.00 10.00
SSTG Toby Gerhart 4.00 10.00
SSTL Thaddeus Lewis 3.00 8.00
SSTP Tony Pike 4.00 10.00
SSTT Tim Tebow 60.00 120.00
SSZR Zac Robinson 3.00 8.00

2010 Press Pass PE Sideline Signatures Ruby

*RUBY/120-150: .5X TO 1.2X GOLD AU
RUBY PRINT RUN 25-150
*RUBY RED INK/20-92: .5X TO 1.2X RUBY AU
RUBY RED INK ANNC'D PRINT RUN 1-92
SSCS C.J. Spiller/50 30.00 60.00
SSJC Jimmy Clausen/25 20.00 50.00
SSSB Sam Bradford/50 50.00 120.00
SSTT Tim Tebow/150 60.00 120.00

2001 Press Pass SE

This 45-card set featured some of the top draft picks from the 2001 NFL Draft. The base set design had an action photo of the player with white borders on the sides and it was highlighted with silver foil markings on its borders. The card backs had their college statistics along with a summary of their abilities that will guide them in the NFL.

COMPLETE SET (45) 20.00 40.00
1 Michael Vick 1.25 3.00
2 Drew Brees 2.00 5.00
3 Quincy Carter .25 .60
4 Marques Tuiasosopo .25 .60
5 Chris Weinke .25 .60
6 Sage Rosenfels .30 .75
7 Jesse Palmer .25 .60
8 Mike McMahon .25 .60
9 Josh Booty .25 .60
10 Josh Heupel .30 .75
11 LaDainian Tomlinson 1.00 2.50
12 Deuce McAllister .30 .75
13 Michael Bennett .25 .60
14 Anthony Thomas .30 .75
15 LaMont Jordan .30 .75
16 Travis Henry .25 .60
17 James Jackson .20 .50
18 Kevan Barlow .25 .60
19 Travis Minor .25 .60
20 Rudi Johnson .30 .75
21 David Terrell .25 .60
22 Koren Robinson .25 .60
23 Rod Gardner .25 .60
24 Santana Moss .40 1.00
25 Freddie Mitchell .20 .50
26 Reggie Wayne .60 1.50
27 Quincy Morgan .25 .60
28 Chris Chambers .30 .75
29 Robert Ferguson .30 .75
30 Chad Johnson .50 1.25
31 Snoop Minnis .20 .50
32 Todd Heap .30 .75
33 Steve Hutchinson .30 .75
34 Leonard Davis .30 .75
35 Kenyatta Walker .20 .50
36 Justin Smith .30 .75
37 Andre Carter .25 .60
38 Jamal Reynolds .20 .50
39 Gerard Warren .25 .60
40 Richard Seymour .30 .75
41 Damione Lewis .25 .60
42 Jamar Fletcher .20 .50
43 Nate Clements .25 .60
44 Derrick Gibson .20 .50
45 David Terrell CL .20 .50

2001 Press Pass SE Gold

COMPLETE SET (45) 50.00 100.00
*GOLDS: .8X TO 2X BASIC CARDS
ONE PER RETAIL PACK

2001 Press Pass SE Autographs Bronze

STATED ODDS 1:1 HOBBY, 1:28 RETAIL
1 Dan Alexander 3.00 8.00
2 Brian Allen 2.00 5.00
3 Jeff Backus 2.50 6.00
4 Kevan Barlow 3.00 8.00
5 Michael Bennett 3.00 8.00
6 Josh Booty 3.00 8.00
7 Drew Brees 50.00 80.00
8 Chris Chambers 4.00 10.00
9 Nate Clements 3.00 8.00
10 Ennis Davis 2.00 5.00
11 Jamar Fletcher 2.50 6.00
12 Rod Gardner 3.00 8.00
13 Casey Hampton 6.00 15.00
14 Todd Heap 4.00 10.00
15 Travis Henry 3.00 8.00
16 Josh Heupel 4.00 10.00
17 Jabari Holloway 2.50 6.00
18 Willie Howard 2.50 6.00
19 Steve Hutchinson 5.00 12.00
20 James Jackson 2.50 6.00
21 Chad Johnson 6.00 15.00
22 Rudi Johnson 4.00 10.00
23 LaMont Jordan 4.00 10.00
24 Ben Leard 2.50 6.00
25 Deuce McAllister 4.00 10.00
26 Mike McMahon 3.00 8.00
27 Snoop Minnis 2.50 6.00
28 Travis Minor 3.00 8.00
29 Freddie Mitchell 2.50 6.00
30 Quincy Morgan 3.00 8.00
31 Santana Moss 5.00 12.00
32 Bobby Newcombe 3.00 8.00
33 Moran Norris 2.00 5.00
34 Jesse Palmer 3.00 8.00
35 Tommy Polley 2.50 6.00
36 Dominic Raiola 2.50 6.00
37 Ken-Yon Rambo 2.50 6.00
38 Jamal Reynolds 2.50 6.00
39 Koren Robinson 3.00 8.00
40 Shaun Rogers 4.00 10.00
41 Sage Rosenfels 4.00 10.00
42 Richard Seymour 4.00 10.00
43 Justin Smith 4.00 10.00
44 David Terrell 3.00 8.00
45 Anthony Thomas 4.00 10.00
46 LaDainian Tomlinson 30.00 60.00
47 Marques Tuiasosopo 3.00 8.00
48 Kenyatta Walker 2.50 6.00
49 Chad Ward 2.50 6.00
50 Gerard Warren 3.00 8.00
51 Reggie Wayne 10.00 25.00
52 Chris Weinke 3.00 8.00
53 Maurice Williams 2.50 6.00
54 Jamie Winborn 3.00 8.00

2001 Press Pass SE Autographs Silver

*SILVER/250: .5X TO 1.2X BRONZE AU
*BLUE/25: .8X TO 2X SILVER AU/250
7 Drew Brees 60.00 120.00

2001 Press Pass SE Class of 2001

COMPLETE SET (9) 6.00 15.00
STATED ODDS 1:6 HOBBY, 1:12 RETAIL
CL1 Michael Vick 1.50 4.00
CL2 LaDainian Tomlinson 1.25 3.00
CL3 David Terrell .30 .75
CL4 Koren Robinson .30 .75
CL5 Santana Moss .50 1.25
CL6 Deuce McAllister .40 1.00
CL7 Freddie Mitchell .25 .60
CL8 Drew Brees 2.50 6.00
CL9 Chris Weinke .30 .75

2001 Press Pass SE Class of 2001 Autographs

STATED PRINT RUN 100 SER.#'d SETS
1 Michael Bennett 5.00 12.00
2 Drew Brees 60.00 120.00
3 Chris Chambers 8.00 20.00
4 Chad Johnson 12.50 30.00
6 Freddie Mitchell 4.00 10.00
7 Santana Moss 8.00 20.00
8 Koren Robinson 5.00 12.00
9 Justin Smith 6.00 15.00
10 David Terrell 5.00 12.00
11 LaDainian Tomlinson 50.00 100.00
12 Michael Vick 60.00 128.00
13 Chris Weinke 5.00 12.00

2001 Press Pass SE Game Jersey

STATED ODDS 1:96 HOB,1:560 RET
STATED PRINT RUN 250 SER.#'d SETS
*UNIF.NUM/25: 1X TO 2.5X BASIC JSY
UNIFORM NUMBER PRINT RUN 25
UNPRICED PATCH VERSION #'d OF 10
JCCW Chris Weinke 6.00 15.00
JCDB Drew Brees 12.00 30.00
JCJS Justin Smith 6.00 15.00
JCKYR Ken-Yon Rambo 6.00 15.00
(2001 National Promo)
JCLT LaDainian Tomlinson 15.00 40.00
JCMB Michael Bennett 6.00 15.00
JCMV Michael Vick 15.00 40.00

2001 Press Pass SE Game Jersey Autographs

STATED PRINT RUN 25 SERIAL #'d SETS
AJCW Chris Weinke 20.00 50.00
AJDB Drew Brees 125.00 200.00
AJJS Justin Smith 20.00 50.00
AJLT LaDainian Tomlinson 100.00 200.00
AJMB Michael Bennett 20.00 50.00

2001 Press Pass SE Old School

COMPLETE SET (27) 12.00 30.00
STATED ODDS 1:2
OS1 Michael Vick 1.50 4.00
OS2 Drew Brees 2.50 6.00
OS3 Chris Weinke .30 .75
OS4 LaDainian Tomlinson 1.25 3.00
OS5 Deuce McAllister .40 1.00
OS6 Michael Bennett .30 .75
OS7 Anthony Thomas .40 1.00
OS8 LaMont Jordan .40 1.00
OS9 Travis Henry .30 .75
OS10 James Jackson .25 .60
OS11 Kevan Barlow .30 .75
OS12 David Terrell .30 .75
OS13 Koren Robinson .30 .75
OS14 Rod Gardner .30 .75
OS15 Santana Moss .50 1.25
OS16 Freddie Mitchell .25 .60
OS17 Reggie Wayne .75 2.00
OS18 Quincy Morgan .30 .75
OS19 Chad Johnson .60 1.50
OS20 Chris Chambers .40 1.00
OS21 Todd Heap .40 1.00
OS22 Justin Smith .40 1.00
OS23 Andre Carter .30 .75
OS24 Leonard Davis .40 1.00
OS25 Kenyatta Walker .25 .60
OS26 Richard Seymour .40 1.00
OS27 Michael Vick CL 1.00 2.50

2001 Press Pass SE Rookievision

COMPLETE SET (12) 8.00 20.00
STATED ODDS 1:3 HOBBY, 1:6 RETAIL
RV1 Michael Vick 1.50 4.00
RV2 LaDainian Tomlinson 1.25 3.00
RV3 David Terrell .30 .75
RV4 Koren Robinson .30 .75
RV5 Rod Gardner .30 .75
RV6 Deuce McAllister .40 1.00
RV7 Santana Moss .50 1.25
RV8 Michael Bennett .30 .75
RV9 Freddie Mitchell .25 .60
RV10 Todd Heap .40 1.00
RV11 Drew Brees 2.50 6.00
RV12 Chad Johnson .60 1.50

2001 Press Pass SE Up Close

COMPLETE SET (6) 6.00 15.00
STATED ODDS 1:9 HOBBY, 1:18 RETAIL
UC1 Michael Vick 1.50 4.00
UC2 Drew Brees 2.50 6.00
UC3 LaDainian Tomlinson 1.25 3.00
UC4 David Terrell .30 .75
UC5 Deuce McAllister .40 1.00
UC6 Santana Moss .50 1.25

2004 Press Pass SE

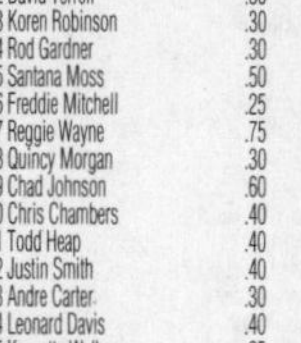

The Press Pass SE (Signature Edition) product was released in early May 2004. The base set consists of 40-cards. Mike Williams made an apearance in this product although he was declared ineligible for the NFL Draft. Hobby boxes contained 12-packs of 5-cards and carried an S.R.P. of $12.99. Each hobby pack also included one autograph or game used jersey card. Retail boxes included 24-packs with 4-cards per packs. The autographs and jersey cards were randomly seeded in retail. One parallel set and a variety of inserts can be found seeded in hobby and retail packs highlighted by the Blue autographs parallel set, Game Used Jerseys Autographs and the Class of 2004 Autographs.

COMPLETE SET (40) 15.00 30.00
1 Shawn Andrews .30 .75
2 Casey Clausen .30 .75
3 Michael Clayton .30 .75
4 Cedric Cobbs .25 .60
5 Devard Darling .25 .60
6 Lee Evans .40 1.00
7 Larry Fitzgerald 1.00 2.50
8 Robert Gallery .40 1.00
9 DeAngelo Hall .40 1.00
10 Tommie Harris .40 1.00
11 Ben Hartsock .25 .60
12 Devery Henderson .40 1.00
13 Steven Jackson .60 1.50
14 Michael Jenkins .40 1.00
15 Greg Jones .25 .60
16 Kevin Jones .30 .75
17 Teddy Lehman .25 .60
18 J.P. Losman .30 .75
19 Eli Manning 2.50 6.00
20 Mewelde Moore .30 .75
21 John Navarre .25 .60
22 Jarrett Payton .30 .75
23 Chris Perry .30 .75
24 Cody Pickett .30 .75
25 Philip Rivers 1.50 4.00
26 Ben Roethlisberger 2.50 6.00
27 Matt Schaub .75 2.00
28 Will Smith .30 .75
29 Ben Troupe .30 .75
30 Michael Turner .50 1.25
31 Ben Watson .40 1.00
32 Darius Watts .25 .60
33 Vince Wilfork .40 1.00
34 Mike Williams .30 .75
35 Reggie Williams .30 .75
36 Roy Williams WR .40 1.00
37 Quincy Wilson .30 .75
38 Rashaun Woods .25 .60
39 Jason Wright .25 .60
40 Eli Manning CL 1.25 3.00
NNO Eli Manning Mini Helmet 60.00 120.00

2004 Press Pass SE First Down Gold

COMPLETE SET (40) 25.00 60.00
*GOLD: .8X TO 2X BASIC CARDS
ONE PER RETAIL PACK

2004 Press Pass SE Class of 2004

COMPLETE SET (9) 10.00 25.00
STATED ODDS 1:3 H, 1:6 R
CL1 Eli Manning 4.00 10.00
CL2 Ben Roethlisberger 4.00 10.00
CL3 Philip Rivers 2.50 6.00
CL4 Mike Williams .50 1.25
CL5 Kevin Jones .50 1.25
CL6 Rashaun Woods .40 1.00
CL7 Steven Jackson 1.00 2.50
CL8 Larry Fitzgerald 1.50 4.00
CL9 Roy Williams WR .60 1.50

2004 Press Pass SE Class of 2004 Autographs

OVERALL SE AUTOGRAPH ODDS 2:3
1 Steven Jackson/50 30.00 80.00
2 Kevin Jones/50 12.00 30.00
3 Eli Manning/200 60.00 120.00
4 Chris Perry/200 10.00 25.00
5 Philip Rivers/200 30.00 60.00
6 Ben Roethlisberger/25 125.00 250.00
7 Ben Troupe/200 7.50 20.00
8 Mike Williams/200 7.50 20.00
9 Rashaun Woods/200 7.50 20.00

2004 Press Pass SE Game Used Jerseys Autographs

STATED PRINT RUN 25 SER.#'d SETS
1 Eli Manning 175.00 300.00
2 Ben Roethlisberger 150.00 300.00

2004 Press Pass SE Game Used Jerseys Bronze

BRONZE STATED PRINT RUN 625-700
*GOLD/100: .6X TO 1.5X BRONZE JSY
GOLD STATED PRINT RUN 100
*NUMBER/25: 1.2X TO 3X BRONZE JSY
NUMBERS STATED PRINT RUN 25
UNPRICED PATCH PRINT RUN 10
*SILVER/330-400: .5X TO 1.2X BRONZE JSY
SILVER PRINT RUN 330-400
OVERALL JERSEY ODDS 1:3H, 1:280R
JCBB Bernard Berrian/700 4.00 10.00
JCBH Ben Hartsock/700 2.50 6.00
JCBR Ben Roethlisberger/700 15.00 40.00
JCCC Casey Clausen/700 3.00 8.00
JCCP Cody Pickett/700 3.00 8.00
JCDD Devard Darling/700 2.50 6.00
JCDW Darius Watts/675 2.50 6.00
JCEM Eli Manning/700 15.00 40.00
JCJG Jermaine Green/700 2.50 6.00
JCJL Jared Lorenzen/700 3.00 8.00
JCJP Jarrett Payton/625 3.00 8.00
JCLM Luke McCown/700 3.00 8.00
JCMM Mewelde Moore/700 3.00 8.00
JCMS Matt Schaub/700 8.00 20.00
JCPR Philip Rivers/700 8.00 20.00
JCSJ Steven Jackson/700 6.00 15.00

2004 Press Pass SE Old School

COMPLETE SET (27) 10.00 25.00
STATED ODDS 1:1 H, 1:2 R
OS1 Casey Clausen .40 1.00
OS2 J.P. Losman .40 1.00
OS3 Eli Manning 3.00 8.00
OS4 John Navarre .30 .75
OS5 Cody Pickett .40 1.00
OS6 Philip Rivers 2.00 5.00
OS7 Ben Roethlisberger 3.00 8.00
OS8 Matt Schaub 1.00 2.50
OS9 Steven Jackson .75 2.00
OS10 Greg Jones .30 .75
OS11 Kevin Jones .40 1.00
OS12 Chris Perry .40 1.00
OS13 Michael Clayton .40 1.00
OS14 Lee Evans .50 1.25
OS15 Larry Fitzgerald 1.25 3.00
OS16 Michael Jenkins .50 1.25
OS17 Mike Williams .40 1.00
OS18 Roy Williams WR .50 1.25
OS19 Rashaun Woods .30 .75
OS20 Ben Troupe .40 1.00
OS21 Ben Watson .50 1.25
OS22 Kellen Winslow .50 1.25
OS23 Robert Gallery .50 1.25
OS24 Tommie Harris .50 1.25
OS25 Will Smith .40 1.00
OS26 Vince Wilfork .50 1.25
OS27 Eli Manning CL 1.50 4.00

2004 Press Pass SE Up Close

COMPLETE SET (6) 7.50 20.00
STATED ODDS 1:4 H, 1:12 R
UC1 Eli Manning 3.00 8.00
UC2 Larry Fitzgerald 1.25 3.00
UC3 Roy Williams WR .50 1.25
UC4 Ben Roethlisberger 3.00 8.00
UC5 Philip Rivers 2.00 5.00
UC6 Kevin Jones .40 1.00

2005 Press Pass SE

Press Pass SE was initially released in mid-May 2005. The base set consists of 40-cards. Hobby boxes contained 12-packs of 5-cards and carried an S.R.P. of $12.99 per pack with one jersey or autographed card inserted per pack. One parallel set and a variety of inserts can be found seeded in packs highlighted by the multi-tiered Game Used Jersey inserts.

COMPLETE SET (40) 10.00 25.00
1 Charlie Frye .40 1.00
2 David Greene .25 .60
3 Gino Guidugli .25 .60
4 Stefan LeFors .25 .60
5 Dan Orlovsky .40 1.00
6 Kyle Orton .40 1.00
7 Aaron Rodgers 3.00 8.00
8 Alex Smith QB .60 1.50
9 Andrew Walter .30 .75
10 Jason White .40 1.00
11 J.J. Arrington .30 .75
12 Marion Barber .40 1.00
13 Ronnie Brown .50 1.25
14 Anthony Davis .25 .60
15 Ciatrick Fason .25 .60
16 T.A. McLendon .25 .60
17 Vernand Morency .30 .75
18 Walter Reyes .25 .60
19 Cadillac Williams .40 1.00
20 Mark Bradley .25 .60
21 Reggie Brown .25 .60
22 Mark Clayton .40 1.00
23 Braylon Edwards .50 1.25
24 Fred Gibson .30 .75
25 Chris Henry .40 1.00
26 Terrence Murphy .25 .60
27 J.R. Russell .25 .60
28 Craphonso Thorpe .25 .60
29 Roddy White .50 1.25
30 Mike Williams .40 1.00
31 Troy Williamson .30 .75
32 Heath Miller .50 1.25
33 Alex Smith TE .25 .60
34 Jammal Brown .40 1.00
35 Marlin Jackson .25 .60
36 Antrel Rolle .40 1.00
37 Dan Cody .30 .75
38 Derrick Johnson .30 .75
39 Thomas Davis .25 .60
40 Aaron Rodgers CL 1.50 4.00

2005 Press Pass SE Gold

COMPLETE SET (40) 40.00 80.00
*GOLD: .8X TO 2X BASIC CARDS
ONE PER RETAIL PACK

2005 Press Pass SE Class of 2005

COMPLETE SET (9) 10.00 25.00
STATED ODDS 1:3 HOB, 1:6 RET
CL1 Aaron Rodgers 5.00 12.00
CL2 Braylon Edwards .75 2.00
CL3 Charlie Frye .60 1.50
CL4 Heath Miller .75 2.00
CL5 Troy Williamson .50 1.25
CL6 Alex Smith QB 1.00 2.50
CL7 Ronnie Brown .75 2.00
CL8 Andrew Walter .50 1.25
CL9 Cadillac Williams .60 1.50

2005 Press Pass SE Class of 2005 Autographs

AR1 Aaron Rodgers/190* 125.00 200.00
BE1 Braylon Edwards/45* 60.00 120.00
CW Cadillac Williams/200 25.00 60.00
DO Dan Orlovsky/200 10.00 25.00
HM Heath Miller/191* 12.00 30.00
RB2 Ronnie Brown/20* Red 40.00 100.00
TW Troy Williamson/200 10.00 25.00

2006 Press Pass SE Class of 2006 Autographs Red Ink

6 Brad Smith/45* 12.00 30.00
9 Vince Young/39* 30.00 80.00

2005 Press Pass SE Game Used Jerseys Silver

SILVER PRINT RUN 450-700 SER.#'d SETS
*GOLD: .5X TO 1.2X SILVER JERSEYS
GOLD PRINT RUN 450-550 SER.#'d SETS
*HOLOFOIL: .6X TO 1.5X SILVER JERSEYS
HOLOFOIL PRINT RUN 100 SER.#'d SETS
*NAMES: 1.2X TO 3X SILVER JERSEYS
NAMES PRINT RUN 25 SER.#'d SETS
UNPRICED PATCH PRINT RUN 1-10 SETS
OVERALL RETAIL ODDS 1:280
JCAS1 Alex Smith TE/700 2.50 6.00
JCAS2 Alex Smith TE/300 2.50 6.00
JCAW Andrew Walter/700 3.00 8.00
JCBB Brock Berlin/700 3.00 8.00
JCCT Craphonso Thorpe/700 2.50 6.00
JCDA Derek Anderson/700 3.00 8.00
JCDG David Greene/700 2.50 6.00
JCDO Dan Orlovsky/700 4.00 10.00
JCJC Jerome Collins/700 3.00 8.00
JCJW Jason White/700 4.00 10.00
JCKO Kyle Orton/700 4.00 10.00
JCMB Mark Bradley/700 2.50 6.00
JCMJ Marlin Jackson/700 2.50 6.00
JCRB Reggie Brown/700 2.50 6.00
JCRW Roddy White/700 5.00 12.00
JCSL Stefan LeFors/700 2.50 6.00
JCTM Terrence Murphy/450 2.50 6.00
JCVM Vernand Morency/700 3.00 8.00

2005 Press Pass SE Game Used Jerseys Autographs

STATED PRINT RUN 25 SER.#'d SETS
JCAW Andrew Walter 25.00 60.00
JCDG David Greene 25.00 60.00
JCDO Dan Orlovsky 25.00 60.00
JCJW Jason White 30.00 80.00
JCKO Kyle Orton 25.00 60.00
JCRB Reggie Brown 25.00 60.00

2005 Press Pass SE Old School

COMPLETE SET (27) 15.00 40.00
STATED ODDS 1:1 HOB, 1:2 RET
COLL.SERIES FACT.SET (28) 12.00 20.00
*COLLECTOR SERIES: .2X TO .5X BASIC INSERTS
COLL.SERIES ISSUED IN FACTORY SET FORM
OS1 Marion Barber .60 1.50
OS2 Reggie Brown .40 1.00
OS3 Ronnie Brown .75 2.00
OS4 Mark Clayton .60 1.50
OS5 Dan Cody .50 1.25
OS6 Anthony Davis .40 1.00
OS7 Braylon Edwards .75 2.00
OS8 Ciatrick Fason .40 1.00
OS9 Charlie Frye .60 1.50
OS10 David Greene .40 1.00
OS11 Gino Guidugli .40 1.00
OS12 Derrick Johnson .50 1.25
OS13 Heath Miller .75 2.00
OS14 Vernand Morency .50 1.25
OS15 Dan Orlovsky .60 1.50
OS16 Kyle Orton .60 1.50
OS17 Aaron Rodgers 5.00 12.00
OS18 Antrel Rolle .60 1.50
OS19 Eric Shelton .40 1.00
OS20 Alex Smith QB 1.00 2.50
OS21 Andrew Walter .50 1.25
OS22 Jason White .60 1.50
OS23 Roddy White .75 2.00
OS24 Cadillac Williams .60 1.50
OS25 Mike Williams .60 1.50
OS26 Troy Williamson .50 1.25
OS27 Braylon Edwards CL .40 1.00

2005 Press Pass SE Up Close

COMPLETE SET (6) 7.50 20.00
STATED ODDS 1:4 HOB, 1:12 RET
UC1 Cadillac Williams .60 1.50
UC2 Aaron Rodgers 5.00 12.00
UC3 Mike Williams .60 1.50
UC4 Ronnie Brown .75 2.00
UC5 Braylon Edwards .75 2.00
UC6 Dan Orlovsky .60 1.50

2006 Press Pass SE

This 40-card set was released in May, 2006. The set was issued into the hobby in five-card packs with an $12.99 which came 12 packs to a box.

COMPLETE SET (40) 12.50 30.00
1 Joseph Addai .40 1.00
2 Jason Avant .25 .60
3 Reggie Bush .75 2.00
4 Dominique Byrd .30 .75
5 Brodie Croyle .40 1.00
6 Jay Cutler .75 2.00
7 Vernon Davis .50 1.25
8 Maurice Drew .60 1.50
9 Anthony Fasano .40 1.00
10 D'Brickashaw Ferguson .40 1.00
11 Bruce Gradkowski .40 1.00
12 Darrell Hackney .30 .75
13 Derek Hagan .30 .75
14 Jerome Harrison .40 1.00
15 A.J. Hawk .40 1.00
16 Santonio Holmes .50 1.25
17 Michael Huff .30 .75
18 Chad Jackson .25 .60
19 Omar Jacobs .25 .60
20 Matt Leinart .40 1.00
21 Marcedes Lewis .40 1.00
22 Laurence Maroney .30 .75
23 Reggie McNeal .30 .75
24 Sinorice Moss .40 1.00
25 Martin Nance .30 .75
26 Haloti Ngata .40 1.00
27 Leonard Pope .40 1.00
28 Michael Robinson .30 .75
29 D.J. Shockley .30 .75
30 Maurice Stovall .25 .60
31 Marcus Vick .25 .60
32 Leon Washington .30 .75
33 LenDale White .30 .75
34 Charlie Whitehurst .40 1.00
35 Jimmy Williams .40 1.00
36 Mario Williams .40 1.00
37 DeAngelo Williams .50 1.25
38 Demetrius Williams .30 .75
39 Vince Young .50 1.25
40 Vince Young CL .25 .60

2006 Press Pass SE Gold

*GOLD: .8X TO 2X BASIC CARDS
GOLD STATED ODDS 1:1 RETAIL

2006 Press Pass SE Class of 2006

COMPLETE SET (9) 12.50 30.00
STATED ODDS 1:3 HOB, 1:6 RET
CL1 Reggie Bush 1.25 3.00
CL2 Brodie Croyle .60 1.50
CL3 A.J. Hawk .60 1.50
CL4 Santonio Holmes .75 2.00
CL5 Matt Leinart .60 1.50
CL6 Sinorice Moss .60 1.50
CL7 LenDale White .50 1.25
CL8 DeAngelo Williams .75 2.00
CL9 Vince Young .75 2.00

2006 Press Pass SE Class of 2006 Autographs

1 Reggie Bush/100 30.00 80.00
2 Brodie Croyle/200 10.00 25.00
3 A.J. Hawk/200 20.00 50.00
4 Omar Jacobs/194* 8.00 20.00
5 Matt Leinart/100 15.00 40.00
6 Brad Smith/155* 10.00 25.00
7 Marcus Vick/50 15.00 40.00
8 LenDale White/190 20.00 50.00
9 Vince Young/61* 25.00 60.00

2006 Press Pass SE Game Used Jerseys Silver

OVERALL JERSEY ODDS 1:3 H, 1:280 R
*GOLD: .5X TO 1.2X SILVER JSYs
*HOLOFOIL: .6X TO 1.5X SILVER JSYs
HOLOFOIL PRINT RUN 99 SER.#'d SETS
*PREMIUM: 1.2X TO 3X SILVER JSYs
PREMIUM PRINT RUN 25 SER.#'d SETS
JCAF Anthony Fasano 5.00 12.00
JCAH A.J. Hawk 12.50 30.00
JCBB Brett Basanez 4.00 10.00
JCBC Brodie Croyle 8.00 20.00
JCBS Brad Smith 4.00 10.00
JCCH Chris Hannon 4.00 10.00
JCCR Cory Rodgers 4.00 10.00
JCCW Charlie Whitehurst 6.00 15.00
JCDA Devin Aromashodu 4.00 10.00
JCDH Darrell Hackney 4.00 10.00
JCDO Drew Olson 4.00 10.00
JCDS D.J. Shockley 5.00 12.00
JCGL Greg Lee 4.00 10.00
JCHN Haloti Ngata 6.00 15.00
JCJH Jerome Harrison 5.00 12.00
JCJK Joe Klopfenstein 4.00 10.00
JCLW LenDale White 8.00 20.00
JCMD Maurice Drew 8.00 20.00
JCMN Martin Nance 4.00 10.00
JCMR Michael Robinson 5.00 12.00
JCOJ Omar Jacobs 5.00 12.00
JCPP Paul Pinegar 5.00 12.00
JCRB Reggie Bush Shirt 10.00 25.00
JCTJ Tarvaris Jackson 6.00 15.00
JCVD Vernon Davis 8.00 20.00
JCMH1 Mike Hass 5.00 12.00
JCMH2 Michael Huff 6.00 15.00
JCML1 Matt Leinart Shirt 6.00 15.00
JCML2 Marcedes Lewis 5.00 12.00
JCDW 1 DeAngelo Williams 6.00 15.00
JCDW 2 Demetrius Williams 5.00 12.00

2006 Press Pass SE Game Used Jerseys Autographs

STATED PRINT RUN 25 SER.#'d SETS
JCAF Anthony Fasano 25.00 50.00
JCAH A.J. Hawk 100.00 175.00
JCBB Brett Basanez 20.00 40.00
JCBS Brad Smith 25.00 60.00
JCCR Cory Rodgers 20.00 40.00
JCCW Charlie Whitehurst 20.00 50.00
JCDA Devin Aromashodu 25.00 50.00
JCDH Darrell Hackney 20.00 40.00
JCDO Drew Olson 25.00 50.00
JCDS D.J. Shockley 25.00 50.00
JCDW Demetrius Williams 25.00 50.00
JCGL Greg Lee 20.00 40.00
JCJH Jerome Harrison 25.00 50.00
JCLW LenDale White 50.00 120.00
JCMD Maurice Drew 50.00 80.00
JCML Marcedes Lewis 25.00 50.00
JCMN Martin Nance 20.00 40.00
JCOJ Omar Jacobs 25.00 50.00

2006 Press Pass SE Old School

COMPLETE SET (27) 15.00 40.00
STATED ODDS 1:1 HOB, 1:2 RET
*COLLECTORS SERIES: .25X TO .6X
COLL.SERIES ISSUED AS FACTORY SET
OS1 Brodie Croyle .60 1.50
OS2 Omar Jacobs .40 1.00
OS3 Charlie Whitehurst .60 1.50
OS4 Chad Jackson .40 1.00
OS5 Ernie Sims .50 1.25
OS6 Leonard Pope .60 1.50
OS7 Chad Greenway .60 1.50
OS8 Joseph Addai .60 1.50
OS9 Vernon Davis .75 2.00
OS10 DeAngelo Williams .75 2.00
OS11 Sinorice Moss .60 1.50
OS12 Laurence Maroney .50 1.25
OS13 Mario Williams .60 1.50
OS14 Anthony Fasano .60 1.50
OS15 Maurice Stovall .40 1.00
OS16 A.J. Hawk .60 1.50
OS17 Santonio Holmes .75 2.00
OS18 Haloti Ngata .60 1.50
OS19 Tamba Hali .60 1.50
OS20 Michael Huff .50 1.25
OS21 Vince Young .75 2.00
OS22 Reggie Bush 1.25 3.00
OS23 Matt Leinart .60 1.50
OS24 LenDale White .50 1.25
OS25 Jay Cutler 1.25 3.00
OS26 Jimmy Williams .60 1.50
OS27 Reggie Bush CL .60 1.50

2007 Press Pass SE

This 50-card set was released in May, 2007. The set was issued into the hobby in five-card packs, with a $12.99 SRP, which came 12 packs to a box.

COMPLETE SET (50) 15.00 40.00
1 Reggie Nelson .30 .75
2 Patrick Willis .75 2.00
3 Brian Leonard .30 .75
4 Sidney Rice .50 1.25
5 Robert Meachem .40 1.00
6 Chris Leak .40 1.00
7 Calvin Johnson 1.25 3.00
8 Charles Johnson .25 .60
9 Kevin Kolb .60 1.50
10 Drew Stanton .40 1.00
11 Antonio Pittman .25 .60
12 Troy Smith .40 1.00
13 Steve Smith USC .40 1.00
14 Leon Hall .30 .75
15 Brandon Jackson .30 .75
16 Ted Ginn Jr. .30 .75
17 Aundrae Allison .50 1.25
18 DeShawn Wynn .30 .75
19 Dwayne Wright .40 1.00
20 Michael Bush .40 1.00
21 Dwayne Bowe 1.25 3.00
22 Adam Carriker .40 1.00
23 Paul Posluszny .40 1.00
24 Aaron Ross .40 1.00
25 Lorenzo Booker .30 .75
26 Jamaal Anderson .40 1.00
27 Zach Miller .40 1.00
28 Dallas Baker .30 .75
29 Adrian Peterson 1.50 4.00
30 Dwayne Jarrett .40 1.00
31 Greg Olsen .40 1.00
32 Darius Walker .30 .75
33 Alan Branch .30 .75
34 Marshawn Lynch .40 1.00
35 JaMarcus Russell .60 1.50
36 Anthony Gonzalez .40 1.00
37 Gaines Adams .40 1.00
38 Craig Buster Davis .30 .75
39 Jason Hill .40 1.00
40 Kenny Irons .25 .60
41 John Beck .40 1.00
42 Lawrence Timmons .40 1.00
43 Trent Edwards .40 1.00
44 Tony Hunt .60 1.50
45 Darrelle Revis .60 1.50
46 Jarvis Moss .30 .75
47 LaRon Landry .40 1.00
48 Brady Quinn .40 1.00
49 Jordan Palmer .75 2.00
50 Rhema McKnight .25 .60

2007 Press Pass SE Gold

*GOLD: .8X TO 2X BASIC CARDS
ONE PER RETAIL PACK

2007 Press Pass SE Class of 2007

COMPLETE SET (10) 15.00 40.00
STATED ODDS 1:6 HOB/RET
1 Brady Quinn .75 2.00
2 JaMarcus Russell .50 1.25
3 Troy Smith .75 2.00
4 Marshawn Lynch .75 2.00
5 Adrian Peterson 3.00 8.00
6 Dwayne Jarrett .60 1.50
7 Calvin Johnson 2.50 6.00
8 Ted Ginn Jr. .60 1.50
9 Robert Meachem .75 2.00
10 Tony Hunt .50 1.25

2007 Press Pass SE Class of 2007 Autographs

STATED PRINT RUN 199 UNLESS NOTED
CLAP Adrian Peterson/75* 75.00 150.00
CLBJ Brandon Jackson/199 8.00 20.00
CLBQ Brady Quinn/198* 30.00 80.00
CLCJ Calvin Johnson/18* 75.00 150.00
CLDW Darius Walker/192* 6.00 15.00
CLJR JaMarcus Russell/188* 15.00 40.00
CLKI Kenny Irons/199 10.00 25.00
CLRM Robert Meachem/199 10.00 25.00
CLSR Sidney Rice/199 8.00 20.00
CLTG Ted Ginn Jr. /199 15.00 40.00
CLTS Troy Smith/20* 30.00 80.00

2007 Press Pass SE Class of 2007 Autographs Red Ink

CLAP Adrian Peterson/25* 75.00 150.00

2007 Press Pass SE Game Day Gear Jerseys Autographs

STATED PRINT RUN 25 SER.#'d SETS
AP Adrian Peterson 200.00 350.00
BL Brian Leonard 20.00 50.00
BQ Brady Quinn 125.00 250.00
GW Garrett Wolfe 25.00 60.00
KD Kenneth Darby 30.00 60.00
KK Kevin Kolb 20.00 50.00
LB Lorenzo Booker 25.00 50.00
MB Michael Bush 20.00 50.00
DB2 Dwayne Bowe 30.00 60.00
DW3 DeShawn Wynn 30.00 60.00
JR2 Jeff Rowe 25.00 50.00

2007 Press Pass SE Game Day Gear Jerseys Silver

*GOLD/299: .5X TO 1.2X SILVER JSYs
GOLD PRINT RUN 299 SER.#'d SETS
*HOLOFOIL/99: .6X TO 1.5X SILVER JSYs
HOLOFOIL PRINT RUN 99 SER.#'d SETS
*HOLO.PLATINUM/25: 1.5X TO 4X SILVER
HOLOFOIL PLATINUM PRINT RUN 25 SER.#'d SETS
OVERALL GD GEAR ODDS 1:3H, 1:280R
AP Adrian Peterson 20.00 50.00
BJ Brandon Jackson 4.00 10.00
BL Brian Leonard 4.00 10.00
BQ Brady Quinn 8.00 20.00
CD Craig Buster Davis 4.00 10.00
CL Chris Leak 5.00 12.00
CS Chansi Stuckey 3.00 8.00
DB2 Dwayne Bowe 5.00 12.00
DJ Dwayne Jarrett 4.00 10.00
DS Drew Stanton 4.00 10.00
DW Darius Walker 4.00 10.00
DW2 Dwayne Wright 3.00 8.00
DW3 DeShawn Wynn 4.00 10.00
GO Greg Olsen 5.00 12.00
GW Garrett Wolfe 4.00 10.00
JF Joel Filani 4.00 10.00
JP Jordan Palmer 4.00 10.00
JR1 JaMarcus Russell 5.00 12.00
JR2 Jeff Rowe 3.00 8.00
KD Kenneth Darby 5.00 12.00
KI Kenny Irons 5.00 12.00
KK Kevin Kolb 4.00 10.00
KS Kolby Smith 4.00 10.00
LB Lorenzo Booker 4.00 10.00
LL LaRon Landry 5.00 12.00
MB Michael Bush 4.00 10.00
ML Marshawn Lynch 5.00 12.00
RB Reggie Bush 10.00 25.00
SS Steve Smith USC 4.00 10.00
ZM Zach Miller 4.00 10.00

2007 Press Pass SE Gridiron Graphs Gold

OVERALL SE AUTO ODDS 2:3
UNPRICED PRINTING PLATES #'d TO 1
*RED INK: .6X TO 1.5X BASIC AUTOS
GGAA Aundrae Allison 4.00 10.00
GGAB Alan Branch 5.00 12.00
GGAG Anthony Gonzalez 6.00 15.00
GGAP Adrian Peterson SP 75.00 150.00
GGAPI Antonio Pittman 4.00 10.00
GGBJ Brandon Jackson 5.00 12.00
GGBL Brian Leonard 5.00 12.00
GGBQ Brady Quinn SP 20.00 50.00
GGCJ Calvin Johnson SP 75.00 150.00
GGCL Chris Leak 5.00 12.00
GGDB1 Dallas Baker 4.00 10.00
GGDB2 Dwayne Bowe 8.00 20.00
GGDS Drew Stanton 4.00 10.00
GGDW1 Darius Walker 4.00 10.00
GGDW2 Dwayne Wright 5.00 12.00
GGGA Gaines Adams 6.00 15.00
GGGO Greg Olsen 5.00 12.00
GGJA Jamaal Anderson 5.00 12.00
GGJB John Beck 6.00 15.00
GGJR JaMarcus Russell SP 12.00 30.00
GGKD Kenneth Darby 5.00 12.00
GGKI Kenny Irons 4.00 10.00
GGKK Kevin Kolb 10.00 25.00
GGLH Leon Hall 5.00 12.00
GGLL LaRon Landry 6.00 15.00
GGLT Lawrence Timmons 6.00 15.00
GGMB Michael Bush 6.00 15.00
GGMM Matt Moore 6.00 15.00
GGRM Robert Meachem 6.00 15.00
GGRN Reggie Nelson 5.00 12.00
GGSR Sidney Rice 8.00 20.00
GGSS Steve Smith USC 6.00 15.00
GGSY Selvin Young 5.00 12.00
GGTG Ted Ginn Jr. SP 15.00 40.00
GGTS Troy Smith SP 15.00 40.00

2007 Press Pass SE Gridiron Graphs Green

*GREEN/25: 1X TO 2.5X GOLD AUTOs
GREEN PRINT RUN 25 SER.#'d SETS
GGAP Adrian Peterson 150.00 300.00
GGBQ Brady Quinn/24* 50.00 120.00
GGCJ Calvin Johnson/19* 125.00 250.00
GGTG Ted Ginn Jr. 30.00 80.00
GGTS Troy Smith/20* 30.00 80.00

2007 Press Pass SE Gridiron Graphs Green Red Ink

RED INK ANNOUNCED PRINT RUN 1-25
GGJA Jamaal Anderson/25 12.00 30.00
GGMB Michael Bush/25 12.00 30.00
GGSY Selvin Young/25 12.00 30.00

2007 Press Pass SE Insider Insight

COMPLETE SET (34) 15.00 40.00
STATED ODDS 1:1 HOB, 1:2 RET
COLL.SERIES ISSUED AS FACTORY SET
1 Gaines Adams .75 2.00
2 Jamaal Anderson .60 1.50
3 Dwayne Bowe 1.00 2.50
4 Alan Branch .60 1.50
5 Michael Bush .75 2.00
6 Adam Carriker .60 1.50
7 Trent Edwards .75 2.00
8 Ted Ginn Jr. .60 1.50
9 Anthony Gonzalez .75 2.00
10 Leon Hall .60 1.50
11 Tony Hunt .50 1.25
12 Kenny Irons .50 1.25
13 Brandon Jackson .60 1.50
14 Dwayne Jarrett .60 1.50
15 Calvin Johnson 2.50 6.00
16 LaRon Landry .75 2.00
17 Brian Leonard .60 1.50
18 Marshawn Lynch .75 2.00
19 Robert Meachem .75 2.00
20 Reggie Nelson .60 1.50
21 Adrian Peterson 3.00 8.00
22 Antonio Pittman .50 1.25
23 Paul Posluszny .75 2.00
24 Brady Quinn .75 2.00
25 Sidney Rice 1.00 2.50
26 Aaron Ross .75 2.00
27 JaMarcus Russell .50 1.25
28 Steve Smith USC .75 2.00
29 Troy Smith .75 2.00
30 Drew Stanton .50 1.25
31 Kevin Kolb 1.25 3.00
32 Lawrence Timmons .75 2.00
33 Darius Walker .50 1.25
34 Brady Quinn CL .40 1.00

2007 Press Pass SE Insider Insight Collectors Series

COMP.FACT.SET (26) 15.00 30.00
COMPLETE SET (25) 10.00 25.00
ISSUED IN FACTORY SET FORM
II1 Gaines Adams .50 1.25
II2 Dwayne Bowe .60 1.50
II3 Michael Bush .50 1.25
II4 Adam Carriker .40 1.00
II5 Trent Edwards .50 1.25
II6 Ted Ginn Jr. .40 1.00
II7 Anthony Gonzalez .50 1.25
II8 Leon Hall .40 1.00
II9 Tony Hunt .30 .75
II10 Brandon Jackson .40 1.00
II11 Dwayne Jarrett .40 1.00
II12 Calvin Johnson 1.50 4.00
II13 LaRon Landry .50 1.25
II14 Brian Leonard .40 1.00
II15 Marshawn Lynch .50 1.25
II16 Robert Meachem .50 1.25
II17 Adrian Peterson 2.00 5.00
II18 Paul Posluszny .50 1.25
II19 Brady Quinn .50 1.25
II20 Sidney Rice .60 1.50
II21 JaMarcus Russell .30 .75
II22 Steve Smith USC .50 1.25
II23 Troy Smith .50 1.25
II24 Drew Stanton .30 .75
II25 Kevin Kolb .75 2.00

2007 Press Pass SE Marquee Matchups

COMPLETE SET (20) 15.00 40.00
STATED ODDS 1:3 HOB/RET
1 JaMarcus Russell 1.00 2.50
Brady Quinn
2 Adrian Peterson 4.00 10.00
Selvin Young
3 Calvin Johnson .75 2.00
David Clowney
4 Ted Ginn Jr. .75 2.00
Leon Hall
5 Dwayne Jarrett .75 2.00
Darius Walker
6 Marshawn Lynch 1.00 2.50
Zach Miller
7 Robert Meachem 1.00 2.50
Dwayne Bowe
8 Sidney Rice 1.25 3.00
Reggie Nelson
9 Tony Hunt .75 2.00
Alan Branch
10 Chris Leak 1.00 2.50
LaRon Landry
11 Anthony Gonzalez 1.00 2.50
Aaron Ross
12 Greg Olsen .75 2.00
Lorenzo Booker
13 Antonio Pittman .60 1.50
Paul Posluszny
14 Brian Leonard 1.00 2.50
Michael Bush
15 Troy Smith 1.00 2.50
Drew Stanton
16 Kenny Irons .75 2.00
Kenneth Darby
17 Matt Moore 1.00 2.50
Steve Smith USC
18 Brandon Jackson .75 2.00
Michael Griffin
19 Trent Edwards 1.00 2.50
Daymeion Hughes
20 Reggie Bush 1.00 2.50
Vince Young

2007 Press Pass SE Teammates Autographs

BQDW Brady Quinn 40.00 100.00
Darius Walker
CLRN Chris Leak 20.00 50.00
Reggie Nelson
JRDB JaMarcus Russell 30.00 80.00
Dwayne Bowe

2007 Press Pass SE Teammates Autographs Red Ink

TSTG Troy Smith 30.00 80.00
Ted Ginn Jr.

2008 Press Pass SE

COMPLETE SET (50) 15.00 20.00
1 Glenn Dorsey .40 1.00
2 Chris Long .40 1.00
3 Dan Connor .40 1.00
4 Aqib Talib .40 1.00
5 Kenny Phillips .40 1.00
6 Erik Ainge .40 1.00
7 John David Booty .30 .75
8 Colt Brennan .40 1.00
9 Brian Brohm .40 1.00
10 Joe Flacco 1.25 3.00
11 Chad Henne .40 1.00
12 Matt Ryan 1.50 4.00
13 Andre Woodson .40 1.00
14 Jamaal Charles .60 1.50
15 Matt Forte .60 1.50
16 Mike Hart .40 1.00
17 Jacob Hester .40 1.00
18 Chris Johnson 1.00 2.50
19 Felix Jones .60 1.50
20 Darren McFadden 1.00 2.50
21 Rashard Mendenhall .75 2.00
22 Ray Rice .75 2.00
23 Steve Slaton .40 1.00
24 Kevin Smith .40 1.00
25 Jonathan Stewart .60 1.50
26 Fred Davis .40 1.00
27 Adrian Arrington .30 .75
28 Earl Bennett .40 1.00
29 Adarius Bowman .30 .75
30 Early Doucet .30 .75
31 James Hardy .30 .75
32 DJ Hall .30 .75
33 DeSean Jackson .75 2.00
34 Malcolm Kelly .30 .75
35 Mario Manningham .40 1.00
36 Limas Sweed .40 1.00
37 Devin Thomas .30 .75
38 Lavelle Hawkins .25 .60
39 Andre Caldwell .30 .75
40 Vernon Gholston .30 .75
41 Derrick Harvey .25 .60
42 Keith Rivers .40 1.00
43 Mike Jenkins .40 1.00
44 Leodis McKelvin .30 .75
45 Dennis Dixon .40 1.00
46 Josh Johnson .40 1.00
47 Tashard Choice .30 .75
48 Chauncey Washington .30 .75
49 John Carlson .40 1.00
50 Donnie Avery .30 .75

2008 Press Pass SE Gold

COMPLETE SET (50) 40.00 80.00
*GOLD: .8X TO 2X BASIC CARDS
ONE GOLD PER RETAIL PACK

2008 Press Pass SE Class of 2008

STATED ODDS 1:6 HOB/RET
CL1 Matt Ryan 3.00 8.00
CL2 Brian Brohm .75 2.00
CL3 Darren McFadden 2.00 5.00
CL4 Jonathan Stewart 1.25 3.00
CL5 DeSean Jackson 1.50 4.00
CL6 Malcolm Kelly .60 1.50
CL7 Limas Sweed .75 2.00
CL8 Glenn Dorsey .75 2.00
CL9 Chris Long .75 2.00
CL10 Rashard Mendenhall 1.50 4.00

2008 Press Pass SE Class of 2008 Autographs

STATED PRINT RUN 142-199
CLAW Andre Woodson/188* 6.00 15.00
CLBB Brian Brohm/199 6.00 15.00
CLCL Chris Long/185* 6.00 15.00
CLDJ DeSean Jackson/172* 12.00 30.00
CLDM Darren McFadden/199 20.00 50.00
CLJS Jonathan Stewart/199 10.00 25.00
CLLS Limas Sweed/142 6.00 15.00
CLMH Mike Hart/196* 6.00 15.00
CLMK Malcolm Kelly/170 5.00 12.00
CLMR Matt Ryan/169* 40.00 80.00
CLRM Rashard Mendenhall/174* 12.00 30.00

2008 Press Pass SE Class of 2008 Autographs Red Ink

*RED INK/14-30: .5X TO 1.2X BASE AU
RED INK ANNOUNCED PRINT RUN 3-30

2008 Press Pass SE Game Day Gear Jerseys Autographs

STATED PRINT RUN 25 SER.#'d SETS
GDGAA Adrian Arrington 12.00 30.00
GDGBB Brian Brohm 15.00 40.00
GDGCB Colt Brennan 15.00 40.00
GDGCH Chad Henne 30.00 80.00
GDGDA Donnie Avery 12.00 30.00
GDGDD Dennis Dixon 15.00 40.00
GDGDH DJ Hall 12.00 30.00
GDGDM Darren McFadden 40.00 100.00
GDGDT Devin Thomas 12.00 30.00
GDGEA Erik Ainge 20.00 50.00
GDGED Early Doucet 12.00 30.00
GDGJC Jamaal Charles 25.00 50.00
GDGJS Jonathan Stewart 25.00 60.00
GDGLS Limas Sweed 15.00 40.00
GDGMH Mike Hart 15.00 40.00
GDGMK Malcolm Kelly 12.00 30.00
GDGMR Matt Ryan 75.00 150.00
GDGRR Ray Rice 40.00 80.00
GDGSS Steve Slaton 15.00 40.00

2008 Press Pass SE Game Day Gear Jerseys Silver

*GOLD/199-299: .5X TO 1.2X BASIC INSERTS
GOLD PRINT RUN 199-299 SER.#'d SETS
*HOLOFOIL/99: .6X TO 1.5X BASIC INSERTS
HOLOFOIL PRINT RUN 99 SER.#'d SETS
*HOLOFOIL PLATINUM/25: 1.5X TO 4X
HOLOFOIL PLATINUM PRINT RUN 25
OVERALL ODDS 1:4 HOB, 1:280 RET
GDGAA Adrian Arrington 3.00 8.00
GDGBB Brian Brohm 4.00 10.00
GDGCB Colt Brennan 4.00 10.00
GDGCH Chad Henne 5.00 12.00
GDGCW Chauncey Washington 2.50 6.00
GDGDA Donnie Avery 2.50 6.00
GDGDB Davone Bess 3.00 8.00
GDGDB Dorien Bryant 3.00 8.00
GDGDC Dan Connor 3.00 8.00
GDGDD Dennis Dixon 3.00 8.00
GDGDH DJ Hall 3.00 8.00
GDGDM Darren McFadden 8.00 20.00
GDGDR Darius Reynaud 3.00 8.00
GDGDS Dantrell Savage 2.50 6.00
GDGDT Devin Thomas 2.50 6.00
GDGEA Erik Ainge 4.00 10.00
GDGED Early Doucet 2.50 6.00
GDGJC Jamaal Charles 4.00 10.00
GDGJDB John David Booty 4.00 10.00
GDGJF Justin Forsett 2.50 6.00
GDGJH Jacob Hester 3.00 8.00
GDGJS Jonathan Stewart 6.00 15.00
GDGJT Jacob Tamme 2.50 6.00
GDGKP Kenny Phillips 3.00 8.00
GDGKS Kevin Smith 3.00 8.00
GDGLH Lavelle Hawkins 2.50 6.00
GDGLS Limas Sweed 3.00 8.00
GDGMF Matt Forte 5.00 12.00
GDGMH Mike Hart 6.00 15.00
GDGMK Malcolm Kelly 4.00 10.00
GDGMR Matt Ryan 8.00 20.00
GDGRL Rafael Little 2.50 6.00
GDGRR Ray Rice 4.00 10.00
GDGSS Steve Slaton 3.00 8.00
GDGTC Tashard Choice 3.00 8.00
GDGVG Vernon Gholston 3.00 8.00

2008 Press Pass SE Gridiron Graphs Gold

UNPRICED PRINT PLATES PRINT RUN 1
GGAA Adrian Arrington 4.00 10.00
GGAB Adarius Bowman 4.00 10.00
GGAC Andre Caldwell 4.00 10.00
GGAC2 Antoine Cason 5.00 12.00
GGAP Allen Patrick 4.00 10.00
GGAW Andre Woodson 5.00 12.00
GGBB Brian Brohm 5.00 12.00
GGCB Colt Brennan 10.00 25.00
GGCC Calais Campbell 4.00 10.00
GGCH Chad Henne 5.00 12.00
GGCJ2 Chris Johnson 12.00 30.00
GGCL Chris Long 5.00 12.00
GGCW Chauncey Washington 4.00 10.00
GGDA Donnie Avery 4.00 10.00
GGDB Dorien Bryant 4.00 10.00
GGDB2 Davone Bess 5.00 12.00
GGDC Dan Connor 5.00 12.00
GGDD Dennis Dixon 5.00 12.00
GGDH DJ Hall 4.00 10.00
GGDJ DeSean Jackson 10.00 25.00
GGDM Darren McFadden 12.00 30.00
GGDR Darius Reynaud 3.00 8.00
GGDS Dantrell Savage 4.00 10.00
GGDT Devin Thomas 4.00 10.00
GGEA Erik Ainge 5.00 12.00
GGEB Earl Bennett 5.00 12.00
GGED Early Doucet 4.00 10.00
GGER Eddie Royal 5.00 12.00
GGFD Fred Davis 5.00 12.00
GGFJ Felix Jones 12.00 30.00
GGHD Harry Douglas 4.00 10.00
GGJC Jamaal Charles 8.00 20.00
GGJC2 John Carlson 5.00 12.00
GGJDB John David Booty 4.00 10.00
GGJF Joe Flacco 20.00 50.00
GGJF2 Justin Forsett 5.00 12.00
GGJH Jacob Hester 5.00 12.00
GGJJ Josh Johnson 5.00 12.00
GGJL J Leman 3.00 8.00
GGJM Josh Morgan 5.00 12.00
GGJN Jordy Nelson 8.00 20.00
GGJS Jonathan Stewart 8.00 20.00
GGJT Jacob Tamme 5.00 12.00
GGKB Keenan Burton 3.00 8.00
GGKP Kenny Phillips 5.00 12.00
GGKR Keith Rivers 5.00 12.00
GGKS Kevin Smith 5.00 12.00
GGLH Lavelle Hawkins 3.00 8.00
GGLM Leodis McKelvin 4.00 10.00
GGLS Limas Sweed 5.00 12.00
GGMF Matt Flynn 10.00 25.00
GGMF2 Matt Forte 8.00 20.00
GGMH Mike Hart 5.00 12.00
GGMH2 Marcus Henry 4.00 10.00
GGMK Malcolm Kelly 4.00 10.00
GGMM2 Mario Manningham 5.00 12.00
GGMR Matt Ryan 30.00 80.00
GGMR2 Martin Rucker 4.00 10.00
GGMS Marcus Smith 4.00 10.00
GGOS Owen Schmitt 5.00 12.00
GGPS Paul Smith 5.00 12.00
GGRL Rafael Little 4.00 10.00
GGRM Rashard Mendenhall 12.00 30.00
GGRR Ray Rice 10.00 25.00
GGSS Steve Slaton 5.00 12.00
GGTC Tashard Choice 4.00 10.00
GGTW Trae Williams 3.00 8.00
GGVG Vernon Gholston 4.00 10.00

2008 Press Pass SE Gridiron Graphs Gold Red Ink

*RED INK/15-149: .6X TO 1.5X BASE GOLD AU
RED INK ANNOUNCED PRINT RUN 1-149

2008 Press Pass SE Gridiron Graphs Green

*GREEN/25: 1X TO 2.5X GOLD AUTO
GREEN PRINT RUN 25 SER.#'d SETS
ANNC'D PRINT RUN ON CARDS W/RED INK VERSION
GGDM Darren McFadden 25.00 60.00
GGJF Joe Flacco 40.00 100.00
GGMR Matt Ryan/24* 75.00 150.00

2008 Press Pass SE Gridiron Graphs Green Red Ink

RED INK ANNOUNCED PRINT RUN 1-50
GGBB Brian Brohm/20* 15.00 40.00
GGCB Colt Brennan/24* 25.00 60.00
GGCW Chauncey Washington/25* 12.00 30.00
GGDT Devin Thomas/22* 12.00 30.00
GGJC Jamaal Charles/21* 25.00 60.00
GGRM Rashard Mendenhall/17* 30.00 80.00
GGSS Steve Slaton/14* 15.00 40.00

2008 Press Pass SE Insider Insight

COMPLETE SET (34) 15.00 40.00
STATED ODDS 1:1 HOB, 1:2 RET
1 Erik Ainge .60 1.50
2 Adrian Arrington .50 1.25
3 Earl Bennett .60 1.50
4 John David Booty .50 1.25
5 Adarius Bowman .50 1.25
6 Colt Brennan .60 1.50
7 Brian Brohm .60 1.50
8 Jamaal Charles 1.00 2.50
9 Fred Davis .60 1.50
10 Glenn Dorsey .60 1.50
11 Early Doucet .50 1.25
12 Joe Flacco 2.00 5.00
13 Matt Forte 1.00 2.50
14 DJ Hall .50 1.25
15 Mike Hart .60 1.50

16 Chad Henne	.60	1.50
17 Jacob Hester	.60	1.50
18 DeSean Jackson	1.25	3.00
19 Chris Johnson	1.50	4.00
20 Felix Jones	1.00	2.50
21 Malcolm Kelly	.50	1.25
22 Chris Long	.60	1.50
23 Mario Manningham	.60	1.50
24 Darren McFadden	1.50	4.00
25 Rashard Mendenhall	1.25	3.00
26 Ray Rice	1.25	3.00
27 Matt Ryan	2.50	6.00
28 Steve Slaton	.60	1.50
29 Kevin Smith	.60	1.50
30 Jonathan Stewart	1.00	2.50
31 Limas Sweed	.60	1.50
32 Aqib Talib	.60	1.50
33 Andre Woodson	.60	1.50
34 Darren McFadden CL	1.50	4.00

2008 Press Pass SE Marquee Matchups

STATED ODDS 1:3 HOB/RET

MM1 Matt Ryan	3.00	8.00
Kenny Phillips		
MM2 Chris Johnson	2.00	5.00
Matt Forte		
MM3 Jonathan Stewart	1.25	3.00
Mike Hart		
MM4 DeSean Jackson	1.50	4.00
Erik Ainge		
MM5 Adrian Arrington	.60	1.50
Andre Caldwell		
MM6 John David Booty	.60	1.50
Rashard Mendenhall		
MM7 Dennis Dixon	.75	2.00
Mario Manningham		
MM8 Andre Woodson	.75	2.00
Brian Brohm		
MM9 Early Doucet	.60	1.50
DJ Hall		
MM10 Darren McFadden	2.00	5.00
Jacob Hester		
MM11 Glenn Dorsey	.75	2.00
Vernon Gholston		
MM12 Jamaal Charles	1.25	3.00
Kevin Smith		
MM13 Malcolm Kelly	.75	2.00
Limas Sweed		
MM14 Adarius Bowman	1.00	2.50
Jordy Nelson		
MM15 Steve Slaton	1.50	4.00
Ray Rice		
MM16 Chad Henne	.75	2.00
Derrick Harvey		
MM17 Keenan Burton	1.25	3.00
Felix Jones		
MM18 Darius Reynaud	.60	1.50
Harry Douglas		
MM19 Devin Thomas	.60	1.50
James Hardy		
MM20 Owen Schmitt	.75	2.00
Allen Patrick		

2008 Press Pass SE Teammates Autographs

STATED PRINT RUN 25 SER.#'d SETS

AWKB Andre Woodson	15.00	40.00
Keenan Burton		
CHMH Chad Henne	40.00	100.00
Mike Hart		
CHMHR Chad Henne Red	40.00	100.00
Mike Hart Red		
DDJS Dennis Dixon	50.00	100.00
Jonathan Stewart		
DJJF DeSean Jackson	25.00	50.00
Justin Forsett		
JCLS Jamaal Charles	25.00	60.00
Limas Sweed		

2009 Press Pass SE

COMPLETE SET (50)	12.50	30.00
1 Nate Davis	.30	.75
2 Josh Freeman	.75	2.00
3 Graham Harrell	.40	1.00
4 Mark Sanchez	1.25	3.00
5 Matthew Stafford	2.00	5.00
6 Pat White	.40	1.00
7 Andre Brown	.25	.60
8 Donald Brown	.40	1.00
9 Glen Coffee	.30	.75
10 Mike Goodson	.40	1.00
11 Shonn Greene	.60	1.50
12 Jeremiah Johnson	.40	1.00
13 LeSean McCoy	.75	2.00
14 Knowshon Moreno	.40	1.00
15 Javon Ringer	.40	1.00
16 Chris Wells	.60	1.50
17 Ramses Barden	.25	.60
18 Kenny Britt	.50	1.25
19 Michael Crabtree	.75	2.00
20 Percy Harvin	.60	1.50
21 Darrius Heyward-Bey	.40	1.00
22 Juaquin Iglesias	.30	.75
23 Jeremy Maclin	.60	1.50
24 Hakeem Nicks	.60	1.50
25 Brian Robiskie	.40	1.00
26 Brandon Tate	.40	1.00
27 Derrick Williams	.30	.75
28 Brandon Pettigrew	.40	1.00
29 Everette Brown	.30	.75
30 Tyson Jackson	.30	.75
31 Aaron Maybin	.30	.75
32 Brian Orakpo	.40	1.00
33 Aaron Curry	.40	1.00
34 Brian Cushing	.40	1.00
35 James Laurinaitis	.40	1.00
36 Rey Maualuga	.40	1.00
37 Vontae Davis	.40	1.00
38 Malcolm Jenkins	.40	1.00
39 D.J. Moore	.30	.75
40 Victor Harris	.40	1.00
41 Alphonso Smith	.30	.75
42 B.J. Raji	.40	1.00
43 Rhett Bomar	.30	.75
44 Ian Johnson	.40	1.00
45 James Davis	.40	1.00
46 Cedric Peerman	.30	.75
47 Jarett Dillard	.40	1.00
48 Louis Murphy	.40	1.00
49 Mike Thomas	.40	1.00
50 Jared Cook	.40	1.00

2009 Press Pass SE Gold

*GOLD: .8X TO 2X BASIC CARDS
ONE GOLD PER RETAIL PACK

2009 Press Pass SE Retail Holofoil

COMPLETE SET (8)	10.00	25.00
RANDOM INSERTS IN RETAIL PACKS		
RE1 Mark Sanchez	2.00	5.00
RE2 Matthew Stafford	3.00	8.00
RE3 LeSean McCoy	1.25	3.00
RE4 Knowshon Moreno	.60	1.50
RE5 Chris Wells	1.00	2.50
RE6 Michael Crabtree	1.25	3.00
RE7 Percy Harvin	1.00	2.50
RE8 Jeremy Maclin	1.00	2.50
RE9 Derrick Williams	.50	1.25
RE10 Donald Brown	.60	1.50

2009 Press Pass SE Class of 2009

STATED ODDS 1:6

CL1 Mark Sanchez	2.50	6.00
CL2 Matthew Stafford	4.00	10.00
CL3 LeSean McCoy	1.50	4.00
CL4 Knowshon Moreno	.75	2.00
CL5 Chris Wells	1.25	3.00
CL6 Michael Crabtree	1.50	4.00
CL7 Percy Harvin	1.25	3.00
CL8 Darrius Heyward-Bey	.75	2.00
CL9 Jeremy Maclin	1.25	3.00
CL10 Donald Brown	.75	2.00

2009 Press Pass SE Class of 2009 Autographs

STATED PRINT RUN 141-199
*HEAD OF CLASS/25: .8X TO 2X BASE AU
HEAD OF CLASS PRINT RUN 1-25

CLDB Donald Brown/199	6.00	15.00
CLJM Jeremy Maclin/141	10.00	25.00
CLJR Javon Ringer/199	6.00	15.00
CLKM Knowshon Moreno/199	12.00	30.00
CLLM LeSean McCoy/191	12.00	30.00
CLMC Michael Crabtree/199	15.00	40.00
CLMS Matthew Stafford/150	40.00	80.00
CLPH Percy Harvin/199	15.00	40.00
CLSG Shonn Greene/199	10.00	25.00
CLDHB Darrius Heyward-Bey/199	6.00	15.00
CLMS2 Mark Sanchez/150	20.00	50.00

2009 Press Pass SE Class of 2009 Autographs Red Ink

CLCW Chris Wells/150	25.00	50.00
CLKM Knowshon Moreno	25.00	60.00

2009 Press Pass SE Double Feature

STATED ODDS 1:3

DF1 Matthew Stafford	4.00	10.00
Percy Harvin		
DF2 Mark Sanchez	2.50	6.00
Jeremiah Johnson		
DF3 Michael Crabtree	1.25	3.00
Jeremy Maclin		
DF4 Knowshon Moreno	.75	2.00
Glen Coffee		
DF5 Chris Wells	1.25	3.00
Aaron Maybin		
DF6 Hakeem Nicks	1.25	3.00
Darrius Heyward-Bey		
DF7 LeSean McCoy	1.50	4.00
Donald Brown		
DF8 Josh Freeman	1.50	4.00
Graham Harrell		
DF9 Shonn Greene	1.25	3.00
Javon Ringer		
DF10 Kenny Britt	1.00	2.50
Brandon Tate		
DF11 Rey Maualuga	.75	2.00
James Laurinaitis		
DF12 Malcolm Jenkins	.75	2.00
Derrick Williams		
DF13 Aaron Curry	.75	2.00
James Davis		
DF14 Arian Foster	1.50	4.00
Kenny McKinley		
DF15 Pat White	.75	2.00
Hunter Cantwell		
DF16 Brian Orakpo	.75	2.00
Stephen McGee		
DF17 Juaquin Iglesias	.60	1.50
Quan Cosby		
DF18 Mohamed Massaquoi	.75	2.00
Louis Murphy		
DF19 Vontae Davis	.75	2.00
Brian Robiskie		
DF20 Brandon Pettigrew	.75	2.00
Mike Goodson		

2009 Press Pass SE Game Day Gear Jerseys Silver

OVERALL GD GEAR ODDS 1:4H, 1:72R
*GOLD/100-299: .5X TO 1.2X SILVER JSY
GOLD JSY PRINT RUN 199-299
*HOLOFOIL/99: .6X TO 1.5X SILVER JSY
HOLOFOIL PRINT RUN 99
*HOLOFOIL PLAT/25: 1.2X TO 3X SLVR JSY
HOLOFOIL PLATINUM PRINT RUN 25

GDGAF Arian Foster	6.00	15.00
GDGBG Brandon Gibson	3.00	8.00
GDGBR Brian Robiskie	3.00	8.00
GDGCD Chase Daniel	3.00	8.00
GDGCH Cullen Harper	3.00	8.00
GDGDB Donald Brown	3.00	8.00
GDGDW Derrick Williams	2.50	6.00
GDGGJ Gartrell Johnson	2.00	5.00
GDGHC Hunter Cantwell	3.00	8.00
GDGIJ Ian Johnson	3.00	8.00
GDGJC James Casey	2.50	6.00
GDGJF Josh Freeman	5.00	12.00
GDGJJ Jeremiah Johnson	3.00	8.00
GDGJL James Laurinaitis	3.00	8.00
GDGJM Jeremy Maclin	6.00	15.00
GDGJR Javon Ringer	3.00	8.00
GDGJW John Parker Wilson	5.00	12.00
GDGKB Kenny Britt	4.00	10.00
GDGKM Kenny McKinley	3.00	8.00
GDGLM LeSean McCoy	6.00	15.00
GDGMC Michael Crabtree	8.00	20.00
GDGMG Mike Goodson	3.00	8.00
GDGML Marlon Lucky	5.00	12.00
GDGMS Mark Sanchez	8.00	20.00
GDGND Nate Davis	2.50	6.00
GDGPH P.J. Hill	2.50	6.00
GDGQC Quan Cosby	2.50	6.00
GDGRB Ramses Barden	2.00	5.00
GDGRM Rey Maualuga	3.00	8.00
GDGSG Shonn Greene	5.00	12.00
GDGSM Stephen McGee	3.00	8.00
GDGDHB Darrius Heyward-Bey	3.00	8.00
GDGLM2 Louis Murphy	3.00	8.00
GDGMS2 Matthew Stafford	8.00	20.00
GDGRB2 Rhett Bomar	2.50	6.00

2009 Press Pass SE Game Day Gear Jerseys Autographs

STATED PRINT RUN 25 SER.#'d SETS

GDGAF Arian Foster	75.00	150.00
GDGBR Brian Robiskie	20.00	50.00
GDGDB Donald Brown	20.00	50.00
GDGIJ Ian Johnson		
GDGJC James Casey	15.00	40.00
GDGJF Josh Freeman	50.00	100.00
GDGJJ Jeremiah Johnson	20.00	50.00
GDGJL James Laurinaitis	20.00	50.00
GDGJM Jeremy Maclin	30.00	80.00
GDGKB Kenny Britt	25.00	60.00
GDGMC Michael Crabtree	50.00	120.00
GDGMG Mike Goodson	20.00	50.00
GDGML Marlon Lucky	15.00	40.00
GDGMS Mark Sanchez	75.00	135.00
GDGPH P.J. Hill	15.00	40.00
GDGSG Shonn Greene	30.00	80.00

2009 Press Pass SE Gridiron Graphs Gold

OVERALL AU ODDS 1:1.5 HOB, 1:72 RET
*GREEN/25: .8X TO 2X GOLD AU
GREEN PRINT RUN 6-25
*RED/100-150: .5X TO 1.2X GOLD AU
RED PRINT RUN 100-150

GGAB Andre Brown	3.00	8.00
GGAC2 Aaron Curry	5.00	12.00
GGAC Austin Collie	6.00	15.00
GGAF Arian Foster	25.00	50.00
GGAS Alphonso Smith	4.00	10.00
GGBC Brian Cushing	5.00	12.00
GGBG Brandon Gibson	5.00	12.00
GGBH Brian Hoyer	5.00	12.00
GGBO Brian Orakpo	5.00	12.00
GGBP Brandon Pettigrew	5.00	12.00
GGBR Brian Robiskie	5.00	12.00
GGBR2 B.J. Raji	5.00	12.00
GGBT Brandon Tate	5.00	12.00
GGCC Chase Coffman	4.00	10.00
GGCD Chase Daniel	5.00	12.00
GGCH Cullen Harper	5.00	12.00
GGCP Cedric Peerman	4.00	10.00
GGCW Chris Wells	8.00	20.00
GGDB Donald Brown	5.00	12.00
GGDHB Darrius Heyward-Bey	5.00	12.00
GGDM D.J. Moore	4.00	10.00
GGDM2 Devin Moore	4.00	10.00
GGDW Derrick Williams	4.00	10.00
GGEB Everette Brown	4.00	10.00
GGGC Glen Coffee	4.00	10.00
GGGH Graham Harrell	8.00	20.00
GGGJ Gartrell Johnson	3.00	8.00
GGHC Hunter Cantwell	5.00	12.00
GGHN Hakeem Nicks	8.00	20.00
GGIJ Ian Johnson	5.00	12.00
GGJC Jared Cook	5.00	12.00
GGJC2 Jeremy Childs	4.00	10.00
GGJD James Davis	5.00	12.00
GGJD2 Jarett Dillard	5.00	12.00
GGJF Josh Freeman	10.00	25.00
GGJI Juaquin Iglesias	4.00	10.00
GGJJ Jeremiah Johnson	5.00	12.00
GGJL James Laurinaitis	5.00	12.00
GGJM Jeremy Maclin	8.00	20.00
GGJR Javon Ringer	5.00	12.00
GGJW John Parker Wilson	5.00	12.00
GGKB Kenny Britt	6.00	15.00
GGKM Knowshon Moreno	15.00	40.00
GGKM2 Kenny McKinley	5.00	12.00
GGKO Kevin Ogletree	5.00	12.00
GGLM LeSean McCoy	10.00	25.00
GGLM2 Louis Murphy	5.00	12.00
GGMC Michael Crabtree	12.00	30.00
GGMG Mike Goodson	5.00	12.00
GGMJ Malcolm Jenkins	5.00	12.00
GGMM Mohamed Massaquoi	4.00	10.00
GGMR Mike Reilly	4.00	10.00
GGMS Matthew Stafford	40.00	80.00
GGMS2 Mark Sanchez	40.00	80.00
GGMT Mike Thomas	5.00	12.00
GGND Nate Davis	4.00	10.00
GGPH Percy Harvin	15.00	40.00
GGPH2 P.J. Hill	4.00	10.00
GGPW Pat White	15.00	30.00
GGQC Quan Cosby	4.00	10.00
GGRB Ramses Barden	3.00	8.00
GGRB2 Rhett Bomar	4.00	10.00
GGRK Rashad Jennings	5.00	12.00
GGRM Rey Maualuga	5.00	12.00
GGSG Shonn Greene	8.00	20.00
GGSM Stephen McGee	5.00	12.00
GGTJ Tyson Jackson	4.00	10.00
GGVD Vontae Davis	5.00	12.00
GGVH Victor Harris	5.00	12.00
GGWM William Moore	5.00	12.00

2009 Press Pass SE Headliners

STATED ODDS 1:2

HL1 Nate Davis	.50	1.25
HL2 Josh Freeman	1.25	3.00
HL3 Graham Harrell	.60	1.50
HL4 Mark Sanchez	2.00	5.00
HL5 Matthew Stafford	3.00	8.00
HL6 Pat White	.60	1.50
HL7 Andre Brown	.40	1.00
HL8 Donald Brown	.60	1.50
HL9 Glen Coffee	.50	1.25
HL10 Shonn Greene	1.00	2.50
HL11 Mike Goodson	.60	1.50
HL12 Knowshon Moreno	.60	1.50
HL13 LeSean McCoy	1.25	3.00
HL14 Javon Ringer	.60	1.50
HL15 Chris Wells	1.00	2.50
HL16 Kenny Britt	.75	2.00
HL17 Michael Crabtree	1.25	3.00
HL18 Percy Harvin	1.00	2.50
HL19 Darrius Heyward-Bey	.60	1.50
HL20 Juaquin Iglesias	.50	1.25
HL21 Jeremy Maclin	1.00	2.50
HL22 Hakeem Nicks	1.00	2.50
HL23 Brandon Tate	.60	1.50
HL24 Derrick Williams	.50	1.25
HL25 Brandon Pettigrew	.60	1.50
HL26 Everette Brown	.50	1.25
HL27 Tyson Jackson	.50	1.25
HL28 Aaron Maybin	.50	1.25
HL29 Brian Orakpo	.60	1.50
HL30 Aaron Curry	.60	1.50
HL31 James Laurinaitis	.60	1.50
HL32 Rey Maualuga	.60	1.50
HL33 Malcolm Jenkins	.60	1.50
HL34 Matthew Stafford CL	2.50	6.00

2009 Press Pass SE Teammates Autographs

STATED PRINT RUN 25 SER.#'d SETS

CWJL Chris Wells	30.00	80.00
James Laurinaitis		
HNBT Hakeem Nicks	25.00	60.00
Brandon Tate		
JMCD Jeremy Maclin	40.00	80.00
Chase Daniel		
MCGH Michael Crabtree	50.00	100.00
Graham Harrell		
MSKS Matthew Stafford	60.00	120.00
Knowshon Moreno		
MSRM Mark Sanchez	60.00	120.00
Rey Maualuga		
PHLM Percy Harvin	40.00	80.00
Louis Murphy		

2012 Press Pass Showcase

STATED PRINT RUN 1-299
RED INK/20-53: .6X TO 1.5X BASIC AU/299

SCAD Alfonzo Dennard/298*	4.00	10.00
SCAJ Alshon Jeffery/299	6.00	15.00
SCAL Andrew Luck/291*	50.00	100.00
SCBO Brock Osweiler/292*	5.00	12.00
SCBW Brandon Weeden/249*	10.00	25.00
SCCG1 Chris Givens/299	3.00	8.00
SCCG2 Cyrus Gray/246*	4.00	10.00
SCCK Case Keenum/299	5.00	12.00
SCCU Courtney Upshaw/299	5.00	12.00
SCDA Dwayne Allen/299	4.00	10.00
SCDH Dan Herron/299	4.00	10.00
SCDM Doug Martin/274*	6.00	15.00
SCDP DeVier Posey/299	4.00	10.00
SCGR Gerell Robinson/299	4.00	10.00
SCIP Isaiah Pead/299	4.00	10.00
SCJF Jeff Fuller/299	5.00	12.00
SCKC Kirk Cousins/249*	6.00	15.00
SCKM Kellen Moore/293*	6.00	15.00
SCKW Kendall Wright/273*	5.00	12.00
SCLJ LaMichael James/289*	8.00	20.00
SCLK Luke Kuechly/272*	5.00	12.00
SCMB Mark Barron/299	6.00	15.00
SCME Michael Egnew/299	3.00	8.00
SCMF Michael Floyd/299	8.00	20.00
SCMI Melvin Ingram/299	5.00	12.00
SCMM Marquis Maze/249*	4.00	10.00
SCMS Mohamed Sanu/249*	4.00	10.00
SCNF Nick Foles/273*	6.00	15.00
SCNT Nick Toon/279*	5.00	12.00
SCOC Orson Charles/299	4.00	10.00
SCRB Ryan Broyles/299	4.00	10.00
SCRL Ryan Lindley/299	4.00	10.00
SCRR Rueben Randle/299	4.00	10.00
SCRW Russell Wilson/299	6.00	15.00
SCSG Stephon Gilmore/299	4.00	10.00
SCSH Stephen Hill/249*	4.00	10.00
SCTG T.J. Graham/299	4.00	10.00

2012 Press Pass Showcase Blue

*BLUE/50: .6X TO 1.5X BASIC AU/299
ANNOUNCED PRINT RUN 3-50

SCLM Lamar Miller	8.00	20.00
SCQC Quinton Coples	6.00	15.00
SCRG Robert Griffin III/24*	125.00	250.00
SCTR Trent Richardson/49*	20.00	50.00
SCTS Tommy Streeter	6.00	15.00

2012 Press Pass Showcase Blue Red Ink

RED INK STATED PRINT RUN 1-47

SCOC Orson Charles/47*	6.00	15.00
SCRG Robert Griffin III/26*	100.00	200.00
SCRR Rueben Randle/47*	6.00	15.00
SCRT Ryan Tannehill/47*	15.00	40.00

2012 Press Pass Showcase Gold

*GOLD/99-149: .5X TO 1.2X BASIC AU/299
GOLD ANNOUNCED PRINT RUN 99-149
GOLD RED INK/23-50: .5X TO 1.2X GLD AU

SCAL Andrew Luck/144*	50.00	100.00
SCQC Quinton Coples	5.00	12.00

2012 Press Pass Showcase End Zone Autographs Blue

BLUE ANNOUNCED PRINT RUN 18-25
*GOLD/99: .25X TO .6X BLUE AU/25
*SILVER/50: .3X TO .8X BLUE AU/25

EZAL Andrew Luck/21*	60.00	120.00
EZBW Brandon Weeden	12.00	30.00
EZJB Justin Blackmon	12.00	30.00
EZKC Case Keenum/18*	8.00	20.00
EZKM Kellen Moore/23*	10.00	25.00
EZKW Kendall Wright	8.00	20.00
EZLJ LaMichael James	12.00	30.00
EZRB Robert Griffin III	60.00	120.00
EZTR Trent Richardson/21*	30.00	60.00

2012 Press Pass Showcase Fantasy Team Autographs Blue

BLUE STATED PRINT RUN 18-25
*GOLD/99: .25X TO .6X BLUE AU/25
*SILVER/50: .3X TO .8X BLUE AU/25

FTAL Andrew Luck	75.00	150.00
FTBW Brandon Weeden	12.00	30.00
FTCK Case Keenum	8.00	20.00
FTGR Gerell Robinson	6.00	15.00
FTJB Justin Blackmon	12.00	30.00
FTKM Kellen Moore	10.00	25.00
FTKW Kendall Wright	8.00	20.00
FTLJ LaMichael James	12.00	30.00
FTLM Lamar Miller	8.00	20.00
FTRB Robert Griffin III	60.00	120.00
FTRW Russell Wilson	10.00	25.00
FTTR Trent Richardson/18*	30.00	60.00

2012 Press Pass Showcase GameDay Threads Silver

ONE JERSEY PER PACK OVERALL
*BLUE/99: .5X TO 1.2X BASIC JSY
*GOLD/199: .5X TO 1.2X BASIC JSY
*GREEN/50: .6X TO 1.5X BASIC JSY

GDTAL Andrew Luck	8.00	20.00
GDTLJ LaMichael James	5.00	12.00
GDTLM Lamar Miller	4.00	10.00
GDTMF Michael Floyd	5.00	12.00
GDTRG Robert Griffin III	8.00	20.00

2012 Press Pass Showcase Making The Cut Autographs Blue

BLUE STATED PRINT RUN 25
*GOLD/99: .25X TO .6X BLUE AU/25
*SILVER/50: .3X TO .8X BLUE AU/25

MCAL Andrew Luck/24*	75.00	150.00
MCAS Alshon Jeffery	10.00	25.00
MCJB Justin Blackmon/24*	12.00	30.00
MCKW Kendall Wright	8.00	20.00
MCMF Michael Floyd	12.00	30.00
MCQC Quinton Coples	6.00	15.00
MCRG Robert Griffin III	60.00	120.00
MCTR Trent Richardson	30.00	60.00

1999 SAGE

The 1999 Sage set was issued in one series totalling 50 cards. The fronts feature borderless color action player photos. The backs carry another player photo with player information, career statistics and a statement about the player's ability. Only 4,200 sets were produced.

COMPLETE SET (50)	12.00	30.00
1 Rahim Abdullah	.25	.60
2 Jerry Azumah	.25	.60
3 Champ Bailey	.75	2.00
4 D'Wayne Bates	.25	.60
5 Michael Bishop	.30	.75
6 David Boston	.30	.75
7 Fernando Bryant	.25	.60
8 Tony Bryant	.25	.60
9 Chris Claiborne	.25	.60
10 Mike Cloud	.25	.60
11 Cecil Collins	.25	.60
12 Tim Couch	.40	1.00
13 Daunte Culpepper	.40	1.00
14 Jared DeVries	.25	.60
15 Adrian Dingle	.25	.60
16 Antuan Edwards	.25	.60
17 Troy Edwards	.30	.75
18 Kevin Faulk	.40	1.00
19 Rufus French	.25	.60
20 Martin Gramatica	.25	.60
21 Torry Holt	.60	1.50
22 Sedrick Irvin	.25	.60
23 Edgerrin James	.50	1.25
24 Jon Jansen	.25	.60
25 Andy Katzenmoyer	.30	.75
26 Jevon Kearse	.40	1.00
27 Patrick Kerney	.30	.75
28 Lamar King	.25	.60
29 Shaun King	.30	.75
30 Jim Kleinsasser	.40	1.00
31 Rob Konrad	.25	.60
32 Brian Kuklick	.25	.60
33 Chris McAlister	.30	.75
34 Darnell McDonald	.25	.60
35 Reggie McGrew	.25	.60
36 Donovan McNabb	1.50	4.00
37 Cade McNown	.30	.75
38 Dat Nguyen	.40	1.00
39 Solomon Page	.25	.60
40 Mike Peterson	.30	.75
41 Anthony Poindexter	.25	.60
42 Peerless Price	.30	.75
43 Mike Rucker	.25	.60
44 L.J. Shelton	.25	.60
45 Akili Smith	.30	.75
46 John Tait	.25	.60
47 Fred Vinson	.25	.60
48 Al Wilson	.40	1.00
49 Antoine Winfield	.25	.60
50 Damien Woody	.25	.60

1999 SAGE Autographs Red

*BRONZE/565-650: .4X TO 1X RED AU
*BRONZE/140-285: .5X TO 1.2X RED AU
RED AUTO/209-999 ODDS 1:2
*SILVER/348-400: .5X TO 1.2X RED AU
*SILVER/75-180: .6X TO 1.5X RED AU
*GOLD/174-200: .6X TO 1.5X RED AU
*GOLD/45-90: .8X TO 2X RED AU
*PLATINUM/13-50: 1X TO 2.5X RED AU
*PLATINUM/13-25: 1.2X TO 3X RED AU
UNPRICED MASTER EDIT/1 ODDS 1:2000

A1 Rahim Abdullah/999	2.50	6.00
A2 Jerry Azumah/999	2.50	6.00
A3 Champ Bailey/999	8.00	20.00
A4 D'Wayne Bates/999	2.50	6.00
A5 Michael Bishop/999	3.00	8.00
A6 David Boston/869	3.00	8.00
A7 Fernando Bryant/999	2.50	6.00
A8 Tony Bryant/999	2.50	6.00
A9 Chris Claiborne/999	2.50	6.00
A10 Mike Cloud/434	2.50	6.00
A11 Cecil Collins/999	2.50	6.00
A12 Tim Couch/999	4.00	10.00
A13 Daunte Culpepper/419	4.00	10.00
A14 Jared DeVries/887	2.50	6.00
A15 Adrian Dingle/999	2.50	6.00
A16 Antuan Edwards/999	2.50	6.00
A17 Troy Edwards/999	3.00	8.00
A18 Kevin Faulk/999	4.00	10.00
A19 Rufus French/999	2.50	6.00
A20 Martin Gramatica/999	2.50	6.00
A21 Torry Holt/999	6.00	15.00
A22 Sedrick Irvin/999	2.50	6.00
A23 Edgerrin James/859	5.00	12.00
A24 Jon Jansen/999	2.50	6.00
A25 Andy Katzenmoyer/209	4.00	10.00
A26 Jevon Kearse/999	4.00	10.00
A27 Patrick Kerney/879	3.00	8.00
A28 Lamar King/999	2.50	6.00
A29 Shaun King/999	3.00	8.00
A30 Jim Kleinsasser/999	4.00	10.00
A31 Rob Konrad/999	2.50	6.00
A32 Brian Kuklick/999	2.50	6.00
A33 Chris McAlister/999	3.00	8.00
A34 Darnell McDonald/999	2.50	6.00
A35 Reggie McGrew/999	2.50	6.00
A36 Donovan McNabb/999	10.00	25.00
A37 Cade McNown/209	4.00	10.00
A38 Dat Nguyen/999	4.00	10.00
A39 Solomon Page/999	2.50	6.00
A40 Mike Peterson/999	3.00	8.00
A41 Anthony Poindexter/999	2.50	6.00
A42 Peerless Price/232	4.00	10.00
A43 Mike Rucker/999	2.50	6.00
A44 L.J. Shelton/999	2.50	6.00
A45 Akili Smith/419	3.00	8.00
A46 John Tait/999	2.50	6.00
A47 Fred Vinson/999	2.50	6.00
A48 Al Wilson/999	4.00	10.00
A49 Antoine Winfield/999	2.50	6.00
A50 Damien Woody/999	2.50	6.00

1999 SAGE Tim Couch

This 9-card set was issued by Sage as a stand alone set; not inserted in packs. Each card features a highlight from the career of Tim Couch. The cards are serial numbered of 1999 on the fronts and include the career highlight below the serial number.

COMPLETE SET (9)	12.50	25.00
COMMON CARD (1-9)	1.25	3.00

2000 SAGE

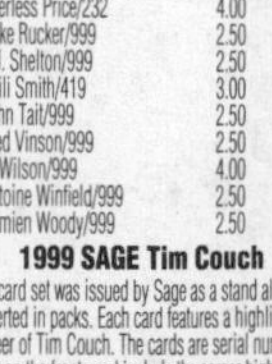

Released as a 50-card set, Sage football showcases top draft picks from the 2000 NFL draft. Packaged in 12-pack boxes, each pack contained three cards, one of which was sequentially numbered and autographed. At the time of it's release, Sage had the only approved LaVar Arrington card.

COMPLETE SET (50)	6.00	15.00
1 John Abraham	.30	.75
2 Shaun Alexander	.40	1.00
3 LaVar Arrington	.50	1.25
4 Courtney Brown	.25	.60
5 Keith Bulluck	.25	.60
6 Plaxico Burress	.30	.75
7 Giovanni Carmazzi	.20	.50
8 Kwame Cavil	.20	.50
9 Cosey Coleman	.20	.50
10 Laveranues Coles	.30	.75
11 Tim Couch	.25	.60
12 Ron Dayne	.30	.75
13 Reuben Droughns	.30	.75
14 Shaun Ellis	.30	.75
15 John Engelberger	.20	.50
16 Danny Farmer	.20	.50
17 Dwayne Goodrich	.20	.50
18 Deon Grant	.20	.50
19 Chris Hovan	.25	.60
20 Darren Howard	.20	.50
21 Todd Husak	.20	.50
22 Thomas Jones	.40	1.00
23 Curtis Keaton	.20	.50
24 Jamal Lewis	.30	.75
25 Anthony Lucas	.20	.50
26 Tee Martin	.30	.75
27 Stockar McDougle	.20	.50
28 Corey Moore	.20	.50
29 Rob Morris	.25	.60
30 Sammy Morris	.25	.60
31 Sylvester Morris	.20	.50
32 Chad Pennington	.50	1.25
33 Todd Pinkston	.20	.50
34 Ahmed Plummer	.20	.50
35 Jerry Porter	.30	.75
36 Travis Prentice	.25	.60
37 Tim Rattay	.25	.60
38 Chris Redman	.25	.60
39 J.R. Redmond	.20	.50
40 Chris Samuels	.25	.60
41 Brandon Short	.20	.50
42 Corey Simon	.25	.60
43 R.Jay Soward	.20	.50
44 Shyrone Stith	.20	.50
45 Raynoch Thompson	.20	.50
46 Brian Urlacher	1.25	3.00
47 Todd Wade	.20	.50
48 Troy Walters	.20	.50
49 Dez White	.25	.60
50 Michael Wiley	.20	.50

2000 SAGE Autographs Red

RED/334-999 STATED ODDS 1:2
RED STATED PRINT RUN 334-999
*BRONZE/225-650: .5X TO 1.2X RED/334-650
BRONZE STATED PRINT RUN 225-650
*GOLD/110-200: .8X TO 2X RED/334-650
GOLD STATED PRINT RUN 110-200
UNPRICED MASTERS PRINT RUN 1 SET
*PLATINUM/20-50: 1X TO 2.5X RED/334-999
PLATINUM STATED PRINT RUN 20-50
*SILVER/140-400: .6X TO 1.5X RED/334-999
SILVER STATED PRINT RUN 140-400

A1 John Abraham/999	3.00	8.00
A2 Shaun Alexander/999	4.00	10.00
A3 LaVar Arrington/534	8.00	30.00
A4 Courtney Brown/554	2.50	6.00
A5 Keith Bulluck/999	2.50	6.00
A6 Plaxico Burress/999	5.00	12.00
A7 Giovanni Carmazzi/999	2.00	5.00
A8 Kwame Cavil/999	2.00	5.00
A9 Cosey Coleman/999	2.00	5.00
A10 Laveranues Coles/999	3.00	8.00
A11 Tim Couch/354	2.50	6.00
A12 Ron Dayne/334	3.00	8.00
A13 Reuben Droughns/999	3.00	8.00
A14 Shaun Ellis/999	3.00	8.00
A15 John Engelberger/999	2.00	5.00
A16 Danny Farmer/999	2.00	5.00
A17 Dwayne Goodrich/999	2.00	5.00
A18 Deon Grant/999	2.00	5.00
A19 Chris Hovan/999	2.50	6.00
A20 Darren Howard/999	2.00	5.00
A21 Todd Husak/999	2.00	5.00
A22 Thomas Jones/999	4.00	10.00
A23 Curtis Keaton/999	2.00	5.00
A24 Jamal Lewis/999	3.00	8.00
A25 Anthony Lucas/999	2.00	5.00
A26 Tee Martin/999	3.00	8.00
A27 Stockar McDougle/999	2.00	5.00
A28 Corey Moore/999	2.00	5.00
A29 Rob Morris/999	2.50	6.00
A30 Sammy Morris/999	2.50	6.00
A31 Sylvester Morris/999	2.00	5.00
A32 Chad Pennington/749	5.00	12.00
A33 Todd Pinkston/999	2.00	5.00
A34 Ahmed Plummer/999	2.00	5.00
A35 Jerry Porter/999	3.00	8.00
A36 Travis Prentice/999	2.50	6.00
A37 Tim Rattay/999	2.50	6.00
A38 Chris Redman/999	2.50	6.00
A39 J.R. Redmond/999	2.00	5.00
A40 Chris Samuels/999	2.50	6.00
A41 Brandon Short/999	2.00	5.00
A42 Corey Simon/999	2.50	6.00
A43 R.Jay Soward/999	2.00	5.00
A44 Shyrone Stith/999	2.00	5.00
A45 Raynoch Thompson/999	2.00	5.00
A46 Brian Urlacher/999	12.00	30.00
A47 Todd Wade/999	2.00	5.00
A48 Troy Walters/999	2.00	5.00
A49 Dez White/999	2.50	6.00
A50 Michael Wiley/999	2.00	5.00

2001 SAGE

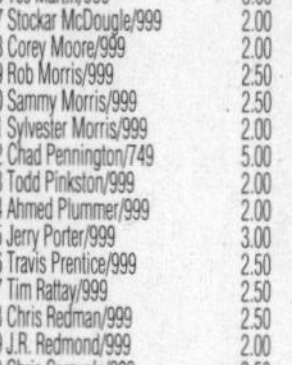

Released as a 50-card set, Sage football showcases top draft picks from the 2001 NFL Draft. Packaged in 12-pack boxes, each pack contained three cards, one of which was sequentially numbered and autographed. These cards were serial numbered to 4500 sets.

COMPLETE SET (50)	7.50	20.00
1 Will Allen	.30	.75
2 Adam Archuleta	.25	.60
3 Jeff Backus	.20	.50
4 Alex Bannister	.20	.50
5 Gary Baxter	.20	.50
6 Michael Bennett	.25	.60
7 Josh Booty	.25	.60
8 Drew Brees	2.00	5.00
9 Correll Buckhalter	.30	.75
10 Quincy Carter	.25	.60
11 Chris Chambers	.30	.75
12 Alge Crumpler	.30	.75
13 Andre Dyson	.20	.50
14 Robert Ferguson	.30	.75
15 Jamar Fletcher	.20	.50
16 Rod Gardner	.25	.60
17 Reggie Germany	.20	.50
18 Derrick Gibson	.20	.50
19 Casey Hampton	.30	.75
20 Tim Hasselbeck	.25	.60
21 Todd Heap	.30	.75
22 Travis Henry	.25	.60
23 Josh Heupel	.30	.75
24 Willie Howard	.20	.50
25 Steve Hutchinson	.30	.75
26 James Jackson	.20	.50
27 Rudi Johnson	.30	.75
28 LaMont Jordan	.30	.75
29 Torrance Marshall	.20	.50
30 Deuce McAllister	.30	.75
31 Willie Middlebrooks	.25	.60
32 Quincy Morgan	.25	.60
33 Santana Moss	.40	1.00
34 Jesse Palmer	.25	.60
35 Carlos Polk	.20	.50
36 Ken-Yon Rambo	.20	.50
37 Jamal Reynolds	.20	.50
38 Koren Robinson	.25	.60
39 Richard Seymour	.30	.75
40 Justin Smith	.30	.75
41 Fred Smoot	.30	.75
42 Marcus Stroud	.25	.60
43 David Terrell	.25	.60
44 LaDainian Tomlinson	1.00	2.50
45 Ja'Mar Toombs	.20	.50
46 Michael Vick	1.25	3.00
47 Kenyatta Walker	.20	.50
48 Gerard Warren	.25	.60
49 Reggie Wayne	.60	1.50
50 Jamie Winborn	.25	.60

2001 SAGE Autographs Red

RED/499-999 ODDS 1:2
RED PRINT RUN 499-999
*BRONZE/325-650: .5X TO 1.2X RED
BRONZE/325-650 ODDS 1:4
BRONZE PRINT RUN 325-650
*GOLD/100-200: .8X TO 2X RED
GOLD/100-200 ODDS 1:12
GOLD PRINT RUN 100-200
UNPRICED MASTER EDIT.PRINT RUN 1
*PLATINUM/25-50: 1.2X TO 3X RED
PLATINUM/25-50 ODDS 1:46
PLATINUM PRINT RUN 25-50
*SILVER/200-400: .6X TO 1.5X RED
SILVER/200-400 ODDS 1:6
SILVER PRINT RUN 200-400

A1 Will Allen	3.00	8.00
A2 Adam Archuleta	2.50	6.00
A3 Jeff Backus/900	2.00	5.00
A4 Alex Bannister	2.00	5.00
A5 Gary Baxter	2.00	5.00
A6 Michael Bennett	2.50	6.00
A7 Josh Booty/900	2.50	6.00
A8 Drew Brees/749	30.00	80.00
A9 Correll Buckhalter	3.00	8.00
A10 Quincy Carter	2.50	6.00
A11 Chris Chambers	3.00	8.00
A12 Alge Crumpler	3.00	8.00
A13 Andre Dyson	2.00	5.00
A14 Robert Ferguson	3.00	8.00
A16 Rod Gardner	2.50	6.00
A17 Reggie Germany	2.00	5.00
A18 Derrick Gibson	2.00	5.00
A19 Casey Hampton	4.00	10.00
A20 Tim Hasselbeck/900	2.50	6.00
A21 Todd Heap	3.00	8.00
A22 Travis Henry/800	2.50	6.00
A23 Josh Heupel	3.00	8.00
A24 Willie Howard/900	2.00	5.00
A25 Steve Hutchinson	3.00	8.00
A26 James Jackson	2.00	5.00
A27 Rudi Johnson	3.00	8.00
A28 LaMont Jordan	3.00	8.00
A29 Torrance Marshall	2.00	5.00
A30 Deuce McAllister/749	3.00	8.00
A31 Willie Middlebrooks	2.50	6.00
A32 Quincy Morgan	2.50	6.00
A33 Santana Moss	4.00	10.00
A34 Jesse Palmer	2.50	6.00
A35 Carlos Polk	2.00	5.00
A36 Ken-Yon Rambo/749	2.00	5.00
A37 Jamal Reynolds	2.00	5.00
A38 Koren Robinson	2.50	6.00
A39 Richard Seymour	3.00	8.00
A40 Justin Smith	3.00	8.00
A41 Fred Smoot	3.00	8.00
A42 Marcus Stroud	2.50	6.00
A43 David Terrell/649	2.50	6.00
A44 LaDainian Tomlinson	15.00	40.00
A45 Ja'Mar Toombs	2.00	5.00
A46 Michael Vick/499	20.00	50.00
A47 Kenyatta Walker	2.00	5.00
A49 Reggie Wayne	6.00	15.00
A50 Jamie Winborn	2.50	6.00

2001 SAGE Jerseys

COMPLETE SET (3)	75.00	150.00
STATED ODDS 1:205		
STATED PRINT RUN 175 SER.#'d SETS		
J1 Michael Vick	12.50	30.00
J2 Drew Brees	12.50	30.00
J3 David Terrell	6.00	15.00

2001 SAGE Michael Vick

COMPLETE SET (2)	60.00	120.00
STATED PRINT RUN 650 SER. #'d SETS		
MV1 Michael Vick JSY	10.00	20.00
MV2 Michael Vick AU	25.00	50.00

2002 SAGE

Released as a 45-card set, Sage football showcases top draft picks from the 2002 NFL Draft. Packaged in 12-pack boxes, each pack contained three cards, one of which was autographed. The base cards read "1 of 3500" cards produced. The SRP was $10.99 per pack.

COMPLETE SET (45)	15.00	40.00
1 Ladell Betts	.60	1.50
2 Antonio Bryant	.60	1.50
3 Reche Caldwell	.60	1.50
4 Kelly Campbell	.50	1.25
5 David Carr	.60	1.50
6 Tim Carter	.50	1.25
7 Eric Crouch	.60	1.50
8 Ronald Curr	.50	1.25

9 Rohan Davey .60 1.50
10 Andre Davis .50 1.25
11 T.J. Duckett .60 1.50
12 Randy Fasani .50 1.25
13 DeShaun Foster .60 1.50
14 Dwight Freeney .75 2.00
15 Jabar Gaffney .60 1.50
16 Lamar Gordon .50 1.25
17 Daniel Graham .50 1.25
18 Joey Harrington .60 1.50
19 Napoleon Harris .50 1.25
20 Albert Haynesworth .60 1.50
21 John Henderson .50 1.25
22 Chad Hutchinson .40 1.00
23 Quentin Jammer .60 1.50
24 Ron Johnson .50 1.25
25 Kurt Kittner .40 1.00
26 Ashley Lelie .50 1.25
27 Bryant McKinnie .40 1.00
28 Maurice Morris .50 1.25
29 David Neill .40 1.00
30 J.T. O'Sullivan .50 1.25
31 Brian Poli-Dixon .40 1.00
32 Clinton Portis .75 2.00
33 Patrick Ramsey .60 1.50
34 Josh Reed .50 1.25
35 Cliff Russell .40 1.00
36 Lito Sheppard .60 1.50
37 Jeremy Shockey 1.00 2.50
38 Luke Staley .40 1.00
39 Donte Stallworth .60 1.50
40 Travis Stephens .40 1.00
41 Chester Taylor .60 1.50
42 Larry Tripplett .40 1.00
43 Javon Walker .60 1.50
44 Marquise Walker .40 1.00
45 Jonathan Wells .60 1.50

2002 SAGE Autographs Red

RED UNL.STARS/110-220 5.00 12.00
RED AUTO/40-860 ODDS 1:2
*BRONZE AU: .5X TO 1.2X RED
BRONZE AU/30-650 ODDS 1:4
*GOLD AU: .8X TO 2X RED
GOLD AU/15-200 ODDS 1:12
*PLATINUM/15-50: 1X TO 2.5X RED
PLATINUM AU/5-50 ODDS 1:48
*SILVER AU: .6X TO 1.5X RED
SILVER AU/20-400 ODDS 1:6
UNPRICED MASTER EDITION PRINT RUN 1
A1 Ladell Betts/40
A2 Antonio Bryant/740 4.00 10.00
A3 Reche Caldwell/630 4.00 10.00
A4 Kelly Campbell/750 3.00 8.00
A5 David Carr/220 5.00 12.00
A6 Tim Carter/720 3.00 8.00
A7 Eric Crouch/220 5.00 12.00
A8 Ronald Curry/800 3.00 8.00
A9 Rohan Davey/650 4.00 10.00
A10 Andre Davis/650 3.00 8.00
A11 T.J. Duckett/860 4.00 10.00
A12 Randy Fasani/700 3.00 8.00
A13 DeShaun Foster/500 4.00 10.00
A14 Dwight Freeney/800 5.00 12.00
A15 Jabar Gaffney/700 4.00 10.00
A16 Lamar Gordon/700 3.00 8.00
A17 Daniel Graham/750 3.00 8.00
A18 Joey Harrington/220 5.00 12.00
A19 Napoleon Harris/770 3.00 8.00
A20 Albert Haynesworth/125 8.00 20.00
A21 John Henderson/625 3.00 8.00
A22 Chad Hutchinson/500 2.50 6.00
A23 Quentin Jammer/300 4.00 10.00
A24 Ron Johnson/720 3.00 8.00
A25 Kurt Kittner/500 2.50 6.00
A26 Ashley Lelie/700 3.00 8.00
A27 Bryant McKinnie/720 2.50 6.00
A28 Maurice Morris/720 3.00 8.00
A29 David Neill/770 2.50 6.00
A30 J.T. O'Sullivan/660 3.00 8.00
A31 Brian Poli-Dixon/700 2.50 6.00
A32 Clinton Portis/70 25.00 60.00
A33 Patrick Ramsey/720 4.00 10.00
A34 Josh Reed/720 3.00 8.00
A35 Cliff Russell/720 2.50 6.00
A36 Lito Sheppard/670 4.00 10.00
A37 Jeremy Shockey/700 6.00 15.00
A38 Luke Staley/750 2.50 6.00
A39 Donte Stallworth/800 4.00 10.00
A40 Travis Stephens/660 2.50 6.00
A41 Chester Taylor/700 4.00 10.00
A42 Larry Tripplett/650 2.50 6.00
A43 Javon Walker/650 4.00 10.00
A44 Marquise Walker/600 2.50 6.00
A45 Jonathan Wells/680 4.00 10.00
VS1 Michael Vick/110 20.00 40.00

2002 SAGE Jerseys Red

RED PRINT RUN 99 SER.#'d SETS
*BRONZE/75: .5X TO 1.2X RED/99
BRONZE PRINT RUN 75 SER.#'d SETS
*SILVER:/50 .6X TO 1.5X RED/99
SILVER PRINT RUN 50 SER.#'d SETS
*GOLD/25: 1X TO 2.5X RED/99
GOLD PRINT RUN 25 SER #'d SETS
UNPRICED MASTER EDIT.PRINT RUN 1
UNPRICED COMBO PRINT RUN 10
1 David Carr 6.00 15.00
2 Eric Crouch 8.00 20.00
3 Rohan Davey 6.00 15.00
4 T.J. Duckett 6.00 15.00
5 DeShaun Foster 6.00 15.00
6 Joey Harrington 6.00 15.00
7 Kurt Kittner 4.00 10.00
8 Clinton Portis 8.00 20.00
9 Patrick Ramsey 6.00 15.00
10 Michael Vick 8.00 20.00

2002 SAGE Jersey Edition Promos

These cards were issued by SAGE direct to dealers one card at a time. Each features one or two top 2002 draft picks with a swatch of jersey on the front and/or back. Each card was also serial numbered as noted below. The cards are not numbered but listed below alphabetically.

STATED PRINT RUN 5-25
4 Eric Crouch/50 4.00 10.00
Rohan Davey
5 Eric Crouch/25 4.00 10.00
Kurt Kittner
6 Eric Crouch/25 4.00 10.00
Patrick Ramsey
7 Eric Crouch/25 5.00 12.00
Clinton Portis
10 Rohan Davey/50 4.00 10.00
Kurt Kittner
13 T.J. Duckett/50 5.00 12.00
Clinton Portis

2003 SAGE

Released as a 45-card set, SAGE football showcases top draft picks from the 2003 NFL Draft. Packaged in 12-pack boxes, each pack contained three cards, including one that was autographed. The base cards were printed in quantities of only 2750. SRP was $10.99 per pack.

COMPLETE SET (45) 10.00 25.00
1 Sam Aiken .40 1.00
2 Boss Bailey .40 1.00
3 Brad Banks .40 1.00
4 Tully Banta-Cain .50 1.25
5 Arnaz Battle .50 1.25
6 Ronald Bellamy .40 1.00
7 Kyle Boller .50 1.25
8 Chris Brown .30 .75
9 Tyrone Calico .40 1.00
10 Dallas Clark .75 2.00
11 Kevin Curtis .50 1.25
12 Sammy Davis .40 1.00
13 Dahrran Diedrick .30 .75
14 Ken Dorsey .40 1.00
15 Justin Fargas .50 1.25
16 Justin Gage .40 1.00
17 Jason Gesser .40 1.00
18 Cie Grant .40 1.00
19 Rex Grossman .50 1.25
20 E.J. Henderson .40 1.00
21 Taylor Jacobs .30 .75
22 Bryant Johnson .50 1.25
23 Larry Johnson .50 1.25
24 Teyo Johnson .40 1.00
25 Kliff Kingsbury .40 1.00
26 Brandon Lloyd .75 2.00
27 Rashean Mathis .40 1.00
28 Jerome McDougle .25 .60
29 Willis McGahee .60 1.50
30 Billy McMullen .30 .75
31 Terence Newman .40 1.00
32 Donnie Nickey .30 .75
33 Terry Pierce .30 .75
34 Dave Ragone .30 .75
35 Charles Rogers .40 1.00
36 Chris Simms .50 1.25
37 Musa Smith .30 .75
38 Lee Suggs .40 1.00
39 Terrell Suggs .50 1.25
40 Marcus Trufant .40 1.00
41 Seneca Wallace .50 1.25
42 Kelley Washington .30 .75
43 Matt Wilhelm .40 1.00
44 Jason Witten 1.25 3.00
45 George Wrighster .30 .75

2003 SAGE Autographs Red

RED STATED ODDS 1:2
*BRONZE: .5X TO 1.2X RED AU
BRONZE STATED ODDS 1:4
*GOLD: .8X TO 2X RED AU
GOLD STATED ODDS 1:12
UNPRICED ME 1/1 ODDS 1:1050
*PLATINUM/30-50: 2X TO 5X RED AU
*PLATINUM/15-20: 2.5X TO 6X RED AU
PLATINUM STATED ODDS 1:45
*PLAY.PROOF/20: 2.5X TO 6X RED AU
PLAYER PROOF/20 ODDS 1:105
*SILVER: .6X TO 1.5X RED AU
SILVER STATED ODDS 1:6
A1 Sam Aiken/379 3.00 8.00
A2 Boss Bailey/370 3.00 8.00
A3 Brad Banks/540 3.00 8.00
A4 Tully Banta-Cain/620 4.00 10.00
A5 Arnaz Battle/910 4.00 10.00
A6 Ronald Bellamy/810 3.00 8.00
A7 Kyle Boller/750 4.00 10.00
A8 Chris Brown/920 2.50 6.00
A9 Tyrone Calico/670 3.00 8.00
A10 Dallas Clark/670 6.00 15.00
A11 Kevin Curtis/930 4.00 10.00
A12 Sammy Davis/799 3.00 8.00
A13 Dahrran Diedrick/250 2.50 6.00
A14 Ken Dorsey/335 3.00 8.00
A15 Justin Fargas/999 4.00 10.00
A16 Justin Gage/690 3.00 8.00
A17 Jason Gesser/799 3.00 8.00
A19 Rex Grossman/395 8.00 20.00
A20 E.J. Henderson/640 3.00 8.00
A21 Taylor Jacobs/700 2.50 6.00
A22 Bryant Johnson/360 4.00 10.00
A23 Larry Johnson/360 5.00 12.00
A24 Teyo Johnson/679 3.00 8.00
A25 Kliff Kingsbury/675 3.00 8.00
A26 Brandon Lloyd/779 6.00 15.00
A27 Rashean Mathis/500 3.00 8.00
A28 Jerome McDougle/930 2.50 6.00
A29 Willis McGahee/360 5.00 12.00
A30 Billy McMullen/690 2.50 6.00
A31 Terence Newman/640 3.00 8.00
A32 Donnie Nickey/290 2.50 6.00
A33 Terry Pierce/930 2.50 6.00
A34 Dave Ragone/210 2.50 6.00
A35 Charles Rogers/220 3.00 8.00
A36 Chris Simms/350 4.00 10.00
A37 Musa Smith/360 2.50 6.00
A38 Lee Suggs/355 3.00 8.00
A39 Terrell Suggs/350 4.00 10.00
A40 Marcus Trufant/930 3.00 8.00
A41 Seneca Wallace/799 4.00 10.00
A42 Kelley Washington/75 15.00 40.00
A43 Matt Wilhelm/650 3.00 8.00
A44 Jason Witten/950 10.00 25.00
A45 George Wrighster/670 2.50 6.00

2003 SAGE Jerseys Red

RED/99 STATED ODDS 1:40
*BRONZE/75: .5X TO 1.2 RED JSY/99
BRONZE/75 STATED ODDS 1:53
*GOLD/25: 1X TO 2.5X RED JSY/99
GOLD/25 STATED ODDS 1:160
*SILVER/50: .6X TO 1.5X RED JSY/99
SILVER/50 STATED ODDS 1:80
UNPRICED ME 1/1 ODDS 1:3950
UNPRICED PLATINUM/10 ODDS 1:395
*PLAY.PROOF/20: 1.2X TO 3X RED JSY/99
PLAYER PROOF/20 ODDS 1:395
SJ1 Brad Banks 4.00 10.00
SJ2 Arnaz Battle 5.00 12.00
SJ3 Kyle Boller 5.00 12.00
SJ4 Chris Brown 3.00 8.00
SJ5 David Carr 4.00 10.00
SJ6 Ken Dorsey 4.00 10.00
SJ7 Rex Grossman 5.00 12.00
SJ8 Taylor Jacobs 3.00 8.00
SJ9 Bryant Johnson 5.00 12.00
SJ10 Larry Johnson 5.00 12.00
SJ11 Willis McGahee 6.00 15.00
SJ12 Dave Ragone 3.00 8.00
SJ13 Charles Rogers 4.00 10.00
SJ14 Chris Simms 5.00 12.00
SJ15 Musa Smith 3.00 8.00
SJ16 Lee Suggs 4.00 10.00
SJ17 Seneca Wallace 5.00 12.00
SJ18 Kelley Washington 3.00 8.00

2003 SAGE First Card

Cards from this set were released directly from SAGE primarily through internet outlets. Each card carried an initial price of either $6.95 or $9.95 and was intended to preview an expected top 2003 NFL Draft pick. A limited number of complete sets were offered at $199.95. Orders for the cards were cut off at the time of the NFL Draft in late April 2003 and SAGE destroyed all unsold cards. The announced final print runs are noted below.

COMPLETE SET (24) 75.00 150.00
FC1 Larry Johnson 2.50 6.00
FC2 Rex Grossman 2.50 6.00
FC3 Kyle Boller 2.50 6.00
FC4 Chris Brown 1.50 4.00
FC5 Lee Suggs 2.00 5.00
FC6 Taylor Jacobs 1.50 4.00
FC7 Justin Fargas 2.50 6.00
FC8 Bryant Johnson 2.50 6.00
FC9 Kliff Kingsbury 2.00 5.00
FC10 Chris Simms 2.50 6.00
FC11 Terence Newman 2.00 5.00
FC12 Musa Smith 1.50 4.00
FC13 Teyo Johnson 2.00 5.00
FC14 Arnaz Battle 2.50 6.00
FC15 Brad Banks 2.00 5.00
FC16 Charles Rogers 2.00 5.00
FC17 Ken Dorsey 2.00 5.00
FC18 Dave Ragone 1.50 4.00
FC19 Seneca Wallace 2.50 6.00
FC20 Kelley Washington 1.50 4.00
FC21 Jason Witten 6.00 15.00
FC22 Terrell Suggs 4.00 10.00
FC23 Jason Gesser 2.00 5.00
FC24 Willis McGahee 3.00 8.00

2004 SAGE

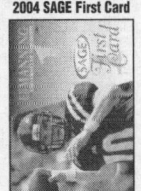

The basic issue SAGE product was released in late May 2004. The base set consists of 46-cards. Maurice Clarett made an apearance in this product although he was declared ineligible for the NFL Draft. Hobby boxes contained 12-packs of 3-cards and carried an S.R.P. of $12.99. Each hobby pack also included one autograph or jersey card which was the primary draw for this product. No other inserts were included in the product.

COMPLETE SET (46) 12.50 30.00
STATED PRINT RUN 3200 SETS
1 Tatum Bell .30 .75
2 Bernard Berrian .40 1.00
3 Michael Boulware .40 1.00
4 Drew Carter .30 .75
5 Maurice Clarett .30 .75
6 Casey Clausen .30 .75
7 Michael Clayton .30 .75
8 Chris Collins .25 .60
9 Karlos Dansby .40 1.00
10 Devard Darling .25 .60
11 Lee Evans .40 1.00
12 Clarence Farmer .25 .60
13 Chris Gamble .30 .75
14 Jake Grove .25 .60
15 DeAngelo Hall .40 1.00
16 Josh Harris .25 .60
17 Tommie Harris .40 1.00
18 Devery Henderson .40 1.00
19 Steven Jackson .60 1.50
20 Michael Jenkins .40 1.00
21 Greg Jones .25 .60
22 Kevin Jones .30 .75
23 Sean Jones .30 .75
24 Derrick Knight .25 .60
25 Craig Krenzel .30 .75
26 Jared Lorenzen .30 .75
27 Eli Manning 2.50 6.00
28 John Navarre .25 .60
29 Chris Perry .30 .75
30 Cody Pickett .30 .75
31 Will Poole .40 1.00
32 Philip Rivers 1.50 4.00
33 Ell Roberson .40 1.00
34 Dunta Robinson .25 .60
35 Ben Roethlisberger 2.50 6.00
36 Rod Rutherford .25 .60
37 P.K. Sam .25 .60
38 Matt Schaub .75 2.00
39 Will Smith .30 .75
40 Jeff Smoker .30 .75
41 Ben Troupe .30 .75
42 Ernest Wilford .30 .75
43 Reggie Williams .30 .75
44 Roy Williams WR .40 1.00
45 Quincy Wilson .30 .75
46 Rashaun Woods .25 .60

2004 SAGE Autographs Red

RED PRINT RUN 300-999
*BRONZE/200-650: .5X TO 1.2X RED
BRONZE PRINT RUN 200-650
*GOLD/60-200: .8X TO 2X RED
GOLD PRINT RUN 60-200
*PLATINUM/15-50: 1.5X TO 4X RED
PLATINUM PRINT RUN 15-50
*PLAY.PROOF/20: 2X TO 5X RED/400-999
*PLAY.PROOF/20: 1.5X TO 4X RED/300-350
PLAYER PROOF PRINT RUN 20
*SILVER/120-400: .6X TO 1.5X RED
SILVER PRINT RUN 120-400
UNPRICED MASTER EDIT.PRIN RUN 1
A1 Tatum Bell/500 3.00 8.00
A2 Bernard Berrian/850 4.00 10.00
A3 Michael Boulware/600 4.00 10.00
A4 Drew Carter/700 3.00 8.00
A5 Maurice Clarett/350 4.00 10.00
A6 Casey Clausen/999 3.00 8.00
A7 Michael Clayton/970 3.00 8.00
A8 Chris Collins/300 3.00 8.00
A9 Karlos Dansby/770 4.00 10.00
A10 Devard Darling/550 2.50 6.00
A11 Lee Evans/770 4.00 10.00
A13 Chris Gamble/750 3.00 8.00
A14 Jake Grove/650 2.50 6.00
A15 DeAngelo Hall/470 4.00 10.00
A16 Josh Harris/770 2.50 6.00
A17 Tommie Harris/500 4.00 10.00
A18 Devery Henderson/700 4.00 10.00
A20 Michael Jenkins/850 4.00 10.00
A21 Greg Jones/750 2.50 6.00
A22 Kevin Jones/750 3.00 8.00
A23 Sean Jones/999 3.00 8.00
A24 Derrick Knight/550 2.50 6.00
A26 Jared Lorenzen/800 3.00 8.00
A27 Eli Manning/400 30.00 60.00
A28 John Navarre/440 2.50 6.00
A29 Chris Perry/750 3.00 8.00
A30 Cody Pickett/600 3.00 8.00
A31 Will Poole/420 4.00 10.00
A32 Philip Rivers/500 15.00 40.00
A33 Ell Roberson/999 4.00 10.00
A34 Dunta Robinson/720 2.50 6.00
A35 Ben Roethlisberger/300 30.00 60.00
A36 Rod Rutherford/500 2.50 6.00
A37 P.K. Sam/850 2.50 6.00
A38 Matt Schaub/600 0.00 20.00
A39 Will Smith/770 3.00 8.00
A40 Jeff Smoker/500 3.00 8.00
A41 Ben Troupe/999 3.00 8.00
A42 Ernest Wilford/350 4.00 10.00
A43 Reggie Williams/600 3.00 8.00
A44 Roy Williams WR/350 5.00 12.00
A45 Quincy Wilson/850 3.00 8.00
A46 Rashaun Woods/777 2.50 6.00

2004 SAGE Jerseys Red

RED PRINT RUN 99 SER.#'d SETS
*BRONZE/75: .4X TO 1X RED/99
BRONZE STATED PRINT RUN 75
*GOLD/25: .8X TO 2X RED/99
GOLD STATED PRINT RUN 25
*PLATINUM/10: 1.2X TO 3X RED/99
PLATINUM PRINT RUN 10
*PLAYER PRF/20: 1X TO 2.5X RED/99
PLAYER PROOF PRINT RUN 20
*SILVER/50: .5X TO 1.2X RED/99
SILVER STATED PRINT RUN 50
UNPRICED MASTER EDITION #'d OF 1
UNPRICED AUTO PRINT RUN 10
J1 Tatum Bell 4.00 10.00
J2 Maurice Clarett 4.00 10.00
J3 Casey Clausen 4.00 10.00
J4 Lee Evans 5.00 12.00
J5 Josh Harris 3.00 8.00
J6 Devery Henderson 5.00 12.00
J7 Michael Jenkins 5.00 12.00
J8 Greg Jones 3.00 8.00
J9 Kevin Jones 4.00 10.00
J10 Jared Lorenzen 4.00 10.00
J11 Eli Manning 15.00 40.00
J12 John Navarre 3.00 8.00
J13 Chris Perry 4.00 10.00
J14 Cody Pickett 4.00 10.00
J15 Philip Rivers 12.00 30.00
J16 Ell Roberson 5.00 12.00
J17 Ben Roethlisberger 15.00 40.00
J18 Rod Rutherford 3.00 8.00
J19 Matt Schaub 10.00 25.00
J20 Jeff Smoker 4.00 10.00
J21 Reggie Williams 4.00 10.00
J22 Roy Williams WR 5.00 12.00
J23 Quincy Wilson 4.00 10.00
J24 Rashaun Woods 3.00 8.00

2004 SAGE Jerseys Combos

UNPRICED COMBOS PRINT RUN 10 SETS

2004 SAGE First Card

These cards represent the first football card releases for 2004 and were sold exclusively through internet channels for $9.99 per. Each card includes the SAGE First Card title as well as a hand serial number. Autographed cards for four of the players were also produced. They originally retailed for $99 each.

1 Maurice Clarett/250 6.00 12.00
2 Casey Clausen/99 6.00 12.00
3 Michael Clayton/99 6.00 12.00
4 Lee Evans/99 6.00 12.00
5 Tommie Harris/99 5.00 10.00
6 Steven Jackson/150 7.50 15.00
7 Michael Jenkins/99 5.00 10.00
8 Greg Jones/99 5.00 10.00
9 Kevin Jones/150 6.00 12.00
10 Eli Manning/250 12.50 25.00
11 John Navarre/99 5.00 10.00
12 Chris Perry/150 6.00 12.00
13 Philip Rivers/150 7.50 15.00
14 Ell Roberson/99 5.00 10.00
15 Ben Roethlisberger/250 12.50 25.00
16 Reggie Williams/99 6.00 12.00
17 Roy Williams WR/150 7.50 15.00
18 Rashaun Woods/99 6.00 12.00

2004 SAGE First Card Autographs

ABR Ben Roethlisberger/99 100.00 200.00
AEM Eli Manning/99 125.00 200.00
AMC Maurice Clarett/99 50.00 80.00
APR Philip Rivers/99 60.00 100.00

2005 SAGE

SAGE was initially released in early-June 2005. The base set consists of 54-cards. Hobby boxes contained 12-packs of 3-cards and carried an S.R.P. of $10.99 per pack with one jersey or autographed card inserted in every pack. A variety of inserts can be found seeded in packs highlighted by the multi-tiered Autograph and Jersey inserts.

COMPLETE SET (54) 12.50 30.00
1 Derek Anderson .40 1.00
2 J.J. Arrington .40 1.00
3 Marion Barber .50 1.25
4 Brock Berlin .40 1.00
5 Jammal Brown .50 1.25
6 Reggie Brown .30 .75
7 Ronnie Brown .60 1.50
8 Jason Campbell .60 1.50
9 Mark Clayton .50 1.25
10 Channing Crowder .40 1.00
11 Anthony Davis .30 .75
12 Josh Davis .30 .75
13 Thomas Davis .00 .75
14 Ciatrick Fason .30 .75
15 Ryan Fitzpatrick .75 2.00
16 Charlie Frye .50 1.25
17 Fred Gibson .40 1.00
18 Johnathan Goddard .40 1.00
19 Frank Gore .75 2.00
20 David Greene .30 .75
21 Kay-Jay Harris .30 .75
22 Marlin Jackson .30 .75
23 Brandon Jacobs .60 1.50
24 Derrick Johnson .40 1.00
25 Matt Jones .50 1.25
26 T.A. McLendon .30 .75
27 Adrian McPherson .30 .75
28 Justin Miller .40 1.00
29 Vernand Morency .40 1.00
30 Terrence Murphy .30 .75
31 Dan Orlovsky .50 1.25
32 Kyle Orton .50 1.25
33 Roscoe Parrish .30 .75
34 Brodney Pool .50 1.25
35 Dante Ridgeway .30 .75
36 Chris Rix .40 1.00
37 Aaron Rodgers 4.00 10.00
38 Carlos Rogers .50 1.25
39 J.R. Russell .30 .75
40 Alex Smith TE .30 .75
41 Alex Smith QB .75 2.00
42 Taylor Stubblefield .30 .75
43 Craphonso Thorpe .30 .75
44 Andrew Walter .40 1.00
45 DeMarcus Ware 1.00 2.50
46 Fabian Washington .40 1.00
47 Corey Webster .40 1.00
48 Jason White .50 1.25
49 Roddy White .60 1.50
50 Cadillac Williams .50 1.25
51 Troy Williamson .40 1.00
52 Maurice Clarett .40 1.00
53 Ben Roethlisberger .75 2.00
54 Antrel Rolle .50 1.25

2005 SAGE Autographs Red

RED/60 000 ODDS 1:2
RED PRINT RUN 50-999
*BRONZE: .5X TO 1.2X REDS
BRONZE/40-650 ODDS 1:4
BRONZE PRINT RUN 40-650
*GOLD/40-200: .8X TO 2X REDS
GOLD/15-200 ODDS 1:12
GOLD PRINT RUN 15-200
*PLATINUM/20-50: 1X TO 2.5X REDS
PLATINUM/5-50 ODDS 1:45
PLATINUM PRINT RUN 5-50
*PLAY.PROOF/20: 1.5X TO 4X RED/770-999
*PLAY.PROOF/20: 1.2X TO 3X RED/400-700
PLAYER PROOF PRINT RUN 20
*SILVER: .6X TO 1.5X REDS
SILVER/25-400 ODDS 1:6
SILVER PRINT RUN 25-400
UNPRICED MASTER EDITION #'d OF 1
A1 Derek Anderson/999 3.00 8.00
A2 J.J. Arrington/650 4.00 10.00
A3 Marion Barber/700 5.00 12.00
A4 Brock Berlin/400 4.00 10.00
A5 Jammal Brown/660 5.00 12.00
A6 Reggie Brown/900 2.50 6.00
A7 Ronnie Brown/999 5.00 12.00
A8 Jason Campbell/600 6.00 15.00
A9 Mark Clayton/600 5.00 12.00
A10 Channing Crowder/700 4.00 10.00
A11 Anthony Davis/900 2.50 6.00
A12 Josh Davis/600 3.00 8.00
A13 Thomas Davis/999 2.50 6.00
A14 Ciatrick Fason/650 3.00 8.00
A15 Ryan Fitzpatrick/799 6.00 15.00
A16 Charlie Frye/550 5.00 12.00
A17 Fred Gibson/900 3.00 8.00
A18 Johnathan Goddard/600 4.00 10.00
A19 Frank Gore/600 12.00 30.00
A20 David Greene/600 3.00 8.00
A21 Kay-Jay Harris/650 3.00 8.00
A22 Marlin Jackson/999 2.50 6.00
A23 Brandon Jacobs/999 10.00 25.00
A24 Derrick Johnson/700 4.00 10.00
A25 Matt Jones/999 4.00 10.00
A26 T.A. McLendon/650 3.00 8.00
A27 Adrian McPherson/770 2.50 6.00
A28 Justin Miller/660 4.00 10.00
A29 Vernand Morency/650 4.00 10.00
A30 Terrence Murphy/900 2.50 6.00
A31 Dan Orlovsky/999 4.00 10.00
A32 Kyle Orton/900 4.00 10.00
A33 Roscoe Parrish/600 3.00 8.00
A34 Brodney Pool/650 5.00 12.00
A35 Dante Ridgeway/600 3.00 8.00
A36 Chris Rix/400 4.00 10.00
A37 Aaron Rodgers/200 100.00 175.00
A38 Carlos Rogers/650 5.00 12.00
A39 J.R. Russell/900 2.50 6.00
A40 Alex Smith TE/900 2.50 6.00
A41 Alex Smith QB/200 15.00 30.00
A42 Taylor Stubblefield/900 2.50 6.00
A43 Craphonso Thorpe/700 3.00 8.00
A44 Andrew Walter/940 3.00 8.00
A45 DeMarcus Ware/910 8.00 20.00
A46 Fabian Washington/900 3.00 8.00
A47 Corey Webster/500 4.00 10.00
A48 Jason White/550 5.00 12.00
A49 Roddy White/50 20.00 50.00
A50 Cadillac Williams/600 10.00 25.00
A51 Troy Williamson/700 4.00 10.00

2005 SAGE Jerseys Red

RED STATED ODDS 1:40
RED PRINT RUN 99 SER.#'d SETS
*BRONZE: .5X TO 1.2X REDS
BRONZE STATED ODDS 1:53
BRONZE PRINT RUN 75 SER.#'d SETS
*GOLD: 1X TO 2.5X REDS
GOLD STATED ODDS 1:160
GOLD PRINT RUN 25 SER.#'d SETS
UNPRICED PLATINUM PRINT RUN 10
UNPRICED JSY AUTO PRINT RUN 10 SETS
*PLAYER PROOF: 1.2X TO 3X REDS
PLAYER PROOF PRINT RUN 20 SER.#'d SETS
*SILVER: .6X TO 1.5X REDS
SILVER STATED ODDS 1:80
SILVER PRINT RUN 50 SER.#'d SETS
UNPRICED MASTER EDITION #'d OF 1
OVERALL JERSEY STATED ODDS 1:15
J1 J.J. Arrington 3.00 8.00
J2 Ronnie Brown 12.00 30.00
J3 Jason Campbell 5.00 12.00
J4 Mark Clayton 4.00 10.00
J5 Anthony Davis 2.50 6.00
J6 Ciatrick Fason 2.50 6.00
J7 Charlie Frye 4.00 10.00
J8 Fred Gibson 3.00 8.00
J9 Frank Gore 8.00 20.00
J10 David Greene 2.50 6.00
J11 Kay-Jay Harris 2.50 6.00
J12 Adrian McPherson 2.50 6.00
J13 Vernand Morency 3.00 8.00
J14 Dan Orlovsky 4.00 10.00
J15 Kyle Orton 4.00 10.00
J16 Roscoe Parrish 2.50 6.00
J17 Chris Rix 3.00 8.00
J18 Aaron Rodgers 20.00 40.00
J19 Alex Smith QB 12.00 30.00
J20 Taylor Stubblefield 2.50 6.00
J21 Craphonso Thorpe 2.50 6.00
J22 Andrew Walter 3.00 8.00
J23 Jason White 4.00 10.00
J24 Cadillac Williams 10.00 25.00

2005 SAGE Jerseys Combos

STATED PRINT RUN 99 SER.#'d SETS
RARE STATED ODDS 1:265
UNPRICED RARE PRINT 10 SER.#'d SETS
JJ1 Alex Smith QB 20.00 50.00
Ronnie Brown
JJ2 Alex Smith QB 20.00 50.00
Aaron Rodgers
JJ3 Alex Smith QB 15.00 40.00
Jason Campbell
JJ4 Aaron Rodgers 20.00 50.00
Jason Campbell
JJ5 Ronnie Brown 25.00 60.00
Cadillac Williams
JJ6 Ronnie Brown 10.00 25.00
Jason Campbell
JJ7 Cadillac Williams 20.00 50.00
Jason Campbell
JJ8 Aaron Rodgers 20.00 50.00
J.J. Arrington
JJ9 Chris Rix 10.00 25.00
Craphonso Thorpe
JJ10 Chris Rix 7.50 20.00
Adrian McPherson
JJ11 Craphonso Thorpe 7.50 20.00
Adrian McPherson
JJ12 David Greene 7.50 20.00
Fred Gibson
JJ13 Roscoe Parrish 12.00 30.00
Frank Gore
JJ14 Mark Clayton 10.00 25.00
Jason White
JJ16 Kylo Orton 10.00 25.00
Taylor Stubblefield
JJ16 Alex Smith QB 12.50 30.00
Jason White
JJ17 David Greene 7.50 20.00
Taylor Stubblefield
JJ18 Aaron Rodgers 20.00 50.00
Andrew Walter
JJ19 Ben Roethlisberger 15.00 40.00
Charlie Frye
JJ20 Eli Manning 12.50 30.00
Alex Smith QB
JJ21 Ben Gordon 12.50 30.00
Dan Orlovsky
JJ22 Emeka Okafor 7.50 20.00
Dan Orlovsky
JJ23 Diana Taurasi 7.50 20.00
Dan Orlovsky
JJ24 Devin Harris 7.50 20.00
Anthony Davis
JJ25 Lee Evans 10.00 25.00
Roscoe Parrish
JJ26 Maurice Clarett 7.50 20.00
Tatum Bell
JJ27 Roy Williams WR 10.00 25.00
Dan Orlovsky
JJ28 Kevin Jones 7.50 20.00
Dan Orlovsky
JJ29 Devery Henderson 7.50 20.00
Adrian McPherson
JJ30 Ben Roethlisberger 15.00 40.00
Fred Gibson
JJ31 Alex Smith QB 20.00 40.00
Frank Gore
JJ32 Rashaun Woods 12.50 30.00
Alex Smith QB
JJ33 Tatum Bell 7.50 20.00
Vernand Morency
JJ34 Lee Evans 7.50 20.00
Anthony Davis
JJ35 Eli Manning 10.00 25.00
Jason Campbell
JJ36 Ben Roethlisberger 15.00 40.00
Alex Smith QB

2005 SAGE Beckett Promos

COMPLETE SET (3) 6.00 15.00
NNO Ronnie Brown 2.00 5.00
NNO Matt Jones 1.25 3.00
NNO Ben Roethlisberger 2.50 6.00

2005 SAGE Beckett

These cards were produced by SAGE and released through Beckett.com in complete set form. Each card includes the SAGE and Beckett Media logos on the front along with a hand serial numbering of either 199 or 25. Three promo cards were inserted into copies of the Summer 2005 issue of Beckett Football Card Plus. Those cards do not include a card number but have a Beckett Football Card Plus logo on the backs. Finally, two autographed cards were sold with the complete set serial numbered to 25.

COMPLETE SET (12) 18.00 30.00
*SERIAL #'d TO 25: 1.2X TO 3X
1 Cadillac Williams .50 1.25
2 Aaron Rodgers 4.00 10.00
3 Alex Smith QB .75 2.00
4 Jason Campbell .60 1.50
5 Troy Williamson .40 1.00
6 Mark Clayton .50 1.25
7 Derrick Johnson .40 1.00
8 DeMarcus Ware 1.00 2.50
9 Charlie Frye .50 1.25
10 Matt Jones .50 1.25
11 Ronnie Brown .60 1.50
12 Ben Roethlisberger 2.50 6.00
A10 Matt Jones AU/25 20.00 50.00
A11 Ronnie Brown AU/25 40.00 80.00

2005 SAGE First Card

These cards represent the first football card releases for 2005. They were originally sold exclusively through internet channels for $9.99 per card. Each card includes the SAGE First Card title as well as a hand serial number. Autographed cards for Alex Smith were also produced and serial numbered of 50.

1 Derrick Johnson/99 5.00 10.00
2 Ronnie Brown/150 7.50 15.00
3 Anthony Davis/99 5.00 10.00
4 Frank Gore/99 6.00 12.00
5 Vernand Morency/99 5.00 10.00
6 Dan Orlovsky/150 5.00 10.00
7 Kyle Orton/150 5.00 10.00
8 Chris Rix/99 5.00 10.00
9 Derek Anderson/99 3.00 12.00
10 Jason White/150 6.00 12.00
11 David Greene/99 5.00 10.00
12 Fred Gibson/99 5.00 10.00
13 Andrew Walter/150 6.00 12.00
14 J.J. Arrington/99 4.00 10.00
15 Cadillac Williams/99 7.50 15.00
16 Ciatrick Fason/99 5.00 10.00
17 Jason Campbell/99 6.00 12.00
18 Mark Clayton/150 3.00 8.00
19 Troy Williamson/99 5.00 10.00
20 Alex Smith QB/250 6.00 12.00
21 Aaron Rodgers/250 10.00 20.00

2005 SAGE First Card Autographs

1 Alex Smith QB/50 50.00 80.00

2006 SAGE

This 60-card set, featuring leading 2006 NFL prospects, was released in July, 2006. The set was issued into the hobby in three-card packs, with an $11.99 SRP, which came 12 packs to a box. The set is sequenced in player alphabetical order.

COMPLETE SET (60) 15.00 30.00
1 Joseph Addai .50 1.25
2 Devin Aromashodu .50 1.25
3 Jason Avant .30 .75
4 Hank Baskett .50 1.25
5 Mike Bell .50 1.25
6 Will Blackmon .40 1.00
7 Daniel Bullocks .50 1.25
8 Reggie Bush 1.00 2.50
9 Dominique Byrd .40 1.00
10 Brian Calhoun .30 .75
11 Bobby Carpenter .30 .75
12 Antonio Cromartie .50 1.25
13 Brodie Croyle .50 1.25
14 Jay Cutler 1.00 2.50
15 Vernon Davis .60 1.50
16 Anthony Fasano .50 1.25
17 D'Brickashaw Ferguson .50 1.25
18 Charles Gordon .40 1.00
19 Bruce Gradkowski .50 1.25
20 Skyler Green .30 .75
21 Jerome Harrison .50 1.25
22 Mike Hass .40 1.00
23 Taurean Henderson .50 1.25
24 Devin Hester .75 2.00
25 Tye Hill .30 .75
26 Michael Huff .40 1.00
27 Tarvaris Jackson .50 1.25
28 Omar Jacobs .30 .75
29 Maurice Drew .75 2.00
30 Winston Justice .40 1.00
31 Matt Leinart .50 1.25
32 Laurence Maroney .40 1.00
33 Reggie McNeal .40 1.00
34 Marcus McNeill .40 1.00
35 Erik Meyer .40 1.00
36 Sinorice Moss .50 1.25
37 Martin Nance .40 1.00
38 Drew Olson .30 .75
39 Jonathan Orr .40 1.00
40 Paul Pinegar .30 .75
41 Leonard Pope .50 1.25
42 Gerald Riggs Jr. .40 1.00
43 Michael Robinson .40 1.00
44 DeMeco Ryans .50 1.25
45 D.J. Shockley .40 1.00
46 Ernie Sims .40 1.00
47 Dwayne Slay .40 1.00
48 Maurice Stovall .30 .75
49 David Thomas .40 1.00
50 Leon Washington .40 1.00
51 Pat Watkins .40 1.00
52 LenDale White .40 1.00
53 Charlie Whitehurst .50 1.25
54 Demetrius Williams .40 1.00
55 Jimmy Williams .50 1.25
56 Mario Williams .50 1.25
57 Rodrique Wright .30 .75
58 Ashton Youboty .30 .75
59 Vince Young .60 1.50
60 Alan Zemaitis .50 1.25

2006 SAGE Autographs Red

RED/100-999 STATED ODDS 1:2
*BRONZE/50-650: .5X TO 1.2X RED AU
BRONZE/50-650 STATED ODDS 1:4
*GOLD/20-200: .8X TO 2X RED AU
GOLD/20-200 STATED ODDS 1:12
UNPRICED ME 1/1 ODDS 1:1050
*PLATINUM/15-50: 1X TO 2.5X RED AU
PLATINUM/5-50 STATED ODDS 1:45
*PLAY.PRF/20: 1.5X TO 4X RED/450-999
*PLAY.PRF/20: 1.2X TO 3X RED/100-300
PLAYER PROOF/20 ODDS 1:105
*SILVER/40-400: .6X TO 1.5X RED AU
SILVER/40-400 STATED ODDS 1:6
OVERALL AUTO/JSY ODDS 1:1
A1 Joseph Addai/999 4.00 10.00
A2 Devin Aromashodu/750 4.00 10.00
A3 Jason Avant/999 2.50 6.00
A4 Hank Baskett/999 4.00 10.00
A5 Mike Bell/999 4.00 10.00

A6 Will Blackmon/200 4.00 10.00
A7 Daniel Bullocks/999 4.00 10.00
A8 Reggie Bush/150 15.00 40.00
A9 Dominique Byrd/999 3.00 8.00
A10 Brian Calhoun/999 2.50 6.00
A11 Bobby Carpenter/999 2.50 6.00
A12 Antonio Cromartie/999 4.00 10.00
A13 Brodie Croyle/700 4.00 10.00
A14 Jay Cutler/200 25.00 50.00
A15 Vernon Davis/700 5.00 12.00
A16 Anthony Fasano/999 4.00 10.00
A17 D'Brickashaw Ferguson/300 5.00 12.00
A18 Charles Gordon/240 4.00 10.00
A19 Bruce Gradkowski/999 4.00 10.00
A20 Skyler Green/999 2.50 6.00
A21 Jerome Harrison/999 4.00 10.00
A22 Mike Hass/999 3.00 8.00
A23 Taurean Henderson/290 5.00 12.00
A25 Tye Hill/999 2.50 6.00
A26 Michael Huff/700 3.00 8.00
A27 Tarvaris Jackson/999 4.00 10.00
A28 Omar Jacobs/700 2.50 6.00
A29 Maurice Drew/999 6.00 15.00
A30 Winston Justice/700 3.00 8.00
A31 Matt Leinart/200 5.00 12.00
A32 Laurence Maroney/700 3.00 8.00
A33 Reggie McNeal/700 3.00 8.00
A34 Marcus McNeill/999 3.00 8.00
A35 Erik Meyer/999 3.00 8.00
A36 Sinorice Moss/999 4.00 10.00
A37 Martin Nance/450 3.00 8.00
A38 Drew Olson/999 2.50 6.00
A39 Jonathan Orr/999 3.00 8.00
A40 Paul Pinegar/999 2.50 6.00
A41 Leonard Pope/650 4.00 10.00
A43 Michael Robinson/600 3.00 8.00
A44 DeMeco Ryans/999 4.00 10.00
A45 D.J. Shockley/999 3.00 8.00
A46 Ernie Sims/150 4.00 10.00
A47 Dwayne Slay/999 3.00 8.00
A48 Maurice Stovall/500 2.50 6.00
A49 David Thomas/999 3.00 8.00
A50 Leon Washington/999 3.00 8.00
A51 Pat Watkins/999 3.00 8.00
A52 LenDale White/900 3.00 8.00
A53 Charlie Whitehurst/700 4.00 10.00
A54 Demetrius Williams/999 3.00 8.00
A55 Jimmy Williams/999 4.00 10.00
A56 Mario Williams/700 4.00 10.00
A57 Rodrique Wright/700 2.50 6.00
A58 Ashton Youboty/999 2.50 6.00
A59 Vince Young/100 15.00 40.00
A60 Alan Zemaitis/999 4.00 10.00

2006 SAGE Jerseys Red

RED PRINT RUN 99 SER.#'d SETS
*BRONZE/75: .4X TO 1X RED JSY/99
BRONZE PRINT RUN 75 SER.#'d SETS
*GOLD/25: .8X TO 2X RED JSY/99
GOLD/25 STATED ODDS 1:160
UNPRICED ME 1/1 ODDS 1:3950
UNPRICED PLATINUM PRINT RUN 10
*PLAYER PRF/20: 1X TO 2.5X RED JSY/99
PLAYER PROOFS PRINT RUN 20
*SILVER/50: .5X TO 1.2X RED JSY/99
SILVER/50 STATED ODDS 1:80
UNPRICED DUAL JSY/10 ODDS 1:265
J1 Joseph Addai 5.00 12.00
J2 Jason Avant 3.00 8.00
J3 Reggie Bush 10.00 25.00
J4 Bobby Carpenter 3.00 8.00
J5 Brodie Croyle 5.00 12.00
J6 Jay Cutler 10.00 25.00
J7 Vernon Davis 6.00 15.00
J8 Omar Jacobs 3.00 8.00
J9 Maurice Drew 8.00 20.00
J10 Matt Leinart 5.00 12.00
J11 Laurence Maroney 4.00 10.00
J12 Reggie McNeal 4.00 10.00
J13 Sinorice Moss 5.00 12.00
J14 Michael Robinson 4.00 10.00
J15 D.J. Shockley 4.00 10.00
J16 LenDale White 4.00 10.00
J17 Charlie Whitehurst 5.00 12.00
J18 Vince Young 6.00 15.00

2006 SAGE Game Exclusive National Draft Swatch Promos

1 Reggie Bush 12.50 30.00
2 Matt Leinart 8.00 20.00
3 Vince Young 10.00 25.00
4 Vince Young 20.00 50.00
Reggie Bush
Matt Leinart

2006 SAGE National 2500 Promos

1 Mario Williams SAGE .40 1.00
2 Reggie Bush SAGE .75 2.00
3 Vince Young Aspire .50 1.25
4 Vernon Davis Aspire .50 1.25
5 Matt Leinart HIT .40 1.00
6 Jay Cutler HIT .75 2.00
7 Triple Threat .75 2.00
LenDale White
Matt Leinart
Reggie Bush
8 Cornerstone QB's .75 2.00
Matt Leinart
Jay Cutler
Vince Young
9 The Big 3 .75 2.00
Matt Leinart
Reggie Bush
Vince Young
10 Top 3 Picks .75 2.00
Mario Williams
Reggie Bush
Vince Young

2006 SAGE National Promos Autographs

NA1 Reggie Bush/20 50.00 120.00
NA2 Matt Leinart/20 30.00 80.00
NA3 LenDale White/20 20.00 40.00

2006 SAGE National VIP Promos

COMPLETE SET (3) 6.00 15.00
1 Reggie Bush 1.50 4.00
2 Matt Leinart .75 2.00
3 Vince Young 1.00 2.50

2007 SAGE

This 62-card set was released in June, 2007. The set was issued into the hobby in three-card packs, with a $12.99 SRP which came 12 packs to a box. The set is sequenced in alphabetical order.

COMPLETE SET (62) 15.00 30.00
1 Gaines Adams .50 1.25
2 Aundrae Allison .30 .75
3 Dallas Baker .30 .75
4 David Ball .40 1.00
5 John Beck .50 1.25
6 Dwayne Bowe .60 1.50
7 Alan Branch .40 1.00
8 Steve Breaston .50 1.25
9 Levi Brown .50 1.25
10 Michael Bush .50 1.25
11 Adam Carriker .40 1.00
12 David Clowney .40 1.00
13 Ken Darby .40 1.00
14 Craig Buster Davis .40 1.00
15 Trent Edwards .50 1.25
16 Earl Everett .40 1.00
17 Yamon Figurs .30 .75
18 Joel Filani .40 1.00
19 Ted Ginn Jr. .40 1.00
20 Anthony Gonzalez .50 1.25
21 Michael Griffin .50 1.25
22 Leon Hall .40 1.00
23 Chris Henry .30 .75
24 Johnnie Lee Higgins .40 1.00
25 Jason Hill .50 1.25
26 David Irons .30 .75
27 Kenny Irons .30 .75
28 Calvin Johnson 1.50 4.00
29 Ryan Kalil .40 1.00
30 Kevin Kolb .75 2.00
31 Chris Leak .40 1.00
32 Brian Leonard .40 1.00
33 Marshawn Lynch .50 1.25
34 Robert Meachem .50 1.25
35 Brandon Meriweather .50 1.25
36 Zach Miller .50 1.25
37 Jarvis Moss .40 1.00
38 Greg Olsen .40 1.00
39 Tyler Palko .40 1.00
40 Jordan Palmer .40 1.00
41 Adrian Peterson 2.00 5.00
42 Antonio Pittman .30 .75
43 Brady Quinn .50 1.25
44 Sidney Rice .60 1.50
45 Aaron Ross .50 1.25
46 Jeff Rowe .30 .75
47 JaMarcus?äRussell .30 .75
48 Kolby Smith .40 1.00
49 Steve Smith USC .50 1.25
50 Troy Smith .50 1.25
51 Jason Snelling .50 1.25
52 Isaiah Stanback .30 .75
53 Drew Stanton .30 .75
54 Courtney Taylor .40 1.00
55 Lawrence Timmons .50 1.25
56 DeMarcus Tank Tyler .30 .75
57 Darius Walker .30 .75
58 Paul Williams .30 .75
59 Patrick Willis 1.00 2.50
60 Garrett Wolfe .30 .75
61 LaMarr Woodley .50 1.25
62 Jared Zabransky .40 1.00

2007 SAGE Autographs Red

*BRONZE: .4X TO 1X RED AUTOS
*SILVER/400: .5X TO 1.2X RED AUTOS
*SILVER/400: .4X TO 1X RED SP AUTOS
SILVER PRINT RUN 400 SER.#'d SETS
*GOLD/200: .6X TO 1.5X RED AUTOS
*GOLD/200: .5X TO 1.2X RED SP AUTOS
GOLD PRINT RUN 200 SER.#'d SETS
*PLATINUM/50: 1X TO 2.5X RED AUTOS
*PLATINUM/50: .6X TO 1.5X RED SP AUTOS
PLATINUM PRINT RUN 50 SER.#'d SETS
UNPRICED MASTER EDITION PRINT RUN 1
A1 Gaines Adams 4.00 10.00
A2 Aundrae Allison 2.50 6.00
A3 Dallas Baker 2.50 6.00
A4 David Ball 3.00 8.00
A5 John Beck 4.00 10.00
A6 Dwayne Bowe 5.00 12.00
A8 Steve Breaston 4.00 10.00
A9 Levi Brown 4.00 10.00
A10 Michael Bush 4.00 10.00
A11 Adam Carriker 3.00 8.00
A12 David Clowney 3.00 8.00
A13 Ken Darby 3.00 8.00
A14 Craig Buster Davis 3.00 8.00
A15 Trent Edwards 4.00 10.00
A16 Earl Everett 3.00 8.00
A17 Yamon Figurs 2.50 6.00
A18 Joel Filani 3.00 8.00
A20 Anthony Gonzalez 4.00 10.00
A21 Michael Griffin 4.00 10.00
A22 Leon Hall 3.00 8.00
A23 Chris Henry 2.50 6.00
A24 Johnnie Lee Higgins 3.00 8.00
A25 Jason Hill 4.00 10.00
A26 David Irons 2.50 6.00
A27 Kenny Irons 2.50 6.00
A29 Ryan Kalil 3.00 8.00
A30 Kevin Kolb 6.00 15.00
A31 Chris Leak SP 4.00 10.00
A32 Brian Leonard 3.00 8.00
A33 Marshawn Lynch SP 10.00 25.00
A34 Robert Meachem 4.00 10.00
A35 Brandon Meriweather 4.00 10.00
A36 Zach Miller 4.00 10.00
A37 Jarvis Moss 3.00 8.00
A38 Greg Olsen 3.00 8.00
A39 Tyler Palko 3.00 8.00
A40 Jordan Palmer 3.00 8.00
A41 Adrian Peterson SP 60.00 120.00
A42 Antonio Pittman 2.50 6.00
A43 Brady Quinn SP 12.00 30.00
A44 Sidney Rice 5.00 12.00
A45 Aaron Ross 4.00 10.00
A46 Jeff Rowe 2.50 6.00
A47 JaMarcus Russell SP 3.00 8.00
A48 Kolby Smith 3.00 8.00
A49 Steve Smith USC 4.00 10.00
A50 Troy Smith SP 12.00 30.00
A51 Jason Snelling 4.00 10.00
A52 Isaiah Stanback 2.50 6.00
A53 Drew Stanton SP 4.00 10.00
A55 Lawrence Timmons 4.00 10.00
A56 DeMarcus Tank Tyler 2.50 6.00
A57 Darius Walker 2.50 6.00
A58 Paul Williams 2.50 6.00
A59 Patrick Willis 8.00 20.00
A60 Garrett Wolfe 2.50 6.00
A61 LaMarr Woodley 4.00 10.00
A62 Jared Zabransky 3.00 8.00

2007 SAGE Jerseys Red

RED PRINT RUN 99 SER.#'d SETS
*BRONZE/75: .4X TO 1X RED JSYs
BRONZE PRINT RUN 75 SER.#'d SETS
*SILVER/50: .5X TO 1.2X RED JSYs
SILVER PRINT RUN 50 SER.#'d SETS
*GOLD/25: .8X TO 2X RED JSYs
GOLD PRINT RUN 25 SER.#'d SETS
*PLATINUM/10: 1X TO 2.5X RED JSYs
PLATINUM PRINT RUN 10 SER.#'d SETS
UNPRICED JSY AUTO PRINT RUN 10
UNPRICED MASTER EDITION PRINT RUN 1
J1 Michael Bush 5.00 12.00
J2 Ken Darby 5.00 12.00
J3 Trent Edwards 5.00 12.00
J4 Anthony Gonzalez 5.00 12.00
J5 Kenny Irons 5.00 12.00
J6 Marshawn Lynch 4.00 10.00
J7 Robert Meachem 8.00 20.00
J8 Brandon Meriweather 5.00 12.00
J9 Greg Olsen 5.00 12.00
J10 Adrian Peterson 15.00 40.00
J11 Antonio Pittman 4.00 10.00
J12 Brady Quinn 12.00 30.00
J13 Sidney Rice 6.00 15.00
J14 JaMarcus Russell 5.00 12.00
J15 Troy Smith 5.00 12.00
J16 Drew Stanton 5.00 12.00
J17 Darius Walker 5.00 12.00

2007 SAGE Jerseys Dual

UNPRICED DUAL AUTO PRINT RUN 10

2007 SAGE First Card

1 Calvin Johnson/99 6.00 15.00
2 Brady Quinn/99 2.00 5.00

2007 SAGE National Convention National Heroes Jerseys

NH1 JaMarcus Russell 1.00 2.50
NH2 Adrian Peterson 6.00 15.00
NH3 Brady Quinn 1.50 4.00
NH4 Troy Smith 1.50 4.00

2007 SAGE Old School Autographs

RANDOM INSERTS IN PACKS
AA Aundrae Allison 4.00 10.00
BL Brian Leonard 5.00 12.00
BQ Brady Quinn 15.00 40.00
CD Craig Buster Davis 5.00 12.00
EE Earl Everett 5.00 12.00
JB John Beck 6.00 15.00
KK Kevin Kolb 10.00 25.00
ML Matt Leinart 5.00 12.00
TS Troy Smith 6.00 15.00
ZM Zach Miller 6.00 15.00
OS1 JaMarcus Russell 4.00 10.00
OS2 Gaines Adams 6.00 15.00
OS5 Dwayne Bowe 8.00 20.00
OS8 Anthony Gonzalez 6.00 15.00
OS12 Chris Henry 4.00 10.00
OS16 Jason Hill 6.00 15.00
OS17 Paul Williams 4.00 10.00
OS19 Garrett Wolfe 4.00 10.00
OS24 Jordan Palmer 5.00 12.00
OS26 David Ball 5.00 12.00
OS28 Chris Leak 5.00 12.00
OS30 Reggie Bush 10.00 25.00

2008 SAGE

COMPLETE SET (60) 20.00 40.00
1 Erik Ainge .50 1.25
2 Adrian Arrington .40 1.00
3 Donnie Avery .40 1.00
4 Sam Baker .30 .75
5 John David Booty .40 1.00
6 Adarius Bowman .40 1.00
7 Brian Brohm .50 1.25
8 Keenan Burton .30 .75
9 Andre Caldwell .40 1.00
10 John Carlson .50 1.25
11 Antoine Cason .50 1.25
12 Jamaal Charles .75 2.00
13 Tashard Choice .40 1.00
14 Ryan Clady .50 1.25
15 Dan Connor .50 1.25
16 Fred Davis .50 1.25
17 Dennis Dixon .50 1.25
18 Early Doucet .40 1.00
19 Sedrick Ellis .50 1.25
20 Joe Flacco 1.50 4.00
21 Brandon Flowers .50 1.25
22 Matt Flynn 1.00 2.50
23 Will Franklin .40 1.00
24 Vernon Gholston .40 1.00
25 James Hardy .40 1.00
26 Mike Hart .50 1.25
27 Derrick Harvey .30 .75
28 Lavelle Hawkins .30 .75
29 Chad Henne .50 1.25
30 Jacob Hester .50 1.25
31 DeSean Jackson 1.00 2.50
32 Lawrence Jackson .40 1.00
33 Mike Jenkins .50 1.25
34 Josh Johnson .50 1.25
35 Felix Jones .75 2.00
36 Dustin Keller .50 1.25
37 Sam Keller .40 1.00
38 Malcolm Kelly .40 1.00
39 Jake Long .50 1.25
40 Darren McFadden 1.25 3.00
41 Leodis McKelvin .40 1.00
42 Rashard Mendenhall 1.00 2.50
43 Jordy Nelson .60 1.50
44 Kevin O'Connell .40 1.00
45 Allen Patrick .40 1.00
46 Kenny Phillips .50 1.25
47 Darius Reynaud .30 .75
48 Ray Rice 1.00 2.50
49 Jason Rivers .40 1.00
50 Keith Rivers .50 1.25
51 Martin Rucker .40 1.00
52 Matt Ryan 2.00 5.00
53 Owen Schmitt .50 1.25
54 Steve Slaton .50 1.25
55 Kevin Smith .50 1.25
56 Paul Smith .50 1.25
57 Jonathan Stewart .75 2.00
58 Limas Sweed .50 1.25
59 Devin Thomas .40 1.00
60 Tom Zbikowski .50 1.25

2008 SAGE Autographs Red

*BRONZE: .4X TO 1X RED AUTO
*SILVER/400: .5X TO 1.2X RED AUTO
*SILVER/400: .4X TO 1X RED AUTO SPs
SILVER PRINT RUN 400 SER.#'d SETS
*GOLD/200: .6X TO 1.5X RED AUTO
*GOLD/200: .5X TO 1.2X RED AUTO SPs
GOLD PRINT RUN 200 SER.#'d SETS
*PLATINUM/50: .8X TO 2X RED AUTO
*PLATINUM/50: .6X TO 1.5X RED AUTO SPs
PLATINUM PRINT RUN 50 SER.#'d SETS
UNPRICED MASTER EDITION PRINT RUN 1
UNPRICED TRIPLE AUTO PRINT RUN 5
1 Erik Ainge 4.00 10.00
2 Adrian Arrington 3.00 8.00
3 Donnie Avery 3.00 8.00
4 Sam Baker 2.50 6.00
5 John David Booty 3.00 8.00
6 Adarius Bowman 3.00 8.00
7 Brian Brohm 4.00 10.00
8 Keenan Burton 2.50 6.00
9 Andre Caldwell 3.00 8.00
10 John Carlson 4.00 10.00
11 Antoine Cason 4.00 10.00
12 Jamaal Charles 6.00 15.00
13 Tashard Choice 3.00 8.00
14 Ryan Clady 4.00 10.00
15 Dan Connor 4.00 10.00
16 Fred Davis 4.00 10.00
17 Dennis Dixon 4.00 10.00
19 Sedrick Ellis 4.00 10.00
20 Joe Flacco 12.00 30.00
21 Brandon Flowers 4.00 10.00
22 Matt Flynn 8.00 20.00
23 Will Franklin 3.00 8.00
24 Vernon Gholston 3.00 8.00
25 James Hardy 3.00 8.00
26 Mike Hart 4.00 10.00
27 Derrick Harvey 2.50 6.00
28 Lavelle Hawkins 2.50 6.00
29 Chad Henne 4.00 10.00
30 Jacob Hester 4.00 10.00
32 Lawrence Jackson 3.00 8.00
33 Mike Jenkins 4.00 10.00
34 Josh Johnson 4.00 10.00
35 Felix Jones 6.00 15.00
36 Dustin Keller 4.00 10.00
37 Sam Keller 3.00 8.00
38 Malcolm Kelly 3.00 8.00
39 Jake Long 4.00 10.00
40 Darren McFadden SP Blue 15.00 40.00
40R Darren McFadden SP Red 20.00 50.00
41 Leodis McKelvin 3.00 8.00
42 Rashard Mendenhall 8.00 20.00
43 Jordy Nelson 6.00 15.00
44 Kevin O'Connell 3.00 8.00
45 Allen Patrick 3.00 8.00
46 Kenny Phillips 4.00 10.00
47 Darius Reynaud 2.50 6.00
48 Ray Rice 8.00 20.00
49 Jason Rivers 3.00 8.00
50 Keith Rivers 4.00 10.00
51 Martin Rucker 3.00 8.00
52 Matt Ryan 30.00 60.00
53 Owen Schmitt 4.00 10.00
54 Steve Slaton 4.00 10.00
55 Kevin Smith 4.00 10.00
56 Paul Smith 4.00 10.00
57 Jonathan Stewart 6.00 15.00
58 Limas Sweed 4.00 10.00
59 Devin Thomas 3.00 8.00
60 Tom Zbikowski 4.00 10.00

2008 SAGE Darren McFadden Road to the Draft

COMPLETE SET (9) 15.00 40.00
COMMON CARD 2.00 5.00

2008 SAGE Darren McFadden Road to the Draft Autographs

COMMON CARD (RD1-RD9) 40.00 100.00

2008 SAGE Jersey Bonus

COMPLETE SET (5) 25.00 60.00
COMMON CARD (MCJ1-MCJ5) 6.00 15.00
MCJ1 Darren McFadden 5.00 12.00
MCJ2 Darren McFadden 5.00 12.00
MCJ3 Darren McFadden 5.00 12.00
MCJ4 Darren McFadden 5.00 12.00
MCJ5 Darren McFadden 5.00 12.00

2009 SAGE

COMPLETE SET (55) 20.00 40.00
1 Tom Brandstater .50 1.25
2 Andre Brown .30 .75
3 Donald Brown .50 1.25
4 Nathan Brown .40 1.00
5 Darius Butler .50 1.25
6 Demetrius Byrd .40 1.00
7 Hunter Cantwell .50 1.25
8 James Casey .40 1.00
9 Chase Coffman .40 1.00
10 Jared Cook .50 1.25
11 Michael Crabtree 1.00 2.50
12 Brian Cushing .50 1.25
13 Nate Davis .40 1.00
14 Jarett Dillard .50 1.25
15 Brooks Foster .30 .75
16 Josh Freeman 1.00 2.50
17 Marcus Freeman .50 1.25
18 Cullen Harper .50 1.25
19 Graham Harrell .50 1.25
20 Darrius Heyward-Bey .50 1.25
21 Brian Hoyer .50 1.25
22 Juaquin Iglesias .40 1.00
23 Cornelius Ingram .30 .75
24 Malcolm Jenkins .50 1.25
25 Rashad Jennings .50 1.25
26 Gartrell Johnson .30 .75
27 Jeremiah Johnson .50 1.25
28 Aaron Kelly .40 1.00
29 James Laurinaitis .50 1.25
30 Jeremy Maclin .75 2.00
31 Clay Matthews 1.25 3.00
32 Rey Maualuga .50 1.25
33 LeSean McCoy 1.00 2.50
34 Stephen McGee .50 1.25
35 Eugene Monroe .30 .75
36 Devin Moore .40 1.00
37 Knowshon Moreno .50 1.25
38 Louis Murphy .50 1.25
39 Hakeem Nicks .75 2.00
40 Brian Orakpo .50 1.25
41 Curtis Painter .50 1.25
42 B.J. Raji .50 1.25
43 Mike Reilly .40 1.00
44 Javon Ringer .50 1.25
45 Brian Robiskie .50 1.25
46 Mark Sanchez 1.50 4.00
47 Clint Sintim .50 1.25
48 Alphonso Smith .40 1.00
49 Jason Smith .40 1.00
50 Matthew Stafford 2.50 6.00
51 Mike Thomas .50 1.25
52 Patrick Turner .40 1.00
53 Chris Wells .75 2.00
54 Pat White .50 1.25
55 John Parker Wilson .50 1.25

2009 SAGE Autographs Red

ONE AUTO PER PACK
*GOLD/200: .6X TO 1.5X RED AUTO
GOLD PRINT RUN 200 SER.#'d SETS
*PLATINUM/50: .8X TO 2X RED AUTO
PLATINUM PRINT RUN 50 SER.#'d SETS
*SILVER/400: .5X TO 1.2X RED AUTO
SILVER PRINT RUN 400 SER.#'d SETS
1 Tom Brandstater 4.00 10.00
2 Andre Brown 2.50 6.00
3 Donald Brown 4.00 10.00
4 Nathan Brown 3.00 8.00
5 Darius Butler 4.00 10.00
6 Demetrius Byrd 3.00 8.00
7 Hunter Cantwell 4.00 10.00
8 James Casey 3.00 8.00
9 Chase Coffman 3.00 8.00
10 Jared Cook 4.00 10.00
11 Michael Crabtree 12.00 30.00
12 Brian Cushing 4.00 10.00
13 Nate Davis 3.00 8.00
14 Jarett Dillard 4.00 10.00
15 Brooks Foster 2.50 6.00
16 Josh Freeman 10.00 25.00
17 Marcus Freeman 4.00 10.00
18 Cullen Harper 4.00 10.00
19 Graham Harrell 6.00 15.00
20 Darrius Heyward-Bey 4.00 10.00
21 Brian Hoyer 4.00 10.00
22 Juaquin Iglesias 3.00 8.00
23 Cornelius Ingram 2.50 6.00
24 Malcolm Jenkins 4.00 10.00
25 Rashad Jennings 4.00 10.00
26 Gartrell Johnson 2.50 6.00
27 Jeremiah Johnson 4.00 10.00
28 Aaron Kelly 3.00 8.00
29 James Laurinaitis 4.00 10.00
30 Jeremy Maclin 6.00 15.00
31 Clay Matthews 15.00 40.00
32 Rey Maualuga 4.00 10.00
33 LeSean McCoy 8.00 20.00
34 Stephen McGee 4.00 10.00
35 Eugene Monroe 2.50 6.00
36 Devin Moore 3.00 8.00
37 Knowshon Moreno 12.00 30.00
38 Louis Murphy 4.00 10.00
39 Hakeem Nicks 6.00 15.00
40 Brian Orakpo 4.00 10.00
41 Curtis Painter 4.00 10.00
42 B.J. Raji 4.00 10.00
43 Mike Reilly 3.00 8.00
44 Javon Ringer 4.00 10.00
45 Brian Robiskie 4.00 10.00
46 Mark Sanchez 25.00 50.00
47 Clint Sintim 4.00 10.00
48 Alphonso Smith 3.00 8.00
49 Jason Smith 3.00 8.00
50 Matthew Stafford 25.00 50.00
51 Mike Thomas 4.00 10.00
52 Patrick Turner 3.00 8.00
53 Chris Wells 12.00 30.00
54 Pat White 4.00 10.00
55 John Parker Wilson 4.00 10.00

2010 SAGE

1 Seyi Ajirotutu .50 1.25
2 Danario Alexander .50 1.25
3 Andre Anderson .40 1.00
4 Joique Bell .40 1.00
5 Arrelious Benn .50 1.25
6 Jahvid Best .75 2.00
7 Sam Bradford 2.00 5.00
8 Dezmon Briscoe .40 1.00
9 Antonio Brown .75 2.00
10 Jarrett Brown .50 1.25
11 Dez Bryant 1.50 4.00
12 Nate Byham .40 1.00
13 Sean Canfield .40 1.00
14 Jimmy Clausen .50 1.25
15 Chris Cook .50 1.25
16 Rennie Curran .40 1.00
17 Anthony Dixon .50 1.25
18 Jonathan Dwyer .50 1.25
19 Toby Gerhart .50 1.25
20 Mardy Gilyard .50 1.25
21 Garrett Graham .40 1.00
22 Jermaine Gresham .60 1.50
23 Rob Gronkowski 1.25 3.00
24 Montario Hardesty .50 1.25
25 Aaron Hernandez .75 2.00
26 Javarris James .50 1.25
27 Stafon Johnson .50 1.25
28 Dan LeFevour .50 1.25
29 Ryan Mathews 1.00 2.50
30 Rolando McClain .50 1.25
31 Colt McCoy 1.00 2.50
32 Gerald McCoy .50 1.25
33 Carlton Mitchell .40 1.00
34 Tony Moeaki .50 1.25
35 Derrick Morgan .40 1.00
36 Colin Peek .50 1.25
37 Jason Pierre-Paul .75 2.00
38 Tony Pike .50 1.25
39 Dennis Pitta .50 1.25
40 Taylor Price .50 1.25
41 Zac Robinson .40 1.00
42 Jordan Shipley .50 1.25
43 John Skelton .50 1.25
44 Jevan Snead .50 1.25
45 Brandon Spikes .50 1.25
46 C.J. Spiller .75 2.00
47 Ndamukong Suh 1.00 2.50
48 Ben Tate .60 1.50
49 Earl Thomas .50 1.25
50 Sean Weatherspoon .50 1.25
51 Joe Webb .50 1.25
52 Blair White .50 1.25
53 Damian Williams .50 1.25
54 Jeremy Williams .30 .75
55 Mike Williams .75 2.00

2010 SAGE Autographs Red

RED STATED ODDS 1:2
*GOLD/200: .5X TO 1.2X RED AUTO
GOLD/200 ODDS 1:6
*PLATINUM/50: .8X TO 2X RED AUTO
PLATINUM/50 ODDS 1:25
*SILVER/400: .4X TO 1X RED AUTO
SILVER/400 ODDS 1:3
1 Seyi Ajirotutu 4.00 10.00
2 Danario Alexander 4.00 10.00
3 Andre Anderson 3.00 8.00
4 Joique Bell SP 3.00 8.00
5 Arrelious Benn SP 4.00 10.00
6 Jahvid Best SP 6.00 15.00
7 Sam Bradford SP 30.00 80.00
8 Dezmon Briscoe SP 3.00 8.00
9 Antonio Brown SP 6.00 15.00
10 Jarrett Brown SP 4.00 10.00
12 Nate Byham 3.00 8.00
13 Sean Canfield 3.00 8.00
14 Jimmy Clausen SP 4.00 10.00
15 Chris Cook 4.00 10.00
16 Rennie Curran 3.00 8.00
17 Anthony Dixon SP 4.00 10.00
18 Jonathan Dwyer SP 4.00 10.00
19 Toby Gerhart SP 6.00 15.00
20 Mardy Gilyard 4.00 10.00
21 Garrett Graham SP 3.00 8.00
22 Jermaine Gresham SP 5.00 12.00
23 Rob Gronkowski SP 10.00 25.00
24 Montario Hardesty 4.00 10.00
25 Aaron Hernandez 6.00 15.00
26 Javarris James 4.00 10.00
27 Stafon Johnson 4.00 10.00
28 Dan LeFevour 4.00 10.00
29 Ryan Mathews 12.00 30.00
30 Rolando McClain SP 4.00 10.00
31 Colt McCoy SP 10.00 25.00
32 Gerald McCoy SP 8.00 20.00
33 Carlton Mitchell SP 3.00 8.00
34 Tony Moeaki 4.00 10.00
35 Derrick Morgan SP 3.00 8.00
36 Colin Peek 4.00 10.00
37 Jason Pierre-Paul 6.00 15.00
38 Tony Pike SP 4.00 10.00
39 Dennis Pitta 4.00 10.00
40 Taylor Price 4.00 10.00
41 Zac Robinson SP 3.00 8.00
42 Jordan Shipley 4.00 10.00
43 John Skelton SP 4.00 10.00
44 Jevan Snead SP 4.00 10.00
45 Brandon Spikes SP 4.00 10.00
46 C.J. Spiller SP 12.00 30.00
47 Ndamukong Suh SP 20.00 40.00
48 Ben Tate 5.00 12.00
49 Earl Thomas SP 4.00 10.00
50 Sean Weatherspoon SP 4.00 10.00
51 Joe Webb 4.00 10.00
52 Blair White 4.00 10.00
53 Damian Williams SP 4.00 10.00
54 Jeremy Williams SP 2.50 6.00
55 Mike Williams 6.00 15.00

2011 SAGE

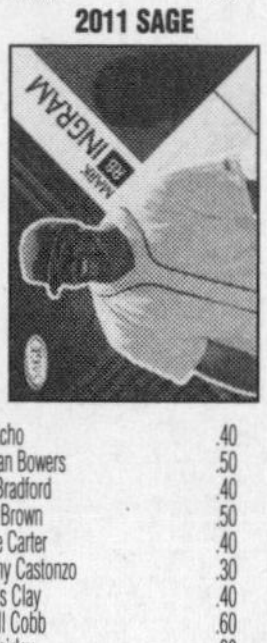

1 Sam Acho .40 1.00
2 Da'Quan Bowers .50 1.25
3 Allen Bradford .40 1.00
4 Curtis Brown .50 1.25
5 Delone Carter .40 1.00
6 Anthony Castonzo .30 .75
7 Charles Clay .40 1.00
8 Randall Cobb .60 1.50
9 Nick Fairley .60 1.50
10 Blaine Gabbert .75 2.00
11 Charlie Gantt .40 1.00
12 Edmond Gates .40 1.00
13 A.J. Green 1.00 2.50
14 Jamie Harper .50 1.25
15 Mark Herzlich .40 1.00
16 Cameron Heyward .50 1.25
17 Rob Housler .40 1.00
18 Mark Ingram 1.00 2.50
19 Lestar Jean .40 1.00
20 Jerrel Jernigan .40 1.00
21 Julio Jones 1.00 2.50
22 Taiwan Jones .50 1.25
23 Jeremy Kerley .50 1.25
24 Ryan Kerrigan .50 1.25
25 Mikel Leshoure .50 1.25
26 Dion Lewis .50 1.25
27 Jake Locker 1.25 3.00
28 Jeff Maehl .50 1.25
29 Ryan Mallett 1.00 2.50
30 Casey Matthews .50 1.25
31 DeAndre McDaniel .40 1.00
32 Von Miller .60 1.50
33 Denarius Moore .60 1.50
34 Rahim Moore .40 1.00
35 DeMarco Murray 1.00 2.50
36 Cam Newton 2.50 6.00
37 Stephen Paea .50 1.25
38 Austin Pettis .40 1.00
39 Christian Ponder 1.00 2.50
40 Taylor Potts .40 1.00
41 Stevan Ridley .50 1.25
42 Jacquizz Rodgers .50 1.25
43 Kyle Rudolph .50 1.25
44 Dane Sanzenbacher .50 1.25
45 Cecil Shorts .40 1.00
46 Aldon Smith .75 2.00
47 Courtney Smith .40 1.00
48 Torrey Smith .60 1.50
49 Nate Solder .50 1.25
50 Ricky Stanzi .60 1.50
51 Luke Stocker .40 1.00
52 Daniel Thomas .50 1.25
53 Jordan Todman .30 .75
54 Shane Vereen .50 1.25
55 J.J. Watt .60 1.50
56 Adam Weber .40 1.00
57 Aaron Williams .40 1.00
58 D.J. Williams .50 1.25
59 Ryan Williams .60 1.50
60 T.J. Yates .60 1.50

2011 SAGE Autographs Red

RED AU STATED ODDS 1:2 HOB
*GOLD/200: .5X TO 1.2X RED AUTO
*PLATINUM/50: .6X TO 1.5X BASIC AU
*SILVER: .4X TO 1X RED AUTO
UNPRICED MAST.EDIT/1 ODDS 1:1255 H
1 Sam Acho 3.00 8.00
2 Da'Quan Bowers 4.00 10.00
3 Allen Bradford 3.00 8.00
4 Curtis Brown 4.00 10.00
5 Delone Carter 3.00 8.00
6 Anthony Castonzo 2.50 6.00
7 Charles Clay 3.00 8.00
8 Randall Cobb 5.00 12.00
9 Nick Fairley 5.00 12.00
10 Blaine Gabbert 12.00 30.00
11 Charlie Gantt 3.00 8.00
12 Edmond Gates 3.00 8.00
13 A.J. Green 8.00 20.00
14 Jamie Harper 4.00 10.00
15 Mark Herzlich 3.00 8.00
16 Cameron Heyward 4.00 10.00
17 Rob Housler 3.00 8.00
18 Mark Ingram 12.00 30.00
19 Lestar Jean 3.00 8.00
20 Jerrel Jernigan 3.00 8.00
21 Julio Jones 12.00 30.00
22 Taiwan Jones 4.00 10.00
23 Jeremy Kerley 4.00 10.00
24 Ryan Kerrigan 4.00 10.00
25 Mikel Leshoure 4.00 10.00
26 Dion Lewis 4.00 10.00
27 Jake Locker 15.00 40.00
28 Jeff Maehl 4.00 10.00
29 Ryan Mallett 12.00 30.00
30 Casey Matthews 4.00 10.00
31 DeAndre McDaniel 3.00 8.00
32 Von Miller 5.00 12.00
33 Denarius Moore 5.00 12.00
34 Rahim Moore 3.00 8.00
35 DeMarco Murray 8.00 20.00
36 Cam Newton 30.00 60.00
37 Stephen Paea 4.00 10.00
38 Austin Pettis 3.00 8.00
39 Christian Ponder 10.00 25.00
40 Taylor Potts 3.00 8.00
41 Stevan Ridley 4.00 10.00
42 Jacquizz Rodgers 4.00 10.00
43 Kyle Rudolph 4.00 10.00
44 Dane Sanzenbacher 4.00 10.00
45 Cecil Shorts 3.00 8.00
46 Aldon Smith 6.00 15.00
47 Courtney Smith 3.00 8.00
48 Torrey Smith 5.00 12.00
49 Nate Solder 4.00 10.00
50 Ricky Stanzi 5.00 12.00
51 Luke Stocker 3.00 8.00
52 Daniel Thomas 4.00 10.00
53 Jordan Todman 2.50 6.00
54 Shane Vereen 4.00 10.00
55 J.J. Watt 5.00 12.00
56 Adam Weber 3.00 8.00
57 Aaron Williams 3.00 8.00
58 D.J. Williams 4.00 10.00
59 Ryan Williams 5.00 12.00
60 T.J. Yates 5.00 12.00

2011 SAGE Through the Lens

RANDOM INSERTS IN PACKS
RF1 Jerrel Jernigan .60 1.50
RF2 Mikel Leshoure .75 2.00
RF3 DeMarco Murray 1.50 4.00
RF4 Jacquizz Rodgers .75 2.00
RF5 Torrey Smith 1.00 2.50
RF6 Ryan Williams 1.00 2.50

2012 SAGE

1 Joe Adams .50 1.25
2 Dwayne Allen .50 1.25
3 Justin Blackmon 1.00 2.50
4 Brandon Bolden .50 1.25
5 Ryan Broyles .50 1.25
6 Vontaze Burfict .40 1.00
7 Orson Charles .50 1.25
8 Quinton Coples .50 1.25
9 Kirk Cousins .75 2.00
10 Jared Crick .50 1.25
11 Juron Criner .40 1.00
12 Alfonzo Dennard .50 1.25
13 Michael Egnew .40 1.00
14 Michael Floyd 1.00 2.50
15 Nick Foles .75 2.00
16 Jeff Fuller .60 1.50
17 Chris Givens .40 1.00
18 Cyrus Gray .50 1.25
19 Ladarius Green .50 1.25
20 Robert Griffin III 2.50 6.00
21 Boom Herron .50 1.25
22 Ronnie Hillman .60 1.50
23 T.Y. Hilton .50 1.25
24 Melvin Ingram .60 1.50
25 LaMichael James 1.00 2.50
26 Alshon Jeffery .75 2.00
27 Janoris Jenkins .50 1.25
28 Matt Kalil .60 1.50
29 Case Keenum .60 1.50
30 Luke Kuechly .60 1.50
31 Ryan Lindley .50 1.25
32 Doug Martin .75 2.00
33 Marvin McNutt .50 1.25
34 Davin Meggett .40 1.00
35 Lamar Miller .60 1.50
36 Kellen Moore .75 2.00
37 Brock Osweiler .60 1.50
38 Eric Page .40 1.00
39 Bernard Pierce .50 1.25
40 Dontari Poe .50 1.25
41 Chris Polk .60 1.50
42 Tauren Poole .40 1.00
43 DeVier Posey .50 1.25
44 Brian Quick .60 1.50
45 Trent Richardson 1.50 4.00
46 Tommy Streeter .50 1.25
47 Ryan Tannehill 1.25 3.00
48 Brandon Weeden 1.00 2.50
49 Jarius Wright .50 1.25
50 Kendall Wright .60 1.50

2012 SAGE Autographs Red

RED AU STATED ODDS 1:2 HOB
*GOLD/100: .5X TO 1.2X RED AU
*PLATINUM/50: .6X TO 1.5X RED AU
*SILVER AU: .4X TO 1X RED AU
A1 Joe Adams 4.00 10.00
A2 Dwayne Allen 4.00 10.00
A3 Justin Blackmon 8.00 20.00
A4 Brandon Bolden 4.00 10.00
A5 Ryan Broyles 4.00 10.00
A6 Vontaze Burfict 3.00 8.00
A7 Orson Charles 4.00 10.00
A8 Quinton Coples 4.00 10.00
A9 Kirk Cousins 6.00 15.00
A10 Jared Crick 4.00 10.00
A11 Juron Criner 3.00 8.00
A12 Alfonzo Dennard 4.00 10.00
A13 Michael Egnew 3.00 8.00
A14 Michael Floyd 6.00 15.00
A15 Nick Foles 6.00 15.00
A16 Jeff Fuller 5.00 12.00
A17 Chris Givens 3.00 8.00
A18 Cyrus Gray 4.00 10.00
A19 Ladarius Green 4.00 10.00
A20 Robert Griffin III 40.00 80.00
A21 Boom Herron 4.00 10.00
A22 Ronnie Hillman 5.00 12.00
A23 T.Y. Hilton 4.00 10.00
A24 Melvin Ingram 5.00 12.00
A25 LaMichael James 8.00 20.00
A26 Alshon Jeffery 6.00 15.00

A27 Janoris Jenkins 4.00 10.00
A28 Matt Kalil 5.00 12.00
A29 Case Keenum 5.00 12.00
A30 Luke Kuechly 5.00 12.00
A31 Ryan Lindley 4.00 10.00
A32 Doug Martin 6.00 15.00
A33 Marvin McNutt 4.00 10.00
A34 Davin Meggett 3.00 8.00
A35 Lamar Miller 5.00 12.00
A36 Kellen Moore 6.00 15.00
A37 Brock Osweiler 5.00 12.00
A38 Eric Page 3.00 8.00
A39 Bernard Pierce 4.00 10.00
A40 Dontari Poe 4.00 10.00
A41 Chris Polk 5.00 12.00
A42 Tauren Poole 3.00 8.00
A43 DeVier Posey 4.00 10.00
A44 Brian Quick 5.00 12.00
A45 Trent Richardson 15.00 40.00
A46 Tommy Streeter 4.00 10.00
A47 Ryan Tannehill 10.00 25.00
A48 Brandon Weeden 8.00 20.00
A49 Jarius Wright 4.00 10.00
A50 Kendall Wright 5.00 12.00

2007 SAGE DECADEnce

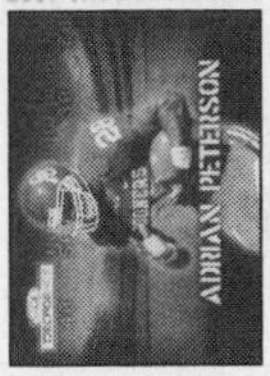

This 56-card set was released in December, 2007. The set was issued into the hobby in three-card packs which came eight to a box.

COMPLETE SET (56) 8.00 20.00
1 JaMarcus Russell .25 .60
2 Calvin Johnson 1.25 3.00
3 Gaines Adams .40 1.00
4 Levi Brown .40 1.00
5 Adrian Peterson 1.50 4.00
6 Ted Ginn Jr. .30 .75
7 Patrick Willis .75 2.00
8 Marshawn Lynch .40 1.00
9 Adam Carriker .30 .75
10 Lawrence Timmons .40 1.00
11 Jarvis Moss .30 .75
12 Leon Hall .30 .75
13 Michael Griffin .40 1.00
14 Aaron Ross .40 1.00
15 Brady Quinn .40 1.00
16 Dwayne Bowe .50 1.25
17 Brandon Meriweather .40 1.00
18 Robert Meachem .40 1.00
19 Craig Buster Davis .30 .75
20 Greg Olsen .30 .75
21 Anthony Gonzalez .40 1.00
22 Alan Branch .30 .75
23 Kevin Kolb .60 1.50
24 Zach Miller .40 1.00
25 John Beck .40 1.00
26 Drew Stanton .25 .60
27 Sidney Rice .50 1.25
28 LaMarr Woodley .40 1.00
29 Kenny Irons .25 .60
30 Chris Henry RB .25 .60
31 Steve Smith USC .40 1.00
32 Brian Leonard .30 .75
33 Ryan Kalil .30 .75
34 Yamon Figurs .25 .60
35 Jason Hill .40 1.00
36 Paul Williams .25 .60
37 Demarcus Tank Tyler .25 .60
38 Trent Edwards .40 1.00
39 Garrett Wolfe .25 .60
40 Johnnie Lee Higgins .30 .75
41 Michael Bush .40 1.00
42 Isaiah Stanback .25 .60
43 Antonio Pittman .25 .60
44 Steve Breaston .40 1.00
45 Aundrae Allison .25 .60
46 Kolby Smith .30 .75
47 Jeff Rowe .25 .60
48 David Clowney .30 .75
49 Troy Smith .40 1.00
50 Joel Filani .30 .75
51 David Irons .25 .60
52 Courtney Taylor .30 .75
53 Jordan Palmer .30 .75
54 Dallas Baker .25 .60
55 Jason Snelling .40 1.00
56 Kenneth Darby .30 .75

2007 SAGE DECADEnce Autographs Bronze

*SILVER/50: .5X TO 1.2X BRONZE AUTO
SILVER PRINT RUN 50 SER.#'d SETS
*GOLD/25: .6X TO 1.5X BRONZE AUTO
GOLD PRINT RUN 25 SER.#'d SETS
UNPRICED EMERALD PRINT RUN 5
UNPRICED PRINT PLATE PRINT RUN 1
UNPRICED RETRO AUTO PRINT RUN 10
A1 JaMarcus Russell 12.00 30.00
A3 Gaines Adams 4.00 10.00
A4 Levi Brown 4.00 10.00
A5 Adrian Peterson 60.00 120.00
A7 Patrick Willis 8.00 20.00
A8 Marshawn Lynch 4.00 10.00
A9 Adam Carriker 3.00 8.00
A10 Lawrence Timmons 4.00 10.00
A11 Jarvis Moss 3.00 8.00
A12 Leon Hall 3.00 8.00
A13 Michael Griffin 4.00 10.00
A14 Aaron Ross 4.00 10.00
A15 Brady Quinn 20.00 50.00
A16 Dwayne Bowe 5.00 12.00
A17 Brandon Meriweather 4.00 10.00
A18 Robert Meachem 4.00 10.00
A19 Craig Buster Davis 3.00 8.00
A20 Greg Olsen 3.00 8.00
A21 Anthony Gonzalez 4.00 10.00
A23 Kevin Kolb 6.00 15.00
A24 Zach Miller 4.00 10.00
A25 John Beck 4.00 10.00
A26 Drew Stanton 2.50 6.00
A27 Sidney Rice 5.00 12.00
A28 LaMarr Woodley 4.00 10.00
A29 Kenny Irons 2.50 6.00
A30 Chris Henry RB 2.50 6.00
A31 Steve Smith USC 4.00 10.00
A32 Brian Leonard 3.00 8.00
A33 Ryan Kalil 3.00 8.00
A34 Yamon Figurs 2.50 6.00
A35 Jason Hill 4.00 10.00
A36 Paul Williams 2.50 6.00
A37 Demarcus Tank Tyler 2.50 6.00
A38 Trent Edwards 4.00 10.00
A39 Garrett Wolfe 2.50 6.00
A40 Johnnie Lee Higgins 3.00 8.00
A41 Michael Bush 4.00 10.00
A42 Isaiah Stanback 2.50 6.00
A43 Antonio Pittman 2.50 6.00
A44 Steve Breaston 4.00 10.00
A45 Aundrae Allison 2.50 6.00
A46 Kolby Smith 3.00 8.00
A47 Jeff Rowe 2.50 6.00
A48 David Clowney 3.00 8.00
A49 Troy Smith 4.00 10.00
A50 Joel Filani 3.00 8.00
A51 David Irons 2.50 6.00
A53 Jordan Palmer 3.00 8.00
A54 Dallas Baker 2.50 6.00
A55 Jason Snelling 4.00 10.00
A56 Kenneth Darby 3.00 8.00

2011 SAGE Five Star

STATED PRINT RUN 50 SER.#'d SETS
SA01 Cam Newton 50.00 100.00
SA02 Von Miller 10.00 25.00
SA03 A.J. Green 15.00 40.00
SA04 Julio Jones 15.00 40.00
SA05 Aldon Smith 10.00 25.00
SA06 Jake Locker 20.00 50.00
SA07 Blaine Gabbert 12.00 30.00
SA08 J.J. Watt 8.00 20.00
SA09 Christian Ponder 25.00 50.00
SA10 Nick Fairley 10.00 25.00
SA11 Ryan Kerrigan 8.00 20.00
SA12 Mark Ingram 15.00 40.00
SA13 Cameron Heyward 8.00 20.00
SA14 Ryan Williams 10.00 25.00
SA15 Shane Vereen 8.00 20.00
SA16 Mikel LeShoure 8.00 20.00
SA17 Daniel Thomas 8.00 20.00
SA18 Randall Cobb 10.00 25.00
SA19 DeMarco Murray 15.00 40.00
SA20 Ryan Mallett 12.00 30.00
SA21 Torrey Smith 10.00 25.00
SA22 Denarius Moore 10.00 25.00
SA23 Terrelle Pryor 15.00 40.00

2011 SAGE Five Star Dual Autographs

STATED PRINT RUN 1-200
A1 Ryan Williams/15 10.00 25.00
Rob Housler
A3 Rob Housler/200 3.00 8.00
Sam Acho
A4 Julio Jones/50 12.00 30.00
Jacquizz Rodgers
A5 DeMarco Murray/200 10.00 25.00
Shaun Chapas
A6 Von Miller/200 8.00 20.00
Rahim Moore
A8 Randall Cobb/200 5.00 12.00
D.J. Williams
A9 J.J. Watt/20 12.00 30.00
T.J. Yates
A12 Daniel Thomas/200 4.00 10.00
Edmund Gates
A13 Daniel Thomas/200 4.00 10.00
Charles Clay
A14 Edmund Gates/200 3.00 8.00
Charles Clay
A15 Christian Ponder/200 20.00 40.00
Kyle Rudolph
A16 Nate Solder/200 4.00 10.00
Shane Vereen
A17 Stevan Ridley/15 15.00 40.00
Ryan Mallett
A18 Shane Vereen/200 5.00 12.00
Stevan Ridley
A21 Nate Solder/200 4.00 10.00
Stevan Ridley
A22 Chimdi Chekwa/200 4.00 10.00
Taiwan Jones
A23 Chimdi Chekwa/200 6.00 15.00
Denarius Moore
A24 Taiwan Jones/200 8.00 20.00
Denarius Moore
A25 Casey Matthews/200 4.00 10.00
Dion Lewis
A26 Cameron Heyward/25 8.00 20.00
Curtis Brown
A27 Marcus Gilchrist/25 5.00 12.00
Jordan Todman
A28 Da'Quan Bowers/200 4.00 10.00
Luke Stocker
A29 Da'Quan Bowers/200 4.00 10.00
Allen Bradford
A30 Luke Stocker/200 6.00 15.00
Allen Bradford
A31 Jake Locker/20 30.00 60.00
Jamie Harper
A32 Jurrell Casey/200 4.00 10.00
Jamie Harper
A33 Mark Ingram/50 30.00 60.00
Julio Jones
A34 Cam Newton/100 40.00 80.00
Nick Fairley
A38 Anthony Castonzo/200 3.00 8.00
Mark Herzlich
A43 Rob Housler/200 3.00 8.00
Jeff Van Camp
A44 Jeff Van Camp/200 3.00 8.00
Lestar Jean
A48 Terrelle Pryor/25 25.00 60.00
Chimdi Chekwa
A49 Terrelle Pryor/25 25.00 60.00
Dane Sanzenbacher
A50 Cameron Heyward/200 4.00 10.00
Dane Sanzenbacher
A51 Casey Matthews/200 4.00 10.00
Jeff Maehl
A52 Stephen Paea/25 8.00 20.00
Jacquizz Rodgers
A53 Luke Stocker/200 8.00 20.00
Denarius Moore
A55 Sam Acho/200 3.00 8.00
Aaron Williams
A57 Curtis Brown/20 8.00 20.00
Aaron Williams
A59 Aaron Williams/200 3.00 8.00
Greg Smith
A60 Kai Forbath/200 3.00 8.00
Rahim Moore
A61 Jurrell Casey/200 3.00 8.00
Allen Bradford
A62 Dane Sanzenbacher/200 8.00 20.00
Stephen Paea
A63 Kai Forbath/200 8.00 20.00
DeMarco Murray
A67 Lestar Jean/200 4.00 10.00
Jeff Maehl
A68 Lestar Jean/200 5.00 12.00
T.J. Yates
A69 Jeff Maehl/200 5.00 12.00
T.J. Yates
A72 Charlie Gantt/200 5.00 12.00
Ricky Stanzi
A74 Mark Herzlich/200 3.00 8.00
Jerrel Jernigan
A75 Courtney Smith/200 4.00 10.00
Jeremy Kerley
A78 Cam Newton/50 50.00 100.00
Jake Locker
A79 Cam Newton/50 50.00 100.00
Blaine Gabbert
A80 Cam Newton/50 50.00 100.00
Christian Ponder
A81 Jake Locker/50 30.00 60.00
Christian Ponder
A82 Cam Newton/100 50.00 100.00
Mark Ingram
A84 Mark Ingram/200 8.00 20.00
Casey Matthews
A85 Cameron Heyward/200 4.00 10.00
Casey Matthews
A86 A.J. Green/50 25.00 50.00
Julio Jones
A87 Cam Newton/50 50.00 100.00
Von Miller
A88 Terrelle Pryor/50 20.00 50.00
Denarius Moore
A89 Torrey Smith/200 5.00 12.00
Courtney Smith
A90 Ryan Kerrigan/200 10.00 25.00
Aldon Smith
A92 Jeremy Kerley/200 4.00 10.00
Cecil Shorts
A95 Jeremy Kerley/200 4.00 10.00
Edmund Gates
A98 Courtney Smith/200 3.00 8.00
Cecil Shorts
A100 Ricky Stanzi/200 5.00 12.00
Taylor Potts
A101 Christian Ponder/200 12.00 30.00
Taylor Potts
A102 Ricky Stanzi/200 5.00 12.00
T.J. Yates
A105 Jordan Todman/200 4.00 10.00
Dion Lewis
A106 D.J. Williams/200 4.00 10.00
Charlie Gantt
A108 Kyle Rudolph/200 4.00 10.00
Charlie Gantt
A109 Luke Stocker/200 3.00 8.00
Charlie Gantt
A110 Kyle Rudolph/200 4.00 10.00
Charles Clay
A111 D.J. Williams/200 4.00 10.00
Charles Clay
A115 Randall Cobb/200 5.00 12.00
Jerrel Jernigan
A116 Delone Carter/200 4.00 10.00
Dion Lewis
A117 Delone Carter/200 3.00 8.00
Jordan Todman
A119 Torrey Smith/200 5.00 12.00
Randall Cobb
A120 Torrey Smith/200 5.00 12.00
Jerrel Jernigan
A122 Von Miller/25 15.00 40.00
Aldon Smith
A123 Randall Cobb/200 5.00 12.00
Stephen Paea
A125 Cameron Heyward/200 4.00 10.00
Nate Solder
A126 Ryan Kerrigan/200 6.00 15.00
Nate Solder
A127 Ryan Kerrigan/200 6.00 15.00
Mark Herzlich
A132 Jerrel Jernigan/200 4.00 10.00
Dane Sanzenbacher
A133 Denarius Moore/200 8.00 20.00
Dane Sanzenbacher
A135 Daniel Thomas/200 4.00 10.00
Shane Vereen
A136 Taiwan Jones/200 6.00 15.00
Delone Carter
A147 Cam Newton/50 50.00 100.00
Randall Cobb

2011 SAGE Five Star Then and Now Autographs

STATED PRINT RUN 25 SER.#'d SETS
TN1 Da'Quan Bowers 10.00 25.00
TN2 Blaine Gabbert 15.00 40.00
TN3 A.J. Green 20.00 50.00
TN4 Julio Jones 25.00 50.00
TN5 Jake Locker 25.00 60.00
TN6 Ryan Mallett 20.00 50.00
TN7 Cam Newton 60.00 120.00
TN8 Austin Pettis 8.00 20.00
TN9 Terrelle Pryor 25.00 50.00
TN10 Kyle Rudolph 10.00 25.00
TN11 Daniel Thomas 10.00 25.00
TN12 Shane Vereen 10.00 25.00
TN13 Casey Matthews 10.00 25.00
TN14 Allen Bradford 8.00 20.00

2011 SAGE Five Star Triple Autographs

STATED PRINT RUN 1-25
TA1 Cam Newton/25 60.00 120.00
Nick Fairley
Mario Fannin
TA2 Cam Newton/15 100.00 175.00
Mark Ingram
Stevan Ridley
TA4 Cameron Heyward/25 15.00 40.00
Chimdi Chekwa
Dane Sanzenbacher
TA5 Aaron Williams/25 10.00 25.00
Sam Acho
Curtis Brown
TA6 Aaron Williams/15 8.00 20.00
Sam Acho
Greg Smith
TA7 Aaron Williams/15 8.00 20.00
Curtis Brown
Greg Smith
TA18 Mark Ingram/25 20.00 50.00
Mikel LeShoure
Daniel Thomas
TA22 Shane Vereen/25 20.00 50.00
Stevan Ridley
Ryan Mallett
TA23 Chimdi Chekwa/25 15.00 40.00
Taiwan Jones
Denarius Moore
TA26 Cam Newton/15 90.00 150.00
Jake Locker
Blaine Gabbert
TA27 Cam Newton/15 100.00 200.00
Jake Locker
Christian Ponder
TA28 Cam Newton/15 100.00 200.00
Blaine Gabbert
Christian Ponder
TA29 Jake Locker/15 40.00 80.00
Blaine Gabbert
Christian Ponder
TA30 Casey Matthews/25 20.00 50.00
Cameron Heyward
Mark Ingram
TA31 Daniel Thomas/25 10.00 25.00
Edmund Gates
Charles Clay
TA38 Cam Newton/15 60.00 120.00
Von Miller
A.J. Green
TA39 Cam Newton/15 100.00 175.00
Mark Ingram
A.J. Green
TA40 Von Miller/25 15.00 40.00
Aldon Smith
J.J. Watt
TA46 Von Miller/25 15.00 40.00
Aldon Smith
Ryan Kerrigan

2006 SAGE Game Exclusive

This 36-card set was released in July, 2006. This set was issued into the hobby in three-card packs, with an $30.99 SRP, which came six packs to a box. Only a few of the select 2006 rookies were featured in this set, with three base cards per player. All the cards of the player are priced the same.

COMPLETE SET (36) 20.00 40.00
1 Mario Williams .50 1.25
2 Mario Williams .50 1.25
3 Mario Williams .50 1.25
4 Reggie Bush 1.00 2.50
5 Reggie Bush 1.00 2.50
6 Reggie Bush 1.00 2.50
7 Vince Young .60 1.50
8 Vince Young .60 1.50
9 Vince Young .60 1.50
10 D'Brickashaw Ferguson .50 1.25
11 D'Brickashaw Ferguson .50 1.25
12 D'Brickashaw Ferguson .50 1.25
13 Vernon Davis .60 1.50
14 Vernon Davis .60 1.50
15 Vernon Davis .60 1.50
16 Michael Huff .40 1.00
17 Michael Huff .40 1.00
18 Michael Huff .40 1.00
19 Donte Whitner .50 1.25
20 Donte Whitner .50 1.25
21 Donte Whitner .50 1.25
22 Ernie Sims .40 1.00
23 Ernie Sims .40 1.00
24 Ernie Sims .40 1.00
25 Matt Leinart .50 1.25
26 Matt Leinart .50 1.25
27 Matt Leinart .50 1.25
28 Jay Cutler 1.00 2.50
29 Jay Cutler 1.00 2.50
30 Jay Cutler 1.00 2.50
31 Reggie Bush 1.00 2.50
Matt Leinart
32 Vince Young Champ .60 1.50
33 Reggie Bush 1.00 2.50
Matt Leinart
Vince Young
34 Mario Williams #1 .50 1.25
35 Matt Leinart Heisman .50 1.25
36 Reggie Bush Heisman 1.00 2.50

2006 SAGE Game Exclusive Autographs Bronze

UNPRICED ELITE 11 SER.#'d TO 11
UNPRICED ELITE 11 MASTERS SER.#'d TO 1
*GOLD/25: .6X TO 1.5X BRONZE
*SILVER/50: .5X TO 1.2X BRONZE
A1 Mario Williams 5.00 12.00
A2 Reggie Bush 10.00 25.00
A4 D'Brickashaw Ferguson 5.00 12.00
A5 Vernon Davis 6.00 15.00
A6 Michael Huff 4.00 10.00
A7 Donte Whitner 5.00 12.00
A8 Ernie Sims 4.00 10.00
A9 Matt Leinart 5.00 12.00
A10 Jay Cutler 10.00 25.00

2006 SAGE Game Exclusive Jersey Combos Bronze

*GOLD/25: .6X TO 1.5X BRONZE
UNPRICED PLATINUM PRINT RUN 5
*SILVER/50: .5X TO 1.2X BRONZE
CG1 Reggie Bush Coll 8.00 20.00
Matt Leinart Coll
CG2 Reggie Bush Coll 12.00 30.00
Vince Young Coll
CG3 Matt Leinart Coll 6.00 15.00
Vince Young Coll
CG4 Reggie Bush NFL 8.00 20.00
Matt Leinart NFL
CG5 Reggie Bush NFL 12.00 30.00
Vince Young NFL
CG6 Matt Leinart NFL 6.00 15.00
Vince Young NFL
LBY1 Reggie Bush Coll 10.00 25.00
Matt Leinart Coll
Vince Young Coll
LBY2 Reggie Bush NFL 10.00 25.00
Matt Leinart NFL
Vince Young NFL

2006 SAGE Game Exclusive Oversized Jerseys Bronze

UNPRICED ELITE 11 SER.#'d TO 11
UNPRICED ELITE 11 MASTERS SER.#'d TO 1
*GOLD/25. .0X TO 1.5X BRONZE
UNPRICED PLATINUM SER.#'d TO 5
*SILVER/50: .5X TO 1.2X BRONZE
SJ1 Reggie Bush 15.00 40.00
SJ2 Matt Leinart 8.00 20.00
SJ3 Vince Young 10.00 25.00
SJ4 Jay Cutler 8.00 20.00
SJ5 Vernon Davis 5.00 12.00

2006 SAGE Game Exclusive Oversized Jersey Combos Bronze

*GOLD/25: .6X TO 1.5X BRONZE
*SILVER/50: .5X TO 1.2X BRONZE
UNPRICED ELITE 11 SER.#'d TO 11
UNPRICED ELITE 11 MASTERS #'d TO 1
UNPRICED PLATINUM SER.#'d TO 5
CS1 Reggie Bush 12.00 30.00
Matt Leinart
CS2 Reggie Bush 12.00 30.00
Vince Young
CS3 Reggie Bush 12.00 30.00
Jay Cutler
CS4 Reggie Bush 10.00 25.00
Vernon Davis
CS5 Matt Leinart 8.00 20.00
Vince Young
CS6 Jay Cutler 8.00 20.00
Matt Leinart
CS7 Vernon Davis 6.00 15.00
Matt Leinart
CS8 Jay Cutler 10.00 25.00
Vince Young
CS9 Vernon Davis 8.00 20.00
Vince Young
CS10 Jay Cutler 6.00 15.00
Vernon Davis

2006 SAGE Game Exclusive Matt Leinart Jerseys Bronze

COMMON CARD (1-10) 4.00 10.00
*GOLD/25: .8X TO 2X BRONZE
UNPRICED PLATINUM PRINT RUN 5 SETS
*SILVER/50: .5X TO 1.2X BRONZE
ML10 Matt Leinart Dual 6.00 15.00

2006 SAGE Game Exclusive Reggie Bush Jerseys Bronze

COMMON CARD (1-10) 6.00 15.00
*GOLD/25: .6X TO 1.5X BRONZE
*SILVER/50: .5X TO 1.2X BRONZE
UNPRICED PLATINUM PRINT RUN 5 SETS
RB10 Reggie Bush Dual 10.00 25.00

2006 SAGE Game Exclusive Vince Young Jerseys Bronze

COMMON CARD (1-10) 5.00 12.00
*GOLD/25: .6X TO 1.5X BRONZE
*SILVER/50: .5X TO 1.2X BRONZE
UNPRICED PLATINUM PRINT RUN 5 SETS
VY10 Vince Young Dual 8.00 20.00

2000 SAGE HIT

Released as a 50-card set, Sage HIT features full color player action photos with a green and black border along the bottom of the card only. The SAGE logo appears in the upper right hand corner of the card front. HIT was packaged in 24-pack boxes where packs contained five cards each.

COMPLETE SET (50) 10.00 25.00
1 Jerry Porter .30 .75
2 Tim Couch .25 .60
3 Chris Samuels .25 .60
4 Plaxico Burress .30 .75
5 Michael Wiley .20 .50
6 Thomas Jones .40 1.00
7 Chris Redman .25 .60
8 Anthony Lucas .20 .50
9 Kwame Cavil .20 .50
10 Chad Pennington .50 1.25
11 LaVar Arrington .50 1.25
12 Giovanni Carmazzi .20 .50
13 Tim Rattay .25 .60
14 Laveranues Coles .30 .75
15 Mario Edwards .20 .50
16 John Engelberger .20 .50
17 Tee Martin .30 .75
18 R.Jay Soward .20 .50
19 Ahmed Plummer .20 .50
20 Na'il Diggs .20 .50
21 J.R. Redmond .20 .50
22 Dez White .25 .60
23 Reuben Droughns .30 .75
24 Sylvester Morris .20 .50
25 Cosey Coleman .20 .50
26 Corey Moore .20 .50
27 Curtis Keaton .20 .50
28 Danny Farmer .20 .50
29 Travis Claridge .20 .50
30 Troy Walters .20 .50
31 Jamal Lewis .30 .75
32 Shaun King .20 .50
33 Ron Dayne .30 .75
34 Keith Bulluck .25 .60
35 Corey Simon .25 .60
36 Deon Dyer .20 .50
37 Shaun Alexander .40 1.00
38 Shyrone Stith .20 .50
39 Shaun Ellis .30 .75
40 Todd Pinkston .20 .50
41 Travis Prentice .25 .60
42 Chris Hovan .25 .60
43 Brandon Short .20 .50
44 Brian Urlacher 1.25 3.00
45 Rob Morris .25 .60
46 Raynoch Thompson .20 .50
47 Deon Grant .20 .50
48 Stockar McDougle .20 .50
49 Darren Howard .20 .50
50 Courtney Brown .25 .60

2000 SAGE HIT NRG

COMPLETE SET (50) 20.00 40.00
*NRG: .6X TO 1.5X BASIC CARDS
NRG STATED ODDS 1:1.5

2000 SAGE HIT Autographs Emerald

EMERALD STATED ODDS 1:12
*EMER.DIE CUT: .6X TO 1.5X EMERALD
EMERALD DIE CUT STATED ODDS 1:40
*DIAMOND: .5X TO 1.2X EMERALD
*DIAM.DIE CUT: 1X TO 2.5X EMERALD
OVERALL AUTOGRAPH ODDS 1:6
1 Jerry Porter 4.00 10.00
2 Tim Couch 3.00 8.00
3 Chris Samuels 3.00 8.00
4 Plaxico Burress 6.00 15.00
5 Michael Wiley 2.50 6.00
6 Thomas Jones 5.00 12.00
7 Chris Redman 3.00 8.00
8 Anthony Lucas 2.50 6.00
9 Kwame Cavil 2.50 6.00
10 Chad Pennington 6.00 15.00
11 LaVar Arrington 6.00 15.00
12 Giovanni Carmazzi 2.50 6.00
13 Tim Rattay 3.00 8.00
14 Laveranues Coles 4.00 10.00
15 Mario Edwards 2.50 6.00
16 John Engelberger 2.50 6.00
17 Tee Martin 4.00 10.00
18 R.Jay Soward 2.50 6.00
19 Ahmed Plummer 2.50 6.00
20 Na'il Diggs 2.50 6.00
21 J.R. Redmond 2.50 6.00
22 Dez White 3.00 8.00
23 Reuben Droughns 4.00 10.00
24 Sylvester Morris 2.50 6.00
25 Cosey Coleman 2.50 6.00
26 Corey Moore 2.50 6.00
27 Curtis Keaton 2.50 6.00
28 Danny Farmer 2.50 6.00
29 Travis Claridge 2.50 6.00
30 Troy Walters 2.50 6.00
31 Jamal Lewis 4.00 10.00
32 Shaun King 2.50 6.00
33 Ron Dayne 4.00 10.00
35 Corey Simon 3.00 8.00
36 Deon Dyer 2.50 6.00
37 Shaun Alexander 5.00 12.00
38 Shyrone Stith 2.50 6.00
39 Shaun Ellis 4.00 10.00
40 Todd Pinkston 2.50 6.00
41 Travis Prentice 3.00 8.00
42 Chris Hovan 3.00 8.00
43 Brandon Short 2.50 6.00
44 Brian Urlacher 15.00 40.00
45 Rob Morris 3.00 8.00
46 Raynoch Thompson UER 2.50 6.00
(name on front misspelled Raynock)
47 Deon Grant 2.50 6.00
48 Stockar McDougle 2.50 6.00
49 Darren Howard 2.50 6.00
50 Courtney Brown 3.00 8.00

2000 SAGE HIT Prospectors Emerald

COMPLETE SET (20) 30.00 60.00
EMERALD/999 ODDS 1:24
EMERALD PRINT RUN 999
*EMER.DIE CUT/300: .6X TO 1.5X EMERALD
EMERALD DIE CUT/300 ODDS 1:80
EMERALD DIE CUT PRINT RUN 300
*DIAMOND/600: .5X TO 1.2X EMERALD
DIAMOND/600 ODDS 1:40
*DIAM.DIE CUT/100: 1.2X TO 3X EMERALD
DIAMOND DIE CUT/100 ODDS 1:240
UNPRICED SOLITAIRE 1/1 ODDS 1:320
OVERALL PROSPECTOR ODDS 1:12
P1 Shaun Alexander 1.25 3.00
P2 LaVar Arrington 1.50 4.00
P3 Courtney Brown .75 2.00
P4 Plaxico Burress 1.00 2.50
P5 Giovanni Carmazzi .60 1.50
P6 Tim Couch .75 2.00
P7 Ron Dayne 1.00 2.50
P8 Thomas Jones 1.25 3.00
P9 Shaun King .60 1.50
P10 Jamal Lewis 1.00 2.50
P11 Tee Martin 1.00 2.50
P12 Sylvester Morris .60 1.50
P13 Chad Pennington 1.50 4.00
P14 Jerry Porter 1.00 2.50
P15 Travis Prentice .75 2.00
P16 Tim Rattay .75 2.00
P17 Chris Redman .75 2.00
P18 R.Jay Soward .60 1.50
P19 Dez White .75 2.00
P20 Michael Wiley .60 1.50

2001 SAGE HIT

Released as a 50-card set, Sage HIT features full color player action photos with a white border. The SAGE logo appears in the upper left hand corner of the card front. HIT was packaged in 16-box cases with 24-pack boxes and packs contained five cards each.

COMPLETE SET (50) 10.00 25.00
1 David Terrell .25 .60
2 Jamar Fletcher .20 .50
3 Koren Robinson .25 .60
4 Ken-Yon Rambo .20 .50
5 LaDainian Tomlinson 1.00 2.50
6 Santana Moss .40 1.00
7 Michael Vick 1.25 3.00
8 Steve Hutchinson .30 .75
9 Robert Ferguson .30 .75
10 Torrance Marshall .20 .50
11 Scotty Anderson .20 .50
12 Derrick Gibson .20 .50
13 Marcus Stroud .25 .60
14 Josh Heupel .30 .75
15 Drew Brees 2.00 5.00
16 Gerard Warren .25 .60
17 Quincy Carter .25 .60
18 Gary Baxter .20 .50
19 Alex Bannister .20 .50
20 Travis Henry .25 .60
21 Andre Dyson .20 .50
22 Deuce McAllister .30 .75
23 Rod Gardner .25 .60
24 Jamie Winborn .25 .60
25 Will Allen .30 .75
26 Kenyatta Walker .20 .50
27 Tim Hasselbeck .25 .60
28 Alge Crumpler .30 .75
29 Michael Bennett .25 .60
30 LaMont Jordan .30 .75
31 Jeff Backus .20 .50
32 Rudi Johnson .30 .75
33 Willie Howard .20 .50
34 Josh Booty .25 .60
35 Todd Heap .30 .75
36 Correll Buckhalter .30 .75
37 Jesse Palmer .25 .60
38 Carlos Polk .20 .50
39 Richard Seymour .30 .75
40 Adam Archuleta .25 .60
41 James Jackson .20 .50
42 Willie Middlebrooks .25 .60
43 Ja'Mar Toombs .20 .50
44 Chris Chambers .30 .75
45 Reggie Germany .20 .50
46 Casey Hampton .30 .75
47 Reggie Wayne .60 1.50
48 Jamal Reynolds .20 .50
49 Justin Smith .30 .75
50 Quincy Morgan .25 .60

2001 SAGE HIT A-Game

COMPLETE SET (9) 20.00 50.00
STATED ODDS 1:42
STATED PRINT RUN 600 SER.#'d SETS
1 Drew Brees 4.00 10.00
2 Drew Brees 4.00 10.00
3 Drew Brees 4.00 10.00
4 David Terrell .50 1.25
5 David Terrell .50 1.25
6 David Terrell .50 1.25
7 Michael Vick 2.50 6.00
8 Michael Vick 2.50 6.00
9 Michael Vick 2.50 6.00

2001 SAGE HIT Autographs

STATED ODDS 1:9
*DIE CUT/250: .6X TO 1.5X BASIC AUTO
DIE CUT/250 STATED ODDS 1:26
*FOILBOARD: .5X TO 1.2X BASIC AUTO
FOILBOARD STATED ODDS 1:13
*FOILBOARD DC/100: .8X TO 2X BASIC AU
FOILBOARD DC PRINT RUN 100 #'d SETS
FOILBOARD DIE CUT/100 ODDS 1:64
OVERALL AUTOGRAPH STATED ODDS 1:4
A1 David Terrell 4.00 10.00
A3 Koren Robinson 4.00 10.00
A4 Ken-Yon Rambo 3.00 8.00
A5 LaDainian Tomlinson 15.00 40.00
A6 Santana Moss 6.00 15.00
A7 Michael Vick 20.00 50.00
A8 Steve Hutchinson 5.00 12.00
A9 Robert Ferguson 5.00 12.00
A10 Torrance Marshall 3.00 8.00
A11 Scotty Anderson 3.00 8.00
A12 Derrick Gibson 3.00 8.00
A13 Marcus Stroud 4.00 10.00
A14 Josh Heupel 5.00 12.00
A15 Drew Brees 30.00 80.00
A17 Quincy Carter 4.00 10.00
A18 Gary Baxter 3.00 8.00
A19 Alex Bannister 3.00 8.00
A20 Travis Henry 4.00 10.00
A21 Andre Dyson 3.00 8.00
A22 Deuce McAllister 5.00 12.00
A23 Rod Gardner 4.00 10.00
A24 Jamie Winborn 4.00 10.00
A25 Will Allen 5.00 12.00
A26 Kenyatta Walker 3.00 8.00
A27 Tim Hasselbeck 4.00 10.00
A28 Alge Crumpler 5.00 12.00
A29 Michael Bennett 4.00 10.00
A30 LaMont Jordan 5.00 12.00
A31 Jeff Backus 3.00 8.00
A32 Rudi Johnson 5.00 12.00
A33 Willie Howard 3.00 8.00
A34 Josh Booty 4.00 10.00
A35 Todd Heap 5.00 12.00
A36 Correll Buckhalter 5.00 12.00
A37 Jesse Palmer 4.00 10.00
A38 Carlos Polk 3.00 8.00
A39 Richard Seymour 5.00 12.00
A40 Adam Archuleta 4.00 10.00
A41 James Jackson 3.00 8.00
A42 Willie Middlebrooks 4.00 10.00
A43 Ja'Mar Toombs 3.00 8.00
A44 Chris Chambers 5.00 12.00
A45 Reggie Germany 3.00 8.00
A46 Casey Hampton 6.00 15.00
A47 Reggie Wayne 10.00 25.00
A48 Jamal Reynolds 3.00 8.00
A49 Justin Smith 5.00 12.00
A50 Quincy Morgan 4.00 10.00
A51 Fred Smoot 5.00 12.00

2001 SAGE HIT Jerseys

STATED ODDS 1:205
STATED PRINT RUN 175 SER.#'d SETS
J1 Michael Vick 12.00 30.00
J2 Michael Vick 12.00 30.00
J3 Michael Vick 12.00 30.00
J4 Drew Brees 20.00 50.00
J5 Drew Brees 20.00 50.00
J6 Drew Brees 20.00 50.00
J7 David Terrell 4.00 10.00
J8 David Terrell 4.00 10.00
J9 David Terrell 4.00 10.00

2001 SAGE HIT Prospectors Emerald

COMPLETE SET (15) 40.00 80.00
STATED ODDS 1:19
EMERALD PRINT RUN 999 SER.#'d SETS
*EMER.DIE CUT/299: .6X TO 1.5X EMERALD
EMERALD DIE CUT/299 ODDS 1:63
EMERALD DC PRINT RUN 299 #'d SETS
*DIAMOND/599: .5X TO 1.2X EMERALD
DIAMOND/599 ODDS 1:32
*DIAM.DIE CUT/99: 1.5X TO 4X EMERALD
DIAMOND DIE CUT/99 ODDS 1:190
P1 Michael Bennett .60 1.50
P2 Drew Brees 5.00 12.00
P3 Quincy Carter .60 1.50
P4 Chris Chambers .75 2.00
P5 Rod Gardner .60 1.50
P6 Josh Heupel .75 2.00
P7 LaMont Jordan .75 2.00
P8 Deuce McAllister .75 2.00
P9 Quincy Morgan .60 1.50
P10 Santana Moss 1.00 2.50
P11 Koren Robinson .60 1.50
P12 David Terrell .60 1.50
P13 LaDainian Tomlinson 2.50 6.00
P14 Michael Vick 3.00 8.00
P15 Reggie Wayne 1.50 4.00

2001 SAGE HIT Rarefied

RAREFIED BRONZE/2001 ODDS 1:3
BRONZE PRINT RUN 2001 SER.#'d SETS
*SILVER/999: 1.2X TO 3X BASIC CARDS
RAREFIED SILVER/999 ODDS 1:6
SILVER PRINT RUN 999 SERIAL #'d SETS
*GOLD/500: 2.5X TO 6X BASIC CARDS
RAREFIED GOLD/500 ODDS 1:11
GOLD PRINT RUN 500 SERIAL #'d SETS

2002 SAGE HIT

Released as a 50-card set, Sage HIT features full color player action photos with a white border. The SAGE logo appears in the bottom left hand corner of the card front. HIT was packaged in 16-box cases with 24-pack boxes where packs contained five cards each.

COMPLETE SET (47) 10.00 25.00
1 John Henderson .30 .75
2 Tim Carter .30 .75
3 Joey Harrington .40 1.00
4 Marquise Walker .25 .60
5 Quentin Jammer .40 1.00
6 Rohan Davey .40 1.00
7A Eric Crouch QB .40 1.00
7B Eric Crouch RB .40 1.00
8 David Carr .40 1.00
9 Maurice Morris .30 .75
10 Jabar Gaffney .40 1.00
11 David Neill .25 .60
12 Randy Fasani .30 .75
13 Alex Brown .40 1.00
14 J.T. O'Sullivan .30 .75
15 Kurt Kittner .25 .60
16 Ashley Lelie .30 .75
17 Reche Caldwell .40 1.00
18 T.J. Duckett .40 1.00
19 Chester Taylor .40 1.00
20 Jonathan Wells .40 1.00
21 Kelly Campbell .30 .75
22 Bryant McKinnie .25 .60
23 Lito Sheppard .40 1.00
24 Donte Stallworth .40 1.00
25 Josh Reed .30 .75
26 DeShaun Foster .40 1.00
27 Patrick Ramsey .40 1.00
28 Clinton Portis .50 1.25
29 Albert Haynesworth .40 1.00
31 Cliff Russell .25 .60
32 Luke Staley .25 .60
33 Ron Johnson .30 .75
34 Travis Stephens .25 .60
35 Chad Hutchinson .25 .60
36 Lamar Gordon .30 .75
37 Larry Tripplett .25 .60
38 Napoleon Harris .30 .75
39 Daniel Graham .30 .75
40 Antonio Bryant .40 1.00
41 Javon Walker .40 1.00
42 Brian Poli-Dixon .25 .60
43 Jeremy Shockey .60 1.50
44 Andre Davis .30 .75
45 Ladell Betts .40 1.00
46 Michael Vick .60 1.50
NNO David Carr CL .30 .75

2002 SAGE HIT Rarefied Emerald

COMPLETE SET (45) 25.00 50.00
*EMERALD: .6X TO 1.5X BASIC CARDS
EMERALD STATED ODDS 1:2
R30 Ronald Curry .50 1.25

2002 SAGE HIT Rarefied Silver

COMPLETE SET (45) 40.00 80.00
*SILVER: 1X TO 2.5X BASIC CARDS
SILVER STATED ODDS 1:5
R30 Ronald Curry .75 2.00

2002 SAGE HIT Autographs Emerald

EMERALD STATED ODDS 1:8
*SILVER AU: .5X TO 1.2X EMERALD AU
SILVER AUTO ODDS 1:16
*GOLD AU/250: .6X TO 1.5X EMERALD AU
*GOLD AU/120-130: 1X TO 2.5X EMER
GOLD AUTO/120-250 ODDS 1:22
GOLD AUTO PRINT RUN 120-250
*RAREFIED GOLD/100: 1X TO 2.5X EMERALD
RAREFIED GOLD/100 ODDS 1:55
H1 John Henderson 3.00 8.00
H2 Tim Carter 3.00 8.00
H3 Joey Harrington 4.00 10.00
H4 Marquise Walker 2.50 6.00
H5 Quentin Jammer 4.00 10.00
H6 Rohan Davey 4.00 10.00
H7A Eric Crouch QB 4.00 10.00
H7B Eric Crouch RB 4.00 10.00
H8 David Carr 4.00 10.00
H9 Maurice Morris 3.00 8.00
H10 Jabar Gaffney 4.00 10.00
H11 David Neill 2.50 6.00
H12 Randy Fasani 3.00 8.00
H14 J.T. O'Sullivan 3.00 8.00
H15 Kurt Kittner 2.50 6.00
H16 Ashley Lelie 3.00 8.00
H17 Reche Caldwell 4.00 10.00
H18 T.J. Duckett 4.00 10.00
H19 Chester Taylor 4.00 10.00
H20 Jonathan Wells 4.00 10.00
H21 Kelly Campbell 3.00 8.00
H22 Bryant McKinnie 2.50 6.00
H23 Lito Sheppard 4.00 10.00
H25 Josh Reed 3.00 8.00
H26 DeShaun Foster 4.00 10.00
H27 Patrick Ramsey 4.00 10.00
H28 Clinton Portis 15.00 30.00
H29 Albert Haynesworth 6.00 15.00
H30 Ronald Curry 3.00 8.00
H31 Cliff Russell 2.50 6.00
H32 Luke Staley 2.50 6.00
H33 Ron Johnson 3.00 8.00
H34 Travis Stephens 2.50 6.00
H35 Chad Hutchinson 2.50 6.00
H36 Lamar Gordon 3.00 8.00
H37 Larry Tripplett 2.50 6.00
H38 Napoleon Harris 3.00 8.00
H39 Daniel Graham 3.00 8.00
H40 Antonio Bryant 4.00 10.00
H41 Javon Walker 4.00 10.00
H42 Brian Poli-Dixon 2.50 6.00
H43 Jeremy Shockey 6.00 15.00
H44 Andre Davis 3.00 8.00
H45 Ladell Betts 4.00 10.00

2002 SAGE HIT Jerseys

STATED ODDS 1:80
*PATCH/25: .8X TO 2X BASIC JSY
PATCH/25 STATED ODDS 1:950
PATCHES PRINT RUN 25 SER.#'d SETS
1 David Carr 6.00 15.00
2 Eric Crouch 8.00 20.00
3 Rohan Davey 6.00 15.00
4 T.J. Duckett 6.00 15.00
5 DeShaun Foster 6.00 15.00
6 Joey Harrington 6.00 15.00
7 Kurt Kittner 4.00 10.00
8 Clinton Portis 8.00 20.00
9 Patrick Ramsey 6.00 15.00

2002 SAGE HIT Write Stuff

COMPLETE SET (15) 12.00 30.00
STATED ODDS 1:20
1 Antonio Bryant 1.00 2.50
2 David Carr 1.00 2.50
3 Eric Crouch 1.00 2.50
4 Rohan Davey 1.00 2.50
5 T.J. Duckett 1.00 2.50
6 DeShaun Foster 1.00 2.50
7 Jabar Gaffney 1.00 2.50
8 Joey Harrington 1.00 2.50
9 Chad Hutchinson .60 1.50
10 Kurt Kittner .60 1.50
11 Ashley Lelie .75 2.00
12 Clinton Portis 1.25 3.00
13 Patrick Ramsey 1.00 2.50
14 Josh Reed .75 2.00
15 Michael Vick 1.50 4.00

2003 SAGE HIT

Released in April 2003, this set consists of 48-cards. Each box contained 30 packs of 5 cards. On average, each box contained nine autographs and one jersey card.

COMPLETE SET (48) 10.00 25.00
1 Charles Rogers .30 .75
2 Willis McGahee .50 1.25
3 Arnaz Battle .40 1.00
4 Terence Newman .30 .75
5 Larry Johnson .40 1.00
6 Taylor Jacobs .25 .60
7 Kyle Boller .40 1.00
8 Rex Grossman .40 1.00
9 Jerome McDougle .25 .60
10 Jason Witten 1.00 2.50
11 Ken Dorsey .30 .75
12 Justin Gage .30 .75
13 Andy Groom .25 .60
14 Seneca Wallace .40 1.00
15 Dave Ragone .25 .60
16 Kliff Kingsbury .30 .75
17 Jason Gesser .30 .75
18 George Wrighster .25 .60
19 Ronald Bellamy .30 .75
20 Donnie Nickey .25 .60
21 Billy McMullen .25 .60
22 Lee Suggs .30 .75
23 Chris Brown .25 .60
24 Bryant Johnson .40 1.00
25 Justin Fargas .40 1.00
26 Brandon Lloyd .60 1.50
27 Tyrone Calico .30 .75
28 Sam Aiken .30 .75
29 Cie Grant .30 .75
30 Dahrran Diedrick .25 .60
31 Kelley Washington .25 .60
32 Musa Smith .25 .60
33 Kevin Curtis .40 1.00
34 Terry Pierce .25 .60
35 Matt Wilhelm .30 .75
36 Rashean Mathis .30 .75
37 Brad Banks .30 .75
38 Tully Banta-Cain .40 1.00
39 Sammy Davis .30 .75
40 Teyo Johnson .30 .75
41 Chris Simms .40 1.00
42 E.J. Henderson .30 .75
43 Terrell Suggs .40 1.00
44 Dallas Clark .60 1.50
45 Marcus Trufant .30 .75
46 Boss Bailey .30 .75
47 David Carr .30 .75
NNO Charles Rogers CL .25 .60

2003 SAGE HIT Autographs Emerald

EMERALD STATED ODDS 1:6
*GOLD/250: .6X TO 1.5X EMERALD
GOLD AUTO/250 ODDS 1:25
*SILVER: .5X TO 1.2X EMERALD
SILVER AUTO ODDS 1:9
A1 Charles Rogers 3.00 8.00
A2 Willis McGahee 5.00 12.00
A3 Arnaz Battle 4.00 10.00
A4 Terence Newman 3.00 8.00
A5 Larry Johnson 4.00 10.00
A6 Taylor Jacobs 2.50 6.00
A7 Kyle Boller 4.00 10.00
A8 Rex Grossman 4.00 10.00
A9 Jerome McDougle 2.50 6.00
A10 Jason Witten 10.00 25.00
A11 Ken Dorsey 3.00 8.00
A12 Justin Gage 3.00 8.00
A13 Andy Groom 2.50 6.00
A14 Seneca Wallace 4.00 10.00
A15 Dave Ragone 2.50 6.00
A16 Kliff Kingsbury 3.00 8.00
A17 Jason Gesser 3.00 8.00
A18 George Wrighster 2.50 6.00
A19 Ronald Bellamy 3.00 8.00
A20 Donnie Nickey 2.50 6.00
A21 Billy McMullen 2.50 6.00
A22 Lee Suggs 3.00 8.00
A23 Chris Brown 2.50 6.00
A24 Bryant Johnson 4.00 10.00
A25 Justin Fargas 4.00 10.00
A26 Brandon Lloyd 6.00 15.00
A27 Tyrone Calico 3.00 8.00
A28 Sam Aiken 3.00 8.00
A29 Cie Grant 3.00 8.00
A30 Dahrran Diedrick 2.50 6.00
A32 Musa Smith 2.50 6.00
A33 Kevin Curtis 4.00 10.00
A34 Terry Pierce 2.50 6.00
A35 Matt Wilhelm 3.00 8.00
A36 Rashean Mathis 3.00 8.00
A37 Brad Banks 3.00 8.00
A38 Tully Banta-Cain 4.00 10.00
A39 Sammy Davis 3.00 8.00
A40 Teyo Johnson 3.00 8.00
A41 Chris Simms 4.00 10.00
A42 E.J. Henderson 3.00 8.00
A43 Terrell Suggs 4.00 10.00
A44 Dallas Clark 6.00 15.00
A45 Marcus Trufant 3.00 8.00
A46 Boss Bailey 3.00 8.00

2003 SAGE HIT Class of 2003 Autographs

*CLASS AU/100: .8X TO 2X EMERALD AU
A31 Kelley Washington 10.00 25.00
A47 David Carr

2003 SAGE HIT Class of 2003 Emerald

COMPLETE SET (46) 25.00 50.00
*EMERALD: .8X TO 2X BASIC CARDS
EMERALD STATED ODDS 1:3

2003 SAGE HIT Class of 2003 Silver

COMPLETE SET (46) 30.00 60.00
*SILVER: 1X TO 2.5X BASIC CARDS
SILVER STATED ODDS 1:5

2003 SAGE HIT Jerseys

*PREMIUM SWATCH/50: .8X TO 2X
PREMIUM SWATCH/50 ODDS 1:460
HJ1 Brad Banks 4.00 10.00
HJ2 Kyle Boller 5.00 12.00
HJ3 Ken Dorsey 4.00 10.00
HJ4 Rex Grossman 5.00 12.00
HJ5 Taylor Jacobs 3.00 8.00
HJ6 Larry Johnson 5.00 12.00
HJ7 Willis McGahee 6.00 15.00
HJ8 Dave Ragone 3.00 8.00
HJ9 Charles Rogers 4.00 10.00
HJ10 Chris Simms 5.00 12.00
HJ11 Lee Suggs 4.00 10.00
HJ12 Kelley Washington 3.00 8.00

2003 SAGE HIT Write Stuff

COMPLETE SET (15) 12.00 30.00
STATED ODDS 1:15
1 Charles Rogers .75 2.00
2 Willis McGahee 1.25 3.00
3 Justin Fargas 1.00 2.50
4 Lee Suggs .75 2.00
5 Larry Johnson 1.00 2.50
6 Kliff Kingsbury .75 2.00
7 Kyle Boller 1.00 2.50
8 Rex Grossman 1.00 2.50
9 Seneca Wallace 1.00 2.50
10 Chris Simms 1.00 2.50
11 Ken Dorsey .75 2.00
12 Chris Brown .60 1.50
13 Musa Smith .60 1.50
14 Brad Banks .75 2.00
15 Dave Ragone .60 1.50

2003 SAGE HIT Write Stuff Autographs

STATED ODDS 1:720
WSA1 Charles Rogers 12.00 30.00
WSA2 Willis McGahee 20.00 50.00
WSA3 Justin Fargas 15.00 40.00
WSA4 Lee Suggs 12.00 30.00
WSA5 Larry Johnson 15.00 40.00
WSA6 Kliff Kingsbury 12.00 30.00
WSA7 Kyle Boller 15.00 40.00
WSA8 Rex Grossman 15.00 40.00
WSA9 Seneca Wallace 15.00 40.00
WSA10 Chris Simms 15.00 40.00
WSA11 Ken Dorsey 12.00 30.00
WSA12 Chris Brown 10.00 25.00
WSA13 Musa Smith 10.00 25.00
WSA14 Brad Banks 12.00 30.00
WSA15 Dave Ragone 10.00 25.00
WSA16 David Carr 15.00 40.00

2004 SAGE HIT

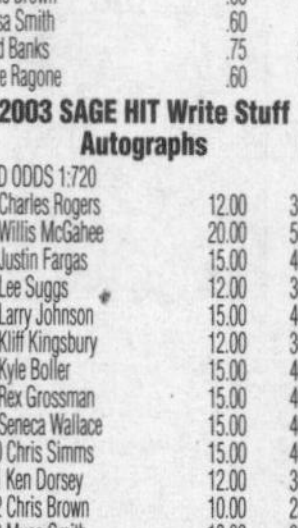

The SAGE HIT product was the first 2004 football card set on the market. It released in mid to late April 2004. The base set consists of 46-cards including an unnumbered Eli Manning checklist card. Maurice Clarett made an apearance in this product although he was declared ineligible for the NFL Draft. Boxes contained 30-packs of 5-cards. A variety of inserts can be found seeded in packs highlighted by the Autographs parallel sets. Two different special retail boxes were produced for Ohio State and the SEC which featured insert sets exclusive to those packs. Note that Craig Krenzel and Rex Grossman appear in the Autograph sets only.

COMPLETE SET (46) 12.50 30.00
1 Reggie Williams .30 .75
2 Bernard Berrian .40 1.00
3 Lee Evans .40 1.00
4 Roy Williams WR .40 1.00
5 Josh Harris .25 .60
6 Greg Jones .25 .60
7 Ben Roethlisberger 2.50 6.00
8 Drew Carter .30 .75
9 Devery Henderson .40 1.00
10 Eli Manning 2.50 6.00
11 Karlos Dansby .40 1.00
12 Michael Jenkins .40 1.00
13 Maurice Clarett .30 .75
14 Michael Clayton .30 .75
15 Casey Clausen .30 .75
16 John Navarre .25 .60
17 Philip Rivers 1.50 4.00
18 Jeff Smoker .30 .75
19 Ernest Wilford .30 .75
20 Derrick Knight .25 .60
21 Chris Gamble .30 .75
22 Jared Lorenzen .30 .75
23 Chris Perry .30 .75
24 Rod Rutherford .25 .60
25 Kevin Jones .30 .75
26 Michael Boulware .40 1.00
27 Tatum Bell .30 .75
28 Will Poole .40 1.00
29 Jake Grove .25 .60
30 Ell Roberson .40 1.00
31 Devard Darling .25 .60
32 Dunta Robinson .25 .60
33 Cody Pickett .30 .75
34 Steven Jackson .60 1.50
35 Matt Schaub .75 2.00
36 Sean Jones .30 .75
37 Tommie Harris .40 1.00
38 Chris Collins .25 .60
39 Will Smith .30 .75
40 DeAngelo Hall .40 1.00
41 Rashaun Woods .25 .60
42 Ben Troupe .30 .75
43 Quincy Wilson .30 .75
44 P.K. Sam .25 .60
45 Clarence Farmer .25 .60
NNO Eli Manning CL 1.25 3.00
EM Eli Manning SEC/30 20.00 50.00

2004 SAGE HIT Autographs Emerald

STATED ODDS 1:10
*SILVER: .5X TO 1.2X EMERALD AU
SILVER AUTO ODDS 1:18
A1 Reggie Williams 3.00 8.00
A2 Bernard Berrian 4.00 10.00
A3 Lee Evans 4.00 10.00
A4 Roy Williams WR SP 4.00 10.00
A5 Josh Harris 2.50 6.00
A6 Greg Jones 2.50 6.00
A7 Ben Roethlisberger 30.00 60.00
A8 Drew Carter 3.00 8.00
A9 Devery Henderson 4.00 10.00
A10 Eli Manning 30.00 60.00
A11 Karlos Dansby 4.00 10.00
A12 Michael Jenkins 4.00 10.00
A13 Maurice Clarett SP 8.00 20.00
A14 Michael Clayton 3.00 8.00
A15 Casey Clausen 3.00 8.00
A16 John Navarre 2.50 6.00
A17 Philip Rivers 12.50 30.00
A18 Jeff Smoker 3.00 8.00
A19 Ernest Wilford 3.00 8.00
A20 Derrick Knight 2.50 6.00
A21 Chris Gamble 3.00 8.00
A22 Jared Lorenzen 3.00 8.00
A23 Chris Perry 3.00 8.00
A24 Rod Rutherford 2.50 6.00
A25 Kevin Jones 3.00 8.00
A26 Michael Boulware 4.00 10.00
A27 Tatum Bell 3.00 8.00
A28 Will Poole 4.00 10.00
A29 Jake Grove 2.50 6.00
A30 Ell Roberson SP
A31 Devard Darling 2.50 6.00
A32 Dunta Robinson 2.50 6.00
A33 Cody Pickett 3.00 8.00
A35 Matt Schaub 8.00 20.00
A36 Sean Jones 3.00 8.00
A37 Tommie Harris 4.00 10.00
A38 Chris Collins 2.50 6.00
A39 Will Smith 3.00 8.00
A40 DeAngelo Hall 4.00 10.00
A41 Rashaun Woods 2.50 6.00
A42 Ben Troupe 3.00 8.00
A43 Quincy Wilson 3.00 8.00
A44 P.K. Sam 2.50 6.00
A46 Craig Krenzel SP
A47 Rex Grossman 3.00 8.00

2004 SAGE HIT Autographs Gold

*GOLD: .6X TO 1.5X EMERALD AU
GOLD/250 ODDS 1:30
GOLD PRINT RUN 250 SER.#'d SETS
A30 Ell Roberson SP 10.00 25.00
A46 Craig Krenzel 10.00 25.00

2004 SAGE HIT Inside the Numbers Silver

*EMERALD: .4X TO 1X SILVERS
*GOLD: .4X TO 1X SILVERS
OVERALL STATED ODDS 1:14
1 Pittsburgh Wide Receiver 1.25 3.00
(Larry Fitzgerald)
2 USC Wide Receiver .75 2.00
(Mike Williams)
3 Mississippi Quarterback 2.50 6.00
(Eli Manning)
4 USC Quarterback 1.00 2.50
(Matt Leinart)
5 Ohio St. Running Back .75 2.00
(Maurice Clarett)
6 Oklahoma Quarterback 1.00 2.50
(Jason White)
7 Auburn Running Back 1.00 2.50
(Cadillac Williams)
8 Texas Running Back 1.00 2.50
(Cedric Benson)
9 Kansas St. Running Back 1.00 2.50
(Darren Sproles)

2004 SAGE HIT Jerseys

STATED ODDS 1:31
*PREM.SWATCH/50: .8X TO 2X
PREMUIM SWATCH PRINT RUN 50
JBR Ben Roethlisberger 12.00 30.00
JCC Casey Clausen 4.00 10.00
JCP Chris Perry 4.00 10.00
JEM Eli Manning 12.00 30.00
JER Ell Roberson 5.00 12.00
JGJ Greg Jones 3.00 8.00
JJL Jared Lorenzen 4.00 10.00
JJN John Navarre 3.00 8.00
JKJ Kevin Jones 4.00 10.00
JLE Lee Evans 5.00 12.00
JMC Maurice Clarett 4.00 10.00
JMJ Michael Jenkins 5.00 12.00
JPR Philip Rivers 10.00 25.00
JRE Reggie Williams 4.00 10.00
JRO Roy Williams WR 5.00 12.00
JRW Rashaun Woods 3.00 8.00
JTB Tatum Bell 4.00 10.00

2004 SAGE HIT Ohio State Autographs

INSERTS IN SPECIAL OHIO STATE BOXES
STATED PRINT RUN 50 SER.#'d SETS
OA1 Drew Carter 12.00 30.00
OA2 Maurice Clarett 12.00 30.00
OA3 Chris Gamble 12.00 30.00
OA4 Michael Jenkins 15.00 40.00
OA5 Craig Krenzel 12.00 30.00
OA6 Will Smith 12.00 30.00

2004 SAGE HIT Q&A Autographs

STATED ODDS 1:70
STATED PRINT RUN 100 SER.#'d SETS
QA1 Reggie Williams 6.00 15.00
QA2 Bernard Berrian 8.00 20.00
QA3 Lee Evans 8.00 20.00
QA4 Roy Williams WR 8.00 20.00
QA5 Josh Harris 5.00 12.00
QA6 Greg Jones 5.00 12.00
QA7 Ben Roethlisberger 50.00 100.00
QA8 Drew Carter 6.00 15.00
QA9 Devery Henderson 8.00 20.00
QA10 Eli Manning 50.00 100.00
QA11 Karlos Dansby 8.00 20.00
QA12 Michael Jenkins 8.00 20.00
QA13 Maurice Clarett 6.00 15.00
QA14 Michael Clayton 6.00 15.00
QA15 Casey Clausen 6.00 15.00
QA16 John Navarre 5.00 12.00
QA17 Philip Rivers 20.00 50.00
QA18 Jeff Smoker 6.00 15.00
QA19 Ernest Wilford 6.00 15.00
QA20 Derrick Knight 5.00 12.00
QA21 Chris Gamble 6.00 15.00
QA22 Jared Lorenzen 6.00 15.00
QA23 Chris Perry 6.00 15.00
QA24 Rod Rutherford 5.00 12.00
QA25 Kevin Jones 6.00 15.00
QA26 Michael Boulware 8.00 20.00
QA27 Tatum Bell 6.00 15.00
QA28 Will Poole 8.00 20.00
QA29 Jake Grove 5.00 12.00
QA30 Ell Roberson SP
QA31 Devard Darling 5.00 12.00
QA32 Dunta Robinson 5.00 12.00
QA33 Cody Pickett 6.00 15.00
QA35 Matt Schaub 12.00 30.00
QA36 Sean Jones 6.00 15.00
QA37 Tommie Harris 8.00 20.00
QA38 Chris Collins 5.00 12.00
QA39 Will Smith 6.00 15.00
QA40 DeAngelo Hall 8.00 20.00
QA41 Rashaun Woods 5.00 12.00
QA42 Ben Troupe 6.00 15.00
QA43 Quincy Wilson 6.00 15.00
QA44 P.K. Sam 5.00 12.00
QA46 Craig Krenzel 6.00 15.00

2004 SAGE HIT Q&A Emerald

COMPLETE SET (46) 20.00 50.00
STATED ODDS 1:2
*SILVER: .5X TO 1.2X EMERALD
SILVER STATED ODDS 1:5
Q1 Reggie Williams .40 1.00
Q2 Bernard Berrian .50 1.25
Q3 Lee Evans .50 1.25
Q4 Roy Williams WR .50 1.25
Q5 Josh Harris .30 .75
Q6 Greg Jones .30 .75
Q7 Ben Roethlisberger 3.00 8.00
Q8 Drew Carter .40 1.00
Q9 Devery Henderson .50 1.25
Q10 Eli Manning 3.00 8.00
Q11 Karlos Dansby .50 1.25
Q12 Michael Jenkins .50 1.25
Q13 Maurice Clarett .40 1.00
Q14 Michael Clayton .40 1.00
Q15 Casey Clausen .40 1.00
Q16 John Navarre .30 .75
Q17 Philip Rivers 2.00 5.00
Q18 Jeff Smoker .40 1.00
Q19 Ernest Wilford .40 1.00
Q20 Derrick Knight .30 .75
Q21 Chris Gamble .40 1.00
Q22 Jared Lorenzen .40 1.00
Q23 Chris Perry .40 1.00
Q24 Rod Rutherford .30 .75
Q25 Kevin Jones .40 1.00
Q26 Michael Boulware .50 1.25
Q27 Tatum Bell .40 1.00
Q28 Will Poole .50 1.25
Q29 Jake Grove .30 .75
Q30 Ell Roberson .50 1.25
Q31 Devard Darling .30 .75
Q32 Dunta Robinson .30 .75
Q33 Cody Pickett .40 1.00
Q34 Steven Jackson .75 2.00
Q35 Matt Schaub 1.00 2.50
Q36 Sean Jones .40 1.00
Q37 Tommie Harris .50 1.25
Q38 Chris Collins .30 .75
Q39 Will Smith .40 1.00
Q40 DeAngelo Hall .50 1.25
Q41 Rashaun Woods .30 .75
Q42 Ben Troupe .40 1.00
Q43 Quincy Wilson .40 1.00
Q44 P.K. Sam .30 .75
Q45 Clarence Farmer .30 .75
Q46 Craig Krenzel .40 1.00

2004 SAGE HIT SEC Autographs

INSERTS IN SPECIAL SEC BOXES
STATED PRINT RUN 50 SER.#'d SETS
S1 Karlos Dansby 15.00 40.00
S2 Ben Troupe 12.00 30.00
S3 Sean Jones 12.00 30.00
S4 Michael Clayton UER 12.00 30.00
(listed as Mark on front)
S5 Devery Henderson 15.00 40.00
S6 Jared Lorenzen 12.00 30.00
S7 Chris Collins 10.00 25.00
S8 Eli Manning 100.00 175.00
S9 Dunta Robinson 10.00 25.00
S10 Casey Clausen 12.00 30.00

2004 SAGE HIT Write Stuff

COMPLETE SET (15) 15.00 40.00
STATED ODDS 1:15
1 Eli Manning 5.00 12.00
2 Ben Roethlisberger 5.00 12.00
3 Philip Rivers 3.00 8.00
4 Matt Schaub 1.50 4.00
5 John Navarre .50 1.25
6 Cody Pickett .60 1.50
7 Roy Williams WR .75 2.00
8 Reggie Williams .60 1.50
9 Lee Evans .75 2.00
10 Rashaun Woods .50 1.25
11 Michael Clayton .60 1.50
12 Greg Jones .50 1.25
13 Maurice Clarett .60 1.50
14 Chris Perry .60 1.50
15 Kevin Jones .60 1.50

2004 SAGE HIT Write Stuff Autographs

STATED ODDS 1:845
STATED PRINT RUN 25 SER.#'d SETS
WSA1 Eli Manning 100.00 175.00
WSA2 Ben Roethlisberger 75.00 150.00
WSA3 Philip Rivers 40.00 100.00
WSA4 Matt Schaub 25.00 60.00
WSA5 John Navarre 12.00 30.00
WSA6 Cody Pickett 15.00 40.00
WSA7 Roy Williams WR 20.00 50.00
WSA8 Reggie Williams 15.00 40.00
WSA9 Lee Evans 20.00 50.00
WSA10 Rashaun Woods 12.00 30.00
WSA11 Michael Clayton 15.00 40.00
WSA12 Greg Jones 12.00 30.00
WSA13 Maurice Clarett 15.00 40.00
WSA14 Chris Perry 15.00 40.00
WSA15 Kevin Jones 15.00 40.00

2005 SAGE HIT

SAGE HIT was initially released in mid-April 2005 as the first football card release of the year. The base set consists of 50-cards including 11-short printed cards. Hobby boxes contained 30-packs of 5-cards and carried an S.R.P. of $3.99 per pack. A variety of inserts can be found seeded in packs highlighted by the multi-tiered Autograph and Reflect Gold Autograph inserts.

COMPLETE SET (50) 10.00 25.00
1 Craphonso Thorpe .25 .60
2 Derrick Johnson .30 .75
3 Frank Gore SP .75 2.00
4 Ciatrick Fason .25 .60
5 Charlie Frye .40 1.00
6 Antrel Rolle .40 1.00
7 Dan Orlovsky .40 1.00
8 Aaron Rodgers 3.00 8.00
9 Mark Clayton .40 1.00
10 Thomas Davis .25 .60
11 Alex Smith QB .60 1.50
12 Fred Gibson SP .40 1.00
13 Maurice Clarett SP .40 1.00
14 David Greene .25 .60
15 Carlos Rogers .40 1.00
16 Andrew Walter .30 .75
17 Jason Campbell .50 1.25
18 Jason White .40 1.00
19 Matt Jones .40 1.00
20 Marion Barber SP .50 1.25
21 Taylor Stubblefield .25 .60
22 Jammal Brown SP .50 1.25
23 Ronnie Brown .50 1.25
24 Cadillac Williams .40 1.00
25 Kay-Jay Harris .25 .60
26 Reggie Brown .25 .60
27 Troy Williamson .30 .75
28 Anthony Davis .25 .60
29 Josh Davis SP .30 .75
30 J.J. Arrington .30 .75
31 Alex Smith TE .25 .60
32 Corey Webster SP .40 1.00
33 Vernand Morency .30 .75
34 Derek Anderson .30 .75
35 DeMarcus Ware SP 1.00 2.50
36 Kyle Orton .40 1.00
37 Brock Berlin .30 .75
38 Marlin Jackson .25 .60
39 Channing Crowder .30 .75
40 Roddy White .50 1.25
41 Roscoe Parrish .25 .60
42 Adrian McPherson .25 .60
43 Brodney Pool .40 1.00
44 T.A. McLendon .25 .60
45 Terrence Murphy .25 .60
46 Chris Rix .30 .75
47 Ben Roethlisberger SP .75 2.00
48 Dante Ridgeway SP .30 .75
49 Justin Miller .30 .75
50 Johnathan Goddard SP .40 1.00
ROY Roethlisberger ROY/100 7.50 20.00

2005 SAGE HIT ACC Autographs

STATED PRINT RUN 50 SER.#'d SETS
ACC2 T.A. McLendon 8.00 20.00
ACC3 Frank Gore 30.00 60.00
ACC4 Roscoe Parrish 10.00 25.00
ACC5 Brock Berlin 10.00 25.00
ACC6 Justin Miller 8.00 20.00
ACC7 Chris Rix 8.00 20.00
ACC8 Craphonso Thorpe 8.00 20.00
ACC9 Adrian McPherson 10.00 25.00

2005 SAGE HIT Autographs Blue

BLUE AUTO STATED ODDS 1:10
*GOLD: .6X TO 1.5X BLUE AUTO
*GOLD: .5X TO 1.2X BLUE SP AUTO
GOLD PRINT RUN 250 SER.#'d SETS
GOLD AUTO STATED ODDS 1:30
*SILVER: .5X TO 1.2X BLUE AUTO
*SILVER: .4X TO 1X BLUE SP AUTO
SILVER AUTO STATED ODDS 1:18
1 Craphonso Thorpe 3.00 8.00
2 Derrick Johnson 4.00 10.00
3 Frank Gore 8.00 20.00
4 Ciatrick Fason 3.00 8.00
5 Charlie Frye 5.00 12.00
7 Dan Orlovsky 5.00 12.00
8 Aaron Rodgers SP 90.00 150.00
9 Mark Clayton 4.00 10.00
10 Thomas Davis 3.00 8.00
11 Alex Smith QB SP 10.00 25.00
12 Fred Gibson 4.00 10.00
14 David Greene 3.00 8.00
15 Carlos Rogers 5.00 12.00
16 Andrew Walter 4.00 10.00
17 Jason Campbell 6.00 15.00
18 Jason White 5.00 12.00
19 Matt Jones 4.00 10.00
20 Marion Barber 5.00 12.00
21 Taylor Stubblefield 3.00 8.00
22 Jammal Brown 5.00 12.00
23 Ronnie Brown 6.00 15.00
24 Cadillac Williams 5.00 12.00
25 Kay-Jay Harris 3.00 8.00
26 Reggie Brown 3.00 8.00
27 Troy Williamson 4.00 10.00
28 Anthony Davis 3.00 8.00
29 Josh Davis 3.00 8.00
30 J.J. Arrington 4.00 10.00
31 Alex Smith TE 3.00 8.00
32 Corey Webster 4.00 10.00
33 Vernand Morency 4.00 10.00
34 Derek Anderson SP 5.00 12.00
35 Demarcus Ware 10.00 25.00
36 Kyle Orton 5.00 12.00
37 Brock Berlin SP 5.00 12.00
38 Marlin Jackson 3.00 8.00
39 Channing Crowder 4.00 10.00
41 Roscoe Parrish 3.00 8.00
42 Adrian McPherson 3.00 8.00
43 Brodney Pool 5.00 12.00
44 T.A. McLendon 3.00 8.00
45 Terrence Murphy 3.00 8.00
46 Chris Rix SP 5.00 12.00
48 Dante Ridgeway 3.00 8.00
49 Justin Miller 4.00 10.00
50 Johnathan Goddard 4.00 10.00

2005 SAGE HIT Ben Roethlisberger

COMPLETE SET (36) 20.00 50.00
COMMON CARD (1-36) 1.00 2.50
ONE PER MAC SPECIAL PACK

2005 SAGE HIT Jerseys

STATED ODDS 1:31
*PREMIUM SWATCH: 1X TO 2.5X BASIC JSY
*PREMIUM SWATCH: .5X TO 1.2X SP JSY
PREMIUM SWATCH STATED ODDS 1:540
PREMIUM SWATCH PRINT RUN 50 SETS
AD Anthony Davis 2.50 6.00
AM Adrian McPherson 2.50 6.00
AR Aaron Rodgers 20.00 40.00
AS Alex Smith QB 12.00 30.00
AW Andrew Walter 3.00 8.00
BR Ben Roethlisberger SP 10.00 25.00
CF Ciatrick Fason 2.50 6.00
CR Chris Rix 3.00 8.00
CW Cadillac Williams 8.00 20.00
DG David Greene 2.50 6.00
DO Dan Orlovsky 4.00 10.00
JA J.J. Arrington 3.00 8.00
JC Jason Campbell 5.00 12.00
JW Jason White 4.00 10.00
KO Kyle Orton 4.00 10.00
MC Mark Clayton 4.00 10.00
MO Maurice Clarett SP 3.00 8.00
RB Ronnie Brown 12.00 30.00
RP Roscoe Parrish 2.50 6.00
VM Vernand Morency 3.00 8.00

2005 SAGE HIT MAC Autographs

STATED PRINT RUN 50 SER.#'d SETS
MAC2 Charlie Frye 10.00 25.00
MAC3 Johnathan Goddard 8.00 20.00
MAC4 Josh Davis 8.00 20.00
MAC5 Dante Ridgeway 8.00 20.00

2005 SAGE HIT Reflect Blue

COMPLETE SET (55) 20.00 50.00
*REFLECT BLUE: .6X TO 1.5X BASIC CARDS
*REFLECT BLUE: .5X TO 1.2X BASIC SP's
*REFLECT BLUE SP's: .8X TO 2X BASIC CARDS
OVERALL REFLECT ODDS 1:1.5
R51 Michigan RB #20 SP 1.50 4.00
(Michael Hart)
R52 Oklahoma RB #28 SP 2.50 6.00
(Adrian Peterson)
R53 Texas QB #10 UER SP 2.50 6.00
(Vince Young)/(Longhorns misspelled on front)
R54 USC RB #5 SP 2.50 6.00
(Reggie Bush)
R55 USC QB #11 SP 2.50 6.00
(Matt Leinart)

2005 SAGE HIT Reflect Silver

COMPLETE SET (55) 20.00 50.00
*REFLECT SILVER: .6X TO 1.5X BASIC CARDS
*REFLECT SILVER: .5X TO 1.2X BASIC SP's
*REFLECT SILV.SP's: .8X TO 2X BASIC CARDS
OVERALL REFLECT ODDS 1:1.5
R51 Michigan RB #20 SP 1.50 4.00
(Michael Hart)
R52 Oklahoma RB #28 SP 2.50 6.00
(Adrian Peterson)
R53 Texas QB #10 SP 2.50 6.00
(Vince Young)
R54 USC RB #5 SP 2.50 6.00
(Reggie Bush)
R55 USC QB #11 SP 2.50 6.00
(Matt Leinart)

2005 SAGE HIT Reflect Gold Autographs

*REFLECT GOLD: .8X TO 2X BLUE AUTO
*REFLECT GOLD: .6X TO 1.5X BLUE SP AUTO
REFLECT GOLD/100 ODDS 1:70

2005 SAGE HIT SEC Autographs

STATED PRINT RUN 50 SER.#'d SETS
SEC2 Cadillac Williams 20.00 50.00
SEC3 Ronnie Brown 30.00 80.00
SEC4 Jason Campbell 15.00 40.00
SEC5 Carlos Rogers 10.00 25.00
SEC6 David Greene 8.00 20.00
SEC7 Reggie Brown 10.00 25.00
SEC8 Fred Gibson 8.00 20.00
SEC9 Thomas Davis 8.00 20.00
SEC10 Troy Williamson 10.00 25.00
SEC11 Matt Jones 12.00 30.00
SEC12 Corey Webster 10.00 25.00
SEC13 Ciatrick Fason 8.00 20.00
SEC14 Channing Crowder 8.00 20.00

2005 SAGE HIT Write Stuff

COMPLETE SET (15) 15.00 40.00
STATED ODDS 1:15
1 Ronnie Brown 1.00 2.50
2 Jason Campbell 1.00 2.50
3 Mark Clayton .75 2.00
4 Ciatrick Fason .50 1.25
5 Charlie Frye .75 2.00
6 David Greene .50 1.25
7 Derrick Johnson .60 1.50
8 Dan Orlovsky .75 2.00
9 Kyle Orton .75 2.00
10 Aaron Rodgers 6.00 15.00
11 Alex Smith QB 1.25 3.00
12 Andrew Walter .60 1.50
13 Jason White .75 2.00
14 Cadillac Williams .75 2.00
15 Troy Williamson .60 1.50

2005 SAGE HIT Write Stuff Autographs

WS AU/25 ODDS 1:845
WSA1 Ronnie Brown 25.00 60.00
WSA2 Jason Campbell 25.00 60.00
WSA3 Mark Clayton 20.00 50.00
WSA4 Ciatrick Fason 12.00 30.00
WSA5 Charlie Frye 20.00 50.00
WSA6 David Greene 12.00 30.00
WSA7 Derrick Johnson 15.00 40.00
WSA8 Dan Orlovsky 20.00 50.00
WSA9 Kyle Orton 20.00 50.00
WSA10 Aaron Rodgers 125.00 200.00
WSA11 Alex Smith QB 40.00 80.00
WSA12 Andrew Walter 15.00 40.00
WSA13 Jason White 20.00 50.00
WSA14 Cadillac Williams 20.00 50.00
WSA15 Troy Williamson 15.00 40.00

2006 SAGE HIT

This 55-card set was released in April, 2006. The set was issued into the hoby in five-card packs with an $3.99 SRP which came 30 packs to a box. A few cards were issued in shorter quantity and we have notated those cards with an SP in our checklist. In addition, card number 56, Jay Cutler, was issued at the 2006 Anaheim National Convention. That card is not considered part of the set.

COMPLETE SET (55) 10.00 25.00
#56 ISSUED AT 2006 ANAHEIM NATIONAL
1 Reggie McNeal .30 .75
2 Jimmy Williams SP .40 1.00
3 D.J. Shockley SP .30 .75
4 Omar Jacobs .25 .60
5 Reggie Bush .75 2.00
6 Charlie Whitehurst .40 1.00
7 Michael Huff .30 .75
8 Tye Hill .25 .60
9 Mario Williams .40 1.00
10 Vince Young .50 1.25
11 Matt Leinart UER .40 1.00
(name misspelled Leinhart)
12 Brodie Croyle .40 1.00
13 Paul Pinegar .25 .60
14 Drew Olson .25 .60
15 Martin Nance .30 .75
16 David Thomas .30 .75
17 Dwayne Slay SP .30 .75
18 Vernon Davis .50 1.25
19 Taurean Henderson SP .40 1.00
20 Maurice Drew .60 1.50
21 LenDale White .30 .75
22 Laurence Maroney .30 .75
23 Leon Washington .30 .75
24 Erik Meyer SP .30 .75
25 Maurice Stovall .25 .60
26 Ashton Youboty .25 .60
27 Devin Aromashodu .40 1.00
28 Mike Hass .30 .75
29 Jonathan Orr .30 .75
30 Joseph Addai .40 1.00
31 Leonard Pope .40 1.00
32 Michael Robinson .30 .75
33 Mike Bell .40 1.00
34 Ernie Sims SP .30 .75
35 Skyler Green .25 .60
36 Demetrius Williams .30 .75
37 Winston Justice .30 .75
38 Sinorice Moss .40 1.00
39 Charles Gordon SP .30 .75
40 Gerald Riggs .30 .75
41 Jerome Harrison .40 1.00
42 Bobby Carpenter .25 .60
43 Dominique Byrd .30 .75
44 Bruce Gradkowski .40 1.00
45 Rodrique Wright .25 .60
46 D'Brickashaw Ferguson .40 1.00
47 Daniel Bullocks SP .40 1.00
48 Jason Avant .25 .60
49 Will Blackmon .30 .75
50 Devin Hester SP .60 1.50
51 Alan Zemaitis SP .40 1.00
52 Hank Baskett .40 1.00
53 Cadillac Williams ROY SP 1.25 3.00
54 Reggie Bush CL SP .60 1.50
Matt Leinart
55 Vince Young CL SP .40 1.00
56 Jay Cutler .75 2.00

2006 SAGE HIT Autographs Blue

BLUE ODDS 1:10 HOB, 1:50 RET
1 Reggie McNeal 4.00 10.00
3 D.J. Shockley 4.00 10.00
4 Omar Jacobs 3.00 8.00
5 Reggie Bush SP 30.00 80.00
6 Charlie Whitehurst 5.00 12.00
7 Michael Huff 4.00 10.00
8 Tye Hill 3.00 8.00
9 Mario Williams 5.00 12.00
10 Vince Young SP 25.00 60.00
11 Matt Leinart SP 12.00 30.00
12 Brodie Croyle 5.00 12.00
13 Paul Pinegar 3.00 8.00
14 Drew Olson 3.00 8.00
15 Martin Nance 4.00 10.00
16 David Thomas 4.00 10.00
17 Dwayne Slay 4.00 10.00
18 Vernon Davis 6.00 15.00
19 Taurean Henderson 5.00 12.00
20 Maurice Drew 10.00 25.00
21 LenDale White SP 15.00 40.00
22 Laurence Maroney 4.00 10.00
24 Erik Meyer 4.00 10.00
25 Maurice Stovall 3.00 8.00
26 Ashton Youboty 3.00 8.00
27 Devin Aromashodu 5.00 12.00
28 Mike Hass 4.00 10.00
29 Jonathan Orr 4.00 10.00
30 Joseph Addai 8.00 20.00
31 Leonard Pope 5.00 12.00
32 Michael Robinson 4.00 10.00
33 Mike Bell 5.00 12.00
34 Ernie Sims 4.00 10.00
35 Skyler Green 3.00 8.00
36 Demetrius Williams 4.00 10.00
37 Winston Justice 4.00 10.00
38 Sinorice Moss 5.00 12.00
39 Charles Gordon 4.00 10.00
41 Jerome Harrison 5.00 12.00
42 Bobby Carpenter 3.00 8.00
43 Dominique Byrd 4.00 10.00
44 Bruce Gradkowski 5.00 12.00
45 Rodrique Wright 3.00 8.00
46 D'Brickashaw Ferguson 5.00 12.00
48 Jason Avant 3.00 8.00
49 Will Blackmon 4.00 10.00
51 Alan Zemaitis 5.00 12.00
52 Hank Baskett 5.00 12.00

2006 SAGE HIT Autographs Gold

*GOLD: .6X TO 1.5X BLUE AUTOS
*GOLD: .5X TO 1.2X BLUE SP AUTOS
GOLD/250 ODDS 1:30 HOB, 1:150 RET
5 Reggie Bush 25.00 60.00
10 Vince Young 25.00 60.00
11 Matt Leinart 10.00 25.00
53 Anthony Fasano 6.00 15.00

2006 SAGE HIT Autographs Silver

*SILVER: .5X TO 1.2X BLUE AUTOS
*SILVER: .4X TO 1X BLUE SP AUTOS
SILVER ODDS 1:18 HOB, 1:90 RET
5 Reggie Bush 30.00 80.00
10 Vince Young 25.00 60.00
11 Matt Leinart 12.00 30.00

2006 SAGE HIT BCS

COMPLETE SET (36) 15.00 40.00
ONE PER SPECIAL BCS PACK
BCS1 Vince Young .50 1.25
BCS2 Michael Robinson .30 .75
BCS3 Bobby Carpenter .25 .60
BCS4 D.J. Shockley .30 .75
BCS5 Vince Young .50 1.25
BCS6 David Thomas .30 .75
BCS7 Michael Huff .30 .75
BCS8 Rodrique Wright .25 .60
BCS9 Matt Leinart .40 1.00
BCS10 Reggie Bush .75 2.00
BCS11 LenDale White .30 .75
BCS12 Dominique Byrd .30 .75
BCS13 Winston Justice .30 .75
BCS14 Michael Robinson .30 .75
BCS15 Alan Zemaitis .40 1.00
BCS16 Leon Washington .30 .75
BCS17 Ernie Sims .30 .75
BCS18 Ashton Youboty .25 .60
BCS19 Maurice Stovall .25 .60
BCS20 Anthony Fasano .40 1.00
BCS21 D.J. Shockley .30 .75
BCS22 Leonard Pope .40 1.00
BCS23 Vince Young .50 1.25
BCS24 Vince Young .50 1.25
BCS25 Vince Young .50 1.25
BCS26 Vince Young .50 1.25
BCS27 Vince Young .50 1.25
BCS28 Vince Young .50 1.25
BCS29 Vince Young .50 1.25
BCS30 Vince Young .50 1.25
BCS31 Matt Leinart .40 1.00
BCS32 Matt Leinart .40 1.00
BCS33 Matt Leinart .40 1.00
BCS34 Reggie Bush .75 2.00
BCS35 Reggie Bush .75 2.00
BCS36 LenDale White .30 .75

2006 SAGE HIT BCS Autographs

TWO PER SPECIAL BCS BOX
STATED PRINT RUN 50 SER.#'d SETS
BCS1 Vince Young
BCS2 Michael Huff 10.00 25.00
BCS3 Rodrique Wright 8.00 20.00
BCS4 David Thomas 10.00 25.00
BCS5 Matt Leinart 12.00 30.00
BCS6 LenDale White 10.00 25.00
BCS7 Reggie Bush 25.00 60.00
BCS8 D.J. Shockley 10.00 25.00
BCS9 Dominique Byrd 10.00 25.00
BCS10 Michael Robinson 10.00 25.00
BCS11 Alan Zemaitis 12.00 30.00
BCS12 Bobby Carpenter 8.00 20.00
BCS13 Ashton Youboty 8.00 20.00
BCS14 Maurice Stovall 8.00 20.00
BCS15 Ernie Sims 10.00 25.00
BCS16 Leonard Pope 12.00 30.00
BCS17 Winston Justice 10.00 25.00
BCS19 Anthony Fasano 12.00 30.00

2006 SAGE HIT BIG-12 Autographs

TWO PER SPECIAL BIG 12 BOX
STATED PRINT RUN 50 SER.#'d SETS
BIG1 Vince Young 15.00 40.00
BIG9 Charles Gordon 10.00 25.00
BIG3 Rodrique Wright 8.00 20.00
BIG4 David Thomas 10.00 25.00
BIG5 Reggie McNeal 10.00 25.00
BIG6 Michael Huff 10.00 25.00
BIG7 Taurean Henderson 12.00 30.00
BIG8 Dwayne Slay 10.00 25.00

2006 SAGE HIT Design for Success Blue

BLUE STATED ODDS 1:2
*GREEN: .3X TO .8X BLUE
GREEN STATED ODDS 14:15 RETAIL
*SILVER: .5X TO 1.2X BLUE
SILVER STATED ODDS 1:5
D1 Reggie McNeal .50 1.25
D2 Jimmy Williams .60 1.50
D3 D.J. Shockley .50 1.25
D4 Omar Jacobs .40 1.00
D5 Reggie Bush 1.25 3.00
D6 Charlie Whitehurst .60 1.50
D7 Michael Huff .50 1.25
D8 Tye Hill .40 1.00
D9 Mario Williams .60 1.50
D10 Vince Young .75 2.00
D11 Matt Leinart .60 1.50
D12 Brodie Croyle .60 1.50
D13 Paul Pinegar .40 1.00
D14 Drew Olson .40 1.00
D15 Martin Nance .50 1.25
D16 David Thomas .50 1.25
D17 Dwayne Slay .50 1.25
D18 Vernon Davis .75 2.00
D19 Taurean Henderson .60 1.50
D20 Maurice Drew 1.00 2.50
D21 LenDale White .50 1.25
D22 Laurence Maroney .50 1.25
D23 Leon Washington .50 1.25
D24 Erik Meyer .50 1.25
D25 Maurice Stovall .40 1.00
D26 Ashton Youboty .40 1.00
D27 Devin Aromashodu .60 1.50
D28 Mike Hass .50 1.25
D29 Jonathan Orr .50 1.25
D30 Joseph Addai .60 1.50
D31 Leonard Pope .60 1.50
D32 Michael Robinson .50 1.25
D33 Mike Bell .60 1.50
D34 Ernie Sims .50 1.25
D35 Skyler Green .40 1.00
D36 Demetrius Williams .50 1.25
D37 Winston Justice .50 1.25
D38 Sinorice Moss .60 1.50
D39 Charles Gordon .50 1.25
D40 Gerald Riggs .50 1.25
D41 Jerome Harrison .60 1.50
D42 Bobby Carpenter .40 1.00
D43 Dominique Byrd .50 1.25
D44 Bruce Gradkowski .60 1.50
D45 Rodrique Wright .40 1.00
D46 D'Brickashaw Ferguson .60 1.50
D47 Daniel Bullocks .60 1.50
D48 Jason Avant .40 1.00
D49 Will Blackmon .50 1.25
D50 Devin Hester 1.00 2.50
D51 Alan Zemaitis .60 1.50
D52 Hank Baskett .60 1.50
D53 Anthony Fasano .60 1.50
D54 Jay Cutler 1.25 3.00
D55 DeMeco Ryans .60 1.50

2006 SAGE HIT Design for Success Gold Autographs

GOLD/100 STATED ODDS 1:70
DA1 Reggie McNeal 10.00 25.00
DA3 D.J. Shockley 10.00 25.00
DA4 Omar Jacobs 10.00 25.00
DA5 Reggie Bush 40.00 100.00
DA6 Charlie Whitehurst 10.00 25.00
DA7 Michael Huff 10.00 25.00
DA8 Tye Hill 10.00 25.00
DA9 Mario Williams 15.00 40.00
DA10 Vince Young 30.00 80.00
DA11 Matt Leinart 15.00 40.00
DA12 Brodie Croyle 12.00 30.00
DA13 Paul Pinegar 8.00 20.00
DA14 Drew Olson 10.00 25.00
DA15 Martin Nance 6.00 15.00
DA16 David Thomas 10.00 25.00
DA17 Dwayne Slay 8.00 20.00
DA18 Vernon Davis 12.00 30.00
DA19 Taurean Henderson 10.00 25.00
DA20 Maurice Drew 20.00 50.00
DA21 LenDale White 25.00 60.00
DA22 Laurence Maroney 8.00 20.00
DA24 Erik Meyer 8.00 20.00
DA25 Maurice Stovall 10.00 25.00
DA26 Ashton Youboty 10.00 25.00
DA27 Devin Aromashodu UER 8.00 20.00
(name misspelled Devon)
DA28 Mike Hass 10.00 25.00
DA29 Jonathan Orr 8.00 20.00
DA30 Joseph Addai 20.00 50.00
DA31 Leonard Pope 12.50 30.00
DA32 Michael Robinson 10.00 25.00
DA33 Mike Bell 10.00 25.00
DA34 Ernie Sims 12.00 30.00
DA35 Skyler Green 10.00 25.00
DA36 Demetrius Williams 10.00 25.00
DA37 Winston Justice 10.00 25.00
DA38 Sinorice Moss 10.00 25.00
DA39 Charles Gordon 8.00 20.00
DA41 Jerome Harrison 10.00 25.00
DA42 Bobby Carpenter 10.00 25.00
DA43 Dominique Byrd 10.00 25.00
DA44 Bruce Gradkowski 12.00 30.00
DA45 Rodrique Wright 6.00 15.00
DA46 D'Brickashaw Ferguson 10.00 25.00
DA48 Jason Avant 10.00 25.00
DA49 Will Blackmon 8.00 20.00
DA51 Alan Zemaitis 10.00 25.00
DA52 Hank Baskett 10.00 25.00
DA53 Anthony Fasano 10.00 25.00
DA55 DeMeco Ryans 12.00 30.00

2006 SAGE HIT Hype

COMPLETE SET (7) 10.00 25.00
1 Jay Cutler 1.00 2.50
2 Reggie Bush 1.00 2.50
3 Vince Young .60 1.50
4 Matt Leinart .50 1.25
5 Vernon Davis .60 1.50
6 Joseph Addai .50 1.25
7 Laurence Maroney .40 1.00

2006 SAGE HIT Jerseys

STATED ODDS 1:31 HOB, 1:90 RET
AV Jason Avant 3.00 8.00
BC Bobby Carpenter 3.00 8.00
CW Charlie Whitehurst 5.00 12.00
DS D.J. Shockley 4.00 10.00
JA Joseph Addai 5.00 12.00
LW LenDale White 4.00 10.00
MD Maurice Drew 8.00 20.00
ML Matt Leinart 5.00 12.00
MR Michael Robinson 4.00 10.00
MS Maurice Stovall 3.00 8.00
OJ Omar Jacobs 3.00 8.00
RB Reggie Bush 10.00 25.00
RM Reggie McNeal 4.00 10.00
VD Vernon Davis 6.00 15.00
VY Vince Young 6.00 15.00

2006 SAGE HIT Jerseys Premium Swatches

*PREMIUM SWATCH: .8X TO 2X JSY
PREM.SWATCH/50 ODDS 1:540 H,1:2700 R
SM Sinorice Moss 10.00 25.00

2006 SAGE HIT PAC-10 Autographs

STATED PRINT RUN 50 SER.#'d SETS
PC1 Matt Leinart 12.00 30.00
PC2 Drew Olson 8.00 20.00
PC3 Reggie Bush 25.00 60.00
PC4 LenDale White 10.00 25.00
PC5 Dominique Byrd 10.00 25.00
PC6 Maurice Drew 20.00 50.00
PC7 Mike Hass 10.00 25.00
PC8 Demetrius Williams 10.00 25.00
PC9 Winston Justice 10.00 25.00
PC10 Mike Bell 12.00 30.00
PC11 Jerome Harrison 12.00 30.00

2006 SAGE HIT QB Autographs

STATED PRINT RUN 50 SER.#'d SETS
QB1 Matt Leinart 12.00 30.00
QB2 Erik Meyer 10.00 25.00
QB3 Vince Young 15.00 40.00
QB4 Omar Jacobs 8.00 20.00
QB5 Brodie Croyle 12.00 30.00
QB6 Michael Robinson 10.00 25.00
QB7 Charlie Whitehurst 12.00 30.00
QB8 D.J. Shockley 10.00 25.00
QB9 Drew Olson 8.00 20.00
QB10 Reggie McNeal 10.00 25.00
QB11 Paul Pinegar 8.00 20.00
QB12 Bruce Gradkowski 12.00 30.00

2006 SAGE HIT Write Stuff

STATED ODDS 1:15
1 Joseph Addai .75 2.00
2 Reggie Bush 1.50 4.00
3 Brodie Croyle .75 2.00
4 Vernon Davis 1.00 2.50
5 Maurice Drew 1.25 3.00
6 Michael Huff .60 1.50
7 Omar Jacobs .50 1.25
8 Matt Leinart .75 2.00
9 Laurence Maroney .60 1.50
10 Sinorice Moss .75 2.00
11 Michael Robinson .60 1.50
12 LenDale White .60 1.50
13 Charlie Whitehurst .75 2.00
14 Mario Williams .75 2.00
15 Vince Young 1.00 2.50

2006 SAGE HIT Write Stuff Autographs

AUTOS/25 ODDS 1:845 HOB, 1:4225 RET
WA1 Joseph Addai 20.00 50.00
WA2 Reggie Bush 40.00 100.00
WA3 Brodie Croyle 20.00 50.00
WA4 Vernon Davis 25.00 60.00
WA5 Maurice Drew 30.00 80.00
WA6 Michael Huff 15.00 40.00
WA7 Omar Jacobs 12.00 30.00
WA8 Matt Leinart 20.00 50.00
WA9 Laurence Maroney 15.00 40.00
WA10 Sinorice Moss 20.00 50.00
WA11 Michael Robinson 15.00 40.00
WA12 LenDale White 15.00 40.00
WA13 Charlie Whitehurst
WA14 Mario Williams 20.00 50.00
WA15 Vince Young 25.00 60.00

2006 SAGE HIT National Promos

These cards were issued at the 2006 National Sports Collector Convention. Each card appears to be from the base SAGE HIT set but for the addition of "/5" after the card number on the backs.

1 Matt Leinart .50 1.25
2 Vince Young .60 1.50
3 Jay Cutler 1.00 2.50
4 LenDale White .40 1.00
5 Reggie Bush 1.00 2.50

2007 SAGE HIT

This 64-card set was released in April, 2007. The set was issued into the hobby in five-card packs with a $3.99 SRP which came 30 packs to a box. The three players listed at the end of this set were all stars of the 2006 NFL Draft.

COMPLETE SET (64) 10.00 25.00
1 Paul Williams .25 .60
2 JaMarcus Russell .25 .60
3 Robert Meachem .40 1.00
4 Sidney Rice .50 1.25
5 Drew Stanton .25 .60
6 Jeff Rowe .25 .60
7 Zach Miller .40 1.00
8 Joel Filani .30 .75
9 Chris Henry .25 .60
10 Brady Quinn .40 1.00
11 Anthony Gonzalez .40 1.00
12 Chris Leak .30 .75
13 David Clowney .30 .75
14 Isaiah Stanback .25 .60
15 Steve Breaston .40 1.00
16 Yamon Figurs .25 .60
17 Lawrence Timmons .40 1.00
18 Greg Olsen .30 .75
19 Michael Bush .40 1.00
20 Alan Branch .30 .75
21 Johnnie Lee Higgins .30 .75
22 Aundrae Allison .25 .60
23 Kenny Irons .25 .60
24 Marshawn Lynch .40 1.00
25 Earl Everett .30 .75
26 Courtney Taylor .30 .75
27 Michael Griffin .40 1.00
28 Adrian Peterson 1.50 4.00
29 Leon Hall .30 .75
30 David Ball .30 .75
31 Aaron Ross .40 1.00
32 John Beck .40 1.00
33 Kolby Smith .30 .75
34 Kenneth Darby .30 .75
35 Trent Edwards .40 1.00
36 Craig Buster Davis .30 .75
37 Ryan Kalil .30 .75
38 Jason Snelling .40 1.00
39 Tyler Palko .30 .75
40 Dwayne Bowe .50 1.25
41 Dallas Baker .25 .60
42 Steve Smith USC .40 1.00
43 Jason Hill .40 1.00
44 Kevin Kolb .60 1.50
45 Jared Zabransky .30 .75
46 Brian Leonard .30 .75
47 Darius Walker .25 .60
48 Adam Carriker .30 .75
49 Patrick Willis .75 2.00
50 Troy Smith .40 1.00
51 Brandon Meriweather .40 1.00
52 Jarvis Moss .30 .75
53 Levi Brown .40 1.00
54 David Irons .25 .60
55 Garrett Wolfe .25 .60
56 LaMarr Woodley .40 1.00
57 DeMarcus Tank Tyler .25 .60
58 Jordan Palmer .30 .75
59 Antonio Pittman .25 .60
60 Gaines Adams .40 1.00
61 Calvin Johnson 1.25 3.00
ML Matt Leinart .50 1.25
RB Reggie Bush .60 1.50
VY Vince Young .50 1.25

2007 SAGE HIT Playmakers Blue

COMPLETE SET (61) 15.00 40.00
*BLUES: .6X TO 1.5X BASIC CARDS
OVERALL PLAYMAKERS ODDS 1:2
*SILVER: .5X TO 1.2X BLUE
SILVER STATED ODDS 1:5

2007 SAGE HIT Playmakers Gold Autographs

*PLAY.GOLD/100: .6X TO 1.5X BASIC AUTOS
PLAYMAKERS GOLD/100 ODDS 1:70
PA10 Brady Quinn 30.00 80.00
PA28 Adrian Peterson 100.00 200.00
PA59 Antonio Pittman 5.00 12.00

2007 SAGE HIT Autographs

BASE AUTO ODDS 1:10
*SILVER: .4X TO 1X BASIC AUTO
SILVER AUTO ODDS 1:18
1 Paul Williams 3.00 8.00
2 JaMarcus Russell SP 10.00 25.00
3 Robert Meachem 5.00 12.00
4 Sidney Rice 6.00 15.00
5 Drew Stanton 3.00 8.00
6 Jeff Rowe 3.00 8.00
7 Zach Miller 5.00 12.00
8 Joel Filani 4.00 10.00
9 Chris Henry 3.00 8.00
10 Brady Quinn SP 15.00 40.00
11 Anthony Gonzalez 5.00 12.00
12 Chris Leak SP 5.00 12.00
13 David Clowney 4.00 10.00
14 Isaiah Stanback 3.00 8.00
15 Steve Breaston 5.00 12.00
16 Yamon Figurs 3.00 8.00
17 Lawrence Timmons 5.00 12.00
18 Greg Olsen 4.00 10.00
19 Michael Bush 5.00 12.00
21 Johnnie Lee Higgins SP 5.00 12.00
22 Aundrae Allison 3.00 8.00
23 Kenny Irons 3.00 8.00
24 Marshawn Lynch SP 6.00 15.00
25 Earl Everett 4.00 10.00
27 Michael Griffin 5.00 12.00
28 Adrian Peterson SP 75.00 150.00
29 Leon Hall 4.00 10.00
30 David Ball 4.00 10.00
31 Aaron Ross 5.00 12.00
32 John Beck 5.00 12.00
33 Kolby Smith 4.00 10.00
34 Kenneth Darby 4.00 10.00
35 Trent Edwards 5.00 12.00
36 Craig Buster Davis SP 4.00 10.00
37 Ryan Kalil 4.00 10.00
38 Jason Snelling SP 6.00 15.00
39 Tyler Palko 4.00 10.00
40 Dwayne Bowe 6.00 15.00
41 Dallas Baker 3.00 8.00
42 Steve Smith USC 5.00 12.00
43 Jason Hill 5.00 12.00
44 Kevin Kolb 8.00 20.00
45 Jared Zabransky 4.00 10.00
46 Brian Leonard 4.00 10.00
47 Darius Walker 3.00 8.00
48 Adam Carriker 4.00 10.00
49 Patrick Willis 10.00 25.00
50 Troy Smith SP 10.00 25.00
51 Brandon Meriweather SP 6.00 15.00
52 Jarvis Moss 4.00 10.00
53 Levi Brown 5.00 12.00
54 David Irons 3.00 8.00
55 Garrett Wolfe 3.00 8.00
56 LaMarr Woodley 5.00 12.00
57 DeMarcus Tank Tyler 3.00 8.00
58 Jordan Palmer 4.00 10.00
59 Antonio Pittman SP
60 Gaines Adams 5.00 12.00
61 Chris Vincent 3.00 8.00

2007 SAGE HIT Autographs Gold

*GOLD/250: .5X TO 1.2X BASIC AUTO
GOLD AUTO/250 ODDS 1:30
10 Brady Quinn 20.00 50.00
28 Adrian Peterson 75.00 150.00

2007 SAGE HIT Big-10

COMPLETE SET (35) 20.00 40.00
INSERTS IN SPECIAL BIG-10 BOXES
1 Troy Smith .60 1.50
2 Troy Smith .60 1.50
3 Troy Smith .60 1.50
4 Antonio Pittman .40 1.00
5 Antonio Pittman .40 1.00
6 Troy Smith .60 1.50
7 Antonio Pittman .40 1.00
8 Anthony Gonzalez .60 1.50
9 Anthony Gonzalez .60 1.50
10 Alan Branch .50 1.25
11 Alan Branch .50 1.25
12 Alan Branch .50 1.25
13 Steve Breaston .60 1.50
14 Steve Breaston .60 1.50
15 Anthony Gonzalez .60 1.50
16 Leon Hall .50 1.25
17 Steve Breaston .60 1.50
18 Steve Breaston .60 1.50
19 Leon Hall .50 1.25
20 Leon Hall .50 1.25
21 Leon Hall .50 1.25
22 LaMarr Woodley .60 1.50
23 LaMarr Woodley .60 1.50
24 LaMarr Woodley .60 1.50
25 LaMarr Woodley .60 1.50
26 Levi Brown .60 1.50
27 Levi Brown .60 1.50
28 Levi Brown .60 1.50
29 Levi Brown .60 1.50
30 Drew Stanton .40 1.00
31 Drew Stanton .40 1.00
32 Drew Stanton .40 1.00
33 Drew Stanton .40 1.00
34 Ted Ginn Jr. .50 1.25
35 Ted Ginn Jr .50 1.25

2007 SAGE HIT Big-10 Autographs

STATED PRINT RUN 50 SER.#'d SETS
BTA1 Leon Hall 12.00 30.00
BTA3 Levi Brown 12.00 30.00
BTA5 Steve Breaston 10.00 25.00
BTA4 Anthony Gonzalez 15.00 40.00
BTA7 Troy Smith 20.00 50.00
BTA8 Drew Stanton 15.00 40.00
BTA9 LaMarr Woodley 15.00 40.00

2007 SAGE HIT Draft Diary

CARDS #1-2 INSERTED IN SAGE HIT 1:15
CARDS #3-4 INSERTED IN ASPIRE 1:20
CARDS #5-6 INSERTED IN SAGE
ALL CARDS FOR EACH PLAYER EQUAL PRICE
AP1 Adrian Peterson CR 2.00 5.00
AP2 Adrian Peterson WO 2.00 5.00
AP3 Adrian Peterson C 2.00 5.00
AP4 Adrian Peterson PD 2.00 5.00
AP5 Adrian Peterson TV 2.00 5.00
AP6 Adrian Peterson DD 2.00 5.00
BQ1 Brady Quinn CR .50 1.25
BQ2 Brady Quinn WO .50 1.25
BQ3 Brady Quinn C .50 1.25
BQ4 Brady Quinn PD .50 1.25
BQ5 Brady Quinn TV .50 1.25
BQ6 Brady Quinn DD .50 1.25
JR1 JaMarcus Russell CR .30 .75
JR2 JaMarcus Russell WO .30 .75
JR3 JaMarcus Russell C .30 .75
JR4 JaMarcus Russell PD .30 .75
JR5 JaMarcus Russell TV .30 .75
JR6 JaMarcus Russell DD .30 .75

2007 SAGE HIT Draft Diary Letter

1-2 LETTER/50 ODDS 1:3200 SAGE HIT
3-4 LETTER/100 ODDS 1:373 ASPIRE
AP1 Adrian Peterson CR/50 12.00 30.00
AP2 Adrian Peterson WO/50 12.00 30.00
AP3 Adrian Peterson C/100 8.00 20.00
AP4 Adrian Peterson PD/100 8.00 20.00
AP5 Adrian Peterson TV/100 8.00 20.00
AP6 Adrian Peterson DD/100 8.00 20.00
BQ1 Brady Quinn CR/50 3.00 8.00
BQ2 Brady Quinn WO/50 3.00 8.00
BQ3 Brady Quinn C/100 2.00 5.00
BQ4 Brady Quinn PD/100 2.00 5.00
BQ5 Brady Quinn TV/100 2.00 5.00
BQ6 Brady Quinn DD/100 2.00 5.00
JR1 JaMarcus Russell CR/50 2.00 5.00
JR2 JaMarcus Russell WO/50 2.00 5.00
JR3 JaMarcus Russell C/100 1.25 3.00
JR4 JaMarcus Russell PD/100 1.25 3.00
JR5 JaMarcus Russell TV/100 1.25 3.00
JR6 JaMarcus Russell DD/100 1.25 3.00

2007 SAGE HIT Jerseys

JERSEY STATED ODDS 1:30
*PREMIUM SWATCH/50: 1X TO 2.5X
PREMIUM SWATCH/50 ODDS 1:425
AD Adrian Peterson 15.00 40.00
AG Anthony Gonzalez 4.00 10.00
AP Antonio Pittman 4.00 10.00
BQ Brady Quinn 10.00 25.00
DS Drew Stanton 4.00 10.00
DW Darius Walker 4.00 10.00
JR JaMarcus Russell 5.00 12.00
KD Kenneth Darby 4.00 10.00
KI Kenny Irons 4.00 10.00
MB Michael Bush 4.00 10.00
ML Marshawn Lynch 5.00 12.00
RB Reggie Bush 8.00 20.00
RL Matt Leinart 5.00 12.00
RM Robert Meachem 5.00 12.00
RY Vince Young 6.00 15.00
SR Sidney Rice 6.00 15.00
TE Trent Edwards 4.00 10.00
TS Troy Smith 4.00 10.00

2007 SAGE HIT Jersey Bonus Red

*GOLD: .8X TO 2X RED
ONE PER RETAIL BOX BLASTER
MLC Matt Leinart College 3.00 8.00
MLP Matt Leinart Pro 3.00 8.00
RBC Reggie Bush College 5.00 12.00
RBP Reggie Bush Pro 5.00 12.00
VYC Vince Young College 4.00 10.00
VYP Vince Young Pro 4.00 10.00

2007 SAGE HIT Write Stuff

STATED ODDS 1:15
1 John Beck .75 2.00
2 Dwayne Bowe 1.00 2.50
3 Calvin Johnson 2.50 6.00
4 Kevin Kolb 1.25 3.00
5 Chris Leak .60 1.50
6 Brian Leonard .60 1.50
7 Marshawn Lynch .75 2.00
8 Robert Meachem .75 2.00
9 Greg Olsen .60 1.50
10 Adrian Peterson 3.00 8.00
11 Antonio Pittman .50 1.25
12 Brady Quinn .75 2.00
13 JaMarcus Russell .50 1.25
14 Troy Smith .75 2.00
15 Drew Stanton .50 1.25

2007 SAGE HIT Write Stuff Autographs

WRITE STUFF AUTO/25 ODDS 1:1000
1 John Beck 25.00 60.00
2 Dwayne Bowe 40.00 100.00
4 Kevin Kolb 30.00 80.00
5 Chris Leak 25.00 60.00
6 Brian Leonard 30.00 80.00
7 Marshawn Lynch 30.00 80.00
8 Robert Meachem 30.00 80.00
9 Greg Olsen 15.00 40.00
10 Adrian Peterson 150.00 300.00
11 Antonio Pittman 12.00 30.00
12 Brady Quinn 50.00 120.00
13 JaMarcus Russell 25.00 60.00
14 Troy Smith 30.00 80.00
15 Drew Stanton 12.00 30.00

2007 SAGE HIT Hype Orange

*BRONZE/550: .4X TO 1X ORANGE
*GOLD/220: .5X TO 1.2X ORANGE
*SILVER/480: .4X TO 1X ORANGE
1 Calvin Johnson 1.00 2.50
2 JaMarcus Russell .20 .50
3 Adrian Peterson 1.25 3.00
4 Brady Quinn .30 .75
5 Marshawn Lynch .30 .75
6 JaMarcus Russell .30 .75
Brady Quinn
7 Adrian Peterson 1.25 3.00
Brady Quinn
8 JaMarcus Russell .30 .75
Brady Quinn
9 JaMarcus Russell .20 .50
Drew Stanton
10 Adrian Peterson 1.25 3.00
Calvin Johnson

2008 SAGE HIT

COMPLETE SET (100) 15.00 40.00
COMP.LOW SERIES (50) 7.50 20.00
COMP.HIGH SERIES (50) 7.50 20.00
1 John David Booty .30 .75
2 Will Franklin .30 .75
3 Danny Woodhead 1.25 3.00
4 Limas Sweed .40 1.00
5 Joe Flacco 1.25 3.00
6 Brian Brohm .40 1.00
7 Chad Henne .40 1.00
8 Marcus Thomas .30 .75
9 Early Doucet .30 .75
10 Dennis Dixon .40 1.00
11 Xavier Adibi .25 .60
12 Matt Ryan 1.50 4.00
13 T.C. Ostrander .30 .75
14 Bernard Morris .30 .75
15 Sam Baker .25 .60
16 Adrian Arrington .30 .75
17 Kevin O'Connell .30 .75
18 Jacob Hester .40 1.00
19 Keenan Burton .25 .60
20 Darius Reynaud .25 .60
21 Keon Lattimore .30 .75
22 Tashard Choice .30 .75
23 Jake Long .40 1.00
24 Paul Smith .40 1.00
25 Jamaal Charles .60 1.50
26 Yvenson Bernard .40 1.00
27 Alex Brink .40 1.00
28 James Hardy .30 .75
29 Martin Rucker .30 .75
30 Steve Slaton .40 1.00
31 Derrick Harvey .25 .60
32 Andre Callender .40 1.00
33 Jabari Arthur .30 .75
34 Bruce Hocker .40 1.00
35 Kalvin McRae .25 .60
36 Lawrence Jackson .30 .75
37 Tyrell Johnson .40 1.00
38 Marcus Howard .40 1.00
39 Sam Keller .30 .75
40 Keith Rivers .40 1.00
41 Brandon Flowers .40 1.00
42 Adarius Bowman .30 .75
43 Ricky Santos .40 1.00
44 Jordon Dizon .40 1.00
45 Robert Jordan .30 .75
46 Maurice Purify .40 1.00
47 Lavelle Hawkins .25 .60
48 Jason Rivers .30 .75
49 John Carlson .40 1.00
50 Vernon Gholston .30 .75
51 Darren McFadden .60 1.50
Felix Jones
52 Matt Ryan 1.00 2.50
Andre Callender
53 DeSean Jackson .50 1.25
Marshawn Lynch
54 Matt Flynn .50 1.25
JaMarcus Russell
55 Brian Brohm .25 .60
Michael Bush
56 Chad Henne .25 .60
Mike Hart
57 Brady Quinn .50 1.25
John Carlson
58 Jonathan Stewart .40 1.00
Dennis Dixon
59 Adrian Peterson .75 2.00
Malcolm Kelly
60 Ray Rice .50 1.25
Brian Leonard
61 John David Booty .20 .50
Fred Davis
62 Jamaal Charles .40 1.00
Limas Sweed
63 Matt Ryan 1.00 2.50
Brian Brohm
64 Darren McFadden .60 1.50
Rashard Mendenhall
65 Malcolm Kelly .50 1.25
DeSean Jackson
66 Joe Flacco .75 2.00
Josh Johnson
67 Adrian Peterson .75 2.00
Patrick Willis
68 Devin Thomas .30 .75
69 Beau Bell .30 .75
70 Owen Schmitt .40 1.00
71 Paul Raymond .30 .75
72 Jordy Nelson .50 1.25
73 Ray Rice .75 2.00
74 Darrell Strong .30 .75
75 Felix Jones .60 1.50
76 Kevin Smith .40 1.00
77 Justin Forsett .40 1.00
78 Antoine Cason .40 1.00
79 Ryan Clady .40 1.00
80 Mike Hart .40 1.00
81 Kenny Phillips .40 1.00
82 Jonathan Stewart .60 1.50
83 Fred Davis .40 1.00
84 Malcolm Kelly .30 .75
85 Matt Flynn .75 2.00
86 Allen Patrick .30 .75
87 Brent Miller .30 .75
88 Andre Caldwell .30 .75
89 Josh Johnson .40 1.00
90 Erik Ainge .40 1.00
91 Tom Zbikowski .40 1.00
92 Dan Connor .40 1.00
93 Leodis McKelvin .30 .75
94 Sedrick Ellis .40 1.00
95 Rashard Mendenhall .75 2.00
96 Mike Jenkins .40 1.00
97 Dustin Keller .40 1.00
98 Donnie Avery .30 .75
99 DeSean Jackson .75 2.00
100 Darren McFadden 1.00 2.50

2008 SAGE HIT Make Ready Black

*BLACK/50: 2.5X TO 6X BASIC CARDS
*CYAN/50: 2.5X TO 6X BASIC CARDS
*MAGENTA/50: 2.5X TO 6X BASIC CARDS
*YELLOW/50: 2.5X TO 6X BASIC CARDS
OVERALL MR/50 ODDS 1:30 LOW, 1:25 HI

2008 SAGE HIT Glossy

*GLOSSY: .6X TO 1.5X BASIC CARDS
ONE GLOSSY PER RETAIL PACK

2008 SAGE HIT Gold

*GOLD: 1X TO 2.5X BASIC CARDS
GOLD ODDS 1:10 LOW/HI

2008 SAGE HIT Silver

*SILVER: .6X TO 1.5X BASIC CARDS
SILVER ODDS 1:3 LOW/HI

2008 SAGE HIT Autographs

BLUE AUTO ODDS 1:10 LOW, 1:14 HI
UNPRICED PRINT PLATE PRINT RUN 1
A1 John David Booty 4.00 10.00
A2 Will Franklin 4.00 10.00
A3 Danny Woodhead 15.00 40.00
A4 Limas Sweed SP 8.00 20.00
A5 Joe Flacco 15.00 40.00
A6 Brian Brohm SP 6.00 15.00
A7 Chad Henne 5.00 12.00
A8 Marcus Thomas 4.00 10.00
A10 Dennis Dixon 5.00 12.00
A11 Xavier Adibi 3.00 8.00
A12 Matt Ryan 25.00 50.00
A13 T.C. Ostrander 4.00 10.00
A14 Bernard Morris 4.00 10.00
A15 Sam Baker 3.00 8.00
A16 Adrian Arrington 4.00 10.00
A17 Kevin O'Connell 4.00 10.00
A18 Jacob Hester 5.00 12.00
A19 Keenan Burton 3.00 8.00
A20 Darius Reynaud 3.00 8.00
A21 Keon Lattimore 4.00 10.00
A22 Tashard Choice 4.00 10.00
A23 Jake Long 5.00 12.00
A24 Paul Smith 5.00 12.00
A25 Jamaal Charles 8.00 20.00
A26 Yvenson Bernard 5.00 12.00
A27 Alex Brink 5.00 12.00
A28 James Hardy 4.00 10.00
A29 Martin Rucker 4.00 10.00
A30 Steve Slaton 5.00 12.00
A31 Derrick Harvey 3.00 8.00
A32 Andre Callender 5.00 12.00
A33 Jabari Arthur 4.00 10.00
A34 Bruce Hocker 5.00 12.00
A35 Kalvin McRae 3.00 8.00
A36 Lawrence Jackson 4.00 10.00
A37 Tyrell Johnson 5.00 12.00
A38 Marcus Howard 5.00 12.00
A39 Sam Keller 4.00 10.00
A40 Keith Rivers 5.00 12.00
A41 Brandon Flowers 5.00 12.00
A42 Adarius Bowman 4.00 10.00
A43 Ricky Santos 5.00 12.00
A44 Jordon Dizon 5.00 12.00
A45 Robert Jordan 4.00 10.00
A46 Maurice Purify 5.00 12.00
A47 Lavelle Hawkins 3.00 8.00
A48 Jason Rivers 4.00 10.00
A49 John Carlson 5.00 12.00
A50 Vernon Gholston 4.00 10.00
A68 Devin Thomas 4.00 10.00

A69 Beau Bell 4.00 10.00
A70 Owen Schmitt 5.00 12.00
A71 Paul Raymond 4.00 10.00
A72 Jordy Nelson 8.00 20.00
A73 Ray Rice 10.00 25.00
A74 Darrell Strong 4.00 10.00
A75 Felix Jones 8.00 20.00
A76 Kevin Smith SP 5.00 12.00
A77 Justin Forsett 5.00 12.00
A78 Antoine Cason 5.00 12.00
A79 Ryan Clady 5.00 12.00
A80 Mike Hart 5.00 12.00
A81 Kenny Phillips 5.00 12.00
A82 Jonathan Stewart SP 12.00 30.00
A83 Fred Davis 5.00 12.00
A84 Malcolm Kelly 4.00 10.00
A85 Matt Flynn 10.00 25.00
A86 Allen Patrick 4.00 10.00
A87 Brent Miller 4.00 10.00
A88 Andre Caldwell 4.00 10.00
A89 Josh Johnson 5.00 12.00
A90 Erik Ainge 5.00 12.00
A91 Tom Zbikowski 5.00 12.00
A92 Dan Connor 5.00 12.00
A93 Leodis McKelvin 4.00 10.00
A94 Sedrick Ellis 5.00 12.00
A95 Rashard Mendenhall SP 15.00 40.00
A96 Mike Jenkins 5.00 12.00
A97 Dustin Keller 5.00 12.00
A98 Donnie Avery 4.00 10.00
A100 Darren McFadden SP 15.00 40.00
A101 Justin McKinney 4.00 10.00
A102 Angelo Craig 3.00 8.00
A103 Larry Grant 3.00 8.00
A104 Nick Hayden 3.00 8.00
A105 Haruki Nakamura 3.00 8.00
A106 Darnell Terrell 3.00 8.00
A107 Nick Hill 3.00 8.00

2008 SAGE HIT Autographs Gold

*GOLD/250: .5X TO 1.2X BASIC AUTO
GOLD/250 ODDS 1:28 LOW, 1:26 HI
GOLD PRINT RUN 250 SER.#'d SETS
A4 Limas Sweed 8.00 20.00
A6 Brian Brohm 8.00 20.00
A7 Chad Henne 8.00 20.00
A12 Matt Ryan 25.00 60.00
A82 Jonathan Stewart 12.00 30.00
A100 Darren McFadden 15.00 40.00

2008 SAGE HIT Autographs Silver

*SILVER: .4X TO 1X BASIC AUTO
SILVER ODDS 1:18 LOW, 1:21 HI
A4 Limas Sweed 8.00 20.00
A6 Brian Brohm 5.00 12.00
A7 Chad Henne 5.00 12.00
A12 Matt Ryan 25.00 60.00
A100 Darren McFadden 12.00 30.00

2008 SAGE HIT Saturday Colors

COMPLETE SET (30) 10.00 25.00
STATED ODDS 1:5 LOW/HI
UNPRICED PRINT PLATE PRINT RUN 1
S1 Matt Ryan 3.00 8.00
S2 Brian Brohm .75 2.00
S3 Chad Henne .75 2.00
S4 Joe Flacco 2.50 6.00
S5 John David Booty .60 1.50
S6 Dennis Dixon .75 2.00
S7 Jamaal Charles 1.25 3.00
S8 Steve Slaton .75 2.00
S9 Early Doucet .60 1.50
S10 James Hardy .60 1.50
S11 Limas Sweed .75 2.00
S12 Vernon Gholston .60 1.50
S13 Derrick Harvey .50 1.25
S14 Keith Rivers .75 2.00
S15 Jake Long .75 2.00
S16 Josh Johnson .75 2.00
S17 Erik Ainge .75 2.00
S18 Darren McFadden 2.00 5.00
S19 Rashard Mendenhall 1.50 4.00
S20 Jonathan Stewart 1.25 3.00
S21 Felix Jones 1.25 3.00
S22 Ray Rice 1.50 4.00
S23 Kevin Smith .75 2.00
S24 Mike Hart .75 2.00
S25 DeSean Jackson 1.50 4.00
S26 Malcolm Kelly .60 1.50
S27 Devin Thomas .60 1.50
S28 Andre Caldwell .60 1.50
S29 Fred Davis .75 2.00
S30 Sedrick Ellis .75 2.00

2008 SAGE HIT Saturday Colors Autographs Gold

AUTO/100 ODDS 1:288 LOW, 1:192 HI
SA1 Matt Ryan 30.00 80.00
SA4 Joe Flacco 25.00 60.00
SA7 Jamaal Charles 12.00 30.00
SA18 Darren McFadden 20.00 50.00
SA19 Rashard Mendenhall 25.00 50.00
SA20 Jonathan Stewart 12.00 30.00
SA21 Felix Jones 15.00 40.00
SA22 Ray Rice 15.00 40.00

2008 SAGE HIT Write Stuff

COMPLETE SET (20) 10.00 25.00
STATED ODDS 1:10 LOW/HI
UNPRICED PRINT PLATE PRINT RUN 1
WS1 John David Booty .60 1.50
WS2 Brian Brohm .75 2.00
WS3 Jamaal Charles 1.25 3.00
WS4 Dennis Dixon .75 2.00
WS5 Early Doucet .60 1.50
WS6 Joe Flacco 2.50 6.00
WS7 James Hardy .60 1.50
WS8 Chad Henne .75 2.00
WS9 Matt Ryan 3.00 8.00
WS10 Steve Slaton .75 2.00
WS11 Erik Ainge .75 2.00
WS12 DeSean Jackson 1.50 4.00
WS13 Josh Johnson .75 2.00
WS14 Felix Jones 1.25 3.00
WS15 Malcolm Kelly .60 1.50
WS16 Darren McFadden 2.00 5.00
WS17 Rashard Mendenhall 1.50 4.00
WS18 Ray Rice 1.50 4.00
WS19 Kevin Smith .75 2.00
WS20 Jonathan Stewart 1.25 3.00

2008 SAGE HIT Write Stuff Autographs

WS AU/25 ODDS 1:1152 LOW, 1:770 HI
WSA1 John David Booty 10.00 25.00
WSA2 Brian Brohm 12.00 30.00
WSA3 Jamaal Charles 20.00 50.00
WSA4 Dennis Dixon 12.00 30.00
WSA6 Joe Flacco 50.00 100.00
WSA7 James Hardy 10.00 25.00
WSA8 Chad Henne 30.00 80.00
WSA9 Matt Ryan 60.00 120.00
WSA10 Steve Slaton 12.00 30.00
WSA11 Erik Ainge 12.00 30.00
WSA13 Josh Johnson 12.00 30.00
WSA14 Felix Jones 25.00 60.00
WSA15 Malcolm Kelly 10.00 25.00
WSA16 Darren McFadden 30.00 80.00
WSA17 Rashard Mendenhall 30.00 80.00
WSA18 Ray Rice 25.00 60.00
WSA19 Kevin Smith 12.00 30.00
WSA20 Jonathan Stewart 30.00 80.00

2009 SAGE HIT

SAGE HIT was issued in two series: low and high. The low series was released on March 18, 2009 and featured 50 cards (#1-50). High series went live on April 20 and featured cards #51-100 plus ten additional first series cards featuring different photos (listed as "B" card numbers below).

COMPLETE SET (110) 15.00 40.00
COMP.LOW SERIES (60) 7.50 20.00
COMP.HIGH SERIES (50) 10.00 25.00
1 Patrick Turner .30 .75
2 Malcolm Jenkins .40 1.00
3 Eugene Monroe .25 .60
4 D.J. Boldin .30 .75
5A Michael Crabtree ball at chest .75 2.00
5B Michael Crabtree ball in air .75 2.00
6A Mark Sanchez facing left 1.25 3.00
6B Mark Sanchez facing right 1.25 3.00
7 Cornelius Ingram .25 .60
8A Darrius Heyward-Bey no ball .40 1.00
8B Darrius Heyward-Bey with ball .40 1.00
9A Jeremy Maclin no helmet visor .60 1.50
9B Jeremy Maclin helmet visor .60 1.50
10 Brian Cushing .40 1.00
11A Josh Freeman hips hidden .75 2.00
11B Josh Freeman hips in view .75 2.00
12 Curtis Painter .40 1.00
13A Nate Davis pointing .30 .75
13B Nate Davis holding ball .30 .75
14 Hunter Cantwell .40 1.00
15A Pat White head shot .40 1.00
15B Pat White running ball .40 1.00
16 Mike Teel .40 1.00
17 Tom Brandstater .40 1.00
18 Jarett Dillard .40 1.00
19 Sammie Stroughter .40 1.00
20 Aaron Kelly .30 .75
21 Darius Passmore .30 .75
22 Alphonso Smith .30 .75
23A Javon Ringer one hand on ball .40 1.00
23B Javon Ringer two hands on ball .40 1.00
24 Jeremiah Johnson .40 1.00
25A LeSean McCoy blu jsy .75 2.00
25B LeSean McCoy white jsy .75 2.00
26 Tim Jamison .30 .75
27 David Bruton .30 .75
28 Worrell Williams .30 .75
29 Matt Shaughnessy .30 .75
30 Nathan Brown .30 .75
31 Mike Reilly .30 .75
32 Darrell Mack .30 .75
33 James Laurinaitis .40 1.00
34A Donald Brown two hands on ball .40 1.00
34B Donald Brown one hand on ball .40 1.00
35 Marlon Lucky .30 .75
36 Roy Miller .30 .75
37 Eric Wood .30 .75
38 Freddie Brown .30 .75
39 Taurus Johnson .30 .75
40 Ryan Purvis .30 .75
41 Darius Butler .40 1.00
42 Ricky Jean-Francois .40 1.00
43 Kaluka Maiava .40 1.00
44 Brandon Underwood .40 1.00
45 Chase Coffman .30 .75
46 Jamon Meredith .30 .75
47 Clay Matthews 1.00 2.50
48 Brian Orakpo .40 1.00
49 Jeremy Childs .30 .75
50 Devin Moore .30 .75
51 Matt Ryan SO .50 1.25
Joe Flacco
52 Matthew Stafford SO 1.25 3.00
Mark Sanchez
53 Knowshon Moreno SO .40 1.00
Chris Wells
54 Michael Crabtree SO .40 1.00
Jeremy Maclin
55 Michael Crabtree TM .50 1.25
Graham Harrell
56 Matthew Stafford TM 1.25 3.00
Knowshon Moreno
57 Mark Sanchez TM .75 2.00
Rey Maualuga
58 Chris Wells TM .40 1.00
James Laurinaitis
59 Matthew Stafford 2.00 5.00
60 Jason Boltus .30 .75
61 Chase Clement .40 1.00
62 Aaron Brown .40 1.00
63 Kevin Ogletree .40 1.00
64 Scott McKillop .30 .75
65 Clint Sintim .40 1.00
66 Andre Brown .25 .60
67 John Parker Wilson .40 1.00
68 Brian Hoyer .40 1.00
69 B.J. Raji .40 1.00
70 Stephen McGee .40 1.00
71 Louis Murphy .40 1.00
72 Jason Smith .30 .75
73 Cullen Harper .40 1.00
74 Johnny Knox .60 1.50
75 Alex Boone .40 1.00
76 Tyrell Fenroy .30 .75
77 Eben Britton .30 .75
78 Chris Wells .60 1.50
79 Mike Mickens .30 .75
80 Brian Robiskie .40 1.00
81 Brooks Foster .25 .60
82 Jamarko Simmons .30 .75
83 Brian Mandeville .30 .75
84 Jared Cook .40 1.00
85 Brandon Williams .40 1.00
86 Rashad Jennings .40 1.00
87 James Casey .30 .75
88 Hakeem Nicks .60 1.50
89 Juaquin Iglesias .30 .75
90 Mike Thomas .40 1.00
91 Jared Bronson .30 .75
92 C.J. Spillman .30 .75
93 Marcus Freeman .40 1.00
94 David Veikune .30 .75
95 Gartrell Johnson .25 .60
96 Graham Harrell .40 1.00
97 Ryan Palmer .40 1.00
98 Demetrius Byrd .30 .75
99 Rey Maualuga .40 1.00
100 Knowshon Moreno .40 1.00
ROY Matt Ryan ROY SP

2009 SAGE HIT Glossy

*GLOSSY: .6X TO 1.5X BASIC CARDS
ONE GLOSSY PER RETAIL PACK

2009 SAGE HIT Gold

COMPLETE SET (110) 50.00 125.00
COMP.LOW SERIES (60) 25.00 60.00
COMP.HIGH SERIES (50) 30.00 80.00
*GOLD 1-100: 1X TO 2.5X BASIC CARDS
1-50 ODDS 1:10 LOW, 51-100 1:27 HIGH

2009 SAGE HIT Make Ready Black

*1-50 BLACK/50: 2.5X TO 6X BASIC CARDS
*1-50 CYAN/50: 2.5X TO 6X BASIC CARDS
*1-50 MAGENTA/50: 2.5X TO 6X BASIC CARDS
*1-50 YELLOW/50: 2.5X TO 6X BASIC CARDS
MAKE READY/50 ODDS 1:30 LOW, 1:13.5 HI

2009 SAGE HIT Silver

COMPLETE SET (110) 40.00 80.00
COMP.LOW SERIES (60) 15.00 40.00
COMP.HIGH SERIES (50) 20.00 50.00
*SILVER 1-100: .6X TO 1.5X BASIC CARDS
1-50 ODDS 1:3 LOW, 51-100 1:4.5 HIGH

2009 SAGE HIT Autographs

BLACK AU ODDS 1:10 LOW, 1:7.2 HIGH
*SILVER: .4X TO 1X BASIC AUTOS
SILVER AU ODDS 1:18 LOW, 1:11 HIGH
*GOLD/250: .5X TO 1.2X BASIC AU
GOLD/250 AU ODDS 1:28 LOW, 1:12 HIGH
OVERALL AUTO ODDS 1:5 LOW, 1:3 HIGH
1 Patrick Turner 4.00 10.00
2 Malcolm Jenkins 5.00 12.00
3 Eugene Monroe 3.00 8.00
4 D.J. Boldin 4.00 10.00
5 Michael Crabtree 25.00 50.00
6 Mark Sanchez SP 25.00 50.00
7 Cornelius Ingram 3.00 8.00
8 Darrius Heyward-Bey 5.00 12.00
9 Jeremy Maclin SP 8.00 20.00
10 Brian Cushing 5.00 12.00
11 Josh Freeman 10.00 25.00
12 Curtis Painter 6.00 15.00
13 Nate Davis 4.00 10.00
14 Hunter Cantwell 5.00 12.00
15 Pat White 5.00 12.00
16 Mike Teel 5.00 12.00
17 Tom Brandstater 5.00 12.00
18 Jarett Dillard 5.00 12.00
19 Sammie Stroughter 5.00 12.00
20 Aaron Kelly 4.00 10.00
22 Alphonso Smith 4.00 10.00
23 Javon Ringer 5.00 12.00
24 Jeremiah Johnson 5.00 12.00
25 LeSean McCoy 10.00 25.00
26 Tim Jamison 4.00 10.00
27 David Bruton 4.00 10.00
28 Worrell Williams 4.00 10.00
29 Matt Shaughnessy 4.00 10.00
30 Nathan Brown 4.00 10.00
31 Mike Reilly 4.00 10.00
32 Darrell Mack 4.00 10.00
33 James Laurinaitis 5.00 12.00
34 Donald Brown 5.00 12.00
35 Marlon Lucky 4.00 10.00
36 Roy Miller 4.00 10.00
37 Eric Wood 4.00 10.00
38 Freddie Brown 4.00 10.00
40 Ryan Purvis 4.00 10.00
41 Darius Butler 5.00 12.00
42 Ricky Jean-Francois 5.00 12.00
43 Kaluka Maiava 5.00 12.00
44 Brandon Underwood 5.00 12.00
45 Chase Coffman 4.00 10.00
46 Jamon Meredith 4.00 10.00
47 Clay Matthews 12.00 30.00
48 Brian Orakpo 5.00 12.00
49 Jeremy Childs 4.00 10.00
50 Devin Moore 4.00 10.00
59 Matthew Stafford SP 25.00 50.00
60 Jason Boltus 4.00 10.00
61 Chase Clement 5.00 12.00
62 Aaron Brown 5.00 12.00
63 Kevin Ogletree 5.00 12.00
64 Scott McKillop 4.00 10.00
65 Clint Sintim 5.00 12.00
66 Andre Brown 3.00 8.00
67 John Parker Wilson 5.00 12.00
68 Brian Hoyer 5.00 12.00
69 B.J. Raji 5.00 12.00
70 Stephen McGee 5.00 12.00
71 Louis Murphy 5.00 12.00
72 Jason Smith 4.00 10.00
73 Cullen Harper 5.00 12.00
74 Johnny Knox 8.00 20.00
75 Alex Boone 5.00 12.00
76 Tyrell Fenroy 4.00 10.00
77 Eben Britton 4.00 10.00
78 Chris Wells SP 20.00 40.00
79 Mike Mickens 4.00 10.00
80 Brian Robiskie 5.00 12.00
81 Brooks Foster 3.00 8.00
82 Jamarko Simmons 4.00 10.00
83 Brian Mandeville 4.00 10.00
84 Jared Cook 5.00 12.00
85 Brandon Williams 5.00 12.00
86 Rashad Jennings 5.00 12.00
87 James Casey 4.00 10.00
88 Hakeem Nicks 8.00 20.00
89 Juaquin Iglesias 4.00 10.00
90 Mike Thomas 5.00 12.00
91 Jared Bronson 4.00 10.00
92 C.J. Spillman 4.00 10.00
93 Marcus Freeman 5.00 12.00
94 David Veikune 4.00 10.00
95 Gartrell Johnson 3.00 8.00
96 Graham Harrell 8.00 20.00
97 Ryan Palmer 5.00 12.00
98 Demetrius Byrd 4.00 10.00
99 Rey Maualuga 5.00 12.00
100 Knowshon Moreno 30.00 50.00
101 Jason Williams 5.00 12.00
102 Jahi Word-Daniels 4.00 10.00
103 DeAndre Levy 5.00 12.00
104 Kyle Moore 4.00 10.00
105 Kory Sperry 3.00 8.00
106 Jarron Gilbert 4.00 10.00
107 Darcel McBath 4.00 10.00
108 Walt Mendenhall 4.00 10.00
109 Pannel Egboh 3.00 8.00
110 Will Johnson 4.00 10.00

2009 SAGE HIT Game Changers

COMPLETE SET (30) 15.00 40.00
COMP.LOW SERIES (15) 8.00 20.00
COMP.HIGH SERIES (15) 8.00 20.00
STATED ODDS 1:5 LOW/HIGH
G1 Michael Crabtree 1.50 4.00
G2 Brian Cushing .75 2.00
G3 Nate Davis .60 1.50
G4 Graham Harrell .75 2.00
G5 Juaquin Iglesias .60 1.50
G6 Malcolm Jenkins .75 2.00
G7 James Laurinaitis .75 2.00
G8 Jeremy Maclin 1.25 3.00
G9 LeSean McCoy 1.50 4.00
G10 Devin Moore .60 1.50
G11 Hakeem Nicks 1.25 3.00
G12 Brian Orakpo .75 2.00
G13 Javon Ringer .75 2.00
G14 Mark Sanchez 2.50 6.00
G15 Pat White .75 2.00
G16 Donald Brown .75 2.00
G17 Chase Coffman .60 1.50
G18 Jared Cook .75 2.00
G19 Josh Freeman 1.50 4.00
G20 Cullen Harper .75 2.00
G21 Darrius Heyward-Bey .75 2.00
G22 Rashad Jennings .75 2.00
G23 Rey Maualuga .75 2.00
G24 Knowshon Moreno .75 2.00
G25 Louis Murphy .75 2.00
G26 B.J. Raji .75 2.00
G27 Brian Robiskie .75 2.00
G28 Matthew Stafford 4.00 10.00
G29 Chris Wells 1.25 3.00
G30 John Parker Wilson .75 2.00

2009 SAGE HIT Game Changers Autographs

AUTO/100 ODDS 1:288 LOW, 1:86 HIGH
G1 Michael Crabtree 30.00 80.00
G2 Brian Cushing 8.00 20.00
G3 Nate Davis 6.00 15.00
G4 Graham Harrell 12.00 30.00
G5 Juaquin Iglesias 6.00 15.00
G6 Malcolm Jenkins 8.00 20.00
G7 James Laurinaitis 8.00 20.00
G8 Jeremy Maclin 12.00 30.00
G9 LeSean McCoy 15.00 40.00
G10 Devin Moore 6.00 15.00
G11 Hakeem Nicks 12.00 30.00
G12 Brian Orakpo 8.00 20.00
G13 Javon Ringer 8.00 20.00
G14 Mark Sanchez 50.00 100.00
G15 Pat White 8.00 20.00
G16 Donald Brown 8.00 20.00
G17 Chase Coffman 6.00 15.00
G18 Jared Cook 8.00 20.00
G19 Josh Freeman 15.00 40.00
G20 Cullen Harper 8.00 20.00
G21 Darrius Heyward-Bey 8.00 20.00
G22 Rashad Jennings 8.00 20.00
G23 Rey Maualuga 8.00 20.00
G24 Knowshon Moreno 30.00 80.00
G25 Louis Murphy 8.00 20.00
G26 B.J. Raji 8.00 20.00
G27 Brian Robiskie 8.00 20.00
G28 Matthew Stafford 50.00 100.00
G29 Chris Wells 25.00 60.00
G30 John Parker Wilson 8.00 20.00

2009 SAGE HIT Write Stuff

COMPLETE SET (20) 15.00 40.00
COMP.LOW SERIES (10) 8.00 20.00
COMP.HIGH SERIES (10) 8.00 20.00
STATED ODDS 1:10 LOW, 1:9 HIGH
WS1 Michael Crabtree 1.50 4.00
WS2 Nate Davis .60 1.50
WS3 Graham Harrell .75 2.00
WS4 Juaquin Iglesias .60 1.50
WS5 Jeremy Maclin 1.25 3.00
WS6 LeSean McCoy 1.50 4.00
WS7 Hakeem Nicks 1.25 3.00
WS8 Javon Ringer .75 2.00
WS9 Mark Sanchez 2.50 6.00
WS10 Pat White .75 2.00
WS11 Donald Brown .75 2.00
WS12 Josh Freeman 1.50 4.00
WS13 Darrius Heyward-Bey .75 2.00
WS14 Rashad Jennings .75 2.00
WS15 James Laurinaitis .75 2.00
WS16 Rey Maualuga .75 2.00
WS17 Knowshon Moreno .75 2.00
WS18 Brian Robiskie .75 2.00
WS19 Matthew Stafford 4.00 10.00
WS20 Chris Wells 1.25 3.00

2009 SAGE HIT Write Stuff Autographs

AUTO/25 ODDS 1:1152 LOW, 1:518 HIGH
WS1 Michael Crabtree 50.00 100.00
WS2 Nate Davis 8.00 20.00
WS3 Graham Harrell 15.00 40.00
WS4 Juaquin Iglesias 8.00 20.00
WS5 Jeremy Maclin 20.00 50.00
WS6 LeSean McCoy 20.00 50.00
WS7 Hakeem Nicks 15.00 40.00
WS8 Javon Ringer 10.00 25.00
WS9 Mark Sanchez 60.00 120.00
WS10 Pat White 10.00 25.00
WS11 Donald Brown 10.00 25.00
WS12 Josh Freeman 20.00 50.00
WS13 Darrius Heyward-Bey 10.00 25.00
WS14 Rashad Jennings 10.00 25.00
WS15 James Laurinaitis 10.00 25.00
WS16 Rey Maualuga 10.00 25.00
WS17 Knowshon Moreno 50.00 100.00
WS18 Brian Robiskie 10.00 25.00
WS19 Matthew Stafford 60.00 120.00
WS20 Chris Wells 40.00 80.00

2010 SAGE HIT

COMP.LOW SERIES (50) 8.00 20.00
COMP.HIGH SERIES (50) 10.00 25.00
1 Mardy Gilyard .30 .75
2 Carlton Mitchell .25 .60
3 Gerald McCoy .30 .75
4 Joe McKnight .30 .75
5 Sean Canfield .25 .60
6 Donovan Warren .30 .75
7 Toby Gerhart DP .30 .75
8 Jordan Shipley .30 .75
9 Thaddeus Lewis .25 .60
10 Blair White .50 1.25
11 Zac Robinson .25 .60
12 Colt McCoy DP .60 1.50
13 Stafon Johnson .30 .75
14 Sam Bradford DP 1.25 3.00
15 Brandon Spikes .30 .75
16 Jarrett Brown .30 .75
17 Sean Weatherspoon .30 .75
18 Damian Williams .30 .75
19 Jermaine Gresham .40 1.00
20 Jeremy Williams .20 .50
21 Ryan Mathews .60 1.50
22 Aaron Hernandez .50 1.25
23 Greg Mathews .25 .60
24 Tony Moeaki .30 .75
25 Rolando McClain .30 .75
26 Joey Elliott .25 .60
27 Antonio Brown .50 1.25
28 C.J. Spiller DP .50 1.25
29 Seyi Ajirotutu .30 .75
30 Javarris James .30 .75
31 Dan LeFevour .30 .75
32 Dennis Pitta .30 .75
33 Andre Anderson .25 .60
34 Colin Peek .30 .75
35 Rennie Curran .25 .60
36 Alabama Program .60 1.50
37 Florida Program .75 2.00
38 Florida State Program .40 1.00
39 Georgia Program .40 1.00
40 LSU Program .40 1.00
41 Miami Program .40 1.00
42 Michigan Program .40 1.00
43 Nebraska Program .75 2.00
44 Notre Dame Program .50 1.25
45 Ohio State Program .50 1.25
46 Oklahoma Program .60 1.50
47 Penn State Program .40 1.00
48 USC Program .50 1.25
49 Tennessee Program .40 1.00
50 Texas Program .40 1.00
51 Jimmy Clausen .30 .75
52 Mike Williams .50 1.25
53 Martell Mallett .25 .60
54 Jevan Snead .30 .75
55 Joe Webb .30 .75
56 Bruce Campbell .25 .60
57 Derrick Morgan .25 .60
58 Montario Hardesty .30 .75
59 NaVorro Bowman .30 .75
60 Earl Thomas .30 .75
61 Jahvid Best IT .40 1.00
62 Dan LeFevour IT .25 .60
63 Tony Pike IT .25 .60
64 C.J. Spiller IT .40 1.00
65 Aaron Hernandez IT .40 1.00
66 Ryan Mathews IT .50 1.25
67 Jonathan Dwyer IT .25 .60
68 Ndamukong Suh IT 1.25 3.00
69 Jimmy Clausen IT .25 .60
70 Sam Bradford IT 1.00 2.50
71 Zac Robinson IT .20 .50
72 Dez Bryant IT .75 2.00
73 Sean Canfield IT .20 .50
74 Damian Williams IT .25 .60
75 Toby Gerhart IT .25 .60
76 Colt McCoy IT .50 1.25
77 Ndamukong Suh 1.50 4.00
78 Anthony Dixon .30 .75
79 Joique Bell .25 .60
80 Jahvid Best .50 1.25
81 Danario Alexander .30 .75
82 Jonathan Dwyer .30 .75
83 Roddrick Muckelroy .25 .60
84 Rob Gronkowski .75 2.00
85 Tony Pike .30 .75
86 Kerry Meier .25 .60
87 Taylor Price .30 .75
88 Nate Byham .25 .60
89 Garrett Graham .25 .60
90 Jason Pierre-Paul .50 1.25
91 John Skelton .30 .75
92 Brandon Lang .25 .60
93 Pat Simonds .25 .60
94 Cameron Sheffield .20 .50
95 C.J. Wilson .25 .60
96 Dezmon Briscoe .25 .60
97 Bryan Bulaga .30 .75
98 Jerry Hughes .30 .75
99 Arrelious Benn .30 .75
100 Dez Bryant 1.00 2.50
CL1 Colt McCoy CL/100 2.50 6.00
C.J. Spiller
Sam Bradford

2010 SAGE HIT Gold

*GOLD: 1.2X TO 3X BASIC CARDS
1-50 GOLD ODDS 1:10 LOW SERIES
51-100 GOLD ODDS 1:10 HIGH SERIES

2010 SAGE HIT Make Ready Black

*MR BLACK: 2X TO 5X BASIC CARDS
*MR CYAN: 2X TO 5X BASIC CARDS
*MR MAGENTA: 2X TO 5 BASIC CARDS
*MR YELLOW: 2X TO 5X BASIC CARDS
MAKE READY/50 ODDS 1:30 LOW
MAKE READY/50 ODDS 1:13 HIGH

2010 SAGE HIT Silver

*SILVER: .8X TO 2X BASIC CARDS
1-50 SILVER ODDS 1:3 LOW SERIES
51-100 SILVER ODDS 1:4 HIGH SERIES

2010 SAGE HIT Autographs

A1-A43 ODDS 1:10 LOW SERIES
A51-A99 ODDS 1:7 HIGH SERIES
*GOLD/250: .5X TO 1.2X BASIC AUTO
*GOLD/250: .4X TO 1X BASIC AU SP
A1-A43 GOLD/250 ODDS 1:28 LOW
A51-A99 GOLD/250 ODDS 1:15 HIGH
*SILVER: .4X TO 1X BASIC AUTO
A1-A43 SILVER ODDS 1:18 LOW SERIES
A51-A99 SILVER ODDS 1:10 HIGH SER.
A1 Mardy Gilyard 5.00 12.00
A2 Carlton Mitchell 4.00 10.00
A3 Gerald McCoy 5.00 12.00
A4 Joe McKnight SP 8.00 20.00
A5 Sean Canfield 4.00 10.00
A6 Donovan Warren 5.00 12.00
A7 Toby Gerhart 5.00 12.00
A8 Jordan Shipley 5.00 12.00
A9 Thaddeus Lewis 4.00 10.00
A10 Blair White 5.00 12.00
A11 Zac Robinson 4.00 10.00
A12 Colt McCoy 8.00 20.00
A13 Stafon Johnson 5.00 12.00
A14 Sam Bradford SP 30.00 80.00
A15 Brandon Spikes 5.00 12.00
A16 Jarrett Brown 5.00 12.00
A17 Sean Weatherspoon 5.00 12.00
A18 Damian Williams 5.00 12.00
A19 Jermaine Gresham 6.00 15.00
A20 Jeremy Williams 3.00 8.00
A21 Ryan Mathews 10.00 25.00
A22 Aaron Hernandez 8.00 20.00
A23 Greg Mathews 4.00 10.00
A24 Tony Moeaki 5.00 12.00
A25 Rolando McClain 5.00 12.00
A26 Joey Elliott 4.00 10.00
A27 Antonio Brown 8.00 20.00
A28 C.J. Spiller SP 10.00 25.00
A29 Seyi Ajirotutu 5.00 12.00
A30 Javarris James 5.00 12.00
A31 Dan LeFevour 5.00 12.00
A32 Dennis Pitta 5.00 12.00
A33 Andre Anderson 4.00 10.00
A34 Colin Peek 5.00 12.00
A35 Rennie Curran 4.00 10.00
A36 Shawn Lauvao 3.00 8.00
A37 Eric Olsen 4.00 10.00
A38 Sam Young 4.00 10.00
A39 Matt Tennant 3.00 8.00
A40 Cam Thomas 4.00 10.00
A41 Chris Cook 5.00 12.00
A42 Kyle McCarthy 5.00 12.00
A43 Shamar Graves 3.00 8.00
A51 Jimmy Clausen 5.00 12.00
A52 Mike Williams 8.00 20.00
A53 Martell Mallett 4.00 10.00
A54 Jevan Snead 5.00 12.00
A55 Joe Webb 5.00 12.00
A56 Bruce Campbell 4.00 10.00
A57 Derrick Morgan 4.00 10.00
A58 Montario Hardesty 5.00 12.00
A59 NaVorro Bowman 5.00 12.00
A60 Earl Thomas 5.00 12.00
A77 Ndamukong Suh SP 20.00 50.00
A78 Anthony Dixon 5.00 12.00
A79 Joique Bell 4.00 10.00
A80 Jahvid Best 8.00 20.00
A81 Danario Alexander 5.00 12.00
A82 Jonathan Dwyer 5.00 12.00
A83 Roddrick Muckelroy 4.00 10.00
A84 Rob Gronkowski 12.00 30.00
A85 Tony Pike 5.00 12.00
A86 Kerry Meier 4.00 10.00
A87 Taylor Price 5.00 12.00
A88 Nate Byham 4.00 10.00
A89 Garrett Graham 4.00 10.00
A90 Jason Pierre-Paul 8.00 20.00
A91 John Skelton 5.00 12.00
A92 Brandon Lang 4.00 10.00
A93 Pat Simonds 4.00 10.00
A94 Cameron Sheffield 3.00 8.00
A95 C.J. Wilson 4.00 10.00
A96 Dezmon Briscoe 4.00 10.00
A97 Bryan Bulaga 5.00 12.00
A98 Jerry Hughes 5.00 12.00
A99 Arrelious Benn 5.00 12.00

2010 SAGE HIT Prospectus

COMPLETE SET (30) 12.00 30.00
COMP.LOW SERIES (15) 6.00 15.00
COMP.HIGH SERIES (15) 6.00 15.00
P1-P15 ODDS 1:5 LOW SERIES
P16-P30 ODDS 1:5 HIGH SERIES
P1 Arrelious Benn 1.00 2.50
P2 Dez Bryant 2.00 5.00
P3 Sean Canfield .50 1.25
P4 Jimmy Clausen .60 1.50
P5 Jonathan Dwyer .60 1.50
P6 Mardy Gilyard .60 1.50
P7 Jermaine Gresham .75 2.00
P8 Montario Hardesty .60 1.50
P9 Aaron Hernandez 1.00 2.50
P10 Dan LeFevour .60 1.50
P11 Ryan Mathews 1.25 3.00
P12 Colt McCoy 1.25 3.00
P13 Joe McKnight .60 1.50
P14 Jevan Snead .60 1.50
P15 Damian Williams .60 1.50
P16 Jahvid Best 1.00 2.50
P17 Sam Bradford 2.50 6.00
P18 Dezmon Briscoe .50 1.25
P19 Jarrett Brown .60 1.50
P20 Anthony Dixon .60 1.50
P21 Toby Gerhart .60 1.50
P22 Rob Gronkowski 1.50 4.00
P23 Carlton Mitchell .50 1.25
P24 Tony Pike .60 1.50
P25 Taylor Price .60 1.50
P26 Zac Robinson .50 1.25
P27 Jordan Shipley .60 1.50
P28 C.J. Spiller 1.00 2.50
P29 Ndamukong Suh 3.00 8.00
P30 Mike Williams 1.00 2.50

2010 SAGE HIT Prospectus Autographs

P1-P15 AU/100 ODDS 1:288 LOW
P16-P20 AU/100 ODDS 1:87 HIGH
P1 Arrelious Benn 8.00 20.00
P3 Sean Canfield 6.00 15.00
P4 Jimmy Clausen 8.00 20.00
P5 Jonathan Dwyer 8.00 20.00
P6 Mardy Gilyard 8.00 20.00
P7 Jermaine Gresham 10.00 25.00
P8 Montario Hardesty 8.00 20.00
P9 Aaron Hernandez 12.00 30.00
P10 Dan LeFevour 8.00 20.00
P11 Ryan Mathews 15.00 40.00
P12 Colt McCoy 25.00 60.00
P13 Joe McKnight 8.00 20.00
P14 Jevan Snead 8.00 20.00
P15 Damian Williams 8.00 20.00
P16 Jahvid Best 12.00 30.00
P17 Sam Bradford 40.00 100.00
P18 Dezmon Briscoe 6.00 15.00
P19 Jarrett Brown 8.00 20.00
P20 Anthony Dixon 8.00 20.00
P21 Toby Gerhart 8.00 20.00
P22 Rob Gronkowski 20.00 50.00
P23 Carlton Mitchell 6.00 15.00
P24 Tony Pike 8.00 20.00
P25 Taylor Price 8.00 20.00
P26 Zac Robinson 6.00 15.00
P27 Jordan Shipley 8.00 20.00
P28 C.J. Spiller 12.00 30.00
P29 Ndamukong Suh 25.00 60.00
P30 Mike Williams 12.00 30.00

2010 SAGE HIT Write Stuff

COMPLETE SET (20) 12.00 30.00
COMP.LOW SERIES (10) 6.00 15.00
COMP.HIGH SERIES (10) 6.00 15.00
WS1-WS10 ODDS 1:10 LOW SERIES
WS11-WS20 ODDS 1:10 HIGH SERIES
WS1 Arrelious Benn 1.00 2.50
WS2 Dez Bryant 2.00 5.00
WS3 Jimmy Clausen .60 1.50
WS4 Jonathan Dwyer .60 1.50
WS5 Mardy Gilyard .60 1.50
WS6 Montario Hardesty .60 1.50
WS7 Colt McCoy 1.25 3.00
WS8 Joe McKnight .60 1.50
WS9 Jevan Snead .60 1.50
WS10 Damian Williams .60 1.50
WS11 Jahvid Best 1.00 2.50
WS12 Sam Bradford 2.50 6.00
WS13 Anthony Dixon .60 1.50
WS14 Toby Gerhart .60 1.50
WS15 Dan LeFevour .60 1.50
WS16 Ryan Mathews 1.25 3.00
WS17 Tony Pike .60 1.50
WS18 Jordan Shipley .60 1.50
WS19 C.J. Spiller 1.00 2.50
WS20 Ndamukong Suh 3.00 8.00

2010 SAGE HIT Write Stuff Autographs

WS1-WS10 AU/25 ODDS 1:1152 LOW
WS11-WS20 AU/25 ODDS 1:208 LOW
WS1 Arrelious Benn 10.00 25.00
WS3 Jimmy Clausen 15.00 40.00
WS4 Jonathan Dwyer 10.00 25.00
WS5 Mardy Gilyard 10.00 25.00
WS6 Montario Hardesty 10.00 25.00
WS7 Colt McCoy 30.00 60.00
WS8 Joe McKnight 10.00 25.00
WS9 Jevan Snead 10.00 25.00
WS10 Damian Williams 10.00 25.00
WS11 Jahvid Best 15.00 40.00
WS12 Sam Bradford 50.00 120.00
WS13 Anthony Dixon 10.00 25.00
WS14 Toby Gerhart 10.00 25.00
WS15 Dan LeFevour 10.00 25.00
WS16 Ryan Mathews 25.00 50.00
WS17 Tony Pike 10.00 25.00
WS18 Jordan Shipley 10.00 25.00
WS19 C.J. Spiller 30.00 60.00
WS20 Ndamukong Suh 30.00 60.00

2011 SAGE HIT

COMPLETE SET (100) 12.00 30.00
COMP.LOW SERIES (50) 6.00 15.00
COMP.HIGH SERIES (50) 6.00 15.00
1 DeMarco Sampson .15 .40
2 Delone Carter .20 .50
3 Jerrel Jernigan .20 .50
4 Aaron Williams .20 .50
5 Chimdi Chekwa .20 .50
6 Jeremy Kerley .25 .60
7 Christian Ponder .50 1.25
8 Julio Jones .50 1.25
9 Kyle Rudolph .25 .60
10 Jake Locker .60 1.50
11 Scotty McKnight .20 .50
12 Dane Sanzenbacher .25 .60
13 Jeff Van Camp .20 .50
14 Anthony Castonzo .15 .40
15 Ryan Mallett .50 1.25
16 Greg Smith .20 .50
17 DeMarco Murray .50 1.25
18 Anthony Allen .15 .40
19 Edmond Gates .20 .50
20 Stephen Skelton .15 .40
21 Allen Bradford .20 .50
22 Mark Ingram .50 1.25
23 Jeff Maehl .25 .60
24 Stephen Paea .25 .60
25 Kai Forbath .15 .40
26 Taylor Potts .20 .50
27 Mario Fannin .25 .60
28 Dion Lewis .25 .60
29 Shaun Chapas .20 .50
30 Sam Acho .20 .50
31 Jurrell Casey .15 .40
32 Torrey Smith .30 .75
33 Rahim Moore .20 .50
34 Rob Housler .20 .50
35 Casey Matthews .25 .60
36 Courtney Smith .20 .50
37 Cameron Heyward .25 .60
38 Daniel Thomas .25 .60
39 Nick Fairley .30 .75
40 Von Miller .30 .75
41 Da'Quan Bowers Art .25 .60
42 Mark Ingram Art .50 1.25
43 Julio Jones Art .50 1.25
44 Jake Locker Art .60 1.50
45 Ryan Mallett Art .50 1.25
46 DeMarco Murray Art .50 1.25
47 Christian Ponder Art .50 1.25
48 Kyle Rudolph Art .25 .60
49 Torrey Smith Art .30 .75
50 Jordan Todman Art .15 .40
51 Randall Cobb Art .30 .75
52 Nick Fairley Art .30 .75
53 Blaine Gabbert Art .40 1.00
54 A.J. Green Art .50 1.25
55 Jerrel Jernigan Art .20 .50
56 Mikel Leshoure Art .25 .60
57 Cam Newton Art 1.25 3.00
58 Daniel Thomas Art .25 .60
59 Shane Vereen Art .25 .60
60 Ryan Williams Art .30 .75
61 Blaine Gabbert .40 1.00
62 Ricky Stanzi .30 .75
63 T.J. Yates .30 .75
64 Stevan Ridley .25 .60
65 Kyle Adams .15 .40
66 Chase Reynolds .15 .40
67 Robert Sands .20 .50
68 Adam Weber .20 .50
69 Cecil Shorts .20 .50
70 James Cleveland .15 .40
71 Jacquizz Rodgers .25 .60
72 Taiwan Jones .25 .60
73 Curtis Brown .25 .60
74 Vai Taua .20 .50
75 D.J. Williams .25 .60
76 Marcus Gilchrist .15 .40
77 Jordan Todman .15 .40
78 Nate Solder .25 .60
79 Armand Robinson .20 .50
80 A.J. Green .50 1.25
81 Randall Cobb .30 .75
82 Austin Pettis .20 .50
83 Charlie Gantt .20 .50
84 Ryan Williams .30 .75
85 Aldon Smith .40 1.00
86 Shane Vereen .25 .60
87 Denarius Moore .30 .75
88 Luke Stocker .20 .50
89 Charles Clay .20 .50
90 Mark Herzlich .20 .50
91 Mikel Leshoure .25 .60
92 Drake Nevis .25 .60
93 Da'Quan Bowers .25 .60
94 Ryan Kerrigan .25 .60
95 Jarvis Williams .15 .40
96 DeAndre McDaniel .20 .50
97 Lestar Jean .20 .50
98 Jamie Harper .25 .60
99 J.J. Watt .30 .75
100A Cam Newton Blue 1.25 3.00
(blue jersey)
100B Cam Newton Blu 1.25 3.00
Org
(blue and orange jersey)

2011 SAGE HIT Gold

*GOLD: 1.2X TO 3X BASIC CARDS
1-50 GOLD ODDS 1:10 LOW SERIES
51-100 GOLD ODDS 1:10 HIGH SERIES

2011 SAGE HIT Make Ready Black

*MR BLACK: 2X TO 5X BASIC CARDS
*MR CYAN: 2X TO 5X BASIC CARDS
*MR MAGENTA: 2X TO 5X BASIC CARDS
*MR YELLOW: 2X TO 5X BASIC CARDS
1-50 MAKE READY/50 ODDS 1:30 LOW
51-100 MAKE READY/50 ODDS 1:30 HIGH

2011 SAGE HIT Silver

*SILVER: .8X TO 2X BASIC CARDS
1-50 SILVER ODDS 1:3 LOW SERIES
51-100 SILVER ODDS 1:3 HIGH SERIES

2011 SAGE HIT Autographs

1-41 AU ODDS 1:10 LOW SERIES
61-100 AU ODDS 1:5 HIGH SERIES
*GOLD/250: .5X TO 1.2X BASIC AUTO

*GOLD/250: .4X TO 1X BASIC AU SP
*SILVER: .4X TO 1X BASIC AUTO
OVERALL AU ODDS 1:5 LOW SERIES
1 DeMarco Sampson 2.50 6.00
2 Delone Carter 3.00 8.00
3 Jerrel Jernigan 3.00 8.00
4 Aaron Williams 3.00 8.00
5 Chimdi Chekwa 3.00 8.00
6 Jeremy Kerley 4.00 10.00
7 Christian Ponder 12.00 30.00
8 Julio Jones 15.00 30.00
9 Kyle Rudolph 4.00 10.00
10 Jake Locker SP 20.00 40.00
11 Scotty McKnight 3.00 8.00
12 Dane Sanzenbacher 4.00 10.00
13 Jeff Van Camp 3.00 8.00
14 Anthony Castonzo 2.50 6.00
15 Ryan Mallett SP 10.00 25.00
16 Greg Smith 3.00 8.00
17 DeMarco Murray 12.00 30.00
18 Anthony Allen 2.50 6.00
19 Edmond Gates 3.00 8.00
20 Stephen Skelton 2.50 6.00
21 Allen Bradford 3.00 8.00
22 Mark Ingram 15.00 30.00
23 Jeff Maehl 4.00 10.00
24 Stephen Paea 4.00 10.00
25 Kai Forbath 2.50 6.00
26 Taylor Potts 3.00 8.00
27 Mario Fannin 4.00 10.00
28 Dion Lewis 4.00 10.00
29 Shaun Chapas 3.00 8.00
30 Sam Acho 3.00 8.00
31 Jurrell Casey 2.50 6.00
32 Torrey Smith 5.00 12.00
33 Rahim Moore 3.00 8.00
34 Rob Housler 3.00 8.00
35 Casey Matthews 4.00 10.00
36 Courtney Smith 3.00 8.00
37 Cameron Heyward 4.00 10.00
38 Daniel Thomas 4.00 10.00
39 Nick Fairley 5.00 12.00
40 Von Miller 5.00 12.00
41 Marcus Cannon 2.50 6.00
61 Blaine Gabbert SP 15.00 40.00
62 Ricky Stanzi 8.00 20.00
63 T.J. Yates 5.00 12.00
64 Stevan Ridley 4.00 10.00
65 Kyle Adams 2.50 6.00
66 Chase Reynolds 2.50 6.00
67 Robert Sands 3.00 8.00
68 Adam Weber 3.00 8.00
69 Cecil Shorts 3.00 8.00
70 James Cleveland 2.50 6.00
71 Jacquizz Rodgers 4.00 10.00
72 Taiwan Jones 4.00 10.00
73 Curtis Brown 4.00 10.00
74 Vai Taua 3.00 8.00
75 D.J. Williams 4.00 10.00
76 Marcus Gilchrist 2.50 6.00
77 Jordan Todman 2.50 6.00
78 Nate Solder 4.00 10.00
79 Armand Robinson 3.00 8.00
80 A.J. Green SP 12.00 30.00
81 Randall Cobb 5.00 12.00
82 Austin Pettis 3.00 8.00
83 Charlie Gantt 3.00 8.00
84 Ryan Williams 5.00 12.00
85 Aldon Smith 5.00 12.00
86 Shane Vereen 4.00 10.00
87 Denarius Moore 5.00 12.00
88 Luke Stocker 3.00 8.00
89 Charles Clay 3.00 8.00
90 Mark Herzlich 3.00 8.00
91 Mikel Leshoure 4.00 10.00
92 Drake Nevis 4.00 10.00
93 Da'Quan Bowers 4.00 10.00
94 Ryan Kerrigan 4.00 10.00
95 Jarvis Williams 2.50 6.00
96 DeAndre McDaniel 3.00 8.00
97 Lestar Jean 3.00 8.00
98 Jamie Harper 4.00 10.00
99 J.J. Watt 5.00 12.00
100 Cam Newton SP 30.00 60.00

2011 SAGE HIT Big Time

COMPLETE SET (30) 12.00 30.00
COMP.LOW SERIES (15) 6.00 15.00
COMP.HIGH SERIES (15) 6.00 15.00
BA1-BA15 ODDS 1:5 LOW SERIES
BA16-BA30 ODDS 1:5 HIGH SERIES
B1 Da'Quan Bowers .50 1.25
B2 Delone Carter .40 1.00
B3 Mark Ingram 1.00 2.50
B4 Jerrel Jernigan .40 1.00
B5 Julio Jones 1.00 2.50
B6 Dion Lewis .50 1.25
B7 Jake Locker 1.25 3.00
B8 Ryan Mallett 1.00 2.50
B9 DeMarco Murray 1.00 2.50
B10 Christian Ponder 1.00 2.50
B11 Kyle Rudolph .50 1.25
B12 Torrey Smith .60 1.50
B13 Ricky Stanzi .60 1.50
B14 Daniel Thomas .50 1.25
B15 Shane Vereen .50 1.25
B16 Randall Cobb .60 1.50
B17 Nick Fairley .60 1.50
B18 Blaine Gabbert .75 2.00
B19 A.J. Green 1.00 2.50
B20 Jamie Harper .50 1.25
B21 Mikel Leshoure .50 1.25
B22 Von Miller .60 1.50
B23 Cam Newton 2.50 6.00
B24 Stevan Ridley .50 1.25
B25 Jacquizz Rodgers .50 1.25
B26 Cecil Shorts .40 1.00
B27 Luke Stocker .40 1.00
B28 Jordan Todman .30 .75
B29 Ryan Williams .60 1.50
B30 T.J. Yates .60 1.50

2011 SAGE HIT Big Time Autographs

BA1-BA15 BIG TIME AU/100 ODDS 1:288 LOW
BA16-BA30 BIG TIME AU/100 ODDS 1:288 HIGH
BA1 Da'Quan Bowers 8.00 20.00
BA2 Delone Carter 6.00 15.00
BA3 Mark Ingram 20.00 50.00
BA4 Jerrel Jernigan 6.00 15.00
BA5 Julio Jones 25.00 50.00
BA6 Dion Lewis 8.00 20.00
BA7 Jake Locker 30.00 60.00
BA8 Ryan Mallett 15.00 40.00
BA9 DeMarco Murray 15.00 40.00
BA10 Christian Ponder 20.00 50.00
BA11 Kyle Rudolph 8.00 20.00
BA12 Torrey Smith 10.00 25.00
BA13 Ricky Stanzi 10.00 25.00
BA14 Daniel Thomas 8.00 20.00
BA15 Shane Vereen 8.00 20.00
BA16 Randall Cobb 10.00 25.00
BA17 Nick Fairley 10.00 25.00
BA18 Blaine Gabbert 15.00 40.00
BA19 A.J. Green 15.00 40.00
BA20 Jamie Harper 8.00 20.00
BA21 Mikel Leshoure 8.00 20.00
BA22 Von Miller 10.00 25.00
BA23 Cam Newton 30.00 80.00
BA24 Stevan Ridley 8.00 20.00
BA25 Jacquizz Rodgers 8.00 20.00
BA26 Cecil Shorts 6.00 15.00
BA27 Luke Stocker 6.00 15.00
BA28 Jordan Todman 5.00 12.00
BA29 Ryan Williams 10.00 25.00
BA30 T.J. Yates 10.00 25.00

2011 SAGE HIT Pre-Rookie

COMP.LOW SERIES (5) 2.50 6.00
COMP.HIGH SERIES (5)
PR1-PR5 INSERTED IN LOW SERIES
PR6-PR10 INSERTED IN HIGH SERIES
*GOLD: 1.2X TO 3X BASIC INSERTS
*SILVER: .8X TO 2X BASIC INSERTS
PR1 Cam Newton 2.00 5.00
PR2 Blaine Gabbert .60 1.50
PR3 Kyle Rudolph .40 1.00
PR4 Julio Jones .75 2.00
PR5 Shane Vereen .40 1.00
PR6 Ryan Mallett .75 2.00
PR7 A.J. Green .75 2.00
PR8 Austin Pettis .30 .75
PR9 Daniel Thomas .40 1.00
PR10 Da'Quan Bowers .40 1.00

2011 SAGE HIT Write Stuff

COMPLETE SET (20) 10.00 25.00
COMP.LOW SERIES (10) 5.00 12.00
COMP.HIGH SERIES (10) 5.00 12.00
WS1-WS10 ODDS 1:10 LOW SERIES
WS11-WS20 ODDS 1:10 HIGH SERIES
WS1 Da'Quan Bowers .60 1.50
WS2 Randall Cobb .75 2.00
WS3 Blaine Gabbert 1.00 2.50
WS4 A.J. Green 1.25 3.00
WS5 Mikel Leshoure .60 1.50
WS6 Cam Newton 3.00 8.00
WS7 Kyle Rudolph .60 1.50
WS8 Jordan Todman .40 1.00
WS9 Shane Vereen .60 1.50
WS10 Ryan Williams .75 2.00
WS11 Nick Fairley .75 2.00
WS12 Mark Ingram 1.25 3.00
WS13 Jerrel Jernigan .50 1.25
WS14 Julio Jones 1.25 3.00
WS15 Jake Locker 1.50 4.00
WS16 Ryan Mallett 1.25 3.00
WS17 DeMarco Murray 1.25 3.00
WS18 Christian Ponder 1.25 3.00
WS19 Torrey Smith .75 2.00
WS20 Daniel Thomas .60 1.50

2011 SAGE HIT Write Stuff Autographs

WSA1-WS10 AU/25 ODDS 1:1152 LOW SER.
WSA11-WS20 AU/25 ODDS 1:1152 HIGH SER.
WSA1 Da'Quan Bowers 10.00 25.00
WSA2 Randall Cobb 12.00 30.00
WSA3 Blaine Gabbert 50.00 100.00
WSA4 A.J. Green 30.00 60.00
WSA5 Mikel Leshoure 10.00 25.00
WSA6 Cam Newton 125.00 200.00
WSA7 Kyle Rudolph 10.00 25.00
WSA8 Jordan Todman 6.00 15.00
WSA9 Shane Vereen 10.00 25.00
WSA10 Ryan Williams 20.00 40.00
WSA11 Nick Fairley 12.00 30.00
WSA12 Mark Ingram 60.00 120.00
WSA13 Jerrel Jernigan 8.00 20.00
WSA14 Julio Jones 30.00 60.00
WSA15 Jake Locker 50.00 100.00
WSA16 Ryan Mallett 40.00 80.00
WSA17 DeMarco Murray 20.00 50.00
WSA18 Christian Ponder
WSA19 Torrey Smith 12.00 30.00
WSA20 Daniel Thomas 12.00 30.00

2012 SAGE HIT

COMPLETE SET (150) 15.00 40.00
COMP.LOW SERIES (75) 8.00 20.00
COMP.HIGH SERIES (75) 8.00 20.00
12R SUBSET CARDS: SAME PRICE
1 Alshon Jeffery .40 1.00
2 Chris Givens .20 .50
3 Michael Floyd .50 1.25
4 T.Y. Hilton .25 .60
5 Stephen Garcia .25 .60
6 Lamar Miller .30 .75
7 Orson Charles .25 .60
8 Nick Foles .40 1.00
9 Jeff Fuller .30 .75
10 Robert Griffin III 3.00 8.00
11 Kellen Moore .40 1.00
12 Jacory Harris .20 .50
13 Davin Meggett .20 .50
14 Ryan Lindley .25 .60
15 Alfonzo Dennard .25 .60
16 Melvin Ingram .30 .75
17 Ryan Tannehill .60 1.50
18 Tommy Streeter .20 .50
19 Thomas Mayo .15 .40
20 Jayron Hosley .25 .60
21 LaMichael James .50 1.25
22 Doug Martin .40 1.00
23 Joe Adams .25 .60
24 Dominique Davis .20 .50
25 Ryan Broyles .25 .60
26 Chaz Powell .15 .40
27 Tony Jerod-Eddie .30 .75
28 Michael Egnew .20 .50
29 Jake Bequette .20 .50
30 Michael Smith .20 .50
31 Sean Spence .20 .50
32 Cyrus Gray .25 .60
33 Derrick Coleman .15 .40
34 Chris Galippo .20 .50
35 Chris Owusu .20 .50
36 Jared Crick .25 .60
37 Jason Ford .20 .50
38 Harrison Smith .25 .60
39 Devon Still .25 .60
40 Luke Kuechly .50 1.25
41 Rhett Ellison .20 .50
42 Keenan Robinson .20 .50
43 Quinton Coples .25 .60
44 David DeCastro 12R .25 .60
45 Matt Kalil 12R .30 .75
46 T.Y. Hilton 12R .25 .60
47 Robert Griffin III 12R 1.25 3.00
48 Case Keenum 12R .30 .75
49 Jeff Fuller 12R .20 .50
50 LaMichael James 12R .50 1.25
51 Jared Crick 12R .25 .60
52 Davin Meggett 12R .20 .50
53 Michael Floyd 12R .50 1.25
54 Devon Still 12R .25 .60
55 Tommy Streeter 12R .25 .60
56 Nick Foles 12R .40 1.00
57 Michael Egnew 12R .20 .50
58 Jacory Harris 12R .20 .50
59 Lamar Miller 12R .30 .75
60 Alfonzo Dennard 12R .25 .60
61 Joe Adams 12R .25 .60
62 Ryan Lindley 12R .25 .60
63 Luke Kuechly 12R .30 .75
64 Chris Givens 12R .20 .50
65 Doug Martin 12R .40 1.00
66 Melvin Ingram 12R .30 .75
67 Ryan Broyles 12R .25 .60
68 Kellen Moore 12R .40 1.00
69 Quinton Coples 12R .25 .60
70 Cyrus Gray 12R .25 .60
71 Dwayne Allen 12R .25 .60
72 Marvin McNutt 12R .25 .60
73 Chris Polk 12R .30 .75
74 Darron Thomas 12R .40 1.00
75 Brandon Weeden 12R .50 1.25
76 Trent Richardson .75 2.00
77 Marvin McNutt .25 .60
78 Brian Quick .30 .75
79 Dontari Poe .25 .60
80 Travis Lewis .20 .50
81 Justin Blackmon .50 1.25
82 Juron Criner .25 .60
83 Dwayne Allen .25 .60
84 Travis Benjamin .25 .60
85 Coryell Judie .20 .50
86 Damaris Johnson .20 .50
87 Cory Harkey .20 .50
88 DeVier Posey .25 .60
89 Ladarius Green .25 .60
90 Dont'a Hightower .40 1.00
91 Boom Herron .20 .50
92 Broderick Green .20 .50
93 B.J. Cunningham .20 .50
94 Jonathan Massaquoi .20 .50
95 Donnie Fletcher .15 .40
96 Tauren Poole .20 .50
97 Vontaze Burfict .20 .50
98 Brandon Bolden .25 .60
99 Chris Polk .30 .75
100 Tim Fugger .20 .50
101 Kendall Wright .30 .75
102 Janoris Jenkins .25 .60
103 Brandon Weeden .50 1.25
104 Jarius Wright .25 .60
105 Darron Thomas .40 1.00
106 Cam Johnson .20 .50
107 Case Keenum .30 .75
108 Kirk Cousins .40 1.00
109 Tyler Hansen .20 .50
110 Markelle Martin .20 .50
111 Alex Tanney .25 .60
112 Eric Page .20 .50
113 Ronnie Hillman .30 .75
114 G.J. Kinne .25 .60
115 Bernard Pierce .25 .60
116 George Iloka .20 .50
117 Brock Osweiler .30 .75
118 Emmanuel Acho .25 .60
119 Mike Willie .20 .50
120 Peter Konz 12R .15 .40
121 Orson Charles 12R .25 .60
122 Dominique Davis 12R .20 .50
123 Rhett Ellison 12R .20 .50
124 Stephen Garcia 12R .25 .60
125 Alshon Jeffery 12R .40 1.00
126 Ryan Tannehill 12R .60 1.50
127 Alex Tanney 12R .25 .60
128 Ronnie Hillman 12R .30 .75
129 Ladarius Green 12R .25 .60
130 Brian Quick 12R .30 .75
131 Boom Herron 12R .20 .50
132 Janoris Jenkins 12R .25 .60
133 DeVier Posey 12R .25 .60
134 Bernard Pierce 12R .25 .60
135 Dont'a Hightower 12R .40 1.00
136 Jarius Wright 12R .25 .60
137 Kirk Cousins 12R .40 1.00
138 Dontari Poe 12R .25 .60
139 Tauren Poole 12R .20 .50
140 Kendall Wright 12R .30 .75
141 Vontaze Burfict 12R .20 .50
142 Eric Page 12R .20 .50
143 Brock Osweiler 12R .30 .75
144 Brandon Bolden 12R .25 .60
145 G.J. Kinne 12R .25 .60
146 Justin Blackmon 12R .50 1.25
147 Tyler Hansen 12R .20 .50
148 Travis Benjamin 12R .25 .60
149 Juron Criner 12R .25 .60
150 Trent Richardson 12R .75 2.00

2012 SAGE HIT Gold

*GOLD: 1.5X TO 4X BASIC CARDS
1-75 STATED ODDS 1:10 HOB LOW
76-150 STATED ODDS 1:10 HOB HIGH

2012 SAGE HIT Red

*RED: 1X TO 2.5X BASIC CARDS
SIX RED PER RETAIL FAT PACK

2012 SAGE HIT Silver

COMPLETE SET (150) 30.00 80.00
COMP. LOW SERIES (75) 15.00 40.00
COMP. HIGH SERIES (75) 15.00 40.00
*SILVER: 1X TO 2.5X BASIC CARDS
1-75 STATED ODDS 1:2.5 HOB LOW
76-150 STATED ODDS 1:3 HOB HIGH

2012 SAGE HIT Artistry

ART1-ART16 SILVER ODDS 1:6 HOB LOW
ART17-ART32 SILVER ODDS 1:6 HOB HIGH
*GOLD: .6X TO 1.5X BASIC INSERTS
ART1 Joe Adams .60 1.50
ART2 Ryan Broyles .60 1.50
ART3 Michael Floyd 1.25 3.00
ART4 Nick Foles 1.00 2.50
ART5 Cyrus Gray .60 1.50
ART6 Robert Griffin III 3.00 8.00
ART7 Jacory Harris .50 1.25
ART8 LaMichael James 1.25 3.00
ART9 Alshon Jeffery 1.00 2.50
ART10 Ryan Lindley .60 1.50
ART11 Doug Martin 1.00 2.50
ART12 Davin Meggett .50 1.25
ART13 Lamar Miller .75 2.00
ART14 Kellen Moore 1.00 2.50
ART15 Cam Newton .50 1.25
ART16 Ryan Tannehill 1.50 4.00
ART17 Dwayne Allen .60 1.50
ART18 Justin Blackmon 1.25 3.00
ART19 Kirk Cousins 1.00 2.50
ART20 Chris Givens .50 1.25
ART21 Boom Herron .50 1.25
ART22 Ronnie Hillman .75 2.00
ART23 Case Keenum .75 2.00
ART24 Marvin McNutt .60 1.50
ART25 Brock Osweiler .75 2.00
ART26 Bernard Pierce .60 1.50
ART27 Chris Polk .75 2.00
ART28 Brian Quick .75 2.00
ART29 Trent Richardson 2.00 5.00
ART30 Darron Thomas 1.00 2.50
ART31 Brandon Weeden 1.25 3.00
ART32 Kendall Wright .75 2.00

2012 SAGE HIT Artistry Autographs

ART1-ART16 AU/100 ODDS 1:288 HOB LOW
ART17-ART32 AU/100 ODDS 1:87 HOB HIGH
ART1 Joe Adams 8.00 20.00
ART2 Ryan Broyles 8.00 20.00
ART3 Michael Floyd 15.00 40.00
ART4 Nick Foles 12.00 30.00
ART5 Cyrus Gray 8.00 20.00
ART6 Robert Griffin III 100.00 200.00
ART7 Jacory Harris 6.00 15.00
ART8 LaMichael James 15.00 40.00
ART9 Alshon Jeffery 12.00 30.00
ART10 Ryan Lindley 8.00 20.00
ART11 Doug Martin 12.00 30.00
ART12 Davin Meggett 6.00 15.00
ART13 Lamar Miller 10.00 25.00
ART14 Kellen Moore 12.00 30.00
ART15 Cam Newton 40.00 80.00
ART16 Ryan Tannehill 20.00 50.00
ART17 Dwayne Allen 8.00 20.00
ART18 Justin Blackmon 25.00 60.00
ART19 Kirk Cousins 12.00 30.00
ART21 Boom Herron 8.00 20.00
ART22 Ronnie Hillman 10.00 25.00
ART23 Case Keenum 10.00 25.00
ART24 Marvin McNutt 8.00 20.00
ART25 Brock Osweiler 10.00 25.00
ART26 Bernard Pierce 8.00 20.00
ART27 Chris Polk 10.00 25.00
ART28 Brian Quick 10.00 25.00
ART29 Trent Richardson 40.00 80.00
ART30 Darron Thomas 12.00 30.00
ART31 Brandon Weeden 15.00 40.00
ART32 Kendall Wright 10.00 25.00

2012 SAGE HIT Autographs

BASIC AU STATED ODDS 1:10 HOB
A1 Alshon Jeffery 6.00 15.00
A2 Chris Givens 3.00 8.00
A3 Michael Floyd 8.00 20.00
A4 T.Y. Hilton 4.00 10.00
A5 Stephen Garcia 4.00 10.00
A6 Lamar Miller 5.00 12.00
A7 Orson Charles 4.00 10.00
A8 Nick Foles 6.00 15.00
A9 Jeff Fuller 5.00 12.00
A10 Robert Griffin III 50.00 100.00
A11 Kellen Moore 6.00 15.00
A12 Jacory Harris 3.00 8.00
A13 Davin Meggett 3.00 8.00
A14 Ryan Lindley 4.00 10.00
A15 Alfonzo Dennard 4.00 10.00
A16 Melvin Ingram 5.00 12.00
A17 Ryan Tannehill 10.00 25.00
A18 Tommy Streeter 4.00 10.00
A19 Thomas Mayo 2.50 6.00
A20 Jayron Hosley 4.00 10.00
A21 LaMichael James 8.00 20.00
A22 Doug Martin 6.00 15.00
A23 Joe Adams 4.00 10.00
A24 Dominique Davis 3.00 8.00
A25 Ryan Broyles 4.00 10.00
A26 Chaz Powell 2.50 6.00
A27 Tony Jerod-Eddie 2.50 6.00
A28 Michael Egnew 3.00 8.00
A29 Jake Bequette 4.00 10.00
A30 Michael Smith 3.00 8.00
A31 Sean Spence 3.00 8.00
A32 Cyrus Gray 4.00 10.00
A33 Derrick Coleman 2.50 6.00
A34 Chris Galippo 3.00 8.00
A35 Chris Owusu 3.00 8.00
A36 Jared Crick 4.00 10.00
A37 Jason Ford 3.00 8.00
A38 Harrison Smith 4.00 10.00
A39 Devon Still 4.00 10.00
A40 Luke Kuechly 5.00 12.00
A41 Rhett Ellison 3.00 8.00
A42 Keenan Robinson 3.00 8.00
A43 Quinton Coples 4.00 10.00
A44 David DeCastro 5.00 12.00
A45 Matt Kalil 5.00 12.00
A46 Garth Gerhart 3.00 8.00
A47 Yoshi Hardrick 3.00 8.00
A48 Joe Long 3.00 8.00
A49 Ryan Miller 3.00 8.00
A50 Kelechi Osemele 4.00 10.00
A51 Moe Petrus 2.50 6.00
A76 Trent Richardson 25.00 50.00
A77 Marvin McNutt 4.00 10.00
A78 Brian Quick 5.00 12.00
A79 Dontari Poe 4.00 10.00
A80 Travis Lewis 3.00 8.00
A81 Justin Blackmon 15.00 40.00
A82 Juron Criner 3.00 8.00
A83 Dwayne Allen 4.00 10.00
A84 Travis Benjamin 4.00 10.00
A85 Coryell Judie 3.00 8.00
A86 Damaris Johnson 3.00 8.00
A87 Cory Harkey 3.00 8.00
A88 DeVier Posey 4.00 10.00
A89 Ladarius Green 4.00 10.00
A90 Dont'a Hightower 6.00 15.00
A91 Boom Herron 4.00 10.00
A92 Broderick Green 3.00 8.00
A93 B.J. Cunningham 3.00 8.00
A94 Jonathan Massaquoi 3.00 8.00
A95 Donnie Fletcher 2.50 6.00
A96 Tauren Poole 3.00 8.00
A97 Vontaze Burfict 3.00 8.00
A98 Brandon Bolden 4.00 10.00
A99 Chris Polk 4.00 10.00
A100 Tim Fugger 3.00 8.00
A101 Kendall Wright 5.00 12.00
A102 Janoris Jenkins 4.00 10.00
A103 Brandon Weeden 8.00 20.00
A104 Jarius Wright 4.00 10.00
A105 Darron Thomas 6.00 15.00
A106 Cam Johnson 3.00 8.00
A107 Case Keenum 5.00 12.00
A108 Kirk Cousins 6.00 15.00
A109 Tyler Hansen 3.00 8.00
A110 Markelle Martin 3.00 8.00
A111 Alex Tanney 4.00 10.00
A112 Eric Page 3.00 8.00
A113 Ronnie Hillman 5.00 12.00
A114 G.J. Kinne 4.00 10.00
A115 Bernard Pierce 4.00 10.00
A116 George Iloka 3.00 8.00
A117 Brock Osweiler 5.00 12.00
A118 Emmanuel Acho 4.00 10.00
A119 Mike Willie 4.00 10.00
A120 Peter Konz 2.50 6.00

2012 SAGE HIT Autographs Gold

*GOLD AU/250: .5X TO 1.2X BASIC AU
GOLD/250 STATED ODDS 1:28 HOB
A10 Robert Griffin III 60.00 120.00

2012 SAGE HIT Autographs Silver

*SILVER AU: .5X TO 1.2X BASIC AU
SILVER AUTO STATED ODDS 1:18 HOB
A10 Robert Griffin III 60.00 120.00

2012 SAGE HIT Sophomore Autographs

RANDOM INSERTS IN PACKS
A1 Da'Quan Bowers 3.00 8.00
A2 Randall Cobb 5.00 12.00
A3 Shane Vereen 4.00 10.00
A4 Blaine Gabbert 6.00 15.00
A5 A.J. Green 8.00 20.00
A6 Cameron Heyward 4.00 10.00
A7 Mark Ingram 8.00 20.00
A8 Jerrel Jernigan 3.00 8.00
A9 Julio Jones 8.00 20.00
A10 Taiwan Jones 4.00 10.00
A11 Jeremy Kerley 4.00 10.00
A12 Ryan Kerrigan 5.00 12.00
A13 Mikel Leshoure 5.00 12.00
A14 Dion Lewis 3.00 8.00
A15 Jake Locker 12.00 30.00
A16 Ryan Mallett 6.00 15.00
A17 Von Miller 5.00 12.00
A18 Denarius Moore 3.00 8.00
A19 DeMarco Murray 15.00 30.00
A20 Cam Newton 25.00 50.00
A21 Jake Locker 12.00 30.00
A22 Christian Ponder 8.00 20.00
A23 Stevan Ridley 4.00 10.00
A24 Jacquizz Rodgers 4.00 10.00
A25 Kyle Rudolph 4.00 10.00
A26 Dean Sanzenbacher 4.00 10.00
A27 Aldon Smith 5.00 12.00
A28 Torrey Smith 6.00 15.00
A29 Ricky Stanzi 4.00 10.00
A30 Daniel Thomas 5.00 12.00
A32 J.J. Watt 5.00 12.00
A33 D.J. Williams 3.00 8.00
A34 Ryan Williams 5.00 12.00

2012 SAGE HIT Write Stuff

COMPLETE SET (20) 12.00 30.00
COMP.LOW SERIES (10) 6.00 15.00
COMP.HIGH SERIES (10) 6.00 15.00
WS1-WS10 SILVER ODDS 1:11 HOB LOW
WS11-WS20 SILVER ODDS 1:11 HOB HIGH
*GOLD: .6X TO 1.5X BASIC INSERTS
WS1 Kirk Cousins 1.00 2.50
WS2 Michael Floyd 1.25 3.00
WS3 Robert Griffin III 3.00 8.00
WS4 Ronnie Hillman .75 2.00
WS5 Alshon Jeffery 1.00 2.50
WS6 Doug Martin 1.00 2.50
WS7 Kellen Moore 1.00 2.50
WS8 Brock Osweiler .75 2.00
WS9 Chris Polk .75 2.00
WS10 Brandon Weeden 1.25 3.00
WS11 Justin Blackmon 1.25 3.00
WS12 Nick Foles 1.00 2.50
WS13 LaMichael James 1.25 3.00
WS14 Case Keenum .75 2.00
WS15 Ryan Lindley .60 1.50
WS16 Lamar Miller .75 2.00
WS17 Bernard Pierce .60 1.50
WS18 Trent Richardson 2.00 5.00
WS19 Ryan Tannehill 1.50 4.00
WS20 Kendall Wright .75 2.00

2012 SAGE HIT Write Stuff Autographs

WS1-WS10 AUTO/25 ODDS 1:1152 HOB LOW
WS11-WS20 AUTO/25 ODDS 1:208 HOB HIGH
WS1 Kirk Cousins 25.00 50.00
WS2 Michael Floyd 20.00 50.00
WS3 Robert Griffin III 125.00 200.00
WS4 Ronnie Hillman 12.00 30.00
WS5 Alshon Jeffery 15.00 40.00
WS6 Doug Martin 15.00 40.00
WS7 Kellen Moore 15.00 40.00
WS8 Brock Osweiler 12.00 30.00
WS9 Chris Polk 12.00 30.00
WS10 Brandon Weeden 20.00 50.00
WS11 Justin Blackmon 30.00 60.00
WS12 Nick Foles 15.00 40.00
WS13 LaMichael James 20.00 50.00
WS14 Case Keenum 12.00 30.00
WS15 Ryan Lindley 10.00 25.00
WS16 Lamar Miller 12.00 30.00
WS17 Bernard Pierce 10.00 25.00
WS18 Trent Richardson 40.00 80.00
WS19 Ryan Tannehill 25.00 60.00
WS20 Kendall Wright 12.00 30.00

2004 SAGE Jersey Update

This product was released in late 2004 with 6-packs per box and one jersey card per pack. Each card in the set features a game used jersey swatch. A Premium Swatch parallel serial numbered to 10 was also produced as well as signed jersey cards numbered to only 5.

*PREM.SWATCH/10: 1.2X TO 3X
PREMIUM SWATCH PRINT RUN 10
UNPRICED AUTO PRINT RUN 5
1 Tatum Bell 3.00 8.00
2 Maurice Clarett 3.00 8.00
3 Casey Clausen 3.00 8.00
4 Lee Evans 4.00 10.00
5 Josh Harris 2.50 6.00
6 Devery Henderson 4.00 10.00
7 Michael Jenkins 3.00 8.00
8 Greg Jones 2.50 6.00
9 Kevin Jones 3.00 8.00
10 Jared Lorenzen 3.00 8.00
11 Eli Manning 12.00 30.00
12 John Navarre 2.50 6.00
13 Chris Perry 3.00 8.00
14 Cody Pickett 3.00 8.00
15 Philip Rivers 10.00 25.00
16 Eli Roberson 4.00 10.00
17 Ben Roethlisberger 12.00 30.00
18 Rod Rutherford 2.50 6.00
19 Matt Schaub 8.00 20.00
20 Jeff Smoker 3.00 8.00
21 Reggie Williams 3.00 8.00
22 Roy Williams WR 4.00 10.00
23 Quincy Wilson 3.00 8.00
24 Rashaun Woods 2.50 6.00

2004 SAGE Jersey Update Roethlisberger

1B Ben Roethlisberger/70 40.00 80.00
1W Ben Roethlisberger/140 30.00 60.00
BR1 Ben Roethlisberger/210 25.00 50.00

2005 SAGE Premium Action Autographs Gold

GOLD PRINT RUN 50 SER.#'d SETS
*BLACK PORTRAIT: .5X TO 1.2X GOLD ACT.
BLACK PORTRAIT PRINT RUN 25 SETS
A1 Aaron Rodgers 150.00 250.00
A2 Adrian McPherson 6.00 15.00
A3 Alex Smith QB
A4 Alex Smith TE 6.00 15.00
A5 Andrew Walter 6.00 15.00
A6 Anthony Davis 5.00 12.00
A7 Brandon Jacobs 10.00 25.00
A8 Brock Berlin 5.00 12.00
A9 Brodney Pool 5.00 12.00
A10 Cadillac Williams 15.00 40.00
A11 Carlos Rogers 6.00 15.00
A12 Channing Crowder 6.00 15.00
A13 Charlie Frye 6.00 15.00
A14 Chris Rix 5.00 12.00
A15 Ciatrick Fason 6.00 15.00
A16 Corey Webster 5.00 12.00
A17 Craphonso Thorpe 5.00 12.00
A18 Dan Orlovsky 6.00 15.00
A19 Dante Ridgeway 5.00 12.00
A20 David Greene 6.00 15.00
A21 DeMarcus Ware 10.00 25.00
A22 Derek Anderson 6.00 15.00
A23 Derrick Johnson 6.00 15.00
A24 Fabian Washington 8.00 20.00
A25 Frank Gore 15.00 40.00
A26 Fred Gibson 5.00 12.00
A27 J.J. Arrington 6.00 15.00
A28 J.R. Russell 5.00 12.00
A29 Jammal Brown 6.00 15.00
A30 Jason Campbell 12.50 30.00
A31 Jason White 6.00 15.00
A32 Johnathan Goddard 5.00 12.00
A33 Josh Davis 5.00 12.00
A34 Justin Miller 5.00 12.00
A35 Kay-Jay Harris 5.00 12.00
A36 Kyle Orton 6.00 15.00
A37 Mark Clayton 6.00 15.00
A38 Marlin Jackson 6.00 15.00
A39 Matt Jones 8.00 20.00
A40 Reggie Brown 6.00 15.00
A41 Roddy White 6.00 15.00
A42 Ronnie Brown 30.00 60.00
A43 Roscoe Parrish 6.00 15.00
A44 Ryan Fitzpatrick 20.00 50.00
A45 T.A. McLendon 3.00 8.00
A46 Taylor Stubblefield 3.00 8.00
A47 Terrence Murphy 6.00 15.00
A48 Thomas Davis 5.00 12.00
A49 Troy Williamson 6.00 15.00
A50 Vernand Morency 6.00 15.00

2005 SAGE Premium Jerseys Black

BLACK PRINT RUN 25 SER.#'d SETS
SJ1 Aaron Rodgers 40.00 100.00
SJ2 Adrian McPherson 6.00 15.00
SJ3 Alex Smith QB 30.00 80.00
SJ4 Andrew Walter 8.00 20.00
SJ5 Cadillac Williams 15.00 40.00
SJ6 Charlie Frye 10.00 25.00
SJ7 Ciatrick Fason 6.00 15.00
SJ8 Dan Orlovsky 10.00 25.00
SJ9 David Greene 6.00 15.00
SJ10 Frank Gore 20.00 50.00
SJ11 J.J. Arrington 8.00 20.00
SJ12 Jason Campbell 12.00 30.00
SJ13 Jason White 10.00 25.00
SJ14 Kyle Orton 10.00 25.00
SJ15 Mark Clayton 10.00 25.00
SJ16 Ronnie Brown 30.00 80.00
SJ17 Roscoe Parrish 6.00 15.00
SJ18 Vernand Morency 8.00 20.00

2008 SAGE Squared

This set was released on August 15, 2008. The base set consists of 87 cards, each of which feature two rookies.

1 Matt Ryan 1.25 3.00
Darren McFadden
2 Matt Ryan 1.25 3.00
Joe Flacco
3 Darren McFadden .75 2.00
Jonathan Stewart
4 Darren McFadden .75 2.00
Felix Jones
5 Darren McFadden .75 2.00
R.Mendenhall
6 Darren McFadden .75 2.00
Kevin Smith
7 Darren McFadden .75 2.00
Ryan Clady
8 Matt Ryan 1.25 3.00
Brian Brohm
9 Matt Ryan 1.25 3.00
Sam Baker
10 Tashard Choice 1.25 3.00
Matt Ryan
11 Matt Ryan 1.25 3.00
Kevin O'Connell
12 Joe Flacco 1.00 2.50
Ray Rice
13 Joe Flacco 1.00 2.50
Josh Johnson
14 Tom Zbikowski 1.00 2.50
Joe Flacco
15 Joe Flacco 1.00 2.50
Allen Patrick
16 Jonathan Stewart .50 1.25
Dennis Dixon
17 Felix Jones .50 1.25
Jonathan Stewart
18 Jonathan Stewart .50 1.25
Dan Connor
19 Rashard Mendenhall .60 1.50
Limas Sweed
20 Tashard Choice .50 1.25
Felix Jones
21 Josh Johnson .30 .75
Sam Keller
22 Dustin Keller .30 .75
Sam Keller
23 Tom Zbikowski .30 .75
John Carlson
24 Tom Zbikowski .60 1.50
Ray Rice
25 Steve Slaton .30 .75
Owen Schmitt
26 Will Franklin .25 .60
Martin Rucker
27 Tashard Choice .30 .75
Mike Jenkins
28 Jordy Nelson .40 1.00
Brian Brohm
29 Matt Flynn .60 1.50
Brian Brohm
30 Brandon Flowers .50 1.25
Jamaal Charles
31 Will Franklin .50 1.25
Jamaal Charles
32 Brandon Flowers .30 .75
Will Franklin
33 Kevin O'Connell .30 .75
Josh Johnson
34 Erik Ainge .30 .75
Dustin Keller
35 Erik Ainge .30 .75
Vernon Gholston
36 Donnie Avery .25 .60
Keenan Burton
37 Paul Smith .30 .75
Derrick Harvey
38 Lawrence Jackson .30 .75
John Carlson
39 Lavelle Hawkins .25 .60
Jason Rivers
40 Darius Reynaud .25 .60
John David Booty
41 Adarius Bowman .25 .60
Malcolm Kelly
42 Ray Rice .60 1.50
Steve Slaton
43 Darius Reynaud .30 .75
Steve Slaton
44 Dustin Keller .30 .75
John Carlson
45 Paul Smith .30 .75
Kevin O'Connell
46 Paul Smith .30 .75
Kevin Smith
47 Adarius Bowman .25 .60
James Hardy
48 Matt Flynn .60 1.50
Erik Ainge
49 Keenan Burton .25 .60
Andre Caldwell
50 Martin Rucker .25 .60
Malcolm Kelly
51 Sam Baker .25 .60
John David Booty
52 Ryan Clady .30 .75
Jake Long
53 Fred Davis .30 .75
John David Booty
54 Devin Thomas .30 .75
Fred Davis
55 Kenny Phillips .30 .75
Leodis McKelvin
56 Kenny Phillips .30 .75
Mike Jenkins
57 Keith Rivers .30 .75
Andre Caldwell
58 Derrick Harvey .25 .60
Andre Caldwell
59 Felix Jones .50 1.25
Mike Jenkins
60 Derrick Harvey .30 .75
Jacob Hester
61 Antoine Cason .30 .75
Jacob Hester
62 Jacob Hester .60 1.50
Matt Flynn
63 Devin Thomas .25 .60
Malcolm Kelly
64 Donnie Avery .25 .60
Devin Thomas
65 Sedrick Ellis .30 .75
Adrian Arrington
66 Adrian Arrington .30 .75
Chad Henne
67 Adrian Arrington .30 .75
Jake Long
68 Limas Sweed .50 1.25
Jamaal Charles
69 Limas Sweed .30 .75
Dennis Dixon
70 Antoine Cason .30 .75
Dan Connor
71 Vernon Gholston .30 .75
Dan Connor
72 Sedrick Ellis .30 .75
Keith Rivers
73 Donnie Avery .40 1.00
Jordy Nelson
74 Leodis McKelvin .25 .60
James Hardy
75 Jordy Nelson .40 1.00
James Hardy
76 Ray Rice .60 1.50
Allen Patrick
77 Malcolm Kelly .25 .60
Allen Patrick
78 Sedrick Ellis .30 .75
Lawrence Jackson
79 Rashard Mendenhall .60 1.50
Dennis Dixon
80 Mike Hart .30 .75
Chad Henne
81 Mike Hart .60 1.50
Rashard Mendenhall
82 Jake Long .30 .75
Mike Hart
83 Jake Long .30 .75
Chad Henne
84 Vernon Gholston .30 .75
Dustin Keller
85 Leodis McKelvin .30 .75
Mike Jenkins
86 Martin Rucker .25 .60
Darrell Terrell
87 Will Franklin .25 .60
Darrell Terrell

2008 SAGE Squared Autographs

ONE SINGLE AUTO PER PACK
A1A Matt Ryan AU 25.00 60.00
Darren McFadden
A1B Darren McFadden AU 12.00 30.00
Matt Ryan
A2A Matt Ryan AU 40.00 80.00
Joe Flacco
A2B Joe Flacco AU 15.00 40.00
Matt Ryan
A3A Darren McFadden AU 12.00 30.00
Jonathan Stewart
A3B Jonathan Stewart AU 6.00 15.00
Darren McFadden
A4A Darren McFadden AU 12.00 30.00
Felix Jones
A4B Felix Jones AU 10.00 25.00
Darren McFadden
A5A Darren McFadden AU 12.00 30.00
Rashard Mendenhall
A5B Rashard Mendenhall AU 6.00 15.00
Darren McFadden

A6A Darren McFadden AU	Kevin Smith	12.00	30.00
A6B Kevin Smith AU	Darren McFadden	4.00	10.00
A7A Darren McFadden AU	Ryan Clady	12.00	30.00
A7B Ryan Clady AU	Darren McFadden	3.00	8.00
A8A Matt Ryan AU	Brian Brohm	40.00	80.00
A8B Brian Brohm AU	Matt Ryan	5.00	12.00
A9A Matt Ryan AU	Sam Baker	40.00	80.00
A9B Sam Baker AU	Matt Ryan	3.00	8.00
A10A Tashard Choice AU	Matt Ryan	5.00	12.00
A10B Matt Ryan AU	Tashard Choice	40.00	80.00
A11A Matt Ryan AU	Kevin O'Connell	40.00	80.00
A11B Kevin O'Connell AU	Matt Ryan	4.00	10.00
A12A Joe Flacco AU	Ray Rice	15.00	40.00
A12B Ray Rice AU	Joe Flacco	8.00	20.00
A13A Joe Flacco AU	Josh Johnson	15.00	40.00
A13B Josh Johnson AU	Joe Flacco	4.00	10.00
A14A Tom Zbikowski AU	Joe Flacco	4.00	10.00
A14B Joe Flacco AU	Tom Zbikowski	15.00	40.00
A15A Joe Flacco AU	Allen Patrick	15.00	40.00
A15B Allen Patrick AU	Joe Flacco	5.00	12.00
A16A Jonathan Stewart AU	Dennis Dixon	6.00	15.00
A16B Dennis Dixon AU	Jonathan Stewart	6.00	15.00
A17A Felix Jones AU	Jonathan Stewart	10.00	25.00
A17B Jonathan Stewart AU	Felix Jones	6.00	15.00
A18A Jonathan Stewart AU	Dan Connor	6.00	15.00
A18B Dan Connor AU	Jonathan Stewart	5.00	12.00
A19A Rashard Mendenhall AU	Limas Sweed	8.00	20.00
A19B Limas Sweed AU	Rashard Mendenhall	4.00	10.00
A20A Tashard Choice AU	Felix Jones	6.00	15.00
A20B Felix Jones AU	Tashard Choice	10.00	25.00
A21A Josh Johnson AU	Sam Keller	4.00	10.00
A21B Sam Keller AU	Josh Johnson	4.00	10.00
A22A Dustin Keller AU	Sam Keller	5.00	12.00
A22B Sam Keller AU	Dustin Keller	4.00	10.00
A23A Tom Zbikowski AU	John Carlson	4.00	10.00
A23B John Carlson AU	Tom Zbikowski	4.00	10.00
A24A Tom Zbikowski AU	Ray Rice	4.00	10.00
A24B Ray Rice AU	Tom Zbikowksi	8.00	20.00
A25A Steve Slaton AU	Owen Schmitt	5.00	12.00
A25B Owen Schmitt AU	Steve Slaton	4.00	10.00
A26A Will Franklin AU	Martin Rucker	3.00	8.00
A26B Martin Rucker AU	Will Franklin	3.00	8.00
A27A Tashard Choice AU	Mike Jenkins	5.00	12.00
A27B Mike Jenkins AU	Tashard Choice	4.00	10.00
A28A Jordy Nelson AU	Brian Brohm	8.00	20.00
A28B Brian Brohm AU	Jordy Nelson	8.00	20.00
A29A Matt Flynn AU	Brian Brohm	10.00	25.00
A29B Brian Brohm AU	Matt Flynn	8.00	20.00
A30A Brandon Flowers AU	Jamaal Charles	4.00	10.00
A30B Jamaal Charles AU	Brandon Flowers	6.00	15.00
A31A Will Franklin AU	Jamaal Charles	3.00	8.00
A31B Jamaal Charles AU	Will Franklin	6.00	15.00
A32A Brandon Flowers AU	Will Franklin	4.00	10.00
A32B Will Franklin AU	Brandon Flowers	3.00	8.00
A33A Kevin O'Connell AU	Josh Johnson	4.00	10.00
A33B Josh Johnson AU	Kevin O'Connell	4.00	10.00
A34A Erik Ainge AU	Dustin Keller	4.00	10.00
A34B Dustin Keller AU	Erik Ainge	5.00	12.00
A35A Erik Ainge AU	Vernon Gholston	4.00	10.00
A35B Vernon Gholston AU	Erik Ainge	4.00	10.00
A36A Donnie Avery AU	Keenan Burton	4.00	10.00
A36B Keenan Burton AU	Donnie Avery	3.00	8.00
A37A Paul Smith AU	Derrick Harvey	3.00	8.00
A37B Derrick Harvey AU	Paul Smith	4.00	10.00
A38A Lawrence Jackson AU	John Carlson	4.00	10.00
A38B John Carlson AU	Lawrence Jackson	5.00	12.00
A39A Lavelle Hawkins AU	Jason Rivers	3.00	8.00
A39B Jason Rivers AU	Lavelle Hawkins	4.00	10.00
A40A Darius Reynaud AU	John David Booty	4.00	10.00
A40B John David Booty AU	Darius Reynaud	4.00	10.00
A41A Adarius Bowman AU	Malcolm Kelly	4.00	10.00
A41B Malcolm Kelly AU	Adarius Bowman	4.00	10.00
A42A Ray Rice AU	Steve Slaton	8.00	20.00
A42B Steve Slaton AU	Ray Rice	5.00	12.00
A43A Darius Reynaud AU	Steve Slaton	4.00	10.00
A43B Steve Slaton AU	Darius Reynard	5.00	12.00
A44A Dustin Keller AU	John Carlson	5.00	12.00
A44B John Carlson AU	Dustin Keller	5.00	12.00
A45A Paul Smith AU	Kevin O'Connell	3.00	8.00
A45B Kevin O'Connell AU	Paul Smith	4.00	10.00
A46A Paul Smith AU	Kevin Smith	3.00	8.00
A46B Kevin Smith AU	Paul Smith	4.00	10.00
A47A Adarius Bowman AU	James Hardy	4.00	10.00
A47B James Hardy AU	Adarius Bowman	4.00	10.00
A48A Matt Flynn AU	Erik Ainge	8.00	20.00
A48B Erik Ainge AU	Matt Flynn	8.00	20.00
A49A Keenan Burton AU	Andre Caldwell	3.00	8.00
A49B Andre Caldwell AU	Keenan Burton	4.00	10.00
A50A Martin Rucker AU	Malcolm Kelly	3.00	8.00
A50B Malcolm Kelly AU	Martin Rucker	4.00	10.00
A51A Sam Baker AU	John David Booty	3.00	8.00
A51B John David Booty AU	Sam Baker	4.00	10.00
A52A Ryan Clady AU	Jake Long	3.00	8.00
A52B Jake Long AU	Ryan Clady	4.00	10.00
A53A Fred Davis AU	John David Booty	4.00	10.00
A53B John David Booty AU	Fred Davis	4.00	10.00
A54A Devin Thomas AU	Fred Davis	4.00	10.00
A54B Fred Davis AU	Devin Thomas	4.00	10.00
A55A Kenny Phillips AU	Leodis McKelvin	3.00	8.00
A55B Leodis McKelvin AU	Kenny Phillips	4.00	10.00
A56A Kenny Phillips AU	Mike Jenkins	3.00	8.00
A56B Mike Jenkins AU	Kenny Phillips	4.00	10.00
A57A Keith Rivers AU	Andre Caldwell	4.00	10.00
A57B Andre Caldwell AU	Keith Rivers	4.00	10.00
A58A Derrick Harvey AU	Andre Caldwell	4.00	10.00
A58B Andre Caldwell AU	Derrick Harvey	4.00	10.00
A59A Felix Jones AU	Mike Jenkins	10.00	25.00
A59B Mike Jenkins AU	Felix Jones	4.00	10.00
A60A Derrick Harvey AU	Jacob Hester	4.00	10.00
A60B Jacob Hester AU	Derrick Harvey	4.00	10.00
A61A Antoine Cason AU	Jacob Hester	4.00	10.00
A61B Jacob Hester AU	Antoine Cason	4.00	10.00
A62A Jacob Hester AU	Matt Flynn	8.00	20.00
A62B Matt Flynn AU	Jacob Hester	8.00	20.00
A63A Devin Thomas AU	Malcolm Kelly	4.00	10.00
A63B Malcolm Kelly AU	Devin Thomas	4.00	10.00
A64A Donnie Avery AU	Devin Thomas	5.00	12.00
A64B Devin Thomas AU	Donnie Avery	4.00	10.00
A65A Sedrick Ellis AU	Adrian Arrington	4.00	10.00
A65B Adrian Arrington AU	Sedrick Ellis	4.00	10.00
A66A Adrian Arrington AU	Chad Henne	4.00	10.00
A66B Chad Henne AU	Adrian Arrington	8.00	20.00
A67A Adrian Arrington AU	Jake Long	4.00	10.00
A67B Jake Long AU	Adrian Arrington	4.00	10.00
A68A Limas Sweed AU	Jamaal Charles	4.00	10.00
A68B Jamaal Charles AU	Limas Sweed	6.00	15.00
A69A Limas Sweed AU	Dennis Dixon	4.00	10.00
A69B Dennis Dixon AU	Limas Sweed	5.00	12.00
A70A Antoine Cason AU	Dan Connor	4.00	10.00
A70B Dan Connor AU	Antoine Cason	4.00	10.00
A71A Vernon Gholston AU	Dan Connor	4.00	10.00
A71B Dan Connor AU	Vernon Gholston	4.00	10.00
A72A Sedrick Ellis AU	Keith Rivers	4.00	10.00
A72B Keith Rivers AU	Sedrick Ellis	4.00	10.00
A73A Donnie Avery AU	Jordy Nelson	6.00	15.00
A73B Jordy Nelson AU	Donnie Avery	8.00	20.00
A74A Leodis McKelvin AU	James Hardy	4.00	10.00
A74B James Hardy AU	Leodis McKelvin	5.00	12.00
A75A Jordy Nelson AU	James Hardy	8.00	20.00
A75B James Hardy AU	Jordy Nelson	6.00	15.00
A76A Ray Rice AU	Allen Patrick	8.00	20.00
A76B Allen Patrick AU	Ray Rice	4.00	10.00
A77A Malcolm Kelly AU	Allen Patrick	4.00	10.00
A77B Allen Patrick AU	Malcolm Kelly	4.00	10.00
A78A Sedrick Ellis AU	Lawrence Jackson	4.00	10.00
A78B Lawrence Jackson AU	Sedrick Ellis	4.00	10.00
A79A Rashard Mendenhall AU	Dennis Dixon	8.00	20.00
A79B Dennis Dixon AU	Rashard Mendenhall	5.00	12.00
A80A Mike Hart AU	Chad Henne	5.00	12.00
A80B Chad Henne AU	Mike Hart	8.00	20.00
A81A Mike Hart AU	Rashard Mendenhall	5.00	12.00
A81B Rashard Mendenhall AU	Mike Hart	8.00	20.00
A82A Jake Long AU	Mike Hart	4.00	10.00
A82B Mike Hart AU	Jake Long	4.00	10.00
A83A Jake Long AU	Chad Henne	4.00	10.00
A83B Chad Henne AU	Jake Long	6.00	15.00
A84A Vernon Gholston AU	Dustin Keller	4.00	10.00
A84B Dustin Keller AU	Vernon Gholston	5.00	12.00
A85A Leodis McKelvin AU	Mike Jenkins	4.00	10.00
A85B Mike Jenkins AU	Leodis McKelvin	4.00	10.00
A86A Martin Rucker AU	Darnell Terrell	3.00	8.00
A86B Darnell Terrell AU	Martin Rucker	4.00	10.00
A87A Will Franklin AU	Darnell Terrell	3.00	8.00
A87B Darnell Terrell AU	Will Franklin	4.00	10.00

2008 SAGE Squared Dual Autographs

ONE DUAL AUTO PER PACK

A1 Matt Ryan	Darren McFadden	50.00	120.00
A2 Matt Ryan	Joe Flacco	50.00	100.00
A3 Darren McFadden	Jonathan Stewart	20.00	50.00
A4 Darren McFadden	Felix Jones	20.00	50.00
A5 Darren McFadden	Rashard Mendenhall	20.00	50.00
A6 Darren McFadden	Kevin Smith	15.00	40.00
A7 Darren McFadden	Ryan Clady	15.00	40.00
A8 Matt Ryan	Brian Brohm	40.00	80.00
A9 Matt Ryan	Sam Baker	40.00	80.00
A10 Tashard Choice	Matt Ryan	40.00	80.00
A11 Matt Ryan	Kevin O'Connell	40.00	80.00
A12 Joe Flacco	Ray Rice	20.00	50.00
A13 Joe Flacco	Josh Johnson	20.00	50.00
A14 Tom Zbikowski	Joe Flacco	20.00	50.00
A15 Joe Flacco	Allen Patrick	20.00	50.00
A16 Jonathan Stewart	Dennis Dixon	8.00	20.00
A17 Felix Jones	Jonathan Stewart	8.00	20.00
A18 Jonathan Stewart	Dan Connor	8.00	20.00
A19 Rashard Mendenhall	Limas Sweed	10.00	25.00
A20 Tashard Choice	Felix Jones	20.00	50.00
A21 Josh Johnson	Sam Keller	5.00	12.00
A22 Dustin Keller	Sam Keller	5.00	12.00
A23 Tom Zbikowski	John Carlson	5.00	12.00
A24 Tom Zbikowski	Ray Rice	10.00	25.00
A25 Steve Slaton	Owen Schmitt	5.00	12.00
A26 Will Franklin	Martin Rucker	4.00	10.00
A27 Tashard Choice	Mike Jenkins	5.00	12.00
A28 Jordy Nelson	Brian Brohm	10.00	25.00
A29 Matt Flynn	Brian Brohm	12.00	30.00
A30 Brandon Flowers	Jamaal Charles	8.00	20.00
A31 Will Franklin	Jamaal Charles	8.00	20.00
A32 Brandon Flowers	Will Franklin	5.00	12.00
A33 Kevin O'Connell	Josh Johnson	5.00	12.00
A34 Erik Ainge	Dustin Keller	5.00	12.00
A35 Erik Ainge	Vernon Gholston	5.00	12.00
A36 Donnie Avery	Keenan Burton	4.00	10.00
A37 Paul Smith	Derrick Harvey	5.00	12.00
A38 Lawrence Jackson	John Carlson	5.00	12.00
A39 Lavelle Hawkins	Jason Rivers	4.00	10.00
A40 Darius Reynaud	John David Booty	4.00	10.00
A41 Adarius Bowman	Malcolm Kelly	4.00	10.00
A42 Ray Rice	Steve Slaton	10.00	25.00
A43 Darius Reynaud	Steve Slaton	5.00	12.00
A44 Dustin Keller	John Carlson	5.00	12.00
A45 Paul Smith	Kevin O'Connell	5.00	12.00
A46 Paul Smith	Kevin Smith	5.00	12.00
A47 Adarius Bowman	James Hardy	4.00	10.00
A48 Matt Flynn	Erik Ainge	10.00	25.00
A49 Keenan Burton	Andre Caldwell	4.00	10.00
A50 Martin Rucker	Malcolm Kelly	4.00	10.00
A51 Sam Baker	John David Booty	4.00	10.00
A52 Ryan Clady	Jake Long	5.00	12.00
A53 Fred Davis	John David Booty	4.00	10.00
A54 Devin Thomas	Fred Davis	5.00	12.00
A55 Kenny Phillips	Leodis McKelvin	5.00	12.00
A56 Kenny Phillips	Mike Jenkins	5.00	12.00
A57 Keith Rivers	Andre Caldwell	5.00	12.00
A58 Derrick Harvey	Andre Caldwell	4.00	10.00
A59 Felix Jones	Mike Jenkins	8.00	20.00
A60 Derrick Harvey	Jacob Hester	5.00	12.00
A61 Antoine Cason	Jacob Hester	5.00	12.00
A62 Jacob Hester	Matt Flynn	10.00	25.00
A63 Devin Thomas	Malcolm Kelly	4.00	10.00
A64 Donnie Avery	Devin Thomas	4.00	10.00
A65 Sedrick Ellis	Adrian Arrington	5.00	12.00
A66 Adrian Arrington	Chad Henne	5.00	12.00
A67 Adrian Arrington	Jake Long	5.00	12.00
A68 Limas Sweed	Jamaal Charles	8.00	20.00
A69 Limas Sweed	Dennis Dixon	5.00	12.00
A70 Antoine Cason	Dan Connor	5.00	12.00
A71 Vernon Gholston	Dan Connor	5.00	12.00
A72 Sedrick Ellis	Keith Rivers	5.00	12.00
A73 Donnie Avery	Jordy Nelson	8.00	20.00
A74 Leodis McKelvin	James Hardy	4.00	10.00
A75 Jordy Nelson	James Hardy	8.00	20.00
A76 Ray Rice	Allen Patrick	10.00	25.00
A77 Malcolm Kelly	Allen Patrick	4.00	10.00
A78 Sedrick Ellis	Lawrence Jackson	5.00	12.00
A79 Rashard Mendenhall	Dennis Dixon	10.00	25.00
A80 Mike Hart	Chad Henne	5.00	12.00
A81 Mike Hart	Rashard Mendenhall	10.00	25.00
A82 Jake Long	Mike Hart	5.00	12.00
A83 Jake Long	Chad Henne	5.00	12.00
A84 Vernon Gholston	Dustin Keller	5.00	12.00
A85 Leodis McKelvin	Mike Jenkins	5.00	12.00
A86 Martin Rucker	Darnell Terrell	4.00	10.00
A87 Will Franklin	Darnell Terrell	4.00	10.00

2009 SAGE Squared

1 Louis Murphy	Cornelius Ingram	.30	.75
2 B.J. Raji	Matt Ryan	.30	.75
3 Matthew Stafford	Knowshon Moreno	1.50	4.00
4 Javon Ringer	Devin Thomas	.30	.75
5 Jeremy Maclin	Chase Coffman	.50	1.25
6 Chris Wells	Brian Robiskie	.50	1.25
7 Chris Wells	Malcolm Jenkins	.50	1.25
8 Juaquin Iglesias	Malcolm Kelly	.25	.60
9 James Casey	Jarett Dillard	.30	.75
10 Brian Orakpo	Roy Miller	.30	.75
11 Michael Crabtree	Graham Harrell	.60	1.50
12 Donald Brown	Darius Butler	.30	.75
13 Brian Cushing	Clay Matthews	.75	2.00
14 Mark Sanchez	Patrick Turner	1.00	2.50
15 Pat White	Steve Slaton	.30	.75
16 Matthew Stafford	Jake Long	1.50	4.00
17 Matthew Stafford	Matt Ryan	1.50	4.00
18 Knowshon Moreno	Darren McFadden	.30	.75
19 Matthew Stafford	Jason Smith	1.50	4.00
20 Matthew Stafford	Mark Sanchez	1.50	4.00
21 Matthew Stafford	Josh Freeman	1.50	4.00
22 Mark Sanchez	Josh Freeman	1.00	2.50
23 Knowshon Moreno	Donald Brown	.30	.75
24 Knowshon Moreno	Chris Wells	.50	1.25
25 Donald Brown	Chris Wells	.50	1.25
26 Darrius Heyward-Bey	Michael Crabtree	.60	1.50
27 Darrius Heyward-Bey	Jeremy Maclin	.50	1.25
28 Darrius Heyward-Bey	Hakeem Nicks	.50	1.25
29 Michael Crabtree	Jeremy Maclin	.50	1.25
30 Michael Crabtree	Hakeem Nicks	.60	1.50
31 Jeremy Maclin	Hakeem Nicks	.50	1.25
32 Rey Maualuga	James Laurinaitis	.30	.75
33 Rey Maualuga	Chase Coffman	.30	.75
34 Knowshon Moreno	Alphonso Smith	.30	.75
35 Matthew Stafford	Kevin Smith	1.50	4.00
36 B.J. Raji	Clay Matthews	.75	2.00
37 Donald Brown	Curtis Painter	.30	.75
38 Pat White	Chad Henne	.30	.75
39 Hakeem Nicks	Andre Brown	.50	1.25
40 Mark Sanchez	Vernon Gholston	1.00	2.50
41 Darrius Heyward-Bey	Louis Murphy	.30	.75
42 Darrius Heyward-Bey	Darren McFadden	.30	.75
43 Jeremy Maclin	LeSean McCoy	.50	1.25
44 Michael Crabtree	Nate Davis	.60	1.50
45 Jason Smith	James Laurinaitis	.30	.75

2009 SAGE Squared Dual Autographs

ONE AUTO PER PACK

1 Louis Murphy	Cornelius Ingram	4.00	10.00
2 Michael Crabtree	Graham Harrell	20.00	50.00
3 Matthew Stafford	Knowshon Moreno	40.00	80.00
4 Rey Maualuga	Brian Cushing	4.00	10.00
5 Jeremy Maclin	Chase Coffman	6.00	15.00
6 Chris Wells	Brian Robiskie	15.00	40.00
7 Patrick Turner	Pat White	4.00	10.00
8 Johnny Knox	Darrius Heyward Bey	6.00	15.00
9 James Casey	Jarett Dillard	4.00	10.00
10 Jason Smith	Eugene Monroe	3.00	8.00
11 LeSean McCoy	Scott McKillop	10.00	25.00
12 Donald Brown	Darius Butler	6.00	15.00
13 Brian Cushing	Clay Matthews	20.00	50.00
14 Mark Sanchez	Patrick Turner	20.00	50.00
15 Knowshon Moreno	Tom Brandstater	8.00	20.00
16 Cullen Harper	Aaron Kelly	5.00	12.00
17 Brian Orakpo	Roy Miller	5.00	12.00
18 Brian Orakpo	Ryan Palmer	5.00	12.00
19 Roy Miller	Ryan Palmer	4.00	10.00
20 Matthew Stafford	Mark Sanchez	75.00	135.00
21 Matthew Stafford	Josh Freeman	40.00	80.00
22 Michael Crabtree	Jeremy Maclin		
23 Knowshon Moreno	Donald Brown	12.00	30.00
24 Chris Wells	Knowshon Moreno		
25 Chris Wells	Donald Brown	15.00	40.00
26 Darrius Heyward Bey	Michael Crabtree	20.00	50.00
27 Darrius Heyward Bey	Jeremy Maclin	12.00	30.00
28 Jared Bronson	Mike Reilly	3.00	8.00
29 Mark Sanchez	Josh Freeman	40.00	80.00
30 Stephen McGee	Brandon Williams	4.00	10.00
31 Ryan Mouton	David Veikune	5.00	12.00
32 Demetrius Byrd	Ricky Jean-Francois	4.00	10.00
33 Rey Maualuga	Chase Coffman	4.00	10.00
34 Mike Teel	Nick Reed	4.00	10.00
35 Freddie Brown	Darrell Mack	3.00	8.00
36 B.J. Raji	Clay Matthews	15.00	40.00
37 Donald Brown	Curtis Painter	8.00	20.00
38 D.J. Boldin	Alphonso Smith	3.00	8.00
39 Hakeem Nicks	Andre Brown	10.00	25.00
40 Juaquin Iglesias	Johnny Knox	6.00	15.00
41 Darrius Heyward Bey	Louis Murphy	4.00	10.00
42 Brian Robiskie	David Veikune	4.00	10.00
43 Jeremy Maclin	LeSean McCoy	15.00	40.00
44 Michael Crabtree	Nate Davis	15.00	40.00
45 Jason Smith	James Laurinaitis	4.00	10.00
46 Clint Sintim	Andre Brown	4.00	10.00
47 Sammie Stroughter	Brandon Hughes	4.00	10.00
48 Javon Ringer	Brian Hoyer	5.00	12.00
49 James Casey	Chase Clement	4.00	10.00
50 Mike Teel	Pat White	4.00	10.00
51 Jarett Dillard	Chase Clement	4.00	10.00
52 Rey Maualuga	Kaluka Maiava	8.00	20.00
53 Eben Britton	Mike Thomas	4.00	10.00
54 Darcel McBath	Alphonso Smith	3.00	8.00
55 Brian Robiskie	Kaluka Maiava	4.00	10.00
56 Eugene Monroe	Eben Britton	3.00	8.00
57 Hunter Cantwell	Eric Wood	4.00	10.00
58 Gartrell Johnson	Kory Sperry	2.50	6.00
59 Jared Cook	Javon Ringer	5.00	12.00
60 Jeremy Maclin	Cornelius Ingram	6.00	15.00
61 LeSean McCoy	Cornelius Ingram	8.00	20.00
62 Hakeem Nicks	Clint Sintim	10.00	25.00
63 Malcolm Jenkins	Marcus Freeman	5.00	12.00
64 Brian Cushing	James Casey	4.00	10.00
65 Marcus Freeman	James Laurinaitis	4.00	10.00
66 Alphonso Smith	David Bruton	3.00	8.00
67 Jarron Gilbert	Juaquin Iglesias	3.00	8.00
68 Mike Thomas	Jarett Dillard	4.00	10.00
69 Eugene Monroe	Clint Sintim	4.00	10.00
70 B.J. Raji	Ryan Purvis	4.00	10.00
71 Hakeem Nicks	Brooks Foster	6.00	15.00
72 Matthew Stafford	DeAndre Levy	30.00	60.00
73 Malcolm Jenkins	James Laurinaitis	8.00	20.00

2010 SAGE Squared

1 Sam Bradford	Ndamukong Suh	1.25	3.00
2 C.J. Spiller	Ryan Mathews	.60	1.50
3 Colt McCoy	Jimmy Clausen	.60	1.50
4 Rolando McClain	Colin Peek	.30	.75
5 Mark Sanchez	Jahvid Best	.75	2.50
6 Dan LeFevour	Antonio Brown	.50	1.25
7 Sam Bradford	C.J. Spiller	1.25	3.00
8 Tony Pike	Mardy Gilyard	.30	.75
9 Josh Freeman	Arrelious Benn	.30	.75
10 Michael Crabtree	Dez Bryant	1.00	2.50
11 Mark Sanchez	Damian Williams	.75	2.00
12 Sam Bradford	Mardy Gilyard	1.25	3.00
13 Darrius Heyward-Bey	Rolando McClain	.30	.75
14 Knowshon Moreno	C.J. Spiller	.50	1.25
15 Colt McCoy	Jordan Shipley	.60	1.50
16 Josh Freeman	Mike Williams	.50	1.25
17 C.J. Spiller	Jonathan Dwyer	.50	1.25
18 Sam Bradford	Gerald McCoy	1.25	3.00
19 Ryan Mathews	Seyi Ajirotutu	.60	1.50
20 Mark Sanchez	Joe McKnight	.60	1.50
21 Jimmy Clausen	Tony Pike	.30	.75
22 Toby Gerhart	Jahvid Best	.50	1.25
23 Colt McCoy	Earl Thomas	.60	1.50
24 Sam Bradford	Jermaine Gresham	1.25	3.00
25 Brandon Spikes	Aaron Hernandez	.50	1.25
26 Mark Sanchez	Sam Bradford	1.25	3.00
27 Josh Freeman	Gerald McCoy	.30	.75
28 C.J. Spiller	Jahvid Best	.50	1.25
29 Arrelious Benn	Mike Williams	.50	1.25
30 Sam Bradford	Colt McCoy	1.25	3.00
31 Toby Gerhart	Chris Cook	.30	.75
32 Mark Sanchez	Jimmy Clausen	.75	2.50
33 Derrick Morgan	Jonathan Dwyer	.30	.75
34 Colt McCoy	Ndamukong Suh	.60	1.50
35 Jason Pierre-Paul	Carlton Mitchell	.50	1.25
36 Knowshon Moreno	Rennie Curran	.40	1.00
37 Mark Sanchez	Jason Pierre-Paul	.75	2.00
38 Michael Crabtree	Anthony Dixon	.50	1.25
39 Darrius Heyward-Bey	Dez Bryant	1.00	2.50
40 Ryan Mathews	Jahvid Best	.60	1.50
41 Josh Freeman	Jevan Snead	.30	.75
42 Colt McCoy	Montario Hardesty	.60	1.50
43 Mark Sanchez	Toby Gerhart	.75	2.50
44 Ndamukong Suh	Gerald McCoy	.60	1.50
45 Sam Bradford	Jimmy Clausen	1.25	3.00

2010 SAGE Squared Dual Autographs

ONE DUAL AUTO PER PACK

A1 Sam Bradford	Matthew Stafford	50.00	100.00
A2 C.J. Spiller	Ryan Mathews	25.00	50.00
A3 C.J. Spiller	Mark Sanchez	25.00	50.00
A4 Rolando McClain	Colin Peek	12.00	30.00
A5 Pat White	Joe Webb	10.00	25.00
A6 Dan LeFevour	Antonio Brown	10.00	25.00
A7 Sam Bradford	C.J. Spiller	40.00	80.00
A8 Tony Pike	Mardy Gilyard	6.00	15.00
A9 Ben Tate	Brian Cushing	8.00	20.00
A10 Darrius Heyward-Bey	Louis Murphy	6.00	15.00
A11 John Skelton	Zac Robinson	6.00	15.00
A12 Sam Bradford	Mardy Gilyard	30.00	60.00
A13 Rolando McClain	Darrius Heyward-Bey	6.00	15.00
A14 C.J. Spiller	Knowshon Moreno	20.00	40.00
A15 Colt McCoy	Jordan Shipley	25.00	50.00
A16 Josh Freeman	Mike Williams	8.00	20.00
A17 C.J. Wilson	Clay Matthews	8.00	20.00
A18 Brian Cushing	Garrett Graham	5.00	12.00
A19 Ryan Mathews	Seyi Ajirotutu	12.00	30.00
A20 Damian Williams	Patrick Turner	6.00	15.00
A21 Jimmy Clausen	Tony Pike	12.00	30.00
A22 Dennis Pitta	Seyi Ajirotutu	6.00	15.00
A23 Colt McCoy	Earl Thomas	12.00	30.00
A24 Donald Brown	Malcolm Jenkins	6.00	15.00
A25 Aaron Hernandez	Brandon Spikes	10.00	25.00
A26 Dan LeFevour	Zac Robinson	6.00	15.00
A27 Josh Freeman	Gerald McCoy	6.00	15.00
A28 Sean Canfield	Sammie Stroughter	5.00	12.00
A29 Arrelious Benn	Mike Williams	10.00	25.00
A30 Sam Young	Kyle McCarthy	6.00	15.00
A31 Toby Gerhart	Chris Cook	6.00	15.00
A32 Andre Anderson	Jeremy Williams	4.00	10.00
A33 Jonathan Dwyer	Derrick Morgan	6.00	15.00
A34 E.J. Wilson	Earl Thomas	6.00	15.00
A35 Blair White	Donald Brown	6.00	15.00
A36 Ryan Mathews	Cam Thomas	12.00	30.00
A37 John Skelton	Chris Wells	10.00	25.00
A38 Anthony Dixon	Michael Crabtree	8.00	20.00
A39 Jeremy Maclin	Sean Weatherspoon	6.00	15.00
A40 Brian Orakpo	Jordan Shipley	6.00	15.00
A41 Cameron Sheffield	Brandon Lang	5.00	12.00
A42 Montario Hardesty	Colt McCoy	12.00	30.00
A43 Rob Gronkowski	Aaron Hernandez	25.00	50.00
A44 Taylor Price	Zac Robinson	6.00	15.00
A45 Sam Bradford	Jimmy Clausen	40.00	80.00
A46 Ndamukong Suh	Jahvid Best	30.00	60.00
A47 Matthew Stafford	Rennie Curran	15.00	40.00
A48 Montario Hardesty	Carlton Mitchell	6.00	15.00
A49 Stafon Johnson	Patrick Turner	6.00	15.00
A50 Andre Anderson	Darrius Heyward-Bey	5.00	12.00
A51 C.J. Wilson	Cameron Sheffield	5.00	12.00
A52 LeSean McCoy	Nate Byham	6.00	15.00
A53 Seyi Ajirotutu	Cam Thomas	6.00	15.00
A54 Sean Weatherspoon	Colin Peek	6.00	15.00
A55 Gerald McCoy	Mike Williams	10.00	25.00
A56 Blair White	Malcolm Jenkins	6.00	15.00
A57 Dezmon Briscoe	Jordan Shipley	6.00	15.00
A58 Rey Maualuga	Jermaine Gresham	8.00	20.00
A59 Ben Tate	Rennie Curran	8.00	20.00
A60 Sam Bradford	Jason Smith	25.00	60.00
A61 Anthony Dixon	Rennie Curran	6.00	15.00
A62 Jevan Snead	Mike Williams	10.00	25.00
A63 Colt McCoy	Carlton Mitchell	10.00	25.00
A64 Toby Gerhart	Joe Webb	6.00	15.00
A65 Mark Sanchez	Zac Robinson	20.00	40.00
A66 Clay Matthews	Brian Orakpo	12.00	30.00
A67 Jonathan Dwyer	Antonio Brown	10.00	25.00
A68 Mardy Gilyard	Jason Smith	6.00	15.00
A69 Louis Murphy	Brandon Spikes	6.00	15.00
A70 C.J. Spiller	Joique Bell	10.00	25.00
A71 Jermaine Gresham	Jordan Shipley	8.00	20.00
A72 Hakeem Nicks	Cam Thomas	5.00	12.00
A73 Tony Moeaki	Cameron Sheffield	6.00	15.00
A74 John Skelton	Joique Bell	6.00	15.00
A75 Dennis Pitta	Ryan Mathews	12.00	30.00

A76 Derrick Morgan	5.00	12.00
Rennie Curran		
A77 Mark Sanchez	20.00	40.00
Clay Matthews		
A78 Pat White	8.00	20.00
Jarrett Brown		
A79 Stafon Johnson		
Clay Matthews		
A80 Dan LeFevour	6.00	15.00
Johnny Knox		
A81 Blair White	6.00	15.00
Jordan Shipley		
A82 E.J. Wilson	5.00	12.00
Cam Thomas		
A83 Brian Orakpo	6.00	15.00
Earl Thomas		
A84 Hakeem Nicks	5.00	12.00
E.J. Wilson		
A85 Ben Tate	8.00	20.00
Garrett Graham		
A86 Anthony Dixon	6.00	15.00
Nate Byham		
A87 Chris Cook	6.00	15.00
Joe Webb		
A88 Jahvid Best	25.00	50.00
Matthew Stafford		
A89 Ndamukong Suh	30.00	60.00
Matthew Stafford		
A90 Jonathan Dwyer	25.00	50.00
Colt McCoy		
A91 Blair White	6.00	15.00
Arrelious Benn		
A92 Matt Tennant	5.00	12.00
Eric Olsen		
A93 Tony Moeaki	6.00	15.00
Dennis Pitta		
A94 Joe McKnight	6.00	15.00
Shawn Lauvao		
A95 Toby Gerhart	6.00	15.00
Chris Wells		
A96 Mark Sanchez		
Jimmy Clausen		

1997 Score Board NFL Rookies

The 1997 Score Board NFL Rookies set was issued in one series totaling 100 standard-size cards. The set was issued in 8-card packs with 36 packs in a box and 12 boxes in a case. Among the topical subsets are: All-Americans (94-98) and Checklists (99-100). The key players in this set are Duce Staley, Tony Gonzalez, Jake Plummer, Warrick Dunn and Corey Dillon.

COMPLETE SET (100)	4.00	10.00
1 Jake Plummer	.50	1.25
2 Tony Gonzalez	.50	1.25
3 Trevor Pryce	.07	.20
4 Greg Jones	.01	.05
5 Koy Detmer	.07	.20
6 Rae Carruth	.01	.05
7 Peter Boulware	.07	.20
8 Warrick Dunn	.40	1.00
9 Antowain Smith	.30	.75
10 Troy Davis	.01	.05
11 David LaFleur	.01	.05
12 Yatil Green	.07	.20
13 Michael Booker	.01	.05
14 Shawn Springs	.02	.10
15 Bryant Westbrook	.02	.10
16 Byron Hanspard	.02	.10
17 Darrell Russell	.01	.05
18 Corey Dillon	.50	1.25
19 Tyrus McCloud	.01	.05
20 Reinard Wilson	.02	.10
21 Adam Meadows	.01	.05
22 Tremain Mack	.01	.05
23 Ricky Parker	.01	.05
24 George Jones	.01	.05
25 Terry Battle	.01	.05
26 Will Blackwell	.02	.10
27 Jerald Sowell	.01	.05
28 Isaac Byrd	.07	.20
29 Chris Naeole	.01	.05
30 Kevin Lockett	.02	.10
31 Freddie Jones	.01	.05
32 Pat Barnes	.02	.10
33 Torrian Gray	.01	.05
34 Brian Manning	.01	.05
35 Dedric Ward	.02	.10
36 Pete Monty	.01	.05
37 Sam Madison	.07	.20
38 Sedrick Shaw	.02	.10
39 Mike Logan	.01	.05
40 Albert Connell	.07	.20
41 Canute Curtis	.01	.05
42 Ronde Barber	.10	.30
43 Orlando Pace	.07	.20
44 Ed Perry	.07	.20
45 Tiki Barber	.75	2.00
46 Kevin Jackson	.01	.05
47 Jerry Wunsch	.01	.05
48 Michael Hamilton	.01	.05
49 Darnell Autry	.02	.10
50 Jim Druckenmiller	.02	.10
51 James Farrior	.07	.20
52 Derrick Mason	.25	.60
53 Ty Howard	.01	.05
54 Jason Taylor	.07	.20
55 Reidel Anthony	.07	.20
56 Bertrand Berry	.30	.75
57 Marc Edwards	.02	.10
58 James Hamilton	.01	.05
59 Ike Hilliard	.15	.40
60 Tommy Knight	.01	.05
61 Walter Jones	.07	.20
62 Chad Levitt	.01	.05
63 Pratt Lyons	.01	.05
64 Greg Clark	.01	.05
65 Ryan Phillips	.01	.05
66 Jason Martin	.01	.05
67 Scott Sanderson	.01	.05
68 Al Singleton	.07	.20
69 Duce Staley	.40	1.00
70 Jared Tomich	.01	.05
71 Ross Verba	.01	.05
72 Derrick Rodgers	.01	.05
73 Mike Vrabel	.75	2.00
74 John Allred	.01	.05
75 Bob Sapp	.07	.20
76 Brad Otton	.01	.05
77 Tarik Glenn	.07	.20
78 Chad Scott	.02	.10
79 Nathan Davis	.01	.05
80 Henri Crockett	.01	.05
81 Tarek Saleh	.01	.05
82 Seth Payne	.01	.05
83 Pete Chryplewicz	.01	.05
84 Reidel Anthony AA	.01	.05
85 Reinard Wilson AA	.01	.05
86 Byron Hanspard AA	.02	.10
87 Shawn Springs AA	.01	.05
88 David LaFleur AA	.01	.05
89 Troy Davis AA	.01	.05
90 Warrick Dunn AA	.20	.50
91 Peter Boulware AA	.02	.10
92 Rae Carruth AA	.01	.05
93 Tony Gonzalez AA	.20	.50
94 Jake Plummer AA	.25	.60
95 Orlando Pace AA	.02	.10
96 Ike Hilliard AA	.07	.20
97 Kevin Jackson AA	.01	.05
98 Jim Druckenmiller AA	.02	.10
99 Shawn Springs CL	.01	.05
100 Warrick Dunn CL	.20	.50

1997 Score Board NFL Rookies Dean's List

COMP.DEAN'S LIST (100)	15.00	40.00
*DEAN'S LIST: 1.5X TO 4X BASIC CARDS		
DEAN'S LIST STATED ODDS 1:5		

1997 Score Board NFL Rookies Varsity Club

COMPLETE SET (30)	30.00	80.00
STATED ODDS 1:36		
V1 Tiki Barber	8.00	20.00
V2 Sedrick Shaw	.40	1.00
V3 Kevin Lockett	.40	1.00
V4 Byron Hanspard	.40	1.00
V5 David LaFleur	.20	.50
V6 Warrick Dunn	4.00	10.00
V7 Yatil Green	.75	2.00
V8 Corey Dillon	5.00	12.00
V9 Orlando Pace	.75	2.00
V10 Tony Gonzalez	5.00	12.00
V11 Darrell Russell	.20	.50
V12 Jake Plummer	5.00	12.00
V13 Peter Boulware	.75	2.00
V14 Shawn Springs	.40	1.00
V15 Bryant Westbrook	.40	1.00
V16 Rae Carruth	.20	.50
V17 Antowain Smith	3.00	8.00
V18 Reidel Anthony	.75	2.00
V19 Michael Booker	.20	.50
V20 Freddie Jones	.20	.50
V21 Pat Barnes	.40	1.00
V22 Troy Davis	.20	.50
V23 Walter Jones	.75	2.00
V24 Reinard Wilson	.40	1.00
V25 George Jones	.20	.50
V26 Terry Battle	.20	.50
V27 Tommy Knight	.20	.50
V28 Tremain Mack	.20	.50
V29 Jim Druckenmiller	.40	1.00
V30 Ike Hilliard	1.50	4.00

1997 Score Board NFL Rookies War Room

COMPLETE SET (20)	60.00	150.00
STATED ODDS 1:100		
W1 Yatil Green	1.50	4.00
W2 Antowain Smith	6.00	15.00
W3 Tony Gonzalez	10.00	25.00
W4 Corey Dillon	10.00	25.00
W5 Jake Plummer	10.00	25.00
W6 Peter Boulware	1.50	4.00
W7 Orlando Pace	1.50	4.00
W8 Darrell Russell	.40	1.00
W9 Reinard Wilson	.75	2.00
W10 Shawn Springs	.75	2.00
W11 Bryant Westbrook	.75	2.00
W12 Rae Carruth	.40	1.00
W13 Warrick Dunn	8.00	20.00
W14 David LaFleur	.40	1.00
W15 Byron Hanspard	.75	2.00
W16 Michael Booker	.40	1.00
W17 Reidel Anthony	1.50	4.00
W18 Troy Davis	.40	1.00
W19 Chris Naeole	.40	1.00
W20 Jim Druckenmiller	.75	2.00

1994 Signature Rookies Autograph Promos

These signed cards were released to promote the 1994 Signature Rookies football set. Each card was signed by the featured player and serial numbered with some player's cards hand numbered on the fronts as well.

C1 Perry Klein/5000	2.50	6.00
(silver hologram on back)		
C2 Marvin Goodwin/5000	2.50	6.00
C3 Toddrick McIntosh/5000	2.50	6.00
C4 Bruce Walker/5000	2.50	6.00
(hand serial numbered)		
PR1 Byron Bam Morris/1000	3.00	8.00
(autographed promo card)		

1994 Signature Rookies

These 60 standard-size cards feature borderless color action shots of top NFL prospects in their college uniforms. A wide gold-foil stripe adorns the left side and carries the words "1 of 45,000" or, for the autographed card included in every six-card pack, "Authentic Signature." The player's name and position appear at the bottom. Production was limited to 12,500 numbered boxes. Special subsets include the five-card Charlie Ward set, 2,500 cards of which were hand signed by the Heisman Trophy winner; the five-card "Hottest Prospect" set, 2,000 of which were hand signed by each of the five players; and also sets of Gale Sayers and Tony Dorsett, of which 2,000 and 1,000 cards, respectively, were autographed.

COMPLETE SET (60)	2.00	5.00
1 Sam Adams	.01	.05
2 Trev Alberts	.01	.05
3 Derrick Alexander WR	.15	.40
4 Larry Allen	.15	.40
5 Aubrey Beavers	.01	.05
6 Lou Benfatti	.01	.05
7 James Bostic	.01	.05
8 Tim Bowens	.01	.05
9 Rich Braham	.01	.05
10 Isaac Bruce	1.00	2.50
11 Vaughn Bryant	.01	.05
12 Brentson Buckner	.01	.05
13 Jeff Burris	.01	.05
14 Carlester Crumpler	.01	.05
15 Lake Dawson	.05	.15
16 Tyronne Drakeford	.01	.05
17 Dan Eichloff	.01	.05
18 Rob Fredrickson	.01	.05
19 Gus Frerotte	.50	1.25
20 William Gaines	.01	.05
21 Wayne Gandy	.01	.05
22 Jason Gildon	.05	.15
23 Lemanski Hall	.01	.05
24 Shelby Hill	.01	.05
25 Willie Jackson	.15	.40
26 LeShon Johnson	.01	.05
27 Tre Johnson	.01	.05
28 Alan Kline	.01	.05
29 Darren Krein	.01	.05
30 Antonio Langham	.01	.05
31 Corey Louchiey	.01	.05
32 Keith Lyle	.01	.05
33 Eric Mahlum	.01	.05
34 Van Malone	.01	.05
35 Chris Maumalanga	.01	.05
36 Jamir Miller	.05	.15
37 Jim Miller	.75	2.00
38 Byron Bam Morris	.05	.15
39 Aaron Mundy	.01	.05
40 Jeremy Nunley	.01	.05
41 Turhon O'Bannon	.01	.05
42 Brad Ottis	.01	.05
43 David Palmer	.05	.15
44 Joe Panos	.01	.05
45 Jim Pyne	.01	.05
46 John Reece	.01	.05
47 Errict Rhett	.15	.40
48 Tony Richardson	.05	.15
49 Sam Rogers	.01	.05
50 Tim Ruddy	.01	.05
51 Corey Sawyer	.05	.15
52 Malcolm Seabron	.01	.05
53 Jason Sehorn	.15	.40
54 John Thierry	.01	.05
55 Jason Winrow	.01	.05
56 Ronnie Woolfork	.01	.05
57 Toby Wright	.01	.05
58 Ryan Yarborough	.01	.05
59 Eric Zomalt	.01	.05
60 Checklist	.01	.05

1994 Signature Rookies Autographs

COMPLETE SET (60)	75.00	200.00
STATED PRINT RUN 7750 SETS		
ONE CARD OR COUPON PER PACK		
1 Sam Adams	1.50	4.00
2 Trev Alberts	1.50	4.00
3 Derrick Alexander WR	4.00	10.00
4 Larry Allen	8.00	20.00
5A Aubrey Beavers	1.50	4.00
5B Trent Pollard	1.50	4.00
6 Lou Benfatti	1.50	4.00
7 James Bostic	1.50	4.00
8 Tim Bowens	1.50	4.00
9 Rich Braham	1.50	4.00
10 Isaac Bruce	7.50	15.00
11 Vaughn Bryant	1.50	4.00
12 Brentson Buckner	1.50	4.00
13 Jeff Burris	1.50	4.00
14 Carlester Crumpler	1.50	4.00
15 Lake Dawson	2.50	6.00
16 Tyronne Drakeford	1.50	4.00
17 Dan Eichloff	1.50	4.00
18 Rob Fredrickson	1.50	4.00
19 Gus Frerotte	8.00	20.00
20 William Gaines	1.50	4.00
21 Wayne Gandy	1.50	4.00
22 Jason Gildon	5.00	12.00
23 Lemanski Hall	1.50	4.00
24 Shelby Hill	1.50	4.00
25 Willie Jackson	4.00	10.00
26 LeShon Johnson	1.50	4.00
27 Tre Johnson	1.50	4.00
28 Alan Kline	1.50	4.00
29 Darren Krein	1.50	4.00
30 Antonio Langham	1.50	4.00
31 Corey Louchiey	1.50	4.00
32 Keith Lyle	1.50	4.00
33 Eric Mahlum	1.50	4.00
34 Van Malone	1.50	4.00
35 Chris Maumalanga	1.50	4.00
36 Jamir Miller	2.50	6.00
37 Jim Miller	6.00	15.00
38 Byron Bam Morris	2.50	6.00
39 Aaron Mundy	1.50	4.00
40 Jeremy Nunley	1.50	4.00
41 Turhon O'Bannon	1.50	4.00
42 Brad Ottis	1.50	4.00
43 David Palmer	2.50	6.00
44 Joe Panos	1.50	4.00
45 Jim Pyne	1.50	4.00
46 John Reece	1.50	4.00
47 Errict Rhett	4.00	10.00
48 Tony Richardson	2.50	6.00
49 Sam Rogers	1.50	4.00
50 Tim Ruddy	1.50	4.00
51 Corey Sawyer	2.50	6.00
52 Malcolm Seabron	1.50	4.00
53 Jason Sehorn	5.00	12.00
54 John Thierry	1.50	4.00
55 Jason Winrow	1.50	4.00
56 Ronnie Woolfork	1.50	4.00
57 Toby Wright	1.50	4.00
58 Ryan Yarborough	1.50	4.00
59 Eric Zomalt	1.50	4.00

1994 Signature Rookies Bonus Autographs

COMPLETE SET (10)	15.00	40.00
STATED PRINT RUN 7750 SETS		
1 Jamal Anderson	7.50	20.00
2 Myron Bell	1.25	3.00
3 Mitch Berger	1.25	3.00
4 Jocelyn Borgella	1.25	3.00
5 Brant Boyer	1.25	3.00
6 Chris Brantley	1.25	3.00
7 Ron Edwards	1.25	3.00
8 Rob Holmberg	1.25	3.00
9 Fred Lester	1.25	3.00
10 Joseph Patton	1.25	3.00
11 Trent Pollard/5000	1.25	3.00
12 Eric Ravotti	1.25	3.00
13 Jim Reid	1.25	3.00
14 Jerry Reynolds	1.25	3.00
15 Bracy Walker	1.25	3.00
16 Gabe Wilkins	1.25	3.00

1994 Signature Rookies Tony Dorsett

COMPLETE SET (2)	1.50	4.00
D1 Tony Dorsett	.75	2.00
Holding ball in left hand		
D1A Tony Dorsett Auto/1000	20.00	40.00
D2 Tony Dorsett	.75	2.00
Holding ball in both hands		
D2A Tony Dorsett Auto/1000	20.00	40.00

1994 Signature Rookies Hottest Prospects

COMPLETE SET (5)	2.50	6.00
STATED PRINT RUN 150,000		
*AUTOGRAPHS: 3X TO 6X BASIC INSERTS		
AUTOGRAPH PRINT RUN 2025 SER.#'d SETS		
*SPECIAL OFFER: .4X TO 1X BASIC INSERTS		
A1 Willie McGinest		
A2 Bryant Young	.75	2.00
A3 Dewayne Washington	.40	1.00
A4 Aaron Taylor	.40	1.00
A5 Charles Johnson	.75	2.00

1994 Signature Rookies Gale Sayers

COMPLETE SET (2)	4.00	4.00
COMMON SAYERS (S1-S2)	2.00	2.00
GALE SAYERS AU/1000	12.50	30.00

1994 Signature Rookies Charlie Ward

COMPLETE SET (5)	2.00	4.00
COMMON WARD (C1-C5)	.40	1.00
CHARLIE WARD AU/525	7.50	20.00
*PROMOS: .4X TO 1X BASIC INSERTS		

1995 Signature Rookies Promos 7500

This set of promos was distributed to announce the release of the 1995 Signature Rookies Draft Preview set. Each card includes a gold foil "Promo 1 of 7500" designation on the cardfront.

COMPLETE SET (3)	.80	2.00
FB1 Ki-Jana Carter	.40	1.00
FB2 Rashaan Salaam	.20	.50
FB3 Kevin Carter	.30	.75

1995 Signature Rookies

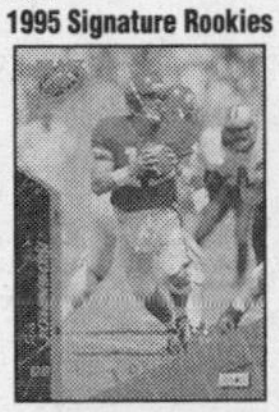

These standard-size six-card packs retailed for $5 and included an autographed card. Each player autographed 7,750 of his own cards, and 39,000 of each card were produced. The fronts display a color action player photo. At the lower left corner, a black marblized stripe outlined in gold foil carries the player's name. The lower right corner has a triangular-shaped green football field design. Edged at the upper right and lower left corners with green grass, the backs show a closeup photo, with a ghosted panel carrying bio and player profile. The cards are numbered in the top right corner. An international version of this set was also issued; in which; players signed 2,750 of their own cards, and 13,500 of each card produced. These cards are similiar to the original set except they are stamped in silver foil with the words international appearing on the card fronts.

COMPLETE SET (80)	5.00	12.00
1 Derrick Alexander DE	.02	.10
2 Kelvin Anderson	.05	.15
3 Antonio Armstrong	.02	.10
4 Jamie Asher	.05	.15
5 Joe Aska	.02	.10
6 Dave Barr	.02	.10
7 Brandon Bennett	.02	.10
8 Tony Berti	.02	.10
9 Mark Birchmeier	.02	.10
10 Tony Boselli	.05	.15
11 Derrick Brooks	.08	.25
12 Anthony Brown	.02	.10
13 Ruben Brown	.08	.25
14 Mark Bruener	.02	.10
15 Ontiwaun Carter	.02	.10
16 Stoney Case	.05	.15
17 Byron Chamberlain	.20	.50
18 Shannon Clavelle	.02	.10
19 Jamal Cox	.02	.10
20 Zack Crockett	.05	.15
21 Terrell Davis	.75	2.00
22 Tyrone Davis	.02	.10
23 Lee DeRamus	.02	.10
24 Ken Dilger	.05	.15
25 Hugh Douglas	.08	.25
26 David Dunn	.02	.10
27 Chad Eaton	.02	.10
28 Hicham El-Mashtoub	.02	.10
29 Christian Fauria	.02	.10
30 Terrell Fletcher	.02	.10
31 Antonio Freeman	.30	.75
32 Eddie Goines	.02	.10
33 Roger Graham	.02	.10
34 Carl Greenwood	.02	.10
35 Ed Hervey	.02	.10
36 Jimmy Hitchcock	.02	.10
37 Darius Holland	.02	.10
38 Torey Hunter	.02	.10
39 Steve Ingram	.02	.10
40 Jack Jackson	.02	.10
41 Trezelle Jenkins	.02	.10
42 Ellis Johnson	.02	.10
43 Eric Johnson RBK	.02	.10
44 Rob Johnson	.15	.40
45 Chris T. Jones	.05	.15
46 Larry Jones	.02	.10
47 Shawn King	.02	.10
48 Scotty Lewis	.02	.10
49 Curtis Martin	.75	2.00
50 Oscar McBride	.02	.10
51 Kez McCorvey	.02	.10
52 Bronzell Miller	.02	.10
53 Pete Mitchell	.02	.10
54 Brent Moss	.02	.10
55 Craig Newsome	.02	.10
56 Herman O'Berry	.02	.10
57 Matt O'Dwyer	.02	.10
58 Tyrone Poole	.08	.25
59 Brian Pruitt	.02	.10
60 Cory Raymer	.02	.10
61 John Sacca	.02	.10
62 Frank Sanders	.08	.25
63 J.J. Smith	.02	.10
64 Brendan Stai	.02	.10
65 Steve Stenstrom	.02	.10
66 James O. Stewart	.30	.75
67 Kordell Stewart	.50	1.25
68 Ben Talley	.02	.10
69 Bobby Taylor	.08	.25
70 Johnny Thomas	.02	.10
71 Orlando Thomas	.02	.10
72 Rodney Thomas	.05	.15
73 Zach Wiegert	.02	.10
74 Jerrott Willard	.02	.10
75 Billy Williams	.02	.10
76 Sherman Williams	.02	.10
77 Jamal Willis	.02	.10
78 Dave Wohlabaugh	.02	.10
79 Eric Zeier	.08	.25
80 Checklist	.02	.10

1995 Signature Rookies International

COMPLETE SET (80)	8.00	20.00
*INTERNATIONALS: .8X TO 2X BASIC CARDS		
STATED PRINT RUN 13,500 SETS		

1995 Signature Rookies Autographs

COMPLETE SET (79)	125.00	250.00
STATED PRINT RUN 7750 SER.#'d SETS		
*INTERNATIONAL: 1X TO 2X BASIC AUTOS		
1 Derrick Alexander DE	1.50	4.00
2 Kelvin Anderson	1.50	4.00
3 Antonio Armstrong	1.50	4.00
4 Jamie Asher	1.50	4.00
5 Joe Aska	1.50	4.00
6 Dave Barr	1.50	4.00
7 Brandon Bennett	1.50	4.00
8 Tony Berti	1.50	4.00
9 Mark Birchmeier	1.50	4.00
10 Tony Boselli	2.00	5.00
11 Derrick Brooks	6.00	15.00
12 Anthony Brown	1.50	4.00
13 Ruben Brown	3.00	8.00
14 Mark Bruener	2.00	5.00
15 Ontiwaun Carter	1.50	4.00
16 Stoney Case	2.00	5.00
17 Byron Chamberlain	3.00	8.00
18 Shannon Clavelle	1.50	4.00
19 Jamal Cox	1.50	4.00
20 Zack Crockett	2.00	5.00
21 Terrell Davis	7.50	20.00
22 Tyrone Davis	1.50	4.00
23 Lee DeRamus	1.50	4.00
24 Ken Dilger	2.00	5.00
25 Hugh Douglas	2.00	5.00
26 David Dunn	1.50	4.00
27 Chad Eaton	1.50	4.00
28 Hicham El-Mashtoub	1.50	4.00
29 Christian Fauria	1.50	4.00
30 Terrell Fletcher	1.50	4.00
31 Antonio Freeman	6.00	15.00
32 Eddie Goines	1.50	4.00
33 Roger Graham	1.50	4.00
34 Carl Greenwood	1.50	4.00
35 Ed Hervey	1.50	4.00
36 Jimmy Hitchcock	1.50	4.00
37 Darius Holland	1.50	4.00
38 Torey Hunter	1.50	4.00
39 Steve Ingram	1.50	4.00
40 Jack Jackson	1.50	4.00
41 Trezelle Jenkins	1.50	4.00
42 Ellis Johnson	1.50	4.00
43 Eric Johnson RBK	1.50	4.00
44 Rob Johnson	5.00	12.00
45 Chris T. Jones	1.50	4.00
46 Larry Jones	1.50	4.00
47 Shawn King	1.50	4.00
48 Scotty Lewis	1.50	4.00
49 Curtis Martin	20.00	40.00
50 Oscar McBride	1.50	4.00
51 Kez McCorvey	1.50	4.00
52 Bronzell Miller	1.50	4.00
53 Pete Mitchell	1.50	4.00
54 Brent Moss	1.50	4.00
55 Craig Newsome	1.50	4.00
56 Herman O'Berry	1.50	4.00
57 Matt O'Dwyer	1.50	4.00
58 Tyrone Poole	3.00	8.00
59 Brian Pruitt	1.50	4.00
60 Cory Raymer	1.50	4.00
61 John Sacca	1.50	4.00
62 Frank Sanders	3.00	8.00
63 J.J. Smith	1.50	4.00
64 Brendan Stai	1.50	4.00
65 Steve Stenstrom	1.50	4.00
66 James O. Stewart	3.00	8.00
67 Kordell Stewart	7.50	20.00
68 Ben Talley	1.50	4.00
69 Bobby Taylor	3.00	8.00
70 Johnny Thomas	1.50	4.00
71 Orlando Thomas	1.50	4.00
72 Rodney Thomas	2.00	5.00
73 Zach Wiegert	1.50	4.00
74 Jerrott Willard	1.50	4.00
75 Billy Williams	1.50	4.00
76 Sherman Williams	1.50	4.00
77 Jamal Willis	1.50	4.00
78 Dave Wohlabaugh	1.50	4.00
79 Eric Zeier	2.00	5.00

1995 Signature Rookies Franchise Rookies

COMPLETE SET (R1-10)	1.50	4.00
OVERALL STATED ODDS 1:8		
*AUTOGRAPHS: 4X TO 10X BASIC INSERTS		
AUTOGRAPH PRINT RUN 2575 SETS		
*INTERNATIONAL: .8X TO 2X BASIC INSERTS		
*SAMPLES: .4X TO 1X BASIC INSERTS		
R1 Kyle Brady	.40	1.00
R2 Kevin Carter	.40	1.00
R3 Ki-Jana Carter	.40	1.00
R4 Luther Elliss	.08	.25
R5 Rashaan Salaam	.20	.50
R6 Warren Sapp	.40	1.00
R7 James A. Stewart	.08	.25
R8 J.J. Stokes	.40	1.00
R9 Michael Westbrook	.40	1.00
R10 Ray Zellars	.08	.25

1995 Signature Rookies International Franchise Duo

COMPLETE SET (10)	6.00	15.00
STATED ODDS 1:8 INTERNATIONAL PACKS		
1 Derrick Alexander DE	.75	2.00
Warren Sapp		
2 Kyle Brady	1.25	3.00
Kerry Collins		
3 Kevin Carter	.75	2.00
Ki-Jana Carter		
4 Ki-Jana Carter	.50	1.25
Rashaan Salaam		
5 Stoney Case	1.00	2.50
Rob Johnson		
6 Kerry Collins	2.00	5.00
Steve McNair		
7 James A. Stewart	1.25	3.00
James O. Stewart		
8 Kordell Stewart	1.25	3.00
Eric Zeier		
9 J.J. Stokes	.75	2.00
Michael Westbrook		
10 Sherman Williams	.30	.75
Ray Zellars		

1995 Signature Rookies International Franchise Duo Autographs

COMPLETE SET (16)	100.00	200.00
RANDOM INSERTS IN INTERNATIONAL PACKS		
1 Derrick Alexander AU/200	2.50	6.00
2 Kyle Brady AU/242	6.00	15.00
3 Kevin Carter AU/315	6.00	15.00
4 Ki-Jana Carter AU/400	4.00	10.00
5 Stoney Case AU/200	4.00	10.00
6 Kerry Collins AU/600	7.50	20.00
7 Rob Johnson AU/309	10.00	25.00
8 Steve McNair AU/300	25.00	50.00
9 Rashaan Salaam AU/299	4.00	10.00
10 Kordell Stewart AU/309	12.50	30.00
11 James O. Stewart AU/200	12.50	30.00
12 J.J. Stokes AU/284	6.00	15.00
13 M. Westbrook AU/282	6.00	15.00
14 Sherman Williams AU/312	2.50	6.00
15 Eric Zeier AU/314	4.00	10.00
16 Ray Zellars AU/310	2.50	6.00

1995 Signature Rookies Masters Of The Mic

COMPLETE SET (5)	1.25	3.00
STATED ODDS 1:4		
STATED PRINT RUN 30,000 SETS		
*INTERNATIONALS: .8X TO 2X BASIC CARDS		
M1 Todd Christensen	.25	.60
M2 Jerry Glanville	.25	.60
M3 Howie Long	.30	.75
M4 Dick Stockton	.25	.60
M5 Joe Theismann UER	.30	.75

1995 Signature Rookies Masters Of The Mic Autographs

COMPLETE SET (5)	15.00	30.00
STATED PRINT RUN 1030 SETS		
OVERALL STATED ODDS 1:4		
M1 Todd Christensen	2.00	5.00
M2 Jerry Glanville	2.00	5.00
M3 Howie Long	12.00	30.00
M4 Dick Stockton	2.00	5.00
M5 Joe Theismann UER	8.00	20.00

1995 Signature Rookies Old Judge Previews

COMPLETE SET (5)	4.00	10.00
OVERALL STATED ODDS 1:24		
STATED PRINT RUN 5000 SETS		
1 Blake Brockermeyer	.50	1.25
2 Kerry Collins	1.50	4.00
3 Steve McNair	2.50	6.00
4 J.J. O'Laughlin	.50	1.25
5 John Walsh	.50	1.25

1995 Signature Rookies Old Judge Previews Autographs

COMPLETE SET (5)	50.00	100.00
STATED PRINT RUN 515 SETS		
OVERALL STATED ODDS 1:24		
1 Blake Brockermeyer	6.00	15.00
2 Kerry Collins	15.00	40.00
3A Steve McNair/515	25.00	60.00
3B Steve McNair	25.00	60.00
4 J.J. O'Laughlin	6.00	15.00
5 John Walsh	6.00	15.00

1996 Signature Rookies Autobilia

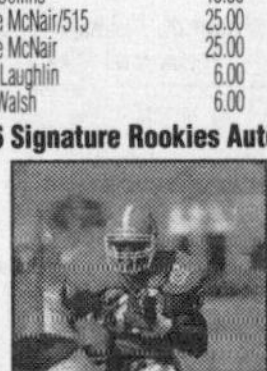

This 55 card standard-size set was issued by Signature Rookies The fronts feature a player photo as well as the words "Autobilia" on the front. The back has vital statistics, seasonal and career information as well as another player photo. Rookies from the 1995 season as well as those for the upcoming 1996 season are featured in this set.

COMPLETE SET (55)	6.00	15.00
1 Ruben Brown	.02	.10
2 Kevin Carter	.07	.20
3 Ki-Jana Carter	.07	.20
4 Stoney Case	.02	.10
5 Kerry Collins	.25	.60
6 Terrell Davis	.50	1.25
7 Antonio Freeman	.25	.60
8 Joey Galloway	.20	.50
9 Darick Holmes	.02	.10
10 Jack Jackson	.02	.10
11 Curtis Martin	.30	.75
12 O.J. McDuffie	.15	.40
13 Steve McNair	.30	.75
14 Byron Bam Morris	.02	.10
15 Craig Newsome	.02	.10
16 Errict Rhett	.07	.20
17 Rashaan Salaam	.07	.20
18 Frank Sanders	.15	.40
19 James O. Stewart	.25	.60
20 Kordell Stewart	.30	.75
21 J.J. Stokes	.15	.40
22 Rodney Thomas	.02	.10
23 Tamarick Vanover	.07	.20
24 Michael Westbrook	.15	.40
25 Sherman Williams	.02	.10
26 Eric Zeier	.15	.40
27 Karim Abdul-Jabbar	.25	.60
28 Mike Alstott	.60	1.50
29 Willie Anderson	.02	.10
30 Tony Banks	.15	.40
31 Marco Battaglia	.02	.10
32 Tim Biakabutuka	.15	.40
33 Stephen Davis	.75	2.00
34 Chris Doering	.02	.10
35 Daryl Gardener	.02	.10
36 Eddie George	1.00	2.50
37 Terry Glenn	.25	.60
38 Randall Godfrey	.02	.10
39 Marvin Harrison	1.25	3.00
40 Aaron Hayden	.02	.10
41 Mercury Hayes	.02	.10
42 Dietrich Jells	.07	.20
43 Cedric Jones	.02	.10
44 Jeff Lewis	.07	.20
45 Derrick Mayes	.15	.40
46 Leland McElroy	.07	.20
47 Jerald Moore	.02	.10
48 Eric Moulds	.60	1.50
49 Kendrick Nord	.02	.10
50 Stanley Pritchett	.02	.10
51 Jon Stark	.02	.10
52 Steve Taneyhill	.02	.10
53 Amani Toomer	.40	1.00
54 Stepfret Williams	.02	.10
55 Checklist	.02	.10

1996 Signature Rookies Autobilia Club Set Autographs

COMPLETE SET (5)	30.00	80.00
ISSUED VIA MAIL PROMOTION		
STATED PRINT RUN 500 SER.#'d SETS		
6 Terrell Davis	12.50	30.00
12 O.J. McDuffie	5.00	12.00
32 Tim Biakabutuka	5.00	12.00
36 Eddie George	12.50	30.00
46 Leeland McElroy	5.00	12.00

1995 Signature Rookies Auto-Phonex Bonus Promos

These cards look very similar to the base Auto-Phonex phone cards except for the words "Bonus Promo" under the Signatures Rookies logo on the card fronts. Each was numbered with a BP prefix as well.

BP2 Derrick Alexander DE	.30	.75
BP11 Ki-Jana Carter	.40	1.00
BP13 Sherman Williams	.30	.75
BP16 Rashaan Salaam	.40	1.00

1995 Signature Rookies Auto-Phonex Phone Card Promos

There were a number of different promo/sample phone cards issued for the 1995 Signature Rookie Tetrad Auto-Phonex product. We've listed below all known versions, any additions to the list are appreciated.

2 Kevin Carter $25	.40	1.00
(reads Sample on back)		
3 Ki-Jana Carter $5/1000	.75	2.00
(reads Promo on front)		
4 Ki-Jana Carter $1000	.80	2.00
(reads Sample on back)		
5 Rashaan Salaam Promo	.40	1.00
(1 of 10,000)		
6 J.J. Stokes $5	1.20	3.00
(reads Sample on back)		

1995 Signature Rookies Auto-Phonex

These 40 standard-size cards feature 1995 NFL Draft picks. The fronts feature triple-exposure color action player photos. The player's name in gold-foil letters appears on a marbleized background above the photo, while "1 of 19,000" is printed on the bottom. The horizontal backs carry another color action player photo with biography and stats. Four hundred and ninety-nine 16-box cases of the product were produced. Each pack contained five regular base cards and one calling card worth either $2.00, $5.00, or $25.00 in phone time. Every case of Auto-Phonex contained randomly inserted Hot Packs, which included an autographed phone card and five additional autographed cards.

COMPLETE SET (40)	3.00	6.00
1 Warren Sapp	.25	.60
2 Kevin Carter	.08	.25
3 Ki-Jana Carter	.08	.25
4 J.J.Stokes	.08	.25
5 Derrick Alexander DE	.01	.05
6 Rashaan Salaam	.02	.10
7 Jamal Willis	.01	.05
8 Frank Sanders	.08	.25
9 Rob Johnson	.20	.50
10 Derrick Brooks	.08	.25
11 Sherman Williams	.01	.05
12 Dave Barr	.01	.05
13 Christian Fauria	.01	.05
14 Stoney Case	.02	.10
15 Rodney Thomas	.02	.10
16 James A. Stewart	.01	.05
17 Ray Zellars	.02	.10
18 Jack Jackson	.01	.05
19 Terrell Davis	.50	1.25
20 Kyle Brady	.08	.25
21 Ruben Brown	.08	.25
22 Brent Moss	.01	.05
23 John Sacca	.01	.05
24 David Dunn	.01	.05
25 Eddie Goines	.01	.05
26 Curtis Martin	.50	1.25
27 Billy Williams	.01	.05
28 Steve Stenstrom	.01	.05
29 Mark Bruener	.01	.05
30 Kelvin Anderson	.08	.25
31 Ellis Johnson	.01	.05
32 Steve Ingram	.01	.05
33 Larry Jones	.01	.05
34 Bobby Taylor	.08	.25
35 Joe Aska	.01	.05
36 Jerrott Willard	.01	.05
37 Chris T. Jones	.01	.05
38 Mark Birchmeier	.01	.05
39 Jimmy Hitchcock	.01	.05
40 Tyrone Davis	.01	.05
NNO Rashaan Salaam CL	.02	.10
(phone card checklist)		
NNO Ki-Jana Carter CL	.02	.10
(base set checkist)		

1995 Signature Rookies Auto-Phonex Autographs

COMPLETE SET (10)	40.00	80.00
FIVE AUTOGRAPHS PER HOT PACK		
STATED PRINT RUN 300 SER.#'d SETS		
3A Ki-Jana Carter	6.00	15.00
6A Rashaan Salaam	3.00	8.00
8A Frank Sanders	6.00	15.00
11A Sherman Williams	2.50	6.00
12A Dave Barr	2.50	6.00
14A Stoney Case	3.00	8.00
16A James A.Stewart	2.50	6.00
17A Ray Zellars	3.00	8.00
20A Kyle Brady	3.00	8.00
23A John Sacca	2.50	6.00

1995 Signature Rookies Auto-Phonex Phone Cards

COMPLETE SET (40)	4.00	10.00
*SINGLES: .6X TO 1.5X BASE CARD HI		
ONE PHONE CARD PER PACK		
STATED PRINT RUN 3750 SER.#'d SETS		
NNO J.J. Stokes/500 $5 PC	1.50	4.00
NNO Kevin Carter/100 $25 PC	4.00	10.00
NNO Warren Sapp $100		
NNO Ki-Jana Carter $1000		
NNO Rashaan Salaam $1000		

1995 Signature Rookies Auto-Phonex Phone Card Autographs

COMPLETE SET (40)	60.00	120.00
STATED PRINT RUN 3750 SER.#'d SETS		
1 Warren Sapp	6.00	15.00
2 Kevin Carter	4.00	8.00
3 Ki-Jana Carter	4.00	8.00
4 J.J.Stokes	4.00	8.00
5 Derrick Alexander DE	1.25	3.00
6 Rashaan Salaam	2.00	5.00
7 Jamal Willis	1.25	3.00
8 Frank Sanders	4.00	8.00
9 Eric Zeier	2.00	5.00
10 Derrick Brooks	2.00	5.00
11 Sherman Williams	1.25	3.00
12 Dave Barr	1.25	3.00
13 Christian Fauria	1.25	3.00
14 Stoney Case	2.00	5.00
15 Rodney Thomas	2.00	5.00
16 James A. Stewart	1.25	3.00
17 Ray Zellars	2.00	5.00
18 Jack Jackson	1.25	3.00
19 Terrell Davis	10.00	25.00
20 Kyle Brady	4.00	8.00
21 Ruben Brown	4.00	8.00
22 Brent Moss	1.25	3.00
23 John Sacca	1.25	3.00
24 David Dunn	1.25	3.00
25 Eddie Goines	1.25	3.00
26 Curtis Martin	20.00	40.00
27 Billy Williams	1.25	3.00
28 Steve Stenstrom	1.25	3.00
29 Mark Bruener	1.25	3.00
30 Kelvin Anderson	1.25	3.00
31 Ellis Johnson	1.25	3.00
32 Steve Ingram	1.25	3.00
33 Larry Jones	1.25	3.00
34 Bobby Taylor	4.00	8.00
35 Joe Aska	1.25	3.00
36 Jerrott Willard	1.25	3.00
37 Chris T. Jones	1.25	3.00
38 Mark Birchmeier	1.25	3.00
39 Jimmy Hitchcock	1.25	3.00
40 Tyrone Davis	1.25	3.00

1994 Signature Rookies Gold Standard

This multi-sport set consists of 100 standard-size cards. The fronts feature color action players photos with a circular gold foil seal at the upper left corner. The player's name appears on a diagonal black stripe edged by yellow. The horizontal backs carry a narrowly-cropped closeup photo and, on a ghosted panel, biography and player profile. The set is subdivided according to sport as follows: basketball (1-25), football (26-50), baseball (51-75), and hockey (76-100). Each sport is sequenced in alphabetical order.

COMPLETE SET (100)	5.00	12.00
26 Sam Adams	.07	.20
27 Trev Alberts	.07	.20
28 Derrick Alexander	.10	.30
29 Mitch Berger	.07	.20
30 Tim Bowens	.07	.20
31 Jeff Burris	.07	.20
32 Shante Carver	.07	.20
33 Lake Dawson	.07	.20
34 Marshall Faulk	.75	2.00
35 Glenn Foley	.07	.20
36 Rob Fredrickson	.07	.20
37 Wayne Gandy	.07	.20
38 Charles Johnson FB	.10	.30
39 Tre Johnson	.07	.20
40 Perry Klein	.07	.20
41 Antonio Langham	.10	.30
42 Eric Mahlum	.07	.20
43 Willie McGinest	.20	.50
44 Jamir Miller	.07	.20
45 Byron Bam Morris	.07	.20
46 Errict Rhett	.10	.30
47 John Thierry	.07	.20
48 Dewayne Washington	.08	.25
49 Dan Wilkinson	.07	.20
50 Bernard Williams	.07	.20

1994 Signature Rookies Gold Standard Facsimile

COMPLETE SET (20)	5.00	12.00
GS1 Marshall Faulk	1.25	3.00
GS2 Josh Booty	.20	.50
GS5 Sam Adams	.30	.75
GS13 Willie McGinest	.40	1.00
GS15 Perry Klein	.30	.75
GS17 Dan Wilkinson	.30	.75

1994 Signature Rookies Gold Standard HOF

COMPLETE SET (24)	8.00	20.00
STATED PRINT RUN 20,000 SETS		
ISSUED VIA MAIL REDEMPTION		
HOF9 Otto Graham	1.00	2.50
HOF10 Jack Ham	.60	1.50
HOF13 Paul Hornung	.75	2.00
HOF14 Sam Huff	.60	1.50
HOF16 Bob Lilly	.60	1.50
HOF17 Don Maynard	.50	1.25
HOF18 Ray Nitschke	.75	2.00
HOF21 Y.A.Tittle	.75	2.00
HOF23 Paul Warfield	.75	2.00
HOF24 Randy White	.75	2.00

1994 Signature Rookies Gold Standard HOF Autographs

9 Otto Graham	20.00	50.00
10 Jack Ham	15.00	30.00
13 Paul Hornung	15.00	40.00
14 Sam Huff	10.00	25.00
16 Bob Lilly	8.00	20.00
17 Don Maynard	6.00	15.00
18 Ray Nitschke	30.00	60.00
21 Y.A.Tittle	15.00	30.00
23 Paul Warfield	10.00	25.00
24 Randy White	10.00	25.00

1994 Signature Rookies Gold Standard Promos

COMPLETE SET (5)	.75	2.00
ANNOUNCED PRINT RUN 10000		
P3 Willie McGinest	.20	.50

1995 Signature Rookies Fame and Fortune

The 1995 Fame and Fortune set was issued in one series totalling 100 cards and featured NBA and NFL draft picks. Cards were distributed in eight-card packs. Five insert card sets were produced with the set and include Collector's Pick, Top 5, Erstad, Star Squad and #1 Pick. The first 48 cards are basketball draft picks and the remaining 52 are football picks. Fronts have full-color action cutout photos with a black background with either a football or basketball. The player's first name is printed in gold foil horizontally while his last name is printed twice vertically in both gold foil and a larger green type on the left side. Backs have another action shot that is seprated with a color screen process. Backs include college statistics, a short biography and a player profile.

COMPLETE SET (100)	5.00	12.00
49 Derrick Alexander DE	.07	.20
50 Joe Aska	.07	.20
51 Dave Barr	.07	.20
52 Tony Boselli	.08	.25
53 Kyle Brady	.07	.20
54 Derrick Brooks	.25	.60
55 Ruben Brown	.07	.20
56 Mark Bruener	.07	.20
57 Kevin Carter	.08	.25
58 Ki-Jana Carter	.08	.25
59 Stoney Case	.07	.20
60 Kerry Collins	.50	1.25
61 Terrell Davis	1.00	2.50
62 Tyrone Davis	.07	.20
63 Hugh Douglas	.08	.25
64 David Dunn	.07	.20
65 Luther Elliss	.07	.20
66 Christian Fauria	.07	.20
67 Mark Fields	.07	.20
68 Joey Galloway	.15	.40
69 Eddie Goines	.07	.20
70 Jimmy Hitchcock	.07	.20
71 Stephen Ingram	.07	.20
72 Jack Jackson	.07	.20
73 Ellis Johnson	.07	.20
74 Chris T. Jones	.07	.20
75 Larry Jones	.07	.20
76 Mike Mamula	.07	.20
77 Curtis Martin	.60	1.50
78 Steve McNair	.60	1.50
79 Brent Moss	.07	.20
80 Craig Newsome	.07	.20
81 Tyrone Poole	.07	.20
82 Rashaan Salaam	.08	.25
83 Frank Sanders	.08	.25
84 Warren Sapp	.20	.50
85 J.J. Smith	.07	.20
86 Steve Stenstrom	.07	.20
87 James A. Stewart	.07	.20
88 James O. Stewart	.20	.50
89 J.J. Stokes	.08	.25
90 Bobby Taylor	.15	.40
91 Rodney Thomas	.08	.25
92 John Walsh	.07	.20
93 Michael Westbrook	.10	.30
94 Zach Wiegert	.07	.20
95 Jerrott Willard	.07	.20
96 Billy Williams	.07	.20
97 Sherman Williams	.07	.20
98 Jamal Willis	.07	.20
99 Eric Zeier	.08	.25
100 Ray Zellars	.08	.25

1995 Signature Rookies Fame and Fortune #1 Pick

COMPLETE SET (5)	1.00	2.50
P2 Ki-Jana Carter	.20	.50
P5 Brian Berard	.30	.75
K-Jana Carter		
Darin Erstad		
Joe Smith		

1995 Signature Rookies Fame and Fortune Collectors Pick

COMPLETE SET (100)	4.00	10.00
B1 Kerry Collins	1.00	2.50
B5 Rashaan Salaam	.30	.75
B6 Warren Sapp	.60	1.50
B9 J.J. Stokes	.30	.75

1995 Signature Rookies Fame and Fortune Darin Erstad

COMMON CARD	.75	2.00

1995 Signature Rookies Fame and Fortune Red Hot Rookies

COMPLTE SET (10)	5.00	12.00
R1 Curtis Martin	1.25	3.00
R3 Terrell Davis	1.50	4.00
R5 Joey Galloway	.40	1.00
R7 Rashaan Salaam	.20	.50
R9 Kerry Collins	.60	1.50

1995 Signature Rookies Fame and Fortune Star Squad

COMPLETE SET (5)	1.50	4.00
S1 Ki-Jana Carter	.20	.50
S2 Kerry Collins	.40	1.00
S3 Steve McNair	1.00	2.50
S4 J.J. Stokes	.20	.50
S5 Eric Zeier	.20	.50

1995 Signature Rookies Peripheral Vision

COMPLETE SET (5)	1.50	3.00
STATED PRINT RUN 5000 SETS		
OVERALL STATED ODDS 1:24		
*INTERNATIONAL: .8X TO 2X BASIC INSERTS		
*SAMPLES: .4X TO 1X BASIC INSERTS		
V1 Rashaan Salaam	.30	.75
V2 Rashaan Salaam	.30	.75
V3 Ki-Jana Carter	.30	.75
V4 Ki-Jana Carter	.30	.75
V5 Ki-Jana Carter	.30	.75
Rashaan Salaam		

1995 Signature Rookies Peripheral Vision Autographs

COMPLETE SET (5)	100.00	200.00
OVERALL STATED ODDS 1:24		
STATED PRINT RUN 105 SETS		
V1 Rashaan Salaam	15.00	40.00
V2 Rashaan Salaam	15.00	40.00
V3 Ki-Jana Carter	15.00	40.00
V4 Ki-Jana Carter	15.00	40.00
V5 Ki-Jana Carter	25.00	60.00
Rashaan Salaam		

1995 Signature Rookies Signature Prime Previews

COMPLETE SET (5)	5.00	8.00
1 Ki-Jana Carter	.50	1.25
2 Kyle Brady	.30	.75
3 J.J. Stokes	.75	2.00
4 Rashaan Salaam	.50	1.25
5 Steve McNair	1.25	5.00

1995 Signature Rookies Signature Prime

This 50-card standard-size set features color player action shots on the fronts. Each player autographed 3,000 of his own cards. These photos are borderless and carries the player's name in gold lettering in a red stripe that appears on the left side of the card. The red stripe starts with the Signature Prime logo and ends with the Signature Rookies logo. The back carries an additional photograph of the player, his position and college stats.

COMPLETE SET (50)	5.00	12.00
1 Justin Armour	.05	.15
2 Joe Aska	.05	.15
3 Henry Bailey	.05	.15
4 Jay Barker	.05	.15
5 Dave Barr	.05	.15
6 Kevin Bouie	.05	.15
7 Mark Bruener	.08	.25
8 Stoney Case	.08	.25
9 Curtis Ceaser	.05	.15
10 Todd Collins QB	.60	1.50
11 Jerry Colquitt	.05	.15
12 Terrell Davis	1.00	2.50
13 David Dunn	.05	.15
14 Omar Ellison	.05	.15
15 Christian Fauria	.05	.15
16 Antonio Freeman	.50	1.25
17 Eddie Goines	.05	.15
18 Aaron Hayden	.05	.15
19 William Henderson	.15	.40
20 Kevin Hickman	.05	.15
21 Jack Jackson	.05	.15
22 Travis Jervey	.05	.15
23 Rob Johnson	.40	1.00
24 Chris T. Jones	.08	.25
25 Larry Jones	.05	.15
26 Curtis Marsh	.05	.15
27 Curtis Martin	1.00	2.50
28 Fred McCrary	.05	.15
29 Mike Miller	.05	.15
30 Shannon Myers	.05	.15
31 Jimmy Oliver	.05	.15
32 Dino Philyaw	.05	.15
33 Lovell Pinkney	.05	.15
34 Michael Roan	.05	.15
35 Chris Sanders	.15	.40
36 Frank Sanders	.15	.40
37 Cory Schlesinger	.08	.25
38 Charlie Simmons	.05	.15
39 David Sloan	.05	.15
40 Steve Stenstrom	.05	.15
41 James A. Stewart	.05	.15
42 Rodney Thomas	.08	.25
43 A.C. Tellison	.05	.15
44 Tamarick Vanover	.08	.25
45 John Walsh	.05	.15
46 Kendell Watkins	.05	.15
47 Charles Way	.08	.25
48 Craig Whelihan	.08	.25
49 Eric Zeier	.15	.40
50 Ray Zellars	.08	.25
NNO Checklist Card	.05	.15
P1 J.J. Stokes Promo	.20	.50

1995 Signature Rookies Signature Prime Autographs

STATED PRINT RUN 3000 SER.#'d SETS		
ONE AUTOGRAPH PER PACK		
1 Justin Armour	2.50	6.00
2 Joe Aska	1.50	4.00
3 Henry Bailey	1.50	4.00
4 Jay Barker	1.50	4.00
5 Dave Barr	1.50	4.00
6 Kevin Bouie	1.50	4.00
7 Mark Bruener	2.50	6.00
8 Stoney Case	2.50	6.00
9 Curtis Ceaser	1.50	4.00
10 Todd Collins QB	5.00	12.00
11 Jerry Colquitt	1.50	4.00
12 Terrell Davis	10.00	25.00
13 David Dunn	1.50	4.00
14 Omar Ellison	1.50	4.00
15 Christian Fauria	4.00	10.00
16 Antonio Freeman	6.00	15.00
17 Eddie Goines	1.50	4.00
18 Aaron Hayden	2.50	6.00
19 William Henderson	7.50	20.00
20 Kevin Hickman	1.50	4.00
21 Jack Jackson	1.50	4.00
22 Travis Jervey	1.50	4.00
23 Rob Johnson	5.00	12.00
24 Chris T. Jones	1.50	4.00
25 Larry Jones	1.50	4.00
26 Curtis Marsh	1.50	4.00
27 Curtis Martin	12.00	30.00
28 Fred McCrary	1.50	4.00
29 Mike Miller	1.50	4.00
30 Shannon Myers	1.50	4.00
31 Jimmy Oliver	1.50	4.00
32 Dino Philyaw	1.50	4.00
33 Lovell Pinkney	1.50	4.00
34 Michael Roan	1.50	4.00
35 Chris Sanders	2.50	6.00
36 Frank Sanders	4.00	10.00
37 Cory Schlesinger	4.00	10.00
38 Charlie Simmons	1.50	4.00
39 David Sloan	1.50	4.00
40 Steve Stenstrom	2.50	6.00
41 James A. Stewart	1.50	4.00
42 Rodney Thomas	2.50	6.00
43 A.C. Tellison	1.50	4.00
44 Tamarick Vanover	2.50	6.00
45 John Walsh	1.50	4.00
46 Kendell Watkins	1.50	4.00
47 Charles Way	2.50	6.00
48 Craig Whelihan	2.50	6.00
49 Eric Zeier	4.00	10.00
50 Ray Zellars	1.50	4.00

1995 Signature Rookies Signature Prime TD Club

COMPLETE SET (10)	3.00	8.00
ONE PER PACK		
OVERALL PRINT RUN 15,000 SETS		
*PREVIEWS: .4X TO 1X BASIC INSERTS		
T1 Kyle Brady	.20	.50
T2 Ki-Jana Carter	.20	.50
T3 Kerry Collins	.60	1.50
T4 Joey Galloway	.50	1.25
T5 Steve McNair	1.00	2.50
T6 Rashaan Salaam	.05	.15
T7 James O. Stewart	.60	1.50
T8 J.J. Stokes	.20	.50
T9 Michael Westbrook	.20	.50
T10 Sherman Williams	.05	.15

1995 Signature Rookies Signature Prime TD Club Autographs

COMPLETE SET (10)	60.00	120.00
STATED PRINT RUN 1000 SER.#'d SETS		
T1 Kyle Brady	4.00	10.00
T2 Ki-Jana Carter	5.00	12.00
T3 Kerry Collins	10.00	25.00
T4 Joey Galloway	6.00	15.00
T5 Steve McNair	12.50	30.00
T6 Rashaan Salaam	4.00	10.00
T7 James O. Stewart	5.00	12.00
T8 J.J. Stokes	4.00	10.00
T9 Michael Westbrook	5.00	12.00
T10 Sherman Williams	3.00	8.00

1995 Signature Rookies Club Promos

S1 Josh Booty	.40	1.00
S2 Ki-Jana Carter	.50	1.25

1995 Signature Rookies Sports Slammers Stackers

Printed on 18-point card stock, this set of 40 stackers and 5 slammers POGs combines football and basketball stars in a game. Each pack contained five sports stackers as well as one rule card.

1 Dave Barr FB	.15	.40
2 Charlie Garner FB	.20	.50
4 James A. Stewart FB	.15	.40
5 Gus Frerotte FB	.30	.75
6 Michael Westbrook FB	.20	.50
7 Ki-Jana Carter FB	.20	.50
10 Tim Bowens FB	.15	.40
11 Kevin Carter FB	.15	.40
13 Rashaan Salaam FB	.30	.75
14 Byron Bam Morris FB	.15	.40
15 Sherman Williams FB	.15	.40
16 Warren Sapp FB	.60	1.50
17 Kyle Brady FB	.20	.50
18 William Floyd FB	.20	.50
19 Rodney Thomas FB	.20	.50
21 Tim Bowens FB	.15	.40
22 Sherman Williams FB	.15	.40
23 Gus Frerotte FB	.30	.75
25 Kyle Brady FB	.20	.50
26 James A. Stewart FB	.15	.40
29 William Floyd FB	.20	.50
30 Michael Westbrook FB	.20	.50
32 Dave Barr FB	.15	.40
33 Byron Bam Morris FB	.15	.40
34 Charlie Garner FB	.20	.50
35 Kevin Carter FB	.15	.40
37 Rodney Thomas FB	.20	.50
38 Ki-Jana Carter FB	.30	.75
39 Warren Sapp FB	.60	1.50
40 Rashaan Salaam FB	.30	.75
S1 Warren Sapp FB Squasher	.75	2.00
S2 Kyle Brady FB Bruiser	.30	.75
S4 Byron Bam Morris FB Bammer	.30	.75

1994 Signature Rookies Tetrad

These 120 standard-size cards feature borderless color player action shots on their fronts. The player's name appears in gold-foil lettering near the bottom. The words "1 of 45,000" appear in vertical gold-foil lettering within a simulated marble column near the left edge. The cards of this four-sport set are numbered on the back in Roman numerals and organized as follows: Football (1-40), Basketball (41-83), Baseball (84-103), and Hockey (104-118).

COMPLETE SET (120)	3.00	8.00
1 Jay Walker	.07	.20
2 Ricky Brady	.07	.20
3 Paul Duckworth	.07	.20
4 Jim Flanigan	.07	.20
5 Brice Adams	.07	.20
6 William Floyd	.10	.30
7 Charlie Garner	.20	.50
8 Pete Bercich	.07	.20
9 Frank Harvey	.07	.20
10 Willie Clark	.07	.20
11 Bernard Williams	.07	.20
12 Kurt Haws	.07	.20
13 Dennis Collier	.07	.20
14 Filmel Johnson	.07	.20
15 Zane Beehn	.07	.20
16 Johnnie Morton	.20	.50
17 Lonnie Johnson	.07	.20
18 Jay Kearney	.07	.20
19 Steve Shine	.07	.20
20 Dexter Nottage	.07	.20
21 Ervin Collier	.07	.20
22 Dorsey Levens	.20	.50
23 Kevin Knox	.07	.20
24 Doug Nussmeier	.07	.20
25 Bill Schroeder	.20	.50
26 Winfred Tubbs	.07	.20
27 Rodney Harrison	.07	.20
28 Rob Waldrop	.07	.20
29 Mike Davis	.07	.20
30 John Burke	.07	.20
31 Allen Aldridge	.07	.20
32 Kevin Mitchell	.07	.20
33 Greg Hill	.10	.30
34 Ernest Jones	.07	.20
35 Kevin Mawae	.10	.30
36 John Covington	.07	.20
37 Mike Wells	.07	.20
38 Thomas Lewis	.07	.20
39 Chad Bratzke	.07	.20
40 Darren Studstill	.07	.20

1994 Signature Rookies Tetrad Autographs

1 Jay Walker	1.50	4.00
2 Ricky Brady	1.50	4.00
3 Paul Duckworth	1.50	4.00
4 Jim Flanigan	1.50	4.00
5 Brice Adams	1.50	4.00
6 William Floyd	2.50	6.00
7 Charlie Garner	3.00	8.00
8 Pete Bercich	1.50	4.00
9 Frank Harvey	1.50	4.00
10 Willie Clark	1.50	4.00
12 Kurt Haws	1.50	4.00
13 Dennis Collier	1.50	4.00
14 Filmel Johnson	1.50	4.00
15 Zane Beehn	1.50	4.00
16 Johnnie Morton	3.00	8.00
17 Lonnie Johnson	1.50	4.00
18 Jay Kearney	1.50	4.00
19 Steve Shine	1.50	4.00
20 Dexter Nottage	1.50	4.00
21 Ervin Collier	1.50	4.00
22 Dorsey Levens	3.00	8.00
23 Kevin Knox	1.50	4.00
24 Doug Nussmeier	1.50	4.00
25 Bill Schroeder	4.00	10.00
26 Winfred Tubbs	1.50	4.00
27 Rodney Harrison	6.00	15.00
28 Rob Waldrop	1.50	4.00
29 Mike Davis	1.50	4.00
30 John Burke	1.50	4.00
31 Allen Aldridge	2.00	5.00
32 Kevin Mitchell	1.50	4.00
33 Greg Hill	2.50	6.00
34 Ernest Jones	1.50	4.00
35 Kevin Mawae	2.50	6.00
36 John Covington	1.50	4.00
37 Mike Wells	1.50	4.00
38 Thomas Lewis	1.50	4.00
39 Chad Bratzke	1.50	4.00
40 Darren Studstill	1.50	4.00

1994 Signature Rookies Tetrad Flip Cards

COMPLETE SET (5)	10.00	25.00
1 Charles Johnson BB Charles Johnson FB	1.25	3.00
2 Tony Dorsett Gale Sayers	3.00	8.00
3 Charlie Ward BK Charlie Ward FB	2.00	5.00

1994 Signature Rookies Tetrad Flip Cards Autographs

AU1 Charles Johnson BB/275	2.00	5.00
AU3 Charlie Ward FB BK/275	6.00	15.00

1994 Signature Rookies Tetrad Previews

COMPLETE SET (7)	1.25	3.00
T6 O.J. Simpson	.60	1.50

1994 Signature Rookies Tetrad Titans

COMPLETE SET (12)	3.00	8.00
129 O.J. Simpson UER (Misnumbered T6)	.40	1.00

1994 Signature Rookies Tetrad Titans Autographs

COMPLETE SET (12)	125.00	250.00
129 O.J. Simpson/2500	20.00	50.00

1994 Signature Rookies Tetrad Top Prospects

COMPLETE SET (4)	1.00	2.50
132 Willie McGinest	.30	.75
133 Shante Carver	.20	.50

1994 Signature Rookies Tetrad Top Prospects Autographs

132A Willie McGinest	4.00	10.00
133A Shante Carver/2025	2.00	5.00

1995 Signature Rookies Tetrad

This 76-card standard-size set features borderless fronts with color action player photos. The named player stands out on a faded background with his name printed in gold below. The backs carry an elongated color action player photo on one side while a head photo, biographical information, position, college, and career statistics round out the backs.

COMPLETE SET (76)	5.00	12.00
1 Kevin Carter	.15	.40
2 Ruben Brown	.08	.25
3 Kyle Brady	.07	.20
4 Tony Boselli	.08	.25
5 Derrick Alexander	.05	.15
6 Mike Mamula	.05	.15
7 Ellis Johnson	.05	.15
8 Mark Fields	.08	.25
9 Luther Elliss	.05	.15
10 Hugh Douglas	.05	.15
51 James O. Stewart	.40	1.00
52 Rashaan Salaam	.08	.25
53 Tyrone Poole	.15	.40
54 Craig Newsome	.05	.15
55 Devin Bush	.05	.15
P3 Kyle Brady Promo	.30	.75

1995 Signature Rookies Tetrad Autographs

SIGS NUMBERED OUT OF 5000		
1 Kevin Carter	1.50	4.00
2 Ruben Brown	1.25	3.00
3 Kyle Brady	1.50	4.00
4 Tony Boselli	2.50	6.00
5 Derrick Alexander	1.50	4.00
6 Mike Mamula	1.25	3.00
7 Ellis Johnson	1.25	3.00
8 Mark Fields	1.25	3.00
9 Luther Ellis	1.25	3.00
10 Hugh Douglas	1.50	4.00
51 James O. Stewart	3.00	8.00
52 Rashaan Salaam	1.50	4.00
53 Tyrone Poole	2.00	5.00
54 Craig Newsome	1.25	3.00
55 Devin Bush	1.25	3.00

1995 Signature Rookies Tetrad Mail-In

This five-card standard size set was available through the mail from Signature Rookies. The set highlights the 1995 first overall draft picks in basketball, football, baseball and hockey. The fronts picture color action photos blended with a fractal-swirling design. In a gold foil stamp, the players name is found vertically on the right, "Mail In" and "#1 Pick" adorn the top and bottom respectively on the left. The back has another color action photo in the upper-right corner. The rest is devoted to a player biography and statistics set on top of the same fractal-swirling design. The cards are numbered with a "P" prefix (P1-P5).

COMPLETE SET (5)	1.50	4.00
P2 Ki-Jana Carter	.40	1.00
P5 Joe Smith	.60	1.50
Ki-Jana Carter		
Darin Erstad		
Bryan Berard		

1995 Signature Rookies Tetrad Previews

COMPLETE SET (5)	1.00	2.50
5 Ki-Jana Carter	.20	.50

1995 Signature Rookies Tetrad SR Force

COMPLETE SET (35)	6.00	15.00
F26 Ki-Jana Carter	.15	.40
F27 Joey Galloway	.20	.50
F28 Michael Westbrook	.15	.40
F29 J.J. Stokes	.20	.50
F30 Eric Zeier	.10	.30
F31 Errict Rhett	.15	.40
F32 Steve McNair	.75	2.00
F33 Kerry Collins	.20	.50
F34 Stoney Case	.10	.30
F35 Mark Bruener	.10	.30

1995 Signature Rookies Tetrad SR Force Autographs

RANDOM INSERTS IN PACKS		
F26 Ki-Jana Carter	1.50	4.00
F27 Joey Galloway	4.00	10.00
F28 Michael Westbrook	2.00	5.00
F29 J.J. Stokes	1.50	4.00
F30 Eric Zeier	1.25	3.00
F31 Errict Rhett	1.50	4.00
F32 Steve McNair	10.00	25.00
F33 Kerry Collins	6.00	15.00
F34 Stoney Case	1.25	3.00
F35 Mark Bruener	1.25	3.00

1995 Signature Rookies Tetrad Titans

COMPLETE SET (5)	2.00	5.00
T5 Bob Griese	.60	1.50

1995 Signature Rookies Tetrad Titans Autographs

T5 Bob Griese	10.00	25.00

1995 Signature Rookies Tetrad Autobilia

The 1995 Signature Rookies Tetrad Autobilia set was issued in one series with a total of 100 cards. The fronts feature a color action player cut-out on a background of a repeated action player photo with the player's name printed in a gold bar at the bottom. The words" Club Set" are printed in gold foil on the fronts as well. The backs carry two player photos with the player's name, position, biographical information, career statistics, and a player fact.

COMPLETE SET (100)	10.00	25.00
*SILVER: .4X TO 1X GOLD		
55 Dave Barr	.08	.25
56 Brandon Bennett	.08	.25
57 Kyle Brady	.10	.30
58 Kevin Carter	.30	.75
59 Terrell Davis	1.25	3.00
60 Luther Ellis	.08	.25
61 Jack Jackson	.08	.25
62 Frank Sanders	.15	.40
63 Ki-Jana Carter	.15	.40
64 Steve Stenstrom	.08	.25
65 James A. Stewart	.08	.25
66 James O. Stewart	.40	1.00
67 Bobby Taylor	.15	.40
68 Michael Westbrook	.15	.40
69 Rashaan Salaam	.15	.40
70 Ray Zellars	.08	.25
75 J.J. Stokes	.15	.40
76 Sherman Williams	.08	.25
80 Kerry Collins	.50	1.25
81 Joey Galloway	.30	.75
82 Steve McNair	.60	1.50
83 Errict Rhett	.10	.30
84 Eric Zeier	.10	.30

1995 Signature Rookies Tetrad Autobilia Auto-Phonex Test

This 3-card set was issued in packs of 1995 Signature Rookies Autobilia packs. Each card follows a similar design to the base cards except for the addition of the words 'Auto-Phonex Test Issue' on the left hand side of the cardfronts. The title 'Autobilia' at the top was also replaced with the word Tetrad.

COMPLETE SET (3)	1.25	3.00
T2 Ki-Jana Carter	.40	1.00

1995 Signature Rookies Tetrad Autobilia Autographed Cards

55 Dave Barr	1.25	3.00
56 Brandon Bennett	1.25	3.00
57 Kyle Brady	1.50	4.00
58 Kevin Carter	2.50	6.00
59 Terrell Davis	12.00	30.00
60 Luther Ellis	1.25	3.00
61 Jack Jackson	1.25	3.00
62 Frank Sanders	1.25	3.00
63 Ki-Jana Carter	2.00	5.00
64 Steve Stenstrom	1.25	3.00
65 James A. Stewart	1.25	3.00
66 James O. Stewart	4.00	10.00
67 Bobby Taylor	2.50	6.00
68 Michael Westbrook	2.50	6.00
69 Rashaan Salaam	2.00	5.00
70 Ray Zellars	1.25	3.00
75 J.J. Stokes	1.50	4.00
76 Sherman Williams	1.50	4.00
80 Kerry Collins	6.00	15.00
81 Joey Galloway	4.00	10.00
82 Steve McNair	10.00	25.00
83 Errict Rhett	1.50	4.00
84 Eric Zeier	1.50	4.00

1995 Signature Rookies Tetrad Autobilia Autographed Photos

ANNOUNCED PRINT RUN 3000		
55 Dave Barr	1.25	3.00
56 Brandon Bennett	1.25	3.00
57 Kyle Brady	1.50	4.00
58 Kevin Carter	2.50	6.00
59 Terrell Davis	12.00	30.00
60 Luther Ellis	1.25	3.00
61 Jack Jackson	1.25	3.00
62 Frank Sanders	1.25	3.00
63 Ki-Jana Carter	2.00	5.00
64 Steve Stenstrom	1.25	3.00
65 James A. Stewart	1.25	3.00
66 James O. Stewart	4.00	10.00
67 Bobby Taylor	2.50	6.00
68 Michael Westbrook	2.50	6.00
69 Rashaan Salaam	2.00	5.00
70 Ray Zellars	1.25	3.00
75 J.J. Stokes	1.50	4.00
76 Sherman Williams	1.50	4.00
80 Kerry Collins	6.00	15.00
81 Joey Galloway	4.00	10.00
82 Steve McNair	10.00	25.00
83 Errict Rhett	1.50	4.00
84 Eric Zeier	1.50	4.00

1991 Star Pics Promos

These promo cards measure the standard size and preview the 1991 Star Pics football set. The cards were distributed in two-card panels with Aaron Craver paired with Mark Carrier and Dan McGwire paired with Eric Turner. These promos were quite plentiful because they were also bound into the Pro Football Weekly annual football preview publication.

COMPLETE SET (4)	.80	2.00
1 Mark Carrier DB	.20	.50
2 Aaron Craver	.20	.50
3 Dan McGwire	.20	.50
4 Eric Turner	.20	.50

1991 Star Pics

This 112-card standard-size set features on the front an action color photo enclosed by a thin white border against a background of footballs. The player's name appears in white print on a maroon-colored box below the picture. The back has a full-color posed photo in the upper left hand corner and the card number (enclosed in a red star) in the upper right hand corner. The biographical information, including accomplishments, strengths, and weaknesses, is printed on a pale green diagram of a football field with a diagrammed play. The set also includes player agents and flashback cards of top young players. Autographed cards were inserted in some of the sets on a random basis. The key players in this set are Brett Favre, Herman Moore, and Ricky Watters.

COMP.FACT.SET (113)	3.00	8.00
1 1991 NFL Draft Overview	.01	.05
2 Barry Sanders FLB	.40	1.00
3 Nick Bell	.01	.05
4 Kelvin Pritchett	.01	.05
5 Huey Richardson	.01	.05
6 Mike Croel	.01	.05
7 Paul Justin	.02	.10
8 Ivory Lee Brown	.01	.05
9 Herman Moore	.08	.25
10 Derrick Thomas FLB	.08	.25
11 Keith Traylor	.01	.05
12 Joe Johnson	.01	.05
13 Dan McGwire	.01	.05
14 Harvey Williams	.02	.10
15 Eric Moten	.01	.05
16 Steve Zucker	.01	.05
17 Randal Hill	.01	.05
18 Browning Nagle	.01	.05
19 Stan Thomas	.01	.05
20 Emmitt Smith FLB	.75	2.00
21 Ted Washington	.01	.05
22 Lamar Rogers	.01	.05
23 Kenny Walker	.01	.05
24 Howard Griffith	.01	.05
25 Reggie Johnson	.01	.05
26 Lawrence Dawsey	.01	.05
27 Joe Garten	.01	.05
28 Moe Gardner	.01	.05
29 Michael Stonebreaker	.01	.05
30 Jeff George FLB	.02	.10
31 Leigh Steinberg	.01	.05
32 John Flannery	.01	.05
33 Pat Harlow	.01	.05
34 Kanavis McGhee	.01	.05
35 Mike Dumas	.01	.05
36 Godfrey Myles	.01	.05
37 Shawn Moore	.01	.05
38 Jeff Graham	.02	.10
39 Ricky Watters	.25	.60
40 Andre Ware	.02	.10
41 Henry Jones	.01	.05
42 Eric Turner	.01	.05
43 Bob Woolf	.01	.05
44 Randy Baldwin	.01	.05
45 Mo Lewis	.01	.05
46 Jerry Evans	.01	.05
47 Derek Russell	.01	.05
48 Merton Hanks	.02	.10
49 Kevin Donnalley	.01	.05
50 Troy Aikman FLB	.30	.75
51 William Thomas	.02	.10
52 Chris Thome	.01	.05
53 Ricky Ervins	.01	.05
54 Jake Reed	.08	.25
55 Jerome Henderson	.01	.05
56 Mark Vander Poel	.01	.05
57 Bernard Ellison	.01	.05
58 Jack Mills	.01	.05
59 Jarrod Bunch	.01	.05
60 Mark Carrier DB	.01	.05
61 Rocen Keeton	.01	.05
62 Louis Riddick	.01	.05
63 Bobby Wilson	.01	.05
64 Steve Jackson	.01	.05
65 Brett Favre	1.25	3.00
66 Ernie Mills	.02	.10
67 Joe Valerio	.01	.05
68 Chris Smith	.01	.05
69 Ralph Cindrich	.01	.05
70 Christian Okoye	.02	.10
71 Charles McRae	.01	.05
72 Jon Vaughn	.01	.05
73 Eric Swann	.02	.10
74 Bill Musgrave	.01	.05
75 Eric Bieniemy	.01	.05
76 Pat Tyrance	.01	.05
77 Vinnie Clark	.01	.05
78 Eugene Williams	.01	.05
79 Rob Carpenter	.01	.05
80 Deion Sanders FLB	.08	.25
81 Roman Phifer	.01	.05
82 Greg Lewis	.01	.05
83 John Johnson	.01	.05
84 Richard Howell	.01	.05
85 Jesse Campbell	.01	.05
86 Stanley Richard	.01	.05
87 Alfred Williams	.01	.05
88 Mike Pritchard	.02	.10
89 Mel Agee	.01	.05
90 Aaron Craver	.01	.05
91 Tim Barnett	.01	.05
92 Wesley Carroll	.02	.10
93 Kevin Scott	.01	.05
94 Darren Lewis	.01	.05
95 Tim Bruton	.01	.05
96 Tim James	.01	.05
97 Darryll Lewis	.01	.05
98 Shawn Jefferson	.08	.25
99 Mitch Donahue	.01	.05
100 Marvin Demoff	.01	.05
101 Adrian Cooper	.01	.05
102 Bruce Pickens	.01	.05
103 Scott Zolak	.01	.05
104 Phil Hansen	.01	.05
105 Ed King	.01	.05
106 Mike Jones DE	.01	.05
107 Alvin Harper	.02	.10
108 Robert Young	.01	.05

109 Favre Bell Harp McRae	.40	1.00
110 Defensive Prospects Mike Croel Eric Swann Eric Turner	.02	.10
111 Checklist 1	.01	.05
112 Checklist 2	.01	.05
NNO Salute Advertisement American Flag background	.01	.05

1991 Star Pics Autographs

RANDOM INSERTS IN FACTORY SETS

2 Barry Sanders FLB	50.00	120.00
3 Nick Bell	2.00	5.00
4 Kelvin Pritchett	2.00	5.00
5 Huey Richardson	2.00	5.00
6 Mike Croel	3.00	8.00
7 Paul Justin	3.00	8.00
8 Ivory Lee Brown	2.00	5.00
9 Herman Moore	6.00	15.00
11 Keith Traylor	2.00	5.00
12 Joe Johnson	2.00	5.00
13 Dan McGwire	3.00	8.00
14 Harvey Williams	3.00	8.00
15 Eric Moten	2.00	5.00
16 Steve Zucker	2.00	5.00
17 Randal Hill	3.00	8.00
18 Browning Nagle	2.00	5.00
19 Stan Thomas	2.00	5.00
20 Emmitt Smith FLB	60.00	150.00
21 Ted Washington	2.00	5.00
22 Lamar Rogers	2.00	5.00
23 Kenny Walker	2.00	5.00
24 Howard Griffith	3.00	8.00
25 Reggie Johnson	2.00	5.00
26 Lawrence Dawsey	2.00	5.00
27 Joe Garten	2.00	5.00
28 Moe Gardner	2.00	5.00
29 Michael Stonebreaker	2.00	5.00
30 Jeff George FLB	6.00	15.00
32 John Flannery	2.00	5.00
33 Pat Harlow	2.00	5.00
34 Kanavis McGhee	2.00	5.00
35 Mike Dumas	2.00	5.00
36 Godfrey Myles	2.00	5.00
37 Shawn Moore	2.00	5.00
38 Jeff Graham	3.00	8.00
39 Ricky Watters	10.00	25.00
40 Andre Ware	3.00	8.00
41 Henry Jones	3.00	8.00
42 Eric Turner	3.00	8.00
43 Bob Woolf	2.00	5.00
44 Randy Baldwin	2.00	5.00
45 Mo Lewis	2.00	5.00
46 Jerry Evans	2.00	5.00
47 Derek Russell	2.00	5.00
48 Merton Hanks	3.00	8.00
49 Kevin Donnalley	2.00	5.00
50 Troy Aikman FLB	50.00	120.00
51 William Thomas	3.00	8.00
52 Chris Thome	2.00	5.00
53 Ricky Ervins	3.00	8.00
54 Jake Reed	6.00	15.00
55 Jerome Henderson	2.00	5.00
56 Mark Vander Poel	2.00	5.00
57 Bernard Ellison	2.00	5.00
58 Jack Mills	2.00	5.00
59 Jarrod Bunch	2.00	5.00
60 Mark Carrier DB	2.00	5.00
61 Rocen Keeton	2.00	5.00
62 Louis Riddick	2.00	5.00
63 Bobby Wilson	2.00	5.00
64 Steve Jackson	2.00	5.00
65 Brett Favre	75.00	150.00
66 Ernie Mills	3.00	8.00
67 Joe Valerio	2.00	5.00
68 Chris Smith	2.00	5.00
69 Ralph Cindrich	2.00	5.00
70 Christian Okoye	3.00	8.00
71 Charles McRae	2.00	5.00
72 Jon Vaughn	2.00	5.00
73 Eric Swann	3.00	8.00
74 Bill Musgrave	2.00	5.00
75 Eric Bieniemy	3.00	8.00
76 Pat Tyrance	2.00	5.00
77 Vinnie Clark	2.00	5.00
78 Eugene Williams	2.00	5.00
79 Rob Carpenter	2.00	5.00
81 Roman Phifer	2.00	5.00
82 Greg Lewis	3.00	8.00
83 John Johnson	2.00	5.00
84 Richard Howell	2.00	5.00
85 Jesse Campbell	2.00	5.00
86 Stanley Richard	2.00	5.00
87 Alfred Williams	2.00	5.00
88 Mike Pritchard	3.00	8.00
89 Mel Agee	2.00	5.00
90 Aaron Craver	2.00	5.00
91 Tim Barnett	2.00	5.00
92 Wesley Carroll	3.00	8.00
93 Kevin Scott	2.00	5.00
94 Darren Lewis	2.00	5.00
95 Tim Bruton	2.00	5.00
96 Tim James	2.00	5.00
97 Darryll Lewis	2.00	5.00
98 Shawn Jefferson	6.00	15.00
99 Mitch Donahue	2.00	5.00
100 Marvin Demoff	2.00	5.00
101 Adrian Cooper	2.00	5.00
102 Bruce Pickens	2.00	5.00
103 Scott Zolak	2.00	5.00
104 Phil Hansen	3.00	8.00
105 Ed King	2.00	5.00
106 Mike Jones DE	2.00	5.00
107 Alvin Harper	3.00	8.00
108 Robert Young	2.00	5.00

1992 Star Pics

This 100-card standard-size set highlights more than 80 of the top college prospects in the country. The set was available in ten-card foil StarPaks and factory sets, with randomly inserted autograph cards in both. It was reported that the production run did not exceed 195,000 factory sets and 12,000 ten-box foil cases. The fronts feature glossy color action photos bordered in white. A color stripe runs the length of the card on the right side, and the player's position and name are printed vertically. The Star Pics logo is superimposed at the lower right corner. The backs present an in-depth scouting report (accomplishments, strengths, and weaknesses), biographical information, and a color head shot in a circular format at the lower right corner. The five-card Flashback subset (10, 20, 30, 50, 70) displays illustrations by sports artist Scott Medlock. The StarStat subset, ten cards in all, compares the top pro prospects' stats to the collegiate stats of NFL greats; two of these were included in each set and eight others were randomly inserted in the foil packs. Autographed cards were inserted in sets and wax on a random basis.

COMPLETE SET (100)	2.00	5.00
COMP.FACT SET (100)	2.00	5.00
1 Steve Emtman SS	.02	.10
2 Chris Hakel	.02	.10
3 Phillippi Sparks	.02	.10
4 Howard Dinkins	.02	.10
5 Robert Brooks	.30	.75
6 Chris Pedersen	.02	.10
7 Bucky Richardson	.02	.10
8 Keith Goganious	.02	.10
9 Robert Porcher	.15	.40
10 Andre Rison FLB	.08	.25
11 Jason Hanson	.08	.25
12 Tommy Vardell	.08	.25
13 Kurt Barber	.02	.10
14 Bernard Dafney	.02	.10
15 Levon Kirkland	.02	.10
16 Corey Widmer	.02	.10
17 Santana Dotson	.08	.25
18 Chris Holder	.02	.10
19 Elbert Turner	.08	.25
20 Mike Croel	.08	.25
21 Darren Perry	.02	.10
22 Troy Vincent	.08	.25
23 Quentin Coryatt	.08	.25
24 John Brown III	.02	.10
25 John Ray	.02	.10
26 Vaughn Dunbar	.02	.10
27 Stacey Dillard	.02	.10
28 Alonzo Spellman	.08	.25
29 Darren Woodson	.15	.40
30 Pat Swilling FLB	.02	.10
31 Eddie Robinson	.02	.10
32 Tyji Armstrong	.02	.10
33 Bill Johnson	.02	.10
34 Eugene Chung	.02	.10
35 Ricardo McDonald	.02	.10
36 Sean Lumpkin	.02	.10
37 Greg Skrepenak	.02	.10
38 Ashley Ambrose	.15	.40
39 Kevin Smith	.02	.10
40 Todd Collins LB	.02	.10
41 Shane Dronett	.02	.10
42 Ronnie West	.02	.10
43 Darryl Williams	.02	.10
44 Rodney Blackshear	.02	.10
45 Dion Lambert	.02	.10
46 Mike Saunders	.20	.50
47 Keo Coleman	.02	.10
48 Dana Hall	.02	.10
49 Arthur Marshall	.02	.10
50 Leonard Russell	.02	.10
51 Matt Rodgers	.02	.10
52 Shane Collins	.02	.10
53 Courtney Hawkins	.08	.25
54 Chuck Smith	.02	.10
55 Joe Bowden	.02	.10
56 Gene McGuire	.02	.10
57 Tracy Scroggins	.02	.10
58 Mark D'Onofrio	.02	.10
59 Jimmy Smith	1.00	2.50
60 Carl Pickens	.20	.50
61 Robert Harris	.02	.10
62 Erick Anderson	.02	.10
63 Doug Rigby	.02	.10
64 Keith Hamilton	.08	.25
65 Vaughn Dunbar	.02	.10
66 Willie Clay	.02	.10
67 Robert Jones	.02	.10
68 Leon Searcy	.02	.10
69 Elliot Pilton	.02	.10
70 Thurman Thomas FLB	.15	.40
71 Mark Wheeler	.02	.10
72 Jeremy Lincoln	.02	.10
73 Tony McCoy	.02	.10
74 Charles Davenport	.02	.10
75 Patrick Rowe	.02	.10
76 Tommy Jeter	.02	.10
77 Rod Smith DB	.02	.10
78 Johnny Mitchell	.02	.10
79 Corey Barlow	.02	.10
80 Scottie Graham	.08	.25
81 Mark Bounds	.02	.10
82 Chester McGlockton	.02	.10
83 Ray Roberts	.02	.10
84 Dale Carter	.08	.25
85 James Patton	.02	.10
86 Tyrone Legette	.02	.10
87 Leodis Flowers	.02	.10
88 Rico Smith	.02	.10
89 Kevin Turner	.02	.10
90 Steve Emtman	.02	.10
91 Rodney Culver	.02	.10
92 Chris Mims	.02	.10
93 Carlos Snow	.02	.10
94 Corey Harris	.02	.10
95 Nate Williams	.02	.10
96 Timothy Roberts	.02	.10
97 Steve Israel	.02	.10
98 Tony Smith WR	.02	.10
99 Dwayne Sabb	.02	.10
100 Checklist	.02	.10
NNO Steve Emtman BC	.15	.40

1992 Star Pics StarStats

COMPLETE SET (8)	2.50	6.00
SS1 Dale Carter	.20	.50
SS2 Carl Pickens	.40	1.00
SS3 Alonzo Spellman	.20	.50
SS4 Jimmy Smith	2.00	5.00
SS5 Quentin Coryatt	.20	.50
SS6 Troy Vincent	.20	.50
SS7 Darryl Williams	.07	.20
SS8 Courtney Hawkins	.20	.50

1994 Superior Rookies Side Line Promos

These two promo cards measure the standard size and feature white-bordered color action shots of the players in their college uniforms. The player's name, the set's title, and a football icon appear within a brownish marbleized bar near the bottom. Aside from the "Promotional Card" disclaimer printed diagonally within a ghosted gray football, the backs are blank. The cards are unnumbered and checklisted below in alphabetical order. The company was previously named Goal Line and Side Line. Both cards can be found with either company name on the cardfronts.

COMPLETE SET (4)	1.60	4.00
1A Rick Mirer Goal Line card	.40	1.00
1B Rick Mirer Side Line Card	.40	1.00
2A Charlie Ward Goal Line card	.50	1.25
2B Charlie Ward Side Line Card	.50	1.25

1994 Superior Rookies

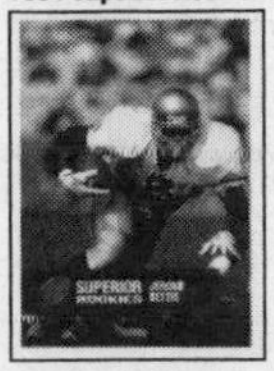

These 80 standard-size cards were issued by Superior Rookies. The white bordered fronts carry color action shots of NFL rookies in their college uniforms. The player's name, set name, and a football icon appear in a color marbleized bar near the bottom. Over a ghosted player photo, the white-bordered back carries the player's name, biography, career highlights, and statistics. The production figures are given as "1 of 26,730". Just 9,900 boxes were produced. Each case included 144 autographed cards and 144 gold foil-stamped cards. The first 300 two-case orders received an individually numbered autographed Jerome Bettis card.

COMPLETE SET (80)	2.50	6.00
1 Rick Mirer FLB	.05	.15
2 Jerome Bettis	.40	1.00
3 Reggie Brooks	.05	.15
4 Trent Pollard	.01	.05
5 Willie Clark	.01	.05
6 Tim Ruddy	.01	.05
7 Lindsey Chapman	.01	.05
8 Van Malone	.01	.05
9 Jeff Burris	.01	.05
10 Charles Johnson	.10	.30
11 Brice Adams	.01	.05
12 Steve Shine	.01	.05
13 Brentson Buckner	.01	.05
14 Marty Moore	.10	.30
15 Ryan Yarborough	.01	.05
16 Aaron Taylor	.01	.05
17 Charlie Ward	.30	.75
18 Aubrey Beavers	.01	.05
19 Zane Beehn	.01	.05
20 Johnnie Morton	.40	1.00
21 Jeremy Nunley	.01	.05
22 Bucky Brooks	.01	.05
23 Dewayne Washington	.01	.05
24 Mario Bates	.05	.15
25 David Palmer	.10	.30
26 Kevin Mawae	.10	.30
27 Chris Brantley	.01	.05
28 Bruce Walker	.01	.05
29 Jamir Miller	.05	.15
30 Thomas Lewis	.01	.05
31 Chad Bratzke	.01	.05
32 Anthony Phillips	.01	.05
33 Errict Rhett	.10	.30
34 Tre Johnson	.01	.05
35 Perry Klein	.01	.05
36 Tyronne Drakeford	.01	.05
37 Bernard Williams	.01	.05
38 Carlester Crumpler	.01	.05
39 Myron Bell	.01	.05
40 Greg Hill	.10	.30
41 James Burton	.01	.05
42 Lloyd Hill	.01	.05
43 Antonio Langham	.01	.05
44 Jim Flanigan	.01	.05
45 Byron Bam Morris	.05	.15
46 Brad Ottis	.01	.05
47 Wayne Gandy	.01	.05
48 Rob Holmberg	.01	.05
49 Bryant Young	.20	.50
50 William Floyd	.05	.15
51 Kevin Mitchell	.01	.05
52 Ervin Collier	.01	.05
53 Winfred Tubbs	.01	.05
54 Mark Montgomery	.01	.05
55 Willie McGinest	.10	.30
56 Jim Miller	.75	2.00
57 Doug Nussmeier	.01	.05
58 Joe Panos	.01	.05
59 Sam Adams	.01	.05
60 Derrick Alexander WR	.10	.30
61 Pete Bercich	.01	.05
62 Eric Ravotti	.01	.05
63 Eric Mahlum	.01	.05
64 Corey Louchiey	.01	.05
65 Lake Dawson	.05	.15
66 Rob Fredrickson	.05	.15
67 Sam Rogers	.01	.05
68 John Covington	.01	.05
69 Larry Allen	.10	.30
70 LeShon Johnson	.01	.05
71 Jerry Reynolds	.01	.05
72 Eric Zomalt	.01	.05
73 Gus Frerotte	.50	1.25
74 Jason Winrow	.01	.05
75 Corey Sawyer	.05	.15
76 Malcolm Seabron	.01	.05
77 Cory Fleming	.01	.05
78 Chris Maumalanga	.01	.05
79 Chris Penn	.01	.05
80 Checklist	.01	.05

1994 Superior Rookies Gold

COMP.GOLD SET (80)	10.00	25.00
*GOLD STARS: 1.5X TO 4X BASIC CARDS		
ONE PER PACK		

1994 Superior Rookies Autographs

COMPLETE SET (79)	75.00	150.00
ONE CARD OR COUPON PER PACK		
1 Rick Mirer FLB/1000	3.00	8.00
2 Jerome Bettis FLB/1000	30.00	60.00
3 Reggie Brooks FLB/1000	1.25	3.00
4 Trent Pollard/6000	.75	2.00
5 Willie Clark/5000	.75	2.00
6 Tim Ruddy/5000	.75	2.00
7 Lindsey Chapman/6000	.75	2.00
8 Van Malone/5000	.75	2.00
9 Jeff Burris/4000	.75	2.00
10 Charles Johnson/5000	2.50	6.00
11 Brice Adams/6000	.75	2.00
12 Steve Shine/6000	.75	2.00
13 Brentson Buckner/4000	.75	2.00
14 Marty Moore/6000	2.50	6.00
15 Ryan Yarborough/5000	.75	2.00
16 Aaron Taylor/4000	.75	2.00
17 Charlie Ward/4000	3.00	8.00
18 Aubrey Beavers/5000	.75	2.00
19 Zane Beehn/6000	.75	2.00
20 Johnnie Morton/4000	6.00	15.00
21 Jeremy Nunley/5000	.75	2.00
22 Bucky Brooks/5000	.75	2.00
23 Dewayne Washington/4000	.75	2.00
24 Mario Bates/5000	1.25	3.00
25 David Palmer/4000	1.25	3.00
26 Kevin Mawae/5000	2.50	6.00
27 Chris Brantley/5000	.75	2.00
28 Bruce Walker/5000	.75	2.00
29 Jamir Miller/4000	.75	2.00
30 Thomas Lewis/5000	.75	2.00
31 Chad Bratzke/6000	.75	2.00
32 Anthony Phillips/5000	.75	2.00
33 Errict Rhett/5000	2.50	6.00
34 Tre Johnson/4000	.75	2.00
35 Perry Klein/5000	.75	2.00
36 Tyronne Drakeford/5000	.75	2.00
37 Bernard Williams/4000	.75	2.00
38 Carlester Crumpler/6000	.75	2.00
39 Myron Bell/6000	.75	2.00
40 Greg Hill/5000	1.25	3.00
41 James Burton/6000	.75	2.00
42 Lloyd Hill/5000	.75	2.00
43 Antonio Langham/4000	.75	2.00
44 Jim Flanigan/5000	.75	2.00
45 Byron Bam Morris/5000	1.25	3.00
46 Brad Ottis/5000	.75	2.00
47 Wayne Gandy/4000	.75	2.00
48 Rob Holmberg/6000	.75	2.00
49 Bryant Young/4000	6.00	15.00
50 William Floyd/5000	.75	2.00
51 Kevin Mitchell/5000	.75	2.00
52 Ervin Collier/5000	.75	2.00
53 Winfred Tubbs/5000	.75	2.00
54 Mark Montgomery/6000	.75	2.00
55 Willie McGinest/4000	4.00	10.00
56 Jim Miller/5000	5.00	12.00
57 Doug Nussmeier/6000	.75	2.00
58 Joe Panos/6000	.75	2.00
59 Sam Adams/5000	.75	2.00
60 Derrick Alexander WR/5000	2.50	6.00
61 Pete Bercich/6000	.75	2.00
62 Eric Ravotti/6000	.75	2.00
63 Eric Mahlum/4000	.75	2.00
64 Corey Louchiey/5000	.75	2.00
65 Lake Dawson/5000	1.25	3.00
66 Rob Fredrickson/4000	.75	2.00
67 Sam Rogers/5000	.75	2.00
68 John Covington/6000	.75	2.00
69 Larry Allen/5000	6.00	15.00
70 LeShon Johnson/5000	.75	2.00
71 Jerry Reynolds/6000	.75	2.00
72 Eric Zomalt/5000	.75	2.00
73 Gus Frerotte/5000	6.00	15.00
74 Jason Winrow/6000	.75	2.00
75 Corey Sawyer/6000	1.25	3.00
76 Malcolm Seabron/5000	.75	2.00
77 Cory Fleming/5000	.75	2.00
78 Chris Maumalanga/5000	.75	2.00
79 Chris Penn/6000	.75	2.00

1994 Superior Rookies Deep Threat

COMPLETE SET (5)	2.50	6.00
ONE CARD PER 10 WRAPPERS VIA MAIL		
*SAMPLE CARDS: SAME PRICE		
1 Charles Johnson	.50	1.25
2 Johnnie Morton	1.50	4.00
3 Derrick Alexander WR	.50	1.25
4 David Palmer	.50	1.25
5 Thomas Lewis	.07	.20

1994 Superior Rookies Instant Impact

COMPLETE SET (10)	5.00	12.00
STATED ODDS 1:12		
1 Rick Mirer	.30	.75
2 Jerome Bettis	2.00	5.00
3 Reggie Brooks	.30	.75
4 Charlie Ward	1.25	3.00
5 Willie McGinest	.60	1.50
6 Greg Hill	.60	1.50
7 William Floyd	.30	.75
8 Bryant Young	1.00	2.50
9 Errict Rhett	.60	1.50
10 Sam Adams	.08	.25

1995 Superior Pix Promos

This 4-card set was issued to preview the 1995 Superior Pix Draft series. The set was mailed out as well as distributed at the National Sports Collectors Convention in St. Louis (July 24-30, 1995). The fronts display full-bleed color action photos, with the player's name in a red variegated diagonal bar across the bottom. A second diagonal bar carries the manufacturer's name. Two versions exist for each of the four-cards. The first release included a write-up about each player on the cardback, while the second version was released at The National and features The National logo. The backs carry a head shot and the National Convention logo.

COMPLETE SET (4)	1.60	4.00
*NATIONAL PROMOS: SAME PRICE		
1 Steve McNair	.50	1.25
2 Kerry Collins	.40	1.00
3 Tyrone Wheatley	.30	.75
4 Joey Galloway	.40	1.00

1995 Superior Pix

These standard-size cards came in eight-card packs with an autographed card in each pack. Each player autographed a number of his own cards. The fronts display a color action player photo with the words '95 Draft in gold foil in either at the top right of left hand corner of the card. The players name and the Superior Pix logo appear on two stripes that appear at an angle across the bottom of the card. The backs includes a box with a head shot photo of the player at the top left hand corner followed by some facts and history on the player.

COMPLETE SET (110)	5.00	12.00
1 Ki-Jana Carter	.08	.25
2 Tony Boselli	.02	.10
3 Steve McNair	.60	1.50
4 Michael Westbrook	.08	.25
5 Kerry Collins	.40	1.00
6 Terrell Davis	.60	1.50
7 Kevin Bouie	.01	.05
8 Brian Williams	.01	.05
9 Kez McCorvey	.01	.05
10 Kyle Brady	.08	.25
11 Rob Johnson	.25	.60
12 Carl Greenwood	.01	.05
13 Mark Fields	.08	.25
14 Andrew Greene	.01	.05
15 Orlando Thomas	.01	.05
16 Don Sasa	.01	.05
17 Brent Moss	.01	.05
18 Jamal Willis	.01	.05
19 Michael Hendricks	.01	.05
20 Rashaan Salaam	.02	.10
21 John Sacca	.01	.05
22 Cory Raymer	.01	.05
23 Kirby Dar Dar	.01	.05
24 Lee DeRamus	.01	.05
25 Joey Galloway	.30	.75
26 Mike Frederick	.01	.05
27 Todd Collins QB	.02	.10
28 Stoney Case	.02	.10
29 Devin Bush	.01	.05
30 Chad May	.01	.05
31 Darick Holmes	.02	.10
32 Johnny Thomas	.01	.05
33 Luther Elliss	.01	.05
34 Tyrone Wheatley	.25	.60
35 Terry Connealy	.01	.05
36 Ruben Brown	.08	.25
37 Kelvin Anderson	.01	.05
38 Tony Berti	.01	.05
39 Steve Ingram	.01	.05
40 Kevin Carter	.08	.25
41 Dave Wohlabaugh	.01	.05
42 Mike Morton	.01	.05
43 Steve Stenstrom	.01	.05
44 Zach Wiegert	.01	.05
45 Rodney Thomas	.02	.10
46 Eddie Goines	.01	.05
47 Kenny Gales	.01	.05
48 Jamal Ellis	.01	.05
49 Demetrius Edwards	.01	.05
50 Justin Armour	.01	.05
51 Billy Williams	.01	.05
52 Ed Hervey	.01	.05
53 Antonio Armstrong	.01	.05
54 Oliver Gibson	.01	.05
55 David Dunn	.01	.05
56 Tyrone Davis	.01	.05
57 Craig Newsome	.01	.05
58 William Strong	.01	.05
59 Sherman Williams	.01	.05
60 James O. Stewart	.25	.60
61 Bryan Schwartz	.01	.05
62 Frank Sanders	.08	.25
63 Barrett Robbins	.01	.05
64 Bronzell Miller	.01	.05
65 Curtis Martin	.60	1.50
66 Chris T. Jones	.02	.10
67 Dave Barr	.01	.05
68 Anthony Brown	.01	.05
69 Ken Dilger	.02	.10
70 Warren Sapp	.25	.60
71 James A. Stewart	.01	.05
72 Corey Fuller	.01	.05
73 Christian Fauria	.02	.10
74 Brian DeMarco	.01	.05
75 J.J. Stokes	.08	.25
76 Hicham El-Mashtoub	.01	.05
77 Anthony Cook	.01	.05
78 Mark Bruener	.02	.10
79 Blake Brockermeyer	.01	.05
80 Derrick Brooks	.08	.25
81 Joe Aska	.01	.05
82 Lance Brown	.01	.05
83 Pete Mitchell	.01	.05
84 Kordell Stewart	.50	1.25
85 Bobby Taylor	.08	.25
86 Jimmy Hitchcock	.01	.05
87 Jack Jackson	.01	.05
88 Ray Zellars	.01	.05
89 Darius Holland	.01	.05
90 Derrick Alexander DE	.01	.05
91 Torey Hunter	.01	.05
92 Scotty Lewis	.01	.05
93 Carl Reeves	.01	.05
94 Terrell Fletcher	.01	.05
95 Ontiwaun Carter	.01	.05
96 Trezelle Jenkins	.01	.05
97 Mark Birchmeier	.01	.05
98 Len Raney	.01	.05
99 Ronald Cherry	.01	.05
100 Tyrone Wheatley	.25	.60
101 John Jones	.01	.05
102 Zack Crockett	.02	.10
103 Larry Jones	.01	.05
104 Michael McCoy	.01	.05
105 Ellis Johnson	.01	.05
106 Jerrott Willard	.01	.05
107 Jason James	.01	.05
108 J.J. Smith	.01	.05
109 Mike Mamula	.01	.05
110 Checklist	.01	.05

1995 Superior Pix Autographs

COMPLETE SET (109)	150.00	300.00
ONE CARD OR COUPON PER PACK		
1 Ki-Jana Carter/1000	3.00	8.00
2 Tony Boselli/4000	2.00	5.00
3 Steve McNair/3000	15.00	30.00
4 Michael Westbrook/4000	2.00	5.00
5 Kerry Collins/3000	6.00	15.00
6 Terrell Davis/5000	7.50	20.00
7 Kevin Bouie/6500	1.50	4.00
8 Brian Williams/6500	1.50	4.00
9 Kez McCorvey/6500	1.50	4.00
10 Kyle Brady/3500	3.00	8.00
11 Rob Johnson/3000	5.00	12.00
12 Carl Greenwood/6500	1.50	4.00
13 Mark Fields/5000	3.00	8.00
14 Andrew Greene/5000	1.50	4.00
15 Orlando Thomas/6000	1.50	4.00
16 Don Sasa/6500	1.50	4.00
17 Brent Moss/4000	1.50	4.00
18 Jamal Willis/5000	1.50	4.00
19 Michael Hendricks/6500	1.50	4.00
20 Rashaan Salaam/3500	2.00	5.00
21 John Sacca/4000	1.50	4.00
22 Cory Raymer/6000	1.50	4.00
23 Kirby Dar Dar/6500	1.50	4.00
24 Lee DeRamus/6500	1.50	4.00
25 Joey Galloway/4000	4.00	10.00
26 Mike Frederick/6000	1.50	4.00
27 Todd Collins/5000	5.00	12.00
28 Stoney Case/4000	2.00	5.00
29 Devin Bush/5000	1.50	4.00
30 Chad May/4000	1.50	4.00
31 Darick Holmes/6500	1.50	4.00
32 Johnny Thomas/6500	1.50	4.00
33 Luther Elliss/5000	1.50	4.00
34 Tyrone Wheatley/5000	3.00	8.00
35 Terry Connealy/6500	1.50	4.00
36 Ruben Brown/3500	3.00	8.00
37 Kelvin Anderson/4000	2.00	5.00
38 Tony Berti/6500	1.50	4.00
39 Steve Ingram/3500	1.50	4.00
40 Kevin Carter/4000	3.00	8.00
41 Dave Wohlabaugh/6500	1.50	4.00
42 Mike Morton/6500	1.50	4.00
43 Steve Stenstrom/5000	1.50	4.00
44 Zach Wiegert/5000	1.50	4.00
45 Rodney Thomas/5000	1.50	4.00
46 Eddie Goines/4000	1.50	4.00
47 Kenny Gales/6500	1.50	4.00
48 Jamal Ellis/6500	1.50	4.00
49 Demetrius Edwards/6500	1.50	4.00
50 Justin Armour/5000	2.00	5.00
51 Billy Williams/5000	1.50	4.00
52 Ed Hervey/6500	1.50	4.00
53 Antonio Armstrong/6500	1.50	4.00
54 Oliver Gibson/6500	1.50	4.00
55 David Dunn/5000	1.50	4.00
56 Tyrone Davis	1.50	4.00
57 Craig Newsome/4000	1.50	4.00
58 William Strong/6500	1.50	4.00
59 Sherman Williams/3500	1.50	4.00
60 James O. Stewart/4000	3.00	8.00
61 Bryan Schwartz/6000	1.50	4.00
62 Frank Sanders/5000	2.00	5.00
63 Barrett Robbins/6000	1.50	4.00
64 Bronzell Miller/6500	1.50	4.00
65 Curtis Martin/4000	20.00	40.00
66 Chris T. Jones/4000	2.00	5.00
67 Dave Barr/5000	1.50	4.00
68 Anthony Brown/6500	1.50	4.00
69 Ken Dilger/6000	3.00	8.00
70 Warren Sapp/4000		
71 James A. Stewart/4000	1.50	4.00
72 Corey Fuller/5000	1.50	4.00
73 Christian Fauria/5000	1.50	4.00
74 Brian DeMarco/6000	1.50	4.00
75 J.J. Stokes/1000	3.00	8.00
76 Hicham El-Mashtoub/6500	1.50	4.00
77 Anthony Cook/6000	1.50	4.00
78 Mark Bruener/4000	2.00	5.00
79 Blake Brockermeyer/4000	1.50	4.00
80 Derrick Brooks/4000	10.00	25.00
81 Joe Aska/4000	2.00	5.00
82 Lance Brown/6500	1.50	4.00
83 Pete Mitchell/6500	2.00	5.00
84 Kordell Stewart/6500	5.00	12.00
85 Bobby Taylor/4000	3.00	8.00
86 Jimmy Hitchcock/4000	1.50	4.00
87 Jack Jackson/5000	1.50	4.00
88 Ray Zellars/4000	1.50	4.00
89 Darius Holland/6000	1.50	4.00
90 Derrick Alexander DE/4000	1.50	4.00
91 Torey Hunter/6000	1.50	4.00
92 Scotty Lewis/6500	1.50	4.00
93 Carl Reeves/6500	1.50	4.00
94 Terrell Fletcher/6000	1.50	4.00
95 Ontiwaun Carter/6500	1.50	4.00
96 Trezelle Jenkins/5000	1.50	4.00
97 Mark Birchmeier/4000	1.50	4.00
98 Len Raney/6500	1.50	4.00
99 Ronald Cherry/6500	1.50	4.00
100 Tyrone Wheatley/6500	3.00	8.00
101 John Jones/6500	1.50	4.00
102 Zack Crockett/6000	2.00	5.00
103 Larry Jones/4000	1.50	4.00
104 Michael McCoy/6500	1.50	4.00
105 Ellis Johnson/3500	1.50	4.00
106 Jerrott Willard/5000	1.50	4.00
107 Jason James/6500	1.50	4.00
108 J.J. Smith/5000	1.50	4.00
109 Mike Mamula/4000	1.50	4.00

1995 Superior Pix Deep Threat

COMPLETE SET (5)	2.50	6.00
STATED ODDS 1:9		
*PROMO CARDS: .25X TO .5X BASIC INSERTS		
1 Michael Westbrook	.25	.60
2 Joey Galloway	.75	2.00
3 J.J. Stokes	.25	.60
4 Kyle Brady	.25	.60
5 Frank Sanders	.25	.60

1995 Superior Pix Instant Impact

COMPLETE SET (5)	3.00	8.00
STATED ODDS 1:18		
*PROMO CARDS: .25X TO .5X BASIC CARDS		
1 Steve McNair	2.00	5.00
2 Kerry Collins	1.25	3.00
3 Tyrone Wheatley	.30	.75
4 Joey Galloway	.60	1.50
5 Tony Boselli	.30	.75

1995 Superior Pix Open Field

COMPLETE SET (5)	2.00	5.00
STATED ODDS 1:18		
*PROMO CARDS: .25X TO .5X BASIC CARDS		
1 Ki-Jana Carter	.25	.60
2 Tyrone Wheatley	.60	1.50
3 James O. Stewart	.60	1.50
4 Rashaan Salaam	.08	.25
5 Ray Zellars	.08	.25

1995 Superior Pix Top Defender

COMPLETE SET (5)	.75	2.00
*PROMO CARDS: .25X TO .5X BASIC CARDS		
1 Kevin Carter	.30	.75
2 Derrick Alexander DE	.05	.15
3 Warren Sapp	.75	2.00
4 Derrick Brooks	.30	.75
5 Mike Mamula	.05	.15

1996 Visions

The 1996 Classic Visions set consists of 150 standard-size cards. The fronts feature full-bleed color action player photos. The player's position and name are presented in blue foil, while the Classic logo and set title "96 Visions" are stamped in gold foil. The back carries a second color photo, college statistics, biography, and a player fact.

COMPLETE SET (150)	6.00	15.00
39 Troy Aikman	.25	.60
40 Emmitt Smith	.40	1.00
41 Marshall Faulk	.15	.40
42 Kerry Collins	.15	.40
43 Michael Westbrook	.08	.25
44 Steve Young	.15	.40
45 Mike Mamula	.05	.15
46 Joey Galloway	.15	.40
47 Kyle Brady	.05	.15
48 J.J. Stokes	.08	.25
49 Steve McNair	.25	.60
50 Kordell Stewart	.15	.40
51 Drew Bledsoe	.15	.40
52 Hugh Douglas	.08	.25
53 Curtis Martin	.20	.50
54 Ki-Jana Carter	.08	.25
55 Tyrone Wheatley	.15	.40
56 Napoleon Kaufman	.15	.40
57 James Stewart	.08	.25
58 Rashaan Salaam	.05	.15
59 Eric Zeier	.08	.25
60 Bobby Taylor	.08	.25
61 Ty Law	.15	.40
62 Mark Bruener	.05	.15
63 Devin Bush	.05	.15
64 Frank Sanders	.08	.25
65 Derrick Brooks	.15	.40
66 Craig Powell	.05	.15
67 Craig Newsome	.05	.15
68 Trent Dilfer	.15	.40
69 Sherman Williams	.05	.15
70 Chris T. Jones	.05	.15
71 Corey Fuller	.05	.15
72 Luther Elliss	.05	.15
73 Warren Sapp	.15	.40
74 Isaac Bruce	.15	.40
75 Tamarick Vanover	.05	.15
76 Terrell Davis	.40	1.00
77 Byron Bam Morris	.08	.25
78 Rodney Thomas	.05	.15
79 Errict Rhett	.08	.25
80 Kevin Carter	.05	.15
81 Darnay Scott	.08	.25
122 Troy Aikman	.25	.60
126 Emmitt Smith	.40	1.00
129 Marshall Faulk	.15	.40
141 Joey Galloway	.15	.40
142 Kerry Collins	.15	.40
143 Michael Westbrook	.08	.25
144 Terrell Davis	.40	1.00
145 Kyle Brady	.05	.15
146 Kordell Stewart	.15	.40
147 Curtis Martin	.20	.50
148 Tyrone Wheatley	.15	.40
149 Napoleon Kaufman	.15	.40
150 Rashaan Salaam	.05	.15

1996 Visions Action 21

1 Troy Aikman	.40	1.00
4 Michael Westbrook	.08	.25
10 Kerry Collins	.20	.50

1996 Visions Signings

The 1996 Visions Signings set consists of 100 standard-size cards. The fronts feature full-bleed color action player photos. The player's position and name are stamped in prismatic foil along with the Classic logo and set title "96 Visions Signings." This set contains standouts from five sports grouped together in this order: basketball, football, hockey, baseball and racing. Cards were distributed in six-card packs. Release date was June 1996. The main allure to this product, in addition to the conventional inserts, were autographed memorabilia redemption cards inserted one per 10 packs.

COMPLETE SET (100)	6.00	15.00
29 Troy Aikman	.30	.75
30 Emmitt Smith	.60	1.50
31 Marshall Faulk	.20	.50
32 Kerry Collins	.15	.40
33 Steve Young	.15	.40
34 Drew Bledsoe	.15	.40
35 Kyle Brady	.05	.15
36 Steve McNair	.15	.40
37 Napoleon Kaufman	.10	.30
38 Karim Abdul-Jabbar	.08	.25
39 Mike Alstott	.15	.40
40 Tim Biakabutuka	.08	.25
41 Duane Clemons	.05	.15
42 Daryl Gardener	.05	.15
43 Joey Galloway	.15	.40
44 Eddie George	.60	1.50
45 Terry Glenn	.08	.25
46 Kevin Hardy	.05	.15
47 Bobby Hoying	.08	.25
48 Keyshawn Johnson	.50	1.25
49 Derrick Mayes	.08	.25
50 Eric Moulds	.30	.75
51 Jonathan Ogden	.10	.30
52 Simeon Rice	.08	.25
53 Orpheus Roye	.05	.15
54 Amani Toomer	.15	.40
55 Chris Doering	.08	.25
56 Jevon Langford	.05	.15
57 Jeff Lewis	.08	.25
58 Jamain Stephens	.08	.25
59 Steve Taneyhill	.05	.15
60 Alex Van Dyke	.05	.15

1996 Visions Signings Artistry

COMPLETE SET (10)	20.00	50.00
2 Emmitt Smith	4.00	10.00
5 Joey Galloway	2.00	5.00
8 Kordell Stewart	3.00	8.00
10 Rashaan Salaam	1.25	3.00

1996 Visions Signings Autographs Gold

1 Karim Abdul-Jabbar	4.00	10.00
5 Mike Alstott	5.00	12.00
7 Tim Biakabutuka	2.50	6.00
10 Jerod Cherry	1.50	4.00
12 Sedric Clark	1.50	4.00
13 Marcus Coleman	1.50	4.00
15 Chris Darkins	1.50	4.00
18 Chris Doering	1.50	4.00
20 Donnie Edwards	1.50	4.00
21 Ray Farmer	1.50	4.00
24 Randall Godfrey	1.50	4.00
25 Scott Greene	1.50	4.00
27 Jeff Hartings	1.50	4.00
28 Jimmy Herndon	1.50	4.00
30 Richard Huntley	1.50	4.00
32 Dietrich Jells	1.50	4.00
36 Jeff Lewis	1.50	4.00
38 Ray Mickens	1.50	4.00
39 Lawyer Milloy	2.50	6.00
40 Bryant Mix	1.50	4.00
41 Alex Molden	1.50	4.00
45 Jason Odom	1.50	4.00
53 Jason Ritchey	1.50	4.00
54 Brian Roche	1.50	4.00
55 Orpheus Roye	1.50	4.00
56 Jon Runyan	1.50	4.00
57 Scott Slutzker	1.50	4.00
59 Jamain Stephens	1.50	4.00
60 Matt Stevens	1.50	4.00
63 Steve Taneyhill	1.50	4.00
64 Zach Thomas	8.00	20.00
65 Alex Van Dyke	1.50	4.00
67 Kyle Wacholtz	1.50	4.00
69 Stepfret Williams	1.50	4.00
70 Jerome Woods	1.50	4.00
71 Dusty Zeigler	1.50	4.00

1996 Visions Signings Autographs Silver

1 Karim Abdul-Jabbar/365	6.00	15.00
2 Troy Aikman/190	20.00	50.00
6 Mike Alstott/345	8.00	20.00
8 Tim Biakabutuka/390	6.00	15.00
9 Drew Bledsoe/110	15.00	40.00
13 Jerod Cherry/355	2.00	5.00
15 Sedric Clark/410	2.00	5.00
16 Marcus Coleman/395	2.00	5.00
18 Chris Darkins/395	2.00	5.00
21 Chris Doering/390	2.00	5.00
23 Donnie Edwards/395	2.00	5.00
24 Ray Farmer/395	2.00	5.00
25 Marshall Faulk/185	12.50	30.00

28 Randall Godfrey/380	2.00	5.00
29 Scott Greene/395	2.00	5.00
31 Jeff Hartings/380	2.00	5.00
32 Jimmy Herndon/380	2.00	5.00
34 Richard Huntley/380	2.00	5.00
37 Dietrich Jells/350	2.00	5.00
41 Jeff Lewis/385	2.00	5.00
44 Ray Mickens/390	2.00	5.00
45 Lawyer Milloy/365	3.00	8.00
46 Bryant Mix/390	2.00	5.00
47 Alex Molden/365	2.00	5.00
51 Jason Odom/390	2.00	5.00
59 Jason Ritchey/360	2.00	5.00
60 Brian Roche/395	2.00	5.00
61 Orpheus Roye/350	2.00	5.00
63 Jon Runyan/430	2.00	5.00
64 Scott Slutzker/385	2.00	5.00
65 Emmitt Smith/90	60.00	120.00
67 Jamain Stephens/380	2.00	5.00
68 Matt Stevens/390	2.00	5.00
71 Steve Taneyhill/420	2.00	5.00
72 Zach Thomas/390	10.00	25.00
74 Alex Van Dyke/385	2.00	5.00
76 Kyle Wacholtz/385	2.00	5.00
79 Stepfret Williams/385	2.00	5.00
80 Jerome Woods/430	2.00	5.00
81 Steve Young/95		50.00
82 Dusty Zeigler/395	2.00	5.00

1997 Visions Signings

Score Board's follow-up to the 1996 Visions Signings debut product was released in June 1997. The second-year product had more of a memorabilia emphasis. According to Score Board, 1,700 sequentially numbered cases were produced with five cards per pack, 16 packs per box and 10 boxes per case. Each pack contains either an autographed card or an insert card. The 50-card regular set includes stars and prospects from all four major team sports. Also, one in every two packs contained a gold parallel card to the base set.

COMPLETE SET (50)	5.00	10.00
4 Steve Young	.30	.75
29 Eddie George	.20	.50
30 Warrick Dunn	.30	.75
31 Darrell Russell	.05	.15
32 Peter Boulware	.05	.15
33 Shawn Springs	.05	.15
34 Yatil Green	.05	.15
35 David LaFleur	.05	.15
36 Bryant Westbrook	.05	.15
37 Rae Carruth	.05	.15
38 Brett Favre	.50	1.25
39 Emmitt Smith	.40	1.00
47 Leeland McElroy	.05	.15
48 Troy Davis	.05	.15
49 Tony Gonzalez	.30	.75
50 Byron Hanspard	.05	.15

1997 Visions Signings Gold

COMPLETE SET (50)	10.00	25.00
*GOLD: .8X TO 2X BASIC CARDS		
GOLD STATED ODDS 1:2		

1997 Visions Signings Artistry

COMPLETE SET (20)	20.00	40.00
A12 Eddie George	1.50	4.00
A13 Warrick Dunn	1.25	3.00
A14 Darrell Russell	.40	1.00
A15 Peter Boulware	.40	1.00
A16 Shawn Springs	.40	1.00
A17 Yatil Green	.40	1.00
A18 Brett Favre	3.00	8.00
A19 Emmitt Smith	2.50	6.00

1997 Visions Signings Artistry Autographs

A12 Eddie George	10.00	25.00
A13 Warrick Dunn	12.50	30.00
A14 Darrell Russell	3.00	8.00
A15 Peter Boulware	3.00	8.00
A16 Shawn Springs	2.50	6.00
A17 Yatil Green	3.00	8.00
A18 Brett Favre	75.00	135.00
A19 Emmitt Smith	40.00	100.00

1997 Visions Signings Autographs

4 Tony Banks	2.50	6.00
5 Michael Booker	1.50	4.00
6 Peter Boulware	1.50	4.00
8 Rae Carruth	2.50	6.00
12 Koy Detmer	2.00	5.00
13 Corey Dillon	10.00	25.00
14 Warrick Dunn	15.00	30.00
19 Yatil Green	1.50	4.00
23 Byron Hanspard	2.00	5.00
24 Kevin Hardy	2.00	5.00
30 DeRon Jenkins	1.50	4.00
31 Andre Johnson	1.50	4.00
32 Greg Jones	1.50	4.00
33 Danny Kanell	2.50	6.00
35 Pete Kendall	1.50	4.00
37 David LaFleur	1.50	4.00
38 Jeff Lewis	1.50	4.00
42 Leeland McElroy	1.50	4.00
43 Ray Mickens	1.50	4.00
46 Trevor Pryce	2.50	6.00
50 Darrell Russell	1.50	4.00
52 Antowain Smith	4.00	10.00
56 Amani Toomer	6.00	15.00
59 Bryant Westbrook	1.50	4.00
61 Stepfret Williams	1.50	4.00

1991 Wild Card Draft National Promos

These cards were given away at the 1991 12th Annual Sports Collectors Convention in Anaheim, California. The fronts of these standard-size cards have high gloss color player photos on a black card face with different colored numbers above and to the right of the picture. Striped versions of these cards with a football-shaped hologram in the upper left corner were also issued. The cards are numbered in the upper right corner of the cardback and begin with Prototype-2.

COMPLETE SET (3)	.60	1.50
*5 STRIPES: SAME PRICE		
*10 STRIPES: .5X TO 1.2X BASIC CARDS		
*20 STRIPES: .6X TO 1.5X BASIC CARDS		
*50 STRIPES: .8X TO 2X BASIC CARDS		
*100 STRIPES: 1.2X TO 3X BASIC CARDS		
*1000 STRIPES: 2X TO 5X BASIC CARDS		
P2 Dan McGwire	.20	.50
P3 Randal Hill	.20	.50
P4 Todd Marinovich	.20	.50

1991 Wild Card Draft

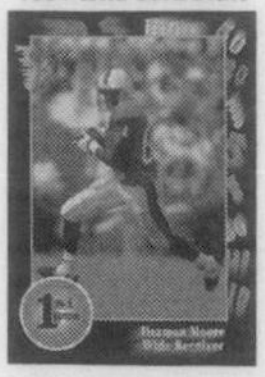

The Wild Card College Football Draft Picks set contains 160 cards measuring the standard size. Reportedly, production quantities were limited to 20,000 numbered cases (or 630,000 sets). The front design features glossy color action player photos on a black card face with an orange frame around the picture and different color numbers appearing in the top and right borders. The words "1st edition" in a circular emblem overlay the lower left corner of the picture. One of out every 100 cards is "wild," with a numbered stripe to indicate how many cards it can be redeemed for. There are 5, 10, 20, 50, 100, and 1000 denominations, with the highest numbers the scarcest. Whatever the "wild" number, the card could be redeemed for that number of regular cards of the same player (plus a redemption fee of $4.95). The set included three surprise wild cards (#1, #15, and #22). If these cards were redeemed before April 30, 1992, the collector received three cards to complete the set (listed below as B versions) and a bonus set of six 1992 collegiate football prototype cards. Collectors who redeemed their cards after April 30 did not receive the prototype cards. Also, Kenny Anderson and Larry Johnson promo cards, numbers P2 and P1 respectively, were randomly inserted, and they could be redeemed after January 2, 1992 for then-unknown player cards. Key cards in this set include Bryan Cox, Craig Erickson, Brett Favre, Alvin Harper, Randal Hill, Rocket Ismail (issued as a surprise card), Herman Moore, Mike Pritchard, Leonard Russell and Ricky Watters.

COMPLETE SET (160)	3.00	8.00
1A Wild Card 1	.01	.05
1B Todd Lyght	.01	.05
2 Kelvin Pritchett	.01	.05
3 Robert Young	.01	.05
4 Reggie Johnson	.01	.05
5 Eric Turner	.02	.10
6 Pat Tyrance	.01	.05
7 Curvin Richards	.01	.05
8 Calvin Stephens	.01	.05
9 Corey Miller	.01	.05
10 Michael Jackson	.02	.10
11 Simmie Carter	.01	.05
12 Roland Smith	.01	.05
13 Pat O'Hara	.01	.05
14 Scott Conover	.01	.05
15A Wild Card 2	.01	.05
15B Russell Maryland	.01	.05
16 Greg Amsler	.01	.05
17 Moe Gardner	.01	.05
18 Howard Griffith	.01	.05
19 David Daniels	.01	.05
20 Henry Jones	.01	.05
21 Don Davey	.01	.05
22A Wild Card 3	.01	.05
22B Rocket Ismail	.15	.40
23 Richie Andrews	.01	.05
24 Shawn Moore	.01	.05
25 Anthony Moss	.01	.05
26 Vince Moore	.01	.05
27 Leroy Thompson	.01	.05
28 Darrick Brown	.01	.05
29 Mel Agee	.01	.05
30 Darryll Lewis	.01	.05
31 Hyland Hickson	.01	.05
32 Leonard Russell	.01	.05
33 Floyd Fields	.01	.05
34 Esera Tuaolo	.01	.05
35 Todd Marinovich	.01	.05
36 Gary Wellman	.01	.05
37 Ricky Ervins	.01	.05
38 Pat Harlow	.01	.05
39 Mo Lewis	.01	.05
40 John Kasay	.01	.05
41 Phil Hansen	.01	.05
42 Kevin Donnalley	.01	.05
43 Dexter Davis	.01	.05
44 Vance Hammond	.01	.05
45 Chris Gardocki	.08	.25
46 Bruce Pickens	.01	.05
47 Godfrey Myles	.01	.05
48 Ernie Mills	.02	.10
49 Derek Russell	.01	.05
50 Chris Zorich	.01	.05
51 Alfred Williams	.01	.05
52 Jon Vaughn	.01	.05
53 Adrian Cooper	.01	.05
54 Eric Bieniemy	.01	.05
55 Robert Bailey	.01	.05
56 Ricky Watters	.25	.60
57 Mark Vander Poel	.01	.05
58 James Joseph	.01	.05
59 Darren Lewis	.01	.05
60 Wesley Carroll	.02	.10
61 Dave Key	.01	.05
62 Mike Pritchard	.02	.10
63 Craig Erickson	.02	.10
64 Browning Nagle	.01	.05
65 Mike Dumas	.01	.05
66 Andre Jones	.01	.05
67 Herman Moore	.08	.25
68 Greg Lewis	.01	.05
69 James Goode	.01	.05
70 Stan Thomas	.01	.05
71 Jerome Henderson	.01	.05
72 Doug Thomas	.01	.05
73 Tony Covington	.01	.05
74 Charles Mincy	.01	.05
75 Kanavis McGhee	.01	.05
76 Tom Backes	.01	.05
77 Fernandus Vinson	.01	.05
78 Marcus Robertson	.01	.05
79 Eric Harmon	.01	.05
80 Rob Selby	.01	.05
81 Ed King	.01	.05
82 William Thomas	.01	.05
83 Mike Jones DE	.01	.05
84 Paul Justin	.01	.05
85 Robert Wilson	.01	.05
86 Jesse Campbell	.01	.05
87 Hayward Haynes	.01	.05
88 Mike Croel	.01	.05
89 Jeff Graham	.02	.10
90 Vinnie Clark	.01	.05
91 Keith Cash	.01	.05
92 Tim Ryan	.01	.05
93 Jarrod Bunch	.01	.05
94 Stanley Richard	.01	.05
95 Alvin Harper	.01	.05
96 Bob Dahl	.01	.05
97 Mark Gunn	.01	.05
98 Frank Blevins	.01	.05
99 Harvey Williams	.02	.10
100 Dixon Edwards	.01	.05
101 Blake Miller	.01	.05
102 Bobby Wilson	.01	.05
103 Chuck Webb	.01	.05
104 Randal Hill	.02	.10
105 Shane Curry	.01	.05
106 Barry Sanders	.40	1.00
107 Richard Fain	.01	.05
108 Joe Garten	.01	.05
109 Dean Dingman	.01	.05
110 Mark Tucker	.01	.05
111 Dan McGwire	.01	.05
112 Paul Glonek	.01	.05
113 Tom Dohring	.01	.05
114 Joe Sims	.01	.05
115 Bryan Cox	.01	.05
116 Bobby Olive	.01	.05
117 Blaise Bryant	.01	.05
118 Charles Johnson	.01	.05
119 Brett Favre	3.00	6.00
120 Luis Cristobal	.01	.05
121 Don Gibson	.01	.05
122 Scott Ross	.01	.05
123 Huey Richardson	.01	.05
124 Chris Smith	.01	.05
125 Duane Young	.01	.05
126 Eric Swann	.02	.10
127 Jeff Fite	.01	.05
128 Eugene Williams	.01	.05
129 Harlan Davis	.01	.05
130 James Bradley	.01	.05
131 Rob Carpenter	.01	.05
132 Dennis Ransom	.01	.05
133 Mike Arthur	.01	.05
134 Chuck Weatherspoon	.01	.05
135 Darrell Malone	.01	.05
136 George Thornton	.01	.05
137 Lamar McGriggs	.01	.05
138 Alex Johnson	.01	.05
139 Eric Moten	.01	.05
140 Joe Valerio	.01	.05
141 Jake Reed	.08	.25
142 Ernie Thompson	.01	.05
143 Roland Poles	.01	.05
144 Randy Bethel	.01	.05
145 Terry Bagsby	.01	.05
146 Tim James	.01	.05
147 Kenny Walker	.01	.05
148 Nolan Harrison	.01	.05
149 Keith Traylor	.01	.05
150 Nick Subis	.01	.05
151 Scott Zolak	.01	.05
152 Pio Sagapolutele	.01	.05
153 James Jones	.01	.05
154 Mike Sullivan	.01	.05
155 Joe Johnson	.01	.05
156 Todd Scott	.01	.05
157 Checklist 1	.01	.05
158 Checklist 2	.01	.05
159 Checklist 3	.01	.05
160 Checklist 4	.01	.05

1991 Wild Card Draft 5 Stripe

*5 STRIPES: 1.2X TO 3X BASIC CARDS		
119 Brett Favre	20.00	40.00

1991 Wild Card Draft 10 Stripe

*10 STRIPES: 2X TO 5X BASIC CARDS		
119 Brett Favre	30.00	80.00

1991 Wild Card Draft 20 Stripe

*20 STRIPES: 3X TO 8X BASIC CARDS		
119 Brett Favre	60.00	120.00

1991 Wild Card Draft 50 Stripe

*50 STRIPES: 6X TO 15X BASIC CARDS		
119 Brett Favre	75.00	200.00

1991 Wild Card Draft 100 Stripe

*100 STRIPES: 10X TO 25X BASIC CARDS		
119 Brett Favre	150.00	300.00

1991 Wild Card Draft 1000 Stripe

*1000 STRIPES: 40X TO 100X BASIC CARDS		
119 Brett Favre	750.00	1,500.00

1991 Wild Card Draft Redemption Prizes

Collectors who redeemed their three 1991 Wild Card Draft Surprise Cards before April 30, 1992 received as a bonus this six-card set of 1992 Wild Card Draft Prototypes. Note that a 1992 Draft set was never issued. These standard-size cards feature glossy color player photos bordered in white. The player's name and position appear in the bottom white border. The backs shade from purple to white and back to purple and carry a color head shot, biography, and statistics. The cards are numbered on the back with a "P" prefix.

COMPLETE SET (6)	1.00	2.50
P1 Edgar Bennett	.20	.50
P2 Jimmy Smith	.75	2.00
P3 Will Furrer	.07	.20
P4 Terrell Buckley	.10	.30
P5 Tommy Vardell	.10	.30
P6 Amp Lee	.07	.20

College

1967 Air Force Team Issue

These 5" by 7" black and white photos were issued by the Air Force Academy. Each features a member of the football team without any player identfiication on the front. The backs were produced blank, however the player's identification is usually hand written on the backs.

COMPLETE SET (7)	25.00	50.00
1 Gerry Cormany	3.00	8.00
2 George Gibson	3.00	8.00
3 Don Heckert	3.00	8.00
4 Mike Mueller	3.00	8.00
5 Neal Starkey	3.00	8.00
6 Paul Stein	3.00	8.00
7 Rich Wolfe	3.00	8.00

1993 Air Force Smokey

This set was produced to honor current and past Air Force Academy athletes and athletic traditions. These 16 standard-size cards feature on their fronts color player action shots set within gray borders with white diagonal stripes. The player's name and position appear on the left side underneath the photo. The team name and logo appear above the photo. The plain white back carries the player's name and position at the top, followed by a Smokey safety tip, and the player's career highlights. The cards are unnumbered and checklisted below in alphabetical order.

COMPLETE SET (16)	6.00	15.00
1 Fisher DeBerry CO FB	.40	1.00
2 Dee Dowis FB	.50	1.25
3 Chad Hennings FB	1.50	4.00
4 Carlton MacDonald FB	.30	.75
5 Terry Maki FB	.30	.75

1994 Air Force Smokey

Similar to the 1993 release, this set was produced to honor current and past Air Force Academy athletes and athletic traditions. These 16 standard-size cards feature on their fronts color player action shots set within gray borders with white diagonal stripes. The player's name and position appear on the left side underneath the photo with the team name and logor above the photo. The cards are unnumbered and checklisted below in alphabetical order.

COMPLETE SET (16)	6.00	15.00
1 Fisher DeBerry FB CO	.40	1.00
2 Dee Dowis	.50	1.25
4 Chad Hennings	1.50	4.00
5 Chris MacInnis	.30	.75
8 Air Force Falcon	.30	.75
9 Air Force Graduation	.30	.75
12 Color Guard	.30	.75
13 Commander-in-Chief's Trophy	.30	.75
15 Falcon Stadium	.30	.75

2006 Akron Schedules

1 Tim Crouch OL	.75	2.00
2 Luke Getsy	.75	2.00
3 Kiki Gonzalez	.75	2.00
4 John Mackey DB	.75	2.00
5 Jermaine Reid	.75	2.00
6 Andy Wills	.75	2.00

1971 Alabama Team Sheets

These six sheets measure approximately 8" by 9". The fronts feature twelve black-and-white player portraits arranged in three rows of four portraits per row. The player's name is printed under the photo. The backs are blank. The sheets are unnumbered and checklisted below in alphabetical order beginning with the player in the upper left hand corner.

COMPLETE SET (6)	40.00	80.00
1 Wayne Adkinson	6.00	12.00
David Bailey		
Marvin Barron		
Jeff Beard		
Andy Cross		
John Croyle		
Bill Davis		
Terry Davis		
Steve Higginbotham		
Ed Hines		
Jimmy Horton		
Wilbur Jackson		
2 Ellis Beck	6.00	12.00
Steve Bisceglia		
Jeff Blitz		
Buddy Brown		
Steve Dean		
Mike Denson		
Joe Doughty		
Mike Eckenrod		
Pat Keever		
David Knapp		
Jim Krapf		
Joe LaBue		
3 Richard Bryan	7.50	15.00
Chip Burke		
Jerry Cash		
Don Cokely		
Greg Gantt		
Jim Grammer		
Wayne Hall		
John Hannah		
Rand Lambert		
Tom Lusk		
Bobby McKinney		
David McMakin		
4 Fred Marshall	6.00	12.00
Noah Miller		
John Mitchell		
Randy Moore		
Gary Reynolds		
Benny Rippetoe		
Ronny Robertson		
John Rogers		
Jim Simmons		
Paul Spivey		
Steve Sprayberry		
Rod Steakley		
5 Johnny Musso	7.50	15.00
Lanny Norris		
Robin Parkhouse		
Jim Patterson		
Steve Root		
Jimmy Rosser		
Jeff Rouzie		
Robby Rowan		
Chuck Strickland		
Tom Surlas		
Steve Wade		
David Watkins		
6 Mike Raines	7.50	15.00
Pat Raines		
Terry Rowell		
Gary Rutledge		
Bubba Sawyer		
Bill Sexton		
Wayne Wheeler		
Jack White		
Steve Williams		
Dexter Wood		

1972 Alabama Playing Cards

This 54-card standard-size set was issued in a box as a playing card deck through the Alabama University bookstore. The cards have rounded corners and the typical playing card finish. The fronts feature black-and-white posed action photos of helmetless players in their uniforms. A white border surrounds each picture and contains the card number and suit designation in the upper left corner and again, but inverted, in the lower right. The player's name and hometown appear just beneath the photo. The white-bordered crimson backs all have the Alabama "A" logo in white and the year of issue, 1972. The name Alabama Crimson Tide also appears on the backs. Since the set is similar to a playing card set, the set is arranged just like a card deck and checklisted below accordingly. In the checklist below S means Spades, D means Diamonds, C means Clubs, H means Hearts, and JK means Joker. The cards are checklisted below in playing card order by suits and numbers are assigned to Aces (1), Jacks (11), Queens (12), and Kings (13). The jokers are unnumbered and listed at the end. Key cards in the set are early cards of coaching legend Paul "Bear" Bryant and lineman John Hannah. This set was available directly from Alabama for $2.50

COMP. FACT SET (54)	90.00	150.00
1C Skip Kubelius	1.00	2.50
1D Terry Davis	1.25	3.00
1H Robert Fraley	1.00	2.50
1S Paul(Bear) Bryant CO	20.00	35.00
2C David Watkins	1.00	2.50
2D Bobby McKinney	1.00	2.50
2H Dexter Wood	1.00	2.50
2S Chuck Strickland	1.00	2.50
3C John Hannah	12.00	20.00
3D Tom Lusk	1.00	2.50
3H Jim Krapf	1.00	2.50
3S Warren Dyar	1.00	2.50
4C Greg Gantt	1.25	3.00
4D Johnny Sharpless	1.00	2.50
4H Steve Wade	1.00	2.50
4S John Rogers	1.00	2.50
5C Doug Faust	1.00	2.50
5D Jeff Rouzie	1.00	2.50
5H Buddy Brown	1.00	2.50
5S Randy Moore	1.00	2.50
6C David Knapp	1.25	3.00
6D Lanny Norris	1.00	2.50
6H Paul Spivey	1.00	2.50
6S Pat Raines	1.00	2.50
7C Pete Pappas	1.00	2.50
7D Ed Hines	1.00	2.50
7H Mike Washington	1.00	2.50
7S David McMakin	1.25	3.00
8C Steve Dean	1.00	2.50
8D Joe LaBue	1.00	2.50
8H John Croyle	1.00	2.50
8S Noah Miller	1.00	2.50
9C Bobby Stanford	1.00	2.50
9D Sylvester Croom	1.50	4.00
9H Wilbur Jackson	4.00	8.00
9S Ellis Beck	1.00	2.50
10C Steve Bisceglia	1.00	2.50
10D Andy Cross	1.00	2.50
10H John Mitchell	1.25	3.00
10S Bill Davis	1.00	2.50
11C Gary Rutledge	1.25	3.00
11D Randy Billingsley	1.00	2.50
11H Randy Hall	1.00	2.50
11S Ralph Stokes	1.00	2.50
12C Jeff Blitz	1.00	2.50
12D Robby Rowan	1.00	2.50
12H Mike Raines	1.00	2.50
12S Wayne Wheeler	1.00	2.50
13C Steve Sprayberry	1.00	2.50
13D Wayne Hall	1.25	3.00
13H Morris Hunt	1.00	2.50
13S Butch Norman	1.00	2.50
JOK1 Denny Stadium	1.00	2.50
JOK2 Memorial Coliseum	1.00	2.50

1973 Alabama Playing Cards

These 54 standard-size playing cards have rounded corners and the typical playing card finish The cards were sold through the Alabama University bookstore. The fronts feature black-and-white posed action photos of helmetless players in their uniforms. A white border surrounds each picture and contains the card number and suit designation in the upper left corner and again, but inverted, in the lower right. The player's name and hometown appear just beneath the photo. The white-bordered crimson backs all have the Alabama "A" logo in white and the year of issue, 1973. The name Alabama Crimson Tide also appears on the backs. Since this is a set of playing cards, the set is checklisted below accordingly. In the checklist below S means Spades, D means Diamonds, C means Clubs, H means Hearts, and JK means Joker. The cards are in playing card order by suits and numbers are assigned to Aces (1), Jacks (11), Queens (12), and Kings (13). The jokers are unnumbered and listed at the end. If a player was in the 1972 set, they have the same pose in this set. This set was originally available from Alabama for $3.50.

COMP. FACT SET (54)	90.00	150.00
1C Skip Kubelius	1.00	2.50
1D Mark Prudhomme	1.00	2.50
1H Robert Fraley	1.00	2.50
1S Paul(Bear) Bryant CO	15.00	30.00
2C David Watkins	1.00	2.50
2D Richard Todd	6.00	12.00
2H Buddy Pope	1.00	2.50
2S Chuck Strickland	1.00	2.50
3C Bob Bryan	1.00	2.50
3D Gary Hanrahan	1.00	2.50
3H Greg Montgomery	1.00	2.50
3S Warren Dyar	1.00	2.50
4C Greg Gantt	1.25	3.00
4D Johnny Sharpless	1.00	2.50
4H Rick Watson	1.00	2.50
4S John Rogers	1.00	2.50
5C George Pugh	1.25	3.00
5D Jeff Rouzie	1.00	2.50
5H Buddy Brown	1.00	2.50
5S Randy Moore	1.00	2.50
6C Ray Maxwell	1.00	2.50
6D Alan Pizzitola	1.00	2.50
6H Paul Spivey	1.00	2.50
6S Ron Robertson	1.00	2.50
7C Pete Pappas	1.00	2.50
7D Steve Kulback	1.00	2.50
7H Mike Washington	1.00	2.50
7S David McMakin	1.25	3.00
8C Steve Dean	1.00	2.50
8D Jerry Brown	1.00	2.50
8H John Croyle	1.00	2.50
8S Noah Miller	1.00	2.50
9C Leroy Cook	1.00	2.50
9D Sylvester Croom	1.50	4.00
9H Wilbur Jackson	3.00	6.00
9S Ellis Beck	1.00	2.50
10C Tyrone King	1.00	2.50
10D Mike Stock	1.00	2.50
10H Mike DuBose	1.00	2.50
10S Bill Davis	1.00	2.50
11C Gary Rutledge	1.25	3.00
11D Randy Billingsley	1.00	2.50
11H Randy Hall	1.00	2.50
11S Ralph Stokes	1.00	2.50
12C Woodrow Lowe	3.00	6.00
12D Marvin Barron	1.00	2.50
12H Mike Raines	1.00	2.50
12S Wayne Wheeler	1.00	2.50
13C Steve Sprayberry	1.00	2.50
13D Wayne Hall	1.25	3.00
13H Morris Hunt	1.00	2.50
13S Butch Norman	1.00	2.50
JOK1 Denny Stadium	1.00	2.50
JOK2 Memorial Coliseum	1.00	2.50

1982 Alabama Team Sheets

The University of Alabama issued these sheets of black-and-white player photos. Each measures roughly 7 7/8" by 10" and was printed on glossy stock with white borders. Each sheet (except the last one) includes photos of 8-players with his name below the image. The photos are blankbacked.

COMPLETE SET (9)	30.00	60.00
1 Mike Adcock	4.00	8.00
Joe Beazley		
Jesse Bendross		
Al Blue		
Steve Booker		
Thomas Boyd		
Dante Bramblett		
Gary Bramblett		
2 Larry Brown	4.00	8.00
Paul Carruth		
Joe Carter		
Jeremiah Castille		
Bob Cayavec		
Tim Clark		
Jackie Cline		
Ken Coley		
3 Earl Collins	4.00	8.00
John Cook		
Bob Dasher		
Randy Edwards		
John Elias		
Jeff Fagan		
Charles Fields		
Paul Fields		
4 Stan Gay	4.00	8.00
Alan Gray		
Jay Grogan		
Jim Bob Harris		
Josh Henderson		
Marcus Hill		
Roosevelt Hill		
Danny Holcombe		
5 Scott Homan	4.00	8.00
Jim Ivy		
Mark Jackson		
Joey Jones		
Robbie Jones		
Peter Kim		
Bart Krout		
Michael Landrum		
6 Walter Lewis	4.00	8.00
Eddie Lowe		
Warren Lyles		
Andy Martin		
Keith Marks		
Tom McCrary		
Mike McQueen		
Scott McRae		
7 Steve Mott	4.00	8.00
Mark Nix		
Ry Ogilvie		
Ben Orcutt		
Benny Perrin		
Mike Pitts		
Dexter Rutherford		
Kurt Schmissrauter		
8 Richard Shinn	4.00	8.00
Malcolm Simmons		
Ken Simon		
Anthony Smiley		
Jerrill Sprinkle		
Paul Trodd		
Doug Vickers		
Jimmy Watts		
9 Darryl White	4.00	8.00
Mike White		
Tommy Wilcox		
Roosevelt Wilder		
Charley Williams		
Russ Wood		
Big Al MASCOT		

1988 Alabama Winners

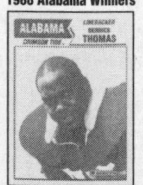

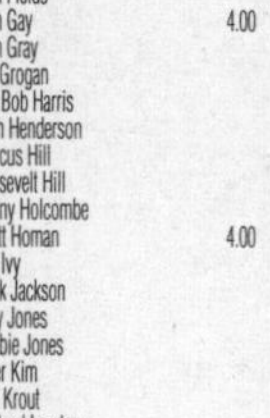

The 1988 Alabama Winners set contains 73 standard-size cards. The fronts have color portrait photos with "Alabama" and name banners in school colors; the vertically oriented backs have brief profiles and Crimson Tide highlights from specific seasons. The card numbering is essentially in order alphabetically by subject's name. The set features an early card of Derrick Thomas.

COMPLETE SET (73)	7.50	15.00
1 Title Card	.08	.25
(Schedule on back)		
2 Charlie Abrams	.05	.15
3 Sam Atkins	.05	.15
4 Marco Battle	.05	.15
5 George Bethune	.05	.15
6 Scott Bolt	.05	.15
7 Tommy Bowden	.40	1.00
8 Danny Cash	.05	.15
9 John Cassimus	.05	.15
10 David Casteal	.05	.15
11 Terrill Chatman	.05	.15
12 Andy Christoff	.05	.15
13 Tommy Cole	.05	.15
14 Tony Cox	.05	.15
15 Howard Cross	.20	.50
16 Bill Curry CO	.08	.25
17 Johnny Davis FB	.08	.25
18 Vantreise Davis	.05	.15
19 Joe Demos	.05	.15
20 Philip Doyle	.08	.25
21 Jeff Dunn	.05	.15
22 John Fruhmorgen	.05	.15
23 Jim Fuller	.05	.15
24 Greg Gilbert	.05	.15
25 Pierre Goode	.08	.25
26 John Guy	.05	.15
27 Spencer Hammond	.05	.15
28 Stacy Harrison	.05	.15
29 Murry Hill	.05	.15
30 Byron Holdbrooks	.05	.15
31 Ben Holt	.05	.15
32 Bobby Humphrey	.20	.50
33 Gene Jelks	.08	.25
34 Kermit Kendrick	.05	.15
35 William Kent	.05	.15
36 David Lenoir	.05	.15
37 Butch Lewis	.05	.15
38 Don Lindsey	.05	.15
39 John Mangum	.08	.25
40 Tim Matheny	.05	.15
41 Mac McWhorter	.08	.25
42 Chris Mohr	.08	.25
43 Larry New	.05	.15
44 Gene Newberry	.05	.15
45 Lee Ozmint	.05	.15
46 Trent Patterson	.05	.15
47 Greg Payne	.05	.15
48 Thomas Rayam	.05	.15
49 Chris Robinette	.05	.15
50 Larry Rose	.05	.15
51 Derrick Rushton	.05	.15
52 Lamonde Russell	.05	.15
53 Craig Sanderson	.05	.15
54 Wayne Shaw	.05	.15
55 Willie Shepherd	.05	.15
56 Roger Shultz	.05	.15
57 David Smith	.05	.15
58 Homer Smith	.05	.15
59 Mike Smith	.05	.15
60 Byron Sneed	.05	.15
61 Robert Stewart	.05	.15
62 Vince Strickland	.05	.15
63 Brian Stutson	.05	.15
64 Vince Sutton	.05	.15
65 Derrick Thomas	4.00	8.00
66 Steve Turner	.05	.15
67 Alan Ward	.05	.15
68 Lorenzo Ward	.05	.15
69 Steve Webb	.05	.15
70 Woody Wilson	.05	.15
71 Chip Wisdom	.05	.15
72 Willie Wyatt	.05	.15
73 Mike Zuga	.05	.15

1989 Alabama 200

The 1989 Alabama football set was produced by Collegiate Collectibles and contains 200 standard-size cards depicting former Crimson Tide greats. The fronts contain vintage photos; the horizontally oriented backs feature player profiles. Both sides have crimson borders. The cards were distributed in sets and in poly packs. These cards were printed on very thin white card stock.

COMPLETE SET (200)	20.00	40.00
1 Paul Bear Bryant	.75	2.00
2 Murray Legg	.05	.15
3 Steve Sprayberry	.05	.15
4 Tony Nathan	.15	.40
5 Howard Cross	.15	.40
6 Scott Homan	.05	.15
7 Rod Nelson	.05	.15
8 John McIntosh	.05	.15
9 Sid Smith	.05	.15
10 Legion Field	.05	.15
11 John Hannah	.20	.50
12 Mike Brock	.05	.15
13 Mike Raines	.05	.15
14 Ricky Tucker	.05	.15
15 Dennis Homan	.15	.40
16 1973 National Champs	.15	.40
17 Jon Hand	.15	.40
18 David McIntyre	.05	.15
19 David Knapp	.08	.25
20 Robert Fraley	.05	.15
21 Fred Sington	.08	.25
22 David McMakin	.08	.25
23 Bob Cryder	.05	.15
24 Randy Scott	.05	.15
25 Ken Stabler	1.00	2.50
26 Mark Prudhomme	.05	.15
27 Lydell Mitchell	.05	.15
28 Steve Patterson	.05	.15
29 Wayne Owen	.05	.15
30 Anthony Smiley	.05	.15
31 Derrick Thomas	.50	1.25
32 Johnny Musso	.15	.40
33 Wayne Wheeler	.05	.15
34 Sylvester Croom	.15	.40
35 Bruce Stephens	.05	.15
36 Tim Hurst	.05	.15
37 Joe LaBue	.05	.15
38 Joe Dismuke	.05	.15

39 Ed Hines .05 .15
40 Jack Smalley Jr. .05 .15
41 Dwight Stephenson .20 .50
42 Woodrow Lowe .08 .25
43 Leroy Cook .05 .15
44 Wes Neighbors .05 .15
45 Donnie Sutton .05 .15
46 Eddie Lowe .05 .15
47 Larry Brown .05 .15
48 Warren Dyar .05 .15
49 Terry Rowell .05 .15
50 Ray Bolden .05 .15
51 Cornelius Bennett .30 .75
52 Paul Bear Bryant .75 2.00
53 Ozzie Newsome .40 1.00
54 Van Tiffin .05 .15
55 1965 National Champs .15 .40
56 William Oliver .05 .15
57 David Smith .05 .15
58 Rich Wingo .08 .25
59 Jeff Beard .05 .15
60 John Fruhmorgen .05 .15
61 Ozzie Newsome .40 1.00
62 John Hannah .20 .50
63 Cornelius Bennett .30 .75
64 Derrick Thomas .50 1.25
65 John Croyle .05 .15
66 Stan Moss .05 .15
67 Linnie Patrick .05 .15
68 Rickey Gilliland .05 .15
69 Vince Boothe .05 .15
70 Ray Perkins CO .15 .40
71 Joe Namath 1.25 3.00
72 John Mitchell .08 .25
73 Bobby Humphrey .20 .50
74 Ray Perkins CO .15 .40
75 Mike Shula .15 .40
76 Tommy Cole .05 .15
77 Eddie Propst .05 .15
78 Rick Neal .05 .15
79 Randy Billingsley .08 .25
80 Scott Allison .05 .15
81 Steve Sloan .15 .40
82 Walter Lewis .08 .25
83 Major Ogilvie .15 .40
84 Mike Stock .05 .15
85 Tom Surlas .05 .15
86 Vince Cowell .05 .15
87 Steve Williams .05 .15
88 Johnny Mosley .05 .15
89 Angelo Stafford .05 .15
90 Vince Sutton .05 .15
91 Bill Curry .08 .25
92 Joey Jones .15 .40
93 Steadman Shealy .15 .40
94 Paul Bear Bryant .75 2.00
95 Steve Booker .05 .15
96 Don Harris .05 .15
97 Paul Bear Bryant .75 2.00
98 Greg Richardson .05 .15
99 Mal Moore .08 .25
100 Jimmy Fuller .05 .15
101 Paul Bear Bryant .75 2.00
102 Freddie Robinson .05 .15
103 Ed Morgan .05 .15
104 Johnny Sullivan .05 .15
105 George Pugh .08 .25
106 Wiley Barnes .05 .15
107 Kurt Schmissrauter .05 .15
108 David Hoss Johnson .05 .15
109 Mike Clements .05 .15
110 Larry Hoberts .08 .25
111 Mascot - Big Al .05 .15
112 Wayne Davis .05 .15
113 E.J. Junior .08 .25
114 Neb Hayden .05 .15
115 Steve Dean .05 .15
116 Craig Epps .05 .15
117 Ray Maxwell .05 .15
118 Hardy Walker .05 .15
119 Wayne Adkinson .05 .15
120 Allen Crumbley .05 .15
121 Scott Hunter .15 .40
122 Randy Barron .05 .15
123 1961 National Champs .08 .25
124 David Bedwell .05 .15
125 Peter Kim .05 .15
126 Larry Abney .05 .15
127 Bob Childs .05 .15
128 Rocky Colburn .05 .15
129 Duffy Boles .05 .15
130 Gary Otten .05 .15
131 Lee Roy Jordan .40 1.00
132 Louis Green .05 .15
133 John David Crow Jr. .08 .25
134 Jim Bob Harris .05 .15
135 David Hannah .05 .15
136 Malcolm Simmons .05 .15
137 David Casteal .05 .15
138 Gene Raburn .05 .15
139 Lou Ikner .05 .15
140 John Mauro .05 .15
141 Walter Lewis .08 .25
142 Derrick Slaughter .05 .15
143 Paul Bear Bryant .75 2.00
144 Major Ogilvie .15 .40
145 Mike Hall .05 .15
146 David Watkins .05 .15
147 Willard Scissum .05 .15
148 Richard Brewer .05 .15
149 Bruce Bolton .05 .15
150 Joe Kelley .05 .15
151 Bobby Humphrey .20 .50
152 Reid Drinkard .05 .15
153 Joe Godwin .05 .15
154 Ricky Thomas .05 .15
155 Randy Moore .05 .15
156 1961 National Champs .08 .25
157 Barry Krauss .08 .25
158 Pete Jilleba .05 .15
159 Wayne Hall .08 .25
160 Bill Curry .08 .25
161 John Mitchell .08 .25
162 Johnny Davis .15 .40
163 Paul Tripoli .05 .15
164 Mike Hodriguez .05 .15
165 Jay Grogan .05 .15
166 Bart Krout .05 .15
167 Jeremiah Castille .08 .25
168 Jimmy Carroll .05 .15
169 Greg Montgomery .08 .25
170 Neil Callaway .05 .15
171 Johnny Musso .15 .40
172 Bill Searcey .05 .15
173 Steve Whitman .05 .15
174 Thornton Chandler .08 .25
175 Britton Cooper .05 .15
176 Jeff Rutledge .15 .40
177 Kerry Goode .08 .25
178 Terry Sanders .05 .15
179 Tom McCrary .05 .15
180 Paul Boschung .05 .15
181 Pat Trammell .15 .40
182 Alan McElroy .05 .15
183 Pete Cavan .05 .15
184 Russ Wood .05 .15
185 Buddy Brown .05 .15
186 Cecil Dowdy .08 .25
187 Darryl White .05 .15
188 Fred Berrey .05 .15
189 David Sadler .05 .15
190 Claude Perry .05 .15
191 Ray Perkins CO .15 .40
192 Todd Richardson .05 .15
193 Bill Davis .05 .15
194 Jerrill Sprinkle .05 .15
195 Bryant-Denney Stadium .05 .15
196 Butch Hobson .20 .50
197 Duff Morrison .05 .15
198 Jug Jenkins .05 .15
199 Russ Mosley .05 .15
200 Hank Crisp .05 .15

1989 Alabama Coke 20

The 1989 Coke University of Alabama football set contains 20 standard-size cards, depicting former Crimson Tide greats. The fronts have vintage photos; the horizontally oriented backs feature player profiles. Both sides have crimson borders. These cards were printed on very thin stock.

COMPLETE SET (20) 5.00 12.00
C1 Paul(Bear) Bryant CO .75 2.00
C2 John Hannah .40 1.00
C3 Fred Sington .15 .40
C4 Derrick Thomas .60 1.50
C5 Dwight Stephenson .40 1.00
C6 Cornelius Bennett .40 1.00
C7 Ozzie Newsome .40 1.00
C8 Joe Namath (Art) 1.25 3.00
C9 Steve Sloan .25 .60
C10 Bill Curry CO .15 .40
C11 Paul(Bear) Bryant CO .75 2.00
C12 Big Al (Mascot) .15 .40
C13 Scott Hunter .20 .50
C14 Lee Roy Jordan .40 1.00
C15 Walter Lewis .15 .40
C16 Bobby Humphrey .15 .40
C17 John Mitchell .15 .40
C18 Johnny Musso .30 .75
C19 Pat Trammell .15 .40
C20 Ray Perkins CO .25 .60

1989 Alabama Coke 580

The 1989 Coke University of Alabama football set contains 580 standard-size cards, depicting former Crimson Tide greats. The fronts contain vintage photos; the horizontally oriented backs feature player profiles. Both sides have crimson borders. The cards were distributed in sets and in poly packs. These cards were printed on very thin stock.

COMPLETE SET (580) 14.00 35.00
1 Paul(Bear) Bryant CO .50 1.25
2 W.T. Van De Graff .02 .10
3 Pooley Hubert .02 .10
4 Bill Buckler .02 .10
5 Hoyt(Wu) Winslett .02 .10
6 Tony Holm .02 .10
7 Fred Sington Sr. .05 .15
8 John Suther .02 .10
9 Johnny Cain .02 .10
10 Tom Hupke .05 .15
11 Dixie Howell .08 .25
12 Steve Wright .02 .10
13 Bill Searcey .02 .10
14 Riley Smith .02 .10
15 Arthur Tarzan White .02 .10
16 Joe Kilgrow .02 .10
17 Leroy Monsky .02 .10
18 James Ryba .02 .10
19 Carey Cox .02 .10
20 Holt Rast .02 .10
21 Joe Domnanovich .02 .10
22 Don Whitmire .05 .15
23 Harry Gilmer .08 .25
24 Vaughn Mancha .02 .10
25 Ed Salem .02 .10
26 Bobby Marlow .10 .30
27 George Mason .02 .10
28 Billy Neighbors .08 .25
29 Lee Roy Jordan .25 .60
30 Wayne Freeman .02 .10
31 Dan Kearley .02 .10
32 Joe Namath .60 1.50
33 David Ray .05 .15
34 Paul Crane .02 .10
35 Steve Sloan .08 .25
36 Richard Cole .02 .10
37 Cecil Dowdy .05 .15
38 Bobby Johns .02 .10
39 Ray Perkins .08 .25
40 Dennis Homan .08 .25
41 Ken Stabler .50 1.25
42 Robert W. Boylston .02 .10
43 Mike Hall .02 .10
44 Alvin Samples .02 .10
45 Johnny Musso .08 .25
Bear Bryant
46 Bryant-Denney Stadium .02 .10
47 Tom Surlas .02 .10
48 John Hannah .10 .30
49 Jim Krapf .02 .10
50 John Mitchell .05 .15
51 Buddy Brown .02 .10
52 Woodrow Lowe .05 .15
53 Wayne Wheeler .02 .10
54 Leroy Cook .02 .10
55 Sylvester Croom .08 .25
56 Mike Washington .02 .10
57 Ozzie Newsome .25 .60
58 Barry Krauss .05 .15
59 Marty Lyons .08 .25
60 Jim Bunch .02 .10
61 Don McNeal .05 .15
62 Dwight Stephenson .10 .30
63 Bill Davis .02 .10
64 E.J. Junior .05 .15
65 Tommy Wilcox .05 .15
66 Jeremiah Castille .05 .15
67 Bobby Swafford .02 .10
68 Cornelius Bennett .20 .50
69 David Knapp .05 .15
70 Bobby Humphrey .10 .30
71 Van Tiffin .02 .10
72 Sid Smith .02 .10
73 Pat Trammell .08 .25
74 Mickey Andrews .02 .10
75 Steve Bowman .02 .10
76 Bob Baumhower .08 .25
77 Bob Cryder .02 .10
78 Byron Braggs .05 .15
79 Warren Lyles .02 .10
80 Steve Mott .02 .10
81 Walter Lewis .05 .15
82 Ricky Moore .02 .10
83 Wes Neighbors .02 .10
84 Derrick Thomas .40 1.00
85 Kermit Kendrick .02 .10
86 Larry Rose .02 .10
87 Charlie Marr .02 .10
88 James Whatley .02 .10
89 Erin Warren .02 .10
90 Charlie Holm .02 .10
91 Fred Davis .02 .10
92 John Wyhonic .02 .10
93 Jimmy Nelson .02 .10
94 Roy Steiner .05 .15
95 Tom Whitley .02 .10
96 John Wozniak .02 .10
97 Ed Holdnak .02 .10
98 Al Lary .02 .10
99 Mike Mizerany .02 .10
100 Pat O'Sullivan .02 .10
101 Jerry Watford .02 .10
102 Hootie Ingram .05 .15
103 Mike Fracchia .02 .10
104 Benny Nelson .02 .10
105 Tommy Tolleson .02 .10
106 Creed Gilmer .02 .10
107 John Calvert .02 .10
108 Derrick Slaughter .02 .10
109 Mike Ford .02 .10
110 Bruce Stephens .02 .10
111 Danny Ford .08 .25
112 Jimmy Grammer .02 .10
113 Steve Higginbotham .02 .10
114 David Bailey .02 .10
115 Greg Gantt .08 .25
116 Terry Davis .05 .15
117 Chuck Strickland .02 .10
118 Bobby McKinney .02 .10
119 Wilbur Jackson .08 .25
120 Mike Raines .02 .10
121 Steve Sprayberry .02 .10
122 David McMakin .05 .15
123 Ben Smith OL .02 .10
124 Steadman Shealy .08 .25
125 John Rogers .02 .10
126 Ricky Davis .05 .15
127 Conley Duncan .02 .10
128 Wayne Rhodes .02 .10
129 Buddy Seay .02 .10
130 Alan Pizzitola .02 .10
131 Richard Todd .08 .25
132 Charlie Ferguson .02 .10
133 Charley Hannah .05 .15
134 Wiley Barnes .02 .10
135 Mike Brock .02 .10
136 Murray Legg .02 .10
137 Wayne Hamilton .02 .10
138 David Hannah .02 .10
139 Jim Bob Harris .02 .10
140 Bart Krout .02 .10
141 Bob Cayavec .02 .10
142 Joe Beazley .02 .10
143 Mike Adcock .02 .10
144 Albert Bell .02 .10
145 Mike Shula .08 .25
146 Curt Jarvis .02 .10
147 Freddie Robinson .02 .10
148 Bill Condon .02 .10
149 Howard Cross .10 .30
150 Joe Demyanovich .02 .10
151 Major Ogilvie .08 .25
152 Perron Shoemaker .02 .10
153 Ralph Jones .02 .10
154 Vic Bradford .02 .10
155 Ed Hickerson .02 .10
156 Mitchell Olenski .02 .10
157 George Hecht .02 .10
158 Russ Craft .02 .10
159 Joey Jones .08 .25
160 Jack Green .02 .10
161 Lowell Tew .05 .15
162 Lamar Moye .02 .10
163 Jesse Richardson .05 .15
164 Harold Lutz .02 .10
165 Travis Hunt .02 .10
166 Ed Culpepper .02 .10
167 Nick Germanos .02 .10
168 Billy Rains .02 .10
169 Don Cochran .02 .10
170 Cotton Clark .02 .10
171 Gaylon McCollogh .02 .10
172 Tim Bates .02 .10
173 Wayne Cook .02 .10
174 Jerry Duncan .02 .10
175 Steve Davis .02 .10
176 Donnie Sutton .02 .10
177 Randy Barron .02 .10
178 Frank Mann .02 .10
179 Jeff Rouzie .02 .10
180 John Croyle .02 .10
181 Skip Kubelius .02 .10
182 Steve Bisceglia .02 .10
183 Gary Rutledge .05 .15
184 Mike DuBose .02 .10
185 Johnny Davis .08 .25
186 K.J. Lazenby .02 .10
187 Jeff Rutledge .08 .25
188 Mike Tucker .02 .10
189 Tony Nathan .08 .25
190 Buddy Aydelette .02 .10
191 Steve Whitman .02 .10
192 Ricky Tucker .02 .10
193 Randy Scott .02 .10
194 Warren Averitte .02 .10
195 Doug Vickers .02 .10
196 Jackie Cline .02 .10
197 Wayne Davis .02 .10
198 Hardy Walker .02 .10
199 Paul Ott Carruth .05 .15
200 Paul(Bear) Bryant CO .50 1.25
201 Randy Rockwell .02 .10
202 Chris Mohr .05 .15
203 Walter Merrill .02 .10
204 Johnny Sullivan .02 .10
205 Harold Newman .02 .10
206 Erskine Walker .02 .10
207 Ted Cook .02 .10
208 Charles Compton .02 .10
209 Bill Cadenhead .02 .10
210 Butch Avinger .02 .10
211 Bobby Wilson .02 .10
212 Sid Youngelman .08 .25
213 Leon Fuller .02 .10
214 Tommy Brooker .05 .15
215 Richard Williamson .05 .15
216 Riggs Stephenson .08 .25
217 Al Clemens .02 .10
218 Grant Gillis .02 .10
219 Johnny Mack Brown .20 .50
220 Major Ogilvie .08 .25
Bear Bryant
221 Fred Pickhard .02 .10
222 Herschel Caldwell .02 .10
223 Emile Barnes .02 .10
224 Mike McQueen .02 .10
225 Ray Abruzzese .05 .15
226 Jesse Bendross .08 .25
227 Lew Bostick .02 .10
228 Jim Bowdoin .02 .10
229 Dave Brown .02 .10
230 Tom Calvin .02 .10
231 Ken Emerson .02 .10
232 Calvin Frey .02 .10
233 Thornton Chandler .05 .15
234 George Weeks .02 .10
235 Randy Edwards .02 .10
236 Phillip Brown .02 .10
237 Clay Whitehurst .02 .10
238 Chris Goode .02 .10
239 Preston Gothard .02 .10
240 Herb Hannah .02 .10
241 John M. Snoderly .02 .10
242 Scott Hunter .08 .25
243 Bobby Jackson .02 .10
244 Bruce Jones .02 .10
245 Robbie Jones .02 .10
246 Terry Jones .02 .10
247 Leslie Kelley .02 .10
248 Larry Lauer .02 .10
249 1961 National Champs .08 .25
(Tommy Brooker,
Pat Trammell,
Lee Roy Jordan,
Paul(Bear) Bryant,
Mike Fracchia,
Billy Neighbors)
250 Bobby Luna .02 .10
251 Keith Pugh .02 .10
252 Alan McElroy .02 .10
253 1925 National Champs .05 .15
(Team Photo)
254 Curtis McGriff .08 .25
255 Norman Mosley .02 .10
256 Herky Mosley .02 .10
257 Ray Ogden .05 .15
258 Pete Jilleba .02 .10
259 Benny Perrin .02 .10
260 Claude Perry .02 .10
261 Tommy Cole .02 .10
262 Ed Versprille .02 .10
263 1930 National Champs .05 .15
(Team Photo)
264 Don Jacobs .02 .10
265 Robert Skelton .02 .10
266 Joe Curtis .02 .10
267 Bart Starr .60 1.50
268 Young Boozer .02 .10
269 Tommy Lewis .05 .15
270 Woody Umphrey .02 .10
271 Carney Laslie .02 .10
272 Russ Wood .02 .10
273 David Smith .02 .10
274 Paul Spivey .02 .10
275 Linnie Patrick .02 .10
276 Ron Durby .02 .10
277 1926 National Champs .05 .15
(Team Photo)
278 Robert Higginbotham .02 .10
279 William Oliver .02 .10
280 Stan Moss .02 .10
281 Eddie Propst .02 .10
282 Laurien Stapp .02 .10
283 Clem Gryska .02 .10
284 Clark Pearce .02 .10
285 Pete Cavan .02 .10
286 Tom Newton .02 .10
287 Rich Wingo .05 .15
288 Rickey Gilliland .02 .10
289 Conrad Fowler .02 .10
290 Rick Neal .02 .10
291 James Blevins .02 .10
292 Dick Flowers .02 .10
293 Marshall Brown .02 .10
294 Jeff Beard .02 .10
295 Pete Moore .02 .10
296 Vince Boothe .02 .10
297 Charley Boswell .02 .10
298 Van Marcus .02 .10
299 Randy Billingsley .05 .15
300 Paul(Bear) Bryant CO .50 1.25
*301 Gene Blackwell .02 .10
302 Johnny Mosley .02 .10
303 Ray Perkins CO .08 .25
304 Harold Drew CO .02 .10
305 Frank Thomas CO .08 .25
(Not the Frank Thomas
that went to Auburn)
306 Wallace Wade CO .05 .15
307 Newton Godfree .02 .10
308 Steve Williams .02 .10
309 Al Lewis .02 .10
310 Fred Grant .02 .10
311 Jerry Brown .02 .10
312 Mal Moore CO .05 .15
with Bear Bryant
313 Tilden Campbell .02 .10
314 Jack Smalley .02 .10
315 Paul(Bear) Bryant CO .50 1.25
316 C.B. Clements .02 .10
317 Billy Piper .02 .10
318 Robert Lee Hamner .02 .10
319 Donnie Faust .02 .10
320 Gary Bramblett .02 .10
321 Peter Kim .02 .10
322 Fred Berrey .02 .10
323 Paul(Bear) Bryant CO .50 1.25
324 John Fruhmorgen .02 .10
325 Jim Fuller .02 .10
Bear Bryant
326 Doug Allen .02 .10
327 Russ Mosley .02 .10
328 Ricky Thomas .02 .10
329 Vince Sutton .02 .10
330 Larry Roberts .05 .15
331 Rick McLain .02 .10
332 Charles Eckerly .02 .10
333 1934 National Champs .05 .15
(Team Photo)
334 Eddie McCombs .02 .10
335 Scott Allison .02 .10
336 Vince Cowell .02 .10
337 David Watkins .02 .10
338 Jim Duke .02 .10
339 Don Harris .02 .10
340 Lanny Norris .02 .10
341 Thad Flanagan .02 .10
342 Albert Elmore Jr. .02 .10
343 Alan Gray .02 .10
344 David Gilmer .02 .10
345 Hal Self .02 .10
346 Ben McLeod .02 .10
347 Clell(Butch) Hobson .10 .30
348 Jimmy Carroll .02 .10
349 Frank Canterbury .02 .10
350 John Byrd Williams .02 .10
351 Marvin Barron .02 .10
352 William J. Stone .02 .10
353 Barry Smith .05 .15
354 Jerrill Sprinkle .02 .10
355 Hank Crisp CO .02 .10
356 Bobby Smith .02 .10
357 Charles Gray .02 .10
358 Marlin Dyess .02 .10
359 1941 National Champs .05 .15
(Team Photo)
360 Robert Moore .02 .10
361 1961 National Champs .05 .15
Billy Neighbors
Pat Trammell
Darwin Holt
362 Tommy White .02 .10
363 Earl Wesley .02 .10
364 John O'Linger .02 .10
365 Bill Battle .02 .10
366 Butch Wilson .02 .10
367 Tim Davis .02 .10
368 Larry Wall .02 .10
369 Hudson Harris .02 .10
370 Mike Hopper .02 .10
371 Jackie Sherrill .10 .30
372 Tom Somerville .02 .10
373 David Chatwood .02 .10
374 George Ranager .02 .10
375 Tommy Wade .08 .25
376 1964 National Champs .40 1.00
(Joe Namath)
377 Reid Drinkard .02 .10
378 Mike Hand .02 .10
379 Ed White .08 .25
380 Angelo Stafford .02 .10
381 Ellis Beck .02 .10
382 Wayne Hall .05 .15
383 Randy Hall .02 .10
384 Jack O'Rear .02 .10
385 Colenzo Hubbard .02 .10
386 Gus White .02 .10
387 Rick Watson .02 .10
388 Steve Allen .02 .10
389 John David Crow Jr. .05 .15
390 Britton Cooper .02 .10
391 Mike Rodriguez .02 .10
392 Steve Wade .02 .10
393 William J. Rice .02 .10
394 Greg Richardson .02 .10
395 Joe Jones .05 .15
396 Todd Richardson .02 .10
397 Anthony Smiley .02 .10
398 Duff Morrison .02 .10
399 Jay Grogan .02 .10
400 Steve Booker .02 .10
401 Larry Abney .02 .10
402 Bill Abston .02 .10
403 Wayne Adkinson .02 .10
404 Charles Allen .02 .10
405 Phil Allman .02 .10
406 1965 National Champs .08 .25
(1965 Seniors)
Steve Sloan
Paul Crane
David Ray
Tommy Tolleson
Ben McLeod
Jackie Sherrill
Tim Bates
Creed Gilmer
Steve Bowman
407 James Angelich .02 .10
408 Troy Barker .02 .10
409 George Bethune .02 .10
410 Bill Blair .02 .10
411 Clark Boler .02 .10
412 Duffy Boles .02 .10
413 Ray Bolden .02 .10
414 Bruce Bolton .02 .10
415 Alvin Davis .02 .10
416 Baxter Booth .02 .10
417 Paul Boschung .02 .10
418 1979 National Champs .08 .25
(Team Photo)
419 Richard Brewer .02 .10
420 Jack Brown .02 .10
421 Larry Brown TE .02 .10
422 David Brungard .02 .10
423 Jim Burkett .02 .10
424 Auxford Burks .02 .10
425 Jim Cain .02 .10
426 Dick Turpin .02 .10
427 Neil Callaway .02 .10
428 David Casteal .02 .10
429 Phil Chaffin .02 .10
430 Howard Chappell .02 .10
431 Bob Childs .02 .10
432 Knute Rockne Christian .02 .10
433 Richard Ciemny .02 .10
434 J.B. Whitworth .02 .10
435 Mike Clements .02 .10
436 1973 National Champs .08 .25
(Coaching Staff)
437 Rocky Colburn .02 .10
438 Danny Collins .02 .10
439 James Taylor .02 .10
440 Joe Compton .02 .10
441 Bob Conway .02 .10
442 Charlie Stephens .02 .10
443 Kerry Goode .05 .15
444 Joe LaBue .02 .10
445 Allen Crumbley .02 .10
446 Bill Curry CO .05 .15
447 David Bedwell .02 .10
448 Jim Davis .02 .10
449 Mike Dean .02 .10
450 Steve Dean .02 .10
451 Vince DeLaurentis .02 .10
452 Gary Deniro .02 .10
453 Jim Dildy .02 .10
454 Joe Dildy .02 .10
455 Jimmy Dill .02 .10
456 Joe Dismuke .02 .10
457 Junior Davis .02 .10
458 Warren Dyar .02 .10
459 Hugh Morrow .02 .10
460 Grady Elmore .02 .10
461 1978 National Champs .08 .25
Jeff Rutledge
Tony Nathan
Barry Krauss
Marty Lyons
Rich Wingo
462 Ed Hines .02 .10
463 D.Joe Gambrell .02 .10
464 Kavanaugh(Kay) Francis .02 .10
465 Robert Fraley .02 .10
466 Milton Frank .02 .10
467 Jim Franko .02 .10
468 Buddy French .02 .10
469 Wayne Rhoads .02 .10
470 Ralph Gandy .02 .10
471 Danny Gilbert .02 .10
472 Greg Gilbert .02 .10
473 Joe Godwin .02 .10
474 Richard Grammer .02 .10
475 Louis Green .02 .10
476 Gary Martin .02 .10
477 Bill Hannah .02 .10
478 Allen Harpole .02 .10
479 Neb Hayden .02 .10
480 Butch Henry .02 .10
481 Norwood Hodges .02 .10
482 Earl Smith .02 .10
483 Darwin Holt .02 .10
484 Scott Homan .02 .10
485 Nathan Rustin .02 .10
486 Gene Raburn .02 .10
487 Ellis Houston .02 .10
488 Frank Howard .02 .10
489 Larry Hughes .02 .10
490 Joe Kelley .02 .10
491 Charlie Harris .02 .10
492 Legion Field .02 .10
493 Tim Hurst .02 .10
494 Hunter Husband .02 .10
495 Lou Ikner .02 .10
496 Craig Epps .02 .10
497 Jug Jenkins .02 .10
498 Billy Johnson .02 .10
499 David Johnson .02 .10
500 Jon Hand .08 .25
501 Max Kelley .02 .10
502 Terry Killgore .02 .10
503 Eddie Lowe .02 .10
504 Noah Langdale .02 .10
505 Ed Lary .02 .10
506 Foy Leach .02 .10
507 Harry Lee .02 .10
508 Jim Loftin .02 .10
509 Curtis Lynch .02 .10
510 John Mauro .02 .10
511 Ray Maxwell .02 .10
512 Frank McClendon .02 .10
513 Tom McCrary .02 .10
514 Sonny McGahey .02 .10
515 John McIntosh .02 .10
516 David McIntyre .02 .10
517 Wes Thompson .02 .10
518 James Melton .02 .10
519 John Miller .02 .10
520 Fred Mims .02 .10
521 Dewey Mitchell .02 .10
522 Lydell Mitchell LB .02 .10
523 Greg Montgomery .05 .15
524 Jimmie Moore .02 .10
525 Randy Moore .02 .10
526 Ed Morgan .02 .10
527 Norris Hamer .02 .10
528 Frank Mosely .02 .10
529 Sidney Neighbors .02 .10
530 Rod Nelson .02 .10
531 James Nisbet .02 .10
532 Mark Nix .02 .10
533 L.W. Noonan .02 .10
534 Louis Thompson .02 .10
535 William Oliver .02 .10
536 Gary Otten .02 .10
537 Wayne Owen .02 .10
538 Steve Patterson .02 .10
539 Charley Pell .08 .25
540 Bob Pettee .02 .10
541 Gordon Pettus .02 .10
542 Gary Phillips .02 .10
543 Clay Walls .02 .10
544 Douglas Potts .02 .10
545 Mike Stock .02 .10
546 John Mark Prudhomme .02 .10
547 George Pugh .05 .15
548 Pat Raines .02 .10
549 Joe Riley .02 .10
550 Wayne Trimble .02 .10
551 Darryl White .02 .10
552 Bill Richardson .02 .10
553 Ray Richeson .02 .10
554 Danny Ridgeway .02 .10
555 Terry Sanders .02 .10
556 Kenneth Roberts .02 .10
557 Jimmy Watts .02 .10
558 Ron Robertson .02 .10
559 Norbie Ronsonet .02 .10
560 Jimmy Lynn Rosser .02 .10
561 Terry Rowell .02 .10
562 Larry Joe Ruffin .02 .10
563 Jack Rutledge .02 .10
564 Al Sabo .02 .10
565 David Sadler .02 .10
566 Donald Sanford .02 .10
567 Hayward Sanford .02 .10
568 Paul Tripoli .02 .10
569 Lou Scales .02 .10
570 Kurt Schmissrauter .02 .10
571 Willard Scissum .02 .10
572 Joe Sewell .05 .15
573 Jimmy Sharpe .02 .10
574 Willie Shepherd .02 .10
575 Jack Smalley Jr. .02 .10
576 Jim Simmons .02 .10
(Tight End)
577 Jim Simmons .02 .10
(Tackle)
578 Malcolm Simmons .02 .10
579 Dave Sington .02 .10
580 Fred Sington Jr. .05 .15
AL1 Joe Namath Promo .75 2.00
AL2 Bart Starr Promo .75 2.00

1992 Alabama All-Century Candidates Hoby

This 42-card standard-size set was issued to commemorate a special Centennial Festival weekend. It is also commonly referred to as "Alabama Greats." It features 42 Team of the Century candidates as selected by the fans. The fronts display a mix of glossy black and white or color player photos with rounded corners on a crimson card face. The "Century of Champions" logo is superimposed at the bottom of the picture over a white and crimson stripe pattern with the "Candidates" tag clearly stated at the card's top. On the crimson-colored backs, "Bama" appears in large block lettering at the top, with the player's name and brief biographical information presented below.

COMPLETE SET (42) 7.50 15.00
1 Bob Baumhower .20 .50
2 Cornelius Bennett .30 .75
3 Buddy Brown .08 .25
4 Paul(Bear) Bryant CO 1.00 2.00
5 Johnny Cain .08 .25
6 Jeremiah Castille .15 .35
7 Leroy Cook .08 .25
8 Paul Crane .15 .35
9 Philip Doyle .08 .25
10 Harry Gilmer .15 .35
11 Jon Hand .20 .50
12 Herb Hannah .08 .25
13 John Hannah .40 1.00
14 Dennis Homan .15 .35
15 Dixie Howell .15 .35
16 Bobby Humphrey .15 .35
17 Don Hutson .40 1.00
18 Curt Jarvis .15 .35
19 Lee Roy Jordan .40 1.00
20 Barry Krauss .15 .35
21 Woodrow Lowe .15 .35
22 Marty Lyons .15 .35
23 Vaughn Mancha .08 .25
24 John Mangum .15 .35
25 Bobby Marlow .15 .35
26 Don McNeal .15 .35
27 Chris Mohr .15 .35
28 Johnny Musso .20 .50
29 Billy Neighbors .15 .35
30 Ozzie Newsome .40 1.00
31 Ray Perkins .20 .50
32 Fred Sington .08 .25
33 Ken Stabler .80 2.00
34 Siran Stacy .15 .35
35 Dwight Stephenson .30 .75
36 Robert Stewart .08 .25
37 Derrick Thomas .80 2.00
38 Van Tiffin .08 .25
39 Mike Washington* .08 .25
40 Arthur Tarzan White .08 .25
41 Tommy Wilcox .15 .35
42 Willie Wyatt .08 .25

1992 Alabama All-Century Team Hoby

This set of cards was produced by Hoby and distributed as a 26-card sheet for the player's selected to the All-Century team. Each card is essentially a re-numbered version of the Candidates Hoby set with the word "Candidates" removed from the cardfronts.

COMPLETE SET (26) 15.00 25.00
1 Johnny Musso .50 1.25
2 Derrick Thomas 2.00 4.00
3 Big Al .20 .50
(mascot)
4 Paul Bear Bryant CO 2.00 4.00
5 Van Tiffin .20 .50
6 Billy Neighbors .30 .75
7 Jon Hand .50 1.25
8 Ozzie Newsome 1.00 2.00
9 Don Hutson 1.00 2.00
10 Bobby Humphrey .30 .75
11 Vaughn Mancha .20 .50
12 John Hannah 1.00 2.00
13 Fred Sington Sr. .20 .50
14 Dwight Stephenson .60 1.50
15 Marty Lyons .30 .75
16 Cornelius Bennett .60 1.50
17 Harry Gilmer .30 .75
18 Jeremiah Castille .30 .75
19 Don McNeal .30 .75
20 Lee Roy Jordan 1.00 2.00
21 Bobby Marlow .30 .75
22 Ken Stabler 2.00 4.00
23 Johnny Cain .20 .50
24 Bob Baumhower .50 1.25
25 Tommy Wilcox .30 .75
26 Barry Krauss .30 .75

1995 Alabama Team Sheets

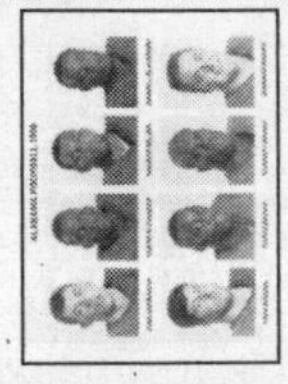

These photos were issued by the school to promote the football program. Unless noted below, each measures roughly 8" by 10" and features either four or eight players with a black and white image for each. The school name and year appear at the top and the backs are blank.

COMPLETE SET (11) 25.00 50.00
1 Thad Abernathy 3.00 6.00
Curtis Alexander
Maurice Belser
Darrell Blackburn
Vann Bodden
Curtis Brown
Elverett Brown
Shannon Brown
2 Tyrell Buckner 3.00 6.00
Brian Burgdorf
Kendrick Burton

Blair Canale		
John Causey		
Jackson Cook		
Travis Crim		
Rhett Crutchfield		
3 Derek Cunningham	3.00	6.00
Fernando Davis		
Pete DiMario		
Anthony Dowdell		
Chris Edwards		
Lamont Floyd		
Brad Ford		
Warren Foust		
4 Will Friend	3.00	6.00
Rondi Gibson		
David Goss		
Calvin Hall		
Patrick Hape		
Steve Harris		
Matt Harrison		
Tracy High		
5 Joel Holliday	3.00	6.00
Chris Hood		
Eddie Hunter		
Kevin Jackson		
Tony Johnson		
Chris Jordan		
Eric Kerley		
Chad Key		
6 Freddie Kitchens	3.00	6.00
Chester Lewis		
Montoya Madden		
Toderick Malone		
Kareem McNeal		
Kelvin Moore		
Josh Niblett		
Franz Odom		
7 Matt Parker	3.00	6.00
Jeremy Pennington		
John David Phillips		
Paul Pickett		
Daniel Pope		
Pzell Powell		
Michael Proctor		
Jeremy Pruitt		
8 Michael Ray	3.00	6.00
Dennis Riddle		
Dwayne Rudd		
Rod Rutledge		
Cedric Samuel		
Ed Scissum		
Andre Short		
Chris Sign		
9 Tito Smith	3.00	6.00
Trevis Smith		
Sage Spree		
Ralph Staten		
Brian Steger		
Hayden Stockton		
Josh Swords		
John Tanks		
10 Bryan Thornton	3.00	6.00
Deshea Townsend		
Lance Tucker		
Eric Turner		
Taurus Turner		
Granison Wagstaff		
Ed Walker		
John Walters		
11 William Watts	3.00	6.00
Marcell West		
Laron White		
Owen Winston		
Team Logo		

1999 Alabama Schedules

COMPLETE SET (12)	3.00	6.00
1 Shaun Alexander	.50	1.25
2 Tim Bowens	.30	.75
3 Shamari Buchanan	.20	.50
4 Jamie Carter	.20	.50
5 Mike DuBose (on players shoulders)	.20	.50
6 Mike DuBose (on sidelines)	.20	.50
7 Cornelius Griffin	.20	.50
8 Reggie Grimes	.20	.50
9 Canary Knight	.20	.50
10 Jason McDonald	.20	.50
11 Miguel Merritt	.20	.50
12 Chris Samuels	.30	.75

2002 Alabama Power

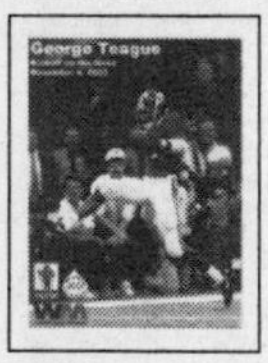

COMPLETE SET (3)	6.00	15.00
1 Travis Hunt	2.00	5.00
2 George Teague	2.50	6.00
3 Bobby Wilson	2.00	5.00

2000 Alabama Schedules

1 Kecalf Bailey	.30	.75
2 Will Cuthbert	.30	.75
3 Tony Dixon (reaching for football)	.40	1.00
4 Tony Dixon (tackling)	.40	1.00
5 Mike DuBose CO	.30	.75
6 Jason Jones	.30	.75
7 Bradley Ledbetter	.30	.75
8 Dustin McClintock	.30	.75
9 Griff Redmill	.30	.75
10 Kelvis White	.30	.75

2003 Alabama

This set was issued by the school at a late season home game in 2003. The cards feature all-time greats from Alabama football and were sponsored on the backs by NBC 13, Golden Flake, The Birmingham News, and the Birmingham Post Herald.

COMPLETE SET (13)	20.00	40.00
1 Cornelius Bennett	2.00	5.00
2 Bear Bryant	2.50	6.00
3 Scott Hunter	1.25	3.00
4 Antonio Langham	1.00	2.50
5 Bobby Marlow	1.00	2.50
6 Johnny Musso	1.00	2.50
7 Joe Namath	2.50	6.00
8 Gary Rutledge Wayne Wheeler	1.00	2.50
9 Mike Shula	1.25	3.00
10 Ken Stabler	2.00	5.00
11 Derrick Thomas	2.00	5.00
12 Van Tiffin	1.25	3.00
13 1948 Alabama vs. Auburn (program cover)	1.25	3.00

2003 Alabama Schedules

1 Dennis Alexander	.30	.75
2 Carlos Andrews	.30	.75
3 Anthony Bryant	.30	.75
4 Antonio Carter	.30	.75
5 Ahmad Childress	.30	.75
6 Donald Clarke	.30	.75
7 Brooks Daniels	.30	.75
8 Dre Fulgham	.30	.75
9 Atlas Herrion	.30	.75
10 Charles Jones RB	.30	.75
11 Matt Lomax	.30	.75
12 Triandos Luke	.40	1.00
13 Nautyn McKay-Loescher	.30	.75
14 Derrick Pope	.40	1.00
15 Nick Ridings	.30	.75
16 Kyle Robinson	.30	.75
17 David Scott	.30	.75
18 Mike Shula CO	.30	.75
19 Lance Taylor	.30	.75
20 Leslie Williams	.30	.75
21 Shaud Williams	.40	1.00

2004 Alabama Power

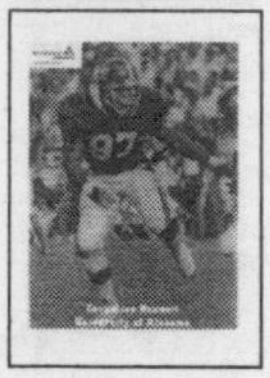

COMPLETE SET (6)	6.00	15.00
1 Cornelius Bennett	1.50	4.00
2 Wayne Freeman	1.25	3.00
3 Bobby Humphrey	1.50	4.00
4 Dan Kearley	1.25	3.00
5 Michael Proctor	1.25	3.00
6 Andrew Zow	1.25	3.00

2004 Alabama Schedules

1 Brian Bostick	.30	.75
2 Wesley Britt	.30	.75
3 Anthony Bryant	.30	.75
4 Antonio Carter	.30	.75
5 Bo Freelend	.30	.75
6 Tarry Givens	.30	.75
7 Ray Hudson	.30	.75
8 Anthony Madison	.30	.75
9 Danny Martz	.30	.75
10 Evan Mathis	.30	.75
11 Mike Shula CO	.30	.75
12 Josh Smith	.30	.75
13 Thurman Ward	.30	.75
14 Cornelius Wortham	.40	1.00

2005 Alabama Schedules

COMPLETE SET (13)	4.00	8.00
1 Jeremy Clark	.30	.75
2 J.B. Closner	.30	.75
3 Brodie Croyle	.75	2.00
4 Kenneth Darby	.50	1.25
5 Roman Harper	.30	.75
6 Anthony Madison	.30	.75
7 Charlie Peprah	.30	.75
8 Tyrone Prothro	.30	.75
9 Freddie Roach	.30	.75
10 DeMeco Ryans	.50	1.25
11 Mike Shula CO (2005 and 2006 scheds on back)	.30	.75
12 Mike Shula CO (2005 sched only on back)	.30	.75
13 Kyle Tatum	.30	.75

2006 Alabama Legends Playing Cards

1C Frank Thomas	.08	.25
1D Wallace Wade	.08	.25
1H Gene Stallings CO	.20	.50
2C Steve Whitman	.08	.25
2D Billy Vandefraaf	.08	.25
2H Hootie Ingram	.08	.25
2S Tarzan White	.08	.25
3C Wilbur Jackson	.15	.40
3D John Mangum	.08	.25
3H Gaylon McCollough	.08	.25
3S Steve Bowman	.08	.25
4C David Bailey	.08	.25
4D Kevin Jackson	.08	.25
4H Terry Davis	.08	.25
4S Tommy Brooker	.08	.25
5C Jeremiah Castille	.08	.25
5D Mike Hall	.08	.25
5H John Croyle	.08	.25
5S Buddy Brown	.08	.25
6C Ricky Moore	.08	.25
6D Scott Hunter	.08	.25
6H Roger Schultz	.08	.25
6S Byron Braggs	.08	.25
7C Jim Krapf	.08	.25
7D Tony Nathan	.20	.50
7H Pat Trammell	.08	.25
7S Bobby Johns	.08	.25
8C Dennis Homan	.08	.25
8D Major Ogilvie	.15	.40
8H Steadman Shealy	.08	.25
8S Mike Washington	.15	.40
9C John Mitchell	.08	.25
9D Bobby Marlow	.08	.25
9H Vaughn Mancha	.08	.25
9S Jeff Rutledge	.08	.25
10C Steve Sloan	.08	.25
10D Tommy Wilcox	.08	.25
10H E.J. Junior	.20	.50
10S Barry Krauss	.08	.25
11C Leroy Cook	.08	.25
11D Johnny Mack Brown	.08	.25
11H Marty Lyons	.08	.25
11S Johnny Cain	.08	.25
12C Dixie Howell	.08	.25
12D Woodrow Lowe	.08	.25
12H Billy Neighbors	.08	.25
12S Don Hutson	.30	.75
13C Fred Sington	.08	.25
13D Johnny Musso	.30	.75
13H Lee Roy Jordan	.20	.50
13S Bobby Humphrey	.15	.40
1S1 Ozzie Newsome (issued in factory set)	.30	.75
1S2 Paul Bear Bryant CO (issued via website only)	.50	1.25
NNO Bryant Museum Ad Card	.08	.25
NNO Legends Collectibles Ad Card	.08	.25
JOK1 Alabama Mascot	.08	.25
JOK2 Alabama Mascot	.08	.25

2006 Alabama Schedules

1 J.P. Adams	.30	.75
2 Danny Barger	.30	.75
3 Jeremy Clark	.30	.75
4 Jeffrey Dukes	.30	.75
5 Mark Guillon	.30	.75
6 Chris Harris	.30	.75
7 Terence Jones	.30	.75
8 Bryan Killpatrick	.30	.75
9 Le'Ron McClain	.75	2.00
10 Ramzee Robinson	.30	.75
11 Juwan Simpson	.30	1.00
12 Kyle Tatum	.30	.75

2007 Alabama Press Pass

This set was issued for the school and released at the Alabama football spring game in early 2007. Four different jersey cards were randomly seeded in the sets with just one featuring an Alabama football player.

COMPLETE SET (25)	12.50	25.00
1 Nick Saban CO	.60	1.50
2 Javier Arenas	.40	1.00
3 Justin Britt	.40	1.00
4 Keith Brown	.60	1.50
5 Antoine Caldwell	.40	1.00
6 Chris Capps	.40	1.00
7 Marcus Carter	.40	1.00
8 Simeon Castille	.40	1.00
9 Jamie Christensen	.40	1.00
10 Matt Collins	.40	1.00
11 P.J. Fitzgerald	.40	1.00
12 Wallace Gilberry	.40	1.00
13 Eric Gray	.40	1.00
14 Bobby Greenwood	.40	1.00
15 DJ Hall	.75	2.00
16 Prince Hall	.40	1.00
17 Jimmy Johns	.60	1.50
18 Travis McCall	.40	1.00
19 Lionel Mitchell	.40	1.00
20 Will Oakley	.40	1.00
21 Tyrone Prothro	.40	1.00
22 Keith Saunders	.40	1.00
23 Zach Schreiber	.40	1.00
24 Andre Smith	.60	1.50
25 John Parker Wilson	1.00	2.50
KD Kenneth Darby JSY	10.00	25.00

2006 Alabama Birmingham

1 Dan Burks	.75	2.00
2 Will McCullars	.75	2.00
3 Orlandus King	.75	2.00
4 Larry McSwain	.75	2.00
5 Corey White	.75	2.00
6 Dr. Henghui Zou	.40	1.00
7 Team Photo	.75	2.00

1996 Alabama State Schedules

COMPLETE SET (8)	3.00	6.00
1 George Bowens	.40	1.00
2 Jeffery Calloway	.40	1.00
3 Antonio Parker B&W	.40	1.00
4 Antonio Parker Color	.40	1.00
5 Reginald Pearson	.40	1.00
6 Harry Seymour	.40	1.00
7 Clarence Thomas	.40	1.00
8 Tim Thurman	.40	1.00

1929 Albert Richard Co. All American Photos

This set of blankbacked photos was issued by the Albert Richard Company to honor the clothing firm's selection of 1929 college All Americans. Each photo measures roughly 8" by 10" and features a sepia toned photo of the player wearing an Albert Richard coat. A thick white border surrounds the image and the player's name and a brief bio is included in the bottom border. Each photo also includes a facsimile autograph. Finally, an additional cover or header sheet accompanied the set.

COMPLETE SET (12)	500.00	800.00
1 George Ackerman	30.00	60.00
2 Chris Cagle	30.00	60.00
3 John Cannon	30.00	60.00
4 Frank Carideo	30.00	60.00
5 Joe Donchess	30.00	60.00
6 Bill Glassgow	30.00	60.00
7 Ray Montgomery	30.00	60.00
8 Bronko Nagurski	250.00	400.00
9 Elmer Sleight	30.00	60.00
10 Francis Tap Tappaan	30.00	60.00
11 Ralph Welch	30.00	60.00
12 Header Sheet	6.00	15.00

1991 Antelope Valley Junior College

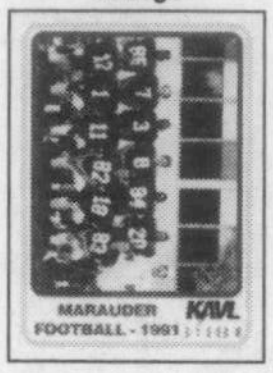

COMPLETE SET (7)	4.00	10.00
1 Joe Watts	.60	1.50
Steve Stokes		
Frank Blua		
Mike Martinez		
Brent Carder		
Dave Gross		
2 Joe Blue	.60	1.50
Richard Cage		
Brian McCalister		
Steve Stokes		
Charley Wright		
Daron Rodgers		
Jon Luna		
Jeremy King		
Eric Cyprian		
Paul Kaplin		
Troy Javadi		
Steve McQuade		
Rick Nickols		
3 Chris Goring	.60	1.50
Richard Pesti		
Robert Haywood		
Hasaan Blunt		
Ronald Bryant		
Wilson Hookfin		
Erik Blake		
Jason Arebalo		
Jason Brown		
Joe Watts (DC)		
4 Nate Williams	.60	1.50
Ryan Callahan		
Marty Washington		
Tony Abrams		
Joseph Arnold		
David Brown		
Dave Gross (OC)		
Brad Cole		
Courtney Miller		
Eric Price		
Brian Porter		
Lemart Cooper		
Jon Furman		
5 Jesse Cartwright	.60	1.50
William Knight		
Mike Martinez CO		
George Murdoch		
Tony Valencia		
John Richards		
Thomas Reimer		
Alex Siler		
Chris Johnson		
Mike Khachatrian		
Chuck Slaton		
6 Frank Blua (OC)	.60	1.50
Gene Washington		
Greg Graham		
Emery Nelson		
David Nelson		
Carey Barnes		
Sid Blackwood		
Jorge Ordaz		
Al Dawkins		
Chris Spivey		
Cash Achziger		
Tom Leite		
Eric Lee		
7 Sid Blackwood (schedule on back)	.60	1.50

1994 Appalachian State Team Sheets

These photos were issued by the school to promote the football program. Each measures roughly 8" by 10" and features eight black and white images of players with the school name and year appearing at the top. The player's name is printed below each image. The backs are blank.

COMPLETE SET (10)	25.00	50.00
1 Nate Abraham	3.00	6.00
Andy Arnold		
Jackie Avery		
Bake Baker		
Ken Barbee		
Craig Barker		
Joel Barrington		
Danny Bentley		
2 Joey Best	3.00	6.00
Don Blue		
Todd Bowers		
Will Burkett		
Kevin Burton		
T.J. Carrington		
Dexter Coakley		
Todd Coates		
3 Jamie Coleman	3.00	6.00
Bryan Cox		
Joe Dibernardo		
Jon Duncan		
J.P. Edwards		
Shawn Elliott		
Dave Evans		
Clyde Everette		
4 Ron Gilliam	3.00	6.00
L.G. Goganious		
Jeff Greene		
Chad Groover		
Allen Guinn		
Kendrick Hall		
Gerard Hardy		
Jason Hatcher		
5 Chip Hooks	3.00	6.00
Dan Horne		
Carlos Horton		
Chad Irvin		
Mark Ivey		
Brian Jean-Mary		
Scott Kadlub		
Aaron Krig		
6 Aldwin Lance	3.00	6.00
Rich Latta		
Jeff Marr		
Jeff McGowan		
Willie McLain		
John McPhaul		
Chip Miller		
Brad Ohrt		
7 Dave Pastusic	3.00	6.00
William Peebles		
Tony Perry		
Adam Perryman		
Bryan Pitts		
John Porter		
Spencer Reeves		
Rob Rice		
9 Jay Sutton	3.00	6.00
Jeff Vollmer		
Trent Wadford		
Lance Ware		
Cubeya Woods		
Brian Wozny		
Jason Yaudes		
Scott Yaudes		
8 Scott Satterfield	3.00	6.00
Jimmy Schimpf		
Damon Scott		
Johnny Smith		
Otis Smith		
Ja		
10 Staff	3.00	6.00
Francis Borkowski Chan.		
Roachel Laney AD		
Dr. Alan Hauser Faculty R		

1995 Appalachian State Team Sheets

COMPLETE SET (8)	20.00	40.00
1 Jackie Avery	2.50	6.00
Bake Baker		
Cameron Ball		
Kenny Barbee		
Craig Barker		
Danny Bentley		
Tony Bequette		
Todd Bowers		
2 Kevin Burton	4.00	10.00
Ben Carlson		
Stephen Carpenter		
Steve Carson		
Shawn Clark		
Dexter Coakley		
Jamie Coleman		
Chad Dalton		
3 Joe Dibernardo	2.50	6.00
Jon Duncan		
Ryan Eichler		
Shawn Elliott		
Clyde Everette		
Jon Fanning		
Gordon Fenderson		
Cliff Fitte		
4 Jason Hatcher	2.50	6.00
Marvin Hodge		
Carlos Horton		
Mark Ivey		
Derek Jarr		
Brian Jean-Mary		
Elando Johnson		
Scott Kadlub		
5 Aaron Krig	2.50	6.00
Aldwin Lance		
Rich Latta		
Mark Maier		
Jeff Marr		
Jeff McGowan		
Willie McLain		
Damon Scott		
6 Chip Miller	2.50	6.00
Adam Neiheisel		
Dave Pastusic		
Tony Perry		
John Pointer		
Spencer Reeves		
David Rogers		
Scott Satterfield		
7 Otis Smith	2.50	6.00
Matt Stevens		
Clarence Sutton		
Jay Sutton		
Rod Thomas		
Sam Vaughan		
Jeff Vollmer		
Will Walker		
8 Lance Ware	2.50	6.00
Josh Wentzel		
Josh Williams		
Scott Williams		
Cuabeya Woods		
Brian Wozny		
Kareem Young		

1980 Arizona Police

The 1980 University of Arizona Police set contains 24 cards measuring approximately 2 7/16" by 3 3/4". The fronts have borderless color player photos, with the player's name and jersey number in a white stripe beneath the picture. The backs have brief biographical information and safety tips. The cards are unnumbered and checklisted below in alphabetical order. Reportedly the Reggie Ware card is very difficult to find.

COMPLETE SET (24)	50.00	100.00
1 Brian Clifford	1.50	3.00
2 Mark Fulcher	1.50	3.00
3 Bob Gareeb	1.50	3.00
4 Marcellus Green	2.00	4.00
5 Drew Hardville	1.50	3.00
6 Neal Harris	1.50	3.00
7 Richard Hersey	1.50	3.00
8 Alfondia Hill	1.50	3.00
9 Tim Holmes	1.50	3.00
10 Jack Housley	1.50	3.00
11 Glenn Hutchinson	1.50	3.00
12 Bill Jensen	1.50	3.00
13 Frank Kalil	1.50	3.00
14 Dave Liggins	1.50	3.00
15 Tom Manno	1.50	3.00
16 Bill Nettling	1.50	3.00
17 Hubie Oliver	3.00	6.00
18 Glenn Perkins	1.50	3.00
19 John Ramseyer	1.50	3.00
20 Mike Robinson	1.50	3.00
21 Chris Schultz	2.00	4.00
22 Larry Smith CO	2.50	5.00
23 Reggie Ware SP	20.00	40.00
24 Bill Zivic	1.50	3.00

1981 Arizona Police

The 1981 University of Arizona Police set contains 27 cards measuring approximately 2 3/8" by 3 1/2". The fronts have borderless color player photos, with the player's name and jersey number in a white stripe beneath the picture. The backs have brief biographical information and safety tips. The cards are unnumbered and checklisted below in alphabetical order.

COMPLETE SET (27)	16.00	40.00
1 Moe Ankney ACO	1.25	3.00
2 Van Brandon	.75	2.00
3 Bob Carter	.75	2.00
4 Brian Christiansen	.75	2.00
5 Mark Fulcher	.75	2.00
6 Bob Gareeb	.75	2.00
7 Gary Gibson	.75	2.00
8 Mark Gobel	.75	2.00
9 Al Gross	.75	2.00
10 Kevin Hardcastle	.75	2.00
11 Neal Harris	.75	2.00
12 Brian Holland	.75	2.00
13 Ricky Hunley	1.50	4.00
14 Frank Kalil	.75	2.00
15 Jeff Kiewel	.75	2.00
16 Chris Knudsen	.75	2.00
17 Ivan Lesnik	.75	2.00
18 Tony Neely	.75	2.00
19 Glenn Perkins	.75	2.00
20 Randy Robbins	.75	2.00
21 Gerald Roper	.75	2.00
22 Chris Schultz	1.25	3.00
23 Gary Shaw	.75	2.00
24 Larry Smith CO	1.25	3.00
25 Tom Tunnicliffe	1.25	3.00
26 Sergio Vega	.75	2.00
27 Brett Weber	1.25	3.00

1982 Arizona Police

The 1982 University of Arizona Police set contains 26 cards. The fronts have borderless color player photos, with the player's name and jersey number in a white stripe beneath the picture. The backs have brief biographical information and safety tips as well as the year of issue 1982-83. The cards are unnumbered and checklisted below in alphabetical order.

COMPLETE SET (26)	14.00	35.00
1 Brad Anderson	.60	1.50
2 Steve Boadway	.60	1.50
3 Bruce Bush	.60	1.50
4 Mike Freeman	.60	1.50
5 Marsharne Graves	.60	1.50
6 Courtney Griffin	.60	1.50
7 Al Gross	.75	2.00
8 Julius Holt	.60	1.50
9 Lamonte Hunley	.75	2.00
10 Ricky Hunley	1.00	2.50
11 Vance Johnson	2.00	5.00
12 Chris Kaesman	.60	1.50
13 John Kaiser	.60	1.50
14 Mark Keel	.60	1.50
15 Jeff Kiewel	.60	1.50
16 Ivan Lesnik	.60	1.50
17 Glenn McCormick	.60	1.50
18 Ray Moret	.60	1.50
19 Tony Neely	.60	1.50
20 Byron Nelson	.75	2.00
21 Glenn Perkins	.60	1.50
22 Randy Robbins	.60	1.50
23 Larry Smith CO	.75	2.00
24 Tom Tunnicliffe	.75	2.00
25 Kevin Ward	.60	1.50
26 David Wood	.60	1.50

1983 Arizona Police

The 1983 University of Arizona Police set contains 24 cards. The fronts have borderless color player photos, with the player's name and jersey number in a white stripe beneath the picture. The backs have brief biographical information and safety tips as well as the year of issue 1983-84. The cards are unnumbered and checklisted below in alphabetical order.

COMPLETE SET (24)	20.00	35.00
1 John Barthalt	.60	1.50
2 Steve Boadway	.60	1.50
3 Chris Brewer	.60	1.50
4 Lynnden Brown	.60	1.50
5 Charlie Dickey	.60	1.50
6 Jay Dobins	.60	1.50
7 Joe Drake	.60	1.50
8 Allen Durden	.75	2.00
9 Byron Evans	1.50	4.00
10 Nils Fox	.60	1.50
11 Mike Freeman	.60	1.50
12 Marsharne Graves	.60	1.50
13 Lamonte Hunley	.75	2.00
14 Vance Johnson	2.00	5.00
15 John Kaiser	.60	1.50
16 Ivan Lesnik	.60	1.50
17 Byron Nelson	.75	2.00
18 Randy Robbins	.60	1.50
19 Craig Schiller	.60	1.50
20 Larry Smith CO	.75	2.00
21 Tom Tunnicliffe	.75	2.00
22 Mark Walczak	.60	1.50
23 David Wood	.60	1.50
24 Max Zendejas	.75	2.00

1984 Arizona Police

The 1984 University of Arizona Police set contains 25 cards measuring approximately 2 1/4" by 3 5/8". The fronts have borderless color photos; the vertically oriented backs have brief bios and safety tips. The cards are unnumbered, so are listed by jersey numbers. These cards are printed on very thin stock. The set is described on the back of each card as 1984-85.

COMPLETE SET (25)	20.00	35.00
1 Alfred Jenkins	1.25	3.00
8 John Connor	.75	2.00
13 Max Zendejas	.75	2.00
15 Gordon Bunch	.60	1.50
19 Allen Durden	.60	1.50
23 Lynnden Brown	.60	1.50
25 Vance Johnson	1.50	4.00
28 Tom Bayse	.60	1.50
35 Brent Wood	.60	1.50
40 Greg Turner	.60	1.50
47 Steve Boadway	.60	1.50
52 Nils Fox	.60	1.50
54 Craig Vesling	.60	1.50
62 David Connor	.60	1.50
67 Charlie Dickey	.60	1.50
71 Brian Denton	.60	1.50
78 John DuBose	.60	1.50
79 Joe Drake	.60	1.50
82 Joy Dobyns	.60	1.50
85 Mark Walczak	.60	1.50
86 Jon Horton	.60	1.50
92 David Wood	.60	1.50
98 Lamonte Hunley	.75	2.00
99 John Barthalt	.60	1.50
NNO Larry Smith CO	.75	2.00

1985 Arizona Police

The 1985 University of Arizona Police set contains 23 cards measuring 2 1/4" by 3 5/8". The fronts have borderless color photos; the vertically oriented backs have brief bios and safety tips. The cards are unnumbered, so are listed by jersey numbers. These cards are printed on very thin stock. The set is described on the back of each card as 1985-86.

COMPLETE SET (23)	15.00	30.00
1 Alfred Jenkins	1.00	2.50
2 David Adams	.50	1.25
6 Chuck Cecil	1.00	2.50
13 Max Zendejas	.60	1.50
15 Gordon Bunch	.50	1.25
18 Jeff Fairholm	.50	1.25
19 Allen Durden	.50	1.25
29 Don Be'ans	.50	1.25
32 Joe Prior	.50	1.25
42 Blake Custer	.50	1.25
44 Boomer Gibson	.50	1.25
48 Byron Evans	1.00	2.50
50 Val Bichekas	.50	1.25
52 Joe Tofflemire	.50	1.25
54 Craig Vesling	.50	1.25
59 Jim Birmingham	.50	1.25
72 Curt DiGiacomo	.50	1.25
73 Lee Brunelli	.50	1.25
78 John DuBose	.50	1.25
83 Gary Parrish	.50	1.25
95 Cliff Thorpe	.50	1.25
96 Glenn Howell	.50	1.25
NNO Larry Smith CO	.60	1.50

1986 Arizona Police

1999 Alabama Schedules

This 24-card set was cosponsored by the Tucson Police Department and Golden Eagle Distributors. The cards measure approximately 2 1/4" by 3 5/8". The fronts feature borderless posed color player photos, with the player's name and uniform number in the white stripe beneath the picture. The backs present player profile, a discussion or definition of some aspect of football, and a safety message. The cards are unnumbered and checklisted below in alphabetical order. The set is described on the back of each card as 1986-87.

COMPLETE SET (24)	15.00	30.00
1 David Adams	.60	1.50
2 Frank Arriola	.60	1.50
3 Val Biehekas	.60	1.50
4 Jim Birmingham	.60	1.50
5 Chuck Cecil	1.00	2.50
6 James Debow	.60	1.50
7 Brian Denton	.60	1.50
8 Byron Evans	.75	2.00
9 Jeff Fairholm	.60	1.50
10 Boomer Gibson	.60	1.50
11 Eugene Hardy	.60	1.50
12 Derek Hill	.75	2.00
13 Jon Horton	.60	1.50
14 Alfred Jenkins	.75	2.00
15 Danny Lockett	.60	1.50
16 Stan Mataele	.60	1.50
17 Chris McLemore	.60	1.50
18 Jeff Rinehart	.60	1.50
19 Ruben Rodriguez	.60	1.50
20 Martin Rudolph	.60	1.50
21 Larry Smith CO	.75	2.00
22 Joe Tofflemire	.60	1.50
23 Dana Wells	.60	1.50
24 Brent Wood	.60	1.50

1987 Arizona Police

The 1987 University of Arizona Police set contains 23 cards measuring approximately 2 1/4" by 3 5/8". The fronts have borderless color photos; the vertically oriented backs have brief bios and safety tips. The cards are unnumbered, so they are listed by jersey numbers. These cards are printed on very thin stock. The set is described on the back of each card as 1987-88.

COMPLETE SET (23)	10.00	20.00
2 Bobby Watters	.40	1.00
3 Doug Pfaff	.40	1.00
6 Chuck Cecil	.75	2.00
11 Gary Coston	.40	1.00
18 Jeff Fairholm	.40	1.00
22 Eugene Hardy	.40	1.00
26 Troy Cephers	.40	1.00
34 Charles Webb	.40	1.00
38 James Debow	.40	1.00
40 Art Greathouse	.40	1.00
43 Jerry Beasley	.40	1.00
44 Boomer Gibson	.40	1.00
47 Gallen Allen	.40	1.00
52 Joe Tofflemire	.40	1.00
60 Jeff Rinehart	.40	1.00
64 Kevin McKinney	.40	1.00
68 Tom Lynch	.40	1.00
82 Derek Hill	.40	1.00
84 Kevin Singleton	.40	1.00
87 Chris Singleton	.50	1.25
97 George Hinkle	.40	1.00
99 Dana Wells	.40	1.00
NNO Dick Tomey CO	.50	1.25

1988 Arizona Police

The 1988 University of Arizona Police set contains 25 cards measuring approximately 2 5/16" by 3 3/4". The fronts have borderless color photos; the vertically oriented backs have brief bios and safety tips. The cards are unnumbered, so they are listed by jersey numbers. These cards are printed on very thin stock. The set is described on the back of each card as 1988-89.

COMPLETE SET (25)	10.00	20.00
2 Bobby Watters	.40	1.00
4 Darryll Lewis UER name misspelled Darryl	.50	1.25
5 Durrell Jones	.40	1.00
8 Reggie McGill	.40	1.00
10 Ronald Veal	.40	1.00
15 Jeff Hammerschmidt	.40	1.00
22 Scott Geyer	.40	1.00
24 Rich Groppenbacher	.40	1.00
25 David Eldridge	.40	1.00
35 Mario Hampton	.40	1.00
38 James Debow	.40	1.00
40 Art Greathouse	.40	1.00
50 Darren Case	.40	1.00
51 Doug Penner	.40	1.00
52 Joe Tofflemire	.40	1.00
63 John Brandom	.40	1.00
65 Ken Hakes	.40	1.00
74 Glenn Parker	.60	1.50
78 Rob Woods	.40	1.00
82 Derek Hill	.50	1.25
84 Kevin Singleton	.40	1.00
87 Chris Singleton	.50	1.25
96 Brad Henke	.40	1.00
99 Dana Wells	.40	1.00
NNO Dick Tomey CO	.40	1.00

1989 Arizona Police

This 26-card set was co-sponsored by the Tucson Police Department and Golden Eagle Distributors. The cards measure approximately 2 1/4" by 3 3/4". The fronts feature borderless posed color player photos, with the player's name and uniform number in the white stripe beneath the picture. The backs present player profile, a discussion or definition of some aspect of football, and a safety message. The cards are unnumbered and checklisted below in alphabetical order. The set is described on the back of each card as 1989-90.

COMPLETE SET (26)	10.00	20.00
1 Zeno Alexander	.40	1.00
2 John Brandom	.40	1.00
3 Todd Burden	.40	1.00
4 Darren Case	.40	1.00
5 David Eldridge	.40	1.00
6 Nick Fineanganofo	.40	1.00
7 Scott Geyer	.40	1.00
8 Art Greathouse	.40	1.00
9 Richard Griffith	.40	1.00
10 Ken Hakes	.40	1.00
11 Jeff Hammerschmidt	.40	1.00
12 Mario Hampton	.40	1.00
13 Darryll Lewis	.50	1.25
14 Kip Lewis	.40	1.00
15 George Malauulu	.40	1.00
16 Reggie McGill	.40	1.00
17 John Nies	.40	1.00
18 Glenn Parker	.50	1.25
19 Mike Parker	.40	1.00
20 Doug Pfaff	.40	1.00
21 David Roney	.40	1.00
22 Pete Russell	.40	1.00
23 Chris Singleton	.50	1.25
24 Paul Tofflemire	.40	1.00
25 Dick Tomey CO	.50	1.25
26 Ronald Veal	.40	1.00

1990-91 Arizona Collegiate Collection

This 125-card standard-size was produced by Collegiate Collection. We've included a sport initial (B-baseball, K-basketball, F-football) for players in the top collected sports.

COMPLETE SET (125)	5.00	12.00
3 Vance Johnson F	.10	.25
5 Chris Singleton F	.10	.25
7 Ricky Hunley F	.05	.15
9 Chuck Cecil F	.10	.25
12 Tommy Tunnicliffe F	.05	.15
14 Theo Bell F	.05	.15
18 Anthony Smith F	.10	.25
24 Chuck Cecil F	.10	.25
26 Allen Durden F	.05	.15
30 Danny Lockett F	.05	.15
31 Dana Wells F	.05	.15
35 David Adams F	.05	.15
37 Vance Johnson F	.10	.25
42 Derek Hill F	.10	.25
43 Hubie Oliver F	.05	.15
44 Scott Geyer F	.05	.15
46 Max Zendejas F	.05	.15
47 Jim Young CO F	.05	.15
48 Mark Arneson F	.05	.15
49 Doug Pfaff F	.05	.15
51 Brad Henke F	.05	.15
52 Bruce Hill F	.10	.25
55 Bryon Evans F	.10	.25
59 David Wood F	.05	.15
62 Ivan Lesnik F	.05	.15
67 Brad Anderson F	.05	.15
68 Chuck Cecil F	.10	.25
69 Mike Dawson F	.05	.15
74 Lamonte Hunley F	.05	.15
84 Jon Abbott F	.05	.15
87 Jeff Kiewel F	.05	.15
90 Ruben Rodriguez F	.05	.15
91 Randy Robbins F	.05	.15
96 Vance Johnson RB F	.10	.25
98 Glenn Parker DT F	.07	.20
102 Dick Tomey CO F	.05	.15
104 Art Luppino F	.05	.15
109 Byron Evans F	.10	.25
112 David Adams F	.05	.15
113 Bobby Thompson F	.05	.15
114 Brad Anderson F	.05	.15
115 Eddie Wilson F	.05	.15
117 Joe Hernandez F	.05	.15
120 Carl Cooper F	.05	.15
122 Robert Lee Thompson F	.05	.15
123 Robert Ruman F	.05	.15
125 John Byrd Salmon F	.05	.15

1990-91 Arizona Collegiate Collection Promos

This ten-card standard size set was produced by Collegiate Collection and features some of the great players of Arizona over the past few years. This set involves players of different sports and we have added a two-letter abbreviation next to the person's name to indicate what sport is pictured on the card. The back of the card either has statistical or biographical information about the player during their college career.

COMPLETE SET (10)	2.00	5.00
1 Chuck Cecil FB	.20	.50
4 Chris Singleton FB	.20	.50
6 Vance Johnson FB	.20	.50
7 Dick Tomey CO FB (Waist)	.10	.25
8 Robert Lee Thompson FB	.10	.25
10 Dick Tomey CO FB (Head and Shoulders)	.10	.25

1992 Arizona Police

This 21-card set was sponsored by the Tucson Police Department and Golden Eagle Distributors. The cards measure approximately 2" by 3 3/4". The fronts feature borderless color photos of the players posed at the football stadium, with bleaches and scoreboard in the background. The player's name and jersey number are printed in the white stripe at the bottom. The backs are white and carry player information, an explanation of some aspect of football, and a safety message. The cards are unnumbered and checklisted below in alphabetical order.

COMPLETE SET (21)	10.00	20.00
1 Tony Bouie	.40	1.00
2 Heath Bray	.40	1.00
3 Charlie Camp	.40	1.00
4 Ontiwaun Carter	.50	1.25
5 Richard Griffith	.40	1.00
6 Sean Harris	.40	1.00
7 Mike Heemsbergen	.40	1.00
8 Jimmy Hopkins	.40	1.00
9 Billy Johnson	.50	1.25
10 Keshon Johnson	.50	1.25
11 Chuck Levy	.60	1.50
12 Richard Maddox	.40	1.00
13 George Malauulu	.40	1.00
14 Darryl Morrison	.40	1.00
15 Mani Ott	.40	1.00
16 Ty Parten	.40	1.00
17 Mike Scurlock	.40	1.00
18 Warner Smith	.40	1.00
19 Dick Tomey CO	.50	1.25
20 Terry Vaughn	.40	1.00
21 Rob Waldrop	.40	1.00

1993 Arizona Police

This set was sponsored by the Tucson Police Department. The cards measure approximately 2" by 3 3/4" and feature borderless color photos of the players posed at the football stadium, with bleaches and the scoreboard in the background. The player's name and jersey number are printed in the white stripe at the bottom. The backs are white and carry player information, an explanation of some aspect of football, and a safety message. This set features the very first card of popular Patriots star Tedy Bruschi. The cards are unnumbered and checklisted below in alphabetical order.

COMPLETE SET (19)	15.00	30.00
1 Tony Bouie	.40	1.00
2 Brant Boyer	.40	1.00
3 Tedy Bruschi	10.00	20.00
4 Charlie Camp	.40	1.00
5 Ontiwaun Carter	.50	1.25
6 Troy Dickey	.40	1.00
7 Hicham El-Mashtoub	.40	1.00
8 Lamar Harris	.40	1.00
9 Sean Harris	.40	1.00
10 Charles Levy	.40	1.00
11 Steve McLaughlin	.40	1.00
12 Brandon Sanders	.40	1.00
13 Joe Smigiel	.40	1.00
14 Warner Smith	.40	1.00
15 Paul Stamer	.40	1.00
16 Terry Vaughn	.40	1.00
17 Rob Waldrop	.40	1.00
18 Dan White	.40	1.00
19 Dick Tomey CO	.50	1.25

1994 Arizona Police

This set was sponsored by the Tucson Police Department. The cards measure approximately 2" by 3 3/4" and feature borderless color photos of the players posed at the football stadium, with bleaches and the scoreboard in the background. The player's name and jersey number are printed in the white stripe at the bottom. The backs are white and carry player information, an explanation of some aspect of football, and a safety message. The cards are unnumbered and checklisted below in alphabetical order.

COMPLETE SET (22)	15.00	25.00
1 Tony Bouie	.40	1.00
2 Tedy Bruschi	7.50	15.00
3 Ontiwaun Carter	.50	1.25
4 Thomas Demps	.40	1.00
5 Richard Dice	.40	1.00
6 Hicham El-Mashtoub	.40	1.00
7 Kevin Gosar	.40	1.00
8 Lamar Harris	.40	1.00
9 Sean Harris	.40	1.00
10 Jim Hoffman	.40	1.00
11 Akil Jackson	.40	1.00
12 Steve McLaughlin	.40	1.00
13 Pulu Poumele	.40	1.00
14 Brandon Sanders	.40	1.00
15 Mike Scurlock	.40	1.00
16 Joe Smigiel	.40	1.00
17 Warner Smith	.40	1.00
18 Cary Taylor	.40	1.00
19 Dick Tomey CO	.50	1.25
20 Dan White	.40	1.00
21 Spencer Wray	.40	1.00
22 Claudius Wright	.40	1.00

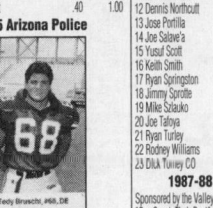

1995 Arizona Police

This set was sponsored by the Tucson Police Department. The cards measure approximately 2" by 3 3/4" and feature borderless color photos of the players posed at the football stadium, with bleaches and the scoreboard in the background. The player's name and jersey number are printed in the white stripe at the bottom. The backs are white and carry player information, an explanation of some aspect of football, and a safety message. The cards are unnumbered and checklisted below in alphabetical order.

COMPLETE SET (22)	15.00	25.00
1 Tedy Bruschi	7.50	15.00
2 Charlie Camp	.40	1.00
3 Thomas Demps	.40	1.00
4 Richard Dice	.40	1.00
5 Kelly Malveaux	.40	1.00
6 Mike Mannelly	.40	1.00
7 Ian McCutcheon	.40	1.00
8 Chuck Osborne	.40	1.00
9 Mani Ott	.40	1.00
10 Shawn Parnell	.40	1.00
11 Matt Peyton	.40	1.00
12 Jonathan Prasuhn	.40	1.00
13 Joe Salave'a	.40	1.00
14 Brandon Sanders	.40	1.00
15 Kevin Schmidtke	.40	1.00
16 Jimmy Sprotte	.40	1.00
17 Mike Szlauko	.40	1.00
18 Gary Taylor	.40	1.00
19 Willie Walker	.40	1.00
20 David Watson	.40	1.00
21 Dan White	.40	1.00
22 Dick Tomey CO	.50	1.25

1996 Arizona Police

This set was sponsored by the Tucson Police Department. The cards measure approximately 2" by 3 3/4" and feature borderless color photos of the players posed at the football stadium, with bleaches and the scoreboard in the background. The player's name and jersey number are printed in the white stripe at the bottom. The backs are white and carry player information, an explanation of some aspect of football, and a safety message. The cards are unnumbered and checklisted below in alphabetical order.

COMPLETE SET (24)	10.00	20.00
1 Brady Batten	.50	1.25
2 Chester Burnett	.40	1.00
3 Richard Dice	.40	1.00
4 Jeremy Evans	.40	1.00
5 Mike Lucky	.50	1.25
6 Kelly Malveaux	.40	1.00
7 Mark McDonald	.40	1.00
8 Frank Middleton	.40	1.00
9 Charles Myles	.40	1.00
10 Matt Peyton	.40	1.00
11 Chuck Rich	.40	1.00
12 Joe Salave'a	.40	1.00
13 Mikal Smith	.40	1.00
14 Jimmy Sprotte	.40	1.00
15 Steve Tatua	.40	1.00
16 Gary Taylor	.40	1.00
17 Van Tuinei	.40	1.00
18 Tevete Usu	.40	1.00
19 Willie Walker	.40	1.00
20 David Watson	.40	1.00
21 Armon Williams	.40	1.00
22 Rodney Williams	.40	1.00
23 Wayne Wyatt	.40	1.00
24 Dick Tomey CO	.50	1.25

1997 Arizona Police

This set was sponsored by the Tucson Police Department. The cards measure approximately 2" by 3 3/4" and feature borderless color photos of the players posed at the football stadium, with bleaches and the scoreboard in the background. The player's name and jersey number are printed in the white stripe at the bottom. The backs are white and carry player information, an explanation of some aspect of football, and a safety message. The cards are unnumbered and checklisted below in alphabetical order.

COMPLETE SET (23)	10.00	20.00
1 Brady Batten	.50	1.25
2 Marcus Bell	.50	1.25
3 Chester Burnett	.40	1.00
4 Trung Canidate	.75	2.00
5 David Fipp	.40	1.00
6 Daniel Greer	.40	1.00
7 Rusty James	.40	1.00
8 Mike Lucky	.50	1.25
9 Kelly Malveaux	.40	1.00
10 Chris McAlister	1.25	3.00
11 Edwin Mulitalo	.40	1.00
12 Dennis Northcutt	.75	2.00
13 Jose Portilla	.40	1.00
14 Joe Salave'a	.40	1.00
15 Yusuf Scott	.40	1.00
16 Keith Smith	.40	1.00
17 Ryan Springston	.40	1.00
18 Jimmy Sprotte	.40	1.00
19 Mike Szlauko	.40	1.00
20 Joe Tafoya	.50	1.25
21 Ryan Turley	.40	1.00
22 Rodney Williams	.40	1.00
23 Dick Tomey CO	.50	1.25

1987-88 Arizona State

Sponsored by the Valley of the Sun Kiwanis Club and "Our Quest: Their Best", this 22-card standard-size was produced by Sports Marketing Inc. The cards feature Arizona State athletes from various sports. The fronts have action color player photos against a white background. A maroon and wider yellow stripe appear below the picture, with the yellow stripe containing the player's name and sport. The words "Arizona State" are printed in maroon block letters above the photo and are underlined by a yellow stripe printed with the word "University". The Sun Devils mascot in the lower right corner rounds out the front. The backs are white with maroon print and include a player profile and a community service announcement from Sparky, the mascot. Sponsors' logos appear at the bottom. The sports represented are basketball, swimming, baseball, football, softball, track, gymnastics, tennis, and volleyball. The cards are unnumbered and checklisted below in alphabetical order.

COMPLETE SET (22)	8.00	20.00
5 John Cooper CO FB	1.50	4.00
6 Aaron Cox FB	1.00	2.50
10 Darryl Harris FB	.40	1.00
14 Randall McDaniel FB	2.00	5.00
16 Anthony Parker FB	1.00	2.50
17 Shawn Patterson FB	.40	1.00
22 Channing Williams FB	.40	1.00

1990-91 Arizona State Collegiate Collection

This 200-card standard-size mulit-sport set was produced by Collegiate Collection. We've included a sport initial (B-baseball, K-basketball, F-football, WK-women's basketball) for players in the top collected sports. The key card is one of the few cards featuring all-time Baseball great Barry Bonds in a college uniform.

COMPLETE SET (200)	6.00	15.00
2 Gerald Higgs F	.08	.25
3 John Jefferson F	.10	.30
5 Charley Taylor F	.15	.40
11 Dan Saleaumua F	.07	.20
14 Doug Allen F	.05	.15
17 Mark Malone F	.08	.25
19 Fair Hooker F	.07	.20
22 Larry Gordon F	.05	.15
24 Bruce Hill F	.05	.15
27 Scott Stephen F	.05	.15
28 Mike Haynes F	.10	.30
30 Vernon Maxwell F	.07	.20
32 Eric Allen F	.10	.30
35 Skip McClendon F	.05	.15
36 David Fulcher F	.07	.20
37 Todd Kalis F	.05	.15
39 Aaron Cox F	.05	.15
40 Bob Kohrs F	.05	.15
42 Mike Richardson F	.05	.15
43 Shawn Patterson F	.07	.20
45 Danny Villa F	.05	.15
47 Mike Pagel F	.07	.20
48 Jim Jeffcoat F	.10	.30
49 John Harris F	.05	.15
51 Jeff Van Raaphorst F	.05	.15
53 Freddie Williams F	.05	.15
55 Brian Noble F	.08	.25
56 Junior Ah You F	.07	.20
58 Tony Lorick F	.05	.15
61 Danny White F	.20	.50
62 John Mistler F	.05	.15
67 Curley Culp F	.10	.30
69 Norris Stevenson F UER (name misspelled Steverson)	.05	.15
72 Al Harris F	.07	.20
75 Bruce Hardy F	.07	.20
78 Ben Malone F	.05	.15
79 Brent McClanahan F	.07	.20
81 Mike Black F	.05	.15
84 Trace Armstrong F	.08	.25
85 Daryl Clack F	.05	.15
86 Steve Holden F	.05	.15
89 Art Malone F	.05	.15
93 Randall McDaniel F	.10	.30
95 Luis Zendejas F	.07	.20
97 J.D. Hill F	.07	.20
99 Bobby Douglass CO	.07	.20
105 Dan Devine CO F	.08	.25
113 Football Team 1957 F	.05	.15
122 Ron Brown F	.05	.15
123 Football Team 1986 F	.05	.15
135 Danny White F	.20	.50
138 Football Team 1975 F	.05	.15
142 Leon Burton F	.05	.15
144 Bob Mulgado F	.05	.15
145 Henry Carr F	.07	.20
155 Bob Breunig F	.10	.30
162 Woody Green F	.05	.15
168 Wilford Whizzer White F with Danny White	.15	.40
174 Mike Haynes F	.10	.30
180 1970 Football Team F	.05	.15
189 Frank Kush CO F	.05	.15
197 Ben Hawkins F	.05	.15

1990-91 Arizona State Collegiate Collection Promos

This ten-card standard size set was issued by Collegiate Collection to honor some of the leading athletes in all sports played at Arizona State. The front features a full-color photo while the back of the card has information or statistical information about the player featured. To help identify the player there is a two-letter abbreviation of the athlete's sport next to the player's name.

COMPLETE SET (10)	1.50	4.00
4 Luis Zendejas FB	.10	.25
8 Brian Noble FB	.10	.25
9 Trace Armstrong FB	.20	.50

2000 Arizona State

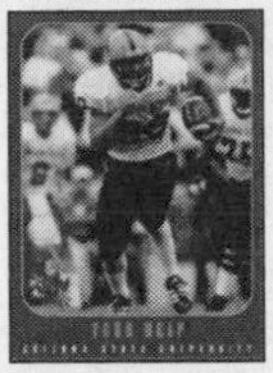

COMPLETE SET (3)	3.00	8.00
1 Willie Daniel	.75	2.00
2 Todd Heap	1.50	4.00
3 Victor Leyva	.75	2.00

1991 Arkansas Collegiate Collection

This 100-card multi-sport standard-size set was produced by Collegiate Collection. The fronts features a mixture of black and white or color player photos with black borders. The player's name is included in a black stripe below the picture. In a horizontal format the backs present biographical information, career summary, or statistics on a white background. Unless noted below, all players are from the sport of football.

COMPLETE SET (100)	6.00	15.00
1 Frank Broyles CO	.15	.40
2 Lance Alworth	.20	.50
5 John Barnhill CO	.05	.15
6 Dan Hampton	.20	.50
10 Clyde Scott	.05	.15
11 Kendall Trainor	.05	.15
16 Derek Russell	.08	.25
18 Jimmy Walker	.05	.15
19 Ben Cowins	.05	.15
21 Tony Cherico	.05	.15
25 Billy Ray Smith Jr.	.08	.25
26 Steve Little	.08	.25
27 Steve Atwater	.10	.30
29 Ron Faurot	.05	.15
32 Dickey Morton	.05	.15
33 Lon Farrell CO	.05	.15
36 Dick Bumpas	.05	.15
39 George Cole CO	.05	.15
40 Bruce Lahay	.05	.15
41 Jim Benton	.05	.15
46 Bill Montgomery	.05	.15
47 Lou Holtz CO	.10	.30
49 Bill McClard	.05	.15
50 Gary Anderson IDK	.08	.25
52 Glen Rose	.05	.15
53 Ronnie Caveness	.05	.15
55 Bobby Joe Edmonds	.07	.20
56 James Shibest	.05	.15
59 Wear Schoonover	.05	.15
60 Bruce James	.05	.15
61 Billy Moore	.05	.15
62 Jim Mabry	.05	.15
63 Ron Calgagni	.05	.15
64 Wilson Matthews CO	.05	.15
65 Martine Bercher	.05	.15
68 Mike Reppond	.05	.15
70 Ish Ordonez	.05	.15
71 Steve Korte	.05	.15
72 Jim Barnes	.05	.15
73 Steve Cox	.05	.15
74 Bud Brooks	.05	.15
75 Roland Sales	.05	.15
76 Chuck Dicus	.05	.15
77 Rodney Brand	.05	.15
78 Wayne Martin	.07	.20
79 Greg Kolenda	.05	.15
81 Brad Taylor	.05	.15
82 Bill Burnett	.05	.15
83 Glen Ray Hines	.07	.20
84 Leotis Harris	.05	.15
86 Joe Ferguson	.08	.25
87 Greg Horne	.05	.15
88 Loyd Phillips	.05	.15
89 James Rouse	.05	.15
90 Ken Hatfield CO	.08	.25
91 Bobby Crockett	.05	.15
92 Quinn Grovey	.05	.15
93 Wayne Harris	.05	.15
94 Jim Mooty	.05	.15
95 Barry Foster	.08	.25
97 Jim Lee Howell	.08	.25
98 Jack Robbins	.05	.15
99 Cliff Powell	.05	.15

1999 Arkansas Coaches JOGO

Released in 1999, this 15-card set pictures the coaching staff of the 1999 Arkansas Razorbacks. Card fronts feature full-color photos and card backs contain a brief blurb about each coach.

COMPLETE SET (15)	6.00	12.00
1 Houston Nutt	.75	2.00
2 Bobby Allen	.30	.75
3 Keith Burns	.30	.75
4 Clifton Ealy	.30	.75
5 Joe Ferguson	.40	1.00
6 Fitz Hill	.40	1.00
7 Mark Hutson	.30	.75
8 Bill Keopple	.30	.75
9 Mike Markuson	.30	.75
10 Danny Nutt	.30	.75
11 Barry Lunney Jr.	.30	.75
12 Chris Vaughn	.30	.75
13 Dean Weber	.30	.75
14 Don Decker	.30	.75
15 Justin Crouse	.30	.75

2002 Arkansas Coaches JOGO

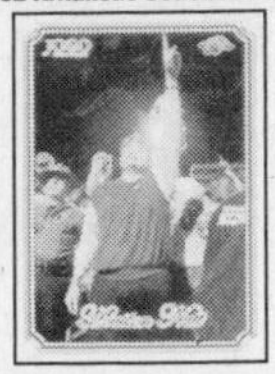

This 11-card set features the coaching staff of the 2002 Arkansas Razorbacks. Each card features a full-color photo and the cardbacks contain a brief bio about the featured coach.

COMPLETE SET (11)	4.00	8.00
1 Houston Nutt	.75	2.00
2 Bobby Allen	.30	.75
3 David Lee	.30	.75
4 Mike Markuson	.30	.75
5 Danny Nutt	.30	.75
6 George Pugh	.40	1.00
7 Kacy Rodgers	.30	.75
8 James Shibest	.30	.75
9 Chris Vaughn	.30	.75
10 Dave Wommack	.30	.75
11 Justin Crouse	.30	.75

1991 Army Smokey

Printed on thin card stock, this set was sponsored by the Forest Service and Pepsi and was issued as a perforated sheet. Both current players and Army Legends were included in the set. The fronts feature color player action shots framed by a black border with yellow lettering. The white backs carry a player bio and a fire prevention cartoon starring Smokey. The cards are unnumbered and checklisted below in alphabetical order.

COMPLETE SET (16)	6.00	12.00
1 Steve Chaloult	.40	1.00
2 Lance Chambers	.40	1.00
3 Mark Dawkins	.40	1.00
4 Pete Dawkins LEG	.60	1.50
5 Trey Gilmore	.40	1.00
6 Mike Mayweather	.60	1.50
7 Willie McMillian	.50	1.25
8 Dan Menendez	.40	1.00
9 Edrian Oliver	.40	1.00
10 Rick Pressel	.40	1.00
11 Aaron Scott	.40	1.00
12 Arlen Smith	.40	1.00
13 Bob Sutton CO	.50	1.25
14 Callian Thomas	.40	1.00
15 Myreon Williams	.40	1.00
16 Michie Stadium	.40	1.00

1992 Army Smokey

Printed on thin card stock, this set was sponsored by the Forest Service and Pepsi and was issued as a perforated sheet. Both current players and Army Legends were included in the set. The fronts of the current player cards feature color action shots and a small black and white photo framed by a black border with yellow and white lettering. The two Legends cards feature a sepia toned photo. The white backs carry a player bio and a fire prevention cartoon starring Smokey. The cards are unnumbered and checklisted below in alphabetical order.

COMPLETE SET (16)	6.00	12.00
1 Red Blaik CO LEG	.50	1.25
2 Doc Blanchard LEG	.60	1.50
3 Bill Currence	.40	1.00
4 Kevin Czarnecki	.40	1.00
5 Chad Davis	.40	1.00
6 Dan Davis	.40	1.00
7 Mark Escobedo	.40	1.00
8 Duncan Johnson	.40	1.00
9 Mike Makovec	.50	1.25
10 Patmon Malcom	.40	1.00
11 Mike McElrath	.40	1.00
12 John Pirog	.40	1.00
13 Bob Sutton CO	.50	1.25
14 Kevin Vaughn	.40	1.00
15 Steve Weber	.40	1.00
16 Michie Stadium	.40	1.00

1993 Army Smokey

Printed on thin card stock, this 15-card standard-size set was sponsored by the USDA, the Forest Service, other state and federal agencies, Pepsi, Freihofer's, and The Times Herald Record. Smokey sets issued in 1993 have a special 50th year anniversary logo on the front. The fronts feature color player action shots framed by thin white and black lines and with gold-colored borders highlighted by oblique white stripes. The team's name appears within the upper margin, and the player's name and position, along with the Smokey 50-year celebration logo, rest in the lower margin. The white backs carry player profile and a fire prevention cartoon starring Smokey. The cards are unnumbered and checklisted below in alphabetical order.

COMPLETE SET (15) 6.00 12.00
1 Paul Andrzejewski .40 1.00
2 Kevin Czarnecki .40 1.00
3 Chad Davis .40 1.00
4 Glenn Davis LEG 1.20 3.00
5 Mark Escobedo .40 1.00
6 Gary Graves .40 1.00
7 Leamon Hall .50 1.25
8 Jason Miller .50 1.25
9 Mike Plaia .40 1.00
10 Rick Roper .50 1.25
11 Jim Slomka .40 1.00
12 Bob Sutton CO .50 1.25
13 Jason Sutton .40 1.00
14 Pat Zelley .40 1.00
15 Army Mule (Mascot) .40 1.00

1972 Auburn Playing Cards

This 54-card standard-size set was issued in a playing card deck box. The cards hate rounded corners and the typical playing card finish. The fronts feature black-and-white posed photos of helmetless players in their uniforms. A white border surrounds each picture and contains the card number and suit designation in the upper left corner and again, but inverted, in the lower right. The player's name and hometown appear just beneath the photo. The white-bordered orange backs all have the Auburn "AU" logo in navy blue and orange and white outlines. The the year of issue, 1972, and the name "Auburn Tigers" also appears on the backs. Since the set is similar to a playing card set, it is arranged just like a card deck and checklisted below accordingly. In the checklist below C means Clubs, D means Diamonds, H means Hearts, S means Spades and JOK means Joker. Numbers are assigned to Aces (1), Jacks (11), Queens (12), and Kings (13). The jokers are unnumbered and listed at the end.

COMP. FACT SET (54) 50.00 100.00
1C Ken Calleja .75 2.00
1D James Owens .75 2.00
1H Mac Lorendo .75 2.00
1S Ralph(Shug) Jordan CO 3.00 6.00
2C Rick Neel .75 2.00
2D Ted Smith .75 2.00
2H Eddie Welch .75 2.00
2S Mike Neel .75 2.00
3C Larry Taylor .75 2.00
3D Rett Davis .75 2.00
3H Rusty Fuller .75 2.00
3S Lee Gross .75 2.00
4C Bruce Evans .75 2.00
4D Rusty Deen .75 2.00
4H Johnny Simmons .75 2.00
4S Bill Newton .75 2.00
5C Dave Beverly 1.25 3.00
5D Dave Lyon .75 2.00
5H Mike Fuller 2.00 5.00
5S Bill Luka .75 2.00
6C Ken Bernich .75 2.00
6D Andy Steele .75 2.00
6H Wade Whatley .75 2.00
6S Bob Newton 1.25 3.00
7C Benny Sivley 1.00 2.50
7D Gardner Jett 1.00 2.50
7H Rob Spivey 1.00 2.50
7S Jay Casey .75 2.00
8C David Langner .75 2.00
8D Terry Henley .75 2.00
8H Thomas Gossom .75 2.00
8S Joe Tanory .75 2.00
9C Chris Linderman .75 2.00
9D Harry Unger .75 2.00
9H Kenny Burks .75 2.00
9S Sandy Cannon .75 2.00
10C Roger Mitchell .75 2.00
10D Jim McKinney .75 2.00
10H Gaines Lanier .75 2.00
10S Dave Beck .75 2.00
11C Bob Farrior .75 2.00
11D Miles Jones .75 2.00
11H Tres Rogers .75 2.00
11S David Hughes .75 2.00
12C Sherman Moon .75 2.00
12D Danny Sanspree .75 2.00
12H Steve Taylor .75 2.00
12S Randy Walls .75 2.00
13C Steve Wilson .75 2.00
13D Bobby Davis .75 2.00
13H Hamlin Caldwell .75 2.00
13S Dan Nugent .75 2.00
JOK1 Joker .75 2.00
  Auburn Memorial Coliseum
JOK2 Joker .75 2.00
  Cliff Hare Stadium

1973 Auburn Playing Cards

This 54-card standard-size set was issued in a playing card deck box. The cards have rounded corners and the typical playing card finish. The fronts feature black-and-white posed photos of helmetless players in their uniforms. A white border surrounds each picture and contains the card number and suit designation in the upper left corner and again, but inverted, in the lower right. The player's name and hometown appear just beneath the photo. The white-bordered navy blue backs all have the Auburn "AU" logo in navy blue and orange and white outlines. The the year of issue, 1973, and the name "Auburn Tigers" also appears on the backs. Since the set is similar to a playing card set, it is arranged just like a card deck and checklisted below accordingly. In the checklist below C means Clubs, D means Diamonds, H means Hearts, S means Spades and JOK means Joker. Numbers are assigned to Aces (1), Jacks (11), Queens (12), and Kings (13). The jokers are unnumbered and listed at the end.

COMP. FACT SET (54) 50.00 100.00
1C Ken Calleja .75 2.00
1D Chris Wilson .75 2.00
1H Lee Hayley .75 2.00
1S Ralph(Shug) Jordan CO 2.50 5.00
2C Rick Neel .75 2.00
2D Johnny Sumner .75 2.00
2H Mitzi Jackson .75 2.00
2S Jim Pitts .75 2.00
3C Steve Stanaland .75 2.00
3D Rett Davis .75 2.00
3H Rusty Fuller .75 2.00
3S Lee Gross .75 2.00
4C Bruce Evans .75 2.00
4D Rusty Deen .75 2.00
4H Liston Eddins .75 2.00
4S Bill Newton .75 2.00
5C Jimmy Sirmans .75 2.00
5D Harry Ward .75 2.00
5H Mike Fuller 1.25 3.00
5S Bill Luka .75 2.00
6C Ken Bernich .75 2.00
6D Andy Steele .75 2.00
6H Wade Whatley .75 2.00
6S Bob Newton 1.00 2.50
7C Benny Sivley 1.00 2.50
7D Rick Telhiard 1.00 2.50
7H Rob Spivey 1.00 2.50
7S David Williams .75 2.00
8C David Langner .75 2.00
8D Chuck Fletcher .75 2.00
8H Thomas Gossom .75 2.00
8S Holley Caldwell .75 2.00
9C Chris Linderman .75 2.00
9D Ed Butler .75 2.00
9H Kenny Burks .75 2.00
9S Mike Flynn .75 2.00
10C Roger Mitchell .75 2.00
10D Jim McKinney .75 2.00
10H Gaines Lanier .75 2.00
10S Carl Hubbard .75 2.00
11C Bob Farrior .75 2.00
11D Ronnie Jones .75 2.00
11H Billy Woods .75 2.00
11S David Hughes .75 2.00
12C Sherman Moon .75 2.00
12D Mike Gates .75 2.00
12H Steve Taylor .75 2.00
12S Randy Walls .75 2.00
13C Roger Pruett .75 2.00
13D Bobby Davis .75 2.00
13H Hamlin Caldwell .75 2.00
13S Dan Nugent .75 2.00
JOK1 Joker .75 2.00
  Auburn Memorial Coliseum
JOK2 Joker .75 2.00
  Cliff Hare Stadium

1987-88 Auburn

This 16-card standard-size set was issued by Auburn University and includes members from different sports programs. Reportedly only 5,000 sets were made by McDag Productions, and the cards were distributed by the Opelika, Alabama police department. The cards feature color player photos on white card stock. The backs present safety tips for children. The last three cards of the set feature "Tiger Greats," former Auburn athletes Bo Jackson, Rowdy Gaines, and Chuck Person. The key card in the set is Frank Thomas. The sports represented in this set are football (1, 3, 5, 11-13, 16), basketball (4, 6, 9-10, 14), baseball (2), and swimming (15). A card of Bo Jackson playing Football has been recently discovered. Since very few of these cards are known it is not considered part of the complete set

COMPLETE SET (16) 70.00 175.00
1 Pat Dye CO FB 1.00 2.50
3 Jeff Burger FB .60 1.50
5 Kurt Crain FB .40 1.00
11 Tracy Rocker FB .60 1.50
12 Brian Shulman FB .40 1.00
13 Lawyer Tillman FB 1.00 2.50
16B Bo Jackson 15.00 40.00
  Playing Football

1989 Auburn Coke 20

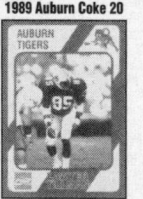

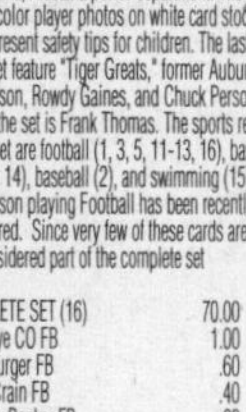

The 1989 Coke Auburn University football set contains 20 standard-size cards, depicting former Auburn greats. The fronts contain vintage photos; the horizontally oriented backs feature player profiles. Both sides have navy borders. These cards were printed on very thin stock.

COMPLETE SET (20) 4.00 10.00
C1 Pat Dye CO .25 .60
C2 Zeke Smith .15 .40
C3 War Eagle (Mascot) .20 .50
C4 Tucker Frederickson .20 .50
C5 John Heisman .20 .50
C6 Ralph(Shug) Jordan CO .20 .50
C7 Pat Sullivan .20 .50
C8 Terry Beasley .15 .40
C9 Punt Bama Punt .20 .50
  Ralph(Shug) Jordan
  and Paul(Bear) Bryant
C10 Retired Jerseys .20 .50
  (Pat Sullivan and
  Terry Beasley)
C11 Bo Jackson 1.00 2.50
C12 Lawyer Tillman .20 .50
C13 Gregg Carr .15 .40
C14 Lionel James .20 .50
C15 Joe Cribbs .30 .75
C16 Heisman Winners .40 1.00
  (Pat Sullivan&
  Bo Jackson&
  and Pat Dye CO)
C17 Aundray Bruce .20 .50
C18 Aubie (Mascot) .15 .40
C19 Tracy Rocker .15 .40
C20 James Brooks .30 .75

1989 Auburn Coke 580

The 1989 Coke Auburn University football set contains 580 standard-size cards, depicting former Auburn greats. The fronts contain vintage photos; the horizontally oriented backs feature player profiles. Both sides have navy borders. The cards were distributed in sets and in poly packs. These cards were printed on very thin stock. This set is notable for its inclusion of several Bo Jackson cards.

COMPLETE SET (580) 12.00 30.00
1 Pat Dye CO .08 .25
  (His First Game)
2 Auburn's First Team .05 .15
  (1892 Team Photo)
3 Pat Sullivan .08 .25
4 Bo (Jackson) .40 1.00
  Over The Top
5 Jimmy Hitchcock .02 .10
6 Walter Gilbert .02 .10
7 Monk Gafford .02 .10
8 Frank D'Agostino .02 .10
9 Joe Childress .05 .15
10 Jim Pyburn .05 .15
11 Tex Warrington .02 .10
12 Travis Tidwell .05 .15
13 Fob James .02 .10
14 Jim Phillips .05 .15
15 Zeke Smith .02 .10
16 Mike Fuller .05 .15
17 Ed Dyas .02 .10
18 Jack Thornton .02 .10
19 Ken Rice .02 .10
20 Freddie Hyatt .02 .10
21 Jackie Burkett .05 .15
22 Jimmy Sidle .05 .15
23 Buddy McClinton .02 .10
24 Larry Willingham .05 .15
25 Bob Harris .02 .10
26 Bill Cody .02 .10
27 Lewis Colbert .02 .10
28 Brent Fullwood .08 .25
29 Tracy Rocker .05 .15
30 Kurt Grain .02 .10
31 Walter Reeves .05 .15
32 Jordan-Hare Stadium .02 .10
33 Ben Tamburello .02 .10
34 Benji Roland .02 .10
35 Chris Knapp .02 .10
36 Dowe Aughtman .02 .10
37 Auburn Tigers Logo .02 .10
38 Tommie Agee .05 .15
39 Bo Jackson .40 1.00
40 Freddy Weygand .05 .15
41 Rodney Garner .02 .10
42 Brian Shulman .02 .10
43 Jim Thompson .02 .10
44 Shan Morris .02 .10
45 Ralph(Shug) Jordan CO .05 .15
46 Stacy Searels .02 .10
47 1957 Champs .05 .15
  (Team Photo)
48 Mike Kolen .05 .15
49 A Challenge Met .05 .15
  (Pat Dye)
50 Mark Dominey .02 .10
51 Greg Staples .02 .10
52 Randy Campbell .02 .10
53 Duke Donaldson .02 .10
54 Yann Cowart .02 .10
55 Second Blocked Punt .05 .15
  (Vs. Alabama 1972)
  Bill Newton
  David Langner
56 Keith Uecker .05 .15
57 David Jordan .02 .10
58 Tim Drinkard .02 .10
59 Connie Frederick .02 .10
60 Pat Arrington .02 .10
61 Willie Howell .02 .10
62 Terry Page .02 .10
63 Ben Thomas .02 .10
64 Ron Stallworth .05 .15
65 Charlie Trotman .02 .10
66 Ed West .05 .15
67 James Brooks .15 .40
68 Changing of the Guard .05 .15
  Doug Barfield and
  Ralph(Shug) Jordan
69 Ken Bernich .02 .10
70 Chris Woods .02 .10
71 Ralph(Shug) Jordan CO .05 .15
72 Steve Dennis CO .02 .10
73 Reggie Herring CO .02 .10
74 Al Del Greco .05 .15
75 Wayne Hall CO .02 .10
76 Langdon Hall .02 .10
77 Donnie Humphrey .02 .10
78 Jeff Burger .05 .15
79 Vernon Blackard .02 .10
80 Larry Blakeney CO .02 .10
81 Doug Smith .02 .10
82 Two Eras Meet .05 .15
  Ralph(Shug) Jordan
  and Vince Dooley
83 Kyle Collins .02 .10
84 Bobby Freeman .02 .10
85 Pat Sullivan CO .08 .25
86 Neil Callaway CO .02 .10
87 William Andrews .08 .25
88 Curtis Kuykendall .02 .10
89 David Campbell .02 .10
90 Seniors of '83 .08 .25
91 Bud Casey CO .02 .10
92 Jay Jacobs CO .02 .10
93 Al Del Greco .05 .15
94 Pate Mote .02 .10
95 Rob Shuler .02 .10
96 Jerry Beasley .02 .10
97 Pat Washington .02 .10
98 Ed Graham .02 .10
99 Leon Myers .02 .10
100 Paul Davis CO .02 .10
101 Tom Banks Jr. .05 .15
102 Mike Simmons .02 .10
103 Alex Bowden .02 .10
104 Jim Bone .02 .10
105 Wincent Harris .02 .10
106 James Daniel CO .02 .10
107 Jimmy Carter .02 .10
108 Leading Passers .08 .25
  (Pat Sullivan)
109 Alvin Mitchell .02 .10
110 Mark Clement .02 .10
111 Bob Brown .02 .10
112 Shot Senn .02 .10
113 Loran Carter .02 .10
114 Pat Dye's First Team .05 .15
  (Team Photo)
115 Bob Hix .02 .10
116 Bo Russell .02 .10
117 Mike Mann .02 .10
118 Mike Shirey .02 .10
119 Pat Dye CO .05 .15
120 Kevin Greene .08 .25
121 Auburn Creed .02 .10
122 Jordan's All-Americans .05 .15
  Ralph(Shug) Jordan
  Tucker Frederickson
  Jimmy Sidle
123 Dave Blanks .02 .10
124 Scott Bolton .02 .10
125 Vince Dooley .08 .25
126 Tim Jessie .02 .10
127 Joe Davis .02 .10
128 Clayton Beauford .02 .10
129 Wilbur Hutsell AD .02 .10
130 Joe Whit CO .02 .10
131 Gary Kelley .02 .10
132 Bo Jackson .40 1.00
133 Aundray Bruce .08 .25
134 Ronny Bellew .02 .10
135 Hindman Wall .02 .10
136 Frank Warren .02 .10
137 Abb Chrietzberg .02 .10
138 Collis Campbell .02 .10
139 Randy Stokes .02 .10
140 Teedy Faulk .02 .10
141 Reese McCall .05 .15
142 Jeff Jackson .02 .10
143 Bill Burgess .02 .10
144 Willie Huntley .02 .10
145 Doug Huntley .02 .10
146 Bacardi Bowl .02 .10
  (Walter Gilbert)
147 Russ Carreker .02 .10
148 Joe Moon .02 .10
149 A Look Ahead .05 .15
  (Pat Dye CO)
150 Joe Sullivan .02 .10
151 Scott Riley .02 .10
152 Larry Ellis .02 .10
153 Jeff Parks .02 .10
154 Gerald Williams .02 .10
155 Lee Griffith .02 .10
156 First Blocked Punt .05 .15
  (Vs. Alabama 1972)
  Bill Newton
157 Bill Beckwith ADMIN .02 .10
158 Celebration .05 .15
  (1957 Action Photo)
159 Tommy Carroll .05 .15
160 John Dailey .02 .10
161 George Stephenson .02 .10
162 Danny Arnold .02 .10
163 Mike Edwards .02 .10
164 1894 Auburn-Alabama .05 .15
  Trophy
165 Don Anderson .02 .10
166 Alvin Briggs .02 .10
167 Herb Waldrop CO .02 .10
168 Jim Skuthan .02 .10
169 Alan Hardin .02 .10
170 Coaching Generations .08 .25
  (Pat Sullivan
  and Bobby Freeman)
171 Georgia Celebration .02 .10
  (1971 Locker Room)
172 Auburn 17, Alabama 16 .05 .15
  (1972 Scoreboard)
173 Nat Ceasar .02 .10
174 Billy Hitchcock .05 .15
175 SEC Championship .05 .15
  Trophy
176 Dr. James E. Martin .02 .10
  PRES
177 Ricky Westbrook .05 .15
178 Fob James .05 .15
179 Stacy Dunn .02 .10
180 Tracy Turner .02 .10
181 Pat Dye CO .05 .15
182 Terry Beasley in the .02 .10
  Record Book
183 Ed(Foots) Bauer .02 .10
184 1984 Sugar Bowl .02 .10
  Scoreboard
185 Mark Robbins .02 .10
186 Paul White CO .02 .10
187 Hindman Wall AD .02 .10
188 Dave Beverly .05 .15
189 Sugar Bowl Trophy .02 .10
190 Edmund Nelson .02 .10
191 Edmund Nelson .02 .10
192 Cliff Hare .02 .10
193 Byron Franklin .05 .15
194 Richard Manry .02 .10
195 Malcolm McCary .02 .10
196 Patrick Waters ADMIN .02 .10
197 Chester Willis .02 .10
198 Alex Dudchock .02 .10
199 Pat Sullivan in the .08 .25
  Record Book
200 Victory Ride .05 .15
  (Pat Dye CO)
201 Dr. George Petrie CO .02 .10
202 D.M. Balliet CO .02 .10
203 G.H. Harvey CO .02 .10
204 F.M. Hall CO .02 .10
205 John Heisman CO .08 .25
206 Billy Watkins CO .02 .10
207 J.R. Kent CO .02 .10
208 Mike Harvey CO .02 .10
209 Billy Bates CO .02 .10
210 Mike Donahue CO .02 .10
211 W.S. Kienholz CO .02 .10
212 Mike Donahue CO .02 .10
213 Boozer Pitts CO .02 .10
214 Dave Morey CO .02 .10
215 George Bohler CO .02 .10
216 John Floyd CO .02 .10
217 Chet Wynne CO .02 .10
218 Jack Meagher CO .02 .10
219 Carl Voyles CO .02 .10
220 Earl Brown CO .02 .10
221 Ralph(Shug) Jordan CO .05 .15
222 Doug Barfield CO .05 .15
223 Most Career Points .15 .40
  (Bo Jackson)
224 Sonny Ferguson .02 .10
225 Ronnie Ross .02 .10
226 Gardner Jett .05 .15
227 Jerry Wilson .02 .10
228 Dick Schmalz .02 .10
229 Morris Savage .02 .10
230 James Owens .02 .10
231 Eddie Welch .02 .10
232 Lee Hayley .02 .10
233 Dick Hayley .02 .10
234 Jeff McCollum .02 .10
235 Rick Freeman .02 .10
236 Bobby Freeman CO .02 .10
237 Auburn 32, Alabama 22 .05 .15
  (Trophy)
238 Chip Powell .02 .10
239 Nick Ardillo .02 .10
240 Don Bristow .02 .10
241 Bucky Waid .02 .10
242 Greg Robert .02 .10
243 Ray Rollins .02 .10
244 Tommy Hicks .02 .10
245 Steve Wallace .05 .15
246 David Hughes .02 .10
247 Chuck Hurston .02 .10
248 Jimmy Long .02 .10
249 John Cochran AD .02 .10
250 Bobby Davis .02 .10
251 G.W. Clapp .02 .10
252 Jere Colley .02 .10
253 Tim James .02 .10
254 Joe Dolan .02 .10
255 Jerry Gordon .02 .10
256 Billy Edge .02 .10
257 Lawyer Tillman .05 .15
258 John McAfee .02 .10
259 Scotty Long .02 .10
260 Billy Austin .02 .10
261 Tracy Rocker .05 .15
262 Mickey Sutton .02 .10
263 Tommy Traylor .02 .10
264 Bill Van Dyke .02 .10
265 Sam McClurkin .02 .10
266 Mike Flynn .02 .10
267 Jimmy Sirmans .02 .10
268 Reggie Ware .05 .15
269 Bill Luka .02 .10
270 Don Machen .02 .10
271 Bill Grisham .02 .10
272 Bruce Evans .02 .10
273 Hank Hall .02 .10
274 Tommy Lunceford .02 .10
275 Pat Thomas .02 .10
276 Marvin Trott .02 .10
277 Brad Everett .02 .10
278 Frank Reeves .02 .10
279 Bishop Reeves .02 .10
280 Carver Reeves .02 .10
281 Billy Haas .02 .10
282 Dye's First AU Bowl .05 .15
  (Pat Dye CO)
283 Nate Hill .02 .10
284 Bucky Howard .02 .10
285 Tim Christian .02 .10
286 Tim Christian CO .02 .10
287 Tom Nettleman .02 .10
288 Carl Hubbard .02 .10
289 Auburn's Biggest Wins .02 .10
  (Chart)
290 Jay Jacobs .02 .10
291 Jimmy Pettus .02 .10
292 Cliff Hare Stadium .02 .10
293 Richard Wood .05 .15
294 Sandy Cannon .02 .10
295 Bill Braswell .02 .10
296 Foy Thompson .02 .10
297 Robert Margeson .02 .10
298 Pipeline to the Pros .08 .25
  (Seven Pro Players)
  Gerald Williams
  Ed West
  Gregg Carr
  Donnie Humphrey
  Al Del Greco
  Ben Thomas
  Edmund Nelson
299 Bill Evans .02 .10
300 Marvin Tucker .02 .10
301 Jack Locklear .02 .10
302 Mike Locklear .02 .10
303 Harry Unger .02 .10
304 Lee Marke Sellers .02 .10
305 Ted Foret .02 .10
306 Bobby Foret .02 .10
307 Mike Neel .02 .10
308 Rick Neel .02 .10
309 Mike Alford .02 .10
310 Mac Crawford .02 .10
311 Bill Cunningham .02 .10
312 Legends .08 .25
  (Pat Sullivan
  and Jeff Burger)
313 Frank LaRussa .02 .10
314 Chris Vacarella .02 .10
315 Gerald Robinson .05 .15
316 Ronnie Baynes .02 .10
317 Dave Edwards .02 .10
318 Steve Taylor .02 .10
319 Phillip Gilchrist .02 .10
320 Ben McCurdy .02 .10
321 Dave Hill .02 .10
322 Jim Reynolds .02 .10
323 Chuck Fletcher .02 .10
324 Bogue Miller .02 .10
325 Dave Beck .02 .10
326 Johnny Simmons .02 .10
327 Howard Simpson .02 .10
328 Benny Sivley .05 .15
329 1987 SEC Champions .05 .15
  (Team Photo)
330 Frank Cox .02 .10
331 Phil Gargis .02 .10
332 Don Webb .02 .10
333 Dan Presley .02 .10
334 Al Giffin .02 .10
335 Don Lewis .02 .10
336 Eric Floyd .05 .15
337 Jordan and Stadium .05 .15
  (Ralph(Shug) Jordan)
338 Terry Hendly .02 .10
339 Bill Atkins .02 .10
340 Tony Long .02 .10
341 Jimmy Clemmer .02 .10
342 John Valentine .02 .10
343 Bruce Bylsma .02 .10
344 Merrill Shirley .02 .10
345 Kenny Howard CO .02 .10
346 Hal Hamrick .02 .10
347 Greg Zipp .02 .10
348 Mac Champion .02 .10
349 Most Tackles in .02 .10
  One Game
  (Kurt Crain)
350 Leading Career .15 .40
  Rushers
  (Bo Jackson)
351 Homer Williams .02 .10
352 Mike Gates .02 .10
353 Rusty Fuller .02 .10
354 Rusty Deen .02 .10
355 Stalwart Defenders .02 .10
  (Bob Harris and
  Mark Dominey)
356 Heroes of '56 .05 .15
  (Ralph(Shug) Jordan
  Jerry Elliott
  Frank Reeves)
357 Road to the Top .05 .15
  (Cartoon)
358 Cleve Wester .02 .10
359 Line Stars .05 .15
  (Jackie Burkett
  and Zeke Smith)
360 Bob Scarbrough .02 .10
361 Jimmy Speigner .02 .10
362 Danny Speigner .02 .10
363 Alvin Bresler .02 .10
364 Wade Whatley .02 .10
365 Lance Hill .02 .10
366 Andy Steele .02 .10
367 John Whatley .02 .10
368 Alton Shell .02 .10
369 Larry Blakeney .02 .10
370 Mickey Zofko .02 .10
371 Gene Lorendo CO .02 .10
372 Mac Lorendo .02 .10
373 Buddy Davidson AD .02 .10
374 Dave Woodward .02 .10
375 Richard Guthrie .02 .10
376 George Rose .02 .10
377 Alan Bollinger .02 .10
378 Danny Sanspree .02 .10
379 Winky Giddens .02 .10
380 Franklin Fuller .02 .10
381 Charlie Collins .02 .10
382 Auburn 23-22 .02 .10
  (Scoreboard)
383 Jeff Weekley .02 .10
384 Larry Haynie .02 .10
385 Miles Jones .02 .10
386 Bobby Wilson .05 .15
387 Bobby Lauder .02 .10
388 Charlie Glenn .02 .10
389 Claude Saia .02 .10
390 Tom Bryan .02 .10
391 Lee Gross .02 .10
392 Jerry Popwell .02 .10
393 Tommy Groat .02 .10
394 Neal Dettmering .02 .10
395 Dr. W.S. Bailey ADMIN .02 .10
396 Jim Pitts .02 .10
397 College Football .02 .10
  History
  (Cliff Hare Stadium)
398 Doc Griffith .02 .10
399 Liston Eddins .02 .10
400 Woody Woodall .02 .10
401 Auburn Helmet .02 .10
402 Skip Johnston .02 .10
403 Trey Gainous .02 .10
404 Randy Walls .02 .10
405 Jimmy Partin .02 .10
406 Dick Ingwerson .02 .10
407 David Shelby .02 .10
408 Harry Ward .02 .10
409 Thomas Gossom .02 .10
410 Samford T. Gower .02 .10
411 Architects of the .05 .15
  Future (Jeff Beard and
  Ralph(Shug) Jordan)
412 Ed Butler .02 .10
413 Bob Butler .02 .10
414 Ben Strickland .02 .10
415 Jeff Lott .02 .10
416 Harris Rabren .02 .10
417 Mike McQuaig .02 .10
418 Steve Wilson .02 .10
419 Jorge Portela .02 .10
420 Dave Middleton .05 .15
421 Tommy Yearout .02 .10
422 Gusty Yearout .02 .10
423 The Auburn Stadium .02 .10
424 Cliff Hare Stadium .02 .10
425 Oscar Burford .02 .10
426 Cliff Hare Stadium .02 .10
427 Cliff Hare Stadium .02 .10
428 Jordan-Hare Stadium .02 .10
429 Jack Meagher CO .02 .10
430 Jeff Beard AD .02 .10
431 Frank Young ADMIN .02 .10
432 Frank Riley .02 .10
433 Ernie Warren .02 .10
434 Brian Atkins .02 .10
435 George Atkins .02 .10
436 Ricky Sanders .08 .25
437 George Kenmore .02 .10
438 Don Heller .02 .10
439 Pat Meagher .02 .10
440 Tim Davis .02 .10
441 Tiger Meat (Cooks) .02 .10
442 Joe Connally CO .02 .10
443 Bob Newton .05 .15
444 Bill Newton .02 .10
445 David Langner .02 .10
446 Charlie Langner .02 .10
447 Brownie Flournoy ADMIN .02 .10
448 Mike Hicks .02 .10
449 Larry Hill .02 .10
450 Tim Baker .02 .10
451 Danny Bentley .02 .10
452 Tommy Lowry .02 .10
453 Jim Price .02 .10
454 Lloyd Nix .02 .10
455 Kenny Burks .02 .10
456 Rusty and Sallie Deen .02 .10
  ADMIN
457 Johnny Sumner .02 .10
458 Scott Blackmon .02 .10
459 Chuck Maxime .02 .10
460 Big SEC Wins (Chart) .02 .10
461 Bo Davis .02 .10
462 George Rose .02 .10
463 Bob Bradley .02 .10
464 Steve Osburne .02 .10
465 George Gross .02 .10
466 Andy Gross .02 .10
467 M.L. Brackett .02 .10
468 Herman Wilkes .02 .10
469 Roger Mitchell .02 .10
470 Bobby Beaird .02 .10
471 Sammy Oates .02 .10
472 Jimmy Ricketts .02 .10
473 Bucky Ayters .02 .10
474 Bill James .02 .10
475 Johnny Wallis .02 .10
476 Chris Jornson .02 .10
477 Joe Overton .02 .10
478 Tommy Lorino .02 .10
479 James Warren .02 .10
480 Lynn Johnson .02 .10
481 Sam Mitchell .02 .10
482 Sedrick McIntyre .02 .10
483 Mike Holtzclaw .02 .10
484 Dave Ostrowski .02 .10
485 Jim Walsh .02 .10
486 Mike Henley .02 .10
487 Roy Tatum .02 .10
488 Al Parks .02 .10
489 Billy Wilson .05 .15
490 Ken Luke .02 .10
491 Phillip Hall .02 .10
492 Bruce Yates .02 .10
493 Dan Hataway .02 .10
494 Joe Leichtnam .02 .10
495 Danny Fulford .02 .10
496 Ken Hardy .02 .10
497 Rob Spivey .02 .10
498 Rick Telhiard .02 .10
499 Ron Yarbrough .02 .10
500 Leo Sexton .02 .10
501 Dick McGowen CO .02 .10
502 Lee Kidd .02 .10
503 Rex McKissick .02 .10
504 Fagen Canzoneri and .02 .10
  Zach Jenkins
505 Jim Bouchillon .02 .10
506 Forrest Blue .08 .25
507 Mike Helms .02 .10
508 Bobby Hunt .05 .15
509 John Liptak .02 .10
510 Jim McKinney .02 .10
511 Ed Baker .02 .10
512 Heisman Trophies .08 .25
513 Eddy Jackson .02 .10
514 Jimmy Powell .02 .10
515 Jerry Elliott .02 .10
516 Jimmy Jones .02 .10
517 Jimmy Laster .02 .10
518 Larry Laster .02 .10
519 Jerry Sansom .02 .10
520 Don Downs .02 .10
521 Danny Skutack .02 .10
522 Keith Green .02 .10
523 Spence McCracken .02 .10
524 Lloyd Cheattom .02 .10
525 Mike Shows .02 .10
526 Spec Kelley .02 .10
527 Dick McGowen .02 .10
528 Jon Kilgore .02 .10
529 Frank Gatski .08 .25
530 Joel Eaves .02 .10
531 John Adcock .02 .10
532 Jimmy Fenton .02 .10
533 Mike McCartney .02 .10
534 Harrison McCraw .02 .10
535 Mailon Kent .02 .10
536 Dickie Flournoy .02 .10
537 Coker Barton .02 .10
538 Scotty Elam .02 .10
539 Tim Wood .02 .10
540 Terry Fuller .02 .10
541 Johnny Kern .02 .10
542 Mike Currier .02 .10
543 Richard Cheek .02 .10
544 Dan Dickerson .02 .10
545 Arnold Fagen .02 .10
546 John Rat Riley .02 .10
547 Jim Burson .05 .15
548 Bob Fleming .02 .10
549 Mike Fitzhugh .02 .10
550 Jim Patton .08 .25
551 Bryant Harvard .02 .10
552 Leon Cochran .02 .10
553 Wayne Frazier .02 .10
554 Phillip Dembowski .02 .10
555 Alex Spurlin and .02 .10
  Ed Spurlin
556 Bill Kilpatrick .02 .10
557 Gaines Lanier .02 .10
558 Johnny McDonald .02 .10
559 Ray Powell .02 .10
560 Jimmy Putman .02 .10
561 Bobby Wasden .02 .10
562 Roger Pruett .02 .10
563 Don Braswell .02 .10
564 Jim Jeffery .02 .10
565 Auburn-A TV Favorite .05 .15
  (Pat Dye CO)
566 Lamar Rawson .02 .10
567 Larry Rawson .02 .10
568 David Rawson .02 .10
569 Hal Herring CO .02 .10
570 Pat Sullivan .08 .25
571 John Cochran .02 .10
572 Jerry Gulledge .02 .10
573 Steve Stanaland .05 .15
574 Greg Zipp .02 .10
575 John Trotman .02 .10
576 Clyde Baumgartner .02 .10
577 Jay Casey .02 .10
578 Ralph O'Gwynne .02 .10
579 Sid Scarborough .02 .10
580 Tom Banks Sr. .05 .15
AU1 Bo Jackson Promo .30 .75

1991 Auburn Hoby

This 42-card standard-size set was produced by Hoby and features the 1991 Auburn football team. Five hundred uncut press sheets were also produced, and they were signed and numbered by Pat Dye. The cards feature on the fronts a mix of posed and action color photos, with thin white borders on a royal blue card face. The school logo occurs in the lower left corner in an orange circle, with the player's name in a gold stripe extending to the right. On a light orange background, the backs carry biography, player profile, or statistics.

COMPLETE SET (42) 4.80 12.00
523 Thomas Bailey .08 .25
524 Corey Barlow .15 .40
525 Reggie Barlow .15 .40
526 Fred Baxter .15 .40
527 Eddie Blake .15 .40
528 Herbert Casey .08 .25
529 Pedro Cherry .08 .25
530 Darrel Crawford .15 .40
531 Tim Cromartie .08 .25
532 Juan Crum .08 .25
533 Karekin Cunningham .08 .25
534 Alonzo Etheridge .08 .25
535 Joe Frazier .08 .25

536 Pat Dye AD/CO	.20	.50
537 Thery George	.08	.25
538 Chris Gray	.15	.40
539 Victor Hall	.08	.25
540 Randy Hart	.08	.25
541 Chris Holland	.08	.25
542 Chuckie Johnson	.08	.25
543 Anthony Judge	.08	.25
544 Corey Lewis	.08	.25
545 Reid McMilion	.08	.25
546 Bob Meeks	.08	.25
547 Dale Overton	.08	.25
548 Mike Pelton	.20	.50
549 Bennie Pierce	.08	.25
550 Mike Pina	.00	.00
551 Anthony Redmon	.08	.25
552 Tony Richardson	.08	.25
553 Richard Shea	.08	.25
554 Fred Smith	.15	.40
555 Otis Mounds	.08	.25
556 Ricky Sutton	.08	.25
557 Alex Thomas	.08	.25
558 Greg Thompson	.08	.25
559 Tim Tillman	.08	.25
560 Jim Von Wyl	.08	.25
561 Stan White	.20	.50
562 Darrell Williams	.08	.25
563 James Willis	.08	.25
564 Jon Wilson	.08	.25

2001 Auburn Team Sheets

These photos were issued by the school to promote the football program. Each measures roughly 8" by 10" and features eight black and white images of players with the school name and year appearing at the top. The player's name is printed below each image. The backs are blank.

COMPLETE SET (8)	25.00	50.00
1 Lamel Ages	6.00	12.00
Jacob Allen		
Ronald Attimy		
Ryan Broome		
Mark Brown		
Ronnie Brown		
Chris Butler		
James Callier		
2 Jason Campbell	5.00	10.00
Tim Carter		
Daniel Cobb		
Monreko Crittenden		
Karlos Dansby		
Lorenzo Diamond		
Damon Duval		
Bret Eddins		
3 Justin Fetsko	3.00	6.00
Nate Grench		
Roshard Gilyard		
Steve Goula		
Deandre Green		
Jamaal Greer		
Brian Henderson		
Roderick Hood		
4 Victor Horn	3.00	6.00
Brandon Johnson		
Marcus Johnson		
Robert Johnson		
Spencer Johnson		
Jeff Klein		
Danny Lindsey		
Michael Lindsey		
5 Hart McGarry	3.00	6.00
Jeris McIntyre		
DeMarco McNeil		
Javor Mills		
Alton Moore		
Casinious Moore		
Dexter Murphy		
Ben Nowland		
6 Michael Owens	3.00	6.00
Phillip Pate		
Mark Pera		
Damien Postell		
Tavarreus Pounds		
Mike Pucillo		
Travaris Robinson		
Junior Rosegreen		
7 Ronald Samuel	3.00	6.00
Kendall Simmons		
Stanford Simmons		
Mayo Sowell		
Jimmy St. Louis		
Dontarrious Thomas		
Allen Tillman		
Reggie Torbor		
8 Rich Trucks	3.00	6.00
Rashaud Walker		
Joe Walkins		
Jeremy Wells		
Marcus White		
Marcel Willis		
Donnay Young		
Phillip Yost		

2003 Auburn Schedules

COMPLETE SET (4)	.75	2.00
1 Karlos Dansby	.30	.75
2 Monreko Crittenden	.20	.50
3 Brandon Johnson	.20	.50
4 Dontarrious Thomas	.20	.50

2004 Auburn Schedules

These "cards" are actually pocket schedules issued by the school. The fronts feature an Auburn player in a color photo with the year noted at the top as well as the player's name. Each one folds and includes the team's 2004 football schedule on the inside and one of a variety of ads on the back.

COMPLETE SET (6)	2.50	6.00
1 Ronnie Brown	.75	2.00
2 Jason Campbell	.50	1.25
3 Danny Lindsay	.20	.50
4 Carlos Rogers	.40	1.00
5 Junior Rosegreen	.20	.50
6 Cadillac Williams	.75	2.00

2006 Auburn Schedules

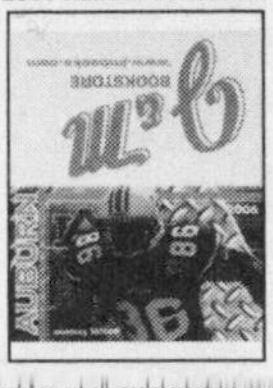

These "cards" are actually pocket schedules issued by the school. The fronts feature an Auburn player in a color photo with the year noted at the top as well as the player's name. Each one folds and includes the team's 2006 football schedule on the inside and one of a variety of ads on the back.

1 Kody Bliss	.20	.50
2 Marquies Gunn	.20	.50
3 Will Herring	.20	.50
4 Kenny Irons	.30	.75
5 Jonathan Palmer	.20	.50
6 Courtney Taylor	.30	.75

2001 Bakersfield College

1 James Brandon	.30	.75
2 Kevin Bryan	.30	.75
3 Sam Campanella	.30	.75
4 Darren Carr	.30	.75
5 Donte Carter	.30	.75
6 Aubrey Dorisme	.30	.75
7 Dallas Grider (HC)	.30	.75
8 Terrence Hall	.30	.75
9 Russell Handy	.30	.75
10 Randy Jordan	.30	.75
11 Ryan Kroeker	.30	.75
12 James McGill	.30	.75
13 Sammy Moore	.30	.75
14 Kenneth Qualls	.30	.75
15 Kyle Rivers	.30	.75
16 Robert Thomas	.30	.75
17 Coaching Staff	.30	.75
Lorenzo Alvarez		
Scott Douglas		
Dallas Grider		
Jeff Arneson		
Chad Grider		
Jeff Chudy		
Brent Damron		
Paul Carrillo		
Kevin Sneed		
Dave Titsworth		

2002 Bakersfield College

1 Ismael Arrenaviz	.40	1.00
2 Nathan Baker	.40	1.00
3 Craig Buckey	.40	1.00
4 Lawrence Figueroa	.40	1.00
5 Kyle Hager	.40	1.00
6 Jason Garcia	.40	1.00
7 Garrett Harker	.40	1.00
8 Josh Lopes	.40	1.00
9 LaRon Mitchell	.40	1.00
10 Tim Neilson	.40	1.00
11 Tim O'Toole	.40	1.00
12 George Valos	.40	1.00
13 Coaching Staff	.40	1.00
Lorenzo Alvarez		
Ryan Geivet		
Dallas Grider		
Jack O'Brien		
Chad Grider		
Jeff Chudy		
Brent Damron		
Paul Carrillo		
Kevin Sneed		
Dave Titsworth		

1987-88 Baylor

This 17-card standard-size set was sponsored by the Hillcrest Baptist Medical Center, the Waco Police Department, and the Baylor University Department of Public Safety. The cards represent several sports: baseball (1-3), basketball (4-6), track (7-10), and football (11-17). The front feature color action shots of the players on white card stock. At the top the words "Baylor Bears 1987-88" are printed between the Hillcrest and Baylor University logos. Player information is given below the picture. The back has more logos, brief career summaries, and "Bear Briefs," which consist of instructional sports information and an anti-drug or crime message.

COMPLETE SET (17)	12.00	30.00
11 Ray Crockett	2.00	5.00
12 Joel Porter	.40	1.00
13 James Francis	2.50	6.00
14 Russell Sheffield	.40	1.00
15 Matt Clark	.40	1.00
16 Eugene Hall	.40	1.00
17 Grant Teaff CO	1.60	4.00

1992 Baylor Program Inserts

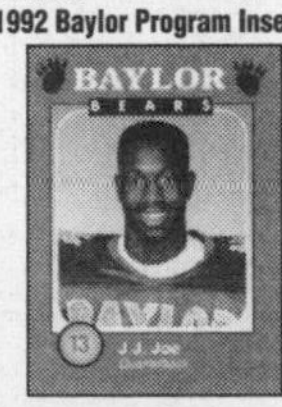

The 21-cards comprising this set were initially issued as game program inserts. Three perforated sheets measuring approximately 7 5/8" by 11" containing seven player cards and a sponsor card were issued in the program. Each perforated player card measures approximately 2 7/16" by 3 5/16" and features green-bordered posed color head shots of helmetless players. The player's name and position appear within the green border at the bottom. The team name, Baylor Bears, appears above the player image and his uniform number is shown in a yellow circle at the lower left. The white back carries the player's name, position, and biography. The cards are unnumbered and checklisted below in alphabetical order.

1 Craig Bellamy	.40	1.00
2 Lee Bruderer	.40	1.00
3 Keith Caldwell	.40	1.00
4 Marvin Callies	.40	1.00
5 Will Davidson	.40	1.00
6 Jeff Deloach	.40	1.00
7 Raynor Finley	.40	1.00
8 Albert Fontenot	.40	1.00
9 Ricky Heard	.40	1.00
10 Ohad Hunter	.40	1.00
11 J.J. Joe	.60	1.50
12 Shawn Lawson	.40	1.00
13 David Leaks	.40	1.00
14 Bradford Lewis	.40	1.00
15 Chris Lewis	.40	1.00
16 Scotty Lewis	.40	1.00
17 Michael McFarland	.40	1.00
18 Reggie Miller	.40	1.00
19 David Mims	.40	1.00
20 Tony Moore	.40	1.00
21 Steve Needham	.40	1.00
22 Chuck Pope	.40	1.00
23 Tyrone Smith	.40	1.00
24 Steve Strahan	.40	1.00
25 Andrew Swasey	.40	1.00
26 John Turner	.40	1.00
27 Trey Weir	.40	1.00
28 Team Mascot	.40	1.00

1993 Baylor

Sponsored by First Waco National Bank, the 21 cards comprising this set were issued as perforated game program insert sheets. The three perforated sheets measure approximately 7 5/8" by 11". Each sheet consists of seven player cards and a sponsor card, which is the size of two player cards. Each perforated player card measures approximately 2 7/16" by 3 5/16" and features green-bordered posed color head shots of helmetless players. The player's name and position appear within an orange banner at the bottom. The team name, Baylor Bears, appears in white lettering within a black bar at the upper right. The player's uniform number is shown in white within a black circle at the upper left. The white back carries the player's name, position, and biography in bold black lettering at the upper right. Previous season highlights follow below. The player's uniform number appears in white within a black icon of a bear's paw at the upper left, but otherwise the cards are unnumbered and so checklisted below in alphabetical order.

COMPLETE SET (21)	10.00	20.00
1 Lamone Alexander	.40	1.00
2 Joseph Asbell	.40	1.00
3 Marvin Callies	.40	1.00
4 Todd Crawford	.40	1.00
5 Earnest Crownover	.40	1.00
6 Will Davidson	.40	1.00
7 Chris Dull	.40	1.00
8 Raynor Finley	.40	1.00
9 J.J. Joe	.60	1.50
10 Phillip Kent	.40	1.00
11 David Leaks	.40	1.00
12 Scotty Lewis	.40	1.00
13 Fred Miller	.40	1.00
14 Bruce Nowak	.40	1.00
15 Mike Oatis	.40	1.00
16 Chuck Pope	.40	1.00
17 Adrian Robinson	.40	1.00
18 Tyrone Smith	.40	1.00
19 Andrew Swasey	.40	1.00
20 Byron Thompson	.40	1.00
21 Tony Tubbs	.40	1.00

1905 Bergman College Postcards

The 1905 J. Borgman postcard series includes various collegiate football teams printed by the Illustrated Post Card Company. Each card features a color art rendering of a generic college co-ed waving the school's pennant against a solid colored background. A copyright date is also included on the cardfront and the cardback is typical postcard style. We've listed the known postcards. Any additions to this list are appreciated.

1 Cornell	25.00	40.00
2 Harvard	25.00	40.00
3 Pennsylvania	25.00	40.00
4 Princeton	25.00	40.00
5 Yale	25.00	40.00

2004 Boise State

COMPLETE SET (20)	7.50	15.00
1 T.J. Acree	.20	.50
2 Andy Avalos	.20	.50
3 Lawrence Bady	.20	.50
4 Chris Carr	.30	.75
5 Daryn Colledge	.30	.75
6 Gabe Franklin	.20	.50
7 Alex Guerrero	.20	.50
8 Korey Hall	.20	.50
9 Drisan James	1.25	3.00
10 Tyler Jones	.20	.50
11 Lee Marks	.20	.50
12 Julius Roberts	.20	.50
13 Derek Schouman	.50	1.25
14 Jared Zabransky	2.50	6.00
15 Dan Hawkins CO	.20	.50
16 Ryan Dinwiddie GR	.20	.50
17 Brock Forsey GR	.20	.50
18 Bart Hendricks GR	.20	.50
19 Jeb Putzier	.75	2.00
20 Cover Card	.20	.50

2005 Boise State

COMPLETE SET (20)	7.50	15.00
1 Jerard Rabb	.75	2.00
2 Gerald Alexander	.40	1.00
3 Legedu Naanee	.20	.50
4 Jared Zabransky	2.00	5.00
5 Antwaun Carter	.30	.75
6 Drisan James	1.00	2.50
7 Lee Marks	.20	.50
8 Marty Tadman	.75	2.00
9 Jeff Carpenter	.20	.50
10 Quinton Jones	.20	.50
11 Korey Hall	.40	1.00
12 Colt Brooks	.30	.75
13 Austin Smith	.20	.50
14 Chris Barrios	.20	.50
15 Andrew Browning	.20	.50
16 Daryn Colledge	.20	.50
17 Derek Schouman	.50	1.25
18 Alex Guerrero	.20	.50
19 Dan Hawkins CO	.20	.50
20 Cover Card	.20	.50

2006 Boise State

This set was released by the school during the 2006 football season. It features members of the undefeated Boise State Broncos. The cards feature a color player image on the front with the team name "Broncos" running vertically down the left hand side.

COMPLETE SET (18)	10.00	20.00
1 Jerard Rabb	1.00	2.50
2 Gerald Alexander	.30	.75
3 Legedu Naanee	.75	2.00
4 Jared Zabransky	2.00	5.00
5 Orlando Scandrick	.75	2.00
6 Drisan James	.75	2.00
7 Marty Tadman	.50	1.25
8 Quinton Jones	.20	.50
9 Korey Hall	.40	1.00
10 Colt Brooks	.30	.75
11 Ian Johnson	1.25	3.00
12 Kyle Stringer	.40	1.00
13 Jeff Cavender	.20	.50
14 Andrew Browning	.20	.50
15 Tad Miller	.20	.50
16 Ryan Clady	.40	1.00
17 Derek Schouman	.40	1.00
18 Dennis Ellis	.20	.50
19 Chris Petersen CO	.75	2.00
20 Carl's Jr. Mascot	.20	.50

2008 Boise State

This set was released by the school during the 2008 football season and features members of the Boise State Broncos. The cards feature a color player image on the front with the school name "Boise State" running vertically down the left hand side.

COMPLETE SET (20)	7.50	15.00
1 Derrell Acrey	.30	.75
2 Jeremy Avery	.40	1.00
3 Tim Brady	.30	.75
4 Richie Brockel	.30	.75
5 Kyle Brotzman	.30	.75
6 Jeremy Childs	.50	1.25
7 Kyle Gingg	.30	.75
8 Julian Hawkins	.30	.75
9 Ian Johnson	.75	2.00
10 Jeron Johnson	.30	.75
11 Kellen Moore	.60	1.50
12 Chris O'Neill	.30	.75
13 Vinny Perretta	.40	1.00
14 Austin Pettis	.40	1.00
15 Ellis Powers	.30	.75
16 Mike Williams	.30	.75
17 Kyle Wilson	.30	.75
18 Ryan Winterswyk	.30	.75
19 Andrew Woodruff	.30	.75
20 Carl's Junior Coupon	.30	.75

2003 Boston College

COMPLETE SET (6)	4.00	8.00
1 Douglas Goodwin	.60	1.50
2 Derrick Knight	.60	1.50
3 Josh Ott	.60	1.50
4 Sean Ryan	.60	1.50
5 Chris Snee	.60	1.50
6 Baldwin (Mascot)	.60	1.50

2004 Boston College

This card set was sponsored by ESPN and features members of the 2004 Boston College team as well as players from the 20th anniversary 1984 team. The cards were issued in 2-different 6-card perforated strips. The cards measure standard size when separated and include a gold border printed on glossy stock.

COMPLETE SET (12)	6.00	12.00
1 Grant Adams	.40	1.00
2 Tim Bulman	.40	1.00
3 Doug Flutie	1.00	2.50
4 Joel Hazard	.40	1.00
5 David Kashetta	.40	1.00
6 Mark MacDonald	.40	1.00
7 Paul Peterson	.40	1.00
8 Gerard Phelan	.60	1.50
9 Mike Ruth	.50	1.25
10 Troy Stradford	.40	1.00
11 TJ Stancil	.40	1.00
12 Tony Thurman	.40	1.00

1999 Buena Vista Schedules

COMPLETE SET (29)	4.00	8.00
1 Dan Bern	.10	.30
2 Jeff Brennah	.10	.30
3 Adam Fast	.10	.30
4 Adam Fast IA	.10	.30
5 Jon Fick	.10	.30
6 Jon Fick IA	.10	.30
7 Shawn Foy	.10	.30
8 Darin Graber	.10	.30
9 Joe Hadachek	.10	.30
10 Jon Ivanovich	.10	.30
11 Jeff Jacobsen	.10	.30
12 Wes Junge	.10	.30
13 Rob Klinkefus	.10	.30
14 Zach Mathers	.10	.30
15 Zach Mathers IA	.10	.30
16 Ryan Meester	.10	.30
17 Wade McInroy	.10	.30
18 Mike Peddicord	.10	.30
19 Mike Peddicord IA	.10	.30
20 Brad Pohlman	.10	.30
21 John Seel	.10	.30
22 John Seel IA	.10	.30
23 Ben Smith	.10	.30
24 Heath Staedtler	.10	.30
25 Jason Steffen	.10	.30
26 Josh Teut	.10	.30
27 Mike Thomas	.10	.30
28 Chris Zimmerman	.10	.30
29 Cheerleaders	.10	.30

2002 Buffalo

This set was distributed at the first home game of the 2002 season. Each card features a member of the 2002 University of Buffalo Bulls football team. The entire set was issued in a collectible mini binder.

COMPLETE SET (6)	12.50	25.00
1 Chad Bartoszek	2.00	5.00
2 Marquis Dwarte	1.50	4.00
3 Andre Forde	1.50	4.00
4 Mark Graham	1.50	4.00
5 Mike Lambert	1.50	4.00
6 Lamar Wilcher	1.50	4.00

1970 BYU Team Issue

These glossy black and white photos measure roughly 8" by 10" and feature members of the BYU football team. Each includes the school name spelled out "Brigham Young University, Provo Utah" below the photo along with a facsimile player signature on the image itself. The backs are blank. Any additions to this list are appreciated.

COMPLETE SET (4)	12.00	20.00
1 Golden Richards	5.00	8.00
2 Pete Van Valkenberg	3.00	5.00
3 Gordon Gravello	3.00	5.00
4 Joe Lilginquist	3.00	5.00

1984 BYU All-Time Greats

This 15-card standard-size set features BYU's all-time great football players since 1958. The sets were sold in a plastic bag, and the back of the attached paper tab indicated that additional sets could be purchased for 2.00 plus 75 cents for postage and handling. On a white card face, the fronts display both close-up and action player photos that have a purple tint. The top reads "All-Time Cougar Greats B.Y.U.," with the words "Cougar Greats" in a purple banner. The player's name is printed in purple in the bottom white border. The horizontal backs are gray and carry biography, BYU career statistics, and a career summary. Steve Young is featured in one of his earliest card appearances.

COMPLETE SET (15)	15.00	25.00
1 Steve Young	10.00	20.00
2 Eldon Fortie	.30	.75
3 Bart Oates	.75	2.00
4 Pete Van Valkenburg	.40	1.00
5 Mike Mees	.30	.75
6 Wayne Baker	.30	.75
7 Gordon Gravelle	.40	1.00
8 Gordon Hudson	.40	1.00
9 Kurt Gunther	.30	.75
10 Todd Shell	.40	1.00
11 Chris Farasopoulos	.50	1.25
12 Paul Howard	.30	.75
13 Dave Atkinson	.30	.75
14 Paul Linford	.30	.75
15 Phil Odle	.40	1.00

1984-85 BYU National Champions

This 15-card standard-size set features the 1984 BYU National Championship team. The bordered front features a player action shot. The back features a banner carrying the phrase "BYU - 1984 National Champions", and a helmet immediately underneath. A player profile completes the back. The cards are unnumbered and checklisted below in alphabetical order.

COMPLETE SET (15)	10.00	25.00
1 Mark Allen	.60	1.50
2 Adam Hysbert	.60	1.50
3 Larry Hamilton	.60	1.50
4 Jim Herrmann	.60	1.50
5 Kyle Morrell	.75	2.00
6 Lee Johnson	.75	2.00
7 David Mills	.60	1.50
8 Dave Wright	1.25	3.00
Craig Garrick		
Trevor Matich		
Robert Anae		
Louis Wong		
9 Jim Herrmann	.75	2.00
Larry Hamilton		
Smith		
10 Louis Wong	.60	1.50
11 Bosco in Holiday Bowl (Robbie Bosco)	2.00	5.00
12 BYU Cougar Stadium	.60	1.50
13 UPI Final Top 20	.60	1.50
14 BYU National Championship Roster	.60	1.50
15 Schedule and Scores For 1984	.60	1.50

1988 BYU

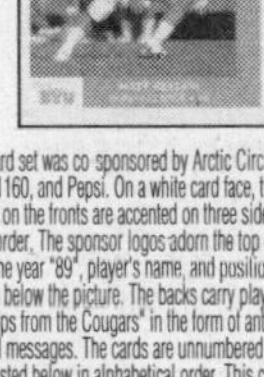

This card set was co sponsored by Arctic Circle, KSL Radio 1160, and Pepsi. On a white card face, the color photos on the fronts are accented on three sides by a blue border. The sponsor logos adorn the top of the card, while the year "89", player's name, and position are printed below the picture. The backs carry player profile and "Tips from the Cougars" in the form of anti-drug and alcohol messages. The cards are unnumbered and checklisted below in alphabetical order. This checklist is very incomplete, and any additions would be welcomed.

COMPLETE SET (16)	12.50	25.00
1 Matt Bellini	1.00	2.50
2 Tim Clark	.75	2.00
3 Sean Covey	.75	2.00
4 Chuck Cutler	.75	2.00
5 Bob Davis	.75	2.00
6 Kirk Davis	.75	2.00
7 Lavell Edwards CO	1.00	2.50
8 Jeff Frandsen	.75	2.00
9 Darren Handley	.75	2.00
10 Regan Hansen	.75	2.00
11 Troy Long	.75	2.00
12 Mike O'Brien	.75	2.00
13 Scott Peterson	.75	2.00
14 Rodney Rice	.75	2.00
15 Pat Thompson	.75	2.00
16 Freddie Whittingham	.75	2.00

1989 BYU

This card set was co-sponsored by Arctic Circle, KSL Radio 1160, and Pepsi. On a white card face, the color photos on the fronts are accented on three sides by a blue border. The sponsor logos adorn the top of the card, while the year "89", player's name, and position are printed below the picture. The backs carry player profile and "Tips from the Cougars" in the form of anti-drug and alcohol messages. The cards are unnumbered and checklisted below in alphabetical order.

COMPLETE SET (16)	12.50	25.00
1 Matt Bellini	.75	2.00
2 Eric Bergeson	.60	1.50
3 Jason Chaffetz	.60	1.50
4 Sean Covey	.60	1.50
5 Bob Davis	.60	1.50
6 Ty Detmer	4.00	10.00
7 Norm Dixon	.60	1.50
8 Lavell Edwards CO	.75	2.00
9 Mo Elewonibi	.60	1.50
10 Jeff Frandsen	.60	1.50
11 Troy Fuller	.60	1.50
12 Duane Johnson	.60	1.50
13 Brian Mitchell	.60	1.50
14 Craig Patterson	.60	1.50
15 Chad Robinson	.60	1.50
16 Freddie Whittingham	.60	1.50

1990 BYU

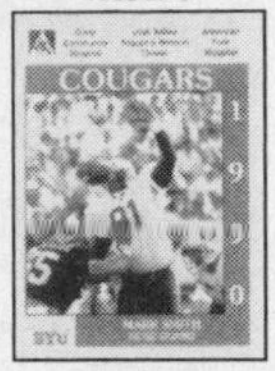

This 16-card standard-size set was issued in Utah in conjunction with three area hospitals to promote safety. The fronts of the cards feature the hospitals' names on the top while underneath them are full-color action shots framed in the blue and white colors of the Cougars. The word "Cougars" is on top of the photo with the year "1990" on the right side and the player's name and position on the bottom of the card. The backs have biographical information as well as various safety tips. The set was issued in four strips of four cards; since the cards are unnumbered, we are listing them in alphabetical order.

COMPLETE SET (16)	10.00	20.00
1 Rocky Beigel	.50	1.25
2 Matt Bellini	.60	1.50
3 Andy Boyce	.50	1.25
4 Stacey Corley	.50	1.25
5 Tony Crutchfield	.50	1.25
6 Ty Detmer	3.00	8.00
7 Norm Dixon	.50	1.25
8 Lavell Edwards CO	.60	1.50
9 Earl Kauffman	.50	1.25
10 Rich Kaufusi	.50	1.25
11 Bryan May	.50	1.25
12 Brian Mitchell	.50	1.25
13 Brent Nyberg	.50	1.25
14 Chris Smith	.60	1.50
15 Mark Smith	.50	1.25
16 Robert Stephens	.50	1.25

1991 BYU

This 16-card standard-size set was sponsored by Orem Community Hospital, Utah Valley Regional Medical Center, and American Fork Hospital. The cards were issued in four-card perforated strips at four different home games. The fronts feature a full-color action shot enclosed by a three-sided blue drop border and a small white border at the left. The name "Cougars" is in white reversed-out letters in the top blue border, while 1991 runs down the right side, and the player's name and position are in the bottom border. Sponsor logos appear in aqua lettering at the top, while the school logo is in blue in the lower left corner. Card backs feature player profile, "Tips from the Cougars" (anti-drug or alcohol messages), and sponsor names. The cards are unnumbered and checklisted below in alphabetical order.

COMPLETE SET (16)	6.00	15.00
1 Josh Arnold	.40	1.00
2 Rocky Biegel	.40	1.00
3 Scott Charlton	.40	1.00
4 Tony Crutchfield	.40	1.00
5 Ty Detmer	2.00	5.00
6 Lavell Edwards CO	.50	1.25
7 Scott Giles	.40	1.00
8 Derwin Gray	.60	1.50
9 Shad Hansen	.40	1.00
10 Brad Hunter	.40	1.00
11 Earl Kauffman	.40	1.00
12 Jared Leavitt	.40	1.00
13 Micah Matsuzaki	.40	1.00
14 Bryan May	.40	1.00
15 Peter Tuipulotu	.40	1.00
16 Matt Zundel	.40	1.00

1992 BYU

This 16-card standard-size set was sponsored by Fillmore Medical Center, an Intermountain Health Care facility. The cards were issued in four-card perforated strips. The fronts feature a glossy full-color action shot enclosed by a three-sided blue border and a small white border at the left. The name "Cougars" is in white lettering in the top blue border, "1992" runs down the right side, and the player's name and position are in the bottom border. The sponsor logo appears in blue lettering at the top, while the school logo is in blue at the lower left corner. The card backs feature a player profile, "Tips from the Cougars" (anti-drug or alcohol messages), and sponsor names. The cards are unnumbered and checklisted below in alphabetical order.

COMPLETE SET (16)	4.00	10.00
1 Tyler Anderson	.30	.75
2 Randy Brock	.30	.75
3 Brad Clark	.30	.75
4 Eric Drage	.40	1.00
5 Lavell Edwards CO	.40	1.00
6 Mike Empey	.30	.75
7 Lenny Gomes	.30	.75
8 Derwin Gray	.50	1.25
9 Shad Hansen	.30	.75
10 Eli Herring	.50	1.25

11 Micah Matsuzaki	.30	.75
12 Patrick Mitchell	.30	.75
13 Garry Pay	.30	.75
14 Greg Pitts	.30	.75
15 Byron Rex	.30	.75
16 Jamal Willis	.40	1.00

1993 BYU

These 20 cards measure 2 3/4" by 3 3/4" and feature on their fronts blue-bordered color player action shots. These photos are offset slightly toward the upper right, making the margins on the top and right narrower. In the wide left margin appears the words "Brigham Young Football '93" in black lettering. The player's name, position, and uniform number rest in the wide lower margin. The gray and white horizontal back carries player biography, career highlights, and statistics. A paper tag on the cello pack carries a handwritten set number out of a total production run of 3,000 sets. The cards are unnumbered and checklisted below in alphabetical order.

COMPLETE SET (20)	5.00	12.00
1 Tyler Anderson	.30	.75
2 Randy Brock	.30	.75
3 Frank Christianson	.30	.75
4 Eric Drage	.40	1.00
5 Lavell Edwards CO	.40	1.00
6 Mike Empey	.30	.75
7 Lenny Gomes	.30	.75
8 Kalin Hall	.30	.75
9 Nathan Hall	.30	.75
10 Hema Heimuli	.40	1.00
11 Todd Herget	.30	.75
12 Eli Herring	.40	1.00
13 Micah Matsuzaki	.30	.75
14 Casey Mazzota	.30	.75
15 Patrick Mitchell	.30	.75
16 Evan Pilgrim	.40	1.00
17 Greg Pitts	.30	.75
18 Vic Tarleton	.30	.75
19 John Walsh	.50	1.25
20 Jamal Willis	.40	1.00

1996 BYU

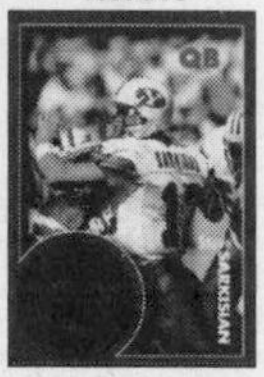

1 LaVell Edwards CO	1.25	3.00
2 Steve Sarkisian	1.25	3.00

1999 BYU Schedules

COMPLETE SET (6)	1.50	4.00
1 Kevin Feterik	.30	.75
2 Brian Gray	.30	.75
3 Margin Hooks	.30	.75
4 Ben Horton	.30	.75
5 Rob Morris	.30	.75
6 Owen Poachman	.30	.75

2001 BYU Schedules

COMPLETE SET (4)	1.00	2.00
1 Ryan Denney	.20	.50
2 Brett Keisel	.30	.75
3 Brian McDonald	.20	.50
4 Mike Rigell	.20	.50

1982 California Postcards

These large (5 1/2" by 8 1/2") postcards were released by the University of California Sports Information Department as promotional pieces for the team's top players. Each features a black and white player photo on the front with a smaller photo on the back along with an extensive player profile.

COMPLETE SET (2)	6.00	10.00
1 David Lewis TE	3.00	5.00
2 Harvey Salem	3.00	5.00

1988 California Smokey

The 1988 California Bears Smokey set contains 12 standard-size cards. The fronts feature color action photos with name, position, and jersey number. The vertically oriented backs have brief career highlights. The cards are unnumbered, so they are listed in alphabetical order by subject's name. The card fronts contain a yellow stripe on the top and bottom that includes the team and player names.

COMPLETE SET (12)	6.00	15.00
1 Rob Bimson	.50	1.25
2 Joel Dickson	.50	1.25
3 Robert DosRemedios	.50	1.25
4 Mike Ford	.50	1.25
5 Darryl Ingram	.60	1.50
6 David Ortega	.50	1.25
7 Chris Richards	.50	1.25
8 Bruce Snyder CO	1.00	2.50
9 Troy Taylor	.50	1.25
10 Natu Tuatagaloa	.75	2.00
11 Majett Whiteside	.50	1.25
12 Dave Zawatson	.50	1.25

1989 California Smokey

The 1989 California Bears Smokey set contains 16 standard-size cards. The fronts feature color action photos with name, position, and jersey number. The vertically oriented backs have brief career highlights. The cards are unnumbered, so they are listed by jersey numbers. The card fronts contain a player photo bordered on the left by a yellow stripe and a blue stripe on the right and below the photo.

COMPLETE SET (16)	6.00	15.00
1 John Hardy	.40	1.00
2 Mike Ford	.40	1.00
10 Robbie Keen	.40	1.00
11 Troy Taylor	.40	1.00
20 Dwayne Jones	.40	1.00
21 Travis Oliver	.40	1.00
34 Darrin Greer	.40	1.00
40 David Ortega	.40	1.00
41 Dan Slevin	.40	1.00
52 Troy Auzenne	1.25	3.00
69 Tony Smith	.40	1.00
80 Junior Tagaloa	.40	1.00
83 Michael Smith	.40	1.00
95 DeWayne Odom	.40	1.00
99 Joel Dickson	.40	1.00
NNO Bruce Snyder CO	.75	2.00

1990 California Smokey

The 1990 California Bears Smokey set contains 16 standard-size cards. The fronts feature a color action photo bordered in yellow on three sides, with the player's name, position, and jersey number below the picture. The backs have brief career highlights and a fire prevention cartoon starring Smokey the Bear. These unnumbered cards are listed in alphabetical order below for convenience. The card fronts contain a player photo bordered on three sides by a yellow stripe.

COMPLETE SET (16)	4.80	12.00
1 Troy Auzenne 52	.80	2.00
2 John Belli 61	.30	.75
3 Joel Dickson 99	.30	.75
4 Ron English 42	.30	.75
5 Rhett Hall 57	.80	2.00
6 John Hardy 1	.30	.75
7 Robbie Keen 10	.30	.75
8 DeWayne Odom 95	.30	.75
9 Mike Pawlawski 9	1.00	2.50
10 Castle Redmond 37	.30	.75
11 James Richards 64	.30	.75
12 Ernie Rogers 68	.30	.75
13 Bruce Snyder CO	.60	1.50
14 Brian Treggs 3	.40	1.00
15 Anthony Wallace 6	.30	.75
16 Greg Zomalt 28	.30	.75

1991 California Smokey

This 16-card standard size set was sponsored by the USDA Forest Service and other agencies. The cards were printed on thin cardboard stock. The card fronts are accented in the team's colors (dark blue and yellow) and have glossy color action player photos. The top of the pictures is curved to resemble an archway, and the team name follows the curve of the arch. The player's name and position appear in a stripe below the picture. The backs present player profile and a fire prevention cartoon starring Smokey. The cards are unnumbered and checklisted below in alphabetical order. An early card of Sean Dawkins is featured in this set.

COMPLETE SET (16)	6.00	15.00
1 Troy Auzenne	.40	1.00
2 Chris Cannon	.30	.75
3 Cornell Collier	.30	.75
4 Sean Dawkins	1.20	3.00
5 Steve Gordon	.30	.75
6 Mike Pawlawski	.40	1.00
7 Bruce Snyder CO	.40	1.00
8 Todd Steussie	.80	2.00
9 Mack Travis	.30	.75
10 Brian Treggs	.30	.75
11 Russell White	.50	1.25
12 Jason Wilborn	.30	.75
13 David Wilson	.30	.75
14 Brent Woodall	.30	.75
15 Eric Zomalt	.40	1.00
16 Greg Zomalt	.30	.75

1992 California Smokey

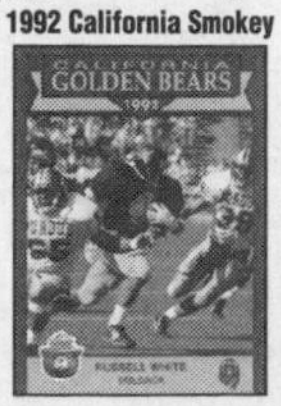

This 16-card standard-size set was sponsored by the USDA Forest Service and other state and federal agencies. The cards are printed on thin card stock. The fronts carry a color action player photo on a navy blue card face. The team name and year appear above the photo in yellow print on a navy blue bar that partially rests on a yellow bar with notched ends. Below the photo, the player's name and sponsor logos appear in a yellow border stripe. The backs carry player profile and a fire prevention cartoon starring Smokey. The cards are unnumbered and checklisted below in alphabetical order.

COMPLETE SET (16)	4.80	12.00
1 Chidi Ahanotu	.40	1.00
2 Wolf Barber	.25	.60
3 Mick Barsala	.25	.60
4 Doug Brien	.50	1.25
5 Al Casner	.25	.60
6 Lindsey Chapman	.25	.60
7 Sean Dawkins	1.00	2.50
8 Keith Gilbertson CO	.30	.75
9 Eric Mahlum	.30	.75
10 Chris Noonan	.25	.60
11 Todd Steussie	.60	1.50
12 Mack Travis	.25	.60
13 Russell White	.30	.75
14 Jerrott Willard	.25	.60
15 Eric Zomalt	.30	.75
16 Greg Zomalt	.25	.60

1993 California Smokey

Printed on thin card stock, this 16-card standard-size set was sponsored by the USDA, the Forest Service, and other state and federal agencies. The fronts feature color player action shots framed by thin white and black lines and with gold-colored borders highlighted by oblique white stripes. The team's name appears within the upper margin, and the player's name and position, along with the Smokey 50-year celebration logo, rest in the lower margin. The white backs carry player profile and a fire prevention cartoon starring Smokey. The cards are unnumbered and checklisted below in alphabetical order.

COMPLETE SET (16)	4.00	10.00
1 Dave Barr	.60	1.50
2 Doug Brien	.40	1.00
3 Mike Caldwell	.30	.75
4 Lindsey Chapman	.25	.60
5 Je'Rod Cherry	.40	1.00
6 Michael Davis	.25	.60
7 Tyrone Edwards	.25	.60
8 Keith Gilbertson CO	.25	.60
9 Jody Graham	.25	.60
10 Marty Holly	.25	.60
11 Paul Joiner	.25	.60
12 Eric Mahlum	.25	.60
13 Damien Semien	.25	.60
14 Todd Steussie	.50	1.25
15 Jerrott Willard	.25	.60
16 Eric Zomalt	.30	.75

1994 California Smokey

This 16-card set of the University of California Golden Bears was sponsored by the USDA, Forest Service and other agencies. The fronts feature color player photos in a gold and blue border. The backs carry player information and a fire prevention cartoon. The cards are unnumbered and checklisted below in alphabetical order.

COMPLETE SET (16)	5.00	10.00
1 Dave Barr	.40	1.00
2 Na'il Benjamin	.40	1.00
3 Brad Bowers	.30	.75
4 Jerod Cherry	.40	1.00
5 Matt Clizbe	.30	.75
6 Dante DePaola	.30	.75
7 Tyrone Edwards	.30	.75
8 Keith Gilbertson CO	.30	.75
9 Artis Houston	.30	.75
10 Ryan Longwell	.40	1.00
11 Reynard Rutherford	.30	.75
12 Ricky Spears	.30	.75
13 Brian Thure	.30	.75
14 Regan Upshaw	.40	1.00
15 Iheanyi Uwaezuoke	.30	.75
16 Jerrott Willard	.30	.75

1995 California Smokey

This 16-card set was sponsored by the USDA Forest Service and other agencies. The cards are printed on thin card stock. The fronts feature color action photos; the phrase "California Football" and player identification are printed in block lettering and reversed out on team color-coded borders. In black print on a white background, the backs present biography, player profile, and a fire prevention cartoon starring Smokey. The cards are unnumbered and checklisted below in alphabetical order.

COMPLETE SET (16)	4.00	8.00
1 Pat Barnes	.50	1.25
2 Na'il Benjamin	.40	1.00
3 Sean Bullard	.30	.75
4 Je'Rod Cherry	.40	1.00
5 Duane Clemons	.40	1.00
6 Dante Depaola	.30	.75
7 Kevin Devine	.30	.75
8 Keith Gilbertson CO	.30	.75
9 Andy Jacobs	.30	.75
10 Ryan Longwell	.40	1.00
11 Ben Lynch	.30	.75
12 Reynard Rutherford	.30	.75
13 James Stallworth	.30	.75
14 Regan Upshaw	.40	1.00
15 Iheanyi Uwaezuoke	.30	.75
16 Brandon Whiting	.40	1.00

1996 California CHP

This 10-card set was sponsored by the California Highway Patrol. The cards are printed on thin card stock and the fronts feature color action photos. The phrase "Cal Golden Bear Football" is printed at the top and the player's name is printed below the photo on the fronts. In blue print on a white background, the backs present a basic player bio and a safety message. The cards are numbered on the backs as well.

COMPLETE SET (10)	5.00	12.00
1 Todd Stewart	.30	.75
2 Kevin Devine	.30	.75
3 Na'il Benjamin	.40	1.00
4 Pat Barnes	.60	1.50
5 Steve Mariucci CO	.75	2.00
6 Brandon Whiting	.40	1.00
7 Tarik Smith	.40	1.00
8 Andy Jacobs	.30	.75
9 Tony Gonzalez	1.50	4.00
10 Tarik Glenn	.30	.75

1997 California CHP

This 16-card set was sponsored by the California Highway Patrol. The cards are printed on thin card stock and the fronts feature color action photos. The phrase "Cal Golden Bears Football '97" and the player's name are printed within a blue border on the fronts. In blue print on a white background, the backs present a basic player bio and a safety message. The cards are numbered on the backs as well.

COMPLETE SET (16)	6.00	12.00
1 Chris Easley	.30	.75
2 Derrick Gardner	.40	1.00
3 Kofi Nartey	.30	.75
4 Jeremy Newberry	.30	.75
5 Drake Parker	.30	.75
6 Andre Rhodes	.30	.75
7 Kato Serwanga	.30	.75
8 Bobby Shaw	.60	1.50
9 Kursten Sheridan	.30	.75
10 Brian Shields	.30	.75
11 Marquis Smith	.40	1.00
12 Tarik Smith	.40	1.00
13 Marc Vera	.30	.75
14 John Welbourn	.30	.75
15 Brandon Whiting	.40	1.00
16 Tom Holmoe CO	.30	.75

2006 California All-Time Leaders

COMPLETE SET (18)	5.00	10.00
1 Pat Barnes	.40	1.00
2 Kyle Boller	.60	1.50
3 Doug Brien	.30	.75
4 Andre Carter	.40	1.00
5 Sean Dawkins	.40	1.00
6 Nick Harris	.30	.75
7 Geoff McArthur	.30	.75
8 Duke Morrison	.30	.75
9 Chuck Muncie	.40	1.00
10 Deltha O'Neal	.40	1.00
11 David Ortega	.30	.75
12 Aaron Rodgers	2.00	5.00
13 Joe Roth	.30	.75
14 Bobby Shaw	.40	1.00
15 Troy Taylor	.30	.75
16 Jeff Tedford CO	.30	.75
17 Ken Wiedemann	.30	.75
18 Russell White	.40	1.00

1991 Canton McKinley High School

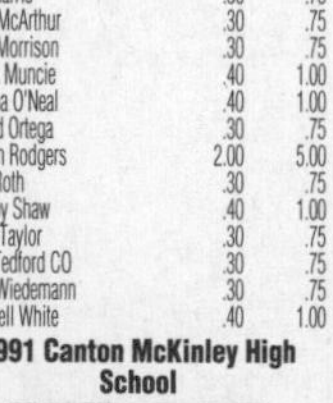

COMPLETE SET (104)	40.00	80.00
1 Domenick Tracy	.40	1.00
2 Bryan Becker	.40	1.00
3 Joe Gallo	.40	1.00
4 Ken Waybright	.40	1.00
5 Paul Mills	.40	1.00
6 Brian Muhleman	.40	1.00
7 Ryan Dragomire	.40	1.00
8 Mike Chevraux	.40	1.00
9 Greg Gilmore	.40	1.00
10 James Printz	.40	1.00
11 Eric Darnley	.40	1.00
12 Paul Popko	.40	1.00
13 Steve Thompson	.40	1.00
14 Brad Shadlie	.40	1.00
15 Jeremy Kirkpatrick	.40	1.00
16 Adam Gallagher	.40	1.00
17 Michael Smith	.40	1.00
18 Adam Roberts	.40	1.00
19 Marlin Smith	.40	1.00
20 Jim Pimpas	.40	1.00
21 Shane Mitchell	.40	1.00
22 Brent McGrady	.40	1.00
23 Dan Dillon	.40	1.00
24 Kevin Yun	.40	1.00
25 Joe Pukansky	.40	1.00
26 Eric Lundquist	.40	1.00
27 Tyrone Moore	.40	1.00
28 Jack Virencio	.40	1.00
29 Tim Gregory	.40	1.00
30 Shaun Curtis	.40	1.00
31 Shawn Strickmaker	.40	1.00
32 Tremaine McElroy	.40	1.00
33 Cory Henderson	.40	1.00
34 Nathon McIntyre	.40	1.00
35 Denell Harris	.40	1.00
36 James Allison	.40	1.00
37 Don Martin	.40	1.00
38 Ronnie Burr	.40	1.00
39 Larry Fields	.40	1.00
40 D.C. Curtis	.40	1.00
41 Chad Wise	.40	1.00
42 Brandon Adams	.40	1.00
43 Jason Bowe	.40	1.00
44 Vinnie Boiano	.40	1.00
45 Patrick Babcock	.40	1.00
46 Marcus Peterson	.40	1.00
47 Eric Gill	.40	1.00
48 Damian Sedlock	.40	1.00
49 Andy Kerekes	.40	1.00
50 Robert Pukansky	.40	1.00
51 Terrell Kindell	.40	1.00
52 Emil Weir	.40	1.00
53 Andy Skalsky	.40	1.00
54 Jason Roberts	.40	1.00
55 Mike Milford	.40	1.00
56 Che Bryant	.40	1.00
57 Tony Calhoun	.40	1.00
58 Bruce Richards	.40	1.00
59 Shawn Fields	.40	1.00
60 Chad Gibbs	.40	1.00
61 C.J. Smith	.40	1.00
62 Josh Plansky	.40	1.00
63 Daniel Terry	.40	1.00
64 Maurice Drayton	.40	1.00
65 Shon Alkire	.40	1.00
66 Tom Hastings	.40	1.00
67 Howard Parker	.40	1.00
68 Alfonso Ash	.40	1.00
69 Gene McElroy	.40	1.00
70 Courtney Burns	.40	1.00
71 Rahsean Toles	.40	1.00
72 Chris Mayle	.40	1.00
73 Terrell Hubbard	.40	1.00
74 R. Claybourne Jr.	.40	1.00
75 Paul Gates	.40	1.00
76 Kristen Thompson	.40	1.00
77 Mark Johnston	.40	1.00
78 Bob Neff CO	.40	1.00
79 John Rinaldi CO	.40	1.00
80 Dave Gable CO	.40	1.00
81 Paul Shimek CO	.40	1.00
82 Ross Rankin CO	.40	1.00
83 Warren Miller CO	.40	1.00
84 Darwin Miller CO	.40	1.00
85 John Twinem CO	.40	1.00
86 Steve Kotema CO	.40	1.00
87 Tom Carver CO	.40	1.00
88 Donald Short CO	.40	1.00
89 Jim Harris CO	.40	1.00
90 Frank Alberta CO	.40	1.00
91 Thom McDaniels CO	.40	1.00
92 Nicole Williams Cheer.	.40	1.00
93 Crystal Johnson Cheer.	.40	1.00
94 Tennille Lemmo Cheer.	.40	1.00
95 Katara Brewer Cheer.	.40	1.00
96 Rebecca Jones Cheer.	.40	1.00
97 Amanda Jacob Cheer.	.40	1.00
98 Keva Massey Cheer.	.40	1.00
99 Larrena Keaton Cheer.	.40	1.00
100 Beth Potter Cheer.	.40	1.00
101 Jonnetta Hubbard Cheer.	.40	1.00
102 Tressa Pride Cheer.	.40	1.00
103 Gina Amigo Cheer.	.40	1.00
104 Marilyn Poulos Advisor	.40	1.00

1907 Christy College Series 7 Postcards

This postcard series features various schools. Each card, measuring roughly 3 1/2" by 5 3/8," includes an embossed artist's rendering of a woman fan with a football player seated at a table with the school's banner underneath. The copyright line reads "COPYRIGHT 1907 F. EARL CHRISTY" and the back features a standard postcard design. The title "College Series No. 7" is included on the cardback as well.

COMPLETE SET (8)	90.00	175.00
1 Chicago	15.00	25.00
2 Columbia	15.00	25.00
3 Cornell	15.00	25.00
4 Harvard	15.00	25.00
5 Michigan	18.00	30.00
6 Penn	15.00	25.00
7 Princeton	15.00	25.00
8 Yale	15.00	25.00

1907 Christy College Series 95 Postcards

Much like the Series 7 set, these postcards feature Ivy League schools. Each card, measuring roughly 3 1/2" by 5 3/8," includes an embossed artist's rendering of a woman fan with a football player sitting on top of a large image of a football with the school's banner being held by the woman fan. The copyright line on the front reads 'COPYRIGHT 1907 Julius Bien and Company' and a card number is printed on the front as well. The backs feature a standard postcard design along with the set name College Series 95.

COMPLETE SET (6)	75.00	125.00
950 Yale	15.00	25.00
951 Harvard	15.00	25.00
952 Columbia	15.00	25.00
953 Penn	15.00	25.00
954 Princeton	15.00	25.00
955 Cornell	15.00	25.00

1958 Cincinnati

These blankbacked cards were issued around 1958 and measure roughly 8 1/2" by 10 5/8." Each features one black and white photo of a University of Cincinnati football player surrounded by a thick red border with the player's name and position below the photo. The backs are blank and the cards were printed on thick white or gray card stock. It is likely that these were issued in more than one year. Any additions to this list are appreciated.

COMPLETE SET (4)	20.00	40.00
1 Ron Couch	5.00	12.00
2 Ed Denk	5.00	12.00
3 Gene Johnson	5.00	12.00
4 Dick Seomin	5.00	12.00

1966 Cincinnati

These oversized (roughly 8 1/2" by 10 1/2") cards were issued around 1966 and feature one black and white photo of a University of Cincinnati football player surrounded by a thick red border with just his name below the photo. The backs are blank and the cards were printed on glossy thick card stock. It is likely that they were issued over a period of years. Any additions to this list are appreciated.

COMPLETE SET (10)	50.00	100.00
1 Jay Bachman	5.00	12.00
1 Bob Amburgey	5.00	12.00
2 Milt Balkum	5.00	12.00
2 Tony Jackson	5.00	12.00
3 Bob Miller	5.00	12.00
3 Ken Jordan	5.00	12.00
4 Lloyd Pate	5.00	12.00
4 Tom Macejko	5.00	12.00
5 Ron Nelson	5.00	12.00
6 Ed Nemann	5.00	12.00

1970 Clemson Team Issue

These photos were issued by the school to promote the football program. Each measures roughly 8" by 10" and features a black and white image of a player. The player's name, position (initials) and school are printed below each photo and the backs are blank.

COMPLETE SET (23)	75.00	150.00
1 Ben Anderson	4.00	8.00
2 Tony Anderson P DB	4.00	8.00
3 Tony Anderson E	4.00	8.00
4 John Bolubasz	4.00	8.00
5 Mike Buckner	4.00	8.00
6 Ralph Daniel	4.00	8.00
7 Heide Davis	4.00	8.00
8 Luke Deanhardt	4.00	8.00
9 Pete Galuska	4.00	8.00
10 Don Kelley	4.00	8.00
11 Tommy Kemdrick	4.00	8.00
12 Larry Lawson	4.00	8.00
13 Steve Lewter	4.00	8.00
14 John McMakin	4.00	8.00
15 Ken Pengitore	4.00	8.00
16 John Price	4.00	8.00
17 Marion Reeves	4.00	8.00
18 Tommy Richardson	4.00	8.00
19 Eddie Seigler	4.00	8.00
20 Jack Sokohl	4.00	8.00
21 Jim Sursavage	4.00	8.00
22 Dave Thompson	4.00	8.00
23 Ray Yauger	4.00	8.00

1989 Clemson

This 32-card standard-size set commemorates the Clemson Tigers as the 1989 Mazda Gator Bowl Champions. It was sponsored by Carolina Pride. The front presents either a posed or action color photo. Two orange bands with black lettering on the top and bottom have the school, player's name, number, classification, and position. The Carolina Pride logo appears in the lower left hand corner and the Tiger pawprint appears in the upper left hand corner. The back has biographical information and a tip from the Tigers in the form of an anti-drug or alcohol message. The cards are unnumbered and are listed below in alphabetical order by subject.

COMPLETE SET (32)	8.00	20.00
1 Wally Ake CO	.30	.75
2 Larry Beckman CO	.30	.75
3 Mitch Belton 32	.30	.75
4 Scott Beville 61	.30	.75
5 Doug Brewster 92	.30	.75
6 Larry Brinson CO	.30	.75
7 Reggie Demps 30	.30	.75
8 Robin Eaves 44	.30	.75
9 Barney Farrar CO	.30	.75
10 Stacy Fields 46	.30	.75
11 Vance Hammond 90	.30	.75
12 Eric Harmon 76	.30	.75
13 Ken Hatfield CO	.60	1.50
14 Jerome Henderson 36	.40	1.00
15 Les Herrin CO	.30	.75
16 Roger Hinshaw CO	.30	.75
17 John Johnson 12	.40	1.00
18 Reggie Lawrence 34	.30	.75
19 Stacy Long 67	.30	.75
20 Eric Mader 82	.30	.75
21 Arlington Nunn 39	.30	.75
22 David Puckett 68	.30	.75
23 Danny Sizer 54	.30	.75
24 Robbie Spector 2	.30	.75
25 Rick Stockstill CO	.30	.75
26 Bruce Taylor 6	.30	.75
27 Doug Thomas 41	.30	.75
28 The Tiger (Mascot)	.30	.75
29 Tiger Paw Title Card	.30	.75
30 Bob Trott CO	.30	.75
31 Larry Van Der Heyden CO	.30	.75
32 Richard Wilson CO	.30	.75

1989 Clemson Team Issue

These photos were issued by the school to promote the football program. Unless noted below, each measures roughly 8" by 10" and features two players with two small black and white images and one larger image for each player The school name and year appear at the top and the player's name, position, and home town are included as well. The backs are blank.

COMPLETE SET (9)	25.00	50.00
1 Terry Allen (three large photos)	5.00	10.00
2 Doug Brewster Vance Hammond	3.00	6.00
3 Gary Cooper Joe Henderson	3.00	6.00
4 David Davis Dexter Davis	3.00	6.00
5 Jeb Flesch Levon Kirkland	3.00	6.00
6 Eric Harmon John Johnson	3.00	6.00
6 Chris Gardocki (two large photos)	4.00	8.00
7 Ed McDaniel Chip Davis	3.00	6.00
8 Otis Moore Chris Morocco	3.00	6.00

1990-91 Clemson Collegiate Collection

This 200-card standard-size set was produced by Collegiate Collection. We've included a sport initial (B-baseball, K-basketball, F-football, G-Golf, WK-women's basketball) for players in the top collected sports.

COMPLETE SET (200)	6.00	15.00
1 William Perry F	.15	.40
2 Kevin Mack F	.08	.25
4 Donald Igwebuike F	.05	.15
5 Michael Dean Perry F	.15	.40
7 Steve Fuller F	.07	.20
9 Frank Howard CO F	.15	.40
10 Orange Bowl Champs F	.07	.20
13 John Phillips F	.05	.15
15 Terry Allen F	.30	.75
16 Chris Morocco F	.05	.15
19 Tracy Johnson F	.05	.15
28 Marvin Sim F	.05	.15
30 Jim Riggs F	.05	.15
34 Banks McFadden F	.05	.15
36 The Kick 1986 F	.05	.15
39 Terrance Flagler F	.07	.20
41 David Treadwell F	.08	.25
42 Perry Tuttle F	.07	.20
44 Homer Jordan F	.05	.15
45 Dale Hatcher F	.07	.20
46 Steve Reese F	.05	.15
48 Obed Ariri F	.05	.15
51 Cliff Austin F	.05	.15
53 Jeff Nunamacher F	.05	.15
54 Steve Berlin F	.05	.15
55 Jess Neely CO F	.05	.15
57 Jeff Bryant F	.07	.20
58 Jerry Butler F	.07	.20
60 Bob Paulling F	.05	.15
62 James Farr F	.05	.15
64 Chuck McSwain F	.05	.15
67 Rodney Williams F	.05	.15
71 Dwight Clark F	.20	.50
73 Kenny Flowers F	.05	.15
78 Gary Cooper F	.05	.15
81 Fred Cone F	.05	.15
84 Donnell Woolford F	.08	.25
87 Frank Howard CO F	.05	.15
89 Terry Kinard F	.07	.20
93 1989 Senior Football F	.05	.15
94 The Clemson Tiger F	.05	.15
95 Howard's Rock F	.05	.15
96 Jeff Davis F	.05	.15
99 Clemson Wins Nebraska F	.05	.15
101 Hill shot from field F	.05	.15
102 Ray Williams F	.05	.15
104 Charlie Waters F	.20	.50
107 Bubba Brown F	.05	.15
108 Ken Hatfield CO F	.07	.20
109 Lester Brown F	.05	.15
110 James Robinson F	.05	.15
111 Michael Dean Perry William Perry F	.10	.30
113 Frank Howard CO F	.15	.40
115 Wesley McFadden F	.05	.15
118 Andy Headen F	.07	.20
120 Hill Shot from Board F	.05	.15
121 Harry Olszewski F	.05	.15
122 CU clinches season F	.05	.15
123 Super Bowl Rings F	.05	.15
124 Otis Moore F	.05	.15
126 Defensive Rankings F	.05	.15
127 Jeff Bostic Joe Bostic F	.08	.25
129 Randy Scott F	.05	.15
131 Clemson VS. Stanford F	.05	.15
133 Danny Ford CO F	.05	.15
139 Clemson vs. Notre Dame F	.05	.15
141 Steve Fuller Jerry Butler F	.08	.25
144 John Phillips Michael Dean Perry F	.07	.20
147 William Perry F	.15	.40
160 Jerry Butler F	.08	.25
170 Joe Blalock F	.05	.15
176 Obed Ariri F	.05	.15

178 Bobby Gage F	.05	.15
179 John Heisman CO F	.08	.25
182 Clemson vs. USC F	.05	.15
189 Lou Cordileone F	.07	.20
190 1949 Gator Bowl F	.05	.15
194 Ray Matthews F	.05	.15

1990-91 Clemson Collegiate Collection Promos

This ten-card standard-size set was issued by Collegiate Collection to honor some of the great athletes who played at Clemson. The front of the card features a full-color photo of the person featured while the back of the card has details about the person pictured. As this set is a multi-sport set we have used a two-letter identification of the sport next to the person's name.

COMPLETE SET (10)	1.50	4.00
C2 CU-USC Series FB	.20	.50
C3 William Perry FB Bio	.30	.75
C4 Michael Dean Perry FB	.30	.75
C5 Orange Bowl FB	.10	.25
C6 Ken Hatfield CO FB	.20	.50
C8 Dwight Clark FB	.40	1.00
C9 William Perry FB Stat	.30	.75
C10 Frank Howard CO FB	.40	1.00

1992-93 Clemson Schedules

COMPLETE SET (11)	1.50	4.00
11 Football Stadium	.20	.50

1993 Clemson Team Issue

These photos were issued by the school to promote the football program. Unless noted below, each measures roughly 8" by 10" and features two players with two small black and white images and one larger image for each player. The school name and year appear at the top and the player's name, position, and home town are included as well. The backs are blank.

COMPLETE SET (10)	25.00	50.00
1 Brentson Buckner	4.00	8.00
Stacy Seegars		
2 Rodney Blunt	3.00	6.00
Terry Smith WR		
3 Derek Burnette	3.00	6.00
Patrick Sapp		
4 Carlos Curry	3.00	6.00
Louis Solomon		
5 Terrance Dixon	3.00	6.00
Andre Humphrey		
6 Warren Forney	3.00	6.00
Tim Jones		
7 Marrio Grier	3.00	6.00
Darnell Stephens		
8 Marcus Hinton	3.00	6.00
Lamarick Simpson		
9 Brent LeJeune	3.00	6.00
Pierre Wilson		
10 Nelson Welch	3.00	6.00
(includes three large photos)		

1994 Clemson Team Issue

These photos were issued by the school to promote the football program. Unless noted below, each measures roughly 8" by 10" and features two players with two small black and white images and one larger image for each player. The school name and year appear at the top and the player's name, position, and home town are included as well. The backs are blank.

COMPLETE SET (11)	25.00	50.00
1 Michael Barber	3.00	6.00
Darnell Stephens		
2 Marvin Cross	3.00	6.00
Andre Humphrey		
3 Brian Dawkins	6.00	12.00
Leomont Evans		
4 Marcus Hinton	3.00	6.00
Louis Solomon		
5 Robert Jackson	3.00	6.00
Will Young		
6 Tim Jones	3.00	6.00
(includes two large photos)		
7 Dexter McCleon	4.00	8.00
(includes two large photos)		
8 Wardell Rouse	3.00	6.00
Antuan Wyatt		
9 Patrick Sapp	3.00	6.00
Warren Forney		
10 Lamarick Simpson	3.00	6.00
Carlos Curry		
11 Emory Smith	3.00	6.00
Brett Williams		

1994 Clemson Team Sheets

These photos were issued by the school to promote the football program. Each measures roughly 8" by 10" and features eight black and white images of players with the school name and year appearing at the top. The player's name is printed below each image. The backs are blank.

1 Brent Banasiewicz	4.00	8.00
Howard Bartley		
Donald Broomfield		
Matt Butler		
Kenya Crooks		
Perez Davis		
Anthony Downs		
Kelton Dunnican		
2 Wesley Ellis	4.00	8.00
Nealon Greene		
Tony Horne		
James Jenkins		
Kevin Laird		
Mark Landry		
Zane Lewis		
Travis Macklin		
3 Dwayne Morgan	4.00	8.00
Lamont Pegues		
Tony Plantin		
Holland Postell		
Raymond Priester		
Undre Williams		
Whitney Jordan AD		
Bruce Warwick AD		

1995 Clemson Team Issue

These photos were issued by the school to promote the football program. Each measures roughly 8" by 10" and features two players with two small black and white images and one larger image for each player. The school name and year appear at the top and the player's name, position, and home town are included as well. The backs are blank.

COMPLETE SET (12)	30.00	60.00
1 Kenya Crooks	3.00	6.00
Nealon Greene		
2 Andy Ford	3.00	6.00
Peter Ford		
3 Warren Forney	3.00	6.00
Marvin Cross		
4 Antwuan Wyatt	4.00	8.00
Dexter McCleon		
5 Lamarick Simpson	3.00	6.00
Carlos Curry		
6 Dwayne Morgan	3.00	6.00
Will Young		
7 Raymond White	3.00	6.00
Mond Wilson		
8 Patrick Sapp	3.00	6.00
Louis Solomon		
9 Glenn Rountree	3.00	6.00
Jim Bundren		
10 Lamont Pegues	3.00	6.00
Raymond Priester		
11 Andre Humphrey	6.00	12.00
Brian Dawkins		
12 Marcus Hinton	3.00	6.00
Andre Carter S		

1998 Clemson Team Issue

These photos were issued by the school to promote the football program. Each measures roughly 8" by 10" and features two players with two small black and white images and one larger image for each player The school name and year appear at the top and the player's name, position, and home town are included as well. The backs are blank.

COMPLETE SET (9)	20.00	40.00
1 Rahim Abdullah	3.00	6.00
DoMarco Fox		
2 Donald Broomfield	3.00	6.00
Chris Jones LB		
3 Robert Carswell	3.00	6.00
Chad Speck		
4 Adrian Dingle	3.00	6.00
Antwan Edwards		
5 Jason Gamble	3.00	6.00
Matt Butler		
6 Mal Lawyer	3.00	6.00
Brian Wofford		
7 Holland Postell	3.00	6.00
Corey Hulsey		
8 Brandon Streeter	3.00	6.00
Harold Means		
9 Terry Witherspoon	3.00	6.00
Javis Austin		

2003 Clemson Bragging Rites

This set was issued together with the South Carolina Bragging Rites card set to promote the 2003 motion picture by the same name. The cards were produced to resemble vintage cards complete with printed on creases, corners wear, and dirt. Black and white player photos were used and the cards were numbered on the front.

COMPLETE SET (12)	10.00	20.00
1 John Heisman CO	1.00	2.50
2 Jess Neely CO	.75	2.00
3 Banks McFadden	.75	2.00
4 Frank Howard CO	.75	2.00
5 Phil Prince	.75	2.00
6 Charlie Bussey	.75	2.00
7 Harvey White	.75	2.00
8 Jerry Butler	1.00	2.50
9 Danny Ford CO	.75	2.00
10 Jeff Davis	.75	2.00
11 Rodney Williams	1.00	2.50
12 Rod Gardner	1.00	2.50

1904 College Captains and Teams Postcards

This set of postcards was issued in 1904. Each card features small black and white photos of two team captains that competed in a college football game that year. The two team's pennants (in school colors) are also included on the cardfronts. Any additions to the below list are appreciated.

1 Wisconsin vs. Michigan	50.00	100.00
(October 29, 1904)		
Bush (Wisconsin)/(Willie Heston (Michigan)		
2 Chicago vs. Michigan	50.00	100.00
(November 12, 1904)		
Frederick Speik (Chicago)/(Willie Heston (Michigan)		
3 Brown vs. Dartmouth	35.00	60.00
(November 19, 1904)		
F. Schwinn (Brown)/(J.W. Knibbs (Dartmouth)		

1905 College Captains and Teams Postcards

This set of postcards was issued in 1905. Each card features small black and white photos of two team captains that competed in a college football game that year. The two team's pennants (in one school color) are also included on the cardfronts along with a blank box score to be filled out upon completion of the game. Any additions to the below list are appreciated.

1 Brown vs. Dartmouth	30.00	50.00
(November 25, 1905)		
G.A. Russ (Brown)/(D.J. Main (Dartmouth)		
2 Wisconsin vs. Chicago	30.00	50.00
(October 21, 1905)		
E. Vanderbloom (Wisconsin)		
Mark Catlin (Chicago)		
3 Wisconsin vs. Michigan	30.00	50.00
(November 18, 1905)		
E. Vanderbloom (Wisconsin)		
Fred Norcross (Michigan)		
4 Chicago vs. Michigan	30.00	50.00
(November 30, 1905)		
Mark Catlin (Chicago)		
Fred Norcross (Michigan)		

1906 College Captains and Teams Postcards

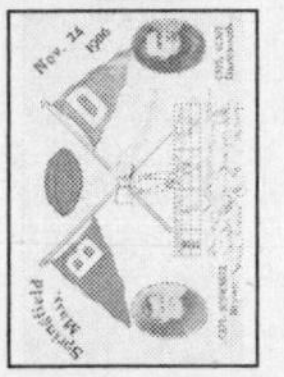

This set of postcards was issued in 1906. Each card features small black and white photos of two team captains that competed in a college game that year. The two team's pennants are also included on the cardfronts along with a blank box score to be filled out upon completion of the game. Any additions to the below list are appreciated.

1 Brown vs. Dartmouth	35.00	60.00
(November 24, 1906)		
V.A. Schwartz (Brown)		
J.B. Glaze (Dartmouth)		
2 Ohio St. vs. Case	40.00	80.00
J.F. Lincoln (OSU)		
Bradford (Case)		
3 Ohio St. vs. Ohio Medical	40.00	80.00
James Lincoln (OSU)		
William Cann (OMU)		

1907 College Captains and Teams Postcards

This set of postcards was issued in 1907 and features small black and white photos of two team captains that competed in a college football game that year. The player's images and date of the game are included on the fronts. The Michigan-Wabash card features the player images within a black and white ink drawing outline of a football while the Notre Dame-Purdue card includes color pennants for both teams. The cardbacks feature a typical postcard design.

1 Michigan vs. Wabash	40.00	80.00
(October 19, 1907)		
Paul Magoffin (Michigan)		
Gipe (Wabash)		
2 Purdue vs. Notre Dame	40.00	80.00
(Nov. 23, 1907)		
Berkheiser (Purdue)		
Callicrate Notre Dame)		

1908 College Captains and Teams Postcards

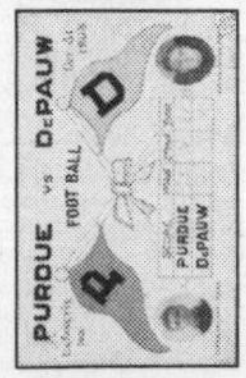

This set of postcards was issued in 1908. Each card features small black and white photos of two team captains that competed in a college game that year. The two team's pennants are also included on the cardfronts with some also including a blank box score to be filled out upon completion of the game. Any additions to the below list are appreciated.

1 Purdue vs. DePauw	35.00	60.00
(October 31, 1908)		
Asher Holloway (Purdue)		
Jackson (DePauw)		
2 Purdue vs. Indiana	35.00	60.00
(November 21, 1908)		
Asher Holloway (Purdue)		
Scott Paddock (Indiana)		
3 Oregon vs. Oregon State	35.00	60.00
(Nov. 21, 1908)		
Fred Moullen (Oregon)		
Carl Wolff (Oregon State)		

1910 College Captains and Teams Postcards

These postcards were issued in 1910 and feature small black and white photos of two team captains that competed in a college game that year. The two team's pennants are also included on the cardfronts with some also including a blank box score to be filled out upon completion of the game. Any additions to the below list are appreciated.

1 Illinois vs. Indiana	30.00	50.00
(November 5, 1910)		
Butzer (Illinois)		
Berndt (Indian		

1911 College Captains and Teams Postcards

These postcards were issued in 1911 and feature small black and white photos of two team captains that competed in a college game that year. The two team's pennants are also included on the cardfronts with some also including a blank box score to be filled out upon completion of the game. Any additions to the below list are appreciated.

1 Purdue vs. Indiana	30.00	50.00
(November 25, 1911)		
Tavey (Purdue)		
Gill (Indiana)		

1912 College Captains and Teams Postcards

These postcards were issued in 1912 and feature small black and white photos of two team captains that competed in a college game that year. The two team's pennants are also included on the cardfronts with some also including a blank box score to be filled out upon completion of the game. Any additions to the below list are appreciated.

1 Purdue vs. Illinois	30.00	50.00
(November 9, 1912)		
Hutchison (Purdue)		
Woolston (Illinois)		

1933 College Captains

These postcard sized cards feature a black and white photo on the fronts with a blank cardback. They were thought to have been released in 1933 as arcade trading cards. Below the photo is a short write-up on the featured college football captain with the college name printed above the photo. The unnumbered cards are listed below alphabetically.

COMPLETE SET (10)	150.00	250.00
1 Gil Berry	15.00	30.00
(Illinois)		
2 Raymond Brown	20.00	35.00
(USC)		
3 Walter Haas	20.00	35.00
(Minnesota)		
4 Lew Hinchman	15.00	30.00
(Ohio)		
5 Paul Host	15.00	30.00
(Notre Dame)		
6 Gregory Kabat	15.00	30.00
(Wisconsin)		
7 John Oehler	15.00	30.00
(Purdue)		
8 Pug Rentner	20.00	35.00
(Northwestern)		
9 Stanley Sokolis	15.00	30.00
(Pennsylvania)		
10 Ivan Williamson	15.00	30.00
(Michigan)		

2009 College Football Hall of Fame

This set of 21 cards was issued by the College Football Hall of Fame in South Bend and sold in their store. Each measures roughly 5 1/2" by 8 1/2" and features a member of the 2009 enshrinement class.

COMPLETE SET (21)	5.00	10.00
1 Troy Aikman	.75	2.00
2 Volney Ashford CO	.20	.50
3 Roger Brown	.20	.50
4 Billy Cannon	.40	1.00
5 John Cooper CO	.20	.50
6 Fred Dean	.30	.75
7 Jim Dombrowski	.20	.50
8 Jim Donnan CO	.20	.50
9 Pat Fitzgerald	.20	.50
10 Lou Holtz CO	.60	1.50
11 Wilber Marshall	.30	.75
12 Rueben Mayes	.30	.75
13 Randall McDaniel	.40	1.00
14 Don McPherson	.20	.50
15 Sam Mills	.30	.75
16 Jay Novacek	.50	1.25
17 Dave Parks	.20	.50
18 Ron Simmons	.20	.50
19 Rod Smith	.40	1.00
20 Thurman Thomas	.50	1.25
21 Arnold Tucker	.20	.50

2010 College Football Hall of Fame

This set of 24 cards was issued by the College Football Hall of Fame in South Bend and sold in their store. Each measures roughly 5 1/2" by 8 1/2" and features a member of the 2010 enshrinement class.

COMPLETE SET (24)	5.00	10.00
1 Pervis Atkins	.30	.75
2 Emerson Boozer	.40	1.00
3 Tim Brown	.60	1.50
4 Troy Brown	.40	1.00
5 Chuck Cecil	.30	.75
6 Ed Dyas	.30	.75
7 Major Harris	.40	1.00
8 Gordon Hudson	.30	.75
9 Willie Jeffries CO	.30	.75
10 Brian Kelly	.30	.75
11 Ted Kessinger CO	.30	.75
12 William Lewis	.30	.75
13 Woodrow Lowe	.30	.75
14 Dick MacPherson	.30	.75
15 Ken Margerum	.30	.75
16 Steve McMichael	.30	.75
17 Milt Morin	.30	.75
18 John Robinson CO	.30	.75
19 Chris Spielman	.50	1.25
20 Larry Station	.30	.75
21 Pat Swilling	.40	1.00
22 Gino Torretta	.40	1.00
23 Curt Warner	.40	1.00
24 Grant Wistrom	.40	1.00

2011 College Football Hall of Fame

This set of 20 cards was issued by the College Football Hall of Fame in South Bend and sold in their store. Each measures roughly 5 1/2" by 8 1/2" and features a member of the 2011 enshrinement class.

COMPLETE SET (20)	10.00	16.00
1 Barry Alvarez CO	.30	.75
2 Dennis Byrd	.30	.75
3 Ronnie Caveness	.30	.75
4 Ray Childress	.40	1.00
5 Dexter Coakley	.30	.75
6 Randy Cross	.40	1.00
7 Sam Cunningham	.40	1.00
8 Mike Favor	.30	.75
9 Charles Haley	.60	1.50
10 Mark Herrmann	.30	.75
11 Clarkston Hines	.30	.75
12 Desmond Howard	.50	1.25
13 Mike Kelly	.30	.75
14 Mickey Kobrosky	.30	.75
15 Bill Manlove CO	.30	.75
16 Chet Moeller	.30	.75
17 Gene Stallings	.40	1.00
18 Jerry Stovall	.30	.75
19 Pat Tillman	1.00	2.50
20 Alfred Williams	.30	.75

1950 C.O.P. Betsy Ross

Subtitled C.O.P.'s Player of the Week, this seven-card set features outstanding players from College of the Pacific. The date of the set is fixed by the Eddie LeBaron card, which listed him as a senior. The oversized cards measure approximately 5" by 7" and are printed on thin paper stock. The fronts feature black-and-white posed action shots that are tilted slightly to the left and have rounded corners. The top stripe carries brief biographical information and career highlights. The bottom stripe notes that these cards were distributed "as a public service by your neighborhood Grocer and Betsy Ross Bread." The bread company's logo is located at the lower right corner. Although LeBaron is the most well known player in the set, he appears to be more plentiful than the others. Additional cards may belong to this set. The backs are blank and the unnumbered cards are listed below in alphabetical order.

COMPLETE SET (7)	400.00	800.00
1 Don Campora	50.00	100.00
2 Don Hardey	50.00	100.00
3 Robert Klein	25.00	60.00
4 Eddie LeBaron	40.00	75.00
5 Eddie Macon	50.00	100.00
6 Walter Polenske SP	175.00	300.00
7 John Rohde	50.00	100.00

1990 Collegiate Collection Say No to Drugs

This multi-sport set was released by Collegiate Collection for the "Say No To Drugs, Yes to Life" campaign. Each card is essentially a re-issue of a standard card from one of the college team sets along with a different card number and different copyright line.

COMPLETE SET (6)	5.00	12.00
AL1 Joe Namath	1.25	4.00
AL2 Bart Starr	1.25	3.00
GA1 Herschel Walker	.40	1.00
LOU1 Johnny Unitas	.75	2.00
AU1 Bo Jackson	.40	1.00

1974 Colorado Playing Cards

This 54-card set of playing cards measures 2 1/4" by 3 1/2". The cardbacks feature the Colorado Buffaloes logo against a black background. The cardfronts feature a black and white player photo with the player's name below. The cards are checklisted below in playing card order by suit (C for Clubs, D for Diamonds, H for Hearts, S for Spades, and JOK for the Jokers) and numbers are assigned to Aces (1), Jacks (11), Queens (12), and Kings (13).

COMPELTE SET (54)	90.00	150.00
1C Doug Payton	1.25	3.00
1D Buck Arnold	1.25	3.00
1H Larry Williams	1.25	3.00
1S Bill Mallory CO	1.25	3.00
2C Whitney Paul	1.25	3.00
2D Pete Brock	1.25	3.00
2H Dave Williams	1.25	3.00
2S Eddie Crowder AD	1.25	3.00
3C Vic Odegard	1.25	3.00
3D Gary Campbell	1.25	3.00
3H Leon White	1.50	4.00
3S Tom Batta Asst.CO	1.25	3.00
4C Emery Moorehead	1.50	4.00
4D Dennis Cimmino	1.25	3.00
4H Billy Waddy	2.00	5.00
4S George Belu COORD	1.25	3.00
5C Mike Metoyer	1.25	3.00
5D Clyde Crutchmer	1.25	3.00
5H Jeff Turcotte	1.25	3.00
5S Ron Corradini Asst.CO	1.25	3.00
6C Jerry Martinez	1.25	3.00
6D Bill Donnell	1.25	3.00
6H Tom Tesone	1.25	3.00
6S Gary Durchik Asst.CO	1.25	3.00
7C David Logan	1.25	3.00
7D Rick Ellwood	1.25	3.00
7H Rick Stearns	1.25	3.00
7S Floyd Keith Asst.CO	1.25	3.00
8C Tom Likovich	1.25	3.00
8D Jeff Geiser	1.25	3.00
8H Mike Spivey	1.25	3.00
8S Bob Reublin COORD	1.25	3.00
9C Terry Kunz	1.25	3.00
9D Harvey Goodman	1.25	3.00
9H Bob Simpson	1.25	3.00
9S Dan Stavely Asst.DIR	1.25	3.00
10C Jeff Kensinger	1.25	3.00
10D Steve Haggerty	1.25	3.00
10H Ed Shoen	1.25	3.00
10S Les Steckel Asst.CO	2.00	5.00
11C Jim Kelleher	1.25	3.00
11D Steve Hakes	1.25	3.00
11H Tom Perry	1.25	3.00
11S Milan Vooletich Asst.CO	1.25	3.00
12C Melvin Johnson	1.25	3.00
12D Brad Harris	1.25	3.00
12H Rod Perry	1.50	4.00
12S Dwight Wallace Asst.CO	1.25	3.00
13C Bobby Hunt	1.25	3.00
13D Don Hasselbeck	1.50	4.00
13H Horace Perkins	1.25	3.00
13S Blake Arnold	1.25	3.00
JOK1 Team Logo Black	1.25	3.00
JOK2 Team Logo Red	1.25	3.00

1990 Colorado Smokey

This 16-card standard-size set was issued to honor the eventual co-National Champion Colorado Buffaloes as well as to promote fire safety. This set was distributed at the final Colorado home game of the 1990 season at Folsom Field. Featured are some of the leading players on the Buffaloes including Eric Bieniemy, Darian Hagan, Charles Johnson, and Butkus Award winner Alfred Williams. The set was issued in a sheet of 16 cards which, when perforated, measure the standard size. The cards feature full-color action photos of the players on the front and a brief biography along with a safety tip featuring the popular safety figure, Smokey the Bear. This unnumbered set has been checklisted below in alphabetical order.

COMPLETE SET (16)	8.00	20.00
1 Eric Bieniemy	.80	2.00
2 Joe Garten	.25	.60
3 Darian Hagan	.60	1.50
4 George Hemingway	.25	.60
5 Garry Howe	.25	.60
6 Tim James	.25	.60
7 Charles Johnson	1.25	3.00
8 Bill McCartney CO	.60	1.50
9 Dave McCloughan	.25	.60
10 Kanavis McGhee	.60	1.50
11 Mike Pritchard	1.25	3.00
12 Tom Rouen	.60	1.50
13 Michael Simmons	.25	.60
14 Mark Vander Poel	.60	1.50
15 Alfred Williams	.60	1.50
16 Ralphie (Mascot)	.25	.60

1992 Colorado Pepsi

Originally issued in perforated sheets, these 12 standard-size cards feature on their fronts color player posed and action shots set within black borders and framed by a yellowish line. The player's name and position, along with the Pepsi logo, appear underneath the photo. The team name and logo appear above the photo. The plain white back carries the player's name and jersey number at the top, followed below by position, height, weight, class, hometown, major, and career highlights. The cards are unnumbered and checklisted below in alphabetical order.

COMPLETE SET (12)	5.00	12.00
1 Greg Biekert	.60	1.50
2 Pat Blottiaux	.30	.75
3 Ronnie Bradford	.40	1.00
4 Chad Brown	1.50	4.00
5 Marcellous Elder	.30	.75
6 Deon Figures	1.00	2.50
7 Jim Hansen	.30	.75
8 Jack Keys	.30	.75
9 Bill McCartney CO	.60	1.50
10 Clint Moles	.30	.75
11 Jason Perkins	.30	.75
12 Scott Starr	.30	.75

1993 Colorado Smokey

Originally issued in perforated sheets, these 12 standard-size cards feature on their fronts color player posed and action shots set within black borders and framed by a yellowish line. The player's name and position, along with the Pepsi logo, appear underneath the photo. The team name and logo appear above the photo. The plain white back carries the player's name and jersey number at the top, followed below by position, height, weight, class, hometown, major, and career highlights. The cards are unnumbered and checklisted below in alphabetical order.

COMPLETE SET (16)	6.00	15.00
1 Craig Anderson	.40	1.00
2 Mitch Berger	.60	1.50
3 Jeff Brunner	.40	1.00
4 Dennis Collier	.40	1.00
5 Dwayne Davis	.40	1.00
6 Brian Dyet	.40	1.00
7 Sean Embree	.40	1.00
8 Garrett Ford	.40	1.00
9 James Hill	.40	1.00
10 Charles Johnson	1.20	3.00
11 Greg Lindsey	.40	1.00
12 Sam Rogers	.40	1.00
13 Mark Smith	.40	1.00
14 Duke Tobin	.40	1.00
15 Ronnie Woolfork	.50	1.25
16 Derek Agnew	.40	1.00

1994 Colorado Smokey

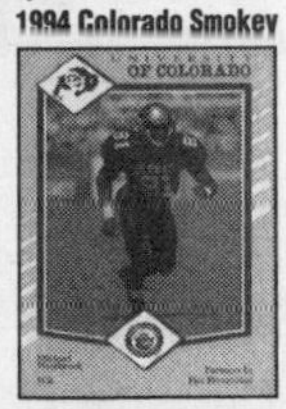

Measuring 10 1/4" by 14 1/4", this perforated sheet consists of sixteen standard-size cards arranged in four 4-card rows. On a yellow card face, the fronts feature color action photos inside black-and-white inner borders. Short white diagonal stripes accent the front on the left and right sides. Player information and the slogan "Partners In Fire Prevention" appear at the bottom. The backs present biographical information and a fire prevention cartoon starring Smokey. The cards are unnumbered and checklisted below in alphabetical order.

COMPLETE SET (16)	8.00	20.00
1 Blake Anderson	.30	.75
2 Norm Barnett	.30	.75
3 Tony Berti	.30	.75
4 Ken Browne	.30	.75
5 Christian Fauria	1.00	2.50
6 Darius Holland	.50	1.25
7 Chris Hudson	.50	1.25
8 Ted Johnson	1.50	4.00
9 Vance Joseph	.30	.75
10 Jon Knutson	.30	.75
11 Bill McCartney CO	.50	1.25
12 Erik Mitchell	.30	.75
13 Kordell Stewart	4.00	10.00
14 Derek West	.30	.75
15 Michael Westbrook	1.00	2.50
16 Team logo	.30	.75

1995 Colorado Smokey

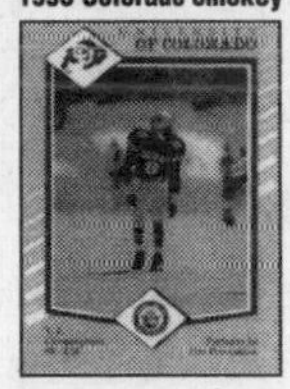

This set was issued by the school as a perforated 12-card sheet. On a yellow card face, the fronts feature color action photos inside black-and-white inner borders. Short white diagonal stripes accent the front on the left and right sides. Player identification and the slogan "Partners In Fire Prevention" appear at the bottom. The backs present biographical information and a fire prevention cartoon starring Smokey. The cards are unnumbered and checklisted below in alphabetical order.

COMPLETE SET (12)	4.00	8.00
1 T.J. Cunningham	.30	.75
2 Kerry Hicks	.30	.75
3 Heath Irwin	.30	.75
4 Donnell Leomiti	.30	.75
5 Clint Moore	.30	.75
6 Rick Neuheisel CO	.40	1.00
7 Daryl Price	.30	.75
8 Bryan Stoltenberg	.30	.75
9 Neil Voskeritchian	.30	.75
10 Mascot Ralphie	.30	.75
11 Mascot Chip	.30	.75
12 Folsom Field	.30	.75

1973 Colorado State Schedules

The 1973 Colorado State football set consists of eight cards, measuring approximately 2 1/2" by 3 3/4". The set was sponsored by Poudre Valley Dairy Foods. The fronts display green-tinted posed action shots with rounded corners and green borders. The words "1973 CSU Football" appear in the top border while the player's name and position are printed in the bottom border. The horizontal backs present the 1973 football schedule. Reportedly, the Stuebbe and Simpson cards are more difficult to obtain because they were given out to the public before hobbyists began to collect the set. Best known among the players is Willie Miller, who played for the Los Angeles Rams. The cards are unnumbered and checklisted below in alphabetical order.

COMPLETE SET (8)	45.00	90.00
1 Wes Cerveny	5.00	10.00
2 Mark Driscoll	5.00	10.00
3 Jimmie Kennedy	5.00	10.00
4 Greg Kuhn	5.00	10.00
5 Willie Miller	10.00	20.00
6 Al Simpson SP	7.50	15.00
7 Jan Stuebbe SP	7.50	15.00
8 Tom Wallace	5.00	10.00

1974 Colorado State Schedules

The 1974 Colorado State football set reportedly consists of just one card measuring roughly 2 1/2" by 3 3/4". Like the 1973 issue, the card was sponsored by Poudre Valley Dairy Foods. The words "1974 CSU Football" appear in the top border while the coach's name printed in the bottom border. The horizontal cardback presents the 1974 football schedule.

1 Sark Arslanian CO	2.50	5.00

1994 Colorado State

This set was issued by the school to promote its football team. Each card measures roughly 2 5/8" by 3 5/8" and was printed with an orange colored border on the front and a typical black-and-white printed cardback.

COMPLETE SET (16)	6.00	15.00
1 Vincent Booker	.40	1.00
2 Leonice Brown	.40	1.00
3 Anthoney Hill	.40	1.00
4 Steve Hodge	.40	1.00
5 Steve Hodge	.40	1.00
Kenya Ragsdale		
6 Kareem Ingram	.40	1.00
7 Scott Lynch	.40	1.00
8 Pat Meyer	.40	1.00
9 Sean Moran	.40	1.00
10 Greg Myers	.40	1.00
11 David Napier	.40	1.00
12 Eric Olsen	.40	1.00
13 Kenya Ragsdale	.40	1.00
14 Andre Strode	.40	1.00
15 Sonny Lubick CO	.40	1.00
16 Team Mascot	.40	1.00

1997 Connecticut

COMPLETE SET (16)	6.00	12.00
1 Carl Bond	.40	1.00
2 Dennis Callaghan	.40	1.00
3 Anthony Carter	.40	1.00
4 Chad Cook	.40	1.00
5 John Fitzsimmons	.40	1.00
6 Kevin Foster	.40	1.00
7 Phil Hunt	.40	1.00
8 Recolon Jumpp	.40	1.00
9 Brad Keatley	.40	1.00
10 Ernie Lowe	.40	1.00
11 Chad Martin	.40	1.00
12 Pat Russo	.40	1.00
13 Mike Sasson	.40	1.00
14 Shane Stafford	.40	1.00
15 Sean Tremblay	.40	1.00
16 Courtney Williams	.40	1.00

1998 Connecticut Legends

COMPLETE SET (16)	6.00	12.00
1 Glenn Antrum	.40	1.00
2 Troy Ashley	.40	1.00
3 Vin Clements	.40	1.00
4 J.O. Christian	.40	1.00
5 Matt DeGennaro	.40	1.00
6 Mark Didio	.40	1.00
7 Bob Donnelly	.40	1.00
8 John Dorsey	.40	1.00
9 Walt Dropo	.40	1.00
10 Nick Giaquinto	.40	1.00
11 Wilbur Gilliard	.40	1.00
12 Vernon Hargreaves	.40	1.00
13 Brian Herosian	.40	1.00
14 Red O.Neill	.40	1.00
15 John Toner	.40	1.00
16 Ted Walton	.40	1.00

1999 Connecticut

This set was sponsored by First Union and issued by the team. Each blue-bordered card includes a color image of a player or team member with the school's name above the photo and the subject's name below.

COMPLETE SET (12)	4.00	10.00
1 Mike Burton	.40	1.00
2 Anthony Carter	.40	1.00
3 Chad Cook	.40	1.00
4 Jeff Delucia	.40	1.00
5 Randy Edsall CO	.40	1.00
6 Ron Gamble	.40	1.00
7 Jamie Harper	.40	1.00
8 Mike Morelli	.40	1.00
9 Mike Sasson	.40	1.00
10 Rob Tritz	.40	1.00
11 Jordan Younger	.40	1.00
12 Team Mascot	.40	1.00

1916 Cornell Postcards

These black and white Cornell Postcards were issued around 1916 by the University. The cards feature a standard postcard style back with the player's last name printed near his photo on the front. Any additions or information on the checklist below would be appreciated.

1 Charles Barrett	30.00	50.00
2 Fritz Shiverick	30.00	50.00

1992 Cotton Bowl Classic Moments

This 24-card set captures "Classic Moments" from the Mobil Cotton Bowl. The fronts feature sepia-toned player photos, edged on the left and below by dark blue borders, and on right and below by pink shadow borders. A red triangle superposed on the picture carries the player's name, school, and the year that he played in the Cotton Bowl game. On a white card face with a ghosted version of the Cotton Bowl logo, the horizontal backs summarize the player's outstanding performance. The cards are numbered on the back "X/24." A Doug Flutie card was also produced but never released.

COMPLETE SET (24)	50.00	100.00
1 The Cotton Bowl	.40	1.00
2 Sammy Baugh	3.00	8.00
3 Doak Walker	2.00	5.00
4 Dick Moegle	.60	1.50
5 Bobby Layne	2.50	6.00
6 Curtis Sanford	.40	1.00
Founder		
7 John Kimbrough	.40	1.00
8 Ernie Davis	4.00	10.00
9 Lance Alworth	2.00	5.00
10 James Street	1.50	4.00
Darrell Royal CO		
11 Mike Singletary	1.50	4.00
12 Roger Staubach	5.00	12.00
13 Earl Campbell	3.00	8.00
14 Wilson Whitley	.40	1.00
15 Jim Swink	.60	1.50
16 Martin Ruby	.40	1.00
17 Davey O'Brien	.75	2.00
18 Gene Stallings CO	2.50	6.00
Paul(Bear) Bryant CO		
19 Bo Jackson	2.50	6.00
20 Joe Theismann	1.50	4.00
21 Field Scovell	.40	1.00
Mr. Cotton Bowl		
22 Ken Hatfield	.40	1.00
23 Joe Montana	15.00	30.00
24 Mobil Cotton Bowl	.40	1.00
Classic Checklist		

1998 Cotton Bowl Hall of Fame Inaugural Class

This set was issued by the Cotton Bowl Foundation in May 1998 to honor the inaugural inductees into the Cotton Bowl Hall of Fame. The cards are the first set in a continuing series to honor members of the Hall of Fame. Each card includes a sepia toned photo on the front against a background of newspaper clippings. The cardbacks feature a simple black printing on white card stock design.

1 Hall of Fame Trophy	1.25	3.00
2 Jim Brown	7.50	15.00
3 Bobby Layne	5.00	10.00
4 Dick Moegle	1.50	4.00
5 Darrell Royal	2.00	5.00
6 Curtis Sanford	1.25	3.00
7 Field Scovell	1.25	3.00
8 Doak Walker	4.00	8.00
9 Cover Card Checklist	1.25	3.00

1999 Cotton Bowl Hall of Fame Class of 1999

This set was released at a Cotton Bowl Association function in 1999. Each card features a famous player or coach from the college classic on the cardfronts against a background of newspaper clippings.

COMPLETE SET (8)	10.00	20.00
1 Stadium Photo	.75	2.00
2 Sammy Baugh	2.50	6.00
3 Frank Broyles CO	.75	2.00
4 Gussie Nell Davis	.75	2.00
5 David Hodge	.75	2.00
6 Felix McKnight	.75	2.00
7 James Street	1.25	3.00
8 Cover Card Checklist	.75	2.00

2000 Cotton Bowl Hall of Fame Class of 2000

This set was issued by the Cotton Bowl Foundation in May 2000 to honor the inductees into the Cotton Bowl Hall of Fame for that year. The cards are part of a continuing series that began in 1998. Each card includes a sepia toned photo on the front and a simple black on white text cardback.

1 Hall of Fame Day	.75	2.00
(Stadium photo)		
2 Paul Bear Bryant	10.00	20.00
3 Duke Carlisle	1.25	3.00
4 Johnny Holland	1.25	3.00
5 John Kimbrough	.75	2.00
6 Lindsey Nelson	.75	2.00
7 Roger Staubach	10.00	20.00
8 Jim Swink	1.25	3.00
9 Cover Card Checklist	.75	2.00

2000 Cotton Bowl Program Covers

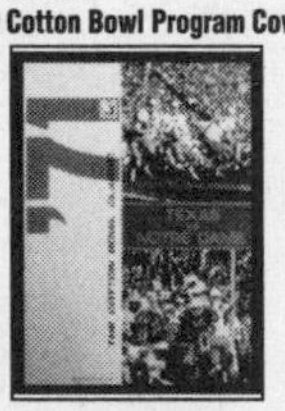

This set was produced by the Cotton Bowl Athletic Association and released at the Emery Award Luncheon in early 2000. The cards feature the game day program covers of each past Cotton Bowl from 1937 through 2000 surrounded by a black border. The cardbacks are simple black and white text with a brief description of that season's game along with a card number. Each card measures slightly larger than standard size at 2 5/8" by 3 5/8".

COMPLETE SET (64)	50.00	100.00
1 1937 TCU 16 - Marquette 6	.75	2.00
2 1938 Rice 28 - Colorado 14	.75	2.00
3 1939 St. Mary's 20	.75	2.00
Texas Tech 13		
4 1940 Clemson 6	.75	2.00
Boston College 3		
5 1941 Texas A&M 13	.75	2.00
Fordham 12		
6 1942 Alabama 29	.75	2.00
Texas A&M 21		
7 1943 Texas 14	.75	2.00
Georgia Tech 7		
8 1944 Randolph Field 7	.75	2.00
Texas 7		
9 1945 Oklahoma St. 34	.75	2.00
TCU 0		
10 1946 Texas 40 - Missouri 27	.75	2.00
11 1947 Arkansas 0 - LSU 0	.75	2.00
12 1948 Penn St. 13 - SMU 13	.75	2.00
13 1949 SMU 21 - Oregon 13	.75	2.00
14 1950 Rice 27	.75	2.00
North Carolina 13		
15 1951 Tennessee 20 - Texas 14	.75	2.00
16 1952 Kentucky 20 - TCU 7	.75	2.00
17 1953 Texas 16	.75	2.00
Tennessee 0		
18 1954 Rice 28 - Alabama 6	.75	2.00
19 1955 Georgia Tech 14	.75	2.00
Arkansas 6		
20 1956 Mississippi 14	.75	2.00
TCU 13		
21 1957 TCU 28 - Syracuse 27	.75	2.00
22 1958 Navy 20 - Rice 7	.75	2.00
23 1959 Air Force 0 - TCU 0	.75	2.00
24 1960 Syracuse 23 - Texas 14	.75	2.00
25 1961 Duke 7 - Arkansas 6	.75	2.00
26 1962 Texas 12 - Mississippi 7	.75	2.00
27 1963 LSU 13 - Texas 0	.75	2.00
28 1964 Texas 28 - Navy 6	.75	2.00
29 1965 Arkansas 10	.75	2.00
Nebraska 7		
30 1966 LSU 14 - Arkansas 7	.75	2.00
31 1967 Georgia 24 - SMU 9	.75	2.00
32 1968 Texas A&M 20	.75	2.00
Alabama 16		
33 1969 Texas 36 - Tennessee 13	.75	2.00
34 1970 Texas 21	.75	2.00
Notre Dame 17		
35 1971 Notre Dame 24	.75	2.00
Texas 11		
36 1972 Penn St. 30 - Texas 6	.75	2.00
37 1973 Texas 17 - Alabama 13	.75	2.00
38 1974 Nebraska 19 - Texas 3	.75	2.00
39 1975 Penn St. 41 - Baylor 20	.75	2.00
40 1976 Arkansas 31	.75	2.00
Georgia 10		
41 1977 Houston 30	.75	2.00
Maryland 21		
42 1978 Notre Dame 38	.75	2.00
Texas 10		
43 1979 Notre Dame 35	.75	2.00
Houston 34		
44 1980 Houston 17	.75	2.00
Nebraska 14		
45 1981 Alabama 30 - Baylor 2	.75	2.00
46 1982 Texas 14 - Alabama 12	.75	2.00
47 1983 SMU 7 - Pittsburgh 3	.75	2.00
48 1984 Georgia 10 - Texas 9	.75	2.00
49 1985 Boston College 45	.75	2.00
Houston 28		
50 1986 Texas A&M 36	.75	2.00
Auburn 16		
51 1987 Ohio St. 28	.75	2.00
Texas A&M 12		
52 1988 Texas A&M 35	.75	2.00
Notre Dame 10		
53 1989 UCLA 17 - Arkansas 3	.75	2.00
54 1990 Tennessee 31	.75	2.00
Arkansas 27		
55 1991 Miami 46 - Texas 3	.75	2.00
56 1992 Florida St. 10 - Texas A&M 2	.75	2.00
57 1993 Notre Dame 28	.75	2.00
Texas A&M 3		
58 1994 Notre Dame 24	.75	2.00
Texas A&M 21		
59 1995 USC 55	.75	2.00
Texas Tech 14		
60 1996 Colorado 38	.75	2.00
Oregon 6		
61 1997 BYU 19	.75	2.00
Kansas St. 15		
62 1998 UCLA 29	.75	2.00
Texas A&M 23		
63 1999 Texas 38#[Mississippi St. 11	.75	2.00
64 2000 Arkansas 27 - Texas 6	.75	2.00

2001 Cotton Bowl Hall of Fame Class of 2001

This set was issued by the Cotton Bowl Foundation in 2001 to honor the inductees into the Cotton Bowl Hall of Fame for that year. The cards are part of a continuing series that began in 1998. Each card includes a sepia toned photo on the front and a simple black on white text cardback.

COMPLETE SET (9)	15.00	25.00
1 Hall of Fame Trophy	.75	2.00
2 Scott Appleton	.75	2.00
3 Ernie Davis	4.00	10.00
4 Russell Maryland	1.25	3.00
5 Jess Neely CO	.75	2.00
6 Loyd Phillips	.75	2.00
7 Cotton Speyrer	.75	2.00
8 Bill Yeoman CO	.75	2.00
9 Cover Card CL	.75	2.00

2003 Cotton Bowl Hall of Fame Class of 2003

This set was issued by the Cotton Bowl Foundation in April 2003 to honor the inductees into the Cotton Bowl Hall of Fame for that year. The cards are essentially an update to the 1999 set. Each card includes a sepia toned photo on the front and a simple black on white text cardback along with a card number in the lower right hand corner.

COMPLETE SET (9)	4.00	10.00
1 Hall of Fame Trophy	.30	.75
2 Robert Cullum	.30	.75
3 Eagle Day	.40	1.00
4 Kent Lawrence	.30	.75
5 Charles McClendon CO	.40	1.00
6 Kyle Rote	.60	1.50
7 Joe Theismann	1.50	4.00
8 Steve Worster	.30	.75
9 Cover Card CL	.30	.75

2005 Cotton Bowl Hall of Fame Class of 2005

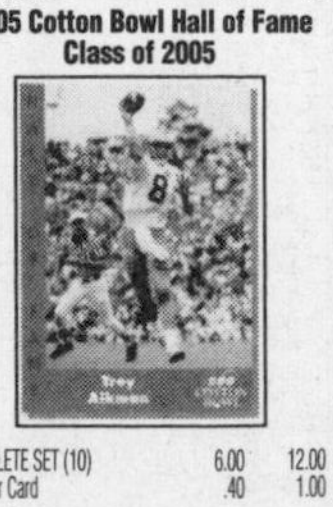

COMPLETE SET (10)	6.00	12.00
1 Cover Card	.40	1.00
2 Troy Aikman	2.00	5.00
3 Lance Alworth	.60	1.50
4 Jim Brock	.40	1.00
5 Mike Dean	.40	1.00
6 Andy Kozar	.40	1.00
7 Lydell Mitchell	.40	1.00
8 Hank Lauricella	.40	1.00
9 Gene Stallings.	.40	1.00
10 Checklist	.40	1.00

2007 Cotton Bowl Hall of Fame

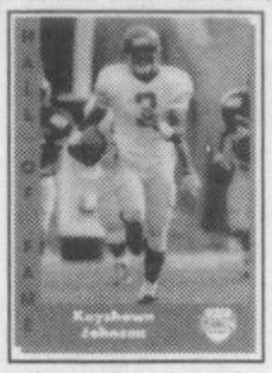

COMPLETE SET (8)	5.00	10.00
1 Class of 2007	.50	1.25
2 Brad Bradley Photo.	.50	1.25
3 Bob Fenimore	.50	1.25
4 Keyshawn Johnson	.60	1.50
5 Dat Nguyen	.60	1.50
6 Ara Parseghian CO	.60	1.50
7 Jerry Sisemore	.50	1.25
8 Cover Card	.50	1.25

1972 Davidson College Team Issue

These photos were issued by the school to promote the football program. Each measures roughly 8" by 10" and features two players with a black and white image for each player. The school name appears at the top and the player's name is included below. The backs are blank.

COMPLETE SET (10)	30.00	60.00
1 John Barbee	4.00	8.00
Greg Sikes		
2 Jim Ellison	4.00	8.00
Randy Parker		
3 Bill Garrett	4.00	8.00
Mike Sikes		
4 Bill Nicklas	4.00	8.00
Larry Spears		
5 Robert Norris	4.00	8.00
Rick Kemmerlin		
6 Johnny Ribet	4.00	8.00
Carl Rizzo		
7 Scotty Shipp	4.00	8.00
Gary Coulter		
8 Scotty Shipp	4.00	8.00
Robert Elliott		
9 Walt Walker	4.00	8.00
John Webel		
10 Terry Woodlief	4.00	8.00
Joe Poteat		

1998 Dayton

COMPLETE SET (22)	12.00	20.00
1 Trevor Andrews	.50	1.25
2 Joel Cutler	.50	1.25
3 Chucky Dauberman	.50	1.25
4 Chad Duff	.50	1.25
5 Sean Gorius	.50	1.25
6 Matt Hershman	.50	1.25
7 Trent Huelsman	.50	1.25
8 Pat Hugar	.50	1.25
9 Ryan Hulme	.50	1.25
10 Kevin Johns	.50	1.25
11 Mike Kelly CO	.50	1.25
12 Bumper McKinley	.50	1.25
13 Matt Moore	.50	1.25
14 Chad Muterspaw	.50	1.25
15 Ryan Rapaszky	.50	1.25
16 Gene Steinke	.50	1.25
17 Jeff Verhoff	.50	1.25
18 Nick Virostko	.50	1.25
19 Peter Wehrman	.50	1.25
20 D.J. Weinert	.50	1.25
21 Dayton Seniors	.50	1.25
22 Cover Card	.50	1.25

1905 Dominoe Postcards

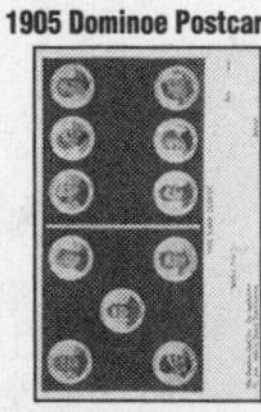

These postcards were issued in 1905 and include small photos of the starting eleven of the featured school. Each was produced by Boston Postcard Company in a typical postcard style on the backs and a dominoe layout on the fronts. Most of the postcards include a space below the images for writing in the score of a game and the date of the game while some include a schedule below the player photos. The Ivy League schools are the easiest to find with the lower level schools generally the most difficult to locate. We've listed the known cards below - any additions to this list are appreciated.

1 Brown	20.00	35.00
Adams		
Curtis		
Westervelt		
Kirley		
Dennie		
Schwartz		
Weikert		
Conklin		
Fletcher		
MacGregor		
Russ		
2 Carlisle	40.00	80.00
Fremont		
Lubo		
Two Dogs in the Snow		
Strong Arm		
Nick Bowen		
Petonga		
Long Horn		
Kennedy		
Little Old Man		
Archiquette		
3 Dartmouth	20.00	35.00
Church		
Bankart		
Thayer		
J. Glaze		
Rich		
Griffin		
R. Glaze		
Lang		
Gage		
Marin		
Herr		
4 Dean Academy	15.00	30.00
5 Harvard	20.00	35.00
Foster		
Starr		
Kersburg		
Squires		
Hall		
Hurley		
Carr		
White		
Burr		
Brill		
6 Penn Captain/Harvard Captain	20.00	35.00
(Torrey - Penn		
Hurley - Harvard		
7 Rindge Training School	15.00	30.00
8 Somerville High School	25.00	50.00
9 Yale	20.00	35.00
Veeder		
Tad Jones		
Hockenberg		
Forbes		
Cates		
Flanders		
Flinn		
Morse		
Tripp		
Turner		
Shevlin		

1976 Duke Team Issue

These photos were issued by the school to promote the football program. Each measures roughly 5" by 8" and features a black and white image of a player with the player's name, position, and school name below each photo. The backs are blank. It is likely that these photos were originally issued as two player panels.

COMPLETE SET (16)	40.00	80.00
1 Mike Barney	3.00	6.00
2 Billy Bryan	3.00	6.00
3 Ernie Clark	3.00	6.00
4 Bob Corbett	3.00	6.00
5 Dave Dusek	3.00	6.00
6 Vince Fusco	3.00	6.00
7 Art Gore	3.00	6.00
8 Jeff Green	3.00	6.00
9 Larry Martinez	3.00	6.00
10 Dave Meier	3.00	6.00
11 Gary Pellom	3.00	6.00
12 Bob Pruitt	3.00	6.00
13 Troy Slade	3.00	6.00
14 Hal Spears	3.00	6.00
15 Larry Upshaw	3.00	6.00
16 Chuck Williamson	3.00	6.00

1987 Duke Police

This 16-card, standard-size set features players on Duke University's 1987 Blue Devils football team. The set was distributed to elementary school children in North Carolina by local law enforcement representatives as part of a drug education program. The front has a color action player photo, with Adolescent CareUnit logos in the upper corners and the player's name, uniform number, and position centered beneath the picture. The back has two Duke helmet logos in the upper corners, biographical information, and an anti-drug tip. The cards are unnumbered and checklisted below in alphabetical order.

COMPLETE SET (16)	20.00	40.00
1 Andy Andreasik 60	.75	2.00
2 Brian Bernard 93	.75	2.00
3 Bob Calamari 31	.75	2.00
4 Jason Cooper 22	.75	2.00
5 Dave Demore 92	.75	2.00
6 Mike Diminick 21	.75	2.00
7 Jim Godfrey 56	.75	2.00
8 Doug Green 5	.75	2.00
9 Stanley Monk 24	.75	2.00
10 Chris Port 73	.75	2.00
11 Steve Ryan 63	.75	2.00
12 Steve Slayden 7	.75	2.00
13 Steve Spurrier CO	6.00	15.00
14 Dewayne Terry 27	.75	2.00
15 Fonda Williams 19	.75	2.00
16 Blue Devil (Mascot)	.75	2.00

1995 FlickBall College Teams

Flickball released a set of 60 college mascot "paper footballs" in 1995. These flickballs were distributed in six count blister packs.

COMPLETE SET (60)	8.00	20.00
1 Alabama	.20	.50
2 Auburn	.20	.50
3 Boston Universary	.08	.25
4 Boston College	.15	.40
5 BYU	.15	.40
6 Citadel	.08	.25
7 Columbia	.08	.25
8 Florida	.20	.50
9 Georgia	.20	.50
10 Houston	.08	.25
11 Illinois	.15	.40
12 Kansas State	.15	.40
13 Kentucky	.15	.40
14 Maine	.08	.25
15 Marquette	.08	.25
16 Memphis	.08	.25
17 Michigan	.20	.50
18 Mississippi	.15	.40
19 Carolina Greensboro	.08	.25
20 North Carolina State	.15	.40
21 Nebraska	.20	.50
22 New Mexico	.08	.25
23 North Carolina	.20	.50
24 Oklahoma State	.15	.40
25 Pittsburgh	.15	.40
26 Purdue	.15	.40
27 Rhode Island	.08	.25
28 Seton Hall	.08	.25
29 South Carolina	.15	.40
30 South Connecticut	.08	.25
31 St. Johns	.08	.25
32 Stony Brook	.08	.25
33 Temple	.08	.25
34 Tennessee	.20	.50
35 Tulane	.08	.25
36 Army	.15	.40
37 Vanderbilt	.15	.40
38 Virginia	.15	.40
39 Wisconsin	.15	.40
40 Wyoming	.08	.25
41 Duke	.15	.40
42 North Carolina Central	.08	.25
43 Georgia Tech	.15	.40
44 New York U.	.08	.25
45 San Francisco State	.08	.25
46 San Diego State	.08	.25
47 Wake Forest	.15	.40
48 Minnesota	.15	.40
49 Penn State	.20	.50
50 Villanova	.08	.25
51 Clemson	.15	.40
52 Fresno State	.08	.25
53 Colorado State	.08	.25
54 LSU	.20	.50
55 Georgetown	.15	.40
56 UNC Charlotte	.08	.25
57 University of San Francisco	.08	.25
58 Arizona	.20	.50
59 Florida State	.20	.50
60 Yale	.08	.25

1973 Florida Playing Cards

This set was issued in a playing card deck box. The cards have rounded corners and the typical playing card format. The fronts feature black-and-white posed photos of helmetless players in their uniforms. A white border surrounds each picture and contains the card number and suit designation in the upper left corner and again, but inverted, in the lower right. The player's name and position initials appear just beneath the photo. The orange backs all feature the "Fighting Gators" logo. The cards were also produced with a blue cardback variation. The year of issue, 1973, is included on the schedule card. Since the set is similar to a playing card set, it is arranged just like a card deck and checklisted below accordingly. In the checklist below C means Clubs, D means Diamonds, H means Hearts, S means Spades and JK means Joker. Numbers are assigned to Aces (1), Jacks (11), Queens (12), and Kings (13). The jokers are unnumbered and listed at the end.

COMPLETE SET (54)	75.00	135.00
1C Kris Anderson	1.00	2.50
1D David Bowden	1.00	2.50
1H Nat Moore	5.00	10.00
1S Doug Dickey CO	1.50	3.00
2C Gary Padgett	1.00	2.50
2D Tom Dolfi	1.00	2.50
2H Sammy Green	1.00	2.50
2S Scott Nugent	1.00	2.50
3C Joel Parker	1.00	2.50
3D Don Gaffney	1.00	2.50
3H Andy Summers	1.00	2.50
3S Joe Wunderly	1.00	2.50
4C George Nicholas	1.00	2.50
4D Hank Foldberg	2.50	5.00
4H Jimmy DuBose	1.00	2.50
4S David Starkey	1.00	2.50
5C Buster Morrison	1.00	2.50
5D Mike Williams	1.00	2.50
5H David Hitchcock	1.00	2.50
5S Glenn Cameron	1.00	2.50
6C Mike Moore DE	1.00	2.50
6D Chan Gailey	3.00	6.00
6H John Williams	1.00	2.50
6S Eddie Sirmons	1.00	2.50
7C Roy Mallory	1.00	2.50
7D Mike Smith DE	1.00	2.50
7H Glenn Sever	1.00	2.50
7S Ward Eastman	1.00	2.50
8C Lee McGriff	1.00	2.50
8D Carey Geiger	1.00	2.50
8H Andy Wade	1.00	2.50
8S Robbie Davis	1.00	2.50
9C Chris McCoun	1.00	2.50
9D Preston Kendrick	1.00	2.50
9H Jim Revels	1.00	2.50
9S Robby Ball	1.00	2.50
10C Burton Lawless	2.50	5.00
10D Clint Griffith	1.00	2.50
10H Alvin Butler	2.50	5.00
10S Thom Clifford	1.00	2.50
11C Jimbo Kynes	1.00	2.50
11D Al Darby	1.00	2.50
11H Hollis Boardman	1.00	2.50
11S Ricky Browne	1.00	2.50
12C Randy Talbot	1.00	2.50
12D Mike Stanfield	1.00	2.50
12H Paul Parker	1.00	2.50
12S John Lacer	1.00	2.50
13C Tyson Sever	1.00	2.50
13D Wayne Fields	1.00	2.50
13H Vince Kendrick	1.00	2.50
13S Ralph Ortega	1.00	2.50
J1 Schedule Card	1.00	2.50
J2 Joker	1.00	2.50

1988 Florida Burger King

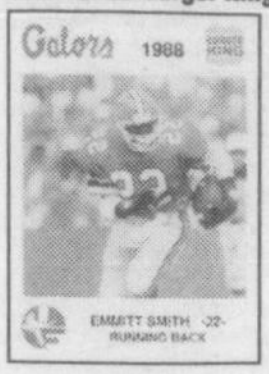

This 16-card standard-size set features then-current football players at the University of Florida. The cards are numbered on the back in the lower right corner. The set was produced by McDag Productions and sponsored by Burger King. The set is also considered to be a police/safety set due to the "Tip from the Gators" on each card back. The Emmitt Smith card from this set has been illegally reprinted; all known reprints (counterfeits) are missing the Burger King logo on the card front. Collectors are urged to be especially cautious when purchasing single Emmitt Smith cards without the rest of the set.

COMPLETE SET (16)	90.00	150.00
1 Florida Gators Team	2.00	5.00
2 Emmitt Smith 22	90.00	150.00
3 David Williams 73	.50	1.25
4 Jeff Roth 96	.40	1.00
5 Rhondy Weston 68	.40	1.00
6 Stacey Simmons 25	.40	1.00
7 Huey Richardson 90	.40	1.00
8 Wayne Williams 23	.40	1.00
9 Charlie Wright 79	.40	1.00
10 Tracy Daniels 63	.40	1.00
11 Ernie Mills 14	1.00	2.50
12 Willie McGrady 38	.40	1.00
13 Chris Bromley 52	.40	1.00
14 Louis Oliver 18	.60	1.50
15 Galen Hall CO	.75	2.00
16 Albert the Alligator	.40	1.00
(Mascot)		

1989 Florida All-Time Greats

The 1989 Florida Gators football set contains 22 standard-size cards of past players, i.e., all-time Gators. The fronts have vintage or color action photos with white borders; the vertically oriented backs have player profiles. These cards were distributed as a complete set. A safety message is included near the bottom of each reverse along with a card number.

COMPLETE SET (22)	20.00	35.00
1 Dale Van Sickle	.40	1.00
2 Cris Collinsworth	.60	1.50
3 Wilber Marshall	.75	2.00
4 Jack Youngblood	.75	2.00
5 Steve Spurrier	5.00	12.00
6 David Little	.50	1.25
7 Bruce Bennett	.40	1.00
8 Charlie LaPradd	.40	1.00
9 John L. Williams	.75	2.00
10 Steve Tannen	.40	1.00
11 Neal Anderson	.75	2.00
12 Larry Dupree	.40	1.00
13 Guy Dennis	.40	1.00
14 Jarvis Williams	.40	1.00
15 Bill Carr	.40	1.00
16 Clifford Charlton	.40	1.00
17 Wes Chandler	.60	1.50
18 David Galloway	.40	1.00
19 Carlos Alvarez	.40	1.00
20 Lomas Brown	.60	1.50
21 Larry Smith	.40	1.00
22 Ricky Nattiel	.50	1.25

1989 Florida Smokey

This 16-card standard size set was issued with the cooperation of the USDA Forest Service, the Florida Division of Forestry, and the BDA and features members of the 1989 Florida Gators. The cards feature the words "Florida Gators 1989" on top of an action photo and a biography of the player and a fire prevention cartoon on the back. We have checklisted this set in alphabetical order and put the uniform number next to the player's name. Sets are sometimes found with only 15 cards, missing the Galen Hall card, which was apparently withdrawn after his termination as coach of the Gators. The key card in this set is Emmitt Smith.

COMPLETE SET (16)	60.00	110.00
1 Chris Bromley 52	.40	1.00
2 Richard Fain 28	.60	1.50
3 John David Francis 7	.40	1.00
4 Galen Hall CO SP	5.00	8.00
5 Tony Lomack 20	.40	1.00
6 Willie McClendon 5	.40	1.00
7 Pat Moorer 45	.40	1.00
8 Kyle Morris 1	.40	1.00
9 Huey Richardson 90	.60	1.50
10 Stacey Simmons 25	.40	1.00
11 Emmitt Smith 22	60.00	100.00
12 Richard Starowesky 75	.40	1.00
13 Kerry Watkins 4	.40	1.00
14 Albert (Mascot)	.40	1.00

15 Cheerleaders	.60	1.50
16 Gator Helmet	.40	1.00

1990 Florida Smokey

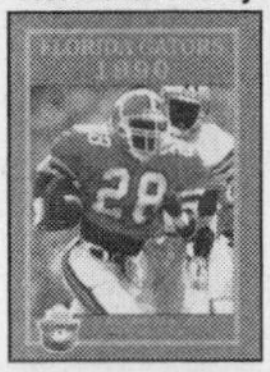

This 12-card standard-size set was sponsored by the USDA Forest Service in conjunction with several other federal agencies. The cards have color action shots, with orange lettering and borders on a purple card face. The back has two Florida helmet icons at the top and features a player profile and a fire prevention cartoon starring Smokey. The cards are unnumbered and checklisted below in alphabetical order, with the uniform number after the name.

COMPLETE SET (12)	6.00	15.00
1 Terence Barber 3	.40	1.00
2 Chris Bromley 52	.40	1.00
3 Richard Fain 28	.40	1.00
4 Willie McClendon 5	.50	1.25
5 Dexter McNabb 21	.50	1.25
6 Ernie Mills 14	1.00	2.50
7 Mark Murray 54	.40	1.00
8 Jerry Odom 57	.40	1.00
9 Huey Richardson 90	.50	1.25
10 Steve Spurrier CO	2.40	6.00
11 Albert and Alberta (Mascots)	.40	1.00
12 Mr. Two-Bits (Fan)	.40	1.00

1991 Florida Smokey

This 12-card standard-size set was sponsored by the USDA Forest Service and other agencies. The cards are printed on thin cardboard stock. The card fronts are accented in the team's colors (blue and red-orange) and have glossy color action player photos. The top of the pictures is curved to resemble an archway, and the team name follows the curve of the arch. The player's name and position appear in a stripe below the picture. The backs present a player profile and a fire prevention cartoon starring Smokey the Bear. The cards are unnumbered and checklisted below in alphabetical order.

COMPLETE SET (12)	6.00	15.00
1 Ephesians Bartley	.50	1.25
2 Michael Brandon	.40	1.00
3 Brad Culpepper	.60	1.50
4 Arden Czyzewski	.40	1.00
5 Cal Dixon	.50	1.25
6 Tre Everett	.40	1.00
7 Hesham Ismail	.40	1.00
8 Shane Matthews	.60	1.50
9 Steve Spurrier CO	3.20	8.00
10 Mark White	.40	1.00
11 Will White	.40	1.00
12 Albert and Alberta (Mascots)	.40	1.00

1994 Florida Team Issue

These photos were issued by the school to promote the football program. Each measures roughly 8" by 10" and features two black and white images (one portrait and one action) of the player with the school name and player's name printed below the portrait. The backs are blank.

COMPLETE SET (11)	25.00	50.00
1 Kevin Carter	4.00	8.00
2 Dexter Daniels	3.00	6.00
3 Judd Davis	3.00	6.00
4 Terry Dean	3.00	6.00
5 Shayne Edge	3.00	6.00
6 Reggie Green	3.00	6.00
7 Jack Jackson	3.00	6.00
8 Ellis Johnson	3.00	6.00
9 Larry Kennedy	3.00	6.00
10 Jason Odom	3.00	6.00
11 Danny Wuerffel	5.00	10.00

2006 Florida All-Americans

This set was produced by Baseline Sports Media and issued by the University of Florida. Each features all-time great Florida football All-Americans and was issued in factory set form.

COMPLETE SET (57)	7.50	15.00
1 Carlos Alvarez	.08	.25
2 Reidel Anthony	.30	.75
3 Trace Armstrong	.15	.40
4 John Barrow	.08	.25
5 Bruce Bennett	.08	.25
6 Alex Brown	.08	.25
7 Lomas Brown	.08	.25
8 Bill Carr	.08	.25
9 Kevin Carter	.15	.40
10 Charley Casey	.08	.25
11 Wes Chandler	.30	.75
12 Clifford Charlton	.08	.25
13 Cris Collinsworth	.40	1.00
14 Brad Culpepper	.08	.25
15 Judd Davis	.08	.25
16 Guy Dennis	.08	.25
17 Larry DuPree	.08	.25
18 Forrest Ferguson	.08	.25
19 Jabar Gaffney	.15	.40
20 Larry Gagner	.08	.25
21 David Galloway	.08	.25
22 Sammy Green	.08	.25
23 Jacquez Green	.30	.75
24 Rex Grossman	.50	1.25
25 Vel Heckman	.08	.25
26 Ike Hilliard	.30	.75
27 Jack Jackson	.15	.40
28 Alonzo Johnson	.08	.25
29 Jevon Kearse	.40	1.00
30 Charlie LaPrado	.08	.25
31 Burton Lawless	.08	.25
32 David Little	.08	.25
33 Wilber Marshall	.15	.40
34 Lynn Matthews	.08	.25
35 Jason Odom	.08	.25
36 Louis Oliver	.08	.25
37 Ralph Ortega	.08	.25
38 Mike Pearson	.08	.25
39 Mike Peterson	.08	.25
40 Kelwan Ratliff	.08	.25
41 John Reaves	.15	.40
42 Errict Rhett	.30	.75
43 Huey Richardson	.08	.25
44 Lito Sheppard	.30	.75
45 Dale Van Sickle	.08	.25
46 Emmitt Smith	1.25	3.00
47 Larry Smith	.08	.25
48 Shannon Snell	.08	.25
49 Steve Spurrier	.60	1.50
50 Steve Tannen	.08	.25
51 Fred Taylor	.50	1.25
52 Fred Weary	.15	.40
53 Will White	.08	.25
54 Jarvis Williams	.08	.25
55 Danny Wuerffel	.40	1.00
56 Jack Youngblood	.30	.75
57 Jeff Zimmerman	.15	.40

2006 Florida Schedules

COMPLETE SET (4)	1.00	2.50
1 Billy Latsko	.20	.50
2 Chris Leak	.40	1.00
3 Brandon Siler	.20	.50
4 Marcus Thomas	.20	.50

1990-91 Florida State Collegiate Collection

This 200-card standard-size set by Collegiate Collection features past and current athletes of Florida State University from a variety of sports.

COMPLETE SET (200)	6.00	15.00
3 Randy White	.05	.15
4 Steve Gabbard	.05	.15
5 Pat Tomberlin	.05	.15
6 Herb Gainer	.05	.15
7 Bobby Jackson	.05	.15
8 Redus Coggin	.05	.15
9 Pat Carter	.07	.20
10 Kevin Grant	.05	.15
11 Peter Tom Willis	.10	.25
12 Phil Carollo	.05	.15
13 Derek Schmidt	.05	.15
14 Rick Stockstill	.05	.15
16 Terry Anthony	.05	.15
17 Darrin Holloman	.05	.15
18 John McLean	.05	.15
19 Rudy Maloy	.05	.15
20 Gary Huff	.07	.20
22 Isaac Williams	.05	.15
23 Weegie Thompson	.07	.20
25 Gerald Nichols	.05	.15
26 John Brown	.05	.15
27 Danny McManus	.07	.20
28 Parrish Barwick	.05	.15
29 Paul McGowan	.05	.15
30 Keith Jones	.05	.15
31 Alphonso Williams	.05	.15
33 Tony Yeomans	.05	.15
34 Michael Tanks	.05	.15
35 Stan Shiver	.05	.15
36 Willie Jones	.05	.15
37 Wally Woodham	.05	.15
38 Chip Ferguson	.05	.15
39 Sam Childers	.05	.15
40 Paul Piurowski	.05	.15
41 Joey Ionata	.05	.15
42 John Hadley	.05	.15
43 Tanner Holloman	.05	.15
44 Fred Jones	.05	.15
45 Terry Warren	.05	.15
46 John Merna	.05	.15
47 Jimmy Jordan	.05	.15
48 Dave Capellen	.05	.15
49 Martin Mayhew	.07	.20
50 Barry Barco	.05	.15
51 Ronald Lewis	.05	.15
52 Tom O'Malley	.05	.15
53 Rick Tuten	.05	.15
56 Bobby Bowden	.20	.50
57 Bobby Bowden	.20	.50
58 Bobby Bowden	.20	.50
59 Bobby Bowden	.20	.50
60 Bobby Bowden	.20	.50
62 Joe Wessel	.05	.15
63 Alphonso Carreker	.07	.20
64 Shelton Thompson	.05	.15
65 Tracy Sanders	.05	.15
66 Bobby Bowden	.20	.50
67 Bobby Bowden	.20	.50
68 Bobby Bowden	.20	.50
69 Bobby Bowden, Jimmy Jordan, Wally Woodham	.20	.50
70 Bobby Bowden	.20	.50
71 David Palmer	.05	.15
72 Jason Kuipers	.05	.15
73 Dayne Williams	.05	.15
74 Mark Salva	.05	.15
75 Bobby Butler	.05	.15
76 Bobby Bowden	.20	.50
77 Bobby Bowden	.20	.50
78 Bobby Bowden	.20	.50
79 Bobby Bowden	.20	.50
80 Bobby Bowden	.20	.50
82 Dexter Carter	.10	.25
83 Dedrick Dodge	.05	.15
84 Greg Allen	.05	.15
86 Bobby Bowden	.20	.50
87 Bobby Bowden	.20	.50
88 Bobby Bowden	.20	.50
89 Bobby Bowden	.20	.50
90 Bobby Bowden	.20	.50
91 Bill Capece	.05	.15
92 Eric Hayes	.05	.15
93 Garth Jax	.07	.20
94 Odell Haggins	.05	.15
95 Leroy Butler	.10	.25
96 Monk Bonasorte	.05	.15
101 Doc Hermann	.05	.15
102 Gary Futch	.05	.15
103 Tony Romeo	.05	.15
104 Lee Corso	.15	.40
105 Steve Bratton	.05	.15
106 Barry Rice	.05	.15
108 John Wachtel	.05	.15
110 Vic Szezepanik	.05	.15
112 Jack Fenwick	.05	.15
114 Mark Meseroll	.05	.15
115 Jimmy Everett	.05	.15
117 Les Murdock	.05	.15
118 Ron Schomburger	.05	.15
119 Scott Warren	.05	.15
120 Eric Williams	.05	.15
121 Buddy Strauss	.05	.15
125 Bill Cappleman	.05	.15
126 Bill Kimber	.05	.15
128 Bill Proctor	.05	.15
129 Kurt Unglaub	.05	.15
132 Lee Nelson	.05	.15
133 Robert Urich	.20	.50
135 Randy Coffield	.05	.15
136 Jimmy Lee Taylor	.05	.15
137 Max Wettstein	.05	.15
138 Brian Williams	.05	.15
139 T.K. Wetherell	.05	.15
140 Dale McCullers	.05	.15
141 Peter Tom Willis	.10	.25
143 J.T. Thomas	.07	.20
144 Hassan Jones	.07	.20
145 Deion Sanders	.75	2.00
146 Barry Smith	.05	.15
148 Bill Moremen	.05	.15
149 Gary Henry	.05	.15
150 John Madden	.50	1.25
151 J.T. Thomas	.07	.20
153 Keith Kinderman	.05	.15
154 Bill Dawson	.05	.15
155 Mike Good	.05	.15
156 Kim Hammond	.05	.15
157 Buddy Blankenship	.05	.15
158 Jimmy Black	.05	.15
159 Vic Prinzi	.05	.15
160 Bobby Renn	.05	.15
161 Mark Macek	.05	.15
162 Wayne McDuffie	.05	.15
163 Joe Avezzano	.10	.25
164 Hector Gray	.05	.15
165 Grant Guthrie	.05	.15
166 Tom Bailey	.05	.15
167 Ron Sellers	.05	.15
168 Dick Hermann	.05	.15
169 Bob Harbison	.05	.15
170 Winfred Bailey	.05	.15
171 James Harris	.05	.15
172 Jerry Jacobs	.05	.15
173 Mike Kincaid	.05	.15
174 Jimmy Heggins	.05	.15
175 Steve Kalenich	.05	.15
176 Del Williams	.05	.15
177 Fred Pickard	.05	.15
178 Walt Sumner	.05	.15
179 Bud Whitehead	.05	.15
180 Bobby Anderson	.05	.15
182 Burt Reynolds	.30	.75
186 Richard Amman	.05	.15
187 Bobby Crenshaw	.05	.15
188 Bill Dawkins	.05	.15
189 Ken Burnett	.05	.15
190 Duane Carrell	.05	.15
191 Gene McDowell	.05	.15
193 Beryl Rice	.05	.15
195 Brian Schmidt	.05	.15
196 Rhett Dawson	.05	.15
197 Greg Futch	.05	.15
198 Joe Majors	.05	.15
199 Stan Dobosz	.05	.15

1992-93 Florida State

COMPLETE SET (80)	15.00	30.00
44 Bobby Bowden CO FB	2.00	5.00
45 Clifton Abraham FB	.07	.20
46 Ken Alexander FB	.07	.20
47 Robbie Baker FB	.07	.20
48 Shannon Baker FB	.20	.50
49 Derrick Brooks FB	1.50	4.00
50 Lavon Brown FB	.07	.20
51 Deondri Clark FB	.07	.20
52 Richard Coes FB	.07	.20
53 Chris Cowart FB	.07	.20
54 John Davis FB	.07	.20
55 Marvin Ferrell FB	.07	.20
56 William Floyd FB	1.25	3.00
57 Dan Footman FB	.20	.50
58 Leon Fowler FB	.07	.20
59 Reggie Freeman FB	.07	.20
60 Matt Frier FB	.07	.20
61 Corey Fuller FB	.07	.20
62 Felix Harris FB	.07	.20
63 Tommy Henry FB	.07	.20
64 Lonnie Johnson FB	.20	.50
65 Marvin Jones FB	.80	2.00
66 Toddrick McIntosh FB	.20	.50
67 Tiger McMillon FB	.07	.20
68 Patrick McNeil FB	.07	.20
69 Sterling Palmer FB	.20	.50
70 Troy Sanders FB	.07	.20
71 Corey Sawyer FB	.40	1.00
72 Carl Simpson FB	.20	.50
73 Robert Stevenson FB	.07	.20
74 Charlie Ward FB	3.20	8.00
75 Seminole Coaches FB	.20	.50

1993 Florida State

These six football "credit" cards each contained 10.00 of food and merchandise value at FSU concession stands specially equipped with scanners to read the value in the cards. The cards were sold for 15.00 each exclusively through the Florida State Athletic Department and could be purchased individually or as a six-card set. Charlie Ward was the first card issued (for the Seminoles' home opener against Clemson) with an additional card issued at each successive home game. Reportedly only 12,000 sets were produced. The cards were manufactured by CollectorCard of America in Minneapolis. The cards have rounded corners and measure 2 1/8" by 3 3/8". The fronts feature borderless color player cutouts superposed upon a background of sky and clouds. The player's name and position appear within a light blue rectangle at the bottom. The horizontal back has a borderless ghosted color photo of an FSU campus building as the background. At the top are shown the FSU opponent and date for the game at which the card was first available. The player's name, position, height, weight, class, hometown, and 1992 season highlights appear on the left side; his career statistics appear on the right. The black scanning stripe appears across the back near the bottom. The cards are unnumbered and checklisted below in alphabetical order.

COMPLETE SET (6)	34.00	85.00
1 Bobby Bowden CO	8.00	20.00
2 Derrick Brooks	4.80	12.00
3 Corey Sawyer	4.00	10.00
4 Tamarick Vanover	6.00	15.00
5 Charlie Ward	6.00	15.00
6 Chief Osceola (Mascot)	2.40	6.00

1996 Florida State

The 1996 Florida State set was produced by Host Communications and handed out in conjunction with program sales made at the various Florida State home games during the 1996 football season. The cards were issued as a complete sheet of 12 cards, which was attached to a cover entitled the "1996 Florida State Football Photo Album". The inside of the "album" had action and practice photos of the Florida State team, while the cover had a defensive action shot with an inset photo of Bobby Bowden. The perforated color front cards measure approximately 3 1/8" by 2 1/2", with the sheet measuring approximately 12 1/2" by 7 1/2". The cards have the players name across the bottom of the card in a red border, while the left side of the card has Florida State in a orange hue with "football" scripted in white over the school name. The backs of the cards are white with black printing and contain the Host Communications logo in the upper right hand corner.The 12 card set is comprised of seniors from the Florida State team, including notable players such as Andre Cooper, Warrick Dunn, Wayne Messam, Connell Spain and Reynard Wilson. The only dual player card in this set features offensive linemen Chad Bates and Todd Fordham. Since the cards are only numbered by jersey number on the back, they are checklisted in alphabetical order below.

COMPLETE SET (12)	6.00	15.00
1 Chad Bates, Todd Fordham	.20	.50
2 Scott Bentley	.20	.50
3 Byron Capers	.20	.50
4 James Colzie	.20	.50
5 Andre Cooper	.60	1.50
6 Henri Crockett	.20	.50
7 Warrick Dunn	6.00	12.00
8 Sean Hamlet	.20	.50
9 Sean Liss	.20	.50
10 Wayne Messam	.30	.75
11 Connell Spain	.30	.75
12 Reinard Wilson	1.25	2.50

1997 Florida State AMA

This 20-card standard-sized set was issued in 1997 by American Marketing Associates to commemorate the '96 Florida State football team. The cards were printed on thick plastic stock with a full bleed photo and facsimile signature on the front with the player's name on the left side of the card. The unnumbered cards are listed below in alphabetical order.

COMPLETE SET (20)	10.00	25.00
1 Chad Bates	.25	.60
2 Harold Battles	.25	.60
3 Scott Bentley	.25	.60
4 Peter Boulware	2.40	6.00
5 Byron Capers	.25	.60
6 Kamari Charlton	.25	.60
7 James Colzie	.25	.60
8 Andre Cooper	.40	1.00
9 Vernon Crawford	.25	.60
10 Henri Crockett	.25	.60
11 Warrick Dunn	6.00	15.00
12 Todd Fordham	.25	.60
13 Sean Hamlet	.25	.60
14 Sean Liss	.25	.60
15 Marcus Long	.25	.60
16 Wayne Messam	.25	.60
17 Kevin Prophete	.25	.60
18 Connell Spain	.25	.60
19 Reinard Wilson	.40	1.00
20 FSU Logo CL	.25	.60

1997 Florida State Host

The 1997 Florida State set was produced by Host Communications and handed out in conjunction with program sales made at the various Florida State home games during the 1997 football season. The cards were issued as a complete sheet of 12 cards, which was attached to a cover entitled the "1997 Florida State Football Photo Album". The inside of the "album" had a space in which to get Florida State signatures, while the cover had a defensive action shot with Sam Cowart sacking Danny Wuerffel. The perforated color front cards measure approximately 3 1/8" by 2 1/2", with the sheet measuring approximately 12 1/2" by 7 1/2". The cards have the players name across the bottom of the card (and sides on the horizontal ones) in a red border, while the left side of the card has Florida State in a orange hue with "football" scripted in white over the school name. The backs of the cards are white with black printing and contain a Universal Sports America logo in the upper right hand corner.The 12 card set is comprised of seniors from the Florida State team, including Thad Busby, Sam Cowart, E. G. Green, Tra Thomas, and Andre Wadsworth. Since the cards are only numbered by jersey number on the back, they are checklisted in alphabetical order below.

COMPLETE SET (12)	4.80	12.00
1 Daryl Bush	.30	.75
2 Thad Busby	.30	.75
3 Sam Cowart	.60	1.50
4 E.G. Green	1.20	3.00
5 Robert Hammond	.20	.50
6 Kevin Long	.20	.50
7 Melvin Pearsall	.20	.50
8 Samari Rolle	.60	1.50
9 Shevin Smith	.20	.50
10 Greg Spires	.20	.50
11 Tra Thomas	.80	2.00
12 Andre Wadsworth	2.40	6.00

1998 Florida State

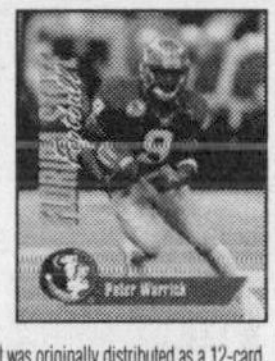

This set was originally distributed as a 12-card perforated uncut sheet. Each card includes a color player photo on the cardfront with a black-and-white printed cardback. The cards measure roughly 2 1/2" by 3 1/8" and are listed alphabetically below.

COMPLETE SET (12)	10.00	20.00
1 Tony Bryant	.40	1.00
2 Dee Feaster	.40	1.00
3 Lamarr Glenn	.40	1.00
4 Lamont Green	.40	1.00
5 Deon Humphrey	.40	1.00
6 Dexter Jackson	.75	2.00
7 Myron Jackson	.40	1.00
8 Billy Rhodes	.40	1.00
9 Troy Saunders	.40	1.00
10 Demetro Stephens	.40	1.00
11 Peter Warrick	2.00	5.00
12 Chris Weinke	1.50	4.00

1999 Florida State

This set was originally distributed as a 12-card perforated uncut sheet. Each card includes a color player photo on the cardfront with a black-and-white printed cardback. A small Poster-sized cover was included attached to the sheet of cards. Each card is unnumbered, measuring roughly 2 1/2" by 3 1/8," and listed alphabetically below.

COMPLETE SET (12)	10.00	20.00
1 Lavernues Coles	1.50	4.00
2 Ron Dugans	.40	1.00
3 Mario Edwards	.40	1.00
4 Sebastian Janikowski	.60	1.50
5 Jerry Johnson	.30	.75
6 Dan Kendra	.30	.75
7 Travis Minor	1.00	2.50
8 Bobby Rhodes	.30	.75
9 Corey Simon	.60	1.50
10 Peter Warrick	1.50	4.00
11 Chris Weinke	1.50	4.00
12 Jason Whitaker	.30	.75
NNO FSU Cover Poster, Peter Warrick, Chris Weinke, Bobby Bowden CO, Jerry Johnson	.40	1.00

2000 Florida State

This set was originally distributed as a 12-card perforated uncut sheet. Each card includes a color player photo on the cardfront, that includes the year of issue, with a black-and-white printed cardback. The cards measure roughly 2 1/2" by 3 1/8" and are listed alphabetically below.

COMPLETE SET (12)	6.00	12.00
1 Brian Allen	.50	1.25
2 Justin Amman	.40	1.00
3 Tay Cody	.50	1.25
4 Derrick Gibson	.40	1.00
5 Travis Minor	.60	1.50
6 Jarad Moon	.40	1.00
7 Marcus Outzen	.40	1.00
8 Tommy Polley	.50	1.25
9 Jamal Reynolds	.40	1.00
10 Clevan Thomas	.40	1.00
11 Tarlos Thomas	.40	1.00
12 Chris Weinke	1.25	3.00

2001 Florida State

This set was originally distributed as a 12-card perforated uncut sheet. Each card includes a color player photo on the cardfron with a black-and-white printed cardback. The cards measure roughly 2 1/2" by 3 1/8" and are listed alphabetically below.

COMPLETE SET (12)	6.00	12.00
1 Atrews Bell	.40	1.00
2 Ronald Boldin	.50	1.25
3 Carver Donaldson	.40	1.00
4 Otis Duhart	.40	1.00
5 Davy Ford	.40	1.00
6 Chris Hope	.50	1.25
7 Abdual Howard	.40	1.00
8 Bradley Jennings	.40	1.00
9 William McCray	.40	1.00
10 Robert Morgan	.40	1.00
11 Javon Walker	1.50	4.00
12 Brett Williams	.40	1.00

1986 Fort Hayes State

This set features 27 standard-size cards. The card fronts feature a player head shot with the team name arcing above. The player's name and position appear below the picture. The back features the player's name, position, and biography at the top with the player's statistics and profile below. The cards are unnumbered and checklisted below in alphabetical order.

COMPLETE SET (27)	12.00	30.00
1 Kelly Barnard	.50	1.25
2 James Bess	.50	1.25
3 Eric Busenbark	.50	1.25
4 Sylvester Butler	.50	1.25
5 Channing Day	.50	1.25
6 Edward Faagai	.50	1.25
7 Randy Fayette	.50	1.25
8 Gerald Hall	.50	1.25
9 Mike Hipp	.50	1.25
10 Sam Holloway	.50	1.25
11 Howard Hood	.50	1.25
12 James Jermon	.50	1.25
13 Randy Jordan	.50	1.25
14 John Kelsh	.50	1.25
15 Randy Knox	.50	1.25
16 Robert Long	.50	1.25
17 Les Miller	.50	1.25
18 Frankie Neal	.50	1.25
19 Paul Nelson	.50	1.25
20 Darryl Pittman	.50	1.25
21 Mike Shoff	.50	1.25
22 Kip Stewart	.50	1.25
23 Rod Timmons	.50	1.25
24 Rob Ukleya	.50	1.25
25 John Vincent CO	.50	1.25
26 Rick Wheeler	.50	1.25
27 Mike Worth	.50	1.25

1987 Fresno State Burger King

This 16-card, standard-size set features past and then-current football players at Fresno State University. The cards are unnumbered and hence are listed below in uniform number order. The set was produced by Sports Marketing Inc. and sponsored by Burger King. The set is also considered to be a police/safety set due to the "Tip from the Bulldogs" on each card back.

COMPLETE SET (16)	10.00	25.00
1 Gene Taylor	.60	1.50
5 Michael Stewart	.75	2.00
9 Kevin Sweeney	.75	2.00
12 Eric Buechele	.60	1.50
19 Rod Webster	.60	1.50
26 Kelly Skipper	.60	1.50
27 Barry Belli	.60	1.50
32 Kelly Brooks	.60	1.50
45 David Grayson	.75	2.00
67 Jethro Franklin	.60	1.50
71 Jeff Truschel	.60	1.50
80 John O'Leary	.60	1.50
81 Stephen Baker	1.25	3.00
83 Henry Ellard	2.50	6.00
86 Stephone Paige	1.25	3.00
NNO Jim Sweeney CO	1.25	3.00

1989 Fresno State Smokey

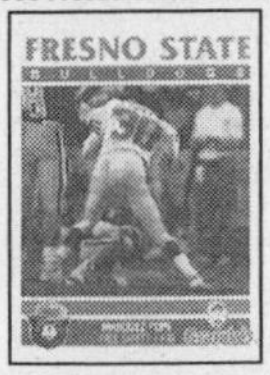

This unnumbered 16-card set measures the standard size. The set was sponsored by the USDA Forest Service and issued with the cooperation of Grandy's restaurants. The fronts feature a color player photo bounded on top and bottom by red and blue-colored strips. At the bottom the player's name, position, and jersey number are sandwiched between the Smokey the Bear picture and Grandy's logo. The back has biographical information and a public service announcement (with cartoon) concerning fire prevention along with the year of issued - - 1989.

COMPLETE SET (16)	8.00	20.00
1 Mark Barsotti	.75	2.00
2 Rich Bartlewski	.50	1.25
3 Ron Cox	1.00	2.50
4 Myron Jones	.50	1.25
5 Steve Loop	.50	1.25
6 Fil Lujan	.50	1.25
7 Darrel Martin	.50	1.25
8 Lance Oberparleiter	.50	1.25
9 Dwight Pickens	.50	1.25
10 Marquez Pope	1.25	3.00
11 Nick Ruggeroli	.50	1.25
12 Jim Sweeney CO	.75	2.00
13 Jeff Thiesen	.50	1.25
14 Paul Vial	.50	1.25
15 James Williams	.75	2.00
16 Bulldog Stadium	.50	1.25

1990 Fresno State Smokey

This unnumbered, 16-card set measures the standard size. The set was sponsored by the USDA Forest Service and issued with the cooperation of Grandy's and the BDA. The front features an action color photo, bounded on top and bottom by red and purple strips. At the bottom the player's name, position, and jersey number are sandwiched between the Smokey the Bear picture and Grandy's logo. The back has biographical information and a public service announcement (with cartoon) concerning fire prevention. Future NFL players included in this set are Ron Cox, Aaron Craver, Marquez Pope, and James Williams.

COMPLETE SET (16)	6.00	15.00
1 Mark Barsotti	.50	1.25
2 Ron Cox	.80	2.00
3 Aaron Craver	.80	2.00
4 DeVonne Edwards	.40	1.00
5 Courtney Griffin	.40	1.00
6 Jesse Hardwick	.40	1.00
7 Melvin Johnson	.40	1.00
8 Brian Lasho	.40	1.00
9 Kelvin Means	.40	1.00
10 Marquez Pope	1.00	2.50
11 Zack Rix	.40	1.00
12 Nick Ruggeroli	.40	1.00
13 Jim Sweeney CO	.60	1.50
14 Erick Ianuvasa	.40	1.00
15 Jeff Thiesen	.40	1.00
16 James Williams	.40	1.00

1981 Georgia Team Sheets

The University of Georgia issued these sheets of black-and-white player photos. Each measures 7 7/8" by 10" and was printed on glossy stock with white borders. Each sheet includes photos of either 10-players or 4-players. Below each player's image is his name and position. These photos also feature the year, Georgia notaion, and sheet number at the top. They are blankbacked.

COMPLETE SET (15)	75.00	125.00
1 Buck Belue, Freddie Gilbert, Joe Happe, Steve Kelly, Jimmy Payne, Lindsay Scott, Ronnie Stewart, Nate Taylor, Herschel Walker, Eddie Weaver	10.00	20.00
2 Matt Arthur, Jim Blakewood, Tim Bobo, Jim Broadway, James Brown, Norris Brown, Lon Buckler, Kevin Butler, Scott Campbell, Gary Cantrell	5.00	10.00
3 Dale Carver, Tim Case, Joe Creamons, Tim Crowe, Roy Curtis, Charlie Dean, Stan Dooley, Landy Ewings, Will Forts, Warren Gray	4.00	8.00
4 Keith Hall, Jimmy Harper, Ronnie Harris, Terry Hoage, Winford Hood, Kevin Jackson, Eric Jarvis, Chuck Jones, Daryll Jones, Mike Jones	4.00	8.00
5 Charles Junior, Clarence Kay, John Lastinger	5.00	10.00

Mel Lattany		
Tommy Lewis		
Dan Leusenring		
Jack Lindsey		
Jay McAlister		
Chris McCarthy		
Guy McIntyre		
6 Mark McKay	4.00	8.00
Todd Milton		
Carnie Norris		
David Painter		
Jeff Paulk		
Wayne Radloff		
Antonio Render		
Tim Reynolds		
Melvin Simmons		
Matt Simon		
7 Richard Singleton	4.00	8.00
Charles Smith		
Guy Stargell		
Jon Tedder		
Tommy Thurson		
Denis Waitley		
Mike Weaver		
Dale Williams		
Scott Williams		
Barry Young		
8 Buck Belue	10.00	20.00
Herschel Walker		
Jimmy Payne		
Eddie Weaver		
9 Jim Blakewood	5.00	10.00
Jim Broadway		
Norris Brown		
Kevin Butler		
10 Dale Carver	4.00	8.00
Tim Crowe		
Freddie Gilbert		
Joe Happe		
11 Jimmy Harper	4.00	8.00
Ronnie Harris		
Terry Hoage		
Winford Hood		
12 Chuck Jones	4.00	8.00
Charles Junior		
Clarence Kay		
Steve Kelly		
13 John Lastinger	4.00	8.00
Mel Lattany		
Carnie Norris		
Jeff Paulk		
14 Wayne Radloff	4.00	8.00
Lindsay Scott		
Ronnie Stewart		
Nate Taylor		
15 Tommy Thurson	4.00	8.00
Denis Waitley		
Dale Williams		
Barry Young		

1988 Georgia McDag

This 16-card set features then-current football players at the University of Georgia. The cards measure approximately 2 1/2" by 3 1/2". The set was produced by McDag Productions. The set is also considered to be a police/safety set due to the "Tip from the Bulldogs" on each card back. The key cards in the set are Rodney Hampton and WCW champion wrestler Bill Goldberg.

COMPLETE SET (16)	30.00	50.00
1 UGA IV (Mascot)	.40	1.00
2 Vince Dooley AD CO	1.25	3.00
3 Steve Crumley	.40	1.00
4 Aaron Chubb	.40	1.00
5 Keith Henderson	.60	1.50
6 Steve Harmon	.40	1.00
7 Terrie Webster	.40	1.00
8 John Kasay	1.25	3.00
9 Wayne Johnson	.40	1.00
10 Tim Worley	.60	1.50
11 Wycliffe Lovelace	.40	1.00
12 Brent Collins	.40	1.00
13 Vince Guthrie	.40	1.00
14 Todd Wheeler	.40	1.00
15 Bill Goldberg	25.00	40.00
16 Rodney Hampton	3.00	8.00

1989 Georgia 200

The 1989 University of Georgia football set contains 200 standard-size cards, depicting former Bulldog greats. The fronts contain vintage photos; the horizontally oriented backs feature player profiles. Both sides have red borders. The cards were distributed in sets and in poly packs. These cards were printed on very thin stock. This set is notable for its inclusion of several Herschel Walker cards.

COMPLETE SET (200)	7.50	20.00
1 Vince Dooley AD	.07	.20
2 Ivy M. Shiver	.02	.10
3 Vince Dooley CO	.07	.20
4 Vince Dooley CO	.07	.20
5 Ray Goff CO	.07	.20
6 Ray Goff CO	.07	.20
7 Wally Butts CO	.07	.20
8 Wally Butts CO	.07	.20
9 Herschel Walker	.30	.75
10 Frank Sinkwich	.15	.40
11 Bob McWhorter	.02	.10
12 Joe Bennett	.02	.10
13 Dan Edwards	.02	.10
14 Tom A. Nash	.02	.10
15 Herb Maffett	.02	.10
16 Ralph Maddox	.02	.10
17 Vernon Smith	.02	.10
18 Bill Hartman Jr.	.02	.10
19 Frank Sinkwich	.07	.20
20 Joe O'Malley	.02	.10
21 Mike Castronis	.02	.10
22 Aschel M. Day	.02	.10
23 Herb St. John	.02	.10
24 Craig Hertwig	.02	.10
25 John Rauch	.07	.20
26 Harry Babcock	.02	.10
27 Bruce Kemp	.02	.10
28 Pat Dye	.07	.20
29 Fran Tarkenton	.75	2.00
30 Larry Kohn	.02	.10
31 Ray Rissmiller	.02	.10
32 George Patton	.07	.20
33 Mixon Robinson	.02	.10
34 Lynn Hughes	.02	.10
35 Bill Stanfill	.07	.20
36 Robert Dicks	.02	.10
37 Lynn Hunnicutt	.02	.10
38 Tommy Lyons	.02	.10
39 Royce Smith	.02	.10
40 Steve Greer	.02	.10
41 Randy Johnson	.15	.40
42 Mike Wilson	.02	.10
43 Joel Parrish	.02	.10
44 Ben Zambiasi	.07	.20
45 Allan Leavitt	.02	.10
46 George Collins	.02	.10
47 Rex Robinson	.02	.10
48 Scott Woerner	.02	.10
49 Herschel Walker	.30	.75
50 Bob Burns	.02	.10
51 Jimmy Payne	.02	.10
52 Fred Brown	.02	.10
53 Kevin Butler	.07	.20
54 Don Porterfield	.02	.10
55 Mac McWhorter	.02	.10
56 John Little	.02	.10
57 Marion Campbell	.15	.40
58 Zeke Bratkowski	.15	.40
59 Buck Belue	.07	.20
60 Duward Pennington	.02	.10
61 Lamar Davis	.02	.10
62 Steve Wilson	.02	.10
63 Leman L. Rosenberg	.02	.10
64 Dennis Hughes	.02	.10
65 Wayne Radloff	.02	.10
66 Lindsay Scott	.07	.20
67 Wayne Swinford	.02	.10
68 Kim Stephens	.02	.10
69 Willie McClendon	.07	.20
70 Ron Jenkins	.02	.10
71 Jeff Lewis	.02	.10
72 Larry Rakestraw	.02	.10
73 Spike Jones	.07	.20
74 Tom Nash Jr.	.02	.10
75 Vassa Cate	.02	.10
76 Theron Sapp	.07	.20
77 Claude Hipps	.07	.20
78 Charley Trippi	.15	.40
79 Mike Weaver	.02	.10
80 Anderson Johnson	.02	.10
81 Matt Robinson	.07	.20
82 Bill Krug	.02	.10
83 Todd Wheeler	.02	.10
84 Mack Guest	.02	.10
85 Frank Ros	.02	.10
86 Jeff Hipp	.02	.10
87 Milton Leathers	.02	.10
88 George Morton	.02	.10
89 Jim Broadway	.02	.10
90 Tim Morrison	.02	.10
91 Homer Key	.02	.10
92 Richard Tardits	.07	.20
93 Tommy Thurson	.02	.10
94 Bob Kelley	.02	.10
95 Bob McWhorter	.02	.10
96 Vernon Smith	.02	.10
97 Eddie Weaver	.02	.10
98 Bill Stanfill	.07	.20
99 Scott Williams	.02	.10
100 Checklist Card	.02	.10
101 Len Hauss	.07	.20
102 Jim Griffith	.02	.10
103 Nat Dye	.02	.10
104 Quinton Lumpkin	.02	.10
105 Mike Garrett	.02	.10
106 Glynn Harrison	.02	.10
107 Aaron Chubb	.02	.10
108 John Brantley	.02	.10
109 Pat Hodgson	.02	.10
110 Guy McIntyre	.15	.40
111 Keith Harris	.02	.10
112 Mike Cavan	.02	.10
113 Kevin Jackson	.02	.10
114 Jim Cagle	.02	.10
115 Charles Whittemore	.02	.10
116 Graham Batchelor	.02	.10
117 Art DeCarlo	.07	.20
118 Kendall Keith	.02	.10
119 Jeff Pyburn	.07	.20
120 James Ray	.02	.10
121 Mack Burroughs	.02	.10
122 Jimmy Vickers	.02	.10
123 Charley Britt	.02	.10
124 Matt Braswell	.02	.10
125 Jake Richardson	.02	.10
126 Ronnie Stewart	.02	.10
127 Tim Crowe	.02	.10
128 Troy Sadowski	.02	.10
129 Robert Honeycutt	.02	.10
130 Warren Gray	.02	.10
131 David Guthrie	.02	.10
132 John Lastinger	.07	.20
133 Chip Wisdom	.02	.10
134 Butch Box	.02	.10
135 Tony Cushenberry	.02	.10
136 Vince Guthrie	.02	.10
137 Floyd Reid Jr.	.07	.20
138 Mark Hodge	.02	.10
139 Joe Happe	.02	.10
140 Al Bodine	.02	.10
141 Gene Chandler	.02	.10
142 Tommy Lawhorne	.02	.10
143 Bobby Walden	.07	.20
144 Douglas McFalls	.02	.10
145 Jim Milo	.02	.10
146 Billy Payne	.30	.75
147 Paul Holmes	.02	.10
148 Bob Clemens	.02	.10
149 Kenny Sims	.02	.10
150 Reid Moseley Jr.	.02	.10
151 Tim Callaway	.02	.10
152 Rusty Russell	.02	.10
153 Jim McCollough	.02	.10
154 Wally Williamson	.02	.10
155 John Bond	.02	.10
156 Charley Trippi	.15	.40
157 The Play (Lindsay Scott)	.07	.20
158 Joe Boland	.02	.10
159 Michael Babb	.02	.10
160 Jimmy Poulos	.02	.10
161 Chris McCarthy	.02	.10
162 Billy Mixon	.02	.10
163 Dicky Clark	.02	.10
164 David Rholetter	.02	.10
165 Chuck Heard	.02	.10
166 Pat Field	.02	.10
167 Preston Ridlehuber	.02	.10
168 Heyward Allen	.02	.10
169 Kirby Moore	.02	.10
170 Chris Welton	.02	.10
171 Bill McKenny	.02	.10
172 Steve Boswell	.02	.10
173 Bob Towns	.02	.10
174 Anthony Towns	.02	.10
175 Porter Payne	.02	.10
176 Bobby Garrard	.02	.10
177 Jack Griffith	.02	.10
178 Herschel Walker	.30	.75
179 Andy Perhach	.02	.10
180 Dr. Charles Herty CO	.02	.10
181 Kent Lawrence	.07	.20
182 David McKnight	.02	.10
183 Joe Tereshinski Jr.	.02	.10
184 Cicero Lucas	.02	.10
185 Pop Warner CO	.07	.20
186 Tony Flack	.02	.10
187 Kevin Butler	.07	.20
188 Bill Mitchell	.02	.10
189 Poulos vs. Tech (Jimmy Poulos)	.02	.10
190 Pete Case	.07	.20
191 Pete Tinsley	.02	.10
192 Joe Tereshinski	.07	.20
193 Jimmy Harper	.02	.10
194 Don Leebern	.02	.10
195 Harry Mehre CO	.02	.10
196 Retired Jerseys (Herschel Walker Theron Sapp Charley Trippi Frank Sinkwich)	.15	.40
197 Terrie Webster	.02	.10
198 George Woodruff CO	.02	.10
199 First Georgia Team (1892 Team Photo)	.02	.10
200 Checklist Card	.02	.10
GA1 Herschel Walker Promo	.30	.75

1989 Georgia Police

This 16-card set was sponsored by Charter Winds Hospital. The cards were issued on an uncut sheet with four rows of four cards each; if cut, the cards would measure the standard size. The color action photos on the fronts are bordered in gray, and card face itself is red. The words "UGA Bulldogs '89" appear in white lettering above the picture. The backs have biography, career summary, and "Tips from the Bulldogs" in the form of anti-drug or alcohol messages. The cards are unnumbered and checklisted below in alphabetical order, with the uniform number after the name. Rodney Hampton and WCW championship wrestler Bill Goldberg are the key cards in this set.

COMPLETE SET (16)	25.00	50.00
1 Hiawatha Berry 58	.40	1.00
2 Brian Cleveland 37	.40	1.00
3 Demetrius Douglas 53	.40	1.00
4 Alphonso Ellis 33	.50	1.25
5 Ray Goff CO	.40	1.00
6 Bill Goldberg 95	20.00	35.00
7 Rodney Hampton 7	2.00	5.00
8 David Hargett 25	.40	1.00
9 Joey Hester 1	.40	1.00
10 John Kasay 3	.75	2.00
11 Mo Lewis 57	.75	2.00
12 Arthur Marshall 12	.60	1.50
13 Curt Mull 50	.40	1.00
14 Ben Smith 26	.40	1.00
15 Greg Talley 11	.40	1.00
16 Kirk Warner 83	.40	1.00

1990 Georgia Police

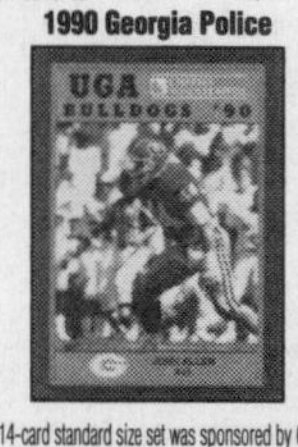

This 14-card standard size set was sponsored by Charter Winds Hospital and features the University of Georgia Bulldogs. The front design has red stripes above and below the color action player photo, with gray borders on a black card face. The back has biographical information, player profile, and "Tips from the Bulldogs" in the form of anti-drug and alcohol messages. The cards are unnumbered and checklisted below in alphabetical order, with the uniform number after the name.

COMPLETE SET (14)	4.00	10.00
1 John Allen 44	.30	.75
2 Brian Cleveland 37	.30	.75
3 Norman Cowins 59	.30	.75
4 Alphonso Ellis 33	.40	1.00
5 Ray Goff CO	.40	1.00
6 David Hargett 25	.30	.75
7 Sean Hunnings 6	.30	.75
8 Preston Jones 14	.40	1.00
9 John Kasay 3	.60	1.50
10 Arthur Marshall 12	.60	1.50
11 Jack Swan 76	.30	.75
12 Greg Talley 11	.30	.75
13 Lemonte Tellis 77	.30	.75
14 Chris Wilson 16	.30	.75

1991 Georgia Police

The 1991 Georgia Bulldog set was sponsored by Charter Winds Hospital, and its company logo appears on both sides of the cards. The cards measure the standard size and were issued on an unperforated sheet. Fronts feature a mix of glossy color action or posed player photos, with a gray border stripe on a red card face. The words "UGA Bulldogs '91" appear in a black stripe above the picture, while player identification is given in a black stripe below the picture. The backs have biography, career summary, and "Tips from the Bulldogs" in the form of anti-drug or alcohol messages. The cards are unnumbered and checklisted below in alphabetical order. The key card in the set is Garrison Hearst.

COMPLETE SET (16)	6.00	15.00
1 John Allen	.30	.75
2 Chuck Carswell	.30	.75
3 Russell DeFoor	.30	.75
4 Ray Goff CO	.40	1.00
5 David Hargett	.30	.75
6 Andre Hastings	1.20	3.00
7 Garrison Hearst	2.40	6.00
8 Arthur Marshall	.40	1.00
9 Kevin Maxwell	.30	.75
10 DeWayne Simmons	.30	.75
11 Jack Swan	.30	.75
12 Greg Talley	.30	.75
13 Lemonte Tellis	.30	.75
14 Chris Wilson	.30	.75
15 George Wynn	.30	.75
16 UGA V (Mascot)	.30	.75

1992 Georgia Police

This 15-card standard-size set was sponsored by Charter Winds Hospital and produced by BD and A cards. The fronts feature color action player photos against a black card face. The top of the picture is arched, and the year and words "Georgia Bulldogs" are printed in red above the arch. The player's name is printed in a gray stripe at the bottom. The backs are white with black print and contain career highlights and "Tips from the Bulldogs." Sponsor logos appear at the bottom. The set features Eric Zeier and Garrison Hearst on early college cards.

COMPLETE SET (15)	4.80	12.00
1 Mitch Davis	.25	.60
2 Damon Evans	.20	.50
3 Torrey Evans	.20	.50
4 Ray Goff CO	.25	.60
5 Andre Hastings	.80	2.00
6 Garrison Hearst	1.60	4.00
7 Donnie Maib	.20	.50
8 Alec Millen	.20	.50
9 Shannon Mitchell	.25	.60
10 Mack Strong	2.00	5.00
11 Jack Swan	.20	.50
12 UGA (Mascot)	.20	.50
13 Bernard Williams	.25	.60
14 Chris Wilson	.20	.50
15 Eric Zeier	1.20	3.00

1993 Georgia Police

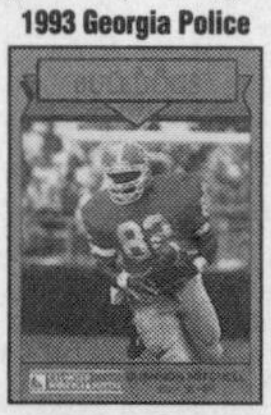

Originally issued in perforated sheets, this 16-card set was sponsored by Charter Winds Hospital and produced by BD and A cards. The cards measure the standard size. The fronts feature color action and posed player photos against a red card face. The year and words "Georgia Bulldogs" are printed in gray lettering above the photo. The player's name, jersey number, position, and class are printed in a gray stripe at the bottom. The plain white backs carry the player's name, position, jersey number, height, weight, and hometown at the top, followed below by career highlights and "Tips from the Bulldogs." The cards are unnumbered and checklisted below in alphabetical order. The set features an early card of Terrell Davis.

COMPLETE SET (16)	14.00	35.00
1 Scot Armstrong	.20	.50
2 Brian Bohannon	.20	.50
3 Carlo Butler	.20	.50
4 Charlie Clemons	1.50	3.00
5 Mitch Davis	.25	.60
6 Terrell Davis	12.00	30.00
7 Randall Godfrey	.80	2.00
8 Ray Goff CO	.25	.60
9 Frank Harvey	.20	.50
10 Travis Jones	.20	.50
11 Shannon Mitchell	.20	.50
12 Greg Tremble	.20	.50
13 Bernard Williams	.25	.60
14 Chad Wilson	.20	.50
15 Eric Zeier	1.20	3.00
16 UGA (Mascot)	.20	.50

2002 Georgia

This set was produced by baselinesportsmedia.com, sponsored by Kroger and Coca-Cola, and features members of the 2002 Georgia football team. Each card includes a color player image on the front with the team logo behind the image and the player's name to the right. The cardbacks are a simple black and white text-filled format with no card numbers.

COMPLETE SET (18)	6.00	12.00
1 Boss Bailey	.40	1.00
2 Billy Bennett	.20	.50
3 Kevin Breedlove	.20	.50
4 Terrence Edwards	.20	.50
5 George Foster	.20	.50
6 Damien Gary	.20	.50
7 Fred Gibson	.60	1.50
8 Antonio Gilbert	.20	.50
9 David Greene	.60	1.50
10 Alex Jackson	.20	.50
11 Jonathan Kilgo	.20	.50
12 David Pollack	.40	1.00
13 Mark Richt CO	.20	.50
14 Musa Smith	.40	1.00
15 Jon Stinchcomb	.30	.75
16 Johnathan Sullivan	.30	.75
17 Bruce Thornton	.30	.75
18 Ben Watson	.75	2.00

2003 Georgia

This set was produced by baselinesportsmedia.com, sponsored by Kroger and Coca-Cola, and features members of the 2003 Georgia football team. Each card includes a color player image on the front with the team name to the left of the photo and the player's name below. The cardbacks are a simple black and white text-filled format with no card numbers.

COMPLETE SET (18)	6.00	12.00
1 Billy Bennett	.20	.50
2 Reggie Brown	.60	1.50
3 Decory Bryant	.20	.50
4 Kentrell Curry	.20	.50
5 Damien Gary	.20	.50
6 Robert Geathers	.20	.50
7 Fred Gibson	.75	2.00
8 David Greene	.60	1.50
9 Michael Johnson	.20	.50
10 Sean Jones	.20	.50
11 Tony Milton	.30	.75
12 David Pollack	.40	1.00
13 Mark Richt CO	.20	.50
14 D.J. Shockley	.40	1.00
15 Will Thompson	.20	.50
16 Bruce Thornton	.30	.75
17 Ken Veal	.20	.50
18 Ben Watson	.75	2.00

2004 Georgia

This set was produced by baselinesportsmedia.com, sponsored by Kroger and Coca-Cola, and features members of the 2004 Georgia football team. Each card includes a color player image on the front with the team logo above the photo and the player's name to the left. The cardbacks are a simple black and white text-filled format with no card numbers.

COMPLETE SET (18)	6.00	12.00
1 Gerald Anderson	.20	.50
2 Josh Brock	.20	.50
3 Reggie Brown	.50	1.25
4 Thomas Davis	.40	1.00
5 Fred Gibson	.75	2.00
6 Max Jean--Gilles	.20	.50
7 Kedric Golston	.40	1.00
8 David Greene	.60	1.50
9 Arnold Harrison	.20	.50
10 Tim Jennings	.20	.50
11 Kregg Lumpkin	.20	.50
12 David Pollack	.40	1.00
13 Mark Richt CO	.20	.50
14 D.J. Shockley	.40	1.00
15 Russ Tanner	.20	.50
16 Jeremy Thomas	.30	.75
17 Will Thompson	.20	.50
18 Odell Thurman	.30	.75

2005 Georgia Legends

COMPLETE SET (42)	6.00	12.00
1 Vince Dooley CO	.20	.50
2 Herschel Walker	.60	1.50
3 Scott Woerner	.20	.50
4 Lindsay Scott	.20	.50
5 Buck Belue	.20	.50
6 Team Card	.20	.50
7 Jim Blakewood	.20	.50
8 Jeff Harper	.20	.50
9 Tim Morrison	.20	.50
10 Wayne Radloff	.20	.50
11 Norris Brown	.20	.50
12 Joe Happe	.20	.50
13 Guy McIntyre	.30	.75
14 Jim Broadway	.20	.50
15 Jimmy Payne	.20	.50
16 Rex Robinson	.20	.50
17 Hugh Nall	.20	.50
18 Eddie Weaver	.20	.50
19 Nate Taylor	.20	.50
20 Nat Hudson	.20	.50
21 Jimmy Womack	.20	.50
22 Ronnie Stewart	.20	.50
23 Frank Ros	.20	.50
24 Amp Arnold	.20	.50
25 Robert Miles	.20	.50
26 Clarence Kay	.20	.50
27 Jeff Hipp	.20	.50
28 Bob Kelley	.20	.50
29 Freddie Gilbert	.20	.50
30 Steve Kelly	.20	.50
31 Joe Creamons	.20	.50
32 Tim Crowe	.20	.50
33 Chris Welton	.20	.50
34 Pat McShae	.20	.50
35 Mike Fisher	.20	.50
36 Tommy Thurson	.20	.50
37 Dale Williams	.20	.50
38 Greg Bell	.30	.75
39 Larry Munson BR	.20	.50
40 Erk Russell DC	.20	.50
41 Team Card	.20	.50
42 Buck Belue Lindsay Scott	.20	.50

2006 Georgia Atlanta Sports Awards

1 D.J. Shockley	1.25	3.00

1991 Georgia Southern

Produced by TJR Marketing, this 45-card set features All-American players and school record holders from Georgia Southern University. Twenty-five hundred numbered sets were printed and sold to the public; each set was accompanied by a certificate of limited edition. One hundred numbered and uncut sheets were also offered. An additional 275 proof sets and another 100 unnumbered uncut sheets with different backs were produced. The 275 proof sets differ from the 2500 limited sets in that the former have a light blue (rather than a dark blue) back border and the word "proof" on the card backs. The fronts feature a full-color photo within a small yellow border enclosed in a turquoise border. A yellow flag pole with a Georgia Southern flag highlights the left side of the card while the player's name is in a white box beneath the photo. The back contains biography, career summary, and statistics.

COMPLETE SET (45)	12.00	30.00
1 Tracy Ham	2.00	5.00
2 Tim Foley	.60	1.50
3 Vance Pike	.25	.60
4 Dennis Franklin	.25	.60
5 Ernie Thompson	.25	.60
6 Giff Smith	.25	.60
7 Flint Matthews	.25	.60
8 Joe Ross	.25	.60
9 Gerald Harris	.25	.60
10 Monty Sharpe	.25	.60
11 The Beginning Erskine(Erk) Russell CO	.40	1.00
12 Mike West	.25	.60
13 Jessie Jenkins	.25	.60
14 '85 Championship (Ring)	.25	.60
15 Erskine(Erk) Russell CO	.40	1.00
16 Tim Brown DT	.30	.75
17 Taz Dixon	.25	.60
18 '86 Championship	.25	.60
19 Sean Gainey	.25	.60
20 James(Peanut) Carter	.30	.75
21 Ricky Harris	.30	.75
22 Fred Stokes	.75	2.00
23 Randell Boone	.25	.60
24 Ronald Warnock	.25	.60
25 Raymond Gross	.25	.60
26 Robert Underwood	.25	.60
27 Frank Johnson	.25	.60
28 Darren Alford	.25	.60
29 Darrell Hendrix	.25	.60
30 Raymond Gross	.25	.60
31 Hugo Rossignol	.25	.60
32 Charles Carper	.25	.60
33 Melvin Bell	.25	.60
34 The Catch (Tracy Ham to Frank Johnson)	.75	2.00
35 Karl Miller	.25	.60
36 Our House Allen E. Paulson Stadium	.25	.60
37 Danny Durham	.25	.60
38 '89 Championship	.25	.60
39 Tony Belser	.25	.60
40 Nay Young	.25	.60
41 Steve Bussoletti	.25	.60
42 Tim Stowers CO	.25	.60
43 Rodney Oglesby	.25	.60
44 '90 Championship	.25	.60
45 Tracy Ham	2.00	5.00

1988 Georgia Tech Team Sheets

These photos were issued by the school to promote the football program. Each measures roughly 8" by 10" and features eight black and white images of players with the school name appearing at the top. The player's name is printed below each image. The backs are blank.

1 Scott Aldredge	4.00	8.00
Gerald Chamblin		
Danny Harrison		
Jay Martin		
Sean McDevitt		
Chuck Owen		
Eric Thomas		
Kenneth Wilson		
2 Thomas Balkcom	4.00	8.00
Orion Cox		
E.A. Grosz		
Keith Holmes		
Mark Hutto		
T.J. Edwards		
Jeff Maloof		
Jerimiah McClary		
3 Scotty Barron	4.00	8.00
Scott Beavers		
Willie Burks		
Darrell Edwards		
David Hicks		
Jessie Marion		
Jeff Mathis		
Steve Mullen		
4 Billy Chubbs	4.00	8.00
Tom Covington		
Will Edwards		
Russell Freeman		
Jim Gallagher		
Jim Mancaruso		
James Merritt		
Darryl Jenkins		
5 Darryl Jenkins	4.00	8.00
Jim Lavin		
Terry Pettis		
Angelo Rush		
Joe Siffri		
Chris Simmons		
Alphanzo Thomas		
Ty Young		
6 Greg Lester	4.00	8.00
Mike Mooney		
Stefen Scotton		
David Stegall		
Darrell Swilling		
Alan Waters		
Lee Williamson/		

1990 Georgia Tech Team Sheets

These photos were issued by the school to promote the football program. Each measures roughly 8" by 10" and features eight black and white images of players with the school name appearing at the top. The player's name is printed below each image. The backs are blank.

COMPLETE SET (10)	30.00	60.00
1 Scott Aldredge	4.00	8.00
Gerald Chamblin		
Danny Harrison		
Jay Martin		
Tim Ewing		
Chuck Owen		
Eric Thomas		
Kenneth Wilson		
2 Boyd Andrews	4.00	8.00
Jason Bender		
Eric Billingslea		
Raleigh Boulware		
Brian Bravy		
Freddie Coger		
Jamal Cox		
Lethon Flowers		
3 Thomas Balkcom	4.00	8.00
Orion Cox		
Frank Scott		
Keith Holmes		
Mark Hutto		
T.J. Edwards		
Carl Lawson		
Jerimiah McClary		
4 Ken Celaj	4.00	8.00
Rich Frost		
Rod Hardin		
Christian Hinish		
Ralph Hughes		
T.J. Johnson		
Gary Joseph		
Harvey Middleton		
5 Billy Chubbs	4.00	8.00
Willie Clay		
Tom Covington		
Russell Freeman		
Jim Gallagher		
Emmett Merchant		
James Merritt		
Ken Swilling		
6 Jimmy Clements	4.00	8.00
James Culbreth		
Mike Dee		
James Easterly		
Scott Florence		
Willie Gonzalez		
Harold Grooms		
Derrick Steagall		
7 Jason Dukes	4.00	8.00
Elliott Fortune		
Rob Garner		
Chris Haney		
Patrick Keuller		
Tommy Luginbill		
Pete Maiello		
Vernon Strickland		
8 Steve Jackson	4.00	8.00
Ryan Jordan		
Chris Leone		
Curtis McGee		
Voel Molina		
Nathan Perryman		
Scott Sharp		
James Singleton		
9 Shawn Jones	4.00	8.00
Jim Kushon		
John Lewis		
James MacKendree		
Woodie Milam		
Kevin Peoples		
Bobby Rodriguez		
Jerrelle Williams		
10 Lashom Mitchell	4.00	8.00
James Richards		
Harie Robinson		
Ron Rogers		
Derrick Shepard		
Steve Shivers		
Sean Wheaton		
C.J. Williams		

1991 Georgia Tech Collegiate Collection

This 200-card set is standard sized. The fronts have a blue border with color action shots on each one. The school name and logo are found across the top border of the card. The featured player's name is found along the bottom border set against a yellow-gold background. The backs carry a small bio of the player and his/her statistics.

COMPLETE SET (200)	4.00	10.00
1 John Dewberry FB	.05	.15
5 Steve Davenport FB	.05	.15
7 Dante Jones FB	.05	.15
8 Cory Collier FB	.05	.15
10 John Ivemeyer FB	.05	.15
11 Ronny Cone FB	.05	.15
12 George Malone FB	.05	.15
13 Darrell Norton FB	.05	.15
14 Roosevelt Isom FB	.05	.15
16 Bobby Dodd FB CO	.20	.50
18 Andre Thomas FB	.05	.15
19 Chuck Easley FB	.05	.15
20 Willie Burks FB	.05	.15
21 Eric Thomas FB	.05	.15
22 Jerry Mays FB	.07	.20
23 Sammy Drummer FB	.05	.15
25 Rob Healy FB	.05	.15
27 Darrell Gast FB	.05	.15
28 David Bell FB	.05	.15
29 Keith Glanton FB	.05	.15
31 Sean Smith FB	.05	.15
32 Cedric Stallworth FB	.05	.15
34 Danny Harrison FB	.05	.15
36 Eric Bearden FB	.05	.15
37 Andy Hearn FB	.05	.15
38 Jim Anderson FB	.05	.15
39 Anthony Harrison FB	.05	.15
41 Dean Weaver FB	.05	.15
43 Mike Kelley FB	.05	.15
44 John Davis FB	.05	.15
45 Mark Hogan FB	.05	.15
47 Kyle Ambrose FB	.05	.15
48 Steve Mullen FB	.05	.15
49 Willis Crockett FB	.05	.15
50 Jeff Mathis FB	.05	.15
51 Ellis Gardner FB	.05	.15
52 Larry Good FB	.05	.15
53 Billy Lothridge FB	.07	.20
54 Bill Kinard FB	.05	.15
55 Brent Cunningham FB	.05	.15
56 Ted Peebles FB	.05	.15
57 Pat Swilling FB	.15	.40
59 Lawrence Lowe FB	.05	.15
61 Cam Bonifay FB	.05	.15

62 George Brodnax FB	.05	.15
63 Fred Braselton FB	.05	.15
64 Joe Auer FB	.07	.20
65 Franklin Brooks FB	.05	.15
66 Rod Stephens FB	.05	.15
67 Bill Curry FB CO	.07	.20
68 Tim Manion FB	.05	.15
69 Rick Strom FB	.05	.15
70 Toby Pearson FB	.05	.15
71 Jim Breland FB	.05	.15
72 Don Bessillieu FB	.05	.15
73 Craig Baynham FB	.07	.20
74 Maxie Baughan FB	.07	.20
75 Wade Mitchell FB	.05	.15
76 Sammy Lilly FB	.05	.15
77 Gary Lee FB	.05	.15
78 Paul Jurgensen FB	.05	.15
79 Robert Lavette FB	.05	.15
80 Robert Jaracz FB	.05	.15
81 Mike Oven FB	.05	.15
82 Paul Menegazzi FB	.05	.15
83 Billy Martin FB	.05	.15
84 Bobby Moorhead FB	.05	.15
85 Buck Martin FB	.05	.15
86 Buzz FB MASCOT	.05	.15
07 Malcolm King FB	.05	.15
88 Bobby Ross FB CO	.07	.20
89 Gary Lanier FB	.05	.15
90 Bill Curry FB CO	.07	.20
92 William Alexander FB CO	.05	.15
93 Rick Lantz FB	.05	.15
94 Eddie McAshan FB	.05	.15
96 Cleve Pounds FB	.05	.15
97 The Rambling Wreck FB	.05	.15
98 Bud Carson FB CO	.05	.15
99 Bobby Dodd Stadium FB	.05	.15
101 Willie Burks FB	.05	.15
102 Sheldon Fox FB	.05	.15
104 Danny Harrison FB	.05	.15
105 Eric Thomas FB	.05	.15
106 Kent Hill FB	.05	.15
112 Ralph Malone FB	.05	.15
113 Jerry Mays FB	.07	.20
114 Mark Bradley FB	.05	.15
115 Thomas Palmer FB	.05	.15
116 Calvin Tiggle FB	.05	.15
118 Thomas Balkcom FB	.05	.15
121 Rod Stephens FB	.05	.15
125 Eddie Lee Ivery FB	.05	.15
126 Darryl Jenkins FB	.05	.15
127 Jerimiah McClary FB	.05	.15
131 Robert Massey FB	.05	.15
132 Cedric Stallworth FB	.05	.15
136 Stefen Scotton FB	.05	.15
137 Jim Lavin FB	.05	.15
138 Joe Siffri FB	.05	.15
143 Kenneth Wilson FB	.05	.15
147 Jay Martin FB	.05	.15
149 Chris Simmons FB	.05	.15
156 Taz Anderson FB	.05	.15
157 Sam Bracken FB	.05	.15
166 Harper Brown FB	.05	.15
160 Bill Flowers FB	.05	.15
180 Tony Daykin FB	.05	.15
186 Donnie Chisholm FB	.05	.15
187 Floyd Faucette FB	.05	.15
189 Drew Hill FB	.05	.15
190 Leon Hardeman FB	.05	.15
196 Mackel Harris FB	.05	.15
197 Eddie Lee Ivery FB	.07	.20
198 Kris Kentera FB	.05	.15
199 Lenny Snow FB	.05	.15

1998 Georgia Tech Team Sheets

These photos were issued by the school to promote the football program. Each measures roughly 8" by 10" and features eight black and white images of players with the school name and year appearing at the top. The player's name and position is printed below each image. The backs are blank.

COMPLETE SET (8)	20.00	40.00
1 Conrad Andrzejewski Brett Basquin Donte Booker Ira Claxton Felipe Claybrooks Bryan Corhen Conrad Daniels Derrick Dudley	3.00	6.00
2 Jason Bostic Chris Brown Jason Burks Jerry Caldwell Delaunta Cameron Jon Carman Brad Chambers Jamara Clark	3.00	6.00
3 Chris Edwards Abe Fernandez John Grantham Sean Gregory Matt Gubba Curtis Hollomon Trotter Hunt Virgil Johnson	3.00	6.00
4 George Godsey Joe Hamilton Brent Key Guenter Kryszon Mike Lillie Matt Miller Jon Muyres Chris Myers	3.00	6.00
5 Brian Meager Dan Mitchell Ross Mitchell Jesse Moody Titus Nelson Marty O'Leary David Powell Craig Page	3.00	6.00
6 Craig Page Justin Robertson Tony Robinson Charlie Rogers Phillip Rogers Mike Sheridan Jesse Tarplin Travares Tillman	3.00	6.00
7 Roderrick Roberts Nick Rogers David Schmidgall DeShaan Simmons Kofi Smith Nate Stimson Mel Whatley Reggie Wilcox	3.00	6.00
8 Troy Tolbert Matt Uremovich Merrix Watson Dez White Ed Wilder Charles Wiley	3.00	6.00

Brian Wilkins
Rodney Williams

2005 Grambling Schedules

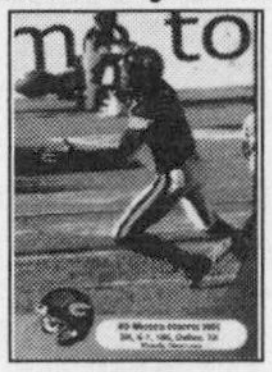

COMPLETE SET (8)	2.50	5.00
1 Bruce Eugene	.30	.75
2 Moses Harris	.30	.75
3 Jason Hatcher	.30	.75
4 Ab Kuuan	.30	.75
5 Jermaine Mills	.30	.75
6 Lennard Patton	.30	.75
7 Charles Wilson	.30	.75
8 Jimmy Zachary	.30	.75

1992 Gridiron Promos

Produced by Lafayette Sportscard Corporation, this four-card promo set was issued to show the design of the 1992 Gridiron set. The standard-size cards feature full-bleed action color player photos. The picture on card number 1P is horizontal. The player's name appears at the lower left in team color-coded lettering; his school and position are at the lower right. On a background of team color-coded panels, the backs display a vertical close-up photo, biography, player profile information, and college statistics.

COMPLETE SET (4)	1.60	4.00
1P Siran Stacy	.20	.50
2P Casey Weldon	.30	.75
3P Mike Saunders	.20	.50
4P Jeff Blake	1.20	3.00

1992 Gridiron

The 1992 Gridiron football set was produced by Lafayette Sportscard Corporation (LSC). The 110 standard-size cards pay tribute to graduating seniors and coaches from the top 25 college teams of 1991. Three players and one coach represent each team included in the set. Reportedly the production run was limited to 50,000 sets or 2,500 numbered cases. The full-bleed glossy color photos dominate the card fronts; the producer's logo, player's name, team name, and position are placed in the corners. In addition to a second color player photo, the back carries biography, career highlights, and statistics (1991 and career), on panels reflecting the team colors. The four Desmond Howard cards (13B, 33B, 105B, and 107B) have a letter suffix after the card number. Questions have been raised as to the proper licensing of this set, but we include it in this volume since the cards are widely accepted in the industry.

COMPLETE SET (110)	10.00	25.00
1 Rob Perez	.05	.15
2 Jason Jones	.02	.10
3 Jason Christ	.02	.10
4 Fisher DeBerry CO	.05	.15
5 Danny Woodson	.02	.10
6 Siran Stacy	.05	.15
7 Robert Stewart	.02	.10
8 Gene Stallings CO	.50	1.25
9 Santana Dotson	.30	.75
10 Curtis Hafford	.02	.10
11 John Turnpaugh	.02	.10
12 Grant Teaff CO	.05	.15
13B Desmond Howard	.30	.75
14 Brian Treggs	.02	.10
15 Troy Auzenne	.05	.15
16 Bruce Snyder CO	.05	.15
17 DeChane Cameron	.02	.10
18 Levon Kirkland	.08	.25
19 Ed McDaniel	.05	.15
20 Ken Hatfield CO	.05	.15
21 Darian Hagan	.05	.15
22 Rico Smith	.05	.15
23 Joel Steed	.05	.15
24 Bill McCartney CO	.40	1.00
25 Jeff Blake	1.20	3.00
26 David Daniels	.02	.10
27 Robert Jones	.05	.15
28 Bill Lewis CO	.05	.15
29 Tim Paulk	.02	.10
30 Arden Czyzewski	.02	.10
31 Cal Dixon	.02	.10
32 Steve Spurrier CO	1.20	3.00
33B Desmond Howard	.25	.60
34 Casey Weldon	.08	.25
35 Kirk Carruthers	.02	.10
36 Bobby Bowden CO	1.00	2.50
37 Mark Barsotti	.02	.10
38 Kelvin Means	.02	.10
39 Marquez Pope	.05	.15
40 Jim Sweeney CO	.08	.25
41 Kameno Bell	.02	.10
42 Elbert Turner	.02	.10
43 Marlon Primous UER (name misspelled Marlin)	.02	.10
44 John Mackovic CO	.08	.25
45 Matt Rodgers	.05	.15
46 Mike Saunders	.05	.15
47 John Derby	.02	.10
48 Hayden Fry CO	.40	1.00
49 Carlos Huerta	.05	.15
50 Leon Searcy	.05	.15
51 Claude Jones	.02	.10
52 Dennis Erickson CO	.40	1.00
53 Erick Anderson	.05	.15
54 J.D. Carlson	.02	.10
55 Greg Skrepenak	.05	.15
56 Gary Moeller CO	.05	.15
57 Keithen McCant	.05	.15
58 Nate Turner	.02	.10
59 Pat Englebert	.02	.10
60 Tom Osborne CO	1.00	2.50
61 Charles Davenport	.02	.10
62 Mark Thomas	.02	.10
63 Clyde Hawley	.02	.10
64 Dick Sheridan CO	.05	.15
65 Derek Brown TE	.05	.15
66 Rodney Culver	.05	.15
67 Tony Smith	.05	.15
68 Lou Holtz CO	.80	2.00
69 Kent Graham	.08	.25
70 Scottie Graham	.40	1.00
71 John Kacherski	.02	.10
72 John Cooper CO	.08	.25
73 Mike Gaddis	.05	.15
74 Joe Bowden	.05	.15
75 Mike McKinley	.02	.10
76 Gary Gibbs CO	.02	.10
77 Sam Gash	.08	.25
78 Keith Goganious	.05	.15
79 Darren Perry	.05	.15
80 Joe Paterno CO	1.25	3.00
81 Steve Israel	.05	.15
82 Eric Seaman	.02	.10
83 Glen Deveaux	.02	.10
84 Paul Hackett CO	.08	.25
85 Tommy Vardell	.08	.25
86 Chris Walsh	.02	.10
87 Jason Palumbis	.02	.10
88 Dennis Green CO	.80	2.00
89 Andy Kelly	.08	.25
90 Dale Carter	.08	.25
91 Shon Walker	.02	.10
92 Johnny Majors CO	.20	.50
93 Bucky Richardson	.05	.15
94 Quentin Coryatt	.40	1.00
95 Kevin Smith	.08	.25
96 R.C. Slocum CO	.30	.75
97 Ed Cunningham	.05	.15
98 Mario Bailey	.05	.15
99 Donald Jones	.02	.10
100 Don James CO	.30	.75
101 Vaughn Dunbar	.05	.15
102 Reggie Yarbrough	.02	.10
103 Matt Blundin	.08	.25
104 Tony Sands	.02	.10
105B Desmond Howard	.25	.60
106 Ty Detmer	.40	1.00
107B Desmond Howard	.25	.60
NNO Mario Bailey CL Jeff Blake	.40	1.00
NNO Mike Gaddis CL Tommy Vardell	.05	.15
NNO Title Card	.02	.10

1973 Harvard Team Sheets

These photos were issued by the school to promote the football program. Each measures roughly 8" by 10" and features ten black and white images of players with the school name and year appearing at the top. The player's name, position, and brief vital stats is printed below each photo. The backs are blank.

1 Joe Restic (HC) Dave Pierre Jim Stoeckel Milt Holt Jeff Bone Mitch Berger Sandy Tennant Bob Kristoff Mike O'Hare Bill Ferry	4.00	8.00

1989 Hawaii

This 25-card set features current football players at the University of Hawaii. The cards are unnumbered, so they are listed below according to uniform number, which is prominently displayed on both sides of the card. The cards measure approximately 2 1/2" by 3 1/2". The set was sponsored by Longs Drugs and Kodak.

COMPLETE SET (25)	10.00	20.00
3 Michael Coulson	.30	.75
4 Walter Briggs	.30	.75
5 Gavin Robertson	.30	.75
7 Jason Elam	2.00	5.00
16 Clayton Mahuka	.30	.75
18 Garrett Gabriel	.30	.75
19 Kim McCloud	.30	.75
27 Kyle Ah Loo	.30	.75
28 Dane McArthur	.30	.75
30 Travis Sims	.30	.75
31 David Maeva	.30	.75
37 Mike Tresler	.30	.75
43 Jamal Farmer	.30	.75
56 Mark Odom	.30	.75
61 Allen Smith	.30	.75
66 Manly Williams	.30	.75
67 Larry Jones	.30	.75
71 Sean Robinson	.30	.75
72 Shawn Alivado	.30	.75
79 Leo Goeas	.40	1.00
86 Larry Khan-Smith	.30	.75
89 Chris Roscoe	.30	.75
91 Augie Apelu	.30	.75
97 Dana Directo	.30	.75
NNO Bob Wagner CO	.30	.75

1990 Hawaii

This 50-card standard size set features members of the 1990 Hawaii Rainbow Warriors Football team. The cards have white borders framing a full-color photo on the front and biographical information on the back of the card. We have checklisted this set in alphabetical order and placed the uniform number of the player next to the name of the player.

COMPLETE SET (50)	20.00	35.00
1 Sean Abreu 40	.30	.75
2 Joaquin Barnett 53	.30	.75
3 Darrick Branch 87	.30	.75
4 David Brantley 9	.30	.75
5 Akili Calhoun 98	.30	.75
6 Michael Carter 3	.30	.75
7 Shawn Ching 72	.30	.75
8 Jason Elam 7	1.50	4.00
9 Jamal Farmer 43	.30	.75
10 Garrett Gabriel 18	.30	.75
11 Brian Gordon 15	.30	.75
12 Kenny Harper 6	.30	.75
13 Mitchell Kaaialii 57	.30	.75
14 Larry Khan-Smith 86	.30	.75
15 Haku Kahoano 95	.30	.75
16 Nuuanu Kaulia 94	.30	.75
17 Eddie Kealoha 38	.30	.75
18 Zerin Khan 14	.30	.75
19 David Maeva 31	.30	.75
20 Dane McArthur 28	.30	.75
21 Kim McCloud 19	.30	.75
22 Jeff Newman 1	.30	.75
23 Mark Odom 56	.30	.75
24 Louis Randall 51	.30	.75
25 Gavin Robertson 5	.30	.75
26 Sean Robinson 71	.30	.75
27 Tavita Sagapolu 77	.30	.75
28 Lyno Samana 45	.30	.75
29 Walter Santiago 12	.30	.75
30 Joe Sardo 21	.30	.75
31 Travis Sims 30	.30	.75
32 Allen Smith 61	.30	.75
33 Jeff Sydner 26	.30	.75
34 Richard Stevenson 33	.30	.75
35 David Tanuvasa 44	.30	.75
36 Mike Tresler 37	.30	.75
37 Lemoe Tua 60	.30	.75
38 Peter Viliamu 69	.30	.75
39 Bob Wagner CO	.30	.75
40 Terry Whitaker 2	.30	.75
41 Manly Williams 66	.30	.75
42 Jerry Winfrey 90	.30	.75
43 Aloha Stadium	.30	.75
44 Assistant Coaches	.30	.75
45 Defense (Nuuanu Kaulia)	.30	.75
46 Offense (Jamal Farmer)	.30	.75
47 Special Teams (Jason Elam)	.30	.75
48 BYU Victory (Jamal Farmer)	.30	.75
49 UH Logo	.30	.75
50 WAC Logo	.30	.75

1996 Hawaii

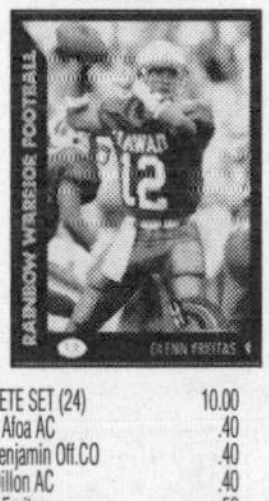

COMPLETE SET (24)	10.00	20.00
1 Ulima Afoa AC	.40	1.00
2 Guy Benjamin Off.CO	.40	1.00
3 Don Dillon AC	.40	1.00
4 Glenn Freitas	.50	1.25
5 Ryan Green	.40	1.00
6 Doe Henderson	.40	1.00
7 Mark Hernandez	.40	1.00
8 Walt Klinker AC	.40	1.00
9 Gerald Lacey	.40	1.00
10 Don Lindsey Def.CO	.40	1.00
11 Lesa Maiava	.40	1.00
12 Ken Margerum AC	.50	1.25
13 Trent Miles AC	.40	1.00
14 Randall Okimoto	.40	1.00
15 Carlton Oswalt	.40	1.00
16 Mike Petersen	.50	1.25
17 Paul Purdy	.40	1.00
18 Greg Roach	.40	1.00
19 Doug Semones AC	.40	1.00
20 Carlos Shaw	.40	1.00
21 Tony Thomas	.40	1.00
22 Fred von Appen CO	.40	1.00
23 C.B. Wentling	.40	1.00
24 Tom Williams AC	.40	1.00

1997 Hawaii

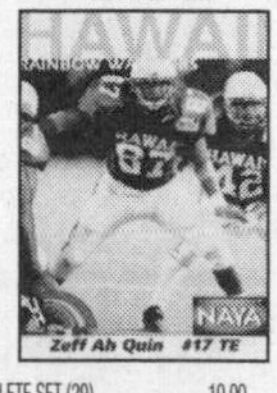

COMPLETE SET (29)	10.00	20.00
1 Zeff Ah Quin	.40	1.00
2 Punahou Aina	.40	1.00
3 Blase Austin	.40	1.00
4 Ryan Battin	.40	1.00
5 Celnell Bobbitt	.40	1.00
6 Tim Carey	.40	1.00
7 Brian Chapman	.40	1.00
8 Sam Collins	.40	1.00
9 Rickey Daley	.40	1.00
10 Gary Ellison	.40	1.00
11 Stephen Gonzales	.40	1.00
12 Gery Graham	.40	1.00
13 Al Hunter	.40	1.00
14 Quincy Jacobs	.40	1.00
15 Mark Jenkins	.40	1.00
16 Lonn Kalama	.40	1.00
17 Ellie Kapihe	.40	1.00
18 Kekoa Kilcoyne	.40	1.00
19 Eddie Klaneski	.40	1.00
20 Johnny Macon	.40	1.00
21 Jason Mane	.40	1.00
22 Shane Oliveira	.40	1.00
23 Conrad Paulo	.40	1.00
24 Bob Pigott	.40	1.00
25 Nick Reuss	.40	1.00
26 Robbie Robinson	.40	1.00
27 Morrie Roe	.40	1.00
28 Doug Rosevold	.40	1.00
29 Chris Shinnick	.40	1.00
30 Larry Slade	.40	1.00
31 Tyler Tanigawa	.40	1.00

2004 Hawaii

This set was sponsored by KKEA Radio and Pizza Hut and was issued by the school. It features members of the 2004 Hawaii football team. Each card was printed with partial green borders on the front along with the school logo in the bottom right corner and the player name at the bottom left. The unnumbered cards have been listed alphabetically below.

COMPLETE SET (29)	7.50	15.00
1 Justin Ayat	.30	.75
2 Mike Bass	.30	.75
3 Ikaika Blackburn	.30	.75
4 Michael Brewster	.40	1.00
5 Timmy Chang	1.25	3.00
6 Jonathan Ekno	.30	.75
7 Abraham Elimimian	.30	.75
8 Matt Faga	.30	.75
9 Thomas Frazier	.30	.75
10 Lui Fuga	.30	.75
11 Watson Ho'ohuli	.30	.75
12 Patrick Jenkins	.30	.75
13 June Jones CO	.40	1.00
14 Chad Kahale	.30	.75
15 Chad Kapanui	.30	.75
16 Phil Kauffman	.30	.75
17 West Keliikipi	.30	.75
18 Britton Komine	.40	1.00
19 Patrick Lavar Harley	.30	.75
20 Paul Lutu-Carroll	.30	.75
21 Matt Manuma	.30	.75
22 Lincoln Manutai	.30	.75
23 Uriah Moenoa	.30	.75
24 Daniel Murray	.30	.75
25 Kilinahe Noa	.30	.75
26 Chad Owens	.50	1.25
27 Se'e Poumele	.40	1.00
28 Darrell Tautofi	.30	.75
29 Gerald Welch	.40	1.00

2007 Hawaii

COMPLETE SET (24)	7.50	15.00
1 Colt Brennan	1.50	4.00
2 Alonzo Chopp	.30	.75
3 C.J. Hawthorne	.30	.75
4 Keenan Jones	.30	.75
5 Brad Kalilimoku	.30	.75
6 Ryan Keomaka	.30	.75
7 Michael Lafaele	.30	.75
8 Micah Lau	.30	.75
9 Jason Laumoli	.30	.75
10 Gerard Lewis	.30	.75
11 Francis Maka	.30	.75
12 A.J. Martinez	.30	.75
13 Myron Newberry	.30	.75
14 Karl Noa	.30	.75
15 Timo Paepule	.30	.75
16 Jacob Patek	.30	.75
17 Amani Purcell	.30	.75
18 Jason Rivers	.30	.75
19 Rustin Saole	.30	.75
20 Hercules Satele	.30	.75
21 Larry Sauafea	.30	.75
22 Siave Seti	.30	.75
23 June Jones CO	.40	1.00
24 Colt Brennan	1.25	3.00

1991 Heisman Collection I

The first series of the Heisman Collection contains 20 standard-size cards honoring former Heisman Trophy winners. One hundred thousand sets were produced, and each set contains a title card with a unique serial number. Each of the 1,000 cases (100 sets per case) contained two personally autographed cards from a former Heisman Trophy winner. The front design features a color posed shot of the player, bordered in gold and black. The player's name appears in a black stripe at the bottom of the picture, with a picture of the Heisman Trophy in the lower right corner of the card face. The horizontally oriented back has a larger picture of the Heisman Trophy and a summary of the player's career. The year the player won the trophy is indicated in a gold stripe on the right side of the card back. The cards are skip-numbered and arranged chronologically from older to more recent Heisman trophy winners. There also exists a promo card of Bo Jackson marked "Sample" on the back. It was issued as part of a 10" by 3 1/2" strip with set and ordering information on it. The sample card is not considered part of the complete set.

COMPLETE SET (21)	2.00	5.00
1 Jay Berwanger	.05	.15
6 Tom Harmon	.08	.25
9 Angelo Bertelli	.05	.15
11 Doc Blanchard	.08	.25
13 Johnny Lujack	.15	.40
15 Leon Hart	.08	.25
16 Vic Janowicz	.15	.40
19 John Lattner	.08	.25
23 John David Crow	.05	.15
26 Joe Bellino	.05	.15
30 John Huarte	.05	.15
32 Steve Spurrier	.40	1.00
36 Jim Plunkett	.15	.40
40 Archie Griffin	.08	.25
42 Tony Dorsett	.30	.75
43 Earl Campbell	.30	.75
45 Charles White	.05	.15
48 Herschel Walker	.25	.60
51 Bo Jackson	.40	1.00
53 Tim Brown	.60	1.50
NNO Title card	.05	.15
SAM Bo Jackson Sample Promo	.40	1.00

1991 Heisman Collection I Autographs

The 1991 series of Heisman Collection cards contained randomly signed cards of 12 of the Heisman Trophy winners pictured in the set. These cards were reportedly inserted at a ratio of 1:50 sets, and at first glance appear identical to the cards within the set, other than the player autograph on the front. However, these cards are printed on a linen finish, with the serial number of the particular card (out of 200) hand written on the Heisman Trophy statute on the reverse of the card. Other differences between the regular cards and the autograph cards include bolder, larger (and sometimes different) text on the back of the autographed cards, no number on the autographed cards, and the copyright listed as College Classics, as opposed to the regular cards, which were copyrighted by The Downtown Athletic Club of New York City, Inc. Since these cards are unnumbered, they are checklisted below in alphabetical order. Some cards surfaced later that did not have the serial numbering on the back. Presumably, these were issued directly to the players for their own use.

COMPLETE SET (12)	300.00	600.00
1 Joe Bellino	20.00	40.00
2 Angelo Bertelli	25.00	50.00
3 Jay Berwanger	30.00	60.00
4 Tim Brown	25.00	50.00
5 Earl Campbell	30.00	60.00
6 Archie Griffin	20.00	40.00
7 Leon Hart	25.00	50.00
8 John Huarte	20.00	40.00
9 Vic Janowicz	30.00	60.00
10 Johnny Lattner	20.00	40.00
11 Jim Plunkett	20.00	40.00
12 Steve Spurrier	40.00	80.00

1992 Heisman Collection II

For the second year, College Classics in association with The Downtown Athletic Club of New York issued a series consisting of 20 cards honoring Heisman Trophy winners. One hundred thousand sets were produced, and each one included a consecutively numbered card from 1-100,000. The set was issued in a sturdy cardboard box with an unnumbered checklist on its back. Two-card strips measuring approximately 3 1/2" by 7 1/2" and featuring either Barry Sanders or Roger Staubach were issued to promote the set. The Sanders and Staubach promos are different in that the card number on the back of the regular issue has been replaced by the word "Sample." The sample cards are not considered part of the set. The front design features a color player portrait bordered in black and gold. The player's name appears in a black stripe that cuts across the bottom of the picture, intersecting a picture of the Heisman Trophy at the lower right corner. The horizontal back has a larger picture of the Heisman Trophy and a summary of the player's career. The year the player won the trophy is printed vertically in a gold stripe running down the right side. The cards are skip-numbered and arranged chronologically from older to more recent Heisman trophy winners.

COMPLETE SET (21)	5.00	12.00
2 Larry Kelley	.20	.50
3 Clint Frank	.20	.50
5 Nile Kinnick	.30	.75
7 Bruce Smith	.20	.50
10 Les Horvath	.20	.50
14 Doak Walker	.50	1.25
17 Dick Kazmaier	.20	.50
20 Alan Ameche	.30	.75
21 Howard Cassady	.20	.50
25 Billy Cannon	.30	.75
27 Ernie Davis	.75	2.00
29 Roger Staubach	.75	2.00
31 Mike Garrett	.20	.50
35 Steve Owens	.30	.75
38 Johnny Rodgers	.30	.75
39 John Cappelletti	.20	.50
44 Billy Sims	.50	1.25
50 Doug Flutie	.75	2.00
52 Vinny Testaverde	.30	.75
54 Barry Sanders	1.50	4.00
NNO Title Card	.20	.50
SAM Barry Sanders	3.00	8.00
SAM Roger Staubach Sample Promo	3.00	8.00

1993 Heisman Collection III

COMPLETE SET (19)	35.00	60.00
4 Davey O'Brien	1.50	4.00
8 Frank Sinkwich	1.00	2.50
12 Glenn Davis	1.50	4.00
18 Billy Vessels	1.00	2.50
22 Paul Hornung	3.00	8.00
24 Pete Dawkins	1.00	2.60
28 Terry Baker	1.00	2.50
33 Gary Beban	1.00	2.50
34 O.J. Simpson	2.50	6.00
37 Pat Sullivan	1.00	2.50
41 Archie Griffin	1.00	2.50
46 George Rogers	1.50	4.00
47 Marcus Allen	4.00	10.00
49 Mike Rozier	1.50	4.00
55 Andre Ware	1.00	2.50
56 Ty Detmer	1.00	2.50
57 Desmond Howard	1.50	4.00
58 Gino Torretta	1.00	2.50
NNO Cover Card	.40	1.00

2004 High School Army All-American

1 Chris Leak	7.50	15.00

2005 High School Army All-American

These cards were issued to promote the January 15, 2005 Army All-American Bowl high school football game held in San Antonio. Each card was produced with a black border at the top and yellow at the bottom and each features a football great who played in a past game. Each measures slightly larger than standard size at 2 7/8" by 3 7/8".

1 Reggie Bush	6.00	15.00
2 Chris Leak	7.50	15.00
3 Brady Quinn	10.00	20.00
4 Adrian Peterson	10.00	20.00

2006 High School Army All-American

These cards were issued to promote the January 7, 2006 Army All-American Bowl high school football game held in San Antonio. Each card was produced with a black border and features a football great who played in a past game. Each measures slightly larger than standard size at 2 7/8" by 3 7/8".

1 Reggie Bush	8.00	20.00
3 Ted Ginn Jr.	10.00	20.00
2 Jamaal Charles	7.50	15.00
4 Vince Young	6.00	15.00

1991 Hoby SEC Stars Samples

These cards are an unsigned version of the Hoby SEC Stars Signature cards. Each is identical to the signed cards with the absence of the signature on the front and with the word "sample" on the cardbacks. These cards are often found in uncut 10-card sheet form.

COMPLETE SET (10)	28.00	70.00
1 Carlos Alvarez	2.00	5.00
2 Zeke Bratkowski	2.40	6.00
3 Jerry Clower	2.00	5.00
4 Condredge Holloway	2.00	5.00
5 Bert Jones	4.00	10.00
6 Archie Manning	4.00	10.00
7 Ken Stabler	6.00	15.00
8 Pat Sullivan	2.40	6.00
9 Jeff Van Note	2.00	5.00
10 Bill Wade	2.40	6.00

1991 Hoby SEC Stars

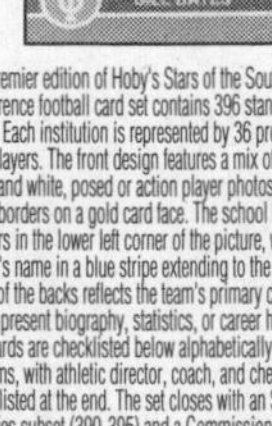

The premier edition of Hoby's Stars of the Southeastern Conference football card set contains 396 standard-size cards. Each institution is represented by 36 prominent past players. The front design features a mix of color or black and white, posed or action player photos, with thin white borders on a gold card face. The school logo appears in the lower left corner of the picture, with the player's name in a blue stripe extending to the right. The color of the backs reflects the team's primary color; the backs present biography, statistics, or career highlights. The cards are checklisted below alphabetically according to teams, with athletic director, coach, and checklist cards listed at the end. The set closes with an SEC Rivalries subset (390-395) and a Commissioner card (396). The numbering below reflects the actual numbering on the cards and checklists. A mistake occurred when Tennessee's players began with 299 rather than 289; thus no cards are numbered 289-298, and both Tennessee and Vanderbilt cards share the numbers 325-334.

COMPLETE SET (396)	36.00	90.00
1 Paul(Bear) Bryant CO	1.00	2.50
2 Johnny Musso	.25	.60
3 Keith McCants	.15	.40
4 Cecil Dowdy	.10	.30
5 Thomas Rayam	.10	.30
6 Van Tiffin	.10	.30
7 Efrum Thomas	.10	.30
8 Jon Hand	.15	.40
9 David Smith	.10	.30
10 Larry Rose	.10	.30
11 Lamonde Russell	.10	.30

12 Mike Washington	.10	.30
13 Tommy Cole	.10	.30
14 Roger Shultz	.10	.30
15 Spencer Hammond	.10	.30
16 John Fruhmorgen	.10	.30
17 Gene Jelks	.15	.40
18 John Mangum	.15	.40
19 George Thornton	.10	.30
20 Billy Neighbors	.15	.40
21 Howard Cross	.20	.50
22 Jeremiah Castille	.15	.40
23 Derrick Thomas	.80	2.00
24 Terrill Chatman	.10	.30
25 Ken Stabler	1.00	2.50
26 Lee Ozmint	.10	.30
27 Philip Doyle	.10	.30
28 Kermit Kendrick	.10	.30
29 Chris Mohr	.10	.30
30 Tommy Wilcox	.10	.30
31 Gary Hollingsworth	.10	.30
32 Sylvester Croom	.20	.50
33 Willie Wyatt	.10	.30
34 Pooley Hubert	.10	.30
35 Bobby Humphrey	.15	.40
36 Vaughn Mancha	.10	.30
37 Reggie Slack	.15	.40
38 Vince Dooley CO	.20	.50
39 Ed King	.15	.40
40 Connie Frederick	.10	.30
41 Jeff Burger	.15	.40
42 Monk Gafford	.10	.30
43 David Rocker	.15	.40
44 Jim Pyburn	.10	.30
45 Bob Harris	.10	.30
46 Travis Tidwell	.10	.30
47 Shug Jordan CO	.15	.40
48 Zeke Smith	.15	.40
49 Terry Beasley	.15	.40
50 Pat Sullivan	.25	.60
51 Stacy Danley	.15	.40
52 Jimmy Hitchcock	.10	.30
53 John Wiley	.10	.30
54 Greg Taylor	.10	.30
55 Lamar Rogers	.15	.40
56 Rob Selby	.10	.30
57 James Joseph	.15	.40
58 Mike Kolen	.10	.30
59 Kevin Greene	.30	.75
60 Ben Thomas	.10	.30
61 Shayne Wasden	.10	.30
62 Tex Warrington	.10	.30
63 Tommie Agee	.15	.40
64 Jim Phillips	.15	.40
65 Lawyer Tillman	.15	.40
66 Mark Dorminey	.10	.30
67 Steve Wallace	.15	.40
68 Ed Dyas	.10	.30
69 Alexander Wright	.15	.40
70 Lionel James	.15	.40
71 Aundray Bruce	.15	.40
72 Edmund Nelson	.10	.30
73 Jack Youngblood	.40	1.00
74 Carlos Alvarez	.15	.40
75 Ricky Nattiel	.15	.40
76 Bill Carr	.10	.30
77 Guy Dennis	.10	.30
78 Charles Casey	.10	.30
79 Louis Oliver	.15	.40
80 John Reaves	.15	.40
81 Wayne Peace	.15	.40
82 Charlie LaPradd	.10	.30
83 Wes Chandler	.20	.50
84 Richard Trapp	.10	.30
85 Ralph Ortega	.10	.30
86 Tommy Durrance	.10	.30
87 Burton Lawless	.10	.30
88 Bruce Bennett	.10	.30
89 Huey Richardson	.15	.40
90 Larry Smith	.10	.30
91 Trace Armstrong	.20	.50
92 Nat Moore	.20	.50
93 James Jones	.15	.40
94 Kay Stephenson	.15	.40
95 Scot Brantley	.10	.30
96 Ray Criswell	.10	.30
97 Steve Tannen	.15	.40
98 Ernie Mills	.20	.50
99 Bruce Vaughn	.10	.30
100 Steve Spurrier	1.20	3.00
101 Crawford Ker	.15	.40
102 David Galloway	.15	.40
103 David Williams	.15	.40
104 Lomas Brown	.20	.50
105 Fernando Jackson	.10	.30
106 Jeff Roth	.10	.30
107 Mark Murray	.10	.30
108 Kirk Kirkpatrick	.10	.30
109 Ray Goff CO	.15	.40
110 Quinton Lumpkin	.10	.30
111 Royce Smith	.10	.30
112 Larry Rakestraw	.15	.40
113 Kevin Butler	.15	.40
114 Aschel M. Day	.10	.30
115 Scott Woerner	.15	.40
116 Herb St. John	.10	.30
117 Ray Rissmiller	.10	.30
118 Buck Belue	.15	.40
119 George Collins	.10	.30
120 Joel Parrish	.10	.30
121 Terry Hoage	.15	.40
122 Frank Sinkwich	.25	.60
123 Billy Payne	.20	.50
124 Zeke Bratkowski	.20	.50
125 Herschel Walker	.60	1.50
126 Pat Dye CO	.20	.50
127 Vernon Smith	.10	.30
128 Rex Robinson	.10	.30
129 Mike Castronis	.10	.30
130 Pop Warner CO	.20	.50
131 George Patton	.15	.40
132 Harry Babcock	.10	.30
133 Lindsay Scott	.15	.40
134 Bill Stanfill	.15	.40
135 Bill Hartman Jr.	.10	.30
136 Eddie Weaver	.10	.30
137 Tim Worley	.20	.50
138 Ben Zambiasi	.15	.40
139 Bob McWhorter	.10	.30
140 Rodney Hampton	.30	.75
141 Len Hauss	.15	.40
142 Wally Butts CO	.15	.40
143 Andy Johnson	.15	.40
144 I.M. Shiver Jr.	.10	.30
145 Clyde Johnson	.10	.30
146 Steve Meilinger	.10	.30
147 Howard Schnellenberger CO	.20	.50
148 Irv Goode	.15	.40
149 Sam Ball	.10	.30
150 Babe Parilli	.20	.50
151 Rick Norton	.15	.40
152 Warren Bryant	.15	.40
153 Mike Pfeifer	.10	.30
154 Sonny Collins	.10	.30
155 Mark Higgs	.20	.50
156 Randy Holleran	.10	.30
157 Bill Ransdell	.10	.30
158 Joey Worley	.10	.30
159 Jim Kovach	.10	.30
160 Joe Federspiel	.15	.40
161 Larry Seiple	.15	.40
162 Darryl Bishop	.10	.30
163 George Blanda	.60	1.50
164 Oliver Barnett	.15	.40
165 Paul Calhoun	.10	.30
166 Dick Lyons	.15	.40
167 Tom Hutchinson	.15	.40
168 George Adams	.15	.40
169 Derrick Ramsey	.15	.40
170 Rick Kestner	.10	.30
171 Art Still	.20	.50
172 Rick Nuzum	.10	.30
173 Richard Jaffe	.10	.30
174 Rodger Bird	.10	.30
175 Jeff Van Note	.20	.50
176 Herschel Turner	.10	.30
177 Lou Michaels	.15	.40
178 Ray Correll	.10	.30
179 Doug Moseley	.10	.30
180 Bob Gain	.15	.40
181 Tommy Casanova	.20	.50
182 Mike Anderson	.10	.30
183 Craig Burns	.10	.30
184 A.J. Duhe	.15	.40
185 Lyman White	.10	.30
186 Paul Dietzel CO	.20	.50
187 Paul Lyons	.10	.30
188 Eddie Ray	.10	.30
189 Roy Winston	.15	.40
190 Brad Davis	.10	.30
191 Mike Williams	.10	.30
192 Karl Wilson	.15	.40
193 Ron Estay	.10	.30
194 Malcolm Scott	.10	.30
195 Greg Jackson	.10	.30
196 Willie Teal	.15	.40
197 Eddie Fuller	.10	.30
198 Ralph Norwood	.10	.30
199 Bert Jones	.25	.60
200 Y.A. Tittle	.40	1.00
201 Jerry Stovall	.20	.50
202 Henry Thomas	.20	.50
203 Lance Smith	.10	.30
204 Doug Moreau	.15	.40
205 Tyler LaFauci	.10	.30
206 George Bevan	.10	.30
207 Robert Dugas	.10	.30
208 Carlos Carson	.15	.40
209 Andy Hamilton	.15	.40
210 James Britt	.10	.30
211 Wendell Davis	.20	.50
212 Ron Sancho	.15	.40
213 Johnny Robinson	.20	.50
214 Eric Martin	.15	.40
215 Michael Brooks	.15	.40
216 Toby Caston	.15	.40
217 Jesse Anderson	.10	.30
218 Jimmy Webb	.10	.30
219 Mardye McDole	.10	.30
220 David Smith	.10	.30
221 Dana Moore	.10	.30
222 Cedric Corse	.10	.30
223 Louis Clark	.10	.30
224 Walter Packer	.10	.30
225 George Wonsley	.10	.30
226 Billy Jackson	.15	.40
227 Bruce Plummer	.10	.30
228 Aaron Pearson	.10	.30
229 Glen Collins	.10	.30
230 Paul Davis CO	.10	.30
231 Wayne Jones	.10	.30
232 John Bond	.10	.30
233 Johnie Cooks	.15	.40
234 Robert Young	.10	.30
235 Don Smith	.10	.30
236 Kent Hull	.15	.40
237 Tony Shell	.10	.30
238 Steve Freeman	.15	.40
239 James Williams	.10	.30
240 Tom Goode	.15	.40
241 Stan Black	.10	.30
242 Bo Russell	.10	.30
243 Richard Byrd	.10	.30
244 Frank Dowsing	.10	.30
245 Wayne Harris	.10	.30
246 Richard Keys	.10	.30
247 Artie Cosby	.10	.30
248 Dave Marler	.10	.30
249 Michael Haddix	.15	.40
250 Jerry Clower	.20	.50
251 Bill Bell	.15	.40
252 Jerry Bouldin	.10	.30
253 Parker Hall	.10	.30
254 Allen Brown	.10	.30
255 Bill Smith	.10	.30
256 Freddie Joe Nunn	.20	.50
257 John Vaught CO	.15	.40
258 Buford McGee	.15	.40
259 Kenny Dill	.10	.30
260 Jim Miller P	.10	.30
261 Doug Jacobs	.10	.30
262 John Dottley	.15	.40
263 Willie Green	.20	.50
264 Tony Bennett	.20	.50
265 Stan Hindman	.10	.30
266 Charles Childers	.10	.30
267 Harry Harrison	.10	.30
268 Todd Sandroni	.10	.30
269 Glynn Griffing	.10	.30
270 Chris Mitchell	.10	.30
271 Shawn Cobb	.10	.30
272 Doug Elmore	.10	.30
273 Dawson Pruett	.10	.30
274 Warner Alford	.10	.30
275 Archie Manning	.60	1.50
276 Kelvin Pritchett	.15	.40
277 Pat Coleman	.10	.30
278 Stevon Moore	.15	.40
279 John Darnell	.10	.30
280 Wesley Walls	.20	.50
281 Billy Brewer	.15	.40
282 Mark Young	.10	.30
283 Andre Townsend	.15	.40
284 Billy Ray Adams	.10	.30
285 Jim Dunaway	.15	.40
286 Paige Cothren	.10	.30
287 Jake Gibbs	.15	.40
288 Jim Urbanek	.10	.30
299 Tony Thompson	.10	.30
300 Johnny Majors CO	.20	.50
301 Roland Poles	.10	.30
302 Alvin Harper	.20	.50
303 Doug Baird	.10	.30
304 Greg Burke	.10	.30
305 Sterling Henton	.10	.30
306 Preston Warren	.10	.30
307 Stanley Morgan	.25	.60
308 Bobby Scott	.15	.40
309 Doug Atkins	.30	.75
310 Bill Young DB	.10	.30
311 Bob Garmon	.10	.30
312 Herman Weaver	.15	.40
313 Dewey Warren	.10	.30
314 John Boynton	.15	.40
315 Bob Davis	.10	.30
316 Pat Ryan	.10	.30
317 Keith DeLong	.15	.40
318 Bobby Dodd CO	.20	.50
319 Ricky Townsend	.10	.30
320 Eddie Brown	.15	.40
321 Herman Hickman CO	.15	.40
322 Nathan Dougherty	.10	.30
323 Mickey Marvin	.10	.30
324 Reggie Cobb	.15	.40
325A Condredge Holloway	.15	.40
325B Josh Cody	.10	.30
326A Anthony Hancock	.15	.40
326B Jack Jenkins	.10	.30
327A Steve Kiner	.10	.30
327B Bob Goodridge	.10	.30
328A Mike Mauck	.10	.30
328B Chris Gaines	.10	.30
329A Bill Bates	.25	.60
329B Willie Geny	.10	.30
330A Austin Denney	.15	.40
330B Bob Laws	.10	.30
331A Robert Neyland CO	.20	.50
331B Rob Monaco	.10	.30
332A Bob Suffridge	.10	.30
332B Chuck Scott	.10	.30
333A Abe Shires	.10	.30
333B Hek Wakefield	.10	.30
334A Robert Shaw	.15	.40
334B Ken Stone	.10	.30
335 Mark Adams	.10	.30
336 Ed Smith	.10	.30
337 Dan McGugin CO	.10	.30
338 Doug Mathews	.10	.30
339 Whit Taylor	.15	.40
340 Gene Moshier	.10	.30
341 Christie Hauck	.10	.30
342 Lee Nalley	.10	.30
343 Wamon Buggs	.10	.30
344 Jim Arnold	.15	.40
345 Buford Ray	.15	.40
346 Will Wolford	.15	.40
347 Steve Bearden	.10	.30
348 Frank Mordica	.10	.30
349 Barry Burton	.10	.30
350 Bill Wade	.20	.50
351 Tommy Woodroof	.10	.30
352 Steve Wade	.10	.30
353 Preston Brown	.10	.30
354 Ben Roderick	.10	.30
355 Charles Horton	.10	.30
356 DeMond Winston	.10	.30
357 John North	.10	.30
358 Don Orr	.10	.30
359 Art Demmas	.10	.30
360 Mark Johnson	.10	.30
361 Hootie Ingram AD	.15	.40
362 Gene Stallings CO	.30	.75
363 Alabama Checklist	.10	.30
364 Pat Dye CO	.20	.50
365 Auburn Checklist	.10	.30
366 Vince Dooley AD	.15	.40
367 Ray Goff CO	.15	.40
368 Georgia Checklist	.10	.30
369 C.M. Newton AD	.15	.40
370 Bill Curry CO	.15	.40
371 Kentucky Checklist	.10	.30
372 Joe Dean AD	.15	.40
373 Curley Hallman CO	.15	.40
374 LSU Checklist	.10	.30
375 Warner Alford AD	.10	.30
376 Billy Brewer CO	.15	.40
377 Ole Miss Checklist	.10	.30
378 Larry Templeton AD	.10	.30
379 Jackie Sherrill CO	.20	.50
380 Miss. State Checklist	.10	.30
381 Bill Arnsparger AD	.15	.40
382 Steve Spurrier CO	1.20	3.00
383 Florida Checklist	.10	.30
384 Doug Dickey AD	.10	.30
385 Johnny Majors CO	.20	.50
386 Tennessee Checklist	.10	.30
387 Paul Hoolahan AD	.10	.30
388 Gerry DiNardo CO	.20	.50
389 Vanderbilt Checklist	.10	.30
390 The Iron Bowl	.15	.40
Alabama vs. Auburn		
391 Largest Outdoor	.10	.30
Cocktail Party		
Florida vs. Georgia		
392 The Egg Bowl	.10	.30
Mississippi State		
vs. Ole Miss		
393 The Beer Barrel	.10	.30
Kentucky vs. Tennessee		
394 Drama on Halloween	.10	.30
LSU vs. Ole Miss		
395 Tennessee Hoedown	.10	.30
Tennessee vs. Vanderbilt		
396 Roy Kramer COMM	.10	.30

1991 Hoby SEC Stars Autographs

These ten specially designed signature series cards feature a prominent player from each SEC institution. They were randomly inserted in the 1991 SEC Stars Hoby gold-foil packs. Each player selected autographed 1,000 cards, and each card bears a unique serial number. The cards are identical in size and design with the corresponding player cards in the regular series, with four exceptions: 1) the stripe at the bottom of the card face is left blank for the player's autograph; 2) the numbering of the complete set has been removed; 3) the pattern of gold and blue borders on the front differs slightly from the regular issue; and 4) the Manning card displays a different photo on the front than its counterpart in the regular set. Since the cards are unnumbered, they are checklisted below in alphabetical order.

COMPLETE SET (10)	250.00	500.00
1 Carlos Alvarez	15.00	30.00
2 Zeke Bratkowski	20.00	40.00
3 Jerry Clower	60.00	100.00
4 Condredge Holloway	15.00	30.00
5 Bert Jones	30.00	60.00
6 Archie Manning	40.00	80.00
7 Ken Stabler	40.00	80.00
8 Pat Sullivan	25.00	50.00
9 Jeff Van Note	15.00	30.00
10 Bill Wade	20.00	40.00

1921 Holy Cross

This set was issued around 1922 and features cards of coaches and team captains for various Holy Cross University sports. The six cards measrue roughly 2 1/2" by 3 3/4" and were issued inside a "wrap-around" style folder that included a photo of the football team. Each card is blankbacked and was printed on thick cream colored stock.

COMPLETE SET (7)	100.00	200.00
2 D.A. Gildea FB	12.50	25.00
6 Cleo O'Donnell CO FB	10.00	20.00
7 Football Team Folder	7.50	15.00

1992 Houston Motion Sports

Produced by Motion Sports Inc., these 66 standard-size cards feature on their fronts black-bordered color player photos, mostly posed, with the player's name and uniform number appearing in white lettering within a red stripe at the top. The back carries a borderless action photo, upon which are ghosted panels that contain the player's biography and Houston highlights.

COMPLETE SET (66)	12.00	30.00
1 Freddie Gilbert	.25	.60
2 Lorenzo Dickson	.20	.50
3 Sherman Smith	.20	.50
4 Brad Whigham	.20	.50
5 Allen Aldridge	.40	1.00
6 Truett Akin	.20	.50
7 Nahala Johnson	.25	.60
8 1980 Garden State Bowl	.20	.50
Terald Clark		
9 1977 Cotton Bowl	.25	.60
10 Tyrone Davis	.20	.50
11 Kevin Bleier	.20	.50
12 Nigel Ventress	.20	.50
13 Darren Woods	.20	.50
14 Linton Weatherspoon	.20	.50
15 John R. Morris	.20	.50
16 Kevin Batiste	.25	.60
17 Kelvin McKnight	.20	.50
18 Stewart Carpenter	.20	.50
19 Ron Peters	.20	.50
20 Stephen Dixon	.25	.60
21 Chandler Evans	.20	.50
22 Tyler Mucho	.20	.50
23 Kevin Labay	.20	.50
24 Steve Clarke	.20	.50
25 Keith Jack	.20	.50
26 Steve Matejka	.20	.50
27 The Astrodome	.20	.50
28 Roman Anderson	.20	.50
29 Quarterback U.	.40	1.00
Andre Ware		
David Klingler		
30 Cougar Pride	.25	.60
Andre Ware		
David Klingler		
31 Bayou Bucket	.20	.50
(Annual Houston		
vs. Rice game)		
32 Jeff Tait	.20	.50
33 Donald Douglas	.20	.50
34 Victor Mamich	.20	.50
35 John W.Brown	.20	.50
36 Zach Chatman	.20	.50
37 Jason Youngblood	.20	.50
38 David Klingler	.60	1.50
39 John H.Brown	.20	.50
40 Tommy Guy	.20	.50
41 1980 Cotton Bowl	.25	.60
(Game action)		
42 1973 Bluebonnet Bowl	.25	.60
(Marshall Johnson)		
43 Chris Pezman	.20	.50
44 Tracy Good	.20	.50
45 Stephen Harris	.20	.50
46 Ryan McCoy	.25	.60
47 Michael Newhouse	.20	.50
48 Jimmy Klingler	.25	.60
49 Joe Wheeler	.20	.50
50 Eric Harrison	.20	.50
51 Craig Hall	.20	.50
52 Shasta (Mascot)	.20	.50
53 NCAA Records	.25	.60
(Passing and Receiving)		
54 Darrell Clapp	.25	.60
55 Eric Blount	.25	.60
56 Tiandre Sanders	.20	.50
57 Kyle Allen	.20	.50
58 Brisket Howard	.20	.50
59 Greg Thornburgh	.20	.50
60 Wilson Whitley	.40	1.00
61 Andre Ware	.60	1.50
62 John Jenkins CO	.25	.60
NNO Ad Card Motion Sports	.20	.50
NNO Front Card	.20	.50
NNO Back Card	.20	.50
NNO Checklist	.20	.50

1988 Humboldt State Smokey

This unnumbered, 11-card standard-size set was issued by the Humboldt State University football team and sponsored by the U. S. Forest Service. The cards feature posed color photos on the front. The cards are bordered right and below in green, with player information below the photo in gold lettering. The Smokey Bear logo is in the lower left corner. The backs have biographical information on the player and a cartoon concerning fire prevention.

COMPLETE SET (11)	5.00	12.00
1 Richard Ashe 1	.50	1.25
2 Darin Bradbury 64	.50	1.25
3 Rodney Dorsett 7	.50	1.25
4 Dave Harper 55	.50	1.25
5 Earl Jackson 6	.50	1.25
6 Derek Mallard 82	.50	1.25
7 Scott Reagan 60	.50	1.25
8 Wesley White 1	.50	1.25
9 Paul Wienecke 40	.50	1.25
10 William Williams 14	.50	1.25
11 Kelvin Windham 30	.50	1.25

1989 Idaho

This 12-card set features then-current football players at the University of Idaho. The cards are unnumbered, so they are listed below according to uniform number, which is displayed on both sides of the card. The photos are in black and white. The cards in the set contain "Tips from the Vandals" on the reverses and measure approximately 2 1/2" by 3 1/2".

COMPLETE SET (12)	5.00	12.00
3 Brian Smith	.30	.75
11 Tim S. Johnson	.30	.75
16 Lee Allen	.30	.75
17 John Friesz	2.00	5.00
20 Todd Hoiness	.30	.75
25 David Jackson	.30	.75
53 Steve Unger	.30	.75
58 John Rust	.30	.75
63 Troy Wright	.30	.75
67 Todd Neu	.30	.75
83 Michael Davis	.30	.75
93 Mike Zeller	.30	.75

1990 Idaho

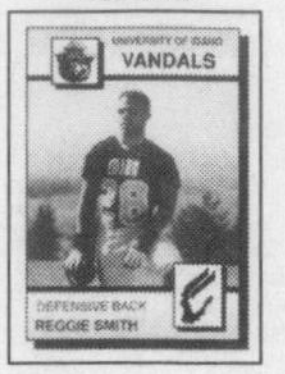

COMPLETE SET (15)	10.00	20.00
1 Joe Carrasco	.60	1.50
2 Roger Cecil	.60	1.50
3 Scott Dahlquist	.60	1.50
4 Kasey Dunn	.60	1.50
5 Bruce Harris	.60	1.50
6 Chris Hoff	.60	1.50
7 Jimmy Jacobs	.60	1.50
8 Mark Matthews	.60	1.50
9 Steve Nolan	.60	1.50
10 Charlie Oliver	.60	1.50
11 Devon Pearce	.60	1.50
12 Mike Rice	.60	1.50
13 John L. Smith CO	.60	1.50
14 Reggie Smith	.60	1.50
15 Chuck Yarbro	.60	1.50

1991 Idaho

COMPLETE (12)	7.50	15.00
1 Elia Ala'ilima-Daley	.60	1.50
2 Thayne Doyle	.60	1.50
3 Kasey Dunn	.60	1.50
4 Jeff Jordan	.60	1.50
5 Robert Monk	.60	1.50
6 Yo Murphy	.60	1.50
7 Doug Nussmeier	.60	1.50
8 Devon Pearce	.60	1.50
9 Jeff Robinson	.60	1.50
10 Will Saffo	.60	1.50
11 Jody Schnug	.60	1.50
12 John Sirmon	.60	1.50

1909-21 Illinois Postcards

A large number of postcards were issued over a period of years between 1910-1921 by Illinois University. Most of them feature campus buildings or scenes, while others feature football players or game action photography. We've cataloged just the postcards below that feature individual football players, team photos, coaches, and game action scenes that are identifiable. The cards feature a standard postcard style back with "U of I Student Life Series, by Strauch Photo Craft House" printed on the backs of some, but not all of the cards. The fronts are printed in sepia or black-and-white with the player's last name typically printed near the photo. Some also include extra data such as the year or "captain." The photographer's name "Lloyde, Aristo, or Strauch" is sometimes printed on the fronts as well. Any additions or information on the checklist below would be appreciated.

1 L.S. Bernstein	30.00	50.00
2 Glenn Butzer	30.00	50.00
3 Arthur Hall CO	30.00	50.00
4 Ralph Jones CO	40.00	75.00
5 Reynold Kraft	30.00	50.00
6 Justa Lindgren CO	30.00	50.00
7 Bart Macomber	75.00	125.00
(hands on hips)		
8 Bart Macomber	50.00	80.00
(Capt. Bart)		
9 J.R. Merriman	30.00	50.00
10 Albert Mohr	30.00	50.00
11 James Richards	30.00	50.00
12 Chester Roberts	30.00	50.00
13 Enos Rowe	30.00	50.00
(Captain Rowe, 1913)		
14 Elmer Rundquist ERR	30.00	50.00
(name misspelled Roundquist)		
15 Otto Seiler	30.00	50.00
16 Dutch Sternaman	125.00	200.00
17 J.O. Tupper	30.00	50.00
18 Forest Van Hook	30.00	50.00
Pom Sinnock		
(The Twins)		
19 John Weiss	30.00	50.00
20 Bob Zuppke CO	75.00	125.00
21 1909 Team Photo	35.00	60.00
22 1910 Team Photo	35.00	60.00
23 1911 Team Photo	35.00	60.00
24 1912 Team Photo	35.00	60.00
(1912 Varsity, U of I)		
25 1912 Team Photo	30.00	50.00
('12 Class team)		
26 1916 Team Photo	60.00	100.00
27 Illinois 6 vs. Indiana 5 (1909)	25.00	40.00
(Butzer's end run)		
28 Illinois 8 vs. Chicago 14 (1909)	25.00	40.00
(action shot near goal line)		
29 Illinois 23 vs. Millikin 0 (1909)	25.00	40.00
(running play)		
30 Illinois 3 vs. Chicago 0, '10	25.00	40.00
(Seiler makes the score)		
31 Illinois 3 vs. Chicago 0	25.00	40.00
(Seiler drops ball over the bars)		
32 Illinois 3 vs. Chicago 0,	25.00	40.00
Oct.15, 1910		
(Seiler's Drop Kick Wins Game)		
33 Chicago 0 vs. Illinois 3,	25.00	40.00
Oct.15, 1910		
(A Near Touchdown by Illinois)		
34 Illinois 3 vs. Chicago 0	25.00	40.00
Oct.15, 1910		
(scrimmage line close-up)		
35 Illinois 29 vs. Drake 0, Oct.8, 1910	25.00	40.00
(Over The Line, Illinois Scores)		
36 Illinois 3 vs. Indiana 0, Nov.5, 1910	25.00	40.00
(tackle action shot)		
37 Illinois 9 vs. St. Louis 0,	25.00	40.00
Oct. 14, 1911		
(action shot, punt in the air)		
38 Illinois 12 vs. Purdue 3,	25.00	40.00
Nov. 4, 1911		
(pass or interception action)		
39 Illinois 12 vs. Purdue 3,	25.00	40.00
Nov. 4, 1911		
(close-up running play action)		
40 Illinois 9 vs. Purdue 9,	25.00	40.00
Nov. 9, 1912		
41 Kentucky 0 vs. Illinois 21, 1913	25.00	40.00
(running play action shot)		
42 Missouri 7 vs. Illinois 25, 1913	25.00	40.00
(passing play action shot)		
43 Illinois 7 vs. Chicago 28, 1913	25.00	40.00
(runner near goal line)		
44 Illinois 21 vs. Chicago 7	25.00	40.00
Homecoming Nov.14 (1914)		
(runner approaching goal line)		
45 Illinois 17 vs. Wisconsin 9	25.00	40.00
Nov. 21, 1914		
(Wisconsin held for downs		
on Illinois 5 yd. line)		
46 Illinois 6 vs. Minnesota 6,	25.00	40.00
Homecoming (1915)		
Holding on the line/4 downs with only foot to gain		
47 Illinois 0 vs. Purdue 0,	25.00	40.00
Nov. 15, 1915		
(Purdue kicking from goal line)		
48 Illinois 17 vs. Wisconsin 3	25.00	40.00
(Bart's Place Kick)		
49 Illinois 17 vs. Wisconsin 3	25.00	40.00
(Wisconsin's Place Kick)		
50 Illinois 17 vs. Wisconsin 3 (1915)	25.00	40.00
The Band		
(band and players warming up)		
51 Illinois vs. Purdue, '16	25.00	40.00
(line of scrimmage action photo)		
52 Illinois 0 vs. Wisconsin 20 (1921)	25.00	40.00
(free kick action shot)		

1974 Illinois Team Sheets

These photos were issued by the school to promote the football program. Each measures roughly 8 by 10 and features eight black and white images of players with the school name appearing at the top. The backs are blank.

1 Bob Blackman CO	4.00	8.00
Lonnie Perrin		
Jim Kopatz		
Tracy Campbell		
Tom Hicks		
Mike McCray		
Dan Beaver		
Mike Gow		
2 Mark Petersen	4.00	8.00
Bruce Beaman		
Steve Greene		
Ty McMillin		
Jim Phillips		
Revie Sorey		
Jeff Hollenbach		
Bill Kleckner		

1990 Illinois Centennial

This 45-card set measures the standard size and was issued to celebrate 100 years of football at the University of Illinois. The set was produced by College Classics and the State Farm Insurance agents in Illinois. The front features either a color or black and white photo of the player with a dark blue border on an orange background. The back has biographical information as well as the card number.

COMPLETE SET (45)	12.00	30.00
1 Red Grange	1.60	4.00
2 Dick Butkus	1.60	4.00
3 Ray Nitschke	.80	2.00
4 Jim Grabowski	.20	.50
5 Alex Agase	.20	.50
6 Buddy Young	.20	.50
7 Scott Studwell	.20	.50
8 Tony Eason	.20	.50
9 John Mackovic	.20	.50
10 Jack Trudeau	.20	.50
11 Jeff George	.60	1.50
12 Rose Bowl Coaches	.15	.40
Ray Eliot		
Pete Elliott		
Mike White		
13 George Huff	.15	.40
14 David Williams	.15	.40
15 Bob Zuppke	.40	1.00
16 George Halas	1.00	2.50
17 Dike Eddleman	.15	.40
18 Dave Wilson	.15	.40
19 Tab Bennett	.15	.40
20 Jim Juriga	.15	.40
21 John Karras	.15	.40
22 Bobby Mitchell	.40	1.00
23 Dan Beaver	.15	.40
24 Joe Rutgens	.20	.50
25 Bill Burrell	.15	.40
26 J.C. Caroline	.20	.50
27 Al Brosky	.15	.40
28 Don Thorp	.15	.40
29 First Football Team	.15	.40
30 Red Grange Retired	1.00	2.50
31 Memorial Stadium	.15	.40
32 Chris White	.15	.40
33 Early Stars	.15	.40
Ralph Chapman		
Perry Graves		
Bart Macomber		
34 Early Stars	.15	.40
John Depler		
Charles Carney		
Jim McMillen		
35 Early Stars	.15	.40
Burt Ingwerson		
Butch Nowack		
Bernie Shively		
36 Great Quarterbacks	.15	.40
Fred Custardo		
Mike Wells		
Tom O'Connell		
37 Great Running Backs	.20	.50
Thomas Rooks		
Abe Woodson		
Keith Jones		
38 Great Receivers	.20	.50
Mike Bellamy		
Doug Dieken		
John Wright		
39 Great Offensive	.15	.40
Forrest Van Hook		
Larry McCarren		
Chris Babyar		
40 Great Defensive Backs	.15	.40
Craig Swope		
George Donnelly		
Mike Gower		
41 Great Linebackers	.15	.40
Charles Boerlo		
Don Hansen		
John Sullivan		
42 Defensive Linemen	.15	.40
Archie Sutton		
Chuck Studley		
Scott Davis		
43 Great Kickers	.15	.40
Mike Bass K		
Bill Brown		
Frosty Peters		
44 Retired Numbers	.80	2.00
Dick Butkus		
45 Football Centennial	.15	.40
Logo		

1992 Illinois

Produced by Flying Color Graphics Inc. and sponsored by WDWS radio station (AM 1400), this 48-card standard-size set features the University of Illinois football team. The cards are printed on thin card stock. The fronts feature a mix of posed or action color player photos. The pictures are bordered on the left by an orange stripe and at the bottom by a purple stripe. The player's name and position are printed in the purple stripe. The backs carry biographical information, the producer's logo, and a brief public service announcement. The cards are unnumbered and checklisted below in alphabetical order.

COMPLETE SET (48)	8.00	20.00
1 Derek Allen	.14	.35
2 Jeff Arneson	.14	.35
3 Randy Bierman	.14	.35
4 Darren Boyer	.14	.35
5 Rod Boykin	.14	.35
6 Mike Cole	.14	.35
7 Chad Copher	.14	.35
8 Fred Cox	.20	.50
9 Robert Crumpton	.14	.35
10 Ken Dilger	1.00	2.50
11 Jason Edwards	.14	.35
12 Greg Engel	.14	.35
13 Steve Feagin	.14	.35
14 Erik Foggey	.14	.35
15 Kevin Hardy	1.60	4.00
16 Jeff Hasenstab	.14	.35
17 John Holecek	.14	.35
18 Brad Hopkins	.20	.50
19 John Horn	.14	.35
20 Dana Howard	.20	.50
21 Filmel Johnson	.14	.35
22 Jon Kerr	.14	.35
23 Jeff Kinney	.20	.50
24 Jim Klein	.14	.35
25 Todd Leach	.14	.35
26 Wagner Lester	.14	.35
27 Lashon Ludington	.14	.35
28 Clinton Lynch	.14	.35
29 Tim McCloud	.14	.35
30 David Olson	.14	.35
31 Antwoine Patton	.14	.35
32 Jim Pesek	.14	.35
33 Alfred Pierce	.14	.35
34 Mark Qualls	.14	.35
35 Phil Rathke	.14	.35
36 Chris Richardson	.14	.35
37 Derrick Rucker	.14	.35
38 Aaron Shelby	.14	.35
39 John Sidari	.14	.35
40 J.J. Strong	.14	.35
41 Mike Suarez	.14	.35
42 Lou Tepper CO	.20	.50
43 Scott Turner	.14	.35
44 Jason Verduzco	.20	.50
45 Tyrone Washington	.14	.35
46 Forry Wells	.14	.35
47 Pat Wendt	.14	.35
48 John Wright	.14	.35

1994 Illinois State

COMPLETE SET (20)	4.00	8.00
1 Danny Barnett	.20	.50
2 Bruce Barro	.20	.50
3 Joel Bosman	.20	.50
4 Dave Connell	.20	.50
5 Herby Demosthenes	.20	.50
6 Kevin Dixon	.20	.50
7 Armandos Fisher	.20	.50
8 Jon Hutton	.20	.50
9 Kevin Johnson	.20	.50
10 Kenneth Lasley	.20	.50
11 Corey Mackey	.20	.50
12 Jon McAvoy	.20	.50
13 Mike O'Sullivan	.20	.50
14 Bennie Radford	.20	.50
15 Leon Smith	.20	.50
16 Damon Turner	.20	.50
17 Franky West	.20	.50
18 Charles Williams	.20	.50
19 Jason Zachery	.20	.50
20 Title Card	.20	.50

1974 Indiana Team Sheets

These photos were issued by the school to promote the football program. Each measures roughly 8" by 10" and features eight black and white images of players with the school name appearing at the top. The backs are blank.

1 Larry Atkinson	4.00	10.00
Rod Lawson		
Mark Deming		
Jim Shuck		
Willie Jones		
Bob Kramer		
Tom Buck		
Rod Harris		
2 Lee Corso CO	4.00	10.00
Trent Smock		
Mike Flanagan		
Dennis Cremeens		
Courtney Snyder		
Larry Jameson		
Mike Glazier		
Donnie Thomas		

2004 Indiana

COMPLETE SET (16)	5.00	10.00
1 Victor Adeyanju	.40	1.00
2 Lance Bennett	.30	.75
3 Jodie Clemons	.30	.75
4 BenJarvus Green-Ellis	.30	.75
5 Aaron Halterman	.30	.75
6 Adam Hines	.30	.75
7 Chris Jahnke	.30	.75
8 Herana-Daze Jones	.30	.75
9 Kenny Kendal	.30	.75
10 Kyle Killion	.30	.75
11 Matt Lovecchio	.30	.75
12 Will Meyers	.30	.75
13 John Pannozzo	.30	.75
14 Courtney Roby	.60	1.50
15 Isaac Sowells	.30	.75
16 Paul Szczesny	.30	.75

2005 Indiana

COMPLETE SET (16)	5.00	10.00
1 Victor Adeyanju	.40	1.00
2 Courtney Clency	.30	.75
3 Brandon Hatcher	.30	.75
4 Adam Hines	.30	.75
5 Ben Ishola	.30	.75
6 Damien Jones	.30	.75
7 Kyle Killion	.30	.75
8 Rhett Kleinschmidt	.30	.75
9 Will Lumpkin	.30	.75
10 Josh Moore	.30	.75
11 Mark Neaman	.30	.75
12 John Pannozzo	.30	.75
13 Russ Richardson	.30	.75
14 Isaac Sowells	.30	.75
15 Chris Taylor	.30	.75
16 Yamar Washington	.30	.75

2006 Indiana

COMPLETE SET (16)	4.00	8.00
1 Scott Anderson	.20	.50
2 Tyson Beattie	.20	.50
3 Lance Bennett	.20	.50
4 Justin Frye	.20	.50
5 Jahkeen Gilmore	.20	.50
6 Troy Grosfield	.20	.50
7 Terry Hoeppner CO	.20	.50
8 Kenny Kendal	.20	.50
9 Chris Manglero	.20	.50
10 Eric McClurg	.20	.50
11 Graeme McFarland	.20	.50
12 Will Meyers	.20	.50
13 Casey Nowinski	.20	.50
14 Matt O'Neal	.20	.50
15 Jake Powers	.20	.50
16 Ryan Skelton	.20	.50

1982-83 Indiana State

This multi-sport set was sponsored by the First National Bank of Terre Haute, 7-Up, and WTHI/TV Channel 10. The cards measure approximately 2 5/8" by 4 1/8". On a bright blue card face, the fronts feature black and white player photos enclosed by a white border. A white diagonal stripe appears beneath the picture, with a drawing of the Sycamores' mascot and the words "Sycamore Rampage." The backs have brief biographical information, a quote about the player, a safety tip, and sponsor logos. Sports represented in this set include wrestling (1), basketball (2-3, 4-10, 12), football (11), and gymnastics (13). Olympic athletes included in the set are Bruce Baumgartner and Kurt Thomas. The key card in the set is NBA superstar Larry Bird. The cards are unnumbered and checklisted below in alphabetical order.

1 David Allen FB	1.25	3.00
2 Doug Arnold FB	1.25	3.00
3 James Banks FB	1.25	3.00
4 Scott Bartel FB	1.25	3.00
6 Kurt Bell FB	1.25	3.00
7 Terry Bell FB	1.25	3.00
8 Steve Bidwell FB	1.25	3.00
10 Keith Bonney FB	1.25	3.00
11 Mark Boster FB	1.25	3.00
12 Bobby Boyce FB	1.25	3.00
14 Steve Brickey CO FB	1.25	3.00
15 Mark Bryson FB	1.25	3.00
16 Steve Buxton FB	1.25	3.00
17 Ed Campbell FB	1.25	3.00
18 Jeff Campbell FB	1.25	3.00
19 Tom Chapman FB	1.25	3.00
21 Darrold Clardy FB	1.25	3.00
23 Wayne Davis FB	1.25	3.00
24 Herbert Dawson FB	1.25	3.00
25 Richard Dawson FB	1.25	3.00
26 Chris Delaplaine FB	1.25	3.00
27 Max Dillon FB	1.25	3.00
28 Rick Dwenger FB	1.25	3.00
30 Ed Foggs FB	1.25	3.00
32 Allen Hartwig FB	1.25	3.00
33 Pat Henderson CO FB	1.25	3.00
34 Don Hitz FB	1.25	3.00
35 Pete Hoener CO FB	1.25	3.00
36 Bob Hopkins FB	1.25	3.00
37 Kris Huber FB	1.25	3.00
38 Leroy Irvin FB	1.25	3.00
39 Mike Johannes FB	1.25	3.00
40 Anthony Kimball FB	1.25	3.00
41 Gregg Kimbrough FB	1.25	3.00
42 Bob Koehne FB	1.25	3.00
43 Jerry Lasko CO FB	1.25	3.00
44 Kevin Lynch FB	1.25	3.00
45 Dan Maher FB	1.25	3.00
46 Ed Martin FB	1.25	3.00
47 Regis Mason FB	1.25	3.00
49 Rob McIntyre FB	1.25	3.00
50 Quintin Mikell FB	1.25	3.00
51 Jeff Miller FB	1.25	3.00
52 Mark Miller FB	1.25	3.00
54 Mike Osborne FB	1.25	3.00
55 Max Payne CO FB	1.25	3.00
56 Scott Piercy FB	1.25	3.00
57 Dennis Raetz CO FB	1.25	3.00
58 Kevin Ramsey FB	1.25	3.00
59 Dean Reader FB	1.25	3.00
60 Eric Robinson FB	1.25	3.00
62 Walter Seaphus FB	1.25	3.00
63 Craig Shaffer FB	1.25	3.00
65 John Spradley FB	1.25	3.00
66 Manual Studway FB	1.25	3.00
67 Sam Suggs FB	1.25	3.00
68 Larry Swart FB	1.25	3.00
70 Bob Tyree FB	1.25	3.00
71 Bob Turner CO FB	1.25	3.00
72 Brad Verdun FB	1.25	3.00
73 Keith Ward FB	1.25	3.00
74 Sean Whiten FB	1.25	3.00
75 Perry Willett FB	1.25	3.00
77 Cheerleaders	1.25	3.00
79 Sparkettes	.75	2.00

1971 Iowa Team Photos

This 32-player University of Iowa photo set was issued as four sheets measuring approximately 8" by 10" featuring eight black and white player portraits. The backs are blank. We have arranged the photos in order alphabetically by the player in the upper left hand corner.

COMPLETE SET (4)	15.00	30.00
1 Geoff Mickelson	5.00	10.00
Craig Clemons		
Frank Holmes		
Levi Mitchell		
Charles Podolak		
Lorin Lynch		
Steve Penney		
Larry Horton		
2 Alan Schaefer	3.50	7.00
Dave Triplett		
John Muller		
Jim Kaiser		
Wendell Bell		
Clark Malmer		
Rich Solomon		
Kelly Disser		
3 Bill Schoonover	3.50	7.00
Frank Sunderman		
Craig Darling		
Tom Cabalka		
Dave Simms		
Bill Rose		
Buster Hoinkes		
Charles Cross		
4 Kyle Skogman	3.50	7.00
Kerry Reardon		
Dave Harris		
Rob Fick		
Mike Dillner		
Ike White		
Mark Nelson		
Harry Kokolus		

1974 Iowa Team Sheets

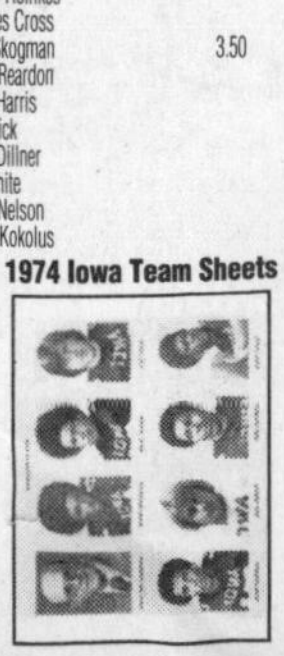

These photos were issued by the school to promote the football program. Each measures roughly 8" by 10" and features eight black and white images of players with the school name appearing at the top. The backs are blank.

1 Bob Commings CO	4.00	8.00
Rodney Wellington		
Andre Jackson		
Rick Penney		
Butch Caldwell		
Bill Schultz		
Earl Douthitt		
Bobby Ousley		
2 Lester Washington	4.00	8.00
Tyrone Dye		
Jim Jensen		
David Bryant		
Mark Fetter		
Lynn Heil		
Sid Thomas		
Doug Reichardt		

1984 Iowa

The 1984 Iowa Hawkeyes set contains 60 standard-size cards. The fronts feature color portrait photos bordered in black. The backs provide brief profiles. The cards are unnumbered and so they are listed in alphabetical order.

COMPLETE SET (60)	40.00	75.00
1 Kevin Angel	.40	1.00
2 Kerry Burt	.40	1.00
3 Fred Bush	.40	1.00
4 Craig Clark	.40	1.00
5 Zane Corbin	.40	1.00
6 Nate Creer	.40	1.00
7 Dave Croston	.40	1.00
8 George Davis	.40	1.00
9 Jeff Drost	.40	1.00
10 Quinn Early	2.00	5.00
11 Mike Flagg	.40	1.00
12 Hayden Fry CO	1.50	3.00
13 Bruce Gear	.40	1.00
14 Owen Gill	.50	1.25
15 Bill Glass	.50	1.25
16 Mike Haight	.50	1.25
17 Bill Happel	.40	1.00
18 Kevin Harmon	.50	1.25
19 Ronnie Harmon	1.50	4.00
20 Craig Hartman	.40	1.00
21 Jonathan Hayes	.60	1.50
22 Erric Hedgeman	.40	1.00
23 Scott Helverson	.40	1.00
24 Mike Hooks	.40	1.00
25 Paul Hufford	.40	1.00
26 Keith Hunter	.40	1.00
27 George Little	.40	1.00
28 Chuck Long	2.00	5.00
29 J.C. Love-Jordan	.40	1.00
30 George Millett	.40	1.00
31 Devon Mitchell	.50	1.25
32 Tom Nichol	.40	1.00
33 Kelly O'Brien	.40	1.00
34 Hap Peterson	.40	1.00
35 Joe Schuster	.50	1.25
36 Tim Sennott	.40	1.00
37 Ken Sims	.40	1.00
38 Mark Sindlinger	.40	1.00
39 Robert Smith	.40	1.00
40 Kevin Spitzig	.40	1.00
41 Larry Station	.40	1.00
42 Mike Stoops	.40	1.00
43 Dave Strobel	.40	1.00
44 Mark Vlasic	.75	2.00
45 Jon Vrieze	.40	1.00
46 Tony Wancket	.40	1.00
47 Herb Webster	.40	1.00
48 Coaching Staff	.50	1.25
49 Captains	.60	1.50
50 Bowl Players	.50	1.25
51 Kevin Harmon	1.00	2.50
Ronnie Harmon		
Harmon Brothers		
52 Cheerleaders	.40	1.00
53 Pompons	.40	1.00
54 Kinnick Stadium	.40	1.00
55 Herky the Hawk	.40	1.00
(Mascot)		
56 Rose Bowl Ring	.40	1.00
57 Peach Bowl Trophy	.40	1.00
58 Gator Bowl Stadium	.40	1.00
59 Floyd of Rosedale	.40	1.00
(Trophy)		
60 Checklist Card	.40	1.00

1985 Iowa

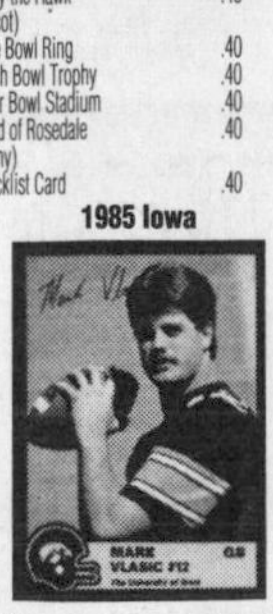

The 1985 Iowa Hawkeyes set contains 60 standard-size cards. The fronts feature color portrait photos bordered in black. The backs provide brief profiles. The cards are unnumbered and listed below in alphabetical order.

COMPLETE SET (60)	40.00	75.00
1 Tim Anderson	.40	1.00
2 Rick Bayless	.40	1.00
3 Mike Bennett	.40	1.00
4 Doug Burrell	.40	1.00
5 Kerry Burt	.40	1.00
6 Fred Bush	.40	1.00
7 Craig Clark	.40	1.00
8 Nate Crer	.40	1.00
9 Dave Croston	.40	1.00
10 George Davis	.40	1.00
11 Jeff Drost	.40	1.00
12 Quinn Early	2.00	5.00
13 Mike Flagg	.40	1.00
14 Chris Gambol	.40	1.00
15 Bruce Gear	.40	1.00
16 Dave Haight	.40	1.00
17 Mike Haight	.50	1.25
18 Bill Happel	.40	1.00
19 Kevin Harmon	.50	1.25
20 Ronnie Harmon	1.50	4.00
21 Scott Helverson	.40	1.00
22 Rob Houghtlin	.40	1.00
23 David Hudson	.40	1.00
24 Tom Humphrey	.40	1.00
25 Lloyd Kimber	.40	1.00
26 Gary Kostrubala	.40	1.00
27 Bob Kratch	.40	1.00
28 Chuck Long	2.00	5.00
29 Chuck Long in Tux	1.00	2.50
30 George Millet	.40	1.00
31 Devon Mitchell	.50	1.25
32 Joe Mott	.40	1.00
33 Jay Norvell	.40	1.00
34 Kelly O'Brien	.40	1.00
35 Hap Peterson	.40	1.00
36 Richard Pryor	.40	1.00
37 Rick Schmidt	.40	1.00
38 Joe Schuster	.50	1.25
39 Ken Sims	.40	1.00
40 Mark Sindlinger	.40	1.00
41 Robert Smith	.40	1.00
42 Mark Spranger	.40	1.00
43 Larry Station	.40	1.00
44 Tyrone Taylor	.40	1.00
45 Mark Vlasic	.75	2.00
46 Jon Vrieze	.40	1.00
47 Herb Wester	.40	1.00
48 Dan Wirth	.40	1.00
49 Captains	.60	1.50
Hap Peterson		
Ronnie Harmon		
Larry Station		
Chuck Long		
Mike Haight		
50 Cheerleaders	.40	1.00
51 Coaches	.50	1.25
Bill Brashier		
Dan McCarney		
Bennie Wyatt		
Barry Alvarez		
Bill Dervrich		
Del Miller		
Don Patterson		
Bill Snyder		
Hayden Fry		
Kirk Ferentz		
Carl Jackson		
52 Floyd of Rosedale Trophy	.40	1.00
53 1984 Freedon Bowl	.40	1.00
54 Gator Bowl Stadium	.40	1.00
55 Hayden Fry CO	1.25	3.00
56 Herky The Hawk	.40	1.00
57 Kinnick Stadium	.40	1.00
58 Peach Bowl Trophy	.40	1.00
59 Pom Pons Squad	.40	1.00
60 Rose Bowl Ring	.40	1.00

1986 Iowa

The 1986 Iowa Hawkeyes set contains 62 standard-size cards. The fronts feature color portrait photos bordered in black. The backs provide brief profiles. The cards are unnumbered and listed below in alphabetical order.

COMPLETE SET (62)	30.00	60.00
1 Dave Alexander	.40	1.00
2 Bill Anderson	.40	1.00
3 Tim Anderson	.40	1.00
4 Rick Bayless	.40	1.00
5 Tyrone Berrie	.40	1.00
6 Mike Bolan	.40	1.00
7 Mike Burke	.40	1.00
8 Kerry Burt	.40	1.00
9 Craig Clark	.40	1.00
10 Marv Cook	.40	1.00
11 Pat Coppinger	.40	1.00
12 Marshal Cotton	.40	1.00
13 Dave Croston	.40	1.00
14 Kyle Crowe	.40	1.00
15 George Davis	.40	1.00
16 Greg Divis	.40	1.00
17 Jeff Drost	.40	1.00
18 Quinn Early	1.50	4.00
19 Mike Flagg	.40	1.00
20 Chris Gambol	.40	1.00
21 Grant Goodman	.40	1.00
22 Robert Grafton	.40	1.00
23 Dave Haight	.50	1.25
24 Deven Harberts	.40	1.00
25 Kevin Harmon	.50	1.25
26 Chuck Hartlied	.40	1.00
27 Tork Hook	.40	1.00
28 Rob Houghtlin	.40	1.00
29 David Hudson	.40	1.00
30 Gary Kostrubala	.40	1.00
31 Bob Kratch	.40	1.00
32 Jim Mauro	.40	1.00
33 Marc Mazzeri	.40	1.00
34 Joe Mott	.50	1.25
35 Tom Poholsky	.40	1.00
36 J.J. Puk	.40	1.00
37 Jim Reilly	.40	1.00
38 Kevin Ringer	.40	1.00
39 Rick Schmidt	.40	1.00
41 Ken Sims	.40	1.00
42 Mark Sindlinger	.40	1.00
43 Keaton Smiley	.40	1.00
44 Robert Smith	.40	1.00
45 Mark Spranger	.40	1.00
46 Steve Thomas	.40	1.00
47 Mark Vlasic	1.00	2.50
48 Jon Vrieze	.40	1.00
49 Herb Wester	.40	1.00
50 Anthony Wright	.40	1.00
51 Captains	.50	1.25
Dave Croston		
Jeff Drost		
Ken Sims		
George Davis		
Mark Vlasic		
52 Cheerleaders	.40	1.00
53 Coaching Staff	.50	1.25
Bill Brashier		
Dan McCarney		
Bennie Wyatt		
Barry Alvarez		
Bill Dervrich		
Del Miller		
Don Patterson		
Bill Snyder		
Hayden Fry		
Kirk Ferentz		
Carl Jackson		
54 Floyd of Rosedale Trophy	.40	1.00
55 Freedom Bowl	.40	1.00
game action		
56 Hayden Fry CO	1.00	2.50
57 Gator Bowl	.40	1.00
game action		
58 Herky The Hawk	.40	1.00
59 Kinnick Stadium	.40	1.00
60 Peach Bowl	.40	1.00
game action		
61 Pom Pons	.40	1.00
62 Rose Bowl	.40	1.00
game action		
63 Rose Bowl Rings	.40	1.00

1987 Iowa

The 1987 Iowa football set contains 63 cards measuring approximately 2 1/2" by 3 9/16". Inside a black border, the fronts display color posed photos shot from the waist up. The Hawkeye helmet appears in the lower left corner, with player information in a yellow stripe extending to the right. The horizontally oriented backs have biographical information, player profile, and bowl game emblems. The cards are unnumbered and checklisted below in alphabetical order, with non-player cards listed at the end.

COMPLETE SET (63)	16.00	40.00
1 Mark Adams	.25	.60
2 Dave Alexander	.30	.75
3 Bill Anderson	.25	.60
4 Tim Anderson	.25	.60
5 Rick Bayless	.25	.60
6 Jeff Beard	.25	.60
7 Mike Burke	.25	.60
8 Kerry Burt	.25	.60
9 Malcolm Christie	.25	.60
10 Craig Clark	.25	.60
11 Marv Cook	.60	1.50
12 Jeff Croston	.25	.60
13 Greg Divis	.25	.60
14 Quinn Early	1.25	3.00
15 Greg Fedders	.25	.60
16 Mike Flagg	.25	.60
17 Melvin Foster	.25	.60
18 Hayden Fry CO	.75	2.00
19 Grant Goodman	.25	.60
20 Dave Haight	.30	.75
21 Merton Hanks	1.25	3.00
22 Deven Harberts	.25	.60
23 Kevin Harmon	.30	.75
24 Chuck Hartlieb	.40	1.00
25 Tork Hook	.25	.60
26 Rob Houghtlin	.25	.60
27 David Hudson	.25	.60
28 Myron Keppy	.25	.60
29 Jeff Koeppel	.25	.60
30 Bob Kratch	.60	1.50
31 Peter Marciano	.25	.60
32 Jim Mauro	.25	.60
33 Marc Mazzeri	.25	.60
34 Dan McGwire	.40	1.00
35 Mike Miller	.25	.60
36 Joe Mott	.30	.75
37 James Pipkins	.25	.60
38 Tom Poholsky	.30	.75
39 Jim Poynton	.25	.60
40 J.J. Puk	.25	.60
41 Brad Quast	.25	.60
42 Jim Reilly	.25	.60
43 Matt Ruhland	.25	.60
44 Bob Schmitt	.25	.60
45 Joe Schuster	.25	.60
46 Dwight Sistrunk	.30	.75
47 Mark Stoops	.25	.60
48 Steve Thomas	.25	.60
49 Kent Thompson	.25	.60
50 Travis Walkins	.25	.60
51 Herb Wester	.25	.60
52 Anthony Wright	.25	.60
53 Big 10 Championship	.25	.60
Ring and Rose Bowl Ring		
54 Cheerleaders	.25	.60
55 Floyd of Rosedale	.25	.60
(Trophy)		
56 Freedom Bowl	.30	.75
(Game Action Photo)		
57 Herky the Hawk	.25	.60
(Mascot)		
58 Holiday Bowl	.30	.75
(Game Action Photo)		
59 Indoor Practice	.25	.60
Facility		
60 Iowa Team Captains	.60	1.50
(Quinn Early and		
five others)		
61 Kinnick Stadium	.25	.60
62 Peach Bowl	.25	.60
(Game Action Photo)		
63 Pom Pons	.25	.60
(Cheerleaders)		

1988 Iowa

The 1988 Iowa Hawkeyes set contains 64 standard-size cards. The fronts feature color portrait photos bordered in black. The horizontally oriented backs show brief profiles. The cards are unnumbered and, therefore, listed by jersey numbers.

COMPLETE SET (64)	12.00	30.00
2 Travis Watkins	.25	.60
4 James Pipkins	.20	.50
5 Mike Burke	.20	.50
8 Chuck Hartlieb	.25	.60
10 Anthony Wright	.20	.50
14 Tom Poholsky	.25	.60
16 Deven Harberts	.20	.50
18 Leroy Smith	.20	.50
20 David Hudson	.20	.50
21 Tony Stewart	.20	.50
22 Sean Smith	.20	.50
23 Richard Bass	.20	.50
26 Peter Marciano	.20	.50
29 Greg Brown	.20	.50
30 Grant Goodman	.20	.50
31 John Derby	.20	.50
32 Mike Saunders	1.25	3.00
35 Brad Quast	.20	.50
38 Chet Davis	.20	.50
40 Marc Mazzeri	.20	.50
41 Mark Stoops	.20	.50
42 Tork Hook	.20	.50
44 Keaton Smiley	.20	.50
45 Merton Hanks	.75	2.00
48 Tyrone Berrie	.20	.50
50 Bill Anderson	.20	.50
51 Jeff Koeppel	.20	.50
53 Greg Fedders	.20	.50
57 Matt Ruhland	.20	.50
58 Greg Davis	.20	.50
60 Bob Schmitt	.20	.50
61 Dave Turner	.20	.50
64 Dave Haight	.25	.60
66 Melvin Foster	.20	.50
67 Jim Poynton	.20	.50
68 Tim Anderson	.20	.50
70 Bob Kratch	.25	.60
71 Jim Johnson	.20	.50
74 George Hawthorne	.20	.50
75 Greg Aegerter	.20	.50
77 Paul Glonek	.20	.50
80 Steve Green	.20	.50
81 Brian Wise	.20	.50
82 Jon Filloon	.20	.50
84 Marv Cook	.40	1.00
85 John Palmer	.25	.60
87 Jeff Skillett	.20	.50
88 Tom Ward	.20	.50
95 Jim Reilly	.20	.50
96 Ron Geater	.20	.50
97 Joe Mott	.25	.60
99 Moses Santos	.20	.50
NNO Team Captains	.30	.75
(Marv Cook and		
four others)		
NNO Hayden Fry CO	.60	1.50
NNO Holiday Bowl 1987	.30	.75
Hayden Fry CO)		
NNO Peach Bowl	.25	.60
(Game Action Photo)		
NNO Holiday Bowl 1986	.25	.60
(Game Action Photo)		
NNO Herky the Hawk(Mascot)	.20	.50
NNO Cheerleaders	.20	.50
NNO Kinnick Stadium	.20	.50
NNO Pom Pons	.20	.50
(Cheerleaders)		
NNO Championship Rings	.20	.50
NNO Indoor Practice	.20	.50
Facility		
NNO Symbolic Tiger Hawk	.20	.50
(Helmet)		

1989 Iowa

The 1989 Iowa football set contains 90 cards measuring approximately 2 1/2" by 3 9/16". Inside a black border, the fronts display color posed photos shot from the waist up. The team helmet appears in the lower left corner, with player information in a yellow stripe extending to the right. The horizontally oriented backs have biographical information, player profile, and bowl game emblems. The cards are unnumbered and checklisted below in alphabetical order, with non-player cards listed at the end.

COMPLETE SET (90)	12.00	30.00
1 Greg Aegerter	.15	.40
2 Kevin Allendorf	.15	.40
3 Bill Anderson	.15	.40
4 Richard Bass	.15	.40
5 Rob Baxley	.15	.40
6 Nick Bell	.40	1.00
7 Phil Bradley	.15	.40
8 Greg Brown	.15	.40
9 Doug Buch	.15	.40
10 Gary Clark	.15	.40
11 Roderick Davis	.15	.40
12 Scott Davis	.40	1.00
13 John Derby	.20	.50
14 Mike Devlin	.15	.40
15 Jason Dumont	.15	.40
16 Mike Ertz	.15	.40
17 Ted Faley	.15	.40
18 Greg Fedders	.15	.40
19 Mike Ferroni	.20	.50
20 Jon Filloon	.15	.40
21 Melvin Foster	.20	.50
22 Hayden Fry CO	.40	1.00
23 Ron Geater	.15	.40
24 Ed Gochenour	.15	.40
25 Merton Hanks	.60	1.50
26 Jim Hartlieb	.20	.50
27 George Hawthorne	.15	.40
28 Tork Hook	.15	.40
29 Danan Hughes	.60	1.50
30 Jim Johnson	.15	.40
31 Jeff Koeppel	.15	.40
32 Marvin Lampkin	.15	.40
33 Peter Marciano	.15	.40
34 Ed Marshall	.15	.40
35 Kirk McGowan	.15	.40
36 Mike Miller	.15	.40
37 Lew Montgomery	.15	.40
38 George Murphy	.15	.40
39 John Palmer	.20	.50
40 James Pipkins	.15	.40
41 Tom Poholsky	.20	.50
42 Eddie Polly	.15	.40
43 Jim Poynton	.15	.40
44 Brad Quast	.15	.40
45 Matt Rodgers	.30	.75
46 Matt Ruhland	.15	.40
47 Ron Ryan	.15	.40
48 Moses Santos	.15	.40
49 Mike Saunders	.75	2.00
50 Doug Scott	.15	.40
51 Jeff Skillett	.15	.40
52 Leroy Smith	.15	.40
53 Sean Smith	.15	.40
54 Sean Snyder	.15	.40
55 Tony Stewart	.15	.40
56 Mark Stoops	.15	.40
57 Dave Turner	.15	.40
58 Darin Vande Zande	.15	.40
59 Ted Velicer	.15	.40
60 Travis Watkins	.15	.40
61 Dusty Weiland	.15	.40
62 Ladd Wessels	.15	.40
63 Matt Whitaker	.15	.40
64 Brian Wise	.15	.40
65 Anthony Wright	.20	.50
66 100 Years of Iowa	.15	.40
Football (Logo)		
67 The Tigerhawk	.15	.40
(School Logo)		
68 Herky The Hawk	.15	.40
(Mascot)		
69 Kinnick Stadium	.15	.40
70 Hawkeye Fans	.15	.40
71 NFL Tradition (Logo)	.15	.40
72 1982 Peach Bowl (Logo)	.15	.40
73 1982 Rose Bowl (Logo)	.15	.40
74 1983 Gator Bowl (Logo)	.15	.40
75 1984 Freedom Bowl	.15	.40
(Logo)		
76 1986 Holiday Bowl	.15	.40
(Logo)		
77 1986 Rose Bowl (Logo)	.15	.40
78 1987 Holiday Bowl	.15	.40
(Logo)		
79 1988 Peach Bowl (Logo)	.15	.40
80 Big Ten Conference	.15	.40
(Logo)		
81 Iowa Marching Band	.15	.40
82 Indoor Practice	.15	.40
Facility		
83 Iowa Locker Rooms	.15	.40
84 Iowa Weight Room	.15	.40
85 Iowa Class Rooms	.15	.40
86 Players' Lounge	.15	.40
87 Floyd of Rosedale	.15	.40
(Trophy)		
88 Medical Facilities	.15	.40
89 Media Coverage	.15	.40
90 Television Coverage	.15	.40
(Camera)		

1990 Iowa

COMPLETE SET (83)	15.00	30.00
1 Greg Aegerter	.15	.40
2 Rob Baxley	.15	.40
3 Nick Bell	.40	1.00
4 Bret Bielema	.15	.40
5 Phillip Bradley	.15	.40
6 Steve Breault	.15	.40
7 Greg Brown	.15	.40
8 Doug Buch	.15	.40
9 Rod Davis	.15	.40
10 Scott Davis	.30	.75
11 John Derby	.20	.50
12 Aubrey Devine	.15	.40
13 Mike Devclin	.15	.40
14 Jason Dumont	.15	.40
15 Forest Evashevski	.15	.40
16 Ted Faley	.15	.40
17 Mike Ferroni	.15	.40
18 Jon Filloon	.15	.40
19 Melvin Foster	.15	.40
20 Hayden Fry CO	.40	1.00
21 Ron Geater	.15	.40
22 Merton Hanks	.60	1.50
23 Jim Hartlieb	.15	.40
24 Danan Hughes	.40	1.00
25 Jim Hujsak	.15	.40
26 Jim Johnson DL	.15	.40
27 Calvin Jones OL	.15	.40
28 Howard Jones CO	.15	.40
29 Alex Karras	.60	1.50
30 Nile Kinnick	.75	2.00
31 Paul Kujawa	.15	.40
32 Marvin Lampkin	.15	.40
33 Bill Lange	.15	.40
34 Chuck Long	.50	1.25
35 Mike Martens	.15	.40
36 Mike Miller	.15	.40
37 Lew Montgomery	.15	.40
38 Jeff Nelson	.15	.40
39 Jason Olejniczak	.15	.40
40 Scott Plate	.15	.40
41 Bob Rees	.15	.40
42 Matt Rodgers	.15	.40
43 Matt Ruhland	.15	.40
44 Ron Ryan	.15	.40
45 Moses Santos	.15	.40
46 Mike Saunders	.75	2.00
47 Doug Scott	.15	.40
48 Jeff Skillett	.15	.40
49 Duke Slater	.30	.75
50 Leroy Smith	.15	.40
51 Jason Soliday	.15	.40
52 Tony Stewart	.15	.40
53 Michael Titley	.15	.40
54 Dave Turner	.15	.40
55 Darin Vande Zande	.15	.40
56 Scott Vang	.15	.40
57 Tewd Velicer	.15	.40
58 Mike Wells	.15	.40
59 Jon Werner	.15	.40
60 Ladd Wessels	.15	.40
61 Matt Whitaker	.15	.40
62 Jason Wilson	.15	.40
63 Brian Wise	.15	.40
64 Kinnick Stadium	.15	.40
65 1939 Ironmen	.40	1.00
(Nile Kinnick)		
66 Floyd of Rosedsale	.15	.40
67 Herky (Mascot)	.15	.40
68 1957 Rose Bowl	.15	.40
69 1982 Peach Bowl	.15	.40
70 1982 Rose Bowl	.15	.40
71 1983 Gator Bowl	.15	.40
72 1984 Freedom Bowl	.15	.40
73 1986 Holiday Bowl	.15	.40
74 1986 Rose Bowl	.15	.40
75 1987 Holiday Bowl	.15	.40
76 1988 Peach Bowl	.15	.40
77 1921 Big 10 Champs	.15	.40
78 1922 Big 10 Champs	.15	.40
79 1956 Big 10 Champs	.15	.40
80 1958 Big 10 Champs	.15	.40
81 1960 Big 10 Champs	.15	.40
82 1981 Big 10 Champs	.15	.40
83 1985 Big 10 Champs	.15	.40

1991 Iowa

COMPLETE SET (63)	15.00	30.00
1 Jeff Antilla	.20	.50
2 Rob Baxley	.20	.50

3 Bret Bielema	.20	.50
4 Larry Blue	.20	.50
5 Bob Bowlsby AD	.20	.50
6 Phillip Bradley	.20	.50
7 Steve Breault	.20	.50
8 Doug Buch	.20	.50
9 Gary Clark DB	.20	.50
10 Alan Cross	.20	.50
11 Mike Dailey	.20	.50
12 Rod Davis DL	.20	.50
13 Scott Davis OL	.30	.75
14 Anthony Dean	.20	.50
15 John Derby	.20	.50
16 Mike Devlin	.20	.50
17 Jason Dumont	.20	.50
18 C.W. Elliott AD	.20	.50
19 Matt Eyde	.20	.50
20 Ted Faley	.20	.50
21 Mike Ferroni	.20	.50
22 Jon Filloon	.20	.50
23 James Freese	.20	.50
24 Hayden Fry CO	.40	1.00
25 Ron Geater	.20	.50
26 Jim Hartlieb	.20	.50
27 Jon Hartlieb	.20	.50
28 Matt Hilliard	.20	.50
29 Brian Honnold	.20	.50
30 Danan Hughes	.40	1.00
31 Jim Hujsak	.20	.50
32 Carlos James	.20	.50
33 Andy Krieder	.20	.50
34 Paul Kujawa	.20	.50
35 Marvin Lampkin	.20	.50
36 Bill Lange	.20	.50
37 Hal Mady	.20	.50
38 Mike Martens	.20	.50
39 Lew Montgomery	.20	.50
40 Jeff Nelson DL	.20	.50
41 Jason Olejniczak	.20	.50
42 Scott Plate	.20	.50
43 Matt Quest	.20	.50
44 Bob Rees	.20	.50
45 Reed Rinderknecht	.20	.50
46 Matt Rodgers	.20	.50
47 Moses Santos	.20	.50
48 Mike Saunders	.75	2.00
49 Doug Scott	.20	.50
50 Jeff Skillett	.20	.50
51 Leroy Smith	.20	.50
52 Dave Turner	.20	.50
53 Ted Velicer	.20	.50
54 Mike Wells	.20	.50
55 Jon Werner	.20	.50
56 Matt Whitaker	.20	.50
57 Jason Wilson DB	.20	.50
58 Brian Wise	.20	.50
59 Herky Mascot	.20	.50
60 Floyd of Rosedale	.20	.50
61 Kinnick Stadium	.20	.50
62 Indoor Practice Facility	.20	.50
63 Big Ten Logo	.20	.50

1992 Iowa

The 1992 Iowa Hawkeyes set contains 90 cards measuring 2 3/4" by 3 5/8". The fronts feature color portrait photos bordered in black. The backs provide player profiles and statistics. The cards are unnumbered and listed below in alphabetical order.

COMPLETE SET (90)	15.00	30.00
1 Jeff Antilla	.15	.40
2 Marty Baldwin	.15	.40
3 George Bennett	.15	.40
4 Bret Bielema	.15	.40
5 Bret Bielema IA	.15	.40
6 Larry Blue	.15	.40
7 Tyrone Boudreaux	.15	.40
8 Bob Bowlsby AD	.15	.40
9 Steve Breault	.15	.40
10 Doug Buch	.15	.40
11 Paul Burmeister	.15	.40
12 Maurea Crain	.15	.40
13 Alan Cross	.15	.40
14 Alan Cross IA	.15	.40
15 Mike Dailey	.15	.40
16 Scott Davis	.40	1.00
17 Scott Davis IA	.40	1.00
18 Anthony Dean	.15	.40
19 Mike Devlin	.15	.40
20 Mike Devlin IA	.15	.40
21 Jason Dumont	.15	.40
22 Matt Eyde	.15	.40
23 Teddy Jo Faley	.15	.40
24 Teddy Jo Faley IA	.15	.40
25 Fritz Ferquiere	.15	.40
26 Mike Ferroni	.15	.40
27 Scott Fisher	.15	.40
28 Chris Frazier	.15	.40
29 James Freese	.15	.40
30 Hayden Fry CO	.40	1.00
31 Shawn Gillen	.15	.40
32 Chris Greene	.15	.40
33 Jim Hartlieb	.15	.40
34 Jim Hartlieb IA	.15	.40
35 John Hartlieb	.15	.40
36 Matt Hilliard	.15	.40
37 Mike Hornaday	.15	.40
38 John Houston	.15	.40
39 Danan Hughes	.30	.75
40 Danan Hughes IA	.30	.75
41 Chris Jackson	.20	.50
42 Carlos James	.15	.40
43 Harold Jasper	.15	.40
44 John Kline	.15	.40
45 Andy Kreider	.15	.40
46 Paul Kujawa	.15	.40
47 Marvin Lampkin	.15	.40
48 Bill Lange	.15	.40
49 Doug Laufenberg	.15	.40
50 Phil Lee	.15	.40
51 Hal Mady	.15	.40
52 Bruce Menzel	.15	.40
53 Lew Montgomery	.15	.40
54 Lew Montgomery IA	.15	.40
55 Jeff Nelson	.15	.40
56 Jason Olejniczak	.15	.40
57 John Oostendorp	.15	.40
58 Scott Plate	.15	.40
59 Marquis Porter	.15	.40
60 Matt Purdy	.15	.40
61 Matt Quest	.15	.40
62 Bob Rees	.15	.40
63 Todd Romano	.15	.40
64 Scott Sether	.15	.40
65 Mike Siebert	.15	.40
66 Ryan Terry	.15	.40
67 Ted Velicer	.15	.40
68 Mike Wells	.15	.40
69 Mike Wells IA	.15	.40
70 Matt Whitaker	.15	.40
71 Matt Whitaker IA	.15	.40
72 Team Mascot	.15	.40
73 Stadium Card	.15	.40
74 Cover Card	.15	.40
75 1957 Rose Bowl	.15	.40
76 1959 Rose Bowl	.15	.40
77 1982 Peach Bowl	.15	.40
78 1982 Rose Bowl	.15	.40
79 1983 Gator Bowl	.15	.40
80 1984 Freedom Bowl	.15	.40
81 1986 Holiday Bowl	.15	.40
82 1986 Rose Bowl	.15	.40
83 1987 Holiday Bowl	.15	.40
84 1988 Peach Bowl	.15	.40
85 1991 Holiday Bowl	.15	.40
86 1991 Rose Bowl	.15	.40
87 Hard Easy Choices	.15	.40
88 Kickoff Classic	.15	.40
89 Night To Remember	.15	.40
90 Checklist	.15	.40

1993 Iowa

The 1993 Iowa set consists of 64 standard-size cards. The fronts feature black-bordered color player photos, mostly posed, with the player's name and uniform number appearing in gold-colored lettering within the top margin. The team name and the player's postion are shown in gold-colored lettering within the bottom margin. The yellow horizontal back carries the player's name, position, and biography in white lettering within the black stripe across the top. Below are the player's high school and college football highlights. The cards are unnumbered and checklisted below in alphabetical order, with nonplayer cards listed at the end.

COMPLETE SET (64)	12.00	30.00
1 Ryan Abraham	.20	.50
2 Greg Allen	.20	.50
3 Jeff Andrews	.20	.50
4 Jeff Anttila	.20	.50
5 Jefferson Bates	.20	.50
6 George Bennett	.20	.50
7 Lloyd Bickham	.20	.50
8 Larry Blue	.20	.50
9 Pat Boone	.20	.50
10 Tyrone Boudreaux	.20	.50
11 Paul Burmeister	.20	.50
12 Tyler Casey	.20	.50
13 Billy Coats	.20	.50
14 Maurea Crain	.20	.50
15 Ernest Crank	.20	.50
16 Mike Dailey	.20	.50
17 Anthony Dean	.20	.50
18 Bobby Diaco	.20	.50
19 Mike Duprey	.20	.50
20 Billy Ennis-Inge	.20	.50
21 Matt Eyde	.20	.50
22 Fritz Fequiere	.30	.75
23 Hayden Fry CO	.40	1.00
24 Willie Guy	.20	.50
25 John Hartlieb	.20	.50
26 Jason Henlon	.20	.50
27 Matt Hilliard	.20	.50
28 Mike Hornaday	.20	.50
29 Rob Huber	.20	.50
30 Chris Jackson	.20	.50
31 Harold Jasper	.20	.50
32 Jamar Jones	.20	.50
33 Kent Kahl	.20	.50
34 Cliff King	.20	.50
35 John Kline	.20	.50
36 Tom Knight	.60	1.50
37 Aaron Kooiker	.20	.50
38 Andy Kreider	.20	.50
39 Bill Lange	.20	.50
40 Doug Laufenberg	.20	.50
41 Hal Mady	.20	.50
42 Brian McCullouch	.20	.50
43 Jason Olejniczak	.20	.50
44 Chris Palmer	.20	.50
45 Scott Plate	.20	.50
46 Marquis Porter	.20	.50
47 Matt Purdy	.20	.50
48 Matt Quest	.20	.50
49 Damien Robinson	.20	.50
50 Todd Romano	.20	.50
51 Mark Roussell	.20	.50
52 Ted Serama	.20	.50
53 Scott Sether	.20	.50
54 Sedrick Shaw	1.00	2.50
55 Scott Slutzker	.20	.50
56 Ryan Terry	.20	.50
57 Mike Wells	.20	.50
58 Casey Wiegmann	.20	.50
59 Parker Wildeman	.20	.50
60 Big Ten Conference (Logo card)	.20	.50
61 Hawkeyes Schedule	.20	.50
62 Herky (Mascot)	.20	.50
63 Indoor Practice Facility	.20	.50
64 Kinnick Stadium	.20	.50

1997 Iowa

This 19-card standard-sized set was issued in 1997 by American Marketing Associates to commemorate the 1996 Alamo Bowl champions. The cards are done in a horizontal fashion, with a full bleed photo and facsimile signature on the front with the player's name on the left side of the card. Reportedly 2,000 sets were produced. The set is listed below in alphabetical order.

COMPLETE SET (19)	12.00	30.00
1 Brett Chambers	.60	1.50
2 Billy Coats	.60	1.50
3 Ryan Driscoll	.60	1.50
4 Bill Ennis-Inge	.80	2.00
5 Rodney Filer	.60	1.50
6 Hayden Fry	1.00	2.50
7 Nick Gallery	.60	1.50
8 Aaron Granquist	.60	1.50
9 Brion Hurley	.60	1.50
10 Tom Knight	1.20	3.00
11 Mark Mitchell	.60	1.50
12 Demo Odems	.60	1.50
13 Jon Ortlieb	.80	2.00
14 Bill Reardon	.60	1.50
15 Damien Robinson	.80	2.00
16 Ted Serama	.60	1.50
17 Ross Verba	1.20	3.00
18 Hawk Watch/1996 Seniors Iowa Hawkeyes Football	.80	2.00
19 Hawkeyes Logo (checklist card)	.60	1.50

1996 Iowa State

Sponsored by Cyclone Clohting First State Bank, the cards in this set measure standard size. The team logo appears on the cardfronts which feature a red border and a full color player photo. The red and white cardbacks include the player's name, a bio, and career stats. The cards are unnumbered and checklisted below in alphabetical order.

COMPLETE SET (6)	3.00	8.00
1 Patrick Augafa	.60	1.50
2 Troy Davis	1.00	2.50
3 Todd Doxzon	.75	2.00
4 Tim Kohn	.60	1.50
5 Dan McCarney CO	.60	1.50
6 Ed Williams	.60	1.50

1907 Gordon Ivy League Postcards

This postcard series features schools of the Ivy League. Each card (3 5/8" by 5 1/2") includes an artist's rendering of a woman's face surrounded by two football action scenes within the outline of a football. The copyright line reads "1907 P.Gordon" and the back features a standard postcard design. The title "No. 5100 Football Series 8 Subjects" is included on the cardback as well.

COMPLETE SET (8)	125.00	200.00
1 Brown	15.00	25.00
2 Columbia	15.00	25.00
3 Cornell	15.00	25.00
4 Dartmouth	15.00	25.00
5 Harvard	18.00	30.00
6 Pennsylvania	15.00	25.00
7 Princeton	18.00	30.00
8 Yale	18.00	30.00

1989 Kansas

The 1989 University of Kansas set contains 40 standard-size cards. The fronts feature color photos bordered in blue. The vertically oriented backs show brief profiles. The cards are numbered on the back in the upper left corner. The set was produced by Leesley, Ltd. for the University of Kansas. The set was originally available from the KU Bookstore for 6.00 plus 1.50 for postage.

COMPLETE SET (40)	6.00	15.00
1 Kelly Donohoe	.30	.75
2 Roger Robben	.15	.40
3 Tony Sands	.15	.40
4 Paul Zaffaroni	.15	.40
5 Lance Flachsbarth	.15	.40
6 Brad Fleeman	.15	.40
7 Chip Budde	.20	.50
8 Bill Hundelt	.15	.40
9 Dan Newbrough	.15	.40
10 Gary Oatis	.15	.40
11 B.J. Lohsen	.15	.40
12 John Fritch	.15	.40
13 Russ Bowen	.15	.40
14 Smith Holland	.15	.40
15 Jason Priest	.20	.50
16 Scott McCabe	.15	.40
17 Jason Tyrer	.15	.40
18 Mongo Allen	.15	.40
19 Glen Mason CO	.60	1.50
20 Deral Boykin	.30	.75
21 Quintin Smith	.15	.40
22 Mark Koncz	.15	.40
23 John Baker	.20	.50
24 Football Staff (schedule on back)	.20	.50
25 Maurice Hooks	.15	.40
26 Frank Hatchett	.15	.40
27 Paul Friday	.15	.40
28 Doug Terry	.15	.40
29 Kenny Drayton	.15	.40
30 Jim New	.15	.40
31 Christopher Perez	.15	.40
32 Maurice Douglas	.30	.75
33 Curtis Moore	.15	.40
34 David Gordon	.15	.40
35 Matt Nolen	.15	.40
36 Dave Walton	.15	.40
37 King Dixon	.20	.50
38 Memorial Stadium	.15	.40
39 Jayhawks in Action (Kelly Donohue)	.20	.50
40 Jayhawks in Action (John Baker OL)	.20	.50
NNO Title Card	.30	.75

1992 Kansas

This 52-card standard-size set features the 1992 Kansas Jayhawks football team. The fronts display either posed or action color player photos inside green and blue borders. The green border has white yard markers as found on a football field. The team helmet, player's name, position, and uniform number are presented in a red bar beneath the picture. The horizontal backs carry a black-and-white head shot, biographical information, player profile, or statistics. The cards are unnumbered and checklisted below in alphabetical order.

COMPLETE SET (52)	10.00	25.00
1 Mark Allison	.15	.40
2 Hassan Bailey	.20	.50
3 Greg Ballard	.15	.40
4 Marlin Blakeney	.15	.40
5 Khristopher Booth	.15	.40
6 Charley Bowen	.15	.40
7 Gilbert Brown	3.00	5.00
8 Dwayne Chandler	.15	.40
9 Brian Christian	.15	.40
10 David Converse	.15	.40
11 Monte Cozzens	.15	.40
12 Don Davis	.15	.40
13 Maurice Douglas	.30	.75
14 Dan Eichloff	.20	.50
15 Chad Fette	.15	.40
16 Matt Gay	.15	.40
17 Harold Harris	.15	.40
18 Rodney Harris	.20	.50
19 Steve Harvey	.15	.40
20 Hessley Hempstead	.15	.40
21 Chip Hilleary	.30	.75
22 Dick Holt	.15	.40
23 Guy Howard	.15	.40
24 Chaka Johnson	.15	.40
25 John Jones	.15	.40
26 Rod Jones	.15	.40
27 Kwamie Lassiter	1.25	2.50
28 Rob Licursi	.15	.40
29 Trace Liggett	.15	.40
30 Keith Loneker	.15	.40
31 Dave Marcum	.15	.40
32 Glen Mason CO	.50	1.25
33 Chris Maumalanga	.40	1.00
34 Gerald McBurrows	.15	.40
35 Robert Mitchell	.15	.40
36 Ty Moeder	.15	.40
37 Kyle Moore	.15	.40
38 Ron Page	.15	.40
39 Chris Powell	.15	.40
40 Dan Schmidt	.15	.40
41 Ashaundai Smith	.15	.40
42 Mike Steele	.16	.40
43 Dana Stubblefield	1.20	3.00
44 Wes Swinford	.15	.40
45 Larry Thiel	.15	.40
46 Fredrick Thomas	.20	.50
47 Pete Vang	.15	.40
48 Robert Vaughn	.15	.40
49 George White	.20	.50
50 Sylvester Wright	.15	.40
NNO Schedule Card	.15	.40
NNO Coaching Staff	.15	.40

1998 Kansas State Greats

COMPLETE SET (10)	5.00	10.00
1 Bill Snyder CO 1989	.40	1.00
2 Bill Snyder CO 1990	.40	1.00
3 Goals For Success	.40	1.00
4 Sean Snyder	.40	1.00
5 Jaime Mendez	.40	1.00
6 Bill Snyder CO 1994	.40	1.00
7 Tim Colston	.40	1.00
8 Chris Canty	.60	1.50
9 Martin Gramatica	.60	1.50
10 Cover Card	.40	1.00

1982 Kentucky Schedules

This 19-card set measures approximately 2 1/4" by 3 3/4". The borderless front features a player head shot with the player's name below. The horizontal back features the 1982 season schedule. The cards are unnumbered and checklisted below in alphabetical order.

COMPLETE SET (19)	18.00	45.00
1 Richard Abraham	1.25	3.00
2 Glenn Amerson	1.25	3.00
3 Effley Brooks	1.25	3.00
4 Shawn Donigan	1.25	3.00
5 Rod Francis	1.25	3.00
6 Terry Henry	1.25	3.00
7 Ben Johnson	1.25	3.00
8 Dave Lyons	1.25	3.00
9 John Maddox	1.25	3.00
10 Rob Mangas	1.50	4.00
11 David(Buzz) Meers	1.25	3.00
12 Andy Molls	1.25	3.00
13 Tom Petty	1.25	3.00
14 Don Roe	1.25	3.00
15 Todd Shadowen	1.25	3.00
16 Gerald Smyth	1.25	3.00
17 Pete Venable	1.25	3.00
18 Allan Watson	1.25	3.00
19 Steve Williams	1.25	3.00

1984 Kentucky Schedules

COMPLETE SET (20)	20.00	40.00
1 George Adams	1.25	3.00
2 Stacy Burrell	1.25	3.00
3 Paul Calhoun	1.25	3.00
4 Frank Hare	1.25	3.00
5 Gordon Jackson	1.25	3.00
6 Cam Jacobs	1.25	3.00
7 Joe Phillips	1.25	3.00
8 Jeff Piecoro	1.25	3.00
9 Don Sabatino	1.25	3.00
10 Bob Shurtleff	1.25	3.00
11 Jeff Smith	1.25	3.00
12 Matt Stein	1.25	3.00
13 Dave Thompson	1.25	3.00
14 D.J. Wallace	1.25	3.00
15 Oliver White	1.25	3.00
16 Jerry Claiborne CO	1.25	3.00
17 Jake Hallum AC	1.25	3.00
18 Dick Redding AC	1.25	3.00
19 Rod Sharpless AC	1.25	3.00
20 Farrell Sheridan AC	1.25	3.00

1986 Kentucky Schedules

Sponsored by several McDonald's restaurants, this four-card schedule set measures approximately 2 1/4" by 3 1/2" and is printed on cardboard stock. Inside black borders, the horizontal fronts feature color photos, with the player's (or coach's) signature inscribed across the picture. The players also wrote their jersey numbers. The backs present the 1986 Wildcat schedule; a sponsor logo at the bottom completes the back. The cards are unnumbered and checklisted below in alphabetical order.

COMPLETE SET (4)	6.00	15.00
1 Jerry Claiborne CO	1.50	4.00
2 Mark Higgs	2.00	5.00
3 Marc Logan	2.00	5.00
4 Bill Ransdell	1.50	4.00

1987 Kentucky Bluegrass State Games

This 24-card set of standard size cards was co-sponsored by Coca-Cola and Valvoline, and their company logos appear on the bottom of the card face. The card sets were originally given out by the Kentucky county sheriff's departments and the Kentucky Highway Patrol. Reportedly about 350 sets were given to the approximately 120 counties in the state of Kentucky. One card per week was given out from May 25 to October 19, 1987. Once all 22 of the numbered cards were collected, they could be turned in to a local sheriff's department for prizes. The front features a color action player photo, on a blue card face with a white outer border. The player's name and the "Champions Against Drugs" insignia appear below the picture. The back has a anti-drug or alcohol tip on a gray background, with white border. The set commemorates Kentucky's hosting of the 1987 Bluegrass State Games and was endorsed by Governor Martha Layne Collins in Kentucky's Champions Against Drugs Crusade for Youth. The set features stars from a variety of sports as well as public figures. The two cards in the set numbered "SC" for special card were not distributed with the regular cards; they were produced in smaller quantities than the 22 numbered cards. The set features the first card of NBA superstar David Robinson. Reportedly the Robinson cards were distributed at the March 1987 Kentucky Boy's State High School Tournament in Rupp Arena, when David Robinson was in attendance.

COMPLETE SET (24)	25.00	60.00
11 Wildcat Mascot	.20	.50
19 Frank Minniefield F	1.25	3.00
20 Mark Higgs F	1.25	3.00

1989-90 Kentucky Schedules

This seven-card multi-sport set features schedule cards each measuring approximately 2 1/4" by 3 3/4". These schedule cards were passed out individually at games by booster clubs. The fronts feature full-bleed color action photos, some horizontally, some vertically oriented. The name "Kentucky" appears in either blue or white letters across the top of the card face on most cards. The backs carry the 1989-90 schedules for the respective sports. The cards are unnumbered and checklisted below with the named individuals listed first.

COMPLETE SET (7)	2.50	6.00
4 Mike Pfeifer FB	.60	1.50

1992-93 Kentucky Schedules

Sponsored by McDonald's, this ten-card multi-sport schedule features schedule cards each measuring 2 1/4" by 3 1/2". These schedule cards were passed out individually at games by booster clubs. The fronts feature a mix of color and black-and-white action player photos. Card numbers 1 and 2 are folded in the middle. The backs (or the insides) carry the 1992-93 schedules for the respective sports. The sponsor's logo appears either on the front or on the back. The cards are unnumbered and checklisted below in alphabetical order, with the schedule cards not featuring athletes listed at the end.

COMPLETE SET (10)	2.50	6.00
3 Pookie Jones FB	.20	.50

1993-94 Kentucky Schedules

3 Marty Moore FB	.20	.50

1924 Lafayette

This blankbacked set of cards was issued by the team and printed on thin cardboard stock with sepia toned player images. The cards measure roughly 2 1/2' by 4 1/4" and include only the player's last name below the photo. They were released as a complete set in a yellow envelope presumably at souvenir stands at home games. The year and team "1924 Lafayette" is printed on the envelope. Several players in the set went on to play in the NFL including Charlie Berry and Jack Ernst who both were major contributors to the Pottsville Maroons disputed NFL championship of 1925.

COMPLETE SET (20)	1,500.00	2,500.00
1 Charlie Berry	250.00	400.00
2 Don Booz	75.00	150.00
3 William Brown	75.00	150.00
4 John Budd	75.00	150.00
5 Frank Chicknoski	75.00	150.00
6 Doug Crate	75.00	150.00
7 Robert Duffy	75.00	150.00
8 Jack Ernst	75.00	150.00
9 Adrian Ford	75.00	150.00
10 Louis Gebhard UER	75.00	150.00
11 Cullen Gourley Asst.CO	75.00	150.00
12 Charles Grantier	75.00	150.00
13 William Highberger	75.00	150.00
14 Frank Kirkleski	75.00	150.00
15 Daniel Lyons	75.00	150.00
16 Herb McCracken CO	75.00	150.00
17 Jim McGarvey	75.00	150.00
18 Bob Millman	75.00	150.00
19 Sheldon Pollock	75.00	150.00
20 Weldon Asst.CO	75.00	150.00

2011 Leaf Army All-American Bowl

UNPRICED BLACK PRINT RUN 10
UNPRICED GOLD PRINT RUN 1

BAAG1 Aaron Green	10.00	25.00
BAAL1 Aaron Lynch	10.00	25.00
BAAR1 Antonio Richardson	4.00	10.00
BAAS1 Anthony Sarao	4.00	10.00
BAASJ Austin Seferian-Jenkins	4.00	10.00
BAAW1 Aundrey Walker	4.00	10.00
BAAW2 Avery Walls	4.00	10.00
BABB1 Brian Bobek	4.00	10.00
BABC1 Blake Countess	4.00	10.00
BABC2 Brent Calloway	5.00	12.00
BABP1 Benjamin Pruitt	4.00	10.00
BABS1 Brandon Shell	4.00	10.00
BABS2 Brennan Scarlett	4.00	10.00
BABS3 Bubba Starling	25.00	50.00
BACF1 Christian French	4.00	10.00
BACG1 Curtis Grant	8.00	20.00
BACJ1 Charles Jackson	4.00	10.00
BACJJ C.J. Johnson	10.00	25.00
BACK1 Cody Kessler	10.00	25.00
BACL1 Colt Lyerla	8.00	20.00
BACM1 Corey Moore	4.00	10.00
BACP1 Charone Peake	8.00	20.00
BADA1 DeAnthony Arnett	5.00	12.00
BADH1 Demetrius Hart	10.00	25.00
BADJ1 Driphus Jackson	4.00	10.00
BADS1 Damian Swann	4.00	10.00
BADS2 Delvon Simmons	4.00	10.00
BADS3 Donovan Smith	4.00	10.00
BADT1 De'Anthony Thomas	30.00	60.00
BADW1 Danny Woodson	6.00	15.00
BAEH1 Ethan Hutson	8.00	20.00
BAGA1 George Atkinson	6.00	15.00
BAGF1 George Farmer	10.00	25.00
BAGF2 Glenn Faulkner	4.00	10.00
BAGG1 Garrett Greenlea	4.00	10.00
BAGH1 Gerod Holliman	4.00	10.00
BAGR1 Gregory Robinson	4.00	10.00
BAHL1 Harvey Langi	4.00	10.00
BAHS1 Herschel Sims	10.00	25.00
BAIW1 Ishaq Williams	6.00	15.00
BAJB1 Jacoby Brissett	8.00	20.00
BAJG1 Jason Gibson	4.00	10.00
BAJK1 Jake Keefer	4.00	10.00
BAJP1 Jeoffrey Pagan	5.00	12.00
BAJP2 Juda Parker	4.00	10.00
BAJR1 Jermauria Rasco	5.00	12.00
BAJR2 Jonathan Rose	4.00	10.00
BAJR3 Jordan Rigsbee	4.00	10.00
BAJS1 James Sample	4.00	10.00
BAJS2 Jaxon Shipley	5.00	12.00
BAJW1 James Wilder	15.00	30.00
BAJWW J.W. Walsh	8.00	20.00
BAKF1 Kris Frost	4.00	10.00
BAKH1 Kenny Hilliard	12.00	30.00
BAKT1 Kendall Thompson	6.00	15.00
BAKW1 Kasen Williams	5.00	12.00
BALD1 Lamar Dawson	5.00	12.00
BALT1 Landon Turner	4.00	10.00
BALT2 Lateek Townsend	4.00	10.00
BAMA1 Marquis Anderson	4.00	10.00
BAMB1 Malcolm Brown	12.00	30.00
BAMB2 Michael Bennett	5.00	12.00
BAMB3 Mike Blakely	6.00	15.00
BAMH1 Matthew Hegarty	5.00	12.00
BAMS1 Miles Shuler	4.00	10.00
BAMS2 Miller Snyder	4.00	10.00
BAMW1 Matthew Wile	4.00	10.00
BANB1 Nickolas Brassell	10.00	25.00
BANOL Nick O'Leary	6.00	15.00
BANS1 Niklas Sade	4.00	10.00
BAOB1 Odell Beckham	6.00	15.00
BAPE1 Phillip Ely	8.00	20.00
BAQR1 Quincy Russell	5.00	12.00
BARC1 Rodney Coe	4.00	10.00
BARD1 Ray Drew	5.00	12.00
BARM1 Ryker Mathews	4.00	10.00
BASB1 Sterling Bailey	4.00	10.00
BASE1 Steve Edmond	5.00	12.00
BASF1 Sedrick Flowers	4.00	10.00
BASM1 Sony Michel	60.00	120.00
BASM2 Stefan McClure	4.00	10.00
BAST1 Stephon Tuitt	6.00	15.00
BASW1 Sammy Watkins	20.00	40.00
BATB1 Teddy Bridgewater	6.00	15.00
BATJ1 Timmy Jernigan	5.00	12.00
BATJ2 Tyler Johnstone	5.00	12.00
BATM1 Tevin Mitchel	4.00	10.00
BATM2 Tony Morales	4.00	10.00
BATM3 Tre Madden	4.00	10.00
BATM4 Trey Metoyer	6.00	15.00
BATM5 Tyler Moore	6.00	15.00
BATP1 Todd Peat	6.00	15.00
BATS1 Tobias Singleton	5.00	12.00
BATS2 Tony Steward	6.00	15.00
BAVB1 Victor Blackwell	5.00	12.00
BAVM1 Viliami Moala	4.00	10.00
BAWL1 Wayne Lyons	4.00	10.00
BAZDB Zach DeBell	4.00	10.00

2011 Leaf Army All-American Bowl Tour Autographs

*TOUR AU: .5X TO 1.2X BASIC AUTO
RANDOM INSERTS IN PACKS
UNPRICED GOLD PRINT RUN 5

2011 Leaf Army All-American Bowl Tour Autographs Black

*TOUR AU BLACK/20: .8X TO 2X BASIC AU
STATED PRINT RUN 20 SER.#'d SETS

2011 Leaf Army All-American Bowl Big Hitters

STATED PRINT RUN 50 SER.#'d SETS
UNPRICED BLACK PRINT RUN 5
UNPRICED GOLD PRINT RUN 1

BAAS1 Anthony Sarao	5.00	12.00
BABC1 Blake Countess	5.00	12.00
BABC2 Brent Calloway	6.00	15.00
BACJ1 Charles Jackson	5.00	12.00
BACM1 Corey Moore	5.00	12.00
BAGA1 George Atkinson	8.00	20.00
BAGF2 Glenn Faulkner	5.00	12.00
BAGH1 Gerod Holliman	5.00	12.00
BAJK1 Jake Keefer	5.00	12.00
BAJS1 James Sample	5.00	12.00
BAKT1 Kendall Thompson	8.00	20.00
BALD1 Lamar Dawson	6.00	15.00
BALT2 Lateek Townsend	5.00	12.00
BAMB2 Michael Bennett	6.00	15.00
BARC1 Rodney Coe	5.00	12.00
BASE1 Steve Edmond	6.00	15.00
BASM2 Stefan McClure	5.00	12.00
BATM1 Tevin Mitchel	5.00	12.00
BATM3 Tre Madden	5.00	12.00

2011 Leaf Army All-American Bowl Bubba Starling

STATED PRINT RUN 25 SER.#'d SETS

BS1 Bubba Starling	90.00	150.00
BS2 Bubba Starling	90.00	150.00

2011 Leaf Army All-American Bowl Dynamic Duos Autographs

UNPRICED DUAL AU PRINT RUN 10
UNPRICED BLACK PRINT RUN 5
UNPRICED GOLD PRINT RUN 1

2011 Leaf Army All-American Bowl Fearsome Foursome Autographs

UNPRICED QUAD AU PRINT RUN 10
UNPRICED BLACK PRINT RUN 5
UNPRICED GOLD PRINT RUN 1

2011 Leaf Army All-American Bowl Touchdown Heroes

STATED PRINT RUN 50 SER.#'d SETS
UNPRICED BLACK PRINT RUN 5
UNPRICED GOLD PRINT RUN 1

TDAG1 Aaron Green	12.00	30.00
TDCP1 Charone Peake	10.00	25.00
TDDA1 DeAnthony Arnett	6.00	15.00
TDDH1 Demetrius Hart	12.00	30.00
TDDS1 Damian Swann	5.00	12.00
TDDW1 Danny Woodson	8.00	20.00
TDGF1 George Farmer	12.00	30.00
TDHL1 Harvey Langi	5.00	12.00
TDHS1 Herschel Sims	12.00	30.00
TDJR2 Jonathan Rose	5.00	12.00
TDJS2 Jaxon Shipley	6.00	15.00
TDJW1 James Wilder	15.00	40.00
TDKF1 Kris Frost	5.00	12.00
TDKH1 Kenny Hilliard	20.00	40.00
TDKW1 Kasen Williams	6.00	15.00
TDMB1 Malcolm Brown	15.00	40.00
TDMB3 Mike Blakely	8.00	20.00
TDMS1 Miles Shuler	5.00	12.00
TDNB1 Nickolas Brassell	12.00	30.00
TDOB1 Odell Beckham	8.00	20.00
TDSW1 Sammy Watkins	30.00	60.00
TDTM4 Trey Metoyer	8.00	20.00
TDTS1 Tobias Singleton	6.00	15.00
TDVB1 Victor Blackwell	6.00	15.00

2011 Leaf Army All-American Bowl Young Guns

STATED PRINT RUN 50 SER.#'d SETS
UNPRICED GOLD PRINT RUN 1
UNPRICED BLACK PRINT RUN 5

YGBS3 Bubba Starling	30.00	60.00
YGCK1 Cody Kessler	12.00	30.00
YGDJ1 Driphus Jackson	5.00	12.00
YGJB1 Jacoby Brissett	10.00	25.00
YGJWW J.W. Walsh	12.00	30.00
YGPE1 Phillip Ely	10.00	25.00
YGTB1 Teddy Bridgewater	8.00	20.00

2011 Leaf Army All-American Bowl Bowl Week Edition

COMPLETE SET (98)	50.00	100.00
E1 Phillip Ely	.60	1.50
E2 Teddy Bridgewater	.75	2.00
E3 Jacoby Brissett	.50	1.25
E4 James Wilder	.50	1.25
E5 Mike Blakely	.75	2.00
E6 Demetrius Hart	.60	1.50
E7 Nick O'Leary	.50	1.25
E8 Charone Peake	.75	2.00
E9 Danny Woodson	.60	1.50
W1 Cody Kessler	1.25	3.00
W2 Bubba Starling	1.25	3.00
W3 J.W. Walsh	.75	2.00
W4 Driphus Jackson	.50	1.25
W5 Malcolm Brown	1.00	2.50
W6 Aaron Green	1.00	2.50
W7 Kenny Hilliard	.75	2.00
W8 Herschel Sims	.60	1.50
W9 De'Anthony Thomas	.75	2.00
E10 Sammy Watkins	1.00	2.50
E11 Tobias Singleton	.60	1.50
E12 Miles Shuler	.50	1.25
E13 Nickolas Brassell	.50	1.25
E14 Donovan Smith	.50	1.25
E15 Tyler Moore	.60	1.50
E16 Aundrey Walker	.50	1.25
E17 Antonio Richardson	.50	1.25
E18 Brian Bobek	.50	1.25
E19 Landon Turner	.50	1.25
E20 Zach DeBell	.50	1.25
E21 Delvon Simmons	.50	1.25
E22 Ray Drew	.60	1.50
E23 Sterling Bailey	.50	1.25
E24 Jeoffrey Pagan	.60	1.50
E25 Aaron Lynch	.75	2.00
E26 Timmy Jernigan	.50	1.25
E27 Stephon Tuitt	.60	1.50
E28 Ishaq Williams	.60	1.50
E29 Michael Bennett	.50	1.25
E30 Curtis Grant	6.00	1.50
E31 Rodney Coe	.50	1.25
E32 C.J. Johnson	.75	2.00
E33 Lateek Townsend	.50	1.25
E34 Kris Frost	.50	1.25
E35 Brent Calloway	.60	1.50
E36 Anthony Sarao	.50	1.25
E37 Tony Steward	.60	1.50
E38 Wayne Lyons	.50	1.25
E39 Gerod Holliman	.50	1.25
E40 Corey Moore	.50	1.25
E41 Avery Walls	.50	1.25
E42 Jonathan Rose	.50	1.25
E43 Blake Countess	.50	1.25
E44 Damian Swann	.50	1.25
E45 Miller Snyder	.50	1.25
E46 Niklas Sade	.50	1.25
E47 Brandon Shell	.50	1.25
W10 Austin Seferian-Jenkins	.50	1.25
W11 DeAnthony Arnett	.60	1.50
W12 Victor Blackwell	.60	1.50
W13 George Farmer	.60	1.50
W14 Trey Metoyer	.75	2.00
W15 Jaxon Shipley	.60	1.50
W16 Kasen Williams	.60	1.50
W17 Ethan Hutson	.50	1.25
W18 Tyler Johnstone	.50	1.25
W19 Sedrick Flowers	.50	1.25
W20 Garrett Greenlea	.50	1.25
W21 Matthew Hegarty	.50	1.25
W22 Ryker Mathews	.50	1.25
W23 Tony Morales	.50	1.25
W24 Jordan Rigsbee	.50	1.25
W25 Gregory Robinson	.50	1.25
W26 Juda Parker	.50	1.25
W27 Jason Gibson	.50	1.25
W28 Jermauria Rasco	.50	1.25
W29 Brennan Scarlett	.50	1.25
W30 Todd Peat	.60	1.50

W31 Marquis Anderson .50 1.25
W32 Viliami Moala .50 1.25
W33 Quincy Russell .50 1.25
W34 Jake Keefer .50 1.25
W35 Kendall Thompson .60 1.50
W36 Colt Lyerla .50 1.25
W37 Tre Madden .50 1.25
W38 Lamar Dawson .60 1.50
W39 Steve Edmond .60 1.50
W40 Christian French .50 1.25
W41 Harvey Langi .50 1.25
W42 Odell Beckham .50 1.25
W43 Stefan McClure .50 1.25
W44 Tevin Mitchel .50 1.25
W45 Charles Jackson .50 1.25
W46 George Atkinson .50 1.25
W47 Glenn Faulkner .50 1.25
W48 James Sample .50 1.25
W49 Ben Pruitt .50 1.25
W50 Matt Wile .60 1.50

2012 Leaf Army All-American Bowl

BAAA1 Anthony Alford SP 5.00 12.00
BAAA2 Arik Armstead 6.00 15.00
BAAB1 Alex Balducci 6.00 15.00
BAAC1 Alex Carter 5.00 12.00
BAAS1 Aziz Shittu 4.00 10.00
BAAW1 Adolphus Washington 5.00 12.00
BABA1 Bralon Addison 5.00 12.00
BABA2 Brooks Abbott 4.00 10.00
BABB1 Brandon Beaver 4.00 10.00
BABK1 Brian Kimbrow 5.00 12.00
BABM1 Byron Marshall SP 5.00 12.00
BABN1 Brian Nance 4.00 10.00
BABP1 Bradley Pinion 5.00 12.00
BABS1 Barry Sanders SP 25.00 50.00
BACD1 Cedric Dozier 5.00 12.00
BACM1 Cyler Miles SP 6.00 15.00
BACM2 Chris Muller 4.00 10.00
BACV1 Chad Voytik 6.00 15.00
BACW1 Carlos Watkins 5.00 12.00
BADB1 Drae Bowles 5.00 12.00
BADB2 Deon Bush 4.00 10.00
BADF1 Devin Fuller SP 4.00 10.00
BADGB Dorial Green-Beckham SP 15.00 40.00
BADH1 Darius Hamilton 6.00 15.00
BADJH D.J. Humphries 5.00 12.00
BADN1 Durron Neal SP 6.00 15.00
BADP1 Dante Phillips 6.00 15.00
BADS1 Dwayne Stanford SP 5.00 12.00
BADV1 Dan Voltz 4.00 10.00
BADW1 Dominique Wheeler 5.00 12.00
BADW2 Derrick Woods SP 5.00 12.00
BAEH1 Eli Harold 6.00 15.00
BAEM1 Erik Magnuson 4.00 10.00
BAEM2 Ellis McCarthy 4.00 10.00
BAEP1 Ethan Perry 4.00 10.00
BAEP2 Edward Pope 5.00 12.00
BAES1 Elijah Shumate 4.00 10.00
BAGH1 Germone Hopper SP 5.00 12.00
BAGK1 Gunner Kiel
BAGS1 Geno Smith 5.00 12.00
BAGS2 Graham Shuler 5.00 12.00
BAHR1 Hassan Ridgeway 4.00 10.00
BAIA1 Ishmael Adams 4.00 10.00
BAJB1 Jonathan Bullard 6.00 15.00
BAJC1 Joel Caleb 6.00 15.00
BAJD1 Jordan Diggs 5.00 12.00
BAJHC Josh Harvey-Clemons 6.00 15.00
BAJJ1 Jarron Jones 4.00 10.00
BAJM1 Javonte Magee 4.00 10.00
BAJMM John Michael McGee 4.00 10.00
BAJP1 Jordan Payton SP 6.00 15.00
BAJR2 James Ross 6.00 15.00
BAJR3 Jabari Ruffin 4.00 10.00
BAJS1 Justin Shanks 4.00 10.00
BAJS2 Jordan Simmons 4.00 10.00
BAJT1 John Theus 4.00 10.00
BAKB1 Keith Brown 4.00 10.00
BAKD1 Kyle Dodson 6.00 15.00
BAKK1 Kyle Kalis 6.00 15.00
BAKM1 Kwontie Moore 4.00 10.00
BAKM2 Kyle Murphy 4.00 10.00
BAKR1 Kei'Varae Russell 6.00 15.00
BAKS1 Kendall Sanders 4.00 10.00
BAKS2 Kevon Seymour 5.00 12.00
BAKT1 Kent Taylor 6.00 15.00
BALC1 Leonte Carroo 5.00 12.00
BALM1 LaDarrell McNeil 4.00 10.00
BAMD1 Mike Davis 6.00 15.00
BAMM1 Mike Matthews 6.00 15.00
BAMS1 Michael Starts 4.00 10.00
BAMT1 Max Tuerk 4.00 10.00
BAND1 Nick Dawson 4.00 10.00
BANJ1 Nick Jordan 4.00 10.00
BAOP1 Ondre Pipkins 6.00 15.00
BARJS Royce Jenkins-Stone 6.00 15.00
BARK1 Raphael Kirby 4.00 10.00
BARW1 Ryan Ward 4.00 10.00
BASD1 Stefon Diggs SP 8.00 20.00
BAST1 Shaq Thompson 6.00 15.00
BATB1 Travis Blanks 5.00 12.00
BATC1 Timothy Cole 4.00 10.00
BATD1 Ty Darlington 5.00 12.00
BATD2 Torshiro Davis 4.00 10.00
BATH1 Tracy Howard 5.00 12.00
BATJY T.J. Yeldon SP 10.00 25.00
BATM1 Tyler Matthews 6.00 15.00
BATM2 Tyriq McCord 6.00 15.00
BATM3 Taylor McNamara 4.00 10.00
BATS1 Tommy Schutt 5.00 12.00
BATW1 Trey Williams 5.00 12.00
BAUE1 Markuss Eligwe 4.00 10.00
BAVB1 Vince Biegel 4.00 10.00
BAYW1 Yuri Wright 4.00 10.00
BAZB1 Zach Banner 5.00 12.00
BAZP1 Zeke Pike 6.00 15.00

2012 Leaf Army All-American Bowl Black

*BLACK/50: .5X TO 1.2X BASIC AUTO
BLACK STATED PRINT RUN 10-50

2012 Leaf Army All-American Bowl Big Hitters Black

STATED PRINT RUN 20 SER.#'d SETS
BHAA2 Arik Armstead 10.00 25.00
BHAB1 Alex Balducci 10.00 25.00
BHAC1 Alex Carter 8.00 20.00
BHAW1 Adolphus Washington 8.00 20.00
BHDB2 Deon Bush 6.00 15.00
BHDF1 Devin Fuller 6.00 15.00
BHDH1 Darius Hamilton 10.00 25.00
BHEH1 Eli Harold 6.00 15.00
BHEM2 Ellis McCarthy 6.00 15.00
BHGS1 Geno Smith 8.00 20.00
BHJB1 Jonathan Bullard 10.00 25.00
BHJHC Josh Harvey-Clemons 6.00 15.00
BHJR3 Jabari Ruffin 6.00 15.00
BHRK1 Raphael Kirby 6.00 15.00
BHST1 Shaq Thompson 10.00 25.00
BHTB1 Travis Blanks 8.00 20.00
BHTH1 Tracy Howard 8.00 20.00
BHTM2 Tyriq McCord 6.00 15.00
BHTS1 Tommy Schutt 8.00 20.00
BHUE1 Markuss Eligwe 6.00 15.00
BHYW1 Yuri Wright 6.00 15.00

2012 Leaf Army All-American Bowl Jersey Autographs Bronze

STATED PRINT RUN 30 SER.#'d SETS
JAAA1 Anthony Alford 8.00 20.00
JABS1 Barry Sanders 30.00 60.00
JACM1 Cyler Miles 10.00 25.00
JADGB Dorial Green-Beckham
JADN1 Durron Neal 10.00 25.00
JADW1 Dominique Wheeler 8.00 20.00
JAGK1 Gunner Kiel 25.00 50.00
JAKT1 Kent Taylor 10.00 25.00
JASD1 Stefon Diggs 12.00 30.00
JATJY T.J. Yeldon 15.00 40.00
JATW1 Trey Williams 8.00 20.00
JAZP1 Zeke Pike 10.00 25.00

2012 Leaf Army All-American Bowl Jersey Patch Autographs Bronze

STATED PRINT RUN 30 SER.#'d SETS
PAAA1 Anthony Alford 12.00 30.00
PAAA2 Arik Armstead 15.00 40.00
PABA1 Bralon Addison 12.00 30.00
PABK1 Brian Kimbrow 12.00 30.00
PABM1 Byron Marshall 12.00 30.00
PABS1 Barry Sanders 40.00 80.00
PACM1 Cyler Miles 25.00 50.00
PACV1 Chad Voytik 15.00 40.00
PADB1 Drae Bowles 12.00 30.00
PADF1 Devin Fuller 10.00 25.00
PADGB Dorial Green-Beckham 40.00 80.00
PADN1 Durron Neal 15.00 40.00
PADS1 Dwayne Stanford 12.00 30.00
PADW1 Dominique Wheeler 12.00 30.00
PADW2 Derrick Woods 12.00 30.00
PAGH1 Germone Hopper 12.00 30.00
PAGK1 Gunner Kiel 40.00 80.00
PAJC1 Joel Caleb 15.00 40.00
PAJP1 Jordan Payton 15.00 40.00
PAKR1 Kei'Varae Russell 15.00 40.00
PAKT1 Kent Taylor 12.00 30.00
PALC1 Leonte Carroo 12.00 30.00
PASD1 Stefon Diggs 20.00 50.00
PATJY T.J. Yeldon 25.00 60.00
PATM1 Tyler Matthews 15.00 40.00
PATM3 Taylor McNamara 10.00 25.00
PATW1 Trey Williams 12.00 30.00
PAZP1 Zeke Pike 15.00 40.00

2012 Leaf Army All-American Bowl Touchdown Kings Black

STATED PRINT RUN 20 SER.#'d SETS
TKBA1 Bralon Addison 8.00 20.00
TKBM1 Byron Marshall 8.00 20.00
TKDB1 Drae Bowles 8.00 20.00
TKDS1 Dwayne Stanford 8.00 20.00
TKDW2 Derrick Woods 8.00 20.00
TKGH1 Germone Hopper 8.00 20.00
TKJC1 Joel Caleb 10.00 25.00
TKJP1 Jordan Payton 10.00 25.00
TKKR1 Kei'Varae Russell 10.00 25.00
TKLC1 Leonte Carroo 8.00 20.00
TKMD1 Mike Davis 10.00 25.00
TKTJY T.J. Yeldon 15.00 40.00
TKTW1 Trey Williams 8.00 20.00

2012 Leaf Army All-American Bowl Tour Autographs Red Ink

*TOUR AUTO/25: .8X TO 2X BASIC AU
STATED PRINT RUN 25 SER.#'d SETS
TADL1 Dillon Lee 12.00 30.00
TALK1 Luke Kaumatule 10.00 25.00
TAPG1 Paul Griggs 8.00 20.00

2012 Leaf Army All-American Bowl Andrew Luck Promos

This card was created in late 2011 and sold initially through eBay direct from Leaf. It carries an announced print run of 500 copies.

AL01 Andrew Luck/500* blk 20.00 40.00
(black border at bottom)

2012 Leaf Army All-American Bowl Retail

INSERTS IN LEAF YOUNG STARS BOXES
1 Brooks Abbott .20 .50
2 Anthony Alford .25 .60
3 Travis Blanks .25 .60
4 Drae Bowles .25 .60
5 Keith Brown .20 .50
6 Jonathan Bullard .30 .75
7 Deon Bush .20 .50
8 Joel Caleb .30 .75
9 Shane Callahan .20 .50
10 Leonte Carroo .25 .60
11 Alex Carter .25 .60
12 Ty Darlington .25 .60
13 Mike Davis .30 .75
14 Nick Dawson .20 .50
15 Jordan Diggs .25 .60
16 Stefon Diggs .40 1.00
17 Kyle Dodson .30 .75
18 Markuss Eligwe .20 .50
19 Devin Fuller .20 .50
20 Paul Griggs .20 .50
21 Darius Hamilton .30 .75
22 Eli Harold .30 .75
23 Josh Harvey-Clemons .30 .75
24 Germone Hopper .25 .60
25 Tracy Howard .25 .60
26 D.J. Humphries .25 .60
27 Jarron Jones .20 .50
28 Kyle Kalis .30 .75
29 Gunner Kiel 1.00 2.50
30 Brian Kimbrow .25 .60
31 Raphael Kirby .20 .50
32 Dillon Lee .30 .75
33 Tyriq McCord .30 .75
34 Kwontie Moore .20 .50
35 Chris Muller .20 .50
36 Dante Phillips .30 .75
37 Bradley Pinion .25 .60
38 Tommy Schutt .25 .60
39 Graham Shuler .25 .60
40 Elijah Shumate .20 .50
41 Geno Smith .20 .50
42 Dwayne Stanford .25 .60
43 Kent Taylor .30 .75
44 John Theus .20 .50
45 Dan Voltz .20 .50
46 Chad Voytik .30 .75
47 Ryan Ward .20 .50
48 Adolphus Washington .25 .60
49 Carlos Watkins .25 .60
50 Yuri Wright .20 .50
51 Ishmael Adams .20 .50
52 Bralon Addison .25 .60
53 Arik Armstead .30 .75
54 Alex Balducci .30 .75
55 Zach Banner .25 .60
56 Brandon Beaver .20 .50
57 Vince Biegel .20 .50
58 Timothy Cole .20 .50
59 Torshiro Davis .20 .50
60 Cedric Dozier .25 .60
61 Dorial Green-Beckham .75 2.00
62 Royce Jenkins-Stone .30 .75
63 Nick Jordan .20 .50
64 Javonte Magee .20 .50
65 John Michael McGee .20 .50
66 Erik Magnuson .30 .75
67 Byron Marshall .25 .60
68 Mike Matthews .30 .75
69 Tyler Matthews .30 .75
70 Ellis McCarthy .30 .75
71 Taylor McNamara .20 .50
72 LaDarrell McNeil .20 .50
73 Cyler Miles .30 .75
74 Kyle Murphy .20 .50
75 Brian Nance .20 .50
76 Durron Neal .30 .75
77 Jordan Payton .30 .75
78 Ethan Perry .20 .50
79 Zeke Pike .30 .75
80 Ondre Pipkins .30 .75
81 Edward Pope .25 .60
82 Hassan Ridgeway .20 .50
83 James Ross .30 .75
84 Jabari Ruffin .20 .50
85 Kei'Varae Russell .30 .75
86 Barry Sanders 1.00 2.50
87 Kendall Sanders .20 .50
88 Kevon Seymour .25 .60
89 Justin Shanks .20 .50
90 Aziz Shittu .20 .50
91 Jordan Simmons .20 .50
92 Michael Starts .20 .50
93 Shaq Thompson .30 .75
94 Max Tuerk .20 .50
95 Dominique Wheeler .25 .60
96 Trey Williams .25 .60
97 Derrick Woods .25 .60
98 T.J. Yeldon .50 1.25

2012 Leaf Metal Army All-American Bowl Andrew Luck Promos

BAL1 Andrew Luck ERR/39* 500.00 800.00
(name misspelled on back)

2008 Liberty Bowl Legends

This set was issued at Autozone stores to commemorate previous Liberty Bowl games. Each card features an artist's rendering of the featured player or coach with a card number on the back.

COMPLETE SET (10) 6.00 12.00
1 Joe Paterno CO .75 2.00
2 Terry Baker .40 1.00
3 Roy Jefferson .40 1.00
4 Archie Manning .60 1.50
5 Paul Bear Bryant CO .75 2.00
6 Doug Flutie .60 1.50
7 Bo Jackson .75 2.00
8 Shaun King .40 1.00
9 Stefan Lefors .40 1.00
10 Sylvester Croom CO .40 1.00

2005 Louisiana Tech Greats

COMPLETE SET (20) 6.00 12.00
1 Larry Anderson .20 .50
2 Terry Bradshaw 1.50 4.00
3 Billy Bundrick .20 .50
4 Roger Carr .30 .75
5 Fred Dean .30 .75
6 Troy Edwards .30 .75
7 Garland Gregory .20 .50
8 Tommy Hinton .20 .50
9 Ed Jackson .20 .50
10 Joe McNeely .20 .50
11 Tim Rattay .40 1.00
12 Willie Roaf .40 1.00
13 Billy Ryckman .20 .50
14 Glennell Sanders .20 .50
15 Leo Sanford .20 .50
16 J.W. Slack .20 .50
17 Mickey Slaughter .20 .50
18 Matt Stover .40 1.00
19 Pat Tilley .30 .75
20 Charles Wyly .20 .50

2006 Louisiana Tech Greats Schedules

COMPLETE SET (20) 5.00 10.00
1 Joe Aillet .20 .50
2 Ronnie Alexander .20 .50
3 Eddie Anglin .20 .50
4 Carroll Dowies .20 .50
5 Matt Dunigan .40 1.00
6 Denny Duron .20 .50
7 Doug Evans .30 .75
8 Bobby Gray .20 .50
9 Roland Harper .20 .50
10 Paul Hynes .20 .50
11 Maxie Lambright .20 .50
12 Luke McCown .40 1.00
13 Charles McDaniel .20 .50
14 Joe Michael .20 .50
15 Ryan Moats .40 1.00
16 Pat Patterson .20 .50
17 Mike Reed .20 .50
18 Josh Scobee .20 .50
19 Bobby Slaughter .20 .50
20 John Henry White .20 .50

1981 Louisville Police

This 64-card set, which measures approximately 2 5/8" by 4 1/8", was sponsored by Pepsi-Cola (Take the Pepsi Challenge), The Louisville Area Chamber of Commerce, and the Greater Louisville Police Departments. The card front features red borders surrounding a black-and-white photo of the player. The backs feature definitions of football terms and a brief safety tip. This set features future professional star Mark Clayton in one of his earliest card appearances. Reportedly the Title/Logo card is very difficult to find. The cards are numbered on the back by safety tips.

COMPLETE SET (64) 50.00 125.00
1 Title Card SP 20.00 50.00
(Catch That
Cardinal Spirit)
2 Bob Weber CO .40 1.00
3 Assistant Coaches .40 1.00
4 Jay Trautwein .40 1.00
5 Darrell Wimberly .40 1.00
6 Jeff Van Camp .40 1.00
7 Joe Welch .40 1.00
8 Fred Blackmon .40 1.00
9 Lamar(Toot) Evans .40 1.00
10 Tom Blair .40 1.00
11 Joe Kader .40 1.00
12 Mike Trainor .40 1.00
13 Richard Tharpe .40 1.00
14 Gene Hagan .40 1.00
15 Greg Jones .40 1.00
16 Leon Williams .40 1.00
17 Ellsworth Larkins .40 1.00
18 Sebastian Curry .40 1.00
19 Frank Minnifield 3.00 8.00
20 Roger Clay .40 1.00
21 Mark Blasinsky .40 1.00
22 Mike Cruz .40 1.00
23 David Arthur .40 1.00
24 Johnny Unitas 10.00 25.00
(In front; background is
list of Cardinals who
played pro ball)
25 John DeMarco .40 1.00
26 Eric Rollins .40 1.00
27 Jack Pok .40 1.00
28 Pete McCartney .40 1.00
29 Mark Clayton 6.00 15.00
30 Jeff Hortort .40 1.00
31 Pete Bowen .40 1.00
32 Robert Niece .40 1.00
33 Todd McMahan .40 1.00
34 John Wall .40 1.00
35 Kelly Stickrod .40 1.00
36 Jim Miller C .40 1.00
37 Tom Moore .40 1.00
38 Kurt Knop .40 1.00
39 Mark Musgrave .40 1.00
40 Tony Campbell .40 1.00
41 Mark Wilson .40 1.00
42 Robert Mitchell .40 1.00
43 Courtney Jeter .40 1.00
44 Wayne Taylor .40 1.00
45 Jeff Speedy .40 1.00
46 Donnie Craft .40 1.00
47 Glenn Hunter .40 1.00
48 1981 Louisville Schedule .40 1.00
49 Greg Hickman .40 1.00
50 Nate Dozier .40 1.00
51 Pat Patterson .40 1.00
52 Scott Gannon .40 1.00
53 Dean May .40 1.00
54 David Hatfield .40 1.00
55 Mike Nuzzolese .40 1.00
56 John Ayers .40 1.00
57 Lamar Cummins .40 1.00
58 Bill Olsen AD .40 1.00
59 Tailgating .40 1.00
60 Football Complex .40 1.00
61 Marching Band .40 1.00
62 Cheerleaders .40 1.00
63 Administration Bldg. .40 1.00
64 Cardinal Mascot .40 1.00

1990 Louisville Smokey

This 16-card standard-size set was sponsored by the USDA Forest Service in cooperation with several other federal agencies. On white card stock, the fronts display color action player photos with rounded bottom corners. The player's name and position appear between two Cardinal logos in a red stripe above the picture. The backs have biographical information and a safety cartoon featuring Smokey the Bear. The cards are unnumbered and checklisted below in alphabetical order.

COMPLETE SET (16) 10.00 25.00
1 Greg Brohm .50 1.25
2 Jeff Brohm 1.00 2.50
3 Pete Burkey .50 1.25
4 Mike Flores .50 1.25
5 Dan Gangwer .50 1.25
6 Reggie Johnson .60 1.50
7 Scott McAllister .50 1.25
8 Ken McKay .50 1.25
9 Browning Nagle .80 2.00
10 Ed Reynolds .50 1.25
11 Mark Sander .50 1.25
12 Howard Schnellenberger CO 1.60 4.00
13 Ted Washington 1.60 4.00
14 Klaus Wilmsmeyer .80 2.00
15 Cardinal Bird Mascot .50 1.25
16 Cardinal Stadium .50 1.25

1992 Louisville Kraft

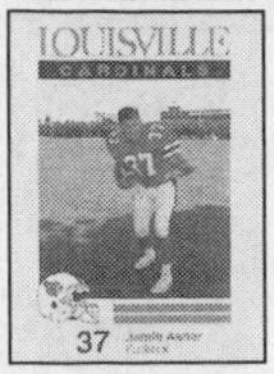

Originally issued in perforated sheets, this 30-card set was sponsored by Kraft. After being cut, the cards measure the standard size. The fronts feature color posed player photos against a white card face. The team's name appears in red above the photo. Below the photo are team helmet, two horizontal red stripes, and the player's name, jersey number, position, and class. The plain white backs carry the player's name, position, jersey number, height, weight, and hometown at the top, followed below by career highlights. The cards are unnumbered and checklisted below in alphabetical order.

COMPLETE SET (30) 8.00 20.00
1 Jamie Asher 1.20 3.00
2 Xzavia Atkins .25 .60
3 Kevin Blumeier .25 .60
4 Greg Brohm .30 .75
5 Jeff Brohm .80 2.00
6 Brandon Brookfield .25 .60
7 Ray Buchanan 2.00 4.00
8 Rawle Bynoe .25 .60
9 Tom Cavallo .25 .60
10 Kevin Cook .25 .60
11 Andy Culley .25 .60
12 Ralph Dawkins .30 .75
13 Dave Debold .25 .60
14 Chris Fitzpatrick .25 .60
15 Kevin Gaines .25 .60
16 Jose Gonzalez .25 .60
17 Jim Hanna .25 .60
18 Ken Harnden .25 .60
19 Ivey Henderson .25 .60
20 Joe Johnson 1.00 2.00
21 Robert Knuutila .25 .60
22 Marty Lowe .30 .75
23 Roman Oben .40 1.00
24 Garin Patrick .25 .60
25 Leonard Ray .25 .60
26 Shawn Rodriguez .25 .60
27 Anthony Shelman .40 1.00
28 Brevin Smith .25 .60
29 Jason Stinson .30 .75
30 Ben Sumpter .25 .60

1993 Louisville Kraft

Originally issued in perforated sheets, this 30-card set was sponsored by Kraft. The cards measure the standard size. The fronts feature color posed player photos against a white card face. The team's name appears in red above the photo. Below the photo are team helmet, two horizontal red stripes, and the player's name, jersey number, position, and class. The plain white backs carry the player's name, position, jersey number, height, weight, and hometown at the top, followed below by career highlights. The cards are unnumbered and checklisted below in alphabetical order.

COMPLETE SET (30) 8.00 20.00
1 Jamie Asher .80 2.00
2 Aaron Bailey .80 2.00
3 Zoe Barney .25 .60
4 Anthony Bridges .25 .60
5 Jeff Brohm .60 1.50
6 Brandon Brookfield .25 .60
7 Kendall Brown .25 .60
8 Tom Carroll .25 .60
9 Tom Cavallo .25 .60
10 Kevin Cook .25 .60
11 Ralph Dawkins .30 .75
12 Dave Debold .25 .60
13 Reggie Ferguson .25 .60
14 Chris Fitzpatrick .25 .60
15 Johnny Frost .25 .60
16 Jim Hanna .25 .60
17 Ivey Henderson .25 .60
18 Marcus Hill .25 .60
19 Shawn Jackson .25 .60
20 Joe Johnson .60 1.50
21 Marty Lowe .30 .75
22 Vertis McKinney .25 .60
23 Greg Minnis .25 .60
24 Roman Oben .50 1.25
25 Garin Patrick .25 .60
26 Terry Quinn .30 .75
27 Leonard Ray .25 .60
28 Anthony Shelman .30 .75
29 Jason Stinson .25 .60
30 Ben Sumpter .25 .60

1994 Louisville Team Issue

These photos were issued by the school to promote the football program. Each measures roughly 8" by 10" and features two black and white images (one portrait and one action) of the player with the school name at the top and the player's name and home town printed below the portrait. The backs are blank.

COMPLETE SET (16) 40.00 80.00
1 Calvin Arrington 3.00 6.00
2 John Bell 3.00 6.00
3 Antonio Bradwell 3.00 6.00
4 Alan Campos 3.00 6.00
5 Rico Clark 3.00 6.00
6 Johnny Frost 3.00 6.00
7 Kendrick Gholston 3.00 6.00
8 Alton Jones 3.00 6.00
9 Derrick Lillard 3.00 6.00
10 Marty Lowe 3.00 6.00
11 Sam Madison 3.00 6.00
12 Tyrus McCloud 3.00 6.00
13 Miguel Montano 3.00 6.00
14 Roman Oben 3.00 6.00
15 Jason Payne 3.00 6.00
16 Jason Stinson 3.00 6.00

2001 Louisville Schedules

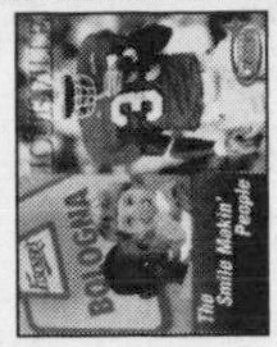

COMPLETE SET (4) .75 2.00
1 Michael Brown LB .20 .50
2 Rob Eble .20 .50
3 Brian Gaines .20 .50
4 Tony Stallings .20 .50

2003 Louisville

COMPLETE SET (27) 6.00 12.00
1 Broderick Clark FB .30 .75
2 Rod Day FB .30 .75
3 Elvis Dumervil FB 1.00 2.50
4 Lionel Gates FB .40 1.00
5 Ronnie Ghent FB .30 .75
6 Victor Glenn FB .30 .75
7 James Greene FB .30 .75
8 Jonathan Jackerson FB .30 .75
9 Kerry Rhodes FB .30 .75
10 J.R. Russell FB .30 .75
11 Tyrone Saterfield FB .30 .75
12 Eric Shelton FB .40 1.00
13 Nate Smith FB .30 .75
14 Jerry Spencer FB .30 .75
15 Jason Spitz FB .30 .75
16 Montavious Stanley FB .30 .75
17 Joshua Tinch FB .30 .75
18 Wade Tydlacka FB .30 .75

1983 LSU Sunbeam

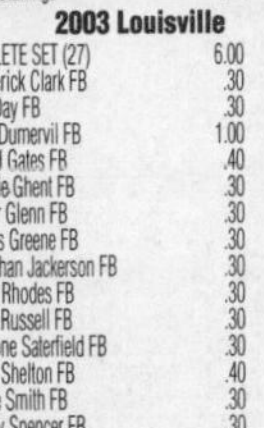

This set features 100 standard-size cards remembering ex-football players from Louisiana State University (LSU). The posed pictures on the front are black and white, bordered on the top and sides by a goal post in the school's colors, purple and gold. The horizontally oriented backs feature purple printing with biographical information and the card number in the upper left hand corner. Some of the former and current NFL stars included in this set are Billy Cannon, Carlos Carson, Tommy Casanova, Tommy Davis, Sid Fournet, Bo Harris, Bert Jones, Leonard Marshall, Jim Taylor, Y.A. Tittle, Steve Van Buren, Roy Winston, and David Woodley. The set was sponsored by Sunbeam Bread in conjunction with McDAG Productions.

COMPLETE SET (100) 10.00 20.00
1 1958 LSU National Championship Team .20 .50
2 Abe Mickal .07 .20
3 Carlos Carson .10 .30
4 Charles Alexander .20 .50
5 Steve Ensminger .07 .20
6 Ken Kavanaugh Sr. .10 .30
7 Bert Jones .30 .75
8 David Woodley .10 .30
9 Jerry Marchand .07 .20
10 Clyde Lindsey .07 .20
11 James Britt .07 .20
12 Warren Rabb .10 .30
13 Mike Hillman .07 .20
14 Nelson Stokley .07 .20
15 Abner Wimberly .07 .20
16 Terry Robiskie .10 .30
17 Steve Van Buren .40 1.00
18 Doug Moreau .10 .30
19 George Tarasovic .10 .30
20 Billy Cannon .30 .75
21 Jerry Stovall .10 .30
22 Joe Labruzzo .07 .20
23 Mickey Mangham .07 .20
24 Craig Burns .07 .20
25 Y.A. Tittle .75 2.00
26 Wendell Harris .10 .30
27 Leroy Labat .07 .20
28 Hokie Gajan .10 .30
29 Mike Williams .07 .20
30 Sammy Grezaffi .10 .30
31 Clinton Burrell .07 .20
32 Orlando McDaniel .07 .20
33 George Bevan .07 .20
34 Johnny Robinson .20 .50
35 Billy Masters .07 .20
36 J.W. Brodnax .07 .20
37 Tommy Casanova .20 .50
38 Fred Miller .07 .20
39 George Rice .07 .20
40 Earl Gros .10 .30
41 Lynn LeBlanc .07 .20
42 Jim Taylor .60 1.50
43 Joe Tuminello .07 .20
44 Tommy Davis .10 .30
45 Alvin Dark .20 .50
46 Richard Picou .07 .20
47 Charlie Percy .07 .20
48 John Garlington .10 .30
49 Mike Morgan DE .07 .20
50 Charles Bo Strange .07 .20
51 Max Fugler .07 .20
52 Don Schwab .07 .20
53 Dennis Gaubatz .10 .30
54 Jimmy Field .07 .20
55 Warren Capone .07 .20
56 Albert Richardson .07 .20
57 Charley Cusimano .07 .20
58 Brad Davis .07 .20
59 Gaynell Kinchen .07 .20
60 Roy Moonie Winston .10 .30
61 Mike Anderson .07 .20
62 Jesse Fatherree .07 .20
63 Gene Red Knight .07 .20
64 Tyler LaFauci .07 .20
65 Emile Fournet .07 .20
66 Gaynell Tinsley .10 .30
67 Remi Prudhomme .07 .20
68 Marvin Moose Stewart .07 .20
69 Jerry Guillot .07 .20
70 Steve Cassidy .07 .20
71 Bo Harris .10 .30
72 Robert Dugas .07 .20
73 Malcolm Scott .07 .20
74 Charles Rohm .07 .20
75 Gerald Keigley .07 .20
76 Don Alexander .07 .20
77 A.J. Duhe .10 .30
78 Ron Estay .07 .20
79 John Wood .07 .20
80 Andy Hamilton .10 .30
81 Jay Michaelson .07 .20
82 Kenny Konz .10 .30
83 Tracy Porter .07 .20
84 Billy Truax .10 .30
85 Alan Risher .07 .20
86 John Adams .07 .20
87 Tommy Neck .07 .20
88 Brad Boyd .07 .20
89 Greg LaFleur .07 .20
90 Bill Elko .07 .20
91 Binks Miciotto .07 .20
92 Lew Sibley .07 .20
93 Willie Teal .07 .20
94 Lyman White .07 .20
95 Chris Williams .07 .20
96 Sid Fournet .07 .20
97 Leonard Marshall .10 .30
98 Ramsey Dardar .07 .20
99 Ken Bordelon .07 .20
100 Fred Hall .07 .20

1985 LSU Police

The 1985 LSU Police set contains 16 standard-size cards. The fronts have color action photos bordered in white; the vertically oriented backs have brief career highlights and safety tips. The cards are unnumbered, so they are listed below alphabetically by subject's name. These cards are printed on very thin stock. The set was produced by McDag Productions. Card backs contain "Tips from the Tigers," while card fronts contain a blue Louisiana Savings logo.

COMPLETE SET (16) 7.50 15.00
1 Mitch Andrews .40 1.00
2 Bill Arnsparger CO .40 1.00
3 Roland Barbay .40 1.00
4 Michael Brooks .60 1.50
5 Shawn Burks .40 1.00
6 Tommy Clapp .40 1.00
7 Matt DeFrank .40 1.00
8 Kevin Guidry .40 1.00
9 Dalton Hilliard .75 2.00
10 Garry James .50 1.25
11 Norman Jefferson .40 1.00
12 Rogie Magee .40 1.00
13 Mike the Tiger(Mascot) .40 1.00
14 Craig Rathjen .40 1.00
15 Jeff Wickersham .40 1.00
16 Karl Wilson .40 1.00

1986 LSU Police

The 1986 LSU Police set contains 16 standard-size cards. The fronts have color action photos bordered in white; the vertically oriented backs have brief career highlights and safety tips. The cards are unnumbered, so they are listed below alphabetically by subject's name. These cards are printed on very thin stock. The set was produced by McDag Productions. Card backs contain "Tips from the Tigers," while card fronts contain logos for The General and the Chemical Dependency Unit of Baton Rouge.

COMPLETE SET (16) 7.50 15.00
1 Nacho Albergamo .40 1.00
2 Eric Andolsek .60 1.50
3 Bill Arnsparger CO .40 1.00
4 Roland Barbay .40 1.00
5 Michael Brooks .40 1.00
6 Chris Carrier .40 1.00
7 Toby Caston .40 1.00
8 Wendell Davis .75 2.00
9 Kevin Guidry .40 1.00
10 John Hazard .40 1.00
11 Oliver Lawrence .40 1.00
12 Rogie Magee .40 1.00
13 Sammy Martin .40 1.00
14 Darrell Phillips .40 1.00
15 Steve Rehage .40 1.00
16 Ron Sancho .40 1.00

1987 LSU Police

The 1987 LSU Police set contains 16 standard-size cards. The fronts have color action photos bordered in white; the vertically oriented backs have brief career highlights and safety tips. These cards are printed on very thin stock. This set was distributed at the Oct. 17, 1987 game vs. Kentucky. The set was produced by McDag Productions. Card backs contain "Tips from the Tigers". The cards are unnumbered, so they are listed below alphabetically by subject's name. The key card in the set is Harvey Williams' first card.

COMPLETE SET (16)	7.50	15.00
2 Nacho Albergamo	.40	1.00
3 Eric Andolsek	.50	1.25
1 Mike Archer CO	.50	1.25
4 David Browndyke	.40	1.00
5 Chris Carrier	.40	1.00
6 Wendell Davis	.60	1.50
7 Matt DeFrank	.40	1.00
8 Nicky Hazard	.40	1.00
9 Eric Hill	.50	1.25
10 Tommy Hodson	.50	1.25
11 Greg Jackson	.50	1.25
12 Brian Kinchen	.60	1.50
13 Darren Malbrough	.40	1.00
14 Sammy Martin	.40	1.00
15 Ron Sancho	.40	1.00
16 Harvey Williams	.75	2.00

1988 LSU Police

The 1988 LSU football set contains 16 standard-size cards. The fronts have color action photos with white borders and black lettering; the vertically oriented backs have career highlights. These cards were distributed as a set, which was produced by McDag Productions. Card backs contain "Tips from the Tigers".

COMPLETE SET (16)	7.50	15.00
1 Mike The Tiger(Mascot)	.40	1.00
2 Mike Archer CO	.60	1.50
3 Tommy Hodson	.50	1.25
4 Harvey Williams	.75	2.00
5 David Browndyke	.40	1.00
6 Karl Dunbar	.40	1.00
7 Eddie Fuller	.40	1.00
8 Mickey Guidry	.40	1.00
9 Greg Jackson	.50	1.25
10 Clint James	.40	1.00
11 Victor Jones	.40	1.00
12 Tony Moss	.40	1.00
13 Ralph Norwood	.40	1.00
14 Darrell Phillips	.40	1.00
15 Ruffin Rodrigue	.40	1.00
16 Ron Sancho	.40	1.00

1988-89 LSU All-Americas

Produced by McDag Productions, this 16-card standard-size set was sponsored by LSU, Baton Rouge General Medical Center, Chemical Dependency Unit of Baton Rouge, and various law enforcement agencies. The General Medical Center and Chemical Dependency Unit logos adorn the bottom of both sides of the card. This set showcases athletes from basketball (1-2), baseball (3-5), track (6), volleyball (7), football (8-15) and golf (16). This set includes early cards of Chris Jackson, who was selected in the first round of the NBA draft by the Denver Nuggets, and of Ben McDonald, who was selected first by the Baltimore Orioles.

COMPLETE SET (16)	5.00	12.00
8 Nacho Albergamo	.20	.50
9 Wendell Davis	.40	1.00
10 Michael Brooks	.60	1.50
11 Lance Smith	.40	1.00
12 Eric Martin	.60	1.50
13 James Britt	.20	.50
14 Albert Richardson	.20	.50
15 Greg Jackson	.40	1.00

1989 LSU Police

The 1989 LSU football set contains 16 standard-size cards. The fronts have color action photos with white borders and black lettering; the vertically oriented backs have career highlights. These cards were distributed as a set, which was produced by McDag Productions. Card backs contain "Tips from the Tigers".

COMPLETE SET (16)	7.50	15.00
1 Mike the Tiger(Mascot)	.40	1.00
2 David Browndyke 4	.40	1.00
3 Mike Archer CO	.60	1.50
4 Ruffin Rodrigue 68	.40	1.00
5 Marc Boutte 95	.50	1.25
6 Clint James 70	.40	1.00
7 Jimmy Young 5	.40	1.00
8 Alvin Lee 26	.40	1.00
9 Eddie Fuller 33	.40	1.00
10 Tiger Stadium	.40	1.00
11 Harvey Williams 22	.75	2.00
12 Verge Ausberry 98	.40	1.00
13 Karl Dunbar 63	.40	1.00
14 Tommy Hodson 13	.50	1.25
15 Tony Moss 6	.40	1.00
16 The Golden Girls (Cheerleaders)	.40	1.00

1990 LSU Collegiate Collection

This 200-card standard-size multi-sport set was produced by Collegiate Collection. Although a few color photos are included, the front features mostly black and white player photos, with borders in the team's colors of gold and purple. Unless noted below, all are football subjects.

COMPLETE SET (200)	6.00	15.00
3 Y.A. Tittle	.30	.75
5 Charles Alexander	.05	.15
7 Billy Cannon	.10	.25
8 Dalton Hilliard	.10	.25
9 Bert Jones	.15	.40
10 Tommy Hodson	.10	.25
12 Mike Archer CO F	.07	.20
15 Brian Kinchen	.10	.25
16 Chris Carrier	.05	.15
17 Jess Fatheree	.05	.15
20 Billy Hendrix	.05	.15
21 Eddie Ray	.05	.15
23 Bo Strange	.05	.15
24 Eric Hill	.10	.25
27 Malcolm Scott	.05	.15
28 A.J. Duhe	.10	.25
29 George Brancato	.05	.15
30 Jim Roshso	.05	.15
31 Karl Wilson	.10	.25
34 Lyman White	.05	.15
36 Michael Brooks	.10	.25
38 Gaynell Tinsley	.05	.15
39 Mike Anderson	.05	.15
41 Jerry Stovall	.10	.25
43 Bill Fortier	.05	.15
44 Mike V-Mascot	.05	.15
45 Richard Granier	.05	.15
47 Pinky Rohm	.05	.15
49 Toby Caston	.10	.25
51 John Ed Bradley	.05	.15
52 Mark Lumpkin	.05	.15
56 Curt Gore	.05	.15
57 Eric Martin	.10	.25
59 Roland Barray	.05	.15
60 Craig Duhe	.05	.15
63 Karl Dunbar	.05	.15
64 Mike Williams	.05	.15
66 Lew Sibley	.05	.15
67 John Sage	.05	.15
68 Craig Burns	.05	.15
70 Wendell Davis	.10	.25
72 Kenny Bordelon	.05	.15
73 Rusty Jackson	.05	.15
75 Garry James	.10	.25
76 Lance Smith	.05	.15
77 Willie Teal	.05	.15
78 John Wood	.05	.15
79 Mike Robichaux	.05	.15
80 Earl Leggett	.05	.15
81 Alex Box Stadium	.05	.15
82 Steve Cassidy	.05	.15
83 Kenny Konz	.05	.15
84 Wendell Harris	.07	.20
85 Alan Risher	.05	.15
86 Gerald Keigley	.05	.15
87 Robert Dugas	.05	.15
88 Chris Williams	.05	.15
89 John DeMarie	.05	.15
90 Eddie Fuller	.05	.15
92 Bo Harris	.05	.15
93 Mel Lyle	.05	.15
94 Greg Jackson	.10	.25
95 Liffort Hobley	.07	.20
96 Shawn Burks	.05	.15
97 David Browndyke	.05	.15
99 Eric Andolsek	.10	.25
101 Jon Streete	.05	.15
102 Barry Wilson	.05	.15
103 Remi Prudhomme	.05	.15
104 Abe Mickal	.05	.15
105 Henry Thomas	.15	.40
106 George Tarasovic	.05	.15
107 Tiger Stadium	.07	.20
108 Benjy Thibodeaux	.05	.15
109 Jeffery Dale	.05	.15
110 Sid Fournet	.05	.15
111 John Adams	.05	.15
112 Dennis Gaubatz	.05	.15
114 Joe Tuminello	.05	.15
115 Billy Truax	.07	.20
116 Warren Rabb	.05	.15
117 Albert Richardson	.05	.15
118 Jay Whitey	.05	.15
119 Clinton Burrell RB	.05	.15
121 Tommy Casanova	.10	.25
122 George Bevan	.05	.15
123 Binks Miciotto	.05	.15
124 Joe Michaelson	.05	.15
125 Mickey Mangham	.05	.15
126 Ronnie Estay	.05	.15
127 John Hazard	.05	.15
128 Darrell Phillips	.05	.15
129 Nacho Albergamo	.05	.15
130 John Garlington	.07	.20
131 Arthur Cantrelle	.05	.15
132 Monk Guillot	.05	.15
133 Gene Knight	.05	.15
134 Gerry Kent	.05	.15
135 Ron Sancho	.05	.15
137 Billy Cannon	.07	.20
139 Mike Vincent	.05	.15
140 Tyler LaFauci	.05	.15
141 Richard Brooks	.05	.15
142 Billy Booth	.05	.15
143 Brad Davis	.05	.15
144 Roy Winston	.05	.15
145 Andy Hamilton	.05	.15
146 Rene Bourgeois	.05	.15
147 Terry Robiskie	.07	.20
148 Godfrey Zaunbrecher	.05	.15
149 George Atiyeh	.05	.15
151 Jeff Wickersham	.07	.20
152 Charlie McClendon CO	.05	.15
153 Hokie Gajan	.10	.25
155 Bill Arnsparger CO	.07	.20
156 Max Fugler	.10	.25
157 Greg Lafleur	.05	.15
158 George Rice	.05	.15
159 Dave McCormick	.05	.15
160 Fred Miller	.05	.15
161 Steve Van Buren	.20	.50
166 Doug Moreau	.05	.15
167 Mike DeMarie	.05	.15
168 James Britt	.05	.15
169 Matt DeFrank	.05	.15
172 Pat Screen	.05	.15
173 Ralph Norwood	.05	.15
174 Marcus Quinn	.05	.15
175 Johnny Robinson	.10	.25
176 Tony Moss	.05	.15
177 Dan Alexander	.05	.15
178 Norman Jefferson	.05	.15
179 Bert Jones	.15	.40
180 Joe LaBruzzo	.05	.15
181 Jimmy Field	.05	.15
182 David Woodley	.07	.20
183 Paul Dietzel CO	.07	.20
184 Abner Wimbley CO	.05	.15
185 Steve Ensminger	.05	.15
186 Carlos Carson	.10	.25
187 Ken Kavanaugh Sr. CO	.05	.15
188 Paul Ziegler	.05	.15
195 Warren Capone	.05	.15
199 Sam Grezaffi	.05	.15

1992 LSU McDag

This 16-card standard-size set was produced for Louisiana State University by McDag Productions Inc. The cards are printed on thin stock and feature on the fronts action color player shots framed in purple on a mustard background. A purple bar at the top contains "LSU" in white lettering with the year and team logo (a tiger's head) immediately below on the mustard top border. The white backs are printed in purple and feature biography, career highlights, statistics, and "Tiger Facts".

COMPLETE SET (16)	3.20	8.00
1 Curley Hallman CO	.30	.75
2 Ray Adams	.20	.50
3 Chad Loup	.20	.50
4 Odell Beckham	.20	.50
5 Wesley Jacob	.20	.50
6 Kevin Mawae	.60	1.50
7 Clayton Mouton	.20	.50
8 Roovelroe Swan	.20	.50
9 Ricardo Washington	.20	.50
10 David Walkup	.20	.50
11 Jessie Daigle	.20	.50
12 Carlton Buckles	.20	.50
13 Anthony Williams	.20	.50
14 Darron Landry	.20	.50
15 Frank Godfrey	.20	.50
16 Pedro Suarez	.20	.50

1986-87 Maine

This 14-card set of Maine Black Bears is part of a "Kids and Kops" promotion, and one card was printed each Saturday in the Bangor Daily News. The cards measure approximately 2 1/2" by 4". The cards were to be collected from any participating plice officer. Once five cards had been collected (including card number 1), they could be turned in at a police station for a University of Maine ID card, which permitted free admission to selected university activities. When all 14 cards had been collected, they could be turned in at a police station to register for the Grand Prize drawing (bicycle) and to pick up a free "Kids and Kops" tee-shirt. The backs have tips in the form of an anti-drug or alcohol message and logos of Burger King, University of Maine and Pepsi across the bottom. With the exception of the rules card, the cards are numbered on the back.

COMPLETE SET (14)	6.00	15.00
4 Doug Dorsey FB	.40	1.00
10 Bob Wilder FB	.40	1.00

1987-88 Maine

This 14-card set of Maine Black Bears is part of a "Kids and Kops" promotion, and one card was printed each Saturday in the Bangor Daily News. The cards measure approximately 2 1/2" by 4". The cards were to be collected from any participating police officer. Once five cards had been collected (including card number 1), they could be turned in at a police station for a University of Maine ID card, which permitted free admission to selected university activities. When all 14 cards had been collected, they could be turned in at a police station to register for the Grand Prize drawing (bicycle) and to pick up a free "Kids and Kops" tee-shirt. The backs have tips in the form of an anti-drug or alcohol message and logos of Burger King, University of Maine, and Pepsi across the bottom. With the exception of the rules card, the cards are numbered on the back. Sports represented in this set include hockey (2), basketball (3, 9, 13), tennis (4), baseball (5), swimming (6), soccer (7), track (8), football (10), field hockey (11), and softball (12).

COMPLETE SET (14)	6.00	15.00
10 David Ingalls FB	.40	1.00

1998 Marshall Chad Pennington

This card was issued by the school to commemorate Marshall's Motor City Bowl game appearance. The cardfront features Chad Pennington in his white jersey along with recognition of Marshall's 1998 Mid-America Conference Championship. The cardback includes a brief history of Marshall's football success during the 1990s along with game-by-game results of the 1998 season.

1 Chad Pennington	2.00	5.00

1999 Marshall Chad Pennington

Issued by Marshall University, this card commemorates Chad Pennington's candidacy for the Heisman Trophy. The standard sized card shows Pennington in a drop back pose holding the football with both hands.

NNO Chad Pennington	2.00	5.00

2000 Marshall Byron Leftwich

This Byron Leftwich card was issued by the school to commemorate the 2000 Motor City Bowl and Marshall's Mid-America Conference Championship . The cardback features only the 2000 Marshall regular season schedule.

1 Byron Leftwich	2.00	5.00

2001 Marshall Byron Leftwich

The first card listed below was issued by the school to commemorate Marshall's appearance in the 2002 GMAC Bowl. It was distributed to fans and purchasers of tickets to the bowl game and measures standard card size. It features a color image of Leftwich on the front and back along with a write-up for Leftwich on the back including his 2001 regular season stats. The jumbo card (measuring roughly 5 7/8" by 9") was issued during the 2001 season and features a large image of Leftwich along with small images of recent past Heisman Trophy candidates Chad Pennington and Randy Moss. The cardback includes a bio and statistics from Byron Leftwich's career.

1 Byron Leftwich	2.00	5.00
2 Byron Leftwich Randy Moss Chad Pennington Jumbo Card	5.00	12.00

2002 Marshall Byron Leftwich

This Byron Leftwich card was issued by the school to commemorate the 2002 season, Byron Leftwich's last at quarterback. The card features Leftwich wearing his green jersey celebrating a victory. A second larger postcard was also issued earlier in the year promoting Leftwich as a 2002 Heisman Trophy candidate.

1 Byron Leftwich	2.00	5.00
2 Byron Leftwich Postcard	4.00	10.00

2003 Marshall Darius Watts

This card was issued by the school to commemorate Marshall's star reciever Darius Watts. They were distributed to fans and purchasers of game tickets and the card measures standard size.

1 Darius Watts	2.00	4.00

2004 Marshall

These two cards were issued by the school to commemorate Marshall's appearance in the 2004 Ft. Worth Bowl. They were distributed to fans and purchasers of tickets to the bowl game and each measures standard card size. They feature a color image of the player on the front and back along with a write-up and his 2004 regular season stats on the back.

1 Josh Davis	1.50	4.00
2 Johnathan Goddard	1.50	4.00

1969 Maryland Team Sheets

These six sheets measure approximately 8" by 10". The fronts feature two rows of four black-and-white player portraits each. The player's name is printed under the photo. The backs are blank. The sheets are unnumbered and checklisted below in alphabetical order according to the first player (or coach) listed.

COMPLETE SET (6)	25.00	50.00
1 Bill Backus	4.00	10.00
Lou Bracken		
Sonny Demczuk		
Roland Merritt		
Rich Slaninka		
Ralph Sonntag		
Mike Stubljar		
Jim Stull		
2 Bill Bell CO	4.00	10.00
George Boutselis CO		
Albert Ferguson CO		
James Kehoe AD		
Roy Lester CO		
Dim Montero CO		
Lee Royer CO		
3 Pat Burke	4.00	10.00
John Dyer		
Craig Gienger		
Tony Greene		
Bob MacBride		
Bill Meister		
Russ Nolan		
Ray Soporowski		
4 Steve Ciambor	4.00	10.00
Kenny Dutton		
Dan Kecman		
Bob Mahnic		
Len Santacroce		
David Seifert		
Len Spicer		
Rick Stoll		
5 Bob Colbert	4.00	10.00
John Dill		
Henry Gareis		
Bill Grant		
Glenn Kubany		
Bill Reilly		
Wally Stalnaker		
Gary Vansickler		
6 Paul Fitzpatrick	4.00	10.00
Larry Marshall		
Tom Miller		
Will Morris		
Dennis O'Hara		
Scott Shank		
Jeff Shugars		
Al Thomas		

1991 Maryland High School Big 33

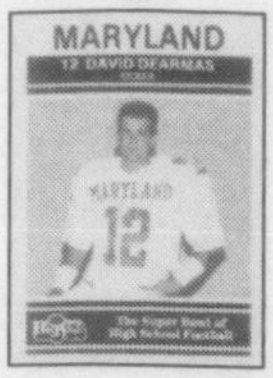

This 34-card standard-size high school football set was issued to commemorate the Big 33 Football Classic. The fronts feature a posed black and white player photo enclosed in a white border. State name appears at top. Player number and position appear as white reversed-out lettering within a black bar. The Big 33 logo and The Super Bowl of High School Football appear at the bottom. The backs feature biographical information and honors received within a thin black border.

COMPLETE SET (34)	50.00	100.00
MD1 Asim Penny	1.50	4.00
MD2 Louis Jason	1.50	4.00
MD3 Mark McCain	1.50	4.00
MD4 Matthew Byrne	1.50	4.00
MD5 Mike Gillespie	1.50	4.00
MD6 Ricky Rowe	1.50	4.00
MD7 David DeArmas	1.50	4.00
MD8 Duane Ashman	1.50	4.00
MD9 James Cunningham	1.50	4.00
MD10 Keith Kormanik	1.50	4.00
MD11 Leonard Green	1.50	4.00
MD12 Larry Washington	1.50	4.00
MD13 Raphael Wall	1.50	4.00
MD14 Kai Hebron	1.50	4.00
MD15 Coy Gibbs	2.50	6.00
MD16 Lenard Marcus	1.50	4.00
MD17 John Taliaferro	1.50	4.00
MD18 J.C. Price	1.50	4.00
MD19 Jamal Cox	1.50	4.00
MD20 Rick Budd	1.50	4.00
MD21 Shaun Marshall	1.50	4.00
MD22 Allan Jenkins	1.50	4.00
MD23 Bryon Turner	1.50	4.00
MD24 Ryan Foran	1.50	4.00
MD25 John Summerday	1.50	4.00
MD26 Joshua Austin	1.50	4.00
MD27 Emile Palmer	1.50	4.00
MD28 John Teter	1.50	4.00
MD29 John Kennedy	1.50	4.00
MD30 Clarence Collins	1.50	4.00
MD31 Daryl Smith	1.50	4.00
MD32 David Wilkins	1.50	4.00
MD33 David Thomas	1.50	4.00
MD34 Russell Thomas	1.50	4.00

1992 Maryland High School Big 33

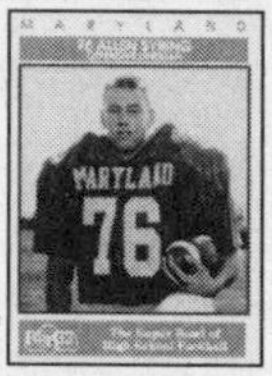

This standard-size high school football set was issued to commemorate the Big 33 Football Classic. The fronts feature posed player photos enclosed by a white border. The state name appears at the top of the card along with the player's name, number, and position. The Big 33 logo appears below the photo. The backs feature the player's biographical information along with a notation to which college he plans to attend. The unnumbered cards are listed below alphabetically.

COMPLETE SET (35)	40.00	80.00
1 George Addison	1.50	4.00
2 Calvin Arrington	1.50	4.00
3 Damon Atwater	1.50	4.00
4 Bruce Ballard	1.50	4.00
5 Mike Bertoni	1.50	4.00
6 Demont Blackmon	1.50	4.00
7 Jason Buckhanan	1.50	4.00
8 Jay Cammon	1.50	4.00
9 James Easterly	1.50	4.00
10 Marlon Evans	1.50	4.00
11 Effrem Gordon	1.50	4.00
12 Ray Gray	1.50	4.00
13 Brent Guyton	1.50	4.00
14 Michael Kelly	1.50	4.00
15 Eric Knight	1.50	4.00
16 Bill Krumpe	1.50	4.00
17 Ted Kwalick Honorary Chairman	1.50	4.00
18 Brandon Lallis	1.50	4.00
19 David Lee	1.50	4.00
20 Jermaine Lewis	2.00	5.00
21 Matt Lilly	1.50	4.00
22 Andre Martin	1.50	4.00
23 Rhad Miles	1.50	4.00
24 Julian Norment	1.50	4.00
25 Steve Oliver	1.50	4.00
26 Jeremy Raley	1.50	4.00
27 Richard Snowden	1.50	4.00
28 Robert St. Pierre	1.50	4.00
29 Jack Sykes	1.50	4.00
30 Allen Syring	1.50	4.00
31 Troy Turner	1.50	4.00
32 David Vernier	1.50	4.00
33 Anthony Walker	1.50	4.00
34 Phillip White	1.50	4.00
35 Joseph Wright	1.50	4.00

1988 McNeese State McDag/Police

This 16-card standard-size set is printed on thin card stock. It is sponsored by the Behavioral Health and Chemical Dependency Units of Lake Charles Memorial Hospital. Card front has a posed picture enclosed in a white border. Team logo appears in upper left while player's name, position, and the year appear in upper right corner. The sponsor logos appear at the bottom. Horizontally oriented backs present biography, player profile, "Tips From the Cowboys" in the form of anti-drug messages, and sponsor logos at the bottom.

COMPLETE SET (16)	2.50	6.00
1 Sonny Jackson CO	.20	.50
2 Lance Wiley	.20	.50
3 Brian McZeal	.20	.50
4 Berwick Davenport	.20	.50
5 Gary Irvin	.20	.50
6 Glenn Koch	.20	.50
7 Chad Habetz	.20	.50
8 Pete Sinclair	.20	.50
9 Tony Citizen	.20	.50
10 Scott Dieterich	.20	.50
11 Hud Jackson	.20	.50
12 Darrin Andrus	.20	.50
13 Jeff Mathews	.20	.50
14 Devin Babineaux	.20	.50
15 Jeff Delhomme	.20	.50
16 Eric LeBlanc Mike Pierce	.20	.50

1989 McNeese State McDag/Police

This 16-card standard-size set is printed on thin card stock. It is sponsored by the Behavioral Health and Chemical Dependency Units of Lake Charles Memorial Hospital. The fronts feature color posed photos enclosed by light blue borders. The player's name, position, year, and school logo are in the top border while the sponsor logo appears beneath the picture. The backs carry biography, player profile, and "Tips From The Cowboys" in the form of anti-drug or mental health messages. The cards are numbered on the back in the upper right corner.

COMPLETE SET (16)	2.50	6.00
1 Marc Stampley	.20	.50
2 Mark LeBlanc	.20	.50
3 Kip Texada	.25	.60
4 Brian Champagne	.20	.50
5 Ronald Scott	.20	.50
6 Jimmy Poirier	.20	.50
7 Cliff Buckner	.20	.50
8 Jericho Loupe	.20	.50
9 Vaughn Calbert	.20	.50
10 Rodney Burks	.20	.50
11 Troy Jones	.20	.50
12 Chris Andrus	.20	.50
13 Robbie Vizier	.20	.50
14 Kenneth Pierce	.20	.50
15 Bobby Smith	.20	.50
16 Trent Lee	.20	.50

1990 McNeese State McDag/Police

The 1990 McNeese State Cowboys football set contains 16 standard-size cards and is basically the same design as previous years. The card front features a posed player photo, with rounded corners and enclosed by a light blue border. The player's name, position, year, and school logo are in the top border while the sponsor's name and logo (Lake Charles Memorial Hospital) are beneath the picture. Backs feature biography, player profile, and "Tips From The Cowboys" in the form of anti-drug or mental health messages.

COMPLETE SET (16)	2.40	6.00
1 Hud Jackson	.20	.50
2 Wes Watts	.20	.50
3 Mark LeBlanc	.20	.50
4 Jeff Delhomme	.20	.50
5 Mike Reed	.20	.50
6 Chuck Esponge	.20	.50
7 Ronald Scott	.20	.50
8 Ken Naquin	.20	.50
9 Steve Aultman	.20	.50
10 Sean Judge	.20	.50
11 Greg Rayson	.20	.50
12 Kip Texada	.20	.50
13 Mike Pierce	.20	.50
14 Jimmy Poirier	.20	.50
15 Ronald Solomon	.20	.50
16 Eric Foster	.20	.50

1991 McNeese State McDag/Police

This 16-card standard-size set was produced by McDag Productions and sponsored by Lake Charles Memorial Hospital. The print run was reportedly limited to 3,500 sets. Each of the cards features a posed color photo of the player kneeling beside the goalpost, with the stadium in the background. The pictures have rounded corners and light blue borders. Player information appears above the picture, while the sponsor's logo adorns the bottom of the card. The backs have biography, player profile, and "Tips from the Cowboys" in the form of anti-drug and alcohol messages.

COMPLETE SET (16)	2.40	6.00
1 Eric Roberts	.20	.50
2 Erwin Brown	.20	.50
3 Marcus Bowie	.20	.50
4 Wes Watts	.20	.50
5 Brian Brumfield	.20	.50
6 Marc Stampley	.20	.50
7 Sean Judge	.20	.50
8 Joey Bernard	.20	.50
9 Ken Naquin	.20	.50
10 Bobby Smith	.20	.50
11 Sam Breaux	.20	.50
12 Ronald Scott	.20	.50
13 Edward Dyer	.20	.50
14 Greg Rayson	.20	.50
15 Eric Kidd	.20	.50
16 Bobby Keasler CO	.20	.50

1992 McNeese State McDag/Police

This 16-card standard-size set was produced by McDag Productions and sponsored by Lake Charles Memorial Hospital. The set is printed on thin card stock. The fronts feature rounded-corner posed color player photos on a mustard card face. The player's name and position appear below the picture. The backs have a white background and carry biographical information, player profile, and anti-drug or alcohol messages under the heading Tips from the Cowboys.

COMPLETE SET (16)	2.40	6.00
1 Eric Acheson	.20	.50
2 Pat Neck	.20	.50
3 Marcus Bowie	.20	.50
4 Marty Posey	.20	.50
5 Brian Brumfield	.20	.50
6 Terry Irving	.30	.75
7 Eric Fleming	.20	.50
8 Lance Guidry	.20	.50
9 Ken Naquin	.20	.50
10 Chris Fontenette	.20	.50
11 Sam Breaux	.20	.50
12 Dana Scott	.20	.50
13 Edward Dyer	.20	.50
14 Blayne Rush	.20	.50
15 Ronald Solomon	.20	.50
16 Steve Aultman	.20	.50

1984 Miami Schedules

These "cards" were printed in the style of a game ticket and feature the team's 1984 football schedule on the back. They were sponsored by Willard Graphics and include a sepia toned player photo on the front. Each measures 2 1/8" by 5 1/2".

COMPLETE SET (8)	2.50	6.00
1 Eddie Brown	.40	1.00
2 Kenny Calhoun	.30	.75
3 Dallas Cameron	.30	.75
4 Juan Comendeiro	.30	.75
5 Alonzo Highsmith	.40	1.00
6 Bernie Kosar	.75	2.00
7 Vic Morris	.30	.75
8 Winston Moss	.40	1.00

1990 Miami

The 1990 Miami Hurricanes Smokey set was issued in a sheet of 16 cards which, when perforated, measure the standard size. The fronts feature color action photos bordered in orange on green background, with the player's name, position, and jersey number below the picture. The backs have biographical information (in English and Spanish) and a fire prevention cartoon starring Smokey. The cards are unnumbered, so they are listed below alphabetically by subject's name. Key players in this set include Craig Erickson, Randal Hill and Russell Maryland.

COMPLETE SET (16)	8.00	20.00
1 Randy Bethel 93	.30	.75
2 Wesley Carroll 81	.80	2.00
3 Rob Chudzinski 84	.30	.75
4 Leonard Conley 28	.40	1.00
5 Luis Cristobal 59	.30	.75
6 Maurice Crum 49	.30	.75
7 Shane Curry 44	.40	1.00
8 Craig Erickson 7	1.20	3.00
9 Dennis Erickson CO	1.00	2.50
10 Darren Handy 66	.30	.75
11 Randal Hill 3	.80	2.00
12 Carlos Huerta 27	.40	1.00
13 Russell Maryland 67	1.00	2.50
14 Stephen McGuire 30	.40	1.00
15 Roland Smith 16	.30	.75
16 Mike Sullivan 79	.30	.75

1991 Miami

This 16-card standard-size set was sponsored by Bounty. Approximately 5,000 sets were issued, and they were given away at the Nov. 9 game against West Virginia at the Orange Bowl. The player action photos on the fronts are enclosed in black, orange, and green borders. College and team name are printed inside top borders while player information appears between the team helmet and Bounty logo at the bottom of the card face. Horizontally oriented backs provide player profile (in

English and Spanish), biographical information, a head shot, and "Tips from the Hurricanes" in form of public service announcements. Sponsor logo and photo credits also appear on the back. The cards are unnumbered and checklisted below in alphabetical order.

COMPLETE SET (16)	8.00	20.00
1 Jessie Armstead	.80	2.00
2 Micheal Barrow	.80	2.00
3 Hurlie Brown	.40	1.00
4 Dennis Erickson CO	.80	2.00
5 Anthony Hamlet	.40	1.00
6 Carlos Huerta	.60	1.50
7 Herbert James	.40	1.00
8 Claude Jones	.40	1.00
9 Stephen McGuire	.60	1.50
10 Eric Miller	.40	1.00
11 Joe Moore	.40	1.00
12 Charles Pharms	.40	1.00
13 Leon Searcy	.80	2.00
14 Darrin Smith	.80	2.00
15 Lamar Thomas	.80	2.00
16 Gino Torretta	1.00	2.50

1992 Miami

This 16-card safety set was sponsored by Bumble Bee Seafoods Inc., and its company logo is found at the bottom of both sides of the card. The cards were issued as an unperforated sheet with four rows of four cards each. If the cards were cut, they would measure the standard size. The color player photos on the fronts bleed off the bottom and right side but are edged by a thick green stripe on the left. The words "Hurricane Football" are printed in orange and green stripes that cut across the top of the front. The backs present biography, career summary, and "What Does It Take to Be a Hurricane" feature, which consists of a quote stressing a positive mental attitude. The cards are unnumbered and checklisted below in alphabetical order. The set features the second collegiate card of 1992 Heismann Trophy winner Gino Torretta as well as a card of wide receiver Kevin Williams.

COMPLETE SET (16)	6.00	15.00
1 Jessie Armstead	.60	1.50
2 Micheal Barrow	.60	1.50
3 Coleman Bell	.30	.75
4 Mark Caesar	.30	.75
5 Horace Copeland UER (Name misspelled Horrace on front)	.60	1.50
6 Mario Cristobal	.30	.75
7 Dennis Erickson CO	.60	1.50
8 Casey Greer	.30	.75
9 Stephen McGuire	.40	1.00
10 Ryan McNeil	1.00	2.00
11 Rusty Medearis	.30	.75
12 Darrin Smith	.60	1.50
13 Darryl Spencer	.30	.75
14 Lamar Thomas	.60	1.50
15 Gino Torretta	.80	2.00
16 Kevin Williams WR	.80	2.00

1993 Miami

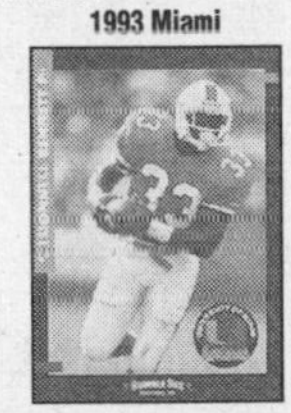

Sponsored by Bumble Bee, the 16 cards comprising this set were issued in one 16-card perforated sheet. The sheet measures approximately 10" by 14" and consists of four rows of four cards each. Each card measures the standard size and carries on its front a black-bordered color player action shot. The player's name, uniform number, and position appear vertically in white lettering within the orange stripe at the upper left. The Hurricanes' logo is displayed within a lower corner of the player photo. The Bumble Bee logo in white lettering rests in the lower black margin. The white back carries the player's name, uniform number, biography, highlights in both English and Spanish, and the player's "Most memorable moment as a Hurricane." The Bumble Bee logo at the bottom rounds out the card. The cards are unnumbered and checklisted below in alphabetical order.

COMPLETE SET (16)	4.80	12.00
1 Rudy Barber	.30	.75
2 Robert Bass	.30	.75
3 Donnell Bennett	1.00	2.50
4 Jason Budroni	.30	.75
5 Marcus Carey	.30	.75
6 Ryan Collins	.30	.75
7 Frank Costa	.40	1.00
8 Dennis Erickson CO	.30	.75
9 Terris Harris	.30	.75
10 Chris T. Jones	.40	1.00
11 Larry Jones	.40	1.00
12 Darren Krein	.40	1.00
13 Kenny Lopez	.30	.75
14 Kevin Patrick	.30	.75
15 Dexter Seigler	.30	.75
16 Paul White	.30	.75

1994 Miami

Sponsored by Bumble Bee, the cards in this set were issued in one 24-card perforated sheet. The sheet consists of six rows of four cards each with each card measuring standard size. The Bumble Bee logo appears on the front of the cards which feature a green border. The white cardback carries the player's name, uniform number, biography and career highlights in both English and Spanish. The cards are unnumbered and checklisted below in alphabetical order. Note that this set features the only card of Dwayne Johnson, better known as "The Rock" in professional wrestling.

COMPLETE SET (24)	40.00	80.00
1 Ryan Collins	.30	.75
2 Frank Costa	.30	.75
3 Dennis Erickson CO	.30	.75
4 Corwin Francis	.30	.75
5 Jammi German	.60	1.50
6 Tirrell Greene	.30	.75
7 Jonathan Harris	.30	.75
8 Dwayne Johnson	25.00	50.00
9 Chris T. Jones	.40	1.00
10 Larry Jones FB	.40	1.00
11 Ray Lewis	7.50	15.00
12 Zev Lumelski	.30	.75
13 Rohan Marley	.30	.75
14 Rusty Medearis	.30	.75
15 Malcolm Pearson	.30	.75
16 Ricky Perry	.30	.75
17 Dane Prewitt	.30	.75
18 C.J. Richardson	.30	.75
19 Patrick Riley	.30	.75
20 Warren Sapp	4.00	10.00
21 Baraka Short	.30	.75
22 James A. Stewart	.40	1.00
23 A.C. Tellison	.40	1.00
24 Chad Wilson CB	.30	.75

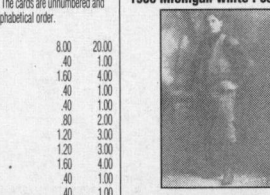

1995 Miami

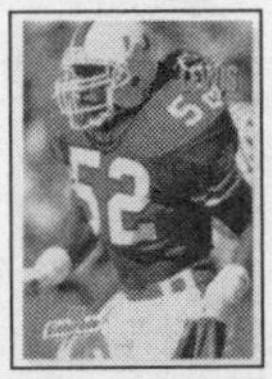

Sponsored by Gatorade, the cards in this set were issued in one 18-card perforated sheet with each card measuring standard size. The Gatorade logo appears on the front of the cards which feature a white border. The white cardback carries the player's name, uniform number, biography and career highlights in both English and Spanish. The cards are unnumbered and checklisted below in alphabetical order.

COMPLETE SET (18)	10.00	20.00
1 Antonio Coley	.30	.75
2 Ryan Collins	.30	.75
3 Mike Crissy	.30	.75
4 Butch Davis CO	.30	.75
5 Marvin Davis	.30	.75
6 Danyell Ferguson	.30	.75
7 Tony Gaiter	.30	.75
8 Jammi German	.60	1.50
9 Yatil Green	.60	1.50
10 Kenny Holmes	.60	1.50
11 K.C. Jones	.30	.75
12 Kenard Lang	.40	1.00
13 Ray Lewis	6.00	12.00
14 Earl Little	.40	1.00
15 Dane Prewitt	.30	.75
16 Eugene Ridgley	.30	.75
17 Twan Russell	.30	.75
18 Syii Tucker	.30	.75

1996 Miami

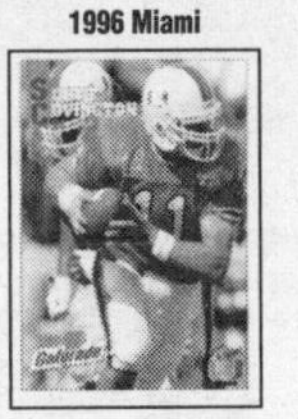

Sponsored by Gatorade, the cards in this set were initially issued as a perforated sheet with each card measuring standard size. The Gatorade logo appears on the front of the cards which feature a white border. The white cardback carries the player's name, uniform number, biography and career highlights in both English and Spanish. The cards are unnumbered and checklisted below in alphabetical order.

COMPLETE SET (27)	7.50	15.00
1 Magic Benton	.30	.75
2 Kerlin Blaise	.30	.75
3 James Burgess	.30	.75
4 Jermaine Chambers	.30	.75
5 Ryan Clement	.40	1.00
6 Tony Coley	.30	.75
7 Scott Covington	.60	1.50
8 Gerard Daphnis	.30	.75
9 Marvin Davis	.30	.75
10 Danyell Ferguson	.30	.75
11 Denny Fortnoy	.30	.75
12 Yatil Green	.60	1.50
13 Jack Hallmon	.30	.75
14 Kenny Holmes	.40	1.00
15 J Ina	.30	.75
16 Carlos Jones	.30	.75
17 Chris T. Jones	.40	1.00
18 K.C. Jones	.30	.75
19 Carlo Joseph	.30	.75
20 Kenard Lang	.40	1.00
21 Earl Little	.40	1.00
22 Tremain Mack	.40	1.00
23 Booker Pickett	.30	.75
24 Twan Russell	.30	.75
25 Duane Starks	.30	.75
26 Marcus Wimberly	.30	.75
27 Sebastian MASCOT	.30	.75

1997 Miami

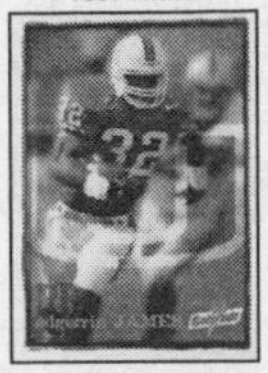

This set was produced for the University of Miami and sponsored by Gatorade. Each card features a color photo of the player on the cardfront along with the Miami logo in the background. The unnumbered backs feature a simple black and white design.

COMPLETE SET (24)	12.50	25.00
1 Yacub Abdul-Matin	.30	.75
2 Kerlin Blaise	.30	.75
3 Freeman Brown	.30	.75
4 Carlos Callejas	.30	.75
5 Ryan Clement	.40	1.00
6 Scott Covington	.60	1.50
7 Andy Crosland	.30	.75
8 Dennis Fortney	.30	.75
9 Derrick Ham	.60	1.50
10 Edgerrin James	6.00	15.00
11 Chris Jones	.40	1.00
12 Trent Jones	.40	1.00
13 Michael Lawson	.30	.75
14 Rod Mack	.30	.75
15 Dyral McMillan	.40	1.00
16 Chad Pegues	.30	.75
17 Eugene Ridgley	.30	.75
18 Nelson Rodriquez	.30	.75
19 Dennis Scott	.30	.75
20 Duane Starks	.30	.75
21 Jeffrey Taylor	.30	.75
22 Nick Ward	.30	.75
23 Mike Wehner	.30	.75
24 Miami Mascot	.30	.75

1999 Miami

Sponsored by Gatorade, the cards in this set were issued in one 30-card perforated sheet with each card measuring standard size. The Gatorade logo appears on the front of the cards which feature a white border. The white cardback carries the player's name, uniform number, biography and career highlights in English only. The cards are unnumbered and checklisted below in alphabetical order.

COMPLETE SET (30)	12.50	25.00
1 Martin Dibla	.30	.75
2 Al Blades	.20	.50
3 Michael Boireau	.20	.50
4 Delvin Brown	.20	.50
5 Andy Crosland	.20	.50
6 Najeh Davenport	.75	2.00
7 Butch Davis CO	.20	.50
8 Pat Del Vecchio	.20	.50
9 Bubba Franks	1.00	2.50
10 Mondriel Fulcher	.20	.50
11 Joaquin Gonzalez	.20	.50
12 Robert Hall	.20	.50
13 James Jackson	.75	2.00
14 Kenny Kelly	.30	.75
15 Andre King	.50	1.25
16 Damione Lewis	.50	1.25
17 Rod Mack	.20	.50
18 Richard Mercier	.20	.50
19 Dan Morgan	1.25	3.00
20 Santana Moss	1.50	4.00
21 Leonard Myers	.20	.50
22 Jeff Popovich	.20	.50
23 Ed Reed	2.50	6.00
24 Eric Schnupp	.20	.50
25 Michael Smith	.20	.50
26 Matt Sweeney	.20	.50
27 Reggie Wayne	2.00	5.00
28 Nate Webster	.20	.50
29 Adrian Wilson	1.25	3.00
30 Ty Wise	.20	.50

2000 Miami

This set was produced for the University of Miami and sponsored by Gatorade. Each card features a color photo of the player on the cardfront along with a simple black and white printed cardback. The cards were originally issued in two 9-panel perforated sheets and the backs were numbered.

COMPLETE SET (18)	10.00	20.00
1 Al Blades	.20	.50
2 Damione Lewis	.50	1.25
3 Freddie Capshaw	.20	.50
4 Ed Reed	1.50	4.00
5 Dan Morgan	1.00	2.50
6 Mike Rumph	.50	1.25
7 Quincy Hipps	.30	.75
8 Chris Campbell	.30	.75
9 Aaron Moser	.20	.50
10 Martin Bibla	.30	.75
11 Najeh Davenport	.60	1.50
12 Ken Dorsey	2.00	5.00
13 Joaquin Gonzalez	.20	.50
14 James Jackson RB	.75	2.00
15 Santana Moss	1.00	2.50
16 Reggie Wayne	2.00	5.00
17 Todd Sievers	.20	.50
18 Andre King	.50	1.25

2001 Miami Schedules

COMPLETE SET (6)	2.00	4.00
1 Joaquin Gonzalez Bryant McKinnie	.20	.50
2 Ken Dorsey (holding ball in both hands)	.30	.75
3 Ed Reed	.50	1.25
4 Jeremy Shockey	.50	1.25
5 Larry Coker	.20	.50
NNO Ken Dorsey (holding ball in one hand)	.30	.75

1997 Miami (OH) Cradle of Coaches

This set was produced by American Marketing Associates and features coaching greats from the University of Miami in Ohio. Football is the focus of the set although it also contains a few coaches from other sports as noted below. The cards are unnumbered and checklisted below in alphabetical order.

COMPLETE SET (19)	8.00	20.00
2 Bill Arnsparger FB	.40	1.00
3 Paul Brown FB	1.60	4.00
4 Carmen Cozza FB	.40	1.00
5 Dick Crum FB	.40	1.00
6 Paul Dietzel FB	.80	2.00
8 Weeb Ewbank FB	1.20	3.00
9 Sid Gillman FB	1.20	3.00
10 Woody Hayes FB	1.60	4.00
12 Bill Mallory FB	.40	1.00
13 John McVay FB	.40	1.00
14 Ara Parseghian FB	1.20	3.00
15 John Pont FB	.40	1.00
16 Bo Schembechler FB	1.20	3.00

2003 Miami (OH)

This set was sponsored by Pepsi and includes members of the 2003 Miami of Ohio University football team. Reportedly just 3000-sets were produced and given away to attendees of the game versus Bowling Green on November 4, 2003. The cardfronts include a red colored border and the backs were printed in black and white. The unnumbered cards are listed below alphabetically.

COMPLETE SET (25)	20.00	35.00
1 Jacob Bell	.20	.50
2 Calvin Blackmon	.20	.50
3 Matt Brandt	.20	.50
4 Larry Burt	.20	.50
5 Jamie Cooper	.20	.50
6 Alan Eyink	.20	.50
7 Ben Herrell	.20	.50
8 Alphonso Hodge	.20	.50
9 Terrell Jones	.20	.50
10 Dan Kosta	.20	.50
11 Michael Larkin	.50	1.25
12 Cal Murray Jr.	.30	.75
13 Matt Pusateri	.20	.50
14 Ben Roethlisberger	15.00	30.00
15 Will Rueff	.20	.50
16 Scott Sagehorn	.20	.50
17 Joe Serina	.20	.50
18 Frank Smith	.20	.50
19 Mike Smith	.20	.50
20 Phil Smith	.20	.50
21 Ryan Sprague	.20	.50
22 Will Stanley	.20	.50
23 J.D. Vonderheide	.20	.50
24 Mike Wafzig	.20	.50
25 Yager Stadium	.20	.50

1905 Michigan Postcards

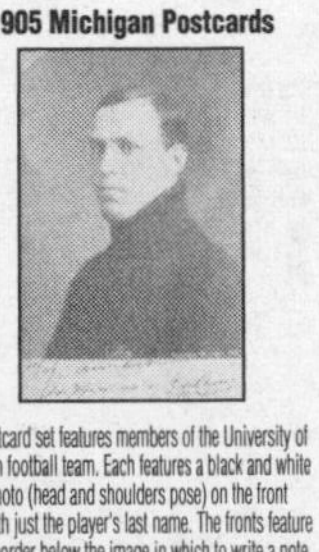

This postcard set features members of the University of Michigan football team. Each features a black and white player photo (head and shoulders pose) on the front along with just the player's last name. The fronts feature a white border below the image in which to write a note. The cardbacks are printed in a generic postcard style with no manufacturer's identification.

1 John Curtis (copyright 1903 on front)	40.00	80.00
2 Tom Hammond	40.00	80.00
3 Fred Norcross	40.00	80.00
4 Germany Schultz	100.00	175.00
5 Fielding Yost CO (Rotograph Series B 469)	125.00	200.00

1907 Michigan Dietsche Postcards

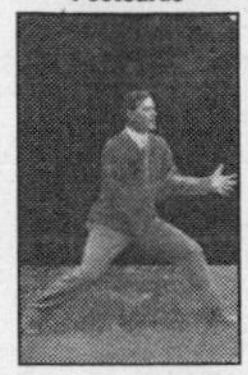

This set features members of the University of Michigan football team on postcard back cards. The ACC catalog designation for this set is PC765-3. Each card features a black and white player photo on front and a postcard back complete with a short player write-up. The A.C. Dietsche copyright line also appears on the back.

COMPLETE SET (15)	1,200.00	1,800.00
1 Dave Allerdice	75.00	125.00
2 William Casey	75.00	125.00
3 William Embs	75.00	125.00
4 Keene Fitzpatrick TR	75.00	125.00
5 Red Flanagan	75.00	125.00
6 Walter Graham	75.00	125.00
7 Harry Hammond	75.00	125.00
8 John Loell	75.00	125.00
9 Paul Magoffin	75.00	125.00
10 James Joy Miller	75.00	125.00
11 Walter Rheinschild	75.00	125.00
12 Mason Rumney	75.00	125.00
13 Adolph (Germany) Schultz	150.00	250.00
14 William Wasmund	75.00	125.00
15 Fielding Yost CO	175.00	300.00

1908 Michigan White Postcards

This postcard set features members of the University of Michigan football team. Most feature a black and white studio photo on the front along with just the player's last name while others feature an action photo with a short caption. The cardbacks are printed in a generic postcard style along with the manufacturer's identification: White Post Card Co., Ann Arbor, Mich.

1 William Casey	40.00	75.00
2 Prentiss Douglas (misspelled Duglas)	40.00	75.00
3 John Loell	40.00	75.00
4 Paul Magoffin (with team mascot)	40.00	75.00
5 Adolph (Germany) Schultz	100.00	175.00
6 William Wasmund	40.00	75.00
7 William Wasmund ACT	35.00	60.00

1913 Michigan Hoppe Postcards

This postcard set features members of the University of Michigan football team. Each features a black and white photo of the player on the field with just the player's last name and photographer's name on the front. The cardbacks are printed in a generic postcard style along with the manufacturer's identification: O.P. Hoppe, 619 E. Liberty St., Ann Arbor, Mich.

1 Capt. Fred Conklin	30.00	60.00
2 Miller Pontius	30.00	60.00
3 Jim Craig	30.00	60.00
4 Harrington	30.00	60.00

1951 Michigan Team Issue

This set of photos was issued in its own envelope and presumaby mailed out to fans. Each photo is blankbacked, black and white and measures roughly 6 1/2" by 9." The player's name is printed in script on the fronts and each has a thin white border on all four sides.

COMPLETE SET (17)	200.00	350.00
1 Harry Allis	12.00	20.00
2 Art Dunne	12.00	20.00
3 John Hess	12.00	20.00
4 David Hill	12.00	20.00
5 Gene Hinton	12.00	20.00
6 Frank Howell	12.00	20.00
7 Tom Johnson	15.00	25.00
8 Tom Kelsey	12.00	20.00
9 Leo Koceski	12.00	20.00
10 Wayne Melchiori	12.00	20.00
11 Terry Nuff	12.00	20.00
12 Bill Ohlenroth	12.00	20.00
13 Bill Putich	15.00	25.00
14 Clyde Reeme	12.00	20.00
15 Robert Timm	12.00	20.00
16 Ted Topor	15.00	25.00
17 James Wolter	12.00	20.00

1977 Michigan Postcards

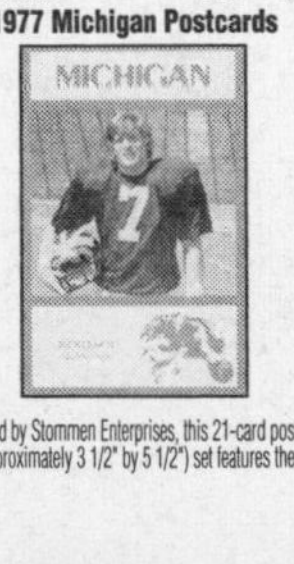

Produced by Stommen Enterprises, this 21-card postcard size (approximately 3 1/2" by 5 1/2") set features the 1977 Michigan Wolverines. Bordered in blue, the fronts divide into three registers. The top register is pale yellow and carries "Michigan" in block lettering. The middle register displays a color posed photo of the player in uniform holding his helmet. The bottom register is pale yellow and has the player's name, position, and a drawing of the mascot, all in blue. The horizontal backs are divided down the middle by two thin bluish-purple stripes, and Michigan's 1977 schedule appears in the same color ink on the upper left. Three cards, those of Giesler, Stephenson, and Szara, have an additional feature on their backs, an order blank printed on the right side. The order blank speaks of the "entire set of 18" and goes on to state "also available at the gates before and after the games." It appears that these three cards may have been produced or distributed later than the other eighteen.

COMPLETE SET (21)	15.00	30.00
1 John Anderson	.60	1.50
2 Russell Davis	.60	1.50
3 Mark Donahue	.50	1.25
4 Walt Downing	.50	1.25
5 Bill Dufek	.60	1.50
6 Jon Giesler SP	1.25	2.50
7 Steve Graves	.50	1.25
8 Curtis Greer	.75	2.00
9 Dwight Hicks	1.25	3.00
10 Derek Howard	.50	1.25
11 Harlan Huckleby	1.00	2.50
12 Gene Johnson	.50	1.25
13 Dale Keitz	.50	1.25
14 Mike Kenn	1.00	2.50
15 Rick Leach	1.50	4.00
16 Mark Schmerge	.50	1.25
17 Ron Simpkins	.60	1.50
18 Curt Stephenson SP	1.25	2.50
19 Gerry Szara SP	1.25	2.50
20 Rick White	.50	1.25
21 Gregg Willner	.50	1.25

1977 Michigan Schedules

These team schedules measure roughly 3 3/8" by 5 3/8" and include a color image of the featured player. Each unnumbered card includes a 1977 Michigan schedule on the back.

COMPLETE SET (4)	10.00	20.00
1 John Anderson	2.50	5.00
2 Walt Downing	2.50	5.00
3 Harlan Huckleby	2.50	5.00
4 Dwight Hicks	4.00	8.00

1989 Michigan

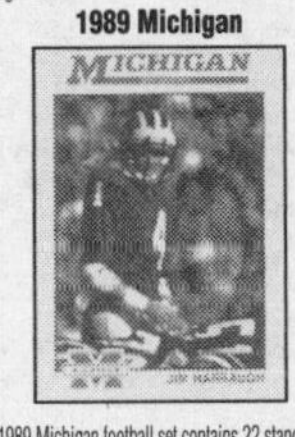

The 1989 Michigan football set contains 22 standard-size cards. The fronts have vintage or color action photos with white borders; the vertically oriented backs have detailed profiles. These cards were distributed as a set.

COMPLETE SET (22)	3.00	8.00
1 H.O.(Fritz) Crisler CO	.30	.75
2 Anthony Carter	.40	1.00
3 Willie Heston	.10	.30
4 Reggie McKenzie	.10	.30
5 Bo Schembechler CO	.75	2.00
6 Dan Dierdorf	.75	2.00
7 Jim Harbaugh	.60	1.50
8 Bennie Oosterbaan	.10	.30
9 Jamie Morris	.20	.50
10 Gerald R. Ford	.75	2.00
11 Curtis Greer	.20	.50
12 Ron Kramer	.20	.50
13 Calvin O'Neal	.10	.30
14 Bob Chappuis	.10	.30
15 Fielding H. Yost CO	.40	1.00
16 Dennis Franklin	.10	.30
17 Benny Friedman	.20	.50
18 Jim Mandich	.20	.50
19 Rob Lytle	.20	.50
20 Bump Elliott	.20	.50
21 Harry Kipke	.10	.30
22 Dave Brown	.20	.50

1991 Michigan

This 56-card multi-sport standard-size set was issued by College Classics. The fronts feature a mix of color or black and white player photos. This set features a card of Gerald Ford, center for the Wolverine football squad from 1932-34. Ford autographed 200 of his cards, one of which was to be included in each of the 200 cases of 50 sets. A letter of authenticity on Gerald Ford stationery accompanies each Ford autographed card. No price has been established for the Ford signed card. The cards are unnumbered and we have checklisted them below according to alphabetical order.

COMPLETE SET (56)	6.00	15.00
6 Dave Brown F	.02	.10
8 Andy Cannavino F	.02	.10
9 Anthony Carter F	.30	.75
10 Gil Chapman F	.02	.10
11 Bob Chappuis F	.02	.10
13 Evan Cooper F	.02	.10
14 Tom Curtis F	.02	.10
16 Dean Dingman F	.08	.25
17 Mark Donahue F	.02	.10
18 Donald Dufek CO F	.08	.25
19 Bump Elliott F	.08	.25
21 Gerald Ford F	.75	2.00
23 Curtis Greer F	.08	.25
24 Ali Haji-Sheikh F	.08	.25
25 Elroy Hirsch F	.30	.75
26 Stefan Humphries F	.02	.10
28 Ron Johnson F	.30	.75
30 Eric Kattus F	.02	.10
31 Ron Kramer F	.08	.25
34 Jim Mandich F	.30	.75
39 Frank Nunley F	.08	.25
40 Calvin O'Neal F	.02	.10
42 Bennie Oosterbaan F	.20	.50
51 Bob Timberlake F	.08	.25
53 John Wangler F	.02	.10
55 Tripp Welborne F	.08	.25
56 Albert Wistert F Alvin Wistert Francis Wistert	.02	.10
AU21 Gerald Ford AU F	150.00	300.00

1998 Michigan

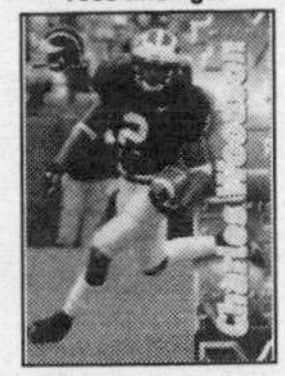

This fully laminated, limited edition set features members of the 1998 Michigan Rose Bowl and National Champions. The set was produced by American Marketing Associates. The fronts feature full color player action shots with the team helmet and player's name. The backs carry brief player information and note the 1997 season record and championship. The cards are unnumbered and checklisted below in alphabetical order. Reportedly the Charles Woodson card was not released with the set initialy but made its way onto the secondary market sometime later.

COMPLETE SET (15)	20.00	40.00
1 Zach Adami	.75	2.00
2 Lloyd Carr CO	.75	2.00
3 David Crispin	.75	2.00
4 Chris Floyd	1.00	2.50
5 Brian Griese	1.50	4.00
6 Chris Howard	1.00	2.50
7 Ben Huff	.75	2.00
8 Colby Keefer	.75	2.00
9 Eric Mayes	1.00	2.50
10 Lance Ostron	.75	2.00
11 Russell Shaw	.75	2.00
12 Glen Steele	.75	2.00
13 Rob Swett	1.00	2.50
14 Charles Woodson	3.00	8.00
15 Michigan Logo CL	.75	2.00

2002 Michigan TK Legacy Promos

These promos were released to promote the 2002 TK Legacy Michigan "The Victors Signature Series" release. The Rick Leach CL card was given away at a Michigan football game. Tom Harmon is featured on a cover or header card that features details about the release.

P1 Bo Schembechler	1.50	4.00
P2 Rick Leach CL	2.00	5.00
P48 Gerald Ford	3.00	8.00
NNO Tom Harmon Cover Card	1.50	4.00

2002-09 Michigan TK Legacy

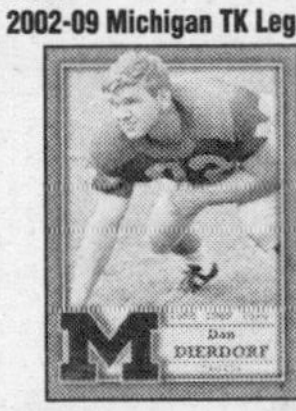

TK Legacy issued seven series of Michigan football cards with the first release in 2002. Series one features 35-base cards (L1-L35), two coaches cards (C1-C2), one broadcaster card (B1), and one unnumbered Harmon/Evashevski checklist card. The other single card inserts are not considered part of the basic issue set. Card #L35 Anthony Carter was released with the purchase of a collector's album to house your set and the Tom Harmon/400 card was issued one per case. The 2002 TK Legacy Michigan series 1 set was issued in 6-card packs with 10-packs per box at an SRP of $80 per box. Series 2 (cards #L36-L66, C3-C4, NNO Wistert Brothers, and P1) was released in 2003. Series 3 was issued in 4-card packs in Fall 2004 and included cards #L67-L99 and CL1-CL2. 2005 saw the relaese of the Michigan series 4 set which included base cards #L100-L116 as well as single card additions to most of the inserts. Series 5 (#L117, L138-L158) was released in late 2007 and the final series (seven) was issued in 2009. One autograph or jersey card was included in every pack for each series.

COMP.SERIES 1 (39)	15.00	30.00
COMP.SERIES 2 (34)	15.00	30.00
COMP.SERIES 3 (35)	15.00	30.00
COMP.SERIES 4 (17)	10.00	20.00
COMP.SERIES 5 (20)	10.00	20.00
L1 Tom Harmon	.75	2.00
L2 Forest Evashevski	.40	1.00
L3 Ed Frutig	.40	1.00
L4 Whitey Wistert	.40	1.00
L5 Francis Wistert	.40	1.00
L6 Alvin Wistert	.40	1.00
L7 Al Wahl	.40	1.00
L8 Bob Chappuis	.40	1.00
L9 Pete Elliott	.40	1.00
L10 Bump Elliott	.40	1.00
L11 Chuck Ortmann	.40	1.00
L12 Don Dufek Sr.	.40	1.00
L13 Bill Putich	.40	1.00
L14 Don Lund	.40	1.00
L15 Ron Kramer	.40	1.00
L16 Bob Timberlake	.40	1.00
L17 Don Moorhead	.40	1.00
L18 Jim Mandich	.40	1.00
L19 Reggie McKenzie	.50	1.25
L20 Dan Dierdorf	.75	2.00
L21 Jim Brandstatter	.40	1.00
L22 Don Dufek Jr.	.40	1.00
L23 Bill Dufek	.40	1.00
L24 Rob Lytle	.75	2.00
L25 Rick Leach	.75	2.00
L26 Harlan Huckleby	.50	1.25
L27 Gerald Ford	1.25	3.00
L28 Tom Slade	.40	1.00
L29 Aaron Shea	.50	1.25
L30 Tai Streets	.75	2.00
L31 Bennie Oosterbaan	.50	1.25

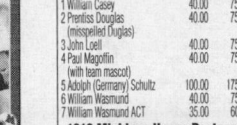

L32 Jack Weisenburger	.40	1.00
L33 Jamie Morris	.50	1.25
L34 Mike Kenn	.40	1.00
L35 Anthony Carter	1.00	2.50
L36 Stu Wilkins SP	2.00	5.00
L37 Dennis Franklin SP	2.00	5.00
L38 John Wangler	.40	1.00
L39 Don Peterson	.50	1.25
L40 Tom Peterson	.40	1.00
L41 Leo Koceski	.40	1.00
L42 Elvis Grbac	.75	2.00
L43 Bill Yearby	.40	1.00
L44 Julius Franks	.40	1.00
L45 Dan Dworsky	.40	1.00
L46 Dick Kempthorn	.40	1.00
L47 Drew Henson	1.25	3.00
L48 Gordon Bell	.40	1.00
L49 Dennis Brown	.40	1.00
L50 Russell Davis	.40	1.00
L51 Mark Messner	.40	1.00
L52 Dave Brown	.40	1.00
L53 Paul Seymour	.40	1.00
L54 Ron Simpkins	.40	1.00
L55 Monte Robbins	.40	1.00
L56 Walt Teninga	.40	1.00
L57 Bob Mann	.40	1.00
L58 Bill Freehan	.75	2.00
L59 Ronald Bellamy	.50	1.25
L60 Bennie Joppru	.50	1.25
L61 Cato June	.50	1.25
L62 B.J. Askew	.50	1.25
L63 William Cunningham	.40	1.00
L64 Joe Ponsetto	.40	1.00
L65 Jack Lousma	.50	1.25
L66 Butch Woolfolk	.50	1.25
L67 Ted Cachey	.40	1.00
L68 Ron Johnson	.40	1.00
L69 Ali Haji-Sheikh	.40	1.00
L70 Terry Barr	.40	1.00
L71 Jim Harbaugh	.75	2.00
L72 Steve Smith	.50	1.25
L73 Garvie Craw	.40	1.00
L74 John Navarre	.75	2.00
L75 Chris Perry	1.25	3.00
L76 Stan Edwards	.40	1.00
L77 Tony Pape	.40	1.00
L78 Greg McMurtry	.40	1.00
L79 Dave Brandon	.40	1.00
L80 Tom Dixon	.40	1.00
L81 Paul Jokisch	.40	1.00
L82 Mike Mallory	.40	1.00
L83 Gil Chapman	.40	1.00
L84 Billy Taylor	.40	1.00
L85 Chris Calloway	.50	1.25
L86 Tom Curtis	.40	1.00
L87 Rick Volk	.40	1.00
L88 Jim Smith	.50	1.25
L89 Curtis Mallory	.40	1.00
L90 Jim Betts	.40	1.00
L91 Bill Kolesar	.40	1.00
L92 John Kolesar	.40	1.00
L93 David Arnold	.40	1.00
L94 Paul Girgash	.40	1.00
L95 Mike Lantry	.40	1.00
L96 Erick Anderson	.40	1.00
L97 Chris Floyd	.50	1.25
L98 Marcus Ray	.40	1.00
L99 Doug Mallory	.40	1.00
L100 Braylon Edwards	1.50	4.00
L101 Dan Jokisch	.40	1.00
L102 Derrick Alexander	.50	1.25
L103 Yale Van Dyne	.40	1.00
L104 David Underwood	.40	1.00
L105 Marlin Jackson	.75	2.00
L106 Marcus Curry	.40	1.00
L107 Mercury Hayes	.50	1.25
L108 Kraig Baker	.40	1.00
L109 J.T. White	.40	1.00
L110 Hercules Renda	.40	1.00
L111 John V. Ghindia	.40	1.00
L112 John R. Ghindia	.40	1.00
L113 Desmond Howard	.75	2.00
L114 Chris Howard	.50	1.25
L115 Dean Dingman	.40	1.00
L116 Sam Sword	.40	1.00
L117 George Lilja	.40	1.00
L118 Thom Darden	.50	1.25
L119 Walt Downing	.40	1.00
L120 Ed Muransky	.40	1.00
L121 Ricky Powers	.40	1.00
L122 Mark Hammerstein	.40	1.00
L123 Mike Hammerstein	.40	1.00
L124 Fred Janke	.40	1.00
L126 Tim Biakabutuka	.75	2.00
L127 Jack Meyer	.40	1.00
L128 Norm Purucker	.40	1.00
L129 Robert Cooper	.40	1.00
L130 Norman Daniels	.40	1.00
L131 Vincent Aug	.40	1.00
L132 David Hall	.40	1.00
L133 Michael Taylor LB	.40	1.00
L134 Rich Hewlett	.40	1.00
L135 Curtis Greer	.40	1.00
L136 Michael Taylor QB	.40	1.00
L137 Jim Maddock	.40	1.00
L138 Carl Tabb	.40	1.00
L139 Chris Zurbrugg	.40	1.00
L140 Darnell Hood	.40	1.00
L141 Eric Kattus	.40	1.00
L142 Garrett Rivas	.40	1.00
L143 Gary Moeller	.40	1.00
L144 Hayden Epstein	.40	1.00
L145 Jeremy Van Alstyne	.40	1.00
L146 Larry Cipa	.40	1.00
L147 Marcus Knight	.40	1.00
L148 Mike Gillette	.40	1.00
L149 Obi Oluigbo	.40	1.00
L150 Paul Staroba	.40	1.00
L151 Remy Hamilton	.40	1.00
L152 Rondell Biggs	.40	1.00
L153 Scott Dreisbach	.60	1.50
L154 Tyler Ecker	.40	1.00
L157 Willis Barringer	.40	1.00
L158 Steve Breaston	.75	2.00
L159 Chad Henne		
L160 Mike Hart		
L161 Jake Long		
L162 Mario Manningham		
L163 Adrian Arrington		
L164 Jamar Adams		
L165 David Gallagher		
L166 Roger Zatkoff		
L167 Mervin Pregulman		
L168 Jarrod Bunch		
L169 Randy Logan		
L170 Tom Mack		
L171 John Henderson		
L172 Russell Rein		
L173 Ben Huff		
L174 Glen Steele		
L175 Ross Ryan		
L176 Adam Kraus		
L177 Marty Huff		
L178 Bob Ptacek		
L179 Stanton Noskin		
L180 Frank Nunley		
L181 Paul Seal		
L183 Leroy Hoard		
NNO T.Harmon	.50	1.25
Evashevski CL		
NNO Tom Harmon/400	3.00	8.00
NNO Wistert Brothers	.75	2.00
B1 Bob Ufer Broadcaster	.40	1.00
C1 Fritz Crisler CO	.40	1.00
C2 Bo Schembechler CO	.50	1.25
C3 Bump Elliott CO	.40	1.00
C4 Langdon Lea CO	.40	1.00
(inserted in 2004 Multi-Sport)		
C5 Coach McCauley	.50	1.25
CL1 Series 3 CL	.40	1.00
CL2 Billy Taylor CL	.40	1.00
CL3 Bennie Oosterbaan CL	.50	1.25
CL4 Bo Schembechler CL	.60	1.50
CL5 Michigan Block M CL	.40	1.00
CL6 Brown Jug CL	.40	1.00
D1 Jake Long/200	3.00	8.00
Mike Hart		
Mario Manningham		
Chad Henne		
Under the Scope		
J1 Aaron Shea JSY	4.00	10.00
J2 Aaron Shea AUTO	10.00	20.00
LBJ1 Little Brown Jug Legend 1	.30	.75
LBJ2 Little Brown Jug Legend 2	.30	.75
P1A Gerald Ford Promo	1.50	4.00
P1B Bo Schembechler Promo	1.25	3.00
P2 Bill Freehan Promo/1000	1.50	4.00
P3 Ron Johnson Promo/500	1.50	4.00
P7A On The Radar Promo		
Mike Hart		
Chad Henne		
Jake Long		
Mario Manningham		
P7B Class of 2007 Promo		
Mike Hart		
Chad Henne		
Jake Long		
Mario Manningham		
Adam Kraus		
Adrian Arrington		
T1 Bob Ufer Broadcaster	.75	2.00
(inserted in 2004 Multi-Sport)		
Z1 Roger Zatkoff AU/100	10.00	20.00

2002-09 Michigan TK Legacy 1969 Autographs

1969A Rich Caldarazzo	7.50	15.00
1969C Frank Gusich	7.50	15.00
1969D John Gabler	7.50	15.00
1969E Dana Coin	7.50	15.00
1969F Mike Hankwitz	7.50	15.00
1969G Jerry Hanlon	7.50	15.00

2002-09 Michigan TK Legacy All-Americans Autographs

3 Anthony Carter	15.00	30.00
4 George Lilja	10.00	20.00
5 Thom Darden	12.50	25.00
6 Walt Downing	10.00	20.00
7 Ed Muransky	10.00	20.00
8 Mike Hammerstein	10.00	20.00
9 Curtis Greer	10.00	20.00
(case insert)		
10 Michael Taylor	10.00	20.00
11 Anthony Carter	15.00	30.00
AA7 Randy Logan	10.00	20.00
AA8 Mervin Pregulman		
AA9 Remy Hamilton	10.00	20.00
AA10 Glen Steele	10.00	20.00
AA12 Tripp Welborne	10.00	20.00

2002-09 Michigan TK Legacy All Century Team

S1-S6 STATED ODDS 1:12
S1-S6 PRINT RUN 300 SER.#'d SETS

S1 Rick Leach	7.50	20.00
S2 Tom Harmon	7.50	20.00
S3 Anthony Carter	7.50	20.00
S4 Bennie Oosterbaan	6.00	15.00
S5 Bo Schembechler	7.50	20.00
S6 Dan Dierdorf	7.50	20.00
S8 Monte Robbins	6.00	15.00
S9 Ron Simpkins	6.00	15.00
S10 Mark Messner	6.00	15.00

2002-09 Michigan TK Legacy Anthony Carter Tribute

COMPLETE SET (8)	6.00	15.00
AC1 Anthony Carter	.75	2.00
AC2 Anthony Carter	.75	2.00
AC3 Anthony Carter	.75	2.00
AC4 Anthony Carter	.75	2.00
AC5 Anthony Carter	.75	2.00
AC6 Anthony Carter	.75	2.00
AC7 Anthony Carter	.75	2.00
AC8 Anthony Carter	.75	2.00

2002-09 Michigan TK Legacy Bennie Oosterbaan Tribute

COMPLETE SET (5)	3.00	8.00
B1 Three-time All-American	1.00	2.50
B2 Benny to Bennie Combination	1.00	2.50
B3 Michigan Stadium Dedication	1.00	2.50
B4 New Michigan Coach	1.00	2.50
B5 Coach Bennie Oosterbaan	1.00	2.50

2002-09 Michigan TK Legacy Captains Autographs

CP1 Jake Long/100	20.00	40.00
CP2 Joe O'Donnell/100	12.50	25.00
CP3 Dave Gallagher/100	12.50	25.00
CP4 Randy Logan/50	15.00	30.00
(case insert)		
CP5 Paul Seal/100	12.50	25.00
CP6 Jarrod Bunch/100	12.50	25.00
CP7 Juaquin Feazell/100	12.50	25.00
CP8 Will Johnson/100	12.50	25.00
CP9 Jarrod Bunch	12.50	25.00

2002-09 Michigan TK Legacy Cover Boys Autographs

SERIES 2 STATED ODDS 1:19
SERIES 3 STATED ODDS 1:37

MC1 Al Wahl 1950	12.50	25.00
MC2 Bill Putich 1951	12.50	25.00
MC3 Bo Schembechler 1982	30.00	60.00
MC4 Alvin Wistert 1949	12.50	25.00
MC5 Ted Cachey 1954	12.50	25.00
MC6 Dick O'Shaughessy 1953	15.00	30.00
MC7 Rick Leach 1977	20.00	40.00
(inserted in 2004 Multi-Sport)		
MC8A John Herrnstein 1958	10.00	25.00
MC8B Steve Smith 1983	12.50	25.00
MC9 George Genyk 1959	12.50	30.00

2002-09 Michigan TK Legacy Game Day Rivalry

COMPLETE SET (10)	5.00	10.00
GR1897 1st Meeting	.30	.75
GR1902 4th Meeting	.30	.75
GR1919 16th Meeting	.30	.75
GR1927 24th meeting	.30	.75
GR1939 36th meeting	.30	.75
GR1940 37th Meeting	.30	.75
GR1941 39th meeting	.30	.75
GR1942 39th Meeting	.30	.75
GR1950 47th Meeting	.30	.75
GR1954 51sth meeting	.30	.75
GR1955 52nd Meeting	.30	.75
GR1969 66th Meeting	.30	.75
GR1970 67th Meeting	.30	.75
GR1972 69th Meeting	.30	.75
GR1975 72nd meeting	.30	.75
GR1978 75th meeting	.30	.75
GR1979 76th meeting	.30	.75
GR1987 84th meeting	.30	.75
GR1994 91st meeting	.30	.75
GR1995 92nd meeting	.30	.75

2002-09 Michigan TK Legacy Go Blue Autographs

MGB1 Ed Frutig	5.00	12.00
MGB2 Al Wahl	5.00	12.00
MGB3 Reggie McKenzie	7.50	20.00
MGB4 Dan Dierdorf	7.50	20.00
MGB5 Don Lund	5.00	12.00
MGB6 Rob Lytle	6.00	15.00
MGB7 Jim Mandich	5.00	12.00
MGB8 Don Dufek Jr	5.00	12.00
MGB9 Bill Dufek	5.00	12.00
MGB10 Ron Kramer	5.00	12.00
MGB11 Bump Elliott	5.00	12.00
MGB12 Chuck Ortmann	5.00	12.00
MGB13 Alvin Wistert	5.00	12.00
MGB14 Aaron Shea	6.00	15.00
MGB15 Tai Streets	7.50	20.00
MGB16 Bill Putich	5.00	12.00
MGB17 Bob Timberlake	5.00	12.00
MGB18 Don Canham	5.00	12.00
MGB19 Don Moorhead	5.00	12.00
MGB20 Jim Brandstatter	5.00	12.00
MGB21 Harlan Huckleby	6.00	15.00
MGB22 Jack Weisenburger	5.00	12.00
MGB23 Jamie Morris	6.00	15.00
MGB24 Mike Kenn	6.00	15.00
MGB25 Bo Schembechler	25.00	50.00
MGB26 Anthony Carter	10.00	25.00
MGB27 Albert Wistert	6.00	15.00
MGB27SP Gerald Ford/50	300.00	500.00
MGB28 Bump Elliott CO	6.00	15.00
(case insert in 2004 Multi-Sport)		
MGB29 Dick Kempthorn	5.00	12.00
MGB30 Tom Peterson	6.00	15.00
MGB31 Don Peterson	7.50	20.00
MGB32 B.J. Askew	7.50	20.00
MGB33 Ronald Bellamy	6.00	15.00
MGB34 Bennie Joppru	6.00	15.00
MGB35 Paul Seymour	5.00	12.00
MGB36 Cato June	6.00	15.00
MGB37 Leo Koceski	5.00	12.00
MGB38 Bill Yearby	5.00	12.00
MGB39 Julius Franks	5.00	12.00
MGB40 Gordon Bell	6.00	15.00
MGB41 John Wangler	6.00	15.00
MGB42 Russell Davis	5.00	12.00
MGB43 Mark Messner	6.00	15.00
MGB44 Forest Evashevski	7.50	20.00
MGB45 Dave Brown	5.00	12.00
MGB46 Jack Lousma	15.00	30.00
MGB47 Dennis Brown	6.00	15.00
MGB48 Bob Mann	5.00	12.00
MGB49 Monte Robbins	5.00	12.00
MGB50 Ron Simpkins	5.00	12.00
MGB51 Walt Teninga	5.00	12.00
MGB52 Bill Freehan	12.50	25.00
MGB53 Joe Ponsetto	5.00	12.00
MGB54 Elvis Grbac SP	15.00	30.00
MGB55 Dan Dworsky	5.00	12.00
MGB57 Ron Johnson	6.00	15.00
MGB58 Stan Edwards SP	5.00	12.00
MGB59 Garvie Craw SP	5.00	12.00
MGB60 Ali Haji-Sheikh SP	5.00	12.00
MGB61 Terry Barr SP	5.00	12.00
MGB62 Jim Harbaugh SP	12.00	30.00
MGB63 Ted Cachey	5.00	12.00
MGB64 John Navarre SP	12.50	25.00
MGB65 Steve Smith	5.00	12.00
MGB66 Dennis Franklin	6.00	15.00
MGB67 Butch Woolfolk	6.00	15.00
MGB68 Chris Perry SP	40.00	80.00
MGB69 Paul Girgash	5.00	12.00
MGB70 Jim Betts	5.00	12.00
MGB71 Tom Dixon	5.00	12.00
MGB72 Mike Mallory	5.00	12.00
MGB73 Doug Mallory	5.00	12.00
MGB74 Erick Anderson	6.00	15.00
MGB75 Rick Volk	5.00	12.00
MGB76 Tom Curtis	5.00	12.00
MGB77 Billy Taylor	5.00	12.00
MGB78 Jim Smith	5.00	12.00
MGB79 Paul Jokisch	6.00	15.00
MGB80 David Arnold	5.00	12.00
MGB81 Chris Calloway	6.00	15.00
MGB82 Greg McMurtry	6.00	15.00
MGB83 Bill Kolesar	5.00	12.00
MGB84 Dave Brandon	5.00	12.00
MGB85 Gil Chapman	5.00	12.00
MGB86 Curtis Mallory	5.00	12.00
MGB87 Mike Lantry	5.00	12.00
MGB88 John Kolesar	5.00	12.00
MGB89 Marcus Ray	5.00	12.00
MGB90 Dan Jokisch	5.00	12.00
MGB91 Chris Floyd	5.00	12.00
MGB92 Marcus Knight	5.00	12.00
MGB93 Derrick Alexander	6.00	15.00
MGB94 Yale Van Dyne	5.00	12.00
MGB95 David Underwood	5.00	12.00
MGB96 Marlin Jackson	8.00	20.00
MGB97 Hayden Epstein	5.00	12.00
MGB98 Mercury Hayes	6.00	15.00
MGB99 Gary Moeller	10.00	20.00
MGB100 Braylon Edwards/150	40.00	80.00
MGB101 J.T. White	10.00	20.00
MGB102 Hercules Renda	6.00	15.00
MGB103 John V. Ghindia	5.00	12.00
MGB104 John R. Ghindia	5.00	12.00
MGB105 Desmond Howard/200	20.00	40.00
MGB106 Chris Howard	5.00	12.00
MGB107 Dean Dingman	5.00	12.00
MGB108 Sam Sword	5.00	12.00
MGB109 Kraig Baker	5.00	12.00
MGB110 George Lilja	5.00	12.00
MGB111 Robert Cooper	5.00	12.00
MGB112 Fred Janke	5.00	12.00
MGB113 Thom Darden	6.00	15.00
MGB114 Walt Downing	5.00	12.00
MGB115 Ed Muransky	5.00	12.00
MGB116 Norman Purucker	5.00	12.00
MGB117 Norman Daniels	5.00	12.00
MGB118 Ricky Powers	5.00	12.00
MGB120 Jack Meyer	5.00	12.00
MGB121 Mark Hammerstein	5.00	12.00
MGB122 Mike Hammerstein	5.00	12.00
MGB123 Tim Biakabutuka	8.00	20.00
MGB124 David Hall	5.00	12.00
MGB125 Michael Taylor LB	5.00	12.00
MGB126 Rich Hewlett	5.00	12.00
MGB127 Curtis Greer	5.00	12.00
MGB128 Michael Taylor QB	5.00	12.00
MGB129 Jim Maddock	5.00	12.00
MGB130 Steve Breaston	8.00	20.00
MGB131 Scott Dreisbach	8.00	20.00
MGB132 Larry Cipa	6.00	15.00
MGB133 Paul Staroba	5.00	12.00
MGB134 Remy Hamilton	5.00	12.00
MGB136 Mike Gillette	5.00	12.00
MGB137 Eric Kattus	5.00	12.00
MGB138 Chris Zurbrugg	5.00	12.00
MGB139 Obi Oluigbo	5.00	12.00
MGB140 Carl Tabb	5.00	12.00
MGB141 Willis Barringer	5.00	12.00
MGB142 Tyler Ecker	5.00	12.00
MGB143 Jeremy Van Alstyne	5.00	12.00
MGB144 Rondell Biggs	5.00	12.00
MGB145 Darnell Hood	5.00	12.00
MGB146 Garrett Rivas	5.00	12.00
MGB147 Mike Hart	15.00	30.00
MGB149 Jake Long	12.50	25.00
MGB150 Adam Kraus	5.00	12.00
MGB151 Chad Henne	30.00	60.00
MGB152 Mario Manningham	15.00	30.00
MGB153 Adrian Arrington	6.00	15.00
MGB154 Jamar Adams	5.00	12.00
MGB155 Marty Huff	5.00	12.00
MGB156 Dave Gallagher	5.00	12.00
MGB157 Joe O'Donnell	5.00	12.00
MGB158 Roger Zatkoff	5.00	12.00
MGB159 Marvin Pregulman	5.00	12.00
MGB160 Tom Mack		
MGB161 Randy Logan	5.00	12.00
MGB162 Glen Steele	5.00	12.00
MGB163 John Henderson	5.00	12.00
MGB164 Leroy Hoard SP	30.00	60.00
MGB165A Bob Ptacek	5.00	12.00
MGB165B Jarrod Bunch	6.00	15.00
MGB166 Tim Jamison	5.00	12.00
MGB167 Paul Seal	5.00	12.00
MGB168 Ross Ryan	5.00	12.00
MGB169 John Gabler	5.00	12.00
MGB170 Rich Caldarazzo	5.00	12.00
MGB171 Mike Hankwitz	5.00	12.00
MGB172 Frank Gusich	5.00	12.00
MGB174 Dana Coin	5.00	12.00
MGB175 Bubba Paris	6.00	15.00
MGB176 Brian Griese	25.00	50.00
MGB179 Jay Riemersma	5.00	12.00
MGB180 Jerry Hanlon CO	5.00	12.00
MGB181 Lawrence Ricks	5.00	12.00

2002-09 Michigan TK Legacy Hand Drawn Sketches

1 Gerald Ford B&W/250	25.00	50.00
2 Tom Harmon Passing	20.00	50.00
3 Tom Harmon Portrait	20.00	50.00
4 Rick Leach	15.00	40.00
5 Michigan Helmet	10.00	25.00
6 Bo Schembechler	20.00	40.00
7 Gerald Ford B&W/100	40.00	80.00
8 Gerald Ford Color/50	90.00	150.00
9 Jim Harbaugh/75	60.00	120.00
10 Michigan Helmet/75	50.00	100.00
11 Braylon Edwards B&W/40	30.00	60.00
12 Braylon Edwards Color		
13 Desmond Howard B&W/40	30.00	60.00
14 Desmond Howard Color		
15 Gerald Ford/10		
16 Pres. Gerald Ford Clr/10		
17 Pres. Gerald Ford Clr/10		
(center pose)		
18 Mike Hammerstein B&W/40	20.00	40.00
19 Bennie Oosterbaan Clr/10		
20 Bennie Oosterbaan CO B&W/40	25.00	50.00
21 Bo Schembechler Clr/10		
22 Bo Schembechler Clr/10		
23 Bo Schembechler Clr/10		
24 Billy Taylor Clr/10		
25 Billy Taylor B&W/40		
26 Tim Biakabatuka Clr/10		
27 Tim Biakabatuka B&W/40	25.00	50.00
28 Butch Woolfolk B&W/40		
29 Butch Woolfolk Clr/10		
30 Thom Darden B&W/40		
31 Anthony Carter Clr/10		
32 Anthony Carter Clr/10		
33 Anthony Carter B&W/40	25.00	50.00
34 Anthony Carter B&W/40	25.00	50.00
35 1949 Rose and Helmet Clr/15		
36 Block M Clr/20		
37 Retired #11 Jersey Clr/15		
38 Retired #47 Jersey Clr/15		
39 Retired #48 Jersey Clr/15		
40 Retired #87 Jersey Clr/15		
41 Retired #98 Jersey Clr/15		
S1 Molinelli CL	.40	1.00
S2 Molinelli CL	.40	1.00
S3 Molinelli CL	.40	1.00
S4 Molinelli CL	.40	1.00
S5 CZOP CL	.40	1.00

2002-09 Michigan TK Legacy Jersey Number Autographs

JN16 Jay Riemersma	10.00	20.00
JN56 Rich Caldarazzo	10.00	20.00
JN59 Frank Nunley	10.00	20.00
JN70 Roger Zatkoff	10.00	20.00
JN96 Tom Mack	12.50	25.00

2002-09 Michigan TK Legacy Mates Autographs

MM1-MM10 DUAL AUTO ODDS 1:20 SER.1
MM1-MM10 TRIPLE AUTO ODDS 1:96 SER.1
MM11-MM15 STATED ODDS 1:28 SER.2
MM16-MM24 DUAL AUTO ODDS 1:22 SER.3
MM16-MM24 TRIPLE AU ODDS 1:112 SER.3

MM1 Rick Leach/250	30.00	60.00
Rob Lytle		
MM2 Pete Elliott/250	20.00	40.00
Bump Elliott		
MM3 Forest Evashevski/250	30.00	60.00
Rick Leach		
MM4 Jim Mandich/250	20.00	40.00
Don Moorhead		
MM5 Bob Chappuis/250	20.00	40.00
Alvin Wistert		
MM6 Jamie Morris/250	20.00	40.00
Rob Lytle		
MM7 Aaron Shea/250	25.00	50.00
Tai Streets		
MM8 Bo Schembechler/250	50.00	100.00
Rick Leach		
MM9 Reggie McKenzie/250	60.00	120.00
Dan Dierdorf		
Bo Schembechler		
MM10 Don Dufek Sr./250	30.00	60.00
Don Dufek Jr.		
Bill Dufek		
MM11 Whitey Wistert/250	40.00	80.00
Alvin Wistert		
MM12 Don Peterson/200	25.00	50.00
Tom Peterson		
MM13 Bill Yearby/200	25.00	50.00
Mark Messner		
MM14 Drew Henson/100	90.00	150.00
Rick Leach		
Elvis Grbac		
MM15 Russell Davis/100	50.00	100.00
Harlan Huckleby		
Rick Leach		
MM16 Steve Smith QB/150	25.00	50.00
Anthony Carter		
MM17 Butch Woolfolk/150	25.00	50.00
Stan Edwards		
MM18 Ron Kramer/150	20.00	120.00
Terry Barr		
MM19 Jim Harbaugh/100	60.00	125.00
John Navarre		
Steve Smith QB		
MM20 John Navarre/100	30.00	60.00
Chris Perry		
MM21 Chris Perry/100	30.00	60.00
Butch Woolfolk		
MM22 Mike Mallory/250	25.00	50.00
Doug Mallory		
Curt Mallory		
MM23 Bill Kolesar/150	20.00	40.00
John Kolesar		
MM24 Paul Jokisch		
Greg McMurtry		
MM25 John V. Ghindia/200	15.00	40.00
John R. Ghindia		
MM26 Chris Howard/150	15.00	40.00
Chris Floyd		
MM27 Paul Jokisch/150	15.00	30.00
Dan Jokisch		
MM28 Mark Hammerstein/150	15.00	30.00
Mike Hammerstein		
MM30 Marcus Knight/100	30.00	60.00
Scott Dreisbach		
MM31 Mike Hart/100	50.00	100.00
Chad Henne		
Mario Manningham		
MM32 Tim Jamison/100	15.00	30.00
Will Johnson		
MM33 Jerry Hanlon/100	15.00	30.00
Mike Hankwitz		
MC1 Braylon Edwards	40.00	80.00
Anthony Carter		
Derrick Alexander WR		
MC2 Mike Gillette/100	20.00	40.00
Remy Hamilton		
Hayden Epstein		
Garrett Rivas		
SP Braylon Edwards/75	60.00	120.00
Stan Edwards		

2002-09 Michigan TK Legacy Mike Hart Tribute

COMPLETE SET (4)	3.00	8.00
COMMON HART (MH1-MH4)	.75	2.00

2002-09 Michigan TK Legacy M-Stat Autographs

ST1 Desmond Howard/100	15.00	30.00
ST2 Butch Woolfolk/100	10.00	20.00
ST3 Billy Taylor/100	10.00	20.00
ST4 Tim Biakabutuka/150	12.50	25.00
ST5 Tim Biakabutuka/150	12.50	25.00
(case insert)		
ST6 Anthony Carter/100	12.50	25.00
ST7 Steve Breaston/100	12.50	25.00
ST8 Steve Breaston/100	12.50	25.00
ST10 Scott Dreisbach/100	15.00	40.00
ST11 Hayden Epstein/100	10.00	20.00
ST12 Marcus Knight/100	10.00	20.00
ST13 Remy Hamilton/100	10.00	20.00
ST18 Mike Gillette/100	10.00	20.00
ST15 Paul Staroba/100	10.00	20.00
ST17 Gary Moeller CO/100	10.00	20.00
ST16 Mike Hart		
ST19 Mario Manningham		
ST20 Chad Henne		
ST21 Stanton Noskin/100	10.00	20.00
ST22 Bob Ptacek/100	10.00	20.00
ST23 Tom Mack		
ST24 Joe O'Donnell/100	10.00	20.00
ST25 Mervin Pregulman	10.00	20.00
ST26 Marty Huff/100	10.00	20.00
ST27A Leroy Hoard	15.00	30.00
ST27B John Henderson/100	10.00	20.00
ST30 Dana Coin/100	10.00	20.00
ST31 Lawrence Ricks/100	10.00	20.00
ST32 John Gabler/100	10.00	20.00

2002-09 Michigan TK Legacy National Champions Autographs

1933A1 Gerald Ford Not #'d 1		
1933A2 Gerald Ford/50 2	300.00	500.00
1947A Bump Elliott 1	7.50	20.00
1947B Bob Chappuis 1	7.50	20.00
1947C Alvin Wistert 1	7.50	20.00
1947D Jack Weisenburger 1	7.50	20.00
1947E Dick Kempthorn 2	7.50	20.00
1947F Dan Dworsky 2	12.50	30.00
1947G Bob Mann 2	10.00	25.00
1947H J.T. White 4		
1948A Pete Elliott 1	7.50	20.00
1948B Al Wahl 1	7.50	20.00
1948C Chuck Ortmann 1	10.00	25.00
1948D Don Dufek Sr. 1	7.50	20.00
1948E Stu Wilkins 2	7.50	20.00
1948F Leo Koceski 2	10.00	25.00
1948G Walt Teninga 2	10.00	25.00
1948H Tom Peterson 2	10.00	25.00
1997A Tai Streets 1	10.00	25.00
1997B Aaron Shea 1	10.00	25.00
1997C Marcus Ray 3	7.50	20.00
1997D Chris Floyd 3	7.50	20.00
1997E Kraig Baker 4	10.00	25.00
1997F Chris Howard 4	7.50	20.00
1997G Sam Sword 4	7.50	20.00
1997S Glen Steele 7		

2002-09 Michigan TK Legacy Playbook Autographs

COMPLETE SET (5)	100.00	200.00
MP1 Bo Schembechler/250	30.00	60.00
MP2 John Wangler/250	10.00	25.00
MP3 Dennis Franklin/250	10.00	25.00
MP4 Forest Evashevski/250	12.50	30.00
MP5 Rick Leach/250	25.00	50.00
MP6 Bump Elliott/250	10.00	25.00
(inserted in 2004 Multi-Sport)		
MP7 Bump Elliott CO/250	10.00	25.00
(inserted in 2004 Multi-Sport)		
MP8 Anthony Carter/300	12.50	30.00
MP9 Larry Cipa/100	12.50	25.00
MP10 Eric Kaltus/100	12.50	25.00

2002-09 Michigan TK Legacy Program Covers

PC1 1897 vs. Chicago	2.50	6.00
PC2 1918 vs. Michigan State	2.50	6.00
PC3 1915 vs. Cornell	2.50	6.00
PC4 1927 vs. Wesleyan	2.50	6.00
PC5 1925 vs. Ohio State	2.50	6.00
PC6 1906 vs. Penn	2.50	6.00
PC7 1920 vs. Chicago	3.00	8.00
PC8 1923 vs. Minnesota	3.00	8.00
PC9 1928 vs. Wisconsin	3.00	8.00
PC10 1926 vs. Minnesota	2.50	6.00
PC11 1926 vs. Wisconsin	2.50	6.00
PC12 1927 vs. Ohio State	2.50	6.00
PC13 1926 vs. Illinois	3.00	8.00
PC14 1928 vs. Indiana	3.00	8.00
PC15 1929 vs. Michigan State	3.00	8.00
PC16 1936 vs. Illinois	3.00	8.00
PC17 1937 vs. Michigan State	3.00	8.00
PC18 1942 vs. Iowa Naval Aviation	3.00	8.00
PC19 1905 vs. Chicago	3.00	8.00
PC20 1894 vs. Cornell	3.00	8.00
PC21 1927 vs. Minnesota	3.00	8.00
PC22 1941 vs. Ohio State	3.00	8.00
PC23 1958 vs. Washington	3.00	8.00
PC24 1889 vs. Minnesota	3.00	8.00
PC25 1900 vs. Kalamazoo	3.00	8.00
PC26 1912 vs. Cornell	3.00	8.00
PC27 1916 vs. Penn	3.00	8.00
PC28 1922 vs. Wisconsin	3.00	8.00
PC29 1935 vs. Ohio State	3.00	8.00
PC30 1943 vs. Notre Dame	3.00	8.00
PC31 1947 vs. Minnesota	3.00	8.00
PC32 1969 vs. Ohio State	3.00	8.00
PC33 1955 vs. Army	3.00	8.00
PC34 1957 vs. Northwestern	3.00	8.00
PC35 1933 vs. Minnesota	3.00	8.00
PC36 1930 vs. Michigan State	3.00	8.00
PC37 1932 vs. Princeton	3.00	8.00
PC38 1961 vs. UCLA	3.00	8.00
PC39 1960 vs. Illinois	3.00	8.00
PC40 1963 vs. Michigan State	3.00	8.00
PC41 1964 vs. Navy	3.00	8.00
PC42 1965 vs. Wisconsin	3.00	8.00
PC43 1961 vs. Michigan State	3.00	8.00
PC44 1962 vs. Minnesota	3.00	8.00
PC45 1965 vs. Michigan State	3.00	8.00
PC48 1972 vs. Minnesota	3.00	8.00
PC51 1975 vs. Indiana	3.00	8.00

2002-09 Michigan TK Legacy Quarterback Club Autographs

QB1 Rick Leach/500	15.00	30.00
QB2 Bob Timberlake/500	10.00	20.00
QB3 Forest Evashevski/500	10.00	20.00
QB4 Pete Elliott/500	10.00	20.00
QB5 Bill Putich/500	10.00	20.00
QB6 Don Moorhead/500	10.00	20.00
QB7 Tom Slade/500	10.00	20.00
QB8 Dennis Franklin/300	12.50	25.00
QB9 Joe Ponsetto/300	12.50	25.00
QB10 John Wangler/300	12.50	25.00
QB11 Dennis Brown/300	12.50	25.00
QB12 Drew Henson/150	30.00	60.00
QB13 Elvis Grbac/300	25.00	50.00
QB14 Jim Harbaugh/200	15.00	40.00
QB15 Steve Smith/300	10.00	20.00
QB16 John Navarre/200	15.00	40.00
QB17 Jack Meyer/200	10.00	20.00
QB18 David Hall/200	10.00	20.00
QB19 Michael Taylor/200	10.00	20.00
QB20 Rich Hewlett/200	10.00	20.00
QB21 Jim Maddock/200	10.00	20.00
QB22 Larry Cipa/200	12.50	25.00
QB23 Scott Dreisbach/100	10.00	25.00
QB24 Chris Zurbrugg		
QB25 Chad Henne		
QB26 Russell Rein		
QB27 Stanton Noskin		
QB28 Bob Ptacek/100	10.00	20.00
QB29 Brian Griese/25	40.00	80.00
QB30 Jay Riemersma/100	15.00	30.00

2002-09 Michigan TK Legacy Quote Autographs

Q1 Bo Schembechler/100	40.00	80.00
Q2 Bo Schembechler/100	40.00	80.00

2002-09 Michigan TK Legacy Retired Numbers

RN1 Ron Kramer	1.25	3.00
RN2 Whitey Wistert	1.25	3.00
RN3 Alvin Wistert	1.25	3.00
RN4 Francis Wistert	1.25	3.00
RN5 Tom Harmon	2.50	6.00
RN6 Bennie Oosterbaan	1.25	3.00
RN7 Gerald Ford	3.00	8.00

2002-09 Michigan TK Legacy Sentry of the Secondary Autographs

SS3 Frank Gusich/40	20.00	40.00
SS4 Tripp Welborne/50	20.00	40.00

2004 Michigan Moments Sheets

COMPLETE SET (6)	5.00	12.00
1 2002 Michigan vs. Wash.	.75	2.00
1995 Michigan vs. Virginia		
(Mercury Hayes)		
2 Award Winners	1.00	2.50
Desmond Howard		
Tom Harmon		
Chris Perry		
Erick Anderson/Cha		
3 Mike Gillette	.75	2.00
Tom Harmon		
4 Michigan vs. Minnesota	.75	2.00
(Trophy)		
5 Rod Woodson	.75	2.00
Chris Perry		
Victor Hobson		
6 Desmond Howard	1.00	2.50
Rod Woodson/1927 Michigan Stadium		
1950 Snow Bowl/Tim Bia		

2004 Michigan Multisport TK Legacy Special Career Autographs

SP1 Jack Lousma/200	20.00	40.00
SP2 Dan Dworsky/250	15.00	30.00
SP3 Jim Brandstatter/150	15.00	30.00
SP4 Dan Dworsky/250	15.00	30.00
SP5 Jack Lousma/200	20.00	40.00
SP6 Gerald Ford/15		

1974 Michigan State Team Sheets

These photos were issued by the school to promote the football program. Each measures roughly 8" by 10" and features eight black and white images of players with the school name appearing at the top. The backs are blank.

1 Mike Hurd	4.00	8.00
Tyrone Willingham		
Tom Hannon		
Tyrone Wilson		
Rich Baes		
Mike Duda		
Charlie Ane		
Greg Croxton		
2 Denny Stolz CO	4.00	8.00
Jim Taubert		
Terry McClowry		
Charles Baggett		
Clarence Bullock		
Mike Cobb		
Charles Wilson		
Greg Schaum		

1990-91 Michigan State Collegiate Collection 200

This 200-card standard-size set was produced by Collegiate Collection. The fronts feature black and white shots for earlier players or color shots for later players, with borders in the team's colors white and green. Since most cards are football, we've noted below which cards feature other sports. Although some players were famous in others sports, like Kirk Gibson and Steve Garvey, they do have football cards in this set.

COMPLETE SET (200)	6.00	15.00
1 Ray Stachowicz	.05	.15
5 Ron Goovert	.05	.15
10 James Ellis	.05	.15
11 Brad Van Pelt FB	.08	.25
12 Andre Rison FB	.15	.40
13 Sherman Lewis FB	.05	.15
14 Eric Allen	.05	.15
16 Earl Morrall FB	.08	.25
19 Lorenzo White FB	.08	.25
20 Dorne Dibble	.05	.15
21 Ronald Saul FB	.05	.15
22 Ed Budde FB	.05	.15
23 Gene Washington FB	.08	.25
25 Morten Andersen FB	.15	.40
26 Lynn Chandnois FB	.08	.25
27 Don Coleman	.05	.15
28 Dave Behrman	.05	.15
29 Bill Simpson	.05	.15
30 LeRoy Bolden	.05	.15
31 Lorenzo White FB	.08	.25
39 George Perles CO FB	.05	.15
40 Mark Brammer	.05	.15
42 Harlon Barnett	.07	.20
43 Charles(Bubba) Smith FB	.15	.40
44 Percy Snow FB	.05	.15
47 Sam Williams	.05	.15
Duffy Daugherty CO FB		
48 Tom Yewcic FB	.05	.15
49 Kirk Gibson FB	.08	.25
50 Clinton Jones	.08	.25
56 Percy Snow	.05	.15
58 Robert W.(Bob) Carey	.05	.15
59 Clarence Biggie Munn CO	.05	.15
60 Dan Currie	.05	.15
61 Al Dorow	.05	.15
63 Joe DeLamielleure FB	.08	.25
67 Eric Allen	.05	.15
71 George Saimes FB	.07	.20
72 Walt Kowalczyk	.05	.15
73 Billy Joe Dupree FB	.08	.25
76 Kirk Gibson FB	.08	.25
77 Andre Rison FB	.15	.40
78 Dean Look FB	.05	.15
79 Hugh(Duffy) Daugherty CO FB	.08	.25
82 Percy Snow FB	.05	.15
83 Carl Banks FB	.08	.25
86 Lorenzo White FB	.08	.25
88 George Webster FB	.08	.25
89 Tony Mandarich FB	.05	.15
90 Ray Stachowicz	.05	.15
91 Blake Miller	.05	.15
92 Billy Joe DuPree	.08	.25
Brad Van Pelt		
Duffy Daugherty CO FB		
93 Morten Andersen FB	.15	.40
96 Andre Rison FB	.15	.40
98 Kirk Gibson	.08	.25
99 Ralf Mojsiejenko FB	.05	.15
105 Steve Garvey FB	.08	.25
130 Pete Gent FB	.08	.25
134 Bobby Reynolds	.05	.15
143 Michael Robinson	.05	.15
156 Robert Ellis	.05	.15
185 Frank Kush FB	.05	.15

1990-91 Michigan State Collegiate Collection Promos

This ten-card standard size set features some of the great athletes from Michigan State History. Most of the cards in the set feature an action photograph on the front of the card along with either statistical or biographical information on the back of the card. Since this set involves more than one sport we have put a two-letter abbreviation to indicate the sport played.

COMPLETE SET (10)	1.50	4.00
3 Percy Snow FB	.10	.30
5 Andre Rison FB	.30	.75
6 Lorenzo White FB	.08	.25
7 Kirk Gibson FB	.30	.75
BB		
8 Tony Mandarich FB	.08	.25

2003 Michigan State TK Legacy

COMPLETE SET (27)	12.00	30.00
F1 Charles Rogers	2.00	5.00
F2 George Webster	.50	1.25
F3 Brad Van Pelt	.50	1.25
F4 Sonny Grandelius	.40	1.00
F5 Kirk Gibson	1.25	3.00
F6 Hank Bullough	.40	1.00
F7 Shane Bullough	.40	1.00
F8 Chuck Bullough	.40	1.00
F9 Ed Budde	.50	1.25
F10 Frank Kush	.40	1.00
F11 Lorenzo White	.75	2.00
F12 Buck Nystrom	.40	1.00
F13 Doug Bobo	.40	1.00
F14 John Wilson	.40	1.00
F15 Jimmy Raye	.40	1.00
F16 James Ellis	.40	1.00
F17 Sam Williams	.40	1.00
F18 Earl Morrall	.60	1.50
F19 Tom Yewcic	.50	1.25
FC1 Duffy Daugherty CO	.75	2.00

2003 Michigan State TK Legacy All-Americans

COMPLETE SET (6)	7.50	15.00
STATED ODDS 1:14		
AA1 Kirk Gibson	2.00	5.00
AA2 Frank Kush	1.25	3.00
AA3 Lorenzo White	.75	2.00
AA4 Brad Van Pelt	.75	2.00
AA5 Charles Rogers	2.00	5.00

2003 Michigan State TK Legacy Autographs

OVERALL AUTO STATED ODDS 1:1		
S1 Charles Rogers/100	15.00	30.00
S2 George Webster	6.00	15.00
S3 Brad Van Pelt	6.00	15.00
S4 Sonny Grandelius	6.00	15.00
S5 Kirk Gibson	15.00	30.00
S6 Hank Bullough	5.00	12.00
S7 Shane Bullough	5.00	12.00
S8 Chuck Bullough	5.00	12.00
S9 Ed Budde	6.00	15.00
S10 Frank Kush	8.00	20.00
S11 Lorenzo White	8.00	20.00
S12 Buck Nystrom	5.00	12.00
S13 Doug Bobo	5.00	12.00
S14 John Wilson	5.00	12.00
S15 James Ellis	5.00	12.00
S16 Sam Williams	5.00	12.00
S17 Earl Morrall	8.00	20.00
S18 Tom Yewcic	6.00	15.00

2003 Michigan State TK Legacy Historical Links Autographs

DOUBLE AUTO STATED ODDS 1:31		
TRIPLE AUTO STATED ODDS 1:100		
HL1 Kirk Gibson	60.00	120.00
C.Rogers/50		
HL2 Sean Bullough	20.00	40.00
Hank Bullough		
Chuck Bullough		
HL4 Frank Kush	25.00	50.00
Hank Bullough/200		
HL5 George Webster		
Brad Van Pelt		

2003 Michigan State TK Legacy National Champions Autographs

STATED ODDS 1:5		
1952A Frank Kush	7.50	15.00
1952C John Wilson	6.00	12.00
1952D Doug Bobo	6.00	12.00
1952E James Ellis	6.00	12.00
1952F Tom Yewcic	6.00	12.00
1966A George Webster	10.00	20.00
1966B Jimmy Raye	6.00	12.00
1966C Hank Bullough	6.00	12.00

2003 Michigan State TK Legacy Quarterback Club Autographs

STATED ODDS 1:25		
STATED PRINT RUN 300 SER.#'d SETS		
QB1 Jimmy Raye	15.00	30.00
QB2 Tom Yewcic	15.00	30.00
QB3 Earl Morrall	20.00	40.00

2003 Michigan State TK Legacy Retired Numbers

STATED ODDS 1:38		
STATED PRINT RUN 300 SER.#'d SETS		
FRN1 George Webster	1.50	4.00

1973 Minnesota Team Issue

These photos were issued by the school to promote the football program. Each measures roughly 8" by 10" and features a black and white image of a player. The backs are blank or sometimes can be found with a typed player identification. Otherwise no player identification is included.

COMPLETE SET (23)	75.00	125.00
1 George Adzick	3.00	6.00
2 Tim Alderson	3.00	6.00
3 Ollie Bakken	3.00	6.00
4 Doug Beaudoin	3.00	6.00
5 Keith Fahnkorst	3.00	6.00
6 Dale Hagland	3.00	6.00
7 Matt Herkenhoff	3.00	6.00
8 Michael Hunt	3.00	6.00
9 Mike Jones	3.00	6.00
10 Doug Kingsriter	3.00	6.00
11 Tom Macleod	3.00	6.00
12 Art Meadowcroft	3.00	6.00
13 Jeff Morrow	3.00	6.00
14 Steve Neils	3.00	6.00
15 J. Dexter Pride	3.00	6.00
16 Jim Ronan	3.00	6.00
17 Keith Simons	3.00	6.00
18 Dave Simonson	3.00	6.00
19 Mark Slater	3.00	6.00
20 Steve Stewart	3.00	6.00
21 Stan Sytsma	3.00	6.00
22 Rick Upchurch	6.00	12.00
23 Mike White	3.00	6.00

1974 Minnesota Team Sheets

These photos were issued by the school to promote the football program. Each measures roughly 8" by 10" and features eight black and white images of players with the school name appearing at the top. The backs are blank.

1 Dan Christensen	5.00	10.00
Orville Gilmore		
Ollie Bakken		
John Jones		
Steve Goldberg		
Greg Shoff		
Vince Fuller		
Jeff Selleck		
2 Cal Stoll CO	5.00	10.00
Paul Giel AD		
Rick Upchurch		
Doug Beaudoin		
Keith Simons		
Tony Dungy		
Paul Glanton		
Greg Engebos		

1988 Mississippi McDag

Apparently, McDag Productions only issued two standard-size cards in this set. Each front displays a color posed head and shoulders shot enclosed by white borders. The school logo, name, and year appear in the top white border while player information is printed beneath the picture. The back has biographical information, a summary of the player's performance in 1987, and "Tips from the Rebels" that consist of anti-drug and alcohol messages.

COMPLETE SET (2)	4.00	10.00
15 Mark Young	2.00	5.00
16 Bryan Owen	2.00	5.00

1991 Mississippi Hoby

This 42-card standard-size set was produced by Hoby and features the 1991 Ole Miss football team. Five hundred uncut press sheets were also produced, and they were signed and numbered by Billy Brewer. The cards feature on the fronts color head and shoulders shots, with thin white borders on a royal blue card face. The school logo occurs in the lower left corner in a red circle, with the player's name in a gold stripe extending to the right. On a light red background, the backs carry biography, player profile, and statistics. The cards are numbered on the back and are ordered alphabetically by player's name.

COMPLETE SET (42)	6.00	15.00
439 Gary Abide	.15	.40
440 Dwayne Amos	.15	.40
441 Tyji Armstrong	.80	2.00
442 Tyrone Ashley	.15	.40
443 Darron Dillings	.15	.40
444 Danny Boyd	.15	.40
445 Billy Brewer CO	.20	.50
446 Chad Brown	.15	.40
447 Tony Brown	.15	.40
448 Vincent Brownlee	.20	.50
449 Jeff Carter	.20	.50
450 Richard Chisolm	.15	.40
451 Clint Conlee	.15	.40
452 Marvin Courtney	.15	.40
453 Cliff Dew	.15	.40
454 Johnny Dixon	.15	.40
455 Artis Ford	.15	.40
456 Chauncey Godwin	.15	.40
457 Brian Harper	.15	.40
458 David Harris	.15	.40
459 Pete Harris	.15	.40
460 David Herring	.15	.40
461 James Holcombe	.15	.40
462 Kevin Ingram	.15	.40
463 Phillip Kent	.30	.75
464 Derrick King	.15	.40
465 Brian Lee	.15	.40
466 Jim Lentz	.15	.40
467 Everett Lindsay	.15	.40
468 Tom Luke	.15	.40
469 Thomas McLeish	.15	.40
470 Wesley Melton	.15	.40
471 Tyrone Montgomery	.20	.50
472 Deano Orr	.15	.40
473 Darrick Owens	.20	.50
474 Lynn Ross	.15	.40
475 Russ Shows	.15	.40
476 Eddie Small	.20	.50
477 Trea Southerland	.15	.40
478 Gerald Vaughn	.15	.40
479 Abner White	.15	.40
480 Sebastian Williams	.15	.40

1991 Mississippi State Hoby

This 42-card standard-size set was produced by Hoby and features the 1991 Mississippi State football team. The cards feature on the fronts color head shots, with thin white borders on a royal blue card face. The school logo occurs in the lower left corner in a maroon circle, with the player's name in a gold stripe extending to the right. On a light maroon background, the backs carry biography, player profile, and statistics. The cards are numbered on the back and are ordered alphabetically by player's name.

COMPLETE SET (42)	6.00	15.00
481 Lance Aldridge	.15	.40
482 Treddis Anderson	.15	.40
483 Shea Bell	.15	.40
484 Chris Bosarge	.15	.40
485 Daniel Boyd	.15	.40
486 Jerome Brown	.15	.40
487 Torrance Brown	.15	.40
488 Keith Carr	.15	.40
489 Herman Carroll	.15	.40
490 Keo Coleman	.30	.75
491 Michael Davis	.15	.40
492 Trenell Edwards	.15	.40
493 Chris Firle	.15	.40
494 Lee Ford	.15	.40
495 Tay Galloway	.15	.40
496 Chris Gardner	.15	.40
497 Arleye Gibson	.15	.40
498 Tony Harris	.15	.40
499 Willie Harris	.15	.40
500 Kevin Henry	.20	.50
501 Jackie Sherrill CO	.30	.75
502 John James	.15	.40
503 Tony James	.15	.40
504 Todd Jordan	.15	.40
505 Keith Joseph	.15	.40
506 Kelvin Knight	.15	.40
507 Lee Lipscomb	.15	.40
508 Juan Long	.15	.40
509 Kyle McCoy	.15	.40
510 Tommy Morrell	.15	.40
511 Kelly Ray	.15	.40
512 Mike Riley	.15	.40
513 Kenny Roberts	.15	.40
514 William Robinson	.15	.40
515 Bill Sartin	.15	.40
516 Kenny Stewart	.15	.40
517 Rodney Stowers	.20	.50
518 Anthony Thames	.15	.40
519 Edward Williams	.15	.40
520 Nate Williams	.15	.40
521 Karl Williamson	.15	.40
522 Marc Woodard	.15	.40

1907 Missouri Postcards

These black and white photo Missouri Postcards were issued in 1907 by the University Co-Operative Store. The cards feature a postcard style back with a brief write-up on the player and closely resemble the 1907 Michigan Dietsche Postcard issue. Just the player's last name or nickname is included on the cardfronts.

1 Aubrey Alexander	30.00	50.00
(ALECK)		
2 William Carothers	30.00	50.00
3 William Deatherage	30.00	50.00
(DEATHERAGE)		
4 William Driver	30.00	50.00
(DRIVER)		
5 Dorcet Graves	30.00	50.00
(TUBBY)		
6 William Jackson	30.00	50.00
7 Edwin Miller	30.00	50.00
(MILLER)		
8 Bill Monilaw CO	30.00	50.00
(COACH)		
9 James Patrick Nixon	30.00	50.00
(NICK)		
10 Carl Ristine	30.00	50.00
(CURLY)		
11 Prewett Roberts	30.00	50.00
(P)		
12 H.K. Rutherford	30.00	50.00
(RUTH)		
13 Melverne Sigler	30.00	50.00
(SIG)		
14 F.L. Williams	30.00	50.00
16 Team Photo	30.00	50.00
(The Tiger Squad 1907)		

1909 Missouri Postcards

These black and white Missouri Postcards were issued in 1909. The cards feature a postcard style back with the player's name and weight printed on the front along with his photo. Any additions or information on the checklist below would be appreciated.

1 James Bluck	25.00	40.00
2 John Clarc	25.00	40.00
3 Henry Crain	25.00	40.00
4 William Deatherage	25.00	40.00
5 H.S. Gove	25.00	40.00
6 Theodore D. Hackney	25.00	40.00
7 Eugene Hall	25.00	40.00
8 Arthur Idler	25.00	40.00
9 Warren Roberts	25.00	40.00
10 William Roper CO	25.00	40.00
11 L.E. Thatcher	25.00	40.00
12 Allen Wilder	25.00	40.00

1913 Missouri Postcards

These black and white Missouri football photo postcards were issued around 1913 by the University. The cards feature a postcard style back and often include a mention of the photographer: Volney McFadden, Student Photographer, Columbia, Mo. on the back or Aristo on the front. The player's last name is printed below his photo on the front or a score and/or caption included for action photos. Any additions or information on the checklist below would be appreciated.

2 Missouri 3, Kansas 0	25.00	40.00
Mc kicks goal (McFadden)		
3 Missouri 20, Oklahoma 17	25.00	40.00
(photo at goal line)		

1914 Missouri Postcards

These black and white photo Missouri Postcards were issued around 1914 by the University. The cards feature a postcard style back with a mention of the photographer: A.M. Finley, Student Photographer, Columbia, Mo. The player's last name is printed below his photo on the front. Any additions or information on the checklist below would be appreciated.

1 Harry Lansing	30.00	50.00
(standing pose)		
2 Missouri 46, W.J. 0	20.00	40.00
(William Jewel; action scene)		

1915 Missouri Postcards

These black and white photo Missouri Postcards were issued around 1915 by the University. The cards feature a postcard style back with a mention of the photographer: A.M. Finley, Volney McFadden, or E.L. Ooker, Student Photographer, Columbia, Mo. The player's last name is printed below his photo on the front. Any additions or information on the checklist below would be appreciated.

1 Frank Herndon	30.00	50.00
2 Capt. Harry Lansing	30.00	50.00
(snapping the ball)		
3 Henry Schulte CO	30.00	50.00
4 Jacob Speelman UER	30.00	50.00
(misspelled Spealman)		
5 Van Dyne	30.00	50.00

1995 Missouri Legends

This set features Missouri Tigers football legends. Each card measures roughly 2 5/8" by 4" and features a black border around an artist's rendering of the player or coach.

1 Paul Christman	.60	1.50
2 Darold Jenkins	.40	1.00
3 Johnny Roland	.40	1.00
4 Bob Steuber	.40	1.00
5 Roger Wehrli	.60	1.50
6 Kellen Winslow	1.00	2.50
7 Dan Devine CO	.60	1.50
8 Don Faurot CO	.40	1.00

1989-90 Montana Smokey

COMPLETE SET (12)	5.00	10.00
2 Jay Fagan	.40	1.00
Men's football		
3 Dwayne Hans	.40	1.00
Men's football		
4 Tim Hauck	.40	1.00
Men's football		
8 Mike Rankin	.40	1.00
Men's football		
11 Kirk Scrafford	.40	1.00
Men's football		

1997 Montana

COMPLETE SET (23)	15.00	25.00
1 Mike Agee FB	.50	1.25
2 Mike Bouchee FB	.50	1.25
3 Joe Douglass FB	.50	1.25
4 Michael Erhardt FB	.50	1.25
5 Corey Falls FB	.50	1.25
6 Sean Goicoechea FB	.50	1.25
7 Mark Hampe FB	.50	1.25
8 Justin Hazel FB	.50	1.25
9 Billy Ivey FB	.50	1.25
10 David Kempfert FB	.50	1.25
11 Andy Larson FB	.50	1.25
12 Blaine McElmurry FB	.50	1.25
13 Randy Riley FB	.50	1.25
14 David Simon FB	.50	1.25
15 Ryan Thompson FB	.50	1.25
16 Brian Toone FB	.50	1.25
17 Jeff Zellick FB	.50	1.25

1910 Murad College Silks S21

Each of these silks was issued by Murad Cigarettes around 1910 with a college emblem and an artist's rendering of a generic athlete on the front. The backs are blank. Each of the S21 silks measures roughly 5" by 7" and there was a smaller version created (roughly 3 1/2" by 5 1/2") of each and cataloged as S22.

*SMALLER S22: .3X TO .8X LARGER S21		
1FB Army (West Point) football	30.00	60.00
2FB Brown football	30.00	60.00
3FB California football	30.00	60.00
4FB Chicago football	30.00	60.00
5FB Colorado football	30.00	60.00
6FB Columbia football	30.00	60.00
7FB Cornell football	30.00	60.00
8FB Dartmouth football	30.00	60.00
9FB Georgetown football	30.00	60.00
10FB Harvard football	30.00	60.00
11FB Illinois football	30.00	60.00
12FB Michigan football	30.00	60.00
13FB Minnesota football	30.00	60.00
14FB Missouri football	30.00	60.00
15FB Navy (Annapolis) football	30.00	60.00
16FB Ohio State football	30.00	60.00
17FB Pennsylvania football	30.00	60.00
18FB Purdue football	30.00	60.00
19FB Stanford football	30.00	60.00
20FB Stanford football	30.00	60.00
21FB Syracuse football	30.00	60.00
22FB Texas football	30.00	60.00
23FB Wisconsin football	30.00	60.00
24FB Yale football	30.00	60.00

1911 Murad College Series T51

These colorful cigarette cards featured several colleges and a variety of sports and recreations of the day and were issued in packs of Murad Cigarettes. The cards measure approximately 2" by 3". Two variations of each of the first 50 cards were produced; one variation says "College Series" on back, the other, "2nd Series". The drawings on cards of the 2nd Series are slightly different from those of the College Series. There are 6 different series of 25 in the College Series and they are listed here in the order that they appear on the checklist on the cardbacks. There is also a larger version (5" x 8") that was available for the first 25 cards as a premium (catalog designation T6) offer that could be obtained in exchange for 15 Murad cigarette coupons; the offers expired June 30, 1911.

*2ND SERIES: .4X TO 1X COLLEGE SERIES		
10 Harvard	25.00	50.00
Football		
13 Michigan#(Football	25.00	50.00
39 S.U.N.D.(Univ. of N.Dakota)	25.00	50.00
Football		
43 Tufts College	25.00	50.00
Football		
54 C (Coalgate)	25.00	50.00
Football		
102 Buchtel	25.00	50.00
Football		

1911 Murad College Series Premiums T6

10 Harvard	250.00	400.00
Football		
13 Michigan#(Football	250.00	400.00

1994 Navy Team Sheets

These photos were issued by the school to promote the football program. Each measures roughly 8" by 10" and features eight players with a black and white image for each along with his name, position, and home town. The school name appears at the top and the backs are blank.

1 George Chaump CO	4.00	8.00
Chris Hart		
Jim Kubiak		
Damon Dixon		
Shane Halloran		
Fernando Harris		
Kevin Hickman		
Joe Speed		
2 Alex Domino	4.00	8.00
Michael Jefferson		
Matt Kaslik		
Andy Person		
Chris Reaghard		
Matt Scornavacchi		
Garrett Smith		
Andy Thompson		
3 Erasto Jackson	4.00	8.00
Greg Emery		
Steve Bellack		
Mark Love		
Omar Nelson		
Cal Quinn		
Tom Neville		
Monty Williams		

1939 Nebraska Don Leon Coffee

These cards were thought to have been produced in the late 1930s and early 1940s and released as a premium for purchasing Don Leon Coffee. Each card measures roughly 1-7/8" by 2-3/4" and features a black and white photo of the player on the cardfront along with just his name, position, and hometown. No height and weight information is included on the 1939 cards. The unnumbered cardbacks containing rules for a card set building contest along with an ad for Don Leon Coffee. Listed below are the known cards, any additions to this list are appreciated.

1 Elmer Dohrmann	125.00	200.00
2 Lowell English	125.00	200.00
3 Perry Franks	125.00	200.00
4 John Richardson	125.00	200.00
5 Fred Shirey	125.00	200.00
6 Kenneth Shindo	125.00	200.00

1940 Nebraska Don Leon Coffee

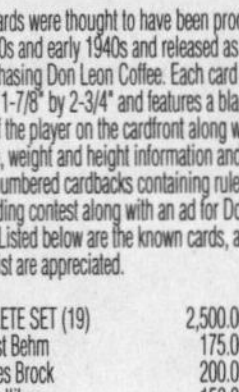

These cards were thought to have been produced in the late 1930s and early 1940s and released as a premium for purchasing Don Leon Coffee. Each card measures roughly 1-7/8" by 2-3/4" and features a black and white photo of the player on the cardfront along with his name, position, weight and height information and hometown. The unnumbered cardbacks containing rules for a card set building contest along with an ad for Don Leon Coffee. Listed below are the known cards, any additions to this list are appreciated.

COMPLETE SET (19)	2,500.00	3,500.00
1 Forrest Behm	175.00	300.00
2 Charles Brock	200.00	350.00
3 Bill Callihan	150.00	250.00
4 Elmer Dohrmann	125.00	200.00
5 Jack Dodd	150.00	250.00
6 Lloyd Grimm	125.00	200.00
7 Lowell English	125.00	200.00
8 Perry Franks	125.00	200.00
9 Harry Hopp	150.00	250.00
10 Robert Kahler	125.00	200.00
11 Royal Kahler	125.00	200.00
12 Vernon Neprud	125.00	200.00
13 E. Nuernberger	125.00	200.00
14 William Pfeiff	125.00	200.00
15 George Porter	150.00	250.00
16 John Richardson	125.00	200.00
17 Fred Preston	125.00	200.00
18 Glen Schluckebier	125.00	200.00
19 Fred Shirey	125.00	200.00
20 Kenneth Shindo	125.00	200.00

1966 Nebraska Team Issue

These 5" by 7" black and white photos were issued by Nebraska. Each features a member of the football team without any player identfiication on the front. The backs were produced blank, however the player's identification is usually hand written or even stamped on the backs.

COMPLETE SET (9)	25.00	50.00
1 LaVerne Allers	3.00	6.00
2 Bob Churchich	4.00	8.00
3 Dick Fitzgerald	3.00	6.00
4 Wayne Meylan	3.00	6.00
5 Bob Pickens	3.00	6.00
6 Lynn Senkbeil	3.00	6.00
7 Pete Tatman	3.00	6.00
8 Larry Wacholtz	3.00	6.00
9 Harry Wilson	4.00	8.00

1973 Nebraska Playing Cards

This 54-card set of playing cards measures 2 1/4" by 3 1/2". The cardbacks feature the words "Go Big Red" and "Nebraska" in the shape of a football helmet against either a red or white background color -- there were two versions of the set in either white or red colored backs. The cardfronts feature a black and white player photo with the player's name below. The cards are checklisted below in playing card order by suit (C for Clubs, D for Diamonds, H for Hearts, S for Spades, and JOK for the Jokers) and numbers are assigned to Aces (1), Jacks (11), Queens (12), and Kings (13). This set was released in 1973 and very closely resembles the 1974 set with a few of the differences as noted below. It also includes the first card of legendary head coach Tom Osborne.

COMP. FACT SET (54)	90.00	150.00
1C Terry Rogers	.75	2.00
1D Richard Duda	1.25	2.50
1H Zaven Yaralian	.75	2.00
1S Tom Osborne CO	35.00	50.00
(reads TOM OSBORNE -- COACH)		
2C Bob Revelle	.75	2.00
2D John Dutton	3.00	5.00
2H Bob Wolfe	.75	2.00
2S Tom Alward	.75	2.00
3C Tom Pate	.75	2.00
3D Pat Fischer	2.50	4.00
3H Steve Wieser	.75	2.00
3S Dan Anderson	.75	2.00
4C Mike O'Holleran	.75	2.00
4D Marvin Crenshaw	1.25	2.50
4H Daryl White	.75	2.00
4S Frosty Anderson	.75	2.00
5C Ron Pruitt	.75	2.00
5D Dean Gissler	.75	2.00
5H Bob Thornton	.75	2.00
5S Al Austin	.75	2.00
6C Bob Nelson	1.25	2.50
6D Dave Goeller	.75	2.00
6H John Starkebaum	.75	2.00
6S Ritch Bahe	.75	2.00
7C Larry Mushinskie	.75	2.00
7D Percy Eichelberger	.75	2.00
7H Dave Shamblin	.75	2.00
7S John Bell	.75	2.00
8C Jeff Moran	.75	2.00
(jersey number visible)		
8D Stan Hegener	.75	2.00
8H Don Westbrook	1.25	2.50
8S Rik Bonness	1.25	2.50
9C Bob Martin	.75	2.00
9D Dave Humm	3.00	5.00
9H Bob Schmit	1.25	2.50
9S Randy Borg	.75	2.00
10C Ralph Powell	.75	2.00
10D Ardell Johnson	.75	2.00
(smiling)		
10H Rich Sanger	.75	2.00
10S Rich Costanzo	.75	2.00
11C Steve Manstedt	.75	2.00
11D Doug Johnson	.75	2.00
11H Willie Thornton	1.25	2.50
11S Maury Damkroger	1.25	2.50
12C Brent Longwell	.75	2.00
12D Chuck Jones	.75	2.00
12H Tom Ruud	1.25	2.50
12S Tony Davis	1.25	2.50
13C George Kyros	.75	2.00
13D Wonder Monds	1.25	2.50
(not smiling)		
13H Steve Runty	.75	2.00
13S Mark Doak	.75	2.00
JOK1 Memorial Stadium	.75	2.00
Black		
(No stadium identification on card)		
JOK2 Memorial Stadium	.75	2.00
Red		
(No stadium identification on card)		

1974 Nebraska Playing Cards

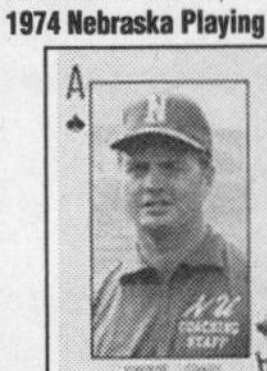

This 54-card set of playing cards measures 2 1/4" by 3 1/2". The cardbacks feature the words "Go Big Red" and "Nebraska" in the shape of a football helmet against either a red or white background color -- there were two versions of the set in either white or red colored backs. The cardfronts feature a black and white player photo with the player's name below. The cards are checklisted below in playing card order by suit (C for Clubs, D for Diamonds, H for Hearts, S for Spades, and JOK for the Jokers) and numbers are assigned to Aces (1), Jacks (11), Queens (12), and Kings (13). This set was released in 1974 and very closely resembles the 1973 set with a few of the differences as noted below. It also includes the first card of legendary head coach Tom Osborne.

COMPLETE SET (54)	75.00	135.00
1C Rik Bonness	1.25	2.50
1D Don Westbrook	.75	2.00
1H Ron Pruitt	.75	2.00
1S Tom Osborne CO	25.00	40.00
(reads OSBORNE COACH)		
2C Mark Doak	.75	2.00
2D Mike Offner	.75	2.00
2H Tony Davis	1.25	2.50
2S Terry Rogers	.75	2.00
3C John Lee	.75	2.00
3D Stan Waldemore	.75	2.00
3H Mike Fultz	.75	2.00
3S Tom Ruud	1.25	2.50
4C Mike Coyle	.75	2.00
4D Stan Hegener	.75	2.00
4H Chad Leonardi	.75	2.00
4S Jeff Schneider	.75	2.00
5C George Kyros	.75	2.00
5D Bobby Thomas	.75	2.00
5H John Starkebaum	.75	2.00
5S Mark Heydorff	.75	2.00
6C Gary Higgs	.75	2.00
6D Bob Martin	.75	2.00
6H Marvin Crenshaw	1.25	2.50
6S Dean Gissler	.75	2.00
7C Dennis Pavelka	.75	2.00
7D Ritch Bahe	.75	2.00
7H Larry Mushinskie	.75	2.00
7S Jim Burrow	.75	2.00
8C Jeff Moran	.75	2.00
(jersey number hidden)		
8D Tom Heiser	.75	2.00
8H Tom Pate	.75	2.00
8S Al Eveland	.75	2.00
9C John O'Leary	.75	2.00
9D Steve Wieser	.75	2.00
9H Dave Humm	3.00	5.00
9S Chuck Jones	.75	2.00
10C Percy Eichelberger	.75	2.00
10D Ardell Johnson	.75	2.00
(not smiling)		
10H Willie Thornton	1.25	2.50
10S Brad Jenkins	.75	2.00
11C Greg Jorgensen	.75	2.00
11D Chuck Malito	.75	2.00
11H Dave Redding	.75	2.00
11S Dave Butterfield	.75	2.00
12C George Mills	.75	2.00
12D Bob Lingenfelter	.75	2.00
12H Dave Shamblin	.75	2.00
12S Rich Duda	1.25	2.50
13C Terry Luck	.75	2.00
13D Wonder Monds	1.25	2.50
(smiling)		
13H Earl Everett	.75	2.00
13S Steve Hoins	.75	2.00
JOK1 Bob Nelson	1.25	2.50
JOK2 Memorial Stadium	1.25	2.50
(Stadium is identified on card)		

1984-85 Nebraska

This 31-card multi-sport set was distributed by the Lincoln Police Department. The cards measure approximately 2 1/4" by 3 5/8" and are printed on thin card stock. The sports represented are football (1-10), volleyball (11-12), gymnastics (13-15), basketball (16-19), baseball (20-24, 26, 28, 30), and track (25, 27, 29, 31).

COMPLETE SET (31)	20.00	40.00
1 Mark Traynowicz	.75	2.00
2 Tom Osborne CO	6.00	15.00
3 Jeff Smith	1.25	3.00
4 Scott Strasburger	1.00	2.50
5 Craig Sundberg	.75	2.00
6 Bill Weber	.75	2.00
7 Shane Swanson	.75	2.00
8 Neil Harris	.75	2.00
9 Mark Behning	1.00	2.50
10 Dave Burke	.75	2.00

1985 Nebraska All Stars Cereal

COMPLETE SET (25)	125.00	250.00
1 Ed Weir	7.50	15.00
2 Bill Callihan	7.50	15.00
4 Tom Novak	6.00	12.00
5 Bob Reynolds	6.00	12.00
6 Jerry Minnick	6.00	12.00
8 Larry L. Wacholtz	6.00	12.00
9 Joe Armstrong	6.00	12.00
12 Jerry Murtaugh	6.00	12.00
13 Dave Humm	7.50	15.00
15 Dave Butterfield	6.00	12.00
16 George Andrews	6.00	12.00
17 Randy Schleusener	6.00	12.00
19 Jim Pillen	6.00	12.00
20 Kelly Saalfeld	6.00	12.00
21 Kris Van Norman	10.00	20.00
22 Brett Clark	6.00	12.00
23 Larry Jacobson	6.00	12.00
24 Craig Sundberg	6.00	12.00
25 Shane Swanson	6.00	12.00

1985 Nebraska Team Sheets

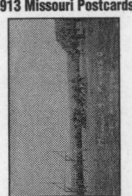

These 8" by 10" sheets were issued primarily to the media for use as player images for print. Each features 8-players with the player's jersey number, name, and position beneath his picture. The sheets are blankbacked and unnumbered.

COMPLETE SET (7)	14.00	35.00
1 McCathorn Clayton	2.50	6.00
Jeff Taylor		
Clete Blakeman		
Doug DuBose		
Paul Miles		
Keith Jones		
Jon Kelley		
Tom Rathman		
2 Todd Frain	2.00	5.00
Tom Banderas		
Tim Roth		
Rob Maggard		
Brian Blankenship		
Ron Galois		
Bill Lewis		
Mark Cooper		
3 Stan Parker	2.00	5.00
John McCormick		
Tom Welter		
Todd Carpenter		
Robb Schnitzler		
Rod Smith		
Hendley Hawkins		
Travis Turner		
4 Ken Kaelin	2.00	5.00
Micah Heibel		
Dan Casterline		
Roger Lindstrom		
Von Sheppard		
Dana Brinson		
Dale Klein		
Dan Wingard		
5 Brad Smith	4.00	10.00
Scott Tucker		
Brad Tyrer		
Chris Spachman		

Neil Smith		
Danny Noonan		
Phil Rogers		
Ken Shead		
6 Gary Schneider	2.00	5.00
Brian Davis		
Bryan Siebler		
Chris Carr		
Dan Thayer		
Brian Washington		
Jeff Tomjack		
Guy Rozier		
7 Steve Forch	2.00	5.00
Marc Munford		
Chad Daffer		
Dennis Watkins		
Brian Pokorny		
John Custard		
Mike Carl		
Cleo Miller		

1985-86 Nebraska

This 37-card multi-sport set measuring 2 1/2" by 4" has on the fronts color action and posed player photos enclosed by a red border. The sports represented are football (2-11), volleyball (12, 14), gymnastics (13, 15-17), track (18, 20, 29-30), basketball (19, 21, 23, 26), baseball (20-24, 31-37), and swimming (22, 24, 27-28). The cards are numbered on the back. The key cards in the set are NBA draftee Rich King and NFL running back Tom Rathman.

COMPLETE SET (37)	20.00	40.00
2 Doug DuBose	1.00	2.50
3 Marc Munford	.75	2.00
4 Travis Turner	.75	2.00
5 Mike Knox	.75	2.00
6 Todd Frain	.75	2.00
7 Danny Noonan	1.50	4.00
8 Tom Rathman	4.00	8.00
9 Jim Skow	1.00	2.50
10 Stan Parker	.75	2.00
11 Bill Lewis	.75	2.00
27 Mark Traynowicz	.20	.50
28 Harry Grimminger	.15	.40
29 Bill Lewis	.20	.50
30 Jim Skow	.20	.50
31 Larry Kramer	.15	.40
32 Tony Jeter	.20	.50
33 Robert Brown	.15	.40
34 Larry Wacholtz	.15	.40
35 Wayne Meylan	.20	.50
36 Bob Newton	.15	.40
37 Willie Harper	.20	.50
38 Bob Martin	.15	.40
39 Jerry Murtaugh	.20	.50
40 Daryl White	.15	.40
41 Larry Jacobson	.15	.40
42 Joe Armstrong	.15	.40
43 Laverne Allers	.15	.40
44 Freeman White	.20	.50
45 Marvin Crenshaw	.20	.50
46 Forrest Behm	.15	.40
47 Jerry Minnick	.15	.40
48 Tom Davis	.15	.40
49 Kelvin Clark	.20	.50
50 Tom Rathman	.40	1.00
51 Sam Francis	.15	.40
52 Joe Orduna	.20	.50
53 Ed Weir	.15	.40
54 Bill Thornton	.15	.40
55 Bob Devaney CO	.60	1.50
56 Bret Clark	.15	.40
57 Frank Solich	.15	.40
58 Tim Smith	.15	.40
59 George Andrews	.15	.40
60 Rick Berns	.20	.50
61 Monte Johnson	.20	.50
62 Walt Barnes	.15	.40
63 Jim McFarland	.15	.40
64 Jimmy Williams	.15	.40
65 Vic Halligan	.15	.40
66 Guy Chamberlin	.15	.40
67 Hugh Rhea	.15	.40
68 George Sauer	.20	.50
69 E.O. Stiehm CO	.15	.40
70 Walter G. Booth CO	.15	.40
71 First Night Game (Memorial Stadium)	.15	.40
72 Memorial Stadium	.15	.40
73 M-Stadium Expansions	.15	.40
74 Andra Franklin	.40	1.00
75 Ron McDole	.20	.50
76 Pat Fischer	.20	.50
77 Dan McMullen	.15	.40
78 Charles Brock	.15	.40
79 Verne Lewellen	.15	.40
80 Bob Nelson	.20	.50
81 Roger Craig	1.00	2.50
82 Fred Shirey	.15	.40
83 Tom Novak	.15	.40
84 Ray Richards	.15	.40
85 Warren Alfson	.15	.40
86 Lawrence Ely	.15	.40
87 Mike Rozier	.60	1.50
88 Dean Steinkuhler	.40	1.00
89 John Dutton	.40	1.00
90 Dave Rimington	.40	1.00
91 Johnny Rodgers	.60	1.50
92 Herbie Husker (Mascot)	.15	.40
93 Tom Osborne CO	1.00	2.50
94 Broderick Thomas	.60	1.50
95 Bob Reynolds	.15	.40
96 Mick Tingelhoff UER (Name misspelled Tinglehoff)	.40	1.00
97 Lloyd Cardwell	.15	.40
98 Johnny Rodgers	.60	1.50
99 '70 National Champs (Team Photo)	.20	.50
100 '71 National Champs (Team Photo)	.20	.50
NNO Title Card (Contest on back)	.20	.50

1986-87 Nebraska

This 30-card multi-sport set was distributed by the Lincoln Police Department. The cards measure approzimately 2 1/2" by 4" and are printed on thin card stock.

COMPLETE SET (30)	20.00	35.00
1 Bob Devaney McGruff the Crime Dog	1.25	3.00
2 Doug DuBose	1.25	3.00
3 Marc Munford	1.00	2.50
4 Von Sheppard	1.00	2.50
5 Dale Klein	1.00	2.50
6 Robb Schnitzler	1.00	2.50
7 Chris Spachman	1.00	2.50
8 Brian Davis	1.00	2.50
9 Ken Kaelin	1.00	2.50

1987-88 Nebraska

This 26-card multi-sport set was distributed by the Lincoln Police Department. The cards measure approximately 2 1/2" by 4" and is printed on this cardboard stock.

COMPLETE SET (26)	20.00	35.00
1 Keith Jones	1.00	2.50
2 Broderick Thomas	2.00	5.00
3 Dana Brinson	1.00	2.50
4 John McCormick	1.00	2.50
5 Steve Taylor	1.00	2.50
6 Lee Jones	1.00	2.50
7 Rod Smith	1.00	2.50
8 Neil Smith	4.00	8.00

1988-89 Nebraska

COMPLETE SET (32)	12.50	30.00
1 Steve Taylor	.75	2.00
2 Broderick Thomas	1.25	3.00
3 LaRoy Etienne	.75	2.00
4 Tyreese Knox	.75	2.00
5 Mark Blazek	.75	2.00
6 Charles Fryar	.75	2.00
7 Tim Jackson	.75	2.00
8 Andy Keeler	.75	2.00
9 John Kroeker	.75	2.00

1989 Nebraska 100

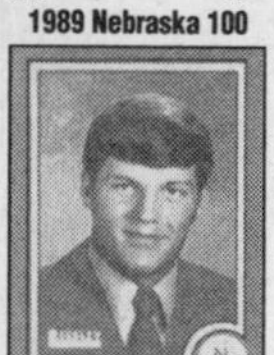

This 100-card standard-size set was sponsored and produced by Leesley Ltd. The set is sometimes subtitled as "100 Years of Nebraska Football" as it features past University of Nebraska football players. Many of the pictures are actually color portrait drawings rather than photos. The cards have thick red borders. The vertically oriented backs have detailed profiles with two slightly different versions. The most common version reads "GO BIG RED 100 Years" at the bottom of the cardback and the tougher versions has corporate logos for "NTV" and "Pizza Hut" at the bottom. These cards were distributed as a complete set and as eight-card cello packs. The cards are numbered on the back in the upper left corner.

COMPLETE SET (100)	15.00	40.00
1 Tony Davis	.20	.50
2 Keith Jones	.15	.40
3 Turner Gill	.40	1.00
4 Dave Butterfield	.15	.40
5 Wonder Monds	.20	.50
6 Dave Rimington	.40	1.00
7 John Dutton	.40	1.00
8 Irving Fryar	1.25	3.00
9 Dean Steinkuhler	.40	1.00
10 Mike Rozier	.60	1.50
11 Jarvis Redwine	.40	1.00
12 Randy Schleusener	.15	.40
13 Junior Miller	.20	.50
14 Broderick Thomas	.60	1.50
15 Steve Taylor	.20	.50
16 Neil Smith	.75	2.00
17 John McCormick	.15	.40
18 Danny Noonan	.20	.50
19 Mike Fultz	.15	.40
20 Vince Ferragamo	.40	1.00
21 Jerry Tagge	.40	1.00
22 Jeff Kinney	.20	.50
23 Rich Glover	.20	.50
24 Johnny Rodgers	.60	1.50
25 Rik Bonness	.20	.50
26 Dave Humm	.20	.50

1989-90 Nebraska

This 33-card multi-sport set measures approximately 2 1/2" by 4" and is printed on thin cardboard stock. The fronts feature color player action photos on a red card face. In black lettering the words "89-90 Huskers" appear over the picture, while the player's name and other information are printed beneath the picture. The backs carry "Husker Tips," which consist of comments about the players combined with crime prevention tips. Sponsor names and logos at the bottom round out the back.

COMPLETE SET (33)	10.00	25.00
1 Ken Clark	.60	1.50
2 Reggie Cooper	.60	1.50
3 Gerry Gdowski	.60	1.50
4 Monte Kratzenstein	.60	1.50
5 Gregg Barrios	.60	1.50
6 Morgan Gregory	.60	1.50
7 Jeff Mills	.60	1.50
8 Richard Bell	.60	1.50
9 Jake Young	.60	1.50
10 Mike Croel	1.25	3.00
11 Bryan Carpenter	.60	1.50
12 Kent Wells	.60	1.50
13 Sam Schmidt	.60	1.50

1990-91 Nebraska

This 28-card set was sponsored by the National Bank of Commerce, the University of Nebraska-Lincoln, and the Lincoln Police Department. Sponsors' logos at the bottom round out the back. The sports represented in this set are football (2-13), volleyball (14-15), wrestling (16), gymnastics (17-20), basketball (21-24), softball (25, 27), and baseball (26, 28). The key cards in the set are these players with NFL experience: Mike Croel, Bruce Pickens, and Kenny Walker.

COMPLETE SET (28)	12.50	30.00
1 Bob Devaney AD	.75	2.00
2 Reggie Cooper	.75	2.00
3 Terry Rodgers	.75	2.00
4 Kenny Walker	1.00	2.50
5 Gregg Barrios	.75	2.00
6 Mike Croel	1.00	2.50
7 Tom Punt	.75	2.00
8 Mike Grant	.75	2.00
9 Joe Sims	.75	2.00
10 Mickey Joseph	.75	2.00
11 Lance Lewis	.75	2.00
12 Bruce Pickens	1.00	2.50
13 Nate Turner	.75	2.00

1991-92 Nebraska

COMPLETE SET (22)	10.00	25.00
1 Mickey Joseph	.75	2.00
2 Pat Englebert	.75	2.00
3 Jon Bostick	.75	2.00
4 Scott Baldwin	.75	2.00
5 Tim Johnk	.75	2.00
6 Tom Haase	.75	2.00
7 Erik Wiegert	.75	2.00
8 Chris Garrett	.75	2.00

1992-93 Nebraska

This 27-card multisport set was sponsored by the National Bank of Commerce, the University of Nebraska-Lincoln, and the Lincoln Police Department. The cards measure approximately 2 5/8" by 3 1/2" and are printed on thin card stock. Sponsor names and logos round out the back. The sports represented are football (1-9), women's volleyball (10, 11), basketball (12-17), gymnastics (18-20), track and field, (21-22) and baseball (23-27).

COMPLETE SET (27)	10.00	25.00
1 Will Shields	1.00	2.50
2 Tyrone Hughes	1.00	2.50
3 Kenny Wilhite	.60	1.50
4 William Washington	.60	1.50
5 Mike Stigge	.60	1.50
6 Tyrone Byrd	.60	1.50
7 Travis Hill	.60	1.50
8 John Parrella	.75	2.00
9 Jim Scott	.60	1.50

1993-94 Nebraska

This 25-card multisport standard-size set was jointly sponsored by the National Bank of Commerce, the Lincoln Police Department, and the university. The cards are unnumbered and checklisted below alphabetically within sport as follows: football (1-9), basketball (men [10-11]; women [12-13]), gymnastics (14-17), baseball (18-19), women's softball (20-21), volleyball (22-23), and wrestling (24-25).

COMPLETE SET (25)	10.00	25.00
1 Trev Alberts	.75	2.00
2 Mike Anderson	.60	1.50
3 Ernie Beler	.50	1.25
4 Byron Bennett	.50	1.25
5 Corey Dixon	.50	1.25
6 Troy Dumas	.50	1.25
7 Calvin Jones	.75	2.00
8 Bruce Moore	.50	1.25
9 David Noonan	.60	1.50

1994-95 Nebraska

This 21-card multi-sport set was jointly sponsored by Union Bank, the Lincoln Police Department and the university. The unnumbered, attractive, full color cards are slightly wider than standard size and printed on very thin stock. Several sports are featured and are listed below alphabetically within sport as follows: baseball (1-2), men's basketball (3-4), women's basketball (5-6), football (7-14), men's gymnastics (15-16), women's gymnastics (17-18), softball (19) and women's volleyball (20-21). Future NBA player Erick Strickland has his first card in this set.

COMPLETE SET (21)	10.00	25.00
7 Terry Connealy	.50	1.25
8 Troy Dumas	.50	1.25
9 Donta Jones	.75	2.00
10 Barron Miles	.50	1.25
11 Cory Schlesinger	1.00	2.50
12 Ed Stewart	.50	1.25
13 Zach Wiegert	.60	1.50
14 Rob Zatechka	.50	1.25

1995 Nebraska Schedules

These "cards" are actually pocket schedules issued by the school. The cardfronts feature a Nebraska player in a color photo with the year and the player's name noted. The cardbacks include the team's 1995 football schedules along with a Star City sponsorship logo.

COMPLETE SET (5)	6.00	15.00
1 Brook Berringer	2.00	5.00
2 Tommie Frazier	2.00	5.00
3 Aaron Graham	1.25	3.00
4 Christian Peter	1.25	3.00
5 Tyrone Williams	2.00	5.00

1995-96 Nebraska

This 21-card multisport set was jointly sponsored by National Bank, Lincoln Police Department and the university. The unnumbered, full-color cards are slightly wider than standard size and feature bold red borders on front. The set contains several sports and is checklisted below alphabetically within sport as follows: men's basketball (1-3), women's basketball (4-6), football (7-13), men's gymnastics (14), women's soccer (15), women's swimming (16), women's volleyball (17-20) and wrestling (21). The set contains early cards of football players Tommy Frazier and Brook Berringer as well as an early card of NBA player Erick Strickland.

COMPLETE SET (21)	12.00	30.00
7 Brook Berringer FB	1.50	4.00
8 Doug Colman FB	.50	1.25
9 Tommie Frazier FB	2.50	6.00
10 Aaron Graham FB	.60	1.50
11 Clester Johnson FB	.50	1.25
12 Jeff Makovicka FB	.60	1.50
13 Tony Veland FB	.50	1.25

1996 Nebraska

The 22-card Nebraska standard-size set was produced by Homeworks Unlimited and was sold in set form. The 21 seniors from the 1995-96 Nebraska National Championship team are included within the set, as well as a checklist card. Key players within this set include Clinton Childs, Tommie Frazier, Aaron Graham, and Jeff Makovicka. In addition, there is a Brook Berringer tribute card, which details his tragic death from a plane crash. While the players' uniform number is listed on each of these cards, they are arranged in alphabetical order below. Each plastic card has a fascimile autograph on the front.

COMPLETE SET (22)	12.00	30.00
1 Jacques Allen	.60	1.50
2 Reggie Baul	.60	1.50
3 Brook Berringer	1.60	4.00
4 Clinton Childs	.80	2.00
5 Doug Colman	.60	1.50
6 Phil Ellis	.60	1.50
7 Tommie Frazier	2.00	5.00
8 Mark Gilman	.60	1.50
9 Aaron Graham	.80	2.00
10 Luther Hardin	.60	1.50
11 Jason Jenkins	.60	1.50
12 Clester Johnson	.60	1.50
13 Jeff Makovicka	.60	1.50
14 Brian Nunns	.60	1.50
15 Steve Ott	.60	1.50
16 Aaron Penland	.60	1.50
17 Christian Peter	.80	2.00
18 Darren Schmadeke	.60	1.50
19 Tony Veland	.60	1.50
20 Steve Volin	.60	1.50
21 Tyrone Williams	.80	2.00
22 Checklist Card Team Logo	.60	1.50

1996 Nebraska Schedules

These "cards" are actually pocket schedules issued by the school. The cardfronts feature a Nebraska player in a color photo with the year and the player's name noted. The cardbacks include the team's 1996 football schedules along with a Star City or JC Penney sponsorship logo.

1 Damon Benning	.40	1.00
2 Michael Booker	.60	1.50
3 Chris Dishman	.60	1.50
4 Terrell Farley	.40	1.00
5 Brendan Holbein	.60	1.50
6 Mike Minter	.40	1.00
7 Tom Osborne CO	1.00	2.50
8 Jared Tomich	.40	1.00
9 Jamel Williams	.40	1.00

1996-97 Nebraska

This 21-card standard-size set was produced by Nebraska and features athletes from all sports. The set features primarily football players, but a variety of other sports as well. We've included initials after each player's name that represent the sport in which they played.

COMPLETE SET (21)	10.00	20.00
1 Damon Benning FB	.50	1.25
2 Michael Booker FB	.60	1.50
3 Chris Dishman FB	.60	1.50
4 Jon Hesse FB	.50	1.25
5 Brendan Holbein FB	.50	1.25
6 Mike Minter FB	.50	1.25
7 Jeff Ogard FB	.50	1.25
8 Scott Saltsman FB	.50	1.25
9 Jared Tomich FB	.50	1.25
10 Matt Turman FB	.50	1.25

1997 Nebraska

The 26-card Nebraska standard-size set was produced by Homeworks Unlimited and was sold in set form. The seniors from the 1996-97 Nebraska team are included in the set, as well as a checklist card. While the players' uniform number is listed on each of these cards, they are arranged in alphabetical order below. Each plastic card has a fascimile autograph on the front.

COMPLETE SET (26)	10.00	25.00
1 David Alderman	.40	1.00
2 Damon Benning	.40	1.00
3 Chad Blahak	.40	1.00
4 Michael Booker	.60	1.50
5 Chris Dishman	.40	1.00
6 Chad Eicher	.40	1.00
7 Terrell Farley	.40	1.00
8 Mike Fullman	.40	1.00
9 Jon Hesse	.40	1.00
10 Brendan Holbein	.40	1.00
11 Kory Mikos	.40	1.00
12 Bryce Miller	.40	1.00
13 Mike Minter	1.25	3.00
14 Jeff Ogard	.40	1.00
15 Mike Roberts	.40	1.00
16 Scott Saltsman	.40	1.00
17 Brian Schuster	.40	1.00
18 Eric Stokes	.40	1.00
19 Ryan Terwilliger	.60	1.50
20 Jared Tomich	.60	1.50
21 Adam Treu	.40	1.00
22 Matt Turman	.60	1.50
23 Jon Vedral	.40	1.00
24 Matt Vrzal	.40	1.00
25 Jamel Williams	.40	1.00
26 Huskers Logo CL	.40	1.00

1997 Nebraska Schedules

These "cards" are actually pocket schedules issued by the school. The cardfronts feature a Nebraska player in a color photo with the year and the player's name noted. The cardbacks include the team's 1997 football schedules along with a Star City or JC Penney sponsorship logo.

COMPLETE SET (8)	5.00	12.00
1 Eric Anderson	.40	1.00
2 Kis Brown Jesse Kosch	.60	1.50
3 Scott Frost	.40	1.00
4 Ahman Green	1.25	3.00
5 Tom Osborne CO	1.00	2.50
6 Jason Peter	.60	1.50
7 Aaron Taylor	.60	1.50
8 Grant Wistrom	.60	1.50

1997-98 Nebraska

This 21-card standard-size set featured players who were seniors at Nebraska. The set features primarily football players, but a variety of other sports as well. We've included initials after each player's name that represent the sport in which they played.

COMPLETE SET (21)	10.00	20.00
1 Eric Anderson FB	.60	1.50
2 Scott Frost FB	.75	2.00
3 Matt Hoskinson FB	.60	1.50
4 Vershan Jackson FB	.60	1.50
5 Jason Peter FB	.75	2.00
6 Fred Pollack FB	.60	1.50
7 Aaron Taylor FB	.60	1.50
8 Eric Warfield FB	.60	1.50
9 Grant Wistrom FB	1.25	3.00
10 Jon Zatechka FB	.60	1.50

1998 Nebraska

The 1998 Nebraska set was produced by Homeworks Unlimited and issued with a total of 25-cards. The cards feature full-bleed color photos with the player's autograph and jersey number on the front. The cards are unnumbered and checklisted below in alphabetical order.

COMPLETE SET (25)	10.00	25.00
1 Eric Anderson	.40	1.00
2 Jason Benes	.40	1.00
3 Tim Carpenter	.40	1.00
4 Jay Gates	.40	1.00
5 Kyle Henson	.40	1.00
6 Matt Hoskinson	.40	1.00
7 Vershan Jackson	.75	2.00
8 Jesse Kosch	.40	1.00
9 Jeff Lake	.40	1.00
10 Curt Lenners	.40	1.00
11 Octavious McFarlin	.40	1.00
12 Tom Osborne CO	1.25	3.00
13 Jason Peter	.75	2.00
14 Fred Pollack	.40	1.00
15 Ted Retzlaff	.40	1.00
16 Doug Seaman	.40	1.00
17 Jay Sims	.40	1.00
18 Aaron Taylor	.75	2.00
19 Mike Van Cleave	.40	1.00
20 Eric Warfield	1.00	2.50
21 Sean Wieting	.40	1.00
22 Grant Wistrom	1.50	4.00
23 Jon Zatechka	.40	1.00
24 Team Photo	.60	1.50
25 Checklist	.40	1.00

1998 Nebraska Schedules

These "cards" are actually pocket schedules issued by the school. The cardfronts feature a Nebraska player in a color photo with the year and the player's name noted. The cardbacks include the team's 1998 football schedules along with a Star City or Nebraska Bankers sponsorship logo.

COMPLETE SET (7)	3.00	8.00
1 Kris Brown	.60	1.50
2 Jay Foreman	.40	1.00
3 Josh Heskew	.40	1.00
4 Chad Kelsay	.60	1.50
5 Joel Makovicka	.60	1.50
6 Mike Rucker	.60	1.50
7 Frank Solich CO	.40	1.00

1998-99 Nebraska

This 21-card set was sponsored by Union Bank and Trust Co, University of Nebraska-Lincoln and the Lincoln Police Department. Each includes a color photo of the player surrounded by a red and gray border with the the year "98 and '99" printed on the front. The unnumbered backs are a simple black print on white card stock. The set features primarily football players, but a variety of other sports as well. We've included initials after each player's name that represent the sport in which they played.

COMPLETE SET (21)	10.00	20.00
1 Kris Brown FB	1.25	3.00
2 Monte Cristo FB	.50	1.25
5 Jay Foreman FB	.50	1.25
7 Josh Heskew FB	.50	1.25
8 Sheldon Jackson FB	.50	1.25
10 Chad Kelsay FB	.60	1.50
11 Bill Lafleur FB	.50	1.25
13 Joel Makovicka FB	.75	2.00
19 Mike Rucker FB	.75	2.00
20 Shevin Wiggins FB	.30	.75

1999 Nebraska

The 1999 Nebraska set was again produced by Homeworks Unlimited and included 28-cards. The cards feature full-bleed color photos with the player's facsimile autograph and the team logo on the front. The cards are unnumbered and checklisted below in alphabetical order.

COMPLETE SET (28)	15.00	25.00
1 Sean Applegate	.40	1.00
2 Matt Baldwin	.40	1.00
3 Mike Brown	.75	2.00
4 Ralph Brown	.40	1.00
5 Ben Buettenback	.40	1.00
6 T.J. DeBates	.40	1.00
7 Aaron Havlovic	.40	1.00
8 Larry Henderson	.60	1.50
9 Julius Jackson	.60	1.50
10 Eric Johnson	.60	1.50
11 Adam Julch	.40	1.00
12 Ben Kingston	.40	1.00
13 Gregg List	.40	1.00
14 Frankie London	.40	1.00
15 Charlie McBride Asst. CO	.40	1.00
16 Greg McGraw	.40	1.00
17 Christopher Moran	.40	1.00
18 Tony Ortiz	.40	1.00
19 Jeff Perino	.40	1.00
20 Steve Raymond	.40	1.00
21 Eric Ryan	.40	1.00
22 Brian Shaw	.40	1.00
23 James Sherman	.40	1.00
24 Frank Solich CO	.60	1.50
25 Steve Warren	.40	1.00
26 Aaron Wills	.40	1.00
27 Stadium Skybox	.40	1.00
28 Checklist Card	.40	1.00

1999 Nebraska Schedules

These "cards" are actually pocket schedules issued by the school. The cardfronts feature a Nebraska player in a color photo with the year noted as well as the player's name. The cardbacks include the team's 1999 football schedule along with a Star City sponsorship logo.

COMPLETE SET (8)	3.00	6.00
1 Mike Brown	.75	2.00
2 Ralph Brown	.40	1.00
3 Eric Johnson	.60	1.50
4 Tony Ortiz	.40	1.00
5 Brian Shaw	.40	1.00
6 Shevin Wiggins	.40	1.00
7 Lil' Red	.40	1.00
8 Offensive Line Russ Hochstein Adam Julch Dominic Raiola Jason Schwab James Sherman Dave Volk	.40	1.00

1999-00 Nebraska

This 19-card set was sponsored by Union Bank and Trust Co, University of Nebraska-Lincoln and the Lincoln Police Department. The set features a variety of sports and we have the put an appropriate initial after each player's name.

COMPLETE SET (19)	6.00	12.00
1 Mike Brown FB	1.50	4.00
2 Ralph Brown FB	.40	1.00
3 T.J. DeBates FB	.40	1.00
7 Julius Jackson FB	.50	1.25
12 Tony Ortiz FB	.40	1.00
15 Brian Shaw FB	.40	1.00
16 James Sherman FB	.40	1.00
19 Steve Warren FB	.40	1.00

2000 Nebraska All-Time Greats

The 2000 Nebraska All-Time Greats set was produced by Homeworks Unlimited and issued with a total of 27-cards. The cards feature full-bleed color photos with the player's autograph on the front. The cards are unnumbered and checklisted below in alphabetical order. Note: #T26 released as #T1.

COMPLETE SET (27)	12.00	30.00
T1 Trev Alberts	.50	1.25
T2 Rik Bonness	.40	1.00
T3 Tommie Frazier	.80	2.00
T4 Turner Gill	.50	1.25
T5 Hugh Rhea	.40	1.00
T6 Johnny Rodgers	.80	2.00
T7 Jason Peter	.50	1.25
T8 Junior Miller	.40	1.00
T9 Steve Taylor	.40	1.00
T10 Aaron Graham	.40	1.00
T11 Forrest Behm	.40	1.00
T12 Guy Chamberlin	.40	1.00
T13 Vince Ferragamo	.80	2.00
T14 David Humm	.40	1.00
T15 Larry Jacobson	.40	1.00
T16 Tony Jeter	.40	1.00
T17 Tom Novak	.40	1.00
T18 Bob Reynolds	.40	1.00
T19 Jerry Tagge	.40	1.00
T20 Ed Weir	.40	1.00
T21 Daryl White	.40	1.00
T22 Dean Steinkuhler	.40	1.00
T23 Jeff Kinney	.40	1.00
T24 Kenny Walker	.40	1.00
T25 Mike Rozier	.50	1.25
T26 Grant Wistrom	.80	2.00
NNO Header Checklist	.40	1.00

2000 Nebraska Legends

This set features Nebraska football all-time greats produced with a red and blue colored artist's rendering of the player. Each card measures roughly 2 5/8" by 3 3/4" and features rounded corners.

COMPLETE SET (8)	4.00	10.00
1 Sam Francis	.40	1.00
2 Ahman Green	.75	2.00
3 Calvin Jones	.50	1.25
4 Jeff Kinney	.40	1.00
5 Bob Reynolds	.40	1.00
6 Tom Rathman	.60	1.50
7 Mike Rozier	.60	1.50
8 Frank Solich	.40	1.00

2000 Nebraska Schedules

These "cards" are actually pocket schedules issued by the school. The cardfronts feature a Nebraska player in a color photo with the year and school noted at the top of the card and the player's name at the bottom. The cardbacks include the team's 2000 and 2001 football schedules along with a Star City or Nebraska Bankers sponsorship logo.

COMPLETE SET (12)	5.00	12.00
1 Dan Alexander	.60	1.50
2 Correll Buckhalter	.75	2.00
3 Matt Davison	.40	1.00
4 Clint Finley	.30	.75
5 Dan Hadenfeldt	.30	.75
6 Russ Hochstein	.30	.75
7 Loran Kaiser	.30	.75
8 Willie Miller	.30	.75
9 Bobby Newcombe	.60	1.50
10 Carlos Polk	.40	1.00
11 Jason Schwab	.30	.75
12 Kyle Vanden Bosch	.75	2.00

2000-01 Nebraska

This 20-card standard-size features star athletes from Nebraska. The set features primarily football players, but a variety of other sports as well. We've included initials after each player's name that represent the sport in which they played.

COMPLETE SET (20)	8.00	20.00
1 Dan Alexander FB	1.00	2.50
2 Matt Davison FB	.60	1.50
3 Russ Hochstein FB	.60	1.50
4 Bobby Newcombe FB	1.00	2.50
5 Carlos Polk FB	.75	2.00

2001 Nebraska

The 2001 Nebraska set was again produced by Homeworks Unlimited and included 24-cards of Husker Seniors. The cards feature full-bleed color photos with the player's facsimile autograph and the team logo on the front. The cards are unnumbered and checklisted below in alphabetical order.

COMPLETE SET (24)	15.00	25.00
1 Steve Altstadt	.40	1.00
2 Mic Boettner	.40	1.00
3 Dion Booker	.60	1.50
4 Jamie Burrow	.40	1.00
5 Keyuo Craver	.60	1.50
6 Eric Crouch	1.50	4.00
7 Eric Crouch Heisman	1.50	4.00
8 Tim Demerath	.40	1.00
9 John Gibson	.40	1.00
10 Nick Gragert	.40	1.00
11 Jeff Hemje	.40	1.00
12 Matt Ickes	.40	1.00
13 Kyle Kollmorgen	.40	1.00
14 Casey Nelson	.40	1.00
15 Jon Rutherford	.40	1.00
16 Carl Scholting	.40	1.00
17 Jeremy Slechta	.40	1.00
18 Erwin Swiney	.40	1.00
19 Mark Vedral	.60	1.50
20 Dave Volk	.40	1.00
21 J.P. Wichmann	.40	1.00
22 Tracey Wistrom	.75	2.00
23 Wes Woodward	.40	1.00
24 Checklist Card	.40	1.00

2001 Nebraska Schedules

These pocket schedules were issued by the school and measure roughly 2 1/4" by 3 5/8." The fronts feature a Nebraska player in a color photo with the year and school logo at the top of the card and the player's name below. The cardbacks include the team's 2001 football schedule along with an Alltel or Star City sponsorship logo.

COMPLETE SET (12)	5.00	12.00
1 Dion Booker	.40	1.00
2 Jamie Burrow	.30	.75
3 Keyuo Craver	.40	1.00
4 Eric Crouch	1.25	3.00
5 John Gibson	.40	1.00
6 Jason Lohr	.30	.75
7 Jon Rutherford	.30	.75
8 Jeremy Slechta	.30	.75
9 Erwin Swiney	.30	.75
10 Mark Vedral	.40	1.00
11 Dave Volk	.30	.75
12 Tracey Wistrom	.60	1.50

2002 Nebraska Schedules

These pocket schedules were issued by the school and measure roughly 2 1/4" by 3 5/8." The fronts feature a Nebraska player in a color photo with the year and school logo at the top of the card along with the player's name. The cardbacks include the team's 2002 football schedule along with an Alltel, Star City, or Nebraska Bankers sponsorship logo.

COMPLETE SET (15)	5.00	12.00
1 Demoine Adams	.30	.75
2 Josh Brown	.30	.75
3 Joe Clanton	.30	.75
4 Wes Cody	.30	.75
5 Thunder Collins	.40	1.00
6 Ben Cornelsen	.30	.75
7 Dahrran Diedrick	.40	1.00
8 John Garrison	.30	.75
9 Aaron Golliday	.30	.75
10 DeJuan Groce	.30	.75
11 Troy Hassebroek	.30	.75
12 Chris Kelsay	.40	1.00
13 Jason Lohr	.30	.75
14 Scott Shanle	.40	1.00
15 Wilson Thomas	.30	.75

2003 Nebraska Schedules

These pocket schedules were issued by the school and measure roughly 2 1/4" by 3 5/8." The fronts feature a Nebraska player in a horizontal format with the year and school logo to the left and the player's name to the right. The cardbacks include the team's 2003 football schedule along with an Alltel, Star City, or Nebraska Bankers sponsorship logo.

COMPLETE SET (12)	5.00	10.00
1 Ryon Bingham	.50	1.25
2 Judd Davies	.60	1.50
3 Josh Davis	.60	1.50
4 T.J. Hollowell	.50	1.25
5 Trevor Johnson	.50	1.25
6 Patrick Kabongo	.50	1.25
7 Kyle Larson	.40	1.00
8 Jason Lohr	.40	1.00
9 Jammal Lord	.50	1.25
10 Pat Ricketts	.40	1.00
11 Dan Vili Waldop	.40	1.00
12 Demorrio Williams	.60	1.50

2004 Nebraska Schedules

These pocket schedules were issued by the school and measure roughly 2 1/4" by 3 5/8." The fronts feature a Nebraska player in a vertical format with the year below the photo and the school logo above. The cardbacks include the team's 2004 football schedule along with sponsorship logos.

COMPLETE SET (5)	1.00	2.50
1 Josh Bullocks	.40	1.25
2 Matt Herian	.30	.75
3 Richie Incognito	.20	.50
4 Lornell McPherson	.20	.50
5 Barrett Ruud	.30	.75

2005 Nebraska Schedules

These pocket schedules were issued by the school and measure roughly 2 1/4" by 3 5/8." The fronts feature a Nebraska player in a vertical format with his name and position below the photo along with the school logo. The cardbacks include the team's 2005 football schedule along with sponsorship logos.

COMPLETE SET (11)	2.00	5.00
1 Titus Adams	.20	.50
2 Stewart Bradley	.30	.75
3 Daniel Bullocks	.30	.75
4 Adam Carriker	.20	.50
5 Seppo Evwaraye	.20	.50
6 Matt Herian	.30	.75
7 Brandon Koch	.20	.50
8 Sam Koch	.20	.50
9 Kurt Mann	.20	.50
10 Cory Ross	.30	.75
11 LeKevin Smith	.20	.50

2006 Nebraska Schedules

These pocket schedules were issued by the school and measure roughly 2 1/4" by 3 5/8." The fronts feature a Nebraska player in a color photo with the player's name and position below. The cardbacks include the team's 2006 football schedule along with various sponsorship logos.

COMPLETE SET (9)	2.00	5.00
1 Greg Austin	.20	.50
2 Zackary Bowman	.20	.50
3 Stewart Bradley	.30	.75
4 Adam Carriker	.20	.50
5 Matt Herian	.20	.50
6 Kurt Mann	.20	.50
7 Jay Moore	.20	.50
8 Zac Taylor	.40	1.00
9 Dane Todd	.20	.50

2007 Nebraska Schedules

These pocket schedules were issued by the school and measure roughly 2 1/4" by 3 5/8." The fronts feature a Nebraska player in a color photo with the player's name and team name as well. The cardbacks include the team's 2007 football schedule along with various sponsorship logos.

COMPLETE SET (10)	2.00	5.00
1 Zachary Bowman	.20	.50
2 Brett Byford	.20	.50
3 Tierre Green	.20	.50
4 Cortney Grixby	.20	.50
5 Andre Jones	.20	.50
6 Corey McKeon	.20	.50
7 Terrence Nunn	.30	.75
8 J.B. Phillips	.20	.50
9 Maurice Purify	.30	.75
10 Bo Ruud	.30	.75

2008 Nebraska Schedules

These pocket schedules were issued by the school and measure roughly 2 1/4" by 3 5/8." The fronts feature a Nebraska player in a color photo with the player's name and team logo. The cardbacks include the team's 2008 football schedule along with various sponsorship logos.

COMPLETE SET (12)	2.50	6.00
1 Joe Ganz	.40	1.00
2 Mike Huff	.20	.50
3 Marlon Lucky	.30	.75
4 Armando Murillo	.20	.50
5 Lydon Murtha	.20	.50
6 Todd Peterson	.30	.75
7 Zach Potter	.20	.50
8 Matt Slauson	.20	.50
9 Ty Steinkuhler	.20	.50
10 Nate Swift	.30	.75
11 Dan Titchener	.20	.50
12 Barry Turner	.20	.50

2008 Nebraska TK Legacy

COMPLETE SET (25)	7.50	15.00
N1 Grant Campbell	.30	.75
N2 Dennis Claridge	.30	.75
N3 Eric Crouch	.50	1.25
N4 Fred Duda	.30	.75
N5 I.M. Hipp	.30	.75
N6 Tony Jeter	.30	.75
N7 Frankie London	.30	.75
N8 Mark Mauer	.30	.75
N9 Maury Damkroger	.30	.75
N10 Jerry Murtaugh	.30	.75
N11 Clete Pillen	.30	.75
N12 Johnny Rodgers	.50	1.25
N13 Mike Rozier	.50	1.25
N14 Freeman White III	.30	.75
N15 Steve Damkroger	.30	.75
N16 Steve Taylor	.30	.75
N17 Craig Sundberg	.30	.75
N18 Jerry Tagge	.40	1.00
N19 Turner Gill	.30	.75
N20 Harry Tolly	.30	.75
N21 Kerry Weinmaster	.30	.75
N22 Freeman White Jr.	.30	.75
N23 Ralph Damkroger	.30	.75
CL1 Checklist 1	.20	.50
CL2 Checklist 2	.20	.50

2008 Nebraska TK Legacy All-American Autographs

AA1 Eric Crouch	20.00	40.00
AA2 Tony Jeter	12.50	25.00
AA3 Jerry Murtaugh	12.50	25.00
AA4 Johnny Rodgers	20.00	40.00
AA5 Mike Rozier	15.00	30.00
AA6 Jerry Tagge	15.00	30.00
AA7 Steve Taylor	12.50	25.00
AA8 Freeman White Jr.	12.50	25.00

2008 Nebraska TK Legacy Black Shirt Brigade Autographs

BS1 Steve Damkroger
BS2 Kerry Weinmaster
BS3 Jerry Murtaugh
BS4 Clete Pillen

2008 Nebraska TK Legacy Eric Crouch Tribute

COMPLETE SET (4)	5.00	12.00
COMMON CROUCH	1.25	3.00

2008 Nebraska TK Legacy Gamebreaker Autographs

GB1 Turner Gill	40.00	80.00
GB2 I.M. Hipp	30.00	60.00
GB3 Mike Rozier	40.00	80.00

2008 Nebraska TK Legacy Heisman Heroes Autographs

HH1 Mike Rozier
Johnny Rodgers
Eric Crouch

2008 Nebraska TK Legacy Huskers Autographs

C1 Grant Campbell	5.00	12.00
C2 Dennis Claridge	5.00	12.00
C3 Eric Crouch	10.00	20.00
C4 Fred Duda	5.00	12.00
C5 I.M. Hipp	5.00	12.00
C6 Tony Jeter	5.00	12.00
C7 Frankie London	5.00	12.00
C8 Mark Mauer	5.00	12.00
C9 Maury Damkroger	5.00	12.00
C10 Jerry Murtaugh	5.00	12.00
C11 Clete Pillen	5.00	12.00
C12 Johnny Rodgers	10.00	20.00
C13 Mike Rozier	6.00	15.00
C14 Freeman White III	5.00	12.00
C15 Steve Damkroger	5.00	12.00
C16 Steve Taylor	5.00	12.00
C17 Craig Sundberg	5.00	12.00
C18 Jerry Tagge	6.00	15.00
C19 Turner Gill	6.00	15.00
C20 Harry Tolly	5.00	12.00
C21 Kerry Weinmaster	5.00	12.00
C22 Freeman White Jr.	5.00	12.00

2008 Nebraska TK Legacy Johnny Rodgers Tribute

COMPLETE SET (4)	5.00	12.00
COMMON RODGERS	1.25	3.00

2008 Nebraska TK Legacy Lincoln Links Autographs

LL1 Fred Duda Freeman White Jr.	15.00	40.00
LL2 Turner Gill Craig Sundberg	25.00	50.00
LL4 Freeman White III Freeman White Jr.	15.00	40.00
LL5 Steve Damkroger Maury Damkroger	15.00	40.00

2008 Nebraska TK Legacy Mike Rozier Tribute

COMPLETE SET (4)	5.00	12.00
COMMON ROZIER	1.25	3.00

2008 Nebraska TK Legacy N-Stat Autographs

ST1 Grant Campbell/100	15.00	30.00
ST2 Eric Crouch/100	25.00	50.00
ST3 Turner Gill/100	20.00	40.00
ST4 I.M. Hipp/100	15.00	30.00
ST5 Clete Pillen/100	15.00	30.00
ST6 Mike Rozier/100	20.00	40.00
ST7 Mike Rozier/100	20.00	40.00
ST9 Steve Taylor/100	15.00	30.00
ST10 Kerry Weinmaster/100	15.00	30.00
ST11 I.M. Hipp/75	15.00	30.00

2008 Nebraska TK Legacy National Titles

COMPLETE SET (5)	4.00	10.00
NC1 1970	.75	2.00
NC2 1971	.75	2.00
NC3 1994	.75	2.00
NC4 1995	.75	2.00
NC5 1997	.75	2.00

2008 Nebraska TK Legacy Nebraska vs. Oklahoma

COMPLETE SET (3)	2.50	6.00
G1 1971 Nebraska Vs. Oklahoma	.75	2.00
G2 1994 Nebraska Vs. Oklahoma	.75	2.00
G3 1996 Nebraska Vs. Oklahoma	.75	2.00

2008 Nebraska TK Legacy Playbook Autographs

PB1 Turner Gill/100 (case insert)	20.00	

2008 Nebraska TK Legacy Quarterback Club Autographs

MM Mark Mauer/100	15.00	30.00
ST Steve Taylor/100	15.00	30.00
HT Harry Tolly		

2008 Nebraska TK Legacy Statistical Leaders

L1 Mike Rozier Johnny Rodgers Eric Crouch	1.50	4.00

2008 Nebraska TK Legacy Turner Gill Tribute

COMPLETE SET (4)	5.00	12.00
COMMON GILL	1.25	3.00

2010 Nebraska Schedules

1 Pierre Allen	.20	.50
2 Tyrone Fahie	.20	.50
3 Thomas Grove	.20	.50
4 Roy Helu	.20	.50
5 Alex Henery	.20	.50
6 Will Henry	.20	.50
7 D.J. Jones	.20	.50
8 Adi Kunalic	.20	.50
9 Latravis Washington	.20	.50
10 Adam Watson	.20	.50
11 Keith Williams	.20	.50
12 Dreu Young	.20	.50

1998 New Mexico

Sponsored by First State Bank, the cards in this set were issued as a perforated sheet with each card measuring standard size went separated. The First State Bank logo appears on the cardfronts which feature a white border on the current players and a wood frame border on the all-time greats. The black and white cardbacks include the player's name, a short bio and career highlights. The cards are unnumbered and checklisted below in alphabetical order.

COMPLETE SET (19)	12.50	25.00
1 Jason Bloom	.20	.50
2 Bill Borchers	.20	.50
3 Stoney Case ATG	.30	.75
4 Robin Cole ATG	.30	.75
5 Barrett Garrison	.20	.50
6 Lennox Gordon	.20	.50
7 Che Johnson	.20	.50
8 Reginal Johnson	.20	.50
9 Graham Leigh	.30	.75
10 Kenny Lewis	.20	.50
11 Rocky Long ATG CO	.20	.50
12 Dion Marion	.20	.50
13 Terance Mathis ATG	.40	1.00
14 Derrick Milner	.20	.50
15 Chad Smith	.20	.50
16 Brian Urlacher	10.00	20.00
17 Chris Wallace	.20	.50
18 1964 Team Photo	.20	.50
19 First State Bank Ad	.20	.50

1999 New Mexico

Sponsored by First State Bank, the cards in this set were issued as a perforated sheet with each card measuring standard size went separated. The First State Bank logo appears on the cardfronts which feature a red border. The black, red and white cardbacks include the player's name, a short bio and career statistics. The cards are unnumbered and checklisted below in alphabetical order.

COMPLETE SET (18)	10.00	20.00
1 Mike Barnett	.20	.50
2 Jarrod Baxter	.30	.75
3 Walter Bernard	.20	.50
4 Josh Brown	.20	.50
5 Jason Carson	.20	.50
6 Eric Jaworsky	.20	.50
7 Reginal Johnson	.20	.50
8 Rocky Long CO	.20	.50
9 Jeff Macrea	.20	.50
10 Marcus McDavid	.20	.50
11 Jason Purvis	.20	.50
12 Henry Stephens	.20	.50
13 Germany Thompson	.20	.50
14 Casey Tisdale	.20	.50
15 Brian Urlacher	7.50	15.00
16 Stacy Washington	.20	.50
17 Martinez Williams	.20	.50
18 Lobos Team	.20	.50

2000 New Mexico

Sponsored by First State Bank, the cards in this set were issued as a perforated sheet with each card measuring standard size went separated. The First State Bank logo appears at the top of the cardfronts which also include a red border and the year 2000 at the bottom. The black, red and white cardbacks include the player's name, a short bio and career statistics. The cards are unnumbered and checklisted below in alphabetical order.

COMPLETE SET (20)	4.00	10.00
1 Mike Barnett	.20	.50
2 Jarrod Baxter	.30	.75
3 Walter Bernard	.20	.50
4 Jonathan Burrough	.20	.50
5 Rob Caston	.20	.50
6 Larry Davis	.20	.50
7 Rantle Harper	.20	.50
8 Ted Lacenda	.20	.50
9 Brian Johnson	.20	.50
10 Rocky Long CO	.20	.50
11 Jeff Macrea	.20	.50
12 David Mauer	.20	.50
13 Rashad McClure	.20	.50
14 Justin Mobley	.20	.50
15 Charles Moss	.20	.50
16 Jon Samuelson	.20	.50
17 Jeremy Sorenson	.20	.50
18 Henry Stephens	.20	.50
19 Holmon Wiggins	.20	.50
20 First State Bank Ad	.20	.50

2001 New Mexico

Sponsored by First State Bank, the cards in this set were issued as a perforated sheet with each card measuring standard size went separated. The First State Bank logo appears at the bottom of the cardfronts which also include a red and black border and the year 2001 at the top. The black, red and white cardbacks include the player's name, a short bio and career statistics. The cards are unnumbered and checklisted below in alphabetical order.

COMPLETE SET (20)	4.00	10.00
1 Jarrod Baxter	.30	.75
2 Vladimir Borombozin	.20	.50
3 Rudy Caamano	.20	.50
4 Dwight Counter	.20	.50
5 Gary Davis	.20	.50
6 Scott Gerhardt	.20	.50
7 Terrell Golden	.20	.50
8 Javier Hanson	.20	.50
9 Brian Johnson	.20	.50
10 Mohammed Konte	.20	.50
11 B.J. Long	.20	.50
12 Rocky Long CO	.20	.50
13 Antonio Manning	.20	.50
14 Tony Mazotti	.20	.50
15 Rashad McClure	.20	.50
16 Charles Moss	.20	.50
17 Stephen Persley	.20	.50
18 Kirk Robbins	.20	.50
19 Jeremy Sorenson	.20	.50
20 Holmon Wiggins	.20	.50

2002 New Mexico

Sponsored by First State Bank, the cards in this set were initially issued as a perforated sheet with each card measuring standard size went separated. The First State Bank logo appears at the bottom of the cardfronts which also include a red and black border with no year mentioned. The black, red and white cardbacks include the player's name, a short bio and career statistics. The cards are unnumbered and checklisted below in alphabetical order.

COMPLETE SET (20)	4.00	10.00
1 Desmar Black	.20	.50
2 Dwight Counter	.20	.50
3 David Crockett	.20	.50
4 Jake Farrel	.20	.50
5 Terrell Golden	.20	.50
6 Brandon Gregory	.20	.50
7 David Hall	.20	.50
8 Hebrews Josue	.20	.50
9 Daniel Kegler	.20	.50
10 Casey Kelly	.30	.75
11 Shannon Kincaid	.20	.50
12 Jason Lenzmeier	.20	.50
13 Joe Manning	.20	.50
14 Justin Millea	.30	.75
15 Charles Moss	.20	.50
16 Bryan Penley	.20	.50
17 D.J. Renteria	.20	.50
18 Nick Speegle	.20	.50
19 Claude Terrell	.20	.50
20 Quincy Wright	.20	.50

2003 New Mexico

Sponsored by First State Bank, the cards in this set were issued as a perforated sheet with each card measuring standard size went separated. The First State Bank logo appears at the bottom of the cardfronts which also include a red and silver border but no year designation. The black, red, silver and white cardbacks include the player's name, a longt bio and career statistics. The cards are unnumbered and checklisted below in alphabetical order.

COMPLETE SET (20)	4.00	10.00
1 Adrian Boyd	.20	.50
2 Justin Colburn	.20	.50
3 Dwight Counter	.20	.50
4 Fola Fashola	.20	.50
5 Daniel Gawronski	.20	.50
6 Terrell Golden	.20	.50
7 Katie Hnida	.40	1.00
8 Daniel Kegler	.20	.50
9 Casey Kelly	.30	.75
10 Jason Lenzmeier	.20	.50
11 DonTrell Moore	.30	.75
12 Bryan Penley	.20	.50
13 Brandon Ratcliff	.20	.50
14 D.J. Renteria	.20	.50
15 Zach Rupp	.20	.50
16 Nick Speegle	.20	.50
17 Billy Strother	.20	.50
18 Claude Terrell	.20	.50
19 Terrence Thomas	.20	.50
20 Sidney Wiley	.20	.50

1988 New Mexico State Greats

This 12-card multi-sport set was sponsored by the Charter Hospital of Santa Teresa. The cards measure approximately 2 5/8" by 4" and are printed on thin cardboard stock. On a white background with a dark red border on three sides, the fronts feature black-and-white posed or action player photos and player information. The backs have brief biographical and statistical information, a cartoon of Chum and a public service announcement. The logo and address of the sponsor round out the backs. The cards are unnumbered and checklisted below in alphabetical order.

COMPLETE SET (12)	9.00	18.00
5 Po James FB	.75	2.00
6 Charley Johnson FB	1.25	3.00
11 Fredd Young FB	.75	2.00

1909 North Carolina State Team Issue

These photos were issued by the school to promote the football program. Each measures roughly 8" by 10" and features a pair of black and white images of players with the player's name, position, and school name below each photo. The backs are blank.

COMPLETE SET (11)	50.00	100.00
1 Bill Clark Don Bradley	5.00	10.00
2 Ed Hoffman Dick Curran	5.00	10.00
3 Don Jordan Dave Rodgers	5.00	10.00
4 Pat Korsnick Pat Kenney	5.00	10.00
5 Mike Mallan Gary Moser	5.00	10.00
6 Robert McLean Gary Yount	5.00	10.00
7 Paul Sharp Jack Whitley	5.00	10.00
8 George Smith Pat Korsnick	5.00	10.00
9 Pete Sowirka Bill Miller	5.00	10.00
10 Van Walker Clyde Chesney	5.00	10.00
11 Bryan Wall Bill Millor	5.00	10.00

1979 North Carolina Schedules

This four card set was apparently issued by the Department of Athletics at North Carolina (Chapel Hill) and partially sponsored by Hardee's. The cards measure approximately 2 3/8" by 3 3/8". The card front features a full-bleed head shot of the player, with the player's name and jersey number burned into the bottom portion of the picture. The backs carry the 1979 varsity football schedule. The cards are unnumbered and checklisted below in alphabetical order.

COMPLETE SET (4)	6.00	12.00
1 Ricky Barden	1.50	3.00
2 Steve Junkman	1.50	3.00
3 Matt Kupec	2.00	4.00
4 Doug Paschal	1.50	3.00

1982 North Carolina Schedules

This eight-card set was apparently issued by the Department of Athletics at North Carolina (Chapel Hill). The cards measure approximately 2 3/8" by 3 3/8". The card front features a full-bleed head shot of the player, with the player's name and jersey number burned into the bottom portion of the picture. The backs carry the 1982 varsity football schedule. The cards are unnumbered and checklisted below in alphabetical order.

COMPLETE SET (8)	15.00	40.00
1 Kelvin Bryant	3.00	8.00
2 Alan Burrus	2.00	5.00
3 David Drechsler	2.00	5.00
4 Rod Elkins	2.00	5.00
5 Jack Parry	2.00	5.00
6 Greg Poole	2.00	5.00
7 Ron Spruill	2.00	5.00
8 Mike Wilcher	2.00	5.00

1986 North Carolina Schedules

This four-card set was apparently issued by the Department of Athletics at North Carolina (Chapel Hill). The cards measure approximately 2 3/8" by 3 3/8". The card front features a full-bleed head shot of the player, with the player's name and jersey number burned into the bottom portion of the picture. The backs carry the 1986 varsity football schedule. The cards are unnumbered and checklisted below in alphabetical order.

COMPLETE SET (4)	6.00	15.00
1 Walter Bailey	1.50	4.00
2 Harris Barton	2.50	6.00
3 C.A. Brooks	1.50	4.00
4 Eric Streater	1.50	4.00

1988 North Carolina

This 16-card set was produced by Sports Marketing and features color player portraits with sponsor logos in the top margin and player's name, jersey number, academic year, and position listed in the bottom border. The backs carry the player's name, position, jersey number, biographical and career information with team tips and sponsors listed below. The cards are unnumbered and checklisted below in alphabetical order.

COMPLETE SET (16)	6.00	15.00
1 Mack Brown CO	1.25	3.00
2 Pat Crowley	.40	1.00
3 Torin Dorn	.75	2.00
4 Jeff Garnica	.40	1.00
5 Antonio Goss	.60	1.50
6 Jonathan Hall	.60	1.50
7 Darrell Hamilton	.40	1.00
8 Creighton Incorminias	.40	1.00
9 John Keller	.40	1.00
10 Randy Marriott	.40	1.00
11 Deems May	.60	1.50
12 John Reed	.40	1.00
13 James Thompson	.60	1.50
14 Steve Steinbacher	.40	1.00
15 Dan Vooletich	.40	1.00
16 Mitch Wike	.40	1.00

1990-91 North Carolina Collegiate Collection Promos

This ten-card set features various sports stars of North Carolina from recent years. Since this set features athletes from more than one sport we have put a two letter abbreviation next to the player's name which identifies the sport he plays. This set includes a Michael Jordan card. All the cards in the set feature full-color photos of the athletes on the front along with either a biography or statistics of the players pictured on the card.

COMPLETE SET (10)	3.00	8.00
NC2 Ethan Horton FB	.10	.30
NC4 Mark Maye FB	.08	.25
NC6 Tyrone Anthony FB	.08	.25
NC8 Kelvin Bryant FB	.10	.30
NC10 Kenan Stadium	.08	.25

1990-91 North Carolina Collegiate Collection Say No to Drugs

This four-card set was released in 1990. It features Herschel Walker, Michael Jordan, Johnny Unitas and Bo Jackson in their college uniforms. This set was produced by the "Collegiate Collection" and the cards state "Say no to Drugs, Yes to Life" on the back of each card. Card backs carry the prefix of the players corresponding college.

AU1 Bo Jackson

1990-91 North Carolina Collegiate Collection Say No to Drugs

GA1 Herschel Walker
LOU1 Johnny Unitas

1991 North Carolina Schedules

This three-card set was apparently issued by the Department of Athletics at North Carolina (Chapel Hill) and partially sponsored by Hardee's. The cards measure approximately 2 3/8" by 3 3/8". The card front features a full-bleed head shot of the player, with the player's name and jersey number burned into the bottom portion of the picture. The backs carry the 1991 varsity football schedule. The cards are unnumbered and checklisted below in alphabetical order.

COMPLETE SET (3)	2.80	7.00
1 Eric Gash	.80	2.00
2 Dwight Hollier	1.60	4.00
3 Tommy Thigpen	.80	2.00

1998 North Carolina

This 12-card set was issued by the school. The cards feature a color player portrait with the player's name, team name, and year listed at the bottom. The backs carry the player's vital statistics and career information. The cards are unnumbered and checklisted below in alphabetical order.

COMPLETE SET (12)	5.00	10.00
1 Dre Bly	.40	1.00
2 Na Brown	.40	1.00
3 Alge Crumpler	.75	2.00
4 Oscar Davenport	.30	.75
5 Russell Davis	.30	.75
6 Ebenezer Ekuban	.40	1.00
7 Keith Newman	.30	.75
8 Jason Peace	.30	.75
9 Mike Pringley	.40	1.00
10 Brandon Spoon	.40	1.00
11 L.C. Stevens	.30	.75
12 Carl Torbush CO	.30	.75

1999 North Carolina

This 12-card set was issued by the school. The cards feature a color player portrait with the player's name, team name, and year listed at the bottom. The backs carry the player's vital statistics and career information. The cards are unnumbered and checklisted below in alphabetical order.

COMPLETE SET (12)	5.00	10.00
1 Kory Bailey	.40	1.00
2 Rufus Brown	.30	.75
3 Alge Crumpler	.75	2.00
4 Ronald Curry	.60	1.50
5 Deon Dyer	.40	1.00
6 Bryan Jones	.30	.75
7 Sedrick Hodge	.40	1.00
8 Josh McGee	.30	.75
9 Jason Peace	.30	.75
10 Sherrod Peace	.30	.75
11 Brian Schmitz	.30	.75
12 Brandon Spoon	.40	1.00

2000 North Carolina

This 12-card set was issued by the school. The cards feature a color player portrait with the player's name below and the team name and year above the photo. The backs carry the player's vital statistics and career information. Julius Peppers appears on his first card in this set. The cards are unnumbered and checklisted below in alphabetical order.

COMPLETE SET (12)	7.50	15.00
1 Kory Bailey	.40	1.00
2 David Bomar	.30	.75
3 Alge Crumpler	.60	1.50
4 Ronald Curry	.60	1.50
5 Billy-Dee Greenwood	.30	.75
6 Sedrick Hodge	.40	1.00
7 Errol Hood	.30	.75
8 Julius Peppers	2.50	6.00
9 Merceda Perry	.30	.75
10 Ryan Sims	.75	2.00
11 Brandon Spoon	.40	1.00
12 Carl Torbush CO	.30	.75

2000 North Carolina Schedules

These "cards" are actually pocket schedules issued by the school. The cardfronts feature a North Carolina player in a color photo with the year and the school noted at the top of the card and the player's name near the bottom. The cardbacks include the team's 2000 football schedule along with a Hardee's ad..

COMPLETE SET (10)	3.00	6.00
1 Kory Bailey	.30	.75
2 David Bomar	.20	.50
3 Alge Crumpler	.50	1.25
4 Ronald Curry	.50	1.25
5 Billy-Dee Greenwood	.20	.50
6 Errol Hood	.20	.50
7 Julius Peppers	1.00	2.50
8 Merceda Perry	.20	.50
9 Ryan Sims	.50	1.25
10 Carl Torbush CO	.20	.50

2001 North Carolina

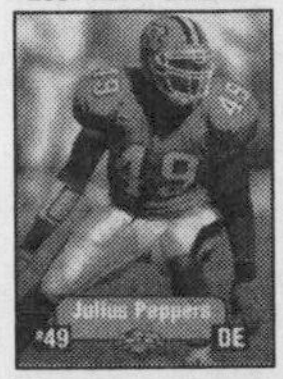

This 12-card set was issued by the school and sponsored by the Wyndham Garden Hotel. The cards feature a color player portrait with the player's name, jersey number, team logo, and position listed at the bottom. The backs carry the player's vital statistics and biographical and career information with the sponsor logo. The cards are unnumbered and checklisted below in alphabetical order.

COMPLETE SET (12)	6.00	12.00
1 Kory Bailey	.30	.75
2 John Bunting CO	.20	.50
3 Ronald Curry	.60	1.50
4 Jocy Evans	.20	.50
5 Errol Hood	.20	.50
6 Adam Metts	.20	.50
7 Quincy Monk	.20	.50
8 Julius Peppers	2.00	5.00
9 Anthony Perkins	.20	.50
10 Merceda Perry	.20	.50
11 Jeff Reed	.20	.50
12 Ryan Sims	.50	1.25

2002 North Carolina

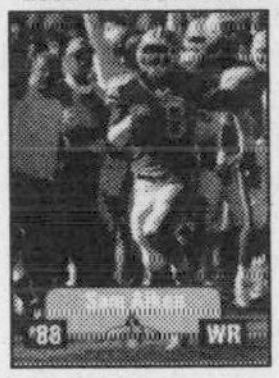

COMPLETE SET (12)	4.00	8.00
1 Sam Aiken	.40	1.00
2 Chesley Borders	.30	.75
3 DeFonte Coleman	.30	.75
4 Eric Davis	.40	1.00
5 Darian Durant	.30	.75
6 Zach Hilton	.30	.75
7 Kevin Knight	.30	.75
8 Dexter Reid	.30	.75
9 C.J. Stephens	.30	.75
10 Malcolm Stewart	.30	.75
11 Michael Waddell	.30	.75
12 John Bunting CO	.30	.75

2002 North Carolina State Philip Rivers

This large card (measuring roughly 5" by 7") was issued by NC State to promote its football program and highly rated quarterback.

1 Philip Rivers	2.00	5.00

2005 North Carolina

COMPLETE SET (12)	4.00	8.00
1 Matt Baker	.30	.75
2 Mahlon Carey	.30	.75

3 Brian Chacos	.30	.75
4 Tommy Davis	.30	.75
5 Cedrick Holt	.30	.75
6 Doug Justice	.30	.75
7 Derrele Mitchell	.30	.75
8 Chase Page	.30	.75
9 Jarwarski Pollack	.30	.75
10 Kyle Ralph	.30	.75
11 Tommy Richardson	.30	.75
12 Skip Seagraves	.30	.75

2006 North Carolina Schedules

COMPLETE SET (5)	1.00	2.50
1 Brian Chacos	.20	.50
2 Larry Edwards	.20	.50
3 Jesse Holley	.20	.50
4 Ronnie McGill	.20	.50
5 Kareen Taylor	.20	.50

2008 North Carolina

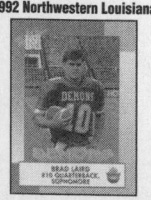

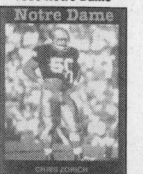

COMPLETE SET (12)	5.00	10.00
1 Terrence Brown	.30	.75
2 Butch Davis CO	.30	.75
3 Brooks Foster	.40	1.00
4 Trimane Goddard	.30	.75
5 Hakeem Nicks	.75	2.00
6 Mark Paschal	.30	.75
7 Garrett Reynolds	.30	.75
8 Chase Rice	.30	.75
9 Brandon Tate	.60	1.50
10 Deunta Williams	.30	.75
11 E.J. Wilson	.30	.75
12 T.J. Yates	.30	.75

1993 North Carolina State

These 56 standard-size cards were produced by Action Graphics. They feature on their fronts color tilted player action and posed shots set within red borders. The team's name appears reversed out of a black bar above the photo. The player's name appears in white lettering within a black bar near the bottom of the photo. The gray-bordered back carries the team name and year at the top. The player's name, position, number, biography, and career highlights follow within a white area below. The cards are unnumbered and checklisted below in alphabetical order.

COMPLETE SET (56)	10.00	25.00
1 John Akins	.20	.50
2 Darryl Beard	.20	.50
3 Ricky Bell	.20	.50
4 Geoff Bender	.20	.50
5 Chuck Browning	.20	.50
6 Chuck Cole	.20	.50
7 Chris Cotton	.20	.50
8 Eric Counts	.20	.50
9 Damien Covington	.60	1.50
10 Dallas Dickerson	.20	.50
11 Gary Downs	.20	.50
12 Brian Fitzgerald	.20	.50
13 Ed Gallon	.20	.50
14 Ledel George	.20	.50
15 Walt Gerard	.20	.50
16 Gregg Giannamore	.20	.50
17 Eddie Goines	.40	1.00
18 Ray Griffis	.20	.50
19 Mike Harrison	.20	.50
20 Terry Harvey	.20	.50
21 George Hegamin	.30	.75
22 Chris Hennie-Roed	.20	.50
23 Adrian Hill	.20	.50
24 Robert Hinton	.20	.50
25 David Inman	.20	.50
26 Dave Janik	.20	.50
27 Shawn Johnson	.20	.50
28 Tyler Lawrence	.20	.50
29 Miller Lawson	.20	.50
30 Sean Maguire	.20	.50
31 Drea Major	.20	.50
32 Mike Moore	.20	.50
33 James Newsome	.20	.50
34 Mike O'Cain CO	.30	.75
35 Loren Pinkney	.20	.50
36 Carlos Pruitt	.20	.50
37 Carl Reeves	.30	.75
38 Jon Rissler	.20	.50
39 Chad Robinson	.20	.50
40 Ryan Schultz	.20	.50
41 William Strong	.30	.75
42 Jimmy Sziksai	.20	.50
43 Eric Taylor	.20	.50
44 Pat Threatt	.20	.50
45 Steve Videtich	.20	.50
46 James Walker	.20	.50
47 Todd Ward	.20	.50
48 Dewayne Washington	1.20	3.00
49 Heath Woods	.20	.50
50 Scott Woods	.20	.50
51 Defensive Coaches	.20	.50
Buddy Green		
Kent Briggs		
Ken Pettus		
Jeff Snipes		
Henry Trevathan		
52 Offensive Coaches	.20	.50
Ted Cain		
Robbie Caldwell		
Jimmy Kiser		
Brette Simmons		
Dick Portee		
53 Tri-Captains	.30	.75
John Akins		
Todd Ward		
Dewayne Washington		
54 Carter-Finley Stadium	.20	.50
55 Checklist	.20	.50
56 Title Card	.20	.50

1994 North Carolina State

These standard-size cards feature color player shots set within red and black borders. The school name appears above the photo and the player's name and position below. The cards are unnumbered and checklisted below in alphabetical order.

COMPLETE SET (42)	7.50	15.00
1 Ricky Bell	.20	.50
2 Geoff Bender	.20	.50
3 Rod Brown	.20	.50
4 Eric Counts	.20	.50
5 Damien Covington	.20	.50
6 Dallas Dickerson	.20	.50
7 Brian Fitzgerald	.20	.50
8 Ed Gallon	.20	.50
9 Eddie Goines	.30	.75
10 Lerone Harper	.20	.50
11 Kenny Harris	.20	.50
12 Mike Harrison	.20	.50
13 Terry Harvey	.20	.50
14 Chris Hennie-Roed	.20	.50
15 Adrian Hill	.20	.50
16 Dave Janik	.20	.50
17 Allen Johnson	.20	.50
18 Steve Keim	.20	.50
19 Carlos King	.20	.50
20 Mark Lawrence	.20	.50
21 Chris Love	.20	.50
22 Drea Major	.20	.50
23 Kevin Matier	.20	.50
24 Jason McGeorge	.20	.50
25 Mike Moore	.20	.50
26 Chad Ray	.20	.50
27 Jonathan Redmond	.20	.50
28 Kenneth Redmond	.20	.50
29 Carl Reeves	.20	.50
30 Jon Rissler	.20	.50
31 Chad Robson	.20	.50
32 William Strong	.30	.75
33 Chris Tortu	.20	.50
34 Steve Videtich	.20	.50
35 James Walker	.20	.50
36 Heath Woods	.20	.50
37 Scott Woods	.20	.50
38 Mike O'Cain CO	.20	.50
39 Defensive Coaches	.20	.50
40 Offensive Coaches	.20	.50
41 Checklist	.20	.50
42 Cover Card	.20	.50

1994 North Carolina State Team Issue

These photos were issued by the school to promote the football program. Each measures roughly 8" by 10" and features two black and white images (one portrait and one action) of the player with the school name and player's name printed below the portrait. The backs are blank.

COMPLETE SET (11)	25.00	50.00
1 Geoff Bender	3.00	6.00
2 Rod Brown	3.00	6.00
3 Damien Covington	3.00	6.00
4 Eddie Goines	3.00	6.00
5 Kenny Harris	3.00	6.00
6 Terry Harvey	3.00	6.00
7 Steve Keim	3.00	6.00
8 Tyler Lawrence	3.00	6.00
9 Carl Reeves	3.00	6.00
10 Jon Rissler	3.00	6.00
11 Steve Videtich	3.00	6.00

1995 North Carolina State

These standard-size cards feature color player shots set within gray and black borders. The school name and year appears above the photo and the player's name and position below. The cards are unnumbered and checklisted below in alphabetical order.

COMPLETE SET (50)	7.50	15.00
1 Greg Addis	.20	.50
2 Ricky Bell	.20	.50
3 Terrence Boykin	.20	.50
4 Morocco Brown	.20	.50
5 Rod Brown	.20	.50
6 Kit Carpenter	.20	.50
7 Brad Collins	.20	.50
8 Bobbie Cotten	.20	.50
9 Larry Daughtry	.20	.50
10 Tom Bombalis	.20	.50
11 Jay Dukes	.20	.50
12 Duan Everett	.20	.50
13 Lonnie Gilbert	.20	.50
14 Jimmy Grissett	.20	.50
15 Mike Guffie	.20	.50
16 Lerone Harper	.20	.50
17 Kenny Harris	.20	.50
18 Mike Harrison	.20	.50
19 Terry Harvey	.20	.50
20 Allen Johnson	.20	.50
21 Steve Keim	.20	.50
22 Carlos King	.20	.50
23 Jose Laureano	.20	.50
24 Mark Lawrence	.20	.50
25 Kevin Matier	.20	.50
26 Lamont McCauley	.20	.50
27 Jason McGeorge	.20	.50
28 Steven McKnight	.20	.50
29 Ron Melnik	.20	.50
30 Seamus Murphy	.20	.50
31 Marc Primanti	.20	.50
32 Jonathan Redmond	.20	.50
33 Kenneth Redmond	.20	.50
34 Jon Rissler	.20	.50
35 Hassan Shamsid-Deen	.30	.75
36 Clayton Simon	.20	.50
37 Devon Smith	.20	.50
38 Tremayne Stephens	.20	.50
39 Mark Thomas	.20	.50
40 Chris Tortu	.20	.50
41 James Walker	.20	.50
42 Alvis Whitted	.40	1.00
43 George Williams	.20	.50
44 Damon Wyche	.20	.50
45 Mike O'Cain CO	.20	.50
46 Coordinators	.20	.50
Ken Pettus		
Ted Cain		
47 Defensive Coaching Staff	.20	.50
Kent Briggs		
Jeff Snipes		
David Turner		
48 Offensive Coaching Staff	.20	.50
Robbie Caldwell		
Jimmy Kiser		
Dick Portee		
Brette Simmons		
49 Checklist	.20	.50
50 Cover Card	.20	.50

1991-92 North Dakota

COMPLETE SET (12)	6.00	12.00
11 Football Team Photo	.40	1.00
12 Shanon Burnell	.40	1.00
Kory Wahl		
Bill Riviere		
football players		

2004 North Dakota State

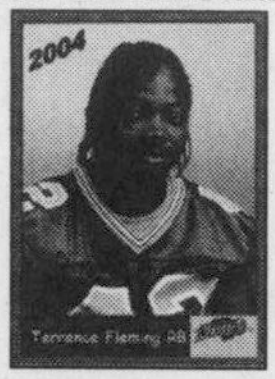

COMPLETE SET (28)	6.00	12.00
1 Allen Burrell	.20	.50
2 Tim Erickson	.20	.50
3 Tony Stauss	.20	.50
4 Charles West	.20	.50
5 Jared Essler	.20	.50
6 Matt Gorman	.20	.50
7 Kyle Ihry	.20	.50
8 Bill Wrigley	.20	.50
9 Stephen Packulak	.20	.50
10 Brian Erenberg	.20	.50
11 Terrance Fleming	.20	.50
12 Matthew Gordon-Jackson	.20	.50
13 Johnny Frank	.20	.50
14 Rob Mamula	.20	.50
15 Travis Ware	.20	.50
16 Mark Sanders	.20	.50
17 Rob Hunt	.20	.50
18 Isaac Snell	.20	.50
19 Nick Zilka	.20	.50
20 Jay Delmedico	.20	.50
21 Dwight Summerville	.20	.50
22 2003 Record	.20	.50
23 Craig Bohl CO	.20	.50
24 Great Western Conf. Logo	.20	.50
25 Assistant Coaches	.20	.50
Jimmy Burrows Jr.		
Casey Bradley		
Nelson Barnes		
Shane Richardson		
26 Assistant Coaches	.20	.50
Tim Albin		
Patrick Perles		
Brent Vigen		
Reggie Moore		
27 FargoDome	.20	.50
HA Phil Hansen	.20	.50

2005 North Dakota State

COMPLETE SET (36)	6.00	12.00
1 Derek Arndt	.20	.50
2 Bobby Babich	.20	.50
3 Craig Bohl CO	.20	.50
4 Casey Bradley Asst.CO	.20	.50
5 Justin Buckwalter	.20	.50
6 Cinque Chapman	.20	.50
7 A.J. Cooper	.20	.50
8 Craig Dahl	.20	.50
9 Andy Delabarre	.20	.50
10 Mike Dragosavich	.20	.50
11 Justin Frick	.20	.50
12 Willie Mack Garza Asst.CO	.20	.50
13 Marques Johnson	.20	.50
14 Steve Laqua Asst.CO	.20	.50
15 Isaac Lavant	.20	.50
16 Joe Mays	.20	.50
17 Hugh Medal	.20	.50
18 Reggie Moore Asst.CO	.20	.50
19 Adam Palczewski	.20	.50
20 Pat Perles	.20	.50
21 Tim Popowski	.20	.50
22 Alvin Robinson	.20	.50
23 Nate Safe	.20	.50
24 Nick Schommer	.20	.50
25 Kyle Steffes	.20	.50
26 Adam Tadisch	.20	.50
27 Rodney Thompson	.20	.50
28 Corey Vartanian	.20	.50
29 Brent Vigen Asst.CO	.20	.50
30 Steve Walker	.20	.50
31 Scott Walter	.20	.50
32 Todd Wash Asst.CO	.20	.50
33 Shamen Washington	.20	.50
34 Travis White	.20	.50
35 Kole Zimmerman	.20	.50
36 Thundar (Mascot)	.20	.50

1989 North Texas McDag

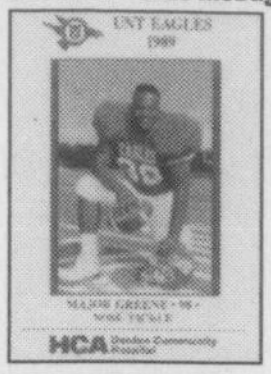

The 1989 University of North Texas McDag set contains 16 standard-size cards. The fronts have color portrait photos bordered in white; the vertically oriented backs have brief career highlights and safety tips. These cards are printed on very thin stock and are numbered on the back in the upper right corner. The cards were produced by McDag Productions and the set was co-sponsored by the Denton Community Hospital. Each card back contains "Tips from the Eagles".

COMPLETE SET (16)	3.00	8.00
1 Clay Bode	.20	.50
2 Scott Bowles	.20	.50
3 Keith Chapman	.20	.50
4 Darrin Collins	.20	.50
5 Tony Cook	.20	.50
6 Scott Davis	.30	.75
7 Byron Gross	.20	.50
8 Larry Green	.20	.50
9 Major Greene	.30	.75
10 Carl Brewer	.20	.50
11 J.D. Martinez	.20	.50
12 Charles Monroe	.20	.50
13 Kregg Sanders	.20	.50
14 Lou Smith	.20	.50
15 Jeff Tutson	.20	.50
16 Trent Touchstone	.20	.50

1990 North Texas McDag

This 16-card standard-size set was sponsored by the HCA Denton Community Hospital, whose company name appears at the bottom on both sides of the card. The front features a color posed photo, with the player in a kneeling posture and the football in his hand. The picture is framed by a thin dark green border on a white card face, with the player's name and position below the picture. In the lower left corner a North Texas Eagles' helmet appears in the school's colors, green and white. The back has biographical information and a tip from the Eagles in the form of an anti-drug or alcohol message. The set features an early card of running back Erric Pegram.

COMPLETE SET (16)	4.00	10.00
1 Scott Davis	.20	.50
2 Byron Gross	.20	.50
3 Tony Cook	.20	.50
4 Walter Casey	.20	.50
5 Erric Pegram	1.20	3.00
6 Clay Bode	.20	.50
7 Scott Bowles	.20	.50
8 Shawn Wash	.20	.50
9 Isaac Barnett	.20	.50
10 Paul Gallamore	.20	.50
11 J.D. Martinez	.20	.50
12 Velton Morgan	.20	.50
13 Major Greene	.30	.75
14 Bart Helsley	.20	.50
15 Jeff Tutson	.20	.50
16 Tony Walker	.20	.50

1974 Northwestern Team Sheets

These photos were issued by the school to promote the football program. Each measures roughly 8" by 10" and features eight black and white images of players with the school name appearing at the top. The backs are blank.

1 Rich Boothe	4.00	8.00
Wayne Frederickson		
Rob Mason		
Carl Patrnchak		
Joe Patrnchak		
Mark Ruff		
Neil Little		
Jim Trimble		
2 John Pont CO	4.00	8.00
Mitch Anderson		
Greg Boykin		
Billy Stevens		
Larry Lilja		
Paul Hiemenz		
Doug Belko		
Kenneth Shaw		

1992 Northwestern Louisiana

This 16-card set was sponsored by the USDA Forest Service, the National Association of State Foresters, and Northwestern State University of Louisiana. The cards measure approximately 2 5/8" by 3 5/8" and are printed on thin card stock. The fronts feature posed color player photos (from the waist up) that are bordered in the team's colors (purple and orange). Player information and the Smokey logo appear in a white box superimposed toward the bottom. In black on white, the backs present basic player information and a fire prevention cartoon starring Smokey. The cards are unnumbered and checklisted below in alphabetical order.

COMPLETE SET (16)	3.20	8.00
1 Darius Adams	.20	.50
2 Paul Arevalo	.20	.50
3 Brad Brown	.20	.50
4 Steve Brown	.25	.60
5 J.J. Eldridge	.20	.50
6 Sam Goodwin CO	.20	.50
7 Adrian Hardy	.25	.60
8 Guy Hedrick	.20	.50
9 Brad Laird	.20	.50
10 Lawann Latson	.20	.50
11 Deon Ridgell	.20	.50
12 Bryan Roussell	.20	.50
13 Brannon Rowlett	.20	.50
14 Marcus Spears	.30	.75
15 Carlos Treadway	.20	.50
16 Vic (Team Mascot)	.20	.50

1923 Notre Dame Postcards

Each of the postcards in this set covers a specific 1923 Notre Dame football game with the date, opponent, and final score included on the cardfront printed in blue along with a gold colored border near the card's edges. The cardbacks feature a typical postcard design with "Souvenir Post Card" printed at the top. The cards are unnumbered and listed below alphabetically. Any additions to this list are appreciated.

1 Elmer Layden	125.00	200.00
2 Don Miller	125.00	200.00
(Nov. 3, 1923)		
3 Gene Oberst	75.00	125.00
(Nov. 17, 1923)		
4 Harry Stuhldreher	125.00	200.00
(Oct. 27, 1923)		

1924 Notre Dame Postcards

Each of the postcards in this set was issued in 1924. The cardfronts were printed in blue along with a thin gold colored border near the card's edges on most. The cardbacks feature a typical postcard design with "Souvenir Post Card" printed at the top and "Published by Jay R. Masenich U.N.D." printed in blue at the bottom. The cards are unnumbered and listed below alphabetically. Any additions to this list are appreciated.

1 Football Player Artwork	30.00	60.00
(Nov.15, 1924, ND vs. Nebraska)		
2 The Four Horseman	150.00	300.00
3 Student Trip to Wisconsin	30.00	60.00
(Nov.8, 1924, ND vs. Wisconsin)		
4 Capt. Adam Walsh	50.00	100.00
(Nov.22, 1924, ND vs. Northwestern)		

1925 Notre Dame Postcards

Each of the postcards in this set was issued in 1925. The cardfronts were printed in black and white along with a thin gold colored border near the card's edges on most. The cardbacks feature a typical postcard design with "Souvenir Post Card" printed at the top. The cards are unnumbered and listed below alphabetically. Any additions to this list are appreciated.

1 Dick Hanousek	50.00	100.00

1926 Notre Dame Postcards

Notre Dame issued postcard sets over a number of years to fans as a momento of each game of the season. They can often be found signed by the player(s) featured. Each of these postcards covers a specific 1926 Notre Dame game with the date and opponent and final score printed on the cardfront. The printing is a single color blue or dark sepia tone. The cards are unnumbered and listed below alphabetically. Any additions to this list are appreciated.

1 Joe Benda	50.00	100.00
Harry O'Boyle		
John Wallace		
2 Bud Boeringer	50.00	100.00
Red Smith		
John Voedisch		
Adam Walsh		
(Spirit of '24))/7-0 vs. Army; no date listed		
3 Joe Boland	175.00	300.00
Fred Collins		
with The Four Horsemen		
(Oct.16 vs. Penn State)		
4 Christie Flanagan	50.00	100.00
(Oct.9 vs. Minnesota)		
5 Tom Hearden	200.00	350.00
Knute Rockne		
Gene Edwards		
(Oct. 2 vs. Beloit)		
6 John Niemiec	50.00	100.00
(Nov.27 vs. Carnegie Tech)		
7 Charlie Riley	50.00	100.00
Vince McNally		
Art Parisien		
Joe Maxwell		
Charles Walsh		
Oct.30 vs. Georgia Tech		

1927 Notre Dame Postcards

Notre Dame issued postcard sets over a number of years to fans as a momento of each game of the season. They can often be found signed by the player featured. Each of these postcards covers a specific 1927 Notre Dame game with the date and opponent included on the cardfront. The printing on the fronts is a single color blue or dark sepia tone. The cards are unnumbered and listed below alphabetically. Any additions to this list are appreciated.

1 Christie Flanagan	50.00	100.00
(October 15)		
2 Bucky Dahman	60.00	120.00
Jack Chevigney		
(October 22)		
3 Knute Rockne	350.00	500.00
(October 1)		
4 Knute Rockne	250.00	400.00
John Smith		
(November 5)		
5 John Niemiec	50.00	100.00
(October 8)		
6 Charlie Riley	50.00	100.00
Fred Collins		
(Nov. 12 vs. Army)		
7 John Frederick	50.00	100.00
John Voedisch		
Charles Walsh		
(October 29)		

1929 Notre Dame Postcards

Each of the postcards in this set covers a specific 1929 Notre Dame football game with the date and opponent included on the cardfront. They are often found with the game's score written on the front and sometimes autographed by the player. The cardbacks are a typical postcards design. The cards are unnumbered and listed below alphabetically. Any additions to this list are appreciated.

1 Jack Cannon	50.00	100.00
2 Eddie Collins	50.00	100.00
3 Jack Elder	50.00	100.00
4 Larry Moon Mullins	60.00	120.00

1930 Notre Dame Postcards

Notre Dame issued this postcard set with the intention of fans to have each card autographed and game score recorded as a momento of the game featured. Each of the postcards covers a specific 1930 Notre Dame game with the date and opponent included on the cardfront. The cards are unnumbered and listed below alphabetically.

COMPLETE SET (25)	1,000.00	1,800.00
1 Marty Brill	40.00	80.00
2 Frank Carideo	60.00	120.00
3 Tom Conley	40.00	80.00
4 Al Culver	40.00	80.00
(October 25)		
5 Dick Donaghue	40.00	80.00
18-Oct		
6 Nordy Hoffman	40.00	80.00
7 Al Howard	40.00	80.00
15-Nov		
8 Chuck Jaskwich	40.00	80.00
22-Nov		
9 Clarence Kaplan	40.00	80.00
18-Oct		
10 Tom Kassis	40.00	80.00
(October 18)		
11 Ed Kosky	40.00	80.00
22-Nov		
12 Joe Kurth	50.00	100.00
13 Bernie Leahy	50.00	100.00
14 Frank Leahy	150.00	250.00
15 Dick Mahoney	40.00	80.00
8-Nov		
16 Art McManmon	40.00	80.00
1-Nov		
17 Bert Metzger	40.00	80.00
18 Larry Moon Mullins	50.00	100.00
19 John O'Brien	40.00	80.00
20 Bucky O'Connor	40.00	80.00
21 Joe Savoldi	60.00	120.00
22 Marchmont Schwartz	50.00	100.00
23 Robert Terlaak	40.00	80.00
8-Nov		
24 George Vlk	40.00	80.00
25-Oct		
25 Tommy Yarr	40.00	80.00

1931 Notre Dame Postcards

Similar to the 1930 release, Notre Dame issued this postcard set with the intention of fans having each card autographed and the game score recorded as a momento of the game featured. Each of the postcards covers a specific 1931 Notre Dame game with the date and opponent included on the cardfront. The cards are unnumbered and listed below alphabetically. The set is thought to contain well over 20-different postcards. Any additions to this list are appreciated.

1 Hunk Anderson CO	60.00	120.00
2 Jack Chevigney CO	50.00	100.00
3 Tommy Yarr	40.00	80.00
4 Knute Rockne	300.00	500.00
(Rock's Last Schedule;/ 1931 Football Schedule)		

1932 Notre Dame Postcards

Similar to previous releases, Notre Dame issued this postcard set with the intention of fans having each card autographed and the game score recorded as a souvenir. Unlike other years, the 1932 issue does not include a specific game on the front, but does have a player photo printed in blue along with a yellow-gold border. The words "Notre Dame Varsity 1932" appear above the player image. The cardbacks feature a typical postcard format. The cards are unnumbered and listed below alphabetically. Any additions to this list are appreciated.

1 Ben Alexander	40.00	80.00
2 Steve Banas	40.00	80.00
3 Ray Brancheau	40.00	80.00
4 Sturla Canale	40.00	80.00
5 Hugh DeVore	40.00	80.00
6 Tom Gorman	40.00	80.00
7 Norman Greeney	40.00	80.00
8 Jim Harris	40.00	80.00
9 Paul Host	50.00	100.00
10 Chuck Jaskwich	40.00	80.00
11 Mike Koken	40.00	80.00
12 Ed Kosky	40.00	80.00
13 Ed Krause	40.00	80.00
14 Joe Kurth	50.00	100.00
15 Mike Leding	40.00	80.00
16 James Leonard	50.00	100.00
17 Nick Lukats	40.00	80.00
18 George Melinkovitch	40.00	80.00
19 Emmett Murphy	40.00	80.00
20 Bill Pierce	50.00	100.00
21 Tom Roach	40.00	80.00
22 Joe Sheeketski	40.00	80.00
23 Laurie Vejar	40.00	80.00
24 Harry Wunsch	40.00	80.00
25 Season Schedule	40.00	80.00

1966 Notre Dame Team Issue

These photos were issued by the school to promote the football program. Each measures roughly 8" by 10" and features a black and white image of a player. The backs are blank or sometimes can be found with a typed player identification. Otherwise no player identification is included.

COMPLETE SET (7)	30.00	60.00
1 John Atamiam	5.00	10.00
2 Alex Bonvechio	5.00	10.00
3 Ken Ivan	5.00	10.00
4 Joseph Kantor	5.00	10.00
5 Marty Olosky	5.00	10.00
6 Tom Talaga	5.00	10.00
7 Bill Wolski	5.00	10.00

1967 Notre Dame Team Issue

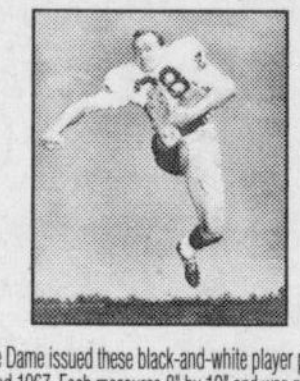

Notre Dame issued these black-and-white player photos around 1967. Each measures 8" by 10" and was printed on glossy stock with white borders. The border below the photo contains the player's position, his name and school name. These photos are blankbacked and unnumbered. Any additions to the below list are appreciated. Some of the players who would later have professional cards include: Rocky Bleier, Pete Duranko, George Goeddeke, Terry Hanratty, Jim Lynch, Tom Regner and Jim Seymour.

COMPLETE SET (15)	75.00	150.00
1 Rocky Bleier	10.00	20.00
2 Larry Conjar	5.00	10.00
3 Pete Duranko	6.00	12.00
4 Don Gmitter	5.00	10.00
5 George Goeddeke	5.00	10.00
6 Terry Hanratty	6.00	12.00
7 Kevin Hardy	5.00	10.00
8 Curt Heneghan	5.00	10.00
9 Jim Lynch	6.00	12.00
10 Dave Martin	5.00	10.00
11 Mike McGill	5.00	10.00
12 Coley O'Brien	5.00	10.00
13 Tom Regner	5.00	10.00
14 Tom Schoen	5.00	10.00
15 Jim Seymour	5.00	10.00

1988 Notre Dame

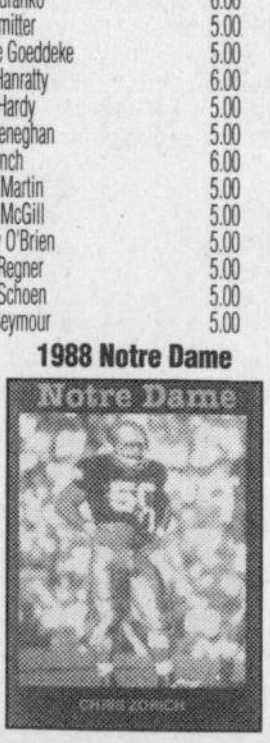

The 1988 Notre Dame football set contains 60 standard-size cards depicting the 1988 National Champions. The fronts have sharp color action photos with dark blue borders and gold lettering; the vertically oriented backs have biographical information. These cards were distributed as a complete set. There are 58 cards of players from the National Championship team, plus one coach card and one for the Golden Dome. The key cards in the set are Raghib Ismail and Ricky Watters.

COMPLETE SET (60)	10.00	25.00
1 Golden Dome	.20	.50
2 Lou Holtz CO	1.00	2.50
3 Mark Green	.08	.25
4 Andy Heck	.30	.75
5 Ned Bolcar	.08	.25
6 Anthony Johnson	.75	2.00
7 Flash Gordon	.08	.25
8 Pat Eilers	.20	.50
9 Rocket Ismail	2.00	5.00
10 Ted FitzGerald	.08	.25
11 Ted Healy	.08	.25
12 Braxston Banks	.20	.50
13 Steve Belles	.08	.25
14 Steve Alaniz	.08	.25
15 Chris Zorich	.60	1.50
16 Kent Graham	.75	2.00
17 Mike Brennan	.08	.25
18 Marty Lippincott	.08	.25
19 Rod West	.08	.25
20 Dean Brown	.08	.25
21 Tom Gorman	.08	.25
22 Tony Rice	.40	1.00
23 Steve Roddy	.08	.25
24 Reggie Ho	.20	.50
25 Pat Terrell	.30	.75
26 Joe Jarosz	.08	.25
27 Mike Stonebreaker	.30	.75
28 David Jandric	.08	.25
29 Jeff Alm	.20	.50
30 Pete Graham	.08	.25
31 Corny Southall	.08	.25
32 Joe Allen	.08	.25
33 Jim Sexton	.08	.25
34 Michael Crounse	.08	.25
35 Kurt Zackrison	.08	.25
36 Stan Smagala	.08	.25
37 Mike Heldt	.08	.25
38 Frank Stams	.30	.75
39 D'Juan Francisco	.08	.25
40 Tim Ryan	.20	.50
41 Arnold Ale	.08	.25
42 Andre Jones DE	.08	.25
43 Wes Pritchett	.08	.25
44 Tim Grunhard	.40	1.00
45 Chuck Killian	.08	.25
46 Scott Kowalkowski	.20	.50
47 George Streeter	.08	.25
48 Donn Grimm	.08	.25
49 Ricky Watters	2.50	6.00
50 Ryan Mihalko	.08	.25
51 Tony Brooks	.30	.75
52 Todd Lyght	.40	1.00
53 Winston Sandri	.08	.25
54 Aaron Robb	.08	.25
55 Derek Brown TE	.40	1.00
56 Bryan Flannery	.08	.25
57 Kevin McShane	.08	.25
58 Billy Hackett	.08	.25
59 George Williams	.08	.25
60 Frank Jacobs	.08	.25

1988 Notre Dame Smokey

This 14-card standard size set was sponsored by the U. S. Forestry Service. The front features a color action photo, with orange and green borders on a purple background. The back has biographical information (or a schedule) and a fire prevention cartoon starring Smokey the Bear. These unnumbered cards are ordered alphabetically within type for convenience. Ricky Walters is featured in this set.

COMPLETE SET (14)	14.00	35.00
1 Braxston Banks 39	1.25	3.00
2 Ned Bolcar 47	1.25	3.00
3 Tom Gorman 87	.75	2.00
4 Mark Green 24	1.25	3.00
5 Andy Heck 66	1.25	3.00
6 Lou Holtz CO	2.00	5.00
7 Anthony Johnson 22	1.50	4.00
8 Wes Pritchett 34	.75	2.00
9 George Streeter 27	.75	2.00
10 Ricky Watters 12	4.00	10.00
11 Brian Piotrowicz BB	.75	2.00
12 Men's Hockey	.60	1.50
13 Men's Soccer	.60	1.50
14 Volleyball	.60	1.50
15 Women's Basketball	.60	1.50
16 Women's Tennis	.60	1.50

1989 Notre Dame 1903-32

The 1989 Notre Dame Football I set contains 22 standard-size cards depicting the Irish stars from 1903-32. The fronts have vintage photos with white borders and gold lettering; the vertically oriented backs have detailed profiles. These cards were distributed as a set.

COMPLETE SET (22)	5.00	10.00
1 Hunk Anderson	.20	.50
2 Bert Metzger	.15	.40
3 Roger Kiley	.15	.40
4 Nordy Hoffman	.15	.40
5 Knute Rockne CO	.75	2.00
6 Elmer Layden	.40	1.00
7 Gus Dorais	.20	.50
8 Ray Eichenlaub	.15	.40
9 Don Miller	.40	1.00
10 Moose Krause	.15	.40
11 Jesse Harper	.15	.40
12 Jack Cannon	.15	.40
13 Eddie Anderson	.15	.40
14 Louis Salmon	.15	.40
15 John Smith	.15	.40
16 Harry Stuhldreher	.40	1.00
17 Joe Kurth	.15	.40
18 Frank Carideo	.20	.50
19 Marchy Schwartz	.20	.50
20 Adam Walsh	.15	.40
21 George Gipp	.75	2.00
22 Jim Crowley	.40	1.00

1989 Notre Dame 1935-59

The 1989 Notre Dame Football II set contains 22 standard-size cards depicting the Irish stars from 1935-59. The fronts have vintage photos with white borders and gold lettering; the vertically oriented backs have detailed profiles. These cards were distributed as a set.

COMPLETE SET (22)	5.00	10.00
1 Frank Leahy CO	.40	1.00
2 John Lattner	.40	1.00
3 Jim Martin	.30	.75
4 Joe Heap	.15	.40
5 Paul Hornung	.75	2.00
6 Bill Shakespeare	.30	.75
7 Bob Dove	.15	.40
8 Bob Williams	.15	.40
9 Al Ecuyer	.15	.40
10 George Connor	.40	1.00
11 Leon Hart	.40	1.00
12 Joe Beinor	.15	.40
13 Bill Fischer	.15	.40
14 Angelo Bertelli	.40	1.00
15 Ralph Guglielmi	.20	.50
16 Pat Filley	.15	.40
17 Emil Sitko	.20	.50
18 Don Schaefer	.15	.40
19 Monty Stickles	.20	.50
20 Creighton Miller	.15	.40
21 Chuck Sweeney	.15	.40
22 Johnny Lujack	.60	1.50

1989 Notre Dame 1964-87

The 1989 Notre Dame Football III set contains 22 standard-size cards depicting the Irish stars from 1964-87. The fronts have vintage and color photos with white borders and gold lettering; the vertically oriented backs have detailed profiles. These cards were distributed as a set.

COMPLETE SET (22)	4.00	10.00
1 Dan Devine CO	.20	.50
2 Joe Theismann	.60	1.50
3 Tom Gatewood	.20	.50
4 Tim Brown	.75	2.00
5 Ara Parseghian CO	.60	1.50
6 Jim Lynch	.20	.50
7 Luther Bradley	.15	.40
8 Ross Browner	.20	.50
9 John Huarte	.40	1.00
10 Bob Crable	.20	.50
11 Ken MacAfee	.20	.50
12 Alan Page	.40	1.00
13 Vagas Ferguson	.20	.50
14 Dick Arrington	.15	.40
15 Bob Golic	.20	.50
16 Mike Townsend	.15	.40
17 Walt Patulski	.20	.50
18 Allen Pinkett	.20	.50
19 Terry Hanratty	.30	.75
20 Dave Casper	.40	1.00
21 Jack Snow	.30	.75
22 Nick Eddy	.20	.50

1990 Notre Dame Promos

This ten-card standard-size set was issued by Collegiate Collection to honor some of the leading figures in Fighting Irish history. This set has a mix of the most famous Notre Dame coaches and some of the offensive stars of Notre Dame's long history. The featured subjects active after 1960 are shown in color photos.

COMPLETE SET (10)	6.00	15.00
1 Knute Rockne CO	.80	2.00
2 Joe Theismann	.60	1.50
3 Joe Montana	2.40	6.00
4 George Gipp	.80	2.00
5 Notre Dame Stadium	.20	.50
6 Ara Parseghian CO	.30	.75
7 Frank Leahy CO	.30	.75
8 Lou Holtz CO	.30	.75
9 Tony Rice	.20	.50
10 Rocky Bleier	.30	.75

1990 Notre Dame 200

This 200-card standard size set was issued by Collegiate Collection in 1990 and features many of the great players and figures of Notre Dame history. The set was available in wax packs and features a mixture of black and white or color photos, posed and action, with a yellow border against a blue background. The horizontally oriented backs are numbered in the upper right hand corner and provide career highlights. There were 2000 special George Gipp cards randomly inserted in wax packs as a bonus.

COMPLETE SET (200)	10.00	25.00
1 Joe Montana	1.00	2.50
2 Tim Brown	.20	.50
3 Reggie Barnett	.08	.25
4 Joe Theismann	.20	.50
5 Bob Clasby	.02	.10
6 Dave Casper	.08	.25
7 George Kunz	.08	.25
8 Vince Phelan	.02	.10
9 Tom Gibbons	.02	.10
10 Tom Thayer	.02	.10
11 Notre Dame Helmet	.02	.10
12 John Scully	.02	.10
13 Lou Holtz CO	.20	.50
14 Larry Dinardo	.08	.25
15 Greg Marx	.02	.10
16 Greg Dingens	.02	.10
17 Jim Seymour	.08	.25
18 1979 Cotton Bowl	.08	.25
(Program)		
19 Mike Kadish	.08	.25
20 Bob Crable	.08	.25
21 Tony Rice	.08	.25
22 Phil Carter	.02	.10
23 Ken MacAfee	.08	.25
24 Nick Eddy	.08	.25
25 1988 National Champs	.08	.25
(Trophies)		
26 Clarence Ellis	.08	.25
27 Joe Restic	.02	.10
28 Dan Devine CO	.08	.25
29 John K. Carney	.02	.10
30 Stacey Toran	.08	.25
31 47th Sugar Bowl	.02	.10
(Program)		
32 Jerome Heavens	.02	.10
33 Mike Fanning	.02	.10
34 Dave Vinson	.02	.10
35 Ralph Guglielmi	.02	.10
36 Reggie Ho	.02	.10
37 Allen Pinkett	.08	.25
38 Jim Browner	.08	.25
39 Blair Kiel	.08	.25
40 Joe Montana	1.00	2.50
41 Rocky Bleier	.20	.50
42 Terry Hanratty	.20	.50
43 Tom Regner	.08	.25
44 Pete Holohan	.02	.10
45 Greg Bell	.08	.25
46 Dave Duerson	.08	.25
47 Frank Varrichione	.08	.25
48 1988 Championship	.08	.25
(Team Photo)		
49 Ted Burgmeier	.02	.10
50 Ara Parseghian CO	.20	.50
51 Mike Townsend	.02	.10
52 Liberty Bowl 1983	.02	.10
(Program)		
53 Tony Furjanic	.02	.10
54 Luther Bradley	.08	.25
55 Steve Niehaus	.08	.25
56 56th Orange Bowl	.02	.10
(Program)		
57 32nd Gator Bowl	.02	.10
(Program)		
58 40th Sugar Bowl	.02	.10
(Program)		
59 52nd Cotton Bowl	.02	.10
(Program)		
60 1975 Orange Bowl	.02	.10
(Program)		
61 Wayne Bullock	.02	.10
62 Larry Moriarty	.02	.10
63 Jim Lynch	.08	.25
64 Mike McCoy	.08	.25
65 Tony Hunter	.08	.25
66 1984 Aloha Bowl	.02	.10
(Program)		
67 Dave Huffman	.02	.10
68 John Lattner	.20	.50
69 Tom Gatewood	.08	.25
70 Knute Rockne CO	.30	.75
71 Phil Pozderac	.02	.10
72 Ross Browner	.08	.25
73 Pete Demmerle	.02	.10
74 Sunkist Fiesta Bowl	.02	.10
(Program)		
75 Walt Patulski	.08	.25
76 George Gipp	.40	1.00
77 Bobby Leopold	.02	.10
78 John Huarte	.20	.50
79 Tony Yelovich CO	.02	.10
80 Johnny Lujack	.20	.50
81 Cotton Bowl Classic	.02	.10
(Program)		
82 Tim Huffman	.02	.10
83 Bob Golic	.08	.25
84 Tom Clements	.08	.25
85 39th Orange Bowl	.02	.10
(Program)		
86 James J. White ADMIN	.02	.10
87 Frank Carideo	.02	.10
88 Vinny Cerrato	.02	.10
89 Louis Salmon	.02	.10
90 Bob Burger	.02	.10
91 Gerry Dinardo	.08	.25
92 Mike Creaney	.02	.10
93 John Krimm	.02	.10
94 Vagas Ferguson	.02	.10
95 Kris Haines	.02	.10
96 Gus Dorais	.08	.25
97 Tom Schoen	.02	.10
98 Jack Robinson	.02	.10
99 Joe Heap	.02	.10
100 Checklist 1-99	.02	.10
101 Gary Darnell CO	.02	.10
102 Peter Vaas CO	.02	.10
103 1924 National Champs	.20	.50
(Team Photo)		
104 Wayne Millner	.20	.50
105 Moose Krause	.08	.25
106 Jack Cannon	.02	.10
107 Christie Flanagan	.02	.10
108 Bob Lehmann	.02	.10
109 1947 Champions	.08	.25
(Team Photo)		
110 Joe Kurth	.02	.10
111 Tommy Yarr	.02	.10
112 Nick Buoniconti	.20	.50
113 Jim Smithberger	.02	.10
114 Joe Beinor	.02	.10
115 Pete Cordelli CO	.02	.10
116 Daryle Lamonica	.20	.50
117 Kevin Hardy	.02	.10
118 Creighton Miller	.08	.25
119 Bob Gladieux	.08	.25
120 Fred Miller	.08	.25
(Later Miller Brewing)		
121 Gary Potempa	.02	.10
122 Bob Kuechenberg	.08	.25
123 Jesse Harper CO	.02	.10
124 1929 National Champs	.08	.25
(Team Photo)		
125 Alan Page	.20	.50
126 Don Miller	.20	.50
127 1943 National Champs	.08	.25
(Team Photo)		
128 Bob Wetoska	.02	.10
129 Skip Holtz CO	.02	.10
130 Hunk Anderson CO	.08	.25
131 Bob Williams	.02	.10
132 1966 National Champs	.08	.25
(Team Photo)		
133 Jim Reilly	.02	.10
134 Earl(Curly) Lambeau	.20	.50
135 Ernie Hughes	.02	.10
136 Dick Bumpas CO	.02	.10
137 Jay Haynes CO	.02	.10
138 Harry Stuhldreher	.20	.50
139 1971 Cotton Bowl	.08	.25
(Game Photo)		
140 1930 National Champs	.08	.25
(Team Photo)		
141 Larry Conjar	.08	.25
142 1977 National Champs	.08	.25
(Team Photo)		
143 Pete Duranko	.08	.25
144 Heisman Winners	.20	.50
Tim Brown		
Johnny Lujack		
Angelo Bertelli		
Leon Hart		
Paul Hornung		
John Huarte		
John Lattner		
145 Bill Fischer	.02	.10
146 Marchy Schwartz	.02	.10
147 Chuck Heater CO	.02	.10
148 Bert Metzger	.02	.10
149 Bill Shakespeare	.08	.25
150 Adam Walsh	.02	.10
151 Nordy Hoffman	.02	.10
152 Ted Gradel	.02	.10
153 Monty Stickles	.08	.25
154 Neil Worden	.02	.10
155 Pat Filley	.02	.10
156 Angelo Bertelli	.08	.25
157 Nick Pietrosante	.08	.25
158 Art Hunter	.02	.10
159 Ziggy Czarobski	.02	.10
160 1925 Rose Bowl	.02	.10
(Program)		
161 Al Ecuyer	.02	.10
162 1949 Notre Dame Champs	.08	.25
(Team Photo)		
163 Elmer Layden	.20	.50
164 Joe Moore CO	.02	.10
165 1946 National Champs	.08	.25
(Team Photo)		
166 Frank Rydzewski	.02	.10
167 Bud Boeringer	.02	.10
168 Jerry Groom	.02	.10
169 Jack Snow	.08	.25
170 Joe Montana	1.00	2.50
171 John Smith	.02	.10
172 Frank Leahy CO	.20	.50
173 Emil Sitko	.08	.25
174 Dick Arrington	.02	.10
175 Eddie Anderson END	.02	.10
176 1928 Army	.02	.10
(Logo and score)		
177 1913 Army	.02	.10
(Logo and score)		
178 1935 Ohio State	.02	.10
(Logo and game score)		
179 1946 Army	.02	.10
(Logo and game score)		
180 1953 Georgia Tech	.02	.10
(Logo and game score)		
181 Don Schaefer	.02	.10
182 1973 Football Team	.08	.25
(Team Photo)		
183 Bob Dove	.02	.10
184 Dick Szymanski	.02	.10
185 Jim Martin	.08	.25
186 1957 Oklahoma	.02	.10
(Logo and game score)		
187 1966 Michigan State	.02	.10
(Logo and game score)		
188 1973 USC	.02	.10
(Logo and game score)		
189 1980 Michigan	.02	.10
(Logo and game score)		
190 1982 Michigan	.02	.10
(Logo and game score)		
191 Chuck Sweeney	.02	.10
192 Notre Dame Stadium	.02	.10
193 Roger Kiley	.02	.10
194 Ray Eichenlaub	.02	.10
195 George Connor	.20	.50
196 1982 Pittsburgh	.02	.10
(Logo and game score)		
197 1986 USC	.02	.10
(Logo and game score)		
198 1988 Miami	.02	.10
(Logo and game score)		
199 1988 USC	.02	.10
(Logo and game score)		
200 Checklist 101-199	.02	.10
NNO George Gipp	.75	2.00
Numbered to 2,000		

1990 Notre Dame 60

This 60-card set measures approximately 2 1/2" by 3 1/2" and was issued to celebrate the 1990 Notre Dame football team. The key cards in this set feature Reggie Brooks, Raghib "Rocket" Ismail, Rick Mirer, and Ricky Watters. There is a full color photo on the front, with the Notre Dame logo in the lower right-hand corner of the card. The back has biographical information about the player. The set was produced by College Classics; reportedly 10,000 sets were produced and distributed.

COMPLETE SET (60)	10.00	25.00
1 Joe Allen	.14	.35
2 William Pollard	.14	.35
3 Tony Smith	.14	.35
4 Tony Brooks	.40	1.00
5 Kenny Spears	.14	.35
6 Mike Heldt	.14	.35
7 Derek Brown TE	.40	1.00
8 Rodney Culver	.40	1.00
9 Ricky Watters	1.60	4.00
10 Rocket Ismail	1.20	3.00
11 Lou Holtz CO	.80	2.00
12 Chris Zorich	.60	1.50
13 Erik Simien	.14	.35
14 Shawn Davis	.14	.35
15 Greg Davis	.14	.35
16 Walter Boyd	.14	.35
17 Tim Ryan	.20	.50
18 Lindsay Knapp	.14	.35
19 Junior Bryant	.14	.35
20 Mike Stonebreaker	.20	.50
21 Randy Scianna	.14	.35
22 Rick Mirer	1.20	3.00
23 Ryan Mihalko	.14	.35
24 Todd Lyght	.40	1.00
25 Andre Jones DE	.20	.50
26 Rod Smith DB	.20	.50
27 Winston Sandri	.14	.35
28 Bob Dahl	.20	.50
29 Stuart Tyner	.14	.35
30 Brian Shannon	.14	.35
31 Shawn Smith	.14	.35
32 Jim Sexton	.14	.35
33 Dorsey Levens	1.60	4.00
34 Lance Johnson	.14	.35
35 George Poorman	.14	.35
36 Irv Smith	.60	1.50
37 George Williams	.14	.35
38 George Marshall	.20	.50
39 Reggie Brooks	.60	1.50
40 Scott Kowalkowski	.20	.50
41 Jerry Bodine	.14	.35
42 Karmeeleyah McGill	.14	.35
43 Donn Grimm	.14	.35
44 Billy Hackett	.14	.35
45 Jordan Halter	.14	.35
46 Mirko Jurkovic	.40	1.00
47 Mike Callan	.14	.35
48 Justin Hall	.14	.35
49 Nick Smith	.14	.35
50 Brian Ratigan	.14	.35
51 Eric Jones	.14	.35
52 Todd Norman	.14	.35
53 Devon McDonald	.20	.50
54 Marc deManigold	.14	.35
55 Bret Hankins	.14	.35
56 Adrian Jarrell	.20	.50
57 Craig Hentrich	.40	1.00
58 Demetrius DuBose	.40	1.00
59 Gene McGuire	.20	.50
60 Ray Griggs	.14	.35

1990 Notre Dame Greats

This 22-card standard-size set celebrates 22 of the All-Americans and past greats who attended Notre Dame. The cards have a mix of color and black and white photos on the front of the card and the back of the card has a biography of the player which describes his career at Notre Dame.

COMPLETE SET (22)	4.00	10.00
1 Clarence Ellis	.20	.50
2 Rocky Bleier	.30	.75
3 Tom Regner	.20	.50
4 Jim Seymour	.10	.30
5 Joe Montana	1.60	4.00
6 Art Hunter	.20	.50
7 Mike McCoy	.20	.50
8 Bud Boeringer	.10	.30
9 Greg Marx	.10	.30
10 Nick Buoniconti	.30	.75
11 Pete Demmerle	.10	.30
12 Fred Miller	.10	.30
13 Tommy Yarr	.10	.30
14 Frank Rydzewski	.10	.30
15 Dave Duerson	.20	.50
16 Ziggy Czarobski	.10	.30
17 Jim White	.20	.50
18 Larry DiNardo	.20	.50
19 George Kunz	.20	.50
20 Jack Robinson	.10	.30
21 Steve Niehaus	.20	.50
22 John Scully	.20	.50

1992 Notre Dame

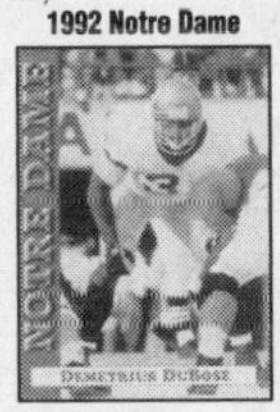

This 59-card standard-size set features color action player photos bordered on the left or right edge by a gray stripe containing the team name. The player's name appears in gold lettering on a white stripe at the bottom. The horizontal backs feature close-up player pictures with shadow box borders. The white background is printed with a profile of the player. The school logo and biographical information appear at the top. The cards are numbered on the back and are arranged alphabetically (with a few exceptions) after leading off with Coach Lou Holtz, Rick Mirer, and Demetrious DuBose. Other noteworthy cards in the set are Jerome Bettis, Reggie Brooks, Lake Dawson and Ray Zellars.

COMPLETE SET (59)	10.00	25.00
1 Lou Holtz CO	.50	1.25
2 Rick Mirer	1.00	2.50
3 Demetrius DuBose	.30	.75
4 Lee Becton	.30	.75
5 Pete Bercich	.20	.50
6 Jerome Bettis	2.40	6.00
7 Reggie Brooks	.50	1.25
8 Junior Bryant	.14	.35
9 Jeff Burris	.60	1.50
10 Tom Carter	.60	1.50
11 Willie Clark	.14	.35
12 John Covington	.20	.50
13 Travis Davis	.14	.35
14 Lake Dawson	.60	1.50
15 Mark Zataveski	.14	.35
16 Paul Failla	.30	.75
17 Jim Flanigan	.30	.75
18 Oliver Gibson	.14	.35
19 Justin Goheen	.20	.50
20 Tracy Graham	.14	.35
21 Ray Griggs	.14	.35
22 Justin Hall	.14	.35
23 Jordan Halter	.14	.35
24 Brian Hamilton	.20	.50
25 Craig Hentrich	.20	.50
26 Germaine Holden	.14	.35
27 Adrian Jarrell	.20	.50
28 Clint Johnson	.20	.50
29 Lance Johnson	.14	.35
30 Lindsay Knapp	.20	.50
31 Ryan Leahy	.20	.50
(Not alphabetical order)		
32 Greg Lane	.20	.50
33 Dean Lytle	.14	.35
34 Bernard Mannelly	.14	.35
35 Oscar McBride	.20	.50
36 Devon McDonald	.30	.75
37 Kevin McDougal	.20	.50
38 Karl McGill	.14	.35
39 Mike McGlinn	.14	.35
40 Mike Miller	.20	.50
41 Jeremy Nau	.14	.35
42 Todd Norman	.20	.50
43 Tim Ruddy	.30	.75
(Not alphabetical order)		
44 William Pollard	.14	.35
45 Brian Ratigan	.14	.35
46 Leshane Saddler	.14	.35
47 Jeremy Sample	.14	.35
48 Irv Smith	.40	1.00
49 Laron Moore	.14	.35
(Not alphabetical order)		
50 Anthony Peterson	.20	.50
(Not alphabetical order)		
51 Charles Stafford	.14	.35
52 Nick Smith	.14	.35
53 Greg Stec	.14	.35
54 John Taliaferro	.14	.35
55 Aaron Taylor	.60	1.50
56 Stuart Tyner	.14	.35
57 Ray Zellars	.60	1.50
(Not alphabetical order)		
58 Tyler Young	.14	.35
(Not alphabetical order)		
59 Bryant Young	.75	2.00

1992 Notre Dame Campus

This set features a variety of subjects related to NotRe Dame football with the images bordered on the left and botton in blue and to the right and top in gold. The word "campus" appears at the bottom along with the subject's name. The cards were issued as a perforated sheet and measure 2 1/2" by 3 3/4' when seperated. They are unnumbered and arranged alphabetically below.

COMPLETE SET (9)	6.00	12.00
1 Lou Holtz	1.50	4.00
Tim Brown		
2 Rocket Ismail	.75	2.00
3 Ronald Reagan	.50	1.25
4 Tony Rice	.50	1.25
5 William Corby Statue	.30	.75
6 Golden Dome	.30	.75
7 No. 1 Moses Statue	.30	.75
8 Touchdown Jesus Mosaic	.30	.75
9 Welsh Mart Ad Card/1992 Schedule on back	.30	
.75		

1993 Notre Dame

These 72 standard-size cards feature on their fronts color player action shots. These photos are bordered in either blue, gold, green, or white, and each variety has its own checklist. All the cards have gold-colored outer borders. The player's name appears vertically in multicolored lettering within a photo of a football stadium near the left side. The horizontal back is bordered in the same color as its front, and carries a color player head shot within a diamond at the upper left, which is framed by a gold-colored line. The player's name, class, position, uniform number, and biography appear within a grayish rectangle at the top. His Notre Dame highlights and stats follow within the greenish panel below. The cards are unnumbered and checklisted below in alphabetical order.

COMPLETE SET (72)	8.00	20.00
1 Jeremy Akers	.14	.35
2 Joe Babey	.08	.25
3 Huntley Bakich	.08	.25
4 Jason Beckwith	.08	.25
5 Lee Becton	.20	.50
6 Pete Bercich	.20	.50
7 Jeff Burris	.40	1.00
8 Pete Chryplewicz	.08	.25
9 Willie Clark	.08	.25
10 John Covington	.14	.35
11 Travis Davis	.08	.25
12 Lake Dawson	.40	1.00
13 Paul Failla	.20	.50
14 Jim Flanigan	.20	.50
15 Reggie Fleurima	.08	.25
16 Ben Foos	.08	.25
17 Herbert Gibson	.08	.25
18 Oliver Gibson	.20	.50
19 Justin Goheen	.14	.35
20 Tracy Graham	.08	.25
21 Paul Grasmanis	.14	.35
22 Jordan Halter	.08	.25
23 Brian Hamilton	.14	.35
24 Germaine Holden	.08	.25
25 Lou Holtz CO	.40	1.00
26 Robert Hughes	.08	.25
27 Adrian Jarrell	.14	.35
28 Clint Johnson	.14	.35
29 Lance Johnson	.08	.25
30 Thomas Knight	.14	.35
31 Jim Kordas	.08	.25
32 Greg Lane	.14	.35
33 Ryan Leahy	.14	.35
34 Will Lyell	.14	.35
35 Dean Lytle	.08	.25
36 Brian Magee	.08	.25
37 Alton Maiden	.08	.25
38 Derrick Mayes	.80	2.00
39 Oscar McBride	.20	.50
40 Mike McCullough	.20	.50
41 Kevin McDougal	.20	.50
42 Mike McGlinn	.08	.25
43 Brian Meter	.08	.25
44 Mike Miller	.20	.50
45 Steve Misetic	.08	.25
46 Jeremy Nau	.08	.25
47 Todd Norman	.14	.35
48 Kevin Pendergast	.14	.35
49 Anthony Peterson	.08	.25
50 David Quist	.08	.25
51 Jeff Riney	.08	.25
52 Tim Ruddy	.20	.50
53 LeShane Saddler	.08	.25
54 Jeremy Sample	.08	.25
55 Charles Stafford	.08	.25
56 Greg Stec	.08	.25
57 Cliff Stroud	.08	.25
58 John Taliaferro	.08	.25
59 Aaron Taylor	.50	1.25
60 Bobby Taylor	1.00	2.50
61 Bill Wagasy	.08	.25
62 Leon Wallace	.08	.25
63 Shawn Wooden	.14	.35
64 Renaldo Wynn	.14	.35
65 Bryant Young	.75	2.00
66 Mark Zataveski	.14	.35
67 Dusty Zeigler	.14	.35
68 Ray Zellars	.50	1.25
69 Blue Roster Checklist	.08	.25
70 Gold Roster Checklist	.08	.25
71 Green Roster Checklist	.08	.25
72 White Roster Checklist	.08	.25

1999 Notre Dame Legendary Irish CD-ROM

This set was produced by Spacemark International to recognize 5-top players and coaches in Notre Dame football history. Each card is actually a CD-ROM with the front including a photo of the featured player/coach and the backs produced as a CD-ROM. In order to use the product the center hole must have been punched-out. A separate paper certificate of authenticity was issued with each CD-ROM and serial numbered of 50,000 produced.

COMPLETE SET (5)	20.00	40.00
1 Lou Holtz	5.00	10.00
2 Knute Rockne	5.00	10.00
3 Ara Parseghian	4.00	8.00
4 Joe Theismann	5.00	10.00
5 Tony Rice	4.00	8.00

2001 Notre Dame Schedules

COMPLETE SET (4)	1.00	2.50
1 Rocky Boiman	.20	.50
2 David Givens	.40	1.00
3 Grant Irons	.20	.50
4 Anthony Weaver	.20	.50

2003-07 Notre Dame TK Legacy

This set of cards was produced by TK Legacy and released in three series. Series one (cards #M1-M41, ALUM1, C1, C2, CL2, and P1-P2) were released in the Fall of 2003, cards #M42-M65 were released as series 2 in Fall 2004, and series three (#M66-M84) was issued in Fall 2007. Each 4-card pack included an autographed card.

COMP SERIES 1 (45)	15.00	30.00
COMP SERIES 2 (24)	10.00	20.00
COMP SERIES 3 (19)	10.00	20.00
M1 Tom Clements	1.25	3.00
M2 Jim Seymour	.75	2.00
M3 Coley O'Brien	.40	1.00
M4 Nick Eddy	.40	1.00
M5 Paul Hornung	1.50	4.00
M6 Bob Golic	.50	1.25
M7 Greg Golic	.40	1.00
M8 Mike Golic	.50	1.25
M9 Bob Williams	.40	1.00
M10 Joe Heap	.50	1.25
M11 Neil Worden	.40	1.00
M12 John Lattner	.50	1.25
M13 Bob Thomas	.40	1.00
M14 Terry Brennan	.40	1.00
M15 Frank Leahy	.50	1.25
M16 Jim Leahy	.40	1.00
M17 Ryan Leahy	.40	1.00
M18 Mike Townsend	.40	1.00
M19 Willie Townsend	.40	1.00
M20 Jerome Heavens	.50	1.25
M21 Vagas Ferguson	.50	1.25
M22 Bob Crable	.40	1.00
M23 Frank Pomarico	.40	1.00
M24 Mike Fanning	.40	1.00
M25 Greg Collins	.40	1.00
M26 John Panelli	.40	1.00
M27 George Kunz	.40	1.00
M28 Bill Gay	.40	1.00
M29 Rudy Ruettiger	2.00	5.00
M30 Tom Lopienski Sr.	.40	1.00
M31 Tom Lopienski Jr.	.75	2.00
M32 George Gipp	.50	1.25
M33 John Ray	.40	1.00
M34 Tony Rice	.50	1.25
M35 Terry Hanratty	.50	1.25
M36 Mike McCoy	.40	1.00
M37 Bob Gladieux	.40	1.00
M38 Ralph Guglielmi	.40	1.00
M39 Jerry Groom	.40	1.00
M40 Alan Page	.75	2.00
M41 Jeff Faine	.75	2.00
(issued with album)		
M42 Ron Powlus	.75	2.00
M43 Monty Stickles	.40	1.00
M44 Gerry DiNardo	.40	1.00
M45 Larry DiNardo	.40	1.00
M46 Jim Lynch	.40	1.00
M47 Frank Tripucka	.75	2.00
M48 Kevin Hardy	.40	1.00
M49 Rocky Bleier	1.25	3.00
M50 Rich Thomann	.40	1.00
M51 Walt Patulski	.40	1.00
M52 Tom Gatewood	.40	1.00
M53 Derrick Mayes	.50	1.25
M54 John Dampeer	.40	1.00
M55 Jim Mutscheller	.40	1.00
M56 Bob Toneff	.40	1.00
M57 Allen Pinkett	.40	1.00
M58 Pat Steenberge	.40	1.00
M59 Jim Browner	.40	1.00
M60 Ross Browner	.50	1.25
M61 Willard Browner	.40	1.00
M62 Dick Swatland	.40	1.00
M63 Gary Potempa	.40	1.00
M64 Clarence Ellis	.40	1.00
M65 Chris Zorich	.50	1.25
M66 Joe Theismann	1.25	3.00
M67 Brady Quinn	2.00	5.00
M68 Rick Mirer	.75	2.00
M69 Reggie Brooks	.50	1.25
M70 Terry Andrysiak	.40	1.00
M71 Joey Getherall	.40	1.00
M72 Ned Bolcar	.40	1.00
M73 Nicholas Setta	.40	1.00
M74 Blair Kiel	.50	1.25
M75 Brian Boulac	.40	1.00
M76 Tim Koegel	.40	1.00
M77 Skip Holtz	.60	1.50
M78 Mirko Jurkovic	.40	1.00
M79 Myron Pottios	.40	1.00

M80 Angelo Dabiero .40 1.00
M81 Joe Carollo .40 1.00
M82 Larry Conjar .40 1.00
M83 Reggie Ho .40 1.00
M84 George Sefcik .40 1.00
ALUM1 Regis Philbin 1.00 2.50
C1 Ara Parseghian CP .50 1.25
C2 Frank Leahy CO .50 1.25
C3 Frank Hering CO .50 1.25
C4 Victor Place CO .50 1.25
C5 Jesse Harper CO .50 1.25
CL1 Frank Leahy CO CL .50 1.25
P1 Paul Hornung Promo/1000 2.50 6.00
P2 Ara Parseghian Promo/800 1.50 4.00

2003-07 Notre Dame TK Legacy All-Americans

COMP.SERIES 2 (6) 20.00 40.00
STATED ODDS 1:8
STATED PRINT RUN 400 SER.#'d SETS
AA1 George Gipp 4.00 10.00
(one per series 1 case)
AA2 Paul Hornung 5.00 12.00
AA3 Alan Page 5.00 12.00
AA4 John Lattner 3.00 8.00
AA5 Vagas Ferguson 4.00 10.00
AA6 Bob Williams 3.00 8.00
AA7 Nick Eddy 3.00 8.00
AA8 Bob Golic 4.00 10.00
AA9 Terry Hanratty 4.00 10.00
AA10 Louis Salmon 3.00 8.00
AA11 Jerry Groom 3.00 8.00
AA12 Chris Zorich 4.00 10.00
(one per series 2 case)
AA13 Clarence Ellis 3.00 8.00
AA14 Larry DiNardo 3.00 8.00
AA15 Gerry DiNardo 3.00 8.00
AA16 Ross Browner 4.00 10.00
AA17 Walt Patulski 3.00 8.00
AA18 Brady Quinn 5.00 12.00
AA20 Luther Bradley 2.00 5.00

2003-07 Notre Dame TK Legacy All-American Autographs

AB1 Luther Bradley 25.00 50.00
AB2 Johnny Lattner/50 40.00 80.00

2003-07 Notre Dame TK Legacy Fighting Irish Autographs

OVERALL AUTO STATED ODDS 1:1
FI1 Jim Seymour 6.00 15.00
FI2 Coley O'Brien 5.00 12.00
FI3 Nick Eddy 5.00 12.00
FI4 Joe Heap 6.00 15.00
FI5 Greg Golic 5.00 12.00
FI6 Mike Golic 6.00 15.00
FI7 Neil Worden 5.00 12.00
FI8 John Lattner 7.50 20.00
FI9 Terry Brennan 6.00 15.00
FI10 Jim Leahy 5.00 12.00
FI11 Ryan Leahy 6.00 15.00
FI12 Mike Townsend 5.00 12.00
FI13 Willie Townsend 6.00 15.00
FI14 Jerome Heavens 6.00 15.00
FI15 Vagas Ferguson 7.50 20.00
FI16 Bob Crable 6.00 15.00
FI17 Jerry Groom 5.00 12.00
FI18 Mike Fanning 5.00 12.00
FI19 Greg Collins 5.00 12.00
FI20 John Panelli 5.00 12.00
FI21 George Kunz 6.00 15.00
FI22 Bill Gay 5.00 12.00
FI23 Rudy Ruettiger 30.00 80.00
FI24 Tom Lopienski Sr. 5.00 12.00
FI25 Tom Lopienski Jr. 6.00 15.00
FI26 Frank Pomarico 5.00 12.00
FI27 John Ray 5.00 12.00
FI28 Terry Hanratty 6.00 15.00
FI29 Bob Gladieux 5.00 12.00
FI30 Ralph Guglielmi 6.00 15.00
FI31 Mike McCoy 6.00 15.00
FI32 Jeff Faine 6.00 15.00
FI33 Monty Stickles 5.00 12.00
FI34 Gerry DiNardo 5.00 12.00
FI35 Jim Lynch 5.00 12.00
FI36 Kevin Hardy 5.00 12.00
FI37 Ron Powlus 7.50 20.00
FI38 Rocky Bleier 12.50 30.00
FI39 Frank Tripucka 7.50 20.00
FI40 Larry DiNardo 5.00 12.00
FI41 Clarence Ellis 5.00 12.00
FI42 Dick Swatland 5.00 12.00
FI43 Pat Steenberge 5.00 12.00
FI44 Ross Browner 6.00 15.00
FI45 Jim Browner 5.00 12.00
FI46 Willard Browner 5.00 12.00
FI47 Gary Potempa 5.00 12.00
FI48 Rick Thomann 5.00 12.00
FI49 Walt Patulski 5.00 12.00
FI50 Tom Gatewood 5.00 12.00
FI51 Derrick Mayes 6.00 15.00
FI52 John Dampeer 5.00 12.00
FI53 Jim Mutscheller 5.00 12.00
FI54 Bob Toneff 5.00 12.00
FI55 Allen Pinkett 6.00 15.00
FI56 Chris Zorich 6.00 15.00
FI57 Joe Theismann/200 15.00 30.00
FI58 Brady Quinn/100 40.00 80.00
FI59 Rick Mirer 8.00 20.00
FI60 Blair Kiel 6.00 15.00
FI61 Ned Bolcar 5.00 12.00
FI62 Reggie Brooks 6.00 15.00
FI63 Reggie Ho 5.00 12.00
FI64 Jarious Jackson 6.00 15.00
FI65 Joey Getherall 5.00 12.00
FI66 Mirko Jurkovic 5.00 12.00
FI67 Tim Koegel 5.00 12.00
FI68 Gene McGuire 5.00 12.00
FI70 Nicholas Setta 5.00 12.00
FI71 Myron Pottios 5.00 12.00
FI72 George Sefcik 5.00 12.00
FI73 Angelo Dabiero 5.00 12.00
FI74 Skip Holtz 6.00 15.00
FI75 Terry Andrysiak 5.00 12.00
FI76 Brian Boulac 5.00 12.00
FI77 Larry Conjar 5.00 12.00
FI78 Joe Carollo 5.00 12.00
FI79 George Izo 6.00 15.00
FI80 Mike McGill 5.00 12.00
FI81 John Pergine 5.00 12.00
FI82 Ken MacAfee 6.00 15.00
FI84 Luther Bradley 5.00 12.00
FI86 Daryle Lamonica 15.00 30.00
FI87 Tom Schoen 5.00 12.00
FI88 Paul Costa 5.00 12.00
FI89 Bob Kuechenberg 6.00 15.00
SP1 Regis Philbin 30.00 80.00

2003-07 Notre Dame TK Legacy Hand Drawn Sketches

NDP1 Notre Dame Helmet/75 20.00 50.00
NDP2 Rudy Ruettiger/75 30.00 60.00
NDP3 George Gipp/75 30.00 60.00

RMS1 Rick Mirer B&W/25 40.00 80.00
BQS1 Brady Quinn Color/1
(close-up portrait)
BQS2 Brady Quinn Color/1
(football at chestt)
JTS1 Joe Theismann B&W/20 25.00 50.00

2003-07 Notre Dame TK Legacy Historical Archives Autographs

STATED PRINT RUN 100 SER.#'d SETS
AR1 Rick Mirer 20.00 40.00
AR2 Reggie Brooks
AR3 Reggie Ho 6.00 15.00
AR4 Nick Setta
AR5 Joey Getherall
AR6 Angelo Dabiero
AR7 Nick Setta
AR8 Blair Kiel 6.00 15.00
AR10 Johnny Lattner 15.00 30.00
AR15 Greg Bell 7.50 20.00

2003-07 Notre Dame TK Legacy Historical Links Autographs

HL1-HL6 DOUBLE AUTO ODDS 1:45
HL1-HL6 TRIPLE AUTO ODDS 1:200
HL7-HL12 DOUBLE AUTO ODDS 1:22
HL7-HL12 TRIPLE AUTO ODDS 1:112
HL1 Jerome Heavens/200 20.00 40.00
Vagas Ferguson
HL2 Mike Townsend/200 20.00 40.00
Willie Townsend
HL3 Tom Lopienski Sr./200 15.00 30.00
Tom Lopienski Jr.
HL4 Jim Leahy/200 20.00 40.00
Ryan Leahy
HL5 John Lattner/100 25.00 50.00
Joe Heap
Neil Worden
HL6 Bob Golic/100 30.00 60.00
Greg Golic
Mike Golic
HL7 Gerry DiNardo/100 15.00 30.00
Larry DiNardo
HL8 Tony Rice/100 30.00 80.00
Frank Tripucka
Terry Hanratty
HL9 Jim Browner/150 20.00 40.00
Ross Browner
Willard Browner
HL10 Joe Ferguson
Allen Pinkett
HL11 Tom Gatewood/100 25.00 50.00
Derrick Mayes
HL12 Chris Zorich/200 30.00 60.00
Walt Patulski
HL13 Nicholas Setta/100 15.00 30.00
Reggie Ho
HL14 George Sefcik/100 15.00 30.00
Angelo Dabiero

2003-07 Notre Dame TK Legacy Joe Theismann Tribute

T1 Joe Theismann
era begins
T2 Joe Theismann
heart of a champion
T3 Joe Theismann
Cotton Bowl heartache
T4 Joe Theismann
Cotton Bowl revenge
T5 Joe Theismann
legacy

2003-07 Notre Dame TK Legacy National Champions Autographs

SERIES 1 STATED ODDS 1:5
SERIES 2 STATED ODDS 1:37
1947A John Panelli 1 7.50 20.00
1947B Terry Brennan 1 10.00 25.00
1949A Bob Williams 1 10.00 25.00
1949B Bill Gay 1 7.50 20.00
1949C Jerry Groom 1 7.50 20.00
1949D Jim Mutscheller 2 7.50 20.00
1949E Bob Toneff 2 7.50 20.00
1966A Alan Page 1 12.50 30.00
1966B Nick Eddy 1 7.50 20.00
1966C Jim Seymour 1 10.00 25.00
1966D Terry Hanratty 1 10.00 25.00
1966E Coley O'Brien 1 7.50 20.00
1966F Bob Gladieux 1 7.50 20.00
1966G Rocky Bleier 2 20.00 40.00
1966H Kevin Hardy 2 7.50 20.00
1966I Jim Lynch 2 7.50 20.00
1966K Mike McGill 7.50 20.00
1966L John Pergine 7.50 20.00
1966N George Goeddeke 7.50 20.00
1973A Ara Parseghian 1 20.00 40.00
1973B Tom Clements 1 10.00 25.00
1973C Mike Townsend 1 7.50 20.00
1973D Greg Collins 1 7.50 20.00
1973E Willie Townsend 1 7.50 20.00
1973F Bob Thomas 1 10.00 25.00
1973G Mike Fanning 1 7.50 20.00
1973H Frank Pomarico 1 7.50 20.00
1973I Tom Lopienski Sr. 1 7.50 20.00
1973J Gary Potempa 2 7.50 20.00
1977A Vagas Ferguson 1 12.50 30.00
1977B Jerome Heavens 1 10.00 25.00
1977C Bob Golic 1 12.50 30.00
1977D Ross Browner 2 10.00 25.00
1977E Jim Browner 2 7.50 20.00
1977G Luther Bradley 7.50 20.00
1977H Ken MacAfee 7.50 20.00
1988A Tony Rice 1 10.00 25.00
1988B Chris Zorich 2 10.00 25.00

2003-07 Notre Dame TK Legacy Playbook Autographs

STATED ODDS 1:37 SERIES 2
STATED PRINT RUN 250 SER.#'d SETS
NDP1 Tony Rice 20.00 40.00
NDP2 Rudy Ruettiger 40.00 80.00

2003-07 Notre Dame TK Legacy QB Club Autographs

QB1-QB7 STATED ODDS 1:22 SER.1
Q81-QB10 STATED ODDS 1:37 SER.2
QB1 Paul Hornung/100 30.00 60.00
QB2 Tom Clements/300 15.00 40.00
QB3 Terry Hanratty/300 12.50 30.00
QB4 Bob Williams/300 15.00 40.00
QB5 Tony Rice/300 12.50 30.00
QB6 Ralph Guglielmi/300 12.50 30.00
QB7 Joe Montana/100 75.00 150.00
QB8 Frank Tripucka/200 20.00 40.00
QB9 Ron Powlus/350 15.00 30.00
QB10 Pat Steenberge/400 12.50 30.00
QB11 Joe Theismann/100 30.00 60.00
QB12 Rick Mirer/100 20.00 40.00
QB13 Tim Andrysiak/100 12.50 25.00
QB14 Blair Kiel/100 12.50 25.00
QB15 Jarious Jackson/100 15.00 30.00
QB16 Tim Koegel/100 12.50 25.00
QB17 George Izo/100 12.50 25.00

2003-07 Notre Dame TK Legacy Sentry of the Secondary Autographs

LB Luther Bradley/40 25.00 50.00

2003-07 Notre Dame TK Legacy Silver Signature Autographs

SP1 Brady Quinn
SP2 Myron Pottios/25 30.00 60.00
SP3 Blair Kiel
SP4 Johnny Lattner/25 50.00 100.00
SP5 Rick Mirer
SP6 Ken MacAfee/25 30.00 60.00

2003-07 Notre Dame TK Legacy Worn With Pride Autographs

GG54 George Goeddeke/100 15.00 30.00
JL14 Johnny Lattner/50 40.00 80.00

2006 Notre Dame Greats Schedules

COMPLETE SET (7) 2.50 5.00
1 Angelo Bertelli .30 .75
2 Tim Brown .40 1.00
3 Leon Hart .30 .75
4 Paul Hornung .40 1.00
5 John Huarte .30 .75
6 John Lattner .30 .75
7 Johnny Lujack .40 1.00

1961 Nu-Card

The 1961 Nu-Card set of 80 standard-size cards features college players. One odd feature of the set is that the card numbers start with the number 101. The set features the first nationally distributed cards of Ernie Davis, Roman Gabriel, and John Hadl.

COMPLETE SET (80) 100.00 200.00
WRAPPER (5-cent) 5.00 10.00
101 Bob Ferguson 2.50 5.00
102 Ron Snidow 1.50 3.00
103 Steve Barnett 1.25 2.50
104 Greg Mather 1.25 2.50
105 Vern Von Sydow 1.25 2.50
106 John Hewitt 1.25 2.50
107 Eddie Johns 1.25 2.50
108 Walt Rappold 1.25 2.50
109 Roy Winston 1.50 3.00
110 Bob Boyda 1.25 2.50
111 Billy Neighbors 1.50 3.00
112 Don Purcell 1.25 2.50
113 Ken Byers 1.25 2.50
114 Ed Pine 1.25 2.50
115 Fred Oblak 1.25 2.50
116 Bobby Iles 1.25 2.50
117 John Hadl 10.00 20.00
118 Charlie Mitchell 1.25 2.50
119 Bill Swinford 1.25 2.50
120 Bill King 1.25 2.50
121 Mike Lucci 3.00 6.00
122 Dave Sarette 1.25 2.50
123 Alex Kroll 1.50 3.00
124 Steve Bauwer 1.25 2.50
125 Jimmy Saxton 1.50 3.00
126 Steve Simms 1.25 2.50
127 Andy Timura 1.25 2.50
128 Gary Collins 6.00 12.00
129 Ron Taylor 1.25 2.50
130 Bobby Dodd 2.50 5.00
131 Curtis McClinton 4.00 8.00
132 Ray Poage 1.50 3.00
133 Gus Gonzales 1.25 2.50
134 Dick Locke 1.25 2.50
135 Larry Libertore 1.25 2.50
136 Stan Sczurek 1.25 2.50
137 Pete Case 1.50 3.00
138 Jesse Bradford 1.25 2.50
139 Coolidge Hunt 1.25 2.50
140 Walter Doleschal 1.25 2.50
141 Bill Williamson 1.25 2.50
142 Pat Trammell 2.50 5.00
143 Ernie Davis 30.00 60.00
144 Chuck Lamson 1.25 2.50
145 Bobby Plummer 1.50 3.00
146 Sonny Gibbs 1.50 3.00
147 Joe Ellers 1.25 2.50
148 Roger Kochman 1.25 2.50
149 Norman Beal 1.25 2.50
150 Sherwyn Torson 1.25 2.50
151 Russ Hepner 1.25 2.50
152 Joe Romig 1.25 2.50
153 Larry Thompson T 1.25 2.50
154 Tom Perdue 1.25 2.50
155 Ken Bolin 1.25 2.50
156 Art Perkins 1.25 2.50
157 Jim Sanderson 1.25 2.50
158 Bob Asack 1.25 2.50
159 Dan Celoni 1.25 2.50
160 Bill McGuirt 1.25 2.50
161 Dave Hoppmann 1.25 2.50
162 Gary Barnes 1.25 2.50
163 Don Lisbon 1.50 3.00
164 Jerry Cross 1.25 2.50
165 George Pierovich 1.25 2.50
166 Roman Gabriel 10.00 20.00
167 Billy White 1.25 2.50
168 Gale Weidner 1.25 2.50
169 Charles Rieves 1.25 2.50
170 Jim Furlong 1.25 2.50
171 Tom Hutchinson 1.50 3.00
172 Galen Hall 5.00 10.00
173 Wilburn Hollis 1.25 2.50
174 Don Kasso 1.25 2.50
175 Bill Miller 1.50 3.00
176 Ron Miller 1.25 2.50
177 Joe Williams 1.25 2.50
178 Mel Mellin 1.25 2.50
179 Tom Vassell 1.25 2.50
180 Mike Cotten 1.50 3.00

1961 Nu-Card Pennant Inserts

This set of pennant sticker pairs was inserted with the 1961 Nu-Card regular issue college football set. These inserts are actually 1 1/2" by 3 7/16" and one pair was to be inserted in each wax pack. The pennant pairs were printed with several different ink colors (orange, light-blue, navy blue, purple, green, black, and red) on several different paper stock colors (white, red, gray, orange, and yellow). The pennant pairs are unnumbered and are ordered below alphabetically according to the lowest alphabetical member of the pair. Many of the teams are available paired with several different other colleges. Any additions to this list below would be welcome.

COMPLETE SET (270) 400.00 750.00
1 Air Force / Georgetown 1.50 4.00
2 Air Force / Queens 1.50 4.00
3 Air Force / Upsala 1.50 4.00
4 Alabama / Boston U. 2.50 5.00
5 Alabama / Cornell 2.50 5.00
6 Alabama / Detroit 2.50 5.00
7 Alabama / Harvard 2.50 5.00
8 Alabama / Miami 2.50 5.00
9 Alabama / North Carolina State 2.50 5.00
10 Alabama / Wisconsin 2.50 5.00
11 Allegheny / Colorado St. 1.50 4.00
12 Allegheny / Oregon 1.50 4.00
13 Allegheny / Piedmont 1.50 4.00
14 Allegheny / Wm.and Mary 1.50 4.00
15 Arizona / Kansas 1.50 4.00
16 Arizona / Mississippi 1.50 4.00
17 Arizona / Pennsylvania 1.50 4.00
18 Arizona / S.M.U. 1.50 4.00
19 Army / Ga.Tech 1.50 4.00
20 Army / Iowa 1.50 4.00
21 Army / Johns Hopkins 1.50 4.00
22 Army / Maryland 1.50 4.00
23 Army / Missouri 1.50 4.00
24 Army / Pratt 1.50 4.00
25 Army / Purdue 1.50 4.00
26 Auburn / Florida 2.00 5.00
27 Auburn / Gettysburg 1.50 4.00
28 Auburn / Illinois 2.00 5.00
29 Auburn / Syracuse 2.00 5.00
30 Auburn / Virginia 2.00 5.00
31 Barnard / Columbia 1.50 4.00
32 Barnard / Maine 1.50 4.00
33 Barnard / N.Carolina 1.50 4.00
34 Baylor / Colorado St. 1.50 4.00
35 Baylor / Drew 1.50 4.00
36 Baylor / Oregon 1.50 4.00
37 Baylor / Piedmont 1.50 4.00
38 Boston Coll. / Minnesota 1.50 4.00
39 Boston Coll. / Norwich 1.50 4.00
40 Boston Coll. / Winthrop 1.50 4.00
41 Boston U. / Cornell 1.50 4.00
42 Boston U. / Rensselaer 1.50 4.00
43 Boston U. / Stanford 1.50 4.00
44 Boston U. / Temple 1.50 4.00
45 Boston U. / Utah State 1.50 4.00
46 Bridgeport / Holy Cross 1.50 4.00
47 Bridgeport / N.Y.U. 1.50 4.00
48 Bridgeport / Northwestrn 1.50 4.00
49 Bucknell / Illinois 1.50 4.00
50 Bucknell / Syracuse 1.50 4.00
51 Bucknell / Virginia 1.50 4.00
52 C.O.P. / Oklahoma St. 1.50 4.00
53 C.O.P. / Oregon St. 1.50 4.00
54 C.O.P. / Princeton 1.50 4.00
55 California / Delaware 1.50 4.00
56 California / Hofstra 1.50 4.00
57 California / Kentucky 1.50 4.00
58 California / Marquette 1.50 4.00
59 California / Michigan 2.50 5.00
60 California / Notre Dame 4.00 8.00
61 California / Wingate 1.50 4.00
62 Charleston / Dickinson 1.50 4.00
63 Charleston / Lafayette 1.50 4.00
64 Charleston / U.of Mass. 1.50 4.00
65 Cincinnati / Maine 1.50 4.00
66 Cincinnati / Ohio Wesl. 1.50 4.00
67 Citadel / Columbia 1.50 4.00
68 Citadel / Maine 1.50 4.00
69 Citadel / N.Carolina 1.50 4.00
70 Coast Guard / Drake 1.50 4.00
71 Coast Guard / Penn St. 1.50 4.00
72 Coast Guard / Yale 1.50 4.00
73 Coker / UCLA 1.50 4.00
74 Coker / Wingate 1.50 4.00
75 Colby / Kings Point 1.50 4.00
76 Colby / Queens 1.50 4.00
77 Colby / Rice 1.50 4.00
78 Colby / Upsala 1.50 4.00
79 Colgate / Dickinson 1.50 4.00
80 Colgate / Lafayette 1.50 4.00
81 Colgate / Springfield 1.50 4.00
82 Colgate / Texas AM 1.50 4.00
83 Colgate / U.of Mass. 1.50 4.00
84 Colo.St. / Drew 1.50 4.00
85 Colo.St. / Oregon 1.50 4.00
86 Colo.St. / Piedmont 1.50 4.00
87 Colo.St. / Wm.and Mary 1.50 4.00
88 Columbia / Dominican 1.50 4.00
89 Columbia / Maine 1.50 4.00
90 Columbia / N.Carolina 1.50 4.00
91 Cornell / Harvard 1.50 4.00
92 Cornell / Rensselaer 1.50 4.00
93 Cornell / Stanford 1.50 4.00
94 Cornell / Wisconsin 1.50 4.00
95 Dartmouth / Mich.St. 1.50 4.00
96 Dartmouth / Ohio U. 1.50 4.00
97 Dartmouth / Wagner 1.50 4.00
98 Davidson / Ohio Wesl. 1.50 4.00
99 Davidson / S.Carolina 1.50 4.00
100 Davidson / Texas Tech 1.50 4.00
101 Delaware / Marquette 1.50 4.00
102 Delaware / Michigan 1.50 4.00
103 Delaware / Notre Dame 4.00 8.00
104 Delaware / UCLA 1.50 4.00
105 Denver / Florida State 2.00 5.00
106 Denver / Indiana 1.50 4.00
107 Denver / Iowa State 1.50 4.00
108 Denver / USC 1.50 4.00
109 Denver / VMI 1.50 4.00
110 Detroit / Harvard 1.50 4.00
111 Detroit / Rensselaer 1.50 4.00
112 Detroit / Stanford 1.50 4.00
113 Detroit / Utah State 1.50 4.00
114 Dickinson / Regis 1.50 4.00
115 Dickinson / Springfield 1.50 4.00
116 Dickinson / Texas AM 1.50 4.00
117 Dickinson / U.of Mass. 1.50 4.00
118 Dominican / North Car. 1.50 4.00
119 Drake / Duke 1.50 4.00
120 Drake / Kentucky 1.50 4.00
121 Drake / Middlebury 1.50 4.00
122 Drake / Penn St. 1.50 4.00
123 Drake / St. Peters 1.50 4.00
124 Drake / Yale 1.50 4.00
125 Drew / Middlebury 1.50 4.00
126 Drew / Oregon 1.50 4.00
127 Drew / Piedmont 1.50 4.00
128 Drew / Wm. and Mary 1.50 4.00
129 Duke / Middlebury 1.50 4.00
130 Duke / Rhode Island 1.50 4.00
131 Duke / Seton Hall 1.50 4.00
133 Duke / Yale 1.50 4.00
134 Finch / Long Island AT 1.50 4.00
135 Finch / Michigan St. 1.50 4.00
136 Finch / Ohio U. 1.50 4.00
137 Finch / Wagner 1.50 4.00
138 Florida St. / Indiana 2.00 5.00
139 Florida St. / Iowa St. 2.00 5.00
140 Florida St. / So.Cal. 2.00 5.00
141 Florida St. / VMI 2.00 5.00
142 Florida / Gettysburg 1.50 4.00
143 Florida / Illinois 2.00 5.00
144 Florida / Syracuse 2.00 5.00
145 Florida / Virginia 2.00 5.00
146 Ga.Tech / Johns Hopkins 1.50 4.00
147 Ga.Tech / Maryland 1.50 4.00
148 Ga.Tech / Missouri 1.50 4.00
149 Georgetown / Kings Point 1.50 4.00
150 Georgetown / Rice 1.50 4.00
151 Georgia / Missouri 2.00 5.00
152 Georgia / Ohio Wesleyan 1.50 4.00
153 Georgia / Rutgers 1.50 4.00
154 Georgia / So.Carolina 2.00 5.00
155 Gettysburg / Syracuse 1.50 4.00
156 Harvard / Miami 2.00 5.00
157 Harvard / NC State 1.50 4.00
158 Harvard / Stanford 1.50 4.00
159 Harvard / Utah State 1.50 4.00
160 Harvard / Wisconsin 1.50 4.00
161 Hofstra / Marquette 1.50 4.00
162 Hofstra / Michigan 2.50 5.00
163 Hofstra / Navy 1.50 4.00
164 Hofstra / Notre Dame 4.00 8.00
165 Hofstra / UCLA 1.50 4.00
166 Holy Cross / Navy 1.50 4.00
167 Holy Cross / New York 1.50 4.00
168 Holy Cross / N'western 1.50 4.00
169 Holy Cross / Nyack 1.50 4.00
170 Howard / Kentucky 1.50 4.00
171 Howard / Villanova 1.50 4.00
172 Illinois / Syracuse 1.50 4.00
173 Indiana / Iowa State 1.50 4.00
174 Indiana / V.M.I. 1.50 4.00
175 Iowa State / So.Cal. 2.00 5.00
176 Iowa / Maryland 1.50 4.00
177 Iowa / Missouri 1.50 4.00
178 Iowa / Pratt 1.50 4.00
179 Johns Hopkins / Pratt 1.50 4.00
180 Johns Hopkins / Purdue 1.50 4.00
181 Kansas State / N.Y.U. 1.50 4.00
182 Kansas State / T.C.U. 1.50 4.00
183 Kansas / S.M.U. 1.50 4.00
184 Kansas / St.Francis 1.50 4.00
185 Kentucky / Maryland 1.50 4.00
186 Kentucky / Middlebury 1.50 4.00
187 Kentucky / New Hampsh. 1.50 4.00
188 Kentucky / Penn State 2.50 5.00
189 Kentucky / Rhode Island 1.50 4.00
190 Kentucky / Seton Hall 1.50 4.00
191 Kentucky / St.Peter's 1.50 4.00
192 Kentucky / Villanova 1.50 4.00
194 Kings Point / Queens 1.50 4.00
195 Kings Point / Rice 1.50 4.00
196 Kings Point / Upsala 1.50 4.00
197 Lafayette / Regis 1.50 4.00
198 Lafayette / U.of Mass. 1.50 4.00
199 Long Isl. AT / Mich.St. 1.50 4.00
200 Long Isl. AT / Ohio U. 1.50 4.00
201 Long Isl. AT / Wagner 1.50 4.00
202 Loyola / Minnesota 1.50 4.00
203 Loyola / Norwich 1.50 4.00
204 Loyola / Winthrop 1.50 4.00
205 Marquette / Michigan 2.50 5.00
206 Marquette / Navy 1.50 4.00
207 Marquette / New Platz 1.50 4.00
208 Marquette / Notre Dame 4.00 8.00
209 Marquette / UCLA 1.50 4.00
210 Maryland / Missouri 1.50 4.00
211 Mass. / Regis 1.50 4.00
212 Mass. / Springfield 1.50 4.00
213 Mass. / Texas AM 1.50 4.00
214 Michigan St. / Ohio U. 1.50 4.00
215 Michigan St. / Wagner 1.50 4.00
216 Michigan / Navy 2.50 5.00
217 Michigan / New Platz 1.50 4.00
218 Michigan / UCLA 2.50 5.00
219 Middlebury / Penn St. 1.50 4.00
220 Middlebury / Yale 1.50 4.00
221 Minnesota / Norwich 1.50 4.00
222 Minnesota / Winthrop 1.50 4.00
223 Mississippi / Penn 1.50 4.00
224 Mississippi / St.Francis 1.50 4.00
225 Missouri / Purdue 1.50 4.00
226 N.Y.U. / Northwestern 1.50 4.00
227 Navy / Notre Dame 4.00 8.00
228 Navy / UCLA 2.00 5.00
229 Navy / Wingate 1.50 4.00
230 NC State / Temple 1.50 4.00
231 NCE / Temple 1.50 4.00
232 NCE / Wisconsin 1.50 4.00
233 New Hamp. / Villanova 1.50 4.00
234 Northwestern / TCU 1.50 4.00
235 Norwich / Winthrop 1.50 4.00
236 Notre Dame / UCLA 4.00 8.00
237 Notre Dame / Wingate 2.50 5.00
238 Ohio U. / Wagner 1.50 4.00
239 Ohio Wesl. / Roberts 1.50 4.00
240 Ohio Wesl. / S.Carolina 1.50 4.00
241 Okla. St. / Pacific 1.50 4.00
242 Okla.St. / Oregon St. 1.50 4.00
243 Okla.St. / Princeton 1.50 4.00
244 Oregon St. / Princeton 1.50 4.00
245 Oregon / Piedmont 1.50 4.00
246 Oregon / Wm.and Mary 1.50 4.00
247 Penn State / Seton Hall 1.50 4.00
248 Penn State / St.Peter's 1.50 4.00
249 Penn State / Yale 1.50 4.00
250 Penn / S.M.U. 1.50 4.00
251 Penn / St.Francis 1.50 4.00
252 Queens / Rice 1.50 4.00
253 Queens / Upsala 1.50 4.00
254 Rensselaer / Stanford 1.50 4.00
255 Rensselaer / Temple 1.50 4.00
256 Rensselaer / Utah State 1.50 4.00
257 Rhode Island / Yale 1.50 4.00
258 Rice / Upsala 1.50 4.00
259 Roberts / So.Carolina 1.50 4.00
260 Roberts / Texas Tech 1.50 4.00
261 Rutgers / So.Carolina 1.50 4.00
262 So.California / VMI 2.00 5.00
263 So.Carolina / Texas Tech 1.50 4.00
264 St.Francis / S.M.U. 1.50 4.00
265 St.Peter's / Villanova 1.50 4.00
266 St.Peter's / Yale 1.50 4.00
267 Syracuse / Virginia 1.50 4.00
268 Temple / Wisconsin 1.50 4.00
269 UCLA / Wingate 2.00 5.00
270 Kentucky / Yale 1.50 4.00
270 Utah State / Wisconsin 1.50 4.00
271 Villanova / Yale 1.50 4.00

1991 Oberlin College Heisman Club

This five-card standard-size set was issued to commemorate 100 years of Oberlin football. The cards feature black-and-white posed and action photos of coaches and players significant to Oberlin's history. The front picture rests on a white card face, and a thin maroon line frames the photo and forms a box around the player's name at the bottom. A football icon in the upper left corner contains the years 1891-1991, and a maroon banner emanating from the football is printed with the words "Celebrating Oberlin Football". The backs are plain cardboard. A thin maroon line forms a box containing information about the front photos. In a smaller box is information about Oberlin College, including the Oberlin Office of Communications' phone number. The cards are unnumbered and checklisted below in alphabetical order.

COMPLETE SET (5)	2.00	5.00
1 50 Years, Two Careers	.40	1.00
C.W.(Doc) Savage		
J.H. Nichols		
(Athletic Directors)		
2 John W. Heisman CO	.80	2.00
3 Oberlin's 1892 Team	.40	1.00
4 Oberlin's Fauver Twins	.40	1.00
Doc Edgar Fauver		
Doc Edwin Fauver		
5 Oberlin's Four Horsemen	.40	1.00
Carl Semple		
Carl Williams		
H.K. Regal		
C.W.(Doc) Savage		

1993 Ohio High School Big 33

This standard-size high school football set was issued to commemorate the annual Big 33 Football Classic. The fronts feature black and white posed player photos enclosed by a white border. The state name appears at the top of the card along with the player's jersey number, name, and position. The Big 33 logo appears below the photo. The backs feature the player's biographical information along with a notation to which college he plans to attend. The unnumbered cards are listed below alphabetically.

COMPLETE SET (36)	75.00	150.00
1 David Baldwin	2.00	5.00
2 Kenya Black	2.00	5.00
3 John Day	2.00	5.00
4 Walt Delong	2.00	5.00
5 Joe Dunn	2.00	5.00
6 Marc Edwards	3.00	8.00
7 Mike Elston	2.00	5.00
8 Matt Finkes	2.00	5.00
9 Mark Fischer	2.00	5.00
10 Anthony Gwinn	2.00	5.00
11 Dan Hackenbracht	2.00	5.00
12 Ben Hall	2.00	5.00
13 Dante Hardy	2.00	5.00
14 Mark Hatgas	2.00	5.00
15 Nakia Hendrix	2.00	5.00
16 Mark Herron	2.00	5.00
17 Bob Houser	2.00	5.00
18 Darnell Howard Jr.	2.00	5.00
19 Tom Hoying	2.00	5.00
20 Brandon L. Jackson	2.00	5.00
21 Carl King	2.00	5.00
22 Pat Krebs	2.00	5.00
23 Scott Loeffler	2.00	5.00
24 Michael Malfatt	2.00	5.00
25 Curt Mellett	2.00	5.00
26 Brian Nicley	2.00	5.00
27 Sylvester Patton	2.00	5.00
28 Charles Purdue	2.00	5.00
29 Derrick Shepard	2.00	5.00
30 Lent Wan Smith	2.00	5.00
31 Jason Stere	2.00	5.00
32 Steve Terry	2.00	5.00
33 Frank Wanat	2.00	5.00
34 Jamon Williams	2.00	5.00
35 Coaches	2.00	5.00
36 Ohio Band	2.00	5.00

1994 Ohio High School Big 33

This standard-size high school football set was issued to commemorate the 37th annual Big 33 Ohio Football Classic. The cardfronts feature posed player photos enclosed by a white border. The state name appears at the top of the card along with the player's name, number, and position. The backs feature player's biographical information and future college plans if known. The cards are unnumbered and listed below alphabetically.

COMPLETE SET (35)	40.00	80.00
1 Ryan Beougher	1.25	3.00
2 Jeremy Beutler	1.25	3.00
3 Chioke Bradley	1.25	3.00
4 Calvin Brown	1.25	3.00
5 Che Bryant	1.25	3.00
6 Brooks Burris	1.25	3.00
7 Todd Bush	1.25	3.00
8 Mike Buzin	1.25	3.00
9 John Cappelletti	1.25	3.00
Honorary Captain		
10 Eric deGroh	1.25	3.00
11 Keith Dimmy	1.25	3.00
12 Chad Duff	1.25	3.00
13 Curtis Enis	3.00	8.00
14 Dennis Fitzgerald	1.25	3.00
15 Eric Gohlstin	1.25	3.00
16 Eric Haddad	1.25	3.00
17 Jason Hughes	1.25	3.00
18 Dontey Hunter	1.25	3.00
19 Kevin Huntley	1.25	3.00
20 Jermon Jackson	1.25	3.00
21 Kevin Jones	1.25	3.00
22 Todd Kollar	1.25	3.00
23 John Lumpkin	1.25	3.00
24 Marvin Major	1.25	3.00
25 Andy McCullough	1.25	3.00
26 Dee Miller	1.50	4.00
27 Damon Moore	1.25	3.00
28 Scott Mutryn	1.25	3.00
29 Orlando Pace	4.00	8.00
30 B.J. Payne	1.25	3.00
31 Pepe Pearson	1.50	4.00
32 Marcus Ray	1.25	3.00
33 Chad Smithberger	1.25	3.00
34 Rasche Sumpter	1.25	3.00
35 Sean Williams	1.25	3.00

1995 Ohio High School Big 33

This standard-size high school football set was issued to commemorate the Big 33 Ohio Football Classic. The cardfronts feature posed player photos enclosed by a white border. The state name and year appear at the top of the card along with the player's name, number, and position. The backs feature player's biographical information and future college plans if known. The cards are unnumbered and listed below alphabetically.

COMPLETE SET (35)	40.00	80.00
1 JoJuan Armour	1.25	3.00
2 Matt Borgmann	1.25	3.00
3 Jason Caswell	1.25	3.00
4 Brian Coleman	1.25	3.00
5 Tony Eisenhard	1.25	3.00
6 Mike Furrey	2.50	6.00
7 Michael Gantous	1.25	3.00
8 Michael Glassmeyer	1.25	3.00
9 Andy Habing	1.25	3.00
10 Brent Hanni	1.25	3.00
11 Murad Holliday	1.25	3.00
12 Chris Huelsman	1.25	3.00
13 Nathaniel Johnson	1.25	3.00
14 Craig Kantz	1.25	3.00
15 Percy King	1.25	3.00
16 Chris Kirk	1.25	3.00
17 Patrick Kratus	1.25	3.00
18 Matthew Lavrar	1.25	3.00
19 Courtney Ledyard	1.25	3.00
20 Tim Lewis	1.25	3.00
Honorary Captain		
21 Jason Lucas	1.25	3.00
22 Rob Majoy	1.25	3.00
23 Josh McDaniels	10.00	25.00
24 Tobey McKee	1.25	3.00
25 Rob Murphy	1.25	3.00
26 Ahmed Plummer	2.00	5.00
27 Vanness Provitt	1.25	3.00
28 Nathan Shaffer	1.25	3.00
29 Eric Smith	1.25	3.00
30 Willie Spencer	1.25	3.00
31 Charles Tincher	1.25	3.00
32 T.J. Upshaw	1.25	3.00
33 Torrence Wilson	1.25	3.00
34 Antoine Winfield	2.00	5.00
35 Steven Wisniewski	1.50	4.00

1996 Ohio High School Big 33

This standard-size high school football set was issued to commemorate the Big 33 Ohio Football Classic. The cardfronts feature posed player photos enclosed by a white border. The state initials and year appear at the top of the card along with the player's name, number, and position. The backs feature player's biographical information and future college plans if known. The cards are unnumbered and listed below alphabetically.

COMPLETE SET (35)	40.00	80.00
1 Mike Austin	1.25	3.00
2 Mike Bath	1.25	3.00
3 Gary Berry	1.25	3.00
4 Kevin Coffey	1.25	3.00
5 Jim Covert	1.25	3.00
Honorary Chairman		
6 Chris Della Vella	1.25	3.00
7 Corey Estell	1.25	3.00
8 Matt Feschak	1.25	3.00
9 Aaron Focht	1.25	3.00
10 Derek Fox	1.25	3.00
11 Ben Gilbert	1.25	3.00
12 Nick Goings	2.00	5.00
13 Kevin Houser	1.25	3.00
14 Chris Hovan	1.50	4.00
15 Robert Johnson	1.25	3.00
16 Andy Katzenmoye ERR	2.50	6.00
(name misspelled Katzemoyer)		
17 Jefferson Kelley	1.25	3.00
18 Marc Kielmeyer	1.25	3.00
19 Jeremy Manns	1.25	3.00
20 Shaun Mason	1.25	3.00
21 Chris Modelski	1.25	3.00
22 Mike Montgomery	1.25	3.00
23 Kurt Murphy	1.25	3.00
24 Daniel Norris	1.25	3.00
25 Danny O'Leary	1.25	3.00
26 Renauld Ray	1.25	3.00
27 Jermaine Sheffield	1.25	3.00
28 Rolland Steele	1.25	3.00
29 Brian Stephan	1.25	3.00
30 Dan Stultz	1.25	3.00
31 Jeremiah Taylor	1.25	3.00
32 Jason Turner	1.25	3.00
33 Tyson Walter	1.25	3.00
34 Shawn Wright	1.25	3.00
35 Eric Zbinovec	1.25	3.00

1997 Ohio High School Big 33

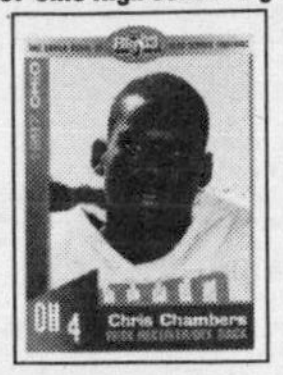

The Ohio Big 33 set consists of 36 cards featuring 34 Ohio High School All-Stars, honorary captain Herb Adderley, and an unnumbered cover card. The color photos are bordered by a reddish-brown outline and the backs are black typeset on a white background. The cards are unnumbered and have been checklisted below alphabetically.

COMPLETE SET (36)	40.00	80.00
1 Herb Adderley	1.50	4.00
2 Rodney Bailey	1.25	3.00
3 Jimmy Barker	1.25	3.00
4 Nathan Bowling	1.25	3.00
5 Jason Boykin	1.25	3.00
6 Jason Brooks	1.25	3.00
7 Terrance Brown	1.25	3.00
8 Chris Chambers	6.00	15.00
9 Tim Cheatwood	1.25	3.00
10 Mike Clinkscale	1.25	3.00
11 Derek Combs	1.50	4.00
12 Joe Cooper	1.25	3.00
13 Scott Donaldson	1.25	3.00
14 Jason Flora	1.25	3.00
15 Joe Hartings	1.50	4.00
16 Cleadous Hawk II	1.25	3.00
17 Chad Huelsman	1.25	3.00
18 Andy Keating	1.25	3.00
19 Matt Kutscher	1.25	3.00
20 Jim Massey	1.25	3.00
21 Milo McGuire	1.25	3.00
22 David Mitchell	1.25	3.00
23 Richard Newsome	1.25	3.00
24 Jason Ott	1.25	3.00
25 David Patton	1.25	3.00
26 Sean Penny	1.25	3.00
27 Ben Pulfer	1.25	3.00
28 Heath Queen	1.25	3.00
29 Mohammad Roman	1.25	3.00
30 Salem Simon	1.25	3.00
31 Greg Simpson	1.25	3.00
32 DeMario Suggs	1.25	3.00
33 Kirk Thompson	1.25	3.00
34 Matthew Wagner	1.25	3.00
35 Greg Zolman	1.25	3.00
30 Big 33 Cover Card	1.25	3.00

1998 Ohio High School Big 33

This standard-size high school football set was issued to commemorate the annual Big 33 Football Classic. The fronts feature posed player photos enclosed by a white border. The state name and year appear to the left of the player photo with the player's name and position below the photo. The Big 33 logo appears at the upper left. The backs feature the player's biographical information along with a notation to which college he plans to attend. The unnumbered cards are listed below alphabetically.

COMPLETE SET (36)	30.00	60.00
1 LeCharles Bentley	1.00	2.50
2 Rocky Boiman	1.00	2.50
3 Jamie Byrum	1.00	2.50
4 Matt Campbell	1.00	2.50
5 Nate Clements	1.50	4.00
6 Lewis Daniels	1.00	2.50
7 Erik Davis	1.00	2.50
8 Matt Edwards	1.00	2.50
9 Antoine Fisher	1.00	2.50
10 Thomas Gholstin	1.00	2.50
11 Cie Grant	1.00	2.50
12 Onaje Grimes	1.00	2.50
13 DeJuan Groce	1.00	2.50
14 Brian Hallett	1.00	2.50
15 Paul Harker	1.00	2.50
16 Heath Hommel	1.00	2.50
17 Jimmy Jones	1.00	2.50
(Honorary Captain)		
18 Sean Kennedy	1.00	2.50
19 Nick Lotz	1.00	2.50
20 Timothy Love	1.00	2.50
21 Jamar Martin	1.25	3.00
22 Gene Mruczkowski	1.00	2.50
23 Sean Nelson	1.00	2.50
24 Nick Newland	1.00	2.50
25 Kenny Peterson	1.00	2.50
26 Dave Petruziello	1.00	2.50
27 Dave Ragone	2.00	5.00
28 Robert Redd	1.00	2.50
29 Shawn Robinson	1.00	2.50
30 DeMarlo Rozier	1.00	2.50
31 Jeff Ryan	1.00	2.50
32 Matt Shook	1.00	2.50
33 Rob Turner	1.00	2.50
34 Tom Ward	1.00	2.50
35 Tommy Weilbacher	1.00	2.50
36 Ryan Wells	1.00	2.50

1999 Ohio High School Big 33

This standard-size high school football set was issued to commemorate the annual Big 33 Football Classic. The fronts feature posed player photos enclosed by a white border. The state name and year appear at the top of the cardfront with the player's name and position below the photo. The Big 33 logo appears just above the player's name. The backs feature the player's biographical information along with a notation to which college he plans to attend. The unnumbered cards are listed below alphabetically.

COMPLETE SET (35)	15.00	30.00
1 Tim Anderson	.60	1.50
2 Leo Bell	.60	1.50
3 Grant Bowman	.60	1.50
4 Carl Diggs	.75	2.00
5 Matt Dudek	.60	1.50
6 Lee Evans	3.00	8.00
7 Anthony Floyd	.60	1.50
8 Timothy Frost	.60	1.50
9 Alex Glantzis	.60	1.50
10 Joe Gonzalez	.60	1.50
11 Richard Hall	.60	1.50
12 Ben Hartsock	.60	1.50
13 Austin King	.60	1.50
14 Scott McMullen	.60	1.50
15 Darrell McMurray	.60	1.50
16 Dave Mentlow	.60	1.50
17 Paul Nixon	.60	1.50
18 Pat O'Neill	.60	1.50
19 Fred Pagac Jr.	.60	1.50
20 Jade Pruitt	.60	1.50
21 B.J. Sander	.60	1.50
22 James Simpson	.60	1.50
23 Jesse Smith	.60	1.50
24 Phillip Smith	.60	1.50
25 Nate Stead	.60	1.50
26 Tony Stemen	.60	1.50
27 Thomas Stephens	.60	1.50
28 Ben Swallow	.60	1.50
29 Derrick Tatum	.60	1.50
30 James Taylor	.60	1.50
31 Blair Thomas Capt.	.60	1.50
32 Ben Timmons	.60	1.50
33 Gary Tisdale	.60	1.50
34 Deryck Toles	.75	2.00
35 Matt Wilhelm	.75	2.00

2000 Ohio High School Big 33

This set was issued to commemorate the annual Big 33 High School Football Classic. The cardfronts feature color player photos along with the outline of the state below the photo and the year to the left. The player's name, jersey number, and position appear within the outline of the state. The cardbacks feature the player's biographical information along with a notation to which college he plans to attend. The unnumbered cards are listed below alphabetically.

COMPLETE SET (36)	75.00	135.00
1 B.J. Barre	.60	1.50
2 Andy Capper	.60	1.50
3 Andy Christopfel	.60	1.50
4 Dan Davis	.60	1.50
5 James Fisher	.60	1.50
6 Ryan Flynn	.60	1.50
7 Steve Gilbert CO	.60	1.50
8 Charles Gilstrap	.60	1.50
9 Jason Harmon	1.00	2.50
10 Brian Heizman	.60	1.50
11 Michael Henry	.60	1.50
12 John Hollins	.60	1.50
13 Jake Holthaus	.60	1.50
14 Josh Huston	.60	1.50
15 Ray Huston	.60	1.50
16 Jorrell Johnson	.60	1.50
17 Jim Kelly	1.25	3.00
(Honorary Captain)		
18 Jeff Kennard	.60	1.50
19 Michael Larkin	.60	1.50
20 Keith Matthews	.60	1.50
21 Sean McHugh	.60	1.50
22 Dan Minocchi	.60	1.50
23 Dan Mooney	.60	1.50
24 Ellery Moore	.60	1.50
25 Nathan Poole	.60	1.50
26 Jon Pressnell	.60	1.50
27 Joe Radich	.60	1.50
28 Dave Rehker	.60	1.50
29 Ben Roethlisberger	60.00	120.00
30 Jason Rollins	.60	1.50
31 Sam Ruhe	.60	1.50
32 James Taylor	.60	1.50
33 Maurice Taylor	.60	1.50
34 Charles Terry	.60	1.50
35 Dennis Thompson	.60	1.50
36 Vinnie West	.60	1.50

2001 Ohio High School Big 33

Pennsylvania and Ohio card sets were again issued in 2001 to commemorate the annual Big 33 High School Football Classic. The cardfronts feature color player photos along with a solid black border. The player's name, jersey number, and position appear below the player's photo. The cardbacks feature the player's biographical information along with a notation to which college he plans to attend. The unnumbered cards are listed below alphabetically.

COMPLETE SET (35)	15.00	30.00
1 Redgie Arden	.60	1.50
2 Chase Blackburn	2.50	6.00
3 Ryan Brown	.60	1.50
4 Jamal Bryant	.60	1.50
5 Angelo Chattams	.60	1.50
6 Blake Dickson	.60	1.50
7 Jared Ellerson	.60	1.50
8 Jameson Evans	.60	1.50
9 Damien Fortson	.60	1.50
10 Dustin Fox	.75	2.00
11 Simon Fraser	.60	1.50
12 Nate Fry	.60	1.50
13 Na'Shan Goddard	.60	1.50
14 Maurice Hall	.75	2.00
15 Ryan Hamby	.60	1.50
16 Chris Harrell	.60	1.50
17 Micah Harris	.60	1.50
18 Blair Kramer	.60	1.50
19 Kyle Magoteaux	.60	1.50
20 Pat Massey	.60	1.50
21 Joe Montana	4.00	8.00
(Honorary Captain)		
22 Tim Murphy	.60	1.50
23 Bryan Panteck	.60	1.50
24 Patrick Ross	.60	1.50
25 Kreg Rotthoff	.60	1.50
26 Brandon Schnittker	.60	1.50
27 Brad Smith	2.00	4.00
28 Jake Sowers	.60	1.50
29 Zach Strief	.60	1.50
30 Matt Turner	.60	1.50
31 Andree Tyree	.60	1.50
32 Ken Williams	.60	1.50
33 Pierre Woods	.60	1.50
34 Jason Wright	.60	1.50
35 Garrett Young	.60	1.50

2002 Ohio High School Big 33

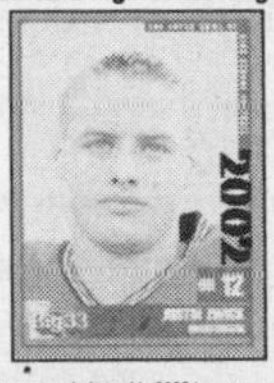

Card sets were again issued in 2002 to commemorate the annual Big 33 High School Football Classic between Ohio and Pennsylvania layers. The cardfronts feature color player photos along with a solid red border. The player's name, jersey number, and position appear below the player's photo. The cardbacks feature the player's vital statistics as well as biographical information. The unnumbered cards are listed below alphabetically.

COMPLETE SET (36)	15.00	30.00
1 David Abdul	.50	1.25
2 Bryan Andrews	.50	1.25
3 Trumaine Banks	.50	1.25
4 Joey Card	.50	1.25
5 Brandon Cornell	.50	1.25
6 T.J. Downing	.50	1.25
7 Joel East	.50	1.25
8 Tyler Everett	.50	1.25
9 Roman Fry	.50	1.25
10 Steven Gunter	.50	1.25
11 A.J. Hawk	2.50	6.00
12 Jeremy Hines	.50	1.25
13 Jeff Hostetler	.50	1.25
(Honorary Chairman)		
14 Mike Kudla	.50	1.25
15 Matt Leininger	.50	1.25
16 Nick Mangold	1.00	2.50
17 Bo Martin	.50	1.25
18 Joel Penton	.50	1.25
19 Erick Phillips	.50	1.25
20 Mark Philmore	.50	1.25
21 P.J. Pope	.50	1.25
22 Robert Price III	.50	1.25
23 Kyle Ralph	.50	1.25
24 Jay Richardson	.50	1.25
25 Jay Rohr	.50	1.25
26 Tim Schafer	.50	1.25
27 John Scott	.50	1.25
28 Robert Sims	.50	1.25
29 Nathan Szep	.50	1.25
30 E.J. Underwood	.50	1.25
31 Steve Vallos	.50	1.25
32 Dave Wannstedt	.50	1.25
(Honorary Chairman)		
33 Ashton Watson	.50	1.25
34 Quentin White	.50	1.25
35 Joshua Williams	.50	1.25
36 Justin Zwick	1.00	2.50

2003 Ohio High School Big 33

A card set was again released in 2003 for the Ohio team in the annual Big 33 High School Football Classic between Ohio and Pennsylvania players. The cardfronts feature color player photos along with a red border. The player's name and position appears below the player's photo along with the Big 33 logo. The cardbacks feature the player's vital statistics as well as biographical information. The unnumbered cards are listed below alphabetically.

COMPLETE SET (36)	15.00	25.00
1 James Addington	.50	1.25
2 Ken Akridge	.50	1.25
3 Tom Anevski	.50	1.25
4 Kirk Barton	.50	1.25
5 Tony Carvitti	.50	1.25
6 Shawn Crable	.50	1.25
7 Michael Daniels	.50	1.25
8 Mike DeLuca	.50	1.25
9 Keilen Dykes	.50	1.25
10 Ray Edwards	.75	2.00
11 Jerrid Gaines	.50	1.25
12 Anthony Gonzalez	2.00	5.00
13 Ty Hall	.50	1.25
14 Louis Irizarry	.50	1.25
15 Derrick Jeffries	.50	1.25
16 Devin Jordan	.50	1.25
17 Curt Lukens	.50	1.25
18 Dan Marino	4.00	8.00
Honorary Chairman		
19 Ben Mauk	.50	1.25
20 Brandon Maupin	.50	1.25
21 Curtis McGhee	.50	1.25
22 Mike McGlynn	.50	1.25
23 Caleb Meyer	.50	1.25
24 Darren Paige	.50	1.25
25 David Patterson	.50	1.25
26 Bill Poland	.50	1.25
27 Ryne Robinson	.50	1.25
28 Zach Slates	.50	1.25
29 Ashley Smith	.50	1.25
30 Reggie Smith	.50	1.25
31 Davanzo Tate	.50	1.25
32 Jon Tobin	.50	1.25
33 Justin Valentine	.50	1.25
34 Ernie Wheelwright	.50	1.25
35 Jarret Woods	.50	1.25
36 Cover Card	.50	1.25
Checklist		

2004 Ohio High School Big 33

This set was released in July 2004 for the Ohio team participating in the annual Big 33 High School Football Classic. The cardfronts feature color player photos along with a border resembling a picture frame. The player's name and position appear below the player's photo along with the Big 33 logo. The cardbacks feature the player's vital statistics as well as biographical information. The unnumbered cards are listed below alphabetically.

COMPLETE SET (36)	15.00	30.00
1 Alex Barrow	.50	1.25
2 Joel Belding	.50	1.25
3 William Brody	.50	1.25
4 Brad Bury	.50	1.25
5 Gerald Cadogan	.50	1.25
6 Tony Davis WR	.50	1.25
7 Andrew Decker	.50	1.25
8 Shawn Donaldson	.50	1.25
9 Jason Giannini	.50	1.25
10 Ted Ginn	2.50	6.00
11 Grant Gregory	.50	1.25
12 Erik Haw	.50	1.25
13 Chad Hoobler	.50	1.25
14 Tony Howard	.50	1.25
15 Brian Hoyer	1.25	3.00
16 Chauncey Incarnato	.50	1.25
17 Josh Kerr	.50	1.25
18 Justin Kershaw	.50	1.25
19 Ryan Marando	.50	1.25
20 Mike Massey	.50	1.25
21 Chad Mayse	.50	1.25
22 Matt Millen	.50	1.25
Honorary Chairman		
23 Nick Moore	.50	1.25
24 Haruki Nakamura	.50	1.25
25 Nii Adjei Oninku	.50	1.25
26 Ben Person	.50	1.25
27 Brandon Smith	.50	1.25
28 K.L. Smith	.50	1.25
29 Ryan Stanchek	.50	1.25
30 Anthony Turner	.50	1.25
31 Brandon Underwood	.50	1.25
32 Sirjo Welch	.50	1.25
33 Asante White	.50	1.25
34 Pernell Williams	.50	1.25
35 Dustin Woods	.50	1.25
36 Cover Card	.50	1.25

2005 Ohio High School Big 33

This set was released in July 2005 for the Ohio team participating in the annual Big 33 High School Football Classic. The cardfronts feature color player photos along with a very thin dark red border. The player's name appears below the player's photo along with the PNC Big 33 logo. The cardbacks feature the player's vital statistics as well as biographical information. The unnumbered cards are listed below alphabetically.

COMPLETE SET (36)	12.50	25.00
1 Andre Amos	.40	1.00
2 Terrill Byrd	.30	.75
3 Rocco Cironi	.30	.75
4 Todd Denlinger	.30	.75
5 Jess East	.30	.75
6 Steve Gawronski	.30	.75
7 Dominic Goodman	.30	.75
8 Brian Hartline	1.25	3.00
9 Rocket Ismail	.50	1.25
10 Brad Jones	.30	.75
11 Brandon Long	.30	.75
12 Dante Love	.30	.75
13 Mario Manningham	3.00	8.00
14 Zach Marshall	.30	.75
15 Jared Martin	.30	.75
16 Brian Mellott	.30	.75
17 Zoltan Mesko	.75	2.00
18 Mike Mickens	.30	.75
19 Derek Moore	.30	.75
20 E.J. Morton-Green	.30	.75
21 Andrew Moses	.30	.75
22 Jim Ramella	.30	.75
23 Tim Reed	.30	.75
24 Javon Ringer	1.25	3.00
25 Brian Robiskie	1.25	3.00
26 Mike Sheridan	.30	.75
27 Robby Shoenhoft	.60	1.50
28 Nick Simon	.30	.75
29 Mister Simpson	.30	.75
30 Curtis Smith	.30	.75
31 Austin Spitler	.30	.75
32 Derrick Stewart	.30	.75
33 Matt Tennant	.30	.75
34 Bryan Williams	.30	.75
35 Lawrence Wilson	.50	1.25
36 Cover Card	.30	.75

2006 Ohio High School Big 33

This set was released in July 2006 for the Ohio team participating in the annual Big 33 High School Football Classic. The cardfronts feature color player photos along with a very thin black border. The player's name appears below the player's photo along with the PNC Big 33 logo. The cardbacks feature the player's vital statistics as well as biographical information. The unnumbered cards are listed below alphabetically.

COMPLETE SET (36)	10.00	20.00
1 Kyle Banna	.30	.75
2 David Brewer	.30	.75
3 Brad Brookbank	.30	.75
4 Bryant Browning	.30	.75
5 Delone Carter	1.00	2.50
6 Chris Condeni	.30	.75
7 Jason Donnal	.30	.75
8 Troy Ellis	.30	.75
9 Anthony Elzy	.50	1.25
10 Kyle Endicott	.30	.75
11 Bill Fralic CO	.30	.75
12 Levi George	.30	.75
13 Thaddeus Gibson	.50	1.25
14 Danny Hall	.30	.75
15 Christen Haywood	.30	.75
16 Jamar Howard	.30	.75
17 Derrell Johnson	.30	.75
18 Drew Kuhn	.30	.75
19 Corey Leggett	.50	1.25
20 Torrance Nicholson Jr.	.30	.75
21 Anthony Oliver	.30	.75
22 Ryan Palmer	.30	.75
23 Troy Pascley	.30	.75
24 Austin Power	.30	.75
25 Zach Pridemore	.30	.75
26 Paul Rice	.30	.75
27 Richard Sandilands	.30	.75
28 Ted Schaible	.30	.75
29 Mike Scherpenberg	.30	.75
30 Zach Slagle	.30	.75
31 Ray Small	.50	1.25
32 Brad Stetler	.30	.75
33 Kallen Wade	.30	.75
34 Mike Welce	.30	.75
35 Robert Williams	.30	.75
36 Cover Card	.30	.75

2007 Ohio High School Big 33

COMPLETE SET (36)	7.50	15.00
1 Disi Alexander	.30	.75
2 Frank Becker	.30	.75
3 Ryan Carter	.30	.75
4 Zach Collaros	.30	.75
5 Zak Crum	.30	.75
6 B.J. Cunningham	.40	1.00
7 Bruce Davis	.30	.75
8 Brady DeMell	.30	.75
9 Frank Edmonds	.30	.75
10 Debo Elias	.30	.75
11 Perci Garner	.30	.75
12 John Hughes	.30	.75
13 Daniel Ifft	.30	.75
14 Kyle Jefferson	.30	.75
15 Will Johnson	.30	.75
16 Kevin Koncelik	.30	.75
17 Caleb Libsey	.30	.75
18 Chris Littleton	.30	.75
19 Charles Matthews	.30	.75
20 Matt Merletti	.30	.75
21 Otis Merrill	.30	.75
22 Julian Miller	.30	.75
23 Diauntae Morrow	.30	.75
24 Chris Rucker	.30	.75
25 Jon Saelinger	.30	.75
26 Marty Schottenheimer	.30	.75
Honorary Chairman		
27 Jeremy Shrieves	.30	.75
28 Nick Spadafore	.30	.75
29 Kenny Staudinger	.30	.75
30 J.B. Strahler	.30	.75
31 George Tabron	.30	.75
32 Jay Triggs	.30	.75
33 Andy Wersel	.30	.75
34 Lorren Womack	.30	.75
35 Anthony Wright	.30	.75
36 Header Card	.30	.75

2008 Ohio High School Big 33

COMPLETE SET (36)	10.00	20.00
1 Phillip Barnett	.30	.75
2 Todd Blackledge HC	.40	1.00
3 D.J. Brown	.30	.75
4 Justin Brown	.30	.75
5 Ben Buchanan	.30	.75
6 Cody Connare	.30	.75
7 Nic Dillo	.30	.75
8 Zac Dysert	.30	.75
9 Steve Gardiner	.30	.75
10 Taylor Hill	.30	.75
11 William Lowe	.30	.75
12 Bijan Machen	.30	.75
13 Joey Madsen	.30	.75
14 Lamar McQueen	.30	.75
15 Matt Mihalik	.30	.75
16 Danny Milligan	.30	.75
17 Brandon Mills	.30	.75
18 Briggs Orsbon	.30	.75
19 Isaiah Pead	.30	.75
20 Andrew Phelan	.30	.75
21 David Plungas	.30	.75
22 Taylor Rice	.30	.75
23 Roy Roundtree	.50	1.25
24 Shawntel Rowell	.30	.75
25 Zebrie Sanders	.30	.75
26 Michael Shaw RB	.50	1.25
27 Bart Tanski	.30	.75
28 Nicholas Truesdell	.30	.75
29 Aaron Van Kuiken	.30	.75
30 Kenny Veal	.30	.75
31 Dawawn Whitner	.30	.75
32 Nathaniel Williams	.30	.75
33 D.J. Woods	.30	.75
34 Jerel Worthy	.75	2.00
35 Michael Zordich ILB	.40	1.00
36 Cover Card	.30	.75

2009 Ohio High School Big 33

COMPLETE SET (36)	7.50	15.00
1 Denicos Allen	.25	.60
2 John Anevski	.25	.60
3 Perez Ashford	.25	.60
4 Adam Bellamy	.25	.60
5 Austin Boucher	.25	.60
6 Kyle Brady HC	.40	1.00
7 Darwin Cook	.25	.60
8 Romel Dismuke	.25	.60
9 Michael Edwards	.25	.60
10 Melvin Fellows	.25	.60

11 Chris Fields	.40	1.00
12 Nate Freese	.25	.60
13 Jeffvon Gill	.25	.60
14 Marcus Hall	.25	.60
15 Mican Hyde	.25	.60
16 Donovan Jarrett	.25	.60
17 Josh Jones	.25	.60
18 Shaun Joplin	.40	1.00
19 Nate Klatt	.25	.60
20 Corey Linsley	.25	.60
21 Sam Longo	.25	.60
22 Tim Moore	.25	.60
23 Johnathan Newsome	.25	.60
24 Patrick Nicely	.25	.60
25 Cody Pettit	.25	.60
26 Jason Pinkston	.25	.60
27 John Prior	.25	.60
28 Adam Replogle	.25	.60
29 Brian Slack	.25	.60
30 Jake Smith	.25	.60
31 Chris Snook	.25	.60
32 Ryan Spiker	.25	.60
33 Will Studlein	.25	.60
34 Fitzgerald Toussaint	.40	1.00
35 Chris Williams	.25	.60
36 Kyle Brady Art Cover	.25	.60

2010 Ohio High School Big 33

COMPLETE SET (36)	7.50	15.00
1 Pete Bachman	.25	.60
2 Darryl Baldwin	.25	.60
3 Shane Belle	.25	.60
4 Devin Brown	.25	.60
5 Christian Bryant	.25	.60
6 Brendan Carozzoni	.25	.60
7 Quintin Cooper	.25	.60
8 Mike Dorsey	.25	.60
9 Te Elias	.25	.60
10 Mark Fackler	.25	.60
11 Darius Gilbert	.25	.60
12 Prince-Tyson Gulley	.30	.75
13 Chase Hammond	.30	.75
14 Chase Hoobler	.25	.60
15 Travis Jackson	.25	.60
16 Andy Jomantas	.25	.60
17 Dwight Macon	.25	.60
18 Greg Mancz	.25	.60
19 Sam Miller	.25	.60
20 J.T. Moore	.25	.60
21 Jeff Myers	.25	.60
22 Mark Myers	.40	1.00
23 Brandon Neal	.25	.60
24 Roosevelt Nix	.25	.60
25 Odis Prunity	.25	.60
26 Verlon Reed	.50	1.25
27 Matt Rotheram	.25	.60
28 Kevin Schloemer	.25	.60
29 Clint Shepherd	.25	.60
30 Lee Skinner	.25	.60
31 Jewone Snow	.25	.60
32 Carey Spear	.25	.60
33 Terrence Talbott	.25	.60
34 Terry Talbott	.25	.60
35 Ricky Watters HC	.30	.75
36 Cover Card	.25	.60

2011 Ohio High School Big 33

COMPLETE SET (36)	7.50	15.00
1 Andrew Bohan	.25	.60
2 Kevin Brewton	.25	.60
3 Kyle Cameron	.25	.60
4 Donavon Clark	.25	.60
5 Frank Clark	.25	.60
6 Connor Cook	.40	1.00
7 Steven Daniels (no player image)	.25	.60
8 Jeremiah Detmer	.25	.60
9 Chris Dukes	.25	.60
10 Trayion Durham	.25	.60
11 Chase Farris	.25	.60
12 Gabe Gilbert	.25	.60
13 Doran Grant	.25	.60
14 Kyle Hammonds	.25	.60
15 Joel Heath	.25	.60
16 Keith Heitzman	.25	.60
17 Brandon Jackson	.25	.60
18 Cardale Jones	.40	1.00
19 Noah Key	.25	.60
20 Ty Law HC	.40	1.00
21 John Lowdermilk	.25	.60
22 Steve Miller	.30	.75
23 Geoff Mogus	.25	.60
24 Cheatham Norrils	.25	.60
25 Justin Olack	.25	.60
26 Antonio Poole	.25	.60
27 Mark Rogers	.25	.60
28 Matt Skura	.25	.60
29 Andrew Smith	.25	.60
30 Devin Smith	.30	.75
31 Akise Teague	.25	.60
32 Chris Thomas	.25	.60
33 Antonio Undrwood	.25	.60
34 Nick Vannett	.25	.60
35 Tyler Williams	.25	.60
36 Cover Card	.25	.60

1955 Ohio University

This set of black and white player photos was released by the University of Ohio. Each was printed on high gloss paper stock and measures roughly 8" by 10." The players are not specifically identified but are often found with a hand typed ID on the backs. The set is unnumbered and checklisted below in alphabetical order.

COMPLETE SET (10)	45.00	90.00
1 Bob Kappes	5.00	10.00
Cliff Heffelfinger		
Joe Dean		
Bill Hess		
Frank Richey		
Frank Elwood		
Bucky Wagner CO		
2 Bob Beach	5.00	10.00
3 James Brown	5.00	10.00
4 Cleve Bryant	5.00	10.00
5 Dick Conley	5.00	10.00
6 Bob Houmard	5.00	10.00
7 Dave LeVeck	5.00	10.00
8 Dave Mueller	5.00	10.00
9 John Smith	5.00	10.00
10 Frank Spolrich	5.00	10.00

1945 Ohio State

This black and white team issue photo set was released by the school in a white envelope that pictured a game action photo from a Minnesota versus OSU contest. Each photo measures roughly 2 3/4" by 3 1/4" and is bankbacked.

COMPLETE SET (18)	200.00	400.00
1 Warren Amling	12.50	25.00
2 Paul Bixler CO	12.50	25.00
3 Matt Brown	12.50	25.00
4 Ollie Cline	12.50	25.00
5 Thornton Dixon	12.50	25.00
6 Bob Dove	12.50	25.00
7 Ernest Godfrey CO	12.50	25.00
8 Bill Hackett	12.50	25.00
9 Dick Jackson	12.50	25.00
10 Jerry Krall	12.50	25.00
11 Jim Lininger	12.50	25.00
12 Ernie Santora	12.50	25.00
13 Paul Sarringhaus	15.00	30.00
14 Russ Thomas	12.50	25.00
15 Alex Verdova	12.50	25.00
16 Carroll Widdoes CO	12.50	25.00
17 Sam Winter	12.50	25.00
18 Ward Wright	12.50	25.00

1974 Ohio State Team Sheets

These photos were issued by the school to promote the football program. Each measures roughly 8" by 10" and features eight black and white images of players with the school name appearing at the top. The backs are blank.

1 Brian Baschnagel	4.00	8.00
Jim Cope		
Dave Purdy		
Tim Fox		
Dick Mack		
Arnie Jones		
Harold Henson		
Pete Johnson		
2 Woody Hayes CO	7.50	15.00
Archie Griffin		
Cornelius Green		
Neal Colzie		
Pete Cusick		
Steve Myers		
Kurt Schumacher		
Van DeCree		

1979 Ohio State Greats 1916-1965

This set features Ohio State football players and coaches who obtained All-American or College Football Hall of Fame status from 1916 through 1965. The cards were issued in playing card format and each card measures approximately 2 1/2" by 3 1/4". The fronts feature a close-up photograph of the player in an octagon frame. The backs feature a collage of Ohio State players within an octagon border with "All-Americans, National Football Hall of Famers" at the bottom. Because this set is similar to a playing card set, the set is arranged just like a card deck and checklisted below as follows: C means Clubs, D means Diamonds, H means Hearts, S means Spades, and JK means Joker. The cards are checklisted below in playing card order by suits and numbers are assigned to Aces (1), Jacks (11), Queens (12), and Kings (13). The joker is listed at the end.

COMPLETE SET (52)	50.00	100.00
1C Howard Cassady 1955	1.25	3.00
1D Wes Fesler 1928	.75	2.00
1H Doug Van Horn	.75	2.00
1S Chic Harley 1916	.75	2.00
2C Dean Dugger	.75	2.00
2D Wes Fesler 1929	.75	2.00
2H Ike Kelley 1965	.75	2.00
2S Robert Karch	.75	2.00
3C Howard Cassady 1954	1.25	3.00
3D Wes Fesler 1930	.75	2.00
3H Jim Davidson	.75	2.00
3S Charles Bolen	.75	2.00
4C Mike Takacs	.75	2.00
4D Joseph Gailus	.75	2.00
4H Ike Kelley 1964	.75	2.00
4S Chic Harley 1917	.75	2.00
5C Robert Momsen	.75	2.00
5D Regis Monahan	.75	2.00
5H Arnold Chonko	.75	2.00
5S Chic Harley 1919	.75	2.00
6C Robert McCullough	.75	2.00
6D Gomer Jones	.75	2.00
6H Bob Ferguson 1961	.75	2.00
6S Iolas Huffman 1920	.75	2.00
7C Vic Janowicz	1.00	2.50
7D Inwood Smith	.75	2.00
7H Bob Ferguson 1960	.75	2.00
7S Gaylord Stinchcomb	.75	2.00
8C Warren Amling 1946	.75	2.00
8D Gust Zarnas	.75	2.00
8H Jim Houston 1959	.75	2.00
8S Iolas Huffman 1921	.75	2.00
9C Warren Amling 1945	.75	2.00
9D Esco Sarkkinen	.75	2.00
9H Jim Marshall	1.25	3.00
9S Harold Cuningham	.75	2.00
10C Bill Willis	1.50	4.00
10D Don Scott	.75	2.00
10H Jim Houston 1958	.75	2.00
10S Edwin Hess 1925	.75	2.00
11C Les Horvath	1.00	2.50
11D Charles Csuri	.75	2.00
11H Aurelius Thomas	.75	2.00
11S Edwin Hess 1926	.75	2.00
12C Bill Hackett	.75	2.00
12D Lindell Houston	.75	2.00
12H Jim Parker 1956	2.00	5.00
12S Martin Karow	.75	2.00
13C Jack Dugger	.75	2.00
13D Bob Shaw	1.00	2.50
13H Jim Parker 1955	2.00	5.00
13S Leo Raskowski	.75	2.00

1979 Ohio State Greats 1966-1978

This 53-card set contains all the Ohio State football players and coaches who obtained All-American or National Football (college) Hall of Fame status from 1966 through 1978. The cards were issued in the playing card format, and each card measures approximately 2 1/2" by 3 1/4". The fronts feature a close-up photograph of the player in an octagon frame. Those cards with two stars in the octagon frame indicate those players voted into the National Football Hall of Fame. The red colored backs feature a collage of Ohio State players within an octagon border with "All-Americans, National Football Hall of Famers" at the bottom. Because this set is similar to a playing card set, the set is arranged just like a card deck and checklisted below as follows: C means Clubs, D means Diamonds, H means Hearts, S means Spades, and JK means Joker. The cards are checklisted below in playing card order by suits and numbers are assigned to Aces (1), Jacks (11), Queens (12), and Kings (13). The joker is listed at the end.

COMPLETE SET (53)	75.00	150.00
1C Chris Ward	.75	2.00
1D Jan White	1.25	2.50
1H Ernest R. Godfrey ACO	.75	2.00
1S Ray Pryor	.75	2.00
2C Ray Griffin	1.25	2.50
2D Tom Deleone	1.25	2.50
2H Francis A. Schmidt CO	1.25	2.50
2S Dave Foley	1.25	2.50
3C Tom Cousineau	2.00	4.00
3D Randy Gradishar	2.50	5.00
3H Jim Parker	3.00	6.00
3S Rufus Mayes	1.25	2.50
4C Aaron Brown	1.25	2.50
4D John Hicks	2.00	4.00
4H Vic Janowicz	2.50	5.00
4S Rex Kern	2.00	4.00
5C Chris Ward	.75	2.00
5D Van Decree	.75	2.00
5H Les Horvath	2.00	5.00
5S Jim Otis	2.00	5.00
6C Tom Skladany	1.25	2.50
6D Randy Gradishar	2.50	5.00
6H Bill Willis	2.00	5.00
6S Ted Provost	.75	2.00
7C Bob Brudzinski	1.25	2.50
7D Archie Griffin	3.00	6.00
7H James Daniell	.75	2.00
7S Jim Stillwagon	1.25	2.50
8C Ted Smith	.75	2.00
8D John Hicks	2.00	4.00
8H Gust Zarnas	.75	2.00
8S Jack Tatum	2.00	5.00
9C Tom Skladany	1.25	2.50
9D Neal Colzie	1.25	2.50
9H Gomer Jones	.75	2.00
9S Tim Anderson	.75	2.00
10C Archie Griffin	3.00	6.00
10D Pete Cusick	.75	2.00
10H Wes Fesler	1.25	2.50
10S John Brockington	2.00	5.00
11C Tim Fox	1.25	2.50
11D Van Decree	.75	2.00
11H Pete Stinchcomb	.75	2.00
11S Mike Sensibaugh	1.25	2.50
12C Tom Skladany	1.25	2.50
12D Archie Griffin	3.00	6.00
12H Chic Harley	.75	2.00
12S Jim Stillwagon	1.25	2.50
13C Kurt Schumacher	1.25	2.50
13D Steve Meyers	1.25	2.50
13H Tom Cousineau	2.00	4.00
13S Jack Tatum	2.00	5.00
JK Howard Jones CO	1.25	2.50

1988 Ohio State

The 1988 Ohio State University football set contains 22 standard-size cards. The fronts have vintage or color action photos with white borders; the vertically oriented backs have detailed profiles. These cards were distributed as a set. The set is unnumbered, so the cards are listed alphabetically.

COMPLETE SET (22)	12.50	25.00
1 Bob Brudzinski	.50	1.25
2 Keith Byars	.75	2.00
3 Hopalong Cassady	.75	2.00
4 Arnold Chonko	.40	1.00
5 Wes Fesler	.40	1.00
6 Randy Gradishar	1.25	3.00
7 Archie Griffin	1.00	2.50
8 Chic Harley	.40	1.00
9 Woody Hayes CO	.50	4.00
10 John Hicks	.40	1.00
11 Les Horvath	.75	2.00
12 Jim Houston	.50	1.25
13 Vic Janowicz	1.00	2.50
14 Pepper Johnson	.60	1.50
15 Ike Kelley	.40	1.00
16 Rex Kern	.50	1.25
17 Jim Lachey	.60	1.50
18 Jim Parker	1.00	2.50
19 Tom Skladany	.40	1.00
20 Chris Spielman	1.00	2.50
21 Jim Stillwagon	.40	1.00
22 Jack Tatum	1.00	2.50

1989 Ohio State

The 1989 Ohio State University football set contains 22 standard-size cards. The fronts have vintage or color action photos with white borders; the vertically oriented backs have detailed profiles. These cards were distributed as a set and are numbered on the backs.

COMPLETE SET (22)	15.00	30.00
1 Mike Tomczak	.60	1.50
2 Paul Warfield	1.25	3.00
3 Kirk Lowdermilk	.50	1.25
4 Bob Ferguson	.50	1.25
5 Jack Graf	.40	1.00
6 Tim Fox	.50	1.25
7 Eric Kumerow	.50	1.25
8 Neal Colzie	.50	1.25
9 Jim Otis	.60	1.50
10 John Brockington	.75	2.00
11 Cornelius Greene	.50	1.25
12 Jim Marshall	1.00	2.50
13 Tim Spencer	.50	1.25
14 Don Scott	.40	1.00
15 Chris Ward	.40	1.00
16 Marcus Marek	.50	1.25
17 Dave Foley	.50	1.25
18 Bill Willis	.75	2.00
19 John Frank	.60	1.50
20 Rufus Mayes	.50	1.25
21 Tom Tupa	.50	1.25
22 Jan White	.50	1.25

1990 Ohio State

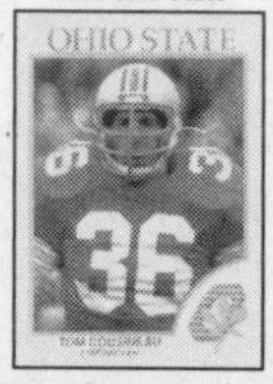

This 22-card set measures the standard size. There is a full color photograph on the front, and the Ohio State logo on the lower right-hand corner. The back has biographical information about the player. The set was produced by College Classics and features past and current players.

COMPLETE SET (22)	10.00	20.00
1 Jeff Uhlenhake	.60	1.50
2 Ray Ellis	.50	1.25
3 Todd Bell	.60	1.50
4 Jeff Logan	.50	1.25
5 Pete Johnson	.75	2.00
6 Van DeCree	.50	1.25
7 Ted Provost	.50	1.25
8 Mike Lanese	.50	1.25
9 Aaron Brown	.60	1.50
10 Pete Cusick	.50	1.25
11 Vlade Janakievski	.50	1.25
12 Steve Myers	.50	1.25
13 Ted Smith	.50	1.25
14 Doug Donley	.60	1.50
15 Ron Springs	.75	2.00
16 Ken Fritz	.50	1.25
17 Jeff Davidson	.50	1.25
18 Art Schlichter	1.00	2.50
19 Tom Cousineau	1.00	2.50
20 Calvin Murray	.50	1.25
21 Brian Baschnagel	.60	1.50
22 Joe Staysniak	.50	1.25

1992 Ohio State

This 1992 Ohio State University football set contains 59 standard-size cards. Packaged in a cardboard sleeve, the cards were available only through the Ohio State Department of Athletics, the Arena Shop and its affiliated University bookstores. They originally sold this card set for 14.00, but the set was later closed out at a lower price. The fronts feature full-bleed action and posed color photos. The player's name is printed in red lettering inside a gray bar at the bottom, and the school logo also appears in different corners on the fronts. On a white background, the backs carry a small color close-up shot, short player biography, a detailed profile, career stats, and the school logo. Robert Smith and Greg Smith were not featured in this 59-card set because they reportedly refused to sign the NCAA waiver that must accompany their appearance in a profit-making endeavor on behalf of their school. Joey Galloway and Eddie George are the key cards in this set, but there are several other NFL draftees and players in this set.

COMPLETE SET (59)	16.00	40.00
1 John Cooper CO	.15	.40
2 Kirk Herbstreit	.08	.25
3 Steve Tovar	.30	.75
4 Chico Nelson	.08	.25
5 Tim Patillo	.08	.25
6 Tito Paul	.15	.40
7 Jim Borchers	.08	.25
8 Craig Powell	.30	.75
9 Deron Brown	.08	.25
10 Alex Rodriguez	.08	.25
11 Chris Sanders	.60	1.50
12 Cedric Saunders	.08	.25
13 Walter Taylor	.08	.25
14 Jack Thrush	.08	.25
15 Brian Stablein	.30	.75
16 Tim Walton	.08	.25
17 Rod Smith	.15	.40
18 Brad Pope	.08	.25
19 William Houston	.08	.25
20 Dan Wilkinson	.60	1.50
21 Jason Winrow	.08	.25
22 Mark Williams	.08	.25
23 Jason Simmons	.08	.25
24 Luke Fickell	.08	.25
25 Tim Williams	.08	.25
26 Raymont Harris	.60	1.50
27 Preston Harrison	.08	.25
28 Len Hartman	.08	.25
29 Eddie George	6.00	15.00
30 Jayson Gwinn	.08	.25
31 Korey Stringer	.75	2.00
32 Tom Lease	.08	.25
33 Randall Brown	.08	.25
34 DeWayne Carter	.08	.25
35 Bryan Cook	.08	.25
36 Allen DeGraffenreid	.08	.25
37 Brian Stoughton	.08	.25
38 Derrick Foster	.08	.25
39 Butler By'not'e	.15	.40
40 Jeff Cothran	.15	.40
41 Robert Davis	.08	.25
42 Joey Galloway	3.20	8.00
43 Roger Harper	.15	.40
44 Bobby Hoying	1.60	4.00
45 C.J. Kelly	.08	.25
46 Brent Johnson	.08	.25
47 Paul Long	.08	.25
48 Joe Metzger	.08	.25
49 Jason Louis	.08	.25
50 Dave Monnot	.08	.25
51 Greg Beatty	.08	.25
52 Pete Beckman	.08	.25
53 Matt Bonhaus	.08	.25
54 Marlon Kerner	.15	.40
55 Alan Kline	.08	.25
56 Greg Kuszmaul	.08	.25
57 Jim Otis Buckeye Flashback October 12, 1968	.15	.40
58 Buckeye Flashback 30-Sep-72	.08	.25
NNO Title Card CL	.08	.25

1997 Ohio State

This fully laminated, limited edition set of the 1997 Ohio State Rose Bowl Champion Buckeyes was distributed by American Marketing Associates. The fronts feature full color player action shots with the team logo and a facsimile autograph printed in red across the bottom. The backs carry player information and the 1996 season record. The cards are unnumbered and checklisted below in alphabetical order. Reportedly 4000 sets were produced.

COMPLETE SET (25)	10.00	25.00
1 Greg Bellisari	.60	1.50
2 Matt Calhoun	.40	1.00
3 Shane Clark	.40	1.00
4 Dan Colson	.40	1.00
5 John Cooper CO	.60	1.50
6 LeShun Daniels	.40	1.00
7 Luke Fickell	.40	1.00
8 Matt Finkes	.80	2.00
9 Anthony Gwinn	.60	1.50
10 Bob Houser	.40	1.00
11 Ty Howard	.40	1.00
12 Josh Jackson	.40	1.00
13 D.J. Jones	.40	1.00
14 Rob Kelly	.60	1.50
15 Heath Knisely	.40	1.00
16 Ryan Miller	.40	1.00
17 Juan Porter	.40	1.00
18 Chad Pulliam	.40	1.00
19 Dimitrious Stanley	.60	1.50
20 Buster Tillman	.60	1.50
21 Mike Vrabel	1.50	4.00
22 American Marketing Associates	.40	1.00
23 1997 Senior Rose Bowl Champions	.60	1.50
24 Team Logo	.40	1.00
25 Sponsor card	.40	1.00

1997-98 Ohio State

This 22-card set is unnumbered and listed below in alphabetical order. The cards feature top athletes from both men's and women's sports at Ohio State.

COMPLETE SET (22)	4.00	10.00
8 Bob Houser FB	.30	.75
9 D.J. Jones FB	.20	.50
11 Ryan Miller FB	.20	.50

2001 Ohio State

This set was issued in four perforated sheets of 8-cards. Each card includes a color photo of a player, mascot or coach along with "Buckeyes" printed down the left side of the cardfront. Two sheets were printed with the cards featuring a red background and 2-sheets with black background cards. The mascot appears on all four sheets. A long strip at the top of the sheet features a team photo on the front side and the team schedule on the back. The cardbacks includes another color player image as well as an extensive player bio.

COMPLETE SET (30)	10.00	20.00
1 Tim Anderson	.50	1.25
2 Steve Bellisari	.75	2.00
3 LeCharles Bentley	.30	.75
4 Bobby Britton	.30	.75
5 Courtland Bullard	.30	.75
6 Tim Cheatwood	.30	.75
7 Adrien Clarke	.30	.75
8 Mike Collins	.50	1.25
9 Joe Cooper	.30	.75
10 Mike Doss	.75	2.00
11 Ben Hartsock	.50	1.25
12 Mike Jacobs	.30	.75
13 Jamar Martin	.50	1.25
14 Scott McMullen	.30	.75
15 Donnie Nickey	.30	.75
16 Shane Olivea	.30	.75
17 Kenny Peterson	.30	.75
18 Robert Reynolds	.30	.75
19 Derek Ross	.50	1.25
20 B.J. Sander	.50	1.25
21 Darnell Sanders	.30	.75
22 Darrion Scott	.50	1.25
23 Will Smith	.75	2.00
24 Alex Stepanovich	.30	.75
25 Jim Tressel CO	.50	1.25
26 Tyson Walter	.50	1.25
27 Jonathan Wells	1.25	3.00
28 Matt Wilhelm	.75	2.00
29 Buckeye Mascot Black	.30	.75
30 Buckeye Mascot Red	.30	.75

2004 Ohio State Greats

The 2004 Ohio State Greats set was produced by American Marketing Associates and issued as a complete set of 32-cards. The cards feature full-bleed color photos with the player's name and the team logo on the front. The backs include a brief bio on the player. The cards are unnumbered and checklisted below in alphabetical order.

COMPLETE SET (32)	10.00	20.00
1 Brian Baschnagel	.20	.50
2 Paul Brown CO	.75	2.00
3 Bob Brudzinski	.20	.50
4 Keith Byars	.30	.75
5 Cris Carter UER	1.00	2.50
6 Howard Cassady	.20	.50
7 John Cooper CO	.20	.50
8 Wes Fesler	.20	.50
9 Dave Foley	.20	.50
10 Tim Fox	.20	.50
11 Joey Galloway	.50	1.25
12 Eddie George	.75	2.00
13 Terry Glenn	.50	1.25
14 Randy Gradishar	.30	.75
15 Cornelius Greene	.20	.50
16 Archie Griffin	.50	1.25
17 Chic Harley	.20	.50
18 Woody Hayes CO	.50	1.25
19 Les Horvath	.20	.50
20 Vic Janowicz	.20	.50
21 Pete Johnson	.20	.50
22 Ike Kelley	.20	.50
23 Rex Kern	.20	.50
24 Rufus Mayes	.20	.50
25 Orlando Pace	.30	.75
26 Tom Skladany	.20	.50
27 Chris Spielman	.30	.75
28 Shawn Springs	.20	.50
29 Jim Stillwagon	.20	.50
30 Jack Tatum	.30	.75
31 Bill Willis	.30	.75
32 Checklist Card	.20	.50

2004-09 Ohio State TK Legacy

This product was released in a number of series that began in Fall 2004. The cards were issued in 8-pack boxes with 14-boxes per case. Each pack included 4-cards with one of those being signed by one or more former OSU players. The first 5-cards in the base set (#L1-L5) could only be originally obtained by purchasing the OSU collector's album designed to house the complete set. The 2004 series 1 release included cards #L6-L35, the Spring 2005 Extension included #L37-L45, the series 2 Encore set (released in Fall 2005) featured cards #L36 and #L46-L97 and the third series was relased in 2006 and featured cards #L98-L123.

COMP.SERIES 1 (30)	15.00	30.00
COMP.SERIES 2 (46)	15.00	30.00
COMP.SPRING SERIES (9)	5.00	10.00
COMP.SERIES 3 (26)	12.50	25.00
COMP.SERIES 4 (29)	12.50	25.00
COMP.SERIES 5 (18)	10.00	20.00
COMP.SERIES 6 (15)	10.00	20.00
L1 Craig Krenzel	1.50	4.00
L2 Cornelius Greene	.75	2.00
L3 Tom Matte	1.25	3.00
L4 Mike Tomczak	1.00	2.50
L5 Joe Germaine	.50	1.25
L6 Ben Hartsock	.75	2.00
L7 Jim Stillwagon	.50	1.25
L8 Jim Karsatos	.40	1.00
L9 George Lynn	.40	1.00
L10 Dave Leggett	.40	1.00
L11 Frank Kremblas	.40	1.00
L12 Jim Otis	.75	2.00
L13 John Brockington	.50	1.25
L14 Tim Fox	.50	1.25
L15 Randy Gradishar	.75	2.00
L16 Tom Cousineau	.75	2.00
L17 Brian Baschnagel	.50	1.25
L18 Calvin Murray	.50	1.25
L19 Kirk Herbstreit	.40	1.00
L20 Gene Fekete	.40	1.00
L21 Hal Dean	.40	1.00
L22 James Herbstreit	.40	1.00
L23 Joe Cannavino	.40	1.00
L24 Matt Snell	.75	2.00
L25 Craig Cassady	.40	1.00
L26 Pete Johnson	.75	2.00
L27 Bob Shaw	.40	1.00
L28 Doug Donley	.40	1.00
L29 Jim Houston	.50	1.25
L30 Tommy James	.40	1.00
L31 Tom Skladany	.40	1.00
L32 Mike Cannavino	.40	1.00
L33 Ted Provost	.40	1.00
L34 Howard Cassady	.75	2.00
L35 Archie Griffin	1.25	3.00
L36 Rex Kern	.50	1.25
L37 Mike Nugent	.50	1.25
L38 Simon Fraser	.40	1.00
L39 Maurice Hall	.50	1.25
L40 Branden Joe	.40	1.00
L41 Kyle Andrews	.40	1.00
L42 Lydell Ross	.40	1.00
L43 Dustin Fox	.40	1.00
L44 Mike Kne	.40	1.00
L45 Bam Childress	.40	1.00
L46 Greg Frey	.40	1.00
L47 Kent Graham	.50	1.25
L48 Bobby Hoying	.75	2.00
L49 Pandel Savic	.50	1.25
L50 John Mummey	.50	1.25
L51 Ray Griffin	.40	1.00
L52 Duncan Griffin	.40	1.00
L54 Jeff Davidson	.40	1.00
L55 James Davidson	.40	1.00
L56 Aaron Brown	.40	1.00
L57 Jim Parker	.75	2.00
L58 Keith Byars	.75	2.00
L59 Chris Ward	.40	1.00
L60 Jan White	.50	1.25
L61 Bruce Jankowski	.40	1.00
L62 Bill Long	.50	1.25
L63 Mike Sensibaugh	.50	1.25
L64 Tim Spencer	.50	1.25
L65 Pepper Johnson	.50	1.25
L67 Rick Middleton	.40	1.00
L68 Andy Groom	.40	1.00
L69 Champ Henson	.40	1.00
L70 Jack Tatum	.75	2.00
L71 J.T. White	.40	1.00
L74 Mark Stier	.40	1.00
L76 Ken Coleman	.40	1.00
L77 Dan Stultz	.40	1.00
L78 Vlade Janakievski	.40	1.00
L79 Gary Berry	.40	1.00
L80 Dimitrious Stanley	.40	1.00
L81 Bob Jabbusch	.40	1.00
L82 Bob McCormick	.40	1.00
L83 Carmen Naples	.40	1.00
L84 Cy Souders	.40	1.00
L85 Dante Lavelli	.75	2.00
L86 Don Steinberg	.40	1.00
L87 Gordon Appleby	.40	1.00
L88 Paul Priday	.40	1.00
L89 Rod Gerald	.40	1.00
L90 Bill Sedor	.40	1.00
L91 Wes Fesler	.40	1.00
L92 Pete Stinchcomb	.50	1.25
L94 Francis Young	.40	1.00
L96 Leo Yasseroff	.40	1.00
L97 Chester Glasser	.40	1.00
L98 John Hicks	.40	1.00
L99 Marcus Marek	.40	1.00
L100 Jim Lachey	.50	1.25
L101 Fred Pagac Sr.	.40	1.00
L102 Fred Pagac Jr.	.40	1.00
L103 Josh Huston	.40	1.00
L104 Mike Kudla	.40	1.00
L105 Rob Sims	.40	1.00
L106 Anthony Schlegel	.50	1.25
L107 Bobby Carpenter	1.00	2.50
L108 A.J. Hawk	1.50	4.00
L109 Pepe Pearson	.40	1.00
L110 Bob Brudzinski	.50	1.25
L111 Matt Finkes	.40	1.00
L112 Ryan Miller	.40	1.00
L113 Stanley Jackson	.40	1.00
L114 Matt Keller	.40	1.00
L115 Luke Fickell	.40	1.00
L116 Steve Bellisari	.50	1.25
L117 Greg Bellisari	.40	1.00
L118 Michael Wiley	.50	1.25
L119 Kurt Schumacher	.40	1.00
L120 Pete Cusick	.40	1.00
L121 D.J. Jones	.40	1.00
L122 Jeff Graham	.50	1.25
L123 Mark Pelini	.40	1.00
L124 Bill Willis	.75	2.00
L125 Doug Datish	.40	1.00
L126 Tim Schafer	.40	1.00
L127 Mike D'Andrea	.40	1.00
L128 Roy Hall	.40	1.00
L129 Justin Zwick	.75	2.00
L130 Antonio Smith	.50	1.25
L131 Brandon Mitchell	.40	1.00
L132 John Kerr	.40	1.00
L133 Drew Norman	.40	1.00
L134 T.J. Downing	.40	1.00
L135 Stan White Jr.	.75	2.00
L136 Bobby Olive	.40	1.00
L137 David Patterson	.40	1.00
L138 Joel Penton	.40	1.00
L139 Dee Miller	.40	1.00
L140 Tim Anderson	.50	1.25
L141 Troy Smith	1.25	3.00
L142 Ted Ginn	1.50	4.00
L143 Mike Datish	.40	1.00
L144 George Jacoby	.40	1.00
L145 Art Schlichter	.50	1.25
L146 Phil Strickland	.40	1.00
L147 Dick Schafrath	.40	1.00
L148 Mike Lanese	.40	1.00
L149 Steve Myers	.40	1.00
L150 Steve Luke	.40	1.00
L151 George Spencer	.40	1.00
L152 Robert Scott	.40	1.00
L154 Vince Workman	.50	1.25
L155 James Langhurst	.40	1.00
L156 Vernon Gholston	.75	2.00
L157 Charles Maag	.40	1.00
L158 Jack Graf	.40	1.00
L159 Campbell Graf	.40	1.00
L160 Billy Ray Anders	.50	1.25
L161 Don Clark	.40	1.00
L163 John Cooper	.40	1.00
L164 Gene Janecko	.40	1.00
L165 Scottie Graham	.60	1.50
L166 Raymont Harris	.60	1.50
L167 Bruce Elia	.40	1.00
L168 Greg Hare	.40	1.00
L169 Don Sutherin	.50	1.25
L170 Stan White Sr.	.50	1.25
L171 Fred Morrison	.50	1.25
L174 Steve Tovar	.50	1.25
L177 Greg Lashutka	.40	1.00
L178 Nick Buonamici	.40	1.00
L179 Tom Tupa	.50	1.25
L180 Carlos Snow	.40	1.00
L181 Galen Cisco	.50	1.25
L182 Bret Powers	.40	1.00
L184 Roger Harper	.40	1.00
L185 Gary Williams	.40	1.00
L186 Mike Collins	.40	1.00
L187 Todd Boeckman	.50	1.25
L188 Chris Wells	1.50	4.00

L189 Ryan Pretorius	.40	1.00
L190 Bill Conley	.40	1.00
L191 A.J. Trapasso	.40	1.00
L192 Tom Backhus	.40	1.00
L193 Brian Donovan	.40	1.00
L194 Mike Polaski	.40	1.00
L195 Dave Brungard	.40	1.00
L196 Alan Jack	.40	1.00
L197 Paul Schmidlin	.40	1.00
L198 Mark Debevc	.40	1.00
L199 Mike Doss	.50	1.25
L200 Stephen O'Dea	.40	1.00
L201 Troian Dendiu	.40	1.00
L202 David Whitfield	.40	1.00
L203 Dirk Worden	.40	1.00
L204 Leo Hayden	.40	1.00
L205 John Muhlbach	.40	1.00
L206 Dave Foley	.40	1.00
L207 Jim Roman	.40	1.00
L208 Tim Anderson	.40	1.00
L209 Brian Robiskie	.75	2.00
NNO Uncut Sheet/250	20.00	40.00
NNO Woody Hayes/500	2.00	5.00
Kneeling pose		
(issued in OSU binder)		
NNO Woody Hayes/500	2.00	5.00
Holding Helmet		
(issued in OSU binder)		
C1 Woody Hayes CO	1.25	3.00
C2 Alexander Lilley CO	.40	1.00
CL1 Checklist 1	.50	1.25
(Woody Hayes with team)		
CL2 Checklist 2	.40	1.00
(1942 vs. Fort Knox)		
P1 Archie Griffin Promo/500	2.50	6.00
P2 Rex Kern Promo/500	3.00	8.00
Woody Hayes		

2004-09 Ohio State TK Legacy All-Americans

COMP.SERIES 1 (11)	30.00	60.00
COMP.SERIES 2 (11)	30.00	60.00
COMP.SERIES 3 (6)	15.00	30.00
STATED ODDS 1:6		
STATED PRINT RUN 400 SER.#'d SETS		
AA1 Howard Cassady 1953	3.00	8.00
AA2 Howard Cassady 1954	3.00	8.00
AA3 Jim Otis	2.50	6.00
AA4 Jim Stillwagon	2.00	5.00
AA5 John Brockington	2.50	6.00
AA6 Tom Cousineau	2.50	6.00
AA7 Randy Gradishar	3.00	8.00
AA8 Tom Skladany	2.00	5.00
AA9 Archie Griffin 1975	3.00	8.00
AA10 Archie Griffin 1974	3.00	8.00
AA11 Chic Harley	2.00	5.00
AA12 Mike Nugent	2.50	6.00
AA13 Pete Stinchcomb	2.50	6.00
AA14 Chic Harley	2.00	5.00
AA16 Andy Groom	2.00	5.00
AA17 Rex Kern	2.50	6.00
AA18 Jack Tatum	3.00	8.00
AA19 Jim Parker	3.00	8.00
AA20 Jan White	2.50	6.00
AA21 Keith Byars	3.00	8.00
AA22 Gene Fekete	2.00	5.00
AA23 Pepper Johnson	2.50	6.00
AA24 Bob Brudzinski	2.50	6.00
AA25 Marcus Marek	2.00	5.00
AA26 John Hicks	2.00	5.00
AA27 Kurt Schumacher	2.00	5.00
AA28 Jim Lachey	2.50	6.00
AA29 Pete Cusick	2.00	5.00
AA31 Tom DeLeone	1.25	3.00
AA33 Steve Tovar	1.25	3.00
AA34 Dave Foley	1.25	3.00
AA35 Mike Doss	1.50	4.00

2004-09 Ohio State TK Legacy All American Autographs

AB1 Steve Tovar/100	15.00	30.00
AB2 Dave Foley/50	20.00	40.00
AB3 Mike Doss	20.00	40.00

2004-09 Ohio State TK Legacy Archie Griffin Rushing Streak

COMPLETE SET (31)	20.00	40.00
G1 1973 vs. Minnesota	.75	2.00
G2 1973 vs. TCU	.75	2.00
G3 1973 vs. Washington State	.75	2.00
G4 1973 vs. Wisconsin	.75	2.00
G5 1973 vs. Indiana	.75	2.00
G6 1973 vs. Northwestern	.75	2.00
G7 1973 vs. Illinois	.75	2.00
G8 1973 vs. Michigan State	.75	2.00
G9 1973 vs. Iowa	.75	2.00
G10 1973 vs. Michigan	.75	2.00
G11 1974 vs. Minnesota	.75	2.00
G12 1974 vs. Oregon State	.75	2.00
G13 1974 vs. SMU	.75	2.00
G14 1974 vs. Washington State	.75	2.00
G15 1974 vs. Wisconsin	.75	2.00
G16 1974 vs. Indiana	.75	2.00
G17 1974 vs. Northwestern	.75	2.00
G18 1974 vs. Illiniois	.75	2.00
G19 1974 vs. Michigan State	.75	2.00
G20 1974 vs. Iowa	.75	2.00
G21 1974 vs. Michigan	.75	2.00
G22 1975 vs. Michigan State	.75	2.00
G23 1975 vs. Penn State	.75	2.00
G24 1975 vs. North Carolina	.75	2.00
G25 1975 vs. UCLA	.75	2.00
G26 1975 vs. Iowa	.75	2.00
G27 1975 vs. Wisconsin	.75	2.00
G28 1975 vs. Purdue	.75	2.00
G29 1975 vs. Indiana	.75	2.00
G30 1975 vs. Illinois	.75	2.00
G31 1975 vs. Minnesota	.75	2.00

2004-09 Ohio State TK Legacy Archie Griffin Rushing Streak Autographs

STATED PRINT RUN 31 SER.#'d SETS		
AG1 1975 vs. Michigan State	20.00	40.00
AG2 1975 vs. Penn State	20.00	40.00
AG3 1975 vs. North Carolina	20.00	40.00
AG4 1975 vs. UCLA	20.00	40.00
AG5 1975 vs. Iowa	20.00	40.00
AG6 1975 vs. Wisconsin	20.00	40.00
AG7 1975 vs. Purdue	20.00	40.00
AG8 1975 vs. Indiana	20.00	40.00
AG9 1975 vs. Illinois	20.00	40.00
AG10 1975 vs. Minnesota	20.00	40.00

2004-09 Ohio State TK Legacy Archives Autographs

AR2 Michael Wiley/100	10.00	25.00
(Sept.12, 1998)		
AR3 Michael Wiley/100	10.00	25.00
(Sept.13, 1997)		
AR10 Jack Graf/150	10.00	20.00
AR12 Fred Morrison/150	12.50	25.00
AR14 Don Sutherin/100	10.00	20.00
AR15 Don Clark/100	10.00	20.00
AR16 John Cooper CO/100	10.00	20.00
AR19 Raymont Harris/100	10.00	20.00
AR20 Stan White Sr./100	12.50	25.00
AR23 Vince Workman/100	12.50	25.00
AR25 Bruce Elia/100	10.00	20.00
AR26 Chris Wells/75	40.00	80.00
AR27 Todd Boeckman/100	12.50	25.00
AR28 Gary Williams/100	10.00	20.00
AR29 Ryan Pretorius/100	10.00	20.00
AR30 A.J. Trapasso/100	10.00	20.00
AR31 Carlos Snow/100	10.00	20.00
AR32 Leo Hayden	10.00	25.00
AR33 Mike Doss/75	12.50	25.00
AR34 Stephen O'Dea/100	10.00	20.00

2004-09 Ohio State TK Legacy Buckeyes Autographs

OVERALL AUTO STATED ODDS 1:1		
B1 Tom Matte SP	10.00	25.00
B2 Joe Germaine SP	7.50	20.00
B3 Cornelius Greene SP	7.50	20.00
B4 Mike Tomczak SP	7.50	20.00
B5 Ben Hartsock	7.50	20.00
B6 Jim Stillwagon	6.00	15.00
B7 Jim Karsatos	5.00	12.00
B8 George Lynn SP	7.50	20.00
B9 Dave Leggett SP	6.00	15.00
B10 Frank Kremblas	5.00	12.00
B11 Jim Otis SP	10.00	25.00
B12 John Brockington	6.00	15.00
B13 Tim Fox	6.00	15.00
B14 Randy Gradishar	7.50	20.00
B15 Tom Cousineau	7.50	20.00
B16 Brian Baschnagel	6.00	15.00
B17 Calvin Murray	6.00	15.00
B18 Kirk Herbstreit	7.50	20.00
B19 Gene Fekete	5.00	12.00
B20 Hal Dean	5.00	12.00
B21 James Herbstreit	5.00	12.00
B22 Joe Cannavino SP	6.00	15.00
B23 Matt Snell	7.50	20.00
B24 Craig Cassady	5.00	12.00
B25 Pete Johnson	7.50	20.00
B26 Bob Shaw	5.00	12.00
B27 Doug Donley	5.00	12.00
B28 Jim Houston	6.00	15.00
B29 Tommy James	5.00	12.00
B30 Tom Skladany	5.00	12.00
B31 Mike Cannavino	5.00	12.00
B32 Ted Provost	5.00	12.00
B33 Howard Cassady SP	75.00	125.00
B34 Archie Griffin/100	50.00	100.00
B35 Mike Nugent	6.00	15.00
B36 Simon Fraser	5.00	12.00
B37 Maurice Hall	6.00	15.00
B38 Branden Joe	5.00	12.00
B39 Kyle Andrews	5.00	12.00
B40 Lydell Ross	5.00	12.00
B41 Dustin Fox	5.00	12.00
B42 Mike Kne	5.00	12.00
B43 Bam Childress	5.00	12.00
B45 Greg Frey	5.00	12.00
B46 Kent Graham	6.00	15.00
B47 Bobby Hoying	7.50	20.00
B48 Pandel Savic	6.00	15.00
B49 John Mummey	7.50	20.00
B50 Ray Griffin	5.00	12.00
B51 Duncan Griffin	5.00	12.00
B52 James Davidson	5.00	12.00
B53 Jeff Davidson	5.00	12.00
B54 James Davidson	5.00	12.00
B55 Aaron Brown	5.00	12.00
B56 Jim Parker/200	30.00	80.00
B57 Keith Byars	7.50	20.00
B58 Chris Ward	5.00	12.00
B59 Jan White	6.00	15.00
B60 Bruce Jankowski	5.00	12.00
B61 Bill Long	6.00	15.00
B62 Mike Sensibaugh	6.00	15.00
B64 Pepper Johnson	6.00	15.00
B65 Vlade Janakievski	5.00	12.00
B66 Rick Middleton	5.00	12.00
B67 Andy Groom	5.00	12.00
B68 Champ Henson	5.00	12.00
B69 Jack Tatum/100	60.00	120.00
B71 Richard Kuhn	5.00	12.00
B72 Ken Kuhn	5.00	12.00
B73 Mark Stier	5.00	12.00
B74 Earle Bruce	5.00	12.00
B75 Rod Gerald	5.00	12.00
B76 Gary Berry	5.00	12.00
B77 Dimitrious Stanley	5.00	12.00
B78 Dan Stultz	5.00	12.00
B79 Don Steinberg	5.00	12.00
B80 Cy Souders	5.00	12.00
B81 Paul Priday	5.00	12.00
B82 Bob McCormick	5.00	12.00
B83 Dante Lavelli	7.50	20.00
B84 Bob Jabbusch	5.00	12.00
B85 Ken Coleman	5.00	12.00
B86 Gordon Appleby	5.00	12.00
B87 Bill Sedor	5.00	12.00
B88 Carmen Naples	5.00	12.00
B89 J.T. White	5.00	12.00
B90 John Hicks	5.00	12.00
B91 Marcus Marek	5.00	12.00
B92 Jim Lachey	6.00	15.00
B93 Fred Pagac Sr.	5.00	12.00
B94 Fred Pagac Jr.	5.00	12.00
B95 Josh Huston	5.00	12.00
B96 Mike Kudla	5.00	12.00
B97 Rob Sims	5.00	12.00
B98 Anthony Schlegel	6.00	15.00
B99 Bobby Carpenter	15.00	30.00
B100 A.J. Hawk/100	25.00	50.00
B101 Pepe Pearson	5.00	12.00
B102 Jeff Graham	6.00	15.00
B103 Bob Brudzinski	6.00	15.00
B104 Matt Finkes	5.00	12.00
B105 Ryan Miller	5.00	12.00
B106 Stanley Jackson	5.00	12.00
B108 D.J. Jones	5.00	12.00
B110 Mark Pelini	5.00	12.00
B111 Steve Bellisari	6.00	15.00
B112 Greg Bellisari	5.00	12.00
B113 Michael Wiley	6.00	15.00
B114 Pete Cusick	5.00	12.00
B115 Kurt Schumacher	5.00	12.00
B116 Bill Willis	8.00	20.00
B117 Doug Datish	5.00	12.00
B118 Tim Schafer	5.00	12.00
B119 Mike D'Andrea	5.00	12.00
B120 Roy Hall	6.00	15.00
B121 Justin Zwick	8.00	20.00
B122 Antonio Smith	8.00	20.00
B123 Brandon Mitchell	5.00	12.00
B124 John Kerr	5.00	12.00
B125 Drew Norman	5.00	12.00
B126 T.J. Downing	5.00	12.00
B127 Stan White Jr.	8.00	20.00
B128 Bobby Olive	5.00	12.00
B129 David Patterson	5.00	12.00
B130 Joel Penton	5.00	12.00
B132 Dee Miller	5.00	12.00
B133 Troy Smith		
B134 Ted Ginn Jr./100		
B135 George Jacoby	5.00	12.00
B136 Art Schlichter	8.00	20.00
B137 Phil Strickland	5.00	12.00
B138 Dick Schafrath	6.00	15.00
B139 Mike Lanese	5.00	12.00
B140 Steve Myers	5.00	12.00
B141 Steve Luke	5.00	12.00
B142 George Spencer	5.00	12.00
B143 Robert Scott	5.00	12.00
B145 Mike Datish Sr.	5.00	12.00
B146 Van DeCree	5.00	12.00
B147A Bill Conley	5.00	12.00
B147B Vernon Gholston	20.00	40.00
B148 Fred Morrison	5.00	15.00
B150 Don Clark	5.00	12.00
B151 Jack Graf	5.00	12.00
B158 Charles Maag	5.00	12.00
B160 Campbell Graf	5.00	12.00
B161 Gene Janecko	5.00	12.00
B163 Billy Ray Anders	5.00	12.00
B164 Galen Cisco	6.00	15.00
B165 Don Sutherin	5.00	12.00
B167 Greg Lashutka	5.00	12.00
B168 Stan White Sr.	6.00	15.00
B170 Greg Hare	5.00	12.00
B172 John Cooper	5.00	12.00
B173 Bruce Elia	5.00	12.00
B174 Nick Buonamici	5.00	12.00
B176 Steve Tovar	6.00	15.00
B177 Raymont Harris	7.50	20.00
B178 Scottie Graham	7.50	20.00
B179 Vince Workman	6.00	15.00
B180 Gary Williams	5.00	12.00
B181 Roger Harper	5.00	12.00
B182 Mike Collins	5.00	12.00
B183 Todd Boeckman	6.00	15.00
B184 Chris Wells	40.00	80.00
B185 Ryan Pretorius	5.00	12.00
B186 A.J. Trapasso	7.50	20.00
B187 Tom Tupa	6.00	15.00
B188 Bret Powers	5.00	12.00
B189 Carlos Snow	5.00	12.00
B190 Mark Debevc	5.00	12.00
B192 Tom Backhus	5.00	12.00
B193 Brian Donovan	5.00	12.00
B196 Leo Hayden	5.00	12.00
B197 Paul Schmidlin	5.00	12.00
B198 Troian Dendiu	5.00	12.00
B199 Stephen O'Dea	5.00	12.00
B200 Dirk Worden	5.00	12.00
B201 Mike Doss	6.00	15.00
B202 David Whitfield	5.00	12.00
B203 Jim Roman	5.00	12.00
B204 John Muhlbach	5.00	12.00
B205 Tim Anderson	5.00	12.00
B206 Brian Robiskie	7.50	20.00
B207 Dave Foley	5.00	12.00

2004-09 Ohio State TK Legacy Buckeye Benchmarks

COMPLETE SET (8)	6.00	15.00
BB1 Don Clark	.60	1.50
BB2 Raymont Harris	1.00	2.50
BB3 John Cooper CO	.60	1.50
BB4 Vince Workman	.75	2.00
BB5 Scottie Graham	.75	2.00
BB6 Vernon Gholston	1.25	3.00
BB7 Carlos Snow	.60	1.50
BB8 Chris Wells	2.00	5.00

2004-09 Ohio State TK Legacy Buckeye Heroes Autographs

BH1 A.J. Hawk/100	30.00	60.00
BH2 Bobby Carpenter/100	20.00	40.00
BH3 Anthony Schlegel/100	15.00	30.00

2004-09 Ohio State TK Legacy Captains Club Autographs

C1 A.J. Hawk/50	40.00	80.00
C2 Rob Sims	10.00	20.00
C3 Jeff Graham	12.50	30.00
C4 Stanley Jackson	10.00	20.00
C5 Matt Keller	10.00	20.00
C6 Greg Bellisari	10.00	20.00
C7 Steve Bellisari	12.50	30.00
C8 Pete Cusick	10.00	20.00
C9 George Jacoby	10.00	20.00
(case insert)		
C10 Mark Pelini	10.00	20.00
C11 Doug Datish	10.00	20.00
C13 David Patterson	10.00	20.00
C14 Art Schlichter	10.00	25.00
C15 Dick Schafrath	12.50	25.00
C16 Mike Lanese	10.00	20.00
C17 Steve Myers	10.00	20.00
C19 Billy Ray Anders/150	10.00	20.00
C20 Galen Cisco/150	10.00	20.00
C21 Greg Lashutka/150	10.00	20.00
C22 Greg Hare/150	10.00	20.00
C23 Steve Tovar/150	10.00	20.00
C24A Mike Collins	10.00	20.00
C24B Scottie Graham	10.00	20.00
C25 Tom DeLeone	10.00	20.00
C26 David Whitfield	10.00	20.00
C27 Alan Jack	10.00	20.00
C28 Dave Foley	10.00	20.00
C29 Dirk Worden	10.00	20.00

2004-09 Ohio State TK Legacy Hand Drawn Sketches

S1 Woody Hayes B&W/50	150.00	250.00
S2 Woody Hayes Clr/50	175.00	300.00
S3 OSU Helmet with leaves	25.00	50.00
S4 OSU Helmet	25.00	50.00
S5 Earle Bruce/30	150.00	250.00
S6 Mike Nugent		
S7 Chic Harley Color		
S8 Chic Harley B&W/50	150.00	250.00
S9 Rex Kern		
S10 Rex Kern	200.00	350.00
Woody Hayes		
S11 Archie Griffin Color/10		
S12 Archie Griffin B&W/50	175.00	300.00
S13 Howard Cassady		
Color/10		
S14 Howard Cassady	175.00	300.00
B&W/50		
S15A Archie Griffin Color/12		
(vs. Michigan State 1975)		
S15B Archie Griffin Color/12		
(vs. Penn State 1975)		
S15C Archie Griffin Color/12		
(vs. North Carolina 1975)		
S15D Archie Griffin Color/12		
(vs. UCLA 1975)		
S15E Archie Griffin Color/12		
(vs. Iowa 1975)		
S15F Archie Griffin Color/12		
(vs. Wisconsin 1975)		
S15G Archie Griffin Color/12		
(vs. Purdue 1975)		
S15H Archie Griffin Color/12		
(vs. Indiana 1975)		
S15I Archie Griffin Color/12		
(vs. Illinois 1975)		
S15J Archie Griffin Color/12		
(vs. Minnesota 1975)		
S16 A.J. Hawk Dual		
S17 Bobby Carpenter Dual		
S18 Anthony Schlegel Dual		
S19 Archie Griffin Color Red Jsy		
S20 Archie Griffin Color Wht Jsy		
S21 Archie Griffin Color Portrait		
S22 Block O Color		
S23 A.J. Hawk B&W/40	50.00	120.00
S24 Art Schlichter Clr		
S25 Troy Smith running		
S26 Troy Smith B&W		
S27 Bill Willis		
S28 OSU Logo		
S29 Brutus Buckeye		
S30 1969 Rose Bowl		
S31 Archie Griffin B&W		
S33 Mike Doss B&W		
S34 Mike Doss Color		
S35 Brian Robiskie B&W		
S36 Brian Robiskie Color		
S37 Fred Morrison Color/10		
S38 Woody Hayes Natl.Champ		
S39 Beanie Wells Color/15		
S40 Vernon Gholston B&W/20		
SK1 Series 2 B&W Checklist	1.25	3.00
SK2 Series 2 Color Checklist	1.25	3.00
NNO Series 1 Checklist	1.25	3.00
Woody Hayes		

2004-09 Ohio State TK Legacy Historical Links Autographs

DUAL AUTO STATED ODDS 1:22		
TRIPLE AUTO STATED ODDS 1:112		
HL1 George Lynn/100	60.00	100.00
Dave Leggett		
Frank Kremblas		
HL2 Tom Matte/100	75.00	125.00
Cornelius Greene		
Mike Tomczak		
HL3 Joe Germaine/100	30.00	60.00
Jim Karsatos		
HL4 Randy Gradishar/200	25.00	50.00
Tom Cousineau		
HL5 John Brockington/100	25.00	50.00
Jim Otis		
HL6 Brian Baschnagel/200	15.00	40.00
Pete Johnson		
HL7 Kirk Herbstreit/200	15.00	40.00
James Herbstreit		
HL8 Calvin Murray/200	12.50	30.00
Doug Donley		
HL9 Joe Cannavino/200	15.00	40.00
Mike Cannavino		
(one per case insert)		
HL10 Howard Cassady/150	75.00	150.00
Craig Cassady		
HL11 Archie Griffin/100	60.00	100.00
Howard Cassady		
HL12 Dustin Fox/100	25.00	50.00
Tim Fox		
HL13 Andy Groom/100	15.00	40.00
Mike Nugent		
HL14 Jim Davidson/100	15.00	40.00
Jeff Davidson		
James Davidson		
HL15 Dick Kuhn/100	12.50	30.00
Ken Kuhn		
HL16 Keith Byars/150	25.00	50.00
Champ Henson		
HL17 Pandel Savic/100	60.00	100.00
John Mummey		
Bill Long		
HL18 Archie Griffin/100	50.00	100.00
Ray Griffin		
Duncan Griffin		
HL19 Dimitrious Stanley/150	25.00	50.00
Joe Germaine		
HL20 Greg Frey/100	40.00	75.00
Kent Graham		
Bobby Hoying		
HL21 Dan Stultz/150	25.00	50.00
Mike Nugent		
Vlade Janakievski		
HL22 Fred Pagac Sr.	12.50	30.00
Fred Pagac Jr.		
HL23 Steve Bellisari		
Greg Bellisari		
HL24 Doug Datish/100	15.00	40.00
Mike Datish		
HL25 Jack Graf	12.50	30.00
Campbell Graf		
HL28 Don Sutherin/100	12.50	30.00
Galen Cisco		
HL30 Tom DeLeone/100	20.00	40.00
Stan White Sr.		
HL32 Bruce Elia/100	15.00	40.00
Steve Tovar		
HL33A John Cooper		
Raymont Harris		
HL34 A.J. Trapasso/100	20.00	40.00
Ryan Pretorius		
HL35 Alan Jack/100	12.50	30.00
David Whitfield		
HL36 Dave Foley/100	12.50	30.00
Dirk Worden		
HL38 Jim Roman/100	20.00	40.00
John Muhlbach		
Tom Backhus		
Alan Jack		
FC1 Dustin Fox/100	25.00	50.00
Tim Fox		
Mark Stier		
Ken Kuhn		
Richard Kuhn		

2004-09 Ohio State TK Legacy Legend of Chris Wells

COMPLETE SET (3)	2.50	6.00
BW1 Chris Wells	.75	2.00
BW2 Chris Wells	.75	2.00
BW3 Chris Wells	.75	2.00

2004-09 Ohio State TK Legacy Milestones

COMPLETE SET (15)	10.00	20.00
OS1 1919 Michigan Win	.75	2.00
OS2 1916 Conference Title	.75	2.00
OS3 1951 Woody Hayes/1st Year	.75	2.00
OS4 1922 Ohio Stadium Opens	.75	2.00
OS5 1942 National Title	.75	2.00
OS6 1890 First Season	.75	2.00
OS7 1890 First Unbeaten Season	.75	2.00
OS8 1949 First Bowl Win	.75	2.00
OS9 1913 Conference Win	.75	2.00
OS10 1917 Fewest Points	.75	2.00
OS11 1944 Heisman Winner	.75	2.00
OS12 1956 Outland Winner	.75	2.00
OS13 1970 Lombardi Winner	.75	2.00
OS14 1975 2-Time	.75	2.00
Heisman Winner		
OS15 2001 Tressel's	.75	2.00
First Season		

2004-09 Ohio State TK Legacy National Champions Autographs

STATED ODDS 1:8		
1942A George Lynn	10.00	25.00
1942B Gene Fekete	7.50	20.00
1942C Hal Dean	7.50	20.00
1942D Bob Shaw	7.50	20.00
1942E Tommy James	7.50	20.00
1942F Paul Priday	7.50	20.00
1942G Cy Souders	7.50	20.00
1942H Dante Lavelli	12.50	30.00
1942I Don Steinberg	7.50	20.00
1942J Gordon Appleby	7.50	20.00
1942K Bob McCormick	7.50	20.00
1942L Ken Coleman	7.50	20.00
1942M Bob Jabbusch	7.50	20.00
1942N Bill Sedor	7.50	20.00
1942O Carmen Naples	7.50	20.00
1942P J.T. White/100	40.00	80.00
1942Q Bill Willis		
1954A Dave Leggett	7.50	20.00
1954B Howard Cassady/125	40.00	80.00
1957A Frank Kremblas	7.50	20.00
1957B Joe Cannavino	7.50	20.00
1957C2 Don Clark	7.50	20.00
1957C1 Jim Houston	10.00	25.00
1957D Don Sutherin	7.50	20.00
1957S Galen Cisco	7.50	20.00
1961A Matt Snell	12.50	30.00
1961B John Mummey	12.50	30.00
1961C Jim Parker/100	20.00	40.00
1968A Jim Stillwagon	7.50	20.00
1968B John Brockington	10.00	25.00
1968C Jim Otis	10.00	25.00
1968D Ted Provost	7.50	20.00
1968E Bruce Jankowski	7.50	20.00
1968F Jan White	7.50	20.00
1968G Mike Sensibaugh	10.00	25.00
1968H Jack Tatum/100	40.00	80.00
1968I Richard Kuhn	7.50	20.00
1968J Mark Stier	7.50	20.00
1968K Bill Long	10.00	25.00
1968L Tom Backhus	7.50	20.00
1968M Dave Foley	7.50	20.00
1968N Mark Debevc	7.50	20.00
1968O Brian Donovan	7.50	20.00
1968P David Brungard	7.50	20.00
1968Q Paul Schmidlin	7.50	20.00
1968R Dirk Worden	7.50	20.00
1968S John Muhlbach	7.50	20.00
1968T Jim Roman	7.50	20.00
1968U Leo Hayden	7.50	20.00
1968V Tim Anderson	7.50	20.00
2002A Ben Hartsock	10.00	25.00
2002B Bam Childress	7.50	20.00
2002C Mike Nugent	7.50	20.00
2002D Kyle Andrews	7.50	20.00
2002E Simon Fraser	10.00	25.00
2002F Maurice Hall	10.00	25.00
2002G Branden Joe	7.50	20.00
2002H Dustin Fox	7.50	20.00
2002I Lydell Ross	7.50	20.00
2002J Mike Kne	7.50	20.00
2002K Andy Groom	7.50	20.00
2002L Fred Pagac Jr.	7.50	20.00
2002M A.J. Hawk/50	40.00	80.00
2002N Bobby Carpenter	10.00	25.00
2002O Mike Kudla	7.50	20.00
2002P Rob Sims	7.50	20.00

2004-09 Ohio State TK Legacy Playbook Autographs

OP1 Earle Bruce/150	15.00	30.00

2004-09 Ohio State TK Legacy Quarterback Collection Autographs

QB1 Tom Matte/500	15.00	40.00
QB2 Craig Krenzel/500	15.00	40.00
QB3 Mike Tomczak/500	12.50	25.00
QB4 Cornelius Greene/500	10.00	20.00
QB5 Joe Germaine/500	12.50	25.00
QB6 Jim Karsatos/300	10.00	25.00
QB7 George Lynn/300	12.50	30.00
QB8 Dave Leggett/300	10.00	25.00
QB9 Frank Kremblas/300	12.50	30.00
QB10 Kirk Herbstreit/300	12.50	30.00
QB11 Bill Long/200	15.00	30.00
QB12 John Mummey/200	15.00	30.00
QB13 Greg Frey/200	12.50	25.00
QB14 Kent Graham/200	15.00	30.00
QB15 Pandel Savic/200	12.50	25.00
QB16 Bobby Hoying/200	15.00	30.00
QB17 Rod Gerald/200	12.50	25.00
QB18 Rex Kern/100	40.00	80.00
QB19 Stanley Jackson	10.00	25.00
QB20 Steve Bellisari	15.00	30.00
QB21 Art Schlichter/100	15.00	30.00
QB22 George Spencer		
QB23 Justin Zwick		
QB24 Greg Hare/200	10.00	20.00
QB25 Todd Boeckman/100	12.50	25.00
QB26 Tom Tupa/100	12.50	25.00
QB27 Bret Powers/100	10.00	20.00

2004-09 Ohio State TK Legacy Silver Special Autographs

SP1 Troy Smith		
SP2 Archie Griffin		
SP3 Archie Griffin		
SP4 Ted Ginn		
SP5 Vernon Gholston/25	30.00	60.00
SP7 Chris Wells		
SP8 Mike Doss		
SP9 Brian Robiskie/25		

2004-09 Ohio State TK Legacy Super Sophomores

SO1 Brian Donovan	2.00	5.00
SO2 Mark Debevc	2.00	5.00
SO3 Leo Hayden	2.00	5.00
SO4 Tim Anderson	2.00	5.00

2004-09 Ohio State TK Legacy Troy Smith Legacy

COMPLETE SET (5)	4.00	10.00
RANDOM INSERTS IN SERIES 4		
LTS1 Troy Smith	.75	2.00
LTS2 Troy Smith	.75	2.00
LTS3 Troy Smith	.75	2.00
LTS4 Troy Smith	.75	2.00
LTS5 Troy Smith	.75	2.00

2005 Ohio State Medallions

This set of medallions was released in 2005 to honor great players and coaches of Ohio State football. Each originally retailed for $3.99 and was produced with a photo of the subject embedded in the coin.

COMPLETE SET (12)	20.00	40.00
1 Howard Cassady	1.50	4.00
2 Eddie George	2.00	5.00
3 Archie Griffin	2.00	5.00
4 Chic Harley	1.50	4.00
5 Woody Hayes	2.00	5.00
6 Les Horvath	1.50	4.00
7 Vic Janowicz	1.50	4.00
8 Rex Kern	1.50	4.00
9 Buckeyes Mascot	1.50	4.00
10 Chris Spielman	2.00	5.00
11 Stadium	1.50	4.00
12 Jack Tatum	2.00	5.00

2006 Ohio State

COMPLETE SET (9)	6.00	12.00
1 Doug Datish	.30	.75
2 Mike D'Andrea	.30	.75
3 Ted Ginn Jr.	1.00	2.50
4 Anthony Gonzalez	.60	1.50
5 Malcolm Jenkins	.50	1.25
6 Quinn Pitcock	.50	1.25
7 Antonio Pittman	.75	2.00
8 Troy Smith	1.25	3.00
9 Jim Tressel CO	.40	1.00

2007 Ohio State

COMPLETE SET (36)	10.00	20.00
1 Andre Amos	.30	.75
2 Jake Ballard	.30	.75
3 Alex Barrow	.30	.75
4 Kirk Barton	.30	.75
5 Alex Boone	.30	.75
6 Kurt Coleman	.30	.75
7 Jim Cordle	.30	.75
8 Todd Denlinger	.30	.75
9 Marcus Freeman	.40	1.00
10 Vernon Gholston	.60	1.50
11 Larry Grant	.30	.75
12 Ross Homan	.30	.75
13 Dionte Johnson	.30	.75
14 James Laurinaitis	1.25	3.00
15 Dimitrios Makridis	.30	.75
16 Rory Nicol	.30	.75
17 Nick Patterson	.30	.75
18 Ben Person	.30	.75
19 Aaron Pettrey	.30	.75
20 Ryan Pretorius	.30	.75
21 Brian Robiskie	.75	2.00
22 Robert Hose	.30	.75
23 Anderson Russell	.30	.75
24 Rob Schoenhoft	.30	.75
25 Brandon Smith	.40	1.00
26 Austin Spitler	.30	.75
27 Curtis Terry	.30	.75
28 Jon Thoma	.30	.75
29 A.J. Trapasso	.40	1.00
30 Jim Tressel CO	.40	1.00
31 Donald Washington	.30	.75
32 Chris Wells	1.50	4.00
33 Maurice Wells	.40	1.00
34 Brutus Buckeye - Mascot	.30	.75
35 Buckeye Trophies	.30	.75
36 Ohio Stadium	.30	.75

2008 Ohio State

COMPLETE SET (45)	10.00	20.00
1 Nader Abdallah	.20	.50
2 Andre Amos	.20	.50
3 Jake Ballard	.20	.50
4 Todd Boeckman	.30	.75
5 Alex Boone	.20	.50
6 Bryant Browning	.20	.50
7 Chimdi Chekwa	.20	.50
8 Kurt Coleman	.20	.50
9 Jim Cordle	.20	.50
10 Todd Dsenlinger	.20	.50
11 Marcus Freeman	.30	.75
12 Brian Hartline	.60	1.50
13 Dan Herron	.20	.50
14 Cameron Heyward	.20	.50
15 Jermale Hines	.20	.50
16 Ross Homan	.20	.50
17 Malcolm Jenkins	.40	1.00
18 Shaun Lane	.20	.50
19 Dexter Larimore	.20	.50
20 James Laurinaitis	1.00	2.50
21 Ryan Lukens	.20	.50
22 Kyle Mitchum	.20	.50
23 Tyler Moeller	.20	.50
24 Andrew Moses	.20	.50
25 Rory Nicol	.20	.50
26 Nick Patterson	.20	.50
27 Ben Person	.20	.50
28 Aaron Pettrey	.20	.50
29 Ryan Pretorius	.20	.50
30 Steve Rehring	.20	.50
31 Brian Robiskie	.75	2.00
32 Rob Rose	.20	.50
33 Anderson Russell	.20	.50
34 Brandon Saine	.20	.50
35 Dane Sanzenbacher	.20	.50
36 Brandon Smith	.30	.75
37 Austin Spitler	.20	.50
38 Curtis Terry	.20	.50
39 A.J. Trapasso	.30	.75
40 Jim Tressel CCO	.30	.75
41 Chris Wells	1.25	3.00
42 Maurice Wells	.20	.50
43 Marcus Williams	.20	.50
44 Lawrence Wilson	.20	.50
45 Doug Worthington	.20	.50

2008 Ohio State Jumbo

This set was issued by the school with each card measuring roughly 5" by 8". A color player photo is included on the fronts along with a blank white area below the photo designed for an autograph.

COMPLETE SET (6)	7.50	15.00
1 Alex Boone	.75	2.00
2 Brian Hartline	1.25	3.00
3 Malcolm Jenkins	.75	2.00
4 James Laurinaitis	1.50	4.00
5 Brian Robiskie	1.25	3.00
6 Chris Wells	2.00	5.00

1962 Oklahoma Team Issue

This set of black and white photos was issued by Oklahoma and released in 1962. Each features a player or coach on a photo measuring roughly 4" by 5" printed on photographic quality paper stock. Each photo is blankbacked and unnumbered.

COMPLETE SET (31)	100.00	200.00
1 Virgil Boll	4.00	8.00
2 Allen Bumgardner	4.00	8.00
3 Newt Burton	4.00	8.00
4 Duane Cook	4.00	8.00
5 Glen Condren	4.00	8.00
6 Jackie Cowan	4.00	8.00
7 Leon Cross	4.00	8.00
8 Monte Deere	4.00	8.00
9 Bud Dempsey	4.00	8.00
10 John Flynn	4.00	8.00
12 Paul Lea	4.00	8.00
13 Alvin Lear	4.00	8.00
14 Wayne Lee	4.00	8.00
15 Joe Don Looney	5.00	10.00
16 Charles Mayhue	4.00	8.00
17 Rick McCurdy	4.00	8.00
18 Ed McQuarters	4.00	8.00
19 Butch Metcalf	4.00	8.00
20 Ralph Neely	7.50	15.00
21 Bobby Page	4.00	8.00
22 John Porterfield	4.00	8.00
23 Mel Sandersfeld	4.00	8.00
24 Wes Skidgel	4.00	8.00
25 Norman Smith	4.00	8.00
26 George Stokes	4.00	8.00
27 Larry Vermillion	4.00	8.00
28 David Voiles	4.00	8.00
29 Dennis Ward	4.00	8.00
30 Bud Wilkinson CO	10.00	20.00
31 Gary Wylie	4.00	8.00

1976 Oklahoma Team Issue

These photos were issued by the school to promote the football program. Each measures roughly 8" by 10" and features a black and white image of a player with the player's name and school name below each photo. The backs are blank.

COMPLETE SET (22)	75.00	150.00
1 Jerry Anderson	4.00	8.00
2 Dean Blevins	4.00	8.00
3 Sidney Brown	4.00	8.00
4 Victor Brown	4.00	8.00
5 Kevin Craig	4.00	8.00
6 Jim Culbreath	4.00	8.00
7 Bill Dalke	4.00	8.00
8 Zac Henderson	4.00	8.00
9 Victor Hicks	4.00	8.00
10 Horace Ivory	5.00	10.00
11 Kenny King	5.00	10.00
12 Reggie Kinlaw	4.00	8.00
13 Thomas Lott	5.00	10.00
14 Jaime Melendez	4.00	8.00
15 Richard Murray	4.00	8.00
16 Elvis Peacock	5.00	10.00
17 Terry Peters	4.00	8.00
18 Mike Phillips	4.00	8.00
19 Jerry Reese	4.00	8.00
20 Greg Roberts	4.00	8.00
21 Myron Shoate	4.00	8.00
22 Uwe Von Schamann	5.00	10.00

1982 Oklahoma Playing Cards

Manufactured for OU by TransMedia, these 56 playing cards measure approximately 2 3/8" by 3 3/8" and have rounded corners and the typical playing card finish. Some of the fronts feature color action shots, some carry black-and-white head shots, and still others have no photos at all, just text. The red backs carry the white OU logo. The set is checklisted below in playing card order by suits, with numbers assigned for Aces (1), Jacks (11), Queens (12), and Kings (13).

COMP. FACT SET (56)	30.00	50.00
C1 Joe Washington	.50	1.25
Action shot		
C2 Coaches 1895-1934	.30	.75
C3 Buddy Burris	.50	1.25
All-Americans 1946-48		
C4 Buck McPhail	.50	1.25
J.D.Roberts		
Max Boydston		
Kurt Burris		
All-Americans 1953-54		
C5 Ralph Neely	.50	1.25
Carl McAdams		
Bob Kalsu		
Steve Owens		
All-Americans 1963-69		

C6 Kyle Davis	.50	1.25
Tinker Owens		
Dewey Selmon		
Lee Roy Selmon		
All-Americans 1974-75		
C7 Jim Weatherall 1951	.50	1.25
C8 Billy Vessels 1952	.50	1.25
C9 NCAA Champions 1955	.50	1.25
C10 Uwe Von Schamann	.30	.75
Action shot		
C11 Tony DiRienzo	.30	.75
Action shot		
C12 Joe Washington	.50	1.25
Action shot		
C13 Tinker Owens	.30	.75
Action shot		
D1 Joe Washington	.50	1.25
Action shot		
D2 Coaches 1935-1982	.30	.75
D3 Jimmy Owens	.50	1.25
Darrell Royal		
All-Americans 1949		
D4 Bo Bolinger	.50	1.25
Ed Gray		
Jerry Tubbs		
Terry McDonald		
All-Americans 1955-56		
D5 Granville Liggins	.50	1.25
Steve Zabel		
Ken Mendenhall		
Jack Mildren		
All-Americans 1966-71		
D6 Terry Webb	.50	1.25
Billy Brooks		
Jimbo Elrod		
Mike Vaughan		
All-Americans 1975-76		
D7 J.D. Roberts 1953	.50	1.25
D8 Steve Owens 1969	.75	2.00
D9 NCAA Champions 1956	.50	1.25
D10 Barry Switzer CO	2.00	5.00
D11 Lucius Selmon	.30	.75
Action shot		
D12 Elvis Peacock	.30	.75
Action shot		
D13 Billy Sims	.50	1.25
Action shot		
H1 Jimbo Elrod	.30	.75
Action shot		
H2 All-Americans 1913-37	.50	1.25
H3 Jim Weatherall	.50	1.25
All-Americans 1949-51		
H4 Bill Krisher	.50	1.25
Clendon Thomas		
Bob Harrison		
Jerry Thompson		
All-Americans 1957-59		
H5 Greg Pruitt	.50	1.25
Tom Brahaney		
Derland Moore		
Rod Shoate		
All-Americans 1971-74		
H6 Zac Henderson	.50	1.25
Greg Roberts		
Daryl Hunt		
George Cumby		
All-Americans 1976-78		
H7 Lee Roy Selmon 1975	2.50	6.00
H8 Billy Sims 1978	1.50	4.00
H9 NCAA Champions 1974	.50	1.25
H10 Lee Roy Selmon	.75	2.00
Action shot		
H11 Tinker Owens	.30	.75
Action shot		
H12 Action shot	.30	.75
H13 Lee Roy Selmon	.75	2.00
Action shot		
S1 Horace Ivory	.30	.75
Action shot		
S2 All-Americans 1938-46	.50	1.25
S3 Tom Catlin	.50	1.25
Billy Vessels		
Eddie Crowder		
All-Americans 1951-52		
S4 Leon Cross	.50	1.25
Wayne Lee		
Jim Grisham		
Joe Don Looney		
All-Americans 1962-63		
S5 Lucius Selmon	.50	1.25
Eddie Foster		
John Roush		
Joe Washington		
All-Americans 1973-75		
S6 Reggie Kinlaw	.50	1.25
Billy Sims		
Louis Oubre		
Terry Crouch		
All-Americans 1978-81		
S7 Greg Roberts 1978	.50	1.25
S8 NCAA Champions 1950	.50	1.25
S9 NCAA Champions 1975	.50	1.25
S10 Bobby Proctor CO	.30	.75
Action shot		
S11 Steve Davis	.30	.75
Action shot		
S12 Greg Pruitt	.50	1.25
Action shot		
S13 Elvis Peacock	.30	.75
Action shot		
JK1 Sooner Schooner	.30	.75
JK2 Sooner Schooner	.30	.75
NNO Mail order card	.30	.75
NNO Mail order card	.30	.75

1986 Oklahoma

The 1986 Oklahoma National Championship set contains 16 unnumbered, standard-size cards. The fronts are "pure" with color photos, thin white borders and no printing; the backs describe the front photos. These cards were printed on very thin stock.

COMPLETE SET (16)	7.50	15.00
1 Championship Ring	.30	.75
1985 National Champs		
2 Orange Bowl	.10	.30
(In Bowl Play)		
3 On the Road to Record	.10	.30
4 Graduation Record	.10	.30
5 Lawrence G. Rawl	.10	.30
President of Exxon		
6 Barry Switzer	1.25	3.00
(Winners)		
7 Win Streaks Hold	.10	.30
Records		
8 Brian Bosworth	3.00	6.00
9 Heisman Trophy	.50	1.25
Billy Vessels 1952		
Steve Owens 1969		
Billy Sims 1978		
10 All-America Sooners	.30	.75
(Tony Casillas)		
11 Jamelle Holieway	.30	.75
12 Sooner Strength	.10	.30
13 Sooner Support	.10	.30
14 Go Sooners	.10	.30
(Crimson and Cream)		
15 Border Battle	.30	.75
(Oklahoma vs. Texas)		
16 Barry Switzer CO SP	2.00	5.00
(Caricature; 'I Want		
You'; '86 OU football		
schedule on back)		

1986 Oklahoma McDag

The 1986 Oklahoma McDag set contains 16 standard-size cards printed on very thin stock. The fronts have color action photos bordered in white; the vertically oriented backs have brief career highlights and safety tips. The cards are unnumbered, so they are listed alphabetically by player's name. The key card in the set features tight end Keith Jackson.

COMPLETE SET (16)	15.00	25.00
1 Brian Bosworth	5.00	10.00
2 Sonny Brown	.40	1.00
3 Steve Bryan	.40	1.00
4 Lydell Carr	.60	1.50
5 Patrick Collins	.60	1.50
6 Jamelle Holieway	.75	2.00
7 Mark Hutson	.40	1.00
8 Keith Jackson	1.50	4.00
9 Troy Johnson	.40	1.00
10 Dante Jones	.75	2.00
11 Tim Lashar	.40	1.00
12 Paul Migliazzo	.40	1.00
13 Anthony Phillips	.40	1.00
14 Darrell Reed	.40	1.00
15 Derrick Shepard	.60	1.50
16 Spencer Tillman	.60	1.50

1987 Oklahoma Police

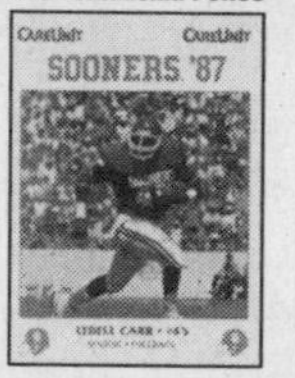

The 1987 Oklahoma Police set consists of 16 standard-size cards printed on thin card stock. The fronts feature color action player photos on a white card face. CareUnit logos and the words "Sooners '87" are printed in the top margin, while player information between two helmets fill the bottom margin. The backs carry biography, career highlights, and "Tips from the Sooners" in the form of anti-crime messages. The cards are unnumbered and checklisted below according to uniform number.

COMPLETE SET (16)	7.50	20.00
1 Eric Mitchel	.50	1.25
4 Jamelle Holieway	.75	2.00
10 David Vickers	.30	.75
25 Anthony Stafford	.50	1.25
29 Rickey Dixon	.75	2.00
33 Patrick Collins	.50	1.25
40 Darrell Reed	.30	.75
45 Lydell Carr	.50	1.25
50 Dante Jones	.60	1.50
66 Jon Phillips and/68 Anthony Phillips	.30	.75
75 Greg Johnson	.30	.75
79 Mark Hutson	.30	.75
80 Troy Johnson	.30	.75
88 Keith Jackson	1.25	3.00
98 Dante Williams	.30	.75
NNO Barry Switzer CO	1.25	3.00

1988 Oklahoma Greats

The 1988 Oklahoma Greats set features 30 standard-size cards. The fronts have color photos bordered in white and red. The vertically oriented backs feature detailed biographical information, statistics, and highlights.

COMPLETE SET (30)	3.00	8.00
1 Jerry Anderson	.10	.30
2 Dee Andros	.15	.40
3 Dean Blevins	.10	.30
4 Rick Bryan	.20	.50
5 Paul(Buddy) Burris	.10	.30
6 Eddie Crowder	.15	.40
7 Jack Ging	.10	.30
8 Jim Grisham	.15	.40
9 Jimmy Harris	.15	.40
10 Scott Hill	.10	.30
11 Eddie Hinton	.15	.40
12 Earl Johnson	.10	.30
13 Don Key	.10	.30
14 Tim Lashar	.10	.30
15 Granville Liggins	.20	.50
16 Thomas Lott	.15	.40
17 Carl McAdams	.15	.40
18 Jack Mitchell	.15	.40
19 Billy Pricer	.10	.30
20 John Roush	.10	.30
21 Darrell Royal	.30	.75
22 Lucious Selmon	.15	.40
23 Ron Shotts	.10	.30
24 Jerry Tubbs	.15	.40
25 Bob Warmack	.10	.30
26 Joe Washington	.20	.50
27 Jim Weatherall	.15	.40
28 '86 Sooner Great Game	.10	.30
29 '75 Sooners	.10	.30
30 Checklist Card	.15	.40

1988 Oklahoma Police

This 16-card standard-size set was produced by Sports Marketing (Seattle, WA). The cards are printed on thin card stock. On a red card face, the fronts display posed color head and shoulders shots accented by black borders. The school and team name are printed above the picture, with player information below the picture. In black print on a white background, the backs have player profile and "Tips from The Sooners," which consist of anti-drug and alcohol messages. The cards are unnumbered and checklisted below in alphabetical order.

COMPLETE SET (16)	7.50	20.00
1 Rotnei Anderson	.60	1.50
2 Eric Bross	.40	1.00
3 Mike Gaddis	.60	1.50
4 Scott Garl	.40	1.00
5 James Goode	.40	1.00
6 Jamelle Holieway	.60	1.50
7 Bob Latham	.40	1.00
8 Ken McMichel	.40	1.00
9 Eric Mitchel	.60	1.50
10 Leon Perry	.60	1.50
11 Anthony Phillips	.40	1.00
12 Anthony Stafford	.60	1.50
13 Barry Switzer CO	1.50	4.00
14 Mark Vankeirsbilck	.40	1.00
15 Curtice Williams	.40	1.00
16 Dante Williams	.40	1.00

1989 Oklahoma Police

This 16-card standard-size set was produced by The C and R Print Shop Inc. and features members of the Oklahoma Sooners football team. The fronts feature posed color player photos inside a black picture frame with white outer borders. The players are pictured in uniform with one knee on the ground. The school name appears above the picture in red print and accented by black horizontal lines; the player's name, number, and the team's logo (a covered wagon) are printed below the picture. The backs present a player profile and, in a black box, a tip for becoming "A Classroom Winner." The team helmet and the producer's logo round out the back. The cards are unnumbered and checklisted below in alphabetical order.

COMPLETE SET (16)	6.00	15.00
1 Tom Backes	.40	1.00
2 Frank Blevins	.40	1.00
3 Eric Bross	.40	1.00
4 Adrian Cooper	.75	2.00
5 Scott Evans	.40	1.00
6 Mike Gaddis	.60	1.50
7 Gary Gibbs CO	.60	1.50
8 James Goode	.40	1.00
9 Ken McMichel	.40	1.00
10 Leon Perry	.60	1.50
11 Mike Sawatzky	.40	1.00
12 Don Smitherman	.40	1.00
13 Kevin Thompson	.40	1.00
14 Mark VanKeirsbilck	.40	1.00
15 Mike Wise	.40	1.00
16 Dante Williams	.40	1.00

1990 Oklahoma Police

This Police set was sponsored by the Bank of Oklahoma and given away during the season. The standard sized cards feature color player photos with many of the players posed with one knee on the ground. The border trim and school name at top were printed in red. The player's name is printed in capital lettering beneath the picture. The cardbacks list career highlights and a player quote in the form of safety messages. The cards are unnumbered and arranged below alphabetically. The set is thought to contain 16-cards. Any additional information on this set would be greatly appreciated.

COMPLETE SET (7)	3.20	8.00
1 Joe Bowden	1.00	2.50
2 Scott Evans	.40	1.00
3 Mike Gaddis	.60	1.50
4 James Goode	.40	1.00
5 Arthur Guess	.40	1.00
6 Mike McKinley	.40	1.00
7 Randy Wallace	.40	1.00

1991 Oklahoma Police

This 16-card Police set was sponsored by the Bank of Oklahoma and given away during the season. The cards were issued on an uncut sheet measuring approximately 10 1/2" by 17". If the cards were cut, each would measure approximately 2 1/2" by 4 1/4". The fronts feature color player photos with the players posed with one knee on the ground. The borders are black. The player's name and team name are printed in large block lettering beneath the picture. The backs list career highlights and a player quote in the form of anti-drug messages. The cards are numbered on the back in a black oval.

COMPLETE SET (16)	6.00	15.00
1 Gary Gibbs CO	.60	1.50
2 Cale Gundy	.60	1.50
3 Charles Franks	.40	1.00
4 Mike Gaddis	.60	1.50
5 Brad Reddell	.40	1.00
6 Brandon Houston	.40	1.00
7 Chris Wilson	.40	1.00
8 Darnell Walker	.40	1.00
9 Mike McKinley	.40	1.00
10 Kenyon Rasheed	.80	2.00
11 Joe Bowden	1.00	2.50
12 Jason Belser	.60	1.50
13 Steve Collins	.40	1.00
14 Reggie Barnes	.40	1.00
15 Randy Wallace	.40	1.00
16 Proctor Land	.40	1.00

2000 Oklahoma

This set of cards was issued in six different seven-card strips and printed on thin white glossy card stock. One of the seven cards on each perforated strip was a cover card with the set number on the front and Conoco and Pizza Hut coupons on the back. The remaining six cards on each strip featured either a great Championship player, coach or event from Oklahoma's football past. Several cards were printed more than once to fill out the strips with two cards having slight variations in the text on the cardbacks. Some of these cards, like Barry Switzer were re-issued with the 2001 Oklahoma set. We've assigned card numbers below to the unnumbered set.

COMPLETE SET (39)	4.00	10.00
1 Brian Bosworth	.50	1.25
2 Tony Casillas	.20	.50
3 Tom Catlin	.08	.25
4 Tony DiRienzo	.08	.25
5 Jimbo Elrod	.08	.25
6 Leon Heath	.08	.25
7 Zac Henderson	.08	.25
8 Jamelle Holieway	.20	.50
9 Mark Hutson	.08	.25
10 Keith Jackson	.30	.75
11 Norman McNabb	.08	.25
12 Kevin Murphy	.08	.25
13 Anthony Phillips	.08	.25
15 Dewey Selmon	.20	.50
15 Darrell Reed	.08	.25
16 Lee Roy Selmon	.40	1.00
17 Barry Switzer CO	1.00	2.50
18 Mike Vaughn	.08	.25
19 Billy Vessels	.20	.50
20 Joe Washington	.20	.50
21 Jim Weatherall	.08	.25
22 Terry Webb	.08	.25
23 Bud Wilkinson CO	.40	1.00
24 1950 Championship Team	.08	.25
25 1975 Championship Team	.08	.25
26 1985 Championship Team	.08	.25
27 Heisman Winners	.20	.50
Billy Vessells		
Steve Owens		
Billy Sims		
28A Memorial Stadium A	.02	.10
(last line reads they		
have played in OMS.)		
28B Memorial Stadium B	.02	.10
(double printed)/(last line reads 77 years		
they have played in OMS.)		
29 Sooner Schooner	.02	.10
(triple printed)		
30A Switzer Center A	.02	.10
(sixth line begins with sports and		
ninth line begins with athletic)		
30B Switzer Center B	.02	.10
(sixth line begins with sports and		
ninth line begins with OU's)		
30C Switzer Center C	.02	.10
(sixth line begins with the)		
31 Set 1 Cover Card	.02	.10
32 Set 2 Cover Card	.02	.10
33 Set 3 Cover Card	.02	.10
34 Set 4 Cover Card	.02	.10
35 Set 5 Cover Card	.02	.10
36 Set 6 Cover Card	.02	.10

2001 Oklahoma

This set of cards was issued in three different seven-card strips and printed on thin white glossy card stock. One of the seven cards on each perforated strip was a cover card with the set number on the front and a Conoco coupon on the back. The remaining six cards on each strip featured a player from the team's 2000 National Championship.

COMPLETE SET (21)	6.00	12.00
1 Matt Anderson	.20	.50
2 Al Baysinger	.20	.50
3 Darryl Bright	.20	.50
4 Bubba Burcham	.20	.50
5 Corey Callens	.20	.50
6 Ryan Fisher	.20	.50
7 Patrick Fletcher	.20	.50
8 Chris Hammons	.20	.50
10 Ontei Jones	.20	.50
9 Josh Heupel	1.25	3.00
11 Scott Kempenich	.20	.50
12 Seth Littrell	.20	.50
13 Torrance Marshall	.50	1.25
14 Ramon Richardson	.20	.50
15 Roger Steffen	.20	.50
16 Bob Stoops CO	.60	1.50
17 J.T. Thatcher	.20	.50
18 Jeremy Wilson-Guest	.20	.50
19 Set 1 Cover Card	.20	.50
20 Set 2 Cover Card	.20	.50
21 Set 3 Cover Card	.20	.50

2003 Oklahoma Program Cards

These cards were issued in 6-card perforated sheets within the programs at OU home games during the 2003 season. When seperated, the card measure between 3" by 4" and 3" by 4 1/8" depending on the size of the sheet. The sheets themselves are numbered 1-6 within the top panel and cards on the first three sheets feature traditional cardbacks. The final three sheets feature a full sized ad on the back instead of cardbacks. We've checklisted the cards below in order of release, or sheet number, with alphabetical characters A-F representing the sheet number.

COMPLETE SET (36)	10.00	20.00
A1 Bennie Owen ATG CO	.20	.50
A2 Claude Reeds	.20	.50
A3 Forest Geyer	.20	.50
A4 Waddy Young	.20	.50
A5 Jim Owens	.20	.50
A6 Memorial Stadium	.20	.50
B1 Bud Wilkinson ATG CO	.40	1.00
B2 Kurt Burris	.20	.50
B3 J.D. Roberts	.20	.50
B4 Jim Weatherall	.20	.50
B5 Cale Gundy Asst. CO	.20	.50
B6 Memorial Stadium	.20	.50
C1 Barry Switzer ATG CO	.75	2.00
C2 Joe Washington	.30	.75
C3 Lee Roy Selmon	.50	1.25
C4 Greg Pruitt	.40	1.00
C5 Jackie Shipp	.20	.50
C6 Memorial Stadium	.20	.50
D1 Bob Stoops CO	.75	2.00
D2 Tommy McDonald	.30	.75
D3 Jerry Tubbs	.20	.50
D4 Billy Sims	.50	1.25
D5 Kevin Sumlin	.20	.50
D6 Memorial Stadium	.20	.50
E1 Chuck Long	.30	.75
E2 Kevin Wilson	.20	.50
E3 Tony Casillas	.30	.75
E4 Keith Jackson	.40	1.00
E5 Darrell Wyatt	.20	.50
E6 Memorial Stadium	.20	.50
F1 Brent Venables	.20	.50
F2 Bobby Jack Wright	.20	.50
F3 Billy Vessels	.20	.50
F4 Steve Owens	.40	1.00
F5 Chris Wilson	.20	.50
F6 Memorial Stadium	.20	.50

1991 Oklahoma State Collegiate Collection

This 100-card multi-sport standard-size set was produced by Collegiate Collection. We've cataloged players from the top three sports using these initials: B-baseball, K-basketball, and F-football.

COMPLETE SET (100)	6.00	15.00
2 Barry Sanders F	.50	1.25
3 Thurman Thomas F	.30	.75
5 Bob Kurland F	.15	.40
10 Allie Reynolds F	.08	.25
11 Rodney Harling F	.05	.15
13 Walt Garrison F	.15	.40
14 Terry Miller F	.07	.20
15 Bob Fenimore F	.05	.15
16 Gerald Hudson F	.05	.15
17 Hart Lee Dykes F	.07	.20
18 1976 Big 8 Conference F	.05	.15
19 Jimmy Johnson CO F	.30	.75
20 Terry Brown F	.05	.15
21 Derrel Gofourth F	.05	.15
22 Paul Blair F	.08	.25
23 John Little F	.05	.15
24 1983 Bluebonnet Bowl F	.05	.15
26 1976 Tangerine Bowl F	.05	.15
27 Gary Cutsinger F	.05	.15
28 Rusty Hilger F	.05	.15
29 Ron Baker F	.05	.15
30 Pat Jones F	.07	.20
31 Phillip Dokes F	.05	.15
32 Neil Armstrong F	.05	.15
34 Jon Kolb F	.05	.15
37 Barry Hanna F	.05	.15
39 1946 Sugar Bowl F	.05	.15
42 Thurman Thomas F	.30	.75
44 1988 Holiday Bowl F	.05	.15
45 Ernest Anderson F	.05	.15
46 Leslie O'Neal F	.08	.25
48 Leonard Thompson F	.05	.15
50 Mike Gundy F	.05	.15
51 Mark Moore F	.05	.15
53 Bum Phillips F	.20	.50
54 John Ward F	.05	.15
55 Larry Roach F	.05	.15
56 Jerry Sherk F	.05	.15
57 Matt Monger F	.05	.15
58 Dick Soergel F	.05	.15
59 Ricky Young F	.05	.15
61 Barry Sanders F	.50	1.25
66 Chris Rockins F	.05	.15
67 Buddy Ryan F	.08	.25
68 Thurman Thomas F	.30	.75
76 Barry Sanders F	.50	1.25
78 Barry Sanders	.40	1.00
Thurman Thomas F		
81 Thurman Thomas F	.30	.75
83 Barry Sanders F	.50	1.25
86 Thurman Thomas F	.30	.75
93 Thurman Thomas F	.30	.75
94 John Washington F	.05	.15
97 1987 Sun Bowl F	.05	.15

2001 Oklahoma State

COMPLETE SET (25)	10.00	20.00
1 Ron Able	.40	1.00
2 Roger Bombach	.40	1.00
3 Chris Calcagni	.40	1.00
4 Michael Cooper	.40	1.00
5 Scott Elder	.40	1.00
6 Robbie Gillem	.40	1.00
7 D.J. Grissom	.40	1.00
8 Matt Henson	.40	1.00
9 George Horton	.40	1.00
10 Jason Howard	.40	1.00
11 Jason Johnson	.40	1.00
12 John Johnston	.40	1.00
13 Marcus Jones	.40	1.00
14 Paul Jones	.40	1.00
15 Dwayne Levels	.40	1.00
16 Jeff Machado	.40	1.00
17 Tarrick McGuire	.40	1.00
18 Bryan Phillips	.40	1.00
19 Jason Rannebarger	.40	1.00
20 Jake Riffe	.40	1.00
21 Chris Tyler	.40	1.00
22 John Vandrell	.40	1.00
23 A.T. Wells	.40	1.00
24 Les Miles CO	.60	1.50
25 Team Mascot	.40	1.00

2002 Oklahoma State

This set was produced for Oklahoma State University and sponsored by Conoco. The set was originally issued as a 24-card perforated sheet that was to be separated by the collector into individual cards. Each card features a color photo of the player along with a silver border on the front and a simple black and white cardback. The unnumbered cards are listed below alphabetically.

COMPLETE SET (24)	10.00	20.00
1 Kobina Amoo	.40	1.00
2 Kyle Beck	.40	1.00
3 Adonis Brewer	.40	1.00
4 LaWaylon Brown	.40	1.00
5 Bullet (mascot)	.40	1.00
6 Michael Cox	.40	1.00
7 Terrance Davis-Bryant	.40	1.00
8 Mike Denard	.40	1.00
9 Kyle Eaton	.40	1.00
10 Ricklan Holmes-Miller	.40	1.00
11 John Lewis	.40	1.00
12 Gabe Lindsay	.40	1.00
13 Chris Massey	.40	1.00
14 Les Miles CO	.75	2.00
15 Kirk Milligan	.40	1.00
16 Jed Newkirk	.40	1.00
17 Pistol Pete (mascot)	.40	1.00
18 Terrence Robinson	.40	1.00
19 Jason Russell	.40	1.00
20 Scott Smith	.40	1.00
21 Saul Talley	.40	1.00
22 Dustin Vanderhoof	.40	1.00
23 Kevin Williams	2.00	5.00
24 Willie Young	.40	1.00

1953 Oregon

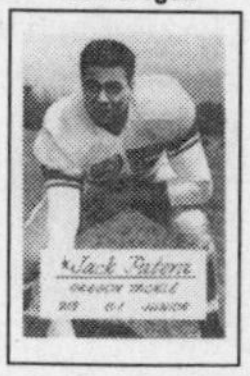

This 20-card set measures roughly 2 1/4" x 3 1/2". The fronts feature a posed action photo, with player information appearing in handwritten script in a white box toward the bottom of the picture. Below the motto "Football is Fun," the backs have a list of locations where adult tickets can be purchased and a Knothole Gang membership offer. The cards are unnumbered and checklisted below in alphabetical order.

COMPLETE SET (20)	600.00	1,000.00
1 Farrell Albright	30.00	50.00
2 Ted Anderson	30.00	50.00
3 Len Berrie	30.00	50.00
4 Tom Elliott	30.00	50.00
5 Tim Flaherty	30.00	50.00
6 Cecil Hodges	30.00	50.00
7 Barney Holland	30.00	50.00
8 Dick James	35.00	60.00
9 Harry Johnson	30.00	50.00
10 Dave Lowe	30.00	50.00
11 Jack Patera	35.00	60.00
12 Ron Pheister	30.00	50.00
13 John Reed	30.00	50.00
14 Hal Reeve	30.00	50.00
15 Larry Rose	30.00	50.00
16 George Shaw	50.00	80.00
17 Lon Stiner Jr.	30.00	50.00
18 Ken Sweitzer	30.00	50.00
19 Keith Tucker	30.00	50.00
20 Dean Van Leuven	30.00	50.00

1956 Oregon

This 19-card set measures the standard size (2 1/2" x 3 1/2"). The fronts feature a posed action photo, with player information appearing in a white box toward the bottom of the picture. Below the motto "Follow the Ducks," the backs have schedule information and a list of locations where adult tickets can be purchased. The cards are unnumbered and checklisted below in alphabetical order.

COMPLETE SET (19)	500.00	800.00
1 Bruce Brenn	30.00	50.00
2 Jack Brown	30.00	50.00
3 Reanous Cochran	30.00	50.00
4 Jack Crabtree	35.00	60.00
5 Tom Crabtree	30.00	50.00
6 Tom Hale	30.00	50.00
7 Spike Hillstrom	30.00	50.00
8 Jim Linden	30.00	50.00
9 Hank Loumena	30.00	50.00
10 Nick Markulis	30.00	50.00
11 Phil McHugh	30.00	50.00
12 Fred Miklancic	30.00	50.00
13 Harry Mondale	30.00	50.00
14 Leroy Phelps	30.00	50.00
15 Jack Pocock	30.00	50.00
16 John Raventos	30.00	50.00
17 Jim Shanley	30.00	50.00
18 Ron Stover	30.00	50.00
19 J.C. Wheeler	30.00	50.00

1958 Oregon

This 20-card set measures approximately 2 1/4" by 3 1/2". The fronts feature a posed action player photo with player information in the white border beneath the picture. The cards are unnumbered and checklisted below in alphabetical order.

COMPLETE SET (20)	500.00	800.00
1 Greg Altenhofen	30.00	50.00
2 Darrel Aschbacher	30.00	50.00
3 Dave Fish	30.00	50.00
4 Sandy Fraser	30.00	50.00
5 Dave Grosz	30.00	50.00
6 Bob Grottkau	30.00	50.00
7 Marlan Holland	30.00	50.00
8 Tom Keele	30.00	50.00
9 Alden Kimbrough	30.00	50.00
10 Don Laudenslager	30.00	50.00
11 Riley Mattson	35.00	60.00
12 Bob Peterson	30.00	50.00
13 Dave Powell	30.00	50.00
14 Len Read	30.00	50.00
15 Will Reeve	30.00	50.00
16 Joe Schaffeld	30.00	50.00
17 Charlie Tourville	30.00	50.00
18 Dave Urell	30.00	50.00
19 Pete Welch	30.00	50.00
20 Willie West	35.00	60.00

1972 Oregon Schedules

COMPLETE SET (16)	125.00	250.00
1 Maurice Anderson	7.50	15.00
2 Steve Bailey	7.50	15.00
3 Chuck Bradley	7.50	15.00
4 Pete Carlson	7.50	15.00
5 Ken Carter	7.50	15.00
6 Charley Cobb	7.50	15.00
7 Steve Herr	7.50	15.00
8 Rick Lessel	7.50	15.00
9 Fred Manuel	7.50	15.00
10 Joe Muse	7.50	15.00
11 Tony Rapolla	7.50	15.00
12 Don Reynolds	7.50	15.00
13 Tim Slapnicka	7.50	15.00
14 Greg Specht	7.50	15.00
15 Marc Traut	7.50	15.00
16 Norv Turner	15.00	30.00

1990 Oregon

This 12-card set was initially issued as a perforated sheet with each card measuring approximately 3" by 4" when separated. Distinctive green and gold cardfronts feature player action photos printed on white card stock. The school name "Oregon" appears at the top of each card while the Smokey logo, player name, position, and number are at the bottom. The cardbacks have biographical information and a fire prevention cartoon starring Smokey the Bear. The cards are unnumbered and checklisted below in alphabetical order.

COMPLETE SET (12)	6.00	15.00
1 Scot Boatright	.50	1.25
2 Peter Brantley	.50	1.25
3 Rich Brooks CO	.60	1.50
4 Andy Conner	.50	1.25
5 Rory Dairy	.50	1.25
6 Joe Farwell	.50	1.25
7 Tony Hargain	.50	1.25
8 Todd Kaanapu	.50	1.25
9 Matt LaBounty	.60	1.50
10 Greg McCallum	.50	1.25
11 Bill Musgrave	1.00	2.50
12 Joe Reitzug	.50	1.25

1991 Oregon

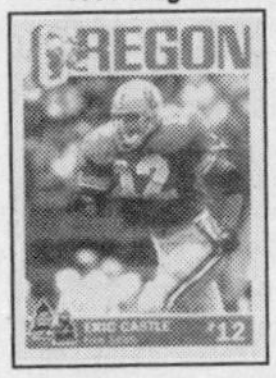

This 12-card set was initially issued as a perforated sheet with each card measuring approximately 3" by 4" when separated. Distinctive green and gold cardfronts feature player action photos printed on white card stock. The school name "Oregon" appears at the top of each card while the Smokey logo, player name, position, and number are at the bottom. The cardbacks have biographical information and a fire prevention cartoon starring Smokey the Bear. The cards are unnumbered and checklisted below in alphabetical order.

COMPLETE SET (12)	5.00	12.00
1 Bud Bowie	.50	1.25
2 Rich Brooks CO	.60	1.50
3 Sean Burwell	.50	1.25
4 Eric Castle	.50	1.25
5 Andy Conner	.50	1.25
0 Joe Farwell	.50	1.25
7 Matt LaBounty	.60	1.50
8 Greg McCallum	.50	1.25
9 Daryle Smith	.50	1.25
10 Jeff Thomason	.60	1.50
11 Tommy Thompson	.50	1.25
12 Marcus Woods	.50	1.25

1992 Oregon

This 12-card set was initially issued as a perforated sheet with each card measuring approximately 3" by 4" when separated. Distinctive green and gold cardfronts feature player action photos printed on white card stock. The school name "Oregon" appears at the top of each card with the year noted within the second "O," while the Smokey logo, the player's name, his position, and jersey number are at the bottom. The cardbacks have biographical information and a fire prevention cartoon starring Smokey the Bear. The cards are unnumbered and checklisted below in alphabetical order.

COMPLETE SET (12)	5.00	12.00
1 Romeo Bandison	.50	1.25
2 Rich Brooks CO	.60	1.50
3 Sean Burwell	.50	1.25
4 Eric Castle	.50	1.25
5 David Collinsworth	.50	1.25
6 Chad Cota	.60	1.50
7 Jeff Cummins	.50	1.25
8 Joe Farwell	.50	1.25
9 Santhony Jones	.50	1.25
10 Danny O'Neil	.50	1.25
11 Jon Tattersall	.50	1.25
12 Tommy Thompson	.50	1.25

1993 Oregon

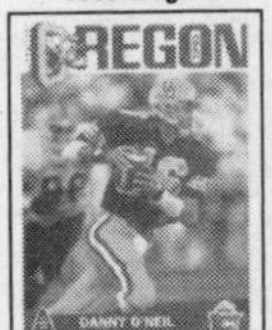

This 12-card set was initially issued as a perforated sheet with each card measuring approximately 3" by 4" when separated. Distinctive green and gold cardfronts feature player action photos printed on white card stock. The school name "Oregon" appears at the top of each card with the year noted within the second "O," while the Smokey logo, the player's name, his position, and jersey number are at the bottom. The cardbacks have biographical information and a fire prevention cartoon starring Smokey the Bear. The cards are unnumbered and checklisted below in alphabetical order.

COMPLETE SET (12)	5.00	12.00
1 Romeo Bandison	.50	1.25
2 Sean Burwell	.50	1.25
3 Chad Cota	.60	1.50
4 Derrick Deadwiler	.50	1.25
5 Mike Difonzo	.50	1.25
6 Ernest Jones	.50	1.25
7 Herman O'Berry	.50	1.25
8 Danny O'Neil	.50	1.25
9 Juan Shedrick	.50	1.25
10 Willie Tate	.50	1.25
11 Tommy Thompson	.50	1.25
12 Gary Williams	.50	1.25

1994 Oregon

This 12-card set was initially issued as a perforated sheet with each card measuring approximately 3" by 4" when separated. Distinctive green and gold cardfronts feature player action photos printed on white card stock. The school name "Oregon" appears at the top of each card with the year noted within the second "O," while the Smokey logo, the player's name, his position, and jersey number are at the bottom. The cardbacks have biographical information and a fire prevention cartoon starring Smokey the Bear. The cards are unnumbered and checklisted below in alphabetical order.

COMPLETE SET (12)	5.00	12.00
1 Jeremy Asher	.50	1.25
2 Chad Cota	.60	1.50
3 Steve Hardin	.50	1.25
4 Dante Lewis	.50	1.25
5 Cristin McLemore	.50	1.25
6 Alex Molden	.60	1.50
7 Silila Malepeai	.50	1.25
8 Herman O'Berry	.50	1.25
9 Danny O'Neil	.50	1.25
10 Dino Philyaw	.60	1.50
11 Jeff Sherman	.50	1.25
12 Ricky Whittle	.50	1.25

1995 Oregon

This 12-card set was initially issued as a perforated sheet with each card measuring approximately 3" by 4" when separated. Distinctive green and gold cardfronts feature player action photos printed on white card stock. The school name "Oregon" appears at the top of each card with the year noted within the second "O," while the Smokey logo, the player's name, his position, and jersey number are at the bottom. The cardbacks have biographical information and a fire prevention cartoon starring Smokey the Bear. The cards are unnumbered and checklisted below in alphabetical order.

COMPLETE SET (12)	5.00	12.00
1 Jeremy Asher	.50	1.25
2 Troy Bailey	.50	1.25
3 Mike Bellotti CO	.50	1.25
4 Tony Graziani	1.00	2.50
5 Reggie Jordan	.50	1.25
6 Dante Lewis	.50	1.25
7 Cristin McLemore	.50	1.25
8 Alex Molden	.60	1.50
9 Rich Ruhl	.50	1.25
10 Kenny Wheaton	.50	1.25
11 Ricky Whittle	.50	1.25
12 Josh Wilcox	.50	1.25

1996 Oregon

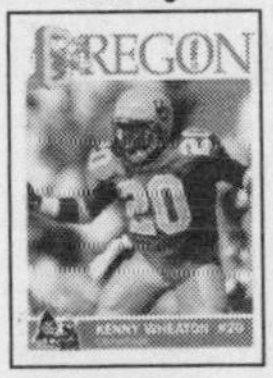

This 12-card set was initially issued as a perforated sheet with each card measuring approximately 3" by 4" when separated. Distinctive green and gold cardfronts feature player action photos printed on white card stock. The school name "Oregon" appears at the top of each card with the year noted within the second "O," while the Smokey logo, the player's name, his position, and jersey number are at the bottom. The cardbacks have biographical information and a fire prevention cartoon starring Smokey the Bear. The cards are unnumbered and checklisted below in alphabetical order.

COMPLETE SET (12)	5.00	10.00
1 Derrick Barnes	.40	1.00
2 Tony Graziani	.75	2.00
3 Mark Gregg	.40	1.00
4 Bryant Jackson	.40	1.00
5 Reggie Jordan	.40	1.00
6 Tasi Malepeai	.40	1.00
7 Dameron Ricketts	.40	1.00
8 Mark Schmidt	.40	1.00
9 Kenny Wheaton	.40	1.00
10 Paul Wiggins	.40	1.00
11 Josh Wilcox	.40	1.00
12 Lamont Woods	.40	1.00

1997 Oregon

This 12-card set was initially issued as a perforated sheet with each card measuring approximately 3" by 4" when separated. Distinctive green and gold cardfronts feature player action photos printed on white card stock. The school name "Oregon" appears at the top of each card with the year noted within the second "O," while the Smokey logo, the player's name, his position, and jersey number are at the bottom. The cardbacks have biographical information and a fire prevention cartoon starring Smokey the Bear. The cards are unnumbered and checklisted below in alphabetical order.

COMPLETE SET (12)	5.00	10.00
1 Josh Bidwell	.40	1.00
2 Desmond Byrd	.40	1.00
3 Seaton Daly	.40	1.00
4 Jaiya Figueras	.40	1.00
5 Damon Griffin	.75	2.00
6 A.J. Jelks	.40	1.00
7 Pat Johnson	.75	2.00
8 Saladin McCullough	.50	1.25
9 Curtis Moore	.40	1.00
10 Blake Spence	.40	1.00
11 David Weber	.40	1.00
12 Eric Winn	.40	1.00

1998 Oregon

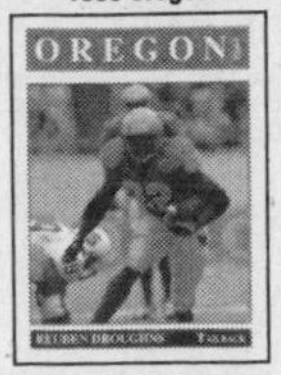

This 12-card set was initially issued as a perforated sheet with each card measuring standard size when separated. Distinctive green and white cardfronts feature player action photos printed on white card stock. The school name "Oregon" appears at the top of each card with the issue year noted. The player's name and position are included below the photo. The cardbacks have biographical information and a Pepsi-Cola logo. The cards are unnumbered and checklisted below in alphabetical order.

COMPLETE SET (12)	7.50	15.00
1 Marco Aguirre	.30	.75
2 Josh Bidwell	.30	.75
3 Stefan DeVries	.30	.75
4 Reuben Droughns	3.00	8.00
5 Eric Edwards	.30	.75
6 Michael Fletcher	.40	1.00
7 Damon Griffin	.40	1.00
8 Dietrich Moore	.40	1.00
9 Kevin Parker	.30	.75
10 Peter Sirmon	.30	.75
11 Akili Smith	1.25	3.00
12 Jed Weaver	.40	1.00

1999 Oregon

This 12-card set was initially issued as a perforated sheet with each card measuring standard size when separated. Green bordered cardfronts feature player action photos on white card stock. The school name "Oregon" appears at the top of each card and the player's name and position are included below the photo. The cardbacks have biographical information, the year of issue and a Pepsi-Cola logo. The cards are unnumbered and checklisted below in alphabetical order.

COMPLETE SET (12)	6.00	12.00
1 Reuben Droughns	2.50	6.00
2 A.J. Feeley	1.50	4.00
3 Michael Fletcher	.30	.75
4 Tony Hartley	.20	.50
5 Brandon McLemore	.20	.50
6 Terry Miller	.20	.50
7 Deke Moen	.20	.50
8 Dietrich Moore	.30	.75
9 Saul Patu	.20	.50
10 Peter Sirmon	.20	.50
11 Nathan Villegas	.20	.50
12 Justin Wilcox	.20	.50

2000 Oregon

This set was produced for the University of Oregon and sponsored by Pepsi. The set was originally issued as a 12-card perforated sheet. Each card features a color photo of the player along with a simple black and white cardback. The unnumbered cards are listed below alphabetically.

COMPLETE SET (12)	7.50	15.00
1 Gary Barker	.20	.50
2 Jed Boice	.20	.50
3 Kurtis Doerr	.20	.50
4 A.J. Feeley	1.25	3.00
5 Josh Frankel	.30	.75
6 Lee Gundy	.20	.50
7 Joey Harrington	2.00	5.00
8 Maurice Morris	1.25	3.00
9 Saul Patu	.20	.50
10 Garrett Sabol	.20	.50
11 Matt Smith	.20	.50
12 Marshaun Tucker	.40	1.00

2001 Oregon

This 12-card set was initially issued as a perforated sheet with each card measuring standard size when separated. Green bordered cardfronts feature player action photos on white card stock. The school name "Oregon" appears at the top of each card and the player's name and position are included below the photo. The cardbacks have biographical information, the year of issue and a Pepsi-Cola logo. The cards are unnumbered and checklisted below in alphabetical order.

COMPLETE SET (12)	6.00	12.00
1 Jim Adams	.20	.50
2 Rashad Bauman	.20	.50
3 Zach Freiter	.20	.50
4 Joey Harrington	1.50	4.00
5 Josh Line	.20	.50
6 Wesley Mallard	.20	.50
7 Seth McEwen	.20	.50
8 Maurice Morris	.75	2.00
9 Justin Peelle	.20	.50
10 Ryan Schmid	.20	.50
11 Steve Smith	.20	.50
12 Rasuli Webster	.20	.50

2002 Oregon

This set was produced for the University of Oregon and sponsored by Pepsi. The set was originally issued as a 12-card perforated sheet that was to be separated by the collector into individual cards. Each card features a color photo of the player along with a simple black and white cardback. The unnumbered cards are listed below alphabetically.

COMPLETE SET (12)	6.00	15.00
1 Allan Amundson	.40	1.00
2 Corey Chambers	.20	.50
3 Jason Fife	.40	1.00
4 Keenan Howry	.40	1.00
5 Keith Lewis	.20	.50
6 Seth McEwen	.20	.50
7 Kevin Mitchell	.30	.75
8 David Moretti	.20	.50
9 Onterrio Smith	3.00	8.00
10 Rasuli Webster	.20	.50
11 George Wrighster	.40	1.00
12 Darrell Wright	.20	.50

2003 Oregon

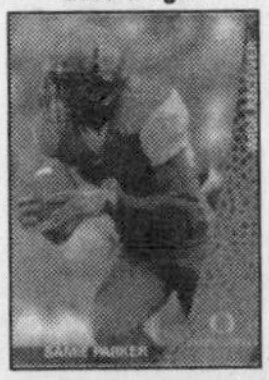

This set was produced for the University of Oregon and sponsored by Pepsi. The set was originally issued as a 12-card perforated sheet that was to be separated by the collector into individual cards. Each card features a color photo of the player printed on high gloss stock. The black and white cardbacks read "2004 Oregon" but the set was issued for the 2003 football season. They are nearly identical to the 2004 release but can be identified by the high glossy card stock and the use of gray on the Oregon team name and logo on the cardback. The unnumbered cards are listed below alphabetically.

COMPLETE SET (12)	4.00	8.00
1 Quinn Dorsey	.20	.50
2 Jason Fife	.40	1.00
3 Matt Floberg	.20	.50
4 Joey Forster	.20	.50
5 Keith Lewis	.20	.50
6 Kevin Mitchell	.30	.75
7 Steven Moore	.30	.75
8 Igor Olshansky	.40	1.00
9 Samie Parker	.75	2.00
10 Junior Slavii	.30	.75
11 Jared Siegel (yellow jersey)	.20	.50
12 Dan Weaver	.30	.75

2004 Oregon

This set was produced for the University of Oregon and sponsored by Pepsi. The set was originally issued as a 12-card perforated sheet that was to be separated by the collector into individual cards. Each card features a color photo of the player printed on a low-gloss stock. They are nearly identical to the 2003 release but can be identified by the low-gloss card stock and the use of black on the Oregon team name and logo on the cardback. The unnumbered cards are listed below alphabetically.

COMPLETE SET (12)	3.00	6.00
1 Kellen Clemens	.75	2.00
2 Tim Day	.30	.75
3 Devan Long	.20	.50
4 Jerry Matson	.20	.50
5 Jared Siegel (green jersey)	.20	.50
6 Adam Snyder	.20	.50
7 Chris Solomona	.20	.50
8 Nick Steitz	.20	.50
9 Marley Tucker	.20	.50
10 Robby Valenzuela	.20	.50
11 Kenny Washington	.20	.50
12 Demetrius Williams	.30	.75

2005 Oregon

This set was produced for the University of Oregon and sponsored by Pepsi. The set was originally issued as a 12-card perforated sheet that was to be separated by the collector into individual cards. Each card features a color photo of the player along with a simple black and white cardback. The unnumbered cards are listed below alphabetically.

COMPLETE SET (12)	5.00	10.00
1 Kellen Clemens	1.00	2.50
2 Tim Day	.30	.75
3 Aaron Gipson	.30	.75
4 Devan Long	.20	.50
5 Enoka Lucas	.20	.50
6 Haloti Ngata	1.00	2.50
7 Justin Phinisee	.20	.50
8 Dante Rosario	.20	.50
9 Matt Toenia	.20	.50
10 Anthony Trucks	.20	.50
11 Terrence Whitehead	.40	1.00
12 Demetrius Williams	.60	1.50

2006 Oregon

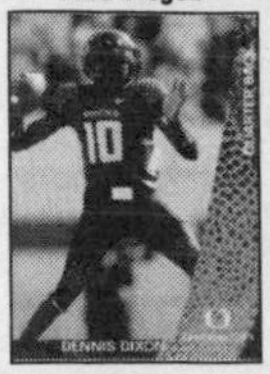

This set was produced for the University of Oregon and sponsored by Pepsi. The set was originally issued as a 12-card perforated sheet that was to be separated by the collector into individual cards. Each card features a color photo of the player along with a simple black and white cardback. The unnumbered cards are listed below alphabetically.

COMPLETE SET (12)	5.00	10.00
1 Dennis Dixon	1.50	4.00
2 Brent Haberly	.20	.50
3 Enoka Lucas	.20	.50
4 Palauni Ma Sun Jr.	.20	.50
5 Paul Martinez	.20	.50
6 J.D. Nelson	.20	.50
7 Blair Phillips	.20	.50
8 Dante Rosario	.30	.75
9 Darius Sanders	.20	.50
10 Jonathan Stewart	1.50	4.00
11 Matt Toeaina	.20	.50
12 Jason Williams	.30	.75

2007 Oregon

This set was produced for the University of Oregon and sponsored by Pepsi. The set was originally issued as a 12-card perforated sheet that was to be separated by the collector into individual cards. Each card features a color photo of the player along with a simple black and white cardback. The unnumbered cards are listed below alphabetically.

COMPLETE SET (12)	6.00	12.00
1 Kwame Agyeman	.20	.50
2 Patrick Chung	.30	.75
3 Dennis Dixon	1.25	3.00
4 David Faaeteete	.20	.50
5 Matthew Harper	.20	.50
6 Jeremiah Johnson	.75	2.00
7 Geoff Schwartz	.20	.50
8 Jonathan Stewart	1.25	3.00
9 Max Unger	.30	.75
10 Cameron Colvin Garren Strong	.20	.50
11 Brian Paysinger A.J. Tuitele	.20	.50
12 Jaison Williams Ed Dickson	.50	1.25

2008 Oregon

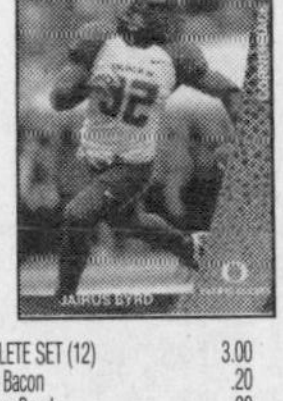

COMPLETE SET (12)	3.00	6.00
1 John Bacon	.20	.50
2 Jerome Boyd	.20	.50
3 Jairus Byrd	.75	2.00
4 Patrick Chung	.30	.75
5 Ed Dickson	.30	.75
6 Matt Evensen	.20	.50
7 Ra'Shon Harris	.30	.75
8 Jeremiah Johnson	.30	.75
9 Nick Reed	.20	.50
10 Terence Scott	.20	.50
11 Walter Thurmond	.20	.50
12 Max Unger	.20	.50

2009 Oregon

COMPLETE SET (12)	3.00	6.00
1 Brandon Bair	.20	.50
2 Ed Dickson	.30	.75
3 Blake Ferras	.20	.50
4 Morgan Flint	.20	.50
5 Willie Glasper	.20	.50
6 Jordan Holmes	.20	.50
7 Jeff Maehl	.40	1.00
8 Jeremiah Masoli	.50	1.25
9 Casey Matthews	.40	1.00
10 Walter Thurmond	.20	.50
11 Will Tukuafu	.20	.50
12 T.J. Ward	.50	1.25

1988 Oregon State

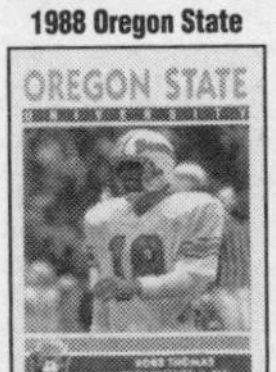

The 1988 Oregon State Smokey set contains 12 standard-size cards. The fronts feature color action photos with name, position, and jersey number. The vertically oriented backs have brief career highlights as well as a brief message from Smokey. The cards are unnumbered, but listed alphabetically below.

COMPLETE SET (12)	5.00	12.00
1 Troy Bussanich	.50	1.25
2 Andre Harris	.50	1.25
3 Teddy Johnson	.50	1.25
4 Jason Kent	.50	1.25
5 Dave Kragthorpe CO	.50	1.25
6 Mike Matthews	.50	1.25
7 Phil Ross	.50	1.25
8 Brian Taylor	.50	1.25
9 Robb Thomas	.50	1.25
10 Esera Tuaolo	.60	1.50
11 Erik Wilhelm	.60	1.50
12 Dowell Williams	.50	1.25

1990 Oregon State

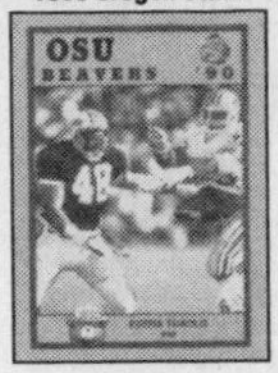

This 16-card set was sponsored by the USDA Forest Service in cooperation with other federal and state agencies. The cards were issued on a sheet with four rows of four cards each; after perforation, they measure the standard size. The fronts feature a mix of color action or posed shots of the players, with black lettering and borders on an orange card face. The backs have player information and a fire prevention cartoon starring Smokey. The cards are unnumbered and checklisted below in alphabetical order.

COMPLETE SET (16)	6.00	15.00
1 Brian Beck	.50	1.25
2 Martin Billings	.50	1.25
3 Matt Booher	.50	1.25
4 George Breland	.50	1.25
5 Brad D'Ancona	.50	1.25
6 Dennis Edwards	.50	1.25
7 Brent Huff	.50	1.25
8 James Jones	.50	1.25
9 Dave Kragthorpe CO	.50	1.25
10 Todd McKinney	.50	1.25
11 Torey Overstreet	.50	1.25
12 Reggie Pitchford	.50	1.25
13 Todd Sahlfeld	.50	1.25
14 Scott Thompson	.50	1.25
15 Esera Tuaolo	.60	1.50
16 Maurice Wilson	.50	1.25

1991 Oregon State

This 12-card set was sponsored by Prime Sports Northwest and other companies to promote fire safety in Oregon. The oversized cards were issued as a perforated sheet and measure approximately 3" by 4". The fronts feature action player photos banded by a black stripe above and an orange stripe below. A Smokey logo and player information are given in the bottom orange stripe. Horizontally oriented backs present career summary and a fire prevention cartoon starring Smokey. The cards are unnumbered and checklisted below in alphabetical order.

COMPLETE SET (12)	5.00	12.00
1 Adam Albaugh	.50	1.25
2 Jamie Burke	.50	1.25
3 Chad de Sully	.50	1.25
4 Dennis Edwards	.50	1.25
5 James Jones	.50	1.25
6 Fletcher Keisler	.50	1.25
7 Tom Nordquist	.50	1.25
8 Tony O'Billovich	.60	1.50
9 Jerry Pettibone CO	.50	1.25
10 Mark Price	.50	1.25
11 Todd Sahlfeld	.50	1.25
12 Earl Zackery	.50	1.25

1992 Oregon State

Sponsored by Prime Sports Northwest, this 12-card set was issued on thin card stock as a perforated sheet; after perforation, each card would measure approximately 3" by 4". The fronts show color player photos bordered in white. The school and team name appear in a black bar above the picture, while the player's name, jersey number, and position are printed within an orange bar beneath the picture. In black print on a white background, the backs feature a player profile and a fire prevention cartoon starring Smokey. The cards are unnumbered and checklisted below in alphabetical order.

COMPLETE SET (12)	5.00	10.00
1 Zechariah Davis	.40	1.00
2 Chad De Sully	.40	1.00
3 Michael Hale	.40	1.00
4 Fletcher Keister	.40	1.00
5 Chad Paulson	.40	1.00
6 Rico Petrini	.40	1.00
7 Jerry Pettibone CO	.40	1.00
8 Sailusi Poulivaati	.40	1.00
9 Tony O'Billovich	.50	1.25
10 Dwayne Owens	.40	1.00
11 Maurice Wilson	.40	1.00
12 J.J. Young	.50	1.25

1993 Oregon State

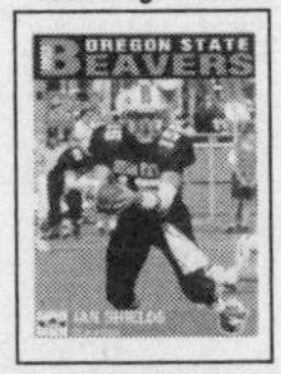

Sponsored by Prime Sports Northwest, this 12-card set was issued on thin card stock as a perforated sheet; after perforation, each card would measure approximately 3" by 4". The fronts show color player photos bordered in white. The year and team name appear in a black bar above the picture, while the player's name, jersey number, and position are printed within an orange bar beneath the picture. In black print on a white background, the backs feature a player profile and a fire prevention cartoon starring Smokey. The cards are unnumbered and checklisted below in alphabetical order.

COMPLETE SET (12)	5.00	10.00
1 Herschel Currie	.40	1.00
2 Chad de Sully	.40	1.00
3 Dennis Edwards	.40	1.00
4 William Ephraim	.40	1.00
5 Johnny Feinga	.40	1.00
6 John Garrett	.40	1.00
7 Tony O'Billovich	.50	1.25
8 Chad Paulson	.40	1.00
9 Rico Petrini	.40	1.00
10 Jerry Pettibone CO	.40	1.00
11 Ian Shields	.40	1.00
12 J.J. Young	.50	1.25

1994 Oregon State

Sponsored by Prime Sports Northwest, this 12-card set was issued on thin card stock as a perforated sheet; after perforation, each card would measure approximately 3" by 4". The fronts show color player photos bordered in white. The school, team name and year appear in a black bar above the picture, while the player's name and position are printed on a orange bar beneath the picture. In black print on a white background, the backs feature a player profile and a fire prevention cartoon starring Smokey. The cards are unnumbered and checklisted below in alphabetical order.

COMPLETE SET (12)	5.00	10.00
1 William Ephraim	.40	1.00
2 Johnny Feinga	.40	1.00
3 John Garrett	.40	1.00
4 Michael Hale	.40	1.00
5 Tom Holmes	.40	1.00
6 Cory Huot	.40	1.00
7 Rico Petrini	.40	1.00
8 Cameron Reynolds	.40	1.00
9 Kane Rogers	.40	1.00
10 Don Shanklin	.40	1.00
11 Reggie Tongue	.75	2.00
12 J.J.Young	.50	1.25

1995 Oregon State

This 12-card set was issued on thin card stock as a perforated sheet. After separated each card measures approximately 3" by 4". The fronts show color player photos bordered in white. The school, team name and year appear in a black bar above the picture, while the player's name and position are printed on a orange bar beneath the picture. In black print on a white background, the backs feature a player profile and a fire prevention cartoon starring Smokey. The cards are unnumbered and checklisted below in alphabetical order.

COMPLETE SET (12)	5.00	10.00
1 Darin Borter	.40	1.00
2 Tim Camp	.40	1.00
3 Tom Holmes	.40	1.00
4 David Kiepke	.40	1.00
5 Mark Olford	.40	1.00
6 Jerry Pettibone CO	.40	1.00
7 Cameron Reynolds	.40	1.00
8 Kane Rogers	.40	1.00
9 Don Shanklin	.40	1.00
10 J.D. Stewart	.40	1.00
11 Sedrick Thomas	.40	1.00
12 Reggie Tongue	.75	2.00

1996 Oregon State

This 16-card set was issued on thin card stock as a perforated sheet. After separated each card measures approximately 2 3/4" by 4". The fronts show color player photos bordered in white. The school, team name and year appear in a black bar above the picture, while the player's name and position are printed on a orange bar beneath the picture. In black print on a white background, the backs feature a player profile and a fire prevention cartoon starring Smokey. The cards are unnumbered and checklisted below in alphabetical order.

COMPLETE SET (16)	6.00	15.00
1 Tim Alexander	.40	1.00
2 Inoke Breckterfield	.40	1.00
3 Larry Bumpus	.40	1.00
4 Jamie Critchlow	.40	1.00
5 Buster Elahee	.40	1.00
6 Grant Forman	.40	1.00
7 Andrae Holland	.40	1.00
8 Tony Huot	.40	1.00
9 Akili King	.40	1.00
10 Bryan Ludwick	.40	1.00
11 Nathan McAtee	.40	1.00
12 Rahim Muhammad	.40	1.00
13 Jerry Pettibone CO	.40	1.00
14 Brian Rogers	.40	1.00
15 Brad Thompson	.40	1.00
16 Marc Williams	.40	1.00

1997 Oregon State

This 16-card set was issued on thin card stock as a perforated sheet. After separated each card measures approximately 2 3/4" by 4". The fronts show color player photos bordered in white. The school, team name and year appear in a black bar above the picture, while the player's name and position are printed on a orange bar beneath the picture. In black print on a white background, the backs feature a player profile and a fire prevention cartoon starring Smokey. The cards are unnumbered and checklisted below in alphabetical order.

COMPLETE SET (16)	6.00	15.00
1 Tim Alexander	.40	1.00
2 Inoke Breckterfield	.40	1.00
3 Larry Bumpus	.40	1.00
4 Terrence Carroll	.40	1.00
5 Basheer Elahee	.40	1.00
6 Armon Hatcher	.40	1.00
7 Andrae Holland	.40	1.00
8 Willis Jenkins	.40	1.00
9 Joe Kuykendall	.40	1.00
10 Nathan McAtee	.40	1.00
11 Freddie Perez	.40	1.00
12 Larry Ramirez	.40	1.00
13 Mike Riley CO	.50	1.25

14 Brian Rogers	.40	1.00
15 Roddy Tompkins	.40	1.00
16 DeShawn Williams	.50	1.25

1998 Oregon State

This 12-card set was issued on thin card stock as a perforated sheet. After separated each card measures approximately 2 3/4" by 4". The fronts show color player photos bordered in white. The school, team name and year appear in a black bar above the picture, while the player's name and position are printed on a orange bar beneath the picture. In black print on a white background, the backs feature a player profile and a fire prevention cartoon starring Smokey. The cards are unnumbered and checklisted below in alphabetical order.

COMPLETE SET (12)	5.00	10.00
1 Greg Ainsworth	.40	1.00
2 Tim Alexander	.40	1.00
3 Inoke Breckterfield	.40	1.00
4 Jose Cortez	.40	1.00
5 Matt Gartung	.40	1.00
6 James Greule	.40	1.00
7 Armon Hatcher	.40	1.00
8 Andrae Holland	.40	1.00
9 Bryan Jones	.40	1.00
10 Joe Kuykendall	.40	1.00
11 Mike Riley CO	.50	1.25
12 Brian Rogers	.40	1.00

1999 Oregon State

This 12-card set was issued on thin card stock as a perforated sheet. After separated each card measures approximately 2 3/4" by 4". The fronts show color player photos bordered in white. The school, team name and year appear in a black bar above the picture, while the player's name and position are printed on a orange bar beneath the picture. In black print on a white background, the backs feature a player profile and a fire prevention cartoon starring Smokey. The cards are unnumbered and checklisted below in alphabetical order.

COMPLETE SET (12)	5.00	10.00
1 Shawn Ball	.40	1.00
2 Terrence Carroll	.40	1.00
3 Keith DiDomenico	.40	1.00
4 Dennis Erickson CO	.50	1.25
5 Jonathan Jackson	.40	1.00
6 Aaron Koch	.40	1.00
7 Martin Maurer	.40	1.00
8 Ken Simonton	.40	1.00
9 Jonathan Smith	.50	1.25
10 Roddy Tompkins	.40	1.00
11 Aaron Wells	.40	1.00
12 Jason White	.40	1.00

2000 Oregon State

This 12-card set was issued on thin card stock as a perforated sheet. After separated each card measures approximately 2 3/4" by 4". The fronts show color player photos bordered in white. The school, team name and year appear in a black bar above the picture, while the player's name and position are printed on a orange bar beneath the picture. In black print on a white background, the backs feature a player profile and a fire prevention cartoon starring Smokey. The cards are unnumbered and checklisted below in alphabetical order.

COMPLETE SET (12)	5.00	10.00
1 James Allen	.30	.75
2 Calvin Carlyle	.30	.75
3 Terrence Carroll	.30	.75
4 Dennis Erickson CO	.40	1.00
5 Delawrence Grant	.30	.75
6 Keith Heyward-Johnson	.30	.75
7 Martin Maurer	.30	.75
8 Tevita Moala	.30	.75
9 Darnell Robinson	.30	.75
10 Ken Simonton	.60	1.50
11 Jonathan Smith	.40	1.00
12 Dennis Weathersby	.40	1.00

2001 Oregon State

This set features members of the Oregon State football team. Each card includes a color player photo on the front and a player bio on back. The set was sponsored by the Oregon State Forester and the Keep Oregon Green Association. The cards were intially issued as a perforated sheet and each measures 2 3/4" by 4" when separated.

COMPLETE SET (12)	5.00	10.00
1 James Allen	.30	.75
2 Calvin Carlyle	.30	.75
3 Jake Cookus	.30	.75
4 Dennis Erickson CO	.40	1.00
5 Chris Gibson	.30	.75
6 Eric Manning	.30	.75
7 Patrick McCall	.30	.75
8 Vincent Sandoval	.30	.75
9 Richard Seigler	.30	.75
10 Ken Simonton	.60	1.50
11 Jonathan Smith	.40	1.00
12 Dennis Weathersby	.40	1.00

1909 Penn State Postcards

These black and white postcards were issued around 1909. The player's name and position are usually included at the bottom of the card front and the backs feature a typical postcard style format. The photographer's ID is also typically included on the fronts and was McNary and Swope.

1 Larry Vorhis (State's Capt.)	35.00	60.00
2 State Varsity 1909	60.00	100.00
3 Team in Offensive Formation	50.00	80.00

1910 Penn State Postcards

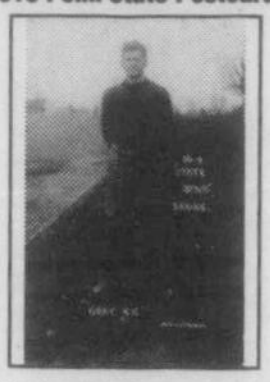

This set of black and white postcards was issued around 1910 and is entitled "State Star Series" as printed on the cardfronts. The player's last name and position are included at the bottom of the card and a card number is included near the set name. The backs feature a typical postcard style format.

1 Bull McCleary	30.00	50.00
4 A.B. Gray	30.00	50.00
11 H.A.Weaver	30.00	50.00

1911 Penn State Postcards

This set of black and white postcards was issued around 1911. The player's name and position are included at the bottom of the card along with "Penn State Varsity." The backs feature a typical postcard style format with a mention of the photographer: Swope and Zerby, College Photographers, State College, PA.

1 Shorty Miller	30.00	50.00

1988 Penn State

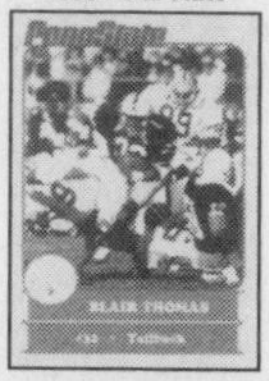

The 1988 Penn State University police/safety set contains 12 standard-size cards. The fronts feature color action photos with name, position, and jersey number. The vertically oriented backs have brief career highlights and "Nittany Lion Tips". The set was produced by McDag Productions. The set is subtitled "The Second Mile" on the front and back of each card. The cards are unnumbered and listed below alphabetically.

COMPLETE SET (12)	50.00	100.00
1 Brian Chizmar	4.00	8.00
2 Andre Collins	4.00	8.00
3 Roger Duffy	4.00	8.00
4 John Greene	4.00	8.00
5 Eddie Johnson	4.00	8.00
6 Keith Karpinski	4.00	8.00
7 Joe Paterno CO	10.00	20.00
8 Rich Schonewolf	4.00	8.00
9 Blair Thomas	5.00	10.00
10 Michael Timpson	4.00	8.00
11 Steve Wisniewski	5.00	10.00
12 Penn State Mascot The Nittany Lion	4.00	8.00

1989 Penn State

This 15-card standard-size set was sponsored by "The Second Mile" (a non-profit organization) in conjunction with IBM. The fronts feature a mix of action and posed player photos, with the player's name and position listed below the picture. The backs carry career highlights and "Nittany Lion Tips." The cards are unnumbered and checklisted below in alphabetical order.

COMPLETE SET (15)	75.00	150.00
1 Brian Chizmar	4.00	8.00
2 Andre Collins	5.00	10.00
3 David Daniels	5.00	10.00
4 Roger Duffy	4.00	8.00
5 Tim Freeman	4.00	8.00
6 Scott Gob	4.00	8.00
7 David Jakob	4.00	8.00
8 Geoff Japchen	4.00	8.00
9 Joe Paterno CO	12.50	25.00
10 Sherrod Rainge	4.00	8.00
11 Rich Schonewolf	4.00	8.00
12 David Szott	5.00	10.00
13 Blair Thomas	6.00	12.00
14 Leroy Thompson	5.00	10.00
15 Nittany Lion Mascot	4.00	8.00

1990 Penn State

This 16-card police/safety standard-size set was sponsored by "The Second Mile," a nonprofit organization that helps needy children. The set was underwritten in part by the Mellon Family Foundation. The cards are printed on thin card stock. The fronts display a mix of posed or action color photos, with solid blue borders above and below, and blue and white striped borders on the sides. The school logo and name are printed in the top blue border while the sponsor's name and player information appear beneath the picture. The backs have brief biographical information, player profile, and "Nittany Lion Tips" in the form of player quotes. A sponsor advertisement at the bottom rounds out the card back. The cards are unnumbered and checklisted below in alphabetical order.

COMPLETE SET (16)	20.00	40.00
1 Gerry Collins	.75	2.00
2 David Daniels	.75	2.00
3 Jim Deter	.75	2.00
4 Mark D'Onofrio	.75	2.00
5 Sam Gash	1.00	2.50
6 Frank Giannetti	.75	2.00
7 Keith Goganious	.75	2.00
8 Doug Helkowski	.75	2.00
9 Hernon Henderson	.75	2.00
10 Matt McCartin	.75	2.00
11 Joe Paterno CO	7.50	15.00
12 Darren Perry	1.25	3.00
13 Tony Sacca	1.00	2.50
14 Terry Smith	.75	2.00
15 Willie Thomas	.75	2.00
16 Leroy Thompson	.75	2.00

1991 Penn State

This set was sponsored by "The Second Mile," a nonprofit organization that helps needy children. The cards were printed on thin card stock and the fronts display a mix of posed or action color photos. The cardbacks have brief biographical information, player profile, and "Nittany Lion Tips" in the form of player quotes. The cards are unnumbered and checklisted below in alphabetical order.

COMPLETE SET (16)	25.00	40.00
1 Lou Benfatti	1.00	2.50
2 Gerry Collins	.75	2.00
3 Jim Deter	.75	2.00
4 Mark D'Onofrio	1.00	2.50
5 Sam Gash	1.50	4.00
6 Reggie Givens	.75	2.00
7 Keith Goganious	1.00	2.50
8 Al Golden	.75	2.00
9 Doug Helkowski	.75	2.00
10 Leonard Humphries	.75	2.00
11 Greg Huntington	.75	2.00
12 O.J. McDuffie	4.00	8.00
13 Rich McKenzie	.75	2.00
14 Darren Perry	1.25	3.00
15 Tony Sacca	1.00	2.50
16 Terry Smith	.75	2.00

1991 Penn State Book Store

The Penn State Book Store offered this 9-card set printed on one perforated sheet. Each unnumbered card includes a Penn State football highlight with the featured player mentioned only on the cardback.

COMPLETE SET (9)	30.00	60.00
1 Anything But the Pits Kenny Jackson	4.00	8.00
2 A Defensive Fiesta Don Graham sacking Vinny Testaverde	5.00	10.00
3 Miracle of Mount Nittany Kirk Bowman	3.00	6.00
4 Nittany Lions Turn the Tide Tim Johnson Shane Conlan	4.00	8.00
5 Orangemen Get Run Over John Shaffer	3.00	6.00
6 Quieting the Echoes Curt Warner	4.00	8.00
7 Run For No. 1 D.J. Dozier	4.00	8.00
8 A Sweet Sugar Bowl Catch Gregg Garrity	3.00	6.00
9 Title Card/1991 Schedule on back	3.00	6.00

1991-92 Penn State Legends

This 50-card standard-size set was produced by Front Row for "The Second Mile," a non-profit organization that helps needy children. The set spotlights All-Americans who played at Penn State from 1923 to 1991. The production run was limited to 20,000 sets. The fronts feature a mix of color and black and white, as well as posed and action, player photos with white borders. Card top carries Penn State in white on a blue border while the bottom has the player's name in a blue border and All-American in red. Front Row's logo appears at the bottom right. Horizontally printed backs have statistics and biography within a red border. An unnumbered insert has a checklist on one side and acknowledgments on the other. The cards are numbered on the back, with the player cards arranged in alphabetical order. Front Row also produced three promo cards prior to the general release of the set; they are distinguished by the fact that "Promo" is stamped diagonally across the back.

COMPLETE SET (51)	10.00	25.00
1 Joe Paterno CO	1.25	3.00
2 Kurt Allerman	.15	.40
3 Chris Bahr	.20	.50
4 Matt Bahr	.20	.50
5 Bruce Bannon	.15	.40
6 Greg Buttle	.20	.50
7 John Cappelletti	.30	.75
8 Bruce Clark	.15	.40
9 Andre Collins	.30	.75
10 Shane Conlan	.30	.75
11 Chris Conlin	.15	.40
12 Randy Crowder	.20	.50
13 Keith Dorney	.20	.50
14 D.J. Dozier	.30	.75
15 Bill Dugan	.15	.40
16 Chuck Fusina	.20	.50
17 Leon Gajecki	.15	.40
18 Jack Ham	.75	2.00
19 Bob Higgins	.15	.40
20 John Hufnagel	.30	.75
21 Kenny Jackson	.20	.50
22 Tim Johnson	.15	.40
23 Dave Joyner	.15	.40
24 Roger Kochman	.15	.40
25 Ted Kwalick	.20	.50
26 Richie Lucas	.30	.75
27 Matt Millen	.30	.75
28 Lydell Mitchell	.30	.75
29 Bob Mitinger	.15	.40
30 John Nessel	.15	.40
31 Ed O'Neil	.20	.50
32 Dennis Onkotz	.15	.40
33 Darren Perry	.20	.50
34 Charlie Pittman	.20	.50
35A Tom Rafferty ERR (Photo actually T. Quinn)	2.00	5.00
35B Tom Rafferty COR	.50	1.25
36 Mike Reid UER (Reversed negative)	.50	1.25
37 Glenn Ressler	.20	.50
38 Dave Robinson	.20	.50
39 Mark Robinson	.15	.40
40 Randy Sidler	.15	.40
41 John Skorupan	.20	.50
42 Neal Smith	.15	.40
43 Steve Suhey	.20	.50
44 Sam Tamburo	.15	.40
45 Blair Thomas	.50	1.25
46 Curt Warner	.60	1.50
47 Steve Wisniewski	.30	.75
48 Chuck Zapiec	.15	.40
49 Michael Zordich	.20	.50
50 Harry Wilson and Joe Bedenk	.15	.40
P1 Joe Paterno CO Promo	2.50	6.00
P10 Shane Conlan Promo	.75	2.00
P18 Jack Ham Promo	1.25	3.00
P46 Curt Warner Promo	1.00	2.50
NNO Checklist Card	.15	.40

1992 Penn State

Sponsored by The Second Mile, this 16-card standard-size set features posed and action color player photos against a royal blue background that is also edged in light blue. White banners, outlined with red and light blue, run across the top and bottom, and behind the middle of the picture. The banners contain the player's position, jersey number, and name. The backs have biographical information, a player profile, and "Nittany Lion Tips" in the form of player quotes. A sponsor message at the bottom rounds out the card back. The cards are unnumbered and checklisted below in alphabetical order. The key cards in the set feature Kyle Brady, Kerry Collins, and O.J. McDuffie.

COMPLETE SET (16)	40.00	80.00
1 Richie Anderson	3.00	6.00
2 Lou Benfatti	1.50	4.00
3 Derek Bochna	1.50	4.00
4 Kyle Brady	3.00	6.00
5 Kerry Collins	7.50	15.00
6 Troy Drayton	2.00	5.00
7 John Gerak	1.50	4.00
8 Reggie Givens	1.50	4.00
9 Shelly Hammonds	1.50	4.00
10 Greg Huntington	1.50	4.00
11 Tyoka Jackson	1.50	4.00
12 O.J. McDuffie	3.00	8.00
13 Lee Rubin	1.50	4.00
14 E.J. Sandusky	1.50	4.00
15 Tisen Thomas	1.50	4.00
16 Brett Wright	1.50	4.00

1992 Penn State Book Store

The Penn State Book Store offered this 9-card set printed on one perforated sheet. Each unnumbered card includes an all-time great Penn State football player light with career highlights mentioned on the cardback.

COMPLETE SET (9)	40.00	80.00
1 Kurt Allerman	5.00	10.00
2 Bruce Bannon	5.00	10.00
3 Todd Blackledge	6.00	12.00
4 John Bruno	5.00	10.00
5 Greg Garrity	5.00	10.00
6 Dave Joyner	5.00	10.00
7 Massimo Manca	5.00	10.00
8 Dennis Onkotz	5.00	10.00
9 Title Card	5.00	10.00

1993 Penn State

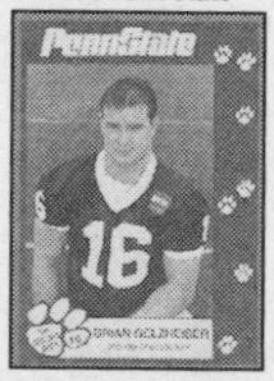

These 25 standard-size cards feature on their fronts color player action and posed shots set within blue and red borders with white paw tracks within the right margin. The school name appears in white lettering within the blue margin above the photo. The player's name, number, and position appear in blue lettering in a white rectangle below the photo. The white back carries the player's name, number, and profile at the top. Below is a Nittany Lions tip given by each player. The cards are unnumbered and checklisted below in alphabetical order.

COMPLETE SET (25)	30.00	60.00
1 Mike Archie Ki-Jana Carter Stephen Pitts	2.50	6.00
2 Lou Benfatti	.75	2.00
3 Derek Bochna	.75	2.00
4 Kyle Brady	1.50	4.00
5 Kerry Collins	7.50	15.00
6 Criag Fayak	.75	2.00
7 Marlon Forbes	.75	2.00
8 Brian Gelzheiser	.75	2.00
9 Bucky Greeley	.75	2.00
10 Ryan Grube	.75	2.00
11 Shelly Hammonds	.75	2.00
12 Jeff Hartings	2.00	5.00
13 Rob Holmberg	.75	2.00
14 Tyoka Jackson	.75	2.00
15 Mike Malinoski	.75	2.00
16 Brian Monaghan	.75	2.00
17 Brian O'Neal	.75	2.00
18 Jeff Perry	.75	2.00
19 Derick Pickett	.75	2.00
20 Tony Pittman	.75	2.00
21 Eric Ravotti	.75	2.00
22 Lee Rubin	.75	2.00
23 Vin Stewart	.75	2.00
24 Tisen Thomas	.75	2.00
25 Phil Yeboah-Kodie	.75	2.00

1994 Penn State

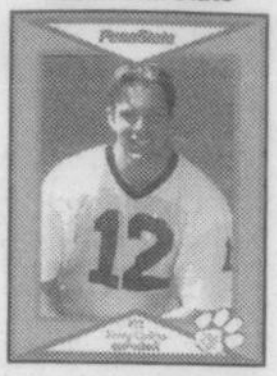

These 25 standard-size cards feature on their fronts color player action and posed shots with a white paw track in the lower right hand corner. The school name appears above the photo. Each card has a thin red front border. The cards are unnumbered and checklisted below in alphabetical order.

COMPLETE SET (25)	30.00	60.00
1 Mike Archie	1.25	3.00
2 Todd Atkins	.75	2.00
3 Kyle Brady	1.25	3.00
4 Ki-Jana Carter	2.00	5.00
5 Eric Clair	.75	2.00
6 Kerry Collins	4.00	8.00
7 Phil Collins	.75	2.00
8 Cliff Dingle	.75	2.00
9 Bobby Engram	2.00	5.00
10 Brian Gelzheiser	.75	2.00
11 Bucky Greeley	.75	2.00
12 Andre Johnson	.75	2.00
13 Josh Kroell	.75	2.00
14 Chris Mazyck	.75	2.00
15 Brian Milne	.75	2.00
16 Jeff Perry	.75	2.00
17 Tony Pittman	.75	2.00
18 Stephen Pitts	.75	2.00
19 Wally Richardson	.75	2.00
20 Marco Rivera	1.00	2.50
21 Freddie Scott	.75	2.00
22 Willie Smith	.75	2.00
23 Vin Stewart	.75	2.00
24 Jon Witman	1.00	2.50
25 Phil Yeboah-Kodie	.75	2.00

1995 Penn State

These 25 standard-size cards feature on their fronts color player action and posed shots with the now common white Lion paw print above the photo with the school name below the photo. Each card has a blue colored border. The cards are unnumbered and checklisted below in alphabetical order.

COMPLETE SET (25)	15.00	30.00
1 Todd Atkins	.40	1.00
2 Mike Archie	.75	2.00
3 Eric Clair	.40	1.00
4 Jason Collins	.40	1.00
5 Keith Conlin	.40	1.00
6 Brett Conway	.40	1.00
7 Jeff Davis	.40	1.00
8 Bobby Engram	.75	2.00
9 Eric Gallman	.40	1.00
10 Carl Gray	.40	1.00
11 Jeff Hartings	.75	2.00
12 Kim Herring	.50	1.25
13 Clint Holes	.40	1.00
14 Andre Johnson	.40	1.00
15 Terry Killens	.40	1.00
16 Brian King	.40	1.00
17 Brian Miller	.40	1.00
18 Brian Milne	.60	1.50
19 Brandon Noble	.60	1.50
20 Stephen Pitts	.40	1.00
21 Wally Richardson	.50	1.25
22 Marco Rivera	.60	1.50
23 Freddie Scott	.50	1.25
24 Mark Tate	.40	1.00
25 Jon Witman	.75	2.00

1996 Penn State

These 25 standard-size cards feature on their fronts color player action and posed shots with a white paw print in the lower right hand corner. The school name appears above the photo. The cards are unnumbered and checklisted below in alphabetical order.

COMPLETE SET (25)	15.00	30.00
1 Aaron Collins	.60	1.50
2 Brett Conway	.40	1.00
3 Chris Eberly	.40	1.00
4 Curtis Enis	1.50	4.00
5 Gerald Filardi	.40	1.00
6 Matt Fornadel	.40	1.00
7 Mike Gonzalez	.40	1.00
8 Jason Henderson	.40	1.00
9 Kim Herring	.50	1.25
10 Joe Jurevicius	3.00	8.00
11 Brad Jones	.40	1.00
12 Darrell Kania	.40	1.00
13 Shawn Lee DB	.50	1.25
14 Brian Miller	.50	1.25
15 Joe Nastasi	.50	1.25
16 Jim Nelson	.40	1.00
17 Brandon Norle	.50	1.25
18 Keith Olsommer	.50	1.25
19 Phil Ostrowski	.40	1.00
20 Chuck Penzenik	.40	1.00
21 Wally Richardson	.50	1.25
22 Jason Sload	.40	1.00
23 Chris Snyder	.40	1.00
24 Mark Tate	.40	1.00
25 Barry Tielsch	.40	1.00

1997 Penn State

This set of 25-cards was sponsored by the Second Mile Foundation. The fronts feature a color player action or posed photo along with a white paw print. The cards are unnumbered and checklisted below in alphabetical order.

COMPLETE SET (25)	20.00	40.00
1 Cuncho Brown	.75	2.00
2 Mike Buzin	.50	1.25
3 Anthony Cleary	.50	1.25
4 Eric Cole	.50	1.25
5 Aaron Collins	1.25	3.00
6 Jason Collins	.50	1.25
7 Kevin Conlin	.50	1.25
8 Maurice Daniels	.50	1.25
9 Chris Eberly	.50	1.25
10 Curtis Enis	1.50	4.00
11 Matt Fornadel	.50	1.25
12 Aaron Harris	.75	2.00
13 Joe Jurevicius	3.00	8.00
14 Shawn Lee DB	.75	2.00
15 Mike McQueary	1.25	3.00
16 Joe Nastasi	.75	2.00
17 Jim Nelson	.50	1.25
18 Phil Ostrowski	.50	1.25
19 Shino Prater	.50	1.25
20 Joe Sabolevski	.75	2.00
21 Brad Scioli	.75	2.00
22 Brandon Short	1.50	4.00
23 Chris Snyder	.50	1.25
24 Bob Stevenson	.50	1.25
25 Floyd Wedderburn	.75	2.00

1998 Penn State

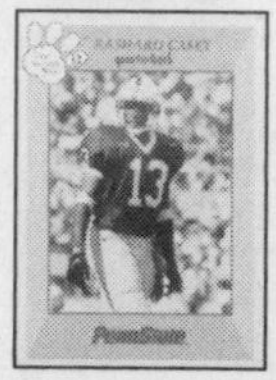

This set of 25-cards was sponsored by the Second Mile Foundation. The fronts feature a color player action or posed photo along with a white paw print. The cards are unnumbered and checklisted below in alphabetical order.

COMPLETE SET (24)	20.00	40.00
1 Imani Bell	.60	1.50
2 John Blick	.40	1.00
3 Courtney Brown	3.00	8.00
4 Mike Buzin	.40	1.00
5 Rashard Casey	1.25	3.00
6 Eric Cole	.40	1.00
7 Maurice Daniels	.40	1.00
8 Ryan Fagan	.40	1.00
9 Chafie Fields	1.50	4.00
10 David Fleischhauer	.60	1.50
11 Derek Fox	1.00	2.50
12 Aaron Gatten	.40	1.00
13 Aaron Harris	1.00	2.50
14 Anthony King	.40	1.00
15 Shawn Lee DB	.60	1.50
16 David Macklin	1.00	2.50
17 Mac Morrison	.40	1.00
18 Joe Nastasi	.60	1.50
19 Brendon Parmer	.40	1.00
20 Brad Scioli	.60	1.50
21 Brandon Short	1.50	4.00
22 Kevin Thompson	1.00	2.50
23 Jason Wallace DL	.40	1.00
24 Kenny Watson	2.00	5.00
25 Floyd Wedderburn	.60	1.50

1999 Penn State

This set was again sponsored by the Second Mile Foundation. The fronts feature a color player action or posed photo along with a white paw print above the photo. The player's name, jersey number, and position appear below the photo. The cards are unnumbered and checklisted below in alphabetical order.

COMPLETE SET (25)	20.00	40.00
1 LaVar Arrington	6.00	15.00
2 Imani Bell	.40	1.00
3 John Blick	.60	1.50
4 Courtney Brown	2.50	6.00
5 Rashard Casey	.75	2.00
6 Mike Cerimele	1.00	2.50
7 Eric Cole	.40	1.00
8 Maurice Daniels	.40	1.00
9 Chafie Fields	1.25	3.00
10 David Fleischhauer	.60	1.50
11 Travis Forney	.40	1.00
12 Derek Fox	1.00	2.50
13 Aaron Harris	1.00	2.50
14 Corey Jones	.40	1.00
15 Anthony King	.40	1.00
16 Justin Kurpeikis	.60	1.50
17 David Macklin	.40	1.00
18 Kareem McKenzie	.60	1.50
19 Cordell Mitchell	1.00	2.50
20 Mac Morrison	.40	1.00
21 Jon Sandusky	.60	1.50
22 Brandon Short	1.25	3.00
23 Rich Stankewicz	.40	1.00
24 Kevin Thompson	.60	1.50
25 Jason Wallace	.40	1.00

2000 Penn State

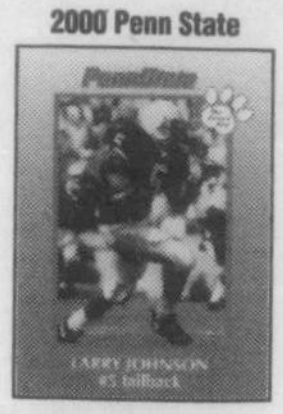

Penn State and the Second Mile Foundation released this set in 2000 featuring the first card for Larry Johnson. The fronts feature a color player action or posed photo along with a white paw print above the photo. The cards are unnumbered and checklisted below in alphabetical order.

COMPLETE SET (25)	15.00	30.00
1 Imani Bell	.30	.75
2 Bruce Branch	.30	.75
3 Jordan Caruso	.30	.75
4 Mike Cerimele	.50	1.25
5 Omar Easy	1.25	3.00
6 Gus Felder	.30	.75
7 Shamar Finney	.30	.75
8 Aaron Gatten	.30	.75
9 John Gilmore	.60	1.50
10 Larry Johnson	4.00	8.00
11 Bob Jones	.30	.75
12 Bhawoh Jue	.40	1.00
13 Jimmy Kennedy	1.25	3.00
14 Justin Kurpeikis	.30	.75
15 Tyler Lenda	.40	1.00
16 Shawn Mayer	.30	.75
17 Eric McCoo	.75	2.00
18 Kareem McKenzie	.40	1.00
19 Josh Mitchell	.30	.75
20 Titcus Pettigrew	.30	.75
21 Matt Schmitt	.30	.75
22 Brandon Steele	.30	.75
23 Tony Stewart	.75	2.00
24 James Sturdifen	.30	.75
25 Kenny Watson	1.25	3.00

2000 Penn State Schedules

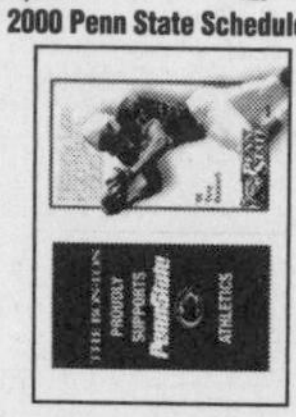

COMPLETE SET (5)	1.25	3.00
1 Mike Cerimele	.30	.75
2 Justin Kurpeikis	.20	.50
3 Kareem McKenzie	.20	.50
4 Tony Stewart	.30	.75
5 Team Huddle	.20	.50

2001 Penn State

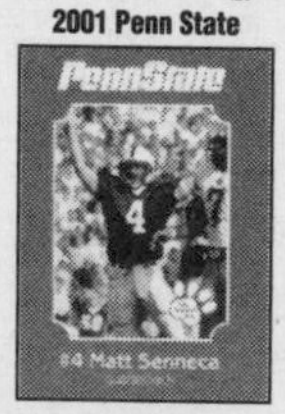

The Second Mile Foundation and Penn State University issued a football set again for 2001. This set includes a wide blue border on the cardfronts along with a color action or posed photo and the typical white paw print Second Mile logo within the photo image. The cards are unnumbered and checklisted below in alphabetical order.

COMPLETE SET (27)	20.00	40.00
1 Anthony Adams	.30	.75
2 Bruce Branch	.30	.75
3 Gino Capone	.30	.75
4 Eddie Drummond	.40	1.00
5 Omar Easy	1.00	2.50
6 Tim Falls	.30	.75
7 Gus Felder	.30	.75
8 Shamar Finney	.30	.75
9 John Gilmore	.30	.75
10 Joe Hartings	.30	.75
11 Michael Haynes DE	1.50	4.00
12 Larry Johnson	3.00	6.00
13 Bob Jones	.30	.75
14 Jimmy Kennedy	1.25	3.00
15 Tyler Lenda	.50	1.25
16 Shawn Mayer	.30	.75
17 Eric McCoo	.40	1.00
18 Joe Paterno CO	2.50	6.00
19 Greg Ransom	.30	.75
20 David Royer	.30	.75
21 Matt Schmitt	.30	.75
22 Bryan Scott	.60	1.50
23 Matt Senneca	1.25	3.00
24 Adam Taliaferro	.30	.75
25 Deryck Toles	.30	.75
26 Tyler Valoczki	.30	.75
27 Yaacov Yisrael	.30	.75

2001 Penn State Greats Mini Posters

This set of small posters (measuring roughly 9" by 12") was issued by Penn State and includes former star football players. Each includes a black and white photo of the player along with a bio to the right of the image. Each also includes the Centre Daily Times sponsorship logo at the bottom and all are blankbacked.

COMPLETE SET (11)	20.00	40.00
1 Chris Bahr	2.00	5.00
2 Courtney Brown	3.00	8.00
3 Greg Buttle	2.00	5.00
4 John Cappelletti	2.00	5.00
5 Shane Conlan	2.00	5.00
6 Jack Ham	3.00	8.00
7 Ted Kwalick	2.00	5.00
8 Matt Millen	2.50	6.00
9 Mike Reid	2.00	5.00
10 Steve Suhey	2.00	5.00
11 Curt Warner	2.50	6.00

2001 Penn State Schedules

COMPLETE SET (5)	1.50	3.00
1 Shamar Finney	.20	.50
2 John Gilmore	.20	.50
3 Bob Jones DE	.20	.50
4 Eric McCoo	.20	.50
5 Joe Paterno	.60	1.50

2002 Penn State

This set was again sponsored by the Second Mile Foundation. The fronts feature a color player action or posed photo along with a white paw print near the photo. The player's name, jersey number, and position appear below the photo. The cards are unnumbered and checklisted below in alphabetical order.

COMPLETE SET (25)	15.00	30.00
1 Anthony Adams	.30	.75
2 Gino Capone	.30	.75
3 Scott Davis	.30	.75
4 Tim Falls	.30	.75
5 Gus Felder	.30	.75
6 Rich Gardner	.50	1.25
7 Michael Haynes DE	1.25	3.00
8 Joe Iorio	.30	.75
9 Bryant Johnson	1.50	4.00
10 Larry Johnson	3.00	6.00
11 Tony Johnson WR	.50	1.25
12 Jimmy Kennedy	1.25	3.00
13 Tyler Lenda	.40	1.00
14 Shawn Mayer	.30	.75
15 Zack Mills	1.00	2.50
16 Sean McHugh	.30	.75
17 Chris McKelvy	.30	.75
18 Eric Rickenbach	.30	.75
19 David Royer	.30	.75
20 Sam Ruhe	.30	.75
21 Matt Schmitt	.30	.75
22 Bryan Scott	.30	.75
23 Doryck Toles	.30	.75
24 Tyler Valoczki	.30	.75
25 Derek Cameron Wake	1.50	4.00

2002 Penn State Schedules

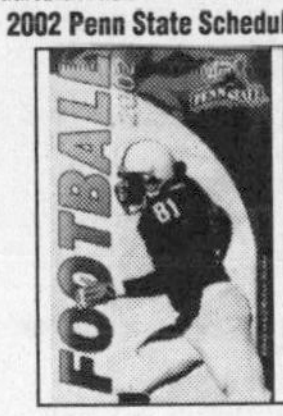

COMPLETE SET (5)	1.25	3.00
1 Anthony Adams	.20	.50
2 Michael Haynes	.30	.75
3 Joe Iorio	.20	.50
4 Tyler Lenda	.30	.75
5 Bryan Scott	.20	.50

2003 Penn State

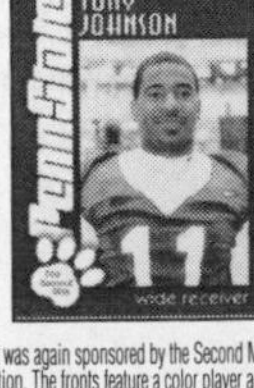

This set was again sponsored by the Second Mile Foundation. The fronts feature a color player action or posed photo along with a white paw print near the photo. The player's name and jersey number appear above the photo and his position is below. The cards are unnumbered and checklisted below in alphabetical order.

COMPLETE SET (25)	12.50	25.00
1 John Bronson	.30	.75
2 Gino Capone	.30	.75
3 David Costlow	.30	.75
4 Paul Cronin	.30	.75
5 Rich Gardner	.40	1.00
6 Mike Gasparato	.30	.75
7 Robbie Gould	1.50	4.00
8 Andrew Guman	.30	.75
9 Tony Johnson	.40	1.00
10 Damone Jones	.30	.75
11 David Kimball	.30	.75
12 Calvin Lowry	.30	.75
13 Mike Lukac	.30	.75
14 Sean McHugh	.30	.75
15 Zack Mills	.60	1.50
16 Kinta Palmer	.30	.75
17 Jason Robinson	.30	.75
18 Michael Robinson	2.00	5.00
19 Sam Ruhe	.30	.75
20 Charles Rush	.30	.75
21 Andy Ryland	.30	.75
22 Ernie Terrell	.30	.75
23 Ricky Upton	.30	.75
24 Derek Cameron Wake	1.25	3.00
25 Casey Williams	.30	.75

2003 Penn State Greats Recruiting Cards

These cards were issued by the University to recruit new athletes and promote the football program. At first glance they appear to follow a greeting card format. They were produced as perforated two-part sections with a traditional trading card being the first part and the second part including minor information about the school's football office and most successful seasons. Each measures roughly 4 1/2" by 6 1/4" when folded. The player's photo was printed in four-color or simple blue and white.

COMPLETE SET (20)	20.00	40.00
1 LaVar Arrington	1.50	4.00
2 Kyle Brady	.75	2.00
3 Courtney Brown	1.00	2.50
4 John Cappelletti	.75	2.00
5 Ki-Jana Carter	.75	2.00
6 Bruce Clark	.60	1.50
7 Kerry Collins	1.25	3.00
8 Keith Dorney	.60	1.50
9 Bobby Engram	1.00	2.50
10 Jeff Hartings	.75	2.00
11 Ted Kwalick	.60	1.50
12 O.J. McDuffie	.75	2.00
13 Lydell Mitchell	.75	2.00
14 Darren Perry	.60	1.50
15 Mike Reid	.60	1.50
16 Dave Robinson	.60	1.50
17 Mark Robinson	.60	1.50
18 Brandon Short	.60	1.50
19 Curt Warner	.75	2.00
20 Stadium Photo	.60	1.50

2003 Penn State Schedules

COMPLETE SET (6)	1.25	3.00
1 David Costlow	.20	.50
2 Rich Gardner	.30	.75
3 Damone Jones	.20	.50
4 Sean McHugh	.20	.50
5 Zack Mills	.20	.50
6 Deryck Toles	.20	.50

2004 Penn State

COMPLETE SET (24)	15.00	30.00
1 Jay Alford	.75	2.00
2 John Bronson	.20	.50
3 Levi Brown	1.00	2.50
4 Scott Davis	.20	.50
5 Chris Ganter	.20	.50
6 Robbie Gould	1.25	3.00
7 Andrew Guman	.20	.50
8 Tamba Hali	2.00	5.00
9 Paul Jefferson	.20	.50
10 Calvin Lowry	.20	.50
11 Zack Mills	.30	.75
12 Paul Posluszny	4.00	8.00
13 Tyler Reed	.20	.50
14 Andrew Richardson	.20	.50
15 Jason Robinson	.20	.50
16 Michael Robinson	1.50	4.00
17 Charles Rush	.20	.50
18 Austin Scott	.30	.75
19 E.Z. Smith	.20	.50
20 Gerald Smith	.20	.50
21 Isaac Smolko	.20	.50
22 Brandon Snow	.20	.50
23 Derek Cameron Wake	1.25	3.00
24 Alan Zemaitis	.75	2.00

2004 Penn State Schedules

COMPLETE SET (7)	1.25	3.00
1 John Bronson	.20	.50
2 Andrew Guman	.20	.50
3 Chris Harrell	.20	.50
4 Paul Jefferson	.20	.50
5 Zack Mills	.20	.50
6 Gerald Smith	.20	.50
7 Derek Cameron Wake	.40	1.00

2005 Penn State

COMPLETE SET (25)	12.50	25.00
1 Jay Alford	.60	1.50
2 Lance Antolick	.20	.50
3 Levi Brown	.60	1.50
4 Lavon Chisley	.20	.50
5 Dan Connor	.75	2.00
6 Paul Cronin	.20	.50
7 Matt Hahn	.20	.50
8 Tamba Hali	1.25	3.00
9 Chris Harrell	.20	.50
10 Tony Hunt	1.00	2.50
11 Jeremy Kapinos	.20	.50
12 Rodney Kinlaw	.20	.50
13 Calvin Lowry	.20	.50
14 Anwar Phillips	.40	1.00
15 Paul Posluszny	3.00	6.00
16 Matthew Rice	.20	.50
17 Michael Robinson	1.25	3.00
18 Mark Rubin	.20	.50
19 Charles Rush	.20	.50
20 Austin Scott	.30	.75
21 Tim Shaw	.40	1.00
22 Isaac Smolko	.20	.50
23 Brandon Snow	.20	.50
24 John Wilson	.20	.50
25 Alan Zemaitis	.60	1.50

2005 Penn State Emmortals Greats CD ROM

These "cards" were produced by Dreamedia Ventures and are entitled Penn State Emmortals. Each is a usable CD ROM that features information and images on the featured player. They were issued in standard card size with slightly rounded corners.

COMPLETE SET (10)	50.00	100.00
1 Gary Brown	8.00	12.00
2 John Cappelletti	8.00	12.00
3 D.J. Dozier	8.00	12.00
4 Franco Harris	8.00	15.00
5 Larry Johnson	8.00	15.00
6 Eric McCoo	8.00	12.00
7 Lydell Mitchell	8.00	12.00
8 Lenny Moore	8.00	12.00
9 Blair Thomas	8.00	12.00
10 Curt Warner	8.00	12.00

2005 Penn State Schedules

COMPLETE SET (7)	2.00	4.00
1 Levi Brown	.20	.50
2 Tamba Hali	.30	.75
3 Calvin Lowry Anwar Phillips	.20	.50
4 Paul Posluszny	.40	1.00
5 Michael Robinson	.30	.75
6 Isaac Smolko	.20	.50
7 Alan Zemaitis	.30	.75

2006 Penn State

This set was sponsored by the Second Mile Foundation. The fronts feature a color player action or posed photo along with a white border and a white paw print near the photo. The player's name and position appear in the border. The cards are unnumbered and checklisted below in alphabetical order.

COMPLETE SET (25)	10.00	20.00
1 Jay Alford	.50	1.25
2 Levi Brown	.50	1.25
3 Deon Butler	.50	1.25
4 Dan Connor	1.25	3.00
5 Jason Ganter	.20	.50
6 Patrick Hall	.20	.50
7 Tony Hunt	1.00	2.50
8 Donnie Johnson	.20	.50
9 Jeremy Kapinos	.20	.50
10 Kevin Kelly	.20	.50
11 Justin King	.30	.75
12 Nolan McCready	.20	.50
13 Anthony Morelli	.60	1.50
14 Jordan Norwood	.50	1.25
15 Brendan Perretta	.30	.75
16 Paul Posluszny	2.00	4.00
17 Elijah Robinson	.20	.50
18 Mark Rubin	.20	.50
19 Tyrell Sales	.20	.50
20 Austin Scott	.60	1.50
21 Jim Shaw	.20	.50
22 Tim Shaw	.30	.75
23 A.Q. Shipley	.20	.50
24 Kevin Suhey	.20	.50
25 Derrick Williams	1.25	3.00

2007 Penn State

This set was sponsored by the Second Mile Foundation. The fronts feature a color player action or posed photo along with a blue and white border and a white paw print near the photo. The player's name and position appear below the photo. The cards are unnumbered and checklisted below in alphabetical order.

COMPLETE SET (25)	7.50	15.00
1 Dontey Brown	.20	.50
2 Deon Butler	.60	1.50
3 Gerald Cadogan	.20	.50
4 Dan Connor	1.00	2.50
5 Tony Davis	.20	.50
6 Maurice Evans	.30	.75
7 Josh Gaines	.20	.50
8 Jason Ganter	.20	.50
9 Terrell Golden	.20	.50
10 Kevin Kelly	.20	.50
11 Matt Hahn	.20	.50
12 Rodney Kinlaw	.20	.50
13 Sean Lee	.75	2.00
14 Anthony Morelli	.60	1.50
15 Jordan Norwood	.40	1.00
16 Brendan Perretta	.30	.75
17 Andrew Quarless	.50	1.25
18 Austin Scott	.60	1.50
19 John Shaw	.20	.50
20 A.Q. Shipley	.40	1.00
21 Kevin Suhey	.40	1.00
22 A.J. Wallace	.20	.50
23 Patrick Weber	.20	.50
24 Derrick Williams	1.00	2.50
25 Team Mascot	.20	.50

2007 Penn State TK Legacy

COMPLETE SET (37)	15.00	30.00
L1 Blair Thomas	.75	2.00
L2 Chris Bahr	.50	1.25
L3 Matt Bahr	.50	1.25
L4 Chuck Fusina	.50	1.25
L5 Glenn Ressler	.40	1.00
L6 Gregg Garrity	.40	1.00
L7 Lenny Moore	.75	2.00
L8 John Cappelletti	.75	2.00
L9 John Shaffer	.40	1.00
L10 Richie Lucas	.50	1.25
L11 Mike Cappelletti	.40	1.00
L12 Michael Zordich	.40	1.00
L13 Ted Kwalick	.40	1.00
L14 Tom Rafferty	.40	1.00
L15 Wally Richardson	.40	1.00
L16 Todd Blackledge	.50	1.25
L17 Shane Conlan	.50	1.25
L18 Tim Manoa	.40	1.00
L19 Curt Warner	.75	2.00
L20 D.J. Dozier	.50	1.25
L21 Zack Mills	.50	1.25
L22 Milt Plum	.40	1.00
L23 Greg Buttle	.40	1.00
L24 Lydell Mitchell	.50	1.25
L25 Mark Battaglia	.40	1.00
L26 Charlie Pittman	.40	1.00
L27 John Sacca	.40	1.00
L28 Tony Sacca	.50	1.25
L29 Pete Liske	.50	1.25
L30 John Hufnagel	.50	1.25
L31 Paul Posluszny	1.25	3.00
L32 Dave Robinson	.50	1.25
L33 Ken Jackson	.40	1.00
CL1 John Cappelletti CL	.50	1.25
CL2 Todd Blackledge CL	.40	1.00
CL3 Curt Warner CL	.50	1.25
CL4 Nittany Lions CL	.40	1.00

2007 Penn State TK Legacy All American Autographs

STATED ODDS 1:7		
AA1 Blair Thomas	12.50	25.00
AA2 Chris Bahr	10.00	20.00
AA3 Matt Bahr	10.00	20.00
AA4 Chuck Fusina	10.00	20.00
AA5 Glenn Ressler	7.50	15.00
AA6 John Cappelletti	12.50	25.00
AA7 Richie Lucas	10.00	20.00
AA8 Michael Zordich	7.50	15.00
AA9 Ted Kwalick	7.50	15.00
AA10 Tom Rafferty	7.50	15.00
AA11 Shane Conlan	10.00	20.00
AA12 Curt Warner	12.50	25.00
AA13 D.J. Dozier	10.00	20.00
AA14 Greg Buttle	7.50	15.00
AA15 Lydell Mitchell	10.00	20.00
AA16 Charlie Pittman	7.50	15.00
AA17 John Hufnagel	7.50	15.00
AA18 Dave Robinson	10.00	20.00
AA19 Paul Posluszny	20.00	40.00

2007 Penn State TK Legacy Fast Stat Autographs

STATED ODDS 1:56		
ST1 John Cappelletti/100	12.50	25.00
ST2 Chris Bahr/100	10.00	20.00
ST3 Lydell Mitchell/100	10.00	20.00
ST4 Paul Posluszny/31		

2007 Penn State TK Legacy Historical Links Autographs

STATED ODDS 1:19		
HL1 Chris Bahr/150 Matt Bahr (case insert)	12.50	25.00
HL2 John Cappelletti/100 Mike Cappelletti	15.00	30.00
HL3 Tony Sacca/100 John Sacca	12.50	25.00
HL4 Todd Blackledge/100 John Shaffer	12.50	25.00
HL5 Todd Blackledge/100 Curt Warner	15.00	30.00
HL7 John Hufnagel/100 Chuck Fusina Richie Lucas	15.00	30.00
HL8 Zach Mills/100 Tony Sacca Wally Richardson	15.00	30.00

2007 Penn State TK Legacy Legends

COMPLETE SET (12)	10.00	20.00
CF1 Chuck Fusina	.75	2.00
CF2 Chuck Fusina	.75	2.00
CF3 Chuck Fusina	.75	2.00
JC1 John Cappelletti	1.00	2.50
JC2 John Cappelletti	1.00	2.50
JC3 John Cappelletti	1.00	2.50
LM1 Lenny Moore	1.00	2.50
LM2 Lenny Moore	1.00	2.50
LM3 Lenny Moore	1.00	2.50
TS1 Tony Sacca	.75	2.00
TS2 Tony Sacca	.75	2.00
TS3 Tony Sacca	.75	2.00

2007 Penn State TK Legacy Milestones

COMPLETE SET (10)	3.00	8.00
PS1 First Season	.40	1.00
PS1 First Homecoming Game	.40	1.00
PS2 First All-American	.40	1.00
PS3 Joe Paterno's First Season	.40	1.00
PS4 First Championship	.40	1.00
PS5 Fisrt Big Ten Season	.40	1.00
PS6 First Top Ten Ranking	.40	1.00
PS7 Fisrt Big Ten Title	.40	1.00
PS8 First Bowl Appearance	.40	1.00
PS9 First Win Over Pittsburgh	.40	1.00

2007 Penn State TK Legacy National Champion Autographs

STATED ODDS 1:10		
1982A Michael Zordich	6.00	15.00
1982B Todd Blackledge	7.50	20.00
1982C Curt Warner	10.00	25.00
1982D Mark Battaglia	6.00	15.00
1986A Blair Thomas	10.00	25.00
1986B John Shaffer	6.00	15.00
1986C Shane Conlan	7.50	20.00
1986D Tim Manoa	6.00	15.00
1986E D.J. Dozier	7.00	20.00

2007 Penn State TK Legacy Quarterback Collection Autographs

QB/150 STATED ODDS 1:8		
QB1 John Shaffer	7.50	15.00
QB2 Richie Lucas	10.00	20.00
QB3 Wally Richardson	7.50	15.00
QB4 Todd Blackledge	10.00	20.00
QB5 John Sacca	7.50	15.00
QB6 Tony Sacca	10.00	20.00
QB7 Zack Mills	10.00	20.00
QB8 Milt Plum	7.50	15.00
QB9 Pete Liske	7.50	15.00
QB10 John Hufnagel	7.50	15.00
QB11 Chuck Fusina	10.00	20.00

2007 Penn State TK Legacy Signature Series

STATED ODDS 1:1		
P1 Blair Thomas	6.00	15.00
P2 Chris Bahr	6.00	15.00
P3 Matt Bahr	6.00	15.00
P4 Chuck Fusina	6.00	15.00
P5 Glenn Ressler	5.00	12.00
P6 Gregg Garrity	5.00	12.00
P7 Lenny Moore	7.50	20.00
P8 John Cappelletti	7.50	20.00
P9 John Shaffer	5.00	12.00
P10 Rich Lucas	6.00	15.00
P11 Mike Cappelletti	5.00	12.00
P12 Michael Zordich	5.00	12.00
P13 Ted Kwalick	5.00	12.00
P14 Tom Rafferty	5.00	12.00
P15 Wally Richardson	5.00	12.00
P16 Todd Blackledge	6.00	15.00
P17 Shane Conlan	6.00	15.00
P18 Tim Manoa	5.00	12.00
P19 Curt Warner	7.50	20.00
P20 D.J. Dozier	6.00	15.00
P21 Zack Mills	6.00	15.00
P22 Milt Plum	5.00	12.00
P23 Greg Buttle	5.00	12.00
P24 Lydell Mitchell	6.00	15.00
P25 Mark Battaglia	5.00	12.00
P26 Charlie Pittman	5.00	12.00
P27 John Sacca	5.00	12.00
P28 Tony Sacca	6.00	15.00
P29 Pete Liske	5.00	12.00
P30 John Hufnagel	5.00	12.00
P31 Paul Posluszny	25.00	50.00
P32 Dave Robinson	6.00	15.00
P33 Ken Jackson	5.00	12.00

2007 Penn State TK Legacy Traditions

T1 The Nittany Lion	.40	1.00
T2 Blue and White Colors	.40	1.00

2008 Penn State

This set was sponsored by the Second Mile Foundation. The fronts feature a color player action or posed photo along with a blue border above and below the image. The player's name and position appear below the photo. The cards are unnumbered and checklisted below in alphabetical order.

COMPLETE SET (25)	7.50	15.00
1 Jeremy Boone	.20	.50
2 Deon Butler	.50	1.25
3 Gerald Cadogan	.20	.50
4 Daryll Clark	1.00	2.50
5 Tony Davis	.20	.50
6 Pat Devlin	.50	1.25
7 Maurice Evans	.20	.50
8 Josh Gaines	.20	.50
9 Josh Hull	.20	.50
10 Kevin Kelly	.20	.50
11 Abe Koroma	.20	.50
12 Dan Lawlor	.30	.75
13 Sean Lee	.60	1.50
14 Mike Lucian	.20	.50
15 Jordan Norwood	.30	.75
16 Jared Odrick	.30	.75
17 Ollie Ogbu	.20	.50
18 Rich Ohrnberger	.20	.50
19 Evan Royster	.50	1.25
20 Mark Rubin	.20	.50
21 Lydell Sargeant	.20	.50
22 Mickey Schuler	.20	.50
23 A.Q. Shipley	.30	.75
24 A.J. Wallace	.20	.50
25 Derrick Williams	.60	1.50

2009 Penn State

This set was sponsored by the Second Mile Foundation. The fronts feature a color player action or posed photo along with a white border above and a blue border below the image. The player's name and position appear above the photo. The cards are unnumbered and checklisted below in alphabetical order.

COMPLETE SET (25)	5.00	10.00
1 Drew Astorino UER (photo actually David Soldner)	.20	.50
2 Jeremy Boone	.20	.50
3 NaVorro Bowman	.40	1.00
4 Brett Brackett	.30	.75
5 Daryll Clark	.75	2.00
6 Chris Colasanti	.20	.50
7 Jack Crawford	.20	.50
8 Andrew Dailey	.20	.50
9 Lou Eliades	.20	.50
10 Bani Gbadyu	.20	.50
11 Tom Golarz	.20	.50
12 Stephon Green	.20	.50
13 Josh Hull	.20	.50
14 Abe Koroma	.20	.50
15 Dennis Landolt	.20	.50
16 Sean Lee	.60	1.50
17 Michael Mauti	.20	.50
18 Patrick Mauti	.20	.50
19 Jared Odrick	.30	.75
20 Ollie Ogbu	.20	.50
21 Evan Royster	.50	1.25
22 Mickey Schulor	.30	.75
23 Devon Still	.20	.50
24 Stefen Wisniewski	.20	.50
25 Nittany Lion Mascot	.20	.50

2010 Penn State

This set was sponsored by the Second Mile Foundation. The fronts feature a color player action or posed photo along with a blue border around the image. The player's name and school name appear above the photo. The cards are unnumbered and checklisted below in alphabetical order.

COMPLETE SET (25)	4.00	8.00
1 Drew Astorino	.20	.50
2 Brandon Beachum	.20	.50
3 Brett Brackett	.30	.75
4 Chris Colasanti	.20	.50
5 Jack Crawford	.20	.50
6 Andrew Dailey	.20	.50
7 Lou Eliades	.20	.50
8 Bani Gbadyu	.20	.50
9 Stephon Green	.20	.50
10 Cedric Jeffries	.20	.50
11 Goug Klopacz	.20	.50
12 Eric Latimore	.20	.50
13 Michael Mauti	.20	.50
14 Kevin Newsome	.20	.50
15 Ollie Ogbu	.20	.50
16 Chimaeze Okoli	.20	.50
17 Chaz Powell	.20	.50
18 Evan Royster	.50	1.25
19 Devon Still	.20	.50
20 Nathan Stupar	.20	.50
21 Nick Sukay	.20	.50
22 Johnnie Troutman	.20	.50
23 Collin Wagner	.20	.50
24 Stefen Wisniewski	.20	.50
25 Graham Zug	.20	.50

1950 Pennsylvania Bulletin Pin-ups

These black and white premium photos measure roughly 8" x 10" and were issued by The Bulletin newspaper in the Philadelphia area. The photos are blankbacked and feature the newspaper's logo in the upper left corner, the school's pennant in the lower left corner and the player's facsimile autograph in the lower right corner.

1 Francis Bagnell	10.00	20.00
2 Bill Deuber	10.00	20.00
3 Bernie Lemonick	10.00	20.00

1991 Pennsylvania High School Big 33

This 36-card standard-size high school football set was issued to commemorate the Big 33 Football Classic, an annual high school football game begun in 1957 and featuring Pennsylvania versus Maryland for the past seven games. The fronts feature posed black and white player photos enclosed by a white border. State name appears at top of card while player name, number, and position appear in white reversed-out lettering in black. The Big 33 logo and The Super Bowl of High School Football appear in same reverse-out fashion at bottom. The backs feature player's biographical information enclosed within a thin black border. The key cards in this set feature Marvin Harrison, Curtis Martin and Ray Zellars.

COMPLETE SET (36)	75.00	150.00
PA1 Dietrich Jells	2.00	5.00
PA2 Mike Archie	3.00	8.00
PA3 Tony Miller	1.50	4.00
PA4 Edmund Robinson	1.50	4.00
PA5 Brian Miller	1.50	4.00
PA6 Marvin Harrison	25.00	50.00
PA7 Mike Cawley	1.50	4.00
PA8 Thomas Marchese	1.50	4.00
PA9 Scott Milanovich	2.00	5.00
PA10 Shawn Wooden	1.50	4.00
PA11 Curtis Martin	30.00	60.00
PA12 William Khayat	1.50	4.00
PA13 Jermell Fleming	1.50	4.00
PA14 Ray Zellars	3.00	8.00
PA15 Jon Witman	2.50	6.00
PA16 Chris McCartney	1.50	4.00
PA17 David Rebar	1.50	4.00
PA18 Mark Zataveski	1.50	4.00
PA19 Todd Atkins	1.50	4.00
PA20 Shannon Stevens	1.50	4.00
PA21 Keith Conlin	1.50	4.00
PA22 John Bowman	1.50	4.00
PA23 Maurice Lawrence	1.50	4.00
PA24 Mike Halapin	1.50	4.00
PA25 Steve Keim	1.50	4.00
PA26 Dennis Martin	1.50	4.00
PA27 Keith Morris	1.50	4.00
PA28 Chris Villarrial	1.50	4.00
PA29 Thomas Tumulty	1.50	4.00
PA30 Jason Augustino	1.50	4.00
PA31 Gregory Delong	1.50	4.00
PA32 James Moore	1.50	4.00
PA33 Eric Clair	1.50	4.00
PA34 Tyler Young	1.50	4.00
PA35 Jeffrey Sauve	1.50	4.00
PA36 Terry Hammons	1.50	4.00

1992 Pennsylvania High School Big 33

This standard-size high school football set was issued to commemorate the Pennsylvania Big 33 Football Classic. The fronts feature posed player photos enclosed by a white border. The state name appears at the top of the card along with the player's name, number, and position. The Big 33 logo appears below the photo. The backs feature the player's biographical information along with a notation to which college he plans to attend. The unnumbered cards are listed below alphabetically.

COMPLETE SET (35)	40.00	80.00
1 Bill Anderson	1.50	4.00
2 Larry Austin	1.50	4.00
3 Brandon Bailey	1.50	4.00
4 Richard Brooks Jr.	1.50	4.00
5 Ken Buczynski	1.50	4.00
6 Jason Chavis	1.50	4.00
7 Matt Cope	1.50	4.00
8 Jeff Craig	1.50	4.00
9 Jamaal Crawford	1.50	4.00
10 Todd Durish	1.50	4.00
11 Jon Dylewski	1.50	4.00
12 Scott Florence	1.50	4.00
13 David Gathman	1.50	4.00
14 Darrell Harding	1.50	4.00
15 Anthony Hardy	1.50	4.00
16 Clinton Holes	1.50	4.00
17 Michael Horn	1.50	4.00
18 Matt Hosilyk	1.50	4.00
19 Jay Jones	1.50	4.00
20 Jason Killian	1.50	4.00
21 Ted Kwalick Honorary Chairman	2.00	5.00
22 Tajuan Law	1.50	4.00
23 Mark Libiano	1.50	4.00
24 Mike Logan	2.50	6.00
25 Michael Mohring	1.50	4.00
26 Justin Morabito	1.50	4.00
27 Mark Nori	1.50	4.00
28 Keith Olsommer	1.50	4.00
29 Harvey Pennypacker	1.50	4.00
30 Cliff Stroud	1.50	4.00
31 Lorenzo Styles	1.50	4.00
32 Mark Tate	1.50	4.00
33 Gerald Thompson	1.50	4.00
34 Barry Tielsch	1.50	4.00
35 Scott Weaver	1.50	4.00

1993 Pennsylvania High School Big 33

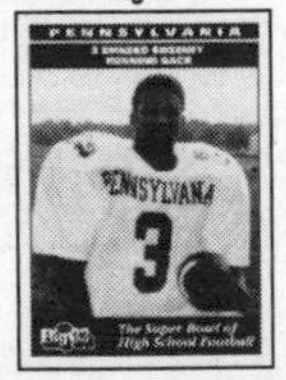

This standard-size high school football set was issued to commemorate the Pennsylvania Big 33 Football Classic. The fronts feature black and white posed player photos enclosed by a white border. The state name appears at the top of the card along with the player's jersey number, name, and position. The Big 33 logo appears below the photo. The backs feature the player's biographical information along with a notation to which college he plans to attend. The unnumbered cards are listed below alphabetically.

COMPLETE SET (36)	75.00	150.00
1 Roger Beckwith	2.00	5.00
2 Trevor Britton	2.00	5.00
3 Omar Brown	2.00	5.00
4 Ahmad Collins	2.00	5.00
5 Bill Coury	2.00	5.00
6 Damon Denson	2.00	5.00
7 Josh Dolbin	2.00	5.00
8 Matt Fornadel	2.00	5.00
9 Dennis Fortney	2.00	5.00
10 Juan Gaddy	2.00	5.00
11 Johnnie Hicks Jr.	2.00	5.00
12 Nate Hobgood-Chittick	2.00	5.00
13 Mark Hondru	2.00	5.00
14 John Jenkins	2.00	5.00
15 Brad Jones	2.00	5.00
16 Jonathan Linton	2.00	5.00
17 Jon Marzock	2.00	5.00

18 Mike McQueary	3.00	8.00
19 Richie Miller	2.00	5.00
20 Adam Myers	2.00	5.00
21 Jeff Nixon	2.00	5.00
22 Chris Orlando	2.00	5.00
23 Phil Ostrowski	2.00	5.00
24 Ron Powlus	5.00	12.00
25 Steve Pratico	2.00	5.00
26 Jon Ritchie	3.00	8.00
27 Keno Shawell	2.00	5.00
28 Geroy Simon	2.50	6.00
29 Jason Soboleski	2.00	5.00
30 Emneko Sweeney	2.00	5.00
31 Robert Swett	2.00	5.00
32 Walter Washington	2.00	5.00
33 Ron White	2.00	5.00
34 Marvin Williams	2.00	5.00
35 Cheerleaders	2.00	5.00
36 Coaching Staff	2.00	5.00

1994 Pennsylvania High School Big 33

This standard-size high school football set was issued to commemorate the 37th annual Pennsylvania Big 33 Football Classic. The fronts feature posed player photos enclosed by a white border. The state name appears at the top of the card along with the player's name, number, and position. The Big 33 logo appears below the photo. The backs feature the player's biographical information along with a notation to which college he plans to attend. The unnumbered cards are listed below alphabetically.

COMPLETE SET (35)	40.00	80.00
1 Lamar Campbell	1.25	3.00
2 John Cappelletti	1.25	3.00
Honorary Chairman		
3 Timothy Cramsey	1.25	3.00
4 Cliff Crosby	1.25	3.00
5 Jon Curry	1.25	3.00
6 Darryl Daniel	1.25	3.00
7 Ted Daniels	1.25	3.00
8 Dan Drogan	1.25	3.00
9 Jamaal Edwards	1.25	3.00
10 Ryan Fagan	1.25	3.00
11 Charles Fisher	1.25	3.00
12 Matt Gubba	1.25	3.00
13 Artrell Hawkins	1.50	4.00
14 Tom Indio	1.25	3.00
15 Isaac Jones	1.25	3.00
16 Eric Kasperowicz	1.25	3.00
17 Brad Keller	1.25	3.00
18 Brian Kuklick	1.25	3.00
19 Shawn Lee	1.25	3.00
20 Frank Lockett	1.25	3.00
21 Troy Logan	1.25	3.00
22 Seamus Murphy	1.25	3.00
23 Joe Nastasi	1.25	3.00
24 Chris Nocco	1.25	3.00
25 Doug Ostrosky	1.25	3.00
26 Darren Oswald	1.25	3.00
27 James Pizano	1.25	3.00
28 Matt Rader	1.25	3.00
29 Jason Richards	1.25	3.00
30 Chris Schneider	1.25	3.00
31 Brad Scioli	1.25	3.00
32 Clint Seace	1.25	3.00
33 Shawn Summerville	1.25	3.00
34 John Thornton UER	1.25	3.00
(spelled Thorton)		
35 Tim Zeglin	1.25	3.00

1995 Pennsylvania High School Big 33

This standard-size high school football set was issued to commemorate the 38th annual Pennsylvania Big 33 Football Classic. The fronts feature posed player photos enclosed by a white border. The state name and year appear at the top of the card along with the player's name, number, and position. The Big 33 logo appears below the photo. The backs feature the player's biographical information along with a notation to which college he plans to attend. The unnumbered cards are listed below alphabetically.

COMPLETE SET (35)	40.00	80.00
1 Askari Adams	1.25	3.00
2 Bryan Arndt	1.25	3.00
3 Michael Bennett	1.25	3.00
4 Bryn Boggs	1.25	3.00
5 Aaron Brady	1.25	3.00
6 Stephen Brominski	1.25	3.00
7 Marc Bulger	6.00	12.00
8 Rich Butcofski	1.25	3.00
9 Anthony Cleary	1.25	3.00
10 Melvin Cobbs	1.25	3.00
11 Eric Cole	1.25	3.00
12 William B. Craver	1.25	3.00
13 Jermaine Cromerdie	1.25	3.00
14 Troy Davidson	1.25	3.00
15 Darnell Dinkins	1.25	3.00
16 Rashonn Drayton	1.25	3.00
17 Chafie Fields	1.50	4.00
18 Joshua George	1.25	3.00
19 Mike Gimbol	1.25	3.00
20 Julian Graham	1.25	3.00
21 Aaron Harris	1.25	3.00
22 Randy Homa	1.25	3.00
23 Corey Jones	1.25	3.00
24 Chad Kroell	1.25	3.00
25 Dan Kreider	4.00	8.00
26 Noel Lamontagne	1.25	3.00
27 Marc Lapadula	1.25	3.00
28 Tim Lewis	1.25	3.00
Honorary Chairman		
29 Matt Mapes	1.25	3.00
30 Vince Pellis	1.25	3.00
31 Hank Poteat	1.25	3.00
32 Brandon Short	1.50	4.00
33 Rich Stankewicz	1.25	3.00
34 Brandon Streeter	1.25	3.00
35 Ethan Weidle	1.25	3.00

1996 Pennsylvania High School Big 33

This standard-size high school football set was issued to commemorate the 39th annual Pennsylvania Big 33 Football Classic. The fronts feature posed player photos enclosed by a white border. The state name and year appear at the top of the card along with the player's name, number, and position. The Big 33 logo appears below the photo. The backs feature the player's biographical information along with a notation to which college he plans to attend. The unnumbered cards are listed below alphabetically.

COMPLETE SET (35)	40.00	80.00
1 Randy Ament	1.25	3.00
2 Imani Bell	1.25	3.00
3 John Blick	1.25	3.00
4 Rick Bolinsky	1.25	3.00
5 Chance Bright	1.25	3.00
6 Mike Cerimele	1.50	4.00
7 Bilal Cook	1.25	3.00
8 David Costa	1.25	3.00
9 Jim Covert	1.25	3.00
Honorary Chairman		
10 Paul Fath	1.25	3.00
11 Aaron Gatten	1.25	3.00
12 Demond Gibson	1.25	3.00
13 Rick Gilliam	1.25	3.00
14 Cullen Hawkins	1.25	3.00
15 Lee Holmes	1.25	3.00
16 Seth Hornacek	1.25	3.00
17 Brad Jones	1.25	3.00
18 Ben Kopp	1.25	3.00
19 Justin Kurpeikis	1.25	3.00
20 Tim Long	1.25	3.00
21 Brian Minehart	1.25	3.00
22 Andy Molinaro	1.25	3.00
23 Robert Mowl	1.25	3.00
24 Jonathan Murphy	1.25	3.00
25 Raki Nelson	1.25	3.00
26 Brian Remley	1.25	3.00
27 David Robbins III	1.25	3.00
28 Sean Ruffing	1.25	3.00
29 Jordan Scott	1.25	3.00
30 Ben Thomas	1.25	3.00
31 Jason Wallace	1.25	3.00
32 Garrett Watkins	1.25	3.00
33 Kenny Watson	2.00	5.00
34 Michael White	1.25	3.00
35 Tony Zimmerman	1.25	3.00

1997 Pennsylvania High School Big 33

This standard-size high school football set was issued to commemorate the 40th annual Pennsylvania Big 33 Football Classic. The fronts feature posed player photos enclosed by a white border. The state name and year appear at the top of the card along with the player's name, number, and position. The Big 33 logo appears below the photo. The backs feature the player's biographical information along with a notation to which college he plans to attend. The unnumbered cards are listed below alphabetically.

COMPLETE SET (35)	40.00	80.00
1 Herb Adderley	1.50	4.00
2 Morgan Anderson	1.25	3.00
3 LaVar Arrington	5.00	10.00
4 Vince Azzolina	1.25	3.00
5 Kevan Barlow	2.50	6.00
6 Jason Bisson	1.25	3.00
7 Travis Blomgren	1.25	3.00
8 Michael Bosnic Jr.	1.25	3.00
9 Dante Coles	1.25	3.00
10 Carlos Daniels	1.25	3.00
11 Dan Ellis	1.25	3.00
12 Ben Erdeljac	1.25	3.00
13 Jim Ferugio	1.25	3.00
14 Delrico Fletcher	1.25	3.00
15 John Gilmore	1.25	3.00
16 Ron Graham	1.25	3.00
17 Richard Hamilton	1.25	3.00
18 Marcus Hoover	1.25	3.00
19 Mycal Jones	1.25	3.00
20 Willie Knapp	1.25	3.00
21 Laban Marsh	1.25	3.00
22 Ryan Mason	1.25	3.00
23 Christopher May	1.25	3.00
24 Ahmound McDonald	1.25	3.00
25 Joe McKinney	1.25	3.00
26 Mike McMahon	2.00	5.00
27 Josh Mitchell	1.25	3.00
28 James Mungro	2.00	5.00
29 Paul Ondrusek	1.25	3.00
30 Vince Scala	1.25	3.00
31 Tony Stewart	1.25	3.00
32 Victor Strader	1.25	3.00
33 Brett Veach	1.25	3.00
34 Matt Wincek	1.25	3.00
35 Coy Wire	1.50	4.00

1998 Pennsylvania High School Big 33

This standard-size high school football set was issued to commemorate the 41st annual Pennsylvania Big 33 Football Classic. The fronts feature posed player photos enclosed by a white border. The state name and year appear to the left of the player photo with the player's name and position below the photo. The Big 33 logo appears at the upper left. The backs feature the player's biographical information along with a notation to which college he plans to attend. The unnumbered cards are listed below alphabetically.

COMPLETE SET (35)	30.00	60.00
1 Bryan Anderson	1.00	2.50
2 Brent Andrew	1.00	2.50
3 Dave Armstrong	1.00	2.50
4 Tim Bennett	1.00	2.50
5 Joshua Bostick	1.00	2.50
6 Aaron Cochran	1.00	2.50
7 Brandon Dewey	1.00	2.50
8 Darnell Greene	1.00	2.50
9 Jason Gross	1.00	2.50
10 Aaron Haddock	1.00	2.50
11 Arlen Harris	1.50	4.00
12 Ben Herbert	1.00	2.50
13 Victor Hobson	1.00	2.50
14 William Hunter	1.00	2.50
15 Larry Johnson	3.00	8.00
16 Jimmy Jones	1.00	2.50
(Honorary Captain)		
17 Rob Kolaczynski	1.00	2.50
18 Dan Koppen	1.25	3.00
19 Tyler Lenda	1.00	2.50
20 Joe Manganello	1.00	2.50
21 Anthony Nastasi	1.00	2.50
22 Brandon Payne	1.00	2.50
23 Amir Purifoy	1.00	2.50
24 Tashun Riddick	1.00	2.50
25 Demetrious Rich	1.00	2.50
26 Kent Rodzwicz	1.00	2.50
27 Ryan Scarola	1.00	2.50
28 Matt Schmitt	1.00	2.50
29 Matt Senneca	1.25	3.00
30 Ryan Smith	1.00	2.50
31 Tyler Valoczki	1.00	2.50
32 Paul Weinacht	1.00	2.50
33 Brandon Williams	1.00	2.50
34 Neal Wood	1.00	2.50
35 Marc Zlotek	1.00	2.50

1999 Pennsylvania High School Big 33

This standard-size high school football set was issued to commemorate the 42nd annual Pennsylvania Big 33 Football Classic. The fronts feature posed player photos enclosed by a white border. The state name and year appear at the top of the cardfront with the player's name and position below the photo. The Big 33 logo appears just above the player's name. The backs feature the player's biographical information along with a notation to which college he plans to attend. The unnumbered cards are listed below alphabetically.

COMPLETE SET (35)	20.00	40.00
1 Mark Bartosic	.60	1.50
2 Rob Blomeier	.60	1.50
3 Tim Brown	.60	1.50
4 Robb-Davon Butler	.60	1.50
5 Gino Capone	.60	1.50
6 Benjamin Carber	.60	1.50
7 Jim Connor	.60	1.50
8 Jaison Cook	.60	1.50
9 Dave Costlow	.60	1.50
10 Vince Crochunis	.60	1.50
11 William Ferguson	.60	1.50
12 John Glass Jr.	.60	1.50
13 Damone Jones	.60	1.50
14 Tony Katic	.60	1.50
15 Mike Kitchen	.60	1.50
16 Geoffrey Lewis	.60	1.50
17 Antoine Lovelace	.60	1.50
18 Jason Malakoski	.60	1.50
19 Matt Morgan	.60	1.50
20 Brad Nida	.60	1.50
21 Bruce Perry	.75	2.00
22 Lousaka Polite	.75	2.00
23 Rod Rutherford	.75	2.00
24 Elly Salamo	.60	1.50
25 Matt Schaub	5.00	10.00
26 Chad Schwenk	.60	1.50
27 Bryan Scott	.75	2.00
28 Art Thomas	.60	1.50
29 Blair Thomas	.60	1.50
(Honorary Captain)		
30 Shane Twyman	.60	1.50
31 Douglas White	.60	1.50
32 Grant Wiley	.60	1.50
33 Jafar Williams	.75	2.00
34 Joe Wilson	.60	1.50
35 Kris Wilson	.60	1.50

2000 Pennsylvania High School Big 33

This set was issued to commemorate the annual Big 33 High School Football Classic. The cardfronts feature color player photos along with the outline of the state below the photo and the year to the left. The player's name, jersey number, and position appear within the outline of the state. The cardbacks feature the player's biographical information along with a notation to which college he plans to attend. The unnumbered cards are listed below alphabetically.

COMPLETE SET (36)	20.00	40.00
1 Dan Acri	.60	1.50
2 Rich Bedesem	.60	1.50
3 Joe Boniewicz	.60	1.50
4 Rondel Bradley	.60	1.50
5 Jonathan Condo	.60	1.50
6 Andrew Elsing	.60	1.50
7 B.J. Evangelista	.60	1.50
8 Justin Geisinger	.60	1.50
9 Pete Gilmore	.60	1.50
10 Jared Hostetler	.60	1.50
11 Paul Jefferson	.60	1.50
12 Hikee Johnson	.60	1.50
13 Tony Johnson	.75	2.00
14 Jim Kelly	2.00	5.00
(Honorary Captain)		
15 David Kimball	.60	1.50
16 Adam Lehnortt	.60	1.50
17 Ben Lynch	.60	1.50
18 Nick Marmo	.60	1.50
19 Jared McClure	.60	1.50
20 Chris McKelvy	.60	1.50
21 Tony Paciotti	.60	1.50
22 Don Patrick	.60	1.50
23 Mike Pettine CO	.60	1.50
24 Dustin Picciotti	.60	1.50
25 Robert Ramsey	.60	1.50
26 Demond Bob Sanders	7.50	15.00
27 Brian Sanks	.60	1.50
28 Kyle Schmitt	.60	1.50
29 Nick Sebes	.60	1.50
30 Jeff Smoker	1.50	3.00
31 Chris Snee	2.50	6.00
32 Shawntae Spencer	.60	1.50
33 Michael Van Aken	.60	1.50
34 Mike Vernillo	.60	1.50
35 Marquis Weeks	.60	1.50
36 Dave Williams	.60	1.50

2001 Pennsylvania High School Big 33

Pennsylvania and Ohio card sets were again issued in 2001 to commemorate the annual Big 33 High School Football Classic. The cardfronts feature color player photos along with a solid black border. The player's name, jersey number, and position appear below the player's photo. The cardbacks feature the player's biographical information along with a notation to which college he plans to attend. The unnumbered cards are listed below alphabetically.

COMPLETE SET (36)	15.00	30.00
1 Troy Banner	.60	1.50
2 Matt Brouse	.60	1.50
3 John Dieser	.60	1.50
4 Adam Fichter	.60	1.50
5 Marcus Furman	.60	1.50
6 Chris Ganter	.60	1.50
7 Dethrell Garcia	.60	1.50
8 Robbie Gould	2.00	5.00
9 John Gross	.60	1.50
10 Chris Hathy	.60	1.50
11 Ed Hinkel	.60	1.50
12 Cecil Howard	.60	1.50
13 Marlin Jackson	.75	2.00
14 Brian Johnson	.60	1.50
15 Kevin Jones	2.00	5.00
16 Bernard Lay	.60	1.50
17 Fred Lee	.60	1.50
18 Tim Massaquoi	.60	1.50
19 Scott McClintock	.60	1.50
20 Joe Montana	4.00	8.00
(Honorary Captain)		
21 Scott Paxson	.60	1.50
22 Terrance Phillips	.60	1.50
23 Tyler Reed	.60	1.50
24 Andrew Richardson	.60	1.50
25 Andy Roland	.60	1.50
26 Charles Rush	.60	1.50
27 Jason Saks	.60	1.50
28 Lamar Stewart	.60	1.50
29 Jeff Vanak	.60	1.50
30 Jonathan Veach	.60	1.50
31 Gio Vendemia	.60	1.50
32 Rian Wallace	.60	1.50
33 Dale Williams	.60	1.50
34 Jason Williams	.60	1.50
35 Joel Yakovac	.60	1.50
36 Tyre Young	.60	1.50

2002 Pennsylvania High School Big 33

Card sets were again issued in 2002 to commemorate the annual Big 33 High School Football Classic between Ohio and Pennsylvania layers. The cardfronts feature color player photos along with a solid blue border. The player's name, jersey number, and position appear below the player's photo. The cardbacks feature the player's vital statistics as well as biographical information. The unnumbered cards are listed below alphabetically.

COMPLETE SET (38)	15.00	30.00
1 Matt Applebaum	.50	1.25
2 Patrick Bedics	.50	1.25
3 Bob Benion	.50	1.25
4 Dwayne Blackman	.50	1.25
5 Brian Borgoyn	.50	1.25
6 Steve Breaston	2.00	5.00
7 Jamar Brittingham	.50	1.25
8 Sam Bryant	.50	1.25
9 Steve Buches	.50	1.25
10 Brandon Darlington	.50	1.25
11 Matt Domonkos	.50	1.25
12 Andy Decker	.50	1.25
13 Keith Ennis	.50	1.25
14 Mark Farris	.50	1.25
15 Ian Firestone	.50	1.25
16 Ryan Gore	.50	1.25
17 Josh Hannum	.50	1.25
18 Jaren Hayes	.50	1.25
19 Jeff Hostetler	.50	1.25
20 Jovon Johnson	.60	1.50
21 Mike Mailey	.50	1.25
22 Dan Melendez	.50	1.25
23 Jermaine Moye	.50	1.25
24 Dan Mozes	.50	1.25
25 Mark Mushel	.50	1.25
26 Tom Parks	.50	1.25
27 Tyler Palko	1.50	4.00
28 Perry Patterson	.50	1.25
29 Gene Rich	.50	1.25
30 Manny Rojas	.50	1.25
31 Eddie Scipio	.50	1.25
32 Rachid Stoury	.50	1.25
33 Maurice Stovall	1.25	3.00
34 Justin Stull	.50	1.25
35 Christopher Thomas	.50	1.25
36 Jawan Walker	.50	1.25
37 Dave Wannstedt	.50	1.25
38 Andre Williams	.50	1.25

2003 Pennsylvania High School Big 33

A card set was again released in 2003 for the Pennsylvania team in the annual Big 33 High School Football Classic between Ohio and Pennsylvania players. The cardfronts feature color player photos along with a blue border. The player's name and position appears below the player's photo along with the Big 33 logo. The cardbacks feature the player's vital statistics as well as biographical information. The unnumbered cards are listed below alphabetically.

COMPLETE SET (36)	20.00	40.00
1 Vincent Beamer	.50	1.25
2 Adam Bednarik	.50	1.25
3 Ardon Bransford	.50	1.25
4 Windell Brown	.50	1.25
5 Lenny Carter	.50	1.25
6 Kevin Cimador	.50	1.25
7 Cody Decker	.50	1.25
8 Jonathan Fowler	.50	1.25
9 Dionte Henry	.50	1.25
10 Michael Hill	.50	1.25
11 Joel Holler	.50	1.25
12 Jeremy Kametz	.50	1.25
13 Andy Lehatto	.50	1.25
14 Mark Malloy	.50	1.25
15 Zach Mariacher	.50	1.25
16 Dan Marino	4.00	8.00
Honorary Chairman		
17 Steve Meister	.50	1.25
18 Cody Morris	.50	1.25
19 Brad Mueller	.50	1.25
20 Ryan Mundy	.75	2.00
21 Jared Palmer	.50	1.25
22 Brendan Perretta	.50	1.25
23 Paul Posluszny	7.50	15.00
24 John Quinn	.50	1.25
25 David Richards	.50	1.25
26 Austin Scott	.75	2.00
27 John Shaw	.50	1.25
28 Kyle Smith	.50	1.25
29 William Starry	.50	1.25
30 Marcus Stone	.50	1.25
31 Travis Thomas	.50	1.25
32 Brian Ushler	.50	1.25
33 Eric Wicks	.50	1.25
34 Brent Wise	.50	1.25
35 Mark Yezovich	.50	1.25
36 Cover Card	.50	1.25
Checklist		

2004 Pennsylvania High School Big 33

This set was released in July 2004 for the Pennsylvania team participating in the annual Big 33 High School Football Classic. The cardfronts feature color player photos along with a border resembling a picture frame. The player's name and position appear below the player's photo along with the Big 33 logo. The cardbacks feature the player's vital statistics as well as biographical information. The unnumbered cards are listed below alphabetically.

COMPLETE SET (36)	20.00	40.00
1 Leyon Azubuike	.50	1.25
2 Curtis Brinkley	.50	1.25
3 Steffan Brinson	.50	1.25
4 Dontey Brown	.50	1.25
5 James Bryant	.50	1.25
6 Dave Brytus	.50	1.25
7 Mike Byrne	.50	1.25
8 Eugene Clay	.50	1.25
9 Kalise Cook	.50	1.25
10 Dave Dalessandro	.50	1.25
11 Chad Henne	6.00	12.00
12 Brian Hentosz	.50	1.25
13 Ben Iannacchione	.50	1.25
14 Mortty Ivy	.50	1.25
15 Andrew Johnson	.50	1.25
16 Dan Lawlor	.60	1.50
17 Devon Lyons	.50	1.25
18 Kevin Mathews	.60	1.50
19 Scott McKillop	.50	1.25
20 Matt Millen	.50	1.25
Honorary Chairman		
21 Kyle Mitchum	.50	1.25
22 Anthony Morelli	1.25	3.00
23 Rory Nicol	.50	1.25
24 Mark Parkhurst	.50	1.25
25 Darrelle Revis	7.50	15.00
26 Chris Rogers	.50	1.25
27 Tyrell Sales	.50	1.25
28 A.Q. Shipley	.75	2.00
29 Jon Skinner	.50	1.25
30 Doug Slavonic	.50	1.25
31 Peter Smith	.50	1.25
32 Tyree Suber	.50	1.25
33 Jaimie Thomas	.50	1.25
34 Nate Waldron	.50	1.25
35 Jai Wilson	.50	1.25
36 Cover Card	.50	1.25

2005 Pennsylvania High School Big 33

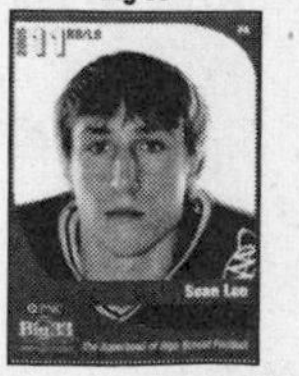

This set was released in July 2005 for the Pennsylvania team participating in the annual Big 33 High School Football Classic. The cardfronts feature color player photos along with a very thin dark red border. The player's name appears below the player's photo along with the PNC Big 33 logo. The cardbacks feature the player's vital statistics as well as biographical information. The unnumbered cards are listed below alphabetically.

COMPLETE SET (36)	12.50	25.00
1 Zachary Anderson	.30	.75
2 Vince Bazzone	.30	.75
3 Joe Blanks	.30	.75
4 Dana Brown	.30	.75
5 Jerry Butler	.30	.75
6 Tommie Campbell	.30	.75
7 James Carson	.30	.75
8 Edward Collington	.30	.75
9 Carmen Connolly	.30	.75
10 C.J. Davis	.30	.75
11 Brad Dawson	.30	.75
12 Ryan Greiser	.30	.75
13 Roger Hall	.30	.75
14 Nate Hartung	.30	.75
15 David Horton	.30	.75
16 Rocket Ismail	.60	1.50
17 Kevin Kelly	.60	1.50
18 Josh Kiner	.30	.75
19 Sean Lee	2.00	5.00
20 Ken Lewis	.30	.75
21 Donnell McKenzie	.30	.75
22 Jordan Mitchell	.30	.75
23 Shane Murray	.40	1.00
24 Malik Newman	.30	.75
25 Osayi Osunde	.30	.75
26 John Pelusi	.30	.75
27 Domenique Price	.30	.75
28 Graham Rihn	.30	.75
29 Jake Serdy	.30	.75
30 Josh Shelton	.30	.75
31 LaRod Stephens-Howling	1.00	2.50
32 Knowledge Timmons	.30	.75
33 LaRondo Tucker	.30	.75
34 Bradley Vierling	.30	.75
35 Ernest Williams	.30	.75
36 Cover Card	.30	.75

2006 Pennsylvania High School Big 33

This set was released in July 2006 for the Pennsylvania team participating in the annual Big 33 High School Football Classic. The cardfronts feature color player photos along with a very thin black border. The player's name appears below the player's photo along with the PNC Big 33 logo. The cardbacks feature the player's vital statistics as well as biographical information. The unnumbered cards are listed below alphabetically.

COMPLETE SET (36)	10.00	20.00
1 Aaron Berry	.30	.75
2 Nate Byham	.40	1.00
3 Barry Church	.30	.75
4 Chris Daino	.30	.75
5 Pat Devlin	.75	2.00
6 Dorin Dickerson	.40	1.00
7 Connor Dixon	.75	2.00
8 Elijah Fields	.30	.75
9 Bill Fralic CO	.30	.75
10 Jeremiha Hunter	.30	.75
11 Alex Johnson	.30	.75
12 Clem Johnson	.30	.75
13 Abe Koroma	.40	1.00
14 Andrew Lee	.30	.75
15 John Malecki	.40	1.00
16 Travis McBride	.40	1.00
17 Tom McEowen	.30	.75
18 Jim McKenzie	.30	.75
19 Andres Morales	.30	.75
20 Chris Neild	.30	.75
21 Josh Neubert	.30	.75
22 Nate Nix	.30	.75
23 Charlie Noonan	.30	.75
24 Jared Odrick	.60	1.50
25 Anthony Parker-Boyd	.30	.75
26 John Plund	.30	.75
27 Da'Rel Scott	.60	1.50
28 Aaron Smith	.50	1.25
29 Tyler Tkach	.30	.75
30 Kevin Uhll	.30	.75
31 Collin Wagner	.30	.75
32 Anthony Walters	.30	.75
33 Greg Webster	.30	.75
34 Dave Williams	.30	.75
35 Nate Williams	.30	.75
36 Aundre Wright	.30	.75

2007 Pennsylvania High School Big 33

COMPLETE SET (36)	10.00	20.00
1 Drew Astorino	.50	1.25
2 Gary Bardzak	.30	.75
3 Jeff Battipaglia	.30	.75
4 Myles Caragein	.30	.75
5 Toney Clemons	.30	.75
6 Dane Conwell	.30	.75
7 Tim Cortazzo	.30	.75
8 Dom DeCicco	.30	.75
9 Andrew Devlin	.30	.75
10 Chris Drager	.30	.75
11 John Fieger	.30	.75
12 Larry Gooden	.30	.75
13 Gino Gradkowski	.30	.75
14 Brad Hallick	.30	.75
15 Henry Hynoski	1.50	4.00
16 Chris Jacobson	.30	.75
17 Devan Johnson	.30	.75
18 Wayne Jones	.30	.75
19 Dominique Joseph	.30	.75
20 Kamryn Keys	.30	.75
21 Tom Kondash	.30	.75
22 C.J. Marck	.30	.75
23 Corey Medina	.30	.75
24 Rontez Miles	.30	.75
25 Derek Moye	.60	1.50
26 Marcus Payton	.30	.75
27 Dan Persa	.50	1.25
28 Daryl Robinson	.30	.75
29 Abe Satterfield	.30	.75
30 Marty Schottenheimer	.40	1.00
Honorary Chairman		
31 Lamont Smith	.30	.75
32 Nathan Stupar	.60	1.50
33 Max Suter	.30	.75
34 Chris Whitney	.30	.75
35 Travis Wolff	.30	.75
36 Header Card	.30	.75

2008 Pennsylvania High School Big 33

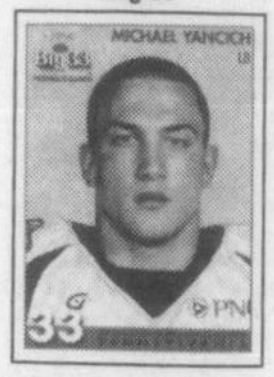

COMPLETE SET (36)	10.00	20.00
1 A.J. Alexander	.40	1.00
2 Jonathan Baldwin	1.00	2.50
3 Todd Blackledge HC	.40	1.00
4 Vaughn Carraway	.30	.75
5 R.J. Dill	.30	.75
6 Nate Eachus	.30	.75
7 Austin Fedell	.30	.75
8 Robert Gumbita	.30	.75
9 Jarred Holley	.30	.75
10 John Jackson TE	.30	.75
11 Chris Johnson DB	.30	.75
12 Mike Jones RB	.30	.75
13 John Laub	.30	.75
14 Phillip Long	.30	.75
15 Pete Massaro	.30	.75
16 Shahid Paulhill	.30	.75
17 Joshua Potts	.30	.75
18 Antwuan Reed	.30	.75
19 Eric Reynolds RB	.30	.75
20 Adrian Robinson	.30	.75
21 Cameron Saddler	.30	.75
22 Michael Shanahan	.30	.75
23 David Soldner	.30	.75
24 Matt Stankiewitch	.30	.75
25 Tino Sunseri	.40	1.00
26 Andrew Taglianetti	.30	.75
27 Wayne Tribue	.30	.75
28 Dan Vaughan	.40	1.00
29 Brandon Ware	.40	1.00
30 Corey Watts	.30	.75
31 Brandon Weaver	.30	.75
32 Mark Wedderburn	.60	1.50
33 Quentin Williams	.30	.75
34 Christian Wilson	.30	.75
35 Michael Yancich	.40	1.00
36 Cover Card	.30	.75

2009 Pennsylvania High School Big 33

COMPLETE SET (36)	7.50	15.00
1 Ronnie Akins	.25	.60
2 Mark Arcidiacono	.25	.60
3 Kyle Brady HC	.40	1.00
4 Dana Brown	.25	.60
5 Josh Bucci	.25	.60
6 James Capello	.25	.60
7 Jay Colbert	.25	.60
8 Brock Decicco	.25	.60
9 Curtis Drake	.30	.75
10 A.J. Fenton	.25	.60
11 Brett Fox	.25	.60
12 Malik Generett	.25	.60
13 Gary Gilliam	.30	.75
14 Steve Greene	.25	.60
15 Brandon Heath	.25	.60
16 Jordan Hill	.25	.60
17 Robert Hollomon	.25	.60
18 Anthony Holmes	.25	.60
19 Chris Houston	.25	.60
20 Horvin Latimer	.25	.60
21 Jermel Lee	.25	.60
22 Jack Lippert	.25	.60
23 Lyle Marsh	.25	.60
24 Dan Mason	.25	.60
25 Brandon McManus	.25	.60
26 Billy Morgan	.25	.60
27 Dave Osei	.25	.60
28 Mike Pinciotti	.25	.60
29 Nick Redden	.25	.60
30 John Schademan	.25	.60
31 Carson Sharbaugh	.25	.60
32 Dan Shorey	.25	.60
33 Jordan Smith	.25	.60
34 Devin Street	.25	.60
35 Rob Stupar	.25	.60
36 Kyle Brady Art Cover	.25	.60

2010 Pennsylvania High School Big 33

COMPLETE SET (36)	7.50	15.00
1 Aaron Achey	.25	.60
2 Taj Alexander	.25	.60
3 Evan Battallio	.25	.60
4 Tyler Beck	.25	.60
5 Seth Betancourt	.25	.60
6 Derrick Burns	.30	.75
7 Andrew Carswell	.30	.75
8 Mike Coccia	.25	.60
9 Sal Conaboy	.25	.60
10 Jack DeBoef	.25	.60
11 Jonathan Duckett	.30	.75
12 J.D. Dzurko	.25	.60
13 Corey Ford	.25	.60
14 Travis Friend	.25	.60
15 Manasseh Garner	.25	.60
16 Anthony Gonzalez	.40	1.00
17 Richard Gray	.25	.60
18 Drake Greer	.25	.60
19 Tim Johnson	.25	.60
20 Ryan Keiser	.25	.60
21 Alex Kenney	.25	.60
22 Joe Laukaitis	.25	.60
23 Adam Metz	.25	.60
24 Khaynin Mosley-Smith	.25	.60
25 Dayonne Nunley	.25	.60
26 Shyquawn Pullium	.25	.60
27 Tyler Smith	.40	1.00
28 Dom Timbers	.25	.60
29 Delbert Tyler	.25	.60
30 Kyle Wallace	.25	.60

31 Ricky Watters HC	.30	.75
32 Colby Way	.25	.60
33 Kevin Weatherspoon	.25	.60
34 Jarrod West	.25	.60
35 Salath Williams	.30	.75
36 Cover Card	.25	.60

2011 Pennsylvania High School Big 33

COMPLETE SET (37)	7.50	15.00
1 Jamal Abdur-Rahman	.25	.60
2 Sean Barowski	.25	.60
3 Dave Bowen	.25	.60
4 Dexter Bridge	.25	.60
5 Julian Campenni	.25	.60
6 Brandon Clemons	.25	.60
7 Devin Cook	.25	.60
8 Daquan Cooper	.25	.60
9 Morgan Craig	.25	.60
10 Tim Cwalina	.25	.60
11 Vincent Czerniewski	.25	.60
12 Steven Finley	.25	.60
13 Jalen Fitzpatrick	.25	.60
14 Desimon Green	.25	.60
15 Justin Haser	.25	.60
16 Brandon Holloman	.25	.60
17 Kyshoen Jarrett	.25	.60
18 Quinton Jefferson	.25	.60
19 Matt Johnson	.25	.60
20 Jordan Kerner	.30	.75
21 Tyler Kroft	.25	.60
22 Ty Law HC	.40	1.00
23 Corey Majors	.25	.60
24 Shane McNeely	.25	.60
25 Shawn Oakman	.25	.60
26 Josh Page	.25	.60
27 Lafayette Pitts	.25	.60
28 Jameel Poteat	.25	.60
29 Ejuan Price	.25	.60
30 Nick Rossi	.25	.60
31 Jeremy Seaman	.25	.60
32 Delvon Simmons	.25	.60
33 Quinton Sullivan	.25	.60
34 Jullian Turner	.25	.60
35 Michael Wainauskis	.25	.60
36 Armstead Williams	.25	.60
37 Cover Card	.25	.60

1989 Pittsburgh Greats

The 1989 Pitt football set contains 22 standard-size cards of past Pitt Panthers greats The fronts have vintage or color action photos with white borders; the vertically oriented backs have detailed profiles. These cards were distributed as a set.

COMPLETE SET (22)	7.50	15.00
1 Tony Dorsett	1.50	4.00
2 Pop Warner CO	.30	.75
3 Hugh Green	.25	.60
4 Matt Cavanaugh	.20	.50
5 Mike Gottfried	.15	.40
6 Jim Covert	.20	.50
7 Bob Peck	.15	.40
8 Gibby Welch	.15	.40
9 Bill Daddio	.15	.40
10 Jock Sutherland CO	.15	.40
11 Joe Walton	.15	.40
12 Dan Marino	5.00	10.00
13 Russ Grimm	.40	1.00
14 Mike Ditka	1.25	3.00
15 Marshall Goldberg	.20	.50
16 Bill Fralic	.20	.50
17 Paul Martha	.15	.40
18 Joe Schmidt	.30	.75
19 Rickey Jackson	.25	.60
20 Ave Daniell	.15	.40
21 Bill Maas	.20	.50
22 Mark May	.20	.50

1990 Pittsburgh Foodland

This 12-card standard-size set was sponsored by Foodland to promote anti-drug involvement in the Pittsburgh area. This set features members of the 1990 Pittsburgh Panthers football team. The front features a color action photo, with the team name, player's name, and position at the top. The Pitt helmet appears at the bottom left hand corner and the Foodland logo below the picture. The back contains biographical information and a tip from the Panthers in the form of an anti-drug message. The set was produced by Bensussen-Deutsch and Association from Redmond, Washington. For convenient reference, these unnumbered cards are checklisted below in alphabetical order.

COMPLETE SET (12)	5.00	10.00
1 Curtis Bray	.20	.50
2 Craig Gob	.20	.50
3 Paul Hackett CO	.30	.75
4 Keith Hamilton	.60	1.50
5 Ricardo McDonald	.60	1.50
6 Ronald Redmon	.20	.50
7 Curvin Richards	.30	.75
8 Louis Riddick	.30	.75
9 Chris Sestili	.20	.50
10 Olanda Truitt	.60	1.50
11 Alex Van Pelt	2.50	5.00
12 Nelson Walker	.20	.50

1991 Pittsburgh Foodland

This 12-card standard-size set was sponsored by Foodland and features the 1991 Pittsburgh Panthers. The cards are printed on thin cardboard stock. The set was issued as individual cards or as an unperforated sheet. The card fronts are accented in the team's colors (blue and yellow) and have glossy color action player photos. The top of the pictures is curved to resemble an archway, and the team name follows the curve of the arch. The player's name and position appear in a yellow stripe below the picture. In black print on white, the backs have the team logo, biography, player profile, and "Tips from the Panthers" in the form of anti-drug messages. The cards are unnumbered and checklisted below in alphabetical order.

COMPLETE SET (12)	4.00	8.00
1 Richard Allen	.30	.75
2 Curtis Bray	.30	.75
3 Jeff Christy	.40	1.00
4 Steve Israel	.40	1.00
5 Scott Kaplan	.30	.75
6 Ricardo McDonald	.40	1.00
7 Dave Moore	.30	.75
8 Eric Seaman	.30	.75
9 Chris Sestili	.30	.75
10 Alex Van Pelt	2.00	4.00
11 Nelson Walker	.30	.75
12 Kevin Williams HB	.30	.75

1991 Pitt State

The 1991 Pitt State Gorillas set consists of 18 standard-size cards. Printed on thin white card stock, fronts show player in either a posed or an action photo placed within an arch design. College and team name appears at top of each card while player's name is in a gold bar at bottom next to a picture of the mascot. The backs present biography and player profile superimposed over a drawing of the mascot. A checklist is included with the set on a paper insert. The key player in this set is NFL running back Ron Moore. Also appearing in the set is Ronnie West, who was the Gorillas' Harlon Hill Award candidate. The cards are unnumbered and listed alphabetically below.

COMPLETE SET (18)	4.80	12.00
1 Chuck Droyles CO	.25	.60
2 Darren Dawson	.25	.60
3 Kendall Gammon	.25	.60
4 Jamie Goodson	.25	.60
5 Brian Hoover	.25	.60
6 James Jenkins	.25	.60
7 Ky Kiger	.25	.60
8 Phil McCoy	.25	.60
9 Kline Minniefield	.25	.60
10 Ronald Moore	1.20	3.00
11 Jeff Mundhenke	.25	.60
12 Brian Pinamonti	.25	.60
13 Michael Rose	.25	.60
14 Shane Tafoya	.25	.60
15 Ronnie West	.40	1.00
16 Michael Wilber	.25	.60
17 Troy Wilson	.60	1.50
18 Team Photo	.50	1.25

1992 Pitt State

Initiated by Students in Free Enterprise (SIFE), this 18-card set was produced to raise funds for the Pitt State athletic department. The cards could be purchased at football games, the University Post Office, or Kelce room 220. The production run figures were 3,000 numbered packaged sets and 750 uncut sheets. One thousand of the packaged sets contained a Ronnie West bonus card. In addition to the 18 standard-size cards, the set included one paper insert providing card history, a checklist, and set serial number, and another paper insert with cartoons about four different "Isms" (socialism, communism, nazism, and capitalism) and a list of examples of "Big Government" waste in spending. The set features full-bleed color action player photos. The backs are plain white card stock printed with black and contain biographies and player profiles. Some cards also carry Pitt State trivia, while others have statistics. The key card in the set features running back Ron Moore.

COMPLETE SET (18)	4.00	10.00
1 Ronald Moore	.80	2.00
2 Craig Jordan	.25	.60
3 Joel Thornton	.25	.60
4 Don Tolar	.25	.60
5 Andy Kesinger	.25	.60
6 Mike Brockel	.25	.60
7 Troy Wilson	.50	1.25
8 Brian Hutchins	.25	.60
9 Chris Hanna	.25	.60
10 Coaching Staff	.25	.60
11 Gus Gorilla (Mascot)	.25	.60
12 Lance Gosch	.25	.60
13 Jerry Boone Chad Watskey	.25	.60
14 Jeff Moreland Scott Lutz	.25	.60
15 Ronnie Fuller Mickey Beagle	.25	.60
16 Todd Hafner Kevin Duncan	.25	.60
17 Duke Palmer Eric Perks	.25	.60
18 Kris Mengarelli	.25	.60

1974 Purdue Team Sheets

These photos were issued by the school to promote the football program. Each measures roughly 8" by 10" and features eight black and white images of players with the school name appearing at the top. The backs are blank.

1 Alex Agase CO Larry Burton Ken Novak Mike Worthington Scott Dierking Ralph Peretta Craig Nagel Mike Terrizzi	4.00	8.00
2 Stan Parker Mark Vitali Steve Schmidt Fred Cooper Randy Clark Pete Gross Mark Gorgal Barry Santini	4.00	8.00

1989 Purdue Legends Smokey

This 16-card set features members of the 1989 Purdue Boilermakers as well as some stars of the past. These sets were distributed at the Purdue/Iowa game in 1989 and have a full-color action photo on the front underneath the Purdue Boilermaker name on top and the player's name, uniform number, and position underneath his photo. The card backs have biographical information as well as a fire safety tip. This set was sponsored by the USDA Forest Service, Indiana Department of Natural Resources, and BDA. We have checklisted this set in alphabetical order and put the initials LEG next to the alumni.

COMPLETE SET (16)	12.00	30.00
1 Fred Akers CO	.60	1.50
2 Jim Everett LEG	1.00	2.50
3 Bob Griese LEG	2.50	6.00
4 Mark Herrmann LEG	.60	1.50
5 Bill Hitchcock	.50	1.25
6 Steve Jackson	.60	1.50
7 Derrick Kelson	.50	1.25
8 Leroy Keyes LEG	.75	2.00
9 Shawn McCarthy	.50	1.25
10 Dwayne O'Connor	.50	1.25
11 Mike Phipps LEG	.75	2.00
12 Darren Trieb	.50	1.25
13 Tony Vinson	.50	1.25
14 Calvin Williams	.75	2.00
15 Rod Woodson LEG	1.50	4.00
16 Dave Young LEG	.50	1.25

1998 Purdue Legends

COMPLETE SET (36)	12.50	25.00
1 Brian Alford	.30	.75
2 Mike Alstott	.60	1.50
3 Otis Armstrong	.40	1.00
4 Jim Beirne	.30	.75
5 Tom Bettis	.30	.75
6 Donald Brumm	.30	.75
7 Dave Butz	.30	.75
8 John Charles	.30	.75
9 Len Dawson	.75	2.00
10 Bob DeMoss	.30	.75
11 Scott Dierking	.30	.75
12 Cris Dishman	.30	.75
13 Jim Everett	.50	1.25
14 Bernie Flowers	.30	.75
15 Tim Foley	.30	.75
16 Bob Griese	1.25	3.00
17 Mark Herrmann	.30	.75
18 Cecil Isbell	.30	.75
19 Leroy Keyes	.40	1.00
20 Chuck Kyle	.30	.75
21 Lamar Lundy	.40	1.00
22 Paul Moss	.30	.75
23 Mike Phipps	.50	1.25
24 Duane Purvis	.30	.75
25 Dave Rankin	.30	.75
26 Dale Samuels	.30	.75
27 Jerry Shay	.30	.75
28 Elmer Sleight	.30	.75
29 Leo Sugar	.30	.75
30 Harry Szulborski	.30	.75
31 Ralph Welch	.30	.75
32 Rod Woodson	.75	2.00
33 Dave Young	.30	.75
34 Jack Mollenkopf CO	.30	.75
35 Joe Tiller CO	.30	.75
36 Cover Card	.30	.75

2000 Purdue Drew Brees

This card was given away to 53,500 fans who attended the Purdue vs. Ohio State football game on October 28, 2000. The card includes a color photo of Brees on the front along with a "don't smoke" message. The cardback contains player stats and biographical information as well as a sponsorship mention. Back variations were created with at least three different sponsors used including: GlaxoWellcome, University Spirit, and Burger King.

1 Drew Brees	6.00	12.00

2004 Purdue Jumbo Heroes

These cards were issued in 4-card panels by the school. Each perforated card when separated measures standard size and features an artist's rendering of the player in super hero style. The cardbacks include an actual player photo, some minor stats, a card number, and list of fictional super powers.

COMPLETE SET (24)	6.00	12.00
1 Kyle Orton	.50	1.25
2 Antwaun Rogers	.20	.50
3 Taylor Stubblefield	.20	.50
4 Ben Jones	.20	.50
5 Jerod Void	.20	.50
6 George Hall	.20	.50
7 Kyle Ingraham	.20	.50
8 Matt Turner	.20	.50
9 Ray Edwards	.30	.75
10 Brandon Jones	.40	.75
11 Brent Grover	.20	.50
12 Mike Otto	.20	.50
13 Tyler Moore	.20	.50
14 Charles Davis	.20	.50
15 Bernard Pollard	.20	.50
16 Bobby Iwuchukwu	.20	.50
17 Ray Williams	.20	.50
18 David Owen	.20	.50
19 Brian Hickman	.20	.50
20 Jon Goldsberry	.20	.50
21 Jerome Brooks	.20	.50
22 Brandon Villarreal	.20	.50
23 Kevin Noel	.20	.50
24 Joe Tiller CO	.20	.50

2005 Purdue Joe Tiller

1 Joe Tiller CO	.40	1.00

2006 Purdue Greats

This set of two cards was issued by the school to honor two famous football alumnus. The unnumbered cards were printed in the style of the 1966 Topps football set.

COMPLETE SET (2)	3.00	8.00
1 Bob Griese	2.00	5.00
2 Leroy Keyes	1.25	3.00

2009 Razor Army All-American Bowl

COMPLETE SET (57)	15.00	30.00
COMP.FACT.SET (58)	20.00	40.00
1 Bryce Brown	1.50	4.00
2 Tajh Boyd	.75	2.00
3 Orson Charles	.40	1.00
4 Roderick McDowell	.40	1.00
5 Aaron Murray	.60	1.50
6 Jeremy Gallon	.60	1.50
7 Je'Ron Stokes	.60	1.50
8 Edwin Baker	.50	1.25
9 Donavan Tate	.50	1.25
10 Donte Moss	.40	1.00
11 Jake Golic	.50	1.25
12 Dorian Bell	.50	1.25
13 Corey Brown	.60	1.50
14 Kevin Newsome	.60	1.50
15 Tom Savage	.60	1.50
16 Kendrick Hardy	.40	1.00
17 Logan Thomas	.40	1.00
18 D.J. Fluker	.40	1.00
19 Kendall Kelly	.50	1.25
20 Dre Kirkpatrick	.40	1.00
21 A.J. McCarron	.50	1.25
22 Adam Hall	.40	1.00
23 Vontaze Burfict	.40	1.00
24 Ronnie Wingo	.40	1.00
25 Tyrik Rollison	.50	1.25
26 Allan Bridgeford	.50	1.25
27 Bryce McNeal	.40	1.00
28 Rueben Randle	.50	1.25
29 Chris Davenport	.40	1.00
30 Sheldon Richardson	.40	1.00
31 Shaquelle Evans	.60	1.50
32 Cierre Wood	.50	1.25
33 Jamarkus McFarland	.40	1.00
34 Patrick Patterson	.40	1.00
35 Greg Timmons	.40	1.00
36 Chris Whaley	.50	1.25
37 Alex Okafor	.40	1.00
38 Christine Michael	.40	1.00
39 Randall Carroll	.60	1.50
40 T.J. McDonald	.40	1.00
41 Koy Detmer Jr.	.40	1.00
42 Ray Lewis III	.40	1.00
43 Christian McCaffrey	.40	1.00
44 Rhett Bomar	.30	.75
45 Brian Brohm	.25	.60
46 Reggie Bush	.40	1.00
47 Josh Freeman	.75	2.00
48 Ted Ginn	.30	.75
49 Percy Harvin	.60	1.50
50 Chad Henne	.30	.75
51 DeSean Jackson	.30	.75
52 Adrian Peterson	.60	1.50
53 Brady Quinn	.30	.75
54 Mark Sanchez	1.25	3.00
55 Chris Wells	.60	1.50
56 Vince Young	.30	.75
MM1 Bryce Brown JSY	6.00	15.00

2009 Razor Army All-American Bowl Autographs

ONE AUTO OR JSY PER FACTORY SET

AU1 Bryce Brown	15.00	40.00
AU2 Larvez Mars	4.00	10.00
AU3 Bryce McNeal	4.00	10.00
AU4 Austin Long	4.00	10.00
AU5 Jackson Rice	4.00	10.00
AU6 Johnny Simon	4.00	10.00
AU7 Tom Savage	8.00	20.00
AU8 Randall Carroll	6.00	15.00
AU9 Brennan Williams	4.00	10.00
AU10 Vontaze Burfict	4.00	10.00
AU11 Darius Winston	4.00	10.00
AU12 Marcus Davis	4.00	10.00
AU13 Devon Kennard	4.00	10.00
AU14 Greg Timmons	4.00	10.00
AU15 D.J. Fluker	4.00	10.00
AU16 Chris Boswell	4.00	10.00
AU17 Kendall Kelly	4.00	10.00
AU18 Dre Kirkpatrick	4.00	10.00
AU19 Sheldon Richardson	4.00	10.00
AU20 Dorian Bell	4.00	10.00
AU21 Corey Brown	4.00	10.00
AU22 Chris Watt	4.00	10.00
AU23 Tyler Stockton	4.00	10.00
AU24 Shaquelle Evans	4.00	10.00
AU25 Xavier Nixon	4.00	10.00
AU26 Tariq Allen	4.00	10.00
AU27 Chris Whaley	4.00	10.00
AU28 Chris Davenport	4.00	10.00
AU29 Allan Bridgford	4.00	10.00
AU30 Nick Alajajian	4.00	10.00
AU31 Byron Moore	4.00	10.00
AU32 Donte Moss	4.00	10.00
AU33 Edwin Baker	4.00	10.00
AU34 Adam Hall	4.00	10.00
AU35 Jon Bostic	4.00	10.00
AU36 Tajh Boyd	6.00	15.00
AU37 Chris Bonds	4.00	10.00
AU38 Patrick Hall	4.00	10.00
AU39 Roderick McDowell	4.00	10.00
AU40 Shayne Skov	4.00	10.00
AU41 Ronnie Wingo	5.00	10.00
AU42 Calvin Howell	4.00	10.00
AU43 Malliciah Goodman	4.00	10.00
AU44 Barkevious Mingo	4.00	10.00

2010 Razor Army All-American Bowl Promo

Cards from this set were issued in 4-card packs at the 2010 Army All-American Bowl game in San Antonio in January 2010. The set consists of 98 player cards for those participating in the 2010 game along with a pair of Tim Tebow cards honoring his appearance the 2006 game. The unnumbered cardbacks mention the cards as being part of a promotional set except for the two Tim Tebow cards that lack the mention of promo and do have card numbers. Each of the 98 basic design cards also include a white area at the bottom of the cardfront to highlight an autograph should the collector get the card signed. At the event there was a postgame signing session so many of the cards can be found on the market with autographs.

1 Keenan Allen	.20	.50
2 Markeith Ambles	.30	.75
3 Latwan Anderson	.20	.50
4 Ross Apo	.25	.60
5 Nate Askew	.25	.60
6 Calvin Barnett	.20	.50
7 Anthony Barr	.25	.60
8 Dillon Baxter	.40	1.00
9 Joe Boisture	.20	.50
10 Barry Brunetti	.60	1.50
11 Christian Bryant	.30	.75
12 Martavis Bryant	.25	.60
13 Chance Carter	.20	.50
14 Cullen Christian	.20	.50
15 Gerald Christian	.20	.50
16 Shon Coleman	.20	.50
17 Austin Collinsworth	.50	1.25
18 Robert Crisp	.20	.50
19 Matt Darr	.20	.50
20 Nick Demien	.20	.50
21 A.J. Derby	.40	1.00
22 Ahmad Dixon	.20	.50
23 Andrew Donnal	.20	.50
24 Matt Elam	.30	.75
25 Dominic Espinosa	.20	.50
26 Ego Ferguson	.20	.50
27 C.J. Fiedorowicz	.25	.60
28 Marquis Flowers	.20	.50
29 Sharrif Floyd	.30	.75
30 Nick Forbes	.20	.50
31 Khairi Fortt	.20	.50
32 Cade Foster	.30	.75
33 Jimmy Gjere	.20	.50
34 Christian Green	.25	.60
35 Will Hagerup	.20	.50
36 Victor Hampton	.20	.50
37 Jake Heaps	1.00	2.50
38 Ricky Heimuli	.20	.50
39 Seantrel Henderson	.30	.75
40 Austin Hinder	.25	.60
41 Trey Hopkins	.20	.50
42 Mike Hull	.30	.75
43 Tevin Jackson	.20	.50
44 Matt James	.20	.50
45 Jackson Jeffcoat	.30	.75
46 Tony Jefferson	.20	.50
47 Malcolm Jones	.25	.60
48 Paul Jones	.25	.60
49 Gabe King	.20	.50
50 Marcus Lattimore	1.25	3.00
51 Brandon Linder	.20	.50
52 Christian Lombard	.20	.50
53 Keanon Lowe	.20	.50
54 Marcus Lucas	.25	.60
55 Blake Lueders	.20	.50
56 Cassius Marsh	.20	.50
57 Chris Martin	.20	.50
58 Dior Mathis	.20	.50
59 Jake Matthews	.20	.50
60 Ivan McCartney	.20	.50
61 Justin McCay	.20	.50
62 D.J. Morgan	.30	.75
63 C.J. Mosley	.20	.50
64 Andrew Norwell	.20	.50
65 Owamagbe Odighizuwa	.20	.50
66 Cedric Ogbuehi	.20	.50
67 Michael Palardy	.20	.50
68 Sean Parker	.20	.50
69 Sione Potoae	.20	.50
70 Ronald Powell	.60	1.50
71 Kyle Prater	.75	2.00
72 Kelcy Quarles	.20	.50
73 Silas Redd	.40	1.00
74 Trovon Reed	.20	.50
75 Eric Reid	.20	.50
76 Damien Robinson	.20	.50
77 Andrew Rodriguez	.30	.75
78 Lache Seastrunk	.60	1.50
79 Traylon Shead	.25	.60
80 Josh Shirley	.20	.50
81 Garrison Smith	.20	.50
82 Jacques Smith	.20	.50
83 Quinton Spain	.20	.50
84 Christian Thomas	.20	.50
85 Carlos Thompson	.40	1.00
86 Spencer Ware	.25	.60
87 Jaylen Watkins	.20	.50
88 Jeff Whitaker	.20	.50
89 Curtis White	.20	.50
90 DeAndrew White	.15	.60
91 Cecil Whiteside	.20	.50
92 Jarrick Williams	.20	.50
93 Brandon Willis	.20	.50
94 Reggie Wilson	.20	.50
95 Connor Wood	.30	.75
96 Robert Woods	.15	.60
97 Demetrius Wright	.20	.50
98 Zach Zwinak	.40	1.00
TB1 Tim Tebow	4.00	10.00
TB2 Tim Tebow	4.00	10.00

2010 Razor Army All-American Bowl

COMPLETE SET (124)	20.00	40.00
1 Seantrel Henderson	.20	.50
2 Kyle Prater	.50	1.25
3 Robert Woods	.15	.40
4 Lache Seastrunk	.40	1.00
5 Ronald Powell	.40	1.00
6 Jackson Jeffcoat	.20	.50
7 Marcus Lattimore	.75	2.00
8 Sharrif Floyd	.20	.50
9 Keenan Allen	.10	.30
10 Robert Crisp	.10	.30
11 Matt Elam	.20	.50
12 Chris Martin	.10	.30
13 Latwan Anderson	.10	.30
14 Ego Ferguson	.10	.30
15 Owa Odighizuwa	.10	.30
16 Anthony Barr	.15	.40
17 Reggie Wilson	.10	.30
18 Dillon Baxter	.25	.60
19 Gabe King	.10	.30
20 Khairi Fortt	.10	.30
21 Tevin Jackson	.10	.30
22 Ivan McCartney	.10	.30
23 Cecil Whiteside	.10	.30
24 Trovon Reed	.10	.30
25 Brandon Willis	.10	.30
26 Kelcy Quarles	.10	.30
27 Martavis Bryant	.15	.40
28 Markeith Ambles	.20	.50
29 Justin McCay	.10	.30
30 Andrew Norwell	.10	.30
31 Garrison Smith	.10	.30
32 Gerald Christian	.10	.30
33 Tony Jefferson	.10	.30
34 Jake Heaps	.60	1.50
35 Silas Redd	.25	.60
36 Matt James	.10	.30
37 Christian Green	.15	.40
38 D.J. Morgan	.20	.50
39 Trey Hopkins	.10	.30
40 Nick Demien	.10	.30
41 Jacques Smith	.10	.30
42 Shakim Phillips	.15	.40
43 Jarrick Williams	.10	.30
44 Eric Reid	.10	.30
45 Nick Forbes	.10	.30
46 Christian Thomas	.10	.30
47 Shon Coleman	.10	.30
48 Malcolm Jones	.15	.40
49 Jake Matthews	.10	.30
50 Andrew Rodriguez	.20	.50
51 Marquis Flowers	.10	.30
52 Cullen Christian	.10	.30
53 Ricky Heimuli	.10	.30
54 Curtis White	.10	.30
55 Jaylen Watkins	.10	.30
56 Ahmad Dixon	.10	.30
57 Dominic Espinosa	.10	.30
58 Demetrius Wright	.10	.30
59 DeAndrew White	.15	.40
60 C.J. Fiedorowicz	.15	.40
61 Connor Wood	.20	.50
62 Carlos Thompson	.25	.60
63 Paul Jones	.15	.40
64 Marcus Lucas	.15	.40
65 Arie Kouandjio	.10	.30
66 Josh Shirley	.10	.30
67 Barry Brunetti	.40	1.00
68 Spencer Ware	.15	.40
69 Austin Hinder	.15	.40
70 Mike Hull	.20	.50
71 Andrew Donnal	.10	.30
72 Keanon Lowe	.10	.30
73 Jimmy Gjere	.10	.30
74 Cedric Ogbuehi	.10	.30
75 Jeff Whitaker	.10	.30
76 Damien Robinson	.10	.30
77 Zach Zwinak	.25	.60
78 Christian Bryant	.20	.50
79 A.J. Derby	.25	.60
80 Sione Potoae	.10	.30
81 Cassius Marsh	.10	.30
82 Quinton Spain	.10	.30
83 Dior Mathis	.10	.30
84 Calvin Barnett	.10	.30
85 C.J. Mosley	.10	.30
86 Brandon Linder	.10	.30
87 Blake Lueders	.10	.30
88 Traylon Shead	.15	.40
89 Ross Apo	.15	.40
90 Nate Askew	.15	.40
91 Joe Boisture	.10	.30
92 Chance Carter	.10	.30
93 Austin Collinsworth	.30	.75
94 V.J. Fehoko	.10	.30
95 Cade Foster	.20	.50
96 Victor Hampton	.10	.30
97 Christian Lombard	.10	.30
98 Cole Marcoux	.15	.40
99 Michael Palardy	.10	.30
100 Sean Parker	.10	.30
101 Will Hagerup	.10	.30
102 Matt Darr	.10	.30
103 Arrelious Benn Alum	.50	1.25
104 Eric Berry Alum	.50	1.25
105 Jimmy Clausen Alum	.50	1.25
106 Perrish Cox Alum	.40	1.00
107 Anthony Davis Alum	.40	1.00
108 Everson Giffen Alum	.50	1.25
109 Brandon Graham Alum	.40	1.00
110 Aaron Hernandez Alum	.75	2.00
111 Stafon Johnson Alum	.50	1.25
112 Sergio Kindle Alum	.50	1.25
113 Taylor Mays Alum	.50	1.25
114 Gerald McCoy Alum	.50	1.25
115 Joe McKnight Alum	.50	1.25
116 Michael Oher Alum	.40	1.00
117 Brian Price Alum	.50	1.25
118 Ricky Sapp Alum	.40	1.00
119 Jordan Shipley Alum	.50	1.25
120 Jevan Snead Alum	.50	1.25
121 Brandon Spikes Alum	.50	1.25
122 C.J. Spiller Alum	.75	2.00
123 Ndamukong Suh Alum	1.00	2.50
124 Tim Tebow Alum	2.00	5.00

2010 Razor Army All-American Bowl Autographs

ONE AUTO OR MEM CARD PER PACK
*GOLD/20: 1X TO 2.5X BASIC AUTO
*GOLD/20: .6X TO 1.5X BASIC AUTO ALUM

AB1 Anthony Barr/169*	4.00	10.00
AC1 Austin Collinsworth/169*	8.00	20.00
AD1 Ahmad Dixon/214*	3.00	8.00
AD2 Andrew Donnal/184*	3.00	8.00
AH1 Austin Hinder/199*	4.00	10.00
AJD A.J. Derby/184*	6.00	15.00
AK1 Arie Kouandjio/244*	3.00	8.00
AN1 Andrew Norwell/184*	3.00	8.00
AR1 Andrew Rodriguez/184*	5.00	12.00
BB1 Barry Brunetti/199*	10.00	25.00
BL1 Brandon Linder/182*	3.00	8.00
BL2 Blake Lueders/184*	3.00	8.00
BW1 Brandon Willis/184*	3.00	8.00
CB1 Calvin Barnett/189*	3.00	8.00
CB2 Christian Bryant/184*	5.00	12.00
CC1 Chance Carter/184*	3.00	8.00
CC2 Cullen Christian/184*	3.00	8.00
CF1 Cade Foster/184*	5.00	12.00
CG1 Christian Green/199*	4.00	10.00
CJF C.J. Fiedorowicz/167*	4.00	10.00
CJM C.J. Mosley/184*	3.00	8.00
CJS C.J. Spiller ALUM/174*	30.00	60.00
CL1 Christian Lombard/184*	3.00	8.00
CM1 Cassius Marsh/214*	3.00	8.00
CM2 Chris Martin/169*	3.00	8.00
CM3 Cole Marcoux/244*	4.00	10.00
CO1 Cedric Ogbuehi/214*	3.00	8.00
CI1 Christian Thomas/169*	3.00	8.00
CT2 Carlos Thompson/184*	6.00	15.00
CW1 Curtis White/184*	3.00	8.00
CW2 Cecil Whiteside/168*	3.00	8.00
CW3 Connor Wood/199*	5.00	12.00
DB1 Dillon Baxter/169*	10.00	25.00
DE1 Dominic Espinosa/214*	3.00	8.00
DJM D.J. Morgan/168*	5.00	12.00
DM1 Dior Mathis/184*	3.00	8.00
DR1 Damien Robinson/214*	3.00	8.00
DW1 DeAndrew White/199*	4.00	10.00
DW2 Demetrius Wright/214*	3.00	8.00
FF1 Ego Ferguson/168*	3.00	8.00
EG1 Everson Giffen/174*	4.00	10.00
ER1 Eric Reid/184*	3.00	8.00
GC1 Gerald Christian/184*	3.00	8.00
GK1 Gabe King/184*	3.00	8.00
GS1 Garrison Smith/213*	3.00	8.00
IM1 Ivan McCartney/214*	3.00	8.00
JB1 Joe Boisture/169*	5.00	12.00
JC1 Jimmy Clausen ALUM/74*	20.00	50.00
JG1 Jimmy Gjere/214*	3.00	8.00
JH1 Jake Heaps/169*	12.00	30.00
JJ1 Jackson Jeffcoat/169*	5.00	12.00
JM1 Jake Matthews/213*	3.00	8.00
JM2 Justin McCay/199*	3.00	8.00
JS1 Josh Shirley/182*	3.00	8.00
JS2 Jacques Smith/183*	3.00	8.00
JS3 Jordan Shipley ALUM/174*	10.00	25.00
JW1 Jaylen Watkins/184*	3.00	8.00
JW2 Jeff Whitaker/184*	3.00	8.00
JW3 Jarrick Williams/184*	3.00	8.00
KA1 Keenan Allen/165*	5.00	12.00
KF1 Khairi Fortt/169*	3.00	8.00
KL1 Keanon Lowe/184*	3.00	8.00
KP1 Kyle Prater/214*	12.00	30.00
KQ1 Kelcy Quarles/184*	3.00	8.00
LA1 Latwan Anderson/198*	3.00	8.00
LS1 Lache Seastrunk/198*	10.00	25.00
MA1 Markeith Ambles/199*	5.00	12.00
MB1 Martavis Bryant/167*	4.00	10.00
MD1 Matt Darr/274*	3.00	8.00
ME1 Matt Elam/169*	5.00	12.00
MF1 Marquis Flowers/244*	3.00	8.00
MH1 Mike Hull/184*	5.00	12.00
MJ1 Matt James/184*	3.00	8.00
MJ2 Malcolm Jones/169*	4.00	10.00
ML1 Marcus Lattimore/169*	15.00	40.00
ML2 Marcus Lucas/169*	4.00	10.00
MP1 Michael Palardy/184*	3.00	8.00
NA1 Nate Askew/214*	4.00	10.00
ND1 Nick Demien/184*	3.00	8.00
NF1 Nick Forbes/214*	3.00	8.00
OO1 Owa Odighizuwa/198*	3.00	8.00
PJ1 Paul Jones/199*	4.00	10.00
QS1 Quinton Spain/184*	3.00	8.00
RA1 Ross Apo/213*	4.00	10.00
RC1 Robert Crisp/169*	3.00	8.00
RH1 Ricky Heimuli/214*	3.00	8.00
RP1 Ronald Powell/199*	10.00	25.00
RW1 Reggie Wilson/199*	3.00	8.00
RW2 Robert Woods/199*	4.00	10.00
SC1 Shon Coleman/214*	3.00	8.00
SF1 Sharrif Floyd/199*	5.00	12.00
SH1 Seantrel Henderson/199*	5.00	12.00
SP1 Sean Parker/184*	3.00	8.00
SP2 Shakim Phillips/229*	4.00	10.00
SP3 Sione Potoae/184*	3.00	8.00
SR1 Silas Redd/199*	4.00	10.00
SW1 Spencer Ware/169*	4.00	10.00
TH1 Trey Hopkins/214*	3.00	8.00

TJ1 Tevin Jackson/199*	3.00	8.00
TJ2 Tony Jefferson/214*	3.00	8.00
TM1 Taylor Mays/174*	8.00	20.00
TR1 Trovon Reed/199*	3.00	8.00
TS1 Traylon Shead/183*	4.00	10.00
VH1 Victor Hampton/184*	3.00	8.00
VJF V.J. Fehoko/213*	3.00	8.00
WH1 Will Hagerup/184*	3.00	8.00
ZZ1 Zach Zwinak/184*	6.00	15.00

2010 Razor Army All-American Bowl Jersey

JERSEY PRINT RUN 150 SER.#'d SETS
*PATCH/25: 1X TO 2.5X BASIC JSY/150

JSAB1 Anthony Barr	3.00	8.00
JSAC1 Austin Collinsworth	4.00	10.00
JSAH1 Austin Hinder	3.00	8.00
JSBB1 Barry Brunetti	4.00	10.00
JSCG1 Christian Green	3.00	8.00
JSCJF C.J. Fiedorowicz	3.00	8.00
JSCM2 Chris Martin	3.00	8.00
JSCT1 Christian Thomas	3.00	8.00
JSCW2 Cecil Whiteside	3.00	8.00
JSCW3 Connor Wood	3.00	8.00
JSDB1 Dillon Baxter	4.00	10.00
JSDJM D.J. Morgan	3.00	8.00
JSDW1 DeAndrew White	3.00	8.00
JSEF1 Ego Ferguson	3.00	8.00
JSJB1 Joe Boisture	3.00	8.00
JSJH1 Jake Heaps	6.00	15.00
JSJJ1 Jackson Jeffcoat	3.00	8.00
JSJM2 Justin McCay	3.00	8.00
JSKA1 Keenan Allen	3.00	8.00
JSKF1 Khairi Fortt	3.00	8.00
JSLA1 Latwan Anderson	3.00	8.00
JSLS1 Lache Seastrunk	5.00	12.00
JSMA1 Markeith Ambles	3.00	8.00
JSMB1 Martavis Bryant	3.00	8.00
JSME1 Matt Elam	3.00	8.00
JSMJ2 Malcolm Jones	3.00	8.00
JSML1 Marcus Lattimore	3.00	8.00
JSML2 Marcus Lucas	3.00	8.00
JSOO1 Owa Odighizuwa	3.00	8.00
JSPJ1 Paul Jones	3.00	8.00
JSRC1 Robert Crisp	3.00	8.00
JSRP1 Ronald Powell	5.00	12.00
JSRW1 Reggie Wilson	3.00	8.00
JSRW2 Robert Woods	3.00	8.00
JSSF1 Sharrif Floyd	3.00	8.00
JSSH1 Seantrel Henderson	3.00	8.00
JSSP2 Shakim Phillips	3.00	8.00
JSSR1 Silas Redd	4.00	10.00
JSSW1 Spencer Ware	3.00	8.00
JSTJ1 Tevin Jackson	3.00	8.00
JSTR1 Trovon Reed	3.00	8.00

2010 Razor Army All-American Bowl Tour Autographs Silver

SILVER PRINT RUN 25 SER.#'d SETS

AB1 Anthony Barr	10.00	25.00
AC1 Austin Collinsworth	20.00	50.00
AD1 Ahmad Dixon	8.00	20.00
AD2 Andrew Donnal	8.00	20.00
AH1 Austin Hinder	10.00	25.00
AJD A.J. Derby	15.00	40.00
AN1 Andrew Norwell	8.00	20.00
AR1 Andrew Rodriguez	12.00	30.00
BB1 Barry Brunetti	25.00	60.00
BL1 Brandon Linder	8.00	20.00
BL2 Blake Lueders	8.00	20.00
BW1 Brandon Willis	8.00	20.00
CB1 Calvin Barnett	8.00	20.00
CB2 Christian Bryant	12.00	30.00
CC1 Chance Carter	8.00	20.00
CC2 Cullen Christian	8.00	20.00
CF1 Cade Foster	12.00	30.00
CG1 Christian Green	10.00	25.00
CJF C.J. Fiedorowicz	10.00	25.00
CJM C.J. Mosley	8.00	20.00
CL1 Christian Lombard	8.00	20.00
CM1 Cassius Marsh	8.00	20.00
CM2 Chris Martin	8.00	20.00
CO1 Cedric Ogbuehi	8.00	20.00
CT1 Christian Thomas	8.00	20.00
CT2 Carlos Thompson	15.00	40.00
CW1 Curtis White	8.00	20.00
CW2 Cecil Whiteside	8.00	20.00
CW3 Connor Wood	12.00	30.00
DB1 Dillon Baxter	25.00	60.00
DE1 Dominic Espinosa	8.00	20.00
DJM D.J. Morgan	12.00	30.00
DM1 Dior Mathis	8.00	20.00
DR1 Damien Robinson	8.00	20.00
DW1 DeAndrew White	10.00	25.00
DW2 Demetrius Wright	8.00	20.00
EF1 Ego Ferguson	8.00	20.00
ER1 Eric Reid	8.00	20.00
GC1 Gerald Christian	8.00	20.00
GK1 Gabe King	8.00	20.00
GS1 Garrison Smith	8.00	20.00
IM1 Ivan McCartney	8.00	20.00
JB1 Joe Boisture	12.00	30.00
JG1 Jimmy Gjere	8.00	20.00
JH1 Jake Heaps	30.00	80.00
JJ1 Jackson Jeffcoat	12.00	30.00
JM1 Jake Matthews	8.00	20.00
JM2 Justin McCay	8.00	20.00
JS1 Josh Shirley	8.00	20.00
JS2 Jacques Smith	8.00	20.00
JW1 Jaylen Watkins	8.00	20.00
JW2 Jeff Whitaker	8.00	20.00
JW3 Jarrick Williams	8.00	20.00
KA1 Keenan Allen	12.00	30.00
KF1 Khairi Fortt	8.00	20.00
KL1 Keanon Lowe	8.00	20.00
KP1 Kyle Prater	30.00	80.00
KQ1 Kelcy Quarles	8.00	20.00
LA1 Latwan Anderson	8.00	20.00
LS1 Lache Seastrunk	25.00	60.00
MA1 Markeith Ambles	12.00	30.00
MB1 Martavis Bryant	10.00	25.00
MD1 Matt Darr	8.00	20.00
ME1 Matt Elam	12.00	30.00
MF1 Marquis Flowers	8.00	20.00
MH1 Mike Hull	12.00	30.00
MJ1 Matt James	8.00	20.00
MJ2 Malcolm Jones	10.00	25.00
ML1 Marcus Lattimore	40.00	100.00
ML2 Marcus Lucas	10.00	25.00
MP1 Michael Palardy	8.00	20.00
NA1 Nate Askew	10.00	25.00
ND1 Nick Demien	8.00	20.00
NF1 Nick Forbes	8.00	20.00
OO1 Owa Odighizuwa	8.00	20.00
PJ1 Paul Jones	10.00	25.00
QS1 Quinton Spain	8.00	20.00
RA1 Ross Apo	10.00	25.00
RC1 Robert Crisp	8.00	20.00
RH1 Ricky Heimuli	8.00	20.00
RP1 Ronald Powell	25.00	60.00
RW1 Reggie Wilson	8.00	20.00
RW2 Robert Woods	10.00	25.00
SC1 Shon Coleman	8.00	20.00
SF1 Sharrif Floyd	12.00	30.00
SH1 Seantrel Henderson	12.00	30.00
SP1 Sean Parker	8.00	20.00
SP3 Sione Potoae	8.00	20.00
SR1 Silas Redd	10.00	25.00
SW1 Spencer Ware	10.00	25.00
TH1 Trey Hopkins	8.00	20.00
TJ1 Tevin Jackson	8.00	20.00
TJ2 Tony Jefferson	8.00	20.00
TR1 Trovon Reed	8.00	20.00
TS1 Traylon Shead	10.00	25.00
VH1 Victor Hampton	8.00	20.00
WH1 Will Hagerup	8.00	20.00
ZZ1 Zach Zwinak	15.00	40.00

1990 Rice Aetna

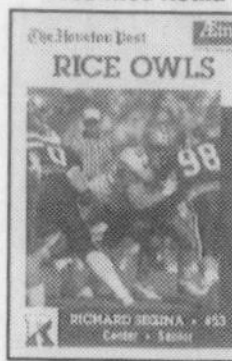

This 12-card standard-size set was sponsored by The Houston Post and Aetna Life and Casualty. The cards feature color action player photos with a navy-blue shadow border on a white card face. The player's name, uniform number, position, and classification appear in the shadow border at the bottom. The team name and sponsor logos are at the top. The backs feature navy-blue print on a white background and include biographical information, player profile, and anti-drug or alcohol messages under the heading "Tips from the Owls". The cards are unnumbered and checklisted below in alphabetical order. The sole distribution of the cards was as giveaways to fans at the Owls' home game against Texas; reportedly 25,000 sets were given away.

COMPLETE SET (12)	4.80	12.00
1 O.J. Brigance	.60	1.50
2 Trevor Cobb	.60	1.50
3 Tim Fitzpatrick	.40	1.00
4 Fred Goldsmith CO	.60	1.50
5 David Griffin	.40	1.00
6 Eric Henley	.60	1.50
7 Donald Hollas	.80	2.00
8 Richard Segina	.40	1.00
9 Matt Sign	.40	1.00
10 Bill Stone	.40	1.00
11 Trey Teichelman UER (Misspelled Tichelman on front and back)	.40	1.00
12 Alonzo Williams	.40	1.00

1991 Rice Aetna

Sponsored by the Houston Post and Aetna Life and Casualty, these 12 standard-size cards feature color action player photos with gray inner borders and white outer borders. The player's name, uniform number, position, and class appear within a navy blue stripe below the photo. The words "Rice Owls '91" appear within a navy blue stripe above the picture. The backs feature navy-colored lettering on a white background and include biographical information, player profile, and anti-drug and alcohol messages under the heading "Tips from the Owls." At the lower right the cards are labeled "series 2." The cards are unnumbered and checklisted below in alphabetical order. The sole distribution of the cards was as giveaways to fans at the Owls' home game against Texas A and M; reportedly 25,000 sets were given away.

COMPLETE SET (12)	4.80	12.00
1 Mike Appelbaum	.40	1.00
2 Louis Balady	.40	1.00
3 Nathan Bennett	.40	1.00
4 Trevor Cobb	.60	1.50
5 Herschel Crowe	.40	1.00
6 David Griffin	.40	1.00
7 Eric Henley	.60	1.50
8 Matt Sign	.40	1.00
9 Larry Stuppy	.40	1.00
10 Trey Teichelman	.40	1.00
11 Alonzo Williams	.40	1.00
12 Greg Willig	.40	1.00

1992 Rice Taco Cabana

This 12-card set was sponsored by The Houston Post and Taco Cabana, and their company logos appear in the top white border. The fronts feature color action player photos bordered in white. A navy blue bar above the picture carries the words "Rice Owls '92", while a navy blue bar below the picture has the school logo and player information. The backs feature navy-blue print on a white background and include biographical information, player profile, and anti-drug or alcohol messages under the heading "Tips from the Owls". The cards are unnumbered and checklisted below in alphabetical order. The sole distribution of the cards was as giveaways to fans at the Owls' home game against Texas; reportedly 25,000 sets were given away.

COMPLETE SET (12)	4.80	12.00
1 Shawn Alberding	.40	1.00
2 Mike Appelbaum	.40	1.00
3 Louis Balady	.40	1.00
4 Nathan Bennett	.40	1.00
5 Trevor Cobb	.60	1.50
6 Josh LaRocca	.40	1.00
7 Jimmy Lee	.50	1.25
8 Corey Seymour	.40	1.00
9 Matt Sign	.40	1.00
10 Emmett Waldron	.50	1.25
11 Alonzo Williams	.40	1.00
12 Taco Cabana (Advertisement)	.40	1.00

1993 Rice Taco Cabana

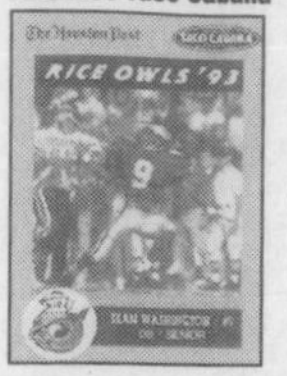

This 12-card standard size set was sponsored by The Houston Post and Taco Cabana. The fronts feature color action player photos against a gray card face. The year and team name are shown in white lettering within a blue bar above the photo. The player's name, jersey number, position, and class are printed in white lettering within a blue bar at the bottom. The horizontal white backs carry the player's name, position, jersey number, height, weight, and hometown at the top, followed below by career highlights and "Tips from the Owls." The cards are unnumbered and checklisted below in alphabetical order. Bert Emanuel is the key player in this set.

COMPLETE SET (12)	6.00	15.00
1 Nathan Bennett	.40	1.00
2 Cris Cooley	.50	1.25
3 Bert Emanuel	2.40	6.00
4 Jimmy Golden	.40	1.00
5 Tom Hetherington	.40	1.00
6 Ed Howard	.40	1.00
7 Jimmy Lee	.50	1.25
8 Corey Seymour	.40	1.00
9 Clemente Torres	.40	1.00
10 Emmett Waldron	.50	1.25
11 Sean Washington	.40	1.00
12 Taco Cabana Ad Card	.40	1.00

1994 Rice

COMPLETE SET (18)	7.50	15.00
1 Chris Cooley	.40	1.00
2 Byron Coston	.40	1.00
3 Bobby Dixon	.40	1.00
4 Yoncy Edmonds	.40	1.00
5 Brynton Goynes	.40	1.00
6 Larry Izzo	.50	1.25
7 Ndukwe Kalu	.40	1.00
8 Josh LaRocca	.40	1.00
9 Jimmy Lee	.40	1.00
10 Jeff Sowells	.40	1.00
11 Emmett Waldron	.40	1.00
12 1934 SWC Champions A.M. Red Bale	.40	1.00
13 1937 SWC Champions Frank Steen	.40	1.00
14 1946 SWC Champions Weldon Humble	.40	1.00
15 1949 SWC Champions Froggie Williams	.40	1.00
16 1953 SWC Champions Dicky Moegle being tackled by Tommy Lewis	.40	1.00
17 1957 SWC Champions Buddy Dial	.40	1.00
18 Cover Card	.40	1.00

1999 Rice

COMPLETE SET (12)	5.00	10.00
1 Rod Beavan	.40	1.00
2 Dan Dawson	.40	1.00
3 Neal Gray	.40	1.00
4 Anthony Griffin	.40	1.00
5 Wesley Kubesch	.40	1.00
6 Travis Ortega	.40	1.00
7 Chad Richardson	.40	1.00
8 Larry Ruffin	.40	1.00
9 Adrian Sadler	.40	1.00
10 Judd Smith	.40	1.00
11 Victor Young Scott Grimes	.40	1.00
12 Ken Hatfield CO	.50	1.25

2000 Rice

COMPLETE SET (12)	5.00	10.00
1 Rod Beavan	.40	1.00
2 Leroy Bradley	.40	1.00
3 Derek Crabtree	.40	1.00
4 Jarrett Erwin	.40	1.00
5 Anthony Griffin	.40	1.00
6 Jason Hebert	.40	1.00
7 Jake Jackson	.40	1.00
8 Josh McMillan	.40	1.00
9 Travis Ortega	.40	1.00
10 Adrian Sadler	.40	1.00
11 Aaron Sandoval	.40	1.00
12 Coaching Staff	.40	1.00

1910 Richmond College Silks S23

These colorful silks were issued around 1910 by Richmond Straight Cut Cigarettes. Each measures roughly 4" by 5 1/2" and are often called "College Flag, Seal, Song, and Yell" due to the content found on each one. More importantly to most sports collectors is the image found in the lower right hand bottom corner. A few feature a mainstream sports' subject such as a generic player or piece of equipment, while most include a realistic image of the school's mascot or image of the founder or the school's namesake.

7 Chicago FB Player	75.00	150.00
29 Pennsylvania Football	60.00	120.00

1995 Roox HS

This 39-card set features football players of various Illinois high schools. Cards 35-39 were not issued. The fronts display color player photos with the player's name and school in a brown marblized stripe at the bottom. The backs carry the player's name, position, biographical information, and a brief Positive Image Point.

COMPLETE SET (39)	8.00	20.00
1 Wesley Crane	.40	1.00
2 Nii Hammond	.40	1.00
3 Daniel Anglin	.40	1.00
4 Ronnie Williams	.40	1.00
5 Harold Blackmon	.40	1.00
6 Tim Lavery	.40	1.00
7 Babatunde Ridley	.40	1.00
8 Fred Wakefield	.50	1.25
9 Bobie Singleton	.40	1.00
10 Chris Janek	.40	1.00
11 Steffan Nicholson	.40	1.00
12 Scott Mullen	.40	1.00
13 Jason Scherer	.40	1.00
14 Kevin Beard, Jr.	.40	1.00
15 Michael Sergeant	.40	1.00
16 Marcus Smith	.40	1.00
17 Eric Garrett	.40	1.00
18 Chris Pickett	.40	1.00
19 Michael Burden	.40	1.00
20 Nick Abruzzo	.40	1.00
21 Stanley Williams	.40	1.00
22 Joey Goodspeed	1.50	4.00
23 Stephen Olien	.40	1.00
24 R.J. Luke	.40	1.00
25 Matt Kelly	.40	1.00
26 Ricardo King	.50	1.25
27 Tamaine Hills	.40	1.00
28 Michael Yarborough	.40	1.00
29 Brian Schmitz	.40	1.00
30 Joe Carroll	.40	1.00
31 Roy Sessions	.40	1.00
32 Marcus Hood	.40	1.00
33 Lorenzo Smith	.50	1.25
34 Karlton Thomas	.40	1.00
40 Carlos Polk	.75	2.00
41 Montinez Williams	.40	1.00
42 Neil Carroll	.40	1.00
43 Shaka Jones	.40	1.00
NNO Cover Card blankbacked	.02	.10

1996 Roox Shrine Bowl HS

Roox Corp. released this 74-card set commemorating the 59th Shrine Bowl between North Carolina and South Carolina High Schools. The cards feature color player photos of members of both teams and measure slightly larger than standard size at 2 5/8" by 3 1/2". Although the cards are not numbered as one set, they are commonly sold as a set of 74.

COMPLETE SET (74)	30.00	50.00
NC1 Rocky Hunt	.40	1.00
NC2 Cam Holland	.40	1.00
NC3 Derrick Chambers	.40	1.00
NC4 Ramondo North	.40	1.00
NC5 Bo Manis	.40	1.00
NC6 Antonio Graham	.40	1.00
NC7 Clayton White	.40	1.00
NC8 Billy Young	.40	1.00
NC9 Josh Tucker	.75	2.00
NC10 Rod Emery	.40	1.00
NC11 Matt Burdick	.40	1.00
NC12 Chad Gathings	.40	1.00
NC13 Brian Ray	.40	1.00
NC14 Brandon Spoon	.50	1.25
NC15 Dauntae Finger	.40	1.00
NC16 Raymond Massey	.40	1.00
NC17 Damien Bennett	.40	1.00
NC18 Bennie Griffin	.40	1.00
NC19 Randolph Galloway	.40	1.00
NC20 Titcus Pettigrew	1.00	2.50
NC21 Chris McCoy	.40	1.00
NC22 Virgil Johnson	.40	1.00
NC23 Marcus Reaves	.40	1.00
NC24 Scottie Stepp	.40	1.00
NC25 Julius Bell	.40	1.00
NC26 Robert Williams	.50	1.25
NC27 Rashad Burke	.40	1.00
NC28 Michael Cox	.40	1.00
NC29 Kwabena Greene	.40	1.00
NC30 Tim Burgess	.40	1.00
NC31 Scott Smith	.40	1.00
NC32 Steven Lindsey	.40	1.00
NC33 Charles Berry	.40	1.00
NC34 Chris Satterfield	.40	1.00
NC35 Eric Leak	.40	1.00
NC36 Nick Means MG	.40	1.00
SC1 Ikie Curry	.40	1.00
SC2 Shaun Ellis	1.50	4.00
SC3 Zabeion McRoy	.40	1.00
SC4 Will McLaurin	.40	1.00
SC5 Jarvis Davis	.40	1.00
SC6 Justin Hill	.40	1.00
SC7 Antwon Black	.40	1.00
SC8 Justin Watts	.40	1.00
SC9 Ray Mazyck	.40	1.00
SC10 Chris McGee	.40	1.00
SC11 Stan Manning	.40	1.00
SC12 Micale Chandler	.40	1.00
SC13 Deveron Harper	.40	1.00
SC14 Brian Wofford	.40	1.00
SC15 Tim Winfield	.40	1.00
SC16 Donovan Norman	.40	1.00
SC17 Chip Brogden	.40	1.00
SC18 Seth Stoddard	.40	1.00
SC19 Nakia Adderson	.40	1.00
SC20 Adam Varnadore	.40	1.00
SC21 Lance Legree	.40	1.00
SC22 Scott Greer	.40	1.00
SC23 B.J. Little	.40	1.00
SC24 Kinte Wilson	.40	1.00
SC25 Rod Joseph	.40	1.00
SC26 Benji Wallace	.40	1.00
SC27 Don Moore	.40	1.00
SC28 Cecil Caldwell	.40	1.00
SC29 Thomas Washington	.40	1.00
SC30 Rory Gallman	.40	1.00
SC31 Courtney Brown	4.00	10.00
SC32 Jermale Kelly	.40	1.00
SC33 Walsh Dingle	.40	1.00
SC34 Mal Lawyer	.40	1.00
SC35 Will Gainey	.40	1.00
SC36 Bird Bourne MG	.40	1.00
NNO South Carolina Title Card	.02	.10
NNO North Carolina Title Card	.02	.10

1996 Roox Prep Stars AT/EA/SE

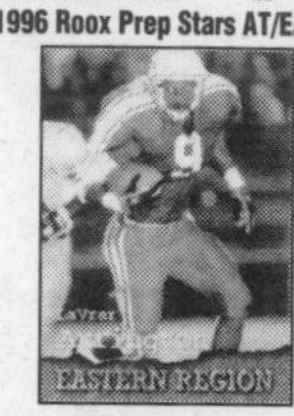

This 143-card standard size boxed set was produced by Roox featuring high school players that played in 1996, and includes standouts from the following states: Alabama, Arkansas, Canada, Connecticut, Delaware, the District of Columbia, Florida, Georgia, Kentucky, Louisiana, Maryland, Massachusetts, Mississippi, New Jersey, New York, North Carolina, Pennsylvania, South Carolina, Virginia, and West Virginia. Reportedly, 1000 sets were produced.

COMPLETE SET (143)	20.00	50.00
AT1 David Garrard	5.00	12.00
AT2 Erik Lipton	.20	.50
AT3 Tim Olmstead	.30	.75
AT4 Craig Powers	.20	.50
AT5 Jason Thompson	.20	.50
AT6 William Combs	.20	.50
AT7 Gil Harris	.20	.50
AT8 Golden Myers	.20	.50
AT9 Chris Willetts	.20	.50
AT10 Chris Ramseur	.20	.50
AT11 Anthony Sanders	.20	.50
AT12 Ali Culpepper	.30	.75
AT13 Dominique Stevenson	.30	.75
AT14 Rondell White	.20	.50
AT15 David Foster	.20	.50
AT16 Luis Moreno	.20	.50
AT17 Sherman Scott	.20	.50
AT18 Doug Bost	.20	.50
AT19 Terry Denoon	.20	.50
AT20 Dave Johnson	.20	.50
AT21 Dain Lewis	.20	.50
AT22 Chris McDaniel	.20	.50
AT23 Chadwick Scott	.20	.50
AT24 Brian Scott	.30	.75
AT25 Bobby Graham	.20	.50
AT26 Steve Shipp	.30	.75
AT27 Jimmy Caldwell	.20	.50
AT28 Rico Gladden	.20	.50
AT29 Evan Kay	.20	.50
AT30 Rashad Slade	.20	.50
AT31 Nate Krill	.30	.75
AT32 Chris Luzar	.30	.75
AT33 Graham Manley	.20	.50
AT34 Neely Page	.20	.50
AT35 David Pugh	.30	.75
AT36 Jason Cox	.20	.50
AT37 Jason McFeasters	.20	.50
AT38 John Miller	.20	.50
AT39 Bobby Dameron	.20	.50
AT40 Keith Esteppe	.20	.50
AT41 Tim Falls	.50	1.25
AT42 Jeman Jacobs	.20	.50
AT43 Scott McLain	.20	.50
AT44 Ty Hunt	.20	.50
AT45 Jeff Chambers	.20	.50
AT46 Nick Gilliland	.20	.50
AT47 Buddy Young	.20	.50
AT48 DeAngelo Lloyd	.40	1.00
AT49 Ben Bacot	.20	.50
AT50 Corey Nelson	.20	.50
AT51 Jimi Massey	.20	.50
AT52 Sam Scott	.20	.50
AT53 Mike Winfield	.20	.50
AT54 Jayvon McKinney	.20	.50
EA1 Luke Richmond	.20	.50
EA2 Mike Gaydosz	.20	.50
EA3 Eddie Campbell	.20	.50
EA4 Dan Ellis	.40	1.00
EA5 Darin Miller	.20	.50
EA6 Ravon Anderson	.20	.50
EA7 Jason Murray	.20	.50
EA8 Brett Aurilla	.20	.50
EA9 Tremayne Bendross	.20	.50
EA10 Sean Fisher	.20	.50
EA11 J.R. Johnson	.20	.50
EA12 Victor Strader	.20	.50
EA13 Dennis Thomas	.20	.50
EA14 Quentin Harris	.20	.50
EA15 Reggie Garrett	.20	.50
EA16 Patrick O'Brien	.20	.50
EA17 Guenter Kryszon	.20	.50
EA18 Kareem McKenzie	.60	1.50
EA19 Martin Bibla	.40	1.00
EA20 Joe Collins	.20	.50
EA21 John Kuchmek	.20	.50
EA22 Greg Ransom	.30	.75
EA23 Tim Sample	.20	.50
EA24 Marty Wensel	.20	.50
EA25 Jack Bloom	.20	.50
EA26 Nate Ritzenhaler	.20	.50
EA27 Charley Powell	.20	.50
EA28 Ron Graham	.40	1.00
EA29 Joe McKinney	.30	.75
EA30 Jeremiah Clarke	.20	.50
EA31 Frank Fodera	.20	.50
EA32 John Yura	.20	.50
EA33 Jonathon Harris	.20	.50
EA34 Ben Martin	.20	.50
EA35 Coy Wire UER name misspelled Cory)	.75	2.00
EA36 Sean Bell	.20	.50
EA37 Brad Eissler	.20	.50
EA38 LaVar Arrington UER (name misspelled LaVrar)	4.00	10.00
SE1 Kenny Kelly	.40	1.00
SE2 Daniel Cobb	.30	.75
SE3 Phillip Deas	.20	.50
SE4 Adam Cox	.30	.75
SE5 Ron Johnson RBK	.20	.50
SE6 Tommy Banks	.20	.50
SE7 Sherrod Dickson	.20	.50
SE8 Davey Ford Jr.	.20	.50
SE9 Travis Henry	2.00	5.00
SE10 William McCray	.20	.50
SE11 Dan Morgan	1.50	4.00
SE12 Adrian Peterson	1.50	4.00
SE13 Darrell Jackson	2.50	6.00
SE14 Orlando Iglesias	.20	.50
SE15 Boo Williams	.60	1.50
SE16 Matt Wright	.20	.50
SE17 Fred Weary C	.60	1.50
SE18 Braxton Anderson	.20	.50
SE19 Romaro Miller	.40	1.00
SE20 Ronald Boldin	.30	.75
SE21 Otis Duhart	.20	.50
SE22 Jabari Ellison	.20	.50
SE23 Tom Hillard	.30	.75
SE24 Ryan Smith	.40	1.00
SE25 Erik Strange	.30	.75
SE26 Sam Matthews	.30	.75
SE27 Thomas Pittman	.30	.75
SE28 Andrew Zow	.60	1.50
SE29 Gerard Warren	.75	2.00
SE30 Adrian Wilson	.30	.75
SE31 Char-Ron Dorsey	.30	.75
SE32 Kennard Ellis	.30	.75
SE33 Jabari Holloway	.60	1.50
SE34 Melvin Richey	.20	.50
SE35 Willie Sams	.20	.50
SE36 Josh Weldon	.40	1.00
SE37 Travis Carroll	.30	.75
SE38 Cortez Allen	.20	.50
SE39 Andra Davis LB	.60	1.50
SE40 Matt Miller	.20	.50
SE41 Whit Smith	.30	.75
SE42 Stanford Simmons	.20	.50
SE43 Tony Dixon	.60	1.50
SE44 Clifton Robinson	.20	.50
SE45 Hugh Holmes	.20	.50
SE46 Abdul Howard	.20	.50
SE47 Rob Pate	.20	.50
SE48 Matt Howard	.20	.50
SE49 Terrence Trammell	.20	.50
SE50 Earl Williams	.20	.50
NNO Jesse Palmer	.75	2.00

1996 Roox Prep Stars C/W

This 144-card standard size boxed set was produced by Roox featuring high school players that played in 1996, and includes standouts from the following states: Arizona, California, Colorado, Hawaii, Idaho, Kansas, Missouri, Nebraska, Nevada, New Mexico, Oklahoma, Oregon, Utah, Washington, and Wyoming. Reportedly, 1000 sets were produced.

COMPLETE SET (144)	15.00	40.00
C1 B.J. Tiger	.30	.75
C2 Ryan Lown	.20	.50
C3 Sherard Poteete	.20	.50
C4 Eric Gooden	.20	.50
C5 Ken Alsop	.20	.50
C6 Levi Mehl	.20	.50
C7 Justin Galimore	.20	.50
C8 Dallas Davis	.20	.50
C9 Ahmed Kabba	.20	.50
C10 Aaron Lockett	.60	1.50
C11 Kevin Wendling	.20	.50
C12 Ryan Humphrey	.20	.50
C13 Brandon Stephens	.20	.50
C14 Dan Engel	.20	.50
C15 Jared Holland	.20	.50
C16 Tango McCauley	.20	.50
C17 Kyle Jenson	.20	.50
C18 Kody Hergert	.20	.50
C19 Jon Rutherford	.20	.50
C20 John Teasdale	.20	.50
C21 Steve Wiedower	.20	.50
C22 Joshua Graham	.20	.50
C23 John Robertson	.20	.50
C24 Austin Lee	.20	.50
C25 Brandon Washington	.20	.50
C26 Andy Wisne	.20	.50
C27 Bary Holleyman	.20	.50
C28 Darren Palladino	.20	.50
C29 Mike Burke	.20	.50
C30 Thomas Fortune	.20	.50
C31 Pete Battisti	.20	.50
C32 Monty Beisel	.75	2.00
C33 John Paul Keserich	.20	.50
C34 Garrett Masters	.20	.50
C35 Bubba Babb	.20	.50
C36 Marlon Guess	.20	.50
C37 Stanley Peters	.20	.50
C38 Harold Burgess	.20	.50
C39 Courtney Hysaw	.20	.50
C40 Darcey Levy	.20	.50
C41 Zach Magalei	.20	.50
C42 Drew Smith	.20	.50
C43 Jeff Ferguson	.20	.50
C44 Eric Rosel	.20	.50
C45 Jeremy Toles	.20	.50
C46 Jason Krause	.20	.50
C47 Jeff Gloy	.20	.50
C48 Brandan Kramer	.20	.50
C49 Marcques Spivey	.30	.75
W1 Randy Fasani	.75	2.00
W2 Todd Mortensen	.30	.75
W3 Spencer Brinton	.20	.50
W4 Greg Cicero	.20	.50
W5 Scott McEwan	.20	.50
W6 Drew Miller	.20	.50
W7 Austin Moherman	.20	.50
W8 David Priestley	.60	1.50
W9 David Carr	5.00	12.00
W10 Chris Czernek	.20	.50
W11 Jared Flint	.20	.50
W12 Josh Rogers	.20	.50
W13 Damion Barton	.20	.50
W14 Eddie Gayles	.20	.50
W15 Mike Rhodes	.20	.50
W16 Donovan Calhoun	.20	.50
W17 Dante Clay	.20	.50
W18 James Creason	.20	.50
W19 Tony Elam	.20	.50
W20 Brian Palmer	.20	.50
W21 Roderick Walker	.20	.50
W22 Terrynce White	.20	.50
W23 Michael Yancy	.20	.50
W24 Ken-Yon Rambo	.60	1.50
W25 Eddie Gorton	.20	.50
W26 Ja'Warren Hooker	.30	.75
W27 Jeff Johnson	.20	.50
W28 Cody Joyce	.20	.50
W29 Rossi Martin	.20	.50
W30 Rashawn Owens	.20	.50
W31 Joey Getherall	.60	1.50
W32 Jamien McCullum	.20	.50
W33 Brandon Nash	.20	.50
W34 Tafiti Uso	.20	.50
W35 Lonnie Ford	.30	.75
W36 Antoine Harris	.20	.50
W37 Corey Lee Smith	.20	.50
W38 Donnell Burch	.20	.50
W39 Lee Turner	.20	.50
W40 Brian Polak	.60	1.50
W41 Mike Souza	.30	.75
W42 Kurt Vollers	.30	.75
W43 Craig Brooks	.20	.50
W44 Ron Price	.20	.50
W45 Mike Wambolt	.20	.50
W46 Ralph Zarate	.20	.50
W47 Jim Adams	.20	.50
W48 Ed Anderson	.20	.50
W49 Justin David	.20	.50
W50 Brian Hart	.20	.50
W51 Nic Hawkins	.20	.50
W52 Brandon Hoopes	.20	.50
W53 Kris Keene	.20	.50
W54 Travis Pfeifer	.20	.50
W55 Langston Walker	.60	1.50
W56 Andre Carter	.75	2.00
W57 John Jackson	.20	.50
W58 Welton Kage	.20	.50
W59 Anthony Thomas	.20	.50
W60 Justin Bannan	.60	1.50
W61 Ryan Nielsen	.20	.50
W62 Brandon Manumaleuna	.75	2.00
W63 Kyle Roselle	.20	.50
W64 Darrell Daniels	.20	.50
W65 Bobby Demars	.20	.50
W66 Tracy Hunt	.20	.50
W67 Zeke Moreno	.75	2.00
W68 Tim Shear	.20	.50
W69 Kori Dickerson	.30	.75
W70 Ty Gregorak	.20	.50
W71 Malachi Keddington	.20	.50
W72 Don Meyers	.20	.50
W73 Tony Thompson	.20	.50
W74 Ifeanyi Ohalete	.75	2.00
W75 Antuan Simmons	.30	.75
W76 Albus Brooks	.20	.50
W77 Dewey Hale	.20	.50
W78 Kameron Jones	.20	.50
W79 Lamont Thompson	.60	1.50
W80 Fred Washington	.20	.50
W81 Shanga Wilson	.20	.50
W82 Marques Anderson	.75	2.00
W83 DeMario Franklin	.20	.50
W84 Melvin Justice	.20	.50
W85 Kris Richard	.60	1.50
W86 Julius Thompson	.20	.50
W87 Wes Tufaga	.20	.50
W88 Zak Haselmo	.20	.50
W89 Jeremy Kelly	.20	.50
W90 John Gonzalez	.20	.50
W91 Bobby Jackson	.75	2.00
W92 Rod Perry Jr.	.30	.75
W93 Charles Tharp	.20	.50
W94 Marcus Brady	.60	1.50
W95 Merle Sango	.20	.50

1996 Roox Prep Stars MW/SW

This 114-card standard size boxed set was produced by Roox featuring high school players that played in 1996, and includes standouts from the following states: Illinois, Indiana, Iowa, Michigan, Minnesota, Ohio, Texas, and Wisconsin. Reportedly, 1000 sets were produced.

COMPLETE SET (114)	15.00	40.00
MW1 Zak Kustok	.40	1.00
MW2 Tyler Evans	.30	.75
MW3 Rob Johnson	.30	.75
MW4 Chris Ludban	.30	.75
MW5 Ken Stopka	.30	.75
MW6 Kyle Van Sluys	.30	.75
MW7 Sean Penny	.30	.75
MW8 Bill Andrews	.30	.75
MW9 James Harrison	10.00	20.00
MW10 De'Wayne Hogan	.40	1.00
MW11 Carlos Honare'	.30	.75
MW12 Ray Jackson	.30	.75
MW13 Greg Simpson	.30	.75
MW14 Israel Thompson	.30	.75
MW15 Ernest Brown	.30	.75
MW16 Sam Crenshaw	.60	1.50
MW17 Adrian Duncan	.30	.75
MW18 Kahlil Hill	.60	1.50
MW19 Teddy Johnson	.30	.75
MW20 Omari Jordan	.30	.75
MW21 Jason Kemble	.30	.75
MW22 Jace Sayler	.30	.75
MW23 Tim Stratton	.40	1.00
MW24 Adam Fay	.30	.75
MW25 Josh Jakubowski	.30	.75
MW26 Ben Mast	.40	1.00
MW27 Mike Collins	.40	1.00
MW28 Oliver King	.30	.75
MW29 Rocky Nease	.30	.75
MW30 Josh Parrish	.30	.75
MW31 Clifton Reta	.30	.75
MW32 Brian Wise	.30	.75
MW33 Maurice Williams	.60	1.50
MW34 Kevin Bell	.30	.75
MW35 Derek Burns	.30	.75
MW36 Anwar Cooper	.30	.75
MW37 Jeremy Dox	.30	.75
MW38 Rasche Hill	.40	1.00
MW39 Jason Ptak	.30	.75
MW40 Ben Pulfer	.30	.75
MW41 Heath Queen	.30	.75
MW42 Bill Seymour	.30	.75
MW43 Demetrius Smith	.30	.75
MW44 Ben Sobieski	.30	.75
MW45 Hubert Thompson	.40	1.00
MW46 Jake Frysinger	.30	.75
MW47 Jason Ott	.30	.75
MW48 Kyle Vanden Bosch	1.50	4.00
MW49 Kurt Anderson	.30	.75
MW50 Napoleon Harris	.40	1.00
MW51 Jason Manson	.30	.75
MW52 Joel Mesman	.30	.75
MW53 Jeff Skibitsky	.30	.75
MW54 T.J. Turner	.30	.75
MW55 Mike Clinkscale	.40	1.00
MW56 Jamie Grant	.30	.75
MW57 Kyle Moffatt	.30	.75
MW58 Abdullah Muhammad	.30	.75
MW59 Eric Parker	1.25	3.00
MW60 Mike Young	.30	.75

MW61 Pat Gibson	.30	.75
MW62 Brendan Rauh	.30	.75
MW63 Antwaan Randle El	2.00	5.00
MW64 Levron Williams	.60	1.50
SW1 Ed Stansbury	.40	1.00
SW2 Grant Elam	.30	.75
SW3 Regan George	.30	.75
SW4 Matt Schobel	.60	1.50
SW5 Hodges Mitchell	.60	1.50
SW6 Twone Simmons	.30	.75
SW7 Donald Williams	.30	.75
SW8 Jason Coffey	.30	.75
SW9 Corey Harris	.30	.75
SW10 Shon Jones	.30	.75
SW11 Burnest Rhodes	.30	.75
SW12 Adrian Thomas	.30	.75
SW13 Robert Williams	.30	.75
SW14 Daniel Belcha	.30	.75
SW15 Damon Daniels	.30	.75
SW16 Raymond Turner	.30	.75
SW17 Chad Irwin	.30	.75
SW18 Ed Kelly	.30	.75
SW19 Miles Koon	.30	.75
SW20 Luke Nichols	.30	.75
SW21 Dennis Jones	.30	.75
SW22 Rodney Endsley	.30	.75
SW23 Norman McKinney	.30	.75
SW24 Terry Williams	.30	.75
SW25 David Warren	.60	1.50
SW26 Lonnie Madison	.30	.75
SW27 Shaun Rogers	1.25	3.00
SW28 Mike Minott	.30	.75
SW29 Evan Perroni	.30	.75
SW30 Grant Irons	.40	1.00
SW31 Josh Spoerl	.30	.75
SW32 Tommy Tull	.30	.75
SW33 Chad Chester	.30	.75
SW34 Devon Lemons	.30	.75
SW35 Antowan Alexander	.30	.75
SW36 Jay Brooks	.30	.75
SW37 Quentin Jammer	1.25	3.00
SW38 Derrick Yates	.30	.75
SW39 Gary Baxter	.60	1.50
SW40 Danny Black	.30	.75
SW41 Brandon Couts	.30	.75
SW42 Derek Dorris	.30	.75
SW43 Michael Jameson	.40	1.00
SW44 Mickey Jones	.30	.75
SW45 Kevon Morton	.30	.75
SW46 Rod Sheppard	.30	.75
SW47 J.R. Pouncey	.30	.75
SW48 Sterlin Gilbert	.30	.75
SW49 Terry Burrell	.30	.75
SW50 Jason Stevenson	.30	.75

1997 Roox Prep Stars

This set was produced and released by Roox in complete set form. It features top high school football players in the country. Each card includes the player's name near the bottom edge with the title "Prep Stars" down the left side. The cardbacks feature a simple black printing on white stock with a "7FPS" prefix on the card numbers. This set features very early cards of noted baseball players Adam Dunn and Drew Henson.

COMP. FACT SET (72)	75.00	150.00
1 Tyler Watts	2.00	5.00
2 Bart Raulston	.75	2.00
3 Marvin Constant	.75	2.00
4 Josh Melton	.75	2.00
5 Harold Harris	1.50	4.00
6 Mike Saffer	1.50	4.00
7 Blake Worley	.75	2.00
8 Charles Dehoney	.75	2.00
9 Emmanuel Evans	.75	2.00
10 Jeremy Wallace	.75	2.00
11 Jafar Williams LB	1.50	4.00
12 Chris Hakim	.75	2.00
13 Ryan Solomona	.75	2.00
14 Michael Jones Jr.	.75	2.00
15 Anthony Kelley	1.50	4.00
16 B'Jay Jones	.75	2.00
17 Joe Weber	1.50	4.00
18 Herman White	.75	2.00
19 Steve Cutlip	1.00	2.50
20 Justin Bates	.75	2.00
21 Dave Jorgensen	.75	2.00
22 Steve Bellisari	1.50	4.00
23 Shawn Bushong	.75	2.00
24 Kawika Mitchell	.75	2.00
25 Lester Norwood	1.00	2.50
26 Keith Stephens	.75	2.00
27 Gary Byrd Jr.	.75	2.00
28 Jason Gesser	3.00	8.00
29 Aaron Kampman	6.00	15.00
30 Dave Diehl	.75	2.00
31 Danny Jordan	.75	2.00
32 Jason Neidigh	.75	2.00
33 Ken Dangerfield	1.50	4.00
34 Brad Smalling	.75	2.00
35 Jamal Burke	1.50	4.00
36 Brian St.Pierre	2.50	6.00
37 James Johnson WR	1.50	4.00
38 Ryan Raley	.75	2.00
39 Drew Henson	4.00	10.00
40 Joe Denay	.75	2.00
41 Larry Foote Jr.	1.50	4.00
42 Bennie Joppru	2.50	6.00
43 Dan Schellhammer	.75	2.00
44 Clarence Jones	.75	2.00
45 Freddie Milons	2.00	5.00
46 Reggie Myles	1.50	4.00
47 Maurice McClain	1.00	2.50
48 Sean O'Connor	1.00	2.50
49 Terrance Howard	1.50	4.00
50 Marc Riley	1.00	2.50
51 Marquise Walker	4.00	10.00
52 Brian Hallett	.75	2.00
53 Christian Morgan	.75	2.00
54 Joe Sellers	.75	2.00
55 Lawson Giddings	1.00	2.50
56 Spencer Marona	.75	2.00
57 Chesley Borders	1.50	4.00
58 Rob Kolaczynski	1.00	2.50
59 Steven Lindsey	.75	2.00
60 Tyler Lenda	1.50	4.00
61 Todd Wike	1.50	4.00
62 Joe Don Reames	1.00	2.50
63 Eric Locke	1.00	2.50
64 Sean Phillips	1.50	4.00
65 Jon Thomas	.75	2.00
66 Antwan Kirk-Hughes	.75	2.00
67 Adam Dunn	20.00	40.00
68 Nathan Woodard	.75	2.00
69 Jake Houseright	1.00	2.50
70 Dominic Smith	.75	2.00
71 Todd Elstrom	1.00	2.50
72 Grant Noel	1.50	4.00

1908 Rotograph Celebrity Series Postcards

The Rotograph Co. of New York issued a Celebrity Series set of postcards in 1908 that included one football subject. The set has an ACC designation of PC438.

1 Fielding Yost	75.00	150.00

1996 Rutgers

COMPLETE SET (14)	5.00	10.00
1 Cameron Chadwick	.30	.75
2 Matt Fleming	.30	.75
3 Brian Sheridan	.30	.75
4 T.J. Spizzo	.30	.75
5 Rusty Swartz	.30	.75
6 Ron Keller	.30	.75
7 Derek Ward	.30	.75
8 Rashod Swinger	.30	.75
9 Shaun Devlin	.30	.75
10 Chad Bosch	.30	.75
11 Jason Curry	.30	.75
12 Robert Seeger	.30	.75
13 Team Mascot	.30	.75
14 Coca-Cola Cover Card	.30	.75

1997 Rutgers

COMPLETE SET (21)	6.00	12.00
1 Chris Cebula	.30	.75
2 Steven Harper	.30	.75
3 Joseph Diggs	.30	.75
4 Joe Donato	.30	.75
5 Reggie Funderburk	.30	.75
6 Norris Crawford	.30	.75
7 Joseph Hynes	.30	.75
8 Brian Sheridan	.30	.75
9 Thomas Kelly	.30	.75
10 Pete Long Mgr	.30	.75
11 Marcus Luna	.30	.75
12 Jack McKiernan	.30	.75
13 Rashied Richardson	.30	.75
14 Bobby Orro	.30	.75
15 Nick Mike-Mayer	.40	1.00
16 Joey Jones	.30	.75
17 Jared Slovan	.30	.75
18 Russell Swanson	.30	.75
19 Kerry Ware	.30	.75
20 Kevin Williams	.30	.75
21 Charles Woolridge	.30	.75

2000 Rutgers

COMPLETE SET (15)	5.00	10.00
1 Tim Baker	.30	.75
2 John Ciurciu	.30	.75
3 Walter King	.30	.75
4 Mike Jones	.30	.75
5 Rich Mazza	.30	.75
6 Dennis McCormack	.30	.75
7 Mike McMahon	1.25	3.00
8 Peter Mendez	.30	.75
9 Mahiri Moody	.30	.75
10 James Pederson	.30	.75
11 Tom Petko	.30	.75
12 Wes Robertson	.30	.75
13 Garrett Shea	.30	.75
14 Randy Smith	.30	.75
15 Shahib White	.30	.75

2005 San Diego State

COMPLETE SET (25)	6.00	12.00
1 Tom Craft CO	.20	.50
2 Jonathan Bailes	.20	.50
3 Donny Baker	.20	.50
4 Brandon Bornes	.20	.50
5 Marcus Demps	.20	.50
6 Marcus Edwards	.20	.50
7 Jacob Elimimian	.20	.50
8 Michael Franklin	.20	.50
9 Reggie Grigsby	.20	.50
10 Lynell Hamilton	.75	2.00
11 Kurt Kahui	.20	.50
12 Freddie Keiaho	.20	.50
13 Lance Louis	.20	.50
14 Joe Martin	.20	.50
15 Eric Miclot	.20	.50
16 Darren Mougey	.20	.50
17 Kevin O'Connell	.75	2.00
18 Robert Ortiz	.20	.50
19 Chris Pino	.20	.50
20 Ramal Porter	.20	.50
21 Will Robinson	.20	.50
22 Chaz Schilens	1.00	2.50
23 Taylor Schmidt	.20	.50
24 Brett Swain	.20	.50
25 Jeff Webb	.20	.50

1990 San Jose State Smokey

This 15-card standard-size set features members of the 1990 San Jose State football team. The front has a color action photo, with the school name above the picture and the player's name, uniform number, and school year below. The picture is enframed by an orange border on a blue background. The back provides information on the player and features a fire prevention cartoon starring Smokey the Bear. For convenient reference, these unnumbered cards are checklisted below in alphabetical order.

COMPLETE SET (15)	4.00	10.00
1 Bob Bleisch 90	.30	.75
2 Sheldon Canley 20	.30	.75
3 Paul Franklin 37	.30	.75
4 Anthony Gallegos 72	.30	.75
5 Steve Hieber 48	.30	.75
6 Everett Lampkins 43	.30	.75
7 Kelly Liebengood 21	.30	.75
8 Ralph Martini 9	.30	.75
9 Lyneil Mayo 62	.30	.75
10 Mike Powers 57	.30	.75
11 Mike Scialabba 46	.30	.75
12 Terry Shea CO	.30	.75
13 Freddie Smith 4	.30	.75
14 Eddie Thomas 26	.30	.75
15 Brian Woods 64	.30	.75

1991 San Jose State

These 20 standard-size cards of the San Jose State Spartans feature posed color "action" shots by Barry Colla on their borderless fronts. The player's name and position appear within a yellow strip in one corner. The white back carries a Spartan helmet logo at the upper left and a 1991 copyright line. The player's jersey number, name, and biography appear alongside the right. The 1992 Spartan game schedule at the bottom rounds out each card. The cards are numbered on the back in alphabetical order as "X of 20".

COMPLETE SET (20)	5.00	12.00
1 Maceo Barbosa	.30	.75
2 Bobby Blackmon	.30	.75
3 David Blakes	.30	.75
4 Walter Brooks Jr.	.30	.75
5 Greg Bruggeman	.30	.75
6 Bryce Burnett	.30	.75
7 Doug Calcagno	.30	.75
8 Gary Charlton	.30	.75
9 Chris Clarke	.30	.75
10 Hesh Colar	.30	.75
11 Jeff Greeney	.30	.75
12 Leon Hawthorne	.30	.75
13 Peni Iosefa	.30	.75
14 Byron Jackson	.30	.75
15 Robbie Miller	.30	.75
16 Freddie Smith	.30	.75
17 Spencer Smith	.30	.75
18 Simon Vaoifi	.30	.75
19 Matt Veatch	.30	.75
20 Blair Zerr	.30	.75

1992 San Jose State

This 18-card set sponsored by Kidder, Peabody and Coca-Cola features borderless photos of the San Jose State Spartans by photographer Barry Colla. The white backs carry player information, a team logo and 1992 copyright line, and a card number printed in blue. Sponsor logos round out the backs.

COMPLETE SET (18)	7.50	15.00
1 Ron Turner CO	.30	.75
2 Jeff Garcia	5.00	10.00
3 Alfred Robinson	.30	.75
4 Anthony Washington	.30	.75
5 Lester Grice	.30	.75
6 Raymond Bowles	.30	.75
7 Nick Trammer	.30	.75
8 Todd Ranney	.30	.75
9 Travis Peterson	.30	.75
10 David Zeishing	.30	.75
11 Mike Fortino	.30	.75
12 Marty Lyon	.30	.75
13 Henry Wright	.30	.75
14 Rich Sarlatte	.30	.75
15 Ricky Jordan	.30	.75
16 Chad Carpenter	.30	.75
17 Kevin O'Connell	.30	.75
18 Sean Neel	.30	.75

1993 San Jose State

This 28-card set sponsored by Bofors Lithography and Matrix Pre-Press features borderless photos of the San Jose State Spartans by photographer Barry Colla. The white backs carry player information, a team logo and 1993 copyright line, and a card number printed in blue. The sponsor logos round out the backs.

COMPLETE SET (28)	7.50	15.00
1 Elliott Franklin	.30	.75
2 Jason Lucky	.30	.75
3 Jeff Garcia	3.00	8.00
4 Troy Jensen	.30	.75
5 Lee Myhre	.30	.75
6 Scott Reese	.30	.75
7 Dexter Burns	.30	.75
8 John Mountain	.30	.75
9 Paul Pitts	.30	.75
10 Nathan DuPree	.30	.75
11 Landon Shaver	.30	.75
12 Tom Petithomme	.30	.75
13 Shon Ellerbe	.30	.75
14 Albert Duncalf	.30	.75
15 Kareeb Harbin	.30	.75
16 Derrick Childs	.30	.75
17 Jim Singleton	.30	.75
18 Joe Simione	.30	.75
19 Tom Cleary	.30	.75
20 Keith Moffatt	.30	.75
21 Matt Earnshaw	.30	.75
22 John Cotti	.30	.75
23 Reuben Johnson	.30	.75
24 Wally Bonnett	.30	.75
25 Peter Platt	.30	.75
26 Mike Gardner	.30	.75
27 Aaron Linen	.30	.75
28 Kenyon Price	.30	.75

1936 Seal Craft Discs

This series of discs was issued by Seal Craft Gum around 1936. The entire set consists of 240-discs featuring various non-sport subjects from animals and american indians to sports oriented college pennants. Each disc featuring a sports theme includes a college pennant in the center with artwork of the team's mascot and a generic representative sport above and below the pennant. The backs feature a brief history of the school and a football icon at the top and artwork of a tennis player at the bottom along with a card number.

91 Stanford (diving)	20.00	40.00
92 Kentucky (polo)	15.00	30.00
93 Pitt (football)	15.00	30.00
94 Vermont (ice hockey)	15.00	30.00
95 Princeton (tennis)	15.00	30.00
96 Fordham football)	15.00	30.00
97 UCLA (track)	20.00	40.00
98 NYU (basketball)	15.00	30.00
99 Notre Dame (football)	40.00	80.00
100 Southern California (track)	20.00	40.00
101 Florida (diving)	20.00	40.00
102 Army (football)	15.00	30.00
103 California (track)	15.00	30.00
104 Columbia (football)	15.00	30.00
105 Cornell (track)	15.00	30.00
106 Yale (track)	15.00	30.00
107 Dartmouth (skiing)	15.00	30.00

1994 Senior Bowl

Cards from this set were given away at the 1994 Senior Bowl in Mobile Alabama. Each is blankbacked and features a black and white player photo on the front with the Coca-Cola logo along with his facsimile autograph below the photo. The cardfronts also include the 1994 Senior Bowl logo near the upper left hand corner. The player's name appears in the upper right hand corner and was printed in either blue or red ink. Each card measures roughly 3" by 5". Any additions to this list are appreciated.

COMPLETE SET	75.00	150.00
1 Joe Allison	1.50	4.00
2 Aubrey Beavers	1.50	4.00
3 Myron Bell	1.50	4.00
4 Bucky Brooks	1.50	4.00
5 Vaughn Bryant	1.50	4.00
6 Brentson Buckner	1.50	4.00
7 James Burton	1.50	4.00
8 Matthew Campbell	1.50	4.00
9 Perry Carter	1.50	4.00
10 Shante Carver	1.50	4.00
11 Dennis Collier	1.50	4.00
12 Carlester Crumpler	1.50	4.00
13 Isaac Davis	1.50	4.00
14 Mitch Davis	1.50	4.00
15 Lake Dawson	2.00	5.00
16 Mark Dixon	1.50	4.00
17 Tyronne Drakeford	1.50	4.00
18 Dan Eichloff	1.50	4.00
19 Bert Emanuel	2.00	5.00
20 Henry Ford	1.50	4.00
21 Rob Fredrickson	2.00	5.00
22 Randy Fuller	1.50	4.00
23 Kevin Gaines	1.50	4.00
24 William Gaines	1.50	4.00
25 Wayne Gandy	1.50	4.00
26 Charlie Garner	2.00	5.00
27 Jason Gildon	2.00	5.00
28 Marvin Graves	1.50	4.00
29 Lemanski Hall	1.50	4.00
30 Raymont Harris	2.00	5.00
31 Tony Harrison	1.50	4.00
32 Shelby Hill	1.25	3.00
33 Sean Jackson	1.50	4.00
34 LeShon Johnson	1.50	4.00
35 Lonnie Johnson	1.50	4.00
36 Tre' Johnson	1.50	4.00
37 Perry Klein	1.50	4.00
38 Darren Krein	1.50	4.00
39 Kevin Lee	1.50	4.00
40 Roderick Lewis	1.50	4.00
41 Corey Louchiey	1.50	4.00
42 Jason Mathews	1.50	4.00
43 Kevin Mawae	2.00	5.00
44 Jaime Mendez	1.50	4.00
45 Jim Miller	3.00	6.00
46 Mark Montgomery	1.50	4.00
47 Jeremy Nunley	1.50	4.00
48 Marlo Perry	1.50	4.00
49 Anthony Phillips	1.50	4.00
50 Trent Pollard	1.50	4.00
51 Damon Primus	1.50	4.00
52 Jim Pyne	1.50	4.00
53 John Reece	1.50	4.00
54 Tony Richardson	2.00	5.00
55 Ron Rivers	1.50	4.00
56 Malcolm Seabron	1.50	4.00
57 Tobie Sheils	1.50	4.00
58 Kelvin Simmons	1.50	4.00
59 Fernando Smith	1.50	4.00
60 Terry Smith	1.50	4.00
61 Marcus Spears	1.50	4.00
62 Todd Steussie	2.00	5.00
63 John Thierry	1.50	4.00
64 Winfred Tubbs	1.50	4.00
65 Tony Vinson	1.50	4.00
66 Rob Waldrop	1.50	4.00
67 Orlando Watters	1.50	4.00
68 Rico White	1.50	4.00
69 Jermaine Younger	1.50	4.00

1995 Senior Bowl

This set was given away at the 1995 Senior Bowl in Mobile Alabama. Each is blankbacked and features a black and white player photo on the front along with his facsimile autograph and Mobile Gas and Coca-Cola sponsorship logos. The cardfronts also include the 1995 Senior Bowl logo near the upper left hand corner. Each card measures roughly 3" by 5". Any additions to this list are appreciated.

COMPLETE SET (54)	60.00	120.00
1 Gerald Collins	1.50	4.00
2 Terry Connealy	1.50	4.00
3 Anthony Cook	1.50	4.00
4 Jamal Cook	1.50	4.00
5 Terry Daniels	1.50	4.00
6 Luther Elliss	1.50	4.00
7 Mike Frederick	1.50	4.00
8 Kenny Gales	1.50	4.00
9 Willie Gaston	1.50	4.00
10 Oliver Gibson	1.50	4.00
11 Brian Hamilton	1.50	4.00
12 Juan Hammonds	1.50	4.00
13 Dana Howard	1.50	4.00
14 Chris Hudson	1.50	4.00
15 Torey Hunter	1.50	4.00
16 Ken Irvin	1.50	4.00
17 Jason James	1.50	4.00
18 Dameian Jeffries	1.50	4.00
19 Melvin Johnson	1.50	4.00
20 Tommy Johnson	1.50	4.00
21 Tony Jones	1.50	4.00
22 Marlon Kerner	1.50	4.00
24 Jason Kyle	1.50	4.00
25 Scott Lewis	1.50	4.00
26 Chad May	1.50	4.00
27 Kevin Mays	1.50	4.00
28 Kez McCorvey	1.50	4.00
29 Steve McNair	6.00	12.00
30 Billy Milner	1.50	4.00
31 Mike Morton	1.50	4.00
32 Craig Newsome	2.00	5.00
33 Matt O'Dwyer	1.50	4.00
34 Mike Pelton	1.50	4.00
35 Marcus Price	1.50	4.00
36 Andre Royal	1.50	4.00
37 Joe Rudolph	1.50	4.00
38 Chris Sanders	2.00	5.00
39 Frank Sanders	2.00	5.00
40 Don Sasa	1.50	4.00
41 Todd Sauerbrun	2.50	6.00
42 Bryan Schwartz	1.50	4.00
43 Chris Shelling	1.50	4.00
44 David Sloan	2.00	5.00
45 Brendan Stai	1.50	4.00
46 Jon Stevenson	1.50	4.00
47 Oscar Sturgis	1.50	4.00
50 Mike Verstegen	1.50	4.00
51 Billy Williams	1.50	4.00
53 Claudius Wright	1.50	4.00
54 Ray Zellars	2.00	5.00

1996 Senior Bowl

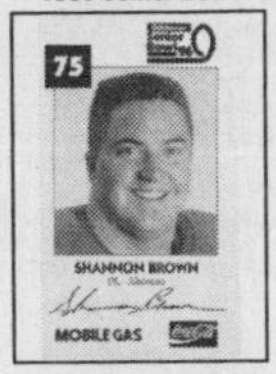

Cards from this set were given away at the 1996 Senior Bowl in Mobile Alabama. Each is blankbacked and features a black and white player photo on the front along with his facsimile autograph and Mobile Gas and Coca-Cola sponsorship logos. The cardfronts also include the 1996 Senior Bowl logo near the upper right hand corner. Each card measures roughly 3" by 5". Any additions to this list are appreciated.

COMPLETE SET (73)	75.00	150.00
1 Eric Abrams	1.50	4.00
2 Kantroy Barber	1.50	4.00
3 Reggie Barlow	1.50	4.00
4 Robert Barr	1.50	4.00
5 Clarence Benford	1.50	4.00
6 Sean Boyd	1.50	4.00
7 Dorain Brew	1.50	4.00
8 Shannon Brown	1.50	4.00
10 Kendrick Burton	1.50	4.00
11 Art Celestine	1.50	4.00
12 Michael Cheever	1.50	4.00
13 Sedric Clark	1.50	4.00
14 Steven Conley	1.50	4.00
15 Dexter Daniels	1.50	4.00
16 Jason Dunn	1.50	4.00
18 Johnny Frost	1.50	4.00
19 Andy Fuller	1.50	4.00
20 Percell Gaskins	1.50	4.00
21 Randall Godfrey	1.50	4.00
22 Lorenzo Green	1.50	4.00
23 Ben Hanks	1.50	4.00
24 Anthony Harris	1.50	4.00
25 Matt Hawkins	1.50	4.00
26 Errick Herrin	1.50	4.00
27 Brice Hunter	1.50	4.00
28 Richard Huntley	1.50	4.00
29 Israel Ifeanyi	1.50	4.00
30 Greg Ivy	1.50	4.00
31 Ray Jackson	1.50	4.00
33 Deron Jenkins	1.50	4.00
34 Darrius Johnson	1.50	4.00
35 Lance Johnstone	1.50	4.00
36 Rod Jones	1.50	4.00
37 Pete Kendall	1.50	4.00
38 Marcus Keyes	1.50	4.00
39 Jason Layman	1.50	4.00
40 Jason Maniecki	1.50	4.00
41 Steve Martin	1.50	4.00
42 Dell McGee	1.50	4.00
43 Johnny McWilliams	1.50	4.00
44 John Michels	1.50	4.00
45 David Millwee	1.50	4.00
46 Bryant Mix	1.50	4.00
47 John Mobley	2.00	5.00
48 Picasso Nelson	1.50	4.00
49 Gabe Northern	1.50	4.00
50 Roman Oben	1.50	4.00
51 Terrell Owens	6.00	12.00
52 Kavika Pittman	1.50	4.00
53 J.C. Price	1.50	4.00
54 Stanley Pritchett	1.50	4.00
55 Albert Reese	1.50	4.00
56 Adrian Robinson	1.50	4.00
57 Shannon Roubique	1.50	4.00
58 Orpheus Roye	1.50	4.00
59 Dwayne Sanders	1.50	4.00
60 Toralno Singleton	1.50	4.00
61 Scott Slutzker	1.50	4.00
62 Jeff Smith	1.50	4.00
63 Greg Spann	1.50	4.00
64 Jamain Stephens	1.50	4.00
65 Rayna Stewart	1.50	4.00
66 Ryan Stewart	1.50	4.00
67 Steve Taneyhill	1.50	4.00
68 Reggie Tongue	1.50	4.00
69 Tom Tumulty	1.50	4.00
70 Kyle Wachholtz	1.50	4.00
71 Stepfret Williams	1.50	4.00
72 Jerome Woods	1.50	4.00
73 Dusty Zeigler	1.50	4.00

1998 Senior Bowl

Cards from this set were given away at the 1998 Senior Bowl in Mobile Alabama. Each is blankbacked and features a black and white player photo on the front along with his facsimile autograph and Mobile Gas and Coca-Cola logos at the bottom. The cardfronts also include the 1998 Senior Bowl logo near the upper right hand corner sponsored by Delchamps. Each card measures roughly 3" by 5". Any additions to this list are appreciated.

COMPLETE SET (108)	75.00	150.00
1 Flozell Adams	1.00	2.50
2 Curtis Alexander	.75	2.00
3 Jamaal Alexander	.75	2.00
4 Stephen Alexander	1.00	2.50
5 John Avery	1.00	2.50
6 Jeff Banks	.75	2.00
7 Shawn Barber	.75	2.00
8 Fred Beasley	.75	2.00
9 Leon Bender	.75	2.00
10 Roosevelt Blackmon	.75	2.00
11 Rob Bohlinger	.75	2.00
12 Dorian Boose	.75	2.00
13 Chris Bordano	.75	2.00
14 Josh Bradley	.75	2.00
15 Keith Brooking	1.00	2.50
16 Eric Brown	.75	2.00
17 Jonathan Brown	.75	2.00
18 Thad Busby	.75	2.00
19 Shane Carwin	.75	2.00
20 Martin Chase	.75	2.00
21 Corey Chavous	1.00	2.50
22 Anthony Clement	.75	2.00
23 Aaron Collins	.75	2.00
24 Chris Conrad	.75	2.00
25 Dameyune Craig	1.00	2.50
26 Germane Crowell	1.00	2.50
27 Donovin Darius	1.00	2.50
28 Phil Dawson	.75	2.00
29 Tim Dwight	1.50	4.00
30 Eric Dotson	.75	2.00
31 Jamie Duncan	.75	2.00
32 John Dutton	.75	2.00
33 Kevin Dyson	1.50	4.00
34 Robert Edwards	1.00	2.50
35 Greg Ellis	.75	2.00
36 Jason Fabini	.75	2.00
37 Terry Fair	.75	2.00
38 Greg Favors	.75	2.00
39 Dan Finn	.75	2.00
40 Chris Floyd	.75	2.00
41 Steve Foley	.75	2.00
42 Darryl Gilliam	.75	2.00
43 Mike Goff	.75	2.00
44 E.G. Green	1.00	2.50
45 Az-Zahir Hakim	1.50	4.00
46 Rob Hallen	.75	2.00
47 Artrell Hawkins	.75	2.00
48 Robert Hicks	.75	2.00
49 Skip Hicks	1.00	2.50
50 Vonnie Holliday	1.00	2.50
51 Jaret Holmes	.75	2.00
52 Brad Jackson	.75	2.00
53 Tebucky Jones	.75	2.00
54 Brian Kelly	1.00	2.50
55 Chad Kessler	.75	2.00
56 Jonathan Linton	1.00	2.50
57 Leonard Little	1.00	2.50
58 Mitch Marrow	.75	2.00
59 Kivuusama Mays	.75	2.00
60 Ramos McDonald	.75	2.00
61 Brian McKenzie	.75	2.00
62 Steve McKinney	.75	2.00
63 Mike McQueary	1.25	3.00
64 Ron Merkerson	.75	2.00
65 Kenny Mixon	.75	2.00
66 Omarr Morgan	.75	2.00
67 Brian Musso	.75	2.00
68 Michael Myers	.75	2.00
69 Deshone Myles	.75	2.00
70 Toby Myles	.75	2.00
71 Tori Noel	.75	2.00
72 Phil Ostrowski	.75	2.00
73 Jerome Pathon	1.50	4.00
74 Julian Pittman	.75	2.00
75 Michael Pittman	2.00	5.00
76 Derrick Ranson	.75	2.00
77 Mikhael Ricks	1.00	2.50
78 Victor Riley	.75	2.00
79 Allen Rossum	1.00	2.50
80 Rod Rutledge	.75	2.00
81 Ephraim Salaam	.75	2.00
82 Kio Sanford	.75	2.00
83 Larry Shannon	.75	2.00
84 Scott Shaw	.75	2.00
85 Rashaan Shehee	1.00	2.50
86 Tony Simmons	1.00	2.50
87 Henry Slay	.75	2.00
88 Travian Smith	.75	2.00
89 Blake Spence	.75	2.00
90 Duane Starks	.75	2.00
91 Nathan Strikwerda	.75	2.00
92 Patrick Surtain	1.50	4.00
93 Aaron Taylor	1.00	2.50
94 Cordell Taylor	.75	2.00
95 Fred Taylor	3.00	8.00
96 Trey Teague	.75	2.00
97 Melvin Thomas	.75	2.00
98 DeShea Townsend	.75	2.00
99 Kyle Turley	1.00	2.50
100 John Wade	.75	2.00
101 Hines Ward	6.00	15.00
102 Todd Washington	.75	2.00
103 Fred Weary	.75	2.00
104 Cory Wedel	.75	2.00
105 Chuck Wiley	.75	2.00
106 Lamanzer Williams	.75	2.00
107 Sammy Williams	.75	2.00
108 Shaun Williams	1.00	2.50

1999 Senior Bowl

Cards from this set were given away at the 1999 Senior Bowl in Mobile Alabama. Each is blankbacked and features a small black and white player photo on the front along with his facsimile autograph. The cardfronts also include the 1999 Senior Bowl logo near the upper left hand corner. Each card measures roughly 3" by 5". Any additions to this list are appreciated.

1 Karsten Bailey	.75	2.00
2 Eric Barton	.75	2.00
3 Cuncho Brown	.75	2.00
4 Larry Brown	.75	2.00
5 Doug Brzezinski	.75	2.00
6 Justin Burroughs	.75	2.00
7 Giovanni Carmazzi	1.00	2.50
8 Mike Cloud	1.00	2.50
9 Tony Coats	.75	2.00
10 Nikia Codie	.75	2.00
11 Jermaine Copeland	1.00	2.50
12 Scott Covington	1.00	2.50
13 Russell Davis	.75	2.00
14 Autry Denson	.75	2.00
15 Troy Edwards	1.00	2.50
16 Ebenezer Ekuban	1.00	2.50
17 Derrick Fletcher	.75	2.00
18 Jason Gamble	.75	2.00
19 Barry Gardner	.75	2.00
20 Joe Germaine	1.00	2.50
21 Phil Glover	.75	2.00
22 Martin Gramatica	1.00	2.50
23 Darran Hall	.75	2.00
24 Matt Hughes	.75	2.00
25 Quincy Jackson	.75	2.00
26 James Johnson	.75	2.00
27 Kevin Johnson	1.00	2.50
28 Gana Joseph	.75	2.00
29 Reggie Kelly	.75	2.00
30 Jim Kleinsasser	1.00	2.50
31 Rob Konrad	1.00	2.50
32 Stacey Mack	.75	2.00
33 Joel Makovicka	1.00	2.50
34 Travis McGriff	.75	2.00

35 Donovan McNabb	7.50	15.00
36 Dee Miller	.75	2.00
37 Kory Minor	.75	2.00
38 Jamar Nesbit	.75	2.00
39 Keith Newman	.75	2.00
40 Jeremy Offutt	.75	2.00
41 Brad Palazzo	.75	2.00
42 Daniel Pope	.75	2.00
43 Peerless Price	1.50	4.00
44 Michael Pringley	.75	2.00
45 Jacoby Rinehart	.75	2.00
46 Chris Sailer	.75	2.00
47 Brian Shay	.75	2.00
48 Derek Smith	.75	2.00
49 Cameron Spikes	.75	2.00
50 Gary Stills	.75	2.00
51 Tai Streets	1.00	2.50
52 Ty Talton	.75	2.00
53 Devin West	.75	2.00
54 Craig Yeast	.75	2.00

2000 Senior Bowl

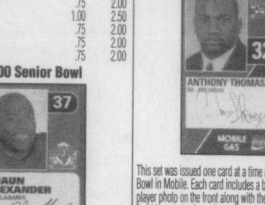

Cards from this set were issued at the 2000 Senior Bowl in Mobile. Each card includes a black and white player photo on the front along with the 2000 Senior Bowl logo, a facsimilie autograph, and a Coca-Cola sponsorship logo. The cardbacks are blank. Any additions to this list are appreciated.

COMPLETE SET (112)	75.00	150.00
1 John Abraham	1.25	3.00
2 Shaun Alexander	3.00	8.00
3 Darnell Alford	.60	1.50
4 Rashard Anderson	.75	2.00
5 Reggie Austin	.60	1.50
6 Mark Baniewicz	.60	1.50
7 David Barrett	.60	1.50
8 William Bartee	.75	2.00
9 Andrew Bayes	.60	1.50
10 Robert Bean	.75	2.00
11 Anthony Becht	1.25	3.00
12 Brad Bedell	.60	1.50
13 Mike Brown	1.00	2.50
14 Ralph Brown	.60	1.50
15 Shamari Buchanan	.60	1.50
16 Keith Bulluck	1.25	3.00
17 David Byrd	.60	1.50
18 Trung Canidate	.75	2.00
19 Giovanni Carmazzi	.75	2.00
20 Leonardo Carson	.60	1.50
21 Tyrone Carter	.75	2.00
22 Chrys Chukwuma	.60	1.50
23 Pedro Cirino	.60	1.50
24 Kendrick Clancy	.60	1.50
25 Travis Claridge	.60	1.50
26 Chad Clifton	.60	1.50
27 Chris Combs	.60	1.50
28 Joe Dean Davenport	.60	1.50
29 Jerry DeLoach	.60	1.50
30 Reuben Droughns	.75	2.00
31 Ron Dugans	.60	1.50
32 Deon Dyer	.75	2.00
33 Paul Edinger	1.25	3.00
34 Mario Edwards	.75	2.00
35 Shaun Ellis	1.25	3.00
36 Danny Farmer	.75	2.00
37 Chafie Fields	.60	1.50
38 Arturo Freeman	.60	1.50
39 Byron Frisch	.60	1.50
40 Trevor Gaylor	.75	2.00
41 Kabeer Gbaja-Biamila	1.50	4.00
42 Sherrod Gideon	.60	1.50
43 Ian Gold	.75	2.00
44 Dwayne Goodrich	.60	1.50
45 Shayne Graham	.60	1.50
46 Barrett Green	.60	1.50
47 Cornelius Griffin	.75	2.00
48 Clark Haggans	.60	1.50
49 Joe Hamilton	.75	2.00
50 Chris Hovan	.75	2.00
51 Darren Howard	.75	2.00
52 Jabari Issa	.60	1.50
53 Jeno James	.60	1.50
54 Dwight Johnson	.60	1.50
55 Jerry Johnson	.60	1.50
56 Leander Jordan	.60	1.50
57 Matt Keller	.60	1.50
58 Kenoy Kennedy	.60	1.50
59 Sean Key	.60	1.50
60 Erron Kinney	1.25	3.00
61 Adrian Klemm	.60	1.50
62 Anthony Lucas	.60	1.50
63 David Macklin	.60	1.50
64 Tee Martin	1.25	3.00
65 Stockar McDougle	.60	1.50
66 Richard Mercier	.60	1.50
67 Corey Moore	.60	1.50
68 Sammy Morris	1.00	2.50
69 Sylvester Morris	.75	2.00
70 Kaulana Noa	.60	1.50
71 Dennis Northcutt	1.25	3.00
72 Matt O'Neal	.60	1.50
73 Terrance Parrish	.60	1.50
74 Chad Pennington	3.00	8.00
75 Julian Peterson	1.25	3.00
76 Mareno Philyaw	.60	1.50
77 Todd Pinkston	1.25	3.00
78 Hank Poteat	.75	2.00
79 Travis Prentice	1.25	3.00
80 Tim Rattay	2.00	5.00
81 Chris Redman	.75	2.00
82 J.R. Redmond	.75	2.00
83 Quinton Reese	.60	1.50
84 Spencer Riley	.60	1.50
85 Rob Riti	.60	1.50
86 Fred Robbins	.60	1.50
87 Chris Samuels	.75	2.00
88 Gari Scott	.60	1.50
89 Aaron Shea	.75	2.00
90 Brandon Short	.75	2.00
91 Mark Simoneau	.75	2.00
92 Peter Sirmon	.60	1.50
93 T.J. Slaughter	.60	1.50
94 Robaire Smith	.60	1.50
95 R.Jay Soward	.75	2.00
96 John St.Clair	.60	1.50
97 Jay Tant	.60	1.50
98 Adalius Thomas	1.25	3.00
99 Michael Thompson	.60	1.50
100 Raynoch Thompson	.75	2.00
101 Jeff Ulbrich	.60	1.50
102 Brian Urlacher	5.00	12.00
103 Todd Wade	.60	1.50
104 Darwin Walker	.60	1.50
105 Jeff Walker	.60	1.50
106 Steve Warren	.60	1.50
107 Marcus Washington	.75	2.00
108 Jason Webster	.60	1.50
109 George White	.60	1.50
110 Michael Wiley	.75	2.00
111 Bobby Williams	.60	1.50
112 Antonio Wilson	.60	1.50

2001 Senior Bowl

This set was issued one card at a time at the 2001 Senior Bowl in Mobile. Each card includes a black and white player photo on the front along with the 2001 Senior Bowl logo and a Coca-Cola sponsorship logo. The cardbacks are blank.

COMPLETE SET (112)	100.00	200.00
1 Dan Alexander	.75	2.00
2 Brian Allen	.75	2.00
3 David Allen	1.00	2.50
4 Will Allen	1.00	2.50
5 Scotty Anderson	1.00	2.50
6 Adam Archuleta	1.25	3.00
7 Jeff Backus	1.00	2.50
8 Alex Bannister	1.00	2.50
9 Kevan Barlow	2.00	5.00
10 Gary Baxter	1.00	2.50
11 Kendrell Bell	2.50	6.00
12 Cory Bird	1.25	3.00
13 Willie Blade	.75	2.00
14 James Boyd	.75	2.00
15 Chris Brown	.75	2.00
16 Derrick Burgess	1.25	3.00
17 Robert Carswell	.75	2.00
18 Rashard Casey	1.00	2.50
19 Larry Casher	1.00	2.50
20 Quinton Caver	1.00	2.50
21 Mike Cerimele	1.00	2.50
22 Tay Cody	.75	2.00
23 Jarrod Cooper	1.25	3.00
24 Alge Crumpler	1.25	3.00
25 Ennis Davis	.75	2.00
26 Ryan Diem	.75	2.00
27 Tony Dixon	1.00	2.50
28 Char-ron Dorsey	.75	2.00
29 Tony Driver	1.00	2.50
30 Andre Dyson	.75	2.00
31 Mario Fatefehi	1.00	2.50
32 Kynan Forney	.75	2.00
33 Mike Gandy	.75	2.00
34 Rod Gardner	2.00	5.00
35 Randy Garner	.75	2.00
36 Robert Garza	.75	2.00
37 Derrick Gibson	1.00	2.50
38 Morlon Greenwood	1.00	2.50
39 Ben Hamilton	.75	2.00
40 Nick Harris	.75	2.00
41 Jamie Henderson	1.00	2.50
42 Travis Henry	1.50	4.00
43 Sedrick Hodge	.75	2.00
44 Paul Hogan	.75	2.00
45 Jabari Holloway	1.00	2.50
46 Margin Hooks	.75	2.00
47 Willie Howard	1.00	2.50
48 Orlando Huff	.75	2.00
49 Steve Hutchinson	1.00	2.50
50 Kris Jenkins	1.25	3.00
51 Jonas Jennings	.75	2.00
52 Ligarius Jennings	.75	2.00
53 Chad Johnson	3.00	8.00
54 Sly Johnson	1.00	2.50
55 LaMont Jordan	2.00	5.00
56 Bhawoh Jue	1.25	3.00
57 Mike Keathley	.75	2.00
58 Ben Leard	1.00	2.50
59 David Leaverton	.75	2.00
60 Alex Lincoln	1.00	2.50
61 Matt Light	1.25	3.00
62 Arther Love	.75	2.00
63 Ken Lucas	1.00	2.50
64 Torrance Marshall	1.25	3.00
65 Dustin McClintock	1.00	2.50
66 Jeff McCurley	.75	2.00
67 Kareem McKenzie	1.00	2.50
68 Mike McMahon	1.00	2.50
69 Snoop Minnis	1.00	2.50
70 Travis Minor	1.00	2.50
71 Zeke Moreno	1.25	3.00
72 Quincy Morgan	1.25	3.00
73 Brian Natkin	.75	2.00
74 Bobby Newcombe	1.00	2.50
75 John Nix	.75	2.00
76 Moran Norris	.75	2.00
77 Jesse Palmer	1.25	3.00
78 Tommy Polley	1.25	3.00
79 Jamie Rheem	.75	2.00
80 Karon Riley	.75	2.00
81 David Rivers	1.00	2.50
82 Bernard Robertson	.75	2.00
83 Kendrick Rogers	.75	2.00
84 Shaun Rogers	1.25	3.00
85 Sage Rosenfels	1.25	3.00
86 John Schlecht	.75	2.00
87 Cedric Scott	1.00	2.50
88 Dwight Smith	.75	2.00
89 Kenny Smith	1.00	2.50
90 Omar Smith	.75	2.00
91 Fred Smoot	1.25	3.00
92 Brandon Spoon	1.25	3.00
93 Daleroy Stewart	.75	2.00
94 Michael Stone	.75	2.00
95 Marcus Stroud	1.25	3.00
96 Marques Sullivan	.75	2.00
97 Joe Tafoya	.75	2.00
98 Anthony Thomas	2.50	6.00
99 LaDainian Tomlinson	10.00	20.00
100 Kyle Vanden Bosch	1.50	4.00
101 Fred Wakefield	1.00	2.50
102 Raymond Walls	.75	2.00
103 Chad Ward	.75	2.00
104 David Warren	.75	2.00
105 Reggie Wayne	2.50	6.00
106 Scott Westerfield	.75	2.00
107 Eric Westmoreland	1.00	2.50
108 Boo Williams	1.00	2.50
109 Maurice Williams	.75	2.00
110 Cedrick Wilson	1.25	3.00
111 Floyd Womack	.75	2.00
112 Ellis Wyms	.75	2.00

2002 Senior Bowl

These cards were given away at the 2002 Senior Bowl in Mobile Alabama. Each is blankbacked and features a small black and white player photo on the front. The cardfronts also include the 2002 Senior Bowl logo near the upper left hand corner. Each card measures roughly 3" by 5".

COMPLETE SET (114)	75.00	150.00
1 P.J. Alexander	.60	1.50
2 James Allen LB	.60	1.50
3 Marques Anderson	1.00	2.50
4 Akin Ayodele	.60	1.50
5 Chris Baker	.60	1.50
6 Justin Bannan	.60	1.50
7 Will Bartholomew	.60	1.50
8 Rashad Bauman	.60	1.50
9 Jarrod Baxter	.75	2.00
10 LeCharles Bentley	.60	1.50
11 Ladell Betts	1.25	3.00
12 Martin Bibla	.60	1.50
13 Deion Branch	2.50	6.00
14 Alex Brown	1.00	2.50
15 Sheldon Brown	1.00	2.50
16 Rocky Calmus	1.00	2.50
17 Kelly Campbell	.75	2.00
18 David Carr	1.25	3.00
19 Tim Carter	.75	2.00
20 Jeff Chandler	.60	1.50
21 Kenyon Coleman	.75	2.00
22 Keyuo Craver	.60	1.50
23 Woody Dantzler	1.00	2.50
24 Rohan Davey	1.00	2.50
25 Andra Davis	1.00	2.50
26 Dorsett Davis	.60	1.50
27 Ryan Denney	.60	1.50
28 Nate Dwyer	.60	1.50
29 Mike Echols	.60	1.50
30 Justin Ena	.60	1.50
31 Hayden Epstein	.75	2.00
32 Bryan Fletcher	.60	1.50
33 Larry Foote	.60	1.50
34 DeShaun Foster	2.00	5.00
35 Melvin Fowler	.60	1.50
36 Eddie Freeman	.60	1.50
37 Dwight Freeney	2.00	5.00
38 David Garrard	2.00	5.00
39 Jonathan Goodwin	.75	2.00
40 Lamar Gordon	1.25	3.00
41 Daniel Graham	1.00	2.50
42 Andre Gurode	.75	2.00
43 Carlos Hall	.60	1.50
44 Alan Harper	.60	1.50
45 Napoleon Harris	1.00	2.50
46 Herb Haygood	.60	1.50
47 Ennis Haywood	.75	2.00
48 Eric Heitman	.60	1.50
49 Charles Hill	.60	1.50
50 Matt Hill	.60	1.50
51 Chris Hope	.75	2.00
52 Joseph Jefferson	.60	1.50
53 Ron Johnson	.75	2.00
54 Levi Jones	1.00	2.50
55 Terry Jones	.60	1.50
56 Brett Keisel	.60	1.50
57 Kurt Kittner	.75	2.00
58 Ken Kocher	.60	1.50
59 Ben Leber	.60	1.50
60 Michael Lewis	.60	1.50
61 Andre Lott	.60	1.50
62 Marquand Manuel	.60	1.50
63 Jason McAddley	.75	2.00
64 Josh McCown	1.50	4.00
65 Nakoa McElrath	.60	1.50
66 Jon McGraw	.60	1.50
67 Seth McKinney	.60	1.50
68 Terrance Metcalf	.60	1.50
69 Freddie Milons	.75	2.00
70 Shannon Money	.60	1.50
71 Brandon Moore	.60	1.50
72 Will Overstreet	.60	1.50
73 Melvin Paige	.60	1.50
74 Scott Peters	.60	1.50
75 Adrian Peterson	1.00	2.50
76 Jermaine Petty	.60	1.50
77 Jermaine Phillips	.60	1.50
78 Chester Pitts	.60	1.50
79 Patrick Ramsey	1.00	2.50
80 Antwaan Randle El	2.00	5.00
81 Victor Rogers	.60	1.50
82 Casey Roussel	.60	1.50
83 Robert Royal	.75	2.00
84 Cliff Russell	.75	2.00
85 Gregory Scott	.60	1.50
86 Antuan Simmons	.60	1.50
87 Kendall Simmons	.75	2.00
88 Ryan Sims	1.00	2.50
89 Raonall Smith	.60	1.50
90 Steve Smith	.60	1.50
91 Charles Stackhouse	.75	2.00
92 Conner Stephens	.60	1.50
93 Travis Stephens	.75	2.00
94 Ed Ta'Amu	.60	1.50
95 Bryan Thomas	1.00	2.50
96 Kevin Thomas	1.00	2.50
97 Lamont Thompson	.75	2.00
98 Josh Thornhill	.60	1.50
99 Larry Tripplett	.75	2.00
100 Kurt Vollers	.75	2.00
101 Javon Walker	2.00	5.00
102 Marquise Walker	1.00	2.50
103 Lenny Walls	.60	1.50
104 Anthony Weaver	.75	2.00
105 Fred Weary	.60	1.50
106 Jonathan Wells	1.00	2.50
107 Brian Westbrook	2.50	6.00
108 Roosevelt Williams	.60	1.50
109 Tank Williams	.60	1.50
110 Coy Wire	1.00	2.50
111 Tracey Wistrom	.75	2.00
112 Will Witherspoon	1.00	2.50
113 Dave Zastudil	.60	1.50
114 Ms. Carrie Colvin (America's Junior Miss)	.60	1.50

2003 Senior Bowl

These cards were given away at the 2003 Senior Bowl in Mobile Alabama. Each is blankbacked and features a small black and white player photo on the front along with Coca-Cola, Bob Baumhower's Wings, and Army National Guard sponsorship logos. The cardfronts also include the 2003 Senior Bowl logo near the lower right hand corner. Each card measures roughly 3" by 5".

COMPLETE SET (98)	75.00	150.00
1 Anthony Adams SP	4.00	10.00
2 Sam Aiken	1.00	2.50
3 Tully Banta-Cain	1.00	2.50
4 Brooks Barnard	.75	2.00
5 Arnaz Battle	1.00	2.50
6 Julian Battle	1.00	2.50
7 Kyle Boller	1.25	3.00
8 Tyler Brayton	1.25	3.00
9 Jeremy Bridges	.75	2.00
10 Lance Briggs	2.00	5.00
11 Chris Brown	1.25	3.00
12 Mark Brown	.75	2.00
13 Tyrone Calico	2.50	6.00
14 Ben Claxton	.75	2.00
15 Colin Cole	.75	2.00
16 Angelo Crowell	1.00	2.50
17 Kevin Curtis	1.25	3.00
18 Anthony Davis	.75	2.00
19 Domanick Davis	2.50	6.00
20 Sammy Davis	1.25	3.00
21 Damon Duval	.75	2.00
22 Nick Eason	.75	2.00
23 Terrence Edwards	1.00	2.50
24 Justin Fargas	1.50	4.00
25 Drayton Florence	.75	2.00
26 George Foster	.75	2.00
27 Doug Gabriel	1.25	3.00
28 Talman Gardner	1.25	3.00
29 Kevin Garrett	.75	2.00
30 Earnest Graham	1.00	2.50
31 Jamaal Green	1.00	2.50
32 Justin Griffith	1.00	2.50
33 DeJuan Groce	1.25	3.00
34 Mario Haggan	.75	2.00
35 Gerald Hayes	.75	2.00
36 Michael Haynes	1.25	3.00
37 Victor Hobson	1.25	3.00
38 Montrae Holland	.75	2.00
39 Terrence Holt	1.00	2.50
40 Taylor Jacobs	1.00	2.50
41 Bradie James	1.25	3.00
42 Al Johnson	.75	2.00
43 Ben Johnson	.75	2.00
44 Bryant Johnson	1.25	3.00
45 Jarret Johnson	1.00	2.50
46 Larry Johnson	4.00	10.00
47 Todd Johnson	.75	2.00
48 Ben Joppru	1.25	3.00
49 Cato June	1.25	3.00
50 Chris Kelsay	.75	2.00
51 Kenny King	1.00	2.50
52 Kliff Kingsbury	1.00	2.50
53 Dan Koppen	1.00	2.50
54 Malaefou MacKenzie	.75	2.00
55 Vince Manuwai	.75	2.00
56 Terrence Martin	.75	2.00
57 Rashean Mathis	1.00	2.50
58 LaMarcus McDonald	.75	2.00
59 Jerome McDougle	1.25	3.00
60 Casey Moore	1.00	2.50
61 Rashad Moore	1.00	2.50
62 Kindal Moorehead	1.00	2.50
63 Ovie Mughelli	.75	2.00
64 Mike Nattiel	1.25	3.00
65 Bruce Nelson	.75	2.00
66 Ben Nowland	.75	2.00
67 Calvin Pace	1.00	2.50
68 Carson Palmer	5.00	12.00
69 Tony Pashos	.75	2.00
70 Kenny Peterson	1.00	2.50
71 Mike Pinkard	.75	2.00
72 Artose Pinner	1.25	3.00
73 Dave Ragone	1.25	3.00
74 Antwoine Sanders	.75	2.00
75 Cecil Sapp	1.00	2.50
76 Steve Sciullo	.75	2.00
77 Bryan Scott	1.00	2.50
78 Mike Seidman	.75	2.00
79 Chris Simms	3.00	8.00
80 Clifton Smith	.75	2.00
81 L.J. Smith	1.00	2.50
82 Eric Steinbach	1.00	2.50
83 Jon Stinchcomb	.75	2.00
84 Pisa Tinoisamoa	1.50	4.00
85 Marcus Trufant	1.25	3.00
86 Torrin Tucker	1.00	2.50
87 Bobby Wade	1.25	3.00
88 Aaron Walker	1.00	2.50
89 Seneca Wallace	1.25	3.00
90 Shane Walton	.75	2.00
91 Seth Wand	.75	2.00
92 Ty Warren	1.25	3.00
93 Matt Wilhelm	1.25	3.00
94 Andrew Williams	1.00	2.50
95 Brett Williams	.75	2.00
96 Kevin Williams	1.25	3.00
97 Eugene Wilson	1.00	2.50
98 Andre Woolfolk	1.25	3.00

2004 Senior Bowl

These cards were given away at the 2004 Senior Bowl in Mobile Alabama. Each is blankbacked and features a small black and white player photo on the front along with Coca-Cola, Bob Baumhower's Wings, and Army National Guard sponsorship logos. The cardfronts also include the 2004 Senior Bowl logo near the lower right hand corner. Most include a printed facsimile autograph on the front inside a white box with the rest simply featuring the large blank white space for the player to actually sign himself. Each card measures roughly 3" by 5".

COMPLETE SET (104)	50.00	100.00
1 Nathaniel Adibi	.50	1.25
2 Will Allen	.60	1.50
3 Tim Anderson	.60	1.50
4 Dave Ball	.60	1.50
5 Jacob Bell	.50	1.25
6 Tatum Bell	.60	1.50
7 Michael Boulware	.75	2.00
8 Greg Brooks	.50	1.25
9 Maurice Brown	.50	1.25
10 Sean Bubin	.50	1.25
11 Darrell Campbell	.50	1.25
12 Jordan Carstens	.50	1.25
13 Kirk Chambers	.50	1.25
14 Adrien Clarke	.50	1.25
15 Cedric Cobbs	.50	1.25
16 Keary Colbert	.50	1.25
17 Ricardo Colclough	.60	1.50
18 Chris Cooley	.75	2.00
19 Jerricho Cotchery	.60	1.50
20 Rod Davis	.50	1.25
21 Darnell Dockett	.50	1.25
22 Dwan Edwards	.50	1.25
23 Brandon Everage	.50	1.25
24 Andrea Finch Jr. MISS	.50	1.25
25 Keyaron Fox	.60	1.50
26 Rich Gardner	.60	1.50
27 Ronnie Ghent	.50	1.25
28 Jake Grove	.50	1.25
29 Nick Hardwick	.50	1.25
30 Josh Harris	.50	1.25
31 Devery Henderson	.75	2.00
32 Bryan Hickman	.50	1.25
33 Justin Jenkins	.50	1.25
34 Michael Jenkins	.75	2.00
35 B.J. Johnson	.50	1.25
36 Brandon Johnson	.50	1.25
37 Donnie Jones	.50	1.25
38 Greg Jones	.50	1.25
39 Julius Jones	.60	1.50
40 Nate Kaeding	.75	2.00
41 Tommy Kelly	.50	1.25
42 Niko Koutouvides	.50	1.25
43 Travis LaBoy	.60	1.50
44 Bo Lacy	.50	1.25
45 Kyle Larson	.50	1.25
46 Chad Lavalais	.50	1.25
47 Nick Leckey	.50	1.25
48 Teddy Lehman	.50	1.25
49 Rodney Leisle	.50	1.25
50 Jeremy LeSueur	.50	1.25
51 Sean Locklear	.50	1.25
52 J.P. Losman	.60	1.50
53 Triandos Luke	.50	1.25
54 Bobby McCray	.50	1.25
55 DeMarco McNeil	.50	1.25
56 Mewelde Moore	.60	1.50
57 Johnnie Morant	.50	1.25
58 John Navarre	.50	1.25
59 James Newson	.75	2.00
60 Shane Olivea	.50	1.25
61 Chris Perry	.60	1.50
62 Stephen Peterman	.75	2.00
63 Shaun Phillips	.75	2.00
64 Cody Pickett	.60	1.50
65 Lousaka Polite	.50	1.25
66 Will Poole	.75	2.00
67 Derrick Pope	.60	1.50
68 Etric Pruitt	.50	1.25
69 Keiwan Ratliff	.50	1.25
70 Alan Reuber	.50	1.25
71 Brian Rimpf	.50	1.25
72 Philip Rivers	3.00	8.00
73 Jacob Rogers	.75	2.00
74 Bob Sanders	2.50	6.00
75 Matt Schaub	1.50	4.00
76 Stuart Schweigert	.60	1.50
77 Guss Scott	.50	1.25
78 Antonio Smith	.60	1.50
79 Brent Smith	.50	1.25
80 Daryl Smith	.50	1.25
81 Keith Smith	.50	1.25
82 Isaac Sopoaga	.50	1.25
83 Max Starks	.60	1.50
84 Alex Stepanovich	.50	1.25
85 Derrick Strait	.50	1.25
86 Thomas Tapeh	.60	1.50
87 Jeb Terry	.50	1.25
88 Dontarrious Thomas	.60	1.50
89 Joey Thomas	.50	1.25
90 Bruce Thornton	.50	1.25
91 Ben Troupe	.60	1.50
92 Michael Turner	1.00	2.50
93 Nathan Vasher	.75	2.00
94 Jonathan Vilma	.75	2.00
95 Ben Watson	.75	2.00
96 Courtney Watson	.50	1.25
97 Scott Wells	.50	1.25
98 Travelle Wharton	.50	1.25
99 Grant Wiley	.50	1.25
100 Ernest Wilford	.60	1.50
101 Demorrio Williams	.75	2.00
102 Madieu Williams	.50	1.25
103 Shaud Williams	.60	1.50
104 Kris Wilson	.60	1.50

2005 Senior Bowl

These cards were given away at the 2005 Senior Bowl in Mobile Alabama. Each is blankbacked and features a small full color player photo on the front along with the Coca-Cola, Bob Baumhower's Wings, and the Alabama Army National Guard sponsorship logos. The cardfronts also include the 2005 Senior Bowl logo near the lower right hand corner. Most include a printed facsimile autograph on the front inside a white box with the rest simply featuring the large blank white space for the player to actually sign himself. Cards of the north squad players include a green border with a blue border on the south squad cards. Each card measures roughly 3" by 5".

COMPLETE SET (102)	50.00	100.00
1 Lorenzo Alexander	.60	1.50
2 J.J. Arrington	1.00	2.50
3 Oshiomogho Atogwe	.60	1.50
4 David Baas	.60	1.50
5 Jonathan Babineaux	.75	2.00
6 Khalif Barnes	.60	1.50
7 Ronald Bartell	.60	1.50
8 Brock Berlin	.75	2.00
9 Michael Boley	.75	2.00
10 Craig Bragg	.75	2.00
11 Jamaal Brimmer	.40	1.00
12 Wesley Britt	.40	1.00
13 Nehemiah Broughton	.40	1.00
14 Elton Brown	.40	1.00
15 Jason Brown	.40	1.00
16 Reggie Brown	1.00	2.50
17 Anthony Bryant	.60	1.50
18 Dan Buenning	.40	1.00
19 James Butler	.60	1.50
20 Jason Campbell	1.25	3.00
21 Mark Clayton	1.00	2.50
22 Jonathan Clinkscale	.40	1.00
23 Shaun Cody	.75	2.00
24 Trent Cole	.40	1.00
25 Dustin Colquitt	.40	1.00
26 Sean Considine	.60	1.50
27 Junius Coston	.40	1.00
28 Travis Daniels	.40	1.00
29 Jim Davis	.40	1.00
30 Joel Dreessen	.60	1.50
31 Abraham Elimimian	.40	1.00
32 Attiyah Ellison	.60	1.50
33 Shannon Essenpreis (Junior Miss)	.40	1.00
34 Cole Farden	.40	1.00
35 Ronald Fields	.60	1.50
36 Alfred Fincher	.60	1.50
37 Charlie Frye	1.00	2.50
38 Vincent Fuller	.60	1.50
39 George Gause	.40	1.00
40 Justin Geisinger	.40	1.00
41 Fred Gibson	1.00	2.50
42 Eric Green	.60	1.50
43 David Greene	.75	2.00
44 Kay-Jay Harris	.60	1.50
45 Anttaj Hawthorne	.60	1.50
46 Noah Herron	.60	1.50
47 Leroy Hill	.60	1.50
48 Alphonso Hodge	.40	1.00
49 Alex Holmes	.40	1.00
50 Cedric Houston	.75	2.00
51 Vincent Jackson	.75	2.00
52 Marcus Johnson	.40	1.00
53 Brandon Jones	.75	2.00
54 Matt Jones	.75	2.00
55 Marcus Lawrence	.40	1.00
56 Logan Mankins	.60	1.50
57 Evan Mathis	.40	1.00
58 Will Matthews	.40	1.00
59 Cody McCarty	.40	1.00
60 Robert McCune	.60	1.50
61 Bryant McFadden	.75	2.00
62 Lance Mitchell	.60	1.50
63 Mike Montgomery	.60	1.50
64 Kirk Morrison	.75	2.00
65 Terrence Murphy	.75	2.00
66 Chris Myers	.40	1.00
67 Jared Newberry	.60	1.50
68 Jonathan Nichols	.40	1.00
69 Mike Nugent	.75	2.00
70 Dan Orlovsky	1.00	2.50
71 Kyle Orton	1.00	2.50
72 Jeremy Parquet	.40	1.00
73 Mike Patterson	.75	2.00
74 Rob Petitti	.60	1.50
75 Courtney Roby	.75	2.00
76 Carlos Rogers	1.00	2.50
77 Michael Roos	.60	1.50
78 Junior Rosegreen	.40	1.00
79 Matt Roth	.75	2.00
80 Barrett Ruud	.75	2.00
81 Alex Smith TE	.75	2.00
82 Adam Snyder	.60	1.50
83 Marcus Spears	1.00	2.50
84 Darren Sproles	1.00	2.50
85 David Stewart	.40	1.00
86 Taylor Stubblefield	.60	1.50
87 Bill Swancutt	.60	1.50
88 Adam Terry	.40	1.00
89 Craphonso Thorpe	.75	2.00
90 Zach Tuiasosopo	.75	2.00
91 Jimmy Verdon	.40	1.00
92 Andrew Walter	1.00	2.50
93 DeMarcus Ware	1.00	2.50
94 Corey Webster	.75	2.00
95 Manuel White	.60	1.50
96 Roddy White	.75	2.00
97 Cadillac Williams	2.50	6.00
98 Darrent Williams	.75	2.00
99 Roydell Williams	.60	1.50
100 Ray Willis	.40	1.00
101 Stanley Wilson	.60	1.50
102 Cornelius Wortham	.60	1.50

2006 Senior Bowl

These cards were given away at the 2006 Senior Bowl in Mobile Alabama. Each is blankbacked and features a small full color player photo on the front along with the Coca-Cola, Bob Baumhower's Wings, and the Alabama Army National Guard sponsorship logos. The cardfronts also include the Senior Bowl logo near the lower left hand corner. Most include a printed facsimile autograph on the front inside a white box with the rest simply featuring the large blank white space for the player to actually sign himself. Each card measures roughly 3" by 5".

COMPLETE SET (99)	50.00	100.00
1 Jahmile Addae	.40	1.00
2 Joseph Addai	1.50	4.00
3 Victor Adeyanju	.40	1.00
4 Will Allen	.40	1.00
5 Jon Alston	.60	1.50
6 Mark Anderson	1.25	3.00
7 Devin Aromashodu	.60	1.50
8 Jason Avant	.50	1.25
9 Hank Baskett	1.00	2.50
10 Mike Bell	.75	2.00
11 Will Blackmon	.60	1.50
12 Greg Blue	.40	1.00
13 Daniel Bullocks	.75	2.00
14 Brodrick Bunkley	.75	2.00
15 Dominique Byrd	.75	2.00
16 Daryn Colledge	.40	1.00
17 Ryan Cook	.40	1.00
18 Brodie Croyle	1.25	3.00
19 Jay Cutler	2.00	5.00
20 Mike Degory	.40	1.00
21 Cody Douglas	.40	1.00
22 Elvis Dumervil	.40	1.00
23 Dusty Dvoracek	.60	1.50
24 D'Brickashaw Ferguson	.75	2.00
25 Stephen Gostkowski	.40	1.00
26 Skyler Green	.75	2.00
27 Chad Greenway	.75	2.00
28 Cedric Griffin	.60	1.50
29 Darrell Hackney	.60	1.50
30 Derek Hagan	.60	1.50
31 Tamba Hali	.75	2.00
32 Andre Hall	.60	1.50
33 Parys Haralson	.40	1.00
34 Roman Harper	.40	1.00
35 Orien Harris	.60	1.50
36 Jerome Harrison	.75	2.00
37 Spencer Havner	.40	1.00
38 Tye Hill	.75	2.00
39 Abdul Hodge	.75	2.00
40 Thomas Howard	.60	1.50
41 Marcus Hudson	.40	1.00
42 Cedric Humes	.75	2.00
43 Darrell Hunter	.40	1.00
44 Clint Ingram	.40	1.00
45 Brian Iwuh	.40	1.00
46 D'Qwell Jackson	.60	1.50
47 Max Jean-Gilles	.40	1.00
48 Kelly Jennings	.60	1.50
49 Tim Jennings	.40	1.00
50 Davin Joseph	.40	1.00
51 Mathias Kiwanuka	.75	2.00
52 Joe Klopfenstein	.60	1.50
53 Manny Lawson	.75	2.00
54 Jonathan Lewis	.60	1.50
55 Marcedes Lewis	.75	2.00
56 Deuce Lutui	.40	1.00
57 Jesse Mahelona	.40	1.00
58 Nick Mangold	.40	1.00
59 Marcus McNeill	.40	1.00
60 Garrett Mills	.40	1.00
61 DeMario Minter	.60	1.50
62 Anthony Mix	.60	1.50
63 Sinorice Moss	.75	2.00
64 Martin Nance	.75	2.00
65 Jerious Norwood	1.25	3.00
66 Ryan O'Callaghan	.40	1.00
67 Ben Obomanu	.60	1.50
68 Thomas Olmsted	.40	1.00
69 Babatunde Oshinowo	.40	1.00
70 Marvin Philip	.40	1.00
71 Anwar Phillips	.75	2.00
72 David Pittman	.40	1.00
73 Freddie Roach	.40	1.00
74 Michael Robinson	.60	1.50
75 DeMeco Ryans	1.00	2.50
76 Jonathan Scott	.40	1.00
77 Mark Setterstrom	.40	1.00
78 D.J. Shockley	.75	2.00
79 Anthony Smith	.75	2.00
80 Charles Spencer	.40	1.00
81 Maurice Stovall	.75	2.00
82 Darryl Tapp	.40	1.00
83 Albert Toeaina	.40	1.00
84 John Torp	.40	1.00
85 Jeremy Trueblood	.40	1.00
86 Lawrence Vickers	.60	1.50
87 Pat Watkins	.40	1.00
88 Gabe Watson	.60	1.50
89 Terrence Whitehead	.60	1.50
90 Charlie Whitehurst	.75	2.00
91 Gerris Wilkinson	.40	1.00
92 DeAngelo Williams	1.25	3.00
93 Demetrius Williams	.60	1.50
94 Kyle Williams	.40	1.00
95 T.J. Williams	.40	1.00
96 Travis Williams	.40	1.00
97 Travis Wilson	.75	2.00
98 Kamerion Wimbley	.60	1.50
99 Eric Winston	.40	1.00
100 Deric Yaussi	.40	1.00

2007 Senior Bowl

COMPLETE SET (102)	40.00	80.00
1 Victor Abiamiri	.60	1.50
2 Rufus Alexander	.50	1.25
3 Aundrae Allison	.40	1.00
4 Dallas Baker	.60	1.50
5 Josh Beekman	.50	1.25
6 Fred Bennett	1.00	2.50
7 H.B. Blades	.40	1.00
8 Justin Blalock	.40	1.00
9 Lorenzo Booker	.50	1.25
10 Dwayne Bowe	.75	2.00
11 Stewart Bradley	.50	1.25
12 Kareem Brown	.50	1.25
13 Levi Brown	.60	1.50
14 Prescott Burgess	.50	1.25
15 Adam Carriker	.50	1.25
16 Scott Chandler	.60	1.50
17 Thomas Clayton	.50	1.25
18 David Clowney	.50	1.25
19 Michael Coe	.40	1.00
20 Mason Crosby	.50	1.25
21 Tim Crowder	.60	1.50
22 Ken Darby	.50	1.25
23 Doug Datish	.40	1.00
24 A.J. Davis	.40	1.00
25 Buster Davis	.50	1.25
26 Chris Davis WR	.40	1.00
27 Tim Duckworth	.40	1.00
28 Earl Everett	.50	1.25
29 Nick Folk	.60	1.50
30 Dustin Fry	.40	1.00
31 Josh Gattis	.40	1.00
32 Brett Goode	.40	1.00
33 Michael Griffin	.60	1.50
34 Ben Grubbs	.50	1.25
35 Leon Hall	.50	1.25
36 Clark Harris	.50	1.25
37 David Harris	.50	1.25
38 Leroy Harris	.40	1.00
39 Ryan Harris	.40	1.00
40 Johnnie Lee Higgins	.50	1.25
41 Jason Hill	.60	1.50

42 Daymeion Hughes	.50	1.25
43 Tony Hunt	.40	1.00
44 David Irons	.50	1.25
45 Kenny Irons	2.00	5.00
46 Tanard Jackson	.40	1.00
47 Antonio Johnson	.40	1.00
48 Ryan Kalil	.50	1.25
49 Kevin Kolb	1.00	2.50
50 Chris Leak	.50	1.25
51 Nicholas Leeson	.40	1.00
52 Brian Leonard	.50	1.25
53 James Marten	.40	1.00
54 Ryan McBean	.60	1.50
55 Marcus McCauley	.50	1.25
56 Le'Ron McClain	.60	1.50
57 Ray McDonald	.50	1.25
58 Rhema McKnight	.40	1.00
59 Kevin McLee	.40	1.00
60 Brandon Mebane	.50	1.25
61 Brandon Meriweather	.60	1.50
62 Martrez Milner	.40	1.00
63 Jay Moore	.50	1.25
64 Quentin Moses	.50	1.25
65 Dan Mozes	.40	1.00
66 Brandon Myles	.50	1.25
67 Joe Newton	.40	1.00
68 Amobi Okoye	.60	1.50
69 Tyler Palko	.50	1.25
70 Jordan Palmer	.50	1.25
71 Ben Patrick	.50	1.25
72 David Patterson	.40	1.00
73 Kevin Payne	.40	1.00
74 Quinn Pitcock	.50	1.25
75 Chase Pittman	.50	1.25
76 Adam Podlesh	.40	1.00
77 Paul Posluszny	.60	1.50
78 Manuel Ramirez	.40	1.00
79 Aaron Ross	.60	1.50
80 Aaron Rouse	.50	1.25
81 Samson Satele	.50	1.25
82 Arron Sears	.50	1.25
83 Daniel Sepulveda	.60	1.50
84 Juwan Simpson	.40	1.00
85 Kolby Smith	.50	1.25
86 Troy Smith	.60	1.50
87 Anthony Spencer	.60	1.50
88 Joe Staley	.50	1.25
89 Drew Stanton	.40	1.00
90 Chansi Stuckey	.60	1.50
91 Courtney Taylor	.50	1.25
92 Tony Taylor	.50	1.25
93 DeMarcus Tank Tyler	.40	1.00
94 Tony Ugoh	.50	1.25
95 Jonathan Wade	.50	1.25
96 Eric Weddle	.60	1.50
97 Paul Williams	.40	1.00
98 Patrick Willis	1.25	3.00
99 Josh Wilson	.60	1.25
100 LaMarr Woodley	.60	1.50
101 Mansfield Wrotto	.40	1.00
102 Marshal Yanda	.40	1.00

2008 Senior Bowl

COMPLETE SET (109)	25.00	50.00
1 Jamar Adams	.25	.60
2 Xavier Adibi	.20	.50
3 Erik Ainge	.30	.75
4 Donnie Avery	.25	.60
5 Cliff Avril	.25	.60
6 Sam Baker	.20	.50
7 Kentwan Balmer	.25	.60
8 Kirk Barton	.20	.50
9 Beau Bell	.25	.60
10 Heath Benedict	.20	.50
11 Yvenson Bernard	.30	.75
12 John David Booty	.25	.60
13 Adarius Bowman	.25	.60
14 Colt Brennan	.30	.75
15 Brian Brohm	.30	.75
16 Durant Brooks	.20	.50
17 Titus Brown	.20	.50
18 Dorien Bryant	.25	.60
19 Red Bryant	.20	.50
20 Tim Bugg	.20	.50
21 Andre Caldwell	.25	.60
22 John Carlson	.30	.75
23 Gosder Cherilus	.25	.60
24 Tashard Choice	.25	.60
25 Dan Connor	.30	.75
26 Brad Cottam	.25	.60
27 Oniel Cousins	.20	.50
28 Brandon Coutu	.20	.50
29 Shawn Crable	.20	.50
30 Bruce Davis	.25	.60
31 Fred Davis	.30	.75
32 Kellen Davis	.20	.50
33 Thomas DeCoud	.20	.50
34 Quintin Demps	.30	.75
35 Jordon Dizon	.30	.75
36 Early Doucet	.25	.60
37 Harry Douglas	.25	.60
38 Mike Dragosavich	.20	.50
39 Chris Ellis	.20	.50
40 Sedrick Ellis	.30	.75
41 Robert Felton	.20	.50
42 Joe Flacco	1.00	2.50
43 Andre Fluellen	.25	.60
44 Justin Forsett	.30	.75
45 Matt Forte	.50	1.25
46 Wallace Gilberry	.20	.50
47 Charles Godfrey	.30	.75
48 Tavares Gooden	.25	.60
49 Marcus Griffin	.20	.50
50 Gary Guyton	.20	.50
51 DJ Hall	.25	.60
52 Marcus Harrison	.25	.60
53 Lavelle Hawkins	.20	.50
54 Chad Henne	.30	.75
55 Jacob Hester	.30	.75
56 Ali Highsmith	.20	.50
57 Peyton Hillis	.40	1.00
58 Chevis Jackson	.20	.50
59 Dexter Jackson	.25	.60
60 Lawrence Jackson	.25	.60
61 Chris Johnson	.75	2.00
62 Jason Jones	.30	.75
63 Steve Justice	.20	.50
64 Kendall Langford	.30	.75
65 Trevor Laws	.30	.75
66 Patrick Lee	.25	.60
67 Kory Lichtensteiger	.20	.50
68 Rafael Little	.25	.60
69 Bryan Mattison	.20	.50
70 Mike McGlynn	.20	.50
71 Leodis McKelvin	.25	.60
72 Ben Moffitt	.20	.50
73 Dre Moore	.25	.60
74 Jordy Nelson	.40	1.00
75 Carl Nicks	.25	.60
76 Jeff Otah	.25	.60
77 Mike Pollak	.20	.50
78 Tracy Porter	.30	.75
79 DeMario Pressley	.25	.60
80 Drew Radovich	.25	.60
81 Barry Richardson	.20	.50
82 Chad Rinehart	.20	.50
83 Keith Rivers	.30	.75
84 Darrell Robertson	.20	.50
85 Dominique Rodgers-Cromartie	.30	.75
86 Eddie Royal	.30	.75
87 Athyba Rubin	.20	.50
88 Martin Rucker	.25	.60
89 Garrison Sanborn	.20	.50
90 Dantrell Savage	.25	.60
91 Owen Schmitt	.30	.75
92 Roy Schuening	.20	.50
93 Alexis Serna	.20	.50
94 Marcus Smith	.25	.60
95 John Sullivan	.25	.60
96 Limas Sweed	.30	.75
97 Jacob Tamme	.30	.75
98 Terrell Thomas	.25	.60
99 Jeremy Thompson	.20	.50
100 DeJuan Tribble	.20	.50
101 Cody Wallace	.20	.50
102 Chauncey Washington	.25	.60
103 Terrence Wheatley	.20	.50
104 Philip Wheeler	.25	.60
105 Chris Williams	.25	.60
106 D.J. Wolfe	.20	.50
107 Andre Woodson	.30	.75
108 Wesley Woodyard	.25	.60
109 Tom Zbikowski	.30	.75

2009 Senior Bowl

1 Robert Ayers	.12	.30
2 Ramses Barden	.12	.30
3 Connor Barwin	.20	.50
4 William Beatty	.12	.30
5 Darry Beckwith	.15	.40
6 Rhett Bomar	.15	.40
7 Ron Brace	.12	.30
8 Andre Brown	.12	.30
9 Cody Brown	.12	.30
10 Nathan Brown	.15	.40
11 David Bruton	.15	.40
12 Darius Butler	.20	.50
13 Antoine Caldwell	.12	.30
14 Trevor Canfield	.12	.30
15 Greg Carr	.12	.30
16 Patrick Chung	.20	.50
17 Quan Cosby	.15	.40
18 Brian Cushing	.20	.50
19 James Davis	.20	.50
20 Will Davis	.12	.30
21 Louis Delmas	.20	.50
22 Larry English	.20	.50
23 Mark Estermyer	.12	.30
24 Tony Fiammetta	.15	.40
25 Moise Fokou	.12	.30
26 Zack Follett	.12	.30
27 Coye Francies	.12	.30
28 Marcus Freeman	.20	.50
29 Xavier Fulton	.12	.30
30 Brandon Gibson	.20	.50
31 Tyronne Green	.12	.30
32 Michael Hamlin	.15	.40
33 Cullen Harper	.20	.50
34 Graham Harrell	.20	.50
35 Victor Macho Harris	.12	.30
36 Anthony Hill	.12	.30
37 Evander Ziggy Hood	.12	.30
38 Kevin Huber	.12	.30
39 Juaquin Iglesias	.15	.40
40 Jake Ingram	.12	.30
41 Corvey Irvin	.12	.30
42 Tim Jamison	.15	.40
43 Rashad Jennings	.20	.50
44 Peria Jerry	.15	.40
45 Domonique Johnson	.12	.30
46 Herman Johnson	.15	.40
47 Jeremiah Johnson	.20	.50
48 Manuel Johnson	.12	.30
49 Quinn Johnson	.15	.40
50 Rashad Johnson	.15	.40
51 Eric Kettani	.12	.30
52 Mitch King	.12	.30
53 Troy Kropog	.12	.30
54 Ellis Lankster	.12	.30
55 Andy Levitre	.12	.30
56 Keenan Lewis	.20	.50
57 Phil Loadholt	.15	.40
58 Jonathan Luigs	.12	.30
59 Alex Mack	.15	.40
60 Alex Magee	.12	.30
61 Sherrod Martin	.15	.40
62 Clay Matthews	.50	1.25
63 Rey Maualuga	.20	.50
64 Patrick McAfee	.12	.30
65 Travis McCall	.12	.30
66 Tyrone McKenzie	.12	.30
67 Scott McKillop	.15	.40
68 Fili Moala	.15	.40
69 Kyle Moore	.15	.40
70 William Moore	.20	.50
71 Thomas Morstead	.12	.30
72 Shawn Nelson	.15	.40
73 Michael Oher	.30	.75
74 Ashlee Palmer	.12	.30
75 John Parker Wilson	.20	.50
76 Cedric Peerman	.15	.40
77 Derek Pegues	.12	.30
78 Brandon Pettigrew	.20	.50
79 John Phillips	.20	.50
80 B.J. Raji	.20	.50
81 Louie Sakoda	.12	.30
82 Kory Sheets	.15	.40
83 Ryan Shuman	.12	.30
84 Lawrence Sidbury	.12	.30
85 Clint Sintim	.20	.50
86 Alphonso Smith	.15	.40
87 DeAngelo Smith	.15	.40
88 Mike Thomas	.20	.50
89 Morgan Trent	.15	.40
90 Patrick Turner	.15	.40
91 Max Unger	.15	.40
92 Kraig Urbik	.15	.40
93 Chip Vaughn	.12	.30
94 David Veikune	.15	.40
95 Vance Walker	.12	.30
96 Mike Wallace	.40	1.00
97 Jason Watkins	.15	.40
98 Pat White	.20	.50
99 Derrick Williams	.15	.40
100 Eric Wood	.15	.40

2010 Senior Bowl

1 Danario Alexander	.20	.50
2 Nate Allen	.20	.50
3 Tyson Alualu	.15	.40
4 Javier Arenas	.20	.50
5 Larry Asante	.12	.30
6 Geno Atkins	.12	.30
7 Zane Beadles	.15	.40
8 Joique Bell	.15	.40
9 Ciron Black	.12	.30
10 Legarrette Blount	.30	.75
11 Chris Brown	.20	.50
12 Jarrett Brown	.20	.50
13 Donald Butler	.12	.30
14 Jeff Byers	.12	.30
15 Sean Canfield	.15	.40
16 Selvish Capers	.12	.30
17 Alex Carrington	.12	.30
18 Jamar Chaney	.12	.30
19 Terrence Cody	.15	.40
20 Justin Cole	.12	.30
21 Antonio Coleman	.12	.30
22 Harry Coleman	.12	.30
23 Kurt Coleman	.20	.50
24 John Conner	.20	.50
25 Chris Cook	.20	.50
26 Riley Cooper	.20	.50
27 Morgan Cox	.12	.30
28 Perrish Cox	.15	.40
29 Dorin Dickerson	.12	.30
30 Ed Dickson	.20	.50
31 Phillip Dillard	.12	.30
32 Anthony Dixon	.20	.50
33 Matt Dodge	.12	.30
34 Vladimir Ducasse	.20	.50
35 A.J. Edds	.20	.50
36 Jacoby Ford	.20	.50
37 Brandon Ghee	.15	.40
38 Mardy Gilyard	.20	.50
39 Brandon Graham	.15	.40
40 Garrett Graham	.15	.40
41 Jimmy Graham	.40	1.00
42 Shay Hodge	.15	.40
43 Mike Hoomanawanui	.20	.50
44 Lamarr Houston	.20	.50
45 Mike Iupati	.20	.50
46 Cory Jackson	.12	.30
47 Rashawn Jackson	.12	.30
48 John Jerry	.12	.30
49 Mike Johnson	.12	.30
50 Stafon Johnson	.20	.50
51 Donald Jones	.20	.50
52 Austen Lane	.12	.30
53 Brandon Lang	.15	.40
54 Ted Larsen	.12	.30
55 Shawn Lauvao	.12	.30
56 Dan Lefevour	.20	.50
57 Trevard Lindley	.12	.30
58 Taylor Mays	.20	.50
59 Kyle McCarthy	.20	.50
60 Dexter McCluster	.20	.50
61 Devin McCourty	.20	.50
62 Anthony McCoy	.15	.40
63 Zoltan Mesko	.12	.30
64 Lonyae Miller	.15	.40
65 Koa Misi	.20	.50
66 Roddrick Muckelroy	.15	.40
67 Jerome Murphy	.15	.40
68 Mike Neal	.20	.50
69 Eric Norwood	.15	.40
70 Jared Odrick	.20	.50
71 Eric Olsen	.15	.40
72 Jeff Owens	.12	.30
73 Colin Peek	.20	.50
74 Mitch Petrus	.12	.30
75 Tony Pike	.20	.50
76 Taylor Price	.20	.50
77 Andre Roberts	.20	.50
78 Patrick Robinson	.20	.50
79 Zac Robinson	.15	.40
80 Myron Rolle	.12	.30
81 Chris Scott	.12	.30
82 George Selvie	.15	.40
83 Darryl Sharpton	.12	.30
84 Cameron Sheffield	.12	.30
85 Terrell Skinner	.12	.30
86 D'Anthony Smith	.12	.30
87 Brett Swenson	.12	.30
88 Ben Tate	.25	.60
89 Tim Tebow	1.50	4.00
90 Matt Tennant	.12	.30
91 Cam Thomas	.15	.40
92 SYD'Quan Thompson	.12	.30
93 Leigh Tiffin	.12	.30
94 Roy Upchurch	.12	.30
95 J.D. Walton	.12	.30
96 Ed Wang	.20	.50
97 Daryl Washington	.15	.40
98 Dekoda Watson	.12	.30
99 Joe Webb	.20	.50
100 Thomas Welch	.12	.30
101 Dan Williams	.15	.40
102 Jeremy Williams	.12	.30
103 C.J. Wilson	.15	.40
104 Kyle Wilson	.20	.50
105 Mike Windt	.12	.30
106 Sean Weatherspoon	.20	.50
107 Sam Young	.15	.40

2011 Senior Bowl

COMPLETE SET (105)		
1 Sam Acho	.15	.40
2 Danny Aiken	.15	.40
3 Anthony Allen	.15	.40
4 Pierre Allen	.20	.50
5 Allen Bailey	.15	.40
6 Christian Ballard	.15	.40
7 Jeremy Beal	.15	.40
8 Ahmad Black	.20	.50
9 Clint Boling	.15	.40
10 James Brewer	.15	.40
11 Curtis Brown	.20	.50
12 Jalil Brown	.15	.40
13 Vincent Brown	.15	.40
14 Kendric Burney	.15	.40
16 Gabe Carimi	.15	.40
18 James Carpenter	.15	.40
19 Quinton Carter	.15	.40
20 Anthony Castonzo	.20	.50
21 Charles Clay	.15	.40
22 Andy Dalton	.40	1.00
23 Noel Devine	.20	.50
24 Preston Dial	.15	.40
25 Zac Etheridge	.15	.40
26 Kai Forbath	.15	.40
27 Mason Foster	.15	.40
28 Sione Fua	.15	.40
29 Brandon Fusco	.15	.40
30 Marcus Gilbert	.15	.40
31 Marcus Gilchrist	.15	.40
32 Eric Hagg	.20	.50
33 Leonard Hankerson	.30	.75
34 Dwayne Harris	.20	.50
35 Roy Helu	.30	.75
36 Alex Henery	.15	.40
37 Chas Henry	.15	.40
38 Mark Herzlich	.15	.40
39 Ross Homan	.20	.50
40 Rodney Hudson	.15	.40
41 Kendall Hunter	.20	.50
42 Nate Irving	.15	.40
43 Jaiquawn Jarrett	.15	.40
44 Josh Jasper	.15	.40
45 Jarvis Jenkins	.15	.40
46 Ronald Johnson	.20	.50
47 Greg Jones	.20	.50
48 Cameron Jordan	.20	.50
49 Colin Kaepernick	.30	.75
50 Lance Kendricks	.20	.50
51 Jeremy Kerley	.15	.40
52 Ryan Kerrigan	.20	.50
53 Jake Kirkpatrick	.15	.40
54 Kevin Kowalski	.15	.40
55 Joe Lefeged	.15	.40
56 Derrick Locke	.15	.40
57 Jake Locker	.60	1.50
58 DeMarcus Love	.15	.40
59 Owen Marecic	.15	.40
60 Casey Matthews	.20	.50
61 Colin McCarthy	.20	.50
62 Terrell McClain	.15	.40
63 DeAndre McDaniel	.20	.50
64 Greg McElroy	.25	.60
65 Mike McNeill	.20	.50
66 Pernell McPhee	.15	.40
67 Von Miller	.25	.60
68 John Moffitt	.15	.40
69 DeMarco Murray	.30	.75
70 Chris Neild	.15	.40
71 Kristofer O'Dowd	.15	.40
72 Johnny Patrick	.15	.40
73 Niles Paul	.25	.60
74 Austin Pettis	.20	.50
75 Jason Pinkston	.15	.40
76 Christian Ponder	.40	1.00
77 Bilal Powell	.15	.40
78 Brooks Reed	.20	.50
79 Greg Salas	.25	.60
80 Jock Sanders	.15	.40
81 Dane Sanzenbacher	.20	.50
82 Stephen Schilling	.15	.40
83 Da'Rel Scott	.15	.40
84 Da'Norris Searcy	.15	.40
85 Kelvin Sheppard	.15	.40
86 Richard Sherman	.15	.40
87 Derek Sherrod	.15	.40
88 Courtney Smith	.15	.40
89 Lee Smith	.15	.40
90 Nate Solder	.20	.50
91 Ricky Stanzi	.30	.75
92 Luke Stocker	.20	.50
93 Phil Taylor	.15	.40
94 Cedric Thornton	.15	.40
95 DeMarcus Van Dyke	.15	.40
96 Danny Watkins	.15	.40
97 Chris White	.15	.40
98 D.J. Williams	.20	.50
99 Ian Williams	.15	.40
100 Lawrence Wilson	.15	.40
101 K.J. Wright	.15	.40
102 Shareece Wright	.15	.40
103 Titus Young	.25	.60
104 Christian Yount	.15	.40

2012 Senior Bowl

1 Emmanuel Acho	0.20	0.50
2 Joe Adams	0.20	0.50
3 Mike Adams	0.20	0.50
4 Antonio Allen	0.15	0.40
5 Jeff Allen	0.15	0.40
6 Vick Ballard	0.15	0.40
7 Dwight Bentley	0.15	0.40
8 Jake Bequette	0.15	0.40
9 Tony Bergstrom	0.15	0.40
10 Will Blackwell	0.15	0.40
11 Philip Blake	0.15	0.40
12 Brandon Boykin	0.20	0.50
13 Nigel Bradham	0.15	0.40
14 Mike Brewster	0.15	0.40
15 James Brown	0.15	0.40
16 Zach Brown	0.15	0.40
17 Randy Bullock	0.15	0.40
18 Drew Butler	0.15	0.40
19 Audie Cole	0.15	0.40
20 Quinton Coples	0.20	0.50
21 Kirk Cousins	0.40	0.75
22 Jack Crawford	0.15	0.40
23 Lennon Creer	0.15	0.40
24 Juron Criner	0.15	0.40
25 Vinny Curry	0.15	0.40
26 Lavonte David	0.25	0.60
27 Demario Davis	0.15	0.40
28 Patrick Edwards	0.20	0.50
29 Michael Egnew	0.15	0.40
30 Bradie Ewing	0.15	0.40
31 Jamell Fleming	0.20	0.50
32 Donnie Fletcher	0.15	0.40
33 Nick Foles	0.30	0.75
34 Jeff Fuller	0.25	0.60
35 Terrance Ganaway	0.15	0.40
36 Cordy Glenn	0.15	0.40
37 T.J. Graham	0.20	0.50
38 Ladarius Green	0.15	0.40
39 Josh Harris	0.15	0.40
40 Casey Hayward	0.20	0.50
41 Dan Herron	0.20	0.50
42 Jaye Howard	0.15	0.40
43 Emil Igwenagu	0.15	0.40
44 George Iloka	0.15	0.40
45 Melvin Ingram	0.25	0.60
46 Asa Jackson	0.15	0.40
47 Malik Jackson	0.15	0.40
48 A.J. Jenkins	0.25	0.60
49 Janoris Jenkins	0.20	0.50
50 Tony Jerod-Eddie	0.15	0.40
51 Cam Johnson	0.15	0.40
52 James-Michael Johnson	0.15	0.40
53 Leonard Johnson	0.15	0.40
54 Rishaw Johnson	0.15	0.40
55 Ben Jones	0.15	0.40
56 Marvin Jones	0.15	0.40
57 Senio Kelemete	0.15	0.40
58 Ryan Lindley	0.15	0.40
59 Brian Linthicum	0.15	0.40
60 D'Anton Lynn	0.15	0.40
61 Doug Martin	0.30	0.75
62 Markelle Martin	0.15	0.40
63 Mike Martin	0.15	0.40
64 Matt McCants	0.15	0.40
65 Shea McClellin	0.20	0.50
66 Marvin McNutt	0.30	0.75
67 DeQuan Menzie	0.15	0.40
68 Kellen Moore	0.30	0.75
69 Alfred Morris	0.15	0.40
70 Josh Norman	0.15	0.40
71 Brad Nortman	0.15	0.40
72 Kelechi Osemele	0.15	0.40
73 Isaiah Pead	0.20	0.50
74 Deangelo Peterson	0.15	0.40
75 Chris Polk	0.15	0.40
76 DeVier Posey	0.20	0.50
77 Tydreke Powell	0.15	0.40
78 Brian Quick	0.20	0.50
79 Chris Rainey	0.15	0.40
80 Kheeston Randall	0.15	0.40
81 Kendall Reyes	0.15	0.40
82 Gerell Robinson	0.15	0.40
83 Keenan Robinson	0.15	0.40
84 Trenton Robinson	0.15	0.40
85 Zebrie Sanders	0.15	0.40
86 Mitchell Schwartz	0.15	0.40
87 Brad Smelley	0.15	0.40
88 Harrison Smith	0.15	0.40
89 Sean Spence	0.15	0.40
90 Ryan Steed	0.15	0.40
91 Alameda Ta'amu	0.15	0.40
92 Brandon Taylor	0.15	0.40
93 Brandon Thompson	0.15	0.40
94 Johnnie Troutman	0.15	0.40
95 Courtney Upshaw	0.15	0.40
96 William Vlachos	0.15	0.40
97 Bobby Wagner	0.15	0.40
98 Brandon Weeden	0.40	1.00
99 Carson Wiggs	0.15	0.40
100 Russell Wilson	0.30	0.75
101 Billy Winn	0.15	0.40
102 Kyle Wojta	0.15	0.40
103 Derek Wolfe	0.15	0.40
104 Kevin Zeitler	0.15	0.40

1969 South Carolina Team Sheets

These six sheets measure approximately 8" by 10". The fronts feature two rows of five black-and white player portraits each. The player's name, position and home town are printed under the photo. The backs are blank. The sheets are unnumbered and checklisted below in alphabetical order according to the first player listed.

COMPLETE SET (6)	25.00	50.00
1 Tim Bice	4.00	8.00
Candler Boyd		
Don Buckner		
Ronald Bunch		
Bob Cole		
Carl Cowart		
Don Dunning		
Mike Fair		
Tony Fusaro		
Benny Galloway		
2 Allen Brown	4.00	8.00
Don Somma		
Billy Tharp		
Scott Townsend		
Pat Watson		
Bob Wehmeyer		
Bob White		
Curtis Williams		
Tom Wingard		
Fred Zeigler		
3 Andy Chavous	4.00	8.00
Wally Orrel		
Ronnie Palmer		
Hyrum Pierce		
Jimmy Poole		
Roy Don Reeves		
Larry Royal		
Gene Schwarting		
Fletcher Spigner		
Frank Tetterton		
4 Paul Dietzel CO	10.00	20.00
Larry Jones CO		
Johnny Menger CO		
Pride Ratterree CO		
Bill Rowe CO		
Bill Shalosky CO		
Lou Holtz CO		
Don Purvis CO		
Jack Powers CO		
Dick Weldon CO		
5 Ben Garnto	4.00	8.00
Gordon Gibson		
Johnny Glass		
Jimmy Gobble		
Dave Grant		
Johnny Gregory		
Bob Harris		
Rudy Holloman		
Earl Hunter		
Jack James		
6 Jimmy Killen	4.00	8.00
Joe Komoroski		
Dave Lucas		
Bob Mauro		
George McCarthy		
Toy McCord		
Wally Medlin		
Bob Morris		
Warren Muir		
Jim Mulvihill		

1991 South Carolina Collegiate Collection

This 200-card set measures standard sized and features cards of all-time great South Carolina athletes. The fronts have a black border with color action shots on each one. The school name and logo are found across the top border of the card. The featured player's name is found along the bottom border set against a red background. The backs carry a small bio of the player and his/her statistics.

COMPLETE SET (200)	5.00	12.00
2 Todd Ellis FB	.05	.15
6 Kent Hagood FB	.05	.15
8 Harold Green FB	.05	.15
10 George Rogers FB	.20	.50
19 James Seawright FB	.05	.15
21 Kevin White FB	.05	.15
25 Derrick Little FB	.05	.15
28 Ron Rabune FB	.05	.15
33 Vic McConnell FB	.05	.15
39 Fitzgerald Davis FB	.05	.15
44 Todd Ellis FB	.05	.15
47 David Poinsett FB	.05	.15
55 Jeff Grantz FB	.05	.15
56 Alfred H. Von Kolnitz FB	.05	.15
57 Mike Caskey FB	.05	.15
58 Tatum Gressette FB	.05	.15
59 Alex Hawkins FB	.07	.20
60 Phil Lavoie FB	.05	.15
61 Lee Collins FB	.05	.15
63 Andrew Provence FB	.05	.15
69 Leon Cunningham FB	.05	.15
76 Dan Reeves FB	.30	.75
77 Tim Lewis FB	.07	.20
79 King Dixon FB	.05	.15
81 Billy Gambrell FB	.05	.15
83 Max Runager FB	.05	.15
91 Del Wilkes FB	.05	.15
93 Johnny Gregory FB	.05	.15
94 Lou Sossamon FB	.05	.15
98 Steve Wadiak FB	.05	.15
101 James Sumpter FB	.05	.15
104 Scott Hagler FB	.05	.15
105 Todd Berry FB	.05	.15
107 Carl Hill FB	.05	.15
109 Earl Johnson FB	.05	.15
110 Dominique Blasingame FB	.05	.15
111 Jim Desmond FB	.05	.15
112 Keith Bing FB	.05	.15
115 Mike Durrah FB	.05	.15
117 Ron Bass FB	.05	.15
118 Charlie Gowan FB	.05	.15
119 Ray Carpenter FB	.05	.15
122 Bryant Gilliard FB	.05	.15
124 Matt McKernan FB	.05	.15
127 Mark Fryer FB	.05	.15
129 Anthony Smith FB	.05	.15
130 Robert Robinson FB	.05	.15
131 Mark Fleetwood FB	.05	.15
134 Rodney Price FB	.05	.15
135 Willie McIntee FB	.05	.15
136 Kenny Haynes FB	.05	.15
138 Willie Scott FB	.05	.15
139 Ricky Daniels FB	.05	.15
140 Bill Barnhill FB	.05	.15
141 Gordon Beckham FB	.05	.15
142 Tim Dyches FB	.05	.15
145 Jim Walsh FB	.05	.15
147 Thomas Dendy FB	.05	.15
149 Bill Bradshaw FB	.05	.15
152 Eric Poole FB	.05	.15
153 Leonard Burton FB	.05	.15
155 Scott Windsor FB	.05	.15
159 Bishop Strickland FB	.05	.15
162 Allen Mitchell FB	.05	.15
164 Paul Vogel FB	.05	.15
165 Norman Floyd FB	.05	.15
166 Carl Brazell FB	.05	.15
168 Fred Zeigler FB	.05	.15
169 Frank Mincevich FB	.05	.15
170 Bobby Bryant FB	.07	.20
171 J.D. Fuller FB	.05	.15
173 Tom O'Connor FB	.05	.15
174 Kevin Hendrix FB	.05	.15
175 Greg Philpot FB	.05	.15
176 Warren Muir FB	.05	.15
179 Tommy Suggs FB	.05	.15
180 Don Bailey FB	.05	.15
181 Jones Andrews FB	.05	.15
182 Chris Major FB	.05	.15
184 Brendan McCormack FB	.05	.15
185 David Taylor FB	.05	.15
187 Bryant Meeks FB	.05	.15
191 Harry Skipper FB	.05	.15
192 Derrick Frazier	.05	.15
193 Raynard Brown FB	.05	.15
194 Quinton Lewis FB	.05	.15
195 Tony Guyton FB	.05	.15
196 John Leheup FB	.05	.15
197 Dick Harris FB	.05	.15

1995 South Carolina Athletic Hall of Fame

This set was issued by the South Carolina Athletic Hall of Fame as part of a fund raising promotion. It features athletes from a variety of sports (primarily football and basketball) with each printed on thick card stock.

2 John McKissick FB	.20	.50
4 Steve Fuller FB	.30	.75
5 Frank Howard FB	.30	.75
7 Art Shell FB	1.00	2.50
8 Dan Reeves FB	1.00	2.50
9 Sam Wyche FB	.50	1.25
10 Bill Hudson FB	.20	.50
12 Jeff Grantz FB	.20	.50
15 Oliver Dawson FB	.20	.50
17 Bobby Bryant FB	.20	.50
18 Fred Cone FB	.20	.50
19 John Small Sr. FB	.20	.50
20 King Dixon FB	.20	.50
21 Pete Tinsley FB	.20	.50
25 Alex Hawkins FB	.30	.75
26 Paul Maguire FB	.50	1.25
31 Charlie Waters FB	.30	.75
32 Marion Campbell FB	.30	.75
34 Thomas Barton FB	.20	.50
36 Doc Blanchard FB	.50	1.25
37 Steve Wadiak FB	.20	.50
38 George Rogers FB	.50	1.25
43 Dom Fusci FB	.20	.50
45 Jim David FB	.20	.50
46 Mac Folger FB	.20	.50
47 Sandy Gilliam FB	.20	.50
48 Bob Sharpe FB	.20	.50
49 Art Gregory FB	.20	.50
50 Tatum Gresselle FB	.20	.50
51 Jimmy Orr FB	.30	.75
55 Frank Howard FB	.30	.75
56 Bill Mathis FB	.30	.75
57 James Moorer FB	.20	.50
58 Marvin Bass FB	.20	.50
63 Tommy Suggs FB	.20	.50
64 Louis Sossamon FB	.20	.50
65 Rex Enright FB	.20	.50
66 Banks McFadden FB	.20	.50
67 Larry Craig FB	.20	.50
68 Cally Gault FB	.20	.50
69 Charlie Bradshaw FB	.20	.50
70 Stanley Morgan FB	.50	1.25
71 John Heisman FB	.50	1.25
74 Danny Ford FB	.20	.50
76 Dwight Clark FB	.50	1.25
77 Joe Morrison FB	.30	.75
79 Barney Chavous FB	.20	.50
81 Dewey Proctor FB	.20	.50
82 Pepper Martin FB	.50	1.25
87 Fred Zeigler FB	.20	.50
88 Bennie Cunningham FB	.20	.50
90 Claude Finney FB	.20	.50
91 Harvey Kirkland FB	.20	.50
92 Bob King FB	.20	.50
93 Bob Hudson FB	.20	.50
95 Joel Wells FB	.20	.50
100 Frank Howard FB	.30	.75
103 June Scott FB	.20	.50
104 John Gilliam FB	.20	.50
105 Todd Ellis FB	.20	.50
106 Bill Seigler FB	.20	.50
107 John Cannady FB	.20	.50

2003 South Carolina Bragging Rites

This set was issued together with the Clemson Bragging Rites card set to promote the 2003 motion picture by the same name. The cards were produced to resemble vintage cards complete with printed on creases, corners wear, and dirt. Black and white player photos were used and the cards were numbered on the front.

COMPLETE SET (12)	10.00	20.00
1 Tatum Gressette	.75	2.00
2 Earl Clary	.75	2.00
3 Rex Enright	.75	2.00
4 Steve Wadiak	.75	2.00
5 1961 Sigma Nu Prank	.75	2.00
6 Tyler Hellams	.75	2.00
7 Tommy Suggs	.75	2.00
8 Jeff Grantz	.75	2.00
9 Mike Hold	.75	2.00
10 Brad Edwards	1.00	2.50
11 Steve Taneyhill	1.00	2.50
12 Brandon Bennett	.75	2.00

1987-88 Southern

This 16-card standard-size set was sponsored by McDonald's, Southern University, and local law enforcement agencies, and was produced by McDag Productions. The McDonald's logo appears at the bottom of both sides of the card. The front features a mix of action or posed, black and white player photos. The pictures are bordered in turquoise on the sides, yellow above, and white below. The school name and player information appear in black lettering in the yellow border. A picture of the school mascot in the lower right corner rounds out the card face. The back presents biographical information, Jag Facts, and "Tips from The Jaguars" in the form of an anti-drug message. The sports represented in this set are football (1-3, 14-16) and basketball (4-13). The key cards in the set feature the first cards of NBA player Avery Johnson and NFL player Gerald Perry.

COMPLETE SET (16)	5.00	12.00
1 Marino Casem CO FB	.20	.50
2 Gerald Perry FB	.80	2.00
3 Michael Ball FB	.20	.50
Toren Robinson		
14 Allan Ratliff FB	.20	.50
15 Eric Foxworth FB	.20	.50
16 Jeff Swain FB	.20	.50

1974 Southern Cal Discs

This 30-disc set was issued inside a miniature plastic football display holder, sitting on a red stand that reads "Trojans 1974". The discs measure approximately 2 5/16" in diameter and feature borderless color glossy player photos, shot from the waist up. The backs have biographical information, including the high school attended in the player's hometown. The discs are unnumbered and are listed alphabetically below. The set was reportedly produced and sold by Photo Sports for $2.50 (under the name Foto Ball) during Southern Cal's homecoming week the Fall of 1974. The miniature football card holder is priced below but is not considered part of the set.

COMPLETE SET (30)	50.00	100.00
1 Bill Bain	1.50	3.00
2 Otha Bradley	1.50	3.00
3 Kevin Bruce	1.00	2.00
4 Mario Celotto	1.00	2.00
5 Marvin Cobb	2.00	4.00
6 Anthony Davis	4.00	8.00
7 Joe Davis	1.00	2.00
8 Shelton Diggs	1.50	3.00
9 Dave Farmer	1.50	3.00
10 Pat Haden	7.50	15.00
11 Donnie Hickman	1.00	2.00
12 Doug Hogan	1.00	2.00
13 Mike Howell	1.00	2.00
14 Gary Jeter	2.00	4.00
15 Steve Knutson	1.00	2.00
16 Chris Limahelu	1.50	3.00
17 Bob McCaffrey	1.00	2.00
18 J.K. McKay	2.00	4.00
19 John McKay CO	4.00	8.00
20 Jim O'Bradovich	2.00	4.00
21 Charles Phillips	1.50	3.00
22 Ed Powell	1.00	2.00
23 Marvin Powell	2.00	4.00
24 Danny Reece	1.50	3.00
25 Art Riley	1.00	2.00
26 Traveller II and Richard Sako	1.50	3.00
27 Tommy Trojan Trojan Statue	1.50	3.00
28 USC Song Girls	1.00	2.00
29 USC Song Girls	1.00	2.00
30 Richard Wood	2.00	4.00
NNO Football Card Holder	10.00	20.00

1988 Southern Cal Smokey

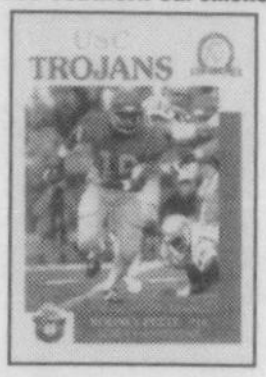

The 1988 Southern Cal Smokey set contains 17 standard-size cards. The fronts feature color photos with name, position, and jersey number. The vertically oriented backs have brief career highlights. The cards are unnumbered, so they are listed alphabetically by subject's name.

COMPLETE SET (17)	7.50	15.00
1 Erik Affholter	.40	1.00
2 Gene Arrington	.30	.75
3 Scott Brennan	.30	.75
4 Jeff Brown	.30	.75
5 Tracy Butts	.30	.75
6 Martin Chesley	.30	.75
7 Paul Green	.30	.75
8 John Guerrero	.30	.75
9 Chris Hale	.30	.75
10 Rodney Peete	1.00	2.50
11 Dave Powroznik	.30	.75
12 Mark Sager	.30	.75
13 Mike Serpa	.30	.75
14 Larry Smith CO	.60	1.50
15 Chris Sperle	.30	.75
16 Joe Walshe	.30	.75
17 Steven Webster	.30	.75

1988 Southern Cal Winners

The 1988 Southern Cal Winners set contains 73 standard-size cards. The fronts have black and white mugshots with USC and name banners in school colors; the vertically oriented backs have brief profiles and Trojan highlights from specific seasons. The set was sold by the USC bookstore. The cards are unnumbered, so they are listed alphabetically by type.

COMPLETE SET (73)	12.50	25.00
1 Title Card (schedule on back)	.10	.30
2 George Achica	.10	.30
3 Marcus Allen	2.00	5.00
4 Jon Arnett	.15	.40
5 Johnny Baker	.10	.30
6 Damon Bame	.10	.30
7 Chip Banks	.15	.40
8 Mike Battle	.10	.30
9 Hal Bedsole	.10	.30
10 Ricky Bell	.15	.40
11 Jeff Bregel	.10	.30
12 Tay Brown	.10	.30
13 Brad Budde	.10	.30
14 Dave Cadigan	.10	.30
15 Pat Cannamela	.10	.30
16 Paul Cleary	.10	.30
17 Sam Cunningham	.15	.40
18 Anthony Davis	.40	1.00
19 Clarence Davis	.10	.30
20 Morley Drury	.10	.30
21 John Ferraro	.10	.30
22 Bill Fisk	.10	.30
23 Roy Foster	.10	.30
24 Mike Garrett	.15	.40
25 Frank Gifford	1.25	3.00
26 Ralph Heywood	.10	.30
27 Pat Howell	.10	.30
28 Gary Jeter	.10	.30
29 Dennis Johnson	.10	.30
30 Mort Kaer	.10	.30
31 Grenny Lansdell	.10	.30
32 Ronnie Lott	1.50	4.00
33 Paul McDonald	.10	.30
34 Tim McDonald	.15	.40
35 Ron Mix	.15	.40
36 Don Mosebar	.15	.40
37 Artimus Parker	.10	.30
38 Charles Phillips	.10	.30
39 Erny Pinckert	.10	.30
40 Marvin Powell	.10	.30
41 Aaron Rosenberg	.10	.30
42 Tim Rossovich	.10	.30
43 Jim Sears	.10	.30
44 Gus Shaver	.10	.30
45 Nate Shaw	.10	.30
46 O.J. Simpson	1.25	3.00
47 Ernie Smith	.10	.30
48 Harry Smith	.10	.30
49 Larry Stevens	.10	.30
50 Lynn Swann	1.50	4.00
51 Brice Taylor	.10	.30
52 Dennis Thurman	.10	.30
53 Keith Van Horne	.10	.30
54 Cotton Warburton	.10	.30
55 Charles White	.60	1.50
56 Elmer Willhoite	.10	.30
57 Richard Wood	.10	.30
58 Ron Yary	.15	.40
59 Adrian Young	.10	.30
60 Charle Young UER (listed as Adrian Young on card front)	.10	.30
61 Pete Adams and John Grant	.10	.30
62 Bill Bain and Jim O'Bradovich	.10	.30
63 Nate Barrager and Francis Tappan	.10	.30
64 Booker Brown and Steve Riley	.10	.30
65 Al Cowlings& Jimmy Gunn& and Charles Weaver	.20	.50
66 Jack Del Rio and Duane Bickett	.20	.50
67 Clay Matthews and Bruce Matthews	.60	1.50
68 Marlin McKeever and Mike McKeever	.15	.40
69 Orv Mohler and Garrett Arbelbide	.10	.30
70 Sid Smith and Marv Montgomery	.10	.30
71 John Vella and Willie Hall	.10	.30
72 Don Williams and Jesse Hibbs	.10	.30
73 Stan Williamson and Tony Slaton	.10	.30

1989 Southern Cal Smokey

The 1989 Smokey USC football set contains 23 standard-size cards. The fronts have color action photos with maroon borders; the vertically oriented backs have fire prevention tips. These cards were distributed as a set. The cards are unnumbered, so the cards are listed below alphabetically by subject.

COMPLETE SET (23)	7.50	15.00
1 Dan Barnes	.30	.75
2 Dwayne Garner	.30	.75
3 Delmar Chesley	.30	.75
4 Cleveland Colter	.30	.75
5 Aaron Emanuel	.40	1.00
6 Scott Galbraith	.50	1.25
7 Leroy Holt	.30	.75
8 Randy Hord	.30	.75
9 John Jackson	.40	1.00
10 Brad Leggett	.30	.75
11 Marching Band	.30	.75
12 Dan Owens	.40	1.00
13 Brent Parkinson	.30	.75
14 Tim Ryan	.40	1.00
15 Bill Schultz	.30	.75
16 Larry Smith CO	.40	1.00
17 Ernest Spears	.30	.75
18 J.P. Sullivan	.30	.75
19 Cordell Sweeney	.30	.75
20 Traveler (Horse Mascot)	.30	.75
21 Marlon Washington	.30	.75
22 Michael Williams	.30	.75
23 Yell Leaders and Song Girls	.30	.75

1990-91 Southern Cal

This 20-card standard-size set was sponsored by the USDA Forest Service in conjunction with several other agencies. The cards have color action shots, with orange borders on a maroon card face with the words "USC Trojans" above the player's picture and his name, uniform number, school year, and position underneath his picture. The back has two Trojan logos at the top and features a player profile and a fire prevention cartoon starring Smokey. The cards are unnumbered and checklisted below in alphabetical order, with the uniform number after the name. Cards 1-2 and 12 feature basketball rather than football players and are so indicated by BKB. The checklist card in the set lists the football players but not the basketball players. The set features the first cards of NFL running back Ricky Ervins and NBA guard Robert Pack.

COMPLETE SET (20)	8.00	20.00
3 Ricky Ervins FB	.75	2.00
4 Shane Foley FB	.20	.50
5 Gene Fruge FB	.20	.50
6 Don Gibson FB	.20	.50
7 Frank Griffin FB	.20	.50
8 Pat Harlow FB	.75	2.00
9 Craig Hartsuyker FB	.20	.50
10 Marcus Hopkins FB	.20	.50
11 Pat O'Hara FB	.20	.50
13 Marc Preston FB	.20	.50
14 Quin Rodriguez FB	.20	.50
15 Scott Ross FB	.20	.50
16 Grant Runnerstrum FB	.30	.75
17 Mark Tucker FB	.20	.50
18 Brian Tuliau FB	.20	.50
19 Gary Wellman FB	.30	.75
20 Checklist Card Smokey Bear	.20	.50

1991 Southern Cal College Classics

Produced by College Classics Inc., this 100-card standard-size set honors former Trojan Athletes of various sports. Most players are football, other sports are designated in the listings below. The complete set comes with a blank-backed white card that carries the set's production number out of a total of 20,000 produced. In addition, 1,400 cards autographed by John Naber, Ron Fairly, Tom Seaver, Charles White, Dave Stockton, Mike Garrett, Anthony Davis, and Fred Lynn were randomly inserted throughout 1,000 of these sets. Since these cards rarely appear in the secondary marketplace, they are not priced.

COMPLETE SET (100)	10.00	25.00
1 Charles White FB	.20	.50
2 Anthony Davis FB	.20	.50
3 Clay Matthews FB	.10	.30
4 Hoby Brenner FB	.07	.20
5 Mike Garrett FB	.20	.50
8 Mike McKeever FB	.02	.10
12 Brad Budde FB	.07	.20
13 Tim Ryan FB	.02	.10
14 Mark Tucker FB	.02	.10
15 Rodney Peete FB	.20	.50
19 Craig Fertig FB	.02	.10
23 Al Cowlings FB	.20	.50
24 Ronnie Lott FB	.60	1.50
28 Tim Rossovich FB	.10	.30
29 Marvin Powell FB	.10	.30
30 Ron Yary FB	.10	.30
31 Ken Ruettgers FB	.07	.20
34 Dave Cadigan FB	.07	.20
35 Jeff Bregel FB	.02	.10
41 Anthony Colorito FB	.02	.10
43 Erik Affholter FB	.07	.20
44 Jim O'Bradovich FB	.02	.10
45 Duane Bickett FB	.10	.30
51 Jack Del Rio FB	.10	.30
53 Pat Haden FB	.40	1.00
55 Pete Beathard FB	.07	.20
58 Don Mosebar FB	.10	.30
59 Don Doll FB	.02	.10
62 Roy Foster FB	.07	.20
63 Bruce Matthews FB	.10	.30
64 Steve Sogge FB	.02	.10
66 Marv Montgomery FB	.02	.10
68 Larry Stevens FB	.02	.10
69 Harry Smith FB	.02	.10
70 Bill Bain FB	.02	.10
73 Richard Wood FB	.02	.10
76 Al Krueger FB	.02	.10
78 Rod Martin FB	.10	.30
85 John Grant FB	.02	.10
89 John McKay CO FB	.10	.30
91 John Jackson FB	.02	.10
92 Paul McDonald FB	.02	.10
93 Jimmy Gunn FB	.02	.10
94 Rod Sherman FB	.02	.10
AU1 Anthony Davis AU FB		
AU3 Mike Garrett AU FB		
AU8 Charles White AU FB		

1991 Southern Cal Smokey

This 16-card standard-size set was sponsored by the USDA Forest Service as well as other federal and state agencies. The front features color action player photos bordered in maroon. The top of the pictures is curved to resemble an archway, and the team name follows the curve of the arch. Player information and logos appear in a mustard stripe beneath the picture. In black on white, the backs carry player profile and a fire prevention cartoon starring Smokey. The cards are unnumbered and checklisted below in alphabetical order.

COMPLETE SET (16)	6.00	12.00
1 Kurt Barber	.40	1.00
2 Ron Dale	.30	.75
3 Derrick Deese	.40	1.00
4 Michael Gaytan	.30	.75
5 Matt Gee	.30	.75
6 Calvin Holmes	.30	.75
7 Scott Lockwood	.30	.75
8 Michael Moody	.30	.75
9 Marvin Pollard	.30	.75
10 Mark Raab	.30	.75
11 Larry Smith CO	.40	1.00
12 Raoul Spears	.30	.75
13 Matt Willig	.30	.75
14 Alan Wilson	.30	.75
15 James Wilson	.30	.75
16 Traveler (The Trojan Horse)	.30	.75

1992 Southern Cal Smokey

This 16-card standard-size set was sponsored by the USDA Forest Service and other state and federal agencies. The cards are printed on thin card stock. The fronts carry a color action player photo on a brick-red card face. The team name and year appear above the photo in gold print on a brick-red bar that partially rests on a gold bar with notched ends. Below the photo, the player's name and sponsor logos appear in a gold border stripe. The backs carry player profile and a fire prevention cartoon starring Smokey. The cards are unnumbered and checklisted below in alphabetical order.

COMPLETE SET (16)	6.00	12.00
1 Wes Bender	.30	.75
2 Estrus Crayton	.30	.75
3 Eric Dixon	.30	.75
4 Travis Hannah	.40	1.00
5 Zuri Hector	.30	.75
6 Lamont Hollinquest	.30	.75
7 Yonnie Jackson	.30	.75
8 Bruce Luizzi	.30	.75
9 Mike Mooney	.30	.75
10 Stephon Pace	.30	.75
11 Joel Scott	.30	.75
12 DeNail Sparks	.30	.75
13 Titus Tuiasosopo	.30	.75
14 Larry Wallace	.30	.75
15 David Webb	.30	.75
16 Title Card ART	.30	.75

1998 Southern Cal CHP

This set was produced for USC and sponsored by the California Highway Patrol. Each card features a color photo of the player along with a simple cardback printed in maroon, black and white. The unnumbered cards are listed below alphabetically.

COMPLETE SET (13)	4.00	8.00
1 Adam Abrams	.30	.75
2 Mike Bastianelli	.30	.75
3 Ken Bowen	.30	.75
4 Rashard Cook	.30	.75
5 Mark Cusano	.30	.75
6 Paul Hackett CO	.30	.75
7 Lawrence Larry	.30	.75
8 Marc Matock	.30	.75
9 Daylon McCutcheon	.40	1.00
10 Billy Miller	.40	1.00
11 Grant Pearsall	.30	.75
12 Marvin Powell	.30	.75
13 David Pratchard	.30	.75

1999 Southern Cal CHP

This set was produced for USC and sponsored by the California Highway Patrol. Each card features a color photo of the player along with a simple cardback printed in black and white. The unnumbered cards are listed below alphabetically.

COMPLETE SET (14)	4.00	8.00
1 Frank Carter	.20	.50
2 Tanqueray Clark	.20	.50
3 Travis Claridge	.20	.50
4 John Fox	.20	.50
5 David Gibson	.30	.75
6 Jason Grain	.20	.50
7 Windrell Hayes	.30	.75
8 Todd Keneley	.20	.50
9 Matt McShane	.20	.50
10 Chad Morton	.40	1.00
11 Petros Papadakis	.30	.75
12 R. Jay Soward	.40	1.00
13 Pat Swanson	.20	.50
14 Aaron Williams	.20	.50

2000 Southern Cal CHP

This set was produced for USC and sponsored by the California Highway Patrol. Each card features a color photo of the player along with a simple cardback printed in school colors. The unnumbered cards are listed below alphabetically.

COMPLETE SET (21)	6.00	12.00
1 Sultan Abdul-Malik	.20	.50
2 Shamsud-Din Abdul-Shaheed	.20	.50
3 Danny Bravo	.20	.50
4 David Bell	.20	.50
5 Matt Childers	.20	.50
6 Ennis Davis	.30	.75
7 Eric Denmon	.20	.50
8 Stanley Guyness	.20	.50
9 Antoine Harris	.20	.50
10 Brent McCaffrey	.20	.50
11 Zeke Moreno	.40	1.00
12 John Morgan	.20	.50
13 David Munoz	.30	.75
14 Matt Nickels	.20	.50
15 Brennan Ochs	.20	.50
16 Ifeanyi Ohalete	.20	.50
17 Petros Papadakis	.30	.75
18 Trevor Roberts	.20	.50
19 Ryan Shapiro	.20	.50
20 Markus Steele	.40	1.00
21 Mike Van Raaphorst	.30	.75

2001 Southern Cal CHP

This set was produced for USC and sponsored by the California Highway Patrol. Each card features a color photo of the player along with the CHP logo on the front. A simple cardback printed in school colors was used that includes a player's bio for each year he played. The unnumbered cards are listed below alphabetically.

1 Sunny Byrd	.40	1.00
2 Chris Cash	.30	.75
3 John Cousins	.30	.75
4 Bobby Demars	.20	.50
5 Kori Dickerson	.30	.75
6 Lonnie Ford	.30	.75
7 Mark Gomez	.30	.75
8 Ryan Kaiser	.20	.50
9 Charlie Landrigan	.30	.75
10 Mike MacGillivray	.20	.50
11 Malaefou MacKenzie	.30	.75
12 Faaesea Mailo	.20	.50
13 David Newbury	.20	.50
14 Ryan Nielson	.30	.75
15 Eric Reese	.20	.50
16 Kris Richard	.40	1.00
17 Antuan Simmons	.30	.75
18 Frank Strong	.20	.50

2002 Southern Cal CHP

The California Highway Patrol (CHP) again sponsored a set of USC football cards in 2002. Each features a color photo of the player designed in school colors. The unnumbered cards are listed below alphabetically. A card of Carson Palmer, the 2002 Heisman Trophy winner and the overall number one NFL draft pick in 2003 is an highlight of this set.

COMPLETE SET (21)	15.00	25.00
1 Doyal Butler	.30	.75
2 Sunny Byrd	.40	1.00
3 David Davis	.20	.50
4 Anthony Daye	.20	.50
5 Phillip Eaves	.20	.50
6 Justin Fargas	.75	2.00
7 Derek Graf	.20	.50
8 Aaron Graham	.20	.50
9 DeShaun Hill	.20	.50
10 Scott Huber	.30	.75
11 Kareem Kelly	.60	1.50
12 Malaefou MacKenzie	.20	.50
13 Grant Mattos	.20	.50
14 Sultan McCullough	.40	1.00
15 Carson Palmer	5.00	10.00
16 Chad Pierson	.30	.75
17 Troy Polamalu	6.00	12.00
18 Mike Pollard	.20	.50
19 Darrell Rideaux	.20	.50
20 Bernard Riley	.20	.50
21 Zach Wilson	.20	.50

2003 Southern Cal CHP Greats

The California Highway Patrol (CHP) sponsored these two cards of former star running backs. They were given away at a USC game in 2003. Each features a color photo of the player designed in school colors. The unnumbered cards are listed below alphabetically.

1 Marcus Allen	3.00	8.00
2 Ricky Bell	1.25	3.00

2005 Southern Cal CHP Greats

The California Highway Patrol (CHP) sponsored these two cards of former star USC players. They were given away at a USC game in 2005. Each features a color photo of the player designed in school colors. The unnumbered cards are listed below alphabetically.

COMPLETE SET (2)	1.50	4.00
1 Anthony Davis	.75	2.00
2 Charles White	.75	2.00

2006 Southern Cal CHP Greats

The California Highway Patrol (CHP) sponsored these two cards of former star USC players. They were given away at a USC game in 2006. Each features a color photo of the player designed in school colors. The unnumbered cards are listed below alphabetically.

1 Anthony Munoz (Nov. 25 vs. Notre Dame)	.75	2.00
2 Lynn Swann (Nov. 11 vs. Cal)	1.50	4.00

2009 Southern Cal Schedules

COMPLETE SET (14)	6.00	15.00
1 Jeff Byers	.50	1.25
2 Pete Carroll CO	.50	1.25
3 C.J. Gable	.50	1.25
4 Everson Griffen	.50	1.25
5 Ronald Johnson	.50	1.25
6 Stafon Johnson	.75	2.00
7 Taylor Mays	.50	1.25
8 Anthony McCoy	.50	1.25
9 Joe McKnight	.60	1.50
10 Kristofer O'Dowd	.50	1.25
11 Josh Pinkard	.50	1.25
12 Kevin Thomas	.50	1.25
13 Damian Williams	.60	1.50
14 Team Trojan Cover Card	.50	1.25

1988 Southwestern Louisiana McDag

Produced by McDag, this standard-size card set features USL action player photos printed on white card stock. Card numbers 1-10 are player cards; cards 11 and 12 feature dance team members. The CDU of Acadiana Adolescent Program logo appears at the top of each card as well as USL Ragin' Cajuns and year. Player's name appears at bottom in white border. The backs carry biographical information, "Tips from the Ragin' Cajuns" in the form of anti-drug messages, and sponsor advertisement.

COMPLETE SET (12)	2.50	6.00
1 Brian Mitchell (QB rolling out)	.75	2.00
2 Brian Mitchell (QB over center)	.75	2.00
3 Chris Gannon (DE signalling sideline)	.20	.50
4 Chris Gannon (DE awaiting snap)	.20	.50
5 Willie Culpepper	.25	.60
6 Greg Eagles	.20	.50
7 Steve McKinney	.20	.50
8 Pat Decuir	.20	.50
9 Leslie Luquette	.20	.50
10 Robert Johnson	.20	.50
11 Lisa McCoy (Cheerleader)	.20	.50
12 Michelle Aubert (Cheerleader)	.20	.50

1984 Sports Soda Big Eight Cans

This set of cans was created in 1984. Each features a college team mascot on one side and the team's 1984 football schedule on the other. A cardboard display and carrying case for the set was also produced.

COMPLETE SET (8)	16.00	40.00
1 Colorado	2.50	6.00
2 Iowa State	2.50	6.00
3 Kansas	2.50	6.00
4 Kansas State	2.50	6.00
5 LSU	2.50	6.00
6 Nebraska	2.50	6.00
7 Oklahoma	2.50	6.00
8 Oklahoma State	2.50	6.00

1984 Sports Soda Big Ten Cans

This set of cans was created in 1984. Each features a college team mascot on one side and the team's 1984 football schedule on the other. A cardboard display and carrying case for the set was also produced.

COMPLETE SET (8)	16.00	40.00
1 Illinios	2.50	6.00
2 Indiana	2.50	6.00
3 Iowa	2.50	6.00
4 Michigan	3.00	8.00
5 Michigan State	2.50	6.00
6 Minnesota	2.50	6.00
7 Northwestern	2.50	6.00
8 Ohio State	2.50	6.00
9 Purdue	2.50	6.00
10 Wisconsin	2.50	6.00

1979 Stanford Playing Cards

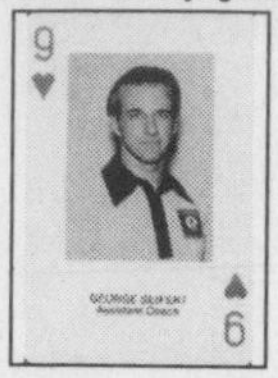

This set was issued as a playing card deck. Each card has rounded corners and a typical playing card format. The fronts feature black-and-white photos with the card number and suit designation in the upper left corner and again, but inverted, in the lower right. The player's name and position initials appear just beneath the photo. The red cardbacks feature the title "The Stanford Cards." A few cards do not feature a player image but simply text about a Stanford football event or record. Since the set is similar to a playing card set, it is arranged just like a card deck and checklisted below accordingly. In the checklist below C means Clubs, D means Diamonds, H means Hearts, S means Spades and JOK means Joker. Numbers are assigned to Aces (1), Jacks (11), Queens (12), and Kings (13).

COMPLETE SET (54)	20.00	40.00
1C 1979 Football Schedule	.30	.75
1D Heisman Winners (text only)	.30	.75
1H Rod Dowhower CO	.30	.75
1S Stanford Stadium	.30	.75
2C 1980 Football Schedule	.30	.75
2D Players in Pro FB (text only)	.30	.75
2H Russel Charles Asst.CO	.30	.75
2S All-Time Leaders (text only; game passing)	.30	.75
3C 1978 Football Results	.30	.75
3D All-Time Leaders (text only; game receptions)	.30	.75
3H Bill Dutton Asst.CO	.30	.75
3S All-Time Leaders (text only; game TD passes)	.30	.75
4C 1978 Team Leaders (text only)	.30	.75
4D All-Time Leaders (text only; season receptions)	.30	.75
4H Jim Fassel Asst.CO	.40	1.00
4S All-Time Leaders (text only; career TD passes)	.30	.75
5C 1978 UPI Football Poll	.30	.75
5D All-Time Leaders (text only; career receptions)	.30	.75
5H John Gooden Asst.CO	.30	.75
5S All-Time Leaders (text only; season passing)	.30	.75
6C 1978 AP Football Poll	.30	.75
6D All-Time Leaders (text only; game rushing)	.30	.75
6H Ray Handley Asst.CO	.30	.75
6S All-Time Leaders (text only; career passing)	.30	.75
7C Football Bowl Record	.30	.75
7D All-Time Leaders (text only; season rushing)	.30	.75
7H Al Lavan Asst.CO	.30	.75
7S All-Time Leaders (text only; season total off.)	.30	.75
8C 1924-1935 All-Americans	.30	.75
8D All-Time Leaders (text only; career rushing)	.30	.75
8H Tom Lovat Asst.CO	.30	.75
8S All-Time Leaders (text only; career total off.)	.30	.75
9C 1940-1959 All-Americans	.30	.75
9D Gordon Banks	.30	.75
9H George Seifert Asst.CO	2.00	5.00
9S All-Time Leaders (text only; career points)	.30	.75
10C 1960-1979 All-Americans	.30	.75
10D Rick Parker	.30	.75
10H 1979 Seniors (text only)	.30	.75
10S All-Time Leaders (text only; career TDs)	.30	.75
11C Andre Tyler	.30	.75
11D Brian Holloway	.40	1.00
11H Turk Schonert	.30	.75
11S All-Time Leaders (text only; long field goal)	.30	.75
12C John MacAulay	.30	.75
12D Milt McColl	.30	.75
12H Ken Margerum	.40	1.00
12S All-Time Leaders (text only; long TD pass)	.30	.75
13C Pat Bowe	.30	.75
13D Chuck Evans	.30	.75
13H Darrin Nelson	.50	1.25
13S All-Time Leaders (text only; long run)	.30	.75
JOK1 Andy Geiger AD	.30	.75
JOK2 Garry Cavalli Assoc.AD	.30	.75

1982 Stanford Team Sheets

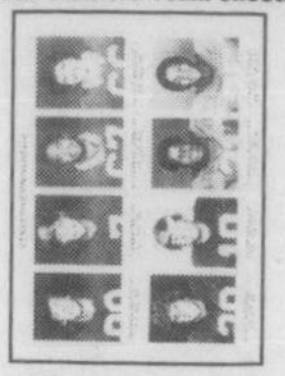

The University of Stanford issued these sheets of black-and-white player photos. Each measures roughly 8" by 10" and was printed on glossy stock with white borders. Each sheet includes photos of 8-players and/or coaches. Below each player's image is his jersey number, name, position, height, weight, and class. They are blankbacked.

COMPLETE SET (2)	25.00	50.00
1 Chris Dressel John Elway Brian Holloway John Macaulay Ken Margerum Ken Naber Darrin Nelson Andre Tyler	20.00	40.00
2 Kevin Bates Duker Drapper Rick Gervais Kevin MacMilan Mile McColl Doug Rogers Craig Zellmer Paul Wiggin CO	5.00	10.00

1991 Stanford All-Century

This 100-card standard-size set is an All-Century commemorative set issued to honor outstanding players at Stanford during the past 100 years. The set was issued in perforated strips of six cards each. The first card of each strip, redeemable at Togo's for a free Pepsi with any purchase, lists the 1991 home schedule on back. Reportedly only 5,000 sets were produced. Card fronts are pale yellow and feature a close-up black and white player photo in a circle surrounded by palm branches. A gold banner with the words "1891 Stanford Football 1991" appears at bottom of picture while "All-Century Team" rounds out the top of picture. The player's name appears in a red stripe at the bottom of the card face. In mauve print on white, card backs have biographical information and sponsor logos at the bottom. The cards are unnumbered and checklisted below in alphabetical order.

COMPLETE SET (100)	100.00	175.00
1 Frankie Albert	.60	1.50
2 Lester Archambeau	.40	1.00
3 Bruno Banducci	.30	.75
4 Benny Barnes	.40	1.00
5 Guy Benjamin	.60	1.50
6 Mike Boryla	.60	1.50
7 Marty Brill	.30	.75
8 John Brodie	3.20	8.00
9 Jackie Brown	.30	.75
10 George Buehler	.40	1.00
11 Don Bunce	.60	1.50
12 Chris Burford	.60	1.50
13 Walter Camp CO	1.00	2.50
14 Gordy Ceresino	.30	.75
15 Jack Chapple	.30	.75
16 Toi Cook	.60	1.50
17 Bill Corbus	.30	.75
18 Steve Dils	1.00	2.50
19 Pat Donovan	.60	1.50
20 John Elway	35.00	60.00
21 Chuck Evans	.30	.75
22 Skip Face	.30	.75
23 Hugh Gallarneau	.30	.75
24 Rod Garcia	.30	.75
25 Bob Garrett	.30	.75
26 Rick Gervais	.30	.75
27 John Gillory	.30	.75
28 Bobby Grayson	.40	1.00
29 Bones Hamilton	.40	1.00
30 Ray Handley	.60	1.50
31 Mark Harmon	.30	.75
32 Marv Harris	.30	.75
33 Emile Harry	.60	1.50
34 Tony Hill	1.00	2.50
35 Brian Holloway	.60	1.50
36 John Hopkins	.30	.75
37 Dick Horn	.30	.75
38 Jeff James	.40	1.00
39 Gary Kerkorian	.30	.75
40 Gordon King	.40	1.00
41 Younger Klippert	.30	.75
42 Pete Kmetovic	.30	.75
43 Jim Lawson	.30	.75
44 Pete Lazetich	.30	.75
45 Dave Lewis	.40	1.00
46 Vic Lindskog	.30	.75
47 James Lofton	3.20	8.00
48 Ken Margerum	.60	1.50
49 Ed McCaffrey	6.00	15.00
50 Charles McCloud	.30	.75
51 Bill McColl	.40	1.00
52 Duncan McColl	.30	.75
53 Milt McColl	.30	.75
54 Jim Merlo	.40	1.00
55 Phil Moffatt	.30	.75
56 Bob Moore	.40	1.00
57 Sam Morley	.30	.75
58 Monk Moscrip	.30	.75
59 Brad Muster	1.00	2.50
60 Ken Naber	.30	.75
61 Darrin Nelson	.80	2.00
62 Ernie Nevers	2.00	5.00
63 Dick Norman	.30	.75
64 Blaine Nye	.60	1.50
65 Don Parish	.30	.75
66 John Paye	.60	1.50
67 Gary Pettigrew	.40	1.00
68 Jim Plunkett	3.20	8.00

69 Randy Poltl	.30	.75
70 Seraphim Post	.30	.75
71 John Ralston CO	.60	1.50
72 Bob Reynolds	.30	.75
73 Don Robesky	.30	.75
74 Doug Robison	.30	.75
75 Greg Sampson	.30	.75
76 John Sande	.30	.75
77 Turk Schonert	.60	1.50
78 Jack Schultz	.30	.75
79 Clark Shaughnessy CO	.60	1.50
80 Ted Shipkey	.30	.75
81 Jeff Siemon	.60	1.50
82 Andy Sinclair	.30	.75
83 Malcolm Snider	.40	1.00
84 Norm Standlee	.40	1.00
85 Roger Stillwell	.30	.75
86 Chuck Taylor CO	.30	.75
87 Dink Templeton	.30	.75
88 Tiny Thornhill CO	.30	.75
89 Dave Tipton	.30	.75
90 Keith Topping	.30	.75
91 Randy Vataha	.40	1.00
92 Garin Veris	.60	1.50
93 Jon Volpe	1.00	2.50
94 Bill Walsh CO	2.40	6.00
95 Pop Warner CO	.60	1.50
96 Gene Washington 49er	.80	2.00
97 Vincent White	.30	.75
98 Paul Wiggin	.60	1.50
99 John Wilbur	.40	1.00
100 David Wyman	.60	1.50

1992 Stanford

This 35-card standard-size set was manufactured by High Step College Football Cards (Turlock, California). The cards were given away individually at home games. Complete sets could be purchased for 10.00 at the Stanford Stadium, the Track House, or by mail order. Production was reportedly limited to 10,000 sets with only 7,500 being sold as complete sets. The cards were also available in five-card packs; the packs were .75 each and could only be purchased in lots of 20 for 15.00. The cards feature posed action color player photos with white borders. The player's name and position appear in the bottom border. The word "Stanford" is printed in brick-red with a white outline either at the top or bottom of the picture. The backs are white and carry biographical and statistical information and career highlights. The player's uniform number appears in a football icon at the upper right corner. The cards are unnumbered and checklisted below in alphabetical order.

COMPLETE SET (35)	12.00	25.00
1 Seyon Albert	.15	.40
2 Estevan Avila	.20	.50
3 Tyler Batson	.15	.40
4 Guy Benjamin ACO	.30	.75
5 David Calomese	.15	.40
6 Mike Cook	.20	.50
7 Chris Dalman	.30	.75
8 Dave Garnett	.15	.40
9 Ron George	.30	.75
10 Darrien Gordon	.60	1.50
11 Tom Holmoe ACO	.30	.75
12 Derron Klafter	.15	.40
13 J.J. Lasley	.20	.50
14 John Lynch	4.00	10.00
15 Glyn Milburn	1.00	2.50
16 Fernando Montes ACO	.20	.50
17 Vince Otoupal	.15	.40
18 Rick Pallow	.15	.40
19 Ron Redell	.15	.40
20 Aaron Rembisz	.15	.40
21 Bill Ring ACO	.20	.50
22 Ellery Roberts	.20	.50
23 Scott Schuhmann ACO	.15	.40
24 Terry Shea ACO	.15	.40
25 Bill Singler ACO	.15	.40
26 Paul Stonehouse	.15	.40
27 Dave Tipton ACO	.15	.40
28 Keena Turner ACO	.40	1.00
29 Fred von Appen ACO	.15	.40
30 Bill Walsh CO	1.20	3.00
31 Ryan Wetnight	.60	1.50
32 Tom Williams	.15	.40
33 Mike Wilson ACO	.20	.50
34 Billy Wittman	.15	.40
35 Checklist Card (J.J. Lasley)	.20	.50

1993 Stanford

These 18 standard-size cards feature on their fronts color player action shots set within white borders. The player's name appears underneath the photo. The white horizonal back carries the player's name, position, number, and biography at the top. On the left is a player head shot, and on the right, the player's career highlights. The cards are unnumbered and checklisted below in alphabetical order.

COMPLETE SET (18)	4.00	10.00
1 Jeff Bailey	.20	.50
2 Parker Bailey	.20	.50
3 Roger Boden	.20	.50
4 Hartwell Brown	.20	.50
5 Vaughn Bryant	.25	.60
6 Brian Cassidy	.20	.50
7 Glen Cavanaugh	.20	.50
8 Kevin Garnett	.20	.50
9 Mark Hatzenbuhler	.20	.50
10 Steve Hoyem	.25	.60
11 Mike Jerich	.20	.50
12 Paul Nickel	.20	.50
13 Toby Norwood	.20	.50
14 Tyrone Parker	.25	.60
15 Ellery Roberts	.20	.50
16 David Shaw	.20	.50
17 Bill Walsh CO	1.00	2.50
18 Josh Wright	.20	.50

1994 Stanford

These standard-size cards feature on their fronts color player action shots set within white borders. The player's name appears underneath the photo. The white horizonal back carries the player's name, position, number, and biography at the top. On the left is a player head shot, and on the right, the player's career highlights. The cards are unnumbered and checklisted below in alphabetical order.

COMPLETE SET (30)	6.00	12.00
1 Ethan Allen	.20	.50
2 Justin Armour	.30	.75
3 Mark Butterfield	.20	.50
4 David Carder	.20	.50
5 Tony Cline	.20	.50
6 Branyon Davis	.20	.50
7 Seth Dittman	.20	.50
8 Jason Fisk	.20	.50
9 Steve Frost	.20	.50
10 Kevin Garnett	.20	.50
11 T.J. Gaynor	.20	.50
12 Coy Gibbs	.40	1.00
13 Allen Gonzalez	.20	.50
14 Dave Grable	.20	.50
15 Ozzie Grenardo	.20	.50
16 Mike Hall LB	.20	.50
17 Jeff Hansen	.20	.50
18 Mark Harris	.20	.50
19 John Hebert	.20	.50
20 John Henton	.20	.50
21 Mike Jerich	.20	.50
22 Lenard Marcus	.20	.50
23 Carl Mennie	.20	.50
24 Aaron Mills	.20	.50
25 Nathan Olson	.20	.50
26 Damon Phillips	.20	.50
27 David Shaw	.20	.50
28 Steve Stenstrom	.40	1.00
29 Ryan Walers	.20	.50
30 Scott Whitt	.20	.50

2001 Stanford

These 35 standard-size cards feature on their fronts color player action photos set within red, black, and white borders. The player's name appears underneath the photo along with his position and team name. The white cardback carries the player's name, position, jersey number, biography, and stats along with a Pepsi sponsorship logo. The cards are unnumbered and checklisted below in alphabetical order.

COMPLETE SET (35)	10.00	20.00
1 Brian Allen	.40	1.00
2 Mike Biselli	.40	1.00
3 Caleb Bowman	.30	.75
4 Colin Branch	.30	.75
5 Kerry Carter	.30	.75
6 Ruben Carter	.40	1.00
7 Kirk Chambers	.30	.75
8 Garry Cobb	.30	.75
9 Randy Fasani	.60	1.50
10 Ryan Fernandez	.30	.75
11 Trey Freeman	.30	.75
12 Matt Friedrichs	.30	.75
13 Kwame Harris	.30	.75
14 Eric Heitmann	.30	.75
15 Simba Hodari	.30	.75
16 Marcus Hoover	.30	.75
17 Eric Johnson	.30	.75
18 Austin Lee	.30	.75
19 Matt Leonard	.30	.75
20 Chris Lewis	.30	.75
21 Jamien McCullum	.30	.75
22 Casey Moore	.30	.75
23 Darin Naatjes	.30	.75
24 Travis Pfeifer	.30	.75
25 Brett Pierce	.30	.75
26 Luke Powell	.30	.75
27 Zack Quaccia	.30	.75
28 Greg Schindler	.30	.75
29 Brian Taylor	.30	.75
30 Paul Weinacht	.30	.75
31 Ryan Wells	.30	.75
32 Jason White	.30	.75
33 Tank Williams	.40	1.00
34 Coy Wire	.60	1.50
35 Matt Wright	.30	.75

1970-86 Sugar Bowl Doubloons

These coins or "Doubloons" were inserted in each program for a number of Sugar Bowl games. Each measures roughly 1 1/2" in diameter and features the two college teams in the contest on one side and a logo, generally of the stadium, on the other. There are color variations on some of the coins. Any additions to the list below are appreciated.

COMPLETE SET (9)	6.00	12.00
1970 Arkansas vs Mississippi	.75	1.50
1972 Auburn vs. Oklahoma	.75	1.50
1973 Oklahoma vs. Penn State (Dec. 1972, blue)	.75	1.50
1973 Oklahoma vs. Penn State (Dec. 1972, gold)	.75	1.50
1974 Alabama vs. Notre Dame (Dec. 1973)	.75	1.50
1975 Florida vs. Nebraska	.75	1.50
1979 Alabama vs. Penn State	.75	1.50
1980 Alabama vs. Arkansas	.75	1.50
1986 Miami vs. Tennessee	.75	1.50

1976 Sunbeam SEC Die Cuts

Produced by Arnold Harris Associates Inc. (Cherry Hill, New Jersey), each one of these twenty standard-size cards was inserted in specially-marked loaves of Sunbeam bread. Sunbeam also issued a 4" by 9" "Stand-up Trading Card Saver Book" to hold the cards. This book features pictures of all the fronts with instructions to put the corners of the cards in the slots indicated by the arrows. The team profile cards display the team helmet, an ink drawing of a football action scene, and the team name. The white backs profile the coach and team. The schedule cards show the mascot, another ink drawing of a football action scene, and the team name. The gray backs carry the 1976 football schedule. Both cards are perforated in an arc. The cards are unnumbered; they are checklisted below alphabetically as presented in the saver book.

COMPLETE SET (20)	100.00	200.00
1 Alabama Crimson Tide Team Profile	6.00	15.00
2 Alabama Crimson Tide Schedule	6.00	15.00
3 Auburn War Eagle Team Profile	4.00	10.00
4 Auburn War Eagle Schedule	4.00	10.00
5 Florida Gators Team Profile	6.00	15.00
6 Florida Gators Schedule	6.00	15.00
7 Georgia Bulldogs Team Profile	4.00	10.00
8 Georgia Bulldogs Schedule	4.00	10.00
9 Kentucky Wildcats Team Profile	4.00	10.00
10 Kentucky Wildcats Schedule	4.00	10.00
11 Louisiana St. Tigers Team Profile	4.00	10.00
12 Louisiana St. Tigers Schedule	4.00	10.00
13 Miss. St. Bulldogs Team Profile	4.00	10.00
14 Miss. St. Bulldogs Schedule	4.00	10.00
15 Ole Miss Rebels Team Profile	4.00	10.00
16 Ole Miss Rebels Schedule	4.00	10.00
17 Tennessee Volunteers Team Profile	5.00	12.00
18 Tennessee Volunteers Schedule	5.00	12.00
19 Vanderbilt Commodores Team Profile	4.00	10.00
20 Vanderbilt Commodores Schedule	4.00	10.00

1977 Syracuse Team Sheets

These photos were issued by the school to promote the football program. Each measures roughly 8" by 10" and features ten black and white images of players with the school name appearing at the top. The player's name, position, and brief vital stats is printed below each photo. The backs are blank.

1 Dan Breznay	4.00	8.00
John Cameron		
Jim Collins		
Ron Farneski		
Warren Harvey		
Willie McCullough		
Aer Monk		
Ron Richardson		
Mandel Robinson		
Greg Williams		
2 Bill Hurley	4.00	8.00
Pete Prather		
Larry Archis		
Rich Rosen		
Mike Jones		
Bill Zanovitch		
Bernie Winters		
Larry King		
Steve Spinney		
Nate Wright		

1989 Syracuse

This 15 card set, featuring cards measuring approximately 2 1/2" by 3 1/2", was produced to honor members of the 1989 Syracuse football team. The fronts of the card have an action photo of the player along with the identification "Syracuse University 1989" and the players name while the back has biography and a safety tip. This set was sponsored by WYSR radio, Burger King, and Pepsi. Since the set is unnumbered, we have checklisted it in alphabetical order. The key card in the set is wide receiver Rob Moore.

COMPLETE SET (15)	8.00	20.00
1 David Bavaro	.60	1.50
2 Blake Bednars	.50	1.25
3 Alban Brown	.50	1.25
4 Dan Burey	.50	1.25
5 Rob Burnett	.75	2.00
6 Fred DeRiggi	.50	1.25
7 John Flannery	.60	1.50
8 Duane Kinnon	.50	1.25
9 Dick MacPherson CO	.60	1.50
10 Rob Moore	1.25	3.00
11 Michael Owens	.50	1.25
12 Bill Scharr	.50	1.25
13 Turnell Sims	.50	1.25
14 Sean Whiteman	.50	1.25
15 Terry Wooden	.75	2.00

1991 Syracuse

The 1991 Syracuse football set was sponsored by Drumlins Travel and available as inserts in Syracuse University football game programs. Each perforated insert measures approximately 8" by 11" and displays three rows of three cards each. The top two rows consist of six approximately 2 5/8" by 3 1/2" player cards, while the third row has three cards with a sponsor advertisement, a 1991-92 basketball schedule, and the university's logo respectively. The player cards feature glossy color action photos bordered in white, with text reversed-out in white in a burnt orange stripe beneath the picture. The backs have biography, career summary, and an "Orange Tip" in the form of an anti-drug message.

COMPLETE SET (36)	15.00	30.00
1 George Rooks	.40	1.00
2 Marvin Graves	1.00	2.50
3 Andrew Dees	.40	1.00
4 Glen Young	.40	1.00
5 Chris Gedney	.75	2.00
6 Paul Pasqualoni CO	.50	1.25
7 Terrence Wisdom	.40	1.00
8 John Biskup	.40	1.00
9 Mark McDonald	.40	1.00
10 Dan Conley	.40	1.00
11 Kevin Mitchell	.75	2.00
12 Qadry Ismail	1.50	4.00
13 John Lusardi	.40	1.00
14 David Walker	.40	1.00
15 John Capachione	.40	1.00
16 Shelby Hill	.50	1.25
17 Dwayne Joseph	.40	1.00
18 Greg Walker	.40	1.00
19 Jerry Sharp	.40	1.00
20 Tim Sandquist	.40	1.00
21 Chuck Bull	.40	1.00
22 Jo Jo Wooden	.40	1.00
23 Terry Richardson	.50	1.25
24 Doug Womack	.40	1.00
25 Reggie Terry	.40	1.00
26 Garland Hawkins	.40	1.00
27 Tony Montemorra	.40	1.00
28 Chip Todd	.40	1.00
29 Pat O'Neill	.50	1.25
30 Kevin Barker	.40	1.00
31 John Reagan	.40	1.00
32 Pat O'Rourke	.40	1.00
33 Jim Wentworth	.40	1.00
34 Ernie Brown	.40	1.00
35 John Nilsen	.40	1.00
36 Al Wooten	.40	1.00

1992 Syracuse

The 1992 Syracuse football set was sponsored by Diet Pepsi and available as inserts in Syracuse University football game programs. Each perforated sheet Included a selection of 2 3/4" by 3 1/2" player cards featuring glossy color action photos bordered in white with the year notated beneath the picture. The backs have a player biography, a career summary, a card number, and an "Orange Tip" in the form of an anti-drug message.

COMPLETE SET (36)	15.00	30.00
1 Glen Young	.40	1.00
2 Pat O'Neill	.50	1.25
3 Ernie Brown	.40	1.00
4 Brian Picucci	.40	1.00
5 Garland Hawkins	.40	1.00
6 Antonio Johnson	.40	1.00
7 Terry Richardson	.50	1.25
8 Marcus Lee	.40	1.00
9 Qadry Ismail	1.25	3.00
10 Matt Greco	.40	1.00
11 John Biskup	.40	1.00
12 Chip Todd	.40	1.00
13 Marvin Graves	.75	2.00
14 Kevin Mitchell	.50	1.25
15 Shelby Hill	.40	1.00
16 Dan Conley	.40	1.00
17 Ousmane Bary	.40	1.00
18 Dwayne Joseph	.40	1.00
19 John Reagan	.40	1.00
20 David Walker	.40	1.00
21 Chris Gedney	.50	1.25
22 Terrance Wisdom	.40	1.00
23 Bob Grosvenor	.40	1.00
24 Tony Jones	.40	1.00
25 Reggie Terry	.40	1.00
26 Al Wooten	.40	1.00
27 James Spencer	.40	1.00
28 Ed Hobson	.40	1.00
29 Jerry Sharp	.40	1.00
30 Melvin Tuten	.50	1.25
31 Chuck Boll	.40	1.00
32 Kerry Ferrell	.40	1.00
33 Scott Langenheim	.40	1.00
34 Jo Jo Wooden	.40	1.00
35 Doug Womack	.40	1.00
36 Kevin Mason	.40	1.00

1993 Syracuse

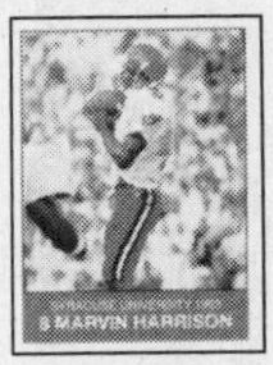

The 1993 Syracuse football set was sponsored by Diet Pepsi and available as inserts in Syracuse University football game programs. Each perforated sheet included a selection of 2 3/4" by 3 1/2" player cards featuring glossy color action photos bordered in white with the year notated beneath the picture. The backs have a player biography, a career summary, a card number, and an "Orange Tip" in the form of an anti-drug message.

COMPLETE SET (30)	15.00	30.00
1 Marvin Graves	.75	2.00
2 Darrell Parker	.40	1.00
3 Kyle Adams	.40	1.00
4 Terry Richardson	.50	1.25
5 Bob Grosvenor	.40	1.00
6 Tony Jones	.40	1.00
7 Kevin Mitchell	.50	1.25
8 Ernie Brown	.40	1.00
9 Al Wooten	.40	1.00
10 John Reagan	.40	1.00
11 Marcus Lee	.40	1.00
12 Chris Marques	.40	1.00
13 Dan Conley	.40	1.00
14 Melvin Tuten	.50	1.25
15 Shelby Hill	.40	1.00
16 Chip Todd	.40	1.00
17 Kevin Mason	.40	1.00
18 Pat O'Neill	.50	1.25
19 Bryce Bevill	.40	1.00
20 Kirby Dar Dar	.50	1.25
21 Marvin Harrison	5.00	10.00
22 Cy Ellsworth	.40	1.00
23 Nate Hemsley	.40	1.00
24 Ed Hobson	.40	1.00
25 Wilky Bazile	.40	1.00
26 Reggie Terry	.40	1.00
27 Dwayne Joseph	.40	1.00
28 Eric Chenoweth	.40	1.00
29 Dave Wohlabaugh	.50	1.25
30 Brian Picucci	.40	1.00

1965 Tennessee Team Sheets

The University of Tennessee issued these sheets of black-and-white player photos in 1865. Each measures roughly 7 7/8" by 10" and was printed on glossy stock with white borders. Each sheet includes photos of 10-players with his position and name printed below the image. The top of the sheets reads "University of Tennessee 1965 Football." The photos are blankbacked.

1 John Boynton	7.50	15.00
Bobby Gratz		
Glenn Gray		
Gerald Woods		
Dewey Warren		
Mike Gooch		
Jimmy Glover		
Bob Johnson		
Terry Bird		
Jim Lowe		
2 Doug Archibald	10.00	20.00
Bill Cameron		
Joe Graham		
Tom Fisher		
Frank Emanuel		
Bob Petrella		
Bobby Morel		
Bobby Frazier		
Paul Naumoff		
Jerry Smith		
3 Charlie Fulton	10.00	20.00
Walter Chadwick		
Stan Mitchell		
Hal Wantland		
Johnny Mills		
Mike Gooch		
Jack Patterson		
David Leake		
Austin Denny		
Art Galiffa		

1975 Tennessee Team Sheets

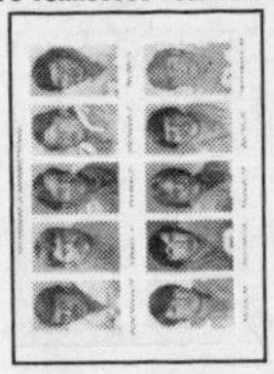

These photos were issued by the school to promote the football program. Each measures roughly 8" by 10" and features ten black and white images of players with the school name and year appearing at the top. The backs are blank.

1 Charles Anderson	4.00	8.00
Keith Autry		
Dave Brady		
Mike Caldwell		
Phil Clabo		
Bill Cole		
Kevin Davis		
Jim Duvall		
Dale Fair		
Tim Fitchpatrick		
2 Joe Gallagher	4.00	8.00
Mike Gayles		
Jim Gaylor		
Mike Huskisson		
Paul Johnson		
Ron McCartney		
Mickey Marvin		
Mike Mauck		
Terry Moore		
Stanley Morgan		
3 John Murphy	4.00	8.00
David Page		
David Parsons		
Steve Poole		
Gary Roach		
Thomas Rowsey		
Pat Ryan		
Chuck Sanford		
Larry Seivers		
Andy Spiva		
4 Al Szawara	4.00	8.00
Randy Verner		
Randy Wallace		
Ernie Ward		
Brent Watson		
Tommy West		
Steve White		
Russ Williams		
Jim Woofter		
John Yarbrough		

1980 Tennessee Police

The 1980 Tennessee Police Set features 19 cards measuring approximately 2 5/8" by 4 3/16". The fronts have color photos bordered in white; the vertically oriented backs feature football terminology and safety tips. The cards are unnumbered, so they are listed alphabetically by subject's name. The key player in this set is longtime Cowboy special team star Bill Bates.

COMPLETE SET (19)	25.00	50.00
1 Bill Bates	7.50	15.00
2 James Berry	.75	2.00
3 Chris Bolton	.75	2.00
4 Mike L. Cofer	3.00	6.00
5 Glenn Ford	.75	2.00
6 Anthony Hancock	1.50	3.00
7 Brian Ingram	.75	2.00
8 Tim Irwin	2.50	5.00
9 Kenny Jones	.75	2.00
10 Wilbert Jones	.75	2.00
11 Johnny Majors CO	3.00	8.00
12 Bill Marren	.75	2.00
13 Danny Martin	.75	2.00
14 Jim Noonan	.75	2.00
15 Lee North	.75	2.00
16 Hubert Simpson	1.50	3.00
17 Danny Spradlin	1.50	3.00
18 John Warren	1.50	3.00
19 Brad White	.75	2.00

1989 Tennessee

This set was released in perforated sheets of cards. The school and team nickname are printed above the player's photo on the front along with the Tennessee helmet logo, the player's name, position and jersey number below. The cardbacks are simply black printing on white stock with a short safety note.

COMPLETE SET (36)	15.00	30.00
1 Mark Adams	.30	.75
2 Greg Amsler	.30	.75
3 Carey Bailey	.30	.75
4 Doug Baird	.30	.75
5 Shazzon Bradley	.30	.75
6 Terence Cleveland	.30	.75
7 Reggie Cobb	.40	1.00
8 Antone Davis	.60	1.50
9 Kelly Days	.30	.75
10 Keith Denson	.30	.75
11 Kent Elmore	.30	.75
12 John Fisher	.30	.75
13 Alvin Harper	.75	2.00
14 Tracy Hayworth	.40	1.00
15 Sterling Henton	.30	.75
16 Marion Hobby	.30	.75
17 Andy Kelly	.40	1.00
18 Jeremy Lincoln	.60	1.50
19 Johnny Majors CO	.60	1.50
20 Chip McCallum	.30	.75
21 Charles McRae	.60	1.50
22 Floyd Miley	.30	.75
23 Mark Moore	.30	.75
24 Anthony Morgan	.75	2.00
25 Carl Pickens	1.50	4.00
26 Roland Poles	.30	.75
27 Von Reeves	.30	.75
28 Eric Still	.30	.75
29 Tony Thompson	.30	.75
30 Preston Warren	.30	.75
31 Martin Williams	.30	.75
32 Thomas Woods	.30	.75
33 Neyland Stadium	.30	.75
34 Smokey Mascot (live dog mascot)	.30	.75
35 Smokey Mascot (puppet mascot)	.30	.75
36 Tennessee Band	.30	.75

1990 Tennessee Centennial

The 1990 Tennessee Volunteers set contains 294 standard-size cards. The fronts feature a mix of color or black and white player photos, enframed by orange borders. The player's name appears in a white stripe above the picture, and a Tennessee insignia with the words "100 Years of Volunteers" is superimposed at the bottom of the picture. In a horizontal format, the backs have player profiles in black lettering overlaying an indistinct version of the same insignia as on the card fronts. The cards are numbered on the backs in both upper corners.

COMPLETE SET (294)	20.00	40.00
1 Vince Moore	.07	.20
2 Steve Matthews	.02	.10
3 Joey Chapman	.02	.10
4 Terence Cleveland	.02	.10
5 Thomas Wood	.02	.10
6 J.J. McCleskey	.02	.10
7 Jason Julian	.02	.10
8 Andy Kelly	.07	.20
9 Derrick Folsom	.02	.10
10 Chip McCallum	.02	.10
11 Lloyd Kerr	.02	.10
12 Cory Fleming	.10	.30
13 Kevin Zurcher	.02	.10
14 Lee England	.02	.10
15 Carl Pickens	.80	2.00
16 Sterling Henton	.02	.10
17 Lee Wood	.02	.10
18 Kent Elmore	.02	.10
19 Craig Faulkner	.02	.10
20 Keith Denson	.02	.10
21 Preston Warren	.02	.10
22 Floyd Miley	.02	.10
23 Earnest Fields	.02	.10
24 Tony Thompson	.02	.10
25 Jeremy Lincoln	.10	.30
26 David Bennett	.02	.10
27 Greg Burke	.02	.10
28 Tavio Henson	.02	.10
29 Kevin Wendelboe	.02	.10
30 Cedric Kline	.02	.10
31 Keith Jeter	.02	.10
32 Chris Russ	.02	.10
33 DeWayne Dotson	.02	.10
34 Mike Rapien	.02	.10
35 Clemons McCroskey	.02	.10
36 Mark Fletcher	.02	.10
37 Chuck Smith	.07	.20
38 Jeff Tullis	.02	.10
39 Kelly Days	.02	.10
40 Shazzon Bradley	.02	.10
41 Reggie Ingram	.02	.10
42 Roland Poles	.02	.10
43 Tracy Smith	.02	.10
44 Chuck Webb	.10	.30
45 Shon Walker	.07	.20
46 Eric Riffer	.02	.10
47 Greg Amsler	.02	.10
48 J.J. Surlas	.02	.10
49 Brian Bradley	.02	.10
50 Tom Myslinski	.07	.20
51 John Fisher	.02	.10
52 Craig Martin	.02	.10
53 Carey Bailey	.02	.10
54 Houston Thomas	.02	.10
55 Ryan Patterson	.02	.10
56 Chad Goodin	.02	.10
57 Brian Spivey	.02	.10
58 Todd Kelly	.02	.10
59 Mike Stowell	.02	.10
60 Jim Fenwick	.02	.10
61 Marc Jones	.02	.10
62 Chris Ragan	.02	.10
63 Rodney Gordon	.02	.10
64 Mark Needham	.02	.10
65 Patrick Lenoir	.02	.10
66 Martin Williams	.02	.10
67 Brad Seiber	.02	.10
68 Larry Smith	.02	.10
69 Jerry Teel	.02	.10
70 Charles McRae	.10	.30
71 Rex Hargrove	.02	.10
72 James Wilson	.02	.10
73 Doug Baird	.02	.10
74 Mark Moore	.02	.10
75 Lance Nelson	.02	.10
76 Robert Todd	.02	.10
77 Greg Gerardi	.02	.10
78 Antone Davis	.10	.30
79 Eric Still	.02	.10
80 Anthony Morgan	.30	.75
81 Alvin Harper	.40	1.00
82 Charles Longmire	.02	.10
83 Mark Adams	.02	.10
84 Chris Benson	.02	.10
85 Horace Morris	.02	.10
86 Harlan Davis	.02	.10
87 Darryl Hardy	.02	.10
88 Tracy Hayworth	.07	.20
89 Von Reeves	.02	.10
90 Marion Hobby	.02	.10
91 John Ward ANN	.02	.10
92 Roderick Lewis	.02	.10

93 Orion McCants	.02	.10
94 James Warren	.02	.10
95 Mario Brunson	.02	.10
96 Joe Davis	.02	.10
97 Shawn Truss	.02	.10
98 Keith Steed	.02	.10
99 Kacy Rodgers	.02	.10
100 Johnny Majors CO	.10	.30
101 Phillip Fulmer CO	.10	.30
102 Larry Lacewell CO	.07	.20
103 Charlie Coe CO	.02	.10
104 Tommy West CO	.02	.10
105 David Cutcliffe CO	.02	.10
106 Jack Sells CO	.02	.10
107 Rex Norris CO	.02	.10
108 John Chavis CO	.02	.10
109 Tim Keane CO	.02	.10
110 Tim Mingey Recruiter	.02	.10
111 Bill Higdon Sr. Admin. Asst.	.02	.10
112 Tim Kerin TR	.02	.10
113 Bruno Pauletto CO	.02	.10
114 Vols 17& Co.State 14 (Chuck Webb)	.07	.20
115 Vols 24& UCLA 6 (Chuck Webb)	.07	.20
116 Vols 28& Duke 6 (Game action photo)	.02	.10
117 Vols 21& Auburn 14 (Game action photo)	.02	.10
118 Vols 17& Georgia 14 (Jason Julian)	.02	.10
119 Vols 30& Alabama 47 (Roland Poles)	.02	.10
120 Vols 45& LSU 39 (Charles McRae)	.07	.20
121 Vols 52& Akron 9 (Brian Spivey)	.02	.10
122 Vols 33& Ole Miss 21 (Alvin Harper)	.10	.30
123 Vols 31& Kentucky 10 (Kelly Days)	.02	.10
124 Vols 17& Vanderbilt 10 (Game action photo)	.02	.10
125 '90 Mobil Cotton Bowl 1 (Jason Julian)	.02	.10
126 '90 Mobil Cotton Bowl-2 (Andy Kelly)	.02	.10
127 '90 Mobil Cotton Bowl 3 (Chuck Webb)	.07	.20
128 '90 Mobil Cotton Bowl 4 (Scoreboard)	.02	.10
129 Eric Still	.02	.10
130 Chris Benson	.02	.10
131 Preston Warren	.02	.10
132 Lee England	.02	.10
133 Kent Elmore	.02	.10
134 Eric Still	.02	.10
135 Chuck Webb	.10	.30
136 Marion Hobby	.02	.10
137 Kent Elmore	.02	.10
138 Antone Davis	.10	.30
139 Thomas Woods	.02	.10
140 Charles McRae	.10	.30
141 Preston Warren	.02	.10
142 Darryl Hardy	.02	.10
143 Offense or Defense (Carl Pickens)	.60	1.50
144 Carl Pickens	.80	2.00
145 Chuck Webb	.10	.30
146 Thomas Woods	.02	.10
147 Total Offense Game (Andy Kelly)	.02	.10
148 The TVA (Offensive Line) Antone Davis Eric Still Tom Myslinski John Fisher	.02	.10
149 Smokey (Mascot)	.02	.10
150 Doug Dickey Director of Athletics	.02	.10
151 Neyland Stadium	.02	.10
152 Neyland-Thompson Ctr	.02	.10
153 Gibbs Hall (Dormitory)	.02	.10
154 Academics and Athletics (Carmen Tegano Asst.AD)	.02	.10
155 Gene McEver HOF	.02	.10
156 Beattie Feathers HOF	.10	.30
157 Robert Neyland HOF CO	.30	.75
158 Herman Hickman HOF	.07	.20
159 Bowden Wyatt HOF	.07	.20
160 Hank Lauricella HOF	.02	.10
161 Doug Atkins HOF	.10	.30
162 Johnny Majors HOF	.10	.30
163 Bobby Dodd HOF	.10	.30
164 Bob Suffridge HOF	.02	.10
165 Nathan Dougherty HOF	.02	.10
166 George Cafego HOF	.02	.10
167 Bob Johnson HOF	.07	.20
168 Ed Molinski HOF	.02	.10
169 Reggie White	1.20	3.00
170 Willie Gault	.25	.60
171 Doug Atkins	.10	.30
172 Keith DeLong	.10	.30
173 Ron Widby	.07	.20
174 Bill Johnson	.07	.20
175 Jack Reynolds	.10	.30
176 Tim McGee	.20	.50
177 Harry Galbreath	.07	.20
178 Roland James	.07	.20
179 Abe Shires	.02	.10
180 Ted Daffer	.02	.10
181 Bob Foxx	.02	.10
182 Richmond Flowers	.10	.30
183 Beattie Feathers	.10	.30
184 Condredge Holloway	.20	.50
185 Larry Sievers	.07	.20
186 Johnnie Jones	.02	.10
187 Carl Zander	.07	.20
188 Dale Jones	.02	.10
189 Bruce Wilkerson	.07	.20
190 Terry McDaniel	.10	.30
191 Craig Colquitt	.07	.20
192 Stanley Morgan	.30	.75
193 Curt Watson	.02	.10
194 Bobby Majors	.02	.10
195 Steve Kiner	.07	.20
196 Paul Naumoff	.07	.20
197 Bud Sherrod	.02	.10
198 Murray Warmath	.07	.20
199 Steve DeLong	.07	.20
200 Bill Pearman	.02	.10
201 Bobby Gordon	.02	.10
202 John Michels	.02	.10
203 Bill Mayo	.02	.10
204 Andy Kozar	.02	.10
205 1892 Volunteers (Team photo)	.02	.10
206 1900 Volunteers (Team photo)	.02	.10
207 1905 Volunteers (Team photo)	.02	.10
208 1907 Volunteers (Individual player photos)	.02	.10
209 1916 Volunteers (Team photo)	.02	.10
210 1914 Volunteers (Team photo)	.02	.10
211 1896 Volunteers (Team photo)	.02	.10
212 1908 Volunteers (Team photo)	.02	.10
213 1926 Volunteers (Team photo)	.02	.10
214 1930 Volunteers (Team photo)	.02	.10
215 1934 Volunteers (Team photo)	.02	.10
216 1938 Volunteers (Team photo)	.02	.10
217 1940 Volunteers (Team photo)	.02	.10
218 1944 Volunteers (Team photo)	.02	.10
219 1945 Volunteers (Team photo)	.02	.10
220 1954 Volunteers (Team photo)	.02	.10
221 1969 Volunteers (Team photo)	.02	.10
222 1962 Volunteers (Team photo)	.02	.10
223 1976 Volunteers (Team photo)	.02	.10
224 1985 Volunteers (Team photo)	.02	.10
225 1978 Volunteers (Team photo)	.02	.10
226 1980 Voluntееers (Team photo)	.02	.10
227 1984 Volunteers (Team photo)	.02	.10
228 1988 Volunteers (Team photo)	.02	.10
229 James Baird	.02	.10
230 Condredge Holloway	.20	.50
231 J.G. Lowe	.02	.10
232 E.A. McLean	.02	.10
233 Lemont Holt Jeffers	.02	.10
234 Howard Johnson	.02	.10
235 Malcolm Aiken	.02	.10
236 Toby Palmer	.02	.10
237 Sam Bartholomew	.02	.10
238 Ray Graves	.02	.10
239 Billy Bevis	.02	.10
240 Bert Rechichar	.07	.20
241 Jim Beutel	.02	.10
242 Mike Lucci	.10	.30
243 Hal Wantland	.02	.10
244 Jackie Walker	.02	.10
245 Ron McCartney	.02	.10
246 Robert Shaw	.10	.30
247 Lee North	.02	.10
248 James Berry	.02	.10
249 Carl Zander	.07	.20
250 Chris White	.02	.10
251 Tommy Sims	.02	.10
252 Tim McGee	.20	.50
253 Keith DeLong	.10	.30
254 1931 NY Charity Game (Program)	.02	.10
255 1941 Sugar Bowl (Program)	.02	.10
256 1945 Rose Bowl (Program)	.02	.10
257 1957 Gator Bowl (Program)	.02	.10
258 1968 Orange Bowl (Program)	.02	.10
259 1972 Bluebonnet Bowl (Program)	.02	.10
260 1981 Garden State Bowl (Program)	.02	.10
261 1968 Sugar Bowl (Program)	.02	.10
262 Checklist 1-76	.02	.10
263 Checklist 77-152	.02	.10
264 Checklist 153-228	.02	.10
265 Checklist 229-294	.02	.10
266 Chris White	.02	.10
267 Kelsey Finch	.02	.10
268 Johnnie Jones	.02	.10
269 Johnnie Jones	.02	.10
270 Curt Watson	.02	.10
271 William Howard	.02	.10
272 Bubba Wyche	.30	.75
273 Tony Robinson	.10	.30
274 Daryl Dickey	.10	.30
275 Alan Cockrell To Willie Gault	.10	.30
276 Alan Cockrell	.10	.30
277 Bobby Scott	.10	.30
278 Tony Robinson	.10	.30
279 Jeff Francis	.07	.20
280 Alvin Harper	.40	1.00
281 Johnny Mills	.02	.10
282 Thomas Woods	.02	.10
283 Bob Lund	.02	.10
284 Gene McEver	.02	.10
285 Stanley Morgan	.30	.75
286 Fuad Reveiz	.10	.30
287 Kent Elmore	.02	.10
288 Jimmy Colquitt	.02	.10
289 Willie Gault	.25	.60
290 100 Years Celebration (Reggie White)	.30	.75
291 The 100 Years Kickoff (Group photo)	.02	.10
292 Like Father& Like Son Keith DeLong Steve DeLong	.10	.30
293 Offense and Defense Raleigh McKenzie Reggie McKenzie	.07	.20
294 It's Football Time (1990 schedule on back)	.07	.20

1991 Tennessee Hoby

This 42-card standard-size set was produced by Hoby and features the 1991 Tennessee football team. Five hundred uncut press sheets were also produced, and they were signed and numbered by Johnny Majors. The cards feature on the fronts a mix of posed and action color photos, with thin white borders on a royal blue card face. The school logo appears in the lower left corner in an orange circle, with the player's name in a gold stripe extending to the right. On a light orange background, the backs carry biography, player profile, or statistics. The cards are numbered on the back and are ordered alphabetically by player. Several NFL players make their first card appearance in this set: Dale Carter, Chris Mims, Carl Pickens, Heath Shuler, and James Stewart.

COMPLETE SET (42)	10.00	25.00
397 Mark Adams	.08	.25
398 Carey Bailey	.08	.25
399 David Bennett	.08	.25
400 Shazzon Bradley	.08	.25
401 Kenneth Campbell	.08	.25
402 Dale Carter	.60	1.50
403 Joey Chapman	.08	.25
404 Jerry Colquitt	.20	.50
405 Bernard Dafney	.20	.50
406 Craig Faulkner	.08	.25
407 Earnest Fields	.08	.25
408 John Fisher	.08	.25
409 Cory Fleming	.20	.50
410 Mark Fletcher	.08	.25
411 Tom Fuhler	.08	.25
412 Johnny Majors CO	.20	.50
413 Darryl Hardy	.08	.25
414 Aaron Hayden	.40	1.00
415 Tavio Henson	.08	.25
416 Reggie Ingram	.08	.25
417 Andy Kelly	.20	.50
418 Todd Kelly	.20	.50
419 Patrick Lenoir	.08	.25
420 Roderick Lewis	.08	.25
421 Jeremy Lincoln	.20	.50
422 J.J. McCleskey	.14	.35
423 Floyd Miley	.08	.25
424 Chris Mims	.30	.75
425 Tom Myslinski	.14	.35
426 Carl Pickens	1.60	4.00
427 Roc Powe	.08	.25
428 Von Reeves	.08	.25
429 Eric Riffer	.08	.25
430 Kacy Rodgers	.08	.25
431 Steve Session	.08	.25
432 Heath Shuler	1.00	2.50
433 Chuck Smith	.14	.35
434 James O. Stewart	3.20	8.00
435 Mike Stowell	.08	.25
436 J.J. Surlas	.08	.25
437 Shon Walker	.14	.35
438 James Wilson	.08	.25

1995 Tennessee

This set was released by the school and sponsored by Hardee's. The name "Best of the Big Orange" is printed above the player's photo on the front along with the Tennessee logo and the player's name below.

COMPLETE SET (12)	6.00	12.00
1 Reggie Cobb	.50	1.25
2 Charlie Garner	1.00	2.50
3 Aaron Hayden	.50	1.25
4 Johnnie Jones	.40	1.00
5 Hank Lauricella	.40	1.00
6 Johnny Majors	.50	1.25
7 Gene McEver	.40	1.00
8 Stanley Morgan	.60	1.50
9 James Stewart	.60	1.50
10 Tony Thompson	.40	1.00
11 Curt Watson	.40	1.00
12 Chuck Webb	.40	1.00

1999 Tennessee Mrs. Winner's

This set was produced for the University of Tennessee and sponsored by Mrs. Winner's Chicken and Bisquits. Each card features a color photo of the player on a horizontally oriented card along with a simple black and white cardback. Several cards feature highlights from past Vols games and one card is simply a coupon for Mrs. Winner's. The unnumbered cards are listed below alphabetically.

COMPLETE SET (31)	6.00	12.00
1 Mikki Allen	.20	.50
2 Matt Blankenship	.20	.50
3 Marcus Carr	.20	.50
4 Chad Clifton	.30	.75
5 Phillip Crosby	.20	.50
6 Derrick Edmonds	.20	.50
7 Shaun Ellis	.40	1.00
8 Dwayne Goodrich	.30	.75
9 Kevin Gregory	.20	.50
10 Gerald Griffin	.20	.50
11 Michael Jackson K	.20	.50
12 Robert Loudermilk	.20	.50
13 Tee Martin	.75	2.00
14 Troy McMaken	.20	.50
15 Robert Moore TE	.20	.50
16 Billy Ratliff	.30	.75
17 Spencer Riley	.20	.50
18 Benson Scott	.20	.50
19 Raynoch Thompson	.30	.75
20 Josh Tucker	.20	.50
21 Darwin Walker	.20	.50
22 Fred White	.20	.50
23 Tennessee vs. FSU (Jan.4, 1999)	.20	.50
24 Tennessee vs. Florida (Sept.19, 1998)	.20	.50
25 Tennessee vs. Auburn (Dec.6, 1997)	.20	.50
26 Tennessee vs. Ohio St. (Jan.1, 1996)	.20	.50
27 Tennessee vs. Alabama -1996	.20	.50
28 Tennessee vs. Georgia -1992	.20	.50
29 Tennessee vs. Notre Dame -1991	.20	.50
30 Tennessee vs. Miami (Jan.1,1986)	.20	.50
31 Tennessee vs. Auburn -1985	.20	.50

1999 Tennessee Mrs. Winner's National Champions

This set was sponsored by Mrs. Winner's Chicken and Biscuits and pays tribute to the 1998 National Championship team. Each card features a color player photo (oriented vertically) with the Mrs. Winner's logo on the cardfronts along with "1998 National Champions" noted on the right side. The unnumbered cardbacks are black and white and orange with player stats and/or a brief bio.

COMPLETE SET (16)	6.00	12.00
1 Chad Clifton	.20	.50
2 Cosey Coleman	.20	.50
3 Shaun Ellis	.40	1.00
4 Dwayne Goodrich	.30	.75
5 Deon Grant	.40	1.00
6 Jamal Lewis	2.50	6.00
7 Tee Martin	.75	2.00
8 Billy Ratliff	.30	.75
9 Spencer Riley	.20	.50
10 Raynoch Thompson	.30	.75
11 Josh Tucker	.20	.50
12 Darwin Walker	.20	.50
13 Eric Westmoreland	.30	.75
14 Fred White	.20	.50
15 Cedrick Wilson	.40	1.00
16 Cover Coupon Card	.20	.50

1999 Tennessee Schedules

COMPLETE SET (7)	1.50	4.00
1 Cosey Coleman	.20	.50
2 Phillip Fulmer CO	.20	.50
3 Dwayne Goodrich	.20	.50
4 Jamal Lewis	.50	1.25
5 Tee Martin	.40	1.00
6 Raynoch Thompson	.20	.50
7 Darwin Walker	.20	.50

2000 Tennessee

This set was produced by Multi Ad Sports and sponsored by Kroger and Coke. It features members of the 2000 Tennessee Volunteers football team with each card including a color player image on front and a black and white text-filled cardback. The cards are also numbered on the back except for the cover card.

COMPLETE SET (16)	6.00	12.00
1 Cover Card	.20	.50
2 Will Bartholomew	.20	.50
3 Teddy Gaines	.20	.50
4 John Henderson	.75	2.00
5 Travis Henry	1.50	4.00
6 Neil Johnson	.20	.50
7 David Leaverton	.20	.50
8 Andre Lott	.20	.50
9 Will Overstreet	.20	.50
10 Leonard Scott	.20	.50
11 Donte Stallworth	1.25	3.00
12 Travis Stephens	.50	1.25
13 Dominique Stevenson	.30	.75
14 Fred Weary	.30	.75
15 Eric Westmoreland	.20	.50
16 Cedrick Wilson	.75	2.00

2000 Tennessee Schedules

COMPLETE SET (7)	1.50	3.00
1 Phillip Fulmer	.20	.50
2 Travis Henry	.50	1.25
3 David Leaverton	.20	.50
4 Andre Lott	.20	.50
5 Will Overstreet	.20	.50
6 Eric Westmoreland	.20	.50
7 Cedrick Wilson	.20	.50

2001 Tennessee

This set was produced by Multi Ad Sports and sponsored by Kroger and Coca-Cola. It features members of the 2001 Tennessee Volunteers football team with each card including a color player image on front and a black and white text-filled cardback. The cards are also numbered on the backs.

COMPLETE SET (16)	5.00	10.00
1 John Henderson	.50	1.25
2 Will Overstreet	.20	.50
3 Andre Lott	.20	.50
4 Casey Clausen	1.00	2.50
5 Travis Stephens	.50	1.25
6 Fred Weary	.30	.75
7 Will Bartholomew	.20	.50
8 Donte Stallworth	.75	2.00
9 Alex Walls	.20	.50
10 Dominique Stevenson	.30	.75
11 Eric Parker	.50	1.25
12 Leonard Scott	.20	.50
13 Reggie Coleman	.20	.50
14 Kelley Washington	.75	2.00
15 Phillip Fulmer CO	.30	.75
NNO Cover Card	.20	.50

2001 Tennessee Schedules

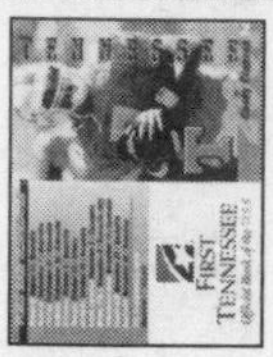

COMPLETE SET (8)	1.50	4.00
1 Will Bartholomew	.20	.50
2 Casey Clausen	.40	1.00
3 Phillip Fulmer CO	.20	.50
4 John Henderson	.20	.50
5 Andre Lott	.20	.50
6 Will Overstreet	.20	.50
7 Alex Walls	.20	.50
8 Fred Weary	.20	.50

2002 Tennessee

This set was produced by Multi Ad Sports, sponsored by Kroger and Coca-Cola, and features members of the 2002 Tennessee Volunteers football team. Each card includes a color player image on front and a black and white text-filled cardback.

COMPLETE SET (15)	5.00	10.00
1 Julian Battle	.30	.75
2 Kevin Burnett	.20	.50
3 Casey Clausen	.75	2.00
4 Troy Fleming	.50	1.25
5 Phillip Fulmer CO	.30	.75
6 Jabari Greer	.20	.50
7 Eddie Moore	.20	.50
8 Rashad Moore	.50	1.25
9 Will Ofenheusle	.20	.50
10 Constantin Ritzmann	.20	.50
11 Leonard Scott	.30	.75
12 Alex Walls	.20	.50
13 Kelley Washington	.60	1.50
14 Scott Wells	.20	.50
15 Jason Witten	1.00	2.50

2002 Tennessee Schedules

COMPLETE SET (8)	2.00	5.00
1 Casey Clausen	.30	.75
2 Casey Clausen Kelley Washington	.30	.75
3 Jabari Greer	.20	.50
4 Eddie Moore	.20	.50
5 Rashad Moore	.20	.50
6 Kelley Washington	.40	1.00
7 Scott Wells	.20	.50
8 Jason Witten	.50	1.25

2003 Tennessee

This set was produced by baselinesportsmedia.com, sponsored by Kroger and Coca-Cola, and features members of the 2003 Tennessee Volunteers football team. Each card includes a color player image on the front with the team name above the photo and the player's name below. The cardbacks are a simple black and white text-filled format.

COMPLETE SET (18)	5.00	10.00
1 Rashad Baker	.50	1.25
2 Tony Brown	.20	.50
3 Kevin Burnett	.20	.50
4 Casey Clausen	.75	2.00
5 Dustin Colquitt	.20	.50
6 Cody Douglas	.20	.50
7 Phillip Fulmer CO	.30	.75
8 Jabari Greer	.20	.50
9 Cedric Houston	.50	1.25
10 Mark Jones	.50	1.25
11 Jason Mitchell	.20	.50
12 Michael Munoz	.30	.75
13 Robert Peace	.20	.50
14 Constantin Ritzmann	.20	.50
15 Kevin Simon	.20	.50
16 Scott Wells	.20	.50
17 Gibril Wilson	.50	1.25
18 Cover Card	.20	.50

2003 Tennessee Schedules

COMPLETE SET (8)	3.00	6.00
1 Rashad Baker	.30	.75
2 Kevin Burnett	.30	.75
3 Casey Clausen	.40	1.00
4 Dustin Colquitt	.30	.75
5 Troy Fleming	.30	.75
6 Phillip Fulmer	.30	.75
7 Michael Munoz	.30	.75
8 Constantin Ritzmann	.30	.75

2004 Tennessee

This set was produced by baselinesportsmedia.com, sponsored by Kroger and Coca-Cola, and features members of the 2004 Tennessee Volunteers football team. Each card includes a color player image on the front with the team logo above the photo and the player's name below. The cardbacks are a simple black and white text-filled format.

COMPLETE SET (16)	4.00	8.00
1 Jason Allen	.30	.75
2 Tony Brown	.30	.75
3 Kevin Burnett	.50	1.25
4 Dustin Colquitt	.30	.75
5 Cody Douglas	.20	.50
6 Phillip Fulmer CO	.20	.50
7 Parys Haralson	.20	.50
8 Cedric Houston	.50	1.25
9 Victor McClure	.20	.50
10 Jason Mitchell	.20	.50
11 Michael Munoz	.20	.50
12 Karlton Neal	.20	.50
13 Jason Respert	.20	.50
14 Kevin Simon	.20	.50
15 Derrick Tinsley	.30	.75
16 Team Schedule	.20	.50

2004 Tennessee Schedules

COMPLETE SET (9)	3.00	6.00
1 Jason Allen	.30	.75
2 Kevin Burnett	.30	.75
3 Dustin Colquitt	.30	.75
4 Phillip Fulmer	.30	.75
5 Parys Haralson	.30	.75
6 Cedric Houston	.30	.75
7 Michael Munoz	.30	.75
8 Kevin Simon	.30	.75
9 James Wilhoit	.30	.75

2005 Tennessee

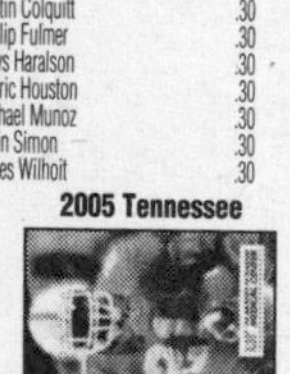

This set was produced by baselinesportsmedia.com and sponsored by The University of Tennessee Medical Center. It features members of the 2005 Tennessee Volunteers football team. Each card includes a color player image on the front with the team logo and the player's name to the left. The cardbacks are a simple black and white text-filled format.

COMPLETE SET (16)	4.00	8.00
1 Jason Allen	.30	.75
2 Cody Douglas	.20	.50
3 Phillip Fulmer CO	.20	.50
4 Omar Gaither	.20	.50
5 Chris Hannon	.20	.50
6 Parys Haralson	.20	.50
7 Jesse Mahelona	.20	.50
8 Robert Meachem	.60	1.50
9 Gerald Riggs Jr.	.40	1.00
10 Arron Sears	.30	.75
11 Kevin Simon	.20	.50
12 Rob Smith	.20	.50
13 Jayson Swain	.20	.50
14 Albert Toeaina	.20	.50
15 James Wilhoit	.20	.50
16 Title Card (2005/2006 Schedules on back)	.20	.50

2005 Tennessee Schedules

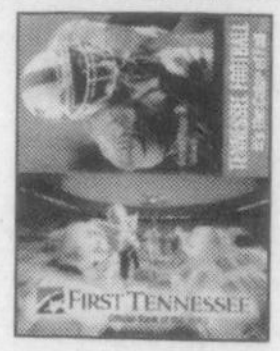

COMPLETE SET (5)	1.00	2.50
1 Jason Allen	.20	.50
2 Cody Douglas	.20	.50
3 Jesse Mahelona	.20	.50
4 Gerald Riggs Jr.	.30	.75
5 Kevin Simon	.20	.50

2006 Tennessee

COMPLETE SET (17)	4.00	8.00
1 Cory Anderson	.20	.50
2 Arian Foster	1.25	3.00
3 Phillip Fulmer CO	.20	.50
4 Justin Harrell	.20	.50
5 Jonathan Hefney	.30	.75
6 David Ligon	.20	.50
7 Turk McBride	.20	.50
8 Matt McGlothlin	.20	.50
9 Robert Meachem	.60	1.50
10 Marvin Mitchell	.20	.50
11 Arron Sears	.30	.75
12 Bret Smith	.20	.50
13 Jayson Swain	.20	.50
14 Jonathan Wade	.20	.50
15 James Wilhoit	.20	.50
16 David Yancey	.20	.50
17 Title Card	.20	.50

2006 Tennessee Schedules

1 Helmet and Football	.20	.50
2 Phillip Fulmer HC	.20	.50
3 Justin Harrell	.20	.50
4 Jonathan Hefney	.20	.50
5 Inquoris Johnson	.20	.50
6 Turk McBride	.20	.50
7 Marvin Mitchell	.20	.50
8 Arron Sears	.30	.75
9 Jayson Swain	.20	.50
10 James Wilhoit	.20	.50

2007 Tennessee

COMPLETE SET (17)	7.50	15.00
1 Erik Ainge	.60	1.50
2 Britton Colquitt	.20	.50
3 Brad Cottam	.30	.75
4 Arian Foster	1.50	4.00
5 Ramon Foster	.20	.50
6 Philip Fulmer CO	.20	.50
7 Montario Hardesty	1.00	2.50
8 Jonathan Hefney	.30	.75
9 Inky Johnson	.20	.50
10 Marsalous Johnson	.20	.50
11 J.T. Mapu	.20	.50
12 Jerod Mayo	1.25	3.00
13 Xavier Mitchell	.20	.50
14 Jarod Parrish	.20	.50
15 Antonio Reynolds	.20	.50
16 Eric Young	.20	.50
17 Title Card	.20	.50

2009 Tennessee

COMPLETE SET (15)	4.00	8.00
1 Eric Berry	.60	1.50
2 Wes Brown	.20	.50
3 Jeff Cottam	.20	.50
4 Jonathan Crompton	.40	1.00
5 Quintin Hancock	.20	.50
6 Montario Hardesty	.60	1.50
7 Marsalous Johnson	.20	.50
8 Lane Kiffin CO	.20	.50
9 Jacques McClendon	.20	.50
10 Rico McCoy	.20	.50
11 Josh McNeil	.20	.50
12 Vladimir Richard	.20	.50
13 Chris Scott	.20	.50
14 Cody Sullins	.20	.50
15 Dan Williams	.20	.50

1990 Texas

Financed by the MOSHANA Foundation and distributed by local law enforcement agencies, this 32-card multi-sport set measures 2 1/2" by 3 1/2" and is printed on thin card stock. The fronts display color action player photos inside a black frame on a white card face. The team name appears in a black bar above the picture, while the player's name and position are printed in the wider bottom border. The backs feature biographical information, player profile, and "A Texas Tip" in the form of anti-drug or alcohol messages. The sports represented are golf (1, 19), basketball (2-4, 8, 25-26, 29, 30), track and field (5-6, 15, 23), tennis (7, 28), baseball (9-10, 16, 32), swimming and diving (11, 13, 20-21), volleyball (12, 14, 18, 31), and football (17, 22, 24, 27). The cards are unnumbered and checklisted below in alphabetical order.

COMPLETE SET (32)	8.00	20.00
17 Ken Hackenmack FB	.30	.75
22 Tony Jones FB	.40	1.00
24 Bobby Lilljedahl FB	.30	.75
27 David McWilliams CO FB	.40	1.00

1991 Texas High School Legends

This 25-card standard-size set was sponsored by Pepsi and issued by the Texas High School Football Hall of Fame. Apparently the set was sold in five five-card packs; each pack featured four player cards and a numbered cover card. On a black card face, the fronts feature sepia-toned player photos. The words "Texas High School Football Legend" and logos adorn the top of the front, while the player's name, high school, and years attended are presented below the picture. In red and blue print on a white panel, the backs carry biographical information, career summary under four subheadings (performance chart; college/pro honors; unforgettable moment; expert opinion), and the player's signature. The cards are unnumbered and checklisted below in alphabetical order, with the cover cards listed at the end.

COMPLETE SET (25)	8.00	20.00
1 Marty Akins	.25	.60
2 Gil Bartosh	.25	.60
3 Bill Bradley	.50	1.25
4 Chris Gilbert	.30	.75
5 Glynn Gregory	.30	.75
6 Charlie Haas	.25	.60
7 Craig James	1.20	3.00
8 Boody Johnson	.25	.60
9 Ernie Koy Jr.	.30	.75
10 Glenn Lippman	.25	.60
11 Jack Pardee	.50	1.25
12 Billy Patterson	.25	.60
13 Billy Sims	1.60	4.00
14 Byron Townsend	.25	.60
15 Doyle Traylor	.25	.60
16 Joe Washington Jr.	.50	1.25
17 Allie White	.25	.60
18 Wilson Whitley	.30	.75
19 Gordon Wood	.30	.75
20 Willie Zapalac	.25	.60
21 Cover Card 1	.25	.60
22 Cover Card 2	.25	.60
23 Cover Card 3	.25	.60
24 Cover Card 4	.25	.60
25 Cover Card 5	.25	.60

1993 Texas Taco Bell

Sponsored by Taco Bell, the 50 cards comprising this set were issued in perforated game program insert sheets. The sheets measure approximately 8" by 10 7/8". Each card measures approximately 2 3/8" by 3 3/8" and carries on its front a white-bordered color player action shot. The player's name and position appear in black lettering within the white border at the bottom. The words "Texas Longhorns" in white lettering, along with the team logo, appear within the vertical black bar along the photo's left side. Each back carries the player's name in orange lettering at the upper left, followed below by his class, position, hometown, and highlights. The Taco Bell logo at the lower left rounds out the card. The cards are unnumbered and checklisted below in alphabetical order.

COMPLETE SET (50)	12.00	30.00
1 Mike Adams	.50	1.25
2 Thomas Baskin	.20	.50
3 Tony Brackens	2.00	5.00
4 Steve Bradley	.20	.50
5 Blake Brockermeyer	.60	1.50
(Wearing home jersey)		
6 Blake Brockermeyer	.60	1.50
(Wearing away jersey)		
7 Phil Brown	.20	.50
8 Chris Carter	.20	.50
9 Stonie Clark	.20	.50
10 Gerald Crawford	.20	.50
12 Trent Elliot	.20	.50
13 Joey Ellis	.30	.75
14 John Elmore	.30	.75
15 Jon Feick	.20	.50
16 Victor Frazier	.20	.50
17 Jimmy Hakes	.20	.50
18 Anthony Holmes	.20	.50
19 Brian Howard	.20	.50
20 Jon Hunter	.20	.50
21 Curtis Jackson	.60	1.50
22 Eric Jackson	.20	.50
23 Bryan Johnson	.30	.75
24 James Lane	.20	.50
25 Doug Livingston	.20	.50
26 Chad Lucas	.20	.50
27 John Mackovic CO	.30	.75
28 Van Malone	.30	.75
29 Justin McLemore	.30	.75
30 Shea Morenz	.50	1.25
31 Dan Neil	.30	.75
32 Cosmo Palmieri	.20	.50
33 Joe Phillips	.20	.50
34 Lovell Pinkney	.30	.75
35 Chris Rapp	.20	.50
36 Robert Reed	.20	.50
37 Jason Reeves	.20	.50
38 Troy Riemer	.20	.50
39 Scott Szeredy	.20	.50
40 Tre Thomas	.50	1.25
41 Winfred Tubbs	.60	1.50
42 Duane Vacek	.30	.75
43 Brian Vasek	.30	.75
44 Rodrick Walker	.30	.75
45 Norman Watkins	.20	.50
46 Kevin Watler	.20	.50
47 Pascal Watty	.20	.50
48 Bryant Westbrook	1.00	2.50
49 Longhorns Band	.20	.50
50 Taco Bell logo card/1993 Texas schedule		.20
.50		

1999 Texas

This set was issued in two 9-card perforated sheets: one for offense and one for defense. Each card features a color photo of the player on the cardfront along with a brown and white colored cardback. The slightly oversized cards (roughly 3" by 4") are unnumbered and listed below alphabetically.

COMPLETE SET (18)	5.00	10.00
1 Major Applewhite	.75	2.00
2 Aaron Babino	.20	.50
3 Mack Brown CO	.30	.75
(carried off the field)		
4 Mack Brown CO	.30	.75
(getting dunked)		
5 Ricky Brown RB	.20	.75
6 Kwame Cavil	.30	.75
7 Leonard Davis	.40	1.00
8 Casey Hampton	.60	1.50
9 Anthony Hicks	.20	.50
10 Aaron Humphrey	.20	.50
11 Quentin Jammer	.75	2.00
12 De'Andre Lewis	.20	.50
13 Hodges Mitchell	.50	1.25
14 Ryan Nunez	.20	.50
15 Roger Roesler	.20	.50
16 Kris Stockton	.20	.50
17 Cedric Woodard	.20	.50
18 Longhorn Defense	.20	.50
(Joe Walker, Aaron Babino)		

2000 Texas

Like the 1999 issue, this set was produced in two 9-card perforated sheets: one for offense and one for defense. Each card features a color photo of the player on the cardfront along with a light brown, orange and white cardback. The 2000 release features the player's jersey number on both the fronts and backs of the cards to differentiate them from the 1999 set. The slightly oversized cards (roughly 3" by 4") are unnumbered and listed below alphabetically.

COMPLETE SET (18)	7.50	15.00
1 Major Applewhite	.60	1.50
2 Greg Brown S	.20	.50
3 Mack Brown CO	.30	.75
(orange shirt)		
4 Mack Brown CO	.30	.75
(white shirt)		
5 Leonard Davis	.40	1.00
6 Casey Hampton	.50	1.25
7 De'Andre Lewis	.20	.50
8 Ryan Long	.20	.50
9 Hodges Mitchell	.40	1.00
10 Cory Quye	.20	.50
11 Cory Redding	.30	.75
13 Chris Simms	2.00	5.00
13 Shaun Rogers	1.25	2.50
14 Kris Stockton	.20	.50
15 Jamel Thompson	.20	.50
16 Joe Walker	.20	.50
17 Defense Domination	.20	.50
(Greg Brown)		
18 Offensive Explosion	.40	1.00
(Major Applewhite)		

2001 Texas

This set was produced in two 9-card perforated sheets: one for offense and one for defense. Each card features a color photo of the player on the cardfront along with a white cardback. This 2001 release features the player's name and the longhorns helmet and team name on the front along with a facsimile autograph. The slightly oversized cards (roughly 3" by 4") are unnumbered and listed below alphabetically.

COMPLETE SET (18)	7.50	15.00
1 Matthew Anderson	.20	.50
2 Major Applewhite	1.00	2.50
3 Ahmad Brooks	.20	.50
4 Mack Brown CO	.30	.75
5 Montrell Flowers	.20	.50
6 Maurice Gordon	.20	.50
7 Ervis Hill	.20	.50
8 Lee Jackson	.20	.50
9 Quentin Jammer	.60	1.50
10 Mike Jones	.20	.50
11 Tyrone Jones	.20	.50
12 Antwan Kirk-Hughes	.20	.50
13 De'Andre Lewis	.20	.50
14 Everick Rawls	.20	.50
15 Chris Simms	1.50	4.00
16 Marcus Wilkins	.20	.50
17 Mike Williams	.30	.75
18 Texas Offense	.30	.75

2002 Texas

This set was produced in two 9-card perforated sheets: one for offense and one for defense. Each card features a color photo of the player on the cardfront along with a dark orange cardback. This 2002 release features the player's position designation on the front along with a facsimile autograph. The slightly oversized cards (roughly 3" by 4") are unnumbered and listed below alphabetically.

COMPLETE SET (18)	7.50	15.00
1 Rod Babers	.30	.75
2 Beau Baker	.20	.50
3 Brian Bradford	.20	.50
4 Mack Brown CO	.30	.75
5 Robbie Doane	.20	.50
6 Derrick Dockery	.20	.50
7 Lee Jackson	.20	.50
8 Miguel McKay	.20	.50
9 Cory Redding	.30	.75
10 Chris Simms	1.25	3.00
11 Chad Stevens	.20	.50
12 Kalen Thornton	.20	.50
13 Beau Trahan	.20	.50
14 Matt Trissel	.20	.50
15 Marcus Tubbs	.50	1.25
16 Michael Ungar	.20	.50
17 Nathan Vasher	1.00	2.50
18 Wide Receivers	1.50	4.00
B.J. Johnson		
Sloan Thomas		
Roy Williams		

2003 Texas

This set was produced in two 9-card perforated sheets: one for offense and one for defense. Each card features a color photo of the player on the cardfront along with a white and orange cardback. This 2003 release features the player's name and the longhorns helmet and team name on the front along with a facsimile autograph. The slightly oversized cards (roughly 3" by 4") are unnumbered and listed below alphabetically.

COMPLETE SET (18)	7.50	15.00
1 Cedric Benson	1.50	4.00
2 Reed Boyd	.20	.50
3 Mack Brown CO	.30	.75
4 Brock Edwards	.20	.50
5 Tillman Holloway	.20	.50
6 B.J. Johnson	.40	1.00
7 Derrick Johnson	1.25	3.00
8 Cullen Loeffler	.20	.50
9 Dakarai Pearson	.20	.50
10 Brett Robin	.20	.50
11 Sloan Thomas	.30	.75
12 Kalen Thornton	.20	.50
13 Marcus Tubbs	.50	1.25
14 Nathan Vasher	.75	2.00
15 Ivan Williams	.30	.75
16 Roy Williams	1.50	4.00
17 Longhorns Defense	.75	2.00
Derrick Johnson		
Reed Boyd		
Marcus Tubbs		
18 Longhorns Offense	1.00	2.50
Cedric Benson		
Brock Edwards		
Jason Glynn		

2004 Texas

This set was produced in two 9-card perforated sheets: one for offense and one for defense/special teams. Each card features a color photo of the player on the cardfront along with a white and burnt orange cardback. This 2004 release features the player's position designation on the front along with a facsimile autograph. The slightly oversized cards (roughly 3" by 4") are unnumbered and listed below alphabetically.

COMPLETE SET (18)	20.00	40.00
1 Trey Bates	.20	.50
2 Cedric Benson	1.25	3.00
3 Mack Brown CO	.30	.75
4 Phillip Geiggar	.20	.50
5 Jason Glynn	.20	.50
6 Cedric Griffin	.40	1.00
7 Michael Huff	1.25	3.00
8 Tony Jeffery	.20	.50
9 Derrick Johnson	1.00	2.50
10 Stevie Lee	.20	.50
11 Dusty Mangum	.20	.50
12 Will Matthews	.20	.50
13 Chance Mock	.40	1.00
14 Bo Scaife	.40	1.00
15 Rodrique Wright	.20	.50
16 Vince Young	10.00	25.00
17 Texas Defense	.20	.50
18 Texas Offense	.30	.75

2005 Texas

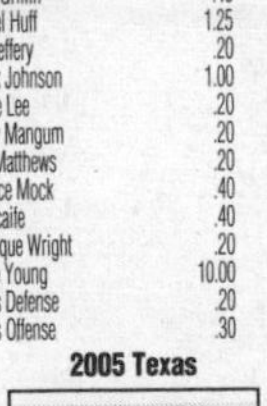

COMPLETE SET (18)	20.00	40.00
1 Will Allen	.20	.50
2 Justin Blalock	.20	.50
3 Mack Brown CO	.30	.75
4 Cedric Griffin	.50	1.25
5 Ahmard Hall	.20	.50
6 Aaron Harris	.20	.50
7 Michael Huff	1.25	3.00
8 Richmond McGee	.20	.50
9 Matt Nordgren	.20	.50
10 Brian Robison	.20	.50
11 Nick Schroeder	.20	.50
12 Jonathan Scott	.20	.50
13 David Thomas	1.50	4.00
14 Rodrique Wright	.30	.75
15 Vince Young	10.00	25.00
16 Mascot - BEVO	.20	.50
17 Texas Defense	.20	.50
18 Texas Offense	.20	.50
(offensive line)		

2006 Texas

COMPLETE SET (12)	4.00	8.00
1 Justin Blalock	.30	.75
2 Tarell Brown	.20	.50
3 Mack Brown CO	.30	.75
4 Tim Crowder	.30	.75
5 Michael Griffin	.75	2.00
6 Greg Johnson	.20	.50
7 Brian Robison	.20	.50
8 Aaron Ross	.75	2.00
9 Lyle Sendlein	.20	.50
10 Kasey Studdard	.20	.50
11 Neale Tweedie	.30	.75
12 Selvin Young	1.50	4.00

2010 Texas

COMPLETE SET (12)	5.00	10.00
1 Sam Acho	.50	1.25
2 Tray Allen	.40	1.00
3 Chykie Brown	.40	1.00
4 Curtis Brown	.40	1.00
5 Mack Brown CO	.40	1.00
6 John Chiles	.40	1.00
7 Dustin Earnest	.40	1.00
8 John Gold	.40	1.00
9 Kyle Hix	.40	1.00
10 Michael Huey	.40	1.00
11 Eddie Jones	.40	1.00
12 James Kirkendoll	.50	1.25

1987 Texas A&M Team Issue

Released by the school, this set features 8X10 dual black and white photos. Each photo has both a portrait shot and an action shot of the featured player and is set up with white borders and a blank back. The photos were not numbered so they appear in alphabetical order below.

COMPLETE SET (57)	50.00	100.00
1 Todd Ariens	1.00	2.50
2 Dana Batiste	1.00	2.50
3 Jayson Black	1.00	2.50
4 Adam Bob	1.00	2.50
5 Chet Brooks	1.00	2.50
6 Guy Broom	1.00	2.50
7 Lovis Cheek	1.00	2.50
8 Melvin Collins	1.00	2.50
9 Kip Corrington	1.00	2.50
10 Gary Coster	1.00	2.50
11 Bryan Edwards	1.00	2.50
12 John Elam	1.00	2.50
13 Jerry Fontenot	1.00	2.50
14 Mike Fouther	1.00	2.50
15 O'Neill Gilbert	1.00	2.50
16 Darren Grudt	1.00	2.50
17 Matt Gurley	1.00	2.50
18 Rod Harris	1.00	2.50
19 Dexter Harrison	1.00	2.50
20 James Howse	1.00	2.50
21 Joe Johnson	1.00	2.50
22 Albert Jones	1.00	2.50
23 Gary Jones	1.00	2.50
24 Tony Jones	1.00	2.50
25 Troy Jones	1.00	2.50
26 Shane Krahl	1.00	2.50
27 Tim Landrum	1.00	2.50
28 Greg Lewis	1.50	3.00
29 Scott Maham	1.00	2.50
30 Trace McGuire	1.00	2.50
31 Sylvester Morgan	1.00	2.50
32 Alex Morris	1.00	2.50
33 Kevin Newton	1.00	2.50
34 Sammy O'Brient	1.00	2.50
35 Lance Pavlas	1.00	2.50
36 Bill Peckman	1.00	2.50
37 Terry Price	1.00	2.50
38 Dennis Ransom	1.00	2.50
39 Derrick Richey	1.00	2.50
40 Jeroy Robinson	1.00	2.50
41 John Roper	1.00	2.50
42 Jeff Shanks	1.00	2.50
43 Jimmy Shelby	1.00	2.50
44 Scott Slater	1.00	2.50
45 Dion Snow	1.00	2.50
46 Craig Stump	1.00	2.50
47 Layne Talbot	1.00	2.50
48 Anthony Taylor	1.00	2.50
49 Lafayette Turner	1.00	2.50
50 Aaron Wallace	2.00	4.00
51 Mickey Washington	1.00	2.50
52 Richmond Webb	2.00	4.00
53 Artis Whetstone	1.00	2.50
54 Matt Wilson	1.00	2.50
55 Sean Wilson	1.00	2.50
56 Keith Woodside	1.00	2.50
57 Chris Work	1.00	2.50

1991 Texas A&M Collegiate Collection

This 100 card standard-size multi-sport set was produced by Collegiate Collection. Although a few color photos are included, the front features mainly black and white player photos with borders in the team's colors. All cards are of football players unless noted.

COMPLETE SET (100)	5.00	10.00
1 Rod Bernstine FB	.05	.15
2 Bear Bryant FB	.60	1.50
4 R.C. Slocum FB	.20	.50
5 Gary Kubiak FB	.07	.20
6 Larry Horton FB	.01	.05
7 Billy Cannon Jr. FB	.02	.10
9 Ray Childress FB	.02	.10
10 John David Crow FB	.30	.75
13 Layne Talbot FB	.01	.05
14 Larry Stegent FB	.01	.05
18 Jimmy Teal FB	.01	.05
20 Lance Pavlas FB	.01	.05
22 Mickey Washington FB	.05	.15
25 Thomas Sanders FB	.02	.10
26 Loyd Taylor FB	.01	.05
29 Curtis Dickey FB	.07	.20
31 Matt McCall FB	.01	.05
34 Brad Dusek FB	.02	.10
36 Gary Oliver FB	.02	.10
37 Charles Milstead FB	.01	.05
43 Jacob Green FB	.07	.20
46 Kevin Monk FB	.01	.05
47 Larry Kelm FB	.01	.05
51 Kent Adams FB	.01	.05
54 Rolf Krueger FB	.05	.15
56 Sylvester Morgan FB	.01	.05
57 Bucky Sams FB	.01	.05
58 Jeff Nelson FB	.01	.05
60 Cary Jones FB	.01	.05
61 Pat Thomas FB	.02	.10
62 Mark Dennard FB	.05	.15
64 Kyle Field	.01	.05
Football Home of the Aggies		
65 Edd Hargett FB	.07	.20
67 Scott Slater FB	.01	.05
68 Louis Cheek FB	.01	.05
69 Ken Ford FB	.01	.05
70 Billy G. Hobbs FB	.01	.05
71 Bob Long FB	.01	.05
72 Jeff Payne FB	.01	.05
73 Garth Tenapel FB	.01	.05
74 David Bandy FB	.01	.05
75 Dennis Swilley FB	.01	.05
76 Mike Whitwell FB	.01	.05
77 Jim Red Cashion FB	.01	.05
80 Texas Aggie Band	.02	.10
81 Bobby Joe Conrad FB	.07	.20
82 Mike Mosley FB	.01	.05
93 Warren Trahan FB	.01	.05
95 Dave Elmendorf FB	.07	.20
99 David Hardy FB	.01	.05

1992 Texas A&M

Produced by Motions Sports Inc., this 64-card standard-size set was sponsored by Pepsi Cola and Chili's restaurants. The cards were to be sold only at the campus bookstore of Texas A and M University. The fronts feature posed color player photos on a black card face. The photo is framed in black and has a white border at the right and bottom and a maroon border at the top and left. The player's name and number appear in the top maroon border and "Texas A and M University" appear in the bottom white border. On a ghosted player photo, the backs present a player profile in a transparent white box. Key cards in this set are Greg Hill and Rodney Thomas.

COMPLETE SET (65)	12.00	30.00
1 Matt Miller	.15	.40
2 Steve Emerson	.15	.40
3 Brad Cooper	.15	.40
4 Mike Hendricks	.20	.50
5 Dexter Wesley	.15	.40
6 Darrell Red	.15	.40
7 Antonio Shorter	.20	.50
8 Larry Wallace	.15	.40
9 Kefa Chatham	.15	.40
10 Billy Mitchell	.15	.40
11 Patrick Bates	.60	1.50
12 Greg Hill	1.50	4.00
13 Tommy Preston	.15	.40
14 Ryan Mathews	.15	.40
15 Steve Kenney	.15	.40
16 John Richard	.15	.40
17 John Ellisor	.15	.40
18 Ryan Kern	.15	.40
19 Jeff Jones	.15	.40
20 Chris Sanders	.15	.40
21 Reggie Graham	.15	.40
22 David Davis	.15	.40
23 Tony Harrison	.20	.50
24 Jason Mathews	.20	.50
25 Otis Nealy	.15	.40
26 Kent Petty	.15	.40
27 Rodney Thomas	.75	2.00
28 Sam Adams	.75	2.00
29 Clif Groce	.20	.50
30 Tyler Harrison	.15	.40
31 Eric England	.15	.40
32 Jason Atkinson	.20	.50
33 Lance Teichelman	.15	.40
34 Marcus Buckley	.60	1.50
35 Steve Solari	.20	.50
36 Aggie Coaches	.20	.50
37 Derrick Frazier	.20	.50
38 James McKeehan	.20	.50
39 Doug Carter	.15	.40
40 Larry Jackson	.15	.40
41 Brian Mitchell	.20	.50
42 Greg Schorp	.20	.50
43 Greg Cook	.15	.40
44 Kyle Maxfield	.15	.40
45 Todd Mathison	.15	.40
46 Chris Dausin	.15	.40
47 Junior White	.15	.40
48 Wilbert Biggens	.15	.40
49 Terry Venetoulias	.15	.40
50 Jessie Cox	.15	.40
51 R.C. Slocum CO	.40	1.00
52 Defensive Coaches	.40	1.00
Bob Davie		
Kirk Doll		
Bill Johnson		
Trent Walters		
53 Offensive Coaches	.40	1.00
Mike Sherman		
Shawn Slocum		
Bob Toledo		
Gary Kubiak		
David Culley		
54 Tim Cassidy	.15	.40
Recruiting Coordinator		
55 Yell Leaders	.15	.40
Steve Scanlon		
Adin Pfeuffer		
Tim Isgitt		
Ronnie McDonald		
Mark Rollins		
56 A and M Band	.15	.40
57 Reveille V	.15	.40
Mascot		
58 Twelfth Man	.20	.50
Statue		
59 Bonfire	.15	.40
60 Training Facility	.15	.40
61 Kyle Field	.15	.40
62 Texas A and M Campus	.15	.40
NNO Front Card	.15	.40
(Texas A and M logo)		
NNO Back Card	.15	.40
NNO Checklist Card	.15	.40

1997 Texas A&M

This 24-card set features color photos of the 1995 and 1996 Aggie senior football players printed on heavy, laminated card stock. The backs carry player information and an inspirational message from the player. The cards are unnumbered and checklisted below in alphabetical order.

COMPLETE SET (24)	10.00	25.00
1 Dennis Allen	.40	1.00
2 Will James Brooks	.40	1.00
3 Reggie Brown LB	.80	2.00
4 Hayward Clay	.40	1.00
5 Calvin Collins	.40	1.00
6 Albert Connell	1.20	3.00
7 Hunter Goodwin	.60	1.50
8 Donovan Greer	.40	1.00
9 Jimmie Irby	.40	1.00
10 Edward Jasper	.40	1.00
11 Gene Lowery	.40	1.00
12 Ray Mickens	.80	2.00
13 Brandon Mitchell	.40	1.00
14 Keith Mitchell	.80	2.00
15 Alcie Peterson	.40	1.00
16 Corey Pullig	.60	1.50
17 Chris Sanders FL	.40	1.00
18 Detron Smith	.80	2.00
19 Sean Terry	.40	1.00
20 Larry Jay Walker	.40	1.00
21 Andre Williams	.40	1.00
22 Pat Williams	1.25	3.00
23 Sherrod Wyatt	.40	1.00
24 Title Card CL	.40	1.00

2005 Texas A&M Schedules

COMPLETE SET (7)	1.50	3.00
1 Jason Carter	.30	.75
2 Aldo De La Garza	.20	.50
3 Jami Hightower	.20	.50
4 Johnny Jolly	.20	.50
5 Archie McDaniel	.20	.50
6 DeQawn Mobley	.20	.50
7 Todd Pegram	.20	.50

2006 Texas Tech Schedules

COMPLETE SET (6)	1.50	3.00
1 Keyunta Dawson (#96)	.20	.50
2 Joel Filani (#8)	.30	.75
Jarrett Hicks (#88)		
3 Chris Hudler (#93)	.20	.50
4 Mike Leach (#HC)	.20	.50
5 Manuel Ramirez (#63)	.20	.50
6 Fletcher Sessions (#42)	.20	.50

1998 Toledo

COMPLETE SET (16)	7.50	15.00
1 James Bates	.40	1.00
2 Loren Burkey	.40	1.00
3 Romain Davis	.40	1.00
4 Matt Fernandez	.40	1.00
5 Chris Holifield	.40	1.00
6 Joey Jones	.40	1.00
7 Kevin Kidd	.40	1.00
8 Mike Lenix	.40	1.00
9 Clarence Love	.40	1.00
10 Marcus Matthews	.40	1.00
11 Sylvester Patton	.40	1.00
12 Gary Pinkel CO	.40	1.00
13 Jason Richards	.40	1.00
14 James Ross	.40	1.00
15 Rasche Sumpter	.40	1.00
16 Wasean Tait	.40	1.00
17 Joe Weaver	.50	1.25
18 Chris Williams	.40	1.00
19 The Glass Bowl	.40	1.00
20 Cover Card	.40	1.00

1995 Tony's Pizza College Mascots

These 20 standard-size cards were issued on the back panels of specially-marked Tony's Italian Pastry and Tony's Pizza D'Primo packages. The cards were not perforated but could be removed from the back panel by cutting along the dotted line. Two cards were featured on each panel as well as an offer for a college sweatshirt. The fronts feature team color-coded drawings of football team mascots, while the backs carry interesting facts and highlights about the college and its football program. The cards are unnumbered and checklisted below in alphabetical order.

COMPLETE SET (20)	12.00	30.00
1 Alabama Crimson Tide	1.20	3.00
2 Auburn Tigers	.60	1.50
3 Arizona Wildcats	.40	1.00
4 Boston College Eagles	.40	1.00
5 Colorado Buffaloes	.60	1.50
6 Florida State Seminoles	1.20	3.00
7 Florida Gators	1.20	3.00
8 Kansas State Wildcats	.40	1.00
9 Miami Hurricanes	1.20	0.00
10 Michigan Wolverines	1.20	3.00
11 Nebraska Cornhuskers	1.20	3.00
12 Notre Dame Fightin' Irish	1.20	3.00
13 Penn State Nittany Lions	1.20	3.00
14 Tennessee Volunteers	1.20	3.00
15 Texas Longhorns	.60	1.50
16 Texas A and M Aggies	.60	1.50
17 UCLA Bruins	.60	1.50
18 USC Trojans	.60	1.50
19 Washington Huskies	.60	1.50
20 Wisconsin Badgers	.40	1.00

2012 Topps AstroTurf NFLPA Collegiate Bowl Autographs

STATED ODDS 1:121 BOWMAN HOB

2012 Topps Under Armour High School All-America

UAAC Amari Cooper
UAAH1 Austin Hardin
UAAH2 Alton Howard
UAAJ1 Angelo Jean-Louis
UAAJ2 Avery Johnson
UAAN Alex Norman
UAAP Andrus Peat
UAAY Avery Young
UABE Bryson Echols
UABG Brandon Greene
UABP Brian Poole
UABS Brock Stadnik
UACB Connor Brewer
UACC Chris Casher
UACE Chaz Elder
UACJ1 Cayleb Jones
UACJ2 Cyrus Jones
UACK Chad Kelly
UACR Curtis Riser
UACT Colin Thompson
UACW Channing Ward
UADB Dakota Ball
UADD Devon Desper
UADF1 Devonte Fields
UADF2 Dante Fowler
UADH1 DeVante Harris
UADH2 Donald Hopkins
UADN Davonte Neal
UADP Darius Powe
UADS1 Deion Sanders Jr.
UADS2 Dalton Santos
UAEB Evan Boehm
UAEG Eddie Goldman
UAEW Eddie Williams
UAIG Issac Gross
UAIO Ifeadi Odenigbo
UAIS Isaac Seaumalo
UAJA John Atkins
UAJB Joe Bolden
UAJC Jalen Cope-Fitzpatrick
UAJD Jessamen Dunker
UAJG1 Josh Garnett
UAJG2 Johnathan Gray
UAJG3 Jay Guillermo
UAJH Joshua Holsey
UAJJ Jordan Jenkins
UAJM Justin Meredith
UAJO Joey O'Connor
UAJT Jonathan Taylor
UAJW Jamels Winston
UAKA Kwon Alexander
UAKE Kennedy Estelle
UAKK Korren Kirven
UAKM Keith Marshall
UALC Landon Collins
UALP LaTroy Pittman
UALT Lucas Thompson
UALW Leonard Williams
UAMB1 Marvin Bracy
UAMB2 Malcom Brown
UAME Mario Edwards Jr.
UAMF Michael Flint
UAMM1 Mike Madaras
UAMM2 Marcus Maye
UAMR Michael Rose
UANA Nelson Agholor
UAND Noor Davis
UANS Noah Spence
UAPD Patrick Destefano
UAPD Peyton Dewey
UAPJ Peter Jinkens
UAPW P.J. Williams
UARD Ronald Darby
UARF1 Ronnie Feist
UARF2 Reid Ferguson
UARJ Randy Johnson
UARL Ricardo Louis
UARM Ross Martin
UARR Reggie Ragland
UASP Sean Price
UASR Shaq Roland
UASS Sterling Shepard
UATE Trae Elston
UATG Trey Griffey
UATJ Thomas Johnson
UATM Tanner Mangum
UATR Terry Richardson
UAVA Vadal Alexander
UAWB Wes Brown
UAZH Zach Hirth
UAZK Zach Kline

1908 Tuck's College Postcards

This set of postcards was issued by Tuck's and features a college co-ed portrait inside the image of a vintage football. The featured school's pennant is prominantly displayed as well on the cardfront. The cardbacks feature a typical postcard design.

COMPLETE SET (6)	60.00	120.00
1 Columbia	10.00	20.00
2 Cornell	10.00	20.00
3 Harvard	10.00	20.00
4 Missouri	10.00	20.00
5 Pennsylvania	10.00	20.00
6 Princeton	10.00	20.00
7 Yale	10.00	20.00

1978 Tulane Team Issue

These photos were issued by the school to promote the football program. Each measures roughly 8" by 10" and features between six and eight black and white images of players with the school name and year appearing at the top. The player's name is printed below each photo. The backs are blank.

COMPLETE SET (9)	30.00	60.00
1 John Ammerman	4.00	8.00
Marcus Anderson		
Steve Athas		
Tommie Barlow		
Bob Becnel		
James Becnel		
Mark Benedetto		
2 Larry Bizzotto	4.00	8.00
Owen Brennan		
Gary Brown		
Willard Browner		
Larry Burke		
Jeff Carnes		
Tom Cheviot		
3 Kevin Cole	4.00	8.00
Terry Daffin		
Darryl Dawkins		
Tony Delaughter		
Arnie Diaz		
Chris Doyle		
Ricky Dunaway		
Joe Dunphy		
4 Carl Duvigneaud	4.00	8.00
Chip Forte		
Jeff Forte		
Nolan Franz		
Nolan Gallo		
Donald Garrett		
Jeff Gates		
George Geishauser		
5 Darrell Griffin	4.00	8.00
Nickie Hall		
Terry Harris		
Fred Hicks		
Tommy Hightower		
Dwain Holland		
Steve Hubbell		
6 Rob Indicott	4.00	8.00
Ken Johnston		
Al Jones		
Clayton Jones		
Clifton Jones		
Jeff Jones		
John Knowlton		
Thad Lee		
7 Donald Louviere	4.00	8.00
Dee Methvin		
Percy Millett		
Mark Montini		
Scott Morrell		
Paul Mudrich		
Chuck Pitcock		
8 Jim Price	4.00	8.00
Nick Ray		
Donnie Rice		
Andre Robert		
Frank Robinson		
Gerry Sheridan		
Joe Silipo		
Wilfred Simon		
9 Mike Sims	4.00	8.00
Ricky Smith		
Rory Stone		
Phil Townsend		
Mike Waslieleski		
Frank Wills		

1995 UCLA Discs

This set of discs were issued together on a perforated panel. The panel includes a Gatorade sponsorship logo and these four discs were part of "Collector Series II" as printed on the panel.

COMPLETE SET (4)	4.00	8.00
1 Jonathan Ogden	1.00	2.50
2 Karim Abdul-Jabbar	1.25	3.00
3 Kevin Jordan	.75	2.00
4 Abdul McCullough	.75	2.00

1997 UCLA

This set was produced for UCLA Florida State University and issued as a 12-card perforated sheet. Each card features a color photo of the player on the cardfront along with a blue and gold colored cardback. The cards are unnumbered and listed below alphabetically.

COMPLETE SET (12)	12.50	25.00
1 Weldon Forde	.40	1.00
2 Javelin Guidry	.40	1.00
3 Skip Hicks	3.00	8.00
4 Jim McElroy	.40	1.00
5 Danjuan McGee	.40	1.00
6 Cade McNown	4.00	10.00
7 Chad Overhauser	.40	1.00
8 Tyrone Pierce	.40	1.00
9 Chad Sauter	.60	1.50
10 Bob Toledo CO	.40	1.00
11 Shaun Williams	.75	2.00
12 Brian Willmer	.40	1.00

1998 UCLA

This 16-card set was originally distributed as a perforated uncut sheet. Each card includes a color player photo on the cardfront with a small black-and-white photo on the back. A Team Photo card, UCLA bear Logo Card, and an ad card for Cal Fed bank were included as three of the 16-cards. Kris Farris' name was misspelled on the card included on the uncut sheet. A corrected card was issued separately. Each card is unnumbered and listed alphabetically below.

COMPLETE SET (16)	5.00	10.00
1 Larry Atkins	.20	.50
2 Brendon Ayanbadejo	.20	.50
3 Danny Farmer	.60	1.50
4A Kris Farris ERR (name spelled Ferris)	.60	1.50
4B Kris Farris COR (name spelled correctly)	.80	2.00
5 Mike Grieb	.20	.50
6 Pete Holland	.20	.50
7 Cade McNown	2.00	5.00
8 Andy Meyers	.20	.50
9 Ryan Neufeld	.30	.75
10 Chris Sailer	.30	.75
11 Shawn Stuart	.20	.50
12 Bob Toledo CO	.20	.50
13 Craig Walendy	.30	.75
14 Team Photo	.30	.75
15 Logo Card	.20	.50
16 Ad Card	.20	.50

1999 UCLA

This set was originally distributed as a perforated uncut sheet. Each card includes a color player photo on the cardfront with a small black-and-white photo on the back. A Team Photo card and an ad card for Met-Rx were included as two of the 16-cards. Each card is unnumbered and listed alphabetically below.

COMPLETE SET (12)	4.00	10.00
1 Jason Bell	.20	.50
2 Pete Holland	.20	.50
3 Danny Farmer	.30	.75
4 Brad Melsby	.30	.75
5 Durell Price	.20	.50
6 Jermaine Lewis RBK	1.00	2.50
7 Brian Polak	.30	.75
8 Keith Brown	.40	1.00
9 Bob Toledo CO	.20	.50
10 DeShaun Foster	1.50	4.00
11 Team Photo	.30	.75
12 Met-Rx Ad Card	.20	.50

2000 UCLA

Like previous UCLA issues, this set was originally distributed as a perforated uncut sheet. Each card includes a color player photo on the cardfront with a small black-and-white photo on the back. An ad card for Met-Rx was also included as one of the 12-cards. Each card is unnumbered and listed alphabetically below.

COMPLETE SET (12)	3.00	8.00
1 Jason Bell	.20	.50
2 Drew Bennett	1.25	3.00
3 Oscar Cabrera	.20	.50
4 Kenyon Coleman	.40	1.00
5 Gabe Grecion	.20	.50
6 Jermaine Lewis RBK	.60	1.50
7 Kory Lombard	.20	.50
8 Brian Polak	.30	.75
9 Mike Vanis	.20	.50
10 Tony White	.20	.50
11 Jason Zdenek	.20	.50
12 Met-Rx Ad Card	.20	.50

2001 UCLA

Like most recent UCLA sets, this one was originally distributed as a perforated uncut sheet. Each card includes a color player photo surrounded by a yellow border. An ad card for Met-Rx was included as one of the 12-cards. Each card is unnumbered and listed alphabetically below.

COMPLETE SET (12)	4.00	10.00
1 Marques Anderson	.60	1.50
2 Kenyon Coleman	.30	.75
3 Troy Danoff	.20	.50
4 Bryan Fletcher	.40	1.00
5 DeShaun Foster	1.25	3.00
6 Ed Stansbury	.30	.75
7 Ken Kocher	.20	.50
8 Ryan Nece	.40	1.00
9 Brian Poli-Dixon	.40	1.00
10 Matt Stanley	.20	.50
11 Robert Thomas LB	.40	1.00
12 Met-Rx Ad Card	.20	.50

2002 UCLA

This set was originally distributed as a perforated uncut sheet. Each card includes a color player photo on the cardfront with a small black-and-white photo on the back against a blue background. An ad card for Met-Rx was also included as one of the 12-cards. Each card is unnumbered and listed alphabetically below.

COMPLETE SET (12)	3.00	8.00
1 Bryce Bohlander	.20	.50
2 Nate Fikse	.20	.50
3 Joe Hunter	.20	.50
4 Ricky Manning	.40	1.00
5 Steve Morgan	.20	.50
6 Cory Paus	.75	2.00
7 Sean Phillips	.30	.75
8 Marcus Reese	.30	.75
9 Mike Saffer	.20	.50
10 Mike Seidman	.20	.50
11 Rusty Williams	.20	.50
12 Met-Rx Ad Card	.20	.50

2003 UCLA

COMPLETE SET (12)	3.00	6.00
1 Dave Ball	.30	.75
2 Mat Ball	.20	.50
3 Brandon Chillar	.30	.75
4 Asi Faoa	.20	.50
5 Akil Harris	.20	.50
6 Shane Lehmann	.20	.50
7 Rodney Leisle	.20	.50
8 Dennis Link	.20	.50
9 Keith Short	.20	.50
10 David Tautofi	.20	.50
11 Karl Dorrell CO	.20	.50
12 Cover Card	.20	.50

2004 UCLA

This set was originally distributed as a perforated uncut sheet. Each card includes a color player photo on the cardfront with a small black-and-white photo on the back against a yellow and white background. An ad card for Met-Rx was also included as one of the 12-cards. Each card is unnumbered and listed alphabetically below.

COMPLETE SET (12)	4.00	8.00
1 Craig Bragg	1.00	2.50
2 Matt Clark	.20	.50
3 Eyoseph Efseaff	.20	.50
4 Ben Emanuel	.30	.75
5 Chris Kluwe	.20	.50
6 Benjamin Lorier	.20	.50
7 Paul Mociler	.20	.50
8 Pat Norton	.20	.50
9 Tab Perry	.30	.75
10 Steven Vieira	.20	.50
11 Manuel White	.40	1.00
12 Met-Rx Ad Card	.20	.50

2005 UCLA

This set was originally distributed as a perforated uncut sheet. Each card includes a color player photo on the cardfront with a small black-and-white photo on the back along with a MET-Rx logo. The cards are unnumbered and listed alphabetically below.

COMPLETE SET (12)	3.00	8.00
1 Ed Blanton	.20	.50
2 Marcus Cassel	.20	.50
3 Robert Cleary	.20	.50
4 Karl Dorrell CO	.20	.50
5 Spencer Havner	.30	.75
6 Marcedes Lewis	.50	1.25
7 Justin London	.20	.50
8 Mike McCloskey	.20	.50
9 Drew Olson	.75	2.00
10 Jarrad Page	.20	.50
11 Wesley Walker	.30	.75
12 Cover Card	.20	.50

2006 UCLA

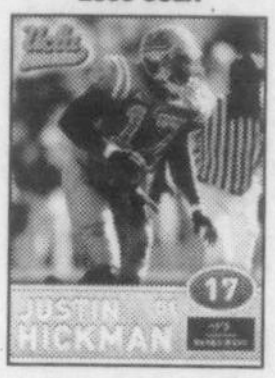

This set was originally distributed as a perforated uncut sheet at the UCLA versus USC game in 2006. Each card includes a color player photo on the cardfront with the player's name below the image along with a Bank of the West logo. The cards are unnumbered and listed alphabetically below.

COMPLETE SET (12)	5.00	10.00
1 Andrew Baumgartner	.30	.75
2 Robert Chai	.30	.75
3 Karl Dorrell CO	.30	.75
4 J.J. Hair	.30	.75
5 Justin Hickman	.60	1.50
6 Riley Jondle	.30	.75
7 Eric McNeal	.40	1.00
8 Justin Medlock	.40	1.00
9 Danny Nelson	.30	.75
10 Will Peddie	.30	.75
11 Junior Taylor	.40	1.00
12 Matt Willis	.30	.75

2007 UCLA

This set was originally distributed as a perforated uncut sheet at a UCLA football game in 2007. Each card includes a color player photo on the cardfront within a football shaped inner border. The cards are unnumbered and listed alphabetically below.

COMPLETE SET (24)	5.00	10.00
1 Brian Abraham	.30	.75
2 Brandon Breazell	.40	1.00
3 Kevin Brown	.30	.75
4 Trey Brown	.30	.75
5 Joe Cowan	.30	.75
6 Bruce Davis	.40	1.00
7 Nikola Dragovic	.30	.75
8 Brigham Harwell	.30	.75
9 Fred Holmes	.30	.75
10 Chris Horton	.50	1.25
11 P.J. Irvin	.30	.75
12 Chris Joseph	.30	.75
13 Dennis Keyes	.30	.75
14 Chris Markey	.30	.75
15 Chad Moline	.30	.75
16 Michael Pitre	.30	.75
17 Brian Rubinstein	.30	.75
18 Matt Slater	.50	1.25
19 William Snead	.30	.75
20 Noah Sutherland	.30	.75
21 Christian Taylor	.30	.75
22 Shannon Tevaga	.30	.75
23 Rodney Van	.30	.75
24 Aaron Whittington	.30	.75

2008 UCLA

This set was originally distributed as a perforated uncut sheet at a UCLA football game in 2007. Each card includes a color player photo on the cardfront within a football shaped inner border. The cards are unnumbered and listed alphabetically below.

COMPLETE SET (20)	5.00	10.00
1 Kahlil Bell	.50	1.25
2 Tom Blake	.20	.50
3 Kyle Bosworth	.20	.50
4 Patrick Cowan	.20	.50
5 Joshua Edwards	.20	.50
6 Marcus Everett	.20	.50
7 Scott Glicksberg	.20	.50
8 Ryan Graves	.20	.50
9 John Hale	.20	.50
10 Brigham Harwell	.20	.50
11 Bret Lockett	.20	.50
12 Chris Meadows	.20	.50
13 Chase Moline	.20	.50
14 Rick Neuheisel CO	.30	.75
15 Michael Norris	.20	.50
16 Ben Olson	.40	1.00
17 Logan Paulsen	.20	.50
18 Aaron Perez	.20	.50
19 Micah Reed	.20	.50
20 Nathaniel Skaggs	.20	.50

1905 Ullman Postcards

The 1905 Ullman Mfg. Co. postcard series includes various collegiate football teams. Each postcard features a color art rendering of a generic football player along with the team's mascot or emblem. A copyright date is also included on the cardfront and the cardback is typical postcard style. We've listed the known postcards. Any additions to this list are appreciated.

COMPLETE SET (7)	75.00	125.00
1 Chicago	12.00	20.00
2 Columbia	12.00	20.00
3 Cornell	12.00	20.00
4 Penn	12.00	20.00
5 Princeton	12.00	20.00
6 Stanford	12.00	20.00
7 Yale	12.00	20.00

1905 University Ivy League Postcards

These cards were issued by the University Post Card Company in 1905. Each card includes a black and white player photo to the left and a smaller football action photo in the upper right corner. The player's name is included in a banner at the top along with a caption for the action photo. The backs feature a very basic postcard style. The notation "Published by University Post Card Company" appears on the card front on the left side. Any additions to this list are appreciated.

1 Robert Folwell	35.00	60.00
2 Harold Gaston	35.00	60.00
3 Daniel Hurley (Harvard)	35.00	60.00
4 Robert Torrey - (Pennsylvania)	35.00	60.00

1906 University Ivy League Postcards

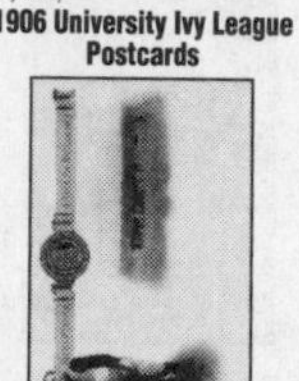

These cards were issued by the University Post Card Company in 1906. Each card includes a black and white player photo to the left and a smaller football action photo in the upper right corner. The player's name is included in a banner at the top along with a caption for the action photo. The backs feature a decorative Post Card style along with the copyright " The University Post Card Company, Andover, Massachusetts" printed on the left side. Any additions to this list are appreciated.

1 Bebee (Yale)	30.00	50.00
2 Edward Bennis (Penn; A Play Through Tackle)	30.00	50.00
3 W.Z. Carr (Harvard)	30.00	50.00
4 Dexter Draper (Pennsylvania)	30.00	50.00
5 MacDonald ERR (Harvard, misspelled McDonald)	30.00	50.00
6 William Rooke (Pennsylvania)	30.00	50.00
7 Howard Roome (Yale)	30.00	50.00
8 Vincent Stevenson (Penn; A Good Start)	50.00	80.00
9 Roswell Tripp (Yale)	30.00	50.00
10 Paul Veeder (Yale)	35.00	60.00
11 John Wendell (Harvard)	30.00	50.00
12 Gus Zeigler (Pennsylvania)	30.00	50.00

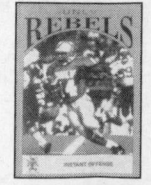

1991 UNLV

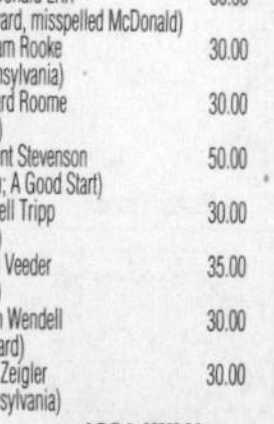

This 12-card standard size set was sponsored by KVVU TV (Fox 5), BDA, and Vons. The cards were printed on thin card stock and issued on a perforated sheet measuring approximately 10" by 10 1/2". The fronts feature color action photos bordered in red. The top of the pictures is curved to resemble an archway, and the team name follows the curve of the arch. The player's name and position appear in a gray stripe below the picture. The backs carry comments, "Drug Tips From The Rebels," sponsor logos, and a phone number for Junior Rebel Club Information. The cards are unnumbered and checklisted below in alphabetical order.

COMPLETE SET (12)	3.20	8.00
1 Cheerleaders and Songleaders	.30	.75
2 Gang Tackle	.30	.75
3 Instant Offense Hernandez Cooper	.30	.75
4 No Escape	.30	.75
5 On the Move	.30	.75
6 Punching It In	.30	.75
7 Ready to Fire Derek Stott	.30	.75
8 Rebel Fever	.30	.75
9 Rebel Sack	.30	.75
10 Sam Boyd Silver Bowl	.30	.75
11 Jim Strong CO	.30	.75
12 Team Photo	.40	1.00

2011 Upper Deck Oklahoma

COMP.SET w/INSERTS (199)	40.00	80.00
COMPLETE SET (99)	8.00	20.00
1 Darrell Royal	.15	.40
2 J.D. Roberts	.12	.30
3 Jerry Tubbs	.12	.30
4 Tommy McDonald	.20	.50
5 Bill Krisher	.12	.30
6 Jerry Thompson	.12	.30
7 Leon Cross	.12	.30
8 Jim Grisham	.12	.30
9 Ralph Neely	.12	.30
10 Carl McAdams	.12	.30
11 Granville Liggins	.12	.30
12 Eddie Hinton	.12	.30
13 Bobby Warmack	.12	.30
14 Barry Switzer CO	.20	.50
15 Steve Owens	.15	.40
16 Steve Zabel	.12	.30
17 Ken Mendenhall	.12	.30
18 Derland Moore	.12	.30
19 Tom Brahaney	.12	.30
20 Greg Pruitt	.15	.40
21 Eddie Foster	.12	.30
22 Kyle Davis	.12	.30
23 John Roush	.12	.30
24 Lucious Selmon	.12	.30
25 Lee Roy Selmon	.20	.50
26 Dewey Selmon	.12	.30
27 Joe Washington	.15	.40
28 Tinker Owens	.12	.30
29 Jimbo Elrod	.12	.30
30 Steve Davis	.12	.30
31 Billy Brooks	.12	.30
32 Mike Vaughan	.12	.30
33 Horace Ivory	.12	.30
34 Zac Henderson	.12	.30
35 Greg Roberts	.12	.30
36 Uwe Von Schamann	.12	.30
37 Reggie Kinlaw	.12	.30
38 Billy Sims	.20	.50
39 George Cumby	.12	.30
40 J.C. Watts	.15	.40
41 Louis Oubre	.12	.30
42 Steve Sewell	.12	.30
43 Tony Casillas	.15	.40
44 Brian Bosworth	.20	.50
45 Lydell Carr	.12	.30
46 Keith Jackson	.15	.40
47 Dante Jones	.12	.30
48 Mark Hutson	.12	.30
49 Rickey Dixon	.12	.30
50 Jamelle Holieway	.15	.40
51 Anthony Phillips	.12	.30
52 Joe Bowden	.12	.30
53 Mike Gaddis	.12	.30
54 Cale Gundy	.15	.40
55 Corey Warren	.12	.30
56 Cedric Jones	.12	.30
57 Josh Heupel	.15	.40
58 Seth Littrell	.12	.30
59 Tim Duncan	.12	.30
60 Rocky Calmus	.12	.30
61 Nate Hybl	.15	.40
62 Quentin Griffin	.15	.40
63 Trent Smith	.12	.30
64 Derrick Strait	.12	.30
65 Teddy Lehman	.12	.30
66 Jason White	.20	.50
67 Antonio Perkins	.12	.30
68 Mark Clayton	.15	.40
69 Vince Carter	.12	.30
70 Paul Thompson	.12	.30
71 Rufus Alexander	.12	.30
72 Adrian Peterson	.40	1.00
73 Lendy Holmes	.12	.30
74 Sam Bradford	.40	1.00
75 Jermaine Gresham	.15	.40
76 Adrian Taylor	.15	.40
77 Jeremy Beal	.15	.40
78 DeMarco Murray	.50	1.25
79 Bob Stoops CO	.20	.50
80 1946-59 Conference Titles MM	.12	.30
81 Tommy McDonald MM	.15	.40
82 Joe Washington MM	.12	.30
83 Lee Roy Selmon MM	.12	.30
84 Uwe Von Schamann kick MM	.12	.30
85 Billy Sims MM	.15	.40
86 J.C. Watts MM	.15	.40
87 Brian Bosworth MM	.15	.40
88 Tony Casillas MM	.12	.30
89 Quentin Griffin MM	.15	.40
90 Josh Heupel MM	.15	.40
91 2001 Whitehouse Visit MM	.12	.30
92 Jason White MM	.15	.40
93 Adrian Peterson MM	.30	.75
94 Adrian Peterson MM	.30	.75
95 Sam Bradford MM	.30	.75
96 Sam Bradford MM	.30	.75
97 Oklahoma Marching Band MM	.12	.30
98 Sooner Schooner MM	.12	.30
99 Memorial Stadium MM	.12	.30

2011 Upper Deck Oklahoma Gold

*GOLD/210: 5X TO 12X BASIC CARDS
STATED PRINT RUN 210 SER.#'d SETS

2011 Upper Deck Oklahoma All-Americans

AAAP Adrian Peterson	.60	1.50
AABB Brian Bosworth	.50	1.25
AABS Billy Sims	.50	1.25
AAGP Greg Pruitt	.40	1.00
AAJG Jermaine Gresham	.40	1.00
AAJH Josh Heupel	.40	1.00
AAJW Joe Washington	.30	.75
AAKJ Keith Jackson	.30	.75
AALS Lee Roy Selmon	.50	1.25
AAMC Mark Clayton	.30	.75
AASB Sam Bradford	.50	1.25
AASO Steve Owens	.30	.75
AATC Tony Casillas	.30	.75
AATM Tommy McDonald	.40	1.00
AATO Tinker Owens	.30	.75
AAWH Jason White	.40	1.00

2011 Upper Deck Oklahoma All-Americans Autographs

STATED PRINT RUN 5-50

AABS Billy Sims/50	25.00	50.00
AAGP Greg Pruitt/50	20.00	40.00
AAJG Jermaine Gresham/50	20.00	40.00
AAJH Josh Heupel/50	25.00	50.00
AAKJ Keith Jackson/50	25.00	50.00
AAMC Mark Clayton/50		
AAWH Jason White/50	25.00	50.00

2011 Upper Deck Oklahoma All-Time Alumni

ATAAP Adrian Peterson	.60	1.50
ATABB Brian Bosworth	.50	1.25
ATABR Billy Brooks	.30	.75
ATABS Billy Sims	.50	1.25
ATABW Bobby Warmack	.30	.75
ATACG Cale Gundy	.40	1.00
ATADM DeMarco Murray	1.00	2.50
ATADS Dewey Selmon	.30	.75
ATAGL Granville Liggins	.30	.75
ATAGP Greg Pruitt	.40	1.00
ATAGR Jim Grisham	.30	.75
ATAHE Josh Heupel	.40	1.00
ATAJC J.C. Watts	.40	1.00
ATAJE Jimbo Elrod	.30	.75
ATAJG Jermaine Gresham	.40	1.00
ATAJH Jamelle Holieway	.40	1.00
ATAJW Joe Washington	.30	.75
ATAKJ Keith Jackson	.40	1.00
ATALS Lee Roy Selmon	.50	1.25
ATALU Lucious Selmon	.30	.75
ATAMC Mark Clayton	.30	.75
ATANH Nate Hybl	.40	1.00
ATAQG Quentin Griffin	.40	1.00
ATARC Rocky Calmus	.30	.75
ATARD Rickey Dixon	.30	.75
ATASB Sam Bradford	.50	1.25
ATASD Steve Davis	.30	.75
ATASO Steve Owens	.40	1.00
ATAST Derrick Strait	.30	.75
ATASZ Steve Zabel	.30	.75
ATATC Tony Casillas	.30	.75
ATATL Teddy Lehman	.30	.75
ATATM Tommy McDonald	.40	1.00
ATATO Tinker Owens	.30	.75
ATAWH Jason White	.50	1.25

2011 Upper Deck Oklahoma All-Time Alumni Autographs

STATED PRINT RUN 5-30

ATABB Brian Bosworth/30		
ATABS Billy Sims/30		
ATABW Bobby Warmack/30		
ATACG Cale Gundy/30		
ATADM DeMarco Murray/30	40.00	80.00
ATADS Dewey Selmon/30	30.00	60.00
ATAGL Granville Liggins/30		
ATAGP Greg Pruitt/30	25.00	50.00
ATAGR Jim Grisham/30		
ATAHE Josh Heupel/30		
ATAJC J.C. Watts/30		
ATAJE Jimbo Elrod/30	20.00	40.00
ATAJG Jermaine Gresham/30	25.00	50.00
ATAJH Jamelle Holieway/30		
ATAJW Joe Washington/30		
ATAKJ Keith Jackson/30		
ATAMC Mark Clayton/30	30.00	60.00
ATANH Nate Hybl/30		
ATAQG Quentin Griffin/30	25.00	50.00
ATARC Rocky Calmus/30		
ATARD Rickey Dixon/30		
ATASD Steve Davis/30		
ATAST Derrick Strait/30	20.00	40.00
ATASZ Steve Zabel/30		
ATATC Tony Casillas/30		
ATATL Teddy Lehman/30		
ATATO Tinker Owens/30		
ATAWH Jason White/30		

2011 Upper Deck Oklahoma All-Time Alumni Duos

ATADBB Barry Switzer Bob Stoops	.60	1.50
ATADBC Tony Casillas Brian Bosworth	.50	1.25
ATADBW Jason White Sam Bradford	.60	1.50
ATADHG Nate Hybl Cale Gundy	.50	1.25
ATADJG Jermaine Gresham Keith Jackson	.50	1.25
ATADOO Steve Owens Tinker Owens	.40	1.00
ATADPB Sam Bradford Adrian Peterson	1.25	3.00
ATADPS Adrian Peterson Billy Sims	.75	2.00
ATADSO Billy Sims Steve Owens	.50	1.25
ATADSP Billy Sims Greg Pruitt	.50	1.25
ATADSS Lee Roy Selmon Dewey Selmon	.50	1.25
ATADSW Billy Sims Joe Washington	.50	1.25

2011 Upper Deck Oklahoma All-Time Alumni Duos Autographs

HG Nate Hybl/20 Cale Gundy	75.00	125.00
JG Jermaine Gresham/20 Keith Jackson		
SP Billy Sims/20 Greg Pruitt		
SW Billy Sims/20 Joe Washington		

2011 Upper Deck Oklahoma All-Time Alumni Trios

BLC Rocky Calmus Teddy Lehman Brian Bosworth	.60	1.50
BWH Jason White Sam Bradford Josh Heupel	.75	2.00
MWP Greg Pruitt Joe Washington Tommy McDonald	.60	1.50
PSM Tommy McDonald Adrian Peterson Billy Sims	1.00	2.50
SOW Billy Sims Jason White Steve Owens	.60	1.50
SSS Dewey Selmon Lee Roy Selmon Lucious Selmon	.60	1.50

2011 Upper Deck Oklahoma Autographs

OVERALL AUTO ODDS 1:24

2 J.D. Roberts	20.00	50.00
4 Tommy McDonald	20.00	50.00

5 Bill Krisher 15.00 40.00
6 Jerry Thompson 20.00 50.00
7 Leon Cross 30.00 60.00
8 Jim Grisham 20.00 50.00
9 Ralph Neely 15.00 40.00
10 Carl McAdams 15.00 40.00
11 Granville Liggins 15.00 40.00
12 Eddie Hinton 20.00 50.00
13 Bobby Warmack 15.00 40.00
14 Barry Switzer 30.00 60.00
15 Steve Owens 30.00 60.00
16 Steve Zabel 15.00 40.00
17 Ken Mendenhall 15.00 40.00
18 Derland Moore 15.00 40.00
19 Tom Brahaney 15.00 40.00
20 Greg Pruitt 75.00 125.00
21 Eddie Foster
22 Kyle Davis
23 John Roush 15.00 40.00
24 Lucious Selmon 15.00 40.00
25 Lee Roy Selmon
26 Dewey Selmon 20.00 50.00
27 Joe Washington
28 Tinker Owens 30.00 60.00
29 Jimbo Elrod 15.00 40.00
30 Steve Davis 30.00 60.00
31 Billy Brooks 15.00 40.00
32 Mike Vaughan 15.00 40.00
33 Horace Ivory 20.00 50.00
34 Zac Henderson 15.00 40.00
35 Greg Roberts
36 Uwe Von Schamann 15.00 40.00
37 Reggie Kinlaw
38 Billy Sims
39 George Cumby 20.00 50.00
40 J.C. Watts 20.00 50.00
41 Louis Oubre 15.00 40.00
42 Steve Sewell
43 Tony Casillas
44 Brian Bosworth 30.00 60.00
45 Lydell Carr 20.00 50.00
46 Keith Jackson 20.00 50.00
47 Dante Jones 15.00 40.00
48 Mark Hutson 15.00 40.00
49 Rickey Dixon 15.00 40.00
50 Jamelle Holieway 30.00 60.00
51 Anthony Phillips 30.00 60.00
52 Joe Bowden 15.00 40.00
53 Mike Gaddis
54 Cale Gundy 20.00 50.00
55 Corey Warren 15.00 40.00
56 Cedric Jones 15.00 40.00
57 Josh Heupel
58 Seth Littrell 15.00 40.00
59 Tim Duncan 15.00 40.00
60 Rocky Calmus 15.00 40.00
61 Nate Hybl
62 Quentin Griffin
63 Trent Smith 15.00 40.00
64 Derrick Strait 15.00 40.00
65 Teddy Lehman
66 Jason White 15.00 40.00
67 Antonio Perkins
68 Mark Clayton 15.00 40.00
69 Vince Carter 15.00 40.00
70 Paul Thompson 20.00 50.00
71 Rufus Alexander 15.00 40.00
72 Adrian Peterson 100.00 175.00
73 Lendy Holmes 15.00 40.00
74 Sam Bradford
75 Jermaine Gresham 20.00 50.00
76 Adrian Taylor 20.00 50.00
77 Jeremy Beal 20.00 50.00
78 DeMarco Murray
79 Bob Stoops 100.00 200.00

2011 Upper Deck Oklahoma Icons

STATED ODDS 1:12
IAP Antonio Perkins 2.00 5.00
IBB Brian Bosworth 3.00 8.00
IBR Billy Brooks 2.00 5.00
IDM DeMarco Murray 6.00 15.00
IDS Derrick Strait 2.00 5.00
IGP Greg Pruitt 2.50 6.00
IJE Jimbo Elrod 2.00 5.00
IJG Jermaine Gresham 2.50 6.00
IJH Josh Heupel 3.00 8.00
IJW Joe Washington 2.00 5.00
IKJ Keith Jackson 2.50 6.00
ILS Lee Roy Selmon 3.00 8.00
IMC Mark Clayton 2.50 6.00
IMH Mark Hutson 2.00 5.00
IPE Adrian Peterson 4.00 10.00
IQG Quentin Griffin 2.50 6.00
IRC Rocky Calmus 2.00 5.00
IRD Rickey Dixon 2.00 5.00
ISB Sam Bradford 3.00 8.00
ISD Steve Davis 2.00 5.00
ISI Billy Sims 3.00 8.00
ISO Steve Owens 2.50 6.00
ISW Barry Switzer 3.00 8.00
ITB Tom Brahaney 2.00 5.00
ITC Tony Casillas 2.00 5.00
ITM Tommy McDonald 2.50 6.00
ITO Tinker Owens 2.00 5.00
IUS Uwe Von Schamann 2.00 5.00
IWH Jason White 3.00 8.00
IZH Zac Henderson 2.00 5.00

2011 Upper Deck Oklahoma National Champions

NCBB Brian Bosworth .50 1.25
NCBK Bill Krisher .30 .75
NCBR Billy Brooks .30 .75
NCBS Bob Stoops .50 1.25
NCDS Dewey Selmon .30 .75
NCHE Josh Heupel .40 1.00
NCHI Horace Ivory .30 .75
NCJE Jimbo Elrod .30 .75
NCJH Jamelle Holieway .40 1.00
NCJT Jerry Tubbs .30 .75
NCJW Joe Washington .30 .75
NCKJ Keith Jackson .30 .75
NCLS Lee Roy Selmon .50 1.25
NCQG Quentin Griffin .40 1.00
NCRC Rocky Calmus .30 .75
NCRD Rickey Dixon .30 .75
NCSD Steve Davis .30 .75
NCSW Barry Switzer .50 1.25
NCTC Tony Casillas .30 .75
NCTM Tommy McDonald .40 1.00
NCTO Tinker Owens .30 .75

2011 Upper Deck Oklahoma National Champions Autographs

STATED PRINT RUN 5-35
NCBR Billy Brooks/35
NCDS Dewey Selmon/35
NCHE Josh Heupel/35
NCHI Horace Ivory/35
NCJE Jimbo Elrod/35 20.00 40.00
NCJH Jamelle Holieway/35 25.00 50.00
NCJW Joe Washington/35
NCKJ Keith Jackson/35
NCQG Quentin Griffin/35 25.00 50.00
NCRC Rocky Calmus/35 15.00 30.00
NCRD Rickey Dixon/35
NCSD Steve Davis/35
NCTC Tony Casillas/35 25.00 50.00
NCTO Tinker Owens/35 20.00 40.00

2011 Upper Deck Oklahoma National Champions Duos

NCDBO Tinker Owens .40 1.00
Billy Brooks
NCDHG Josh Heupel .50 1.25
Quentin Griffin
NCDMT Tommy McDonald .50 1.25
Jerry Tubbs
NCDSB Barry Switzer .60 1.50
Brian Bosworth
NCDSH Bob Stoops .60 1.50
Josh Heupel
NCDWI Joe Washington .40 1.00
Horace Ivory

2011 Upper Deck Oklahoma National Champions Duos Autographs

BO Tinker Owens/15
Billy Brooks
HG Josh Heupel/15
Quentin Griffin
SB Barry Switzer/15
Brian Bosworth
WI Joe Washington/15
Horace Ivory

2011 Upper Deck Oklahoma National Champions Trios

DWO Joe Washington .50 1.25
Tinker Owens
Steve Davis
HGC Josh Heupel .60 1.50
Quentin Griffin
Rocky Calmus
HJB Brian Bosworth .75 2.00
Keith Jackson
Jamelle Holieway
MTK Jerry Tubbs .60 1.50
Bill Krisher
Tommy McDonald

2011 Upper Deck Texas

COMPLETE SET (100) 8.00 20.00
1 Bobby Dillon .12 .30
2 Darrell Royal CO .20 .50
3 Jimmy Saxton .12 .30
4 Jack Collins .12 .30
5 Mike Cotten .12 .30
6 Don Talbert .12 .30
7 Johnny Treadwell .12 .30
8 Charlie Talbert .12 .30
9 Ernie Koy .12 .30
10 Diron Talbert .12 .30
11 Bill Bradley .15 .40
12 Ted Koy .12 .30
13 James Street .15 .40
14 Bob McKay .12 .30
15 Bobby Wuensch .12 .30
16 Tom Campbell .12 .30
17 Bill Atessis .12 .30
18 Scott Henderson .12 .30
19 Steve Worster .12 .30
20 Happy Feller .12 .30
21 Cotton Speyrer .12 .30
22 Jim Bertelsen .12 .30
23 Eddie Phillips .12 .30
24 Alan Lowry .12 .30
25 Roosevelt Leaks .12 .30
26 Doug English .12 .30
27 Marty Akins .12 .30
28 Bill Hamilton .12 .30
29 Earl Campbell .20 .50
30 Brad Shearer .12 .30
31 Russell Erxleben .12 .30
32 Johnny Ham Jones .12 .30
33 Randy McEachern .12 .30
34 Steve McMichael .15 .40
35 Johnnie Johnson .12 .30
36 Johnny Lam Jones .15 .40
37 Bill Acker .12 .30
38 Robin Sendlein .12 .30
39 Mike Baab .12 .30
40 A.J. Jam Jones .12 .30
41 Terry Tausch .12 .30
42 Doug Shankle .12 .30
43 Doug Dawson .12 .30
44 Jerry Gray .12 .30
45 Tony Degrate .12 .30
46 Kiki DeAyala .12 .30
47 Bret Stafford .12 .30
48 Eric Metcalf .15 .40
49 Britt Hager .12 .30
50 Brian Jones .12 .30
51 Keith Cash .12 .30
52 Kerry Cash .12 .30
53 Johnny Walker .12 .30
54 Peter Gardere .12 .30
55 Adrian Walker .12 .30
56 Blake Brockermeyer .12 .30
57 Tony Brackens .12 .30
58 Shea Morenz .12 .30
59 Priest Holmes .20 .50
60 Dan Neil .12 .30
61 Shon Mitchell .12 .30
62 Chris Carter .15 .40
63 Bryant Westbrook .12 .30
64 James Brown .15 .40
65 Ricky Williams .20 .50
66 Wane McGarity .12 .30
67 Kwame Cavil .12 .30
68 Roger Roesler .12 .30
69 Hodges Mitchell .12 .30
70 Major Applewhite .20 .50
71 Tillman Holloway .12 .30
72 B.J. Johnson .12 .30
73 Dusty Mangum .12 .30
74 Vince Young .20 .50
75 Rodrique Wright .12 .30
76 Jamaal Charles .20 .50
77 Colt McCoy .30 .75
78 Chykie Brown .12 .30
79 James Kirkendoll .12 .30
80 Aaron Williams .15 .40
81 Mack Brown CO .15 .40
82 1943 Cotton Bowl MM .12 .30
83 1964 Cotton Bowl MM .12 .30
84 Ernie Koy MM .12 .30
85 James Street MM .15 .40
86 James Street MM .15 .40
87 Cotton Speyrer MM .12 .30
88 Earl Campbell MM .20 .50
89 James Brown MM .15 .40
90 Ricky Williams MM .15 .40
91 Ricky Williams MM .15 .40
92 Major Applewhite MM .20 .50
93 Vince Young MM .15 .40
94 Vince Young MM .15 .40
95 Vince Young MM .15 .40
96 2005 Team visits White House .12 .30
97 Colt McCoy MM .25 .60
98 Longhorn Band MM .12 .30
99 Bevo MM .12 .30
100 Darrell Royal Stadium MM .12 .30

2011 Upper Deck Texas Gold

*GOLD/210: 5X TO 12X BASIC CARDS
GOLD PRINT RUN 210 SER.#'d SETS

2011 Upper Deck Texas All-Americans

AABA Bill Atessis .30 .75
AABW Bryant Westbrook .30 .75
AACM Colt McCoy .40 1.00
AACS Cotton Speyrer .30 .75
AAEC Earl Campbell .50 1.25
AAJG Jerry Gray .30 .75
AAJJ Johnnie Johnson .30 .75
AALJ Johnny Lam Jones .40 1.00
AAMA Marty Akins .30 .75
AARE Russell Erxleben .30 .75
AARL Roosevelt Leaks .30 .75
AASH Scott Henderson .30 .75
AASM Steve McMichael .40 1.00
AASW Steve Worster .30 .75
AAVY Vince Young .50 1.25
AAWI Ricky Williams .50 1.25

2011 Upper Deck Texas All-Americans Autographs

STATED PRINT RUN 10-35
AABW Bryant Westbrook/35
AACS Cotton Speyrer/35
AAJG Jerry Gray/35
AAJJ Johnnie Johnson/35
AALJ Johnny Lam Jones/35
AAMA Marty Akins/35
AARE Russell Erxleben/35
AARL Roosevelt Leaks/35
AASM Steve McMichael/35
AASW Steve Worster/35

2011 Upper Deck Texas All-Time Alumni

ATAAP Major Applewhite .50 1.25
ATABA Bill Atessis .30 .75
ATABE Jim Bertelsen .30 .75
ATABJ B.J. Johnson .30 .75
ATABR Bret Stafford .30 .75
ATABS Brad Shearer .30 .75
ATABW Bryant Westbrook .30 .75
ATACM Colt McCoy .40 1.00
ATACS Cotton Speyrer .30 .75
ATADE Doug English .30 .75
ATAEC Earl Campbell .50 1.25
ATAEK Ernie Koy .30 .75
ATAEM Eric Metcalf .40 1.00
ATAEP Eddie Phillips .30 .75
ATAHJ Johnny Ham Jones .30 .75
ATAJB James Brown .40 1.00
ATAJC Jamaal Charles .50 1.25
ATAJG Jerry Gray .30 .75
ATAJJ Johnnie Johnson .30 .75
ATAJS Jimmy Saxton .30 .75
ATAJT Johnny Treadwell .30 .75
ATAKC Kwame Cavil .30 .75
ATALJ Johnny Lam Jones .40 1.00
ATAMA Marty Akins .30 .75
ATAPG Peter Gardere .30 .75
ATAPH Priest Holmes .50 1.25
ATARE Russell Erxleben .30 .75
ATARL Roosevelt Leaks .30 .75
ATASM Steve McMichael .40 1.00
ATAST James Street .40 1.00
ATASW Steve Worster .30 .75
ATATD Tony Degrate .30 .75
ATATK Ted Koy .30 .75
ATAVY Vince Young .40 1.00
ATAWI Ricky Williams .50 1.25

2011 Upper Deck Texas All-Time Alumni Autographs

STATED PRINT RUN 10-30
ATAAP Major Applewhite/30
ATABA Bill Atessis/30
ATABE Jim Bertelsen/30
ATABJ B.J. Johnson/30
ATABR Bret Stafford/30
ATABS Brad Shearer/30
ATABW Bryant Westbrook/30
ATACS Cotton Speyrer/30
ATADE Doug English/30
ATAEM Eric Metcalf/30 25.00 50.00
ATAEP Eddie Phillips/30 25.00 50.00
ATAHJ Johnny Ham Jones/30
ATAJB James Brown/30 30.00 60.00
ATAJG Jerry Gray/30
ATAJJ Johnnie Johnson/30
ATAJT Johnny Treadwell/30
ATAKC Kwame Cavil/30
ATALJ Johnny Lam Jones/30
ATAMA Marty Akins/30
ATAPG Peter Gardere/30
ATARL Roosevelt Leaks/30
ATASM Steve McMichael/30 25.00 50.00
ATAST James Street/30
ATASW Steve Worster/30 30.00 60.00
ATATD Tony Degrate/30
ATATK Ted Koy/30

2011 Upper Deck Texas All-Time Alumni Duos

AB James Brown .60 1.50
Major Applewhite
AG Major Applewhite .60 1.50
Peter Gardere
CC Kerry Cash .40 1.00
Keith Cash
CJ Johnny Ham Jones .60 1.50
Earl Campbell
CL Earl Campbell .60 1.50
Roosevelt Leaks
CW Earl Campbell .60 1.50
Ricky Williams
KK Ted Koy .40 1.00
Ernie Koy
MA Major Applewhite .75 2.00
Colt McCoy
WB Steve Worster .40 1.00
Jim Bertelsen
WC Ricky Williams .60 1.50
Jamaal Charles
YC Jamaal Charles .60 1.50
Vince Young
YM Colt McCoy .75 2.00
Vince Young

2011 Upper Deck Texas All-Time Alumni Duos Autographs

STATED PRINT RUN 5-20
AG Major Applewhite/20
Peter Gardere
CC Kerry Cash/20
Keith Cash
CJ Johnny Ham Jones/20
Earl Campbell
KK Ted Koy/20
Ernie Koy
WB Steve Worster/20
Jim Bertelsen

2011 Upper Deck Texas All-Time Alumni Trios

BAG James Brown .75 2.00
Major Applewhite
Peter Gardere
CJL A.J. Jam Jones .75 2.00
Roosevelt Leaks
Earl Campbell
CWC Earl Campbell .75 2.00
Ricky Williams
Jamaal Charles
CWY Vince Young .75 2.00
Ricky Williams
Earl Campbell
YMA Vince Young 1.00 2.50
Colt McCoy
Major Applewhite
YSM James Street 1.00 2.50
Colt McCoy
Vince Young

2011 Upper Deck Texas Autographs

OVERALL AUTO ODDS 1:24
1 Bobby Dillon
2 Darrell Royal CO 40.00 80.00
4 Jack Collins
5 Mike Cotten 12.00 30.00
6 Don Talbert 12.00 30.00
7 Johnny Treadwell
8 Charlie Talbert
9 Ernie Koy
10 Diron Talbert 12.00 30.00
11 Bill Bradley 15.00 40.00
12 Ted Koy 12.00 30.00
13 James Street 40.00 80.00
14 Bob McKay
15 Bobby Wuensch 12.00 30.00
16 Tom Campbell 12.00 30.00
17 Bill Atessis
18 Scott Henderson 12.00 30.00
19 Steve Worster 20.00 50.00
20 Happy Feller
21 Cotton Speyrer
22 Jim Bertelsen
23 Eddie Phillips 12.00 30.00
24 Alan Lowry
25 Roosevelt Leaks
26 Doug English 12.00 30.00
27 Marty Akins
28 Bill Hamilton 12.00 30.00
29 Earl Campbell
30 Brad Shearer 12.00 30.00
31 Russell Erxleben 12.00 30.00
32 Johnny Ham Jones 12.00 30.00
33 Randy McEachern 15.00 40.00
34 Steve McMichael
35 Johnnie Johnson 12.00 30.00
36 Johnny Lam Jones
37 Bill Acker
38 Robin Sendlein 12.00 30.00
39 Mike Baab 12.00 30.00
40 A.J. Jam Jones 12.00 30.00
41 Terry Tausch 12.00 30.00
42 Doug Shankle 20.00 50.00
43 Doug Dawson 12.00 30.00
44 Jerry Gray
45 Tony Degrate 12.00 30.00
46 Kiki DeAyala
47 Bret Stafford 12.00 30.00
48 Eric Metcalf
49 Britt Hager 12.00 30.00
50 Brian Jones 12.00 30.00
51 Keith Cash 12.00 30.00
52 Kerry Cash 12.00 30.00
53 Johnny Walker 12.00 30.00
54 Peter Gardere 12.00 30.00
55 Adrian Walker 12.00 30.00
56 Blake Brockermeyer
57 Tony Brackens 12.00 30.00
58 Shea Morenz
59 Priest Holmes
60 Dan Neil 12.00 30.00
61 Shon Mitchell
62 Chris Carter
63 Bryant Westbrook
64 James Brown
65 Ricky Williams
66 Wane McGarity 12.00 30.00
67 Kwame Cavil 12.00 30.00
68 Roger Roesler
69 Hodges Mitchell
70 Major Applewhite 40.00 80.00
71 Tillman Holloway 12.00 30.00
72 B.J. Johnson 12.00 30.00
73 Dusty Mangum
74 Vince Young
75 Rodrique Wright
76 Jamaal Charles 20.00 50.00
77 Colt McCoy 50.00 100.00
78 Chykie Brown 12.00 30.00
79 James Kirkendoll 12.00 30.00
80 Aaron Williams 15.00 40.00
81 Mack Brown CO

2011 Upper Deck Texas Icons

IAJ A.J. Jam Jones 2.00 5.00
IBA Bill Atessis 2.00 5.00
IBH Britt Hager 2.00 5.00
IBJ B.J. Johnson 2.00 5.00
IBW Bobby Wuensch 2.00 5.00
ICA Kwame Cavil 2.00 5.00
ICM Colt McCoy 2.50 6.00
ICS Cotton Speyrer 2.00 5.00
IDR Darrell Royal CO 3.00 8.00
IEC Earl Campbell 3.00 8.00
IEM Eric Metcalf 2.50 6.00
IJB James Brown 2.50 6.00
IJC Jamaal Charles 3.00 8.00
IJG Jerry Gray 2.00 5.00
IJJ Johnnie Johnson 2.00 5.00
IJS James Street 2.50 6.00
IKC Kerry Cash 2.00 5.00
IKD Kiki DeAyala 2.00 5.00
ILJ Johnny Lam Jones 2.50 6.00
IMA Major Applewhite 3.00 8.00
IMB Mike Baab 2.00 5.00
IRE Russell Erxleben 2.00 5.00
IRL Roosevelt Leaks 2.00 5.00
IRW Ricky Williams 3.00 8.00
ISA Jimmy Saxton 2.00 5.00
ISM Steve McMichael 2.50 6.00
ISW Steve Worster 2.00 5.00
ITD Tony Degrate 2.00 5.00
IVY Vince Young 3.00 8.00
IWM Wane McGarity 2.00 5.00

2011 Upper Deck Texas National Champions

NCAL Alan Lowry .30 .75
NCBA Bill Atessis .30 .75
NCBE Jim Bertelsen .30 .75
NCBM Bob McKay .30 .75
NCBW Bobby Wuensch .30 .75
NCCS Cotton Speyrer .30 .75
NCDA Darrell Royal CO .50 1.25
NCDR Darrell Royal CO .50 1.25
NCEP Eddie Phillips .30 .75
NCHF Happy Feller .30 .75
NCJB Jim Bertelsen .30 .75
NCJC Jamaal Charles .50 1.25
NCJS James Street .40 1.00
NCMB Mack Brown CO .40 1.00
NCRO Darrell Royal CO .50 1.25
NCSH Scott Henderson .30 .75
NCSW Steve Worster .30 .75
NCTC Tom Campbell .30 .75
NCTK Ted Koy .30 .75
NCVY Vince Young .50 1.25
NCWO Steve Worster .30 .75

2011 Upper Deck Texas National Champions Autographs

NCAL Alan Lowry/30
NCBA Bill Atessis/30
NCBE Jim Bertelsen/30
NCBM Bob McKay/30
NCCS Cotton Speyrer/30
NCDA Darrell Royal/30
NCDR Darrell Royal/30
NCEP Eddie Phillips/30
NCHF Happy Feller/30
NCJB Jim Bertelsen/30
NCJS James Street/30
NCRO Darrell Royal CO/30
NCSH Scott Henderson/30
NCSW Steve Worster/30
NCTC Tom Campbell/30 20.00 40.00
NCTK Ted Koy/30 20.00 40.00
NCWO Steve Worster/30

2011 Upper Deck Texas National Champions Duos

BY Mack Brown CO .60 1.50
Vince Young
RS Darrell Royal CO .50 1.25
James Street
SS James Street .50 1.25
Cotton Speyrer
SW Cotton Speyrer .40 1.00
Steve Worster
WB Jim Bertelsen .40 1.00
Steve Worster
YC Vince Young .60 1.50
Jamaal Charles

2011 Upper Deck Texas National Champions Duos Autographs

SS James Street/15
Cotton Speyrer
SW Cotton Speyrer/15
Steve Worster
WB Steve Worster/15
Jim Bertelsen

2011 Upper Deck Texas National Champions Trios

PWB Jim Bertelsen .50 1.25
Steve Worster
Eddie Phillips
RSS Cotton Speyrer .60 1.50
James Street
Darrell Royal CO
SWS James Street .60 1.50
Cotton Speyrer
Steve Worster
YCB Mack Brown CO .75 2.00
Jamaal Charles
Vince Young

2012 Upper Deck USA Football

COMP.FACTORY SET (48) 35.00 50.00
COMPLETE SET (45) 8.00 20.00
1 Jabriel Washington .30 .75
2 Ty Montgomery .30 .75
3 George Atkinson .40 1.00
4 Aaron Green .40 1.00
5 Anthony Sarao .25 .60
6 Stephon Tuitt .30 .75
7 Hakeem Flowers .25 .60
8 Tacoi Sumler .25 .60
9 Kevin Hogan .40 1.00
10 Conner Floyd .25 .60
11 Ryan Simmons .25 .60
12 Kiehl Frazier .30 .75
13 Manoa Pikula .25 .60
14 Josh Turner .25 .60
15 Tyler Wright .25 .60
16 Ronald Tanner .30 .75
17 Wayne Lyons .25 .60
18 Kellen Jones .30 .75
19 Savon Huggins .25 .60
20 Joe Bergeron .30 .75
21 Kenny Williams .25 .60
22 Devon Cajuste .30 .75
23 Kevin McReynolds .25 .60
24 Jesse Hayes .25 .60
25 Josh Atkinson .30 .75
26 Graham Stewart .25 .60
27 Nick Lifka .25 .60
28 Anthony Rabasa .30 .75
29 Bobby Thompson .25 .60
30 Matt Freeman .25 .60
31 Michael Bennett .25 .60
32 Jarrett Hudson .25 .60
33 Chris Merlene .25 .60
34 Kiaro Holts .25 .60
35 Matt Wofford .25 .60
36 Matt Hegarty .25 .60
37 Hunter Goodwin .25 .60
38 Jamelle Naff .25 .60
39 Jaxon Shipley .30 .75
40 Jack Konopka .25 .60
41 Will Monday .25 .60
42 Taniela Tupou .25 .60
43 Kris Harley .25 .60
44 Avery Walls .25 .60
45 Cody Keith .25 .60

2012 Upper Deck USA Football Autographs

ONE AUTO PER FACTORY SET
1 Jabriel Washington 4.00 10.00
2 Ty Montgomery 4.00 10.00
3 George Atkinson 5.00 12.00
4 Aaron Green 5.00 12.00
5 Anthony Sarao 3.00 8.00
6 Stephon Tuitt 4.00 10.00
7 Hakeem Flowers 3.00 8.00
8 Tacoi Sumler 3.00 8.00
9 Kevin Hogan 5.00 12.00
10 Conner Floyd 3.00 8.00
11 Ryan Simmons 3.00 8.00
12 Kiehl Frazier 4.00 10.00
13 Manoa Pikula 3.00 8.00
14 Josh Turner 3.00 8.00
15 Tyler Wright 3.00 8.00
16 Ronald Tanner 4.00 10.00
17 Wayne Lyons 3.00 8.00
19 Savon Huggins 3.00 8.00
20 Joe Bergeron 4.00 10.00
21 Kenny Williams 3.00 8.00
22 Devon Cajuste 4.00 10.00
23 Kevin McReynolds 3.00 8.00
24 Jesse Hayes 3.00 8.00
25 Josh Atkinson 4.00 10.00
26 Graham Stewart 3.00 8.00
27 Nick Lifka 3.00 8.00
28 Anthony Rabasa 4.00 10.00
29 Bobby Thompson 3.00 8.00
30 Matt Freeman 3.00 8.00
31 Michael Bennett 3.00 8.00
32 Jarrett Hudson 3.00 8.00
33 Chris Merlene 3.00 8.00
34 Kiaro Holts 3.00 8.00
35 Matt Wofford 3.00 8.00
36 Matt Hegarty 3.00 8.00
37 Hunter Goodwin 3.00 8.00
38 Jamelle Naff 3.00 8.00
39 Jaxon Shipley 4.00 10.00
40 Jack Konopka 3.00 8.00
41 Will Monday 3.00 8.00
42 Taniela Tupou 3.00 8.00
43 Kris Harley 3.00 8.00
44 Avery Walls 3.00 8.00
45 Cody Keith 3.00 8.00

2012 Upper Deck USA Football Future Swatch

TWO MEM CARDS PER FACTORY SET
*PATCH: .6X TO 1.5X BASIC JSY

1991 Utah State Schedules

These Utah State schedules were distributed during the 1991 season. They are listed below in alphabetical order. If there are any additions to the players checklisted below, that information would be appreciated.

COMPLETE SET (7) 4.00 10.00
1 Warren Bowers .60 1.50
2 Floyd Foreman .60 1.50
3 Ron Lopez .60 1.50
4 Del Lyles .60 1.50
5 Charlie Smith .60 1.50
6 Toby Tyler .60 1.50
7 Rob Van De Pol .60 1.50

2000 Vanderbilt Schedules

These "cards" are actually pocket schedules issued by the school. The cardfronts feature a Vanderbilt player in a color photo with the year noted at the bottom and the school noted at the top of the card. No player name is identified on the cards so we've included the player's jersey number to aid in identification. The cardbacks include the team's 2000 football schedule.

COMPLETE SET (4) .75 2.00
1 Ryan Aulds .30 .75
(jersey #98)
2 Elliott Carson .20 .50
3 Michael Faltsman .20 .50
4 Brian Gruber .20 .50
(jersey #64)
5 John Markham .20 .50
(jersey #19)
6 Jared McGrath .20 .50
7 Russ Nicoll .20 .50
8 Jimmy Williams .40 1.00
9 Jamie Winborn .40 1.00
(jersey #42)

2004 Vanderbilt Schedules

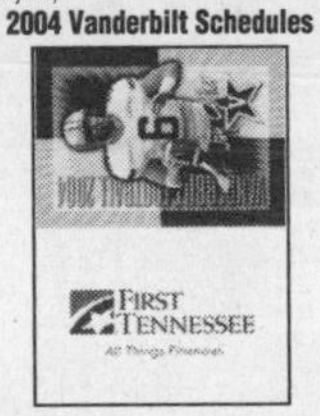

COMPLETE SET (4) 1.25 3.00
1 Jay Cutler .75 2.00
2 Justin Geisinger .20 .50
3 Jovan Haye .20 .50
4 Chris Young .20 .50

1990 Versailles High School

This 20-card set features the Versailles Tigers, the 1990 State Champions of Division 4 Ohio Football. The set was issued as a perforated sheet consisting of five rows of four cards each; after perforation, each individual card measures the standard size. On a white card face, the fronts feature black and white action game shots. The player's name team name above the photo and the player's name below it are printed in orange lettering; other information on the fronts is in black lettering. The backs are dominated by a black and white head shot with biography and a list of sponsors immediately below the pictures. The cards are unnumbered and checklisted below alphabetically.

COMPLETE SET (20) 3.20 8.00
1 Kevin Bergman .20 .50
2 A.J. Bey .20 .50
3 Brad Bey .20 .50
4 Ed Dingman .30 .75
5 Brian Griesdorn .20 .50
6 Al Hetrick CO .30 .75
7 Garth Hoellrich .20 .50
8 Trent Huff .20 .50
9 Brian Keiser .20 .50
10 Lane Knore .20 .50
11 Brian Kunk .20 .50
12 Keenan Leichty .20 .50
13 Marc Litten .20 .50
14 Craig Oliver .20 .50
15 Jon Pothast .20 .50
16 Joe Rush .20 .50
17 Shane Schultz .20 .50
18 Mark Siekman .20 .50
19 Matt Stall .20 .50
20 Nathan Subler .20 .50

1998 Versailles High School

COMPLETE SET (63) 10.00 25.00
1 Tim Agne .20 .50
2 Jason Ahrens .20 .50
3 Jeremy Baker .20 .50
4 Josh Baker .20 .50
5 Kyle Barga .20 .50
6 T.J. Barga .20 .50
7 Chris Barnhardt .20 .50
8 Nick Beasley .20 .50
9 Ryan Beisner .20 .50
10 Matt Bensman .20 .50
11 Ryan Bergman .20 .50
12 Brian Berfke .20 .50
13 Scott Borchers .20 .50
14 Sean Borchers .20 .50
15 Jacob Broerman .20 .50
16 Josh Bruns .20 .50
17 Matthew Curtis .20 .50
18 Matt Folkerth .20 .50
19 David Francis .20 .50
20 Eric Francis .20 .50
21 Greg Garland .20 .50
22 Kevin Grieshop .20 .50
23 Mitch Heitkamp .20 .50
24 Matt Heitkamp .20 .50
25 Josh Henderson .20 .50
26 Charlie Henry .20 .50
27 B.J. Hill .20 .50
28 Jason Hoelscher .20 .50
29 Dusty Johns .20 .50
30 Kurt Keiser .20 .50
31 Joe Klosterman .20 .50
32 Steve Langston .20 .50
33 Lee Link .20 .50
34 Matt Magoteaux .20 .50
35 John Magoto .20 .50
36 Ben Mescher .20 .50
37 Jeremy Mescher .20 .50
38 John Monnin .20 .50
39 Michael Paulus .20 .50
40 T.J. Phlipot .20 .50
41 Ben Poeppelman .20 .50
42 Lee Poeppelman .20 .50
43 Kevin Pohlman .20 .50
44 Joe Raterman .20 .50
45 Kyle Rhoades .20 .50
46 Nick Rhoades .20 .50
47 Zach Roll .20 .50
48 Hayden Roush .20 .50
49 Ryan Ruchty .20 .50
50 Mitch Schlaler .20 .50
51 Jason Schutz .20 .50
52 Dustin Shadoan .20 .50
53 Brian Shappie .20 .50
54 Jason Shardo .20 .50
55 Craig Stammen .40 1.00
56 Kevin Stauffer .20 .50
57 Bill Streib .20 .50
58 Tyler Treon .20 .50
59 Shane Unger .20 .50
60 Jason Voisard .20 .50
61 Ken Wagner .20 .50
62 Joe Wagner .20 .50
63 Ken York .20 .50

1971 Virginia Team Sheets

The University of Virginia issued these sheets of black-and-white player photos. Each measures roughly 8" by 10 1/4" and was printed on glossy stock with white borders. Each sheet includes photos of 10-players and/or coaches. Below each player's image is his name and position. The photos are blankbacked.

COMPLETE SET (7) 25.00 50.00
STATED ODDS
1 Athletic Staff 4.00 8.00
Bill Gibson-Basketball
Chip Conner-Basketball
Joe Gieck-Trainer
Glenn Thiel-Lacrosse
George Edwards-Wrestling
Jim West-Baseball
Lou Onesty-Track
Jim Stephens-Soccer
Gordon Burris-Tennis
Ron Good-Swimming
2 Defensive Soph Performers 4.00 8.00
Craig Critchley
Harry Gehr
Dan Blakley
Rick Duffalo
Gerard Mullins
Bill Kuykendall
Stanley Land
Ronnie Burgess
Joe Ryan
Leroy Still
3 Defensive Sophomores 4.00 8.00
Kent Merritt
John Rainey
Steve Sroba
Paul Ryczek
Steve Shawley
Greg Godfrey
Harrison Davis
Dale Dickerson
Ed Sabornie
Billy Maxwell

4 Defensive Veterans	4.00	8.00
Robbie Gustafson		
Bill Kettunen		
Chris Brown		
Billy Williams		
Dennis Scott		
Bob Bressan		
Bob McGrail		
Kevin Michales		
Chuck Belic		
Andy Selfridge		
5 U. of Virginia Cavaliers	4.00	8.00
Billy League		
John Beattie		
Ken Golder		
Phil Cerpanya		
Rick McFarland		
Gary Ham		
Ron Similo		
Mike Silvester		
Fred Kaspick		
Terry McGovern		
6 Veteran Off.Backs-Ends	4.00	8.00
U. of Virginia Cavaliers		
Gary Helman		
Greg Dickerhoff		
Jim Lacey		
Dave Bratt		
Bill Troup		
Larry Albert		
Dave Sullivan		
Brian Kitchen		
Bill Davis		
Joe Smith		
7 Veteran Offensive Linemen	4.00	8.00
Bill Farrell		
Tom Kennedy		
Jamie Davis		
Tom Goss		
Bob Burkley		
Abby Sailenger		
Bob Kasonik		
Tommy Viar		
Stormy Costas		
Hal Trentham		

1972 Virginia Team Sheets

The University of Virginia issued these sheets of black-and-white player photos. Each measures roughly 8" by 10 1/8" and was printed on glossy stock with white borders. Each sheet includes photos of 2-players. Below each player's image is his name, position, and school. The photos are blankbacked.

COMPLETE SET (8)	30.00	60.00
1 Bill Davis	4.00	8.00
Joe Smith		
2 Harrison Davis	4.00	8.00
Dave Sullivan		
3 Tom Kennedy	4.00	8.00
Bill Maxwell		
4 Jimmy Lacey	4.00	8.00
Gary Helman		
5 Steve Shawley	4.00	8.00
Greg Godfrey		
6 Leroy Still	4.00	8.00
Gerald Mullins		
7 Dennis Scott	4.00	8.00
Billy Williams		
8 Kent Merritt	4.00	8.00
Stanley Land		

1988 Virginia Team Sheets

These photos were issued by the school to promote the football program. Each measures roughly 8" by 10" and features eight (except for one sheet) black and white images of players with the school name and year appearing at the top. The player's name, position, and school are printed below each image. The backs are blank.

COMPLETE SET (11)	25.00	50.00
1 Jeff Allen	4.00	10.00
Matt Blake		
Matt Blundin		
Chris Borsari		
Derrick Boyd		
Roy Brown		
Donald Bryant		
Ron Carey		
2 Joe Carnuche	3.00	6.00
Charles Carridine		
Fred Carter		
Chip Cathey		
James Chaplin		
Chris Churovia		
Brad Collins		
Paul Collins		
3 Kevin Cook	3.00	6.00
Tony Covington		
David Delk		
Joel Dempsey		
Derek Dooley		
Doug Duenkel		
Steve Ewers		
Dennis Fields		
4 Tim Finkelston	3.00	6.00
Randy Foley		
John Ford		
Keith Fuller		
Ed Garno		
Doug Glagola		
Paul Gollinge		
Benson Goodwyn		
5 John Gowen	3.00	6.00
Durwin Greggs		
Scott Griese		
David Griggs		
Joe Hall		
Preston Hicks		
Doonie Hunt		
Mark Inderlied		
6 Phil Intinar	3.00	6.00
Scott Kemp		
Billy Keys		
Walter Kulp		
Jeff Lageman		
Rip Leonard		
Tyrone Lewis		
Bruce McGonnigal		
7 Jake McInerney	3.00	6.00
Keith McMeans		
Herman Moore		
Shawn Moore		
Kevin Morgan		
Tim Morris		
Tony Morton		
Rodger Moss		
8 Tim O'Connor	3.00	6.00
Ken Plumb		
Lenny Pritchard		
Matt Quigley		
Jim Redmond		
Donald Reynolds		
Ray Roberts		
John Runyon		
9 Trevor Ryals	3.00	6.00
Jim Sanford		
Brian Satola		
Ray Savage		
Mike Smith		
Bryan Snyder		
Chris Stearns		
Lance Terry		
10 Phil Thomas	3.00	6.00
Jerome Thompson		
Elton Toliver		
Rob Toney		
Jason Wallace		
Mike Williams		
Johnnie Wilson		
Marcus Wilson		
11 Matt Woods	3.00	6.00
Large Team Logo		

1989 Virginia Team Sheets

These photos were issued by the school to promote the football program. Each measures roughly 8" by 10" and features eight (except for one sheet with just five players) black and white images of players with the school name and year appearing at the top. The player's name, position, and school are printed below each image. The backs are blank.

COMPLETE SET (11)	25.00	50.00
1 Matt Blundin	4.00	8.00
Chros Borsari		
Derrick Boyd		
David Brown		
Roy Brown		
Don Bryant		
Geoff Carey		
Ron Carey		
2 Charles Carridine	3.00	6.00
Chip Cathey		
James Chaplin		
Brad Collins		
Paul Collins		
Kevin Cook		
Tony Covington		
Errin Crowell		
3 David Delk	3.00	6.00
Derek Dooley		
Doug Duenkel		
Lloyd Falshaw		
Tim Finkelston		
Nikki Fisher		
Randy Foley		
Chris Galloway		
4 Ed Garno	3.00	6.00
Bobby Goodman		
Benson Goodwyn		
John Gowen		
Blake Grant		
Durwin Greggs		
Scott Griese		
Erick Hackenberg		
5 Joe Hall	3.00	6.00
Clifton Harris		
Michael Husted		
Yusef Jackson		
Charles Keiningham		
Billy Keys		
Matt Klinger		
Walter Kulp		
6 Rip Leonard	3.00	6.00
Tyrone Lewis		
Eril Mace		
Bruce McConnigal		
Jake McInerney		
Keith McMeans		
Ken Miles		
Herman Moore		
7 Shawn Moore	3.00	6.00
Tim Morris		
Tim Moss		
Ed Myers		
Tim o'Connor		
Buddy Omohundro		
James Pearson		
Rickie Peete		
8 Colin Preis	3.00	6.00
Larry Pritchard		
Matt Quigley		
Jim Redmond		
Don Reynolds		
Ray Roberts		
John Runyon		
Trevor Ryals		
9 Tim Samec	3.00	6.00
Brian Satola		
Ray Savage		
Carlos Shippy		
Mike Smith		
Alvin Snead		
Chris Stearns		
Gary Steele		
10 Dave Sweeney	3.00	6.00
Phil Thomas		
Elton Toliver		
Jeff Tomlin		
Terry Tomlin		
Rob Toney		
Jason Wallace		
Dave Ware		
11 Mike Williams	3.00	6.00
Johnnie Wilson		
Marcus Wilson		
Matt Woods		
Marc Yavinsky		

1990 Virginia Team Sheets

These photos were issued by the school to promote the football program. Each measures roughly 8" by 10" and features eight black and white images of players with the school name and year appearing at the top. The player's name, position, and school are printed below each image. The backs are blank.

COMPLETE SET (8)	20.00	40.00
1 Daymon Anderson	4.00	8.00
Randolph Austin		
Matt Blundin		
Chris Borsari		
David Brown		
Geoff Carey		
Ron Carey		
Charles Carridine		
2 Chip Cathey	3.00	6.00
James Chaplin		
Brad Collins		
Paul Collins		
Peter Collins		
Matt Cooke		
Tony Covington		
Bill Curry		
3 David Delk	3.00	6.00
Mark Dixon		
Derek Dooley		
Bill Edwards		
Lloyd Falshaw		
Nikki Fisher		
Chuck Fiveash		
Randy Foley		
4 Chris Galloway	3.00	6.00
Ed Garno		
Andreas Gaynor		
Bobby Goodman		
Benson Goodwyn		
Blake Grant		
Scott Griese		
Erick Hackenberg		
5 Terry Kirby	3.00	6.00
Matt Klinger		
Walter Kulp		
Tyrone Lewis		
Jim Lundy		
Myron Martin		
Greg McClellan		
Bruce McGonnigal		
6 Jake McInerney	3.00	6.00
Keith McMeans		
Matthew Mikeska		
Kenneth Miles		
Herman Moore		
Shawn Moore		
Tim Moss		
Buddy Omohundro		
7 Eugene Rodgers	3.00	6.00
Trevor Ryals		
Tim Samec		
Brian Satola		
Josh Schrader		
Carlos Shippy		
Chris Slade		
Alvin Snead		
8 Brian Snyder	3.00	6.00
Chris Stearns		
Gary Steele		
Dave Sweeney		
Sean Thompson		
Gene Toliver		
Jeff Tomlin		
Terrence Tomlin		

1990 Virginia

This 16-card standard size set was issued to celebrate the 1990 Virginia Cavalier team, which contended for the National Title. This set features a good mix of action photography and portrait shots on the front with biographical information on the back. The set was issued as a perforated sheet with four rows of four cards each. This set was sponsored by the Charter Hospital of Charlottesville and was given out to those fans in attendance at the Sept. 29, 1990 game against William and Mary. The cards are unnumbered and listed below in alphabetical order. The key card in this set is wide receiver Herman Moore.

COMPLETE SET (16)	10.00	25.00
1 Chris Borsari	.50	1.25
2 Ron Carey	.50	1.25
3 Paul Collins	.50	1.25
4 Tony Covington	.80	2.00
5 Derek Dooley	.50	1.25
6 Joe Hall	.50	1.25
7 Myron Martin	.50	1.25
8 Bruce McGonnigal	.50	1.25
9 Jake McInerney	.50	1.25
10 Keith McMeans	.50	1.25
11 Herman Moore	2.50	6.00
12 Shawn Moore	1.00	2.50
13 Trevor Ryals	.50	1.25
14 Chris Stearns	.50	1.25
15 Jason Wallace	.50	1.25
16 George Welsh CO	.80	2.00

1991 Virginia

This set was issued to celebrate the 1991 Virginia Cavalier football team. The cards were issued as a perforated sheet and was sponsored by Coca-Cola. The cards are unnumbered and listed below in alphabetical order.

COMPLETE SET (16)	7.50	15.00
1 Matt Blundin	.75	2.00
2 Nikki Fisher	.40	1.00
3 Ed Garno	.40	1.00
4 Terry Kirby	.75	2.00
5 Tyrone Lewis	.50	1.25
6 Matt Quigley	.40	1.00
7 Don Reynolds	.40	1.00
8 Ray Roberts	.40	1.00
9 Eugene Rodgers	.40	1.00
10 Brian Satola	.40	1.00
11 Chris Slade	.50	1.25
12 George Welsh CO	.40	1.00
13 All-American Bowl	.40	1.00
14 Citrus Bowl	.40	1.00
15 Peach Bowl	.40	1.00
16 Sugar Bowl	.40	1.00

1992 Virginia Coca-Cola

Sponsored by Coca-Cola, the 16 cards comprising this set were issued in one 16-card insert sheet. The perforated sheet measures approximately 10" by 14" and consists of four rows of four cards each. Each card measures the standard size and carries on its front a blue-bordered color player action shot. The player's name and position appear in white lettering within a dark blue bar set off by white lines at the bottom of the player photo. "Virginia" appears in orange lettering within the blue border above the photo. The Cavaliers logo is shown in one corner of the photo, and the word "Cavs" appears in orange lettering within a white rectangle at the lower left corner of the player photo. The Coca-Cola logo rests within the blue border at the bottom. The white back carries the player's name, position, biography, and highlights. The Coca-Cola logo at the bottom rounds out the card. The cards are unnumbered and checklisted below in alphabetical order. The key card in this set is running back Terry Kirby.

COMPLETE SET (16)	6.00	15.00
1 Bobby Goodman	.40	1.00
2 Michael Husted	.80	2.00
3 Greg Jeffries	.40	1.00
4 Charles Keiningham	.40	1.00
5 Terry Kirby	2.00	5.00
6 Kenneth Miles	.40	1.00
7 Tim Samec	.40	1.00
8 Chris Slade	1.20	3.00
9 Alvin Snead	.40	1.00
10 Gary Steele	.40	1.00
11 Jeff Tomlin	.40	1.00
12 Terrence Tomlin	.40	1.00
13 David Ware	.40	1.00
14 George Welsh CO	.50	1.25
15 Virginia 20 vs. Clemson 7 (Sept. 8, 1990)	.40	1.00
16 Virginia 20 vs. N.Carolina 17 (Nov. 14, 1987)	.40	1.00

1993 Virginia Coca-Cola

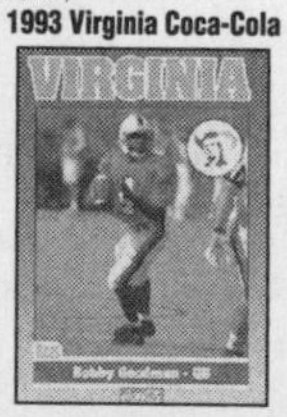

Sponsored by Coca-Cola, the 16 cards comprising this set were issued in one 16-card game program insert sheet. The perforated sheet measures approximately 10" by 14" and consists of four rows of four cards each. Each card measures the standard size and carries on its front an elliptical color player action shot bordered in blue with black vertical stirpes. The player's name and position appear in white lettering within a dark blue stripe at the bottom. The team name appears in orange and white lettering above the photo. The Coca-Cola logo appears at the lower right. The white back carries the player's name, position, biography, and highlights. The Coca-Cola logo at the bottom rounds out the card. The cards are unnumbered and checklisted below in alphabetical order.

COMPLETE SET (16)	6.00	15.00
1 Tom Burns	.40	1.00
2 Peter Collins	.40	1.00
3 Bill Curry	.40	1.00
4 Mark Dixon	.40	1.00
5 Bill Edwards	.40	1.00
6 P.J. Killian	.40	1.00
7 Keith Lyle	.50	1.25
8 Greg McClellan	.40	1.00
9 Matt Mikeska	.40	1.00
10 Aaron Mundy	.40	1.00
11 Jim Reid	.40	1.00
12 Josh Schrader	.40	1.00
13 Jerrod Washington	.40	1.00
14 George Welsh CO	.50	1.25
15 Cavalier Spirit (Cheerleaders)	.40	1.00
16 Cavalier Mascot	.40	1.00

1994 Virginia Team Sheets

These photos were issued by the school to promote the football program. Each measures roughly 8" by 10" and features eight black and white images of players with the school name and year appearing at the top. The player's name, position, and school are printed below each image. The backs are blank.

COMPLETE SET (7)	20.00	40.00
1 Joe Aben	3.00	6.00
Scott Allanson		
Demetrius Allen		
Duane Ashman		
Jason Augustino		
Jesse Ayres		
Ronde Barber		
Tiki Barber		
2 Joe Crocker	3.00	6.00
Andrew Dausch		
Marcus Davis		
Tyrone Davis		
Walt Derey		
Percy Ellsworth		
James farrior		
Mike Frederick		
3 Patrick Jeffers	3.00	6.00
Skeet Jones		
Ray Kane		
Doug Karczewski		
Mike Kelly		
Brendan Kilfeather		
Charles Kirby		
Kyle Kirkeide		
4 Ray McKenzie	3.00	6.00
Sam McKiver		
Kendall Meade		
Darrell Medley		
Randy Neal		
Bobby Neely		
Bryan Owen		
Stephen Phelan		
5 Jeremy Raley	3.00	6.00
C.E. Rhodes		
John Allen Roberts		
Eddie Robertson		
Jason Robinson		
Frank Rotella		
Jow Rowe		
Jamie Sharper		
6 Tim Sherman	3.00	6.00
Barry Simmons		
John Slocum		
Carl Smith		
Bobby Spencer		
Jay Strath		
Greg Terry		
Mike Wardlaw		
7 Charles Way	3.00	6.00
Damon White		
Todd White		
Joe Williams		
Julius Williams		
Symmion Willis		
Erich Wiltsee		
Team Logo		

1995 Virginia Team Sheets

These photos were issued by the school to promote the football program. Each measures roughly 8" by 10" and features eight black and white images of players with the school name and year appearing at the top. The player's name, position, and school are printed below each image. The backs are blank.

COMPLETE SET (10)	25.00	50.00
1 Joe Aben	3.00	6.00
Tony Agee		
Scott Allanson		
Demetrius Allen		
Duane Ashman		
Jason Augustino		
Ronde Barber		
Tiki Barber		
2 Jimm Bonk	3.00	6.00
Charles Bostek		
Matt Bressan		
Will Brice		
Trevor Britton		
Aaron Brooks		
Kevin Brooks		
Brandon Brucker		
3 Ken Buczynski	3.00	6.00
Adrian Burnim		
Derick Byrd		
Fady Chamoun		
Joe Crocker		
Germane Crowell		
Walt Derey		
Percy Ellsworth		
4 James Farrior	3.00	6.00
Rafael Garcia		
Darren Garland		
Dave Gathman		
Styart Greene		
Mike Groh		
Jon Harris		
Chris Harrison		
5 Antawan Holmes	3.00	6.00
Robert Hunt		
Patrick Jeffers		
Skeet Jones		
Doug Karczewski		
Mike Kelly		
Charles Kirby		
Kyle Kirkeide		
6 Wayne Lineburg	3.00	6.00
Matt Link		
Tom Locklin		
Paul London		
Whitney Magers		
Faraji Mason		
Brian McCarthy		
Ray McKenzie		
7 Sam McKiver	3.00	6.00
Darrell Medley		
Bobby Neely		
Joshua Nowocin		
Bryan Owen		
Stephen Phelan		
Maurice Philogene		
Anthony Poindexter		
8 Greg Powell	3.00	6.00
Charles Preston		
Jeremy Raley		
C.E. Rhodes		
John Allen Roberts		
Eddie Robertson		
Jason Robinson		
Frank Rotella		
9 Joe Rowe	3.00	6.00
Jamie Sharper		
Tim Sherman		
Barry Simmons		
John Slocum		
Jay Strath		
Greg Terry		
Eric Tracy		
10 Chris White	3.00	6.00
Todd White		
Terrence Wilkins		
Kirk Willett		
Joe Williams		
Julius Williams		
Symmion Willis		
Erich Wiltsee		

1996 Virginia Team Issue

COMPLETE SET (12)	30.00	60.00
1 Maurice Anderson	4.00	10.00
Duane Ashman		
Ronde Barber		
Tiki Barber		
Jason Barker		
Jeremy Bird		
James Bonk		
Charles Bostek		
2 Will Brice	2.50	6.00
Trevor Britton		
Aaron Brooks		
Marcus Bullett		
Derick Byrd		
Pady Chamoun		
Casey Crawford		
Germane Crowell		
3 Walt Derey	2.00	5.00
Tony Dingle		
Brad Dittman		
Wally Elegbe		
James Farrior		
Rafael Garcia		
Darren Garland		
Travis Griffith		
4 Jon Harris	2.00	5.00
Kevin Hillerich		
Antawan Holmes		
Evan Hunt		
Robert Hunt		
Ewill Jackson		
Tim Johnson		
Shawn Jones		
5 Doug Karczewski	2.00	5.00
Andreas Karelis		
Mike Kelly		
Patrick Kerney		
Charles Kirby		
Noel LaMontagne		
Mark Lindsey		
Matt Link		
6 Tom Locklin	2.00	5.00
Whitney Magers		
Brian McCarthy		
Matthew McClelland		
Ray McKenzie		
Sam McKiver		
Andre McNeal		
Darrell Medley		
7 Colin Mulligan	2.00	5.00
Joshua Nowocin		
Bryan Owen		
Stephan Phelan		
Anthony Poindexter		
Jami'h Rainer		
Wali Rainer		
Jeremy Raley		
8 John Allen Roberts	2.00	5.00
Frank Rotella		
Joe Rowe		
George Seals		
Jamie Sharper		
Tim Sherman		
Johnny Shivers		
Anthony Southern		
9 John St. Clair	2.00	5.00
Jay Strath		
Dwayne Stukes		
Dillon Taylor		
Shannon Taylor		
Will Thompson		
Chris White		
Todd White		
10 Terrence Wilkins	2.50	6.00
Kirk Willett		
Joe Williams		
Julius Williams		
Shannon Wilson		
11 Will Brice (two photos)	2.00	5.00
12 George Welsh CO (two photos)	2.00	5.00

1998 Virginia Team Sheets

COMPLETE SET (16)	30.00	60.00
1 Mike Abrams	2.50	6.00
Maurice Anderson		
Billy Baber		
Brad Barnes		
Kofi Bawuah		
Todd Braverman		
Aaron Brooks		
Paul Burke		
2 Adrian Burnim	2.00	5.00
Fady Chamoun		
Scooter Clark		
Kevin Coffey		
Casey Crawford		
Kenny Crawford		
Matt D'Acunto		
Ian Dawson		
3 Antonio Dingle	2.00	5.00
Brad Dittman		
John Duckett		
Wale Elegbe		
Dan Ellis		
Duane Fisher		
Alec Fleming		
Tyree Foreman		
4 Michael Graviss	2.00	5.00
Donny Green		
David Greene		
Travis Griffith		
Antwan Harris		
Ahmad Hawkins		
Kevin Hillerich		
Robert Hunt		
5 Yubrenal Isabelle	2.00	5.00
Will Jackson		
O.J. Johnson		
Tim Johnson		
Jermese Jones		
Thomas Jones		
Andreas Karelis		
Dustin Keith		
6 Patrick Kerney	2.50	6.00
Noel LaMontagne		
Parker Lange		
Josh Lawson		
Chris Luzar		
Ryan Mickles		
Colin Mulligan		
Greg Owens		
7 Bill Pattisall	2.00	5.00
Anthony Poindexter		
Johnny Ponder		
Monsanto Pope		
Jami'h Rainer		
Wali Rainer		
Ben Richardson		
8 David Rivers	2.00	5.00
Tremayne Robertson		
Michael Robinson		
Evan Routzahn		
Darryl Sanders		
Donald Scott		
George Seals		
9 Johnny Shivers	2.00	5.00
Devon Simmons		
Earl Sims		
Jason Small		
Anthony Southern		
Tim Spruill		
John St. Clair		
10 Ljubomir Stamenich	2.00	5.00
Dwayne Stukes		
Dillon Taylor		
Shannon Taylor		
Will Thompson		
Byron Thweatt		
Brian Walsh		
11 Patrick Washington	2.50	6.00
Adam Westcott		
Terrence Wilkins		
Antwoine Womack		
Jared Woodson		
Rick Lantz Asst.CO		
Art Markos Asst.CO		
12 Bob Petchel Asst.CO	2.00	5.00
Andre' Powell Asst.CO		
Bob Price Asst.CO		
Paul Schudel Asst.CO		
David Turner Asst.CO		
Danny Wilmer Asst.CO		
Sparky Woods Asst.CO		
13 George Welsh Asst.CO	2.00	5.00
14 Aaron Brooks	2.00	5.00
15 Antonio Dingle	2.00	5.00
16 Anthony Poindexter	2.00	5.00

2005 Virginia

COMPLETE SET (6)	6.00	12.00
1 Marques Hagans	.60	1.50
2 Wali Lundy	1.25	3.00
3 Team Card	.60	1.50
4 Al Groh CO	.60	1.50
5 D'Brickashaw Ferguson	1.25	3.00
6 Ahmad Brooks	.75	2.00

2006 Virginia Schedules

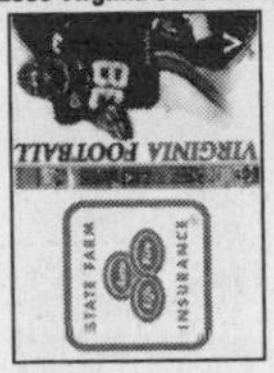

COMPLETE SET (5) 2.00 4.00
1 Marcus Hamilton .30 .75
2 Chris Long .30 .75
3 Tom Santi .30 .75
4 Jason Snelling .40 1.00
5 Deyon Williams .30 .75

1992-93 Virginia Tech

COMPLETE SET (12) 5.00 12.00
2 Will Furrer FB .60 1.50
5 Eugene Chung FB .40 1.00
10 Tony Kennedy FB .20 .50
11 Vaughn Hebron FB .80 2.00

2000 Virginia Tech Schedules

COMPLETE SET (4) 1.25 3.00
1 Frank Beamer CO .20 .50
2 Chad Beasley .20 .50
3 Andre Davis .30 .75
4 Michael Vick .60 1.50

1927 W560 Black

Cards in this set feature athletes from baseball and college football, along with an assortment of other sports and non-sports. The cards were issued in strips and full sheets and follow a standard playing card design. Quite a few Joker cards were produced. We've numbered the cards below according to the suit and playing card number (face cards were assigned numbers as well). It is thought there were at least three different printings and that the baseball and football players were added in the second printing replacing other subjects. All are baseball players below unless otherwise noted. Many cards were printed in a single color red, single color black, and a black/red dual color printing, thereby creating up to three versions. The full set, with just one of each different subject, contains 88-different cards. It is thought that the two-color cards are slightly tougher to find than the single color version.

COMPLETE SET (63) 900.00 1,500.00
*RED: .4X TO 1X BLACK
*BLACK/RED: .5X TO 1.2X BLACK
D1 Dutch Loud (football) 4.00 8.00
D2 Chris Cagle (football) 7.50 15.00
D10 D.A. Lowry (misspelled Lowery (football) 4.00 8.00
H6 Bruce T. Dumont (football) 4.00 8.00
H9 Al Lassman (football) 4.00 8.00
H12 M.E. Sprague (football) 4.00 8.00
JOK Ken Strong 10.00 20.00

1967 Wake Forest Team Issue

These photos were issued by the school to promote the football program. Each measures roughly 8" by 10" and features a pair of black and white images of players with the school name and year appearing at the top and the player's name and position below each photo. The backs are blank.

COMPLETE SET (9) 40.00 80.00
1 Fred Angerman, Rick Decker 5.00 10.00
2 Eddie Arrington, Don Hensley 5.00 10.00
3 Phil Cheatwood, Larry Hambrick 5.00 10.00
4 Ken Erickson, Roman Wszelaki 5.00 10.00
5 Chick George, Bob Flynn 5.00 10.00
6 Robert Grant, Caryle Pate 5.00 10.00
7 Lloyd Halvorson, Tom Deacon 5.00 10.00
8 Ron Jurewicz, Jimmy Clack 5.00 10.00
9 Bill Overton, Joe Theriault 5.00 10.00

1967 Wake Forest Team Sheets

These photos were issued by the school to promote the football program. Each measures roughly 8" by 10" and features ten black and white images of players with the school name and year appearing at the top. The backs are blank.

COMPLETE SET (3) 20.00 35.00
1 Jack Dolbin, Rick White, Fred Angerman, Phil Cheatwood, Fred Barden, Tom Deacon, Jimmy Johnson, Don Lobos, Roman Waselaki, Joe Theriault 6.00 12.00
2 Ron Jurewicz, Eddie Arrington, Buz Leavitt, Ken Erickson, Butch Henry, Rick Decker, lloyd Halvorson, Don Hensley, Larry Hambrick, Howard Stanback 0.00 12.00
3 Howard Stanback, Ed Atkinson, Digit Laughridge, Carlton Baker, Jimmy Clack, Caryle Pate, Bob Flynn, Chick George, John McQueeney, Robert Grant 6.00 12.00

1968 Wake Forest Team Sheets

These photos were issued by the school to promote the football program. Each measures roughly 8" by 10" and features ten black and white images of players with the school name and year appearing at the top. The backs are blank.

COMPLETE SET (3) 20.00 35.00
1 Jack Dolbin, Rick White, Fred Augerman, Jon Schubert, Dick Bozoian, Tom Deacom, Jimmy Johnson, Don Kobos, Roman Wazelaki, John Mazalewski 6.00 12.00
2 Ron Jurewicz, Eddie Arrington, Buz Leavitt, Dave Connors, Larry Russell, Joe Dobner, Lloyd Halvorson, Freddie Summers, Fred Cooke, Larry Hambrick 6.00 12.00
3 Howard Stanback, Tom Gavin, Digit Laughridge, Ed George, Jimmy Clack, Caryle Pate, Win Headley, Chick George, John McQueeney, Gary Willard 6.00 12.00

1987 Wake Forest Team Sheets

These photos were issued by the school to promote the football program. Each measures roughly 8" by 10" and features eight black and white images of players with the school name and year appearing at the top. The backs are blank.

1 Mark Agientas, Tony Watt, Randy Burrows, Randy Whiting, Steve Fleming, David Jarvis, Rob Watson, Rodney Ferguson 4.00 8.00
2 Louis Altobelli, Marco Pickett, Tony Rogers, Stafford Moser, Mike Smith, Warren Belin, Brian Johnson, Jerome Rice 4.00 8.00
3 Dwayne Brown, James DuBose, Joe Ellison, Ralph Godic, Spencer Jenkins, Rodney Hogue, Willie Robinson, Bradford Benson 4.00 8.00
4 Steve Brown, Chip Rives, David Braxton, Tony Mosley, Mark Young, Mike Hooten, Dexter Victor, Kelly Vaughan 4.00 8.00
5 Jay Deaver, Phil Barnhill, Wilson Hoyle, Terry Smith, Joe Walker, James Phillips, Tony Mayberry, Martin Bailey 4.00 8.00
6 Ricky Proehl, Ernie Purnsley, Paul Mann, Darryl McGill, Greg Scales, Jimmie Simmons, Mike Elkins, A.j. Greene 4.00 8.00
7 Warren Smith, Roger Foltz, Joe Kenn, Jeff Miller, Carl Nesbit, David Whitley, Kyle White, Kevin Graham 4.00 8.00

1994 Wake Forest Team Sheets

1 Doug Marsigli, Jerome Simpkins, Tony Yarnall, Dan Ballou, Gardell Chavis, Major Griffey, Jeremiah Williams, Harold Gragg 3.00 6.00
2 Eddie McKeel, Roger Pettus, Maurice Gravely, Semmajh Taylor, Jimmy Quander, Kevin Giles, Richard Goodpasture, Rhett Blancgard 3.00 6.00
3 Matt McNeel, Sherron Gudger, Jones Holcomb, Austin Crowder, Bill Leeder, Aljamony Joyner, Bobby Fatzinger, Kai Snead 3.00 6.00
4 Brent Morehead, John Lewis, Rusty LaRue, Ticker Grace, Mike Neubeiser, Elton Ndoma-Ogar, Tom Stuetzer, Rick Gardner 3.00 6.00
5 Myles Savage, Tim Hailstock, Hgeorge Kinney, Greg MvCracken, Bo Loy, Tim Goodson, William Clark, Rojah Rhodes 3.00 6.00
6 Alexis Sockwell, Stacie Gredham, Terrence Suber, David Cerchio, Adam Dolder, Bill Hollows, Andre Mason, LaDwaun Harrison 3.00 6.00
7 Rusty LaRue, Elton Ndoma-Ogar 3.00 6.00

1995 Wake Forest Team Sheets

These photos were issued by the school to promote the football program. Unless noted below, each measures roughly 8" by 10" and features either two or eight players with a black and white image for each. The school name and year appear at the top and the backs are blank.

COMPLETE SET (5) 15.00 30.00
1 Chad Alexander, Darrell Braswell, David Cerchio, LaDwaun Harrison, Aljamont Joyner, Brandon Perry, Myles Savage, Joe Zelenka 3.00 6.00
2 Austin Crowder, Harold Gragg, Jones Holcomb, Bill Leeder, D'Angelo Solomon, Tom Stuetzer, Steve Vaughan, David Zadel 3.00 6.00
3 Bill Hollows, Herman Lewis, John Lewis, Jon Mannon, Doug Marsigli, Kelvin Moses, Terrence Suber, Tony Yarnall 3.00 6.00
4 Rusty LaRue, Elton Ndoma-Ogar 3.00 6.00
5 Tucker Grace, Rick Gardner 3.00 6.00

1997 Wake Forest Team Sheets

These photos were issued by the school to promote the football program. Unless noted below, each measures roughly 8" by 10" and features one, two, or eight players with a black and white image for each. The school name and year appear at the top and the backs are blank.

COMPLETE SET (6) 15.00 30.00
1 Taris Clark, Pat Depenbrock, Herman Lewis, Spencer Wagner, Kai Snead, Myles Savage, Joe Zelenka, Brian Wolverton 3.00 6.00
2 Thabiti Davis, Robert Fatzinger, Chris Gaskell, Aljamont Joyner, D'Angelo Solomon, David Zadel, Terrence Suber, Chad Alexander 3.00 6.00
3 Tripp Moore, Matthew Burdick, Dameon Daniel, Jeffrey Muyres, Fred Robbins, Ben Sankey, Kelvin Jones, Clinton Wilburn 3.00 6.00
4 Jim Caldwell CO 3.00 6.00
5 Robert Fatzinger, Kelvin Moses 3.00 6.00
6 Brian Kuklick, Thabiti Davis 3.00 6.00

1999 Wake Forest Team Sheets

These photos were issued by the school to promote the football program. Unless noted below, each measures roughly 8" by 10" and features one, two, or eight players with a black and white image for each. The school name and year appear at the top and the backs are blank.

COMPLETE SET (10) 25.00 50.00
1 Marvin Chalmers, Jammie Deese, DaLawn Parrish, Reggie Austin, Brian Wolverton, Dustin Lyman, Morgan Kane, Kelvin Moses 3.00 6.00
2 Kelvin Jones, William Merritt, Abdul Guice, Matt Brennie, Chris McCoy, Da'Vaughn Mellerson, Vince Azzolina, Mat Petz 3.00 6.00
3 Ed Kargbookorogie, Tehran Carpenter, Tyler Ashe, Willie Lam, Chris Justice, Roderick Stephen, Clinton Wilburn, John Stone 3.00 6.00
4 Bryan Ray, Ira Williams, Marlon Curtis, Michael Clinkscale, Jimmy Caldwell, Michael Collins, Mark DeOrio, Nathan Bolling 3.00 6.00
5 Fred Robbins, Sam Settar, Ben Sankey, Kelvin Shackleford, David Moore, James Lik, Kito Gray, Matt Burdick 3.00 6.00
6 Jim Caldwell CO 3.00 6.00
7 Morgan Kane, Ben Sankey 3.00 6.00
8 Dustin Lyman, Kelvin Moses 3.00 6.00
9 Dalawn Parrish, Fred Robbins 3.00 6.00
10 Sam Settar, Jammie Deese 3.00 6.00

2008 Wake Forest Schedules

COMPLETE SET (19) 6.00 12.00
1 Josh Adams .30 .75
2 Stanley Arnoux .30 .75
3 Rich Belton .30 .75
4 Demir Boldin .30 .75
5 Chip Brinkman .30 .75
6 Andrew Conroy .30 .75
7 Aaron Curry .60 1.50
8 Anthony Davis .30 .75
9 Jim Grobe CO .30 .75
10 Kerry Major .30 .75
11 Chantz McClinic .30 .75
12 Kevin Patterson .30 .75
13 Matt Robinson .30 .75
14 Riley Skinner .50 1.25
15 Alphonso Smith .40 1.00
16 Sam Swank .30 .75
17 Chip Vaughn .30 .75
18 Antonio Wilson .30 .75
19 Andrew Wright .30 .75

1973 Washington KFC

Sponsored by Kentucky Fried Chicken and KIRO (Radio Northwest 710), these 30 cards measure approximately 3" by 4" and are printed on thick card stock. The fronts feature posed black-and-white head shots with white borders. The Kentucky Fried Chicken logo is in the top border, while player information is printed in the bottom border. The backs are blank. The cards are unnumbered and checklisted below in alphabetical order. The cards were given out by KFC with purchase of their product. Also distributed to purchasers of 5.00 or more was a color team photo or coaches picture measuring approximately 8" by 10".

COMPLETE SET (30) 225.00 450.00
1 Jim Anderson 7.50 15.00
2 Jim Andrilenas 7.50 15.00
3 Glen Bonner 7.50 15.00
4 Bob Boustead 7.50 15.00
5 Skip Boyd 7.50 15.00
6 Gordie Bronson 7.50 15.00
7 Reggie Brown 7.50 15.00
8 Dan Celoni CO 7.50 15.00
9 Brian Daheny 7.50 15.00
10 Fred Dean 7.50 15.00
11 Pete Elswick 7.50 15.00
12 Dennis Fitzpatrick 7.50 15.00
13 Bob Graves 7.50 15.00
14 Pedro Hawkins 7.50 15.00
15 Rick Hayes 7.50 15.00
16 Barry Houlihan 7.50 15.00
17 Roberto Jourdan 7.50 15.00
18 Washington Keenan 7.50 15.00
19 Eddie King 7.50 15.00
20 Jim Kristoff 7.50 15.00
21 Murphy McFarland 7.50 15.00
22 Walter Oldes 7.50 15.00
23 Louis Quinn 7.50 15.00
24 Frank Reed 7.50 15.00
25 Dain Rodwell 7.50 15.00
26 Ron Stanley 7.50 15.00
27 Joe Tabor 7.50 15.00
28 Pete Taggares 7.50 15.00
29 John Whitacre 7.50 15.00
30 Hans Woldseth 7.50 15.00
NNO Color Team Photo (Large 8x10) 10.00 20.00
NNO Coaches Photo (Large 8x10) 12.50 25.00

1988 Washington Smokey

The 1988 University of Washington Smokey set contains 16 standard-size cards. The fronts feature color photos bordered in deep purple, with name, position, and jersey number. The vertically oriented backs have fire prevention cartoons. The cards are unnumbered and are listed below in alphabetical order.

COMPLETE SET (16) 6.00 15.00
1 Ricky Andrews .40 1.00
2 Bern Brostek .60 1.50
3 Dennis Brown .60 1.50
4 Cary Conklin .40 1.00
5 Tony Covington .40 1.00
6 Darryl Hall .40 1.00
7 Martin Harrison .40 1.00
8 Don James CO .75 2.00
9 Aaron Jenkins .40 1.00
10 Le-Lo Lang .60 1.50
11 Art Malone .40 1.00
12 Andre Riley .40 1.00
13 Brian Slater .40 1.00
14 Vince Weathersby .40 1.00
15 Brett Wiese .40 1.00
16 Mike Zandofsky .40 1.00

1990 Washington Smokey

This 16-card standard size set was issued to promote fire safety. The fronts of the cards are purple bordered with "1990 Washington Huskies" on the top of the card. A full-color action photo is in the middle of the card and the player's name, uniform number, and position are underneath. On the lower left hand corner is the Smokey symbol and in the lower right-hand corner is the Washington Huskies logo. On the back is biographical information about the player and a fire safety tip. The set was issued with cooperation from the USDI Bureau of Land Management, the National Park Service, the National Association of State Foresters, Keep Washington Green, BDA, and KOMO Radio. We have checklisted this set alphabetically within player type and put the uniform number, where applicable, next to the player's name. The set was also issued in an unperforated sheet with four rows of four cards each. The last row of cards features women volleyball players. The key card in this set is quarterback Mark Brunell.

COMPLETE SET (16) 16.00 40.00
1 Eric Briscoe 28 .30 .75
2 Mark Brunell 11 12.50 30.00
3 James Clifford 53 .30 .75
4 John Cook 93 .30 .75
5 Ed Cunningham 79 .80 2.00
6 Dana Hall 5 1.00 2.50
7 Don James CO .80 2.00
8 Donald Jones 48 .30 .75
9 Dean Kirkland 51 .30 .75
10 Greg Lewis 20 .60 1.50
11 Orlando McKay 4 .30 .75
12 Travis Richardson 58 .30 .75
13 Kelley Larsen (Women's volleyball) .30 .75
14 Michelle Reid (Women's volleyball) .30 .75
15 Ashleigh Robertson (Women's volleyball) .30 .75
16 Gail Thorpe (Women's volleyball) .30 .75

1991 Washington Smokey

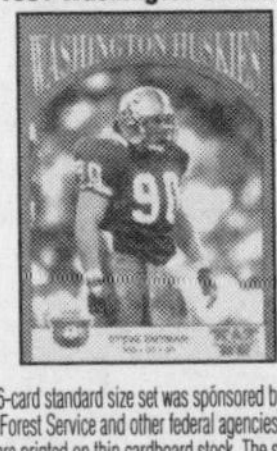

This 16-card standard size set was sponsored by the USDA Forest Service and other federal agencies. The cards are printed on thin cardboard stock. The set was issued in two different forms. Ten thousand 12-card sets were distributed at the Huskies' home game against the University of Toledo. This set was also issued as a 16-card unperforated sheet, with the final row featuring four women volleyball players. The card fronts are accented in the team's colors (purple and gold) and have glossy color action player photos. The top of the pictures is curved to resemble an archway, and the team name follows the curve of the arch. The player's name and position appear in a stripe below the picture. The backs present statistics and a fire prevention cartoon starring Smokey. The cards are unnumbered and checklisted below in alphabetical order, with the women volleyball players listed at the end. The key card in this set is quarterback Billy Joe Hobert.

COMPLETE SET (16) 6.00 15.00
1 Mario Bailey .50 1.25
2 Beno Bryant .30 .75
3 Brett Collins .30 .75
4 Ed Cunningham .30 .75
5 Steve Emtman .80 2.00
6 Dana Hall .80 2.00
7 Billy Joe Hobert 2.00 5.00
8 Dave Hoffmann .30 .75
9 Don James CO .60 1.50
10 Donald Jones .30 .75
11 Siupeli Malamala .30 .75
12 Orlando McKay .30 .75
13 Diane Flick (Women's volleyball) .30 .75
14 Kelley Larsen (Women's volleyball) .30 .75
15 Ashleigh Robertson (Women's volleyball) .30 .75
16 Dana Thompson (Women's volleyball) .30 .75

1992 Washington Greats Pacific

This 110-card standard-size set highlights 100 years of Huskies football. The cards were produced by Pacific Trading Cards, who donated a portion of the proceeds from their sale to the University of Washington and the Don James Endowment Fund for athletic scholarships. Reportedly the production run was limited to 2,500 numbered cases; moreover, 1,000 serial numbered cards autographed by Hugh McElhenny were randomly inserted in the ten-card foil packs. On a white card face, the fronts display a mix of color or black and white player photos enclosed by thin gold and purple borders. The team helmet appears in the lower left corner, with the player's name and position in a gold stripe extending to the right. The backs carry biography and career summary. The checklist card was randomly inserted at a reported rate of one every one or two wax boxes; it is not included in the complete set price listed below.

COMPLETE SET (110) 8.00 20.00
1 Don James CO .20 .50
2 Cary Conklin .20 .50
3 Tom Cowan .05 .15
4 Thane Cleland .06 .15
5 Steve Pelluer .20 .50
6 Sonny Sixkiller .20 .50
7 Koll Hagen .05 .15
8 Danny Greene .05 .15
9 George Black .05 .15
10 Mike Baldassin .05 .15
11 Bill Douglas .05 .15
12 Tom Flick .05 .15
13 Brian Slater .05 .15
14 Dick Sprague .05 .15
15 Bob Schloredt .08 .25
16 Bill Smith .05 .15
17 Marv Bergmann .05 .15
18 Sam Mitchell .05 .15
19 Bill Earley .05 .15
20 Clarence Dirks .05 .15
21 Jimmie Cain .05 .15
22 Don Heinrich .08 .25
23 Paul(Socko) Sulkosky .05 .15
24 By Haines .05 .15
25 Joe Steele .05 .15
26 Bob Monroe .05 .15
27 Roy McKasson .05 .15
28 Charlie Mitchell .05 .15
29 Ernie Steele .05 .15
30 Kyle Heinrich .05 .15
31 Travis Richardson .05 .15
32 Hugh McElhenny .40 1.00
33 George Wildcat Wilson .05 .15
34 Merle Hufford .05 .15
35 Steve Thompson .05 .15
36 Jim Krieg .05 .15
37 Chuck Olson .05 .15
38 Charley Russell .05 .15
39 Duane Wardlow .05 .15
40 Jay MacDowell .05 .15
41 Alf Hemstad .05 .15
42 Max Starcevich .05 .15
43 Ray Mansfield .05 .15
44 Brooks Biddle .05 .15
45 Toussaint Tyler .08 .25
46 Randy Van Diver .05 .15
47 John Cook .05 .15
48 Paul Skansi .08 .25
49 Tim Meamber .05 .15
50 Milt Bohart .05 .15
51 Curt Marsh .05 .15
52 Antowaine Richardson .05 .15
53 Jim Rodgers .05 .15
54 Mike Rohrbach .05 .15
55 Dan Agen .05 .15
56 Tom Turnure .05 .15
57 Ron Medved .05 .15
58 Vic Markov .05 .15
59 Carl(Bud) Ericksen .05 .15
60 Bill Kinnune .05 .15
61 Karsten(Corky) Lewis .05 .15
62 Sam Robinson .05 .15
63 Dave Nisbet .05 .15
64 Barry Bullard .05 .15
65 Norm Dicks .05 .15
66 Rick Redman .05 .15
67 Mark Jerue .05 .15
68 Jeff Toews .05 .15
69 Fletcher Jenkins .05 .15
70 Ray Horton .05 .15
71 Tom Erlandson .05 .15
72 Steve Alvord .05 .15
73 Dean Browning .05 .15
74 Scott Greenwood .05 .15
75 Bo Yates .05 .15
76 Jake Kupp .08 .25
77 Jim Owens CO .05 .15
78 Don McKeta .05 .15
79 Ben Davidson .20 .50
80 Tim Bullard .05 .15
81 Bill Albrecht .05 .15
82 Jim Cope .05 .15
83 Earl Monlux .05 .15
84 Paul Schwegler .05 .15
85 Steve Bramwell .05 .15
86 Ted Holzknecht .05 .15
87 Larry Hatch .05 .15
88 John Brady .05 .15
89 Bob Hivner .05 .15
90 Chuck Nelson .05 .15
91 Jeff Jaeger .08 .25
92 Rich Camarillo .08 .25
93 Jim Houston .05 .15
94 Jim Skaggs .05 .15
95 John Cherberg CO .05 .15
96 Bo Cornell .05 .15
97 Bill Cahill .05 .15
98 Dean McAdams .05 .15
99 Gil Dobie CO .05 .15
100 Walter Shiel .05 .15
101 Enoch Bagshaw CO .05 .15
102 Ray Eckmann .05 .15
103 Luther Carr .05 .15
104 Jimmy Bryan .05 .15
105 Darrell Royal .20 .50
106 Ray Frankowski .05 .15
107 Ray Pinney .05 .15
108 Skip Boyd .05 .15
109 Al Burleson .05 .15
110 Dennis Fitzpatrick .05 .15
NNO Checklist Card 1.20 3.00
AU32 Hugh McElhenny (AU/1000) 20.00 50.00

1992 Washington Little Sun

COMPLETE SET (8) 3.00 8.00
2 Mark Rypien .30 .75
8 Dana Hall .20 .50

1992 Washington Pay Less

This 16-card standard-size set was sponsored by Pay Less Drug Stores and Prime Sports Northwest. The cards are printed on thin card stock. The fronts carry a color action player photo on a purple card face. The team name and year appear above the photo in gold print on a purple bar that partially rests on a gold bar with notched ends. Below the photo, the player's name and sponsor logos appear in a gold border stripe. The backs carry statistics and sponsor advertisements. The cards are unnumbered and checklisted below in alphabetical order. The Billy Joe Hobart card was reportedly pulled from circulation after his suspension from the team.

COMPLETE SET (16) 12.00 30.00
1 Walter Bailey .30 .75
2 Jay Barry .30 .75
3 Mark Brunell 8.00 20.00
4 Beno Bryant .30 .75
5 James Clifford .30 .75
6 Jaime Fields .40 1.00
7 Travis Hanson .30 .75
8 Billy Joe Hobert SP 2.00 5.00
9 Dave Hoffmann .30 .75
10 Matt Jones .30 .75
11 Lincoln Kennedy .80 2.00
12 Andy Mason .30 .75
13 Shane Pahukoa .30 .75
14 Tommie Smith .30 .75
15 Darius Turner .30 .75
16 Team Photo (Schedule) .30 .75

1993 Washington Safeway

The 16 standard-size cards comprising this Huskies set sponsored by Safeway food stores, Pepsi, and Prime Sports Northwest, were printed on thin card stock and feature on their fronts purple- and gold-bordered color player action shots. The player's name and position, along with the sponsors' logos, appear within the gold margin at the bottom. The words "Huskies 1993" appear in purple lettering within a gold bar at the upper left. The player's uniform number appears in white lettering at the upper right. The white back carries the player's name at the top, followed below by a stat table or player highlights. The sponsors' logos at the bottom round out the card. The cards are unnumbered and checklisted below in alphabetical order. The key cards in this set are Damon Huard and Napoleon Kaufman.

COMPLETE SET (16) 8.00 20.00
1 Beno Bryant .30 .75
2 Hillary Butler .30 .75
3 D'Marco Farr .60 1.50
4 Jamal Fountaine .30 .75
5 Tom Gallagher .30 .75
6 Travis Hanson .30 .75
7 Damon Huard 3.00 8.00
8 Matt Jones .30 .75
9 Pete Kaligis .30 .75
10 Napoleon Kaufman 3.20 8.00
11 Joe Kralik .30 .75
12 Andy Mason .30 .75
13 Jim Nevelle .30 .75
14 Pete Pierson .30 .75
15 Steve Springstead .30 .75
16 John Werdel .30 .75

1994 Washington

Produced by BD&A Cards, this 12-card standard-size set was jointly sponsored by Pepsi and PSN (Prime Sports Northwest) Cable T.V. Printed on thin card stock, the fronts display color player photos that are framed by purple and gold borders. The player's name is printed in the top border, his position in the right border, and sponsor logos in the bottom border. In black print on a white background, the backs present career statistics. The cards are unnumbered and checklisted below in alphabetical order. The set was also issued as a 10 3/8" by 10 3/4" uncut sheet.

COMPLETE SET (12)	8.00	20.00
1 Eric Bjornson	.80	2.00
2 Mark Bruener	.80	2.00
3 Richie Chambers	.25	.60
4 Frank Garcia	.25	.60
5 Russell Hairston	.25	.60
6 Damon Huard	2.50	6.00
7 Napoleon Kaufman	2.40	6.00
8 David Killpatrick	.25	.60
9 Lamar Lyons	.25	.60
10 Andrew Peterson	.25	.60
11 Donovan Schmidt	.25	.60
12 Richard Thomas	.25	.60

1995 Washington

This 16-card set released by the University of Washington Huskies features color action player photos with a team-color partial border containing the player's name and position. The backs carry player career highlights. The cards are unnumbered and checklisted below in alphabetical order.

COMPLETE SET (16)	10.00	25.00
1 Ink Aleaga	.60	1.50
2 Eric Battle	.60	1.50
3 Ernie Conwell	.40	1.00
4 Deke Devers	.40	1.00
5 Mike Ewaliko	.40	1.00
6 Scott Greenlaw	.40	1.00
7 Trevor Highfield	.40	1.00
8 Stephen Hoffmann	.40	1.00
9 Damon Huard	2.50	6.00
10 Dave Janoski	.40	1.00
11 Patrick Kesi	.40	1.00
12 Jim Lambright CO	.60	1.50
13 Lawyer Milloy	2.50	6.00
14 Leon Neal	.40	1.00
15 Reggie Reser	.40	1.00
16 Richard Thomas	.40	1.00

1996 Washington

This 16-card set released by the University of Washington Huskies features color action player photos with the player's name below and the school name to the right. The backs are unnumbered and carry player career highlights. We've listed the cards below in alphabetical order.

COMPLETE SET (16)	7.50	15.00
1 Ink Aleaga	.30	.75
2 Jason Chorak	.30	.75
3 Cameron Cleeland	.50	1.25
4 Fred Coleman	.30	.75
5 John Fiala	.30	.75
6 Shane Fortney	.30	.75
7 Brock Huard	1.50	4.00
8 Dave Janoski	.30	.75
9 Jerry Jensen	.30	.75
10 Benji Olson	.30	.75
11 Jerome Pathon	1.25	3.00
12 Mike Reed	.30	.75
13 David Richie	.30	.75
14 Bob Sapp	.30	.75
15 Rashaan Shehee	.75	2.00
16 Jim Lambright CO	.40	1.00

1997 Washington

This 16-card set released by the University of Washington Huskies features color action player photos with a team-color partial border containing the player's name and position. The backs are unnumbered and carry player career highlights. We've listed the cards below in alphabetical order.

COMPLETE SET (16)	7.50	15.00
1 Nigel Burton	.30	.75
2 Chris Campbell	.30	.75
3 Jason Chorak	.30	.75
4 Cameron Cleeland	.50	1.25
5 Tony Coats	.30	.75
6 Fred Coleman	.30	.75
7 Brock Huard	1.50	4.00
8 Jerry Jensen	.30	.75
9 Olin Kreutz	1.50	4.00
10 Jim Lambright CO	.40	1.00
11 Mel Miller	.30	.75
12 Benji Olson	.30	.75
13 Tony Parrish	.40	1.00
14 Jerome Pathon	1.00	2.50
15 Rashaan Shehee	.60	1.50
16 Jermaine Smith	.30	.75

1997 Washington Homeworks

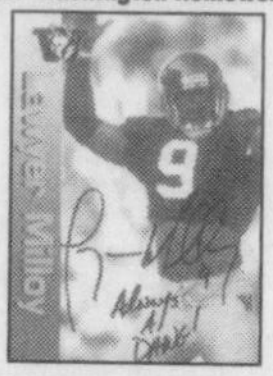

This 18-card set features color photos of the top 1996 and 1997 Huskies football players printed on heavy, laminated card stock. The backs carry basic player information and details on how to order the set from Homeworks Unlimited. The cards are unnumbered and checklisted below in alphabetical order.

COMPLETE SET (18)	8.00	20.00
1 Ink Aleaga	.80	2.00
2 Brooks Beaupain	.50	1.25
3 Jesse Binkley	.50	1.25
4 Eddie Burrell	.50	1.25
5 John Fiala	.50	1.25
6 Chris Hoffman	.50	1.25
7 Dave Janoski	.50	1.25
8 Lynn Johnson OL	.50	1.25
9 Cam Kissel	.50	1.25
10 Jim Lambright CO	.80	2.00
11 Ikaika Malloe	.50	1.25
12 Lawyer Milloy	1.20	3.00
13 Geoffrey Prince	.50	1.25
14 David J. Richie	.50	1.25
15 Bob Sapp	1.20	3.00
16 John Wales	.50	1.25
17 Team Schedule	.50	1.25
18 Team Checklist	.50	1.25

1998 Washington

This set was distributed at home football games during the 1998 season. Each card features a color player photo on the front along with "Husky Football 1998." The cardbacks include a complete write-up on the player featured and are unnumbered.

COMPLETE SET (16)	6.00	15.00
1 Nigel Burton	.30	.75
2 Tony Coats	.30	.75
3 Aaron Dalan	.30	.75
4 Reggie Davis	.30	.75
5 Marques Hairston	.30	.75
6 Ja'Warren Hooker	.40	1.00
7 Brock Huard	2.00	4.00
8 Jabari Issa	.30	.75
9 Todd Johnson	.30	.75
10 Jim Lambright CO	.30	.75
11 Jeremiah Pharms	.30	.75
12 Jermaine Smith	.40	1.00
13 Josh Smith	.30	.75
14 Lester Towns	.50	1.25
15 Mac Tuiaea	.30	.75
16 Marques Tuiasosopo	2.50	6.00

1999 Washington

This 16-card set released by the University of Washington Huskies features color action player photos with a team-color border containing the player's name, position, and team name. The backs are unnumbered and carry player career highlights. We've listed the cards below in alphabetical order.

COMPLETE SET (16)	6.00	12.00
1 Kurth Connell	.30	.75
2 Renard Edwards	.30	.75
3 Ryan Fleming	.30	.75
4 Marques Hairston	.30	.75
5 Gerald Harris	.30	.75
6 Jabari Issa	.30	.75
7 Joe Jarzynka	.30	.75
8 Dane Looker	.50	1.25
9 Toalei Mulitauaopele	.30	.75
10 Jeremiah Pharms	.30	.75
11 Elliot Silvers	.30	.75
12 Jermaine Smith	.30	.75
13 Lester Towns	.30	.75
14 Mac Tuiaea	.30	.75
15 Marques Tuiasosopo	1.25	3.00
16 Rick Neuheisel CO	.40	1.00

2000 Washington

This set was released by the University of Washington. Each card features a full-bleed color action player photo on the front with "Husky Football" printed to the left of the player image. The backs are unnumbered and carry player career highlights. We've listed the cards below in alphabetical order.

COMPLETE SET (16)	6.00	12.00
1 Hakim Akbar	.40	1.00
2 Paul Arnold	.50	1.25
3 Pat Conniff	.30	.75
4 Darrell Daniels	.30	.75
5 Dominic Daste	.30	.75
6 Todd Elstom	.30	.75
7 Matt Fraize	.30	.75
8 Rick Neuheisel CO	.40	1.00
9 Jeremiah Pharms	.30	.75
10 Elliott Silvers	.30	.75
11 Jerramy Stevens	.75	2.00
12 Larry Tripplett	.30	.75
13 Marques Tuiasosopo	1.25	3.00
14 Anthony Vontoure	.30	.75
15 Chad Ward	.30	.75
16 Curtis Williams	.30	.75

2001 Washington

This set was released by the University of Washington. Each card features a color action player photo on the front with the school name above the player image. The unnumbered backs are printed in color and carry player career highlights. We've listed the cards below in alphabetical order.

COMPLETE SET (17)	6.00	12.00
1 Rich Alexis	.30	.75
2 John Anderson	.30	.75
3 Paul Arnold	.40	1.00
4 Kyle Benn	.30	.75
5 Braxton Cleman	.30	.75
6 Wondame Davis	.30	.75
7 Todd Elstom	.30	.75
8 Willie Hurst	.30	.75
9 Anthony Kelley	.30	.75
10 Omare Lowe	.30	.75
11 Ben Mahdavi	.30	.75
12 Rick Neuheisel CO	.40	1.00
13 Cody Pickett	1.25	3.00
14 Marcus Roberson	.30	.75
15 Jerramy Stevens	.60	1.50
16 Larry Tripplett	.30	.75
17 Jamaun Willis	.30	.75

2002 Washington

This set was printed by High Step, released by the University of Washington, and sponsored by Red Robin and Pepsi. Each card features a color action player photo on the front with the Washington name above the image. The backs are unnumbered (except the player's jersey number) and carry player career highlights. We've listed the cards below in alphabetical order.

COMPLETE SET (16)	6.00	12.00
1 John Anderson	.30	.75
2 Paul Arnold	.40	1.00
3 Taylor Barton	.30	.75
4 Greg Carothers	.30	.75
5 Braxton Cleman	.30	.75
6 Kai Ellis	.30	.75
7 Wilbur Hooks Jr.	.40	1.00
8 Anthony Kelley	.40	1.00
9 Ben Mahdavi	.30	.75
10 Rick Neuheisel CO	.40	1.00
11 Cody Pickett	.75	2.00
12 Patrick Reddick	.30	.75
13 Kevin Ware	.40	1.00
14 Jafar Williams	.30	.75
15 Reggie Williams	1.50	4.00
16 Elliott Zajac	.30	.75

2003 Washington

This set was released by the University of Washington. Each card features a color action player photo on the front with the Washington name above the image. The backs are unnumbered and carry an extensive player bio and statistics. We've listed the cards below in alphabetical order.

COMPLETE SET (16)	6.00	12.00
1 Roc Alexander	.50	1.25
2 Rich Alexis	.30	.75
3 Todd Bachert	.30	.75
4 Khalif Barnes	.50	1.25
5 Greg Carothers	.30	.75
6 Marquis Cooper	.75	2.00
7 Charles Frederick	.30	.75
8 Keith Gilbertson CO	.30	.75
9 Derrick Johnson	.30	.75
10 Tank Johnson	.50	1.25
11 Chris Massey	.30	.75
12 Jimmy Newell	.30	.75
13 Nick Newton	.30	.75
14 Cody Pickett	.75	2.00
15 Jerome Stevens	.30	.75
16 Reggie Williams	1.25	3.00

2004 Washington

This set was produced by High Step and released by the University of Washington. Each card features a color action player photo on the front with the school logo above the player image. The backs are unnumbered and carry player career highlights. We've listed the cards below in alphabetical order.

COMPLETE SET (16)	5.00	10.00
1 Khalif Barnes	.50	1.25
2 Sam Cunningham	.30	.75
3 Ty Ericks	.30	.75
4 Charles Frederick	.40	1.00
5 Tim Galloway	.30	.75
6 Keith Gilbertson CO	.30	.75
7 Dashon Goldson	.40	1.00
8 Kenny James	.50	1.25
9 Derrick Johnson CB	.30	.75
10 Joe Lobendahn	.30	.75
11 Jon Lyon	.30	.75
12 Jimmy Newell	.30	.75
13 Shelton Sampson	.40	1.00
14 Joe Toledo	.50	1.25
15 Zach Tuiasosopo	.40	1.00
16 Corey Williams	.40	1.00

2005 Washington

This set was produced by High Step and released by the University of Washington. Each card features a color action player photo on the front with the school name above the player image. The backs are unnumbered and carry player career highlights. We've listed the cards below in alphabetical order.

COMPLETE SET (16)	7.50	15.00
1 Evan Benjamin	.30	.75
2 Sean Douglas	.30	.75
3 Johnny DuRocher	.30	.75
4 Ty Eriks	.30	.75
5 Dashon Goldson	.30	.75
6 Greyson Gunheim	.30	.75
7 Manase Hopoi	.30	.75
8 Kenny James	.60	1.50
9 Evan Knudson	.30	.75
10 Joe Lobendahn	.30	.75
11 Robin Meadow	.30	.75
12 Tusi Sa'au	.30	.75
13 Isaiah Stanback	.60	1.50
14 Joe Toledo	.40	1.00
15 Scott White	.30	.75
16 Tyrone Willingham CO	.30	.75

2006 Washington

This set was produced by High Step and released by the University of Washington. Each card features a color action player photo on the front withion a blue oval with the school logo above the player image. The backs are unnumbered and carry player career highlights. We've listed the cards below in alphabetical order.

COMPLETE SET (19)	6.00	12.00
1 Tahj Bomar	.30	.75
2 Michael Braunstein	.30	.75
3 Stanley Daniels	.30	.75
4 Sean Douglas	.30	.75
5 Dashon Goldson	.30	.75
6 Greyson Gunheim	.30	.75
7 Dan Howell	.30	.75
8 Kenny James	.40	1.00
9 Roy Lewis	.30	.75
10 Donny Mateaki	.30	.75
11 Warren Moon ATG	.30	.75
12 Louis Rankin	.40	1.00
13 Anthony Russo	.40	1.00
14 Sonny Shackelford	.30	.75
15 Isaiah Stanback	.60	1.50
16 Clay Walker	.30	.75
17 C.J. Wallace	.30	.75
18 Scott White	.30	.75
19 Tyrone Willingham CO	.30	.75

2007 Washington

This set was produced by High Step and released by the University of Washington. Each card features a color action player photo on the front with unnumbered cardbacks. We've listed the cards below in alphabetical order.

COMPLETE SET (16)	5.00	10.00
1 Wilson Afoa	.30	.75
2 Carl Bonnell	.30	.75
3 Cody Ellis	.30	.75
4 Juan Garcia	.30	.75
5 Greyson Gunheim	.30	.75
6 Dan Howell	.30	.75
7 Johnie Kirton	.30	.75
8 Roy Lewis	.30	.75
9 Chad Macklin	.30	.75
10 Louis Rankin	.30	.75
11 Caesar Rayford	.30	.75
12 Marcel Reese	.30	.75
13 Jordan Reffett	.30	.75
14 Anthony Russo	.30	.75
15 Corey Williams	.30	.75
16 Ty Willingham CO	.30	.75

2008 Washington

This set was released by the University of Washington. Each card features a color action player photo on the front along with the player's name, jersey number, and the school logo. The backs are unnumbered and carry player career highlights. We've listed the cards below in alphabetical order.

COMPLETE SET (16)	5.00	10.00
1 Jared Ballman	.30	.75
2 Casey Bulyca	.30	.75
3 Donald Butler	.30	.75
4 Byron Davenport	.30	.75
5 Mesphin Forrester	.30	.75
6 Juan Garcia	.30	.75
7 Michael Gottlieb	.30	.75
8 Darin Harris	.30	.75
9 Johnie Kirton	.30	.75
10 Luke Kravitz	.30	.75
11 Jake Locker	1.25	3.00
12 Ryan Perkins	.30	.75
13 Chris Stevens	.30	.75
14 Daniel Te'o-Nesheim	.30	.75
15 Jordan White-Frisbee	.30	.75
16 Spirit MASCOT	.30	.75

2009 Washington

COMPLETE SET (13)	4.00	8.00
1 Donald Butler	.30	.75
2 Mason Foster	.30	.75
3 Cody Habben	.30	.75
4 Nick Holt CO	.30	.75
5 Paul Homer	.30	.75
6 Jermaine Kearse	.40	1.00
7 Jake Locker	1.00	2.50
8 Doug Nussmeier CO	.30	.75
9 Ben Ossai	.30	.75
10 Steve Sarkisian CO	.30	.75
11 Daniel Te'o-Nesheim	.40	1.00
12 Nate Williams	.30	.75
13 Dubs MASCOT	.30	.75

2010 Washington

COMPLETE SET (15)	4.00	8.00
1 Devin Aguilar	.40	1.00
2 Cameron Elisara	.30	.75
3 Mason Foster	.30	.75
4 D'Andre Goodwin	.40	1.00
5 Cody Habben	.30	.75
6 Nick Holt Def.CO	.30	.75
7 Jermaine Kearse	.40	1.00
8 Jake Locker	.75	2.00
9 Doug Nussmeier Off.CO	.30	.75
10 Chris Polk	.60	1.50
11 Steve Sarkisian CO	.30	.75
12 Ryan Tolar	.30	.75
13 Desmond Trufant	.30	.75
14 Nate Williams	.30	.75
15 Dubs Mascot	.30	.75

1988 Washington State Smokey

The 1988 Washington State University Smokey set contains 12 standard-size cards. The fronts feature color photos bordered in white and maroon, with name, position, and jersey number. The vertically oriented backs have fire prevention cartoons. The cards are unnumbered, so are listed by jersey numbers. The set is also noteworthy in that it contains one of the few cards of Mike Utley, the courageous Detroit Lions' lineman, who was paralyzed as a result of an on-field injury during a NFL game in 1991.

COMPLETE SET (12)	7.50	15.00
3 Timm Rosenbach	.75	2.00
18 Shawn Landrum	.40	1.00
19 Artie Holmes	.40	1.00
31 Steve Broussard	1.25	3.00
42 Ron Lee	.40	1.00
55 Tuineau Alipate	.40	1.00
60 Mike Utley	1.50	4.00
68 Chris Dyko	.40	1.00
74 Jim Michalczik	.40	1.00
75 Tony Savage	.40	1.00
76 Ivan Cook	.40	1.00
82 Doug Wellsandt	.40	1.00

1990 Washington State Smokey

This 16-card standard-size set was sponsored by the USDA Forest Service in cooperation with several other federal agencies. Apart from four female volleyball players (2, 11, 13, and 14), the set features football players. The front presents an action color photo with text and borders in the school's colors maroon and silver. The Smokey the Bear picture appears in the lower left hand corner. The back includes biographical information and a public service announcement (with cartoon) concerning fire prevention. The cards are unnumbered, so they are listed alphabetically by subject's name.

COMPLETE SET (16)	4.00	10.00
1 Lewis Bush 48	.30	.75
2 Carrie Couturier (Women's volleyball)	.30	.75
3 Steve Cromer 70	.30	.75
4 C.J. Davis 1	.30	.75
5 John Diggs 22	.30	.75
6 Alvin Dunn 27	.30	.75
7 Aaron Garcia 9	.30	.75
8 Bob Garman 74	.30	.75
9 Brad Gossen 12	.30	.75
10 Calvin Griggs 5	.30	.75
11 Kelly Hankins (Women's volleyball)	.30	.75
12 Jason Hanson 4	1.00	2.50
13 Kristen Hovde (Women's volleyball)	.30	.75
14 Keri Killebrew (Women's volleyball)	.30	.75
15 Chris Moton 6	.30	.75
16 Ron Ricard 26	.30	.75

1991 Washington State Smokey

This 16-card standard-size set was sponsored by the USDA Forest Service and other federal agencies. The cards are printed on thin cardboard stock. The set was issued as a perforated sheet and as an uncut sheet without perforations. The final row of the sheet features four women volleyball players. The card fronts are accented in the team's colors (dark red and gray) and have either glossy color action or posed player photos. The top of the pictures is curved to resemble an archway, and the team name follows the curve of the arch. The player's name and position appear in a stripe below the picture. The backs present statistics and a fire prevention cartoon starring Smokey. The cards are unnumbered and checklisted below in alphabetical order, with the women volleyball players

COMPLETE SET (16)	4.00	10.00
1 Lewis Bush	.30	.75
2 Chad Cushing	.30	.75
3 C.J. Davis	.30	.75
4 Bob Garman	.30	.75
5 Jason Hanson	.80	2.00
6 Gabriel Oladipo	.30	.75
7 Anthony Prior	.30	.75
8 Jay Reyna	.30	.75
9 Lee Tilleman	.30	.75
10 Kirk Westerfield	.30	.75
11 Butch Williams	.30	.75
12 Michael Wright	.30	.75
13 Carrie Couturier (Women's volleyball)	.30	.75
14 Kelly Hankins (Women's volleyball)	.30	.75
15 Kristen Hovde (Women's volleyball)	.30	.75
16 Keri Killebrew (Women's volleyball)	.30	.75

1992 Washington State Smokey

This 20-card standard size set was sponsored by the USDA Forest Service and other federal agencies. The cards are printed on thin cardboard stock. The set was issued as a perforated sheet. The last two rows of the sheet feature women volleyball players. The card fronts are accented in the team's colors (brick-red and gray) and have color action player photos. The team name and year appear above the photo in gray print on a brick-red bar that partially rests on a gray bar with notched ends. Below the photo, the player's name and sponsor logos appear in a gray border stripe. The cards are unnumbered and checklisted below in alphabetical order with the volleyball players listed at the end. The key card is Drew Bledsoe, featured in his first card appearence.

COMPLETE SET (20)	16.00	40.00
1 Drew Bledsoe	12.00	30.00
2 Phillip Bobo	.30	.75
3 Lewis Bush	.25	.60
4 C.J. Davis	.25	.60
5 Shaumbe Wright-Fair	.30	.75
6 Bob Garman	.25	.60
7 Ray Hall	.25	.60
8 Torey Hunter	.30	.75
9 Kurt Loertscher	.25	.60
10 Anthony McClanahan	.25	.60
11 John Rushing	.25	.60
12 Clarence Williams	.40	1.00
13 Betty Bartram (Women's volleyball)	.25	.60
14 Krista Beightol (Women's volleyball)	.25	.60
15 Carrie Gilley (Women's volleyball)	.25	.60
16 Shannan Griffin (Women's volleyball)	.25	.60
17 Becky Howlett (Women's volleyball)	.25	.60
18 Kristen Hovde (Women's volleyball)	.25	.60
19 Keri Killebrew (Women's volleyball)	.25	.60
20 Cindy Fredrick CO M. Farokhmanesh ACO Gweyn Leabo ACO (Women's volleyball)	.25	.60

1967 Western Michigan Team Issue

These photos were issued by the school to promote the football program. Each measures roughly 5" by 7" and features a black and white image of a player. The backs are blank or sometimes can be found with a typed player identification. Otherwise no player identification is included.

COMPLETE SET (20)	75.00	150.00
1 Sam Antonazzo	4.00	8.00
2 Marty Barski	4.00	8.00
3 Dennis Bridges	4.00	8.00
4 Larry Butler	4.00	8.00
5 Glenn Cherup	4.00	8.00
6 Bill Devine	4.00	8.00
7 Clarence Harville	4.00	8.00
8 John Messenger	4.00	8.00
9 Pete Mitchell	4.00	8.00
10 Steve Mitchell	4.00	8.00
11 Gary Parent	4.00	8.00
12 Terry Pierce	4.00	8.00
13 Gary Rowe	4.00	8.00
14 Tom Randolph	4.00	8.00
15 Tom Saewert	4.00	8.00
16 Orv Schneider	4.00	8.00
17 Ron Seifert	4.00	8.00
18 Michael Sobol	4.00	8.00
19 Rolf Strout	4.00	8.00
20 Rick Trudeau	4.00	8.00

1999 West Texas A&M

COMPLETE SET (56)	12.50	25.00
1 Ricko Aguirre	.30	.75
2 Jimmy Arias	.30	.75
3 John Ayers	.30	.75
4 Richard Bailey	.30	.75
5 Aaron Bassett	.30	.75
6 Michael Becker	.30	.75
7 Todd Billings	.30	.75
8 Kevin Brinkley	.30	.75
9 Chris Brown	.30	.75
10 John Burnett	.30	.75
11 Derrick Caldwell	.30	.75
12 Kyle Clark	.30	.75
13 Kaleb Clay	.30	.75
14 Dustin Cleavenger	.30	.75
15 Nathan Cook	.30	.75
16 Brandon Crump	.30	.75
17 Asanti Danzie	.30	.75
18 Larry Dickerson	.30	.75
19 Kyle Duncan	.30	.75
20 Tony Frescaz	.30	.75
21 Jimmy Gaston	.30	.75
22 Otis Griffin	.30	.75
23 Ed Grission-Lipsky	.30	.75
24 Chris Harbin	.30	.75
25 Antonio Harrison	.30	.75
26 Vic Henning	.30	.75
27 Jason Hernandez	.30	.75
28 Luke Inman	.30	.75
29 Will James	.30	.75
30 Mario King	.30	.75
31 Jodie LaFrance	.30	.75
32 Kareem Larrimore	.30	.75
33 Tony Lawson	.30	.75
34 Rick Leach	.30	.75
35 Michael Lusby	.30	.75
36 Stan McGravey CO	.30	.75
37 Terrance Meks	.30	.75
38 DeWayne Miles	.30	.75
39 Jud Moller	.30	.75
40 Uduak Joe Ntuk	.30	.75
41 Nick Pasquale	.30	.75
42 Gleen Pope	.30	.75
43 Andrew Reagon	.30	.75
44 Matt Sardello	.30	.75
45 Justin Schantz	.30	.75
46 Mark Simmons	.30	.75
47 Rick Solis	.30	.75
48 Cody Stovall	.30	.75
49 Patrick Strambler	.30	.75
50 Raymond Talpule	.30	.75
51 Peter Tawil	.30	.75
52 Brian Thompson	.30	.75
53 Chaun Thompson	.30	.75
54 Drew Thorn	.30	.75
55 Angel Vega	.30	.75
56 Schedule Card	.30	.75

1974 West Virginia Playing Cards

This 54-card set was sponsored by the Student Foundation, a non-profit campus development group. The cards were issued in the playing card format, and each card measures approximately 2 1/8" by 3 1/8". The fronts feature either close-ups or posed action shots of the players. Card backs feature a line drawing of a West Virginia Mountaineer, with the four corners cut off to create triangles. There are two different card backs, same design, but either blue or gold. The set is arranged just like a card deck and checklisted below as follows: C means Clubs, D means Diamonds, H means Hearts, S means Spades, and JOK means Joker. The cards are checklisted below in playing card order by suits and numbers are assigned to Aces (1), Jacks (11), Queens (12), and Kings (13). The jokers are listed at the end. The key card in the set is coach Bobby Bowden.

COMPLETE SET (54)	60.00	120.00
1C Stu Wolpert	.60	1.50
1D Mountaineer Coaches	2.50	5.00
1H Leland Byrd AD	.60	1.50
1S Bobby Bowden CO	20.00	40.00
2C Jay Sheehan	.60	1.50
2D Tom Brandner	.60	1.50
2H Tommy Bowden	6.00	12.00

2S Chuck Smith	.60	1.50
3C Ray Marshall	.60	1.50
3D Randy Swinson	.60	1.50
3H Tom Loadman	.60	1.50
3S Bob Kaminski	.75	2.00
4C Ron Lee	1.50	3.00
4D Kirk Lewis	.60	1.50
4H Greg Dorn	.60	1.50
4S Emil Ros	.60	1.50
5C Mark Burke	.60	1.50
5D Rory Fields	.60	1.50
5H Gary Lombard	.60	1.50
5S Brian Gates	.60	1.50
6C John Schell	.60	1.50
6D Paul Jordan	.60	1.50
6H Mike Hubbard	.60	1.50
6S Chuck Kelly	.60	1.50
7C Rick Pennypacker	.75	2.00
7D Heywood Smith	.60	1.50
7H Jack Eastwood	.60	1.50
7S Andy Peters	.60	1.50
8C Steve Dunlap	.60	1.50
8D Dave Wilcher	.75	2.00
8H Greg Anderson	.60	1.50
8S Ken Culbertson	.60	1.50
9C David Van Halanger	.60	1.50
9D Rick Shaffer	.60	1.50
9H Rich Lukowski	.60	1.50
9S Al Gluchoski	.60	1.50
10C Dwayne Woods	.60	1.50
10D Ben Williams	.75	2.00
10H John Adams	.60	1.50
10S Tom Florence	.60	1.50
11C Marcus Mauney	.60	1.50
11D John Spraggins	.60	1.50
11H Bruce Huffman	.60	1.50
11S Bernie Kirchner	.60	1.50
12C Artie Owens	.75	2.00
12D Charlie Miller	.60	1.50
12H 1974 Cheerleaders	.60	1.50
12S Eddie Russell	.60	1.50
13C Danny Buggs	2.50	5.00
13D Marshall Mills	.60	1.50
13H John Everly	.60	1.50
13S Jeff Merrow	2.00	4.00
JOK1 Student Foundation Logo	.60	1.50
JOK2 Student Foundation Info	.60	1.50

1988 West Virginia

The 1988 West Virginia University set contains 16 standard-size cards. The fronts feature color photos bordered in white, with name, position, and jersey number. The vertically oriented backs have brief biographical information and "Tips from the Mountaineers." The cards are unnumbered and are listed alphabetically by subject. The set was sponsored by West Virginia University Hospitals.

COMPLETE SET (16)	8.00	20.00
1 Charlie Baumann	.50	1.25
2 Anthony Brown	.50	1.25
3 Willie Edwards	.50	1.25
4 Theron Ellis	.50	1.25
5 Chris Haering	.50	1.25
6 Major Harris	1.50	4.00
7 Undra Johnson	.60	1.50
8 Kevin Koken	.50	1.25
9 Pat Marlatt	.50	1.25
10 Eugene Napoleon	.50	1.25
11 Don Nehlen CO	.60	1.50
12 Bo Orlando	1.25	3.00
13 Chris Parker	.50	1.25
14 Robert Pickett	.50	1.25
15 Brian Smider	.50	1.25
16 John Stroia	.50	1.25

1990 West Virginia Postcards

This unnumbered set of post cards was issued by the school to promote the football program.

COMPLETE SET (5)	10.00	20.00
1 Defensive Line of Scrimmage	1.50	4.00
2 Defensive Dog Pile against Louisville	1.50	4.00
3 Mike Fox Reggie Rembert Renaldo Turnbull	2.00	5.00
4 Major Harris	2.50	6.00
5 Ron Wolfley Darryl Talley Jeff Hostetler	2.00	5.00

1990 West Virginia Program Cards

Sponsored by Gatorade Thirst Quencher, the 1990 West Virginia Mountaineers football set consists of 49 standard-size cards printed on thin card stock. The set was available as a complete set or in seven-card perforated sheets featured in issues of Mountaineer Illustrated Magazine. The fronts feature posed color action shots bordered in white. The words "West Virginia Mountaineers" is shown in the team's colors above the picture. Below the picture are the team helmet, a green broken stripe, and player information. The back has biographical information, player profile, and "Mountaineer Tips" that consist of encouragements to stay in school. The cards are unnumbered and checklisted below in alphabetical order. Key cards in the set include James Jett and baseball's Darrell Whitmore.

COMPLETE SET (49)	25.00	40.00
1 Tarris Alexander	.40	1.00
2 Leroy Axem	.40	1.00
3 Michael Beasley	.40	1.00
4 Calvin Bell	.40	1.00
5 Matt Bland	.40	1.00
6 John Brown	.40	1.00
7 Brad Carroll	.40	1.00
8 Mike Collins	.40	1.00
9 Mike Compton	.60	1.50
10 Cecil Doggette	.40	1.00
11 Rick Dolly	.40	1.00
12 Theron Ellis	.40	1.00
13 Charlie Fedorco	.40	1.00
14 Garrett Ford	.40	1.00
15 Scott Gaskins	.40	1.00
16 Boris Graham	.40	1.00
17 Keith Graley	.40	1.00
18 Chris Gray	.40	1.00
19 Greg Hertzog	.40	1.00
20 Ed Hill	.40	1.00
21 Verne Howard	.40	1.00
22 James Jett	1.20	3.00
23 Greg Jones	.40	1.00
24 Jon Jones	.40	1.00
25 Ted Kester	.40	1.00
26 Darroll Mitchell	.40	1.00
27 John Murphy	.40	1.00
28 Don Nehlen CO	1.00	2.50
29 Tim Newsom	.40	1.00
30 Joe Pabian	.40	1.00
31 John Ray	.40	1.00
32 Steve Redd	.40	1.00
33 Joe Ruth	.40	1.00
34 Alex Shook	.40	1.00
35 Jeff Sniffen	.40	1.00
36 Ray Staten	.40	1.00
37 Rick Stead	.40	1.00
38 Darren Studstill	.60	1.50
39 Lorenzo Styles	.60	1.50
40 Gary Tillis	.40	1.00
41 Rico Tyler	.40	1.00
42 Darrell Whitmore	.60	1.50
43 E.J. Wheeler	.40	1.00
44 Darrick Wiley	.40	1.00
45 Tim Williams	.40	1.00
46 Sam Wilson	.40	1.00
47 Dale Wolfley	.40	1.00
48 Rob.Yachini	.40	1.00
49 Mountaineer Field	.40	1.00

1991 West Virginia ATG

The 1991 West Virginia All-Time Greats football set was produced by College Classics to celebrate the university's 100th year anniversary. It was sponsored and sold by 7-Eleven Stores. The 50 standard-size cards display action photos, with the team name above and the player's name in the white border beneath the picture. A "100 Years" emblem is superimposed at the lower right corner. The backs have biographical information, career statistics, and "Mountaineer Tips" in the form of "stay in school" messages.

COMPLETE SET (50)	8.00	20.00
1 Jeff Hostetler	.80	2.00
2 Tom Allman	.14	.35
3 Russ Bailey	.14	.35
4 Paul Bischoff	.14	.35
5 Bruce Bosley	.20	.50
6 Jim Braxton	.20	.50
7 Danny Buggs	.14	.35
8 Harry Clarke	.14	.35
9 Ken Culbertson	.14	.35
10 Willie Drewrey	.20	.50
11 Steve Dunlap	.14	.35
12 Garrett Ford	.14	.35
13 Dennis Fowlkes	.14	.35
14 Bob Gresham	.14	.35
15 Chris Haering	.14	.35
16 Major Harris	.60	1.50
17 Steve Hathaway	.14	.35
18 Rick Hollins	.14	.35
19 Chuck Howley	.40	1.00
20 Sam Huff	1.00	2.50
21 Brian Jozwiak	.14	.35
22 Gene Lamone	.14	.35
23 Oliver Luck	.20	.50
24 Kerry Marbury	.14	.35
25 Joe Marconi	.20	.50
26 Jeff Merrow	.14	.35
27 Steve Newberry	.14	.35
28 Bob Orders	.14	.35
29 Artie Owens	.14	.35
30 Tom Pridemore	.20	.50
31 Mark Raugh	.14	.35
32 Reggie Rembert	.20	.50
33 Ira Rodgers	.14	.35
34 Mike Sherwood	.14	.35
35 Joe Stydahar	.20	.50
36 Renaldo Turnbull	.50	1.25
37 Paul Woodside	.14	.35
38 Fred Wyant	.14	.35
39 Carl Leatherwood	.14	.35
40 Darryl Talley	.40	1.00
41 David Grant	.14	.35
42 Bobby Bowden CO	1.00	2.50
43 Jim Carlen CO	.14	.35
44 Frank Cignetti CO	.14	.35
45 Gene Corum CO	.14	.35
46 Art Lewis CO	.14	.35
47 Don Nehlen CO	.20	.50
48 New Mountaineer Field	.14	.35
49 Old Mountaineer Field	.14	.35
50 Lambert Trophy	.14	.35

1991 West Virginia Program Cards

This 42-card standard-size set was printed on thin card stock with white borders; the card fronts carry a posed action player photo against a screened blue background with blue and gold diagonal lines. West Virginia Mountaineers is imprinted over blue background at top while jersey number, name, and position appear at bottom. The backs have biography, "Mountaineer Tips" consisting of school advice, and the Gatorade Thirst Quencher logo. The cards are numbered on the back; the numbering is essentially alphabetical by player's name. Seven different cards were featured in each of the team's six home game Mountaineer Illustrated programs.

COMPLETE SET (42)	12.00	30.00
1 Tarris Alexander	.40	1.00
2 Johnathan Allen	.40	1.00
3 Leroy Axem	.40	1.00
4 Joe Ayuso	.40	1.00
5 Michael Beasley	.40	1.00
6 Rich Braham	.40	1.00
7 Tom Briggs	.40	1.00
8 John Cappa	.40	1.00
9 Mike Collins	.40	1.00
10 Mike Compton	.50	1.25
11 Doug Cooley	.40	1.00
12 Cecil Doggette	.40	1.00
13 Rick Dolly	.40	1.00
14 Garrett Ford	.40	1.00
15 Scott Gaskins	.40	1.00
16 Boris Graham	.40	1.00
17 Keith Graley	.40	1.00
18 Chris Gray	.40	1.00
19 Barry Hawkins	.40	1.00
20 Ed Hill	.40	1.00
21 James Jett	1.20	3.00
22 Jon Jones	.40	1.00
23 Jim LeBlanc	.40	1.00
24 David Mayfield	.40	1.00
25 Adrian Murrell	2.00	5.00
26 Sam Mustipher	.40	1.00
27 Tim Newsom	.40	1.00
28 Tommy Orr	.40	1.00
29 Joe Pabian	.40	1.00
30 John Ray	.40	1.00
31 Wes Richardson	.40	1.00
32 Nate Rine	.40	1.00
33 Joe Ruth	.40	1.00
34 Alex Shook	.40	1.00
35 Kwame Smith	.40	1.00
36 Darren Studstill	.50	1.25
37 Lorenzo Styles	.50	1.25
38 Gary Tillis	.40	1.00
39 Ron Weaver	.40	1.00
40 Darrell Whitmore	.50	1.25
41 Darrick Wiley	.40	1.00
42 Rodney Woodard	.40	1.00

1992 West Virginia Program Cards

This 49-card standard-size set was available in the team's home game Mountaineer Illustrated Programs. The cards were printed on thin stock. The white-bordered fronts carry a posed action player photo on an orange-yellow background with short diagonal maroon and gray lines. West Virginia Mountaineers is imprinted at the top above the player's photo. The jersey number, name and position appear at the bottom. The backs have biography, "Mountaineer Tips," consisting of school advice, and the Gatorade logo.

COMPLETE SET (49)	12.00	30.00
1 Tarris Alexander	.40	1.00
2 Joe Avila	.40	1.00
3 Leroy Axem	.40	1.00
4 Mike Baker	.40	1.00
5 Sean Biser	.40	1.00
6 Mike Booth	.40	1.00
7 Rich Braham	.40	1.00
8 Tom Briggs	.40	1.00
9 Tim Brown	.40	1.00
10 Darius Burwell	.40	1.00
11 John Cappa	.40	1.00
12 Matt Ceglie	.40	1.00
13 Mike Collins	.40	1.00
14 Mike Compton	.40	1.00
15 Rick Dolly	.40	1.00
16 Garrett Ford	.40	1.00
17 Scott Gaskins	.40	1.00
18 Boris Graham	.40	1.00
19 Dan Harless	.40	1.00
20 Barry Hawkins	.40	1.00
21 Ed Hill	.40	1.00
22 James Jett	1.00	2.50
23 Mark Johnson	.40	1.00
24 Jon Jones	.40	1.00
25 Jake Kelchner	.50	1.25
26 Harold Kidd	.40	1.00
27 Jim LeBlanc	.40	1.00
28 David Mayfield	.40	1.00
29 Brian Moore	.40	1.00
30 Adrian Murrell	2.00	4.00
31 Robert Nelson	.40	1.00
32 Tommy Orr	.40	1.00
33 Joe Pabian	.40	1.00
34 Brett Parise	.40	1.00
35 Steve Perkins	.40	1.00
36 Steve Redd	.40	1.00
37 Wes Richardson	.40	1.00
38 Nate Rine	.40	1.00
39 Tom Robsock	.40	1.00
40 Kwame Smith	.40	1.00
41 Darren Studstill	.50	1.25
42 Lorenzo Styles	.50	1.25
43 Matt Taffoni	.40	1.00
44 Mark Ulmer	.40	1.00
45 Mike Vanderjagt	.50	1.25
46 Darrick Wiley	.40	1.00
47 Dale Williams	.40	1.00
48 Rodney Woodard	.40	1.00
49 James Wright	.40	1.00

1993 West Virginia

These 49 standard-size cards feature on their fronts posed color player photos set within blue marbleized borders. The player's name and position appear in a yellowish rectangle underneath the photo. The gray bordered back carries the player's name, position, uniform number and biography at the top, followed by the player's career highlights. Two different sets were issued. The fronts are identical in both sets but the backs differ slightly. The first set was the program set sponsored by Gatorade; the second set was the Big East Champions set. The WVU Sports Information office originally sold the program set for 5.00 and the Big East Champions sets for 7.00. Also there was a variation in these sets. In the program set, card number 13 is Daymeian Gallimore; in the Big East set, he is replaced by the Big East Trophy.

COMPLETE SET (49)	15.00	30.00
1 Zach Abraham	.30	.75
2 Tarris Alexander	.30	.75
3 Mike Baker	.30	.75
4 Aaron Beasley	.30	.75
5 Derrick Bell	.30	.75
6 Mike Booth	.30	.75
7 Rich Braham	.30	.75
8 Tim Brown LB	.30	.75
9 Mike Collins	.30	.75
10 Doug Costin	.30	.75
11 Calvin Edwards	.30	.75
12 Jim Freeman	.30	.75
13A Big East Trophy	.60	1.50
13B Daymeian Gallimore	.30	.75
14 Jimmy Gary	.30	.75
15 Scott Gaskins	.30	.75
16 Buddy Hager	.30	.75
17 Dan Harless	.30	.75
18 John Harper	.30	.75
19 Barry Hawkins	.30	.75
20 Ed Hill	.30	.75
21 Jon Jones	.30	.75
22 Jay Kearney	.30	.75
23 Jake Kelchner	.30	.75
24 Harold Kidd	.30	.75
25 Chris Klick	.30	.75
26 Jim LeBlanc	.30	.75
27 Chris Ling	.30	.75
28 David Mayfield	.30	.75
29 Keith Morris	.30	.75
30 Tommy Orr	.30	.75
31 Joe Pabian	.30	.75
32 Ken Painter	.30	.75
33 Steve Perkins	.30	.75
34 Maurice Richards	.30	.75
35 Wes Richardson	.30	.75
36 Nate Rine	.30	.75
37 Tom Robsock	.30	.75
38 Todd Sauerbrun	.60	1.50
39 Darren Studstill	.40	1.00
40 Matt Taffoni	.30	.75
41 Keith Taparausky	.30	.75
42 Mark Ulmer	.30	.75
43 Robert Walker	.30	.75
44 Charles Washington	.30	.75
45 Darrick Wiley	.30	.75
46 Dale Williams	.30	.75
47 James(Puppy) Wright	.30	.75
48 Don Nehlen CO	.30	.75
49 Mountaineer Field	.30	.75

2003 West Virginia Greats

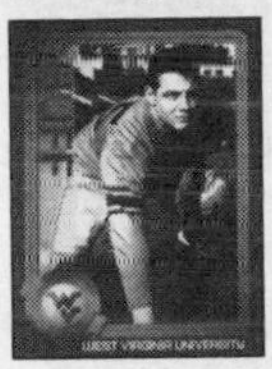

This set was available in the team's home football game programs throughout the season. The slightly oversized (roughly 2 5/8" by 3 5/8") cards were printed on thin stock and issued in perforated sheets of nine cards. The blue-bordered fronts carry a posed action player photo with the team name below the image. The unnumbered cards are listed below alphabetically.

COMPLETE SET (63)	12.50	25.00
1 Zach Abraham	.20	.50
2 Tom Allman	.20	.50
3 Mike Baker	.20	.50
4 Charlie Baumann	.20	.50
5 Aaron Beasley	.20	.50
6 Kittie Blakemore CO BK	.20	.50
7 Bruce Bosley	.20	.50
8 Rich Braham	.20	.50
9 Jim Braxton	.30	.75
10 Tim Brown	.20	.50
11 Marc Bulger	.75	2.00
12 Danny Buggs	.20	.50
13 Avon Cobourne	.20	.50
14 Mike Collins	.20	.50
15 Mike Compton	.20	.50
16 Tony Constantine Writer	.20	.50
17 Canute Curtis	.20	.50
18 Willie Drewrey	.20	.50
19 Dennis Fowlkes	.20	.50
20 Garrett Ford Sr.	.20	.50
21 James Davis	.20	.50
22 John Doyle	.20	.50
23 Steve Grant	.20	.50
24 Major Harris	.30	.75
25 Ed Hill	.20	.50
26 Jeff Hostetler	.30	.75
27 Chuck Howley	.30	.75
28 Sam Huff	.40	1.00
29 James Jett	.20	.50
30 Brian Jozwiak	.20	.50
31 Kyle Kayden	.20	.50
32 Jake Kelchner	.20	.50
33 Gene Lamone	.20	.50
34 Sam Littlepage Boxer	.20	.50
35 Mike Logan	.20	.50
36 Oliver Luck	.20	.50
37 John Mallory	.20	.50
38 Joe Marconi	.20	.50
39 Bob Moss	.20	.50
40 Don Nehlen	.20	.50
41 Steve Newberry	.20	.50
42 Bob Orders	.20	.50
43 Tom Pridemore	.20	.50
44 Ira Rogers	.20	.50
45 Rich Rodriguez	.20	.50
46 Todd Sauerbrun	.30	.75
47 David Saunders	.20	.50
48 Jack Stone	.20	.50
49 Darren Studstill	.30	.75
50 Joe Stydahar	.30	.75
51 Steve Superick	.20	.50
52 Darryl Talley	.30	.75
53 Jay Taylor	.20	.50
54 John Thornton	.20	.50
55 Renaldo Turnbull	.30	.75
56 Robert Walker	.20	.50
57 Paul Woodside	.20	.50
58 Fred Wyant	.20	.50
59 Amos Zereoue	.40	1.00
60 Old Mountaineer Field	.20	.50
61 New Mountaineer Field	.20	.50
62 1953 Team	.20	.50
63 1993 Team	.20	.50

1933 Wheaties College Photo Premiums

This series of team photos was apparently issued as a premium from Wheaties in 1933. Each includes a college football team photo printed on parchment style paper stock. The backs are blank.

NNO Loyola U.	50.00	80.00
NNO San Francisco U.	50.00	80.00
NNO Stanford	50.00	80.00

1994 William and Mary

This set was sponsored by Dominos Pizza and includes greats from recent William and Mary football to celebrate their 100th anniversary. The cards were printed with black and white photos with a dark green tint in a strip of 4-player or coach cards along with a Dominos Pizza advertising card.

COMPLETE SET (4)	2.40	6.00
1 Robert Green	.40	1.00
2 Lou Holtz	1.60	4.00
3 Mark Kelso	.80	2.00
4 Jimmye Laycock	.40	1.00

1908-09 Wisconsin Postcards

These black and white postcards was issued from roughly 1908-1909. The player's last name is included below the photo and the backs feature a typical postcard style format. Any additions to the list below are appreciated.

1 F.E. Boyle	30.00	50.00
2 John Moll	30.00	50.00
3 Oscar Osthoff	30.00	50.00
4 Ewald Jumbo Stiehm	35.00	60.00
5 John Wilce	30.00	50.00

1915-20 Wisconsin Photoart Postcards

These black and white postcards was issued from roughly 1915-1920 primarily by the Photoart House in Madison, Wisconsin. The player's name is typically included in small letters across his chest with the company name appearing at his belt. A number of different game action shots were also produced and we've cataloged those that include players on them along with the card's printed description. The backs feature a typical postcard style format with the manufacturer's name and address. Any additions to the list below are appreciated.

1 Cub Buck	200.00	350.00
2 George Bunge	30.00	50.00
3 D.J. Byers (Photoart)	30.00	50.00
4 D.J. Byers (McKillop Photo)	30.00	50.00
5 Rowdy Elliott	30.00	50.00
6 W. Juneau CO	30.00	50.00
7 L.G. Kreuz	30.00	50.00
8 Arlie Mucks	30.00	50.00
9 L.H. Smith	30.00	50.00
10 G.E. Taylor	30.00	50.00
11 Smith - Wis. with ball (action shot of L.H. Smith)	30.00	50.00

1951-53 Wisconsin Hall of Fame Postcards

These 12 postcards were issued by the Wisconsin Hall of Fame and feature some of the leading athletes out of Milwaukee. The sepia illustrations have a relief of the player as well as some information about them. Since these cards are unnumbered, we have sequenced them in alphabetical order.

COMPLETE SET (12)	175.00	350.00
6 Ernie Nevers FB	40.00	80.00
8 Pat O'Dea FB	15.00	30.00
9 Dave Schreiner FB	7.50	15.00
12 Bob Zuppke CO FB	20.00	40.00

1972 Wisconsin Team Sheets

The University of Wisconsin issued these sheets of black-and-white player photos. Each measures roughly 8" by 10" and was printed on glossy stock with white borders. Each sheet includes photos of 10-players and/or coaches. Below each player's image is his jersey number, name, school class, position, height, and weight. The photos are blankbacked.

COMPLETE SET (2)	15.00	30.00
1 Rick Jakious Mike Webster Mark Zakula Dennis Lick John Jardine CO Mike Seifert Rick Koeck Alvin Peabody Duane Johnson Tony Davis	10.00	20.00
2 Rufus Ferguson Dave Lokanc John Jardine CO K.Nosbusch Rudy Steiner Gary Lund Jack Novak Jeff Mack Bob Johnson J.Schymanski	5.00	10.00

1974 Wisconsin Team Sheets

These photos were issued by the school to promote the football program. Each measures roughly 8" by 10" and features eight black and white images of players with the school name appearing at the top. The backs are blank.

1 John Jardine CO Dennis Lick Bill Marek Gregg Bohlig Art Sanger Jeff Mack Jack Novak Ron Pollard	4.00	8.00
2 Rodney Rhodes Ken Starch Larry Canada Mark Zakula Rick Jarious Terry Stieve Randy Rose Mike Jenkins	4.00	8.00

1992 Wisconsin Program Cards

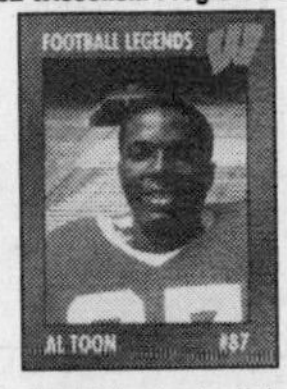

This 27-card standard-size set was issued in three Badger game programs in October 1992, each containing one nine-card sheet. The fronts feature former Badger football legends pictured in various poses, some in color, others in black and white, on a red-bordered card that has the red Wisconsin "W" logo in the top right. The player's name and uniform number appear in white in the bottom margin. The back has the player's name in white on a red stripe at the top. Another red stripe at the bottom contains the "W" logo and the logo of the sponsor, Bucky's Locker Room. Between the red stripes, a brief player biography appears in the white middle portion.

COMPLETE SET (27)	12.50	25.00
1 Troy Vincent	.80	2.00
2 Tim Krumrie	.50	1.25
3 Barry Alvarez CO	.60	1.50
4 Pat Richter	.50	1.25
5 Nate Odomes	.50	1.25
6 Ron Vander Kelen	.60	1.50
7 Don Davey	.50	1.25
8 Alan Ameche	.80	2.00
9 Randy Wright	.50	1.25
10 Ken Bowman	.40	1.00
11 Chuck Belin	.30	.75
12 Elroy Hirsch	1.00	2.50
13 Paul Gruber	.50	1.25
14 Al Toon	.60	1.50
15 Richard Johnson	.40	1.00
16 Pat Harder	.40	1.00
17 Gary Casper	.30	.75
18 Rufus Ferguson	.30	.75
19 Pat O'Donahue	.30	.75
20 Dennis Lick	.30	.75
21 Jeff Dellenbach	.40	1.00
22 Jim Bakken	.40	1.00
23 Milt Bruhn CO	.30	.75
24 Mike Webster	1.00	2.50
25 Dave McClain CO	.30	.75
26 Bill Marek	.30	.75
27 Rick Graf	.30	.75

1993 Wisconsin Milwaukee Journal

The "cards" were actually printed in the Milwaukee Journal newspaper and intended to be cut out and folded to form a standard sized trading card.

COMPLETE SET (18)	7.50	15.00
1 Barry Alvarez CO	.50	1.25
2 Darrell Bevell	.40	1.00
3 Yusef Burgess	.40	1.00
4 J.C. Dawkins	.40	1.00
5 Lee DeRamus	.40	1.00
6 Terrell Fletcher	.50	1.25
7 Reggie Holt	.40	1.00
8 Jeff Messenger	.40	1.00
9 Mark Montgomery FB	.40	1.00
10 Brent Moss	.40	1.00
11 Scott Nelson	.40	1.00
12 Joe Panos	.40	1.00
13 Cory Raymer	.50	1.25
14 Michael Roan	.40	1.00
15 Joe Rudolph	.40	1.00
16 Rick Schnetzky	.40	1.00
17 Lamar Shackerford	.40	1.00
18 Mike Thompson	.40	1.00

2003 Wisconsin

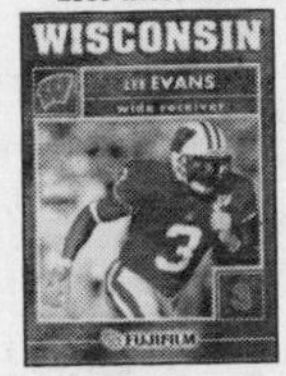

This set was released by the school and originally issued as a perforated sheet with each card measuring standard size when separated. The cards feature red borders with the school name above the player photo and the sponsor logo (Fujifilm) below. The cardbacks feature black and red printing on white stock with a card number near the bottom.

COMPLETE SET (28)	7.50	15.00
1 Jim Leonhard	.30	.75
2 Jonathan Orr	.30	.75
3 Jonathan Welsh	.20	.50
4 Morgan Davis	.20	.50
5 Erasmus James	.50	1.25
6 Mike Allen	.20	.50
7 Donovan Raiola	.20	.50
8 Kyle McCorison	.20	.50
9 Jeff Mack	.20	.50
10 Matt Bernstein	.20	.50
11 Mike Lorenz	.20	.50
12 Alex Lewis	.50	1.25
13 Barry Alvarez CO	.20	.50
14 Darrin Charles	.20	.50
15 Jonathan Clinkscale	.20	.50
16 Jason Jefferson	.20	.50
17 Anthony Davis	1.00	2.50
18 Scott Starks	.20	.50
19 Darius Jones	.20	.50
20 Dan Buenning	.30	.75
21 Anttaj Hawthorne	.50	1.25
22 Brett Bell	.20	.50
23 Brandon Williams	.30	.75
24 Jim Sorgi	.75	2.00
25 Ryan Aiello	.30	.75
26 LaMarr Watkins	.20	.50
27 Dwayne Smith	.30	.75
28 Lee Evans	1.50	4.00

2004 Wisconsin

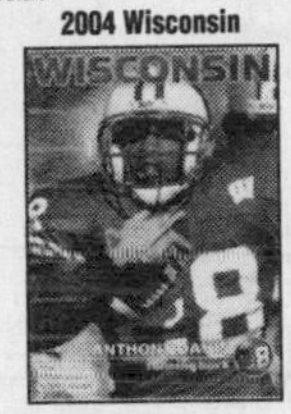

This set was released by the university book store and produced by Litho Productions. Each card measures standard size and is borderless. The school name appears above the player photo and his name below. The cardbacks feature black and red printing on a gray background with a card number near the bottom.

COMPLETE SET (24)	6.00	12.00
1 Barry Alvarez CO	.20	.50
2 Anthony Davis	.75	2.00
3 Morgan Davis	.20	.50
4 Jason Jefferson	.20	.50
5 Mike Allen	.20	.50
6 Dan Buenning	.30	.75
7 Brandon Williams	.30	.75
8 Matt Bernstein	.20	.50
9 John Stocco	.30	.75
10 R.J. Morse	.20	.50
11 Jonathan Welsh	.20	.50
12 Levonne Rowan	.20	.50
13 Darrin Charles	.20	.50
14 Tony Paciotti	.20	.50
15 Donovan Raiola	.20	.50
16 Anttaj Hawthorne	.50	1.25
17 Jonathan Orr	.20	.50
18 Jonathan Clinkscale	.20	.50
19 Erasmus James	.50	1.25
20 Scott Starks	.20	.50
21 Mike Lorenz	.20	.50
22 Lamarr Watkins	.20	.50
23 Robert Brooks	.20	.50
24 Jim Leonhard	.30	.75

2005 Wisconsin

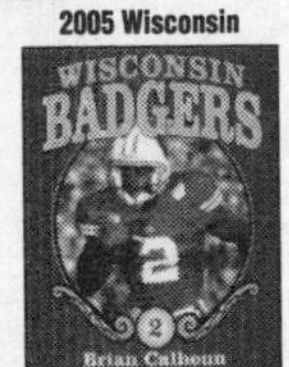

This set was released by the school with each borderless card measuring standard size. The school name appears above the player photo and his name below. The cardbacks feature black and red printing on a gray background with a card number near the bottom.

COMPLETE SET (24)	7.50	15.00
1 Jamal Cooper	.30	.75
2 Roderick Rogers	.30	.75
3 John Stocco	.60	1.50
4 Jason Pociask	.30	.75
5 Johnny White	.40	1.00
6 Mark Zalewski	.30	.75
7 Matt Lawrence	.30	.75
8 Jason Palermo	.30	.75
9 Andy Crooks	.30	.75
10 Ken DeBauche	.30	.75
11 Brandon Williams	.40	1.00
12 Brian Calhoun	1.00	2.50
13 Levonne Rowan	.30	.75
14 Joe Monty	.30	.75
15 Brandon White	.30	.75
16 Booker Stanley	.30	.75
17 Justin Ostrowski	.30	.75
18 Brett Bell	.30	.75
19 Donovan Raiola	.30	.75
20 Matt Bernstein	.30	.75
21 Joe Thomas	.30	.75

22 Jonathan Orr	.60	1.50
23 Owen Daniels	.60	1.50
24 Barry Alvarez CO	.40	1.00

2006 Wisconsin

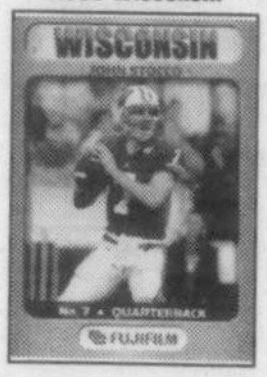

This set was released by the school in perforated strips of 4-cards. Each card measures standard size and includes a gray border on the front with the school name above the photo and a U.S. Cellular sponsorship logo below. The unumbered cardbacks feature black and red printing on a gray background along with a small photo of the featured player.

COMPLETE SET (28)	7.50	15.00
1 Bret Bielema CO	.30	.75
2 Jonathan Casillas	.30	.75
3 Jason Chapman	.30	.75
4 Marcus Coleman	.30	.75
5 Jamal Cooper	.30	.75
6 Ken DeBauche	.30	.75
7 Zach Hampton	.30	.75
8 Nick Hayden	.30	.75
9 P.J. Hill	1.00	2.50
10 Paul Hubbard	.40	1.00
11 Jack Ikegwuonu	.40	1.00
12 Andy Kemp	.30	.75
13 Allen Langford	.30	.75
14 DeAndre Levy	.30	.75
15 Taylor Mehlhaff	.30	.75
16 Jarvis Minton	.40	1.00
17 Joe Monty	.30	.75
18 Justin Ostrowski	.30	.75
19 Chris Pressley	.30	.75
20 Roderick Rogers	.30	.75
21 Matt Shaughnessy	.30	.75
22 Joe Stellmacher	.30	.75
23 John Stocco	.40	1.00
24 Joe Thomas	.75	2.00
25 Kraig Urbik	.30	.75
26 Eric Vanden Heuvel	.30	.75
27 Johnny White	.40	1.00
28 Mark Zalewski	.30	.75

2008 Wisconsin

This set was released by the school in perforated strips of 4-cards. Each card measures standard size and includes a full-bleed photo on the front with the player's name in the upper left corner, A Coca-Cola sponsorship logo is also on the cardfronts The unumbered cardbacks feature black and red printing on a gray background along with a small photo of the featured player.

COMPLETE SET (28)	7.50	15.00
1 Travis Beckum	.50	1.25
2 Bret Bielema	.30	.75
3 Zach Brown	.30	.75
4 Gabe Carimi	.30	.75
5 Shane Carter	.30	.75
6 Jonathan Casillas	.30	.75
7 Jason Chapman	.30	.75
8 Kirk DeCremer	.30	.75
9 Allan Evridge	.40	1.00
10 David Gilreath	.30	.75
11 Garrett Graham	.30	.75
12 Aaron Henry	.30	.75
13 P.J. Hill	.50	1.25
14 Elijah Hodge	.30	.75
15 Kyle Jefferson	.30	.75
16 Andy Kemp	.30	.75
17 Allen Langford	.30	.75
18 DeAndre Levy	.30	.75
19 John Moffitt	.30	.75
20 Mike Newkirk	.30	.75
21 Chris Pressley	.30	.75
22 Bill Rentmeester	.30	.75
23 O'Brien Schofield	.30	.75
24 Matt Shaughnessy	.30	.75
25 Culmer St.Jean	.30	.75
26 Kraig Urbik	.30	.75
27 Jay Valai	.30	.75
28 Eric Vanden Heuvel	.30	.75

2009 Wisconsin

This set was released by the school in perforated strips of 4-cards. Each card measures standard size and includes a color photo on the front with the player's name in the upper left corner along with the school's logo.

COMPLETE SET (27)	6.00	15.00
1 Isaac Anderson	.30	.75
2 Bret Bielema	.30	.75
3 Zach Brown	.30	.75
4 Gabe Carimi	.30	.75
5 John Clay	.30	.75
6 David Gilreath	.30	.75
7 Garrett Graham	.50	1.25
8 Aaron Henry	.30	.75
9 Kyle Jefferson	.30	.75
10 Lance Kendricks	.30	.75
11 Chris Maragos	.30	.75
12 Jaevery McFadden	.30	.75
13 John Moffitt	.30	.75
14 Dan Moore	.30	.75
15 Brad Nortman	.30	.75
16 Josh Oglesby	.30	.75
17 Curt Phillips	.30	.75
18 O'Brien Schofield	.30	.75
19 Dustin Sherer	.30	.75
20 Devin Smith	.30	.75
21 Blake Sorensen	.30	.75
22 Culmer St. Jean	.30	.75
23 Jeff Stehle	.30	.75
24 Nick Toon	.30	.75
25 Jay Valai	.30	.75
26 J.J. Watt	.30	.75
27 Philip Welch	.30	.75

2010 Wisconsin

This set was released by the school in perforated strips of 4-cards. Each card measures standard size and includes a full-bleed photo on the front with the player's name ibelow the photo and the school's name on the right side. The unumbered cardbacks feature black and red printing on a gray background along with a small black and white photo of the featured player.

COMPLETE SET (28)	10.00	20.00
1 Isaac Anderson	.30	.75
2 Montee Ball	.30	.75
3 Bret Bielema	.30	.75
4 Chris Borland	.30	.75
5 Niles Brinkley	.30	.75
6 Zach Brown	.30	.75
7 Patrick Butrym	.30	.75
8 Gabe Carimi	.30	.75
9 John Clay	.30	.75
10 Antonio Fenelus	.30	.75
11 David Gilreath	.30	.75
12 Aaron Henry	.30	.75
13 Lance Kendricks	.30	.75
14 Peter Konz	.30	.75
15 John Moffitt	.30	.75
16 Brad Nortman	.30	.75
17 Louis Nzegwu	.30	.75
18 Josh Oglesby	.30	.75
19 Devin Smith	.30	.75
20 Blake Sorensen	.30	.75
21 Culmer St. Jean	.30	.75
22 Mike Taylor	.30	.75
23 Scott Tolzien	.30	.75
24 Nick Toon	.30	.75
25 Jay Valai	.30	.75
26 J.J. Watt	.30	.75
27 Philip Welch	.30	.75
28 Kevin Zeitler	.30	.75

1989 Wyoming Leesley

COMPLETE SET (90)	25.00	50.00
1 Richard Sauls	.30	.75
2 Jim Scifres	.30	.75
3 Craig Schlichting	.30	.75
4 Rick Donnelly	.30	.75
5 Anthony Sargent	.30	.75
6 Joe Wahlgren	.30	.75
7 Mitch Donahue	.30	.75
8 Sean Fleming	.30	.75
9 Paul Toscano	.30	.75
10 Jack Weil	.30	.75
11 Jay Novacek	1.50	4.00
12 Galand Thaxton	.30	.75
13 Darrell Perkins	.30	.75
14 Willie Wright	.30	.75
15 Peter Gunn	.30	.75
16 Gordy Wood	.30	.75
17 Steve Slay	.30	.75
18 Steve Addison	.30	.75
19 Melvin Wells	.30	.75
20 Paul Wallace	.30	.75
21 Doug Rigby	.30	.75
22 Matt O'Brien	.30	.75
23 Tom Kramer	.30	.75
24 Dwaine Jones	.30	.75
25 Darryl Harris	.30	.75
26 Shawn Dostal	.30	.75
27 Ted Gilmore	.30	.75
28 Pete Gosar	.30	.75
29 Vaughn Henderson	.30	.75
30 Eric Worden	.30	.75
31 Quenton Skinner	.30	.75
32 Jeff Leick	.30	.75
33 Shawn Wiggins	.30	.75
34 Mitch Rosebrough	.30	.75
35 Pete Rowe	.30	.75
36 Brady Jacobson	.30	.75
37 Tyrone Fittje	.30	.75
38 Bobby Fresques	.30	.75
39 George Dozier	.30	.75
40 Dan Cudworth	.30	.75
41 Jeff Chadiha	.30	.75
42 Tom Corontzos	.30	.75
43 Carl Bruere	.30	.75
44 Kevin Lowe	.30	.75
45 Steve Bena	.30	.75
46 Scott Gibson	.30	.75
47 Mark Foos	.30	.75
48 Robert Midgett	.30	.75
49 Mark Timmer	.30	.75
50 Craig Burnett	.30	.75
51 Bill Hoffman	.30	.75
52 Ron Dean	.30	.75
53 Gerald Abraham	.30	.75
54 Steve Martinez	.30	.75
55 Phil Davis	.30	.75
56 Vic Washington	.50	1.25
57 Cowboy Joe III (Mascot)	.30	.75
58 Bowden Wyatt CO	.30	.75
59 Lloyd Eaton CO	.30	.75
60 Phil Dickens CO	.30	.75
61 Bob Devaney CO	.30	.75
62 Scott Downing CO	.30	.75
63 Mark Tommerdahl CO	.30	.75
64 Gregg Brandon CO	.30	.75
65 Bill Cockreham CO	.30	.75
66 Dave Butterfield CO	.30	.75
67 Del Wight CO	.30	.75
68 Tom Everson CO	.30	.75
69 Tom Lovat CO	.30	.75
70 Paul Swenson CO	.30	.75
71 War Memorial Stadium	.30	.75
72 1988 Holiday Bowl	.30	.75
73 Wac Championship	.30	.75
74 1987 Holiday Bowl	.30	.75
75 Randy Welniak	.30	.75
76 Paul Roach CO	.30	.75
77 Eddie Talboom	.30	.75
78 Dewey McConnell	.30	.75
79 Jim Crawford	.30	.75
80 Jim Walden	.30	.75
81 Mike Dirks	.30	.75
82 Jerry Depoyster	.30	.75
83 Bob Jacobs	.30	.75
84 Steve Cockreham	.30	.75
85 Dennis Baker	.30	.75
86 Ken Fantetti	.30	.75
87 Pat Rabold	.30	.75
88 Dabby Dawson	.30	.75
89 Dabby Dawson	.30	.75
90 Greg Brown	.30	.75

1990 Wyoming Smokey

The 1990 Wyoming Cowboys Smokey set was issued in a sheet of 16 cards which, when perforated, measure the standard size. The fronts feature color photos with the player's name, position, and jersey number below the picture. The backs have biographical information and a fire prevention cartoon starring Smokey. The cards are unnumbered, so they are listed below in alphabetical order by subject.

COMPLETE SET (16)	8.00	20.00
1 Tom Corontzos 18	.60	1.50
2 Jay Daffer 34	.60	1.50
3 Mitch Donahue 49	.60	1.50
4 Sean Fleming 42	.60	1.50
5 Pete Gosar 53	.60	1.50
6 Robert Midgett 57	.60	1.50
7 Bryan Mooney 9	.60	1.50
8 Doug Rigby 77	.60	1.50
9 Paul Roach CO	.80	2.00
10 Mark Timmer 48	.60	1.50
11 Paul Wallace 29	.60	1.50
12 Shawn Wiggins 15	.60	1.50
13 Gordy Wood 95	.60	1.50
14 Willie Wright 96	.60	1.50
15 Cowboy Joe Mascot	.60	1.50
16 Title Card Cowboy logo	.60	1.50

1993 Wyoming Smokey

These 16 standard-size cards feature on their fronts color player action shots set within yellow borders. The player's name and position appear on the left side beneath the photo; the team name and logo appear above the photo. The plain white back carries the player's name and position at the top, followed by a Smokey safety tip, and the player's career highlights. The cards are unnumbered and checklisted below in alphabetical order.

COMPLETE SET (16)	4.00	10.00
1 John Burrough	.30	.75
2 Wade Constance	.30	.75
3 Mike Fitzgerald	.30	.75
4 Jarrod Heidmann	.30	.75
5 Joe Hughes	.30	.75
6 Kenny Johnson	.40	1.00
7 Mike Jones	.40	1.00
8 Cody Kelly	.30	.75
9 Rob Levin	.30	.75
10 Prentice Rhone	.30	.75
11 Greg Scanlan	.40	1.00
12 Cory Talich	.30	.75
13 Kurt Whitehead	.30	.75
14 Thomas Williams	.30	.75
15 Tyrone Williams	.30	.75
16 Ryan Yarborough	1.00	2.50

1995 Wyoming

COMPLETE SET (16)	5.00	10.00
1 Jason Bartlett	.30	.75
2 Ken Boris	.30	.75
3 Mark Brook	.30	.75
4 Joe Cummings	.30	.75
5 Jeremy Gilstrap	.30	.75
6 Brian Gragert	.30	.75
7 Marcus Harris	.30	.75
8 Jason Holanda	.30	.75
9 Patrick Larson	.30	.75
10 Steve Scifres	.30	.75
11 Jim Talich	.30	.75
12 Brent Tillman	.30	.75
13 Lee Vaughn	.30	.75
14 Josh Wallwork	.30	.75
15 Aaron Wilson	.30	.75
16 Cover Card	.30	.75

1996 Wyoming

COMPLETE SET (8)	3.00	6.00
1 Marcus Harris	.30	.75
2 Jay Jenkins	.30	.75
3 Brent Leu	.30	.75
4 Waymon Levingston	.30	.75
5 Steve Scifres Jay Korth	.30	.75
6 Len Sexton	.30	.75
7 Lee Vaughn	.30	.75
8 Cory Wedel	.30	.75

2004 Wyoming

COMPLETE SET (30)	7.50	15.00
1 Josh Barge	.30	.75
2 Jacob Bonde	.30	.75
3 Jovon Bouknight	.30	.75
4 Corey Bramlet	.40	1.00
5 Terrance Butler	.30	.75
6 Chris Cox	.30	.75
7 C.R. Davis	.30	.75
8 John Flora	.30	.75
9 Trenton Franz	.30	.75
10 Kevin Fulton	.30	.75
11 Austin Hall	.30	.75
12 Ivan Harrison	.30	.75
13 Chase Johnson	.30	.75
14 Jason Karcher	.30	.75
15 Derrick Martin	.30	.75
16 Jay McNeal	.30	.75
17 Zach Morris	.30	.75
18 John Prater	.30	.75
19 Aaron Robbins	.30	.75
20 Marcial Rosales	.30	.75
21 Drew Severn	.30	.75
22 Jeff Tatnall	.30	.75
23 Randy Tscharner	.30	.75
24 Guy Tuell	.30	.75
25 John Wendling	.30	.75
26 Deric Yaussi	.40	1.00
27 Joe Glenn CO	.30	.75
28 Team Mascot	.30	.75
29 Cover Card	.30	.75
30 Cover Card	.30	.75

2005 Wyoming

COMPLETE SET (6)	4.00	8.00
1 Jovon Bouknight	.60	1.50
2 Corey Bramlet	.60	1.50
3 Dusty Hoffschneider	.60	1.50
4 Derrick Martin	.60	1.50
5 John Wendling	.60	1.50
6 Deric Yaussi	.75	2.00

1909 Yale Postcards

These postcards were issued in 1909 and feature members of the Yale football team. The fronts include a large black and white image of the player with his name, position, and school identified below the photo. The backs featue a standard "private mailing card" style design with the publisher's name: B. B. Steiber.

COMPLETE SET (14)	300.00	500.00
1 Ham Andrus	30.00	50.00
2 Biddle	30.00	50.00
3 Bob Burch	30.00	50.00
4 Art Brides	30.00	50.00
5 Carrol Cooney	30.00	50.00
6 Ted Coy	30.00	50.00
7 Bill Goebel	30.00	50.00
8 Haines	30.00	50.00
9 Henry Hobbs	30.00	50.00
10 Tad Jones CO	30.00	50.00
11 Reed Kilpatrick	30.00	50.00
12 W.S. Logan	30.00	50.00
13 Steve Philbin	30.00	50.00
14 Wheaton	30.00	50.00

2002 Yale Greats

This set was produced for and sold by the Yale Athletic Dept. The cards were printed in blue ink on white paper and feature a heavy laminate coating. The set features great Yale football players from the past 100+ years of the program.

COMPLETE SET (36)	15.00	25.00
1 Malcolm Aldrich	.30	.75
2 Doug Bomeisler	.30	.75
3 Albie Booth	.30	.75
4 Gordon Brown	.30	.75
5 Walter Camp	.40	1.00
6 Pa Corbin	.30	.75
7 Ted Coy	.30	.75
8 Carm Cozza CO	.30	.75
9 Brian Dowling	.30	.75
10 Gary Fencik	.30	.75
11 Clint Frank	.30	.75
12 Pudge Heffelfinger	.40	1.00
13 William Hickok	.30	.75
14 Calvin Hill	.40	1.00
15 Frank Hinkey	.40	1.00
16 Jim Hogan	.30	.75
17 Art Howe	.30	.75
18 Levi Jackson	.40	1.00
19 Dick Jauron	.40	1.00
20 Howard Jones Tad Jones	.30	.75
21 Larry Kelley	.30	.75
22 Henry Ketcham	.30	.75
23 John Reed Kilpatrick	.30	.75
24 William Mallory	.30	.75
25 Thomas McClung	.30	.75
26 Century Milstead	.30	.75
27 Mike Pyle	.30	.75
28 Tom Shevlin	.30	.75
29 Amos Alonzo Stagg	.60	1.50
30 Mal Stevens	.30	.75
31 Herbert Sturhahn	.30	.75
32 Brinck Thorne	.30	.75
33 George Woodruff	.30	.75
34 Yale's First Team	.30	.75
35 Yale's Greatest Team	.30	.75
36 Yale Logo Checklist	.30	.75

1992 Youngstown State

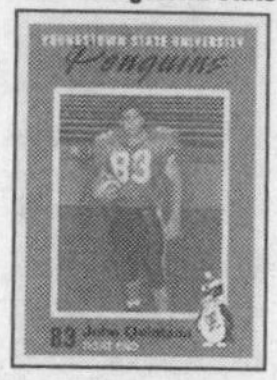

These 54 standard-size cards feature on their fronts posed black-and-white player photos set within red borders. The player's name, position, and jersey number appear beneath the photo. The gray-bordered back carries the player's name, position, uniform number and biography at the top, followed by the player's career highlights. The cards are unnumbered and checklisted below in alphabetical order.

COMPLETE SET (54)	10.00	20.00
1 Ramon Amill	.20	.50
2 Dan Black	.20	.50
3 Trent Boykin	.20	.50
4 Reginald Brown	.20	.50
5 Mark Brungard	.30	.75
6 Larry Bucciarelli	.20	.50
7 David Burch	.20	.50
8 Nick Cochran	.20	.50
9 Brian Coman	.20	.50
10 Ken Conatser ACO	.20	.50
11 Darnell Clark	.30	.75
12 Dave DelBoccio	.20	.50
13 Tom Dillingham	.20	.50
14 John Englehardt	.20	.50
15 Marcus Evans	.20	.50
16 Malcolm Everette	.20	.50
17 Drew Gerber	.20	.50
18 Michael Ghent	.20	.50
19 Aaron Green	.20	.50
20 Jon Heacock ACO	.20	.50
21 Alfred Hill	.20	.50
22 Terica Jones	.20	.50
23 Craig Kertesz	.20	.50
24 Paul Kokos Jr.	.20	.50
25 Reginald Lee	.20	.50
26 Raymond Miller	.20	.50
27 Brian Moore ACO	.20	.50
28 Mike Nezbeth	.20	.50
29 William Norris	.20	.50
30 James Panozzo	.20	.50
31 Derek Pixley	.20	.50
32 Jeff Powers	.20	.50
33 David Quick	.20	.50
34 John Quintana	.20	.50
35 Mike Rekstis	.20	.50
36 Demario Ridgeway	.20	.50
37 Dave Roberts	.20	.50
38 Chris Sammarone	.20	.50
39 Randy Smith	.20	.50
40 Tamron Smith	.20	.50
41 John Steele	.20	.50
42 Jim Tressel CO	.80	2.00
43 Chris Vecchione	.20	.50
44 Lester Weaver	.20	.50
45 Jeff Wilkins	.50	1.25
46 Herb Williams	.20	.50
47 Ryan Wood	.20	.50
48 Don Zwisler	.20	.50
49 Penguin Pros Card 1	.20	.50
50 Penguin Pros Card 2	.20	.50
51 First-Team All-American	.20	.50
52 Did You Know 1	.20	.50
53 Did You Know 2	.20	.50
54 Did You Know 3	.20	.50

1998 Youngstown State

COMPLETE SET (11)	4.00	8.00
1 Jake Anderson	.30	.75
2 Jake Andreadis	.30	.75
3 Eric Brown	.30	.75
4 Jarritt Goode	.30	.75
5 Jack Crews	.30	.75
6 Chris Jones	.30	.75
7 Matt Panigutti	.30	.75
8 Tony Pannunzio	.30	.75
9 Matt Richardson	.30	.75
10 Mike Stanec	.30	.75
11 Jim Tressel CO	.40	1.00

2000 Youngstown State

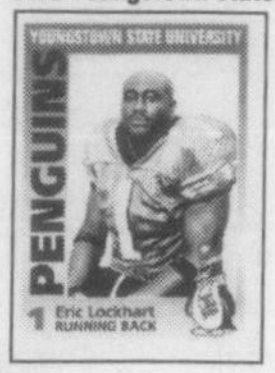

COMPLETE SET (14)	5.00	10.00
1 Ed Blizzard	.30	.75
2 Bryan Hawthorne	.30	.75
3 Tim Johnson	.30	.75
4 Troy LeFever	.30	.75
5 Eric Lockhart	.30	.75
6 Robert McGinty	.30	.75
7 Fon Nanji	.30	.75
8 Jason Paris	.30	.75
9 Steve Rovnak	.30	.75
10 Luke Schumacher	.30	.75
11 Montrial Thomas	.30	.75
12 Denver Williams	.30	.75
13 Jim Tressel CO	.40	1.00
14 Team Mascots	.30	.75

2003 Youngstown State

COMPLETE SET (15)	5.00	10.00
1 Mike Burns	.30	.75
2 Josh Davis	.30	.75
3 Justin Dellarose	.30	.75
4 Chris DiMauro	.30	.75
5 Josiah Doby	.30	.75
6 Steve Durbin	.30	.75
7 Luis Gonzalez	.30	.75
8 Sherod Holmes	.30	.75
9 Keland Logan	.30	.75
10 Waymann Peters	.30	.75
11 Darius Peterson	.30	.75
12 Will Sanders	.30	.75
13 Scott Thiessen	.30	.75
14 Jon Heacock CO	.30	.75
15 Team Mascots	.30	.75

Canadian

1991 All World CFL

The premier edition of the 1991 All World Canadian Football set contains of 110 standard-size cards. The cards were produced in both set and foil cases, and in both English and French versions. This set includes legends of the CFL (designated below by LEG) and an eight-card "Rocket" subset. In addition, 2,000 personally signed Rocket Ismail cards were randomly inserted in the packs: 1600 in the English foil cases and 400 in the French foil cases. The cards are numbered from 1-1600 in the English and 1-400 in the French. The front design has high gloss color action photos trimmed in red, on a royal blue background with diagonal white pinstripes. The player's name appears in red lettering in the lower left corner, and the CFL helmet logo is in the lower right corner. The backs are horizontally oriented and have royal blue borders. While the veteran player cards have head and shoulders color shots and player information on the backs, the rookie, coach, All Star, "Rocket," and legend cards omit the picture and have personal information framed by red borders. The following cards are designated as "Rookie" on the card front: 4, 16, 28, 33, 53, 63, 66, 68, 78, 84, 92, 101, and 110. The premium for the French version is very slight, just ten percent above the prices listed below. A Rocket Ismail promo card was released and is priced below.

COMPLETE SET (110)	1.20	3.00
1 Rocket Ismail	.08	.25
2 Bruce McNall Owner	.02	.04
3 Ray Alexander	.03	.08
4 Matt Clark	.05	.15
5 Bobby Jurasin	.08	.25
6 Dieter Brock LEG	.05	.15
7 Doug Flutie	.50	1.25
8 Stewart Hill	.03	.08
9 James Mills	.05	.15
10 Raghib(Rocket) Ismail (With Bruce McNall)	.08	.25
11 Tom Clements LEG	.05	.15
12 Lui Passaglia	.05	.15
13 Ian Sinclair	.03	.08
14 Chris Skinner	.03	.08
15 Joe Theismann LEG	.05	.15
16 Jon Volpe	.20	.50
17 Deatrich Wise	.02	.04
18 Danny Barrett	.05	.15
19 Warren Moon LEG	.08	.25
20 Leo Blanchard	.02	.04
21 Derrick Crawford	.03	.08
22 Lloyd Fairbanks	.02	.04
23 David Beckman CO	.02	.04
24 Matt Finlay	.02	.04
25 Darryl Hall	.03	.08
26 Ron Hopkins	.02	.04
27 Wally Buono CO	.02	.04
28 Kenton Leonard	.03	.08
29 Brent Matich	.02	.04
30 Greg Peterson	.02	.04
31 Steve Goldman CO	.02	.04
32 Allen Pitts	.25	.60
33 Rocket Ismail	.08	.25
34 Danny Bass	.05	.15
35 John Gregory CO	.02	.04
36 Rod Connop	.02	.04
37 Craig Ellis	.03	.08
38 Rocket Ismail	.08	.25
39 Ron Lancaster CO	.05	.15
40 Tracy Ham	.15	.40
41 Ray Macoritti	.02	.04
42 Willie Pless	.08	.25
43 Bob O'Billovich CO	.02	.04
44 Michael Soles	.03	.08
45 Reggie Taylor	.03	.08
46 Gizmo Williams	.10	.30
47 Adam Rita CO	.02	.04
48 Larry Wruck	.03	.08
49 Grover Covington	.05	.15
50 Rocky DiPietro	.05	.15
51 Darryl Rogers CO	.02	.04
52 Peter Giftopoulus	.03	.08
53 Herman Heard	.03	.08
54 Mike Kerrigan	.08	.25
55 Reggie Barnes AS	.03	.08
56 Derrick McAdoo	.03	.08
57 Paul Osbaldiston	.03	.08
58 Earl Winfield	.05	.15
59 Greg Battle AS	.03	.08
60 Damon Allen	.15	.40
61 Reggie Barnes	.05	.15
62 Bob Molle	.02	.04
63 Rocket Ismail	.08	.25
64 Irv Daymond	.02	.04
65 Andre Francis	.02	.04
66 Bart Hull	.03	.08
67 Stephen Jones	.05	.15
68 Rocket Ismail	.08	.25
69 Glenn Kulka	.02	.04
70 Loyd Lewis	.02	.04
71 Rob Smith	.02	.04
72 Roger Aldag	.03	.08
73 Kent Austin	.08	.25
74 Ray Elgaard	.08	.25
75 Mike Clemons AS	.20	.50
76 Jeff Fairholm	.05	.15
77 Richie Hall	.02	.04
78 Willis Jacox	.05	.15
79 Eddie Lowe	.02	.04
80 Ray Elgaard AS	.03	.08
81 Donald Narcisse	.15	.40
82 James Mills AS	.03	.08
83 Dave Ridgway	.05	.15
84 Ted Wahl	.03	.08
85 Carl Brazley	.03	.08
86 Mike Clemons	.30	.75
87 Matt Dunigan	.10	.30
88 Grey Cup Checklist 1	.02	.04
89 Harold Hallman	.03	.08
90 Rodney Harding	.02	.04
91 Don Moen	.03	.08
92 Rocket Ismail	.08	.25
93 Reggie Pleasant	.03	.08
94 Darrell Smith UER (One L on front& two on back)	.05	.15
95 Group Shot Checklist 2	.02	.04
96 Chris Schultz	.03	.08
97 Don Wilson	.02	.04
98 Greg Battle	.05	.15
99 Lyle Bauer	.02	.04
100 Less Browne	.03	.08
101 Rocket Ismail	.08	.25
102 Tom Burgess	.05	.15
103 Mike Gray	.02	.04
104 Rod Hill	.02	.04
105 Warren Hudson	.03	.08
106 Tyrone Jones	.03	.08
107 Stan Mikawos	.02	.04
108 Robert Mimbs	.07	.20
109 James West	.05	.15
110 Rocket Ismail	.08	.25
NNO Rocket Ismail AUTO (numbered of 1600)	16.00	40.00
P1 Rocket Ismail Promo (numbered P)	.40	1.00

1991 All World CFL French

COMPLETE SET (110)	5.00	10.00
*FRENCH CARDS: 1.2X TO 3X		
NNO Rocket Ismail AUTO (numbered of 400)	20.00	40.00

1992 All World CFL

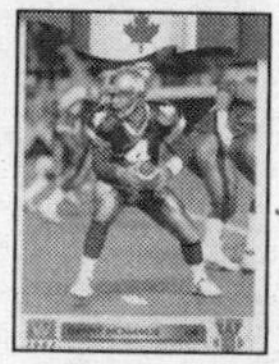

The 1992 All World CFL set consists of 180 standard-size cards. The reported production run was 4000 individually numbered foil cases and 8000 numbered factory sets. Foil embossed maple leaf cards and (reportedly) 1000 autographed Doug Flutie cards were randomly inserted into foil packs. It is thought that Flutie did not sign all 1000-cards since a number of them can be found unsigned. Special subsets focus on Rookies (eight cards), Trophy Winners (12 cards), Road to the Cup (four cards), and Memorable Grey Cups (four cards). The color action player photos on the fronts are accented above by a Canadian flag that bleeds off the card top. The backs present statistics, another player photo, biography, and an import designation to indicate a player is non-Canadian. Two Promo cards were produced and are priced below.

COMPLETE SET (180)	8.00	20.00
1 Checklist 1-90	.01	.05
2 Draft Picks Checklist	.01	.05
3 Western Final	.01	.05
4 Eastern Final	.01	.05
5 79th Grey Cup	.01	.05
6 Grey Cup Most Outstanding Player Rocket Ismail	.07	.20
7 Memorable Grey Cups/1909	.01	.05
8 Memorable Grey Cups/1969	.01	.05
9 Memorable Grey Cups/1982	.01	.05
10 Memorable Grey Cups/1989	.01	.05
11 Jeff Braswell	.02	.10
12 Glenn Kulka	.02	.10
13 Will Johnson	.02	.10
14 Lance Chomyc	.01	.05
15 Stan Mikawos	.01	.05
16 Bobby Jurasin	.10	.30
17 Terry Baker	.02	.10
18 Tracy Ham	.25	.60
19 Todd Wiseman	.01	.05
20 Rob Crifo	.01	.05
21 Chris Morris	.02	.10
22 Jon Volpe	.20	.50

23 Donald Narcisse .10 .30
24 David Williams .07 .20
25 Paul Clatney .01 .05
26 Willie Pless .07 .20
27 Rickey Foggie .10 .30
28 Denny Chronopoulos .01 .05
29 Darryl Sampson .01 .05
30 Patrick Wayne .01 .05
31 Terrence Jones .07 .20
32 Larry Wruck .02 .10
33 Angelo Snipes .07 .20
34 Tony Champion .07 .20
35 Steve Taylor .07 .20
36 Lorne King .01 .05
37 Roger Aldag .02 .10
38 Damon Allen .15 .40
39 Chris Walby .07 .20
40 Doug Davies .01 .05
41 Dan Rashovich .01 .05
42 Mark Scott .01 .05
43 Reggie Pleasant .02 .10
44 Bob Cameron .07 .20
45 Danny McManus .20 .50
46 Matt Clark .07 .20
47 Bart Hull .02 .10
48 Hank Ilesic .07 .20
49 Pee Wee Smith .10 .30
50 Irv Daymond .01 .05
51 Greg Battle .07 .20
J.P. McCaffrey Trophy
52 Will Johnson .02 .10
Norm Fieldgate Trophy
53 Lance Chomyc .01 .05
Lew Hayman Trophy
54 Jim Mills .02 .10
DeMarco-Becket
Memorial Trophy
55 Jon Volpe .07 .20
Jackie Parker Trophy
56 Rocket Ismail .10 .30
Frank M. Gibson Trophy
57 Dave Ridgway .07 .20
David Dryburgh
Memorial Trophy
58 Chris Walby .07 .20
Leo Dandurand Trophy
59 Doug Flutie .80 2.00
Jeff Nicklin
Memorial Trophy
60 Robert Mimbs .15 .40
Jeff Russell
Memorial Trophy
61 Jon Volpe .07 .20
Eddie James
Memorial Trophy
62 Blake Marshall .02 .10
Dr. Beattie Martin Trophy
63 Eric Streater .02 .10
64 Carl Brazley .01 .05
65 Kent Warnock .02 .10
66 Brian Bonner .01 .05
67 Tom Burgess .07 .20
68 Bob Gordon .01 .05
69 Milson Jones .02 .10
70 Todd Dillon .02 .10
71 Keyvan Jenkins .07 .20
72 Ken Evraire .02 .10
73 Willis Jacox .02 .10
74 Carl Bland .01 .05
75 Daniel Hunter .01 .05
76 Chris Schultz .02 .10
77 Earl Winfield .07 .20
78 Gizmo Williams .30 .75
79 Matt Dunigan .20 .50
80 Mark McLoughlin .07 .20
81 Craig Ellis .02 .10
82 Rodney Harding .02 .10
83 Scott Douglas .01 .05
84 Ray Elgaard .10 .30
85 Doug Flutie 1.60 4.00
86 Gary Lewis .01 .05
87 Rod Hill .01 .05
88 Gregg Stumon .01 .05
89 Ray Alexander .02 .10
90 Blake Dermott .02 .10
91 Checklist 91-180 .01 .05
92 Trophy Winners CL .02 .10
93 British Columbia CL .01 .05
94 Calgary CL .01 .05
95 Edmonton CL .01 .05
96 Saskatchewan CL .01 .05
97 Hamilton CL .01 .05
98 Ottawa CL .01 .05
99 Toronto CL .01 .05
100 Winnipeg CL .01 .05
101 James West .07 .20
102 Jeff Fairholm .02 .10
103 Mike Campbell .02 .10
104 Darren Flutie 1.00 2.50
105 Blake Marshall .07 .20
106 Loyd Lewis .01 .05
107 Enis Jackson .01 .05
108 John Motton .10 .30
109 Ken Walcott .01 .05
110 Richie Hall .01 .05
111 Greg Peterson .01 .05
112 Wally Zatylny .02 .10
113 Lui Passaglia .10 .30
114 Darryl Hall .01 .05
115 Michael Soles .02 .10
116 Doug Brewster .01 .05
117 Mike Gray .01 .05
118 Mike Trevathan .07 .20
119 Don Moen .02 .10
120 Chris Armstrong .10 .30
121 Lucius Floyd .07 .20
122 Ken Pettway .01 .05
123 Anthony Drawhorn .02 .10
124 Brian Walling .07 .20
125 Troy Westwood .07 .20
126 Reggie Barnes .07 .20
127 Rocket Ismail .20 .50
128 Rod Connop .01 .05
129 Chris Major .07 .20
130 Dave Bovell .01 .05
131 Quency Williams .01 .05
132 Michel Bourgeau .01 .05
133 Harold Hallman .02 .10
134 Junior Thurman .07 .20
135 Stewart Hill .02 .10
136 Brent Matich .01 .05
137 Leroy Blugh .02 .10
138 Nick Mazzoli .01 .05
139 Dave Ridgway .07 .20
140 Matt Finlay .01 .05
141 Mike Clemons .60 1.50
142 Jason Riley .01 .05
143 Stacey Hairston .01 .05
144 Jim Mills .02 .10
145 Paul Randolph .01 .05
146 David Sapunjis .10 .30
147 Charles Gordon .01 .05
148 Chris Tsangaris .01 .05
149 Darrell K. Smith .07 .20
150 Leo Groenewegen .01 .05
151 Greg Battle .07 .20
152 Bruce Covernton .08 .25
153 Paul Osbaldiston .02 .10
154 Don Wilson .01 .05
155 Kent Austin .10 .30
156 Jamie Morris .07 .20
157 Andre Francis .02 .10
158 O.J. Brigance .10 .30
159 Less Browne .02 .10
160 Alondra Johnson .02 .10
161 Dexter Manley .02 .10
162 Bob Poley .01 .05
163 Ed Berry .01 .05
164 Peter Giftopoulus .02 .10
165 Glen Suitor .02 .10
166 Eddie Thomas .01 .05
167 Danny Barrett .07 .20
168 Robert Mimbs .10 .30
169 Jim Sandusky .07 .20
170 Maurice Smith .01 .05
171 David Conrad .01 .05
172 Larry Willis .02 .10
173 Ian Sinclair .02 .10
174 Allen Pitts .20 .50
175 Don McPherson .07 .20
176 Ray Bernard .01 .05
177 Dale Sanderson .01 .05
178 Dan Ferrone .02 .10
179 Vic Stevenson .01 .05
180 Rob Smith .01 .05
A Doug Flutie AUTO/1000 30.00 60.00
A Doug Flutie Unsigned 4.00 10.00
P1 Doug Flutie Promo .80 2.00
(Numbered P)
P2 Rocket Ismail Promo .40 1.00
(Numbered P)

1992 All World CFL Foils

COMP.FOIL SET (180) 30.00 60.00
*FOIL CARDS: 1.2X TO 3X BASIC CARDS

1992 Arena Holograms CFL

Arena Trading Cards produced this Grey Cup Trophy hologram card. It was released at the 1992 Toronto Sky Dome card show.

1 Grey Cup Trophy 2.40 6.00

2003 Atomic CFL

COMPLETE SET (100) 20.00 40.00
1 Kelvin Anderson .75 2.00
2 Chris Brazzell .30 .75
3 Jason Clermont .75 2.00
4 Frank Cutolo .50 1.25
5 Dave Dickenson 1.00 2.50
6 Lyle Green .20 .50
7 Curtis Head .20 .50
8 Casey Printers 1.25 3.00
9 Geroy Simon .50 1.25
10 Herman Smith .20 .50
11 Mark Washington .30 .75
12 Spergon Wynn .30 .75
13 Andre Arlain .10 .30
14 Marcus Crandell .60 1.50
15 Blake Machan .30 .75
16 Saladin McCullough .20 .50
17 Darnell McDonald .20 .50
18 Wane McGarity .30 .75
19 Scott Milanovich .30 .75
20 Aries Monroe .30 .75
21 Lawrence Phillips .75 2.00
22 Latario Rachal .20 .50
23 Scott Regimbald .20 .50
24 Davis Sanchez .10 .30
25 Kojo Aidoo .20 .50
26 Kory Bailey .20 .50
27 Darrel Crutchfield .10 .30
28 Bart Hendricks .20 .50
29 Ed Hervey .30 .75
30 Troy Mills .20 .50
31 Winston October .50 1.25
32 Mike Pringle .75 2.00
33 Brock Ralph .20 .50
34 Ricky Ray 1.50 4.00
35 Jason Tucker .30 .75
36 Terry Vaughn .50 1.25
37 Tony Akins .20 .50
38 Archie Amerson .60 1.50
39 David Corley .20 .50
40 Troy Davis .30 .75
41 Tyree Davis .20 .50
42 Pete Gonzalez .20 .50
43 Danny McManus 1.00 2.50
44 Joe Montford .30 .75
45 Chad Plummer .20 .50
46 Julian Radlein .20 .50
47 Thyron Anderson .30 .75
48 Adrian Archie .20 .50
49 Ben Cahoon .50 1.25
50 Anthony Calvillo 1.00 2.50
51 Jermaine Copeland .50 1.25
52 D.J. Johnson .10 .30
53 Richard Karikari .10 .30
54 Eric Lapointe .20 .50
55 Dave Stala .30 .75
56 Keith Stokes .50 1.25
57 Demetris Bendross .20 .50
58 Darren Davis .60 1.50
59 D.J. Flick .20 .50
60 John Grace .30 .75
61 Reggie Jones .20 .50
62 Kerry Joseph .50 1.25
63 Andre Kirwan .20 .50
64 Mike Maurer .20 .50
65 Romaro Miller .30 .75
66 Denis Montana .20 .50
67 Ian Butler .30 .75
68 Matt Dominguez .20 .50
69 Corey Grant .20 .50
70 Nealon Greene .50 1.25
71 Corey Holmes .20 .50
72 Kenton Keith .75 2.00
73 Jason Mallett .10 .30
74 LaDouphyous McCalla .10 .30
75 Travis Moore .60 1.50
76 Brian Roberson .20 .50
77 Sedrick Shaw .30 .75
78 Chris Szarka .20 .50
79 Damon Allen .75 2.00
80 Marcus Brady .20 .50
81 Kevin Eiben .10 .30
82 Michael Jenkins .75 2.00
83 Lal Knight .20 .50
84 Bashir Levingston .40 1.00
85 Tony Miles .30 .75
86 Derrell Mitchell .50 1.25
87 Mike Morreale .30 .75
88 Michael Palmer .20 .50
89 Antonio Banks .10 .30
90 Geoff Drover .10 .30
91 Robert Gordon .30 .75
92 Markus Howell .20 .50
93 Khari Jones 1.00 2.50
94 Terry Ray .20 .50
95 Charles Roberts .40 1.00
96 Mike Sellers .20 .50
97 Brian Stallworth .75 2.00
98 Milt Stegall .75 2.00
99 Jamie Stoddard .20 .50
100 LaDaris Vann .20 .50

2003 Atomic CFL Gold

*SINGLES: 3X TO 8X BASIC CARDS
STATED ODDS 1:11
STATED PRINT RUN 175 SER. #'d SETS

2003 Atomic CFL Red

*SINGLES: 1.2X TO 3X BASIC CARDS

2003 Atomic CFL Core Players

COMPLETE SET (6) 15.00 30.00
STATED ODDS 1:33
1 Dave Dickenson 3.00 8.00
2 Ricky Ray 4.00 10.00
3 Danny McManus 3.00 8.00
4 Anthony Calvillo 3.00 8.00
5 Damon Allen 2.50 6.00
6 Khari Jones 2.50 6.00

2003 Atomic CFL Friday Knights

COMPLETE SET (10) 20.00 40.00
STATED ODDS 1:17
1 Dave Dickenson 2.50 6.00
2 Lawrence Phillips 2.00 5.00
3 Ricky Ray 3.00 8.00
4 Terry Vaughn 1.25 3.00
5 Danny McManus 2.50 6.00
6 Anthony Calvillo 2.50 6.00
7 Darren Davis 1.50 4.00
8 Nealon Greene 1.25 3.00
9 Khari Jones 2.50 6.00
10 Milt Stegall 2.00 5.00

2003 Atomic CFL Fusion Force

COMPLETE SET (8) 7.50 15.00
STATED ODDS 1:17
1 Albert Connell .60 1.50
2 Mike Pringle 1.50 4.00
3 Troy Davis .75 2.00
4 Jermaine Copeland 1.00 2.50
5 Darren Davis 1.00 2.50
6 Travis Moore 1.00 2.50
7 Michael Jenkins 1.50 4.00
8 Milt Stegall 1.50 4.00

2003 Atomic CFL Game Worn Jerseys

STATED ODDS 1:17
1 Robert Drummond 6.00 15.00
2 Marcus Crandell 7.50 20.00
3 Ed Hervey 6.00 15.00
4 Terry Vaughn 6.00 15.00
5 Danny McManus 7.50 20.00
6 Joe Montford 6.00 15.00
7 Paul Osbaldiston 5.00 12.00
8 Ben Cahoon 6.00 15.00
9 Anthony Calvillo 10.00 25.00
10 Eric LaPointe 5.00 12.00
11 Henry Burris 10.00 25.00
12 Nealon Greene 10.00 25.00
13 Chris Szarka 5.00 12.00
14 Noah Cantor 5.00 12.00
16 Noel Prefontaine 5.00 12.00
17 Khari Jones 7.50 20.00
18 Charles Roberts 10.00 25.00

1982 Bantam/FBI CFL Discs

The discs in this set measure approximately 2 7/8" in diameter and two were available on the bottoms of specially marked Bantam Orange Drink and FBI Juice product boxes. The discs were perforated for removal. Each carries a black-and-white photo of the player's face against a white background. The player's name and team are printed on either side of the photo, while the player's position is printed below. The backs are blank and the discs are checklisted below in alphabetical order. It is thought that many of the discs were issued in more than one year as slight variations have been found on some and additional players have been reported. One variation is that the oval shaped FBI logo at the top of the disc can be found with a badge or shield shape within the oval on some cards. We've listed known discs below. Any additions to the list below are appreciated.

COMPLETE SET (39) 600.00 1,000.00
1 Junior Ah You 20.00 35.00
2 Zenon Andrusyshyn 18.00 30.00
3 Joe Barnes 25.00 40.00
4 Leon Bright 18.00 30.00
5 Bob Cameron 20.00 35.00
6 Tom Clements 30.00 50.00
7 Jim Corrigall 18.00 30.00
8 Tom Cousineau 30.00 50.00
9 Carl Crennell 18.00 30.00
10 Dave Cutler 20.00 35.00
11 Peter Dalla Riva 20.00 35.00
12 Gerry Dattilio 20.00 35.00
13 Dave Fennell 18.00 30.00
14 Vince Ferragamo 30.00 50.00
15 Tom Forzani 18.00 30.00
16 Tony Gabriel 20.00 35.00
17 Gabriel Gregoire 18.00 30.00
18 Billy Hardee 18.00 30.00
19 Larry Highbaugh 18.00 30.00
20 Condredge Holloway 30.00 50.00
21 Richard Holmes 18.00 30.00
22 Mark Jackson QB 18.00 30.00
23 Billy Johnson 25.00 40.00
(White Shoes)
24 Larry Key 18.00 30.00
25 Marc Lacelle 18.00 30.00
26 Willie Martin 18.00 30.00
(shield design)
27 Gerry McGrath 18.00 30.00
28 Ian Mofford 18.00 30.00
29 Peter Muller 18.00 30.00
(shield design)
30 Mike Murphy 18.00 30.00
31 Gerry Organ 18.00 30.00
32 Tony Petruccio 18.00 30.00
33 Tony Proudfoot 18.00 30.00
34 Randy Rhino 20.00 35.00
35 Ian Santer 18.00 30.00
36 Jerry Tagge 25.00 40.00
37 Larry Uteck 18.00 30.00
38 Jim Washington 18.00 30.00
39 Tom Wilkinson 20.00 35.00

1955 B.C. Lions Team Issue

These 8" by 10" photos feature members of the B.C. Lions and were issued by the team. Each includes the player's name and position along with the team name and photographer (Artray Ltd.) notation. The photo backs are generally blank except for those that can often by found with the photographer's (Artray Ltd.) stamp.

COMPLETE SET (8) 50.00 100.00
1 By Bailey 12.50 25.00
2 Ron Baker 5.00 10.00
3 Ken Higgs 5.00 10.00
4 Laurie Niemi 5.00 10.00
5 Al Pollard 5.00 10.00
6 Mac Speedie 10.00 20.00
7 Primo Villanueva 5.00 10.00
8 Arnie Weinmeister 12.50 25.00

1956 B.C. Lions Team Issue

These 8" by 10" sepia toned photos feature members of the B.C. Lions and were issued by the team. Each includes the player's name, height, weight, position, team name and year in the border below the image. The photo backs are generally blank except for those that can often by found with the photographer's (Graphic Industries Ltd.) stamp.

COMPLETE SET (38) 175.00 300.00
1 Ken Arkell 5.00 10.00
2 By Bailey 12.50 25.00
3 Ron Baker 5.00 10.00
4 Bob Brady 5.00 10.00
5 Paul Cameron 5.00 10.00
6 Vic Chapman 5.00 10.00
7 Glen Christian 5.00 10.00
8 Ron Clinkscale 5.00 10.00
9 Chuck Dubuque 5.00 10.00
10 Dan Edwards 5.00 10.00
11 Norm Fieldgate 10.00 20.00
12 Arnie Galiffa 6.00 12.00
13 Jerry Gustafson 5.00 10.00
14 Bob Hantla 5.00 10.00
15 Ken Higgs 5.00 10.00
16 Bill Hortie 5.00 10.00
17 John Jankins 5.00 10.00
18 Roy Jenson 5.00 10.00
19 Ivan Livingstone 6.00 12.00
20 Don Lord 5.00 10.00
21 Rommie Loudd 5.00 10.00
22 Norm Masters 6.00 12.00
23 Carl Mayes 5.00 10.00
24 Jim Mitchener 5.00 10.00
25 Brian Mulhern 5.00 10.00
26 Steve Palmer 5.00 10.00
27 Doug Peters 5.00 10.00
28 Al Pollard 5.00 10.00
29 Chuck Quilter 5.00 10.00
30 Fred Robinson 5.00 10.00
31 Don Ross 5.00 10.00
32 Rae Ross 5.00 10.00
33 Frank Smith 5.00 10.00
34 Ken Stallwell 5.00 10.00
35 Bill Stuart 5.00 10.00
36 Tony Teresa 5.00 10.00
37 Primo Villanueva 5.00 10.00
38 Ron Watton 5.00 10.00

1957 B.C. Lions Team Issue 5x8

These 5" by 8" photos feature members of the B.C. Lions and were issued by the team. Each includes the player's name, position, team name and year in the border below the image. The photo backs are blank. A larger size photo was also issued for each player.

COMPLETE SET (64) 250.00 400.00
1 Tom Allman 4.00 10.00
2 Ken Arkell 4.00 10.00
3 By Bailey 10.00 20.00
4 Emery Barnes 4.00 10.00
5 Bob Brady 4.00 10.00
6 Rudy Brooks 4.00 10.00
7 Mike Cacic 4.00 10.00
8 Paul Cameron 4.00 10.00
9 Bill Carrington 4.00 10.00
10 Vic Chapman 4.00 10.00
11 Glen Christian 4.00 10.00
12 Bob Dickie 4.00 10.00
13 Chuck Dubuque 4.00 10.00
14 Jerry Duncan 5.00 12.00
15 Maury Duncan 4.00 10.00
16 Dan Edwards 4.00 10.00
17 Norm Fieldgate 7.50 15.00
18 Dick Foster 4.00 10.00
19 Chuck Frank 4.00 10.00
20 Mel Gillett 4.00 10.00
21 Vern Hallback 4.00 10.00
22 Bob Hantla 4.00 10.00
23 Sherman Hood 4.00 10.00
24 Ted Hunt 4.00 10.00
25 Jerry Janes 4.00 10.00
26 John Jankins 4.00 10.00
27 Roy Jenson 4.00 10.00
28 Rick Kaser 4.00 10.00
29 Al Kopare 4.00 10.00
30 Cas Krol 4.00 10.00
31 Ray Lackner 4.00 10.00
32 Paul Larson 4.00 10.00
33 Henry Laughlin 4.00 10.00
34 Wally Lencz 4.00 10.00
35 Vic Lindskog 4.00 10.00
36 Vern Lofstrom 4.00 10.00
37 Don Lord 4.00 10.00
38 Rommie Loudd 4.00 10.00
39 Walt Mazur 4.00 10.00
40 Harrison McDonald 4.00 10.00
41 Jim Mitchener 4.00 10.00
42 Steve Palmer 4.00 10.00
43 Matt Phillips 4.00 10.00
44 Joe Poirier 5.00 12.00
45 Chuck Quilter 4.00 10.00
46 Lorne Reid 4.00 10.00
47 Don Ross 4.00 10.00
48 Rae Ross 4.00 10.00
49 Leo Rucka 4.00 10.00
50 Art Shannon 4.00 10.00
51 Ed Sharkey 4.00 10.00
52 Frank Smith 4.00 10.00
53 Hal Sparrow 4.00 10.00
54 Ian Stewart 4.00 10.00
55 Tony Teresa 4.00 10.00
56 Toppy Vann 4.00 10.00
57 Don Vicic 4.00 10.00
58 Primo Villanueva 4.00 10.00
59 Ron Watton 4.00 10.00
60 Dave West 4.00 10.00
61 Ken Whitten 4.00 10.00
62 Phil Wright 4.00 10.00
63 Joe Yamauchi 4.00 10.00
64 Team Photo 5.00 10.00

1957 B.C. Lions Team Issue 8x10

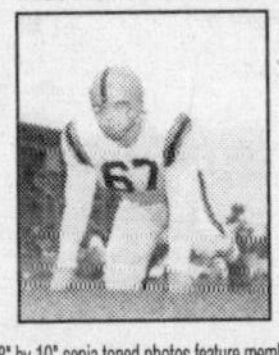

These 8" by 10" sepia toned photos feature members of the B.C. Lions and were issued by the team. Each includes the player's name, position, team name and year in the border below the image. The photo backs are generally blank except for those that can often by found with the photographer's (Graphic Industries Ltd.) stamp. A smaller size photo was also issued for each player.

COMPLETE SET (64) 300.00 500.00
1 Tom Allman 5.00 10.00
2 Ken Arkell 5.00 10.00
3 By Bailey 12.50 25.00
4 Emery Barnes 5.00 10.00
5 Bob Brady 5.00 10.00
6 Rudy Brooks 5.00 10.00
7 Mike Cacic 5.00 10.00
8 Paul Cameron 5.00 10.00
9 Bill Carrington 5.00 10.00
10 Vic Chapman 5.00 10.00
11 Glen Christian 5.00 10.00
12 Bob Dickie 5.00 10.00
13 Chuck Dubuque 5.00 10.00
14 Jerry Duncan 6.00 12.00
15 Maury Duncan 5.00 10.00
16 Dan Edwards 5.00 10.00
17 Norm Fieldgate 10.00 20.00
18 Dick Foster 5.00 10.00
19 Chuck Frank 5.00 10.00
20 Mel Gillett 5.00 10.00
21 Vern Hallback 5.00 10.00
22 Bob Hantla 5.00 10.00
23 Sherman Hood 5.00 10.00
24 Ted Hunt 5.00 10.00
25 Jerry Janes 5.00 10.00
26 John Jankins 5.00 10.00
27 Roy Jenson 5.00 10.00
28 Rick Kaser 5.00 10.00
29 Al Kopare 5.00 10.00
30 Cas Krol 5.00 10.00
31 Ray Lackner 5.00 10.00
32 Paul Larson 5.00 10.00
33 Henry Laughlin 5.00 10.00
34 Wally Lencz 5.00 10.00
35 Vic Lindskog 5.00 10.00
36 Vern Lofstrom 5.00 10.00
37 Don Lord 5.00 10.00
38 Rommie Loudd 5.00 10.00
39 Walt Mazur 5.00 10.00
40 Harrison McDonald 5.00 10.00
41 Jim Mitchener 5.00 10.00
42 Steve Palmer 5.00 10.00
43 Matt Phillips 5.00 10.00
44 Joe Poirier 6.00 12.00
45 Chuck Quilter 5.00 10.00
46 Lorne Reid 5.00 10.00
47 Don Ross 5.00 10.00
48 Rae Ross 5.00 10.00
49 Leo Rucka 5.00 10.00
50 Art Shannon 5.00 10.00
51 Ed Sharkey 5.00 10.00
52 Frank Smith 5.00 10.00
53 Hal Sparrow 5.00 10.00
54 Ian Stewart 5.00 10.00
55 Tony Teresa 5.00 10.00
56 Toppy Vann 5.00 10.00
57 Don Vicic 5.00 10.00
58 Primo Villanueva 5.00 10.00
59 Ron Watton 5.00 10.00
60 Dave West 5.00 10.00
61 Ken Whitten 5.00 10.00
62 Phil Wright 5.00 10.00
63 Joe Yamauchi 5.00 10.00
64 Team Photo 6.00 12.00

1958 B.C. Lions Clearbrook Farms

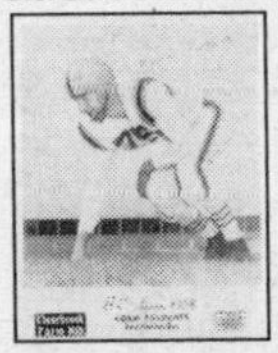

Measuring 3 3/4" by 5", these cards were sponsored by Clearbrook Farm Milk and House of Shannon. The fronts feature black-and-white photos with the player's name, position, team name, and year below the photo. The cards are unnumbered and checklisted below in alphabetical order.

1 By Bailey 15.00 30.00
2 John Bayuk 10.00 20.00
3 Don Bingham 10.00 20.00
4 Bob Brady 10.00 20.00
5 Bill Britton 10.00 20.00
6 Pete Brown 10.00 20.00
7 Mike Cacic 10.00 20.00
8 Paul Cameron 81 10.00 20.00
9 Paul Cameron 90 10.00 20.00
10 Vic Chapman 10.00 20.00
11 Gord Chiarot 10.00 20.00
12 Dick Chrobak 10.00 20.00
13 Mike Davies 10.00 20.00
14 Bob Dickie 10.00 20.00
15 Hugh Drake 10.00 20.00
16 Chuck Dubuque 10.00 20.00
17 Jerry Duncan 10.00 20.00
18 Dan Edwards 10.00 20.00
19 Alvie Elliott 10.00 20.00
20 Maurice Elias 10.00 20.00
21 Ed Enos 10.00 20.00
22 Norm Fieldgate 12.50 25.00
23 Chuck Frank 10.00 20.00
24 Mel Gillett 10.00 20.00
25 Larry Goble 10.00 20.00
26 John Groom 10.00 20.00
27 Jerry Gustafson 10.00 20.00
28 Urban Henry 10.00 20.00
29 George Herring 10.00 20.00
30 Tom Hinton 10.00 20.00
31 Laurie Hodgson 10.00 20.00
32 Sonny Homer 10.00 20.00
33 Ted Hunt 10.00 20.00
34 Curt Iaukea 10.00 20.00
35 Jerry Janes 10.00 20.00
36 Jerry Johnson 10.00 20.00
37 Steve Kapasky 10.00 20.00
38 Rick Kaser 10.00 20.00
39 Earl Keeley 10.00 20.00
40 Ray Lackner 10.00 20.00
41 Vern Lofstrom 10.00 20.00
42 Don Lord 10.00 20.00
43 Marty Martinello 10.00 20.00
44 Norm Masters 10.00 20.00
45 Gordie Mitchell 10.00 20.00
46 Gordie MacDonald 10.00 20.00
47 Baz Nagle 10.00 20.00
48 Pete Neft 10.00 20.00
49 Rod Pantages 10.00 20.00
50 Matt Phillips 10.00 20.00
51 Joe Poirier 10.00 20.00
52 Roger Power 10.00 20.00
53 Chuck Quilter 10.00 20.00
54 Howard Schnellenberger 12.50 25.00
55 Art Shannon 10.00 20.00
56 Ed Sharkey 10.00 20.00
57 Billy Clyde Smith 10.00 20.00
58 Harold Sparrow 10.00 20.00
59 Ed Vereb 10.00 20.00
60 Don Vicic 10.00 20.00
61 Primo Villanueva 10.00 20.00
62 Bob Ward 10.00 20.00
63 Duke Washington 10.00 20.00
64 Ron Watton 10.00 20.00
65 Hall Whitley 10.00 20.00
66 Bob Winters 10.00 20.00
67 Joe Yamauchi 10.00 20.00

1958 B.C. Lions Puritan Meats

Measuring 2 1/4 by 3 3/8", these cards were distributed with Puritan canned meat products in late 1958. The fronts feature black-and-white posed action photos inside white borders. In bold black lettering, the player's name, position, height, and weight are given. Immediately after in italic print is a player profile. In addition to a team logo, the back carries an offer for a 1958 B.C. Lions album for three Puritan product wrappers and 20 cents. The cards are unnumbered and checklisted below in alphabetical order. Although the album contains spaces for just 33-cards, more than that have been confirmed.

COMPLETE SET (46) 600.00 1,000.00
1 By Bailey 30.00 50.00
2 Bob Brady 15.00 25.00
3 Curt Iaukea 15.00 25.00
3 Bill Britton 15.00 25.00
4 Pete Brown 15.00 25.00
5 Mike Cacic 15.00 25.00
6 Paul Cameron 15.00 25.00
7 Vic Chapman 15.00 25.00
8 Gord Chiarot 15.00 25.00
9 Mike Davies 15.00 25.00
10 Chuck Dubuque 15.00 25.00
11 Dan Edwards 15.00 25.00
12 Ed Enos 15.00 25.00
13 Norm Fieldgate 20.00 35.00
14 Chuck Frank 15.00 25.00
15 Mel Gillett 15.00 25.00
16 Larry Goble 15.00 25.00
17 Urban Henry 15.00 25.00
18 George Herring 15.00 25.00
19 Tom Hinton 15.00 25.00
20 Laurie Hodgson 15.00 25.00
21 Sonny Homer 15.00 25.00
22 Ted Hunt 15.00 25.00
24 Gerry James 25.00 40.00
25 Steve Kapasky 15.00 25.00
26 Rick Kaser 15.00 25.00
27 Earl Keeley 15.00 25.00
28 Roy Lackner 15.00 25.00
29 Don Lord 15.00 25.00
30 Gordie MacDonald 15.00 25.00
31 Marty Martinello 15.00 25.00
32 Gordie Mitchell 15.00 25.00
33 Baz Nagle 15.00 25.00
34 Pete Neft 15.00 25.00
35 Matt Phillips 15.00 25.00
36 Joe Poirier 15.00 25.00
37 Roger Power 15.00 25.00
38 Chuck Quilter 15.00 25.00
39 Howard Schnellenberger 25.00 40.00
40 Ed Sharkey 15.00 25.00
41 Billy Clyde Smith 15.00 25.00
42 Ed Vereb 15.00 25.00
43 Don Vicic 15.00 25.00
44 Primo Villanueva 15.00 25.00
45 Bob Ward 15.00 25.00
46 Duke Washington 15.00 25.00
47 Ron Watton 15.00 25.00
48 Hall Whitley 15.00 25.00
49 Bob Winters 15.00 25.00
50 Joe Yamauchi 15.00 25.00

1959 B.C. Lions Program Inserts

Cards from this set were inserted in 1959 Lions programs - one per program. Each measures roughly 4" by 5" and features a black and white player image with his name, position, and year printed below the photo. The blankbacked photos do not feature any sponsorship logos.

COMPLETE SET (42) 250.00 400.00
1 By Bailey 10.00 20.00
2 Bob Brady 5.00 10.00
3 Bill Britton 5.00 10.00
4 Bruce Claridge 5.00 10.00
5 Chuck Diamond 5.00 10.00
6 Al Dorow 10.00 20.00
7 Chuck Dubuque 5.00 10.00
8 Randy Duncan 10.00 20.00
9 Norm Fieldgate 10.00 20.00
10 Willie Fleming 12.50 25.00
11 Jim Furey 5.00 10.00
12 Chuck Gavin 5.00 10.00
13 Mel Gillett 5.00 10.00
14 Urban Henry 6.00 12.00
15 Tom Hinton 6.00 12.00
16 Sonny Homer 6.00 12.00
17 Curt Iaukea 5.00 10.00
18 Gerry James 12.50 25.00
19 Bill Jessup 5.00 10.00
20 Roy Jokanovich 5.00 10.00
21 Earl Keeley 6.00 12.00
22 Vic Kristopaitis 5.00 10.00
23 Lavern Lofstrom 5.00 10.00
24 Don Lord 5.00 10.00
25 Marty Martinello 5.00 10.00
26 Gordie Mitchell 5.00 10.00
27 Baz Nagle 5.00 10.00
28 Chuck Quilter 5.00 10.00
29 Ted Roman 5.00 10.00
30 Vince Scorsone 5.00 10.00
31 Hal Sparrow 5.00 10.00
32 Ed Sullivan 5.00 10.00
33 Ted Tully 5.00 10.00
34 Don Vassos 5.00 10.00
35 Ed Vereb 5.00 10.00
36 Don Vicic 5.00 10.00
37 Ron Watton 5.00 10.00
38 Hank Whitley 5.00 10.00
39 Jim Wood 5.00 10.00
40 Joe Yamauchi 5.00 10.00
41 Coaches 5.00 10.00
Dave Skrien
Ken Snyder
Wayne Robinson
42 Team Photo 6.00 12.00
(measures 5" by 8")

1959 B.C. Lions Woodward's

These 4" by 5" photos are virtually identical to the 1959 B.C. Lions Team Issue photos with the addition of the "Woodward's" logo in the lower right hand corner. Each photo features a facsimile autograph printed in blue ink across the player image.

COMPLETE SET (4) 25.00 50.00
1 By Bailey 12.50 25.00
2 Don Vassos 5.00 10.00
3 Baz Nagle 5.00 10.00
4 Hank Whitley 5.00 10.00

1960 B.C. Lions CKWX Program Inserts

Cards from this set were inserted in 1960 Lions programs one card per program. Each measures roughly 4" by 5" and features a black and white player image with his name, position, and year printed below the photo. The photos were sponsored by CKWX radio and feature a facsimilie player autograph. At the time, a complete set of 40-photos could be ordered for $2 via a program offer.

COMPLETE SET (40)	175.00	300.00
1 By Bailey	10.00	20.00
2 Dave Barrus	4.00	8.00
3 Nub Beamer	4.00	8.00
4 Neil Beaumont	5.00	10.00
5 Bill Britton	4.00	8.00
6 Mike Cacic	4.00	8.00
7 Roy Cameron	4.00	8.00
8 Jim Carphin	4.00	8.00
9 Joe Carruthers	4.00	8.00
10 Bruce Claridge	4.00	8.00
11 Steve Cotter	4.00	8.00
12 Lonnie Dennis	4.00	8.00
13 Randy Duncan	7.50	15.00
14 Norm Fieldgate	7.50	15.00
15 Willie Fleming	10.00	20.00
16 Jim Furey	4.00	8.00
17 Frank Gilliam	4.00	8.00
18 George Grant	4.00	8.00
19 Urban Henry	5.00	10.00
20 Bill Herron	4.00	8.00
21 Tom Hinton	5.00	10.00
22 Sonny Homer	5.00	10.00
23 Bob Jeter	7.50	15.00
24 Jim Jones	4.00	8.00
25 Earl Keeley	5.00	10.00
26 Vic Kristopaitis	4.00	8.00
27 John Land	4.00	8.00
28 Vern Lofstrom	4.00	8.00
29 Doug Mitchell	4.00	8.00
30 Gordie Mitchell	4.00	8.00
31 Baz Nagle	4.00	8.00
32 Ted Roman	4.00	8.00
33 Harold Sparrow	4.00	8.00
34 Ed Sullivan	5.00	10.00
35 Don Vassos	4.00	8.00
36 Don Vicic	4.00	8.00
37 Jim Walden	4.00	8.00
38 Ron Watton	4.00	8.00
39 Joe Yamauchi	4.00	8.00
40 Coaches Photo	4.00	8.00
Don Branby		
Wayne Robinson		
Dave Skrien		

1961 B.C. Lions CKNW Program Inserts

Each of these photos measure approximately 3 7/8" by 5 1/2". Inside white borders, the fronts feature black-and-white posed action photos. The player's facsimile autograph is written across the picture in either black or orange colored ink. Immediately below the picture in small print are player information and "Graphic Industries Limited Photo." The wider white bottom border also carries sponsor information and a five- or six-digit serial number. Apparently the photos were primarily sponsored by CKNW (a radio station), which appears on every photo, and various other co-sponsors that may vary from card to card. The photos show signs of perforation as they were originally issued in game programs. The backs display various advertisements. The photos are unnumbered and checklisted below in alphabetical order. The co-sponsors (listed on the card front) are also listed below. The set can be distinguished from the set of the following year by the presence of the set's date in the lower left corner of the cardfront.

COMPLETE SET (32)	125.00	200.00
1 By Bailey	7.50	15.00
King's Drive-in		
2 Nub Beamer	3.00	6.00
Nestle's Quik		
3 Bob Belak	3.00	6.00
Kings Drive-In		
4 Neil Beaumont	4.00	8.00
Kings Drive-In		
5 Bill Britton	3.00	6.00
Nestle's Quik		
6 Tom Brown	4.00	8.00
Kings Drive-In		
7 Mike Cacic	3.00	6.00
Kings Drive-In		
8 Jim Carphin	3.00	6.00
Kings Drive-In		
9 Bruce Claridge	3.00	6.00
10 Pat Claridge	3.00	6.00
Nestle's Quik		
11 Steve Cotter	3.00	6.00
Nestle's Quik		
12 Lonnie Dennis	3.00	6.00
Nestle's Quik		
13 Norm Fieldgate	5.00	8.00
14 Willie Fleming	10.00	20.00
15 George Grant	3.00	6.00
16 Tom Hinton	4.00	8.00
17 Sonny Homer	4.00	8.00
Nestle's Quik		
18 Bob Jeter	5.00	10.00
19 Dick Johnson	3.00	6.00
Kings Drive-In		
20 Joe Kapp	10.00	20.00
King's Drive-in		
21 Earl Keeley	4.00	8.00
Nestle's Quik		
22 Vic Kristopaitis	3.00	6.00
Nestle's Quik		
23 Vern Lofstrom	3.00	6.00
24 Gordie Mitchell	3.00	6.00
Nestle's Quik		
25 Rae Ross	3.00	6.00
Nestle's Quik		
26 Bob Schloredt	4.00	8.00
Kings Drive-In		
27 Mel Semenko	3.00	6.00
Kings Drive-In		
28 Ed Sullivan	4.00	8.00
Nestle's Quik		
29 Barney Therrien	3.00	6.00
Nestle's Quik		
30 Ed Vereb	3.00	6.00
King's Drive-in		
31 Don Vicic	3.00	6.00
King's Drive-in		
32 Ron Watton	3.00	6.00
Kings Drive-In		

1961 B.C. Lions Team Issue

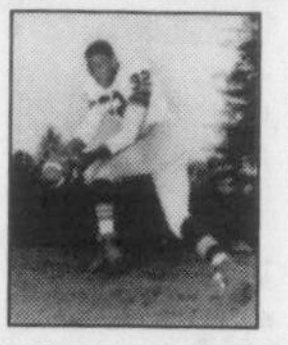

These 8" by 10" black and white photos feature members of the B.C. Lions and were issued by the team. Each photo includes the player's name, position, team name and year in the border below the image. The photo backs are blank.

COMPLETE SET (32)	150.00	300.00
1 By Bailey	10.00	20.00
2 Nub Beamer	5.00	10.00
3 Neil Beaumont	6.00	12.00
4 Bob Belak	5.00	10.00
5 Bill Britton	5.00	10.00
6 Tom Brown	6.00	12.00
7 Mike Cacic	5.00	10.00
8 Jim Carphin	5.00	10.00
9 Bruce Claridge	5.00	10.00
10 Pat Claridge	5.00	10.00
11 Lonnie Dennis	5.00	10.00
12 Norm Fieldgate	7.50	15.00
13 Willie Fleming	10.00	20.00
14 George Grant	5.00	10.00
15 Tom Hinton	6.00	12.00
16 Sonny Homer	6.00	12.00
17 Bob Jeter	7.50	15.00
18 Dick Johnson	5.00	10.00
19 Jim Jones	5.00	10.00
20 Earl Keeley	6.00	12.00
21 Vic Kristopaitis	5.00	10.00
22 Vern Lofstrom	5.00	10.00
23 Gordie Mitchell	5.00	10.00
24 Ed O'Bradovich	6.00	12.00
25 Bob Schloredt	6.00	12.00
26 Mel Semenko	5.00	10.00
27 Barney Therrien	5.00	10.00
28 Don Vicic	5.00	10.00
29 Jim Walden	5.00	10.00
30 Ron Watton	5.00	10.00
31 Joe Wendryhoski	5.00	10.00
32 Coaches	5.00	10.00
Don Branby		
Wayne Robinson		
Dave Skrien		

1962 B.C. Lions CKNW Program Inserts

Each of these photos measure approximately 3 7/8" by 5 1/2". Inside white borders, the fronts feature black-and-white posed action photos. The player's facsimile autograph is written across the picture; on most of the cards it is in red ink. Immediately below the picture in small print are player information and "Graphic Industries Limited Photo." The wider white bottom border also carries sponsor information and a five- or six-digit serial number. Apparently the photos were primarily sponsored by CKNW (a radio station), which appears on every photo, and various other co-sponsors that may vary from card to card. The photos show signs of perforation as they were originally issued in game programs. The backs display various advertisements. The photos are unnumbered and checklisted below in alphabetical order. The co-sponsors are also listed below. The set can be distinguished from the set of the previous year by the presence of the set's date in the lower left corner of the cardfront.

COMPLETE SET (32)	125.00	200.00
1 By Bailey	7.50	15.00
Shop-Easy		
2 Nub Beamer	3.50	6.00
3 Neil Beaumont	5.00	8.00
Shop-Easy		
4 Bob Belak	3.50	6.00
Shop-Easy		
5 Walt Bilicki	3.50	6.00
6 Tom Brown	5.00	8.00
Shop-Easy		
7 Mack Burton	5.00	8.00
Shop-Easy		
8 Mike Cacic	3.50	6.00
9 Jim Carphin	3.50	6.00
10 Pat Claridge	3.50	6.00
11 Steve Cotter	3.50	6.00
12 Lonnie Dennis	3.50	6.00
13 Norm Fieldgate	3.50	6.00
14 Willie Fleming	10.00	20.00
Shop-Easy		
15 Dick Fouts	5.00	8.00
16 George Grant	3.50	6.00
17 Ian Hagemoen	3.50	6.00
18 Tommy Hinton	5.00	8.00
Shop-Easy		
19 Sonny Homer	5.00	8.00
20 Joe Kapp	10.00	20.00
21 Earl Keeley	5.00	8.00
Shop-Easy		
22 Vic Kristopaitis	3.50	6.00
Shop-Easy		
23 Tom Larscheid	3.50	6.00
24 Mike Martin	3.50	6.00
25 Gordie Mitchell	3.50	6.00
26 Baz Nagle	3.50	6.00
27 Bob Schloredt	5.00	8.00
28 Gary Schwertfeger	3.50	6.00
29 Willie Taylor	5.00	8.00
30 Barney Therrien	3.50	6.00
31 Don Vicic	3.50	6.00
32 Tom Walker	3.50	6.00

1962 B.C. Lions Team Issue

These 4 1/2" by 6" black and white photos feature members of the B.C. Lions and were issued by the team. Each includes the player's name, position, team name and year in the border below the image. The photo backs are blank.

COMPLETE SET (12)	75.00	125.00
1 By Bailey	7.50	15.00
2 Neil Beaumont	5.00	10.00
3 Walt Bilicki	4.00	8.00
4 Tom Brown	5.00	10.00
5 Pat Claridge	4.00	8.00
6 Norm Fieldgate	7.50	15.00
7 Willie Fleming	10.00	20.00
8 Dick Fouts	5.00	10.00
9 Joe Kapp	10.00	20.00
10 Vic Kristopaitis	4.00	8.00
11 Gordie Mitchell	4.00	8.00
12 Don Vicic	4.00	8.00

1963 B.C. Lions Photo Gallery Program Inserts

These photo gallery sheets were actually page inserts into 1963 Lions game programs. Each features four Lions players on the front under the title "B.C. Lions Photo Gallery -- 1963." The backs feature another page from the program with advertising or other game related text. We've listed them below as uncut sheets in order by game program date.

COMPLETE SET (10)	60.00	100.00
1 1-Aug	10.00	20.00
Sonny Homer		
Joe Kapp		
Norris Stephenson		
Tom Hinton		
2 12-Aug	7.50	15.00
Neil Beaumont		
Willie Fleming		
Tom Brown		
Steve Cotter		
3 19-Aug	6.00	12.00
By Bailey		
Dick Fouts		
Pat Claridge		
Norm Fieldgate		
4 7-Sep	4.00	8.00
Nub Beamer		
Bill Frank		
Mack Burton		
Mike Martin		
5 16-Sep	4.00	8.00
Barney Therrien		
Tom Larscheid		
Bill Lasseter		
Gary Schwertfeger		
6 30-Sep	5.00	10.00
Bill Munsey		
Lonnie Dennis		
Peter Kempf		
Walt Bilicki		
7 12-Oct	6.00	12.00
Ian Hagemoen		
Gerry James		
Paul Seale		
Pete Ohler		
8 19-Oct	4.00	8.00
Emery Barnes		
Don Vicic		
Steve Shafer		
Harvey Scott		
9 3-Nov	4.00	8.00
Ron Morris		
Greg Findlay		
Mel Melin		
Mike Cacic		
10 November 20,23	10.00	20.00
Trophy Winners		
Tom Brown		
Joe Kapp		
Peter Kempf		
Neil Beaumont		

1963 B.C. Lions Team Issue

These 4 1/2" by 5 1/2" black and white photos feature members of the B.C. Lions and were issued by the team. Each includes the player's name and year in the border below the image. The photo backs are blank.

COMPLETE SET (10)	50.00	100.00
1 By Bailey	7.50	15.00
2 Neil Beaumont	5.00	10.00
3 Walt Bilicki	4.00	8.00
4 Tom Brown	5.00	10.00
5 Pat Claridge	4.00	8.00
6 Steve Cotter	4.00	8.00
7 Norm Fieldgate	6.00	12.00
8 Willie Fleming	7.50	15.00
9 Dick Fouts	5.00	10.00
10 Joe Kapp	10.00	20.00

1964 B.C. Lions CKWX Program Inserts

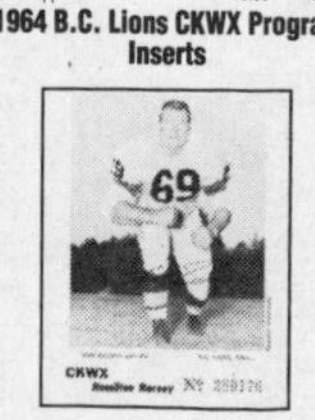

Each of these photos was sponsored by CKWX radio and measure roughly 3 7/8" by 5 1/4". The fronts feature black-and-white photos of B.C. Lions players. The player's facsimile autograph is written across the picture in red ink. Immediately below the picture in small print is the player's name, position, jersey number, team and year of issue. The wider bottom border carries the sponsor information and a five- or six-digit serial number. The photos were primarily sponsored by CKWX and other co-sponsors on the card fronts that may vary from card to card. The photos show signs of perforation as they were originally issued 4-per page in Lions game programs. The backs display various advertisements. The photos are unnumbered and checklisted below in alphabetical order. Any additions to this list are appreciated.

COMPLETE SET (35)	125.00	200.00
1 By Bailey	7.50	15.00
2 Emery Barnes	3.00	6.00
3 Neil Beaumont	4.00	8.00
4 Walt Bilicki	3.00	6.00
5 Tom Brown	4.00	8.00
6 Mack Burton	4.00	8.00
7 Mike Cacic	3.00	6.00
8 Jim Carphin	3.00	6.00
9 Pat Claridge	3.00	6.00
10 Steve Cotter	3.00	6.00
11 Lonnie Dennis	3.00	6.00
12 Norm Fieldgate	5.00	10.00
13 Greg Findlay	3.00	6.00
14 Willie Fleming	7.50	15.00
15 Dick Fouts	4.00	8.00
16 Bill Frank	3.00	6.00
17 Tom Hinton	4.00	8.00
18 Lou Holland	3.00	6.00
19 Sonny Homer	4.00	8.00
20 Joe Kapp	7.50	15.00
21 Gus Kasapis	3.00	6.00
22 Peter Kempf	3.00	6.00
23 Bill Lasseter	3.00	6.00
24 Mike Martin	3.00	6.00
25 Mel Mellin	3.00	6.00
26 Ron Morris	3.00	6.00
27 Bill Munsey	4.00	8.00
28 Pete Ohler	3.00	6.00
29 Gary Schwertfeger	3.00	6.00
30 Paul Seale	3.00	6.00
31 Steve Shafer	3.00	6.00
32 Ken Sugarman	3.00	6.00
33 Bob Swift	3.00	6.00
34 Don Vicic	3.00	6.00
35 Jesse Williams	3.00	6.00

1964 B.C. Lions Team Issue

These 8" by 10" photos feature members of the B.C. Lions and were issued by the team. Each includes two photos of the featured player along with an extensive bio on the front. The photo backs are blank.

COMPLETE SET (35)	125.00	250.00
1 By Bailey	7.50	15.00
2 Emery Barnes	4.00	8.00
3 Neil Beaumont	5.00	10.00
4 Walt Bilicki	4.00	8.00
5 Tom Brown	5.00	10.00
6 Mack Burton	5.00	10.00
7 Mike Cacic	4.00	8.00
8 Jim Carphin	4.00	8.00
9 Pat Claridge	4.00	8.00
10 Steve Cotter	4.00	8.00
11 Lonnie Dennis	4.00	8.00
12 Norm Fieldgate	6.00	12.00
13 Greg Findlay	4.00	8.00
14 Willie Fleming	7.50	15.00
15 Dick Fouts	5.00	10.00
16 Bill Frank	4.00	8.00
17 Tom Hinton	5.00	10.00
18 Louie Holland	4.00	8.00
19 Sonny Homer	5.00	10.00
20 Joe Kapp	10.00	20.00
21 Gus Kasapis	4.00	8.00
22 Peter Kempf	4.00	8.00
23 Bill Lasseter	4.00	8.00
24 Mike Martin	4.00	8.00
25 Mel Mellin	4.00	8.00
26 Ron Morris	4.00	8.00
27 Bill Munsey	5.00	10.00
28 Pete Ohler	4.00	8.00
29 Gary Schwertfeger	4.00	8.00
30 Paul Seale	4.00	8.00
31 Steve Shafer	4.00	8.00
32 Ken Sugarman	4.00	8.00
33 Bob Swift	4.00	8.00
34 Don Vicic	4.00	8.00
35 Jesse Williams	4.00	8.00

1965 B.C. Lions Program Inserts

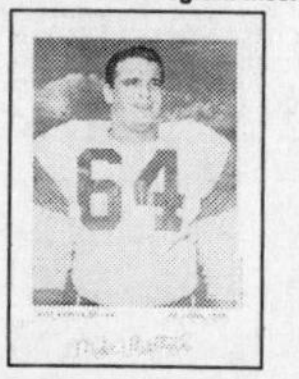

Each of these photos did not include a sponsor like previous years and measure roughly 3 7/8" by 5 1/4". The fronts feature black-and-white photos of B.C. Lions players. The player's facsimile autograph is written below the player photo along with the player's name, position, jersey number, team and year of issue. The photos show signs of perforation as they were originally issued 4-per page in Lions game programs. The backs display various advertisements. The photos are unnumbered and checklisted below in alphabetical order. Any additions to this list are appreciated.

COMPLETE SET (30)	125.00	200.00
1 Ernie Allen	3.00	6.00
2 Neil Beaumont	4.00	8.00
3 Walt Bilicki	3.00	6.00
4 Tom Brown	4.00	8.00
5 Mack Burton	4.00	8.00
6 Mike Cacic	3.00	6.00
7 Jim Carphin	3.00	6.00
8 Pat Claridge	3.00	6.00
9 Steve Cotter	3.00	6.00
10 Lonnie Dennis	3.00	6.00
11 Norm Fieldgate	6.00	12.00
12 Greg Findlay	3.00	6.00
13 Willie Fleming	7.50	15.00
14 Dick Fouts	4.00	8.00
15 Tom Hinton	4.00	8.00
16 Sonny Homer	4.00	8.00
17 Joe Kapp	7.50	15.00
18 Gus Kasapis	3.00	6.00
19 Peter Kempf	3.00	6.00
20 Bill Lasseter	3.00	6.00
21 Mike Martin	3.00	6.00
22 Ron Morris	3.00	6.00
23 Bill Munsey	4.00	8.00
24 Gary Schwertfeger	3.00	6.00
25 Paul Seale	3.00	6.00
26 Steve Shafer	3.00	6.00
27 Roy Shatzko	3.00	6.00
28 Ken Sugarman	3.00	6.00
29 Bob Swift	3.00	6.00
30 Jesse Williams	3.00	6.00

1966 B.C. Lions Program Inserts

The B.C. Lions continued their tradition of inserting player photos into game programs in 1966. However, this was the first year for color player images. Each also measured a much larger 7 3/4" by 10 1/2" and the set featured only 8-players. Each included a sponsor notation below the image as well as a page number as any other page from the program.

COMPLETE SET (8)	35.00	60.00
1 Neil Beaumont	4.00	8.00
2 Tom Brown	4.00	8.00
3 Mike Cacic	3.50	6.00
4 Norm Fieldgate	6.00	12.00
5 Willie Fleming	7.50	15.00
6 Dick Fouts	4.00	8.00
7 Tom Hinton	4.00	8.00
8 Joe Kapp	7.50	15.00

1967 B.C. Lions Team Issue

These 8" by 10" photos feature members of the B.C. Lions and were issued by the team. Each includes two photos of the featured player along with an extensive bio on the front. The photo backs are blank.

COMPLETE SET (26)	100.00	175.00
1 Ernie Allen	4.00	8.00
2 Neil Beaumont	5.00	10.00
3 Tom Brown	5.00	10.00
4 Mike Cacic	4.00	8.00
5 Dwayne Czupka	4.00	8.00
6 Lonnie Dennis	4.00	8.00
7 Larry Eilmes	5.00	10.00
8 Bernie Faldney	4.00	8.00
9 Norm Fieldgate	6.00	12.00
10 Greg Findlay	4.00	8.00
11 Wayne Foster	4.00	8.00
12 Ted Gerela	5.00	10.00
13 Sonny Homer	5.00	10.00
14 Bill Lasseter	4.00	8.00
15 Mike Martin	4.00	8.00
16 Bill Mitchell	4.00	8.00
17 Dave Moton	4.00	8.00
18 Bill Munsey	5.00	10.00
19 Craig Murray	4.00	8.00
20 Rudy Resche	4.00	8.00
21 Henry Schichtle	4.00	8.00
22 Steve Shafer	4.00	8.00
23 Leroy Sledge	4.00	8.00
24 Ken Sugarman	4.00	8.00
25 Jerry West	4.00	8.00
26 Jim Young	10.00	20.00

1968 B.C. Lions Team Issue

These photos feature members of the B.C. Lions and were issued by the team. Each measures 8" by 10" and includes two photos of the featured player along with an extensive bio on the front. The photo backs are blank.

COMPLETE SET (14)	50.00	10.00
1 Paul Brothers	4.00	8.00
2 Bill Bufton	4.00	8.00
3 Jim Carphin	4.00	8.00
4 Skip Diaz	4.00	8.00
5 Jim Evenson	4.00	8.00
6 Ted Gerela	5.00	10.00
7 John Griffin	4.00	8.00
8 Lynn Hendrickson	4.00	8.00
9 Lach Heron	4.00	8.00
10 Sonny Homer	5.00	10.00
11 Bill Lasseter	4.00	8.00
12 Mike Martin	4.00	8.00
13 Jim Sioie	4.00	8.00
14 Leroy Sledge	4.00	8.00

1971 B.C. Lions Chevron

This card set of the British Columbia Lions measures approximately 3" by 4 1/2" and was distributed by Standard Oil Company. The unnumbered cards were originally attached in complete sheet form. The fronts feature color player portraits and player information on a white background. The backs carry information about the Canadian Football League. A plastic folded "wallet" was produced to house the set with the words "Chevron Touchdown Cards" on the cover. Cards 3,7,11,22, 27,28,33,44 and 46 were bonus cards added later and therefore considered tougher to find.

COMPLETE SET (50)	175.00	300.00
1 George Anderson	3.00	6.00
2 Josh Ashton	4.00	8.00
3 Ross Boice SP	10.00	20.00
4 Paul Brothers	3.00	6.00
5 Tom Cassese	3.00	6.00
6 Roy Cavallin	3.00	6.00
7 Rusty Clark SP	10.00	20.00
8 Owen Dejanovich CO	3.00	6.00
9 Dave Denny	3.00	6.00
10 Brian Donnelly	3.00	6.00
11 Steve Duich SP	10.00	20.00
12 Jim Duke	3.00	6.00
13 Dave Easley	3.00	6.00
14 Trevor Ekdahl	4.00	8.00
15 Jim Evenson	4.00	8.00
16 Greg Findlay	3.00	6.00
17 Ted Gerela	3.00	6.00
18 Dave Golinsky	3.00	6.00
19 Lefty Hendrickson	3.00	6.00
20 Lach Heron	4.00	8.00
21 Gerry Herron	3.00	6.00
22 Larry Highbaugh SP	10.00	20.00
23 Wayne Holm	3.00	6.00
24 Bob Howes	3.00	6.00
25 Max Huber	3.00	6.00
26 Garrett Hunsperger	3.00	6.00
27 Lawrence James SP	10.00	20.00
28 Brian Kelsey SP	10.00	20.00
29 Eagle Keys CO	4.00	8.00
30 Mike Leveille	3.00	6.00
31 John Love	3.00	6.00
32 Ray Lychak	3.00	6.00
33 Dick Lyons SP	10.00	20.00
34 Wayne Matherne	3.00	6.00
35 Ken McCullough CO	3.00	6.00
36 Don Moorhead	3.00	6.00
37 Pete Palmer	3.00	6.00
38 Jackie Parker GM	6.00	12.00
39 Ken Phillips	3.00	6.00
40 Cliff Powell	3.00	6.00
41 Gary Robinson	3.00	6.00
42 Ken Sugarman	4.00	8.00
43 Bruce Taupier	3.00	6.00
44 Jim Tomlin SP	10.00	20.00
45 Bud Tynes CO	3.00	6.00
46 Carl Weathers SP	10.00	20.00
47 Jim White	3.00	6.00
48 Mike Wilson	3.00	6.00
49 Jim Young	5.00	10.00
50 Contest Card	3.00	6.00
For Chevron		

1971 B.C. Lions Royal Bank

This 16-photo set of the CFL's British Columbia Lions was sponsored by Royal Bank. Each black-and-white, blank-backed picture measures approximately 5" by 7" and features a white-bordered posed action photo and a facsimile autograph inscribed across it. The sponsor logo appears in black in each corner of the bottom margin. The photos are unnumbered and checklisted below in alphabetical order.

COMPLETE SET (16)	50.00	100.00
1 George Anderson	3.00	6.00
2 Paul Brothers	3.00	6.00
3 Brian Donnelly	3.00	6.00
4 Dave Easley	3.00	6.00
5 Trevor Ekdahl	4.00	8.00
6 Jim Evenson	4.00	8.00
7 Greg Findlay	3.00	6.00
8 Lefty Hendrickson	3.00	6.00
9 Bob Howes	3.00	6.00
10 Garrett Hunsperger	3.00	6.00
11 Wayne Matherne	3.00	6.00
12 Don Moorhead	3.00	6.00
13 Ken Phillips	3.00	6.00
14 Ken Sugarman	4.00	8.00
15 Tom Wilkinson	5.00	10.00
16 Jim Young	5.00	10.00

1972 B.C. Lions Royal Bank

This set of 16 photos was sponsored by Royal Bank. They measure approximately 5" by 7" and are printed on thin glossy paper. The color posed player photos are bordered in white. A facsimile autograph is inscribed across the picture. At the bottom of the front, the words "Royal Bank Leo's Leaders, B.C. Lions Player of the Week" are printed between the sponsor's logo and the Lions' logo. The backs are blank. The photos are unnumbered and checklisted below in alphabetical order. One noteworthy card in the set is Carl Weathers, who went on to acting fame as Apollo Creed in Sylvester Stallone's popular "Rocky" movies.

COMPLETE SET (16)	60.00	120.00
1 George Anderson	3.00	6.00
2 Brian Donnelly	3.00	6.00
3 Dave Easley	3.00	6.00
4 Trevor Ekdahl	4.00	8.00
5 Ron Estay	3.00	6.00
6 Jim Evenson	4.00	8.00
7 Dave Golinsky	3.00	6.00
8 Larry Highbaugh	4.00	8.00
9 Garrett Hunsperger	3.00	6.00
10 Don Moorhead	3.00	6.00
11 Johnny Musso	6.00	12.00
12 Ray Nettles	3.00	6.00
13 Willie Postler	3.00	6.00
14 Carl Weathers	7.50	15.00
15 Jim Young	5.00	10.00
16 Coaching Staff	4.00	8.00
Bud Tynes		
Ken McCullough		
Owen Dejanovich		
Eagle Keys		

1973 B.C. Lions Royal Bank

This set of 18-photos (including all variations) was sponsored by Royal Bank. They measure approximately 5" by 7" and were printed on thin glossy paper. The color posed action shots are bordered in white. A facsimile autograph is inscribed across the picture. At the bottom of the front, the words "Royal Leaders, B.C. Lions Player of the Week" are printed between the sponsor's logo and the Lions' logo. The set includes three Don Moorhead cards, and two of these have borders around the picture. The third Moorhead photo and one of the Matherne photos has a black stripe at the bottom to cover up a wrong signature. The backs are blank, unnumbered and checklisted below in alphabetical order.

COMPLETE SET (18)	60.00	120.00
1 Barry Ardern	3.00	6.00
2 Monroe Eley	4.00	8.00
3 Bob Friend	3.00	6.00
4 Eric Guthrie	3.00	6.00
5 Garrett Hunsperger	3.00	6.00
6 Wayne Matherne	3.00	6.00
7 Wayne Matherne	3.00	6.00
(black stripe across photo)		
8 Don Moorhead	3.00	6.00
(Black border)		
9 Don Moorhead	3.00	6.00
(Silver border)		
10 Don Moorhead	3.00	6.00
(black stripe across photo)		
11 Johnny Musso	6.00	12.00
(running pose)		
12 Ray Nettles	3.00	6.00
13 Pete Palmer	3.00	6.00
14 Gary Robinson SP	12.00	20.00
15 Al Wilson	3.00	6.00
16 Mike Wilson	3.00	6.00
17 Jim Young	5.00	10.00
18 Coaches	4.00	8.00
Bud Tynes		
Ken McCullough		
Owen Dejanovich		
Eagle Keys		

1974 B.C. Lions Royal Bank

This blank-backed 14-photo color set was sponsored by Royal Bank. Each posed and bordered CFL Lions player's photo measures approximately 5" by 7" and carries a facsimile autograph across it. The sponsor logo appears in the lower left corner while the team logo is in the lower right corner. The photos are unnumbered and checklisted below in alphabetical order.

COMPLETE SET (14)	40.00	80.00
1 Bill Baker	4.00	8.00
2 Karl Douglas	2.50	5.00
3 Layne McDowell	2.50	5.00
4 Ivan MacMillan	2.50	5.00
5 Bud Magrum	2.50	5.00
6 Don Moorhead	2.50	5.00
7 Johnny Musso	5.00	10.00
(standing pose)		
8 Ray Nettles	2.50	5.00
9 Brian Sopatyk	2.50	5.00
10 Curtis Wester	3.00	6.00
11 Slade Willis	2.50	5.00
12 Al Wilson	2.50	5.00
13 Jim Young	4.00	8.00
14 Coaching Staff	3.00	6.00

1974 B.C. Lions Team Issue

These black and white photos were issued by the B.C. Lions around 1974. Each includes the player's name and team name below the photo on the front and the backs are blank. The photos measure roughly 5" by 8".

COMPLETE SET (25)	50.00	100.00
1 Barry Ardern	2.00	5.00
2 Brock Ansley	2.00	5.00
3 Terry Bailey	2.00	5.00
4 Bill Baker	3.00	6.00
5 Elton Baker	2.00	5.00
6 Grady Cavness	3.00	6.00
7 Brian Donnelly	2.00	5.00
8 Karl Douglas	2.00	5.00
9 Joe Fourqurean	2.00	5.00
10 Lou Harris	3.00	6.00
11 Garrett Hunsperger	2.00	5.00
12 Mike Lahood	2.00	5.00
13 Ivan MacMillan	2.00	5.00
14 Bud Magrum	2.00	5.00
15 Wayne Matherne	2.00	5.00
16 Don Moorhead	2.00	5.00
17 Johnny Musso	4.00	8.00
18 Ray Nettles	2.00	5.00
19 Peter Palmer	2.00	5.00
20 Brian Sopatyk	2.00	5.00
21 Slade Willis	2.00	5.00
22 Carl Winfrey	2.00	5.00
23 Al Wilson	2.00	5.00
24 Mike Wilson	2.00	5.00
25 Jim Young	4.00	8.00

1975 B.C. Lions Royal Bank

Royal Bank sponsored this 14-photo set. Each photo measures approximately 5 1/4" by 6". The photos are unnumbered and checklisted below in alphabetical order.

COMPLETE SET (14)	30.00	60.00
1 Brock Ansley	2.50	5.00
2 Terry Bailey	2.50	5.00
3 Bill Baker	4.00	8.00
4 Elton Brown	2.50	5.00
5 Grady Cavness	3.00	6.00
6 Ross Clarkson	2.50	5.00
7 Joe Fourqurean	2.50	5.00
8 Lou Harris	3.00	6.00
9 Layne McDowell	2.50	5.00
10 Don Moorhead	2.50	5.00
11 Tony Moro	2.50	5.00
12 Ray Nettles	2.50	5.00
13 Curtis Wester	3.00	6.00
14 Jim Young	4.00	8.00

1976 B.C. Lions Team Issued Buttons

These buttons were issued by the B.C. Lions and feature members of the team. Each measures roughly 2 1/4" in diameter and includes a black and white player photo against an orange background. A "nickname" for the player is included along with his jersey number, but no other identification is given.

COMPLETE SET (36)	125.00	200.00
1 Barry Ardern (jersey #10)	3.00	5.00
2 Brock Ansley (jersey #17)	3.00	5.00
3 Bill Baker (jersey #76)	8.00	12.00
4 Larry Cameron (jersey #37)	5.00	8.00
5 Elton Brown (jersey #69)	3.00	5.00
6 Doug Carlson (jersey #28)	3.00	5.00
7 Grady Cavness (jersey #32)	5.00	8.00
8 Ross Clarkson (jersey #20)	3.00	5.00
9 Jerry Ellison (jersey #64)	3.00	5.00
10 Allen Gallagher (jersey #64)	3.00	5.00
11 Paul Giroday (jersey #78)	3.00	5.00
12 Eric Guthrie (jersey #18)	3.00	5.00
13 Lou Harris (jersey #31)	5.00	8.00
14 Bob Hornes (jersey #21)	3.00	5.00
15 Barry Houlihan (jersey #21)	3.00	5.00
16 Andy Jonassen (jersey #44)	3.00	5.00
17 Pete Liske (jersey #12)	8.00	12.00
18 Rocky Long (jersey #16)	3.00	5.00
19 Ivan MacMillan (jersey #28)	3.00	5.00
20 Dan McDonough (jersey #79)	3.00	5.00
21 Layne McDowell (jersey #62)	3.00	5.00
22 Don Moorhead (jersey #27)	3.00	5.00
23 Tony Moro (jersey #11)	3.00	5.00
24 Wayne Moseley (jersey #34)	3.00	5.00
25 Ray Nettles (jersey #51)	3.00	5.00
26 Pete Palmer (jersey #47)	5.00	8.00
27 Gary Robinson (jersey #67)	3.00	5.00
28 Wally Saunders (jersey #22)	3.00	5.00
29 Jim Schneitz (jersey #65)	3.00	5.00
30 Brian Sopatyk (jersey #50)	3.00	5.00
31 Michael Strickland (jersey #4)	3.00	5.00
32 Lorne Watters (jersey #79)	3.00	5.00
33 Curtis Wester (jersey #61)	5.00	8.00
34 Slade Willis (jersey #74)	3.00	5.00
35 Don Wunderley (jersey #60)	3.00	5.00
36 Jim Young (jersey #30)	10.00	15.00

1975 B.C. Lions Team Sheets

This group of 32-players and coaches of the B.C. Lions was produced on four glossy sheets each measuring approximately 8" by 10". The fronts feature black-and-white player portraits with eight pictures to a sheet. The year and the "CP" (printer) logo appears at the top of each sheet. The backs are blank. The cards are unnumbered and checklisted below in alphabetical order, with the player pictured in the upper left hand corner of the sheet listed first.

COMPLETE SET (4)	12.50	25.00
1 Brock Aynsley	2.50	5.00
Tony Moro		
Lorne Watters		
Grady Cavness		
Slade Willis		
Joe Fourqurean		
Curtis Wester		
Don Moorhead		
2 Luther Howard	3.00	6.00
Brian Sopatyk		
Ross Clarkson		
Ivan MacMillan		
Dan Dever		
Barry Ardern		
Gary Robinson		
Pete Liske		
3 Eagle Keys CO	5.00	10.00
Dan McDonough		
Lou Harris		
Terry Bailey		
Alan Wilson		
Elton Brown		
Mike La Hood		
Jim Young		
4 Don Wunderly	3.00	6.00
Eric Guthrie		
Bob Hornes		
Bill Baker		
Ray Nettles		
Ken Johnson		
Pete Palmer		
Layne McDowell		

1976 B.C. Lions Royal Bank

This set of 15 photos was sponsored by Royal Bank. They measure approximately 5 1/4" by 6" and are printed on thin glossy paper. The color posed player shots (from the waist up) are bordered in white. A facsimile autograph is inscribed across the picture. At the bottom of the front, the words "1976 Royal Leaders, B.C. Lions Player of the Week" are printed between the sponsor's logo and the Lions' logo. The backs are blank. The photos are unnumbered and checklisted below in alphabetical order.

COMPLETE SET (15)	40.00	80.00
1 Terry Bailey	2.50	5.00
2 Bill Baker	4.00	8.00
3 Ted Dushinski	2.50	5.00
4 Eric Guthrie	2.50	5.00
5 Lou Harris	3.00	6.00
6 Glen Jackson	2.50	5.00
7 Rocky Long	2.50	5.00
8 Layne McDowell	2.50	5.00
9 Ray Nettles	2.50	5.00
10 Gary Robinson	2.50	5.00
11 John Sciarra	4.00	8.00
12 Wayne Smith	2.50	5.00
13 Michael Strickland	2.50	5.00
14 Al Wilson	2.50	5.00
15 Jim Young	4.00	8.00

1977 B.C. Lions Royal Bank

This set of 12 photos was sponsored by Royal Bank. They measure approximately 4 3/4" by 5 3/8" and are printed on thin glossy paper. The color head and shoulders shots are bordered in white. A facsimile autograph is inscribed across the picture. At the bottom of the front, the words "Royal Leaders, B.C. Lions Player of the Week" are printed between the Lions' logo and the sponsor's logo. The backs are blank. The photos are unnumbered and checklisted below in alphabetical order.

COMPLETE SET (12)	30.00	60.00
1 Doug Carlson	2.50	5.00
2 Sam Cvijanovich	2.50	5.00
3 Ted Dushinski	2.50	5.00
4 Paul Giroday	2.50	5.00
5 Glen Jackson	2.50	5.00
6 Frank Landy	2.50	5.00
7 Lui Passaglia	4.00	8.00
8 John Sciarra	3.00	6.00
9 Michael Strickland	2.50	5.00
10 Jerry Tagge	4.00	8.00
11 Al Wilson	2.50	5.00
12 Jim Young	4.00	8.00

1977-78 B.C. Lions Team Sheets

This group of 32-players and coaches of the B.C. Lions was produced on four glossy sheets each measuring approximately 8" by 10". The fronts feature black-and-white player portraits with eight pictures to a sheet. The year, the Lions logo, and the CFL logo appear at the top of each sheet. The backs are blank. The cards are unnumbered and checklisted below in alphabetical order, with the player pictured in the upper left hand corner of the sheet listed first.

COMPLETE SET (4)	12.50	25.00
1 Bob Ackles	3.00	6.00
Jack Farley		
Vince Tobin		
Vic Rapp		
Max McCartney		
Bill Quinter		
Don Wunderly		
Richard Appleby		
2 Gerry Inglis	2.50	5.00
Glen Jackson		
Gary Keithley		
Tom Kudaba		
Frank Landy		
Glen Leach		
Rocky Long		
Layne McDowell		
3 Rob McLaren	4.00	8.00
Jesse O'Neal		
Lui Passaglia		
Gary Robinson		
Jim Schnietz		
John Sciarra		
Doug Seymour		
Henry Sovio		
4 Jerry Tagge	4.00	8.00
Mike Strickland		
Tuufuli Uperesa		
Larry Watkins		
Alan Wilson		
Don Ratliff		
Terry Bailey		
Jim Harrison		

1978 B.C. Lions Royal Bank

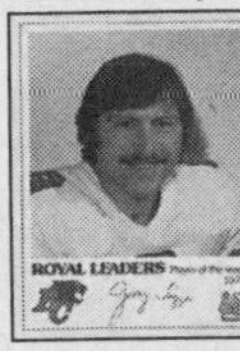

Royal Bank sponsored this 12-photo set again featuring the player's of the week as chosen by Royal Bank. Each photo measures approximately 4 1/4" by 5 1/2". The photos are unnumbered and checklisted below in alphabetical order.

COMPLETE SET (12)	30.00	60.00
1 Terry Bailey	2.00	4.00
2 Leon Bright	3.00	6.00
3 Doug Carlson	2.00	4.00
4 Grady Cavness	2.50	5.00
5 Al Charuk	2.00	4.00
6 Paul Giroday	2.00	4.00
7 Larry Key	2.00	4.00
8 Frank Landy	2.00	4.00
9 Lui Passaglia	4.00	8.00
10 Jerry Tagge	4.00	8.00
11 Al Wilson	2.00	4.00
12 Jim Young	4.00	8.00

1979 B.C. Lions Team Sheets

This group of 32-players and coaches of the B.C. Lions was produced on four glossy sheets each measuring approximately 8" by 10". The fronts feature black-and-white player portraits with eight pictures to a sheet. The year, the Lions logo, and the CFL logo appear at the top of each sheet. The backs are blank. The cards are unnumbered and checklisted below in alphabetical order, with the player pictured in the upper left hand corner of the sheet listed first.

COMPLETE SET (4)	10.00	25.00
1 Andre Anderson	3.00	6.00
Terry Bailey		
John Beaton		
John Blain		
John Blake		
Leon Bright		
Sam Britts		
Doug Carlson		
2 Alan Charuk	3.00	6.00
Joe Fourqurean		
Devon Ford		
Paul Giroday		
Rick Goltz		
Nick Hebeler		
Ken Hinton		
Harry Holt		
3 Mark Houghton	2.50	5.00
Glen Jackson		
Larry Key		
Tom Kudaba		
Frank Landy		
Glenn Leonhard		
Jim Lohmann		
Ron Morehouse		
4 John Henry White	4.00	8.00
Al Wilson		
Jim Young		
Bob Ackles		
Bill Quinter		
Jack Farley		
Vic Rapp		

1983 B.C. Lions Mohawk Oil

This 24-card set of the CFL's British Columbia Lions was only issued in British Columbia by Mohawk Oil as a premium at its gas stations. Posed color player's photos appear on a white card face. The cards measure approximately 2 1/2" by 3 5/8". A thin black line forms a box at the bottom that contains the player's name, jersey number, position, team logo, and sponsor logo. Each card has a facsimile autograph of the player on the front. The backs have biographical information and career notes printed in blue. The cards are unnumbered and checklisted below in alphabetical order.

COMPLETE SET (24)	8.00	20.00
1 John Blain	.30	.75
2 Tim Cowan	.40	1.00
3 Larry Crawford	.40	1.00
4 Tyrone Crews	.30	.75
5 James Curry	.40	1.00
6 Roy Dewalt	.60	1.50
7 Mervyn Fernandez	1.00	2.50
8 Sammy Greene	.30	.75
9 Jo Jo Heath	.30	.75
10 Nick Hebeler	.40	1.00
11 Glen Jackson	.30	.75
12 Tim Kearse	.30	.75
13 Rick Klassen	.40	1.00
14 Kevin Konar	.40	1.00
15 Glenn Leonhard	.30	.75
16 Nelson Martin	.30	.75
17 Mack Moore	.30	.75
18 John Pankratz	.30	.75
19 Joe Paopao	.50	1.25
20 Lui Passaglia	1.00	2.50
21 Don Taylor	.30	.75
22 Mike Washburn	.30	.75
23 John Henry White	.30	.75
24 Al Wilson	.30	.75

1984 B.C. Lions Mohawk Oil

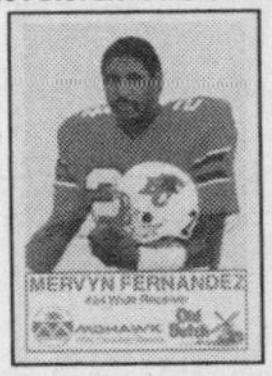

This 32-card set was co-sponsored by Mohawk and Old Dutch, and only issued in British Columbia by Mohawk Oil as a premium at its gas stations. The set features members of the British Columbia Lions of the CFL. The cards measure approximately 2 1/2" by 3 5/8". The front features a posed color player photo, with white borders and a facsimile autograph across the picture. Player information and sponsors' logos appear in a rectangle below the picture. In blue print on white, the back has biography and player profile. The cards are unnumbered and checklisted below in alphabetical order.

COMPLETE SET (32)	8.00	20.00
1 Ned Armour	.40	1.00
2 John Blain	.25	.60
3 Melvin Byrd	.40	1.00
4 Darnell Clash	.40	1.00
5 Tim Cowan	.40	1.00
6 Larry Crawford	.40	1.00
7 Tyrone Crews	.25	.60
8 Roy DeWalt	.60	1.50
9 Mervyn Fernandez	1.00	2.50
10 Bernie Glier	.25	.60
11 Dennis Guevin	.25	.60
12 Nick Hebeler	.25	.60
13 Bryan Illerbrun	.25	.60
14 Glen Jackson	.25	.60
15 Andre Jones DB	.25	.60
16 Rick Klassen	.40	1.00
17 Kevin Konar	.40	1.00
18 Glenn Leonhard	.25	.60
19 Nelson Martin	.25	.60
20 Billy McBride	.25	.60
21 Mack Moore	.25	.60
22 John Pankratz	.25	.60
23 James Parker	.60	1.50
24 Lui Passaglia	1.00	2.50
25 Ryan Potter	.25	.60
26 Gerald Roper	.25	.60
27 Jim Sandusky	.75	2.00
28 Don Taylor	.25	.60
29 John Henry White	.25	.60
30 Al Wilson	.25	.60
31 Team Card	.40	1.00
32 Checklist	.40	1.00

1985 B.C. Lions Mohawk Oil

This 32-card set was co-sponsored by Mohawk and Old Dutch, and only issued in British Columbia by Mohawk Oil as a premium at its gas stations. Measuring approximately 2 1/2" by 3 5/8", the card fronts feature posed, color player photos with white borders. A facsimile autograph is inscribed across the picture. At the bottom, a white box that is outlined by a thin black line carries the player's name, jersey number, position, and sponsor logos. In blue print, the backs carry biographical information and a player profile. The cards are unnumbered and checklisted below in alphabetical order.

COMPLETE SET (32)	8.00	20.00
1 John Blain	.20	.50
2 Jamie Buis	.20	.50
3 Melvin Byrd	.30	.75
4 Darnell Clash	.40	1.00
5 Tim Cowan	.30	.75
6 Tyrone Crews	.20	.50
7 Mark DeBrueys	.20	.50
8 Roy Dewalt	.60	1.50
9 Mervyn Fernandez	1.00	2.50
10 Bernie Glier	.20	.50
11 Keith Gooch	.20	.50
12 Dennis Guevin	.20	.50
13 Nick Hebeler	.20	.50
14 Bryan Illerbrun	.20	.50
15 Glen Jackson	.20	.50
16 Keyvan Jenkins	.40	1.00
17 Andre Jones DB	.20	.50
18 Rick Klassen	.30	.75
19 Kevin Konar	.30	.75
20 Glenn Leonhard	.20	.50
21 Nelson Martin	.20	.50
22 John Pankratz	.20	.50
23 James Parker	.50	1.25
24 Lui Passaglia	1.00	2.50
25 Ryan Potter	.20	.50
26 Ron Robinson	.30	.75
27 Gerald Roper	.20	.50
28 Jim Sandusky	.75	2.00
29 John Henry White	.20	.50
30 Al Wilson	.20	.50
31 Team Photo	.30	.75
32 Checklist	.30	.75

1988 B.C. Lions Bootlegger

This 13-card standard-size safety set features members of the British Columbia Lions and was co-sponsored by Bootlegger and PS Pharmasave, whose company logos adorn the bottom of the card face. These cards display posed color player photos, shot from the waist up against a sky blue background. The photos are framed by white borders, with player information immediately below the pictures. The backs have an icon of the team helmet, biography, and an anti-drug message. A different "Just Say No To Drugs" message is included on each card. The sponsor title card lists a total of 36 different companies who financed the drug awareness program. The cards are unnumbered and checklisted below in alphabetical order.

COMPLETE SET (13)	8.00	20.00
1 Jamie Buis	.50	1.25
2 Jan Carinci	.50	1.25
3 Dwayne Derban	.50	1.25
4 Roy Dewalt	1.25	3.00
5 Andre Francis	.60	1.50
6 Rick Klassen	.75	2.00
7 Kevin Konar	.60	1.50
8 Scott Lecky	.50	1.25
9 James Parker	1.25	3.00
10 John Ulmer	.50	1.25
11 Peter VandenBos	.50	1.25
12 Todd Wiseman	.50	1.25
NNO Title Card Corporate Sponsors	.60	1.50

1994 B.C. Lions Forty Years of Pride

These cards were issued in one perforated sheet to Lions season ticket holders in 1994. Each unnumbered card when separated measures roughly 2 1/4" by 3 3/4" and includes a color player photo on front and brief player bio on back.

COMPLETE SET (8)	7.50	15.00
1 By Bailey	1.50	4.00
2 Danny Barrett	1.00	2.50
3 Mervyn Fernandez	1.00	2.50
4 Willie Fleming	1.00	2.50
5 Sean Millington	1.00	2.50
6 Lui Passaglia	1.50	4.00
7 Cory Philpot	1.50	4.00
8 Rob Smith	.60	1.50

1997 B.C. Lions SmartLease

This set was issued by the Lions for members of their official fan club. Each card measures a large 3 3/4" by 8 1/2" and features a color image of the player with his jersey number and name above the photo. The cards are blankbacked and were sponsored by SmartLease.

COMPLETE SET (8)	10.00	20.00
1 Paul Blackwood	1.25	3.00
2 Giulio Caravatta	1.25	3.00
3 Dave Chaytors	1.25	3.00
4 Tony Collier	1.25	3.00
5 Greg Frers	1.25	3.00
6 Steven Glenn	1.25	3.00
7 Cory Philpot	2.50	6.00
8 Eddie Thomas	1.25	3.00

1954 Blue Ribbon Tea

The 1954 Blue Ribbon Tea set contains 80 color cards of CFL players. The cards measure 2 1/4" by 4" and the pictures on the front are posed rather than action shots. The backs of the cards contain biographical data in both English and French. An album for this set was produced to house the cards. The set was printed in Canada by a firm called Colorgraphic.

COMPLETE SET (80)	5,000.00	9,000.00
1 Jack Jacobs	100.00	200.00
2 Neill Armstrong	60.00	100.00
3 Lorne Benson	50.00	80.00
4 Tom Casey	60.00	100.00
5 Vinnie Drake	50.00	80.00
6 Tommy Ford	50.00	80.00
7 Bud Grant	350.00	600.00
8 Dick Huffman	60.00	100.00
9 Gerry James	75.00	150.00
10 Bud Korchak	50.00	80.00
11 Thomas Lumsden	50.00	80.00
12 Steve Patrick	50.00	80.00
13 Keith Pearce	50.00	80.00
14 Jesse Thomas	50.00	80.00
15 Buddy Tinsley	60.00	100.00
16 Alan Scott Wiley	50.00	80.00
17 Winty Young	50.00	80.00
18 Joseph Zaleski	50.00	80.00
19 Ron Vaccher	50.00	80.00
20 John Gramling	50.00	80.00
21 Bob Simpson	75.00	150.00
22 Bruno Bitkowski	60.00	100.00
23 Kaye Vaughan	60.00	100.00
24 Don Carter	50.00	80.00
25 Gene Roberts	50.00	80.00
26 Howie Turner	50.00	80.00
27 Avatus Stone	50.00	80.00
28 Tom McHugh	50.00	80.00
29 Clyde Bennett	50.00	80.00
30 Bill Berezowski	50.00	80.00
31 Eddie Bevan	50.00	80.00
32 Dick Brown	50.00	80.00
33 Bernie Custis	60.00	100.00
34 Merle Hapes	60.00	100.00
35 Tip Logan	50.00	80.00
36 Vince Mazza	60.00	100.00
37 Pete Neumann	60.00	100.00
38 Vince Scott	60.00	100.00
39 Ralph Toohy	50.00	80.00
40 Frank Anderson	50.00	80.00
41 Bob Dean	50.00	80.00
42 Leon Manley	50.00	80.00
43 Bill Zock	60.00	100.00
44 Frank Morris	75.00	150.00
45 Jim Quondamatteo	50.00	80.00
46 Eagle Keys	75.00	150.00
47 Bernie Faloney	200.00	400.00
48 Jackie Parker	300.00	500.00
49 Ray Willsey	50.00	80.00
50 Mike King	50.00	80.00
51 Johnny Bright	200.00	350.00
52 Gene Brito	60.00	100.00
53 Stan Heath	60.00	100.00
54 Roy Jenson	50.00	80.00
55 Don Loney	50.00	80.00
56 Eddie Macon	50.00	80.00
57 Peter Maxwell-Muir	50.00	80.00
58 Tom Miner	50.00	80.00
59 Jim Prewett	50.00	80.00
60 Lowell Wagner	50.00	80.00
61 Red O'Quinn	60.00	100.00
62 Ray Poole	60.00	100.00
63 Jim Staton	50.00	80.00
64 Alex Webster	100.00	200.00
65 Al Dekdebruin	50.00	80.00
66 Ed Bradley	50.00	80.00
67 Tex Coulter	75.00	150.00
68 Sam Etcheverry	300.00	500.00
69 Larry Grigg	50.00	80.00
70 Tom Hugo	50.00	80.00
71 Chuck Hunsinger	50.00	80.00
72 Herb Trawick	75.00	150.00
73 Virgil Wagner	60.00	100.00
74 Phil Adrian	50.00	80.00
75 Bruce Coulter	50.00	80.00
76 Jim Miller	50.00	80.00
77 Jim Mitchener	50.00	80.00
78 Tom Moran	50.00	80.00
79 Doug McNichol	50.00	80.00
80 Joey Pal	50.00	80.00
NNO Card Album	175.00	350.00

1969 Calgary Stampeders Team Issue

The Stampeders issued this set of player photos around 1969. Each includes two black-and-white player photos with one being a posed action shot along with a smaller portrait image. The roughly 8" by 10 1/8" photos include the player's name, a short bio and team logo on the cardfronts. The backs are blank and unnumbered.

COMPLETE SET (28)	100.00	200.00
1 Frank Andruski	4.00	8.00
2 Lanny Boleski	4.00	8.00
3 Ron Capham	4.00	8.00
4 Terry Evanshen	7.50	15.00
5 Joe Forzani	5.00	10.00
6 Jim Furlong	4.00	8.00
7 Wayne Harris	7.50	15.00
8 Herman Harrison	6.00	12.00
9 John Helton	6.00	12.00
10 Fred James	4.00	8.00
11 Jerry Keeling	6.00	12.00
12 Roger Kramer	5.00	10.00
13 Granville Liggins	5.00	10.00
14 Rudy Linterman	5.00	10.00
15 Bob Lueck	4.00	8.00
16 Don Luzzi	4.00	8.00
17 Bob McCarthy	4.00	8.00
18 Ron Payne	4.00	8.00
19 Larry Robinson	5.00	10.00
20 Billy Roy	4.00	8.00
21 Herb Schumm	4.00	8.00
22 Gerry Shaw	4.00	8.00
23 Rick Shaw	4.00	8.00
24 Jim Sillye	4.00	8.00
25 Ward Smith	4.00	8.00
26 Howard Starks	4.00	8.00
27 Terry Wilson	4.00	8.00
28 Ted Woods	4.00	8.00

1971 Calgary Stampeders Team Issue

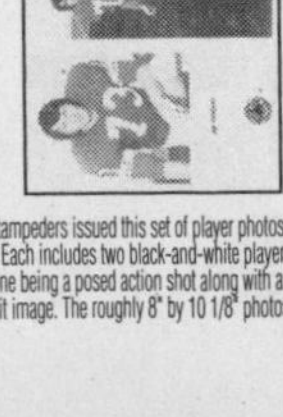

The Stampeders issued this set of player photos around 1971. Each includes two black-and-white player photos with one being a posed action shot along with a smaller portrait image. The roughly 8" by 10 1/8" photos include the player's name and team logo on the cardfronts. The backs are blank and unnumbered.

COMPLETE SET (22)	75.00	150.00
1 Frank Andruski	4.00	8.00
2 Basil Bark	4.00	8.00
3 Lanny Boleski	4.00	8.00
4 Jim Bond	4.00	8.00
5 Joe Forzani	5.00	10.00
6 John Forzani	4.00	8.00
7 Jim Furlong	4.00	8.00
8 Wayne Harris	6.00	12.00
9 Herman Harrison	6.00	12.00
10 John Helton	5.00	10.00
11 Fred James	4.00	8.00
12 Jerry Keeling	6.00	12.00
13 Craig Koinzan	4.00	8.00
14 Granville Liggins	5.00	10.00
15 Jim Lindsey	4.00	8.00
16 Rudy Linterman	5.00	10.00
17 Brian Marcil	4.00	8.00
18 Hugh McInnis	4.00	8.00
19 Herb Schumm	4.00	8.00
20 John Senst	4.00	8.00
21 Gerry Shaw	4.00	8.00
22 Howard Starks	4.00	8.00

1973 Calgary Stampeders Team Issue

The Stampeders issued this set of player photos around 1973. Each includes two black-and-white player photos with one being a posed action shot along with a smaller portrait image. The roughly 8" by 10 1/8" photos include the player's name and team logo on the cardfronts. The backs are blank and unnumbered.

COMPLETE SET (18)	60.00	120.00
1 Frank Andruski	4.00	8.00
2 Lanny Boleski	4.00	8.00
3 John Forzani	4.00	8.00
4 Jim Furlong	4.00	8.00
5 John Helton	5.00	10.00
6 Dave Herbert	4.00	8.00
7 Fred James	4.00	8.00
8 Blain Lamoureaux	4.00	8.00
9 Marion Latimore	4.00	8.00
10 Jim Lindsey	4.00	8.00
11 Pete Liske	10.00	20.00
12 John Senst	4.00	8.00
13 Larry Robinson	5.00	10.00
14 Fritz Seyferth	4.00	8.00
15 Gerry Shaw	4.00	8.00
16 Jim Sillye	4.00	8.00
17 Howard Starks	4.00	8.00
18 Bob Wyatt	4.00	8.00

1975 Calgary Stampeders Team Sheets

This group of 32-players and coaches of the Stampeders was produced on four glossy sheets each measuring approximately 8" by 10". The fronts feature black-and-white player portraits with eight pictures to a sheet with the year printed at the top. The backs are blank. The cards are unnumbered and checklisted below in alphabetical order, with the player pictured in the upper left hand corner of the sheet listed first.

COMPLETE SET (4)	15.00	30.00
1 John Forzani	4.00	8.00
Moody Jackson		
Karl Douglas		
Fred James		
Ted Bachman		
Bill Line		
Geary Murdock		
Rick Galbos		
2 John Helton	4.00	8.00
Willie Burden		
Paul McKay		
Blain Lamoureux		
Gord Stewart		
Joe Forzani		
Basil Bark		
Tom Forzani		
3 Cyril McFall	5.00	10.00
Joe Pisarcik		
Roger Goree		
Ozell Collier		
Lorne Sherbina		
Jim Sillye		
Rudy Linterman		
Jim Wood		
4 Dick Wesolowski	4.00	8.00
Henry Sovio		
Octavis Morgan		
Don Moulton		
Jim Bond		
Howard Starks		
Larry Cates		
Harold Holton		

1977-78 Calgary Stampeders Team Sheets

This group of 40-players and coaches of the Stampeders was produced on five glossy sheets each measuring approximately 8" by 10". The fronts feature black-and-white player portraits with eight pictures to a sheet with the year printed at the top. The backs are blank. The cards are unnumbered and checklisted below in alphabetical order, with the player pictured in the upper left hand corner of the sheet listed first.

COMPLETE SET (5)	12.50	25.00
1 Alvin Burleson	3.00	6.00
Brian Gervais		
Willie Armstead		
Blain Lamoureux		
Doug Falconer		
Ollie Bakken		
John Palazeti		
Larry Leathem		
2 Art Evans	2.50	5.00
Ardell Wiegandt		
Jim Spavital		
Jack Gotta		
Ernie Zwahlen		
Lloyd Fairbanks		
Rick Galbos		
Basil Bark		
3 Bob Martin	3.00	6.00
John Jones		
Jody Medford		

Rod Woodward
Tom Forzani
Cyril McFall
Dennis Meyer
Willie Thomas
4 Ray Odums 2.50 5.00
Jim Harris
Harold Holton
Jim Baker
Rudy Linterman
Bob Viccars
Geary Murdock
John Helton
5 Laurent Tittley 3.00 6.00
Lorne Sherbina
Bill Palmer
Andy Jonassen
Willie Burden
Bryan McLaughlin
Melvin Wilson
John Hufnagel

1978 Calgary Stampeders Team Sheets

This group of 40-players and coaches of the Stampeders was produced on five glossy sheets each measuring approximately 8" by 10". The fronts feature black-and-white player portraits with eight pictures to a sheet with the year printed at the top. The backs are blank. The cards are unnumbered and checklisted below in alphabetical order, with the player pictured in the upper left hand corner of the sheet listed first.

COMPLETE SET (5) 15.00 30.00
1 Ollie Bakken 4.00 8.00
Matthew Reed
Reggie Lewis
Jim Baker
Lloyd Fairbanks
Ed McAleney
Larry Tittley
Alex Morris
2 John Helton 4.00 8.00
Willie Burden
Alvin Burleson
Terry Irvin
Blain Lamoureux
Ray Odums
Harold Holton
Willie Armstead
3 Dave Kirzinger 4.00 8.00
Andy Jonassen
Anthony Dickerson
Doug Falconer
John Palazeti
Tom Reimer
Tom Forzani
John Hufnagel
4 Rick Koswin 3.00 6.00
Art Evans
Jack Gotta
Joe Tiller
Willie Thomas
Miles Gorrell
Andre Johnson
Bob Lubig
5 John Malinosky 4.00 8.00
Cyril McFall
Alan MacLean
Kelvin Kirk
Robin Harber
Rob Kochel
Gene Sykes
Bob Viccars

1980 Calgary Stampeders Team Sheets

This group of 40-players and coaches of the Stampeders was produced on five glossy sheets each measuring approximately 8" by 10". The fronts feature black-and-white player portraits with eight pictures to a sheet with the year printed at the top. The backs are blank. The cards are unnumbered and checklisted below in alphabetical order, with the player pictured in the upper left hand corner of the sheet listed first.

COMPLETE SET (5) 12.50 25.00
1 Willie Armstead 3.00 6.00
Doug Battershill
Willie Burden
John Palazeti
Ken Dombrowski
Lloyd Fairbanks
Rob Forbes
Tim Gillespie
2 Miles Gorrell 3.00 6.00
Jack Gotta CO
John T. Hay
Tyrone Hicks
Mike Horton
Jeff Inglis
Terry Irvin
Ken Johnson
3 Steve Kearns 3.00 6.00
Kelvin Kirk
Dave Kirzinger
Tom Krebs
Leo Lewis
Reggie Lewis
Robert Lubig
Darrell Moir
4 Ed McAleney 2.50 5.00
Mike McTague
Mark Nelson
Ray Odums
Ronnie Paggett
Robert Sparks
James Sykes
Bruce Threadgill
5 Bob Viccars 2.50 5.00
Mervin Walker
Lyall Woznesensky
Ardell Wiegandt
Rob Kochel
Stan Schwartz CO
Dennis Meyer CO
Marvin Bass CO

1981 Calgary Stampeders Red Rooster

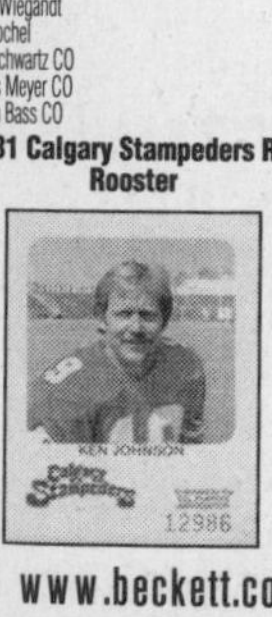

This 40-card set, distributed by Red Rooster Food Stores, measures approximately 2 3/4" by 3 5/8" and features posed, color player photos with rounded corners on a white card face. Since the card edges are perforated, the cards were apparently issued as a sheet. The player's name is printed below the photo, as is the team name and a CFL Players Association endorsement. (Some of the cards have a serial number below the endorsement). The backs carry biographical information and a player profile. Sponsor logos and names are printed at the bottom. The cards are unnumbered and checklisted below in alphabetical order.

COMPLETE SET (40) 10.00 25.00
1 Willie Armstead .25 .60
2 Doug Battershill .25 .60
3 Willie Burden 1.00 2.50
(From waist up)
4 Willie Burden 1.00 2.50
(Head and shoulders)
5 Scott Burk UER .25 .60
(Misspelled Burke/4th line of bio)
6 Al Burleson .25 .60
7 Ken Dombrowski .25 .60
8 Lloyd Fairbanks .50 1.25
9 Rob Forbes .25 .60
10 Tom Forzani .40 1.00
11 Miles Gorrell .25 .60
12 J.T. Hay .25 .60
13 John Holland .40 1.00
14 Norm Hopely .25 .60
15 Jeff Inglis .40 1.00
16 Lepoleon Ingram .25 .60
17 Terry Irvin .25 .60
18 Ken Johnson .40 1.00
19 Franklin King .25 .60
20 Dave Kirzinger .25 .60
21 Frank Kosec .25 .60
22 Tom Krebs .25 .60
23 Reggie Lewis .25 .60
24 Robert Lubig .25 .60
25 Scott MacArthur .25 .60
26 Ed McAleney .25 .60
27 Mike McTague .40 1.00
28 Mark Moors .40 1.00
29 Bernie Morrison .25 .60
30 Mark Nelson .25 .60
31 Ray Odums .25 .60
32 Ronnie Paggett .25 .60
33 John Palazeti .25 .60
34 John Prassas .25 .60
35 Tom Reimer .25 .60
36 James Sykes 1.00 2.50
(Close-up)
37 James Sykes 1.00 2.50
(From waist up)
38 Bruce Threadgill .25 .60
39 Bob Viccars .25 .60
40 Merv Walker .25 .60

1989 Calgary Stampeders KFC

The 1989 KFC Calgary Stampeders set contains 24 cards measuring approximately 2 7/16" by 3 5/16". The fronts have color portrait photos bordered in white; the vertically oriented backs have detailed profiles and statistics. The cards come as perforated strips of four player cards and one discount card for 2.00 off any 1989 Stampeder home game ticket purchase. The cards are ordered on the strips by uniform number such that by looking at the reverse of each strip, the cards are in almost perfect numerical order. The only exception is that card 9 comes before 8.

COMPLETE SET (24) 4.00 10.00
3 David McCrary .15 .40
4 Brent Matich .25 .60
8 Danny Barrett .60 1.50
9 Terrence Jones .60 1.50
12 Tim Petros .25 .60
13 Mark McLoughlin .15 .40
15 Ron Hopkins .25 .60
20 Chris Major .50 1.25
24 Greg Peterson .15 .40
25 Shawn Faulkner .15 .40
32 Darcy Kopp .15 .40
34 Andy McVey .15 .40
39 Doug(Tank) Landry .40 1.00
59 Leo Blanchard .15 .40
61 Tom Spoletini .15 .40
65 Mike Palumbo .15 .40
66 Dan Ferrone .25 .60
74 Mitchell Price .25 .60
76 Marshall Toner .15 .40
84 Eugene Belliveau .25 .60
85 Brock Smith .15 .40
89 Larry Willis .30 .75
93 Kent Warnock .30 .75
97 Ken Ford .15 .40

1990 Calgary Stampeders KFC

The 1990 KFC Calgary Stampeders set contains 24 cards measuring approximately 2 7/16" by 3 5/16". The fronts have color portrait photos bordered in white. The cards come as perforated strips of four player cards and one discount card for 2.00 off any 1990 Stampeder home game ticket purchase. The cards are ordered alphabetically in the list below.

COMPLETE SET (24) 4.00 10.00
1 Walter Ballard .20 .50
2 Danny Barrett .60 1.50
3 Eddie Brown .60 1.50
4 Joe Clausi .20 .50
5 Lloyd Fairbanks .30 .75
6 Matt Finlay .30 .75
7 Ken Ford .20 .50
8 Ron Hopkins .30 .75
9 Keyvan Jenkins .40 1.00
10 Will Johnson .30 .75
11 Terrence Jones .60 1.50
12 David McCrary .20 .50
13 Mark McLoughlin .20 .50
14 Andy McVey .20 .50
15 Brent Matich .20 .50
16 Mike Palumbo .20 .50
17 Greg Peterson .20 .50
18 Tim Petros .30 .75
19 Mitchell Price .30 .75
20 Brock Smith .20 .50
21 Tom Spoletini .20 .50
22 Junior Thurman .40 1.00
23 Marshall Toner .20 .50
24 Kent Warnock .30 .75

1993 Calgary Stampeders Sport Chek

Measuring approximately 12 1/2" by 19 1/2", this perforated sheet displays twenty-four player cards and six coupons. After perforation, the individual cards measure approximately 2 1/2" by 3 1/4". The fronts show posed color shots inside white borders. Some of these photos are overexposed. The upper corners hold sponsor logos, while at the bottom the team logo and player identification are provided. In black print on a white background, the backs carry biography, season summary, and personal information. The sheets were given away to fans at two Stampeder home games during the season. Also four-card mini-sheets, depicting Flutie, Thurman, Zizakovic, and Sapunjis, were included in each 1993 Grey Cup Fan Fest welcome package. The cards are unnumbered and checklisted below in alphabetical order.

COMPLETE SET (24) 8.00 20.00
1 Karl Anthony .25 .60
2 Raymond Biggs .25 .60
3 Douglas Craft .25 .60
4 Doug Davies .25 .60
5 Mark Dube .25 .60
6 Matt Finlay .25 .60
7 Doug Flutie 3.20 8.00
8 Fred Gatlin .25 .60
9 Keyvan Jenkins .40 1.00
10 Alondra Johnson .40 1.00
11 Pat Mahon .25 .60
12 Tony Martino .25 .60
13 Mark McLoughlin .25 .60
14 Andy McVey .25 .60
15 Will Moore .60 1.50
16 Mark Pearce .25 .60
17 Allen Pitts 1.20 3.00
18 David Sapunjis .60 1.50
19 Junior Thurman .40 1.00
20 Gerald Vaughn .25 .60
21 Ken Watson .25 .60
22 Brian Wiggins .40 1.00
23 Blair Zerr .25 .60
24 Srecko Zizakovic .25 .60

1999 Calgary Stampeders Kraft

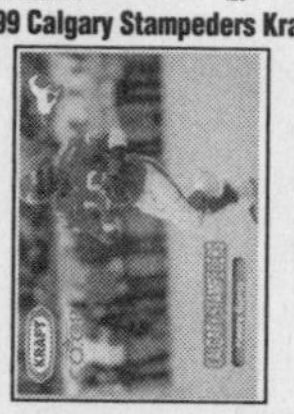

This set of 12-cards was sponsored by Kraft Co-Op and produced for the Calgary Stampeders. Each card includes a full color player photo on the front along with the Stampeders name, the team logo, and player name on the cardfront.

COMPLETE SET (12) 15.00 30.00
1 Allen Pitts 1.50 4.00
2 Alondra Johnson .60 1.50
3 Aubrey Cummings 1.00 2.50
4 Darryl Hall .60 1.50
5 Dave Dickenson 2.00 5.00
6 Henry Burris 2.00 5.00
7 Kelvin Anderson 1.50 4.00
8 Mark McLoughlin .60 1.50
9 Marvin Coleman .60 1.50
10 Rocco Romano .60 1.50
11 Travis Moore 1.00 2.50
12 Vince Danielsen 1.00 2.50

2000 Calgary Stampeders Kraft

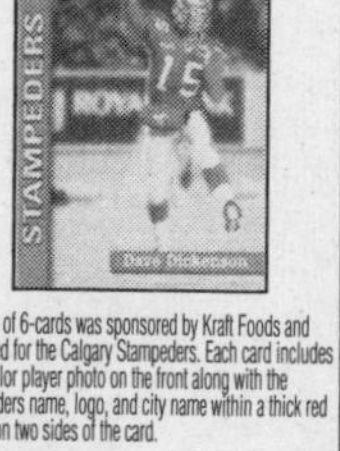

This set of 6-cards was sponsored by Kraft Foods and produced for the Calgary Stampeders. Each card includes a full color player photo on the front along with the Stampeders name, logo, and city name within a thick red border on two sides of the card.

COMPLETE SET (6) 4.00 8.00
1 Marvin Coleman .40 1.00
2 Vince Danielsen .75 2.00
3 Dave Dickenson 2.00 4.00
4 Darryl Hall .40 1.00
5 Travis Moore .75 2.00
6 Allen Pitts 1.50 3.00

1971 Chiquita CFL All-Stars

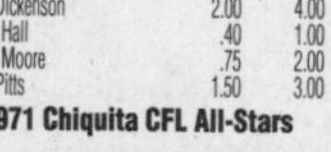

This set of CFL All-Stars actually consists of 13 slides which were intended to be viewed by a special yellow Chiquita viewer. Each slide measures approximately 1 3/4" by 3 5/8" and contains four small color slides showing two views of two players. Each side has a player summary on its middle portion, with two small color action slides at each end stacked one above the other. When the slide is placed in the viewer, the two bottom slides, which are identical, reveal the first player. Flipping the slide over reveals the other player biography and enables one to view the other two slides, which show the second player. Each side of the slides is numbered as listed below. The set is considered complete without the yellow viewer.

COMPLETE SET (13) 100.00 200.00
1 Bill Baker/2 Ken Sugarman 6.00 15.00
3 Wayne Giardino/4 Peter Dalla Riva 6.00 15.00
5 Leon McQuay/6 Jim Thorpe 7.50 20.00
7 George Reed/8 Jerry Campbell 6.00 15.00
9 Tommy Joe Coffey/10 Terry Evanshen 7.50 20.00
11 Jim Young/12 Mark Kosmos 6.00 15.00
13 Ron Forwick/14 Jack Abendschan 5.00 12.00
15 Don Jonas/16 Al Marcellin 6.00 15.00
17 Joe Theismann/18 Jim Corrigall 15.00 40.00
19 Ed George/20 Dick Dupuis 5.00 12.00
21 Ted Dushinski/22 Bob Swift 5.00 12.00
23 John Lagrone/24 Bill Danychuk 5.00 12.00
25 Garney Henley/26 John Williams 6.00 15.00
NNO Yellow Viewer 6.00 15.00

1965 Coke Caps CFL

This set of 230 Coke caps was issued on bottled soft drinks and featured CFL players. The caps measure approximately one inch in diameter. The outside of the cap exhibits a black-and-white photo of the player's face, with a Coke (or Sprite) advertisement below the picture. Sprite caps are harder to find and are valued using the multiplier line below. The player's team name is written vertically on the left side, following the curve of the bottle cap, and likewise for the player's name on the right side. The players are listed in alphabetical order within their teams, and the teams are arranged alphabetically. Three players appear twice with two different teams, Don Fuell, Hal Ledyard, and L. Tomlinson. A plastic holder measuring approximately 14" by 16" was also available. The caps were available in French and English, the difference being "Drink Coke" or "Bovez Coke" under the player photo.

COMPLETE SET (230) 600.00 1,000.00
*SPRITE CAPS: 1.5X TO 2.5X
*FRENCH CAPS: 1.25X TO 2X
1 Neil Beaumont 3.00 6.00
2 Tom Brown 4.00 8.00
3 Mack Burton 2.50 5.00
4 Mike Cacic 2.50 5.00
5 Pat Claridge 2.50 5.00
6 Steve Cotter 2.50 5.00
7 Norm Fieldgate 4.00 8.00
8 Greg Findlay 2.50 5.00
9 Willie Fleming 8.00 12.00
10 Dick Fouts 2.50 5.00
11 Tom Hinton 4.00 8.00
12 Sonny Homer 3.00 6.00
13 Joe Kapp 15.00 25.00
14 Gus Kasapis 2.50 5.00
15 Peter Kempf 2.50 5.00
16 Bill Lasseter 2.50 5.00
17 Mike Martin 2.50 5.00
18 Ron Morris 2.50 5.00
19 Bill Munsey 2.50 5.00
20 Paul Seale 2.50 5.00
21 Steve Shafer 2.50 5.00
22 Ken Sugarman 3.00 6.00
23 Bob Swift 2.50 5.00
24 Jesse Williams 2.50 5.00
25 Ron Albright UER 2.50 5.00
(misspelled Allbright)
26 Lu Bain 2.50 5.00
27 Frank Budd 2.50 5.00
28 Lovell Coleman 3.00 6.00
29 Eagle Day 5.00 10.00
30 Paul Dudley 2.50 5.00
31 Jim Furlong 2.50 5.00
32 George Hansen 2.50 5.00
33 Wayne Harris 8.00 12.00
34 Herman Harrison 4.00 8.00
35 Pat Holmes 2.50 5.00
36 Art Johnson 2.50 5.00
37 Jerry Keeling 4.00 8.00
38 Roger Kramer 3.00 6.00
39 Hal Krebs 2.50 5.00
40 Don Luzzi 4.00 8.00
41 Pete Manning 2.50 5.00
42 Dale Parsons 2.50 5.00
43 Ron Payne 2.50 5.00
44 Larry Robinson 3.00 6.00
45 Gerry Shaw 2.50 5.00
46 Don Stephenson 2.50 5.00
47 Bob Taylor 3.00 6.00
48 Ted Woods 2.50 5.00
49 Jon Anabo 2.50 5.00
50 Ray Ash 2.50 5.00
51 Jim Battle 2.50 5.00
52 Charlie Brown 2.50 5.00
53 Tommy Joe Coffey 10.00 15.00
54 Marcel Deleeuw 2.50 5.00
55 Al Ecuyer 2.50 5.00
56 Ron Forwick 2.50 5.00
57 Jim Higgins 2.50 5.00
58 Henry Huth 2.50 5.00
59 Randy Kerbow 2.50 5.00
60 Oscar Kruger 2.50 5.00
61 Tom Machan 2.50 5.00
62 Grant McKee 2.50 5.00
63 Bill Mitchell 2.50 5.00
64 Barry Mitchelson 2.50 5.00
65 Roger Nelson 4.00 8.00
66 Bill Redell 2.50 5.00
67 Morley Rohliser 2.50 5.00
68 Howie Schumm 2.50 5.00
69 E.A. Sims 2.50 5.00
70 John Sklopan 2.50 5.00
71 Jim Stinnette 2.50 5.00
72 Barney Therrien 2.50 5.00
73 Jim Thomas 2.50 5.00
74 Neil Thomas 2.50 5.00
75 Bill Tobin 3.00 6.00
76 Terry Wilson 2.50 5.00
77 Art Baker 4.00 8.00
78 John Barrow 4.00 8.00
79 Gene Ceppetelli 2.50 5.00
80 John Cimba 2.50 5.00
81 Dick Cohee 2.50 5.00
82 Frank Cosentino 3.00 6.00
83 Johnny Counts 2.50 5.00
84 Stan Crisson 2.50 5.00
85 Tommy Grant 4.00 8.00
86 Garney Henley 4.00 8.00
87 Ed Hoerster 2.50 5.00
88 Zeno Karcz 3.00 6.00
89 Ellison Kelly 4.00 8.00
90 Bob Krouse 2.50 5.00
91 Billy Ray Locklin 2.50 5.00
92 Chet Miksza 2.50 5.00
93 Angelo Mosca 12.00 20.00
94 Bronko Nagurski Jr. 4.00 8.00
95 Ted Page 2.50 5.00
96 Don Sutherin 5.00 10.00
97 Dave Viti 2.50 5.00
98 Dick Walton 2.50 5.00
99 Billy Wayte 2.50 5.00
100 Joe Zuger 2.50 5.00
101 Jim Andreotti 3.00 6.00
102 John Baker 3.00 6.00
103 Gino Beretta 2.50 5.00
104 Bill Bewley 3.00 6.00
105 Garland Boyette 3.00 6.00
106 Doug Daigneault 2.50 5.00
107 George Dixon 4.00 8.00
108 D. Dolatri 2.50 5.00
109 Ted Elsby 2.50 5.00
110 Don Estes 2.50 5.00
111 Terry Evenshen 8.00 12.00
112 Clare Exelby 2.50 5.00
113 Larry Fairholm 3.00 6.00
114 Bernie Faloney 12.00 20.00
115 Don Fuell 2.50 5.00
116 Mike Gibbons 2.50 5.00
117 Ralph Goldston 3.00 6.00
118 Al Irwin 2.50 5.00
119 John Kennerson 2.50 5.00
120 Ed Learn 2.50 5.00
121 Moe Levesque 2.50 5.00
122 Bob Minihane 2.50 5.00
123 Jim Reynolds 2.50 5.00
124 Billy Roy 2.50 5.00
125 Larry Tomlinson 2.50 5.00
126 Ernie White 2.50 5.00
127 Rick Black 2.50 5.00
128 Mike Blum 2.50 5.00
129 Billy Joe Booth 2.50 5.00
130 Jim Cain 2.50 5.00
131 Bill Cline 2.50 5.00
132 Merv Collins 2.50 5.00
133 Jim Conroy 3.00 6.00
134 Larry DeGraw 2.50 5.00
135 Jim Dillard 2.50 5.00
136 Gene Gaines 4.00 8.00
137 Don Gilbert 2.50 5.00
138 Russ Jackson 12.00 20.00
139 Ken Lehmann 3.00 6.00
140 Bob O'Billovich 2.50 5.00
141 John Pentecost 2.50 5.00
142 Joe Poirier 3.00 6.00
143 Moe Racine 2.50 5.00
144 Sam Scoccia 2.50 5.00
145 Bo Scott 5.00 10.00
146 Jerry Selinger 2.50 5.00
147 Marshall Shirk 2.50 5.00
148 Bill Siekierski 2.50 5.00
149 Ron Stewart 5.00 10.00
150 Whit Tucker 4.00 8.00
151 Ron Atchison 5.00 10.00
152 Al Benecick 2.50 5.00
153 Clyde Brock 2.50 5.00
154 Ed Buchanan 2.50 5.00
155 Roy Cameron 2.50 5.00
156 Hugh Campbell 4.00 8.00
157 Henry Dorsch 2.50 5.00
158 Larry Dumelie 2.50 5.00
159 Garner Ekstran 3.00 6.00
160 Martin Fabi 2.50 5.00
161 Bob Good 2.50 5.00
162 Bob Kosid 2.50 5.00
163 Ron Lancaster 12.00 20.00
164 Hal Ledyard 2.50 5.00
165 Len Legault 2.50 5.00
166 Ron Meadmore 2.50 5.00
167 Bob Ptacek 3.00 6.00
168 George Reed 8.00 12.00
169 Dick Schnell 2.50 5.00
170 Wayne Shaw 2.50 5.00
171 Ted Urness 4.00 8.00
172 Dale West 3.00 6.00
173 Reg Whitehouse 2.50 5.00
174 Gene Wlasiuk 2.50 5.00
175 Jim Worden 2.50 5.00
176 Dick Aldridge 2.50 5.00
177 Walt Balasiuk 2.50 5.00
178 Ron Brewer 2.50 5.00
179 W. Dickey 2.50 5.00
180 Bob Dugan 3.00 6.00
181 Larry Ferguson 3.00 6.00
182 Don Fuell 2.50 5.00
183 Ed Harrington 3.00 6.00
184 Ron Howell 2.50 5.00
185 Francis LaRoue 2.50 5.00
186 Sherman Lewis 3.00 6.00
187 Marv Luster 4.00 8.00
188 Dave Mann 3.00 6.00
189 Pete Martin 2.50 5.00
190 Marty Martinello 2.50 5.00
191 Lamar McHan 4.00 8.00
192 Danny Nykoluk 2.50 5.00
193 Jackie Parker 15.00 25.00
194 Dave Pivec 2.50 5.00
195 Jim Rountree 2.50 5.00
196 Dick Shatto 4.00 8.00
197 Billy Shipp 2.50 5.00
198 Len Sparks 2.50 5.00
199 Dave Still 2.50 5.00
200 Norm Stoneburgh 2.50 5.00
201 Dave Thelen 5.00 10.00
202 John Vilanus 2.50 5.00
203 Jim Walter 2.50 5.00
204 Pat Watson 2.50 5.00
205 John Wydareny 3.00 6.00
206 Billy Cooper 2.50 5.00
207 Wayne Dennis 2.50 5.00
208 Paul Desjardins 3.00 6.00
209 Noel Dunford 2.50 5.00
210 Farrell Funston 3.00 6.00
211 Herb Gray 4.00 8.00
212 Roger Hamelin 2.50 5.00
213 Barrie Hansen 2.50 5.00
214 Henry Janzen 3.00 6.00
215 Hal Ledyard 2.50 5.00
216 Leo Lewis 5.00 10.00
217 Brian Palmer 2.50 5.00
218 Art Perkins 2.50 5.00
219 Cornel Piper 2.50 5.00
220 Ernie Pitts 2.50 5.00
221 Kenny Ploen 5.00 10.00
222 Dave Raimey 3.00 6.00
223 Norm Rauhaus 3.00 6.00
224 Frank Rigney 4.00 8.00
225 Roger Savoie 2.50 5.00
226 Jackie Simpson 4.00 8.00
227 Dick Thornton 3.00 6.00
228 Sherwyn Thorson 2.50 5.00
229 Ed Ulmer 2.50 5.00
230 Bill Whisler 2.50 5.00

1952 Crown Brand Photos

This set of 48 pictures was distributed by Crown Brand Corn Syrup. The collection of the complete set of pictures involved a mail-in offer: one label or cone top from a tin of Crown Brand Corn Syrup and 10 cents for two pictures; or two labels and 25 cents for seven pictures. The photos measure approximately 7" by 8 1/4" and feature a posed photo of the player, with player information below. The back has a checklist of all 48 players included in the set. Hall of Famers included in this set are Tom Casey, Dick Huffman, Jack Jacobs, Martin Ruby, Buddy Tinsley, and Frank Morris. The photos are listed below in alphabetical order according to their teams.

COMPLETE SET (48) 1,000.00 2,000.00
1 John Brown 25.00 50.00
2 Tom Casey 37.50 75.00
3 Tommy Ford 25.00 50.00
4 Ian Gibb 25.00 50.00
5 Dick Huffman 37.50 75.00
6 Jack Jacobs 50.00 100.00
7 Thomas Lumsden 25.00 50.00
8 George McPhail 25.00 50.00
9 Jim McPherson 25.00 50.00
10 Buddy Tinsley 37.50 75.00
11 Ron Vaccher 25.00 50.00
12 Al Wiley 25.00 50.00
13 Ken Charlton 37.50 75.00
14 Glenn Dobbs 37.50 75.00
15 Sully Glasser 25.00 50.00
16 Nelson Greene 25.00 50.00
17 Bert Iannone 25.00 50.00
18 Art McEwan 25.00 50.00
19 Jimmy McFaul 25.00 50.00
20 Bob Pelling 25.00 50.00
21 Chuck Radley 25.00 50.00
22 Martin Ruby 37.50 75.00
23 Jack Russell 25.00 50.00
24 Roy Wright 25.00 50.00
25 Paul Alford 25.00 50.00
26 Sugarfoot Anderson 25.00 50.00
27 Dick Bradley 25.00 50.00
28 Bob Bryant 25.00 50.00
29 Cliff Cyr 25.00 50.00
30 Cal Green 25.00 50.00
31 Stan Heath 37.50 75.00
32 Stan Kaluznick 25.00 50.00
33 Guss Knickerhm 25.00 50.00
34 Paul Salata 25.00 50.00
35 Murry Sullivan 25.00 50.00
36 Dave West 25.00 50.00
37 Joe Aguirre 25.00 50.00
38 Claude Arnold 25.00 50.00
39 Bill Briggs 25.00 50.00
40 Mario DeMarco 25.00 50.00
41 Mike King 25.00 50.00
42 Donald Lord 25.00 50.00
43 Frank Morris 37.50 75.00
44 Gayle Pace 25.00 50.00
45 Rod Pantages 25.00 50.00
46 Rollin Prather 25.00 50.00
47 Chuck Quilter 25.00 50.00
48 Jim Quondamatteo 25.00 50.00

1972-83 Dimanche/Derniere Heure

The blank-backed photo sheets in this multi-sport set measure approximately 8 1/2" by 11" and feature white-bordered color sports star photos from Dimanche Derniere Heure, a Montreal newspaper. The player's name, position and biographical information appear within the lower white margin. All text is in French. A white vinyl album was available for storing the photo sheets. Printed on the album's spine are the words, "Mes Vedettes du Sport" (My Stars of Sport).The photos are unnumbered and are checklisted below in alphabetical order according to sport or team as follows: Montreal Expos baseball players (1-117; National League baseball players (118-130); Montreal Canadiens hockey players (131-177); wrestlers (178-202); prize fighters (203-204); auto racing drivers (205-208); women's golf (209); Patof the circus clown (210); and CFL (211-278).

214 Peter Dalla Riva 10/23/77 2.00 5.00
215 Don Sweet 10/30/77 2.00 5.00
216 Mark Jackson 11/6/77 2.00 5.00
217 Tony Proudfoot 11/13/77 2.00 5.00
218 Dan Yochum 11/20/77 2.00 5.00
219 1977 Team Photo 11/27/77 2.00 5.00
220 Wayne Conrad 12/77 2.00 5.00
221 Vernon Perry 12/11/77 2.50 6.00
222 Carl Crennel 12/17/77 2.00 5.00
223 Sonny Wade 5.00 10.00
Marv Levy 12/25/77
224 John O'Leary 8/6/78 2.00 5.00
225 Dickie Harris 8/13/78 2.50 6.00
226 Glen Weir 8/20/78 2.00 5.00
227 Gabriel Gregoire 8/27/78 2.00 5.00
228 Larry Smith 9/3/78 2.00 5.00
229 Gerry Dattilio 9/10/78 2.00 5.00
230 Ken Starch 9/17/78 2.00 5.00
231 Larry Uteck 9/24/78 2.00 5.00
232 Jim Burrow 10/1/78 2.50 6.00
233 Randy Rhino 10/8/78 2.00 5.00
234 Chuck McMann 10/15/78 2.00 5.00
235 Gordon Judges 10/22/78 2.00 5.00
236 Doug Payton 10/29/78 2.00 5.00
237 Ty Morris 11/5/78 2.00 5.00
238 Wally Buono 11/12/78 2.00 5.00
239 1978 Team Photo 11/19/78 2.50 6.00
240 Ray Watrin 11/26/78 2.00 5.00
241 Junior Ah You 12/3/78 3.00 8.00
242 David Green 10/7/79 2.50 6.00
243 Ron Calgagni 10/14/79 2.00 5.00
244 Bobby Husea 10/21/79 2.00 5.00
245 Nick Arakgi 10/28/79 2.00 5.00
246 Joe Barnes 11/4/79 3.00 8.00
247 Keith Baker 11/11/79 2.00 5.00
248 Tony Petruccio 11/18/79 2.00 5.00
249 Tom Cousineau 11/25/79 3.00 8.00
250 Doug Scott 10/5/80 2.00 5.00
251 Dickie Harris 10/12/80 2.50 6.00
252 Gabriel Gregoire 10/19/80 2.00 5.00
253 Fred Biletnikoff 10/26/80 10.00 20.00
254 Tom Cousineau 11/2/80 3.00 8.00
255 Chuck McMann 11/9/80 2.00 5.00
256 Junior Ah You 11/16/80 3.00 8.00
257 Gerry Dattilio 11/23/80 2.00 5.00
258 Vince Ferragamo 7/19/81 3.00 8.00
259 Joe Scannella 7/26/81 2.00 5.00
260 Billy Johnson 8/2/81 3.00 8.00
261 Joe Hawco 8/9/81 2.00 5.00
262 Gerry McGrath 8/16/81 2.00 5.00
263 Joe Taylor 8/23/81 2.00 5.00
264 Doug Scott 8/30/81 2.00 5.00
265 Tom Cousineau 9/6/81 3.00 8.00
266 Nick Arakgi 9/13/81 2.00 5.00
267 Mike Hameluck 8/20/81 2.00 5.00
268 Doug Payton 9/27/81 2.00 5.00
269 James Scott 10/4/81 2.50 6.00
270 Keith Gary 10/11/81 2.00 5.00
271 David Overstreet 10/18/81 3.00 8.00
272 Peter Dalla Riva 10/25/81 2.00 5.00
273 Marc Lacelle 11/1/81 2.00 5.00
274 Luc Tousignant 9/19/82 2.00 5.00
275 Denny Ferdinand 9/26/82 2.00 5.00
276 Joe Galat 10/3/82 2.00 5.00
277 Lester Brown 10/10/82 2.00 5.00
278 Dom Vetro 10/17/82 2.00 5.00
279 Preston Young 10/24/82 2.00 5.00
280 Eugene Beliveau 10/31/82 2.00 5.00
281 Ken Miller 11/7/82 2.00 5.00

1962 Edmonton Eskimos Program Inserts

Each of these photos measures approximately 3 7/8" by 5 3/8". Inside white borders, the fronts feature black-and-white posed action photos. The player's facsimile autograph is written across the photo in red ink. Immediately below the picture is the player's name and position. The wider white bottom border also carries some sponsor information and a red ink printed serial number. The photos were primarily sponsored by CFRN radio and/or A&W Drive-in. The photos were initially issued in perforated sheets of four per Eskimos game programs. The backs display various advertisements. The photos are unnumbered and checklisted below in alphabetical order.

COMPLETE SET (32) 125.00 225.00
1 Ray Baillie 3.00 6.00
2 Johnny Bright 6.00 12.00
3 Tommy Joe Coffey 6.00 12.00
4 Toby Deese 3.00 6.00
5 Don Duncalfe 3.00 6.00
6 Nat Dye 3.00 6.00
7 Pat Dye 12.00 20.00
8 Al Ecuyer 3.00 6.00
9 Larry Fleisher 3.00 6.00
10 Gino Fracas 4.00 8.00
11 Ted Frechette 3.00 6.00
12 Don Getty 6.00 12.00
13 Ed Gray 3.00 6.00
14 Dunc Harvey 4.00 8.00
15 Tony Kehrer 3.00 6.00
16 Mike Kmeche 3.00 6.00
17 Oscar Kruger 4.00 8.00
18 Jack Lamb 3.00 6.00
19 Mike Lashuk 3.00 6.00
20 Jim Letcavits 3.00 6.00
21 Bill McKenny 3.00 6.00
22 Roger Nelson 6.00 12.00
23 Jackie Parker 12.00 20.00
24 Howie Schumm 3.00 6.00
25 E.A. Sims 3.00 6.00
26 Bill Smith 3.00 6.00
27 Don Stephenson 3.00 6.00
28 Roy Stevenson 3.00 6.00
29 Ted Tully 3.00 6.00
30 Len Vella 3.00 6.00
31 Mike Volcan 3.00 6.00
32 Bobby Walden 4.00 8.00

1962 Edmonton Eskimos Team Issue 4x5

This set of photos was issued by the Eskimos to fill fan requests. Each photo measures roughly 4" by 5" and includes a black and white photo of the player in street clothes instead of in uniform. There is no identification on the fronts, but the player's name is usually included on the backs of the photos. The unnumbered photos are listed alphabetically below.

COMPLETE SET (20) 75.00 150.00
1 Don Barry 4.00 8.00
2 Steve Bendiak 4.00 8.00
3 Johnny Bright 6.00 12.00
4 Gino Fracas 4.00 8.00
5 Don Getty 5.00 10.00
6 Ed Gray 4.00 8.00
7 Mike Kmeche 4.00 8.00
8 Oscar Kruger 4.00 8.00
9 Mike Lashuk 4.00 8.00
10 Jim Letcavits 4.00 8.00
11 Rollie Miles 4.00 8.00
12 Jackie Parker 7.50 15.00
13 Roger Nelson 5.00 10.00
14 Jim Shipka 4.00 8.00
15 Bill Smith 4.00 8.00
16 Joe-Bob Smith 4.00 8.00
17 Roy Stevenson 4.00 8.00
18 Don Stephenson 4.00 8.00
19 Mike Volcan 4.00 8.00
20 Art Walker 4.00 8.00

1962 Edmonton Eskimos Team Issue 8x10

This set of Eskimos player photos was issued by the team to fill fan requests. Each photo measures roughly 8" by 10" and includes the player's name, position (spelled out), height, and weight to the far left below the photo. The Eskimo logo appears in the lower right hand corner. The unnumbered backs are blank.

COMPLETE SET (6)	30.00	60.00
1 Ray Baillie	5.00	10.00
2 Gino Fracas	6.00	12.00
3 Ted Frechette	5.00	10.00
4 Tony Kehrer	5.00	10.00
5 E.A. Sims	5.00	10.00
6 Mike Volcan	5.00	10.00

1963 Edmonton Eskimos Team Issue

This set of Eskimos player photos was issued by the team to fill fan requests and looks nearly identical to the 1962 photos. Each photo measures roughly 8" by 10" and includes the player's name, position (spelled out), height, and weight below the photo but about 1 1/2" from the left edge. The Eskimo logo appears in the lower right hand corner. The unnumbered backs are blank.

COMPLETE SET (7)	25.00	50.00
1 Charlie Brown	4.00	8.00
2 Marcel Deleeuw	4.00	8.00
3 Ted Frechette	4.00	8.00
4 Sammie Harris	4.00	8.00
5 Dunc Harvey	5.00	10.00
6 Ken Reed	4.00	8.00
7 James Earl Wright	4.00	8.00

1964 Edmonton Eskimos Team Issue

This set of Eskimos player photos was issued by the team to fill fan requests. Each photo measures roughly 8" by 10" and includes the player's name, position (initials), height, and weight to the left below the photo. The Eskimo logo appears in the lower right hand corner. The unnumbered backs are blank.

COMPLETE SET (5)	20.00	40.00
1 Clair Branch	4.00	8.00
2 Junior Hawthorne	4.00	8.00
3 Ken Sigaty	4.00	8.00
4 Jim Stinnette	4.00	8.00
5 Jim Thibert	4.00	8.00

1965 Edmonton Eskimos Team Issue

This set of Eskimos player photos was issued by the team to fill fan requests. Each photo measures roughly 8" by 10" and includes the player's name, position (initials), height, and weight centered below the photo. The Eskimo logo appears in the lower right hand corner. The unnumbered backs are blank.

COMPLETE SET (9)	30.00	60.00
1 Charlie Brown	4.00	8.00
2 Ron Forwick	4.00	8.00
3 Bill Mitchell	4.00	8.00
4 Barry Mitchelson	4.00	8.00
5 John Sklopan	5.00	10.00
6 Jim Stinnette	4.00	8.00
7 Barney Therrien	4.00	8.00
8 Norman Thomas	4.00	8.00
9 Terry Wilson	4.00	8.00

1966 Edmonton Eskimos Program Inserts

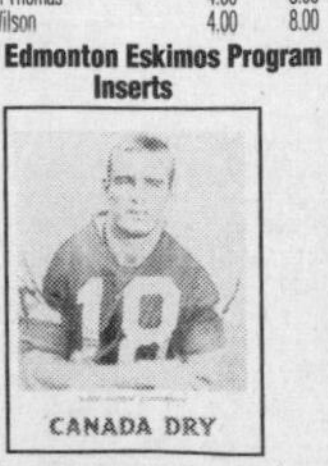

Each of these photos measures approximately 3 7/8" by 5 1/8". Inside white borders, the fronts feature black-and-white posed action photos with the player's name and position below the image. The wider white bottom border carries the sponsor -- Canada Dry. The photos were initially issued in perforated sheets of four in each Eskimos game program for the season. The unnumbered backs include various advertisements.

COMPLETE SET (32)	75.00	125.00
1 Neill Armstrong CO	2.50	5.00
2 Mickey Bitsko	2.00	4.00
3 Ron Brewer	2.50	5.00
4 Ron Capham	2.00	4.00
5 Tommy Joe Coffey	4.00	8.00
6 Merv Collins	2.00	4.00
7 Steve Cotter	2.00	4.00
8 Ron Forwick	2.00	4.00
9 Ed Husmann	2.00	4.00
10 Art Johnson	2.00	4.00
11 Randy Kerbow	2.00	4.00
12 Garry Lefebvre	2.00	4.00
13 Ian MacLeod	2.00	4.00
14 Rusty Martin	2.00	4.00
15 Barry Mitchelson	2.00	4.00
16 Roger Nelson	4.00	8.00
17 Ken Perkins	2.00	4.00
18 Edgar Poles	2.00	4.00
19 Bill Redell	2.00	4.00
20 Billy Roy	2.00	4.00
21 Howie Schumm	2.00	4.00
22 Ken Sigaty	2.00	4.00
23 E.A. Sims	2.00	4.00
24 Bob Spanach	2.00	4.00
25 Marshall Starks	2.00	4.00
26 Jim Stinnette	2.00	4.00
27 Barney Therrien	2.00	4.00
28 Jim Thomas	2.00	4.00
29 Ed Turek	2.00	4.00
30 Trent Walters	2.00	4.00
31 Terry Wilson	2.00	4.00
32 John Wydareny	2.50	5.00

1966 Edmonton Eskimos Team Issue

This set of Eskimos player photos was issued by the team to fill fan requests and is very similar to the 1964 and 1965 issues. Each photo measures roughly 8" by 10" and includes the player's name, position (initials), height, and weight to the far left below the photo. The Eskimo logo appears in the lower right hand corner. The unnumbered backs are blank.

COMPLETE SET (11)	40.00	80.00
1 Mickey Bitsko	4.00	8.00
2 Ron Capham	4.00	8.00
3 Merv Collins	4.00	8.00
4 Steve Cotter	4.00	8.00
5 Norm Kimball GM	4.00	8.00
6 Rusty Martin	4.00	8.00
7 Willie Shine	4.00	8.00
8 Bob Spanach	4.00	8.00
9 Jon Sterling	4.00	8.00
10 Trent Walters	4.00	8.00
11 Terry Wilson	4.00	8.00

1967 Edmonton Eskimos Team Issue

The Eskimos issued this set of player photos around 1967. Each includes two black-and-white player photos with one being an action shot along with a smaller portrait image. The roughly 8" by 10 1/8" photos include the player's name, position underneath the name, college, vital stats, years pro, and team logo on the cardfronts. The coaches and GM photos measure a smaller 5" by 10 1/4" and include only his position, name, and team logo below the photo. The backs are blank and unnumbered.

COMPLETE SET (24)	75.00	150.00
1 Neill Armstrong CO	5.00	10.00
2 Brent Berry	4.00	8.00
3 David Campbell	4.00	8.00
4 Frank Cosentino	4.00	8.00
5 Steve Cotter	4.00	8.00
6 Doug Dersch	4.00	8.00
7 Earl Edwards	5.00	10.00
8 Charles Fulton	4.00	8.00
9 Jerry Griffin	4.00	8.00
10 Joe Hernandez	4.00	8.00
11 Ray Jauch CO	4.00	8.00
12 Peter Kempf	4.00	8.00
13 Randy Kerbow	4.00	8.00
14 Norm Kimball GM	4.00	8.00
15 Garry Lefebvre	4.00	8.00
16 Don Lisbon	4.00	8.00
17 Gordon Lund	4.00	8.00
18 Art Perkins	4.00	8.00
19 Edgar Poles	4.00	8.00
20 E.A. Sims	4.00	8.00
21 Bob Spanach	4.00	8.00
22 Phil Tucker	4.00	8.00
23 Trent Walters	4.00	8.00
24 John Wilson	4.00	8.00

1971 Edmonton Eskimos Team Issue

The Eskimos issued this set of player photos around 1971. Each includes two black-and-white player photos with one being an action shot along with a smaller portrait image. The roughly 8" by 10 1/8" photos include the player's name, position, vital stats, and team logo on the cardfronts. The backs are blank and unnumbered.

COMPLETE SET (13)	35.00	60.00
1 Rusty Clark	3.00	6.00
2 Fred Dunn	3.00	6.00
3 Mike Eben	3.00	6.00
4 Dave Fahrner	3.00	6.00
5 Ken Ferguson	3.00	6.00
6 James Henshal	3.00	6.00
7 Chip Kell	3.00	6.00
8 Henry King	3.00	6.00
9 Larry Kerychuk	3.00	6.00
10 Lance Olssen	3.00	6.00
11 Peter Travis	3.00	6.00
12 Don Trull	4.00	8.00
13 Willie Young	3.00	6.00

1972 Edmonton Eskimos Team Issue

The Eskimos issued this set of player photos. Each includes a black-and-white player photo on thin card stock. The photos measure roughly 7" by 9" and include the player's name, vital stats, college, and team logo on the cardfronts. The cardbacks are blank.

COMPLETE SET (10)	30.00	60.00
1 Ron Forwick	3.00	6.00
2 Gene Foster	3.00	6.00
3 Jim Henshall	3.00	6.00
4 Garry Lefebvre	3.00	6.00
5 Ed Molstad	3.00	6.00
6 Rayne Norrie	3.00	6.00
7 Dave Syme	3.00	6.00
8 Peter Travis	3.00	6.00
9 Charlie Turner	3.00	6.00
10 Tom Wilkinson	5.00	10.00

1981 Edmonton Eskimos Red Rooster

This 40-card set, distributed by Red Rooster Food Stores, measures approximately 2 3/4" by 3 1/2" and features posed, color player photos with rounded corners on a white card face. Since the card edges are perforated, the cards were apparently issued as a sheet. The player's name is printed below the photo, as is the team name and a CFL Players Association endorsement. The backs carry biographical information and a player profile. Sponsor logos and names are printed at the bottom. The cards are unnumbered and checklisted below in alphabetical order.

COMPLETE SET (40)	35.00	60.00
1 Leo Blanchard	.30	.75
2 David Boone	.30	.75
3 Brian Broomell	.30	.75
4 Hugh Campbell CO	.60	1.50
5 Dave Cutler	1.25	3.00
6 Marco Cyncar	.50	1.25
7 Ron Estay	.30	.75
8 Dave Fennell	.50	1.25
9 Emilio Fraietta	.30	.75
10 Brian Fryer	.30	.75
11 Jim Germany	.50	1.25
12 Gary Hayes	.30	.75
13 Larry Highbaugh	.60	1.50
14 Joe Hollimon	.30	.75
15 Hank Ilesic	.60	1.50
16 Ed Jones	.30	.75
17 Dan Kearns	.30	.75
18 Sean Kehoe	.30	.75
19 Brian Kelly	1.00	2.50
20 Dan Kepley	.60	1.50
21 Stu Lang	.50	1.25
22 Pete Lavorato	.30	.75
23 Neil Lumsden	.50	1.25
24 Bill Manchuk	.30	.75
25 Mike McLeod	.30	.75
26 Ted Milian	.30	.75
27 Warren Moon	15.00	30.00
28 James Parker	1.00	2.50
29 John Pointer	.30	.75
30 Hector Pothier	.30	.75
31 Dale Potter	.30	.75
32 Angelo Santucci	.30	.75
33 Tom Scott	.50	1.25
34 Waddell Smith	.50	1.25
35 Bill Stevenson	.50	1.25
36 Tom Towns	.30	.75
37 Eric Upton	.30	.75
38 Mark Wald	.30	.75
39 Ken Walter	.30	.75
40 Tom Wilkinson	1.50	4.00

1981 Edmonton Eskimos Red Rooster Cups

Red Rooster Food Stores sponsored a series of 10-cups featuring the 1981 Edmonton Eskimos. Each cup included four black and white photos of Edmonton players, except for the coaches cup that included five coaches. Warren Moon is the key player in the set.

COMPLETE SET (10)	20.00	50.00
1 Neil Lumsden	8.00	20.00
Warren Moon		
Hector Pothier		
Dale Potter		
2 Eric Upton	3.00	8.00
Don Warrington		
Tom Wilkinson		
Mike Wilson		
3 Coaches	1.25	3.00
Dan Daniel		
Joe Faragalli		
Don Matthews		
Hugh Campbell		
Cal Murphy		
4 Stu Lang	1.25	3.00
Pete Lavorato		
Tod Milian		
Dave Fennell		
5 Ed Jones	2.00	5.00
Brian Kelly		
Dan Kepley		
John Konihowski		
6 Dan Kearns	2.00	5.00
James Parker		
Angelo San Tucci		
Tom Scott		
7 Waddell Smith	1.25	3.00
Bill Stevenson		
Tom Towns		
Hank Ilesic		
8 David Boone	2.00	5.00
Gregg Butler		
Dave Cutler		
Ron Estay		
9 Emilio Fraietta	1.25	3.00
Brian Fryer		
Jim Germany		
York Hentschel		
10 Larry Highbaugh UER(Laray)	1.25	3.00
Joe Hollimon		
Bob Howes		
Leo Blanchard		

1983 Edmonton Eskimos Edmonton Journal

This 26-card set measures approximately 3" by 5" and was sponsored by the Edmonton Journal. The set features black-and-white posed player photos with white borders. The player's name and position is printed at the bottom. The Edmonton helmet icon is printed at the bottom. The backs are blank. The cards are unnumbered and checklisted below in alphabetical order. Warren Moon is featured in one of his earliest card appearances.

COMPLETE SET (26)	150.00	250.00
1 David Boone	2.50	5.00
2 Dave Cutler	7.50	15.00
3 Marco Cyncar	3.00	6.00
4 Mark DeBrueys	2.50	5.00
5 Harry Doering	2.50	5.00
6 Dave Fennell	5.00	10.00
7 Brian Fryer	2.50	5.00
8 Jim Germany	3.00	6.00
9 Gary Hayes	2.50	5.00
10 Larry Highbaugh	5.00	10.00
11 Joe Hollimon	2.50	5.00
12 Ed Jones	2.50	5.00
13 Dan Kearns	2.50	5.00
14 Brian Kelly	7.50	15.00
15 Dan Kepley	5.00	10.00
16 Pete Kettela CO	2.50	5.00
17 Neil Lumsden	3.00	6.00
18 Warren Moon	50.00	80.00
19 James Parker	7.50	15.00
20 Tom Scott	5.00	10.00
21 Waddell Smith	2.50	5.00
22 Bill Stevenson	3.00	6.00
23 Tom Towns	2.50	5.00
24 Eric Upton	2.50	5.00
25 Kenneth Walter	2.50	5.00
26 Wendell Williams	2.50	5.00

1984 Edmonton Eskimos Edmonton Journal

This set measures approximately 3" by 5" and was sponsored by the Edmonton Journal. The set features black-and-white posed player photos with white borders. The player's name and position is printed at the bottom. The sponsor's logo and a Edmonton helmet icon are printed at the top. The backs are blank. The cards are unnumbered and checklisted below in alphabetical order.

COMPLETE SET (58)	175.00	300.00
1 Kevin Allen	2.50	5.00
2 Frank Balkovec	2.50	5.00
3 Leo Blanchard	2.50	5.00
4 David Boone	2.50	5.00
5 Paul Boudreau ACO	2.50	5.00
6 Bruce Bush	2.50	5.00
7 Gio Chisotti	2.50	5.00
8 Dennis Clay	2.50	5.00
9 Larry Cowan	2.50	5.00
10 Dave Cutler	7.50	15.00
11 Marco Cyncar	3.00	6.00
12 Blake Dermott	3.00	6.00
13 Ralph Dixon	2.50	5.00
14 Matt Dunigan	12.50	25.00
15 Marcus Fisher	2.50	5.00
16 Emilio Fraietta	2.50	5.00
17 Brian Fryer	2.50	5.00
18 John Godry	2.50	5.00
19 Harry Gosier	2.50	5.00
20 Darryl Green	2.50	5.00
21 Darryl Hall	3.00	6.00
22 Peter Harvey	2.50	5.00
23 Paul Hickie	2.50	5.00
24 Joe Hollimon	2.50	5.00
25 James Hunter	2.50	5.00
26 Kevin Ingram	2.50	5.00
27 Terry Irvin	3.00	6.00
28 Milson Jones	2.50	5.00
29 Wayne Jones	2.50	5.00
30 Brian Kelly	7.50	15.00
31 Danny Kepley	2.50	5.00
32 Terry Leschuk	2.50	5.00
33 Neil Lumsden	2.50	5.00
34 Leon Lyszkiewicz	2.50	5.00
35 Greg Marshall	3.00	6.00
36 Sheldon Martin	2.50	5.00
37 Mike McLeod	2.50	5.00
38 Mike Nelson ACO	2.50	5.00
39 Jackie Parker CO	10.00	20.00
40 Jerry Philip	3.00	6.00
41 Hector Pothier	2.50	5.00
42 Dale Potter	2.50	5.00
43 Billy Record	2.50	5.00
44 Paul G. Rudzinski ACO	2.50	5.00
45 Daniel Runge	2.50	5.00
46 John Samuelson	2.50	5.00
47 Angelo Santucci	2.50	5.00
48 Danny Saso	2.50	5.00
49 Tom Scott	5.00	10.00
50 Chris Skinner	2.50	5.00
51 Harold Smith	2.50	5.00
52 Scott Stauch	2.50	5.00
53 Bill Stevenson	3.00	6.00
54 Ronnie Stiger	2.50	5.00
55 Cliff Toney	2.50	5.00
56 Tom Towns	2.50	5.00
57 Tom Tuinei	3.00	6.00
58 Eric Upton	2.50	5.00

2007 Extreme Sports CFL

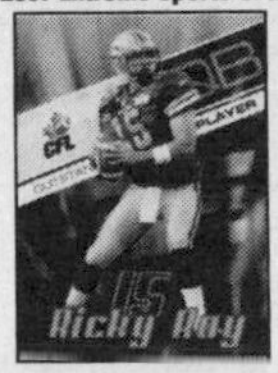

This set was produced by Extreme Sports and released in Fall 2007. Each wax box included 20-packs with 5-cards per pack. Each box also promised one full set.

COMPLETE SET (100)	15.00	30.00
1 Anthony Calvillo	1.00	2.50
2 Ben Cahoon	.60	1.50
3 Etienne Boulay	.30	.75
4 Damon Duval	.20	.50
5 Kerry Watkins	.40	1.00
6 Bryan Chiu	.40	1.00
7 Robert Edwards	.60	1.50
8 Davis Sanchez	.20	.50
9 Anwar Stewart	.20	.50
10 Timothy Strickland	.20	.50
11 Scott Flory	.20	.50
12 Diamond Ferri	.30	.75
13 Byron Parker	.20	.50
14 Arland Bruce	.40	1.00
15 Michael Fletcher	.20	.50
16 Orlondo Steinauer	.20	.50
17 Michael Bishop	.60	1.50
18 Kevin Eiben	.20	.50
19 Mike O'Shea	.40	1.00
20 Noel Prefontaine	.20	.50
21 Jeff Johnson	.20	.50
22 Jonathan Brown	.20	.50
23 Chad Folk	.20	.50
24 Andre Durie	.20	.50
25 Jesse Lumsden	.60	1.50
26 Corey Holmes	.40	1.00
27 Brock Ralph	.20	.50
28 George Hudson	.30	.75
29 JoJuan Armour	.30	.75
30 Richard Karikari	.20	.50
31 Jason Maas	.50	1.25
32 Nautyn McKay-Loescher	.20	.50
33 Tay Cody	.30	.75
34 Talman Gardner	.20	.50
35 Zeke Moreno	.50	1.25
36 Timmy Chang	.60	1.50
37 Milt Stegall	.75	2.00
38 Charles Roberts	.60	1.50
39 Kevin Glenn	.40	1.00
40 Doug Brown	.20	.50
41 Terrence Edwards	.40	1.00
42 Ibrahim Khan	.20	.50
43 Derick Armstrong	.20	.50
44 Tom Canada	.20	.50
45 Barrin Simpson	.20	.50
46 Gavin Walls	.30	.75
47 Kyries Hebert	.30	.75
48 Corey Jenkins	.20	.50
49 Matt Dominguez	.50	1.25
50 Fred Perry	.20	.50
51 Kerry Joseph	.75	2.00
52 D.J. Flick	.30	.75
53 Luca Congi	.20	.50
54 Jason Armstead	.50	1.25
55 Reggie Hunt	.20	.50
56 Scott Schultz	.30	.75
57 Andy Fantuz	.30	.75
58 Jeremy O'Day	.30	.75
59 Gene Makowsky	.20	.50
60 David McKoy	.20	.50
61 Ricky Ray	1.25	3.00
62 Adam Braidwood	.20	.50
63 Jason Tucker	.40	1.00
64 Kamau Peterson	.30	.75
65 Dan Comiskey	.20	.50
66 Robert Brown	.20	.50
67 Joe McGrath	.20	.50
68 Sean Fleming	.30	.75
69 Kevin Lefsrud	.20	.50
70 Pat Woodcock	.40	1.00
71 J.R. LaRose	.20	.50
72 Tyler Ebell	.20	.50
73 Sandro DeAngelis	.20	.50
74 Joffrey Reynolds	.60	1.50
75 Henry Burris	.60	1.50
76 Jermaine Copeland	.30	.75
77 Jay McNeil	.20	.50
78 Marc Boerigter	.40	1.00
79 Scott Coe	.20	.50
80 Trey Young	.20	.50
81 Shannon James	.20	.50
82 Brian Clark	.20	.50
83 Nikolas Lewis	.30	.75
84 Rob Cote	.20	.50
85 Geroy Simon	.40	1.00
86 Brent Johnson	.30	.75
87 Dave Dickenson	1.00	2.50
88 Jason Clermont	.60	1.50
89 Javier Glatt	.20	.50
90 Barron Miles	.30	.75
91 Otis Floyd	.20	.50
92 Korey Banks	.20	.50
93 Buck Pierce	.40	1.00
94 Aaron Hunt	.20	.50
95 Paris Jackson	.40	1.00
96 Cameron Wake	1.25	3.00
97 Mike Pringle FHOF	.50	1.25
98 Damon Allen FHOF	.75	2.00
99 Danny McManus FHOF	.60	1.50
100 Terry Vaughn FHOF	.50	1.25

2008 Extreme Sports CFL

COMPLETE SET (100)	15.00	30.00
1 Anthony Calvillo	.75	2.00
2 Ben Cahoon	.40	1.00
3 Bryan Chiu	.30	.75
4 Avon Cobourne	.40	1.00
5 Chip Cox	.20	.50
6 Damon Duval	.30	.75
7 Diamond Ferri	.20	.50
8 Scott Flory	.20	.50
9 Reggie Hunt	.20	.50
10 Jamel Richardson	.40	1.00
11 Davis Sanchez	.30	.75
12 Anwar Stewart	.20	.50
13 Kerry Watkins	.30	.75
14 Korey Banks	.20	.50
15 Kelly Bates	.20	.50
16 Jason Clermont	.50	1.25
17 Javier Glatt	.20	.50
18 Paris Jackson	.20	.50
19 Jarious Jackson	.50	1.25
20 Brent Johnson	.30	.75
21 Paul McCallum	.30	.75
22 Barron Miles	.30	.75
23 Rob Murphy	.30	.75
24 Geroy Simon	.40	1.00
25 Cameron Wake	1.25	3.00
26 Mike O'Shea	.30	.75
27 Adriano Belli	.20	.50
28 Jonathan Brown	.20	.50
29 Dominique Dorsey	.20	.50
30 Kevin Eiben	.30	.75
31 Michael Fletcher	.20	.50
32 Chad Folk	.20	.50
33 Riall Johnson	.20	.50
34 Kerry Joseph	.60	1.50
35 Byron Parker	.20	.50
36 Jude St John	.20	.50
37 Andre Talbot	.20	.50
38 Mike Vanderjagt	.30	.75
39 Chris Bauman	.20	.50
40 Terry Caulley	.20	.50
41 Ryan Glasper	.20	.50
42 Marwan Hage	.20	.50
43 George Hudson	.30	.75
44 Markeith Knowlton	.20	.50
45 Jesse Lumsden	.50	1.25
46 Ray Mariuz	.20	.50
47 Tony Miles	.30	.75
48 Casey Printers	.30	.75
49 Nicholas Setta	.20	.50
50 Richie Williams	.30	.75
51 Milt Stegall	.60	1.50
52 Derick Armstrong	.20	.50
53 Doug Brown	.20	.50
54 Romby Bryant	.30	.75
55 Tom Canada	.20	.50
56 Terrence Edwards	.30	.75
57 Arjei Franklin	.20	.50
58 Kevin Glenn	.40	1.00
59 Dan Goodspeed	.20	.50
60 Cam Hall	.20	.50
61 Anthony Malbrough	.20	.50
62 Kelly Malveaux	.20	.50
63 Gavin Walls	.20	.50
64 Wes Cates	.30	.75
65 John Chick	.20	.50
66 Eddie Davis	.20	.50
67 Darian Durant	.40	1.00
68 Andy Fantuz	.30	.75
69 D.J. Flick	.30	.75
70 Neal Hughes	.20	.50
71 James Johnson	.30	.75
72 Maurice Lloyd	.20	.50
73 Gene Makowsky	.20	.50
74 Jeremy O'Day	.30	.75
75 Scott Schultz	.30	.75
76 Tom Pate	.30	.75
77 Augustin Barrenechea	.20	.50
78 Mathieu Bertrand	.20	.50
79 Shannon Garrett	.20	.50
80 Jason Goss	.20	.50
81 Tristan Jackson	.30	.75
82 Fred Perry	.20	.50
83 Kamau Peterson	.30	.75
84 Noel Prefontaine	.20	.50
85 Ricky Ray	.50	1.25
86 Dario Romero	.30	.75
87 Jason Tucker	.40	1.00
88 Jordan Younger	.20	.50
89 Henry Burris	.50	1.25
90 Jermaine Copeland	.40	1.00
91 Sandro DeAngelis	.20	.50
92 Markus Howell	.20	.50
93 Rob Lazeo	.20	.50
94 Nik Lewis	.40	1.00
95 Wes Lysack	.20	.50
96 Jeff Pilon	.20	.50
97 Brett Ralph	.20	.50
98 Ken-Yon Rambo	.50	1.25
99 Joffrey Reynolds	.30	.75
100 Ryan Thelwell	.20	.50

2008 Extreme Sports CFL Signatures

1 Anthony Calvillo	15.00	30.00
2 Jason Clermont	25.00	50.00
3 Jesse Lumsden	15.00	30.00
4 Gene Makowsky	15.00	30.00
5 Mike O'Shea	20.00	40.00
6 Kamau Peterson	15.00	30.00
7 Milt Stegall	25.00	50.00

2009 Extreme Sports CFL

COMPLETE SET (160)	15.00	30.00
1 Jarious Jackson	.50	1.25
2 Buck Pierce	.50	1.25
3 Alexis Bwenge	.20	.50
4 Jason Arakgi	.20	.50
5 Korey Banks	.20	.50
6 Ricky Foley	.20	.50
7 Geroy Simon	.40	1.00
8 Javier Glatt	.20	.50
9 Sherko Haji-Rasouli	.20	.50
10 Aaron Hunt	.20	.50
11 Ian Smart	.20	.50
12 Jason Jimenez	.20	.50
13 Brent Johnson	.30	.75
14 Lyle Green	.20	.50
15 Dante Marsh	.20	.50
16 Ryan Phillips		
17 Paris Jackson	.20	.50
18 Paul McCallum	.30	.75
19 Ryan Phillips	.20	.50
20 Angus Reid	.20	.50
21 Henry Burris	.50	1.25
22 Dwight Anderson	.20	.50
23 Barrick Nealy	.20	.50
24 Brett Ralph	.20	.50
25 Burke Dales	.20	.50
26 Dwaine Carpenter	.20	.50
27 J.R. Ruffin	.20	.50
28 Jermaine Copeland	.40	1.00
29 Joffrey Reynolds	.30	.75
30 Ken-Yon Rambo	.50	1.25
31 Rob Lazeo	.20	.50
32 Wes Lysack	.20	.50
33 Marc Calixte	.20	.50
34 Markus Howell	.20	.50
35 Nik Lewis	.30	.75
36 Jeff Pilon	.20	.50
37 Rob Cote	.20	.50
38 Ryan Thelwell	.20	.50
39 Sandro DeAngelis	.20	.50
40 Teyo Johnson	.40	1.00
41 Ricky Ray	.50	1.25
42 Andrew Nowacki	.20	.50
43 Arkee Whitlock	.60	1.50
44 Calvin McCarty	.20	.50
45 Kai Ellis	.20	.50
46 Aaron Fiacconi	.20	.50
47 Fred Stamps	.40	1.00
48 Jason Goss	.20	.50
49 T.J. Hill	.20	.50
50 Taylor Inglis	.30	.75
51 Jamaica Rector	.30	.75
53 Kamau Peterson	.30	.75
54 Mathieu Bertrand	.20	.50
55 Maurice Mann	.20	.50
56 Noel Prefontaine	.20	.50
57 Byron Parker	.20	.50
58 Greg Peach	.20	.50
59 Mark Restelli	.20	.50
60 Tristan Jackson	.30	.75
61 Darian Durant	.40	1.00
62 Marcus Adams	.20	.50
63 Andy Fantuz	.30	.75
64 Stevie Baggs	.20	.50
65 John Chick	.20	.50
66 Chris Szarka	.30	.75
67 Eddie Davis	.20	.50
68 Jorrell Freeman	.20	.50
69 Jason Armstead	.40	1.00
70 Jason Clermont	.50	1.25
71 Tad Kornegay	.20	.50
72 Luca Congi	.20	.50
73 Gene Makowsky	.20	.50
74 Mike McCullough	.20	.50
75 Omarr Morgan	.20	.50
76 Luc Mullinder	.20	.50
77 Jeremy O'Day	.30	.75
78 Wes Cates	.30	.75
79 Weston Dressler	.40	1.00
80 Renaud Williams	.20	.50
81 Michael Bishop	.50	1.25
82 Stefan Lefors	.20	.50
83 Adarius Bowman	.30	.75
84 Alexis Serna	.20	.50
85 Doug Brown	.20	.50
86 Brady Browne	.20	.50
87 Ike Charlton	.20	.50
88 Keyuo Craver	.30	.75
89 Fred Perry	.20	.50
90 Fred Reid	.30	.75
91 Johnathon Hefney	.20	.50
92 Jovon Johnson	.20	.50
93 Jon Oosterhuis	.20	.50
94 Ibrahim Khan	.20	.50
95 Lenny Walls	.20	.50
96 Joe Lobendahn	.20	.50
97 Ian Logan	.20	.50
98 Mike Renaud	.30	.75
99 Siddeeg Shabazz	.20	.50
100 Terrence Edwards	.30	.75
101 Kevin Glenn	.40	1.00
102 Sandy Beveridge	.20	.50
103 Jykine Bradley	.20	.50
104 Yannick Carter	.20	.50
105 Chris Bauman	.20	.50
106 Dave Stala	.30	.75
107 DeAndra Cobb	.40	1.00
108 Otis Floyd	.20	.50
109 Marwan Hage	.20	.50
110 Kevin Justin Hickman	.20	.50
111 George Hudson	.30	.75
112 Jordan Matechuk	.20	.50
113 Matt Kirk	.20	.50
114 Markeith Knowlton	.20	.50
115 Lawrence Gordon	.20	.50
116 Nick Setta	.20	.50
117 Prechae Rodriguez	.20	.50
118 Quinton Porter	.20	.50
119 Chris Thompson	.20	.50
120 Arland Bruce III	.40	1.00
121 Kerry Joseph	.60	1.50
122 Adriano Belli	.20	.50
123 Andre Durie	.20	.50
124 Andre Talbot	.20	.50
125 Bryan Crawford	.20	.50
126 Chad Lucas	.20	.50
127 Cody Pickett	.30	.75
128 Kevin Eiben	.30	.75
129 Jamal Robertson	.40	1.00
130 Jeff Johnson	.20	.50
131 Justin Medlock	.30	.75
132 Mike Bradwell	.20	.50
133 Zeke Moreno	.30	.75
134 Willie Pile	.30	.75
135 Will Poole	.30	.75
136 Brian Ramsay	.20	.50
137 Rob Murphy	.30	.75
138 Steve Schmidt	.20	.50
139 Tyler Scott	.20	.50
140 Jordan Younger	.20	.50
141 Anthony Calvillo	.75	2.00
142 Avon Cobourne	.40	1.00
143 Ben Cahoon	.40	1.00
144 Etienne Boulay	.30	.75
145 Brian Bratton	.20	.50
146 Jerald Brown	.20	.50
147 Bryan Chiu	.30	.75
148 Chip Cox	.20	.50
150 Damon Duval	.30	.75
151 Davis Sanchez	.30	.75
152 Shea Emry	.20	.50
153 Scott Flory	.20	.50
154 Jamel Richardson	.40	1.00
155 Keron Williams	.20	.50
156 Kerry Watkins	.30	.75
157 Paul Lambert	.20	.50
158 Larry Taylor	.20	.50
159 Matthieu Proulx	.20	.50
160 S.J. Green	.20	.50

1960-61 Hamilton Tiger-Cats Team Issue

These 5" by 7" black and white photos were issued by the team to fill fan requests for souvenirs. Each photo was printed on glossy stock and includes the player's name, position, height, weight, and team name below the photo. The backs are blank and unnumbered.

COMPLETE SET (8)	30.00	60.00
1 Geno DeNobile	4.00	8.00
2 Jamie Colet	4.00	8.00
3 Grant McKee	4.00	8.00
4 Bob Minihane	4.00	8.00
5 Tom Moulton	4.00	8.00
6 Ron Ray	4.00	8.00
7 Butch Rogers	4.00	8.00
8 Willie Taylor	5.00	10.00

1962 Hamilton Tiger-Cats Team Issue

These 5" by 8" black and white photos were issued by the team to fill fan requests for souvenirs. Each photo was printed on glossy stock and includes the player's name, position, height, weight, and team name below the photo. In addition to the difference in length, the print size used for the 1962 photos is much larger than that used for 1960-61. Otherwise, the photos appear to be very similar. The backs are blank and unnumbered.

COMPLETE SET (12)	40.00	80.00
1 Art Baker	5.00	10.00
2 Don Caraway	4.00	8.00
3 Dick Cohee	5.00	10.00
4 Dick Easterly	4.00	8.00

5 Sam Fernandez	4.00	8.00
6 Larry Hickman	4.00	8.00
7 Willie McClung	4.00	8.00
8 Tom Moran	4.00	8.00
9 Jim Pace	4.00	8.00
10 Tim Reid	4.00	8.00
11 Milam Wall	4.00	8.00
12 Dave Viti	4.00	8.00

1964 Hamilton Tiger-Cats Team Issue

These 5" by 7" black and white photos were issued by the team to fill fan requests for souvenirs. Each photo was printed on glossy stock and includes the player's name, position, height, weight, and team name below the photo. Note there is no "--" between the player's name and position like exists on the 1960-61 photos. The backs are blank and unnumbered.

COMPLETE SET (6)	20.00	40.00
1 Joe Cannavino UER (name misspelled Loe)	4.00	8.00
2 Gene Ceppetelli	4.00	8.00
3 John Cimba	4.00	8.00
4 Stan Crisson	4.00	8.00
5 Bob Gaiters	5.00	10.00
6 Steve Hmiel	4.00	8.00

1965 Hamilton Tiger-Cats Team Issue

These 5" by 8" black and white photos were issued by the team to fill fan requests for souvenirs. Each photo was printed on glossy stock and includes the player's name, height and weight in a single line below the photo followed by the team name in the lower right corner. The backs are blank and unnumbered.

1 Dick Cohee	5.00	10.00
2 Billy Ray Locklin	4.00	8.00
3 Ted Page	4.00	8.00
4 Jim Reynolds	4.00	8.00
5 Dave Viti	4.00	8.00
6 Billy Wayte	4.00	8.00

1966 Hamilton Tiger-Cats Team Issue

These 5" by 8" black and white photos were issued by the team to fill fan requests for souvenirs. Each photo was printed on glossy stock and includes the player's name, position, height and weight in two lines of type below the photo followed by the team name in the lower right corner. The backs are blank and unnumbered.

COMPLETE SET (3)	10.00	20.00
1 Gene Ceppetelli	4.00	8.00
2 Billy Ray Locklin	4.00	8.00
3 Bob Steiner	4.00	8.00

1967 Hamilton Tiger-Cats Team Issue

These 5" by 8" black and white photos were issued by the team to fill fan requests for souvenirs. Each photo was printed on glossy stock and includes the player's name, height and weight in a single line below the photo followed by the team name in the lower right corner. The backs are blank and unnumbered.

COMPLETE SET (5)	20.00	40.00
1 Gordan Christian	4.00	8.00
2 Barrie Hansen	4.00	8.00
3 Doug Mitchell	4.00	8.00
4 Bob Storey	5.00	10.00
5 Ted Watkins	4.00	8.00

1977-78 Hamilton Tiger-Cats Team Sheets

This group of 32-players and coaches of the Tiger-Cats was produced on four glossy sheets each measuring approximately 8" by 10". The fronts feature black-and-white player portraits with eight pictures to a sheet with the year printed at the top. The backs are blank. The cards are unnumbered and checklisted below in alphabetical order, with the player pictured in the upper left hand corner of the sheet listed first.

COMPLETE SET (4)	10.00	20.00
1 Bart Evans	2.50	5.00
Sam Britts		
Jimmy Jones		
Nick Jambrosic		
Larry Butler		
Dave Shaw		
Mike Harris		
Paul Sheridan		
2 Frank Gibson	3.00	6.00
Bob Shaw		
Ralph Sazio		
Walter Bauer		
Mike Wilson		
Lewis Porter		
Mark Perrelli		
Pat Donley		
3 Craig Jensen	2.50	5.00
Gary Shaw		
Ken Strayhorn		
John Martini		
Lawrie Skolrood		
John Kinch		
Joe Worobec		
Tim Berryman		
4 Alan Moffat	2.50	5.00
Kent Carter		
Larry Brune		
Barry Finlay		
Steve Gelley		
Mike Samples		
Henry Waszczuk		
Ken Clark		

1980 Hamilton Tiger-Cats Team Sheets

This group of 40-players and coaches of the Tiger-Cats was produced on five glossy sheets each measuring approximately 8" by 10". The fronts feature black-and-white player portraits with eight pictures to a sheet with the year printed at the top. The backs are blank. The cards are unnumbered and checklisted below in alphabetical order, with the player pictured in the upper left hand corner of the sheet listed first.

COMPLETE SET (5)	12.50	25.00
1 Jerry Anderson	3.00	6.00
Brock Aynsley		
Jack Blair		
Woodrow Carter		
Phil Colwell		
Rufus Crawford		
Carl Crennel		
Chris Curran		
2 Linden Davidson	2.50	5.00
Bill Dutton CO		
Rocky DiPietro		
Al Dosant		
Robert Gaddis		
Ed George		
Randy Graham		
Joe Haering CO		
3 John Holland	2.50	5.00
Craig Labbett		
Bruce Lemmerman		
Dave Marler		
Willie Martin		
Jim Muller		
Frank Moffatt		
Bob Macauley		
4 Billy McBride	2.50	5.00
Emil Nielsen		
Gord Paterson		
Leroy Paul		
Leif Pettersen		
Ron Rowland		
Bob Rozier		
Bernie Ruoff		
5 Dave Shaw	3.00	6.00
Gene Thiessen		
Gene Wall		
Henry Waszczuk		
Harold Woods		
Ben Zambiasi		
Ray Honey		
Marco Cyncar		

1982 Hamilton Tiger-Cats Safety

This 35-card safety standard-size set was co-sponsored by the Hamilton Tiger-Cats, The Spectator (newspaper), and the Hamilton Fire Department. These cards were printed on thin cardboard stock and feature posed color player photos, shot from the waist up against a light blue background. The surrounding card face is gold, with player information in black below the picture. The backs have biography, a fire safety tip in the form of a player quote, as well as team and sponsor logos. The cards are unnumbered and checklisted below in alphabetical order. Four additional cards were produced but not released as part of the set (since the players were released from the team at mid-season) and hence are not included below in the complete set price. These four cards (Mike Horton, Joe Kuklo, Peter Martell, and Alan Moffat) are quite scarce as they were only issued to press members and a few distinguished guests at a Hamilton Tiger-Cat game.

COMPLETE SET (35)	10.00	20.00
1 Marv Allemang	.20	.50
2 Jeff Arp	.20	.50
3 Keith Baker	.20	.50
4 Gerald Bess	.30	.75
5 Mark Bragagnolo	.20	.50
6 Carmelo Carteri	.20	.50
7 Tom Clements	3.00	8.00
8 Grover Covington	1.25	3.00
9 Rocky DiPietro	1.25	3.00
10 Howard Fields	.20	.50
11 Ross Francis	.20	.50
12 Ed Fulton	.20	.50
13 Peter Gales	.20	.50
14 Ed Gataveckas	.20	.50
15 Dave Graffi	.20	.50
16 Obie Graves	.20	.50
17 Hazen Henderson	.20	.50
18 Mike Horton SP	15.00	25.00
19 Ron Johnson	.50	1.25
20 Joe Kuklo SP	15.00	25.00
21 Peter Martell SP	15.00	25.00
22 Dave Marler	.30	.75
23 Alan Moffat SP	15.00	25.00
24 Jim Muller	.20	.50
25 Leroy Paul	.20	.50
26 John Priestner	.30	.75
27 Dave Purves	.20	.50
28 James Ramey	.20	.50
29 Doug Redl	.20	.50
30 Bernie Ruoff	.30	.75
31 David Sauve	.20	.50
32 David Shaw	.20	.50
33 Kerry Smith	.20	.50
34 Steve Stapler	.30	.75
35 Kyle Stevens	.20	.50
36 Mike Walker	.75	2.00
37 Henry Waszczuk	.20	.50
38 Harold Woods	.20	.50
39 Ben Zambiasi	1.00	2.50

1983 Hamilton Tiger-Cats Safety

This 37-card police standard-size set was jointly sponsored by the Hamilton Tiger-Cats, The Spectator (a newspaper), and the Hamilton Fire Department. The cards are printed on thin card stock and feature posed color player photos, shot from the waist up against a black background. The surrounding card face is gold, with player information in black print below the picture. The backs have biographical information, a fire safety tip in the form of a player quote, as well as team and sponsor logos. The cards are unnumbered and checklisted below in alphabetical order. Two cards were pulled early in production (marked below as SP) and are not considered part of the complete set price.

COMPLETE SET (37)	8.00	20.00
1 Marv Allemang	.20	.50
2 Jeff Arp	.20	.50
3 Keith Baker	.20	.50
4 Harold E. Ballard PRES	.75	2.00
5 Mike Barker	.20	.50
6 Gerald Bess	.30	.75
7 Pat Brady	.20	.50
8 Mark Bragagnolo	.20	.50
9 Tom Clements	3.00	8.00
10 Grover Covington	1.25	3.00
11 Rufus Crawford	.75	2.00
12 Rocky DiPietro	1.25	3.00
13 Leo Ezerins	.20	.50
14 Howard Fields	.20	.50
15 Ross Francis	.20	.50
16 Peter Gales	.20	.50
17 Ed Gataveckas	.20	.50
18 Paul Gohier	.20	.50
19 Dave Graffi	.20	.50
20 Ron Johnson	.50	1.25
21 Steve Kearns	.20	.50
22 Wayne Lee	.20	.50
23 Terry Lehne SP	15.00	25.00
24 Claude Mathews SP	15.00	25.00
25 Mike McIntyre	.20	.50
26 Paul Palma	.20	.50
27 George Piva	.20	.50
28 Mitchell Price	.30	.75
29 John Priestner	.30	.75
30 Bernie Ruoff	.30	.75
31 David Sauve	.20	.50
32 Johnny Shepherd	.20	.50
33 Steve Stapler	.40	1.00
34 Mark Streeter	.20	.50
35 Jeff Tedford	.20	.50
36 Mike Walker	.75	2.00
37 Henry Waszczuk	.20	.50
38 Felix Wright	1.00	2.50
39 Ben Zambiasi	1.00	2.50

1984 Hamilton Tiger-Cats Postcards

This series of postcards was issued by the Tiger-Cats likely over the course of a number of years. Each card is oversized (roughly 3 1/2" by 5 1/2") and produced in one of two styles: with a yellow border on the bottom of the card front and borderless on the other three sides or with a thin yellow border all the way around the card and a thick yellow border at the bottom. The team logo is included inside the photo area or inside the yellow bottom portion and each features a standard postcard style cardback. Any additions to this checklist are appreciated.

1 Paul Bennett	3.00	8.00
2 Dieter Brock	6.00	15.00
3 Grover Covington	3.00	8.00
4 Ken Hobart	4.00	10.00
5 Johnny Shepherd	3.00	8.00
6 Steve Stapler	3.00	8.00
7 Mike Walker	3.00	8.00
8 Henry Waszczuk	3.00	8.00
9 Ben Zambiasi	3.00	8.00
10 Team Mascot	3.00	8.00

1998 Hamilton Tiger-Cats Police

This set was distributed by the Hamilton-Wentworth Regional Police. Each card includes a black border on the front along with the Police and Tiger-Cats' logos. The unnumbered cardbacks feature player vital statistics, sponsor logos, and a short safety tip.

COMPLETE SET (40)	7.50	15.00
1 Archie Amerson	.30	.75
2 Chris Burns	.10	.30
3 Eric Carter	.20	.50
4 Carl Coulter	.10	.30
5 Jeff Cummins	.20	.50
6 Seth Dittman	.10	.30
7 Tim Fleiszer	.10	.30
8 Gonzalo Floyd	.10	.30
9 Darren Flutie	1.25	2.50
10 Derek Grier	.10	.30
11 Andrew Grigg	.20	.50
12 Dave Hack	.10	.30
13 Joe Hagins	.10	.30
14 Cooper Harris	.10	.30
15 Rob Hitchcock	.10	.30
16 Ron Lancaster CO	.30	.75
17 Cody Ledbetter	.20	.50
18 Danny McManus	.75	2.00
19 Joe Montford	.40	1.00
20 Mike Morreale	.30	.75
21 Bobby Olive	.10	.30
22 Paul Osbaldiston	.10	.30
23 Mike Philbrick	.10	.30
24 Tim Prinsen	.10	.30
25 Dan Pronyk	.10	.30
26 Justin Ring	.10	.30
27 Frank Rocca	.10	.30
28 Trevor Shaw	.10	.30
29 Jarrett Smith	.10	.30
30 Obie Spanic	.10	.30
31 Orlondo Steinauer	.10	.30
32 Val St.Germain	.10	.30
33 Calvin Tiggle	.10	.30
34 Gerald Vaughn	.10	.30
35 Kyle Walters	.10	.30
36 Frank West	.10	.30
37 Willie Whitehead	.30	.75
38 Ronald Williams	.60	1.50
39 Team Mascot	.10	.30
40 Team Logo	.10	.30

1999 Hamilton Tiger-Cats Police

This set was produced to celebrate the Tiger-Cats 1999 Grey Cup Championship. The cards (slightly oversized at 2 5/8" by 3 5/8") were distributed by local law enforcement officers and each card includes a color player photo with a yellow border. The unnumbered cardbacks include a small player photo, vital statistics and sponsor logos.

COMPLETE SET (42)	4.00	10.00
1 Archie Amerson	.25	.60
2 Tony Akins	.25	.60
3 Chris Burns	.08	.25
4 Mike Campbell	.08	.25
5 Carl Coulter	.08	.25
6 Jeff Cummins	.15	.40
7 Seth Dittman	.08	.25
8 Gonzalo Floyd	.08	.25
9 Darren Flutie	.75	2.00
10 Mace Freeman	.08	.25
11 Corey Grant	.08	.25
12 Andrew Grigg	.15	.40
13 Dave Hack	.08	.25
14 Joe Hagins	.08	.25
15 Cooper Harris	.08	.25
16 Rob Hitchcock	.08	.25
17 Eric Lapointe	.25	.60
18 Cody Ledbetter	.15	.40
19 Lamar McGriggs	.08	.25
20 Danny McManus	.60	1.50
21 Joe Montford	.25	.60
22 Mike Morreale	.25	.60
23 Warren Muzika	.08	.25
24 Paul Osbaldiston	.08	.25
25 Eurosius Parker	.08	.25
26 Mike Philbrick	.08	.25
27 Tim Prinsen	.08	.25
28 Frank Rocca	.08	.25
29 Trevor Shaw	.08	.25
30 Chris Shelling	.08	.25
31 Jarrett Smith	.08	.25
32 Obie Spanic	.08	.25
33 Orlondo Steinauer	.08	.25
34 Calvin Tiggle	.08	.25
35 Jason Van Geel	.08	.25
36 Gerald Vaughn	.08	.25
37 Kyle Walters	.08	.25
38 Frank West	.08	.25
39 Ronald Williams	.40	1.00
40 Kids, Cats & Cops	.08	.25
41 McDonad's Coupon	.08	.25
42 Pre-season Coupon	.08	.25

1981 JOGO Black and White

This Canadian Football League set consists of 50 numbered black and white cards with blue printing on the backs of the cards. Cards were printed in Canada and measure 3 1/2" by 5". J.C. Watts (card number 4) was added to the set after he was the MVP of the Grey Cup in 1981 replacing Greg Marshall. According to the producer, there were three press runs (500 sets, 500 sets, and 300 sets) for this set; only the third contained the J.C. Watts card. The set price below includes both number 4's. The key card in the set is Warren Moon, representing his first card of any kind.

COMPLETE SET (51)	150.00	250.00
1 Richard Crump	1.00	2.50
2 Tony Gabriel	3.00	8.00
3 Gerry Organ	1.50	4.00
4A Greg Marshall	1.00	2.50
4B J.C. Watts SP	35.00	60.00
5 Mike Raines	.75	2.00
6 Larry Brune	.75	2.00
7 Randy Rhino	1.00	2.50
8 Bruce Clark	1.50	4.00
9 Condredge Holloway	7.50	15.00
10 Dave Newman	.75	2.00
11 Cedric Minter	.75	2.00
12 Peter Muller	.75	2.00
13 Vince Ferragamo	7.50	15.00
14 James Scott	1.50	4.00
15 Billy Johnson (White Shoes)	4.00	8.00
16 David Overstreet	4.00	8.00
17 Keith Gary	.75	2.00
18 Tom Clements	6.00	15.00
19 Keith Baker	.75	2.00
20 David Shaw	.75	2.00
21 Ben Zambiasi	1.50	4.00
22 John Priestner	1.00	2.50
23 Warren Moon	60.00	120.00
24 Tom Wilkinson	2.00	5.00
25 Brian Kelly	2.50	6.00
26 Dan Kepley	1.50	4.00
27 Larry Highbaugh	1.00	2.50
28 David Boone	.75	2.00
29 John Henry White	.75	2.00
30 Joe Paopao	1.50	4.00
31 Larry Key	.75	2.00
32 Glen Jackson	.75	2.00
33 Joe Hollimon	.75	2.00
34 Dieter Brock	3.00	8.00
35 Mike Holmes	.75	2.00
36 William Miller	.75	2.00
37 John Helton	1.25	3.00
38 Joe Poplawski	1.00	2.50
39 Joe Barnes	1.50	4.00
40 John Hufnagel	4.00	8.00
41 Bobby Thompson T	.75	2.00
42 Steve Stapler	1.00	2.50
43 Tom Cousineau	5.00	10.00
44 Bruce Threadgill	.75	2.00
45 Ed McAleney	.75	2.00
46 Leif Petterson	.75	2.00
47 Paul Bennett	.75	2.00
48 James Reed	.75	2.00
49 Gerry Dattilio	.75	2.00
50 Checklist Card	1.50	4.00

1982 JOGO Ottawa

These 24 large (approximately 3 1/2" by 5") cards featuring the Ottawa Rough Riders of the CFL have full color fronts while the backs are printed in red and black on white stock. Cards are numbered inside a leaf in the middle of the back of the card; player's uniform number is also given on the back of the card. A sample card of Rick Sowieta (with blank back) is also available with overstruck "Collector's Series" in red ink diagonally across the front of the card. These cards were endorsed by the CFL Players Association and produced by JOGO and were available for sale in some confectionary stores.

COMPLETE SET (24)	5.00	12.00
1 Jordan Case	.30	.75
2 Larry Brune	.20	.50
3 Val Belcher	.20	.50
4 Greg Marshall	.30	.75
5 Mike Raines	.20	.50
6 Rick Sowieta	.20	.50
7 John Glassford	.20	.50
8 Bruce Walker	.20	.50
9 Jim Reid	.60	1.50
10 Kevin Powell	.30	.75
11 Jim Piaskoski	.20	.50
12 Kelvin Kirk	.20	.50
13 Gerry Organ	.60	1.50
14 Carl Brazley	.20	.50
15 William Mitchell	.20	.50
16 Billy Hardee	.20	.50
17 Jonathan Sutton	.20	.50
18 Doug Seymour	.20	.50
19 Pat Staub	.20	.50
20 Larry Tittley	.20	.50
21 Pat Stoqua	.20	.50
22 Sam Platt	.20	.50
23 Gary Dulin	.60	1.50
24 John Holland	.30	.75

1982 JOGO Ottawa Past

This set consists of 16 black and white numbered cards measuring approximately 3 1/2" by 5." They feature ex-Ottawa players with the front of the card giving the position and years that the player played for the Rough Riders. The cards are numbered on the front in the lower right corner and the backs are blank except for the words "Printed in Canada by The Runge Press Limited." The first series (1-12) was issued as an insert to the 1982 color set of Rough Riders; the next series of four (13-16) were added later. In the first series, six of the cards were double printed; these are designated with a DP in the checklist below. The cards were also re-issued in 1984 as inserts in the Ottawa Rough Rider game programs. These 1984 cards are part of the Ottawa Yesterday's Heroes set and contain a different cardback complete with sponsor logos and a player write-up.

COMPLETE SET (16)	12.00	30.00
1 Tony Gabriel	1.25	3.00
2 Whit Tucker DP	.50	1.25
3 Dave Thelen	1.00	2.50
4 Ron Stewart DP	.75	2.00
5 Russ Jackson DP	1.50	4.00
6 Kaye Vaughan	.75	2.00
7 Bob Simpson	.75	2.00
8 Ken Lehmann	.60	1.50
9 Lou Bruce	.60	1.50
10 Wayne Giardino DP	.50	1.25
11 Moe Racine	.60	1.50
12 Gary Schreider	.60	1.50
13 Don Sutherin	2.00	5.00
14 Mark Kosmos DP	.50	1.25
15 Jim Foley DP	.50	1.25
16 Jim Conroy	.75	2.00

1983 JOGO Limited

This unnumbered set of 110 color cards was printed in very limited quantities (only 600 sets of which 500 were numbered according to the producer) and features players in the Canadian Football League. The backs of the cards appear to be on off-white card stock. The checklist below is organized in alphabetical order within each team, although the player's uniform number is given on the back of the cards. The Cards are listed by team order. Cards of Warren Moon and Dieter Brock are especially difficult to find since both of these players purchased quantities of their own card directly from the producer for distribution to their fans. Each of the registered sets is numbered on the Darrell Moir (Calgary number 110) card.

COMPLETE SET (110)	400.00	800.00
1 Steve Ackroyd	2.00	5.00
2 Joe Barnes	5.00	12.00
3 Bob Bronk	2.00	5.00
4 Jan Carinci	2.00	5.00
5 Gordon Elser	2.00	5.00
6 Dan Ferrone	2.50	6.00
7 Terry Greer	5.00	12.00
8 Mike Hameluck	2.00	5.00
9 Condredge Holloway	12.50	25.00
10 Greg Holmes	2.00	5.00
11 Hank Ilesic	4.00	10.00
12 John Malinosky	2.00	5.00
13 Cedric Minter	2.00	5.00
14 Don Moen	2.50	6.00
15 Rick Mohr	2.00	5.00
16 Darrell Nicholson	2.00	5.00
17 Paul Pearson	2.50	6.00
18 Matthew Teague	2.00	5.00
19 Geoff Townsend	2.00	5.00
20 Tom Trifaux	2.00	5.00
21 Darrell Wilson	2.00	5.00
22 Earl Wilson	2.00	5.00
23 Ricky Barden	2.00	5.00
24 Roger Cattelan	2.00	5.00
25 Michael Collymore	2.00	5.00
26 Charles Cornelius	2.00	5.00
27 Mariet Ford	2.00	5.00
28 Tyron Gray	3.00	8.00
29 Steve Harrison	2.00	5.00
30 Tim Hook	2.00	5.00
31 Greg Marshall	3.00	8.00
32 Ken Miller	2.00	5.00
33 Dave Newman	2.00	5.00
34 Rudy Phillips	4.00	10.00
35 Jim Reid	3.00	8.00
36 Junior Robinson	2.00	5.00
37 Mark Seale	2.00	5.00
38 Rick Sowieta	2.00	5.00
39 Pat Stoqua	2.00	5.00
40 Skip Walker	4.00	10.00
41 Al Washington	2.00	5.00
42 J.C. Watts	60.00	100.00
43 Keith Baker	2.00	5.00
44 Dieter Brock	15.00	30.00
45 Rocky DiPietro	6.00	15.00
46 Howard Fields	2.00	5.00
47 Ron Johnson	2.50	6.00
48 John Priestner	2.00	5.00
49 Johnny Shepherd	2.50	6.00
50 Mike Walker	2.50	6.00
51 Ben Zambiasi	5.00	12.00
52 Nick Arakgi	2.50	6.00
53 Brian DeRoo	2.00	5.00
54 Denny Ferdinand	2.00	5.00
55 Willie Hampton	2.00	5.00
56 Kevin Starkey	2.00	5.00
57 Glen Weir	2.00	5.00
58 Larry Crawford	3.00	8.00
59 Tyrone Crews	2.00	5.00
60 James Curry	4.00	10.00
61 Roy DeWalt	5.00	12.00
62 Mervyn Fernandez	15.00	30.00
63 Sammy Green	2.00	5.00
64 Glen Jackson	2.00	5.00
65 Glenn Leonhard	2.00	5.00
66 Nelson Martin	2.00	5.00
67 Joe Paopao	3.00	8.00
68 Lui Passaglia	6.00	12.00
69 Al Wilson	2.00	5.00
70 Nick Bastaja	2.00	5.00
71 Paul Bennett	2.00	5.00
72 John Bonk	4.00	8.00
73 Aaron Brown	2.00	5.00
74 Bob Cameron	4.00	10.00
75 Tom Clements	25.00	50.00
76 Rick House	2.50	6.00
77 John Hufnagel	10.00	25.00
78 Sean Kehoe	2.00	5.00
79 James Murphy	5.00	12.00
80 Tony Norman	2.00	5.00
81 Joe Poplawski	2.00	5.00
82 Willard Reaves	5.00	12.00
83 Bobby Thompson T	2.00	5.00
84 Wylie Turner	2.00	5.00
85 Dave Fennell	3.00	8.00
86 Jim Germany	2.50	6.00
87 Larry Highbaugh	3.00	8.00
88 Joe Hollimon	2.00	5.00
89 Dan Kepley	4.00	10.00
90 Neil Lumsden	2.50	6.00
91 Warren Moon	200.00	350.00
92 James Parker	4.00	10.00
93 Dale Potter	2.00	5.00
94 Angelo Santucci	2.00	5.00
95 Tom Towns	2.00	5.00
96 Tom Tuinei	2.50	6.00
97 Danny Bass	5.00	12.00
98 Ray Crouse	2.00	5.00
99 Gerry Dattilio	3.00	8.00
100 Tom Forzani	2.00	5.00
101 Mike Levenseller	2.00	5.00
102 Mike McTague	2.50	6.00
103 Bernie Morrison	2.00	5.00
104 Darrell Toussaint	2.00	5.00
105 Chris DeFrance	2.00	5.00
106 Dwight Edwards	2.50	6.00
107 Vince Goldsmith	4.00	10.00
108 Homer Jordan	2.00	5.00
109 Mike Washington	2.00	5.00
110A Darrell Moir (Set number on back)	5.00	12.00
110B Darrell Moir (Without set number)	15.00	30.00

1983 JOGO Hall of Fame A

This 25-card standard-size set features members of the Canadian Football Hall of Fame. Cards were produced by JOGO Novelties. These black and white standard sized cards have a red border. On the back they are numbered (with the prefix A) and contain biographical information.

COMPLETE SET (25)	25.00	50.00
A1 Russ Jackson	3.00	6.00
A2 Harvey Wylie	.30	.75
A3 Kenny Ploen	.75	2.00
A4 Garney Henley	.75	2.00
A5 Hal Patterson	1.00	2.50
A6 Carl Cronin	.30	.75
A7 Bob Simpson	.30	.75
A8 Dick Shatto	.50	1.25
A9 John Red O'Quinn	.30	.75
A10 Johnny Bright	.75	2.00
A11 Ernest Cox	.30	.75
A12 Rollie Miles	.30	.75
A13 Leo Lewis	1.25	3.00
A14 Bud Grant	5.00	12.00
A15 Herb Trawick	.30	.75
A16 Wayne Harris	.60	1.50
A17 Earl Lunsford	.30	.75
A18 Tony Golab	.30	.75
A19 George Reed	1.50	4.00
A20 By Bailey	.40	1.00
A21 Harry Batstone	.30	.75
A22 Ron Atchison	.50	1.25
A23 Willie Fleming	.50	1.25
A24 Frank Leadlay	.30	.75
A25 Lionel Conacher	1.50	4.00

1983 JOGO Hall of Fame B

This 25-card standard-size set features members of the Canadian Football Hall of Fame. Cards were produced by JOGO Novelties. These black and white standard-sized cards have a red border. On the back they are numbered (with the prefix B) and contain biographical information. The title card is not required (or considered below) as part of the complete set. However the title card is indeed somewhat harder to find separately as there were reportedly only half as many title cards printed as there were cards for each player.

COMPLETE SET (25)	25.00	50.00
B1 Bernie Faloney	2.00	5.00
B2 George Dixon	.75	2.00
B3 John Barrow	.75	2.00
B4 Jackie Parker	2.50	6.00
B5 Jack Jacobs	.30	.75
B6 Sam Etcheverry	3.00	8.00
B7 Norm Fieldgate	.50	1.25
B8 John Ferrard	.30	.75
B9 Tommy Joe Coffey	.75	2.00
B10 Martin Ruby	.50	1.25
B11 Ted Reeve	.30	.75
B12 Kaye Vaughan	.30	.75
B13 Ron Lancaster	1.50	4.00
B14 Smirle Lawson	.30	.75
B15 Fritz Hanson	.30	.75
B16 Vince Scott	.30	.75
B17 Frank Morris	.30	.75
B18 Normie Kwong	1.00	2.50
B19 Dr. Tom Casey	.50	1.25
B20 Herb Gray	.75	2.00
B21 Gerry James	.50	1.25
B22 Pete Neumann	.30	.75
B23 Joe Krol	.30	.75
B24 Ron Stewart	.50	1.25
B25 Buddy Tinsley	.30	.75
NNO Title Card SP (Map to HOF on back)	2.50	6.00

1983 JOGO Quarterbacks

This nine-card black and white (with red border) standard-size set contains several well-known quarterbacks performing in the CFL. The cards are unnumbered although each player's uniform number is given on the back of his card. The cards are numbered in alphabetical order in the checklist below for convenience.

COMPLETE SET (9)	50.00	100.00
1 Dieter Brock	1.50	4.00
2 Tom Clements	4.00	8.00
3 Gerry Dattilio	.75	2.00
4 Roy DeWalt	1.25	3.00
5 Johnny Evans	.75	2.00
6 Condredge Holloway	4.00	10.00
7 John Hufnagel	2.50	5.00
8 Warren Moon	25.00	50.00
9 J.C. Watts	15.00	30.00

1984 JOGO

This full-color set of 160 standard-size cards produced by JOGO consists of two series: the first series is 1-110 and the second series runs from 111-160. According to the producer, there were 400 more sets of the first series printed than were printed of the second series; hence the second series is slightly more valuable per card. The cards are numbered on the back; the backs contain printing in red and black ink. The second series was printed on a gray cardboard stock whereas the first series is on a cream-colored stock. Photos were taken by F. Scott Grant, who is credited on the fronts of the cards. The cards feature players in the Canadian Football League. Some players are featured in both series.

COMPLETE SET (160)	150.00	300.00
COMP.SERIES 1 (110)	75.00	150.00
COMP.SERIES 2 (50)	75.00	150.00
1 Mike Hameluck	.60	1.50
2 Bob Bronk	.75	2.00
3 Paul Pearson	.40	1.00
4 Dan Ferrone	.60	1.50
5 Paul Bennett	.40	1.00
6 Joe Barnes	2.00	4.00
7 Condredge Holloway	4.00	8.00
8 Terry Greer	2.50	5.00
9 Vince Goldsmith	1.00	2.50
10 Darrell Wilson	.40	1.00
11 Tom Trifaux	.40	1.00
12 Kelvin Pruenster	.40	1.00
13 Earl Wilson	.40	1.00
14 Hank Ilesic	1.00	2.50
15 Stephen Del Col	.40	1.00
16 Lamont Meacham	.40	1.00
17 Lester Brown	.75	2.00
18 Rob Forbes	.40	1.00
19 Darrell Nicholson	.40	1.00
20 James Curry	1.00	2.50
21 Skip Walker	1.00	2.50
22 J.C. Watts	20.00	40.00
23 Kevin Powell	.40	1.00
24 Dean Dorsey	1.00	2.50
25 Tyron Gray	1.00	2.50
26 Mike Hudson	.60	1.50
27 Dan Rashovich	.40	1.00
28 Rudy Phillips	.60	1.50
29 Larry Tittley	.40	1.00
30 Ricky Barden UER (Number missing)	.40	1.00
31 Mark Seale	.40	1.00
32 Prince McJunkins	.60	1.50
33 Kevin Dalliday	.40	1.00
34 Rick Sowieta	.40	1.00
35 Roger Cattelan	.40	1.00
36 Damir Dupin	.40	1.00
37 Jack Williams	.40	1.00
38 Dave Newman	.40	1.00
39 Maurice Doyle	.40	1.00
40 Tim Hook	.40	1.00
41 Dieter Brock	5.00	10.00
42 Rufus Crawford	2.50	5.00
43 Steve Kearns	.40	1.00
44 Ross Francis	.40	1.00
45 Henry Waszczuk	.40	1.00
46 Mark Streeter	.40	1.00
47 Mike McIntyre	.40	1.00
48 John Priestner	.40	1.00
49 Paul Palma	.40	1.00
50 Mike Walker	.60	1.50
51 Mike Barker	.40	1.00
52 Todd Brown	.40	1.00
53 Andre Francis	1.00	2.50
54 Glenn Keeble	.40	1.00
55 Turner Gill	5.00	10.00
56 Eugene Belliveau	.40	1.00
57 Willie Hampton	.40	1.00
58 Ken Ciancone	.40	1.00
59 Preston Young	.40	1.00
60 Stanley Washington	.40	1.00
61 Denny Ferdinand	.40	1.00
62 Steve Smith	.40	1.00
63 Rick Klassen	.60	1.50
64 Larry Crawford	.60	1.50
65 John Henry White	.40	1.00
66 Bernie Glier	.40	1.00
67 Don Taylor	.40	1.00
68 Roy DeWalt	2.50	5.00
69 Mervyn Fernandez	6.00	12.00
70 John Blain	.40	1.00
71 James Parker	2.00	4.00
72 Henry Vereen	.40	1.00
73 Gerald Roper	.40	1.00
74 Jim Sandusky	5.00	10.00
75 John Pankratz	.40	1.00
76 Tom Clements	6.00	12.00
77 Vernon Pahl	.40	1.00
78 Trevor Kennerd	1.00	2.50
79 Stan Mikawos	.40	1.00
80 Ken Hailey	.40	1.00
81 James Murphy	2.00	4.00
82 Jeff Boyd	1.00	2.50

83 Bob Cameron	2.00	4.00
84 Jerome Erdman	.60	1.50
85 Tyrone Jones	1.00	2.50
86 John Bonk	.40	1.00
87 John Sturdivant	.60	1.50
88 Dan Huclack	.40	1.00
89 Tony Norman	.40	1.00
90 Kevin Neiles	.40	1.00
91 Dave Kirzinger	.40	1.00
92 Kevin Molle	.40	1.00
93 Jerry Debrouolny	.40	1.00
94 Larry Hogue	.40	1.00
95 Ken Moore	.40	1.00
96 Jerry Friesen	.40	1.00
97 Mike McTague	.60	1.50
98 Jason Riley	.40	1.00
99 Roger Aldag	1.00	2.50
100 Dave Ridgway	2.00	4.00
101 Eric Upton	.40	1.00
102 Laurent DesLauriers	.40	1.00
103 Brian Fryer	.40	1.00
104 Brian DeRoo	.40	1.00
105 Neil Lumsden	.40	1.00
106 Hector Pothier	.40	1.00
107 Brian Kelly	4.00	8.00
108 Dan Kepley	2.00	4.00
109 Danny Bass	3.00	6.00
110 Nick Arakgi	.60	1.50
111 Lyle Bauer	1.50	4.00
112 Al Washington	.75	2.00
113 Michel Bourgeau	1.50	4.00
114 Keith Gooch	.75	2.00
115 Sean Kehoe	.40	1.00
116 Ken Clark	1.00	2.50
117 Orlando Flanagan	.75	2.00
118 Greg Vavra	.75	2.00
119 Mark Bragagnolo	.75	2.00
120 Dave Cutler	4.00	8.00
121 Nick Hebeler	.75	2.00
122 Harry Skipper	2.50	5.00
123 Frank Robinson	1.00	2.50
124 DeWayne Jett	1.00	2.50
125 Mark Young	.75	2.00
126 Felix Wright	7.50	15.00
127 Bob Poley	.75	2.00
128 Leo Ezerins	.75	2.00
129 Johnny Shepherd	1.00	2.50
130 Jeff Inglis	.75	2.00
131 Dwaine Wilson	.75	2.00
132 Aaron Hill	.75	2.00
133 Brian Dudley	1.00	2.50
134 Ned Armour	.75	2.00
135 Darryl Hall	1.00	2.50
136 Vince Phason	.75	2.00
137 Terry Lymon	.75	2.00
138 Jerry Dobrovolny	.75	2.00
139 Richard Nemeth	.75	2.00
140 Matt Dunigan	20.00	40.00
141 Rick Mohr	.75	2.00
142 Lawrie Skolrood	.75	2.00
143 Craig Ellis	2.00	4.00
144 Steve Johnson	.75	2.00
145 Glen Suitor	1.50	3.00
146 Jeff Roberts	.75	2.00
147 Greg Fieger	.75	2.00
148 Sterling Hinds	.75	2.00
149 Willard Reaves	4.00	8.00
150 John Pitts	.75	2.00
151 Delbert Fowler	1.00	2.50
152 Mark Hopkins	.75	2.00
153 Pat Cantner	.75	2.00
154 Scott Flagel	1.00	2.50
155 Donovan Rose	.75	2.00
156 David Shaw	.75	2.00
157 Mark Moors	.75	2.00
158 Chris Walby	3.00	8.00
159 Eugene Belliveau	.75	2.00
160 Trevor Kennerd	4.00	8.00

1984 JOGO Ottawa Yesterday's Heroes

JOGO released this 22-card set as inserts into 1984 Ottawa Rough Rider game programs. The first 16-cards of this set were re-issued from the 1982 Jogo Ottawa Past set, with the primary difference being the complete player write-up on the cardbacks. The title "Yesterday's Heroes" as well as sponsor logos also are included on the cardbacks.

COMPLETE SET (22)	60.00	120.00
1 Tony Gabriel	2.50	6.00
2 Whit Tucker	1.50	4.00
3 Dave Thelen	1.50	4.00
4 Ron Stewart	1.50	4.00
5 Russ Jackson	7.50	15.00
6 Kaye Vaughan	1.50	4.00
7 Bob Simpson	1.50	4.00
8 Ken Lehmann	1.50	4.00
9 Lou Bruce	1.50	4.00
10 Wayne Giardino	1.50	4.00
11 Moe Racine	1.50	4.00
12 Gary Schreider	1.50	4.00
13 Don Sutherin	2.50	6.00
14 Mark Kosmos	1.50	4.00
15 Jim Foley	1.50	4.00
16 Jim Conroy	1.50	4.00
17 George Brancato	2.00	5.00
18 Art Green	2.00	5.00
19 Rudy Sims	2.00	5.00
20 Jim Coode	5.00	10.00
21 Jerry Campbell	2.00	5.00
22 Jim Piaskoski	7.50	15.00

1985 JOGO

The 1985 JOGO CFL set is standard size and was distributed as a single series of 110 cards, numbered 1-110. With some exceptions, the number ordering of the set is by teams.

COMPLETE SET (110)	75.00	150.00
1 Mike Hameluck	.75	2.00
2 Michel Bourgeau	.50	1.25
3 Waymon Alridge	.30	.75
4 Daric Zeno	.30	.75
5 J.C. Watts	10.00	20.00
6 Kevin Gray	.30	.75
7 Steve Harrison	.30	.75
8 Ralph Dixon	.30	.75
9 Jo Jo Heath	.30	.75
10 Rick Sowieta	.30	.75
11 Brad Fawcett	.30	.75
12 Lamont Meacham	.30	.75
13 Dean Dorsey	.50	1.25
14 Bernard Quarles	.30	.75
15 Mike Caterbone	.30	.75
16 Bob Stephen	.30	.75
17 Nick Benjamin	.50	1.25
18 Tim McCray	.75	2.00
19 Chris Sigler	.30	.75
20 Tony Johns	.30	.75
21 Jason Riley	.30	.75
22 Ralph Scholz	.30	.75
23 Ken Hobart	1.25	3.00
24 Paul Bennett	.30	.75
25 Dan Ferrone	.50	1.25
26 Jim Kalafat	.30	.75
27 William Mitchell	.30	.75
28 Denny Ferdinand	.30	.75
29 James Curry	.75	2.00
30 Jeff Inglis	.30	.75
31 Bob Bronk	.60	1.50
32 Dan Petschenig	.30	.75
33 Terry Greer	1.50	4.00
34 Condredge Holloway	3.00	6.00
35 Ian Beckstead	.30	.75
36 James Parker	1.25	3.00
37 Tim Cowan	.50	1.25
38 Roy DeWalt	.75	2.00
39 Mervyn Fernandez	4.00	8.00
40 Bernie Glier	.30	.75
41 Keyvan Jenkins	1.25	3.00
42 Melvin Byrd	.75	2.00
43 Ron Robinson	.75	2.00
44 Andre Jones DB	.30	.75
45 Jim Sandusky	1.50	4.00
46 Darnell Clash	.75	2.00
47 Rick Klassen	.50	1.25
48 Brian Kelly	2.00	5.00
49 Rick House	.50	1.25
50 Stewart Hill	1.25	3.00
51 Chris Woods	1.25	3.00
52 Darryl Hall	.50	1.25
53 Laurent DesLauriers	.30	.75
54 Larry Cowan	.30	.75
55 Matt Dunigan	7.50	15.00
56 Andre Francis	.50	1.25
57 Roy Kurtz	.30	.75
58 Steve Raquet	.30	.75
59 Turner Gill	2.00	5.00
60 Sandy Armstrong	.30	.75
61 Nick Arakgi	.50	1.25
62 Mike McTague	.50	1.25
63 Aaron Hill	.50	1.25
64 Brett Williams	.75	2.00
65 Trevor Bowles	.50	1.25
66 Mark Hopkins	.30	.75
67 Frank Kosec	.30	.75
68 Ken Ciancone	.30	.75
69 Dwaine Wilson	.30	.75
70 Mark Stevens	.30	.75
71 George Voelk	.30	.75
72 Doug Scott	.30	.75
73 Rob Smith	.75	2.00
74 Alan Reid	.30	.75
75 Rick Mohr	.30	.75
76 Dave Ridgway	1.25	3.00
77 Homer Jordan	.30	.75
78 Terry Leschuk	.30	.75
79 Rick Goltz	.30	.75
80 Neil Quilter	.30	.75
81 Joe Paopão	.50	1.25
82 Stephen Jones	.75	2.00
83 Scott Redl	.30	.75
84 Tony Dennis	.30	.75
85 Glen Suitor	.75	2.00
86 Mike Anderson	.30	.75
87 Stewart Fraser	.30	.75
88 Fran McDermott	.30	.75
89 Craig Ellis	1.25	3.00
90 Eddie Ray Walker	.50	1.25
91 Trevor Kennerd	1.50	4.00
92 Pat Cantner	.30	.75
93 Tom Clements	4.00	8.00
94 Glen Steele	.30	.75
95 Willard Reaves	1.50	4.00
96 Tony Norman	.30	.75
97 Tyrone Jones	.75	2.00
98 Jerome Erdman	.30	.75
99 Sean Kehoe	.30	.75
100 Kevin Neiles	.30	.75
101 Ken Hailey	.30	.75
102 Scott Flagel	.50	1.25
103 Mark Moors	.30	.75
104 Gerry McGrath	.30	.75
105 James Hood	.30	.75
106 Randy Ambrosie	.50	1.25
107 Terry Irvin	.50	1.25
108 Joe Barnes	1.25	3.00
109 Richard Nemeth	.30	.75
110 Darrell Patterson	.75	2.00

1985 JOGO Ottawa Program Inserts

These inserts were featured in Ottawa home game programs. The cards are black-and-white with a white border and measure approximately 3 3/8" by 5 1/8". They are numbered in the lower right hand corner.

COMPLETE SET (9)	14.00	35.00
1 1960 Grey Cup Team	2.00	4.00
2 Russ Jackson	5.00	10.00
3 Angelo Mosca	4.00	8.00
4 Joe Poirier	2.00	4.00
5 Sam Scoccia	2.00	4.00
6 Gilles Archambeault	2.00	4.00
7 Ron Lancaster	3.00	6.00
8 Tom Jones	2.00	4.00
9 Gerry Nesbitt	2.00	5.00

1986 JOGO

The 1986 JOGO CFL set is standard size. These numbered cards were issued in two different series, 1-110 and 111-169. A few players appear in both series. This year's set from JOGO has a distinctive black border on the front of the card. Card backs are printed in red and black on white card stock. The player's name and uniform number are given on the front of the card. The player's team is not explicitly listed anywhere on the card. An interesting card in this is set is #83 Brian Pillman, who later went on to fame as wrestler "Flyin Brian".

COMPLETE SET (169)	75.00	150.00
COMP.SERIES 1 (110)	50.00	100.00
COMP.SERIES 2 (59)	25.00	50.00
1 Ken Hobart	.75	2.00
2 Tom Porras	.75	2.00
3 Jason Riley	.25	.60
4 Ron Ingram	.25	.60
5 Steve Stapler	.40	1.00
6 Mike Derks	.25	.60
7 Grover Covington	1.25	3.00
8 Lance Shields	.40	1.00
9 Mike Robinson	.25	.60
10 Mark Napiorkowski	.25	.60
11 Romel Andrews	.25	.60
12 Ed Gataveckas	.25	.60
13 Tony Champion	1.50	4.00
14 Dale Sanderson	.25	.60
15 Mark Barousse	.25	.60
16 Nick Benjamin	.40	1.00
17 Reginal Butts	.25	.60
18 Tom Burgess	1.25	3.00
19 Todd Dillon	1.25	3.00
20 Jim Reid	.75	2.00
21 Robert Reid	.25	.60
22 Roger Cattelan	.25	.60
23 Kevin Powell	.25	.60
24 Randy Fabi	.25	.60
25 Gerry Hornett	.25	.60
26 Rick Sowieta	.25	.60
27 Warren Hudson	.40	1.00
28 Steven Cox	.25	.60
29 Dean Dorsey	.40	1.00
30 Michel Bourgeau	.40	1.00
31 Ken Joiner	.25	.60
32 Mark Seale	.25	.60
33 Condredge Holloway	2.50	5.00
34 Bob Bronk	.50	1.25
35 Jeff Inglis	.25	.60
36 Lance Chomyc	.75	2.00
37 Craig Ellis	.75	2.00
38 Marcellus Greene	.25	.60
39 David Marshall	.25	.60
40 Kerry Parker	.25	.60
41 Darrell Wilson	.25	.60
42 Walter Lewis	.75	2.00
43 Sandy Armstrong	.25	.60
44 Ken Ciancone	.25	.60
45 Steve Raquet	.25	.60
46 Lemont Jeffers	.25	.60
47 Paul Gray	.25	.60
48 Jacques Chapdelaine	.25	.60
49 Rick Ryan	.25	.60
50 Mark Hopkins	.25	.60
51 Glenn Keeble	.25	.60
52 Roy Kurtz	.25	.60
53 Brian Dudley	.25	.60
54 Mike Gray	.25	.60
55 Tyrone Crews	.25	.60
56 Roy DeWalt	.75	2.00
57 Mervyn Fernandez	1.50	4.00
58 Bernie Glier	.25	.60
59 James Parker	1.25	3.00
60 Bruce Barnett	.25	.60
61 Keyvan Jenkins	.75	2.00
62 Al Wilson	.25	.60
63 Delbert Fowler	.40	1.00
64 James Jefferson	1.50	4.00
65 James West	2.50	6.00
66 Laurent DesLauriers	.25	.60
67 Damon Allen	8.00	20.00
68 Roy Bennett	1.25	3.00
69 Hasson Arbubakrr	.25	.60
70 Tom Clements	2.50	6.00
71 Trevor Kennerd	.75	2.00
72 Perry Tuttle	1.25	3.00
73 Pat Cantner	.25	.60
74 Mike Hameluck	.40	1.00
75 Rob Prodanovic	.25	.60
76 James Bell	.40	1.00
77 Hector Pothier	.25	.60
78 Milson Jones	.75	2.00
79 Craig Shaffer	.25	.60
80 Chris Skinner	.40	1.00
81 Matt Dunigan	3.00	8.00
82 Tom Dixon	.25	.60
83 Brian Pillman	8.00	20.00
84 Randy Ambrosie	.25	.60
85 Rick Johnson	1.25	3.00
86 Larry Hogue	.25	.60
87 Garrett Doll	.40	1.00
88 Stu Laird	.75	2.00
89 Greg Fieger	.25	.60
90 Sean McKeown	.25	.60
91 Rob Bresciani	.25	.60
92 Harold Hallman	1.25	3.00
93 Jamie Harris	.25	.60
94 Dan Rashovich	.25	.60
95 David Conrad	.25	.60
96 Glen Suitor	.75	2.00
97 Mike Siroishka	.25	.60
98 Mike McGruder	.75	2.00
99 Brad Calip	.25	.60
100 Mike Anderson	.25	.60
101 Trent Bryant	.25	.60
102 Gary Lewis	.25	.60
103 Tony Dennis	.25	.60
104 Paul Tripoli	.25	.60
105 Daric Zeno	.25	.60
106 Michael Elarms	.25	.60
107 Donohue Grant	.25	.60
108 Ray Elgaard	3.00	8.00
109 Joe Paopao	.75	2.00
110 Dave Ridgway	1.00	2.50
111 Rudy Phillips	.75	2.00
112 Carl Brazley	.40	1.00
113 Andre Francis	.40	1.00
114 Mitchell Price	.40	1.00
115 Wayne Lee	.25	.60
116 Tim McCray	.75	2.00
117 Scott Virkus	.25	.60
118 Nick Hebeler	.25	.60
119 Eddie Ray Walker	.25	.60
120 Bobby Johnson	.25	.60
121 Mike McTague	.25	.60
122 Jeff Inglis	.25	.60
123 Joe Fuller	.25	.60
124 Steve Crane	.25	.60
125 Bill Henry	.25	.60
126 Ron Brown	.25	.60
127 Henry Taylor	.25	.60
128 Greg Holmes	.25	.60
129 Steve Harrison	.25	.60
130 Paul Osbaldiston	1.25	3.00
131 Craig Walls	.25	.60
132 Clorindo Grilli	.25	.60
133 Marty Palazeti	.25	.60
134 Darryl Hall	.40	1.00
135 David Black	.25	.60
136 Bennie Thompson	1.00	2.50
137 Darryl Sampson	.25	.60
138 James Murphy	1.00	2.50
139 Scott Flagel	.25	.60
140 Trevor Kennerd	.75	2.00
141 Bob Molle	.25	.60
142 Darrell Patterson	.25	.60
143 Stan Mikawos	.25	.60
144 John Sturdivant	.25	.60
145 Tyrone Jones	.75	2.00
146 Jim Zorn	3.00	8.00
147 Steve Howlett	.25	.60
148 Jeff Volpe	.25	.60
149 Jerome Erdman	.25	.60
150 Ned Armour	.25	.60
151 Rick Klassen	.40	1.00
152 Brett Williams	.75	2.00
153 Richie Hall	.75	2.00
154 Ray Alexander	1.00	2.50
155 Willie Pless	2.50	6.00
156 Marlon Jones	.25	.60
157 Danny Bass	1.25	3.00
158 Frank Balkovec	.25	.60
159 Less Browne	1.25	3.00
160 Paul Osbaldiston	.75	2.00
161 Trevor Bowles	.25	.60
162 David Daniels	.25	.60
163 Kevin Konar	.40	1.00
164 Gary Allen	.75	2.00
165 Karlton Watson	.25	.60
166 Ron Hopkins	.40	1.00
167 Rob Smith	.40	1.00
168 Garrett Doll	.25	.60
169 Rod Skillman	.60	1.50
170 Scott Grant Phot. SP	10.00	20.00

1987 JOGO

The 1987 JOGO CFL set is standard size. These numbered cards were issued essentially in team order. A color photo is framed by a blue border. Card backs are printed in black on white card stock except for the CFLPA (Canadian Football League Players' Association) logo in the upper right corner which is red and black.

COMPLETE SET (110)	50.00	100.00
1 Jim Reid	.40	1.00
2 Nick Benjamin	.30	.75
3 Dean Dorsey	.30	.75
4 Hasson Arbubakrr	.20	.50
5 Gerald Alphin	2.50	6.00
6 Larry Willis	1.25	3.00
7 Rick Wolkensperg	.20	.50
8 Roy DeWalt	.40	1.00
9 Michel Bourgeau	.30	.75
10 Anthony Woodson	.20	.50
11 Marv Allemang	.20	.50
12 Jerry Dobrovolny	.20	.50
13 Larry Mohr	.20	.50
14 Kyle Hall	.20	.50
15 Irv Daymond	.20	.50
16 Ken Ford	.20	.50
17 Leo Groenewegen	.20	.50
18 Michael Cline	.20	.50
19 Gilbert Renfroe	1.25	3.00
20 Danny Barrett	2.50	6.00
21 Dan Petschenig	.20	.50
22 Gill Fenerty UER (Misspelled Gil on card front)	4.00	10.00
23 Lance Chomyc	.30	.75
24 Jake Vaughan	.20	.50
25 John Congemi	.60	1.50
26 Kelvin Pruenster	.20	.50
27 Mike Siroishka	.20	.50
28 Dwight Edwards	.30	.75
29 Darnell Clash	.40	1.00
30 Glenn Kulka	.40	1.00
31 Jim Kardash	.20	.50
32 Selwyn Drain	.20	.50
33 Ian Sinclair	.40	1.00
34 Pat Cantner	.20	.50
35 Trevor Kennerd	.40	1.00
36 Bob Cameron	.60	1.50
37 Willard Reaves	1.25	3.00
38 Jeff Treftlin	.20	.50
39 David Black	.20	.50
40 Chris Walby	1.00	2.50
41 Tom Clements	1.25	3.00
42 Mike Gray	.20	.50
43 Bennie Thompson	.40	1.00
44 Tyrone Jones	.30	.75
45 Ken Winey	.20	.50
46 Nick Arakgi	.30	.75
47 James West	1.00	2.50
48 Ken Pettway	.20	.50
49 James Murphy	1.00	2.50
50 Carl Fodor	.20	.50
51 Tom Muecke	.60	1.50
52 Alvis Satele	.20	.50
53 Grover Covington	.60	1.50
54 Tom Porras	.30	.75
55 Jason Riley	.20	.50
56 Jed Tommy	.20	.50
57 Bernie Ruoff	.30	.75
58 Ed Gataveckas	.20	.50
59 Wayne Lee	.20	.50
60 Ken Hobart	.30	.75
61 Frank Robinson	.30	.75
62 Mike Robinson	.20	.50
63 Ben Zambiasi UER (No team listed on front of card)	.60	1.50
64 Byron Williams	.20	.50
65 Lance Shields	.30	.75
66 Ralph Scholz	.20	.50
67 Earl Winfield	1.25	3.00
68 Terry Lehne	.20	.50
69 Alvin Bailey	.20	.50
70 David Sauve	.20	.50
71 Bernie Glier	.20	.50
72 Nelson Martin	.20	.50
73 Kevin Konar	.40	1.00
74 Greg Peterson	.20	.50
75 Harold Hallman	.40	1.00
76 Sandy Armstrong	.20	.50
77 Glenn Harper	.20	.50
78 Rick Worman	.40	1.00
79 Darrell Toussaint	.20	.50
80 Larry Hogue	.20	.50
81 Rick Johnson	1.00	2.50
82 Richie Hall	.30	.75
83 Stu Laird	.30	.75
84 Mike Emery	.20	.50
85 Cliff Toney	.20	.50
86 Matt Dunigan	2.00	5.00
87 Hector Pothier	.20	.50
88 Stewart Hill	.40	1.00
89 Stephen Jones	.40	1.00
90 Dan Huclack	.20	.50
91 Mark Napiorkowski	.20	.50
92 Mike Derks	.20	.50
93 Mike Walker	.40	1.00
94 Mike McGruder	1.00	2.50
95 Terry Baker	1.25	3.00
96 Bobby Jurasin	1.25	3.00
97 James Curry	.40	1.00
98 Tracey Mack	.20	.50
99 Tom Burgess	1.00	2.50
100 Steve Crane	.20	.50
101 Glen Suitor	.30	.75
102 Walter Bender	.20	.50
103 Jeff Bentrim	.75	2.00
104 Eric Florence	.20	.50
105 Terry Cochrane	.20	.50
106 Tony Dennis	.20	.50
107 David Albright	.20	.50
108 David Sidoo	.20	.50
109 Harry Skipper	.40	1.00
110 Dave Ridgway	1.00	2.50

1988 JOGO

The 1988 JOGO CFL set is standard size. These numbered cards were issued essentially in team order. A color photo is framed by a blue border with a white inner outline. Card backs are printed in black on white card stock, except for the CFLPA (Canadian Football League Players' Association) logo in the upper right corner which is red and black. The cards are arranged according to teams.

COMPLETE SET (110)	45.00	80.00
1 Roy DeWalt	.50	1.25
2 Jim Reid	.50	1.25
3 Patrick Wayne	.20	.50
4 Jerome Erdman	.20	.50
5 Tom Dixon	.20	.50
6 Brad Fawcett	.20	.50
7 Tom Muecke	.50	1.25
8 Mike Hudson	.20	.50
9 Orville Lee	.50	1.25
10 Michel Bourgeau	.30	.75
11 Dan Sellers	.20	.50
12 Rob Pavan	.20	.50
13 Rae Robirtis	.20	.50
14 Rod Brown	.20	.50
15 Ken Evraire	.50	1.25
16 Irv Daymond	.20	.50
17 Tim Jessie	.50	1.25
18 Jim Sandusky	.75	2.00
19 Blake Dermott	.50	1.25
20 Brian Warren	.20	.50
21 Mike Walker	.75	2.00
22 Tom Porras	.30	.75
23 Less Browne	.75	2.00
24 Paul Osbaldiston	.50	1.25
25 Vernell Quinn	.20	.50
26 Mike Derks	.20	.50
27 Arnold Grevious	.20	.50
28 Tim Lorenz	.20	.50
29 Mike Robinson	.20	.50
30 Doug Davies	.20	.50
31 Earl Winfield	.75	2.00
32 Wally Zatylny	.75	2.00
33 Martin Sartin	.20	.50
34 Lee Knight	.20	.50
35 Jason Riley	.20	.50
36 Darrell Corbin	.20	.50
37 Tony Champion	1.00	2.50
38 Steve Stapler	.20	.50
39 Scott Flagel	.20	.50
40 Grover Covington	.75	2.00
41 Mark Napiorkowski	.20	.50
42 Jacques Chapdelaine	.20	.50
43 Lance Shields	.30	.75
44 Donohue Grant	.20	.50
45 Gizmo Williams	8.00	20.00
46 Trevor Bowles	.20	.50
47 Don Wilson	.20	.50
48 Tracy Ham	6.00	15.00
49 Richie Hall	.30	.75
50 Rob Bresciani	.20	.50
51 James Curry	.50	1.25
52 Kent Austin	4.00	10.00
53 Jeff Bentrim	.50	1.25
54 Dave Ridgway	.75	2.00
55 Terry Baker	.75	2.00
56 Lance Chomyc	.30	.75
57 Paul Sandor	.20	.50
58 Kevin Cummings	.20	.50
59 John Congemi	.50	1.25
60 Gilbert Renfroe	.60	1.50
61 Jake Vaughan	.20	.50
62 Doran Major	.20	.50
63 Dwight Edwards	.30	.75
64 Bruce Elliott	.20	.50
65 Lorenzo Graham	.30	.75
66 Jim Kardash	.20	.50
67 Reggie Pleasant	1.00	2.50
68 Carl Brazley	.30	.75
69 Gill Fenerty	2.00	5.00
70 Selwyn Drain	.20	.50
71 Warren Hudson	.30	.75
72 Willie Fears	.50	1.25
73 Randy Ambrosie	.20	.50
74 George Ganas	.20	.50
75 Glenn Kulka	.30	.75
76 Kelvin Pruenster	.20	.50
77 Darrell Smith	.75	2.00
78 Jearld Baylis	.50	1.25
79 Blaine Schmidt	.20	.50
80 Tony Visco	.50	1.25
81 Carl Fodor	.20	.50
82 Rudy Phillips	.30	.75
83 Craig Watson	.30	.75
84 Kent Warnock	.30	.75
85 Ken Ford	.20	.50
86 Blake Marshall	.75	2.00
87 Terry Cochrane	.20	.50
88 Shawn Faulkner	.20	.50
89 Marshall Toner	.20	.50
90 Darren Yewshyn	.20	.50
91 Eugene Belliveau	.20	.50
92 Jay Christensen	.50	1.25
93 Anthony Parker	.75	2.00
94 Walter Ballard	.20	.50
95 Matt Dunigan	2.00	5.00
96 Andre Francis	.30	.75
97 Rickey Foggie	2.00	5.00
98 Delbert Fowler	.30	.75
99 Michael Allen	.50	1.25
100 Greg Battle	1.50	4.00
101 Mike Gray	.20	.50
102 Dan Wicklum	.20	.50
103 Paul Shorten	.20	.50
104 Paul Clatney	.20	.50
105 Rod Hill	.30	.75
106 Steve Rodehutskors	.50	1.25
107 Sean Salisbury	2.00	5.00
108 Vernon Pahl	.20	.50
109 Trevor Kennerd	.50	1.25
110 David Williams	1.00	2.50

1988 JOGO League

This 106-card set was produced and distributed before the CFL season started. The set was produced expressly for the league. There were to be 13 players for each of the eight teams with, reportedly, 3000 complete sets printed. Since the cards were intended for promotional purposes, each team was responsible for distributing their own cards making complete sets rather difficult. After the cards were printed, roster changes caused some of the cards to be withdrawn. All the cards were distributed by the players and teams except for three cards. Tom Clements number 105 (retired), Nick Arakgi number 54 (retired), and the checklist number 106, which were only available from hobby distributors of JOGO products. In addition, players who were victims of early trades or injuries, are also more difficult to find, e.g., Kevin Powell (traded to Edmonton), Greg Marshall (injured and retired), Willard Reaves (signed with Washington Redskins), Milson Jones (traded to Saskatchewan), Scott Flagel (traded to Hamilton), and Jim Sandusky (traded to Edmonton). Cards are unnumbered except for uniform number which is prominently displayed on both sides of the card. The cards are ordered below alphabetically within team.

COMPLETE SET (106)	100.00	200.00
1 Walter Ballard	.40	1.00
2 Jan Carinci	.40	1.00
3 Larry Crawford	.60	1.50
4 Tyrone Crews	.40	1.00
5 Andre Francis	.60	1.50
6 Bernie Glier	.40	1.00
7 Keith Gooch	.40	1.00
8 Kevin Konar	.60	1.50
9 Scott Lecky	.40	1.00
10 James Parker	1.25	3.00
11 Jim Sandusky (Traded)	4.00	8.00
12 Gregg Stumon	.75	2.00
13 Todd Wiseman (Not listed on checklist card)	.40	1.00
14 Gary Allen	.60	1.50
15 Scott Flagel (Traded)	.75	2.00
16 Harold Hallman	.75	2.00
17 Larry Hogue UER (Misspelled Hoque)	.40	1.00
18 Ron Hopkins	.40	1.00
19 Stu Laird	.60	1.50
20 Andy McVey	.40	1.00
21 Bernie Morrison	.40	1.00
22 Tim Petros	.75	2.00
23 Bob Poley	.40	1.00
24 Tom Spoletini	.40	1.00
25 Emanuel Tolbert	1.25	3.00
26 Larry Willis	.60	1.50
27 Damon Allen	6.00	12.00
28 Danny Bass	1.50	4.00
29 Stanley Blair	.40	1.00
30 Marco Cyncar	.60	1.50
31 Tracy Ham	15.00	30.00
32 Milson Jones (Traded)	1.25	3.00
33 Stephen Jones	.75	2.00
34 Jerry Kauric	.75	2.00
35 Hector Pothier	.40	1.00
36 Tom Richards	1.25	3.00
37 Chris Skinner	.60	1.50
38 Gizmo Williams	20.00	40.00
39 Larry Wruck	.60	1.50
40 Pat Brady	.40	1.00
41 Grover Covington	.75	2.00
42 Rocky DiPietro	1.25	3.00
43 Howard Fields	.40	1.00
44 Miles Gorrell	.40	1.00
45 Johnnie Jones	.40	1.00
46 Tom Porras	.60	1.50
47 Jason Riley	.40	1.00
48 Dale Sanderson	.40	1.00
49 Ralph Scholz	.40	1.00
50 Lance Shields	.60	1.50
51 Steve Stapler	.40	1.00
52 Mike Walker	1.25	3.00
53 Gerald Alphin	1.50	4.00
54 Nick Arakgi SP (Retired before season)	10.00	20.00
55 Nick Benjamin	.60	1.50
56 Tom Dixon	.40	1.00
57 Leo Groenewegen	.40	1.00
58 Will Lewis	.60	1.50
59 Greg Marshall (Injured and retired)	1.50	4.00
60 Larry Mohr	.40	1.00
61 Kevin Powell (Traded)	.75	2.00
62 Jim Reid	.75	2.00
63 Art Schlichter	4.00	8.00
64 Rick Wolkensperg	.40	1.00
65 Anthony Woodson	.40	1.00
66 David Albright	.40	1.00
67 Roger Aldag	.60	1.50
68 Mike Anderson	.40	1.00
69 Kent Austin	10.00	20.00
70 Tom Burgess	1.50	4.00
71 James Curry	.75	2.00
72 Ray Elgaard	3.00	6.00
73 Denny Ferdinand	.40	1.00
74 Bobby Jurasin	2.50	5.00
75 Gary Lewis	.40	1.00
76 Dave Ridgway	1.25	3.00
77 Harry Skipper	.60	1.50
78 Glen Suitor	.60	1.50
79 Ian Beckstead	.40	1.00
80 Lance Chomyc	.60	1.50
81 John Congemi	.75	2.00
82 Gill Fenerty	4.00	8.00
83 Dan Ferrone	.60	1.50
84 Warren Hudson	.60	1.50
85 Hank Ilesic	.75	2.00
86 Jim Kardash	.40	1.00
87 Glenn Kulka	.60	1.50
88 Don Moen	.60	1.50
89 Gilbert Renfroe	.75	2.00
90 Chris Schultz	.60	1.50
91 Darrell Smith	.75	2.00
92 Lyle Bauer	.40	1.00
93 Nick Bastaja	.40	1.00
94 David Black	.40	1.00
95 Bob Cameron	.75	2.00
96 Randy Fabi	.40	1.00
97 James Jefferson	2.50	5.00
98 Stan Mikawos	.40	1.00
99 James Murphy	.75	2.00
100 Ken Pettway	.40	1.00
101 Willard Reaves (Signed with Redskins)	5.00	10.00
102 Darryl Sampson	.40	1.00
103 Chris Walby	1.25	3.00
104 James West	1.50	4.00
105 Tom Clements SP (Retired before season)	10.00	20.00
106 Checklist Card SP	3.00	6.00

1989 JOGO

The 1989 JOGO CFL set contains 160 standard-size cards. The cards were issued in two series, 1-110 and 111-160. Except for the card numbering, the two series are indistinguishable. The fronts have color action photos with dark blue borders and yellow lettering; the vertically oriented backs have biographical information and career highlights. The first 200 sets of the first series cards came out with purple borders creating a series 1 parallel variation. The cards are numbered on the back and checklisted below according to teams.

COMPLETE SET (160)	50.00	100.00
COMP.SERIES 1 (110)	30.00	60.00
COMP.SERIES 2 (50)	20.00	40.00
1 Mike Kerrigan	1.00	2.50
2 Ian Beckstead	.25	.60
3 Lance Chomyc	.40	1.00
4 Gill Fenerty	1.50	4.00
5 Lee Morris	.25	.60
6 Todd Wiseman	.25	.60
7 John Congemi	.75	2.00
8 Harold Hallman	.40	1.00
9 Jim Kardash	.25	.60
10 Kelvin Pruenster	.25	.60
11 Blaine Schmidt	.25	.60
12 Bruce Holmes	.25	.60
13 Ed Berry	.25	.60
14 Bobby McAllister	1.00	2.50
15 Frank Robinson	.40	1.00
16 Darrell Corbin	.25	.60
17 Jason Riley	.25	.60
18 Darrell Patterson	.25	.60
19 Darrell Harle	.25	.60
20 Mark Napiorkowski	.25	.60
21 Derrick McAdoo	.75	2.00
22 Sam Loucks	.25	.60
23 Ronnie Glanton	.25	.60
24 Lance Shields	.25	.60
25 Tony Champion	.75	2.00
26 Floyd Salazar	.25	.60
27 Tony Visco	.40	1.00
28 Glenn Kulka	.40	1.00
29 Reggie Pleasant	.75	2.00
30 Rod Skillman	.25	.60
31 Grover Covington	1.00	2.50
32 Gerald Alphin	1.00	2.50
33 Gerald Wilcox	.75	2.00
34 Daniel Hunter	.25	.60
35 Tony Kimbrough	.40	1.00
36 Willie Fears	.40	1.00
37 Tyrone Thurman	1.00	2.50
38 Dean Dorsey	.40	1.00
39 Tom Schimmer	.25	.60
40 Ken Evraire	.40	1.00
41 Steve Wiggins	.25	.60
42 Donovan Wright	.25	.60
43 Tuineau Alipate	.40	1.00
44 Richie Hall	.25	.60
45 Rob Bresciani	.25	.60
46 Tom Burgess	.75	2.00
47 Jeff Fairholm	1.00	2.50
48 John Hoffman	.25	.60
49 Dave Ridgway	1.00	2.50
50 Terry Baker	1.25	3.00
51 Mike Hildebrand	.25	.60
52 Danny Bass	1.00	2.50
53 Jeff Braswell	.40	1.00
54 Michel Bourgeau	.40	1.00
55 Ken Ford	.25	.60
56 Enis Jackson	.25	.60

57 Tony Hunter	.75	2.00
58 Andre Francis	.40	1.00
59 Larry Wruck	.40	1.00
60 Pierre Vercheval	1.00	2.50
61 Keith Wright	.25	.60
62 Andrew McConnell	.25	.60
63 Gregg Stumon	.40	1.00
64 Steve Taylor	1.00	2.50
65 Brett Williams	.40	1.00
66 Tracy Ham	4.00	10.00
67 Stewart Hill	.75	2.00
68 Eugene Belliveau	.25	.60
69 Tom Porras	.40	1.00
70 Jay Christensen	.40	1.00
71 Michael Soles	.75	2.00
72 John Mandarich	.40	1.00
73 Dan Wicklum	.25	.60
74 Shawn Daniels	.25	.60
75 Marshall Toner	.25	.60
76 Kent Warnock	.40	1.00
77 Terrence Jones	1.25	3.00
78 Damon Allen	2.50	6.00
79 Kevin Konar	.40	1.00
80 Phillip Smith	.25	.60
81 Marcus Thomas	.25	.60
82 Jamie Taras	.75	2.00
83 Rob Moretto	.25	.60
84 Eugene Mingo	.25	.60
85 Matt Dunigan	1.50	4.00
86 Jan Carinci	.25	.60
87 Anthony Parker	1.00	2.50
88 Keith Gooch	.25	.60
89 Ron Howard	.25	.60
90 David Williams	.75	2.00
91 Less Browne	.40	1.00
92 Quency Williams	.25	.60
93 Tim McCray	.40	1.00
94 Jeff Croonen	.25	.60
95 Greg Battle	1.00	2.50
96 Moustafa Ali	.40	1.00
97 Michael Allen	.40	1.00
98 David Black	.25	.60
99 Paul Randolph	.25	.60
100 Trevor Kennerd	.75	2.00
101 Ken Pettway	.25	.60
102 Sean Salisbury	2.00	5.00
103 Bob Cameron	.75	2.00
104 Tim Jessie	.40	1.00
105 Leon Hatziioannou	.25	.60
106 Matt Pearce	.25	.60
107 Paul Clatney	.25	.60
108 Randy Fabi	.25	.60
109 Mike Gray	.25	.60
110 James Murphy	1.25	3.00
111 Danny Barrett	1.25	3.00
112 Wally Zatylny	.75	2.00
113 Tony Truelove	.25	.60
114 Leroy Blugh	.75	2.00
115 Reggie Taylor	.75	2.00
116 Mark Zeno	1.00	2.50
117 Paul Wetmore	.25	.60
118 Mark McLoughlin	.75	2.00
119 Randy Ambrosie	.25	.60
120 Will Johnson	.75	2.00
121 Brock Smith	.25	.60
122 Willie Gillus	.25	.60
123 Andy McVey	.25	.60
124 Wes Cooper	.25	.60
125 Tyrone Pope	.25	.60
126 Craig Ellis	.75	2.00
127 Darrel Hopper	.25	.60
128 Brad Fawcett	.25	.60
129 Pat Miller	.25	.60
130 Irv Daymond	.25	.60
131 Bob Molle	.25	.60
132 James Mills	1.00	2.50
133 Darrell Wallace	.40	1.00
134 Jerry Beasley	.25	.60
135 Loyd Lewis	.25	.60
136 Bernie Glier	.25	.60
137 Eric Streater	1.00	2.50
138 Gerald Roper	.25	.60
139 Brad Tierney	.25	.60
140 Patrick Wayne	.25	.60
141 Craig Watson	.25	.60
142 Doug(Tank) Landry	1.00	2.50
143 Orville Lee	.75	2.00
144 Rocco Romano	.75	2.00
145 Todd Dillon	.75	2.00
146 Michel Lamy	.25	.60
147 Tony Cherry	1.00	2.50
148 Flint Fleming	.25	.60
149 Kennard Martin	.25	.60
150 Lorenzo Graham	.25	.60
151 Junior Thurman	.75	2.00
152 Darnell Graham	.25	.60
153 Dan Ferrone	.40	1.00
154 Matt Finlay	.25	.60
155 Brent Matich	.25	.60
156 Kent Austin	2.00	5.00
157 Will Lewis	.25	.60
158 Mike Walker	.75	2.00
159 Tim Petros	.40	1.00
160 Stu Laird	.40	1.00

1989 JOGO Purple

COMPLETE SET (110)	100.00	200.00
*PURPLES: 1.5X TO 4X BASIC CARDS		

1990 JOGO

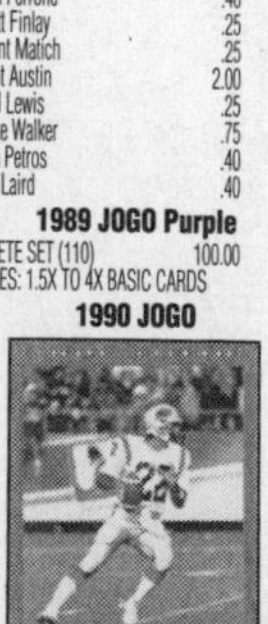

This 220-card standard-size set of JOGO Canadian Football League cards was issued in two series of 110 cards. The first series card fronts feature an action shot of the player, enframed by a thin red border on blue background, with team name above the photo and player's name below. The second series card fronts feature solid blue borders surrounding an action shot of the player with the team's name on the top of the card and the player's name underneath. The card number and player information are found on the back. Three British Columbia players featured in the set that are of interest to American collectors are Doug Flutie, Mark Gastineau, and Major Harris. The complete set price below includes only one of the variations of card 84. First series cards are arranged according to teams.

COMPLETE SET (220)	15.00	40.00
COMP.SERIES 1 (110)	8.00	20.00
COMP.SERIES 2 (110)	8.00	20.00
1A Grey Cup Champs ERR (Roughriders because...)	.40	1.00
1B Grey Cup Champs COR (Roughriders became...)	1.60	4.00
2 Kent Austin	.60	1.50
3 James Ellingson	.25	.60
4 Vince Goldsmith	.25	.60
5 Gary Lewis	.08	.25
6 Bobby Jurasin	.40	1.00
7 Tim McCray	.15	.40
8 Chuck Klingbeil	.15	.40
9 Albert Brown	.08	.25
10 Dave Ridgway	.40	1.00
11 Tony Rice	1.00	2.50
12 Richie Hall	.08	.25
13 Jeff Fairholm	.25	.60
14 Ray Elgaard	.60	1.50
15 Sonny Gordon	.08	.25
16 Peter Giftopoulus	.25	.60
17 Mike Kerrigan	.40	1.00
18 Jason Riley	.08	.25
19 Wally Zatylny	.15	.40
20 Derrick McAdoo	.15	.40
21 Dale Sanderson	.08	.25
22 Paul Osbaldiston	.15	.40
23 Todd Dillon	.15	.40
24 Miles Gorrell	.08	.25
25 Earl Winfield	.25	.60
26 Bill Henry	.08	.25
27 Darrell Harle	.08	.25
28 Ernie Schramayr	.08	.25
29 Greg Peterson	.08	.25
30 Marshall Toner	.08	.25
31 Danny Barrett	.60	1.50
32 Mike Palumbo	.08	.25
33 Ken Ford	.08	.25
34 Brock Smith	.08	.25
35 Tom Spoletini	.08	.25
36 Will Johnson	.25	.60
37 Terrence Jones	.25	.60
38 Darcy Kopp	.08	.25
39 Tim Petros	.15	.40
40 Mitchell Price	.08	.25
41 Junior Thurman	.25	.60
42 Kent Warnock	.15	.40
43 Darrell Smith	.25	.60
44 Chris Schultz UER (No team on back)	.15	.40
45 Kelvin Pruenster	.08	.25
46 Matt Dunigan	.80	2.00
47 Lance Chomyc	.08	.25
48 John Congemi	.15	.40
49 Mike Clemons	6.00	12.00
50 Glenn Harper	.08	.25
51 Branko Vincic	.08	.25
52 Tom Porras	.15	.40
53 Reggie Pleasant	.15	.40
54 Randy Marriott	.08	.25
55 James Parker	.25	.60
56 Don Moen	.15	.40
57 James West	.25	.60
58 Trevor Kennerd	.25	.60
59 Warren Hudson	.15	.40
60 Tom Burgess	.25	.60
61 David Black	.08	.25
62 Matt Pearce	.08	.25
63 Steve Rodehutskors	.15	.40
64 Rod Hill	.08	.25
65 Nick Benjamin	.15	.40
66 Bob Cameron	.25	.60
67 Leon Hatziioannou	.08	.25
68 Robert Mimbs	1.00	2.50
69 Mike Gray	.08	.25
70 Ken Winey	.08	.25
71 Mike Hildebrand	.08	.25
72 Brett Williams	.15	.40
73 Tracy Ham	1.60	4.00
74 Danny Bass	.40	1.00
75 Mark Norman	.08	.25
76 Andre Francis	.15	.40
77 Todd Storme	.08	.25
78 Gizmo Williams	1.60	4.00
79 Kevin Clark	.25	.60
80 Enis Jackson	.08	.25
81 Leroy Blugh	.15	.40
82 Jeff Braswell	.08	.25
83 Larry Wruck	.15	.40
84A Mike McLean ERR (Photo actually/24 Mike Hildebrand)	.80	2.00
84B Mike McLean COR (Two players shown)	1.60	4.00
85 Leo Groenewegen UER (Misspelled Groenewegan on card back)	.08	.25
86 Mark Gastineau	.40	1.00
87 Rocco Romano	.08	.25
88 Major Harris	.60	1.50
89 Ray Alexander	.25	.60
90 Joe Paopao	.25	.60
91 Ian Sinclair	.15	.40
92 Tony Visco UER (British Columbia on front& correctly has team as Toronto on front)	.08	.25
93 Lui Passaglia	.40	1.00
94 Doug Flutie	4.00	10.00
95 Glenn Kulka	.15	.40
96 Bruce Holmes	.08	.25
97 Stacey Dawsey	.08	.25
98 Damon Allen	.80	2.00
99 Ken Evraire	.15	.40
100 David Williams	.25	.60
101 Gregg Stumon	.15	.40
102 Scott Flagel	.08	.25
103 Gerald Roper	.08	.25
104 Tony Cherry	.25	.60
105 Jim Mills	.15	.40
106 Dean Dorsey	.15	.40
107 Patrick Wayne	.08	.25
108 Reggie Barnes	.25	.60
109 Kari Yli-Renko	.08	.25
110 Ken Hobart	.15	.40
111 Doug Flutie	4.00	10.00
112 Grover Covington	.25	.60
113 Michael Allen	.08	.25
114 Mike Walker	.25	.60
115 Danny McManus	3.00	6.00
116 Greg Battle	.40	1.00
117 Quency Williams	.08	.25
118 Jeff Croonen	.08	.25
119 Paul Randolph	.08	.25
120 Rick House	.15	.40
121 Rob Smith	.15	.40
122 Mark Napiorkowski	.08	.25
123 Ed Berry	.08	.25
124 Rob Crifo	.08	.25
125 Gord Weber	.08	.25
126 Jeff Boyd	.15	.40
127 Paul McGowan	.15	.40
128 Reggie Taylor	.15	.40
129 Warren Jones	.15	.40
130 Blake Marshall	.25	.60
131 Darrell Corbin	.08	.25
132 Jim Rockford	.15	.40
133 Richard Nurse	.08	.25
134 Bryan Illerbrun	.08	.25
135 Mark Waterman	.08	.25
136 Doug(Tank) Landry	.40	1.00
137 Ronnie Glanton	.08	.25
138 Mark Guy	.15	.40
139 Mike Anderson	.08	.25
140 Remi Trudel	.08	.25
141 Stephen Jones	.25	.60
142 Mike Derks	.08	.25
143 Michel Bourgeau	.15	.40
144 Jeff Bentrim	.15	.40
145 Roger Aldag	.15	.40
146 Donald Narcisse	1.20	3.00
147 Troy Wilson	.08	.25
148 Glen Suitor	.15	.40
149 Stewart Hill	.25	.60
150 Chris Johnstone	.08	.25
151 Mark Mathis	.08	.25
152 Blaine Schmidt	.08	.25
153 Craig Ellis	.25	.60
154 John Mandarich	.08	.25
155 Steve Zatylny	.08	.25
156 Michel Lamy	.08	.25
157 Irv Daymond	.08	.25
158 Tom Porras	.15	.40
159 Rick Worman	.25	.60
160 Major Harris	.40	1.00
161 Darryl Hall	.15	.40
162 Terry Andrysiak	.15	.40
163 Harold Hallman	.15	.40
164 Carl Brazley	.15	.40
165 Kevin Smellie	.08	.25
166 Mark Campbell	.15	.40
167 Andy McVey	.08	.25
168 Derrick Crawford	.15	.40
169 Howard Dell	.08	.25
170 Dave Van Belleghem	.08	.25
171 Don Wilson	.08	.25
172 Robert Smith	.15	.40
173 Keith Browner	.15	.40
174 Chris Munford	.08	.25
175 Gary Wilkerson	.08	.25
176 Rickey Foggie UER (Misspelled Foogie on card front)	.40	1.00
177 Robin Belanger	.08	.25
178 Andrew Murray	.08	.25
179 Paul Masotti	.40	1.00
180 Chris Gaines	.08	.25
181 Joe Clausi	.08	.25
182 Greg Harris	.08	.25
183 Dave Bovell	.08	.25
184 Eric Streater	.25	.60
185 Larry Hogue	.08	.25
186 Jan Carinci	.08	.25
187 Floyd Salazar	.08	.25
188 Alondra Johnson	.15	.40
189 Jay Christensen UER (Misspelled Christenson on card front)	.15	.40
190 Rick Ryan	.08	.25
191 Willie Pless	.50	1.25
192 Walter Ballard	.08	.25
193 Lee Knight	.08	.25
194 Ray Macoritti	.15	.40
195 Dan Payne	.08	.25
196 Dan Sellers	.08	.25
197 Rae Robirtis	.08	.25
198 Dave Mossman	.08	.25
199 Sam Loucks	.08	.25
200 Derek MacCready	.08	.25
201 Tony Cherry	.25	.60
202 Moustafa Ali	.08	.25
203 Terry Baker	.40	1.00
204 Matt Finlay	.08	.25
205 Daniel Hunter	.08	.25
206 Chris Major	.60	1.50
207 Henry Smith	.08	.25
208 David Sapunjis	1.20	3.00
209 Darrell Wallace	.15	.40
210 Mark Singer	.08	.25
211 Tuineau Alipate	.08	.25
212 Tony Champion	.25	.60
213 Mike Lazecki	.08	.25
214 Larry Clarkson	.08	.25
215 Lorenzo Graham	.08	.25
216 Tony Martino	.08	.25
217 Ken Watson	.08	.25
218 Paul Clatney	.08	.25
219 Ken Pettway	.08	.25
220 Tyrone Jones	.15	.40

1991 JOGO

The 1991 JOGO CFL football set contains 220 standard-size cards. The set was released in two series, 1-110 and 111-220. The set was distributed in factory sets and in foil packs (10 cards per pack). The front design has glossy color action shots, with thin gray and red borders against a royal blue card face. The team name appears above.the picture, while the CFL helmet logo and the player's name appear at the bottom of the card face. The backs have red, green, and yellow lettering on a black background. They feature biography and career summary. The team logo and card number round out the back. The cards are numbered on the back and checklisted below according to teams. It is estimated that 30,000 sets were produced. Rocket Ismail was originally planned for inclusion in the set, but was removed based on litigation. Ismail had signed an exclusive with All World, which apparently took precedence over JOGO's attempt to include him in the set based on his membership in the CFL Players' Association.

COMPLETE SET (220)	4.00	10.00
COMP.SERIES 1 (110)	2.00	5.00
COMP.SERIES 2 (110)	2.00	5.00
1 Tracy Ham	.20	.50
2 Larry Wruck	.02	.10
3 Pierre Vercheval	.05	.15
4 Rod Connop	.01	.05
5 Michel Bourgeau	.01	.05
6 Leroy Blugh	.02	.10
7 Mike Walker	.02	.10
8 Ray Macoritti	.01	.05
9 Michael Soles	.02	.10
10 Brett Williams	.02	.10
11 Blake Marshall	.05	.15
12 David Williams	.02	.10
13 Enis Jackson	.01	.05
14 Craig Ellis	.02	.10
15 Reggie Taylor	.02	.10
16 Mike McLean	.01	.05
17 Blake Dermott	.02	.10
18 Gizmo Williams	.20	.50
19 Jordan Gaertner	.01	.05
20 Willie Pless	.08	.25
21 Danny Bass	.10	.30
22 Trevor Bowles	.01	.05
23 Rob Davidson	.01	.05
24 Mark Norman	.01	.05
25 Ron Lancaster CO	.05	.15
26 Chris Johnstone	.01	.05
27 Randy Ambrosie	.01	.05
28 Glenn Kulka	.01	.05
29 Gerald Wilcox	.02	.10
30 Kari Yli-Renko	.01	.05
31 Daniel Hunter	.01	.05
32 Bryan Illerbrun	.01	.05
33 Terry Baker	.07	.20
34 Jeff Braswell	.01	.05
35 Andre Francis	.01	.05
36 Irv Daymond	.01	.05
37 Sean Foudy	.01	.05
38 Brad Tierney	.01	.05
39 Gregg Stumon	.01	.05
40 Scott Flagel	.01	.05
41 Gerald Roper	.01	.05
42 Charles Wright	.01	.05
43 Rob Smith	.01	.05
44 James Ellingson	.02	.10
45 Damon Allen	.40	1.00
46 John Congemi	.02	.10
47 Reggie Barnes	.05	.15
48 Stephen Jones	.05	.15
49 Rob Prodanovic	.01	.05
50 Steve Goldman	.01	.05
51 Patrick Wayne	.01	.05
52 David Conrad	.01	.05
53 John Kropke	.01	.05
54 Loyd Lewis	.01	.05
55 Tony Cherry	.05	.15
56 Terrence Jones	.08	.25
57 Dan Wicklum	.01	.05
58 Allen Pitts	.40	1.00
59 Junior Thurman	.01	.05
60 Ron Hopkins	.01	.05
61 Andy McVey	.01	.05
62 Leo Blanchard	.01	.05
63 Mark Singer	.01	.05
64 Darryl Hall	.02	.10
65 David McCrary	.01	.05
66 Mark Guy	.01	.05
67 Marshall Toner	.01	.05
68 Derrick Crawford	.02	.10
69 Danny Barrett	.05	.15
70 Kent Warnock	.02	.10
71 Brent Matich	.01	.05
72 Mark McLoughlin	.05	.15
73 Joe Clausi	.01	.05
74 Wally Buono CO	.01	.05
75 Will Johnson	.02	.10
76 Walter Ballard	.01	.05
77 Matt Finlay	.01	.05
78 David Sapunjis	.15	.40
79 Greg Peterson	.01	.05
80 Paul Clatney	.01	.05
81 Lloyd Fairbanks	.01	.05
82 Herman Heard	.02	.10
83 Richard Nurse	.01	.05
84 Dave Richardson	.01	.05
85 Ernie Schramayr	.01	.05
86 Todd Dillon	.02	.10
87 Tuineau Alipate	.01	.05
88 Peter Giftopoulus	.02	.10
89 Miles Gorrell	.01	.05
90 Earl Winfield	.05	.15
91 Paul Osbaldiston	.02	.10
92 Dale Sanderson	.01	.05
93 Jason Riley	.01	.05
94 Ken Evraire	.01	.05
95 Lee Knight	.01	.05
96 Tim Lorenz	.01	.05
97 Derrick McAdoo	.02	.10
98 Bobby Dawson	.01	.05
99 Rickey Royal	.01	.05
100 Ronald Veal	.05	.15
101 Grover Covington	.05	.15
102 Mike Kerrigan	.08	.25
103 Rocky DiPietro	.05	.15
104 Mark Dennis	.05	.15
105 Tony Champion	.05	.15
106 Tony Visco	.01	.05
107 Darrell Harle	.01	.05
108 Wally Zatylny	.02	.10
109 David Beckman CO	.01	.05
110 Checklist 1-110	.01	.05
111 Jeff Fairholm	.05	.15
112 Roger Aldag	.02	.10
113 David Albright	.01	.05
114 Gary Lewis	.01	.05
115 Dan Rashovich	.01	.05
116 Lucius Floyd	.05	.15
117 Bob Poley	.01	.05
118 Donald Narcisse	.30	.75
119 Bobby Jurasin	.08	.25
120 Orville Lee	.02	.10
121 Stacey Hairston	.01	.05
122 Richie Hall	.01	.05
123 John Gregory CO	.01	.05
124 Rick Worman	.02	.10
125 Dave Ridgway	.05	.15
126 Wayne Drinkwalter	.02	.10
127 Eddie Lowe	.01	.05
128 Mike Hogue	.01	.05
129 Larry Hogue	.01	.05
130 Milson Jones	.02	.10
131 Ray Elgaard	.10	.30
132 Dave Pitcher	.01	.05
133 Vic Stevenson	.01	.05
134 Albert Brown	.01	.05
135 Mike Anderson	.01	.05
136 Glen Suitor	.02	.10
137 Kent Austin	.10	.30
138 Mike Gray	.01	.05
139 Steve Rodehutskors	.02	.10
140 Eric Streater	.02	.10
141 David Black	.01	.05
142 James West	.05	.15
143 Danny McManus	.30	.75
144 Darryl Sampson	.01	.05
145 Bob Cameron	.05	.15
146 Tom Burgess	.05	.15
147 Rick House	.01	.05
148 Chris Walby	.05	.15
149 Michael Allen	.01	.05
150 Warren Hudson	.01	.05
151 Dave Bovell	.01	.05
152 Rob Crifo	.01	.05
153 Lyle Bauer	.01	.05
154 Trevor Kennerd	.05	.15
155 Troy Johnson	.01	.05
156 Less Browne	.02	.10
157 Nick Benjamin	.01	.05
158 Matt Pearce	.01	.05
159 Tyrone Jones	.02	.10
160 Rod Hill	.01	.05
161 Bob Molle	.01	.05
162 Lee Hull	.01	.05
163 Greg Battle	.05	.15
164 Robert Mimbs	.20	.50
165 Giulio Caravatta	.01	.05
166 James Mills	.05	.15
167 Ian Sinclair	.02	.10
168 Robin Belanger	.01	.05
169 Deatrich Wise	.01	.05
170 Chris Skinner	.02	.10
171 Norman Jefferson	.01	.05
172 Larry Clarkson	.01	.05
173 Chris Major	.08	.25
174 Stewart Hill	.02	.10
175 Tony Hunter	.01	.05
176 Stacey Dawsey	.01	.05
177 Doug Flutie	1.00	2.50
178 Mike Trevathan	.08	.25
179 Jearld Baylis	.02	.10
180 Matt Clark	.05	.15
181 Ken Pettway	.01	.05
182 Lloyd Joseph	.01	.05
183 Jon Volpe	.30	.75
184 Leo Groenewegen	.01	.05
185 Carl Coulter	.01	.05
186 O.J. Brigance	.30	.75
187 Ryan Hanson	.01	.05
188 Rocco Romano	.01	.05
189 Ray Alexander	.02	.10
190 Bob O'Billovich CO	.01	.05
191 Paul Wetmore	.01	.05
192 Harold Hallman	.02	.10
193 Ed Berry	.01	.05
194 Brian Warren	.01	.05
195 Matt Dunigan	.15	.40
196 Kelvin Pruenster	.01	.05
197 Ian Beckstead	.01	.05
198 Carl Brazley	.02	.10
199 Trevor Kennerd	.05	.15
200 Reggie Pleasant	.02	.10
201 Kevin Smellie	.01	.05
202 Don Moen	.02	.10
203 Blaine Schmidt	.01	.05
204 Chris Schultz	.02	.10
205 Lance Chomyc	.01	.05
206 Darrell Smith	.05	.15
207 Dan Ferrone	.02	.10
208 Chris Gaines	.01	.05
209 Keith Castello	.01	.05
210 Chris Munford	.01	.05
211 Rodney Harding	.01	.05
212 Darryl Ford	.01	.05
213 Rickey Foggie	.15	.40
214 Don Wilson	.01	.05
215 Andrew Murray	.01	.05
216 Jim Kardash	.01	.05
217 Mike Clemons	.50	1.25
218 Bruce Elliott	.01	.05
219 Mike McCarthy	.01	.05
220 Checklist Card	.01	.05

1991 JOGO Stamp Card Inserts

These three standard-size insert cards have photos on their fronts within a white postage stamp border. In red, green, and yellow print on a black background, the backs present commentary to the front pictures. The first two cards are numbered on the back, while the card picturing the Grey Cup Trophy is unnumbered.

COMPLETE SET (3)	14.00	35.00
1 Albert Henry George Grey	4.00	10.00
2 Trevor Kennerd	4.80	12.00
NNO Grey Cup Trophy (Grey Cup Winners listed on card back)	6.00	15.00

1992 JOGO Promos

JOGO produced the first two of the five Promo cards with a color action player photo on a silver cardfront. The team helmet and player's name appear in the bottom silver border. The third card features Rocket Rat, the JOGO Card Company "mascot." The back presents his biography and closes with an educational message ("Education Equals More Freedom"). Reportedly only 6,000 of each card were released. Two other cards (P1-P2) were inserted into the second edition of the Charlton CFL Football Card Price Guide as an uncut sheet of two. Reportedly, 5500 of the two card sheets were produced. The two Ken Danby Collector's Classic Library cards were produced to promote the Libraries series as well as a Ken Danby Grey Cup lithograph.

COMPLETE SET (7)	4.80	12.00
A1 Mike Clemons	.80	2.00
A2 Jon Volpe	.80	2.00
A3 Rocket Rat (Cartoon character)	.30	.75
P1 Mike Clemons	1.20	3.00
P2 Jon Volpe	1.20	3.00
CC1 Ken Danby Art Collector's Classic Library	.30	.75
CC2 Ken Danby Art Collector's Classic Library	.30	.75

1992 JOGO

The 1992 JOGO CFL set contains 220 standard-size cards. Reportedly there were less than 1200 cases produced. The cards feature color action player photos on a silver card face. The team helmet and player's name appear in the bottom silver border. In yellow, red, and green print on a silver background, the back has biography and player profile. The cards are numbered on the back and checklisted below according to teams.

COMPLETE SET (220)	8.00	20.00
1 Dave Bovell	.01	.05
2 Don Moen	.02	.10
3 Ian Beckstead	.01	.05
4 David Williams	.07	.20
5 Hank Ilesic	.07	.20
6 Brian Warren	.01	.05
7 Paul Masotti	.10	.30
8 Kelvin Pruenster	.01	.05
9 Mike Clemons	.80	2.00
10 Chris Schultz	.02	.10
11 Andrew Murray	.01	.05
12 Lance Chomyc	.01	.05
13 Ed Berry	.01	.05
14 Harold Hallman	.02	.10
15 Dave Van Belleghem	.01	.05
16 Rodney Harding	.02	.10
17 Rickey Foggie	.15	.40
18 Darrell Smith	.07	.20
19 Bob Skemp	.01	.05
20 Carl Brazley	.01	.05
21 J.P. Izquierdo	.01	.05
22 Mike Campbell	.02	.10
23 Reggie Pleasant	.02	.10
24 Dan Ferrone	.02	.10
25 Kevin Smellie	.01	.05
26 Don Wilson	.01	.05
27 Adam Rita CO	.01	.05
28 Greg Peterson	.01	.05
29 David Sapunjis	.20	.50
30 Srecko Zizakovic	.02	.10
31 Carl Bland	.01	.05
32 Errol Tucker	.01	.05
33 Allen Pitts	.40	1.00
34 Pee Wee Smith	.10	.30
35 Will Johnson	.02	.10
36 Kent Warnock	.02	.10
37 Brent Matich	.01	.05
38 Stu Laird	.02	.10
39 Shawn Beals	.01	.05
40 Darcy Kopp	.01	.05
41 Ken Moore	.01	.05
42 Alondra Johnson	.02	.10
43 Matt Finlay	.01	.05
44 Andy McVey	.01	.05
45 Paul Clatney	.01	.05
46 Karl Anthony	.01	.05
47 Bruce Covernton	.14	.35
48 Mark McLoughlin UER (Name misspelled several times on the card back)	.07	.20
49 Pat Hinds	.01	.05
50 Eric Mitchel UER (Misspelled Mitchell on both sides)	.07	.20
51 Dan Wicklum	.01	.05
52 Tim Cofield	.20	.50
53 Steve Taylor	.07	.20
54 Darryl Hall	.01	.05
55 Angelo Snipes	.15	.40
56 Shawn Daniels	.01	.05
57 Terrence Jones	.07	.20
58 Brian Bonner	.01	.05
59 Kari Yli-Renko	.01	.05
60 Denny Chronopoulos	.01	.05
61 Damon Allen	.50	1.25
62 Reggie Barnes	.07	.20
63 Andre Francis UER (Misspelled Frances on card front)	.01	.05
64 Rob Smith	.01	.05
65 Anthony Drawhorn	.02	.10
66 David Conrad	.01	.05
67 Irv Daymond	.01	.05
68 Terry Baker	.07	.20
69 Daniel Hunter	.01	.05
70 Gord Weber	.01	.05
71 Tom Burgess	.07	.20
72 Charles Gordon	.01	.05
73 Bobby Gordon	.01	.05
74 Jock Climie	.20	.50
75 Patrick Wayne	.01	.05
76 Sean Foudy	.01	.05
77 James Ellingson	.02	.10
78 Gregg Stumon	.01	.05
79 John Kropke	.02	.10
80 Stephen Jones	.07	.20
81 Ron Smeltzer	.01	.05
82 Scott Campbell	.20	.50
83 Gizmo Williams	.50	1.25
84 Willie Pless	.10	.30
85 Dan Murphy	.01	.05
86 Chris Armstrong	.25	.60
87 Tracy Ham	.30	.75
88 Larry Wruck	.02	.10
89 Rod Connop	.01	.05
90 Jim Sandusky	.08	.25
91 Randy Ambrosie	.01	.05
92 Michel Bourgeau	.01	.05
93 Bennie Goods UER (Misspelled Benny)	.08	.25
94 Rob Davidson	.01	.05
95 Leroy Blugh	.02	.10
96 Brian Walling	.07	.20
97 Michael Soles	.02	.10
98 Craig Ellis	.02	.10
99 Pierre Vercheval	.02	.10
100 Matt Dunigan	.30	.75
101 Enis Jackson	.01	.05
102 Tom Muecke	.07	.20
103 Jed Roberts	.01	.05
104 Steve Krupey	.01	.05
105 Blake Marshall	.07	.20
106 Trevor Bowles	.01	.05
107 Eddie Thomas	.01	.05
108 Rocket Rat (JOGO Mascot)	.01	.05
109 Checklist 1-110 UER (50 Eric Mitchell/93 Benny Goods)	.02	.10
110 Tom Burgess	.07	.20
111 Bob Cameron	.07	.20
112 James West	.07	.20
113 Chris Walby	.07	.20
114 David Black	.01	.05
115 Nick Benjamin	.01	.05
116 Matt Pearce	.01	.05
117 Bob Molle	.01	.05
118 Rod Hill	.01	.05
119 Kyle Hall	.01	.05
120 Danny McManus	.50	1.25
121 Cal Murphy	.02	.10
122 Stan Mikawos	.01	.05
123 Bobby Evans	.01	.05
124 Larry Willis	.02	.10
125 Eric Streater	.02	.10
126 Perry Tuttle	.07	.20
127 Leon Hatziioannou	.01	.05
128 Sammy Garza	.07	.20
129 Greg Battle	.07	.20
130 Elfrid Payton	.10	.30
131 Troy Westwood	.07	.20
132 Mike Gray	.01	.05
133 Dave Vankoughnett	.01	.05
134 Paul Randolph	.01	.05
135 Darryl Sampson	.01	.05
136 Less Browne	.02	.10
137 Quency Williams	.01	.05
138 Robert Mimbs	.20	.50
139 Matt Dunigan	.30	.75
140 Dan Rashovich	.01	.05
141 Dan Farthing	.20	.50
142 Bruce Boyko	.01	.05
143 Kim McCloud	.01	.05
144 Richie Hall	.01	.05
145 Paul Vajda	.01	.05
146 Willis Jacox	.08	.25
147 Glen Scrivener	.01	.05
148 Dave Ridgway	.07	.20
149 Lucius Floyd	.07	.20
150 James King	.01	.05
151 Kent Austin	.15	.40
152 Jeff Fairholm	.02	.10
153 Roger Aldag	.02	.10
154 Albert Brown	.01	.05
155 Chris Gioskos	.01	.05
156 Stacey Hairston	.01	.05
157 Glen Suitor	.02	.10
158 Milson Jones	.02	.10
159 Vic Stevenson	.01	.05
160 Bob Poley	.01	.05
161 Bobby Jurasin	.10	.30
162 Gary Lewis	.01	.05
163 Donald Narcisse	.25	.60
164 Mike Anderson	.01	.05
165 Nick Mazzoli	.01	.05
166 Lance Trumble	.01	.05
167 Dale Sanderson	.01	.05
168 Todd Wiseman	.01	.05
169 Mark Dennis	.02	.10
170 Peter Giftopoulus	.02	.10
171 Ken Evraire	.02	.10
172 Darrell Harle	.01	.05
173 Terry Wright	.01	.05
174 Jamie Morris	.07	.20
175 Corris Ervin	.01	.05
176 Don McPherson	.07	.20
177 Jason Riley	.01	.05
178 Tim Jackson	.01	.05
179 Todd Dillon	.02	.10
180 Lee Knight	.01	.05
181 Scott Douglas	.01	.05
182 Dave Richardson	.01	.05
183 Wally Zatylny	.02	.10
184 Rickey Martin	.01	.05
185 John Motton	.10	.30
186 Mark Waterman	.01	.05
187 Ernie Schramayr	.01	.05
188 Miles Gorrell	.01	.05
189 Tony Champion	.07	.20
190 Earl Winfield	.07	.20
191 John Zajdel	.01	.05
192 Danny Barrett	.07	.20
193 Ian Sinclair	.02	.10
194 Norman Jefferson	.01	.05
195 Ryan Hanson	.01	.05
196 Matt Clark	.07	.20
197 Leo Groenewegen	.01	.05
198 Ray Alexander	.02	.10
199 James Mills	.07	.20
200 Jon Volpe	.30	.75
201 Doug Hocking	.01	.05
202 Tony Kimbrough	.01	.05
203 Lui Passaglia	.15	.40
204 Bruce Holmes	.01	.05
205 Jamie Taras	.02	.10
206 Derek MacCready	.01	.05
207 Jay Christensen	.02	.10
208 O.J. Brigance	.20	.50
209 Robin Belanger	.01	.05
210 Stewart Hill	.02	.10
211 Mike Marasco	.01	.05
212 Mike Trevathan	.07	.20
213 Chris Major	.07	.20
214 Steve Rodehutskors	.01	.05
215 Paul Wetmore	.01	.05
216 Ken Pettway	.01	.05
217 Darren Flutie	2.40	6.00
218 Giulio Caravatta	.01	.05
219 Murray Pezim	.02	.10
220 Checklist 111-220	.02	.10

1992 JOGO Missing Years

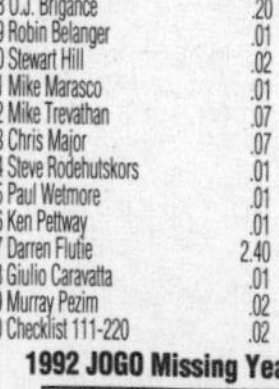

Since no major CFL sets were produced from 1972 to 1981, JOGO created this set of "Missing Years" players to provide CFL fans with memories of their favorite players of the 70's. This 22-card standard-size set was randomly inserted in the packs. The fronts carry action black-and-white player photos on a gold metallic face. A red, blue, and orange stripe borders the bottom of the picture. A blue helmet with the JOGO "J" is in the lower left corner and the player's name appears in red in the bottom border. The backs are metallic gold with red and green print. They carry biographical information and a player profile. The cards are numbered on the back with an "A" suffix.

COMPLETE SET (22)	8.00	20.00
1 Larry Smith	.60	1.50
2 Mike Nelms	.60	1.50

3 John Sciarra	.80	2.00
4 Ed Chalupka	.40	1.00
5 Mike Rae	.60	1.50
6 Terry Metcalf UER	1.00	2.50
(His CFL years were/78-80& not 78-90)		
7 Chuck Ealey	1.60	4.00
8 Junior Ah-You	.60	1.50
9 Mike Samples	.40	1.00
10 Ray Nettles	.40	1.00
11 Dickie Harris	.40	1.00
12 Willie Burden	1.20	3.00
13 Johnny Rodgers	2.00	5.00
14 Anthony Davis	1.20	3.00
15 Joe Pisarcik UER	.60	1.50
(His CFL years were/74-70& not 74 76)		
16 Jim Washington	.40	1.00
17 Tom Scott UER	.60	1.50
(11 years in CFL& not 10)		
18 Butch Norman	.40	1.00
19 Steve Molnar	.40	1.00
20 Jerry Tagge	1.00	2.50
21 Leon Bright UER	1.00	2.50
(His CFL years were/77-80& not 77-79)		
22 Waddell Smith	.80	2.00

1992 JOGO Stamp Cards

This five-card standard-size set was randomly inserted in foil packs. There were only two sets per foil case and only 1,200 cases of foil made according to JOGO. The fronts feature color photos with white postage stamp borders. In green, yellow, and red print on a silver metallic background, the backs provide information about the pictures on the front.

COMPLETE SET (5)	20.00	40.00
1 CFL Hall of Fame Museum and Statue	4.00	8.00
2 Toronto Argonauts/1991 Grey Cup Champs 10.00		5.00
3 Tom Pate Memorial Trophy	4.00	8.00
4 Russ Jackson MVP	5.00	10.00
5 Oldest Trophy in The Hall of Fame (Montreal Football Challenge Cup)	4.00	8.00

1993 JOGO

The 1993 JOGO CFL set consists of 220 standard-size cards. Just 1,300 numbered sets and 440 sets for the players were produced. The fronts feature color action player photos on a light gray card face with ghosted JOGO CFL lettering. A team-color coded stripe highlights the bottom edge of the picture. The team helmet and player's name appear in the bottom border. The white backs contain biography and player profiles which are printed in red and black. The cards are numbered on the back according to teams.

COMPLETE SET (220)	20.00	50.00
COMP.SERIES 1 (110)	10.00	25.00
COMP.SERIES 2 (110)	10.00	25.00
1 Stephen Jones	.20	.50
2 Chris Gioskos	.07	.20
3 Treamelle Taylor	.07	.20
4 Irv Daymond	.07	.20
5 Gord Weber	.07	.20
6 James Ellingson	.07	.20
7 Lybrant Robinson	.07	.20
8 Michael Allen	.07	.20
9 Gregg Stumon	.07	.20
10 Darren Joseph	.20	.50
11 Terry Baker	.20	.50
12 Denny Chronopoulos	.07	.20
13 Tom Burgess	.20	.50
14 Wayne Walker WR	.20	.50
15 Brendan Rogers	.07	.20
16 Matt Pearce	.07	.20
17 Chris Tsangaris	.07	.20
18 Leon Hatziioannou	.07	.20
19 Bob Cameron	.20	.50
20 Donald Smith	.07	.20
21 Michael Richardson	.60	1.50
22 Jayson Dzikowicz	.07	.20
23 Matt Dunigan	.50	1.25
24 Steve Grant	.07	.20
25 Rob Crifo	.07	.20
26 Dave Vankoughnett	.07	.20
27 Paul Masotti	.20	.50
28 Blaine Schmidt	.07	.20
29 Dave Van Belleghem	.07	.20
30 Brian Warren	.07	.20
31 Reggie Pleasant	.10	.30
32 Tracy Ham	.60	1.50
33 Mike Clemons	1.50	4.00
34 Lance Chomyc	.07	.20
35 Ken Benson	.07	.20
36 Chris Green	.07	.20
37 Mike Campbell	.07	.20
38 Chris Schultz	.10	.30
39 Reggie Rogers	.10	.30
40 John Hood	.10	.30
41 Dave Richardson	.07	.20
42 Mike Jovanovich	.10	.30
43 Joey Jauch	.10	.30
44 Lubo Zizakovic	.07	.20
45 Don McPherson	.10	.30
46 Brett Williams	.10	.30
47 Todd Wiseman	.07	.20
48 Jim Jauch	.07	.20
49 Eros Sanchez	.10	.30
50 Scott Walker	.07	.20
51 Roger Hennig	.07	.20
52 Glen Suitor	.10	.30
53 Bobby Jurasin	.20	.50
54 Scott Hendrickson	.07	.20
55 Ventson Donelson	.07	.20
56 Dan Rashovich	.07	.20
57 Kent Austin	.25	.60
58 Ray Elgaard	.25	.60
59 Dave Ridgway	.20	.50
60 Byron Williams	.07	.20
61 Larry Ryckman PRES	.07	.20
62 Karl Anthony	.07	.20
63 Greg Knox	.07	.20
64 Ken Moore	.07	.20
65 Allen Pitts	.50	1.25
66 Matt Finlay	.10	.30
67 Tony Martino	.20	.50
68 Harald Hasselback	.50	1.25
69 David Sapunjis	.40	1.00
70 Andy McVey	.07	.20
71 Stu Laird	.10	.30
72 Derrick Crawford	.10	.30
73 Mark McLoughlin	.10	.30
74 Will Johnson UER	.40	1.00
(Eskimo logo on front; Calgary on back)		
75 Don Wilson	.07	.20
76 J.P. Izquierdo	.07	.20
77 Gizmo Williams	1.00	2.50
78 Larry Wruck	.10	.30
79 David Shelton	.10	.30
80 Damion Lyons	.07	.20
81 Jed Roberts	.07	.20
82 Trent Brown	.07	.20
83 Michel Bourgeau	.07	.20
84 Blake Dermott	.10	.30
85 Willie Pless	.25	.60
86 Leroy Blugh	.10	.30
87 Steve Krupey	.07	.20
88 Jim Sandusky	.20	.50
89 Danny Barrett	.20	.50
90 James West	.20	.50
91 Glen Scrivener	.07	.20
92 Tyrone Jones	.10	.30
93A Jon Volpe ERR	.25	.60
(Photo has poor color)		
93B Jon Volpe COR	.80	2.00
94 Less Browne	.10	.30
95 Matt Clark	.10	.30
96 Andre Francis	.07	.20
97 Darren Flutie	2.00	5.00
98 Ray Alexander	.10	.30
99 Rob Smith	.07	.20
100 Fred Anderson	.10	.30
Managing General Partner		
101 Robb White UER	.07	.20
Rob on front and back		
102 Bobby Humphery	.07	.20
103 Willie Bouyer	.07	.20
104 Titus Dixon	.10	.30
105 John Wiley	.07	.20
106 Kerwin Bell	1.00	2.50
107 Carl Parker	.07	.20
108 Mike Oliphant	.30	.75
109 David Archer	1.20	3.00
110 Freeman Baysinger	.10	.30
111 Gerald Alphin	.20	.50
112 Gerald Wilcox	.10	.30
113 Reggie Barnes	.20	.50
114 Michel Raby	.07	.20
115 Charles Wright	.07	.20
116 Brott Young	.10	.30
117 Charles Gordon	.07	.20
118 Anthony Drawhorn	.10	.30
119 Daved Benefield	.60	1.50
120 Patrick Burke	.07	.20
121 Joe Sardo	.07	.20
122 Dexter Manley	.10	.30
123 Bruce Beaton	.07	.20
124 Joe Fuller	.07	.20
125 Michel Lamy	.07	.20
126 Terrence Jones	.20	.50
127 Jeff Croonen	.07	.20
128 Leonard Johnson	.07	.20
129 Dan Payne	.07	.20
130 Carlton Lance	.07	.20
131 Errol Brown	.07	.20
132 Wayne Drinkwalter	.07	.20
133 Malvin Hunter	.25	.60
134 Maurice Crum	.07	.20
135 Brooks Findlay	.07	.20
136 Ray Bernard	.07	.20
137 Paul Osbaldiston	.10	.30
138 Mark Dennis	.10	.30
139 Glenn Kulka	.07	.20
140 Lee Knight	.07	.20
141 Mike O'Shea	.80	2.00
142 Paul Bushey	.07	.20
143 Nick Mazzoli	.07	.20
144 Earl Winfield	.20	.50
145 Gary Wilkerson	.07	.20
146 Jason Riley	.07	.20
147 Bob MacDonald	.07	.20
148 Dale Sanderson	.07	.20
149 Bobby Dawson	.07	.20
150 Rod Connop	.07	.20
151 Tony Woods	.10	.30
152 Dan Murphy	.07	.20
153 Mike DuMaresq	.07	.20
154 Allan Boyko	.07	.20
155 Vaughn Booker	.50	1.25
156 Elfrid Payton	.20	.50
157 Mike Kerrigan	.25	.60
158 Charles Anthony	.07	.20
159 Brent Matich	.07	.20
160 Craig Hendrickson	.07	.20
161 Dave Pitcher	.07	.20
162 Stewart Hill	.10	.30
163 Terryl Ulmer	.07	.20
164 Paul Cranmer	.07	.20
165 Mike Saunders	1.50	3.00
166 Doug Flutie	2.40	6.00
167 Keilan Matthews	.07	.20
168 Kip Texada	.07	.20
169 Jonathan Wilson	.07	.20
170 Bruce Dickson	.07	.20
171 Mike Trevathan	.20	.50
172 Vic Stevenson	.07	.20
173 Keith Powe	.07	.20
174 Eddie Taylor	.07	.20
175 Tim Lorenz	.07	.20
176 Sean Millington	.75	2.00
177 Ryan Hanson	.07	.20
178 Ed Berry	.07	.20
179 Kent Warnock	.10	.30
180 Spencer McLennan	.07	.20
181 Brian Walling	.10	.30
182 Danny McManus	.50	1.25
183 Donovan Wright	.07	.20
184 Giulio Caravatta	.07	.20
185 Derek MacCready	.07	.20
186 Greg Eaglin	.07	.20
187 Jim Mills	.07	.20
188 Tom Europe	.07	.20
189 Zock Allen	.07	.20
190 Ian Sinclair	.10	.30
191 O.J. Brigance	.60	1.50
192 Steve Rodehutskors	.07	.20
193 Lou Cafazzo	.07	.20
194 Mark Dube	.07	.20
195 Srecko Zizakovic	.07	.20
196 Alondra Johnson	.10	.30
197 Rocco Romano	.07	.20
198 Raymond Biggs	.07	.20
199 Frank Marof	.07	.20
200 Brian Wiggins	.10	.30
201 Marvin Pope	.07	.20
202 Gerald Vaughn	.07	.20
203 Todd Storme	.07	.20
204 Blair Zerr	.07	.20
205 Eric Johnson	.10	.30
206 Mark Pearce	.07	.20
207 Will Moore	.50	1.25
208 Bruce Plummer	.07	.20
209 Kari Yli-Renko	.07	.20
210 Doug Parrish	.07	.20
211 Warren Hudson	.07	.20
212 Kevin Whitley	.07	.20
213 Enis Jackson	.07	.20
214 Wally Zatylny	.10	.30
215 Bruce Elliott	.07	.20
216 Harold Hallman	.10	.30
217 Glenn Rogers	.07	.20
218 Manny Hazard	.20	.50
219 Robert Clark	.10	.30
220 Doug Flutie UER	2.40	6.00
(Three misspelled Tree on back)		

1993 JOGO Missing Years

For the second year, JOGO created a "Missing Years" set to provide CFL fans with memories of their favorite players of the '70s, since no major CFL sets were produced from 1972 to 1981. These cards were randomly inserted in packs. The 22 standard-size cards feature on their fronts black-and-white player photos with metallic gold borders. Blue, white, and orange stripes border the bottom of the picture. A blue helmet with the JOGO "J" is in the lower left corner, and the player's name appears in red lettering within the lower gold margin. The white back has black and red lettering and carries the player's name, uniform number, position, biography, team name, and career highlights. The cards are numbered on the back with a "B" suffix.

COMPLETE SET (22)	7.50	15.00
1B Jimmy Edwards	.40	1.00
2B Lou Harris	.25	.60
3B George Mira	.50	1.25
4B Fred Biletnikoff	5.00	10.00
5B Randy Halsall	.25	.60
6B Don Sweet	.25	.60
7B Jim Coode	.25	.60
8B Steve Mazurak	.30	.75
9B Wayne Allison	.25	.60
10B Paul Williams	.25	.60
11B Eric Allen	.50	1.25
12B M.L. Harris	.30	.75
13B James Sykes	.60	1.50
14B Chuck Zapiec	.30	.75
15B George McGowan	.25	.60
16B Bob Macoritti	.30	.75
17B Chuck Walton	.25	.60
18B Willie Armstead	.30	.75
19B Rocky Long	.25	.60
20B Gene Mack	.25	.60
21B David Green	.60	1.50
22B Don Warrington	.30	.75

1994 JOGO Caravan

These 22 standard-size cards feature white-bordered color player action shots framed by a black line. Black, white, and red stripes border the bottom of the picture. The player's name appears in red lettering within the bottom white margin; his team helmet rests at the lower left. The white back has black and red lettering and carries the player's name, uniform number, position, biography, nationality, and team name. Below is the show schedule that lists the North American cities and dates for "Caravan 1994." The cards are numbered on the back as "X of 22." The cards are organized by team.

COMPLETE SET (22)	20.00	40.00
1 Glenn Kulka	.40	1.00
2 Jock Climie	1.60	4.00
3 Danny Barrett	.80	2.00
4 Stephen Jones	.80	2.00
5 Mike Clemons	3.20	8.00
6 Pierre Vercheval	.60	1.50
7 Ken Evraire	.60	1.50
8 Brett Williams UER	.60	1.50
(Misspelled Willians on card front)		
9 Wally Zatylny	.40	1.00
10 Mike O'Shea	1.25	3.00
11 Earl Winfield	.80	2.00
12 Mike Oliphant	.80	2.00
13 Matt Dunigan	1.60	4.00
14 Chris Walby	.80	2.00
15 Tracy Ham	2.00	5.00
16 Darrell K. Smith	.80	2.00
17 Glen Suitor	.60	1.50
18 Mark McLoughlin	.60	1.50
19 Bruce Covernton	.80	2.00
20 Willie Pless	.80	2.00
21 Gizmo Williams	2.00	5.00
22 Lui Passaglia	1.20	3.00

1994 JOGO

The 1994 JOGO set consists of 310 standard-size cards released in three series. Reportedly 2,000 numbered sets were produced. The fronts feature color action player photos on a white card face, with a team color-coded jagged stripe on the bottom. The team helmet, player's name and position appear under the picture. The white backs contain biography and player profiles which are printed in red and black. The cards are numbered on the back according to teams.

COMPLETE SET (310)	40.00	100.00
COMP.SERIES 1 (110)	8.00	20.00
COMP.SERIES 2 (110)	8.00	20.00
COMP.SERIES 3 (90)	25.00	60.00
1 Danny Barrett	.20	.50
2 Remi Trudel	.07	.20
3 Terry Baker	.20	.50
4 Paul Clatney	.07	.20
5 Michael Richardson	.30	.75
6 John Kropke	.10	.30
7 Glenn Kulka	.07	.20
8 Daved Benefield	.40	1.00
9 Derek MacCready	.07	.20
10 Jessie Small	.10	.30
11 Chris Gioskos	.07	.20
12 Gregg Stumon	.07	.20
13 Lee Johnson	.10	.30
14 Michael Jefferson Jr.	.07	.20
15 Mario Perry	.07	.20
16 Joe Mero	.07	.20
17 Reggie Barnes	.10	.30
18 Mike Stowell	.07	.20
19 Tony Moss	.07	.20
20 Antoine Worthman	.07	.20
21 Joe Fuller	.07	.20
22 Daniel Hunter	.07	.20
23 Doug Flutie	3.00	6.00
24 Douglas Craft	.20	.50
25 Lubo Zizakovic	.07	.20
26 Srecko Zizakovic	.07	.20
27 Stu Laird	.10	.30
28 Brian Wiggins	.10	.30
29 Will Johnson	.10	.30
30 David Sapunjis	.30	.75
31 Rocco Romano	.07	.20
32 Raymond Biggs	.07	.20
33 Ken Moore	.07	.20
34 Matt Finlay	.10	.30
35 Ian Sinclair	.10	.30
36 Glen Scrivener	.07	.20
37 Less Browne	.10	.30
38 Darren Flutie	1.50	4.00
39 Freeman Baysinger	.07	.20
40 Kent Austin	.20	.50
41 Donovan Wright	.07	.20
42 Cory Philpot	.75	2.00
43 Tom Europe	.07	.20
44 Giulio Caravatta	.07	.20
45 Mike Clemons	1.25	3.00
46 Leon Hatziioannou	.07	.20
47 Blaine Schmidt	.07	.20
48 Reggie Pleasant	.10	.30
49 Paul Masotti	.20	.50
50 Pierre Vercheval	.10	.30
51 Duane Forde	.07	.20
52 Jeff Fairholm	.10	.30
53 Carl Coulter	.07	.20
54 Bobby Gordon	.07	.20
55 Mike Jovanovich	.07	.20
56 Chris Johnstone	.07	.20
57 Matt Pearce	.07	.20
58 Bob Cameron	.20	.50
59 Brett MacNeil	.07	.20
60 Blaise Bryant	.20	.50
61 Chris Tsangaris	.07	.20
62 Dave Vankoughnett	.07	.20
63 Gerald Alphin	.20	.50
64 Alfred Jackson	1.25	3.00
65 Jayson Dzikowicz	.07	.20
66 Bobby Evans	.07	.20
67 Dave Ridgway	.20	.50
68 Bobby Jurasin	.20	.50
69 Dan Payne	.07	.20
70 Ray Elgaard	.25	.60
71 Dan Farthing	.30	.75
72 Glen Suitor	.10	.30
73 Mike Saunders	.50	1.25
74 Brent Matich	.07	.20
75 Scott Hendrickson	.07	.20
76 Dan Rashovich	.07	.20
77 Wayne Drinkwalter	.07	.20
78 Larry Wruck	.10	.30
79 J.P. Izquierdo	.07	.20
80 Jed Roberts	.07	.20
81 Michel Bourgeau	.07	.20
82 Malvin Hunter	.20	.50
83 Bruce Dickson	.07	.20
84 Jim Sandusky	.20	.50
85 Mike DuMaresq	.07	.20
86 Tracy Gravely	.20	.50
87 Tracy Ham	.75	2.00
88 John Congemi	.10	.30
89 Darrell Corbin	.07	.20
90 Maurice Kelly	.20	.50
91 Doug Flutie MVP	3.00	6.00
92 Alfred Jordan	.10	.30
93 Curtis Mayfield	.40	1.00
94 David Hollis	.07	.20
95 James Blake	.07	.20
96 Anthony Blue	.10	.30
97 Jeffrey Sawyer	.07	.20
98 Al Whiting	.07	.20
99 Brad LaCombe	.07	.20
100 Wally Zatylny	.07	.20
101 Bob Torrance	.07	.20
102 Jeffery Fields	.07	.20
103 John G. Motton Jr.	.10	.30
104 Todd Wiseman	.07	.20
105 Mike O'Shea	.20	.50
106 Scott Douglas	.07	.20
107 Dale Sanderson	.07	.20
108 David Diaz-Infante	.10	.30
109 Michael Kiselak	.07	.20
110 Chris Thieneman	.07	.20
111 Horace Brooks	.10	.30
112 Andre Francis	.07	.20
113 Nick Mazzoli	.07	.20
114 Irv Daymond	.07	.20
115 Alfred Smith	.07	.20
116 Stephen Jones	.20	.50
117 Bruce Beaton	.07	.20
118 Corey Dowden	.20	.50
119 Gerald Collins	.07	.20
120 Joe Washington	.10	.30
121 Irvin Smith	.07	.20
122 Harold Nash Jr.	.10	.30
123 Ray Savage Jr.	.07	.20
124 Billy Scott	.07	.20
125 Aaron Kanner	.07	.20
126 Ben Williams	.10	.30
127 Keith Browner	.07	.20
128 Eros Sanchez	.10	.30
129 Don Caparotti	.07	.20
130 Earnest Fields	.07	.20
131 O.J. Brigance	1.00	2.50
132 Walter Wilson	.10	.30
133 Allen Pitts	.60	1.50
134 Tony Stewart	.20	.50
135 Marvin Pope	.07	.20
136 Tony Martino	.20	.50
137 Vince Danielsen	.75	2.00
138 Pee Wee Smith	.20	.50
139 Bruce Covernton	.20	.50
140 Greg Knox	.07	.20
141 Gerald Vaughn	.07	.20
142 Jay McNeil	.07	.20
143 Larry Ryckman OWN	.07	.20
144 Blair Zerr	.07	.20
145 Danny McManus	.50	1.25
146 Jamie Taras	.10	.30
147 Kelly Sims	.10	.30
148 Denny Chronopoulos	.07	.20
149 Enis Jackson	.07	.20
150 Virgil Robertson	.20	.50
151 Tyrone Chatman	.07	.20
152 Brian Forde	.07	.20
153 Andrew Stewart	.10	.30
154 Ryan Hanson	.07	.20
155 Francois Belanger	.07	.20
156 Tony O'Billovich	.07	.20
157 Erik White	.10	.30
158 Kevin Whitley	.07	.20
159 Chris Schultz	.10	.30
160 Mike Campbell	.07	.20
161 Wayne Lammle	.07	.20
162 Keith Ballard	.07	.20
163 Neal Fort	.20	.50
164 Charles Anthony	.07	.20
165 John Buddenberg	.07	.20
166 Allan Boyko	.07	.20
167 Paul Randolph	.07	.20
168 Gerald Wilcox	.10	.30
169 Brendan Rogers	.07	.20
170 Kim Phillips	.07	.20
171 David Williams	.10	.30
172 James Pruitt	.10	.30
173 Kevin O'Brien	.07	.20
174 Tre Everett	.10	.30
175 Hurlie Brown	.07	.20
176 Malcolm Frank	.07	.20
177 Sean Brantley	.07	.20
178 Aaron Ruffin	.07	.20
179 Anthony Drawhorn	.10	.30
180 Larry Thompson	.30	.75
181 Brooks Findlay	.07	.20
182 Dallas Rysavy	.07	.20
183 Ray Bernard	.07	.20
184 Donald Narcisse	.50	1.25
185 Warren Jones	.07	.20
186 Tom Gerhart	.07	.20
187 David Robinson Jr.	.20	.50
188 Damon Allen	1.00	2.50
189 Gizmo Williams	.75	2.00
190 Jay Christensen	.10	.30
191 Trent Brown	.07	.20
192 Rod Connop	.07	.20
193 Michael Soles	.10	.30
194 Vance Hammond	.07	.20
195 Maurice Miller	.07	.20
196 Shar Pourdanesh	.50	1.25
197 Elfrid Payton	.20	.50
198 Ken Benson	.07	.20
199 David Maeva	.07	.20
200 Carlos Huerta	.10	.30
201 Prince Wimbley III	.25	.60
202 Anthony Calvillo	3.00	8.00
203 Kenny Wilhite	.20	.50
204 Peter Shorts	.07	.20
205 Willie Fears	.10	.30
206 Rod Harris	.30	.75
207 Terry Wright	.07	.20
208 Stephen Bates	.10	.30
209 John Hood	.10	.30
210 Steven McKee	.07	.20
211 Richard Nurse	.07	.20
212 Lee Knight	.07	.20
213 Joey Jauch	.10	.30
214 Dave Richardson	.07	.20
215 Paul Bushey	.07	.20
216 Lou Cafazzo	.07	.20
217 Don Odegard	.07	.20
218 Mark Ledbetter	.07	.20
219 Curtis Moore	.07	.20
220 CFL Team Helmets	.15	.40
(Set number card)		
221 Patrick Burke	.40	1.00
222 Dean Noel	.25	.60
223 Leonard Johnson	.15	.40
224 Darren Joseph	.15	.40
225 Adam Rita CO	.15	.40
226 Fred Ward	.25	.60
227 Tony Bailey	.15	.40
228 Frank Marof	.15	.40
229 Andrew Thomas	.25	.60
230 Peter Tuipulotu	.25	.60
231 Shawn Beals	.15	.40
232 Ken Watson	.15	.40
233 Robert Holland	.15	.40
234 John Terry	.15	.40
235 Michael Philbrick	.15	.40
236 Reggie Slack	1.25	3.00
237 Gary Wilkerson UER	.15	.40
(First name misspelled Garry on back)		
238 Brett Young	.25	.60
239 Eric Carter	.40	1.00
240 Sheldon Canley	.25	.60
241 Lester Smith	.40	1.00
242 Donald Igwebuike	.25	.60
243 Keith Ballard	.15	.40
244 Roger Reinson	.15	.40
245 Duane Dmytryshyn	.15	.40
246 Marvin Coleman	.15	.40
247 Ken Burress	.15	.40
248 Jearld Baylis	.25	.60
249 Rickey Foggie	.60	1.50
250 Dave Dinnall	.25	.60
251 Darrell Harle	.15	.40
252 P.J. Martin	.25	.60
253 Val St. Germain	.15	.40
254 Tim Cofield	.40	1.00
255 Charles Gordon	.15	.40
256 Keilly Rush	.15	.40
257 James Pruitt	.25	.60
258 Brian McCurdy	.25	.60
259 Joe Johnson UER	.25	.60
(Front says last name is Jackson)		
260 Joe Burgos	.15	.40
261 Tim Jackson	.15	.40
262 George Nimako	.25	.60
263 Hency Charles	.15	.40
264 Eric Drage	.25	.60
265 Joe Sardo	.15	.40
266 Norm Casola	.15	.40
267 Dave Irwin	.25	.60
268 Tommy Henry	.15	.40
269 Taly Williams	.15	.40
270 Swift Burch III	.15	.40
271 Keita Crespina	.15	.40
272 Michael Brooks	.25	.60
273 Chris Armstrong	.30	.75
274 Karl Anthony	.15	.40
275 David Archer	2.50	6.00
276 Kevin Robson	.15	.40
277 Jamie Holland	.25	.60
278 Donald Smith	.15	.40
279 Norris Thomas	.25	.60
280 Matt Dunigan	.50	1.25
281 Greg Clark	.15	.40
282 Del Lyles	.15	.40
283 Alan Wetmore	.15	.40
284 Errol Brown	.15	.40
285 Ryan Carey	.15	.40
286 Rob Davidson	.15	.40
287 Ed Kucy SP	2.50	6.00
288 Tom Burgess	.40	1.00
289 Peter Miller	.15	.40
290 Dale Joseph	.15	.40
291 Chris Burns	.15	.40
292 Nathaniel Bolton	.25	.60
293 Byron Williams	.15	.40
294 David Harper	.15	.40
295 Jason Wallace	.07	.20
296 Greg Joelson	.15	.40
297 Doug Parrish	.15	.40
298 Sean Fleming	.15	.40
299 Mike Lee	.25	.60
300 Chris Morris	.40	1.00
301 Eddie Brown	.75	2.00
302 Blake Dermott	.15	.40
303 Brian Walling	.25	.60
304 Charles Miles	.25	.60
305 Robin Crifo	.25	.60
306 Nick Benjamin	.15	.40
307 Jim Speros PR OWN	.25	.60
308 Robert Presbury	.15	.40
309 Mike Pringle	4.00	10.00
310 Jon Volpe	2.00	5.00

1994 JOGO Hall of Fame C

These 25 cards measure the standard size. The fronts feature black-and-white player photos with metallic gold borders. Red, white, and blue stripes edge the bottom of the picture. The player's name appears in red lettering within the lower gold margin. On a white background, the backs carry the player's career years along with awards and honors he received.

COMPLETE SET (25)	7.20	18.00
C1 Leo Lewis	.80	2.00
C2 Tom Brown	.30	.75
C3 Samuel Berger	.30	.75
C4 Dave Fennell	.50	1.25
C5 Arthur Chipman	.30	.75
C6 Tony Gabriel	.50	1.25
C7 Frank Clair	.30	.75
C8 Dean Griffing	.30	.75
C9 Hec Crighton	.30	.75
C10 Eddie James	.30	.75
C11 Andrew Currie	.30	.75
C12 Ab Box	.30	.75
C13 Gord Perry	.30	.75
C14 Terry Evanshen	.80	2.00
C15 Syd Halter	.30	.75
C16 Don Luzzi	.50	1.25
C17 Norm Kimball	.30	.75
C18 Percival Molson	.30	.75
C19 Bob Kramer	.30	.75
C20 Angelo Mosca	1.00	2.50
C21 Ralph Cooper	.30	.75
C22 Ken Charlton	.30	.75
C23 Jim Young	.50	1.25
C24 Joe Tubman	.30	.75
C25 Virgil Wagner	.50	1.25

1994 JOGO Hall of Fame D

These 25 cards measure the standard size. The fronts feature black-and-white player photos with metallic gold borders. Red, white, and blue stripes edge the bottom of the picture. The player's name appears in red lettering within the lower gold margin. On a white background, the backs carry the player's career years along with awards and honors he received.

COMPLETE SET (25)	10.00	18.00
D1 Teddy Morris	.30	.75
D2 John Ferraro	.30	.75
D3 Len Back	.30	.75
D4 Harold Ballard	.50	1.25
D5 Seppi DuMoulin	.30	.75
D6 Herm Harrison	.50	1.25
D7 William Foulds	.30	.75
D8 Peter Dalla Riva	.50	1.25
D9 John Metras	.30	.75
D10 Don Sutherin	.50	1.25
D11 Ken Preston	.30	.75
D12 Ellison Kelly	.50	1.25
D13 Annis Stukus	.30	.75
D14 Brian Timmis	.30	.75
D15 Ralph Sazio	.30	.75
D16 Hugh Stirling	.30	.75
D17 Jimmie Simpson	.30	.75
D18 Russ Rebholz	.30	.75
D19 Seymour Wilson	.30	.75
D20 Paul Rowe	.30	.75
D21 Jeff Russel	.30	.75
D22 Art Stevenson	.30	.75
D23 Whit Tucker	.50	1.25
D24 Dave Thelen	.50	1.25
D25 Tom Wilkinson	.80	2.00

1994 JOGO Hall of Fame Inductees

This five-card standard-size set honors the 1994 inductees of the Canadian Football Hall of Fame. The fronts feature black-and-white player photos with metallic gold borders. Red, white, and black stripes edge the bottom of the picture. The player's name appears in red lettering within the lower gold margin. On a white background, the backs carry the player's career years along with awards and honors he received.

COMPLETE SET (5)	2.00	5.00
1 Bill Baker	.40	1.00
2 Tom Clements	1.00	2.50
3 Gene Gaines	.40	1.00
4 Don McNaughton	.30	.75
5 Title Card	.30	.75

1994 JOGO Missing Years

For the third year, JOGO created a "Missing Link" set to provide CFL fans with memories of their favorite players of the 1970s, since no major CFL sets were produced from 1972-1981. JOGO produced 1,700 sets, of which 500 were broken to provide individual players with cards. Of the 1,200 complete sets, 200 were used for press and promotional give-aways. The 20-card set measures the standard size. The fronts feature black-and-white player photos with metallic gold borders. Red, white, and blue stripes edge the bottom of the picture. A blue helmet with the JOGO "J" is in the lower left corner, and the player's name appears in red lettering within the lower gold margin. On a white background, the backs carry player biography and career highlights.

COMPLETE SET (20)	5.00	10.00
C1 Steve Ferrughelli UER	.60	1.50
(Photo actually John O'Leary)		
C2 Rhome Nixon	.20	.50
C3 Don Moorhead	.20	.50
C4 Mike Widger	.20	.50
C5 Pete Catan	.20	.50
C6 Ron Meeks	.20	.50
C7 Ezzret Anderson	.50	1.25
C8 Bill Hatanaka	.20	.50
C9 Joe Jackson	.30	.75
C10 Tom Campana	.20	.50
C11 Vernon Perry	.40	1.00
C12 Ian Mofford	.30	.75
C13 Wally Highsmith	.20	.50
C14 Jake Dunlop	.20	.50
C15 Bill Stevenson	.20	.50
C16 Pete Lavorato	.20	.50
C17 Cyril McFall	.20	.50
C18 Maurice Butler	.20	.50
C19 Tom Pate	.50	1.25
C20 Eugene Clark	.50	1.25

1995 JOGO

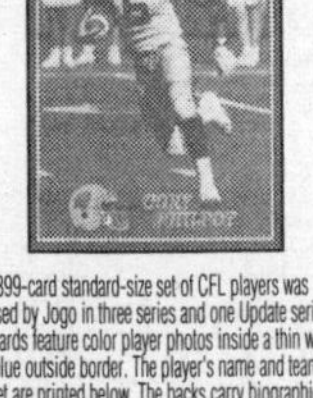

This 399-card standard-size set of CFL players was released by Jogo in three series and one Update series. The cards feature color player photos inside a thin white and blue outside border. The player's name and team helmet are printed below. The backs carry biographical and career information. Jogo reports there were 1000 numbered sets of series 1-3 produced for sale to the hobby and 200 additional sets distributed to the players. The Update set was limited to 850 sets produced. The Doug Flutie M.V.P. card (#330) carries the set number.

COMPLETE SET (399)	170.00	340.00
COMP.SERIES 1 (110)	50.00	100.00
COMP.SERIES 2 (110)	50.00	100.00
COMP.SERIES 3 (110)	50.00	100.00
COMP.UPDATE SET (69)	20.00	40.00
1 Doug Flutie	7.50	15.00
2 Lubo Zizakovic	.15	.40
3 Srecko Zizakovic	.15	.40
4 Greg Knox	.15	.40
5 Kenny Walker	.20	.50
6 Raymond Biggs	.15	.40
7 Stu Laird	.20	.50
8 Jeff Garcia	20.00	40.00
9 Alfred Jordan	.20	.50
10 Tracy Gravely	.20	.50
11 Tracy Ham	1.25	3.00
12 O.J. Brigance	.60	1.50

13 Mike Pringle 3.00 6.00
14 Nick Subis .15 .40
15 Irvin Smith .15 .40
16 Shar Pourdanesh .30 .75
17 Lester Smith .15 .40
18 Josh Miller .15 .40
19 Jamie Taras .20 .50
20 Darren Flutie 1.25 3.00
21 Danny McManus .75 2.00
22 Spencer McLennan .15 .40
23 Tony Collier .15 .40
24 Cory Philpot .60 1.50
25 Ian Sinclair .20 .50
26 Dave Chaytors .30 .75
27 Dave Ritchie UER .15 .40
Richie on front
28 Rob Wallow .15 .40
29 Brad Breedlove .30 .75
30 Adrion Smith .15 .40
31 Stephen Bates .15 .40
32 Don Odegard .15 .40
33 Eric Nelson .15 .40
34 Danton Barto .15 .40
35 Donald Smith .15 .40
36 Gary Morris .15 .40
37 Michael Jovanovich .15 .40
38 Danny Barrett .30 .75
39 Ray Alexander .20 .50
40 John Kropke .20 .50
41 Remi Trudel .15 .40
42 Ray Bernard .15 .40
43 Pat Mahon .15 .40
44 Dan Murphy .15 .40
45 Stefen Reid .15 .40
46 Marcus Gates .15 .40
47 Tom Gerhart .15 .40
48 Mike Kiselak .60 1.50
49 David Archer 2.00 5.00
50 Tommie Smith .15 .40
51 Roman Anderson .15 .40
52 Tony Burse .30 .75
53 Todd Jordan .15 .40
54 Peter Shorts .15 .40
55 Jimmy Klingler .20 .50
56 Mark Ledbetter .15 .40
57 Thomas Rayam .15 .40
58 Andre Strode .15 .40
59 Eddie Davis .15 .40
60 Jimmie Reed .15 .40
61 Fernando Thomas .15 .40
62 Craig Gibson .15 .40
63 Akaba Delaney .15 .40
64 Mike Clemons 1.50 4.00
65 Kent Austin .30 .75
66 Joe Burgos .15 .40
67 John Terry .15 .40
68 Don Wilson .15 .40
69 Eric Blount DE .30 .75
70 Reggie Barnes .20 .50
71 Darrick Branch .15 .40
72 P.J. Gleason .15 .40
73 Rod Connop .15 .40
74 J.P. Izquierdo .15 .40
75 Jed Roberts .15 .40
76 Jim Sandusky .30 .75
77 Chris Vargas .30 .75
78 Gizmo Williams 1.25 3.00
79 Michael Soles .15 .40
80 Robert Holland .15 .40
81 Larry Wruck .20 .50
82 Dale Sanderson .15 .40
83 Anthony Calvillo 2.50 5.00
84 Kalin Hall .15 .40
85 Sam Rogers .15 .40
86 Lee Knight .15 .40
87 Wally Zatylny .15 .40
88 Earl Winfield .30 .75
89 Dave Richardson .15 .40
90 Mike O'Shea .30 .75
91 Bruce Boyko .15 .40
92 Dave Ridgway .30 .75
93 Dave Van Belleghem .15 .40
94 Mike Anderson .15 .40
95 Ray Elgaard .60 1.50
96 Dan Rashovich .15 .40
97 Wayne Drinkwalter .15 .40
98 Brent Matich .15 .40
99 Joe Fuller .15 .40
100 Freeman Baysinger Jr. .15 .40
101 Billy Joe Tolliver .50 1.25
102 Martin Patton .15 .40
103 Wayne Walker .20 .50
104 Bjorn Nittmo .30 .75
105 Alan Wetmore .15 .40
106 K.D. Williams .15 .40
107 Bob Cameron .30 .75
108 Ken Burress .15 .40
109 Chris Johnstone .15 .40
110 Allan Boyko .15 .40
111 David Sapunjis .60 1.50
112 Matt Finlay .20 .50
113 Jamie Crysdale .15 .40
114 Marvin Pope .15 .40
115 Craig Brenner .15 .40
116 Vince Danielsen .75 2.00
117 Will Johnson .20 .50
118 Tony Stewart .20 .50
119 Chris Wright .30 .75
120 Grant Carter .20 .50
121 Karl Anthony .15 .40
122 Elfrid Payton .20 .50
123 Ken Watson .15 .40
124 Cory Mantyka .15 .40
125 Todd Furdyk .15 .40
126 Keithen McCant .20 .50
127 Ryan Hanson .15 .40
128 Glen Scrivener .15 .40
129 Mike Trevathan .30 .75
130 Tom Europe .15 .40
131 Giulio Caravatta .15 .40
132 Eddie Lee Thomas .15 .40
133 Shelton Quarles .75 2.00
134 Robert E. Davis II .15 .40
135 Damon Allen 1.25 3.00
136 Derek Brown .20 .50
137 Joe Horn 10.00 20.00
138 John Tweet Martin .20 .50
139 Greg Battle .30 .75
140 Ed Berry .15 .40
141 Irv Daymond .15 .40
142 Jay Christensen .20 .50
143 Michael Richardson .30 .75
144 James Ellingson .15 .40
145 Brett Young .20 .50
146 Kai Bjorn .15 .40
147 James Monroe .15 .40
148 Eric Geter .15 .40
149 Emanuel Martin .15 .40
150 DeWayne Knight .15 .40
151 Mike Saunders .60 1.50
152 David Harper .15 .40
153 Bobby Humphery .15 .40
154 Charles Franks .15 .40
155 Jeff Sawyer .15 .40
156 John Buddenberg .15 .40
157 Willie Fears .20 .50
158 Jason Wallace .15 .40
159 Robert Gordon 1.00 2.50
160 Scott Player .20 .50
161 York Kurinsky .15 .40
162 Stephen Anderson .15 .40
163 Shonte Peoples .30 .75
164 Angelo Snipes .20 .50
165 Ted Long .15 .40
166 Anthony Drawhorn .20 .50
167 Marvin Graves .15 .40
168 Joe Sardo .15 .40
169 Duane Forde .15 .40
170 P.J. Martin .15 .40
171 Jock Climie .75 2.00
172 Jeff Fairholm .20 .50
173 Tommy Henry .15 .40
174 Paul Masotti .30 .75
175 Chris Green .15 .40
176 Bruce Dickson .15 .40
177 Darian Hagan .15 .40
178 Malvin Hunter .20 .50
179 Steve Krupey .15 .40
180 Sean Fleming .15 .40
181 Blake Dermott .15 .40
182 Leroy Blugh .20 .50
183 Steve Taylor .30 .75
184 Eric Carter .30 .75
185 Jessie Small .20 .50
186 Blaine Schmidt .15 .40
187 Lou Cafazzo .15 .40
188 Doug Davies .15 .40
189 Kelvin Means .15 .40
190 Derek Grier .15 .40
191 Darren Joseph .15 .40
192 Aaron Ruffin .15 .40
193 Dan Farthing .60 1.50
194 Dan Payne .15 .40
195 Brooks Findlay .15 .40
196 Paul Vajda .15 .40
197 Ron Goetz .15 .40
198 Tim Broady .15 .40
199 Terryl Ulmer .15 .40
200 Harold Nash Jr. 1.00 2.50
201 Mike Stowell .15 .40
202 Ben Williams .30 .75
203 Curtis Mayfield .30 .75
204 Reggie Rogers .20 .50
205 Donnell Johnson .15 .40
206 Jon Heidenreich .15 .40
207 Ronald Perry .15 .40
208 Robbie Keen .15 .40
209 Alex Mash Jr. .15 .40
210 Jason Mallett .15 .40
211 Miles Gorrell .15 .40
212 Juran Bolden .20 .50
213 Greg Clark .15 .40
214 Ryan Carey .15 .40
215 Del Lyles .15 .40
216 Brendan Rogers .15 .40
217 Kevin Robson .15 .40
218 Paul Randolph .15 .40
219 Shannon Garrett .15 .40
220 Charlie Clemons .75 2.00
221 Matt Dunigan 1.00 2.50
222 Jay McNeil .15 .40
223 Denny Chronopoulos .15 .40
224 Bobby Pandelidis .15 .40
225 Bruce Beaton .15 .40
226 Mark Pearce .15 .40
227 Rocco Romano .15 .40
228 Alondra Johnson .20 .50
229 Tony Martino .30 .75
230 John James .15 .40
231 Courtney Griffin .15 .40
232 Robert Davis .15 .40
233 Manny Hazard. .20 .50
234 Joe Mero .15 .40
235 Maurice Kelly .20 .50
236 Mike Morreale 1.50 4.00
237 Reggie Slack 1.00 2.50
238 Greg Eaglin .15 .40
239 Noah Cantor .15 .40
240 Shawn Daniels .15 .40
241 Charles Gordon .15 .40
242 Enis Jackson .15 .40
243 Matt Clark .20 .50
244 David Lucas .15 .40
245 Roger Hennig .15 .40
246 Leonard Nelson .15 .40
247 George Bethune .15 .40
248 Maurice Miller .15 .40
249 Kenny Walker .20 .50
250 Andre Ware 1.25 3.00
251 Jay Macias .15 .40
252 Mark Ricks .15 .40
253 Chris Tsangaris .15 .40
254 Wayne Lammle .15 .40
255 Derek MacCready .15 .40
256 Paul Yatkowski .15 .40
257 Horace Brooks .20 .50
258 Kerry Brown .15 .40
259 Jude St. John .15 .40
260 Mike Schad .75 2.00
261 Malcolm Frank .15 .40
262 Kenny Wilhite .20 .50
263 Billy Hess .15 .40
264 Grady Cavness .20 .50
265 Roosevelt Collins Jr. .15 .40
266 Darren Muilenberg .15 .40
267 Kitrick Taylor .30 .75
268 Chuck Esty .15 .40
269 Myron M. Wise .15 .40
270 James King .15 .40
271 Jimmy Kemp .50 1.25
272 Oscar Giles .30 .75
273 Dave Ritchie CO .15 .40
274 Joe Kralik .15 .40
275 Troy Mills .75 2.00
276 Mark Stock .15 .40
277 Pierre Vercheval .20 .50
278 Terry Baker .50 1.25
279 Scott Douglas .15 .40
280 Leon Hatziioannou .15 .40
281 Jeff Cummins .30 .75
282 Allen Pitts .75 2.00
283 Ken Walcott .15 .40
284 Swift Burch III .15 .40
285 Charles Davis .15 .40
286 Leo Groenewegen .15 .40
287 Bennie Goods .20 .50
288 Craig Hendrickson .15 .40
289 John Kalin .15 .40
290 Trent Brown .15 .40
291 Marc Tobert .15 .40
292 Nick Mazzoli .15 .40
293 Singor Mobley .15 .40
294 Dondre Owens .15 .40
295 Kerwin Bell .60 1.50
296 Mike Kerrigan .30 .75
297 Hassan Bailey .15 .40
298 Frank Marof .15 .40
299 Derrick McAdoo .20 .50
300 Brian McCurdy .20 .50
301 Larry Thompson .30 .75
302 Errol Brown .15 .40
303 Troy Alexander .30 .75
304 Dave Pitcher .15 .40
305 Joey Jauch .20 .50
306 Gene Makowsky .15 .40
307 Ventson Donelson .15 .40
308 Gary Rogers .15 .40
309 Carl Coulter .15 .40
310 Chris Gioskos .15 .40
311 Michael DuMaresq .15 .40
312 Rob Crifo .15 .40
313 Terry Smith .15 .40
314 Don Robinson .15 .40
315 Uzooma Okeke .15 .40
316 Eldonta Osborne .15 .40
317 Rob Hitchcock .15 .40
318 Ray Savage Jr. .15 .40
319 Terry Beauford .15 .40
320 Cliff Baskerville .15 .40
321 David Gamble .15 .40
322 Darrius Watson .15 .40
323 Tim Daniel .15 .40
324 Len Johnson .15 .40
325 Blaise Bryant .20 .50
326 Doug Hocking .15 .40
327 Sean Graham .15 .40
328 Jamie Holland .20 .50
329 Matt Pearce .15 .40
330 Doug Flutie MVP 3.00 6.00
331 Donald Narcisse .75 2.00
332 Chuck Reed .15 .40
333 Sheldon Benoit .15 .40
334 John Motton .20 .50
335 Franco Grilla .15 .40
336 Brett MacNeil .15 .40
337 Wade Miller .15 .40
338 Steven McKee .15 .40
339 Brad Elberg .15 .40
340 Greg Patrick .15 .40
341 Andrew Grigg .75 2.00
342 Kevin McDougal .15 .40
343 Prince Wimbley III .30 .75
344 Sam Hairston .15 .40
345 Curtis Gordon .20 .50
346 Chris Keneally .30 .75
347 Michael Philbrick .15 .40
348 Keith Embray .15 .40
349 Steve Grant .15 .40
350 Taly Williams .15 .40
351 Garry Sawatzky .15 .40
352 Dean Noel .20 .50
353 Mike Armstrong .15 .40
354 David Pool .15 .40
355 Tyrone Edwards .15 .40
356 Tim Cofield .30 .75
357 Gerald Vaughn .15 .40
358 Mark McLoughlin .20 .50
359 Robert Dougherty .15 .40
360 Norm Casola .15 .40
361 Shawn Knight .15 .40
362 Kelvin Means .15 .40
363 Reggie Pleasant .20 .50
364 Jim Smyrl .15 .40
365 Fred Montgomery .15 .40
366 Ron Perry .15 .40
367 Jami Anderson .15 .40
368 Jeff Reinebold .15 .40
369 Steve Brannon .15 .40
370 Jimmy Cunningham .75 2.00
371 Damion Lyons .15 .40
372 John Tweet Martin .20 .50
373 Mike Campbell .15 .40
374 Jonathan Wilson .15 .40
375 Sandy Annunziata .15 .40
376 Brian Walling .20 .50
377 Eric Blount RB 1.00 2.50
378 Tom Gerhart .15 .40
379 Milt Stegall 5.00 10.00
380 Bob Kronenberg .15 .40
381 Barry Rose .15 .40
382 Tim Walton .15 .40
383 Kelvin Harris .15 .40
384 Dwayne Provo .15 .40
385 Jayson Dzikowicz .15 .40
386 Melendez Byrd .15 .40
387 Val St. Germain .15 .40
388 Dave Vankoughnett .15 .40
389 Aaron Kanner .15 .40
390 Nick Richards .15 .40
391 Rohan Marley 1.00 2.50
392 Chris Burns .15 .40
393 Joe Fuller .15 .40
394 Donovan Gans .15 .40
395 Jermaine Chaney .15 .40
396 Jackie Kellogg .15 .40
397 Ray Savage Jr. .15 .40
398 Oscar Giles .30 .75
399 Jeff Neal .50 1.25

1995 JOGO Athletes in Action

This 21-card standard-size set of players in the Canadian Football League features front color action player photos with the AIA logo. The backs carry a small black-and-white head photo of the player with biographical information and the importance of religion in that player's life in his own words.

COMPLETE SET (21) 7.50 15.00
1 Kelly Sims .30 .75
2 Craig Hendrickson .20 .50
3 Kerwin Bell .50 1.25
4 Glenn Harper .20 .50
5 Jim Sandusky .40 1.00
6 Eldonta Osborne .20 .50
7 Guy Earle .20 .50
8 Charles Anthony .20 .50
9 O.J. Brigance .60 1.50
10 Junior Thurman .30 .75
11 Erik White .30 .75
12 Henry Newby .20 .50
13 Darryl Sampson .20 .50
14 Tony Woods .30 .75
15 Sean Brantley .20 .50
16 Shalon Baker .20 .50
17 Greg Frers .20 .50
18 Danny Barrett .30 .75
19 John Earle .20 .50
20 Tracy Ham 1.25 3.00
21 Jimmy Klingler .30 .75

1995 JOGO Missing Years

For the fourth year, JOGO created a Missing Link set to provide CFL fans with collectibles of their favorite former players from seasons not covered on JOGO cards. JOGO reportedly produced 1200 sets, of which 200 were broken to provide individual players with cards. This 20-card set features black-and-white player photos with metallic gold borders. The player's name and a blue helmet with the Jogo logo round out the fronts. The backs carry the player's name, jersey number, position, team, biography and career highlights.

COMPLETE SET (20) 4.80 12.00
1D Jimmy Jones .30 .75
2D Charlie Brandon .20 .50
3D Erik Kramer UER 1.20 3.00
name spelled Krammer
4D Jeff Avery .20 .50
5D Wally Buono .20 .50
6D Mike Strickland .30 .75
7D Bob Toogood .30 .75
8D Joe Hernandez .20 .50
9D Doug Battershill .20 .50
10D Al Brenner .20 .50
11D Tim Anderson .20 .50
12D Ted Provost .20 .50
13D Eugene Goodlow .50 1.25
14D Rudy Florio .20 .50
15D Joey Walters 1.25 3.00
16D Bob Viccars .20 .50
17D Tyrone Walls .30 .75
18D John Harvey .30 .75
19D Dick Aldridge .20 .50
20D Grady Cavness .30 .75

1996 JOGO

For the 16th year, JOGO Inc. produced a set of CFL cards. This year's set was released in two 110-card series. Just 500-sets were produced for distributed to the hobby with each having the final card in the set hand numbered of 500. One hundred additional sets were produced for distribution to league players.

COMPLETE SET (220) 60.00 120.00
COMP.SERIES 1 (110) 30.00 60.00
COMP.SERIES 2 (110) 30.00 60.00
1 Jeff Garcia 12.50 25.00
2 Jeff Cummins .20 .50
3 Terry Baker .50 1.25
4 Jamie Taras .15 .40
5 Eric Blount RB .50 1.25
6 Dan Rashovich .15 .40
7 Dale Sanderson .15 .40
8 Paul Masotti .20 .50
9 Giulio Caravatta .15 .40
10 Stefen Reid .15 .40
11 Lee Knight .15 .40
12 Dave Vankoughnett .15 .40
13 Stu Laird .20 .50
14 Todd Storme .15 .40
15 Glenn Rogers Jr. .15 .40
16 Miles Gorrell .15 .40
17 Mike Kiselak .30 .75
18 Mike Trevathan .20 .50
19 Troy Westwood .15 .40
20 Michael Jovanovich .15 .40
21 Alan Wetmore .15 .40
22 Bruce Covernton .20 .50
23 Ryan Carey .15 .40
24 Larry Wruck .20 .50
25 Lou Cafazzo .15 .40
26 Mac Cody .40 1.00
27 Todd Furdyk .15 .40
28 Shannon Garrett .15 .40
29 Kenny Wilhite .20 .50
30 Bruce Beaton .15 .40
31 Tony Martino .20 .50
32 Brooks Findlay .15 .40
33 Matt Dunigan 1.00 2.50
34 Ed Kucy .15 .40
35 Mike Clemons 1.25 3.00
36 Cory Philpot .40 1.00
37 Steve Taylor 1.00 2.50
38 Jackie Kellogg .15 .40
39 Spencer McLennan .15 .40
40 Jason Mallett .15 .40
41 Robert Mimbs .40 1.00
42 Doug Davies .15 .40
43 Malvin Hunter .20 .50
44 Wayne Lammle .15 .40
45 David Maeva .15 .40
46 Jay McNeil .15 .40
47 Ed Berry .15 .40
48 Irvin Smith .15 .40
49 Wade Miller .15 .40
50 Dan Farthing .20 .50
51 Tom Gerhart .15 .40
52 Ray Bernard .15 .40
53 Jude St. John .15 .40
54 Terry Vaughn 1.50 3.00
55 Shelton Quarles .60 1.50
56 Kelvin Anderson 2.00 5.00
57 Mike Withycombe .15 .40
58 Sean Graham .15 .40
59 Errol Brown .15 .40
60 Swift Burch III .15 .40
61 Jed Roberts .15 .40
62 Ted Long .15 .40
63 Mike Morreale .75 2.00
64 Tyrone Chatman .15 .40
65 Anthony McClanahan .15 .40
66 David Pitcher .30 .75
67 Shannon Baker .15 .40
68 Fred Childress .40 1.00
69 John Terry .15 .40
70 Chris Morris .30 .75
71 Andrew Grigg .30 .75
72 Reggie Givens .30 .75
73 Cory Mantyka .15 .40
74 Alfred Jordan .20 .50
75 Harold Nash Jr. .15 .40
76 Brett MacNeil .15 .40
77 Brent Matich .15 .40
78 Gerry Collins .15 .40
79 Johnson Joseph .15 .40
80 Jimmy Cunningham .40 1.00
81 Eddie Davis .15 .40
82 Tom Europe .15 .40
83 Darryl Hall .15 .40
84 Tracy Gravely .20 .50
85 Bob Cameron .30 .75
86 Paul McCallum .15 .40
87 Tyrone Williams .15 .40
88 Maurice Kelly .15 .40
89 Sammie Brennan .15 .40
90 Ken Benson .15 .40
91 Sean Millington .50 1.25
92 Greg Knox .15 .40
93 Kevin Robson .15 .40
94 Rod Harris .30 .75
95 Charles Gordon .15 .40
96 Donald Smith .15 .40
97 Joe Mero .15 .40
98 Reggie Slack .60 1.50
99 Garry Sawatzky .15 .40
100 Adrion Smith .30 .75
101 Allan Boyko .15 .40
102 Scott Hendrickson .15 .40
103 Eddie Britton .15 .40
104 Will Johnson .20 .50
105 John Raposo .15 .40
106 Chris Tsangaris .15 .40
107 Cooper Harris .15 .40
108 Quinn Magnuson .15 .40
109 Blaine Schmidt .15 .40
110 David Archer 1.00 2.50
111 David Sapunjis .30 .75
112 Stephen Anderson .15 .40
113 Raymond Biggs .15 .40
114 Jean-Agnes Charles .15 .40
115 Vince Danielsen .50 1.25
116 Wayne Drinkwalter .15 .40
117 Farell Duclair .15 .40
118 Duane Forde .15 .40
119 Rohn Meyer .15 .40
120 Travis Moore 2.00 4.00
121 Kevin Reid .15 .40
122 Roger Reinson .15 .40
123 Gonzalo Floyd .15 .40
124 Dwayne Provo .15 .40
125 Peter Tuipulotu .15 .40
126 Curtis Mayfield .30 .75
127 Ray Elgaard .30 .75
128 John James .15 .40
129 Dave Van Belleghem .15 .40
130 J.P. Izquierdo .15 .40
131 Darren Joseph .15 .40
132 Frank Jagas .15 .40
133 Heath Rylance .15 .40
134 Rick Walters .30 .75
135 Michael Philbrick .15 .40
136 Val St. Germain .15 .40
137 Justin Ring .15 .40
138 Mike Campbell .15 .40
139 Burt Thornton .15 .40
140 Jason Kaiser .15 .40
141 Tim Brown LB .15 .40
142 Ken Watson .15 .40
143 Tommie Frasier 15.00 30.00
144 Tyrone Rodgers .30 .75
145 Craig Hendrickson .15 .40
146 Johnny Scott .30 .75
147 Mark Pimiskern .15 .40
148 Frank Pimiskern .15 .40
149 Carl Coulter .15 .40
150 Reggie Carthon .15 .40
151 Ronald Williams .75 2.00
152 Ted Alford 1.25 3.00
153 Dave Chaytors .20 .50
154 Robert Gordon .40 1.00
155 Jayson Dzikowicz .15 .40
156 Lubo Zizakovic .15 .40
157 Mike Hendricks .15 .40
158 Obie Spanic .15 .40
159 Andre Bolduc .15 .40
160 Robert Drummond 1.00 2.50
161 Chuck Esty .15 .40
162 Tommy Henry .15 .40
163 Nick Richards .15 .40
164 Profail Grier .15 .40
165 Melvin Aldridge .15 .40
166 Uzooma Okeke .15 .40
167 Courtney Griffin .15 .40
168 Leonard Humphries .15 .40
169 Jason Wallace .15 .40
170 Derek MacCready .15 .40
171 Frank West .15 .40
172 Kelvin Means .15 .40
173 David Harper .15 .40
174 Rob Stevenson .15 .40
175 John Kalin .15 .40
176 Nigel Williams .15 .40
177 Chris Armstrong .20 .50
178 Douglas Craft .30 .75
179 Michael Soles .15 .40
180 Mike Saunders .50 1.25
181 Michel Lamy .15 .40
182 Jock Climie .30 .75
183 Grant Carter .20 .50
184 Hency Charles .15 .40
185 Jason Bryant .15 .40
186 Dexter Dawson .15 .40
187 Glen Scrivener .15 .40
188 K.D. Williams .15 .40
189 Dean Lytle .15 .40
190 Donovan Wright .15 .40
191 Andrew Henry .15 .40
192 Doug Flutie 4.00 8.00
193 Brendan Rogers .15 .40
194 Darian Hagan .15 .40
195 Jeff Fairholm .20 .50
196 Marcello Simmons .15 .40
197 Oscar Giles .20 .50
198 Chris Gioskos .15 .40
199 Dan Murphy .15 .40
200 Norm Casola .15 .40
201 Vic Stevenson .15 .40
202 Duane Dmytryshyn .20 .50
203 Christopher Perez .15 .40
204 Noah Cantor .15 .40
205 Mike Vanderjagt 1.25 3.00
206 George Nimako .20 .50
207 Andrew Stewart .40 1.00
208 Pierre Vercheval .15 .40
209 Chris Green .15 .40
210 Maurice Miller .15 .40
211 Leroy Blugh .20 .50
212 Jim Sandusky .30 .75
213 Thomas Rayam .15 .40
214 Cody Ledbetter 1.00 2.00
215 Mike Sellers .30 .75
216 Reggie Pleasant .20 .50
217 Errol Martin .15 .40
218 Trent Brown .15 .40
219 Bruce Dickson .15 .40
220 Dan Payne .50 1.25

1997 JOGO

For the 17th year, JOGO Inc. produced a set of CFL cards. The 1997 set was released in two 110-card series. Just 500-sets were produced for distributed to the hobby with each having the final card in the set hand numbered of 500. One hundred additional sets were produced for distribution to league players.

COMPLETE SET (220) 50.00 100.00
COMP.SERIES 1 (110) 25.00 50.00
COMP.SERIES 2 (110) 25.00 50.00
1 Terry Baker .50 1.25
2 Douglas Craft .20 .50
3 Tracy Gravely .20 .50
4 Irvin Smith .15 .40
5 Mike Soles .15 .40
6 Doug Petersen .15 .40
7 Tracy Ham 1.25 3.00
8 Ryan Coughlin .15 .40
9 Nigel Williams .15 .40
10 Neal Fort .30 .75
11 Michael Sutherland .15 .40
12 Uzooma Okeke .40 1.00
13 Chris Wright .20 .50
14 Chris Armstrong .30 .75
15 Harold Nash Jr. .75 2.00
16 Ken Benson .15 .40
17 Duane Dmytryshyn .20 .50
18 Johnnie Harris .15 .40
19 Jeremy O'Day .15 .40
20 Robert Drummond .50 1.25
21 Mike O'Shea .30 .75
22 Brendan Rogers .15 .40
23 Adrion Smith .20 .50
24 Lester Smith .15 .40
25 Donald Smith .15 .40
26 Mike Kiselak .20 .50
27 Noah Cantor .15 .40
28 Lee Knight .15 .40
29 Paul Osbaldiston .20 .50
30 Eric Carter .20 .50
31 Mike Morreale .50 1.25
32 Rob Hitchcock .15 .40
33 Joe Montford 1.50 4.00
34 Jude St. John .15 .40
35 Tim Prinsen .15 .40
36 Orlondo Steinauer .15 .40
37 Andrew Grigg .30 .75
38 Mike Campbell .15 .40
39 Pete Shorts .15 .40
40 Blaine Schmidt .15 .40
41 Dave Vankoughnett .15 .40
42 Kai Bjorn .15 .40
43 Sean Graham .15 .40
44 Craig Hendrickson .15 .40
45 Brett MacNeil .15 .40
46 Greg Battle .30 .75
47 Bruce Boyko .15 .40
48 Shonte Peoples .20 .50
49 Franco Rocca .15 .40
50 Chris Vargas .20 .50
51 Jeff Reinebold .15 .40
52 Ronald Williams .75 2.00
53 Harry Van Hofwegen .15 .40
54 Leonard Jean-Pierre .15 .40
55 David Pitcher .20 .50
56 Jed Roberts .15 .40
57 Trent Brown .15 .40
58 Malvin Hunter .20 .50
59 Darren Flutie 1.25 3.00
60 Leroy Blugh .20 .50
61 Danny McManus .75 2.00
62 Derek MacCready .15 .40
63 Leo Groenewegen .15 .40
64 Chris Morris .20 .50
65 Jimmy Kemp .30 .75
66 Don Blair .40 1.00
67 Andre Bolduc .15 .40
68 Chris Hardy .15 .40
69 Patrice Denis .15 .40
70 Mark Farraway .15 .40
71 Jamie Taras .15 .40
72 David Maeva .15 .40
73 Sean Millington .40 1.00
74 Maurice Kelly .15 .40
75 Frank Pimiskern .15 .40
76 Alfred Shipman .15 .40
77 Mike Trevathan .20 .50
78 Steven Glenn .15 .40
79 Johnny Scott .20 .50
80 Peter Miller .15 .40
81 Mo Elewonibi .20 .50
82 Dave Chaytors .15 .40
83 Joe Fleming 1.25 3.00
84 Larry Thompson .20 .50
85 Dan Rashovich .15 .40
86 Ryan Carey .15 .40
87 Jason Mallett .15 .40
88 Terryl Ulmer .15 .40
89 Bobby Jurasin .30 .75
90 Henry Newby .15 .40
91 Donald Narcisse .60 1.50
92 Ray Elgaard .30 .75
93 Patrick Burke .15 .40
94 Dan Farthing .20 .50
95 Gene Makowsky .15 .40
96 Dale Joseph .15 .40
97 Fred Bailey .15 .40
98 Duane Forde .15 .40
99 Greg Knox .15 .40
100 Fred Childress .40 1.00
101 Raymond Biggs .15 .40
102 Ernie Brown .15 .40
103 Chris Burns .15 .40
104 Marvin Coleman .15 .40
105 Eddie Davis .15 .40
106 Marvin Pope .15 .40
107 Jay McNeil .15 .40
108 Jeff Garcia 10.00 20.00
109 Tony Martino .20 .50
110 Mike Clemons 1.25 3.00
111 Marvin Graves .15 .40
112 Rahsaan Giddings .15 .40
113 Bruno Heppell .15 .40
114 Lawrence McSeed .15 .40
115 Bryan Chiu .15 .40
116 Torey Hunter .15 .40
117 Hency Charles .15 .40
118 Spencer McLennan .15 .40
119 Steve Charbonneau .15 .40
120 Swift Burch .15 .40
121 Thomas Hipsz .15 .40
122 Marcus T. Wall .15 .40
123 Denis Montana .15 .40
124 Alan Wetmore .15 .40
125 Bruce Beaton .15 .40
126 Chad Folk .15 .40
127 Andre Kirwan .30 .75
128 Kelly Wiltshire .15 .40
129 John Raposo .15 .40
130 Dan Payne .15 .40
131 Norm Casola .15 .40
132 Marcello Simmons .15 .40
133 Antonious Bonner .15 .40
134 Paul Masotti .20 .50
135 Doug Flutie 3.00 6.00
136 Mike Clemons 1.25 3.00
137 Derrell Mitchell 1.50 4.00
138 Doug Davies .15 .40
139 Tom Nutten .15 .40
140 Cooper Harris .15 .40
141 Justin Ring .15 .40
142 Joe Rumolo .15 .40
143 Archie Amerson .40 1.00
144 Frank West .15 .40
145 Colin Quiney .15 .40
146 Kenny Wilhite .20 .50
147 Kyle Walters .15 .40
148 Prince Wimbley .20 .50
149 Michael Philbrick .15 .40
150 Val St. Germain .15 .40
151 Mike Mihelic .15 .40
152 Dexter Dawson .15 .40
153 Joseph Rogers .30 .75
154 Tyrone Rodgers .20 .50
155 Glen Scrivener .15 .40
156 Colin Scrivener .15 .40
157 Troy Westwood .20 .50
158 Wade Miller .15 .40
159 Bob Cameron .20 .50
160 Reggie Carthon .15 .40
161 Christopher Perez .15 .40
162 Turhon O'Bannon .15 .40
163 Dan Comiskey .15 .40
164 Nick Ferguson .15 .40
165 Melvin Aldridge .15 .40
166 Reggie Pleasant .20 .50
167 Malcolm Frank .15 .40
168 Tommy Henry .15 .40
169 Derrick Beatty .15 .40
170 Eric Blount RB .40 1.00
171 Cory Mantyka .15 .40
172 Carl Coulter .15 .40
173 Donovan Wright .15 .40
174 Shannon Myers .15 .40
175 Brandon Hamilton .15 .40
176 Reggie Givens .20 .50
177 Vince Danielsen .40 1.00
178 Brian Clark .15 .40
179 Mill Coleman .15 .40
180 Don Wilson .15 .40
181 B.J. Gallis .15 .40
182 Brad Yamaoka .15 .40
183 Brooks Findlay .15 .40
184 Pierre Vercheval .15 .40
185 Todd Furdyk .15 .40
186 Trevor Shaw .15 .40
187 Damon Allen 1.00 2.50
188 Mark Hatfield .15 .40
189 Less Browne .20 .50
190 Dean Noel .20 .50
191 Willie Brown .15 .40
192 Willie Whitehead .50 1.25
193 Burt Thornton .15 .40
194 Aaron Ruffin .15 .40
195 Greg Clark .15 .40
196 Paul Frlan .15 .40
197 Bryce K. Bevill .15 .40
198 Profail Grier .15 .40
199 Ventson Donelson .15 .40
200 Todd McMillon .15 .40
201 Kevin Mason .30 .75
202 Doug Hocking .15 .40
203 Robert Mimbs .30 .75
204 John Terry .15 .40
205 Travis Moore 1.00 2.00
206 John Kalin .15 .40
207 William Hampton .15 .40
208 Shannon Garrett .15 .40
209 Alondra Johnson .20 .50
210 Dewayne Patterson .20 .50
211 Roger Reinson .15 .40
212 Jason Clemett .15 .40
213 Jeff Traversy .15 .40
214 J.P. Izquierdo .15 .40
215 Larry Jusdanis .15 .40
216 Tom Europe .15 .40
217 Elfrid Payton .20 .50
218 Paul Randolph .15 .40
219 Stefen Reid .15 .40
220 Ray Bernard .50 1.25

1997 JOGO Betty Crocker

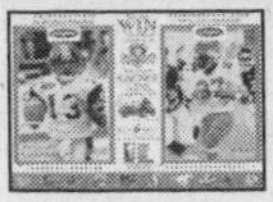

This set of 12-cards was released on boxes of Betty Cocker pop corn in Canada. Each box featured two player cards designed after the 1997 JOGO set but with different photos. Although the cards are numbered, we've listed them below in uncut box or panel form (6-boxes) since that is how they are most commonly traded.

COMPLETE SET (6)	25.00	50.00
1 Terry Baker	6.00	12.00
Troy Westwood		
2 Leroy Blugh	3.00	6.00
Jock Climie		
3 Anthony Calvillo	6.00	12.00
Robert Mimbs		
4 Bob Cameron	3.00	6.00
Jamie Taras		
5 Pinball Clemons	7.50	15.00
Jeff Garcia		
6 Bobby Jurasin	3.00	6.00
Paul Masotti		

1998 JOGO

JOGO Inc. produced a set of CFL cards for the 18th year in 1998. Just 500-sets were produced for distributed to the hobby with each having the final advertising card in the set hand numbered of 500.

COMPLETE SET (220)	50.00	100.00
COMP.SERIES 1 (110)	25.00	50.00
COMP.SERIES 2 (110)	25.00	50.00
1 Danny McManus	.75	2.00
2 Mike Morreale	.30	.75
3 Val St. Germain	.15	.40
4 Franco Rocca	.15	.40
5 Darren Flutie	1.25	3.00
6 Frank West	.15	.40
7 Orlondo Steinauer	.30	.75
8 Michael Philbrick	.15	.40
9 Cooper Harris	.15	.40
10 Jarrett Smith	.15	.40
11 Justin Ring	.15	.40
12 Rob Hitchcock	.15	.40
13 Andrew Grigg	.20	.50
14 Jeff Cummins	.30	.75
15 Obie Spanic	.15	.40
16 Tim Fleiszer	.15	.40
17 David Hack	.15	.40
18 Tarek Jayoussi	.30	.75
19 Tim Prinsen	.15	.40
20 Derek Grier	.15	.40
21 Terry Baker	.50	1.25
22 Tom Europe	.15	.40
23 Bryan Chiu	.15	.40
24 Chris Wright	.20	.50
25 Irvin Smith	.15	.40
26 Tracy Gravely	.20	.50
27 Swift Burch	.15	.40
28 Alan Wetmore	.15	.40
29 Uzooma Okeke	.15	.40
30 Jock Climie	.30	.75
31 Michael Soles	.15	.40
32 Pierre Vercheval	.15	.40
33 Anthony Calvillo	1.50	4.00
34 Mike Pringle	2.50	5.00
35 Douglas Craft	.15	.40
36 Dwayne Provo	.15	.40
37 Michael Sutherland	.15	.40
38 Thomas Haskins Jr.	.30	.75
39 Dave Ritchie CO	.15	.40
40 Jim Popp GM	.15	.40
41 Elfrid Payton	.20	.50
42 Brendan Rogers	.15	.40
43 Chad Folk	.15	.40
44 Maurice Miller	.15	.40
45 Lester Smith	.15	.40
46 Derrell Mitchell	1.25	3.00
47 Kato Hitson	.15	.40
48 Mike O'Shea	.30	.75
49 Jayson Hansen	.15	.40
50 Jude St. John	.15	.40
51 Byron Capers	.15	.40
52 Roger Dunbrack	.75	2.00
53 Duane Dmytryshyn	.20	.50
54 Noel Prefontaine	.15	.40
55 Kerwin Bell	.75	2.00
56 Kelly Wiltshire	.15	.40
57 Andre Kirwan	.20	.50
58 Jeremy O'Day	.15	.40
59 Dave Vankoughnett	.15	.40
60 Glen Scrivener	.15	.40
61 Eric Blount RB	.40	1.00
62 T.J. Rubley	.30	.75
63 Troy Westwood	.15	.40
64 Mike Mihelic	.15	.40
65 Sean Millington	.30	.75
66 Brad Elberg	.15	.40
67 Grant Carter	.20	.50
68 Matt Dubuc	.15	.40
69 Chris Vargas	.20	.50
70 Jeff Reinebold	.15	.40
71 Patrick McNerney	.15	.40
72 Joe Fleming	1.25	3.00
73 Brandon Hamilton	.15	.40
74 Greg Battle	.30	.75
75 Ted Long	.15	.40
76 Tyrone Rodgers	.30	.75
77 Maurice Kelly	.15	.40
78 Bob Cameron	.20	.50
79 Greg Knox	.15	.40
80 Tony Martino	.20	.50
81 Anthony McClanahan	.15	.40
82 Jeff Garcia	5.00	10.00
83 Kelvin Anderson	2.00	4.00
84 Terry Vaughn	.50	1.25
85 Jamie Crysdale	.15	.40
86 Eddie Davis	.15	.40
87 Rocco Romano	.15	.40
88 Darryl Hall	.15	.40
89 William Hampton	.15	.40
90 Stephen Anderson	.15	.40
91 Raymond Biggs	.15	.40
92 Jay McNeil	.15	.40
93 Ryan Carey	.15	.40
94 Reggie Slack	.60	1.50
95 Dan Rashovich	.15	.40
96 Gene Makowsky	.15	.40
97 Scott Deibert	.15	.40
98 A.J. Gass	.15	.40
99 Malvin Hunter	.20	.50
100 Ken Benson	.15	.40
101 Patrice Denis	.15	.40
102 Derek MacCready	.15	.40
103 Jed Roberts	.15	.40
104 Bret Anderson	.30	.75
105 Mo Elewonibi	.20	.50
106 Rashid Gayle	.15	.40
107 Alfred Shipman	.15	.40
108 Jamie Taras	.15	.40
109 Mike Clemons	1.25	3.00
110 Travis Moore	.60	1.50
111 Reggie Carthon	.15	.40
112 Eric Carter	.20	.50
113 Shannon Myers	.15	.40
114 Chris Burns	.15	.40
115 Carl Coulter	.15	.40
116 B.J. Gallis	.15	.40
117 Dan Pronyk	.15	.40
118 Todd Furdyk	.15	.40
119 Darnell Small	.15	.40
120 Andre Bolduc	.15	.40
121 Todd McMillon	.15	.40
122 Rob Lazeo	.15	.40
123 Ben Fairbrother	.15	.40
124 Dan Farthing	.20	.50
125 Shawn Daniels	.15	.40
126 Randy Srochenski	.15	.40
127 Rick Walters	.20	.50
128 Paul McCallum	.15	.40
129 Mike Saunders	.40	1.00
130 Colin Scrivener	.15	.40
131 Bruno Heppell	.15	.40
132 Ryan Coughlin	.15	.40
133 Mac Cody	.30	.75
134 William Loftus	.15	.40
135 Lance Funderburk	.15	.40
136 Steve Charbonneau	.15	.40
137 Stefen Reid	.15	.40
138 Hency Charles	.15	.40
139 Barron Miles	.15	.40
140 Thomas Hipsz	.15	.40
141 Neal Fort	.30	.75
142 Brett MacNeil	.15	.40
143 Eric Sutton	.15	.40
144 Shannon Garrett	.15	.40
145 Terryl Ulmer	.15	.40
146 R-Kal Truluck	.20	.50
147 Cody Ledbetter	.20	.50
148 Scott Hendrickson	.15	.40
149 Sean Graham	.15	.40
150 Andre Strode	.15	.40
151 Johnny Scott	.20	.50
152 Noah Cantor	.15	.40
153 Paul Masotti	.20	.50
154 Jay Barker	1.20	3.00
155 Larry Thompson	.20	.50
156 Charles Assmann	.15	.40
157 Antonious Bonner	.15	.40
158 Chris Gioskos	.15	.40
159 John Raposo	.15	.40
160 Khari Jones	3.00	8.00
161 Dave Chaytors	.15	.40
162 Glenn Rogers Jr.	.15	.40
163 Cory Mantyka	.15	.40
164 Gizmo Williams	.80	2.00
165 Harry Van Hofwegen	.15	.40
166 Fred Childress	.30	.75
167 Stu Laird	.15	.40
168 Trevor Shaw	.15	.40
169 Dale Joseph	.15	.40
170 Jason Van Geel	.15	.40
171 Nick Ferguson	.15	.40
172 Spencer McLennan	.15	.40
173 Jean-Daniel Roy	.15	.40
174 Sandy Annunziata	.15	.40
175 Rob Robinson	.15	.40
176 Christopher Perez	.15	.40
177 John Terry	.15	.40
178 Morris Lolar	.15	.40
179 John Kalin	.15	.40
180 Wayne Weathers	.15	.40
181 Wade Miller	.15	.40
182 David Maeva	.15	.40
183 Deland McCullough	.80	2.00
184 Jimmy Kemp	.30	.75
185 Jackie Kellogg	.15	.40
186 Aldi Henry	.15	.40
187 Willis Marshall	.15	.40
188 Jeff Traversy	.15	.40
189 Henry Burris	2.00	5.00
190 Dave Van Belleghem	.15	.40
191 Jason Clemett	.15	.40
192 Jung-Yul Kim	.15	.40
193 Bobby Olive	.15	.40
194 Rohn Meyer	.15	.40
195 Tarrence McEvans	.15	.40
196 Mark Washington	.15	.40
197 Bronzell Miller	.15	.40
198 Jermaine Miles	.15	.40
199 Vince Danielsen	.40	1.00
200 Duane Forde	.15	.40
201 Dave Dickenson	4.00	8.00
202 Roger Reinson	.15	.40
203 Dewayne Knight	.15	.40
204 Steven Glenn	.15	.40
205 Tracy Ham	1.20	3.00
206 C.J. Williams	.15	.40
207A Robert Brown ERR	.80	2.00
Calgary on Back		
207B Robert Brown COR	.15	.40
(Edmonton on back)		
208 Samir Chahine	.15	.40
209 Philippe Girard	.15	.40
210 Troy Mills	.40	1.00
211 Andrew English	.30	.75
212 Jamie Richardson	.15	.40
213 Rio Wells	.15	.40
214 Dan Payne	.15	.40
215 Dave Donaldson	.40	1.00
216 Steven Salter	.15	.40
217 Brad Yamaoka	.15	.40
218 Mike Crumb	.30	.75
219 Reggie Love	.15	.40
NNO CSC AD Card	.20	.50
(contains set number)		

1999 JOGO

Released by JOGO incorporated, this 221-card set features the stars of the Canadian Football League. Card fronts have a white border and contain a full-color action shot while card backs have a black and white portrait and short player bio. This set also contains a non-numbered card featuring Doug and Darren Flutie

COMPLETE SET (220)	50.00	100.00
COMP.SERIES 1 (110)	25.00	50.00
COMP.SERIES 2 (110)	25.00	50.00
1 Damon Allen	1.00	2.50
2 Cory Mantyka	.15	.40
3 Glen Scrivener	.15	.40
4 Daved Benefield	.30	.75
5 Robert Drummond	.40	1.00
6 Rod Harris	.20	.50
7 Alfred Jackson	.60	1.50
8 Herman Smith	.30	.75
9 Johnny Scott	.20	.50
10 Jamie Taras	.15	.40
11 Kelvin Anderson	1.25	2.50
12 Marvin Coleman	.15	.40
13 Jay McNeil	.15	.40
14 Dave Dickenson	2.50	5.00
15 Aubrey Cummings	.30	.75
16 Rohn Meyer	.15	.40
17 Travis Moore	.60	1.50
18 Allen Pitts	.80	2.00
19 Nealon Greene	4.00	10.00
20 Malvin Hunter	.20	.50
21 Troy Mills	.30	.75
22 Kavis Reed	.15	.40
23 Gizmo Williams	.80	2.00
24 Darren Flutie	1.00	2.50
25 Danny McManus	.75	2.00
26 Joe Montford	.75	2.00
27 Mike Morreale	.30	.75
28 Frank West	.15	.40
29 Archie Amerson	.30	.75
30 Ronald Williams	.50	1.25
31 Terry Baker	.50	1.25
32 Michael Soles	.15	.40
33 Tracy Ham	1.25	3.00
34 Elfrid Payton	.20	.50
35 Mike Pringle	1.50	4.00
36 Curtis Mayfield	.20	.50
37 Bret Anderson	.20	.50
38 Mike Saunders	.40	1.00
39 John Terry	.15	.40
40 Reggie Slack	.60	1.50
41 Jay Barker	.60	1.50
42 Andrew Grigg	.20	.50
43 Mike Clemons	1.25	3.00
44 Paul Masotti	.20	.50
45 Mike O'Shea	.30	.75
46 Kerwin Bell	.75	2.00
47 Bob Cameron	.20	.50
48 Gene Makowsky	.15	.40
49 Dave Vankoughnett	.15	.40
50 Milt Stegall	1.50	4.00
51 Anthony Calvillo	1.00	2.50
52 Bryan Chiu	.30	.75
53 Swift Burch	.15	.40
54 Tracy Gravely	.20	.50
55 Pierre Vercheval	.15	.40
56 Winston October	.40	1.00
57 Tyree Davis	.50	1.25
58 Ryan Coughlin	.15	.40
59 Uzooma Okeke	.15	.40
60 Jason Richards	.15	.40
61 Stefen Reid	.15	.40
62 Mark Washington	.15	.40
63 Thomas Haskins Jr.	.20	.50
64 Lester Smith	.15	.40
65 Irvin Smith	.15	.40
66 Rob Hitchcock	.15	.40
67 Chris Burns	.15	.40
68 Kyle Walters	.15	.40
69 Cody Ledbetter	.20	.50
70 Mike Campbell	.15	.40
71 Seth Dittman	.15	.40
72 Jeff Cummins	.20	.50
73 Carl Coulter	.15	.40
74 Jimmy Kemp	.30	.75
75 Chad Folk	.15	.40
76 Jermaine Haley	.15	.40
77 Noel Prefontaine	.15	.40
78 Donald Smith	.15	.40
79 Alundis Brice	.15	.40
80 Adrion Smith	.20	.50
81 Dan Giancola	.15	.40
82 Tony Burse	.20	.50
83 Kelly Wiltshire	.15	.40
84 J.P. Darche	.15	.40
85 Darren Joseph	.15	.40
86 Steve Sarkisian	.50	1.25
87 Todd McMillon	.15	.40
88 Dan Rashovich	.15	.40
89 Mike Maurer	.15	.40
90 Mark Tate	.15	.40
91 Shannon Garrett	.15	.40
92 Douglas Craft	.15	.40
93 Brandon Hamilton	.15	.40
94 Mike Mihelic	.15	.40
95 R.T. Swinton	.40	1.00
96 Tom Europe	.15	.40
97 Charles Assmann	.15	.40
98 Patrice Denis	.15	.40
99 Bruce Beaton	.15	.40
100 Scott Deibert	.20	.50
101 B.J. Gallis	.15	.40
102 Val St. Germain	.15	.40
103 Frantz Clarkson	.15	.40
104 Chris Hardy	.15	.40
105 Antonio Armstrong	.15	.40
106 Jason Kralt	.15	.40
107 E. Rafael Robinson	.15	.40
108 Reggie Carthon	.15	.40
109 Mark Hatfield	.15	.40
110 Steve Asad Muhammad	.15	.40
111 Don Blair	.30	.75
112 Eric Carter	.20	.50
113 Dave Chaytors	.15	.40
114 Mike Crumb	.20	.50
115 Doug Davies	.15	.40
116 Dave Donaldson	.20	.50
117 Sean Graham	.15	.40
118 Steve Hardin	.15	.40
119 Khari Jones	1.25	3.00
120 Dale Joseph	.15	.40
121 Jason Clemett	.15	.40
122 Jackie Kellogg	.15	.40
123 Greg Frers	.15	.40
124 Jeff Traversy	.15	.40
125 Stephen Anderson	.15	.40
126 Rocco Romano	.15	.40
127 Raymond Biggs	.15	.40
128 Eddie Davis	.15	.40
129A Robert Brown	.15	.40
Calgary		
129B Robert Brown	.15	.40
Edmonton		
130 Dave Heasman	.15	.40
131 Eric Johnson	.15	.40
132 Ousmane Tounkara	.20	.50
133 Danny Crowley	.60	1.50
134 Keith Cobb	.15	.40
135 Tim Prinsen	.15	.40
136 Jason Van Geel	.15	.40
137 Ryan Carruthers	.15	.40
138 Orlondo Steinauer	.15	.40
139 Cooper Harris	.15	.40
140 David Hack	.15	.40
141 Andre Bolduc	.15	.40
142 Bruno Heppell	.15	.40
143 Michael Sutherland	.15	.40
144 William Loftus	.15	.40
145 Neal Fort	.30	.75
146 Steve Charbonneau	.15	.40
147 Brendan Rogers	.15	.40
148 Dan Farthing	.20	.50
149 Neal Bradley Smith	.30	.75
150 Trevis Lerone Smith	.15	.40
151 Cameron Chance	.15	.40
152 Fred Perry	.30	.75
153 Michael Philbrick	.15	.40
154 Jim Ballard	.20	.50
155 David De La Perralle	.15	.40
156 Brad Elberg	.15	.40
157 Wade Miller	.15	.40
158 Paul Blackwood	.15	.40
159 Christopher Perez	.15	.40
160 Troy Westwood	.15	.40
161 Rahsaan Giddings	.15	.40
162 Thomas Hipsz	.15	.40
163 Stanley Jackson	.75	2.00
164 Ben Cahoon	2.00	4.00
165 Harold Nash Jr.	.15	.40
166 Davis Sanchez	.75	2.00
167 Alfonzo Browning	1.00	2.00
168 Tim Fleiszer	.15	.40
169 Jude St. John	.15	.40
170 William Hampton	.15	.40
171 Cameron Legault	.15	.40
172 Andre Arlain	.15	.40
173 Aldi Henry	.15	.40
174 Craig Hendrickson	.15	.40
175 Steven Glenn	.15	.40
176 Byron Thomas	.15	.40
177 Tyrone Rodgers	.20	.50
178 Ray Jacobs	.15	.40
179 Shad Criss	.15	.40
180 Jim Popp GM	.15	.40
181 Jermaine Miles	.15	.40
182 Roger Reinson	.15	.40
183 Franco Rocca	.15	.40
184 Robert Gordon	.30	.75
185 Justin Ring	.15	.40
186 Duane Dmytryshyn	.20	.50
187 Steven Salter	.15	.40
188 Wayne Shaw	.15	.40
189 Andre Kirwan	.20	.50
190 Inoke Breckterfield	.15	.40
191 Jung-Yul Kim	.15	.40
192 Vince Danielson	.40	1.00
193 Kevin Johnson	.75	2.00
194 T.J. Ackerman	.15	.40
195 Pulu Tolo Poumele	.15	.40
196 Nelson VanWaes	.15	.40
197 Stephane Fortin	.15	.40
198 Sheldon Benoit	.15	.40
199 Hency Charles	.15	.40
200 Edward Thomas	.15	.40
201 Chris Hoople	.15	.40
202 Corby Jones	.30	.75
203 Geroy Simon	1.50	4.00
204 Wayne Weathers	.15	.40
205 Brad Yamaoka	.15	.40
206 Garry Sawatzky	.15	.40
207 Terry Ray	.30	.75
208 Andre Batson	.15	.40
209 Jed Roberts	.15	.40
210 Matt Kellett	.15	.40
211 Rock Preston	.20	.50
212 Willie Pless	.30	.75
213 Ken Benson	.15	.40
214 Paul Girdo	.15	.40
215 Troy Kopp	.30	.75
216 Paul Lacoste	.20	.50
217 Derrick Lewis	.15	.40
218 Dan Payne	.15	.40
219 Noah Cantor	.15	.40
220 Jeremy O'Day	.15	.40
NNO Doug Flutie	1.50	4.00
Darren Flutie		

1999 JOGO Boston Pizza

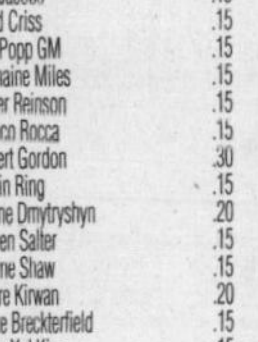

This set was distributed in 12-card packs over the course of 5-weeks in the Fall of 1999 at participating Boston Pizza restaurants in the Vancouver area for 99-cents. Each pack of cards included one checklist/cover card and one 99.3 The Fox radio personality card (A-E) as well as 10-player cards. Each card follows the typical JOGO design and contains a unique card number.

COMPLETE SET (60)	8.00	20.00
1 Damon Allen	.30	.75
2 Cory Mantyka	.05	.15
3 Eddie Brown	.20	.50
4 Daved Benefield	.10	.30
5 Robert Drummond	.20	.50
6 Rod Harris	.10	.30
7 Alfred Jackson	.20	.50
8 Lui Passaglia	.20	.50
9 Johnny Scott	.05	.15
10 Jamie Taras	.05	.15
11 Kelvin Anderson	.20	.50
12 Marvin Coleman	.05	.15
13 Vince Danielsen	.20	.50
14 Dave Dickenson	.20	.50
15 Alondra Johnson	.10	.30
16 Mark McLoughlin	.05	.15
17 Travis Moore	.20	.50
18 Allen Pitts	.40	1.00
19 Leroy Blugh	.10	.30
20 Malvin Hunter	.05	.15
21 Troy Mills	.20	.50
22 Kavis Reed	.05	.15
23 Gizmo Williams	.40	1.00
24 Darren Flutie	.60	1.50
25 Danny McManus	.30	.75
26 Joe Montford	.20	.50
27 Mike Morreale	.10	.30
28 Paul Osbaldiston	.10	.30
29 Archie Amerson	.20	.50
30 Ronald Williams	.20	.50
31 Terry Baker	.30	.75
32 Jock Climie	.20	.50
33 Tracy Ham	.60	1.50
34 Elfrid Payton	.10	.30
35 Mike Pringle	.80	2.00
36 Curtis Mayfield	.20	.50
37 Donald Narcisse	.40	1.00
38 Mike Saunders	.25	.60
39 John Terry	.05	.15
40 Reggie Slack	.20	.50
41 Jay Barker	.30	.75
42 Eric Blount RB	.20	.50
43 Mike Clemons	.40	1.00
44 Paul Masotti	.20	.50
45 Mike O'Shea	.20	.50
46 Kerwin Bell	.25	.60
47 Bob Cameron	.10	.30
48 Grant Carter	.10	.30
49 Dave Vankoughnett	.05	.15
50 Milt Stegall	.20	.50
A Larry and Willy	.01	.05
(with cheerleaders)		
B Steve Dunbar	.01	.05
C The Bill Courage Show	.20	.50
D Jeff O'Neil	.01	.05
E Mr. Fox	.01	.05
CL1 Checklist	.01	.05
Cover Card 1		
CL2 Checklist	.01	.05
Cover Card 2		
CL3 Checklist	.01	.05
Cover Card 3		
CL4 Checklist	.01	.05
Cover Card 4		
CL5 Checklist	.01	.05
Cover Card 5		

2000 JOGO

Released in 2000 by JOGO, this set features the stars of the Canadian Football League. The cards were issued in three series. Series 1 card fronts have a red border, series 2 feature a white border with a blue frame around the player photo and series 3 have white borders with a red frame.

COMPLETE SET (240)	60.00	120.00
COMP.SERIES 1 (110)	25.00	50.00
COMP.SERIES 2 (110)	25.00	50.00
COMP.SERIES 3 (20)	10.00	20.00
1 Malvin Hunter	.20	.50
2 Singor Mobley	.15	.40
3 Rick Walters	.20	.50
4 Hency Charles	.15	.40
5 Philippe Girard	.15	.40
6 Charles Assmann	.15	.40
7 Craig Carr	.30	.75
8 Tim Prinsen	.15	.40
9 Anthony Calvillo	1.25	3.00
10 Terry Baker	.50	1.25
11 Sheldon Benoit	.15	.40
12 Stanley Jackson	.40	1.00
13 Jamie Barnette	.40	1.00
14 Thomas Haskins Jr.	.20	.50
15 Alphonso Roundtree	.15	.40
16 Ben Cahoon	1.25	3.00
17 Mercury Hayes	.30	.75
18 Edmond Philion	.15	.40
19 Jason Richards	.15	.40
20 Lester Smith	.15	.40
21 Bryan Chiu	.30	.75
22 Neal Fort	.30	.75
23 Mike Sutherland	.15	.40
24 Davis Sanchez	.40	1.00
25 Chris Hoople	.15	.40
26 Winston October	.30	.75
27 Jamie Taras	.15	.40
28 Kelly Lochbaum	.20	.50
29 Cory Mantyka	.15	.40
30 Steve Hardin	.15	.40
31 Mike Crumb	.15	.40
32 Keith Franklin	.20	.50
33 Eric Carter	.20	.50
34 Jason Kralt	.15	.40
35 Doug Nussmeier	.20	.50
36 Dan Payne	.15	.40
37 Noah Cantor	.15	.40
38 Sean Graham	.15	.40
39 Derrick Lewis	.15	.40
40 Bret Anderson	.20	.50
41 Jimmy Kemp	.30	.75
42 Andrew English	.20	.50
43 Jacob Marini	.15	.40
44 Ryan Terry	1.50	3.00
45 Fred Perry	.15	.40
46 Greg Hill QB	.30	.75
47 Sandy Annunziata	.15	.40
48 Andre Kirwan	.20	.50
49 Derrell Mitchell	.75	2.00
50 Roger Dunbrack	.30	.75
51 Donnavan Carter	.20	.50
52 Brad Elberg	.15	.40
53 Glen Scrivener	.15	.40
54 Jude St. John	.15	.40
55 Adrion Smith	.20	.50
56 Dave Vankoughnett	.15	.40
57 Markus Howell	.20	.50
58 Ryland Wickman	.30	.75
59 Harold Nash Jr.	.15	.40
60 Troy Westwood	.15	.40
61 Brian Clark	.15	.40
62 Steven Glenn	.15	.40
63 Brett MacNeil	.15	.40
64 Dave Mudge	.15	.40
65 Garry Sawatzky	.15	.40
66 Mo Elewonibi	.20	.50
67 Mike Abou-Mechrek	.15	.40
68 Albert Johnson	.20	.50
69 Khari Jones	1.00	2.50
70 Robert Gordon	.30	.75
71 Dave Ritchie CO	.15	.40
72 Milt Stegall	1.00	2.50
73 Doug Hocking	.15	.40
74 Eric Lapointe	1.25	2.50
75 Jay Barker	.40	1.50
76 Greg Frers	.15	.40
77 Rocco Romano	.15	.40
78 Kelvin Anderson	1.25	2.50
79 Dave Dickenson	2.00	4.00
80 Troy Kopp	.20	.50
81 Aubrey Cummings	.20	.50
82 Eric Sutton	.15	.40
83 Marc Pilon	.20	.50
84 Dan Giancola	.15	.40
85 Denis Montana	.20	.50
86 Mike Adams	.30	.75
87 Christopher Perez	.15	.40
88 Dwayne Morgan	.15	.40
89 Mark Verbeek	.15	.40
90 David Hack	.15	.40
91 Mike Morreale	.30	.75
92 Cody Ledbetter	.20	.50
93 Danny McManus	1.00	2.50
94 Jarrett Smith	.15	.40
95 Jerry Urias	.15	.40
96 Chris Burns	.15	.40
97 Darren Flutie	.75	2.00
98 Andrew Grigg	.20	.50
99 Jeff Cummins	.20	.50
100 Mike O'Shea	.30	.75
101 Jeff Johnson RBK	.20	.50
102 Joel Becker	.15	.40
103 Chris Shelling	.15	.40
104 Warren Kyle Muzika	.15	.40
105 Ben Fairbrother	.15	.40
106 Henry Burris	1.50	4.00
107 Danny Barrett CO	.20	.50
108 Jeremy O'Day	.15	.40
109 Marcus McDavid	.20	.50
110 Dan Farthing	.20	.50
111 Danny Crowley	.40	1.00
112 Jason Maas	1.50	4.00
113 Jed Roberts	.15	.40
114 Terry Vaughn	.40	1.00
115 Frantz Clarkson	.15	.40
116 Terry Ray	.20	.50
117 Albert Reese	.15	.40
118 Rio Wells	.15	.40
119 Tracy Gravely	.20	.50
120 John Grace Jr.	.15	.40
121 Eric Riddick	.15	.40
122 Tito Hannah	.15	.40
123 Will Loftus	.15	.40
124 Pierre Vercheval	.15	.40
125 Stefen Reid	.15	.40
126 Allonzo Drowning	.30	.75
127 Barron Miles	.30	.75
128 Kevin Lefsrud	.15	.40
129 Kelly Wiltshire	.15	.40
130 Steve Charbonneau	.15	.40
131 Irvin Smith	.15	.40
132 Mark Washington	.15	.40
133 Scott Flory	.15	.40
134 Swift Burch	.15	.40
135 Selvesta Miller	.20	.50
136 Tim Fleiszer	.15	.40
137 Jason Crumb	.30	.75
138 Craig Hendrickson	.15	.40
139 Centrai McClellion	.60	1.50
140 Michael Fletcher	.20	.50
141 Scott Hendrickson	.15	.40
142 Raphaol Ball	.15	.40
143 Nate Sparks	.30	.75
144 Lui Passaglia	.40	1.00
145 Damon Allen	1.00	2.50
146 Paul Lacoste	.15	.40
147 Trevor Ludtke	.15	.40
148 Chuck Levy	.30	.75
149 Mike Philbrick	.15	.40
150 Carl Coulter	.15	.40
151 Chad Folk	.15	.40
152 Frank Rocca	.15	.40
153 Dave Henrey	.15	.40
154 O.T. Sampson	.30	.75
155 Byron Capers	.15	.40
156 Darren Joseph	.15	.40
157 Jim Cooper	.15	.40
158 Dave Heasman	.15	.40
159 Vernon Mitchell	.15	.40
160 Wayne Shaw	.15	.40
161 Jimmy Haley	.20	.50
162 Johnny Scott	.20	.50
163 Tyrone Rodgers	.20	.50
164 Jason Clemett	.15	.40
165 Scott Deibert	.15	.40
166 George White	.30	.75
167 Aaron Williams	.15	.40
168 Samir Chahine	.15	.40
169 Bob Cameron	.20	.50
170 Wade Miller	.15	.40
171 Antonio Armstrong	.15	.40
172 Spencer McLennan	.15	.40
173 Brad Yamaoka	.15	.40
174 Tom Europe	.15	.40
175 Brandon Hamilton	.15	.40
176 Phillip Curry	.15	.40
177 Daved Benefield	.30	.75
178 Elfrid Payton Sr.	.20	.50
179 Bruno Heppell	.15	.40
180 Michael McCoy	.20	.50
181 Rock Preston	.15	.40
182 Geroy Simon	.60	1.50
183 Mike Clemons	1.25	3.00
184 Mike Clemons CO	.60	1.50
185 Tony Martino	.20	.50
186 Marc Boerigter	4.00	8.00
187 Jay McNeil	.15	.40
188 Eddie Davis	.15	.40
189 Vince Danielsen	.40	1.00
190 Jamie Crysdale	.15	.40
191 Duane Forde	.15	.40
192 Raymond Biggs	.15	.40
193 Joe Fleming	1.25	3.00
194 Ibrahim Tounkara	.40	1.00
195 Jackie Kellogg	.15	.40
196 Herman Smith	.20	.50
197 Rob Hitchcock	.15	.40
198 Trevor Shaw	.15	.40
199 Donald Smith	.15	.40
200 Mike Mihelic	.15	.40
201 Joe Hagins	.20	.50
202 Joe Montford	.50	1.25
203 Aaron Collins	.40	1.00
204 John Terry	.15	.40
205 Marcel Desjardins DIR	.15	.40
206 Jim Popp GM	.15	.40
207 Andre Bolduc	.15	.40
208 Jock Climie	.30	.75
209 Sylvain Girard	.20	.50
210 Tyree Davis	.30	.75
211 Bamidele Ali	.15	.40
212 Andre Arlain	.15	.40
213 Roger Dunbrack	.30	.75
214 John Rayborn	.20	.50
215 Curtis Marsh	.75	2.00
216 Duane Dmytryshyn	.20	.50
217 Shawn Gallant	.15	.40
218 Dylan Ching	.20	.50
219 Jackie Mitchell	.15	.40
220 Umarr Morgan	.20	.50
221 Dwayne Provo	.15	.40
222 Chris Hardy	.15	.40
223 Shawn Daniels	.15	.40
224 A.J. Gass	.15	.40
225 Jerome Peterson	.15	.40
226 Dave Donaldson	.20	.50
227 Marcello Simmons	.15	.40
228 Julian Graham	.15	.40
229 Michael Jenkins	.75	2.00
230 Harvey Stables	.20	.50
231 Colin Scrivener	.15	.40
232 Val St. Germain	.15	.40
233 Orlando Bowen	.15	.40
234 Shonte Peoples	.20	.50
235 Nealon Greene	1.50	4.00
236 Carl Kidd	.60	1.50
237 Mike Maurer	.20	.50
238 Dave Dickenson MOP	.75	2.00
239 Damon Allen	1.00	2.50
Lui Passaglia		
(2000 Grey Cup)		
240 The Guess Who	1.50	4.00

2000 JOGO Hall of Fame E

After a six year hiatus, JOGO produced two sets of cards for the Hall of Fame in 2000. The cards measure standard size and the fronts feature black-and-white player photos with a red border on all four sides. The player's name appears in red lettering within the lower portion of the photo. On a white background, the backs carry the player's career years along with awards and honors he received. The card numbers identify this set as "E."

COMPLETE SET (25)	10.00	20.00
E1 Junior Ah-You	.75	2.00
E2 Donald Barker	.30	.75
E3 Danny Bass	.50	1.25
E4 Ormond Beach	.30	.75
E5 Al Benecick	.30	.75
E6 Dieter Brock	1.50	3.00
E7 Hugh Campbell	.30	.75
E8 Jerry Campbell	.30	.75
E9 Bill Clarke	.30	.75
E10 Royal Copeland	.30	.75
E11 Jim Corrigall	.30	.75
E12 Bruce Coulter	.30	.75
E13 Grover Covington	.30	.75
E14 Ross Craig	.30	.75
E15 Bernie Custis	.30	.75
E16 Dave Cutler	.50	1.25
E17 Rocky Dipietro	.75	2.00
E18 Paul Dojack	.30	.75
E19 Eric Duggan	.30	.75
E20 A.H. Fear	.30	.75
E21 Greg Fulton	.30	.75
E22 Jake Gaudaur	.30	.75
E23 Tommy Grant	.50	1.25
E24 Harry Griffith	.30	.75
E25 Dickie Harris	.30	.75

2000 JOGO Hall of Fame F

After a six year hiatus, JOGO produced two sets of cards for the Hall of Fame in 2000. The cards measure standard size and the fronts feature black-and-white player photos with a red border on all four sides. The player's name appears in red lettering within the lower portion of the photo. On a white background, the backs carry the player's career years along with awards and honors he received. The card numbers identify this set as "F."

COMPLETE SET (25)	10.00	20.00
F1 Condredge Holloway	2.00	4.00
F2 Dick Huffman	.30	.75
F3 Bob Isbister	.30	.75
F4 Jerry Keeling	.50	1.25
F5 Brian Kelly	.50	1.25
F6 Danny Kepley	.30	.75
F7 Eagle Keys	.50	1.25
F8 Les Lear	.30	.75
F9 Moe Lieberman	.30	.75
F10 Ed McQuarters	.30	.75
F11 James Murphy	.75	2.00
F12 Roger Nelson	.30	.75
F13 Tony Pajaczkowski	.30	.75
F14 Norm Perry	.50	1.25
F15 Joe Poplawski	.50	1.25
F16 Dave Raimey	.30	.75
F17 Frank Rigney	.30	.75
F18 Larry Robinson	.30	.75
F19 Joe Ryan	.30	.75
F20 Tom Scott	.75	2.00

F21 Bill Symons	.30	.75
F22 Frank Tindall	.30	.75
F23 Ted Urness	.30	.75
F24 Al Wilson	.30	.75
F25 Bill Zock	.30	.75

2001 JOGO

JOGO Inc. again issued a set of cards for 2001 featuring players of the CFL. Reportedly 500 sets were made for hobby distribution with 100-additional sets being issued directly to the players themselves. The cards feature a light tan border along with the standard JOGO cardback format. Card #71 was initially produced with the incorrect player jersey number on the back but was later corrected.

COMPLETE SET (240)	55.00	110.00
COMP.SERIES 1 (110)	25.00	50.00
COMP.SERIES 2 (110)	25.00	50.00
COMP.SERIES 3 (20)	6.00	12.00
1 Jamie Taras	.15	.40
2 Bret Anderson	.20	.50
3 Lee Vaughn	.15	.40
4 Daved Benefield	.30	.75
5 Noah Cantor	.20	.50
6 Tony Corbin	.20	.50
7 Jason Crumb	.15	.40
8 Mike Crumb	.15	.40
9 Michael Fletcher	.20	.50
10 Sean Graham	.15	.40
11 Lyle Green	.20	.50
12 Steve Hardin	.15	.40
13 Matt Kellett	.15	.40
14 Jason Kralt	.15	.40
15 Toya Jones	.15	.40
16 Mike Maurer	.20	.50
17 Alfred Jackson	.50	1.25
18 Barrin Simpson	.15	.40
19 Irvin Smith	.15	.40
20 Demeco Archangel	.20	.50
21 Terry Baker	.50	1.25
22 Ed Philion	.15	.40
23 William Loftus	.15	.40
24 Stefen Reid	.15	.40
25 Tito Hannah	.15	.40
26 Jason Richards	.15	.40
27 Kelly Wiltshire	.15	.40
28 Mat Petz	.15	.40
29 Bryan Chiu	.30	.75
30 Bruno Heppell	.15	.40
31 Uzooma Okeke	.15	.40
32 Pierre Vercheval	.15	.40
33 Mark Washington	.50	1.25
34 Glen Young	.15	.40
35 Ben Sankey	.30	.75
36 Ricky Bell	.15	.40
37 Kelly Lochbaum	.15	.40
38 Mark Pilon	.15	.40
39 Jeff Pilon	.15	.40
40 Jay McNeil	.15	.40
41 Marcus Crandell	.75	2.00
42 Farwan Zubedi	.20	.50
43 James Cotton	.15	.40
44 Antonio Warren	.75	2.00
45 Marc Boerigter	2.00	5.00
46 Greg Frers	.15	.40
47 Jimmy Kemp	.30	.75
48 Chad Folk	.15	.40
49 Jude St. John	.15	.40
50 Michel Dupuis	.15	.40
51 Elfrid Payton	.20	.50
52 Darren Joseph	.15	.40
53 Alfonzo Browning	.30	.75
54 Leroy Blugh	.15	.40
55 Derrell Mitchell	.75	2.00
56 Ted Alford	.30	.75
57 Warren Muzika	.15	.40
58 Darren Flutie	.75	2.00
59 Corey Grant	.20	.50
60 Andrew Grigg	.20	.50
61 David Hack	.15	.40
62 Idris Haroon	.15	.40
63 Byron Capers	.15	.40
64 Danny McManus	1.00	2.50
65 Chris Shelling	.15	.40
66 Paul Lambert	.15	.40
67 Sean Woodson	.15	.40
68 Pascal Cheron	.15	.40
69 Matt Robichaud	.15	.40
70 Mike Morreale	.30	.75
71A Jon Nielsen ERR 18 (Jersey number 18 on back)	.30	.75
71B Jon Nielsen COR (Jersey number 19 on back)	.75	2.00
72 Wayne Shaw	.15	.40
73 Roger Reinson	.15	.40
74 Tim Prinsen	.15	.40
75 Frantz Clarkson	.15	.40
76 Jason Maas	1.00	2.50
77 Singor Mobley	.15	.40
78 Bruce Beaton	.15	.40
79 Jed Roberts	.15	.40
80 Rob Harrod	.20	.50
81 Ed Hervey	.50	1.25
82 Albert Reese	.15	.40
83 Rick Walters	.20	.50
84 Terry Ray	.20	.50
85 Raphaol Ball	.15	.40
86 Mo Elewonibi	.20	.50
87 Wade Miller	.15	.40
88 Brett MacNeil	.15	.40
89 Khari Jones	1.25	3.00
90 Harold Nash Jr.	.15	.40
91 Brad Yamaoka	.15	.40
92 Troy Westwood	.15	.40
93 Dave Mudge	.15	.40
94 Eric Blount	.40	1.00
95 Troy Mills	.30	.75
96 Julian Graham	.15	.40
97 Jamie Stoddard	.20	.50
98 Donnie Ruiz	.15	.40
99 Milt Stegall	.75	2.00
100 Brandon Dyson	.15	.40
101 Dan Comiskey	.15	.40
102 Dylan Ching	.20	.50
103 Shawn Gallant	.15	.40
104 George White	.15	.40
105 Dan Farthing	.20	.50
106 Andrew Greene	.75	2.00
107 Jeremy O'Day	.15	.40
108 Eddie Davis	.15	.40
109 Shonte Peoples	.20	.50
110 John H. Terry III	.15	.40
111 Thomas Rayam	.15	.40
112 Aubrey Cummings	.20	.50
113 Lawrence Deck	.15	.40
114 Kelvin Anderson	.75	2.00
115 Duncan O'Mahony	.15	.40
116 Scott Deibert	.15	.40
117 Joe Fleming	1.25	3.00
118 David Heasman	.15	.40
119 Anthony Calvillo	1.25	3.00
120 Ibrahim Tounkara	.30	.75
121 William Fields	.15	.40
122 Bob Cameron	.20	.50
123 Cory Mantyka	.15	.40
124 Tyrone Bell	.30	.75
125 Sedrick Curry	.15	.40
126 Herman Smith	.20	.50
127 Tyrone Taylor	.15	.40
128 Ben Fairbrother	.15	.40
129 Jamie Barnette	.30	.75
130 Andre Bolduc	.15	.40
131 Ben Cahoon	.75	2.00
132 Josh Cochran	.15	.40
133 Tyree Davis	.30	.75
134 Marcel Desjardins DIR	.15	.40
135 Tim Fleiszer	.15	.40
136 Scott Flory	.15	.40
137 Neal Fort	.30	.75
138 Sylvain Girard	.20	.50
139 Tracy Gravely	.20	.50
140 Thomas Haskins	.20	.50
141 Chris Hoople	.15	.40
142 Eric Lapointe	.40	1.00
143 Kevin Lefsrud	.15	.40
144 Jim Popp GM	.15	.40
145 Don Wnek	.15	.40
146 Eric Riddick	.15	.40
147 Ray Jacobs	.15	.40
148 Aldi Henry	.15	.40
149 Scott Regimbald	.20	.50
150 Willie Fells	.15	.40
151 Kamau Peterson	.30	.75
152 Chris Hardy	.15	.40
153 Donnavan Carter	.20	.50
154 Kent Ring	.15	.40
155 Anthony E. Prior	.15	.40
156 Kerwin Bell	.75	2.00
157 Samir Chahine	.15	.40
158 Marcello Simmons	.15	.40
159 Tyrone Rodgers	.30	.75
160 Andre Talbot	.20	.50
161 Adrion Smith	.20	.50
162 Orlondo Steinauer	.15	.40
163 Mike O'Shea	.30	.75
164 Sandy Annunziata	.15	.40
165 Dan Giancola	.15	.40
166 Rob Hitchcock	.15	.40
167 Dario Romero	.15	.40
168 Jeff Johnson	.15	.40
169 Randy Bowles	.20	.50
170 Carl Coulter	.15	.40
171 Chris Nofo	.15	.40
172 Kyle Walters	.15	.40
173 Terry Billups	.15	.40
174 Mark Verbeek	.15	.40
175 Michael Philbrick	.15	.40
176 Gary Brown	.15	.40
177 Roger Dunbrack	.20	.50
178 Michael Jenkins	.60	1.50
179 Brad Elberg	.15	.40
180 Orlando Bowen	.15	.40
181 Paul LaPolice ASST CO	.15	.40
182 Fabian Rayne	.20	.50
183 Sheldon Benoit	.15	.40
184 Yves Dossous	.15	.40
185 A.J. Gass	.15	.40
186 Perry Carter	.15	.40
187 Shannon Garrett	.15	.40
188 Ronald Williams	.40	1.00
189 Jackie Kellogg	.15	.40
190 Joe Barnes	.15	.40
191 Otis Floyd	.15	.40
192 Fred Childress	.30	.75
193 Jeff Traversy	.15	.40
194 Rob Lazeo	.15	.40
195 Steven Glenn	.15	.40
196 Mike Abou-Mechrek	.15	.40
197 Tom Europe	.15	.40
198 Arland Bruce III	.60	1.50
199 Juran Bolden	.15	.40
200 Robert Gordon	.30	.75
201 Dave Ritchie CO	.15	.40
202 Stanley Jackson	.30	.75
203 Kevin Feterik	1.00	2.50
204 Torey Hunter	.15	.40
205 Mike Sutherland	.15	.40
206 Germaine Jones	.15	.40
207 Chris Burns	.15	.40
208 Jackie Mitchell	.15	.40
209 Trevis Smith	.15	.40
210 Tyson St. James	.15	.40
211 Rock Preston	.15	.40
212 Darren Davis	1.00	2.50
213 Keith Smith	.20	.50
214 Val St. Germain	.15	.40
215 James Epps	.30	.75
216 Omar Evans	.15	.40
217 Andrew Moore	.15	.40
218 Jason A. Mallett	.15	.40
219 Teddy Neptune	.15	.40
220 Danny Barrett CO	.20	.50
221 Troy Davis	1.00	2.50
222 Andre Kirwan	.20	.50
223 Ian Williams	.15	.40
224 Daaron McField	.15	.40
225 Cordell Taylor	.15	.40
226 Fred Perry	.15	.40
227 Jermaine Copeland	.75	2.00
228 Cody Ledbetter	.20	.50
229 Aaron Williams	.15	.40
230 Bill Lafleur	.30	.75
231 Pat Woodcock	.60	1.50
232 Glen Scrivener	.15	.40
233 Tony Martino	.20	.50
234 Vince Danielsen	.30	.75
235 Dave Donaldson	.20	.50
236 Charles Roberts	2.00	5.00
237 Tyrone Rodgers	.30	.75
238 Joe Montford	.50	1.25
NNO Rik Fedyck PHOTO	.15	.40

2002 JOGO

JOGO produced this set for 2002 featuring players of the CFL. Reportedly 500 sets were made for hobby distribution with 100-additional sets being issued directly to the players themselves. The cards feature a colored border along with the standard JOGO cardback format. Several cards were produced with errors that were later corrected. The corrected cards are much more difficult to find than the errors.

COMPLETE SET (220)	60.00	120.00
COMP.SERIES 1 (110)	30.00	60.00
COMP.SERIES 2 (110)	30.00	60.00
1 Marcus Crandell	.60	1.50
2 Scott Regimbald	.20	.50
3 Aldi Henry	.15	.40
4 Jayson Bray	.15	.40
5 Da'Shann Austin	.15	.40
6 Raymonn Adams	.15	.40
7 William Fields	.15	.40
8 Greg Frers	.15	.40
9 Willie Fells	.15	.40
10 Duncan O'Mahony	.15	.40
11 Kamau Peterson	.30	.75
12 Jeff Pilon	.15	.40
13 Scott Deibert	.15	.40
14 David Heasman	.15	.40
15 Alondra Johnson	.60	1.50
16 James Burgess	.15	.40
17 Kevin Feterik	.75	2.00
18 Ibrahim Tounkara	.30	.75
19 Don Blair	.20	.50
20 Bobby Singh	.15	.40
21 Sean Spender	.15	.40
22 Kevin Johnson	.30	.75
23 Kevin Lefsrud	.15	.40
24 Uzo Okeke	.15	.40
25 Stefen Reid	.15	.40
26 Reggie Durden	.30	.75
27 William Loftus	.15	.40
28 Bryan Chiu	.30	.75
29A Stephane Fortin ERR (daughter's name Trinity on back)	.15	.40
29B Stephane Fortin COR (daughter's name Tainaly on back)	.75	2.00
30 Scott Flory	.15	.40
31 Keith Stokes	1.25	3.00
32 Mat Petz	.15	.40
33 Wayne Shaw	.15	.40
34 Barron Miles	.30	.75
35 Reggie Lowe	.15	.40
36 Marc L. Megna	.15	.40
37 Rob Brown	.15	.40
38 Chris Jones CO	.15	.40
39 Don Matthews CO	.30	.75
40 Ricky Ray	6.00	12.00
41 Chris Hardy	.15	.40
42 Sheldon Benoit	.15	.40
43 Thomas A. Haskins Jr.	.15	.40
44 Fabian Burke	.15	.40
45 Tim Prinsen	.15	.40
46 Rick Walters	.20	.50
47 Elfrid Payton	.20	.50
48 A.J. Gass	.15	.40
49 Jackie Kellogg	.15	.40
50 Jason Maas	.75	2.00
51 Wade Miller	.15	.40
52 Mike Sutherland	.15	.40
53 Bob Cameron	.20	.50
54 Brian Clark	.15	.40
55 Jamie Stoddard	.20	.50
56 Mo Elewonibi	.20	.50
57 Milt Stegall	.75	2.00
58 Khari Jones	1.25	3.00
59 Dave Mudge	.15	.40
60 Wayne Weathers	.15	.40
61 Steve Alexandre	.15	.40
62 Mace Freeman	.15	.40
63 Chris Shelling	.15	.40
64 Randy Bowles	.20	.50
65 Pascal Cheron	.15	.40
66 Brandon Hamilton	.15	.40
67 Andrew Grigg	.20	.50
68 Sean Woodson	.15	.40
69 Daaron McField	.15	.40
70 Danny McManus	1.00	2.50
71 Jamie Taras	.15	.40
72 Jason Clermont	1.00	2.50
73 Steve Hardin	.15	.40
74 Cory Mantyka	.15	.40
75 Tony Martino	.20	.50
76 Dan Payne	.15	.40
77 Matt Kellett	.15	.40
78 Geroy Simon	1.50	4.00
79 Damon Allen	1.00	2.50
80 Michael Fletcher	.20	.50
81 Mike Morreale	.30	.75
82 Bruno Heppell	.15	.40
83 Joe Montford	.40	1.00
84 Derrell Mitchell	.40	1.00
85 Jude St. John	.15	.40
86 Mike O'Shea	.30	.75
87 Johnny Scott	.20	.50
88 Orlondo Steinauer	.15	.40
89 Adrion Smith	.20	.50
90 Chad Folk	.15	.40
91 Jeremy O'Day	.15	.40
92 Jason A. Mallett	.15	.40
93 Nealon Greene	1.00	2.50
94 Simon Baffoe	.15	.40
95 Dylan Ching	.20	.50
96 Reggie Hunt	.15	.40
97 Paul McCallum	.30	.75
98 Danny Barrett CO	.20	.50
99 Mike Abou-Mechrek	.15	.40
100 Seth Dittman	.15	.40
101 Donnavan Carter	.20	.50
102 Jason Kralt	.15	.40
103 Dan Crowley	.30	.75
104 Shawn Gallant	.15	.40
105 Glenn Harper	.15	.40
106 Mike Vilimek	.15	.40
107 Mike Maurer	.20	.50
108 George Hudson	.20	.50
109 Mike Boireau	.30	.75
110 Donnie Ruiz	.15	.40
111 Lawrence Phillips	1.50	4.00
112 Stephen Anderson	.15	.40
113 Tyrone Rodgers	.30	.75
114 Joe Barnes	.15	.40
115 Travis Moore	.60	1.50
116 Chris Hoople	.15	.40
117 Darnell Kennedy	.15	.40
118 Rob Johnson	.15	.40
119 Mike Clemons CO	.60	1.50
120 Scott Gordon	.15	.40
121 Jay McNeil	.15	.40
122 Brian S. Stallworth	.50	1.25
123 Jackie Mitchell	.15	.40
124 Dan Gyetvai	.15	.40
125 Ryland Wickman	.30	.75
126 Andre Arlain	.15	.40
127 Arland Bruce III	.30	.75
128 Carl Coulter	.15	.40
129 Rob Lazeo	.15	.40
130 Jonathan Beasley	1.00	2.50
131 Patrick Dorvelus	.15	.40
132 Perry Carter	.15	.40
133 Ed Philion	.15	.40
134 Timothy Strickland	.15	.40
135 Eric Lapointe	.30	.75
136 Noel Thorpe CO	.15	.40
137 Corey Grant	.20	.50
138 Terry Vaughn	.40	1.00
139 Adriano Belli	.15	.40
140 Pat Woodcock	.40	1.00
141 Tim Fleiszer	.15	.40
142 Neal Fort	.30	.75
143 Sylvain Girard	.20	.50
144 Jason Richards	.15	.40
145 Benedict Ibisi	.15	.40
146 Terry Baker	.40	1.00
147 Barrin Simpson	.15	.40
148 Corey Holmes	1.25	3.00
149 Michel Dupuis	.15	.40
150 Kevin Eiben	.15	.40
151 Chuck Walsh	.15	.40
152 Steve Charbonneau	.15	.40
153 Mike Bradley	.15	.40
154 Jed Roberts	.15	.40
155 John Avery	1.00	2.50
156 Quincy Coleman	.15	.40
157 Marc Pilon	.20	.50
158 Scott Robinson	.15	.40
159 Donald Brady	.15	.40
160 Kelvin Powell	.15	.40
161 Dave Ritchie CO	.15	.40
162 Dennis Fortney	.15	.40
163 Geoffrey Drover	.30	.75
164 Darren Flutie	1.25	3.00
165 Jason Congdon	.15	.40
166 Garry Sawatzky	.15	.40
167 Harold Nash Jr.	.15	.40
168 Tom Europe	.15	.40
169 Brad Yamaoka	.15	.40
170 Anthony Calvillo	1.25	3.00
171 Mark Verbeek	.15	.40
172 Rob Hitchcock	.15	.40
173 John MacDonald	.15	.40
174 Marcus Spencer	.15	.40
175 Warren Muzika	.15	.40
176 Ryan Donnelly	.15	.40
177 Scott Coe	.15	.40
178 Mike Mihelic	.15	.40
179 Pene Talamaivao	.15	.40
180 Shannon Garrett	.15	.40
181 Bret Anderson	.20	.50
182A Jason Crumb (half body photo on front)	.15	.40
182B Jason Crumb (full body photo on front)	.50	1.25
183 Mike Crumb	.15	.40
184 Ben Fairbrother	.15	.40
185 Ron Ockimey	.15	.40
186 Willie Hurst	.30	.75
187 Anthony E. Prior	.15	.40
188 John Williams	.15	.40
189 Paul Cheng	.15	.40
190 Clifford Ivory	.15	.40
191 Shawn Daniels	.15	.40
192 Roger Dunbrack	.20	.50
193 Alexis Sanschagrin	.15	.40
194 Charles Assmann	.15	.40
195 Andre Talbot	.20	.50
196A Matt McKnight (text on back starts: The Argonauts...)	.15	.40
196B Matt McKnightMatt McKnight (text on back starts: Matt was the Argonauts...)	.75	2.00
197 Darryl Ray	.15	.40
198 Juan Johnson	.15	.40
199 Jeff Johnson	.15	.40
200 Leroy Blugh	.15	.40
201 Jim Popp VP	.15	.40
202 Tony Akins	.30	.75
203 Andrew Greene	.30	.75
204 Chris Cvetkovic	.15	.40
205 Chris Wright	.15	.40
206 Shawn Gifford	.15	.40
207A Eddie Davis (standing photo on front)	.15	.40
207B Eddie Davis (cutting to the right in photo on front)	.75	2.00
208 Chris Szarka	.20	.50
209 Aubrey Cummings	.20	.50
210 David De La Perralle	.15	.40
211 Demitris Scouras	.15	.40
212 Kelly Wiltshire	.30	.75
213 Mike Moten	.30	.75
214 Steven Glenn	.15	.40
215 Keaton Cromartie	.15	.40
216 Denis Montana	.20	.50
217 Derrick Ford	.15	.40
218 David Thomas	.15	.40
219 Dan Giancola	.15	.40
220 Jerome Haywood	.60	1.50

2002 JOGO Additions

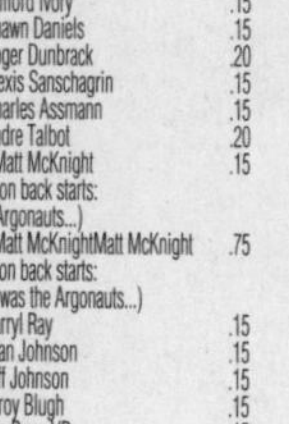

These 6-cards were created after the initial 220-card JOGO set was released. The format is essentially the same as the 2002 JOGO release with just a slight change in the border that surrounds the player photo. None of the cards were numbered.

NNO Bruce Beaton	4.00	8.00
NNO Alexandre Gauthier	4.00	8.00
NNO F.Scott Grant Photographer	4.00	8.00
NNO Lal Knight	4.00	8.00
NNO Tony Miles	4.00	8.00
NNO Ross Saunders Official	4.00	8.00

2003 JOGO

JOGO once again produced a CFL card set for 2003. Reportedly 500 sets were made for hobby distribution with 100-additional sets being issued directly to the players themselves. The cards feature a colored border along with the standard JOGO cardback format. Several cards were produced with errors that were later corrected. The corrected cards are much more difficult to find than the errors.

COMPLETE SET (269)	60.00	120.00
COMP.SERIES 1 (110)	25.00	50.00
COMP.SERIES 2 (110)	25.00	50.00
COMP.SERIES 3 (49)	10.00	20.00
1 Dave Dickenson	1.00	2.50
2 Dan Payne	.15	.40
3 Curtis Head	.30	.75
4 Wes White	.30	.75
5 Cory Mantyka	.15	.40
6 Matt McKnight	.15	.40
7 Bret Anderson	.20	.50
8 Kelly Bates	.15	.40
9 Adrian Archie	.20	.50
10 Neal Fort	.30	.75
11 Matt Kellett	.15	.40
12 Adriano Belli	.15	.40
13 William Loftus	.15	.40
14 Bruno Heppell	.15	.40
15 Mat Petz	.15	.40
16 Keith Stokes	.75	2.00
17 Jim Popp CO	.15	.40
18 Daniel Pugh	.20	.50
19 Brad Collinson	.15	.40
20 Dave Stala	.30	.75
21 Paul Lambert	.15	.40
22 D.J. Johnson	.15	.40
23 Bryan Chiu	.30	.75
24 Uzooma Okeke	.15	.40
25 Philippe Girard	.15	.40
26 Mark Thompson	.15	.40
27 Ricky Ray	1.50	4.00
28 A.J. Gass	.15	.40
29 Bruce Beaton	.15	.40
30 Malcolm Frank	.15	.40
31 Sheldon Benoit	.15	.40
32 Scott Robinson	.15	.40
33 Mike Bradley	.15	.40
34 Quincy Coleman	.15	.40
35 Rashad Jeanty	.15	.40
36A Rob Grant ERR (wrong photo; player is in white jeresey)	.30	.75
36B Rob Grant COR (correct photo; player is in green jeresey)	.60	1.50
37 Chris Burns	.15	.40
38 Josh Ranek	2.00	5.00
39 D.J. Flick	.50	1.25
40 Mike Vilimek	.15	.40
41 Darren Davis	.60	1.50
42 Kerry Joseph	.50	1.25
43 Tim Fleiszer	.15	.40
44 Demetris Bendross	.20	.50
45 Patrick Fleming	.15	.40
46 Seth Dittman	.15	.40
47 Darryl Ray	.15	.40
48 Mike Maurer	.20	.50
49 Andrew Greene	.30	.75
50 Jeremy O'Day	.15	.40
51 Nealon Greene	.60	1.50
52 Rocky Henry	.20	.50
53 Paul McCallum	.30	.75
54 Eric Carter	.15	.40
55 Chris Szarka	.20	.50
56 Reggie Hunt	.15	.40
57 Terrence Melton	.20	.50
58 Dennis Mavrin	.15	.40
59 Donald Heaven	.15	.40
60 Rob Lazeo	.15	.40
61 Kevin Glenn	.60	1.50
62 Jackie Mitchell	.15	.40
63 Gene Makowsky	.15	.40
64 Corey Grant	.20	.50
65 Jason French	.15	.40
66 Charles Thomas	.15	.40
67 Andre Arlain	.15	.40
68 Kevin Feterik	.50	1.25
69 Don Blair	.20	.50
70 Joe Fleming	.75	2.00
71 David Heasman	.15	.40
72 Jay McNeil	.15	.40
73 Charles Assmann	.15	.40
74 Scott Regimbald	.20	.50
75 Joey Boese	.20	.50
76 Anthony E. Prior	.15	.40
77 Lawrence Deck	.15	.40
78 Samir Chahine	.15	.40
79 Michel Dupuis	.15	.40
80 Lawrence Phillips	.60	1.50
81 Damon Allen	1.00	2.50
82 Noah Cantor	.20	.50
83 Sandy Annunziata	.15	.40
84 Jude St. John	.15	.40
85 Adrion Smith	.20	.50
86 Luke Fritz	.15	.40
87 Bashir Levingston	.60	1.50
88 Tim Prinsen	.15	.40
89 Eric Wilson	.15	.40
90 Terry Ray	.20	.50
91 Jamie Stoddard	.20	.50
92 Brian Clark	.15	.40
93A Scott Harper ERR (wrong photo on back; player has no beard)	.20	.50
93B Scott Harper COR (correct photo on back; player has a beard)	.60	1.50
94 Jason Congdon	.15	.40
95 Wade Miller	.15	.40
96 Maurice Kelly	.15	.40
97 Dave Mudge	.15	.40
98 Ricky Bell	.15	.40
99 Khari Jones	1.00	2.50
100 Marvin Coleman	.20	.50
101 Mike Sellers	.60	1.50
102 Matt Sheridan	.15	.40
103 Troy Westwood	.15	.40
104 Dave Ritchie CO	.15	.40
105 Danny McManus	1.00	2.50
106 Emmerson Phillips	.20	.50
107 Archie Amerson	.40	1.00
108 Troy Davis	.50	1.25
109 Pete Gonzalez	.20	.50
110 Carl Coulter	.15	.40
111 Jason Clermont	.75	2.00
112 Steve Hardin	.15	.40
113 Bill Chamberlain	.20	.50
114 Mark Washington	.30	.75
115 Spergon Wynn	.30	.75
116 Tyrone Williams	.15	.40
117 Javier Glatt	.15	.40
118 Ray Jacobs	.15	.40
119 Brent Johnson	.50	1.25
120 Kelly Lochbaum	.15	.40
121 Ron Ockimey	.15	.40
122 Geroy Simon	.50	1.25
123 Scott Flory	.15	.40
124 Wayne Shaw	.15	.40
125 Ben Cahoon	.75	2.00
126 Sylvain Girard	.20	.50
127 Steve Fisher	.20	.50
128 Aaron Fiacconi	.15	.40
129 Anwar Stewart	.40	1.00
130 Eric Lapointe	.20	.50
131 Marc Megna	.40	1.00
132 Barron Miles	.30	.75
133 Donald Brady	.15	.40
134 Kory Bailey	.20	.50
135 Brock Balog	.15	.40
136 Dan Comiskey	.15	.40
137 Cory Annett	.15	.40
138 Randy Chevrier	.15	.40
139 Rick Walters	.20	.50
140 Kevin Lefsrud	.15	.40
141 Dounia Whitehouse	.20	.50
142 Roger Reinson	.15	.40
143 Steve Charbonneau	.15	.40
144 Sean Spender	.15	.40
145 Carlo Panaro	.15	.40
146 Shannon Garrett	.15	.40
147 Travis Moore	.60	1.50
148 George Hudson	.20	.50
149 Chase Raynock	.15	.40
150 Mike Moten	.15	.40
151 Donnavan Carter	.20	.50
152 Mike Sutherland	.15	.40
153 Roger Dunbrack	.20	.50
154 Alexandre Gauthier	.15	.40
155 Fred Perry	.15	.40
156 Val St. Germain	.15	.40
157 Shawn Gallant	.15	.40
158 Keaton Cromartie	.15	.40
159 Frank Cutolo	1.50	4.00
160 Philip Gibson	.15	.40
161 Jason A. Mallett	.15	.40
162 Chris Hoople	.15	.40
163 Scott Schultz	.20	.50
164 Matt Dominguez	.75	2.00
165 Marcus Adams	.15	.40
166 Kelvin Anderson	.75	2.00
167 Wes Lysack	.20	.50
168 Davis Sanchez	.30	.75
169 Kenyatte Morgan	.20	.50
170 Blake Machan	.30	.75
171 Anthony Malbrough	.20	.50
172 Scott Deibert	.15	.40
173 Jeff Pilon	.15	.40
174 Bobby Singh	.15	.40
175 Chad Folk	.15	.40
176 Marvin L. Thomas	.15	.40
177 Jeff Johnson	.15	.40
178 Mike Crumb	.15	.40
179 Ray Mariuz	.15	.40
180 Danny Barrett CO	.20	.50
181 Randy Bowles	.20	.50
182 Shawn Gifford	.15	.40
183 Tony Miles	.50	1.25
184 Orlondo Steinauer	.15	.40
185 Mike O'Shea	.30	.75
186 Lal Knight	.20	.50
187 John Feugill	.15	.40
188 Michael Fletcher	.20	.50
189 Chuck Walsh	.15	.40
190 Milt Stegall	.75	2.00
191 Robert Gordon	.30	.75
192 Tom Europe	.15	.40
193 Tyson St. James	.15	.40
194 Brad Yamaoka	.15	.40
195 Markus Howell	.20	.50
196 Andrew Carter	.15	.40
197 Jon Oosterhuis	.15	.40
198 Dan Gyetvai	.15	.40
199 Ryland Wickman	.30	.75
200 Sebastien Roy	.15	.40
201 Johnny R. Scott	.20	.50
202 Chris Shelling	.15	.40
203 Joe Rumolo	.15	.40
204 Mark Verbeek	.15	.40
205 Karim Grant	.15	.40
206 John MacDonald	.15	.40
207 Jarrett Smith	.20	.50
208 Angus Reid	.15	.40
209 Ryan Donnelly	.15	.40
210 Mike Mihelic	.15	.40
211 Sean Woodson	.15	.40
212 Orlando Bowen	.15	.40
213 Kourtney Young	.15	.40
214 Joe Montford	.30	.75
215 Sandy Beveridge	.15	.40
216 Ibrahim Tounkara	.20	.50
217 Scott Coe	.15	.40
218 Julian Radlein	.20	.50
219 Ryan Thelwell	.60	1.50
220 Marc Pilon	.20	.50
221 Jermaine Copeland	.50	1.25
222 Eddie Davis	.15	.40
223 Charles Roberts	1.00	2.50
224 Kenton Keith	2.00	5.00
225 Jason Tucker	.30	.75
226 Anthony Calvillo	1.00	2.50
227 Chris Jones CO	.15	.40
228 Duncan O'Mahony	.15	.40
229 Harvey Stables	.20	.50
230 Steve Glenn	.15	.40
231 Tim Cheatwood	.20	.50
232 Da'Shann Austin	.15	.40
233 Ben Fairbrother	.15	.40
234 Jocelyn Frenette	.15	.40
235 Randy Spencer	.20	.50
236 Jason Crumb	.15	.40
237 Troy Mills	.20	.50
238 Olanzo Jarrett	.15	.40
239 Jerome Haywood	.30	.75
240 Terry Vaughn	.40	1.00
241 Jason Kralt	.15	.40
242 Mike Morreale	.30	.75
243 Corey Holmes	.60	1.50
244 Clinton Wayne	.15	.40
245 Andre Kirwan	.20	.50
246 Bart Hendricks	.20	.50
247 Darren Joseph	.15	.40
248 David De La Perralle	.15	.40
249 Eric Lee	.15	.40
250 Saladin McCullough	.20	.50
251 Wes White	.30	.75
252 Kelly Wiltshire	.15	.40
253 Derrick Ford	.15	.40
254 Kelvin Kinney	.20	.50
255 Stephen Young	.15	.40
256 Aubrey Cummings	.20	.50
257 Rob Hitchcock	.15	.40
258 Trevor Shaw	.15	.40
259 Mike Abou-Mechrek	.15	.40
260 Wane McGarity	.30	.75
261 Frantz Clarkson	.15	.40
262 Wayne Weathers	.15	.40
263 Darnell Edwards	.15	.40
264 Bobby Perry	.15	.40
265 Terry Baker	.40	1.00
266 Michael Palmer	.20	.50
267 Kevin Johnson	.30	.75
268 Andrew Greene	.30	.75
269 Ricky Ray Grey Cup	1.50	4.00
270 Bryan Adams Singer	5.00	10.00
NNO Rodney Sassi TR	.20	.50
NNO Ronnie James MGR	.20	.50

2003 JOGO CSC Promos

These 2-cards were produced to honor the 150th issue of the Canadian Sports Collector magazine as well as the Sports Collector Day in Canada held March 1, 2003. Each card features a white border on front along with the 150th Issue logo.

NNO Jason Clermont	2.00	4.00
NNO Pat Woodcock	2.00	4.00

2004 JOGO

One of the longest running annual card sets continued in 2004 as JOGO once again produced a CFL card set. Reportedly 500 sets were made for hobby distribution with 100-additional sets being issued directly to the players themselves. The cards feature a yellow border along with the standard JOGO cardback format printed on yellow as well. Three different series were again produced in 2004 with the third series being issued with both a white cardback and a yellow cardback. Five additional black bordered cards were released throughout the year for special occasions.

COMPLETE SET (270)	60.00	120.00
COMP.SERIES 1 (110)	25.00	50.00
COMP.SERIES 2 (110)	25.00	50.00
COMP.SERIES 3 (50)	12.50	25.00
1 Kerry Joseph	.50	1.25
2 Tony White	.15	.40
3 Mike Vilimek	.15	.40
4 Kelly Wiltshire	.15	.40
5 Jerome Haywood	.30	.75
6 Raymonn Adams	.15	.40
7 George Hudson	.20	.50
8 Jason Armstead	.60	1.50
9 Tim Fleiszer	.15	.40
10 Mike Maurer	.20	.50
11 Patrick Fleming	.15	.40
12 Shawn Gallant	.15	.40
13 Darryl Ray	.15	.40
14 Jeremy O'Day	.15	.40
15 Jackie Mitchell	.15	.40
16 Eddie Davis	.15	.40
17 Davin Bush	.15	.40
18 Darnell Edwards	.15	.40
19 Reggie Hunt	.15	.40
20 Scott Gordon	.15	.40
21 Travis Moore	.50	1.25
22 Kevin Nickerson	.15	.40
23 Rob Lazeo	.15	.40
24 Chris Szarka	.20	.50
25 Walter Spencer-Robinson	.15	.40
26 Donald Heaven	.15	.40
27 Jocelyn Frenette	.15	.40
28 Nathan Davis	.20	.50
29 Luke Fritz	.15	.40
30 Neal Fort	.30	.75
31 Bruno Heppell	.15	.40
32 Sylvain Girard	.20	.50
33 Eric Lapointe	.20	.50
34 Matt Kellett	.15	.40
35 Timothy Strickland	.15	.40
36 Scott Flory	.15	.40
37 Reggie Durden	.30	.75
38 Jason Congdon	.15	.40
39 Mike Botterill	.15	.40
40 Robert Brown	.20	.50
41 D.J. Johnson	.15	.40
42 Ben Cahoon	.75	2.00
43 Dave Dickenson	1.00	2.50
44 Bo Lewis	.15	.40
45 Mark Washington	.20	.50
46 Jason Gavadza	.15	.40
47 Geroy Simon	.50	1.25
48 Kelly Bates	.15	.40
49 Cory Mantyka	.15	.40
50 Freddie Moore	.15	.40
51 Chris Brazzell	.20	.50
52 Mawuko Tugbenyoh	.15	.40
53 Javier Glatt	.15	.40
54 Dimitrius Breedlove	.15	.40
55 Jamie Boreham	.15	.40
56 Montrell Lowe	.15	.40
57 Wayne Smith	.15	.40
58 Mat Petz	.15	.40
59 Carl Coulter	.15	.40
60 D.J. Flick	.30	.75
61 Mike Morreale	.30	.75
62 Marcus Brady	.30	.75

63 Wayne Shaw .15 .40
64 Danny McManus .75 2.00
65 David Hack .15 .40
66 Agustin Barrenechea .15 .40
67 Marcus Crandell .40 1.00
68 Jay McNeil .15 .40
69 Scott Deibert .15 .40
70 John Grace .50 1.25
71 Michael Juhasz .15 .40
72 Matt McKnight .15 .40
73 Joseph Bonaventura .15 .40
74 Tyler Lynem .15 .40
75 Selucio Sanford .15 .40
76 Seth Dittman .15 .40
77 Nikolas Lewis .40 1.00
78 Marc Mitchell .15 .40
79 Joe Fleming .60 1.50
80 Keith Stokes .50 1.25
81 Eric Carter .15 .40
82 Troy Westwood .15 .40
83 Jon Ryan .15 .40
84 Chris Cvetkovic .15 1.00
85 Cory Olynick .15 .40
86 Tom Canada .15 .40
87 Dave Ritchie CO .15 .40
88 Orlando Bobo .15 .40
89 Cory Annett .15 .40
90 Jermese Jones .15 .40
91 Todd Krenbrink .15 .40
92 Dan Gyetvai .15 .40
93 Mo Elewonibi .20 .50
94 Noah Cantor .20 .50
95 Andre Talbot .20 .50
96 Raphael Ball .15 .40
97 Chad Folk .15 .40
98 Bashir Levingston .30 .75
99 Tony Miles .30 .75
100 Jude St. John .15 .40
101 Scott Krause .30 .75
102 Gabe Robinson .15 .40
103 Jeff Johnson .15 .40
104 Sandy Annunziata .15 .40
105 Jason Maas .60 1.50
106 Shannon Garrett .15 .40
107 A.J. Gass .15 .40
108 Mike Bradley .15 .40
109 Glen Carson .15 .40
110 Ed Hervey .40 1.00
111 Josh Ranek .75 2.00
112 Roger Dunbrack .20 .50
113 Dave Donaldson .20 .50
114 Ibrahim Khan .15 .40
115 Val St. Germain .15 .40
116 Gerald Vaughn .15 .40
117 Steven Glenn .15 .40
118 Mike Abou-Mechrek .15 .40
119 Serge Darryl-Sejour .15 .40
120 Mike Sutherland .15 .40
121 Donnie Ruiz .15 .40
122 Anthony Malbrough .20 .50
123 Kyries Hebert .20 .50
124 Nealon Greene .50 1.25
125 Ducarmel Augustin .15 .40
126 Henry Burris 1.25 3.00
127 Lawrence Deck .15 .40
128 Jason French .15 .40
129 Corey Holmes .60 1.50
130 Omarr Morgan .15 .40
131 Corey Grant .20 .50
132 Santino Hall .15 .40
133 Dennis Mavrin .15 .40
134 Elijah Thurmon .15 .40
135 Paul McCallum .30 .75
136 Mike McCullough .15 .40
137 Trevis Smith .15 .40
138 Bryan Chiu .30 .75
139 Duane Butler .15 .40
140 Almondo Curry .15 .40
141 Brian Nugent .15 .40
142 Dave Stala .30 .75
143 William Loftus .15 .40
144 Paul Lambert .15 .40
145 Uzooma Okeke .15 .40
146 Ezra Landry .60 1.50
147 Stephen McAdoo CO .15 .40
148 Jason Clermont .75 2.00
149 Otis D. Floyd Jr. .15 .40
150 Charles Thomas .15 .40
151 Dante Booker .15 .40
152 Bret Anderson .20 .50
153 Duncan O'Mahony .15 .40
154 Dave Heasman .15 .40
155 Frank Cutolo 1.00 2.50
156 Dante Marsh .15 .40
157 Tyrone Williams .15 .40
158 Eddie A. Linscomb .15 .40
159 Jason Crumb .15 .40
160 Carl Kidd .30 .75
161 Casey Printers 2.00 5.00
162 Da'Shann Austin .15 .40
163 Wally Buono CO .15 .40
164 Paris Jackson .15 .40
165 Ibrahim Tounkara .20 .50
166 Ryan Donnelly .15 .40
167 Julian Radlein .20 .50
168 Sandy Beveridge .15 .40
169 Rob Hitchcock .15 .40
170 Ray Thomas .15 .40
171 Frantz Clarkson .15 .40
172 Adriano Belli .15 .40
173 Charles Assmann .15 .40
174 Matt Robichaud .15 .40
175 Joey Boese .20 .50
176 Greg Schaefer .15 .40
177 Taylor Robertson .15 .40
178 William Fields .15 .40
179 Brian Clark .15 .40
180 George R. White .15 .40
181 Scott Coe .15 .40
182 Michael Fletcher .20 .50
183 Jamie Crysdale .20 .50
184 Jeff Pilon .15 .40
185 Charlie Hebert .15 .40
186 Wade Miller .15 .40
187 Robert Gordon .30 .75
188 Melvin Bradley .15 .40
189 Markus Howell .20 .50
190 Dave Mudge .15 .40
191 Derrick J. Smith .15 .40
192 Marcel Smith .15 .40
193 Milt Stegall .60 1.50
194 Jamie Stoddard .20 .50
195 Elfrid Payton .20 .50
196 Kevin Glenn .30 .75
197 Charles Roberts .75 2.00
198 Noel Prefontaine .15 .40
199 Mike Mihelic .15 .40
200 Orlondo Steinauer .15 .40
201 Adrion Smith .20 .50
202 Damon Allen .75 2.00
203 Danny Frame .15 .40
204 John Williams II .15 .40
205 David Costa .15 .40
206 Mark Moroz .15 .40
207 Frank Hoffmann .15 .40
208 John Feugill .15 .40
209 Aaron Fiacconi .15 .40
210 Jason Johnson .15 .40
211 Mike Pringle .75 2.00
212 Harold Nash Jr. .15 .40
213 Scott Schultz .20 .50
214 Gilles Lezi .15 .40
215 Tim Prinsen .15 .40
216 Kevin Lefsrud .15 .40
217 Scott Robinson .15 .40
218 Andrew Nowacki .15 .40
219 Dan Comiskey .15 .40
220 Marc Pilon .20 .50
221 Anthony Calvillo 1.00 2.50
222 Fred Childress .20 .50
223 Barron Miles .30 .75
224 Anwar Stewart .30 .75
225 Kwame Cavil .30 .75
226 Chris Burns .15 .40
227 David Azzi .15 .40
228 Jason Kralt .15 .40
229 Pat Woodcock .30 .75
230 Samir Chahine .15 .40
231 Daved Benefield .30 .75
232 Philip Gibson .15 .40
233 Dennis Gile .15 .40
234 Andrew Greene .30 .75
235 Kennedy Nkeyasen .15 .40
236 Ryan Folk .15 .40
237 Terrell Jurineack .15 .40
238 Neal Hughes .15 .40
239 Kenton Keith .75 2.00
240 Matt Dominguez .60 1.50
241 Mathieu Bertrand .15 .40
242 Benjamin Sankey .15 .40
243 Sean Spender .15 .40
244 Imokhai Atogwe .15 .40
245 Thyron Anderson .30 .75
246 Arland Bruce .30 .75
247 Mike O'Shea .30 .75
248 Chuck Walsh .15 .40
249 Clifford Ivory .15 .40
250 Kenny Wheaton .15 .40
251 Mike Crumb .15 .40
252 Joe Fleming .60 1.50
253 Pascal Masson .15 .40
254 Randy Bowles .20 .50
255 Stanley Jackson .30 .75
256 Khari Jones .75 2.00
257 Wes Lysack .15 .40
258 Bobby Singh .15 .40
259 Mike Benevides CO .15 .40
260 Chris Hoople .15 .40
261 Marques McFadden .15 .40
262 Angus Reid .15 .40
263 Carl Gourgues .15 .40
264 Gerald Harris .15 .40
265 Patrick Dorvelus .15 .40
266 Tim Kearse CO .15 .40
267 Antonio Wilson .15 .40
268 A.K. Keyes .15 .40
269 Tim Gilligan .15 .40
270 Mike Homewood .15 .40
NNO Admiral Renbow Co. Promo .20 .50
NNO Damon Allen Grey Cup MVP 1.50 4.00
NNO Neil McEvoy CO .20 .50
NNO Marc & Jeff Pilon's Camp .30 .75
NNO Geroy Simon 2.00 5.00

2005 JOGO

JOGO celebrated its 25th year in 2005 as one of the longest running annual card sets. Reportedly 400 numbered sets were made for hobby distribution with 100-additional sets being issued directly to the players themselves. The cards feature a white border along with the standard JOGO cardback format printed within a brown frame. Three different series were produced along with a black bordered gold foil parallel version of each card.

COMPLETE SET (200) 60.00 110.00
*GOLD: .8X TO 2X BASIC CARDS
1A Ezra Landry .60 1.50
1B Ezra Landry 1.00 2.50
(mentions Hurricane Katrina on back)
2 Uzooma Okeke .20 .50
3 Ed Philion .20 .50
4 Mawuko Tugbenyoh .20 .50
5 Mike Vilimek .20 .50
6 Scott Flory .20 .50
7 Luke Fritz .20 .50
8 Sean Weston .20 .50
9 Paul Lambert .20 .50
10 Dave Stala .30 .75
11 Dave Mudge .20 .50
12 O'Neil Wilson .20 .50
13A Robert Edwards .60 1.50
(white jersey photo)
13B Robert Edwards .75 2.00
(red jersey photo)
14 Kerry Watkins .75 2.00
15 Ben Cahoon .75 2.00
16 Jason Armstead .50 1.25
17 Anthony Collier .50 1.25
18 Jason Kralt .20 .50
19 Quincy Coleman .20 .50
20 Donnie Ruiz .20 .50
21 Jerome Haywood .40 1.00
22 Kyries Hebert .30 .75
23 Mike Crumb .20 .50
24 Jude St.John .20 .50
25 Jon Landon .20 .50
26 Noah Cantor .30 .75
27 Kris Aiken .20 .50
28 Chad Folk .20 .50
29 David Costa .20 .50
30 Tony Miles .40 1.00
31A Damon Allen ERR 2.00 5.00
(Hamilton)
31B Damon Allen COR .75 2.00
(Toronto)
32 Wayne Shaw .20 .50
33 Rob Hitchcock .20 .50
34 David Hack .20 .50
35 Jon'ta Woodard .20 .50
36 Mat Petz .20 .50
37 Wayne Smith .20 .50
38 Danny McManus .60 1.50
39 Mike Morreale .40 1.00
40 Roger Dunbrack .30 .75
41 Jamie Boreham .20 .50
42 D.J. Flick .40 1.00
43A Agustin Barrenechea .20 .50
(last line on back reads:/ including one for...)
43B Agustin Barrenechea .75 2.00
(last line on back reads:/ touchdown)
44 DeVonte Peterson .20 .50
45 Jason Goss .20 .50
46 Marwan Hage .20 .50
47 Renard Cox .20 .50
48 Chris Martin .20 .50
49 Aaron Fiacconi .20 .50
50 Mike Abou-Mechrek .20 .50
51 Martin Lapostolle .20 .50
52A Kevin Glenn .40 1.00
(white jersey photo)
52B Kevin Glenn .60 1.50
(gold jersey photo)
53 Joe Fleming .60 1.50
54 Shawn Gallant .20 .50
55 Wes Lysack .20 .50
56 Keith Stokes .50 1.25
57 Stanford Samuels .20 .50
58 Omar Evans .20 .50
59 Matt Sheridan .20 .50
60 Sean Woodson .20 .50
61 Troy Westwood .20 .50
62 Gilles Colon .20 .50
63 Chris Cvetkovic .50 1.25
64 Jon Ryan .60 1.50
65 Gavin Walls .75 2.00
66 Jeremy O'Day .30 .75
67 Eddie Davis .20 .50
68 Rob Lazeo .20 .50
69 Gene Makowsky .20 .50
70 Chris Szarka .30 .75
71 Davin Bush .20 .50
72 Reggie Hunt .20 .50
73 Scott Gordon .20 .50
74A Corey Holmes .60 1.50
(both hands on ball)
74B Corey Holmes 1.00 2.50
(football in right hand)
75A Kenton Keith .60 1.50
(white jersey photo)
75B Kenton Keith 1.00 2.50
(green jersey photo)
76 Nealon Greene .60 1.50
77 Jay McNeil .20 .50
78 George White .20 .50
79 Marc Mitchell .20 .50
80 Pascal Masson .20 .50
81 Taylor Robertson .20 .50
82 Jamie Crysdale .30 .75
83 Sandro DeAngelis .20 .50
84 Sheldon Napastuk .20 .50
85 Bobby Singh .20 .50
86 Marc-Falande Calixte .20 .50
87 Godfrey Ellis .20 .50
88 Burke Dales .20 .50
89 Duncan O'Mahony .20 .50
90 Ryan Phillips .20 .50
91 Moe Elewonibi .30 .75
92 Tyson Craiggs .20 .50
93 Paris Jackson .75 2.00
94 Javier Glatt .20 .50
95 Jason Crumb .20 .50
96A Cory Mantyka ERR .20 .50
(last line of text/ cut off on back)
96B Cory Mantyka COR .75 2.00
(last line of text on/ back ends: ...in my life)
97 Angus Reid .20 .50
98 Jamal Powell .20 .50
99 Tony Tiller .20 .50
100 Jason Gavadza .20 .50
101 Antico Dalton .20 .50
102 Geroy Simon .60 1.50
103 Anwar Stewart .50 1.25
104 Matt Kellett .20 .50
105 Anthony Calvillo 1.00 2.50
106 Kerry Joseph .75 2.00
107A Dave Dickenson 1.25 3.00
(orange jersey photo)
107B Dave Dickenson 1.50 4.00
(black jersey photo)
108 Henry Burris .75 2.00
109A Casey Printers 1.00 2.50
(orange jersey photo)
109B Casey Printers 1.50 4.00
(white jersey photo)
110A Milton Stegall .60 1.50
(white jersey photo)
110B Milton Stegall 1.00 2.50
(gold jersey photo)
111 Bryan Chiu .40 1.00
112 Don Matthews .40 1.00
113 Sylvain Girard .30 .75
114 Richard Karikari .20 .50
115 Clinton Wayne .20 .50
116 Trey Young .20 .50
117 Brian Clark .20 .50
118 Randy Chevrier .20 .50
119 Joey Boese .30 .75
120 Eric Lapointe .30 .75
121 Corey Grant .30 .75
122 Jeff Pilon .20 .50
123 Lawrence Deck .20 .50
124 Joffrey Reynolds 1.25 3.00
125 Jeff Johnson .20 .50
126 Val St.Germain .20 .50
127 Darryl Ray .20 .50
128 Marc Pilon .30 .75
129 David Azzi .20 .50
130 Marc Parenteau .20 .50
131 Josh Ranek .60 1.50
132 Mike Sutherland .20 .50
133 John Williams .20 .50
134 Mike O'Shea .40 1.00
135 Ray Mariuz .20 .50
136 Adrion Smith .30 .75
137 Jesse Lumsden 1.00 2.50
138 Tom Menas CO .20 .50
139 Arland Bruce .60 1.50
140 Khari Jones .60 1.50
141 Tim Cheatwood .40 1.00
142 Jon Beutjer .20 .50
143 Jykine Bradley .20 .50
144 Antwoine Sanders .20 .50
145 James Cotton .50 1.25
146 Ryan Donnelly .20 .50
147 Marcus Crandell .50 1.25
148 Elijah Thurmon .40 1.00
149 Scott Schultz .30 .75
150 Karsten Bailey .20 .50
151 Andrew Greene .40 1.00
152 Dustin Cherniawski .20 .50
153 Darnell Edwards .20 .50
154 Marcus Adams .20 .50
155 Santino Hall .20 .50
156 Steven Glenn .20 .50
157 Ibrahim Tounkara .30 .75
158 Charles Roberts .60 1.50
159 Wade Miller .20 .50
160 Jamie Stoddard .30 .75
161 William Fields .20 .50
162 Airabin Justin .20 .50
163 Boyd Barrett .20 .50
164 John Sullivan .20 .50
165 Dan Gyetvai .20 .50
166 Scott Robinson .20 .50
167 Tom Canada .20 .50
168 Cedric Dickerson .20 .50
169 John Feugill .20 .50
170 Brad Franklin .20 .50
171 Barron Miles .40 1.00
172 Kelly Bates .20 .50
173A Buck Pierce .75 2.00
(white jersey photo)
173B Buck Pierce 1.25 3.00
(black jersey photo)
174 Aaron Lockett .20 .50
175 Antonio Warren .20 .50
176 Dante Marsh .20 .50
177 Otis Floyd .20 .50
178 Clifford Ivory .20 .50
179 Tim Fleiszer .20 .50
180 Kelly Wiltshire .20 .50
181 Andrew Nowacki .20 .50
182 Bruce Beaton .20 .50
183 Shannon Garrett .20 .50
184 Kevin Lefsrud .20 .50
185 Sandy Annunziata .20 .50
186 Ronald McClendon .60 1.50
187 Steve Charbonneau .20 .50
188 Tony Tompkins .60 1.50
189 Joe Montford .40 1.00
190A Ricky Ray 1.50 4.00
(white jersey photo)
190B Ricky Ray 2.50 6.00
(green jersey photo)
191 Mike Bradley .20 .50
192 Crance Clemons .20 .50
193 A.J. Gass .20 .50
194 Trevor Gaylor .50 1.25
195 Jason Clermont .75 2.00
196 Carl Kidd .60 1.50
197 Bryan Crawford .20 .50
198 Tony White .20 .50
199 Vinny Sutherland .30 .75
200 Carl Gourgues .20 .50
NNO Jason Gavadza .60 1.50
(RE
MAX Realty Promo)
NNO Rik Fedyck Photo. .50 1.25
NNO John Sokolowski Photo. .50 1.25

2005 JOGO Athletes in Action

This 8-card set was produced by JOGO for Athletes in Action. Each card includes the AIA logo on the front and a religious message on the back. A Black Border Gold version of each card was also produced with a stated print run of 125.

COMPLETE SET (7) 4.00 8.00
*GOLD: .8X TO 2X BASIC CARDS
1 Anthony Calvillo .60 1.50
2 Anwar Stewart .60 1.50
3 Kerry Joseph .60 1.50
4 Kelly Malveaux .40 1.00
5 Rob Brown .40 1.00
6 Steve Kearns Chap. .20 .50
7 Ryan Dawson Chaplain .20 .50
8 Mark Washington .75 2.00

2006 JOGO

COMPLETE SET (165) 60.00 110.00
*WHITE BORDER: .8X TO 2X BLACK BORDER
1 Milton Stegall .75 2.00
2 Kevin Glenn .40 1.00
3 Gavin Walls .30 .75
4 Matt Sheridan .20 .50
5 Ron Warner .20 .50
6 Donnavan Carter .20 .50
7 Charles Roberts .60 1.50
8 Val St.Germain .20 .50
9 Adrian Baird .20 .50
10 Kyries Hebert .30 .75
11 Barrin Simpson .20 .50
12 Omar Evans .20 .50
13 Tom Canada .20 .50
14 Albert Johnson .20 .50
15 Ron Ockimey .20 .50
16 Shawn Gallant .20 .50
17 Stanford Samuels .20 .50
18 Chris Brazzell .30 .75
19 Chris Cvetkovic .50 1.25
20 Graeme Bell .20 .50
21 Mike Quinn .40 1.00
22 Arjei Franklin .30 .75
23 Terrence Edwards .30 1.00
24 Sylvain Girard .30 .75
25 Jeff Piercy .20 .50
26 Dave Mudge .20 .50
27 Eric Lapointe .20 .50
28 Dario Romero .20 .50
29 Ed Philion .20 .50
30 Paul Lambert .20 .50
31 Anthony Calvillo 1.00 2.50
32 Luke Fritz .20 .50
33 Scott Flory .20 .50
34 Kai Ellis .30 .75
35 Dave Stala .30 .75
36 Matthieu Proulx .20 .50
37 Jerome Haywood .40 1.00
38 Uzo Okeke .20 .50
39 Mike Vilimek .20 .50
40 Bryan Chiu .40 1.00
41 Kenton Keith .60 1.50
42 Ryan Phillips .20 .50
43 Donnie Ruiz .20 .50
44 Ibrahim Tounkara .30 .75
45 Scott Schultz .30 .75
46 Luca Congi .20 .50
47 Marcus Crandell .50 1.25
48 Rob Lazeo .20 .50
49 Jason Armstead .50 1.25
50 Corey Grant .30 .75
51 Kerry Joseph .60 2.00
52 Jeremy O'Day .30 .75
53 Jason French .20 .50
54 Dustin Cherniawski .20 .50
55 Gene Makowsky .20 .50
56 Jackie Mitchell .20 .50
57 Andrew Greene .40 1.00
58 Chris Szarka .30 .75
59 Jamel Richardson .75 2.00
60 Reggie Hunt .20 .50
61 Jocelyn Frenette .20 .50
62 Neal Hughes .20 .50
63 Eddie Davis .20 .50
64 Matt Dominguez .50 1.25
65 Tristan Clovis .20 .50
66 Kitwana Jones .20 .50
67 Luc Mullinder .20 .50
68 Fred Perry .20 .50
69 Mike Mahoney .20 .50
70 Dominique Dorsey .75 2.00
71 Freddie Childress .20 .50
72 Andy Fantuz .40 1.00
73 Joffrey Reynolds 1.00 2.50
74 Jeff Pilon .20 .50
75 Pascal Masson .20 .50
76 Jay McNeil .20 .50
77 Elijah Thurmon .40 1.00
78 Tony Tiller .20 .50
79 Brian Clark .20 .50
80 John Comiskey .20 .50
81 Sandro DeAngelis .20 .50
82 Trey Young .20 .50
83 Nik Lewis .75 2.00
84 Danny McManus .60 1.50
85 Taylor Robertson .20 .50
86 Marc Mitchell .20 .50
87 Wes Lysack .20 .50
88 Henry Burris .60 1.50
89 Wes Cates 1.25 3.00
90 J.R. Ruffin .20 .50
91 John Grace 1.25
92 Khalid Abdullah .20 .50
93 Jermaine Chatman .20 .50
94 Angus Reid .20 .50
95 Paul McCallum .40 1.00
96 Tim Bakker .20 .50
97 Malcolm Frank .20 .50
98 Mike Maurer .30 .75
99 Kelly Wiltshire .20 .50
100 Shannon Garrett .20 .50
101 Pat Woodcock .40 1.00
102 Ricky Ray 1.25 3.00
103 Marcus Winn .20 .50
104 Rob Brown .20 .50
105 Adam Braidwood .20 .50
106 Jonte' Buhl .20 .50
107 Anthony Malbrough .30 .75
108 Rob LeBlanc .20 .50
109 Ibrahim Obby Khan .20 .50
110 John Jenkins CO .30 .75
111 John Sullivan .20 .50
112 Ian Logan .20 .50
113 Shockmain Davis .20 .50
114 Marc Parenteau .20 .50
115 Jean-Philippe Abraham .20 .50
116 Damon Allen .75 2.00
117 David Azzi .20 .50
118 Chad Folk .20 .50
119 David Costa .20 .50
120 Orlondo Steinauer .20 .50
121 Jude St.John .20 .50
122 Byron Parker .20 .50
123 Mike O'Shea .40 1.00
124 J.D. Davis .20 .50
125 Matthew Kudu .20 .50
126 Ricky Williams 1.50 4.00
127 Clifford Ivory .20 .50
128 Agustin Barrenechea .20 .50
129 Ryan Folk .20 .50
130 Etienne Boulay .20 1.00
131 Davis Sanchez .20 .50
132 R-Kal Truluck .20 .50
133 Jim Popp VP .20 .50
134 Roger Dunbrack .30 .75
135 Richard Karikari .20 .50
136 Bobby Singh .20 .50
137 Geroy Simon .50 1.25
138 Aaron Lockett .30 .75
139 Mark Washington .30 .75
140 Miguel Robede .20 .50
141 Walter Spencer-Robinson .20 .50
142 Kelly Bates .20 .50
143 Brent Johnson .30 .75
144 Korey Banks .20 .50
145 Carl Kidd .40 1.00
146 Rob Murphy .20 .75
147 Aaron Hunt .20 .50
148 Tony Simmons .30 .75
149 Jason Jimenez .20 .50
150 Ricky Foley .20 .50
151 Dave Dickenson 1.25 3.00
152 Rob Pikula .20 .50
153 William Loftus .20 .50
154 Richard Dwight Alston .20 .50
155 James Cotton .50 1.25
156 Cornelius Anthony .20 .50
157 Jason Maas .50 1.25
158 Ray Mariuz .20 .50
159 DeVonte Peterson .20 .50
160 Jason Tucker .40 1.00
161 Steven Jyles .30 .75
162 Corey Holmes .40 1.00
163 Jarious Jackson .60 1.50
164 George Hudson .30 .75
165 Marwan Hage .20 .50
NNO Damon Allen/100* 10.00 20.00
Marcus Allen
Warren Moon

2006 JOGO Rookies

COMPLETE SET (14) 15.00 30.00
1R Joe Smith 1.25 3.00
2R Chip Cox 1.25 3.00
3R Kendrick Jones 2.00 5.00
4R Eric Crouch 1.25 3.00
5R Kahlil Carter 1.25 3.00
6R Coby Rhinehart 1.25 3.00
7R Dahrran Diedrick 1.25 3.00
8R Jordan Younger 1.25 3.00
9R Rontarius Robinson 1.50 4.00
10R Shermar Bracey 1.50 4.00
11R Robert Bean 1.25 3.00
12R Avon Cobourne 1.25 3.00
13R Cedrick Williams 1.25 3.00
14R DaVon Fowlkes 1.25 3.00

2006 JOGO Variations and Short Prints

COMPLETE SET (15) 15.00 30.00
1V Milt Stegall 1.50 4.00
2V Ricky Williams 2.50 6.00
6V Brent Johnson 1.25 3.00
10V Ricky Ray 2.00 5.00
15V Geroy Simon 1.25 3.00
3SP Arland Bruce 1.00 2.50
4SP Ben Cahoon 1.00 2.50
5SP Keyuo Craver 1.00 2.50
7SP Ken-Yon Rambo 1.25 3.00
8SP Barron Miles 1.00 2.50
9SP Buck Pierce .75 2.00
11SP Rocky Butler 1.00 2.50
12SP Jesse Lumsden 1.00 2.50
13SP Jermaine Copeland 1.25 3.00
14SP Terry Vaughn 1.25 3.00

2007 JOGO

COMPLETE SET (175) 60.00 110.00
1 Bryan Chiu .40 1.00
2 Luke Fritz .30 .75
3 Scott Flory .30 .75
4 Matthieu Proulx .30 .75
5 Mike Vilimek .30 .75
6 Dave Mudge .30 .75
7 Paul Lambert .30 .75
8 Etienne Boulay .40 1.00
9 Shawn Gallant .30 .75
10 Jeff Perrett .30 .75
11 T.J. Hill .30 .75
12 Danny Desriveaux .30 .75
13 Brian Bratton .30 .75
14 Skip Seagraves .30 .75
15 Cory Huclack .30 .75
16 Marcus Brady .30 .75
17 Ashlan Davis .30 .75
18 Devone Claybrooks .30 .75
19 Jarrett Payton .60 1.50
20 John Bowman .30 .75
21 Chris Vrantsis .30 .75
22 Jesse Hendrix .30 .75
23 Rob Murphy .40 1.00
24 Angus Reid .30 .75
25 Jason Clermont .60 1.50
26 Barron Miles .40 1.00
27 Geroy Simon .50 1.25
28 Tyson Craiggs .30 .75
29 Buck Pierce .60 1.50
30 Javier Glatt .30 .75
31 Sebastian Clovis .30 .75
32 Ryan Phillips .30 .75
33 Tad Crawford .30 .75
34 Jason Pottinger .30 .75
35 Sherko Rasouli .30 .75
36 Brent Johnson .40 1.00
37 Kelly Bates .30 .75
38 Chad Folk .30 .75
39 Jude St.John .30 .75
40 Orlondo Steinauer .30 .75
41 David Costa .30 .75
42 Bryan Crawford .30 .75
43 Tony Miles .40 1.00
44 Taylor Robertson .30 .75
45 Glenn January .30 .75
46 Brian Ramsay .30 .75
47 Jay McNeil .30 .75
48 Burke Dales .30 .75
49 Pat McDonald .30 .75
50 J.R. Ruffin .30 .75
51 Ken-Yon Rambo .75 2.00
52 Henry Burris .60 1.50
53 Bobby Singh .30 .75
54 Wes Lysack .30 .75
55 Sandro DeAngelis .30 .75
56 Brian Clark .30 .75
57 Scott Coe .30 .75
58 Jeff Pilon .30 .75
59 Pascal Masson .30 .75
60 Justin Phillips .30 .75
61 Sadrick Williams .30 .75
62 Rob Lazeo .30 .75
63 Rob Cote .30 .75
64 Terrence Patrick .30 .75
65 Crance Clemons .30 .75
66 Trey Young .30 .75
67 John Comiskey .30 .75
68 Marwan Hage .30 .75
69 Tay Cody .40 1.00
70 George Hudson .40 1.00
71 Jermaine Reid .30 .75
72 Chris Bauman .30 .75
73 Julian Radlein .30 .75
74 Jason French .30 .75
75 Nate Curry .30 .75
76 Joseph Walker .30 .75
77 Brock Ralph .30 .75
78 Jason Armstead .50 1.25
79 Jesse Lumsden .60 1.50
80 Peter Dyakowski .30 .75
81 Pascal Cheron .30 .75
82 Ryan Donnelly .30 .75
83 Kori Dickerson .30 .75
84 Sandy Beveridge .30 .75
85 JoJuan Armour .40 1.00
86 Dwight Anderson .30 .75
87 Shannon Garrett .30 .75
88 Stefan Lefors .30 .75
89 Scott Gordon .30 .75
90 Tyler Ebell .30 .75
91 Jean-Francois Romeo .30 .75
92 Raleigh Roundtree .30 .75
93 Matt Dominguez .50 1.25
94 Jason Goss .30 .75
95 Kenny Onatolu .30 .75
96 Siddeeq Shabazz .30 .75
97 David McKoy .30 .75
98 Sean Fleming .30 .75
99 Steven Jyles .40 1.00
100 Marcus Adams .30 .75
101 Jeremy O'Day .40 1.00
102 D.J. Flick .40 1.00
103 Kerry Joseph .75 2.00
104 Marcus Crandell .50 1.25
105 Reggie Hunt .30 .75
106 Luca Congi .30 .75
107 Chris Szarka .40 1.00
108 Fred Perry .30 .75
109 Gene Makowsky .30 .75
110 Milt Stegall .75 2.00
111 Adrian Baird .30 .75
112 Chris Brazzell .40 1.00
113 Davin Bush .30 .75
114 Tom Canada .30 .75
115 Ryan Dinwiddie 1.00 2.50
116 Terrence Edwards .40 1.00
117 Arjei Franklin .40 1.00
118 Kevin Glenn .40 1.25
119 Dan Goodspeed .30 .75
120 Andrew Greene .30 .75
121 Brian Guebert .30 .75
122 Cam Hall .30 .75
123 Jerome Haywood .40 1.00
124 Corey Jenkins .30 .75
125 Gilles Lezi .30 .75
126 Ian Logan .30 .75
127 Patrick Kabongo .30 .75
128 Anthony Malbrough .30 .75
129 Kelly Malveaux .30 .75
130 Neil McKinlay .30 .75
131 Greg Moss .30 .75
132 Jason Nugent .30 .75
133 Chijioke Onyenegecha .30 .75
134 Jon Oosterhuis .30 .75
135 Dominic Picard .30 .75
136 Rob Pikula .30 .75
137 Fred Reid .30 1.00
138 Matt Sheridan .30 .75
139 Jamie Stoddard .40 1.00
140 Gavin Walls .40 1.00
141 Troy Westwood .30 .75
142 O'Neil Wilson .30 .75
143 Corey Grant .40 1.00
144 James Johnson .40 1.00
145 Dustin Cherniawski .30 .75
146 Rontarius Robinson .30 .75
147 Aaron Fiacconi .30 .75
148 Randy Chevrier .30 .75
149 Eddie Davis .30 .75
150 Jamie Boreham .30 .75
151 Neal Hughes .30 .75
152 Michael Roberts .30 .75
153 Tim Fleiszer .30 .75
154 Kitwana Jones .30 .75
155 Maurice Lloyd .30 .75
156 Wayne Smith .30 .75
157 Jermese Jones .30 .75
158 Mark Parenteau .30 .75
159 Jocelyn Frenette .30 .75
160 Ibrahim Khan .30 .75
161 Mike Abou-Mechrek .30 .75
162 Michael Washington .30 .75
163 Andy Fantuz .40 1.00
164 Kamau Peterson .40 1.00
165 Nathan Hoffart .30 .75
166 Khalil Carter .30 .75
167 Scott Schultz .40 1.00
168 Randy Spencer .30 .75
169 Chris Jones CO .30 .75
170 Jim Popp GM .30 .75
171 Elijah Thurmon .40 1.00
172 Chip Cox .30 .75
173 Aaron Wagner .30 .75
174 Richie Williams .40 1.00
175 Mark Estelle .40 1.00

2007 JOGO Autographs

1 Bryan Chiu 12.50 25.00
2 Jeremy O'Day 12.50 25.00
3 Jay McNeil 12.50 25.00
4 Jarrett Payton 12.50 25.00
5 Brent Johnson 12.50 25.00
6 Geroy Simon 15.00 30.00
7 Kerry Joseph/65 20.00 40.00

2007 JOGO Rookies

COMPLETE SET (14) 15.00 30.00
1R Jarrett Payton 1.25 3.00
2R Barrick Nealy .75 2.00
3R Pat Johnson 1.25 3.00
4R Terry Caulley 1.00 2.50
5R Ian Smart .75 2.00
6R Frank Murphy 1.00 2.50
7R Obed Cetoute .75 2.00
8R Derek Cameron Wake 2.50 6.00
9R Zeke Moreno 1.25 3.00
10R Chris Thompson .75 2.00
11R Josh Bodon .75 2.00
12R Willie Pile 1.00 2.50
13R David Lofton .75 2.00
14R Timmy Chang 1.25 3.00

2007 JOGO Short Prints

COMPLETE SET (15) 15.00 30.00
1SP Jarious Jackson 1.50 4.00
2SP Ricky Ray 2.00 5.00
3SP Nikolas Lewis 1.00 2.50
4SP Ben Cahoon 1.00 2.50
5SP Joe Smith 1.00 2.50
6SP Barrin Simpson 1.00 2.50
7SP Derick Armstrong 1.00 2.50
8SP Anthony Calvillo 1.00 2.50
9SP Wes Cates 1.50 4.00
10SP Casey Printers 1.00 2.50
11SP Corey Holmes 1.00 2.50
12SP Charles Roberts 1.00 2.50
13SP Joffrey Reynolds 1.50 4.00
14SP Michael Bishop 1.25 3.00
15SP T.J. Acree 1.00 2.50

2007 JOGO Where Are They Now

COMPLETE SET (9) 5.00 10.00
1W Khari Jones 1.25 3.00
2W Gord Weber .50 1.25
3W Trevor Kennerd .50 1.25
4W Michel Bourgeau .50 1.25
5W Bob Young .50 1.25
6W Greg Battle .50 1.25
7W Darren Flutie .50 1.25
8W Rocco Romano .50 1.25
9W Pierre Vercheval .75 2.00

2008 JOGO

COMPLETE SET (180) 60.00 110.00
1 Jeremy O'Day .40 1.00
2 Corey Grant .40 1.00
3 Omarr Morgan .30 .75
4 Darian Durant .30 1.25
5 Marcus Crandell .50 1.25
6 Steven Jyles .40 1.00
7 Luca Congi .30 .75
8 Tad Kornegay .30 .75
9 Denatay Heard .30 .75
10 Stuart Foord .30 .75
11 Scott Gordon .30 .75
12 Eddie Davis .30 .75
13 Neal Hughes .30 .75
14 Chris Szarka .40 1.00
15 Brandon Lynch .30 .75
16 Anton McKenzie .30 .75
17 Mike McCullough .30 .75
18 Kitwana Jones .30 .75
19 Maurice Lloyd .30 .75
20 Renauld Williams .30 .75
21 Yannick Carter .30 .75

22 Marcus Adams .30 .75
23 Wayne Smith .30 .75
24 Scott Schultz .40 1.00
25 Marc Parenteau .30 .75
26 Jocelyn Frenette .30 .75
27 Gene Makowsky .30 .75
28 Steve Morley .30 .75
29 Chris Best .30 .75
30 Mike Abou-Mechrek .30 .75
31 Glenn January .30 .75
32 Michael Palmer .30 .75
33 Andy Fantuz .40 1.00
34 Dek Bake .30 .75
35 Luc Mullinder .30 .75
36 John Chick .30 .75
37 James Johnson CB .40 1.00
38 Jamie Boreham .30 .75
39 Sandro DeAngelis .30 .75
40 Dave Dickenson 1.25 3.00
41 Brett Ralph .30 .75
42 Rob Lazeo .30 .75
43 Nik Lewis .50 1.25
44 Justin Phillips .30 .75
45 Tim O'Neill .30 .75
46 Jeff Pilon .30 .75
47 Antonio Hall .30 .75
48 Jesse Newman .30 .75
49 Burke Dales .30 .75
50 Wes Lysack .30 .75
51 Miguel Robede .30 .75
52 Patrick McDonald .30 .75
53 Dimitri Tsoumpas .30 .75
54 Randy Chevrier .30 .75
55 Marc-Falande Calixte .30 .75
56 Andrew Nowacki .30 .75
57 Markus Howell .30 .75
58 Ryan Thelwell .30 .75
59 Mike Labinjo .30 .75
60 Charleston Hughes .30 .75
61 Eddie Freeman .30 .75
62 JoJuan Armour .40 1.00
63 Derek Armstrong .30 .75
64 Ben Archibald .30 .75
65 Shannon Garrett .30 .75
66 Damien Anderson .30 .75
67 Agustin Barrenechea .30 .75
68 Kevin Challenger .30 .75
69 Chris Ciezki .30 .75
70 John Comiskey .30 .75
71 Justin Cooper .30 .75
72 Jason Goss .30 .75
73 J.R. Larose .30 .75
74 Bradley Robinson .30 .75
75 Siddeeq Shabazz .30 .75
76 Tim St.Pierre .30 .75
77 Keith Williams DB .30 .75
78 Pierre-Luc Yao .30 .75
79 Trey Young .30 .75
80 Jordan Younger .30 .75
81 Fred Perry .30 .75
82 Adrian Baird .30 .75
83 Bryan Chiu .40 1.00
84 Jeff Perrett .30 .75
85 Scott Flory .30 .75
86 Josh Bourke .30 .75
87 Paul Lambert .30 .75
88 Dave Mudge .30 .75
89 Luke Fritz .30 .75
90 Alain Kashama .30 .75
91 Jeff Robertshaw .30 .75
92 Dwayne Taylor .30 .75
93 Brian Bratton .30 .75
94 Shea Emry .30 .75
95 Keron Williams .30 .75
96 Randee Drew .30 .75
97 Cory Huclack .30 .75
98 Shawn Gallant .30 .75
99 Eric Deslauriers .30 .75
100 Diamond Ferri .30 .75
101 Kai Ellis .30 .75
102 Walter Spencer .30 .75
103 Jamel Richardson .50 1.25
104 Stevie Baggs .30 .75
105 Anthony Calvillo 1.00 2.50
106 Chad Folk .30 .75
107 Jude St.John .30 .75
108 Orlondo Steinauer .30 .75
109 Byron Parker .30 .75
110 Kerry Joseph .75 2.00
111 Brian Ramsey .30 .75
112 Richard Seigler .30 .75
113 Randy Srochenski .30 .75
114 Mark Dewitt .30 .75
115 Chuck Winters .30 .75
116 Aaron Wagner .30 .75
117 Obed Cetoute .30 .75
118 Andre Durie .30 .75
119 Delroy Clarke .30 .75
120 Nathan Hoffart .30 .75
121 Arland Bruce III .50 1.25
122 Taylor Robertson .30 .75
123 Jean-Nicolas Carriere .30 .75
124 Tyler Scott .30 .75
125 Steve Schmidt .30 .75
126 Mike O'Shea .40 1.00
127 Ross Weaver .30 .75
128 Sebastian Clovis .30 .75
129 Jeff Johnson RB .30 .75
130 Milt Stegall .75 2.00
131 Gavin Walls .30 .75
132 Fred Reid .30 1.00
133 Steven Balarama Holness .30 .75
134 Ryan Dinwiddie .60 1.50
135 Anthony Malbrough .30 .75
136 Marcus Winn .30 .75
137 Chris Cvetkovic .50 1.25
138 Derick Armstrong .30 .75
139 Jerome Haywood .40 1.00
140 Pierre-Luc Labbe .30 .75
141 Arjei Franklin .30 .75
142 Kyle Koch .30 .75
143 Jamie Stoddard .40 1.00
144 Anthony Maggiacomo .30 .75
145 Ian Logan .30 .75
146 Graeme Bell .30 .75
147 Jovon Johnson .30 .75
148 Ryan Donnelly .30 .75
149 Aaron Hargreaves .30 .75
150 Brian Guebert .30 .75
151 Shawn Mayne .30 .75
152 Brendon LaBatte .30 .75
153 Angus Reid .30 .75
154 Kelly Bates .30 .75
155 Dean Valli .30 .75
156 Jarious Jackson .60 1.50
157 Tyrone Williams DT .30 .75
158 Otis Floyd .30 .75
159 Paul McCallum .40 1.00
160 Lavar Glover .30 .75
161 Javier Glatt .30 .75
162 Dante Marsh .30 .75
163 Korey Banks .30 .75
164 Dan McCullough .30 .75
165 Jerome Dennis .30 .75
166 Tad Crawford .30 .75
167 Rolly Lumbala .30 .75
168 George Hudson .40 1.00
169 Jason Nedd .30 .75
170 Richie Williams .40 1.00
171 Ray Mariuz .30 .75
172 Chris Thompson .30 .75
173 Jykine Bradley .30 .75
174 Lawrence Gordon .30 .75
175 Marko Cavka .30 .75
176 Markeith Knowlton .30 .75
177 Peter Dyakowski .30 .75
178 Marwan Hage .30 .75
179 Jim Popp CO .30 .75
180 Tony Miles .40 1.00
NNO Weston Dressler 1.25 3.00

2008 JOGO Autographs

1S Angus Reid/118 12.50 25.00
2S Buck Pierce/124 20.00 40.00
3S Sandro DeAngelis/127 12.50 25.00
4S George Hudson/124 12.50 25.00
5S Shannon Garrett/118 12.50 25.00
6S Ricky Ray/116 20.00 40.00
7S Wes Cates/121 15.00 30.00
8S Kerry Joseph/124 20.00 40.00
9S Ben Cahoon/117 15.00 30.00
10S Jesse Lumsden/111 12.50 25.00

2008 JOGO Rookies

COMPLETE SET (15) 15.00 30.00
1R Stefan Logan 1.25 3.00
2R Adarius Bowman 1.00 2.50
3R James Patrick 1.25 3.00
4R Brandon Smith .75 2.00
5R Demetris Summers .75 2.00
6R A.J. Harris .75 2.00
7R Tristan Jackson 1.25 3.00
8R Zac Champion .75 2.00
9R Bryan Randall .75 2.00
10R Quinton Porter 1.25 3.00
11R Romby Bryant 1.25 3.00
12R Kelly Campbell 1.00 2.50
13R Adrian McPherson 1.00 2.50
14R Jamal Robertson 1.00 2.50
15R Larry Taylor 2.00

2008 JOGO Short Prints

COMPLETE SET (15) 20.00 35.00
1SP Jesse Lumsden 1.25 2.50
2SP Ken-Yon Rambo 1.50 4.00
3SP Henry Burris 1.50 4.00
4SP Michael Bishop 1.50 4.00
5SP Wes Cates 1.50 4.00
6SP Fred Stamps 1.00 2.50
7SP Ricky Ray 1.50 4.00
8SP Geroy Simon 1.25 3.00
9SP Avon Cobourne 1.25 3.00
10SP Doug Brown 1.00 2.50
11SP Dominique Dorsey 1.50 4.00
12SP Calvin McCarty 1.00 2.50
13SP Buck Pierce 1.50 4.00
14SP Joffrey Reynolds 1.00 2.50
15SP Matt Dominguez 3.00

2009 JOGO

COMPLETE SET (180) 60.00 110.00
1 Ricky Ray .60 1.50
2 Aaron Fiacconi .30 .75
3 Kyle Koch .30 .75
4 Jesse Lumsden .60 1.50
5 Taylor Inglis .40 1.00
6 Jonte Buhl .30 .75
7 Justin Cooper .30 .75
8 Lenny Williams .30 .75
9 Kitwana Jones .30 .75
10 Kevin Challenger .30 .75
11 Elliott Richardson .30 .75
12 Maurice Lloyd .30 .75
13 Dario Romero .40 1.00
14 Jason Nugent .30 .75
15 Calvin McCarty .30 .75
16 Graeme Bell .30 .75
17 Joe McGrath .30 .75
18 Eric Taylor .30 .75
19 Mark Restelli .30 .75
20 Kamau Peterson .40 1.00
21 John Comiskey .30 .75
22 Fred Stamps .50 1.25
23 Bryan Chiu .40 1.00
24 John N. Bowman .30 .75
25 Etienne Boulay .40 1.00
26 Matthieu Proulx .30 .75
27 Paul Lambert .30 .75
28 Jerald Brown .30 .75
29 Skip Seagraves .30 .75
30 Josh Bourke .30 .75
31 Jeff Perrett .30 .75
32 Kerry Ocei Carter .30 .75
33 Scott Flory .30 .75
34 Jeff Robertshaw .30 .75
35 Paul Woldu .30 .75
36 Jermaine McElveen .30 .75
37 S.J. Green .30 .75
38 Shea Emry .30 .75
39 Cory Huclack .30 .75
40 Doug Goldsby .30 .75
41 Brian Bratton .30 .75
42 Martin Bedard .30 .75
43 Billy Parker .30 .75
44 Luc Brodeur-Jourdain .30 .75
45 Jeremy O'Day .40 1.00
46 Renauld Williams .30 .75
47 Denatay Heard .30 .75
48 Eddie Davis .30 .75
49 Darian Durant .50 2.00
50 Rob Bagg .30 .75
51 Marc Parenteau .30 .75
52 Weston Dressler .50 1.25
53 Kye Stewart .30 .75
54 Chris Szarka .40 1.00
55 Chris Best .30 .75
56 Stevie Baggs .30 .75
57 Chris Jones .30 .75
58 Marcus Adams .30 .75
59 Andy Fantuz .40 1.00
60 Stuart Foord .30 .75
61 Hugh Charles .30 .75
62 Jerrell Freeman .30 .75
63 Chris McKenzie .30 .75
64 Aaron Wagner .30 .75
65 Nick Hutchins .30 .75
66 Jamie Boreham .30 .75
67 Wes Cates .40 1.00
68 Scott Schultz .40 1.00
69 John Chick .30 .75
70 Tad Kornegay .30 .75
71 Keith Shologan .30 .75
72 Chris Getzlaf .30 .75
73 Jocelyn Frenette .30 .75
74 Gene Makowsky .30 .75
75 James Patrick .40 1.00
76 Neal Hughes .30 .75
77 Bryan Crawford .30 .75
78 Kerry Joseph .75 2.00
79 Mike Bradwell .30 .75
80 Taylor Robertson .30 .75
81 Dominic Picard .30 .75
82 Jonta Woodard .30 .75
83 Jason Shivers .30 .75
84 Kevin Huntley .30 .75
85 Jeff Keeping .30 .75
86 Jeff Johnson .30 .75
87 Brian Ramsay .30 .75
88 Jason Pottinger .30 .75
89 Will Poole .40 1.00
90 Jordan Younger .30 .75
91 James Green .30 .75
92 Etienne Legare .30 .75
93 Andre Durie .30 .75
94 Chad Rempel .30 .75
95 Mark Dewitt .30 .75
96 Matthew Black .30 .75
97 Adrian Davis .30 .75
98 Lin-J Sheil .30 .75
99 Claude Harriott .30 .75
100 Joel Lipinski .30 .75
101 Justin Sorensen .30 .75
102 O'Neil Wilson .30 .75
103 Korey Banks .30 .75
104 James Yurichuk .30 .75
105 Sean Whyte .30 .75
106 Sherko Rasouli .30 .75
107 Dean Valli .30 .75
108 Buck Pierce .60 1.50
109 Jerome Dennis .30 .75
110 Angus Reid .30 .75
111 Emmanuel Arceneaux .30 .75
112 Anton McKenzie .30 .75
113 Dante Marsh .30 .75
114 Rufus Skillern .30 .75
115 Bobby Singh .30 .75
116 Ryan Grice-Mullen .40 1.00
117 Sandro DeAngelis .30 .75
118 Justin Phillips .30 .75
119 Ronnie Amadi .30 .75
120 Tim O'Neill .30 .75
121 Rob Lazeo .30 .75
122 Tristan Black .30 .75
123 Keon Raymond .30 .75
124 Randy Chevrier .30 .75
125 Ben Archibald .30 .75
126 Tom Johnson .30 .75
127 Wes Lysack .30 .75
128 Markus Howell .30 .75
129 Jesse Newman .30 .75
130 Miguel Robede .30 .75
131 Jeff Pilon .30 .75
132 Kelly Bates .30 .75
133 Steve Morley .30 .75
134 Ryan Donnelly .30 .75
135 Shawn Gallant .30 .75
136 Ian Logan .30 .75
137 Michael Bishop .60 1.50
138 Daryl Stephenson .30 .75
139 Jon Oosterhuis .30 .75
140 Mike Renaud .40 1.00
141 Aaron Hargreaves .30 .75
142 Brock Ralph .30 .75
143 Alexis Serna .30 .75
144 Siddeeq Shabazz Sr. .30 .75
145 Bryan Randall .30 .75
146 Romby Bryant .40 1.00
147 Arjei Franklin .30 .75
148 Gavin Walls .30 .75
149 Fred Reid .40 1.00
150 Chris Cvetkovic .50 1.25
151 Glenn January Jr. .30 .75
152 Luke Fritz .30 .75
153 Ray Mariuz .30 .75
154 Chris Davis .30 .75
155 Geoff Tisdale .30 .75
156 Agustin Barrenechea .30 .75
157 Markeith Knowlton .30 .75
158 Nicholas Setta .30 .75
159 Yannick Carter .30 .75
160 Jordan Matechuk .30 .75
161 Marc Beswick .30 .75
162 John Williams .30 .75
163 Dennis Haley .30 .75
164 Sandy Beveridge .30 .75
165 Chris Bauman .30 .75
166 Marwan Hage .30 .75
167 George Hudson .40 1.00
168 Robert Pavlovic .30 .75
169 Matt Robichaud .30 .75
170 Otis Floyd .30 .75
171 Peter Dyakowski .30 .75
172 Shannon Boatman .30 .75
173 Jarious Jackson .60 1.50
174 Scott Gordon .30 .75
175 Ben Cahoon .50 1.25
176 Bo Smith .30 .75
177 Jamel Richardson .50 1.25
178 Jim Popp .30 .75
179 Ron Skoler .30 .75
180 Corey Grant .40 1.00

2009 JOGO White

*WHITE: .8X TO 2X BASIC CARDS

2009 JOGO Autographs

1 Dante Marsh/126 10.00 25.00
2 Nik Lewis/124 10.00 25.00
3 Avon Cobourne/134 10.00 25.00
4 Eddie Davis
5 Fred Reid/130 12.00 30.00
6 Kevin Glenn
7 Jesse Lumsden/133 10.00 25.00
8 John Comiskey/134 8.00 20.00
9 Andy Fantuz
10 Jim Popp

2009 JOGO Rookies

COMPLETE SET (15) 15.00 30.00
*WHITE: .8X TO 2X BASIC CARDS
1R Casey Bramlet .75 2.00
2R DeAndra Cobb 1.00 2.50
3R Martell Mallett .75 2.00
4R Arkee Whitlock 1.25 3.00
5R Brandon Browner .75 2.00
6R Jermaine Jackson .75 2.00
7R Jamaica Rector 1.00 2.50
8R Marquay McDaniel .75 2.00
9R Adam Tafralis .75 2.00
10R Travis Lulay 1.00 2.50
11R Johnny Quinn .75 2.00
12R Hank Edwards .75 2.00
13R Andrew Hawkins .75 2.00
14R Chris Leak 1.25 3.00
15R Dudley Guice .75 2.00

2009 JOGO Short Prints

COMPLETE SET (15) 20.00 35.00
*WHITE: .8X TO 2X BASIC CARDS
1SP Anthony Calvillo 1.50 4.00
2SP Cody Pickett 1.25 3.00
3SP Henry Burris 1.50 4.00
4SP Avon Cobourne 1.25 3.00
5SP Maurice Mann 1.00 2.50
6SP Kerry Watkins 1.00 2.50
7SP Jamal Robertson 1.25 3.00
8SP Jermaine Copeland 1.25 3.00
9SP Geroy Simon 1.25 3.00
10SP Terrence Edwards 1.25 3.00
11SP Paris Jackson 1.00 2.50
12SP Quinton Porter 1.25 3.00
13SP Prechae Rodriguez 1.00 2.50
14SP Joffrey Reynolds 1.25 3.00
15SP Arland Bruce 1.25 3.00

2010 JOGO

COMPLETE SET (215) 75.00 140.00
COMP.SERIES 1 (190) 60.00 110.00
COMP.UPDATE SET (25) 15.00 30.00
*WHITE BORDER: .8X TO 2X BASIC CARDS
ANNOUNCED PRINT RUN 300
1 Darian Durant .75 2.00
2 Jeremy O'Day .40 1.00
3 Gene Makowsky .30 .75
4 Jocelyn Frenette .30 .75
5 Dominique Dorsey .40 1.00
6 Luc Mullinder .30 .75
7 Steve Morley .30 .75
8 Donovan Alexander .30 .75
9 Chris Szarka .40 1.00
10 Neal Hughes .30 .75
11 Wes Cates .40 1.00
12 Chris Best .30 .75
13 Ryan Dinwiddie .30 .75
14A Marc Parenteau ERR .30 .75
14B Marc Parenteau COR .75 2.00
15 Shomari Williams .30 .75
16 Rob Bagg .30 .75
17 Keith Shologan .30 .75
18 Chris Getzlaf .30 .75
19 Marcus Adams .30 .75
20 Hugh Charles .30 .75
21 Jerrell Freeman .30 .75
22 Nick Hutchins .30 .75
23 Kelly Bates .30 .75
24 Luca Congi .30 .75
25 Jason Clermont .30 .75
26A Tad Kornegay ERR .30 .75
26B Tad Kornegay COR .75 2.00
27 Stuart Foord .30 .75
28 Brent Hawkins .30 .75
29 Kitwana Jones .30 .75
30 Tamon George .30 .75
31 Bryan Crawford .30 .75
32 Jamie Boreham .30 .75
33 Jason Pottinger .30 .75
34 Taylor Robertson .30 .75
35 Jonathan St.Pierre .30 .75
36 Shannon Boatman .30 .75
37 Chad Rempel .30 .75
38 Grant Shaw .30 .75
39 Kevin Huntley .30 .75
40 Chad Lucas .30 .75
41 Ejiro Kuale .30 .75
42 Dominic Picard .30 .75
43 Peter Quinney .30 .75
44 Jordan Younger .30 .75
45 Tang Bacheyie .30 .75
46 Andre Durie .30 .75
47 Cleo Lemon .75 2.00
48 Chad Owens .30 .75
49 Ryan Christian .30 .75
50 Jeff Johnson .30 .75
51 Lin-J Shell .30 .75
52 Byron Parker .40 1.50
53 Mike Bradwell .30 .75
54 Eric Taylor .30 .75
55 Chris Van Zeyl .30 .75
56 Danny Brannagan .30 .75
57 Joe Eppele .30 .75
58 Cos DeMatteo CO .30 .75
59 Jamie Elizondo CO .40 1.00
60 Stephen McAdoo CO .30 .75
61 Orlondo Steinauer CO .40 1.00
62 Greg Quick CO .30 .75
63 Danny Webb Eq. Mgr .30 .75
64 Aaron Fiacconi .30 .75
65 Lenny Walls .30 .75
66 Chris Thompson .30 .75
67 Kyle Koch .30 .75
68 Calvin Armstrong .30 .75
69 Justin Cooper .30 .75
70 Gord Hinse .30 .75
71 Saleem Borhot .30 .75
72 Weldon Brown .60 1.50
73 Jason Nugent .30 .75
74 Lawrence Gordon .30 .75
75 Rod Williams .30 .75
76 Tristan Jackson .30 .75
77 Chris Ciezki .30 .75
78 Greg Wojt .30 .75
79 Maurice Lloyd .30 .75
80 Graeme Bell .30 .75
81 Elliott Richardson .30 .75
82 Corbin Sharun .30 .75
83 Randee Drew .30 .75
84 Rob Lazeo .30 .75
85 Dan Comiskey .30 .75
86 Ryan Thelwell .30 .75
87 Eric Fraser .30 .75
88 Keon Raymond .30 .75
89 Burke Dales .30 .75
90 Dwight Anderson .30 .75
91 Edwin Harrison .30 .75
92 Wes Lysack .30 .75
93 Justin Phillips .30 .75
94 Karl McCartney .30 .75
95 Randy Chevrier .30 .75
96A Tim O'Neill .30 .75
96B Miguel Robede ERR .30 .75
(card slated to be #102)
97 Rob Maver .30 .75
98 Arjei Franklin .30 .75
99 Michael Cornell .30 .75
100 Tristan Black .30 .75
101 DeVone Claybrooks .30 .75
103 Rob Cote .30 .75
104 Ben Archibald .30 .75
105 Romby Bryant .40 1.25
106 Jabari Arthur .30 .75
107 Corey Chamblin CO .30 .75
108 Cornell Brown CO .30 .75
109 Angus Reid .30 .75
110 Dean Valli .30 .75
111 Dan McCullough .30 .75
112 Andrew Jones .30 .75
113 Damane Duckett .30 .75
114 Justin Sorensen .30 .75
115 Aaron Hunt .30 .75
116 Anton McKenzie .30 .75
117 Dante Marsh .30 .75
118 J.R. Larose .30 .75
119 Davis Sanchez .40 1.00
120 Ryan Phillips .30 .75
121 Sherko Rasouli .30 .75
122 Korey Banks .40 1.00
123 Keron Williams .30 .75
124 Jerome Messam .30 3.00
125 Dominie Pittman .30 .75
126 Montrell Craft .30 .75
127 Paris Jackson .30 .75
128 Jon Hameister-Ries .30 .75
129 James Yurichuk .30 .75
130 Andrew Harris .30 .75
131 Travis Lulay .30 1.25
132 Akeem Foster .30 .75
133 Jovan Olafioye .30 1.25
134 Cauchy Muamba .30 .75
135 Sean Ortiz .30 .75
136 Jason Arakgi .30 .75
137 Paul Lapolice .30 .75
138 Shawn Gallant .30 .75
139 Ian Logan .30 .75
140 Pierre-Luc Labbe .30 .75
141 LaVar Grover .30 .75
142 Mike Renaud .40 1.00
143 Luke Fritz .30 .75
144 Aaron Hargreaves .30 .75
145 Clinton Kent .30 .75
146 Don Oramasionwu .30 .75
147 Taylor Inglis .40 1.00
148 Jovon Johnson .30 .75
149 Odell Willis .30 .75
150 Scott Flory .30 .75
151 Etienne Boulay .40 1.00
152 De'Audra Dix .30 .75
153 Jermaine McElveen .30 .75
154 Eric Wilson .30 .75
155 Luc Brodeur-Jourdain .30 .75
156 Josh Bourke .30 .75
157 S.J. Green .30 .75
158 Martin Bedard .30 .75
159 Jerald Brown .30 .75
160 Mark Estelle .30 .75
161 Jeff Perrett .30 .75
162 Patrick MacDonald .30 .75
163 Dahrran Diedrick .30 .75
164 Mike Giffin .30 .75
165A Diamond Ferri .30 .75
165B Diamond Ferri .75 2.00
166 Paul Woldu .30 .75
167 Jamel Richardson .60 1.50
168 Jim Popp .30 .75
169 Sandro DeAngelis .30 .75
170 Jykine Bradley .30 .75
171 Ryan Hinds .30 .75
172 Geoff Tisdale .30 .75
173 DeAndra Cobb .40 1.00
174 William Heyward .30 .75
175 Raymond Wladichuk .30 .75
176 Marquay McDaniel .30 .75
177 Samuel Fournier .30 .75
178 Ray Mariuz .30 .75
179 Jordan Matechuk .30 .75
180 Belton Johnson .30 .75
181 Brian Ramsay .30 .75
182 Garrett McIntyre .30 .75
183 Matt Carter .30 .75
184 Chris Bauman .30 .75
185 Eric Wilbur .30 .75
186 Yannick Carter .30 .75
187 Buck Pierce .60 1.50
188 Arkee Whitlock .75 2.00
189 Kelly Campbell .75 2.00
190 Moton Hopkins .40 1.00
191 Stu Laird .40 1.00
192 Edward Molstad .40 1.00
193 Mike Morreale .40 1.00
194 Jon Volpe .75 2.00
195 Bill Baker .40 1.00
196 Dimitri Tsoumpas .40 1.00
197A Jeff Jacobs SUPP .30 .75
197B Jeff Jacobs w/logo 30.00 50.00
198 Phillip Hunt .75 2.00
199 Jarious Jackson .50 1.25
200 Steven Jyles .40 1.25
201 Nik Lewis .40 1.00
202 Greg Carr .40 1.00
203 James Patrick .60 1.50
204 Juwan Simpson .40 1.00
205 Canadian HOF .30 .75
206 Jeff Solinski SUPP .30 .75
207 Glenn Ominski SUPP .30 .75
208 Wayne Scott SUPP .30 .75
209 Dan Moran SUPP .30 .75
210 2007 Grey Cup Winners .30 .75
211 2008 Grey Cup Winners .30 .75
212 1993 Grey Cup Winners .30 .75
213 2009 Grey Cup Winners .30 .75
214 Gord Weber PHOTO .30 .75
215 Beckett Publications .30 .75

2010 JOGO Autographs

COMPLETE SET (8) 50.00 100.00
1 Weston Dressler 6.00 15.00
2 Hugh Charles 5.00 12.00
3 Arland Bruce 5.00 12.00
4 Maurice Lloyd 5.00 12.00
5 Romby Bryant 6.00 15.00
6 Travis Lulay 6.00 15.00
7 Cleo Lemon 8.00 20.00
8 Anthony Calvillo 8.00 20.00

2010 JOGO Rookies

COMPLETE SET (15) 20.00 35.00
*WHITE BORDER: .8X TO 2X BASIC CARDS
1R Cory Boyd 1.50 4.00
2R Marcus Thigpen 1.25 3.00
3R Terence Jeffers-Harris 1.50 4.00
4R Brandon Isaac 1.25 3.00
5R Brandon Rideau 1.25 3.00
6R Deon Murphy 1.25 3.00
7R Jason Barnes 1.25 3.00
8R Steven Black 1.25 3.00
9R Cole Bergquist 1.25 3.00
10R Stanley Franks 1.25 3.00
11R Jared Zabransky 1.50 4.00
12R Dalton Bell 1.25 3.00
13R Tim Maypray 1.25 3.00
14R Alex Brink 1.25 3.00
15R Yonus Davis 1.50 4.00

2010 JOGO Short Prints

COMPLETE SET (15) 20.00
*WHITE BORDER: .8X TO 2X BASIC CARDS
1SP Weston Dressler 1.50 4.00
2SP Fred Reid 1.00 2.50
3SP Henry Burris 2.00 5.00
4SP Avon Cobourne 1.50 4.00
5SP Kevin Glenn 1.00 2.50
6SP Andy Fantuz 2.00 5.00
7SP Stevie Baggs 1.00 2.50
8SP Willie Pile 1.00 2.50
9SP Geroy Simon 1.00 2.50
10SP Terrence Edwards 1.00 2.50
11SP Ricky Ray 1.25 3.00
12SP Fred Stamps 1.00 2.50
13SP Anthony Calvillo 1.50 4.00
14SP Joffrey Reynolds 1.25 3.00
15SP Arland Bruce 1.50 4.00

2011 JOGO

ANNOUNCED PRINT RUN 300
WHITE BORDER/59: .8X TO 2X BASIC CARDS
1 Bryan Crawford .60 1.50
2 Matthew Black .40 1.00
3 Spencer Watt .40 1.00
4 Kevin Huntley .40 1.00
5 Zander Robinson .40 1.00
6 Wes Lysack .40 1.00
7 Ron Flemons .40 1.00
8 Joe Eppele .40 1.00
9 Dee Webb .40 1.00
10 Djems Kouame .40 1.00
11 Lin-J Shell .40 1.00
12 Cory Boyd .40 1.00
13 Mike Bradwell .40 1.00
14 Byron Parker .60 1.50
15 Jeff Johnson .40 1.00
16 Andre Durie .40 1.00
17 Cleo Lemon .75 2.00
18 Noel Prefontaine .40 1.00
19 Sammy Tranks .40 1.00
20 Willie Pile .40 1.00
21 Taylor Robertson .40 1.00
22 Ejiro Kuale .40 1.00
23 Tristan Black .40 1.00
24 Nick Clement .40 1.00
25A B.J. Hall .40 1.00
25B Ben Ishola UER .40 1.00
(intended to be card #26)
27 Jonathan St.Pierre .40 1.00
28 Jamel Richardson .60 1.50
29 Neal Hughes .40 1.00
30 Graeme Bell .40 1.00
31 Chris Best .40 1.00
32 Craig Butler .40 1.00
33 Wes Cates .40 1.00
34 Hugh Charles .40 1.00
35 Jason Clermont .40 1.00
36 Ryan Dinwiddie .40 1.00
37 Weston Dressler .60 1.50
38 Stu Foord .40 1.00
39 John Bowman .40 1.00
40 Chris Graham .40 1.00
41 Efrem Hill .40 1.00
42 Cory Huclack .40 1.00
43 Nick Hutchins .40 1.00
44 Tristan Jackson .40 1.00
45 Cary Koch .40 1.00
46 Chima Ihekwoaba .40 1.00
47 Gene Makowsky .40 1.00
48 Mike McCullough .40 1.00
49 Christopher Milo .40 1.00
50 John Surla .40 1.00
51A Fernand Kashama?áERR 20.00 40.00
(wrong photo, blocking)
51B Fernand Kashama?áCOR .60 1.50
(correct photo, running)
52 Marc Parenteau .40 1.00
53 Darian Durant .75 2.00
54 Dario Romero .40 1.00
55 Eddie Russ Jr. .40 1.00
56 Keith Shologan .40 1.00
57 Jordan Sisco .40 1.00
58 Brandon West .40 1.00
59 Henry Burris .40 1.00
60 Justin Phillips .40 1.00
61 Geoff Tisdale .40 1.00
62 Samuel Scott .40 1.00
63 Anthony Parker .40 1.00
64 Randy Chevrier .40 1.00
65 Adrian Davis .40 1.00
66 Johnny Forzani .40 1.00
67 Dimitri Tsoumpas .40 1.00
68 Burke Dales .40 1.00
69 Corey Mace .40 1.00
70 Gerald Cadogan .40 1.00
71 Larry Taylor .40 1.00
72 Brandon Smith .40 1.00
73 Rene Paredes .40 1.00
74 Romby Bryant .50 1.25
75 Tim O'Neill .40 1.00
76 Daren Stone .40 1.00
77 Eric Fraser .40 1.00
78 Tim St.Pierre .40 1.00
79 Karl McCartney .40 1.00
80 Arjei Franklin .40 1.00
81 George Hopkins Eqp Mgr .40 1.00
82 Johnnie Dixon .40 1.00
83 Greg Fassitt .40 1.00
84 Terrance Lee .40 1.00
85 Stevie Baggs .40 1.00
86 Ivan Brown .40 1.00
87 Belton Johnson .40 1.00
88 Al Smith .40 1.00
89 Marcell Young .40 1.00
90 Carlos Thomas .40 1.00
91 Peter Dyakowski .40 1.00
92 Eddie Steele .40 1.00
93 Glenn MacKay .40 1.00
94 Yannick Carter .40 1.00
95 Nathan Kanya .40 1.00
96 Renauld Williams .40 1.00
97 Ken-Yon Rambo .40 1.00
98 Agustin Barrenechea .40 1.00
99 Khari Jones CO .40 1.00
100 Jason Boltus .40 1.00
101 Kevin Glenn .40 1.00
102 Bo Smith .40 1.00
103 Marwan Hage .40 1.00
104 Jason Jimenez .40 1.00
105 Marc Beswick .40 1.00
106 Ryan Hinds .40 1.00
107 Corey Chamblin CO .40 1.00
108 Darcy Brown .40 1.00
109 Wayne Smith .40 1.00
110 Matt Carter .40 1.00
111 James Yurichuk .40 1.00
112 Runako Reth .75 2.00
113 Adam Bighill .40 1.00
114 Aaron Fiacconi .40 1.00
115 Kerry Joseph .40 1.00
116 Kyle Koch .40 1.00
117 Nate Coehoorn .40 1.00
118 Greg Wojt .40 1.00
119A Corbin Sharun .40 1.00
(photo from knees up)
119B Corbin Sharun .75 2.00
(full body photo)
120 Taylor Inglis .40 1.00
121 Donovan Alexander .40 1.00
122 Michael Cornell .40 1.00
123 Andrew Nowacki .40 1.00
124 Jermaine Reid .40 1.00
125 Greg Peach .40 1.00
126 Brian Ramsay .40 1.00
127 Tyler Scott .40 1.00
128 Jykine Bradley .40 1.00
129 Weldon Brown .60 1.50
130 Samuel Fournier .40 1.00
131 Chris Thompson .40 1.00
132 Andrew Woodruff .40 1.00
133 Jerome Messam 1.25 3.00
134 Ian Logan .40 1.00
135 Doug Brown .40 1.00
136 Jade Etienne .40 1.00
137 Terrence Edwards .40 1.00
138 James Green .40 1.00
139 Henoc Muamba .40 1.00
140 Jerry-Ralph Jules .40 1.00
141 Clint Kent .40 1.00
142 Carl Volny .40 1.00
143 Aaron Hargreaves .40 1.00
144 Johnny Sears Jr. .40 1.00
145 Terence Jeffers-Harris .40 1.00
146 Brady Browne .40 1.00
147 Buck Pierce .60 1.50
148 Angus Reid .40 1.00
149 Dan McCullough .40 1.00
150 Ben Archibald .40 1.00
151 Jovan Olafioye .50 1.25
152 Jamal Robertson .40 1.00
153 Anton McKenzie .40 1.00
154 Solomon Elimimian .40 1.00
155 Akeem Foster .40 1.00
156 Andrew Harris .40 1.00
157 Keron Williams .40 1.00
158 J.R. Ruffin .40 1.00
159 Cauchy Muamba .40 1.00
160 Brent Johnson .40 1.00
161 Paris Jackson .40 1.00
162 J.R. Larose .40 1.00
163 Hugh O'Neill .40 1.00
164 Paul McCallum .50 1.25
165 Eric Taylor .40 1.00
166 Davis Sanchez .40 1.00
167 Andrew Jones .40 1.00
168 Joash Gesse .40 1.00
169 Dean Valli .40 1.00
170 Jesse Newman .40 1.00
171 Rolly Lumbala .40 1.00
172 Jason Arakgi .40 1.00
173 Adam Leonard .40 1.00
174 Scott Flory .40 1.00
175 Greg Laybourn .40 1.00
176 Tim Maypray .40 1.00
178 Walter Spencer-Robinson .40 1.00
179 Shea Emry .40 1.00
180 Kitwana Jones .40 1.00
181 Etienne Boulay .40 1.00
182 Jeff Perrett .40 1.00
183 Dwight Anderson .40 1.00
184 Sean Whyte .40 1.00
185 Tad Crawford .40 1.00
186 Emmanuel Marc .40 1.00
187 Brian Ridgeway .40 1.00
188 Jeff Hecht .40 1.00
189 Martin Bedard .40 1.00
190 Jim Popp EXEC .40 1.00
191 Justin Conn .40 1.00
192 Jabari Arthur .40 1.00
193 Drew Tate .40 1.00
194 Moton Hopkins .40 1.00
SP1 Anthony Calvillo/150 5.00 12.00
SP2 Anthony Calvillo/25* No SER

2011 JOGO Autographs

ANNOUNCED PRINT RUN 92 SETS
1S Henry Burris 10.00 25.00
2S Terrence Edwards 6.00 15.00
3S Stevie Baggs 6.00 15.00
4S S.J. Green 6.00 15.00
5S Gene Makowsky 6.00 15.00
6S Chad Owens 8.00 20.00

2011 JOGO Lifetime Supporters

ANNOUNCED PRINT RUN 100 SETS
1C Terry Lodge .60 1.50
2C Larry Oleskiw .60 1.50
3C Garry Hlady .60 1.50
4C Jean-Philippe Dutremble .60 1.50
5C Byron Smith .60 1.50
6C Allan Radomske .60 1.50
7C Tommy Smith .60 1.50
8C Paul McCarney .60 1.50
9C Irwin Family .60 1.50

2011 JOGO Rookies

ANNOUNCED PRINT RUN 175
WHITE BORDER/59: .8X TO 2X BASIC CARDS
1R Chad Kackert 1.50 4.00
2R Bakari Grant 1.25 3.00
3R Chris Williams 1.50 4.00
4R Kenny Mainor 1.25 3.00
5R Eric Ward 1.25 3.00
6R Mike Reilly 1.25 3.00
7R Marcus Henry 1.25 3.00
8R Marco Iannuzzi 1.25 3.00
9R Terrence Nunn 1.25 3.00
10R Tim Brown 1.25 3.00
11R J.C. Sherritt 1.25 3.00
12R Clarence Denmark 1.25 3.00
13R Brandon Whitaker 1.25 3.00
14R Perry Floyd 1.25 3.00
15R Shawn Gore 1.50 4.00

2011 JOGO Short Prints

ANNOUNCED PRINT RUN 175 SETS
WHITE BORDER/59: .8X TO 2X BASIC CARDS
1SP Anthony Calvillo 1.50 4.00
2SP Fred Reid 1.25 3.00
3SP Deon Beasley 1.50 4.00
4SP S.J. Green 1.25 3.00
5SP Andy Fantuz 1.25 3.00
6SP Nik Lewis 1.50 4.00
7SP Jonathan Hefney 1.25 3.00
8SP Alex Suber 1.25 3.00
9SP Geroy Simon 1.25 3.00
10SP Chris Getzlaf 1.25 3.00
11SP Ricky Ray 1.25 3.00
12SP Fred Stamps 1.25 3.00
13SP Chad Owens 2.00 5.00
14SP Jon Cornish 1.25 3.00
15SP Travis Lulay 1.25 3.00

1971 Mac's Milk CFL Cloth Stickers

These, roughly 3" in diameter, cloth sticker discs feature a color image of a CFL player or team helmet. The backs are blank and the discs are thought to have been issued by Mac's Milk.

COMPLETE SET (20) 75.00 150.00
1 Greg Barton 3.00 8.00
2 Tommy Joe Coffey 5.00 12.00
3 Garney Henley 3.00 8.00
4 Marv Luster 3.00 8.00
5 Leon McQuay 3.00 8.00
6 Angelo Mosca 5.00 12.00

7 Mel Profit	3.00	8.00
8 Dave Raimey	3.00	8.00
9 Joe Theismann	7.50	15.00
10 John Williams	3.00	8.00
11 Alouettes Helmet	3.00	8.00
12 Argonauts Helmet	3.00	8.00
13 B.C. Lions Helmet	3.00	8.00
14 Blue Bombers Helmet	3.00	8.00
15 CFL Helmet	3.00	8.00
16 Eskimos Helmet	3.00	8.00
17 Rough Riders Helmet	3.00	8.00
18 Roughriders Helmet	3.00	8.00
19 Stampeders Helmet	3.00	8.00
20 Tiger-Cats Helmet	3.00	8.00

1963 Montreal Alouettes Bank of Montreal

Each of these photos measure approximately 3 7/8" by 5 3/8". Inside white borders, the fronts feature black-and-white posed action photos. Immediately below the picture in small print is the player's name. The wider white bottom border carries the sponsor (Bank of Montreal) information. The photos were perforated as they were originally issued in game programs as pairs. The backs display various advertisements. The photos are unnumbered and checklisted below in alphabetical order.

COMPLETE SET (14)	50.00	100.00
1 Dick Aboud	4.00	10.00
2 Jim Andreotti	4.00	10.00
3 Ross Buckle	4.00	10.00
4 Don Clark	4.00	10.00
5 Tom Cloutier	4.00	10.00
6 Ted Elsby	4.00	10.00
7 Jack Espenship	4.00	10.00
8 Bob Geary	4.00	10.00
9 Robert LeBlanc	4.00	10.00
10 Billy Ray Locklin	4.00	10.00
11 Ron Maddocks	5.00	12.00
12 Don Paquette	4.00	10.00
13 Dick Schnell	4.00	10.00
14 Billy Wayte	4.00	10.00

1970-72 Montreal Alouettes Matin Sports Weekend Posters

These posters were actually newspaper page cut-outs. Each is oversized and features a color photo of the featured player surrounded by cardlike graphics. The posters were printed on newsprint type stock or a period of years. The backs are simply another page from the newspaper. Any additions to the below checklist are appreciated.

1 Bruce Van Ness	7.50	15.00
2 Terry Evanshen 1970	15.00	30.00
3 Terry Evanshen 1971	15.00	30.00
4 Gene Gaines	15.00	30.00
5 Gino Cappelletti	15.00	30.00
6 Pierre Desjardins	7.50	15.00
7 Dennis Duncan	7.50	15.00
8 Russ Jackson	15.00	30.00
9 Joe Theismann	25.00	50.00
10 Sam Etcheverry	15.00	30.00
Sonny Wade		
Tony Passander		
11 Moses Denson	10.00	20.00
12 Jim Chasey	7.50	15.00

1974-76 Montreal Alouettes Team Issue

These oversized (roughly 3 1/2" by 5 1/2") photos feature black and white player photos and were issued by the Alouettes for player appearances and fan mail. Each is blankbacked and features the team name and logo below the photo with only a facsimile player signature to help identify the athlete. The photos were likely issued over a number of years. Any additions to this list are appreciated.

COMPLETE SET (38)	125.00	200.00
1 Junior Ah-You	6.00	10.00
2 Brock Ansley	3.00	5.00
3 Joe Barnes	6.00	10.00
4 Pat Bonnet	3.00	5.00
5 Dave Braggins	3.00	5.00
6 Wally Buono	3.00	5.00
7 Gary Chown	3.00	5.00
8 Wayne Conrad	3.00	5.00
9 Carl Crennell	3.00	5.00
10 Peter Dalla Riva	3.50	6.00
11 Gerry Dattilio	3.00	5.00
12 Marvin Davis	3.00	5.00
13 Rudy Florio	3.00	5.00
14 Gene Gaines	6.00	10.00
15 Pierre Gelesiar	3.00	5.00
16 Gabriel Gregoire	3.00	5.00
17 Dickie Harris	3.00	5.00
18 Andy Hopkins	3.00	5.00
19 Gordon Judges	3.00	5.00
20 Glen Leach	3.00	5.00
21 Chuck McMann	3.00	5.00
22 Ian Mofford	3.00	5.00
23 Joe Petty	3.00	5.00
24 Frank Pomarico	3.00	5.00
25 Phil Price	3.00	5.00
26 Barry Randall	3.00	5.00
27 Randy Rhino	3.00	5.00
28 Johnny Rodgers	6.00	10.00
(sitting on helmet,		
signed Johnny R.Superstar)		
29 Johnny Rodgers	6.00	10.00
(running photo,		
signed Johnny R.Superstar)		
30 Doug Smith	3.00	5.00
31 Larry Smith	3.00	5.00
32 Don Sweet	3.00	5.00
33 John Tanner	3.00	5.00
34 Sonny Wade	3.00	5.00
35 Glen Weir	3.00	5.00
36 Mike Widger	3.00	5.00
37 Dan Yochum	3.00	5.00
38 Chuck Zapiec	3.00	5.00

1978 Montreal Alouettes Redpath Sugar

Redpath Sugar produced small (roughly 1 5/8" by 2 1/2") sugar packets featuring Alouette players for distribution in the Montreal area. Each is unnumbered and includes a small color photo of the player on the front along with his name, position, and vital information in both French and English. The back of the sugar packet includes an Alouettes logo and a short player bio. Any additions to this checklist are appreciated.

COMPLETE SET (11)	25.00	50.00
1 Jim Burrow	3.75	7.50
2 Gary Chown	2.50	5.00
3 Dan Diebert	2.50	5.00
Trainer		
4 Gabriel Gregoire	2.50	5.00
5 Dickie Harris	3.75	7.50
6 Max Huber	2.50	5.00
7 Mark Jackson	3.75	7.50
8 Larry Pasquale	2.50	5.00
9 Craig Thomson	2.50	5.00
10 Sonny Wade	2.50	5.00
11 Alouettes	2.50	5.00
Mascot		

1978 Montreal Alouettes Team Sheets

This group of 32-players of the Montreal Alouettes was produced on four glossy sheets each measuring approximately 8" by 10". The fronts feature black-and-white player portraits with eight pictures to a sheet. The backs are blank. The cards are unnumbered and checklisted below in alphabetical order, with the player pictured in the upper left hand corner of the sheet listed first.

COMPLETE SET (4)	10.00	20.00
1 Gerry Dattilio	3.00	6.00
Peter Dalla Riva		
Wayne Conrad		
Jim Burrow		
Wally Buono		
Pat Bonnett		
Joe Barnes		
Chuck Zapiec		
2 Jerry Friesen	3.00	6.00
John Olenchalk		
Clifton Alapa		
Carl Crennel		
Junior Ah You		
Eletise Fiatoa		
Brent Watson		
Glen Weir		
3 Bob Gaddis	2.50	5.00
Vernon Perry		
Gabriel Gregoire		
Dickie Harris		
Craig Labbett		
Chuck McMann		
Ty Morris		
John O'Leary		
4 Ray Watrin	2.50	5.00
Sonny Wade		
Larry Uteck		
John Taylor		
Ken Starch		
Larry Smith		
Don Sweet		
Doug Payton		

2003 Montreal Alouettes JOGO Natrel

This set features players of the Montreal Alouettes. Each card was printed by JOGO and sponsored by Natrel Milk. A complete set could be had by collectors through a mail-in redemption offer on Natrel Milk products. Reportedly, 6500 sets were produced.

COMPLETE SET (10)	5.00	10.00
1 Barron Miles	.60	1.50
2 Ben Cahoon	1.00	2.50
3 Bryan Chiu	.30	.75
4 Bruno Heppell	.30	.75
5 Eric LaPointe	.60	1.50
6 Stephane Fortin	.30	.75
7 Sylvain Girard	.40	1.00
8 Marc Megna	.40	1.00
9 Ed Philion	.30	.75
10 Mat Petz	.30	.75

2005 Montreal Alouettes Team of the Decade JOGO

COMPLETE SET (27)	12.50	25.00
1 Terry Baker	.50	1.25
2 Thomas Haskins	.40	1.00
3 William Loftus	.40	1.00
4 Anwar Stewart	.50	1.25
5 Ed Philion	.50	1.25
6 Doug Petersen	.40	1.00
7 Elfrid Payton	.40	1.00
8 Tracy Gravely	.40	1.00
9 Timothy Strickland	.40	1.00
10 Kevin Johnson	.40	1.00
11 Davis Sanchez	.40	1.00
12 Reggie Durden	.40	1.00
13 Barron Miles	.40	1.00
14 Mark Washington	.50	1.25
15 Irv Smith	.40	1.00
16 Neal Fort	.40	1.00
17 Pierre Vercheval	.40	1.00
18 Bryan Chiu	.40	1.00
19 Scott Flory	.40	1.00
20 Uzooma Okeke	.40	1.00
21 Chris Armstrong	.40	1.00
22 Jock Climie	.40	1.00
23 Jermaine Copeland	.50	1.25
24 Ben Cahoon	.75	2.00
25 Bruno Heppell	.50	1.25
26 Mike Pringle	1.00	2.50
27 Anthony Calvillo	1.50	4.00

1982 Montreal News

This 21-card set was cut out of the Montreal News and features various size color player photos of stars of different sports. The paper is printed in French. The cards are unnumbered and checklisted below in alphabetical order.

COMPLETE SET (21)	16.00	40.00
17 Luc Tousignant FB	.40	1.00

1963 Nalley's Coins

This 160 coin set is difficult to complete due to the fact that within every team grouping, the last ten coins are much tougher to find. The back of the coin is hard plastic, but also see-through. The coins can be found with sponsors Nalley's Potato Chips, Hunter's Potato Chips, Krun-Chee Potato Chips, and Humpty Dumpty Potato Chips. Humpty Dumpty coins were printed in French and English, instead of just English. The coins can also be found without sponsor names. There are no price differences between the variations. Eight of the nine CFL teams are represented. The coins measure approximately 1 3/8" in diameter. Shields to hold the coins were also issued; these shields are also very collectible and are listed at the end of the list below, with the prefix S. The shields are not included in the complete set price.

COMPLETE SET (160)	1,500.00	3,000.00
1 Jackie Parker	10.00	20.00
2 Dick Shatto	4.00	8.00
3 Dave Mann	3.00	6.00
4 Danny Nykoluk	2.50	5.00
5 Billy Shipp	2.50	5.00
6 Doug McNichol	2.50	5.00
7 Jim Rountree	2.50	5.00
8 Art Johnson	2.50	5.00
9 Walt Radzick	2.50	5.00
10 Jim Andreotti	3.00	6.00
11 Gerry Philip	10.00	20.00
12 Lynn Bottoms	10.00	20.00
13 Ron Morris SP	40.00	80.00
14 Nobby Wirkowski CO	10.00	20.00
15 John Wydareny	10.00	20.00
16 Gerry Wilson	10.00	20.00
17 Gerry Patrick SP	25.00	50.00
18 Aubrey Linne	10.00	20.00
19 Norm Stoneburgh	10.00	20.00
20 Ken Bock	10.00	20.00
21 Russ Jackson	7.50	15.00
22 Kaye Vaughan	4.00	8.00
23 Dave Thelen	4.00	8.00
24 Ron Stewart	4.00	8.00
25 Moe Racine	2.50	5.00
26 Jim Conroy	3.00	6.00
27 Joe Poirier	3.00	6.00
28 Mel Seminko	2.50	5.00
29 Whit Tucker	4.00	8.00
30 Ernie White	2.50	5.00
31 Frank Clair CO	10.00	20.00
32 Merv Bevan	10.00	20.00
33 Jerry Selinger	10.00	20.00
34 Jim Cain	10.00	20.00
35 Mike Snodgrass	10.00	20.00
36 Ted Smale	10.00	20.00
37 Billy Joe Booth	10.00	20.00
38 Len Chandler	10.00	20.00
39 Rick Black	10.00	20.00
40 Allen Schau	10.00	20.00
41 Bernie Faloney	7.50	15.00
42 Bobby Kuntz	3.00	6.00
43 Joe Zuger	3.00	6.00
44 Hal Patterson	6.00	12.00
45 Bronko Nagurski Jr.	5.00	10.00
46 Zeno Karcz	3.00	6.00
47 Hardiman Cureton	2.50	5.00
48 John Barrow	4.00	8.00
49 Tommy Grant	4.00	8.00
50 Garney Henley	4.00	8.00
51 Dick Easterly	10.00	20.00
52 Frank Cosentino	10.00	20.00
53 Geno DeNobile	10.00	20.00
54 Ralph Goldston	10.00	20.00
55 Chet Miksza	10.00	20.00
56 Bob Minihane	10.00	20.00
57 Don Sutherin	20.00	40.00
58 Ralph Sazio CO	10.00	20.00
59 Dave Viti SP	17.50	35.00
60 Angelo Mosca SP	62.50	125.00
61 Sandy Stephens	4.00	8.00
62 George Dixon	4.00	8.00
63 Don Clark	3.00	6.00
64 Don Paquette	2.50	5.00
65 Billy Wayte	2.50	5.00
66 Ed Nickla	2.50	5.00
67 Marv Luster	4.00	8.00
68 Joe Stracini	2.50	5.00
69 Bobby Jack Oliver	3.00	6.00
70 Ted Elsby	2.50	5.00
71 Jim Trimble CO	5.00	10.00
72 Bob Leblanc	5.00	10.00
73 Dick Schnell	5.00	10.00
74 Milt Crain	5.00	10.00
75 Dick Dalatri	5.00	10.00
76 Billy Roy	5.00	10.00
77 Dave Hoppmann	5.00	10.00
78 Billy Ray Locklin	5.00	10.00
79 Ed Learn SP	75.00	150.00
80 Meco Poliziani SP	20.00	40.00
81 Leo Lewis	4.00	8.00
82 Kenny Ploen	4.00	8.00
83 Steve Patrick	2.50	5.00
84 Farrell Funston	3.00	6.00
85 Charlie Shepard	3.00	6.00
86 Ronnie Latourelle	2.50	5.00
87 Gord Rowland	3.00	6.00
88 Frank Rigney	3.00	6.00
89 Cornel Piper	2.50	5.00
90 Ernie Pitts	2.50	5.00
91 Roger Hagberg	7.50	15.00
92 Herb Gray	15.00	30.00
93 Jack Delveaux	5.00	10.00
94 Roger Savoie	5.00	10.00
95 Nick Miller	5.00	10.00
96 Norm Rauhaus	5.00	10.00
97 Cec Luining	5.00	10.00
98 Hal Ledyard	5.00	10.00
99 Neil Thomas	5.00	10.00
100 Bud Grant CO	40.00	80.00
101 Eagle Keys CO	4.00	8.00
102 Mike Wicklum	2.50	5.00
103 Bill Mitchell	2.50	5.00
104 Mike Lashuk	2.50	5.00
105 Tommy Joe Coffey	4.00	8.00
106 Zeke Smith	2.50	5.00
107 Joe Hernandez	2.50	5.00
108 Johnny Bright	4.00	8.00
109 Don Getty	4.00	8.00
110 Nat Dye	2.50	5.00
111 James Earl Wright	5.00	10.00
112 Mike Volcan SP	17.50	35.00
113 Jon Rechner	5.00	10.00
114 Len Vella	5.00	10.00
115 Ted Frechette	5.00	10.00
116 Larry Fleisher	5.00	10.00
117 Oscar Kruger	5.00	10.00
118 Ken Petersen	5.00	10.00
119 Bobby Walden	5.00	10.00
120 Mickey Ording	5.00	10.00
121 Pete Manning	2.50	5.00
122 Harvey Wylie	3.00	6.00
123 Tony Pajaczkowski	4.00	8.00
124 Wayne Harris	5.00	10.00
125 Earl Lunsford	4.00	8.00
126 Don Luzzi	3.00	6.00
127 Ed Buckanan	2.50	5.00
128 Lovell Coleman	3.00	6.00
129 Hal Krebs	2.50	5.00
130 Eagle Day	4.00	8.00
131 Bobby Dobbs CO	5.00	10.00
132 George Hansen	5.00	10.00
133 Roy Jokanovich SP	40.00	80.00
134 Jerry Keeling	15.00	30.00
135 Larry Anderson	5.00	10.00
136 Bill Crawford	5.00	10.00
137 Ron Albright	5.00	10.00
138 Bill Britton	5.00	10.00
139 Jim Dillard	5.00	10.00
140 Jim Furlong	5.00	10.00
141 Dave Skrien CO	2.50	5.00
142 Willie Fleming	5.00	10.00
143 Nub Beamer	2.50	5.00
144 Norm Fieldgate	4.00	8.00
145 Joe Kapp	17.50	35.00
146 Tom Hinton	4.00	8.00
147 Pat Claridge	2.50	5.00
148 Bill Munsey	2.50	5.00
149 Mike Martin	2.50	5.00
150 Tom Brown	4.00	8.00
151 Ian Hagemoen	5.00	10.00
152 Jim Carphin	5.00	10.00
153 By Bailey	15.00	30.00
154 Steve Cotter	5.00	10.00
155 Mike Cacic	5.00	10.00
156 Neil Beaumont	5.00	10.00
157 Lonnie Dennis	5.00	10.00
158 Barney Therrien	5.00	10.00
159 Sonny Homer	5.00	10.00
160 Walt Bilicki	5.00	10.00
S1 Toronto Shield	25.00	50.00
S2 Ottawa Shield	25.00	50.00
S3 Hamilton Shield	25.00	50.00
S4 Montreal Shield	25.00	50.00
S5 Winnipeg Shield	25.00	50.00
S6 Edmonton Shield	25.00	50.00
S7 Calgary Shield	25.00	50.00
S8 British Columbia Shield	25.00	50.00

1964 Nalley's Coins

This 100-coin set is very similar to the set from the previous year except that there are no real distribution scarcities. The backs of the coins are plastic, but not see-through. No specific information about the player, as in the previous year, is included. The coins were sponsored by Nalley's Potato Chips and packaged one per box of chips. The set numbering is in team order. The coins measure approximately 1 3/8" in diameter. Shields to hold the coins were also issued; these shields are also very collectible and are listed at the end of the list below with the prefix "S". The shields are not included in the complete set price. Only teams from the Western Conference of the CFL were included.

COMPLETE SET (100)	375.00	750.00
1 Joe Kapp	15.00	30.00
2 Willie Fleming	5.00	10.00
3 Norm Fieldgate	4.00	8.00
4 Bill Murray	2.50	5.00
5 Tom Brown	5.00	10.00
6 Neil Beaumont	3.00	6.00
7 Sonny Homer	3.00	6.00
8 Lonnie Dennis	2.50	5.00
9 Dave Skrien	2.50	5.00
10 Dick Fouts CO	2.50	5.00
11 Paul Seale	2.50	5.00
12 Peter Kempf	2.50	5.00
13 Steve Shafer	2.50	5.00
14 Tom Hinton	4.00	8.00
15 Pat Claridge	2.50	5.00
16 By Bailey	4.00	8.00
17 Nub Beamer	3.00	6.00
18 Steve Cotter	2.50	5.00
19 Mike Cacic	2.50	5.00
20 Mike Martin	2.50	5.00
21 Eagle Day	7.50	15.00
22 Jim Dillard	2.50	5.00
23 Pete Murray	2.50	5.00
24 Tony Pajaczkowski	4.00	8.00
25 Don Luzzi	3.00	6.00
26 Wayne Harris	5.00	10.00
27 Harvey Wylie	3.00	6.00
28 Bill Crawford	2.50	5.00
29 Jim Furlong	2.50	5.00
30 Lovell Coleman	3.00	6.00
31 Pat Haines	2.50	5.00
32 Bob Taylor	3.00	6.00
33 Ernie Danjean	2.50	5.00
34 Jerry Keeling	4.00	8.00
35 Larry Robinson	3.00	6.00
36 George Hansen	2.50	5.00
37 Ron Albright	2.50	5.00
38 Larry Anderson	2.50	5.00
39 Bill Miller	2.50	5.00
40 Bill Britton	2.50	5.00
41 Lynn Amadee	4.00	8.00
42 Mike Lashuk	2.50	5.00
43 Tommy Joe Coffey	4.00	8.00
44 Junior Hawthorne	2.50	5.00
45 Nat Dye	2.50	5.00
46 Al Ecuyer	2.50	5.00
47 Howie Schumm	2.50	5.00
48 Zeke Smith	2.50	5.00
49 Mike Wicklum	2.50	5.00
50 Mike Volcan	2.50	5.00
51 E.A. Sims	2.50	5.00
52 Bill Mitchell	2.50	5.00
53 Ken Reed	2.50	5.00
54 Len Vella	2.50	5.00
55 Johnny Bright	4.00	8.00
56 Don Getty	4.00	8.00
57 Oscar Kruger	2.50	5.00
58 Ted Frechette	2.50	5.00
59 James Earl Wright	2.50	5.00
60 Roger Nelson	2.50	5.00
61 Ron Lancaster	6.00	12.00
62 Bill Clarke	2.50	5.00
63 Bob Shaw	2.50	5.00
64 Ray Purdin	2.50	5.00
65 Ron Atchison	4.00	8.00
66 Ted Urness	4.00	8.00
67 Bob Ptacek	2.50	5.00
68 Neil Habig	2.50	5.00
69 Garner Ekstran	3.00	6.00
70 Gene Wlasiuk	2.50	5.00
71 Jack Gotta	3.00	6.00
72 Dick Cohee	2.50	5.00
73 Ron Meadmore	2.50	5.00
74 Martin Fabi	2.50	5.00
75 Bob Good	2.50	5.00
76 Len Legault	2.50	5.00
77 Al Benecick	2.50	5.00
78 Dale West	3.00	6.00
79 Reg Whitehouse	2.50	5.00
80 George Reed	5.00	10.00
81 Kenny Ploen	4.00	8.00
82 Leo Lewis	6.00	12.00
83 Dick Thornton	3.00	6.00
84 Steve Patrick	2.50	5.00
85 Frank Rigney	3.00	6.00
86 Cornel Piper	2.50	5.00
87 Sherwyn Thorson	2.50	5.00
88 Ernie Pitts	2.50	5.00
89 Roger Hagberg	3.00	6.00
90 Bud Grant CO	25.00	50.00
91 Jack Delveaux	2.50	5.00
92 Farrell Funston	3.00	6.00
93 Ronnie Latourelle	2.50	5.00
94 Roger Hamelin	2.50	5.00
95 Gord Rowland	3.00	6.00
96 Herb Gray	5.00	10.00
97 Nick Miller	2.50	5.00
98 Norm Rauhaus	3.00	6.00
99 Bill Whisler	2.50	5.00
100 Hal Ledyard	2.50	5.00
S1 British Columbia	22.50	45.00
Shield		
S2 Calgary Shield	22.50	45.00
S3 Edmonton Shield	22.50	45.00
S4 Saskatchewan Shield	22.50	45.00
S5 Winnipeg Shield	22.50	45.00

1976 Nalley's Chips

This 31-card set was distributed in Western Canada in boxes of Nalley's Plain or Salt 'n Vinegar potato chips. The cards measure approximately 3 3/8" by 5 1/2" and feature posed color photos of the player, with the Nalley company name and player's signature below the picture. These blank-backed, unnumbered cards are listed below in alphabetical order.

COMPLETE SET (31)	250.00	400.00
1 Bill Baker	12.50	25.00
2 Willie Burden	20.00	35.00
3 Larry Cates	5.00	10.00
4 Dave Cutler	10.00	20.00
5 Lloyd Fairbanks	7.50	15.00
6 Joe Forzani	6.00	12.00
7 Tom Forzani	5.00	10.00
8 Rick Galbos	5.00	10.00
9 Eric Guthrie	5.00	10.00
10 Lou Harris	6.00	12.00
11 John Helton	10.00	20.00
12 Larry Highbaugh	7.50	15.00
13 Harold Holton	5.00	10.00
14 John Konihowski	5.00	10.00
15 Bruce Lemmerman	6.00	12.00
16 Rudy Linterman	7.50	15.00
17 Layne McDowell	5.00	10.00
18 George McGowan	7.50	15.00
19 Ray Nettles	5.00	10.00
20 Lui Passaglia	15.00	30.00
21 Joe Pisarcik	10.00	20.00
22 Dale Potter	5.00	10.00
23 John Sciarra	10.00	20.00
24 Wayne Smith	5.00	10.00
25 Michael Strickland	5.00	10.00
26 Charlie Turner	5.00	10.00
27 Tyrone Walls	6.00	12.00
28 Don Warrington	5.00	10.00
29 Tom Wilkinson	15.00	30.00
30 Jim Young	15.00	30.00
31 Cover Card	5.00	10.00

1953 Northern Photo Services Giant Postcards

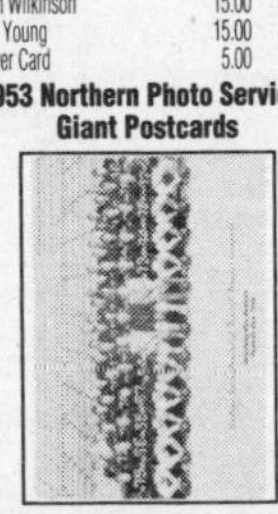

These large (roughly) postcards were produced by Northern Photo Services and feature the four teams of the Western Interprovincial Football Union of the CFL. Each was produced in Ektachrome color, features rounded corners, and includes a postcard style cardback.

NNO Winnipeg Blue Bombers	90.00	150.00
NNO Edmonton Eskimos	90.00	150.00
NNO Sask. Roughriders	90.00	150.00
NNO Calgary Stampeders	90.00	150.00

1968 O-Pee-Chee CFL

The 1968 O-Pee-Chee CFL set of 132 standard-size cards received limited distribution and is considered by some to be a test set. The card backs are written in English and French in green ink on yellowish card stock. The cards are ordered by teams. A complete checklist is given on card number 132. The card front design is similar to the design of the 1968 Topps NFL set.

COMPLETE SET (132)	900.00	1,500.00
1 Roger Murphy	6.00	12.00
2 Charlie Parker	5.00	10.00
3 Mike Webster	5.00	10.00
4 Carroll Williams	5.00	10.00
5 Phil Brady	5.00	10.00
6 Dave Lewis	5.00	10.00
7 John Baker	5.00	10.00
8 Basil Bark	5.00	10.00
9 Donnie Davis	5.00	10.00
10 Pierre Desjardins	5.00	10.00
11 Larry Fairholm	5.00	10.00
12 Peter Paquette	5.00	10.00
13 Ray Lychak	5.00	10.00
14 Ted Collins	5.00	10.00
15 Margene Adkins	6.00	12.00
16 Ron Stewart	10.00	20.00
17 Russ Jackson	20.00	35.00
18 Bo Scott	7.50	15.00
19 Joe Poirier	5.00	10.00
20 Wayne Giardino	5.00	10.00
21 Gene Gaines	7.50	15.00
22 Billy Joe Booth	5.00	10.00
23 Whit Tucker	7.50	15.00
24 Rick Black	5.00	10.00
25 Ken Lehmann	6.00	12.00
26 Bob Brown	5.00	10.00
27 Moe Racine	5.00	10.00
28 Dick Thornton	5.00	10.00
29 Bob Taylor	5.00	10.00
30 Mel Profit	6.00	12.00
31 Dave Mann	6.00	12.00
32 Marv Luster	6.00	12.00
33 Ed Buchanan	5.00	10.00
34 Ed Harrington	5.00	10.00
35 Jim Dillard	5.00	10.00
36 Bob Taylor	5.00	10.00
37 Ron Arends	5.00	10.00
38 Mike Wadsworth	5.00	10.00
39 Wally Gabler	6.00	12.00
40 Pete Martin	5.00	10.00
41 Danny Nykoluk	5.00	10.00
42 Bill Frank	5.00	10.00
43 Gordon Christian	5.00	10.00
44 Tommy Joe Coffey	10.00	20.00
45 Ellison Kelly	10.00	20.00
46 Angelo Mosca	15.00	30.00
47 John Barrow	10.00	20.00
48 Bill Danychuk	6.00	12.00
49 Jon Hohman	5.00	10.00
50 Bill Redell	5.00	10.00
51 Joe Zuger	5.00	10.00
52 Willie Bethea	6.00	12.00
53 Dick Cohee	5.00	10.00
54 Tommy Grant	7.50	15.00
55 Garney Henley	10.00	20.00
56 Ted Page	5.00	10.00
57 Bob Krouse	5.00	10.00
58 Phil Minnick	5.00	10.00
59 Butch Pressley	5.00	10.00
60 Dave Raimey	5.00	10.00
61 Sherwyn Thorson	5.00	10.00
62 Bill Whisler	5.00	10.00
63 Roger Hamelin	5.00	10.00
64 Chuck Harrison	5.00	10.00
65 Ken Nielsen	6.00	12.00
66 Ernie Pitts	5.00	10.00
67 Mitch Zainasky	5.00	10.00
68 John Schneider	5.00	10.00
69 Ron Kirkland	5.00	10.00
70 Paul Desjardins	5.00	10.00
71 Luther Selbo	5.00	10.00
72 Don Gilbert	5.00	10.00
73 Bob Lueck	5.00	10.00
74 Gerry Shaw	5.00	10.00
75 Chuck Zickefoose	5.00	10.00
76 Frank Andruski	5.00	10.00
77 Lanny Boleski	5.00	10.00
78 Terry Evanshen	10.00	20.00
79 Jim Furlong	5.00	10.00
80 Wayne Harris	10.00	20.00
81 Jerry Keeling	6.00	12.00
82 Roger Kramer	5.00	10.00
83 Pete Liske	10.00	20.00
84 Dick Suderman	6.00	12.00
85 Granville Liggins	10.00	20.00
86 George Reed	12.50	25.00
87 Ron Lancaster	15.00	30.00
88 Alan Ford	5.00	10.00
89 Gordon Barwell	5.00	10.00
90 Wayne Shaw	5.00	10.00
91 Bruce Bennett	7.50	15.00
92 Henry Dorsch	5.00	10.00
93 Ken Reed	5.00	10.00
94 Ron Atchison	7.50	15.00
95 Clyde Brock	5.00	10.00
96 Al Benecick	5.00	10.00
97 Ted Urness	6.00	12.00
98 Wally Dempsey	5.00	10.00
99 Don Gerhardt	5.00	10.00
100 Ted Dushinski	5.00	10.00
101 Ed McQuarters	6.00	12.00
102 Bob Kosid	5.00	10.00
103 Gary Brandt	5.00	10.00
104 John Wydareny	5.00	10.00
105 Jim Thomas	5.00	10.00
106 Art Perkins	5.00	10.00
107 Frank Cosentino	6.00	12.00
108 Earl Edwards	5.00	10.00
109 Garry Lefebvre	5.00	10.00
110 Greg Pipes	5.00	10.00
111 Ian MacLeod	5.00	10.00
112 Dick Dupuis	5.00	10.00
113 Ron Forwick	5.00	10.00
114 Jerry Griffin	5.00	10.00
115 John LaGrone	6.00	12.00
116 E.A. Sims	5.00	10.00
117 Greenard Poles	5.00	10.00
118 Leroy Sledge	5.00	10.00
119 Ken Sugarman	5.00	10.00
120 Jim Young	12.50	25.00
121 Garner Ekstran	5.00	10.00
122 Jim Evenson	6.00	12.00
123 Greg Findlay	5.00	10.00
124 Ted Gerela	5.00	10.00
125 Lach Heron	5.00	10.00
126 Mike Martin	5.00	10.00
127 Craig Murray	5.00	10.00
128 Pete Ohler	5.00	10.00
129 Sonny Homer	5.00	10.00
130 Bill Lasseter	5.00	10.00
131 John McDowell	5.00	10.00
132 Checklist Card	60.00	120.00

1968 O-Pee-Chee CFL Poster Inserts

This 16-card set of color posters featuring all-stars of the Canadian Football League was inserted in wax packs along with the regular issue of 1968 O-Pee-Chee CFL cards. These (approximately) 5" by 7" posters were folded twice in order to fit in the wax packs. They are unnumbered and are blank on the back. They were printed on very thin paper. These posters are similar in appearance to the 1967 Topps baseball and 1968 Topps football poster inserts.

COMPLETE SET (16)	150.00	300.00
1 Margene Adkins	9.00	18.00
2 Tommy Joe Coffey	12.50	25.00
3 Frank Cosentino	9.00	18.00
4 Terry Evanshen	12.50	25.00
5 Larry Fairholm	7.50	15.00
6 Wally Gabler	7.50	15.00
7 Russ Jackson	17.50	35.00
8 Ron Lancaster	17.50	35.00
9 Pete Liske	12.50	25.00
10 Dave Mann	9.00	18.00
11 Ken Nielsen	9.00	18.00
12 Dave Raimey	9.00	18.00
13 George Reed	15.00	30.00
14 Carroll Williams	7.50	15.00
15 Jim Young	15.00	30.00
16 Joe Zuger	7.50	15.00

1970 O-Pee-Chee CFL

The 1970 O-Pee-Chee CFL set features 115 standard-size cards ordered by teams. The design of these cards is very similar to the 1969 Topps NFL football issue. The card backs are written in French and English; the card back is predominantly black with white lettering and green accent. Six miscellaneous special feature cards comprise cards numbered 110-115.

COMPLETE SET (115)	175.00	350.00
1 Ed Harrington	2.00	4.00
2 Danny Nykoluk	1.25	2.50
3 Marv Luster	2.50	5.00
4 Dave Raimey	2.00	4.00
5 Bill Symons	2.50	5.00
6 Tom Wilkinson	10.00	20.00
7 Mike Wadsworth	1.25	2.50
8 Dick Thornton	2.00	4.00
9 Jim Tomlin	1.25	2.50
10 Mel Profit	2.00	4.00
11 Bob Taylor	2.50	5.00
12 Dave Mann	2.00	4.00
13 Tommy Joe Coffey	3.00	6.00
14 Angelo Mosca	9.00	18.00
15 Joe Zuger	2.00	4.00
16 Garney Henley	5.00	10.00
17 Mike Strofolino	1.25	2.50
18 Billy Ray Locklin	1.25	2.50
19 Ted Page	1.25	2.50
20 Bill Danychuk	2.00	4.00
21 Bob Krouse	1.25	2.50
22 John Reid	1.25	2.50
23 Dick Wesolowski	1.25	2.50
24 Willie Bethea	2.00	4.00
25 Ken Sugarman	2.00	4.00
26 Rich Robinson	1.25	2.50
27 Dave Tobey	1.25	2.50
28 Paul Brothers	1.25	2.50
29 Charlie Brown RB	1.25	2.50
30 Jerry Bradley	1.25	2.50
31 Ted Gerela	2.00	4.00
32 Jim Young	4.00	8.00
33 Gary Robinson	1.25	2.50
34 Bob Howes	1.25	2.50
35 Greg Findlay	1.25	2.50
36 Trevor Ekdahl	2.00	4.00
37 Ron Stewart	3.00	6.00
38 Joe Poirier	2.00	4.00
39 Wayne Giardino	1.25	2.50
40 Tom Schuette	1.25	2.50
41 Roger Perdrix	1.25	2.50
42 Jim Mankins	1.25	2.50
43 Jay Roberts	1.25	2.50
44 Ken Lehmann	2.00	4.00
45 Jerry Campbell	2.00	4.00
46 Billy Joe Booth	2.00	4.00
47 Whit Tucker	3.00	6.00
48 Moe Racine	1.25	2.50
49 Corey Colehour	2.00	4.00
50 Dave Gasser	1.25	2.50
51 Jerry Griffin	1.25	2.50
52 Greg Pipes	2.00	4.00
53 Roy Shatzko	1.25	2.50
54 Ron Forwick	1.25	2.50
55 Ed Molstad	1.25	2.50
56 Ken Ferguson	1.25	2.50
57 Terry Swarn	3.00	6.00
58 Tom Nettles	1.25	2.50
59 John Wydareny	2.00	4.00
60 Bayne Norrie	1.25	2.50
61 Wally Gabler	2.00	4.00
62 Paul Desjardins	1.25	2.50

63 Peter Francis	1.25	2.50
64 Bill Frank	1.25	2.50
65 Chuck Harrison	1.25	2.50
66 Gene Lakusiak	1.25	2.50
67 Phil Minnick	1.25	2.50
68 Doug Strong	1.25	2.50
69 Glen Schapansky	1.25	2.50
70 Ed Ulmer	1.25	2.50
71 Bill Whisler	1.25	2.50
72 Ted Collins	1.25	2.50
73 Larry DeGraw	1.25	2.50
74 Henry Dorsch	1.25	2.50
75 Alan Ford	1.25	2.50
76 Ron Lancaster	10.00	20.00
77 Bob Kosid	1.25	2.50
78 Bobby Thompson	1.25	2.50
79 Ted Dushinski	1.25	2.50
80 Bruce Bennett	2.50	5.00
81 George Reed	7.50	15.00
82 Wayne Shaw	1.25	2.50
83 Cliff Shaw	1.25	2.50
84 Jack Abendschan	2.00	4.00
85 Ed McQuarters	3.00	6.00
86 Jerry Keeling	3.00	6.00
87 Gerry Shaw	1.25	2.50
88 Basil Bark UER (Misspelled Back)	1.25	2.50
89 Wayne Harris	4.00	8.00
90 Jim Furlong	1.25	2.50
91 Larry Robinson	2.50	5.00
92 John Helton	5.00	10.00
93 Dave Cranmer	1.25	2.50
94 Lanny Boleski UER (Misspelled Larry)	1.25	2.50
95 Herman Harrison	3.00	6.00
96 Granville Liggins	2.50	5.00
97 Joe Forzani	2.00	4.00
98 Terry Evanshen	4.00	8.00
99 Sonny Wade	3.00	6.00
100 Dennis Duncan	1.25	2.50
101 Al Phaneuf	2.00	4.00
102 Larry Fairholm	1.25	2.50
103 Moses Denson	2.50	5.00
104 Gino Baretta	1.25	2.50
105 Gene Ceppetelli	1.25	2.50
106 Dick Smith	1.25	2.50
107 Gordon Judges	1.25	2.50
108 Harry Olszewski	1.25	2.50
109 Mike Webster	1.25	2.50
110 Checklist 1-115	15.00	30.00
111 Outstanding Player (list from 1953-1969)	4.00	8.00
112 Player of the Year (list from 1954-1969)	4.00	8.00
113 Lineman of the Year (list from 1955-1969)	3.00	6.00
114 CFL Coaches (listed on card front)	3.00	6.00
115 Identifying Player (explanation of uniform numbering system)	7.50	15.00

1970 O-Pee-Chee CFL Push-Out Inserts

This attractive set of 16 push-out inserts features players in the Canadian Football League. The cards are standard size, but are actually stickers, if the backs are moistened. The cards are numbered at the bottom and the backs are blank. Instructions on the front (upper left corner) are written in both English and French. Each player's team is identified on his card under his name. The player is shown superimposed over a football; the push-out area is essentially the football.

COMPLETE SET (16)	150.00	300.00
1 Ed Harrington	7.50	15.00
2 Danny Nykoluk	7.50	15.00
3 Tommy Joe Coffey	12.50	25.00
4 Angelo Mosca	20.00	35.00
5 Ken Sugarman	10.00	20.00
6 Jay Roberts	7.50	15.00
7 Joe Poirier	10.00	20.00
8 Corey Colehour	7.50	15.00
9 Dave Gasser	7.50	15.00
10 Wally Gabler	10.00	20.00
11 Paul Desjardins	7.50	15.00
12 Larry DeGraw	7.50	15.00
13 Jerry Keeling	12.50	25.00
14 Gerry Shaw	7.50	15.00
15 Terry Evanshen	12.50	25.00
16 Sonny Wade	10.00	20.00

1971 O-Pee-Chee CFL

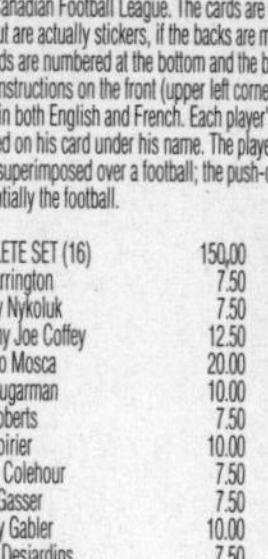

The 1971 O-Pee-Chee CFL set features 132 standard-size cards ordered by teams. The card fronts feature a bright red border. The card backs are written in French and English. A complete checklist is given on card number 132. The key card in the set is Joe Theismann, which is his first professional card and predates his entry into the NFL.

COMPLETE SET (132)	200.00	400.00
1 Bill Symons	1.25	3.00
2 Mel Profit	1.25	3.00
3 Jim Tomlin	1.00	2.50
4 Ed Harrington	1.25	3.00
5 Jim Corrigall	1.50	4.00
6 Chip Barrett	1.00	2.50
7 Marv Luster	1.25	3.00
8 Ellison Kelly	1.50	4.00
9 Charlie Bray	1.00	2.50
10 Pete Martin	1.00	2.50
11 Tony Moro	1.00	2.50
12 Dave Raimey	1.25	3.00
13 Joe Theismann	30.00	60.00
14 Greg Barton	3.00	6.00
15 Leon McQuay	3.00	6.00
16 Don Jonas	3.00	6.00
17 Doug Strong	1.00	2.50
18 Paul Brule	1.00	2.50
19 Bill Frank	1.00	2.50
20 Joe Critchlow	1.00	2.50
21 Chuck Liebrock	1.00	2.50
22 Rob McLaren	1.00	2.50
23 Bob Swift	1.00	2.50
24 Rick Shaw	1.00	2.50
25 Ross Richardson	1.00	2.50
26 Benji Dial	1.00	2.50
27 Jim Heighton	1.00	2.50
28 Ed Ulmer	1.00	2.50
29 Glen Schapansky	1.00	2.50
30 Larry Slagle	1.00	2.50
31 Tom Cassese	1.00	2.50
32 Ted Gerela	1.00	2.50
33 Bob Howes	1.00	2.50
34 Ken Sugarman	1.25	3.00
35 A.D. Whitfield	1.25	3.00
36 Jim Young	3.00	6.00
37 Tom Wilkinson	4.00	8.00
38 Lefty Hendrickson	1.00	2.50
39 Dave Golinsky	1.00	2.50
40 Gerry Herron	1.00	2.50
41 Jim Evenson	1.25	3.00
42 Greg Findlay	1.00	2.50
43 Garrett Hunsperger	1.00	2.50
44 Jerry Bradley	1.00	2.50
45 Trevor Ekdahl	1.25	3.00
46 Bayne Norrie	1.00	2.50
47 Henry King	1.00	2.50
48 Terry Swarn	1.25	3.00
49 Jim Thomas	1.25	3.00
50 Bob Houmard	1.00	2.50
51 Don Trull	1.25	3.00
52 Dave Cutler	4.00	8.00
53 Mike Law	1.00	2.50
54 Dick Dupuis	1.25	3.00
55 Dave Gasser	1.00	2.50
56 Ron Forwick	1.00	2.50
57 John LaGrone	1.25	3.00
58 Greg Pipes	1.25	3.00
59 Ted Page	1.00	2.50
60 John Wydareny	1.25	3.00
61 Joe Zuger	1.25	3.00
62 Tommy Joe Coffey	3.00	6.00
63 Rensi Perdoni	1.00	2.50
64 Bob Taylor	1.25	3.00
65 Garney Henley	3.00	6.00
66 Dick Wesolowski	1.00	2.50
67 Dave Fleming	1.00	2.50
68 Bill Danychuk	1.25	3.00
69 Angelo Mosca	7.50	15.00
70 Bob Krouse	1.00	2.50
71 Tony Gabriel	7.50	15.00
72 Wally Gabler	1.25	3.00
73 Bob Steiner	1.00	2.50
74 John Reid	1.00	2.50
75 Jon Hohman	1.00	2.50
76 Barry Ardern	1.00	2.50
77 Jerry Campbell	1.25	3.00
78 Billy Cooper	1.00	2.50
79 Dave Braggins	1.00	2.50
80 Tom Schuette	1.00	2.50
81 Dennis Duncan	1.00	2.50
82 Moe Racine	1.00	2.50
83 Rod Woodward	1.00	2.50
84 Al Marcelin	1.25	3.00
85 Gary Wood	2.50	5.00
86 Wayne Giardino	1.00	2.50
87 Roger Perdrix	1.00	2.50
88 Hugh Oldham	1.00	2.50
89 Rick Cassatta	1.25	3.00
90 Jack Abendschan	1.25	3.00
91 Don Bahnuik	1.00	2.50
92 Bill Baker	4.00	8.00
93 Gordon Barwell	1.00	2.50
94 Gary Brandt	1.00	2.50
95 Henry Dorsch	1.00	2.50
96 Ted Dushinski	1.00	2.50
97 Alan Ford	1.00	2.50
98 Ken Frith	1.00	2.50
99 Ralph Galloway	1.00	2.50
100 Bob Kosid	1.00	2.50
101 Ron Lancaster	6.00	12.00
102 Silas McKinnie	1.00	2.50
103 George Reed	4.00	8.00
104 Gene Ceppetelli	1.00	2.50
105 Merl Code	1.00	2.50
106 Peter Dalla Riva	4.00	8.00
107 Moses Denson	1.25	3.00
108 Pierre Desjardins	1.00	2.50
109 Terry Evanshen	3.00	6.00
110 Larry Fairholm	1.25	3.00
111 Gene Gaines	2.50	5.00
112 Ed George	1.25	3.00
113 Gordon Judges	1.00	2.50
114 Garry Lefebvre	1.00	2.50
115 Al Phaneuf	1.25	3.00
116 Steve Smear	2.50	5.00
117 Sonny Wade	1.50	4.00
118 Frank Andruski	1.00	2.50
119 Basil Bark	1.00	2.50
120 Lanny Boleski	1.00	2.50
121 Joe Forzani	1.25	3.00
122 Jim Furlong	1.00	2.50
123 Wayne Harris	3.00	6.00
124 Herman Harrison	2.50	5.00
125 John Helton	1.50	4.00
126 Wayne Holm	1.00	2.50
127 Fred James	1.00	2.50
128 Jerry Keeling	2.50	5.00
129 Rudy Linterman	1.25	3.00
130 Larry Robinson	1.50	4.00
131 Gerry Shaw	1.00	2.50
132 Checklist Card	15.00	30.00

1971 O-Pee-Chee CFL Poster Inserts

This 16-card set of posters featuring all-stars of the Canadian Football League was inserted in wax packs along with the regular issue of O-Pee-Chee cards. These 5" by 7" posters were folded twice in order to fit in the wax packs. They are numbered at the bottom and are blank on the back. These posters are somewhat similar in appearance to the Topps football poster inserts of 1971.

COMPLETE SET (16)	75.00	150.00
1 Tommy Joe Coffey	6.00	12.00
2 Herman Harrison	6.00	12.00
3 Bill Frank	4.00	8.00
4 Ellison Kelly	5.00	10.00
5 Charlie Bray	4.00	8.00
6 Bill Danychuk	5.00	10.00
7 Ron Lancaster	7.50	15.00
8 Bill Symons	5.00	10.00
9 Steve Smear	5.00	10.00
10 Angelo Mosca	7.50	15.00
11 Wayne Harris	6.00	12.00
12 Greg Findlay	4.00	8.00
13 John Wydareny	5.00	10.00
14 Garney Henley	6.00	12.00
15 Al Phaneuf	5.00	10.00
16 Ed Harrington	5.00	10.00

1972 O-Pee-Chee CFL

The 1972 O-Pee-Chee CFL set of 132 standard-size cards is the last O-Pee-Chee CFL issue to date. Cards are ordered by teams. The card backs are written in French and English; card back is blue and green print on white card stock. Fourteen Pro-Action cards (118-131) and a checklist card (132) complete the set. The key card in the set is Joe Theismann. The cards were originally sold in ten-cent wax packs with eight cards and a piece of bubble gum.

COMPLETE SET (132)	125.00	250.00
1 Bob Krouse	1.50	3.00
2 John Williams	.50	1.25
3 Garney Henley	3.00	6.00
4 Dick Wesolowski	.50	1.25
5 Paul McKay	.50	1.25
6 Bill Danychuk	.75	2.00
7 Angelo Mosca	5.00	10.00
8 Tommy Joe Coffey	2.50	5.00
9 Tony Gabriel	4.00	8.00
10 Mike Blum	.50	1.25
11 Doug Mitchell	.50	1.25
12 Emery Hicks	.50	1.25
13 Max Anderson	.50	1.25
14 Ed George	.75	2.00
15 Mark Kosmos	.75	2.00
16 Ted Collins	.50	1.25
17 Peter Dalla Riva	2.50	5.00
18 Pierre Desjardins	.50	1.25
19 Terry Evanshen	3.00	6.00
20 Larry Fairholm	.75	2.00
21 Jim Foley	.75	2.00
22 Gordon Judges	.50	1.25
23 Barry Randall	.50	1.25
24 Brad Upshaw	.50	1.25
25 Jorma Kuisma	.50	1.25
26 Mike Widger	.50	1.25
27 Joe Theismann	15.00	30.00
28 Greg Barton	2.00	4.00
29 Bill Symons	1.50	3.00
30 Leon McQuay	2.00	4.00
31 Jim Corrigall	2.00	4.00
32 Jim Stillwagon	2.50	5.00
33 Dick Thornton	.75	2.00
34 Marv Luster	2.00	4.00
35 Paul Desjardins	.50	1.25
36 Mike Eben	.50	1.25
37 Eric Allen	2.50	5.00
38 Chip Barrett	.50	1.25
39 Noah Jackson	1.50	3.00
40 Jim Young	3.00	6.00
41 Trevor Ekdahl	.75	2.00
42 Garrett Hunsperger	.50	1.25
43 Willie Postler	.50	1.25
44 George Anderson	.50	1.25
45 Ron Estay	.50	1.25
46 Johnny Musso	6.00	12.00
47 Eric Guthrie	.50	1.25
48 Monroe Eley	.50	1.25
49 Don Bunce	2.50	5.00
50 Jim Evenson	.75	2.00
51 Ken Sugarman	.75	2.00
52 Dave Golinsky	.50	1.25
53 Wayne Harris	2.50	5.00
54 Jerry Keeling	2.00	4.00
55 Herman Harrison	2.00	4.00
56 Larry Robinson	1.50	3.00
57 John Helton	2.00	4.00
58 Gerry Shaw	.50	1.25
59 Frank Andruski	.50	1.25
60 Basil Bark	.50	1.25
61 Joe Forzani	.75	2.00
62 Jim Furlong	.50	1.25
63 Rudy Linterman	.75	2.00
64 Granville Liggins	1.50	3.00
65 Lanny Boleski	.50	1.25
66 Hugh Oldham	.50	1.25
67 Dave Braggins	.50	1.25
68 Jerry Campbell	.75	2.00
69 Al Marcelin	.75	2.00
70 Tom Pullen	.50	1.25
71 Rudy Sims	.50	1.25
72 Marshall Shirk	.50	1.25
73 Tom Laputka	.50	1.25
74 Barry Ardern	.50	1.25
75 Billy Cooper	.50	1.25
76 Dan Deever	.50	1.25
77 Wayne Giardino	.50	1.25
78 Terry Wellesley	.50	1.25
79 Ron Lancaster	5.00	10.00
80 George Reed	4.00	8.00
81 Bobby Thompson	.50	1.25
82 Jack Abendschan	.75	2.00
83 Ed McQuarters	1.50	3.00
84 Bruce Bennett	1.50	3.00
85 Bill Baker	2.50	5.00
86 Don Bahnuik	.50	1.25
87 Gary Brandt	.50	1.25
88 Henry Dorsch	.50	1.25
89 Ted Dushinski	.50	1.25
90 Alan Ford	.50	1.25
91 Bob Kosid	.50	1.25
92 Greg Pipes	.75	2.00
93 John LaGrone	.75	2.00
94 Dave Gasser	.50	1.25
95 Bob Taylor	.75	2.00
96 Dave Cutler	3.00	6.00
97 Dick Dupuis	.50	1.25
98 Ron Forwick	.50	1.25
99 Bayne Norrie	.50	1.25
100 Jim Henshall	.50	1.25
101 Charlie Turner	.50	1.25
102 Fred Dunn	.50	1.25
103 Sam Scarber	.50	1.25
104 Bruce Lemmerman	3.00	6.00
105 Don Jonas	2.50	5.00
106 Doug Strong	.50	1.25
107 Ed Williams	.50	1.25
108 Paul Markle	.50	1.25
109 Gene Lakusiak	.50	1.25
110 Bob LaRose	.50	1.25
111 Rob McLaren	.50	1.25
112 Pete Ribbins	.50	1.25
113 Bill Frank	.50	1.25
114 Bob Swift	.50	1.25
115 Chuck Liebrock	.50	1.25
116 Joe Critchlow	.50	1.25
117 Paul Williams	.50	1.25
118 Pro Action Max Anderson	.50	1.25
119 Pro Action Max Anderson	.50	1.25
120 Pro Action	.50	1.25
121 Pro Action	.50	1.25
122 Pro Action Emery Hicks Frank Andruski	.50	1.25
123 Pro Action Greg Barton	.50	1.25
124 Pro Action	.50	1.25
125 Pro Action Paul Markle	.50	1.25
126 Pro Action	.50	1.25
127 Pro Action Don Jonas	.75	2.00
128 Pro Action Don Jonas	.75	2.00
129 Pro Action	.50	1.25
130 Pro Action Joe Theismann	6.00	12.00
131 Pro Action Paul McKay	.50	1.25
132 Checklist Card	15.00	30.00

1972 O-Pee-Chee CFL Trio Sticker Inserts

Issued with the 1972 CFL regular cards was this 24-card set of trio peel-off sticker inserts. These blank-backed panels of three small stickers are 2 1/2" by 3 1/2" and have a distinctive black border around an inner white border. Each individual player is numbered in the upper corner of his card; the player's name and team are given below the player's picture in the black border. The copyright notation (O.P.C. Printed in Canada) is overprinted in the picture area of the card.

COMPLETE SET (24)	125.00	225.00
1 Johnny Musso/2 Ron Lancaster 3 Don Jonas	15.00	30.00
4 Jerry Campbell/5 Bill Symons 6 Ted Collins	4.00	8.00
7 Dave Cutler/8 Paul McKay/9 Rudy Sims	5.00	10.00
10 Wayne Harris/11 Greg Pipes 12 Chuck Ealey	10.00	20.00
13 Ron Estay/14 Jack Abendschan 15 Paul Markle	4.00	8.00
16 Jim Stillwagon/17 Terry Evanshen 18 Willie Postler	7.50	15.00
19 Hugh Oldham/20 Joe Theismann 21 Ed George	17.50	35.00
22 Larry Robinson23 Bruce Lemmerman 24 Garney Henley	5.00	10.00
25 Bill Baker/26 Bob LaRose 27 Frank Andruski	5.00	10.00
28 Don Bunce/29 George Reed 30 Doug Strong	6.00	12.00
31 Al Marcelin/32 Leon McQuay/ 33 Peter Dalla Riva	5.00	10.00
34 Dick Dupuis/35 Bill Danychuk 36 Marshall Shirk	4.00	8.00
37 Jerry Keeling/38 John LaGrone 39 Bob Krouse	5.00	10.00
40 Jim Young/41 Ed McQuarters 42 Gene Lakusiak	5.00	10.00
43 Dick Thornton/44 Larry Fairholm 45 Garrett Hunsperger	4.00	8.00
46 Dave Braggins/47 Greg Barton 48 Mark Kosmos	5.00	10.00
49 John Helton/50 Bobby Taylor 51 Dick Wesolowski	5.00	10.00
52 Don Bahnuik/53 Rob McLaren 54 Granville Liggins	4.00	8.00
55 Monroe Eley/56 Bob Thompson 57 Ed Williams	4.00	8.00
58 Tom Pullen/59 Jim Corrigall 60 Pierre Desjardins	4.00	8.00
61 Ron Forwick/62 Angelo Mosca 63 Tom Laputka	10.00	20.00
64 Herman Harrison/65 Dave Gasser 66 John Williams	4.00	8.00
67 Trevor Ekdahl/68 Bruce Bennett 69 Gerry Shaw	4.00	8.00
70 Jim Foley/71 Pete Ribbins 72 Marv Luster	4.00	8.00

1951 Ottawa Rough Riders Team Issue

This set of Rough Riders player photos was issued by the team to fill fan requests. Each photo measures roughly 8 1/2" by 11" and includes the player's name and position (spelled out) below the photo. The unnumbered backs are blank.

COMPLETE SET (12)	100.00	200.00
1 Alton Baldwin	12.50	25.00
2 Bruce Cummings	12.50	25.00
3 Jake Dunlop	12.50	25.00
4 Bob Gain	12.50	25.00
5 Steve Hatfield	12.50	25.00
6 Bill Larochelle	12.50	25.00
7 Benny MacDonnell	12.50	25.00
8 Tom O'Malley	12.50	25.00
9 Bob Simpson	12.50	25.00
10 Bill Stanton	12.50	25.00
11 Howie Turner	12.50	25.00
12 John Wagoner	12.50	25.00

1960 Ottawa Rough Riders Team Issue

This set of Rough Riders player photos was issued by the team to fill fan requests. Each photo measures roughly 8" by 10" and includes the player's name, position (spelled out), height, and weight slightly to the left below the photo. The Rough Riders logo appears in the lower right hand corner. The unnumbered backs are blank.

COMPLETE SET (4)	25.00	50.00
1 Jim Conroy	7.50	15.00
2 Joe Poirier	7.50	15.00
3 Gary Schreider	6.00	12.00
4 George Terlep GM	6.00	12.00

1961 Ottawa Rough Riders Team Issue

This set of Rough Riders player photos was issued by the team to fill fan requests. Each photo measures roughly 8" by 10" and includes the player's name, position (spelled out), height, and weight to the far left below the photo. The Rough Riders logo appears in the lower right hand corner. The unnumbered backs are blank.

COMPLETE SET (40)	200.00	400.00
1 Gilles Archambeault	6.00	12.00
2 Merv Bevan	7.50	15.00
3 Bruno Bitkowski	6.00	12.00
4 Billy Joe Booth	6.00	12.00
5 George Brancato	6.00	12.00
6 Jim Cain	6.00	12.00
7 Len Chandler	6.00	12.00
8 Edward Chlebek	6.00	12.00
9 Merv Collins	6.00	12.00
10 Jim Conroy	6.00	12.00
11 Doug Daigneault	6.00	12.00
12 Paul D'Arras	6.00	12.00
13 Dick Desmarais	6.00	12.00
14 Millard Flemming	6.00	12.00
15 David Herne	6.00	12.00
16 Ron Koes	6.00	12.00
17 Russ Jackson	15.00	25.00
18 Tom Jones	6.00	12.00
19 Ron Lancaster	18.00	30.00
20 Donald Scott Maentz	6.00	12.00
21 Joe Poirier	6.00	12.00
22 Moe Racine	6.00	12.00
23 Jim Reynolds	6.00	12.00
24 Tom Rodgers	6.00	12.00
25 Norb Roy	6.00	12.00
26 Sam Scoccia	6.00	12.00
27 Jerry Selinger	6.00	12.00
28 Bob Simpson	12.00	20.00
29 Ted Smale	6.00	12.00
30 Mike Snodgras	6.00	12.00
31 Ron Stewart	15.00	25.00
32 Chuck Stanley	6.00	12.00
33 Dave Thelen	12.00	20.00
34 Whit Tucker	7.50	15.00
35 Kaye Vaughan	7.50	15.00
36 Ernie White	6.00	12.00
37 Chuck Wood	6.00	12.00
38 Coaches Don Branby Frank Clair Bill Smyth	6.00	12.00
39 Frank Clair CO	6.00	12.00
40 Bill Smyth CO	6.00	12.00

1962 Ottawa Rough Riders Team Issue

This set of Rough Riders player photos was issued by the team to fill fan requests. Each photo measures roughly 8" by 10 1/4" and includes the player's name, position, height, and weight in large letters below the photo. The Rough Riders logo appears in the lower right hand corner. The unnumbered backs are blank.

COMPLETE SET (30)	150.00	300.00
1 Merv Bevan	7.50	15.00
2 Rick Black	6.00	12.00
3 Don Branby ASST. CO	6.00	12.00
4 Billy Joe Booth	6.00	12.00
5 Jim Cain	6.00	12.00
6 Frank Clair Head CO	6.00	12.00
7 Merv Collins	6.00	12.00
8 Larry DeGraw	6.00	12.00
9 Gene Gaines	7.50	15.00
10 Russ Jackson	15.00	25.00
11 Bill Johnson	6.00	12.00
12 Roger Kramer	6.00	12.00
13 Tommy Lee	6.00	12.00
14 Bob O'Billovich	6.00	12.00
15 Joe Poirier	6.00	12.00
16 Peter Quinn	6.00	12.00
17 Bill Quinter	6.00	12.00
18 Moe Racine	6.00	12.00
19 Sam Scoccia	6.00	12.00
20 Jerry Selinger	6.00	12.00
21 Mel Semenko	6.00	12.00
22 Bill Siekierski	6.00	12.00
23 Billy Smyth ASST. CO	6.00	12.00
24 Ron Stewart	15.00	25.00
25 Dave Thelen	12.00	20.00
26 Oscar Thorsland	6.00	12.00
27 Whit Tucker	7.50	15.00
28 Kaye Vaughan	7.50	15.00
29 Ted Watkins	6.00	12.00
30 Ernie White	6.00	12.00

1967 Ottawa Rough Riders Rideau Trust

These photos measure roughly 4" by 6" and feature three members of the 1967 Ottawa Rough Riders. The Rideau Trust Company logo appears below each player's black and white photo. A facsimile autograph also appears below the photo for each player as well. The unnumbered backs feature a bio for each of the three players. We've cataloged the photos with the player on the far left listed first on each card.

COMPLETE SET (12)	175.00	300.00
1 Mike Blum Russ Jackson Chuck Harrison	20.00	35.00
2 Billy Joe Booth Russ Jackson Jay Roberts	25.00	40.00
3 Al Bruno Kelley Mote Frank Clair Coaches	10.00	20.00
4 Jim Cain Bo Scott Larry DeGraw	20.00	35.00
5 Bill Cline Whit Tucker Ted Collins	12.50	25.00
6 Wayne Giardino Margene Adkins Moe Levesque	10.00	20.00
7 Roger Pardin Ken Lehmann Doug Specht	10.00	20.00
8 Joe Poirier Rick Black Bob Brown	12.50	25.00
9 Tom Schuette Moe Racine Jerry Selinger	10.00	20.00
10 Don Sutherlin Ron Stewart Jim Conroy	20.00	35.00
11 Peter Thompson Bob O'Billovich Don Gilbert	10.00	20.00
12 Mike Walderzak Gene Gaines Marshall Shirk	12.50	25.00

1967 Ottawa Rough Riders Team Issue

The Rough Riders issued this set of player photos around 1967. Each includes two black-and-white player photos with one being a posed action shot along with a smaller portrait image. The roughly 8" by 10 1/8" photos include the player's name, position, college, age, birthplace, a short bio, and team logo on the cardfronts. The backs are blank and unnumbered.

COMPLETE SET (14)	60.00	120.00
1 Rick Black	5.00	10.00
2 Terry Black	5.00	10.00
3 Mike Blum	5.00	10.00
4 Jim Cain	5.00	10.00
5 Bill Cline	5.00	10.00
6 Ted Collins	5.00	10.00
7 Gene Gaines	6.00	12.00
8 Don Gilbert	5.00	10.00
9 Chuck Harrison	5.00	10.00
10 Ed Joyner	5.00	10.00
11 Moe Levesque	5.00	10.00
12 Bob O'Billovich	5.00	10.00
13 Jerry Selinger	5.00	10.00
14 Mike Walderzak	5.00	10.00

1970 Ottawa Rough Riders Team Issue

The Rough Riders issued this set of player photos around 1970. Each includes two black-and-white player photos with one being a larger posed action shot and the other a smaller portrait image. The roughly 8" by 10 1/8" photos include only the player's name and team logo on the cardfronts below the smaller image. The backs are blank and unnumbered.

COMPLETE SET (32)	100.00	200.00
1 Dick Adams	4.00	8.00
2 Barry Ardern	4.00	8.00
3 Allan Barclay	4.00	8.00
4 Charles Brandon	4.00	8.00
5A Paul Brothers (black jersey)	4.00	8.00
5B Paul Brothers (white jersey)	4.00	8.00
6 Jerry Campbell	4.00	8.00
7 Arthur Cantrelle	4.00	8.00
8 Rick Cassatta	4.00	8.00
9 Marcel Deleeuw	4.00	8.00
10 Dennis Duncan	4.00	8.00
11A Skip Eaman (black jersey)	4.00	8.00
11B Skip Eaman (white jersey)	4.00	8.00
12 James Elder	4.00	8.00
13 Bob Houmard	4.00	8.00
14 John Kennedy	4.00	8.00
15 John Kruspe	4.00	8.00
16 Tom Laputka	4.00	8.00
17 Art Laster	4.00	8.00
18 Richard Lolotai	4.00	8.00
19 Bob McKeown	4.00	8.00
20 Rhome Nixon	4.00	8.00
21 Gerry Organ	5.00	10.00
22 Jim Piaskoski	4.00	8.00
23 Dave Pivec	4.00	8.00
24 Gus Revenberg	4.00	8.00
25 Rudy Sims	4.00	8.00
26 Tom Schultz	4.00	8.00
27 Wayne Tosh	4.00	8.00
28 Bill Van Burkleo	4.00	8.00
29 Gary Wood	5.00	10.00
30 Rod Woodward	4.00	8.00
31 Ulysses Young	4.00	8.00
32 Coaches: Kelley Mote Frank Clair Jack Gotta	4.00	8.00

1971 Ottawa Rough Riders Royal Bank

These photos were issued by Royal Bank and feature members of the Rough Riders. Each photo measures roughly 5" by 7" and includes a black and white photo of the player with his jersey number and name above the picture. The Royal Bank logo and set title "Royal Bank Leo's Leaders Rough Riders Player of the Week" appear below the photo in French and English. The photo backs are blank.

COMPLETE SET (7)	18.00	30.00
1 Billy Cooper	2.50	5.00
2 Wayne Giardino	2.50	5.00
3 Al Marcelin	2.50	5.00
4 Bob McKeown	2.50	5.00
5 Rhome Nixon	2.50	5.00
6 Hugh Oldham	2.50	5.00
7 Moe Racine	2.50	5.00

1971 Ottawa Rough Riders Team Issue

The Rough Riders issued this set of player photos around 1971. Each includes two black-and-white player photos with one being a posed action shot along with a smaller portrait image. The roughly 8" by 10 1/8" photos include the player's name, position, college, vital stats, a lengthy bio, and team logo on the cardfronts. The backs are blank and unnumbered.

COMPLETE SET (18)	40.00	80.00
1 Irby Augustine	4.00	8.00
2 Bob Brown	4.00	8.00
3 Lovell Coleman	5.00	10.00
4 Tom Deacon	4.00	8.00
5 Ivan MacMillan	4.00	8.00
6 Jim Mankins	4.00	8.00
7 Allen Marcelin	4.00	8.00
8 Hugh Oldham	4.00	8.00
9 LeVerle Pratt	4.00	8.00
10 Tom Pullen	4.00	8.00
11 Frank Reid	4.00	8.00
12 Gus Revenberg	4.00	8.00
13 Ken Shaw	4.00	8.00
14 Greg Thompson	4.00	8.00
15 Bill Van Burkleo	4.00	8.00
16 Joe Vijuk	4.00	8.00
17 Terry Wellesley	4.00	8.00
18 Gary Wood	5.00	10.00

1984 Ottawa Rough Riders McDonald's Jogo

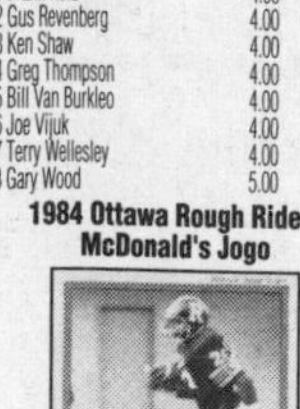

This 4 panel (12 card) full-color set was issued in panels of three over a four-week period as a promotion of McDonald's and radio station CFRA 58 AM. It was reported that 210,000 panels were given away at McDonald's. Cards were produced in conjunction with JOGO Novelties. The cards can be separated as they are perforated. The cards are unnumbered although the player's uniform number is given on the back of the card. The numbering below refers to the week (of the promotion) during which the panel was distributed. Photos were taken by F. Scott Grant, who is credited on the fronts of the cards. The cards measure approximately 2 1/2" by 3 1/2" when separated.

COMPLETE SET (4)	7.50	15.00
1 Ken Miller Rudy Phillips Jim Reid	.75	2.00

2 Gary Dulin	.75	2.00
Greg Marshall		
Junior Robinson		
3 Kevin Powell	.75	2.00
Tyron Gray		
Skip Walker		
4 Rick Sowieta	5.00	10.00
Bruce Walker		
J.C. Watts		

1984 Ottawa Rough Riders Police

This ten-card full-color set was given away over a ten-week period. The sponsors were Kiwanis, several Police Forces, and radio station CFRA 58 AM. Cards were produced in conjunction with JOGO Inc. The cards are unnumbered although the player's uniform number is given on the front of the card. The numbering below is in alphabetical order for convenience. The cards measure approximately 2 1/2" by 3 1/2". Photos were taken by F. Scott Grant, who is credited on the fronts of the cards. Mark Seale was the card for the tenth and final week; he was printed in a much smaller quantity than the other cards. It was reported that 6,000 of each of the first nine players were given away, whereas only 500 Mark Seale cards were given out.

COMPLETE SET (10)	25.00	50.00
1 Greg Marshall	.50	1.25
2 Dave Newman	.30	.75
3 Rudy Phillips	1.50	4.00
4 Jim Reid	.50	1.25
5 Mark Seale SP	8.00	20.00
6 Rick Sowieta	.50	1.25
7 Pat Sloqua	.50	1.25
8 Skip Walker	.30	.75
9 Al Washington	.30	.75
10 J.C. Watts	10.00	20.00

1985 Ottawa Rough Riders Police

This ten-card set was also sponsored by Burger King as indicated on the front of each card and JOGO Inc. as indicated on the back. The cards measure approximately 2 1/2" by 3 1/2". Card photos (by photographer F. Scott Grant) all show Ottawa Rough Riders in game action. The numbering below is in alphabetical order for convenience.

COMPLETE SET (10)	2.50	6.00
1 Ricky Barden	.10	.30
2 Michel Bourgeau	.20	.50
3 Roger Cattolan	.10	.30
4 Ken Clark	.20	.50
5 Dean Dorsey	.20	.50
6 Greg Marshall	.20	.50
7 Kevin Powell	.10	.30
8 Jim Reid	.20	.50
9 Rick Sowieta	.20	.50
10 J.C. Watts	1.50	4.00

1985 Ottawa Rough Riders Yesterday's Heroes

Cards from this set were inserted in Rough Riders game programs in 1985. Each card measures roughly 3 1/2" by 5" and features two former players with one player identified and one player featured as the "Name the Rider" player. The following week's card would identify the previous week's mystery player along with a new mystery. The cardbacks include a bio of the primary player along with various advertising sponsorships. We've cataloged the cards below with the featured (identified) player listed first.

COMPLETE SET (9)	18.00	30.00
1 1960 Rough Riders Team	1.25	3.00
2 Russ Jackson	3.00	6.00
Angelo Mosca		
3 Angelo Mosca	2.50	5.00
Joe Poirier		
4 Joe Poirier	1.25	3.00
Sam Scoccia		
5 Sam Scoccia	.75	2.00
Gilles Archambeault		
6 Gilles Archambeault	2.50	5.00
Ron Lancaster		
7 Ron Lancaster	2.50	5.00
Tom Jones		
8 Tom Jones	.75	2.00
Gerry Nesbitt		
9 Gerry Nesbitt/	.75	2.00

2003 Pacific CFL Promos

*SINGLES: .6X TO 1.5X BASIC CARDS

2003 Pacific CFL

This set marks the first Pacific Trading Cards CFL release and the first major card manufacturer to produce cards for the league in more than 10-years. Most of the top stars of the league are included in the set with the first ever CFL jersey card inserts as highlights. The cards were packaged 5-cards per pack with 30-packs in a box. A 10-card Update set was issued later in the year featuring ten rookies not included in the base set. Reportedly, only 499-Update sets were produced.

COMPLETE SET (120)	25.00	50.00
COMP.SERIES 1 SET (110)	20.00	40.00
COMP.UPDATE SET (10)	12.00	20.00
1 Bret Anderson	.15	.40
2 Chris Brazzell	.25	.60
3 Eric Carter	.08	.25
4 Jason Clermont	.50	1.25
5 Dave Dickenson	.60	1.50
6 Willie Hurst	.25	.60
7 Carl Kidd	.25	.60
8 Bo Lewis	.08	.25
9 Mark Nohra	.15	.40
10 Geroy Simon	.40	1.00
11 Barrin Simpson	.08	.25
12 Ryan Thelwell	.40	1.00
13 Spergon Wynn	.25	.60
14 Kelvin Anderson	.50	1.25
15 Don Blair	.15	.40
16 Albert Connell	.25	.60
17 Marcus Crandell	.40	1.00
18 Kevin Feterik	.30	.75
19 Joe Fleming	.40	1.00
20 Alondra Johnson	.25	.60
21 Demetrious Maxie	.15	.40
22 Wane McGarity	.25	.60
23 Mark McLoughlin	.08	.25
24 Lawrence Phillips	.50	1.25
25 Reidel Anthony	.25	.60
26 Mike Bradley	.08	.25
27 Sean Fleming	.08	.25
28 Ed Hervey	.30	.75
29 Jason Maas	.40	1.00
30 Singor Mobley	.08	.25
31 Winston October	.30	.75
32 Elfrid Payton	.15	.40
33 Mike Pringle	.60	1.50
34 Ricky Ray	1.00	2.50
35 Jason Tucker	.25	.60
36 Terry Vaughn	.30	.75
37 Rick Walters	.15	.40
38 Tony Akins	.15	.40
39 Archie Amerson	.40	1.00
40 Troy Davis	.40	1.00
41 Tyree Davis	.15	.40
42 Pete Gonzalez	.15	.40
43 Rob Hitchcock	.08	.25
44 Danny McManus	.60	1.50
45 Joe Montford	.25	.60
46 Paul Osbaldiston	.08	.25
47 Chris Shelling	.08	.25
48 Jarrett Smith	.15	.40
49 Tavares Bolden	.08	.25
50 Robert Brown	.08	.25
51 Ben Cahoon	.75	2.00
52 Anthony Calvillo	.60	1.50
53 Jermaine Copeland	.30	.75
54 Sylvain Girard	.15	.40
55 Bruno Heppell	.08	.25
56 Kevin Johnson	.25	.60
57 Eric Lapointe	.15	.40
58 Marc Megna	.30	.75
59 Barron Miles	.25	.60
60 Demetris Bendross	.15	.40
61 Donnavan Carter	.15	.40
62 Dameyune Craig	.15	.40
63 Danny Crowley	.25	.60
64 Aubrey Cummings	.15	.40
65 Darren Davis	.40	1.00
66 John Grace	.25	.60
67 Andre Kirwan	.15	.40
68 Denis Montana	.15	.40
69 Josh Ranek	1.00	2.50
70 Lawrence Tynes	.08	.25
71 Gerald Vaughn	.08	.25
72 Kelly Wiltshire	.08	.25
73 Jason French	.08	.25
74 Kevin Glenn	.50	1.25
75 Nealon Greene	.40	1.00
76 Rocky Henry	.15	.40
77 Corey Holmes	.50	1.25
78 Reggie Hunt	.08	.25
79 Paul McCallum	.25	.60
80 Travis Moore	.40	1.00
81 Omarr Morgan	.08	.25
82 Shonte Peoples	.15	.40
83 Sedrick Shaw	.25	.60
84 Damon Allen	.50	1.25
85 Michael Bishop	.25	.60
86 Marcus Brady	.15	.40
87 Clifford Ivory	.08	.25
88 Alfred Jackson	.40	1.00
89 Michael Jenkins	.50	1.25
90 Tony Miles	.40	1.00
91 Derrell Mitchell	.30	.75
92 Mike Morreale	.25	.60
93 Jimmy Oliver	.25	.60
94 Mike O?ÇÖShea	.25	.60
95 Johnny Scott	.08	.25
96 Adrion Smith	.15	.40
97 Doug Brown	.08	.25
98 Tom Europe	.08	.25
99 Dennis Fortney	.08	.25
100 Robert Gordon	.25	.60
101 Markus Howell	.15	.40
102 Khari Jones	.60	1.50
103 Maurice Kelly	.08	.25
104 Lamar McGriggs	.08	.25
105 Harold Nash Jr.	.08	.25
106 Chad Plummer	.15	.40
107 Charles Roberts	.75	2.00
108 Mike Sellers	.15	.40
109 Milt Stegall	.50	1.25
110 Troy Westwood	.08	.25
111 Frank Cutolo	1.25	3.00
112 Curtis Head	.60	1.50
113 Blake Machan	1.00	2.50
114 Brock Ralph	.60	1.50
115 Julian Radlein	.60	1.50
116 Thyron Anderson	1.00	2.50
117 Dave Stala	.25	.60
118 Pat Fleming	1.00	2.50
119 Kenton Keith	1.25	3.00
120 LaDaris Vann	.60	1.50

2003 Pacific CFL Red

COMPLETE SET (110)	60.00	120.00

*RED: 1.2X TO 3X BASIC CARDS
STATED ODDS ONE PER PACK

2003 Pacific CFL Division Collision

COMPLETE SET (9)	12.50	30.00
STATED ODDS 1:11		
1 Damon Allen	2.00	5.00
2 Marcus Crandell	2.00	5.00
3 Ricky Ray	2.50	6.00
4 Danny McManus	2.50	6.00
5 Anthony Calvillo	2.50	6.00
6 John Grace	.75	2.00
7 Nealon Greene	1.25	3.00
8 Derrell Mitchell	1.25	3.00
9 Khari Jones	2.50	6.00

2003 Pacific CFL Game Worn Jerseys

1 Marcus Crandell	7.50	20.00
2 Ed Hervey	6.00	15.00
3 Terry Vaughn	6.00	15.00
4 Danny McManus	10.00	25.00
5 Anthony Calvillo	10.00	25.00
6 John Grace	5.00	12.00
7 Khari Jones	10.00	25.00
8 Charles Roberts	7.50	20.00

2003 Pacific CFL Grey Cup Heroes

RANDOM INSERTS IN PACKS

1 Doug Flutie	6.00	15.00
2 Jeff Garcia	6.00	15.00

2003 Pacific CFL Grey Expectations

COMPLETE SET (7)	12.50	30.00
1 Damon Allen	2.00	5.00
2 Mike Pringle	2.00	5.00
3 Ricky Ray	2.50	6.00
4 Danny McManus	2.50	6.00
5 Anthony Calvillo	2.50	6.00
6 Khari Jones	2.50	6.00
7 Milt Stegall	2.00	5.00

2003 Pacific CFL Maximum Overdrive

COMPLETE SET (8)	10.00	25.00
STATED ODDS 1:16		
1 Mike Pringle	2.50	6.00
2 Terry Vaughn	1.50	4.00
3 Troy Davis	1.25	3.00
4 Ben Cahoon	1.50	4.00
5 Corey Holmes	.75	2.00
6 Michael Jenkins	2.50	6.00
7 Charles Roberts	1.50	4.00
8 Milt Stegall	2.50	6.00

2004 Pacific CFL

Pacific CFL initially released in mid-June 2004. The base set consists of 110-cards and boxes contained 30-packs of 5-cards with an S.R.P. of $2.99 per pack. One parallel set and a variety of inserts can be found seeded in packs highlighted by the Game Worn Jerseys inserts.

COMPLETE SET (110)	15.00	30.00
1 Angus Reid	.08	.25
Ben Fairbrother		
Bobby Singh		
Cory Mantyka		
Fred Moore		
2 Chris Brazzell	.25	.60
3 Jason Clermont	.50	1.25
4 Frank Cutolo	.60	1.50
5 Dave Dickenson	.60	1.50
6 Ray Jacobs	.08	.25
7 Carl Kidd	.15	.40
8 Cam Legault	.08	.25
9 Ron Ockimey	.08	.25
10 Geroy Simon	.40	1.00
11 Barrin Simpson	.08	.25
12 Mark Washington	.15	.40
13 Spergon Wynn	.25	.60
14 Jamie Crysdale	.08	.25
Jay McNeil		
Seth Dittman		
Jeff Pilon		
Taylor Robertson		
15 Don Blair	.08	.25
16 Joey Boese	.15	.40
17 Marcus Crandell	.40	1.00
18 Willie Fells	.08	.25
19 Saladin McCullough	.15	.40
20 Darnell McDonald	.15	.40
21 Wane McGarity	.25	.60
22 Scott Regimbald	.15	.40
23 Antwone Young	.08	.25
24 Tim Prinzen	.08	.25
Kevin Lefsrud		
Bruce Beaton		
Dan Comiskey		
Chris Morris		
25 Donny Brady	.15	.40
26 Steve Charbonneau	.08	.25
27 Sean Fleming	.08	.25
28 Shannon Garrett	.08	.25
29 A.J. Gass	.08	.25
30 Bart Hendricks	.15	.40
31 Ed Hervey	.25	.60
32 Jason Maas	.25	.60
33 Winston October	.25	.60
34 Mike Pringle	.50	1.25
35 Ricky Ray	.75	2.00
30 Terry Vaughn	.30	.75
37 Carl Coulter	.08	.25
Mike Mihelic		
Pascal Cheron		
Dave Hack		
Chase Raynock		
38 Archie Amerson	.40	1.00
39 Archie Amerson	.15	.40
40 Jason Currie	.15	.40
41 Troy Davis	.25	.60
42 Danny McManus	.60	1.50
43 Joe Montford	.25	.60
44 Paul Osbaldiston	.08	.25
45 Julian Radlein	.15	.40
46 Ray Thomas	.15	.40
47 Ibrahim Tounkara	.15	.40
48 Craig Yeast	.15	.40
49 Bryan Chiu	.15	.40
Scott Flory		
Neal Fort		
Uzooma Okeke		
Paul Lambert		
50 Robert Brown	.08	.25
51 Ben Cahoon	.30	.75
52 Anthony Calvillo	.60	1.50
53 Kwame Cavil	.15	.40
54 Jermaine Copeland	.30	.75
55 Sylvain Girard	.15	.40
56 Bruno Heppell	.08	.25
57 Kevin Johnson	.25	.60
58 Barron Miles	.25	.60
59 Ed Philion	.08	.25
60 Anwar Stewart	.15	.40
61 Timothy Strickland	.08	.25
62 Mike Abou-Mechrek	.15	.40
Chris Burns		
Mike Sutherland		
George Hudson		
Val St. Germain		
63 Raymonn Adams	.08	.25
64 Keaton Cromartie	.08	.25
65 Pat Fleming	.25	.60
66 Sherrod Gideon	.15	.40
67 Jerome Haywood	.08	.25
68 Kerry Joseph	.40	1.00
69 Denis Montana	.15	.40
70 Yo Murphy	.15	.40
71 Josh Ranek	.75	2.00
72 Clinton Wayne	.08	.25
73 Kelly Wiltshire	.08	.25
74 Jeremy O?ÇÖDay	.08	.25
Andrew Greene		
Donald Heaven		
Gene Makowsky		
Charles Thomas		
75 Nathan Davis	.08	.25
76 Corey Grant	.15	.40
77 Nealon Greene	.40	1.00
78 Corey Holmes	.15	.40
79 Reggie Hunt	.08	.25
80 Kenton Keith	.15	.40
81 Paul McCallum	.25	.60
82 Jackie Mitchell	.08	.25
83 Travis Moore	.40	1.00
84 Omarr Morgan	.08	.25
85 Jamol Richardson	.08	.25
86 Chris Szarka	.15	.40
87 Chad Folk	.08	.25
Sandy Annunziata		
Jude St. John		
Bernard Williams		
John Feugill		
88 Damon Allen	.50	1.25
89 Marcus Brady	.15	.40
90 Eric England	.15	.40
91 Clifford Ivory	.08	.25
92 Michael Jenkins	.50	1.25
93 Bashir Levingston	.30	.75
94 Tony Miles	.25	.60
95 Derrell Mitchell	.30	.75
96 Adrion Smith	.15	.40
97 Orlondo Steinauer	.08	.25
98 Mo Elewonibi	.08	.25
Eric Wilson		
Dave Mudge		
Matt Sheridan		
Dan Gyetvai		
99 Daved Benefield	.25	.60
100 Doug Brown	.08	.25
101 Tim Carter	.15	.40
102 Markus Howell	.15	.40
103 Stanley Jackson	.25	.60
104 Reggie Jones	.08	.25
105 Lamar McGriggs	.08	.25
106 Charles Roberts	.30	.75
107 Milt Stegall	.50	1.25
108 Jamie Stoddard	.15	.40
109 Troy Westwood	.08	.25
110 Ryland Wickman	.25	.60

2004 Pacific CFL Red

COMPLETE SET (110)	60.00	120.00

*REDS: 1.2X TO 3X BASIC CARDS
ONE RED PER PACK

2004 Pacific CFL Division Collision

COMPLETE SET (9)	10.00	25.00
STATED ODDS 1:11		
1 Dave Dickenson	2.00	5.00
2 Marcus Crandell	1.25	3.00
3 Mike Pringle	1.50	4.00
4 Danny McManus	2.00	5.00
5 Ben Cahoon	1.00	2.50
6 Kerry Joseph	1.25	3.00
7 Nealon Greene	1.25	3.00
8 Damon Allen	1.50	4.00
9 Milt Stegall	1.50	4.00

2004 Pacific CFL Game Worn Jerseys

TWO JERSEY CARDS PER BOX
STATED PRINT RUN 800 SER.#'d SETS

1 Dave Dickenson	10.00	25.00
2 Geroy Simon	6.00	15.00
3 Don Blair	4.00	10.00
4 Joe Fleming	5.00	12.00
5 Ed Hervey	6.00	15.00
6 Troy Davis	6.00	15.00
7 Danny McManus	10.00	25.00
8 Ben Cahoon	5.00	12.00
9 Anthony Calvillo	10.00	25.00
10 Jeremaine Copeland	6.00	15.00
11 Kevin Johnson	5.00	12.00
12 Grayson Shillingford	5.00	12.00
13 Nealon Greene	6.00	15.00
14 Khari Jones	10.00	25.00
15 Charles Roberts	5.00	12.00

2004 Pacific CFL Grey Expectations

COMPLETE SET (6)	5.00	12.00
STATED ODDS 1:16		
1 Dave Dickenson	2.00	5.00
2 Jason Maas	.75	2.00
3 Anthony Calvillo	2.00	5.00
4 Nealon Greene	1.25	3.00
5 Damon Allen	1.50	4.00
6 Khari Jones	.75	2.00

2004 Pacific CFL Maximum Overdrive

COMPLETE SET (8)	5.00	12.00
STATED ODDS 1:16		
1 Geroy Simon	1.25	3.00
2 Darnell McDonald	.50	1.25
3 Mike Pringle	1.50	4.00
4 Troy Davis	.75	2.00
5 Jermaine Copeland	1.00	2.50
6 Pat Woodcock	.50	1.25
7 Derrell Mitchell	1.00	2.50
8 Charles Roberts	1.00	2.50

1952 Parkhurst

The 1952 Parkhurst CFL set of 100 cards is the earliest known CFL issue. Features include the four Eastern teams: Toronto Argonauts (20-40), Montreal Alouettes (41-61), Ottawa Rough Riders (63-78, 100), and Hamilton Tiger-Cats (79-99), as well as 19 instructional artwork cards (1-19). These small cards measure approximately 1 7/8" by 2 3/4". There are two different number 58's and card number 62 does not exist.

COMPLETE SET (100)	1,800.00	3,000.00
1 Watch the games	30.00	50.00
2 Teamwork	12.50	25.00
3 Football Equipment	12.50	25.00
4 Hang onto the ball	12.50	25.00
5 The head on tackle	12.50	25.00
6 The football field	12.50	25.00
7 The Lineman's Stance	12.50	25.00
8 Centre's spiral pass	12.50	25.00
9 The lineman	12.50	25.00
10 The place kick	12.50	25.00
11 The cross-body block	12.50	25.00
12 T formation	12.50	25.00
13 Falling on the ball	12.50	25.00
14 The throw	12.50	25.00
15 Breaking from tackle	12.50	25.00
16 How to catch a pass	12.50	25.00
17 The punt	12.50	25.00
18 Shifting the ball	12.50	25.00
19 Penalty signals	12.50	25.00
20 Leslie Ascott	18.00	30.00
21 Robert Marshall	18.00	30.00
22 Tom Harpley	18.00	30.00
23 Robert McClelland	18.00	30.00
24 Rod Smylie	18.00	30.00
25 Bill Bass	18.00	30.00
26 Fred Black	18.00	30.00
27 Jack Carpenter	18.00	30.00
28 Bob Hack	18.00	30.00
29 Ulysses Curtis	18.00	30.00
30 Nobby Wirkowski	30.00	50.00
31 George Arnett	18.00	30.00
32 Lorne Parkin	18.00	30.00
33 Alex Toogood	18.00	30.00
34 Marshall Haymes	18.00	30.00
35 Shanty McKenzie	18.00	30.00
36 Byron Karrys	18.00	30.00
37 George Rooks	18.00	30.00
38 Red Ettinger	18.00	30.00
39 Al Bruno	25.00	40.00
40 Stephen Karrys	18.00	30.00
41 Herb Trawick	30.00	50.00
42 Sam Etcheverry	200.00	350.00
43 Marv Melrowitz	18.00	30.00
44 John Red O'Quinn	30.00	50.00
45 Jim Ostendarp	18.00	30.00
46 Tom Tofaute	18.00	30.00
47 Joey Pal	18.00	30.00
48 Ray Cicia	18.00	30.00
49 Bruce Coulter	25.00	40.00
50 Jim Mitchener	18.00	30.00
51 Lally Lalonde	18.00	30.00
52 Jim Staton	18.00	30.00
53 Glenn Douglas	18.00	30.00
54 Dave Tomlinson	18.00	30.00
55 Ed Salem	18.00	30.00
56 Virgil Wagner	30.00	50.00
57 Dawson Tilley	18.00	30.00
58A Cec Findlay	25.00	40.00
58B Tommy Manastersky	25.00	40.00
59 Frank Nable	18.00	30.00
60 Chuck Anderson	18.00	30.00
61 Charlie Hubbard	18.00	30.00
63 Benny MacDonnell	18.00	30.00
64 Peter Karpuk	18.00	30.00
65 Tom O'Malley	18.00	30.00
66 Bill Stanton	18.00	30.00
67 Matt Anthony	18.00	30.00
68 John Morneau	18.00	30.00
69 Howie Turner	18.00	30.00
70 Alton Baldwin	18.00	30.00
71 John Bovey	18.00	30.00
72 Bruno Bitkowski	25.00	40.00
73 Gene Roberts	18.00	30.00
74 John Wagoner	18.00	30.00
75 Ted MacLarty	18.00	30.00
76 Jerry Lefebvre	18.00	30.00
77 Buck Rogers	18.00	30.00
78 Bruce Cummings	18.00	30.00
79 Hal Wagner	25.00	40.00
80 Joe Shinn	18.00	30.00
81 Eddie Bevan	18.00	30.00
82 Ralph Sazio	30.00	50.00
83 Bob McDonald	18.00	30.00
84 Vince Scott	25.00	40.00
85 Jack Stewart	18.00	30.00
86 Ralph Bartolini	18.00	30.00
87 Blake Taylor	18.00	30.00
88 Richard Brown	18.00	30.00
89 Douglas Gray	18.00	30.00
90 Alex Muzyka	18.00	30.00
91 Pete Neumann	30.00	50.00
92 Jack Rogers	18.00	30.00
93 Bernie Custis	25.00	40.00
94 Cam Fraser	18.00	30.00
95 Vince Mazza	25.00	40.00
96 Peter Wooley	18.00	30.00
97 Earl Valiquette	18.00	30.00
98 Floyd Cooper	18.00	30.00
99 Louis DiFrancisco	18.00	30.00
100 Robert Simpson	90.00	150.00

1956 Parkhurst

The 1956 Parkhurst CFL set of 50 cards features ten players from each of five teams: Edmonton Eskimos (1-10), Saskatchewan Roughriders (11-20), Calgary Stampeders (21-30), Winnipeg Blue Bombers (31-40), and Montreal Alouettes (41-50). Cards are numbered on the front. The cards measure approximately 1 3/4" by 1 7/8". The cards were sold in wax boxes of 48 five-cent wax packs each containing cards and gum. The set features an early card of Bud Grant, who later coached the Minnesota Vikings.

COMPLETE SET (50)	2,000.00	3,500.00
1 Art Walker	50.00	80.00
2 Frank Anderson	25.00	40.00
3 Normie Kwong	90.00	150.00
4 Johnny Bright	90.00	150.00
5 Jackie Parker	250.00	400.00
6 Bob Dean	25.00	40.00
7 Don Getty	75.00	125.00
8 Rollie Miles	60.00	100.00
9 Ted Tully	25.00	40.00
10 Frank Morris	60.00	100.00
11 Martin Ruby	35.00	60.00
12 Mel Becket	50.00	80.00
13 Bill Clarke	25.00	40.00
14 John Wozniak	25.00	40.00
15 Larry Isbell	25.00	40.00
16 Ken Carpenter	50.00	80.00
17 Sully Glasser	25.00	40.00
18 Bobby Marlow	60.00	100.00
19 Paul Anderson	35.00	60.00
20 Gord Sturtridge	50.00	80.00
21 Alex Macklin	25.00	40.00
22 Duke Cook	25.00	40.00
23 Bill Stevenson	25.00	40.00
24 Lynn Bottoms	50.00	80.00
25 Aramis Dandoy	25.00	40.00
26 Peter Muir	35.00	60.00
27 Harvey Wylie	50.00	80.00
28 Joe Yamauchi	25.00	40.00
29 John Alderton	25.00	40.00
30 Bill McKenna	25.00	40.00
31 Edward Kotowich	25.00	40.00
32 Herb Gray	60.00	100.00
33 Calvin Jones	90.00	150.00
34 Herman Day	25.00	40.00
35 Buddy Leake	25.00	40.00
36 Robert McNamara	25.00	40.00
37 Bud Grant	300.00	500.00
38 Gord Rowland	35.00	60.00
39 Glen McWhinney	25.00	40.00
40 Lorne Benson	25.00	40.00
41 Sam Etcheverry	175.00	300.00
42 Joey Pal	25.00	40.00
43 Tom Hugo	25.00	40.00
44 Tex Coulter	35.00	60.00
45 Doug McNichol	25.00	40.00
46 Tom Moran	25.00	40.00
47 Red O'Quinn	50.00	80.00
48 Hal Patterson	125.00	200.00
49 Jacques Belec	25.00	40.00
50 Pat Abruzzi	60.00	100.00

1962 Post Cereal CFL

The 1962 Post Cereal CFL set is the first of two Post Cereal Canadian Football issues. The cards measure the standard size. The cards were issued on the backs of boxes of Post Cereals distributed in Canada. Cards were not available directly from the company via a send-in offer as with other Post Cereal issues. Cards which are marked as SP are considered somewhat shorter printed and more limited in supply. Many of these short-printed cards have backs that are not the typical brown color but rather white. The cards are arranged according to teams.

COMPLETE SET (137)	750.00	1,500.00
1A Don Clark (Brown back)	12.00	20.00
1B Don Clark SP (White back)	30.00	60.00
2 Ed Meadows	4.00	8.00
3 Meco Poliziani	4.00	8.00
4 George Dixon	12.00	20.00
5 Bobby Jack Oliver	5.00	10.00
6 Ross Buckle	4.00	8.00
7 Jack Espenship	4.00	8.00
8 Howard Cissell	4.00	8.00
9 Ed Nickla	4.00	8.00
10 Ed Learn	4.00	8.00
11 Billy Ray Locklin	4.00	8.00
12 Don Paquette	4.00	8.00
13 Milt Crain	5.00	10.00
14 Dick Schnell	4.00	8.00
15 Dick Cohee	5.00	10.00
16 Joe Francis	5.00	10.00
17 Gilles Archambeault	4.00	8.00
18 Angelo Mosca	18.00	30.00
19 Ernie White	4.00	8.00
20 George Brancato	5.00	10.00
21 Ron Lancaster	18.00	30.00
22 Jim Cain	4.00	8.00
23 Gerry Nesbitt	4.00	8.00
24 Russ Jackson	18.00	30.00
25 Bob Simpson	10.00	20.00
26 Sam Scoccia	4.00	8.00
27 Tom Jones	4.00	8.00
28 Kaye Vaughan	7.50	15.00
29 Chuck Stanley	4.00	8.00
30 Dave Thelen	7.50	15.00
31 Gary Schreider	4.00	8.00
32 Jim Reynolds	4.00	8.00
33 Doug Daigneault	4.00	8.00
34 Joe Poirier	4.00	8.00
35 Clare Exelby	4.00	8.00
36 Art Johnson	4.00	8.00
37 Menan Schriewer	4.00	8.00
38 Art Darch	4.00	8.00
39 Cookie Gilchrist	18.00	30.00
40 Brian Aston	4.00	8.00
41 Bobby Kuntz SP	25.00	50.00
42 Gerry Patrick	4.00	8.00
43 Norm Stoneburgh	4.00	8.00
44 Billy Shipp	5.00	10.00
45 Jim Andreotti	7.50	15.00
46 Tobin Rote	12.00	20.00
47 Dick Shatto	7.50	15.00
48 Dave Mann	5.00	10.00
49 Ron Morris	4.00	8.00
50 Lynn Bottoms	5.00	10.00
51 Jim Rountree	5.00	10.00
52 Bill Mitchell	4.00	8.00
53 Wes Gideon SP	25.00	50.00
54 Boyd Carter	4.00	8.00
55 Ron Howell	5.00	10.00
56 John Barrow	7.50	15.00
57 Bernie Faloney	18.00	30.00
58 Ron Ray	4.00	8.00
59 Don Sutherin	7.50	15.00
60 Frank Cosentino	5.00	10.00
61 Hardiman Cureton	4.00	8.00
62 Hal Patterson	10.00	20.00
63 Ralph Goldston	5.00	10.00
64 Tommy Grant	7.50	15.00
65 Larry Hickman	5.00	10.00
66 Zeno Karcz	5.00	10.00
67 Garney Henley	10.00	20.00
68 Gerry McDougall	5.00	10.00
69 Vince Scott	6.00	12.00
70 Gerry James	7.50	15.00
71 Roger Hagberg	5.00	10.00
72 Gord Rowland	5.00	10.00
73 Ernie Pitts	4.00	8.00
74 Frank Rigney	6.00	12.00
75 Norm Rauhaus	6.00	12.00
76 Leo Lewis	10.00	20.00
77 Mike Wright	4.00	8.00
78 Jack Delveaux	5.00	10.00
79 Steve Patrick	4.00	8.00
80 Dave Burkholder	4.00	8.00
81 Charlie Shepard	5.00	10.00
82 Kenny Ploen	10.00	20.00
83 Ronnie Latourelle	4.00	8.00
84 Herb Gray	7.50	15.00
85 Hal Ledyard	4.00	8.00
86 Cornel Piper SP	25.00	50.00
87 Farrell Funston	5.00	10.00
88 Ray Smith	4.00	8.00
89 Clair Branch	4.00	8.00
90 Fred Burket	4.00	8.00
91 Dave Grosz	4.00	8.00
92 Bob Golic	5.00	10.00
93 Billy Gray	4.00	8.00
94 Neil Habig	4.00	8.00
95 Reg Whitehouse	4.00	8.00
96 Jack Gotta	5.00	10.00
97 Bob Ptacek	6.00	12.00
90 Jerry Kooling	7.50	15.00
99 Ernie Danjean	4.00	8.00
100 Don Luzzi	6.00	12.00
101 Wayne Harris	12.00	20.00
102 Tony Pajaczkowski	7.50	15.00
103 Earl Lunsford	7.50	15.00
104 Ernie Warlick	6.00	12.00
105 Gene Filipski	6.00	12.00
106 Eagle Day	10.00	20.00
107 Bill Crawford	4.00	8.00
108 Oscar Kruger	4.00	8.00
109 Gino Fracas	5.00	10.00
110 Don Stephenson	4.00	8.00
111 Jim Letcavits	4.00	8.00
112 Howie Schumm	4.00	8.00
113 Jackie Parker	20.00	40.00
114 Rollie Miles	7.50	15.00
115 Johnny Bright	15.00	25.00
116 Don Getty	7.50	15.00
117 Bobby Walden	5.00	10.00
118 Roger Nelson	7.50	15.00
119 Al Ecuyer	4.00	8.00
120 Ed Gray	4.00	8.00
121 Vic Chapman SP	25.00	50.00
122 Earl Keeley	4.00	8.00
123 Sonny Homer	4.00	8.00
124 Bob Jeter	10.00	20.00
125 Jim Carphin	4.00	8.00
126 By Bailey	10.00	20.00
127 Norm Fieldgate	7.50	15.00
128 Vic Kristopaitis	4.00	8.00
129 Willie Fleming	10.00	20.00
130 Don Vicic	4.00	8.00
131 Tom Brown SP	25.00	50.00
132 Tom Hinton SP	25.00	50.00
133 Pat Claridge	4.00	8.00
134 Bill Britton	4.00	8.00
135 Neil Beaumont	6.00	12.00
136 Nub Beamer SP	25.00	50.00
137 Joe Kapp	30.00	60.00

1963 Post Cereal CFL

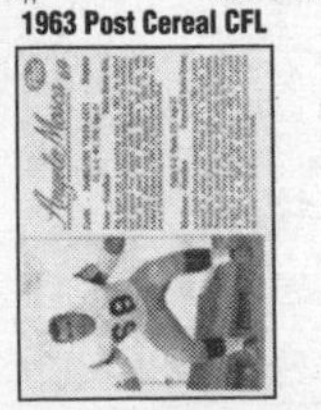

The 1963 Post Cereal CFL set was issued on backs of boxes of Post Cereals in Canada. The cards measure 2 1/2" by 3 1/2". Cards could also be obtained from an order-by-number offer during 1963 from Post's Canadian affiliate. Cards are numbered and ordered within the set according to team. An album for the cards was also produced for this set and is relatively hard to find.

COMPLETE SET (160)	400.00	800.00
1 Larry Hickman	4.00	8.00
2 Dick Schnell	2.50	5.00
3 Don Clark	4.00	8.00
4 Ted Page	2.50	5.00
5 Milt Crain	4.00	8.00

6 George Dixon 7.50 15.00
7 Ed Nickla 2.50 5.00
8 Barrie Hansen 2.50 5.00
9 Ed Learn 2.50 5.00
10 Billy Ray Locklin 2.50 5.00
11 Bobby Jack Oliver 4.00 8.00
12 Don Paquette 2.50 5.00
13 Sandy Stephens 6.00 12.00
14 Billy Wayte 2.50 5.00
15 Jim Reynolds 2.50 5.00
16 Ross Buckle 2.50 5.00
17 Bob Geary 2.50 5.00
18 Bobby Lee Thompson 2.50 5.00
19 Mike Snodgrass 2.50 5.00
20 Billy Joe Booth 4.00 8.00
21 Jim Cain 2.50 5.00
22 Kaye Vaughan 5.00 10.00
23 Doug Daigneault 2.50 5.00
24 Millard Flemming 4.00 8.00
25 Russ Jackson 12.50 25.00
26 Joe Poirier 4.00 8.00
27 Moe Racine 2.50 5.00
28 Norb Roy 2.50 5.00
29 Ted Smale 2.50 5.00
30 Ernie White 2.50 5.00
31 Whit Tucker 5.00 10.00
32 Dave Thelen 5.00 10.00
33 Len Chandler 2.50 5.00
34 Jim Conroy 4.00 8.00
35 Jerry Selinger 2.50 5.00
36 Ron Stewart 6.00 12.00
37 Jim Andreotti 4.00 8.00
38 Jackie Parker 12.50 25.00
39 Lynn Bottoms 4.00 8.00
40 Gerry Patrick 2.50 5.00
41 Gerry Philip 2.50 5.00
42 Art Johnson 2.50 5.00
43 Aubrey Linne 2.50 5.00
44 Dave Mann 4.00 8.00
45 Marty Martinello 2.50 5.00
46 Doug McNichol 2.50 5.00
47 Ron Morris 2.50 5.00
48 Walt Radzick 2.50 5.00
49 Jim Rountree 4.00 8.00
50 Dick Shatto 5.00 10.00
51 Billy Shipp 4.00 8.00
52 Norm Stoneburgh 2.50 5.00
53 Gerry Wilson 2.50 5.00
54 Danny Nykoluk 2.50 5.00
55 John Barrow 5.00 10.00
56 Frank Cosentino 4.00 8.00
57 Hardiman Cureton 2.50 5.00
58 Bobby Kuntz 4.00 8.00
59 Bernie Faloney 10.00 20.00
60 Garney Henley 6.00 12.00
61 Zeno Karcz 4.00 8.00
62 Dick Easterly 2.50 5.00
63 Bronko Nagurski Jr. 6.00 12.00
64 Hal Patterson 7.50 15.00
65 Ron Ray 2.50 5.00
66 Don Sutherin 4.00 8.00
67 Dave Viti 2.50 5.00
68 Joe Zuger 4.00 8.00
69 Angelo Mosca 10.00 20.00
70 Ralph Goldston 4.00 8.00
71 Tommy Grant 5.00 10.00
72 Geno DeNobile 2.50 5.00
73 Dave Burkholder 2.50 5.00
74 Jack Delveaux 4.00 8.00
75 Farrell Funston 4.00 8.00
76 Herb Gray 5.00 10.00
77 Roger Hagberg 4.00 8.00
78 Henry Janzen 4.00 8.00
79 Ronnie Latourelle 2.50 5.00
80 Leo Lewis 5.00 10.00
81 Cornel Piper 2.50 5.00
82 Ernie Pitts 2.50 5.00
83 Kenny Ploen 5.00 10.00
84 Norm Rauhaus 4.00 8.00
85 Charlie Shepard 4.00 8.00
86 Gar Warren 2.50 5.00
87 Dick Thornton 4.00 8.00
88 Hal Ledyard 2.50 5.00
89 Frank Rigney 4.00 8.00
90 Gord Rowland 4.00 8.00
91 Don Walsh 2.50 5.00
92 Bill Burrell 2.50 5.00
93 Ron Atchison 5.00 10.00
94 Billy Gray 2.50 5.00
95 Neil Habig 2.50 5.00
96 Bob Ptacek 4.00 8.00
97 Ray Purdin 2.50 5.00
98 Ted Urness 4.00 8.00
99 Dale West 4.00 8.00
100 Reg Whitehouse 2.50 5.00
101 Clair Branch 2.50 5.00
102 Bill Clarke 2.50 5.00
103 Garner Ekstran 4.00 8.00
104 Jack Gotta 4.00 8.00
105 Len Legault 2.50 5.00
106 Larry Dumelie 2.50 5.00
107 Bill Britton 2.50 5.00
108 Ed Buchanan 2.50 5.00
109 Lovell Coleman 4.00 8.00
110 Bill Crawford 2.50 5.00
111 Ernie Danjean 2.50 5.00
112 Eagle Day 5.00 10.00
113 Jim Furlong 2.50 5.00
114 Wayne Harris 7.50 15.00
115 Roy Jakanovich 2.50 5.00
116 Phil Lohmann 2.50 5.00
117 Earl Lunsford 4.00 8.00
118 Don Luzzi 4.00 8.00
119 Tony Pajaczkowski 4.00 8.00
120 Pete Manning 4.00 8.00
121 Harvey Wylie 4.00 8.00
122 George Hansen 2.50 5.00
123 Pat Holmes 4.00 8.00
124 Larry Robinson 4.00 8.00
125 Johnny Bright 7.50 15.00
126 Jon Rechner 2.50 5.00
127 Al Ecuyer 2.50 5.00
128 Don Getty 6.00 12.00
129 Ed Gray 2.50 5.00
130 Oscar Kruger 2.50 5.00
131 Jim Letcavits 2.50 5.00
132 Mike Lashuk 2.50 5.00
133 Don Duncalfe 2.50 5.00
134 Bobby Walden 4.00 8.00
135 Tommy Joe Coffey 6.00 12.00
136 Nat Dye 4.00 8.00
137 Roy Stevenson 2.50 5.00
138 Howie Schumm 2.50 5.00
139 Roger Nelson 4.00 8.00
140 Larry Fleisher 4.00 8.00
141 Dunc Harvey 2.50 5.00
142 James Earl Wright 4.00 8.00
143 By Bailey 6.00 12.00
144 Nub Beamer 2.50 5.00
145 Neil Beaumont 4.00 8.00
146 Tom Brown 4.00 8.00
147 Pat Claridge 4.00 8.00
148 Lonnie Dennis 4.00 8.00
149 Norm Fieldgate 4.00 8.00
150 Willie Fleming 6.00 12.00
151 Dick Fouts 4.00 8.00
152 Tom Hinton 4.00 8.00
153 Sonny Homer 4.00 8.00
154 Joe Kapp 12.50 25.00
155 Tom Larscheid 2.50 5.00
156 Mike Martin 2.50 5.00
157 Mel Mellin 2.50 5.00
158 Mike Cacic 2.50 5.00
159 Walt Bilicki 2.50 5.00
160 Earl Keeley 2.50 5.00
NNO Post Album English 20.00 40.00
NNO Post Album French 20.00 40.00
NNO Checklist 60.00 100.00
(measures 5 1/2 x 6)

1991 Queen's University

This 52-card standard-size set, produced by Breakaway Graphics, Inc., commemorates the sesquicentennial year of Queen's University. This Golden Gaels football set is the first ever to be issued by a Canadian college football organization. Reportedly only 5,725 sets and 275 uncut sheets were printed. The card fronts feature color player photos inside a gold border, with a pale green strip running down the left side of the picture. On a pale green background, the backs have a color head shot, biography, player profile, and statistics. Five special promotional cards were also included with this commemorative set. Five hundred autographed promo cards were randomly inserted in the production run, including 100 by Mike Schad and Jock Climie and 300 by Ron Stewart.

COMPLETE SET (52) 4.80 12.00
1 First Rugby Team .30 .75
Team photo
2 Grey Cup Years .30 .75
Harry Batstone
Frank R. Leadlay
3 1978 Vanier Cup Champs .10 .30
4 1978 Vanier Cup Champs .10 .30
5 Tim Pendergast .10 .30
6 Brad Elberg .10 .30
7 Ken Kirkwood .10 .30
8 Kyle Wanzel .10 .30
9 Brian Alford .10 .30
10 Paul Kozan .10 .30
11 Paul Beresford .10 .30
12 Ron Herman .10 .30
13 Mike Ross .10 .30
14 Tom Black .10 .30
15 Steve Yovetich .10 .30
16 Mark Robinson T .10 .30
17 Don Rorwick .10 .30
18 Ed Kidd .10 .30
19 Jamie Galloway .10 .30
20 Dan Wright .10 .30
21 Scott Gray .10 .30
22 Dan McCullough .10 .30
23 Steve Othen .10 .30
24 Doug Hargreaves CO .10 .30
25 Sue Bolton CO .10 .30
26 Coaching Staff .20 .50
27 Joel Dagnone .10 .30
28 Mark Morrison .10 .30
29 Rob Krog .10 .30
30 Dan Pawliw .10 .30
31 Greg Bryk .10 .30
32 Eric Dell .10 .30
33 Mike Boone .10 .30
34 James Paterson .10 .30
35 Jeff Yach .10 .30
36 Peter Pain .10 .30
37 Aron Campbell .10 .30
38 Chris McCormick .10 .30
39 Jason Moller .10 .30
40 Terry Huhtala .10 .30
41 Matt Zarowny .10 .30
42 David St. Amour .10 .30
43 Frank Tindall .10 .30
44 Ron Stewart .50 1.25
45 Jim Young .60 1.50
46 Bob Howes .10 .30
47 Stu Lang .10 .30
48 Mike Schad .30 .75
(In college uniform)
49 Mike Schad .30 .75
(In Philadelphia
Eagles uniform)
50 Jock Climie .60 1.50
51 Checklist .10 .30
P1 Jock Climie 1.20 3.00
P1AU Jock Climie AU/100 12.00 30.00
P2 Ron Stewart 1.60 4.00
P2AU Ron Stewart AU/300 12.00 30.00
P3 Jim Young 1.60 4.00
P4 Stu Lang 1.20 3.00
P5 Mike Schad 1.20 3.00
P5AU Mike Schad AU/100 12.00 30.00
NNO Title Card .30 .75

1987 Regina Rams Royal Studios

This standard sized set features members of the Regina Rams. Each card includes a color photo with a white and green striped border. The player's name and jersey number also appears on the cardfront. The unnumbered cardbacks were printed on white paper stock with a short bio of the featured player.

COMPLETE SET (20) 14.00 35.00
1 Jami Anderson .75 2.00
2 Tim Burnie .75 2.00
3 Doug Dorsch .75 2.00
4 Brian Eltom .75 2.00
5 Dave Gebert .75 2.00
6 Ryan Hall .75 2.00
7 Dan Johnston .75 2.00
8 Sam Khuber .75 2.00
9 Lance Lascue .75 2.00
10 Mike Lazecki .75 2.00
11 Dean Mihalicz .75 2.00
12 Ken Neiszner .75 2.00
13 Dean Picton .75 2.00
14 Tim Relke .75 2.00
15 Cliff Rusconi .75 2.00
16 Rob Sillinger .75 2.00
17 Richard Sutcliffe .75 2.00
18 Wendell Toth .75 2.00
19 Steve Tunison .75 2.00
20 Jim Warnecke .75 2.00

1995 R.E.L.

This 250-card set of the CFL was produced by Hammer Slammer Canada and Robindale Enterprises LTD. The cards feature color action player photos with the player's name in the left team-colored border above a small black-and-white player action photo. The team and card logos at the bottom round out the front. The backs carry a black-and-white player portrait with the team name, position, jersey number, and biographical and career information on a background of blended team colors. Reportedly, 3999 individually numbered sets were produced and distributed in 10-set cases. Each case also included an individually numbered (of 399) Doug Flutie signed card. The 14 logo cards near the end of the set listing are actually unnumbered, but have been assigned numbers below according to the checklist card. A Doug Flutie Promo card was issued as well to promote the new set.

COMPLETE SET (250) 12.00 30.00
1 Doug Flutie 2.40 6.00
2 Bruce Covernton .02 .10
3 Jamie Crysdale .01 .05
4 Matt Finlay .02 .10
5 Alondra Johnson .02 .10
6 Will Johnson .02 .10
7 Greg Knox .01 .05
8 Stu Laird .02 .10
9 Kenton Leonard .01 .05
10 Tony Martino .01 .05
11 Mark McLoughlin .01 .05
12 Allen Pitts .30 .75
13 Marvin Pope .01 .05
14 Rocco Romano .01 .05
15 David Sapunjis .20 .50
16 Pee Wee Smith .07 .20
17 Tony Stewart .02 .10
18 Srecko Zizakovic .01 .05
19 Kerwin Bell .15 .40
20 Leroy Blugh .02 .10
21 Rod Connop .01 .05
22 Blake Dermott .01 .05
23 Lucius Floyd .02 .10
24 Bennie Goods .02 .10
25 Glenn Harper .01 .05
26 Craig Hendrickson .01 .05
27 Robert Holland .01 .05
28 Malvin Hunter .01 .05
29 John Kalin .01 .05
30 Nick Mazzoli .01 .05
31 Willie Pless .15 .40
32 Jim Sandusky .07 .20
33 Michael Soles .02 .10
34 Marc Tobert .01 .05
35 Gizmo Williams .30 .75
36 Larry Wruck .02 .10
37 Lee Knight .01 .05
38 Shawn Prendergast .01 .05
39 Richard Nurse .01 .05
40 Eric Carter .07 .20
41 Frank Marof .01 .05
42 Roger Hennig .01 .05
43 Derek Grier .01 .05
44 Kelvin Means .01 .05
45 Michael Philbrick .01 .05
46 Jessie Small .02 .10
47 Mike O'Shea .07 .20
48 Marcus Cotton .01 .05
49 Hassan Bailey .01 .05
50 Anthony Calvillo 1.25 2.50
51 Mike Kerrigan .10 .30
52 Hank Ilesic .07 .20
53 Paul Osbaldiston .02 .10
54 Earl Winfield .07 .20
55 Danton Barto .01 .05
56 Tim Cofield .07 .20
57 Bruce Perkins .01 .05
58 Damion Lyons .01 .05
59 Joe Horn 2.50 5.00
60 Rickey Foggie .30 .75
61 Bobby Dawson .01 .05
62 Eddie Brown .40 1.00
63 Vance Hammond .01 .05
64 Ed Berry .01 .05
65 Stephen Bates .01 .05
66 Greg Battle .07 .20
67 Gary Anderson .01 .05
68 Donald Smith .01 .05
69 Adrion Smith .01 .05
70 Rodney Harding .02 .10
71 Damon Allen .30 .75
72 Junior Robinson .01 .05
73 Ken Watson .01 .05
74 Nick Subis .01 .05
75 Mike Pringle 1.20 3.00
76 Shar Pourdanesh .07 .20
77 Elfrid Payton .07 .20
78 Josh Miller .01 .05
79 Carlos Huerta .02 .10
80 Tracy Ham .25 .60
81 Tracey Gravely .01 .05
82 Matt Goodwin .01 .05
83 Neal Fort .07 .20
84 O.J. Brigance .25 .60
85 Jearld Baylis .02 .10
86 Mike Alexander .01 .05
87 Shannon Culver .02 .10
88 Robert Clark .02 .10
89 Courtney Griffin .01 .05
90 Demetrious Maxie .01 .05
91 Dave Ridgway .07 .20
92 Terryl Ulmer .01 .05
93 Lybrant Robinson .01 .05
94 Troy Alexander .01 .05
95 Darren Joseph .01 .05
96 Warren Jones .02 .10
97 Dan Rashovich .01 .05
98 Glenn Kulka .02 .10
99 Dale Joseph .01 .05
100 Scott Hendrickson .01 .05
101 Ron Goetz .01 .05
102 Ventson Donelson .01 .05
103 Mike Anderson .01 .05
104 Brent Matich .01 .05
105 Donald Narcisse .15 .40
106 Tom Burgess .07 .20
107 Bobby Jurasin .07 .20
108 Ray Elgaard .10 .30
109 Brian Bonner .07 .20
110 Robbie Keen .01 .05
111 Bjorn Nittmo .14 .35
112 Martin Patton .01 .05
113 Rod Harris .07 .20
114 Mike Johnson .01 .05
115 Billy Joe Tolliver .08 .25
116 Curtis Mayfield .07 .20
117 Ben Jefferson .01 .05
118 Jon Heidenreich .01 .05
119 Mike Stowell .01 .05
120 Alex Mash .01 .05
121 Ray Savage .01 .05
122 Mario Perry .01 .05
123 Ron Perry .01 .05
124 Joe Fuller .01 .05
125 Jonathan Wilson .01 .05
126 Anthony Shelton .01 .05
127 Emanuel Martin .01 .05
128 Ray Alexander .02 .10
129 Michael Richardson .15 .40
130 Irv Daymond .01 .05
131 Terry Baker .02 .10
132 Danny Barrett .07 .20
133 James Ellingson .02 .10
134 John Kropke .02 .10
135 Garry Lewis .01 .05
136 James Monroe .01 .05
137 Brett Young .02 .10
138 Remi Trudel .01 .05
139 Jed Tommy .01 .05
140 Odessa Turner .02 .10
141 David Black .01 .05
142 Eric Geter .01 .05
143 Sammy Garza .02 .10
144 Loyd Lewis .01 .05
145 Enis Jackson .01 .05
146 Danny McManus .20 .50
148 Cory Philpot .40 1.00
149 Glen Scrivener .01 .05
150 Ian Sinclair .02 .10
151 Vic Stevenson .01 .05
152 Andrew Stewart .02 .10
153 Jamie Taras .02 .10
154 Robert Gordon .07 .20
155 Tom Europe .01 .05
156 Spencer McLennan .01 .05
157 Mike Trevathan .07 .20
158 Matt Clark .02 .10
159 Daved Benefield .02 .10
160 Darren Flutie 1.20 3.00
161 Charles Gordon .01 .05
162 Ryan Hanson .01 .05
163 Kent Austin .07 .20
164 Reggie Barnes .02 .10
165 Mike Clemons .50 1.25
166 Jock Climie .07 .20
167 Duane Forde .01 .05
168 Leon Hatziioannou .01 .05
169 Wayne Lammle .01 .05
170 Paul Masotti .07 .20
171 George Nimako .02 .10
172 Calvin Tiggle .01 .05
173 Don Wilson .01 .05
174 Chris Tsangaris .01 .05
174 Lui Passaglia .15 .40
175 Darrick Branch .01 .05
176 Carl Coulter .01 .05
177 P.J. Martin .02 .10
178 Eric Blount DE .01 .05
179 Norm Casola .01 .05
180 Joe Burgos .01 .05
181 John Buddenberg .01 .05
182 George Bethune .01 .05
183 Oscar Giles .02 .10
184 Myron Wise .01 .05
185 Roman Anderson .01 .05
186 Dave Harper .01 .05
187 Mike Saunders .20 .50
188 Roosevelt Collins .01 .05
189 Peter Shorts .01 .05
190 Willie Fears .02 .10
191 Mike Kiselak .01 .05
192 Malcolm Frank .01 .05
193 Joe Kralik .01 .05
194 David Archer .60 1.50
195 Billy Hess .01 .05
196 Mark Stock .01 .05
197 James King .01 .05
198 Tony Burse .01 .05
199 Donovan Gans .01 .05
200 Keith Woodside .01 .05
201 Anthony Drawhorn .02 .10
202 Jimmy Klingler .07 .20
203 Matt Dunigan .25 .60
204 John Motton .02 .10
205 Scott Player .02 .10
206 Franco Grilla .01 .05
207 Shonte Peoples .01 .05
208 Derrick Crawford .02 .10
209 Fernando Thomas .01 .05
210 Delius Morris .01 .05
211 Roosevelt Patterson .01 .05
212 Willie McClendon .01 .05
213 Jason Phillips .01 .05
214 Mike James .01 .05
215 Andre Strode .01 .05
216 Chris Dyko .01 .05
217 Chris Walby .07 .20
218 Miles Gorrell .01 .05
219 Dave Vankoughnett .01 .05
220 Del Lyles .01 .05
221 Bob Cameron .07 .20
222 Troy Westwood .07 .20
223 Reggie Slack .30 .75
224 Blaise Bryant .07 .20
225 Gerald Wilcox .02 .10
226 David Williams .02 .10
227 Keilly Rush .01 .05
228 Stan Mikawos .01 .05
229 Paul Randolph .01 .05
230 Greg Clark .01 .05
231 Jason Mallett .01 .05
232 Juran Bolden .07 .20
233 Brett MacNeil .01 .05
234 Chris Johnstone .01 .05
235 Toronto Argonauts Logo .01 .05
236 Ottawa Rough Riders Logo .01 .05
237 Hamilton Tiger-Cats Logo .01 .05
238 Winnipeg Blue Bombers Logo .01 .05
239 Saskatchewan Roughriders Logo .01 .05
240 Calgary Stampeders Logo .01 .05
241 Edmonton Eskimos Logo .01 .05
242 B.C. Lions Logo .01 .05
243 Memphis Mad Dogs Logo .01 .05
244 Birmingham Barracudas Logo .01 .05
245 San Antonio Texans Logo .01 .05
246 Shreveport Pirates Logo .01 .05
247 Baltimore Stallions Logo .01 .05
248 Grey Cup Logo .01 .05
249 Checklist #1 .02 .10
250 Checklist #2 .02 .10
P1 Doug Flutie Promo 2.00 5.00
numbered one of 2500
AU1 Doug Flutie AUTO 35.00 60.00
(signed card; numbered of 399)

1995 R.E.L. Pogs

R.E.L. issued this set of CFL milkcaps (Pogs) in 1995. The coins were distributed on a thick cardboard mount with each featuring the team's logo on the front and team stadium stats on the back.

COMPLETE SET (15) 6.00 15.00
1 Toronto Argonauts .50 1.25
2 Birmingham Barracudas .50 1.25
3 Winnipeg Blue Bombers .50 1.25
4 Edmonton Eskimos .50 1.25
5 B.C. Lions .50 1.25
6 Memphis Mad Dogs .50 1.25
7 Shreveport Pirates .50 1.25
8 Saskatchewan Roughriders .50 1.25
9 Ottawa Rough Riders .50 1.25
10 Baltimore Stallions .50 1.25
11 Calgary Stampeders .50 1.25
12 San Antonio Texans .50 1.25
13 Hamilton Tiger-Cats .50 1.25
14 CFL Helmet Logo .50 1.25
15 Grey Cup Logo .50 1.25

1994 Sacramento Gold Miners Smokey

This Smokey sponsored set features members of the Sacramento Gold Miners and measures approximately 2 1/4" by 3 1/2." The cardfronts include a color player photo with the team name above the photo and the player's name, position and vital statistics below. Cardbacks contain a fire prevention message from Smokey.

COMPLETE SET (18) 12.00 30.00
1 Fred Anderson CEO .60 1.50
2 David Archer 3.00 6.00
3 George Bethune .50 1.25
4 David Diaz-Infante .60 1.50
5 Willie Fears .75 2.00
6 Corian Freeman .50 1.25
7 Pete Gardere .60 1.50
8 Tom Gerhart .50 1.25
9 Rod Harris .75 2.00
10 Bobby Humphery .75 2.00
11 Mike Kiselak .50 1.25
12 Mark Ledbetter .50 1.25
13 Maurice Miller .50 1.25
14 Troy Mills .50 1.25
15 Mike Oliphant 1.00 2.50
16 James Pruitt .60 1.50
17 Junior Robinson .50 1.25
18 Kay Stephenson CO .50 1.25

1971 Sargent Promotions Stamps

This photo album, measuring approximately 10 3/4" by 13", features 225 players from nine Canadian Football League teams. The set was sponsored by Eddie Sargent Promotions and is completely bi-lingual. The collector completed the set by purchasing a different picture packet from a participating food store each week. There were 16 different picture packets, with 14 color stickers per packet. After a general introduction, the album is divided into team sections, with two pages devoted to each team. A brief history of each team is presented, followed by 25 numbered sticker slots. Each sticker measures approximately 2" by 2 1/2" and has a posed color player photo with white borders. The player's name and team affiliation are indicated in the bottom white border. Biographical information and career summary appear below each sticker slot on the page itself. The stickers are numbered on the front and checklisted below alphabetically according to teams.

COMPLETE SET (225) 300.00 600.00
1 Jim Young 7.50 15.00
2 Trevor Ekdahl 1.50 3.00
3 Ted Gerela 1.50 3.00
4 Jim Evenson 1.50 3.00
5 Ray Lychak 1.00 2.00
6 Dave Golinsky 1.00 2.00
7 Ted Warkentin 1.00 2.00
8 A.D. Whitfield 1.50 3.00
9 Lach Heron 1.50 3.00
10 Ken Phillips 1.00 2.00
11 Lefty Hendrickson 1.00 2.00
12 Paul Brothers 1.00 2.00
13 Eagle Keys CO 2.00 4.00
14 Garrett Hunsperger 1.00 2.00
15 Greg Findlay 1.00 2.00
16 Dave Easley 1.00 2.00
17 Barrie Hansen 1.00 2.00
18 Wayne Dennis 1.00 2.00
19 Jerry Bradley 1.00 2.00
20 Gerry Herron 1.00 2.00
21 Gary Robinson 1.00 2.00
22 Bill Whisler 1.00 2.00
23 Bob Howes 1.00 2.00
24 Tom Wilkinson 6.00 12.00
25 Tom Cassese 1.00 2.00
26 Dick Suderman 1.50 3.00
27 Jerry Keeling 3.00 6.00
28 John Helton 3.00 6.00
29 Jim Furlong 1.00 2.00
30 Fred James 1.00 2.00
31 Howard Starks 1.00 2.00
32 Craig Koinzan 1.00 2.00
33 Frank Andruski 1.00 2.00
34 Joe Forzani 1.50 3.00
35 Herb Schumn 1.00 2.00
36 Gerry Shaw 1.00 2.00
37 Lanny Boleski 1.00 2.00
38 Jim Duncan CO 1.00 2.00
39 Hugh McKinnis 1.00 2.00
40 Basil Bark 1.00 2.00
41 Herman Harrison 3.00 6.00
42 Larry Robinson 1.50 3.00
43 Larry Lawrence 1.00 2.00
44 Granville Liggins 2.00 4.00
45 Wayne Harris 3.00 6.00
46 John Atamian 1.00 2.00
47 Wayne Holm 1.00 2.00
48 Rudy Linterman 1.50 3.00
49 Jim Sillye 1.00 2.00
50 Terry Wilson 1.00 2.00
51 Don Trull 2.00 4.00
52 Rusty Clark 1.00 2.00
53 Ted Page 1.00 2.00
54 Ken Ferguson 1.00 2.00
55 Alan Pitcaithley 1.00 2.00
56 Bayne Norrie 1.00 2.00
57 Dave Gasser 1.00 2.00
58 Jim Thomas 1.00 2.00
59 Terry Swarn 1.50 3.00
60 Ron Forwick 1.00 2.00
61 Henry King 1.00 2.00
62 John Wydareny 1.50 3.00
63 Ray Jauch CO 1.50 3.00
64 Jim Henshall 1.00 2.00
65 Dave Cutler 3.00 6.00
66 Fred Dunn 1.00 2.00
67 Dick Dupuis 1.50 3.00
68 Fritz Greenlee 1.00 2.00
69 Jerry Griffin 1.50 3.00
70 Allen Ische 1.00 2.00
71 John LaGrone 1.50 3.00
72 Mike Law 1.00 2.00
73 Ed Molstad 1.00 2.00
74 Greg Pipes 1.50 3.00
75 Roy Shatzko 1.00 2.00
76 Joe Zuger 1.50 3.00
77 Wally Gabler 1.50 3.00
78 Tony Gabriel 6.00 12.00
79 John Reid 1.00 2.00
80 Dave Fleming 1.00 2.00
81 Jon Hohman 1.00 2.00
82 Tommy Joe Coffey 4.00 8.00
83 Dick Wesolowski 1.00 2.00
84 Gordon Christian 1.00 2.00
85 Steve Worster 5.00 10.00
86 Bob Taylor 1.50 3.00
87 Doug Mitchell 1.00 2.00
88 Al Dorow CO 1.50 3.00
89 Angelo Mosca 10.00 20.00
90 Bill Danychuk 1.50 3.00
91 Mike Blum 1.00 2.00
92 Garney Henley 5.00 10.00
93 Bob Steiner 1.00 2.00
94 John Manel 1.00 2.00
95 Bob Krouse 1.00 2.00
96 John Williams 1.00 2.00
97 Scott Henderson 1.00 2.00
98 Ed Chalupka 1.00 2.00
99 Paul McKay 1.00 2.00
100 Rensi Perdoni 1.00 2.00
101 Ed George 1.50 3.00
102 Al Phaneuf 1.50 3.00
103 Sonny Wade 2.00 4.00
104 Moses Denson 2.00 4.00
105 Terry Evanshen 5.00 10.00
106 Pierre Desjardins 1.00 2.00
107 Larry Fairholm 1.00 2.00
108 Gene Gaines 3.00 6.00
109 Bobby Lee Thompson 1.00 2.00
110 Mike Widger 1.00 2.00
111 Gene Ceppetelli 1.00 2.00
112 Barry Randall 1.00 2.00
113 Sam Etcheverry CO 2.00 4.00
114 Mark Kosmos 1.50 3.00
115 Peter Dalla Riva 2.00 4.00
116 Ted Collins 1.00 2.00
117 John Couture 1.00 2.00
118 Tony Passander 1.00 2.00
119 Garry Lefebvre 1.00 2.00
120 George Springate 1.00 2.00
121 Gordon Judges 1.00 2.00
122 Steve Smear 2.00 4.00
123 Tom Pullen 1.00 2.00
124 Merl Code 1.00 2.00
125 Steve Booras 1.00 2.00
126 Hugh Oldham 1.00 2.00
127 Moe Racine 1.00 2.00
128 John Kruspe 1.00 2.00
129 Ken Lehmann 1.50 3.00
130 Billy Cooper 1.00 2.00
131 Marshall Shirk 1.00 2.00
132 Tom Schuette 1.00 2.00
133 Doug Specht 1.00 2.00
134 Dennis Duncan 1.00 2.00
135 Jerry Campbell 1.50 3.00
136 Wayne Giardino 1.00 2.00
137 Roger Perdrix 1.00 2.00
138 Jack Gotta CO 1.50 3.00
139 Terry Wellesley 1.00 2.00
140 Dave Braggins 1.00 2.00
141 Dave Pivec 1.00 2.00
142 Rod Woodward 1.00 2.00
143 Gary Wood 2.00 4.00
144 Al Marcelin 1.50 3.00
145 Dan Dever 1.00 2.00
146 Ivan MacMillan 1.00 2.00
147 Wayne Smith 1.00 2.00
148 Barry Ardern 1.00 2.00
149 Rick Cassatta 1.50 3.00
150 Bill Van Burkleo 1.00 2.00
151 Ron Lancaster 6.00 12.00
152 Wayne Shaw 1.00 2.00
153 Bob Kosid 1.00 2.00
154 George Reed 7.50 15.00
155 Don Bahnuik 1.00 2.00
156 Gordon Barwell 1.00 2.00
157 Clyde Brock 1.00 2.00
158 Alan Ford 1.00 2.00
159 Jack Abendschan 1.50 3.00
160 Steve Molnar 1.00 2.00
161 Al Rankin 1.00 2.00
162 Bobby Thompson 1.00 2.00
163 Dave Skrien CO 1.00 2.00
164 Nolan Bailey 1.00 2.00
165 Bill Baker 4.00 8.00
166 Bruce Bennett 2.00 4.00
167 Gary Brandt 1.00 2.00
168 Charlie Collins 1.00 2.00
169 Henry Dorsch 1.00 2.00
170 Ted Dushinski 1.00 2.00
171 Bruce Gainer 1.00 2.00
172 Ralph Galloway 1.00 2.00
173 Ken Frith 1.00 2.00
174 Cliff Shaw 1.00 2.00
175 Silas McKinnie 1.00 2.00
176 Mike Eben 1.00 2.00
177 Greg Barton 2.00 4.00
178 Joe Theismann 25.00 50.00
179 Charlie Bray 1.00 2.00
180 Roger Scales 1.00 2.00
181 Bob Hudspeth 1.00 2.00
182 Bill Symons 1.50 3.00
183 Dave Raimey 1.50 3.00
184 Dave Cranmer 1.50 3.00
185 Mel Profit 1.50 3.00
186 Paul Desjardins 1.00 2.00
187 Tony Moro 1.00 2.00
188 Leo Cahill CO 1.00 2.00
189 Chip Barrett 1.00 2.00
190 Pete Martin 1.00 2.00
191 Walt Balasiuk 1.00 2.00
192 Jim Corrigall 1.50 3.00
193 Ellison Kelly 4.00 8.00
194 Jim Tomlin 1.00 2.00
195 Marv Luster 2.00 4.00
196 Jim Thorpe 2.00 4.00
197 Jim Stillwagon 3.00 6.00
198 Ed Harrington 1.00 2.00
199 Jim Dye 1.00 2.00
200 Leon McQuay 2.00 4.00
201 Rob McLaren 1.00 2.00
202 Benji Dial 1.00 2.00
203 Chuck Liebrock 1.00 2.00
204 Glen Schapansky 1.00 2.00
205 Ed Ulmer 1.00 2.00
206 Ross Richardson 1.00 2.00
207 Lou Andrus 1.00 2.00
208 Paul Robson 1.00 2.00
209 Paul Brule 1.00 2.00
210 Doug Strong 1.00 2.00
211 Dick Smith 1.00 2.00
212 Bill Frank 1.00 2.00
213 Jim Spavital CO 1.00 2.00
214 Rick Shaw 1.00 2.00
215 Joe Critchlow 1.00 2.00
216 Don Jonas 2.00 4.00
217 Bob Swift 1.00 2.00
218 Larry Kerychuk 1.00 2.00
219 Bob McCarthy 1.00 2.00
220 Gene Lakusiak 1.00 2.00
221 Jim Heighton 1.00 2.00
222 Chuck Harrison 1.00 2.00
223 Lance Fletcher 1.00 2.00
224 Larry Slagle 1.00 2.00
225 Wayne Giesbrecht 1.00 2.00

1970-71 Saskatchewan Roughriders Gulf

Gulf Canada gasoline stations issued this set of player photos during both the 1970 and 1971 seasons. Each measures roughly 8" by 10" and features a black and white player photo to the right. Both the Roughriders and Gulf Canada logos are included on the cardfronts to the left. The cardbacks are blank. Three players were issued only for the 1971 and were thought to be printed in shorter supply. We've marked those three as short prints (SP).

COMPLETE SET (37) 75.00 150.00
1 Jack Abendschan 2.50 5.00
2 Barry Aldag 2.50 5.00
3 Don Bahnuik 2.00 4.00
4 Nolan Bailey 2.00 4.00
5 Bill Baker 6.00 12.00
6 Gord Barwell 2.00 4.00
7 Bruce Bennett 3.00 6.00
8 Gary Brandt 2.00 4.00
9 Clyde Brock 2.00 4.00
10 Larry DeGraw 2.00 4.00
11 Dave Denny 2.00 4.00
12 Henry Dorsch 2.00 4.00
13 Ted Dushinski 2.00 4.00
14 Alan Ford 2.00 4.00
15 Ken Frith 2.00 4.00
16 Bruce Gainer 2.00 4.00
17 Ralph Galloway 2.00 4.00
18 Eagle Keys CO 3.00 6.00
19 Bob Kosid 2.00 4.00
20 Chuck Kyle 2.00 4.00
21 Ron Lancaster 7.50 15.00
22 Gary Lane SP 7.50 15.00
23 Ken McCullough CO 2.00 4.00
24 Silas McKinnie 2.00 4.00
25 Ed McQuarters 2.00 4.00
26 Steve Molnar 2.00 4.00
27 Bob Pearce SP 7.50 15.00
28 Al Rankin 2.00 4.00
29 George Reed 10.00 20.00
30 Ken Reed 2.00 4.00
31 Don Seaman 2.00 4.00
32 Cliff Shaw 2.00 4.00
33 Wayne Shaw 2.00 4.00
34 Dave Skrien CO 2.00 4.00
35 Bobby Thompson 2.00 4.00
36 Ted Urness 3.00 6.00
37 Jim Walter SP 7.50 15.00

1975 Saskatchewan Roughriders Team Sheets

This group of 32-players and coaches of the Roughriders was produced on four glossy sheets each measuring approximately 8" by 10". The fronts feature black-and-white player portraits with eight pictures to a sheet with the year printed at the top. The backs are blank. The cards are unnumbered and checklisted below in alphabetical order, with the player pictured in the upper left hand corner of the sheet listed first.

COMPLETE SET (4) 10.00 20.00
1 Lee Benard 2.50 5.00
Charlie Collins
Bill Manchuk
Randy Mattingly
Clyde Brock
Terry Bulych
Frank Landy
Peter Watson
2 Mike Dirks 2.50 5.00
Tom Campana
Ted Dushinski
Rhett Dawson
Steve Mazurak
Steve Molnar
Ralph Galloway
Steve Smear

3 Leif Peterson	4.00	8.00
Al Ford		
George Reed		
Lorne Richardson		
Brian Berg		
Tim Roth		
Jim Hopson		
Ron Lancaster		
4 George Wells	3.00	6.00
Ken McEachern		
Bob Pearce		
Larry Bird		
Ted Provost		
James Elder		
Bob Richardson		
Gary Brandt		

1976 Saskatchewan Roughriders Team Sheets

This group of 40-players and coaches of the Roughriders was produced on five glossy sheets each measuring approximately 8" by 10". The fronts feature black-and-white player portraits with eight pictures to a sheet with the year printed at the top. The backs are blank. The cards are unnumbered and checklisted below in alphabetical order, with the player pictured in the upper left hand corner of the sheet listed first.

COMPLETE SET (5)	12.50	25.00
1 Larry Bird	4.00	8.00
Ken McEachern		
Bob Richardson		
Gary Brandt		
Steve Mazurak		
Ralph Galloway		
Tom Campana		
Ron Lancaster		
2 Steve Mazurak	2.50	5.00
John Washington		
Brian Bertefeuille		
George Wells		
Jim Hopson		
Randy Graham		
Peter Van Valkenburg		
Cleveland Vann		
3 Lorne Richardson	2.50	5.00
Bob Macoritti		
Ted McEachern		
Ron Cherkas		
Rhett Dawson		
Al Ford		
Brian O'Hara		
Leif Pettersen		
4 Dalton Smarsh	2.50	5.00
Tim Roth		
Steve Molnar		
Jim Marshall		
Roger Goree		
Bill Manchuk		
Ray Odums		
Sam Holden		
5 Dave Syme	3.00	6.00
Ted Provost		
Mike Dirks		
Jesse O'Neal		
Paul Williams		
John Payne		
Ken Preston		
Bruce Cowie		

1977-78 Saskatchewan Roughriders Team Sheets

This group of 40-players and coaches of the Roughriders was produced on five glossy sheets each measuring approximately 8" by 10". The fronts feature black-and-white player portraits with eight pictures to a sheet with the year printed at the top. The backs are blank. The cards are unnumbered and checklisted below in alphabetical order, with the player pictured in the upper left hand corner of the sheet listed first.

COMPLETE SET (5)	12.50	25.00
1 Barry Ardern	4.00	8.00
Bob Richardson		
Gary Brandt		
Tom Campana		
Ron Lancaster		
Eric Guthrie		
Phil Price		
Lewis Cook		
2 Lou Clare	2.50	5.00
Ken McEachern		
Ted Provost		
Ron Cherkas		
Sylvester McGee		
Randy Graham		
Joe Miller		
Steve Mazurak		
3 Steve Dennis	3.00	6.00
Ralph Galloway		
Carl Roaches		
Mike Dirks		
Leif Pettersen		
Cleveland Vann		
Dave Hadden		
Roger Goree		
4 Bob Macoritti	3.00	6.00
Paul Williams		
Bill Baker		
Roger Aldag		
Sam Holden		
Brian O'Hara		
Emil Nielsen		
Bill Manchuk		
5 Ken Preston	2.50	5.00
Bill Clarke		
Bruce Cowie		
Jim Eddy		
Larry Bird		
Tim Roth		
Steve Molnar		
George Wells		

1978 Saskatchewan Roughriders Team Sheets

This group of 40-players and coaches of the Roughriders was produced on five glossy sheets each measuring approximately 8" by 10". The fronts feature black-and-white player portraits with eight pictures to a sheet with the year printed at the top. The backs are blank. The cards are unnumbered and checklisted below in alphabetical order, with the player pictured in the upper left hand corner of the sheet listed first.

COMPLETE SET (5)	12.50	25.00
1 Bill Clarke	4.00	8.00
Bruce Cowie		
Jim Eddy		
Henry Dorsch		
Preston Young		
Rod Wellington		
Joey Walters		
Ron Lancaster		
2 Steve Dennis	2.50	5.00
James Wolf		
Cleveland Vann		
Roger Goree		
Brian O'Hara		
Larry Dick		
Craig Thomson		
Joe Worobec		
3 Steve Molnar	2.50	5.00
George Wells		
Louis Clare		
Joe Miller		
Ron Cherkas		
Mike Strickland		
Sam Holden		
Ken McEachern		
4 Bob Richardson	3.00	6.00
Emil Nielsen		
Bill Manchuk		
Roger Aldag		
Bill Baker		
Paul Williams		
Bob Macoritti		
Larry Bird		
5 Harold Woods	2.50	5.00
Ralph Galloway		
Steve Mazurak		
Mike Dirks		
Bob Bruer		
Sylvester McGee		
Eary Jones		
Steve Gelley		

1980 Saskatchewan Roughriders Team Sheets

This group of 40-players and coaches of the Roughriders was produced on five glossy sheets each measuring approximately 8" by 10". The fronts feature black-and-white player portraits with eight pictures to a sheet with the year printed at the top. The backs are blank. The cards are unnumbered and checklisted below in alphabetical order, with the player pictured in the upper left hand corner of the sheet listed first.

COMPLETE SET (5)	12.50	25.00
1 Roger Aldag	2.50	5.00
Vickey Anderson		
Carmelo Carteri		
Al Chorney		
Frank Dark		
Steve Dennis		
Gerry Fellner		
Stewart Fraser		
2 Randy Gill	3.00	6.00
Roger Goree		
Gary Harris		
Ken Helms		
Curtis Henderson		
Tim Hook		
Gerry Hornett		
John Hufnagel		
3 Bryan Illerbrun	2.50	5.00
Alan Johns		
Zackery Jones		
John Kinch		
Dlaine Lamouroux		
Bob Macoritti		
Bill Manchuk		
Steve Mazurak		
4 Joe Miller	2.50	5.00
Ray Milo		
Ken McEachern		
Doug McIver		
Dave Petzke		
Bob Poley		
Neil Quilter		
Tim Roberts		
5 Dave Robey	2.50	5.00
Tom Rozantz		
Mike Samples		
Danny Sanders		
Kerry Smith		
Jim Spavital CO		
Cleveland Vann		
Alvin Walker		

1981 Saskatchewan Roughriders Police

The 1981 Police Saskatchewan set is very similar to other Roughriders police issues. The cards measure approximately 2 5/8" by 4 1/8" and were printed on thin white stock. The unnumbered cards are listed below alphabetically with the player's jersey number also included.

COMPLETE SET (10)	7.50	15.00
1 Roger Aldag 44	.60	1.50
2 Joe Barnes 7	1.00	2.50
3 Lester Brown 22	.40	1.00
4 Dwight Edwards 33	.60	1.50
5 Vince Goldsmith 78	.60	1.50
6 John Hufnagel 12	2.50	6.00
7 Ken McEachern 20	.40	1.00
8 Mike Samples 66	.40	1.00
9 Joey Walters 17	.40	1.00
10 Lyall Woznesensky 76	.40	1.00

1982 Saskatchewan Roughriders Police

The 1982 Police SUMA (Saskatchewan Urban Municipalities Association) Saskatchewan Roughriders set contains 16 cards measuring approximately 2 5/8" by 4 1/8". The fronts have color action photos bordered in white; the vertically oriented backs have career highlights and safety tips. The card backs have black printing with green accent on white card stock. The cards are printed on thin stock. The cards are unnumbered, so they are listed below by uniform number.

COMPLETE SET (16)	7.50	15.00
2 Greg Fieger	.40	1.00
7 Joe Adams	.30	.75
12 John Hufnagel	2.50	6.00
17 Joey Walters	.30	.75
20 Ken McEachern	.30	.75
21 Marcellus Greene	.30	.75
25 Steve Dennis	.30	.75
29 Fran McDermott	.30	.75
37 Frank Robinson	.40	1.00
44 Roger Aldag	.60	1.50
57 Bob Poley	.40	1.00
66 Mike Samples	.30	.75
69 Don Swafford	.30	.75
74 Chris DeFrance	.30	.75
76 Lyall Woznesensky	.30	.75
78 Vince Goldsmith	.75	2.00

1983 Saskatchewan Roughriders Police

The 1983 Police SUMA (Saskatchewan Urban Municipalities Association) Saskatchewan Roughriders set contains 16 cards measuring approximately 2 5/8" by 4 1/8". The fronts have color action photos bordered in white; the vertically oriented backs have career highlights and safety tips. The card backs have black printing with green accent on white card stock. The cards are printed on thin stock. The cards are unnumbered, so they are listed below by uniform number. The 1983 set is distinguished from the similar 1982 SUMA set by the presence of facsimile autographs on the 1983 version.

COMPLETE SET (16)	7.50	15.00
9 Ron Robinson	.40	1.00
12 John Hufnagel	2.00	5.00
13 Ken Clark	.40	1.00
18 Mike Washington	.30	.75
24 Marshall Hamilton	.30	.75
25 Mike Emery	.30	.75
30 Duane Galloway	.30	.75
33 Dwight Edwards	.40	1.00
36 Dave Ridgway	.75	2.00
42 Eddie Lowe	.40	1.00
58 J.C. Pelusi	.30	.75
60 Karl Morgan	.30	.75
61 Bryan Illerbrun	.30	.75
65 Neil Quilter	.30	.75
72 Ray Elgaard	1.25	3.00
74 Chris DeFrance	.30	.75

1987 Saskatchewan Roughriders Royal Studios

This 40-card standard-size set features members of the Saskatchewan Roughriders. The card fronts are in color with a white and green striped border and the player's name and uniform number at the bottom. The cardbacks are on white card stock with the player's name, number, position, team, and bio at the top. The cards are unnumbered and are listed below in alphabetical order.

COMPLETE SET (40)	12.00	30.00
1 Dave Albright	.40	1.00
2 Roger Aldag	.60	1.50
3 Mike Anderson	.30	.75
4 Tron Armstrong	.30	.75
5 Terry Baker	.60	1.50
6 Walter Bender	.40	1.00
7 Jeff Bentrim	.40	1.00
8 Todd Brown	.30	.75
9 Tom Burgess	1.25	3.00
10 Coaching Staff	.75	2.00
John Hufnagel		
Dick Adams		
John Gregory		
Ted Heath		
Gary Hoffman		
M. Samples		
11 Terry Cochrane	.30	.75
12 David Conrad	.30	.75
13 Steve Crane	.30	.75
14 James Curry	.75	2.00
15 Tony Dennis	.30	.75
16 Ray Elgaard	1.25	3.00
17 Denny Ferdinand	.30	.75
18 Roderick Fisher	.30	.75
19 Joe Fuller	.30	.75
20 Gainer The Gopher (Team Mascot)	.30	.75
21 Norris Gibbs	.30	.75
22 Nick Hebeler	.30	.75
23 Bryan Illerbrun	.40	1.00
24 Alan Johns	.30	.75
25 Bobby Jurasin	1.25	3.00
26 Eddie Lowe	.40	1.00
27 Tracey Mack	.30	.75
28 Tim McCray	.60	1.50
29 Mike McGruder	.40	1.00
30 Ken Moore	.30	.75
31 Dan Rashovich	.30	.75
32 Scott Redl	.30	.75
33 Dave Ridgway	.60	1.50
34 Dave Sidoo	.30	.75
35 Harry Skipper	.40	1.00
36 Lawrie Skolrood	.40	1.00
37 Vic Stevenson	.30	.75
38 Glen Suitor	.60	1.50
39 Brendan Taman	.30	.75
Asst.EQ MG		
Ivan Gutfriend		
Athletic Therapist		
Norm Fong EQ MG		
40 Mark Urness	.30	.75

1988 Saskatchewan Roughriders McDonald's JOGO

This set was produced by JOGO and features members of the Saskatchewan Roughriders. Each card was produced with a black border, includes the McDonald's sponsorship logo on the back, and is unnumbered.

COMPLETE SET (12)	15.00	30.00
1 David Albright	.75	2.00
2 Roger Aldag	1.00	2.50
3 Mike Anderson	.75	2.00
4 Tom Burgess	2.50	6.00
5 James Curry	1.50	4.00
6 Ray Elgaard	2.00	5.00
7 Denny Ferdinand	.75	2.00
8 Bobby Jurasin	2.50	6.00
9 Gary Lewis	.75	2.00
10 Dave Ridgway	2.50	6.00
11 Harry Skipper	1.00	2.50
12 Glen Suitor	1.50	4.00

1988 Saskatchewan Roughriders Royal Studios

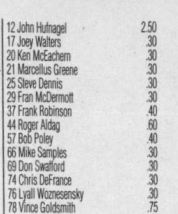

This 54-card standard-size set features members of the Saskatchewan Roughriders. The card fronts are in color, with a white and green striped border, with the player's name and number at the bottom. The card backs are black on white card stock, with the player's name, number, position, team, and resume at the top. The cards are unnumbered and are listed below in alphabetical order by subject. The cards were printed on three different 20-card sheets, necessitating six double-printed cards as noted below.

COMPLETE SET (54)	16.00	40.00
1 Dave Albright	.20	.50
2 Roger Aldag DP	.30	.75
3 Mike Anderson	.20	.50
4 Kent Austin DP	1.25	3.00
5 Terry Baker	.40	1.00
6 Jeff Bentrim	.30	.75
7 Rob Bresciani	.20	.50
8 Albert Brown	.30	.75
9 Tom Burgess DP	1.00	2.50
10 Coaching Staff	.30	.75
Gary Hoffman		
Dick Adams		
Dan Daniel		
Ted Heath		
John Gregory		
Steve Goldman		
11 Dick Cohee and The Store	.20	.50
12 David Conrad	.20	.50
13 Steve Crane	.20	.50
14 James Curry DP	.50	1.25
15 Dream Team (Cheerleaders)	.50	1.25
16 Ray Elgaard	1.00	2.50
17 James Ellingson	.30	.75
18 Jeff Fairholm	.50	1.25
19 Denny Ferdinand	.20	.50
20 The Flame (Team Mascot)	.20	.50
21 Norm Fong and Ivan Gulfriend (Equipment Trainer)	.20	.50
22 Joe Fuller	.20	.50
23 Gainer The Gopher (Team Mascot)	.20	.50
24 Vince Goldsmith	.40	1.00
25 John Gregory CO	.30	.75
26 Richie Hall	.20	.50
27 Bill Henry	.20	.50
28 James Hood	.20	.50
29 Bryan Illerbrun UER (Name misspelled Brian on front and back)	.30	.75
30 Milson Jones	.50	1.25
31 Bobby Jurasin DP	1.00	2.50
32 Tim Kearse	.20	.50
33 Rick Klassen	.30	.75
34 Gary Lewis	.20	.50
35 Eddie Lowe	.30	.75
36 Greg McCormack	.20	.50
37 Tim McCray	.40	1.00
38 Ray McDonald	.30	.75
39 Mike McGruder	.30	.75
40 Ken Moore	.20	.50
41 Donald Narcisse	1.00	2.50
42 Dan Rambo and Brendan Taman (Rider Scouting)	.20	.50
43 Dan Rashovich	.20	.50
44 Dameon Reilly	.30	.75
45 Dave Ridgway DP	.40	1.00
46 Rocco Romano	.20	.50
47 Harry Skipper	.30	.75
48 Vic Stevenson	.20	.50
49 Glen Suitor	.50	1.25
50 Jeff Treftlin	.20	.50
51 Mark Urness	.20	.50
52 Eddie Ray Walker	.30	.75
53 John Walker	.30	.75
54 Jeff Watson	.20	.50

1989 Saskatchewan Roughriders Royal Studios

This 54-card standard-size set features members of the Saskatchewan Roughriders. The card fronts are in color, with white and green striped border, with the player's name and uniform number at the bottom. The card backs are black on white card stock, with the player's name, number, position, team, and resume at the top. The cards are unnumbered and are listed below in alphabetical order by subject. The cards were printed on three different 20-card sheets, necessitating six double-printed cards as noted below.

COMPLETE SET (54)	14.00	35.00
1 Dave Albright	.20	.50
2 Roger Aldag DP	.30	.75
3 Tuineau Alipate	.30	.75
4 Mike Anderson	.20	.50
5 Kent Austin	1.25	3.00
6 Terry Baker	.40	1.00
7 Jeff Bentrim	.30	.75
8 Rob Bresciani	.20	.50
9 Albert Brown	.30	.75
10 Tom Burgess DP	1.00	2.50
11 Coaching Staff	.30	.75
12 Steve Crane	.20	.50
13 James Curry	.50	1.25
14 Kevin Dixon	.20	.50
15 Dream Team (Cheerleaders sponsored by CKRM)	.20	.50
16 Wayne Drinkwalter	.30	.75
17 Ray Elgaard	.75	2.00
18 James Ellingson	.30	.75
19 Jeff Fairholm	.30	.75
20 The Flame	.20	.50
21 Norm Fong and Ivan Gutfriend (Equipment Trainer)	.20	.50
22 Gainer The Gopher DP (Team Mascot)	.20	.50
23 John Gregory CO	.30	.75
24 Vince Goldsmith	.30	.75
25 Mark Guy	.30	.75
26 Richie Hall DP	.20	.50
27 John Hoffman	.20	.50
28 Bryan Illerbrun UER (Name misspelled Brian on front and back)	.30	.75
29 Milson Jones	.30	.75
30 Bobby Jurasin DP	.75	2.00
31 Chuck Klingbeil	.30	.75
32 Gary Lewis	.30	.75
33 Eddie Lowe	.30	.75
34 Greg McCormack	.20	.50
35 Tim McCray	.40	1.00
36 Ray McDonald	.20	.50
37 Ken Moore	.20	.50
38 Cedric Moses	.20	.50
39 Donald Narcisse	.75	2.00
40 Dan Payne	.20	.50
41 Bob Poley	.20	.50
42 Dan Rashovich	.20	.50
43 Dave Ridgway DP	.40	1.00
44 Junior Robinson	.30	.75
45 Harry Skipper	.30	.75
46 Vic Stevenson	.20	.50
47 Glen Suitor	.50	1.25
48 Jeff Treftlin	.20	.50
49 Kelly Trithart	.30	.75
50 Mark Urness	.20	.50
51 Lionel Vital	.20	.50
52 Eddie Ray Walker	.30	.75
53 Steve Wiggins	.20	.50
54 Donovan Wright	.20	.50

1990 Saskatchewan Roughriders Royal Studios

This 60-card standard size set features members of the Saskatchewan Roughriders. The card fronts are in color, with white and green striped border, with the player's name and uniform number at the bottom. The card backs are black on white card stock, with the player's name, number, position, team, and resume at the top. The cards are unnumbered and are listed below in alphabetical order by subject.

COMPLETE SET (60)	14.00	35.00
1 Dick Adams CO	.20	.50
2 Dave Albright	.20	.50
3 Roger Aldag	.30	.75
4 Tuineau Alipate	.30	.75
5 Mike Anderson	.20	.50
6 Kent Austin	1.00	2.50
7 Tony Belser	.20	.50
8 Jeff Bentrim	.30	.75
9 Bruce Boyko	.30	.75
10 Albert Brown	.30	.75
11 Paul Bushey	.20	.50
12 Larry Donovan CO	.20	.50
13 Dream Team (Cheerleaders sponsored by CKRM)	.30	.75
14 Wayne Drinkwalter	.30	.75
15 Sean Dykes	.20	.50
16 Ray Elgaard	1.00	2.50
17 Jeff Fairholm	.40	1.00
18 Norman Fong MG Ivan Gutfriend MG	.20	.50
19 Alan Ford GM	.20	.50
20 Lucius Floyd	.40	1.00
21 Gainer The Gopher (Team Mascot)	.20	.50
22 Chris Gioskos	.20	.50
23 Vince Goldsmith	.40	1.00
24 John Gregory CO	.30	.75
25 Mark Guy	.30	.75
26 Stacey Hairston	.30	.75
27 Richie Hall	.30	.75
28 Greg Harris	.20	.50
29 Ted Heath CO	.20	.50
30 Gary Hoffman CO	.20	.50
31 John Hoffman	.20	.50
32 Larry Hogue	.30	.75
33 Bobby Jurasin	.80	2.00
34 Milson Jones	.40	1.00
35 James King	.20	.50
36 Chuck Klingbeil	.40	1.00
37 Mike Lazecki	.20	.50
38 Orville Lee	.60	1.50
39 Gary Lewis	.30	.75
40 Eddie Lowe	.30	.75
41 Greg McCormack	.20	.50
42 Tim McCray	.40	1.00
43 Ken Moore	.20	.50
44 Donald Narcisse	.80	2.00
45 Dave Pitcher	.20	.50
46 Bob Poley	.20	.50
47 Brent Pollack	.20	.50
48 Dan Rashovich	.20	.50
49 Tony Rice	.80	2.00
50 Dave Ridgway	.40	1.00
51 Pal Sartori	.20	.50
52 Saskatchewan Roughriders	.40	1.00
53 Glen Scrivener	.20	.50
54 Tony Simmons DE	.20	.50
55 Vic Stevenson	.20	.50
56 Glen Suitor	.40	1.00
57 Jeff Treftlin	.20	.50
58 Kelly Trithart UER (Name misspelled Trihart on front and back)	.30	.75
59 Lionel Vital	.20	.50
60 Slater Zaleski	.20	.50

1991 Saskatchewan Roughriders Royal Studios

This 66-card standard-size set features members of the Saskatchewan Roughriders. The card fronts are in color, borderless, and without the player identification except through the photo. The card backs are black on white card stock, with the player's name, number, position, team, and resume at the top. The cards are unnumbered and are listed below in alphabetical order by subject.

COMPLETE SET (66)	14.00	35.00
1 Dick Adams CO	.20	.50
2 Dave Albright	.20	.50
3 Roger Aldag	.30	.75
4 Mike Anderson	.20	.50
5 Kent Austin	1.20	3.00
6 John Bankhead	.30	.75
7 Kerry Beutler/1990 Miss Grey Cup	.30	.75
8 Allan Boyko	.30	.75
9 Bruce Boyko	.30	.75
10 Doug Brewster	.20	.50
11 Albert Brown	.30	.75
12 Paul Bushey	.20	.50
13 Coaching Staff	.20	.50
14 Larry Donovan CO	.20	.50
15 Wayne Drinkwalter	.30	.75
16 Sean Dykes	.20	.50
17 Ray Elgaard	.80	2.00
18 Jeff Fairholm	.40	1.00
19 Dan Farthing	.20	.50
20 Lucius Floyd	.40	1.00
21 Gainer The Gopher Team Mascot	.20	.50
22 Chris Gioskos UER (Name misspelled Gioskas on front)	.20	.50
23 Sonny Gordon	.20	.50
24 John Gregory CO	.30	.75
25 Stacey Hairston	.30	.75
26 Richie Hall	.30	.75
27 Greg Harris	.20	.50
28 Major Harris	.60	1.50
29 Ted Heath CO	.20	.50
30 Gary Hoffman CO	.20	.50
31 John Hoffman	.20	.50
32 Larry Hogue	.30	.75
33 Willis Jacox	.60	1.50
34 Ray Jauch CO	.30	.75
35 Gene Jelks	.60	1.50
36 Milson Jones	.40	1.00
37 Bobby Jurasin	.80	2.00
38 James King	.20	.50
39 Mike Lazecki	.20	.50
40 Orville Lee	.40	1.00
41 Gary Lewis	.30	.75
42 Eddie Lowe	.30	.75
43 Paul Maines	.20	.50
44 Don Matthews CO	.20	.50
45 Dane McArthur	.20	.50
46 David McCrary	.20	.50
47 Donald Narcisse	.60	1.50
48 Offensive Line	.20	.50
49 Dave Pitcher	.20	.50
50 Bob Poley	.20	.50
51 Brent Pollack	.20	.50
52 Basil Proctor	.20	.50
53 Dan Rashovich	.20	.50
54 Dave Ridgway UER (Name misspelled Ridgeway on back)	.40	1.00
55 Roughriders vs. Rocket	.40	1.00
56 Roughriders Team	.30	.75
57 Glen Scrivener	.20	.50
58 Keith Stephens	.20	.50
59 Vic Stevenson	.20	.50
60 Glen Suitor	.50	1.25
61 Chris Thieneman	.20	.50
62 Jeff Treftlin	.20	.50
63 Kelly Trithart	.30	.75
64 Paul Vajda	.20	.50
65 Ted Wahl	.20	.50
66 Rick Worman	.40	1.00

1991 Saskatchewan Roughriders Royal Studios Grey Cup 1966-91

This set was distributed by Royal Studios and honors the Roughriders Grey Cup years of 1966-91. Each card is standard sized with the cardfront featuring a color photo of the player with a white and silver border. The player's name, jersey number and brief bio appear on the backs of these unnumbered cards.

COMPLETE SET (40)	12.00	30.00
1 Jack Abendschan	.30	.75
2 Sandy Archer TR	.20	.50
3 Ron Atchison	1.20	3.00
4 Gord Barwell	.20	.50
5 Al Benecick	.20	.50
6 Bruce Bennett	.30	.75
7 Tom Beynon	.20	.50
8 Clyde Brock	.20	.50
9 Ed Buchanan	.20	.50
10 Hugh Campbell	.30	.75
11 Wally Dempsey	.20	.50
12 Henry Dorsch	.20	.50
13 Paul Dudley	.20	.50
14 Larry Dumelie	.20	.50
15 Ted Dushinski	.20	.50
16 Garner Ekstran	.30	.75
17 Alan Ford	.30	.75
18 Alan Ford The Catch	.30	.75
19 Don Gerhardt	.20	.50
20 Eagle Keys CO	.80	2.00
21 Bob Kosid	.20	.50
22 Ron Lancaster	1.60	4.00
23 Ron Lancaster Hugh Campbell	1.00	2.50
24 Moe Levesque	.20	.50
25 Ed McQuarters	.30	.75
26 Gil Petmanis	.20	.50
27 Ken Preston GM	.50	1.25
28 George Reed	.60	1.50
29 Ken Reed	.20	.50
30 Cliff Shaw	.20	.50
31 Wayne Shaw	.20	.50
32 Ted Urness	.30	.75
33 Galen Wahlmeier	.20	.50
34 Dale West	.30	.75
35 Reg Whitehouse	.30	.75
36 Gene Wlasiuk	.20	.50
37 Jim Worden	.20	.50
38 Roughriders '66 Cup Lineup	.20	.50
39 Grey Cup 40th Annual Ticket	.20	.50
40 Grey Cup 40th Annual	.20	.50

1992 Saskatchewan Roughriders Sid's Sunflowers

This set of standard-sized cards was sponsored by Sid's Sunflowers and features members of the Saskatchewan Roughriders. The cards feature a solid green border on the front and a standard black and white unnumbered cardback.

COMPLETE SET (12)	5.00	10.00
1 Roger Aldag	.30	.75
2 Kent Austin	1.00	2.50
3 Jearld Baylis	.30	.75
4 Ray Elgaard	.75	2.00
5 Jeff Fairholm	.30	.75
6 Lucius Floyd	.40	1.00
7 Willis Jacox	.50	1.25
8 Tyrone Jones	.30	.75
9 Bobby Jurasin	.30	.75
10 Gary Lewis DT	.30	.75
11 Dave Ridgway	.30	.75
12 Glen Suitor	.20	.50

1993 Saskatchewan Roughriders Dairy Lids

Issued in Saskatchewan and featuring 1993 Roughriders players, these six 1993 Dairy Producers Ice Cream collector lids were issued on four-liter ice cream cartons. Each white plastic lid measures approximately 8 1/4" in diameter. Inside a black border, the circular lids display a head shot, team helmet, and facsimile autograph on the upper portion, with information about the ice cream on the lower portion. The lids are unnumbered and checklisted below in alphabetical order.

COMPLETE SET (6)	8.00	20.00
1 Kent Austin	3.00	6.00
2 Ray Elgaard	2.00	5.00
3 Jeff Fairholm	1.50	3.50
4 Bobby Jurasin	1.50	3.50
5 Dave Ridgway UER (Misspelled Ridgeway)	1.50	3.50
6 Glen Suitor	1.00	2.50

1993 Saskatchewan Roughriders Coke

This set of standard-sized cards was sponsored by Coca-Cola Cards and features members of the Saskatchewan Roughriders. The cards feature a green border and two Coca-Cola logos on the front. The cardbacks were produced in simple black and white with a player photo and no card number.

COMPLETE SET (4)	3.00	8.00
1 Kent Austin	1.25	3.00
2 Ray Elgaard	1.00	2.50
3 Bobby Jurasin	.60	1.50
4 Dave Ridgway	.60	1.50

1993 Saskatchewan Roughriders Dream Cards

This set of standard-sized cards was sponsored and produced by Dream Cards and features members of the Saskatchewan Roughriders. The cards feature a white border on the front and a color cardback complete with a second player photo and card number.

COMPLETE SET (24)	7.50	15.00
1 Kent Austin	1.00	2.50
2 Albert Brown	.20	.50
3 Barry Wilburn	.20	.50
4 Bobby Jurasin	.30	.75
5 Bruce Boyko	.20	.50
6 Charles Anthony	.20	.50
7 Craig Hendrickson	.20	.50
8 Dan Payne	.20	.50
9 Dave Ridgway	.30	.75
10 Dave Pitcher	.20	.50
11 Donald Narcisse	.20	.50
12 Gary Lewis	.30	.75
13 Glen Suitor	.30	.75
14 Jearld Baylis	.30	.75
15 Jeff Fairholm	.30	.75
16 Maurice Crum	.20	.50
17 Mike Anderson	.20	.50
18 Mike Saunders	1.50	4.00
19 Paul Vajda	.20	.50
20 Ray Bernard	.20	.50
21 Ray Elgaard	.75	2.00
22 Scott Hendrickson	.20	.50
23 Stewart Hill	.30	.75
24 Ventson Donelson	.20	.50

1993 Saskatchewan Roughriders Royal Studios Team Health

This 7-card standard-size set features members of the Saskatchewan Roughriders. The card fronts are in color with the player's name, position, Team Health title, and team name below the photo. The cardbacks were printed in black on white card stock and are unnumbered.

COMPLETE SET (7)	1.50	4.00
1 Jearld Baylis	.30	.75
2 Bruce Boyko	.20	.50
3 Ventson Donelson	.20	.50
4 Dan Farthing	.40	1.00
5 Dan Johnston	.40	1.00
6 Dan Rashovich	.20	.50
7 Team Photo	.20	.50

1994 Saskatchewan Roughriders Royal Studios Team Health

This 12-card standard-size set features members of the Saskatchewan Roughriders. The card fronts are in color with the player's name, position, Team Health title, and team name below the photo and Royal Studios name above. The cardbacks were printed in black on white card stock and are unnumbered.

COMPLETE SET (12)	2.50	5.00
1 Mike Anderson	.20	.50
2 Bruce Boyko	.20	.50
3 Ventson Donelson	.20	.50
4 Wayne Drinkwalter	.20	.50
5 Dan Farthing	.40	1.00
6 Scott Hendrickson	.20	.50
7 Quinn Magnuson	.20	.50
8 Dan Rashovich	.20	.50
9 Aaron Ruffin	.20	.50
10 Dallas Rysavy	.20	.50
11 Randy Srochenski	.20	.50
12 Team Photo	.20	.50

1995 Saskatchewan Roughriders Royal Studios Team Health

This 11-card standard-size set features members of the Saskatchewan Roughriders. The cardfronts are in color with only the player's name and Team Health title included. The cardbacks were printed in black on white card stock and are unnumbered.

COMPLETE SET (11)	2.50	5.00
1 Troy Alexander	.30	.75
2 Bruce Boyko	.20	.50
3 Ventson Donelson	.20	.50
4 Dan Farthing	.40	1.00
5 Gene Makowsky	.20	.50
6 Dan Payne	.20	.50
7 Dave Pitcher	.20	.50
8 Dan Rashovich	.20	.50
9 Aaron Ruffin	.20	.50
10 Dave Van Belleghem	.30	.75
11 Team Photo	.20	.50

1997 Saskatchewan Roughriders Price Watchers

This 30-card set of the Saskatchewan Roughriders was sponsored by Price Watchers drug stores and features color action player photos with inner green and outer black borders. The backs carry player information and a health message. The cards are unnumbered and checklisted below in alphabetical order.

COMPLETE SET (30)	4.00	10.00
1 Troy Alexander	.20	.50
2 Patrick Burke	.08	.25
3 Carl Coulter	.08	.25
4 Jim Daley CO	.08	.25
5 Shawn Daniels	.08	.25
6 Ventson Donelson	.08	.25
7 Dan Farthing	.30	.75
8 Profail Grier	.08	.25
9 Rod Harris	.08	.25
10 Scott Hendrickson	.08	.25
11 Dale Joseph	.08	.25
12 Darren Joseph	.08	.25
13 Bobby Jurasin	.30	.75
14 John Kropke	.08	.25
15 Gene Makowsky	.08	.25
16 Kevin Mason	.30	.75
17 Curtis Mayfield	.08	.25
18 Paul McCallum	.08	.25
19 Lamar McGriggs	.08	.25
20 Robert Mimbs	.50	1.25
21 Donald Narcisse	.50	1.25
22 Henry Newby	.08	.25
23 Dan Rashovich	.08	.25
24 Steve Sarkisian	.50	1.25
25 Reggie Slack	.80	2.00
26 John Terry	.08	.25
27 K.D. Williams	.08	.25
28 Dream Team Cheerleaders	.08	.25
29 Gainer (Mascot)	.08	.25
30 Title Card CL	.08	.25

1999 Saskatchewan Roughriders Police

This set was produced by Signature Graphics and distributed by local law enforcement officers. The cards feature a green border with the year 1999 clearly printed on the fronts. The unnumbered cardbacks feature a safety message, brief player vital statistics and sponsor logos.

COMPLETE SET (24)	5.00	12.00
1 Ken Benson	.10	.30
2 Dan Comiskey	.10	.30
3 Douglas Craft	.10	.30
4 Ben Fairbrother	.10	.30
5 Dan Farthing	.20	.50
6 Shannon Garrett	.10	.30
7 Eric Guliford	.10	.30
8 Curtis Mayfield	.20	.50
9 Gene Makowsky	.10	.30
10 Todd McMillon	.10	.30
11 Cal Murphy CO	.10	.30
12 Don Narcisse	.40	1.00
13 Kennedy Nkeyason	.10	.30
14 Willie Pless	.30	.75
15 John Rayborn	.50	1.25
16 Steve Sarkisian	.50	1.25
17 Mike Saunders	.40	1.00
18 Reggie Slack	.60	1.50
19 Neal Smith	.10	.30
20 Chris Szarka	.10	.30
21 John Terry	.10	.30
22 R-Kal Truluck	.20	.50
23 Cheerleaders	.10	.30
24 Team Mascot	.10	.30

2000 Saskatchewan Roughriders Legends of the Game

This set of cards was printed on 2-uncut sheets of 6-cards each. They feature members of the 1966 Grey Cup Champ Roughriders and were issued for a player reunion on February 5, 2000. The sheets can sometimes be found signed by every player in attendence at the event.

COMPLETE SET (2)	7.50	15.00
1 Garner Ekstran, Gene Wlasiuk	2.50	5.00
Sandy Archer		
Al Benecick		
Hank Dorsch		
Dale West		
2 George Reed	5.00	10.00
Ron Lancaster		
Dale Laird		
Ron Atchison		
Alan Ford		
Wayne Shaw		

1956 Shredded Wheat

The 1956 Shredded Wheat CFL football card set contains 105 cards portraying CFL players. The cards measure 2 1/2" by 3 1/2". The fronts of the cards contain a black and white portrait photo of the player on a one-color striped background. The lower 1/2" of the front contains the card number and the player's name below a dashed line. This lower portion of the card was presumably connected with a premium offer, as the back indicates such an offer, in both English and French, on the bottom. The backs contain brief biographical data in both English and French. Each letter prefix corresponds to a team, e.g., A: Calgary Stampeders, B: Edmonton Eskimos, C: Winnipeg Blue Bombers, D: Hamilton Tiger-Cats, E: Toronto Argonauts, F: Saskatchewan Roughriders, and G: Ottawa Rough Riders.

COMPLETE SET (105)	5,000.00	9,000.00
A1 Peter Muir	60.00	100.00
A2 Harry Langford	50.00	80.00
A3 Tony Pajaczkowski	90.00	150.00
A4 Bob Morgan	50.00	80.00
A5 Baz Nagle	50.00	80.00
A6 Alex Macklin	50.00	80.00
A7 Bob Geary	50.00	80.00
A8 Don Klosterman	75.00	125.00
A9 Bill McKenna	50.00	80.00
A10 Bill Stevenson	50.00	80.00
A11 Ray Baillie	50.00	80.00
A12 Berdett Hess	50.00	80.00
A13 Lynn Bottoms	60.00	100.00
A14 Doug Brown	50.00	80.00
A15 Jack Hennemier	50.00	80.00
B1 Frank Anderson	50.00	80.00
B2 Don Barry	50.00	80.00
B3 Johnny Bright	125.00	200.00
B4 Kurt Burris	50.00	80.00
B5 Bob Dean	50.00	80.00
B6 Don Getty	90.00	150.00
B7 Normie Kwong	125.00	200.00
B8 Earl Lindley	50.00	80.00
B9 Art Walker	60.00	100.00
B10 Rollie Miles	75.00	125.00
B11 Frank Morris	75.00	125.00
B12 Jackie Parker	175.00	300.00
B13 Ted Tully	50.00	80.00
B14 Frank Ivy	60.00	100.00
B15 Bill Rowekamp	50.00	80.00
C1 Allie Sherman	60.00	100.00
C2 Larry Cabrelli	50.00	80.00
C3 Ron Kelly	50.00	80.00
C4 Edward Kotowich	50.00	80.00
C5 Buddy Leake	60.00	100.00
C6 Thomas Lumsden	50.00	80.00
C7 Bill Smitiuk	50.00	80.00
C8 Buddy Tinsley	75.00	125.00
C9 Ron Vaccher	50.00	80.00
C10 Eagle Day	90.00	150.00
C11 Buddy Allison	50.00	80.00
C12 Bob Haas	60.00	100.00
C13 Steve Patrick	50.00	80.00
C14 Keith Pearce UER	50.00	80.00
(Misspelled Pierce		
on front)		
C15 Lorne Benson	50.00	80.00
D1 George Arnett	50.00	80.00
D2 Eddie Bevan	50.00	80.00
D3 Art Darch	50.00	80.00
D4 John Fedosoff	50.00	80.00
D5 Cam Fraser	50.00	80.00
D6 Ron Howell	60.00	100.00
D7 Alex Muzyka	60.00	100.00
D8 Chet Miksza	50.00	80.00
D9 Walt Nikorak	50.00	80.00
D10 Pete Neumann	75.00	125.00
D11 Steve Oneschuk	50.00	80.00
D12 Vince Scott	75.00	125.00
D13 Ralph Toohy	50.00	80.00
D14 Ray Truant	50.00	80.00
D15 Nobby Wirkowski	60.00	100.00
E1 Pete Bennett	50.00	80.00
E2 Fred Black	50.00	80.00
E3 Jim Copeland	50.00	80.00
E4 Al Pfeifer	60.00	100.00
E5 Ron Albright	50.00	80.00
E6 Tom Dublinski	60.00	100.00
E7 Billy Shipp	60.00	100.00
E8 Baz Mackie	50.00	80.00
E9 Bill McFarlane	50.00	80.00
E10 John Sopinka	60.00	100.00
E11 Dick Brown	50.00	80.00
E12 Gerry Doucette	50.00	80.00
E13 Dan Shaw	50.00	80.00
E14 Dick Shatto	100.00	175.00
E15 Bill Swiacki	60.00	100.00
F1 Ray Syrnyk	50.00	80.00
F2 Martin Ruby	90.00	150.00
F3 Bobby Marlow	75.00	125.00
F4 Doug Kiloh	50.00	80.00
F5 Gord Sturtridge	60.00	100.00
F6 Stan Williams	50.00	80.00
F7 Larry Isbell	50.00	80.00
F8 Ken Casner	50.00	80.00
F9 Mel Becket	60.00	100.00
F10 Reg Whitehouse	50.00	80.00
F11 Harry Lampman	50.00	80.00
F12 Mario DeMarco	60.00	100.00
F13 Ken Carpenter	60.00	100.00
F14 Frank Filchock	60.00	100.00
F15 Frank Tripucka	90.00	150.00
G1 Tom Tracy	90.00	150.00
G2 Pete Ladygo	50.00	80.00
G3 Sam Scoccia	50.00	80.00
G4 Joe Upton	50.00	80.00
G5 Bob Simpson	90.00	150.00
G6 Bruno Bitkowski	60.00	100.00
G7 Joe Stracini UER	50.00	80.00
(Misspelled Straccini		
on card front)		
G8 Hal Ledyard	50.00	80.00
G9 Milt Graham	50.00	80.00
G10 Bill Sowalski	50.00	80.00
G11 Avatus Stone	50.00	80.00
G12 John Boich	60.00	100.00
G13 Don Pinhey UER	50.00	80.00
(Misspelled Bob Pinkney		
on card front)		
G14 Peter Karpuk	50.00	80.00
G15 Frank Clair	75.00	125.00

1952 Star Weekly Posters

These posters were actually pages from a newspaper weekly magazine. Each measures roughly 11" by 14" and features a color photo of a top CFL player. The posters were printed on newsprint type stock and unnumbered. The backs are simply another page from the magazine. We've arranged them below in order of their publication date which can be found along the top or bottom edge. Additions to this list are appreciated.

1 Herb Trawick	25.00	50.00
(October 12, 1952 issue)		
2 Ed Salem	15.00	30.00
(November 2, 1952 issue)		
3 Lally Lalonde	15.00	30.00
(November 23, 1952 issue)		

1958 Star Weekly Posters

These posters were actually pages from a newspaper weekly magazine. Each measures roughly 11" by 14" and features two color photos of top CFL players at the bottom and a "Stars of the Canadian Gridiron" title at the top. The posters were printed on newsprint type stock and each was not numbered. The backs are simply another page from the magazine.

1 Pat Abbruzzi	15.00	30.00
Herb Gray		
(November 15)		
2 Johnny Bright	20.00	40.00
Dean Renfro		
(September 13)		
3 Jerry Doucette	15.00	30.00
Steve Oneschuk		
(October 11)		
4 Sam Etcheverry	25.00	50.00
Gerry James		
(October 18)		
5 Cookie Gilchrist	20.00	40.00
Fran Rogel		
(November 8)		
6 Ted Hunt	15.00	30.00
Milt Graham		
(September 20)		
7 Larry Isbell	15.00	30.00
Dick Shatto		
(October 25)		
8 Gerry McDougall	25.00	50.00
Buddy Tinsley		
(November 22)		
9 Roger Nelson	15.00	30.00
Jack Gotta		
(September 20)		
10 Jackie Parker	20.00	50.00
Charlie Zickefoose		
(September 6)		
11 Hal Patterson	15.00	30.00
Ken Ploen		
(November 1)		
12 Ed Sharkey	25.00	50.00
Normie Kwong		
(October 4)		

1959 Star Weekly Posters

These posters were actually magazine page cut-outs designed to form a football player photo album. Each uncut page measures roughly 11" by 14" and features two color photos of top CFL players at the bottom and a "Great Moments in Canadian Football" note at the top. The posters were printed on newsprint type stock and each was not numbered. The backs are simply another page from the magazine.

COMPLETE SET (7)	125.00	200.00
1 Bernie Faloney	25.00	50.00
Randy Duncan		
(October 31, 1959)		
2 Jack Hill	15.00	30.00
Russ Jackson		
(October 3, 1959)		
3 Gerry James	20.00	40.00
Frank Tripucka		
4 Ronnie Knox	12.50	25.00
Jim Van Pelt		
(October 24, 1959)		
5 Bobby Kuntz	15.00	30.00
Bruce Claridge		
(September 27, 1959)		
6 Tony Pajaczkowski	12.50	25.00
Ron Howell		
(October 10, 1959)		
7 Billy Shipp	12.50	25.00
Don Getty		
(October 17, 1959)		

1963 Star Weekly Posters

These small posters were actually newspaper color magazine page cut-outs measuring roughly 11" by 14." The posters feature a color photo of a top CFL player to the right and a detailed player bio to the left. The posters were printed on newsprint type stock and not numbered. The backs are simply another page from the magazine.

1 George Dixon	12.50	25.00
2 Willie Fleming	20.00	40.00
3 Leo Lewis	12.50	25.00
4 Ray Purdin	10.00	20.00
5 Jim Rountree	10.00	20.00
6 Whit Tucker	15.00	30.00
7 James Earl Wright	10.00	20.00
8 Harvey Wylie	10.00	20.00

1958 Topps CFL

The 1958 Topps CFL set features eight of the nine Canadian Football League teams, excluding Montreal. The cards measure the standard size. This first Topps Canadian issue is very similar in format to the 1958 Topps NFL issue. The cards were sold in wax boxes containing 36 five-cent wax packs. The card backs feature a "Rub-a-coin" quiz along with the typical biographical and statistical information. The set features the first card of Cookie Gilchrist, who later led the AFL in rushing twice.

COMPLETE SET (88)	500.00	900.00
1 Paul Anderson	5.00	10.00
2 Leigh McMillan	4.00	8.00
3 Vic Chapman	4.00	8.00
4 Bobby Marlow	7.50	15.00
5 Mike Cacic	4.00	8.00
6 Ron Pawlowski	4.00	8.00
7 Frank Morris	5.00	10.00
8 Earl Keeley	4.00	8.00
9 Don Walsh	4.00	8.00
10 Bryan Engram	4.00	8.00
11 Bobby Kuntz	4.00	8.00
12 Jerry Janes	4.00	8.00
13 Don Bingham	4.00	8.00
14 Paul Fedor	4.00	8.00
15 Tommy Grant	6.00	12.00
16 Don Getty	7.50	15.00
17 George Brancato	4.00	8.00
18 Jackie Parker	20.00	40.00
19 Alan Valdes	4.00	8.00
20 Paul Dekker	4.00	8.00
21 Frank Tripucka	6.00	12.00
22 Gerry McDougall	5.00	10.00
23 Willard Dewveall	5.00	10.00
24 Ted Smale	4.00	8.00
25 Tony Pajaczkowski	6.00	12.00
26 Don Pinhey	4.00	8.00
27 Buddy Tinsley	6.00	12.00
28 Cookie Gilchrist	20.00	40.00
29 Larry Isbell	4.00	8.00
30 Bob Kelley	4.00	8.00
31 Thomas(Corky) Tharp	5.00	10.00
32 Steve Patrick	4.00	8.00
33 Hardiman Cureton	4.00	8.00
34 Joe Mobra	4.00	8.00
35 Harry Lunn	4.00	8.00
36 Gord Rowland	4.00	8.00
37 Herb Gray	7.50	15.00
38 Bob Simpson	7.50	15.00
39 Cam Fraser	4.00	8.00
40 Kenny Ploen	10.00	20.00
41 Lynn Bottoms	4.00	8.00
42 Bill Stevenson	4.00	8.00
43 Jerry Selinger	4.00	8.00
44 Oscar Kruger	5.00	10.00
45 Gerry James	7.50	15.00
46 Dave Mann	6.00	12.00
47 Tom Dimitroff	5.00	10.00
48 Vince Scott	6.00	12.00
49 Fran Rogel	5.00	10.00
50 Henry Hair	4.00	8.00
51 Bob Brady	4.00	8.00
52 Gerry Doucette	4.00	8.00
53 Ken Carpenter	5.00	10.00
54 Bernie Faloney	12.50	25.00
55 John Barrow	10.00	20.00
56 George Druxman	4.00	8.00
57 Rollie Miles	6.00	12.00
58 Jerry Cornelison	4.00	8.00
59 Harry Langford	4.00	8.00
60 Johnny Bright	10.00	20.00
61 Ron Clinkscale	4.00	8.00
62 Jack Hill	4.00	8.00
63 Ron Quillian	4.00	8.00
64 Ted Tully	4.00	8.00
65 Pete Neft	5.00	10.00
66 Arvyd Buntins	4.00	8.00
67 Normie Kwong	10.00	20.00
68 Matt Phillips	4.00	8.00
69 Pete Bennett	4.00	8.00
70 Vern Lofstrom	4.00	8.00
71 Norm Stoneburgh	4.00	8.00
72 Danny Nykoluk	4.00	8.00
73 Chuck Dubuque	4.00	8.00
74 John Varone	4.00	8.00
75 Bob Kimoff	4.00	8.00
76 John Pyeatt	4.00	8.00
77 Pete Neumann	6.00	12.00
78 Ernie Pitts	5.00	10.00
79 Steve Oneschuk	4.00	8.00
80 Kaye Vaughan	6.00	12.00
81 Joe Yamauchi	4.00	8.00
82 Harvey Wylie	5.00	10.00
83 Berdett Hess	4.00	8.00
84 Dick Shatto	10.00	20.00
85 Floyd Harrawood	4.00	8.00
86 Ron Atchison	6.00	12.00
87 Bobby Judd	4.00	8.00
88 Keith Pearce	5.00	10.00
NNO Free Felt Initial Card	7.50	15.00
(Canadian Bazooka ad on back)		

1959 Topps CFL

The 1959 Topps CFL set features cards grouped by teams. The cards measure the standard size. Checklists are given on the backs of card number 15 (1-44) and card number 44 (45-88). The issue is very similar to the Topps 1959 NFL issue. The cards were originally sold in five-cent wax packs with gum.

COMPLETE SET (88)	400.00	750.00
1 Norm Rauhaus	5.00	10.00
2 Cornel Piper UER	3.00	6.00
(Misspelled Cornell		
on both sides)		
3 Leo Lewis	10.00	20.00
4 Roger Savoie	3.00	6.00
5 Jim Van Pelt	5.00	10.00
6 Herb Gray	5.00	10.00
7 Gerry James	5.00	10.00
8 By Bailey	6.00	15.00
9 Tom Hinton	4.00	8.00
10 Chuck Quilter	3.00	6.00
11 Mel Gillett	3.00	6.00
12 Ted Hunt	3.00	6.00
13 Sonny Homer	3.00	6.00
14 Bill Jessup	3.00	6.00
15 Al Dorow	12.00	20.00
(Checklist 1-44 back)		
16 Norm Fieldgate	6.00	12.00
17 Urban Henry	3.00	6.00
18 Paul Cameron	3.00	6.00
19 Bruce Claridge	3.00	6.00
20 Jim Bakhtiar	3.00	6.00
21 Earl Lunsford	6.00	12.00
22 Walt Radzick	3.00	6.00
23 Ron Albright	4.00	8.00
24 Art Scullion	3.00	6.00
25 Ernie Warlick	5.00	10.00
26 Nobby Wirkowski	3.00	6.00
27 Harvey Wylie	4.00	8.00
28 Gordon Brown	3.00	6.00
29 Don Luzzi	5.00	10.00
30 Hal Patterson	10.00	20.00
31 Jackie Simpson	7.50	15.00
32 Doug McNichol	3.00	6.00
33 Bob MacLellan	3.00	6.00
34 Ted Elsby	3.00	6.00
35 Mike Kovac	3.00	6.00
36 Bob Leary	3.00	6.00
37 Hal Krebs	3.00	6.00
38 Steve Jennings	3.00	6.00
39 Don Getty	6.00	12.00
40 Normie Kwong	7.50	15.00
41 Johnny Bright	7.50	15.00
42 Art Walker	4.00	8.00
43 Jackie Parker UER	17.50	35.00
(Incorrectly listed as		
Tackle on card front)		
44 Don Barry	10.00	20.00
(Checklist 45-88 back)		
45 Tommy Joe Coffey	12.50	25.00
46 Mike Volcan	3.00	6.00
47 Stan Renning	3.00	6.00
48 Gino Fracas	4.00	8.00
49 Ted Smale	3.00	6.00
50 Mack Yoho	4.00	8.00
51 Bobby Gravens	3.00	6.00
52 Milt Graham	3.00	6.00
53 Lou Bruce	3.00	6.00
54 Bob Simpson	6.00	15.00
55 Bill Sowalski	3.00	6.00
56 Russ Jackson	20.00	40.00
57 Don Clark	4.00	8.00
58 Dave Thelen	5.00	10.00
59 Larry Cowart	3.00	6.00
60 Dave Mann	3.00	6.00
61 Norm Stoneburgh UER	3.00	6.00
(Misspelled Stoneburg)		
62 Ronnie Knox	4.00	8.00
63 Dick Shatto	6.00	12.00
64 Bobby Kuntz	3.00	6.00
65 Phil Muntz	3.00	6.00
66 Gerry Doucette	3.00	6.00
67 Sam DeLuca	4.00	8.00
68 Boyd Carter	3.00	6.00
69 Vic Kristopaitis	4.00	8.00
70 Gerry McDougall UER	4.00	8.00
(Misspelled Jerry)		
71 Vince Scott	5.00	10.00
72 Angelo Mosca	17.50	35.00
73 Chet Miksza	3.00	6.00
74 Eddie Macon	3.00	6.00
75 Harry Lampman	3.00	6.00
76 Bill Graham	3.00	6.00
77 Ralph Goldston	3.00	6.00
78 Cam Fraser	3.00	6.00
79 Ron Dundas	3.00	6.00
80 Bill Clarke	3.00	6.00
81 Len Legault	3.00	6.00
82 Reg Whitehouse	3.00	6.00
83 Dale Parsons	3.00	6.00
84 Doug Kiloh	3.00	6.00
85 Tom Whitehouse	3.00	6.00
86 Mike Hagler	3.00	6.00
87 Paul Anderson	3.00	6.00
88 Danny Banda	3.00	6.00

1960 Topps CFL

The 1960 Topps CFL set features cards grouped by teams. The cards measure the standard size. Checklists are given on the backs of card number 14 (1-44) and card number 45 (45-88). The issue is very similar in format to the Topps NFL issue of 1960. The set features a card of Gerry James, who also played in the National Hockey League.

COMPLETE SET (88)	400.00	750.00
1 By Bailey	7.50	15.00
2 Paul Cameron	2.50	5.00
3 Bruce Claridge	2.50	5.00
4 Chuck Dubuque	2.50	5.00
5 Randy Duncan	6.00	12.00
6 Norm Fieldgate	5.00	10.00
7 Urban Henry	3.00	6.00
8 Ted Hunt	2.50	5.00
9 Bill Jessup	2.50	5.00
10 Ted Tully	2.50	5.00
11 Vic Chapman	2.50	5.00
12 Gino Fracas	3.00	6.00
13 Don Getty	5.00	10.00
14 Ed Gray	2.50	5.00
15 Oscar Kruger	10.00	20.00
(Checklist 1-44 back)		
16 Rollie Miles	5.00	10.00
17 Jackie Parker	15.00	30.00
18 Joe-Bob Smith UER	2.50	5.00
(Misspelled Bob-Joe		
on both sides)		
19 Mike Volcan	2.50	5.00
20 Art Walker	4.00	8.00
21 Ron Albright	3.00	6.00
22 Jim Bakhtiar	2.50	5.00
23 Lynn Bottoms	3.00	6.00
24 Jack Gotta	4.00	8.00
25 Joe Kapp	25.00	50.00
26 Earl Lunsford	4.00	8.00
27 Don Luzzi	4.00	8.00
28 Art Scullion	2.50	5.00
29 Hugh Simpson	2.50	5.00
30 Ernie Warlick	5.00	10.00
31 John Barrow	6.00	12.00
32 Paul Dekker	2.50	5.00
33 Bernie Faloney	12.50	25.00
34 Cam Fraser	2.50	5.00
35 Ralph Goldston	3.00	6.00
36 Ron Howell	5.00	10.00
37 Gerry McDougall UER	3.00	6.00
(Misspelled Jerry)		
38 Angelo Mosca	10.00	20.00
39 Pete Neumann	4.00	8.00
40 Vince Scott	4.00	8.00
41 Ted Elsby	2.50	5.00
42 Sam Etcheverry	15.00	30.00
43 Mike Kovac	2.50	5.00
44 Ed Learn	2.50	5.00
45 Ivan Livingstone	10.00	20.00
(Checklist 45-88 back)		
46 Hal Patterson	10.00	20.00
47 Jackie Simpson	6.00	12.00
48 Veryl Switzer	2.50	5.00
49 Bill Bewley	4.00	8.00
50 Joel Wells	2.50	5.00
51 Ron Atchison	4.00	8.00
52 Ken Carpenter	3.00	6.00
53 Bill Clarke	2.50	5.00
54 Ron Dundas	2.50	5.00
55 Mike Hagler	2.50	5.00
56 Jack Hill	2.50	5.00
57 Doug Kiloh	2.50	5.00
58 Bobby Marlow	6.00	12.00
59 Bob Mulgado	2.50	5.00
60 George Brancato	3.00	6.00
61 Lou Bruce	2.50	5.00
62 Hardiman Cureton	2.50	5.00
63 Russ Jackson	15.00	30.00
64 Gerry Nesbitt	2.50	5.00
65 Bob Simpson	5.00	12.00
66 Ted Smale	2.50	5.00
67 Dave Thelen	5.00	10.00
68 Kaye Vaughan	4.00	8.00
69 Pete Bennett	2.50	5.00
70 Boyd Carter	2.50	5.00
71 Gerry Doucette	2.50	5.00
72 Bobby Kuntz	3.00	6.00
73 Alex Panton	2.50	5.00
74 Tobin Rote	12.50	25.00
75 Jim Rountree	3.00	6.00
76 Dick Shatto	5.00	10.00
77 Norm Stoneburgh	2.50	5.00
78 Thomas(Corky) Tharp	4.00	8.00
79 George Druxman	2.50	5.00
80 Herb Gray	5.00	10.00
81 Gerry James	5.00	10.00
82 Leo Lewis	5.00	10.00
83 Ernie Pitts	3.00	6.00
84 Kenny Ploen	7.50	15.00
85 Norm Rauhaus	3.00	6.00
86 Gord Rowland	3.00	6.00
87 Charlie Shepard	3.00	6.00
88 Don Clark	4.00	8.00

1961 Topps CFL

The 1961 Topps CFL set features cards grouped by teams with the team picture last in the sequence. The cards measure the standard size. Card number 102 gives the full set checklist. Although the T.C.G. trademark appears on these cards, they were printed in Canada by O-Pee-Chee.

COMPLETE SET (132)	700.00	1,200.00
1 By Bailey	7.50	15.00
2 Bruce Claridge	3.00	6.00
3 Norm Fieldgate	6.00	12.00
4 Willie Fleming	10.00	20.00
5 Urban Henry	4.00	8.00
6 Bill Herron	3.00	6.00
7 Tom Hinton	5.00	10.00
8 Sonny Homer	4.00	8.00
9 Bob Jeter	7.50	15.00
10 Vic Kristopaitis	3.00	6.00
11 Baz Nagle	3.00	6.00
12 Ron Watton	3.00	6.00
13 Joe Yamauchi	3.00	6.00
14 Bob Schloredt	7.50	15.00
15 B.C. Lions Team	6.00	12.00
16 Ron Albright	4.00	8.00
17 Gordon Brown	3.00	6.00
18 Gerry Doucette	3.00	6.00
19 Gene Filipski	6.00	12.00
20 Joe Kapp	15.00	30.00
21 Earl Lunsford	6.00	12.00
22 Don Luzzi	6.00	12.00
23 Bill McKenna	3.00	6.00
24 Ron Morris	3.00	6.00
25 Tony Pajaczkowski	6.00	12.00
26 Lorne Reid	3.00	6.00
27 Art Scullion	3.00	6.00
28 Ernie Warlick	6.00	12.00
29 Stampeders Team	6.00	12.00
30 Johnny Bright	7.50	15.00
31 Vic Chapman	3.00	6.00
32 Gino Fracas	4.00	8.00
33 Tommy Joe Coffey	9.00	18.00
34 Don Getty	7.50	15.00
35 Ed Gray	3.00	6.00
36 Oscar Kruger	4.00	8.00
37 Rollie Miles	6.00	12.00
38 Roger Nelson	6.00	12.00
39 Jackie Parker	20.00	35.00
40 Howie Schumm	3.00	6.00
41 Joe-Bob Smith UER	3.00	6.00
(Misspelled Bob-Joe		
on both sides)		
42 Art Walker	5.00	10.00
43 Eskimos Team	6.00	12.00
44 John Barrow	7.50	15.00
45 Paul Dekker	3.00	6.00
46 Tom Dublinski	4.00	8.00
47 Bernie Faloney	12.50	25.00
48 Cam Fraser	3.00	6.00
49 Ralph Goldston	4.00	8.00
50 Ron Howell	5.00	10.00
51 Gerry McDougall	4.00	8.00
52 Pete Neumann	6.00	12.00
53 Bronko Nagurski Jr.	7.50	15.00
54 Vince Scott	5.00	10.00
55 Steve Oneschuk	4.00	8.00
56 Hal Patterson	10.00	20.00
57 Jim Taylor LB	4.00	8.00
58 Hamilton Tiger-Cats	6.00	12.00
Team		
59 Ted Elsby	3.00	6.00
60 Don Clark	5.00	10.00
61 Dick Cohee	5.00	10.00
62 George Dixon	10.00	20.00
63 Wes Gideon	3.00	6.00
64 Harry Lampman	3.00	6.00
65 Meco Poliziani	3.00	6.00
66 Ray Baillie	3.00	6.00
67 Howard Cissell	3.00	6.00
68 Ed Learn	3.00	6.00
69 Tom Moran	3.00	6.00
70 Jackie Simpson	6.00	12.00
71 Bill Bewley	4.00	8.00
72 Tom Hugo	3.00	6.00
73 Alouettes Team	7.50	15.00
74 Gilles Archambeault	3.00	6.00
75 Lou Bruce	3.00	6.00
76 Russ Jackson	15.00	30.00
77 Tom Jones	3.00	6.00
78 Gerry Nesbitt	3.00	6.00
79 Ron Lancaster	20.00	40.00
80 Joe Kelley	3.00	6.00
81 Joe Poirier	4.00	8.00
82 Doug Daigneault	3.00	6.00
83 Kaye Vaughan	5.00	10.00
84 Dave Thelen	7.50	15.00
85 Ron Stewart	12.50	25.00
86 Ted Smale	3.00	6.00
87 Bob Simpson	7.50	15.00
88 Ottawa Rough Riders	6.00	12.00
Team		
89 Don Allard	3.00	6.00
90 Ron Atchison	6.00	12.00
91 Bill Clarke	3.00	6.00
92 Ron Dundas	3.00	6.00
93 Jack Gotta	5.00	10.00
94 Bob Golic	4.00	8.00
95 Jack Hill	3.00	6.00
96 Doug Kiloh	3.00	6.00
97 Len Legault	3.00	6.00
98 Doug McKenzie	3.00	6.00
99 Bob Ptacek	4.00	8.00
100 Roy Smith	3.00	6.00
101 Saskatchewan	6.00	12.00
Roughriders Team UER		
(photo actually the Cleveland Browns)		
102 Checklist 1-132	50.00	100.00
103 Jim Andreotti	4.00	8.00
104 Boyd Carter	3.00	6.00
105 Dick Fouts	4.00	8.00
106 Cookie Gilchrist	12.50	25.00
107 Bobby Kuntz	4.00	8.00
108 Jim Rountree	4.00	8.00
109 Dick Shatto	7.50	15.00
110 Norm Stoneburgh	3.00	6.00
111 Dave Mann	4.00	8.00
112 Ed Ochiena	3.00	6.00
113 Bill Stribling	3.00	6.00
114 Tobin Rote	10.00	20.00
115 Stan Wallace	3.00	6.00
116 Billy Shipp	4.00	8.00
117 Argonauts Team	7.50	15.00
118 Dave Burkholder	3.00	6.00
119 Jack Delveaux	4.00	8.00
120 George Druxman	3.00	6.00
121 Farrell Funston	4.00	8.00
122 Herb Gray	6.00	12.00
123 Gerry James	6.00	12.00
124 Ronnie Latourelle	3.00	6.00
125 Leo Lewis	7.50	15.00
126 Steve Patrick	4.00	8.00
127 Ernie Pitts	4.00	8.00
128 Kenny Ploen	7.50	15.00
129 Norm Rauhaus	4.00	8.00
130 Gord Rowland	4.00	8.00
131 Charlie Shepard	4.00	8.00
132 Winnipeg Blue Bombers	10.00	20.00
Team Card		

1961 Topps CFL Transfers

There were 27 transfers inserted in Topps CFL wax packs issued in 1961. The transfers measure approximately 2" by 3" and feature players, logos, and pennants of the CFL teams. After placing the transfer against any surface, the collector could apply the transfer by rubbing the top side with a coin. The top side carried instructions for applying the transfers. The pictures on the transfers are done in five basic colors: reddish orange, yellow, blue, black, and green. The transfers are unnumbered and are checklisted below alphabetically according to players (1-15) and teams (19-27). The set price below is only for the 24 players and team cards that we currently list. Three Transfers (#16-18) are yet to be identified. Any additional information on the other players that were contained in this set would be appreciated.

COMPLETE SET (24)	375.00	750.00
1 Don Clark	17.50	35.00
2 Gene Filipski	17.50	35.00
3 Willie Fleming	20.00	40.00
4 Cookie Gilchrist	25.00	50.00
5 Jack Hill	15.00	30.00
6 Bob Jeter	17.50	35.00
7 Joe Kapp	30.00	60.00
8 Leo Lewis	20.00	40.00
9 Gerry McDougall	17.50	35.00
10 Jackie Parker	30.00	60.00
11 Hal Patterson	20.00	40.00
12 Kenny Ploen	20.00	40.00
13 Bob Ptacek	17.50	35.00
14 Ron Stewart	20.00	40.00
15 Dave Thelen	20.00	40.00
19 British Columbia Lions	10.00	20.00
Logo		
Pennant		
20 Calgary Stampeders	10.00	20.00
Logo		
Pennant		

21 Edmonton Eskimos	10.00	20.00
Logo		
Pennant		
22 Hamilton Tiger-Cats	10.00	20.00
Logo		
Pennant		
23 Montreal Alouettes	10.00	20.00
Logo		
Pennant		
24 Ottawa Rough Riders	10.00	20.00
Logo		
Pennant		
25 Saskatchewan Roughriders	10.00	20.00
Logo		
Pennant		
26 Toronto Argonauts	10.00	20.00
Logo		
Pennant		
27 Winnipeg Blue Bombers	10.00	20.00
Logo		
Pennant		

1962 Topps CFL

This 1962 Topps CFL set features 169-different numbered cards originally issued in perforated pairs. We've priced the cards below as separate cards; pairs are worth up to a slight premium over the value of both cards. Note that there are many variations on which two cards were paired together. Each card measures 1 1/4" by 2,1/2" individually and 2 1/2" by 3 1/2" as a pair. The team cards contain a team checklist on the reverse side and the players preceding the team cards belong to the respective teams. Although the T.C.G. trademark appears on the cards, they were printed in Canada by O-Pee-Chee.

COMPLETE SET (169)	400.00	700.00
1 By Bailey	4.00	8.00
2 Nub Beamer	1.00	2.50
3 Tom Brown	4.00	8.00
4 Mack Burton	1.00	2.50
5 Mike Cacic	1.00	2.50
6 Pat Claridge	1.00	2.50
7 Steve Cotter	1.00	2.50
8 Lonnie Dennis	1.00	2.50
9 Norm Fieldgate	2.50	5.00
10 Willie Fleming	5.00	10.00
11 Tom Hinton	2.00	4.00
12 Sonny Homer	1.50	3.00
13 Joe Kapp	7.50	15.00
14 Tom Larscheid	1.00	2.50
15 Gordie Mitchell	1.00	2.50
16 Baz Nagle	1.00	2.50
17 Norris Stevenson	1.00	2.50
18 Barney Therrion UER	1.00	2.50
(Misspelled Therien		
on card front)		
19 Don Vicic	2.00	4.00
20 B.C. Lions Team	4.00	8.00
21 Ed Buchanan	1.00	2.50
22 Joe Carruthers	1.00	2.50
23 Lovell Coleman	1.50	3.00
24 Barrie Cyr	1.00	2.50
25 Ernie Danjean	1.00	2.50
26 Gene Filipski	2.00	4.00
27 George Hansen	1.00	2.50
28 Earl Lunsford	2.50	5.00
29 Don Luzzi	1.50	3.00
30 Bill McKonna	1.00	2.50
31 Tony Pajaczkowski	2.00	4.00
32 Chuck Quilter	1.00	2.50
33 Lorne Reid	1.00	2.50
34 Art Scullion	1.00	2.50
35 Jim Walden	1.00	2.50
36 Harvey Wylie	2.00	4.00
37 Calgary Stampeders	4.00	8.00
Team Card		
38 Johnny Bright	5.00	10.00
39 Vic Chapman	1.00	2.50
40 Marion Drew Deese	1.00	2.50
41 Al Ecuyer	1.00	2.50
42 Gino Fracas	1.50	3.00
43 Don Getty	3.00	6.00
44 Ed Gray	1.00	2.50
45 Urban Henry	1.50	3.00
46 Bill Hill	1.00	2.50
47 Mike Kmeche	1.00	2.50
48 Oscar Kruger	1.50	3.00
49 Mike Lashuk	1.00	2.50
50 Jim Letcavits	1.00	2.50
51 Roger Nelson	2.00	4.00
52 Jackie Parker	7.50	15.00
53 Howie Schumm	1.00	2.50
54 Jim Shipka	1.00	2.50
55 Bill Smith	1.00	2.50
56 Joe-Bob Smith	1.00	2.50
57 Art Walker	2.00	4.00
58 Edmonton Eskimos	4.00	8.00
Team card		
59 John Barrow	4.00	8.00
60 Hardiman Cureton	1.00	2.50
61 Geno DeNobile	1.00	2.50
62 Tom Dublinski	1.50	3.00
63 Bernie Faloney	6.00	12.00
64 Cam Fraser	1.00	2.50
65 Ralph Goldston	1.50	3.00
66 Tommy Grant	3.50	7.00
67 Garney Henley	7.50	15.00
68 Ron Howell	2.00	5.00
69 Zeno Karcz	1.50	3.00
70 Gerry McDougall UER	1.50	3.00
(Misspelled Jerry)		
71 Chet Miksza	1.00	2.50
72 Bronko Nagurski Jr.	3.00	6.00
73 Hal Patterson	5.00	10.00
74 George Scott	1.00	2.50
75 Vince Scott	2.00	4.00
76 Hamilton Tiger-Cats	4.00	8.00
Team card		
77 Ron Brewer	1.50	3.00
78 Ron Brooks	1.00	2.50
79 Howard Cissell	1.00	2.50
80 Don Clark	2.00	4.00
81 Dick Cohee	1.50	3.00
82 John Conroy	1.00	2.50
83 Milt Crain	1.50	3.00
84 Ted Elsby	1.00	2.50
85 Joe Francis	1.50	3.00
86 Gene Gaines	4.00	8.00
87 Barrie Hansen	1.00	2.50
88 Mike Kovac	1.00	2.50
89 Ed Learn	1.00	2.50
90 Billy Ray Locklin	1.00	2.50
91 Marv Luster	3.00	6.00
92 Bobby Jack Oliver	1.50	3.00
93 Sandy Stephens	4.00	8.00
94 Montreal Alouettes	5.00	10.00
Team Card		
95 Gilles Archambeault	1.00	2.50
96 Bruno Bitkowski	1.50	3.00
97 Jim Conroy	1.50	3.00
98 Doug Daigneault	1.00	2.50
99 Dick Desmarais	1.00	2.50
100 Russ Jackson	7.50	15.00
101 Tom Jones	1.00	2.50
102 Ron Lancaster	10.00	20.00
103 Angelo Mosca	7.50	15.00
104 Gerry Nesbitt	1.00	2.50
105 Joe Poirier	1.50	3.00
106 Moe Racine	1.00	2.50
107 Gary Schreider	1.00	2.50
108 Bob Simpson	3.00	6.00
109 Ted Smale	1.00	2.50
110 Ron Stewart	3.50	7.00
111 Dave Thelen	3.00	6.00
112 Kaye Vaughan	2.00	4.00
113 Ottawa Rough Riders	4.00	8.00
Team card		
114 Ron Atchison UER	2.00	4.00
(Misspelled Atcheson		
on card front)		
115 Danny Banda	1.00	2.50
116 Al Benecick	1.00	2.50
117 Clair Branch	1.00	2.50
118 Fred Burket	1.00	2.50
119 Bill Clarke	1.00	2.50
120 Jim Copeland	1.00	2.50
121 Ron Dundas	1.00	2.50
122 Bob Golic	1.50	3.00
123 Jack Gotta	2.00	4.00
124 Dave Grosz	1.00	2.50
125 Neil Habig	1.50	3.00
126 Jack Hill	1.00	2.50
127 Len Legault	1.00	2.50
128 Bob Ptacek	1.00	2.50
129 Roy Smith	1.00	2.50
130 Saskatchewan Rough-	4.00	8.00
riders Team Card		
131 Lynn Bottoms	1.50	3.00
132 Dick Fouts	1.50	3.00
133 Wes Gideon	1.00	2.50
134 Cookie Gilchrist	7.50	15.00
135 Art Johnson	1.00	2.50
136 Bobby Kuntz	1.50	3.00
137 Dave Mann	1.50	3.00
138 Marty Martinello	1.00	2.50
139 Doug McNichol	1.00	2.50
140 Bill Mitchell	1.00	2.50
141 Danny Nykoluk	1.00	2.50
142 Walt Radzick	1.00	2.50
143 Tobin Rote	5.00	10.00
144 Jim Rountree	1.50	3.00
145 Dick Shatto	4.00	8.00
146 Billy Shipp	1.50	3.00
147 Norm Stoneburgh	1.00	2.50
148 Toronto Argonauts	5.00	10.00
Team Card		
149 Dave Burkholder	1.00	2.50
150 Jack Delveaux	1.50	3.00
151 George Druxman	1.00	2.50
152 Farrell Funston	1.50	3.00
153 Herb Gray	2.50	5.00
154 Roger Hagberg	1.50	3.00
155 Gerry James	3.00	6.00
156 Henry Janzen	1.50	3.00
157 Ronnie Latourelle	1.00	2.50
158 Hal Ledyard	1.00	2.50
159 Leo Lewis	3.00	6.00
160 Steve Patrick	1.50	3.00
161 Cornel Piper	1.00	2.50
162 Ernie Pitts	1.50	3.00
163 Kenny Ploen	4.00	8.00
164 Norm Rauhaus	1.50	3.00
165 Frank Rigney	3.00	6.00
166 Gord Rowland	1.50	3.00
167 Roger Savoie	1.00	2.50
168 Charlie Shepard	1.50	3.00
169 Winnipeg Blue	10.00	20.00
Bombers Team Card		

1963 Topps CFL

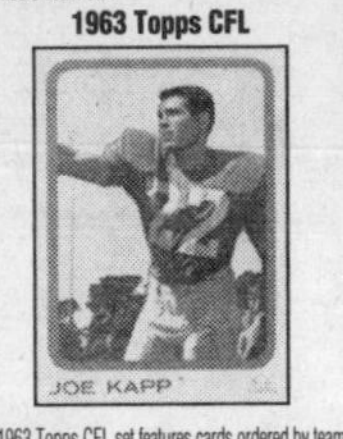

The 1963 Topps CFL set features cards ordered by teams (which are in alphabetical order) with players preceding . their respective team cards. Although the T.C.G. trademark appears on the cards, they were printed in Canada by O-Pee-Chee.

COMPLETE SET (88)	300.00	500.00
1 Willie Fleming	6.00	12.00
2 Dick Fouts	2.00	4.00
3 Joe Kapp	7.50	15.00
4 Nub Beamer	1.25	2.50
5 By Bailey	3.00	6.00
6 Tom Walker	1.25	2.50
7 Sonny Homer	2.00	4.00
8 Tom Hinton	2.50	5.00
9 Lonnie Dennis	1.25	2.50
10 British Columbia Lions	4.00	8.00
Team Card		
11 Ed Buchanan	1.25	2.50
12 Ernie Danjean	1.25	2.50
13 Eagle Day	3.00	6.00
14 Earl Lunsford	2.50	5.00
15 Don Luzzi	2.50	5.00
16 Tony Pajaczkowski	2.50	5.00
17 Jerry Keeling	7.50	15.00
18 Pat Holmes	2.00	4.00
19 Wayne Harris	7.50	15.00
20 Calgary Stampeders	4.00	8.00
Team Card		
21 Tommy Joe Coffey	4.00	8.00
22 Mike Lashuk	1.25	2.50
23 Bobby Walden	2.00	4.00
24 Don Getty	4.00	8.00
25 Len Vella	1.25	2.50
26 Ted Frechette	1.25	2.50
27 E.A. Sims	1.25	2.50
28 Nat Dye	1.25	2.50
29 Edmonton Eskimos	4.00	8.00
Team Card		
30 Bernie Faloney	5.00	10.00
31 Hal Patterson	4.00	8.00
32 John Barrow	3.00	6.00
33 Sam Fernandez	1.25	2.50
34 Garney Henley	6.00	12.00
35 Joe Zuger	2.00	4.00
36 Hardiman Cureton	1.25	2.50
37 Zeno Karcz	2.00	4.00
38 Bobby Kuntz	2.00	4.00
39 Hamilton Tiger-Cats	4.00	8.00
Team Card		
40 George Dixon	3.00	6.00
41 Don Clark	2.50	5.00
42 Marv Luster	3.00	6.00
43 Bobby Jack Oliver	2.00	4.00
44 Billy Ray Locklin	1.25	2.50
45 Sandy Stephens	3.00	6.00
46 Milt Crain	2.00	4.00
47 Meco Poliziani	1.25	2.50
48 Ted Elsby	1.25	2.50
49 Montreal Alouettes	4.00	8.00
Team Card		
50 Russ Jackson	7.50	15.00
51 Ron Stewart	4.00	8.00
52 Dave Thelen	3.00	6.00
53 Kaye Vaughan	2.50	5.00
54 Joe Poirier	2.00	4.00
55 Moe Racine	1.25	2.50
56 Whit Tucker	5.00	10.00
57 Ernie White	1.25	2.50
58 Ottawa Rough Riders	4.00	8.00
Team Card		
59 Bob Ptacek	1.25	2.50
60 Ray Purdin	1.25	2.50
61 Dale West	2.00	4.00
62 Neil Habig	1.25	2.50
63 Jack Gotta	2.00	4.00
64 Billy Gray	1.25	2.50
65 Don Walsh	1.25	2.50
66 Bill Clarke	1.25	2.50
67 Saskatchewan Rough-	4.00	8.00
riders Team Card		
68 Jackie Parker	7.50	15.00
69 Dave Mann	2.00	4.00
70 Dick Shatto	3.00	6.00
71 Norm Stoneburgh UER	1.25	2.50
(Misspelled Stoneburg		
on card front)		
72 Clare Exelby	1.25	2.50
73 Art Johnson	1.25	2.50
74 Doug McNichol	1.25	2.50
75 Danny Nykoluk	1.25	2.50
76 Walt Radzick	1.25	2.50
77 Toronto Argonauts	4.00	8.00
Team Card		
78 Leo Lewis	3.00	6.00
79 Kenny Ploen	4.00	8.00
80 Henry Janzen	2.00	4.00
81 Charlie Shepard	2.00	4.00
82 Roger Hagberg	2.00	4.00
83 Herb Gray	3.00	6.00
84 Frank Rigney	2.50	5.00
85 Jack Delveaux	2.00	4.00
86 Ronnie Latourelle	1.25	2.50
87 Winnipeg Blue Bombers	4.00	8.00
Team Card		
88 Checklist Card	30.00	60.00

1964 Topps CFL

The 1964 Topps CFL set features cards ordered by teams (which are in alphabetical order) with players preceding their respective team cards. Although the T.C.G. trademark appears on the cards, they were printed in Canada by O-Pee-Chee.

COMPLETE SET (88)	300.00	500.00
1 Willie Fleming	6.00	12.00
2 Dick Fouts	2.00	4.00
3 Joe Kapp	7.50	15.00
4 Nub Beamer	1.25	2.50
5 Tom Brown	2.50	5.00
6 Tom Walker	1.25	2.50
7 Sonny Homer	2.00	4.00
8 Tom Hinton	2.50	5.00
9 Lonnie Dennis	1.25	2.50
10 B.C. Lions Team	4.00	8.00
11 Lovell Coleman	2.00	4.00
12 Ernie Danjean	1.25	2.50
13 Eagle Day	2.50	5.00
14 Jim Furlong	1.25	2.50
15 Don Luzzi	2.50	5.00
16 Tony Pajaczkowski	2.50	5.00
17 Jerry Keeling	3.00	6.00
18 Pat Holmes	2.00	4.00
19 Wayne Harris	4.00	8.00
20 Calgary Stampeders	4.00	8.00
Team Card		
21 Tommy Joe Coffey	4.00	8.00
22 Al Ecuyer	1.25	2.50
23 Checklist Card	20.00	40.00
24 Don Getty	3.00	6.00
25 Len Vella	1.25	2.50
26 Ted Frechette	1.25	2.50
27 E.A. Sims	1.25	2.50
28 Nat Dye	1.25	2.50
29 Edmonton Eskimos	4.00	8.00
Team Card		
30 Bernie Faloney	7.50	15.00
31 Hal Patterson	4.00	8.00
32 John Barrow	3.00	6.00
33 Tommy Grant	3.00	6.00
34 Garney Henley	4.00	8.00
35 Joe Zuger	2.00	4.00
36 Hardiman Cureton	1.25	2.50
37 Zeno Karcz	2.00	4.00
38 Bobby Kuntz	2.00	4.00
39 Hamilton Tiger-Cats	4.00	8.00
Team Card		
40 George Dixon	4.00	8.00
41 Dave Hoppmann	1.25	2.50
42 Dick Walton	1.25	2.50
43 Jim Andreotti	2.00	4.00
44 Billy Ray Locklin	1.25	2.50
45 Fred Burket	1.25	2.50
46 Milt Crain	2.00	4.00
47 Meco Poliziani	1.25	2.50
48 Ted Elsby	1.25	2.50
49 Montreal Alouettes	5.00	10.00
Team Card		
50 Russ Jackson	7.50	15.00
51 Ron Stewart	4.00	8.00
52 Dave Thelen	2.50	5.00
53 Kaye Vaughan	2.50	5.00
54 Joe Poirier	2.00	4.00
55 Moe Racine	1.25	2.50
56 Whit Tucker	3.00	6.00
57 Ernie White	1.25	2.50
58 Ottawa Rough Riders	4.00	8.00
Team Card		
59 Bob Ptacek	1.25	2.50
60 Ray Purdin	1.25	2.50
61 Dale West	2.00	4.00
62 Neil Habig	1.25	2.50
63 Jack Gotta	2.00	4.00
64 Billy Gray	1.25	2.50
65 Don Walsh	1.25	2.50
66 Bill Clarke	1.25	2.50
67 Saskatchewan Rough-	4.00	8.00
riders Team Card		
68 Jackie Parker	7.50	15.00
69 Dave Mann	2.00	4.00
70 Dick Shatto	3.00	6.00
71 Norm Stoneburgh	1.25	2.50
72 Clare Exelby	1.25	2.50
73 Jim Christopherson	1.25	2.50
74 Sherman Lewis	3.00	6.00
75 Danny Nykoluk	1.25	2.50
76 Walt Radzick	1.25	2.50
77 Toronto Argonauts	5.00	10.00
Team Card		
78 Leo Lewis	3.00	6.00
79 Kenny Ploen	3.00	6.00
80 Henry Janzen	2.00	4.00
81 Charlie Shepard	2.00	4.00
82 Roger Hagberg	2.00	4.00
83 Herb Gray	3.00	6.00
84 Frank Rigney	2.50	5.00
85 Jack Delveaux	2.00	4.00
86 Ronnie Latourelle	1.25	2.50
87 Winnipeg Blue	4.00	8.00
Bombers Team Card		
88 Checklist Card	25.00	50.00

1965 Topps CFL

The 1965 Topps CFL set features 132 cards ordered by teams (which are in alphabetical order) with players also in alphabetical order. Card numbers 60 (1-60) and 132 (61-132) are checklist cards. Don Sutherlin, number 57, has number 51 on the back. Although the T.C.G. trademark appears on the cards, they were printed in Canada by O-Pee-Chee.

COMPLETE SET (132)	350.00	600.00
1 Neil Beaumont	3.00	6.00
2 Tom Brown	3.00	6.00
3 Mike Cacic	1.25	2.50
4 Pat Claridge	1.25	2.50
5 Steve Cotter	1.25	2.50
6 Lonnie Dennis	1.25	2.50
7 Norm Fieldgate	2.50	5.00
8 Willie Fleming	6.00	12.00
9 Dick Fouts	2.00	4.00
10 Tom Hinton	2.50	5.00
11 Sonny Homer	2.00	4.00
12 Joe Kapp	7.50	15.00
13 Paul Seale	1.25	2.50
14 Steve Shafer	1.25	2.50
15 Bob Swift	1.25	2.50
16 Larry Anderson	1.25	2.50
17 Lu Bain	1.25	2.50
18 Lovell Coleman	2.00	4.00
19 Eagle Day	2.50	5.00
20 Jim Furlong	1.25	2.50
21 Wayne Harris	3.50	7.00
22 Herman Harrison	6.00	12.00
23 Jerry Keeling	3.00	6.00
24 Hal Krebs	1.25	2.50
25 Don Luzzi	2.50	5.00
26 Tony Pajaczkowski	2.50	5.00
27 Larry Robinson	2.50	5.00
28 Bob Taylor	2.00	4.00
29 Ted Woods	1.25	2.50
30 Jon Anabo	1.25	2.50
31 Jim Battle	1.25	2.50
32 Charlie Brown	1.25	2.50
33 Tommy Joe Coffey	5.00	10.00
34 Marcel Deleeuw	1.25	2.50
35 Al Ecuyer	1.25	2.50
36 Jim Higgins	1.25	2.50
37 Oscar Kruger	2.00	4.00
38 Barry Mitchelson	1.25	2.50
39 Roger Nelson	2.50	5.00
40 Bill Redell	1.25	2.50
41 E.A. Sims	1.25	2.50
42 Jim Stinnette	1.25	2.50
43 Jim Thomas	1.25	2.50
44 Terry Wilson	1.25	2.50
45 Art Baker	2.00	4.00
46 John Barrow	3.00	6.00
47 Dick Cohee	2.00	4.00
48 Frank Cosentino	2.50	5.00
49 Johnny Counts	1.25	2.50
50 Tommy Grant	2.50	5.00
51 Garney Henley	4.00	8.00
(See also number 57)		
52 Zeno Karcz	2.00	4.00
53 Ellison Kelly	6.00	12.00
54 Bobby Kuntz	2.00	4.00
55 Angelo Mosca	7.50	15.00
56 Bronko Nagurski Jr.	3.50	7.00
57 Don Sutherin UER	6.00	12.00
(number 51 on back)		
58 Dave Viti	1.25	2.50
59 Joe Zuger	2.00	4.00
60 Checklist 1-60	17.50	35.00
61 Jim Andreotti	2.00	4.00
62 Harold Cooley	1.25	2.50
63 Nat Craddock	1.25	2.50
64 George Dixon	3.00	6.00
65 Ted Elsby	1.25	2.50
66 Clare Exelby	1.25	2.50
67 Bernie Faloney	7.50	15.00
68 Al Irwin	1.25	2.50
69 Ed Learn	1.25	2.50
70 Moe Levesque	1.25	2.50
71 Bob Minihane	1.25	2.50
72 Jim Reynolds	1.25	2.50
73 Billy Roy	1.25	2.50
74 Billy Joe Booth	2.00	4.00
75 Jim Cain	1.25	2.50
76 Larry DeGraw	1.25	2.50
77 Don Estes	1.25	2.50
78 Gene Gaines	2.50	5.00
79 John Kennerson	1.25	2.50
80 Roger Kramer	2.00	4.00
81 Ken Lehmann	2.00	4.00
82 Bob O'Billovich	1.25	2.50
83 Joe Poirier	2.00	4.00
84 Bill Quinter	1.25	2.50
85 Jerry Selinger	1.25	2.50
86 Bill Siekierski	1.25	2.50
87 Len Sparks	1.25	2.50
88 Whit Tucker	2.50	5.00
89 Ron Atchison	2.50	5.00
90 Ed Buchanan	1.25	2.50
91 Hugh Campbell	5.00	10.00
92 Henry Dorsch	1.25	2.50
93 Garner Ekstran	2.00	4.00
94 Martin Fabi	1.25	2.50
95 Bob Good	1.25	2.50
96 Ron Lancaster	7.50	15.00
97 Bob Ptacek	1.25	2.50
98 George Reed	12.50	25.00
99 Wayne Shaw	1.25	2.50
100 Dale West	2.00	4.00
101 Reg Whitehouse	1.25	2.50
102 Jim Worden	1.25	2.50
103 Ron Brewer	2.00	4.00
104 Don Fuell	1.25	2.50
105 Ed Harrington	2.00	4.00
106 George Hughley	1.25	2.50
107 Dave Mann	2.00	4.00
108 Marty Martinello	1.25	2.50
109 Danny Nykoluk	1.25	2.50
110 Jackie Parker	10.00	20.00
111 Dave Pivec	1.25	2.50
112 Walt Radzick	1.25	2.50
113 Lee Sampson	1.25	2.50
114 Dick Shatto	2.50	5.00
115 Norm Stoneburgh	1.25	2.50
116 Jim Vollenweider	1.25	2.50
117 John Wydareny	2.00	4.00
118 Billy Cooper	1.25	2.50
119 Farrell Funston	2.00	4.00
120 Herb Gray	2.50	5.00
121 Henry Janzen	2.00	4.00
122 Leo Lewis	3.50	7.00
123 Brian Palmer	1.25	2.50
124 Cornel Piper	1.25	2.50
125 Ernie Pitts	1.25	2.50
126 Kenny Ploen	3.50	7.00
127 Norm Rauhaus	2.00	4.00
128 Frank Rigney	2.50	5.00
129 Roger Savoie	1.25	2.50
130 Dick Thornton	2.50	5.00
131 Bill Whisler	1.25	2.50
132 Checklist 61-132	25.00	50.00

1965 Topps CFL Transfers

These four-color transfers were inserts in the 1965 Topps CFL packs. They measure approximately 2" by 3". These 1965 inserts are distinguished from the 1961 inserts by the notation "Printed in U.S.A." on the 1965 inserts.

COMPLETE SET (27)	250.00	500.00
1 British Columbia Lions Crest	10.00	20.00
2 British Columbia Lions Pennant	10.00	20.00
3 Calgary Stampeders Crest	10.00	20.00
4 Calgary Stampeders Pennant	10.00	20.00
5 Edmonton Eskimos Crest	10.00	20.00
6 Edmonton Eskimos Pennant	10.00	20.00
7 Hamilton Tiger-Cats	10.00	20.00
Crest		
8 Hamilton Tiger-Cats Pennant	10.00	20.00
9 Montreal Alouettes Crest	10.00	20.00
10 Montreal Alouettes Pennant	10.00	20.00
11 Ottawa Rough Riders Crest	10.00	20.00
12 Ottawa Rough Riders Pennant	10.00	20.00
13 Saskatch.Roughriders Crest	10.00	20.00
14 Saskatch.Roughriders Pennant	10.00	20.00
15 Toronto Argonauts Crest	10.00	20.00
16 Toronto Argonauts Pennant	10.00	20.00
17 Winnipeg Blue Bombers Crest	10.00	20.00
18 Win.Blue Bombers Pennant	10.00	20.00
19 Quebec Provincial Crest	10.00	20.00
20 Ontario Provincial Crest	10.00	20.00
21 Manitoba Provincial Crest	10.00	20.00
22 Saskatchewan Provincial Crest	10.00	20.00
23 Alberta Provincial Crest	10.00	20.00
24 British Columbia Prov. Crest	10.00	20.00
25 Northwest Territories Crest	10.00	20.00
26 Yukon Territory Territorial Crest	10.00	20.00
27 Canada	12.50	25.00

1970 Toronto Argonauts Team Issue

The Argonauts issued this set of player photos around 1970. Each includes two black-and-white player photos with one being a posed action shot along with a smaller portrait image. The roughly 8" by 10 1/8" photos include the player's name and team logo on the cardfronts. The backs are blank and unnumbered.

COMPLETE SET (41)	125.00	250.00
1 Harry Abofs	4.00	8.00
2 Dick Aldridge	4.00	8.00
3 Eric Allen	6.00	12.00
4 Wayne Allison	4.00	8.00
5 Zenon Andrusyshyn	5.00	10.00
6 Chip Barrett	4.00	8.00
7 Greg Barton	6.00	12.00
8 Bruce Borgey	4.00	8.00
9 Charlie Bray	4.00	8.00
10 Leo Cahill CO	4.00	8.00
11 Jim Corrigall	6.00	12.00
12 Paul Desjardins	4.00	8.00
13 Jimmy Dye	4.00	8.00
14 Mike Eben	4.00	8.00
15 Barry Finlay	4.00	8.00
16 Stewart Francis	4.00	8.00
17 Jim Henderson	4.00	8.00
18 Noah Jackson	5.00	10.00
19 Ellison Kelly	5.00	10.00
20 Dave Knechtel	4.00	8.00
21 Gary Kuzyk	4.00	8.00
22 Marv Luster	5.00	10.00
23 Leon McQuay	6.00	12.00
24 Gene Mack	4.00	8.00
25 Peter Martin	4.00	8.00
26 Ron Mikolajczyk	4.00	8.00
27 Tony Moro	4.00	8.00
28 Peter Muller	4.00	8.00
29 Peter Paquette	4.00	8.00
30 Mike Rae	4.00	8.00
31 Dave Raimey	4.00	8.00
32 John Rauch GM	4.00	8.00
33 Roger Scales	4.00	8.00
34 Elmars Sprogis	4.00	8.00
35 Jim Stillwagon	6.00	12.00
36 Bill Symons	5.00	10.00
37 Joe Theismann	15.00	25.00
38 Dick Thornton	5.00	10.00
39 John Trainor	4.00	8.00
40 Coaches	4.00	8.00
Frank Johnston		
Gordon Ackerman		
41 Coaches	4.00	8.00
Jim Rountree		
Robert Gibson		

1970 Toronto Argonauts Team Sheets

This group of 40-players and coaches of the Argonauts was produced on five glossy sheets each measuring approximately 8" by 10". The fronts feature black-and-white player portraits with eight pictures to a sheet with the year printed at the top. The backs are blank. The cards are unnumbered and checklisted below in alphabetical order, with the player pictured in the upper left hand corner of the sheet listed first.

COMPLETE SET (5)	15.00	30.00
1 George Anderson	3.00	6.00
Stewart Francis		
Peter Muller		
Mike Eben		
Doyle Orange		
L.J. Clayton		
Jim Corrigal		
Granville Liggins		
2 Roy Beechey	4.00	8.00
Barry Finlay		
Morris Zubkewych		
Larry Uteck		
Ecomet Burley		
Steve Dennis		
Al Charuk		
Doug MacIver		
3 Ron Foxx	3.00	6.00
Neil Lumsden		
Bruce Smith		
Gail Clark		
Terry Shelsta		
Tom Chandler		
Bill Belk		
Zenon Andrushyshyn		
4 Wonderful Monds	4.00	8.00
Wayne Allison		
Sam Cvijanovich		
Anthony Davis		
John Kennedy		
Chuck Ealey		
Matthew Reed		
Eugene Clark		
5 Tom Terhart	3.00	6.00
Wally Highsmith		
Al Bloomingdale		
Dave Hadden		
Joe Moss CO		
Lamar Leachman CO		
Russ Jackson CO		
Bob Ward CO		

1977-78 Toronto Argonauts Team Sheets

This group of 40 players and coaches of the Argonauts was produced on five glossy sheets each measuring approximately 8" by 10". The fronts feature black-and-white player portraits with eight pictures to a sheet with the year printed at the top. The backs are blank. The cards are unnumbered and checklisted below in alphabetical order, with the player pictured in the upper left hand corner of the sheet listed first.

COMPLETE SET (5)	15.00	30.00
1 Granville Liggins	3.00	6.00
Wally Highsmith		
Stew Francis		
Wayne Allison		
Zonon Andrushyshyn		
Eric Harris		
Paul Bennett		
Doug MacIver		
2 Jim Marshall	3.00	6.00
Ward Smith		
Wayne Smith		
Eugene Clark		
Tom Chandler		
Matthew Reed		
Mark Bragagnola		
Nick Bastaja		
3 Dick Shatto CO	3.00	6.00
Leo Cahill CO		
Gordon Knowlton		
Bruce Smith		
Richard Holmes		
Peter Muller		
Neil Lumsden		
Alan MacLean		
4 Peter Sorensen	3.00	6.00
Rick Sowieta		
Tony Hill		
Alex Morris		
Ron Foxx		
Lorne Richardson		
Dennis Franklin		
Kelvin Kirk		
5 Mike Wilson	4.00	8.00
Joel Parrish		
Ray Nettles		
Ecomet Burley		
Ike Thomas		
Jim Corrigall		
Chuck Ealey		
George Mira CO		

1981 Toronto Argonauts Toronto Sun

The television schedule portion of the Toronto Sun included one-sided large color portraits of Argonauts' players throughout the season. Each was designed to be cut from the publication, thus each includes a newsprint type back. The player's name and a brief write-up appear below the photo along with the team logo and "Meet the Argos" title line. The checklist below includes the known copies and is thought to be incomplete.

COMPLETE SET (11)	8.00	20.00
1 Zenon Andrusyshyn	1.25	3.00
2 Danny Bass	1.50	4.00
3 Dan Ferrone	1.25	3.00
4 Billy Hardee	.75	2.00
5 Condredge Holloway	2.00	5.00
6 Gordon Judges	.75	2.00
7 Leon Lyszkiewicz	.75	2.00
8 Dan Manucci	.75	2.00
9 Peter Muller	.75	2.00
10 Dave Newman	.75	2.00
11 Paul Pearson	.75	2.00

1996 Toronto Argonauts Team Issue

This set was issued by the Argonauts. Each card includes a color player photo surrounded by a blue border. The unnumbered cardbacks include a player bio.

COMPLETE SET (18)	8.00	20.00
1 Mike Clemons	1.20	3.00
2 Tim Cofield	.15	.40
3 Jimmy Cunningham	.08	.25
4 Robert Drummond	.50	1.25
5 Jeff Fairholm	.08	.25
6 Doug Flutie	6.00	15.00
7 Paul Masotti	.30	.75
8 Don Matthews CO	.08	.25
9 Dan Murphy	.08	.25
10 Andrew Stewart	.08	.25
11 Tyrone Williams	.15	.40
12 Grey Cup Champs 1914/21	.08	.25
13 Grey Cup Champs 1933/37	.08	.25
14 Grey Cup Champs 1938/45	.08	.25
15 Grey Cup Champs 1946-47	.08	.25
16 Grey Cup Champs 1950/52	.08	.25
17 Grey Cup Champs 1983/91	.08	.25
18 Cover Card	.08	.25
Checklist		

1988 Vachon

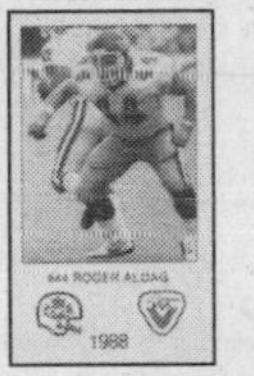

The 1988 Vachon CFL set contains 160 cards measuring 2" by 3 1/2", that is, standard business card size. The fronts have color action photos bordered in white; the vertically oriented backs have brief biographies and career highlights. These cards were printed on very thin stock. Since the cards are unnumbered, they have been ordered below alphabetically for reference. The card fronts contain the Vachon logo and the CFL logo.

COMPLETE SET (160)	150.00	250.00
1 David Albright	.40	1.00
2 Roger Aldag	.50	1.25
3 Marv Allemang	.40	1.00
4 Damon Allen	12.00	20.00
5 Gary Allen	.50	1.25
6 Randy Ambrosie	.40	1.00
7 Mike Anderson	.40	1.00
8 Kent Austin	7.50	15.00
9 Terry Baker	1.50	3.00
10 Danny Bass	2.00	5.00
11 Nick Bastaja	.40	1.00
12 Greg Battle	2.50	6.00
13 Lyle Bauer	.40	1.00
14 Jearld Baylis	.75	2.00
15 Ian Beckstead	.40	1.00
16 Walter Bender	.75	2.00
17 Nick Benjamin	.50	1.25
18 David Black	.40	1.00
19 Leo Blanchard	.40	1.00
20 Trevor Bowles	.50	1.25
21 Ken Braden	.40	1.00
22 Rod Brown	.40	1.00
23 Less Browne	.75	2.00
24 Jamie Buis	.40	1.00
25 Tom Burgess	2.50	6.00
26 Bob Cameron	.75	2.00
27 Jan Carinci	.40	1.00
28 Tony Champion	1.50	4.00
29 Jacques Chapdelaine	.40	1.00
30 Tony Cherry	.75	2.00
31 Lance Chomyc	.50	1.25
32 John Congemi	.75	2.00
33 Rod Connop	.40	1.00
34 David Conrad	.40	1.00
35 Grover Covington	.75	2.00
36 Larry Crawford	.75	2.00
37 James Curry	.75	2.00
38 Marco Cyncar	.50	1.25
39 Gabriel DeLaGarza	.40	1.00
40 Mike Derks	.40	1.00
41 Blake Dermott	.75	2.00
42 Roy DeWalt SP	1.50	4.00
43 Todd Dillon	.75	2.00
44 Rocky DiPietro	.75	2.00
45 Kevin Dixon SP	.75	2.00
46 Tom Dixon	.40	1.00
47 Selwyn Drain	.40	1.00
48 Matt Dunigan	3.00	8.00
49 Ray Elgaard	1.50	4.00
50 Jerome Erdman	.40	1.00
51 Randy Fabi	.40	1.00
52 Gill Fenerty	3.00	8.00
53 Denny Ferdinand	.40	1.00
54 Dan Ferrone	.50	1.25
55 Howard Fields	.40	1.00
56 Matt Finlay	.50	1.25
57 Rickey Foggie	3.00	8.00
58 Delbert Fowler	.50	1.25
59 Ed Gataveckas	.40	1.00

60 Keith Gooch	.40	1.00
61 Miles Gorrell	.40	1.00
62 Mike Gray	.40	1.00
63 Leo Groenewegen	.40	1.00
64 Ken Hailey	.40	1.00
65 Harold Hallman	.75	2.00
66 Tracy Ham	15.00	25.00
67 Rodney Harding	.75	2.00
68 Glenn Harper	.40	1.00
69 J.T. Hay	.40	1.00
70 Larry Hogue	.40	1.00
71 Ron Hopkins SP	.75	2.00
72 Hank Ilesic	.75	2.00
73 Bryan Illerbrun	.40	1.00
74 Lemont Jeffers	.40	1.00
75 James Jefferson	.75	2.00
76 Rick Johnson	.75	2.00
77 Chris Johnstone	.40	1.00
78 Johnnie Jones	.40	1.00
79 Milson Jones	.50	1.25
80 Stephen Jones	.75	2.00
81 Bobby Jurasin	1.50	4.00
82 Jerry Kauric	.50	1.25
83 Dan Kearns	.40	1.00
84 Trevor Kennerd	.75	2.00
85 Mike Kerrigan	2.50	6.00
86 Rick Klassen	.75	2.00
87 Lee Knight	.40	1.00
88 Kevin Konar	.50	1.25
89 Glenn Kulka	.50	1.25
90 Doug(Tank) Landry	.75	2.00
91 Scott Lecky	.40	1.00
92 Orville Lee	.75	2.00
93 Marc Lewis	.50	1.25
94 Eddie Lowe	.50	1.25
95 Lynn Madsen	.40	1.00
96 Chris Major	1.50	4.00
97 Doran Major	.40	1.00
98 Tony Martino	.40	1.00
99 Tim McCray	.75	2.00
100 Mike McGruder	.50	1.25
101 Sean McKeown SP	1.50	4.00
102 Andy McVey	.40	1.00
103 Stan Mikawos	.40	1.00
104 James Mills	.75	2.00
105 Larry Mohr	.40	1.00
106 Bernie Morrison	.40	1.00
107 James Murphy	.75	2.00
108 Paul Osbaldiston	.50	1.25
109 Anthony Parker	2.00	5.00
110 James Parker	.75	2.00
111 Greg Peterson	.40	1.00
112 Tim Petros	.75	2.00
113 Reggie Pleasant	1.25	3.00
114 Willie Pless	.75	2.00
115 Bob Poley	.40	1.00
116 Tom Porras	.50	1.25
117 Hector Pothier	.40	1.00
118 Jim Reid	.75	2.00
119 Robert Reid	.40	1.00
120 Gilbert Renfroe	.75	2.00
121 Tom Richards	.75	2.00
122 Dave Ridgway	1.50	4.00
123 Rae Robirtis	.40	1.00
124 Gerald Roper	.40	1.00
125 Darryl Sampson	.40	1.00
126 Jim Sandusky	1.50	4.00
127 David Sauve	.40	1.00
128 Art Schlichter	1.25	3.00
129 Ralph Scholz	.40	1.00
130 Mark Seale	.40	1.00
131 Dan Sellers	.40	1.00
132 Lance Shields	.50	1.25
133 Ian Sinclair	.50	1.25
134 Mike Siroishka	.40	1.00
135 Chris Skinner	.50	1.25
136 Harry Skipper	.50	1.25
137 Darrell Smith	1.50	4.00
138 Tom Spoletini	.40	1.00
139 Steve Stapler	.50	1.25
140 Bill Stevenson	.40	1.00
141 Gregg Stumon	.50	1.25
142 Glen Suitor	.75	2.00
143 Emanuel Tolbert	1.25	3.00
144 Perry Tuttle SP	2.00	5.00
145 Peter VandenBos	.40	1.00
146 Jake Vaughan	.40	1.00
147 Chris Walby	.75	2.00
148 Mike Walker	1.25	3.00
149 Patrick Wayne	.40	1.00
150 James West	.75	2.00
151 Brett Williams	.75	2.00
152 David Williams	1.50	4.00
153 Gizmo Williams	15.00	30.00
154 Tommie Williams	.40	1.00
155 Larry Willis	.50	1.25
156 Don Wilson	.40	1.00
157 Earl Winfield	1.50	4.00
158 Rick Worman	.75	2.00
159 Larry Wruck	.50	1.25
160 Kari Yli-Renko	.40	1.00

1989 Vachon

The 1989 Vachon CFL set consists of 160 cards. The cards were issued on 6" by 7" perforated panels, consisting of five player cards and one "Instant Prize Card" featuring instructions on how to play the contest. After perforation, the cards measure approximately 2" by 3 1/2". Starting in September 1989, these panels were inserted inside 6 million specially-marked packages of Vachon Cakes. (The collector could also send a self-addressed stamped envelope to receive an additional player card.) Prize cards carrying the following words were to be mailed in and made the holder eligible to receive the certain prizes: 1) Touchdown (one of ten V.I.P. trips for two to the 1989 Grey Cup game in the SkyDome in Toronto, with 250.00 spending money); 2) Field Goal (CFL game jersey); 3) Convert (ticket to the game of your choice); and 4) Single Point (.50 off your next purchase of Vachon family pack snack cakes). No prize was awarded for cards marked "Goal Line Stand." The fronts feature white-bordered color player photos; the CFL football helmet logo and Vachon's logo appear in the wider white border beneath the picture. The backs present biographical information, the card number, and the team helmet. The cards are checklisted below according to teams.

COMPLETE SET (160)	125.00	200.00
1 Tony Williams	.50	1.25
2 Sean Foudy	.40	1.00
3 Tom Schimmer	.40	1.00
4 Ken Evraire	.50	1.25
5 Gerald Wilcox	.75	2.00
6 Damon Allen	6.00	12.00
7 Tony Kimbrough	.50	1.25
8 Dean Dorsey	.50	1.25
9 Rocco Romano	.40	1.00
10 Ken Braden	.40	1.00
11 Kari Yli-Renko	.40	1.00
12 Darrel Hopper	.40	1.00
13 Irv Daymond	.40	1.00
14 Orville Lee	.75	2.00
15 Steve Howlett	.40	1.00
16 Kyle Hall	.40	1.00
17 Reggie Ward	.40	1.00
18 Gerald Alphin	1.25	3.00
19 Troy Wilson	.40	1.00
20 Patrick Wayne	.40	1.00
21 Harold Hallman	.75	2.00
22 John Congemi	.75	2.00
23 Doran Major	.40	1.00
24 Hank Ilesic	.75	2.00
25 Gilbert Renfroe	.75	2.00
26 Rodney Harding	.75	2.00
27 Todd Wiseman	.40	1.00
28 Chris Schultz	.50	1.25
29 Carl Brazley	.50	1.25
30 Darrell Smith	2.00	4.00
31 Glenn Kulka	.50	1.25
32 Bob Skemp	.40	1.00
33 Don Moen	.50	1.25
34 Jearld Baylis	.75	2.00
35 Lorenzo Graham	.40	1.00
36 Lance Chomyc	.50	1.25
37 Warren Hudson	.50	1.25
38 Gill Fenerty	2.50	5.00
39 Paul Masotti	1.00	2.50
40 Reggie Pleasant	.75	2.00
41 Scott Flagel	.50	1.25
42 Mike Kerrigan	2.00	4.00
43 Frank Robinson	.50	1.25
44 Jacques Chapdelaine	.40	1.00
45 Miles Gorrell	.40	1.00
46 Mike Walker	.75	2.00
47 Jason Riley	.40	1.00
48 Grover Covington	.75	2.00
49 Ralph Scholz	.40	1.00
50 Mike Derks	.40	1.00
51 Derrick McAdoo	.75	2.00
52 Rocky DiPietro	.75	2.00
53 Lance Shields	.50	1.25
54 Dale Sanderson	.40	1.00
55 Tim Lorenz	.40	1.00
56 Rod Skillman	.50	1.25
57 Jed Tommy	.40	1.00
58 Paul Osbaldiston	.50	1.25
59 Darrell Corbin	.40	1.00
60 Tony Champion	1.25	3.00
61 Romel Andrews	.40	1.00
62 Bob Cameron	.75	2.00
63 Greg Battle	2.00	4.00
64 Rod Hill	.50	1.25
65 Steve Rodehutskors	.50	1.25
66 Trevor Kennerd	.75	2.00
67 Moustafa Ali	.50	1.25
68 Mike Gray	.40	1.00
69 Bob Molle	.40	1.00
70 Tim Jessie	.50	1.25
71 Matt Pearce	.40	1.00
72 Will Lewis	.50	1.25
73 Sean Salisbury	1.25	3.00
74 Chris Walby	.75	2.00
75 Jeff Croonen	.40	1.00
76 David Black	.40	1.00
77 Buster Rhymes	1.25	3.00
78 James Murphy	.75	2.00
79 Stan Mikawos	.40	1.00
80 Lee Saltz	.75	2.00
81 Bryan Illerbrun	.40	1.00
82 Donald Narcisse	2.50	5.00
83 Milson Jones	.50	1.25
84 Dave Ridgway	2.00	4.00
85 Glen Suitor	.75	2.00
86 Terry Baker	.75	2.00
87 James Curry	.75	2.00
88 Harry Skipper	.50	1.25
89 Bobby Jurasin	2.00	4.00
90 Gary Lewis	.40	1.00
91 Roger Aldag	.50	1.25
92 Jeff Fairholm	1.25	3.00
93 David Albright	.40	1.00
94 Ray Elgaard	2.00	4.00
95 Kent Austin	4.00	8.00
96 Tom Burgess	1.25	3.00
97 Richie Hall	.40	1.00
98 Eddie Lowe	.50	1.25
99 Vince Goldsmith	.50	1.25
100 Tim McCray	.75	2.00
101 Leo Blanchard	.40	1.00
102 Tom Spoletini	.40	1.00
103 Dan Ferrone	.50	1.25
104 Doug(Tank) Landry	.75	2.00
105 Chris Major	1.25	3.00
106 Mike Palumbo	.40	1.00
107 Terrence Jones	2.50	5.00
108 Larry Willis	.50	1.25
109 Kent Warnock	.50	1.25
110 Tim Petros	.75	2.00
111 Marshall Toner	.40	1.00
112 Ken Ford	.40	1.00
113 Ron Hopkins	.50	1.25
114 Erik Kramer	4.00	8.00
115 Stu Laird	.50	1.25
116 Vernell Quinn	.40	1.00
117 Lemont Jeffers	.40	1.00
118 Derrick Taylor	.40	1.00
119 Jay Christensen	.50	1.25
120 Mitchell Price	.50	1.25
121 Rod Connop	.40	1.00
122 Mark Norman	.40	1.00
123 Andre Francis	.50	1.25
124 Reggie Taylor	.75	2.00
125 Rick Worman	.75	2.00
126 Marco Cyncar	.50	1.25
127 Blake Dermott	.75	2.00
128 Jerry Kauric	.50	1.25
129 Steve Taylor	1.25	3.00
130 Dave Richardson	.40	1.00
131 John Mandarich	.50	1.25
132 Gregg Stumon	.50	1.25
133 Tracy Ham	7.50	15.00
134 Danny Bass	2.00	4.00
135 Blake Marshall	.75	2.00
136 Jeff Braswell	.50	1.25
137 Larry Wruck	.50	1.25
138 Warren Jones	.50	1.25
139 Stephen Jones	.75	2.00
140 Tom Richards	.75	2.00
141 Tony Cherry	1.25	3.00
142 Anthony Parker	2.50	5.00
143 Gerald Roper	.40	1.00
144 Lui Passaglia	2.00	4.00
145 Mack Moore	.40	1.00
146 Jamie Taras	.50	1.25
147 Rickey Foggie	4.00	8.00
148 Matt Dunigan	3.00	6.00
149 Anthony Drawhorn	.50	1.25
150 Eric Streater	.75	2.00
151 Marcus Thomas	.40	1.00
152 Wes Cooper	.40	1.00
153 James Mills	1.25	3.00
154 Peter VandenBos	.40	1.00
155 Ian Sinclair	.50	1.25
156 James Parker	.75	2.00
157 Andrew Murray	.40	1.00
158 Larry Crawford	.75	2.00
159 Kevin Konar	.50	1.25
160 David Williams	2.00	4.00

1957 Weekend Magazine Posters

These posters were actually magazine page cut-outs. Each measures roughly 11" by 15" and features a color photo of the featured player on the left and a bio of the player on the right. The posters were printed on newsprint type stock and each was numbered in the lower right hand corner. The backs are simply another page from the magazine. Any additions to the below checklist are appreciated.

COMPLETE SET (11)	125.00	200.00
35 Normie Kwong	20.00	35.00
36 Hal Patterson	12.00	20.00
37 Dick Huffman	12.00	20.00
38 Bob Simpson	12.00	20.00
39 By Bailey	20.00	35.00
40 Vince Scott	12.00	20.00
41 Ken Carpenter	15.00	25.00
42 Sam Etcheverry	15.00	25.00
43 Bob McNamara	12.00	20.00
44 Jackie Parker	20.00	35.00
45 Kaye Vaughan	12.00	20.00

1958 Weekend Magazine Posters

These posters were actually magazine page cut-outs. Each measures roughly 11" by 15" and features a color photo of the featured player. The numbered posters were printed on newsprint stock. The poster backs are simply another page from the magazine.

37 Tony Curcillo	10.00	20.00
38 Gerry James	15.00	30.00
39 Johnny Bright	20.00	40.00
40 Pat Abruzzi	12.50	25.00
41 Ted Hunt	10.00	20.00
42 Bobby Judd	10.00	20.00
43 Reg Whitehouse	10.00	20.00
44 Ernie Warlick	12.50	25.00
45 Dave Mann	12.50	25.00
46 Ken Carpenter	12.50	25.00

1959 Weekend Magazine Posters

These posters were actually magazine page cut-outs. Each measures roughly 11" by 15" and features a color art portrait, by former player Tex Coulter, of the featured player on the left and a bio of the player on the right. The posters were printed on newsprint type stock and each was numbered on the right hand side. The backs are simply another page from the magazine.

33 Jim Van Pelt	12.50	25.00
34 Ron Howell	10.00	20.00
35 Jackie Parker	25.00	40.00
36 Dick Shatto	12.50	25.00
37 Don Luzzi	12.50	25.00
38 Sam Etcheverry	15.00	30.00
39 Bob Simpson	10.00	20.00
40 By Bailey	20.00	35.00
41 Jack Hill	10.00	20.00

1959 Wheaties CFL

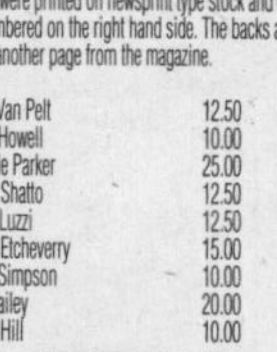

The 1959 Wheaties CFL set contains 48 cards, each measuring 2 1/2" by 3 1/2". The fronts contain a black and white photo on a one-colored striped field, with the player's name and team in black within a white rectangle at the lower portion. The back contains the player's name and team, his position, and brief biographical data in both English and French. The cards are quite similar in appearance to the 1956 Shredded Wheat set. These unnumbered cards are ordered below in alphabetical order. Every 1959 CFL game program contained a full-page ad for the Wheaties Grey Cup Game Contest. The ad detailed the card program which indicated that each specially marked package of Wheaties contained four cards.

COMPLETE SET (48)	3,000.00	4,500.00
1 Ron Adam	35.00	60.00
2 Bill Bewley	45.00	80.00
3 Lynn Bottoms	45.00	80.00
4 Johnny Bright	90.00	150.00
5 Ken Carpenter	45.00	80.00
6 Tony Curcillo	45.00	80.00
7 Sam Etcheverry	150.00	250.00
8 Bernie Faloney	125.00	200.00
9 Cam Fraser	45.00	80.00
10 Don Getty	75.00	125.00
11 Jack Gotta	45.00	80.00
12 Milt Graham	35.00	60.00
13 Jack Hill	35.00	60.00
14 Ron Howell	45.00	80.00
15 Russ Jackson	125.00	200.00
16 Gerry James	75.00	125.00
17 Doug Kiloh	35.00	60.00
18 Ronnie Knox	45.00	80.00
19 Vic Kristopaitis	35.00	60.00
20 Oscar Kruger	35.00	60.00
21 Bobby Kuntz	45.00	80.00
22 Normie Kwong	100.00	175.00
23 Leo Lewis	90.00	150.00
24 Harry Lunn	35.00	60.00
25 Don Luzzi	60.00	100.00
26 Dave Mann	45.00	80.00
27 Bobby Marlow	60.00	100.00
28 Gerry McDougall	45.00	80.00
29 Doug McNichol	35.00	60.00
30 Rollie Miles	60.00	100.00
31 Red O'Quinn	60.00	100.00
32 Jackie Parker	175.00	300.00
33 Hal Patterson	90.00	150.00
34 Don Pinhey	35.00	60.00
35 Kenny Ploen	75.00	125.00
36 Gord Rowland	45.00	80.00
37 Vince Scott	60.00	100.00
38 Art Scullion	35.00	60.00
39 Dick Shatto	75.00	125.00
40 Bob Simpson	75.00	125.00
41 Jackie Simpson UER (Misspelled Jacki)	60.00	100.00
42 Bill Sowalski	35.00	60.00
43 Norm Stoneburgh	35.00	60.00
44 Buddy Tinsley	60.00	100.00
45 Frank Tripucka	75.00	125.00
46 Jim Van Pelt	45.00	80.00
47 Ernie Warlick	60.00	100.00
48 Nobby Wirkowski	60.00	100.00

1962 Wheaties Great Moments in Canadian Sports

This 25 card set, which measure approximately 3 1/2" by 2 1/2" was issued in Canada one per cereal box. The fronts have a color drawing of an important event in Canadian sport history while the backs have a description in both English and French as to what the significance of the event was.

COMPLETE SET (25)		
4 McGill Player Introduction of Football to America	2.00	5.00
6 Jackie Parker/1954 Grey Cup	3.00	8.00
13 Red Storey/1938 Grey Cup	2.00	5.00
18 Ron Stewart/1960 Grey Cup	2.50	6.00

1976 Winnipeg Blue Bombers Team Sheets

This group of 40-players and coaches of the Blue Bombers was produced on five glossy sheets each measuring approximately 8" by 10". The fronts feature black-and-white player portraits with eight pictures to a sheet with the year printed at the top. The backs are blank. The cards are unnumbered and checklisted below in alphabetical order, with the player pictured in the upper left hand corner of the sheet listed first.

COMPLETE SET (5)	12.50	25.00
1 Lee Benard Bob Swift Marion Reeves Steve Williams Mike Hoban Bob Toogood Ralph Brock Bob LaRose	2.50	5.00
2 Darryl Craig Chuck Liebrock Brian Herosian Joe Jackson Gary Anderson Steve Beaird Don Bowman Mark McDonald	3.00	6.00
3 Randy Halsall Jim Heighton Buddy Brown Gord Paterson Chuck Wills Richard Crump Harry Knight Bernie Ruoff	2.50	5.00
4 Ron Southwick Ollie Bakken Rick Koswin Harry Walters John Bonk Butch Norman Earl Lunsford Bud Riley	2.50	5.00
5 Jim Washington Bill Frank Tom Scott Brian Jack Tom Walker Merv Walker Dave Knechtel Peter Ribbins	3.00	6.00

1977-78 Winnipeg Blue Bombers Team Sheets

This group of 32-players and coaches of the Blue Bombers was produced on four glossy sheets each measuring approximately 8" by 10". The fronts feature black-and-white player portraits with eight pictures to a sheet with the year printed at the top. The backs are blank. The cards are unnumbered and checklisted below in alphabetical order, with the player pictured in the upper left hand corner of the sheet listed first.

COMPLETE SET (4)	10.00	20.00
1 John Bonk John Babinecz Don Hubbard Richard Crump Jim Heighton Steve Scully Ray Honey Chuck Wills	3.00	6.00
2 Mark McDonald Brian Herosian Chuck Liebrock Harry Walters Ron Southwick Butch Norman Ralph Brock Tom Walker	2.50	5.00
3 Merv Walker Elton Brown Jim Washington Bob Swift Rick Koswin Gary Rosolowich Tom Scott Lee Benard	3.00	6.00
4 Slade Willis Harry Knight Lyall Woznesensky Vince Phason Bernie Ruoff Gary Krahn Joey Walters Gord Paterson	2.50	5.00

1978 Winnipeg Blue Bombers Team Sheets

This group of 40-players and coaches of the Blue Bombers was produced on five glossy sheets each measuring approximately 8" by 10". The fronts feature black-and-white player portraits with eight pictures to a sheet with the year printed at the top. The backs are blank. The cards are unnumbered and checklisted below in alphabetical order, with the player pictured in the upper left hand corner of the sheet listed first.

COMPLETE SET (5)	12.50	25.00
1 Elton Brown Buddy Hardeman Randy Halsall John McCorquindale Wayne Allison Mark McDonald Dave Knechtel Reggie Pierson	2.50	5.00
2 Brian Herosian Harry Walters Buddy Brown Bernie Morrison Earle Hiebert Earl Lunsford Ray Jauch Mike Holmes	2.50	5.00
3 Harry Knight Butch Norman Billy Howard Gordon Paterson Jim Washington Ralph Brock Merv Walker Jim Heighton	3.00	6.00
4 Ira Watley Bernie Ruoff Lyall Woznesensky Vince Phason Richard Crump Steve Okoniewski Ray Clark Bob Toogood	3.00	6.00
5 Chuck Wills Gary Rosolowich Duncan MacKinlay Ron Southwick Jeff Hart Tom Walker John Bonk Leo Ezerins	2.50	5.00

1980 Winnipeg Blue Bombers Team Sheets

This group of 32-players and coaches of the Blue Bombers was produced on four glossy sheets each measuring approximately 8" by 10". The fronts feature black-and-white player portraits with eight pictures to a sheet with the year printed at the top. The backs are blank. The cards are unnumbered and checklisted below in alphabetical order, with the player pictured in the upper left hand corner of the sheet listed first.

COMPLETE SET (4)	10.00	20.00
1 Marv Allemang Nick Bastaja John Bonk Mark Bragagnolo Ralph Brock Ecomet Burley Larry Butler Bob Cameron	3.00	6.00
2 Brian Gervais Charles Williams John Helton Bruce Holland Mike Holmes Rick House Jim Krohn Harry Kruger	2.50	5.00
3 John Martini Butch Norman Walt Passaglia Vince Phason Trevor Kennerd Reggie Pierson Joe Poplawski Mike Rieker	3.00	6.00
4 Gary Rosolowich Tom Schulz Chris Cobb George Seidel Willie Thomas Bob Toogood Jim Washington Ricky Wesson	3.00	6.00

1982 Winnipeg Blue Bombers Police

This 24-card Police set was sponsored by the Union of Manitoba Municipalities, all Police Forces in Manitoba, and The Optimist Clubs of Manitoba. The cards measure approximately 2 5/8" by 3 7/8" and were issued in two-card perforated panels one per week over a 12-week period. The panel pairs were Kennerd/Phason, Jackson/Walby, Pierson/House, Miller/Mikawos, Goodlow/Bennett, Bonk/Helton, Catan/Ezerins, Norman/Jones, Smith/Williams, Thompson/Poplawski, Bastaja/Reed, and Jauch/Brock. The fronts have posed color player photos, bordered in white with player information below the picture. The backs have "Bomber Tips" that consist of public safety announcements. These thin-stock cards are unnumbered and checklisted below in alphabetical order.

COMPLETE SET (24)	6.00	15.00
1 Nick Bastaja	.20	.50
2 Paul Bennett	.20	.50
3 John Bonk	.20	.50
4 Dieter Brock	1.25	3.00
5 Pete Catan	.20	.50
6 Leo Ezerins	.20	.50
7 Eugene Goodlow	.30	.75
8 John Helton	.60	1.50
9 Rick House	.30	.75
10 Mark Jackson	.30	.75
11 Ray Jauch CO	.20	.50
12 Milson Jones	.40	1.00
13 Trevor Kennerd	.60	1.50
14 Stan Mikawos	.20	.50
15 William Miller	.30	.75
16 Tony Norman	.20	.50
17 Vince Phason	.20	.50
18 Reggie Pierson	.20	.50
19 Joe Poplawski	.30	.75
20 James Reed	.20	.50
21 Franky Smith	.20	.50
22 Bobby Thompson T	.20	.50
23 Chris Walby	.40	1.00
24 Charles Williams	.20	.50

1985 Winnipeg Blue Bombers CFRW

These oversized cards (roughly 3 3/4" by 5 3/4") were sponsored by CFRW radio and feature members of the Winnipeg Blue Bombers. The cardfronts include a color photo with the sponsor logo at the top and the subject's name below. The cardbacks carry a schedule of 1986 Blue Bomber off-season events. Any additions to the list below are appreciated.

COMPLETE SET (15)	20.00	40.00
1 Bob Cameron	1.50	4.00
2 Tom Clements	5.00	10.00
3 Scott Flagel	1.25	3.00
4 John Gregory Asst CO	1.25	3.00
5 Ken Hailey	1.25	3.00
6 Tyrone Jones	1.50	4.00
7 Ray Koshiola	1.25	3.00
8 Stan Mikawos	1.25	3.00
9 Tony Norman	1.25	3.00
10 Vernon Pahl	1.25	3.00
11 Darrell Patterson	1.25	3.00
12 Willard Reaves	1.25	3.00
13 Mike Riley CO	1.50	4.00
14 Chris Walby	1.25	3.00
15 Buzz the Mascot	1.25	3.00

1986 Winnipeg Blue Bombers Silverwood Dairy

These oversized cards (roughly 3 3/4" by 5 3/4") were sponsored by Silverwood's and feature members of the Winnipeg Blue Bombers. The cardfronts include a color photo with the sponsor logo at the top and the subject's name below. The cardbacks carry a schedule of 1986 Blue Bomber off-season events. Any additions to the list below are appreciated.

1 Trevor Kennerd	1.50	4.00

1988 Winnipeg Blue Bombers Silverwood Dairy

Silverwood Dairy issued these player profiles on the sides of its milk cartons in 1988. Each includes a player photo printed in red with his vital statistics underneath followed by two questions about the player. When neatly cut, each measures roughly 2 3/4" by 4 1/2" in size. Any additions to this list are appreciated.

1 James West	3.00	8.00

1993 Winnipeg Blue Bombers Dream Cards

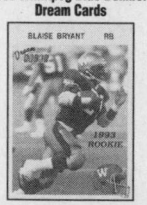

Printed on thin card stock, these 12 standard-size cards feature on their fronts white-bordered color player action shots. The player's name and position appear in black lettering within the wide upper margin. The white-bordered horizontal back is framed by a blue line and carries a color player head shot at the upper left. The player's name and biography appear below, and his career highlights are shown to the right.

COMPLETE SET (12)	1.60	4.00
1 Matt Dunigan	.50	1.25
2 Greg Battle	.30	.75
3 Nathaniel Bolton	.10	.30
4 Stan Mikawos	.10	.30
5 Miles Gorrell	.10	.30
6 Troy Westwood	.30	.75
7 Michael Richardson	.60	1.50
8 David Black	.10	.30
9 Chris Walby	.20	.50
10 David Williams	.20	.50
11 Blaise Bryant	.20	.50
12 Bob Cameron	.20	.50

1994 Winnipeg Blue Bombers Double D

This set of cards was sponsored by Double D and features members of the Blue Bombers. The sponsor's logo appears at the top of the cardfront with the player's name, position, and Blue Bomber logo at the bottom. A second photo is included on the cardbacks along with a brief player bio.

COMPLETE SET (16)	2.50	6.00
1 Matt Dunigan	.50	1.25
2 David Black	.10	.30
3 Bob Cameron	.20	.50
4 Blaise Bryant	.20	.50
5 Gerald Wilcox	.20	.50
6 Chris Walby	.20	.50
7 Troy Westwood	.30	.75
8 Miles Gorrell	.10	.30
9 Stan Mikawos	.10	.30
10 Donald Smith	.10	.30
11 Paul Randolph	.10	.30
12 Del Lyles	.10	.30
13 Sammy Garza	.20	.50
14 Keithen McCant	.20	.50
15 Team Mascots	.10	.30
16 Cover Card	.10	.30

1997 Winnipeg Blue Bombers All Pro Readers Club

This set of bookmarks was released through Winnipeg area schools and libraries and features top Blue Bombers players. Each includes a color photo on the olive colored front along with the player's name, jersey number and a short educational quote. The backs are blue with sponsor logos and the year 1996-97 at the top.

COMPLETE SET (4)	3.20	8.00
1 Mike Richardson	1.20	3.00
2 Dave Vankoughnett	.80	2.00
3 Chris Walby	.80	2.00
4 Troy Westwood	.80	2.00

1998 Winnipeg Blue Bombers All Pro Readers Club

This set of bookmarks was released through Winnipeg area schools and libraries and features top Blue Bombers players. Each includes a color photo on the front along with the player's jersey number and a short quote. The backs are blue with sponsor logos and the year at the top.

COMPLETE SET (4)	3.20	8.00
1 Grant Carter	1.60	4.00
2 Brett McNeil	.80	2.00
3 Wade Miller	.80	2.00
4 Chris Vargas	1.60	4.00

1999 Winnipeg Blue Bombers SAAN

The set of cards was issued on 2-perforated sheets of 18-cards each. Each sheet also contained a group of coupons good for various offers from local company sponsors and the team. The fronts feature color player images with the Blue Bombers logo and the SAAN sponsor logo.

COMPLETE SET (36)	6.00	12.00
1 Kerwin Bell	1.00	2.50
2 Bruce Boyko	.10	.30
3 Bob Cameron	.20	.50
4 Grant Carter	.20	.50
5 Matt Dubuc	.10	.30
6 Brad Elberg	.10	.30
7 Tom Europe	.10	.30
8 Nick Ferguson	.10	.30
9 Joe Fleming	.30	.75
10 Rashid Gayle	.10	.30
11 Bennie Goods	.10	.30
12 Robert Gordon	.30	.75
13 Brandon Hamilton	.10	.30
14 Craig Hendrickson	.10	.30
15 Doug Hocking	.10	.30
16 Eric Johnson	.10	.30
17 Maurice Kelly	.10	.30
18 Troy Kopp	.30	.75
19 David Maeva	.10	.30
20 Deland McCullough	.30	.75
21 Spencer McLennan	.10	.30
22 Mike Mihelic	.10	.30
23 Sean Millington	.10	.30
24 Harold Nash	.10	.30
25 Henry Newby	.10	.30
26 Chris Perez	.10	.30
27 Dave Ritchie CO	.10	.30
28 Don Robinson	.10	.30
29 Tyrone Rodgers	.20	.50
30 Glen Scrivener	.10	.30
31 Milt Stegall	.75	2.00
32 Eddie Thomas	.10	.30
33 Larry Thompson	.10	.30
34 Dave Vankoughnett	.10	.30
35 Wayne Weathers	.10	.30
36 Troy Westwood	.10	.30

1946-49 AAFC Championship Press Pins

1 1946 Browns vs Yankees		
2 1947 Browns vs Yankees	300.00	500.00
3 1948 Browns vs Bills	300.00	500.00
4 1949 Browns vs 49ers	250.00	400.00

1946-49 AAFC Championship Programs

The All-America Football Conference began play in 1946 and folded after the 1949 season. The AAFC was the brainchild of Chicago Sportswriter and sports promoter, Arch Ward. The AAFC was comprised of eight teams representing the cities of: Cleveland (Browns), San Francisco (49ers), Los Angeles (Dons), Chicago (Rockets, Hornets), New York (Yankees), Brooklyn (Dodgers), Buffalo (Bills) and Miami. The Miami Seahawks folded after the 1946 season and were replaced by the Baltimore Colts. The Cleveland Browns, with a combined record of 47-4-3, won the AAFC title game in each of the league's four seasons. Three AAFC franchises, the San Francisco 49ers, Baltimore Colts and Cleveland Browns merged with the NFL for the 1950 season.

1 1946 Browns vs Yankees	350.00	600.00
2 1947 Browns vs Yankees	350.00	600.00
3 1948 Browns vs Bills	350.00	600.00
4 1949 Browns vs 49ers	350.00	600.00

1946-49 AAFC Championship Ticket Stubs

Complete AAFC Championship tickets are nearly impossible to obtain and would command a premium above and beyond the values below.

1 1946 Browns vs Yankees	200.00	350.00
2 1947 Browns vs Yankees	200.00	325.00
3 1948 Browns vs Bills	200.00	325.00
4 1949 Browns vs 49ers	200.00	325.00

1947-49 AAFC Record Manuals

These guides or manuals were issued by the league and include AAFC records, lists of league leaders, championship teams, etc. Most years also include a basic league rules section. We've noted the subject matter on each front cover when known.

1947 Record Manual	40.00	80.00
(Glenn Dobbs photo)		
1948 Record Manual	50.00	100.00
(Otto Graham photo)		
1949 Record Manual	40.00	80.00
Frank Albert		
Otto Graham photos		

1960-69 AFL Championship Programs

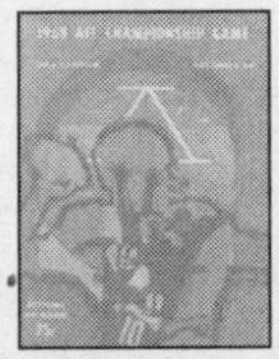

1 1960 Chargers vs Oilers	200.00	400.00
2 1961 Oilers vs Chargers	175.00	350.00
3 1962 Texans vs Oilers	162.50	325.00
4 1963 Patriots vs Chargers	150.00	300.00
5 1964 Chargers vs Bills	125.00	250.00
6 1965 Bills vs Chargers	75.00	150.00
7 1966 Chiefs vs Bills	75.00	150.00
8 1967 Oilers vs Raiders	75.00	150.00
9 1968 Raiders vs Jets	100.00	200.00
10 1969 Chiefs vs Raiders	75.00	150.00

1960-69 AFL Championship Ticket Stubs

Complete AFL Championship tickets are valued 2 to 4 times the stub prices listed below.

1 1960 Chargers vs Oilers	75.00	150.00
2 1961 Oilers vs Chargers	62.50	125.00
3 1962 Texans vs Oilers	62.50	125.00
4 1963 Patriots vs Chargers	50.00	100.00
5 1964 Chargers vs Bills	37.50	75.00
6 1965 Bills vs Chargers	37.50	75.00
7 1966 Chiefs vs Bills	30.00	60.00
8 1967 Oilers vs Raiders	30.00	60.00
9 1968 Raiders vs Jets	25.00	50.00
10 1969 Chiefs vs Raiders	25.00	50.00

1933-69 NFL Championship Programs

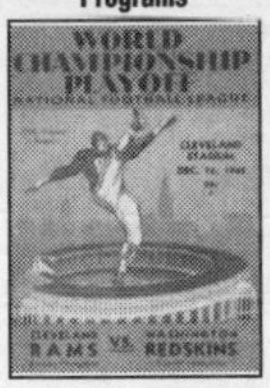

Pre-War programs are difficult to obtain in top condition and are graded Vg-Ex below. Post-War programs are priced in Ex-Mt condition.

1 1933 Giants vs Bears	3,000.00	4,500.00
2 1934 Bears vs Giants	2,000.00	3,000.00
3 1935 Giants vs Lions	2,000.00	3,000.00
4 1936 Packers vs Redskins	2,500.00	3,500.00
5 1937 Redskins vs Bears	1,800.00	3,000.00
6 1938 Giants vs Packers	1,800.00	3,000.00
7 1939 Packers vs Giants	1,500.00	2,500.00
8 1940 Bears vs Redskins	1,200.00	2,000.00
9 1941 Bears vs Giants	1,000.00	1,800.00
10 1942 Redskins vs Bears	1,000.00	1,600.00
11 1943 Bears vs Redskins	800.00	1,200.00
12 1944 Packers vs Giants	800.00	1,200.00
13 1945 Rams vs Redskins	500.00	800.00
14 1946 Bears vs Giants	350.00	600.00
15 1947 Cardinals vs Eagles	300.00	500.00
16 1948 Eagles vs Cardinals	300.00	500.00
17 1949 Eagles vs Rams	250.00	400.00
18 1950 Browns vs Rams	250.00	400.00
19 1951 Rams vs Browns	175.00	300.00
20 1952 Lions vs Browns	175.00	300.00
21 1953 Browns vs Lions	175.00	300.00
22 1954 Lions vs Browns	175.00	300.00
23 1955 Browns vs Rams	150.00	250.00
24 1956 Bears vs Giants	150.00	250.00
25 1957 Browns vs Lions	150.00	250.00
26 1958 Colts vs Giants	175.00	300.00
27 1959 Giants vs Colts	125.00	200.00
28 1960 Packers vs Eagles	175.00	300.00
29 1961 Giants vs Packers	150.00	250.00
30 1962 Giants vs Packers	150.00	250.00
31 1963 Giants vs Bears	100.00	175.00
32 1964 Colts vs Browns	100.00	175.00
33 1965 Browns vs Packers	150.00	250.00
34 1966 Packers vs Cowboys	150.00	250.00
35 1967 Cowboys vs Packers	175.00	300.00
36 1968 Colts vs Browns	75.00	125.00
37 1969 Browns vs Vikings	60.00	100.00

1933-69 NFL Championship Ticket Stubs

Pre-war ticket stubs are difficult to obtain in top condition and are graded Vg-Ex and Ex-Mt below. Complete tickets are valued 3 to 5 times that of a stub.

1 1933 Giants vs Bears	250.00	500.00
2 1934 Bears vs Giants	225.00	450.00
3 1935 Giants vs Lions	225.00	450.00
4 1936 Packers vs (Redskins	175.00	350.00
5 1937 Redskins vs Bears	150.00	300.00
6 1938 Giants vs Packers	125.00	250.00
7 1939 Packers vs Giants	125.00	250.00
8 1940 Bears vs Redskins	175.00	350.00
9 1941 Bears vs Giants	125.00	250.00
10 1942 Redskins vs Bears	125.00	250.00
11 1943 Bears vs Redskins	125.00	250.00
12 1944 Packers vs Giants	125.00	250.00
13 1945 Rams vs Redskins	112.50	225.00
14 1946 Bears vs Giants	100.00	200.00
15 1947 Cardinals vs (Eagles	87.50	175.00
16 1948 Eagles vs (Cardinals	75.00	150.00
17 1949 Eagles vs Rams	75.00	150.00
18 1950 Browns vs Rams	75.00	150.00
19 1951 Rams vs Browns	75.00	150.00
20 1952 Lions vs Browns	75.00	150.00
21 1953 Browns vs Lions	75.00	150.00
22 1954 Lions vs Browns	62.50	125.00
23 1955 Browns vs Rams	62.50	125.00
24 1956 Bears vs Giants	62.50	125.00
25 1957 Browns vs Lions	62.50	125.00
26 1958 Colts vs Giants	75.00	150.00
27 1959 Giants vs Colts	50.00	100.00
28 1960 Packers vs Eagles	62.50	125.00
29 1961 Giants vs Packers	62.50	125.00
30 1962 Giants vs Packers	50.00	100.00
31 1963 Giants vs Bears	50.00	100.00
32 1964 Colts vs Browns	62.50	125.00
33 1965 Browns vs (Packers	50.00	100.00
34 1966 Packers vs (Cowboys	75.00	150.00
35 1967 Cowboys vs (Packers	37.50	75.00
36 1968 Colts vs (Browns	30.00	60.00
37 1969 Browns vs (Vikings	30.00	60.00

1941-63 NFL Record Manuals

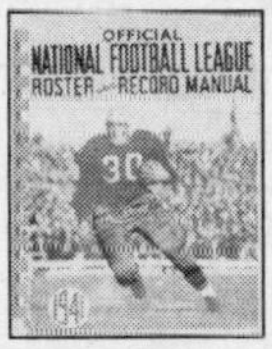

These guides or manuals were issued by the league and include historical NFL records, lists of past league leaders, championship teams, etc. Most years also include a basic league rules section. We've noted the subject matter on each front cover when known.

1941 Roster and Record Manual	60.00	100.00
(Clarke Hinkle photo)		
1942 Roster and Record Manual	60.00	100.00
1943 Roster and Record Manual	60.00	100.00
1944 Record and Rules Manual	60.00	100.00
(Sid Luckman photo)		
1945 Record and Rules Manual	60.00	100.00
(Frank Sinkwich photo)		
1946 Record and Rules Manual	50.00	80.00
(Bob Waterfield photo)		
1947 Record and Rules Manual	50.00	80.00
(Chicago Bears Logo)		
1948 Record and Rules Manual	35.00	60.00
(Chicago Cardinals Logo)		
1949 Record and Rules Manual	35.00	60.00
1950 Record and Rules Manual	35.00	60.00
1951 Record and Rules Manual	35.00	60.00
1952 Record and Rules Manual	35.00	60.00
1953 Record and Rules Manual	30.00	50.00
(Detroit Lions Logo)		
1954 Record and Rules Manual	30.00	50.00
(Detroit Lions logo)		
1955 Record and Rules Manual	35.00	60.00
(Cleveland Browns Logo)		
1956 Record and Rules Manual	35.00	60.00
(Cleveland Browns Logo)		
1957 Record and Rules Manual	30.00	50.00
(New York Giants Logo)		
1958 Record and Rules Manual	25.00	50.00
(Detroit Lions Logo)		
1959 Record and Rules Manual	25.00	50.00
(Baltimore Colts Logo)		
1960 Record and Rules Manual	25.00	50.00
1961 Record and Rules Manual	25.00	50.00
(Philadelphia Eagles Logo)		
1962 Record Manual	100.00	175.00
(Green Bay Packers logo)		
1963 Record Manual	40.00	80.00
Jim Taylor photo)		
1964 Record Manual	25.00	50.00
1965 Record Manual	20.00	40.00
(Frank Ryan photo)		
1966 Record Manual	20.00	40.00
1967 Record Manual	25.00	50.00
(Vince Lombardi photo)		
1968 Record Manual	25.00	50.00
(Bart Starr Ice Bowl photo)		
1969 Record Manual	20.00	40.00
(Earl Morrall photo)		

1935-40 Spalding NFL Guides

These guides were issued by Spalding and include historical NFL records, lists of past league leaders, championship teams, please photos and bios of then current NFL teams. Most years also include a basic league rules section and a cover photo from the previous year's championship game. We've noted the subject matter on each front cover when known.

1935 Guide and Pro/ Football Rules	45.00	80.00
1936 Guide and Pro/ Football Rules	45.00	80.00
1937 Guide and Pro/ Football Rules	45.00	80.00
1938 Pro Football Rules	45.00	80.00
(Bears vs. Redskins photo)		
1939 Guide and Pro/ Football Rules	35.00	60.00
1940 Pro Football Rules	35.00	60.00
(Packers vs. Giants photo)		

1946-50 Spink NFL Guides

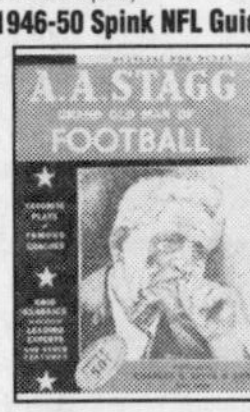

These guides and manuals were published by the Charles Spink and Son Company and include historical NFL records, lists of past league leaders, championship teams, etc. Most years also include a feature on one significant football player or contributor. We've noted the subject matter on each front cover when known.

1946 Official Pro Rules	20.00	40.00
(Amos Alonzo Stagg art)		
1947 Official Pro Rules	20.00	40.00
(Pop Warner art)		
1948 NFL Record and Rule Book	20.00	40.00
(Frank Leahy art)		
1949 NFL Record and Rule Book	20.00	40.00
(Sammy Baugh art)		
1950 NFL Record and Rule Book	20.00	40.00
(Greasy Neale art)		

1962-70 Sporting News AFL Football Guide

1 1962 Game Action	37.50	75.00
2 1963 Game Action	30.00	60.00
3 1964 Game Action	25.00	50.00
4 1965 Tobin Rote	20.00	40.00
5 1966 Sherrill Headrick	17.50	35.00
6 1967 Bobby Burnett	17.50	35.00
7 1968 Multi-Players	17.50	35.00
8 1969 Game Action	15.00	30.00
9 1970 Lance Alworth	15.00	30.00

1970-03 Sporting News NFL Football Guide

1 1970 Hank Stram	25.00	50.00
2 1971 Jim Bakken	20.00	40.00
3 1972 Roger Staubach	15.00	30.00
4 1973 Mercury Morris	12.50	25.00
5 1974 Larry Csonka	12.50	25.00
6 1975 Franco Harris	12.50	25.00
7 1976 Lynn Swann	10.00	20.00
8 1977 Kenny Stabler	10.00	20.00
9 1978 Roger Staubach	10.00	20.00
10 1979 Terry Bradshaw	10.00	20.00
11 1980 Lynn Swann	10.00	20.00
John Stallworth		
12 1981 Billy Simms	7.50	15.00
13 1982 Kenny Anderson	7.50	15.00
14 1983 Mark Moesley	7.50	15.00
15 1984 Eric Dickerson	7.50	15.00
16 1985 Dan Marino	10.00	20.00
17 1986-PRESENT	5.00	10.00

1966-03 Sporting News NFL Football Register

1 1966 St. Louis Cardinals	25.00	50.00
2 1967 Mike Garrett	20.00	40.00
3 1968 Cleveland Browns	20.00	40.00
San Francisco 49ers		
4 1969 Dick Butkus	20.00	40.00
Bart Starr		
5 1970 Roman Gabriel	15.00	30.00
6 1971 Sonny Jurgensen	15.00	30.00
7 1972 Larry Wilson	15.00	30.00
8 1973 Terry Bradshaw	15.00	30.00
9 1974 O.J. Simpson	12.50	25.00
10 1975 Kenny Stabler	10.00	20.00
11 1976 Fran Tarkenton	10.00	20.00
12 1977 Bert Jones	10.00	20.00
13 1978 Walter Payton	12.50	25.00
14 1979 Earl Campbell	12.50	25.00
15 1980 Dan Fouts	10.00	20.00
16 1981 Brian Sipe	7.50	15.00
17 1982 Geroge Rogers	7.50	15.00
18 1983 Marcus Allen	7.50	15.00
19 1984 Dan Marino	10.00	20.00
20 1985 Walter Payton	10.00	20.00
21 1986 -PRESENT	5.00	10.00

1963-03 Street and Smith's Pro Football Yearbook

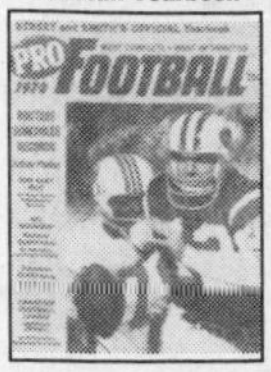

Street and Smith's was one of the first sports magazines to feature regional covers.

1 1963 Milt Plum	30.00	60.00
2 1963 Roman Gabriel	30.00	60.00
3 1963 Y.A. Tittle	37.50	75.00
4 1964 Terry Baker	25.00	50.00
5 1964 Jim Katcavage	25.00	50.00
6 1964 Bart Starr	30.00	60.00
7 1965 Johnny Unitas	25.00	50.00
8 1965 Frank Ryan	20.00	40.00
9 1965 Dick Bass	20.00	40.00
10 1966 Charley Johnson	17.50	35.00
11 1966 Ken Willard	17.50	35.00
12 1966 LaLonde	17.50	35.00
Hillebrand		
13 1967 Vogel	15.00	30.00
Lorick		
14 1967 Dick Bass	15.00	30.00
15 1967 Gale Sayers	20.00	40.00
16 1968 Norm Snead	15.00	30.00
17 1968 Raiders (action)	15.00	30.00
18 1968 Don Meredith	17.50	35.00
19 1969 John Brodie	15.00	30.00
20 1969 Joe Namath	22.50	45.00
21 1969 Jack Concannon	12.50	25.00
22 1970 Joe Namath	20.00	40.00
23 1970 Roman Gabriel	12.50	25.00
24 1970 Joe Kapp	12.50	25.00
25 1971 Earl Morrall	12.50	25.00
26 1971 Duane Thomas	12.50	25.00
Ralph Neely		
27 1971 John Brodie	12.50	25.00
Ken Willard		
28 1972 Roger Staubach	15.00	30.00
29 1972 John Hadl	10.00	20.00
30 1972 Bob Griese	12.50	25.00
31 1973 Larry Csonka	12.50	25.00
32 1973 Chester Marcol	10.00	20.00
33 1973 Steve Spurrier	12.50	25.00
34 1974 Roger Staubach	12.50	25.00
35 1974 O.J. Simpson	12.50	25.00
36 1974 Jim Bertelsen	10.00	20.00
37 1975 Jim Hart	10.00	20.00
38 1975 Franco Harris	12.50	25.00
39 1975 Lawrence McCutchen	10.00	20.00
40 1976 Roger Staubach	10.00	20.00
41 1976 Terry Bradshaw	10.00	20.00
42 1976 Ken Stabler	10.00	20.00
43 1977 Walter Payton	10.00	20.00
44 1977 Bert Jones	7.50	15.00
45 1977 John Cappelletti	7.50	15.00
46 1978 Bob Griese	10.00	20.00
47 1978 Mark Van Eeghen	7.50	15.00
48 1978 Tony Dorsett	10.00	20.00
49 1979 Jim Zorn	7.50	15.00
50 1979 Terry Bradshaw	10.00	20.00
51 1979 Roger Staubach	10.00	20.00
52 1980 Terry Bradshaw	10.00	20.00
53 1980 Walter Payton	10.00	20.00
54 1980 Dan Fouts	7.50	15.00
55 1981 Earl Campbell	10.00	20.00
Steve Bartkowski		
56 1981 Jim Plunkett	7.50	15.00
Jim Zorn		
57 1981 Brian Sipe	7.50	15.00
Tommy Kramer		
58 1982 Joe Montana	12.50	25.00
59 1982 Ken Anderson	7.50	15.00
60 1982 Lawrence Taylor	7.50	15.00
61 1982 Tony Dorsett	7.50	15.00
62 1983 Marcus Allen	7.50	15.00
63 1983 Ken Anderson	6.00	12.00
64 1983 Joe Theismann	7.50	15.00
65 1983 A.J. Duhe	6.00	12.00
66 1984 Walter Payton	7.50	15.00
67 1984 Dan Marino	10.00	20.00
68 1984 Marcus Allen	7.50	15.00
69 1984 John Riggins	7.50	15.00
70 1985 Walter Payton	7.50	15.00
71 1985 Phil Simms	6.00	12.00
72 1985 Dan Marino	10.00	20.00
73 1985 Joe Montana	10.00	20.00
74 1986-PRESENT	5.00	10.00

1967-04 Super Bowl Media Guides

1 1967 (I)	150.00	450.00
(Green Bay Packers		
Kansas City Chiefs		
2 1968 (II)	150.00	400.00
(Green Bay Packers		
Oakland Raiders		
3 1969 (III)	200.00	400.00
(New York Jets		
Baltimore Colts		
4 1970 (IV)	150.00	300.00
(Kansas City Chiefs		
Minnesota Vikings (game)		
5 1971 (V)	150.00	300.00
(Baltimore Colts		
Dallas Cowboys		
6 1972 (VI)	125.00	250.00
(Dallas Cowboys		
Miami Dolphins		
7 1973 (VII)	125.00	250.00
(Miami Dolphins		
Washington Redskins		
8 1974 (VIII)	125.00	250.00
(Miami Dolphins		
Minnesota Vikings		
9 1975 (IX)	75.00	150.00
Pittsburgh Steelers		
Minnesota Vikings		
10 1976 (X)	75.00	150.00
Pittsburgh Steelers		
Dallas Cowboys		
11 1977 (XI)	50.00	100.00
Oakland Raiders		
Minnesota Vikings		
12 1978 (XII)	50.00	100.00
Denver Broncos		
Dallas Cowboys		
13 1979 (XIII)	37.50	75.00
Pittsburgh Steelers		
Dallas Cowboys		
14 1980 (XIV)	37.50	75.00
Pittsburgh Steelers		
Los Angeles Rams		
15 1981 (XV)	25.00	50.00
Philadelphia Eagles		
Oakland Raiders		
16 1982 (XVI)	25.00	50.00
San Francisco 49ers		
Cincinnati Bengals		
17 1983 (XVII)	25.00	50.00
Washington Redskins		
Miami Dolphins		
18 1984 (XVIII)	25.00	50.00
Oakland Raiders		
Washington Redskins		
19 1985 (XIX)	25.00	50.00
San Francisco 49ers		
Miami Dolphins		
20 1986 (XX)	25.00	50.00
Chicago Bears		
New England Patriots		
21 1987 (XXI)	20.00	40.00
New York Giants		
Denver Broncos		
22 1988 (XXII)	20.00	40.00
Washington Redskins		
Denver Broncos		
23 1989 (XXIII)	20.00	40.00
San Francisco 49ers		
Denver Bengals		
24 1990 (XXIV)	20.00	40.00
San Francisco 49ers		
Denver Broncos		
25 1991 (XXV)	12.50	25.00
New York Giants		
Buffalo Bills		
26 1992 (XXVI)	12.50	25.00
Washington Redskins		
Buffalo Bills		
27 1993 (XXVII)	12.50	25.00
Buffalo Bills		
Dallas Cowboys		
28 1994 (XXVIII)	12.50	25.00
Buffalo Bills		
Dallas Cowboys		
29 1995 (XXIX)	12.50	25.00
San Francisco 49ers		
San Diego Chargers		
30 1996 (XXX)	12.50	25.00
Pittsburgh Steelers		
Dallas Cowboys		
31 1997 (XXXI)	12.50	25.00
Green Bay Packers		
New England Patriots		
32 1998 (XXXII)	12.50	25.00
Denver Broncos		
Green Bay Packers		
33 1999 (XXXIII)	12.50	25.00
Denver Broncos		
Atlanta Falcons		
34 2000 (XXXIV)	12.50	25.00
St Louis Rams		
Tennessee Titans		
35 2001 (XXXV)	25.00	40.00
Baltimore Ravens		
New York Giants		
36 2002 (XXXVI)	15.00	30.00
New England Patriots		
St.Louis Rams		
37 2003 (XXXVII)	15.00	30.00
Tampa Bay Buccaneers		
Oakland Raiders		
38 2004 (XXXVIII)	15.00	30.00
Carolina Panthers		
New England Patriots		
39 2005 (XXXIX)	15.00	30.00
New England Patriots		
Philadelphia Eagles		
40 2006 (XL)	15.00	30.00
Pittsburgh Steelers		
Seattle Seahawks		

1967-04 Super Bowl Patches

Super Bowl patches were intended to be sold at each Super Bowl venue as a souvenir. In recent years most patches have been reprinted. It's difficult to differentiate original Super Bowl patches from reprints. However, original patches prior to Super Bow XIV do not have the plastic coating applied to the backside like the current patches do.

1 1967 (I)	40.00	80.00
(Green Bay Packers		
Kansas City Chiefs		
2 1968 (II)	40.00	80.00
(Green Bay Packers		
Oakland Raiders		
3 1969 (III)	30.00	60.00
(New York Jets		
Baltimore Colts		
4 1970 (IV)	25.00	50.00
(Kansas City Chiefs		
Minnesota Vikings		
5 1971 (V)	25.00	50.00
(Baltimore Colts		
Dallas Cowboys		
6 1972 (VI)	25.00	50.00
(Dallas Cowboys		
Miami Dolphins		
7 1973 (VII)	20.00	40.00
(Miami Dolphins		
Washington Redskins		
8 1974 (VIII)	10.00	25.00
(Miami Dolphins		
Minnesota Vikings		
9 1975 (IX)	10.00	25.00
(Pittsburgh Steelers		
Minnesota Vikings		
10 1976 (X)	10.00	25.00
(Pittsburgh Steelers		
Dallas Cowboys		
11 1977 (XI)	10.00	25.00
(Oakland Raiders		
Minnesota Vikings		
12 1978 (XII)	10.00	25.00
(Denver Broncos		
Dallas Cowboys		
13 1979 (XIII)	10.00	25.00
Pittsburgh Steelers		
Dallas Cowboys		
14 1980 (XIV)	10.00	25.00
Pittsburgh Steelers		
Los Angeles Rams		
15 1981 (XV)	10.00	25.00
Philadelphia Eagles		
Oakland Raiders		
16 1982 (XVI)	10.00	25.00
San Francisco 49ers		
Cincinnati Bengals		
17 1983 (XVII)	10.00	25.00
Washington Redskins		
Miami Dolphins		
18 1984 (XVIII)	10.00	25.00
Los Angeles Raiders		
Washington Redskins		
19 1985 (XIX)	10.00	25.00
San Francisco 49ers		
Miami Dolphins		
20 1986 (XX)	10.00	25.00
Chicago Bears		
New England Patriots		
21 1987 (XXI)	7.50	20.00
(New York Giants		
Denver Broncos		
22 1988 (XXII)	7.50	20.00
Washington Redskins		
Denver Broncos		
23 1989 (XXIII)	7.50	20.00
San Francisco 49ers		
Cincinnati Bengals		
24 1990 (XXIV)	7.50	20.00
San Francisco 49ers		
Denver Broncos		
25 1991 (XXV)	7.50	20.00
(New York Giants		
Buffalo Bills		
26 1992 (XXVI)	7.50	20.00
Washington Redskins		
Buffalo Bills		
27 1993 (XXVII)	7.50	20.00
(Buffalo Bills		
Dallas Cowboys		
28 1994 (XXVIII)	7.50	20.00
(Buffalo Bills		
Dallas Cowboys		
29 1995 (XXIX)	7.50	20.00
San Francisco 49ers		
San Diego Chargers		
30 1996 (XXX)	6.00	15.00
Pittsburgh Steelers		
Dallas Cowboys		
31 1997 (XXXI)	6.00	15.00
Green Bay Packers		
New England Patriots		
32 1998 (XXXII)	6.00	15.00
(Denver Broncos		
Green Bay Packers		
33 1999 (XXXIII)	6.00	15.00
(Denver Broncos		
Atlanta Falcons		
34 2000 (XXXIV)	6.00	15.00
(Tennessee Titans		
St Louis Rams		
35 2001 (XXXV)	6.00	15.00
Baltimore Ravens		
New York Giants		
36 2002 (XXXVI)	7.50	15.00
New England Patriots		
St.Louis Rams		
37A 2003 (XXXVII)	20.00	40.00
Tampa Bay Buccaneers		
Oakland Raiders		
37B 2003 (XXXVII)	7.50	20.00
Media Version		
Tampa Bay Buccaneers		
Oakland Raiders		
(larger 4 x 5 format)		
38 2004 (XXXVIII)	7.50	20.00
Carolina Panthers		
New England Patriots		
39 2005 (XXXIX)	10.00	20.00
New England Patriots		
Philadelphia Eagles		
40 2006 (XL)	10.00	20.00
Pittsburgh Steelers		
Seattle Seahawks		

1967-04 Super Bowl Press Pins

Press pins are given to members of the media attending the Super Bowl. The value for Super Bowl I pin includes the tie-bar and cuff links. The value of the Super Bowl I pin by itself would be $900. There was no pin issued for Super Bowl II. The media received a charm. Also, the media attending Super Bowl III were given a tie-clasp rather than the traditional press pin. There were no press pins issued for either Super Bowl IV or V.

1 1967 (I) (Tie Clasp)	1,200.00	2,000.00
Green Bay Packers		
Kansas City Chiefs		
2 1968 (II)	1,000.00	2,000.00
Green Bay Packers		
Oakland Raiders		
3 1969 (III) (Tie Clasp)	750.00	1,500.00
New York Jets		
Baltimore Colts		
4 1970 (IV)		
(Kansas City Chiefs		
Minnesota Vikings		
5 1971 (V)		
(Baltimore Colts		
Dallas Cowboys		
6 1972 (VI)	250.00	400.00
(Dallas Cowboys		
Miami Dolphins		
7 1973 (VII)	200.00	350.00
(Miami Dolphins		
Washington Redskins		
8 1974 (VIII)	200.00	350.00
(Miami Dolphins		
Minnesota Vikings		
9 1975 (IX)	175.00	300.00
Pittsburgh Steelers		
Minnesota Vikings		
10 1976 (X)	175.00	300.00
Pittsburgh Steelers		
Dallas Cowboys		
11 1977 (XI)	150.00	250.00
(Oakland Raiders		
Minnesota Vikings		
12 1978 (XII)	150.00	250.00
(Denver Broncos		
Dallas Cowboys		
13 1979 (XIII)	125.00	225.00
Pittsburgh Steelers		
Dallas Cowboys		
14 1980 (XIV)	125.00	225.00
Pittsburgh Steelers		
Los Angeles Rams		
15 1981 (XV)	125.00	200.00
Philadelphia Eagles		
Oakland Raiders		
16 1982 (XVI)	175.00	300.00
(San Francisco 49ers		
Cincinnati Bengals		
17 1983 (XVII)	125.00	250.00
Washington Redskins		
Miami Dolphins		
18 1984 (XVIII)	75.00	150.00
(Los Angeles Raiders		
Washington Redskins		
19 1985 (XIX)	62.50	125.00
San Francisco 49ers		
Miami Dolphins		
20 1986 (XX)	62.50	125.00
(Chicago Bears		
New England Patriots		
21 1987 (XXI)	62.50	125.00
(New York Giants		
Denver Broncos		
22 1988 (XXII)	50.00	100.00
Washington Redskins		
Denver Broncos		
23 1989 (XXIII)	50.00	100.00
(San Francisco 49ers		
Cincinnati Bengals		
24 1990 (XXIV)	50.00	100.00
San Francisco 49ers		
Denver Broncos		
25 1991 (XXV)	50.00	100.00
New York Giants		
Buffalo Bills		
26 1992 (XXVI)	62.50	125.00
(Washington Redskins		
Buffalo Bills		
27 1993 (XXVII)	62.50	125.00
(Buffalo Bills		
Dallas Cowboys		
28 1994 (XXVIII)	62.50	125.00
(Buffalo Bills		
Dallas Cowboys		
29 1995 (XXIX)	62.50	125.00
(San Francisco 49ers		
San Diego Chargers		
30 1996 (XXX)	75.00	150.00
Pittsburgh Steelers		
Dallas Cowboys		
31 1997 (XXXI)	62.50	125.00
Green Bay Packers		
New England Patriots		
32 1998 (XXXII)	62.50	125.00
Denver Broncos		
Green Bay Packers		
33 1999 (XXXIII)	62.50	125.00
Denver Broncos		
Atlanta Falcons		
34 2000 (XXXIV)	62.50	125.00
St. Louis Rams		
Tennessee Titans		
35 2001 (XXXV)	62.50	125.00
Baltimore Ravens		
New York Giants		
36 2002 (XXXVI)	50.00	100.00
New England Patriots		
St Louis Rams		
37 2003 (XXXVII)/5225	25.00	50.00
Tampa Bay Buccaneers		
Oakland Raiders		
38 2004 (XXXVIII)/5000	50.00	100.00
Carolina Panthers		
New England Patriots		

1967-07 Super Bowl Programs

The program for Super Bowl V is sold at a premium due to a limited number being available on game day. Reportedly, a semi-truck carrying a quantity of programs crashed and overturned in route to the stadium. These programs were later destroyed. Beginning with Super Bowl X, game programs were available through the mail, thus the drop-off in values.

1 1967 (I)	200.00	350.00
(Green Bay Packers		
Kansas City Chiefs		
2 1968 (II)	250.00	400.00
(Green Bay Packers		
Oakland Raiders		
3 1969 (III)	175.00	300.00
(New York Jets		
Baltimore Colts		
4 1970 (IV)	150.00	250.00
(Kansas City Chiefs		
Minnesota Vikings (game)		
4A 1970 (IV)	50.00	100.00
Kansas City Chiefs		
Minnesota Vikings (newsstand)		
5 1971 (V)	150.00	300.00
(Baltimore Colts		
Dallas Cowboys		
6 1972 (VI)	125.00	200.00
(Dallas Cowboys		
Miami Dolphins		
7 1973 (VII)	100.00	175.00
(Miami Dolphins		
Washington Redskins		
8 1974 (VIII)	100.00	175.00
(Miami Dolphins		
Minnesota Vikings		
9 1975 (IX)	60.00	100.00
Pittsburgh Steelers		
Minnesota Vikings		
10 1976 (X)	75.00	125.00
Pittsburgh Steelers		
Dallas Cowboys		

11 1977 (XI) 40.00 75.00
Oakland Raiders
Minnesota Vikings
12 1978 (XII) 40.00 75.00
Denver Broncos
Dallas Cowboys
13 1979 (XIII) 35.00 60.00
Pittsburgh Steelers
Dallas Cowboys
14 1980 (XIV) 30.00 50.00
Pittsburgh Steelers
Los Angeles Rams
15 1981 (XV) 17.50 35.00
Philadelphia Eagles
Oakland Raiders
16 1982 (XVI) 17.50 35.00
San Francisco 49ers
Cincinnati Bengals
17 1983 (XVII) 15.00 30.00
Washington Redskins
Miami Dolphins
18 1984 (XVIII) 15.00 30.00
Oakland Raiders
Washington Redskins
19 1985 (XIX) 15.00 30.00
San Francisco 49ers
Miami Dolphins
20 1986 (XX) 15.00 30.00
Chicago Bears
New England Patriots
21 1987 (XXI) 12.50 25.00
New York Giants
Denver Broncos
22 1988 (XXII) 12.50 25.00
Washington Redskins
Denver Broncos
23 1989 (XXIII) 12.50 25.00
San Francisco 49ers
Denver Bengals
24 1990 (XXIV) 10.00 20.00
San Francisco 49ers
Denver Broncos
25 1991 (XXV) 10.00 20.00
New York Giants
Buffalo Bills
26 1992 (XXVI) 10.00 20.00
Washington Redskins
Buffalo Bills
27 1993 (XXVII) 10.00 20.00
Buffalo Bills
Dallas Cowboys
28 1994 (XXVIII) 10.00 20.00
Buffalo Bills
Dallas Cowboys
29 1995 (XXIX) 10.00 20.00
San Francisco 49ers
San Diego Chargers
30 1996 (XXX) 10.00 20.00
Pittsburgh Steelers
Dallas Cowboys
31 1997 (XXXI) 10.00 20.00
Green Bay Packers
New England Patriots
32 1998 (XXXII) 10.00 20.00
Denver Broncos
Green Bay Packers
33 1999 (XXXIII) 10.00 20.00
Denver Broncos
Atlanta Falcons
34 2000 (XXXIV) 10.00 20.00
St Louis Rams
Tennessee Titans
35 2001 (XXXV) 10.00 20.00
Baltimore Ravens
New York Giants
36 2002 (XXXVI) 10.00 20.00
New England Patriots
St.Louis Rams
37 2003 (XXXVII) 10.00 20.00
Tampa Bay Buccaneers
Oakland Raiders
38A 2004 (XXXVIII) 10.00 20.00
Carolina Panthers
New England Patriots
(Holographic Cover Stadium Version)
38B 2004 (XXXVIII) 6.00 15.00
Carolina Panthers
New England Patriots
(Mass Market Version)
39 2005 (XXXIX) 10.00 20.00
New England Patriots
Philadelphia Eagles
40 2006 (XL) 10.00 20.00
Pittsburgh Steelers
Seattle Seahawks
41 2007 (XLI) 10.00 20.00
Indianapolis Colts
Chicago Bears

1967-04 Super Bowl Full Tickets

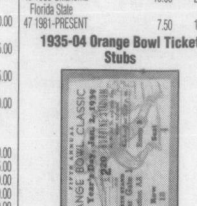

Prices below are for full game tickets. Note that full tickets for some recent Super Bowls are much easier to obtain since the NFL began scanning full tickets at some games instead of tearing them.

1 1967 (I) 1,250.00 3,000.00
Green Bay Packers
Kansas City Chiefs
2 1968 (II) 1,750.00 6,000.00
Green Bay Packers
Oakland Raiders
3 1969 (III) 1,600.00 5,000.00
{New York Jets
Baltimore Colts
4 1970 (IV) 600.00 1,200.00
Kansas City Chiefs
Minnesota Vikings
5 1971 (V) 1,400.00 2,800.00
{Baltimore Colts
Dallas Cowboys
6 1972 (VI) 600.00 1,200.00
{Dallas Cowboys
Miami Dolphins
7 1973 (VII) 375.00 750.00
{Miami Dolphins
Washington Redskins
8 1974 (VIII) 375.00 750.00
{Miami Dolphins
Minnesota Vikings
9 1975 (IX) 250.00 500.00
Pittsburgh Steelers
Minnesota Vikings
10 1976 (X) 175.00 350.00
Pittsburgh Steelers
Dallas Cowboys
11 1977 (XI) 175.00 350.00
{Oakland Raiders
Minnesota Vikings
12 1978 (XII) 750.00 1,500.00
Denver Broncos
Dallas Cowboys
13 1979 (XIII) 200.00 400.00
Pittsburgh Steelers
Dallas Cowboys
14 1980 (XIV) 150.00 300.00
Pittsburgh Steelers
Los Angeles Rams
15 1981 (XV) 175.00 350.00
{Philadelphia Eagles
Oakland Raiders
16 1982 (XVI) 175.00 350.00
San Francisco 49ers
Cincinnati Bengals
17 1983 (XVII) 200.00 400.00
Washington Redskins
Miami Dolphins
18 1984 (XVIII) 150.00 300.00
Los Angeles Raiders
Washington Redskins
19 1985 (XIX) 162.50 325.00
San Francisco 49ers
Miami Dolphins
20 1986 (XX) 150.00 300.00
{Chicago Bears
New England Patriots
21 1987 (XXI) 150.00 300.00
New York Giants
Denver Broncos
22 1988 (XXII) 125.00 250.00
Washington Redskins
Denver Broncos
23 1989 (XXIII) 125.00 250.00
San Francisco 49ers
Cincinnati Bengals
24 1990 (XXIV) 150.00 300.00
San Francisco 49ers
Denver Broncos
25 1991 (XXV) 100.00 200.00
New York Giants
Buffalo Bills
26 1992 (XXVI) 100.00 200.00
Washington Redskins
Buffalo Bills
27 1993 (XXVII) 112.50 225.00
Buffalo Bills
Dallas Cowboys
28 1994 (XXVIII) 125.00 250.00
{Buffalo Bills
Dallas Cowboys
29 1995 (XXIX) 150.00 300.00
San Francisco 49ers
San Diego Chargers
30 1996 (XXX) 125.00 225.00
Pittsburgh Steelers
Dallas Cowboys
31 1997 (XXXI) 125.00 225.00
Green Bay Packers
New England Patriots
32 1998 (XXXII) 125.00 225.00
Denver Broncos
Green Bay Packers
33 1999 (XXXIII) 125.00 225.00
Denver Broncos
Atlanta Falcons
34 2000 (XXXIV) 125.00 225.00
St Louis Rams
Tennessee Titans
35 2001 (XXXV) 125.00 225.00
Baltimore Raven
New York Giants
36 2002 (XXXVI) 125.00 225.00
New England Patriots
St.Louis Rams
37 2003 (XXXVII) 125.00 225.00
Tampa Bay Buccaneers
Oakland Raiders
38 2004 (XXXVIII) 125.00 225.00
New England Patriots
Carolina Panthers
39 2005 (XXXIX) 125.00 225.00
New England Patriots
Philadelphia Eagles
40 2006 (XL) 125.00 225.00
Pittsburgh Steelers
Seattle Seahawks

1967-07 Super Bowl Ticket Stubs

Prices below are for game stubs. The stub for Super Bowl IV is sold at a premium because many of Tulane Stadiums ticket takers tore the tickets in half instead of ripping them at the perforation. Note that Ticket Stubs for some recent Super Bowls essentially do not exist since the NFL began scanning full tickets at some games instead of tearing them.

1 1967 (I) 500.00 800.00
{Green Bay Packers
Kansas City Chiefs
2 1968 (II) 500.00 800.00
{Green Bay Packers
Oakland Raiders
3 1969 (III) 500.00 800.00
{New York Jets
Baltimore Colts
4 1970 (IV) 350.00 600.00
Kansas City Chiefs
Minnesota Vikings
5 1971 (V) 175.00 300.00
{Baltimore Colts
Dallas Cowboys
6 1972 (VI) 150.00 250.00
{Dallas Cowboys
Miami Dolphins
7 1973 (VII) 150.00 250.00
{Miami Dolphins
Washington Redskins
8 1974 (VIII) 87.50 175.00
{Miami Dolphins
Minnesota Vikings
9 1975 (IX) 75.00 150.00
{Pittsburgh Steelers
Minnesota Vikings
10 1976 (X) 87.50 175.00
Pittsburgh Steelers
Dallas Cowboys
11 1977 (XI) 50.00 125.00
{Oakland Raiders
Minnesota Vikings
12 1978 (XII) 50.00 125.00
{Denver Broncos
Dallas Cowboys
13 1979 (XIII) 50.00 125.00
Pittsburgh Steelers
Dallas Cowboys
14 1980 (XIV) 50.00 125.00
Pittsburgh Steelers
Los Angeles Rams
15 1981 (XV) 50.00 125.00
Philadelphia Eagles
Oakland Raiders
16 1982 (XVI) 50.00 125.00
San Francisco 49ers
Cincinnati Bengals
17 1983 (XVII) 50.00 125.00
{Washington Redskins
Miami Dolphins
18 1984 (XVIII) 50.00 125.00
Los Angeles Raiders
Washington Redskins
19 1985 (XIX) 50.00 125.00
{San Francisco 49ers
Miami Dolphins
20 1986 (XX) 50.00 125.00
{Chicago Bears
New England Patriots
21 1987 (XXI) 50.00 125.00
{New York Giants
Denver Broncos
22 1988 (XXII) 50.00 125.00
{Washington Redskins
Denver Broncos
23 1989 (XXIII) 50.00 125.00
San Francisco 49ers
Cincinnati Bengals
24 1990 (XXIV) 50.00 125.00
San Francisco 49ers
Denver Broncos
25 1991 (XXV) 50.00 125.00
New York Giants
Buffalo Bills
26 1992 (XXVI) 50.00 100.00
Washington Redskins
Buffalo Bills
27 1993 (XXVII) 50.00 100.00
{Buffalo Bills
Dallas Cowboys
28 1994 (XXVIII) 50.00 100.00
{Buffalo Bills
Dallas Cowboys
29 1995 (XXIX) 50.00 100.00
San Francisco 49ers
San Diego Chargers
30 1996 (XXX) 50.00 100.00
Pittsburgh Steelers
Dallas Cowboys
31 1997 (XXXI) 40.00 80.00
Green Bay Packers
New England Patriots
32 1998 (XXXII) 40.00 80.00
Denver Broncos
Green Bay Packers
33 1999 (XXXIII) 40.00 80.00
Denver Broncos
Atlanta Falcons
34 2000 (XXXIV) 40.00 80.00
St Louis Rams
Tennessee Titans
35 2001 (XXXV) 40.00 80.00
{Baltimore Ravens
New York Giants
36 2002 (XXXVI) 40.00 80.00
New England Patriots
St.Louis Rams
37 2003 (XXXVII) 40.00 80.00
Tampa Bay Buccaneers
Oakland Raiders
38 2004 (XXXVIII) 40.00 80.00
Carolina Panthers
New England Patriots
39 2005 (XXXIX) 40.00 80.00
New England Patriots
Philadelphia Eagles
40 2006 (XL) 40.00 80.00
Pittsburgh Steelers
Seattle Seahawks
41 2007 (XLI) 40.00 80.00
Indianapolis Colts
Chicago Bears

1967-04 Super Bowl Proof Tickets

Super Bowl proof tickets are officially licensed by the NFL and are given to NFL sponsors and league VIPs as a memento. Super Bowl proof tickets are indistinguishable from the real thing and many times are sold as the genuine article. Generally, proof tickets are printed with a fictitious seating location. Our suggestion to readers is to check the seating diagram on the reverse of the ticket to make sure the seat location on the front actually exists. The original ticket for Super Bowl I was printed by Dillingham, while the reverse of the proof ticket lists Weldon, William of Little Rock, Ark. as the printer. The original Super Bowl II and III tickets were printed by Globe Ticket Company. Beginning with Super Bowl IV, both the originals and proofs were printed by Weldon, William & Lick. All known fictitious sealing locations are listed in parentheses.

1 1967 (I) 20.00 40.00
{Green Bay Packers
Kansas City Chiefs
2 1968 (II) 25.00 50.00
{Green Bay Packers
Oakland Raiders
NA-76-99
3 1969 (III) 17.50 35.00
{New York Jets
Baltimore Colts
NA-76-99
4 1970 (IV) 15.00 30.00
{Kansas City Chiefs
Minnesota Vikings
Z-4-11
5 1971 (V) 12.50 25.00
{Baltimore Colts
Dallas Cowboys
Z
6 1972 (VI) 12.50 25.00
{Dallas Cowboys
Miami Dolphins
Z-58-50
7 1973 (VII) 12.50 25.00
{Miami Dolphins
Washington Redskins/50-90-51
8 1974 (VIII) 10.00 20.00
{Miami Dolphins
Minnesota Vikings
9 1975 (IX) 10.00 20.00
{Pittsburgh Steelers
Minnesota Vikings
Z-68-50
10 1976 (X) 10.00 20.00
{Pittsburgh Steelers
Dallas Cowboys
Z-75-81
11 1977 (XI) 7.50 15.00
{Oakland Raiders
Minnesota Vikings/100-80-40
12 1978 (XII) 10.00 20.00
{Denver Broncos
Dallas Cowboys/465-4-8
13 1979 (XIII) 10.00 20.00
{Pittsburgh Steelers
Dallas Cowboys
Z-75-81
14 1980 (XIV) 7.50 15.00
{Pittsburgh Steelers
Los Angeles Rams/100-80-40
15 1981(XV) 7.50 15.00
{Philadelphia Eagles
Oakland Raiders/561-1-4
16 1982 (XVI) 10.00 20.00
San Francisco 49ers
Cincinnati Bengals/600-A-20
17 1983 (XVII) 7.50 15.00
Washington Redskins
Miami Dolphins
18 1984 (XVIII) 7.50 15.00
Los Angeles Raiders
Washington Redskins
19 1985 (XIX) 10.00 20.00
San Francisco 49ers
Miami Dolphins
20 1986 (XX) 7.50 15.00
{Chicago Bears
New England Patriots
21 1987 (XXI) 7.50 15.00
{New York Giants
Denver Broncos
Z-30-90-45
22 1988 (XXII) 10.00 20.00
Washington Redskins
Denver Broncos
23 1989 (XXIII) 10.00 20.00
San Francisco 49ers
Cincinnati Bengals
24 1990 (XXIV) 7.50 15.00
San Francisco 49ers
Denver Broncos
25 1991 (XXV) 7.50 15.00
{New York Giants
Buffalo Bills
26 1992 (XXVI) 10.00 20.00
Washington Redskins
Buffalo Bills
27 1993 (XXVII) 10.00 20.00
{Buffalo Bills
Dallas Cowboys
28 1994 (XXVIII) 10.00 20.00
{Buffalo Bills
Dallas Cowboys
29 1995 (XXIX) 10.00 20.00
San Fransisco 49ers
San Diego Chargers
30 1996 (XXX) 10.00 20.00
Pittsburgh Steelers
Dallas Cowboys
31 1997 (XXXI) 10.00 20.00
Green Bay Packers
New England Patriots
32 1998 (XXXII) 10.00 20.00
{Denver Broncos
Green Bay Packers
33 1999 (XXXIII) 10.00 20.00
{Denver Broncos
Atlanta Falcons
34 2000 (XXXIV) 10.00 20.00
{St Louis Rams
Tennessee Titans
35 2001 (XXXV) 10.00 20.00
{Baltimore Ravens
New York Giants
36 2002 (XXXVI) 10.00 20.00
New England Patriots
St.Louis Rams

1937-04 Cotton Bowl Programs

1 1937 TCU 200.00 400.00
Marquette
2 1938 Rice 150.00 300.00
Colorado
3 1939 Texas Tech 150.00 300.00
St. Mary's (Cal)
4 1940 Clemson 150.00 300.00
Boston College
5 1941 Texas A and M 162.50 325.00
Fordham
6 1942 Texas A and M 150.00 300.00
Alabama
7 1943 Texas 150.00 300.00
Georgia Tech
8 1944 Texas 125.00 250.00
Randolph Field
9 1945 Oklahoma State 125.00 250.00
TCU
10 1946 Texas 112.50 225.00
Missouri
11 1947 Arkansas 112.50 225.00
LSU
12 1948 SMU 100.00 200.00
Penn State
13 1949 SMU 100.00 200.00
Oregon
14 1950 Rice 75.00 150.00
North Carolina
15 1951 Texas 75.00 150.00
Tennessee
16 1952 TCU 62.50 125.00
Kentucky
17 1953 Texas 60.00 120.00
Tennessee
18 1954 Rice 60.00 120.00
Alabama
19 1955 Arkansas 50.00 100.00
Georgia Tech
20 1956 TCU 50.00 100.00
Mississippi
21 1957 TCU 50.00 100.00
Rice
22 1958 Rice 50.00 100.00
Navy
23 1959 TCU 37.50 75.00
Air Force
24 1960 Texas 50.00 100.00
Syracuse
25 1961 Arkansas 37.50 75.00
Duke
26 1962 Texas 37.50 75.00
Mississippi
27 1963 Texas 37.50 75.00
LSU
28 1964 Texas 37.50 75.00
Navy
29 1965 Arkansas 30.00 60.00
Nebraska
30 1966 Arkansas 30.00 60.00
LSU
31 1967 Georgia 30.00 60.00
Wyoming
32 1968 Texas A and M 25.00 50.00
Alabama
33 1969 Texas 25.00 50.00
Tennessee
34 1970 Texas 37.50 75.00
Notre Dame
35 1971 Texas 37.50 75.00
Notre Dame
36 1972 Texas 30.00 60.00
Penn State
37 1973 Texas 25.00 50.00
Alabama
38 1974 Texas 25.00 50.00
Nebraska
39 1975 Baylor 20.00 40.00
Penn State
40 1976 Arkansas 25.00 50.00
Georgia
41 1977 Houston 25.00 50.00
Notre Dame
42 1978 Texas 37.50 75.00
Notre Dame
43 1979 Houston 50.00 100.00
Notre Dame
44 1980 Houston 12.50 25.00
Nebraska
45 1981-PRESENT 7.50 15.00

1937-04 Cotton Bowl Ticket Stubs

Complete tickets are valued double the prices listed below. Pre-War complete tickets are valued even higher.

1 1937 TCU 150.00 250.00
Marquette
2 1938 Rice 100.00 175.00
Colorado
3 1939 Texas Tech 100.00 175.00
St. Mary's (Cal)
4 1940 Clemson 100.00 175.00
Boston College
5 1941 Texas A and M 100.00 175.00
Fordham
6 1942 Texas A and M 100.00 175.00
Alabama
7 1943 Texas 90.00 150.00
Georgia Tech
8 1944 Texas 90.00 150.00
Randolph Field
9 1945 Oklahoma State 75.00 125.00
TCU
10 1946 Texas 60.00 100.00
Missouri
11 1947 Arkansas 75.00 125.00
LSU
12 1948 SMU 40.00 75.00
Penn State
13 1949 SMU 40.00 75.00
Oregon
14 1950 Rice 30.00 60.00
North Carolina
15 1951 Texas 35.00 60.00
Tennessee
16 1952 TCU 30.00 60.00
Kentucky
17 1953 Texas 30.00 60.00
Tennessee
18 1954 Rice 30.00 60.00
Alabama
19 1955 Arkansas 25.00 50.00
Georgia Tech
20 1956 TCU 30.00 60.00
Mississippi
21 1957 TCU 30.00 60.00
Rice
22 1958 Rice 37.50 75.00
Navy
23 1959 TCU 25.00 50.00
Air Force
24 1960 Texas 37.50 75.00
Syracuse
25 1961 Arkansas 25.00 50.00
Duke
26 1962 Texas 25.00 50.00
Mississippi
27 1963 Texas 25.00 50.00
LSU
28 1964 Texas 25.00 50.00
Navy
29 1965 Arkansas 20.00 40.00
Nebraska
30 1966 Arkansas 25.00 50.00
LSU
31 1967 Georgia 25.00 50.00
Wyoming
32 1968 Texas A and M 20.00 40.00
Alabama
33 1969 Texas 17.50 35.00
Tennessee
34 1970 Texas 40.00 80.00
Notre Dame
35 1971 Texas 40.00 80.00
Notre Dame
36 1972 Texas 25.00 50.00
Penn State
37 1973 Texas 25.00 50.00
Alabama
38 1974 Texas 25.00 50.00
Nebraska
39 1975 Baylor 15.00 30.00
Penn State
40 1976 Arkansas 12.50 25.00
Georgia
41 1977 Houston 12.50 25.00
Notre Dame
42 1978 Texas 25.00 50.00
Notre Dame
43 1979 Houston 37.50 75.00
Notre Dame
44 1980 Houston 12.50 25.00
Nebraska
45 1981-PRESENT 10.00 20.00

1931-53 Football Illustrated (College)

1 1931 Illustration 90.00 150.00
2 1932 Illustration 40.00 75.00
3 1933 Illustration 35.00 60.00
4 1934 Illustration 25.00 50.00
5 1935 Illustration 25.00 50.00
6 1936 Illustration 25.00 40.00
7 1937 Illustration 25.00 40.00
8 1938 Illustration 25.00 40.00
9 1939 Illustration 25.00 40.00
10 1940 Illustration 20.00 35.00
11 1941 Illustration 20.00 35.00
12 1942 Frank Sinkwich 20.00 35.00
13 1943 Doug Kenna 20.00 35.00
14 1944 Joe Sullivan 20.00 35.00
15 1945 Joe Haskett 20.00 35.00
16 1946 Herman Wedemeyer 20.00 35.00
17 1947 Bobby Layne 30.00 50.00
18 1948 Chuck Bednarik 30.00 50.00
19 1949 Jim Owens 20.00 40.00
20 1950 Billy Cox 20.00 35.00
21 1951 Les Richter 20.00 35.00
22 1952 Bob Kennedy 20.00 35.00
23 1953 Illustration 18.00 30.00

1935-04 Orange Bowl Programs

1 1935 Bucknell 250.00 500.00
Miami
2 1936 Mississippi 150.00 300.00
Catholic U.
3 1937 Mississippi State 137.50 275.00
Duquesne
4 1938 Auburn 125.00 250.00
Michigan State
5 1939 Tennessee 150.00 300.00
Oklahoma
6 1940 Georgia Tech 137.50 275.00
Missouri
7 1941 Mississippi St. 125.00 250.00
Georgetown
8 1942 Georgia 125.00 250.00
TCU
9 1943 Alabama 125.00 250.00
Boston College
10 1944 LSU 112.50 225.00
Texas A and M
11 1945 Georgia Tech 100.00 200.00
Tulsa
12 1946 Miami 100.00 200.00
Holy Cross
13 1947 Tennessee 75.00 150.00
Rice
14 1948 Georgia Tech 62.50 125.00
Kansas
15 1949 Georgia 50.00 100.00
Texas
16 1950 Kentucky 50.00 100.00
Santa Clara
17 1951 Miami 62.50 125.00
Clemson
18 1952 Georgia Tech 50.00 100.00
Baylor
19 1953 Alabama 50.00 100.00
Syracuse
20 1954 Maryland 50.00 100.00
Oklahoma
21 1955 Duke 75.00 150.00
Nebraska
22 1956 Maryland 50.00 100.00
Oklahoma
23 1957 Clemson 50.00 100.00
Colorado
24 1958 Duke 50.00 100.00
Oklahoma
25 1959 Syracuse 50.00 100.00
Oklahoma
26 1960 Georgia 37.50 75.00
Missouri
27 1961 Navy 37.50 75.00
Missouri
28 1962 LSU 37.50 75.00
Colorado
29 1963 Alabama 30.00 60.00
Oklahoma
30 1964 Auburn 30.00 60.00
Nebraska
31 1965 Alabama 50.00 100.00
Texas
32 1966 Alabama 30.00 60.00
Nebraska
33 1967 Florida 25.00 50.00
Georgia Tech
34 1968 Tennessee 25.00 50.00
Oklahoma
35 1969 Penn State 25.00 50.00
Kansas
36 1970 Penn State 20.00 40.00
Missouri
37 1971 LSU 17.50 35.00
Nebraska
38 1972 Alabama 17.50 35.00
Nebraska
39 1973 Notre Dame 17.50 35.00
Nebraska
40 1974 LSU 17.50 35.00
Penn State
41 1975 Alabama 17.50 35.00
Notre Dame
42 1976 Oklahoma 15.00 30.00
Michigan
43 1977 Ohio State 15.00 30.00
Colorado
44 1978 Arkansas 12.50 25.00
Oklahoma
45 1979 Oklahoma 10.00 20.00
Nebraska
46 1980 Oklahoma 10.00 20.00
Florida State
47 1981-PRESENT 7.50 15.00

1935-04 Orange Bowl Ticket Stubs

1 1935 Bucknell 150.00 300.00
Miami
2 1936 Mississippi 75.00 150.00
Catholic U.
3 1937 Mississippi State 75.00 150.00
Duquesne
4 1938 Auburn 75.00 150.00
Michigan State
5 1939 Tennessee 87.50 175.00
Oklahoma
6 1940 Georgia Tech 62.50 125.00
Missouri
7 1941 Mississippi St. 50.00 100.00
Georgetown
8 1942 Georgia 62.50 125.00
TCU
9 1943 Alabama 62.50 125.00
Boston College
10 1944 LSU 50.00 100.00
Texas A and M
11 1945 Georgia Tech 37.50 75.00
Tulsa
12 1946 Miami 37.50 75.00
Holy Cross
13 1947 Tennessee 37.50 75.00
Rice
14 1948 Georgia Tech 37.50 75.00
Kansas
15 1949 Georgia 30.00 60.00
Texas
16 1950 Kentucky 30.00 60.00
Santa Clara
17 1951 Miami 30.00 60.00
Clemson
18 1952 Georgia Tech 30.00 60.00
Baylor
19 1953 Alabama 30.00 60.00
Syracuse
20 1954 Maryland 30.00 60.00
Oklahoma
21 1955 Duke 37.50 75.00
Nebraska
22 1956 Maryland 30.00 60.00
Oklahoma
23 1957 Clemson 30.00 60.00
Colorado
24 1958 Duke 30.00 60.00
Oklahoma
25 1959 Syracuse 37.50 75.00
Oklahoma
26 1960 Georgia 25.00 50.00
Missouri
27 1961 Navy 25.00 50.00
Missouri
28 1962 LSU 25.00 50.00
Colorado
29 1963 Alabama 25.00 50.00
Oklahoma
30 1964 Auburn 20.00 40.00
Nebraska
31 1965 Alabama 37.50 75.00
Texas
32 1966 Alabama 30.00 60.00
Nebraska
33 1967 Florida 20.00 40.00
Georgia Tech
34 1968 Tennessee 20.00 40.00
Oklahoma
35 1969 Penn State 20.00 40.00
Kansas
36 1970 Penn State 15.00 30.00
Missouri
37 1971 LSU 15.00 30.00
Nebraska
38 1972 Alabama 15.00 30.00
Nebraska
39 1973 Notre Dame 20.00 40.00
Nebraska
40 1974 LSU 17.50 35.00
Penn State
41 1975 Alabama 20.00 40.00
Notre Dame
42 1976 Oklahoma 12.50 25.00
Michigan
43 1977 Ohio State 12.50 25.00
Colorado
44 1978 Arkansas 12.50 25.00
Oklahoma
45 1979 Oklahoma 12.50 25.00
Nebraska
46 1980 Oklahoma 12.50 25.00
Florida State
47 1981-PRESENT 10.00 20.00

1902-07 Rose Bowl Programs

Pre-war bowl programs and ticket stubs are rarely found in Nr-Mt condition. These programs and ticket stubs are graded at Ex-Mt and Ex condition.

1 1902 Stanford Michigan	1,000.00	15,000.00
2 1916 Wash. State Brown	1,250.00	2,500.00
3 1917 Oregon Penn.	750.00	1,500.00
4 1918 Mare Isle. Camp Lewis	600.00	1,200.00
5 1919 Mare Isle Great Lakes	600.00	1,200.00
6 1920 Oregon Harvard	500.00	1,000.00
7 1921 California Ohio State	600.00	1,200.00
8 1922 California Washington and Jefferson	500.00	1,000.00
9 1923 USC Penn State	750.00	1,500.00
10 1924 Washington Navy	500.00	1,000.00
11 1925 Stan. Notre Dame	900.00	1,800.00
12 1926 Washington Alabama	600.00	1,200.00
13 1927 Stanford Alabama	600.00	1,000.00
14 1928 Stanford Pittsburgh	350.00	700.00
15 1929 Cal. Georgia Tech	500.00	1,000.00
16 1930 USC Pittsburgh	400.00	750.00
17 1931 Wash. St Alabama	900.00	1,400.00
18 1932 USC Tulane	250.00	500.00
19 1933 USC Pittsburgh	250.00	500.00
20 1934 Stanford Columbia	300.00	600.00
21 1935 Stanford Alabama	250.00	500.00
22 1936 Stanford LSU	175.00	350.00
23 1937 Washington Pittsburgh	150.00	300.00
24 1938 California Alabama	150.00	300.00
25 1939 USC Duke	125.00	250.00
26 1940 USC Tennessee	125.00	250.00
27 1941 Stanford Nebraska	125.00	250.00
28 1942 Oregon State Duke	400.00	800.00
29 1943 UCLA Georgia	150.00	300.00
30 1944 USC Washington	100.00	200.00
31 1945 USC Tennessee	87.50	175.00
32 1946 USC Alabama	75.00	150.00
33 1947 UCLA Illinois	75.00	150.00
34 1948 USC Michigan	75.00	150.00
35 1949 Cal. Northwestern	62.50	125.00
36 1950 California Ohio State	62.50	125.00
37 1951 California Michigan	62.50	125.00
38 1952 Stanford Illinois	50.00	100.00
39 1953 UCLA Wisconsin	50.00	100.00
40 1954 UCLA Michigan State	50.00	100.00
41 1955 USC Ohio State	50.00	100.00
42 1956 UCLA Michigan State	37.50	75.00
43 1957 Oregon State Iowa	30.00	60.00
44 1958 Oregon Ohio State	37.50	75.00
45 1959 California Iowa	30.00	60.00
46 1960 Washington Wisconsin	30.00	60.00
47 1961 Washington Minnesota	25.00	50.00
48 1962 UCLA Minnesota	25.00	50.00
49 1963 USC Wisconsin	37.50	75.00
50 1964 Washington Illinois	25.00	50.00
51 1965 Oregon State Michigan	25.00	50.00
52 1966 UCLA Michigan State	30.00	60.00
53 1967 USC Purdue	25.00	50.00
54 1968 USC Indiana	37.50	75.00
55 1969 USC Ohio State	25.00	50.00
56 1970 USC Michigan	17.50	35.00
57 1971 Stanford Ohio State	17.50	35.00
58 1972 Stanford Michigan	17.50	35.00
59 1973 USC Ohio State	17.50	35.00
60 1974 USC Ohio State	17.50	35.00
61 1975 USC Ohio State	17.50	35.00
62 1976 UCLA Ohio State	12.50	25.00
63 1977 USC Michigan	12.50	25.00
64 1978 Washington Michigan	12.50	25.00
65 1979 USC Michigan	10.00	20.00
66 1980 USC Ohio State	10.00	20.00
67 1981-PRESENT	7.50	15.00

1902-04 Rose Bowl Ticket Stubs

1 1902 Stanford Michigan	1,500.00	3,000.00
2 1916 Wash. State Brown	600.00	1,200.00
3 1917 Oregon Penn.	375.00	750.00
4 1918 Mare Isle Camp Lewis	300.00	600.00
5 1919 Mare Isle Great Lakes	300.00	600.00
6 1920 Oregon Harvard	250.00	500.00
7 1921 California Ohio State	300.00	600.00
8 1922 Cal. Wash.&Jeff.	250.00	500.00
9 1923 USC Penn State	375.00	750.00
10 1924 Washington Navy	250.00	500.00
11 1925 Stan. Notre Dame	450.00	900.00
12 1926 Washington Alabama	250.00	500.00
13 1927 Stanford Alabama	175.00	350.00
14 1928 Stanford Pittsburgh	150.00	300.00
15 1929 Cal. Georgia Tech	150.00	300.00
16 1930 USC Pittsburgh	150.00	300.00
17 1931 Wash. St. alabama	250.00	500.00
18 1932 USC Tulane	125.00	250.00
19 1933 USC Pittsburgh	125.00	250.00
20 1934 Stanford Columbia	125.00	250.00
21 1935 Stanford Alabama	100.00	200.00
22 1936 Stanford LSU	75.00	150.00
23 1937 Wash Pittsburgh	50.00	100.00
24 1938 California Alabama	62.50	125.00
25 1939 USC Duke	62.50	125.00
26 1940 USC Tennessee	50.00	100.00
27 1941 Stanford Nebraska	200.00	400.00
28 1942 Oregon State Duke	100.00	200.00
29 1943 UCLA Georgia	37.50	75.00
30 1944 USC Washington	37.50	75.00
31 1945 USC Tennessee	37.50	75.00
32 1946 USC Alabama	37.50	75.00
33 1947 UCLA Illinois	37.50	75.00
34 1948 USC Michigan	30.00	60.00
35 1949 Cal. Northwestern	30.00	60.00
36 1950 California Ohio State	37.50	75.00
37 1951 California Michigan	37.50	75.00
38 1952 Stanford Illinois	30.00	60.00
39 1953 UCLA Wisconsin	30.00	60.00
40 1954 UCLA Michigan State	30.00	60.00
41 1955 USC Ohio State	30.00	60.00
42 1956 UCLA Michigan State	25.00	50.00
43 1957 Oregon State Iowa	20.00	40.00
44 1958 Oregon Ohio State	25.00	50.00
45 1959 California Iowa	25.00	50.00
46 1960 Washington Wisconsin	25.00	50.00
47 1961 Washington Minnesota	20.00	40.00
48 1962 UCLA Minnesota	20.00	40.00
49 1963 USC Wisconsin	25.00	50.00
50 1964 Washington Illinois	20.00	40.00
51 1965 Oregon State Michigan	20.00	40.00
52 1966 UCLA Michigan State	20.00	40.00
53 1967 USC Purdue	15.00	30.00
54 1968 USC Indiana	25.00	50.00
55 1969 USC Ohio State	25.00	50.00
56 1970 USC Michigan	15.00	30.00
57 1971 Stanford Ohio State	15.00	30.00
58 1972 Stanford Michigan	15.00	30.00
59 1973 USC Ohio State	15.00	30.00
60 1974 USC Ohio State	12.50	25.00
61 1975 USC Ohio State	12.50	25.00
62 1976 UCLA Ohio State	12.50	25.00
63 1977 USC Michigan	12.50	25.00
64 1978 Washington Michigan	12.50	25.00
65 1979 USC Michigan	12.50	25.00
66 1980 USC Ohio State	12.50	25.00
67 1981-PRESENT	10.00	20.00

1940-04 Street and Smith's College Football Yearbook

1 1940 Illustration	125.00	250.00
2 1941 Frankie Albert	62.50	125.00
3 1942 Allen Cameron	50.00	100.00
4 1943 Steve Juzwik	37.50	75.00
5 1944 Bob Kelly	37.50	75.00
6 1945 Bob Jenkins	37.50	75.00
7 1946 John Ferraro	30.00	60.00
8 1947 George Connor	37.50	75.00
9 1948 Jack Cloud	30.00	60.00
10 1949 Charley Justice	37.50	75.00
11 1950 Leon Heath	25.00	50.00
12 1951 Bob Smith	25.00	50.00
13 1952 Johnny Olszewski	25.00	50.00
14 1953 Ike Eisenhower	25.00	50.00
15 1954 Ralph Guglielmi	25.00	50.00
16 1955 Howard Cassidy	25.00	50.00
17 1956 Jim Swink	20.00	40.00
18 1957 Clendon Thomas	20.00	40.00
19 1958 Bob White	20.00	40.00
20 1959 Notre Dame	25.00	50.00
21 1960 Rich Mayo	20.00	40.00
22 1961 Ronnie Bull	20.00	40.00
23 1962 Jay Wilkerson	17.50	35.00
24 1963 Pete Beathard	17.50	35.00
25 1963 Paul Martha	17.50	35.00
26 1963 Tom Myers	15.00	30.00
27 1964 Dick Butkus	20.00	40.00
28 1964 Craig Morton	15.00	30.00
29 1964 Roger Staubach	20.00	40.00
30 1965 Roger Bird	12.50	25.00
31 1965 Ray Handley	12.50	25.00
32 1965 Phil Sheridan	12.50	25.00
33 1966 Bob Griese	15.00	30.00
34 1967 Ron Drake	12.50	25.00
35 1967 Terry Hanratty	12.50	25.00
36 1967 Ted Hendricks	15.00	30.00
37 1968 Chris Gilbert	12.50	25.00
38 1968 Larry Smith	12.50	25.00
39 1969 Rex Kern	12.50	25.00
40 1969 Steve Kiner	12.50	25.00
41 1970 Archie Manning	15.00	30.00
42 1970 Jim Plunkett	15.00	30.00
43 1970 Steve Worcester	10.00	20.00
44 1971 Joe Ferguson	10.00	20.00
45 1971 Sonny Sixkiller	10.00	20.00
46 1971 Pat Sullivan	10.00	20.00
47 1972 Pete Adams	10.00	20.00
48 1972 John Hufnagel	10.00	20.00
49 1972 Brad Van Pelt	10.00	20.00
50 1973 Champ Henson	7.50	15.00
51 1973 Kermit Johnson	7.50	15.00
52 1973 Wayne Wheeler	7.50	15.00
53 1974 Tom Clements	7.50	15.00
54 1974 Brad Davis	7.50	15.00
55 1974 Pat Haden	9.00	18.00
56 1975 Archie Griffin	10.00	20.00
57 1975 Richard Todd	7.50	15.00
58 1975 John Sciarra	7.50	15.00
59 1976 Ricky Bell	7.50	15.00
60 1976 Tony Dorsett	10.00	20.00
61 1976 Rob Lytle	7.50	15.00
62 1977 Guy Benjamin	7.50	15.00
63 1977 Ken McAfee	7.50	15.00
64 1977 Ben Zambiasi	7.50	15.00
65 1978 Rick Leach	7.50	15.00
66 1978 Jeff Rutledge	7.50	15.00
67 1978 Jack Thompson	7.50	15.00
68 1979 Mark Hermann	7.50	15.00
69 1979 Jeff Pyburn	6.00	12.00
70 1979 Charles White	7.50	15.00
71 1980 Rick Campbell	6.00	12.00
72 1980 Art Schlichter	6.00	12.00
73 1980 Scott Woener	6.00	12.00
74 1981 Anthony Carter Bob Crable	7.50	15.00
75 1981 John Elway	12.50	25.00
76 1981 Dan Marino Joe Morris	12.50	25.00
77 1981 Herschel Walker Bear Bryant	10.00	20.00
78 1982 Tony Eason Marcus Marek	7.50	15.00
79 1982 John Elway	12.50	25.00
80 1982 Dan Marino Curt Warner	10.00	20.00
81 1982 Herschel Walker	7.50	15.00
82 1983 Marcus Dupree	6.00	12.00
83 1983 Ken Jackson	6.00	12.00
84 1983 Johnny Robinson	6.00	12.00
85 1983 Mike Rozier	6.00	12.00
86 1984 Jack Del Rio	6.00	12.00
87 1984 Doug Flutie	7.50	15.00
88 1984 Bo Jackson	7.50	15.00
89 1984 Jack Trudeau	6.00	12.00
90 1985 Robie Bosco	5.00	10.00
91 1985 Keith Byers	5.00	10.00
92 1985 D.J. Dozier	5.00	10.00
93 1985 Jeff Wickersham	5.00	10.00
94 1986-PRESENT	5.00	10.00

1935-04 Sugar Bowl Programs

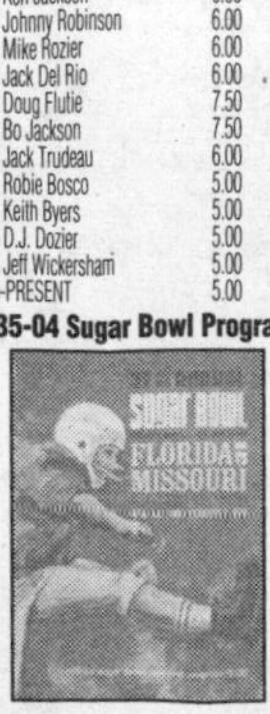

1 1935 Tulane Temple	450.00	900.00
2 1936 LSU TCU	300.00	600.00
3 1937 LSU Santa Clara	300.00	600.00
4 1938 LSU Santa Clara	250.00	500.00
5 1939 TCU Carnegie Tech.	175.00	350.00
6 1940 Texas A and M Tulane	150.00	300.00
7 1941 Tennessee Boston College	125.00	250.00
8 1942 Missouri Fordham	87.50	175.00
9 1943 Tennessee Tulsa	87.50	175.00
10 1944 Georgia Tech Tulsa	87.50	175.00
11 1945 Alabama Duke	75.00	150.00
12 1946 Oklahoma A and M St. Mary's	75.00	150.00
13 1947 Georgia North Carolina	75.00	150.00
14 1948 Alabama Texas	87.50	175.00
15 1949 Oklahoma North Carolina	75.00	150.00
16 1950 Oklahoma LSU	62.50	125.00
17 1951 Oklahoma Kentucky	62.50	125.00
18 1952 Tennessee Maryland	50.00	100.00
19 1953 Mississippi Georgia Tech	50.00	100.00
20 1954 Georgia Tech West Virginia	50.00	100.00
21 1955 Mississippi Navy	37.50	100.00
22 1956 Georgia Tech Pittsburgh	37.50	100.00
23 1957 Tennessee Baylor	37.50	100.00
24 1958 Mississippi LSU	60.00	100.00
25 1959 LSU Clemson	37.50	100.00
26 1960 Mississippi LSU	60.00	100.00
27 1961 Mississippi Rice	30.00	75.00
28 1962 Alabama Arkansas	30.00	75.00
29 1963 Mississippi Arkansas	25.00	60.00
30 1964 Mississippi Alabama	30.00	60.00
31 1965 LSU Syracuse	25.00	50.00
32 1966 Florida Missouri	25.00	60.00
33 1967 Alabama Nebraska	30.00	60.00
34 1968 LSU Wyoming	20.00	40.00
35 1969 Georgia Arkansas	20.00	40.00
36 1970 Mississippi Arkansas	20.00	40.00
37 1971 Tennessee Air Force	17.50	35.00
38 1972 Auburn Oklahoma	17.50	35.00
39 1973 Oklahoma Penn State	17.50	35.00
40 1974 Alabama Notre Dame	20.00	40.00
41 1975 Florida Nebraska	15.00	30.00
42 1976 Alabama Penn State	15.00	30.00
43 1977 Georgia Pittsburgh	15.00	30.00
44 1978 Alabama Ohio State	10.00	20.00
45 1979 Alabama Penn State	15.00	30.00
46 1980 Alabama Arkansas	10.00	20.00
47 1981-PRESENT	7.50	15.00

1935-04 Sugar Bowl Ticket Stubs

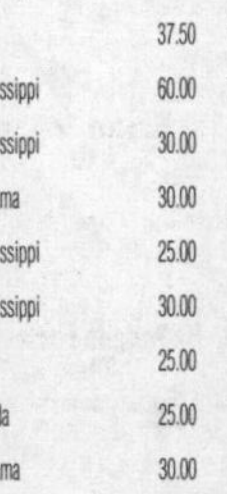

1 1935 Tulane Temple	250.00	500.00
2 1936 LSU TCU	150.00	300.00
3 1937 LSU Santa Clara	125.00	250.00
4 1938 LSU Santa Clara	75.00	150.00
5 1939 TCU Carnegie Tech.	75.00	150.00
6 1940 Texas A and M Tulane	62.50	125.00
7 1941 Tennessee Boston College	50.00	100.00
8 1942 Missouri Fordham	62.50	125.00
9 1943 Tennessee Tulsa	50.00	100.00
10 1944 Georgia Tech Tulsa	37.50	75.00
11 1945 Alabama Duke	37.50	75.00
12 1946 Okla. A & M St. Mary's	37.50	75.00
13 1947 Georgia North Carolina	37.50	75.00
14 1948 Alabama Texas	50.00	100.00
15 1949 Oklahoma North Carolina	37.50	75.00
16 1950 Oklahoma LSU	37.50	75.00
17 1951 Oklahoma Kentucky	30.00	60.00
18 1952 Tennessee Maryland	30.00	60.00
19 1953 Mississippi Georgia Tech	30.00	60.00
20 1954 Georgia Tech West Virginia	30.00	60.00
21 1955 Mississippi Navy	25.00	50.00
22 1956 Georgia Tech Pittsburgh	30.00	60.00
23 1957 Tennessee Baylor	25.00	50.00
24 1958 Mississippi LSU	30.00	60.00
25 1959 LSU Clemson	37.50	75.00
26 1960 Mississippi LSU	25.00	50.00
27 1961 Mississippi Rice	20.00	40.00
28 1962 Alabama Arkansas	25.00	50.00
29 1963 Mississippi Arkansas	25.00	50.00
30 1964 Mississippi Alabama	25.00	50.00
31 1965 LSU Syracuse	25.00	50.00
32 1966 Florida Missouri	25.00	50.00
33 1967 Alabama Nebraska	25.00	50.00
34 1968 LSU Wyoming	20.00	40.00
35 1969 Georgia Arkansas	20.00	40.00
36 1970 Mississippi Arkansas	20.00	40.00
37 1971 Tennessee Air Force	15.00	30.00
38 1972 Auburn Oklahoma	15.00	30.00
39 1973 Oklahoma Penn State	20.00	40.00
40 1974 Alabama Notre Dame	20.00	40.00
41 1975 Florida Nebraska	15.00	30.00
42 1976 Alabama Penn State	15.00	30.00
43 1977 Georgia Pittsburgh	15.00	30.00
44 1978 Alabama Ohio State	12.50	25.00
45 1979 Alabama Penn State	12.50	25.00
46 1980 Alabama Arkansas	12.50	25.00
47 1981-PRESENT	10.00	20.00

1997 All-Star MVPs Football

10 Dallas Cowboys	15.00	30.00
Jay Novacek		
Troy Aikman		
Emmitt Smith		
Michael Irving		
Deion Sanders		
20 Denver Broncos	10.00	20.00
John Elway		
Shannon Sharpe		
Terrell Davis		
Steve Atwater		
Bill Romanowski		
30 Green Bay Packers	10.00	20.00
Reggie White		
Brett Favre		
Edgar Bennett		
Mark Chmura		
Keith Jackson		
40 Kansas City Chiefs	10.00	20.00
Marcus Allen		
Elvis Grbac		
Keith Cash		
Kimble Anders		
Derrick Thomas		
50 Miami Dolphins	10.00	20.00
O.J. McDuffie		
Dan Marino		
Karim Abdul-Jabbar		
Tim Bowens		
Keith Sims		
60 New England Patriots	10.00	20.00
Drew Bledsoe		
Keith Byars		
Dave Meggett		
Curtis Martin		
Ben Coates		
70 Pittsburgh Steelers	10.00	20.00
Greg Lloyd		
Yancey Thigpen		
Rod Woodson		
Kordell Stewart		
Jerome Bettis		
80 San Francisco 49ers	10.00	20.00
Merton Hanks		
Steve Young		
Ken Norton Jr.		
Jerry Rice		
Brent Jones		

1966 Aurora Sports Model Kits

This set of six plastic models was released in 1966. Each model, when fully assembled, measures approx. 6" high. Prices below are for complete, unbuilt models accompanied by the box. Model kits still in factory wrapped boxes are considered to be Nr-Mt-Mt . Built-up models minus the box are valued at 20 to 50 percent of the Nr-Mt prices below.

1 Jim Brown	60.00	150.00
2 Jack Dempsey	30.00	75.00
5 Johnny Unitas	40.00	100.00

1997 Best Heroes of the Gridiron

1 Ki-Jana Carter	3.00	8.00
2 Marshall Faulk	6.00	15.00
3 Brett Favre	6.00	15.00
4 Desmond Howard	5.00	12.00
5 Dan Marino	8.00	20.00
6 Herman Moore	3.00	8.00
7 Errict Rhett	3.00	8.00
8 Deion Sanders	5.00	12.00
9 Derrick Thomas	5.00	12.00
10 Herschel Walker	4.00	10.00
11 Reggie White	4.00	10.00
12 Rod Woodson	3.00	8.00

1961-62 Bobbin Heads Football AFL Toes Up

This set is identified by the distinctive "toes up" pose of the players. The Dolls are standing on a ceramic round base painted in the color of the jersey. A city name and team name decal is usually applied with one on the jersey and the other on the base. However, they can often be found with only one or no decal(s) at all. Dolls still in original boxes are worth approximately 1.5 times the value of loose pieces.

1 Boston Patriots	350.00	600.00
2 Buffalo Bills	350.00	600.00
3 Dallas Texans	1,000.00	1,800.00
4 Denver Broncos	350.00	600.00
5 Houston Oilers	350.00	600.00
6 New York Titans	1,000.00	1,800.00
7 Oakland Raiders	500.00	800.00
8 San Diego Chargers	350.00	600.00

1961-62 Bobbin Heads Football NFL Square Base Ceramic

The statues in this series feature boy-like faces and have a ceramic molded base painted in varying colors. There are two distinct varieties of ceramic base dolls in this group. The first version includes a raised molded lettering on the "N.F.L." notation on the base. The second includes a gold NFL shield decal on top of the base instead of the molded raised lettering. Both versions of each team are valued roughly the same. Note that the Vikings were added to this second and third version of the initial NFL Bobbin Heads. Dolls still in original boxes are worth approximately 1.5 times the value of loose pieces.

1 Baltimore Colts	75.00	150.00
2 Chicago Bears	75.00	150.00
3 Cleveland Browns	100.00	200.00
4 Dallas Cowboys	150.00	250.00
5 Detroit Lions	75.00	150.00
6 Green Bay Packers	75.00	150.00
7 Los Angeles Rams	75.00	150.00
8 Minnesota Vikings	100.00	200.00
9 New York Giants	75.00	150.00
10 Philadelphia Eagles	75.00	125.00
11 Pittsburgh Steelers	100.00	200.00
12 San Francisco 49ers	75.00	150.00
13 St.Louis Cardinals	75.00	150.00
14 Washington Redskins	175.00	300.00

1960-61 Bobbin Heads Football NFL Square Base Wood

The statues in this series feature boy-like faces and various colored bases. Each were produced with a wooden base glued onto the figure. Dolls still in original boxes are worth approximately 1.5 times the value of loose pieces.

1 Baltimore Colts	90.00	150.00
2 Chicago Bears	90.00	150.00
3 Cleveland Browns	125.00	200.00
4 Dallas Cowboys	175.00	300.00
5 Detroit Lions	90.00	150.00
6 Green Bay Packers	150.00	250.00
7 Los Angeles Rams	90.00	150.00
8 Minnesota Vikings	90.00	150.00
9 New York Giants	90.00	150.00
10 Philadelphia Eagles	90.00	150.00
11 Philadelphia Eagles (1960 Champions)	125.00	200.00
12 Pittsburgh Steelers	125.00	200.00
13 San Francisco 49ers	90.00	150.00
14 St.Louis Cardinals	90.00	150.00
15 Washington Redskins	200.00	350.00

1962-64 Bobbin Heads Football NFL Square Base Black Player

These statues are similar to the 1961-62 NFL Square Ceramic Base set, albeit much tougher to find. Note that not all teams were issued in the black player version. Dolls still in original boxes are worth approximately 1.5 times the value of loose pieces.

1 Baltimore Colts	350.00	600.00
2 Chicago Bears	500.00	800.00
3 Cleveland Browns	400.00	750.00
4 Dallas Cowboys	800.00	1,200.00
5 Detroit Lions	400.00	750.00
6 Green Bay Packers	600.00	1,000.00
7 Los Angeles Rams	350.00	600.00
8 Minnesota Vikings	350.00	600.00
9 New York Giants	350.00	600.00
10 Philadelphia Eagles	350.00	600.00
11 Pittsburgh Steelers	400.00	750.00
12 San Francisco 49ers	350.00	600.00
13 St. Louis Cardinals	350.00	600.00
14 Washington Redskins	1,000.00	1,800.00

1962-64 Bobbin Heads Football NFL Toes Up

This set is identified by the distinctive "toes up" pose of the players. These bobbin' heads were issued over a period of years with at least 4-distinct production runs or versions. The first and second groups were produced with a painted base that matches the team colors. A city name decal was affixed to the base and printed in slightly smaller letters than the third and fourth versions. The player can be found holding the football vertically (first version) or horizontally (second version). The third and fourth groups feature the same doll with a gold painted base and a slightly larger print on the city name decal. The doll's face is also slightly different between the first two versions and third and fourth. The player can be found holding the football vertically (third version) or horizontally (fourth version). Dolls still in original boxes are worth approximately 1.5 times the value of loose pieces.

1 Baltimore Colts	150.00	250.00
2 Chicago Bears	150.00	250.00
3 Cleveland Browns	250.00	350.00
4 Dallas Cowboys	400.00	700.00
5 Detroit Lions	150.00	250.00
6 Green Bay Packers	300.00	450.00
7 Los Angeles Rams	150.00	250.00
8 Minnesota Vikings	150.00	300.00
9 New York Giants	150.00	300.00
10 Philadelphia Eagles	150.00	300.00
11 Pittsburgh Steelers	150.00	300.00
12 San Francisco 49ers	150.00	300.00
13 St.Louis Cardinals	150.00	300.00
14 Washington Redskins	400.00	750.00

1965-67 Bobbin Heads: AFL 00 Gold Base

1 Boston Patriots	70.00	125.00
2 Buffalo Bills	90.00	150.00
3 Denver Broncos	75.00	125.00
4 Houston Oilers	75.00	125.00
5 Kansas City Chiefs	75.00	125.00
6 New York Jets	90.00	150.00
7 Oakland Raiders	90.00	150.00
8 San Diego Chargers	75.00	125.00

1965-67 Bobbin Heads: NFL 00 Gold Base

These statues feature a gold painted ceramic base along with the jersey number "00" on the player's shoulders. The manufacturer's sticker was produced in a football shaped design. Dolls still in original boxes are worth approximately 1.5 times the value of loose pieces.

1 Atlanta Falcons	60.00	100.00
2 Baltimore Colts	75.00	125.00
3 Chicago Bears	60.00	100.00
4 Cleveland Browns	125.00	200.00
5 Dallas Cowboys	150.00	250.00
6 Detroit Lions	60.00	100.00
7 Green Bay Packers	75.00	125.00
8 Los Angeles Rams	175.00	300.00
9 Minnesota Vikings	75.00	125.00
10 New Orleans Saints	60.00	100.00
11 New York Giants	60.00	100.00
12 Philadelphia Eagles	90.00	160.00
13 Pittsburgh Steelers	90.00	150.00
14 San Francisco 49ers	125.00	200.00
15 St.Louis Cardinals	60.00	100.00
16 Washington Redskins	150.00	250.00

1965-67 Bobbin Heads: NFL Realistic Face

This set of bobbin' heads feature more realistically sculpted faces than previous issues. They feature a gold painted base and a "00" jersey number on the shoulder. Dolls still in original boxes are worth approximately 1.5 times the value of loose pieces.

1 Atlanta Falcons	150.00	250.00
2 Baltimore Colts	175.00	300.00
3 Chicago Bears	175.00	300.00
4 Cleveland Browns	175.00	300.00
5 Dallas Cowboys	250.00	400.00
6 Detroit Lions	175.00	300.00
7 Green Bay Packers	250.00	400.00
8 Minnesota Vikings	175.00	300.00
9 New Orleans Saints	150.00	250.00
10 New York Giants	175.00	300.00
11 Philadelphia Eagles	150.00	250.00
12 St.Louis Cardinals	150.00	250.00
13 Washington Redskins	300.00	500.00

1965 Bobbin Heads Football AFL Ear Pads

This set of AFL Team Bobbin Heads includes a gold ceramic base with distinctive ear pads on the player's helmet. Dolls still in original boxes are worth approximately 1.5 times the value of loose pieces.

1 Boston Patriots	350.00	500.00
2 Buffalo Bills	400.00	600.00
3 Denver Broncos	500.00	800.00
4 Houston Oilers	350.00	500.00
5 Kansas City Chiefs	400.00	600.00
6 Miami Dolphins	400.00	600.00
7 New York Jets	400.00	600.00
8 Oakland Raiders	500.00	800.00
9 San Diego Chargers	350.00	500.00

1965 Bobbin Heads Football AFL Kissing Pairs

1 Boston Patriots	250.00	400.00
2 Buffalo Bills	300.00	500.00

1965 Bobbin Heads Football NFL Kissing Pairs

These dolls were issued two to a team, one boy (or team mascot) and one girl in a kissing pose. Prices below reflect that of a pair of dolls for each team. The girl doll can be found with either black or red hair variations on most pieces. She also is most commonly wearing a majorette's hat, but can also be found with a chef's hat variation as well. Dolls still in original boxes are worth approximately 1.5 times the value of loose pieces.

1 Baltimore Colts	250.00	400.00
2 Chicago Bears	200.00	350.00
3 Cleveland Browns (with mascot)	400.00	750.00
4 Dallas Cowboys	300.00	500.00
5 Detroit Lions	200.00	350.00
6 Green Bay Packers	300.00	500.00
7 Los Angeles Rams	200.00	350.00
8 Minnesota Vikings	250.00	400.00
9 New York Giants	250.00	400.00
10 Philadelphia Eagles	200.00	350.00
11 Pittsburgh Steelers (with mascot)	300.00	500.00
12 San Francisco 49ers	300.00	500.00
13 St.Louis Cardinals	200.00	350.00
14 Washington Redskins	350.00	600.00

1968-70 Bobbin Heads: AFL-NFL Merger Series

This series is generally considered the easiest to find of the original ceramic bobbin' head dolls. It was also the last series imported from Japan. Each features a more realistic face than many earlier sets with longer legs and smaller shoes than previous issues. The initial production run included an NFL decal between the feet of the doll. Some were issued later with an AFC decal logo instead. The manufacturer's identification sticker was produced in the shape of an circle. Dolls still in original boxes are worth approximately 1.5 times the value of loose pieces.

1 Atlanta Falcons	50.00	100.00
2 Baltimore Colts AFC	75.00	150.00
3 Baltimore Colts NFL	50.00	100.00
4 Boston Patriots	75.00	150.00
5 Buffalo Bills	100.00	200.00
6 Chicago Bears	50.00	100.00
7 Cincinnati Bengals	50.00	100.00
8 Cleveland Browns AFC	100.00	200.00
9 Cleveland Browns NFL	50.00	100.00
10 Dallas Cowboys	100.00	175.00
11 Denver Broncos	75.00	150.00
12 Detroit Lions	50.00	100.00
13 Green Bay Packers	75.00	125.00
14 Houston Oilers	50.00	100.00
15 Kansas City Chiefs	50.00	100.00
16 Los Angeles Rams	50.00	100.00
17 Miami Dolphins	100.00	200.00
18 Minnesota Vikings	50.00	100.00
19 New England Patriots	50.00	100.00
20 New Orleans Saints	50.00	100.00
21 New York Giants	50.00	100.00
22 New York Jets AFL	75.00	125.00
23 New York Jets NFL	50.00	100.00
24 Oakland Raiders	100.00	175.00
25 Philadelphia Eagles	75.00	150.00
26 Pittsburgh Steelers AFC	100.00	200.00
27 Pittsburgh Steelers NFL	75.00	150.00
28 San Diego Chargers	50.00	100.00
29 San Francisco 49ers	75.00	125.00
30 St.Louis Cardinals	50.00	100.00
31 Washington Redskins	100.00	200.00

1959-63 Hartland Statues Football

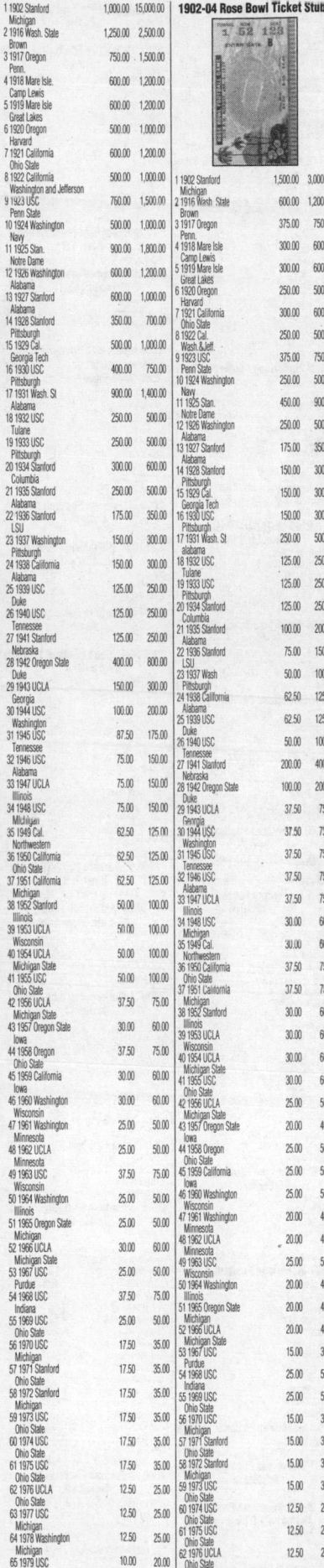

The Hartland Plastics Company of Hartland, Wisconsin first released, around 1959, a series of plastic NFL football statues similar to the ones the company had issued for baseball and TV western stars. Hartland produced 5000 Baltimore Colt quarterback figurines of Johnny Unitas -- the only quarterback produced by Hartland. Jon Arnett, the Los Angeles Rams star running back, also had 5000 statues minted and both players sold very well in their respective home markets but seemingly no where else. Therefore Hartland introduced 28 additional football players. At the time there were only 14 teams in the NFL and Hartland made a running back and a lineman each adorned in their respective team colors. They each stand on a green base that has the NFL logo and team named embossed in gold on the front of the base. In total, 5000 of each were manufactured between 1959 and 1963. The football statues were sold in a plain white cardboard box with blue and red ink printing, sketches and logos. The front panel tore away to reveal a cello panel through which one could see the figure. The top flap of the box was then stamped with a black label indicating RUNNINGBACK or LINEMAN. A sheet of uniform numbers and team decals were included inside each box. In 1958 LSU won the NCAA football championship and their star running back, Billy Cannon won the Heisman Trophy in 1959. Hartland used its running back mold and in 1962 created an LSU running back with the purple and gold emblems of the school on each shoulder as well as the orange pants. The university ordered 10,000 figures that were completely sold out by the end of the first semester. The LSU Statue is rarely seen in the hobby. A prototype quarterback from the University of Wisconsin was also produced but rejected and subsequently returned to Hartland from the university. A running back prototype was also sent to Notre Dame for consideration but the university never got back to Hartland and kept the "Fighting Irish" figurine. Prices below reflect that of loose stautes. Statues in clean boxes are worth approximately double the price of a single loose statue.

1 Bears Lineman 125.00 250.00
2 Bears Running Back 175.00 300.00
3 Browns Lineman 200.00 350.00
4 Browns Running Back 200.00 400.00
5 Cardinals Lineman 125.00 250.00
6 Cardinals Running Back 500.00 800.00
7 Colts Lineman 300.00 500.00
8 Colts Running Back 200.00 350.00
9 Cowboys Lineman 350.00 600.00
10 Cowboys Running Back 400.00 700.00
11 Eagles Lineman 125.00 250.00
12 Eagles Running Back 150.00 300.00
13 Forty-Niners Lineman 175.00 300.00
14 Forty-Niners Running Back 500.00 800.00
15 Giants Lineman 125.00 250.00
16 Giants Running Back 150.00 300.00
17 Lions Lineman 125.00 250.00
18 Lions Running Back 350.00 600.00
19 Packers Lineman 150.00 300.00
20 Packers Running Back 200.00 400.00
21 Rams Lineman 125.00 250.00
22 Rams Rinning Back 150.00 300.00
23 Redskins Lineman 600.00 1,000.00
24 Redskins Running Back 400.00 700.00
25 Steelers Lineman 175.00 300.00
26 Steelers Running Back 200.00 350.00
27 Vikings Lineman 125.00 250.00
28 Vikings Running Back 150.00 300.00
29 Jon Arnett 250.00 400.00
30 Johnny Unitas 350.00 600.00
31 LSU Lineman 1,000.00 1,500.00
32 LSU Running Back 1,200.00 2,000.00

1958-62 Kail Football 10-Inch Standing

Each figure in this series features the standing lineman pose and was produced in Japan for Fred Kail Jr. Each figure is wearing a number "00" jersey with a football at his feet, and includes a metal facemask. The bases are often found with the team name decaled on or a local sponsor name or even blank. These statues were also called "Big Joe Jolter." A smaller 5" version of each statue was also produced as well as a 10" bank and a 10" decanter version of each piece.

*BANKS: ADD $25-$50
*DECANTERS: ADD $100-$200
1 Chicago Bears 125.00 250.00
2 Cleveland Browns 125.00 250.00
3 St. Louis Cardinals 125.00 250.00
4 Baltimore Colts 125.00 250.00
5 Dallas Cowboys 400.00 600.00
6 Philadelphia Eagles 125.00 250.00
7 San Francisco 49ers 150.00 300.00
8 New York Giants 125.00 250.00
9 Detroit Lions 125.00 250.00
10 Green Bay Packers 125.00 250.00
11 Los Angeles Rams 125.00 250.00
12 Washington Redskins 500.00 800.00
13 Pittsburgh Steelers 125.00 250.00
14 Minnesota Vikings 125.00 250.00

1958-62 Kail Football 5-Inch Standing

1 Chicago Bears 100.00 200.00
2 Cleveland Browns 100.00 200.00
3 St. Louis Cardinals 100.00 200.00
4 Baltimore Colts 100.00 200.00
5 Dallas Cowboys 300.00 500.00
6 Philadelphia Eagles 100.00 200.00
7 San Francisco 49ers 125.00 250.00
8 New York Giants 100.00 200.00
9 Detroit Lions 100.00 200.00
10 Green Bay Packers 100.00 200.00
11 Los Angeles Rams 100.00 200.00
12 Washington Redskins 250.00 500.00
13 Pittsburgh Steelers 100.00 200.00
14 Minnesota Vikings 100.00 200.00

1958-62 Kail Football Large 3-Point Stance

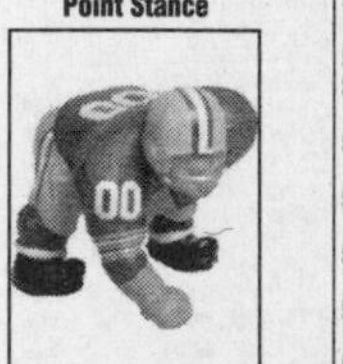

Each figure in this series features a lineman in a 3-point stance pose with each produced in Japan for Fred Kail Jr. Each figure is wearing a number "00" jersey. The bases are often found with the team name decaled on or a local sponsor name or even blank. These statues were also called "Bruce Bruiser." A smaller version of the stautues was also produced.

1 Chicago Bears 400.00 600.00
2 Cleveland Browns 400.00 600.00
3 St. Louis Cardinals 400.00 600.00
4 Baltimore Colts 400.00 600.00
5 Dallas Cowboys 1,100.00 1,800.00
6 Philadelphia Eagles 400.00 600.00
7 San Francisco 49ers 500.00 800.00
8 New York Giants 400.00 600.00
9 Detroit Lions 400.00 600.00
10 Green Bay Packers 400.00 600.00
11 Los Angeles Rams 400.00 600.00
12 Washington Redskins 1,500.00 2,000.00
13 Pittsburgh Steelers 500.00 800.00
14 Minnesota Vikings 500.00 800.00

1958-62 Kail Football Small 3-Point Stance

1 Chicago Bears 125.00 250.00
2 Cleveland Browns 125.00 250.00
3 St. Louis Cardinals 125.00 250.00
4 Baltimore Colts 125.00 250.00
5 Dallas Cowboys 400.00 600.00
6 Philadelphia Eagles 125.00 250.00
7 San Francisco 49ers 150.00 300.00
8 New York Giants 125.00 250.00
9 Detroit Lions 125.00 250.00
10 Green Bay Packers 125.00 250.00
11 Los Angeles Rams 125.00 250.00
12 Washington Redskins 500.00 800.00
13 Pittsburgh Steelers 125.00 250.00
14 Minnesota Vikings 125.00 250.00

1958-62 Kail Football Ashtrays

1 Chicago Bears 250.00 400.00
2 Cleveland Browns 250.00 400.00
3 St. Louis Cardinals 250.00 400.00
4 Baltimore Colts 250.00 400.00
5 Dallas Cowboys 600.00 1,000.00
6 Philadelphia Eagles 250.00 400.00
7 San Francisco 49ers 250.00 450.00
8 New York Giants 250.00 400.00
9 Detroit Lions 250.00 400.00
10 Green Bay Packers 250.00 400.00
11 Los Angeles Rams 250.00 400.00
12 Washington Redskins 600.00 1,000.00
13 Pittsburgh Steelers 250.00 450.00
14 Minnesota Vikings 250.00 400.00

2001 McFarlane Football Series 1-2

McFarlane's first fully licensed product, this is also the company's debut football set, comprised of twelve figures (released in two series of six figures each). Multiple variations exist, namely home and away uniforms as well as a clean (no mud/grass stains) uniform with no helmet. In Series II, a production error led to numerous clean uniform pieces being produced for standard and variant jerseys.

10 Eddie George Blue Dirty 10.00 20.00
11 Eddie George Blue Clean Variant 50.00 100.00
12 Eddie George White Dirty Variant 40.00 60.00
13 Eddie George White Clean Variant 150.00 300.00
14 Eddie George No Helmet Dirty Variant 75.00 120.00
15 Eddie George No Helmet Clean Variant 150.00 250.00
20 Edgerrin James White Dirty 12.00 30.00
21 Edgerrin James White Clean Variant 20.00 40.00
24 Edgerrin James Blue Dirty Variant 25.00 50.00
25 Edgerrin James Blue Clean Variant 75.00 150.00
26 Edgerrin James No Helmet Dirty Variant 60.00 120.00
27 Edgerrin James No Helmet Clean Variant 80.00 160.00
28 Randy Moss Purple Dirty Moss on Nameplate 10.00 20.00
29 Randy Moss Purple Clean Moss on Nameplate Variant 15.00 30.00
30 Randy Moss Purple Dirty R.Moss on Nameplate Variant 20.00 40.00
31 Randy Moss Purple Clean R.Moss on Nameplate Variant 10.00 20.00
32 Randy Moss White Dirty Moss on Nameplate Variant 20.00 40.00
33 Randy Moss White Clean Moss on Nameplate Variant 75.00 150.00
34 Randy Moss White Dirty R.Moss on Nameplate Variant
35 Randy Moss White Clean R.Moss on Nameplate Variant 50.00 80.00
36 Randy Moss Purple Dirty No Helmet Moss on Nameplate Variant 100.00 175.00
37 Randy Moss Purple Clean No Helmet Moss on Name Variantplate 150.00 250.00
38 Randy Moss White Dirty No Helmet R.Moss on Nameplate Variant
39 Randy Moss White Clean No Helmet R.Moss on Nameplate Variant
40 Warren Sapp Red Dirty 10.00 25.00
41 Warren Sapp Red Clean Variant 40.00 60.00
43 Warren Sapp White Dirty Variant 40.00 60.00
44 Warren Sapp White Clean Variant 75.00 150.00
46 Warren Sapp No Helmet Dirty Variant 50.00 100.00
47 Warren Sapp No Helmet Clean Variant 75.00 150.00
50 Emmitt Smith White Dirty 30.00 70.00
51 Emmitt Smith White Clean Variant 30.00 80.00
53 Emmitt Smith Blue with Star Dirty Variant 80.00 200.00
54 Emmitt Smith Blue with Star Clean Variant 300.00 600.00
55 Emmitt Smith Blue No Star Dirty Variant 200.00 275.00
56 Emmitt Smith Blue No Star Clean Variant 75.00 150.00
57 Emmitt Smith No Helmet Dirty Variant 300.00 425.00
58 Emmitt Smith No Helmet Clean Variant 150.00 300.00
60 Kurt Warner White Dirty 10.00 25.00
61 Kurt Warner White Clean Variant 15.00 30.00
63 Kurt Warner Blue Dirty Variant 25.00 50.00
64 Kurt Warner Blue Clean Variant 125.00 225.00
66 Kurt Warner No Helmet Dirty Variant 100.00 175.00
67 Kurt Warner No Helmet Clean Variant 125.00 200.00
100 Mark Brunell Blue 6.00 12.00
101 Mark Brunell White Variant 15.00 30.00
102 Mark Brunell No Helmet Dirty Variant 50.00 100.00
103 Mark Brunell No Helmet Clean Variant 50.00 100.00
110 Wayne Chrebet White 10.00 25.00
111 Wayne Chrebet Green Variant 30.00 60.00
112 Wayne Chrebet No Helmet Dirty Variant 60.00 120.00
113 Wayne Chrebet No Helmet Clean Variant 75.00 150.00
120 Daunte Culpepper White 6.00 12.00
121 Daunte Culpepper Purple Variant 25.00 50.00
122 Daunte Culpepper No Helmet Dirty Variant 50.00 100.00
123 Daunte Culpepper No Helmet Clean Variant 60.00 120.00
130 Marshall Faulk Blue 12.50 25.00
131 Marshall Faulk White Variant 60.00 120.00
132 Marshall Faulk No Helmet Dirty Variant 125.00 200.00
133 Marshall Faulk No Helmet Clean Variant 125.00 250.00
140 Marvin Harrison Blue 6.00 12.00
141 Marvin Harrison White Variant 30.00 50.00
142 Marvin Harrison No Helmet Dirty Variant 60.00 120.00
143 Marvin Harrison No Helmet Clean Variant 75.00 150.00
150 Brian Urlacher Blue FP 25.00 60.00
151 Brian Urlacher White Variant 100.00 200.00
152 Brian Urlacher No Helmet Dirty Variant 300.00 400.00
153 Brian Urlacher No Helmet Clean Variant 250.00 400.00

2002 McFarlane Football Series 4-5

Continuing from the 2001 Football and 2002 Rookies Sets, the 2002 season's initial offering began with the fourth officially licensed series from McFarlane. The lone First Piece in Series IV is Michael Vick, but Series V includes several: Tom Brady, Jeff Garcia, Ray Lewis, and Anthony Thomas.

COMMON PIECE 5.00 10.00
10 Brett Favre Green 10.00 20.00
11 Brett Favre White with Green Sleeves Variant 20.00 40.00
12 Brett Favre White with White Sleeves Variant 50.00 90.00
20 Peyton Manning White 10.00 25.00
21 Peyton Manning Blue Variant 12.50 25.00
30 Curtis Martin Green 8.00 20.00
31 Curtis Martin White Variant 12.50 25.00
40 Donovan McNabb Green 6.00 12.00
41 Donovan McNabb White Variant 20.00 35.00
50 Terrell Owens Red 6.00 12.00
51 Terrell Owens White Variant 20.00 40.00
60 Jason Sehorn White with Red Socks 5.00 10.00
61 Jason Sehorn White with Blue Socks Variant 12.50 25.00
62 Jason Sehorn Blue Variant 10.00 25.00
70 Michael Vick White FP 10.00 25.00
71 Michael Vick Black Variant 40.00 80.00
80 Ricky Williams Dolphins 8.00 20.00
81 Ricky Williams Saints White Socks Variant 25.00 60.00
82 Ricky Williams Saints Striped Sock Variant 150.00 300.00
100 Jerome Bettis Black 15.00 40.00
101 Jerome Bettis White Variant 40.00 100.00
110 Tom Brady White FP 20.00 50.00
111 Tom Brady Blue Variant 30.00 80.00
112 Tom Brady Blue with Snow Base Variant 175.00 350.00
120 Stephen Davis White 5.00 10.00
121 Stephen Davis Maroon Variant 30.00 60.00
130 Jeff Garcia White FP 7.50 15.00
131 Jeff Garcia Red 25.00 50.00
140 Tony Gonzalez Red FP 8.00 20.00
141 Tony Gonzalez White Variant 20.00 35.00
150 Ray Lewis White FP 15.00 30.00
151 Ray Lewis Purple Variant 50.00 90.00
160 Jerry Rice Raiders 8.00 20.00
161 Jerry Rice 49ers Black Belt Variant 60.00 120.00
162 Jerry Rice 49ers Gold Belt Variant 80.00 200.00
163 Jerry Rice 49ers Gold Belt Reebok Logos Variant 800.00 1,000.00
170 Anthony Thomas Blue/Black Mouth Piece 5.00 10.00
171 Anthony Thomas Blue/White Mouth Piece Variant 6.00 12.00
172 Anthony Thomas White Variant 10.00 25.00

2002 McFarlane Football 2001 Rookies Series 3

A continuation of the 2001 McFarlane football product, series 3 featured four 2001 NFL rookies.

10 Michael Bennett FP 8.00 20.00
20 James Jackson FP 7.50 15.00
30 LaDainian Tomlinson FP 15.00 30.00
40 Chris Weinke FP 7.50 15.00

2003 McFarlane Football Series 6-7

McFarlane's sixth football series debuted shortly after the start of the 2003 NFL season, and featured FPs of Rich Gannon, Joey Harrington, Priest Holmes, and Deuce McAllister. Variant jerseys and retro pieces of Emmitt Smith, Brett Favre, and Stephen Davis also added to the allure of the set. Series VII debuted in November with seven pieces in the set and adding a retro piece of Marshall Faulk and Jason Sehorn in a Rams uniform. Marshall Faulk and Jason Sehorn are not part of the set. First pieces included Chad Pennington, Clinton Portis, David Carr, Hines Ward, Jeremy Shockey and Julius Peppers.

10 Shaun Alexander White Pants 6.00 15.00
12 Shaun Alexander Blue Pants Variant 12.00 30.00
20 Mike Alstott Red 6.00 15.00
22 Mike Alstott White Variant 15.00 30.00
30 Drew Bledsoe Blue 6.00 15.00
32 Drew Bledsoe White Variant 15.00 30.00
40 Rich Gannon Raiders FP 8.00 20.00
42 Rich Gannon Chiefs Variant 15.00 30.00
50 Joey Harrington Blue FP 6.00 12.00
52 Joey Harrington White Variant 15.00 30.00
60 Priest Holmes White FP 8.00 20.00
62 Priest Holmes Red Variant 20.00 40.00
64 Priest Holmes Red with White Pants Variant 75.00 150.00
70 Deuce McAllister White FP 6.00 12.00
72 Deuce McAllister Black Variant 12.00 30.00
74 Deuce McAllister Black with Eye Paint Variant 25.00 50.00
80 Emmitt Smith Cardinals White with White Gloves 6.00 12.00
82 Emmitt Smith Cards White with Red Gloves Variant 6.00 12.00
84 Emmitt Smith Cards Red with White Gloves Variant 12.00 20.00
85 Emmitt Smith Cards Red with Red Gloves Variant 12.00 20.00
86 Emmitt Smith Cowboys White Variant 25.00 50.00
100 Stephen Davis Panthers 15.00 30.00
110 Brett Favre Falcons 35.00 70.00
111 Brett Favre Falcons with Hand Warmer Variant 175.00 300.00
120 David Carr FP 6.00 15.00
122 David Carr Blue Variant 20.00 40.00
130 Marshall Faulk Retro 12.00 30.00
140 Brett Favre Green 10.00 25.00
142 Brett Favre White Variant 25.00 50.00
150 Chad Pennington FP 8.00 20.00
152 Chad Pennington Green Variant 20.00 40.00
160 Julius Peppers FP 6.00 15.00
162 Julius Peppers White Variant 15.00 40.00
170 Clinton Portis FP 6.00 15.00
172 Clinton Portis White Variant 25.00 50.00
180 Jason Sehorn Rams 15.00 30.00
190 Jeremy Shockey FP 8.00 20.00
192 Jeremy Shockey White Variant 15.00 30.00
200 Michael Vick 10.00 25.00
202 Michael Vick Red Variant 15.00 40.00
210 Hines Ward FP 10.00 20.00
212 Hines Ward White Variant 15.00 40.00

2003 McFarlane Football 12-Inch

This set featured the usual high detail associated with McFarlane pieces, but on large-scale 12-inch figures.

10 Brett Favre 25.00 60.00
11 Brett Favre Shopko 30.00 60.00
20 Jerry Rice 30.00 80.00
30 Emmitt Smith Cowboys 50.00 120.00
32 Emmitt Smith Cardinals 50.00 120.00
40 Michael Vick 20.00 50.00
50 Ricky Williams 20.00 50.00

2003 McFarlane Football 2-Pack

10 Brett Favre / Brian Urlacher 15.00 40.00
20 Rich Gannon / Derrick Brooks 12.00 30.00
30 Ed McCaffrey / Zach Thomas 12.00 30.00

2003 McFarlane Football Hall of Fame

This William Green exclusive was sold at the 2003 NFL Hall of Fame in early August, 2003.

10 William Green 12.50 30.00

2003 McFarlane Football Superbowl XXXVII Exclusive

This 2-figure set was exclusively sold at the Superbowl XXXVII Experience Card Show. Just 2500 sets were produced, and the figures sold out rapidly. The Tomlinson piece is a repaint of the his previous figure, this time sporting a powder blue jersey.

10 Junior Seau 40.00 100.00
20 LaDainian Tomlinson 40.00 100.00

2003 McFarlane Multi-Sport National Convention Exclusive

Sold only at the 2003 National Sports Collector's Convention in Atlantic City (in July of 2003), this set featured New Jersey Net Kenyon Martin and New York Giant Tiki Barber.

10 Tiki Barber 15.00 35.00

2004 McFarlane Football Series 8-10

COMMON PIECE 6.00 12.00
10 Tim Brown 10.00 25.00
11 Tim Brown No Towel Variant 30.00 60.00
12 Tim Brown White Variant 20.00 35.00
20 Ahman Green FP 7.50 15.00
22 Ahman Green White Variant 12.50 25.00
30 Torry Holt FP 6.00 12.00
31 Torry Holt Retro Variant 12.50 25.00
40 Jamal Lewis FP 7.50 15.00
41 Jamal Lewis White Variant 15.00 30.00
50 Peyton Manning 6.00 12.00
51 Peyton Manning White Variant 12.50 25.00
60 Steve McNair 6.00 12.00
61 Steve McNair White Variant 12.50 25.00
110 Kendrell Bell FP 6.00 12.00
111 Kendrell Bell Black Variant 10.00 20.00
120 Daunte Culpepper 6.00 12.00
121 Daunte Culpepper White Variant 12.50 25.00
130 Priest Holmes 6.00 12.00
131 Priest Holmes Red with White Socks Variant 10.00 20.00
132 Priest Holmes White Variant 10.00 25.00
140 Chad Johnson FP 8.00 20.00
141 Chad Johnson Black Variant 12.50 30.00
150 Jake Plummer 6.00 12.00
151 Jake Plummer White Variant 7.50 15.00
160 Brian Urlacher FP 8.00 20.00
161 Brian Urlacher Blue Pants Variant 12.50 25.00
210 Jake Delhomme FP 7.50 15.00
211 Jake Delhomme 3-Bar Facemask Variant 15.00 30.00
212 Jake Delhomme Teal Variant 12.50 25.00
213 Jake Delhomme Teal 3-Bar Facemask Variant 15.00 30.00
220 Trent Green FP 6.00 12.00
221 Trent Green White Variant 10.00 20.00
230 Randy Moss 7.50 15.00
231 Randy Moss White Variant 12.50 25.00
240 Terrell Owens 7.50 15.00
241 Terrell Owens Retro 49ers Variant 10.00 25.00
242 Terrell Owens Retro 49ers Missing SF Logo on Pants Variant 40.00 80.00
250 LaDainian Tomlinson 6.00 12.00
251 LaDainian Tomlinson Small Sock Stain Variant 12.50 25.00
252 LaDainian Tomlinson White Variant 12.50 25.00
253 LaDainian Tomlinson White with Small Sock Stain Variant 15.00 30.00
260 Ricky Williams 7.50 15.00
261 Ricky Williams Light Blue Facemask Variant 12.50 25.00
262 Ricky Williams Orange Variant 15.00 30.00
270 Roy Williams FP 7.50 15.00
271 Roy Williams Blue Retro Variant 20.00 40.00
280 Adam Vinatieri FP 8.00 20.00
281 Adam Vinatieri 3-Bar Facemask Variant 12.50 25.00
290 Warren Sapp 12.50 30.00

2004 McFarlane Football 12-Inch

COMMON PIECE 15.00 40.00
10 Brett Favre 25.00 60.00
20 Priest Holmes 15.00 40.00
30 Peyton Manning Blue 25.00 60.00
31 Peyton Manning White 40.00 70.00
40 Donovan McNabb 20.00 50.00
50 Steve McNair 15.00 40.00
51 Steve McNair Blue 25.00 50.00
60 Randy Moss 15.00 40.00
70 Brian Urlacher 25.00 50.00
80 Michael Vick 15.00 40.00

2004 McFarlane Football 3-Inch Duals

10 Jake Delhomme / Marshall Faulk 4.00 8.00
20 Brett Favre / Tony Gonzalez 5.00 10.00
30 Jeff Garcia / Terrell Owens 5.00 10.00
40 Randy Moss / Drew Bledsoe 4.00 8.00
50 Brian Urlacher / Duce McAllister 4.00 8.00
60 Michael Vick / Shaun Alexander 5.00 10.00

2004 McFarlane Football 2-Pack

10 Donovan McNabb / Michael Strahan 15.00 30.00
20 Peyton Manning / Eli Manning 15.00 40.00
30 Clinton Portis / Ray Lewis 15.00 30.00

2004 McFarlane Football Collector's Club

10 Shannon Sharpe 25.00 60.00
11 Shannon Sharpe Retro 25.00 60.00
20 Clinton Portis PB 12.00 30.00

2004 McFarlane Football Super Bowl XXXVIII Exclusive

STATED PRINT RUN 5000 SETS
10 David Carr 25.00 60.00
20 Eddie George 25.00 60.00

2005 McFarlane Football Series 11-12

COMMON PIECE 6.00 15.00
10 Tiki Barber 6.00 15.00
11 Tiki Barber White Variant 10.00 20.00
20 Tom Brady 10.00 20.00
21 Tom Brady White Variant 20.00 40.00
22 Tom Brady White No Helmet Variant 100.00 180.00
30 Joe Horn FP 10.00 25.00
31 Joe Horn White Variant 20.00 35.00
40 Julius Jones FP 8.00 20.00
41 Julius Jones Blue with Star Variant 15.00 30.00
50 Willis McGahee FP 6.00 15.00
51 Willis McGahee White Variant 12.50 25.00
60 Randy Moss 6.00 15.00
70 Willie Roaf FP 6.00 15.00
80 Ben Roethlisberger FP 10.00 25.00
81 Ben Roethlisberger White Variant 15.00 40.00
90 Alex Smith FP 10.00 25.00
100 LaVar Arrington FP 8.00 20.00
101 LaVar Arrington White Variant 12.00 30.00
110 Drew Brees FP 20.00 50.00
120 Corey Dillon 6.00 15.00
121 Corey Dillon Gray Belt Variant 6.00 15.00
130 Brett Favre 10.00 20.00
131 Brett Favre Sholder Towel Variant 15.00 30.00
140 Marvin Harrison 8.00 20.00
141 Marvin Harrison Blue Variant 10.00 20.00
150 Kevin Mawae FP 6.00 15.00
160 Donovan McNabb 6.00 15.00
161 Donovan McNabb Black Variant 15.00 30.00
170 LaDainian Tomlinson 6.00 15.00
180 Jason Elam FP 30.00 60.00

2005 McFarlane Football 12-Inch

10 Troy Aikman 30.00 60.00
20 Jerome Bettis 50.00 120.00
30 Tom Brady 50.00 90.00
40 John Elway 25.00 60.00
50 Terrell Owens 20.00 50.00
60 LaDainian Tomlinson 40.00 80.00

2005 McFarlane Football Collector's Club

10 Deion Sanders Falcons 20.00 50.00
11 Deion Sanders Ravens 20.00 50.00

2005 McFarlane Football Legends Series 1

10 Troy Aikman White 12.50 25.00
11 Troy Aikman Blue Variant 20.00 40.00
20 John Elway Orange 12.50 25.00
21 John Elway White Variant 15.00 30.00
30 Franco Harris 20.00 50.00
31 Franco Harris Misspelled Name Variant 25.00 60.00
40 Barry Sanders 12.50 30.00
41 Barry Sanders Retro Variant 25.00 50.00
50 Lawrence Taylor Blue 15.00 40.00
51 Lawrence Taylor Blue No Name Variant 35.00 75.00
52 Lawrence Taylor White Variant 30.00 60.00
60 Johnny Unitas Blue 15.00 30.00
62 Johnny Unitas White Variant 30.00 60.00

2005 McFarlane Football 2-Pack

10 Jerry Rice / Deion Sanders 40.00 100.00
20 Brian Dawkins / Michael Vick 25.00 50.00

2005 McFarlane Football Super Bowl XXXIX Exclusive

10 Byron Leftwich 12.50 30.00
20 Fred Taylor 12.50 30.00

2006 McFarlane Football Series 13-14

10 Drew Bledsoe 7.50 15.00
20 Tedy Bruschi FP 10.00 25.00
30 Eli Manning Blue FP 10.00 25.00
31 Eli Manning Red Variant 10.00 25.00
40 Randy Moss Raiders 7.50 15.00
41 Randy Moss Vikings Afro Variant 20.00 40.00
50 Carson Palmer Black FP 10.00 20.00
51 Carson Palmer Orange Variant 15.00 30.00
60 Cadillac Williams FP 7.50 15.00
100 Shaun Alexander FP 7.50 15.00
110 Reggie Bush Black FP 10.00 25.00
111 Reggie Bush White Variant 25.00 45.00
120 Antonio Gates Navy FP 10.00 25.00
121 Antonio Gates Light Blue Variant 12.50 30.00
130 Larry Johnson FP 7.50 15.00
140 Troy Polamalu FP 12.50 30.00
141 Troy Polamalu Snow Variant 20.00 40.00
150 Steve Smith White 10.00 25.00
151 Steve Smith Blue Variant 20.00 40.00

2006 McFarlane Football 2-Pack

10 Troy Polamalu / Matt Hasselbeck 15.00 30.00

2006 McFarlane Football 3-Inch Series 4

10 Shaun Alexander 4.00 8.00
20 Drew Bledsoe 4.00 8.00
30 Tom Brady 5.00 10.00
40 Chad Johnson 5.00 10.00
50 Eli Manning 4.00 8.00
60 Peyton Manning 6.00 12.00
70 Donovan McNabb 4.00 8.00
80 Randy Moss 5.00 10.00
90 Ben Roethlisberger 6.00 15.00
100 Ladainian Tomlinson 4.00 8.00
110 Brian Urlacher 4.00 8.00
120 Michael Vick 4.00 8.00

2006 McFarlane Football 3-Pack

10 Drew Bledsoe / Julius Jones / Roy Williams 20.00 45.00
20 Tom Brady / Corey Dillion / Tedy Bruschi 15.00 40.00
30 Tiki Barber / Michael Strahan / Plaxico Burress 15.00 40.00
40 Ben Roethlisberger / Hines Ward / Joey Porter 25.00 55.00

2006 McFarlane Football Collector's Club

10 Matt Leinart White 10.00 25.00
11 Matt Leinart Red Variant 40.00 70.00
20 Deion Sanders Falcons RC Year 20.00 50.00
21 Deion Sanders Ravens Alt. 20.00 50.00

2006 McFarlane Football Hall of Fame

Limited to 3000 figures.

10 Troy Aikman Blue 20.00 50.00
11 Troy Aikman White 25.00 60.00

2006 McFarlane Football Legends Series 2

10 Jim Brown 10.00 25.00
20 Joe Greene 10.00 25.00
30 Ronnie Lott 49ers 10.00 25.00
31 Ronnie Lott Raiders Variant 25.00 50.00
*40 Joe Montana Red 10.00 25.00
41 Joe Montana White Variant 15.00 40.00
50 Ray Nitschke 12.50 30.00
60 Walter Payton Navy 20.00 50.00
61 Walter Payton White Variant 40.00 70.00

2006 McFarlane Football Super Bowl XL

Limited to 3000 copies.

10 Barry Sanders 40.00 75.00

2007 McFarlane Football Series 15-16

10 Cedric Benson FP 10.00 20.00
20 Ray Lewis Black Variant 15.00 40.00
20 Ray Lewis Purple 12.50 25.00
30 Peyton Manning 10.00 20.00
40 Tony Romo White FP 12.50 25.00
41 Tony Romo Blue Variant 20.00 40.00
50 William Thomas FP 12.50 25.00
60 Brian Westbrook FP 10.00 20.00
70 Vince Young White FP 10.00 20.00
71 Vince Young Blue Pants Variant 10.00 20.00
100 Champ Bailey FP 10.00 20.00
110 Frank Gore Red FP 10.00 20.00
111 Frank Gore White Variant 15.00 30.00
120 Steve McNair Ravens 10.00 20.00
121 Steve McNair Oilers Variant 15.00 30.00
130 Terrell Owens 10.00 20.00
140 Brady Quinn FP 10.00 20.00
150 LaDainian Tomlinson Blue 10.00 20.00
151 LaDainian Tomlinson White Variant 20.00 40.00

2007 McFarlane Football 3-Inch Series 5

10 Tom Brady 6.00 12.00
20 Plaxico Burress 6.00 12.00
30 Reggie Bush 7.50 15.00
40 Brett Favre 7.50 15.00
50 Terrell Owens 6.00 12.00
60 Ladainian Tomlinson 6.00 12.00

2007 McFarlane Football 3-Pack

10 Tony Romo / Roger Staubach / Troy Aikman 30.00 80.00
20 Donovan McNabb / Brian Westbrook / (Brian Dawkins 15.00 40.00
30 Joe Montana / Ronnie Lott / Jerry Rice 25.00 60.00
40 Larry Johnson / Shaun Alexander / LaDainian Tomlinson 15.00 40.00

2007 McFarlane Football 12-Inch

10 Walter Payton Dk Blue 40.00 80.00
11 Walter Payton White Variant 40.00 80.00

2007 McFarlane Football Canton Exclusive

10 Jim Brown/3000* 40.00 80.00

2007 McFarlane Football Collector's Club 3-Pack

10 Joe Montana / Ronnie Lott / Jerry Rice 25.00 60.00

2007 McFarlane Football Collector's Edition

10 Peyton Manning 12.50 25.00
20 Brian Urlacher 10.00 20.00

2007 McFarlane Football Hall of Fame

10 Jim Brown 12.50 25.00

2007 McFarlane Football Legends Series 3

10 Earl Campbell 10.00 25.00
11 Earl Campbell White Variant 10.00 25.00
20 John Elway 10.00 25.00
21 John Elway Orange Variant 15.00 30.00
22 John Elway White Variant 15.00 30.00
30 Bo Jackson 15.00 40.00
40 Dan Marino 10.00 25.00
50 Roger Staubach 15.00 30.00
60 Reggie White Eagles 10.00 25.00
70 Reggie White Packers 15.00 40.00

2007 McFarlane Football Super Bowl XLI

10 Jason Taylor 20.00 50.00

2007 McFarlane Football Ultimate Team Sets

10 Chicago Bears 15.00 30.00
20 Dallas Cowboys 15.00 30.00
30 Denver Broncos 15.00 30.00
40 New York Giants 15.00 30.00

2008 McFarlane Football 12-Inch

10 LaDanainian Tomlinson 25.00 50.00

2008 McFarlane Football 3-Pack

10 Tom Brady / Ben Roethlisberger / Peyton Manning 20.00 40.00
20 Joe Greene / Jerome Bettis / Jack Lambert 30.00 60.00
30 Eli Manning / Michael Strahan / Plaxico Burress 40.00 80.00

2008 McFarlane Football Arizona Exclusive

10 Anquan Boldin 10.00 25.00

2008 McFarlane Football Collector's Club

10 Brett Favre 15.00 40.00
20 Matt Leinart 12.50 25.00
30 Terrell Owens 20.00 50.00

2008 McFarlane Football Hall of Fame

10 John Riggins 15.00 40.00

2008 McFarlane Football Legends Series 4

10 Jack Lambert 10.00 25.00
11 Jack Lambert Black Variant 25.00 60.00
20 Howie Long 12.50 30.00
30 Joe Montana 10.00 25.00
31 Joe Montana Clean Variant 15.00 30.00
32 Joe Montana Left Hand Variant
40 Warren Moon 10.00 25.00
*41 Warren Moon Blue Sleeve Variant 10.00 25.00
50 John Riggins 10.00 25.00
51 John Riggins Red Variant 10.00 25.00
60 Fran Tarkenton 12.50 30.00
61 Fran Tarkenton White Sleeve Variant 12.50 30.00

2008 McFarlane Football Super Bowl XLII

10 Larry Fitzgerald 12.50 30.00

2008 McFarlane Football Ultimate Team Sets

10 Green Bay Packers 20.00 50.00
20 New England Patriots 12.50 30.00
30 Oakland Raiders 12.50 30.00
40 Pittsburgh Steelers 12.50 30.00
50 New York Giants 12.50 30.00

2008 McFarlane Football Wave 1 Series 17

COMMON PIECE 10.00 20.00
10 Joseph Addai FP 10.00 20.00
11 Joseph Addai Dirty Variant 10.00 20.00
20 Reggie Bush 10.00 20.00
21 Reggie Bush Clean Variant 12.50 25.00
30 Brett Favre 10.00 20.00
31 Brett Favre No C Variant 12.50 25.00
40 Randy Moss 10.00 20.00
41 Randy Moss Red Band Variant 12.50 25.00
50 Willie Parker FP 10.00 20.00
51 Willie Parker Black Tape Variant 12.50 25.00
60 JaMarcus Russell FP 10.00 20.00
61 JaMarcus Russell Clean Variant 12.50 25.00
70 Tony Romo 10.00 25.00
71 Tony Romo Clean Variant 15.00 30.00

2008 McFarlane Football Wave 2 Series 18

COMMON PIECE 10.00 20.00
10 Tom Brady 10.00 20.00
11 Tom Brady Clean Variant 10.00 20.00
12 Tom Brady Tattoo Variant 50.00 100.00
20 Devin Hester FP 10.00 25.00
21 Devin Hester Arm Bands Variant 15.00 40.00
30 Brandon Jacobs FP 10.00 20.00
31 Brandon Jacobs Black Gloves Variant 12.50 25.00
40 Adrian Peterson FP 12.50 25.00
41 Adrian Peterson Black Wrist Variant 20.00 40.00
50 LaDainian Tomlinson 10.00 20.00
51 LaDainian Tomlinson Black Bands Variant 12.50 25.00
60 Ben Roethlisberger 10.00 20.00
61 Ben Roethlisberger Clean Variant 12.50 25.00
70 DeMarcus Ware FP 12.50 30.00

2008 McFarlane Football Wave 3 Series 19

COMMON PIECE 7.50 15.00
10 Marion Barber FP 7.50 15.00
11 Marion Barber Blue Variant 15.00 40.00
20 Jay Cutler FP 10.00 20.00
21 Jay Cutler White Pants Variant 15.00 30.00
25 Donald Driver FP 12.50 30.00
30 Brett Favre Green 12.50 25.00
40 Brett Favre White 10.00 20.00
50 Clinton Portis 7.50 15.00
51 Clinton Portis Clean Variant 12.50 25.00

2008 McFarlane Football Williams Davis Collectibles

10 Hines Ward	20.00	35.00

2009 McFarlane Football 3-Inch Series 6-7

10 Tom Brady	6.00	12.00
20 Eli Manning	6.00	12.00
30 Peyton Manning	6.00	12.00
40 Terrell Owens	6.00	12.00
50 Ben Roethlisberger	6.00	12.00
60 LaDainian Tomlinson	6.00	12.00
100 Tom Brady	7.50	15.00
110 Eli Manning	6.00	12.00
120 Peyton Manning	6.00	12.00
130 Donovan McNabb	6.00	12.00
140 Adrian Peterson	20.00	40.00
150 Philip Rivers	6.00	12.00
160 Aaron Rodgers	6.00	12.00
170 Ben Roethlisberger	6.00	12.00
180 Tony Romo	6.00	12.00
190 Matt Ryan	6.00	12.00
200 Brian Urlacher	6.00	12.00
210 Jason Witten	6.00	12.00

2009 McFarlane Football 12-Inch

10 Ben Roethlisberger	25.00	50.00
20 Tony Romo	25.00	50.00

2009 McFarlane Football 2-Pack

10 Ben Roethlisberger Santonio Holmes	15.00	30.00
20 Tony Romo Jason Witten	15.00	40.00
30 Troy Polamalu Hines Ward	20.00	40.00

2009 McFarlane Football 3-Pack

10 Archie Manning Peyton Manning Eli Manning	40.00	80.00

2009 McFarlane Football College Series 1

10 Tom Brady	15.00	30.00
20 Ray Lewis	25.00	60.00
30 Peyton Manning	15.00	30.00
40 Adrian Peterson	15.00	30.00
41 Adrian Peterson White Variant	15.00	30.00
50 JaMarcus Russell	15.00	30.00
51 JaMarcus Russell Blue Variant	15.00	30.00
60 Hines Ward	15.00	30.00
61 Hines Ward White Variant	15.00	30.00

2009 McFarlane Football Legends Series 5

10 Randall Cunningham	20.00	40.00
20 Archie Manning	12.50	30.00
30 Dan Marino	12.50	25.00
31 Dan Marino White Variant	10.00	20.00
40 Joe Montana Chiefs	10.00	20.00
50 Joe Montana 49ers	12.50	30.00
60 Barry Sanders	10.00	25.00
61 Barry Sanders Blue Pants/20 Variant	1,400.00	1,800.00
70 Bart Starr	10.00	25.00
71 Bart Starr White Variant	15.00	30.00
80 Steve Young	10.00	20.00

2009 McFarlane Football Series 20-22

COMMON PIECE	10.00	20.00
10 Larry Fitzgerald FP	12.50	25.00
20 Eli Manning	12.50	25.00
21 Eli Manning Variant Red	15.00	30.00
30 Philip Rivers FP	10.00	25.00
31 Philip Rivers White Variant	15.00	30.00
40 Ben Roethlisberger	12.50	25.00
50 Tony Romo	12.50	25.00
51 Tony Romo Blue Variant	20.00	40.00
60 Michael Turner FP	12.50	25.00
61 Michael Turner Red Variant	15.00	30.00
62 Michael Turner/33 Variant		
100 Drew Brees	12.50	25.00
110 Jay Cutler	12.50	25.00
111 Jay Cutler White Variant	20.00	35.00
120 Joe Flacco FP	10.00	25.00
130 Thomas Jones FP	10.00	20.00
131 Thomas Jones/500 Variant	75.00	150.00
140 Peyton Manning	12.50	25.00
141 Peyton Manning White Variant	20.00	40.00
150 Troy Polamalu	12.50	25.00
160 Aaron Rodgers FP	15.00	40.00
161 Aaron Rodgers White Variant	20.00	50.00
170 Jason Witten FP	15.00	40.00
200 Tom Brady	10.00	20.00
201 Tom Brady Red/1000 Variant	50.00	120.00
210 Matt Cassel FP	10.00	20.00
211 Matt Cassel White Variant	15.00	30.00
220 Matt Forte FP	12.50	25.00
221 Matt Forte White/2000 Variant	20.00	40.00
230 Adrian Peterson	12.50	25.00
231 Adrian Peterson White/500 Variant	75.00	150.00
240 Matt Ryan FP	12.50	30.00
241 Matt Ryan Black Variant	25.00	50.00
242 Matt Ryan Black/200 Variant	150.00	250.00
250 Brett Favre Exclusive Purple	10.00	20.00
251 Brett Favre Exclusive White	10.00	20.00
260 Kurt Warner Exclusive	40.00	100.00

2010 McFarlane Football Series 24

10 Adrian Peterson	10.00	20.00
11 Adrian Peterson White Jsy/3000 Variant	12.50	30.00
20 Felix Jones FP	10.00	20.00
21 Felix Jones Alternate Jsy/500 Variant	75.00	150.00
30 DeSean Jackson FP	10.00	20.00
31 DeSean Jackson Black Jsy/3000 Variant	12.50	30.00
40 Chris Johnson FP	10.00	25.00
41 Chris Johnson Dark Jsy/1000 Variant	20.00	40.00
42 Chris Johnson Throwback Jsy Variant	10.00	25.00
50 Ed Reed FP	10.00	20.00
51 Ed Reed Purple Jsy/500 Variant	40.00	80.00
60 Peyton Manning	10.00	20.00
61 Peyton Manning White Jsy/3000 Variant	12.50	30.00
70 Hines Ward	12.50	30.00
71 Hines Ward White Jsy Variant	12.50	30.00
80 Jeff Saturday Variant Only/3000	17.50	35.00
90 Robbie Gould/2500	12.50	30.00

2010 McFarlane Football Series 23

10 Miles Austin FP	10.00	25.00
11 Miles Austin Blue/White Uniform/250 Variant	125.00	250.00
20 Drew Brees	8.00	20.00
21 Drew Brees White Jsy Variant	15.00	40.00
22 Drew Brees Black Pants/500 Variant	100.00	200.00
30 Michael Crabtree FP	10.00	25.00
31 Michael Crabtree White/1000 Variant	25.00	60.00
40 Brett Favre	8.00	20.00
41 Brett Favre White/3000 Variant	15.00	30.00
42 Brett Favre White GB Excl Variant	10.00	25.00
50 Donovan McNabb	10.00	25.00
51 Donovan McNabb Red Pants/1000 VAR	20.00	40.00
60 Rashard Mendenhall FP	10.00	25.00
61 Rashard Mendenhall White/1000 Variant	25.00	50.00
70 Mark Sanchez FP	10.00	25.00
71 Mark Sanchez Green Pants Variant	10.00	25.00
80 Tim Tebow FP	15.00	40.00
81 Tim Tebow Orange/2500 Variant	50.00	100.00
90 Beanie Wells Exclusive	12.00	30.00

2010 McFarlane Football College Series 2

10 Marion Barber Red	8.00	20.00
11 Marion Barber White/500 Variant	40.00	80.00
20 Drew Brees Black	10.00	25.00
21 Drew Brees White/3000 Variant	15.00	30.00
30 Larry Fitzgerald Black	8.00	20.00
31 Larry Fitzgerald White/3000 Variant	15.00	30.00
40 Eli Manning Red	8.00	20.00
41 Eli Manning Black/3000 Variant	12.00	30.00
50 Tony Romo Blue	8.00	20.00
51 Tony Romo White/3000 Variant	12.00	30.00
60 Matt Ryan Red	8.00	20.00
61 Matt Ryan White/100 Variant	100.00	200.00
70 Jason Witten Orange	8.00	20.00
71 Jason Witten White/2500 Variant	15.00	40.00

2010 McFarlane Football Legends Series 6

10 Marcus Allen Black	10.00	25.00
11 Marcus Allen White/1000 Variant	25.00	60.00
20 Jerome Bettis Black	10.00	25.00
21 Jerome Bettis White/500 Variant	60.00	120.00
30 Dick Butkus Blue	15.00	40.00
31 Dick Butkus White/1000 Variant	35.00	70.00
40 Randall Cunningham Purple/1000	35.00	70.00
50 Tony Dorsett White	10.00	25.00
51 Tony Dorsett Blue/2000 Variant	25.00	50.00
60 Warren Moon Purple/3000	15.00	30.00
70 John Riggins Green/2500	20.00	40.00
80 Phil Simms Blue	10.00	25.00
81 Phil Simms White/100 Variant	200.00	275.00
90 Steve Young 49ers	10.00	25.00
91 Steve Young Bucs/500 Variant	75.00	150.00

2010 McFarlane Football Playmakers Series 1

10 Tom Brady	6.00	15.00
20 Drew Brees	6.00	15.00
30 Jay Cutler	6.00	15.00
40 Brett Favre	6.00	15.00
50 Larry Fitzgerald	6.00	15.00
60 Eli Manning	6.00	15.00
70 Peyton Manning	6.00	15.00
80 Adrian Peterson	6.00	15.00
90 Troy Polamalu	6.00	15.00
100 Aaron Rodgers	6.00	15.00
110 Ben Roethlisberger	6.00	15.00
120 Tony Romo	6.00	15.00
130 Mark Sanchez	6.00	15.00
140 Jason Witten	6.00	15.00

2010 McFarlane Football 2-Pack

10 Brett Favre Vikings	12.50	30.00
20 Troy Polamalu Rashard Mendenhall	10.00	25.00
30 Aaron Rodgers Greg Jennings	15.00	40.00
40 Tony Romo Miles Austin	15.00	30.00
50 Mark Sanchez Shonn Greene	10.00	25.00

2010 McFarlane Football 3-Pack

10 Drew Brees Reggie Bush Jeremy Shockey	40.00	80.00

2011 McFarlane Football Series 25

10 Troy Polamalu	8.00	20.00
11 Troy Polamalu Black Jsy Variant	12.50	30.00
20 LeSean McCoy FP	8.00	20.00
21 LeSean McCoy White Jsy/1500 Variant	20.00	50.00
30 LaDainian Tomlinson	8.00	20.00
31 LaDainian Tomlinson White Jsy/3000 Variant	12.50	30.00
32 LaDainian Tomlinson SD Uniform/250 Variant	200.00	350.00
40 Ray Rice FP	10.00	25.00
41 Ray Rice Black Jsy/100 Variant	200.00	400.00
50 Julius Peppers	8.00	20.00
51 Julius Peppers White Jsy/1000 Variant	30.00	80.00
60 Percy Harvin FP	8.00	20.00
70 Charles Woodson Oakland/1000 Variant	60.00	150.00
80 Charles Woodson GB FP	15.00	40.00
81 Charles Woodson GB Green Jsy/3000 Variant	20.00	40.00

2011 McFarlane Football Series 26

10 Jerome Bettis	10.00	25.00
11 Jerome Bettis Blue/1000 Variant	25.00	60.00
20 Terry Bradshaw	10.00	25.00
21 Terry Bradshaw White/3000 Variant	20.00	40.00
22 Terry Bradshaw All Wht/600 Variant	60.00	120.00
30 James Harrison CS Exlsv FP	10.00	20.00
40 Ray Lewis	10.00	20.00
41 Ray Lewis Black/1000 Variant	35.00	70.00
50 Eli Manning	10.00	20.00
51 Eli Manning White/2500 Variant	12.00	30.00
60 Brandon Marshall FP	10.00	25.00
61 Brandon Marshall White/3000 Variant	20.00	40.00
70 Adrian Peterson	10.00	20.00
71 Adrian Peterson Retro/3000 Variant	12.50	25.00
80 Wes Welker FP	10.00	25.00
81 Wes Welker Red/350 Variant	100.00	200.00

2011 McFarlane Football Series 27

10 Marcus Allen	8.00	20.00
11 Marcus Allen White/1000 Variant	15.00	40.00
20 Miles Austin	8.00	20.00
21 Miles Austin Jersey #14/500 Variant	75.00	150.00
30 Tom Brady	8.00	20.00
31 Tom Brady White/2000 Variant	25.00	60.00
32 Tom Brady Short Hair/1000 Variant	40.00	80.00
40 Eric Dickerson	10.00	25.00
41 Eric Dickerson Colts Uniform/3000 Variant	20.00	40.00
50 Larry Fitzgerald	8.00	20.00
51 Larry Fitzgerald White/1000 Variant	20.00	40.00
60 Heath Miller FP	8.00	20.00
61 Heath Miller White/3000 Variant	15.00	30.00
70 Aaron Rodgers	12.00	30.00
71 Aaron Rodgers Clark Exclusive Acme TB Variant	15.00	30.00

2011 McFarlane Football Series 28

10 Drew Brees	8.00	20.00
11 Drew Brees Black Pant/100 Variant	400.00	700.00
20 Dez Bryant FP	10.00	25.00
21 Dez Bryant Blue/2000 Variant	25.00	50.00
22 Dez Bryant Throwback Variant	30.00	60.00
30 Peyton Hillis FP	8.00	20.00
40 Andre Johnson FP	10.00	25.00
41 Andre Johnson Blue/2000 Variant	20.00	40.00
50 Clay Matthews FP	10.00	25.00
51 Clay Matthews Throwback/900 Variant	50.00	100.00
60 Cam Newton/3000 FP	40.00	70.00
70 Ben Roethlisberger	8.00	20.00
71 Ben Roethlisberger Throwback/1000 Variant	30.00	60.00
80 Barry Sanders	8.00	20.00
81 Barry Sanders White/2000 Variant	20.00	40.00
90 Michael Vick	8.00	20.00
91 Michael Vick Black/500 Variant	75.00	200.00

2011 McFarlane Football 2-pack

10 Dick Butkus Brian Urlacher	20.00	40.00
20 Joe Greene James Harrison	20.00	40.00
30 Howie Long Terry Bradshaw	20.00	35.00

2011 McFarlane Football 3-pack

10 Clay Matthews Aaron Rodgers Greg Jennings	30.00	60.00

2011 McFarlane Football Elite Series 2

10 Jared Allen	10.00	25.00
20 Anquan Boldin	12.50	25.00
30 Maurice Jones-Drew	10.00	20.00
40 Darren McFadden	10.00	25.00
41 Darren McFadden White/2500 Variant	15.00	40.00
50 Troy Polamalu	10.00	20.00
60 Aaron Rodgers	10.00	20.00
70 Tony Romo	10.00	20.00
71 Tony Romo Alt.Uniform/3000 Variant	15.00	30.00
80 Mark Sanchez	10.00	20.00
81 Mark Sanchez White Pants/3000 Variant	12.50	25.00

2011 McFarlane Football Playmakers Series 2

10 Miles Austin	6.00	15.00
20 Tom Brady	6.00	15.00
30 Reggie Bush	6.00	15.00
40 Eli Manning	6.00	15.00
50 Peyton Manning	6.00	15.00
60 Rashard Mendenhall	6.00	15.00
70 Adrian Peterson	6.00	15.00
80 Ben Roethlisberger	6.00	15.00
90 Aaron Rodgers	6.00	15.00
100 Matt Ryan	6.00	15.00
110 Tim Tebow	12.00	30.00
120 LaDainian Tomlinson	6.00	15.00
130 Tom Brady EXT	6.00	15.00
140 Drew Brees EXT	6.00	15.00
150 Devin Hester EXT	6.00	15.00
160 DeSean Jackson EXT	6.00	15.00
170 Ray Lewis EXT	6.00	15.00
180 Darren McFadden EXT	6.00	15.00
190 Troy Polamalu EXT	8.00	20.00
200 Tony Romo EXT	6.00	15.00

2011 McFarlane Football College Series 3

10 Joseph Addai	8.00	20.00
11 Joseph Addai Purple/500 Variant	40.00	100.00
20 Adrian Peterson	8.00	20.00
21 Adrian Peterson Red/750 Variant	25.00	50.00
30 Troy Polamalu	10.00	25.00
31 Troy Polamalu Red/1250 Variant	10.00	25.00
40 Ray Rice	15.00	40.00
50 Ndamukong Suh	10.00	25.00
60 Tim Tebow	15.00	40.00
61 Tim Tebow Blue Pants/2500 Variant	20.00	50.00
70 Beanie Wells	8.00	20.00
71 Beanie Wells White/625 Variant	25.00	60.00
80 Charles Woodson	12.00	30.00
81 Charles Woodson White/1000 Variant	25.00	60.00

2012 McFarlane Football 2-pack

10 Terry Bradshaw Ben Roethlisberger	20.00	35.00

2012 McFarlane Football Series 29

10 Rob Gronkowski FP	8.00	20.00
11 Rob Gronkowski Autograph/100 Variant	400.00	650.00
12 Rob Gronkowski Retro Variant	30.00	60.00
20 Troy Polamalu	8.00	20.00
21 Troy Polamalu Retro/2000 Variant	10.00	25.00
30 Aaron Rodgers	8.00	20.00
31 Aaron Rodgers Retro/1000 Variant	40.00	80.00
40 Tony Romo	8.00	20.00
41 Tony Romo Blue/1500 Variant	20.00	40.00
50 Matt Ryan	8.00	20.00
60 Ken Stabler	8.00	20.00
61 Ken Stabler White/1500 Variant	30.00	60.00
70 Matthew Stafford FP	25.00	50.00

2012 McFarlane Football College Series 4

10 Marcus Allen	10.00	25.00
20 Champ Bailey	10.00	25.00
21 Champ Bailey White/400 Variant	40.00	80.00
30 Sam Bradford	10.00	25.00
40 Peyton Manning	10.00	25.00
50 Cam Newton	10.00	25.00
51 Cam Newton White/100 Variant	250.00	450.00
60 Tim Tebow	12.00	30.00
61 Tim Tebow White/2000 Variant	20.00	40.00
70 Ricky Williams	10.00	25.00
71 Ricky Williams White/2000 Variant	20.00	40.00

2012 McFarlane Football Playmakers Series 3

10 Tom Brady	6.00	15.00
20 Drew Brees	6.00	15.00
30 Victor Cruz	6.00	15.00
40 Larry Fitzgerald	6.00	15.00
50 Calvin Johnson	6.00	15.00
60 Eli Manning	6.00	15.00
70 Peyton Manning	8.00	20.00
80 LeSean McCoy	6.00	15.00
90 Darrelle Revis	6.00	15.00
100 Philip Rivers	6.00	15.00
110 Aaron Rodgers	6.00	15.00
120 Ben Roethlisberger	6.00	15.00
130 Ray Rice	6.00	15.00
140 Tony Romo	6.00	15.00
150 Tim Tebow	8.00	20.00
160 Brian Urlacher	6.00	15.00
170 Mike Wallace	6.00	15.00
180 DeMarcus Ware	6.00	15.00
190 Patrick Willis	6.00	15.00
200 Charles Woodson	6.00	15.00

1988 SLU Football

This set of 137 football figurines and collectors cards was issued by Cincinnati-based Kenner Toy Company. The statues feature top NFL stars in action poses and are accompanied by a standard-size card. The front of the card has either a posed or action color shot with a white border. The back has biographical and statistical information and a facsimile signature. The values listed below refer to unopened packages. The cards are unnumbered and checklisted below in alphabetical order. The four modes of distribution for the '88 Football set were team cases (24 pieces) issued in each teams respective region, All-Star cases (24 pieces) issued nationwide, retail catalogs and a 1-800 number. The individual player assortments within the team cases were not equal and caused certain pieces to be short prints. The Bills, Chargers, Cowboys and Raiders are the toughest teams to complete. The following players made up the All-Star case assortments: Marcus Allen (2 per case), Brian Bosworth (2), Eric Dickerson (2), John Elway (2), Dan Marino (3), Jim McMahon (3), Joe Montana (20, Phil Simms (2), Lawrence Taylor (3), Herschel Walker (2) and Reggie White (1). Three players, Tony Dorsett, Willie Gault and Marc Wilson were only made available through Sears and J.C. Penney's catalogs. Sears offered all three pieces while J.C. Penney's offered only the Willie Gault. Finally, in 1989, a company in conjunction with Kenner set up a 1-800 mail order business that sold all Kenner products made through 1989. The 1988 football sets were made available at approximately $7.00 per piece through this company.

BLUE SHWCSE	30.00	50.00
GRN DSPLY.STND	40.00	60.00
1 Marcus Allen	15.00	40.00
2 Neal Anderson	12.00	30.00
3 Chip Banks	40.00	100.00
4 Mark Bavaro	15.00	40.00
5 Cornelius Bennett	40.00	100.00
6 Albert Bentley	25.00	60.00
7 Duane Bickett	40.00	100.00
8 Todd Blackledge	20.00	50.00
9 Brian Bosworth	12.00	30.00
10 Brian Brennan	25.00	60.00
11 Bill Brooks	30.00	80.00
12 James Brooks	25.00	60.00
13 Eddie Brown	25.00	60.00
14 Joey Browner	30.00	80.00
15 Aundray Bruce	20.00	50.00
16 Chris Burkett	65.00	125.00
17 Keith Byars	20.00	50.00
18 Scott Campbell	40.00	100.00
19 Carlos Carson	40.00	100.00
20 Harry Carson	25.00	60.00
21 Anthony Carter	40.00	100.00
22 Gerald Carter	20.00	50.00
23 Michael Carter	20.00	50.00
24 Tony Casillas	30.00	80.00
25 Jeff Chadwick	12.00	30.00
26 Deron Cherry	15.00	40.00
27 Ray Childress	40.00	100.00
28 Todd Christensen	30.00	80.00
29 Gary Clark	25.00	60.00
30 Mark Clayton	40.00	100.00
31 Cris Collinsworth	40.00	100.00
32 Doug Cosbie	65.00	125.00
33 Roger Craig	15.00	40.00
34 Randall Cunningham	15.00	40.00
35 Jeff Davis	25.00	60.00
36 Kenneth Davis	65.00	125.00
37 Richard Dent	15.00	40.00
38 Eric Dickerson	20.00	50.00
39 Floyd Dixon	20.00	50.00
40 Tony Dorsett	100.00	250.00
41 Mark Duper	30.00	80.00
42 Tony Eason	40.00	100.00
43 Carl Ekern	25.00	60.00
44 Henry Ellard	25.00	60.00
45 John Elway	30.00	80.00
46 Phillip Epps	50.00	120.00
47 Boomer Esiason	30.00	80.00
48 Jim Everett	20.00	50.00
49 Brent Fullwood	40.00	100.00
50 Mark Gastineau	15.00	40.00
51 Willie Gault	40.00	100.00
52 Bob Golic	40.00	100.00
53 Jerry Gray	20.00	50.00
54 Darrell Green	100.00	250.00
55 Jacob Green	40.00	100.00
56 Roy Green	30.00	80.00
57 Steve Grogan	40.00	100.00
58 Ronnie Harmon	65.00	125.00
59 Bobby Hebert	30.00	80.00
60 Alonzo Highsmith	12.00	30.00
61 Drew Hill	12.00	30.00
62 Earnest Jackson	25.00	60.00
63 Rickey Jackson	40.00	100.00
64 Vance Johnson	20.00	50.00
65 Ed Jones	50.00	120.00
66 James Jones	20.00	50.00
67 Rod Jones	15.00	40.00
68 Rulon Jones	25.00	60.00
69 Steve Jordan	80.00	200.00
70 E.J. Junior	25.00	60.00
71 Jim Kelly	75.00	200.00
72 Bill Kenney	30.00	80.00
73 Bernie Kosar	20.00	50.00
74 Tommy Kramer	40.00	100.00
75 Dave Krieg	40.00	100.00
76 Tim Krumrie	65.00	125.00
77 Mark Lee	40.00	100.00
78 Ronnie Lippett	20.00	50.00
79 Louis Lipps	40.00	100.00
80 Neil Lomax	30.00	80.00
81 Chuck Long	20.00	50.00
82 Howie Long	30.00	80.00
83 Ronnie Lott	40.00	100.00
84 Kevin Mack	15.00	40.00
85 Mark Malone	60.00	150.00
86 Dexter Manley	15.00	40.00
87 Dan Marino	30.00	80.00
88 Eric Martin	15.00	40.00
89 Rueben Mayes	15.00	40.00
90 Jim McMahon	20.00	50.00
91 Freeman McNeil	15.00	40.00
92 Karl Mecklenburg	20.00	50.00
93 Mike Merriweather	30.00	80.00
94 Stump Mitchell	25.00	60.00
95 Art Monk	75.00	150.00
96 Joe Montana	40.00	100.00
97 Warren Moon	40.00	100.00
98 Stanley Morgan	25.00	60.00
99 Joe Morris	20.00	50.00
100 Darrin Nelson	30.00	80.00
101 Ozzie Newsome	40.00	100.00
102 Ken O'Brien	15.00	40.00
103 John Offerdahl	40.00	100.00
104 Christian Okoye	20.00	50.00
105 Mike Quick	15.00	40.00
106 Jerry Rice	75.00	200.00
107 Gerald Riggs	15.00	40.00
108 Reggie Rogers	15.00	40.00
109 Mike Rozier	20.00	50.00
110 Jay Schroeder	15.00	40.00
111 Mickey Shuler	15.00	40.00
112 Phil Simms	15.00	40.00
113 Mike Singletary	20.00	50.00
114 Billy Ray Smith	50.00	120.00
115 Bruce Smith	60.00	150.00
116 J.T. Smith	30.00	80.00
117 Troy Stradford	30.00	80.00
118 Lawrence Taylor	15.00	40.00
119 Vinny Testaverde	25.00	60.00
120 Andre Tippett	25.00	60.00
121 Anthony Toney	15.00	40.00
122 Al Toon	15.00	40.00
123 Jack Trudeau	65.00	125.00
124 Herschel Walker	25.00	60.00
125 Curt Warner	15.00	40.00
126 Dave Waymer	40.00	100.00
127 Charles White	20.00	50.00
128 Danny White	30.00	80.00
129 Randy White	40.00	100.00
130 Reggie White	20.00	50.00
131 James Wilder	25.00	60.00
132 Doug Williams	20.00	50.00
133 Marc Wilson	125.00	300.00
134 Sammy Winder	25.00	60.00
135 Kellen Winslow	100.00	250.00
136 Rod Woodson	75.00	200.00
137 Randy Wright	65.00	125.00

1989 SLU Football

This set of 122 football figurines and collectors cards was issued by Cincinnati-based Kenner Toy Company. The statues feature top NFL stars in action poses and are accompanied by a standard-size card. The front has either a posed or action color shot with a black border. The back has biographical and statistical information and a facsimile signature of the player. The four modes of distribution for the '89 Football set were team cases issued in each teams respective region, All-Star cases issued nationwide, Superbowl Twenty-four, and a 1-800 number. Team cases consisted of 24 pieces and were issued in the regional area for that particular team. The individual player assortmetns within the team cases were not equal and caused certain pieces to be short prints. The Buffalo Bills and Philadelphia Eagles teams were the shortest printed teams. The Bill Bates, Jerome Brown, and Chris Spielman, are the three toughest figures in the set to currently find. This has also been the only time these three players have been issued. There were two nationwide All-Star case assortments, a AFC and a NFC. Each conferences' All-Star cases consisted of 15 different players making up the 24 piece assortments. The All-Star case players were, Marcus Allen, Neal Anderson, Cornelius Bennett, Bubby Brister, Eddie Brown, Tim Brown, Anthony Carter, Roger Craig, Randall Cunningham, John Elway, Boomer Esiason, Jim Everett, Keith Jackson, Neil Lomax, Howie Long, Dan Marino, Freeman McNeil, Joe Montana, Warren Moon, Jerry Rice, Phil Simms, Mike Singletary, John Stephens, Lawrence Taylor, Vinny Testaverde, Andre Tippett, Al Toon, Herschel Walker, Curt Warner, Reggie White. Also, approximately 25,000 of the Jerry Rice piece was given out at Superbowl XXIV. In 1989, a company in conjunction with Kenner set up a 1-800 mail order business that sold all Kenner products made through 1989. The 1989 football sets were made available at approximately $8.00 per piece through this company. Key first pieces of Bill Bates, Jerome Brown, Shane Conlan, Charles Haley, Michael Irvin, James Lofton, Anthony Munoz, Andre Reed, Chris Spielman, Thurman Thomas, and Steve Young combine to make this Kenner's best first piece class. There is one variation in the set. Ken O'Brien's name is misspelled (O'Brian) on the front of the collector card. This error came in team cases only and was corrected early in production. This misspelled name variation is considerably shorter than the corrected version. The error is not part of the complete set price. The values listed below refer to unopened packages. The cards are unnumbered and checklisted below in alphabetical order.

1 Marcus Allen	20.00	50.00
2 Neal Anderson	12.00	30.00
3 Carl Banks FP	30.00	80.00
4 Bill Bates FP	150.00	300.00
5 Mark Bavaro	15.00	40.00
6 Cornelius Bennett	15.00	40.00
7 Duane Bickett	25.00	60.00
8 Bennie Blades FP	40.00	100.00
9 Bubby Brister FP	25.00	60.00
10 Bill Brooks FP	30.00	80.00
11 James Brooks	20.00	50.00
12 Eddie Brown	20.00	50.00
13 Jerome Brown FP	75.00	200.00
14 Tim Brown FP	30.00	80.00
15 Joey Browner	25.00	60.00
16 Kelvin Bryant FP	12.00	30.00
17 Jim Burt FP	60.00	150.00
18 Keith Byars	75.00	200.00
19 Dave Cadigan FP	125.00	300.00
20 Anthony Carter	12.00	30.00
21 Michael Carter	20.00	50.00
22 Chris Chandler FP	20.00	50.00
23 Gary Clark	15.00	40.00
24 Shane Conlan FP	65.00	125.00
25 Jimbo Covert FP	100.00	250.00
26 Roger Craig	15.00	40.00
27 Randall Cunningham	15.00	40.00
28 Richard Dent	12.00	30.00
29 Hanford Dixon FP	40.00	100.00
30 Chris Doleman FP	30.00	80.00
31 Tony Dorsett	30.00	80.00
32 Dave Duerson FP	40.00	100.00
33 John Elway	65.00	125.00
34 Boomer Esiason	15.00	40.00
35 Jim Everett	12.00	30.00
36 Thomas Everett FP	40.00	100.00
37 Sean Farrell FP	75.00	200.00
38 Bill Fralic FP	100.00	250.00
39 Irving Fryar FP	40.00	100.00
40 David Fulcher FP	25.00	60.00
41 Ernest Givins FP	20.00	50.00
42 Alex Gordon FP	40.00	100.00
43 Charles Haley FP	50.00	120.00
44 Bobby Hebert	20.00	50.00
45 Johnny Hector FP	40.00	100.00
46 Drew Hill	20.00	50.00
47 Dalton Hilliard FP	15.00	40.00
48 Bryan Hinkle FP	150.00	300.00
49 Michael Irvin FP	40.00	100.00
50 Keith Jackson FP	15.00	40.00
51 Garry James FP	20.00	50.00
52 Sean Jones FP	30.00	80.00
53 Jim Kelly	40.00	100.00
54 Joe Kelly FP	20.00	50.00
55 Bernie Kosar	12.00	30.00
56 Tim Krumrie	40.00	100.00
57 Louis Lipps	60.00	150.00
58 Eugene Lockhart FP	65.00	125.00
59 James Lofton FP	30.00	80.00
60 Neil Lomax	15.00	40.00
61 Chuck Long	25.00	60.00
62 Howie Long	30.00	80.00
63 Ronnie Lott	40.00	100.00
64 Kevin Mack	15.00	40.00
65 Pete Mandley FP	15.00	40.00
66 Dexter Manley	15.00	40.00
67 Charles Mann FP	25.00	60.00
68 Lionel Manuel FP	20.00	50.00
69 Dan Marino	50.00	120.00
70 Leonard Marshall FP	30.00	80.00
71 Eric Martin	12.00	30.00
72 Rueben Mayes	12.00	30.00
73 Vann McElroy FP	30.00	80.00
74 Dennis McKinnon FP	25.00	60.00
75 Jim McMahon	15.00	40.00
76 Steve McMichael FP	50.00	125.00
77 Erik McMillan FP	30.00	80.00
78 Freeman McNeil	15.00	40.00
79 Keith Millard FP	30.00	80.00
80 Chris Miller FP	30.00	80.00
81 Frank Minnifield FP	30.00	80.00
82 Art Monk	30.00	80.00
83 Joe Montana	30.00	80.00
84 Warren Moon	15.00	40.00
85 Joe Morris	20.00	50.00
86 Anthony Munoz FP	150.00	300.00
87 Ricky Nattiel FP	15.00	40.00
88 Darrin Nelson	25.00	60.00
89 Danny Noonan FP	60.00	150.00
90 Ken O'Brien Misspelled Name	40.00	100.00
91 Ken O'Brien	15.00	40.00
92 Steve Pelluer FP	40.00	100.00
93 Mike Quick	15.00	40.00
94 Andre Reed FP	40.00	100.00
95 Jerry Rice	20.00	50.00
96 Mike Rozier	15.00	40.00
97 Jay Schroeder	25.00	60.00
98 John Settle FP	25.00	60.00
99 Mickey Shuler	20.00	50.00
100 Phil Simms	15.00	40.00
101 Mike Singletary	15.00	40.00
102 Webster Slaughter FP	15.00	40.00
103 Bruce Smith	65.00	125.00
104 Chris Spielman FP	100.00	250.00
105 John Stephens FP	12.00	30.00
106 Kelly Stouffer FP	15.00	40.00
107 Pat Swilling FP	25.00	60.00
108 Lawrence Taylor	12.00	30.00
109 Vinny Testaverde	12.00	30.00
110 Thurman Thomas FP	40.00	100.00
111 Andre Tippett	12.00	30.00
112 Anthony Toney	25.00	60.00
113 Al Toon	12.00	30.00
114 Garin Veris FP	100.00	250.00
115 Herschel Walker	15.00	40.00
116 Curt Warner	12.00	30.00
117 Reggie White	20.00	50.00
118 Doug Williams	20.00	50.00
119 John Williams FP	40.00	100.00
120 Wade Wilson FP	25.00	60.00
121 Ickey Woods FP	12.00	30.00
122 Rod Woodson	75.00	200.00
123 Steve Young FP	125.00	300.00

1989 SLU Legends Series *

The 1989 Legends series focused on legendary players from the sports of Football and Basketball. The figures were carded on a light background card with a player card included.

SET CONSIDERED COMPLETE WITH EITHER UNITAS OR SAYERS VERSION

1 Terry Bradshaw	25.00	60.00
3 Mike Ditka	20.00	50.00
5 Joe Greene	25.00	60.00
8 Gale Sayers w mustache	15.00	40.00
9 Gale Sayers w o mustache	15.00	40.00
10 Johnny Unitas w high tops	20.00	50.00
11 Johnny Unitas w o high tops	15.00	40.00

1989 SLU One-On-One *

The 1989 One-On-One series featured baseball, basketball, and football figures in posed action scenes.

9 John Elway Howie Long	60.00	150.00
10 Jim McMahon Chris Doleman	20.00	50.00
11 Ken O'Brien Lawrence Taylor	25.00	60.00
12 Mike Singletary Mike Quick	20.00	50.00
13 Herschel Walker Dexter Manley	20.00	50.00

1990 SLU Football

This set of 66 different football figurines and collectors cards was issued by Cincinnati-based Kenner Toy Company. The statues feature top NFL stars in action poses and are accompanied by two standard size cards. Each player has a posed and an action color shot card. The back has biographical and statistical information and a facsimile signature of the player. The values listed below refer to unopened packages. The cards are unnumbered and checklisted below in alphabetical order. Figures were issued in All-Star case assortments and team case (16 pieces) assortments. There were two nationwide All-Star case assortments, an AFC and an NFC. The AFC All-Star case assortment consisted of 10 players comprising of 16 pieces. The breakdown for the AFC case is John Elway (2 per case), Boomer Esiason, Bo Jackson (4), Jim Kelly (2), Bernie Kosar, Dan Marino, Warren Moon, Christian Okoye, Bruce Smith, and Ickey Woods (2). The Marino figure was the 1989 piece packaged in a 1990 box. The NFC All-Star case assortment consisted of 13 players making up the 16 piece case. The breakdown for the NFC case is Troy Aikman, Neal Anderson, Roger Craig, Randall Cunningham (2), Jim Everett, Don Majkowski, Keith Millard, Joe Montana (2), Barry Sanders, Deion Sanders, Mike Singletary, Herschel Walker (2) and Reggie White. The Jim Everett figure was the 1989 piece packaged in a 1990 box. There are eight jersey variations in this set. Neal Anderson, Roger Craig, John Elway, Boomer Esiason, Bernie Kosar, Joe Montana, Mike Singletary, and Reggie White all have a white jersey variation and a team color jersey variation. All the while jersey variations except the Boomer Esiason black jersey variation were distributed through All-Star cases. All the colored jersey variations except the Boomer Esiason white jersey variation were distributed through team cases. With these variations the set is 74 pieces. There is confirmation of a Randall Cunningham white jersey variation existing. The piece is the 1989 Cunningham figure in a 1990 package. Only a few of these have been reported. The set price only includes the road jersey variations.

1 Troy Aikman FP	10.00	25.00
2A Neal Anderson Blue Uniform	10.00	25.00
2B Neal Anderson White Uniform	10.00	25.00
3 Mark Bavaro	12.00	30.00
4 Steve Beuerlein FP	15.00	40.00
5 Bubby Brister	40.00	100.00
6 James Brooks	12.00	30.00
7 Tim Brown	25.00	60.00
8 Cris Carter FP	40.00	100.00
9A Roger Craig Red Uniform	10.00	25.00
9B Roger Craig White Uniform	10.00	25.00
10 Randall Cunningham Green	12.00	30.00
10B Randall Cunningham White	12.00	30.00
11 Hart Lee Dykes FP	15.00	40.00
12A John Elway Orange Uniform	25.00	60.00
12B John Elway White Uniform	25.00	60.00
13A Boomer Esiason Black Uniform	10.00	25.00
13B Boomer Esiason White Uniform	10.00	25.00
14 Jim Everett	10.00	25.00
15 Simon Fletcher FP	30.00	80.00
16 Doug Flutie FP	30.00	80.00
17 Dennis Gentry FP	12.00	30.00
18 Dan Hampton FP	25.00	60.00
19 Jim Harbaugh FP	25.00	60.00
20 Rodney Holman FP	20.00	50.00
21 Bobby Humphrey FP	12.00	30.00
22 Michael Irvin	25.00	60.00
23 Bo Jackson FP	12.00	30.00
24 Keith Jackson	10.00	25.00
25 Vance Johnson	25.00	60.00
26 Jim Kelly	12.00	30.00
27A Bernie Kosar Brown Uniform	12.00	30.00
27B Bernie Kosar White Uniform	12.00	30.00
28 Louis Lipps	40.00	100.00
29 Don Majkowski FP	10.00	25.00
30 Charles Mann	15.00	40.00
31 Lionel Manuel	10.00	25.00
32 Dan Marino	30.00	80.00
33 Tim McGee FP	10.00	25.00
34 Dave Meggett FP	10.00	25.00
35 Mike Merriweather	25.00	60.00
36 Eric Metcalf FP	10.00	25.00
37 Keith Millard	10.00	25.00
38A Joe Montana Red Uniform	20.00	50.00
38B Joe Montana White Uniform	20.00	50.00
39 Warren Moon	10.00	25.00
40 Christian Okoye	10.00	25.00

769.49 Beckett 2012-13 4/13

41 Tom Rathman FP	20.00	50.00
42 Andre Reed	10.00	25.00
43 Gerald Riggs	10.00	25.00
44 Mark Rypien FP	10.00	25.00
45 Barry Sanders FP	20.00	50.00
46 Deion Sanders FP	15.00	40.00
47 Ricky Sanders FP	10.00	25.00
48 Clyde Simmons FP	30.00	80.00
49 Phil Simms	10.00	25.00
50A Mike Singletary Blue Uniform	12.00	30.00
50B Mike Singletary White Uniform	12.00	30.00
51 Webster Slaughter	15.00	40.00
52 Bruce Smith	20.00	50.00
53 John Stephens	10.00	25.00
54 John Taylor FP	12.00	30.00
55 Thurman Thomas	12.00	30.00
56 Mike Tomczak FP	15.00	40.00
57 Greg Townsend FP	20.00	50.00
58 Odessa Turner FP	10.00	25.00
59 Herschel Walker	10.00	25.00
60 Steve Walsh FP	20.00	50.00
61A Reggie White Green Uniform	12.00	30.00
61B Reggie White White Uniform	12.00	30.00
62 Wade Wilson	12.00	30.00
63 Ickey Woods	10.00	25.00
64 Donnell Woolford FP	15.00	40.00
65 Tim Worley FP	30.00	80.00
66 Felix Wright FP	25.00	60.00

1991 SLU Football

This set of 26 football figurines and collectors cards was issued by Cincinnati-based Kenner Toy Company. The statues feature top NFL stars in action poses and are accompanied by a standard-size card and a coin. The front of the card has either a posed or action color shot. The back has biographical and statistical information and a facsimile signature of the player. The values listed below refer to unopened packages. The cards are unnumbered and checklisted below in alphabetical order. Kenner cut the size of this set considerably compared to previous years. There were only three teams, the Bears, Bengals and Giants to have team cases in 1991. Everything else was released through a twenty-four piece All-Star case assortment. Steel and aluminum versions of the coin that comes with the figures also exists.

1 Troy Aikman	12.00	30.00
2 Flipper Anderson FP	6.00	15.00
3 Neal Anderson	6.00	15.00
4 James Brooks	6.00	15.00
5 Eddie Brown	6.00	15.00
6 Mark Carrier FP	8.00	20.00
7 Boomer Esiason	6.00	15.00
8 James Francis FP	10.00	25.00
9 Jeff George FP	10.00	25.00
10 Rodney Hampton FP	8.00	20.00
11 Jim Harbaugh	10.00	25.00
12 Jeff Hostetler FP	8.00	20.00
13 Bobby Humphrey	8.00	20.00
14 Don Majkowski	6.00	15.00
15 Dan Marino	20.00	50.00
16 Dave Meggett	6.00	15.00
17 Joe Montana	12.00	30.00
18 Warren Moon	8.00	20.00
19 Christian Okoye	6.00	15.00
20 Jerry Rice	12.00	30.00
21 Andre Rison FP	6.00	15.00
22 Barry Sanders	10.00	25.00
23 Phil Simms	6.00	15.00
24 Emmitt Smith FP	40.00	100.00
25 Thurman Thomas	6.00	15.00
26 Herschel Walker.	8.00	20.00

1991 SLU Football Headline Collection

This set of six football figurines and collectors cards was issued by Cincinnati-based Kenner Toy Company. The statues feature top NFL stars in action poses and are accompanied by a authentic newspaper article and a high gloss, black base used to insert the figurine and article into. The article is framed and describes a memorable moment from the previous season. The pieces came in a 12 piece case assortment. The case breakdown is John Elway (1), Boomer Esiason (2), Dan Marino (1), Joe Montana (4), Jerry Rice (1), and Barry Sanders (3). The values listed below refer to unopened packages. They are unnumbered and checklisted below in alphabetical order.

1 John Elway	20.00	50.00
2 Boomer Esiason	6.00	15.00
3 Dan Marino	30.00	80.00
4 Joe Montana	10.00	25.00
5 Jerry Rice	10.00	25.00
6 Barry Sanders	12.00	30.00

1992 SLU Football

This set of 26 football figurines and collectors cards was issued by Cincinnati-based Kenner Toy Company. The statues feature top NFL stars in action poses and are accompanied by a standard size card and a poster. The front of the card has either a posed or action color shot. The back has biographical and statistical information and a facsimile signature of the player. The poster folds out to be 11" X 14". The pieces came in two 16-piece case assortments. The values listed below refer to unopened packages. They are unnumbered and checklisted below in alphabetical order.

1 Troy Aikman	12.00	30.00
2 Earnest Byner FP	8.00	20.00
3 Randall Cunningham	5.00	12.00
4 Rodney Hampton	5.00	12.00
5 Bobby Hebert	5.00	12.00
6 Jeff Hostetler	6.00	15.00
7 Michael Irvin	6.00	15.00
8 Bo Jackson	5.00	12.00
9 Haywood Jeffires FP	5.00	12.00
10 Seth Joyner FP	6.00	15.00
11 Jim Kelly	8.00	20.00
12 Ronnie Lott	15.00	40.00
13 Dan Marino	25.00	60.00
14 Joe Montana	12.00	30.00
15 Warren Moon	6.00	15.00
16 Rob Moore FP	5.00	12.00
17 Jerry Rice	10.00	25.00
18 Andre Rison	5.00	12.00
19 Mark Rypien	5.00	12.00
20 Barry Sanders	10.00	25.00
21 Deion Sanders	8.00	20.00
22 Emmitt Smith	12.00	30.00
23 Pat Swilling	6.00	15.00
24 Derrick Thomas FP	12.00	30.00
25 Thurman Thomas	6.00	15.00
26 Steve Young	15.00	40.00

1992 SLU Football Headline Collection

his set of six football figurines and collectors cards was issued by Cincinnati-based Kenner Toy Company. The statues feature top NFL stars in action poses and are accompanied by a authentic newspaper article and a high gloss, black base used to insert the figurine and article into. The article is framed and describes a memorable moment from the previous season. The pieces came in a 12-count case assortment. The values listed below refer to unopened packages. They are unnumbered and listed below in alphabetical order.

1 Joe Montana	12.00	30.00
2 Warren Moon	8.00	20.00
3 Mark Rypien	6.00	15.00
4 Barry Sanders	15.00	40.00
5 Emmitt Smith	15.00	40.00
6 Thurman Thomas	6.00	15.00

1993 SLU Football

This set of 27 football figurines and collectors cards was issued by Cincinnati-based Kenner Toy Company. The statues feature top NFL stars in action poses and are accompanied by two standard size cards. Each player has a posed and an action color shot card. The back has biographical and statistical information and a facsimile signature of the player. The pieces came in two different 24-count case assortments. The values listed below refer to unopened packages. Since the pieces are unnumbered, we have listed this set in alphabetical order.

1 Troy Aikman	8.00	20.00
2 Cornelius Bennett	4.00	10.00
3 Randall Cunningham	4.00	10.00
4 Chris Doleman	12.00	30.00
5 John Elway	15.00	40.00
6 Barry Foster FP	4.00	10.00
7 Michael Irvin	8.00	20.00
8 Rickey Jackson	4.00	10.00
9 Cortez Kennedy FP	5.00	12.00
10 David Klingler FP	4.00	10.00
11 Chip Lohmiller FP	6.00	15.00
12 Russell Maryland FP	8.00	20.00
13 Anthony Miller FP	4.00	10.00
14 Chris Miller	5.00	12.00
15 Joe Montana	12.00	30.00
16 Warren Moon Blue Uniform	6.00	15.00
17 Warren Moon White Uniform	6.00	15.00
18 Andre Reed	4.00	10.00
19 Barry Sanders	10.00	25.00
20 Deion Sanders	6.00	15.00
21 Junior Seau FP	6.00	15.00
22 Sterling Sharpe FP	12.00	30.00
23 Emmitt Smith	12.00	30.00
24 Neil Smith FP	10.00	25.00
25 Pete Stoyanovich FP	5.00	12.00
26 Ricky Watters FP	8.00	20.00
27 Rod Woodson	10.00	25.00
28 Steve Young	10.00	25.00

1994 SLU Football

This set of 32 football figurines and collectors cards was issued by Cincinnati-based Kenner Toy Company. The statues feature top NFL stars in action poses and are accompanied by a standard-size card. The front of the card has either a posed or action color shot. The back has biographical and statistical information and a facsimile signature of the player. The pieces came in two different 24-count case assortments. The values listed below refer to unopened packages. They are unnumbered and checklisted below in alphabetical order.

1 Troy Aikman	4.00	10.00
2 Jerome Bettis FP	8.00	20.00
3 Drew Bledsoe FP	12.00	30.00
4 Randall Cunningham	4.00	10.00
5 Boomer Esiason	4.00	10.00
6 Brett Favre FP	25.00	60.00
7 Barry Foster	4.00	10.00
8 Rodney Hampton	4.00	10.00
9 Ronnie Harmon	4.00	10.00
10 Garrison Hearst FP	5.00	12.00
11 Rocket Ismail FP	6.00	15.00
12 Brent Jones FP	8.00	20.00
13 Cortez Kennedy	4.00	10.00
14 Nick Lowery FP	8.00	20.00
15 Dan Marino	15.00	40.00
16 Eric Metcalf	6.00	15.00
17 Rick Mirer FP	5.00	12.00
18 Joe Montana	10.00	25.00
19 Ken Norton FP	6.00	15.00
20 Jerry Rice	6.00	15.00
21 Andre Rison	4.00	10.00
22 Barry Sanders	10.00	25.00
23 Deion Sanders	6.00	15.00
24 Junior Seau	4.00	10.00
25 Phil Simms	4.00	10.00
26 Emmitt Smith	10.00	25.00
27 Lawrence Taylor	8.00	20.00
28 Chris Warren	4.00	10.00
29 Lorenzo White FP	4.00	10.00
30 Reggie White	8.00	20.00
31 Rod Woodson	8.00	20.00
32 Steve Young	8.00	20.00

1995 SLU Football

This set of 33 football figurines and collectors cards was issued by Cincinnati-based Kenner Toy Company. The statues feature top NFL stars in action poses and are accompanied by a standard-size card. The front of the card has either a posed or action color shot. The back has biographical and statistical information and a facsimile signature of the player. The pieces came in three different 16-count case assortments. The set is highlighted by the Joe Montana retirement piece. The values listed below refer to unopened packages. They are unnumbered and checklisted below in alphabetical order.

1 Troy Aikman	6.00	15.00
2 Jerome Bettis	6.00	15.00
3 Drew Bledsoe	10.00	25.00
4 Steve Christie FP	6.00	15.00
5 Ben Coates FP	6.00	15.00
6 Randall Cunningham	5.00	12.00
7 Willie Davis FP	4.00	10.00
8 Jim Everett	4.00	10.00
9 Marshall Faulk FP	12.00	30.00
10 Brett Favre	10.00	25.00
11 Irving Fryar	6.00	15.00
12 Jeff George	5.00	12.00
13 Stan Humphries FP	4.00	10.00
14 Michael Irvin	8.00	20.00
15 Johnny Johnson FP	4.00	10.00
16 Seth Joyner	4.00	10.00
17 Greg Lloyd FP	10.00	25.00
18 Dan Marino	10.00	25.00
19 Terry McDaniel FP	8.00	20.00
20 Natrone Means FP	8.00	20.00
21 Scott Mitchell FP	4.00	10.00
22 Joe Montana Retirement	10.00	25.00
23 Warren Moon	6.00	15.00
24 Hardy Nickerson FP	8.00	20.00
25 Michael Dean Perry FP	6.00	15.00
26 Jerry Rice	6.00	15.00
27 Barry Sanders	12.00	30.00
28 Deion Sanders	8.00	20.00
29 Shannon Sharpe FP	10.00	25.00
30 Emmitt Smith	8.00	20.00
31 Dan Wilkinson FP	4.00	10.00
32 Steve Young	6.00	15.00
33 Chris Zorich FP	6.00	15.00

1996 SLU Football

This set of 38 football figurines and collectors cards was issued by Cincinnati-based Kenner Toy Company. The statues feature top NFL stars in action poses and are accompanied by a standard-size card. The front of the card has either a posed or action color shot. The back has biographical and statistical information and a facsimile signature of the player. The set is highlighted by the first pieces of Mark Brunell, Kerry Collins, Steve McNair and Kordell Stewart. The set is considered complete without the Troy Aikman White Chest Double Star variation, the Troy Aikman Nations Mark and the Brett Favre Shopko. The values listed below refer to unopened packages. They are unnumbered and checklisted below in alphabetical order.

1A Troy Aikman	6.00	15.00
1B Troy Aikman Nations Mark	8.00	20.00
1C Troy Aikman White Chest Double Star	60.00	150.00
2 Terry Allen FP	5.00	12.00
3 Steve Beuerlein	6.00	15.00
4 Jeff Blake FP	5.00	12.00
5 Drew Bledsoe	6.00	15.00
6 Steve Bono FP	5.00	12.00
7 Kyle Brady FP	5.00	12.00
8 Robert Brooks FP	8.00	20.00
9 Dave Brown FP	5.00	12.00
10 Isaac Bruce FP	8.00	20.00
11 Mark Brunell FP	8.00	20.00
12 Mark Carrier FP	5.00	12.00
13 Cris Carter	10.00	25.00
14 Kerry Collins FP	6.00	15.00
15 John Elway	10.00	25.00
16 Marshall Faulk	6.00	15.00
17 Brett Favre Shopko	12.00	30.00
18 Joey Galloway FP	5.00	12.00
19 Kevin Greene FP	5.00	12.00
20 Dan Marino	10.00	25.00
21 Steve McNair FP	10.00	25.00
22 Eric Metcalf	5.00	12.00
23 Jay Novacek FP	8.00	20.00
24 Bryce Paup FP	5.00	12.00
25 Carl Pickens FP	6.00	15.00
26 Frank Reich FP	5.00	12.00
27 Errict Rhett FP	5.00	12.00
28 Jerry Rice	6.00	15.00
29 Rashaan Salaam FP	5.00	12.00
30 Barry Sanders	15.00	40.00
31 Deion Sanders	6.00	15.00
32 Junior Seau	5.00	12.00
33 Emmitt Smith	10.00	25.00
34 Chris Spielman	5.00	12.00
35 Kordell Stewart FP	10.00	25.00
36 Ricky Watters	5.00	12.00
37 Reggie White	6.00	15.00
38 Harvey Williams FP	5.00	12.00
39 Steve Young	6.00	15.00

1997 SLU Football

This 43-piece set was released in late August by the Kenner Toy Company and features a posed shot of the player with an accompanying card. The pieces came in 5 different case assortments. There are two pieces that were exclusives and are not considered part of the set - the Terry Bradshaw Hill's Exclusive and the Emmitt Smith Albertson's Exclusive. Notable first pieces include Karim Abdul-Jabbar, Terrell Davis, Eddie George, Keyshawn Johnson, Curtis Martin and Herman Moore. The values listed below refer to unopened packages. The figures are unnumbered and checklisted below in alphabetical order. Complete sets were also available through the JC Penney catalog late in 1997.

1 Karim Abdul-Jabbar FP	5.00	12.00
2 Troy Aikman	6.00	15.00
3 Jamal Anderson FP	8.00	20.00
4 Jerome Bettis	8.00	20.00
5 Jeff Blake	3.00	8.00
6 Drew Bledsoe	5.00	12.00
7 Terry Bradshaw Hill's Exclusive	8.00	20.00
8 Mark Brunell	6.00	15.00
9 Dale Carter FP	5.00	12.00
10 Larry Centers FP	5.00	12.00
11 Mark Chmura FP	4.00	10.00
12 Kerry Collins	3.00	8.00
13 Brian Cox FP	5.00	12.00
14 Terrell Davis FP	10.00	25.00
15 Quinn Early FP	5.00	12.00
16 John Elway	8.00	20.00
17A Brett Favre	8.00	20.00
17B Brett Favre MVP Sticker	8.00	20.00
18 Eddie George FP	10.00	25.00
19 Jeff George	5.00	12.00
20 Elvis Grbac FP	5.00	12.00
21 Kevin Greene	3.00	8.00
22 Marvin Harrison FP	10.00	25.00
23 Jim Harbaugh	3.00	8.00
24 Brad Johnson FP	8.00	20.00
25 Keyshawn Johnson FP	10.00	25.00
26 Daryl Johnston FP	6.00	15.00
27 Dan Marino	8.00	20.00
28 Curtis Martin FP	10.00	25.00
29 Tony Martin FP	4.00	10.00
30 Herman Moore FP	8.00	20.00
31 Jerry Rice	5.00	12.00
32 Willie Roaf FP	5.00	12.00
33 Deion Sanders	5.00	12.00
34 Bruce Smith	6.00	15.00
35 Emmitt Smith	6.00	15.00
36 Emmitt Smith Albertson's Exclusive	8.00	20.00
37 Phillipi Sparks FP	5.00	12.00
38 Kordell Stewart	5.00	12.00
39 Vinny Testaverde	4.00	10.00
40 Eric Turner FP	4.00	10.00
41 Chris Warren	3.00	8.00
42 Ricky Watters	3.00	8.00
43 Michael Westbrook FP	5.00	12.00
44 Reggie White	6.00	15.00
45 Steve Young	6.00	15.00

1997 SLU Football Classic Doubles

This 8-piece set was distributed in two different assortments in late 1997. The package features two pieces and highlights some of the best double tandems (both past and present) in the NFL.

SET ONLY INC.ONE FAVRE/STARR

1 Fred Biletnikoff Tim Brown	15.00	40.00
2 Tony Dorsett Emmitt Smith	12.00	30.00
3A Brett Favre Bart Starr	10.00	25.00
3B Brett Favre Bart Starr Super Bowl Sticker	10.00	25.00
4 Dan Marino Bob Griese	10.00	25.00
5 Joe Montana Dwight Clark	10.00	25.00
6 Joe Montana Jerry Rice	10.00	25.00
7 Walter Payton Barry Sanders	30.00	80.00
8 Roger Staubach Troy Aikman	10.00	25.00

1997 SLU Football Gridiron Greats

This 9-piece set was distributed in two assortments and features the first NFL set very similar to the Baseball Stadium Stars. Each figure is 8" and is suspended above a football field with facsimile signatures.

1 Brett Favre	12.00	30.00
2 Kevin Greene	5.00	12.00
3 Dan Marino	12.00	30.00
4 Joe Montana	12.00	30.00
5 Jerry Rice	10.00	25.00
6 Deion Sanders	12.00	30.00
7 Emmitt Smith	10.00	25.00
8 Thurman Thomas	8.00	20.00
9 Ricky Watters	5.00	12.00

1997 SLU Football Heisman Collection

This 9-piece set was distributed in two different assortments and features Heisman Trophy winners. Each package includes a figure and a trophy, rather than a card. Prices are for pieces in the package. The set is listed below alphabetically.

1 Tony Dorsett	5.00	12.00
2 Doug Flutie	5.00	12.00
3 Eddie George	8.00	20.00
4 Archie Griffin	8.00	20.00
5 Bo Jackson	4.00	10.00
6 Steve Owens	4.00	10.00
7 Johnny Rodgers	4.00	10.00
8 Barry Sanders	10.00	25.00
9 Danny Wuerffel	6.00	15.00

1998 SLU Football

This 52-piece set was released by the Kenner Toy Company and features a posed shot of the player with an accompanying card. The pieces came in 6 different case assortments. The Kordell Stewart pieces was a Hills exclusive and the Barry Sanders was a Meijers exclusive. They are not considered part of the set. The corrected Elvis Grbac piece was only available in the JC Penney 42 piece set, which didn't include the extended pieces. Notable first pieces include Trent Dilfer, Corey Dillon, Terry Glenn and Antowain Smith. The extended series was released for the first time in football in one assortment. The key players in the extended series were Peyton Manning and Charles Woodson. The values listed below refer to unopened packages. The figures are unnumbered and checklisted below in alphabetical order.

1 Troy Aikman	4.00	10.00
2 Terry Allen	3.00	8.00
4 Jerome Bettis	5.00	12.00
5 Drew Bledsoe	3.00	8.00
6 Tony Boselli FP	5.00	12.00
7 Derrick Brooks FP	8.00	20.00
8 Mark Brunell	3.00	8.00
9 Kerry Collins	3.00	8.00
10 Terrell Davis	3.00	8.00
12 Trent Dilfer FP	4.00	10.00
13 Corey Dillon FP	6.00	15.00
14 John Elway	5.00	12.00
15 Brett Favre	4.00	10.00
16 Antonio Freeman FP	5.00	12.00
17 Gus Frerotte FP	3.00	8.00
18 Joey Galloway	4.00	10.00
19 Eddie George	6.00	15.00
20 Terry Glenn FP	4.00	10.00
21 Elvis Grbac COR	10.00	25.00
21A Elvis Grbac ERR	4.00	10.00
23 Raymont Harris FP	3.00	8.00
24 Bobby Hoying FP	3.00	8.00
25 Carnell Lake FP	6.00	15.00
26 Lamar Lathon FP	3.00	8.00
29 Dan Marino	6.00	15.00
31 Randall McDaniel FP	6.00	15.00
32 Chester McGlockton FP	6.00	15.00
34 Scott Mitchell	3.00	8.00
35 Adrian Murrell FP	3.00	8.00
36 Nate Newton FP	8.00	20.00
37 Jonathan Ogden FP	6.00	15.00
38 Orlando Pace FP	6.00	15.00
39 Carl Pickens	3.00	8.00
40 Jerry Rice	4.00	10.00
41 Simeon Rice FP	4.00	10.00
42 Barry Sanders Meijer	10.00	25.00
43 Deion Sanders	4.00	10.00
46 Antowain Smith FP	3.00	8.00
47 Emmitt Smith	4.00	10.00
48 Kordell Stewart Hills	6.00	15.00
49 Dana Stubblefield FP	5.00	12.00
50 Vinny Testaverde	3.00	8.00
51 Tyrone Wheatley FP	4.00	10.00
52 Reggie White	3.00	8.00
54 Steve Young	3.00	8.00

1998 SLU Football 12-inch Figures

This is the first year that Kenner has produced 12" figures for football. The set was released in one assortment and contains key members of the NFL Quarterback Club. The pieces are not numbered and listed below in alphabetical order. These pieces also have no cards to go with the statues.

1 Drew Bledsoe	5.00	12.00
2 John Elway	15.00	40.00
3 Brett Favre	12.00	30.00
4 Dan Marino	12.00	30.00
5 Jerry Rice	6.00	15.00

1998 SLU Football Classic Doubles

Produced for the second year in a row by Kenner, this 8-piece set was distributed in two assortments.

1 Herb Adderley Deion Sanders	6.00	15.00
2 Troy Aikman Emmitt Smith	10.00	25.00
3 Marcus Allen Mike Garrett	6.00	15.00
4 John Elway Dan Marino	12.00	30.00
5 Joe Namath Don Maynard	8.00	20.00
6 Jerry Rice Steve Young	6.00	15.00
7 Junior Seau Dick Butkus	6.00	15.00
8 Y.A.Title Sam Huff	6.00	15.00

1998 SLU Football Classic Doubles Quarterback Club

Produced exclusively for Wal-Mart by the Cincinatti based Kenner Company, this 6-figure set was released in one assortment. The figures feature only six players, with one figure in their pro uniform and the other in their college uniform. The pieces are not numbered and listed below in alphabetical order.

1 Drew Bledsoe	6.00	15.00
2 John Elway	12.00	30.00
3 Jim Harbaugh	6.00	15.00
4 Dan Marino	12.00	30.00
5 Emmitt Smith	12.00	30.00
6 Steve Young	8.00	20.00

1998 SLU Football Extended

This 10-piece extended set was issued by Cincinnati-based Kenner Toy Company. The statues feature top National Football League stars in action poses and are accompanied by a standard-size card of each player. This was the first extended product for the football market. The values listed below refer to unopened packages. The figures are unnumbered and checklisted below in alphabetical order. Some of the more popular first pieces from this set include Peyton Manning, Mike Alstott, and Charles Woodson.

10 Mike Alstott FP	5.00	12.00
20 Terrell Davis	6.00	15.00
30 Jim Harbaugh	3.00	8.00
40 Ryan Leaf FP	3.00	8.00
50 Peyton Manning FP EXT	20.00	40.00
60 Curtis Martin	3.00	8.00
70 Steve McNair	5.00	12.00
80 Deion Sanders	4.00	10.00
90 Shannon Sharpe	5.00	12.00
100 Charles Woodson FP EXT	10.00	25.00

1998 SLU Football Gridiron Greats

This 7-piece set was distributed in two assortments and features the second year for this line. Each figure is 8" and is suspended above a football field with facsimile signatures. Prices refer to in box pieces. Each piece is not numbered and listed below in alphabetical order.

1 Troy Aikman	6.00	15.00
2 Drew Bledsoe	8.00	20.00
3 Mark Brunell	6.00	15.00
4 John Elway	10.00	25.00
5 Barry Sanders	10.00	25.00
6 Junior Seau	6.00	15.00
7 Steve Young	8.00	20.00

1998 SLU Football Hall of Fame

The first release of this set features NFL Hall of Fame greats. The figures were released in two assortments. Prices below are for in package pieces. These pieces are 7" and have no cards to go with them.

1 Dick Butkus	5.00	12.00
2 Larry Csonka	5.00	12.00
3 Joe Greene	5.00	12.00
4 Deacon Jones	5.00	12.00
5 Bob Lilly	6.00	15.00
6 Vince Lombardi	12.50	30.00
7 Ray Nitschke	10.00	25.00
8 Gale Sayers	5.00	12.00
9 Bart Starr	8.00	20.00
10 Y.A. Tittle	5.00	12.00
11 Gene Upshaw	5.00	12.00

1998 SLU Football Heisman Collection

Released for the second consecutive year by Kenner, this 10-piece set features Heisman Winners in their college uniforms. The pieces were released in two assortments. Prices below refer to in package pieces.

1 Marcus Allen	5.00	12.00
2 Earl Campbell	6.00	15.00
3 John Cappelletti	4.00	10.00
4 Glenn Davis	4.00	10.00
5 Paul Hornung	5.00	12.00
6 Desmond Howard	4.00	10.00
7 Rashaan Salaam	4.00	10.00
8 Roger Staubach	6.00	15.00
9 Herschel Walker	4.00	10.00
10 Charles Woodson	10.00	25.00

1999 SLU Football

This 39-piece SLU Football series was released by Hasbro in six assortments throughout the year. Five regular assortments were released during the season. The statues feature top National Football League stars in action poses and are accompanied by a standard-size card of each player. The values listed below refer to unopened packages. The figures are unnumbered and checklisted below in alphabetical order. Some of the more popular first pieces from this set include Zach Thomas, Randy Moss and Jake Plummer.

1 Troy Aikman	3.00	8.00
4 Drew Bledsoe	3.00	8.00
5 Mark Brunell	3.00	8.00
6 Chris Chandler	3.00	8.00
7 Wayne Chrebet FP	8.00	20.00
8 Randall Cunningham	3.00	8.00
9 Terrell Davis	3.00	8.00
10 Dermontti Dawson FP	10.00	25.00
11 Corey Dillon	3.00	8.00
12 Warrick Dunn FP	5.00	12.00
13 John Elway	6.00	15.00
14 Curtis Enis FP	6.00	15.00
15 Brett Favre	3.00	8.00
16 Doug Flutie	3.00	8.00
17 Eddie George Oilers	5.00	12.00
18 Eddie George Titans	8.00	20.00
20 Napoleon Kaufman FP	8.00	20.00
21 Jim Kelly	8.00	20.00
22 Ryan Leaf	3.00	8.00
23 Dorsey Levens FP	5.00	12.00
24 Peyton Manning	8.00	20.00
26 Dan Marino	6.00	15.00
27 Curtis Martin	3.00	8.00
28 Randy Moss FP	10.00	25.00
29 Jake Plummer FP	4.00	10.00
31 Jerry Rice	4.00	10.00
32 Andre Rison	4.00	10.00
33 Barry Sanders	5.00	12.00
34 Barry Sanders Meijer	10.00	25.00
35 Warren Sapp FP	10.00	25.00
36 Emmitt Smith	6.00	15.00
37 Jimmy Smith FP	6.00	15.00
38 Neil Smith	6.00	15.00
39 Robert Smith FP	6.00	15.00
40 Kordell Stewart	3.00	8.00
41 Eric Swann FP	5.00	12.00
43 Zach Thomas FP	8.00	20.00
44 Ricky Walters	3.00	8.00
46 Steve Young	3.00	8.00

1999 SLU Football 12-inch Figures

This 5-piece Kenner Football series was released by Hasbro. The figures feature top National Football League Stars and measure 12" in size. Each comes with comes detailed, with real cloth material uniforms.

10 Mark Brunell	12.00	30.00
20 Terrell Davis	15.00	40.00
30 Curtis Martin	12.00	30.00
40 Barry Sanders	15.00	40.00
50 Steve Young	15.00	40.00

1999 SLU Football Classic Doubles

The 1999 Football Classic Doubles series was a continuation series to previous years. In addition, all but two of the pieces are focusing this year on teammates.

1 Cris Carter Randy Moss	8.00	20.00
2 Jack Lambert Jack Ham	6.00	15.00
3 Earl Campbell Eddie George	6.00	15.00
4 Anthony Munoz Boomer Esiason	5.00	12.00
5 John Elway Terrell Davis	6.00	15.00
6 Mike Alstott Warrick Dunn	5.00	12.00
7 Ken Stabler Dave Casper	6.00	15.00
8 Archie Manning Peyton Manning	10.00	25.00
9 Johnny Unitas Raymond Berry	5.00	12.00
10 Franco Harris Jerome Bettis	6.00	15.00

1999 SLU Football Classic Doubles Quarterback Club

The 1999 Football Classic Doubles feature Quarterback Club members and continue the Wal-Mart exclusive first issued in 1998. Each player's package has two figurines and two cards showing him in both his college and pro uniforms.

1 Troy Aikman	6.00	15.00
2 Terrell Davis	6.00	15.00
3 Brett Favre	10.00	20.00
4 Jake Plummer	6.00	15.00
5 Kordell Stewart	6.00	15.00

1999 SLU Football Extended

This 8-piece extended set was issued by Cincinnati-based Hasbro Toy Company. The statues feature top National Football League stars in action poses and are accompanied by a standard-size card of each player. The values listed below refer to unopened packages. The figures are unnumbered and checklisted below in alphabetical order. Some of the more popular first pieces from this set include Tim Couch and Ricky Williams.

10 Jamal Anderson	3.00	8.00
20 Charlie Batch FP	3.00	8.00
30 Tim Couch FP	8.00	20.00
40 Ed McCaffrey FP	6.00	15.00
50 Donovan McNabb FP	12.00	30.00
60 John Randle FP	5.00	12.00
70 Fred Taylor FP	5.00	12.00
80 Ricky Williams FP	6.00	15.00

1999 SLU Football Gridiron Greats

The 1999 Football Gridiron Greats series was issued for the third year in a row. Each figure is 8" tall and is suspended above a football field with facsimile signatures. Prices refer to in-box pieces. Each piece is unnumbered and listed below in alphabetical order.

1 Dick Butkus	5.00	12.00
2 Terrell Davis	8.00	20.00
3 Warrick Dunn	5.00	12.00
4 Eddie George	6.00	15.00
5 Dan Marino	8.00	20.00
6 Curtis Martin	10.00	25.00
7 Barry Sanders	8.00	20.00
8 Kordell Stewart	6.00	15.00

1999 SLU Football Hall of Fame Legends

For 1999, only three pieces were issued that contained pieces similar to the 1998 Hall of Fame issue. The Fouts and Unitas are basic pieces while the Staubach was a Nationmark exclusive. Lastly, Joe Namath single cards hit the secondary without a figurine included.

1 Dan Fouts-Internet	6.00	15.00
2 Johnny Unitas-Internet	6.00	15.00
3 Roger Staubach NatMark	6.00	15.00

1999 SLU Football Heroes of the Gridiron

Heroes of the Gridiron features some of the best current and former players in the NFL in their college uniform. Each figure includes a helmet and replicas of either a Heisman Trophy or college pennant.

1 Charlie Batch	5.00	12.00
2 Mark Brunell	3.00	8.00
3 Ernie Davis	3.00	8.00
4 Warrick Dunn	3.00	8.00
5 Curtis Martin	3.00	8.00
6 Randy Moss	8.00	20.00
7 Jim Plunkett	3.00	8.00
8 Charlie Ward	4.00	10.00
9 Ricky Williams	8.00	20.00

1999 SLU Football Pro Action

This seven-piece set was released by the Hasbro Toy Company and features a posed shot of the player. Each figure comes complete with several accessories such as football and helmets. Each has real action movement related to their position. The figure's card-back can be cut out to form a target for the figure's related action movement. Listed below are prices for figures still mint in package.

1 John Elway	3.00	8.00
2 Jerry Rice	2.50	6.00
3 Barry Sanders	3.00	8.00
4 Deion Sanders	2.50	6.00
5 Emmitt Smith	3.00	8.00
6 Neil Smith	2.00	5.00
7 Steve Young	2.50	6.00

1999 SLU Football Pro Action Deluxe

This three-piece set was released by the Hasbro Toy Company and features a posed shot of the player slightly bigger than the regular Pro Action figures. Each comes complete with several accessories such as football and helmets. Each has real action movement related to their position. The figure's card-back can be cut out to form a target for the figure's related action movement. Listed below are prices for figures still mint in package.

10 Jason Elam	2.50	6.00
20 Brett Favre	3.00	8.00
30 Kordell Stewart	2.50	6.00

2000 SLU Football

This 46-piece set was issued by Cincinnati-based Hasbro Toy Company. The statues feature top NFL stars in action posed figures accompanied by a standard-size trading card. The values listed below refer to unopened packages. The figures are unnumbered and checklisted below in alphabetical order.

10 Troy Aikman	5.00	12.00
20 Mike Alstott	4.00	10.00
30 Jesse Armstead FP	8.00	20.00
40 Champ Bailey FP	6.00	15.00
50 Drew Bledsoe	4.00	10.00
60 Tony Brackens FP	6.00	15.00
70 Mark Brunell	4.00	10.00
80 Tim Couch	6.00	15.00
81 Tim Couch Ames	6.00	15.00
85 Daunte Culpepper FP	15.00	40.00
90 Stephen Davis FP	6.00	15.00
100 Terrell Davis	4.00	10.00
110 John Elway	6.00	15.00
115 Marshall Faulk	10.00	25.00
120 Brett Favre	5.00	12.00
130 Doug Flutie	4.00	10.00
140 Antonio Freeman	4.00	10.00
160 Tony Gonzalez FP	6.00	15.00
170 Brian Griese FP	8.00	20.00
180 Torry Holt FP	6.00	15.00
190 Edgerrin James FP	10.00	25.00
200 Brad Johnson	4.00	10.00
210 Keyshawn Johnson Jets	5.00	12.00
211 Keyshawn Johnson Bucs	8.00	20.00
220 Shaun King FP	8.00	20.00
230 Jon Kitna FP	5.00	12.00
240 Peyton Manning	5.00	12.00
245 Peyton Manning	5.00	12.00
250 Dan Marino	12.00	30.00
260 Steve McNair	8.00	20.00
270 Joe Montana	8.00	20.00
280 Randy Moss	6.00	15.00
285 Randy Moss	6.00	15.00
290 Ozzie Newsome	6.00	15.00
300 Jim Otto FP	12.00	30.00
310 Terrell Owens FP	6.00	15.00
320 Jake Plummer	4.00	10.00
330 Takeo Spikes FP	6.00	15.00
335 Akili Smith FP	6.00	15.00
340 Fred Taylor	4.00	10.00
350 Vinny Testaverde	4.00	10.00
360 Kurt Warner New Uni FP	10.00	25.00
365 Kurt Warner Old Uni FP	10.00	25.00
366 Kurt Warner Wal	10.00	25.00
370 Ricky Williams New Uni	5.00	12.00
371 Ricky Williams Old Uni	5.00	12.00
375 Ricky Williams	5.00	12.00
380 Darren Woodson FP	8.00	20.00

2000 SLU Football Classic Doubles

The 2000 Football Classic Doubles series was a continuation series to previous years. This set pairs two NFL greats at the same position.

10 John Elway Brett Favre	8.00	20.00
20 Terrell Davis Jamal Anderson	8.00	20.00
30 Troy Aikman Jim Kelly	8.00	20.00
40 Marshall Faulk Eddie George	10.00	25.00
50 Phil Simms John Elway	8.00	20.00
60 Brett Favre Drew Bledsoe	8.00	20.00
70 Joe Montana Dan Marino	15.00	40.00

2000 SLU Football Classic Doubles Quarterback Club

This Peyton Manning piece was released directly through one distributor. It was intended to be part of a larger set issue that was never released.

10 Peyton Manning	8.00	20.00

2000 SLU Football Elite

The Elite series features slightly larger figures in more realistic poses and likenesses. Each blister pack is accompanied by an SLU trading card produced by Pacific.

10 Terrell Davis	8.00	20.00
20 Brett Favre	12.00	30.00
30 Peyton Manning	8.00	20.00
40 Joe Montana	15.00	40.00
50 Randy Moss	8.00	20.00
60 Emmitt Smith	10.00	25.00

2000 SLU Football Extended

This 10-piece extended set was issued by Cincinnati-based Hasbro Toy Company. The statues feature top National Football League stars in action poses and are accompanied by a standard-size card of each player. The values listed below refer to unopened packages. The figures are unnumbered and checklisted below in alphabetical order. Some of the more popular first pieces from this set include Ron Dayne, Jevon Kearse and Peter Warrick.

10 Shaun Alexander FP	8.00	20.00
20 Isaac Bruce	6.00	15.00
30 Cris Carter	6.00	15.00
40 Ron Dayne FP	8.00	20.00
50 Marvin Harrison	5.00	12.00
60 Jevon Kearse FP	6.00	15.00
70 Jason Sehorn FP	6.00	15.00
80 Shawn Springs FP	5.00	12.00
90 Peter Warrick Home FP	6.00	15.00
100 Peter Warrick Away FP	6.00	15.00

2000 Wheaties Series I

Sponsored by Wheaties, this set featured four top NFL stars.

10 John Elway	8.00	20.00
20 Brett Favre	8.00	20.00
30 Jerry Rice	8.00	20.00
40 Steve Young	8.00	20.00

2000 Wheaties Series II

Carrying on from the first Wheaties set, this expanded to include classic baseball players as well.

10 Dan Marino	8.00	20.00